BECKETT THE #1 AUTHORITY ON COLLECTIBLES

BASEBALL CARD PRICE GUIDE

43rd EDITION - 2021

THE HOBBY'S MOST RELIABLE AND RELIED UPON SOURCE ™

Founder: Dr. James Beckett III

Edited by the Price Guide Staff of BECKETT MEDIA LLC

BECKETT is a registered trademark of BECKETT MEDIA LLC, DALLAS, TEXAS
Manufactured in the United States of America | Published by Beckett Media LLC

Beckett Media LLC
4635 McEwen Dr.
Dallas, TX 75244
972.991.6657
beckett.com

First Printing
ISBN: 978-1-953801-00-5

BASEBALL CARD PRICE GUIDE

NUMBER 43

BECKETT - THE #1 AUTHORITY ON COLLECTIBLES

EDITORIAL
Mike Payne - Editorial Director

COVER DESIGN
Eric Knagg - Graphic Designer

ADVERTISING
Ted Barker - Advertising Director
972.448.9147, tbarker@beckett.com
Alex Soriano - Advertising Sales
619.392.5299, alex@beckett.com

COLLECTIBLES DATA PUBLISHING
Brian Fleischer
Manager, | Sr. Market Analyst
Lloyd Almonguera, Matt Bible, Jeff Camay, Steve Dalton, Justin Grunert, Badz Mercader, Eric Norton, Kristian Redulla, Sam Zimmer
Price Guide Staff
Daniel Moscoso - Digital Studio

BECKETT GRADING SERVICES
Jeromy Murray
VP, Grading & Authentication
jmurray@beckett.com
4635 McEwen Road, Dallas, TX 75244
Grading Sales – 972-448-9188 |
grading@beckett.com

BECKETT GRADING SALES/ SHOW STAFF
DALLAS OFFICE
4635 McEwen, Dallas, TX 75244
Derek Ficken - Midwest/Southeast Regional Sales Manager
dficken@beckett.com
972.448.9144

NEW YORK OFFICE
Charles Stabile - Northeast Regional Sales Manager
484 White Plains Rd, 2nd Floor, Eastchester, N.Y. 10709
cstabile@beckett.com
914.268.0533

ASIA OFFICE
Dongwoon Lee - Asia/Pacific Sales Manager, Seoul, Korea
dongwoonl@beckett.com
Cell: +82.10.6826.6868

GRADING CUSTOMER SERVICE:
972-448-9188 or grading@beckett.com

OPERATIONS
Alberto Chavez - Sr. Logistics & Facilities Manager

EDITORIAL, PRODUCTION & SALES OFFICE
4635 McEwen Road,
Dallas TX 75244
972.991.6657
www.beckett.com

CUSTOMER SERVICE
Beckett Media, LLC
4635 Mc Ewen Road.
Dallas, TX 75244
Subscriptions, Address Changes, Renewals, Missing or Damaged Copies
866.287.9383 · 239.653.0225

FOREIGN INQUIRES
subscriptions@beckett.com
Back Issues: www.beckettmedia.com

BOOKS, MERCHANDISE, REPRINTS
239.280.2380
Dealer Sales & Production
dealers@beckett.com

BECKETT MEDIA, LLC
Sandeep Dua: President
Kevin Isaacson: Chief Operating Officer

COVER IMAGE: GETTY IMAGES

CONTENTS

BASEBALL CARD PRICE GUIDE - NUMBER 43

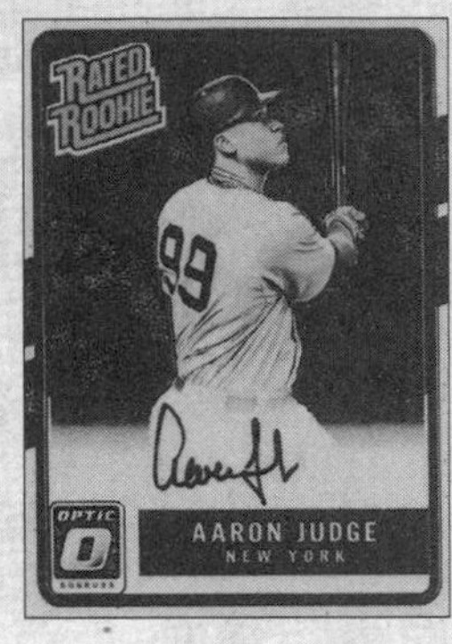

ABOUT THE AUTHOR

Based in Dallas, Beckett Media LLC is the leading publisher of sports and specialty market collectible products in the U.S. Beckett operates Beckett.com and is the premier publisher of monthly sports and entertainment collectibles magazines.

The growth of Beckett Media's sports magazines, ***Beckett Baseball, Beckett Sports Card Monthly, Beckett Basketball, Beckett Football, Beckett Hockey*** and ***Beckett Vintage Collector***, is another indication of the unprecedented popularity of sports cards. Founded in 1984 by Dr. James Beckett, Beckett sports magazines contain the most extensive and accepted Price Guide, collectible superstar covers, colorful feature articles, the Hot List, tips for beginners, information on errors and varieties, autograph collecting tips and profiles of the sport's hottest stars. Published 12 times a year, ***Beckett Baseball*** is the hobby's largest baseball periodical.

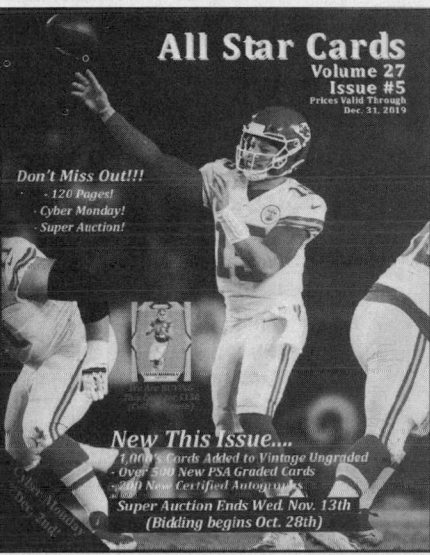

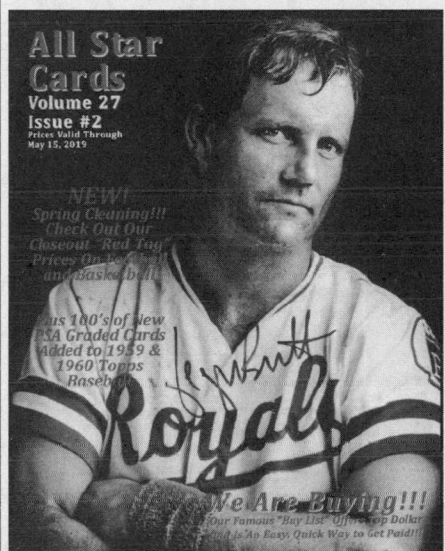

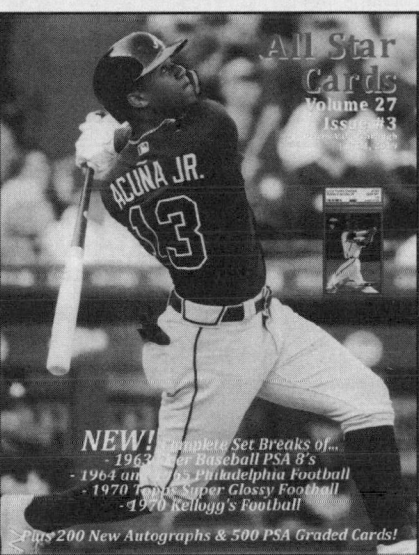

HOW TO USE & CONDITION GUIDE

BECKETT BASEBALL CARD PRICE GUIDE - NUMBER 43

Every year, this book gets better and better. This edition has been enhanced from the previous volume with new releases, updated prices and additions to older listings. This must-have reference book is filled with extensive checklists and prices for the most important and popularly traded baseball card sets, including all of the flagship Donruss, Fleer, Panini, Topps and Upper Deck brands as well as all of the newly released products from the last several years.

Unfortunately, space restrictions don't allow us to run checklists and pricing for every set cataloged in our database. So what's not listed in the Beckett Baseball Card Price Guide? Many of the ancillary brands released over the last decade that never gained a strong foothold in the hobby, brands from defunct manufacturers such as Collector's Edge, Pacific and Pinnacle, stadium giveaway sets, regional teams sets, and obscure vintage releases, among others. Collectors interested in checklists and pricing for cards not listed in this guide should reference the Online Price Guide on Beckett.com or the Beckett Almanac of Baseball Cards & Collectibles. Both of these sources are more complete representations of our immense baseball card database.

The Beckett Baseball Card Price Guide has been successful where other attempts have failed because it is complete, current, and valid. The prices were added to the card lists just prior to printing and reflect not the author's opinions or desires, but the going retail prices for each card based on the marketplace – sports memorabilia conventions and shows, sports card shops, online trading, auction results and other firsthand reports of realized prices.

What is the best price guide available on the market today? Of course sellers will prefer the price guide with the highest prices, while buyers will naturally prefer the one with the lowest prices. Accuracy, however, is the true test. Compared to other price guides, the Beckett Baseball Card Price Guide may not always have the highest or lowest values, but the accuracy of both our checklists and pricing – produced with the utmost integrity – has made it the most widely used reference book in the industry.

To facilitate your use of this book, please read the complete introductory section before going to the pricing pages, paying special attention to the section on grading and card conditions, as the condition of the card greatly affects its value. We hope you find the book both interesting and useful in your collecting pursuits.

HOW TO COLLECT

Each collection is personal and reflects the individuality of its owner. There are no set rules on how to collect cards. Since card collecting is a hobby or leisure pastime, what you collect, how much you collect, and how much time and money you spend collecting are entirely up to you. The funds you have available for collecting and your own personal taste should determine how you collect.

It is impossible to collect every card ever produced. Therefore, beginners as well as intermediate and advanced collectors usually specialize in some way. One of the reasons this hobby is popular is that individual collectors can define and tailor their collecting methods to match their own tastes.

Many collectors select complete sets from particular years, acquire only certain players, some collectors are only interested in the first cards or Rookie Cards of certain players, and others collect cards by team.

Remember, this is a hobby, so pick a style of collecting that appeals to you.

GLOSSARY/ LEGEND

Our glossary defines terms most frequently used in the card collecting hobby. Many of these terms are common to other types of sports memorabilia collecting. Some terms may have several meanings depending on the use and context.

AU – Certified autograph.

AS – All-Star card. A card portraying an All-Star Player that says "All-Star" on its face.
ATG – All-Time Great card.

BRICK – A group of 50 or more cards having common characteristics that is intended to be bought, sold or traded as a unit.

CABINET CARD – Popular and highly valuable photographs on thick card stock produced in the 19th and early 20th century.

CHECKLIST – A list of the cards contained in a particular set. The list is always in numerical order if the cards are numbered. Some unnumbered sets are artificially numbered in

Continued on page 8

HOW TO USE & CONDITION GUIDE

UNDERSTANDING CARD VALUES

Why are some cards more valuable than others? Obviously, the economic laws of supply and demand are applicable to card collecting just as they are to any other field where a commodity is bought, sold or traded in a free, unregulated market.

Supply (the number of cards available on the market) is less than the total number of cards originally produced since attrition diminishes that original quantity. Each year a percentage of cards is typically thrown away, destroyed or otherwise lost to collectors. This percentage is much, much smaller today than it was in the past because more and more people have become increasingly aware of the value of their cards.

For those who collect only Mint condition cards, the supply of older cards can be quite small indeed. Until recently, collectors were not so conscious of the need to preserve the condition of their cards. For this reason, it is difficult to know exactly how many 1953 Topps are currently available, Mint or otherwise. It is generally accepted that there are fewer 1953 Topps available than 1963, 1973 or 1983 Topps cards. If demand were equal for each of these sets, the law of supply and demand would increase the price for the least available sets. Demand, however, is never equal for all sets, so price correlations can be complicated. The demand for a card is influenced by many factors. These include the age of the card, the number of cards printed, the player(s) portrayed on the card, the attractiveness and popularity of the set and the physical condition of the card.

In general, the older the card, the fewer the number of the cards printed, the more famous, popular and talented the player, the more attractive and popular the set, and the better the condition of the card, the higher the value of the card will be. There are exceptions to all but one of these factors: the condition of the card. Given two cards similar in all respects except condition, the one in the best condition will always be valued higher.

While those guidelines help to establish the value of a card, the countless exceptions and peculiarities make any simple, direct mathematical formula to determine card values impossible.

WHAT THE COLUMNS MEAN

The LO and HI columns reflect a range of current retail selling prices and are listed in U.S. dollars. The HI column represents the typical full retail selling price while the LO column represents the lowest price one could expect to find through extensive shopping. Both columns represent the same condition for the card listed. Keep in mind that market conditions can change quickly up and down based on extreme levels of demand.

PRICING PREMIUMS

Some cards can trade at premium price levels compared to values listed in this issue. Those include but are not limited to: cards of players who became hot since this book went to press, regional stars or fan favorites in high demand locally and memorabilia cards with unusually dramatic swatches or patches.

ONLY A REFERENCE

The data and pricing information contained within this publication is intended for reference only and is not to be used as an endorsement of any specific product(s) or as a recommendation to buy or sell any product(s). Beckett's goal is to provide the most accurate and verifiable information in the industry. However, Beckett cannot guarantee the accuracy of all data published. Typographical errors occasionally occur and unverifiable information may reach print from time to time. Buyers and sellers of sports collectibles should be aware of this and handle their personal transactions at their own risk. If you discover an error or misprint in this book, please notify us via email at baseballmag@beckett.com.

Continued from page 6

alphabetical order or by team.

CL – Checklist card. A card that lists, in order, the cards and players in the set or series.

CO – Coach.

COMMON CARD – The typical card of any set. It has no premium value accruing from the subject matter, numerical scarcity, popular demand, or anomaly.

CONVENTION – A gathering of dealers and collectors at a single location with the purpose of buying, selling and trading sports memorabilia items. Conventions are open to the public and sometimes feature autograph guests, door prizes, contests, or seminars. They are frequently referred to as "shows."

COR – Corrected.

DEALER – A person who engages in the buying, selling and trading of sports collectibles or supplies. A dealer may also be a collector, but as a dealer, his main goal it to earn a profit.

DIE-CUT – A card with part of its stock partially cut, allowing one or more parts to be folded or removed. After removal or appropriate folding, the remaining part of the card can frequently be made to stand up.

DK – Diamond King.

DP – Draft pick or double print. A double print is a card that was printed in double the quantity compared to other cards in the same series.

DUFEX- A method of manufacturing technology patented by Pinnacle Brands, Inc. It involves refractive quality to a card with a foil coating.

HOW TO USE & CONDITION GUIDE

MULTIPLIERS

Some parallel sets and lightly traded insert sets are listed with multipliers to provide values of unlisted cards. Multiplier ranges (i.e. 10X to 20X HI) apply only to the HI column. Example: If basic-issue card A or the insert card in question lists for 20 to 50 cents, and the multiplier is "20X to 40X HI", then the parallel version of card A or the insert card in question is valued at $10 to $20. Please note that the term "basic card" used in the Price Guide refers to a player's standard regular-issue card. A "basic card" cannot be an insert or parallel card.

STATED ODDS AND PRINT RUNS

Odds of pulling insert cards are often listed as a ratio (1:12 – one in 12 packs). If the odds vary by pack type, they are generally listed separately. Stated print runs are also included in the set header lines or after the player's name for many serial numbered cards or for sets which the manufacturer has chosen to announce print runs. Stated odds and print runs are provided by the manufacturer based on the entire print run and should be considered very close estimates and not exact figures. The data provided in this book has been verified by Beckett to the best of our ability. Neither the stated odds nor print runs should be viewed as a guarantee by either Beckett or the manufacturer.

CONDITION GUIDE

Much of the value of your card is dependent on the condition or "grade" of your card. Prices in this issue reflect the highest raw condition (i.e. not professionally graded by a third party) of the card most commonly found at shows, shops, on the internet and right out of the pack for brand new releases. This generally means Near Mint-Mint condition for modern era cards. Use the chart below as a guide to estimate the value of your cards in a variety of condition using the prices found in this Annual. A complete condition guide follows.

The most widely used grades are defined on page 14. Obviously, many cards will not perfectly fit one of the definitions. Therefore, categories between the major grades known as in-between grades are used, such as Good to Very Good (G-Vg), Very Good to Excellent (VgEx), and Excellent-Mint to Near Mint (Ex-Mt-NrMt). Such grades indicate a card with all qualities of the lower category but with at least a few qualities of the higher category.

CONDITION CHART

	Pre-1930	1930-47	1948-59	1960-80	1981-89	1990-Present
MT	N/A	300+%	300+%	250+%	100-150%	100-125%
NRMT-MT	300+%	150-300%	150-250%	125-200%	100%	100%
NRMT	150-300%	150%	100%	100%	30-50%	30-50%
EX-MT	100%	100%	50-75%	40-60%	25-40%	20-30%
EX	50-75%	50-75%	30-50%	20-40%	15-25%	10-20%
VG	30-50%	30-50%	15-30%	10-20%	5-15%	5-10%
G/F/P	10-30%	10-30%	5-15%	5-10%	5%	5%

ERR – Error card. A card with erroneous information, spelling or depiction on either side of the card. Most errors are not corrected by the manufacturer.

EXCH – Exchange.

HIGH NUMBER – The cards in the last series of a set in a year in which such high-numbered cards were printed or distributed in significantly less amounts than the lower numbered cards. Not all years have high numbers in terms of this definition.

HOF – Hall of Fame or a card that pictures of Hall of Famer (HOFer).

HOR – Horizonal pose on a card as opposed to the standart vertical orientation found on most cards.

IA – In action.

INSERT – A card or any other sports collectible contained and sold in the same package along with a card or cards from a major set. An insert card may or may not be numbered in the same sequence as the major set. Many times the inserts are randomly inserted in packs.

ISSUE – Synonymous with set, but usually used in conjunction with a manufacturer, e.g. a Topps issue.

JSY – Jersey.

MAJOR SET – A set produced by a national manufacturer of cards.

MINI – A small card; for example a 1975 Topps card of identical desing but smaller dimensions than the regular 1975 Topps issue.

MULTI-PLAYER CARD – A single card depicting two or more players.

HOW TO USE & CONDITION GUIDE

Unopened packs, boxes and factory-collated sets are considered mint in their unknown (and presumed perfect) state. Once opened, however, each card can be graded (and valued) in its own right by taking into account any defects that may be present in spite of the fact that the card has never been handled.

GENERAL CARD FLAWS

Centering

Current centering terminology uses numbers representing the percentage of border on either side of the main design. Obviously, centering is diminished in importance for borderless cards.

SLIGHTLY OFF-CENTER (60/40)

A slightly off-center card is one that upon close inspection is found to have one border bigger than the opposite border. This degree once was offensive to only purists, but now some hobbyists try to avoid cards that are anything other than perfectly centered.

OFF-CENTER (70/30)

An off-center card has one border that is noticeably more than twice as wide as the opposite border.

BADLY OFF-CENTER (80/20 OR WORSE)

A badly off-center card has virtually no border on one side of the card.

MISCUT

A miscut card actually shows part of the adjacent card in its larger border and consequently a corresponding amount of its card is cut off.

CORNER WEAR

Corner wear is the most scrutinized grading criteria in the hobby.

CORNER WITH A SLIGHT TOUCH OF WEAR

The corner still is sharp, but there is a slight touch of wear showing. On a dark-bordered card, this shows as a dot of white.

FUZZY CORNER

The corner still comes to a point, but the point has just begun to fray. A slightly "dinged" corner is considered the same as a fuzzy corner.

SLIGHTLY ROUNDED CORNER

The fraying of the corner has increased to where there is only a hint of a point. Mild layering may be evident. A "dinged" corner is considered the same as a slightly rounded corner.

ROUNDED CORNER

The point is completely gone. Some layering is noticeable.

BADLY ROUNDED CORNER

The corner is completely round and rough. Severe layering is evident.

Creases

A third common defect is the crease. The degree of creasing in a card is difficult to show in a drawing or picture. On giving the specific condition of an expensive card for sale, the seller should note any creases additionally. Creases can be categorized as to severity according to the following scale.

LIGHT CREASE

A light crease is a crease that is barely noticeable upon close inspection. In fact, when cards are in plastic sheets or holders, a light crease may not be seen (until the card is taken out of the holder). A light crease on the front is much more serious than a light crease on the card back only.

MEDIUM CREASE

A medium crease is noticeable when held and studied at arm's length by the naked eye, but does not overly detract from the appearance of the card. It is an obvious crease, but not one that breaks the picture surface of the card.

HEAVY CREASE

A heavy crease is one that has torn or broken through the card's surface, e.g., puts a tear in the photo surface.

Alterations

DECEPTIVE TRIMMING

This occurs when someone alters the card in order to shave off edge wear, to improve the sharpness of the corners, or to improve centering — obviously their objective is to falsely increase the perceived value of the card to an unsuspecting buyer. The shrinkage usually is

NNO – Unnumbered.

NNOF – No Name On Front.

PACKS – A means by which cards are issued in terms of pack type (wax, cello, foil, rack, etc.) and channel of distribution (hobby, retail, etc.).

PARALLEL – A card that is similar in design to its counterpart from a basic set, but offers a distinguishing quality.

PREMIUM – A card that is obtained in conjunction with, or redemption for, another card or product. The premium is not packaged in the same unit as the primary item.

(RC) – Rookie Logo Card. These cards feature the official MLBPA Rookie Logo. However, the player depicted on the card has already had a Rookie Card(s) issued in a previous year.

RC – Rookie Card.

REDEMPTION – A program established by multiple card manufacturers that allows collectors to mail in a special card (usually a random insert) in return for special cards, sets, or other prizes not available through conventional channels.

REFRACTOR – A card that features a design element that enhances its color or appearance by deflecting light.

ROY – Rookie of the Year.

SERIES – The entire set of cards issued by a particular manufacturer in a particular year. Within a particular set, a series can refer to a group of consecutively numbered cards printed at the same time.

HOW TO USE & CONDITION GUIDE

evident only if the trimmed card is compared to an adjacent full-sized card or if the trimmed card is itself measured.

OBVIOUS TRIMMING

Trimming is noticeable. It is usually performed by non-collectors who give no thought to the present or future value of their cards.

DECEPTIVELY RETOUCHED BORDERS

This occurs when the borders (especially on those cards with dark borders) are touched up on the edges and corners with magic marker or crayons of appropriate color in order to make the card appear to be Mint.

Miscellaneous Card Flaws

The following are common minor flaws that, depending on severity, lower a card's condition by one to four grades and often render it no better than Excellent-Mint: bubbles (lumps in surface), gum and wax stains, diamond cutting (slanted borders), notching, off-centered backs, paper wrinkles, scratched-off cartoons or puzzles on back, rubber band marks, scratches, surface impressions and warping.

The following are common serious flaws that, depending on severity, lower a card's condition at least four grades and often render it no better than Good: chemical or sun fading, erasure marks, mildew, miscutting (severe off-centering), holes, bleached or retouched borders, tape marks, tears, trimming, water or coffee stains and writing.

Grades

MINT (MT)

A card with no flaws or wear. The card has four perfect corners, 55/45 or better centering from top to bottom and from left to right, original gloss, smooth edges and original color borders. A Mint card does not have print spots, color or focus imperfections.

NEAR MINT-MINT (NRMT-MT)

A card with one minor flaw. Any one of the following would lower a Mint card to Near Mint-Mint: one corner with a slight touch of wear, barely noticeable print spots, color or focus imperfections. The card must have 60/40 or better centering in both directions, original gloss, smooth edges and original color border.

NEAR MINT (NRMT)

A card with one minor flaw. Any one of the following would lower a Mint card to Near Mint: one fuzzy corner or two to four corners with slight touches of wear, 70/30 to 60/40 centering, slightly rough edges, minor print spots, color or focus imperfections. The card must have original gloss and original color borders.

EXCELLENT-MINT (EXMT)

A card with two or three fuzzy, but not rounded, corners and centering no worse than 80/20. The card may have no more than two of the following: slightly rough edges, slightly discolored borders, minor print spots, color or focus imperfections. The card must have original gloss.

EXCELLENT (EX)

A card with four fuzzy but definitely not rounded corners and centering no worse than 70/30. The card may have a small amount of original gloss lost, rough edges, slightly discolored borders and minor print spots, color or focus imperfections.

VERY GOOD (VG)

A card that has been handled but not abused: slightly rounded corners with slight layering, slight notching on edges, a significant amount of gloss lost from the surface but no scuffing and moderate discoloration of borders. The card may have a few light creases.

GOOD (G), FAIR (F), POOR (P)

A well-worn, mishandled or abused card: badly rounded and layered corners, scuffing, most or all original gloss missing, seriously discolored borders, moderate or heavy creases, and one or more serious flaws. The grade of Good, Fair or Poor depends on the severity of wear and flaws. Good, Fair and Poor cards generally are used only as fillers.

SET – One of each of the entire run of cards of the same type produced by a particular manufacturer during a single year.

SKIP-NUMBERED – A set that has many unissued card numbers between the lowest and highest number in the set. A major set in which onlya few numbers were not printed is not considered to be skip-numbered.

SP – Single or Short Print. A short print is a card that was printed in less quantity compared to the other cards in the same series.

TC – Team card.

TP – Triple print. A card that was printed in triple the quantity compared to the other cards in the same series.

UER – Uncorrected error.

UNI – Uniform.

VAR – Variation card. One of two or more cards from the same series, with the same card number, that differ from one and other in some way. This sometimes occurs when the manufacture notices an error in one or more of the cards, corrects the mistake, and then resumes the printing process. In some cases, on of the variations may be relatively scarce.

XRC – Extended Rookie Card.

* – Used to denote an announced print run.

Note: Nearly all other abbreviations signify various subsets (i.e. B, G and S in 1996 Finest are short for Bronze, Gold and Silver. WS in the 1960s and 1970s Topps sets is short for World Series as examples).

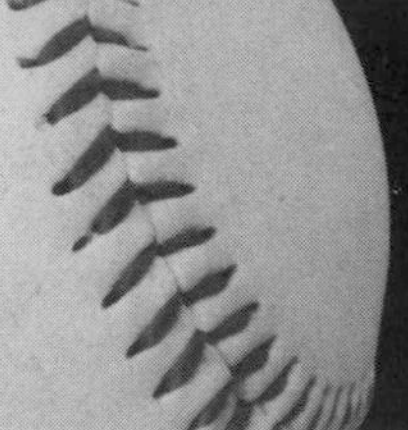

2017 Absolute
INSERTED IN '17 CHRONICLES PACKS
STATED PRINT RUN 99 SER.#'d SETS
*BLUE: .25X TO .6X BASIC
*SPEC.RED/49: .4X TO 1X BASIC
*SPEC.GRN/25: .6X TO 1.5X BASIC
1 Aaron Judge 10.00 25.00
2 Cody Bellinger 12.00 30.00
3 Yoan Moncada 2.50 6.00
4 Andrew Benintendi 2.50 6.00
5 Christian Arroyo 1.25 3.00
6 Dansby Swanson 2.00 5.00
7 Carson Fulmer .75 2.00
8 Ryon Healy 1.00 2.50
9 Mitch Haniger 1.25 3.00
10 Antonio Senzatela .75 2.00
11 Ian Happ 1.50 4.00
12 Trey Mancini 1.50 4.00
13 Jordan Montgomery 1.25 3.00
14 Bradley Zimmer 1.00 2.50
15 Hunter Renfroe 1.00 2.50
16 Jorge Bonifacio .75 2.00
17 Lewis Brinson 1.25 3.00
18 Jacoby Jones 1.00 2.50
19 Alex Bregman 3.00 8.00
20 Josh Bell 2.00 5.00
21 Derek Fisher 1.00 2.50
22 Austin Slater .75 2.00
23 Paul DeJong 2.50 6.00
24 Franklin Barreto .75 2.00
25 Sam Travis .75 2.00

2017 Absolute Rookie Premiere Materials Autographs
INSERTED IN '17 CHRONICLES PACKS
PRINT RUNS B/WN 20-99 COPIES PER
EXCHANGE DEADLINE 5/22/2019
1 Aaron Judge/99 100.00 250.00
2 Cody Bellinger/49 60.00 150.00
3 Andrew Benintendi/99 20.00 50.00
4 Dansby Swanson/20 12.00 30.00
5 Alex Bregman/20 20.00 50.00
6 Franklin Barreto/99 4.00 10.00
7 Yoan Moncada/20
8 Ian Happ/99 8.00 20.00
9 Hunter Renfroe/99 5.00 12.00
10 Mitch Haniger/99 6.00 15.00
11 Josh Bell/99 8.00 20.00
12 Lewis Brinson/99 6.00 15.00
13 Sam Travis/99 4.00 10.00
14 Ryon Healy/99 5.00 12.00
15 Bradley Zimmer/99 8.00 20.00
16 Antonio Senzatela/99 4.00 10.00
17 Jorge Bonifacio/99 4.00 10.00
18 Trey Mancini/99 6.00 15.00
19 Jordan Montgomery/99 4.00 10.00
20 Dinelson Lamet/99 4.00 10.00
21 Derek Fisher/99 8.00 20.00
22 Magneuris Sierra/99 6.00 15.00
23 Francis Martes/99 4.00 10.00
24 Orlando Arcia/99 6.00 15.00
25 Jacoby Jones/99 5.00 12.00

2017 Absolute Tools of the Trade Materials Double
INSERTED IN '17 CHRONICLES PACKS
PRINT RUNS B/WN 25-99 COPIES PER
*DBL PRIME/25: .5X TO 1.2X BASIC
1 Aaron Judge/99 25.00 60.00
2 Cody Bellinger/99 8.00 20.00
3 Yoan Moncada/99 5.00 12.00
4 Dansby Swanson/99 4.00 10.00
5 Alex Bregman/99 4.00 10.00
6 Lewis Brinson/99 3.00 8.00
7 Mickey Mantle/25 30.00 80.00
8 Bradley Zimmer/99 2.50 6.00
9 Hunter Renfroe/99 2.50 6.00
10 Franklin Barreto/99 2.00 5.00
11 Ian Happ/99 4.00 10.00
12 Albert Pujols/99 4.00 10.00
13 Sam Travis/99 2.00 5.00
14 Mike Trout/25 20.00 50.00
15 Bryce Harper/25 6.00 15.00
16 Kris Bryant/25 5.00 12.00
17 Buster Posey/49 4.00 10.00
18 Tony Gwynn/25 12.00 30.00
19 Rickey Henderson/25 15.00 40.00
20 Alex Rodriguez/99 4.00 10.00
21 Nomar Garciaparra/99 2.50 6.00
22 Miguel Sano/99 2.50 6.00
23 David Ortiz/49 3.00 8.00
24 Manny Machado/99 3.00 8.00
25 Joey Votto/99 3.00 8.00

2017 Absolute Tools of the Trade Materials Quad
INSERTED IN '17 CHRONICLES PACKS
PRINT RUNS B/WN 10-25 COPIES PER
NO PRICING ON QTY 10
2 Cody Bellinger/25 12.00 30.00
3 Aaron Judge/25 30.00 80.00
5 Cal Ripken/25 12.00 30.00

2017 Absolute Tools of the Trade Materials Triple
INSERTED IN '17 CHRONICLES PACKS
PRINT RUNS B/WN 25-99 COPIES PER
1 Aaron Judge/99 25.00 60.00
2 Cody Bellinger/99 8.00 20.00
3 Dansby Swanson/99 4.00 10.00
4 Alex Bregman/99 4.00 10.00
5 Yoan Moncada/99 5.00 12.00
6 Amed Rosario/99 3.00 8.00
7 Mickey Mantle/25 30.00 80.00
8 Alex Reyes/99 2.50 6.00
9 David Dahl/99 2.50 6.00
10 Don Mattingly/25 12.00 30.00
11 Salvador Perez/99 5.00 12.00
12 Francisco Lindor/99 3.00 8.00
13 Ken Griffey Jr./49 12.00 30.00
14 Lewis Brinson/99 3.00 8.00
15 Kirby Puckett/25 50.00 120.00

2019 Absolute Rookie Autographs
RANDOM INSERTS IN PACKS
EXCHANGE DEADLINE 2/21/2021
*GOLD: .5X TO 1.2X
*RED: .6X TO 1.5X
*HOLO SLVR: .75X TO 2X
1 Adam Kolarek 2.50 6.00
2 Pablo Lopez 2.50 6.00
3 Dean Deetz 2.50 6.00
4 Thomas Pannone 4.00 10.00
5 Nick Martini 2.50 6.00
6 Isaac Galloway 2.50 6.00
7 Trevor Richards 2.50 6.00
8 Scott Barlow 2.50 6.00
9 Ryan Meisinger 2.50 6.00
10 Dawel Lugo 4.00 10.00
11 Michael Perez 2.50 6.00
12 Rosell Herrera 2.50 6.00
13 DJ Stewart 3.00 8.00
14 Austin Dean 2.50 6.00
15 Meibrys Viloria 2.50 6.00
16 Gabriel Guerrero 2.50 6.00
17 Nick Ciuffo 2.50 6.00
18 Austin Wynns 2.50 6.00
19 Richie Martin 2.50 6.00
20 C.D. Pelham 2.50 6.00
21 Harold Castro 3.00 8.00
22 James Norwood 2.50 6.00
23 Tanner Rainey 2.50 6.00
24 Heath Fillmyer 5.00 12.00
25 Jalen Beeks 2.50 6.00
26 Brett Kennedy 2.50 6.00
27 Ty Buttrey 4.00 10.00
28 Yency Almonte 2.50 6.00
29 Connor Sadzeck 2.50 6.00
30 Austin Voth 2.50 6.00
31 Edmundo Sosa 3.00 8.00
32 Jefry Rodriguez 2.50 6.00
33 Chad Sobotka 2.50 6.00
34 Victor Reyes 2.50 6.00
35 Duane Underwood 2.50 6.00
36 Justin Williams 2.50 6.00
37 Abiatal Avelino 2.50 6.00
38 Pablo Reyes 2.50 6.00
39 Andrew Velazquez 2.50 6.00
40 Eric Haase 2.50 6.00
41 Daniel Ponce de Leon 4.00 10.00
42 Josh Naylor 3.00 8.00
43 Steven Duggar 3.00 8.00
44 Jake Cave 3.00 8.00
45 Cionel Perez 2.50 6.00
46 Rowdy Tellez 4.00 10.00
47 Kyle Wright 4.00 10.00
48 Dakota Hudson 5.00 12.00

2019 Absolute Triple Memorabilia
RANDOM INSERTS IN PACKS
*GOLD/99: .5X TO 1.2X
*GOLD/50: .6X TO 1.5X
*GOLD/25: .75X TO 2X
*BLUE/25: .75X TO 2X
1 Vladimir Guerrero Jr. 10.00 25.00
2 Fernando Tatis Jr. 15.00 40.00
3 Eloy Jimenez 6.00 15.00
4 Kyle Tucker 3.00 8.00
5 Yusei Kikuchi 2.50 6.00
6 Michael Kopech 3.00 8.00
7 Touki Toussaint 2.00 5.00
8 Justus Sheffield 2.50 6.00
9 Pete Alonso 6.00 15.00
10 Ramon Laureano 3.00 8.00
11 Christin Stewart 2.00 5.00
12 Jeff McNeil 4.00 10.00
13 Mike Trout 12.00 30.00
14 Jose Altuve 2.00 5.00
15 Aaron Judge 6.00 15.00
16 Yasiel Puig 2.50 6.00
17 Marcell Ozuna 2.50 6.00
18 Gleyber Torres 5.00 12.00

19 Miguel Andujar 2.50 6.00
20 Victor Robles 3.00 8.00
21 Alex Rodriguez 3.00 8.00
22 Adrian Beltre 2.50 6.00
23 George Brett 5.00 12.00
24 Vladimir Guerrero 10.00 25.00
25 Don Mattingly 5.00 12.00

2020 Absolute
101-166 RANDOMLY INSERTED
101-166 PRINT RUN 149 SER.#'d SETS
EXCHANGE DEADLINE 1/8/2022
1 Bryce Harper .60 1.50
2 Alex Verdugo .30 .75
3 Adalberto Mondesi .40 1.00
4 Yogi Berra .40 1.00
5 Gerrit Cole .60 1.50
6 Andrew Benintendi .40 1.00
7 Mickey Mantle 1.25 3.00
8 Jose Berrios .30 .75
9 Ronald Acuna Jr. 1.50 4.00
10 Manny Machado .40 1.00
11 Kris Bryant .50 1.25
12 Pete Alonso 1.00 2.50
13 Anthony Rizzo .60 1.50
14 Josh Bell .30 .75
15 Stephen Strasburg .40 1.00
16 Luis Arraez .50 1.25
17 Ramon Laureano .40 1.00
18 Charlie Morton .40 1.00
19 Corey Kluber .30 .75
20 Christian Yelich .50 1.25
21 Aaron Nola .40 1.00
22 Zack Greinke .30 .75
23 Jorge Polanco .30 .75
24 Tim Anderson .40 1.00
25 Juan Soto 1.25 3.00
26 Jose Ramirez .30 .75
27 Brian Anderson .25 .60
28 Mookie Betts .75 2.00
29 Javier Baez .50 1.25
30 Marco Gonzales .25 .60
31 Ozzie Albies .40 1.00
32 Clayton Kershaw .75 2.00
33 Ketel Marte .30 .75
34 Jose Altuve .30 .75
35 Byron Buxton .30 .75
36 Jorge Soler .40 1.00
37 Mike Soroka .40 1.00
38 Trevor Story .40 1.00
39 Nolan Arenado .50 1.25
40 Jack Flaherty .30 .75
41 Joe DiMaggio .75 2.00
42 Josh Donaldson .30 .75
43 Nicholas Castellanos .40 1.00
44 Max Scherzer .40 1.00
45 Nick Senzel .40 1.00
46 Victor Robles .50 1.25
47 Walker Buehler .50 1.25
48 Trea Turner .30 .75
49 Alex Bregman .40 1.00
50 Jose Abreu .40 1.00
51 Ted Williams .75 2.00
52 Rhys Hoskins .50 1.25
53 Fernando Tatis Jr. 1.50 4.00
54 Xander Bogaerts .40 1.00
55 Gleyber Torres .75 2.00
56 Sandy Alcantara .25 .60
57 Giancarlo Stanton .40 1.00
58 Cavan Biggio .50 1.25
59 Jacob deGrom .60 1.50
60 Hyun-Jin Ryu .30 .75
61 Stan Musial .60 1.50
62 Yasmani Grandal .25 .60
63 Whit Merrifield .40 1.00
64 Anthony Rendon .40 1.00
65 Justin Verlander .40 1.00
66 Franmil Reyes .25 .60
67 Rafael Devers .50 1.25
68 Austin Meadows .30 .75
69 Will Smith .25 .60
70 Eugenio Suarez .30 .75
71 Shane Bieber .40 1.00
72 Yadier Molina .40 1.00
73 Tommy Edman .40 1.00
74 Paul Goldschmidt .40 1.00
75 Cody Bellinger .75 2.00
76 Jimmie Foxx .40 1.00
77 Buster Posey .50 1.25
78 Vladimir Guerrero Jr. .75 2.00
79 Yoan Moncada .40 1.00
80 Chris Paddack .40 1.00
81 Trey Mancini .40 1.00
82 Nelson Cruz .40 1.00
83 Keston Hiura .50 1.25
84 Eloy Jimenez .75 2.00
85 Amed Rosario .30 .75
86 Aaron Judge 1.00 2.50
87 Ken Griffey Jr. 1.50 4.00
88 Roberto Clemente 2.00 5.00
89 David Dahl .25 .60
90 Babe Ruth 1.00 2.50
91 Miguel Cabrera .40 1.00
92 Marcus Semien .25 .60
93 Freddie Freeman .50 1.25
94 Shohei Ohtani .50 1.25
95 DJ LeMahieu .40 1.00
96 Francisco Lindor .40 1.00
97 Miguel Andujar .40 1.00
98 Mike Trout 2.00 5.00
99 Joey Gallo .40 1.00
100 J.T. Realmuto .40 1.00
101 Bryan Abreu AU RC 3.00 8.00
102 Mauricio Dubon AU RC 4.00 10.00
103 Isan Diaz AU RC 8.00 20.00
104 Domingo Leyba AU RC 4.00 10.00
105 Sean Murphy AU RC 6.00 15.00
106 Kwang-Hyun Kim AU RC 20.00 50.00
107 Brock Burke AU RC 3.00 8.00
108 Adrian Morejon AU RC 3.00 8.00
109 Tony Gonsolin AU RC 10.00 25.00
110 Danny Mendick AU RC 4.00 10.00
111 Josh Rojas AU RC 3.00 8.00
112 Zac Gallen AU RC 8.00 20.00
113 Luis Robert AU RC EXCH 75.00 200.00
114 Yonathan Daza AU RC 4.00 10.00
115 Yoshitomo Tsutsugo AU RC 4.00 10.00
116 Gavin Lux AU RC 25.00 60.00
117 Jordan Yamamoto AU RC 4.00 10.00
118 Trent Grisham AU RC 10.00 25.00
119 Sheldon Neuse AU RC 4.00 10.00
120 Justin Dunn AU RC 4.00 10.00
121 Matt Thaiss AU RC 4.00 10.00
122 Logan Webb AU RC 4.00 10.00
123 Jake Fraley AU RC 4.00 10.00
124 Anthony Kay AU RC 3.00 8.00
125 Donnie Walton AU RC 8.00 20.00
126 Willi Castro AU RC 5.00 12.00
127 Jaylin Davis AU RC 5.00 12.00
128 Brendan McKay AU RC 5.00 12.00
129 Sam Hilliard AU RC 8.00 20.00
130 Deivy Grullon AU RC 3.00 8.00
131 Dustin May AU RC 15.00 40.00
132 Abraham Toro AU RC 4.00 10.00
133 Nico Hoerner AU RC 12.00 30.00
134 Joe Palumbo AU RC 3.00 8.00
135 Ronald Bolanos AU RC 5.00 12.00
136 Logan Allen AU RC 3.00 8.00
137 Michel Baez AU RC 3.00 8.00
138 Nick Solak AU RC 8.00 20.00
139 Aaron Civale AU RC 8.00 20.00
140 Jonathan Hernandez AU RC 3.00 8.00
141 Brusdar Graterol AU RC 5.00 12.00
142 Rico Garcia AU RC 5.00 12.00
143 Shogo Akiyama AU RC 15.00 40.00
144 T.J. Zeuch AU RC 3.00 8.00
145 Dylan Cease AU RC 6.00 15.00
146 Kyle Lewis AU RC 25.00 60.00
147 Randy Arozarena AU RC 25.00 60.00
148 Bobby Bradley AU RC 4.00 10.00
149 Zack Collins AU RC 4.00 10.00
150 Aristides Aquino AU RC 6.00 15.00
151 Yu Chang AU RC 12.00 30.00
152 Yordan Alvarez AU RC 15.00 40.00
153 Michael King AU RC 10.00 25.00
154 Patrick Sandoval AU RC 5.00 12.00
155 Tres Barrera AU RC 6.00 15.00
156 Jake Rogers AU RC 6.00 15.00
157 Adbert Alzolay AU RC 6.00 15.00
158 Edwin Rios AU RC 12.00 30.00
159 Tyrone Taylor AU RC 3.00 8.00
160 A.J. Puk AU RC 6.00 15.00
161 Jesus Luzardo AU RC 6.00 15.00
162 Lewis Thorpe AU RC 3.00 8.00
163 Shun Yamaguchi AU RC 6.00 15.00
164 Travis Demeritte AU RC 4.00 10.00
165 Andres Munoz AU RC 6.00 15.00
166 Bo Bichette AU RC 40.00 100.00

2020 Absolute Black
*BLACK/125: .5X TO 1.2X BASIC
RANDOM INSERTS IN PACKS
STATED PRINT RUN 125 SER.#'d SETS
EXCHANGE DEADLINE 1/8/22

2020 Absolute Black Gold
*BLK GOLD/25: .8X TO 2X BASIC
RANDOM INSERTS IN PACKS
STATED PRINT RUN 25 SER.#'d SETS
EXCHANGE DEADLINE 1/8/22
103 Isan Diaz AU 20.00 50.00
106 Kwang-Hyun Kim AU 50.00 120.00
109 Tony Gonsolin AU 20.00 50.00
113 Luis Robert AU EXCH 150.00 400.00
126 Willi Castro AU 15.00 40.00
128 Brendan McKay AU 25.00 60.00
133 Nico Hoerner AU 40.00 100.00
139 Aaron Civale AU 20.00 50.00
146 Kyle Lewis AU 40.00 100.00
150 Aristides Aquino AU 25.00 60.00
161 Jesus Luzardo AU 25.00 60.00
166 Bo Bichette AU 75.00 200.00

2020 Absolute Blue
*BLUE/99: .5X TO 1.2X BASIC
RANDOM INSERTS IN PACKS
STATED PRINT RUN 99 SER.#'d SETS
EXCHANGE DEADLINE 1/8/22

2020 Absolute Light Blue
*LGHT BLUE/50: .5X TO 1.2X BASIC
*LGHT BLUE/19: .8X TO 2X BASIC
RANDOM INSERTS IN PACKS
PRINT RUNS B/WN 19-50 COPIES PER
EXCHANGE DEADLINE 1/8/22
113 Luis Robert AU/50 EXCH 100.00 250.00
126 Willi Castro AU/50 10.00 25.00
128 Brendan McKay AU/50 12.00 30.00
150 Aristides Aquino AU/50 15.00 40.00
161 Jesus Luzardo AU/50 15.00 40.00
166 Bo Bichette AU/50 50.00 120.00

2020 Absolute Pink
*PINK/75: .5X TO 1.2X BASIC
RANDOM INSERTS IN PACKS
STATED PRINT RUN 99 SER.#'d SETS
EXCHANGE DEADLINE 1/8/22
113 Luis Robert AU EXCH 100.00 250.00
150 Aristides Aquino AU 15.00 40.00
161 Jesus Luzardo AU 15.00 40.00

2020 Absolute 500 HR Club Bats
RANDOM INSERTS IN PACKS
1 Eddie Mathews 30.00 80.00
2 Rafael Palmeiro
3 Jimmie Foxx
4 Mark McGwire 20.00 50.00
6 Babe Ruth 150.00 400.00
8 Alex Rodriguez 20.00 50.00
9 Mike Schmidt 12.00 30.00

2020 Absolute Absolute Heroes
RANDOM INSERTS IN PACKS
*SP BLUE: .6X TO 1.5X BASIC
*SP SILVER/99: .8X TO 2X BASIC
*SP PURPLE/25: 1.2X TO 3X BASIC
1 Mike Trout 3.00 8.00
2 Ronald Acuna Jr. 2.50 6.00
3 Pete Alonso 1.50 4.00
4 Vladimir Guerrero Jr. 1.25 3.00
5 Cody Bellinger 1.25 3.00
6 Juan Soto 2.00 5.00
7 Christian Yelich .75 2.00
8 Mookie Betts 1.25 3.00
9 Aaron Judge 1.50 4.00
10 Fernando Tatis Jr. 2.50 6.00
11 Nolan Arenado .75 2.00
12 Rafael Devers .75 2.00
13 Francisco Lindor .60 1.50
14 Javier Baez .75 2.00
15 Max Scherzer .60 1.50

2020 Absolute Absolute Heroes Material Signatures
RANDOM INSERTS IN PACKS
PRINT RUNS B/WN 10-99 COPIES PER
NO PRICING ON QTY 15 OR LESS
EXCHANGE DEADLINE 1/8/22
1 Darryl Strawberry/25 15.00 40.00
4 Josh Bell/49 10.00 25.00
6 Andy Pettitte/49 10.00 25.00
7 Cliff Lee/25 8.00 20.00
9 Cavan Biggio/99 12.00 30.00
10 Chris Paddack/99 5.00 12.00
11 Dale Murphy/25 20.00 50.00
16 Juan Soto/99 EXCH 30.00 80.00
17 Paul Molitor/25 15.00 40.00
21 Keston Hiura/99 10.00 25.00
23 Ronald Acuna Jr./25 50.00 120.00
25 Michael Chavis/99 8.00 20.00
29 Fergie Jenkins/49 10.00 25.00
30 Eloy Jimenez/49 EXCH 20.00 50.00
31 Chris Sale/25 15.00 40.00
34 Adam Haseley/99 5.00 12.00
35 Bert Blyleven/25 10.00 25.00
37 Ketel Marte/49 15.00 40.00
40 Adrian Beltre/25 20.00 50.00

2020 Absolute Absolute Heroes Material Signatures Spectrum Purple
*PURPLE/25: .6X TO 1.5X p/r 49-99
RANDOM INSERTS IN PACKS
PRINT RUNS B/WN 5-25 COPIES PER
NO PRICING ON QTY 15 OR LESS
3 Paul Konerko/25 12.00 30.00
14 Goose Gossage/25 6.00 15.00
21 Keston Hiura/25 40.00 100.00
24 Pete Alonso/25 EXCH 50.00 120.00
25 Michael Chavis/25 25.00 60.00

2020 Absolute Absolute Heroes Materials
RANDOM INSERTS IN PACKS
PRINT RUNS B/WN 10-199 COPIES PER
NO PRICING ON QTY 10 OR LESS
1 Barry Larkin/99 6.00 15.00
2 Cal Ripken/99 10.00 25.00
3 Frank Thomas/99 6.00 15.00
4 George Brett/25 20.00 50.00
5 Reggie Jackson/25 6.00 15.00
6 Billy Martin/49 8.00 20.00
7 Robin Yount/99 3.00 8.00
8 Tom Seaver/49 3.00 8.00
9 Mike Trout/49 25.00 60.00
10 Ted Williams/25 20.00 50.00
11 Aaron Judge/199 6.00 15.00
12 Joe DiMaggio/10
13 Ken Griffey Jr./99 8.00 20.00
14 Ichiro/49 6.00 15.00
15 Ron Santo/49 10.00 25.00
16 Roberto Clemente/10
17 Randy Johnson/49 5.00 12.00
18 Tony Gwynn/49 10.00 25.00
19 Greg Maddux/49 5.00 12.00
20 Chipper Jones/49 8.00 20.00

2020 Absolute Absolute Heroes Materials Spectrum Purple
*PURPLE/25: .6X TO 1.5X p/r 99-199
*PURPLE/25: .5X TO 1.2X p/r 49
RANDOM INSERTS IN PACKS
STATED PRINT RUN 25 SER.#'d SETS
2 Cal Ripken/25 30.00 80.00
13 Ken Griffey Jr./25 20.00 50.00

2020 Absolute Absolute Heroes Materials Spectrum Red
RANDOM INSERTS IN PACKS
PRINT RUNS B/WN 5-49 COPIES PER
NO PRICING ON QTY 15 OR LESS
13 Ken Griffey Jr./49 12.00 30.00
14 Ichiro/25 15.00 40.00
15 Ron Santo/25 15.00 40.00
17 Randy Johnson/25 10.00 25.00

2020 Absolute Absolute Ink
RANDOM INSERTS IN PACKS
PRINT RUNS B/WN 10-199 COPIES PER
EXCHANGE DEADLINE 1/8/22
*PURPLE/25: .6X TO 1.5X p/r 49-99
*PURPLE/25: .4X TO 1X p/r 25
1 Mike Soroka/99 12.00 30.00
2 Jordan Hicks/99 4.00 10.00
3 Nathaniel Lowe/99 3.00 8.00
4 Miguel Tejada/25 5.00 12.00
5 Nomar Mazara/99 3.00 8.00
6 Josh Donaldson/25 6.00 15.00
7 Chris Paddack/99 5.00 12.00
8 Alex Verdugo/71 12.00 30.00
9 Luis Urias/99 10.00 25.00
10 Gleyber Torres/49 25.00 60.00
11 Cole Hamels/25 6.00 15.00
12 Trey Mancini/75 5.00 12.00
13 Salvador Perez/99 8.00 20.00
14 Willie Calhoun/99 3.00 8.00
16 Josh Bell/49 4.00 10.00
17 Whit Merrifield/99 5.00 12.00
18 Corey Seager/49 12.00 30.00
19 Justin Turner/99 10.00 25.00
20 Ben Zobrist/99 4.00 10.00
21 Rafael Devers/49 6.00 15.00
22 Ramon Laureano/99 5.00 12.00
23 Max Muncy/99 4.00 10.00
24 Matt Carpenter/99 8.00 20.00
25 Harold Baines/49 8.00 20.00
26 Ketel Marte/25 6.00 15.00
28 Eloy Jimenez/25 15.00 40.00
29 Bobby Bradley/99 4.00 10.00
30 Matt Thaiss/99 3.00 8.00
31 Keston Hiura/25 10.00 25.00
32 Nick Solak/99 5.00 12.00
33 Tommy Edman/99 12.00 30.00
34 Zack Collins/25 6.00 15.00
35 A.J. Puk/99 6.00 15.00
36 Kwang-Hyun Kim/49 10.00 25.00
37 Shun Yamaguchi/99 4.00 10.00
38 Yoshitomo Tsutsugo/49 12.00 30.00
39 Shogo Akiyama/99 5.00 12.00
40 Luis Robert/25 75.00 200.00
41 Evan White/99 3.00 8.00
42 Mauricio Dubon/25 6.00 15.00
43 Isan Diaz/75 8.00 20.00
44 Jesus Luzardo/25 10.00 25.00
45 Eugenio Suarez/99 12.00 30.00
46 Brendan McKay/25 8.00 20.00
48 Kyle Lewis/99 25.00 60.00
49 Aroldis Chapman/49 25.00 60.00
50 Nico Hoerner/25 20.00 50.00

2020 Absolute Absolute Jersey Signatures
RANDOM INSERTS IN PACKS
PRINT RUNS B/WN 25-199 COPIES PER
EXCHANGE DEADLINE 1/8/22
1 Jorge Posada/49 15.00 40.00
3 Andres Munoz/199 4.00 10.00
4 Bryan Abreu/140 3.00 8.00
5 Danny Mendick/140 4.00 10.00
6 Jaylin Davis/140 5.00 12.00
7 Joe Palumbo/140 3.00 8.00
8 Jonathan Hernandez/125 3.00 8.00
9 Justin Dunn/99 4.00 10.00
10 Lewis Thorpe/140 3.00 8.00
11 Logan Allen/149 3.00 8.00
13 Rico Garcia/140 5.00 12.00
14 Sheldon Neuse/140 4.00 10.00
15 T.J. Zeuch/140 3.00 8.00
16 Travis Demeritte/140 4.00 10.00
23 Dansby Swanson/109 10.00 25.00
24 Cody Bellinger/25 30.00 80.00

2020 Absolute Absolute Jersey Signatures Spectrum Purple
*PURPLE/25: .6X TO 1.5X p/r 49-199
PRINT RUNS B/WN 5-25 COPIES PER
NO PRICING ON QTY 15 OR LESS
EXCHANGE DEADLINE 1/8/22
2 Adrian Morejon/25 8.00 20.00
6 Jaylin Davis/25 12.00 30.00
14 Sheldon Neuse/25 10.00 25.00
17 Trent Grisham/25 20.00 50.00
19 Walker Buehler/25 30.00 80.00
21 Miguel Andujar/25 25.00 60.00

2020 Absolute Absolute Jersey Signatures Spectrum Red
*RED/49-99: .4X TO 1X p/r 49-199
*RED/25: .6X TO 1.5X p/r 49-199
PRINT RUNS B/WN 10-99 COPIES PER
NO PRICING ON QTY 15 OR LESS
EXCHANGE DEADLINE 1/8/22
6 Jaylin Davis/49 8.00 20.00
17 Trent Grisham/99 12.00 30.00
19 Walker Buehler/49 15.00 40.00
20 Vladimir Guerrero Jr./25 25.00 60.00
21 Miguel Andujar/49 15.00 40.00

2020 Absolute Absolute Jersey Signatures Spectrum Silver
*SLVR/43-99: .4X TO 1X p/r 49-199
*SLVR/25: .6X TO 1.5X p/r 49-199
PRINT RUNS B/WN 15-99 COPIES PER
NO PRICING ON QTY 15 OR LESS
EXCHANGE DEADLINE 1/8/22
6 Jaylin Davis/75 6.00 15.00
18 Victor Robles/43 6.00 15.00
19 Walker Buehler/99 15.00 40.00

2020 Absolute Absolute Legends
RANDOM INSERTS IN PACKS
*SP BLUE: .6X TO 1.5X BASIC
*SP SILVER/99: .8X TO 2X BASIC
*SP PURPLE/25: 1.2X TO 3X BASIC
1 Babe Ruth 1.50 4.00
2 Gil Hodges .50 1.25
3 Billy Martin .50 1.25
4 Ron Santo .50 1.25
5 Joe DiMaggio 1.25 3.00
6 Ted Williams 4.00 10.00
7 Mickey Mantle 4.00 10.00
8 Yogi Berra .60 1.50
9 Jimmie Foxx .60 1.50
10 Roberto Clemente 3.00 8.00
11 Stan Musial 1.00 2.50
12 Cal Ripken 1.50 4.00
13 George Brett 1.25 3.00
14 Nolan Ryan 2.00 5.00
15 Harmon Killebrew .60 1.50
16 Reggie Jackson 2.50 6.00
17 Tony Gwynn 2.00 5.00
18 Warren Spahn .50 1.25
19 Jim Palmer .50 1.25
20 Babe Ruth 1.50 4.00

2020 Absolute Absolute Rookie Materials
RANDOM INSERTS IN PACKS
*SP RED/99: .5X TO 1.2X BASIC
*SP PURPLE/25: .8X TO 2X BASIC
1 Brendan McKay 2.50 6.00
2 Jonathan Hernandez 1.50 4.00
3 Kyle Lewis 6.00 15.00
4 Bo Bichette 6.00 15.00
5 Jordan Yamamoto 2.00 5.00
6 Bobby Bradley 2.00 5.00
7 Domingo Leyba 2.00 5.00
8 Zac Gallen 4.00 10.00
9 Deivy Grullon 1.50 4.00
10 Matt Thaiss 2.00 5.00
11 Aaron Civale 2.50 6.00
12 Brock Burke 1.50 4.00
14 Andres Munoz 2.00 5.00
15 Jaylin Davis 2.50 6.00
16 Dylan Cease 3.00 8.00
17 Tres Barrera 3.00 8.00
18 Rico Garcia 5.00 12.00
19 Josh Rojas 1.50 4.00
20 Bryan Abreu 1.50 4.00
21 Gavin Lux 5.00 12.00
22 Ronald Bolanos 2.50 6.00
23 Logan Allen 1.50 4.00
24 Donnie Walton 4.00 10.00
25 Travis Demeritte 2.00 5.00

26 T.J. Zeuch 1.50 4.00
28 Yordan Alvarez 4.00 10.00
29 Shun Yamaguchi 2.00 5.00
30 Aristides Aquino 3.00 8.00

2020 Absolute Baseball Material Signatures

RANDOM INSERTS IN PACKS
PRINT RUNS B/WN 6-149 COPIES PER
NO PRICING ON QTY 15 OR LESS
EXCHANGE DEADLINE 1/8/22
*BLK GOLD/25: .6X TO 1.5X p/r 33-149
1 Omar Vizquel/25 20.00 50.00
2 Barry Larkin/24 25.00 60.00
3 Bobby Richardson/100 10.00 25.00
4 Ken Griffey Jr./25 125.00 300.00
5 Cal Ripken/26 40.00 100.00
6 Dave Winfield/43 8.00 20.00
7 Shohei Ohtani/20 100.00 250.00
8 Don Sutton/50 8.00 20.00
11 Pedro Martinez/25 30.00 80.00
12 Paul Konerko/25 15.00 40.00
13 Frank Robinson/57 15.00 40.00
14 Dustin Pedroia/28 20.00 50.00
15 Jeff Bagwell/38 25.00 60.00
16 Ozzie Smith/55 30.00 80.00
17 Reggie Jackson/33 25.00 60.00
18 Rickey Henderson/50 60.00 150.00
20 Don Mattingly/25 40.00 100.00
21 Dylan Carlson/149 12.00 30.00
23 Vladimir Guerrero/50 25.00 60.00
24 Wade Boggs/40 15.00 40.00
26 Chipper Jones/25 50.00 120.00
27 Rafael Palmeiro/20 6.00 15.00
28 Roger Clemens/26 25.00 60.00
29 Randy Johnson/25 30.00 80.00
30 John Smoltz/27 20.00 50.00
31 Evan White/149 10.00 25.00
32 Frank Thomas/25 30.00 80.00
33 Whitey Ford/21 30.00 80.00

2020 Absolute Baseball Material Signatures Black

*BLACK/124-125: .4X TO 1X p/r 33-149
*BLACK/20: .6X TO 1.5X p/r 33-149
*BLACK/20: .4X TO 1X p/r 20-28
RANDOM INSERTS IN PACKS
PRINT RUNS B/WN 10-125 COPIES PER
NO PRICING ON QTY 15 OR LESS
EXCHANGE DEADLINE 1/8/22
9 Dwight Gooden/124 8.00 20.00

2020 Absolute Baseball Material Signatures Blue

*BLUE/50-99: .4X TO 1X p/r 33-149
RANDOM INSERTS IN PACKS
PRINT RUNS B/WN 50-99 COPIES PER
EXCHANGE DEADLINE 1/8/22
9 Dwight Gooden/50 8.00 20.00

2020 Absolute Baseball Material Signatures Light Blue

*LGHT BLUE/20-25: .6X TO 1.5X p/r 33-149
RANDOM INSERTS IN PACKS
PRINT RUNS B/WN 10-25 COPIES PER
NO PRICING ON QTY 15 OR LESS
EXCHANGE DEADLINE 1/8/22
9 Dwight Gooden/25 12.00 30.00

2020 Absolute Baseball Material Signatures Pink

*PINK/50-75: .4X TO 1X p/r 33-149
RANDOM INSERTS IN PACKS
PRINT RUNS B/WN 50-75 COPIES PER
EXCHANGE DEADLINE 1/8/22
9 Dwight Gooden/50 8.00 20.00

2020 Absolute Grip It-N-Rip It Materials

RANDOM INSERTS IN PACKS
PRINT RUNS B/WN 49-199 COPIES PER
1 Adrian Beltre/49 6.00 15.00
3 Fernando Tatis Jr./149 10.00 25.00
4 Eloy Jimenez/149 6.00 15.00
6 Manuel Margot/199 2.00 5.00
7 Ozzie Albies/145 8.00 20.00
9 Victor Robles/99 4.00 10.00
10 Vladimir Guerrero Jr./149 6.00 15.00
11 Alex Verdugo/99 2.50 6.00
12 Andrew Benintendi/149 6.00 15.00
15 Aristides Aquino/199 4.00 10.00
18 Bo Bichette/149 8.00 20.00
20 Luis Robert/199 15.00 40.00

2020 Absolute Grip It-N-Rip It Materials Spectrum Purple

RANDOM INSERTS IN PACKS
PRINT RUNS B/WN 10-25 COPIES PER
NO PRICING ON QTY 15 OR LESS

2020 Absolute Grip It-N-Rip It Materials Spectrum Red

RANDOM INSERTS IN PACKS
PRINT RUNS B/WN 35-99 COPIES PER
14 Nico Hoerner/99 6.00 15.00
16 Yordan Alvarez/99 6.00 15.00
17 Gavin Lux/49 8.00 20.00
19 Isan Diaz/49 4.00 10.00

2020 Absolute Hall Bound Materials

RANDOM INSERTS IN PACKS
1 Larry Walker 2.00 5.00
2 Ichiro 4.00 10.00
3 Albert Pujols 3.00 8.00
4 Adrian Beltre 2.50 6.00
5 Justin Verlander 2.50 6.00
6 Clayton Kershaw 5.00 12.00
7 Mike Trout 12.00 30.00
8 Miguel Cabrera 2.50 6.00
9 Alex Rodriguez 3.00 8.00
10 Robinson Cano 2.00 5.00

2020 Absolute Hall Bound Materials Spectrum Purple

*PURPLE/25: .8X TO 2X BASIC
RANDOM INSERTS IN PACKS
STATED PRINT RUN 25 SER.#'d SETS
3 Albert Pujols 20.00 50.00

2020 Absolute Hall Bound Materials Spectrum Red

*RED/49: .6X TO 1.5X BASIC
*RED/25: .8X TO 2X BASIC
RANDOM INSERTS IN PACKS
PRINT RUNS B/WN 25-49 COPIES PER
3 Albert Pujols/49 8.00 20.00

2020 Absolute Iconic Ink

RANDOM INSERTS IN PACKS
PRINT RUNS B/WN 10-99 COPIES PER
NO PRICING ON QTY 15 OR LESS
EXCHANGE DEADLINE 1/8/22
*PURPLE/25: .6X TO 1.5X p/r 49-99
*PURPLE/25: .4X TO 1X p/r 25
1 Brooks Robinson/25 15.00 40.00
3 Jose Canseco/49 6.00 15.00
5 Robin Yount/25 20.00 50.00
6 Willie McGee/25 10.00 25.00
14 Cody Bellinger/25 20.00 50.00
17 Anthony Rendon/96 20.00 50.00
19 Matt Chapman/49 EXCH 5.00 12.00
21 Fernando Tatis Jr./99 50.00 120.00
22 Vladimir Guerrero Jr./49 20.00 50.00
24 Paul Goldschmidt/25 12.00 30.00
25 Jose Ramirez/49 8.00 20.00
26 Yoenis Cespedes/25 8.00 20.00
30 Yordan Alvarez/25 EXCH 40.00 100.00

2020 Absolute Iconic Ink Dual Materials

RANDOM INSERTS IN PACKS
PRINT RUNS B/WN 15-99 COPIES PER
NO PRICING ON QTY 15 OR LESS
EXCHANGE DEADLINE 1/8/22
*PURPLE/25: .6X TO 1.5X p/r 49
1 Jim Rice/49 12.00 30.00
3 Darryl Strawberry/49 15.00 40.00
4 Dave Concepcion/49 20.00 50.00
6 Kenny Lofton/25 30.00 80.00
10 Omar Vizquel/49 6.00 15.00
11 Tommy Lasorda/25
15 Brooks Robinson/25 25.00 60.00
19 CC Sabathia/25 25.00 60.00

2020 Absolute Iconic Ink Duals

RANDOM INSERTS IN PACKS
PRINT RUNS B/WN 15-49 COPIES PER
NO PRICING ON QTY 15 OR LESS
EXCHANGE DEADLINE 1/8/22
*PURPLE/25: .6X TO 1.5X p/r 49
*PURPLE/25: .4X TO 1X p/r 25
1 S.Akiyama/Y.Tsutsugo/25 EXCH 30.00 80.00
2 S.Yamaguchi/K.Kim/25 20.00 50.00
3 J.Adell/L.Robert/15
4 X.Bogaerts/R.Devers/15
5 R.Acuna Jr./J.Soto/15
6 E.Jimenez/F.Thomas/15
7 V.Guerrero/V.Guerrero Jr./15
8 F.Lindor/J.Ramirez/25 8.00 20.00
9 W.Franco/J.Dominguez/25 EXCH 400.00 800.00
10 T.Story/F.Tatis Jr./49 50.00 120.00

2020 Absolute Iconic Ink Materials

RANDOM INSERTS IN PACKS
PRINT RUNS B/WN 10-99 COPIES PER
NO PRICING ON QTY 15 OR LESS
EXCHANGE DEADLINE 1/8/22
*PURPLE/25: .6X TO 1.5X p/r 40-99
12 Brooks Robinson/25 10.00 25.00
14 Tony Perez/49 15.00 40.00
17 Steve Garvey/25 25.00 60.00
21 Dale Murphy/49 15.00 40.00
22 Trevor Hoffman/25 12.00 30.00
23 Harold Baines/40 10.00 25.00
25 Paul Molitor/25 15.00 40.00
29 Jose Canseco/49 20.00 50.00
30 Goose Gossage/49 8.00 20.00
33 Kerry Wood/99 10.00 25.00
34 Mark Grace/40 25.00 60.00
40 Andre Dawson/49 10.00 25.00

2020 Absolute Iconic Ink Triples

RANDOM INSERTS IN PACKS
PRINT RUNS B/WN 7-25 COPIES PER
NO PRICING ON QTY 15 OR LESS
EXCHANGE DEADLINE 1/8/22
2 Murphy/Puk/Luzardo/25 20.00 50.00
3 Rutschman/Bart/Ruiz/25 30.00 80.00
4 Vaughn/White/Mountcastle/25 30.00 80.00
6 Aquino/Bichette/Alvarez/25 EXCH 100.00 250.00
10 Cease/McKay/May/25 20.00 50.00

2020 Absolute Introductions

RANDOM INSERTS IN PACKS
*SP.BLUE: .6X TO 1.5X BASIC
1 Pete Alonso 1.50 4.00
2 Vladimir Guerrero Jr. 1.25 3.00
3 Shohei Ohtani .75 2.00
4 Eloy Jimenez 1.25 3.00
5 Fernando Tatis Jr. 2.50 6.00
6 Luis Robert 4.00 10.00
7 Mike Soroka .60 1.50
8 Walker Buehler .75 2.00
9 Ronald Acuna Jr. 2.50 6.00
10 Juan Soto 2.00 5.00
11 Gleyber Torres 1.25 3.00
12 Jack Flaherty .50 1.25
13 Shohei Ohtani .75 2.00
14 Yordan Alvarez 2.00 5.00
15 Bo Bichette 3.00 8.00

2020 Absolute Introductions Spectrum Purple

1 Pete Alonso 12.00 30.00

2020 Absolute Introductions Spectrum Silver

*SP.SILVER/99: .8X TO 2X BASIC
RANDOM INSERTS IN PACKS
STATED PRINT RUN 99 SER.#'d SETS
1 Pete Alonso 4.00 10.00

2020 Absolute One Two Punch

RANDOM INSERTS IN PACKS
*SP.BLUE: .6X TO 1.5X BASIC
*SP.SILVER/99: .8X TO 2X BASIC
*SP.PURPLE/25: 1.2X TO 3X BASIC
1 M.Scherzer/S.Strasburg .60 1.50
2 Z.Greinke/J.Verlander .60 1.50
3 M.Clevinger/S.Bieber .60 1.50
4 J.deGrom/N.Syndergaard .60 1.50
5 W.Buehler/C.Kershaw 1.25 3.00
6 L.Castillo/S.Gray .50 1.25
7 B.Snell/C.Morton .60 1.50
8 E.Rodriguez/C.Sale .60 1.50
9 M.Tanaka/G.Cole 1.00 2.50
10 R.Johnson/C.Schilling .60 1.50

2020 Absolute Rookie Round Up

RANDOM INSERTS IN PACKS
1 Bo Bichette 3.00 8.00
2 Luis Robert 4.00 10.00
3 Brendan McKay .60 1.50
4 Yordan Alvarez 2.00 5.00
5 Gavin Lux 2.50 6.00
6 Dustin May 1.50 4.00
7 Aristides Aquino .75 2.00
8 Nico Hoerner 1.50 4.00
9 Jesus Luzardo .75 2.00
10 Trent Grisham 1.50 4.00
11 A.J. Puk .75 2.00
12 Yoshitomo Tsutsugo .50 1.25
14 Zac Gallen 1.00 2.50
15 Sean Murphy .60 1.50
16 Kwang-Hyun Kim 1.25 3.00
17 Shun Yamaguchi .50 1.25
18 Dylan Cease .75 2.00
19 Adbert Alzolay .50 1.25
20 Isan Diaz .60 1.50
21 Brendan McKay .60 1.50
22 Sam Hilliard .60 1.50
23 Abraham Toro .50 1.25
24 Kyle Lewis 1.50 4.00
25 Bobby Bradley .50 1.25

2020 Absolute Rookie Round Up Spectrum Blue

*SP.BLUE: .6X TO 1.5X BASIC
RANDOM INSERTS IN PACKS
24 Kyle Lewis 4.00 10.00

2020 Absolute Rookie Round Up Spectrum Purple

*SP.PURPLE/25: 1.2X TO 3X BASIC
RANDOM INSERTS IN PACKS
STATED PRINT RUN 25 SER.#'d SETS
24 Kyle Lewis 15.00 40.00

2020 Absolute Rookie Round Up Spectrum Silver

*SP.SILVER/99: .8X TO 2X BASIC
RANDOM INSERTS IN PACKS
STATED PRINT RUN 99 SER.#'d SETS
24 Kyle Lewis 10.00 25.00

2020 Absolute Rookie Threads

RANDOM INSERTS IN PACKS
*SP.RED/99: .5X TO 1.2X BASIC
*SP.PURPLE/25: .8X TO 2X BASIC
1 Brendan McKay 2.50 6.00
2 Adrian Morejon 1.50 4.00
4 Michel Baez 1.50 4.00
5 Jake Rogers 1.50 4.00
6 Brusdar Graterol 2.50 6.00
7 Trent Grisham 6.00 15.00
8 Adbert Alzolay 2.00 5.00
9 Nico Hoerner 4.00 10.00
10 Zack Collins 2.00 5.00
11 Sean Murphy 2.50 6.00
12 Jesus Luzardo 3.00 8.00
13 Mauricio Dubon 2.00 5.00
14 Joe Palumbo 1.50 4.00
15 Randy Arozarena 5.00 12.00
16 Kwang-Hyun Kim 5.00 12.00
17 Sheldon Neuse 2.00 5.00
18 Nick Solak 2.50 6.00
19 A.J. Puk 3.00 8.00
20 Justin Dunn 2.00 5.00
21 Tony Gonsolin 6.00 15.00
22 Sam Hilliard 2.50 6.00
23 Yordan Alvarez 8.00 20.00
24 Logan Webb 2.00 5.00
25 Jake Fraley 2.00 5.00
26 Anthony Kay 1.50 4.00
27 Lewis Thorpe 1.50 4.00
28 Aristides Aquino 4.00 10.00
30 Danny Mendick 2.00 5.00
31 Abraham Toro 2.00 5.00
33 Yonathan Daza 2.00 5.00
34 Tyrone Taylor 1.50 4.00
35 Willi Castro 2.50 6.00
36 Dustin May 6.00 15.00
37 Edwin Rios 4.00 10.00
38 Patrick Sandoval 2.50 6.00
39 Isan Diaz 2.50 6.00
40 Michael King 2.50 6.00

2020 Absolute Rookie Threads Duals

RANDOM INSERTS IN PACKS
*SP.RED/99: .5X TO 1.2X BASIC
*SP.PURPLE/25: .8X TO 2X BASIC
1 Nico Hoerner 4.00 10.00
2 Aristides Aquino 4.00 10.00
3 Gavin Lux 5.00 12.00
4 Bo Bichette 6.00 15.00
5 Dylan Cease 3.00 8.00
7 Yu Chang 2.50 6.00
8 Sam Hilliard 2.50 6.00
9 Jake Fraley 2.00 5.00
10 Jordan Yamamoto 2.00 5.00

2020 Absolute Rookie Threads Duals Spectrum Purple

*SP.PURPLE/25: .8X TO 2X BASIC
RANDOM INSERTS IN PACKS
STATED PRINT RUN 25 SER.#'d SETS
4 Bo Bichette 15.00 40.00

2020 Absolute Rookie Threads Duals Spectrum Red

*SP.RED/99: .5X TO 1.2X BASIC
RANDOM INSERTS IN PACKS
STATED PRINT RUN 99 SER.#'d SETS
4 Bo Bichette 12.00 30.00

2020 Absolute Team Tandem Materials

RANDOM INSERTS IN PACKS
1 F.Freeman/R.Acuna Jr. 8.00 20.00
3 M.Trout/J.Adell 12.00 30.00
4 J.Ramirez/F.Lindor 2.50 6.00
5 C.Yelich/K.Hiura 3.00 8.00
6 N.Arenado/T.Story 3.00 8.00
7 T.Williams/D.DiMaggio 15.00 40.00
8 K.Bryant/A.Rizzo 3.00 8.00
9 J.Soto/V.Robles 6.00 15.00
10 M.Mantle/Y.Berra 30.00 80.00

2020 Absolute Team Tandem Materials Spectrum Purple

*PURPLE/25: .8X TO 2X BASIC
RANDOM INSERTS IN PACKS
PRINT RUNS B/WN 10-25 COPIES PER
NO PRICING ON QTY 15 OR LESS
1 Freddie Freeman 20.00 50.00
Ronald Acuna Jr./25
8 Kris Bryant 12.00 30.00
Anthony Rizzo/25

2020 Absolute Team Tandem Materials Spectrum Red

*RED/99: .5X TO 1.2X BASIC
*RED/49: .6X TO 1.5X BASIC
*RED/25: .8X TO 2X BASIC
RANDOM INSERTS IN PACKS
PRINT RUNS B/WN 25-99 COPIES PER
8 Kris Bryant 8.00 20.00
Anthony Rizzo/99

2020 Absolute Tools of the Trade Dual Swatch Signatures

RANDOM INSERTS IN PACKS
PRINT RUNS B/WN 49-199 COPIES PER
EXCHANGE DEADLINE 1/8/22
2 Bo Bichette/149 25.00 60.00
8 Jake Fraley/140 4.00 10.00
10 Tony Gonsolin/149 12.00 30.00
13 Deivy Grullon/149 3.00 8.00
16 Bert Blyleven/49 4.00 10.00
17 Josh Rojas/125 3.00 8.00
18 Kyle Lewis/99 25.00 60.00
20 Michael King/140 5.00 12.00
21 Michel Baez/125 3.00 8.00
22 Patrick Sandoval/140 5.00 12.00
24 Tyrone Taylor/132 3.00 8.00
25 Willi Castro/125 5.00 12.00
26 Tres Barrera/93 6.00 15.00
28 Yu Chang/149 5.00 12.00
29 Sam Hilliard/140 5.00 12.00

2020 Absolute Tools of the Trade Dual Swatch Signatures Spectrum Purple

*PURPLE/25: .6X TO 1.5X BASIC
PRINT RUNS B/WN 5-25 COPIES PER
NO PRICING ON QTY 15 OR LESS
EXCHANGE DEADLINE 1/8/22
1 Yordan Alvarez/25 EXCH 40.00 100.00
3 Aristides Aquino/25 25.00 60.00
4 Luis Robert/25 150.00 400.00
5 Brendan McKay/20 20.00 50.00
7 Dustin May/25 40.00 100.00

2020 Absolute Tools of the Trade Dual Swatch Signatures Spectrum Red

*RED/35-49: .4X TO 1X BASIC
*RED/25: .6X TO 1.5X BASIC
PRINT RUNS B/WN 10-49 COPIES PER
NO PRICING ON QTY 15 OR LESS
EXCHANGE DEADLINE 1/8/22
1 Yordan Alvarez/49 EXCH 25.00 60.00
2 Bo Bichette/25 60.00 150.00
4 Luis Robert/49 100.00 250.00
5 Brendan McKay/35 12.00 30.00
19 Goose Gossage/25 15.00 40.00

2020 Absolute Tools of the Trade Dual Swatch Signatures Spectrum Silver

*SLVR: .4X TO 1X BASIC
PRINT RUNS B/WN 15-99 COPIES PER
NO PRICING ON QTY 15 OR LESS
EXCHANGE DEADLINE 1/8/22
2 Bo Bichette/49 40.00 100.00

2020 Absolute Tools of the Trade Quad Swatch Signatures

RANDOM INSERTS IN PACKS
PRINT RUNS B/WN 99-199 COPIES PER
EXCHANGE DEADLINE 1/8/22
6 Dylan Carlson/149 25.00 60.00
8 Royce Lewis/99 12.00 30.00
9 Brock Burke/99 3.00 8.00
10 Sean Murphy/150 6.00 15.00
11 Mauricio Dubon/149 4.00 10.00
12 Jordan Yamamoto/199 4.00 10.00
13 Aaron Civale/140
14 Dylan Cease/99 6.00 15.00
15 Donnie Walton/149 8.00 20.00

2020 Absolute Tools of the Trade Quad Swatch Signatures Spectrum Purple

*PURPLE/25: .6X TO 1.5X BASIC
PRINT RUNS B/WN 5-25 COPIES PER
NO PRICING ON QTY 15 OR LESS
EXCHANGE DEADLINE 1/8/22
4 Pete Alonso/25 75.00 200.00
6 Dylan Carlson/25 50.00 120.00
7 Hunter Greene/25 25.00 60.00

2020 Absolute Tools of the Trade Quad Swatch Signatures Spectrum Red

*RED/49-99: .4X TO 1X BASIC
*RED/25: .6X TO 1.5X BASIC
PRINT RUNS B/WN 10-99 COPIES PER
NO PRICING ON QTY 15 OR LESS
EXCHANGE DEADLINE 1/8/22
3 Phil Niekro/25 15.00 40.00
4 Pete Alonso/49 50.00 120.00
6 Dylan Carlson/49 30.00 80.00
7 Hunter Greene/49 15.00 40.00

2020 Absolute Tools of the Trade Quad Swatch Signatures Spectrum Silver

*SLVR/49-149: .4X TO 1X BASIC
*SLVR/25: .6X TO 1.5X BASIC
PRINT RUNS B/WN 25-149 COPIES PER
EXCHANGE DEADLINE 1/8/22
7 Hunter Greene/75 12.00 30.00

2020 Absolute Tools of the Trade Quad Swatches

RANDOM INSERTS IN PACKS
STATED PRINT RUN 99 SER.#'d SETS
1 Christin Stewart 2.00 5.00
2 Domingo Leyba 2.50 6.00
3 Vladimir Guerrero Jr. 6.00 15.00
4 Adbert Alzolay 2.50 6.00
5 David Fletcher 3.00 8.00
6 Ronald Acuna Jr. 12.00 30.00
7 Aaron Civale 3.00 8.00
8 Estevan Florial 3.00 8.00
9 Yu Chang 3.00 8.00
10 Taylor Ward 3.00 8.00
11 Sam Hilliard 3.00 8.00
12 Nick Williams 2.00 5.00
13 Jake Rogers 2.00 5.00
14 Orlando Arcia 2.00 5.00
15 Abraham Toro 2.50 6.00
16 Patrick Wisdom 2.00 5.00
17 Edwin Rios 5.00 12.00
18 Miguel Sano 2.50 6.00
19 Jordan Yamamoto 2.50 6.00
20 Jesus Sanchez 2.00 5.00

2020 Absolute Tools of the Trade Quad Swatches Spectrum Purple

*PURPLE/25: .6X TO 1.5X BASIC
RANDOM INSERTS IN PACKS
STATED PRINT RUN 25 SER.#'d SETS
3 Vladimir Guerrero Jr. 15.00 40.00

2020 Absolute Tools of the Trade Quad Swatches Spectrum Red

*RED/49: .5X TO 1.2X BASIC
RANDOM INSERTS IN PACKS
STATED PRINT RUN 49 SER.#'d SETS
3 Vladimir Guerrero Jr. 12.00 30.00

2020 Absolute Tools of the Trade Six Swatch Signatures

RANDOM INSERTS IN PACKS
PRINT RUNS B/WN 140-299 COPIES PER
EXCHANGE DEADLINE 1/8/22
*SLVR/75-199: .4X TO 1X BASIC
*RED/49-99: .4X TO 1X BASIC
*PURPLE/25: .6X TO 1.5X BASIC
1 Yonathan Daza/199 4.00 10.00
2 Domingo Leyba/149 4.00 10.00
3 Brandon Lowe/299 5.00 12.00
5 Tyler Mahle/149 8.00 20.00
7 Randy Arozarena/149 50.00 120.00
8 Edwin Rios/140 10.00 25.00
10 Cavan Biggio/199 15.00 40.00

2020 Absolute Tools of the Trade Six Swatches

RANDOM INSERTS IN PACKS
STATED PRINT RUN 99 SER.#'d SETS
*RED/49: .5X TO 1.2X BASIC
*PURPLE/25: .6X TO 1.5X BASIC
1 Kyle Tucker 2.50 6.00
2 Evan White 2.00 5.00
3 Aristides Aquino 4.00 10.00
4 Yordan Alvarez 12.00 30.00
5 Bo Bichette 12.00 30.00
6 Gavin Lux 12.00 30.00
7 Isan Diaz 3.00 8.00
8 Eloy Jimenez 6.00 15.00
9 Jake Bauers 2.50 6.00
10 Jeff McNeil 2.50 6.00

2020 Absolute Tools of the Trade Triple Swatch Signatures

RANDOM INSERTS IN PACKS
PRINT RUNS B/WN 49-149 COPIES PER
EXCHANGE DEADLINE 1/8/22
1 Kwang-Hyun Kim/99 15.00 40.00
2 Ronald Bolanos/140 5.00 12.00
3 Zac Gallen/99 8.00 20.00
4 Brusdar Graterol/140 5.00 12.00
9 J.D. Martinez/49 5.00 12.00
11 Adbert Alzolay/149 4.00 10.00
12 Troy Glaus/49 12.00 30.00
14 Jake Rogers/140 3.00 8.00
16 Abraham Toro/149 4.00 10.00
17 Gavin Lux/99 25.00 60.00

2020 Absolute Tools of the Trade Triple Swatch Signatures Spectrum Purple

*PURPLE/25: .6X TO 1.5X BASIC
PRINT RUNS B/WN 5-25 COPIES PER
NO PRICING ON QTY 15 OR LESS
EXCHANGE DEADLINE 1/8/22
13 Luis Robert/25 150.00 400.00
18 Nico Hoerner/25 20.00 50.00
20 Ryan Zimmerman/25 10.00 25.00

2020 Absolute Tools of the Trade Triple Swatch Signatures Spectrum Red

*RED/35-99: .4X TO 1X BASIC
*RED/25-30: .6X TO 1.5X BASIC
PRINT RUNS B/WN 10-99 COPIES PER
NO PRICING ON QTY 15 OR LESS
EXCHANGE DEADLINE 1/8/22
13 Luis Robert/49 100.00 250.00
18 Nico Hoerner/49 12.00 30.00
20 Ryan Zimmerman/30 10.00 25.00

2020 Absolute Tools of the Trade Triple Swatch Signatures Spectrum Silver

*SLVR/49-125: .4X TO 1X BASIC
*SLVR/25: .6X TO 1.5X BASIC
PRINT RUNS B/WN 15-125 COPIES PER
NO PRICING ON QTY 15 OR LESS
EXCHANGE DEADLINE 1/8/22
19 Paul Molitor/25 15.00 40.00

2020 Absolute Tools of the Trade Triple Swatches

RANDOM INSERTS IN PACKS
PRINT RUNS B/WN 49-99 COPIES PER
1 Sheldon Neuse/99 2.50 6.00
2 Dustin Pedroia/49 5.00 12.00
3 Adrian Morejon/99 2.00 5.00
4 Ryan McMahon/99 2.00 5.00
5 Jaylin Davis/99 3.00 8.00
6 Fernando Tatis Jr./99 12.00 30.00
7 Donnie Walton/99 5.00 12.00
8 Ryan O'Hearn/99 2.00 5.00
9 Willie Calhoun/99 2.00 5.00
10 Wander Franco/99 15.00 40.00
11 Nick Solak/99 3.00 8.00
12 Max Kepler/99 2.50 6.00
13 Tres Barrera/99 4.00 10.00
14 Kyle Tucker/99 2.50 6.00
15 Jake Fraley/99 2.50 6.00
16 Kevin Kramer/99 2.00 5.00
18 Kevin Newman/99 2.50 6.00

2020 Absolute Tools of the Trade Triple Swatches Spectrum Purple

*PURPLE/25: .6X TO 1.5X p/r 99
RANDOM INSERTS IN PACKS
STATED PRINT RUN 25 SER.#'d SETS
17 Stan Musial 15.00 40.00
19 Gil Hodges 10.00 25.00
20 Kirby Puckett 30.00 80.00

2020 Absolute Tools of the Trade Triple Swatches Spectrum Red

*RED/49: .5X TO 1.2X p/r 99
*RED/25: .5X TO 1.2X p/r 49
RANDOM INSERTS IN PACKS
PRINT RUNS B/WN 25-49 COPIES PER
2 Dustin Pedroia/25 12.00 30.00

2020 Absolute Unsung Heroes

RANDOM INSERTS IN PACKS
*SP.BLUE: .6X TO 1.5X BASIC
*SP.SILVER/99: .8X TO 2X BASIC
*SP.PURPLE/25: 1.2X TO 3X BASIC
1 Mike Clevinger .50 1.25
2 Jorge Soler .60 1.50
3 Andrew Benintendi .60 1.50
4 Tommy Pham .40 1.00
5 Mark Canha .40 1.00
6 Yoan Moncada .60 1.50
7 Jonathan Villar .40 1.00
8 Yuli Gurriel .50 1.25
9 Kyle Schwarber .60 1.50
10 Ozzie Albies .60 1.50
11 Elvis Andrus .50 1.25
12 Starling Marte .50 1.25
13 Eddie Rosario .50 1.25
14 Gio Urshela .60 1.50
15 Justin Turner .50 1.25

1948 Bowman

The 48-card Bowman set of 1948 was the first major set of the post-war period. Each 2 1/16" by 2 1/2" card had a black and white photo of a current player, with his biographical information printed in black ink on a gray back. Due to the printing process and the 36-card sheet size upon which Bowman was then printing, the 12 cards marked with an SP in the checklist are scarcer numerically, as they were removed from the printing sheet in order to make room for the 12 high numbers (37-48). Cards were issued in one-card penny packs. Many cards are found with over-printed, transposed, or blank backs. The set features the Rookie Cards of Hall of Famers Yogi Berra, Ralph Kiner, Stan Musial, Red Schoendienst, and Warren Spahn. Half of the cards in the set feature New York Yankees or Giants players.

COMPLETE SET (48) 3000.00 5000.00
WRAPPER (5-CENT) 600.00 700.00
CARDS PRICED IN NM CONDITION !
1 Bob Elliott RC 75.00 125.00
2 Ewell Blackwell RC 35.00 60.00
3 Ralph Kiner RC 100.00 250.00
4 Johnny Mize RC 50.00 120.00
5 Bob Feller RC 125.00 250.00
6 Yogi Berra RC 500.00 1000.00
7 Pete Reiser SP RC 75.00 125.00
8 Phil Rizzuto SP RC 150.00 300.00
9 Walker Cooper RC 10.00 20.00
10 Buddy Rosar RC 10.00 20.00
11 Johnny Lindell RC 12.50 25.00
12 Johnny Sain RC 20.00 50.00
13 Willard Marshall SP RC 20.00 40.00
14 Allie Reynolds RC 30.00 80.00
15 Eddie Joost 10.00 20.00
16 Jack Lohrke SP RC 20.00 40.00
17 Enos Slaughter RC 60.00 150.00
18 Warren Spahn RC 200.00 500.00
19 Tommy Henrich 20.00 50.00
20 Buddy Kerr SP RC 20.00 40.00
21 Ferris Fain RC 20.00 50.00
22 Floyd Bevens SP RC 30.00 50.00
23 Larry Jansen RC 12.50 25.00
24 Dutch Leonard SP 20.00 40.00
25 Barney McCosky 10.00 20.00
26 Frank Shea SP RC 30.00 50.00
27 Sid Gordon RC 20.00 50.00
28 Emil Verban SP RC 20.00 40.00
29 Joe Page SP RC 25.00 60.00
30 Whitey Lockman SP RC 30.00 50.00
31 Bill McCahan RC 10.00 20.00
32 Bill Rigney RC 10.00 20.00
33 Bill Johnson RC 12.50 25.00
34 Sheldon Jones SP RC 20.00 40.00
35 Snuffy Stirnweiss RC 20.00 40.00
36 Stan Musial RC 1000.00 2000.00
37 Clint Hartung RC 15.00 30.00
38 Red Schoendienst RC 150.00 400.00
39 Augie Galan RC 15.00 30.00
40 Marty Marion RC 50.00 80.00
41 Rex Barney RC 35.00 60.00
42 Ray Poat RC 15.00 30.00
43 Bruce Edwards RC 20.00 40.00
44 Johnny Wyrostek RC 15.00 30.00
45 Hank Sauer RC 35.00 60.00
46 Herman Wehmeier RC 15.00 30.00
47 Bobby Thomson RC 60.00 100.00
48 Dave Koslo RC 50.00 80.00

1949 Bowman

The cards in this 240-card set measure approximately 2 1/16" by 2 1/2". In 1949 Bowman took an intermediate step between black and white and full color with this set of tinted photos on colored backgrounds. Collectors should note the series price variations, which reflect some inconsistencies in the printing process. There are four major varieties in name printing, which are noted in the checklist below: NOF: name on front; NNOF: no name on front; PR: printed name on back; and SCR: script name on back. Cards were issued in five card nickel packs which came 24 packs to a box. These variations resulted when Bowman used twelve of the lower numbers to fill out the last press sheet of 36 cards, adding to numbers 217-240. Cards 1-3 and 5-73 can be found with either gray or white backs. Certain cards have been seen with a "gray" or "slate" background on the front. These cards are a result of a color printing error and are rarely seen on the secondary market so no value is established for them. Not all numbers are known to exist in this fashion. However, within the numbers between 75 and 107, slightly more of these cards have appeared on the market. Within the high numbers series (145-240), these cards have been seen but the appearance of these cards are very rare. Other cards are known to be extant with double printed backs. The set features the Rookie Cards of Hall of Famers Richie Ashburn, Roy Campanella, Bob Lemon, Robin Roberts, Duke Snider, and Early Wynn as well as Rookie Card of Gil Hodges.

COMP. MASTER SET (252)	10000.00	16000.00
COMPLETE SET (240)	10000.00	15000.00
WRAPPER (5-CENT, GR.)	200.00	250.00
WRAPPER (5-CENT, BL.)	150.00	200.00
CARDS PRICED IN NM CONDITION		
1 Vern Bickford RC	75.00	125.00
2 Whitey Lockman	20.00	40.00
3 Bob Porterfield RC	7.50	15.00
4A Jerry Priddy NNOF RC	7.50	15.00
4B Jerry Priddy NOF	30.00	50.00
5 Hank Sauer	20.00	40.00
6 Phil Cavarretta RC	20.00	40.00
7 Joe Dobson RC	7.50	15.00
8 Murry Dickson RC	7.50	15.00
9 Ferris Fain	20.00	40.00
10 Ted Gray RC	7.50	15.00
11 Lou Boudreau MG RC	25.00	60.00
12 Cass Michaels RC	7.50	15.00
13 Bob Chesnes RC	7.50	15.00
14 Curt Simmons RC	20.00	40.00
15 Ned Garver RC	7.50	15.00
16 Al Kozar RC	7.50	15.00
17 Earl Torgeson RC	7.50	15.00
18 Bobby Thomson	20.00	40.00
19 Bobby Brown RC	35.00	60.00
20 Gene Hermanski RC	7.50	15.00
21 Frank Baumholtz RC	12.50	25.00
22 Peanuts Lowrey RC	7.50	15.00
23 Bobby Doerr	50.00	80.00
24 Stan Musial	300.00	600.00
25 Carl Scheib RC	7.50	15.00
26 George Kell RC	50.00	80.00
27 Bob Feller	200.00	300.00
28 Don Kolloway RC	7.50	15.00
29 Ralph Kiner	75.00	125.00
30 Andy Seminick RC	20.00	40.00
31 Dick Kokos RC	7.50	15.00
32 Eddie Yost RC	35.00	60.00
33 Warren Spahn	100.00	250.00
34 Dave Koslo	7.50	15.00
35 Vic Raschi RC	35.00	60.00
36 Pee Wee Reese	125.00	200.00
37 Johnny Wyrostek	7.50	15.00
38 Emil Verban	7.50	15.00
39 Billy Goodman RC	12.50	25.00
40 George Munger RC	7.50	15.00
41 Lou Brissie RC	7.50	15.00
42 Hoot Evers RC	7.50	15.00
43 Dale Mitchell RC	20.00	40.00
44 Dave Philley RC	7.50	15.00
45 Wally Westlake RC	7.50	15.00
46 Robin Roberts RC	250.00	500.00
47 Johnny Sain	35.00	60.00
48 Willard Marshall	7.50	15.00
49 Frank Shea	12.50	25.00
50 Jackie Robinson RC	2000.00	4000.00
51 Herman Wehmeier	7.50	15.00
52 Johnny Schmitz RC	7.50	15.00
53 Jack Kramer RC	7.50	15.00
54 Marty Marion	35.00	60.00
55 Eddie Joost	7.50	15.00
56 Pat Mullin RC	7.50	15.00
57 Gene Bearden RC	20.00	40.00
58 Bob Elliott	20.00	40.00
59 Jack Lohrke	7.50	15.00
60 Yogi Berra	250.00	500.00
61 Rex Barney	20.00	40.00
62 Grady Hatton RC	7.50	15.00
63 Andy Pafko RC	20.00	40.00
64 Dom DiMaggio	40.00	100.00
65 Enos Slaughter	50.00	80.00
66 Elmer Valo RC	7.50	15.00
67 Alvin Dark RC	20.00	40.00
68 Sheldon Jones	7.50	15.00
69 Tommy Henrich	20.00	40.00
70 Carl Furillo RC	90.00	150.00
71 Vern Stephens RC	7.50	15.00
72 Tommy Holmes RC	20.00	40.00
73 Billy Cox RC	20.00	40.00
74 Tom McBride RC	7.50	15.00
75 Eddie Mayo RC	7.50	15.00
76 Bill Nicholson RC	12.50	25.00
77 Ernie Bonham RC	7.50	15.00
78A Sam Zoldak NNOF RC	7.50	15.00
78B Sam Zoldak NOF	30.00	50.00
79 Ron Northey RC	7.50	15.00
80 Bill McCahan	7.50	15.00
81 Virgil Stallcup RC	7.50	15.00
82 Joe Page	35.00	60.00
83A Bob Scheffing NNOF RC	7.50	15.00
83B Bob Scheffing NOF	30.00	50.00
84 Roy Campanella RC	400.00	1000.00
85A Johnny Mize NNOF	60.00	100.00
85B Johnny Mize NOF	90.00	150.00
86 Johnny Pesky RC	35.00	60.00
87 Randy Gumpert RC	7.50	15.00
88A Bill Salkeld NNOF RC	7.50	15.00
88B Bill Salkeld NOF	30.00	50.00
89 Mizell Platt RC	7.50	15.00
90 Gil Coan RC	7.50	15.00
91 Dick Wakefield RC	7.50	15.00
92 Willie Jones RC	20.00	40.00
93 Ed Stevens RC	7.50	15.00
94 Mickey Vernon RC	20.00	40.00
95 Howie Pollet RC	7.50	15.00
96 Taft Wright	7.50	15.00
97 Danny Litwhiler RC	7.50	15.00
98A Phil Rizzuto NNOF	125.00	200.00
98B Phil Rizzuto NOF	150.00	250.00
99 Frank Gustine RC	7.50	15.00
100 Gil Hodges RC	150.00	250.00
101 Sid Gordon	7.50	15.00
102 Stan Spence RC	7.50	15.00
103 Joe Tipton RC	7.50	15.00
104 Eddie Stanky RC	20.00	40.00
105 Bill Kennedy RC	7.50	15.00
106 Jake Early RC	7.50	15.00
107 Eddie Lake RC	7.50	15.00
108 Ken Heintzelman RC	7.50	15.00
109A Ed Fitzgerald Script RC	7.50	15.00
109B Ed Fitzgerald Print	35.00	60.00
110 Early Wynn RC	100.00	250.00
111 Red Schoendienst	60.00	100.00
112 Sam Chapman	20.00	40.00
113 Ray LaManno RC	7.50	15.00
114 Allie Reynolds	35.00	60.00
115 Dutch Leonard	7.50	15.00
116 Joe Hatten RC	7.50	15.00
117 Walker Cooper	7.50	15.00
118 Sam Mele RC	7.50	15.00
119 Floyd Baker RC	7.50	15.00
120 Cliff Fannin RC	7.50	15.00
121 Mark Christman RC	7.50	15.00
122 George Vico RC	7.50	15.00
123 Johnny Blatnik UER	7.50	15.00
Name misspelled		
124A D.Murtaugh Script RC	20.00	40.00
124B D.Murtaugh Print	35.00	60.00
125 Ken Keltner RC	12.50	25.00
126A Al Brazle Script RC	7.50	15.00
126B Al Brazle Print	35.00	60.00
127A Hank Majeski Script RC	7.50	15.00
127B Hank Majeski Print	35.00	60.00
128 Johnny VanderMeer	35.00	60.00
129 Bill Johnson	20.00	40.00
130 Harry Walker RC	7.50	15.00
131 Paul Lehner RC	7.50	15.00
132A Al Evans Script RC	7.50	15.00
132B Al Evans Pint	35.00	60.00
133 Aaron Robinson RC	7.50	15.00
134 Hank Borowy RC	7.50	15.00
135 Stan Rojek RC	7.50	15.00
136 Hank Edwards RC	7.50	15.00
137 Ted Wilks RC	7.50	15.00
138 Buddy Rosar	7.50	15.00
139 Hank Arft RC	7.50	15.00
140 Ray Scarborough RC	7.50	15.00
141 Tony Lupien RC	7.50	15.00
142 Eddie Waitkus RC	20.00	40.00
143A Bob Dillinger Script RC	12.50	25.00
143B Bob Dillinger Print	35.00	60.00
144 Mickey Haefner RC	7.50	15.00
145 Sylvester Donnelly RC	30.00	50.00
146 Mike McCormick RC	30.00	50.00
147 Bert Singleton RC	30.00	50.00
148 Bob Swift RC	30.00	50.00
149 Roy Partee RC	30.00	50.00
150 Allie Clark RC	30.00	50.00
151 Mickey Harris RC	30.00	50.00
152 Clarence Maddern RC	30.00	50.00
153 Phil Masi RC	30.00	50.00
154 Clint Hartung	35.00	60.00
155 Mickey Guerra RC	30.00	50.00
156 Al Zarilla RC	30.00	50.00
157 Walt Masterson RC	30.00	50.00
158 Harry Brecheen RC	35.00	60.00
159 Glen Moulder RC	30.00	50.00
160 Jim Blackburn RC	30.00	50.00
161 Jocko Thompson RC	30.00	50.00
162 Preacher Roe RC	75.00	125.00
163 Clyde McCullough RC	30.00	50.00
164 Vic Wertz RC	50.00	80.00
165 Snuffy Stirnweiss	50.00	80.00
166 Mike Tresh RC	30.00	50.00
167 Babe Martin RC	30.00	50.00
168 Doyle Lade RC	30.00	50.00
169 Jeff Heath RC	35.00	60.00
170 Bill Rigney	35.00	60.00
171 Dick Fowler RC	30.00	50.00
172 Eddie Pellagrini RC	30.00	50.00
173 Eddie Stewart RC	30.00	50.00
174 Terry Moore RC	50.00	80.00
175 Luke Appling	75.00	200.00
176 Ken Raffensberger RC	30.00	50.00
177 Stan Lopata RC	35.00	60.00
178 Tom Brown RC	35.00	60.00
179 Hugh Casey	50.00	80.00
180 Connie Berry	30.00	50.00
181 Gus Niarhos RC	30.00	50.00
182 Hal Peck RC	30.00	50.00
183 Lou Stringer RC	30.00	50.00
184 Bob Chipman RC	30.00	50.00
185 Pete Reiser	50.00	80.00
186 Buddy Kerr	30.00	50.00
187 Phil Marchildon RC	30.00	50.00
188 Karl Drews RC	30.00	50.00
189 Earl Wooten RC	30.00	50.00
190 Jim Hearn RC	30.00	50.00
191 Joe Haynes RC	30.00	50.00
192 Harry Gumbert	30.00	50.00
193 Ken Trinkle RC	30.00	50.00
194 Ralph Branca RC	50.00	120.00
195 Eddie Bockman RC	30.00	50.00
196 Fred Hutchinson RC	35.00	60.00
197 Johnny Lindell	35.00	60.00
198 Steve Gromek RC	30.00	50.00
199 Tex Hughson RC	30.00	50.00
200 Jess Dobernic RC	30.00	50.00
201 Sibby Sisti RC	30.00	50.00
202 Larry Jansen	35.00	60.00
203 Barney McCosky	30.00	50.00
204 Bob Savage RC	30.00	50.00
205 Dick Sisler RC	35.00	60.00
206 Bruce Edwards	30.00	50.00
207 Johnny Hopp RC	30.00	50.00
208 Dizzy Trout	35.00	60.00
209 Charlie Keller	40.00	100.00
210 Joe Gordon RC	50.00	80.00
211 Boo Ferriss RC	30.00	50.00
212 Ralph Hamner RC	30.00	50.00
213 Red Barrett RC	30.00	50.00
214 Richie Ashburn RC	400.00	800.00
215 Kirby Higbe	30.00	50.00
216 Schoolboy Rowe	35.00	60.00
217 Marino Pieretti RC	30.00	50.00
218 Dick Kryhoski RC	30.00	50.00
219 Virgil Trucks RC	35.00	60.00
220 Johnny McCarthy	30.00	50.00
221 Bob Muncrief RC	30.00	50.00
222 Alex Kellner RC	30.00	50.00
223 Bobby Hofman RC	30.00	50.00
224 Satchel Paige RC	2000.00	4000.00
225 Jerry Coleman RC	50.00	80.00
226 Duke Snider RC	600.00	1200.00
227 Fritz Ostermueller	30.00	50.00
228 Jackie Mayo RC	30.00	50.00
229 Ed Lopat RC	90.00	150.00
230 Augie Galan	35.00	60.00
231 Earl Johnson RC	30.00	50.00
232 George McQuinn	35.00	60.00
233 Larry Doby RC	400.00	800.00
234 Rip Sewell RC	30.00	50.00
235 Jim Russell RC	30.00	50.00
236 Fred Sanford RC	30.00	50.00
237 Monte Kennedy RC	30.00	50.00
238 Bob Lemon RC	250.00	500.00
239 Frank McCormick	30.00	50.00
240 Babe Young UER	60.00	100.00

1950 Bowman

The cards in this 252-card set measure approximately 2 1/16" by 2 1/2". This set, marketed in 1950 by Bowman, represented a major improvement in terms of quality over their previous efforts. Each card was a beautifully colored line drawing developed from a simple photograph. The first 72 cards are the scarcest in the set, while the final 72 cards may be found with or without the copyright line. This was the only Bowman sports set to carry the famous "5-Star" logo. Cards were issued in five-card nickel packs. Key rookies in this set are Hank Bauer, Don Newcombe, and Al Rosen.

COMPLETE SET (252)	6000.00	8500.00
COMMON CARD (1-72)	30.00	50.00
WRAPPER (1-CENT)	200.00	250.00
WRAPPER (5-CENT)	200.00	250.00
CARDS PRICED IN NM CONDITION		
1 Mel Parnell RC	90.00	150.00
2 Vern Stephens	35.00	60.00
3 Dom DiMaggio	50.00	80.00
4 Gus Zernial RC	20.00	50.00
5 Bob Kuzava RC	30.00	50.00
6 Bob Feller	100.00	250.00
7 Jim Hegan	35.00	60.00
8 George Kell	50.00	80.00
9 Vic Wertz	35.00	60.00
10 Tommy Henrich	40.00	100.00
11 Phil Rizzuto	125.00	300.00
12 Joe Page	20.00	50.00
13 Ferris Fain	35.00	60.00
14 Alex Kellner	20.00	50.00
15 Al Kozar	30.00	50.00
16 Roy Sievers RC	40.00	100.00
17 Sid Hudson	30.00	50.00
18 Eddie Robinson RC	30.00	50.00
19 Warren Spahn	100.00	250.00
20 Bob Elliott	35.00	60.00
21 Pee Wee Reese	100.00	250.00
22 Jackie Robinson	1500.00	3000.00
23 Don Newcombe RC	100.00	250.00
24 Johnny Schmitz	30.00	50.00
25 Hank Sauer	35.00	60.00
26 Grady Hatton	30.00	50.00
27 Herman Wehmeier	30.00	50.00
28 Bobby Thomson	50.00	80.00
29 Eddie Stanky	35.00	60.00
30 Eddie Waitkus	35.00	60.00
31 Del Ennis	50.00	80.00
32 Robin Roberts	75.00	200.00
33 Ralph Kiner	60.00	150.00
34 Murry Dickson	30.00	50.00
35 Enos Slaughter	30.00	80.00
36 Eddie Kazak RC	35.00	60.00
37 Luke Appling	40.00	100.00
38 Bill Wight RC	30.00	50.00
39 Larry Doby	60.00	150.00
40 Bob Lemon	50.00	80.00
41 Hoot Evers	30.00	50.00
42 Art Houtteman RC	30.00	50.00
43 Bobby Doerr	50.00	80.00
44 Joe Dobson	30.00	50.00
45 Al Zarilla	30.00	50.00
46 Yogi Berra	300.00	600.00
47 Jerry Coleman	20.00	50.00
48 Lou Brissie	30.00	50.00
49 Elmer Valo	15.00	40.00
50 Dick Kokos	30.00	50.00
51 Ned Garver	35.00	60.00
52 Sam Mele	30.00	50.00
53 Clyde Vollmer RC	30.00	50.00
54 Gil Coan	30.00	50.00
55 Buddy Kerr	30.00	50.00
56 Del Crandall RC	35.00	60.00
57 Vern Bickford	30.00	50.00
58 Carl Furillo	50.00	80.00
59 Ralph Branca	50.00	80.00
60 Andy Pafko	35.00	60.00
61 Bob Rush RC	30.00	50.00
62 Ted Kluszewski	30.00	80.00
63 Ewell Blackwell	35.00	60.00
64 Alvin Dark	20.00	50.00
65 Dave Koslo	30.00	50.00
66 Larry Jansen	35.00	60.00
67 Willie Jones	35.00	60.00
68 Curt Simmons	35.00	60.00
69 Wally Westlake	30.00	50.00
70 Bob Chesnes	30.00	50.00
71 Red Schoendienst	50.00	80.00
72 Howie Pollet	30.00	50.00
73 Willard Marshall	7.50	15.00
74 Johnny Antonelli RC	35.00	60.00
75 Roy Campanella	125.00	300.00
76 Rex Barney	20.00	40.00
77 Duke Snider	100.00	250.00
78 Mickey Owen	10.00	25.00
79 Johnny VanderMeer	20.00	50.00
80 Howard Fox RC	6.00	15.00
81 Ron Northey	6.00	15.00
82 Whitey Lockman	10.00	25.00
83 Sheldon Jones	6.00	15.00
84 Richie Ashburn	75.00	125.00
85 Ken Heintzelman	7.50	15.00
86 Stan Rojek	7.50	15.00
87 Bill Werle RC	7.50	15.00
88 Marty Marion	20.00	50.00
89 George Munger	7.50	15.00
90 Harry Brecheen	20.00	40.00
91 Cass Michaels	7.50	15.00
92 Hank Majeski	7.50	15.00
93 Gene Bearden	20.00	40.00
94 Lou Boudreau MG	35.00	60.00
95 Aaron Robinson	7.50	15.00
96 Virgil Trucks	12.50	25.00
97 Maurice McDermott RC	7.50	15.00
98 Ted Williams	400.00	800.00
99 Billy Goodman	12.50	25.00
100 Vic Raschi	35.00	60.00
101 Bobby Brown	15.00	40.00
102 Billy Johnson	12.50	25.00
103 Eddie Joost	7.50	15.00
104 Sam Chapman	7.50	15.00
105 Bob Dillinger	7.50	15.00
106 Cliff Fannin	7.50	15.00
107 Sam Dente RC	7.50	15.00
108 Ray Scarborough	10.00	25.00
109 Sid Gordon	7.50	15.00
110 Tommy Holmes	12.50	25.00
111 Walker Cooper	7.50	15.00
112 Gil Hodges	75.00	125.00
113 Gene Hermanski	7.50	15.00
114 Wayne Terwilliger RC	7.50	15.00
115 Roy Smalley	7.50	15.00
116 Virgil Stallcup	7.50	15.00
117 Bill Rigney	7.50	15.00
118 Clint Hartung	7.50	15.00
119 Dick Sisler	12.50	25.00
120 John Thompson	7.50	15.00
121 Andy Seminick	12.50	25.00
122 Johnny Hopp	12.50	25.00
123 Dino Restelli RC	7.50	15.00
124 Clyde McCullough	7.50	15.00
125 Del Rice RC	7.50	15.00
126 Al Brazle	7.50	15.00
127 Dave Philley	7.50	15.00
128 Phil Masi	7.50	15.00
129 Joe Gordon	20.00	50.00
130 Dale Mitchell	12.50	25.00
131 Steve Gromek	7.50	15.00
132 Mickey Vernon	12.50	25.00
133 Don Kolloway	7.50	15.00
134 Paul Trout	7.50	15.00
135 Pat Mullin	7.50	15.00
136 Buddy Rosar	7.50	15.00
137 Johnny Pesky	12.50	25.00
138 Allie Reynolds	20.00	50.00
139 Johnny Mize	40.00	100.00
140 Pete Suder RC	7.50	15.00
141 Joe Coleman RC	12.50	25.00
142 Sherman Lollar RC	20.00	40.00
143 Eddie Stewart	7.50	15.00
144 Al Evans	7.50	15.00
145 Jack Graham RC	7.50	15.00
146 Floyd Baker	7.50	15.00
147 Mike Garcia RC	20.00	40.00
148 Early Wynn	40.00	100.00
149 Bob Swift	7.50	15.00
150 George Vico	7.50	15.00
151 Fred Hutchinson	12.50	25.00
152 Ellis Kinder RC	7.50	15.00
153 Walt Masterson	10.00	25.00
154 Gus Niarhos	7.50	15.00
155 Frank Shea	12.50	25.00
156 Fred Sanford	12.50	25.00
157 Mike Guerra	7.50	15.00
158 Paul Lehner	7.50	15.00
159 Joe Tipton	7.50	15.00
160 Mickey Harris	7.50	15.00
161 Sherry Robertson RC	7.50	15.00
162 Eddie Yost	12.50	25.00
163 Earl Torgeson	7.50	15.00
164 Sibby Sisti	7.50	15.00
165 Bruce Edwards	7.50	15.00
166 Joe Hatten	7.50	15.00
167 Preacher Roe	15.00	40.00
168 Bob Scheffing	7.50	15.00
169 Hank Edwards	7.50	15.00
170 Dutch Leonard	7.50	15.00
171 Harry Gumbert	7.50	15.00
172 Peanuts Lowrey	7.50	15.00
173 Lloyd Merriman RC	7.50	15.00
174 Hank Thompson RC	20.00	40.00
175 Monte Kennedy	7.50	15.00
176 Sylvester Donnelly	7.50	15.00
177 Hank Borowy	7.50	15.00
178 Ed Fitzgerald	7.50	15.00
179 Chuck Diering RC	7.50	15.00
180 Harry Walker	12.50	25.00
181 Marino Pieretti	7.50	15.00
182 Sam Zoldak	7.50	15.00
183 Mickey Haefner	7.50	15.00
184 Randy Gumpert	7.50	15.00
185 Howie Judson RC	7.50	15.00
186 Ken Keltner	12.50	25.00
187 Lou Stringer	7.50	15.00
188 Earl Johnson	7.50	15.00
189 Owen Friend RC	12.00	30.00
190 Ken Wood RC	7.50	15.00
191 Dick Starr RC	7.50	15.00
192 Bob Chipman	7.50	15.00
193 Pete Reiser	20.00	40.00
194 Billy Cox	35.00	60.00
195 Phil Cavarretta	20.00	40.00
196 Doyle Lade	7.50	15.00
197 Johnny Wyrostek	7.50	15.00
198 Danny Litwhiler	7.50	15.00
199 Jack Kramer	7.50	15.00
200 Kirby Higbe	12.50	25.00
201 Pete Castiglione RC	7.50	15.00
202 Cliff Chambers RC	7.50	15.00
203 Danny Murtaugh	12.50	25.00
204 Granny Hamner RC	20.00	40.00
205 Mike Goliat RC	7.50	15.00
206 Stan Lopata	12.50	25.00
207 Max Lanier RC	7.50	15.00
208 Jim Hearn	7.50	15.00
209 Johnny Lindell	7.50	15.00
210 Ted Gray	7.50	15.00
211 Charlie Keller	20.00	40.00
212 Jerry Priddy	7.50	15.00
213 Carl Scheib	7.50	15.00
214 Dick Fowler	7.50	15.00
215 Ed Lopat	35.00	60.00
216 Bob Porterfield	12.50	25.00
217 Casey Stengel MG	40.00	100.00
218 Cliff Mapes RC	12.50	25.00
219 Hank Bauer RC	25.00	60.00
220 Leo Durocher MG	35.00	60.00
221 Don Mueller RC	20.00	40.00
222 Bobby Morgan RC	7.50	15.00
223 Jim Russell	7.50	15.00
224 Jack Banta RC	7.50	15.00
225 Eddie Sawyer MG RC	12.50	25.00
226 Jim Konstanty RC	35.00	60.00
227 Bob Miller RC	12.50	25.00
228 Bill Nicholson	12.50	30.00
229 Frankie Frisch MG	35.00	60.00
230 Bill Serena RC	7.50	15.00
231 Preston Ward RC	7.50	15.00
232 Al Rosen RC	35.00	60.00
233 Allie Clark	7.50	15.00
234 Bobby Shantz RC	35.00	60.00
235 Harold Gilbert RC	7.50	15.00
236 Bob Cain RC	7.50	15.00
237 Bill Salkeld	7.50	15.00
238 Nippy Jones RC	7.50	15.00
239 Bill Howerton RC	7.50	15.00
240 Eddie Lake	7.50	15.00
241 Neil Berry RC	7.50	15.00
242 Dick Kryhoski	7.50	15.00
243 Johnny Groth RC	7.50	15.00
244 Dale Coogan RC	7.50	15.00
245 Al Papai RC	7.50	15.00
246 Walt Dropo RC	20.00	40.00
247 Irv Noren RC	12.50	25.00
248 Sam Jethroe RC	20.00	50.00
249 Snuffy Stirnweiss	12.50	25.00
250 Ray Coleman RC	7.50	15.00
251 Les Moss RC	7.50	15.00
252 Billy DeMars RC	35.00	60.00

1951 Bowman

The cards in this 324-card set measure approximately 2 1/16" by 3 1/8". Many of the obverses of the cards appearing in the 1951 Bowman set are enlargements of those appearing in the previous year. The high number series (253-324) is highly valued and contains the true Rookie Cards of Mickey Mantle and Willie Mays. Card number 195 depicts Paul Richards in caricature. George Kell's card (number 46) incorrectly lists him as being in the "1941" Bowman series. Cards were issued either in one card penny packs which came 120 to a box or in six-card nickel packs which came 24 to a box. Player names are found printed in a panel on the front of the card. These cards were supposedly also sold in sheets in variety stores in the Philadelphia area.

COMPLETE SET (324)	20000.00	40000.00
COMMON CARD (1-252)	10.00	20.00
WRAPPER (1-CENT)	150.00	200.00
WRAPPER (5-CENT)	200.00	250.00
CARDS PRICED IN NM CONDITION		
1 Whitey Ford RC	600.00	1500.00
2 Yogi Berra	250.00	500.00
3 Robin Roberts	40.00	100.00
4 Del Ennis	20.00	50.00
5 Dale Mitchell	10.00	25.00
6 Don Newcombe	30.00	80.00
7 Gil Hodges	50.00	120.00
8 Paul Lehner	8.00	20.00
9 Sam Chapman	8.00	20.00
10 Red Schoendienst	25.00	60.00
11 George Munger	8.00	20.00
12 Hank Majeski	8.00	20.00
13 Eddie Stanky	10.00	25.00
14 Alvin Dark	15.00	40.00
15 Johnny Pesky	10.00	25.00
16 Maurice McDermott	8.00	20.00
17 Pete Castiglione	8.00	20.00
18 Gil Coan	8.00	20.00
19 Sid Gordon	8.00	20.00
20 Del Crandall UER	10.00	25.00
21 Snuffy Stirnweiss	10.00	25.00
22 Hank Sauer	10.00	25.00
23 Hoot Evers	8.00	20.00
24 Ewell Blackwell	15.00	40.00
25 Vic Raschi	25.00	60.00
26 Phil Rizzuto	60.00	150.00
27 Jim Konstanty	10.00	25.00
28 Eddie Waitkus	8.00	20.00
29 Allie Clark	8.00	20.00
30 Bob Feller	75.00	200.00
31 Roy Campanella	100.00	250.00
32 Duke Snider	100.00	250.00
33 Bob Hooper RC	8.00	20.00
34 Marty Marion MG	15.00	40.00
35 Al Zarilla	8.00	20.00
36 Joe Dobson	8.00	20.00
37 Whitey Lockman	15.00	40.00
38 Al Evans	8.00	20.00
39 Ray Scarborough	8.00	20.00
40 Gus Bell RC	25.00	60.00
41 Eddie Yost	10.00	25.00
42 Vern Bickford	10.00	25.00
43 Billy DeMars	8.00	20.00
44 Roy Smalley	8.00	20.00
45 Art Houtteman	8.00	20.00
46 George Kell UER	25.00	60.00
47 Grady Hatton	8.00	20.00
48 Ken Raffensberger	8.00	20.00
49 Jerry Coleman	10.00	25.00
50 Johnny Mize	30.00	80.00
51 Andy Seminick	8.00	20.00
52 Dick Sisler	15.00	40.00
53 Bob Lemon	25.00	60.00
54 Ray Boone RC	15.00	40.00
55 Gene Hermanski	8.00	20.00
56 Ralph Branca	25.00	60.00
57 Alex Kellner	8.00	20.00
58 Enos Slaughter	25.00	60.00
59 Randy Gumpert	10.00	25.00
60 Chico Carrasquel RC	25.00	60.00
61 Jim Hearn	10.00	25.00
62 Lou Boudreau MG	25.00	60.00
63 Bob Dillinger	8.00	20.00
64 Bill Werle	8.00	20.00
65 Mickey Vernon	15.00	40.00
66 Bob Elliott	10.00	25.00
67 Roy Sievers	15.00	30.00
68 Dick Kokos	8.00	20.00
69 Johnny Schmitz	8.00	20.00
70 Ron Northey	8.00	20.00
71 Jerry Priddy	8.00	20.00
72 Lloyd Merriman	8.00	20.00
73 Tommy Byrne RC	8.00	20.00
74 Billy Johnson	10.00	25.00
75 Russ Meyer RC	10.00	25.00
76 Stan Lopata	10.00	25.00
77 Mike Goliat	8.00	20.00
78 Early Wynn	25.00	60.00
79 Jim Hegan	10.00	25.00
80 Pee Wee Reese	50.00	120.00
81 Carl Furillo	25.00	60.00
82 Joe Tipton	8.00	20.00
83 Carl Scheib	8.00	20.00
84 Barney McCosky	8.00	20.00
85 Eddie Kazak	8.00	20.00
86 Harry Brecheen	10.00	25.00
87 Floyd Baker	8.00	20.00
88 Eddie Robinson	8.00	20.00
89 Hank Thompson	10.00	25.00
90 Dave Koslo	8.00	20.00
91 Clyde Vollmer	15.00	30.00
92 Vern Stephens	10.00	25.00
93 Danny O'Connell RC	10.00	25.00
94 Clyde McCullough	8.00	20.00
95 Sherry Robertson	8.00	20.00
96 Sandy Consuegra RC	8.00	20.00
97 Bob Kuzava	8.00	20.00
98 Willard Marshall	8.00	20.00
99 Earl Torgeson	8.00	20.00
100 Sherm Lollar	10.00	25.00
101 Owen Friend	8.00	20.00
102 Dutch Leonard	8.00	20.00
103 Andy Pafko	15.00	40.00
104 Virgil Trucks	8.00	20.00
105 Don Kolloway	8.00	20.00
106 Pat Mullin	8.00	20.00
107 Johnny Wyrostek	8.00	20.00
108 Virgil Stallcup	8.00	20.00
109 Allie Reynolds	25.00	60.00
110 Bobby Brown	15.00	40.00
111 Curt Simmons	15.00	40.00
112 Willie Jones	8.00	20.00
113 Bill Nicholson	8.00	20.00
114 Sam Zoldak	8.00	20.00
115 Steve Gromek	8.00	20.00
116 Bruce Edwards	8.00	20.00
117 Eddie Miksis RC	8.00	20.00
118 Preacher Roe	25.00	60.00
119 Eddie Joost	8.00	20.00
120 Joe Coleman	10.00	25.00
121 Gerry Staley RC	8.00	20.00
122 Joe Garagiola RC	30.00	80.00
123 Howie Judson	8.00	20.00
124 Gus Niarhos	8.00	20.00
125 Bill Rigney	10.00	25.00
126 Bobby Thomson	25.00	60.00
127 Sal Maglie RC	20.00	50.00
128 Ellis Kinder	8.00	20.00
129 Matt Batts	8.00	20.00
130 Tom Saffell RC	8.00	20.00
131 Cliff Chambers	8.00	20.00
132 Cass Michaels	8.00	20.00
133 Sam Dente	8.00	20.00
134 Warren Spahn	60.00	150.00
135 Walker Cooper	8.00	20.00
136 Ray Coleman	8.00	20.00
137 Dick Starr	8.00	20.00
138 Phil Cavarretta	10.00	25.00
139 Doyle Lade	8.00	20.00
140 Eddie Lake	8.00	20.00
141 Fred Hutchinson	10.00	25.00
142 Aaron Robinson	8.00	20.00
143 Ted Kluszewski	25.00	60.00
144 Herman Wehmeier	8.00	20.00
145 Fred Sanford	10.00	25.00
146 Johnny Hopp	10.00	25.00
147 Ken Heintzelman	8.00	20.00
148 Granny Hamner	8.00	20.00
149 Bubba Church RC	8.00	20.00
150 Mike Garcia	10.00	25.00
151 Larry Doby	50.00	120.00
152 Cal Abrams RC	8.00	20.00
153 Rex Barney	10.00	25.00
154 Pete Suder	8.00	20.00
155 Lou Brissie	8.00	20.00
156 Del Rice	8.00	20.00
157 Al Brazle	8.00	20.00
158 Chuck Diering	8.00	20.00
159 Eddie Stewart	8.00	20.00
160 Phil Masi	8.00	20.00
161 Wes Westrum RC	10.00	25.00
162 Larry Jansen	10.00	25.00
163 Monte Kennedy	8.00	20.00
164 Bill Wight	8.00	20.00
165 Ted Williams UER	300.00	600.00
166 Stan Rojek	8.00	20.00
167 Murry Dickson	8.00	20.00
168 Sam Mele	8.00	20.00
169 Sid Hudson	8.00	20.00
170 Sibby Sisti	8.00	20.00
171 Buddy Kerr	8.00	20.00
172 Ned Garver	8.00	20.00
173 Hank Arft	10.00	25.00
174 Mickey Owen	10.00	25.00
175 Wayne Terwilliger	8.00	20.00
176 Vic Wertz	15.00	40.00
177 Charlie Keller	10.00	25.00
178 Ted Gray	8.00	20.00
179 Danny Litwhiler	8.00	20.00
180 Howie Fox	8.00	20.00
181 Casey Stengel MG	40.00	100.00
182 Tom Ferrick RC	8.00	20.00
183 Hank Bauer	20.00	50.00
184 Eddie Sawyer MG	15.00	40.00
185 Jimmy Bloodworth	8.00	20.00
186 Richie Ashburn	40.00	100.00
187 Al Rosen	15.00	40.00
188 Bobby Avila RC	10.00	25.00
189 Erv Palica RC	8.00	20.00
190 Joe Hatten	8.00	20.00
191 Billy Hitchcock RC	8.00	20.00
192 Hank Wyse RC	8.00	20.00
193 Ted Wilks	8.00	20.00
194 Peanuts Lowrey	8.00	20.00
195 Paul Richards MG	10.00	25.00
196 Billy Pierce RC	25.00	60.00
197 Bob Cain	8.00	20.00
198 Monte Irvin RC	100.00	250.00
199 Sheldon Jones	8.00	20.00
200 Jack Kramer	8.00	20.00
201 Steve O'Neill MG RC	8.00	20.00
202 Mike Guerra	8.00	20.00
203 Vernon Law RC	25.00	60.00
204 Vic Lombardi RC	8.00	20.00
205 Mickey Grasso RC	8.00	20.00
206 Conrado Marrero RC	8.00	20.00
207 Billy Southworth MG RC	20.00	50.00
208 Blix Donnelly	8.00	20.00
209 Ken Wood	8.00	20.00
210 Les Moss	8.00	20.00
211 Hal Jeffcoat RC	8.00	20.00
212 Bob Rush	8.00	20.00
213 Neil Berry	10.00	25.00
214 Bob Swift	8.00	20.00
215 Ken Peterson	8.00	20.00
216 Connie Ryan RC	8.00	20.00
217 Joe Page	10.00	25.00
218 Ed Lopat	25.00	60.00

Card	Low	High
219 Gene Woodling RC	15.00	40.00
220 Bob Miller	8.00	20.00
221 Dick Whitman RC	8.00	20.00
222 Thurman Tucker RC	10.00	25.00
223 Johnny VanderMeer	15.00	40.00
224 Billy Cox	10.00	25.00
225 Dan Bankhead RC	15.00	40.00
226 Jimmy Dykes MG	8.00	20.00
227 Bobby Shantz UER	10.00	25.00
228 Cloyd Boyer RC	10.00	25.00
229 Bill Howerton	8.00	20.00
230 Max Lanier	8.00	20.00
231 Luis Aloma RC	8.00	20.00
232 Nellie Fox RC	125.00	300.00
233 Leo Durocher MG	25.00	60.00
234 Clint Hartung	10.00	25.00
235 Jack Lohrke	8.00	20.00
236 Buddy Rosar	8.00	20.00
237 Billy Goodman	10.00	25.00
238 Pete Reiser	15.00	40.00
239 Bill MacDonald RC	8.00	20.00
240 Joe Haynes	8.00	20.00
241 Irv Noren	10.00	25.00
242 Sam Jethroe	10.00	25.00
243 Johnny Antonelli	10.00	25.00
244 Cliff Fannin	8.00	20.00
245 John Berardino RC	8.00	20.00
246 Bill Serena	8.00	20.00
247 Bob Ramazzotti RC	8.00	20.00
248 Johnny Klippstein RC	8.00	20.00
249 Johnny Groth	8.00	20.00
250 Hank Borowy	8.00	20.00
251 Willard Ramsdell RC	15.00	40.00
252 Dixie Howell RC	8.00	20.00
253 Mickey Mantle RC	15000.00	25000.00
254 Jackie Jensen RC	40.00	100.00
255 Milo Candini RC	20.00	50.00
256 Ken Silvestri RC	20.00	50.00
257 Birdie Tebbetts RC	25.00	60.00
258 Luke Easter RC	25.00	60.00
259 Chuck Dressen MG	25.00	60.00
260 Carl Erskine RC	40.00	100.00
261 Wally Moses	25.00	60.00
262 Gus Zernial	25.00	60.00
263 Howie Pollet	20.00	50.00
264 Don Richmond RC	20.00	50.00
265 Steve Bilko RC	20.00	50.00
266 Harry Dorish RC	20.00	50.00
267 Ken Holcombe RC	20.00	50.00
268 Don Mueller	25.00	60.00
269 Ray Noble RC	20.00	50.00
270 Willard Nixon RC	15.00	40.00
271 Tommy Wright RC	20.00	50.00
272 Billy Meyer MG RC	20.00	50.00
273 Danny Murtaugh	25.00	60.00
274 George Metkovich RC	20.00	50.00
275 Bucky Harris MG	30.00	80.00
276 Frank Quinn RC	20.00	50.00
277 Roy Hartsfield RC	20.00	50.00
278 Norman Roy RC	20.00	50.00
279 Jim Delsing RC	20.00	50.00
280 Frank Overmire	20.00	50.00
281 Al Widmar RC	20.00	50.00
282 Frank Frisch MG	30.00	80.00
283 Walt Dubiel RC	20.00	50.00
284 Gene Bearden	25.00	60.00
285 Johnny Lipon RC	20.00	50.00
286 Bob Usher RC	20.00	50.00
287 Jim Blackburn	20.00	50.00
288 Bobby Adams	20.00	50.00
289 Cliff Mapes	25.00	60.00
290 Bill Dickey CO	50.00	120.00
291 Tommy Henrich CO	30.00	80.00
292 Eddie Pellagrini	20.00	50.00
293 Ken Johnson RC	20.00	50.00
294 Jocko Thompson	20.00	50.00
295 Al Lopez MG RC	50.00	120.00
296 Bob Kennedy RC	25.00	60.00
297 Dave Philley	20.00	50.00
298 Joe Astroth RC	15.00	30.00
299 Clyde King RC	20.00	50.00
300 Hal Rice RC	15.00	40.00
301 Tommy Glaviano RC	20.00	50.00
302 Jim Busby RC	20.00	50.00
303 Marv Rotblatt RC	20.00	50.00
304 Al Gettell RC	20.00	50.00
305 Willie Mays RC	6000.00	12000.00
306 Jim Piersall RC	30.00	80.00
307 Walt Masterson	20.00	50.00
308 Ted Beard RC	20.00	50.00
309 Mel Queen RC	20.00	50.00
310 Erv Dusak RC	20.00	50.00
311 Mickey Harris	20.00	50.00
312 Gene Mauch RC	25.00	60.00
313 Ray Mueller RC	20.00	50.00
314 Johnny Sain	25.00	60.00
315 Zack Taylor MG	20.00	50.00
316 Duane Pillette RC	20.00	50.00
317 Smoky Burgess RC	30.00	80.00
318 Warren Hacker RC	20.00	50.00
319 Red Rolfe MG	25.00	60.00
320 Hal White RC	20.00	50.00
321 Earl Johnson	20.00	50.00
322 Luke Sewell MG	25.00	60.00
323 Joe Adcock RC	30.00	80.00
324 Johnny Pramesa RC	50.00	120.00

1952 Bowman

The cards in this 252-card set measure approximately 2 1/16" by 3 1/8". While the Bowman set of 1952 retained the card size introduced in 1951, it employed a modification of color tones from the two preceding years. The cards also appeared with a facsimile autograph on the front and, for the first time since 1949, premium advertising on the back. The 1952 set was apparently sold in sheets as well as in gum packs. Artwork for 15 cards that were never issued was discovered in the early 1980s. Cards were issued in one card penny packs or five card nickel packs. The five cent packs came 24 to a box. Notable Rookie Cards in this set are Lew Burdette, Gil McDougald, and Minnie Minoso.

Card	Low	High
COMPLETE SET (252)	5000.00	10000.00
WRAPPER (1-CENT)	150.00	200.00
WRAPPER (5-CENT)	75.00	100.00
CARDS PRICED IN NM CONDITION		
1 Yogi Berra	300.00	600.00
2 Bobby Thomson	15.00	40.00
3 Fred Hutchinson	10.00	25.00
4 Robin Roberts	30.00	80.00
5 Minnie Minoso RC	50.00	120.00
6 Virgil Stallcup	6.00	15.00
7 Mike Garcia	10.00	25.00
8 Pee Wee Reese	60.00	150.00
9 Vern Stephens	10.00	25.00
10 Bob Hooper	6.00	15.00
11 Ralph Kiner	30.00	80.00
12 Max Surkont RC	6.00	15.00
13 Cliff Mapes	6.00	15.00
14 Cliff Chambers	6.00	15.00
15 Sam Mele	6.00	15.00
16 Turk Lown RC	6.00	15.00
17 Ed Lopat	15.00	40.00
18 Don Mueller	10.00	25.00
19 Bob Cain	6.00	15.00
20 Willie Jones	6.00	15.00
21 Nellie Fox	40.00	100.00
22 Willard Ramsdell	6.00	15.00
23 Bob Lemon	25.00	60.00
24 Carl Furillo	25.00	60.00
25 Mickey McDermott	6.00	15.00
26 Eddie Joost	6.00	15.00
27 Joe Garagiola	15.00	40.00
28 Roy Hartsfield	6.00	15.00
29 Ned Garver	6.00	15.00
30 Red Schoendienst	25.00	60.00
31 Eddie Yost	10.00	25.00
32 Eddie Miksis	6.00	15.00
33 Gil McDougald RC	30.00	80.00
34 Alvin Dark	10.00	25.00
35 Granny Hamner	6.00	15.00
36 Cass Michaels	6.00	15.00
37 Vic Raschi	10.00	25.00
38 Whitey Lockman	10.00	25.00
39 Vic Wertz	10.00	25.00
40 Bubba Church	6.00	15.00
41 Chico Carrasquel	10.00	25.00
42 Johnny Wyrostek	6.00	15.00
43 Bob Feller	75.00	200.00
44 Roy Campanella	75.00	200.00
45 Johnny Pesky	10.00	25.00
46 Carl Scheib	6.00	15.00
47 Pete Castiglione	6.00	15.00
48 Vern Bickford	6.00	15.00
49 Jim Hearn	6.00	15.00
50 Gerry Staley	6.00	15.00
51 Gil Coan	6.00	15.00
52 Phil Rizzuto	60.00	150.00
53 Richie Ashburn	30.00	80.00
54 Billy Pierce	10.00	25.00
55 Ken Raffensberger	6.00	15.00
56 Clyde King	10.00	25.00
57 Clyde Vollmer	6.00	15.00
58 Hank Majeski	6.00	15.00
59 Murry Dickson	6.00	15.00
60 Sid Gordon	6.00	15.00
61 Tommy Byrne	6.00	15.00
62 Joe Presko RC	6.00	15.00
63 Irv Noren	6.00	15.00
64 Roy Smalley	6.00	15.00
65 Hank Bauer	15.00	40.00
66 Sal Maglie	10.00	25.00
67 Johnny Groth	6.00	15.00
68 Jim Busby	10.00	25.00
69 Joe Adcock	10.00	25.00
70 Carl Erskine	15.00	40.00
71 Vern Law	10.00	25.00
72 Earl Torgeson	6.00	15.00
73 Jerry Coleman	10.00	25.00
74 Wes Westrum	10.00	25.00
75 George Kell	25.00	60.00
76 Del Ennis	10.00	25.00
77 Eddie Robinson	6.00	15.00
78 Lloyd Merriman	6.00	15.00
79 Lou Brissie	6.00	15.00
80 Gil Hodges	40.00	100.00
81 Billy Goodman	10.00	25.00
82 Gus Zernial	10.00	25.00
83 Howie Pollet	6.00	15.00
84 Sam Jethroe	10.00	25.00
85 Marty Marion CO	10.00	25.00
86 Cal Abrams	6.00	15.00
87 Mickey Vernon	10.00	25.00
88 Bruce Edwards	6.00	15.00
89 Billy Hitchcock	6.00	15.00
90 Larry Jansen	10.00	25.00
91 Don Kolloway	6.00	15.00
92 Eddie Waitkus	10.00	25.00
93 Paul Richards MG	10.00	25.00
94 Luke Sewell MG	10.00	25.00
95 Luke Easter	10.00	25.00
96 Ralph Branca	15.00	30.00
97 Willard Marshall	6.00	15.00
98 Jimmie Dykes MG	10.00	25.00
99 Clyde McCullough	6.00	15.00
100 Sibby Sisti	6.00	15.00
101 Mickey Mantle	3000.00	6000.00
102 Peanuts Lowrey	6.00	15.00
103 Joe Haynes	6.00	15.00
104 Hal Jeffcoat	6.00	15.00
105 Bobby Brown	10.00	25.00
106 Randy Gumpert	6.00	15.00
107 Del Rice	6.00	15.00
108 George Metkovich	6.00	15.00
109 Tom Morgan RC	15.00	40.00
110 Max Lanier	6.00	15.00
111 Hoot Evers	6.00	15.00
112 Smoky Burgess	10.00	25.00
113 Al Zarilla	6.00	15.00
114 Frank Hiller RC	6.00	15.00
115 Larry Doby	25.00	60.00
116 Duke Snider	75.00	200.00
117 Bill Wight	6.00	15.00
118 Ray Murray RC	6.00	15.00
119 Bill Howerton	6.00	15.00
120 Chet Nichols RC	6.00	15.00
121 Al Corwin RC	6.00	15.00
122 Billy Johnson	6.00	15.00
123 Sid Hudson	6.00	15.00
124 Birdie Tebbetts	6.00	15.00
125 Howie Fox	6.00	15.00
126 Phil Cavarretta	25.00	50.00
127 Dick Sisler	6.00	15.00
128 Don Newcombe	25.00	60.00
129 Gus Niarhos	6.00	15.00
130 Allie Clark	6.00	15.00
131 Bob Swift	6.00	15.00
132 Dave Cole RC	6.00	15.00
133 Dick Kryhoski	6.00	15.00
134 Al Brazle	6.00	15.00
135 Mickey Harris	6.00	15.00
136 Gene Hermanski	6.00	15.00
137 Stan Rojek	6.00	15.00
138 Ted Wilks	6.00	15.00
139 Jerry Priddy	6.00	15.00
140 Ray Scarborough	6.00	15.00
141 Hank Edwards	6.00	15.00
142 Early Wynn	25.00	60.00
143 Sandy Consuegra	6.00	15.00
144 Joe Hatten	6.00	15.00
145 Johnny Mize	25.00	60.00
146 Leo Durocher MG	25.00	50.00
147 Marlin Stuart RC	6.00	15.00
148 Ken Heintzelman	6.00	15.00
149 Howie Judson	6.00	15.00
150 Herman Wehmeier	6.00	15.00
151 Al Rosen	10.00	25.00
152 Billy Cox	6.00	15.00
153 Fred Hatfield RC	15.00	30.00
154 Ferris Fain	10.00	25.00
155 Billy Meyer MG	6.00	15.00
156 Warren Spahn	60.00	150.00
157 Jim Delsing	6.00	15.00
158 Bucky Harris MG	15.00	30.00
159 Dutch Leonard	10.00	25.00
160 Eddie Stanky	10.00	25.00
161 Jackie Jensen	25.00	50.00
162 Monte Irvin	30.00	80.00
163 Johnny Lipon	6.00	15.00
164 Connie Ryan	6.00	15.00
165 Saul Rogovin RC	6.00	15.00
166 Bobby Adams	6.00	15.00
167 Bobby Avila	10.00	25.00
168 Preacher Roe	10.00	25.00
169 Walt Dropo	10.00	25.00
170 Joe Astroth	6.00	15.00
171 Mel Queen	6.00	15.00
172 Ebba St.Claire RC	6.00	15.00
173 Gene Bearden	6.00	15.00
174 Mickey Grasso	6.00	15.00
175 Randy Jackson RC	6.00	15.00
176 Harry Brecheen	10.00	25.00
177 Gene Woodling	10.00	25.00
178 Dave Williams RC	10.00	25.00
179 Pete Suder	6.00	15.00
180 Ed Fitzgerald	6.00	15.00
181 Joe Collins RC	10.00	25.00
182 Dave Koslo	6.00	15.00
183 Pat Mullin	6.00	15.00
184 Curt Simmons	10.00	25.00
185 Eddie Stewart	6.00	15.00
186 Frank Smith RC	6.00	15.00
187 Jim Hegan	10.00	25.00
188 Chuck Dressen MG	10.00	25.00
189 Jimmy Piersall	15.00	40.00
190 Dick Fowler	6.00	15.00
191 Bob Friend RC	10.00	25.00
192 John Cusick RC	6.00	15.00
193 Bobby Young RC	6.00	15.00
194 Bob Porterfield	6.00	15.00
195 Frank Baumholtz	6.00	15.00
196 Stan Musial	300.00	600.00
197 Charlie Silvera RC	6.00	15.00
198 Chuck Diering	6.00	15.00
199 Ted Gray	6.00	15.00
200 Ken Silvestri	6.00	15.00
201 Ray Coleman	6.00	15.00
202 Harry Perkowski RC	6.00	15.00
203 Steve Gromek	6.00	15.00
204 Andy Pafko	15.00	40.00
205 Walt Masterson	6.00	15.00
206 Elmer Valo	6.00	15.00
207 George Strickland RC	6.00	15.00
208 Walker Cooper	6.00	15.00
209 Dick Littlefield RC	6.00	15.00
210 Archie Wilson RC	6.00	15.00
211 Paul Minner RC	6.00	15.00
212 Solly Hemus RC	15.00	40.00
213 Monte Kennedy	6.00	15.00
214 Ray Boone	15.00	40.00
215 Sheldon Jones	6.00	15.00
216 Matt Batts	6.00	15.00
217 Casey Stengel MG	50.00	120.00
218 Willie Mays	1000.00	2000.00
219 Neil Berry	25.00	60.00
220 Russ Meyer	25.00	60.00
221 Lou Kretlow RC	25.00	60.00
222 Dixie Howell	25.00	60.00
223 Harry Simpson RC	25.00	60.00
224 Johnny Schmitz	25.00	60.00
225 Del Wilber RC	25.00	60.00
226 Alex Kellner	25.00	60.00
227 Clyde Sukeforth CO RC	25.00	60.00
228 Bob Chipman	25.00	60.00
229 Hank Arft	25.00	60.00
230 Frank Shea	25.00	60.00
231 Dee Fondy RC	25.00	60.00
232 Enos Slaughter	40.00	100.00
233 Bob Kuzava	25.00	60.00
234 Fred Fitzsimmons CO	25.00	60.00
235 Steve Souchock RC	25.00	60.00
236 Tommy Brown	25.00	60.00
237 Sherm Lollar	25.00	60.00
238 Roy McMillan RC	25.00	60.00
239 Dale Mitchell	25.00	60.00
240 Billy Loes RC	25.00	60.00
241 Mel Parnell	25.00	60.00
242 Everett Kell RC	25.00	60.00
243 George Munger	25.00	60.00
244 Lew Burdette RC	40.00	100.00
245 George Schmees RC	25.00	60.00
246 Jerry Snyder RC	25.00	60.00
247 Johnny Pramesa	25.00	60.00
248 Bill Werle Full Name	25.00	60.00
248A Bill Werle No W	25.00	60.00
249 Hank Thompson	25.00	60.00
250 Ike Delock RC	25.00	60.00
251 Jack Lohrke	25.00	60.00
252 Frank Crosetti CO	60.00	150.00

1953 Bowman Black and White

The cards in this 64-card set measure approximately 2 1/2" by 3 3/4". Some collectors believe that the high cost of producing the 1953 color series forced Bowman to issue this set in black and white, since the two sets are identical in design except for the element of color. This set was also produced in fewer numbers than its color counterpart, and is popular among collectors for the challenge involved in completing it and the lack of short prints. Cards were issued in one-card penny packs which came 120 to a box and five-card nickel packs. There are no key Rookie Cards in this set. Card #43, Hal Bevan, exists with him being born in either 1930 or 1950. The 1950 version seems to be is much more difficult to find.

Card	Low	High
COMPLETE SET (64)	1250.00	2500.00
WRAPPER (1-CENT)	300.00	350.00
CARDS PRICED IN NM CONDITION !		
1 Gus Bell	75.00	125.00
2 Willard Nixon	25.00	40.00
3 Bill Rigney	25.00	40.00
4 Pat Mullin	25.00	40.00
5 Dee Fondy	25.00	40.00
6 Ray Murray	25.00	40.00
7 Andy Seminick	25.00	40.00
8 Pete Suder	25.00	40.00
9 Walt Masterson	25.00	40.00
10 Dick Sisler	35.00	60.00
11 Dick Gernert	25.00	40.00
12 Randy Jackson	25.00	40.00
13 Joe Tipton	25.00	40.00
14 Bill Nicholson	35.00	60.00
15 Johnny Mize	75.00	125.00
16 Stu Miller RC	35.00	60.00
17 Virgil Trucks	35.00	60.00
18 Billy Hoeft	25.00	40.00
19 Paul LaPalme	25.00	40.00
20 Eddie Robinson	25.00	40.00
21 Clarence Podbielan	25.00	40.00
22 Matt Batts	25.00	40.00
23 Wilmer Mizell	35.00	60.00
24 Del Wilber	25.00	40.00
25 Johnny Sain	50.00	80.00
26 Preacher Roe	50.00	80.00
27 Bob Lemon	100.00	175.00
28 Hoyt Wilhelm	75.00	125.00
29 Sid Hudson	25.00	40.00
30 Walker Cooper	25.00	40.00
31 Gene Woodling	50.00	80.00
32 Rocky Bridges	25.00	40.00
33 Bob Kuzava	25.00	40.00
34 Ebba St.Claire	25.00	40.00
35 Johnny Wyrostek	25.00	40.00
36 Jimmy Piersall	50.00	80.00
37 Hal Jeffcoat	25.00	40.00
38 Dave Cole	25.00	40.00
39 Casey Stengel MG	200.00	350.00
40 Larry Jansen	35.00	60.00
41 Bob Ramazzotti	25.00	40.00
42 Howie Judson	25.00	40.00
43 Hal Bevan ERR RC	25.00	40.00
43A Hal Bevan COR	25.00	40.00
44 Jim Delsing	25.00	40.00
45 Irv Noren	35.00	60.00
46 Bucky Harris MG	50.00	80.00
47 Jack Lohrke	25.00	40.00
48 Steve Ridzik RC	25.00	40.00
49 Floyd Baker	25.00	40.00
50 Dutch Leonard	25.00	40.00
51 Lou Burdette	50.00	80.00
52 Ralph Branca	50.00	80.00
53 Morrie Martin	25.00	40.00
54 Bill Miller	25.00	40.00
55 Don Johnson	25.00	40.00
56 Roy Smalley	25.00	40.00
57 Andy Pafko	35.00	60.00
58 Jim Konstanty	35.00	60.00
59 Duane Pillette	25.00	40.00
60 Billy Cox	50.00	80.00
61 Tom Gorman RC	25.00	40.00
62 Keith Thomas RC	25.00	40.00
63 Steve Gromek	25.00	40.00
64 Andy Hansen	50.00	80.00

1953 Bowman Color

The cards in this 160-card set measure approximately 2 1/2" by 3 3/4". The 1953 Bowman Color set features Kodachrome photographs with no names or facsimile autographs on the face. Cards were issued in five-card nickel packs in a 24 pack box with each pack having gum in it. The entire low number run were also printed in three card strips; it is believed that these three card strips in numerical order were box toppers to retailers. The box features an endorsement from Joe DiMaggio. Numbers 113 to 160 are somewhat more difficult to obtain, with numbers 113 to 128 being the most difficult. There are two cards of Al Corwin (126 and 149). There are no key Rookie Cards in this set.

Card	Low	High
COMPLETE SET (160)	6000.00	12000.00
WRAPPER (1-CENT)	300.00	400.00
WRAPPER (5-CENT)	250.00	300.00
CARDS PRICED IN NM CONDITION !		
1 Davey Williams	50.00	120.00
2 Vic Wertz	30.00	50.00
3 Sam Jethroe	30.00	50.00
4 Art Houtteman	20.00	40.00
5 Sid Gordon	20.00	40.00
6 Joe Ginsberg	20.00	40.00
7 Harry Chiti RC	20.00	40.00
8 Al Rosen	30.00	50.00
9 Phil Rizzuto	60.00	150.00
10 Richie Ashburn	50.00	120.00
11 Bobby Shantz	30.00	50.00
12 Carl Erskine	30.00	80.00
13 Gus Zernial	30.00	50.00
14 Billy Loes	12.00	30.00
15 Jim Busby	20.00	40.00
16 Bob Friend	30.00	50.00
17 Gerry Staley	20.00	40.00
18 Nellie Fox	40.00	100.00
19 Alvin Dark	30.00	50.00
20 Don Lenhardt	20.00	40.00
21 Joe Garagiola	15.00	40.00
22 Bob Porterfield	20.00	40.00
23 Herman Wehmeier	20.00	40.00
24 Jackie Jensen	15.00	40.00
25 Hoot Evers	20.00	40.00
26 Roy McMillan	30.00	50.00
27 Vic Raschi	35.00	60.00
28 Smoky Burgess	30.00	50.00
29 Bobby Avila	30.00	50.00
30 Phil Cavarretta	30.00	50.00
31 Jimmy Dykes MG	30.00	50.00
32 Stan Musial	200.00	500.00
33 Pee Wee Reese	400.00	800.00
34 Gil Coan	20.00	40.00
35 Maurice McDermott	20.00	40.00
36 Minnie Minoso	50.00	80.00
37 Jim Wilson	20.00	40.00
38 Harry Byrd RC	20.00	40.00
39 Paul Richards MG	30.00	50.00
40 Larry Doby	50.00	120.00
41 Sammy White	20.00	40.00
42 Tommy Brown	20.00	40.00
43 Mike Garcia	30.00	50.00
44 Bauer/Berra/Mantle	300.00	600.00
45 Walt Dropo	30.00	50.00
46 Roy Campanella	100.00	250.00
47 Ned Garver	20.00	40.00
48 Hank Sauer	30.00	50.00
49 Eddie Stanky MG	30.00	50.00
50 Lou Kretlow	20.00	40.00
51 Monte Irvin	40.00	100.00
52 Marty Marion MG	30.00	50.00
53 Del Rice	20.00	40.00
54 Chico Carrasquel	20.00	40.00
55 Leo Durocher MG	50.00	80.00
56 Bob Cain	20.00	40.00
57 Lou Boudreau MG	25.00	60.00
58 Willard Marshall	20.00	40.00
59 Mickey Mantle	1500.00	2500.00
60 Granny Hamner	20.00	40.00
61 George Kell	40.00	100.00
62 Ted Kluszewski	60.00	100.00
63 Gil McDougald	50.00	80.00
64 Curt Simmons	30.00	80.00
65 Robin Roberts	60.00	150.00
66 Mel Parnell	20.00	50.00
67 Mel Clark RC	20.00	40.00
68 Allie Reynolds	40.00	100.00
69 Charlie Grimm MG	30.00	50.00
70 Clint Courtney RC	20.00	40.00
71 Paul Minner	20.00	40.00
72 Ted Gray	20.00	40.00
73 Billy Pierce	30.00	50.00
74 Don Mueller	30.00	50.00
75 Saul Rogovin	20.00	40.00
76 Jim Hearn	20.00	40.00
77 Mickey Grasso	20.00	40.00
78 Carl Furillo	30.00	80.00
79 Ray Boone	30.00	50.00
80 Ralph Kiner	30.00	80.00
81 Enos Slaughter	40.00	100.00
82 Joe Astroth	20.00	40.00
83 Jack Daniels RC	20.00	40.00
84 Hank Bauer	35.00	60.00
85 Solly Hemus	20.00	40.00
86 Harry Simpson	20.00	40.00
87 Harry Perkowski	20.00	40.00
88 Joe Dobson	20.00	40.00
89 Sandy Consuegra	20.00	40.00
90 Joe Nuxhall	30.00	50.00
91 Steve Souchock	20.00	40.00
92 Gil Hodges	75.00	200.00
93 P.Rizzuto/B.Martin	100.00	250.00
94 Bob Addis	20.00	40.00
95 Wally Moses CO	30.00	50.00
96 Sal Maglie	30.00	50.00
97 Eddie Mathews	100.00	250.00
98 Hector Rodriguez RC	20.00	40.00
99 Warren Spahn	100.00	250.00
100 Bill Wight	20.00	40.00
101 Red Schoendienst	60.00	150.00
102 Jim Hegan	30.00	50.00
103 Del Ennis	25.00	60.00
104 Luke Easter	40.00	100.00
105 Eddie Joost	20.00	40.00
106 Ken Raffensberger	20.00	40.00
107 Alex Kellner	20.00	40.00
108 Bobby Adams	20.00	40.00
109 Ken Wood	20.00	40.00
110 Bob Rush	20.00	40.00
111 Jim Dyck RC	20.00	40.00
112 Toby Atwell	20.00	40.00
113 Karl Drews	40.00	100.00
114 Bob Feller	150.00	400.00
115 Cloyd Boyer	50.00	80.00
116 Eddie Yost	60.00	100.00
117 Duke Snider	250.00	500.00
118 Billy Martin	125.00	300.00
119 Dale Mitchell	60.00	100.00
120 Marlin Stuart	40.00	100.00
121 Yogi Berra	400.00	800.00
122 Bill Serena	50.00	80.00
123 Johnny Lipon	50.00	80.00
124 Charlie Dressen MG	60.00	100.00
125 Fred Hatfield	50.00	80.00
126 Al Corwin	50.00	80.00
127 Dick Kryhoski	50.00	80.00
128 Whitey Lockman	60.00	150.00
129 Russ Meyer	40.00	100.00
130 Cass Michaels	40.00	100.00
131 Connie Ryan	45.00	75.00
132 Fred Hutchinson	40.00	100.00
133 Willie Jones	45.00	75.00
134 Johnny Pesky	40.00	100.00
135 Bobby Morgan	40.00	100.00
136 Jim Brideweser RC	45.00	75.00
137 Sam Dente	20.00	50.00
138 Bubba Church	45.00	75.00
139 Pete Runnels	60.00	90.00
140 Al Brazle	25.00	60.00
141 Frank Shea	45.00	75.00
142 Larry Miggins RC	45.00	75.00
143 Al Lopez MG	50.00	120.00
144 Warren Hacker	50.00	80.00
145 George Shuba	40.00	100.00
146 Early Wynn	50.00	120.00
147 Clem Koshorek	45.00	75.00
148 Billy Goodman	60.00	90.00
149 Al Corwin	20.00	50.00
150 Carl Scheib	45.00	75.00
151 Joe Adcock	40.00	100.00
152 Clyde Vollmer	45.00	75.00
153 Whitey Ford	250.00	500.00
154 Turk Lown	30.00	80.00
155 Allie Clark	30.00	80.00
156 Max Surkont	45.00	75.00
157 Sherm Lollar	60.00	90.00
158 Howard Fox	25.00	80.00
159 Mickey Vernon UER	40.00	100.00
160 Cal Abrams	100.00	250.00

1954 Bowman

The cards in this 224-card set measure approximately 2 1/2" by 3 3/4". The set was distributed in two separate series: 1-128 in first series and 129-224 in second series. A contractual problem apparently resulted in the deletion of the number 66 Ted Williams card from this Bowman set, thereby creating a scarcity that is highly valued among collectors. The set price below does NOT include number 66 Williams but does include number 66 Jim Piersall, the apparent replacement for Williams in spite of the fact that Piersall was already number 210 to appear later in the set. Many errors in players' statistics exist (and some were corrected) while a few players' names were printed on the front, instead of appearing as a facsimile autograph. Most of these differences are so minor that there is no price differential for either card. The cards which changes were made on are numbers 12, 22,25,26,35,38,41,43,47,53,61,67,80,81,82,85,93,94,99,103,105,124,138,139, 140,145,153,156,174,179,185,212,216 and 217. The set was issued in seven-card nickel packs and one-card penny packs. The penny packs were issued 120 to a box while the nickel packs were issued 24 to a box. The notable Rookie Cards in this set are Harvey Kuenn and Don Larsen.

Card	Low	High
COMPLETE SET (224)	2500.00	4000.00
WRAP.(1-CENT, DATED)	100.00	150.00
WRAP.(1-CENT, UNDAT)	150.00	200.00
WRAP.(5-CENT, DATED)	100.00	150.00
WRAP.(5-CENT, UNDAT)	50.00	60.00
1 Phil Rizzuto	50.00	120.00
2 Jackie Jensen	15.00	30.00
3 Marion Fricano	6.00	12.00
4 Bob Hooper	6.00	12.00
5 Billy Hunter	6.00	12.00
6 Nellie Fox	50.00	80.00
7 Walt Dropo	10.00	20.00
8 Jim Busby	6.00	12.00
9 Dave Williams	6.00	12.00
10 Carl Erskine	12.00	30.00
11 Sid Gordon	6.00	12.00
12A Roy McMillan 551/1290 At Bat	10.00	20.00
12B Roy McMillan 557/1296 At Bat	10.00	20.00
13 Paul Minner	6.00	12.00
14 Gerry Staley	6.00	12.00
15 Richie Ashburn	25.00	60.00
16 Jim Wilson	6.00	12.00
17 Tom Gorman	6.00	12.00
18 Hoot Evers	6.00	12.00
19 Bobby Shantz	10.00	20.00
20 Art Houtteman	6.00	12.00
21 Vic Wertz	10.00	20.00
22A Sam Mele 213/1661 Putouts	6.00	12.00
22B Sam Mele 217/1665 Putouts	6.00	12.00
23 Harvey Kuenn RC	15.00	30.00
24 Bob Porterfield	6.00	12.00
25A Wes Westrum 1.000/.987 Fielding Avg.	10.00	20.00
25B Wes Westrum .982/.986 Fielding Avg.	10.00	20.00
26A Billy Cox 1.000/.960 Fielding Avg.	10.00	20.00
26B Billy Cox .972/.960 Fielding Avg.	10.00	20.00
27 Dick Cole RC	6.00	12.00
28A Jim Greengrass Birthplace Addison, NJ	6.00	12.00
28B Jim Greengrass Birthplace Addison, NY	6.00	12.00
29 Johnny Klippstein	6.00	12.00
30 Del Rice	6.00	12.00
31 Smoky Burgess	10.00	20.00
32 Del Crandall	10.00	20.00
33A Vic Raschi No Trade	10.00	20.00
33B Vic Raschi Traded to St.Louis	15.00	30.00
34 Sammy White	6.00	12.00
35A Eddie Joost Quiz Answer is 8	6.00	12.00
35B Eddie Joost Quiz Answer is 33	6.00	12.00
36 George Strickland	6.00	12.00
37 Dick Kokos	6.00	12.00
38A Minnie Minoso .895/.961 Fielding Avg.	15.00	30.00
38B Minnie Minoso .963/.963 Fielding Avg.	15.00	30.00
39 Ned Garver	6.00	12.00
40 Gil Coan	6.00	12.00
41A Alvin Dark .986/960 Fielding Avg.	10.00	20.00
41B Alvin Dark	10.00	20.00

.968/.960 Fielding Avg.		
42 Billy Loes	10.00	20.00
43A Bob Friend 20 Shutouts in Quiz	10.00	20.00
43B Bob Friend 16 Shutouts in Quiz	10.00	20.00
44 Harry Perkowski	6.00	12.00
45 Ralph Kiner	15.00	40.00
46 Rip Repulski	6.00	12.00
47A Granny Hamner	6.00	12.00
.970/.953 Fielding Avg.		
47B Granny Hamner	6.00	12.00
.953/.951 Fielding Avg.		
48 Jack Dittmer	6.00	12.00
49 Harry Byrd	6.00	12.00
50 George Kell	15.00	40.00
51 Alex Kellner	6.00	12.00
52 Joe Ginsberg	6.00	12.00
53A Don Lenhardt	6.00	12.00
.969/.984 Fielding Avg.		
53B Don Lenhardt	6.00	12.00
.966/.983 Fielding Avg.		
54 Chico Carrasquel	6.00	12.00
55 Jim Delsing	6.00	12.00
56 Maurice McDermott	6.00	12.00
57 Hoyt Wilhelm	15.00	40.00
58 Pee Wee Reese	40.00	100.00
59 Bob Schultz	6.00	12.00
60 Fred Baczewski RC	6.00	12.00
61A Eddie Miksis	6.00	12.00
.954/.962 Fielding Avg.		
61B Eddie Miksis	6.00	12.00
.954/.961 Fielding Avg.		
62 Enos Slaughter	20.00	50.00
63 Earl Torgeson	6.00	12.00
64 Eddie Mathews	40.00	100.00
65 Mickey Mantle	1250.00	2500.00
66A Ted Williams	1250.00	2500.00
66B Jimmy Piersall	50.00	80.00
67A Carl Scheib .306 Pct.		
Two Lines under Bio	6.00	12.00
67B Carl Scheib .306 Pct.		
One Line under Bio	6.00	12.00
67C Carl Scheib .300 Pct.	6.00	12.00
68 Bobby Avila	10.00	20.00
69 Clint Courtney	6.00	12.00
70 Willard Marshall	6.00	12.00
71 Ted Gray	6.00	12.00
72 Eddie Yost	10.00	20.00
73 Don Mueller	10.00	20.00
74 Jim Gilliam	15.00	30.00
75 Max Surkont	6.00	12.00
76 Joe Nuxhall	10.00	20.00
77 Bob Rush	6.00	12.00
78 Sal Yvars	6.00	12.00
79 Curt Simmons	10.00	20.00
80A Johnny Logan 106 Runs	6.00	12.00
80B Johnny Logan 100 Runs	6.00	12.00
81A Jerry Coleman	10.00	20.00
1.000/.975 Fielding Avg.		
81B Jerry Coleman	10.00	20.00
.952/.975 Fielding Avg.		
82A Bill Goodman	10.00	20.00
.965/.986 Fielding Avg.		
82B Bill Goodman	10.00	20.00
.972/.985 Fielding Avg.		
83 Ray Murray	6.00	12.00
84 Larry Doby	25.00	50.00
85A Jim Dyck	6.00	12.00
.926/.956 Fielding Avg.		
85B Jim Dyck	6.00	12.00
.947/.960 Fielding Avg.		
86 Harry Dorish	6.00	12.00
87 Don Lund	6.00	12.00
88 Tom Umphlett RC	6.00	12.00
89 Willie Mays	250.00	600.00
90 Roy Campanella	50.00	120.00
91 Cal Abrams	6.00	12.00
92 Ken Raffensberger	6.00	12.00
93A Bill Serena	6.00	12.00
.983/.966 Fielding Avg.		
93B Bill Serena	6.00	12.00
.977/.966 Fielding Avg.		
94A Solly Hemus	6.00	12.00
476/1343 Assists		
94B Solly Hemus	6.00	12.00
477/1343 Assists		
95 Robin Roberts	25.00	50.00
96 Joe Adcock	10.00	20.00
97 Gil McDougald	10.00	20.00
98 Ellis Kinder	6.00	12.00
99A Peter Suder	6.00	12.00
.985/.974 Fielding Avg.		
99B Peter Suder	6.00	12.00
.978/.974 Fielding Avg.		
100 Mike Garcia	10.00	20.00
101 Don Larsen RC	25.00	60.00
102 Billy Pierce	10.00	20.00
103A Stephen Souchock	6.00	12.00
144/1192 Putouts		
103B Stephen Souchock	6.00	12.00
147/1195 Putouts		
104 Frank Shea	6.00	12.00
105A Sal Maglie Quiz Answer is 8	10.00	20.00
105B Sal Maglie Quiz Answer is 1904	10.00	20.00
106 Clem Labine	10.00	20.00
107 Paul LaPalme	6.00	12.00
108 Bobby Adams	6.00	12.00
109 Roy Smalley	6.00	12.00
110 Red Schoendienst	25.00	50.00
111 Murry Dickson	6.00	12.00
112 Andy Pafko	10.00	20.00
113 Allie Reynolds	20.00	50.00
114 Willard Nixon	6.00	12.00
115 Don Bollweg	6.00	12.00
116 Luke Easter	10.00	20.00
117 Dick Kryhoski	6.00	12.00
118 Bob Boyd	6.00	12.00
119 Fred Hatfield	6.00	12.00
120 Mel Hoderlein RC	6.00	12.00
121 Ray Katt RC	6.00	12.00
122 Carl Furillo	15.00	30.00
123 Toby Atwell	6.00	12.00
124A Gus Bell	10.00	20.00
15/27 Errors		
124B Gus Bell	10.00	20.00
11/26 Errors		
125 Warren Hacker	6.00	12.00
126 Cliff Chambers	6.00	12.00
127 Del Ennis	10.00	20.00
128 Ebba St.Claire	6.00	12.00
129 Hank Bauer	15.00	30.00
130 Milt Bolling	6.00	12.00
131 Joe Astroth	6.00	12.00
132 Bob Feller	40.00	100.00
133 Duane Pillette	6.00	12.00
134 Luis Aloma	6.00	12.00
135 Johnny Pesky	10.00	20.00
136 Clyde Vollmer	6.00	12.00
137 Al Corwin	6.00	12.00
138A Hodges .993/.991 Field.Avg.	50.00	80.00
138B Hodges .992/.991 Field.Avg.	50.00	80.00
139A Preston Ward	6.00	12.00
.961/.992 Fielding Avg.		
139B Preston Ward	6.00	12.00
.990/.992 Fielding Avg.		
140A Saul Rogovin	6.00	12.00
7-12 W-L 2 Strikeouts		
140B Saul Rogovin	6.00	12.00
7-12 W-L 62 Strikeouts		
140C Saul Rogovin 8-12 W-L	6.00	12.00
141 Joe Garagiola	15.00	30.00
142 Al Brazle	6.00	12.00
143 Willie Jones	6.00	12.00
144 Ernie Johnson RC	15.00	30.00
145A Martin .985/.983 Field.Avg.	50.00	80.00
145B Martin .983/.982 Field.Avg.	50.00	80.00
146 Dick Gernert	6.00	12.00
147 Joe DeMaestri	6.00	12.00
148 Dale Mitchell	10.00	20.00
149 Bob Young	6.00	12.00
150 Cass Michaels	6.00	12.00
151 Pat Mullin	6.00	12.00
152 Mickey Vernon	10.00	20.00
153A Whitey Lockman	10.00	20.00
100/331 Assists		
153B Whitey Lockman	10.00	20.00
102/333 Assists		
154 Don Newcombe	15.00	30.00
155 Frank Thomas RC	10.00	20.00
156A Rocky Bridges	6.00	12.00
320/467 Assists		
156B Rocky Bridges	6.00	12.00
328/475 Assists		
157 Turk Lown	6.00	12.00
158 Stu Miller	10.00	20.00
159 Johnny Lindell	6.00	12.00
160 Danny O'Connell	6.00	12.00
161 Yogi Berra	60.00	150.00
162 Ted Lepcio	6.00	12.00
103A Dave Philley No Trade 152 Games	10.00	20.00
163B Dave Philley Traded to		
Cleveland 152 Games	15.00	30.00
163C Dave Philley Traded to		
Cleveland 157 Games	15.00	30.00
164 Early Wynn	20.00	50.00
165 Johnny Groth	6.00	12.00
166 Sandy Consuegra	6.00	12.00
167 Billy Hoeft	6.00	12.00
168 Ed Fitzgerald	6.00	12.00
169 Larry Jansen	10.00	20.00
170 Duke Snider	50.00	120.00
171 Carlos Bernier	6.00	12.00
172 Andy Seminick	6.00	12.00
173 Dee Fondy	6.00	12.00
174A Pete Castiglione	6.00	12.00
.966/.959 Fielding Avg.		
174B Pete Castiglione	6.00	12.00
.970/.959 Fielding Avg.		
175 Mel Clark	6.00	12.00
176 Vern Bickford	6.00	12.00
177 Whitey Ford	50.00	120.00
178 Del Wilber	6.00	12.00
179A Morris Martin 44 ERA	6.00	12.00
179B Morris Martin 4.44 ERA	6.00	12.00
180 Joe Tipton	6.00	12.00
181 Les Moss	6.00	12.00
182 Sherm Lollar	10.00	20.00
183 Matt Batts	6.00	12.00
184 Mickey Grasso	6.00	12.00
185A Daryl Spencer	6.00	12.00
.941/.944 Fielding Avg. RC		
185B Daryl Spencer .933		
.936 Fielding Avg.	6.00	12.00
186 Russ Meyer	6.00	12.00
187 Vern Law	10.00	20.00
188 Frank Smith	6.00	12.00
189 Randy Jackson	6.00	12.00
190 Joe Presko	6.00	12.00
191 Karl Drews	6.00	12.00
192 Lew Burdette	10.00	20.00
193 Eddie Robinson	6.00	12.00
194 Sid Hudson	6.00	12.00
195 Bob Cain	6.00	12.00
196 Bob Lemon	25.00	50.00
197 Lou Kretlow	6.00	12.00
198 Virgil Trucks	6.00	12.00
199 Steve Gromek	6.00	12.00
200 Conrado Marrero	6.00	12.00
201 Bobby Thomson	15.00	30.00
202 George Shuba	10.00	20.00
203 Vic Janowicz	10.00	20.00
204 Jack Collum RC	6.00	12.00
205 Hal Jeffcoat	6.00	12.00
206 Steve Bilko	6.00	12.00
207 Stan Lopata	6.00	12.00
208 Johnny Antonelli	10.00	20.00
209 Gene Woodling UER		
Reversed Photo	6.00	12.00
210 Jimmy Piersall	15.00	30.00
211 Al Robertson RC	6.00	12.00
212A Owen Friend	6.00	12.00
.964/.957 Fielding Avg.		
212B Owen Friend	6.00	12.00
.967/.958 Fielding Avg.		
213 Dick Littlefield	6.00	12.00
214 Ferris Fain	10.00	20.00
215 Johnny Bucha	6.00	12.00
216A Jerry Snyder	6.00	12.00
.988/.988 Fielding Avg.		
216B Jerry Snyder	6.00	12.00
.968/.968 Fielding Avg.		
217A Henry Thompson	10.00	20.00
.956/.951 Fielding Avg.		
217B Henry Thompson	10.00	20.00
.958/.952 Fielding Avg.		
218 Preacher Roe	10.00	20.00
219 Hal Rice	6.00	12.00
220 Hobie Landrith RC	6.00	12.00
221 Frank Baumholtz	6.00	12.00
222 Memo Luna RC	6.00	12.00
223 Steve Ridzik	6.00	12.00
224 Bill Bruton	25.00	50.00

1955 Bowman

The cards in this 320-card set measure approximately 2 1/2" by 3 3/4". The Bowman set of 1955 is known as the "TV set" because each player photograph is cleverly shown within a television set design. The set contains umpire cards, some transposed pictures (e.g., Johnsons and Bollings), an incorrect spelling for Harvey Kuenn, and a traded line for Palica (all of which are noted in the checklist below). Some three-card advertising strips exist, the backs of these panels contain advertising for Bowman products. Print advertisments for these cards featured Willie Mays along with publicizing the great value in nine cards for a nickel. Advertising panels seen include Nellie Fox/Carl Furillo/Carl Erskine; Hank Aaron/Johnny Logan/Eddie Miksis; Bob Rush/Ray Katt/Willie Mays; Steve Gromek/Milt Bolling/Vern Stephens, Russ Kemmemer/ Hal Jeffcoat/Dee Fondy and a Bob Darnell/Early Wynn/Pee Wee Reese. Cards were issued either in nine-card nickel packs or one card penny packs. Cello packs containing approximately 20 cards have also been seen, albeit on a very limited basis. The notable Rookie Cards in this set are Elston Howard and Don Zimmer. Hall of Fame umpires pictured in the set are Al Barlick, Jocko Conlon and Cal Hubbard. Undated five cent wrappers are also known to exist for this set.

COMPLETE SET (320)	3500.00	6000.00
COMMON CARD (1-96)	6.00	12.00
COM. CARD (97-224)	5.00	10.00
COM. CARD (225-320)	7.50	15.00
COM. UMPIRE (225-320)	18.00	30.00
WRAPPER (1-CENT)	50.00	60.00
WRAPPER (5-CENT)	50.00	60.00
1 Hoyt Wilhelm	60.00	100.00
2 Alvin Dark	7.50	15.00
3 Joe Coleman	7.50	15.00
4 Eddie Waitkus	7.50	15.00
5 Jim Robertson	6.00	12.00
6 Pete Suder	6.00	12.00
7 Gene Baker RC	6.00	12.00
8 Warren Hacker	6.00	12.00
9 Gil McDougald	10.00	20.00
10 Phil Rizzuto	30.00	80.00
11 Bill Bruton	7.50	15.00
12 Andy Pafko	7.50	15.00
13 Clyde Vollmer	6.00	12.00
14 Gus Keriazakos RC	6.00	12.00
15 Frank Sullivan RC	6.00	12.00
16 Jimmy Piersall	12.00	30.00
17 Del Ennis	7.50	15.00
18 Stan Lopata	6.00	12.00
19 Bobby Avila	7.50	15.00
20 Al Smith	7.50	15.00
21 Don Hoak	6.00	12.00
22 Roy Campanella	40.00	100.00
23 Al Kaline	40.00	100.00
24 Al Aber	6.00	12.00
25 Minnie Minoso	15.00	30.00
26 Virgil Trucks	7.50	15.00
27 Preston Ward	6.00	12.00
28 Dick Cole	6.00	12.00
29 Red Schoendienst	15.00	30.00
30 Bill Sarni	6.00	12.00
31 Johnny Temple RC	7.50	15.00
32 Wally Post	7.50	15.00
33 Nellie Fox	30.00	50.00
34 Clint Courtney	6.00	12.00
35 Bill Tuttle RC	6.00	12.00
36 Wayne Belardi RC	6.00	12.00
37 Pee Wee Reese	30.00	80.00
38 Early Wynn	20.00	50.00
39 Bob Darnell RC	7.50	15.00
40 Vic Wertz	7.50	15.00
41 Mel Clark	6.00	12.00
42 Bob Greenwood RC	6.00	12.00
43 Bob Buhl	7.50	15.00
44 Danny O'Connell	6.00	12.00
45 Tom Umphlett	6.00	12.00
46 Mickey Vernon	7.50	15.00
47 Sammy White	6.00	12.00
48A Milt Bolling ERR	10.00	20.00
48B Milt Bolling COR	10.00	20.00
49 Jim Greengrass	6.00	12.00
50 Hobie Landrith	6.00	12.00
51 Elvin Tappe RC	6.00	12.00
52 Hal Rice	6.00	12.00
53 Alex Kellner	6.00	12.00
54 Don Bollweg	6.00	12.00
55 Cal Abrams	6.00	12.00
56 Billy Cox	7.50	15.00
57 Bob Friend	7.50	15.00
58 Frank Thomas	7.50	15.00
59 Whitey Ford	40.00	100.00
60 Enos Slaughter	12.00	30.00
61 Paul LaPalme	6.00	12.00
62 Royce Lint RC	6.00	12.00
63 Irv Noren	7.50	15.00
64 Curt Simmons	7.50	15.00
65 Don Zimmer RC	20.00	50.00
66 George Shuba	10.00	20.00
67 Don Larsen	25.00	60.00
68 Elston Howard RC	50.00	80.00
69 Billy Hunter	6.00	12.00
70 Lew Burdette	10.00	20.00
71 Dave Jolly	6.00	12.00
72 Chet Nichols	6.00	12.00
73 Eddie Yost	7.50	15.00
74 Jerry Snyder	6.00	12.00
75 Brooks Lawrence RC	6.00	12.00
76 Tom Poholsky	6.00	12.00
77 Jim McDonald RC	6.00	12.00
78 Gil Coan	8.00	20.00
79 Willie Miranda	6.00	12.00
80 Lou Limmer	6.00	12.00
81 Bobby Morgan	6.00	12.00
82 Lee Walls RC	6.00	12.00
83 Max Surkont	6.00	12.00
84 George Freese RC	6.00	12.00
85 Cass Michaels	6.00	12.00
86 Ted Gray	6.00	12.00
87 Randy Jackson	6.00	12.00
88 Steve Bilko	6.00	12.00
89 Lou Boudreau MG	15.00	30.00
90 Art RC	6.00	12.00
91 Dick Marlowe RC	6.00	12.00
92 George Zuverink	6.00	12.00
93 Andy Seminick	6.00	12.00
94 Hank Thompson	7.50	15.00
95 Sal Maglie	7.50	15.00
96 Ray Narleski RC	6.00	12.00
97 Johnny Podres	20.00	50.00
98 Jim Gilliam	10.00	20.00
99 Jerry Coleman	7.50	15.00
100 Tom Morgan	5.00	10.00
101A Don Johnson ERR	10.00	20.00
101B Don Johnson COR	10.00	20.00
102 Bobby Thomson	7.50	15.00
103 Eddie Mathews	50.00	120.00
104 Bob Porterfield	5.00	10.00
105 Johnny Schmitz	5.00	10.00
106 Del Rice	5.00	10.00
107 Solly Hemus	5.00	10.00
108 Lou Kretlow	5.00	10.00
109 Vern Stephens	7.50	15.00
110 Bob Miller	5.00	10.00
111 Steve Ridzik	5.00	10.00
112 Granny Hamner	5.00	10.00
113 Bob Hall RC	5.00	10.00
114 Vic Janowicz	7.50	15.00
115 Roger Bowman RC	5.00	10.00
116 Sandy Consuegra	5.00	10.00
117 Johnny Groth	5.00	10.00
118 Bobby Adams	5.00	10.00
119 Joe Astroth	5.00	10.00
120 Ed Burtschy RC	5.00	10.00
121 Rufus Crawford RC	5.00	10.00
122 Al Corwin	5.00	10.00
123 Marv Grissom RC	5.00	10.00
124 Johnny Antonelli	12.00	30.00
125 Paul Giel RC	7.50	15.00
126 Billy Goodman	7.50	15.00
127 Hank Majeski	5.00	10.00
128 Mike Garcia	7.50	15.00
129 Hal Naragon RC	5.00	10.00
130 Richie Ashburn	25.00	60.00
131 Willard Marshall	6.00	15.00
132A Harvey Kueen ERR	30.00	50.00
132B Harvey Kuenn COR	15.00	30.00
133 Charles King RC	5.00	10.00
134 Bob Feller	40.00	100.00
135 Lloyd Merriman	5.00	10.00
136 Rocky Bridges	5.00	10.00
137 Bob Talbot	5.00	10.00
138 Davey Williams	7.50	15.00
139 W.Shantz/B.Shantz	7.50	15.00
140 Bobby Shantz	7.50	15.00
141 Wes Westrum	7.50	15.00
142 Rudy Regalado RC	5.00	10.00
143 Don Newcombe	20.00	50.00
144 Art Houtteman	5.00	10.00
145 Bob Nieman RC	5.00	10.00
146 Don Liddle	5.00	10.00
147 Sam Mele	5.00	10.00
148 Bob Chakales	5.00	10.00
149 Cloyd Boyer	5.00	10.00
150 Billy Klaus RC	5.00	10.00
151 Jim Brideweser	5.00	10.00
152 Johnny Klippstein	5.00	10.00
153 Eddie Robinson	5.00	10.00
154 Frank Lary RC	7.50	15.00
155 Gerry Staley	5.00	10.00
156 Jim Hughes	7.50	15.00
157A Ernie Johnson ERR	10.00	20.00
157B Ernie Johnson COR	10.00	20.00
158 Gil Hodges	25.00	60.00
159 Harry Byrd	5.00	10.00
160 Bill Skowron	10.00	20.00
161 Matt Batts	5.00	10.00
162 Charlie Maxwell	5.00	10.00
163 Sid Gordon	7.50	15.00
164 Toby Atwell	5.00	10.00
165 Maurice McDermott	5.00	10.00
166 Jim Busby	10.00	25.00
167 Bob Grim RC	10.00	20.00
168 Yogi Berra	75.00	200.00
169 Carl Furillo	15.00	40.00
170 Carl Erskine	15.00	40.00
171 Robin Roberts	25.00	60.00
172 Willie Jones	5.00	10.00
173 Chico Carrasquel	5.00	10.00
174 Sherm Lollar	7.50	15.00
175 Wilmer Shantz RC	5.00	10.00
176 Joe DeMaestri	5.00	10.00
177 Willard Nixon	5.00	10.00
178 Tom Brewer RC	5.00	10.00
179 Hank Aaron	300.00	600.00
180 Johnny Logan	7.50	15.00
181 Eddie Miksis	5.00	10.00
182 Bob Rush	5.00	10.00
183 Ray Katt	5.00	10.00
184 Willie Mays	200.00	500.00
185 Vic Raschi	5.00	10.00
186 Alex Grammas	5.00	10.00
187 Fred Hatfield	5.00	10.00
188 Ned Garver	5.00	10.00
189 Jack Collum	5.00	10.00
190 Fred Baczewski	5.00	10.00
191 Bob Lemon	20.00	50.00
192 George Strickland	5.00	10.00
193 Howie Judson	5.00	10.00
194 Joe Nuxhall	7.50	15.00
195A Erv Palica	7.50	15.00
195B Erv Palica TR	20.00	40.00
196 Russ Meyer	7.50	15.00
197 Ralph Kiner	20.00	50.00
198 Dave Pope RC	5.00	10.00
199 Vern Law	7.50	15.00
200 Dick Littlefield	8.00	20.00
201 Allie Reynolds	15.00	40.00
202 Mickey Mantle UER	600.00	1500.00
203 Steve Gromek	5.00	10.00
204A Frank Bolling ERR RC	10.00	20.00
204B Frank Bolling COR	10.00	20.00
205 Rip Repulski	5.00	10.00
206 Ralph Beard RC	5.00	10.00
207 Frank Shea	5.00	10.00
208 Ed Fitzgerald	5.00	10.00
209 Smoky Burgess	7.50	15.00
210 Earl Torgeson	5.00	10.00
211 Sonny Dixon RC	5.00	10.00
212 Jack Dittmer	5.00	10.00
213 George Kell	15.00	30.00
214 Billy Pierce	7.50	15.00
215 Bob Kuzava	5.00	10.00
216 Preacher Roe	10.00	20.00
217 Del Crandall	7.50	15.00
218 Joe Adcock	7.50	15.00
219 Whitey Lockman	7.50	15.00
220 Jim Hearn	5.00	10.00
221 Hector Brown	5.00	10.00
222 Russ Kemmerer RC	5.00	10.00
223 Hal Jeffcoat	5.00	10.00
224 Dee Fondy	5.00	10.00
225 Paul Richards MG	7.50	15.00
226 Bill McKinley UMP	18.00	30.00
227 Frank Baumholtz	7.50	15.00
228 John Phillips RC	7.50	15.00
229 Jim Brosnan RC	10.00	20.00
230 Al Brazle	7.50	15.00
231 Jim Konstanty	10.00	20.00
232 Birdie Tebbetts MG	10.00	20.00
233 Bill Serena	7.50	15.00
234 Dick Bartell CO	10.00	20.00
235 Joe Paparella UMP	18.00	30.00
236 Murry Dickson	7.50	15.00
237 Johnny Wyrostek	7.50	15.00
238 Eddie Stanky MG	10.00	20.00
239 Edwin Rommel UMP	20.00	40.00
240 Billy Loes	10.00	20.00
241 Johnny Pesky	10.00	20.00
242 Ernie Banks	150.00	400.00
243 Gus Bell	10.00	20.00
244 Duane Pillette	7.50	15.00
245 Bill Miller	7.50	15.00
246 Hank Bauer	15.00	30.00
247 Dutch Leonard CO	7.50	15.00
248 Harry Dorish	7.50	15.00
249 Billy Gardner RC	10.00	20.00
250 Larry Napp UMP	18.00	30.00
251 Stan Jok	7.50	15.00
252 Roy Smalley	7.50	15.00
253 Jim Wilson	7.50	15.00
254 Bennett Flowers RC	7.50	15.00
255 Pete Runnels	10.00	20.00
256 Owen Friend	7.50	15.00
257 Tom Alston RC	7.50	15.00
258 John Stevens UMP	18.00	30.00
259 Don Mossi RC	15.00	30.00
260 Edwin Hurley UMP	18.00	30.00
261 Walt Moryn RC	10.00	20.00
262 Jim Lemon FBC	7.50	15.00
263 Eddie Joost	7.50	15.00
264 Bill Henry RC	7.50	15.00
265 Al Barlick UMP	50.00	80.00
266 Mike Fornieles	7.50	15.00
267 J.Honochick UMP	15.00	40.00
268 Roy Lee Hawes RC	7.50	15.00
269 Joe Amalfitano RC	10.00	20.00
270 Chico Fernandez RC	10.00	20.00
271 Bob Hooper	7.50	15.00
272 John Flaherty UMP	18.00	30.00
273 Bubba Church	7.50	15.00
274 Jim Delsing	7.50	15.00
275 William Grieve UMP	18.00	30.00
276 Ike Delock	7.50	15.00
277 Ed Runge UMP	18.00	30.00
278 Charlie Neal RC	20.00	40.00
279 Hank Soar UMP	20.00	40.00
280 Clyde McCullough	7.50	15.00
281 Charles Berry UMP	20.00	40.00
282 Phil Cavarretta MG	10.00	20.00
283 Nestor Chylak UMP	50.00	80.00
284 Bill Jackowski UMP	18.00	30.00
285 Walt Dropo	10.00	20.00
286 Frank Secory UMP	18.00	30.00
287 Ron Mrozinski RC	7.50	15.00
288 Dick Smith RC	7.50	15.00
289 Arthur Gore UMP	18.00	30.00
290 Hershell Freeman RC	7.50	15.00
291 Frank Dascoli UMP	18.00	30.00
292 Marv Blaylock RC	7.50	15.00
293 Thomas Gorman UMP	20.00	40.00
294 Wally Moses CO	7.50	15.00
295 Lee Ballanfant UMP	18.00	30.00
296 Bill Virdon RC	15.00	30.00
297 Dusty Boggess UMP	18.00	30.00
298 Charlie Grimm	10.00	20.00
299 Lon Warneke UMP	20.00	40.00
300 Tommy Byrne	10.00	20.00
301 William Engeln UMP	18.00	30.00
302 Frank Malzone RC	15.00	30.00
303 Jocko Conlan UMP	50.00	80.00
304 Harry Chiti	7.50	15.00
305 Frank Umont UMP	18.00	30.00
306 Bob Cerv	10.00	20.00
307 Babe Pinelli UMP	20.00	40.00
308 Al Lopez MG	30.00	50.00
309 Hal Dixon UMP	18.00	30.00
310 Ken Lehman RC	7.50	15.00
311 Lawrence Goetz UMP	18.00	30.00
312 Bill Wight	7.50	15.00
313 Augie Donatelli UMP	30.00	50.00
314 Dale Mitchell	10.00	20.00
315 Cal Hubbard UMP	25.00	60.00
316 Marion Fricano	7.50	15.00
317 William Summers UMP	10.00	20.00
318 Sid Hudson	7.50	15.00
319 Al Schroll RC	7.50	15.00
320 George Susce RC	30.00	50.00

1989 Bowman

The 1989 Bowman set, produced by Topps, contains 484 slightly oversized cards (measuring 2 1/2" by 3 3/4"). The cards were released in midseason 1989 in wax, rack, cello and factory set formats. The fronts have white-bordered color photos with facsimile autographs and small Bowman logos. The backs feature charts detailing 1988 player performances vs. each team. The cards are ordered alphabetically according to teams in the AL and NL. Cards 258-261 form a father/son subset. Rookie Cards in this set include Sandy Alomar Jr., Steve Finley, Ken Griffey Jr., Tino Martinez, Gary Sheffield, John Smoltz and Robin Ventura.

COMPLETE SET (484)	10.00	25.00
COMP.FACT.SET (484)	10.00	25.00
1 Oswald Peraza RC	.01	.05
2 Brian Holton	.01	.05
3 Jose Bautista RC	.02	.10
4 Pete Harnisch RC	.08	.25
5 Dave Schmidt	.01	.05
6 Gregg Olson RC	.08	.25
7 Jeff Ballard	.01	.05
8 Bob Melvin	.01	.05
9 Cal Ripken	.30	.75
10 Randy Milligan	.01	.05
11 Juan Bell RC	.02	.10
12 Billy Ripken	.01	.05
13 Jim Traber	.01	.05
14 Pete Stanicek	.01	.05
15 Steve Finley RC	.30	.75
16 Larry Sheets	.01	.05
17 Phil Bradley	.01	.05
18 Brady Anderson RC	.15	.40
19 Lee Smith	.02	.10
20 Tom Fischer	.01	.05
21 Mike Boddicker	.01	.05
22 Rob Murphy	.01	.05
23 Wes Gardner	.01	.05
24 John Dopson	.01	.05
25 Bob Stanley	.01	.05
26 Roger Clemens	.40	1.00
27 Rich Gedman	.01	.05
28 Marty Barrett	.01	.05
29 Luis Rivera	.01	.05
30 Jody Reed	.01	.05
31 Nick Esasky	.01	.05
32 Wade Boggs	.05	.15
33 Jim Rice	.02	.10
34 Mike Greenwell	.01	.05
35 Dwight Evans	.05	.15
36 Ellis Burks	.02	.10
37 Chuck Finley	.02	.10
38 Kirk McCaskill	.01	.05
39 Jim Abbott RC	.40	1.00
40 Bryan Harvey RC *	.08	.25
41 Bert Blyleven	.02	.10
42 Mike Witt	.01	.05
43 Bob McClure	.01	.05
44 Bill Schroeder	.01	.05
45 Lance Parrish	.02	.10
46 Dick Schofield	.01	.05
47 Wally Joyner	.02	.10
48 Jack Howell	.01	.05
49 Johnny Ray	.01	.05
50 Chili Davis	.02	.10
51 Tony Armas	.02	.10
52 Claudell Washington	.01	.05
53 Brian Downing	.02	.10
54 Devon White	.02	.10
55 Bobby Thigpen	.01	.05
56 Bill Long	.01	.05
57 Jerry Reuss	.01	.05
58 Shawn Hillegas	.01	.05
59 Melido Perez	.01	.05
60 Jeff Bittiger	.01	.05
61 Jack McDowell	.02	.10
62 Carlton Fisk	.05	.15
63 Steve Lyons	.01	.05
64 Ozzie Guillen	.02	.10
65 Robin Ventura RC	.30	.75
66 Fred Manrique	.01	.05
67 Dan Pasqua	.01	.05
68 Ivan Calderon	.01	.05
69 Ron Kittle	.01	.05
70 Daryl Boston	.01	.05
71 Dave Gallagher	.01	.05
72 Harold Baines	.02	.10
73 Charles Nagy RC	.08	.25
74 John Farrell	.01	.05
75 Kevin Wickander	.01	.05
76 Greg Swindell	.01	.05
77 Mike Walker	.01	.05
78 Doug Jones	.01	.05
79 Rich Yett	.01	.05
80 Tom Candiotti	.01	.05
81 Jesse Orosco	.01	.05
82 Bud Black	.01	.05
83 Andy Allanson	.01	.05
84 Pete O'Brien	.01	.05
85 Jerry Browne	.01	.05
86 Brook Jacoby	.01	.05
87 Mark Lewis RC	.08	.25
88 Luis Aguayo	.01	.05
89 Cory Snyder	.01	.05
90 Oddibe McDowell	.01	.05
91 Joe Carter	.02	.10
92 Frank Tanana	.02	.10
93 Jack Morris	.02	.10
94 Doyle Alexander	.01	.05
95 Steve Searcy	.01	.05
96 Randy Bockus	.01	.05
97 Jeff M. Robinson	.01	.05
98 Mike Henneman	.01	.05
99 Paul Gibson	.01	.05
100 Frank Williams	.01	.05
101 Matt Nokes	.01	.05
102 Rico Brogna RC	.15	.40
103 Lou Whitaker	.02	.10
104 Al Pedrique	.01	.05
105 Alan Trammell	.02	.10
106 Chris Brown	.01	.05
107 Pat Sheridan	.01	.05
108 Chet Lemon	.02	.10
109 Keith Moreland	.01	.05
110 Mel Stottlemyre Jr.	.01	.05
111 Bret Saberhagen	.02	.10
112 Floyd Bannister	.01	.05
113 Jeff Montgomery	.01	.05
114 Steve Farr	.01	.05
115 Tom Gordon UER RC	.15	.40
116 Charlie Leibrandt	.01	.05
117 Mark Gubicza	.01	.05
118 Mike Macfarlane RC *	.08	.25
119 Bob Boone	.02	.10
120 Kurt Stillwell	.01	.05
121 George Brett	.25	.60
122 Frank White	.02	.10
123 Kevin Seitzer	.01	.05
124 Willie Wilson	.02	.10
125 Pat Tabler	.01	.05
126 Bo Jackson	.08	.25
127 Hugh Walker RC	.02	.10
128 Danny Tartabull	.01	.05
129 Teddy Higuera	.01	.05

130 Don August .01 .05
131 Juan Nieves .01 .05
132 Mike Birkbeck .01 .05
133 Dan Plesac .01 .05
134 Chris Bosio .01 .05
135 Bill Wegman .01 .05
136 Chuck Crim .01 .05
137 B.J. Surhoff .02 .10
138 Joey Meyer .01 .05
139 Dale Sveum .01 .05
140 Paul Molitor .02 .10
141 Jim Gantner .01 .05
142 Gary Sheffield RC .60 1.50
143 Greg Brock .01 .05
144 Robin Yount .15 .40
145 Glenn Braggs .01 .05
146 Rob Deer .01 .05
147 Fred Toliver .01 .05
148 Jeff Reardon .02 .10
149 Allan Anderson .01 .05
150 Frank Viola .02 .10
151 Shane Rawley .01 .05
152 Juan Berenguer .01 .05
153 Johnny Ard .01 .05
154 Tim Laudner .01 .05
155 Brian Harper .01 .05
156 Al Newman .01 .05
157 Kent Hrbek .02 .10
158 Gary Gaetti .02 .10
159 Wally Backman .01 .05
160 Gene Larkin .01 .05
161 Greg Gagne .01 .05
162 Kirby Puckett .08 .25
163 Dan Gladden .01 .05
164 Randy Bush .01 .05
165 Dave LaPoint .01 .05
166 Andy Hawkins .01 .05
167 Dave Righetti .02 .10
168 Lance McCullers .01 .05
169 Jimmy Jones .01 .05
170 Al Leiter .08 .25
171 John Candelaria .01 .05
172 Don Slaught .01 .05
173 Jamie Quirk .01 .05
174 Rafael Santana .01 .05
175 Mike Pagliarulo .01 .05
176 Don Mattingly .25 .60
177 Ken Phelps .01 .05
178 Steve Sax .01 .05
179 Dave Winfield .02 .10
180 Stan Jefferson .01 .05
181 Rickey Henderson .08 .25
182 Bob Brower .01 .05
183 Roberto Kelly .01 .05
184 Curt Young .01 .05
185 Gene Nelson .01 .05
186 Bob Welch .02 .10
187 Rick Honeycutt .01 .05
188 Dave Stewart .02 .10
189 Mike Moore .01 .05
190 Dennis Eckersley .05 .15
191 Eric Plunk .01 .05
192 Storm Davis .01 .05
193 Terry Steinbach .02 .10
194 Ron Hassey .01 .05
195 Stan Royer RC .02 .10
196 Walt Weiss .01 .05
197 Mark McGwire .40 1.00
198 Carney Lansford .02 .10
199 Glenn Hubbard .01 .05
200 Dave Henderson .01 .05
201 Jose Canseco .08 .25
202 Dave Parker .02 .10
203 Scott Bankhead .01 .05
204 Tom Niedenfuer .01 .05
205 Mark Langston .01 .05
206 Erik Hanson RC .08 .25
207 Mike Jackson .01 .05
208 Dave Valle .01 .05
209 Scott Bradley .01 .05
210 Harold Reynolds .02 .10
211 Tino Martinez RC .75 2.00
212 Rich Renteria .01 .05
213 Rey Quinones .01 .05
214 Jim Presley .01 .05
215 Alvin Davis .01 .05
216 Edgar Martinez .08 .25
217 Darnell Coles .01 .05
218 Jeffrey Leonard .01 .05
219 Jay Buhner .02 .10
220 Ken Griffey Jr. RC 2.50 6.00
221 Drew Hall .01 .05
222 Bobby Witt .01 .05
223 Jamie Moyer .02 .10
224 Charlie Hough .02 .10
225 Nolan Ryan .40 1.00
226 Jeff Russell .01 .05
227 Jim Sundberg .02 .10
228 Julio Franco .02 .10
229 Buddy Bell .02 .10
230 Scott Fletcher .01 .05
231 Jeff Kunkel .01 .05
232 Steve Buechele .01 .05
233 Monty Fariss .01 .05
234 Rick Leach .01 .05
235 Ruben Sierra .02 .10
236 Cecil Espy .01 .05
237 Rafael Palmeiro .08 .25
238 Pete Incaviglia .01 .05
239 Dave Stieb .02 .10
240 Jeff Musselman .01 .05
241 Mike Flanagan .01 .05
242 Todd Stottlemyre .01 .05
243 Jimmy Key .02 .10
244 Tony Castillo RC .02 .10
245 Alex Sanchez RC .01 .05
246 Tom Henke .01 .05
247 John Cerutti .01 .05
248 Ernie Whitt .01 .05
249 Bob Brenly .01 .05
250 Rance Mulliniks .01 .05
251 Kelly Gruber .01 .05
252 Ed Sprague RC .08 .25
253 Fred McGriff .05 .15
254 Tony Fernandez .01 .05
255 Tom Lawless .01 .05
256 George Bell .02 .10
257 Jesse Barfield .02 .10
258 Roberto Alomar w Dad .05 .15
259 Ken Griffey Sr. Jr. .40 1.00
260 Cal Ripken Sr. Jr. .08 .25
261 M.Stottlemyre Jr. Sr. .01 .05
262 Zane Smith .01 .05
263 Charlie Puleo .01 .05
264 Derek Lilliquist RC .02 .10
265 Paul Assenmacher .01 .05
266 John Smoltz RC .60 1.50
267 Tom Glavine .08 .25
268 Steve Avery RC .08 .25
269 Pete Smith .01 .05
270 Jody Davis .01 .05
271 Bruce Benedict .01 .05
272 Andres Thomas .01 .05
273 Gerald Perry .01 .05
274 Ron Gant .02 .10
275 Darrell Evans .02 .10
276 Dale Murphy .05 .15
277 Dion James .01 .05
278 Lonnie Smith .01 .05
279 Geronimo Berroa .01 .05
280 Steve Wilson RC .02 .10
281 Rick Sutcliffe .02 .10
282 Kevin Coffman .01 .05
283 Mitch Williams .01 .05
284 Greg Maddux .20 .50
285 Paul Kilgus .01 .05
286 Mike Harkey RC .02 .10
287 Lloyd McClendon .01 .05
288 Damon Berryhill .01 .05
289 Ty Griffin .01 .05
290 Ryne Sandberg .15 .40
291 Mark Grace .08 .25
292 Curt Wilkerson .01 .05
293 Vance Law .01 .05
294 Shawon Dunston .01 .05
295 Jerome Walton RC .08 .25
296 Mitch Webster .01 .05
297 Dwight Smith RC .08 .25
298 Andre Dawson .02 .10
299 Jeff Sellers .01 .05
300 Jose Rijo .01 .05
301 John Franco .02 .10
302 Rick Mahler .01 .05
303 Ron Robinson .01 .05
304 Danny Jackson .01 .05
305 Rob Dibble RC .15 .40
306 Tom Browning .01 .05
307 Bo Diaz .01 .05
308 Manny Trillo .01 .05
309 Chris Sabo RC .15 .40
310 Ron Oester .01 .05
311 Barry Larkin .05 .15
312 Todd Benzinger .01 .05
313 Paul O'Neill .05 .15
314 Kal Daniels .01 .05
315 Joel Youngblood .01 .05
316 Eric Davis .02 .10
317 Dave Smith .01 .05
318 Mark Portugal .01 .05
319 Brian Meyer .01 .05
320 Jim Deshaies .01 .05
321 Juan Agosto .01 .05
322 Mike Scott .02 .10
323 Rick Rhoden .01 .05
324 Jim Clancy .01 .05
325 Larry Andersen .01 .05
326 Alex Trevino .01 .05
327 Alan Ashby .01 .05
328 Craig Reynolds .01 .05
329 Bill Doran .01 .05
330 Rafael Ramirez .01 .05
331 Glenn Davis .01 .05
332 Willie Ansley RC .02 .10
333 Gerald Young .01 .05
334 Cameron Drew .01 .05
335 Jay Howell .01 .05
336 Tim Belcher .01 .05
337 Fernando Valenzuela .02 .10
338 Ricky Horton .01 .05
339 Tim Leary .01 .05
340 Bill Bene .01 .05
341 Orel Hershiser .02 .10
342 Mike Scioscia .01 .05
343 Rick Dempsey .01 .05
344 Willie Randolph .02 .10
345 Alfredo Griffin .01 .05
346 Eddie Murray .08 .25
347 Mickey Hatcher .01 .05
348 Mike Sharperson .01 .05
349 John Shelby .01 .05
350 Mike Marshall .01 .05
351 Kirk Gibson .02 .10
352 Mike Davis .01 .05
353 Bryn Smith .01 .05
354 Pascual Perez .01 .05
355 Kevin Gross .01 .05
356 Andy McGaffigan .01 .05
357 Brian Holman RC * .02 .10
358 Dave Wainhouse RC .02 .10
359 Dennis Martinez .02 .10
360 Tim Burke .01 .05
361 Nelson Santovenia .01 .05
362 Tim Wallach .01 .05
363 Spike Owen .01 .05
364 Rex Hudler .01 .05
365 Andres Galarraga .02 .10
366 Otis Nixon .01 .05
367 Hubie Brooks .01 .05
368 Mike Aldrete .01 .05
369 Tim Raines .02 .10
370 Dave Martinez .01 .05
371 Bob Ojeda .01 .05
372 Ron Darling .02 .10
373 Wally Whitehurst RC .02 .10
374 Randy Myers .02 .10
375 David Cone .02 .10
376 Dwight Gooden .02 .10
377 Sid Fernandez .01 .05
378 Dave Proctor .01 .05
379 Gary Carter .02 .10
380 Keith Miller .01 .05
381 Gregg Jefferies .01 .05
382 Tim Teufel .01 .05
383 Kevin Elster .01 .05
384 Dave Magadan .01 .05
385 Keith Hernandez .02 .10
386 Mookie Wilson .02 .10
387 Darryl Strawberry .02 .10
388 Kevin McReynolds .01 .05
389 Mark Carreon .01 .05
390 Jeff Parrett .01 .05
391 Mike Maddux .01 .05
392 Don Carman .01 .05
393 Bruce Ruffin .01 .05
394 Ken Howell .01 .05
395 Steve Bedrosian .01 .05
396 Floyd Youmans .01 .05
397 Larry McWilliams .01 .05
398 Pat Combs RC * .02 .10
399 Steve Lake .01 .05
400 Dickie Thon .01 .05
401 Ricky Jordan RC * .08 .25
402 Mike Schmidt .20 .50
403 Tom Herr .01 .05
404 Chris James .01 .05
405 Juan Samuel .01 .05
406 Von Hayes .01 .05
407 Ron Jones .02 .10
408 Curt Ford .01 .05
409 Bob Walk .01 .05
410 Jeff D. Robinson .01 .05
411 Jim Gott .01 .05
412 Scott Medvin .01 .05
413 John Smiley .01 .05
414 Bob Kipper .01 .05
415 Brian Fisher .01 .05
416 Doug Drabek .01 .05
417 Mike LaValliere .01 .05
418 Ken Oberkfell .01 .05
419 Sid Bream .01 .05
420 Austin Manahan .01 .05
421 Jose Lind .01 .05
422 Bobby Bonilla .02 .10
423 Glenn Wilson .01 .05
424 Andy Van Slyke .05 .15
425 Gary Redus .01 .05
426 Barry Bonds .60 1.50
427 Don Heinkel .01 .05
428 Ken Dayley .01 .05
429 Todd Worrell .02 .10
430 Brad DuVall .01 .05
431 Jose DeLeon .01 .05
432 Joe Magrane .01 .05
433 John Ericks .01 .05
434 Frank DiPino .01 .05
435 Tony Pena .02 .10
436 Ozzie Smith .15 .40
437 Terry Pendleton .02 .10
438 Jose Oquendo .01 .05
439 Tim Jones .01 .05
440 Pedro Guerrero .02 .10
441 Milt Thompson .01 .05
442 Willie McGee .02 .10
443 Vince Coleman .01 .05
444 Tom Brunansky .01 .05
445 Walt Terrell .01 .05
446 Eric Show .01 .05
447 Mark Davis .01 .05
448 Andy Benes RC .15 .40
449 Ed Whitson .01 .05
450 Dennis Rasmussen .01 .05
451 Bruce Hurst .01 .05
452 Pat Clements .01 .05
453 Benito Santiago .02 .10
454 Sandy Alomar Jr. RC .15 .40
455 Garry Templeton .02 .10
456 Jack Clark .02 .10
457 Tim Flannery .01 .05
458 Roberto Alomar .08 .25
459 Carmelo Martinez .01 .05
460 John Kruk .02 .10
461 Tony Gwynn .10 .30
462 Jerald Clark RC .02 .10
463 Don Robinson .01 .05
464 Craig Lefferts .01 .05
465 Kelly Downs .01 .05
466 Rick Reuschel .02 .10
467 Scott Garrelts .01 .05
468 Wil Tejada .01 .05
469 Kirt Manwaring .01 .05
470 Terry Kennedy .01 .05
471 Jose Uribe .01 .05
472 Royce Clayton RC .15 .40
473 Robby Thompson .01 .05
474 Kevin Mitchell .02 .10
475 Ernie Riles .01 .05
476 Will Clark .05 .15
477 Donell Nixon .01 .05
478 Candy Maldonado .01 .05
479 Tracy Jones .01 .05
480 Brett Butler .02 .10
481 Checklist 1-121 .01 .05
482 Checklist 122-242 .01 .05
483 Checklist 243-363 .01 .05
484 Checklist 364-484 .01 .05

1989 Bowman Tiffany

COMP.FACT.SET (495) 200.00 400.00
*STARS: 6X TO 15X BASIC CARDS
*ROOKIES: 6X TO 15X BASIC CARDS
DISTRIBUTED ONLY IN FACTORY SET FORM
211 Tino Martinez 6.00 15.00
220 Ken Griffey Jr. 75.00 200.00
266 John Smoltz 10.00 25.00

1989 Bowman Reprint Inserts

The 1989 Bowman Reprint Inserts set contains 11 cards measuring approximately 2 1/2" by 3 3/4". The fronts depict reproduced actual size "classic" Bowman cards, which are noted as reprints. The backs are devoted to a sweepstakes entry form. One of these reprint cards was included in each 1989 Bowman wax pack thus making these "reprints" quite easy to find. Since the cards are unnumbered, they are ordered below in alphabetical order by player's name and year within player.

COMPLETE SET (11) .75 2.00
ONE PER PACK
*TIFFANY: 10X TO 20X HI COLUMN
ONE TIFF.REP.SET PER TIFF.FACT.SET
1 Richie Ashburn 49 .15 .40
2 Yogi Berra 48 .08 .25
3 Whitey Ford 51 .15 .40
4 Gil Hodges 49 .20 .50
5 Mickey Mantle 51 .40 1.00
6 Mickey Mantle 53 .40 1.00
7 Willie Mays 51 .20 .50
8 Satchel Paige 49 .20 .50
9 Jackie Robinson 50 .20 .50
10 Duke Snider 49 .08 .25
11 Ted Williams 54 .20 .50

1990 Bowman

The 1990 Bowman set (produced by Topps) consists of 528 standard-size cards. The cards were issued in wax packs and factory sets. Each wax pack contained one of 11 different 1950's retro art cards. Unlike most sets, player selection focused primarily on rookies instead of proven major leaguers. The cards feature a white border with the player's photo inside and the Bowman logo on top. The card numbering is in team order with the teams themselves being ordered alphabetically within each league. Notable Rookie Cards include Moises Alou, Travis Fryman, Juan Gonzalez, Chuck Knoblauch, Ray Lankford, Sammy Sosa, Frank Thomas, Mo Vaughn, Larry Walker, and Bernie Williams.

COMPLETE SET (528) 10.00 25.00
COMP.FACT.SET (528) 10.00 25.00
ART CARDS: RANDOM INSERTS IN PACKS
1 Tommy Greene RC .02 .10
2 Tom Glavine .05 .15
3 Andy Nezelek .01 .05
4 Mike Stanton RC .08 .25
5 Rick Luecken RC .01 .05
6 Kent Mercker RC .08 .25
7 Derek Lilliquist .01 .05
8 Charlie Leibrandt .01 .05
9 Steve Avery .01 .05
10 John Smoltz .08 .25
11 Mark Lemke .01 .05
12 Lonnie Smith .01 .05
13 Oddibe McDowell .01 .05
14 Tyler Houston RC .08 .25
15 Jeff Blauser .01 .05
16 Ernie Whitt .01 .05
17 Alexis Infante .01 .05
18 Jim Presley .01 .05
19 Dale Murphy .05 .15
20 Nick Esasky .01 .05
21 Rick Sutcliffe .02 .10
22 Mike Bielecki .01 .05
23 Steve Wilson .01 .05
24 Kevin Blankenship .01 .05
25 Mitch Williams .01 .05
26 Dean Wilkins RC .01 .05
27 Greg Maddux .15 .40
28 Mike Harkey .01 .05
29 Mark Grace .05 .15
30 Ryne Sandberg .15 .40
31 Greg Smith RC .01 .05
32 Dwight Smith .01 .05
33 Damon Berryhill .01 .05
34 Earl Cunningham UER RC .02 .10
35 Jerome Walton .01 .05
36 Lloyd McClendon .01 .05
37 Ty Griffin .01 .05
38 Shawon Dunston .01 .05
39 Andre Dawson .02 .10
40 Luis Salazar .01 .05
41 Tim Layana RC .01 .05
42 Rob Dibble .02 .10
43 Tom Browning .01 .05
44 Danny Jackson .01 .05
45 Jose Rijo .01 .05
46 Scott Scudder .01 .05
47 Randy Myers UER .02 .10
(Career ERA .274, should be 2.74
48 Brian Lane RC .02 .10
49 Paul O'Neill .05 .15
50 Barry Larkin .05 .15
51 Reggie Jefferson RC .08 .25
52 Jeff Branson RC .02 .10
53 Chris Sabo .01 .05
54 Joe Oliver .01 .05
55 Todd Benzinger .01 .05
56 Rolando Roomes .01 .05
57 Hal Morris .01 .05
58 Eric Davis .02 .10
59 Scott Bryant RC .01 .05
60 Ken Griffey Sr. .02 .10
61 Darryl Kile RC .20 .50
62 Dave Smith .01 .05
63 Mark Portugal .01 .05
64 Jeff Juden RC .02 .10
65 Bill Gullickson .01 .05
66 Danny Darwin .01 .05
67 Larry Andersen .01 .05
68 Jose Cano RC .01 .05
69 Dan Schatzeder .01 .05
70 Jim Deshaies .01 .05
71 Mike Scott .01 .05
72 Gerald Young .01 .05
73 Ken Caminiti .02 .10
74 Ken Oberkfell .01 .05
75 Dave Rohde RC .01 .05
76 Bill Doran .01 .05
77 Andujar Cedeno RC .02 .10
78 Craig Biggio .08 .25
79 Karl Rhodes RC .08 .25
80 Glenn Davis .01 .05
81 Eric Anthony RC .02 .10
82 John Wetteland .08 .25
83 Jay Howell .01 .05
84 Orel Hershiser .02 .10
85 Tim Belcher .01 .05
86 Kiki Jones RC .01 .05
87 Mike Hartley RC .01 .05
88 Ramon Martinez .01 .05
89 Mike Scioscia .01 .05
90 Willie Randolph .02 .10
91 Juan Samuel .01 .05
92 Jose Offerman RC .08 .25
93 Dave Hansen RC .08 .25
94 Jeff Hamilton .01 .05
95 Alfredo Griffin .01 .05
96 Tom Goodwin RC .08 .25
97 Kirk Gibson .02 .10
98 Jose Vizcaino RC .08 .25
99 Kal Daniels .01 .05
100 Hubie Brooks .01 .05
101 Eddie Murray .08 .25
102 Dennis Boyd .01 .05
103 Tim Burke .01 .05
104 Bill Sampen RC .01 .05
105 Brett Gideon .01 .05
106 Mark Gardner RC .02 .10
107 Howard Farmer RC .01 .05
108 Mel Rojas RC .02 .10
109 Kevin Gross .01 .05
110 Dave Schmidt .01 .05
111 Dennis Martinez .02 .10
112 Jerry Goff RC .01 .05
113 Andres Galarraga .02 .10
114 Tim Wallach .01 .05
115 Marquis Grissom RC .20 .50
116 Spike Owen .01 .05
117 Larry Walker RC .40 1.00
118 Tim Raines .02 .10
119 Delino DeShields RC .08 .25
120 Tom Foley .01 .05
121 Dave Martinez .01 .05
122 Frank Viola UER .01 .05
(Career ERA .384 should be 3.84
123 Julio Valera RC .01 .05
124 Alejandro Pena .01 .05
125 David Cone .02 .10
126 Dwight Gooden .02 .10
127 Kevin D. Brown RC .01 .05
128 John Franco .02 .10
129 Terry Bross RC .01 .05
130 Blaine Beatty RC .01 .05
131 Sid Fernandez .01 .05
132 Mike Marshall .01 .05
133 Howard Johnson .01 .05
134 Jaime Roseboro RC .01 .05
135 Alan Zinter RC .02 .10
136 Keith Miller .01 .05
137 Kevin Elster .01 .05
138 Kevin McReynolds .01 .05
139 Barry Lyons .01 .05
140 Gregg Jefferies .02 .10
141 Darryl Strawberry .02 .10
142 Todd Hundley RC .08 .25
143 Scott Service .01 .05
144 Chuck Malone RC .01 .05
145 Steve Ontiveros .01 .05
146 Roger McDowell .01 .05
147 Ken Howell .01 .05
148 Pat Combs .01 .05
149 Jeff Parrett .01 .05
150 Chuck McElroy RC .02 .10
151 Jason Grimsley RC .02 .10
152 Len Dykstra .02 .10
153 Mickey Morandini RC .08 .25
154 John Kruk .02 .10
155 Dickie Thon .01 .05
156 Ricky Jordan .01 .05
157 Jeff Jackson RC .02 .10
158 Darren Daulton .02 .10
159 Tom Herr .01 .05
160 Von Hayes .01 .05
161 Dave Hollins RC .08 .25
162 Carmelo Martinez .01 .05
163 Bob Walk .01 .05
164 Doug Drabek .01 .05
165 Walt Terrell .01 .05
166 Bill Landrum .01 .05
167 Scott Ruskin RC .01 .05
168 Bob Patterson .01 .05
169 Bobby Bonilla .02 .10
170 Jose Lind .01 .05
171 Andy Van Slyke .05 .15
172 Mike LaValliere .01 .05
173 Willie Greene RC .02 .10
174 Jay Bell .02 .10
175 Sid Bream .01 .05
176 Tom Prince .01 .05
177 Wally Backman .01 .05
178 Moises Alou RC .30 .75
179 Steve Carter .01 .05
180 Gary Redus .01 .05
181 Barry Bonds .40 1.00
182 Don Slaught UER .01 .05
(Card back shows headings for a pitcher
183 Joe Magrane .01 .05
184 Bryn Smith .01 .05
185 Todd Worrell .01 .05
186 Jose DeLeon .01 .05
187 Frank DiPino .01 .05
188 John Tudor .01 .05
189 Howard Hilton RC .01 .05
190 John Ericks .01 .05
191 Ken Dayley .01 .05
192 Ray Lankford RC .20 .50
193 Todd Zeile .02 .10
194 Willie McGee .02 .10
195 Ozzie Smith .15 .40
196 Milt Thompson .01 .05
197 Terry Pendleton .02 .10
198 Vince Coleman .01 .05
199 Paul Coleman RC .02 .10
200 Jose Oquendo .01 .05
201 Pedro Guerrero .01 .05
202 Tom Brunansky .01 .05
203 Roger Smithberg RC .01 .05
204 Eddie Whitson .01 .05
205 Dennis Rasmussen .01 .05
206 Craig Lefferts .01 .05
207 Andy Benes .02 .10
208 Bruce Hurst .01 .05
209 Eric Show .01 .05
210 Rafael Valdez RC .01 .05
211 Joey Cora .02 .10
212 Thomas Howard .01 .05
213 Rob Nelson .01 .05
214 Jack Clark .02 .10
215 Garry Templeton .01 .05
216 Fred Lynn .01 .05
217 Tony Gwynn .10 .30
218 Benito Santiago .02 .10
219 Mike Pagliarulo .01 .05
220 Joe Carter .02 .10
221 Roberto Alomar .05 .15
222 Bip Roberts .01 .05
223 Rick Reuschel .01 .05
224 Russ Swan RC .01 .05
225 Eric Gunderson RC .01 .05
226 Steve Bedrosian .01 .05
227 Mike Remlinger RC .01 .05
228 Scott Garrelts .01 .05
229 Ernie Camacho .01 .05
230 Andres Santana RC .01 .05
231 Will Clark .05 .15
232 Kevin Mitchell .01 .05
233 Robby Thompson .01 .05
234 Bill Bathe .01 .05
235 Tony Perezchica .01 .05
236 Gary Carter .02 .10
237 Brett Butler .02 .10
238 Matt Williams .02 .10
239 Ernie Riles .01 .05
240 Kevin Bass .01 .05
241 Terry Kennedy .01 .05
242 Steve Hosey RC .02 .10
243 Ben McDonald RC .08 .25
244 Jeff Ballard .01 .05
245 Joe Price .01 .05
246 Curt Schilling .40 1.00
247 Pete Harnisch .01 .05
248 Mark Williamson .01 .05
249 Gregg Olson .02 .10
250 Chris Myers RC .01 .05
251A David Segui ERR .20 .50
Missing vital stats at top of card back under name)
251B David Segui COR RC .20 .50
252 Joe Orsulak .01 .05
253 Craig Worthington .01 .05
254 Mickey Tettleton .01 .05
255 Cal Ripken .30 .75
256 Bill Ripken .01 .05
257 Randy Milligan .01 .05
258 Brady Anderson .02 .10
259 Chris Hoiles RC UER .08 .25
Baltimore is spelled Balitmore
260 Mike Devereaux .01 .05
261 Phil Bradley .01 .05
262 Leo Gomez RC .02 .10
263 Lee Smith .02 .10
264 Mike Rochford .01 .05
265 Jeff Reardon .02 .10
266 Wes Gardner .01 .05
267 Mike Boddicker .01 .05
268 Roger Clemens .40 1.00
269 Rob Murphy .01 .05
270 Mickey Pina RC .01 .05
271 Tony Pena .01 .05
272 Jody Reed .01 .05
273 Kevin Romine .01 .05
274 Mike Greenwell .01 .05
275 Mo Vaughn RC .40 1.00
276 Danny Heep .01 .05
277 Scott Cooper RC .02 .10
278 Greg Blosser RC .02 .10
279 Dwight Evans UER .05 .15
(* by 1990 Team Breakdown)
280 Ellis Burks .05 .15
281 Wade Boggs .05 .15
282 Marty Barrett .01 .05
283 Kirk McCaskill .01 .05
284 Mark Langston .01 .05
285 Bert Blyleven .02 .10
286 Mike Fetters RC .08 .25
287 Kyle Abbott RC .01 .05
288 Jim Abbott .05 .15
289 Chuck Finley .02 .10
290 Gary DiSarcina RC .08 .25
291 Dick Schofield .01 .05
292 Devon White .02 .10
293 Bobby Rose .01 .05
294 Brian Downing .01 .05
295 Lance Parrish .01 .05
296 Jack Howell .01 .05
297 Claudell Washington .01 .05
298 John Orton RC .02 .10
299 Wally Joyner .02 .10
300 Lee Stevens .02 .10
301 Chili Davis .02 .10
302 Johnny Ray .01 .05
303 Greg Hibbard RC .02 .10
304 Eric King .01 .05
305 Jack McDowell .01 .05
306 Bobby Thigpen .01 .05
307 Adam Peterson .01 .05
308 Scott Radinsky RC .08 .25
309 Wayne Edwards RC .01 .05
310 Melido Perez .01 .05
311 Robin Ventura .08 .25
312 Sammy Sosa RC 1.25 3.00
313 Dan Pasqua .01 .05
314 Carlton Fisk .05 .15
315 Ozzie Guillen .02 .10
316 Ivan Calderon .01 .05
317 Daryl Boston .01 .05
318 Craig Grebeck RC .08 .25
319 Scott Fletcher .01 .05
320 Frank Thomas RC .75 2.00
321 Steve Lyons .01 .05
322 Carlos Martinez .01 .05
323 Joe Skalski .01 .05
324 Tom Candiotti .01 .05
325 Greg Swindell .01 .05
326 Steve Olin RC .08 .25
327 Kevin Wickander .01 .05
328 Doug Jones .01 .05
329 Jeff Shaw .01 .05
330 Kevin Bearse RC .01 .05
331 Dion James .01 .05
332 Jerry Browne .01 .05
333 Albert Belle .08 .25
334 Felix Fermin .01 .05
335 Candy Maldonado .01 .05
336 Cory Snyder .01 .05
337 Sandy Alomar Jr. .02 .10
338 Mark Lewis .01 .05
339 Carlos Baerga RC .08 .25
340 Chris James .01 .05
341 Brook Jacoby .01 .05
342 Keith Hernandez .02 .10
343 Frank Tanana .01 .05
344 Scott Aldred RC .01 .05
345 Mike Henneman .01 .05

346 Steve Wapnick RC .01 .05
347 Greg Gohr RC .02 .10
348 Eric Stone RC .01 .05
349 Brian DuBois RC .01 .05
350 Kevin.Ritz RC .01 .05
351 Rico Brogna .08 .25
352 Mike Heath .01 .05
353 Alan Trammell .02 .10
354 Chet Lemon .01 .05
355 Dave Bergman .01 .05
356 Lou Whitaker .02 .10
357 Cecil Fielder UER .02 .10
* by 1990 Team Breakdown
358 Milt Cuyler RC .02 .10
359 Tony Phillips .01 .05
360 Travis Fryman RC .20 .50
361 Ed Romero .01 .05
362 Lloyd Moseby .01 .05
363 Mark Gubicza .01 .05
364 Bret Saberhagen .02 .10
365 Tom Gordon .02 .10
366 Steve Farr .01 .05
367 Kevin Appier .02 .10
368 Storm Davis .01 .05
369 Mark Davis .01 .05
370 Jeff Montgomery .02 .10
371 Frank White .02 .10
372 Brent Mayne RC .08 .25
373 Bob Boone .02 .10
374 Jim Eisenreich .01 .05
375 Danny Tartabull .01 .05
376 Kurt Stillwell .01 .05
377 Bill Pecota .01 .05
378 Bo Jackson .08 .25
379 Bob Hamelin RC .08 .25
380 Kevin Seitzer .01 .05
381 Rey Palacios .01 .05
382 George Brett .25 .60
383 Gerald Perry .01 .05
384 Teddy Higuera .01 .05
385 Tom Filer .01 .05
386 Dan Plesac .01 .05
387 Cal Eldred RC .08 .25
388 Jaime Navarro .01 .05
389 Chris Bosio .01 .05
390 Randy Veres .01 .05
391 Gary Sheffield .08 .25
392 George Canale RC .01 .05
393 B.J. Surhoff .02 .10
394 Tim McIntosh RC .01 .05
395 Greg Brock .01 .05
396 Greg Vaughn .01 .05
397 Darryl Hamilton .01 .05
398 Dave Parker .02 .10
399 Paul Molitor .02 .10
400 Jim Gantner .01 .05
401 Rob Deer .01 .05
402 Billy Spiers .01 .05
403 Glenn Braggs .01 .05
404 Robin Yount .15 .40
405 Rick Aguilera .02 .10
406 Johnny Ard .01 .05
407 Kevin Tapani RC .08 .25
408 Park Pittman RC .01 .05
409 Allan Anderson .01 .05
410 Juan Berenguer .01 .05
411 Willie Banks RC .02 .10
412 Rich Yett .01 .05
413 Dave West .01 .05
414 Greg Gagne .01 .05
415 Chuck Knoblauch RC .20 .50
416 Randy Bush .01 .05
417 Gary Gaetti .02 .10
418 Kent Hrbek .02 .10
419 Al Newman .01 .05
420 Danny Gladden .01 .05
421 Paul Sorrento RC .08 .25
422 Derek Parks RC .02 .10
423 Scott Leius RC .02 .10
424 Kirby Puckett .08 .25
425 Willie Smith .01 .05
426 Dave Righetti .01 .05
427 Jeff D. Robinson .01 .05
428 Alan Mills RC .02 .10
429 Tim Leary .01 .05
430 Pascual Perez .01 .05
431 Alvaro Espinoza .01 .05
432 Dave Winfield .02 .10
433 Jesse Barfield .01 .05
434 Randy Velarde .01 .05
435 Rick Cerone .01 .05
436 Steve Balboni .01 .05
437 Mel Hall .01 .05
438 Bob Geren .01 .05
439 Bernie Williams RC .60 1.50
440 Kevin Maas RC .08 .25
441 Mike Blowers RC .02 .10
442 Steve Sax .01 .05
443 Don Mattingly .25 .60
444 Roberto Kelly .01 .05
445 Mike Moore .01 .05
446 Reggie Harris RC .02 .10
447 Scott Sanderson .01 .05
448 Dave Otto .01 .05
449 Dave Stewart .02 .10
450 Rick Honeycutt .01 .05
451 Dennis Eckersley .02 .10
452 Carney Lansford .02 .10
453 Scott Hemond RC .02 .10
454 Mark McGwire .40 1.00
455 Felix Jose .01 .05
456 Terry Steinbach .01 .05
457 Rickey Henderson .08 .25
458 Dave Henderson .01 .05
459 Mike Gallego .01 .05
460 Jose Canseco .05 .15
461 Walt Weiss .01 .05
462 Ken Phelps .01 .05
463 Darren Lewis RC .02 .10
464 Ron Hassey .01 .05
465 Roger Salkeld RC .02 .10
466 Scott Bankhead .01 .05
467 Keith Comstock .01 .05
468 Randy Johnson .20 .50
469 Erik Hanson .01 .05
470 Mike Schooler .01 .05
471 Gary Eave RC .01 .05
472 Jeffrey Leonard .01 .05
473 Dave Valle .01 .05
474 Omar Vizquel .08 .25
475 Pete O'Brien .01 .05
476 Henry Cotto .01 .05
477 Jay Buhner .02 .10
478 Harold Reynolds .02 .10
479 Alvin Davis .01 .05
480 Darnell Coles .01 .05
481 Ken Griffey Jr. .40 1.00
482 Greg Briley .01 .05
483 Scott Bradley .01 .05
484 Tino Martinez .20 .50
485 Jeff Russell .01 .05
486 Nolan Ryan .40 1.00
487 Robb Nen RC .20 .50
488 Kevin Brown .02 .10
489 Brian Bohanon RC .02 .10
490 Ruben Sierra .02 .10
491 Pete Incaviglia .01 .05
492 Juan Gonzalez RC .40 1.00
493 Steve Buechele .01 .05
494 Scott Coolbaugh .01 .05
495 Geno Petralli .01 .05
496 Rafael Palmeiro .05 .15
497 Julio Franco .02 .10
498 Gary Pettis .01 .05
499 Donald Harris RC .01 .05
500 Monty Fariss .01 .05
501 Harold Baines .02 .10
502 Cecil Espy .01 .05
503 Jack Daugherty RC .01 .05
504 Willie Blair RC .02 .10
505 Dave Stieb .02 .10
506 Tom Henke .01 .05
507 John Cerutti .01 .05
508 Paul Kilgus .01 .05
509 Jimmy Key .02 .10
510 John Olerud RC .40 1.00
511 Ed Sprague .02 .10
512 Manuel Lee .01 .05
513 Fred McGriff .08 .25
514 Glenallen Hill .01 .05
515 George Bell .01 .05
516 Mookie Wilson .02 .10
517 Luis Sojo RC .08 .25
518 Nelson Liriano .01 .05
519 Kelly Gruber .01 .05
520 Greg Myers .01 .05
521 Pat Borders .01 .05
522 Junior Felix .01 .05
523 Eddie Zosky RC .02 .10
524 Tony Fernandez .01 .05
525 Checklist 1-132 UER .01 .05
(No copyright mark on the back)
526 Checklist 133-264 .01 .05
527 Checklist 265-396 .01 .05
528 Checklist 397-528 .01 .05

1990 Bowman Tiffany

COMP.FACT.SET (539) 100.00 200.00
*STARS: 6X TO 15X BASIC CARDS
*ROOKIES: 4X TO 10X BASIC CARDS

1990 Bowman Art Inserts

These standard-size cards were included as an insert in every 1990 Bowman pack. This set, which consists of 11 superstars, depicts drawings by Craig Pursley with the backs being descriptions of the 1990 Bowman sweepstakes. We have checklisted the set alphabetically by player. All the cards in this set can be found with either one asterisk or two on the back.

COMPLETE SET (11) .75 2.00
ONE PER PACK
*TIFFANY: 8X TO 20X BASIC ART INSERT
ONE TIFF.REP.SET PER TIFF.FACT.SET
1 Will Clark .05 .15
2 Mark Davis .01 .05
3 Dwight Gooden .02 .10
4 Bo Jackson .08 .25
5 Don Mattingly .25 .60
6 Kevin Mitchell .01 .05
7 Gregg Olson .02 .10
8 Nolan Ryan .40 1.00
9 Bret Saberhagen .02 .10
10 Jerome Walton .01 .05
11 Robin Yount .15 .40

1990 Bowman Insert Lithographs

These 11" by 14" lithographs were issued through both Topps dealer network and through a pack/wrapper redemption. The fronts of the lithographs are larger versions of the 1990 Bowman insert sets. These lithos were drawn by Craig Pursley and are signed by the artist and are come either with or without serial numbering to 500. The backs are blank but we are sequencing them in the same order as the 1990 Bowman inserts. The lithos which the artist signed are worth approximately 2X to 3X the regular lithographs.

COMPLETE SET (11) 300.00 600.00
1 Will Clark 20.00 50.00
2 Mark Davis 10.00 25.00
3 Dwight Gooden 12.50 30.00
4 Bo Jackson 20.00 50.00
5 Don Mattingly 40.00 100.00
6 Kevin Mitchell 10.00 25.00
7 Gregg Olson 10.00 25.00
8 Nolan Ryan 100.00 250.00
9 Bret Saberhagen 12.50 30.00
10 Jerome Walton 10.00 25.00
11 Robin Yount 25.00 60.00

1991 Bowman

This single-series 704-card standard-size set marked the third straight year that Topps issued a set weighted towards prospects using the Bowman name. Cards were issued in wax packs and factory sets. The cards share a design very similar to the 1990 Bowman set with white borders enframing a color photo. The player name, however, is more prominent than in the previous year set. The cards are arranged in team order by division as follows: AL East, AL West, NL East, and NL West. Subsets include Rod Carew Tribute (1-5), Minor League MVP's (180-185/693-698), AL Silver Sluggers (367-375), NL Silver Sluggers (376-384) and checklists (699-704). Rookie Cards in this set include Jeff Bagwell, Jeromy Burnitz, Carl Everett, Chipper Jones, Eric Karros, Ryan Klesko, Kenny Lofton, Javier Lopez, Raul Mondesi, Mike Mussina, Ivan "Pudge" Rodriguez, Tim Salmon, Jim Thome, and Rondell White. There are two instances of misnumbering in the set, Ken Griffey (should be 255) and Ken Griffey Jr. are both numbered 246 and Donovan Osborne (should be 406) and Thomson/Branca share number 410.

COMPLETE SET (704) 15.00 40.00
COMP.FACT.SET (704) 15.00 40.00
1 Rod Carew I .05 .15
2 Rod Carew II .05 .15
3 Rod Carew III .05 .15
4 Rod Carew IV .05 .15
5 Rod Carew V .05 .15
6 Willie Fraser .01 .05
7 John Olerud .02 .10
8 William Suero RC .01 .05
9 Roberto Alomar .05 .15
10 Todd Stottlemyre .01 .05
11 Joe Carter .02 .10
12 Steve Karsay RC .20 .50
13 Mark Whiten .01 .05
14 Pat Borders .01 .05
15 Mike Timlin RC .20 .50
16 Tom Henke .01 .05
17 Eddie Zosky .01 .05
18 Kelly Gruber .01 .05
19 Jimmy Key .02 .10
20 Jerry Schunk RC .01 .05
21 Manuel Lee .01 .05
22 Dave Stieb .01 .05
23 Pat Hentgen RC .20 .50
24 Glenallen Hill .01 .05
25 Rene Gonzales .01 .05
26 Ed Sprague .01 .05
27 Ken Dayley .01 .05
28 Pat Tabler .01 .05
29 Denis Boucher RC .05 .15
30 Devon White .02 .10
31 Dante Bichette .02 .10
32 Paul Molitor .02 .10
33 Greg Vaughn .01 .05
34 Dan Plesac .01 .05
35 Chris George RC .05 .15
36 Tim McIntosh .01 .05
37 Franklin Stubbs .01 .05
38 Bo Dodson RC .05 .15
39 Ron Robinson .01 .05
40 Ed Nunez .01 .05
41 Greg Brock .01 .05
42 Jaime Navarro .01 .05
43 Chris Bosio .01 .05
44 B.J. Surhoff .02 .10
45 Chris Johnson RC .01 .05
46 Willie Randolph .02 .10
47 Narciso Elvira RC .01 .05
48 Jim Gantner .01 .05
49 Kevin Brown .01 .05
50 Julio Machado .01 .05
51 Chuck Crim .01 .05
52 Gary Sheffield .02 .10
53 Angel Miranda RC .05 .15
54 Ted Higuera .01 .05
55 Robin Yount .15 .40
56 Cal Eldred .01 .05
57 Sandy Alomar Jr. .01 .05
58 Greg Swindell .01 .05
59 Brook Jacoby .01 .05
60 Efrain Valdez RC .01 .05
61 Ever Magallanes RC .01 .05
62 Tom Candiotti .01 .05
63 Eric King .01 .05
64 Alex Cole .01 .05
65 Charles Nagy .01 .05
66 Mitch Webster .01 .05
67 Chris James .01 .05
68 Jim Thome RC 3.00 8.00
69 Carlos Baerga .01 .05
70 Mark Lewis .01 .05
71 Jerry Browne .01 .05
72 Jesse Orosco .01 .05
73 Mike Huff .01 .05
74 Jose Escobar RC .01 .05
75 Jeff Manto .01 .05
76 Turner Ward RC .05 .15
77 Doug Jones .01 .05
78 Bruce Egloff RC .01 .05
79 Tim Costo RC .05 .15
80 Beau Allred .01 .05
81 Albert Belle .02 .10
82 John Farrell .01 .05
83 Glenn Davis .01 .05
84 Joe Orsulak .01 .05
85 Mark Williamson .01 .05
86 Ben McDonald .01 .05
87 Billy Ripken .01 .05
88 Leo Gomez UER .01 .05
Baltimore is spelled Balitmore
89 Bob Melvin .01 .05
90 Jeff M. Robinson .01 .05
91 Jose Mesa .01 .05
92 Gregg Olson .01 .05
93 Mike Devereaux .01 .05
94 Luis Mercedes RC .05 .15
95 Arthur Rhodes RC .20 .50
96 Juan Bell .01 .05
97 Mike Mussina RC 2.00 5.00
98 Jeff Ballard .01 .05
99 Chris Hoiles .01 .05
100 Brady Anderson .02 .10
101 Bob Milacki .01 .05
102 David Segui .01 .05
103 Dwight Evans .05 .15
104 Cal Ripken .30 .75
105 Mike Linskey RC .01 .05
106 Jeff Tackett RC .05 .15
107 Jeff Reardon .02 .10
108 Dana Kiecker .01 .05
109 Ellis Burks .02 .10
110 Dave Owen .01 .05
111 Danny Darwin .01 .05
112 Mo Vaughn .02 .10
113 Jeff McNeely RC .05 .15
114 Tom Bolton .01 .05
115 Greg Blosser .01 .05
116 Mike Greenwell .01 .05
117 Phil Plantier RC .05 .15
118 Roger Clemens .30 .75
119 John Marzano .01 .05
120 Jody Reed .01 .05
121 Scott Taylor RC .05 .15
122 Jack Clark .02 .10
123 Derek Livernois RC .01 .05
124 Tony Pena .01 .05
125 Tom Brunansky .01 .05
126 Carlos Quintana .01 .05
127 Tim Naehring .01 .05
128 Matt Young .01 .05
129 Wade Boggs .05 .15
130 Kevin Morton RC .01 .05
131 Pete Incaviglia .01 .05
132 Rob Deer .01 .05
133 Bill Gullickson .01 .05
134 Rico Brogna .01 .05
135 Lloyd Moseby .01 .05
136 Cecil Fielder .02 .10
137 Tony Phillips .01 .05
138 Mark Leiter RC .05 .15
139 John Cerutti .01 .05
140 Mickey Tettleton .01 .05
141 Milt Cuyler .01 .05
142 Greg Gohr .01 .05
143 Tony Bernazard .01 .05
144 Dan Gakeler RC .01 .05
145 Travis Fryman .02 .10
146 Dan Petry .01 .05
147 Scott Aldred .01 .05
148 John DeSilva RC .01 .05
149 Rusty Meacham RC .05 .15
150 Lou Whitaker .02 .10
151 Dave Haas RC .01 .05
152 Luis de los Santos .01 .05
153 Ivan Cruz RC .01 .05
154 Alan Trammell .02 .10
155 Pat Kelly RC .01 .05
156 Carl Everett RC .60 1.50
157 Greg Cadaret .01 .05
158 Kevin Maas .01 .05
159 Jeff Johnson RC .01 .05
160 Willie Smith .01 .05
161 Gerald Williams RC .20 .50
162 Mike Humphreys RC .05 .15
163 Alvaro Espinoza .01 .05
164 Matt Nokes .01 .05
165 Wade Taylor RC .01 .05
166 Roberto Kelly .01 .05
167 John Habyan .01 .05
168 Steve Farr .01 .05
169 Jesse Barfield .01 .05
170 Steve Sax .01 .05
171 Jim Leyritz .01 .05
172 Robert Eenhoorn RC .05 .15
173 Bernie Williams .08 .25
174 Scott Lusader .01 .05
175 Torey Lovullo .01 .05
176 Chuck Cary .01 .05
177 Scott Sanderson .01 .05
178 Don Mattingly .25 .60
179 Mel Hall .01 .05
180 Juan Gonzalez .08 .25
181 Hensley Meulens .01 .05
182 Jose Offerman .01 .05
183 Jeff Bagwell RC 1.25 3.00
184 Jeff Conine RC .40 1.00
185 Henry Rodriguez RC .20 .50
186 Jimmy Reese CO .02 .10
187 Kyle Abbott .01 .05
188 Lance Parrish .02 .10
189 Rafael Montalvo RC .01 .05
190 Floyd Bannister .01 .05
191 Dick Schofield .01 .05
192 Scott Lewis RC .01 .05
193 Jeff D. Robinson .01 .05
194 Kent Anderson .01 .05
195 Wally Joyner .02 .10
196 Chuck Finley .02 .10
197 Luis Sojo .01 .05
198 Jeff Richardson RC .01 .05
199 Dave Parker .02 .10
200 Jim Abbott .05 .15
201 Junior Felix .01 .05
202 Mark Langston .01 .05
203 Tim Salmon RC .60 1.50
204 Cliff Young .01 .05
205 Scott Bailes .01 .05
206 Bobby Rose .01 .05
207 Gary Gaetti .02 .10
208 Ruben Amaro RC .05 .15
209 Luis Polonia .01 .05
210 Dave Winfield .02 .10
211 Bryan Harvey .01 .05
212 Mike Moore .01 .05
213 Rickey Henderson .08 .25
214 Steve Chitren RC .01 .05
215 Bob Welch .01 .05
216 Terry Steinbach .01 .05
217 Earnest Riles .01 .05
218 Todd Van Poppel RC .20 .50
219 Mike Gallego .01 .05
220 Curt Young .01 .05
221 Todd Burns .01 .05
222 Vance Law .01 .05
223 Eric Show .01 .05
224 Don Peters RC .01 .05
225 Dave Stewart .02 .10
226 Dave Henderson .01 .05
227 Jose Canseco .05 .15
228 Walt Weiss .01 .05
229 Dann Howitt .01 .05
230 Willie Wilson .01 .05
231 Harold Baines .02 .10
232 Scott Hemond .01 .05
233 Joe Slusarski RC .01 .05
234 Mark McGwire .30 .75
235 Kirk Dressendorfer RC .05 .15
236 Craig Paquette RC .20 .50
237 Dennis Eckersley .02 .10
238 Dana Allison RC .01 .05
239 Scott Bradley .01 .05
240 Brian Holman .01 .05
241 Mike Schooler .01 .05
242 Rich DeLucia RC .01 .05
243 Edgar Martinez .05 .15
244 Henry Cotto .01 .05
245 Omar Vizquel .05 .15
246 Ken Griffey Jr. .25 .60
(See also 255)
247 Jay Buhner .02 .10
248 Bill Krueger .01 .05
249 Dave Fleming RC .05 .15
250 Patrick Lennon RC .01 .05
251 Dave Valle .01 .05
252 Harold Reynolds .02 .10
253 Randy Johnson .10 .30
254 Scott Bankhead .01 .05
255 Ken Griffey Sr. UER .01 .05
(Card number is 246)
256 Greg Briley .01 .05
257 Tino Martinez .08 .25
258 Alvin Davis .01 .05
259 Pete O'Brien .01 .05
260 Erik Hanson .01 .05
261 Bret Boone RC .60 1.50
262 Roger Salkeld .01 .05
263 Dave Burba RC .20 .50
264 Kerry Woodson RC .05 .15
265 Julio Franco .02 .10
266 Dan Peltier RC .05 .15
267 Jeff Russell .01 .05
268 Steve Buechele .01 .05
269 Donald Harris .01 .05
270 Robb Nen .05 .15
271 Rich Gossage .02 .10
272 Ivan Rodriguez RC 1.50 4.00
273 Jeff Huson .01 .05
274 Kevin Brown .02 .10
275 Dan Smith RC .05 .15
276 Gary Pettis .01 .05
277 Jack Daugherty .01 .05
278 Mike Jeffcoat .01 .05
279 Brad Arnsberg .01 .05
280 Nolan Ryan .40 1.00
281 Eric McCray RC .01 .05
282 Scott Chiamparino .01 .05
283 Ruben Sierra .02 .10
284 Geno Petralli .01 .05
285 Monty Fariss .01 .05
286 Rafael Palmeiro .05 .15
287 Bobby Witt .01 .05
288 Dean Palmer UER .02 .10
Photo is Dan Peltier
289 Tony Scruggs RC .01 .05
290 Kenny Rogers .02 .10
291 Bret Saberhagen .02 .10
292 Brian McRae RC .20 .50
293 Storm Davis .01 .05
294 Danny Tartabull .01 .05
295 David Howard RC .01 .05
296 Mike Boddicker .01 .05
297 Joel Johnston RC .05 .15
298 Tim Spehr RC .01 .05
299 Hector Wagner RC .01 .05
300 George Brett .25 .60
301 Mike Macfarlane .01 .05
302 Kirk Gibson .02 .10
303 Harvey Pulliam RC .05 .15
304 Jim Eisenreich .01 .05
305 Kevin Seitzer .01 .05
306 Mark Davis .01 .05
307 Kurt Stillwell .01 .05
308 Jeff Montgomery .01 .05
309 Kevin Appier .02 .10
310 Bob Hamelin .01 .05
311 Tom Gordon .01 .05
312 Kerwin Moore RC .05 .15
313 Hugh Walker .01 .05
314 Terry Shumpert .01 .05
315 Warren Cromartie .01 .05
316 Gary Thurman .01 .05
317 Steve Bedrosian .01 .05
318 Danny Gladden .01 .05
319 Jack Morris .02 .10
320 Kirby Puckett .08 .25
321 Kent Hrbek .02 .10
322 Kevin Tapani .01 .05
323 Denny Neagle RC .20 .50
324 Rich Garces RC .05 .15
325 Larry Casian RC .01 .05
326 Shane Mack .01 .05
327 Allan Anderson .01 .05
328 Junior Ortiz .01 .05
329 Paul Abbott RC .05 .15
330 Chuck Knoblauch .02 .10
331 Chili Davis .02 .10
332 Todd Ritchie RC .20 .50
333 Brian Harper .01 .05
334 Rick Aguilera .02 .10
335 Scott Erickson .01 .05
336 Pedro Munoz RC .05 .15
337 Scott Leius .01 .05
338 Greg Gagne .01 .05
339 Mike Pagliarulo .01 .05
340 Terry Leach .01 .05
341 Willie Banks .01 .05
342 Bobby Thigpen .01 .05
343 Roberto Hernandez RC .20 .50
344 Melido Perez .01 .05
345 Carlton Fisk .05 .15
346 Norberto Martin RC .01 .05
347 Johnny Ruffin RC .05 .15
348 Jeff Carter .01 .05
349 Lance Johnson .01 .05
350 Sammy Sosa .08 .25
351 Alex Fernandez .01 .05
352 Jack McDowell .01 .05
353 Bob Wickman RC .60 1.50
354 Wilson Alvarez .01 .05
355 Charlie Hough .02 .10
356 Ozzie Guillen .02 .10
357 Cory Snyder .01 .05
358 Robin Ventura .02 .10
359 Scott Fletcher .01 .05
360 Cesar Bernhardt RC .01 .05
361 Dan Pasqua .01 .05
362 Tim Raines .02 .10
363 Brian Drahman RC .01 .05
364 Wayne Edwards .01 .05
365 Scott Radinsky .01 .05
366 Frank Thomas .08 .25
367 Cecil Fielder SLUG .01 .05
368 Julio Franco SLUG .01 .05
369 Kelly Gruber SLUG .01 .05
370 Alan Trammell SLUG .02 .10
371 Rickey Henderson SLUG .05 .15
372 Jose Canseco SLUG .02 .10
373 Ellis Burks SLUG .01 .05
374 Lance Parrish SLUG .01 .05
375 Dave Parker SLUG .01 .05
376 Eddie Murray SLUG .05 .15
377 Ryne Sandberg SLUG .08 .25
378 Matt Williams SLUG .01 .05
379 Barry Larkin SLUG .02 .10
380 Barry Bonds SLUG .20 .50
381 Bobby Bonilla SLUG .01 .05
382 Darryl Strawberry SLUG .01 .05
383 Benny Santiago SLUG .01 .05
384 Don Robinson SLUG .01 .05
385 Paul Coleman .01 .05
386 Milt Thompson .01 .05
387 Lee Smith .02 .10
388 Ray Lankford .02 .10
389 Tom Pagnozzi .01 .05
390 Ken Hill .01 .05
391 Jamie Moyer .02 .10
392 Greg Carmona RC .01 .05
393 John Ericks .01 .05
394 Bob Tewksbury .01 .05
395 Jose Oquendo .01 .05
396 Rheal Cormier RC .05 .15
397 Mike Milchin RC .01 .05
398 Ozzie Smith .15 .40
399 Aaron Holbert RC .05 .15
400 Jose DeLeon .01 .05
401 Felix Jose .01 .05
402 Juan Agosto .01 .05
403 Pedro Guerrero .02 .10
404 Todd Zeile .01 .05
405 Gerald Perry .01 .05
406 Donovan Osborne UER RC .05 .15
407 Bryn Smith .01 .05
408 Bernard Gilkey .01 .05
409 Rex Hudler .01 .05
410 Bobby Thomson .08 .25
Ralph Branca
Shot Heard Round the World
See also 406
411 Lance Dickson RC .05 .15
412 Danny Jackson .01 .05
413 Jerome Walton .01 .05
414 Sean Cheetham RC .01 .05
415 Joe Girardi .01 .05
416 Ryne Sandberg .15 .40
417 Mike Harkey .01 .05
418 George Bell .01 .05
419 Rick Wilkins RC .05 .15
420 Earl Cunningham .01 .05
421 Heathcliff Slocumb RC .05 .15
422 Mike Bielecki .01 .05
423 Jessie Hollins RC .05 .15
424 Shawon Dunston .01 .05
425 Dave Smith .01 .05
426 Greg Maddux .15 .40
427 Jose Vizcaino .01 .05
428 Luis Salazar .01 .05
429 Andre Dawson .02 .10
430 Rick Sutcliffe .02 .10
431 Paul Assenmacher .01 .05
432 Erik Pappas RC .01 .05
433 Mark Grace .05 .15
434 Dennis Martinez .02 .10
435 Marquis Grissom .02 .10
436 Wil Cordero RC .20 .50
437 Tim Wallach .01 .05
438 Brian Barnes RC .01 .05
439 Barry Jones .01 .05
440 Ivan Calderon .01 .05
441 Stan Spencer RC .01 .05
442 Larry Walker .08 .25
443 Chris Haney RC .05 .15
444 Hector Rivera RC .01 .05
445 Delino DeShields .02 .10
446 Andres Galarraga .02 .10
447 Gilberto Reyes .01 .05
448 Willie Greene .01 .05
449 Greg Colbrunn RC .20 .50
450 Rondell White RC .40 1.00
451 Steve Frey .01 .05
452 Shane Andrews RC .05 .15
453 Mike Fitzgerald .01 .05
454 Spike Owen .01 .05
455 Dave Martinez .01 .05
456 Dennis Boyd .01 .05
457 Eric Bullock .01 .05
458 Reid Cornelius RC .05 .15
459 Chris Nabholz .01 .05
460 David Cone .02 .10
461 Hubie Brooks .01 .05
462 Sid Fernandez .01 .05
463 Doug Simons RC .01 .05
464 Howard Johnson .01 .05
465 Chris Donnels RC .01 .05
466 Anthony Young RC .05 .15
467 Todd Hundley .01 .05
468 Rick Cerone .01 .05
469 Kevin Elster .01 .05
470 Wally Whitehurst .01 .05
471 Vince Coleman .01 .05
472 Dwight Gooden .02 .10
473 Charlie O'Brien .01 .05
474 Jeromy Burnitz RC .40 1.00
475 John Franco .02 .10
476 Daryl Boston .01 .05
477 Frank Viola .02 .10
478 D.J. Dozier .01 .05
479 Kevin McReynolds .01 .05
480 Tom Herr .01 .05
481 Gregg Jefferies .01 .05
482 Pete Schourek RC .05 .15
483 Ron Darling .01 .05
484 Dave Magadan .01 .05
485 Andy Ashby RC .20 .50
486 Dale Murphy .05 .15

487 Von Hayes .01 .05
488 Kim Batiste RC .05 .15
489 Tony Longmire RC .05 .15
490 Wally Backman .01 .05
491 Jeff Jackson .01 .05
492 Mickey Morandini .01 .05
493 Darrel Akerfelds .01 .05
494 Ricky Jordan .01 .05
495 Randy Ready .01 .05
496 Darrin Fletcher .01 .05
497 Chuck Malone .01 .05
498 Pat Combs .01 .05
499 Dickie Thon .01 .05
500 Roger McDowell .01 .05
501 Len Dykstra .02 .10
502 Joe Boever .01 .05
503 John Kruk .02 .10
504 Terry Mulholland .01 .05
505 Wes Chamberlain RC .05 .15
506 Mike Lieberthal RC .40 1.00
507 Darren Daulton .02 .10
508 Charlie Hayes .01 .05
509 John Smiley .01 .05
510 Gary Varsho .01 .05
511 Curt Wilkerson .01 .05
512 Orlando Merced RC .05 .15
513 Barry Bonds .40 1.00
514 Mike LaValliere .01 .05
515 Doug Drabek .01 .05
516 Gary Redus .01 .05
517 William Pennyfeather RC .05 .15
518 Randy Tomlin RC .05 .15
519 Mike Zimmerman RC .05 .15
520 Jeff King .01 .05
521 Kurt Miller RC .05 .15
522 Jay Bell .02 .10
523 Bill Landrum .01 .05
524 Zane Smith .01 .05
525 Bobby Bonilla .02 .10
526 Bob Walk .01 .05
527 Austin Manahan .01 .05
528 Joe Ausanio RC .01 .05
529 Andy Van Slyke .05 .15
530 Jose Lind .01 .05
531 Carlos Garcia RC .05 .15
532 Don Slaught .01 .05
533 Gen.Colin Powell .20 .50
534 Frank Bolick RC .05 .15
535 Gary Scott RC .01 .05
536 Nikco Riesgo RC .01 .05
537 Reggie Sanders RC .60 1.50
538 Tim Howard RC .05 .15
539 Ryan Bowen RC .05 .15
540 Eric Anthony .01 .05
541 Jim Deshaies .01 .05
542 Tom Nevers RC .05 .15
543 Ken Caminiti .02 .10
544 Karl Rhodes .01 .05
545 Xavier Hernandez .01 .05
546 Mike Scott .01 .05
547 Jeff Juden .01 .05
548 Darryl Kile .02 .10
549 Willie Ansley .01 .05
550 Luis Gonzalez RC .60 1.50
551 Mike Simms RC .01 .05
552 Mark Portugal .01 .05
553 Jimmy Jones .01 .05
554 Jim Clancy .01 .05
555 Pete Harnisch .01 .05
556 Craig Biggio .05 .15
557 Eric Yelding .01 .05
558 Dave Rohde .01 .05
559 Casey Candaele .01 .05
560 Curt Schilling .08 .25
561 Steve Finley .02 .10
562 Javier Ortiz .01 .05
563 Andujar Cedeno .01 .05
564 Rafael Ramirez .01 .05
565 Kenny Lofton RC .60 1.50
566 Steve Avery .01 .05
567 Lonnie Smith .01 .05
568 Kent Mercker .01 .05
569 Chipper Jones RC 5.00 12.00
570 Terry Pendleton .02 .10
571 Otis Nixon .01 .05
572 Juan Berenguer .01 .05
573 Charlie Leibrandt .01 .05
574 David Justice .02 .10
575 Keith Mitchell RC .05 .15
576 Tom Glavine .05 .15
577 Greg Olson .01 .05
578 Rafael Belliard .01 .05
579 Ben Rivera RC .05 .15
580 John Smoltz .05 .15
581 Tyler Houston .01 .05
582 Mark Wohlers RC .20 .50
583 Ron Gant .02 .10
584 Ramon Caraballo RC .05 .15
585 Sid Bream .01 .05
586 Jeff Treadway .01 .05
587 Javy Lopez RC 1.25 3.00
588 Deion Sanders .05 .15
589 Mike Heath .01 .05
590 Ryan Klesko RC .40 1.00
591 Bob Ojeda .01 .05
592 Alfredo Griffin .01 .05
593 Raul Mondesi RC .40 1.00
594 Greg Smith .01 .05
595 Orel Hershiser .02 .10
596 Juan Samuel .01 .05
597 Brett Butler .02 .10
598 Gary Carter .02 .10
599 Stan Javier .01 .05
600 Kal Daniels .01 .05
601 Jamie McAndrew RC .05 .15
602 Mike Sharperson .01 .05
603 Jay Howell .01 .05
604 Eric Karros RC .60 1.50
605 Tim Belcher .01 .05
606 Dan Opperman RC .01 .05
607 Lenny Harris .01 .05
608 Tom Goodwin .01 .05
609 Darryl Strawberry .02 .10
610 Ramon Martinez .01 .05
611 Kevin Gross .01 .05
612 Zakary Shinall RC .01 .05
613 Mike Scioscia .01 .05
614 Eddie Murray .08 .25
615 Ronnie Walden RC .05 .15
616 Will Clark .05 .15
617 Adam Hyzdu RC .20 .50
618 Matt Williams .02 .10
619 Don Robinson .01 .05
620 Jeff Brantley .01 .05
621 Greg Litton .01 .05
622 Steve Decker RC .01 .05
623 Robby Thompson .01 .05
624 Mark Leonard RC .01 .05
625 Kevin Bass .01 .05
626 Scott Garrelts .01 .05
627 Jose Uribe .01 .05
628 Eric Gunderson .01 .05
629 Steve Hosey .01 .05
630 Trevor Wilson .01 .05
631 Terry Kennedy .01 .05
632 Dave Righetti .02 .10
633 Kelly Downs .01 .05
634 Johnny Ard .01 .05
635 Eric Christopherson RC .05 .15
636 Kevin Mitchell .01 .05
637 John Burkett .01 .05
638 Kevin Rogers RC .05 .15
639 Bud Black .01 .05
640 Willie McGee .02 .10
641 Royce Clayton .01 .05
642 Tony Fernandez .01 .05
643 Ricky Bones RC .05 .15
644 Thomas Howard .01 .05
645 Dave Staton RC .05 .15
646 Jim Presley .01 .05
647 Tony Gwynn .10 .30
648 Marty Barrett .01 .05
649 Scott Coolbaugh .01 .05
650 Craig Lefferts .01 .05
651 Eddie Whitson .01 .05
652 Oscar Azocar .01 .05
653 Wes Gardner .01 .05
654 Bip Roberts .01 .05
655 Robbie Beckett RC .05 .15
656 Benito Santiago .02 .10
657 Greg W.Harris .01 .05
658 Jerald Clark .01 .05
659 Fred McGriff .05 .15
660 Larry Andersen .01 .05
661 Bruce Hurst .01 .05
662 Steve Martin UER RC .05 .15
663 Rafael Valdez .01 .05
664 Paul Faries RC .01 .05
665 Andy Benes .01 .05
666 Randy Myers .01 .05
667 Rob Dibble .02 .10
668 Glenn Sutko RC .01 .05
669 Glenn Braggs .01 .05
670 Billy Hatcher .01 .05
671 Joe Oliver .01 .05
672 Freddie Benavides RC .05 .15
673 Barry Larkin .05 .15
674 Chris Sabo .01 .05
675 Mariano Duncan .01 .05
676 Chris Jones RC .01 .05
677 Gino Minutelli RC .01 .05
678 Reggie Jefferson .01 .05
679 Jack Armstrong .01 .05
680 Chris Hammond .01 .05
681 Jose Rijo .01 .05
682 Bill Doran .01 .05
683 Terry Lee RC .01 .05
684 Tom Browning .01 .05
685 Paul O'Neill .05 .15
686 Eric Davis .02 .10
687 Dan Wilson RC .20 .50
688 Ted Power .01 .05
689 Tim Layana .01 .05
690 Norm Charlton .01 .05
691 Hal Morris .01 .05
692 Rickey Henderson RB .05 .15
693 Sam Militello RC .05 .15
694 Matt Mieske RC .05 .15
695 Paul Russo RC .05 .15
696 Domingo Mota MVP .01 .05
697 Todd Guggiana RC .05 .15
698 Marc Newfield RC .05 .15
699 Checklist 1-122 .01 .05
700 Checklist 123-244 .01 .05
701 Checklist 245-366 .01 .05
702 Checklist 367-471 .01 .05
703 Checklist 472-593 .01 .05
704 Checklist 594-704 .01 .05

1992 Bowman

This 705-card standard-size set was issued in one comprehensive series. Unlike the previous Bowman issues, the 1992 set was radically upgraded to slick stock with gold foil subset cards in an attempt to reposition the brand as a premium level product. It initially stumbled out of the gate, but its superior selection of prospects enabled it to eventually gain acceptance in the hobby and now stands as one of the more important issues of the 1990's. Cards were distributed in plastic wrap packs, retail jumbo packs and special 80-card retail carton packs. Card fronts feature posed and action color player photos on a UV-coated white card face. . Forty-five foil cards inserted at a stated rate of one per wax pack and two per jumbo (23 regular cards) pack. These foil cards feature past and present Team USA players and minor league POY Award winners. Each foil card has an extremely slight variation in that the photos are cropped differently. There is no additional value to either version. Some of the regular and special cards picture prospects in civilian clothing who were still in the farm system. Rookie Cards in this set include Garret Anderson, Carlos Delgado, Mike Hampton, Brian Jordan, Mike Piazza, Manny Ramirez and Mariano Rivera.

COMPLETE SET (705) 60.00 120.00
ONE FOIL PER PACK/TWO PER JUMBO
FIVE FOILS PER 80-CARD CARTON

1 Ivan Rodriguez .50 1.25
2 Kirk McCaskill .20 .50
3 Scott Livingstone .20 .50
4 Salomon Torres RC .20 .50
5 Carlos Hernandez .20 .50
6 Dave Hollins .20 .50
7 Scott Fletcher .20 .50
8 Jorge Fabregas RC .20 .50
9 Andujar Cedeno .20 .50
10 Howard Johnson .20 .50
11 Trevor Hoffman RC 8.00 20.00
12 Roberto Kelly .20 .50
13 Gregg Jefferies .20 .50
14 Marquis Grissom .20 .50
15 Mike Ignasiak .20 .50
16 Jack Morris .20 .50
17 William Pennyfeather .20 .50
18 Todd Stottlemyre .20 .50
19 Chito Martinez .20 .50
20 Roberto Alomar .30 .75
21 Sam Militello .20 .50
22 Hector Fajardo RC .20 .50
23 Paul Quantrill RC .20 .50
24 Chuck Knoblauch .20 .50
25 Reggie Jefferson .20 .50
26 Jeremy McGarity RC .20 .50
27 Jerome Walton .20 .50
28 Chipper Jones 5.00 12.00
29 Brian Barber RC .20 .50
30 Ron Darling .20 .50
31 Roberto Petagine RC .20 .50
32 Chuck Finley .20 .50
33 Edgar Martinez .30 .75
34 Napoleon Robinson .20 .50
35 Andy Van Slyke .30 .75
36 Bobby Thigpen .20 .50
37 Travis Fryman .20 .50
38 Eric Christopherson .20 .50
39 Terry Mulholland .20 .50
40 Darryl Strawberry .20 .50
41 Manny Alexander RC .20 .50
42 Tracy Sanders RC .20 .50
43 Pete Incaviglia .20 .50
44 Kim Batiste .20 .50
45 Frank Rodriguez .20 .50
46 Greg Swindell .20 .50
47 Delino DeShields .20 .50
48 John Ericks .20 .50
49 Franklin Stubbs .20 .50
50 Tony Gwynn .60 1.50
51 Clifton Garrett RC .20 .50
52 Mike Gardella .20 .50
53 Scott Erickson .20 .50
54 Gary Caraballo RC .20 .50
55 Jose Oliva RC .20 .50
56 Brook Fordyce .20 .50
57 Mark Whiten .20 .50
58 Joe Slusarski .20 .50
59 J.R. Phillips RC .20 .50
60 Barry Bonds 1.50 4.00
61 Bob Milacki .20 .50
62 Keith Mitchell .20 .50
63 Angel Miranda .20 .50
64 Raul Mondesi .20 .50
65 Brian Koelling RC .20 .50
66 Brian McRae .20 .50
67 John Patterson RC .20 .50
68 John Wetteland .20 .50
69 Wilson Alvarez .20 .50
70 Wade Boggs .30 .75
71 Darryl Ratliff RC .20 .50
72 Jeff Jackson .20 .50
73 Jeremy Hernandez RC .20 .50
74 Darryl Hamilton .20 .50
75 Rafael Belliard .20 .50
76 Rick Trlicek RC .20 .50
77 Felipe Crespo RC .20 .50
78 Carney Lansford .20 .50
79 Ryan Long RC .20 .50
80 Kirby Puckett .50 1.25
81 Earl Cunningham .20 .50
82 Pedro Martinez 6.00 15.00
83 Scott Hatteberg RC .40 1.00
84 Juan Gonzalez UER .30 .75
65 doubles vs. Tigers
85 Robert Nutting RC .20 .50
86 Pokey Reese RC .40 1.00
87 Dave Silvestri .20 .50
88 Scott Ruffcorn RC .20 .50
89 Rick Aguilera .20 .50
90 Cecil Fielder .20 .50
91 Kirk Dressendorfer .20 .50
92 Jerry DiPoto RC .20 .50
93 Mike Felder .20 .50
94 Craig Paquette .20 .50
95 Elvin Paulino RC .20 .50
96 Donovan Osborne .20 .50
97 Hubie Brooks .20 .50
98 Derek Lowe RC 1.50 4.00
99 David Zancanaro .20 .50
100 Ken Griffey Jr. 1.00 2.50
101 Todd Hundley .20 .50
102 Mike Trombley RC .20 .50
103 Ricky Gutierrez RC .40 1.00
104 Braulio Castillo .20 .50
105 Craig Lefferts .20 .50
106 Rick Sutcliffe .20 .50
107 Dean Palmer .20 .50
108 Henry Rodriguez .20 .50
109 Mark Clark RC .40 1.00
110 Kenny Lofton .30 .75
111 Mark Carreon .20 .50
112 J.T. Bruett .20 .50
113 Gerald Williams .20 .50
114 Frank Thomas .50 1.25
115 Kevin Reimer .20 .50
116 Sammy Sosa .50 1.25
117 Mickey Tettleton .20 .50
118 Reggie Sanders .20 .50
119 Trevor Wilson .20 .50
120 Cliff Brantley .20 .50
121 Spike Owen .20 .50
122 Jeff Montgomery .20 .50
123 Alex Sutherland .20 .50
124 Brien Taylor RC .40 1.00
125 Brian Williams RC .20 .50
126 Kevin Seitzer .20 .50
127 Carlos Delgado RC 3.00 8.00
128 Gary Scott .20 .50
129 Scott Cooper .20 .50
130 Domingo Jean RC .20 .50
131 Pat Mahomes RC .40 1.00
132 Mike Boddicker .20 .50
133 Roberto Hernandez .20 .50
134 Dave Valle .20 .50
135 Kurt Stillwell .20 .50
136 Brad Pennington RC .20 .50
137 Jermaine Swinton RC .20 .50
138 Ryan Hawblitzel RC .20 .50
139 Tito Navarro RC .20 .50
140 Sandy Alomar Jr. .20 .50
141 Todd Benzinger .20 .50
142 Danny Jackson .20 .50
143 Melvin Nieves RC .20 .50
144 Jim Campanis .20 .50
145 Luis Gonzalez .20 .50
146 Dave Doorneweerd RC .20 .50
147 Charlie Hayes .20 .50
148 Greg Maddux .75 2.00
149 Brian Harper .20 .50
150 Brent Miller RC .20 .50
151 Shawn Estes RC .40 1.00
152 Mike Williams RC .40 1.00
153 Charlie Hough .20 .50
154 Randy Myers .20 .50
155 Kevin Young RC .40 1.00
156 Rick Wilkins .20 .50
157 Terry Shumpert .20 .50
158 Steve Karsay .20 .50
159 Gary DiSarcina .20 .50
160 Deion Sanders .30 .75
161 Tom Browning .20 .50
162 Dickie Thon .20 .50
163 Luis Mercedes .20 .50
164 Riccardo Ingram .20 .50
165 Tavo Alvarez RC .20 .50
166 Rickey Henderson .50 1.25
167 Jaime Navarro .20 .50
168 Billy Ashley RC .20 .50
169 Phil Dauphin RC .20 .50
170 Ivan Cruz .20 .50
171 Harold Baines .20 .50
172 Bryan Harvey .20 .50
173 Alex Cole .20 .50
174 Curtis Shaw RC .20 .50
175 Matt Williams .20 .50
176 Felix Jose .20 .50
177 Sam Horn .20 .50
178 Randy Johnson .50 1.25
179 Ivan Calderon .20 .50
180 Steve Avery .20 .50
181 William Suero .20 .50
182 Bill Swift .20 .50
183 Howard Battle RC .20 .50
184 Ruben Amaro .20 .50
185 Jim Abbott .30 .75
186 Mike Fitzgerald .20 .50
187 Bruce Hurst .20 .50
188 Jeff Juden .20 .50
189 Jeromy Burnitz .20 .50
190 Dave Burba .20 .50
191 Kevin Brown .20 .50
192 Patrick Lennon .20 .50
193 Jeff McNeely .20 .50
194 Wil Cordero .20 .50
195 Chili Davis .20 .50
196 Milt Cuyler .20 .50
197 Von Hayes .20 .50
198 Todd Revenig RC .20 .50
199 Joel Johnston .20 .50
200 Jeff Bagwell .50 1.25
201 Alex Fernandez .20 .50
202 Todd Jones RC 1.00 2.50
203 Charles Nagy .20 .50
204 Tim Raines .20 .50
205 Kevin Maas .20 .50
206 Julio Franco .20 .50
207 Randy Velarde .20 .50
208 Lance Johnson .20 .50
209 Scott Leius .20 .50
210 Derek Lee .20 .50
211 Joe Sondrini RC .20 .50
212 Royce Clayton .20 .50
213 Chris George .20 .50
214 Gary Sheffield .20 .50
215 Mark Gubicza .20 .50
216 Mike Moore .20 .50
217 Rick Huisman RC .20 .50
218 Jeff Russell .20 .50
219 D.J. Dozier .20 .50
220 Dave Martinez .20 .50
221 Alan Newman RC .20 .50
222 Nolan Ryan 1.50 4.00
223 Teddy Higuera .20 .50
224 Damon Buford RC .20 .50
225 Ruben Sierra .20 .50
226 Tom Nevers .20 .50
227 Tommy Greene .20 .50
228 Nigel Wilson RC .20 .50
229 John DeSilva .20 .50
230 Bobby Witt .20 .50
231 Greg Cadaret .20 .50
232 John Vander Wal RC .40 1.00
233 Jack Clark .20 .50
234 Bill Doran .20 .50
235 Bobby Bonilla .20 .50
236 Steve Olin .20 .50
237 Derek Bell .20 .50
238 David Cone .20 .50
239 Victor Cole RC .20 .50
240 Rod Bolton RC .20 .50
241 Tom Pagnozzi .20 .50
242 Rob Dibble .20 .50
243 Michael Carter RC .20 .50
244 Don Peters .20 .50
245 Mike LaValliere .20 .50
246 Joe Perona RC .20 .50
247 Mitch Williams .20 .50
248 Jay Buhner .20 .50
249 Andy Benes .20 .50
250 Alex Ochoa RC .20 .50
251 Greg Blosser .20 .50
252 Jack Armstrong .20 .50
253 Juan Samuel .20 .50
254 Terry Pendleton .20 .50
255 Ramon Martinez .20 .50
256 Rico Brogna .20 .50
257 John Smiley .20 .50
258 Carl Everett .30 .75
259 Tim Salmon .30 .75
260 Will Clark .30 .75
261 Ugueth Urbina RC .40 1.00
262 Jason Wood RC .20 .50
263 Dave Magadan .20 .50
264 Dante Bichette .20 .50
265 Jose DeLeon .20 .50
266 Mike Neill RC .40 1.00
267 Paul O'Neill .30 .75
268 Anthony Young .20 .50
269 Greg W. Harris .20 .50
270 Todd Van Poppel .20 .50
271 Pedro Castellano RC .20 .50
272 Tony Phillips .20 .50
273 Mike Gallego .20 .50
274 Steve Cooke RC .20 .50
275 Robin Ventura .20 .50
276 Kevin Mitchell .20 .50
277 Doug Linton RC .20 .50
278 Robert Eenhoorn .20 .50
279 Gabe White RC .20 .50
280 Dave Stewart .20 .50
281 Mo Sanford .20 .50
282 Greg Perschke .20 .50
283 Kevin Flora RC .20 .50
284 Jeff Williams RC .40 1.00
285 Keith Miller .20 .50
286 Andy Ashby .20 .50
287 Doug Dascenzo .20 .50
288 Eric Karros .20 .50
289 Glenn Murray RC .20 .50
290 Troy Percival RC 1.25 3.00
291 Orlando Merced .20 .50
292 Peter Hoy .20 .50
293 Tony Fernandez .20 .50
294 Juan Guzman .20 .50
295 Jesse Barfield .20 .50
296 Sid Fernandez .20 .50
297 Scott Cepicky .20 .50
298 Garret Anderson RC 2.00 5.00
299 Cal Eldred .20 .50
300 Ryne Sandberg 1.00 2.50
301 Jim Gantner .20 .50
302 Mariano Rivera RC 40.00 100.00
303 Ron Lockett RC .20 .50
304 Jose Offerman .20 .50
305 Dennis Martinez .20 .50
306 Luis Ortiz RC .20 .50
307 David Howard .20 .50
308 Russ Springer RC .40 1.00
309 Chris Howard .20 .50
310 Kyle Abbott .20 .50
311 Aaron Sele RC .40 1.00
312 David Justice .20 .50
313 Pete O'Brien .20 .50
314 Greg Hansell RC .20 .50
315 Dave Winfield .20 .50
316 Lance Dickson .20 .50
317 Eric King .20 .50
318 Vaughn Eshelman RC .20 .50
319 Tim Belcher .20 .50
320 Andres Galarraga .20 .50
321 Scott Bullett RC .20 .50
322 Doug Strange .20 .50
323 Jerald Clark .20 .50
324 Dave Righetti .20 .50
325 Greg Hibbard .20 .50
326 Eric Hillman RC .20 .50
327 Shane Reynolds RC .40 1.00
328 Chris Hammond .20 .50
329 Albert Belle .20 .50
330 Rich Becker RC .20 .50
331 Ed Williams .20 .50
332 Donald Harris .20 .50
333 Dave Smith .20 .50
334 Steve Fireovid .20 .50
335 Steve Buechele .20 .50
336 Mike Schooler .20 .50
337 Kevin McReynolds .20 .50
338 Hensley Meulens .20 .50
339 Benji Gil RC .40 1.00
340 Don Mattingly 1.25 3.00
341 Alvin Davis .20 .50
342 Alan Mills .20 .50
343 Kelly Downs .20 .50
344 Leo Gomez .20 .50
345 Tarrik Brock RC .20 .50
346 Ryan Turner RC .20 .50
347 John Smoltz .30 .75
348 Bill Sampen .20 .50
349 Paul Byrd RC 1.25 3.00
350 Mike Bordick .20 .50
351 Jose Lind .20 .50
352 David Wells .20 .50
353 Barry Larkin .30 .75
354 Bruce Ruffin .20 .50
355 Luis Rivera .20 .50
356 Sid Bream .20 .50
357 Julian Vasquez RC .20 .50
358 Jason Bere RC .40 1.00
359 Ben McDonald .20 .50
360 Scott Stahoviak RC .20 .50
361 Kirt Manwaring .20 .50
362 Jeff Johnson .20 .50
363 Rob Deer .20 .50
364 Tony Pena .20 .50
365 Melido Perez .20 .50
366 Clay Parker .20 .50
367 Dale Sveum .20 .50
368 Mike Scioscia .20 .50
369 Roger Salkeld .20 .50
370 Mike Stanley .20 .50
371 Jack McDowell .20 .50
372 Tim Wallach .20 .50
373 Billy Ripken .20 .50
374 Mike Christopher .20 .50
375 Paul Molitor .20 .50
376 Dave Stieb .20 .50
377 Pedro Guerrero .20 .50
378 Russ Swan .20 .50
379 Bob Ojeda .20 .50
380 Donn Pall .20 .50
381 Eddie Zosky .20 .50
382 Darnell Coles .20 .50
383 Tom Smith RC .20 .50
384 Mark McGwire 1.25 3.00
385 Gary Carter .20 .50
386 Rich Amaral RC .20 .50
387 Alan Embree RC .40 1.00
388 Jonathan Hurst RC .20 .50
389 Bobby Jones RC .40 1.00
390 Rico Rossy .20 .50
391 Dan Smith .20 .50
392 Terry Steinbach .20 .50
393 Jon Farrell RC .20 .50
394 Dave Anderson .20 .50
395 Benny Santiago .20 .50
396 Mark Wohlers .20 .50
397 Mo Vaughn .20 .50
398 Randy Kramer .20 .50
399 John Jaha RC .40 1.00
400 Cal Ripken 1.50 4.00
401 Ryan Bowen .20 .50
402 Tim McIntosh .20 .50
403 Bernard Gilkey .20 .50
404 Junior Felix .20 .50
405 Cris Colon RC .20 .50
406 Marc Newfield .20 .50
407 Bernie Williams .30 .75
408 Jay Howell .20 .50
409 Zane Smith .20 .50
410 Jeff Shaw .20 .50
411 Kerry Woodson .20 .50
412 Wes Chamberlain .20 .50
413 Dave Mlicki RC .40 1.00
414 Benny Distefano .20 .50
415 Kevin Rogers .20 .50
416 Tim Naehring .20 .50
417 Clemente Nunez RC .20 .50
418 Luis Sojo .20 .50
419 Kevin Ritz .20 .50
420 Omar Olivares .20 .50
421 Manuel Lee .20 .50
422 Julio Valera .20 .50
423 Omar Vizquel .30 .75
424 Darren Burton RC .20 .50
425 Mel Hall .20 .50
426 Dennis Powell .20 .50
427 Lee Stevens .20 .50
428 Glenn Davis .20 .50
429 Willie Greene .20 .50
430 Kevin Wickander .20 .50
431 Dennis Eckersley .20 .50
432 Joe Orsulak .20 .50
433 Eddie Murray .50 1.25
434 Matt Stairs RC .40 1.00
435 Wally Joyner .20 .50
436 Rondell White .20 .50
437 Rob Maurer RC .20 .50
438 Joe Redfield .20 .50
439 Mark Lewis .20 .50
440 Darren Daulton .20 .50
441 Mike Henneman .20 .50
442 John Cangelosi .20 .50
443 Vince Moore RC .20 .50
444 John Wehner .20 .50
445 Kent Hrbek .20 .50
446 Mark McLemore .20 .50
447 Bill Wegman .20 .50
448 Robby Thompson .20 .50
449 Mark Anthony RC .20 .50
450 Archi Cianfrocco RC .20 .50
451 Johnny Ruffin .20 .50
452 Javy Lopez .75 2.00
453 Greg Gohr .20 .50
454 Tim Scott .20 .50
455 Stan Belinda .20 .50
456 Darrin Jackson .20 .50
457 Chris Gardner .20 .50
458 Esteban Beltre .20 .50
459 Phil Plantier .20 .50
460 Jim Thome 3.00 8.00
461 Mike Piazza RC 15.00 40.00
462 Matt Sinatro .20 .50
463 Scott Servais .20 .50
464 Brian Jordan RC .75 2.00
465 Doug Drabek .20 .50
466 Carl Willis .20 .50
467 Bret Barberie .20 .50
468 Hal Morris .20 .50
469 Steve Sax .20 .50
470 Jerry Willard .20 .50
471 Dan Wilson .20 .50
472 Chris Hoiles .20 .50
473 Rheal Cormier .20 .50
474 John Morris .20 .50
475 Jeff Reardon .20 .50
476 Mark Leiter .20 .50
477 Tom Gordon .20 .50
478 Kent Bottenfield RC .40 1.00
479 Gene Larkin .20 .50
480 Dwight Gooden .20 .50
481 B.J. Surhoff .20 .50
482 Andy Stankiewicz .20 .50
483 Tino Martinez .30 .75
484 Craig Biggio .30 .75
485 Denny Neagle .20 .50
486 Rusty Meacham .20 .50
487 Kal Daniels .20 .50
488 Dave Henderson .20 .50
489 Tim Costo .20 .50
490 Doug Davis .20 .50
491 Frank Viola .20 .50
492 Cory Snyder .20 .50
493 Chris Martin RC .20 .50
494 Dion James .20 .50
495 Randy Tomlin .20 .50
496 Greg Vaughn .20 .50
497 Dennis Cook .20 .50
498 Rosario Rodriguez .20 .50
499 Dave Staton .20 .50
500 George Brett 1.25 3.00
501 Brian Barnes .20 .50
502 Butch Henry RC .20 .50
503 Harold Reynolds .20 .50
504 David Nied RC .20 .50
505 Lee Smith .20 .50
506 Steve Chitren .20 .50
507 Ken Hill .20 .50
508 Robbie Beckett .20 .50
509 Troy Afenir .20 .50
510 Kelly Gruber .20 .50
511 Bret Boone .30 .75
512 Jeff Branson .20 .50
513 Mike Jackson .20 .50
514 Pete Harnisch .20 .50
515 Chad Kreuter .20 .50
516 Joe Vitko RC .20 .50
517 Orel Hershiser .20 .50
518 John Doherty RC .20 .50
519 Jay Bell .20 .50
520 Mark Langston .20 .50
521 Dann Howitt .20 .50
522 Bobby Reed RC .20 .50
523 Bobby Munoz RC .20 .50

524 Todd Ritchie .20 .50
525 Bip Roberts .20 .50
526 Pat Listach RC .40 1.00
527 Scott Brosius RC .75 2.00
528 John Roper RC .20 .50
529 Phil Hiatt RC .20 .50
530 Denny Walling .20 .50
531 Carlos Baerga .20 .50
532 Manny Ramirez RC 3.00 8.00
533 Pat Clements UER .20 .50
Mistakenly numbered 553
534 Ron Gant .20 .50
535 Pat Kelly .20 .50
536 Bill Spiers .20 .50
537 Darren Reed .20 .50
538 Ken Caminiti .20 .50
539 Butch Huskey RC .20 .50
540 Matt Nokes .20 .50
541 John Kruk .20 .50
542 John Jaha FOIL .20 .50
543 Justin Thompson RC .20 .50
544 Steve Hosey .20 .50
545 Joe Kmak .20 .50
546 John Franco .20 .50
547 Devon White .20 .50
548 Elston Hansen FOIL SP RC .20 .50
549 Ryan Klesko .20 .50
550 Danny Tartabull .20 .50
551 Frank Thomas FOIL .50 1.25
552 Kevin Tapani .20 .50
553 Willie Banks .20 .50
See also 533
554 B.J.Wallace FOIL RC .20 .50
555 Orlando Miller RC .20 .50
556 Mark Smith RC .20 .50
557 Tim Wallach FOIL .20 .50
558 Bill Gullickson .20 .50
559 Derek Bell FOIL .20 .50
560 Joe Randa FOIL RC 1.25 3.00
561 Frank Seminara RC .20 .50
562 Mark Gardner .20 .50
563 Rick Greene FOIL RC .20 .50
564 Gary Gaetti .20 .50
565 Ozzie Guillen .20 .50
566 Charles Nagy FOIL .20 .50
567 Mike Milchin .20 .50
568 Ben Shelton RC .20 .50
569 Chris Roberts FOIL .20 .50
570 Ellis Burks .20 .50
571 Scott Scudder .20 .50
572 Jim Abbott FOIL .30 .75
573 Joe Carter .20 .50
574 Steve Finley .20 .50
575 Jim Olander FOIL .20 .50
576 Carlos Garcia .20 .50
577 Gregg Olson .20 .50
578 Greg Swindell FOIL .20 .50
579 Matt Williams FOIL .20 .50
580 Mark Grace .30 .75
581 Howard House FOIL RC .20 .50
582 Luis Polonia .20 .50
583 Erik Hanson .20 .50
584 Salomon Torres FOIL .20 .50
585 Carlton Fisk .30 .75
586 Bret Saberhagen .20 .50
587 Chad McConnell FOIL RC .20 .50
588 Jimmy Key .20 .50
589 Mike Macfarlane .20 .50
590 Barry Bonds FOIL 1.50 4.00
591 Jamie McAndrew .20 .50
592 Shane Mack .20 .50
593 Kerwin Moore .20 .50
594 Joe Oliver .20 .50
595 Chris Sabo .20 .50
596 Alex Gonzalez RC .40 1.00
597 Brett Butler .20 .50
598 Mark Hutton RC .20 .50
599 Andy Benes FOIL .20 .50
600 Jose Canseco .30 .75
601 Darryl Kile .20 .50
602 Matt Stairs FOIL .20 .50
603 Rob Butler FOIL RC .20 .50
604 Willie McGee .20 .50
605 Jack McDowell FOIL .20 .50
606 Tom Candiotti .20 .50
607 Ed Martel RC .20 .50
608 Matt Mieske FOIL .20 .50
609 Darrin Fletcher .20 .50
610 Rafael Palmeiro .30 .75
611 Bill Swift FOIL .20 .50
612 Mike Mussina .50 1.25
613 Vince Coleman .20 .50
614A Scott Cepicky FOIL
ERR(BATS LEFLT on back .20 .50
614B Scott Cepicky COR .20 .50
615 Mike Greenwell .20 .50
616 Kevin McGehee RC .20 .50
617 Jeffrey Hammonds FOIL .20 .50
618 Scott Taylor .20 .50
619 Dave Otto .20 .50
620 Mark McGwire FOIL 1.25 3.00
621 Kevin Tatar RC .20 .50
622 Steve Farr .20 .50
623 Ryan Klesko FOIL .20 .50
624 Dave Fleming .20 .50
625 Andre Dawson .20 .50
626 Tino Martinez FOIL SP .30 .75
627 Chad Curtis RC .40 1.00
628 Mickey Morandini .20 .50
629 Gregg Olson FOIL SP .20 .50
630 Lou Whitaker .20 .50
631 Arthur Rhodes .20 .50
632 Brandon Wilson RC .20 .50
633 Lance Jennings RC .20 .50
634 Allen Watson RC .20 .50
635 Len Dykstra .20 .50
636 Joe Girardi .20 .50
637 Kiki Hernandez FOIL RC .20 .50
638 Mike Hampton RC .75 2.00
639 Al Osuna .20 .50
640 Kevin Appier .20 .50
641 Rick Helling FOIL .20 .50
642 Jody Reed .20 .50
643 Ray Lankford .20 .50
644 John Olerud .20 .50
645 Paul Molitor FOIL .20 .50
646 Pat Borders .20 .50
647 Mike Morgan .20 .50
648 Larry Walker .30 .75
649 Pedro Castellano FOIL .20 .50
650 Fred McGriff .30 .75
651 Walt Weiss .20 .50
652 Calvin Murray FOIL RC .40 1.00
653 Dave Nilsson .20 .50
654 Greg Pirkl RC .20 .50
655 Robin Ventura FOIL .20 .50
656 Mark Portugal .20 .50
657 Roger McDowell .20 .50
658 Rick Hirtensteiner FOIL RC .20 .50
659 Glenallen Hill .20 .50
660 Greg Gagne .20 .50
661 Charles Johnson FOIL .20 .50
662 Brian Hunter .20 .50
663 Mark Lemke .20 .50
664 Tim Belcher FOIL SP .20 .50
665 Rich DeLucia .20 .50
666 Bob Walk .20 .50
667 Joe Carter FOIL .20 .50
668 Jose Guzman .20 .50
669 Otis Nixon .20 .50
670 Phil Nevin FOIL .20 .50
671 Eric Davis .20 .50
672 Damion Easley RC .40 1.00
673 Will Clark FOIL .30 .75
674 Mark Kiefer RC .20 .50
675 Ozzie Smith .75 2.00
676 Manny Ramirez FOIL 3.00 8.00
677 Gregg Olson .20 .50
678 Cliff Floyd RC 1.25 3.00
679 Duane Singleton RC .20 .50
680 Jose Rijo .20 .50
681 Willie Randolph .20 .50
682 Michael Tucker FOIL RC .40 1.00
683 Darren Lewis .20 .50
684 Dale Murphy .30 .75
685 Mike Pagliarulo .20 .50
686 Paul Miller RC .20 .50
687 Mike Robertson RC .20 .50
688 Mike Devereaux .20 .50
689 Pedro Astacio RC .40 1.00
690 Alan Trammell .20 .50
691 Roger Clemens 1.00 2.50
692 Bud Black .20 .50
693 Turk Wendell RC .40 1.00
694 Barry Larkin FOIL .30 .75
695 Todd Zeile .20 .50
696 Pat Hentgen .20 .50
697 Eddie Taubensee RC .40 1.00
698 Guillermo Velasquez RC .20 .50
699 Tom Glavine .30 .75
700 Robin Yount .75 2.00
701 Checklist 1-141 .20 .50
702 Checklist 142-282 .20 .50
703 Checklist 283-423 .20 .50
704 Checklist 424-564 .20 .50
705 Checklist 565-705 .20 .50

1993 Bowman

This 708-card standard-size set (produced by Topps) was issued in one series and features one of the more comprehensive selection of prospects and rookies available that year. Cards were distributed in 14-card plastic wrapped packs and jumbo packs. Each 14-card pack contained one silver foil bordered subset card. The basic issue card fronts feature white-bordered color action player photos. The 48 foil subset cards (339-374 and 693-704) feature sixteen 1992 MVPs of the Minor Leagues, top prospects and a few father/son combinations. Rookie Cards in this set include James Baldwin, Roger Cedeno, Derek Jeter, Jason Kendall, Andy Pettitte, Jose Vidro and Preston Wilson.

COMPLETE SET (708) 15.00 40.00
ONE FOIL PER PACK/2 PER JUMBO
1 Glenn Davis .05 .15
2 Hector Roa RC .08 .25
3 Ken Ryan RC .08 .25
4 Derek Wallace RC .08 .25
5 Jorge Fabregas .05 .15
6 Joe Oliver .05 .15
7 Brandon Wilson .05 .15
8 Mark Thompson RC .08 .25
9 Tracy Sanders .05 .15
10 Rich Renteria .05 .15
11 Lou Whitaker .10 .30
12 Brian L. Hunter RC .20 .50
13 Joe Vitiello .05 .15
14 Eric Karros .10 .30
15 Joe Kmak .05 .15
16 Tavo Alvarez .05 .15
17 Steve Dunn RC .08 .25
18 Tony Fernandez .05 .15
19 Melido Perez .05 .15
20 Mike Lieberthal .10 .30
21 Terry Steinbach .05 .15
22 Stan Belinda .05 .15
23 Jay Buhner .10 .30
24 Allen Watson .05 .15
25 Daryl Henderson RC .08 .25
26 Ray McDavid RC .08 .25
27 Shawn Green .40 1.00
28 Bud Black .05 .15
29 Sherman Obando RC .08 .25
30 Mike Hostetler RC .08 .25
31 Nate Minchey RC .08 .25
32 Randy Myers .05 .15
33 Brian Grebeck .05 .15
34 John Roper .05 .15
35 Larry Thomas .05 .15
36 Alex Cole .05 .15
37 Tom Kramer RC .08 .25
38 Matt Whisenant RC .08 .25
39 Chris Gomez RC .20 .50
40 Luis Gonzalez .10 .30
41 Kevin Appier .10 .30
42 Omar Daal RC .08 .25
43 Duane Singleton .05 .15
44 Bill Risley .05 .15
45 Pat Meares RC .20 .50
46 Butch Huskey .05 .15
47 Bobby Munoz .05 .15
48 Juan Bell .05 .15
49 Scott Lydy RC .08 .25
50 Dennis Moeller .05 .15
51 Marc Newfield .05 .15
52 Tripp Cromer RC .08 .25
53 Kurt Miller .05 .15
54 Jim Pena .05 .15
55 Juan Guzman .05 .15
56 Matt Williams .10 .30
57 Harold Reynolds .10 .30
58 Donnie Elliott RC .08 .25
59 Jon Shave RC .08 .25
60 Kevin Roberson RC .08 .25
61 Hilly Hathaway RC .08 .25
62 Jose Rijo .05 .15
63 Kerry Taylor RC .05 .15
64 Ryan Hawblitzel .05 .15
65 Glenallen Hill .05 .15
66 Ramon Martinez RC .08 .25
67 Travis Fryman .10 .30
68 Tom Nevers .05 .15
69 Phil Hiatt .05 .15
70 Tim Wallach .05 .15
71 B.J. Surhoff .10 .30
72 Rondell White .10 .30
73 Denny Hocking RC .20 .50
74 Mike Oquist RC .08 .25
75 Paul O'Neill .20 .50
76 Willie Banks .05 .15
77 Bob Welch .05 .15
78 Jose Sandoval RC .08 .25
79 Bill Haselman .05 .15
80 Rheal Cormier .05 .15
81 Dean Palmer .10 .30
82 Pat Gomez RC .08 .25
83 Steve Karsay .05 .15
84 Carl Hanselman RC .08 .25
85 T.R. Lewis RC .08 .25
86 Chipper Jones .30 .75
87 Scott Hatteberg .05 .15
88 Greg Hibbard .05 .15
89 Lance Painter RC .08 .25
90 Chad Mottola RC .20 .50
91 Jason Bere .05 .15
92 Dante Bichette .10 .30
93 Sandy Alomar Jr. .05 .15
94 Carl Everett .10 .30
95 Danny Bautista RC .20 .50
96 Steve Finley .10 .30
97 David Cone .10 .30
98 Todd Hollandsworth .05 .15
99 Matt Mieske .05 .15
100 Larry Walker .10 .30
101 Shane Mack .05 .15
102 Aaron Ledesma RC .08 .25
103 Andy Pettitte RC 4.00 10.00
104 Kevin Stocker .05 .15
105 Mike Mohler RC .08 .25
106 Tony Menendez .05 .15
107 Derek Lowe .10 .30
108 Basil Shabazz .05 .15
109 Dan Smith .05 .15
110 Scott Sanders RC .20 .50
111 Todd Stottlemyre .05 .15
112 Benji Simonton RC .08 .25
113 Rick Sutcliffe .05 .15
114 Lee Heath RC .08 .25
115 Jeff Russell .05 .15
116 Dave Stevens RC .08 .25
117 Mark Holzemer RC .08 .25
118 Tim Belcher .05 .15
119 Bobby Thigpen .05 .15
120 Roger Bailey RC .08 .25
121 Tony Mitchell RC .08 .25
122 Junior Felix .05 .15
123 Rich Robertson RC .08 .25
124 Andy Cook RC .08 .25
125 Brian Bevil RC .08 .25
126 Darryl Strawberry .10 .30
127 Cal Eldred .05 .15
128 Cliff Floyd .10 .30
129 Alan Newman .05 .15
130 Howard Johnson .05 .15
131 Jim Abbott .20 .50
132 Chad McConnell .05 .15
133 Miguel Jimenez RC .08 .25
134 Brett Backlund RC .08 .25
135 John Cummings RC .08 .25
136 Brian Barber .05 .15
137 Rafael Palmeiro .20 .50
138 Tim Worrell RC .08 .25
139 Jose Pett RC .08 .25
140 Barry Bonds .75 2.00
141 Damon Buford .05 .15
142 Jeff Blauser .05 .15
143 Frankie Rodriguez .05 .15
144 Mike Morgan .05 .15
145 Gary DiSarcina .05 .15
146 Pokey Reese .05 .15
147 Johnny Ruffin .05 .15
148 David Nied .05 .15
149 Charles Nagy .05 .15
150 Mike Myers RC .08 .25
151 Kenny Carlyle RC .08 .25
152 Eric Anthony .05 .15
153 Jose Lind .05 .15
154 Pedro Martinez .60 1.50
155 Mark Kiefer .05 .15
156 Tim Laker RC .08 .25
157 Pat Mahomes .05 .15
158 Bobby Bonilla .10 .30
159 Domingo Jean .05 .15
160 Darren Daulton .10 .30
161 Mark McGwire .75 2.00
162 Jason Kendall RC .75 2.00
163 Desi Relaford .05 .15
164 Ozzie Canseco .05 .15
165 Rick Helling .05 .15
166 Steve Pegues RC .08 .25
167 Paul Molitor .10 .30
168 Larry Carter RC .05 .15
169 Arthur Rhodes .05 .15
170 Damon Hollins RC .20 .50
171 Frank Viola .10 .30
172 Steve Trachsel RC .40 1.00
173 J.T.Snow RC .40 1.00
174 Keith Gordon RC .08 .25
175 Carlton Fisk .20 .50
176 Jason Bates RC .08 .25
177 Mike Crosby RC .08 .25
178 Benny Santiago .10 .30
179 Mike Moore .05 .15
180 Jeff Juden .05 .15
181 Darren Burton .05 .15
182 Todd Williams RC .20 .50
183 John Jaha .05 .15
184 Mike Lansing RC .20 .50
185 Pedro Grifol RC .08 .25
186 Vince Coleman .05 .15
187 Pat Kelly .05 .15
188 Clemente Alvarez RC .08 .25
189 Ron Darling .05 .15
190 Orlando Merced .05 .15
191 Chris Bosio .05 .15
192 Steve Dixon RC .08 .25
193 Doug Dascenzo .05 .15
194 Ray Holbert RC .08 .25
195 Howard Battle .05 .15
196 Willie McGee .10 .30
197 John O'Donoghue RC .08 .25
198 Steve Avery .05 .15
199 Greg Blosser .05 .15
200 Ryne Sandberg .50 1.25
201 Joe Grahe .05 .15
202 Dan Wilson .10 .30
203 Domingo Martinez RC .08 .25
204 Andres Galarraga .10 .30
205 Jamie Taylor RC .08 .25
206 Darrell Whitmore RC .08 .25
207 Ben Blomdahl RC .08 .25
208 Doug Drabek .05 .15
209 Keith Miller .05 .15
210 Billy Ashley .05 .15
211 Mike Farrell RC .08 .25
212 John Wetteland .10 .30
213 Randy Tomlin .05 .15
214 Sid Fernandez .05 .15
215 Quilvio Veras RC .20 .50
216 Dave Hollins .05 .15
217 Mike Neill .05 .15
218 Andy Van Slyke .20 .50
219 Bret Boone .10 .30
220 Tom Pagnozzi .05 .15
221 Mike Welch RC .08 .25
222 Frank Seminara .05 .15
223 Ron Villone .20 .50
224 D.J.Thielen RC .08 .25
225 Cal Ripken 1.00 2.50
226 Pedro Borbon Jr. RC .08 .25
227 Carlos Quintana .05 .15
228 Tommy Shields .05 .15
229 Tim Salmon .20 .50
230 John Smiley .05 .15
231 Ellis Burks .10 .30
232 Pedro Castellano .05 .15
233 Paul Byrd .10 .30
234 Bryan Harvey .05 .15
235 Scott Livingstone .05 .15
236 James Mouton RC .08 .25
237 Joe Randa .10 .30
238 Pedro Astacio .05 .15
239 Darryl Hamilton .05 .15
240 Joey Eischen RC .08 .25
241 Edgar Herrera RC .08 .25
242 Dwight Gooden .10 .30
243 Sam Militello .05 .15
244 Ron Blazier RC .08 .25
245 Ruben Sierra .10 .30
246 Al Martin .05 .15
247 Mike Felder .05 .15
248 Bob Tewksbury .05 .15
249 Craig Lefferts .05 .15
250 Luis Lopez RC .08 .25
251 Devon White .10 .30
252 Will Clark .20 .50
253 Mark Smith .05 .15
254 Terry Pendleton .10 .30
255 Aaron Sele .05 .15
256 Jose Viera RC .08 .25
257 Damion Easley .05 .15
258 Rod Lofton RC .08 .25
259 Chris Snopek RC .08 .25
260 Quinton McCracken RC .20 .50
261 Mike Matthews RC .08 .25
262 Hector Carrasco RC .08 .25
263 Rick Greene .05 .15
264 Chris Holt RC .20 .50
265 George Brett .75 2.00
266 Rick Gorecki RC .08 .25
267 Francisco Gamez RC .08 .25
268 Marquis Grissom .10 .30
269 Kevin Tapani UER .05 .15
Misspelled Tapan
on card front
270 Ryan Thompson .05 .15
271 Gerald Williams .05 .15
272 Paul Fletcher RC .08 .25
273 Lance Blankenship .05 .15
274 Marty Neff RC .08 .25
275 Shawn Estes .05 .15
276 Rene Arocha RC .20 .50
277 Scott Eyre RC .08 .25
278 Phil Plantier .05 .15
279 Paul Spoljaric RC .08 .25
280 Chris Gambs .05 .15
281 Harold Baines .10 .30
282 Jose Oliva .05 .15
283 Matt Whiteside RC .08 .25
284 Brant Brown RC .20 .50
285 Russ Springer .05 .15
286 Chris Sabo .05 .15
287 Ozzie Guillen .10 .30
288 Marcus Moore RC .08 .25
289 Chad Ogea .05 .15
290 Walt Weiss .05 .15
291 Brian Edmondson .05 .15
292 Jimmy Gonzalez .05 .15
293 Danny Miceli RC .20 .50
294 Jose Offerman .05 .15
295 Greg Vaughn .05 .15
296 Frank Bolick .05 .15
297 Mike Maksudian RC .08 .25
298 John Franco .10 .30
299 Danny Tartabull .05 .15
300 Len Dykstra .10 .30
301 Bobby Witt .05 .15
302 Trey Beamon RC .08 .25
303 Tino Martinez .20 .50
304 Aaron Holbert .05 .15
305 Juan Gonzalez .10 .30
306 Billy Hall RC .08 .25
307 Duane Ward .05 .15
308 Rod Beck .05 .15
309 Jose Mercedes RC .08 .25
310 Otis Nixon .05 .15
311 Gettys Glaze RC .08 .25
312 Candy Maldonado .05 .15
313 Chad Curtis .05 .15
314 Tim Costo .05 .15
315 Mike Robertson .05 .15
316 Nigel Wilson .05 .15
317 Greg McMichael RC .08 .25
318 Scott Pose RC .08 .25
319 Ivan Cruz .05 .15
320 Greg Swindell .05 .15
321 Kevin McReynolds .05 .15
322 Tom Candiotti .05 .15
323 Rob Wishnevski RC .08 .25
324 Ken Hill .05 .15
325 Kirby Puckett .30 .75
326 Tim Bogar RC .08 .25
327 Mariano Rivera 5.00 12.00
328 Mitch Williams .05 .15
329 Craig Paquette .05 .15
330 Jay Bell .10 .30
331 Jose Martinez RC .08 .25
332 Rob Deer .05 .15
333 Brook Fordyce .05 .15
334 Matt Nokes .05 .15
335 Derek Lee .05 .15
336 Paul Ellis RC .08 .25
337 Desi Wilson RC .08 .25
338 Roberto Alomar .20 .50
339 Jim Tatum FOIL RC .08 .25
340 J.T.Snow FOIL .40 1.00
341 Tim Salmon FOIL .20 .50
342 Russ Davis FOIL RC .20 .50
343 Javy Lopez FOIL .20 .50
344 Troy O'Leary FOIL RC .20 .50
345 Marty Cordova FOIL RC .20 .50
346 Bubba Smith RC FOIL .08 .25
347 Chipper Jones FOIL .30 .75
348 Jessie Hollins FOIL .05 .15
349 Willie Greene FOIL .05 .15
350 Mark Thompson FOIL .05 .15
351 Nigel Wilson FOIL .05 .15
352 Todd Jones FOIL .10 .30
353 Raul Mondesi FOIL .10 .30
354 Cliff Floyd FOIL .10 .30
355 Bobby Jones FOIL .10 .30
356 Kevin Stocker FOIL .05 .15
357 Midre Cummings FOIL .05 .15
358 Allen Watson FOIL .05 .15
359 Ray McDavid FOIL .05 .15
360 Steve Hosey FOIL .05 .15
361 Brad Pennington FOIL .05 .15
362 Frankie Rodriguez FOIL .05 .15
363 Troy Percival FOIL .20 .50
364 Jason Bere FOIL .05 .15
365 Manny Ramirez FOIL .50 1.25
366 Justin Thompson FOIL .05 .15
367 Joe Vitiello FOIL .05 .15
368 Tyrone Hill FOIL .05 .15
369 David McCarty FOIL .05 .15
370 Brien Taylor FOIL .05 .15
371 Todd Van Poppel FOIL .05 .15
372 Marc Newfield FOIL .05 .15
373 Terrell Lowery FOIL RC .20 .50
374 Alex Gonzalez FOIL .05 .15
375 Ken Griffey Jr. .60 1.50
376 Donovan Osborne .05 .15
377 Ritchie Moody RC .08 .25
378 Shane Andrews .05 .15
379 Carlos Delgado .30 .75
380 Bill Swift .05 .15
381 Leo Gomez .05 .15
382 Ron Gant .10 .30
383 Scott Fletcher .05 .15
384 Matt Walbeck RC .20 .50
385 Chuck Finley .10 .30
386 Kevin Mitchell .05 .15
387 Wilson Alvarez UER .05 .15
Misspelled Alverez
on card front
388 John Burke RC .08 .25
389 Alan Embree .05 .15
390 Trevor Hoffman .30 .75
391 Alan Trammell .10 .30
392 Todd Jones .10 .30
393 Felix Jose .05 .15
394 Orel Hershiser .10 .30
395 Pat Listach .05 .15
396 Gabe White .05 .15
397 Dan Serafini RC .08 .25
398 Todd Hundley .05 .15
399 Wade Boggs .20 .50
400 Tyler Green .05 .15
401 Mike Bordick .05 .15
402 Scott Bullett .05 .15
403 LaGrande Russell RC .08 .25
404 Ray Lankford .10 .30
405 Nolan Ryan 1.25 3.00
406 Robbie Beckett .05 .15
407 Brent Bowers RC .08 .25
408 Adell Davenport RC .08 .25
409 Brady Anderson .10 .30
410 Tom Glavine .20 .50
411 Doug Hecker RC .08 .25
412 Jose Guzman .05 .15
413 Luis Polonia .05 .15
414 Brian Williams .05 .15
415 Bo Jackson .30 .75
416 Eric Young .05 .15
417 Kenny Lofton .10 .30
418 Orestes Destrade .05 .15
419 Tony Phillips .05 .15
420 Jeff Bagwell .20 .50
421 Mark Gardner .05 .15
422 Brett Butler .10 .30
423 Graeme Lloyd RC .20 .50
424 Delino DeShields .05 .15
425 Scott Erickson .05 .15
426 Jeff Kent .30 .75
427 Jimmy Key .10 .30
428 Mickey Morandini .05 .15
429 Marcos Armas RC .08 .25
430 Don Slaught .05 .15
431 Randy Johnson .30 .75
432 Omar Olivares .05 .15
433 Charlie Leibrandt .05 .15
434 Kurt Stillwell .05 .15
435 Scott Brow RC .08 .25
436 Robby Thompson .05 .15
437 Ben McDonald .05 .15
438 Deion Sanders .20 .50
439 Tony Pena .05 .15
440 Mark Grace .20 .50
441 Eduardo Perez .10 .30
442 Tim Pugh RC .08 .25
443 Scott Ruffcorn .05 .15
444 Jay Gainer RC .08 .25
445 Albert Belle .10 .30
446 Bret Barberie .05 .15
447 Justin Mashore .05 .15
448 Pete Harnisch .05 .15
449 Greg Gagne .05 .15
450 Eric Davis .10 .30
451 Dave Mlicki .05 .15
452 Moises Alou .10 .30
453 Rick Aguilera .05 .15
454 Eddie Murray .30 .75
455 Bob Wickman .05 .15
456 Wes Chamberlain .05 .15
457 Brent Gates .05 .15
458 Paul Wagner .05 .15
459 Mike Hampton .05 .15
460 Ozzie Smith .50 1.25
461 Tom Henke .05 .15
462 Ricky Gutierrez .05 .15
463 Jack Morris .10 .30
464 Joel Chimelis .05 .15
465 Gregg Olson .05 .15
466 Javy Lopez .20 .50
467 Scott Cooper .05 .15
468 Willie Wilson .05 .15
469 Mark Langston .05 .15
470 Barry Larkin .20 .50
471 Rod Bolton .05 .15
472 Freddie Benavides .05 .15
473 Ken Ramos RC .08 .25
474 Chuck Carr .05 .15
475 Cecil Fielder .10 .30
476 Eddie Taubensee .05 .15
477 Chris Eddy RC .08 .25
478 Greg Hansell .05 .15
479 Kevin Reimer .05 .15
480 Dennis Martinez .10 .30
481 Chuck Knoblauch .10 .30
482 Mike Draper .05 .15
483 Spike Owen .05 .15
484 Terry Mulholland .05 .15
485 Dennis Eckersley .10 .30
486 Blas Minor .05 .15
487 Dave Fleming .05 .15
488 Dan Cholowsky .05 .15
489 Ivan Rodriguez .20 .50
490 Gary Sheffield .10 .30
491 Ed Sprague .05 .15
492 Steve Hosey .05 .15
493 Jimmy Haynes RC .20 .50
494 John Smoltz .20 .50
495 Andre Dawson .10 .30
496 Rey Sanchez .05 .15
497 Ty Van Burkleo .05 .15
498 Bobby Ayala RC .08 .25
499 Tim Raines .10 .30
500 Charlie Hayes .05 .15
501 Paul Sorrento .05 .15
502 Richie Lewis RC .08 .25
503 Jason Pfaff RC .08 .25
504 Ken Caminiti .10 .30
505 Mike Macfarlane .05 .15
506 Jody Reed .05 .15
507 Bobby Hughes RC .08 .25
508 Wil Cordero .05 .15
509 George Tsamis RC .08 .25
510 Bret Saberhagen .10 .30
511 Derek Jeter RC 12.00 30.00
512 Gene Schall .05 .15
513 Curtis Shaw .05 .15
514 Steve Cooke .05 .15
515 Edgar Martinez .20 .50
516 Mike Milchin .05 .15
517 Billy Ripken .05 .15
518 Andy Benes .05 .15
519 Juan de la Rosa RC .08 .25
520 John Burkett .05 .15
521 Alex Ochoa .05 .15
522 Tony Tarasco RC .20 .50
523 Luis Ortiz .05 .15
524 Rick Wilkins .05 .15
525 Chris Turner RC .08 .25
526 Rob Dibble .10 .30
527 Jack McDowell .05 .15
528 Daryl Boston .05 .15
529 Bill Wertz RC .08 .25
530 Charlie Hough .10 .30
531 Sean Bergman .05 .15
532 Doug Jones .05 .15
533 Jeff Montgomery .05 .15
534 Roger Cedeno RC .20 .50
535 Robin Yount .50 1.25
536 Mo Vaughn .10 .30
537 Brian Harper .05 .15
538 Juan Castillo RC .08 .25
539 Steve Farr .05 .15
540 John Kruk .10 .30
541 Troy Neel .05 .15
542 Danny Clyburn RC .08 .25
543 Jim Converse RC .08 .25
544 Gregg Jefferies .05 .15
545 Jose Canseco .20 .50
546 Julio Bruno RC .08 .25
547 Rob Butler .05 .15
548 Royce Clayton .05 .15
549 Chris Hoiles .05 .15
550 Greg Maddux .50 1.25
551 Joe Ciccarella RC .08 .25
552 Ozzie Timmons .05 .15
553 Chili Davis .10 .30
554 Brian Koelling .05 .15
555 Frank Thomas .30 .75
556 Vinny Castilla .30 .75
557 Reggie Jefferson .05 .15
558 Rob Natal .05 .15
559 Mike Henneman .05 .15
560 Craig Biggio .20 .50
561 Billy Brewer .05 .15
562 Dan Melendez .05 .15
563 Kenny Felder RC .08 .25
564 Miguel Batista RC .40 1.00
565 Dave Winfield .10 .30
566 Al Shirley .05 .15
567 Robert Eenhoorn .05 .15
568 Mike Williams .05 .15
569 Tanyon Sturtze RC .20 .50
570 Tim Wakefield .30 .75
571 Greg Pirkl .05 .15
572 Sean Lowe RC .08 .25

573 Terry Burrows RC .08 .25
574 Kevin Higgins .05 .15
575 Joe Carter .10 .30
576 Kevin Rogers .05 .15
577 Manny Alexander .05 .15
578 David Justice .10 .30
579 Brian Conroy RC .08 .25
580 Jessie Hollins .05 .15
581 Ron Watson RC .08 .25
582 Bip Roberts .05 .15
583 Tom Urbani RC .08 .25
584 Jason Hutchins RC .08 .25
585 Carlos Baerga .05 .15
586 Jeff Mutis .05 .15
587 Justin Thompson .05 .15
588 Orlando Miller .05 .15
589 Brian McRae .05 .15
590 Ramon Martinez .05 .15
591 Dave Nilsson .05 .15
592 Jose Vidro RC .75 2.00
593 Rich Becker .05 .15
594 Preston Wilson RC .60 1.50
595 Don Mattingly .75 2.00
596 Tony Longmire .05 .15
597 Kevin Seitzer .05 .15
598 Midre Cummings RC .08 .25
599 Omar Vizquel .20 .50
600 Lee Smith .10 .30
601 David Hulse RC .08 .25
602 Darrell Sherman RC .08 .25
603 Alex Gonzalez .05 .15
604 Geronimo Pena .05 .15
605 Mike Devereaux .05 .15
606 Sterling Hitchcock RC .20 .50
607 Mike Greenwell .05 .15
608 Steve Buechele .05 .15
609 Troy Percival .20 .50
610 Roberto Kelly .05 .15
611 James Baldwin RC .20 .50
612 Jerald Clark .05 .15
613 Albie Lopez RC .08 .25
614 Dave Magadan .05 .15
615 Mickey Tettleton .05 .15
616 Sean Runyan RC .08 .25
617 Bob Hamelin .05 .15
618 Raul Mondesi .10 .30
619 Tyrone Hill .05 .15
620 Darrin Fletcher .05 .15
621 Mike Trombley .05 .15
622 Jeromy Burnitz .10 .30
623 Bernie Williams .20 .50
624 Mike Farmer RC .08 .25
625 Rickey Henderson .30 .75
626 Carlos Garcia .05 .15
627 Jeff Darwin RC .08 .25
628 Todd Zeile .05 .15
629 Benji Gil .05 .15
630 Tony Gwynn .40 1.00
631 Aaron Small RC .40 1.00
632 Joe Rosselli RC .08 .25
633 Mike Mussina .20 .50
634 Ryan Klesko .10 .30
635 Roger Clemens .60 1.50
636 Sammy Sosa .30 .75
637 Orlando Palmeiro RC .08 .25
638 Willie Greene .05 .15
639 George Bell .05 .15
640 Garvin Alston RC .08 .25
641 Pete Janicki RC .08 .25
642 Chris Sheff RC .08 .25
643 Felipe Lira RC .08 .25
644 Roberto Petagine .05 .15
645 Wally Joyner .10 .30
646 Mike Piazza 1.25 3.00
647 Jaime Navarro .05 .15
648 Jeff Hartsock .05 .15
649 David McCarty .05 .15
650 Bobby Jones .10 .30
651 Mark Hutton .05 .15
652 Kyle Abbott .05 .15
653 Steve Cox RC .08 .25
654 Jeff King .05 .15
655 Norm Charlton .05 .15
656 Mike Gulan RC .08 .25
657 Julio Franco .10 .30
658 Cameron Cairncross RC .08 .25
659 John Olerud .10 .30
660 Salomon Torres .05 .15
661 Brad Pennington .05 .15
662 Melvin Nieves .05 .15
663 Ivan Calderon .05 .15
664 Turk Wendell .05 .15
665 Chris Pritchett .05 .15
666 Reggie Sanders .10 .30
667 Robin Ventura .10 .30
668 Joe Girardi .05 .15
669 Manny Ramirez .50 1.25
670 Jeff Conine .10 .30
671 Greg Gohr .05 .15
672 Andujar Cedeno .05 .15
673 Les Norman RC .08 .25
674 Mike James RC .08 .25
675 Marshall Boze RC .08 .25
676 B.J.Wallace .05 .15
677 Kent Hrbek .10 .30
678 Jack Voigt RC .08 .25
679 Brien Taylor .05 .15
680 Curt Schilling .10 .30
681 Todd Van Poppel .05 .15
682 Kevin Young .10 .30
683 Tommy Adams .05 .15
684 Bernard Gilkey .05 .15
685 Kevin Brown .10 .30
686 Fred McGriff .20 .50
687 Pat Borders .05 .15
688 Kirt Manwaring .05 .15
689 Sid Bream .05 .15
690 John Valentin .05 .15
691 Steve Olsen RC .08 .25
692 Roberto Mejia RC .08 .25
693 Carlos Delgado FOIL .30 .75
694 Steve Gibralter FOIL RC .08 .25
695 Gary Mota FOIL RC .08 .25
696 Jose Malave FOIL RC .08 .25
697 Larry Sutton FOIL RC .08 .25
698 Dan Frye FOIL RC .08 .25
699 Tim Clark FOIL RC .08 .25
700 Brian Rupp FOIL RC .08 .25
701 Felipe Alou FOIL .10 .30
Moises Alou
702 Barry Bonds FOIL .40 1.00
Bobby Bonds
703 Ken Griffey Sr. FOIL .40 1.00
Ken Griffey Jr.
704 Brian McRae FOIL .05 .15
Hal McRae
705 Checklist 1 .05 .15
706 Checklist 2 .05 .15
707 Checklist 3 .05 .15
708 Checklist 4 .05 .15

1994 Bowman Previews

This 10-card standard-size set served as a preview to the 1994 Bowman set. The cards were randomly inserted one in every 24 1994 Stadium Club second series pack. The backs are identical to the basic issue with a horizontal layout containing a player photo, text and statistics.

COMPLETE SET (10) 10.00 25.00
STATED ODDS 1:24 SER.2 STADIUM CLUB
1 Frank Thomas 2.00 5.00
2 Mike Piazza 4.00 10.00
3 Albert Belle .75 2.00
4 Javier Lopez .75 2.00
5 Cliff Floyd .75 2.00
6 Alex Gonzalez .50 1.25
7 Ricky Bottalico .30 .75
8 Tony Clark 1.25 3.00
9 Mac Suzuki .75 2.00
10 James Mouton FOIL .50 1.25

1994 Bowman

The 1994 Bowman set consists of 682 standard-size, full-bleed cards primarily distributed in plastic wrap packs and jumbo packs. There are 52 Foil cards (337-388) that include a number of top young stars and prospects. These foil cards were issued one per foil pack and two per jumbo. Rookie Cards of note include Edgardo Alfonzo, Tony Clark, Jermaine Dye, Brad Fullmer, Richard Hidalgo, Derrek Lee, Chan Ho Park, Jorge Posada, Edgar Renteria and Billy Wagner.

COMPLETE SET (682) 20.00 50.00
1 Joe Carter .15 .40
2 Marcus Moore .08 .25
3 Doug Creek RC .08 .25
4 Pedro Martinez .40 1.00
5 Ken Griffey Jr. .75 2.00
6 Greg Swindell .08 .25
7 J.J. Johnson .08 .25
8 Homer Bush RC .15 .40
9 Arquimedez Pozo RC .15 .40
10 Bryan Harvey .08 .25
11 J.T. Snow .15 .40
12 Alan Benes RC .40 1.00
13 Chad Kreuter .08 .25
14 Eric Karros .15 .40
15 Frank Thomas .40 1.00
16 Bret Saberhagen .15 .40
17 Terrell Lowery .08 .25
18 Rod Bolton .08 .25
19 Harold Baines .15 .40
20 Matt Walbeck .08 .25
21 Tom Glavine .25 .60
22 Todd Jones .08 .25
23 Alberto Castillo RC .15 .40
24 Ruben Sierra .15 .40
25 Don Mattingly 1.00 2.50
26 Mike Morgan .08 .25
27 Jim Musselwhite RC .15 .40
28 Matt Brunson RC .15 .40
29 Adam Meinershagen RC .15 .40
30 Joe Girardi .08 .25
31 Shane Halter .08 .25
32 Jose Paniagua RC .40 1.00
33 Paul Perkins RC .15 .40
34 John Hudek RC .15 .40
35 Frank Viola .15 .40
36 David Lamb RC .15 .40
37 Marshall Boze .08 .25
38 Jorge Posada RC 5.00 12.00
39 Brian Anderson RC .40 1.00
40 Mark Whiten .08 .25
41 Sean Bergman .08 .25
42 Jose Parra RC .15 .40
43 Mike Robertson .08 .25
44 Pete Walker RC .15 .40
45 Juan Gonzalez .15 .40
46 Cleveland Ladell RC .15 .40
47 Mark Smith .08 .25
48 Kevin Jarvis UER .15 .40
team listed as Yankees on back
49 Amaury Telemaco RC .15 .40
50 Andy Van Slyke .25 .60
51 Rikkert Faneyte RC .15 .40
52 Curtis Shaw .08 .25
53 Matt Drews RC .15 .40
54 Wilson Alvarez .08 .25
55 Manny Ramirez .40 1.00
56 Bobby Munoz .08 .25
57 Ed Sprague .08 .25
58 Jamey Wright RC .40 1.00
59 Jeff Montgomery .08 .25
60 Kirk Rueter .08 .25
61 Edgar Martinez .25 .60
62 Luis Gonzalez .15 .40
63 Tim Vanegmond RC .15 .40
64 Bip Roberts .08 .25
65 John Jaha .08 .25
66 Chuck Carr .08 .25
67 Chuck Finley .15 .40
68 Aaron Holbert .08 .25
69 Cecil Fielder .15 .40
70 Tom Engle RC .15 .40
71 Ron Karkovice .08 .25
72 Joe Orsulak .08 .25
73 Duff Brumley RC .15 .40
74 Craig Clayton RC .15 .40
75 Cal Ripken 1.25 3.00
76 Brad Fullmer RC .40 1.00
77 Tony Tarasco .08 .25
78 Terry Farrar RC .15 .40
79 Matt Williams .15 .40
80 Rickey Henderson .40 1.00
81 Terry Mulholland .08 .25
82 Sammy Sosa .40 1.00
83 Paul Sorrento .08 .25
84 Pete Incaviglia .08 .25
85 Darren Hall RC .15 .40
86 Scott Klingenbeck .08 .25
87 Dario Perez RC .15 .40
88 Ugueth Urbina .08 .25
89 Dave Vanhof RC .15 .40
90 Domingo Jean .08 .25
91 Otis Nixon .08 .25
92 Andres Berumen .08 .25
93 Jose Valentin .08 .25
94 Edgar Renteria RC 2.50 6.00
95 Chris Turner .08 .25
96 Ray Lankford .15 .40
97 Danny Bautista .08 .25
98 Chan Ho Park RC .60 1.50
99 Glenn DiSarcina RC .15 .40
100 Butch Huskey .08 .25
101 Ivan Rodriguez .25 .60
102 Johnny Ruffin .08 .25
103 Alex Ochoa .08 .25
104 Torii Hunter RC 2.00 5.00
105 Ryan Klesko .15 .40
106 Jay Bell .15 .40
107 Kurt Peltzer RC .15 .40
108 Miguel Jimenez .08 .25
109 Russ Davis .08 .25
110 Derek Wallace .08 .25
111 Keith Lockhart RC .40 1.00
112 Mike Lieberthal .15 .40
113 Dave Stewart .15 .40
114 Tom Schmidt .08 .25
115 Brian McRae .08 .25
116 Moises Alou .15 .40
117 Dave Fleming .08 .25
118 Jeff Bagwell .25 .60
119 Luis Ortiz .08 .25
120 Tony Gwynn .50 1.25
121 Jaime Navarro .08 .25
122 Benito Santiago .15 .40
123 Darrell Whitmore .08 .25
124 John Mabry RC .40 1.00
125 Mickey Tettleton .08 .25
126 Tom Candiotti .08 .25
127 Tim Raines .15 .40
128 Bobby Bonilla .15 .40
129 John Dettmer .08 .25
130 Hector Carrasco .08 .25
131 Chris Hoiles .08 .25
132 Rick Aguilera .08 .25
133 David Justice .15 .40
134 Esteban Loaiza RC .60 1.50
135 Barry Bonds 1.00 2.50
136 Bob Welch .08 .25
137 Mike Stanley .08 .25
138 Roberto Hernandez .08 .25
139 Sandy Alomar Jr. .08 .25
140 Darren Daulton .15 .40
141 Angel Martinez RC .15 .40
142 Howard Johnson .08 .25
143 Bob Hamelin UER .08 .25
(name and card number colors don't match
144 J.J.Thobe RC .15 .40
145 Roger Salkeld .08 .25
146 Orlando Miller .08 .25
147 Dmitri Young .15 .40
148 Tim Hyers RC .15 .40
149 Mark Loretta RC 2.00 5.00
150 Chris Hammond .08 .25
151 Joel Moore RC .15 .40
152 Todd Zeile .08 .25
153 Wil Cordero .08 .25
154 Chris Smith .08 .25
155 James Baldwin .08 .25
156 Edgardo Alfonzo RC .40 1.00
157 Kym Ashworth RC .15 .40
158 Paul Bako RC .15 .40
159 Rick Krivda RC .15 .40
160 Pat Mahomes .08 .25
161 Damon Hollins .08 .25
162 Felix Martinez RC .15 .40
163 Jason Myers RC .15 .40
164 Izzy Molina RC .15 .40
165 Brien Taylor .08 .25
166 Kevin Orie RC .15 .40
167 Casey Whitten RC .15 .40
168 Tony Longmire .08 .25
169 John Olerud .15 .40
170 Mark Thompson .08 .25
171 Jorge Fabregas .08 .25
172 John Wetteland .15 .40
173 Dan Wilson .08 .25
174 Doug Drabek .08 .25
175 Jeff McNeely .08 .25
176 Melvin Nieves .08 .25
177 Doug Glanville RC .40 1.00
178 Javier De La Hoya RC .15 .40
179 Chad Curtis .08 .25
180 Brian Barber .08 .25
181 Mike Henneman .08 .25
182 Jose Offerman .08 .25
183 Robert Ellis RC .15 .40
184 John Franco .15 .40
185 Benji Gil .08 .25
186 Hal Morris .08 .25
187 Chris Sabo .08 .25
188 Blaise Ilsley RC .15 .40
189 Steve Avery .08 .25
190 Rick White RC .15 .40
191 Rod Beck .08 .25
192 Mark McGwire UER 1.00 2.50
No card number on back
193 Jim Abbott .25 .60
194 Randy Myers .08 .25
195 Kenny Lofton .15 .40
196 Mariano Duncan .08 .25
197 Lee Daniels RC .15 .40
198 Armando Reynoso .08 .25
199 Joe Randa .15 .40
200 Cliff Floyd .15 .40
201 Tim Harkrider RC .15 .40
202 Kevin Gallaher RC .15 .40
203 Scott Cooper .08 .25
204 Phil Stidham RC .15 .40
205 Jeff D'Amico RC .15 .40
206 Matt Whisenant .08 .25
207 De Shawn Warren .08 .25
208 Rene Arocha .08 .25
209 Tony Clark RC .60 1.50
210 Jason Jacome RC .15 .40
211 Scott Christman RC .15 .40
212 Bill Pulsipher .15 .40
213 Dean Palmer .15 .40
214 Chad Mottola .08 .25
215 Manny Alexander .08 .25
216 Rich Becker .08 .25
217 Andre King RC .15 .40
218 Carlos Garcia .08 .25
219 Ron Pezzoni RC .15 .40
220 Steve Karsay .08 .25
221 Jose Musset RC .15 .40
222 Karl Rhodes .08 .25
223 Frank Cimorelli RC .15 .40
224 Kevin Jordan RC .15 .40
225 Duane Ward .08 .25
226 John Burke .08 .25
227 Mike Macfarlane .08 .25
228 Mike Lansing .08 .25
229 Chuck Knoblauch .15 .40
230 Ken Caminiti .15 .40
231 Gar Finnvold RC .15 .40
232 Derrek Lee RC 3.00 8.00
233 Brady Anderson .15 .40
234 Vic Darensbourg RC .15 .40
235 Mark Langston .08 .25
236 T.J.Mathews RC .15 .40
237 Lou Whitaker .15 .40
238 Roger Cedeno .08 .25
239 Alex Fernandez .08 .25
240 Ryan Thompson .08 .25
241 Kerry Lacy RC .15 .40
242 Reggie Sanders .15 .40
243 Brad Pennington .08 .25
244 Bryan Eversgerd RC .15 .40
245 Greg Maddux .60 1.50
246 Jason Kendall .15 .40
247 J.R. Phillips .08 .25
248 Bobby Witt .08 .25
249 Paul O'Neill .25 .60
250 Ryne Sandberg .60 1.50
251 Charles Nagy .08 .25
252 Kevin Stocker .08 .25
253 Shawn Green .40 1.00
254 Charlie Hayes .08 .25
255 Donnie Elliott .08 .25
256 Rob Fitzpatrick RC .15 .40
257 Tim Davis .08 .25
258 James Mouton .08 .25
259 Mike Greenwell .08 .25
260 Ray McDavid .08 .25
261 Mike Kelly .08 .25
262 Andy Larkin RC .15 .40
263 Marquis Riley UER .08 .25
No card number on back
264 Bob Tewksbury .08 .25
265 Brian Edmondson .08 .25
266 Eduardo Lantigua RC .15 .40
267 Brandon Wilson .08 .25
268 Mike Welch .08 .25
269 Tom Henke .08 .25
270 Pokey Reese .08 .25
271 Gregg Zaun RC .40 1.00
272 Todd Ritchie .08 .25
273 Javier Lopez .15 .40
274 Kevin Young .08 .25
275 Kirt Manwaring .08 .25
276 Bill Taylor RC .15 .40
277 Robert Eenhoorn .08 .25
278 Jessie Hollins .08 .25
279 Julian Tavarez RC .40 1.00
280 Gene Schall .08 .25
281 Paul Molitor .15 .40
282 Neifi Perez RC .40 1.00
283 Greg Gagne .08 .25
284 Marquis Grissom .15 .40
285 Randy Johnson .40 1.00
286 Pete Harnisch .08 .25
287 Joel Bennett RC .15 .40
288 Derek Bell .08 .25
289 Darryl Hamilton .08 .25
290 Gary Sheffield .15 .40
291 Eduardo Perez .08 .25
292 Basil Shabazz .08 .25
293 Eric Davis .15 .40
294 Pedro Astacio .08 .25
295 Robin Ventura .15 .40
296 Jeff Kent .25 .60
297 Rick Helling .08 .25
298 Joe Oliver .08 .25
299 Lee Smith .15 .40
300 Dave Winfield .15 .40
301 Deion Sanders .25 .60
302 Ravelo Manzanillo RC .15 .40
303 Mark Portugal .08 .25
304 Brent Gates .08 .25
305 Wade Boggs .25 .60
306 Rick Wilkins .08 .25
307 Carlos Baerga .08 .25
308 Curt Schilling .15 .40
309 Shannon Stewart .40 1.00
310 Darren Holmes .08 .25
311 Robert Toth RC .15 .40
312 Gabe White .08 .25
313 Mac Suzuki RC .40 1.00
314 Alvin Morman RC .15 .40
315 Mo Vaughn .15 .40
316 Bryce Florie RC .15 .40
317 Gabby Martinez RC .15 .40
318 Carl Everett .15 .40
319 Kerwin Moore .08 .25
320 Tom Pagnozzi .08 .25
321 Chris Gomez .08 .25
322 Todd Williams .08 .25
323 Pat Hentgen .08 .25
324 Kirk Presley RC .15 .40
325 Kevin Brown .15 .40
326 Jason Isringhausen RC 1.25 3.00
327 Rick Forney RC .15 .40
328 Carlos Pulido RC .15 .40
329 Terrell Wade RC .15 .40
330 Al Martin .08 .25
331 Dan Carlson RC .15 .40
332 Mark Acre RC .15 .40
333 Sterling Hitchcock .08 .25
334 Jon Ratliff RC .15 .40
335 Alex Ramirez RC .15 .40
336 Phil Geisler RC .08 .25
337 Eddie Zambrano FOIL RC .15 .40
338 Jim Thome FOIL .25 .60
339 James Mouton FOIL .08 .25
340 Cliff Floyd FOIL .15 .40
341 Carlos Delgado FOIL .25 .60
342 Roberto Petagine FOIL .08 .25
343 Tim Clark FOIL .08 .25
344 Bubba Smith FOIL .08 .25
345 Randy Curtis FOIL RC .15 .40
346 Joe Biasucci FOIL RC .15 .40
347 D.J. Boston FOIL RC .15 .40
348 Ruben Rivera FOIL RC .15 .40
349 Bryan Link FOIL RC .15 .40
350 Mike Bell FOIL RC .15 .40
351 Marty Watson FOIL RC .15 .40
352 Jason Myers FOIL .08 .25
353 Chipper Jones FOIL .40 1.00
354 Brooks Kieschnick FOIL .15 .40
355 Pokey Reese FOIL .08 .25
356 John Burke FOIL .08 .25
357 Kurt Miller FOIL .08 .25
358 Orlando Miller FOIL .08 .25
359 Todd Hollandsworth FOIL .08 .25
360 Rondell White FOIL .15 .40
361 Bill Pulsipher FOIL .15 .40
362 Tyler Green FOIL .08 .25
363 Midre Cummings FOIL .08 .25
364 Brian Barber FOIL .08 .25
365 Melvin Nieves FOIL .08 .25
366 Salomon Torres FOIL .08 .25
367 Alex Ochoa FOIL .08 .25
368 Frankie Rodriguez FOIL .08 .25
369 Brian Anderson FOIL .15 .40
370 James Baldwin FOIL .08 .25
371 Manny Ramirez FOIL .40 1.00
372 Justin Thompson FOIL .08 .25
373 Johnny Damon FOIL .25 .60
374 Jeff D'Amico FOIL .15 .40
375 Rich Becker FOIL .08 .25
376 Derek Jeter FOIL 1.25 3.00
377 Steve Karsay FOIL .08 .25
378 Mac Suzuki FOIL .15 .40
379 Benji Gil FOIL .08 .25
380 Alex Gonzalez FOIL .08 .25
381 Jason Bere FOIL .08 .25
382 Brett Butler FOIL .15 .40
383 Jeff Conine FOIL .15 .40
384 Darren Daulton FOIL .15 .40
385 Jeff Kent FOIL .25 .60
386 Don Mattingly FOIL 1.00 2.50
387 Mike Piazza FOIL .75 2.00
388 Ryne Sandberg FOIL .60 1.50
389 Rich Amaral .08 .25
390 Craig Biggio .25 .60
391 Jeff Suppan RC .75 2.00
392 Andy Benes .08 .25
393 Cal Eldred .08 .25
394 Jeff Conine .15 .40
395 Tim Salmon .25 .60
396 Ray Suplee RC .15 .40
397 Tony Phillips .08 .25
398 Ramon Martinez .08 .25
399 Julio Franco .15 .40
400 Dwight Gooden .15 .40
401 Kevin Loman RC .15 .40
402 Jose Rijo .08 .25
403 Mike Devereaux .08 .25
404 Mike Zolecki RC .15 .40
405 Fred McGriff .25 .60
406 Danny Clyburn .08 .25
407 Robby Thompson .08 .25
408 Terry Steinbach .08 .25
409 Luis Polonia .08 .25
410 Mark Grace .25 .60
411 Albert Belle .15 .40
412 John Kruk .15 .40
413 Scott Spiezio RC .40 1.00
414 Ellis Burks UER .15 .40
Name spelled Elkis on front
415 Joe Vitiello .08 .25
416 Tim Costo .08 .25
417 Marc Newfield .08 .25
418 Oscar Henriquez RC .15 .40
419 Matt Perisho RC .15 .40
420 Julio Bruno .08 .25
421 Kenny Felder .08 .25
422 Tyler Green .08 .25
423 Jim Edmonds .40 1.00
424 Ozzie Smith .60 1.50
425 Rick Greene .08 .25
426 Todd Hollandsworth .08 .25
427 Eddie Pearson RC .15 .40
428 Quilvio Veras .08 .25
429 Kenny Rogers .15 .40
430 Willie Greene .08 .25
431 Vaughn Eshelman .08 .25
432 Pat Meares .08 .25
433 Jermaine Dye RC 2.50 6.00
434 Steve Cooke .08 .25
435 Bill Swift .08 .25
436 Fausto Cruz RC .15 .40
437 Mark Hutton .08 .25
438 Brooks Kieschnick RC .15 .40
439 Yorkis Perez .08 .25
440 Len Dykstra .15 .40
441 Pat Borders .08 .25
442 Doug Walls RC .15 .40
443 Wally Joyner .15 .40
444 Ken Hill .08 .25
445 Eric Anthony .08 .25
446 Mitch Williams .08 .25
447 Cory Bailey RC .15 .40
448 Dave Staton .08 .25
449 Greg Vaughn .08 .25
450 Dave Magadan .08 .25
451 Chili Davis .15 .40
452 Gerald Santos RC .15 .40
453 Joe Perona .08 .25
454 Delino DeShields .08 .25
455 Jack McDowell .08 .25
456 Todd Hundley .08 .25
457 Ritchie Moody .08 .25
458 Bret Boone .15 .40
459 Ben McDonald .08 .25
460 Kirby Puckett .40 1.00
461 Gregg Olson .08 .25
462 Rich Aude RC .15 .40
463 John Burkett .08 .25
464 Troy Neel .08 .25
465 Jimmy Key .15 .40
466 Ozzie Timmons .08 .25
467 Eddie Murray .40 1.00
468 Mark Tranberg RC .15 .40
469 Alex Gonzalez .08 .25
470 David Nied .08 .25
471 Barry Larkin .25 .60
472 Brian Looney RC .15 .40
473 Shawn Estes .08 .25
474 A.J.Sager RC .15 .40
475 Roger Clemens .75 2.00
476 Vince Moore .08 .25
477 Scott Karl RC .15 .40
478 Kurt Miller .08 .25
479 Garret Anderson .40 1.00
480 Allen Watson .08 .25
481 Jose Lima RC .40 1.00
482 Rick Gorecki .08 .25
483 Jimmy Hurst RC .15 .40
484 Preston Wilson .15 .40
485 Will Clark .25 .60
486 Mike Ferry RC .15 .40
487 Curtis Goodwin RC .15 .40
488 Mike Myers .08 .25
489 Chipper Jones .40 1.00
490 Jeff King .08 .25
491 W.VanLandingham RC .15 .40
492 Carlos Reyes RC .15 .40
493 Andy Pettitte .40 1.00
494 Brant Brown .08 .25
495 Daron Kirkreit .08 .25
496 Ricky Bottalico RC .15 .40
497 Devon White .15 .40
498 Jason Johnson RC .40 1.00
499 Vince Coleman .08 .25
500 Larry Walker .15 .40
501 Bobby Ayala .08 .25
502 Steve Finley .15 .40
503 Scott Fletcher .08 .25
504 Brad Ausmus .25 .60
505 Scott Talanoa RC .15 .40
506 Orestes Destrade .08 .25
507 Gary DiSarcina .08 .25
508 Willie Smith RC .15 .40
509 Alan Trammell .15 .40
510 Mike Piazza .75 2.00
511 Ozzie Guillen .15 .40
512 Jeromy Burnitz .15 .40
513 Darren Oliver RC .40 1.00
514 Kevin Mitchell .08 .25
515 Rafael Palmeiro .25 .60
516 David McCarty .08 .25
517 Jeff Blauser .08 .25
518 Trey Beamon .08 .25
519 Royce Clayton .08 .25
520 Dennis Eckersley .15 .40
521 Bernie Williams .25 .60
522 Steve Buechele .08 .25
523 Dennis Martinez .15 .40
524 Dave Hollins .08 .25
525 Joey Hamilton .08 .25
526 Andres Galarraga .15 .40
527 Jeff Granger .08 .25
528 Joey Eischen .08 .25
529 Desi Relaford .08 .25
530 Roberto Petagine .08 .25
531 Andre Dawson .15 .40
532 Ray Holbert .08 .25
533 Duane Singleton .08 .25
534 Kurt Abbott RC .15 .40
535 Bo Jackson .40 1.00
536 Gregg Jefferies .08 .25
537 David Mysel .08 .25
538 Raul Mondesi .15 .40
539 Chris Snopek .08 .25
540 Brook Fordyce .08 .25
541 Ron Frazier RC .15 .40
542 Brian Koelling .08 .25
543 Jimmy Haynes .08 .25
544 Marty Cordova .08 .25
545 Jason Green RC .15 .40
546 Orlando Merced .08 .25
547 Lou Pote RC .15 .40
548 Todd Van Poppel .08 .25
549 Pat Kelly .08 .25
550 Turk Wendell .08 .25
551 Herbert Perry RC .15 .40
552 Ryan Karp RC .15 .40
553 Juan Guzman .08 .25
554 Bryan Rekar RC .15 .40
555 Kevin Appier .15 .40
556 Chris Schwab RC .15 .40
557 Jay Buhner .15 .40
558 Andujar Cedeno .08 .25
559 Ryan McGuire RC .15 .40
560 Ricky Gutierrez .08 .25
561 Keith Kimsey RC .15 .40
562 Tim Clark .08 .25
563 Damion Easley .08 .25
564 Clint Davis RC .15 .40
565 Mike Moore .08 .25
566 Orel Hershiser .15 .40
567 Jason Bere .08 .25
568 Kevin McReynolds .08 .25
569 Leland Macon RC .15 .40
570 John Courtright RC .15 .40
571 Sid Fernandez .08 .25
572 Chad Roper .08 .25
573 Terry Pendleton .15 .40
574 Danny Miceli .08 .25
575 Joe Rosselli .08 .25
576 Mike Bordick .08 .25
577 Danny Tartabull .08 .25
578 Jose Guzman .08 .25
579 Omar Vizquel .25 .60
580 Tommy Greene .08 .25
581 Paul Spoljaric .08 .25
582 Walt Weiss .08 .25
583 Oscar Jimenez RC .15 .40
584 Rod Henderson .08 .25
585 Derek Lowe .15 .40
586 Richard Hidalgo RC .40 1.00
587 Shayne Bennett RC .15 .40
588 Tim Belk RC .15 .40
589 Matt Mieske .08 .25
590 Nigel Wilson .08 .25
591 Jeff Knox RC .15 .40
592 Bernard Gilkey .08 .25

593 David Cone .15 .40
594 Paul LoDuca RC 2.00 5.00
595 Scott Ruffcorn .08 .25
596 Chris Roberts .08 .25
597 Oscar Munoz RC .15 .40
598 Scott Sullivan RC .15 .40
599 Matt Jarvis RC .15 .40
600 Jose Canseco .25 .60
601 Tony Graffanino RC .60 1.50
602 Don Slaught .08 .25
603 Brett King RC .15 .40
604 Jose Herrera RC .15 .40
605 Melido Perez .08 .25
606 Mike Hubbard RC .15 .40
607 Chad Ogea .08 .25
608 Wayne Gomes RC .40 1.00
609 Roberto Alomar .25 .60
610 Angel Echevarria RC .15 .40
611 Jose Lind .08 .25
612 Darrin Fletcher .08 .25
613 Chris Bosio .08 .25
614 Darryl Kile .15 .40
615 Frankie Rodriguez .08 .25
616 Phil Plantier .08 .25
617 Pat Listach .08 .25
618 Charlie Hough .15 .40
619 Ryan Hancock RC .15 .40
620 Darrel Deak RC .15 .40
621 Travis Fryman .15 .40
622 Brett Butler .15 .40
623 Lance Johnson .08 .25
624 Pete Smith .08 .25
625 James Hurst RC .15 .40
626 Roberto Kelly .08 .25
627 Mike Mussina .25 .60
628 Kevin Tapani .08 .25
629 John Smoltz .25 .60
630 Midre Cummings .08 .25
631 Salomon Torres .08 .25
632 Willie Adams .08 .25
633 Derek Jeter 1.25 3.00
634 Steve Trachsel .08 .25
635 Albie Lopez .08 .25
636 Jason Moler .08 .25
637 Carlos Delgado .25 .60
638 Roberto Mejia .08 .25
639 Darren Burton .08 .25
640 B.J. Wallace .08 .25
641 Brad Clontz RC .15 .40
642 Billy Wagner RC 1.50 4.00
643 Aaron Sele .08 .25
644 Cameron Cairncross .08 .25
645 Brian Harper .08 .25
646 Marc Valdes UER .08 .25
No card number on back
647 Mark Ratekin .08 .25
648 Terry Bradshaw RC .15 .40
649 Justin Thompson .08 .25
650 Mike Busch RC .15 .40
651 Joe Hall RC .15 .40
652 Bobby Jones .08 .25
653 Kelly Stinnett RC .40 1.00
654 Rod Steph RC .15 .40
655 Jay Powell RC .40 1.00
656 Keith Garagozzo RC UER .15 .40
No card number on back
657 Todd Dunn .08 .25
658 Charles Peterson RC .15 .40
659 Darren Lewis .08 .25
660 John Wasdin RC .15 .40
661 Tate Seefried RC .15 .40
662 Hector Trinidad RC .15 .40
663 John Carter RC .15 .40
664 Larry Mitchell .08 .25
665 David Catlett RC .15 .40
666 Dante Bichette .15 .40
667 Felix Jose .08 .25
668 Rondell White .15 .40
669 Tino Martinez .25 .60
670 Brian L.Hunter .08 .25
671 Jose Malave .08 .25
672 Archi Cianfrocco .08 .25
673 Mike Matheny RC .60 1.50
674 Bret Barberie .08 .25
675 Andrew Lorraine RC .15 .40
676 Brian Jordan .15 .40
677 Tim Belcher .08 .25
678 Antonio Osuna RC .15 .40
679 Checklist .08 .25
680 Checklist .08 .25
681 Checklist .08 .25
682 Checklist .08 .25

1994 Bowman Superstar Samplers

1 Joe Carter .60 1.50
5 Ken Griffey Jr. 4.00 10.00
15 Frank Thomas 2.00 5.00
21 Tom Glavine 1.50 4.00
25 Don Mattingly 1.50 4.00
45 Juan Gonzalez 1.25 3.00
50 Andy Van Slyke .40 1.00
55 Manny Ramirez 2.00 5.00
69 Cecil Fielder .60 1.50
75 Cal Ripken 6.00 15.00
79 Matt Williams 1.00 2.50
118 Jeff Bagwell 2.00 5.00
120 Tony Gwynn 3.00 8.00
128 Bobby Bonilla .60 1.50
133 David Justice 1.25 3.00
135 Barry Bonds 3.00 8.00
140 Darren Daulton .60 1.50
169 John Olerud .60 1.50

200 Cliff Floyd 1.00 2.50
245 Greg Maddux 4.00 10.00
250 Ryne Sandberg 2.50 6.00
281 Paul Molitor 1.50 4.00
284 Marquis Grissom .60 1.50
285 Randy Johnson 2.50 6.00
290 Gary Sheffield 2.00 5.00
307 Carlos Baerga .40 1.00
315 Mo Vaughn .60 1.50
395 Tim Salmon .60 1.50
405 Fred McGriff 1.00 2.50
410 Mark Grace 1.00 2.50
411 Albert Belle .60 1.50
440 Len Dykstra .40 1.00
455 Jack McDowell .40 1.00
460 Kirby Puckett 2.00 5.00
471 Barry Larkin 1.25 3.00
475 Roger Clemens 3.00 8.00
485 Will Clark 1.25 3.00
505 Larry Walker 1.50 4.00
510 Mike Piazza 3.00 8.00
515 Rafael Palmeiro 1.50 4.00
526 Andres Galarraga 1.25 3.00
536 Gregg Jefferies .40 1.00
538 Raul Mondesi .60 1.50
600 Jose Canseco 2.00 5.00
609 Roberto Alomar 1.25 3.00

1995 Bowman

Cards from this 439-card standard-size prospect-oriented set were primarily issued in plastic wrapped packs and jumbo packs. Card fronts feature white borders enframing full color photos. The left border is a reversed negative of the photo. The set includes 54 silver foil subset cards (221-274). The foil subset, largely comprising of minor league stars, have embossed borders and are found one per pack and two per jumbo pack. Rookie Cards of note include Bob Abreu, Bartolo Colon, Vladimir Guerrero, Andruw Jones, Hideo Nomo and Scott Rolen.

COMPLETE SET (439) 30.00 60.00
ONE SILVER FOIL PER PACK/TWO PER JUMBO
1 Billy Wagner .30 .75
2 Chris Widger .08 .25
3 Brent Bowers .08 .25
4 Bob Abreu RC 3.00 8.00
5 Lou Collier RC .40 1.00
6 Juan Acevedo RC .20 .50
7 Jason Kelley RC .20 .50
8 Brian Sackinsky .08 .25
9 Scott Christman .08 .25
10 Damon Hollins .08 .25
11 Willis Otanez RC .20 .50
12 Jason Ryan RC .20 .50
13 Jason Giambi .30 .75
14 Andy Taulbee RC .20 .50
15 Mark Thompson .08 .25
16 Hugo Pivaral RC .20 .50
17 Brien Taylor .08 .25
18 Antonio Osuna .08 .25
19 Edgardo Alfonzo .08 .25
20 Carl Everett .20 .50
21 Matt Drews .08 .25
22 Bartolo Colon RC 1.25 3.00
23 Andruw Jones RC 8.00 20.00
24 Robert Person RC .40 1.00
25 Derrek Lee .50 1.25
26 John Ambrose RC .20 .50
27 Eric Knowles RC .20 .50
28 Chris Roberts .08 .25
29 Don Wengert .08 .25
30 Marcus Jensen RC .40 1.00
31 Brian Barber .08 .25
32 Kevin Brown C .20 .50
33 Benji Gil .08 .25
34 Mike Hubbard .08 .25
35 Bart Evans RC .20 .50
36 Enrique Wilson RC .20 .50
37 Brian Buchanan RC .20 .50
38 Ken Ray RC .20 .50
39 Micah Franklin RC .20 .50
40 Ricky Otero RC .20 .50
41 Jason Kendall .20 .50
42 Jimmy Hurst .08 .25
43 Jerry Wolak RC .20 .50
44 Jayson Peterson RC .20 .50
45 Allen Battle RC .20 .50
46 Scott Stahoviak .08 .25
47 Steve Schrenk RC .20 .50
48 Travis Miller RC .20 .50
49 Eddie Rios RC .20 .50
50 Mike Hampton .20 .50
51 Chad Frontera RC .20 .50
52 Tom Evans .08 .25
53 C.J. Nitkowski .08 .25
54 Clay Caruthers RC .20 .50
55 Shannon Stewart .20 .50
56 Jorge Posada .50 1.25
57 Aaron Holbert .08 .25
58 Harry Berrios RC .20 .50
59 Steve Rodriguez .08 .25
60 Shane Andrews .08 .25
61 Will Cunnane RC .20 .50
62 Richard Hidalgo .08 .25
63 Bill Selby RC .20 .50
64 Jay Cranford RC .20 .50
65 Jeff Suppan .20 .50
66 Curtis Goodwin .08 .25
67 John Thomson RC .40 1.00
68 Justin Thompson .08 .25
69 Troy Percival .20 .50
70 Matt Wagner RC .20 .50
71 Terry Bradshaw .08 .25
72 Greg Hansell .08 .25
73 John Burke .08 .25
74 Jeff D'Amico .08 .25
75 Ernie Young .08 .25
76 Jason Bates .08 .25
77 Chris Stynes .08 .25
78 Cade Gaspar RC .20 .50
79 Melvin Nieves .08 .25
80 Rick Gorecki .08 .25
81 Felix Rodriguez RC .20 .50
82 Ryan Hancock .08 .25
83 Chris Carpenter RC 3.00 8.00
84 Ray McDavid .08 .25
85 Chris Wimmer .08 .25
86 Doug Glanville .08 .25
87 DeShawn Warren .08 .25
88 Damian Moss RC .20 .50
89 Rafael Orellano RC .20 .50
90 Vladimir Guerrero RC ! 10.00 25.00
91 Raul Casanova RC .20 .50
92 Karim Garcia RC .20 .50
93 Bryce Florie .08 .25
94 Kevin Orie .08 .25
95 Ryan Nye RC .20 .50
96 Matt Sachse RC .20 .50
97 Ivan Arteaga RC .20 .50
98 Glenn Murray .08 .25
99 Stacy Hollins RC .20 .50
100 Jim Pittsley .08 .25
101 Craig Mattson RC .20 .50
102 Neifi Perez .08 .25
103 Keith Williams .08 .25
104 Roger Cedeno .08 .25
105 Tony Terry RC .20 .50
106 Jose Malave .08 .25
107 Joe Rosselli .08 .25
108 Kevin Jordan .08 .25
109 Sid Roberson RC .20 .50
110 Alan Embree .08 .25
111 Terrell Wade .08 .25
112 Bob Wolcott .08 .25
113 Carlos Perez RC .40 1.00
114 Mike Bovee RC .20 .50
115 Tommy Davis RC .20 .50
116 Jeremey Kendall RC .20 .50
117 Rich Aude .08 .25
118 Rick Huisman .08 .25
119 Tim Belk .08 .25
120 Edgar Renteria .20 .50
121 Calvin Maduro RC .20 .50
122 Jerry Martin RC .20 .50
123 Ramon Fermin RC .20 .50
124 Kimera Bartee RC .20 .50
125 Mark Farris .08 .25
126 Frank Rodriguez .08 .25
127 Bob Higginson RC .75 2.00
128 Bret Wagner .08 .25
129 Edwin Diaz RC .20 .50
130 Jimmy Haynes .08 .25
131 Chris Weinke RC QB .40 1.00
132 Damian Jackson RC .20 .50
133 Felix Martinez .20 .50
134 Edwin Hurtado RC .20 .50
135 Matt Raleigh RC .20 .50
136 Paul Wilson .08 .25
137 Ron Villone .08 .25
138 Eric Stuckenschneider RC .20 .50
139 Tate Seefried .08 .25
140 Rey Ordonez RC .75 2.00
141 Eddie Pearson .08 .25
142 Kevin Gallaher .08 .25
143 Torii Hunter .30 .75
144 Daron Kirkreit .08 .25
145 Craig Wilson .08 .25
146 Ugueth Urbina .08 .25
147 Chris Snopek .08 .25
148 Kym Ashworth .08 .25
149 Wayne Gomes .08 .25
150 Mark Loretta .20 .50
151 Ramon Morel RC .20 .50
152 Trot Nixon .20 .50
153 Desi Relaford .08 .25
154 Scott Sullivan .08 .25
155 Marc Barcelo .08 .25
156 Willie Adams .08 .25
157 Derrick Gibson RC .20 .50
158 Brian Meadows RC .20 .50
159 Julian Tavarez .08 .25
160 Bryan Rekar .08 .25
161 Steve Gibralter .08 .25
162 Esteban Loaiza .08 .25
163 John Wasdin .08 .25
164 Kirk Presley .08 .25
165 Mariano Rivera 1.25 3.00
166 Andy Larkin .08 .25
167 Sean Whiteside RC .20 .50
168 Matt Apana RC .20 .50
169 Shawn Senior RC .20 .50
170 Scott Gentile .08 .25
171 Quilvio Veras .08 .25
172 Eli Marrero RC .60 1.50
173 Mendy Lopez RC .20 .50
174 Homer Bush .08 .25
175 Brian Stephenson RC .20 .50
176 Jon Nunnally .08 .25
177 Jose Herrera .08 .25
178 Corey Avrard RC .20 .50
179 David Bell .08 .25
180 Jason Isringhausen .20 .50
181 Jamey Wright .08 .25
182 Lonell Roberts RC .20 .50
183 Marty Cordova .08 .25
184 Amaury Telemaco .08 .25
185 John Mabry .08 .25
186 Andrew Vessel RC .20 .50
187 Jim Cole RC .20 .50
188 Marquis Riley .08 .25
189 Todd Dunn .08 .25
190 John Carter .08 .25
191 Donnie Sadler RC .40 1.00
192 Mike Bell .08 .25
193 Chris Cumberland RC .20 .50
194 Jason Schmidt .50 1.25
195 Matt Brunson .08 .25
196 James Baldwin .08 .25
197 Bill Simas RC .20 .50
198 Gus Gandarillas .08 .25
199 Mac Suzuki .08 .25
200 Rick Holifield RC .20 .50
201 Fernando Lunar RC .20 .50
202 Kevin Jarvis .08 .25
203 Everett Stull .08 .25
204 Steve Wojciechowski .08 .25
205 Shawn Estes .08 .25
206 Jermaine Dye .20 .50
207 Marc Kroon .08 .25
208 Peter Munro RC .40 1.00
209 Pat Watkins .08 .25
210 Matt Smith .08 .25
211 Joe Vitiello .08 .25
212 Gerald Witasick Jr. .08 .25
213 Freddy Adrian Garcia RC .20 .50
214 Glenn Dishman RC .20 .50
215 Jay Canizaro RC .20 .50
216 Angel Martinez .08 .25
217 Yamil Benitez RC .20 .50
218 Fausto Macey RC .20 .50
219 Eric Owens .08 .25
220 Checklist .08 .25
221 Dwayne Hosey FOIL RC .20 .50
222 Brad Woodall FOIL RC .20 .50
223 Billy Ashley FOIL .08 .25
224 Mark Grudzielanek FOIL RC .75 2.00
225 Mark Johnson FOIL RC .40 1.00
226 Tim Unroe FOIL RC .20 .50
227 Todd Greene FOIL .08 .25
228 Larry Sutton FOIL .08 .25
229 Derek Jeter FOIL 1.50 4.00
230 Sal Fasano FOIL RC .20 .50
231 Ruben Rivera FOIL .08 .25
232 Chris Truby FOIL RC .20 .50
233 John Donati FOIL .08 .25
234 Decomba Conner FOIL RC .20 .50
235 Sergio Nunez FOIL RC .20 .50
236 Ray Brown FOIL RC .20 .50
237 Juan Melo FOIL RC .20 .50
238 Hideo Nomo FOIL RC 2.00 5.00
239 Jaime Bluma RC FOIL .20 .50
240 Jay Payton FOIL RC .75 2.00
241 Paul Konerko FOIL 1.50 4.00
242 Scott Elarton FOIL RC .40 1.00
243 Jeff Abbott FOIL RC .40 1.00
244 Jim Brower FOIL RC .20 .50
245 Geoff Blum FOIL RC .75 2.00
246 Aaron Boone FOIL RC .75 2.00
247 J.R. Phillips FOIL .08 .25
248 Alex Ochoa FOIL .08 .25
249 Nomar Garciaparra FOIL 1.50 4.00
250 Garret Anderson FOIL .20 .50
251 Ray Durham FOIL .20 .50
252 Paul Shuey FOIL .08 .25
253 Tony Clark FOIL .08 .25
254 Johnny Damon FOIL .30 .75
255 Duane Singleton FOIL .08 .25
256 LaTroy Hawkins FOIL .08 .25
257 Andy Pettitte FOIL .30 .75
258 Ben Grieve FOIL .08 .25
259 Marc Newfield FOIL .08 .25
260 Terrell Lowery FOIL .08 .25
261 Shawn Green FOIL .20 .50
262 Chipper Jones FOIL .50 1.25
263 Brooks Kieschnick FOIL .08 .25
264 Pokey Reese FOIL .08 .25
265 Doug Million FOIL .08 .25
266 Marc Valdes FOIL .08 .25
267 Brian L.Hunter FOIL .08 .25
268 Todd Hollandsworth FOIL .08 .25
269 Rod Henderson FOIL .08 .25
270 Bill Pulsipher FOIL .08 .25
271 Scott Rolen FOIL RC 5.00 12.00
272 Trey Beamon FOIL .08 .25
273 Alan Benes FOIL .08 .25
274 Dustin Hermanson FOIL .08 .25
275 Ricky Bottalico .08 .25
276 Albert Belle .20 .50
277 Deion Sanders .30 .75
278 Matt Williams .20 .50
279 Jeff Bagwell .30 .75
280 Kirby Puckett .50 1.25
281 Dave Hollins .08 .25
282 Don Mattingly 1.25 3.00
283 Joey Hamilton .08 .25
284 Bobby Bonilla .20 .50
285 Moises Alou .20 .50
286 Tom Glavine .30 .75
287 Brett Butler .20 .50
288 Chris Hoiles .08 .25
289 Kenny Rogers .20 .50
290 Larry Walker .20 .50
291 Tim Raines .20 .50
292 Kevin Appier .20 .50
293 Roger Clemens 1.00 2.50
294 Chuck Carr .08 .25
295 Randy Myers .08 .25
296 Dave Nilsson .08 .25
297 Joe Carter .20 .50
298 Chuck Finley .20 .50
299 Ray Lankford .20 .50
300 Roberto Kelly .08 .25
301 Jon Lieber .08 .25
302 Travis Fryman .20 .50
303 Mark McGwire 1.25 3.00
304 Tony Gwynn .60 1.50
305 Kenny Lofton .20 .50
306 Mark Whiten .08 .25
307 Doug Drabek .08 .25
308 Terry Steinbach .08 .25
309 Ryan Klesko .20 .50
310 Mike Piazza .75 2.00
311 Ben McDonald .08 .25
312 Reggie Sanders .20 .50
313 Alex Fernandez .08 .25
314 Aaron Sele .08 .25
315 Gregg Jefferies .08 .25
316 Rickey Henderson .50 1.25
317 Brian Anderson .08 .25
318 Jose Valentin .08 .25
319 Rod Beck .08 .25
320 Marquis Grissom .20 .50
321 Ken Griffey Jr. 1.00 2.50
322 Bret Saberhagen .20 .50
323 Juan Gonzalez .20 .50
324 Paul Molitor .20 .50
325 Gary Sheffield .20 .50
326 Darren Daulton .20 .50
327 Bill Swift .08 .25
328 Brian McRae .08 .25
329 Robin Ventura .20 .50
330 Lee Smith .20 .50
331 Fred McGriff .30 .75
332 Delino DeShields .08 .25
333 Edgar Martinez .30 .75
334 Mike Mussina .30 .75
335 Orlando Merced .08 .25
336 Carlos Baerga .08 .25
337 Wil Cordero .08 .25
338 Tom Pagnozzi .08 .25
339 Pat Hentgen .08 .25
340 Chad Curtis .08 .25
341 Darren Lewis .08 .25
342 Jeff Kent .20 .50
343 Bip Roberts .08 .25
344 Ivan Rodriguez .30 .75
345 Jeff Montgomery .08 .25
346 Hal Morris .08 .25
347 Danny Tartabull .08 .25
348 Raul Mondesi .20 .50
349 Ken Hill .08 .25
350 Pedro Martinez .30 .75
351 Frank Thomas .50 1.25
352 Manny Ramirez .30 .75
353 Tim Salmon .30 .75
354 W. VanLandingham .08 .25
355 Andres Galarraga .20 .50
356 Paul O'Neill .30 .75
357 Brady Anderson .20 .50
358 Ramon Martinez .20 .50
359 John Olerud .20 .50
360 Ruben Sierra .20 .50
361 Cal Eldred .08 .25
362 Jay Buhner .20 .50
363 Jay Bell .20 .50
364 Wally Joyner .20 .50
365 Chuck Knoblauch .20 .50
366 Len Dykstra .20 .50
367 John Wetteland .20 .50
368 Roberto Alomar .30 .75
369 Craig Biggio .30 .75
370 Ozzie Smith .75 2.00
371 Terry Pendleton .20 .50
372 Sammy Sosa .50 1.25
373 Carlos Garcia .08 .25
374 Jose Rijo .08 .25
375 Chris Gomez .08 .25
376 Barry Bonds 1.25 3.00
377 Steve Avery .08 .25
378 Rick Wilkins .08 .25
379 Pete Harnisch .08 .25
380 Dean Palmer .20 .50
381 Bob Hamelin .08 .25
382 Jason Bere .08 .25
383 Jimmy Key .20 .50
384 Dante Bichette .20 .50
385 Rafael Palmeiro .30 .75
386 David Justice .20 .50
387 Chili Davis .20 .50
388 Mike Greenwell .08 .25
389 Todd Zeile .08 .25
390 Jeff Conine .20 .50
391 Rick Aguilera .08 .25
392 Eddie Murray .50 1.25
393 Mike Stanley .08 .25
394 Cliff Floyd UER .20 .50
395 Randy Johnson .50 1.25
396 David Nied .08 .25
397 Devon White .20 .50
398 Royce Clayton .08 .25
399 Andy Benes .08 .25
400 John Hudek .08 .25
401 Bobby Jones .08 .25
402 Eric Karros .20 .50
403 Will Clark .30 .75
404 Mark Langston .08 .25
405 Kevin Brown .20 .50
406 Greg Maddux .75 2.00
407 David Cone .20 .50
408 Wade Boggs .30 .75
409 Steve Trachsel .08 .25
410 Greg Vaughn .08 .25
411 Mo Vaughn .20 .50
412 Wilson Alvarez .20 .50
413 Cal Ripken 1.50 4.00
414 Rico Brogna .08 .25
415 Barry Larkin .30 .75
416 Cecil Fielder .20 .50
417 Jose Canseco .30 .75
418 Jack McDowell .08 .25
419 Mike Lieberthal .20 .50
420 Andrew Lorraine .08 .25
421 Rich Becker .08 .25
422 Tony Phillips .08 .25
423 Scott Ruffcorn .08 .25
424 Jeff Granger .08 .25
425 Greg Pirkl .08 .25
426 Dennis Eckersley .20 .50
427 Jose Lima .08 .25
428 Russ Davis .08 .25
429 Armando Benitez .08 .25
430 Alex Gonzalez .08 .25
431 Carlos Delgado .20 .50
432 Chan Ho Park .20 .50
433 Mickey Tettleton .08 .25
434 Dave Winfield .20 .50
435 John Burkett .08 .25
436 Orlando Miller .08 .25
437 Rondell White .20 .50
438 Jose Oliva .08 .25
439 Checklist .08 .25

1995 Bowman Gold Foil

COMPLETE SET (54) 75.00 150.00
*STARS: .6X TO 1.5X BASIC CARDS
*ROOKIES: .5X TO 1.2X BASIC
STATED ODDS 1:6
229 Derek Jeter 12.00 30.00

1996 Bowman

The 1996 Bowman set was issued in one series totalling 385 cards. The 11-card packs retailed for $2.50 each. The fronts feature color action player photos in a tan-checkered frame with the player's name printed in silver foil at the bottom. The backs carry another color player photo with player information, 1995 and career player statistics. Each pack contained 10 regular issue cards plus either one foil parallel or an insert card. In a special promotional program, Topps offered collector's a $100 guarantee on complete sets. To get the guarantee, collectors had to mail in a Guaranteed Value Certificate request form, found in packs, along with a $5 processing and registration fee before the December 31st, 1996 deadline. Collectors would then receive a $100 Guaranteed Value Certificate, of which they could mail back to Topps between August 31st, 1999 and December 31st, 1999, along with their complete set, to receive $100. A reprint version of the 1952 Bowman Mickey Mantle card was randomly inserted into packs. Rookie Cards in this set include Russell Branyan, Mike Cameron, Luis Castillo, Ryan Dempster, Livan Hernandez, Geoff Jenkins, Ben Petrick and Mike Sweeney.

COMPLETE SET (385) 20.00 50.00
MANTLE STATED ODDS 1:48
1 Cal Ripken 1.00 2.50
2 Ray Durham .10 .30
3 Ivan Rodriguez .20 .50
4 Fred McGriff .20 .50
5 Hideo Nomo .30 .75
6 Troy Percival .10 .30
7 Moises Alou .10 .30
8 Mike Stanley .10 .30
9 Jay Buhner .10 .30
10 Shawn Green .10 .30
11 Ryan Klesko .10 .30
12 Andres Galarraga .10 .30
13 Dean Palmer .10 .30
14 Jeff Conine .10 .30
15 Brian L.Hunter .10 .30
16 J.T. Snow .10 .30
17 Larry Walker .10 .30
18 Barry Larkin .20 .50
19 Alex Gonzalez .10 .30
20 Edgar Martinez .20 .50
21 Mo Vaughn .10 .30
22 Mark McGwire .75 2.00
23 Jose Canseco .20 .50
24 Jack McDowell .10 .30
25 Dante Bichette .10 .30
26 Wade Boggs .20 .50
27 Mike Piazza .50 1.25
28 Ray Lankford .10 .30
29 Craig Biggio .20 .50
30 Rafael Palmeiro .20 .50
31 Ron Gant .10 .30
32 Javy Lopez .10 .30
33 Brian Jordan .10 .30
34 Paul O'Neill .20 .50
35 Mark Grace .20 .50
36 Matt Williams .10 .30
37 Pedro Martinez .20 .50
38 Rickey Henderson .30 .75
39 Bobby Bonilla .10 .30
40 Todd Hollandsworth .10 .30
41 Jim Thome .20 .50
42 Gary Sheffield .30 .75
43 Tim Salmon .20 .50
44 Gregg Jefferies .10 .30
45 Roberto Alomar .20 .50
46 Carlos Baerga .10 .30
47 Mark Grudzielanek .10 .30
48 Randy Johnson .30 .75
49 Tino Martinez .20 .50
50 Robin Ventura .10 .30
51 Ryne Sandberg .50 1.25
52 Jay Bell .10 .30
53 Jason Schmidt .20 .50
54 Frank Thomas .30 .75
55 Kenny Lofton .10 .30
56 Ariel Prieto .10 .30
57 David Cone .10 .30
58 Reggie Sanders .10 .30
59 Michael Tucker .10 .30
60 Vinny Castilla .10 .30
61 Len Dykstra .10 .30
62 Todd Hundley .10 .30
63 Brian McRae .10 .30
64 Dennis Eckersley .10 .30
65 Rondell White .10 .30
66 Eric Karros .10 .30
67 Greg Maddux .50 1.25
68 Kevin Appier .10 .30
69 Eddie Murray .30 .75
70 John Olerud .10 .30
71 Tony Gwynn .40 1.00
72 David Justice .10 .30
73 Ken Caminiti .10 .30
74 Terry Steinbach .10 .30
75 Alan Benes .10 .30
76 Chipper Jones .30 .75
77 Jeff Bagwell .20 .50
78 Barry Bonds .75 2.00
79 Ken Griffey Jr. .75 2.00
80 Roger Cedeno .10 .30
81 Joe Carter .10 .30
82 Henry Rodriguez .10 .30
83 Jason Isringhausen .10 .30
84 Chuck Knoblauch .10 .30
85 Manny Ramirez .20 .50
86 Tom Glavine .20 .50
87 Jeffrey Hammonds .10 .30
88 Paul Molitor .10 .30
89 Roger Clemens .60 1.50
90 Greg Vaughn .10 .30
91 Marty Cordova .10 .30
92 Albert Belle .10 .30
93 Mike Mussina .20 .50
94 Garret Anderson .10 .30
95 Juan Gonzalez .10 .30
96 John Valentin .10 .30
97 Jason Giambi .10 .30
98 Kirby Puckett .30 .75
99 Jim Edmonds .10 .30
100 Cecil Fielder .10 .30
101 Mike Aldrete .10 .30
102 Marquis Grissom .10 .30
103 Derek Bell .10 .30
104 Raul Mondesi .10 .30
105 Sammy Sosa .30 .75
106 Travis Fryman .10 .30
107 Rico Brogna .10 .30
108 Will Clark .20 .50
109 Bernie Williams .20 .50
110 Brady Anderson .10 .30
111 Torii Hunter .10 .30
112 Derek Jeter .75 2.00
113 Mike Kusiewicz RC .20 .50
114 Scott Rolen .30 .75
115 Ramon Castro .10 .30
116 Jose Guillen RC 1.25 3.00
117 Wade Walker RC .20 .50
118 Shawn Senior .10 .30
119 Onan Masaoka RC .40 1.00
120 Marlon Anderson RC .40 1.00
121 Katsuhiro Maeda RC .40 1.00
122 Garrett Stephenson RC .20 .50
123 Butch Huskey .10 .30
124 D'Angelo Jimenez RC .40 1.00
125 Tony Mounce RC .20 .50
126 Jay Canizaro .10 .30
127 Juan Melo .10 .30
128 Steve Gibralter .10 .30
129 Freddy Adrian Garcia .10 .30
130 Julio Santana .10 .30
131 Richard Hidalgo .10 .30
132 Jermaine Dye .10 .30
133 Willie Adams .10 .30
134 Everett Stull .10 .30
135 Ramon Morel .10 .30
136 Chan Ho Park .10 .30
137 Jamey Wright .10 .30
138 Luis R.Garcia RC .20 .50
139 Dan Serafini .10 .30
140 Ryan Dempster RC .75 2.00
141 Tate Seefried .10 .30

1996 Bowman

Card	Low	High
142 Jimmy Hurst	.10	.30
143 Travis Miller	.10	.30
144 Curtis Goodwin	.10	.30
145 Rocky Coppinger RC	.20	.50
146 Enrique Wilson	.10	.30
147 Jaime Bluma	.10	.30
148 Andrew Vessel	.10	.30
149 Damian Moss	.10	.30
150 Shawn Gallagher RC	.20	.50
151 Pat Watkins	.10	.30
152 Jose Paniagua	.10	.30
153 Danny Graves	.10	.30
154 Bryon Gainey RC	.20	.50
155 Steve Soderstrom	.10	.30
156 Cliff Brumbaugh RC	.20	.50
157 Eugene Kingsale RC	.20	.50
158 Lou Collier	.10	.30
159 Todd Walker	.10	.30
160 Kris Detmers RC	.20	.50
161 Josh Booty RC	.20	.50
162 Greg Whiteman RC	.20	.50
163 Damian Jackson	.10	.30
164 Tony Clark	.10	.30
165 Jeff D'Amico	.10	.30
166 Johnny Damon	.20	.50
167 Rafael Orellano	.10	.30
168 Ruben Rivera	.10	.30
169 Alex Ochoa	.10	.30
170 Jay Powell	.10	.30
171 Tom Evans	.10	.30
172 Ron Villone	.10	.30
173 Shawn Estes	.10	.30
174 John Wasdin	.10	.30
175 Bill Simas	.10	.30
176 Kevin Brown	.10	.30
177 Shannon Stewart	.10	.30
178 Todd Greene	.10	.30
179 Bob Wolcott	.10	.30
180 Chris Snopek	.10	.30
181 Nomar Garciaparra	.60	1.50
182 Cameron Smith RC	.20	.50
183 Matt Drews	.10	.30
184 Jimmy Haynes	.10	.30
185 Chris Carpenter	.20	.50
186 Desi Relaford	.10	.30
187 Ben Grieve	.10	.30
188 Mike Bell	.10	.30
189 Luis Castillo RC	.60	1.50
190 Ugueth Urbina	.10	.30
191 Paul Wilson	.10	.30
192 Andruw Jones	.50	1.25
193 Wayne Gomes	.10	.30
194 Craig Counsell RC	.60	1.50
195 Jim Cole	.10	.30
196 Brooks Kieschnick	.10	.30
197 Trey Beamon	.10	.30
198 Marino Santana RC	.20	.50
199 Bob Abreu	.30	.75
200 Pokey Reese	.10	.30
201 Dante Powell	.10	.30
202 George Arias	.10	.30
203 Jorge Velandia RC	.20	.50
204 George Lombard RC	.20	.50
205 Byron Browne RC	.20	.50
206 John Frascatore	.10	.30
207 Terry Adams	.10	.30
208 Wilson Delgado RC	.20	.50
209 Billy McMillon	.10	.30
210 Jeff Abbott	.10	.30
211 Trot Nixon	.10	.30
212 Amaury Telemaco	.10	.30
213 Scott Sullivan	.10	.30
214 Justin Thompson	.10	.30
215 Decomba Conner	.10	.30
216 Ryan McGuire	.10	.30
217 Matt Luke	.10	.30
218 Doug Million	.10	.30
219 Jason Dickson RC	.20	.50
220 Ramon Hernandez RC	.75	2.00
221 Mark Bellhorn RC	.75	2.00
222 Eric Ludwick RC	.20	.50
223 Luke Wilcox RC	.20	.50
224 Marty Malloy RC	.20	.50
225 Gary Coffee RC	.20	.50
226 Wendell Magee RC	.20	.50
227 Brett Tomko RC	.40	1.00
228 Derek Lowe	.10	.30
229 Jose Rosado RC	.20	.50
230 Steve Bourgeois RC	.20	.50
231 Neil Weber RC	.20	.50
232 Jeff Ware	.10	.30
233 Edwin Diaz	.10	.30
234 Greg Norton	.10	.30
235 Aaron Boone	.10	.30
236 Jeff Suppan	.10	.30
237 Bret Wagner	.10	.30
238 Elieser Marrero	.10	.30
239 Will Cunnane	.10	.30
240 Brian Barkley RC	.20	.50
241 Jay Payton	.10	.30
242 Marcus Jensen	.10	.30
243 Ryan Nye	.10	.30
244 Chad Mottola	.10	.30
245 Scott McClain RC	.20	.50
246 Jesse Ibarra RC	.20	.50
247 Mike Darr RC	.20	.50
248 Bobby Estalella RC	.20	.50
249 Michael Barrett	.10	.30
250 Jamie Lopiccolo RC	.20	.50
251 Shane Spencer RC	.40	1.00
252 Ben Petrick RC	.20	.50
253 Jason Bell RC	.20	.50
254 Arnold Gooch RC	.20	.50
255 T.J. Mathews	.10	.30
256 Jason Ryan	.10	.30
257 Pat Cline RC	.20	.50
258 Rafael Carmona RC	.20	.50
259 Carl Pavano RC	.75	2.00
260 Ben Davis	.10	.30
261 Matt Lawton RC	.40	1.00
262 Kevin Sefcik RC	.20	.50
263 Chris Fussell RC	.20	.50
264 Mike Cameron RC	.60	1.50
265 Marty Janzen RC	.20	.50
266 Livan Hernandez RC	.75	2.00
267 Raul Ibanez RC	2.00	5.00
268 Juan Encarnacion	.10	.30
269 David Yocum RC	.20	.50
270 Jonathan Johnson RC	.20	.50
271 Reggie Taylor	.10	.30
272 Danny Buxbaum RC	.20	.50
273 Jacob Cruz	.10	.30
274 Bobby Morris RC	.20	.50
275 Andy Fox RC	.20	.50
276 Greg Keagle	.10	.30
277 Charles Peterson	.10	.30
278 Derrek Lee	.20	.50
279 Bryant Nelson RC	.20	.50
280 Antone Williamson	.10	.30
281 Scott Elarton	.10	.30
282 Shad Williams RC	.20	.50
283 Rich Hunter RC	.20	.50
284 Chris Sheff	.10	.30
285 Derrick Gibson	.10	.30
286 Felix Rodriguez	.10	.30
287 Brian Banks RC	.20	.50
288 Jason McDonald	.10	.30
289 Glendon Rusch RC	.40	1.00
290 Gary Rath	.10	.30
291 Peter Munro	.10	.30
292 Tom Fordham	.10	.30
293 Jason Kendall	.10	.30
294 Russ Johnson	.10	.30
295 Joe Long	.10	.30
296 Robert Smith RC	.20	.50
297 Jarrod Washburn RC	.60	1.50
298 Dave Coggin RC	.20	.50
299 Jeff Yoder RC	.20	.50
300 Jed Hansen RC	.20	.50
301 Matt Morris RC	1.00	2.50
302 Josh Bishop RC	.20	.50
303 Dustin Hermanson	.10	.30
304 Mike Gulan	.10	.30
305 Felipe Crespo	.10	.30
306 Quinton McCracken	.10	.30
307 Jim Bonnici RC	.20	.50
308 Sal Fasano	.10	.30
309 Gabe Alvarez RC	.20	.50
310 Heath Murray RC	.20	.50
311 Javier Valentin RC	.20	.50
312 Bartolo Colon	.30	.75
313 Olmedo Saenz	.10	.30
314 Norm Hutchins RC	.20	.50
315 Chris Holt	.10	.30
316 David Doster RC	.20	.50
317 Robert Person	.10	.30
318 Donne Wall RC	.20	.50
319 Adam Riggs RC	.20	.50
320 Homer Bush	.10	.30
321 Brad Rigby RC	.20	.50
322 Lou Merloni RC	.20	.50
323 Neifi Perez	.10	.30
324 Chris Cumberland	.10	.30
325 Alvie Shepherd RC	.20	.50
326 Jarrod Patterson RC	.20	.50
327 Ray Ricken RC	.20	.50
328 Danny Klassen RC	.20	.50
329 David Miller RC	.20	.50
330 Chad Alexander RC	.20	.50
331 Matt Beaumont	.10	.30
332 Damon Hollins	.10	.30
333 Todd Dunn	.10	.30
334 Mike Sweeney RC	.75	2.00
335 Richie Sexson	.20	.50
336 Billy Wagner	.10	.30
337 Ron Wright RC	.20	.50
338 Paul Konerko	.30	.75
339 Tommy Phelps RC	.20	.50
340 Karim Garcia	.10	.30
341 Mike Grace RC	.20	.50
342 Russell Branyan RC	.40	1.00
343 Randy Winn RC	.60	1.50
344 A.J. Pierzynski RC	1.50	4.00
345 Mike Busby RC	.20	.50
346 Matt Beech RC	.20	.50
347 Jose Cepeda RC	.20	.50
348 Brian Stephenson	.10	.30
349 Rey Ordonez	.10	.30
350 Rich Aurilia RC	.40	1.00
351 Edgard Velazquez RC	.20	.50
352 Raul Casanova	.10	.30
353 Carlos Guillen RC	.75	2.00
354 Bruce Aven RC	.20	.50
355 Ryan Jones RC	.20	.50
356 Derek Aucoin RC	.20	.50
357 Brian Rose RC	.20	.50
358 Richard Almanzar RC	.20	.50
359 Fletcher Bates RC	.20	.50
360 Russ Ortiz RC	.60	1.50
361 Wilton Guerrero RC	.20	.50
362 Geoff Jenkins RC	.60	1.50
363 Pete Janicki	.10	.30
364 Yamil Benitez	.10	.30
365 Aaron Holbert	.10	.30
366 Tim Belk	.10	.30
367 Terrell Wade	.10	.30
368 Terrence Long	.10	.30
369 Brad Fullmer	.10	.30
370 Matt Wagner	.10	.30
371 Craig Wilson RC	.20	.50
372 Mark Loretta	.10	.30
373 Eric Owens	.10	.30
374 Vladimir Guerrero	.60	1.50
375 Tommy Davis	.10	.30
376 Donnie Sadler	.10	.30
377 Edgar Renteria	.10	.30
378 Todd Helton	.60	1.50
379 Ralph Milliard RC	.20	.50
380 Darin Blood RC	.20	.50
381 Shayne Bennett	.10	.30
382 Mark Redman	.10	.30
383 Felix Martinez	.10	.30
384 Sean Watkins RC	.20	.50
385 Oscar Henriquez	.10	.30
M20 52 Bowman Mantle	2.00	5.00
NNO Unnumbered Checklists	.10	.30

1996 Bowman Foil

	Low	High
COMPLETE SET (385)	150.00	300.00
*STARS: 1X TO 2.5X BASIC CARDS		
*ROOKIES: .6X TO 1.5X BASIC CARDS		
ONE FOIL OR INSERT CARD PER HOBBY PACK		
TWO FOILS PER RETAIL PACK		
267 Raul Ibanez	4.00	10.00

1996 Bowman Minor League POY

Randomly inserted in packs at a rate of one in 12, this 15-card set features top minor league prospects for Player of the Year Candidates. The fronts carry a color player photo with red-and-silver foil printing. The backs display player information including his career bests.

	Low	High
COMPLETE SET (15)	10.00	25.00
STATED ODDS 1:12		
1 Andruw Jones	1.25	3.00
2 Derrick Gibson	.30	.75
3 Bob Abreu	.75	2.00
4 Todd Walker	.30	.75
5 Jamey Wright	.30	.75
6 Wes Helms	.60	1.50
7 Karim Garcia	.30	.75
8 Bartolo Colon	.75	2.00
9 Alex Ochoa	.30	.75
10 Mike Sweeney	.75	2.00
11 Ruben Rivera	.30	.75
12 Gabe Alvarez	.20	.50
13 Billy Wagner	.30	.75
14 Vladimir Guerrero	1.50	4.00
15 Edgard Velazquez	.20	.50

1997 Bowman

The 1997 Bowman set was issued in two series (series one numbers 1-221, series two numbers 222-441) and was distributed in 10 card packs with a suggested retail price of $2.50. The 441-card set features color photos of 300 top prospects with silver and blue foil stamping and 140 veteran stars designated by silver and red foil stamping. An unannounced Hideki Irabu red bordered card (number 441) was also included in series two packs. Players that were featured for the first time on a Bowman card also carried a blue foil "1st Bowman Card" logo on the card front. Topps offered collectors a $125 guarantee on complete sets. To get the guarantee, collectors had to mail in the Guaranteed Certificate Request Form which was found in every three packs of either series along with a $5 registration and processing fee. To redeem the guarantee, collectors had to send a complete set of Bowman regular cards (441 cards in both series) along with the certificate to Topps between August 31 and December 31 in the year 2000. Rookie Cards in this set include Adrian Beltre, Kris Benson, Eric Chavez, Jose Cruz Jr, Travis Lee, Aramis Ramirez, Miguel Tejada and Kerry Wood. Please note that cards 155 and 158 don't exist. Calvin "Pokey" Reese and George Arias are both numbered 156 (Reese is an uncorrected error - should be numbered 155). Chris Carpenter and Eric Milton are both numbered 159 (Carpenter is an uncorrected error - should be numbered 158).

Card	Low	High
COMPLETE SET (441)	10.00	25.00
COMPLETE SERIES 1 (221)	5.00	12.00
COMPLETE SERIES 2 (220)	5.00	12.00
CARDS 155 AND 158 DON'T EXIST		
REESE AND ARIAS BOTH NUMBERED 156		
CARPENTER 'N MILTON BOTH NUMBER 159		
CONDITION SENSITIVE SET		
1 Derek Jeter	.75	2.00
2 Edgar Renteria	.10	.30
3 Chipper Jones	.30	.75
4 Hideo Nomo	.30	.75
5 Tim Salmon	.20	.50
6 Jason Giambi	.10	.30
7 Robin Ventura	.10	.30
8 Tony Clark	.10	.30
9 Barry Larkin	.20	.50
10 Paul Molitor	.10	.30
11 Bernard Gilkey	.10	.30
12 Jack McDowell	.10	.30
13 Andy Benes	.10	.30
14 Ryan Klesko	.10	.30
15 Mark McGwire	.75	2.00
16 Ken Griffey Jr.	.60	1.50
17 Robb Nen	.10	.30
18 Cal Ripken	1.00	2.50
19 John Valentin	.10	.30
20 Ricky Bottalico	.10	.30
21 Mike Lansing	.10	.30
22 Ryne Sandberg	.50	1.25
23 Carlos Delgado	.10	.30
24 Craig Biggio	.20	.50
25 Eric Karros	.10	.30
26 Kevin Appier	.10	.30
27 Mariano Rivera	.30	.75
28 Vinny Castilla	.10	.30
29 Juan Gonzalez	.10	.30
30 Al Martin	.10	.30
31 Jeff Cirillo	.10	.30
32 Eddie Murray	.30	.75
33 Ray Lankford	.10	.30
34 Manny Ramirez	.20	.50
35 Roberto Alomar	.20	.50
36 Will Clark	.20	.50
37 Chuck Knoblauch	.10	.30
38 Harold Baines	.10	.30
39 Trevor Hoffman	.10	.30
40 Edgar Martinez	.20	.50
41 Geronimo Berroa	.10	.30
42 Rey Ordonez	.10	.30
43 Mike Stanley	.10	.30
44 Mike Mussina	.20	.50
45 Kevin Brown	.10	.30
46 Dennis Eckersley	.10	.30
47 Henry Rodriguez	.10	.30
48 Tino Martinez	.20	.50
49 Eric Young	.10	.30
50 Bret Boone	.10	.30
51 Raul Mondesi	.10	.30
52 Sammy Sosa	.30	.75
53 John Smoltz	.20	.50
54 Billy Wagner	.10	.30
55 Jeff D'Amico	.10	.30
56 Ken Caminiti	.10	.30
57 Jason Kendall	.10	.30
58 Wade Boggs	.20	.50
59 Andres Galarraga	.10	.30
60 Jeff Brantley	.10	.30
61 Mel Rojas	.10	.30
62 Brian L. Hunter	.10	.30
63 Bobby Bonilla	.10	.30
64 Roger Clemens	.60	1.50
65 Jeff Kent	.10	.30
66 Matt Williams	.10	.30
67 Albert Belle	.10	.30
68 Jeff King	.10	.30
69 John Wetteland	.10	.30
70 Deion Sanders	.20	.50
71 Bubba Trammell RC	.25	.60
72 Felix Heredia RC	.15	.40
73 Billy Koch RC	.40	1.00
74 Sidney Ponson RC	.40	1.00
75 Ricky Ledee RC	.25	.60
76 Brett Tomko	.10	.30
77 Braden Looper RC	.15	.40
78 Damian Jackson	.10	.30
79 Jason Dickson	.10	.30
80 Chad Green RC	.15	.40
81 R.A. Dickey RC	1.25	3.00
82 Jeff Liefer	.10	.30
83 Matt Wagner	.10	.30
84 Richard Hidalgo	.10	.30
85 Adam Riggs	.10	.30
86 Robert Smith	.10	.30
87 Chad Hermansen RC	.15	.40
88 Felix Martinez	.10	.30
89 J.J. Johnson	.10	.30
90 Todd Dunwoody	.10	.30
91 Katsuhiro Maeda	.10	.30
92 Darin Erstad	.10	.30
93 Elieser Marrero	.10	.30
94 Bartolo Colon	.10	.30
95 Chris Fussell	.10	.30
96 Ugueth Urbina	.10	.30
97 Josh Paul RC	.15	.40
98 Jaime Bluma	.10	.30
99 Seth Greisinger RC	.15	.40
100 Jose Cruz Jr. RC	.25	.60
101 Todd Dunn	.10	.30
102 Joe Young RC	.15	.40
103 Jonathan Johnson	.10	.30
104 Justin Towle RC	.15	.40
105 Brian Rose	.10	.30
106 Jose Guillen	.10	.30
107 Andruw Jones	.20	.50
108 Mark Kotsay RC	.60	1.50
109 Wilton Guerrero	.10	.30
110 Jacob Cruz	.10	.30
111 Mike Sweeney	.10	.30
112 Julio Mosquera	.10	.30
113 Matt Morris	.10	.30
114 Wendell Magee	.10	.30
115 John Thomson	.10	.30
116 Javier Valentin	.10	.30
117 Tom Fordham	.10	.30
118 Ruben Rivera	.10	.30
119 Mike Drumright RC	.15	.40
120 Chris Holt	.10	.30
121 Sean Maloney	.10	.30
122 Michael Barrett	.10	.30
123 Tony Saunders RC	.15	.40
124 Kevin Brown C	.10	.30
125 Richard Almanzar	.10	.30
126 Mark Redman	.10	.30
127 Anthony Sanders RC	.15	.40
128 Jeff Abbott	.10	.30
129 Eugene Kingsale	.10	.30
130 Paul Konerko	.20	.50
131 Randall Simon RC	.25	.60
132 Andy Larkin	.10	.30
133 Rafael Medina	.10	.30
134 Mendy Lopez	.10	.30
135 Freddy Adrian Garcia	.10	.30
136 Karim Garcia	.10	.30
137 Larry Rodriguez RC	.15	.40
138 Carlos Guillen	.10	.30
139 Aaron Boone	.10	.30
140 Donnie Sadler	.10	.30
141 Brooks Kieschnick	.10	.30
142 Scott Spiezio	.10	.30
143 Everett Stull	.10	.30
144 Enrique Wilson	.10	.30
145 Milton Bradley RC	.75	2.00
146 Kevin Orie	.10	.30
147 Derek Wallace	.10	.30
148 Russ Johnson	.10	.30
149 Joe Lagarde RC	.15	.40
150 Luis Castillo	.10	.30
151 Jay Payton	.10	.30
152 Joe Long	.10	.30
153 Livan Hernandez	.10	.30
154 Vladimir Nunez RC	.25	.60
155 Pokey Reese UER	.10	.30
156 George Arias	.10	.30
157 Homer Bush	.10	.30
158 Chris Carpenter UER	.10	.30
159 Eric Milton RC	.25	.60
160 Richie Sexson	.10	.30
161 Carl Pavano	.10	.30
162 Chris Gissell RC	.15	.40
163 Mac Suzuki	.10	.30
164 Pat Cline	.10	.30
165 Ron Wright	.10	.30
166 Dante Powell	.10	.30
167 Mark Bellhorn	.10	.30
168 George Lombard	.10	.30
169 Pee Wee Lopez RC	.15	.40
170 Paul Wilder RC	.15	.40
171 Brad Fullmer	.10	.30
172 Willie Martinez RC	.15	.40
173 Dario Veras RC	.15	.40
174 Dave Coggin	.10	.30
175 Kris Benson RC	.40	1.00
176 Torii Hunter	.10	.30
177 D.T. Cromer	.10	.30
178 Nelson Figueroa RC	.15	.40
179 Hiram Bocachica RC	.15	.40
180 Shane Monahan	.10	.30
181 Jimmy Anderson RC	.15	.40
182 Juan Melo	.10	.30
183 Pablo Ortega RC	.15	.40
184 Calvin Pickering RC	.15	.40
185 Reggie Taylor	.10	.30
186 Jeff Farnsworth RC	.15	.40
187 Terrence Long	.10	.30
188 Geoff Jenkins	.10	.30
189 Steve Rain RC	.15	.40
190 Nerio Rodriguez RC	.15	.40
191 Derrick Gibson	.10	.30
192 Darin Blood	.10	.30
193 Ben Davis	.10	.30
194 Adrian Beltre RC	8.00	20.00
195 Damian Sapp RC UER	.15	.40
196 Kerry Wood RC	2.00	5.00
197 Nate Rolison RC	.15	.40
198 Fernando Tatis RC	.15	.40
199 Brad Penny RC	1.25	3.00
200 Jake Westbrook RC	.40	1.00
201 Edwin Diaz	.10	.30
202 Joe Fontenot RC	.25	.60
203 Matt Halloran RC	.15	.40
204 Blake Stein RC	.15	.40
205 Onan Masaoka	.10	.30
206 Ben Petrick	.10	.30
207 Matt Clement RC	.40	1.00
208 Todd Greene	.10	.30
209 Ray Ricken	.10	.30
210 Eric Chavez RC	1.50	4.00
211 Edgard Velazquez	.10	.30
212 Bruce Chen RC	.40	1.00
213 Danny Patterson	.10	.30
214 Jeff Yoder	.10	.30
215 Luis Ordaz RC	.15	.40
216 Chris Widger	.10	.30
217 Jason Brester	.10	.30
218 Carlton Loewer	.10	.30
219 Chris Reitsma RC	.25	.60
220 Neifi Perez	.10	.30
221 Hideki Irabu RC	.25	.60
222 Ellis Burks	.10	.30
223 Pedro Martinez	.20	.50
224 Kenny Lofton	.10	.30
225 Randy Johnson	.30	.75
226 Terry Steinbach	.10	.30
227 Bernie Williams	.20	.50
228 Dean Palmer	.10	.30
229 Alan Benes	.10	.30
230 Marquis Grissom	.10	.30
231 Gary Sheffield	.10	.30
232 Curt Schilling	.10	.30
233 Reggie Sanders	.10	.30
234 Bobby Higginson	.10	.30
235 Moises Alou	.10	.30
236 Tom Glavine	.20	.50
237 Mark Grace	.20	.50
238 Ramon Martinez	.10	.30
239 Rafael Palmeiro	.20	.50
240 John Olerud	.10	.30
241 Dante Bichette	.10	.30
242 Greg Vaughn	.10	.30
243 Jeff Bagwell	.20	.50
244 Barry Bonds	.75	2.00
245 Pat Hentgen	.10	.30
246 Jim Thome	.20	.50
247 Jermaine Allensworth	.10	.30
248 Andy Pettitte	.20	.50
249 Jay Bell	.10	.30
250 John Jaha	.10	.30
251 Jim Edmonds	.10	.30
252 Ron Gant	.10	.30
253 David Cone	.10	.30
254 Jose Canseco	.20	.50
255 Jay Buhner	.10	.30
256 Greg Maddux	.50	1.25
257 Brian McRae	.10	.30
258 Lance Johnson	.10	.30
259 Travis Fryman	.10	.30
260 Paul O'Neill	.20	.50
261 Ivan Rodriguez	.20	.50
262 Gregg Jefferies	.10	.30
263 Fred McGriff	.20	.50
264 Derek Bell	.10	.30
265 Jeff Conine	.10	.30
266 Mike Piazza	.50	1.25
267 Mark Grudzielanek	.10	.30
268 Brady Anderson	.10	.30
269 Marty Cordova	.10	.30
270 Ray Durham	.10	.30
271 Joe Carter	.10	.30
272 Brian Jordan	.10	.30
273 David Justice	.10	.30
274 Tony Gwynn	.40	1.00
275 Larry Walker	.10	.30
276 Cecil Fielder	.10	.30
277 Mo Vaughn	.10	.30
278 Alex Fernandez	.10	.30
279 Michael Tucker	.10	.30
280 Jose Valentin	.10	.30
281 Sandy Alomar Jr.	.10	.30
282 Todd Hollandsworth	.10	.30
283 Rico Brogna	.10	.30
284 Rusty Greer	.10	.30
285 Roberto Hernandez	.10	.30
286 Hal Morris	.10	.30
287 Johnny Damon	.20	.50
288 Todd Hundley	.10	.30
289 Rondell White	.10	.30
290 Frank Thomas	.30	.75
291 Don Denbow RC	.15	.40
292 Derrek Lee	.20	.50
293 Todd Walker	.10	.30
294 Scott Rolen	.20	.50
295 Wes Helms	.10	.30
296 Bob Abreu	.20	.50
297 John Patterson RC	.60	1.50
298 Alex Gonzalez RC	.40	1.00
299 Grant Roberts RC	.15	.40
300 Jeff Suppan	.10	.30
301 Luke Wilcox	.10	.30
302 Marlon Anderson	.10	.30
303 Ray Brown	.10	.30
304 Mike Caruso RC	.15	.40
305 Sam Marsonek RC	.15	.40
306 Brady Raggio RC	.15	.40
307 Kevin McGlinchy RC	.25	.60
308 Roy Halladay RC	8.00	20.00
309 Jeremi Gonzalez RC	.15	.40
310 Aramis Ramirez RC	1.50	4.00
311 Dee Brown RC	.15	.40
312 Justin Thompson	.10	.30
313 Jay Tessmer RC	.15	.40
314 Mike Johnson RC	.15	.40
315 Danny Clyburn	.10	.30
316 Bruce Aven	.10	.30
317 Keith Foulke RC	.60	1.50
318 Jimmy Osting RC	.25	.60
319 Valerio De Los Santos RC	.15	.40
320 Shannon Stewart	.10	.30
321 Willie Adams	.10	.30
322 Larry Barnes RC	.15	.40
323 Mark Johnson RC	.15	.40
324 Chris Stowers RC	.15	.40
325 Brandon Reed	.10	.30
326 Randy Winn	.10	.30
327 Steve Chavez RC	.15	.40
328 Nomar Garciaparra	.50	1.25
329 Jacque Jones RC	.60	1.50
330 Chris Clemons	.10	.30
331 Todd Helton	.30	.75
332 Ryan Brannan RC	.15	.40
333 Alex Sanchez RC	.25	.60
334 Arnold Gooch	.10	.30
335 Russell Branyan	.10	.30
336 Daryle Ward	.15	.40
337 John LeRoy RC	.15	.40
338 Steve Cox	.10	.30
339 Kevin Witt	.10	.30
340 Norm Hutchins	.10	.30
341 Gabby Martinez	.10	.30
342 Kris Detmers	.10	.30
343 Mike Villano RC	.15	.40
344 Preston Wilson	.10	.30
345 James Manias RC	.15	.40
346 Deivi Cruz RC	.25	.60
347 Donzell McDonald RC	.15	.40
348 Rod Myers RC	.15	.40
349 Shawn Chacon RC	.40	1.00
350 Elvin Hernandez RC	.25	.60
351 Orlando Cabrera RC	.60	1.50
352 Brian Banks	.10	.30
353 Robbie Bell	.15	.40
354 Brad Rigby	.10	.30
355 Scott Elarton	.10	.30
356 Kevin Sweeney RC	.15	.40
357 Steve Soderstrom	.10	.30
358 Ryan Nye	.10	.30
359 Marlon Allen RC	.15	.40
360 Donny Leon RC	.15	.40
361 Garrett Neubart RC	.25	.60
362 Abraham Nunez RC	.25	.60
363 Adam Eaton RC	.40	1.00
364 Octavio Dotel RC	.25	.60
365 Dean Crow RC	.15	.40
366 Jason Baker RC	.15	.40
367 Sean Casey	.40	1.00
368 Joe Lawrence RC	.15	.40
369 Adam Johnson RC	.15	.40
370 Scott Schoeneweis RC	.25	.60
371 Gerald Witasick Jr.	.10	.30
372 Ronnie Belliard RC	.50	1.25
373 Russ Ortiz	.10	.30
374 Robert Stratton RC	.25	.60
375 Bobby Estalella	.10	.30
376 Corey Lee RC	.15	.40
377 Carlos Beltran	.75	2.00
378 Mike Cameron	.10	.30
379 Scott Randall RC	.15	.40
380 Corey Erickson RC	.15	.40
381 Jay Canizaro	.10	.30
382 Kerry Robinson RC	.15	.40
383 Todd Noel RC	.15	.40
384 A.J. Zapp RC	.15	.40
385 Jarrod Washburn	.10	.30
386 Ben Grieve	.10	.30
387 Javier Vazquez RC	.60	1.50
388 Tony Graffanino	.10	.30
389 Travis Lee RC	.25	.60
390 DaRond Stovall	.10	.30
391 Dennis Reyes RC	.25	.60
392 Danny Buxbaum	.10	.30
393 Marc Lewis RC	.15	.40
394 Kelvim Escobar RC	.40	1.00
395 Danny Klassen	.10	.30
396 Ken Cloude RC	.15	.40
397 Gabe Alvarez	.10	.30
398 Jaret Wright RC	.25	.60
399 Raul Casanova	.10	.30
400 Clayton Bruner RC	.15	.40
401 Jason Marquis RC	.60	1.50
402 Marc Kroon	.10	.30
403 Jamey Wright	.10	.30
404 Matt Snyder RC	.15	.40
405 Josh Garrett RC	.15	.40
406 Juan Encarnacion	.10	.30
407 Heath Murray	.10	.30
408 Brett Herbison RC	.25	.60
409 Brent Butler RC	.15	.40
410 Danny Peoples RC	.15	.40
411 Miguel Tejada RC	2.00	5.00
412 Damian Moss	.10	.30
413 Jim Pittsley	.10	.30
414 Dmitri Young	.10	.30
415 Glendon Rusch	.10	.30
416 Vladimir Guerrero	.30	.75
417 Cole Liniak RC	.25	.60
418 Ramon Hernandez	.10	.30
419 Cliff Politte RC	.15	.40
420 Mel Rosario RC	.15	.40
421 Jorge Carrion RC	.15	.40
422 John Barnes RC	.15	.40
423 Chris Stowe RC	.15	.40
424 Vernon Wells RC	2.00	5.00
425 Brett Caradonna RC	.15	.40
426 Scott Hodges RC	.25	.60
427 Jon Garland RC	1.00	2.50
428 Nathan Haynes RC	.15	.40
429 Geoff Goetz RC	.15	.40
430 Adam Kennedy RC	.40	1.00
431 T.J. Tucker RC	.15	.40
432 Aaron Akin RC	.15	.40
433 Jayson Werth RC	2.00	5.00
434 Glenn Davis RC	.15	.40
435 Mark Mangum RC	.15	.40
436 Troy Cameron RC	.15	.40
437 J.J. Davis RC	.15	.40
438 Lance Berkman RC	4.00	10.00
439 Jason Standridge RC	.15	.40
440 Jason Dellaero RC	.25	.60
441 Hideki Irabu	.25	.60

1997 Bowman International

COMPLETE SET (441) 75.00 150.00
COMPLETE SERIES 1 (221) 30.00 80.00
COMPLETE SERIES 2 (220) 30.00 80.00
*STARS: 1X TO 2.5X BASIC CARDS
*ROOKIES: .5X TO 1.2X BASIC CARDS
ONE INT'L OR INSERT PER PACK

1997 Bowman 1998 ROY Favorites

Randomly inserted in 1997 Bowman Series two packs at the rate of one in 12, this 15-card set features color photos of prospective 1998 Rookie of the Year candidates.

COMPLETE SET (15) 6.00 15.00
SER.2 STATED ODDS 1:12
ROY1 Jeff Abbott .40 1.00
ROY2 Karim Garcia .40 1.00
ROY3 Todd Helton 1.00 2.50
ROY4 Richard Hidalgo .40 1.00
ROY5 Geoff Jenkins .40 1.00
ROY6 Russ Johnson .40 1.00
ROY7 Paul Konerko .60 1.50
ROY8 Mark Kotsay .75 2.00
ROY9 Ricky Ledee .30 .75
ROY10 Travis Lee .30 .75
ROY11 Derrek Lee .60 1.50
ROY12 Elieser Marrero .40 1.00
ROY13 Juan Melo .40 1.00
ROY14 Brian Rose .40 1.00
ROY15 Fernando Tatis .20 .50

1997 Bowman Certified Blue Ink Autographs

Randomly inserted in first and second series packs at a rate of one in 96 and ANCO packs at one in 115, this 90-card set features color player photos of top prospects with blue ink autographs and printed on sturdy 16 pt. card stock with the Topps Certified Autograph Issue Stamp. The Derek Jeter blue ink and green ink versions are seeded in every 1,928 packs.

STATED ODDS 1:96, ANCO 1:115
*BLACK INK: .5X TO 1.2X BLUE INK
BLACK STATED ODDS 1:503, ANCO 1:600
*GOLD INK: 1X TO 2.5X BLUE INK
GOLD: STATED ODDS 1:1509, ANCO 1:1795
*GREEN JETER: SAME VALUE AS BLUE INK
D.JETER BLUE SER.1 ODDS 1:1928
D.JETER GREEN SER.2 ODDS 1:1928
SKIP-NUMBERED SET
CA1 Jeff Abbott 5.00 12.00
CA2 Bob Abreu 6.00 15.00
CA3 Willie Adams 3.00 8.00
CA4 Brian Banks 3.00 8.00
CA5 Kris Benson 5.00 12.00
CA6 Darin Blood 3.00 8.00
CA7 Jaime Bluma 3.00 8.00
CA8 Kevin L. Brown 3.00 8.00
CA9 Ray Brown 3.00 8.00
CA10 Homer Bush 3.00 8.00
CA11 Mike Cameron 3.00 8.00
CA12 Jay Canizaro 3.00 8.00
CA13 Luis Castillo 5.00 12.00
CA14 Dave Coggin 5.00 12.00
CA15 Bartolo Colon 3.00 8.00
CA16 Rocky Coppinger 3.00 8.00
CA17 Jacob Cruz 3.00 8.00
CA18 Jose Cruz Jr. 3.00 8.00
CA19 Jeff D'Amico 3.00 8.00
CA20 Ben Davis 3.00 8.00
CA21 Mike Drumright 3.00 8.00
CA22 Scott Elarton 3.00 8.00
CA23 Darin Erstad 5.00 12.00
CA24 Bobby Estalella 3.00 8.00
CA25 Joe Fontenot 3.00 8.00
CA26 Tom Fordham 3.00 8.00
CA27 Brad Fullmer 3.00 8.00
CA28 Chris Fussell 3.00 8.00
CA29 Karim Garcia 3.00 8.00
CA30 Kris Detmers 3.00 8.00
CA31 Todd Greene 3.00 8.00
CA32 Ben Grieve 3.00 8.00
CA33 Vladimir Guerrero 15.00 40.00
CA34 Jose Guillen 5.00 12.00
CA36 Wes Helms 3.00 8.00
CA37 Chad Hermansen 3.00 8.00
CA38 Richard Hidalgo 5.00 12.00
CA39 Todd Hollandsworth 3.00 8.00
CA40 Damian Jackson 3.00 8.00
CA41 Derek Jeter 125.00 300.00
CA42 Andruw Jones 5.00 12.00
CA43 Brooks Kieschnick 3.00 8.00
CA44 Eugene Kingsale 3.00 8.00
CA45 Paul Konerko 8.00 20.00
CA46 Marc Kroon 5.00 12.00
CA47 Derrek Lee 6.00 15.00
CA48 Travis Lee 3.00 8.00
CA49 Terrence Long 3.00 8.00
CA50 Curt Lyons 5.00 12.00
CA51 Eli Marrero 3.00 8.00
CA52 Rafael Medina 3.00 8.00
CA53 Juan Melo 3.00 8.00
CA54 Shane Monahan 3.00 8.00
CA55 Julio Mosquera 3.00 8.00
CA56 Heath Murray 3.00 8.00
CA57 Ryan Nye 3.00 8.00
CA58 Kevin Orie 3.00 8.00
CA59 Russ Ortiz 5.00 12.00
CA60 Carl Pavano 5.00 12.00
CA61 Jay Payton 3.00 8.00
CA62 Neifi Perez 3.00 8.00
CA63 Sidney Ponson 5.00 12.00
CA64 Pokey Reese 5.00 12.00
CA65 Ray Ricken 3.00 8.00
CA66 Brad Rigby 3.00 8.00
CA67 Adam Riggs 3.00 8.00
CA68 Ruben Rivera 5.00 10.00
CA69 J.J. Johnson 3.00 8.00
CA70 Scott Rolen 6.00 15.00
CA71 Tony Saunders 3.00 8.00
CA72 Donnie Sadler 3.00 8.00
CA73 Richie Sexson 5.00 12.00
CA74 Scott Spiezio 3.00 8.00
CA75 Everett Stull 3.00 8.00
CA76 Mike Sweeney 5.00 12.00
CA77 Fernando Tatis 5.00 12.00
CA78 Miguel Tejada 6.00 15.00
CA79 Justin Thompson 3.00 8.00
CA80 Justin Towle 3.00 8.00
CA81 Billy Wagner 5.00 12.00
CA82 Todd Walker 5.00 12.00
CA83 Luke Wilcox 3.00 8.00
CA84 Paul Wilder 3.00 8.00
CA85 Enrique Wilson 3.00 8.00
CA86 Kerry Wood 10.00 25.00
CA87 Jamey Wright 3.00 8.00
CA88 Ron Wright 5.00 10.00
CA89 Dmitri Young 4.00 10.00
CA90 Nelson Figueroa 3.00 8.00

1997 Bowman International Best

Randomly inserted in series two packs at the rate of one in 12, this 20-card set features color photos of both prospects and veterans from far and wide who have made an impact on the game.

COMPLETE SET (20) 20.00 50.00
SER.2 STATED ODDS 1:12
*ATOMIC: 1.5X TO 4X BASIC INT.BEST
ATOMIC SER.2 STATED ODDS 1:96
*REFRACTORS: .75X TO 2X BASIC INT.BEST
REFRACTOR SER.2 STATED ODDS 1:48
BBI1 Frank Thomas 1.25 3.00
BBI2 Ken Griffey Jr. 2.50 6.00
BBI3 Juan Gonzalez .50 1.25
BBI4 Bernie Williams .75 2.00
BBI5 Hideo Nomo 1.25 3.00
BBI6 Sammy Sosa 1.25 3.00
BBI7 Larry Walker .50 1.25
BBI8 Vinny Castilla .50 1.25
BBI9 Mariano Rivera 1.25 3.00
BBI10 Rafael Palmeiro .75 2.00
BBI11 Nomar Garciaparra 2.00 5.00
BBI12 Todd Walker .50 1.25
BBI13 Andruw Jones .75 2.00
BBI14 Vladimir Guerrero 1.25 3.00
BBI15 Ruben Rivera .50 1.25
BBI16 Bob Abreu .75 2.00
BBI17 Karim Garcia .50 1.25
BBI18 Katsuhiro Maeda .50 1.25
BBI19 Jose Cruz Jr. .50 1.25
BBI20 Damian Moss .50 1.25

1997 Bowman Scout's Honor Roll

Randomly inserted in first series packs at a rate of one in 12, this 15-card set features color photos of top prospects and rookies printed on double-etched foil cards.

COMPLETE SET (15) 10.00 25.00
SER.1 STATED ODDS 1:12
1 Dmitri Young .30 .75
2 Bob Abreu .50 1.25
3 Vladimir Guerrero .75 2.00
4 Paul Konerko .50 1.25
5 Kevin Orie .30 .75
6 Todd Walker .30 .75
7 Ben Grieve .30 .75
8 Darin Erstad .30 .75
9 Derrek Lee .50 1.25
10 Jose Cruz Jr. .30 .75
11 Scott Rolen .50 1.25
12 Travis Lee .30 .75
13 Andruw Jones .50 1.25
14 Wilton Guerrero .30 .75
15 Nomar Garciaparra 1.25 3.00

1998 Bowman Previews

Randomly inserted in Stadium Club first series hobby and retail packs at the rate of one in 12 and first series Home Team Advantage packs at a rate of one in four, this 10-card set is a sneak preview of the Bowman series and features color photos of top players. The cards are numbered with a BP prefix on the backs.

COMPLETE SET (10) 10.00 25.00
SER.1 STATED ODDS 1:12 H/R, 1:4 HTA
BP1 Nomar Garciaparra 1.50 4.00
BP2 Scott Rolen .60 1.50
BP3 Ken Griffey Jr. 2.00 5.00
BP4 Frank Thomas 1.00 2.50
BP5 Larry Walker .40 1.00
BP6 Mike Piazza 1.50 4.00
BP7 Chipper Jones 1.00 2.50
BP8 Tino Martinez .60 1.50
BP9 Mark McGwire 2.50 6.00
BP10 Barry Bonds 2.50 6.00

1998 Bowman Prospect Previews

Randomly seeded in Stadium Club second series hobby and retail packs at a rate of one in twelve and second series Home Team Advantage packs at a rate of one in four, this ten card set previewed the upcoming 1998 Bowman brand, featuring a selection of top youngsters expected to make an impact in 1998.

COMPLETE SET (10) 4.00 10.00
SER.2 STATED ODDS 1:12 H/R, 1:4 HTA
BP1 Ben Grieve .40 1.00
BP2 Brad Fullmer .40 1.00
BP3 Ryan Anderson .40 1.00
BP4 Mark Kotsay .50 1.25
BP5 Bobby Estalella .40 1.00
BP6 Juan Encarnacion .40 1.00
BP7 Todd Helton .60 1.50
BP8 Mike Lowell 2.00 5.00
BP9 A.J. Hinch .40 1.00
BP10 Richard Hidalgo .40 1.00

1998 Bowman

The complete 1998 Bowman set was distributed amongst two series with a total of 441 cards. The 10-card packs retailed for $2.50 each. Series one contains 221 cards while series two contains 220 cards. Each player's facsimile signature taken from the contract they signed with Topps is also on the left border. Players new to Bowman are marked with the new Bowman Rookie Card stamp. Notable Rookie Cards include Ryan Anderson. Jack Cust, Troy Glaus, Orlando Hernandez, Gabe Kapler, Ruben Mateo, Kevin Millwood and Magglio Ordonez. The 1991 BBM (Major Japanese Card set) cards of Shigetoshi Hasegawa, Hideki Irabu and Hideo Nomo (All of which are considered Japanese Rookie Cards) were randomly inserted into these packs.

COMPLETE SET (441) 20.00 50.00
COMPLETE SERIES 1 (221) 10.00 25.00
COMPLETE SERIES 2 (220) 10.00 25.00
91 BBM'S RANDOM INSERTS IN PACKS
1 Nomar Garciaparra .50 1.25
2 Scott Rolen .20 .50
3 Andy Pettitte .20 .50
4 Ivan Rodriguez .20 .50
5 Mark McGwire .75 2.00
6 Jason Dickson .10 .30
7 Jose Cruz Jr. .10 .30
8 Jeff Kent .10 .30
9 Mike Mussina .20 .50
10 Jason Kendall .10 .30
11 Brett Tomko .10 .30
12 Jeff King .10 .30
13 Brad Radke .10 .30
14 Robin Ventura .10 .30
15 Jeff Bagwell .20 .50
16 Greg Maddux .50 1.25
17 John Jaha .10 .30
18 Mike Piazza .50 1.25
19 Edgar Martinez .20 .50
20 David Justice .10 .30
21 Todd Hundley .10 .30
22 Tony Gwynn .40 1.00
23 Larry Walker .10 .30
24 Bernie Williams .20 .50
25 Edgar Renteria .10 .30
26 Rafael Palmeiro .20 .50
27 Tim Salmon .20 .50
28 Matt Morris .10 .30
29 Shawn Estes .10 .30
30 Vladimir Guerrero .30 .75
31 Fernando Tatis .10 .30
32 Justin Thompson .10 .30
33 Ken Griffey Jr. .60 1.50
34 Edgardo Alfonzo .10 .30
35 Mo Vaughn .10 .30
36 Marty Cordova .10 .30
37 Craig Biggio .20 .50
38 Roger Clemens .60 1.50
39 Mark Grace .20 .50
40 Ken Caminiti .10 .30
41 Tony Womack .10 .30
42 Albert Belle .10 .30
43 Tino Martinez .20 .50
44 Sandy Alomar Jr. .10 .30
45 Jeff Cirillo .10 .30
46 Jason Giambi .10 .30
47 Darin Erstad .10 .30
48 Livan Hernandez .10 .30
49 Mark Grudzielanek .10 .30
50 Sammy Sosa .30 .75
51 Curt Schilling .10 .30
52 Brian Hunter .10 .30
53 Neifi Perez .10 .30
54 Todd Walker .10 .30
55 Jose Guillen .10 .30
56 Jim Thome .20 .50
57 Tom Glavine .20 .50
58 Todd Greene .10 .30
59 Rondell White .10 .30
60 Roberto Alomar .20 .50
61 Tony Clark .10 .30
62 Vinny Castilla .10 .30
63 Barry Larkin .20 .50
64 Hideki Irabu .10 .30
65 Johnny Damon .20 .50
66 Juan Gonzalez .10 .30
67 John Olerud .10 .30
68 Gary Sheffield .10 .30
69 Raul Mondesi .10 .30
70 Chipper Jones .30 .75
71 David Ortiz 1.00 2.50
72 Warren Morris RC .15 .40
73 Alex Gonzalez .10 .30
74 Nick Bierbrodt .10 .30
75 Roy Halladay .60 1.50
76 Danny Buxbaum .10 .30
77 Adam Kennedy .10 .30
78 Jared Sandberg .10 .30
79 Michael Barrett .10 .30
80 Gil Meche .25 .60
81 Jayson Werth .10 .30
82 Abraham Nunez .10 .30
83 Ben Petrick .10 .30
84 Brett Caradonna .10 .30
85 Mike Lowell RC 1.25 3.00
86 Clayton Bruner .10 .30
87 John Curtice RC .25 .60
88 Bobby Estalella .10 .30
89 Juan Melo .10 .30
90 Arnold Gooch .10 .30
91 Kevin Millwood RC .60 1.50
92 Richie Sexson .10 .30
93 Orlando Cabrera .10 .30
94 Pat Cline .10 .30
95 Anthony Sanders .10 .30
96 Russ Johnson .10 .30
97 Ben Grieve .10 .30
98 Kevin McGlinchy .10 .30
99 Paul Wilder .10 .30
100 Russ Ortiz .10 .30
101 Ryan Jackson RC .15 .40
102 Heath Murray .10 .30
103 Brian Rose .10 .30
104 Ryan Radmanovich RC .15 .40
105 Ricky Ledee .10 .30
106 Jeff Wallace RC .15 .40
107 Ryan Minor RC .15 .40
108 Dennis Reyes .10 .30
109 James Manias .10 .30
110 Chris Carpenter .10 .30
111 Daryle Ward .10 .30
112 Vernon Wells .10 .30
113 Chad Green .10 .30
114 Mike Stoner RC .15 .40
115 Brad Fullmer .10 .30
116 Adam Eaton .10 .30
117 Jeff Liefer .10 .30
118 Corey Koskie RC .40 1.00
119 Todd Helton .20 .50
120 Jaime Jones RC .15 .40
121 Mel Rosario .10 .30
122 Geoff Goetz .10 .30
123 Adrian Beltre .10 .30
124 Jason Dellaero .10 .30
125 Gabe Kapler RC .40 1.00
126 Scott Schoeneweis .10 .30
127 Ryan Brannan .10 .30
128 Aaron Akin .10 .30
129 Ryan Anderson RC .15 .40
130 Brad Penny .10 .30
131 Bruce Chen .10 .30
132 Eli Marrero .10 .30
133 Eric Chavez .10 .30
134 Troy Glaus RC 1.50 4.00
135 Troy Cameron .10 .30
136 Brian Sikorski RC .15 .40
137 Mike Kinkade RC .15 .40
138 Braden Looper .10 .30
139 Mark Mangum .10 .30
140 Danny Peoples .10 .30
141 J.J. Davis .10 .30
142 Ben Davis .10 .30
143 Jacque Jones .10 .30
144 Derrick Gibson .10 .30
145 Bronson Arroyo .60 1.50
146 Luis De Los Santos RC .15 .40
147 Jeff Abbott .10 .30
148 Mike Cuddyer RC .60 1.50
149 Jason Romano .10 .30
150 Shane Monahan .10 .30
151 Ntema Ndungidi RC .15 .40
152 Alex Sanchez .10 .30
153 Jack Cust RC .75 2.00
154 Brent Butler .10 .30
155 Ramon Hernandez .10 .30
156 Norm Hutchins .10 .30
157 Jason Marquis .10 .30
158 Jacob Cruz .10 .30
159 Rob Burger RC .15 .40
160 Dave Coggin .10 .30
161 Preston Wilson .10 .30
162 Jason Fitzgerald RC .15 .40
163 Dan Serafini .10 .30
164 Peter Munro .10 .30
165 Trot Nixon .10 .30
166 Homer Bush .10 .30
167 Dermal Brown .10 .30
168 Chad Hermansen .10 .30
169 Julio Moreno RC .15 .40
170 John Roskos RC .15 .40
171 Grant Roberts .10 .30
172 Ken Cloude .10 .30
173 Jason Brester .10 .30
174 Jason Conti .10 .30
175 Jon Garland .10 .30
176 Robbie Bell .10 .30
177 Nathan Haynes .10 .30
178 Ramon Ortiz RC .25 .60
179 Shannon Stewart .10 .30
180 Pablo Ortega .10 .30
181 Jimmy Rollins RC 2.00 5.00
182 Sean Casey .10 .30
183 Ted Lilly RC .40 1.00
184 Chris Enochs RC .15 .40
185 Magglio Ordonez UER RC 2.00 5.00
186 Mike Drumright .10 .30
187 Aaron Boone .10 .30
188 Matt Clement .10 .30
189 Todd Dunwoody .10 .30
190 Larry Rodriguez .10 .30
191 Todd Noel .10 .30
192 Geoff Jenkins .10 .30
193 George Lombard .10 .30
194 Lance Berkman .10 .30
195 Marcus McCain .10 .30
196 Ryan McGuire .10 .30
197 Jhensy Sandoval .10 .30
198 Corey Lee .10 .30
199 Mario Valdez .10 .30
200 Robert Fick RC .25 .60
201 Donnie Sadler .10 .30
202 Marc Kroon .10 .30
203 David Miller .10 .30
204 Jarrod Washburn .10 .30
205 Miguel Tejada .30 .75
206 Raul Ibanez .10 .30
207 John Patterson .10 .30
208 Calvin Pickering .10 .30
209 Felix Martinez .10 .30
210 Mark Redman .10 .30
211 Scott Elarton .10 .30
212 Jose Amado RC .15 .40
213 Kerry Wood .10 .30
214 Dante Powell .10 .30
215 Aramis Ramirez .10 .30
216 A.J. Hinch .10 .30
217 Dustin Carr RC .15 .40
218 Mark Kotsay .10 .30
219 Jason Standridge .10 .30
220 Luis Ordaz .10 .30
221 Orlando Hernandez RC .75 2.00
222 Cal Ripken 1.00 2.50
223 Paul Molitor .10 .30
224 Derek Jeter .75 2.00
225 Barry Bonds .75 2.00
226 Jim Edmonds .10 .30
227 John Smoltz .20 .50
228 Eric Karros .10 .30
229 Ray Lankford .10 .30
230 Rey Ordonez .10 .30
231 Kenny Lofton .10 .30
232 Alex Rodriguez .50 1.25
233 Dante Bichette .10 .30
234 Pedro Martinez .20 .50
235 Carlos Delgado .10 .30
236 Rod Beck .10 .30
237 Matt Williams .10 .30
238 Charles Johnson .10 .30
239 Rico Brogna .10 .30
240 Frank Thomas .30 .75
241 Paul O'Neill .20 .50
242 Jaret Wright .10 .30
243 Brant Brown .10 .30
244 Ryan Klesko .10 .30
245 Chuck Finley .10 .30
246 Derek Bell .10 .30
247 Delino DeShields .10 .30
248 Chan Ho Park .10 .30
249 Wade Boggs .20 .50
250 Jay Buhner .10 .30
251 Butch Huskey .10 .30
252 Steve Finley .10 .30
253 Will Clark .20 .50
254 John Valentin .10 .30
255 Bobby Higginson .10 .30
256 Darryl Strawberry .10 .30
257 Randy Johnson .30 .75
258 Al Martin .10 .30
259 Travis Fryman .10 .30
260 Fred McGriff .20 .50
261 Jose Valentin .10 .30
262 Andruw Jones .20 .50
263 Kenny Rogers .10 .30
264 Moises Alou .10 .30
265 Denny Neagle .10 .30
266 Ugueth Urbina .10 .30
267 Derrek Lee .20 .50
268 Ellis Burks .10 .30
269 Mariano Rivera .30 .75
270 Dean Palmer .10 .30
271 Eddie Taubensee .10 .30
272 Brady Anderson .10 .30
273 Brian Giles .10 .30
274 Quinton McCracken .10 .30
275 Henry Rodriguez .10 .30
276 Andres Galarraga .10 .30
277 Jose Canseco .20 .50
278 David Segui .10 .30
279 Bret Saberhagen .10 .30
280 Kevin Brown .20 .50
281 Chuck Knoblauch .10 .30
282 Jeromy Burnitz .10 .30
283 Jay Bell .10 .30
284 Manny Ramirez .20 .50
285 Rick Helling .10 .30
286 Francisco Cordova .10 .30
287 Bob Abreu .10 .30
288 J.T. Snow .10 .30
289 Hideo Nomo .30 .75
290 Brian Jordan .10 .30
291 Javy Lopez .10 .30
292 Travis Lee .10 .30
293 Russell Branyan .10 .30
294 Paul Konerko .10 .30
295 Masato Yoshii RC .25 .60
296 Kris Benson .10 .30
297 Juan Encarnacion .10 .30
298 Eric Milton .10 .30
299 Mike Caruso .10 .30
300 Ricardo Aramboles RC .15 .40
301 Bobby Smith .10 .30
302 Billy Koch .10 .30
303 Richard Hidalgo .10 .30
304 Justin Baughman RC .15 .40
305 Chris Gissell .10 .30
306 Donnie Bridges RC .15 .40
307 Nelson Lara RC .15 .40
308 Randy Wolf RC .25 .60
309 Jason LaRue RC .25 .60
310 Jason Gooding RC .15 .40
311 Edgard Clemente .10 .30
312 Andrew Vessel .10 .30
313 Chris Reitsma .10 .30
314 Jesus Sanchez RC .15 .40
315 Buddy Carlyle RC .15 .40
316 Randy Winn .10 .30
317 Luis Rivera RC .15 .40
318 Marcus Thames RC 1.00 2.50
319 A.J. Pierzynski .10 .30
320 Scott Randall .10 .30
321 Damian Sapp .10 .30
322 Ed Yarnall RC .15 .40
323 Luke Allen RC .15 .40
324 J.D. Smart .10 .30
325 Willie Martinez .10 .30
326 Alex Ramirez .10 .30
327 Eric DuBose RC .15 .40
328 Kevin Witt .10 .30
329 Dan McKinley RC .15 .40
330 Cliff Politte .10 .30
331 Vladimir Nunez .10 .30
332 John Halama RC .15 .40
333 Nerio Rodriguez .10 .30
334 Desi Relaford .10 .30
335 Robinson Checo .10 .30
336 John Nicholson .20 .50
337 Tom LaRosa RC .15 .40
338 Kevin Nicholson RC .15 .40
339 Javier Vazquez .10 .30
340 A.J. Zapp .10 .30
341 Tom Evans .10 .30
342 Kerry Robinson .10 .30
343 Gabe Gonzalez RC .15 .40
344 Ralph Milliard .10 .30
345 Enrique Wilson .10 .30
346 Elvin Hernandez .10 .30
347 Mike Lincoln RC .15 .40
348 Cesar King RC .15 .40
349 Cristian Guzman RC .25 .60
350 Donzell McDonald .10 .30
351 Jim Parque RC .15 .40
352 Mike Saipe RC .15 .40
353 Carlos Febles RC .25 .60
354 Dernell Stenson RC .15 .40
355 Mark Osborne RC .15 .40
356 Odalis Perez RC .60 1.50
357 Jason Dewey RC .15 .40
358 Joe Fontenot .10 .30
359 Jason Grilli RC .15 .40
360 Kevin Haverbusch RC .15 .40
361 Jay Yennaco RC .15 .40
362 Brian Buchanan .10 .30
363 John Barnes .10 .30
364 Chris Fussell .10 .30
365 Kevin Gibbs RC .15 .40
366 Joe Lawrence .10 .30
367 DaRond Stovall .10 .30
368 Brian Fuentes RC .15 .40
369 Jimmy Anderson .10 .30
370 Lariel Gonzalez RC .15 .40
371 Scott Williamson RC .15 .40
372 Milton Bradley .10 .30
373 Jason Halper RC .15 .40
374 Brent Billingsley RC .15 .40
375 Joe DePastino RC .15 .40
376 Jake Westbrook .10 .30
377 Octavio Dotel .10 .30
378 Jason Williams RC .15 .40
379 Julio Ramirez RC .15 .40
380 Seth Greisinger .10 .30
381 Mike Judd RC .15 .40
382 Ben Ford RC .15 .40
383 Tom Bennett RC .15 .40
384 Adam Butler RC .15 .40
385 Wade Miller RC .40 1.00
386 Kyle Peterson RC .15 .40
387 Tommy Peterman RC .15 .40
388 Onan Masaoka .10 .30
389 Jason Rakers RC .15 .40
390 Rafael Medina .10 .30
391 Luis Lopez RC .15 .40
392 Jeff Yoder .10 .30
393 Vance Wilson RC .15 .40
394 Fernando Seguignol RC .15 .40
395 Ron Wright .10 .30
396 Ruben Mateo RC .15 .40
397 Steve Lomasney RC .25 .60
398 Damian Jackson .10 .30
399 Mike Jerzembeck RC .15 .40
400 Luis Rivas RC .40 1.00
401 Kevin Burford RC .15 .40
402 Glenn Davis .10 .30
403 Robert Luce RC .15 .40
404 Cole Liniak .10 .30
405 Matt LeCroy RC .25 .60
406 Jeremy Giambi RC .25 .60
407 Shawn Chacon .10 .30
408 Dewayne Wise RC .15 .40
409 Steve Woodard .10 .30
410 Francisco Cordero RC .40 1.00
411 Damon Minor RC .15 .40
412 Lou Collier .10 .30
413 Justin Towle .10 .30
414 Juan LeBron .10 .30
415 Michael Coleman .10 .30
416 Felix Rodriguez .10 .30
417 Paul Ah Yat RC .15 .40
418 Kevin Barker RC .15 .40
419 Brian Meadows .10 .30
420 Darnell McDonald RC .15 .40
421 Matt Kinney RC .15 .40
422 Mike Vavrek RC .15 .40
423 Courtney Duncan RC .15 .40
424 Kevin Millar RC .60 1.50
425 Ruben Rivera .10 .30
426 Steve Shoemaker RC .15 .40
427 Dan Reichert RC .15 .40
428 Carlos Lee RC 1.25 3.00
429 Rod Barajas .40 1.00
430 Pablo Ozuna RC .25 .60
431 Todd Belitz RC .15 .40
432 Sidney Ponson .10 .30
433 Steve Carver RC .15 .40
434 Esteban Yan RC .25 .60
435 Cedrick Bowers .10 .30
436 Marlon Anderson .10 .30
437 Carl Pavano .10 .30
438 Jae Weong Seo RC .25 .60
439 Jose Taveras RC .15 .40
440 Matt Anderson RC .15 .40
441 Darron Ingram RC .15 .40
CL1 Series 1 CL 1 .10 .30
CL2 Series 1 CL 2 .10 .30
CL3 Series 2 CL 1 .10 .30
CL4 Series 2 CL 2 .10 .30
NNO S.Hasegawa '91 BBM 4.00 10.00
NNO H.Irabu '91 BBM 4.00 10.00
NNO H.Nomo '91 BBM 10.00 25.00

1998 Bowman Golden Anniversary

*STARS: 12.5X TO 30X BASIC CARDS
*ROOKIES: 10X TO 20X BASIC CARDS
SER.1 STATED ODDS 1:237
SER.2 STATED ODDS 1:194
STATED PRINT RUN 50 SERIAL #'d SETS
424 Kevin Millar 15.00 30.00

1998 Bowman International

COMPLETE SET (441) 75.00 150.00
COMPLETE SERIES 1 (221) 30.00 80.00
COMPLETE SERIES 2 (220) 30.00 80.00
*STARS: 1.25X TO 3X BASIC CARDS
*ROOKIES: .6X TO 1.5X BASIC CARDS
ONE PER PACK

1998 Bowman 1999 ROY Favorites

Randomly inserted in second series packs at a rate of one in 12, this 10-card insert features color action photography on borderless, double-etched foil cards. The players featured on these cards were among the leading early candidates for the 1999 ROY award.

COMPLETE SET (10)	8.00	20.00
SER.2 STATED ODDS 1:12		
ROY1 Adrian Beltre	.50	1.25
ROY2 Troy Glaus	1.50	4.00
ROY3 Chad Hermansen	.50	1.25
ROY4 Matt Clement	.50	1.25
ROY5 Eric Chavez	.50	1.25
ROY6 Kris Benson	.50	1.25
ROY7 Richie Sexson	.50	1.25
ROY8 Randy Wolf	1.00	2.50
ROY9 Ryan Minor	.60	1.50
ROY10 Alex Gonzalez	.50	1.25

1998 Bowman Certified Blue Autographs

Randomly inserted in first series packs at a rate of one in 149 and second series packs at a rate of one in 122.

SER.1 STATED ODDS 1:149
SER.2 STATED ODDS 1:122
*GOLD FOIL: 1.5X TO 4X BLUE AU'S
SER.1 GOLD FOIL STATED ODDS 1:2976
SER.2 GOLD FOIL STATED ODDS 1:2445
*SILVER FOIL: .75X TO 2X BLUE AU'S
SER.1 SILVER FOIL STATED ODDS 1:992
SER.2 SILVER FOIL STATED ODDS 1:815

1 Adrian Beltre	100.00	250.00
2 Brad Fullmer	4.00	10.00
3 Ricky Ledee	4.00	10.00
4 David Ortiz	15.00	40.00
5 Fernando Tatis	4.00	10.00
6 Kerry Wood	4.00	10.00
7 Mel Rosario	4.00	10.00
8 Cole Liniak	4.00	10.00
9 A.J. Hinch	4.00	10.00
10 Jhensy Sandoval	4.00	10.00
11 Jose Cruz Jr.	4.00	10.00
12 Richard Hidalgo	4.00	10.00
13 Geoff Jenkins	6.00	15.00
14 Carl Pavano	8.00	20.00
15 Richie Sexson	6.00	15.00
16 Tony Womack	4.00	10.00
17 Scott Rolen	4.00	10.00
18 Ryan Minor	4.00	10.00
19 Eli Marrero	4.00	10.00
20 Jason Marquis	6.00	15.00
21 Mike Lowell	6.00	15.00
22 Todd Helton	5.00	12.00
23 Chad Green	4.00	10.00
24 Scott Elarton	4.00	10.00
25 Russell Branyan	4.00	10.00
26 Mike Drumright	4.00	10.00
27 Ben Grieve	4.00	10.00
28 Jacque Jones	6.00	15.00
29 Jared Sandberg	4.00	10.00
30 Grant Roberts	4.00	10.00
31 Mike Stoner	4.00	10.00
32 Brian Rose	4.00	10.00
33 Randy Winn	4.00	10.00
34 Justin Towle	4.00	10.00
35 Anthony Sanders	4.00	10.00
36 Rafael Medina	4.00	10.00
37 Corey Lee	4.00	10.00
38 Mike Kinkade	4.00	10.00
39 Norm Hutchins	4.00	10.00
40 Jason Brester	4.00	10.00
41 Ben Davis	4.00	10.00
42 Nomar Garciaparra	10.00	25.00
43 Jeff Liefer	4.00	10.00
44 Eric Milton	4.00	10.00
45 Preston Wilson	6.00	15.00
46 Miguel Tejada	15.00	40.00
47 Luis Ordaz	4.00	10.00
48 Travis Lee	4.00	10.00
49 Kris Benson	6.00	15.00
50 Jacob Cruz	4.00	10.00
51 Dermal Brown	4.00	10.00
52 Marc Kroon	4.00	10.00
53 Chad Hermansen	4.00	10.00
54 Roy Halladay	40.00	100.00
55 Eric Chavez	4.00	10.00
56 Jason Conti	4.00	10.00
57 Juan Encarnacion	6.00	15.00
58 Paul Wilder	4.00	10.00
59 Aramis Ramirez	8.00	20.00
60 Cliff Politte	4.00	10.00
61 Todd Dunwoody	4.00	10.00
62 Paul Konerko	10.00	25.00
63 Shane Monahan	4.00	10.00
64 Alex Sanchez	4.00	10.00
65 Jeff Abbott	4.00	10.00
66 John Patterson	6.00	15.00
67 Peter Munro	4.00	10.00
68 Jarrod Washburn	4.00	10.00
69 Derrek Lee	10.00	25.00
70 Ramon Hernandez	4.00	10.00

1998 Bowman Minor League MVP's

Randomly inserted in second series packs at a rate of one in 12, this 11-card insert features former Minor League MVP award winners in color action photography.

COMPLETE SET (11)	10.00	25.00
SER.2 STATED ODDS 1:12		
MVP1 Jeff Bagwell	.60	1.50
MVP2 Andres Galarraga	.40	1.00
MVP3 Juan Gonzalez	.40	1.00
MVP4 Tony Gwynn	1.25	3.00
MVP5 Vladimir Guerrero	1.00	2.50
MVP6 Derek Jeter	2.50	6.00
MVP7 Andruw Jones	.60	1.50
MVP8 Tino Martinez	.60	1.50
MVP9 Manny Ramirez	.60	1.50
MVP10 Gary Sheffield	.40	1.00
MVP11 Jim Thome	.60	1.50

1998 Bowman Scout's Choice

Randomly inserted in first series packs at a rate of one in 12, this borderless 21-card set is an insert featuring leading minor league prospects.

COMPLETE SET (21)	10.00	25.00
SER.1 STATED ODDS 1:12		
SC1 Paul Konerko	.75	2.00
SC2 Richard Hidalgo	.75	2.00
SC3 Mark Kotsay	.75	2.00
SC4 Ben Grieve	.75	2.00
SC5 Chad Hermansen	.75	2.00
SC6 Matt Clement	.75	2.00
SC7 Brad Fullmer	.75	2.00
SC8 Eli Marrero	.75	2.00
SC9 Kerry Wood	1.00	2.50
SC10 Adrian Beltre	.75	2.00
SC11 Ricky Ledee	.75	2.00
SC12 Travis Lee	.75	2.00
SC13 Abraham Nunez	.75	2.00
SC14 Brian Rose	.75	2.00
SC15 Dermal Brown	.75	2.00
SC16 Juan Encarnacion	.75	2.00
SC17 Aramis Ramirez	.75	2.00
SC18 Todd Helton	1.25	3.00
SC19 Kris Benson	.75	2.00
SC20 Russell Branyan	.75	2.00
SC21 Mike Stoner	1.00	2.50

1999 Bowman

The 1999 Bowman set was issued in two series and was distributed in 10 card packs with a suggested retail price of $3.00. The 440-card set featured the newest faces and potential talent that would carry Major League Baseball into the next millennium. This set features 300 top prospects and and 140 veterans. Prospect cards are designated with a silver and blue design while the veteran cards are shown with a silver and red design. Prospects making their debut on a Bowman card each featured a "Bowman Rookie Card" stamp on front. Notable Rookie Cards include Pat Burrell, Sean Burroughs, Carl Crawford, Adam Dunn, Rafael Furcal, Tim Hudson, Nick Johnson, Austin Kearns, Corey Patterson, Wily Mo Pena, Adam Piatt and Alfonso Soriano.

COMPLETE SET (440)	20.00	50.00
COMPLETE SERIES 1 (220)	8.00	20.00
COMPLETE SERIES 2 (220)	12.50	30.00
COMMON CARD (1-440)	.10	.30
COMMON RC	.15	.40
1 Ben Grieve	.12	.30
2 Kerry Wood	.12	.30
3 Ruben Rivera	.12	.30
4 Sandy Alomar Jr.	.12	.30
5 Cal Ripken	1.00	2.50
6 Mark McGwire	.50	1.25
7 Vladimir Guerrero	.20	.50
8 Moises Alou	.12	.30
9 Jim Edmonds	.20	.50
10 Greg Maddux	.40	1.00
11 Gary Sheffield	.12	.30
12 John Valentin	.12	.30
13 Chuck Knoblauch	.12	.30
14 Tony Clark	.12	.30
15 Rusty Greer	.12	.30
16 Al Leiter	.12	.30
17 Travis Lee	.12	.30
18 Jose Cruz Jr.	.12	.30
19 Pedro Martinez	.20	.50
20 Paul O'Neill	.20	.50
21 Todd Walker	.12	.30
22 Vinny Castilla	.12	.30
23 Barry Larkin	.20	.50
24 Curt Schilling	.12	.30
25 Jason Kendall	.12	.30
26 Scott Erickson	.12	.30
27 Andres Galarraga	.20	.50
28 Jeff Shaw	.12	.30
29 John Olerud	.12	.30
30 Orlando Hernandez	.12	.30
31 Larry Walker	.20	.50
32 Andruw Jones	.12	.30
33 Jeff Cirillo	.12	.30
34 Barry Bonds	.50	1.25
35 Manny Ramirez	.30	.75
36 Mark Kotsay	.12	.30
37 Ivan Rodriguez	.20	.50
38 Jeff King	.12	.30
39 Brian Hunter	.12	.30
40 Ray Durham	.12	.30
41 Bernie Williams	.20	.50
42 Darin Erstad	.12	.30
43 Chipper Jones	.30	.75
44 Pat Hentgen	.12	.30
45 Eric Young	.12	.30
46 Jaret Wright	.12	.30
47 Juan Guzman	.12	.30
48 Jorge Posada	.20	.50
49 Bobby Higginson	.12	.30
50 Jose Guillen	.12	.30
51 Trevor Hoffman	.20	.50
52 Ken Griffey Jr.	.60	1.50
53 David Justice	.12	.30
54 Matt Williams	.12	.30
55 Eric Karros	.12	.30
56 Derek Bell	.12	.30
57 Ray Lankford	.12	.30
58 Mariano Rivera	.40	1.00
59 Brett Tomko	.12	.30
60 Mike Mussina	.20	.50
61 Kenny Lofton	.12	.30
62 Chuck Finley	.12	.30
63 Alex Gonzalez	.12	.30
64 Mark Grace	.20	.50
65 Raul Mondesi	.12	.30
66 David Cone	.12	.30
67 Brad Fullmer	.12	.30
68 Andy Benes	.12	.30
69 John Smoltz	.20	.50
70 Shane Reynolds	.12	.30
71 Bruce Chen	.12	.30
72 Adam Kennedy	.12	.30
73 Jack Cust	.12	.30
74 Matt Clement	.12	.30
75 Derrick Gibson	.12	.30
76 Darnell McDonald	.12	.30
77 Adam Everett RC	.25	.60
78 Ricardo Aramboles	.12	.30
79 Mark Quinn RC	.15	.40
80 Jason Rakers	.12	.30
81 Seth Etherton RC	.15	.40
82 Jeff Urban RC	.15	.40
83 Manny Aybar	.12	.30
84 Mike Nannini RC	.15	.40
85 Onan Masaoka	.12	.30
86 Rod Barajas	.12	.30
87 Mike Frank	.12	.30
88 Scott Randall	.12	.30
89 Justin Bowles RC	.15	.40
90 Chris Haas	.12	.30
91 Arturo McDowell RC	.15	.40
92 Matt Belisle RC	.15	.40
93 Scott Elarton	.12	.30
94 Vernon Wells	.12	.30
95 Pat Cline	.12	.30
96 Ryan Anderson	.12	.30
97 Kevin Barker	.12	.30
98 Ruben Mateo	.12	.30
99 Robert Fick	.12	.30
100-Corey Koskie	.12	.30
101 Ricky Ledee	.12	.30
102 Rick Elder RC	.15	.40
103 Jack Cressend RC	.15	.40
104 Joe Lawrence	.12	.30
105 Mike Lincoln	.12	.30
106 Kit Pellow RC	.15	.40
107 Matt Burch RC	.15	.40
108 Cole Liniak	.12	.30
109 Jason Dewey	.12	.30
110 Cesar King	.12	.30
111 Julio Ramirez	.12	.30
112 Jake Westbrook	.12	.30
113 Eric Valent RC	.15	.40
114 Roosevelt Brown RC	.15	.40
115 Choo Freeman RC	.15	.40
116 Juan Melo	.12	.30
117 Jason Grilli	.12	.30
118 Jared Sandberg	.12	.30
119 Glenn Davis	.12	.30
120 David Riske RC	.15	.40
121 Jacque Jones	.12	.30
122 Corey Lee	.12	.30
123 Michael Barrett	.12	.30
124 Lariel Gonzalez	.12	.30
125 Mitch Meluskey	.12	.30
126 F.Adrian Garcia	.12	.30
127 Tony Torcato RC	.15	.40
128 Jeff Liefer	.12	.30
129 Ntema Ndungidi	.12	.30
130 Andy Brown RC	.15	.40
131 Ryan Mills RC	.15	.40
132 Andy Abad RC	.15	.40
133 Carlos Febles	.12	.30
134 Jason Tyner RC	.15	.40
135 Mark Osborne	.12	.30
136 Phil Norton RC	.15	.40
137 Nathan Haynes	.12	.30
138 Roy Halladay	.20	.50
139 Juan Encarnacion	.12	.30
140 Brad Penny	.12	.30
141 Grant Roberts	.12	.30
142 Aramis Ramirez	.12	.30
143 Cristian Guzman	.12	.30
144 Mamon Tucker RC	.15	.40
145 Ryan Bradley	.12	.30
146 Brian Simmons	.12	.30
147 Dan Reichert	.12	.30
148 Russ Branyan	.12	.30
149 Victor Valencia RC	.15	.40
150 Scott Schoeneweis	.12	.30
151 Sean Spencer RC	.15	.40
152 Odalis Perez	.12	.30
153 Joe Fontenot	.12	.30
154 Milton Bradley	.12	.30
155 Josh McKinley RC	.15	.40
156 Terrence Long	.12	.30
157 Danny Klassen	.12	.30
158 Paul Hoover RC	.15	.40
159 Ron Belliard	.12	.30
160 Armando Rios	.12	.30
161 Ramon Hernandez	.12	.30
162 Jason Conti	.12	.30
163 Chad Hermansen	.12	.30
164 Jason Standridge	.12	.30
165 Jason Dellaero	.12	.30
166 John Curtice	.12	.30
167 Clayton Andrews RC	.15	.40
168 Jeremy Giambi	.12	.30
169 Alex Ramirez	.12	.30
170 Gabe Molina RC	.15	.40
171 Mario Encarnacion RC	.15	.40
172 Mike Zywica RC	.15	.40
173 Chip Ambres RC	.15	.40
174 Trot Nixon	.12	.30
175 Pat Burrell RC	.60	1.50
176 Jeff Yoder	.12	.30
177 Chris Jones RC	.15	.40
178 Kevin Witt	.12	.30
179 Keith Luuloa RC	.15	.40
180 Billy Koch	.12	.30
181 Damaso Marte RC	.15	.40
182 Ryan Glynn RC	.15	.40
183 Calvin Pickering	.12	.30
184 Michael Cuddyer	.12	.30
185 Nick Johnson RC	.40	1.00
186 Doug Mientkiewicz RC	.25	.60
187 Nate Cornejo RC	.15	.40
188 Octavio Dotel	.12	.30
189 Wes Helms	.12	.30
190 Nelson Lara	.12	.30
191 Chuck Abbott RC	.15	.40
192 Tony Armas Jr.	.12	.30
193 Gil Meche	.12	.30
194 Ben Petrick	.12	.30
195 Chris George RC	.15	.40
196 Scott Hunter RC	.15	.40
197 Ryan Brannan	.12	.30
198 Amaury Garcia RC	.15	.40
199 Chris Gissell	.12	.30
200 Austin Kearns RC	.60	1.50
201 Alex Gonzalez	.12	.30
202 Wade Miller	.12	.30
203 Scott Williamson	.12	.30
204 Chris Enochs	.12	.30
205 Fernando Seguignol	.12	.30
206 Marlon Anderson	.12	.30
207 Todd Sears RC	.15	.40
208 Nate Bump RC	.15	.40
209 J.M. Gold RC	.15	.40
210 Matt LeCroy	.12	.30
211 Alex Hernandez	.12	.30
212 Luis Rivera	.12	.30
213 Troy Cameron	.12	.30
214 Alex Escobar RC	.15	.40
215 Jason LaRue	.12	.30
216 Kyle Peterson	.12	.30
217 Brent Butler	.12	.30
218 Dernell Stenson	.12	.30
219 Adrian Beltre	.30	.75
220 Daryle Ward	.12	.30
221 Jim Thome	.20	.50
222 Cliff Floyd	.12	.30
223 Rickey Henderson	.30	.75
224 Garret Anderson	.12	.30
225 Ken Caminiti	.12	.30
226 Bret Boone	.12	.30
227 Jeromy Burnitz	.12	.30
228 Steve Finley	.12	.30
229 Miguel Tejada	.20	.50
230 Greg Vaughn	.12	.30
231 Jose Offerman	.12	.30
232 Andy Ashby	.12	.30
233 Albert Belle	.12	.30
234 Fernando Tatis	.12	.30
235 Todd Helton	.20	.50
236 Sean Casey	.12	.30
237 Brian Giles	.12	.30
238 Andy Pettitte	.20	.50
239 Fred McGriff	.20	.50
240 Roberto Alomar	.20	.50
241 Edgar Martinez	.20	.50
242 Lee Stevens	.12	.30
243 Shawn Green	.12	.30
244 Ryan Klesko	.12	.30
245 Sammy Sosa	.30	.75
246 Todd Hundley	.12	.30
247 Shannon Stewart	.12	.30
248 Randy Johnson	.30	.75
249 Rondell White	.12	.30
250 Mike Piazza	.30	.75
251 Craig Biggio	.20	.50
252 David Wells	.12	.30
253 Brian Jordan	.12	.30
254 Edgar Renteria	.12	.30
255 Bartolo Colon	.12	.30
256 Frank Thomas	.30	.75
257 Will Clark	.20	.50
258 Dean Palmer	.12	.30
259 Dmitri Young	.12	.30
260 Scott Rolen	.20	.50
261 Jeff Kent	.12	.30
262 Dante Bichette	.12	.30
263 Nomar Garciaparra	.20	.50
264 Tony Gwynn	.30	.75
265 Alex Rodriguez	.40	1.00
266 Jose Canseco	.20	.50
267 Jason Giambi	.12	.30
268 Jeff Bagwell	.20	.50
269 Carlos Delgado	.12	.30
270 Tom Glavine	.20	.50
271 Eric Davis	.12	.30
272 Edgardo Alfonzo	.12	.30
273 Tim Salmon	.12	.30
274 Johnny Damon	.20	.50
275 Rafael Palmeiro	.20	.50
276 Denny Neagle	.12	.30
277 Neifi Perez	.12	.30
278 Roger Clemens	.40	1.00
279 Brant Brown	.12	.30
280 Kevin Brown	.12	.30
281 Jay Bell	.12	.30
282 Jay Buhner	.12	.30
283 Matt Lawton	.12	.30
284 Robin Ventura	.12	.30
285 Juan Gonzalez	.12	.30
286 Mo Vaughn	.12	.30
287 Kevin Millwood	.12	.30
288 Tino Martinez	.12	.30
289 Justin Thompson	.12	.30
290 Derek Jeter	.75	2.00
291 Ben Davis	.12	.30
292 Mike Lowell	.12	.30
293 Calvin Murray	.12	.30
294 Micah Bowie RC	.15	.40
295 Lance Berkman	.20	.50
296 Jason Marquis	.12	.30
297 Chad Green	.12	.30
298 Dee Brown	.12	.30
299 Jerry Hairston Jr.	.12	.30
300 Gabe Kapler	.12	.30
301 Brent Stentz RC	.15	.40
302 Scott Mullen RC	.15	.40
303 Brandon Reed	.12	.30
304 Shea Hillenbrand RC	.25	.60
305 J.D. Closser RC	.15	.40
306 Gary Matthews Jr.	.12	.30
307 Toby Hall RC	.15	.40
308 Jason Phillips RC	.15	.40
309 Jose Macias RC	.15	.40
310 Jung Bong RC	.15	.40
311 Ramon Soler RC	.15	.40
312 Kelly Dransfeldt RC	.15	.40
313 Carlos E. Hernandez RC	.15	.40
314 Kevin Haverbusch	.12	.30
315 Aaron Myette RC	.15	.40
316 Chad Harville RC	.15	.40
317 Kyle Farnsworth RC	.15	.40
318 Gookie Dawkins RC	.15	.40
319 Willie Martinez	.12	.30
320 Carlos Lee	.12	.30
321 Carlos Pena RC	.50	1.25
322 Peter Bergeron RC	.15	.40
323 A.J. Burnett RC	.25	.60
324 Bucky Jacobsen RC	.15	.40
325 Mo Bruce RC	.15	.40
326 Reggie Taylor	.12	.30
327 Jackie Rexrode	.12	.30
328 Alvin Morrow RC	.15	.40
329 Carlos Beltran	.20	.50
330 Eric Chavez	.12	.30
331 John Patterson	.12	.30
332 Jayson Werth	.20	.50
333 Richie Sexson	.12	.30
334 Randy Wolf	.12	.30
335 Eli Marrero	.12	.30
336 Paul LoDuca	.12	.30
337 J.D Smart	.12	.30
338 Ryan Minor	.12	.30
339 Kris Benson	.12	.30
340 George Lombard	.12	.30
341 Troy Glaus	.12	.30
342 Eddie Yarnall	.12	.30
343 Kip Wells RC	.15	.40
344 C.C. Sabathia RC	1.25	3.00
345 Sean Burroughs RC	.15	.40
346 Felipe Lopez RC	.25	.60
347 Ryan Rupe RC	.15	.40
348 Orber Moreno RC	.15	.40
349 Rafael Roque RC	.15	.40
350 Alfonso Soriano RC	1.50	4.00
351 Pablo Ozuna	.12	.30
352 Corey Patterson RC	.40	1.00
353 Braden Looper	.12	.30
354 Robbie Bell	.12	.30
355 Mark Mulder RC	.50	1.25
356 Angel Pena	.12	.30
357 Kevin McGlinchy	.12	.30
358 Michael Restovich RC	.15	.40
359 Eric DuBose	.12	.30
360 Geoff Jenkins	.12	.30
361 Mark Harriger RC	.15	.40
362 Junior Herndon RC	.15	.40
363 Tim Raines Jr. RC	.15	.40
364 Rafael Furcal RC	.50	1.25
365 Marcus Giles RC	.40	1.00
366 Ted Lilly	.12	.30
367 Jorge Toca RC	.15	.40
368 David Kelton RC	.15	.40
369 Adam Dunn RC	.60	1.50
370 Guillermo Mota RC	.15	.40
371 Brett Laxton RC	.15	.40
372 Travis Harper RC	.15	.40
373 Tom Davey RC	.15	.40
374 Darren Blakely RC	.15	.40
375 Tim Hudson RC	.60	1.50
376 Jason Romano	.12	.30
377 Dan Reichert	.12	.30
378 Julio Lugo RC	.25	.60
379 Jose Garcia RC	.15	.40
380 Erubiel Durazo RC	.15	.40
381 Jose Jimenez	.12	.30
382 Chris Fussell	.12	.30
383 Steve Lomasney	.12	.30
384 Juan Pena RC	.15	.40
385 Allen Levrault RC	.15	.40
386 Juan Rivera RC	.40	1.00
387 Steve Colyer RC	.15	.40
388 Joe Nathan RC	.40	1.00
389 Ron Walker RC	.15	.40
390 Nick Bierbrodt	.12	.30
391 Luke Prokopec RC	.15	.40
392 Dave Roberts RC	.40	1.00
393 Mike Darr	.12	.30
394 Abraham Nunez RC	.15	.40
395 Giuseppe Chiaramonte RC	.15	.40
396 Jermaine Van Buren RC	.15	.40
397 Mike Kusiewicz	.12	.30
398 Matt Wise RC	.15	.40
399 Joe McEwing RC	.15	.40
400 Matt Holliday RC	.75	2.00
401 Willi Mo Pena RC	.50	1.25
402 Ruben Quevedo RC	.15	.40
403 Rob Ryan RC	.15	.40
404 Freddy Garcia RC	.40	1.00
405 Kevin Eberwein RC	.15	.40
406 Jesus Colome RC	.15	.40
407 Chris Singleton	.12	.30
408 Bubba Crosby RC	.15	.40
409 Jesus Cordero RC	.15	.40
410 Donny Leon	.12	.30
411 Goefrey Tomlinson RC	.15	.40
412 Jeff Winchester RC	.15	.40
413 Adam Piatt RC	.15	.40
414 Robert Stratton	.12	.30
415 T.J. Tucker	.12	.30
416 Ryan Langerhans RC	.25	.60
417 Anthony Shumaker RC	.15	.40
418 Matt Miller RC	.15	.40
419 Doug Clark RC	.15	.40
420 Kory DeHaan RC	.15	.40
421 David Eckstein RC	.50	1.25
422 Brian Cooper RC	.15	.40
423 Brady Clark RC	.15	.40
424 Chris Magruder RC	.15	.40
425 Bobby Seay RC	.15	.40
426 Aubrey Huff RC	.40	1.00
427 Mike Jerzembeck	.15	.40
428 Matt Blank RC	.15	.40
429 Benny Agbayani RC	.15	.40
430 Kevin Beirne RC	.15	.40
431 Josh Hamilton RC	1.25	3.00
432 Josh Girdley RC	.15	.40
433 Kyle Snyder RC	.15	.40
434 Mike Paradis RC	.15	.40
435 Jason Jennings RC	.25	.60
436 David Walling RC	.15	.40
437 Omar Ortiz RC	.15	.40
438 Jay Gehrke RC	.15	.40
439 Casey Burns RC	.15	.40
440 Carl Crawford RC	.75	2.00

1999 Bowman Gold

*GOLD: 10X TO 25X BASIC
*GOLD RC: 8X TO 20X BASIC RC
SER.1 STATED ODDS 1:111
SER.2 STATED ODDS 1:59
STATED PRINT RUN 99 SERIAL #'d SETS

1999 Bowman International

*INT: 1X TO 2.5X BASIC
*INT RC: .75X TO 2X BASIC RC
ONE PER PACK

1999 Bowman Autographs

This set contains a selection of top young prospects, all of whom participated by signing their cards in blue ink. Card rarity is differentiated by either a blue, silver or gold foil Topps Certified Autograph Issue Stamp. The insert rates for Blue are at a rate of one in 162; Silver one in 485 and Gold one in 1,194.

BLUE FOIL SER.1 ODDS 1:162
BLUE FOIL SER.2 ODDS 1:85
SILVER FOIL SER.1 ODDS 1:485
SILVER FOIL SER.2 ODDS 1:256
GOLD FOIL SER.1 ODDS 1:1941
GOLD FOIL SER.2 ODDS 1:1024

BA1 Ruben Mateo B	4.00	10.00
BA2 Troy Glaus G	6.00	15.00
BA3 Ben Davis G	6.00	15.00
BA4 Jayson Werth B	6.00	15.00
BA5 Jerry Hairston Jr. S	4.00	10.00
BA6 Darnell McDonald B	4.00	10.00
BA7 Calvin Pickering S	6.00	15.00
BA8 Ryan Minor S	6.00	15.00
BA9 Alex Escobar B	4.00	10.00
BA10 Grant Roberts B	4.00	10.00
BA11 Carlos Guillen B	6.00	15.00
BA12 Ryan Anderson S	6.00	15.00
BA13 Gil Meche S	6.00	15.00
BA14 Russell Branyan S	6.00	15.00
BA15 Alex Ramirez S	6.00	15.00
BA16 Jason Rakers S	6.00	15.00
BA17 Eddie Yarnall B	4.00	10.00
BA18 Freddy Garcia B	4.00	10.00
BA19 Jason Conti B	4.00	10.00
BA20 Corey Koskie B	6.00	15.00
BA21 Roosevelt Brown B	4.00	10.00
BA22 Willie Martinez B	4.00	10.00
BA23 Mike Jerzembeck B	4.00	10.00
BA24 Lariel Gonzalez B	4.00	10.00
BA25 Fernando Seguignol B	6.00	15.00
BA26 Robert Fick S	6.00	15.00
BA27 J.D. Smart B	4.00	10.00
BA28 Ryan Mills B	4.00	10.00
BA29 Chad Hermansen G	6.00	15.00
BA30 Jason Grilli B	4.00	10.00
BA31 Michael Cuddyer B	6.00	15.00
BA32 Jacque Jones S	10.00	25.00
BA33 Reggie Taylor B	4.00	10.00
BA34 Richie Sexson G	6.00	15.00
BA35 Michael Barrett B	4.00	10.00
BA36 Paul LoDuca B	6.00	15.00
BA37 Adrian Beltre G	15.00	40.00
BA38 Peter Bergeron B	4.00	10.00
BA39 Joe Fontenot B	4.00	10.00
BA40 Randy Wolf B	6.00	15.00
BA41 Nick Johnson B	4.00	10.00
BA42 Ryan Bradley B	4.00	10.00
BA43 Mike Lowell S	4.00	10.00
BA44 Ricky Ledee G	4.00	10.00
BA45 Mike Lincoln S	6.00	15.00
BA46 Jeremy Giambi B	4.00	10.00
BA47 Dermal Brown S	6.00	15.00
BA48 Derrick Gibson B	4.00	10.00
BA49 Scott Randall B	4.00	10.00
BA50 Ben Petrick S	6.00	15.00
BA51 Jason LaRue B	6.00	15.00
BA52 Cole Liniak B	4.00	10.00
BA53 John Curtice B	4.00	10.00
BA54 Jackie Rexrode B	4.00	10.00
BA55 John Patterson B	6.00	15.00

BA56 Brad Penny S 10.00 25.00
BA57 Jared Sandberg B 6.00 15.00
BA58 Kerry Wood G 10.00 25.00
BA59 Eli Marrero S 6.00 15.00
BA60 Jason Marquis B 6.00 15.00
BA61 George Lombard S 6.00 15.00
BA62 Bruce Chen S 6.00 15.00
BA63 Kevin Witt S 6.00 15.00
BA64 Vernon Wells B 6.00 15.00
BA65 Billy Koch B 6.00 15.00
BA66 Roy Halladay G 20.00 50.00
BA67 Nathan Haynes B 4.00 10.00
BA68 Ben Grieve G 4.00 10.00
BA69 Eric Chavez G 4.00 10.00
BA70 Lance Berkman S 15.00 40.00

1999 Bowman 2000 ROY Favorites

Randomly inserted in second series packs at a rate of one in twelve, this 10-card insert set features borderless, double-etched foil cards and feature players that had serious potential to win the 2000 Rookie of the Year award.

COMPLETE SET (10) 2.50 6.00
SER.2 STATED ODDS 1:12
ROY1 Ryan Anderson .20 .50
ROY2 Pat Burrell .75 2.00
ROY3 A.J. Burnett .30 .75
ROY4 Ruben Mateo .20 .50
ROY5 Alex Escobar .20 .50
ROY6 Pablo Ozuna .20 .50
ROY7 Mark Mulder .60 1.50
ROY8 Corey Patterson .50 1.25
ROY9 George Lombard .20 .50
ROY10 Nick Johnson .50 1.25

1999 Bowman Early Risers

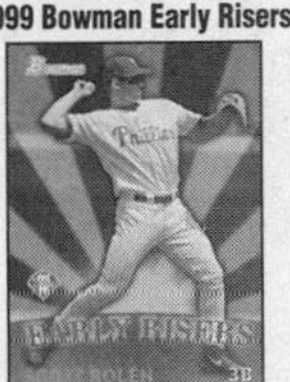

Randomly inserted in second series packs at a rate of one in twelve, this 11-card insert set features current superstars who have already won a ROY award and who continue to prove their worth on the diamond.

COMPLETE SET (11) 5.00 12.00
SER.2 STATED ODDS 1:12
ER1 Mike Piazza .60 1.50
ER2 Cal Ripken 2.00 5.00
ER3 Jeff Bagwell .40 1.00
ER4 Ben Grieve .25 .60
ER5 Kerry Wood .25 .60
ER6 Mark McGwire 1.00 2.50
ER7 Nomar Garciaparra .40 1.00
ER8 Derek Jeter 1.50 4.00
ER9 Scott Rolen .40 1.00
ER10 Jose Canseco .40 1.00
ER11 Raul Mondesi .25 .60

1999 Bowman Late Bloomers

Randomly inserted in first series packs at a rate of one in twelve, this 10-card insert set features late round picks from previous drafts. Players featured include Mike Piazza and Jim Thome.

COMPLETE SET (10) 2.50 6.00
SER.1 STATED ODDS 1:12
LB1 Mike Piazza .60 1.50
LB2 Jim Thome .40 1.00
LB3 Larry Walker .40 1.00
LB4 Vinny Castilla .25 .60
LB5 Andy Pettitte .40 1.00
LB6 Jim Edmonds .40 1.00
LB7 Kenny Lofton .25 .60
LB8 John Smoltz .40 1.00
LB9 Mark Grace .40 1.00
LB10 Trevor Hoffman .40 1.00

1999 Bowman Scout's Choice

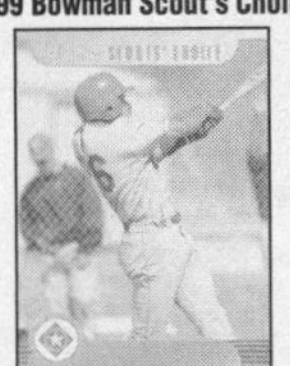

Randomly inserted in first series packs at a rate of one in twelve, this 21-card insert set features a selection of gifted prospects.

COMPLETE SET (21) 6.00 15.00
SER.1 STATED ODDS 1:12
SC1 Ruben Mateo .40 1.00
SC2 Ryan Anderson .40 1.00
SC3 Pat Burrell 1.50 4.00
SC4 Troy Glaus .40 1.00
SC5 Eric Chavez .40 1.00
SC6 Adrian Beltre 1.00 2.50
SC7 Bruce Chen .40 1.00
SC8 Carlos Beltran .60 1.50
SC9 Alex Gonzalez .40 1.00
SC10 Carlos Lee .40 1.00
SC11 George Lombard .40 1.00
SC12 Matt Clement .40 1.00
SC13 Calvin Pickering .40 1.00
SC14 Marlon Anderson .40 1.00
SC15 Chad Hermansen .40 1.00
SC16 Russell Branyan .40 1.00
SC17 Jeremy Giambi .40 1.00
SC18 Ricky Ledee .40 1.00
SC19 John Patterson .40 1.00
SC20 Roy Halladay .60 1.50
SC21 Michael Barrett .40 1.00

2000 Bowman Pre-Production

This three card set of sample cards was distributed within a sealed, clear, cello poly-wrap to dealers and hobby media several weeks prior to the national release of 2000 Bowman.

COMPLETE SET (3) 1.50 4.00
PP1 Chipper Jones 1.00 2.50
PP2 Adam Piatt .40 1.00
PP3 Josh Hamilton 1.25 3.00

2000 Bowman

The 2000 Bowman product was released in May, 2000 as a 440-card set. The set features 140 veteran players and 300 rookies and prospects. Each pack contained 10 cards and carried a suggested retail price of $3.00. Rookie Cards include Rick Asadoorian, Bobby Bradley, Kevin Mench, Nick Neugebauer, Ben Sheets and Barry Zito.

COMPLETE SET (440) 20.00 50.00
COMMON CARD (1-440) .12 .30
COMMON RC .12 .30
1 Vladimir Guerrero .20 .50
2 Chipper Jones .30 .75
3 Todd Walker .12 .30
4 Barry Larkin .20 .50
5 Bernie Williams .20 .50
6 Todd Helton .20 .50
7 Jermaine Dye .12 .30
8 Brian Giles .12 .30
9 Freddy Garcia .12 .30
10 Greg Vaughn .12 .30
11 Alex Gonzalez .12 .30
12 Luis Gonzalez .12 .30
13 Ron Belliard .12 .30
14 Ben Grieve .12 .30
15 Carlos Delgado .12 .30
16 Brian Jordan .12 .30
17 Fernando Tatis .12 .30
18 Ryan Rupe .12 .30
19 Miguel Tejada .20 .50
20 Mark Grace .20 .50
21 Kenny Lofton .12 .30
22 Eric Karros .12 .30
23 Cliff Floyd .12 .30
24 John Halama .12 .30
25 Cristian Guzman .12 .30
26 Scott Williamson .12 .30
27 Mike Lieberthal .12 .30
28 Tim Hudson .20 .50
29 Warren Morris .12 .30
30 Pedro Martinez .20 .50
31 John Smoltz .30 .75
32 Ray Durham .12 .30
33 Chad Allen .12 .30
34 Tony Clark .12 .30
35 Tino Martinez .12 .30
36 J.T. Snow .12 .30
37 Kevin Brown .12 .30
38 Bartolo Colon .12 .30
39 Rey Ordonez .12 .30
40 Jeff Bagwell .20 .50
41 Ivan Rodriguez .20 .50
42 Eric Chavez .12 .30
43 Eric Milton .12 .30
44 Jose Canseco .20 .50
45 Shawn Green .12 .30
46 Rich Aurilia .12 .30
47 Roberto Alomar .20 .50
48 Brian Daubach .12 .30
49 Magglio Ordonez .20 .50
50 Derek Jeter .75 2.00
51 Kris Benson .12 .30
52 Albert Belle .12 .30
53 Rondell White .12 .30
54 Justin Thompson .12 .30
55 Nomar Garciaparra .20 .50
56 Chuck Finley .12 .30
57 Omar Vizquel .20 .50
58 Luis Castillo .12 .30
59 Richard Hidalgo .12 .30
60 Barry Bonds .50 1.25
61 Craig Biggio .20 .50
62 Doug Glanville .12 .30
63 Gabe Kapler .12 .30
64 Johnny Damon .20 .50
65 Pokey Reese .12 .30
66 Andy Pettitte .20 .50
67 B.J. Surhoff .12 .30
68 Richie Sexson .12 .30
69 Javy Lopez .12 .30
70 Raul Mondesi .12 .30
71 Darin Erstad .12 .30
72 Kevin Millwood .12 .30
73 Ricky Ledee .12 .30
74 John Olerud .12 .30
75 Sean Casey .12 .30
76 Carlos Febles .12 .30
77 Paul O'Neill .20 .50
78 Bob Abreu .12 .30
79 Neifi Perez .12 .30
80 Tony Gwynn .30 .75
81 Russ Ortiz .12 .30
82 Matt Williams .12 .30
83 Chris Carpenter .20 .50
84 Roger Cedeno .12 .30
85 Tim Salmon .12 .30
86 Billy Koch .12 .30
87 Jeromy Burnitz .12 .30
88 Edgardo Alfonzo .12 .30
89 Jay Bell .12 .30
90 Manny Ramirez .30 .75
91 Frank Thomas .30 .75
92 Mike Mussina .20 .50
93 J.D. Drew .12 .30
94 Adrian Beltre .30 .75
95 Alex Rodriguez .40 1.00
96 Larry Walker .20 .50
97 Juan Encarnacion .12 .30
98 Mike Sweeney .12 .30
99 Rusty Greer .12 .30
100 Randy Johnson .30 .75
101 Jose Vidro .12 .30
102 Preston Wilson .12 .30
103 Greg Maddux .40 1.00
104 Jason Giambi .12 .30
105 Cal Ripken 1.00 2.50
106 Carlos Beltran .20 .50
107 Vinny Castilla .12 .30
108 Mariano Rivera .40 1.00
109 Mo Vaughn .12 .30
110 Rafael Palmeiro .20 .50
111 Shannon Stewart .12 .30
112 Mike Hampton .12 .30
113 Joe Nathan .12 .30
114 Ben Davis .12 .30
115 Andruw Jones .12 .30
116 Robin Ventura .12 .30
117 Damion Easley .12 .30
118 Jeff Cirillo .12 .30
119 Kerry Wood .12 .30
120 Scott Rolen .20 .50
121 Sammy Sosa .30 .75
122 Ken Griffey Jr. .60 1.50
123 Shane Reynolds .12 .30
124 Troy Glaus .12 .30
125 Tom Glavine .20 .50
126 Michael Barrett .12 .30
127 Al Leiter .12 .30
128 Jason Kendall .12 .30
129 Roger Clemens .40 1.00
130 Juan Gonzalez .12 .30
131 Corey Koskie .12 .30
132 Curt Schilling .20 .50
133 Mike Piazza .30 .75
134 Gary Sheffield .12 .30
135 Jim Thome .20 .50
136 Orlando Hernandez .12 .30
137 Ray Lankford .12 .30
138 Geoff Jenkins .12 .30
139 Jose Lima .12 .30
140 Mark McGwire .50 1.25
141 Adam Piatt .12 .30
142 Pat Manning RC .12 .30
143 Marcos Castillo RC .12 .30
144 Lesli Brea RC .12 .30
145 Humberto Cota RC .12 .30
146 Ben Petrick .12 .30
147 Kip Wells .12 .30
148 Wily Pena .12 .30
149 Chris Wakeland RC .12 .30
150 Brad Baker RC .12 .30
151 Robbie Morrison RC .12 .30
152 Reggie Taylor .12 .30
153 Matt Ginter RC .12 .30
154 Peter Bergeron .12 .30
155 Roosevelt Brown .12 .30
156 Matt Cepicky RC .12 .30
157 Ramon Castro .12 .30
158 Brad Baisley RC .12 .30
159 Jeff Goldbach RC .12 .30
160 Mitch Meluskey .12 .30
161 Chad Harville .12 .30
162 Brian Cooper .12 .30
163 Marcus Giles .12 .30
164 Jim Morris 1.50 4.00
165 Geoff Goetz .12 .30
166 Bobby Bradley RC .12 .30
167 Rob Bell .12 .30
168 Joe Crede .12 .30
169 Michael Restovich .12 .30
170 Quincy Foster RC .12 .30
171 Enrique Cruz RC .12 .30
172 Mark Quinn .12 .30
173 Nick Johnson .12 .30
174 Jeff Liefer .12 .30
175 Kevin Mench RC .30 .75
176 Steve Lomasney .12 .30
177 Jayson Werth .20 .50
178 Tim Drew .12 .30
179 Chip Ambres .12 .30
180 Ryan Anderson .12 .30
181 Matt Blank .12 .30
182 Giuseppe Chiaramonte .12 .30
183 Corey Myers RC .12 .30
184 Jeff Yoder .12 .30
185 Craig Dingman RC .12 .30
186 Jon Hamilton RC .12 .30
187 Toby Hall .12 .30
188 Russell Branyan .12 .30
189 Brian Falkenborg RC .12 .30
190 Aaron Harang RC .75 2.00
191 Juan Pena .12 .30
192 Travis Thompson RC .12 .30
193 Alfonso Soriano .30 .75
194 Alejandro Diaz RC .12 .30
195 Carlos Pena .20 .50
196 Kevin Nicholson .12 .30
197 Mo Bruce .12 .30
198 C.C. Sabathia .20 .50
199 Carl Crawford .20 .50
200 Rafael Furcal .20 .50
201 Andrew Beinbrink RC .12 .30
202 Jimmy Osting .12 .30
203 Aaron McNeal RC .12 .30
204 Brett Laxton .12 .30
205 Chris George .12 .30
206 Felipe Lopez .12 .30
207 Ben Sheets RC .30 .75
208 Mike Meyers RC .20 .50
209 Jason Conti .12 .30
210 Milton Bradley .12 .30
211 Chris Mears RC .12 .30
212 Carlos Hernandez RC .12 .30
213 Jason Romano .12 .30
214 Geofrey Tomlinson .12 .30
215 Jimmy Rollins .20 .50
216 Pablo Ozuna .12 .30
217 Steve Cox .12 .30
218 Terrence Long .12 .30
219 Jeff DaVanon RC .12 .30
220 Rick Ankiel .20 .50
221 Jason Standridge .12 .30
222 Tony Armas Jr. .12 .30
223 Jason Tyner .12 .30
224 Ramon Ortiz .12 .30
225 Daryle Ward .12 .30
226 Enger Veras RC .12 .30
227 Chris Jones .12 .30
228 Eric Cammack RC .12 .30
229 Ruben Mateo .12 .30
230 Ken Harvey RC .12 .30
231 Jake Westbrook .12 .30
232 Rob Purvis RC .12 .30
233 Choo Freeman .12 .30
234 Aramis Ramirez .12 .30
235 A.J. Burnett .12 .30
236 Kevin Barker .12 .30
237 Chance Caple RC .12 .30
238 Jarrod Washburn .12 .30
239 Lance Berkman .20 .50
240 Michael Wenner RC .12 .30
241 Alex Sanchez .12 .30
242 Pat Daneker .12 .30
243 Grant Roberts .12 .30
244 Mark Ellis RC .20 .50
245 Donny Leon .12 .30
246 David Eckstein .12 .30
247 Dicky Gonzalez RC .12 .30
248 John Patterson .12 .30
249 Chad Green .12 .30
250 Scot Shields RC .12 .30
251 Troy Cameron .12 .30
252 Jose Molina .12 .30
253 Rob Pugmire RC .12 .30
254 Rick Elder .12 .30
255 Sean Burroughs .12 .30
256 Josh Kalinowski RC .12 .30
257 Matt LeCroy .12 .30
258 Alex Graman RC .12 .30
259 Tomo Ohka RC .12 .30
260 Brady Clark .12 .30
261 Rico Washington RC .12 .30
262 Gary Matthews Jr. .12 .30
263 Matt Wise .12 .30
264 Keith Reed RC .12 .30
265 Santiago Ramirez RC .12 .30
266 Ben Broussard RC .20 .50
267 Ryan Langerhans .12 .30
268 Juan Rivera .12 .30
269 Shawn Gallagher .12 .30
270 Jorge Toca .12 .30
271 Brad Lidge .12 .30
272 Leoncio Estrella RC .12 .30
273 Ruben Quevedo .12 .30
274 Jack Cust .12 .30
275 T.J. Tucker .12 .30
276 Mike Colangelo .12 .30
277 Brian Schneider .12 .30
278 Calvin Murray .12 .30
279 Josh Girdley .12 .30
280 Mike Paradis .12 .30
281 Chad Hermansen .12 .30
282 Ty Howington RC .12 .30
283 Aaron Myette .12 .30
284 D'Angelo Jimenez .12 .30
285 Dernell Stenson .12 .30
286 Jerry Hairston Jr. .12 .30
287 Gary Majewski RC .12 .30
288 Derrin Ebert .12 .30
289 Steve Fish RC .12 .30
290 Carlos E. Hernandez .12 .30
291 Allen Levrault .12 .30
292 Sean McNally RC .12 .30
293 Randey Dorame RC .12 .30
294 Wes Anderson RC .12 .30
295 B.J. Ryan .12 .30
296 Alan Webb RC .12 .30
297 Brandon Inge RC .75 2.00
298 David Walling .12 .30
299 Sun Woo Kim RC .12 .30
300 Pat Burrell .12 .30
301 Rick Guttormson RC .12 .30
302 Gil Meche .12 .30
303 Carlos Zambrano RC .75 2.00
304 Eric Byrnes UER RC .12 .30
305 Robb Quinlan RC .12 .30
306 Jackie Rexrode .12 .30
307 Nate Bump .12 .30
308 Sean DePaula RC .12 .30
309 Matt Riley .12 .30
310 Ryan Minor .12 .30
311 J.J. Davis .12 .30
312 Randy Wolf .12 .30
313 Jason Jennings .12 .30
314 Scott Seabol RC .12 .30
315 Doug Davis .12 .30
316 Todd Moser RC .12 .30
317 Rob Ryan .12 .30
318 Bubba Crosby .12 .30
319 Lyle Overbay RC .20 .50
320 Mario Encarnacion .12 .30
321 Francisco Rodriguez RC .75 2.00
322 Michael Cuddyer .12 .30
323 Ed Yarnall .12 .30
324 Cesar Saba RC .12 .30
325 Gookie Dawkins .12 .30
326 Alex Escobar .12 .30
327 Julio Zuleta RC .12 .30
328 Josh Hamilton .40 1.00
329 Nick Neugebauer RC .12 .30
330 Matt Belisle .12 .30
331 Kurt Ainsworth RC .12 .30
332 Tim Raines Jr. .12 .30
333 Eric Munson .12 .30
334 Donzell McDonald .12 .30
335 Larry Bigbie RC .12 .30
336 Matt Watson RC .12 .30
337 Aubrey Huff .12 .30
338 Julio Ramirez .12 .30
339 Jason Grabowski RC .12 .30
340 Jon Garland .12 .30
341 Austin Kearns .12 .30
342 Josh Pressley RC .12 .30
343 Miguel Olivo RC .20 .50
344 Julio Lugo .12 .30
345 Roberto Vaz .12 .30
346 Ramon Soler .12 .30
347 Brandon Phillips RC .50 1.25
348 Vince Faison RC .12 .30
349 Mike Venafro .12 .30
350 Rick Asadoorian RC .12 .30
351 B.J. Garbe RC .12 .30
352 Dan Reichert .12 .30
353 Jason Stumm RC .12 .30
354 Ruben Salazar RC .12 .30
355 Francisco Cordero .12 .30
356 Juan Guzman RC .12 .30
357 Mike Bacsik RC .12 .30
358 Jared Sandberg .12 .30
359 Rod Barajas .12 .30
360 Junior Brignac RC .12 .30
361 J.M. Gold .12 .30
362 Octavio Dotel .12 .30
363 David Kelton .12 .30
364 Scott Morgan .12 .30
365 Wascar Serrano RC .12 .30
366 Wilton Veras .12 .30
367 Eugene Kingsale .12 .30
368 Ted Lilly .12 .30
369 George Lombard .12 .30
370 Chris Haas .12 .30
371 Wilton Pena RC .12 .30
372 Vernon Wells .12 .30
373 Jason Royer RC .12 .30
374 Jeff Heaverlo RC .12 .30
375 Calvin Pickering .12 .30
376 Mike Lamb RC .12 .30
377 Kyle Snyder .12 .30
378 Javier Cardona RC .12 .30
379 Aaron Rowand RC .60 1.50
380 Dee Brown .12 .30
381 Brett Myers RC .40 1.00
382 Abraham Nunez .12 .30
383 Eric Valent .12 .30
384 Jody Gerut RC .12 .30
385 Adam Dunn .20 .50
386 Jay Gehrke .12 .30
387 Omar Ortiz .12 .30
388 Darnell McDonald .12 .30
389 Tony Schrager RC .12 .30
390 J.D. Closser .12 .30
391 Ben Christensen RC .12 .30
392 Adam Kennedy .12 .30
393 Nick Green RC .12 .30
394 Ramon Hernandez .12 .30
395 Roy Oswalt RC 2.00 5.00
396 Andy Tracy RC .12 .30
397 Eric Gagne .12 .30
398 Michael Tejera RC .12 .30
399 Adam Everett .12 .30
400 Corey Patterson .12 .30
401 Gary Knotts RC .12 .30
402 Ryan Christianson RC .12 .30
403 Eric Ireland RC .12 .30
404 Andrew Good RC .12 .30
405 Brad Penny .12 .30
406 Jason LaRue .12 .30
407 Kit Pellow .12 .30
408 Kevin Beirne .12 .30
409 Kelly Dransfeldt .12 .30
410 Jason Grilli .12 .30
411 Scott Downs RC .12 .30
412 Jesus Colome .12 .30
413 John Sneed RC .12 .30
414 Tony McKnight .12 .30
415 Luis Rivera .12 .30
416 Adam Eaton .12 .30
417 Mike MacDougal RC .20 .50
418 Mike Nannini .12 .30
419 Barry Zito RC 1.00 2.50
420 DeWayne Wise .12 .30
421 Jason Dellaero .12 .30
422 Chad Moeller .12 .30
423 Jason Marquis .12 .30
424 Tim Redding RC .20 .50
425 Mark Mulder .12 .30
426 Josh Paul .12 .30
427 Chris Enochs .12 .30
428 Wilfredo Rodriguez RC .12 .30
429 Kevin Witt .12 .30
430 Scott Sobkowiak RC .12 .30
431 McKay Christensen .12 .30
432 Jung Bong .12 .30
433 Keith Evans RC .12 .30
434 Garry Maddox Jr. RC .12 .30
435 Ramon Santiago RC .12 .30
436 Alex Cora .20 .50
437 Carlos Lee .12 .30
438 Jason Repko RC .12 .30
439 Matt Burch .12 .30
440 Shawn Sonnier RC .12 .30

2000 Bowman Gold

*GOLD: 10X TO 25X BASIC
STATED ODDS 1:64 HOB/RET, 1:31 HTC
STATED PRINT RUN 99 SERIAL #'d SETS

2000 Bowman Retro/Future

COMPLETE SET (440) 75.00 200.00
*RETRO: 1X TO 2.5X BASIC
ONE PER PACK

2000 Bowman Autographs

Randomly inserted into packs, this 40-card insert features autographed cards from young players like Corey Patterson, Ruben Mateo, and Alfonso Soriano. Please note that this is a three tiered autographed set. Cards that are marked with a "B" are part of the Blue Tier (1:144 HOB/RET, 1:69 HTC). Cards marked with an "S" are part of the Silver Tier (1:312 HOB/RET, 1:148 HTC), and cards marked with a "G" are part of the Gold Tier (1:1604 HOB/RET, 1:762 HTC).

BLUE ODDS 1:144 HOB/RET, 1:69 HTC
BLUE: ONE CHIP-TOPPER PER HTC BOX
SILVER ODDS 1:312 HOB/RET, 1:148 HTC
GOLD ODDS 1:1604 HOB/RET, 1:762 HTC
AD Adam Dunn B 3.00 8.00
AH Aubrey Huff B 2.00 5.00
AK Austin Kearns B 2.00 5.00
AP Adam Piatt S 2.50 6.00
AS Alfonso Soriano S 6.00 15.00
BP Ben Petrick G 3.00 8.00
BS Ben Sheets B 5.00 12.00
BWP Brad Penny B 2.00 5.00
CA Chip Ambres B 2.00 5.00
CB Carlos Beltran G 20.00 50.00
CF Choo Freeman B 2.00 5.00
CP Corey Patterson S 2.50 6.00
DB Dee Brown S 2.50 6.00
DK David Kelton B 2.00 5.00
EV Eric Valent B 2.00 5.00
EY Ed Yarnall S 2.50 6.00
JC Jack Cust S 2.50 6.00
JDC J.D. Closser B 2.00 5.00
JDD J.D. Drew G 3.00 8.00
JJ Jason Jennings B 2.00 5.00
JR Jason Romano B 2.00 5.00
JV Jose Vidro S 2.50 6.00
JZ Julio Zuleta B 2.00 5.00
KJW Kevin Witt S 2.50 6.00
KLW Kerry Wood S 2.50 6.00
LB Lance Berkman S 4.00 10.00
MC Michael Cuddyer S 2.50 6.00
MJR Mike Restovich B 2.00 5.00
MM Mike Meyers B 3.00 8.00
MQ Mark Quinn S 2.50 6.00
MR Matt Riley S 2.50 6.00
NJ Nick Johnson S 2.50 6.00
RA Rick Ankiel G 5.00 12.00
RF Rafael Furcal S 4.00 10.00
RM Ruben Mateo G 3.00 8.00
SB Sean Burroughs S 2.50 6.00
SC Steve Cox B 2.00 5.00
SD Scott Downs S 2.50 6.00
SW Scott Williamson G 3.00 8.00
VW Vernon Wells G 3.00 8.00

2000 Bowman Early Indications

Randomly inserted into hobby/retail packs at one in 24, this 10-card insert features players that put up big numbers early on in their careers. Card backs carry an "E" prefix.

COMPLETE SET (10) 10.00 25.00
STATED ODDS 1:24 HOB/RET, 1:9 HTC
E1 Nomar Garciaparra .60 1.50
E2 Cal Ripken 3.00 8.00
E3 Derek Jeter 2.50 6.00
E4 Mark McGwire 1.50 4.00
E5 Alex Rodriguez 1.25 3.00
E6 Chipper Jones 1.00 2.50
E7 Todd Helton .60 1.50
E8 Vladimir Guerrero .60 1.50
E9 Mike Piazza 1.00 2.50
E10 Jose Canseco .60 1.50

2000 Bowman Major Power

Randomly inserted into hobby/retail packs at one in 24, this 10-card insert features the major league's top sluggers. Card backs carry a "MP" prefix.

COMPLETE SET (10) 8.00 20.00
STATED ODDS 1:24 HOB/RET, 1:9 HTC
MP1 Mark McGwire 1.50 4.00
MP2 Chipper Jones 1.00 2.50
MP3 Alex Rodriguez 1.25 3.00
MP4 Sammy Sosa 1.00 2.50
MP5 Rafael Palmeiro .60 1.50
MP6 Ken Griffey Jr. 2.00 5.00
MP7 Nomar Garciaparra .60 1.50
MP8 Barry Bonds 1.50 4.00
MP9 Derek Jeter 2.50 6.00
MP10 Jeff Bagwell .60 1.50

2000 Bowman Tool Time

Randomly inserted into hobby/retail packs at one in eight, this 20-card insert set grades the major league's top prospects on their batting, power, speed, arm strength, and defensive skills. Card backs carry a "TT" prefix.

COMPLETE SET (20) 6.00 15.00
STATED ODDS 1:8 HOB/RET, 1:3 HTC
TT1 Pat Burrell .40 1.00
TT2 Aaron Rowand 2.00 5.00
TT3 Chris Wakeland .40 1.00
TT4 Ruben Mateo .40 1.00

TT5 Pat Burrell .40 1.00
TT6 Adam Piatt .40 1.00
TT7 Nick Johnson .40 1.00
TT8 Jack Cust .40 1.00
TT9 Rafael Furcal .60 1.50
TT10 Julio Ramirez .40 1.00
TT11 Gookie Dawkins .40 1.00
TT12 Corey Patterson .40 1.00
TT13 Ruben Mateo .40 1.00
TT14 Jason Dellaero .40 1.00
TT15 Sean Burroughs .40 1.00
TT16 Ryan Langerhans .40 1.00
TT17 D'Angelo Jimenez .40 1.00
TT18 Corey Patterson .40 1.00
TT19 Troy Cameron .40 1.00
TT20 Michael Cuddyer .40 1.00

2000 Bowman Draft

The 2000 Bowman Draft Picks set was released in November, 2000 as a 110-card set. Each factory set was initially distributed in a tight, clear cello wrap and contained the 110-card set plus one of 60 different autographs. Topps announced that due to the unavailability of certain players previously scheduled to sign autographs, a small quantity (less than ten percent) of autographed cards from the 2000 Topps Baseball Rookies/Traded set were be included into its 2000 Bowman Baseball Draft Picks set. Rookie Cards include Chin-Feng Chen, Adrian Gonzalez, Kazuhiro Sasaki, Grady Sizemore and Chin-Hui Tsao.

COMP.FACT.SET (111) 12.50 30.00
COMPLETE SET (110) 8.00 20.00
COMMON CARD (1-110) .12 .30
COMMON RC .12 .30
1 Pat Burrell .12 .30
2 Rafael Furcal .20 .50
3 Grant Roberts .12 .30
4 Barry Zito 1.00 2.50
5 Julio Zuleta .12 .30
6 Mark Mulder .12 .30
7 Rob Bell .12 .30
8 Adam Piatt .12 .30
9 Mike Lamb .12 .30
10 Pablo Ozuna .12 .30
11 Jason Tyner .12 .30
12 Jason Marquis .12 .30
13 Eric Munson .12 .30
14 Seth Etherton .12 .30
15 Milton Bradley .12 .30
16 Nick Green .12 .30
17 Chin-Feng Chen RC .40 1.00
18 Matt Boone RC .12 .30
19 Kevin Gregg RC .12 .30
20 Eddy Garabito RC .12 .30
21 Aaron Capista RC .12 .30
22 Esteban German RC .12 .30
23 Derek Thompson RC .12 .30
24 Phil Merrell RC .12 .30
25 Brian O'Connor RC .12 .30
26 Yamid Haad .12 .30
27 Hector Mercado RC .12 .30
28 Jason Woolf RC .12 .30
29 Eddy Furniss RC .12 .30
30 Cha Sueng Baek RC .12 .30
31 Colby Lewis RC .30 .75
32 Pasqual Coco RC .12 .30
33 Jorge Cantu RC .20 .50
34 Erasmo Ramirez RC .12 .30
35 Bobby Kielty RC .12 .30
36 Joaquin Benoit RC .12 .30
37 Brian Esposito RC .12 .30
38 Michael Wenner .12 .30
39 Juan Rincon RC .12 .30
40 Yorvit Torrealba RC .20 .50
41 Chad Durham RC .12 .30
42 Jim Mann RC .12 .30
43 Shane Loux RC .12 .30
44 Luis Rivas .12 .30
45 Ken Chenard RC .12 .30
46 Mike Lockwood RC .12 .30
47 Yovanny Lara RC .12 .30
48 Bubba Carpenter RC .12 .30
49 Ryan Dittfurth RC .12 .30
50 John Stephens RC .12 .30
51 Pedro Feliz RC .30 .75
52 Kenny Kelly RC .12 .30
53 Neil Jenkins RC .12 .30
54 Mike Glendenning RC .12 .30
55 Bo Porter .12 .30
56 Eric Byrnes .12 .30
57 Tony Alvarez RC .12 .30
58 Kazuhiro Sasaki RC .30 .75
59 Chad Durbin RC .12 .30
60 Mike Bynum RC .12 .30
61 Travis Wilson RC .12 .30
62 Jose Leon RC .12 .30
63 Ryan Vogelsong RC 1.25 3.00
64 Geraldo Guzman RC .12 .30
65 Craig Anderson RC .12 .30
66 Carlos Silva RC .12 .30
67 Brad Thomas RC .12 .30
68 Chin-Hui Tsao RC .30 .75
69 Mark Buehrle RC 2.00 5.00
70 Juan Salas RC .12 .30
71 Denny Abreu RC .12 .30
72 Keith McDonald RC .12 .30
73 Chris Richard RC .12 .30
74 Tomas De la Rosa RC .12 .30
75 Vicente Padilla RC .30 .75
76 Justin Brunette RC .12 .30
77 Scott Linebrink RC .12 .30
78 Jeff Sparks RC .12 .30
79 Tike Redman RC .12 .30
80 John Lackey RC .75 2.00
81 Joe Strong RC .12 .30
82 Brian Tollberg RC .12 .30
83 Steve Sisco RC .12 .30
84 Chris Clapinski RC .12 .30
85 Augie Ojeda RC .12 .30
86 Adrian Gonzalez RC 4.00 10.00
87 Mike Stodolka RC .12 .30
88 Adam Johnson RC .12 .30
89 Matt Wheatland RC .12 .30
90 Corey Smith RC .12 .30
91 Rocco Baldelli RC .30 .75
92 Keith Bucktrot RC .12 .30
93 Adam Wainwright RC 1.25 3.00
94 Blaine Boyer RC .12 .30
95 Aaron Herr RC .20 .50
96 Scott Thorman RC .20 .50
97 Bryan Digby RC .12 .30
98 Josh Shortslef RC .12 .30
99 Sean Smith RC .12 .30
100 Alex Cruz RC .12 .30
101 Marc Love RC .12 .30
102 Kevin Lee RC .12 .30
103 Victor Ramos RC .12 .30
104 Jason Kaanoi RC .12 .30
105 Luis Escobar RC .12 .30
106 Tripper Johnson RC .12 .30
107 Phil Dumatrait RC .12 .30
108 Bryan Edwards RC .12 .30
109 Grady Sizemore RC 2.50 6.00
110 Thomas Mitchell RC .12 .30

2000 Bowman Draft Autographs

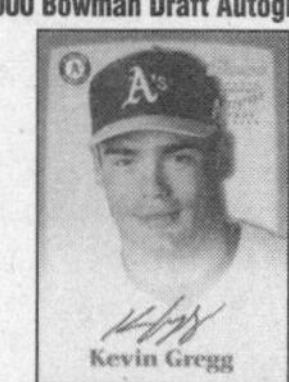

Inserted into 2000 Bowman Draft Pick sets at one per set, this 55-card insert features autographed cards of some of the hottest prospects in baseball. Card backs carry a "BDPA" prefix. Please note that cards BDPA16, BDPA32, BDPA34, BDPA45, BDPA56 do not exist.

ONE AUTOGRAPH PER FACTORY SET
CARDS 16, 32, 34, 45 AND 56 DO NOT EXIST
BDPA1 Pat Burrell 3.00 8.00
BDPA2 Rafael Furcal 5.00 12.00
BDPA3 Grant Roberts 3.00 8.00
BDPA4 Barry Zito 8.00 20.00
BDPA5 Julio Zuleta 3.00 8.00
BDPA6 Mark Mulder 3.00 8.00
BDPA7 Rob Bell 3.00 8.00
BDPA8 Adam Piatt 3.00 8.00
BDPA9 Mike Lamb 3.00 8.00
BDPA10 Pablo Ozuna 3.00 8.00
BDPA11 Jason Tyner 3.00 8.00
BDPA12 Jason Marquis 3.00 8.00
BDPA13 Eric Munson 3.00 8.00
BDPA14 Seth Etherton 3.00 8.00
BDPA15 Milton Bradley 3.00 8.00
BDPA17 Michael Wenner 3.00 8.00
BDPA18 Mike Glendenning 3.00 8.00
BDPA19 Tony Alvarez 3.00 8.00
BDPA20 Adrian Gonzalez 20.00 50.00
BDPA21 Corey Smith 3.00 8.00
BDPA22 Matt Wheatland 3.00 8.00
BDPA23 Adam Johnson 3.00 8.00
BDPA24 Mike Stodolka 3.00 8.00
BDPA25 Rocco Baldelli 8.00 20.00
BDPA26 Juan Rincon 3.00 8.00
BDPA27 Chad Durbin 3.00 8.00
BDPA28 Yorvit Torrealba 5.00 12.00
BDPA29 Nick Green 3.00 8.00
BDPA30 Derek Thompson 3.00 8.00
BDPA31 John Lackey 8.00 20.00
BDPA33 Kevin Gregg 3.00 8.00
BDPA35 Denny Abreu 3.00 8.00
BDPA36 Brian Tollberg 3.00 8.00
BDPA37 Yamid Haad 3.00 8.00
BDPA38 Grady Sizemore 12.00 30.00
BDPA39 Carlos Silva 3.00 8.00
BDPA40 Jorge Cantu 5.00 12.00
BDPA41 Bobby Kielty 3.00 8.00
BDPA42 Scott Thorman 5.00 12.00
BDPA43 Juan Salas 3.00 8.00
BDPA44 Phil Dumatrait 3.00 8.00
BDPA46 Mike Lockwood 3.00 8.00
BDPA47 Yovanny Lara 3.00 8.00
BDPA48 Tripper Johnson 3.00 8.00
BDPA49 Colby Lewis 8.00 20.00
BDPA50 Neil Jenkins 3.00 8.00
BDPA51 Keith Bucktrot 3.00 8.00
BDPA52 Eric Byrnes 3.00 8.00
BDPA53 Aaron Herr 5.00 12.00
BDPA54 Erasmo Ramirez 3.00 8.00
BDPA55 Chris Richard 3.00 8.00
BDPA57 Mike Bynum 3.00 8.00
BDPA58 Brian Esposito 3.00 8.00
BDPA59 Chris Clapinski 3.00 8.00
BDPA60 Augie Ojeda 3.00 8.00

2001 Bowman Promos

This three-card set was distributed in a sealed plastic cello wrap to dealers and hobby media a few months prior to the release of 2001 Bowman to allow a sneak preview of the upcoming brand. The promos can be readily identified from base issue cards by their PP prefixed numbering on back.

COMPLETE SET (3) 2.40 6.00
PP1 Barry Bonds .80 2.00
PP2 Roger Clemens 1.20 3.00
PP3 Adrian Gonzalez 4.00 10.00

2001 Bowman

Issued in one series, this 440 card set features a mix of 140 veteran cards along with 300 cards of young players. The cards were issued in either 10-card retail or hobby packs or 21-card hobby collector packs. The 10 card packs had an SRP of $3 while the jumbo packs had an SRP of $6. The 10 card packs were inserted 24 packs to a box and 12 boxes to a case. The 21 card packs were inserted 12 packs per box and eight boxes per case. An exchange card with a redemption deadline of May 31st, 2002, good for a signed Sean Burroughs baseball, was randomly seeded into packs at a miniscule rate of 1:30,432. Only eighty exchange cards were produced. In addition, a special card featuring game-used jersey swatches of A.L. and N.L. Rookie of the Year winners Kazuhiro Sasaki and Rafael Furcal was randomly seeded into packs at the following rates; hobby 1:2,202 and Home Team Advantage 1:1,045.

COMPLETE SET (440) 40.00 100.00
COMMON CARD (1-440) .10 .30
COMMON RC .15 .40
SASAKI/FURCAL JSY ODDS 1:2202 HOB
SASAKI/FURCAL JSY ODDS 1:1045 HTA
BURROUGHS BALL EXCH ODDS 1:30,432
1 Jason Giambi .10 .30
2 Rafael Furcal .10 .30
3 Rick Ankiel .10 .30
4 Freddy Garcia .10 .30
5 Magglio Ordonez .10 .30
6 Bernie Williams .20 .50
7 Kenny Lofton .10 .30
8 Al Leiter .10 .30
9 Albert Belle .10 .30
10 Craig Biggio .20 .50
11 Mark Mulder .10 .30
12 Carlos Delgado .10 .30
13 Darin Erstad .10 .30
14 Richie Sexson .10 .30
15 Randy Johnson .30 .75
16 Greg Maddux .50 1.25
17 Cliff Floyd .10 .30
18 Mark Buehrle .20 .50
19 Chris Singleton .10 .30
20 Orlando Hernandez .10 .30
21 Javier Vazquez .10 .30
22 Jeff Kent .10 .30
23 Jim Thome .20 .50
24 John Olerud .10 .30
25 Jason Kendall .10 .30
26 Scott Rolen .20 .50
27 Tony Gwynn .40 1.00
28 Edgardo Alfonzo .10 .30
29 Pokey Reese .10 .30
30 Todd Helton .20 .50
31 Mark Quinn .10 .30
32 Dan Tosca RC .15 .40
33 Dean Palmer .10 .30
34 Jacque Jones .10 .30
35 Ray Durham .10 .30
36 Rafael Palmeiro .20 .50
37 Carl Everett .10 .30
38 Ryan Dempster .10 .30
39 Randy Wolf .10 .30
40 Vladimir Guerrero .30 .75
41 Livan Hernandez .10 .30
42 Mo Vaughn .10 .30
43 Shannon Stewart .10 .30
44 Preston Wilson .10 .30
45 Jose Vidro .10 .30
46 Fred McGriff .20 .50
47 Kevin Brown .10 .30
48 Peter Bergeron .10 .30
49 Miguel Tejada .10 .30
50 Chipper Jones .30 .75
51 Edgar Martinez .20 .50
52 Tony Batista .10 .30
53 Jorge Posada .20 .50
54 Ricky Ledee .10 .30
55 Sammy Sosa .30 .75
56 Steve Cox .10 .30
57 Tony Armas Jr. .10 .30
58 Gary Sheffield .10 .30
59 Bartolo Colon .10 .30
60 Pat Burrell .10 .30
61 Jay Payton .10 .30
62 Sean Casey .10 .30
63 Larry Walker .10 .30
64 Mike Mussina .20 .50
65 Nomar Garciaparra .50 1.25
66 Darren Dreifort .10 .30
67 Richard Hidalgo .10 .30
68 Troy Glaus .10 .30
69 Ben Grieve .10 .30
70 Jim Edmonds .10 .30
71 Raul Mondesi .10 .30
72 Andruw Jones .20 .50
73 Luis Castillo .10 .30
74 Mike Sweeney .10 .30
75 Derek Jeter .75 2.00
76 Ruben Mateo .10 .30
77 Carlos Lee .10 .30
78 Cristian Guzman .10 .30
79 Mike Hampton .10 .30
80 J.D. Drew .10 .30
81 Matt Lawton .10 .30
82 Moises Alou .10 .30
83 Terrence Long .10 .30
84 Geoff Jenkins .10 .30
85 Manny Ramirez Sox .20 .50
86 Johnny Damon .20 .50
87 Barry Larkin .20 .50
88 Pedro Martinez .20 .50
89 Juan Gonzalez .10 .30
90 Roger Clemens .60 1.50
91 Carlos Beltran .10 .30
92 Brad Radke .10 .30
93 Orlando Cabrera .10 .30
94 Roberto Alomar .20 .50
95 Barry Bonds .75 2.00
96 Tim Hudson .10 .30
97 Tom Glavine .20 .50
98 Jeromy Burnitz .10 .30
99 Adrian Beltre .10 .30
100 Mike Piazza .50 1.25
101 Kerry Wood .10 .30
102 Steve Finley .10 .30
103 Alex Cora .10 .30
104 Bob Abreu .10 .30
105 Neifi Perez .10 .30
106 Mark Redman .10 .30
107 Paul Konerko .10 .30
108 Jermaine Dye .10 .30
109 Brian Giles .10 .30
110 Ivan Rodriguez .20 .50
111 Vinny Castilla .10 .30
112 Adam Kennedy .10 .30
113 Eric Chavez .10 .30
114 Billy Koch .10 .30
115 Shawn Green .10 .30
116 Matt Williams .10 .30
117 Greg Vaughn .10 .30
118 Gabe Kapler .10 .30
119 Jeff Cirillo .10 .30
120 Frank Thomas .30 .75
121 David Justice .10 .30
122 Cal Ripken 1.00 2.50
123 Rich Aurilia .10 .30
124 Curt Schilling .10 .30
125 Barry Zito .20 .50
126 Brian Jordan .10 .30
127 Chan Ho Park .10 .30
128 J.T. Snow .10 .30
129 Kazuhiro Sasaki .10 .30
130 Alex Rodriguez .40 1.00
131 Mariano Rivera .30 .75
132 Eric Milton .10 .30
133 Andy Pettitte .20 .50
134 Scott Elarton .10 .30
135 Ken Griffey Jr. .60 1.50
136 Bengie Molina .10 .30
137 Jeff Bagwell .20 .50
138 Kevin Millwood .10 .30
139 Tino Martinez .20 .50
140 Mark McGwire .75 2.00
141 Larry Barnes .10 .30
142 John Buck RC 1.50 4.00
143 Freddie Bynum RC .15 .40
144 Abraham Nunez .10 .30
145 Felix Diaz RC .15 .40
146 Horacio Estrada .10 .30
147 Ben Diggins .10 .30
148 Tsuyoshi Shinjo RC .40 1.00
149 Rocco Baldelli .10 .30
150 Rod Barajas .10 .30
151 Luis Terrero .10 .30
152 Milton Bradley .10 .30
153 Kurt Ainsworth .10 .30
154 Russell Branyan .10 .30
155 Ryan Anderson .10 .30
156 Mitch Jones RC .25 .60
157 Chip Ambres .10 .30
158 Steve Bennett RC .15 .40
159 Ivanon Coffie .10 .30
160 Sean Burroughs .10 .30
161 Keith Bucktrot .10 .30
162 Tony Alvarez .10 .30
163 Joaquin Benoit .10 .30
164 Rick Asadoorian .10 .30
165 Ben Broussard .10 .30
166 Ryan Madson RC .50 1.25
167 Dee Brown .10 .30
168 Sergio Contreras RC .25 .60
169 John Barnes .10 .30
170 Ben Washburn RC .15 .40
171 Erick Almonte RC .15 .40
172 Shawn Fagan RC .15 .40
173 Gary Johnson RC .15 .40
174 Brady Clark .10 .30
175 Grant Roberts .10 .30
176 Tony Torcato .10 .30
177 Ramon Castro .10 .30
178 Esteban German .10 .30
179 Joe Hamer RC .25 .60
180 Nick Neugebauer .10 .30
181 Dernell Stenson .10 .30
182 Yhency Brazoban RC .40 1.00
183 Aaron Myette .10 .30
184 Juan Sosa .10 .30
185 Brandon Inge .10 .30
186 Domingo Guante RC .15 .40
187 Adrian Brown .10 .30
188 Deivi Mendez RC .15 .40
189 Luis Matos .10 .30
190 Pedro Liriano RC .25 .60
191 Donnie Bridges .10 .30
192 Alex Cintron .10 .30
193 Jace Brewer .10 .30
194 Ron Davenport RC .25 .60
195 Jason Belcher RC .15 .40
196 Adrian Hernandez RC .15 .40
197 Bobby Kielty .10 .30
198 Reggie Griggs RC .25 .60
199 Reggie Abercrombie RC .40 1.00
200 Troy Farnsworth RC .25 .60
201 Matt Belisle .10 .30
202 Miguel Villilo RC .25 .60
203 Adam Everett .10 .30
204 John Lackey .10 .30
205 Pasqual Coco .10 .30
206 Adam Wainwright .25 .60
207 Matt White RC .25 .60
208 Chin-Feng Chen .10 .30
209 Jeff Andra RC .15 .40
210 Willie Bloomquist .20 .50
211 Wes Anderson .10 .30
212 Enrique Cruz .10 .30
213 Jerry Hairston Jr. .10 .30
214 Mike Bynum .10 .30
215 Brian Hitchcox RC .15 .40
216 Ryan Christianson .10 .30
217 J.J. Davis .10 .30
218 Jovanny Cedeno .10 .30
219 Elvin Nina .10 .30
220 Alex Graman .10 .30
221 Arturo McDowell .10 .30
222 Deivis Santos RC .15 .40
223 Jody Gerut .10 .30
224 Sun Woo Kim .10 .30
225 Jimmy Rollins .10 .30
226 Ntema Ndungidi .10 .30
227 Ruben Salazar .10 .30
228 Josh Girdley .10 .30
229 Carl Crawford .10 .30
230 Luis Montanez RC .30 .75
231 Ramon Carvajal RC .25 .60
232 Matt Riley .10 .30
233 Ben Davis .10 .30
234 Jason Grabowski .10 .30
235 Chris George .10 .30
236 Hank Blalock RC 1.00 2.50
237 Roy Oswalt .30 .75
238 Eric Reynolds RC .15 .40
239 Brian Cole .10 .30
240 Denny Bautista RC .40 1.00
241 Hector Garcia RC .15 .40
242 Joe Thurston RC .25 .60
243 Brad Cresse .10 .30
244 Corey Patterson .10 .30
245 Brett Evert RC .15 .40
246 Elpidio Guzman RC .15 .40
247 Vernon Wells .10 .30
248 Roberto Miniel RC .25 .60
249 Brian Bass RC .15 .40
250 Mark Burnett RC .25 .60
251 Juan Silvestre .10 .30
252 Pablo Ozuna .10 .30
253 Jayson Werth .10 .30
254 Russ Jacobson .10 .30
255 Chad Hermansen .10 .30
256 Travis Hafner RC 4.00 10.00
257 Brad Baker .10 .30
258 Gookie Dawkins .10 .30
259 Michael Cuddyer .10 .30
260 Mark Buehrle .20 .50
261 Ricardo Aramboles .10 .30
262 Esix Snead RC .15 .40
263 Wilson Betemit RC 1.25 3.00
264 Albert Pujols RC 20.00 50.00
265 Joe Lawrence .10 .30
266 Ramon Ortiz .10 .30
267 Ben Sheets .20 .50
268 Luke Lockwood RC .25 .60
269 Toby Hall .10 .30
270 Jack Cust .10 .30
271 Pedro Feliz .10 .30
272 Noel Devarez RC .25 .60
273 Josh Beckett .20 .50
274 Alex Escobar .10 .30
275 Doug Gredvig RC .15 .40
276 Marcus Giles .10 .30
277 Jon Rauch .10 .30
278 Brian Schmitt RC .15 .40
279 Seung Song RC .25 .60
280 Kevin Mench .10 .30
281 Adam Eaton .10 .30
282 Shawn Sonnier .10 .30
283 Andy Van Hekken RC .15 .40
284 Aaron Rowand .10 .30
285 Tony Blanco RC .25 .60
286 Ryan Kohlmeier .10 .30
287 C.C. Sabathia .10 .30
288 Bubba Crosby .10 .30
289 Josh Hamilton .25 .60
290 Dee Haynes RC .15 .40
291 Jason Marquis .10 .30
292 Julio Zuleta .10 .30
293 Carlos Hernandez .10 .30
294 Matt Lecroy .10 .30
295 Andy Beal RC .15 .40
296 Carlos Pena .10 .30
297 Reggie Taylor .10 .30
298 Bob Keppel RC .15 .40
299 Miguel Cabrera UER 2.50 6.00
300 Ryan Franklin .10 .30
301 Brandon Phillips .10 .30
302 Victor Hall RC .25 .60
303 Tony Pena Jr. .10 .30
304 Jim Journell RC .25 .60
305 Cristian Guerrero .10 .30
306 Miguel Olivo .10 .30
307 Jin Ho Cho .10 .30
308 Choo Freeman .10 .30
309 Danny Borrell RC .15 .40
310 Doug Mientkiewicz .10 .30
311 Aaron Herr .10 .30
312 Keith Ginter .10 .30
313 Felipe Lopez .10 .30
314 Jeff Goldbach .10 .30
315 Travis Harper .10 .30
316 Paul LoDuca .10 .30
317 Joe Torres .10 .30
318 Eric Byrnes .10 .30
319 George Lombard .10 .30
320 Dave Krynzel .10 .30
321 Ben Christensen .10 .30
322 Aubrey Huff .10 .30
323 Lyle Overbay .10 .30
324 Sean McGowan .10 .30
325 Jeff Heaverlo .10 .30
326 Timo Perez .10 .30
327 Octavio Martinez RC .25 .60
328 Vince Faison .10 .30
329 David Parrish RC .15 .40
330 Bobby Bradley .10 .30
331 Jason Miller RC .15 .40
332 Corey Spencer RC .15 .40
333 Craig House .10 .30
334 Maxim St. Pierre RC .25 .60
335 Adam Johnson .10 .30
336 Joe Crede .10 .30
337 Greg Nash RC .15 .40
338 Chad Durbin .10 .30
339 Pat Magness RC .25 .60
340 Matt Wheatland .10 .30
341 Julio Lugo .10 .30
342 Grady Sizemore .60 1.50
343 Adrian Gonzalez .75 2.00
344 Tim Raines Jr. .10 .30
345 Ranier Olmedo RC .25 .60
346 Phil Dumatrait .10 .30
347 Brandon Mims RC .15 .40
348 Jason Jennings .10 .30
349 Phil Wilson RC .25 .60
350 Jason Hart .10 .30
351 Cesar Izturis .10 .30
352 Matt Butler RC .25 .60
353 David Kelton .10 .30
354 Luke Prokopec .10 .30
355 Corey Smith .10 .30
356 Joel Pineiro .25 .60
357 Ken Chenard .10 .30
358 Keith Reed .10 .30
359 David Walling .10 .30
360 Alexis Gomez RC .15 .40
361 Justin Morneau RC 4.00 10.00
362 Josh Fogg RC .25 .60
363 J.R. House .10 .30
364 Andy Tracy .10 .30
365 Kenny Kelly .10 .30
366 Aaron McNeal .10 .30
367 Nick Johnson .10 .30
368 Brian Esposito .10 .30
369 Charles Frazier RC .15 .40
370 Scott Heard .10 .30
371 Pat Strange .10 .30
372 Mike Meyers .10 .30
373 Ryan Ludwick RC 3.00 8.00
374 Brad Wilkerson .10 .30
375 Allen Levrault .10 .30
376 Seth McClung RC .25 .60
377 Joe Nathan .10 .30
378 Rafael Soriano RC .25 .60
379 Chris Richard .10 .30
380 Jared Sandberg .10 .30
381 Tike Redman .10 .30
382 Adam Dunn .20 .50
383 Jared Abruzzo RC .15 .40
384 Jason Richardson RC .15 .40
385 Matt Holliday .25 .60
386 Darwin Cubillan RC .15 .40
387 Mike Nannini .10 .30
388 Blake Williams RC .15 .40
389 Valentino Pascucci RC .25 .60
390 Jon Garland .10 .30
391 Josh Pressley .15 .40
392 Jose Ortiz .10 .30
393 Ryan Hannaman RC .25 .60
394 Steve Smyth RC .25 .60
395 John Patterson .10 .30
396 Chad Petty RC .15 .40
397 Jake Peavy UER RC 1.25 3.00
398 Onix Mercado RC .25 .60
399 Jason Romano .10 .30
400 Luis Torres RC .25 .60
401 Casey Fossum RC .15 .40
402 Eduardo Figueroa RC .15 .40
403 Bryan Barnowski RC .15 .40
404 Tim Redding .10 .30
405 Jason Standridge .10 .30
406 Marvin Seale RC .25 .60
407 Todd Moser .10 .30
408 Alex Gordon .10 .30
409 Steve Smitherman RC .25 .60
410 Ben Petrick .10 .30
411 Eric Munson .10 .30
412 Luis Rivas .10 .30
413 Matt Ginter .10 .30
414 Alfonso Soriano .20 .50
415 Rafael Boitel RC .15 .40
416 Dany Morban RC .15 .40
417 Justin Woodrow RC .25 .60
418 Wilfredo Rodriguez .10 .30
419 Derrick Van Dusen RC .15 .40
420 Josh Spoerl RC .25 .60
421 Juan Pierre .10 .30
422 J.C. Romero .10 .30
423 Ed Rogers RC .15 .40
424 Tomo Ohka .10 .30
425 Ben Hendrickson RC .15 .40
426 Carlos Zambrano .20 .50
427 Brett Myers .10 .30
428 Scott Seabol .10 .30
429 Thomas Mitchell .10 .30
430 Jose Reyes RC 5.00 12.00
431 Kip Wells .10 .30
432 Donzell McDonald .10 .30
433 Adam Pettyjohn RC .15 .40
434 Austin Kearns .10 .30
435 Rico Washington .10 .30
436 Doug Nickle RC .15 .40
437 Steve Lomasney .10 .30
438 Jason Jones RC .15 .40
439 Bobby Seay .10 .30
440 Justin Wayne RC .25 .60
ROYR Sasaki/Furcal ROY Jsy 6.00 15.00
NNO Sean Burroughs Ball/80 6.00 15.00

2001 Bowman Gold

*STARS: 1.25X TO 3X BASIC CARDS
*ROOKIES: .6X TO 1.5X BASIC
ONE PER PACK
430 Jose Reyes 6.00 15.00

2001 Bowman Autographs

Inserted at a rate of one in 74 hobby packs and one in 35 HTA packs, these 40 cards feature autographs from some of the leading prospects in the Bowman set. Dustin McGowan did not return his cards in time for inclusion in the product and exchange cards with a redemption deadline of April 30th, 2003 were seeded into packs in their place.

STATED ODDS 1:74 HOBBY, 1:35 HTA
BAAE Alex Escobar 3.00 8.00
BAAG Adrian Gonzalez 10.00 25.00
BAAJ Adam Johnson 3.00 8.00
BAAP Albert Pujols 250.00 450.00
BAADP Adam Piatt 3.00 8.00
BAAJG Alex Graman 3.00 8.00
BAAKG Alex Gordon 3.00 8.00
BABB Brian Barnowski 3.00 8.00
BABD Ben Diggins 3.00 8.00
BABS Ben Sheets 3.00 8.00
BABW Brad Wilkerson 3.00 8.00
BABZ Barry Zito 5.00 12.00
BACG Cristian Guerrero 3.00 8.00
BADK Dave Krynzel 3.00 8.00
BADM Dustin McGowan 3.00 8.00
BADWK David Kelton 3.00 8.00
BAFB Freddie Bynum 3.00 8.00
BAJB Jason Botts 3.00 8.00
BAJD Jose Diaz 3.00 8.00
BAJH Josh Hamilton 6.00 15.00
BAJM Justin Morneau 3.00 8.00
BAJP Josh Pressley 3.00 8.00
BAJRH J.R. House 3.00 8.00
BAJWH Jason Hart 3.00 8.00
BAKM Kevin Mench 3.00 8.00
BALM Luis Montanez 3.00 8.00
BALO Lyle Overbay 3.00 8.00
BAMV Miguel Villilo 3.00 8.00
BAND Noel Devarez 3.00 8.00
BAPL Pedro Liriano 3.00 8.00
BARF Rafael Furcal 3.00 8.00
BARJ Russ Jacobson 3.00 8.00

BASB Sean Burroughs 3.00 8.00
BASM Sean McGowan 3.00 8.00
BASS Shawn Sonnier 3.00 8.00
BASU Sixto Urena 3.00 8.00
BASDS Steve Smyth 3.00 8.00
BATH Travis Hafner 5.00 12.00
BATJ Tripper Johnson 3.00 8.00
BAWB Wilson Betemit 5.00 12.00

2001 Bowman AutoProofs

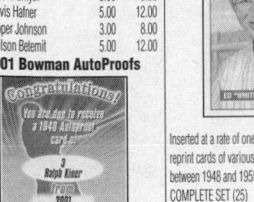

Inserted at a rate of 1 in 18,239 hobby packs and 1 in 8,306 HTA packs; these 10 cards feature players signing their actual Bowman Rookie Cards. Each player signed 25 cards for this promotion. Hank Bauer, Pat Burrell, Carlos Delgado, Chipper Jones, Ralph Kiner, Gil McDougald, and Ivan Rodriguez did not return their cards in time for inclusion in this product and exchange cards with a redemption deadline of April 30th, 2003 were seeded in to packs in their place.

2001 Bowman Futures Game Relics

Inserted at overall odds of one in 82 hobby packs and one in 39 HTA packs, these 34 cards feature relics used by the featured players in the futures game. These cards were inserted at different ratios and our checklist provides that information as to what group each insert belongs to.

GROUP A ODDS 1:293 HOB, 1:139 HTA
GROUP B ODDS 1:365 HOB, 1:174 HTA
GROUP C ODDS 1:418 HOB, 1:199 HTA
GROUP D ODDS 1:274 HOB, 1:130 HTA
OVERALL ODDS 1:82 HOBBY, 1:39 HTA
FGRAE Alex Escobar A 2.00 5.00
FGRAM Aaron Myette B 2.00 5.00
FGRBB Bobby Bradley B 2.00 5.00
FGRBP Ben Petrick C 2.00 5.00
FGRBS Ben Sheets B 2.00 5.00
FGRBW Brad Wilkerson C 2.00 5.00
FGRBZ Barry Zito B 3.00 8.00
FGRCA Craig Anderson B 2.00 5.00
FGRCC Chin-Feng Chen A 6.00 15.00
FGRCG Chris George D 2.00 5.00
FGRCH Carlos Hernandez D 2.00 5.00
FGRCP Corey Patterson A 2.00 5.00
FGRCP Carlos Pena A 2.00 5.00
FGRCT Chin-Hui Tsao D 6.00 15.00
FGREM Eric Munson A 2.00 5.00
FGRFL Felipe Lopez A 2.00 5.00
FGRGR Grant Roberts D 2.00 5.00
FGRJC Jack Cust A 2.00 5.00
FGRJH Josh Hamilton 3.00 8.00
FGRJR Jason Romano C 2.00 5.00
FGRJZ Julio Zuleta A 2.00 5.00
FGRKA Kurt Ainsworth B 2.00 5.00
FGRMB Mike Bynum D 2.00 5.00
FGRMG Marcus Giles A 2.00 5.00
FGRNN Ntema Ndungidi A 2.00 5.00
FGRRA Ryan Anderson B 2.00 5.00
FGRRC Ramon Castro C 2.00 5.00
FGRRD Randey Dorame D 2.00 5.00
FGRRO Ramon Ortiz D 2.00 5.00
FGRSK Sun Woo Kim D 2.00 5.00
FGRTD Travis Dawkins C 2.00 5.00
FGRTO Tomokazu Ohka B 2.00 5.00
FGRTW Travis Wilson A 2.00 5.00
FGRVW Vernon Wells C 2.00 5.00

2001 Bowman Multiple Game Relics

Issued at overall odds of one in 1,476 hobby packs and one in 701 HTA packs, these cards have three different pieces of memorabilia on them. These cards feature a piece of a jersey, helmet and a base fragment.

GROUP A ODDS 1:1883 HOB, 1:895 HTA
GROUP B ODDS 1:6842 HOB, 1:3230 HTA
OVERALL ODDS 1:1476 HOBBY, 1:701 HTA
MGRAE Alex Escobar B 10.00 25.00
MGRBP Ben Petrick A 10.00 25.00
MGRBW Brad Wilkerson B 10.00 25.00
MGRCC Chin-Feng Chen A 75.00 150.00
MGRCP Carlos Pena A 10.00 25.00
MGREM Eric Munson B 10.00 25.00
MGRFL Felipe Lopez A 12.00 30.00
MGRJC Jack Cust A 10.00 25.00
MGRJH Josh Hamilton 20.00 50.00
MGRJR Jason Romano A 10.00 25.00
MGRJZ Julio Zuleta A 10.00 25.00
MGRMG Marcus Giles A 12.00 30.00
MGRNN Ntema Ndungidi A 10.00 25.00
MGRRC Ramon Castro A 10.00 25.00
MGRTD Travis Dawkins A 10.00 25.00
MGRTW Travis Wilson A 10.00 25.00
MGRVW Vernon Wells A 12.50 30.00
MGRDCP Corey Patterson B 10.00 25.00

2001 Bowman Multiple Game Relics Autograph

Inserted in packs at a rate of one in 18,259 Hobby and one in 8,306 HTA packs, these five cards feature not only three pieces of memorabilia from the featured players but also included an authentic signature.

2001 Bowman Rookie Reprints

Inserted at a rate of one in 12, these 25 cards feature reprint cards of various stars who made their debut between 1948 and 1955.

COMPLETE SET (25) 25.00 60.00
STATED ODDS 1:12
1 Yogi Berra 2.00 5.00
2 Ralph Kiner 1.25 3.00
3 Stan Musial 4.00 10.00
4 Warren Spahn 1.25 3.00
5 Roy Campanella 2.00 5.00
6 Bob Lemon 1.25 3.00
7 Robin Roberts 1.25 3.00
8 Duke Snider 1.25 3.00
9 Early Wynn 1.25 3.00
10 Richie Ashburn 1.25 3.00
11 Gil Hodges 2.00 5.00
12 Hank Bauer 1.25 3.00
13 Don Newcombe 1.25 3.00
14 Al Rosen 1.25 3.00
15 Willie Mays 5.00 12.00
16 Joe Garagiola 1.25 3.00
17 Whitey Ford 1.25 3.00
18 Lew Burdette 1.25 3.00
19 Gil McDougald 1.25 3.00
20 Minnie Minoso 1.25 3.00
21 Eddie Mathews 2.00 5.00
22 Harvey Kuenn 1.25 3.00
23 Don Larsen 1.25 3.00
24 Elston Howard 1.25 3.00
25 Don Zimmer 1.25 3.00

2001 Bowman Rookie Reprints Autographs

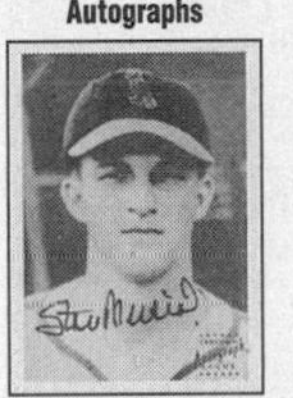

Inserted at a rate of one in 2,467 hobby packs and one in 1,162 HTA packs, these 10 cards feature the players signing their rookie reprint cards. Duke Snider did not return his card in time for inclusion in packs. His card was redeemable until April 30, 2003. Please note that card number 7 does not exist. Though the cards are serial-numbering, Topps did announce that only 100 sets were produced. Card number 7 does not exist.

1 Yogi Berra 40.00 100.00
2 Willie Mays 175.00 350.00
3 Stan Musial 75.00 150.00
4 Duke Snider 30.00 60.00
5 Warren Spahn 20.00 50.00
6 Ralph Kiner 20.00 50.00
8 Don Larsen 10.00 25.00
9 Don Zimmer 10.00 25.00
10 Minnie Minoso 10.00 25.00

2001 Bowman Rookie Reprints Relic Bat

Issued at a rate of one in 1,954 hobby packs and one in 928 HTA packs, these five cards feature not only the rookie reprint of these players but also a piece of a bat they used during their career.

STATED ODDS 1:1954 HOBBY, 1:928 HTA
1 Willie Mays 10.00 25.00
2 Duke Snider 10.00 25.00
3 Minnie Minoso 6.00 15.00
4 Hank Bauer 6.00 15.00
5 Gil McDougald 6.00 15.00

2001 Bowman Rookie Reprints Relic Bat Autographs

Issued at a rate of one in 18,259 hobby packs and one in 8,306 HTA packs, these five cards feature not only the rookie reprint of these players but also a piece of a bat they used during their career as well as an authentic autograph.

2001 Bowman Draft

Issued as a 112-card factory set with a SRP of $45.99, these sets feature 100 cards of young players along with an autograph and relic card in each box. Twelve sets were included in each case. Cards BDP51 and BDP71 featuring Alex Herrera and Brad Thomas are uncorrected errors in that the card backs were switched for each player.

COMP.FACT.SET (112) 12.00 30.00
COMPLETE SET (110) 8.00 20.00
CARDS 51 AND 71 HAVE SWITCHED BACKS
BDP1 Alfredo Amezaga RC .10 .30
BDP2 Andrew Good .10 .30
BDP3 Kelly Johnson RC 1.25 3.00
BDP4 Larry Bigbie .10 .30
BDP5 Matt Thompson RC .15 .40
BDP6 Wilton Chavez RC .15 .40
BDP7 Joe Borchard RC .15 .40
BDP8 David Espinosa .10 .30
BDP9 Zach Day RC .15 .40
BDP10 Brad Hawpe RC 1.00 2.50
BDP11 Nate Cornejo .10 .30
BDP12 Matt Cooper RC .15 .40
BDP13 Brad Lidge .10 .30
BDP14 Angel Berroa RC .25 .60
BDP15 Lamont Matthews RC .15 .40
BDP16 Jose Garcia .10 .30
BDP17 Grant Balfour RC .10 .30
BDP18 Ron Chiavacci RC .10 .30
BDP19 Jae Seo .10 .30
BDP20 Juan Rivera .10 .30
BDP21 D'Angelo Jimenez .10 .30
BDP22 Juan A.Pena RC .15 .40
BDP23 Marlon Byrd RC .15 .40
BDP24 Sean Burnett .10 .30
BDP25 Josh Pearce RC .15 .40
BDP26 Brandon Duckworth RC .10 .30
BDP27 Jack Taschner RC .10 .30
BDP28 Marcus Thames .10 .30
BDP29 Brent Abernathy .10 .30
BDP30 David Elder RC .10 .30
BDP31 Scott Cassidy RC .15 .40
BDP32 Dennis Tankersley RC .10 .30
BDP33 Denny Stark .10 .30
BDP34 Dave Williams RC .10 .30
BDP35 Boof Bonser RC .10 .30
BDP36 Kris Foster RC .10 .30
BDP37 Luis Garcia RC .15 .40
BDP38 Shawn Chacon .10 .30
BDP39 Mike Rivera RC .15 .40
BDP40 Will Smith RC .15 .40
BDP41 Morgan Ensberg RC .75 2.00
BDP42 Ken Harvey .10 .30
BDP43 Ricardo Rodriguez RC .15 .40
BDP44 Jose Mieses RC .15 .40
BDP45 Luis Maza RC .10 .30
BDP46 Julio Perez RC .15 .40
BDP47 Dustan Mohr RC .15 .40
BDP48 Randy Flores RC .10 .30
BDP49 Covelli Crisp RC 2.00 5.00
BDP50 Kevin Reese RC .15 .40
BDP51 Brad Thomas UER .10 .30
BDP52 Xavier Nady .10 .30
BDP53 Ryan Vogelsong .10 .30
BDP54 Carlos Silva .10 .30
BDP55 Dan Wright .10 .30
BDP56 Brent Butler .10 .30
BDP57 Brandon Knight RC .10 .30
BDP58 Brian Reith RC .10 .30
BDP59 Mario Valenzuela RC .15 .40
BDP60 Bobby Hill RC .15 .40
BDP61 Rich Rundles RC .15 .40
BDP62 Rick Elder .10 .30
BDP63 J.D. Closser .10 .30
BDP64 Scot Shields .10 .30
BDP65 Miguel Olivo .10 .30
BDP66 Stubby Clapp RC .10 .30
BDP67 Jerome Williams RC .25 .60
BDP68 Jason Lane RC .25 .60
BDP69 Chase Utley RC 6.00 15.00
BDP70 Erik Bedard RC 2.00 5.00
BDP71 Alex Herrera UER RC .10 .30
BDP72 Juan Cruz RC .15 .40
BDP73 Billy Martin RC .10 .30
BDP74 Ronnie Merrill RC .15 .40
BDP75 Jason Kinchen RC .10 .30
BDP76 Wilkin Ruan RC .15 .40
BDP77 Cody Ransom RC .10 .30
BDP78 Bud Smith RC .10 .30
BDP79 Wily Mo Pena .10 .30
BDP80 Jeff Nettles RC .15 .40
BDP81 Jamal Strong RC .10 .30
BDP82 Bill Ortega RC .10 .30
BDP83 Mike Bell .10 .30
BDP84 Ichiro Suzuki RC 4.00 10.00
BDP85 Fernando Rodney RC .10 .30
BDP86 Chris Smith RC .10 .30
BDP87 John VanBenschoten RC .15 .40
BDP88 Bobby Crosby RC 1.50 4.00
BDP89 Kenny Baugh RC .10 .30
BDP90 Jake Gautreau RC .10 .30
BDP91 Gabe Gross RC .25 .60
BDP92 Kris Honel RC .15 .40
BDP93 Dan Denham RC .10 .30
BDP94 Aaron Heilman RC .15 .40
BDP95 Irvin Guzman RC 1.50 4.00
BDP96 Mike Jones RC .25 .60
BDP97 John-Ford Griffin RC .15 .40
BDP98 Macay McBride RC .40 1.00
BDP99 John Rheinecker RC .40 1.00
BDP100 Bronson Sardinha RC .10 .30
BDP101 Jason Weintraub RC .10 .30
BDP102 J.D. Martin RC .10 .30
BDP103 Jayson Nix RC .15 .40
BDP104 Noah Lowry RC 1.00 2.50
BDP105 Richard Lewis RC .15 .40
BDP106 Brad Hennessey RC .25 .60
BDP107 Jeff Mathis RC .25 .60
BDP108 Jon Skaggs RC .15 .40
BDP109 Justin Pope RC .15 .40
BDP110 Josh Burrus RC .15 .40

2001 Bowman Draft Autographs

Inserted one per Bowman draft pick factory set, these 37 cards feature autographs of some of the leading players from the Bowman Draft Pick set.

ONE PER SEALED FACTORY SET
BDPAAA Alfredo Amezaga 4.00 10.00
BDPAAC Alex Cintron 4.00 10.00
BDPAAE Adam Everett 4.00 10.00
BDPAAF Alex Fernandez 4.00 10.00
BDPAAG Alexis Gomez 4.00 10.00
BDPAAH Aaron Herr 4.00 10.00
BDPAAK Austin Kearns 6.00 15.00
BDPABB Bobby Bradley 4.00 10.00
BDPABH Beau Hale 4.00 10.00
BDPABP Brandon Phillips 4.00 10.00
BDPABS Bud Smith 4.00 10.00
BDPACG Cristian Guerrero 4.00 10.00
BDPACI Cesar Izturis 4.00 10.00
BDPACP Christian Parra 4.00 10.00
BDPAER Ed Rogers 4.00 10.00
BDPAFL Felipe Lopez 4.00 10.00
BDPAGA Garrett Atkins 4.00 10.00
BDPAGJ Gary Johnson 4.00 10.00
BDPAJA Jared Abruzzo 4.00 10.00
BDPAJK Joe Kennedy 4.00 15.00
BDPAJL John Lackey 8.00 20.00
BDPAJP Joel Pineiro 6.00 15.00
BDPAJT Joe Torres 4.00 10.00
BDPANJ Nick Johnson 6.00 15.00
BDPANR Nick Regilio 4.00 10.00
BDPARC Ryan Church 6.00 15.00
BDPARD Ryan Dittfurth 4.00 10.00
BDPARL Ryan Ludwick 4.00 10.00
BDPARO Roy Oswalt 6.00 15.00
BDPASH Scott Heard 4.00 10.00
BDPASS Scott Seabol 4.00 10.00
BDPATO Tomo Ohka 6.00 15.00
BDPAANC Antoine Cameron 4.00 10.00
BDPABJS Brian Specht 4.00 10.00
BDPAJMW Justin Wayne 4.00 10.00
BDPARMM Ryan Madson 4.00 15.00
BDPAROC Ramon Carvajal 4.00 10.00

2001 Bowman Draft Futures Game Relics

Inserted one per factory set, these 26 cards feature relics from the futures game.

ONE RELIC PER FACTORY SET
FGRAA Alfredo Amezaga 2.00 5.00
FGRAD Adam Dunn 3.00 8.00
FGRAG Adrian Gonzalez 6.00 15.00
FGRAH Alex Herrera 2.00 5.00
FGRBM Brett Myers 2.00 5.00
FGRCD Cody Ransom 2.00 5.00
FGRCG Chris George 2.00 5.00
FGRCH Carlos Hernandez 2.00 5.00
FGRCU Chase Utley 8.00 20.00
FGREB Erik Bedard 2.00 5.00
FGRGB Grant Balfour 2.00 5.00
FGRHB Hank Blalock 3.00 8.00
FGRJB Joe Borchard 2.00 5.00
FGRJC Juan Cruz 2.00 5.00
FGRJP Josh Pearce 2.00 5.00
FGRJR Juan Rivera 2.00 5.00
FGRJAP Juan A.Pena 2.00 5.00
FGRLG Luis Garcia 2.00 5.00
FGRMC Miguel Cabrera 10.00 25.00
FGRMR Mike Rivera 2.00 5.00
FGRRR Ricardo Rodriguez 2.00 5.00
FGRSC Scott Chiasson 2.00 5.00
FGRSS Seung Song 2.00 5.00
FGRTB Toby Hall 2.00 5.00
FGRWB Wilson Betemit 3.00 8.00
FGRWP Wily Mo Pena 2.00 5.00

2001 Bowman Draft Relics

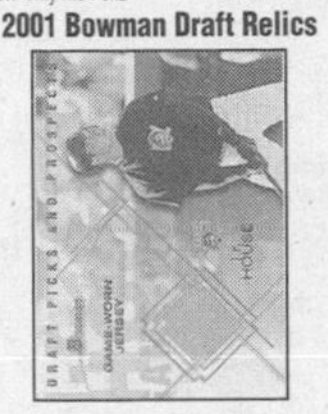

Inserted one per factory set, these six cards feature relics from some of the most popular prospects in the Bowman Draft Pick set.

ONE RELIC PER FACTORY SET
BDPRCI Cesar Izturis 2.00 5.00
BDPRGJ Gary Johnson 2.00 5.00
BDPRNR Nick Regilio 2.00 5.00
BDPRRC Ryan Church 2.00 5.00
BDPRBJS Brian Specht 2.00 5.00
BDPRJRH J.R. House 2.00 5.00

2002 Bowman

This 440 card set was issued in May, 2002. It was issued in 10 card packs which were packed 24 packs to a box and 12 boxes per case. These packs had an SRP of $3 per pack. The first 110 cards of this set featured veterans while the rest of the set featured rookies and prospects.

COMPLETE SET (440) 20.00 50.00
1 Adam Dunn .20 .50
2 Derek Jeter .75 2.00
3 Alex Rodriguez .40 1.00
4 Miguel Tejada .20 .50
5 Nomar Garciaparra .20 .50
6 Toby Hall .12 .30
7 Brandon Duckworth .12 .30
8 Paul LoDuca .12 .30
9 Brian Giles .12 .30
10 C.C. Sabathia .20 .50
11 Curt Schilling .20 .50
12 Tsuyoshi Shinjo .12 .30
13 Ramon Hernandez .12 .30
14 Jose Cruz Jr. .12 .30
15 Albert Pujols .60 1.50
16 Joe Mays .12 .30
17 Javy Lopez .12 .30
18 J.T. Snow .12 .30
19 David Segui .12 .30
20 Jorge Posada .20 .50
21 Doug Mientkiewicz .12 .30
22 Jerry Hairston Jr. .12 .30
23 Bernie Williams .20 .50
24 Mike Sweeney .12 .30
25 Jason Giambi .12 .30
26 Ryan Dempster .12 .30
27 Ryan Klesko .12 .30
28 Mark Quinn .12 .30
29 Jeff Kent .12 .30
30 Eric Chavez .12 .30
31 Adrian Beltre .30 .75
32 Andruw Jones .12 .30
33 Alfonso Soriano .20 .50
34 Aramis Ramirez .12 .30
35 Greg Maddux .50 1.25
36 Andy Pettitte .20 .50
37 Bartolo Colon .12 .30
38 Ben Sheets .12 .30
39 Bobby Higginson .12 .30
40 Ivan Rodriguez .20 .50
41 Brad Penny .12 .30
42 Carlos Lee .12 .30
43 Damion Easley .12 .30
44 Preston Wilson .12 .30
45 Jeff Bagwell .20 .50
46 Eric Milton .12 .30
47 Rafael Palmeiro .20 .50
48 Gary Sheffield .12 .30
49 J.D. Drew .12 .30
50 Jim Thome .20 .50
51 Ichiro Suzuki .40 1.00
52 Bud Smith .12 .30
53 Chan Ho Park .20 .50
54 D'Angelo Jimenez .12 .30
55 Ken Griffey Jr. .60 1.50
56 Wade Miller .12 .30
57 Vladimir Guerrero .20 .50
58 Troy Glaus .12 .30
59 Shawn Green .12 .30
60 Kerry Wood .12 .30
61 Jack Wilson .12 .30
62 Kevin Brown .12 .30
63 Marcus Giles .12 .30
64 Pat Burrell .12 .30
65 Larry Walker .20 .50
66 Sammy Sosa .30 .75
67 Raul Mondesi .12 .30
68 Tim Hudson .20 .50
69 Lance Berkman .20 .50
70 Mike Mussina .20 .50
71 Barry Zito .12 .30
72 Jimmy Rollins .20 .50
73 Barry Bonds .50 1.25
74 Craig Biggio .20 .50
75 Todd Helton .20 .50
76 Roger Clemens .40 1.00
77 Frank Catalanotto .12 .30
78 Josh Towers .12 .30
79 Roy Oswalt .20 .50
80 Chipper Jones .30 .75
81 Cristian Guzman .12 .30
82 Darin Erstad .12 .30
83 Freddy Garcia .12 .30
84 Jason Tyner .12 .30
85 Carlos Delgado .12 .30
86 Jon Lieber .12 .30
87 Juan Pierre .12 .30
88 Matt Morris .12 .30
89 Phil Nevin .12 .30
90 Jim Edmonds .20 .50
91 Magglio Ordonez .20 .50
92 Mike Hampton .12 .30
93 Rafael Furcal .12 .30
94 Richie Sexson .12 .30
95 Luis Gonzalez .12 .30
96 Scott Rolen .20 .50
97 Tim Redding .12 .30
98 Moises Alou .12 .30
99 Jose Vidro .12 .30
100 Mike Piazza .30 .75
101 Pedro Martinez .20 .50
102 Geoff Jenkins .12 .30
103 Johnny Damon Sox .20 .50
104 Mike Cameron .12 .30
105 Randy Johnson .30 .75
106 David Eckstein .12 .30
107 Javier Vazquez .12 .30
108 Mark Mulder .12 .30
109 Robert Fick .12 .30
110 Roberto Alomar .20 .50
111 Wilson Betemit .12 .30
112 Chris Tritle RC .25 .60
113 Ed Rogers .12 .30
114 Juan Pena .12 .30
115 Josh Beckett .12 .30
116 Juan Cruz .12 .30
117 Noochie Varner RC .25 .60
118 Taylor Buchholz RC .25 .60
119 Mike Rivera .12 .30
120 Hank Blalock .12 .30
121 Hansel Izquierdo RC .25 .60
122 Orlando Hudson .12 .30
123 Bill Hall .12 .30
124 Jose Reyes .30 .75
125 Juan Rivera .12 .30
126 Eric Valent .12 .30
127 Scotty Layfield RC .25 .60
128 Austin Kearns .12 .30
129 Nic Jackson RC .25 .60
130 Chris Baker RC .25 .60
131 Chad Qualls RC .40 1.00
132 Marcus Thames .12 .30
133 Nathan Haynes .12 .30
134 Brett Evert .12 .30
135 Joe Borchard .12 .30
136 Ryan Christianson .12 .30
137 Josh Hamilton .20 .50
138 Corey Patterson .12 .30
139 Travis Wilson .12 .30
140 Alex Escobar .12 .30
141 Alexis Gomez .12 .30
142 Nick Johnson .12 .30
143 Kenny Kelly .12 .30
144 Marlon Byrd .12 .30
145 Kory DeHaan .12 .30
146 Matt Belisle .12 .30
147 Carlos Hernandez .12 .30
148 Sean Burroughs .12 .30
149 Angel Berroa .12 .30
150 Aubrey Huff .12 .30
151 Travis Hafner .12 .30
152 Brandon Berger .12 .30
153 David Krynzel .12 .30
154 Ruben Salazar .12 .30
155 J.R. House .12 .30
156 Juan Silvestre .12 .30
157 Dewon Brazelton .12 .30
158 Jayson Werth .20 .50
159 Larry Barnes .12 .30
160 Elvis Pena .12 .30
161 Ruben Gotay RC .25 .60
162 Tommy Marx RC .25 .60
163 John Suomi RC .25 .60
164 Javier Colina .12 .30
165 Greg Sain RC .25 .60
166 Robert Cosby RC .25 .60
167 Angel Pagan RC .60 1.50
168 Ralph Santana RC .25 .60
169 Joe Orloski RC .25 .60
170 Shayne Wright RC .25 .60
171 Jay Caligiuri RC .25 .60
172 Greg Montalbano RC .25 .60
173 Rich Harden RC .75 2.00
174 Rich Thompson RC .25 .60
175 Fred Bastardo RC .25 .60
176 Alejandro Giron RC .25 .60
177 Jesus Medrano RC .25 .60
178 Kevin Deaton RC .25 .60
179 Mike Rosamond RC .25 .60
180 Jon Guzman RC .25 .60
181 Gerard Oakes RC .25 .60
182 Francisco Liriano RC 1.25 3.00
183 Matt Allegra RC .25 .60
184 Mike Snyder RC .25 .60
185 James Shanks RC .25 .60
186 Anderson Hernandez RC .25 .60
187 Dan Trumble RC .25 .60
188 Luis DePaula RC .25 .60
189 Randall Shelley RC .25 .60
190 Richard Lane RC .25 .60
191 Antwon Rollins RC .25 .60
192 Ryan Bukvich RC .25 .60
193 Derrick Lewis .12 .30
194 Eric Miller RC .25 .60
195 Justin Schuda RC .25 .60
196 Brian West RC .25 .60
197 Adam Roller RC .25 .60
198 Neal Frendling RC .25 .60
199 Jeremy Hill RC .25 .60
200 James Barrett RC .25 .60
201 Brett Kay RC .25 .60
202 Ryan Mottl RC .25 .60
203 Brad Nelson RC .25 .60
204 Juan M. Gonzalez RC .25 .60
205 Curtis Legendre RC .25 .60
206 Ronald Acuna RC .25 .60
207 Chris Flinn RC .25 .60
208 Nick Alvarez RC .25 .60
209 Jason Ellison RC .25 .60
210 Blake McGinley RC .25 .60
211 Dan Phillips RC .25 .60
212 Demetrius Heath RC .25 .60
213 Eric Bruntlett RC .25 .60
214 Joe Jiannetti RC .25 .60
215 Mike Hill RC .25 .60
216 Ricardo Cordova RC .25 .60
217 Mark Hamilton RC .25 .60
218 David Mattox RC .25 .60
219 Jose Morban RC .25 .60
220 Scott Wiggins RC .25 .60
221 Steve Green .12 .30
222 Brian Rogers .12 .30
223 Chin-Hui Tsao .12 .30
224 Kenny Baugh .12 .30
225 Nate Teut .12 .30
226 Josh Wilson RC .25 .60
227 Christian Parker .12 .30
228 Tim Raines Jr. .12 .30
229 Anastacio Martinez RC .25 .60
230 Richard Lewis .12 .30
231 Tim Kalita RC .25 .60
232 Edwin Almonte RC .25 .60
233 Hee-Seop Choi .12 .30
234 Ty Howington .12 .30
235 Victor Alvarez RC .25 .60
236 Morgan Ensberg .12 .30
237 Jeff Austin RC .12 .30
238 Luis Terrero .12 .30
239 Adam Wainwright .20 .50
240 Clint Weibl RC .25 .60
241 Eric Cyr .12 .30
242 Marlyn Tisdale RC .25 .60
243 John VanBenschoten .12 .30
244 Ryan Raburn RC .40 1.00
245 Miguel Cabrera 3.00 8.00
246 Jung Bong .12 .30
247 Raul Chavez RC .25 .60
248 Erik Bedard .12 .30
249 Chris Snelling RC .25 .60
250 Joe Rogers RC .25 .60
251 Nate Field RC .25 .60
252 Matt Herges RC .25 .60
253 Matt Childers RC .25 .60
254 Erick Almonte .12 .30
255 Nick Neugebauer .12 .30
256 Ron Calloway RC .12 .30
257 Seung Song .12 .30
258 Brandon Phillips .12 .30
259 Cole Barthel RC .25 .60
260 Jason Lane .12 .30
261 Jae Seo .12 .30
262 Randy Flores .12 .30
263 Scott Chiasson .12 .30
264 Chase Utley .50 1.25
265 Tony Alvarez .12 .30
266 Ben Howard RC .25 .60
267 Nelson Castro RC .25 .60
268 Mark Lukasiewicz .25 .60
269 Eric Glaser RC .25 .60
270 Rob Henkel RC .25 .60
271 Jose Valverde RC .40 1.00
272 Ricardo Rodriguez .12 .30
273 Chris Smith .12 .30
274 Mark Prior .20 .50
275 Miguel Olivo .12 .30
276 Ben Broussard .12 .30
277 Zach Sorensen .12 .30
278 Brian Mallette RC .25 .60
279 Brad Wilkerson .12 .30
280 Carl Crawford .20 .50
281 Chone Figgins RC .40 1.00
282 Jimmy Alvarez RC .25 .60
283 Gavin Floyd RC .60 1.50
284 Josh Bonifay RC .25 .60
285 Garrett Guzman RC .25 .60
286 Blake Williams .12 .30
287 Matt Holliday .30 .75
288 Ryan Madson .12 .30
289 Luis Torres .12 .30
290 Jeff Verplancke RC .25 .60
291 Nate Espy RC .25 .60
292 Jeff Lincoln RC .25 .60
293 Ryan Snare RC .25 .60
294 Jose Ortiz .12 .30

295 Eric Munson .12 .30
296 Denny Bautista .12 .30
297 Willy Aybar .12 .30
298 Kelly Johnson .30 .75
299 Justin Morneau .30 .75
300 Derrick Van Dusen .12 .30
301 Chad Petty .12 .30
302 Mike Restovich .12 .30
303 Shawn Fagan .12 .30
304 Yurendell DeCaster RC .25 .60
305 Justin Wayne .12 .30
306 Mike Peeples RC .25 .60
307 Joel Guzman .12 .30
308 Ryan Vogelsong .60 1.50
309 Jorge Padilla RC .25 .60
310 Grady Sizemore .20 .50
311 Joe Jester RC .25 .60
312 Jim Journell .12 .30
313 Bobby Seay .12 .30
314 Ryan Church RC .25 .60
315 Grant Balfour .12 .30
316 Mitch Jones .12 .30
317 Travis Foley RC .25 .60
318 Bobby Crosby .30 .75
319 Adrian Gonzalez .30 .75
320 Ronnie Merrill .12 .30
321 Joel Pineiro .12 .30
322 John-Ford Griffin .12 .30
323 Brian Forystek RC .25 .60
324 Sean Douglass .12 .30
325 Manny Delcarmen RC .25 .60
326 Donnie Bridges .12 .30
327 Jim Kavourias RC .25 .60
328 Gabe Gross .12 .30
329 Jon Rauch .12 .30
330 Bill Ortega .12 .30
331 Joey Hammond RC .25 .60
332 Ramon Moreta RC .25 .60
333 Ron Davenport .12 .30
334 Brett Myers .12 .30
335 Carlos Pena .20 .50
336 Ezequiel Astacio RC .25 .60
337 Edwin Yan RC .25 .60
338 Josh Girdley .12 .30
339 Shaun Boyd .12 .30
340 Juan Rincon .12 .30
341 Chris Duffy RC .25 .60
342 Jason Kinchen .12 .30
343 Brad Thomas .12 .30
344 David Kelton .12 .30
345 Rafael Soriano .12 .30
346 Colin Young RC .25 .60
347 Eric Byrnes .12 .30
348 Chris Narveson RC .25 .60
349 John Rheinecker .12 .30
350 Mike Wilson RC .25 .60
351 Justin Sherrod RC .25 .60
352 Deivi Mendez .12 .30
353 Wily Mo Pena .12 .30
354 Brett Roneberg RC .25 .60
355 Trey Lunsford RC .25 .60
356 Jimmy Gobble RC .25 .60
357 Brent Butler .12 .30
358 Aaron Heilman .12 .30
359 Wilkin Ruan .12 .30
360 Brian Wolfe RC .25 .60
361 Cody Ransom .12 .30
362 Koyie Hill .12 .30
363 Scott Cassidy .12 .30
364 Tony Fontana RC .25 .60
365 Mark Teixeira .20 .50
366 Doug Sessions RC .25 .60
367 Victor Hall .12 .30
368 Josh Cisneros RC .25 .60
369 Kevin Mench .12 .30
370 Tike Redman .12 .30
371 Jeff Heaverlo .12 .30
372 Carlos Brackley RC .25 .60
373 Brad Hawpe .12 .30
374 Jesus Colome .12 .30
375 David Espinosa .12 .30
376 Jesse Foppert RC .25 .60
377 Ross Peeples RC .25 .60
378 Alex Requena RC .25 .60
379 Joe Mauer RC 5.00 12.00
380 Carlos Silva .12 .30
381 David Wright RC 4.00 10.00
382 Craig Kuzmic RC .25 .60
383 Pete Zamora RC .25 .60
384 Matt Parker RC .25 .60
385 Keith Ginter .12 .30
386 Gary Cates Jr. RC .25 .60
387 Justin Reid RC .25 .60
388 Jake Mauer RC .25 .60
389 Dennis Tankersley .12 .30
390 Josh Barfield RC .40 1.00
391 Luis Maza .12 .30
392 Henry Pichardo RC .25 .60
393 Michael Floyd RC .25 .60
394 Clint Nageotte RC .25 .60
395 Raymond Cabrera RC .25 .60
396 Mauricio Lara RC .25 .60
397 Alejandro Cadena RC .25 .60
398 Jonny Gomes RC .75 2.00
399 Jason Bulger RC .25 .60
400 Bobby Jenks RC .40 1.00
401 David Gil RC .25 .60
402 Joel Crump RC .25 .60
403 Kazuhisa Ishii RC .40 1.00
404 So Taguchi RC .40 1.00
405 Ryan Doumit RC .40 1.00
406 Macay McBride .12 .30
407 Brandon Claussen .12 .30
408 Chin-Feng Chen .12 .30
409 Josh Phelps .12 .30
410 Freddie Money RC .25 .60
411 Cliff Bartosh RC .25 .60
412 Josh Pearce .12 .30
413 Lyle Overbay .12 .30
414 Ryan Anderson .12 .30
415 Terrance Hill RC .25 .60
416 John Rodriguez RC .25 .60
417 Richard Stahl .12 .30
418 Brian Specht .12 .30
419 Chris Latham RC .25 .60
420 Carlos Cabrera RC .25 .60
421 Jose Bautista RC 2.00 5.00
422 Kevin Frederick RC .25 .60
423 Jerome Williams .12 .30
424 Napoleon Calzado RC .25 .60
425 Benito Baez .12 .30
426 Xavier Nady .12 .30
427 Jason Botts RC .25 .60
428 Steve Bechler RC .25 .60
429 Reed Johnson RC .40 1.00
430 Mark Outlaw RC .25 .60
431 Billy Sylvester .12 .30
432 Luke Lockwood .12 .30
433 Jake Peavy .12 .30
434 Alfredo Amezaga .12 .30
435 Aaron Cook RC .25 .60
436 Josh Shaffer RC .25 .60
437 Dan Wright .12 .30
438 Ryan Gripp RC .25 .60
439 Alex Herrera .12 .30
440 Jason Bay RC 1.25 3.00

2002 Bowman Gold

COMPLETE SET (440) 75.00 200.00
*GOLD VET: 1.2X TO 3X BASIC
*GOLD RC: .6X TO 1.5X BASIC
ONE PER PACK
245 Miguel Cabrera 5.00 12.00

2002 Bowman Uncirculated

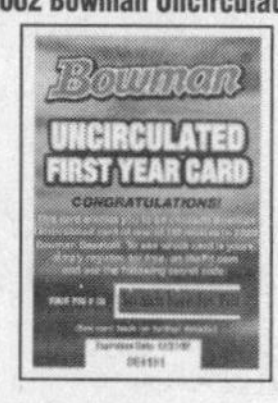

ONE EXCHANGE CARD PER BOX
STATED PRINT RUN 672 SETS
EXCHANGE DEADLINE 12/31/02
CARD DELIVERY OPTION AVAIL. 07/07/02
112 Chris Tritle .40 1.00
117 Noochie Varner .40 1.00
118 Taylor Buchholz .40 1.00
121 Hansel Izquierdo .40 1.00
123 Bill Hall .40 1.00
127 Scotty Layfield .40 1.00
129 Nic Jackson .40 1.00
130 Chris Baker .40 1.00
131 Chad Qualls .60 1.50
161 Ruben Gotay .40 1.00
162 Tommy Marx .40 1.00
163 John Suomi .40 1.00
164 Javier Colina .40 1.00
165 Greg Sain .40 1.00
222 Brian Rogers .40 1.00
229 Anastacio Martinez .40 1.00
230 Richard Lewis .40 1.00
231 Tim Kalita .40 1.00
232 Edwin Almonte .40 1.00
235 Victor Alvarez .40 1.00
237 Jeff Austin .40 1.00
240 Clint Weibl .40 1.00
244 Ryan Raburn .60 1.50
249 Chris Snelling .40 1.00
250 Joe Rogers .40 1.00
251 Nate Field .40 1.00
253 Matt Childers .40 1.00
256 Ron Calloway .40 1.00
259 Cole Barthel .40 1.00
266 Ben Howard .40 1.00
267 Nelson Castro .40 1.00
269 Eric Glaser .40 1.00
270 Rob Henkel .40 1.00
271 Jose Valverde .60 1.50
278 Brian Mallette .40 1.00
281 Chone Figgins .60 1.50
282 Jimmy Alvarez .40 1.00
283 Gavin Floyd 1.00 2.50
284 Josh Bonifay .40 1.00
285 Garrett Guzman .40 1.00
290 Jeff Verplancke .40 1.00
291 Nate Espy .40 1.00
293 Ryan Snare .40 1.00
304 Yurendell De Caster .40 1.00
306 Mike Peeples .40 1.00
309 Jorge Padilla .40 1.00
311 Joe Jester .40 1.00
314 Ryan Church .40 1.00
317 Travis Foley .40 1.00
323 Brian Forystek .40 1.00
325 Manny Delcarmen .40 1.00
327 Jim Kavourias .40 1.00
331 Joey Hammond .40 1.00
336 Ezequiel Astacio .40 1.00
337 Edwin Yan .40 1.00
341 Chris Duffy .40 1.00
348 Chris Narveson .40 1.00
351 Justin Sherrod .40 1.00
354 Brett Roneberg .40 1.00
355 Trey Lunsford .40 1.00
356 Jimmy Gobble .40 1.00
360 Brian Wolfe .40 1.00
362 Koyie Hill .40 1.00
364 Tony Fontana .40 1.00
366 Doug Sessions .40 1.00
372 Carlos Brackley .40 1.00
376 Jesse Foppert .40 1.00
377 Ross Peeples .40 1.00
378 Alex Requena .40 1.00
379 Joe Mauer 4.00 10.00
381 David Wright 3.00 8.00
382 Craig Kuzmic .40 1.00
383 Pete Zamora .40 1.00
384 Matt Parker .40 1.00
386 Gary Cates Jr .40 1.00
387 Justin Reid .40 1.00
388 Jake Mauer .40 1.00
390 Josh Barfield .60 1.50
392 Henry Pichardo .40 1.00
393 Michael Floyd .40 1.00
394 Clint Nageotte .40 1.00
395 Raymond Cabrera .40 1.00
396 Mauricio Lara .40 1.00
397 Alejandro Cadena .40 1.00
398 Jonny Gomes 1.25 3.00
399 Jason Bulger .40 1.00
400 Bobby Jenks .60 1.50
401 David Gil .40 1.00
402 Joel Crump .40 1.00
403 Kazuhisa Ishii .60 1.50
404 So Taguchi .60 1.50
405 Ryan Doumit .60 1.50
410 Freddie Money .40 1.00
411 Cliff Bartosh .40 1.00
415 Terrance Hill .40 1.00
416 John Rodriguez .40 1.00
419 Chris Latham .40 1.00
420 Carlos Cabrera .40 1.00
421 Jose Bautista 3.00 8.00
422 Kevin Frederick .40 1.00
424 Napoleon Calzado .40 1.00
425 Benito Baez .40 1.00
427 Jason Botts .40 1.00
428 Steve Bechler .40 1.00
429 Reed Johnson .60 1.50
430 Mark Outlaw .40 1.00
436 Josh Shaffer .40 1.00
437 Dan Wright .40 1.00
438 Ryan Gripp .40 1.00
440 Jason Bay 2.00 5.00

2002 Bowman Autographs

Inserted in packs at overall odds of one in 40 hobby packs, one in 24 HTA packs and one in 53 retail packs, this 45 card set featured autographs of leading rookies and prospects.

GROUP A 1:67 H, 1:39 HTA, 1:89 R
GROUP B 1:129 H, 1:74 HTA, 1:170 R
GROUP C 1:881 H, 1:507 HTA, 1:1165 R
GROUP D 1:1558 H, 1:896 HTA, 1:2060 R
GROUP E 1:1685 H, 1:968 HTA, 1:2238 R
OVERALL ODDS 1:40 H, 1:24 HTA, 1:53 R
ONE ADD'L AUTO PER SEALED HTA BOX
BAAA Alfredo Amezaga A 4.00 10.00
BAAH Aubrey Huff A 4.00 10.00
BABA Brandon Claussen A 4.00 10.00
BABC Ben Christensen A 4.00 10.00
BABD Brian Cardwell A 4.00 10.00
BABBC Boof Bonser A 4.00 10.00
BABJC Brian Specht C 4.00 10.00
BABSS Bud Smith B 4.00 10.00
BACK Charles Kegley A 4.00 10.00
BACR Cody Ransom B 4.00 10.00
BACS Chris Smith B 4.00 10.00
BACT Chris Tritle B 4.00 10.00
BACU Chase Utley A 40.00 100.00
BADV Domingo Valdez A 4.00 10.00
BADW Dan Wright B 4.00 10.00
BAGA Garrett Atkins A 8.00 20.00
BAGJ Gary Johnson C 4.00 10.00
BAHB Hank Blalock B 6.00 15.00
BAJB Josh Beckett B 6.00 15.00
BAJD Jeff Davanon A 4.00 10.00
BAJL Jason Lane A 6.00 15.00
BAJP Juan Pena A 4.00 10.00
BAJS Juan Silvestre A 4.00 10.00
BAJAB Jason Botts B 6.00 15.00
BAJLW Jerome Williams A 4.00 10.00
BAKG Keith Ginter B 4.00 10.00
BALB Larry Bigbie A 6.00 15.00
BAMB Marlon Byrd B 4.00 10.00
BAMC Matt Cooper A 4.00 10.00
BAMD Manny Delcarmen A 4.00 10.00
BAME Morgan Ensberg A 6.00 15.00
BAMP Mark Prior B 6.00 15.00
BANJ Nick Johnson B 6.00 15.00
BANN Nick Neugebauer E 4.00 10.00
BANV Noochie Varner B 4.00 10.00
BARF Randy Flores D 4.00 10.00
BARF Ryan Franklin B 4.00 10.00
BARH Ryan Hannaman A 4.00 10.00
BARO Roy Oswalt B 6.00 15.00
BARV Ryan Vogelsong B 6.00 15.00
BATB Tony Blanco A 4.00 10.00
BATH Toby Hall B 4.00 10.00
BATS Termel Sledge B 4.00 10.00
BAWB Wilson Betemit B 4.00 10.00
BAWS Will Smith A 4.00 10.00

2002 Bowman Futures Game Autograph Relics

Inserted at overall odds of one in 196 hobby packs, one in 113 HTA packs and one in 259 retail packs for jersey cards and one in 126 HTA packs for base cards, these cards feature pieces of memorabilia and the player's autograph from the 2001 Futures Game.

GROUP A JSY 1:2193 H, 1:1262 HTA, 1:2898 R
GROUP B JSY 1:1599 H, 1:923 HTA, 1:2125 R
GROUP C JSY 1:522 H, 1:301 HTA, 1:688 R
GROUP D JSY 1:1533 H, 1:882 HTA, 1:2028 R
GROUP E JSY 1:1425 H, 1:822 HTA, 1:1882 R
GROUP F JSY 1:1316 H, 1:759 HTA, 1:1738 R
OVERALL JSY 1:196 H, 1:113 HTA, 1:259 R
BASE ODDS 1:126 HTA
CH Carlos Hernandez Jsy B 5.00 12.00
CP Carlos Pena Jsy D 5.00 12.00
DT Dennis Tankersley Jsy E 5.00 12.00
JRH J.R. House Jsy C 5.00 12.00
JW Jerome Williams Jsy F 5.00 12.00
NJ Nick Johnson Jsy C 5.00 12.00
RL Ryan Ludwick Jsy C 8.00 20.00
TH Toby Hall Base 5.00 12.00
WB Wilson Betemit Jsy A 5.00 12.00

2002 Bowman Game Used Relics

Inserted at an overall stated odd of one in 74 hobby packs, one in 43 HTA packs and one in 99 retail packs, these 26 cards features some of the leading prospects from the set along a piece of game-used memorabilia.

GROUP A BAT 1:3236 H,1:1866 HTA,1:4331 R
GROUP B BAT 1:1472 H, 1:849 HTA, 1:1949 R
GROUP C BAT 1:1647 H, 1:948 HTA, 1:2180 R
GROUP D BAT 1:894 H, 1:515 HTA, 1:1180 R
GROUP E BAT 1:375 H, 1:216 HTA, 1:496 R
GROUP F BAT 1:1042 H, 1:601 HTA, 1:1381 R
GROUP G BAT 1:939 H, 1:541 HTA, 1:1237 R
OVERALL BAT 1:135 H, 1:78 HTA, 1:179 R
GROUP A JSY 1:2085 H,1:1202 HTA,1:2762 R
GROUP B JSY 1:1916 H, 1:528 HTA, 1:1213 R
GROUP C JSY 1:223 H, 1:129 HTA, 1:295 R
OVERALL JSY 1:165 H, 1:95 HTA, 1:219 R
OVERALL RELIC 1:74 H, 1:43 HTA, 1:99 R
BRAB Angel Berroa Bat B 4.00 10.00
BRAC Antoine Cameron Bat C 4.00 10.00
BRAE Adam Everett Bat E 3.00 8.00
BRAF Alex Fernandez Bat B 4.00 10.00
BRAF Alex Fernandez Jsy C 3.00 8.00
BRAG Alexis Gomez Bat A 4.00 10.00
BRAK Austin Kearns Bat E 3.00 8.00
BRALC Alex Cintron Bat E 3.00 8.00
BRCG Cristian Guerrero Bat E 3.00 8.00
BRCI Cesar Izturis Bat D 3.00 8.00
BRCP Corey Patterson Bat B 4.00 10.00
BRCY Colin Young Jsy C 3.00 8.00
BRDJ D'Angelo Jimenez Bat C 4.00 10.00
BRFJ Forrest Johnson Bat G 3.00 8.00
BRGA Garrett Atkins Bat F 4.00 10.00
BRJA Jared Abruzzo Bat D 3.00 8.00
BRJA Jared Abruzzo Jsy C 3.00 8.00
BRJL Jason Lane Jsy B 3.00 8.00
BRJS Jamal Strong Jsy A 3.00 8.00
BRNC Nate Cornejo Jsy C 3.00 8.00
BRNN Nick Neugebauer Jsy C 3.00 8.00
BRRC Ryan Church Bat D 3.00 8.00
BRRD Ryan Dittfurth Jsy C 3.00 8.00
BRRM Ryan Madson Bat E 3.00 8.00
BRRS Ruben Salazar Bat A 4.00 10.00
BRRST Richard Stahl Jsy B 3.00 8.00

2002 Bowman Draft

This 165 card set was issued in December, 2002. These cards were issued in seven card packs which came 24 packs to a box and 10 boxes to a case. Each pack contained four regular Bowman Draft Pick Cards, two Bowman Chrome Draft cards and one Bowman gold card.

COMPLETE SET (165) 15.00 40.00
BDP1 Clint Everts RC .12 .30
BDP2 Fred Lewis RC .12 .30
BDP3 Jon Broxton RC .30 .75
BDP4 Jason Anderson RC .12 .30
BDP5 Mike Eusebio RC .12 .30
BDP6 Zack Greinke RC 2.00 5.00
BDP7 Joe Blanton RC .20 .50
BDP8 Sergio Santos RC .12 .30
BDP9 Jason Cooper RC .12 .30
BDP10 Delwyn Young RC .12 .30
BDP11 Jeremy Hermida RC .20 .50
BDP12 Dan Ortmeier RC .12 .30
BDP13 Kevin Jepsen RC .12 .30
BDP14 Russ Adams RC .12 .30
BDP15 Mike Nixon RC .12 .30
BDP16 Nick Swisher RC .75 2.00
BDP17 Cole Hamels RC 1.50 4.00
BDP18 Brian Dopirak RC .12 .30
BDP19 James Loney RC .30 .75
BDP20 Denard Span RC .20 .50
BDP21 Billy Petrick RC .12 .30
BDP22 Jared Doyle RC .12 .30
BDP23 Jeff Francoeur RC .75 2.00
BDP24 Nick Bourgeois RC .12 .30
BDP25 Matt Cain RC .75 2.00
BDP26 John McCurdy RC .12 .30
BDP27 Mark Kiger RC .12 .30
BDP28 Bill Murphy RC .12 .30
BDP29 Matt Craig RC .12 .30
BDP30 Mike Megrew RC .12 .30
BDP31 Ben Crockett RC .12 .30
BDP32 Luke Hagerty RC .12 .30
BDP33 Matt Whitney RC .12 .30
BDP34 Dan Meyer RC .12 .30
BDP35 Jeremy Brown RC .12 .30
BDP36 Doug Johnson RC .12 .30
BDP37 Steve Obenchain RC .12 .30
BDP38 Matt Clanton RC .12 .30
BDP39 Mark Teahen RC .12 .30
BDP40 Tom Carrow RC .12 .30
BDP41 Micah Schilling RC .12 .30
BDP42 Blair Johnson RC .12 .30
BDP43 Jason Pridie RC .12 .30
BDP44 Joey Votto RC 6.00 15.00
BDP45 Taber Lee RC .12 .30
BDP46 Adam Peterson RC .12 .30
BDP47 Adam Donachie RC .12 .30
BDP48 Josh Murray RC .12 .30
BDP49 Brent Clevlen RC .12 .30
BDP50 Chad Pleiness RC .12 .30
BDP51 Zach Hammes RC .12 .30
BDP52 Chris Snyder RC .12 .30
BDP53 Chris Smith RC .12 .30
BDP54 Justin Maureau RC .12 .30
BDP55 David Bush RC .12 .30
BDP56 Tim Gilhooly RC .12 .30
BDP57 Blair Barbier RC .12 .30
BDP58 Zach Segovia RC .12 .30
BDP59 Jeremy Reed RC .12 .30
BDP60 Matt Pender RC .12 .30
BDP61 Eric Thomas RC .12 .30
BDP62 Justin Jones RC .12 .30
BDP63 Brian Slocum RC .12 .30
BDP64 Larry Broadway RC .12 .30
BDP65 Bo Flowers RC .12 .30
BDP66 Scott White RC .12 .30
BDP67 Steve Stanley RC .12 .30
BDP68 Alex Merricks RC .12 .30
BDP69 Josh Womack RC .12 .30
BDP70 Dave Jensen RC .12 .30
BDP71 Curtis Granderson RC 1.50 4.00
BDP72 Pat Osborn RC .12 .30
BDP73 Nic Carter RC .12 .30
BDP74 Mitch Talbot RC .12 .30
BDP75 Don Murphy RC .12 .30
BDP76 Val Majewski RC .12 .30
BDP77 Javy Rodriguez RC .12 .30
BDP78 Fernando Pacheco RC .12 .30
BDP79 Steve Russell RC .12 .30
BDP80 Jon Slack RC .12 .30
BDP81 John Baker RC .12 .30
BDP82 Aaron Coonrod RC .12 .30
BDP83 Josh Johnson RC .75 2.00
BDP84 Jake Blalock RC .12 .30
BDP85 Alex Hart RC .12 .30
BDP86 Wes Bankston RC .12 .30
BDP87 Josh Rupe RC .12 .30
BDP88 Dan Cevette RC .12 .30
BDP89 Kiel Fisher RC .12 .30
BDP90 Alan Rick RC .12 .30
BDP91 Charlie Morton RC 1.00 2.50
BDP92 Chad Spann RC .12 .30
BDP93 Kyle Boyer RC .12 .30
BDP94 Bob Malek RC .12 .30
BDP95 Ryan Rodriguez RC .12 .30
BDP96 Jordan Renz RC .12 .30
BDP97 Randy Frye RC .12 .30
BDP98 Rich Hill RC .30 .75
BDP99 B.J. Upton RC .60 1.50
BDP100 Dan Christensen RC .12 .30
BDP101 Casey Kotchman RC .20 .50
BDP102 Eric Good RC .12 .30
BDP103 Mike Fontenot RC .12 .30
BDP104 John Webb RC .12 .30
BDP105 Jason Dubois RC .12 .30
BDP106 Ryan Kibler RC .12 .30
BDP107 Jhonny Peralta RC .20 .50
BDP108 Kirk Saarloos RC .12 .30
BDP109 Rhett Parrott RC .12 .30
BDP110 Jason Grove RC .12 .30
BDP111 Colt Griffin RC .12 .30
BDP112 Dallas McPherson RC .12 .30
BDP113 Oliver Perez RC .30 .75
BDP114 Marshall McDougall RC .12 .30
BDP115 Mike Wood RC .12 .30
BDP116 Scott Hairston RC .12 .30
BDP117 Jason Simontacchi RC .12 .30
BDP118 Taggert Bozied RC .12 .30
BDP119 Shelley Duncan RC .30 .75
BDP120 Dontrelle Willis RC .30 .75
BDP121 Sean Burnett .12 .30
BDP122 Aaron Cook .12 .30
BDP123 Brett Evert .12 .30
BDP124 Jimmy Journell .12 .30
BDP125 Brett Myers .12 .30
BDP126 Brad Baker .12 .30
BDP127 Billy Traber RC .12 .30
BDP128 Adam Wainwright .20 .50
BDP129 Jason Young RC .12 .30
BDP130 John Buck .30 .75
BDP131 Kevin Cash RC .12 .30
BDP132 Jason Stokes RC .12 .30
BDP133 Drew Henson .12 .30
BDP134 Chad Tracy RC .20 .50
BDP135 Orlando Hudson .12 .30
BDP136 Brandon Phillips .12 .30
BDP137 Joe Borchard .12 .30
BDP138 Marlon Byrd .12 .30
BDP139 Carl Crawford .20 .50
BDP140 Michael Restovich .12 .30
BDP141 Corey Hart RC .60 1.50
BDP142 Edwin Almonte .12 .30
BDP143 Francis Beltran RC .12 .30
BDP144 Jorge De La Rosa RC .12 .30
BDP145 Gerardo Garcia RC .12 .30
BDP146 Franklyn German RC .12 .30
BDP147 Francisco Liriano .60 1.50
BDP148 Francisco Rodriguez .20 .50
BDP149 Ricardo Rodriguez .12 .30
BDP150 Seung Song .12 .30
BDP151 John Stephens .12 .30
BDP152 Justin Huber RC .12 .30
BDP153 Victor Martinez .20 .50
BDP154 Hee Seop Choi .12 .30
BDP155 Justin Morneau .30 .75
BDP156 Miguel Cabrera 3.00 8.00
BDP157 Victor Diaz RC .12 .30
BDP158 Jose Reyes .30 .75
BDP159 Omar Infante .30 .75
BDP160 Angel Berroa .12 .30
BDP161 Tony Alvarez .12 .30
BDP162 Shin Soo Choo RC 1.00 2.50
BDP163 Wily Mo Pena .12 .30
BDP164 Andres Torres .12 .30
BDP165 Jose Lopez RC .20 .50

2002 Bowman Draft Gold

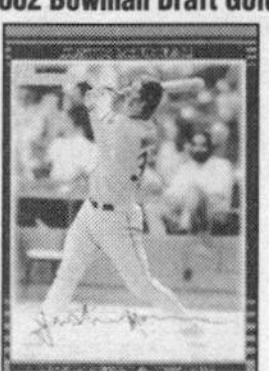

COMPLETE SET (165) 30.00 80.00
*GOLD: 1.2X TO 3X BASIC
*GOLD RC'S: 1.2X TO 3X BASIC
ONE PER PACK
BDP156 Miguel Cabrera 5.00 12.00

2002 Bowman Draft Fabric of the Future Relics

Inserted at a stated rate of one in 55, these 28 cards feature prospects from the 2002 All-Star Futures Game who are very close to be major leaguers. All of these cards have a game-worn jersey relic piece on them.

STATED ODDS 1:55
ALL CARDS FEATURE JERSEY SWATCHES
AB Angel Berroa 3.00 8.00
AT Andres Torres 3.00 8.00
AW Adam Wainwright 5.00 12.00
BM Brett Myers 3.00 8.00
BT Billy Traber 2.00 5.00
CC Carl Crawford 4.00 10.00
CH Corey Hart 4.00 10.00
CT Chad Tracy 3.00 8.00
DH Drew Henson 3.00 8.00
EA Edwin Almonte 2.00 5.00
FB Francis Beltran 2.00 5.00
FG Franklyn German 2.00 5.00
FL Francisco Liriano 4.00 10.00
GG Gerardo Garcia 2.00 5.00
HC Hee Seop Choi 4.00 10.00
JH Justin Huber 3.00 8.00
JK Josh Karp 2.00 5.00
JL Jose Lopez 3.00 8.00
JR Jorge De La Rosa 2.00 5.00
JS1 Jason Stokes 2.00 5.00
JS2 John Stephens 3.00 8.00
KC Kevin Cash 2.00 5.00
MR Michael Restovich 3.00 8.00
SB Sean Burnett 3.00 8.00
SC Shin Soo Choo 6.00 15.00
TA Tony Alvarez 3.00 8.00
VD Victor Diaz 3.00 8.00
WP Wily Mo Pena 4.00 10.00

2002 Bowman Draft Freshman Fiber

Issued at a stated rate of one in 605 for the bat cards and one in 45 for the jersey cards, these 13 cards feature some of the leading young players in the game along with a game-worn piece.

BAT STATED ODDS 1:605
JERSEY STATED ODDS 1:45
AH Aubrey Huff Jsy 2.00 5.00
AK Austin Kearns Bat 3.00 8.00
BA Brent Abernathy Jsy 2.00 5.00
DB Dewon Brazelton Jsy 2.00 5.00
JH Josh Hamilton 6.00 15.00
JK Joe Kennedy Jsy 2.00 5.00
JS Jared Sandberg Jsy 2.00 5.00
JV John VanBenschoten Jsy 2.00 5.00
JWS Jason Standridge Jsy 2.00 5.00
MB Marlon Byrd Bat 3.00 8.00
MT Mark Teixeira Bat 6.00 15.00
NB Nick Bierbrodt Jsy 2.00 5.00
TH Toby Hall Jsy 2.00 5.00

2002 Bowman Draft Signs of the Future

Inserted at different odds depending on what group the player belonged to, these 21 cards feature authentic autographs of the featured player.

GROUP A ODDS 1:100
GROUP B ODDS 1:110
GROUP C ODDS 1:1028
GROUP D ODDS 1:1103
GROUP E ODDS 1:386
GROUP F ODDS 1:2807
BI Brandon Inge E 5.00 12.00
BK Bob Keppel C 4.00 10.00
BP Brandon Phillips B 4.00 10.00
BS Bud Smith E 4.00 10.00
CP Christian Parra D 4.00 10.00
CT Chad Tracy A 6.00 15.00
DD Dan Denham A 4.00 10.00
EB Erik Bedard A 6.00 15.00
JEM Justin Morneau B 6.00 15.00
JM Jake Mauer B 4.00 10.00
JR Juan Rivera B 4.00 10.00
JW Jerome Williams F 4.00 10.00
KH Kris Honel A 4.00 10.00
LB Larry Bigbie E 4.00 10.00
LN Lance Niekro A 6.00 15.00
ME Morgan Ensberg E 4.00 10.00
MF Mike Fontenot A 4.00 10.00
MJ Mitch Jones A 4.00 10.00
NJ Nic Jackson B 4.00 10.00
TB Taylor Buchholz B 4.00 10.00
TL Todd Linden B 6.00 15.00

2003 Bowman

This 330 card set was released in May, 2003. These cards were mixed between veteran cards with red borders on the bottom (1-155) and rookie/prospect cards with blue on the bottom (156-330). This set was issued in 10 card packs which came 24 packs to a box and 12 boxes to a case with an $3 SRP per pack. A special card was inserted featured game-used relics of the two 2002 Major League Rookie of the Years.

COMPLETE SET (330) 15.00 40.00
HINSKE/JENNINGS 1:765 H,1:246 HTA,1:1416 R
1 Garret Anderson .12 .30
2 Derek Jeter .75 2.00
3 Gary Sheffield .12 .30
4 Matt Morris .12 .30
5 Derek Lowe .12 .30
6 Andy Van Hekken .12 .30
7 Sammy Sosa .30 .75
8 Ken Griffey Jr. .60 1.50
9 Omar Vizquel .20 .50
10 Jorge Posada .20 .50
11 Lance Berkman .20 .50

12 Mike Sweeney .12 .30
13 Adrian Beltre .30 .75
14 Richie Sexson .12 .30
15 A.J. Pierzynski .12 .30
16 Bartolo Colon .12 .30
17 Mike Mussina .20 .50
18 Paul Byrd .12 .30
19 Bobby Abreu .12 .30
20 Miguel Tejada .20 .50
21 Aramis Ramirez .12 .30
22 Edgardo Alfonzo .12 .30
23 Edgar Martinez .20 .50
24 Albert Pujols .40 1.00
25 Carl Crawford .20 .50
26 Eric Hinske .12 .30
27 Tim Salmon .12 .30
28 Luis Gonzalez .12 .30
29 Jay Gibbons .12 .30
30 John Smoltz .30 .75
31 Tim Wakefield .20 .50
32 Mark Prior .20 .50
33 Magglio Ordonez .20 .50
34 Adam Dunn .20 .50
35 Larry Walker .20 .50
36 Luis Castillo .12 .30
37 Wade Miller .12 .30
38 Carlos Beltran .20 .50
39 Odalis Perez .12 .30
40 Alex Sanchez .12 .30
41 Torii Hunter .12 .30
42 Cliff Floyd .12 .30
43 Andy Pettitte .20 .50
44 Francisco Rodriguez .20 .50
45 Eric Chavez .12 .30
46 Kevin Millwood .12 .30
47 Dennis Tankersley .12 .30
48 Hideo Nomo .30 .75
49 Freddy Garcia .12 .30
50 Randy Johnson .30 .75
51 Aubrey Huff .12 .30
52 Carlos Delgado .12 .30
53 Troy Glaus .12 .30
54 Junior Spivey .12 .30
55 Mike Hampton .12 .30
56 Sidney Ponson .12 .30
57 Aaron Boone .12 .30
58 Kerry Wood .12 .30
59 Runelvys Hernandez .12 .30
60 Nomar Garciaparra .20 .50
61 Todd Helton .20 .50
62 Mike Lowell .12 .30
63 Roy Oswalt .20 .50
64 Raul Ibanez .20 .50
65 Brian Jordan .12 .30
66 Geoff Jenkins .12 .30
67 Jermaine Dye .12 .30
68 Tom Glavine .20 .50
69 Bernie Williams .20 .50
70 Vladimir Guerrero .20 .50
71 Mark Mulder .12 .30
72 Jimmy Rollins .20 .50
73 Oliver Perez .12 .30
74 Rich Aurilia .12 .30
75 Joel Pineiro .12 .30
76 J.D. Drew .12 .30
77 Ivan Rodriguez .20 .50
78 Josh Phelps .12 .30
79 Darin Erstad .12 .30
80 Curt Schilling .20 .50
81 Paul Lo Duca .12 .30
82 Marty Cordova .12 .30
83 Manny Ramirez .30 .75
84 Bobby Hill .12 .30
85 Paul Konerko .20 .50
86 Austin Kearns .12 .30
87 Jason Jennings .12 .30
88 Brad Penny .12 .30
89 Jeff Bagwell .20 .50
90 Shawn Green .12 .30
91 Jason Schmidt .12 .30
92 Doug Mientkiewicz .12 .30
93 Jose Vidro .12 .30
94 Bret Boone .12 .30
95 Jason Giambi .12 .30
96 Barry Zito .20 .50
97 Roy Halladay .20 .50
98 Pat Burrell .12 .30
99 Sean Burroughs .12 .30
100 Barry Bonds .50 1.25
101 Kazuhiro Sasaki .12 .30
102 Fernando Vina .12 .30
103 Chan Ho Park .20 .50
104 Andruw Jones .12 .30
105 Adam Kennedy .12 .30
106 Shea Hillenbrand .12 .30
107 Greg Maddux .40 1.00
108 Jim Edmonds .20 .50
109 Pedro Martinez .20 .50
110 Moises Alou .12 .30
111 Jeff Weaver .12 .30
112 C.C. Sabathia .20 .50
113 Robert Fick .12 .30
114 A.J. Burnett .12 .30
115 Jeff Kent .12 .30
116 Kevin Brown .12 .30
117 Rafael Furcal .12 .30
118 Cristian Guzman .12 .30
119 Brad Wilkerson .12 .30
120 Mike Piazza .30 .75
121 Alfonso Soriano .20 .50
122 Mark Ellis .12 .30
123 Vicente Padilla .12 .30
124 Eric Gagne .12 .30
125 Ryan Klesko .12 .30
126 Ichiro Suzuki .40 1.00
127 Tony Batista .12 .30
128 Roberto Alomar .20 .50
129 Alex Rodriguez .40 1.00
130 Jim Thome .20 .50
131 Jarrod Washburn .12 .30
132 Orlando Hudson .12 .30
133 Chipper Jones .30 .75
134 Rodrigo Lopez .12 .30
135 Johnny Damon .20 .50
136 Matt Clement .12 .30
137 Frank Thomas .30 .75
138 Ellis Burks .12 .30
139 Carlos Pena .20 .50
140 Josh Beckett .12 .30
141 Joe Randa .12 .30
142 Brian Giles .12 .30
143 Kazuhisa Ishii .12 .30
144 Corey Koskie .12 .30
145 Orlando Cabrera .12 .30
146 Mark Buehrle .20 .50
147 Roger Clemens .40 1.00
148 Tim Hudson .20 .50
149 Randy Wolf .12 .30
150 Josh Fogg .12 .30
151 Phil Nevin .12 .30
152 John Olerud .12 .30
153 Scott Rolen .20 .50
154 Joe Kennedy .12 .30
155 Rafael Palmeiro .20 .50
156 Chad Hutchinson .12 .30
157 Quincy Carter XRC .12 .30
158 Hee Seop Choi .12 .30
159 Joe Borchard .12 .30
160 Brandon Phillips .12 .30
161 Wily Mo Pena .12 .30
162 Victor Martinez .20 .50
163 Jason Stokes .12 .30
164 Ken Harvey .12 .30
165 Juan Rivera .12 .30
166 Jose Contreras RC .30 .75
167 Dan Haren RC .60 1.50
168 Michel Hernandez RC .12 .30
169 Eider Torres RC .12 .30
170 Chris De La Cruz RC .12 .30
171 Ramon Nivar-Martinez RC .12 .30
172 Mike Adams RC .20 .50
173 Justin Arneson RC .12 .30
174 Jamie Athas RC .12 .30
175 Dwaine Bacon RC .12 .30
176 Clint Barmes RC .30 .75
177 B.J. Barns RC .12 .30
178 Tyler Johnson RC .12 .30
179 Bobby Dasham RC .12 .30
180 T.J. Bohn RC .12 .30
181 J.D. Durbin RC .12 .30
182 Brandon Bowe RC .12 .30
183 Craig Brazell RC .12 .30
184 Dusty Brown RC .12 .30
185 Brian Bruney RC .12 .30
186 Greg Bruso RC .12 .30
187 Jaime Bubela RC .12 .30
188 Bryan Bullington RC .12 .30
189 Brian Burgamy RC .12 .30
190 Eny Cabreja RC .50 1.25
191 Daniel Cabrera RC .20 .50
192 Ryan Cameron RC .12 .30
193 Lance Caracciolo RC .12 .30
194 David Cash RC .12 .30
195 Bernie Castro RC .12 .30
196 Ismael Castro RC .12 .30
197 Daryl Clark RC .12 .30
198 Jeff Clark RC .12 .30
199 Chris Colton RC .12 .30
200 Dexter Cooper RC .12 .30
201 Callix Crabbe RC .12 .30
202 Chien-Ming Wang RC .50 1.25
203 Eric Crozier RC .12 .30
204 Nook Logan RC .12 .30
205 David DeJesus RC .30 .75
206 Matt DeMarco RC .12 .30
207 Chris Duncan RC .40 1.00
208 Eric Eckenstahler .12 .30
209 Willie Eyre RC .12 .30
210 Evel Bastida-Martinez RC .12 .30
211 Chris Fallon RC .12 .30
212 Mike Flannery RC .12 .30
213 Mike O'Keefe RC .12 .30
214 Ben Francisco RC .12 .30
215 Kason Gabbard RC .12 .30
216 Mike Gallo RC .12 .30
217 Jairo Garcia RC .12 .30
218 Angel Garcia RC .12 .30
219 Michael Garciaparra RC .12 .30
220 Joey Gomes RC .12 .30
221 Dusty Gomon RC .12 .30
222 Bryan Grace RC .12 .30
223 Tyson Graham RC .12 .30
224 Henry Guerrero RC .12 .30
225 Franklin Gutierrez RC .30 .75
226 Carlos Guzman RC .12 .30
227 Matthew Hagen RC .12 .30
228 Josh Hall RC .12 .30
229 Rob Hammock RC .12 .30
230 Brendan Harris RC .12 .30
231 Gary Harris RC .12 .30
232 Clay Hensley RC .12 .30
233 Michael Hinckley RC .12 .30
234 Luis Hodge RC .12 .30
235 Donnie Hood RC .12 .30
236 Travis Ishikawa RC .30 .75
237 Edwin Jackson RC .20 .50
238 Ardley Jansen RC .12 .30
239 Ferenc Jongejan RC .12 .30
240 Matt Kata RC .12 .30
241 Kazuhiro Takeoka RC .12 .30
242 Beau Kemp RC .12 .30
243 Il Kim RC .12 .30
244 Brennan King RC .12 .30
245 Chris Kroski RC .12 .30
246 Jason Kubel RC .40 1.00
247 Pete LaForest RC .12 .30
248 Wil Ledezma RC .12 .30
249 Jeremy Bonderman RC .50 1.25
250 Gonzalo Lopez RC .12 .30
251 Brian Luderer RC .12 .30
252 Ruddy Lugo RC .12 .30
253 Wayne Lydon RC .12 .30
254 Mark Malaska RC .12 .30
255 Andy Marte RC .12 .30
256 Tyler Martin RC .12 .30
257 Branden Florence RC .12 .30
258 Aneudis Mateo RC .12 .30
259 Derell McCall RC .12 .30
260 Brian McCann RC 1.00 2.50
261 Mike McNutt RC .12 .30
262 Jacobo Meque RC .12 .30
263 Derek Michaelis RC .12 .30
264 Aaron Miles RC .12 .30
265 Jose Morales RC .12 .30
266 Dustin Moseley RC .12 .30
267 Adrian Myers RC .12 .30
268 Dan Neil RC .12 .30
269 Jon Nelson RC .12 .30
270 Mike Neu RC .12 .30
271 Leigh Neuage RC .12 .30
272 Wes O'Brien RC .12 .30
273 Trent Oeltjen RC .12 .30
274 Tim Olson RC .12 .30
275 David Pahucki RC .12 .30
276 Nathan Panther RC .12 .30
277 Arnie Munoz RC .12 .30
278 Dave Pember RC .12 .30
279 Jason Perry RC .12 .30
280 Matthew Peterson RC .12 .30
281 Ryan Shealy RC .12 .30
282 Jorge Piedra RC .12 .30
283 Simon Pond RC .12 .30
284 Aaron Rakers RC .12 .30
285 Hanley Ramirez RC 1.00 2.50
286 Manuel Ramirez RC .12 .30
287 Kevin Randel RC .12 .30
288 Darrell Rasner RC .12 .30
289 Prentice Redman RC .12 .30
290 Eric Reed RC .12 .30
291 Wilton Reynolds RC .12 .30
292 Eric Riggs RC .12 .30
293 Carlos Rijo RC .12 .30
294 Rajai Davis RC .12 .30
295 Aron Weston RC .12 .30
296 Arturo Rivas RC .12 .30
297 Kyle Roat RC .12 .30
298 Bubba Nelson RC .12 .30
299 Levi Robinson RC .12 .30
300 Ray Sadler RC .12 .30
301 Gary Schneidmiller RC .12 .30
302 Jon Schuerholz RC .12 .30
303 Corey Shafer RC .12 .30
304 Brian Shackelford RC .12 .30
305 Bill Simon RC .12 .30
306 Haj Turay RC .12 .30
307 Sean Smith RC .12 .30
308 Ryan Spataro RC .12 .30
309 Jemel Spearman RC .12 .30
310 Keith Stamler RC .12 .30
311 Luke Steidlmayer RC .12 .30
312 Adam Stern RC .12 .30
313 Jay Sitzman RC .12 .30
314 Thomari Story-Harden RC .12 .30
315 Terry Tiffee RC .12 .30
316 Nick Trzesniak RC .12 .30
317 Denny Tussen RC .12 .30
318 Scott Tyler RC .12 .30
319 Shane Victorino RC .40 1.00
320 Doug Waechter RC .12 .30
321 Brandon Watson RC .12 .30
322 Todd Wellemeyer RC .12 .30
323 Eli Whiteside RC .12 .30
324 Josh Willingham RC .40 1.00
325 Travis Wong RC .12 .30
326 Brian Wright RC .12 .30
327 Kevin Youkilis RC .75 2.00
328 Andy Sisco RC .12 .30
329 Dustin Yount RC .12 .30
330 Andrew Dominique RC .12 .30
NNO Hinske/Jennings ROY Relic 6.00 15.00

2003 Bowman Gold

COMPLETE SET (330) 75.00 150.00
*RED 1-155: 1.25X TO 3X BASIC
*BLUE 156-330: 1.25X TO 3X BASIC
*BLUE ROOKIES: 1.25X TO 3X BASIC
ONE PER PACK

2003 Bowman Uncirculated Metallic Gold

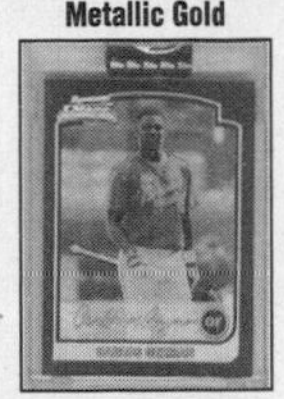

*UNC.GOLD 1-155: 2.5X TO 6X BASIC
*UNC.GOLD 156-330: 2.5X TO 6X BASIC
*UNC.GOLD ROOKIES: 2.5X TO 6X BASIC
ONE EXCH.CARD PER SEALED SILVER PACK
ONE SILVER PACK PER SEALED HOBBY BOX
STATED ODDS 1:49 RETAIL
STATED PRINT RUN 230 SETS
EXCHANGE DEADLINE 04/30/04

2003 Bowman Uncirculated Silver

*UNC.SILVER 1-155: 2.5X TO 6X BASIC
*UNC.SILVER 156-330: 2.5X TO 6X BASIC
*UNC.SILVER ROOKIES: 2.5X TO 6X BASIC
ONE PER SEALED SILVER PACK
ONE SILVER PACK PER SEALED HOBBY BOX
STATED PRINT RUN 250 SERIAL #'d SETS
SET EXCH.CARD ODDS 1:8589 H, 1:5576 HTA
SET EXCHANGE CARD DEADLINE 04/30/04
202 Chien-Ming Wang 5.00 12.00

2003 Bowman Future Fiber Bats

GROUP A ODDS 1:96 H, 1:34 HTA, 1:196 R
GROUP B ODDS 1:393 H, 1:140 HTA, 1:803 R
AG Adrian Gonzalez A 3.00 8.00
AH Aubrey Huff A 3.00 8.00
AK Austin Kearns A 3.00 8.00
BS Bud Smith B 3.00 8.00
CD Chris Duffy B 3.00 8.00
CK Casey Kotchman A 3.00 8.00
DH Drew Henson A 3.00 8.00
DW David Wright A 10.00 25.00
ES Esix Snead A 3.00 8.00
EY Edwin Yan B 3.00 8.00
FS Freddy Sanchez A 3.00 8.00
HB Hank Blalock A 3.00 8.00
JB Jason Botts A 2.00 5.00
JDM Jake Mauer A 3.00 8.00
JG Jason Grove A 3.00 8.00
JH Josh Hamilton 6.00 15.00
JM Joe Mauer A 6.00 15.00
JW Justin Wayne B 3.00 8.00
KC Kevin Cash B 3.00 8.00
KD Kory DeHaan A 3.00 8.00
MR Michael Restovich A 3.00 8.00
NH Nathan Haynes A 3.00 8.00
PF Pedro Feliz A 3.00 8.00
RB Rocco Baldelli B 3.00 8.00
RJ Reed Johnson A 3.00 8.00
RK Ryan Langerhans A 3.00 8.00
RS Randall Shelley A 3.00 8.00
SB Sean Burroughs A 3.00 8.00
ST So Taguchi A 3.00 8.00
TW Travis Wilson A 3.00 8.00
WB Wilson Betemit A 3.00 8.00
WR Wilkin Ruan B 3.00 8.00
XN Xavier Nady A 3.00 8.00

2003 Bowman Futures Game Base Autograph

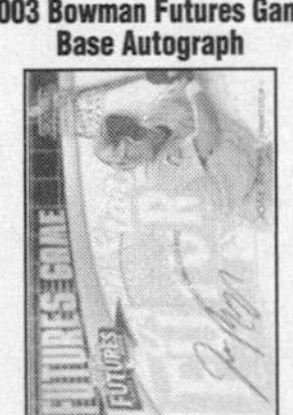

STATED ODDS 1:141 HTA
JR Jose Reyes 8.00 20.00

2003 Bowman Futures Game Gear Jersey Relics

STATED ODDS 1:26 H, 1:9 HTA, 1:52 R
AC Aaron Cook 3.00 8.00
AW Adam Wainwright 3.00 8.00
BB Brad Baker 3.00 8.00
BE Brett Evert 3.00 8.00
BH Bill Hall 3.00 8.00
BM Brett Myers 3.00 8.00
BP Brandon Phillips 3.00 8.00
BT Billy Traber 3.00 8.00
CC Carl Crawford 3.00 8.00
CH Corey Hart 3.00 8.00
CT Chad Tracy 3.00 8.00
DH Drew Henson 3.00 8.00
EA Edwin Almonte 3.00 8.00
FB Francis Beltran 3.00 8.00
FL Francisco Liriano 6.00 15.00
FR Francisco Rodriguez 3.00 8.00
GG Gerardo Garcia 3.00 8.00
HC Hee Seop Choi 3.00 8.00
JB John Buck 3.00 8.00
JDR Jorge De La Rosa 3.00 8.00
JEB Joe Borchard 3.00 8.00
JH Justin Huber 3.00 8.00
JJ Jimmy Journell 3.00 8.00
JK Josh Karp 3.00 8.00
JL Jose Lopez 4.00 10.00
JM Justin Morneau 3.00 8.00
JMS John Stephens 3.00 8.00
JR Jose Reyes 3.00 8.00
JS Jason Stokes 3.00 8.00
JY Jason Young 3.00 8.00
KC Kevin Cash 3.00 8.00
LO Lyle Overbay 3.00 8.00
MB Marlon Byrd 3.00 8.00
MC Miguel Cabrera 10.00 25.00
MR Michael Restovich 3.00 8.00
OH Orlando Hudson 3.00 8.00
OI Omar Infante 3.00 8.00
RD Ryan Dittfurth 3.00 8.00
RR Ricardo Rodriguez 3.00 8.00
SB Sean Burnett 3.00 8.00
SC Shin Soo Choo 3.00 8.00
SS Seung Song 3.00 8.00
TA Tony Alvarez 3.00 8.00
VD Victor Diaz 3.00 8.00
VM Victor Martinez 4.00 10.00
WP Wily Mo Pena 3.00 8.00

2003 Bowman Signs of the Future

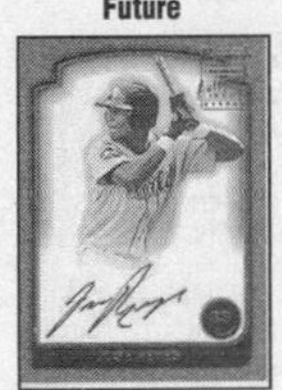

GROUP A ODDS 1:39 H, 1:13 HTA, 1:79 R
GROUP B ODDS 1:183 H, 1:65 HTA, 1:374 R
GROUP C ODDS 1:2288 H,1:816 HTA,1:4720 R
*RED INK: 1.25X TO 3X GROUP A
*RED INK: 1.25X TO 3X GROUP B
*RED INK: .75X TO 2X GROUP C
RED INK ODDS 1:687 H, 1:245 HTA, 1:1402 R
AV Andy Van Hekken A 4.00 10.00
BB Bryan Bullington A 3.00 8.00
BJ Bobby Jenks B 6.00 15.00
BK Ben Kozlowski A 4.00 10.00
BL Brandon League B 4.00 10.00
BS Brian Slocum A 4.00 10.00
CH Cole Hamels A 15.00 40.00
CJH Corey Hart A 6.00 15.00
CMH Chad Hutchinson C 4.00 10.00
CP Chris Piersoll B 4.00 10.00
DG Doug Gredvig A 4.00 10.00
DHM Dustin McGowan A 4.00 10.00
DL Donald Levinski A 3.00 8.00
DS Doug Sessions B 4.00 10.00
FL Fred Lewis A 4.00 10.00
FS Freddy Sanchez B 6.00 15.00
HR Hanley Ramirez A 4.00 10.00
JA Jason Arnold B 4.00 10.00
JB John Buck A 4.00 10.00
JC Jesus Cota B 4.00 10.00
JG Jason Grove B 4.00 10.00
JGU Jeremy Guthrie A 3.00 8.00
JL James Loney A 6.00 15.00
JOG Jonny Gomes B 6.00 15.00
JR Jose Reyes A 6.00 15.00
JRH Joel Hanrahan A 4.00 10.00
JSC Jason St. Clair B 4.00 10.00
KG Khalil Greene A 4.00 10.00
KH Koyie Hill B 4.00 10.00
MT Mitch Talbot A 4.00 10.00
NC Nelson Castro B 4.00 10.00
OV Oscar Villareal A 3.00 8.00
PR Prentice Redman A 3.00 8.00
QC Quincy Carter C 6.00 15.00
RC Ryan Church B 6.00 15.00
RS Ryan Snare B 4.00 10.00
TL Todd Linden B 4.00 10.00
VM Val Majewski A 4.00 10.00
ZG Zack Greinke A 15.00 40.00
ZS Zach Segovia A 4.00 10.00

2003 Bowman Signs of the Future Dual

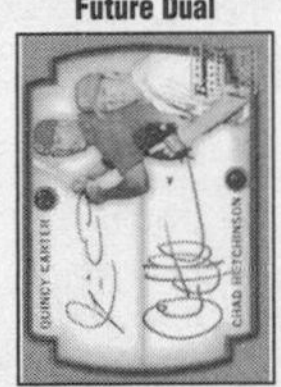

STAT.ODDS 1:9220 H,1:3264 HTA,1:20,390 R
CH Q.Carter/C.Hutchinson 20.00 50.00

2003 Bowman Draft

This 165-card standard-size set was released in December, 2003. The set was issued in 10 card packs with a $2.99 SRP which came 24 packs to a box and 10 boxes to a case. Please note that each Draft pack included 2 Chrome cards.

COMPLETE SET (165) 20.00 50.00
1 Dontrelle Willis .12 .30
2 Freddy Sanchez .12 .30
3 Miguel Cabrera 1.50 4.00
4 Ryan Ludwick .12 .30
5 Ty Wigginton .12 .30
6 Mark Teixeira .20 .50
7 Trey Hodges .12 .30
8 Laynce Nix .12 .30
9 Antonio Perez .12 .30
10 Jody Gerut .12 .30
11 Jae Weong Seo .12 .30
12 Erick Almonte .12 .30
13 Lyle Overbay .12 .30
14 Billy Traber .12 .30
15 Andres Torres .12 .30
16 Jose Valverde .12 .30
17 Aaron Heilman .12 .30
18 Brandon Larson .12 .30
19 Jung Bong .12 .30
20 Jesse Foppert .12 .30
21 Angel Berroa .12 .30
22 Jeff DaVanon .12 .30
23 Kurt Ainsworth .12 .30
24 Brandon Claussen .12 .30
25 Xavier Nady .12 .30
26 Travis Hafner .12 .30
27 Jerome Williams .12 .30
28 Jose Reyes .30 .75
29 Sergio Mitre RC .12 .30
30 Bo Hart RC .12 .30
31 Adam Miller RC .50 1.25
32 Brian Finch RC .12 .30
33 Taylor Mattingly RC .12 .30
34 Daric Barton RC .20 .50
35 Chris Ray RC .20 .50
36 Jarrod Saltalamacchia RC .60 1.50
37 Dennis Dove RC .12 .30
38 James Houser RC .12 .30
39 Clint King RC .12 .30
40 Lou Palmisano RC .12 .30
41 Dan Moore RC .12 .30
42 Craig Stansberry RC .12 .30
43 Jo Jo Reyes RC .12 .30
44 Jake Stevens RC .12 .30
45 Tom Gorzelanny RC .20 .50
46 Brian Marshall RC .12 .30
47 Scott Beerer RC .12 .30
48 Javi Herrera RC .12 .30
49 Steve LeRud RC .12 .30
50 Josh Banks RC .12 .30
51 Jon Papelbon RC 1.25 3.00
52 Juan Valdes RC .12 .30
53 Beau Vaughan RC .12 .30
54 Matt Chico RC .12 .30
55 Todd Jennings RC .12 .30
56 Anthony Gwynn RC .12 .30
57 Matt Harrison RC .50 1.25
58 Aaron Marsden RC .12 .30
59 Casey Abrams RC .12 .30
60 Cory Stuart RC .12 .30
61 Mike Wagner RC .12 .30
62 Jordan Pratt RC .12 .30
63 Andre Randolph RC .12 .30
64 Blake Balkcom RC .12 .30
65 Josh Muecke RC .12 .30
66 Jamie D'Antona RC .12 .30
67 Cole Seifrig RC .12 .30
68 Josh Anderson RC .12 .30
69 Matt Lorenzo RC .12 .30
70 Nate Spears RC .12 .30
71 Chris Goodman RC .12 .30
72 Brian McFall RC .12 .30
73 Billy Hogan RC .12 .30
74 Jamie Romak RC .12 .30
75 Jeff Cook RC .12 .30
76 Brooks McNiven RC .12 .30
77 Xavier Paul RC .12 .30
78 Bob Zimmerman RC .12 .30
79 Mickey Hall RC .12 .30
80 Shaun Marcum RC .12 .30
81 Matt Nachreiner RC .12 .30
82 Chris Kinsey RC .12 .30
83 Jonathan Fulton RC .12 .30
84 Edgardo Baez RC .12 .30
85 Robert Valido RC .12 .30
86 Kenny Lewis RC .12 .30
87 Trent Peterson RC .12 .30
88 Johnny Woodard RC .12 .30
89 Wes Littleton RC .12 .30
90 Sean Rodriguez RC .20 .50
91 Kyle Pearson RC .12 .30
92 Josh Rainwater RC .12 .30
93 Travis Schlichting RC .12 .30
94 Tim Battle RC .12 .30
95 Aaron Hill RC .40 1.00
96 Bob McCrory RC .12 .30
97 Rick Guarno RC .12 .30
98 Brandon Yarbrough RC .12 .30
99 Peter Stonard RC .12 .30
100 Darin Downs RC .12 .30
101 Matt Bruback RC .12 .30
102 Danny Garcia RC .12 .30
103 Cory Stewart RC .12 .30
104 Ferdin Tejeda RC .12 .30
105 Kade Johnson RC .12 .30
106 Andrew Brown RC .12 .30
107 Aquilino Lopez RC .12 .30
108 Stephen Randolph RC .12 .30
109 Dave Matranga RC .12 .30
110 Dustin McGowan RC .12 .30
111 Juan Camacho RC .12 .30
112 Cliff Lee .75 2.00
113 Jeff Duncan RC .12 .30
114 C.J. Wilson 1.00 2.50
115 Brandon Roberson RC .12 .30
116 David Corrente RC .12 .30
117 Kevin Beavers RC .12 .30
118 Anthony Webster RC .12 .30
119 Oscar Villarreal RC .12 .30
120 Hong-Chih Kuo RC .60 1.50
121 Josh Barfield .12 .30
122 Denny Bautista .12 .30
123 Chris Burke RC .12 .30
124 Robinson Cano RC 5.00 12.00
125 Jose Castillo .12 .30
126 Neal Cotts .12 .30
127 Jorge De La Rosa .12 .30
128 J.D. Durbin .12 .30
129 Edwin Encarnacion 1.00 2.50
130 Gavin Floyd .12 .30
131 Alexis Gomez .12 .30
132 Edgar Gonzalez RC .12 .30
133 Khalil Greene .20 .50
134 Zack Greinke .30 .75
135 Franklin Gutierrez .30 .75
136 Rich Harden .20 .50
137 J.J. Hardy RC 1.00 2.50
138 Ryan Howard RC 1.00 2.50
139 Justin Huber .12 .30
140 David Kelton .12 .30
141 Dave Krynzel .12 .30
142 Pete LaForest .12 .30
143 Adam LaRoche .12 .30
144 Preston Larrison RC .12 .30
145 John Maine RC .20 .50
146 Andy Marte .12 .30
147 Jeff Mathis .12 .30
148 Joe Mauer .30 .75
149 Clint Nageotte .12 .30
150 Chris Narveson .12 .30
151 Ramon Nivar .12 .30
152 Felix Pie RC .20 .50
153 Guillermo Quiroz RC .12 .30
154 Rene Reyes .12 .30
155 Royce Ring .12 .30
156 Alexis Rios .12 .30
157 Grady Sizemore .20 .50
158 Stephen Smitherman .12 .30
159 Seung Song .12 .30
160 Scott Thorman .12 .30
161 Chad Tracy .12 .30
162 Chin-Hui Tsao .12 .30
163 John VanBenschoten .12 .30
164 Kevin Youkilis .75 2.00
165 Chien-Ming Wang .50 1.25

2003 Bowman Draft Gold

COMPLETE SET (165) 50.00 100.00
*GOLD: 1.25X TO 3X BASIC
*GOLD RC'S: 1.25X TO 3X BASIC
*GOLD RC YR: 1.25X TO 3X BASIC
ONE PER PACK
124 Robinson Cano 6.00 15.00

2003 Bowman Draft Fabric of the Future Jersey Relics

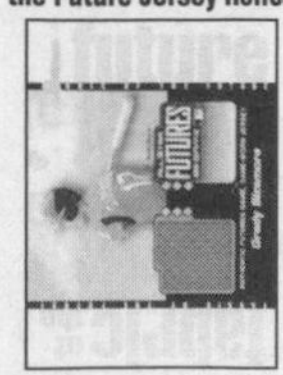

GROUP A ODDS 1:721 H, 1:720 R		
GROUP B ODDS 1:315 H/R		
GROUP C ODDS 1:98 H/R		
GROUP D ODDS 1:81 H, 1:82 R		
GROUP E ODDS 1:263 H/R		
GROUP F ODDS 1:241 H, 1:240 R		
AL Adam LaRoche D	2.00	5.00
AM Andy Marte D	4.00	10.00
CN Chris Narveson C	2.00	5.00
EG Edgar Gonzalez D	2.00	5.00
FG Franklin Gutierrez C	3.00	8.00
FP Felix Pie A	4.00	10.00
GF Gavin Floyd E	2.00	5.00
GS Grady Sizemore D	4.00	10.00
JB Josh Barfield B	3.00	8.00
JD J.D. Durbin D	2.00	5.00
JH Justin Huber D	2.00	5.00
JM Joe Mauer C	8.00	20.00
JSM Jeff Mathis B	2.00	5.00
KG Khalil Greene D	4.00	10.00
RC Robinson Cano C	10.00	25.00
RH Rich Harden C	4.00	10.00
RJH Ryan Howard F	4.00	10.00
RR Rene Reyes E	2.00	5.00
RRR Royce Ring F	2.00	5.00
ZG Zack Greinke C	5.00	12.00

2003 Bowman Draft Prospect Premiums Relics

GROUP A ODDS 1:216 H/R		
GROUP B ODDS 1:470 H, 1:469 R		
AK Austin Kearns Jsy B	2.00	5.00
BH Brendan Harris Bat A	3.00	8.00
BM Brett Myers Jsy B	2.00	5.00
CC Carl Crawford Bat A	3.00	8.00
CS Chris Snelling Bat A	3.00	8.00
CU Chase Utley Bat A	8.00	20.00
HB Hank Blalock Bat A	3.00	8.00
JM Justin Morneau Bat A	3.00	8.00
JT Joe Thurston Bat A	3.00	8.00
NH Nathan Haynes Bat A	3.00	8.00
RB Rocco Baldelli Bat A	3.00	8.00
TH Travis Hafner Bat A	3.00	8.00

2003 Bowman Draft Signs of the Future

GROUP A ODDS 1:385 H, 1:720 R		
GROUP B ODDS 1:491 H, 1:491 R		
GROUP C ODDS 1:2160 H, 1:12,185 R		
AT Andres Torres A	4.00	10.00
CS Cory Stewart B	4.00	10.00
DT Dennis Tankersley A	4.00	10.00
JA Jason Arnold B	4.00	10.00
ZG Zack Greinke C	25.00	60.00

2004 Bowman

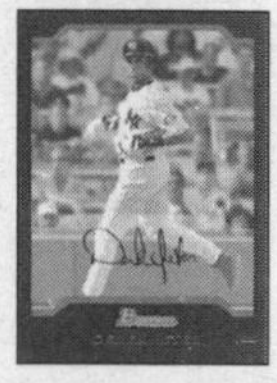

This 330-card set was released in May, 2004. The set was issued in hobby, retail and HTA versions. The hobby version was 10 card packs with an $3 SRP which came 24 packs to a box and 12 boxes to a case. The HTA version had 21 card packs with an $6 SRP which came 12 packs to a box and eight boxes to a case. Meanwhile the Retail version consisted of seven card packs with an $3 SRP which came 24 packs to a box and 12 boxes to a case. Cards numbered 1 through 144 feature veterans while cards cards 145 through 165 feature prospects and cards numbered 166 through 330 feature Rookie Cards. Please note that there is a special card featuring memorabilia pieces from 2003 ROY's Dontrelle Willis and Angel Berroa which we have notated at the end of our checklist.

COMPLETE SET (330)	20.00	50.00
COMMON CARD (1-165)	.10	.30
COMMON CARD (166-330)	.10	.30
ROY ODDS 1:829 H, 1:284 HTA, 1:1632 R		
1 Garret Anderson	.12	.30
2 Larry Walker	.20	.50
3 Derek Jeter	.75	2.00
4 Curt Schilling	.20	.50
5 Carlos Zambrano	.20	.50
6 Shawn Green	.12	.30
7 Manny Ramirez	.30	.75
8 Randy Johnson	.30	.75
9 Jeremy Bonderman	.12	.30
10 Alfonso Soriano	.20	.50
11 Scott Rolen	.20	.50
12 Kerry Wood	.12	.30
13 Eric Gagne	.12	.30
14 Ryan Klesko	.12	.30
15 Kevin Millar	.12	.30
16 Ty Wigginton	.12	.30
17 David Ortiz	.30	.75
18 Luis Castillo	.12	.30
19 Bernie Williams	.20	.50
20 Edgar Renteria	.12	.30
21 Matt Kata	.12	.30
22 Bartolo Colon	.12	.30
23 Derrek Lee	.12	.30
24 Gary Sheffield	.12	.30
25 Nomar Garciaparra	.20	.50
26 Kevin Millwood	.12	.30
27 Corey Patterson	.12	.30
28 Carlos Beltran	.20	.50
29 Mike Lieberthal	.12	.30
30 Troy Glaus	.12	.30
31 Preston Wilson	.12	.30
32 Jorge Posada	.20	.50
33 Bo Hart	.12	.30
34 Mark Prior	.20	.50
35 Hideo Nomo	.30	.75
36 Jason Kendall	.12	.30
37 Roger Clemens	.40	1.00
38 Dmitri Young	.12	.30
39 Jason Giambi	.12	.30
40 Jim Edmonds	.20	.50
41 Ryan Ludwick	.12	.30
42 Brandon Webb	.12	.30
43 Todd Helton	.20	.50
44 Jacque Jones	.12	.30
45 Jamie Moyer	.12	.30
46 Tim Salmon	.12	.30
47 Kelvim Escobar	.12	.30
48 Tony Batista	.12	.30
49 Nick Johnson	.12	.30
50 Jim Thome	.20	.50
51 Casey Blake	.12	.30
52 Trot Nixon	.12	.30
53 Luis Gonzalez	.12	.30
54 Dontrelle Willis	.12	.30
55 Mike Mussina	.20	.50
56 Carl Crawford	.20	.50
57 Mark Buehrle	.20	.50
58 Scott Podsednik	.12	.30
59 Brian Giles	.12	.30
60 Rafael Furcal	.12	.30
61 Miguel Cabrera	.30	.75
62 Rich Harden	.12	.30
63 Mark Teixeira	.20	.50
64 Frank Thomas	.30	.75
65 Johan Santana	.20	.50
66 Jason Schmidt	.12	.30
67 Aramis Ramirez	.12	.30
68 Jose Reyes	.20	.50
69 Magglio Ordonez	.20	.50
70 Mike Sweeney	.12	.30
71 Eric Chavez	.12	.30
72 Rocco Baldelli	.12	.30
73 Sammy Sosa	.30	.75
74 Javy Lopez	.12	.30
75 Roy Oswalt	.20	.50
76 Raul Ibanez	.20	.50
77 Ivan Rodriguez	.20	.50
78 Jerome Williams	.12	.30
79 Carlos Lee	.12	.30
80 Geoff Jenkins	.12	.30
81 Sean Burroughs	.12	.30
82 Marcus Giles	.12	.30
83 Mike Lowell	.12	.30
84 Barry Zito	.20	.50
85 Aubrey Huff	.12	.30
86 Esteban Loaiza	.12	.30
87 Torii Hunter	.12	.30
88 Phil Nevin	.12	.30
89 Andruw Jones	.12	.30
90 Josh Beckett	.12	.30
91 Mark Mulder	.12	.30
92 Hank Blalock	.12	.30
93 Jason Phillips	.12	.30
94 Russ Ortiz	.12	.30
95 Juan Pierre	.12	.30
96 Tom Glavine	.20	.50
97 Gil Meche	.12	.30
98 Ramon Ortiz	.12	.30
99 Richie Sexson	.12	.30
100 Albert Pujols	.40	1.00
101 Javier Vazquez	.12	.30
102 Johnny Damon	.20	.50
103 Alex Rodriguez Yanks	.40	1.00
104 Omar Vizquel	.20	.50
105 Chipper Jones	.30	.75
106 Lance Berkman	.20	.50
107 Tim Hudson	.20	.50
108 Carlos Delgado	.12	.30
109 Austin Kearns	.12	.30
110 Orlando Cabrera	.12	.30
111 Edgar Martinez	.20	.50
112 Melvin Mora	.12	.30
113 Jeff Bagwell	.20	.50
114 Marlon Byrd	.12	.30
115 Vernon Wells	.12	.30
116 C.C. Sabathia	.20	.50
117 Cliff Floyd	.12	.30
118 Ichiro Suzuki	.40	1.00
119 Miguel Olivo	.12	.30
120 Mike Piazza	.30	.75
121 Adam Dunn	.20	.50
122 Paul Lo Duca	.12	.30
123 Brett Myers	.12	.30
124 Michael Young	.12	.30
125 Sidney Ponson	.12	.30
126 Greg Maddux	.40	1.00
127 Vladimir Guerrero	.20	.50
128 Miguel Tejada	.20	.50
129 Andy Pettitte	.20	.50
130 Rafael Palmeiro	.20	.50
131 Ken Griffey Jr.	.60	1.50
132 Shannon Stewart	.12	.30
133 Joel Pineiro	.12	.30
134 Luis Matos	.12	.30
135 Jeff Kent	.12	.30
136 Randy Wolf	.12	.30
137 Chris Woodward	.12	.30
138 Jody Gerut	.12	.30
139 Jose Vidro	.12	.30
140 Bret Boone	.12	.30
141 Bill Mueller	.12	.30
142 Angel Berroa	.12	.30
143 Bobby Abreu	.12	.30
144 Roy Halladay	.20	.50
145 Delmon Young	.20	.50
146 Jonny Gomes	.12	.30
147 Rickie Weeks	.12	.30
148 Edwin Jackson	.12	.30
149 Neal Cotts	.12	.30
150 Jason Bay	.20	.50
151 Khalil Greene	.20	.50
152 Joe Mauer	.25	.60
153 Bobby Jenks	.12	.30
154 Chin-Feng Chen	.12	.30
155 Chien-Ming Wang	.50	1.25
156 Mickey Hall	.12	.30
157 James Houser	.12	.30
158 Jay Sborz	.12	.30
159 Jonathan Fulton	.12	.30
160 Steven Lerud	.12	.30
161 Grady Sizemore	.20	.50
162 Felix Pie	.12	.30
163 Dustin McGowan	.12	.30
164 Chris Lubanski	.12	.30
165 Tom Gorzelanny	.12	.30
166 Rudy Guillen FY RC	.12	.30
167 Bobby Brownlie FY RC	.12	.30
168 Conor Jackson FY RC	.40	1.00
169 Matt Moses FY RC	.20	.50
170 Ervin Santana FY RC	.30	.75
171 Merkin Valdez FY RC	.12	.30
172 Erick Aybar FY RC	.30	.75
173 Brad Sullivan FY RC	.12	.30
174 David Aardsma FY RC	.12	.30
175 Brad Snyder FY RC	.12	.30
176 Alberto Callaspo FY RC	.30	.75
177 Brandon Medders FY RC	.12	.30
178 Zach Miner FY RC	.20	.50
179 Charlie Zink FY RC	.12	.30
180 Adam Greenberg FY RC	.60	1.50
181 Kevin Howard FY RC	.12	.30
182 Wanell Severino FY RC	.12	.30
183 Kevin Kouzmanoff FY RC	.75	2.00
184 Joel Zumaya FY RC	.50	1.25
185 Skip Schumaker FY RC	.20	.50
186 Nic Ungs FY RC	.12	.30
187 Todd Self FY RC	.12	.30
188 Brian Steffek FY RC	.12	.30
189 Brock Peterson FY RC	.12	.30
190 Greg Thissen FY RC	.12	.30
191 Frank Brooks FY RC	.12	.30
192 Estee Harris FY RC	.12	.30
193 Chris Mabeus FY RC	.12	.30
194 Dan Giese FY RC	.12	.30
195 Jared Wells FY RC	.12	.30
196 Carlos Sosa FY RC	.12	.30
197 Bobby Madritsch FY	.12	.30
198 Calvin Hayes FY RC	.12	.30
199 Omar Quintanilla FY RC	.12	.30
200 Chris O'Riordan FY RC	.12	.30
201 Tim Hutting FY RC	.12	.30
202 Carlos Quentin FY RC	.50	1.25
203 Brayan Pena FY RC	.12	.30
204 Jeff Salazar FY RC	.12	.30
205 David Murphy FY RC	.20	.50
206 Alberto Garcia FY RC	.12	.30
207 Ramon Ramirez FY RC	.12	.30
208 Luis Bolivar FY RC	.12	.30
209 Rodney Choy Foo FY RC	.12	.30
210 Kyle Sleeth FY RC	.12	.30
211 Anthony Acevedo FY RC	.12	.30
212 Chad Santos FY RC	.12	.30
213 Jason Frasor FY RC	.12	.30
214 Jesse Roman FY RC	.12	.30
215 James Tomlin FY RC	.12	.30
216 Josh Labandeira FY RC	.12	.30
217 Joaquin Arias FY RC	.30	.75
218 Don Sutton FY UER RC	.12	.30
219 Danny Gonzalez FY RC	.12	.30
220 Javier Guzman FY RC	.12	.30
221 Anthony Lerew FY RC	.12	.30
222 Jon Knott FY RC	.12	.30
223 Jesse English FY RC	.12	.30
224 Felix Hernandez FY RC	2.00	5.00
225 Travis Hanson FY RC	.12	.30
226 Jesse Floyd FY RC	.12	.30
227 Nick Gorneault FY RC	.12	.30
228 Craig Ansman FY RC	.12	.30
229 Wardell Starling FY RC	.12	.30
230 Carl Loadenthal FY RC	.12	.30
231 Dave Crouthers FY RC	.12	.30
232 Harvey Garcia FY RC	.12	.30
233 Casey Kopitzke FY RC	.12	.30
234 Ricky Nolasco FY RC	.20	.50
235 Miguel Perez FY RC	.12	.30
236 Ryan Mulhern FY RC	.12	.30
237 Chris Aguila FY RC	.12	.30
238 Brooks Conrad FY RC	.12	.30
239 Damaso Espino FY RC	.12	.30
240 Jereme Milons FY RC	.12	.30
241 Luke Hughes FY RC	.30	.75
242 Kory Casto FY RC	.12	.30
243 Jose Valdez FY RC	.12	.30
244 J.T. Stotts FY RC	.12	.30
245 Lee Gwaltney FY RC	.12	.30
246 Yoann Torrealba FY RC	.12	.30
247 Omar Falcon FY RC	.12	.30
248 Jon Coutlangus FY RC	.12	.30
249 George Sherrill FY RC	.12	.30
250 John Santor FY RC	.12	.30
251 Tony Richie FY RC	.12	.30
252 Kevin Richardson FY RC	.12	.30
253 Tim Bittner FY RC	.12	.30
254 Dustin Nippert FY RC	.12	.30
255 Jose Capellan FY RC	.12	.30
256 Donald Levinski FY RC	.12	.30
257 Jerome Gamble FY RC	.12	.30
258 Jeff Keppinger FY RC	.20	.50
259 Jason Szuminski FY RC	.12	.30
260 Akinori Otsuka FY RC	.12	.30
261 Ryan Budde FY RC	.12	.30
262 Shingo Takatsu FY RC	.12	.30
263 Jeff Allison FY RC	.12	.30
264 Hector Gimenez FY RC	.12	.30
265 Tim Frend FY RC	.12	.30
266 Tom Farmer FY RC	.12	.30
267 Shawn Hill FY RC	.12	.30
268 Lastings Milledge FY RC	.20	.50
269 Scott Proctor FY RC	.12	.30
270 Jorge Mejia FY RC	.12	.30
271 Terry Jones FY RC	.12	.30
272 Zach Duke FY RC	.20	.50
273 Tim Stauffer FY RC	.20	.50
274 Luke Anderson FY RC	.12	.30
275 Hunter Brown FY RC	.12	.30
276 Matt Lemanczyk FY RC	.12	.30
277 Fernando Cortez FY RC	.12	.30
278 Vince Perkins FY RC	.12	.30
279 Tommy Murphy FY RC	.12	.30
280 Mike Gosling FY RC	.12	.30
281 Paul Bacot FY RC	.12	.30
282 Matt Capps FY RC	.12	.30
283 Juan Gutierrez FY RC	.12	.30
284 Teodoro Encarnacion FY RC	.12	.30
285 Juan Cedeno FY RC	.12	.30
286 Matt Creighton FY RC	.12	.30
287 Ryan Hankins FY RC	.12	.30
288 Leo Nunez FY RC	.12	.30
289 Dave Wallace FY RC	.12	.30
290 Rob Tejeda FY RC	.12	.30
291 Lincoln Holdzkom FY RC	.12	.30
292 Jason Hirsh FY RC	.12	.30
293 Tydus Meadows FY RC	.12	.30
294 Khalid Ballouli FY RC	.12	.30
295 Benji DeQuin FY RC	.12	.30
296 Tyler Davidson FY RC	.12	.30
297 Brant Colamarino FY RC	.12	.30
298 Marcus McBeth FY RC	.12	.30
299 Brad Eldred FY RC	.12	.30
300 David Pauley FY RC	.20	.50
301 Yadier Molina FY RC	1.50	4.00
302 Chris Shelton FY RC	.12	.30
303 Travis Blackley FY RC	.12	.30
304 Jon DeVries FY RC	.12	.30
305 Sheldon Fulse FY RC	.12	.30
306 Vito Chiaravalloti FY RC	.12	.30
307 Warner Madrigal FY RC	.12	.30
308 Reid Gorecki FY RC	.12	.30
309 Sung Jung FY RC	.12	.30
310 Pete Shier FY RC	.12	.30
311 Michael Mooney FY RC	.12	.30
312 Kenny Perez FY RC	.12	.30
313 Michael Mallory FY RC	.12	.30
314 Ben Himes FY RC	.12	.30
315 Ivan Ochoa FY RC	.12	.30
316 Donald Kelly FY RC	.20	.50
317 Logan Kensing FY RC	.12	.30
318 Kevin Davidson FY RC	.12	.30
319 Brian Pilkington FY RC	.12	.30
320 Alex Romero FY RC	.12	.30
321 Chad Chop FY RC	.12	.30
322 Dioner Navarro FY RC	.20	.50
323 Casey Myers FY RC	.12	.30
324 Mike Rouse FY RC	.12	.30
325 Sergio Silva FY RC	.12	.30
326 J.J. Furmaniak FY RC	.12	.30
327 Brad Vericker FY RC	.12	.30
328 Blake Hawksworth FY RC	.12	.30
329 Brock Jacobsen FY RC	.12	.30
330 Alec Zumwalt FY RC	.12	.30
BW Berroa Bat/Willis Jsy ROY	6.00	15.00

2004 Bowman 1st Edition

*1ST EDITION 1-165: .75X TO 2X BASIC
*1ST EDITION 166-330: .75X TO 2X BASIC
ISSUED IN FIRST EDITION PACKS

2004 Bowman Gold

COMPLETE SET (330)	60.00	150.00
*GOLD 1-165: 1.25X TO 3X BASIC		
*GOLD 166-330: 1X TO 2.5X BASIC		
ONE PER HOBBY PACK		
ONE PER HTA PACK		
ONE PER RETAIL PACK		

2004 Bowman Uncirculated Gold

ONE EXCH.CARD PER SILVER PACK		
ONE SILVER PACK PER SEALED HOBBY BOX		
ONE SILVER PACK PER SEALED HTA BOX		
STATED ODDS 1:44 RETAIL		
STATED PRINT RUN 210 SETS		
SEE WWW.THEPIT.COM FOR PRICING		
NNO Exchange Card	2.00	5.00

2004 Bowman Uncirculated Silver

*UNC.SILVER 1-165: 4X TO 10X BASIC
*UNC.SILVER 166-330: 3X TO 8X BASIC
ONE PER SILVER PACK
ONE SILVER PACK PER SEALED HOBBY BOX
ONE SILVER PACK PER SEALED HTA BOX
SET EXCH.CARD ODDS 1:9159 H, 1:3718 HTA
STATED PRINT RUN 245 SERIAL #'d SETS
1ST 100 SETS PRINTED HELD FOR EXCH.
LAST 145 SETS PRINTED DIST.IN BOXES
EXCHANGE DEADLINE 05/31/06

2004 Bowman Autographs

STATED ODDS 1:72 H, 1:24 HTA, 1:139 R		
RED INK ODDS 1:1466 H,1:501 HTA,1:2901 R		
RED INK PRINT RUN 25 SETS		
RED INK ARE NOT SERIAL-NUMBERED		
RED INK PRINT RUN PROVIDED BY TOPPS		
NO RED INK PRICING DUE TO SCARCITY		
161 Grady Sizemore	4.00	10.00
162 Felix Pie	4.00	10.00
163 Dustin McGowan	3.00	8.00
164 Chris Lubanski	4.00	10.00
165 Tom Gorzelanny	3.00	8.00
166 Rudy Guillen	4.00	10.00
167 Bobby Brownlie	4.00	10.00
168 Conor Jackson	4.00	10.00
169 Matt Moses	4.00	10.00
170 Ervin Santana	4.00	10.00
171 Merkin Valdez	4.00	10.00
172 Erick Aybar	4.00	10.00
173 Brad Sullivan	4.00	10.00
174 David Aardsma	4.00	10.00
175 Brad Snyder	4.00	10.00

2004 Bowman Relics

GROUP A 1:346 H, 1:118 HTA, 1:1685 R		
GROUP B 1:133 H, 1:44 HTA, 1:269 R		
HS JSY MEANS HIGH SCHOOL JERSEY		
154 Chin-Feng Chen Jsy B	6.00	15.00
155 Chien-Ming Wang Uni B	6.00	15.00
156 Mickey Hall HS Jsy B	3.00	8.00
157 James Houser HS Jsy A	3.00	8.00
158 Jay Sborz HS Jsy B	3.00	8.00
159 Jonathan Fulton HS Jsy B	3.00	8.00
160 Steve Lerud HS Jsy A	3.00	8.00
164 Chris Lubanski HS Jsy B	3.00	8.00
192 Estee Harris HS Jsy A	3.00	8.00
221 Anthony Lerew Jsy B	3.00	8.00

2004 Bowman Base of the Future Autograph

STATED ODDS 1:110 HTA		
RED INK ODDS 1:5112 HTA		
RED INK PRINT RUN 25 SERIAL #'d CARDS		
NO RED INK PRICING DUE TO SCARCITY		
GS Grady Sizemore	6.00	15.00

2004 Bowman Futures Game Gear Jersey Relics

GROUP A 1:167 H, 1:58 HTA, 1:333 R		
GROUP B 1:71 H, 1:23 HTA, 1:148 R		
GROUP C 1:181 H, 1:63 HTA, 1:362 R		
GROUP D 1:173 H, 1:59 HTA, 1:341 R		
GROUP E 1:145 H, 1:70 HTA, 1:318 R		
AR Alexis Rios A	3.00	8.00
CB Chris Burke B	3.00	8.00
CN Clint Nageotte B	3.00	8.00
CT Chad Tracy B	3.00	8.00
CW Chien-Ming Wang C	15.00	40.00
DB Denny Bautista D	3.00	8.00
DBK Dave Krynzel B	3.00	8.00
DK David Kelton E	3.00	8.00
EE Edwin Encarnacion A	3.00	8.00
EJ Edwin Jackson C	3.00	8.00
ES Ervin Santana D	4.00	10.00
GQ Guillermo Quiroz A	3.00	8.00
JC Jose Castillo E	3.00	8.00
JD Jorge De La Rosa C	3.00	8.00
JH J.J. Hardy A	3.00	8.00
JM John Maine B	4.00	10.00
JV John VanBenschoten B	3.00	8.00
KY Kevin Youkilis E	3.00	8.00
MV Merkin Valdez E	3.00	8.00
NC Neal Cotts D	3.00	8.00
PL Pete LaForest B	3.00	8.00
PWL Preston Larrison B	3.00	8.00
RN Ramon Nivar A	3.00	8.00
SH Shawn Hill D	3.00	8.00
SJS Seung Song B	3.00	8.00
SS Stephen Smitherman B	3.00	8.00
ST Scott Thorman C	3.00	8.00
TB Travis Blackley B	3.00	8.00

2004 Bowman Signs of the Future

GROUP A 1:75 H, 1:25 HTA, 1:147 R		
GROUP B 1:847 H, 1:289 HTA, 1:1675 R		
GROUP C 1:582 H, 1:198 HTA, 1:1148 R		
GROUP D 1:315 H, 1:105 HTA, 1:605 R		
RED INK ODDS 1:1466 H,1:501 HTA,1:2901 R		
RED INK PRINT RUN 25 SETS		
RED INK CARDS ARE NOT SERIAL #'d		
RED INK PRINT RUN PROVIDED BY TOPPS		
NO RED INK PRICING DUE TO SCARCITY		
AH Aaron Hill A	5.00	12.00
BC Brent Clevlen A	8.00	20.00
BF Brian Finch D	4.00	10.00
BM Brandon Medders A	3.00	8.00
BS Brian Snyder D	4.00	10.00
BW Brandon Wood B	8.00	20.00
CS Corey Shafer A	3.00	8.00
DS Denard Span A	4.00	10.00
ED Eric Duncan D	6.00	15.00
GS Grady Sizemore D	10.00	25.00
IC Ismael Castro A	3.00	8.00
JB Justin Backsmeyer D	4.00	10.00
JH James Houser A	3.00	8.00
JV Joey Votto A	60.00	150.00
MM Matt Murton D	6.00	15.00
NM Nick Markakis C	3.00	8.00
RH Ryan Harvey C	4.00	10.00
TJ Tyler Johnson A	3.00	8.00
TL Todd Linden A	3.00	8.00

2004 Bowman Draft

This 165-card set was released in November-December, 2004. The set was issued in seven-card hobby and retail packs, both with an $3 SRP which were issued 24 packs to a box and 10 boxes to a case. The hobby and retial packs can be differentiated by the insert odds.

COMPLETE SET (165)	15.00	40.00
COMMON CARD (1-165)	.12	.30
COMMON RC (1-165)	.12	.30
COMMON RC YR	.12	.30
PLATES ODDS 1:559 HOBBY		
PLATES PRINT RUN 1 SERIAL #'d SET		
BLACK-CYAN-MAGENTA-YELLOW EXIST		
NO PLATES PRICING DUE TO SCARCITY		
1 Lyle Overbay	.12	.30
2 David Newhan	.12	.30
3 J.R. House	.12	.30
4 Chad Tracy	.12	.30
5 Humberto Quintero	.12	.30
6 Dave Bush	.12	.30
7 Scott Hairston	.12	.30
8 Mike Wood	.12	.30
9 Alexis Rios	.12	.30
10 Sean Burnett	.12	.30
11 Wilson Valdez	.12	.30
12 Lew Ford	.12	.30
13 Freddy Thon RC	.12	.30
14 Zack Greinke	.30	.75
15 Bucky Jacobsen	.12	.30
16 Kevin Youkilis	.12	.30
17 Grady Sizemore	.20	.50
18 Denny Bautista	.12	.30
19 David DeJesus	.12	.30
20 Casey Kotchman	.12	.30
21 David Kelton	.12	.30
22 Charles Thomas RC	.12	.30
23 Kazuhito Tadano RC	.12	.30
24 Justin Leone RC	.12	.30
25 Eduardo Villacis RC	.12	.30
26 Brian Dallimore RC	.12	.30
27 Nick Green	.12	.30
28 Sam McConnell RC	.12	.30
29 Brad Halsey RC	.12	.30
30 Roman Colon RC	.12	.30
31 Josh Fields RC	.20	.50
32 Cody Bunkelman RC	.12	.30
33 Jay Rainville RC	.12	.30
34 Richie Robnett RC	.12	.30
35 Jon Poterson RC	.12	.30
36 Huston Street RC	.20	.50
37 Erick San Pedro RC	.12	.30
38 Cory Dunlap RC	.12	.30
39 Kurt Suzuki RC	.20	.50
40 Anthony Swarzak RC	.20	.50
41 Ian Desmond RC	.20	.50
42 Chris Covington RC	.12	.30
43 Christian Garcia RC	.20	.50
44 Gaby Hernandez RC	.20	.50
45 Steven Register RC	.12	.30
46 Eduardo Morlan RC	.20	.50
47 Collin Balester RC	.12	.30
48 Nathan Phillips RC	.12	.30
49 Dan Schwartzbauer RC	.12	.30
50 Rafael Gonzalez RC	.12	.30
51 K.C. Herren RC	.12	.30
52 William Susdorf RC	.12	.30
53 Rob Johnson RC	.12	.30
54 Louis Marson RC	.20	.50
55 Joe Koshansky RC	.12	.30
56 Jamar Walton RC	.12	.30
57 Mark Lowe RC	.20	.50
58 Matt Macri RC	.20	.50
59 Donny Lucy RC	.12	.30
60 Mike Ferris RC	.12	.30
61 Mike Nickeas RC	.12	.30
62 Eric Hurley RC	.12	.30
63 Scott Elbert RC	.12	.30
64 Blake DeWitt RC	.20	.50
65 Danny Putnam RC	.12	.30
66 J.P. Howell RC	.12	.30
67 John Wiggins RC	.12	.30
68 Justin Orenduff RC	.20	.50
69 Ray Liotta RC	.12	.30
70 Billy Buckner RC	.12	.30
71 Eric Campbell RC	.12	.30
72 Olin Wick RC	.12	.30
73 Sean Gamble RC	.12	.30
74 Seth Smith RC	.20	.50
75 Wade Davis RC	.30	.75
76 Joe Jacobitz RC	.12	.30
77 J.A. Happ RC	.30	.75
78 Eric Ridener RC	.12	.30
79 Matt Tuiasosopo RC	.30	.75
80 Brad Bergesen RC	.12	.30
81 Javy Guerra RC	.30	.75
82 Buck Shaw RC	.12	.30
83 Paul Janish RC	.20	.50
84 Sean Kazmar RC	.12	.30
85 Josh Johnson RC	.12	.30
86 Angel Salome RC	.12	.30

87 Jordan Parraz RC .20 .50
88 Kelvin Vazquez RC .12 .30
89 Grant Hansen RC .12 .30
90 Matt Fox RC .12 .30
91 Trevor Plouffe RC .30 .75
92 Wes Whisler RC .12 .30
93 Curtis Thigpen RC .12 .30
94 Donnie Smith RC .12 .30
95 Luis Rivera RC .12 .30
96 Jesse Hoover RC .12 .30
97 Jason Vargas RC .20 .50
98 Clary Carlsen RC .12 .30
99 Mark Robinson RC .12 .30
100 J.C. Holt RC .12 .30
101 Chad Blackwell RC .12 .30
102 Daryl Jones RC .12 .30
103 Jonathan Tierce RC .12 .30
104 Patrick Bryant RC .12 .30
105 Eddie Prasch RC .12 .30
106 Mitch Einertson RC .12 .30
107 Kyle Waldrop RC .12 .30
108 Jeff Marquez RC .12 .30
109 Zach Jackson RC .12 .30
110 Josh Wahpepah RC .12 .30
111 Adam Lind RC .20 .50
112 Kyle Bloom RC .12 .30
113 Ben Harrison RC .12 .30
114 Taylor Tankersley RC .12 .30
115 Steven Jackson RC .12 .30
116 David Purcey RC .20 .50
117 Jacob McGee RC .20 .50
118 Lucas Harrell RC .12 .30
119 Brandon Allen RC .12 .30
120 Van Pope RC .12 .30
121 Jeff Francis .12 .30
122 Joe Blanton .12 .30
123 Wil Ledezma .12 .30
124 Bryan Bullington .12 .30
125 Jairo Garcia .12 .30
126 Matt Cain .75 2.00
127 Arnie Munoz .12 .30
128 Clint Everts .12 .30
129 Jesus Cota .12 .30
130 Gavin Floyd .12 .30
131 Edwin Encarnacion .30 .75
132 Koyie Hill .12 .30
133 Ruben Gotay .12 .30
134 Jeff Mathis .12 .30
135 Andy Marte .12 .30
136 Dallas McPherson .12 .30
137 Justin Morneau .20 .50
138 Rickie Weeks .12 .30
139 Joel Guzman .12 .30
140 Shin Soo Choo .20 .50
141 Yusmeiro Petit RC .30 .75
142 Jorge Cortes RC .12 .30
143 Val Majewski .12 .30
144 Felix Pie .12 .30
145 Aaron Hill .12 .30
146 Jose Capellan .12 .30
147 Dioner Navarro .20 .50
148 Fausto Carmona RC .20 .50
149 Robinzon Diaz RC .12 .30
150 Felix Hernandez 2.00 5.00
151 Andres Blanco RC .12 .30
152 Jason Kubel .12 .30
153 Willy Taveras RC .30 .75
154 Merkin Valdez .12 .30
155 Robinson Cano .40 1.00
156 Bill Murphy .12 .30
157 Chris Burke .12 .30
158 Kyle Sleeth .12 .30
159 B.J. Upton .20 .50
160 Tim Stauffer .20 .50
161 David Wright .25 .60
162 Conor Jackson .40 1.00
163 Brad Thompson RC .20 .50
164 Delmon Young .20 .50
165 Jeremy Reed .12 .30

2004 Bowman Draft Gold

COMPLETE SET (165) 25.00 60.00
*GOLD RC's: .6X TO 1.5X BASIC
*GOLD RC YR: .6X TO 1.5X BASIC
ONE PER PACK

2004 Bowman Draft Red

STATED ODDS 1:4471 HOBBY
STATED PRINT RUN 1 SERIAL #'d SET
NO PRICING DUE TO SCARCITY

2004 Bowman Draft AFLAC Promos

Little is known about how many of these six cards have appeared on the secondary market. A few of these cards surfaced in the AFLAC redemption packs issued to dealers. These cards were issued instead of some of the standard 12 cards in those packs. If you know of other cards issued this way or can provide extra information, that would be very appreciated.

DISTRIBUTED TO DEALERS
11 Cameron Maybin
15 Ryan DeLaughter
17 Jeremy Hellickson
18 Austin Jackson
19 Ryan Mitchell
30 Ralphie Henriquez
38 Kent Matthes

2004 Bowman Draft AFLAC

COMP.FACT.SET (12) 8.00 20.00
ONE SET VIA MAIL PER AFLAC EXCH.CARD
ONE EXCH.PER '04 BOW.DRAFT HOBBY BOX
EXCH.CARD DEADLINE WAS 11/30/05
SETS ACTUALLY SENT OUT JANUARY, 2006
RED PRINT RUN 1 SERIAL #'d SET
NO RED PRICING DUE TO SCARCITY
1 C.J. Henry .20 .50
2 John Drennen .20 .50
3 Beau Jones .20 .50
4 Jeff Lyman .20 .50
5 Andrew McCutchen 3.00 8.00
6 Chris Volstad .30 .75
7 Jonathan Egan .20 .50
8 P.J. Phillips .20 .50
9 Steve Johnson .20 .50
10 Ryan Tucker .20 .50
11 Cameron Maybin .60 1.50
12 Shane Funk .20 .50

2004 Bowman Draft Futures Game Jersey Relics

STATED ODDS 1:31 HOBBY, 1:30 RETAIL
146 Jose Capellan 3.00 8.00
147 Dioner Navarro 3.00 8.00
148 Fausto Carmona 2.00 5.00
149 Robinzon Diaz 2.00 5.00
150 Felix Hernandez 10.00 25.00
151 Andres Blanco 2.00 5.00
152 Jason Kubel 2.00 5.00
153 Willy Taveras 3.00 8.00
154 Merkin Valdez 3.00 8.00
155 Robinson Cano 6.00 15.00
156 Bill Murphy 2.00 5.00
157 Chris Burke 2.00 5.00
158 Kyle Sleeth 3.00 8.00
159 B.J. Upton 3.00 8.00
160 Tim Stauffer 3.00 8.00
161 David Wright 8.00 20.00
162 Conor Jackson 3.00 8.00
163 Brad Thompson 3.00 8.00
164 Delmon Young 3.00 8.00
165 Jeremy Reed 2.00 5.00

2004 Bowman Draft Prospect Premiums Relics

GROUP A ODDS 1:145 H, 1:153 R
GROUP B ODDS 1:387 H, 1:411 R
AB Angel Berroa Bat A 2.00 5.00
BU B.J. Upton Bat B 3.00 8.00
CJ Conor Jackson Bat B 3.00 8.00
CQ Carlos Quentin Bat B 3.00 8.00
DN Dioner Navarro Bat A 2.00 5.00
DY Delmon Young Bat A 3.00 8.00
EJ Edwin Jackson Jsy A 2.00 5.00
JR Jeremy Reed Bat A 2.00 5.00
KC Kevin Cash Bat B 2.00 5.00
LM Lastings Milledge Bat A 4.00 10.00
NS Nick Swisher Bat B 2.00 5.00
RH Ryan Harvey Bat A 2.00 5.00

2004 Bowman Draft Signs of the Future

GROUP A ODDS 1:127 H, 1:127 R
GROUP B ODDS 1:509 H, 1:511 R
EXCHANGE DEADLINE 11/30/05
AL Adam Loewen A 6.00 15.00
CC Chad Cordero B 6.00 15.00
JH James Houser B 4.00 10.00
PM Paul Maholm A 4.00 10.00
TP Tyler Pelland A 4.00 10.00
TT Terry Tiffee A 4.00 10.00

2005 Bowman

This 330-card set was released in May, 2005. The set was issued in 10-card hobby and retail packs which had an $3 SRP and which came 24 packs to a box and 12 boxes to a case. These cards were also issued in "HTA" or jumbo packs with an $6 SRP which had 21 cards per pack and came 12 packs to a box and eight boxes to a case. The first 140 cards in this set feature active veterans while cards number 141 through 165 feature leading prospects and cards 166 through 330 feature Rookie Cards. There was also a card randomly inserted into packs featuring game-used relics of the 2004 Rookies of the Year.

COMPLETE SET (330) 20.00 50.00
COMMON CARD (1-140) .10 .30
COMMON CARD (141-165) .15 .40
COMMON CARD (166-330) .15 .40
PLATE ODDS 1:695 HOBBY, 1:177 HTA
PLATE PRINT RUN 1 SET PER COLOR
BLACK-CYAN-MAGENTA-YELLOW ISSUED
NO PLATE PRICING DUE TO SCARCITY
ROY ODDS 1:668 H, 1:248 HTA, 1:1535 R
1 Gavin Floyd .12 .30
2 Eric Chavez .12 .30
3 Miguel Tejada .20 .50
4 Dmitri Young .12 .30
5 Hank Blalock .12 .30
6 Kerry Wood .12 .30
7 Andy Pettitte .20 .50
8 Pat Burrell .12 .30
9 Johnny Estrada .12 .30
10 Frank Thomas .30 .75
11 Juan Pierre .12 .30
12 Tom Glavine .20 .50
13 Lyle Overbay .12 .30
14 Jim Edmonds .20 .50
15 Steve Finley .12 .30
16 Jermaine Dye .12 .30
17 Omar Vizquel .20 .50
18 Nick Johnson .12 .30
19 Brian Giles .12 .30
20 Justin Morneau .20 .50
21 Preston Wilson .12 .30
22 Wily Mo Pena .12 .30
23 Rafael Palmeiro .20 .50
24 Scott Kazmir .30 .75
25 Derek Jeter .75 2.00
26 Barry Zito .20 .50
27 Mike Lowell .12 .30
28 Jason Bay .12 .30
29 Ken Harvey .12 .30
30 Nomar Garciaparra .20 .50
31 Roy Halladay .20 .50
32 Todd Helton .20 .50
33 Mark Kotsay .12 .30
34 Jake Peavy .12 .30
35 David Wright .25 .60
36 Dontrelle Willis .12 .30
37 Marcus Giles .12 .30
38 Chone Figgins .12 .30
39 Sidney Ponson .12 .30
40 Randy Johnson .30 .75
41 John Smoltz .30 .75
42 Kevin Millar .12 .30
43 Mark Teixeira .20 .50
44 Alex Rios .12 .30
45 Mike Piazza .30 .75
46 Victor Martinez .20 .50
47 Jeff Bagwell .20 .50
48 Shawn Green .12 .30
49 Ivan Rodriguez .20 .50
50 Alex Rodriguez .40 1.00
51 Kazuo Matsui .12 .30
52 Mark Mulder .12 .30
53 Michael Young .12 .30
54 Javy Lopez .12 .30
55 Johnny Damon .20 .50
56 Jeff Francis .12 .30
57 Rich Harden .12 .30
58 Bobby Abreu .12 .30
59 Mark Loretta .12 .30
60 Gary Sheffield .12 .30
61 Jamie Moyer .12 .30
62 Garret Anderson .12 .30
63 Vernon Wells .12 .30
64 Orlando Cabrera .12 .30
65 Magglio Ordonez .20 .50
66 Ronnie Belliard .12 .30
67 Carlos Lee .12 .30
68 Carl Pavano .12 .30
69 Jon Lieber .12 .30
70 Aubrey Huff .12 .30
71 Rocco Baldelli .12 .30
72 Jason Schmidt .12 .30
73 Bernie Williams .20 .50
74 Hideki Matsui .50 1.25
75 Ken Griffey Jr. .60 1.50
76 Josh Beckett .12 .30
77 Mark Buehrle .20 .50
78 David Ortiz .30 .75
79 Luis Gonzalez .12 .30
80 Scott Rolen .20 .50
81 Joe Mauer .25 .60
82 Jose Reyes .20 .50
83 Adam Dunn .20 .50
84 Greg Maddux .40 1.00
85 Bartolo Colon .12 .30
86 Bret Boone .12 .30
87 Mike Mussina .20 .50
88 Ben Sheets .12 .30
89 Lance Berkman .20 .50
90 Miguel Cabrera .30 .75
91 C.C. Sabathia .20 .50
92 Mike Maroth .12 .30
93 Andruw Jones .12 .30
94 Jack Wilson .12 .30
95 Ichiro Suzuki .40 1.00
96 Geoff Jenkins .12 .30
97 Zack Greinke .30 .75
98 Jorge Posada .20 .50
99 Travis Hafner .12 .30
100 Barry Bonds .50 1.25
101 Aaron Rowand .12 .30
102 Aramis Ramirez .12 .30
103 Curt Schilling .20 .50
104 Melvin Mora .12 .30
105 Albert Pujols .40 1.00
106 Austin Kearns .12 .30
107 Shannon Stewart .12 .30
108 Carl Crawford .20 .50
109 Carlos Zambrano .20 .50
110 Roger Clemens .40 1.00
111 Javier Vazquez .12 .30
112 Randy Wolf .12 .30
113 Chipper Jones .30 .75
114 Larry Walker .20 .50
115 Alfonso Soriano .20 .50
116 Brad Wilkerson .12 .30
117 Bobby Crosby .12 .30
118 Jim Thome .20 .50
119 Oliver Perez .12 .30
120 Vladimir Guerrero .20 .50
121 Roy Oswalt .20 .50
122 Torii Hunter .12 .30
123 Rafael Furcal .12 .30
124 Luis Castillo .12 .30
125 Carlos Beltran .20 .50
126 Mike Sweeney .12 .30
127 Johan Santana .20 .50
128 Tim Hudson .20 .50
129 Troy Glaus .12 .30
130 Manny Ramirez .30 .75
131 Jeff Kent .12 .30
132 Jose Vidro .12 .30
133 Edgar Renteria .12 .30
134 Russ Ortiz .12 .30
135 Sammy Sosa .30 .75
136 Carlos Delgado .12 .30
137 Richie Sexson .12 .30
138 Pedro Martinez .20 .50
139 Adrian Beltre .30 .75
140 Mark Prior .20 .50
141 Omar Quintanilla .15 .40
142 Carlos Quentin .25 .60
143 Dan Johnson .15 .40
144 Jake Stevens .15 .40
145 Nate Schierholtz .15 .40
146 Neil Walker .25 .60
147 Bill Bray .15 .40
148 Taylor Tankersley .15 .40
149 Trevor Plouffe .40 1.00
150 Felix Hernandez .50 1.25
151 Philip Hughes .40 1.00
152 James Houser .15 .40
153 David Murphy .25 .60
154 Ervin Santana .15 .40
155 Anthony Whittington .15 .40
156 Chris Lambert .15 .40
157 Jeremy Sowers .15 .40
158 Giovanny Gonzalez .25 .60
159 Blake DeWitt .25 .60
160 Thomas Diamond .15 .40
161 Greg Golson .15 .40
162 David Aardsma .15 .40
163 Paul Maholm .15 .40
164 Mark Rogers .15 .40
165 Homer Bailey .15 .40
166 Chip Cannon FY RC .15 .40
167 Tony Giarratano FY RC .15 .40
168 Darren Fenster FY RC .15 .40
169 Elvys Quezada FY RC .15 .40
170 Glen Perkins FY RC .15 .40
171 Ian Kinsler FY RC .75 2.00
172 Mike Bourn FY RC .40 1.00
173 Jeremy West FY RC .15 .40
174 Justin Verlander FY RC 3.00 8.00
175 Kevin West FY RC .15 .40
176 Luis Hernandez FY RC .15 .40
177 Matt Campbell FY RC .15 .40
178 Nate McLouth FY RC .25 .60
179 Ryan Goleski FY RC .15 .40
180 Matthew Lindstrom FY RC .15 .40
181 Matt DeSalvo FY RC .15 .40
182 Kole Strayhorn FY RC .15 .40
183 Jose Vaquedano FY RC .15 .40
184 James Jurries FY RC .15 .40
185 Ian Bladergroen FY RC .15 .40
186 Eric Nielsen FY RC .15 .40
187 Chris Vines FY RC .15 .40
188 Chris Denorfia FY RC .15 .40
189 Kevin Melillo FY RC .15 .40
190 Melky Cabrera FY RC .50 1.25
191 Ryan Sweeney FY RC .25 .60
192 Sean Marshall FY RC .40 1.00
193 Andy LaRoche FY RC .15 .40
194 Tyler Pelland FY RC .15 .40
195 Mike Morse FY RC .50 1.25
196 Wes Swackhamer FY RC .15 .40
197 Wade Robinson FY RC .15 .40
198 Dan Santin FY RC .15 .40
199 Steve Doetsch FY RC .15 .40
200 Shane Costa FY RC .15 .40
201 Scott Mathieson FY RC .15 .40
202 Ben Jones FY RC .15 .40
203 Michael Rogers FY RC .15 .40
204 Matt Rogelstad FY RC .15 .40
205 Luis Ramirez FY RC .15 .40
206 Landon Powell FY RC .15 .40
207 Erik Cordier FY RC .15 .40
208 Chris Seddon FY RC .15 .40
209 Chris Roberson FY RC .15 .40
210 Thomas Oldham FY RC .15 .40
211 Dana Eveland FY RC .15 .40
212 Cody Haerther FY RC .15 .40
213 Danny Core FY RC .15 .40
214 Craig Tatum FY RC .15 .40
215 Elliot Johnson FY RC .15 .40
216 Ender Chavez FY RC .15 .40
217 Errol Simonitsch FY RC .15 .40
218 Matt Van Der Bosch FY RC .15 .40
219 Eulogio de la Cruz FY RC .15 .40
220 C.J. Smith FY RC .15 .40
221 Adam Boeve FY RC .15 .40
222 Adam Harben FY RC .15 .40
223 Baltazar Lopez FY RC .15 .40
224 Russ Martin FY RC .50 1.25
225 Brian Bannister FY RC .25 .60
226 Brian Miller FY RC .15 .40
227 Casey McGehee FY RC .25 .60
228 Humberto Sanchez FY RC .25 .60
229 Javon Moran FY RC .15 .40
230 Brandon McCarthy FY RC .25 .60
231 Danny Zell FY RC .15 .40
232 Jake Postlewait FY RC .15 .40
233 Juan Tejeda FY RC .15 .40
234 Keith Ramsey FY RC .15 .40
235 Lorenzo Scott FY RC .15 .40
236 Wladimir Balentien FY RC .25 .60
237 Martin Prado FY RC 1.00 2.50
238 Matt Albers FY RC .15 .40
239 Brian Schweiger FY RC .15 .40
240 Brian Stavisky FY RC .15 .40
241 Pat Misch FY RC .15 .40
242 Pat Osborn FY .15 .40
243 Ryan Feierabend FY RC .15 .40
244 Shaun Marcum FY .40 1.00
245 Kevin Collins FY RC .15 .40
246 Stuart Pomeranz FY RC .15 .40
247 Tetsu Yofu FY RC .15 .40
248 Hernan Iribarren FY RC .15 .40
249 Mike Spidale FY RC .15 .40
250 Tony Americh FY RC .15 .40
251 Manny Parra FY RC .40 1.00
252 Drew Anderson FY RC .15 .40
253 T.J. Beam FY RC .15 .40
254 Pedro Lopez FY RC .15 .40
255 Andy Sides FY RC .15 .40
256 Bear Bay FY RC .15 .40
257 Bill McCarthy FY RC .15 .40
258 Daniel Haigwood FY RC .15 .40
259 Brian Sprout FY RC .15 .40
260 Bryan Triplett FY RC .15 .40
261 Steven Bondurant FY RC .15 .40
262 Darwinson Salazar FY RC .15 .40
263 David Shepard FY RC .15 .40
264 Johan Silva FY RC .15 .40
265 J.B. Thurmond FY RC .15 .40
266 Brandon Moorhead FY RC .15 .40
267 Kyle Nichols FY RC .15 .40
268 Jonathan Sanchez FY RC .60 1.50
269 Mike Esposito FY RC .15 .40
270 Erik Schindewolf FY RC .15 .40
271 Peeter Ramos FY RC .15 .40
272 Juan Senreiso FY RC .15 .40
273 Matthew Kemp FY RC .75 2.00
274 Vinny Rottino FY RC .15 .40
275 Micah Furtado FY RC .15 .40
276 George Kottaras FY RC .25 .60
277 Billy Butler FY RC .75 2.00
278 Buck Coats FY RC .15 .40
279 Kenny Durost FY RC .15 .40
280 Nick Touchstone FY RC .15 .40
281 Jerry Owens FY RC .15 .40
282 Stefan Bailie FY RC .15 .40
283 Jesse Gutierrez FY RC .15 .40
284 Chuck Tiffany FY RC .40 1.00
285 Brendan Ryan FY RC .15 .40
286 Hayden Penn FY RC .15 .40
287 Shawn Bowman FY RC .15 .40
288 Alexander Smit FY RC .15 .40
289 Micah Schnurstein FY RC .15 .40
290 Jared Gothreaux FY RC .15 .40
291 Jair Jurrjens FY RC .75 2.00
292 Bobby Livingston FY RC .15 .40
293 Ryan Speier FY RC .15 .40
294 Zach Parker FY RC .15 .40
295 Christian Colonel FY RC .15 .40
296 Scott Mitchinson FY RC .15 .40
297 Neil Wilson FY RC .15 .40
298 Chuck James FY RC .40 1.00
299 Heath Totten FY RC .15 .40
300 Sean Tracey FY RC .15 .40
301 Ismael Ramirez FY RC .15 .40
302 Matt Brown FY RC .15 .40
303 Franklin Morales FY RC .25 .60
304 Brandon Sing FY RC .15 .40
305 D.J. Houlton FY RC .15 .40
306 Jayce Tingler FY RC .15 .40
307 Mitchell Arnold FY RC .15 .40
308 Jim Burt FY RC .15 .40
309 Jason Motte FY RC .25 .60
310 David Gassner FY RC .15 .40
311 Andy Santana FY RC .15 .40
312 Kelvin Pichardo FY RC .15 .40
313 Carlos Carrasco FY RC .40 1.00
314 Willy Mota FY RC .15 .40
315 Frank Mata FY RC .15 .40
316 Carlos Gonzalez FY RC 1.25 3.00
317 Jeff Niemann FY RC .40 1.00
318 Chris B.Young FY RC .50 1.25
319 Billy Sadler FY RC .15 .40
320 Ricky Barrett FY RC .15 .40
321 Ben Harrison FY .15 .40
322 Steve Nelson FY RC .15 .40
323 Daryl Thompson FY RC .15 .40
324 Philip Humber FY RC .40 1.00
325 Jeremy Harts FY RC .15 .40
326 Nick Masset FY RC .15 .40
327 Mike Rodriguez FY RC .15 .40
328 Mike Garber FY RC .15 .40
329 Kennard Bibbs FY RC .15 .40
330 Ryan Garko FY RC .15 .40
BC Bay Bat 6.00 15.00
Crosby Bat ROY

2005 Bowman 1st Edition

*1ST EDITION 1-165: .75X TO 2X BASIC
*1ST EDITION 166-330: .75X TO 2X BASIC
ISSUED IN 1ST EDITION PACKS

2005 Bowman Gold

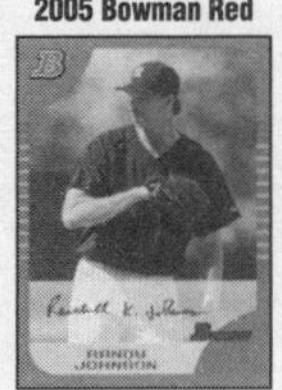

COMPLETE SET (330) 75.00 150.00
*GOLD 1-165: 1.25X TO 3X BASIC
*GOLD 166-330: .75X TO 2X BASIC
ONE PER HOBBY PACK
ONE PER HTA PACK
ONE PER RETAIL PACK

2005 Bowman Red

STATED ODDS 1:2768 H, 1:708 HTA
STATED PRINT RUN 1 SERIAL #'d SET
NO PRICING DUE TO SCARCITY

2005 Bowman White

*WHITE 1-165: 4X TO 10X BASIC
*WHITE 166-330: 3X TO 8X BASIC
STATED ODDS 1:23 HOBBY, 1:6 HTA
STATED PRINT RUN 240 SERIAL #'d SETS
UNCIRCULATED EXCH.ODDS 1:94 H, 1:23 R
FOUR PIT.COM CARDS PER UNCIRC.EXCH
UNCIRCULATED EXCH DEADLINE 12/31/05
50% OF PRINT SEEDED INTO PACKS
50% OF PRINT AVAIL VIA PIT.COM EXCH

2005 Bowman Autographs

GROUP A ODDS 1:74 H, 1:26 HTA, 1:118 R
GROUP B ODDS 1:95 H, 1:33 HTA, 1:212 R
RED INK ODDS 1:1599 H, 1:599 HTA, 1:3672 R
RED INK PRINT RUN 25 SETS
RED INK ARE NOT SERIAL-NUMBERED
RED INK PRINT RUN PROVIDED BY TOPPS
NO RED INK PRICING DUE TO SCARCITY
GROUP A IS CARDS 141-151
GROUP B IS CARDS 152-165
EXCHANGE DEADLINE 05/31/07
141 Omar Quintanilla A 4.00 10.00
142 Carlos Quentin A 6.00 15.00
143 Dan Johnson A 4.00 10.00
144 Jake Stevens A 4.00 10.00
145 Nate Schierholtz A 4.00 10.00
146 Neil Walker A 4.00 10.00
147 Bill Bray A 4.00 10.00
148 Taylor Tankersley A 4.00 10.00
149 Trevor Plouffe A 4.00 10.00
150 Felix Hernandez A 20.00 50.00
151 Philip Hughes A 6.00 15.00
152 James Houser B 4.00 10.00
153 David Murphy B 4.00 10.00
154 Ervin Santana B 4.00 10.00
155 Anthony Whittington B 4.00 10.00
156 Chris Lambert B 4.00 10.00
157 Jeremy Sowers B 6.00 15.00
158 Giovanny Gonzalez B 6.00 15.00
159 Blake DeWitt B 6.00 15.00
160 Thomas Diamond B 6.00 15.00
161 Greg Golson B 4.00 10.00
163 Paul Maholm B 4.00 10.00
164 Mark Rogers B 6.00 15.00
165 Homer Bailey B 6.00 15.00

2005 Bowman Relics

STATED ODDS 1:50 H, 1:19 HTA, 1:114 R
2 Eric Chavez Jsy 3.00 8.00
5 Hank Blalock Bat 3.00 8.00
23 Rafael Palmeiro Bat 4.00 10.00
43 Mark Teixeira Bat 4.00 10.00
49 Ivan Rodriguez Bat 4.00 10.00
50 Alex Rodriguez Bat 6.00 15.00
60 Gary Sheffield Bat 3.00 8.00
65 Magglio Ordonez Bat 3.00 8.00
78 David Ortiz Bat 4.00 10.00
83 Adam Dunn Jsy 3.00 8.00
90 Miquel Cabrera Bat 4.00 10.00
93 Andruw Jones Bat 4.00 10.00
100 Barry Bonds Jsy 10.00 25.00
104 Melvin Mora Jsy 3.00 8.00
105 Albert Pujols Bat 6.00 15.00
115 Alfonso Soriano Bat 3.00 8.00
120 Vladimir Guerrero Bat 4.00 10.00
125 Carlos Beltran Bat 3.00 8.00
130 Manny Ramirez Bat 4.00 10.00
135 Sammy Sosa Bat 4.00 10.00

2005 Bowman A-Rod Throwback

COMPLETE SET (4) 3.00 8.00
STATED ODDS 1:12 HOBBY
94 Alex Rodriguez 1994 .60 1.50
95 Alex Rodriguez 1995 .60 1.50
96 Alex Rodriguez 1996 .60 1.50
97 Alex Rodriguez 1997 .60 1.50

2005 Bowman A-Rod Throwback Autographs

1994 BOW ODDS 1:108,288 HTA
1995 BOW ODDS 1:27,684 H, 1:13,536 HTA
1996 BOW ODDS 1:9039 H, 1:4922 HTA
1996 BOW.DRAFT ODDS 1:44,837 H
1997 BOW ODDS 1:6815 H, 1:3734 HTA
1997 BOW.DRAFT ODDS 1:8664 H
1994 PRINT RUN 1 SERIAL #'d CARD
1995 PRINT RUN 25 SERIAL #'d CARDS
1996 PRINT RUN 75 SERIAL #'d CARDS
1997 PRINT RUN 225 SERIAL #'d CARDS
NO PRICING ON QTY OF 25 OR LESS
75 OF 99 1996 CARDS ARE IN BOWMAN

25 OF 99 1996 CARDS ARE IN BOW.DRAFT
100 OF 225 1997 CARDS ARE IN BOWMAN
125 OF 225 1997 CARDS ARE IN BOW.DRAFT
96A Alex Rodriguez 1996/99 100.00 175.00
97A Alex Rodriguez 1997/225 50.00 100.00

2005 Bowman A-Rod Throwback Jersey Relics

1994 ODDS 1:108,288 HTA
1995 ODDS 1:27,684 H, 1:13,536 HTA
1996 ODDS 1:6815 H, 1:3734 HTA
1997 ODDS 1:849 H, 1:461 HTA
1994 PRINT RUN 1 SERIAL #'d CARD
1995 PRINT RUN 25 SERIAL #'d CARDS
1996 PRINT RUN 99 SERIAL #'d CARDS
1997 PRINT RUN 800 SERIAL #'d CARDS
NO PRICING ON QTY OF 25 OR LESS
96R Alex Rodriguez 1996/99 15.00 40.00
97R Alex Rodriguez 1997/800 6.00 15.00

2005 Bowman A-Rod Throwback Posters

ONE PER SEALED HOBBY BOX
05 POSTER ISSUED IN BECKETT MONTHLY
1994 Alex Rodriguez 1994 .30 .75
1995 Alex Rodriguez 1995 .30 .75
1996 Alex Rodriguez 1996 .30 .75
1997 Alex Rodriguez 1997 .30 .75
2005 Alex Rodriguez 2005 .30 .75

2005 Bowman Base of the Future Autograph Relic

STATED ODDS 1:106 HTA
RED INK ODDS 1:4708 HTA
RED INK PRINT RUN 25 CARDS
RED INK IS NOT SERIAL-NUMBERED
RED INK PRINT RUN PROVIDED BY TOPPS
NO RED INK PRICING DUE TO SCARCITY
AH Aaron Hill 6.00 15.00

2005 Bowman Futures Game Gear Jersey Relics

STATED ODDS 1:36 H, 1:14 HTA, 1:83 R
AH Aaron Hill 2.00 5.00
AM Arnie Munoz 2.00 5.00
AMA Andy Marte 3.00 8.00
BB Bryan Bullington 2.00 5.00
CE Clint Everts 2.00 5.00
DM Dallas McPherson 2.00 5.00
EE Edwin Encarnacion 3.00 8.00
FP Felix Pie 3.00 8.00
GF Gavin Floyd 2.00 5.00
JB Joe Blanton 2.00 5.00
JC Jesus Cota 2.00 5.00
JCO Jorge Cortes 2.00 5.00
JF Jeff Francis 2.00 5.00
JG Jairo Garcia 2.00 5.00
JGU Joel Guzman 3.00 8.00
JM Jeff Mathis 2.00 5.00
JMO Justin Morneau 3.00 8.00
KH Koyie Hill 2.00 5.00
MC Matt Cain 4.00 10.00
RG Ruben Gotay 2.00 5.00
RW Rickie Weeks 3.00 8.00
SC Shin Soo Choo 2.00 5.00
VM Val Majewski 2.00 5.00
WL Wilfredo Ledezma 2.00 5.00
YP Yusmeiro Petit 3.00 8.00

2005 Bowman Signs of the Future

GROUP A ODDS 1:252 H, 1:93 HTA, 1:571 R
GROUP B ODDS 1:219 H, 1:82 HTA, 1:502 R
GROUP C ODDS 1:167 H, 1:63 HTA, 1:382 R
GROUP D ODDS 1:636 H, 1:239 HTA, 1:1448 R
D.WRIGHT PRINT RUN 100 CARDS
D.WRIGHT IS NOT SERIAL-NUMBERED
D.WRIGHT PRINT RUN GIVEN BY TOPPS
EXCHANGE DEADLINE 05/31/07
AL Adam Loewen C 4.00 10.00
AW Anthony Whittington B 4.00 10.00
BB Brian Bixler B 4.00 10.00
BC Bobby Crosby B 6.00 15.00
BD Blake DeWitt C 6.00 15.00
BS Brad Sullivan C 4.00 10.00
CC Chad Cordero D 4.00 10.00
CG Christian Garcia C 4.00 10.00
DM Dallas McPherson B 4.00 10.00
DP Dan Putnam B 4.00 10.00
DW David Wright D/100 * 30.00 60.00
ES Ervin Santana D 4.00 10.00
HS Huston Street C 8.00 20.00
JR Jay Rainville C 4.00 10.00
JS Jay Sborz C 4.00 10.00
KW Kyle Waldrop B 4.00 10.00
MC Melky Cabrera C 6.00 15.00
PH Philip Hughes C 6.00 15.00
PM Paul Maholm C 4.00 10.00
RC Robinson Cano D 12.00 30.00
RR Richie Robnett A 4.00 10.00
RW Ryan Wagner C 4.00 10.00
SK Scott Kazmir D 8.00 20.00
SO Scott Olson D 4.00 10.00
TG Tom Gorzelanny C 4.00 10.00
TH Tim Hutting A 3.00 8.00
TP Trevor Plouffe D 8.00 20.00
TT Taylor Tankersley D 4.00 10.00

2005 Bowman Two of a Kind Autographs

STATED ODDS 1:55,368 H, 1:21,658 HTA
STATED PRINT RUN 13 SERIAL #'d CARDS
NO PRICING DUE TO SCARCITY

2005 Bowman Draft

This 165-card set was released in November, 2005. The set was issued in seven-card packs (which included two Bowman Chrome Draft Cards) with an $2 SRP which came 24 packs to a box and 10 boxes to a case.

COMPLETE SET (165) 15.00 40.00
COMMON CARD (1-165) .10 .30
COMMON RC .10 .30
COMMON RC YR .10 .30
OVERALL PLATE ODDS 1:826 HOBBY
PLATE PRINT RUN 1 SET PER COLOR
BLACK-CYAN-MAGENTA-YELLOW ISSUED
NO PLATE PRICING DUE TO SCARCITY
1 Rickie Weeks .12 .30
2 Kyle Davies .12 .30
3 Garrett Atkins .12 .30
4 Chien-Ming Wang .50 1.25
5 Dallas McPherson .12 .30
6 Dan Johnson .12 .30
7 Andy Sisco .12 .30
8 Ryan Doumit .12 .30
9 J.P. Howell .12 .30
10 Tim Stauffer .12 .30
12 Aaron Hill .20 .50
13 Victor Diaz .12 .30
14 Wilson Betemit .12 .30
15 Ervin Santana .12 .30
16 Mike Morse .40 1.00
17 Yadier Molina .30 .75
18 Kelly Johnson .12 .30
19 Clint Barmes .12 .30
20 Robinson Cano .40 1.00
21 Brad Thompson .12 .30
22 Jorge Cantu .12 .30
23 Brad Halsey .12 .30
24 Lance Niekro .12 .30
25 D.J. Houlton .12 .30
26 Ryan Church .12 .30
27 Hayden Penn .12 .30
28 Chris Young .20 .50
29 Chad Orvella RC .12 .30
30 Mark Teahen .12 .30
31 Mark McCormick FY RC .12 .30
32 Jay Bruce FY RC 1.00 2.50
33 Beau Jones FY RC .30 .75
34 Tyler Greene FY RC .12 .30
35 Zach Ward FY RC .12 .30
36 Josh Bell FY RC .20 .50
37 Josh Wall FY RC .20 .50
38 Nick Webber FY RC .12 .30
39 Travis Buck FY RC .12 .30
40 Kyle Winters FY RC .12 .30
41 Mitch Boggs FY RC .12 .30
42 Tommy Mendoza FY RC .12 .30
43 Brad Corley FY RC .12 .30
44 Drew Butera FY RC .12 .30
45 Ryan Mount FY RC .12 .30
46 Tyler Herron FY RC .12 .30
47 Nick Weglarz FY RC .12 .30
48 Brandon Erbe FY RC .40 1.00
49 Cody Allen FY RC .12 .30
50 Eric Fowler FY RC .12 .30
51 James Boone FY RC .12 .30
52 Josh Flores FY RC .12 .30
53 Brandon Monk FY RC .12 .30
54 Kieron Pope FY RC .12 .30
55 Kyle Cofield FY RC .12 .30
56 Brent Lillibridge FY RC .12 .30
57 Daryl Jones FY RC .12 .30
58 Eli Iorg FY RC .12 .30
59 Brett Hayes FY RC .12 .30
60 Mike Durant FY RC .12 .30
61 Michael Bowden FY RC .20 .50
62 Paul Kelly FY RC .12 .30
63 Andrew McCutchen FY RC 1.50 4.00
64 Travis Wood FY RC .30 .75
65 Cesar Ramos FY RC .12 .30
66 Chaz Roe FY RC .12 .30
67 Matt Torra FY RC .12 .30
68 Kevin Slowey FY RC .60 1.50
69 Trayvon Robinson FY RC .30 .75
70 Reid Engel FY RC .12 .30
71 Kris Harvey FY RC .12 .30
72 Craig Italiano FY RC .12 .30
73 Matt Maloney FY RC .12 .30
74 Sean West FY RC .20 .50
75 Henry Sanchez FY RC .20 .50
76 Scott Blue FY RC .12 .30
77 Jordan Schafer FY RC .60 1.50
78 Chris Robinson FY RC .12 .30
79 Chris Hobdy FY RC .12 .30
80 Brandon Durden FY RC .12 .30
81 Clay Buchholz FY RC .60 1.50
82 Josh Geer FY RC .12 .30
83 Sam LeCure FY RC .12 .30
84 Justin Thomas FY RC .12 .30
85 Brett Gardner FY RC .40 1.00
86 Tommy Manzella FY RC .12 .30
87 Matt Green FY RC .12 .30
88 Yunel Escobar FY RC .50 1.25
89 Mike Costanzo FY RC .12 .30
90 Nick Hundley FY RC .12 .30
91 Zach Simons FY RC .12 .30
92 Jacob Marceaux FY RC .12 .30
93 Jed Lowrie FY RC .12 .30
94 Brandon Snyder FY RC .30 .75
95 Matt Goyen FY RC .12 .30
96 Jon Egan FY RC .12 .30
97 Drew Thompson FY RC .12 .30
98 Bryan Anderson FY RC .12 .30
99 Clayton Richard FY RC .12 .30
100 Jimmy Shull FY RC .12 .30
101 Mark Pawelek FY RC .12 .30
102 P.J. Phillips FY RC .12 .30
103 John Drennen FY RC .12 .30
104 Nolan Reimold FY RC .50 1.25
105 Troy Tulowitzki FY RC 1.25 3.00
106 Kevin Whelan FY RC .12 .30
107 Wade Townsend FY RC .12 .30
108 Micah Owings FY RC .12 .30
109 Ryan Tucker FY RC .12 .30
110 Jeff Clement FY RC .12 .30
111 Josh Sullivan FY RC .12 .30
112 Jeff Lyman FY RC .12 .30
113 Brian Bogusevic FY RC .12 .30
114 Trevor Bell FY RC .12 .30
115 Brent Cox FY RC .12 .30
116 Michael Billek FY RC .12 .30
117 Garrett Olson FY RC .12 .30
118 Steven Johnson FY RC .12 .30
119 Chase Headley FY RC .20 .50
120 Daniel Carte FY RC .12 .30
121 Francisco Liriano PROS .30 .75
122 Fausto Carmona PROS .12 .30
123 Zach Jackson PROS .12 .30
124 Adam Loewen PROS .12 .30
125 Chris Lambert PROS .12 .30
126 Scott Mathieson FY .12 .30
127 Paul Maholm PROS .12 .30
128 Fernando Nieve PROS .12 .30
129 Justin Verlander FY 2.50 6.00
130 Yusmeiro Petit PROS .12 .30
131 Joel Zumaya PROS .30 .75
132 Merkin Valdez PROS .12 .30
133 Ryan Garko FY .12 .30
134 Edison Volquez FY RC .40 1.00
135 Russ Martin FY .40 1.00
136 Conor Jackson PROS .20 .50
137 Miguel Montero FY RC .40 1.00
138 Josh Barfield PROS .20 .50
139 Delmon Young PROS .30 .75
140 Andy LaRoche FY .12 .30
141 William Bergolla PROS .12 .30
142 B.J. Upton PROS .20 .50
143 Hernan Iribarren FY .12 .30
144 Brandon Wood PROS .20 .50
145 Jose Bautista PROS .50 1.25
146 Edwin Encarnacion PROS .30 .75
147 Javier Herrera FY RC .12 .30
148 Jeremy Hermida PROS .20 .50
149 Frank Diaz PROS RC .12 .30
150 Chris B.Young FY .40 1.00
151 Shin-Soo Choo PROS .20 .50
152 Kevin Thompson PROS RC .12 .30
153 Hanley Ramirez PROS .20 .50
154 Lastings Milledge PROS .12 .30
155 Luis Montanez PROS .12 .30
156 Justin Huber PROS .12 .30
157 Zach Duke PROS .12 .30
158 Jeff Francoeur PROS .30 .75
159 Melky Cabrera FY .40 1.00
160 Bobby Jenks PROS .12 .30
161 Ian Snell PROS .12 .30
162 Fernando Cabrera PROS .12 .30
163 Troy Patton PROS .12 .30
164 Anthony Lerew PROS .12 .30
165 Nelson Cruz FY RC 1.00 2.50

2005 Bowman Draft Gold

COMPLETE SET (165) 25.00 60.00
*GOLD: 1.25X TO 3X BASIC
*GOLD: .6X TO 1.5X BASIC RC
*GOLD: .6X TO 1.5X BASIC RC YR
ONE PER PACK

2005 Bowman Draft Red

STATED ODDS 1:6609 HOBBY
STATED PRINT RUN 1 SERIAL #'d SET
NO PRICING DUE TO SCARCITY

2005 Bowman Draft White

*WHITE: 4X TO 10X BASIC
*WHITE: 3X TO 8X BASIC RC
*WHITE: 2.5X TO 6X BASIC RC YR
STATED ODDS 1:35 HOBBY, 1:72 RETAIL
STATED PRINT RUN 225 SERIAL #'d SETS

2005 Bowman Draft Futures Game Jersey Relics

STATED ODDS 1:24 HOBBY
121 Francisco Liriano 3.00 8.00
122 Fausto Carmona 1.25 3.00
123 Zach Jackson 1.25 3.00
124 Adam Loewen 1.50 4.00
125 Chris Lambert 1.25 3.00
126 Scott Mathieson 1.25 3.00
127 Paul Maholm 1.25 3.00
128 Fernando Nieve 1.25 3.00
129 Justin Verlander 6.00 15.00
130 Yusmeiro Petit 1.25 3.00
131 Joel Zumaya 3.00 8.00
132 Merkin Valdez 1.25 3.00
133 Ryan Garko 1.25 3.00
134 Edison Volquez 4.00 10.00
135 Russ Martin 4.00 10.00
136 Conor Jackson 2.00 5.00
137 Miguel Montero 4.00 10.00
138 Josh Barfield 2.00 5.00
139 Delmon Young 3.00 8.00
140 Andy LaRoche 1.25 3.00
141 William Bergolla 1.25 3.00
142 B.J. Upton 2.00 5.00
143 Hernan Iribarren 1.25 3.00
144 Brandon Wood 2.00 5.00
145 Jose Bautista 5.00 12.00
146 Edwin Encarnacion 4.00 10.00
147 Javier Herrera 1.25 3.00
148 Jeremy Hermida 2.00 5.00
149 Frank Diaz 1.25 3.00
150 Chris B.Young 4.00 10.00

2005 Bowman Draft A-Rod Throwback Autograph

SEE 2005 BOWMAN A-ROD AU'S FOR INFO

2005 Bowman Draft Signs of the Future

GROUP A ODDS 1:232 H, 1:232 R
GROUP B ODDS 1:823 H, 1:819 R
GROUP C ODDS 1:232 H, 1:232 R
GROUP D ODDS 1:1157 H, 1:1166 R
GROUP E ODDS 1:348 H, 1:349 R
GROUP F ODDS 1:1746 H, 1:1749 R
AG Angel Guzman E 3.00 8.00
BB Bill Bray E 3.00 8.00
DL Donald Lucey F 3.00 8.00
DM David Murphy E 3.00 8.00
DP David Purcey C 3.00 8.00
GG Greg Golson C 3.00 8.00
HB Homer Bailey D 3.00 8.00
JF Jeff Frazier C 3.00 8.00
JH Justin Hoyman A 3.00 8.00
JJ Justin Jones B 3.00 8.00
JP Jonathan Poterson C 3.00 8.00
JS Jeremy Sowers E 3.00 8.00
RR Richie Robnett A 3.00 8.00
TL Tyler Lumsden A 3.00 8.00

2005 Bowman Draft AFLAC Exchange Cards

STATED ODDS 1:32 HOBBY
PLATES PRINT RUN 1 SET PER COLOR
NO PLATES PRICING DUE TO SCARCITY
EXCHANGE DEADLINE 12/25/06
1 Basic Set 3.00 8.00

2005 Bowman Draft AFLAC

COMP.FACT.SET (14) 4.00 10.00
STATED ODDS 1:32 '05 BOW.DRAFT HOB.
EXCHANGE DEADLINE 12/26/06
ONE SET VIA MAIL PER AFLAC EXCH.CARD
SETS ACTUALLY SENT OUT JANUARY, 2007
PLATE PRINT RUN 1 SET PER COLOR
BLACK-CYAN-MAGENTA-YELLOW ISSUED
NO PLATE PRICING DUE TO SCARCITY
1 Billy Rowell .75 2.00
2 Kasey Kiker .50 1.25
3 Chris Marrero 1.00 2.50
4 Jeremy Jeffress .30 .75
5 Kyle Drabek .50 1.25
6 Chris Parmelee .50 1.25
7 Colton Willems .30 .75
8 Cody Johnson .30 .75
9 Hank Conger .50 1.25
10 Cory Rasmus .30 .75
11 David Christensen .30 .75
12 Chris Tillman .50 1.25
13 Torre Langley .30 .75
14 Robby Alcombrack .30 .75

2006 Bowman

This 231-card set was released in May, 2006. The first 200 cards in the set consist of veterans while the last 31 cards in the set are players who were Rookie Cards under the then-new rules used in 2006. Cards number 219 and 220 come either signed or unsigned. The cards were issued in 10-card hobby packs with an $3 SRP which came 24 packs to a box and 12 boxes to a case. In addition, these cards were issued in 21-card HTA packs with an $6 SRP which were produced in 12-pack boxes which came eight boxes to a case and also in 10-card retail packs with an $3 SRP which came 24 packs to a box and 12 boxes to a case.

COMP.SET w/o AU's (220) 15.00 40.00
COMP.SET w/PROS (330) 40.00 80.00
COMMON CARD (1-200) .10 .30
COMMON ROOKIE (201-220) .15 .40
219-220 AU ODDS 1:1150 HOBBY, 1:699 HTA
COMMON AUTO (221-231) 4.00 10.00
221-231 AU ODDS 1:82 HOBBY, 1:40 HTA
1-220 PLATE ODDS 1:588 HOBBY, 1:575 HTA
221-231 AU PLATES 1:15,700 H, 1:4100 HTA
PLATE PRINT RUN 1 SET PER COLOR
BLACK-CYAN-MAGENTA-YELLOW ISSUED
NO PLATE PRICING DUE TO SCARCITY
1 Nick Swisher .20 .50
2 Ted Lilly .12 .30
3 John Smoltz .30 .75
4 Lyle Overbay .12 .30
5 Alfonso Soriano .20 .50
6 Javier Vazquez .12 .30
7 Ronnie Belliard .12 .30
8 Jose Reyes .20 .50
9 Brian Roberts .12 .30
10 Curt Schilling .20 .50
11 Adam Dunn .20 .50
12 Zack Greinke .20 .50
13 Carlos Guillen .12 .30
14 Jon Garland .12 .30
15 Robinson Cano .20 .50
16 Chris Burke .12 .30
17 Barry Zito .20 .50
18 Russ Adams .12 .30
19 Chris Capuano .12 .30
20 Scott Rolen .20 .50
21 Kerry Wood .12 .30
22 Scott Kazmir .20 .50
23 Brandon Webb .20 .50
24 Jeff Kent .12 .30
25 Albert Pujols .40 1.00
26 C.C. Sabathia .20 .50
27 Adrian Beltre .30 .75
28 Brad Wilkerson .12 .30
29 Randy Wolf .12 .30
30 Jason Bay .12 .30
31 Austin Kearns .12 .30
32 Clint Barmes .12 .30
33 Mike Sweeney .12 .30
34 Justin Verlander 1.00 2.50
35 Justin Morneau .20 .50
36 Scott Podsednik .12 .30
37 Jason Giambi .12 .30
38 Steve Finley .12 .30
39 Morgan Ensberg .12 .30
40 Eric Chavez .12 .30
41 Roy Halladay .20 .50
42 Horacio Ramirez .12 .30
43 Ben Sheets .12 .30
44 Chris Carpenter .20 .50
45 Andruw Jones .12 .30
46 Carlos Zambrano .20 .50
47 Jonny Gomes .12 .30
48 Shawn Green .12 .30
49 Moises Alou .12 .30
50 Ichiro Suzuki .40 1.00
51 Juan Pierre .12 .30
52 Grady Sizemore .20 .50
53 Kazuo Matsui .12 .30
54 Jose Vidro .12 .30
55 Jake Peavy .12 .30
56 Dallas Mcpherson .12 .30
57 Ryan Howard .25 .60
58 Zach Duke .12 .30
59 Michael Young .12 .30
60 Todd Helton .20 .50
61 David Dejesus .12 .30
62 Ivan Rodriguez .20 .50
63 Johan Santana .20 .50
64 Danny Haren .12 .30
65 Derek Jeter .75 2.00
66 Greg Maddux .40 1.00
67 Jorge Cantu .12 .30
68 Conor Jackson .20 .50
69 Victor Martinez .20 .50
70 David Wright .25 .60
71 Ryan Church .12 .30
72 Khalil Greene .12 .30
73 Jimmy Rollins .20 .50
74 Hank Blalock .12 .30
75 Pedro Martinez .20 .50
76 Jon Papelbon .75 2.00
77 Felipe Lopez .12 .30
78 Jeff Francis .12 .30
79 Andy Sisco .12 .30
80 Hideki Matsui .30 .75
81 Ken Griffey Jr. .60 1.50
82 Nomar Garciaparra .20 .50
83 Kevin Millwood .12 .30
84 Paul Konerko .20 .50
85 A.J. Burnett .12 .30
86 Mike Piazza .30 .75
87 Brian Giles .12 .30
88 Johnny Damon .20 .50
89 Jim Thome .20 .50
90 Roger Clemens .40 1.00
91 Aaron Rowand .12 .30
92 Rafael Furcal .12 .30
93 Gary Sheffield .12 .30
94 Mike Cameron .12 .30
95 Carlos Delgado .12 .30
96 Jorge Posada .20 .50
97 Denny Bautista .12 .30
98 Mike Maroth .12 .30
99 Brad Radke .12 .30
100 Alex Rodriguez .40 1.00
101 Freddy Garcia .12 .30
102 Oliver Perez .12 .30
103 Jon Lieber .12 .30
104 Melvin Mora .12 .30
105 Travis Hafner .12 .30
106 Matt Cain .75 2.00
107 Derek Lowe .12 .30
108 Luis Castillo .12 .30
109 Livan Hernandez .12 .30
110 Tadahito Iguchi .12 .30
111 Shawn Chacon .12 .30
112 Frank Thomas .30 .75
113 Josh Beckett .12 .30
114 Aubrey Huff .12 .30
115 Derrek Lee .12 .30
116 Chien-Ming Wang .20 .50
117 Joe Crede .12 .30
118 Torii Hunter .12 .30
119 J.D. Drew .12 .30
120 Troy Glaus .12 .30
121 Sean Casey .12 .30
122 Edgar Renteria .12 .30
123 Craig Wilson .12 .30
124 Adam Eaton .12 .30
125 Jeff Francoeur .30 .75
126 Bruce Chen .12 .30
127 Cliff Floyd .12 .30
128 Jeremy Reed .12 .30
129 Jake Westbrook .12 .30
130 Wily Mo Pena .12 .30
131 Toby Hall .12 .30
132 David Ortiz .30 .75
133 David Eckstein .12 .30
134 Brady Clark .12 .30
135 Marcus Giles .12 .30
136 Aaron Hill .12 .30
137 Mark Kotsay .12 .30
138 Carlos Lee .12 .30
139 Roy Oswalt .20 .50
140 Chone Figgins .12 .30
141 Mike Mussina .20 .50
142 Orlando Hernandez .12 .30
143 Magglio Ordonez .20 .50
144 Jim Edmonds .20 .50
145 Bobby Abreu .12 .30
146 Nick Johnson .12 .30
147 Carlos Beltran .20 .50
148 Jhonny Peralta .12 .30
149 Pedro Feliz .12 .30
150 Miguel Tejada .20 .50
151 Luis Gonzalez .12 .30
152 Carl Crawford .20 .50
153 Yadier Molina .30 .75
154 Rich Harden .12 .30
155 Tim Wakefield .20 .50
156 Rickie Weeks .12 .30
157 Johnny Estrada .12 .30
158 Gustavo Chacin .12 .30
159 Dan Johnson .12 .30
160 Willy Taveras .12 .30
161 Garret Anderson .12 .30
162 Randy Johnson .30 .75
163 Jermaine Dye .12 .30
164 Joe Mauer .20 .50
165 Ervin Santana .12 .30
166 Jeremy Bonderman .12 .30
167 Garrett Atkins .12 .30
168 Manny Ramirez .30 .75
169 Brad Eldred .12 .30
170 Chase Utley .20 .50
171 Mark Loretta .12 .30
172 John Patterson .12 .30
173 Tom Glavine .20 .50
174 Dontrelle Willis .12 .30
175 Mark Teixeira .20 .50
176 Felix Hernandez .20 .50
177 Cliff Lee .20 .50
178 Jason Schmidt .12 .30
179 Chad Tracy .12 .30
180 Rocco Baldelli .12 .30
181 Aramis Ramirez .12 .30
182 Andy Pettitte .20 .50
183 Mark Mulder .12 .30
184 Geoff Jenkins .12 .30
185 Chipper Jones .30 .75
186 Vernon Wells .12 .30
187 Bobby Crosby .12 .30
188 Lance Berkman .20 .50
189 Vladimir Guerrero .20 .50
190 Jose Capellan .12 .30
191 Brad Penny .12 .30
192 Jose Guillen .12 .30
193 Brett Myers .12 .30
194 Miguel Cabrera .30 .75
195 Bartolo Colon .12 .30
196 Craig Biggio .20 .50
197 Tim Hudson .20 .50
198 Mark Prior .20 .50
199 Mark Buehrle .20 .50
200 Barry Bonds .50 1.25
201 Anderson Hernandez (RC) .15 .40
202 Charlton Jimerson (RC) .15 .40
203 Jeremy Accardo RC .15 .40
204 Hanley Ramirez (RC) .25 .60
205 Matt Capps (RC) .15 .40
206 John-Ford Griffin (RC) .15 .40
207 Chuck James (RC) .15 .40
208 Jaime Bubela (RC) .15 .40
209 Mark Woodyard (RC) .15 .40
210 Jason Botts (RC) .15 .40
211 Chris Demaria RC .15 .40
212 Miguel Perez (RC) .15 .40
213 Tom Gorzelanny (RC) .15 .40
214 Adam Wainwright (RC) .25 .60
215 Ryan Garko (RC) .15 .40
216 Jason Bergmann RC .15 .40
217 J.J. Furmaniak (RC) .15 .40
218 Francisco Liriano (RC) .40 1.00
219 Kenji Johjima RC .40 1.00
219a Kenji Johjima AU 6.00 15.00
220 Craig Hansen RC .40 1.00
220a Craig Hansen AU 4.00 10.00
221 Ryan Zimmerman AU (RC) 8.00 20.00
222 Joey Devine AU RC 4.00 10.00
223 Scott Olsen AU (RC) 4.00 10.00
224 Darrel Rasner AU (RC) 4.00 10.00
225 Craig Breslow AU RC 4.00 10.00
226 Reggie Abercrombie AU (RC) 4.00 10.00
227 Dan Uggla AU (RC) 4.00 10.00
228 Willie Eyre AU (RC) 4.00 10.00
229 Joel Zumaya AU (RC) 4.00 10.00
230 Ricky Nolasco AU (RC) 4.00 10.00
231 Ian Kinsler AU (RC) 5.00 12.00

2006 Bowman Blue

*BLUE 1-200: 2X TO 5X BASIC
*BLUE 76/201-220: 2X TO 5X BASIC

*BLUE 221-231: 4.X TO 1X BASIC AU
1-220 ODDS 1:8 HOBBY, 1:4 HTA
221-231 AU ODDS 1:225 HOBBY, 1:115 HTA
STATED PRINT RUN 500 SERIAL #'d SETS
227 Dan Uggla AU 4.00 10.00

2006 Bowman Gold

*GOLD 1-200: 1.25X TO 3X BASIC
*GOLD 201-220: 1X TO 2.5X BASIC
ONE PER HOBBY PACK
ONE PER HTA PACK

2006 Bowman Red

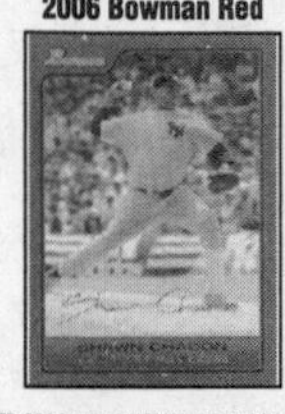

STATED ODDS 1:3750 HOBBY, 1:1754 HTA
221-231 AU ODDS 1:114,583 H, 1:58,464 HTA
STATED PRINT RUN 1 SERIAL #'d SET
NO PRICING DUE TO SCARCITY

2006 Bowman White

*WHITE 1-200: 3X TO 8X BASIC
*WHITE 76/201-220: 3X TO 8X BASIC
*WHITE 221-231: .6X TO 1.5X BASIC AU
1-220 ODDS 1:32 HOBBY, 1:15 HTA
221-231 AU ODDS 1:1020 HOBBY, 1:500 HTA
STATED PRINT RUN 120 SERIAL #'d SETS
227 Dan Uggla AU 30.00 80.00

2006 Bowman Prospects

For the first time, the non-major league prospects in Bowman had their own seperate set. These cards were inserted at a stated rate of two cards for every Bowman hobby pack and four cards for every HTA pack. The final 14 cards in this insert set were signed and were inserted at a stated rate of one in 62 hobby and one in 35 HTA.

COMP.SET w/o AU's (110) 25.00 50.00
COMMON CARD (B1-B110) .15 .40
B1-B110 STATED ODDS 2:1 HOBBY, 4:1 HTA
B111-B124 AU ODDS 1:62 HOBBY, 1:35 HTA
B1-B110 PLATE ODDS 1:588 H, 1:575 HTA
B111-B124 AU PLATE 1:15,700 H, 1:4100 HTA
PLATE PRINT RUN 1 PER COLOR
BLACK-CYAN-MAGENTA-YELLOW ISSUED
NO PLATE PRICING DUE TO SCARCITY
B1 Alex Gordon .50 1.25
B2 Jonathan George .15 .40
B3 Scott Walter .15 .40
B4 Brian Holliday .15 .40
B5 Ben Copeland .15 .40
B6 Bobby Wilson .15 .40
B7 Mayker Sandoval .15 .40
B8 Alejandro de Aza .25 .60
B9 David Munoz .15 .40
B10 Josh LeBlanc .15 .40
B11 Philippe Valiquette .15 .40
B12 Edwin Bellorin .15 .40
B13 Jason Quarles .15 .40
B14 Mark Trumbo .40 1.00
B15 Steve Kelly .15 .40
B16 Jamie Hoffman .15 .40
B17 Joe Bauserman .15 .40
B18 Nick Adenhart .15 .40
B19 Mike Butia .15 .40
B20 Jon Weber .15 .40
B21 Luis Valdez .15 .40
B22 Rafael Rodriguez .15 .40
B23 Wyatt Toregas .15 .40
B24 John Vanden Berg .15 .40
B25 Mike Connolly .15 .40
B26 Mike O'Connor .15 .40
B27 Garrett Mock .15 .40
B28 Bill Layman .15 .40
B29 Luis Pena .15 .40
B30 Billy Killian .15 .40
B31 Ross Ohlendorf .15 .40
B32 Mark Kaiser .15 .40
B33 Ryan Costello .15 .40
B34 Dale Thayer .15 .40
B35 Steve Garrabrants .15 .40
B36 Samuel Deduno .15 .40
B37 Juan Portes .15 .40
B38 Javier Martinez .15 .40
B39 Clint Sammons .15 .40
B40 Andrew Kown .15 .40
B41 Matt Tolbert .15 .40
B42 Michael Ekstrom .15 .40
B43 Shawn Norris .15 .40
B44 Diory Hernandez .15 .40
B45 Chris Maples .15 .40
B46 Aaron Hathaway .15 .40
B47 Steven Baker .15 .40
B48 Greg Creek .15 .40
B49 Collin Mahoney .15 .40
B50 Corey Ragsdale .15 .40
B51 Ariel Nunez .15 .40
B52 Max Ramirez .25 .60
B53 Eric Rodland .15 .40
B54 Dante Brinkley .15 .40
B55 Casey Craig .15 .40
B56 Ryan Spilborghs .15 .40
B57 Fredy Deza .15 .40
B58 Jeff Frazier .15 .40
B59 Vince Cordova .15 .40
B60 Oswaldo Navarro .15 .40
B61 Jarod Rine .15 .40
B62 Jordan Tata .15 .40
B63 Ben Julianel .15 .40
B64 Yung-Chi Chen .25 .60
B65 Carlos Torres .15 .40
B66 Juan Francia .15 .40
B67 Brett Smith .15 .40
B68 Francisco Leandro .15 .40
B69 Chris Turner .15 .40
B70 Matt Joyce .75 2.00
B71 Jason Jones .15 .40
B72 Jose Diaz .15 .40
B73 Kevin Ool .15 .40
B74 Nate Bumstead .15 .40
B75 Omir Santos .15 .40
B76 Shawn Riggans .15 .40
B77 Ofilio Castro .15 .40
B78 Mike Rozier .15 .40
B79 Wilkin Ramirez .25 .60
B80 Yobal Duenas .15 .40
B81 Adam Bourassa .15 .40
B82 Tony Granadillo .15 .40
B83 Brad McCann .15 .40
B84 Dustin Majewski .15 .40
B85 Kelvin Jimenez .15 .40
B86 Mark Reed .15 .40
B87 Asdrubal Cabrera .75 2.00
B88 James Barthmaier .15 .40
B89 Brandon Boggs .15 .40
B90 Raul Valdez .15 .40
B91 Jose Campusano .15 .40
B92 Henry Owens .15 .40
B93 Tug Hulett .15 .40
B94 Nate Gold .15 .40
B95 Lee Mitchell .15 .40
B96 John Hardy .15 .40
B97 Aaron Wideman .15 .40
B98 Brandon Roberts .15 .40
B99 Lou Santangelo .15 .40
B100 Kyle Kendrick .40 1.00
B101 Michael Collins .15 .40
B102 Camilo Vazquez .15 .40
B103 Mark McLemore .15 .40
B104 Alexander Peralta .15 .40
B105 Josh Whitesell .15 .40
B106 Carlos Guevara .15 .40
B107 Michael Aubrey .25 .60
B108 Brandon Chaves .15 .40
B109 Leonard Davis .15 .40
B110 Kendry Morales .40 1.00
B111 Koby Clemens AU 4.00 10.00
B112 Lance Broadway AU 6.00 15.00
B113 Cameron Maybin AU 4.00 10.00
B114 Mike Aviles AU 6.00 15.00
B115 Kyle Blanks AU 10.00 25.00
B116 Chris Dickerson AU 6.00 15.00
B117 Sean Gallagher AU 10.00 25.00
B118 Jamar Hill AU 4.00 10.00
B119 Garrett Mock AU 4.00 10.00
B120 Kendry Morales AU 6.00 15.00
B121 Russ Rohlicek AU 4.00 10.00
B122 Clete Thomas AU 4.00 10.00
B123 Josh Kinney AU 4.00 10.00
B124 Justin Huber AU 4.00 10.00

2006 Bowman Prospects Blue

*BLUE B1-B110: 1.5X TO 4X BASIC
*BLUE B111-B124: .4X TO 1X BASIC
B1-B110 ODDS 1:8 HOBBY, 1:4 HTA
B111-B124 AU ODDS 1:170 H, 1:100 HTA
STATED PRINT RUN 500 SERIAL #'d SETS

2006 Bowman Prospects Gold

*GOLD B1-B110: .75X TO 2X BASIC
ONE PER HOBBY PACK
ONE PER HTA PACK

2006 Bowman Prospects Red

B1-B110 ODDS 1:3750 HOBBY, 1:1754 HTA
111-124 AU ODDS 1:80,208 H, 1:56,464 HTA
STATED PRINT RUN 1 SERIAL #'d SET
NO PRICING DUE TO SCARCITY

2006 Bowman Prospects White

*WHITE B1-B110: 2.5X TO 6X BASIC
*WHITE B111-B124: .6X TO 1.5X BASIC
B1-B110 ODDS 1:32 HOBBY, 1:15 HTA
B111-B124 AU ODDS 1:750 H, 1:450 HTA
STATED PRINT RUN 120 SERIAL #'d SETS

2006 Bowman Base of the Future

STATED ODDS 1:173 HTA
RED INK ODDS 1:7800 HTA
NO RED INK PRICING DUE TO SCARCITY
JH Justin Huber 4.00 10.00

2006 Bowman Signs of the Future

ONE PER SEALED HTA BOX
GROUP A ODDS 1:5 HTA BOXES, 1:150 RETAIL
GROUP B ODDS 1:4 HTA BOXES, 1:105 RETAIL
GROUP C-D ODDS 1:6 HTA BOXES, 1:200 R
GROUP E ODDS 1:19 HTA BOXES, 1:1050 R
AT Aaron Thompson D 4.00 10.00
BB Brian Bogusevic A 4.00 10.00
BC Ben Copeland C 4.00 10.00
CR Cesar Ramos E 4.00 10.00
DS Denard Span B 6.00 15.00
GO Garrett Olson C 6.00 15.00
HS Henry Sanchez D 4.00 10.00
JC Jeff Clement B 4.00 10.00
JD John Drennen C 4.00 10.00
JE Jacoby Ellsbury D 5.00 12.00
JM John Mayberry Jr. E 4.00 10.00
MB Michael Bowden B 6.00 15.00
MC Mike Costanzo D 4.00 10.00
RB Ryan Braun E 6.00 15.00
RR Ricky Romero B 6.00 15.00
RT Ryan Tucker C 4.00 10.00
SW Sean West D 4.00 10.00
TB Travis Buck D 6.00 15.00
TC Trevor Crowe B 4.00 10.00
TT Troy Tulowitzki A 4.00 10.00
YE Yunel Escobar A 4.00 10.00

2006 Bowman Draft

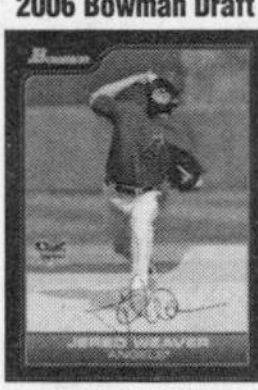

COMPLETE SET (55) 6.00 15.00
COMMON RC (1-55) .15 .40
APPX. TWO PER HOBBY/RETAL PACK
ODDS INFO PROVIDED BY BECKETT
OVERALL PLATE ODDS 1:990 HOBBY
PLATE PRINT RUN 1 SET PER COLOR
BLACK-CYAN-MAGENTA-YELLOW ISSUED
NO PLATE PRICING DUE TO SCARCITY
1 Matt Kemp (RC) .40 1.00
2 Taylor Tankersley (RC) .15 .40
3 Mike Napoli RC .25 .60
4 Brian Bannister (RC) .15 .40
5 Melky Cabrera (RC) .25 .60
6 Bill Bray (RC) .15 .40
7 Brian Anderson (RC) .15 .40
8 Jered Weaver (RC) .50 1.25
9 Chris Duncan (RC) .25 .60
10 Boof Bonser (RC) .25 .60
11 Mike Rouse (RC) .15 .40
12 David Pauley (RC) .15 .40
13 Russ Martin (RC) .25 .60
14 Jeremy Sowers (RC) .15 .40
15 Kevin Reese (RC) .15 .40
16 John Rheinecker (RC) .15 .40
17 Tommy Murphy (RC) .15 .40
18 Sean Marshall (RC) .15 .40
19 Jason Kubel (RC) .15 .40
20 Chad Billingsley (RC) .25 .60
21 Kendry Morales (RC) .40 1.00
22 Jon Lester RC .60 1.50
23 Brandon Fahey RC .15 .40
24 Josh Johnson (RC) .40 1.00
25 Kevin Frandsen (RC) .15 .40
26 Casey Janssen RC .15 .40
27 Scott Thorman (RC) .15 .40
28 Scott Mathieson (RC) .15 .40
29 Jeremy Hermida (RC) .15 .40
30 Dustin Nippert (RC) .15 .40
31 Kevin Thompson (RC) .15 .40
32 Bobby Livingston (RC) .15 .40
33 Travis Ishikawa (RC) .25 .60
34 Jeff Mathis (RC) .15 .40
35 Charlie Haeger RC .25 .60
36 Josh Willingham (RC) .25 .60
37 Taylor Buchholz (RC) .15 .40
38 Joel Guzman (RC) .15 .40
39 Zach Jackson (RC) .15 .40
40 Howie Kendrick (RC) .30 .75
41 T.J. Beam (RC) .15 .40
42 Ty Taubenheim RC .25 .60
43 Erick Aybar (RC) .15 .40
44 Anibal Sanchez (RC) .15 .40
45 Michael Pelfrey RC .40 1.00
46 Shawn Hill (RC) .15 .40
47 Chris Roberson (RC) .15 .40
48 Carlos Villanueva RC .15 .40
49 Andre Ethier (RC) .50 1.25
50 Anthony Reyes (RC) .15 .40
51 Franklin Gutierrez (RC) .15 .40
52 Angel Guzman (RC) .15 .40
53 Michael O'Connor RC .15 .40
54 James Shields RC .50 1.25
55 Nate McLouth (RC) .15 .40

2006 Bowman Draft Gold

COMPLETE SET (55) 8.00 20.00
*GOLD: .75X TO 2X BASIC
APPX. ODDS 1:3 HOBBY, 1:3 RETAIL
ODDS INFO PROVIDED BY BECKETT

2006 Bowman Draft Red

STATED ODDS 1:7934 HOBBY
STATED PRINT RUN 1 SERIAL #'d SET
NO PRICING DUE TO SCARCITY

2006 Bowman Draft White

*WHITE: 2.5X TO 6X BASIC
STATED ODDS 1:43 H,1:93 R
STATED PRINT RUN 225 SER.#'d SETS

2006 Bowman Draft Draft Picks

COMPLETE SET (65) 8.00 20.00
APPX. ODDS 1:1 HOBBY, 1:1 RETAIL
ODDS INFO PROVIDED BY BECKETT
OVERALL PLATE ODDS 1:990 HOBBY
PLATE PRINT RUN 1 SET PER COLOR
BLACK-CYAN-MAGENTA-YELLOW ISSUED
NO PLATE PRICING DUE TO SCARCITY
1 Tyler Colvin .25 .60
2 Chris Marrero .25 .60
3 Hank Conger .25 .60
4 Chris Parmelee .25 .60
5 Jason Place .15 .40
6 Billy Rowell .40 1.00
7 Travis Snider .50 1.25
8 Colton Willems .15 .40
9 Chase Fontaine .15 .40
10 Jon Jay .25 .60
11 Wade Leblanc .25 .60
12 Justin Masterson .25 .60
13 Gary Daley .15 .40
14 Justin Edwards .15 .40
15 Charlie Yarbrough .15 .40
16 Cyle Hankerd .15 .40
17 Zach McAllister .15 .40
18 Tyler Robertson .15 .40
19 Joe Smith .15 .40
20 Nate Culp .15 .40
21 John Holdzkom .15 .40
22 Patrick Bresnehan .15 .40
23 Chad Lee .15 .40
24 Ryan Morris .15 .40
25 D'Arby Myers .15 .40
26 Garrett Olson .15 .40
27 Jon Still .15 .40
28 Brandon Rice .15 .40
29 Chris Davis .30 .75
30 Zack Daeges .15 .40
31 Bobby Henson .15 .40
32 George Kontos .15 .40
33 Jermaine Mitchell .15 .40
34 Adam Coe .15 .40
35 Dustin Richardson .15 .40
36 Allen Craig .40 1.00
37 Austin McClune .15 .40
38 Doug Fister .25 .60
39 Corey Madden .15 .40
40 Justin Jacobs .15 .40
41 Jim Negrych .15 .40
42 Tyler Norrick .15 .40
43 Adam Davis .15 .40
44 Brett Logan .15 .40
45 Brian Omogrosso .15 .40
46 Kyle Drabek .25 .60
47 Jamie Ortiz .15 .40
48 Alex Presley .25 .60
49 Terrance Warren .15 .40
50 David Christensen .15 .40
51 Helder Velazquez .15 .40
52 Matt McBride .15 .40
53 Quintin Berry .40 1.00
54 Michael Eisenberg .15 .40
55 Dan Garcia .15 .40
56 Scott Cousins .15 .40
57 Sean Land .15 .40
58 Kristopher Medlen .75 2.00
59 Tyler Reves .15 .40
60 John Shelby .15 .40
61 Jordan Newton .15 .40
62 Ricky Orta .15 .40
63 Jason Donald .15 .40
64 David Huff .15 .40
65 Brett Sinkbeil .15 .40

2006 Bowman Draft Draft Picks Gold

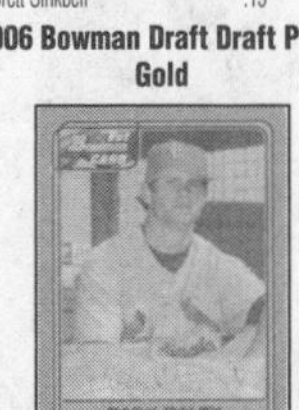

*GOLD: .75X TO 2X BASIC
APPX. ODDS 1:2 HOBBY, 1:2 RETAIL
ODDS INFO PROVIDED BY BECKETT

2006 Bowman Draft Draft Picks Red

STATED ODDS 1:7934 HOBBY
STATED PRINT RUN 1 SERIAL #'d SET
NO PRICING DUE TO SCARCITY

2006 Bowman Draft Draft Picks White

*WHITE: 2.5X TO 6X BASIC
STATED ODDS 1:43 H,1:93 R
STATED PRINT RUN 225 SER.#'d SETS

2006 Bowman Draft Future's Game Prospects

COMPLETE SET (45) 6.00 15.00
APPX. ODDS 1:1 HOBBY, 1:1 RETAIL
ODDS INFO PROVIDED BY BECKETT
OVERALL PLATE ODDS 1:990 HOBBY
PLATE PRINT RUN 1 SET PER COLOR
BLACK-CYAN-MAGENTA-YELLOW ISSUED
NO PLATE PRICING DUE TO SCARCITY
1 Nick Adenhart .15 .40
2 Joel Guzman .15 .40
3 Ryan Braun .75 2.00
4 Carlos Carrasco .25 .60
5 Neil Walker .25 .60
6 Pablo Sandoval .60 1.50
7 Gio Gonzalez .25 .60
8 Joey Votto 1.00 2.50
9 Luis Cruz .15 .40
10 Nolan Reimold .25 .60
11 Juan Salas .15 .40
12 Josh Fields .15 .40
13 Yovani Gallardo .50 1.25
14 Radhames Liz .15 .40
15 Eric Patterson .15 .40
16 Cameron Maybin .50 1.25
17 Edgar Martinez .15 .40
18 Hunter Pence .60 1.50
19 Philip Hughes .40 1.00
20 Trent Oeltjen .15 .40
21 Nick Pereira .15 .40
22 Wladimir Balentien .15 .40
23 Stephen Drew .30 .75
24 Davis Romero .15 .40
25 Joe Koshansky .15 .40
26 Chin Lung Hu .15 .40
27 Jason Hirsh .15 .40
28 Jose Tabata .25 .60
29 Eric Hurley .15 .40
30 Yung Chi Chen .25 .60
31 Howie Kendrick .30 .75
32 Humberto Sanchez .15 .40
33 Alex Gordon .50 1.25
34 Yunel Escobar .15 .40
35 Travis Buck .15 .40
36 Billy Butler .40 1.00
37 Homer Bailey .40 1.00
38 George Kottaras .15 .40
39 Kurt Suzuki .15 .40
40 Joaquin Arias .15 .40
41 Matt Lindstrom .15 .40
42 Sean Smith .15 .40
43 Carlos Gonzalez .40 1.00
44 Jaime Garcia .75 2.00
45 Jose Garcia .15 .40

2006 Bowman Draft Future's Game Prospects Gold

*GOLD: 1X TO 2.5X BASIC
APPX. ODDS 1:6 HOBBY, 1:6 RETAIL
ODDS INFO PROVIDED BY BECKETT

2006 Bowman Draft Future's Game Prospects Red

STATED ODDS 1:7934 HOBBY
STATED PRINT RUN 1 SERIAL #'d SET
NO PRICING DUE TO SCARCITY

2006 Bowman Draft Future's Game Prospects White

*WHITE: 2.5X TO 6X BASIC
STATED ODDS 1:43 H,1:93 R
STATED PRINT RUN 225 SER.#'d SETS

2006 Bowman Draft Future's Game Prospects Relics

GROUP A ODDS 1:285 H,1:285 R
GROUP B ODDS 1:26 H,1:25 R
PRICES LISTED FOR JSY SWATCHES
PRIME SWATCHES MAY SELL FOR A PREMIUM
1 Nick Adenhart Jsy B 4.00 10.00
2 Joel Guzman Jsy B 2.50 6.00
3 Ryan Braun Jsy B 5.00 12.00
4 Carlos Carrasco Jsy B 2.50 6.00
6 Pablo Sandoval Jsy B 8.00 20.00
7 Gio Gonzalez Jsy B 2.50 6.00
8 Joey Votto Jsy B 6.00 15.00
9 Luis Cruz Jsy B 2.50 6.00
10 Nolan Reimold Jsy B 3.00 8.00
11 Juan Salas Jsy B 2.50 6.00
12 Josh Fields Jsy B 2.50 6.00
13 Yovani Gallardo Jsy B 6.00 15.00
14 Radhames Liz Jsy B 2.50 6.00
15 Eric Patterson Jsy A 2.50 6.00
16 Cameron Maybin Jsy B 3.00 8.00
17 Edgar Martinez Jsy B 2.50 6.00
18 Hunter Pence Jsy B 3.00 8.00
19 Philip Hughes Jsy B 4.00 10.00
20 Trent Oeltjen Jsy B 2.50 6.00
21 Nick Pereira Jsy B 2.50 6.00
22 Wladimir Balentien Jsy B 2.50 6.00
23 Stephen Drew Jsy B 3.00 8.00
24 Davis Romero Jsy A 2.50 6.00
25 Joe Koshansky Jsy B 2.50 6.00
26 Chin-Lung Hu Jsy Black B 10.00 25.00
26b Chin-Lung Hu Jsy Red 60.00 120.00
26c Chin-Lung Hu Jsy Yellow 50.00 100.00
27 Jason Hirsh Jsy B 2.50 6.00
28 Jose Tabata Jsy B 3.00 8.00
29 Eric Hurley Jsy B 2.50 6.00
30 Yung-Chi Chen Jsy Black B 10.00 25.00
30b Yung-Chi Chen Jsy Red 60.00 120.00
30c Yung-Chi Chen Jsy Yellow 50.00 100.00
31 Howie Kendrick Jsy A 3.00 8.00
32 Humberto Sanchez Jsy B 2.50 6.00
33 Alex Gordon Jsy B 3.00 8.00
34 Yunel Escobar Jsy A 6.00 15.00
35 Travis Buck Jsy B 6.00 15.00
36 Billy Butler Jsy B 4.00 10.00
37 Homer Bailey Jsy B 4.00 10.00
38 George Kottaras Jsy B 2.50 6.00
39 Kurt Suzuki Jsy B 2.50 6.00
40 Joaquin Arias Jsy B 2.50 6.00
43 Carlos Gonzalez Jsy B 4.00 10.00
44 Jaime Garcia Jsy B 3.00 8.00
45 Jose Garcia Jsy B 2.50 6.00

2006 Bowman Draft Head of the Class Dual Autograph

STATED ODDS 1:7640 HOBBY
STATED PRINT RUN 174 SER.#'d SETS
GOLD REF. ODDS 1:56,000 HOBBY
GOLD REF. PRINT RUN 25 SER.#'d SETS
NO GOLD PRICING DUE TO SCARCITY
SUPERFRAC. ODDS 1:261,680 HOBBY
SUPERFRAC. PRINT RUN 1 SER.#'d SET
NO SUPERFRAC.PRICING DUE TO SCARCITY
RU A.Rodriguez/J.Upton 100.00 200.00

2006 Bowman Draft Head of the Class Dual Autograph Refractor

STATED ODDS 1:27,000 HOBBY
STATED PRINT RUN 50 SERIAL #'d SETS
RU A.Rodriguez/J.Upton 125.00 250.00

2006 Bowman Draft Signs of the Future

GROUP A ODDS 1:973 H, 1:973 R
GROUP B ODDS 1:324 H, 1:323 R
GROUP C ODDS 1:430 H, 1:431 R
GROUP D ODDS 1:1140 H, 1:1140 R
GROUP E ODDS 1:322 H, 1:323 R
GROUP F ODDS 1:387 H, 1:388 R
AG Alex Gordon A 6.00 15.00
BJ Beau Jones B 3.00 8.00
BS Brandon Snyder A 3.00 8.00
CDR Chaz Roe C 3.00 8.00
CI Chris Iannetta A 4.00 10.00
CR Clayton Richard B 3.00 8.00
CRA Cesar Ramos F 3.00 8.00
CTI Craig Italiano C 3.00 8.00
DJ Daryl Jones B 6.00 15.00
HS Henry Sanchez E 3.00 8.00
JB Jay Bruce D 6.00 15.00
JC Jeff Clement B 6.00 15.00
JM Jacob Marceaux C 3.00 8.00
KC Koby Clemens A 8.00 20.00
MC Mike Costanzo F 3.00 8.00
MM Mark McCormick E 3.00 8.00
MO Micah Owings B 6.00 15.00
TB Travis Buck B 4.00 10.00
WT Wade Townsend E 3.00 8.00

2007 Bowman

This 237-card set was released in June, 2007. This set was issued through both hobby and retail channels. The hobby version came in 10-card packs with an $3 SRP which came 24 packs to a box and 12 boxes to a case. In addition, hobby HTA packs were also produced and those packs contained 32 cards with an $10 SRP. Those packs were issued 12 to a box and eight boxes to a case. Card #219, Hideki Okajima comes in three versions; a standard version, an signed version in English and a signed Japanese version. In addition, card number 234 was never issued. Cards number 1-200 feature veteran, cards numbered 201-219 feature 2007 rookies and the aforementioned Okajima signed versions and cards numbered 221-236 are signed. Those cards were inserted into packs at a stated rate of one in 98 hobby and one in 25 HTA packs.

COMP.SET w/o AU's (221) 20.00 50.00
COMMON CARD (1-200) .12 .30
COMMON ROOKIE (201-220) .15 .40
COMMON AUTO (221-236) 4.00 10.00
219/221-236 AU ODDS 1:98 HOBBY, 1:25 HTA
BONDS ODDS 1:51 HTA, 1:610 RETAIL
1-220 PLATE ODDS 1:1468 H, 1:212 HTA
221-231 AU PLATES 1:8200 H, 1:1150 HTA
BONDS PLATE ODDS 1:106,000 HTA
PLATE PRINT RUN 1 SET PER COLOR
BLACK-CYAN-MAGENTA-YELLOW ISSUED
NO PLATE PRICING DUE TO SCARCITY
1 Hanley Ramirez .20 .50
2 Justin Verlander .30 .75
3 Ryan Zimmerman .20 .50
4 Jered Weaver .20 .50
5 Stephen Drew .12 .30
6 Jonathan Papelbon .30 .75
7 Melky Cabrera .12 .30
8 Francisco Liriano .12 .30
9 Prince Fielder .20 .50
10 Dan Uggla .12 .30
11 Jeremy Sowers .12 .30
12 Carlos Quentin .12 .30
13 Chuck James .12 .30
14 Andre Ethier .20 .50
15 Cole Hamels UER .25 .60
16 Kenji Johjima .30 .75
17 Chad Billingsley .20 .50
18 Ian Kinsler .20 .50
19 Jason Hirsh .12 .30
20 Nick Markakis .25 .60
21 Jeremy Hermida .12 .30
22 Ryan Shealy .12 .30
23 Scott Olsen .12 .30
24 Russell Martin .12 .30
25 Conor Jackson .12 .30
26 Erik Bedard .12 .30
27 Brian McCann .12 .30
28 Michael Barrett .12 .30
29 Brandon Phillips .12 .30
30 Garrett Atkins .12 .30
31 Freddy Garcia .12 .30
32 Mark Loretta .12 .30
33 Craig Biggio .20 .50
34 Jeremy Bonderman .12 .30
35 Johan Santana .20 .50
36 Jorge Posada .20 .50
37 Brian Bannister .12 .30
38 Carlos Delgado .12 .30
39 Gary Matthews Jr. .12 .30
40 Mike Cameron .12 .30
41 Adrian Beltre .30 .75
42 Freddy Sanchez .12 .30
43 Austin Kearns .12 .30
44 Mark Buehrle .20 .50
45 Miguel Cabrera .30 .75
46 Josh Beckett .12 .30
47 Chone Figgins .12 .30
48 Edgar Renteria .12 .30
49 Derek Lowe .12 .30
50 Ryan Howard .25 .60
51 Shawn Green .12 .30
52 Jason Giambi .12 .30
53 Ervin Santana .12 .30
54 Jack Wilson .12 .30
55 Roy Oswalt .20 .50
56 Dan Haren .12 .30
57 Jose Vidro .12 .30
58 Kevin Millwood .12 .30
59 Jim Edmonds .20 .50
60 Carl Crawford .20 .50
61 Randy Wolf .12 .30
62 Paul LoDuca .12 .30
63 Johnny Estrada .12 .30
64 Brian Roberts .12 .30
65 Manny Ramirez .30 .75
66 Jose Contreras .12 .30
67 Josh Barfield .12 .30
68 Juan Pierre .12 .30
69 David DeJesus .12 .30
70 Gary Sheffield .12 .30
71 Jon Lieber .12 .30
72 Randy Johnson .30 .75
73 Rickie Weeks .12 .30
74 Brian Giles .12 .30
75 Ichiro Suzuki .40 1.00
76 Nick Swisher .20 .50
77 Justin Morneau .20 .50
78 Scott Kazmir .20 .50
79 Lyle Overbay .12 .30
80 Alfonso Soriano .20 .50
81 Brandon Webb .20 .50
82 Joe Crede .12 .30
83 Corey Patterson .12 .30
84 Kenny Rogers .12 .30
85 Ken Griffey Jr .60 1.50
86 Cliff Lee .20 .50
87 Mike Lowell .12 .30
88 Marcus Giles .12 .30
89 Orlando Cabrera .12 .30
90 Derek Jeter .75 2.00
91 Josh Johnson .30 .75
92 Carlos Guillen .12 .30
93 Bill Hall .12 .30
94 Michael Cuddyer .12 .30
95 Miguel Tejada .20 .50
96 Todd Helton .20 .50
97 C.C. Sabathia .20 .50
98 Tadahito Iguchi .12 .30
99 Jose Reyes .20 .50
100 David Wright .25 .60
101 Barry Zito .20 .50
102 Jake Peavy .12 .30
103 Richie Sexson .12 .30
104 A.J. Burnett .12 .30
105 Eric Chavez .12 .30
106 Jorge Cantu .12 .30
107 Grady Sizemore .20 .50
108 Bronson Arroyo .12 .30
109 Mike Mussina .20 .50
110 Magglio Ordonez .20 .50
111 Anibal Sanchez .12 .30
112 Jeff Francoeur .30 .75
113 Kevin Youkilis .12 .30
114 Aubrey Huff .12 .30
115 Carlos Zambrano .20 .50
116 Mark Teahen .12 .30
117 Carlos Silva .12 .30
118 Pedro Martinez .20 .50
119 Hideki Matsui .30 .75
120 Mike Piazza .30 .75
121 Jason Schmidt .12 .30
122 Greg Maddux .40 1.00
123 Joe Blanton .12 .30
124 Chris Carpenter .20 .50
125 David Ortiz .30 .75
126 Alex Rios .12 .30
127 Nick Johnson .12 .30
128 Carlos Lee .12 .30
129 Pat Burrell .12 .30
130 Ben Sheets .12 .30
131 Kazuo Matsui .12 .30
132 Adam Dunn .20 .50
133 Jermaine Dye .12 .30
134 Curt Schilling .20 .50
135 Chad Tracy .12 .30
136 Vladimir Guerrero .20 .50
137 Melvin Mora .12 .30
138 John Smoltz .30 .75
139 Craig Monroe .12 .30
140 Dontrelle Willis .12 .30
141 Jeff Francis .12 .30
142 Chipper Jones .30 .75
143 Frank Thomas .30 .75
144 Brett Myers .12 .30
145 Xavier Nady .12 .30
146 Robinson Cano .20 .50
147 Jeff Kent .12 .30
148 Scott Rolen .20 .50
149 Roy Halladay .20 .50
150 Joe Mauer .25 .60
151 Bobby Abreu .12 .30
152 Matt Cain .20 .50
153 Hank Blalock .12 .30
154 Chris Capuano .12 .30
155 Jake Westbrook .12 .30
156 Javier Vazquez .12 .30
157 Garret Anderson .12 .30
158 Aramis Ramirez .12 .30
159 Mark Kotsay .12 .30
160 Matt Kemp .25 .60
161 Adrian Gonzalez .25 .60
162 Felix Hernandez .20 .50
163 David Eckstein .12 .30
164 Curtis Granderson .25 .60
165 Paul Konerko .20 .50
166 Orlando Hudson .12 .30
167 Tim Hudson .20 .50
168 J.D. Drew .12 .30
169 Chien-Ming Wang .20 .50
170 Jimmy Rollins .20 .50
171 Matt Morris .12 .30
172 Raul Ibanez .20 .50
173 Mark Teixeira .20 .50
174 Ted Lilly .12 .30
175 Albert Pujols .40 1.00
176 Carlos Beltran .20 .50
177 Lance Berkman .20 .50
178 Ivan Rodriguez .20 .50
179 Torii Hunter .12 .30
180 Johnny Damon .20 .50
181 Chase Utley .20 .50
182 Jason Bay .20 .50
183 Jeff Weaver .12 .30
184 Troy Glaus .12 .30
185 Rocco Baldelli .12 .30
186 Rafael Furcal .12 .30
187 Jim Thome .20 .50
188 Travis Hafner .12 .30
189 Matt Holliday .30 .75
190 Andruw Jones .12 .30
191 Ramon Hernandez .12 .30
192 Victor Martinez .20 .50
193 Aaron Hill .12 .30
194 Michael Young .12 .30
195 Vernon Wells .12 .30
196 Mark Mulder .12 .30
197 Derrek Lee .12 .30
198 Tom Glavine .20 .50
199 Chris Young .12 .30
200 Alex Rodriguez .40 1.00
201 Delmon Young (RC) .25 .60
202 Alexi Casilla RC .25 .60
203 Shawn Riggans (RC) .15 .40
204 Jeff Baker (RC) .15 .40
205 Hector Gimenez (RC) .15 .40
206 Ubaldo Jimenez (RC) .50 1.25
207 Adam Lind (RC) .15 .40
208 Joaquin Arias (RC) .15 .40
209 David Murphy (RC) .15 .40
210 Daisuke Matsuzaka RC 2.00 5.00
211 Jerry Owens (RC) .15 .40
212 Ryan Sweeney (RC) .15 .40
213 Kei Igawa RC .60 1.50
214 Fred Lewis (RC) .25 .60
215 Philip Humber (RC) .15 .40
216 Kevin Hooper (RC) .15 .40
217 Jeff Fiorentino (RC) .15 .40
218 Michael Bourn (RC) .25 .60
219 Hideki Okajima RC .75 2.00
219b H.Okajima English AU 4.00 10.00
219c H.Okajima Japan AU 10.00 25.00
220 Josh Fields (RC) .15 .40
221 Andrew Miller AU RC 6.00 15.00
222 Troy Tulowitzki AU (RC) 6.00 15.00
223 Ryan Braun AU RC 4.00 10.00
224 Oswaldo Navarro AU RC 4.00 10.00
225 Philip Humber AU (RC) 4.00 10.00
226 Mitch Maier AU RC 4.00 10.00
227 Jerry Owens AU (RC) 4.00 10.00
228 Mike Rabelo AU RC 4.00 10.00
229 Delwyn Young AU (RC) 4.00 10.00
230 Miguel Montero AU (RC) 4.00 10.00
231 Akinori Iwamura AU RC 4.00 10.00
232 Matt Lindstrom AU (RC) 4.00 10.00
233 Josh Hamilton AU (RC) 6.00 15.00
235 Elijah Dukes AU RC 4.00 10.00
236 Sean Henn AU (RC) 4.00 10.00
237 Barry Bonds .50 1.25

2007 Bowman Blue

*BLUE 1-200: 2X TO 5X BASIC
*BLUE 201-220: 2X TO 5X BASIC
*BLUE 219 AU/221-236: .4X TO 1X BASIC AU
1-220 ODDS 1:17 HOB, 1:3 HTA, 1:30 RET
221-236 AU ODDS 1:241 HOBBY, 1:60 HTA
BONDS ODDS 1:1261 HTA, 1:15,500 RETAIL
STATED PRINT RUN 500 SERIAL #'d SETS
221 Andrew Miller AU 6.00 15.00

2007 Bowman Gold

*GOLD 1-200: 1.2X TO 3X BASIC
*GOLD 201-220: 1.2X TO 3X BASIC
OVERALL GOLD ODDS 1 PER PACK

2007 Bowman Orange

*ORANGE 1-200: 3X TO 8X BASIC
*ORANGE 201-220: 3X TO 8X BASIC
*ORANGE 219 AU/221-236: .5X TO 1.2X BASIC AU
1-220 ODDS 1:33 HOB, 1:6 HTA, 1:65 RET
221-236 AU ODDS 1:486 HOBBY, 1:119 HTA
BONDS ODDS 1:2521 HTA, 1:30,000 RETAIL
STATED PRINT RUN 250 SERIAL #'d SETS
219b H.Okajima English AU 15.00 40.00
221 Andrew Miller AU 8.00 20.00

2007 Bowman Red

1-220 ODDS 1:6036 HOBBY, 1:1400 HTA
221-236 AU ODDS 1:222,220 H, 1:27,000 HTA
BONDS ODDS 1:211,776 HTA
STATED PRINT RUN 1 SER.#'d SET
NO PRICING DUE TO SCARCITY

2007 Bowman Prospects

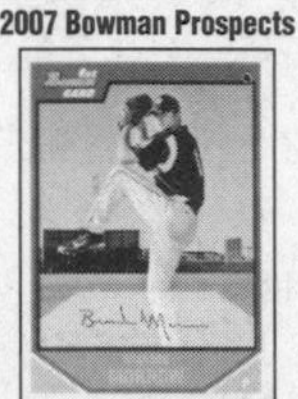

COMP.SET w/o AU's (110) 20.00 50.00
111-135 AU ODDS 1:64 HOBBY, 1:16 HTA
1-110 PLATE ODDS 1:1468 H, 1:212 HTA
111-135 AU PLATES 1:8200 H, 1:1150 HTA
PLATE PRINT RUN 1 SET PER COLOR
BLACK-CYAN-MAGENTA-YELLOW ISSUED
NO PLATE PRICING DUE TO SCARCITY
BP1 Cooper Brannon .20 .50
BP2 Jason Taylor .20 .50
BP3 Shawn O'Malley .20 .50
BP4 Robert Alcombrack .20 .50
BP5 Dellin Betances .60 1.50
BP6 Jeremy Papelbon .20 .50
BP7 Adam Carr .20 .50
BP8 Matthew Clarkson .20 .50
BP9 Darin McDonald .20 .50
BP10 Brandon Rice .20 .50
BP11 Matthew Sweeney .60 1.50
BP12 Scott Deal .20 .50
BP13 Brennan Boesch .60 1.50
BP14 Scott Taylor .20 .50
BP15 Michael Brantley .50 1.25
BP16 Yahmed Yema .20 .50
BP17 Brandon Morrow 1.00 2.50
BP18 Cole Garner .20 .50
BP19 Erik Lis .30 .75
BP20 Lucas French .20 .50
BP21 Aaron Cunningham .30 .75
BP22 Ryan Schreppel .20 .50
BP23 Kevin Russo .20 .50
BP24 Yohan Pino .30 .75
BP25 Michael Sullivan .20 .50
BP26 Trey Shields .20 .50
BP27 Daniel Matienzo .20 .50
BP28 Chuck Lofgren .50 1.25
BP29 Gerrit Simpson .20 .50
BP30 David Haehnel .20 .50
BP31 Marvin Lowrance .20 .50
BP32 Kevin Ardoin .20 .50
BP33 Edwin Maysonet .20 .50
BP34 Derek Griffith .20 .50
BP35 Sam Fuld .60 1.50
BP36 Chase Wright .50 1.25
BP37 Brandon Roberts .20 .50
BP38 Kyle Aselton .20 .50
BP39 Steven Sollmann .20 .50
BP40 Mike Devaney .20 .50
BP41 Charlie Fermaint .20 .50
BP42 Jesse Litsch .30 .75
BP43 Bryan Hansen .20 .50
BP44 Ramon Garcia .20 .50
BP45 John Otness .20 .50
BP46 Trey Hearne .20 .50
BP47 Habelito Hernandez .20 .50
BP48 Edgar Garcia .20 .50
BP49 Seth Fortenberry .20 .50
BP50 Reid Brignac .30 .75
BP51 Derek Rodriguez .20 .50
BP52 Ervin Alcantara .20 .50
BP53 Thomas Hottovy .20 .50
BP54 Jesus Flores .20 .50
BP55 Matt Palmer .20 .50
BP56 Brian Henderson .20 .50
BP57 John Gragg .20 .50
BP58 Jay Garthwaite .20 .50
BP59 Esmerling Vasquez .20 .50
BP60 Gilberto Mejia .20 .50
BP61 Aaron Jensen .20 .50
BP62 Cedric Brooks .20 .50
BP63 Brandon Mann .20 .50
BP64 Myron Leslie .20 .50
BP65 Ray Aguilar .20 .50
BP66 Jesus Guzman .30 .75
BP67 Sean Thompson .20 .50
BP68 Jarrett Hoffpauir .20 .50
BP69 Matt Goodson .20 .50
BP70 Neal Musser .20 .50
BP71 Tony Abreu .50 1.25
BP72 Tony Peguero .20 .50
BP73 Michael Bertram .20 .50
BP74 Randy Wells .50 1.25
BP75 Bradley Davis .20 .50
BP76 Jay Sawatski .20 .50
BP77 Vic Buttler .20 .50
BP78 Jose Oyervidez .20 .50
BP79 Doug Deeds .20 .50
BP80 Dan Dement .20 .50
BP81 Spike Lundberg .20 .50
BP82 Ricardo Nanita .20 .50
BP83 Brad Knox .20 .50
BP84 Will Venable .30 .75
BP85 Greg Smith .30 .75
BP86 Pedro Powell .20 .50
BP87 Gabriel Medina .20 .50
BP88 Duke Sardinha .20 .50
BP89 Mike Madsen .20 .50
BP90 Rayner Bautista .20 .50
BP91 T.J. Nall .20 .50
BP92 Neil Sellers .20 .50
BP93 Andrew Dobies .20 .50
BP94 Leo Daigle .20 .50
BP95 Brian Duensing .30 .75
BP96 Vincent Blue .20 .50
BP97 Fernando Rodriguez .20 .50
BP98 Derin McMains .20 .50
BP99 Adam Bass .20 .50
BP100 Justin Ruggiano .30 .75
BP101 Jared Burton .20 .50
BP102 Mike Parisi .20 .50
BP103 Aaron Peel .20 .50
BP104 Evan Englebrook .20 .50
BP105 Sendy Vasquez .20 .50
BP106 Desmond Jennings .75 2.00
BP107 Clay Harris .20 .50
BP108 Cody Strait .20 .50
BP109 Ryan Mullins .20 .50
BP110 Ryan Webb .20 .50
BP111 Kyle Drabek AU 4.00 10.00
BP112 Evan Longoria AU 8.00 20.00
BP113 Tyler Colvin AU 6.00 15.00
BP114 Matt Long AU 4.00 10.00
BP115 Jeremy Jeffress AU 3.00 8.00
BP116 Kasey Kiker AU 4.00 10.00
BP117 Hank Conger AU 5.00 12.00
BP118 Cody Johnson AU 4.00 10.00
BP119 David Huff AU 4.00 10.00
BP120 Tommy Hickman AU 4.00 10.00
BP121 Chris Parmelee AU 4.00 10.00
BP122 Dustin Evans AU 4.00 10.00
BP123 Brett Sinkbeil AU 4.00 10.00
BP124 Andrew Carpenter AU 4.00 10.00
BP125 Colten Willems AU 4.00 10.00
BP126 Matt Antonelli AU 4.00 10.00
BP127 Marcus Sanders AU 4.00 10.00
BP128 Joshua Rodriguez AU 4.00 10.00
BP129 Keith Weiser AU 4.00 10.00
BP130 Chad Tracy AU 4.00 10.00
BP131 Matthew Sulentic AU 6.00 15.00
BP132 Adam Ottavino AU 4.00 10.00
BP133 Jarrod Saltalamacchia AU 4.00 10.00
BP134 Kyle Blanks AU 5.00 12.00
BP135 Brad Eldred AU 4.00 10.00

2007 Bowman Prospects Blue

*BLUE 1-110: 2X TO 5X BASIC
*BLUE 111-135: .4X TO 1X BASIC AU
1-110 ODDS 1:17 HOB, 1:3 HTA, 1:30 RET
111-135 AU ODDS 1:156 HOBBY, 1:38 HTA
STATED PRINT RUN 500 SERIAL #'d SETS

2007 Bowman Prospects Gold

*GOLD 1-110: .75X TO 2X BASIC
OVERALL GOLD ODDS 1 PER PACK

2007 Bowman Prospects Orange

*ORANGE 1-110: 2.5X TO 6X BASIC
*ORANGE 111-135: .5X TO 1.2X BASIC AU
1-110 ODDS 1:33 HOB, 1:6 HTA, 1:65 RET
111-135 AU ODDS 1:311 HOBBY, 1:77 HTA
STATED PRINT RUN 250 SERIAL #'d SETS
BP111 Kyle Drabek AU 10.00 25.00
BP115 Jeremy Jeffress AU 5.00 12.00
BP121 Chris Parmelee AU 10.00 25.00
BP131 Matthew Sulentic AU 10.00 25.00

2007 Bowman Prospects Red

1-110 ODDS 1:6036 HOBBY, 1:1400 HTA
111-135 AU ODDS 80,000 H, 1:19,252 HTA
STATED PRINT RUN 1 SER.#'d SET
NO PRICING DUE TO SCARCITY

2007 Bowman Signs of the Future

GROUP A ODDS 1:2725 RETAIL
GROUP B ODDS 1:385 RETAIL
GROUP C ODDS 1:268 RETAIL
GROUP D ODDS 1:82 RETAIL
GROUP E ODDS 1:83 RETAIL
GROUP F ODDS 1:89 RETAIL
PRINTING PLATE ODDS 1:8200 H, 1:1150 HTA
PLATE PRINT RUN 1 SET PER COLOR
BLACK-CYAN-MAGENTA-YELLOW ISSUED
NO PLATE PRICING DUE TO SCARCITY
AM Andrew McCutchen 12.00 30.00
AR Adam Russell 3.00 8.00
BB Brian Bixler 3.00 8.00
BM Brandon Moss 3.00 8.00
CG Chris Gelz 3.00 8.00
CJS Chris Seddon 3.00 8.00
CL Chris Lubanski 3.00 8.00
CM Chris McConnell 3.00 8.00
JW Jared Wells 3.00 8.00
CS Chad Santos 3.00 8.00
DB Dellin Betances 12.00 30.00
DS Denard Span 3.00 8.00
EH Estee Harris 3.00 8.00
ER Eric Reed 3.00 8.00
FP Felix Pie 3.00 8.00
JB John Baker 3.00 8.00
CR Chris Robinson 3.00 8.00
JBC J. Brent Cox 3.00 8.00
JC Jesus Cota 3.00 8.00
JCB Jordan Brown 3.00 8.00
JD John Drennen 3.00 8.00
JBB John Bowker 3.00 8.00
JJ Jair Jurrjens 5.00 12.00
MM Matt Merricks 3.00 8.00
BF Ben Fritz 3.00 8.00
KC Koby Clemens 5.00 12.00
KD Kyle Drabek 5.00 12.00
KS Kurt Suzuki 3.00 8.00
MA Mike Aviles 3.00 8.00
ME Mike Edwards 3.00 8.00
JDA Jaime D'Antona 3.00 8.00
MN Mike Neu 3.00 8.00
MR Michael Rogers 3.00 8.00
RB Reid Brignac 5.00 12.00
RG Richie Gardner 3.00 8.00
RO Ross Ohlendorf 5.00 12.00
SG Sean Gallagher 3.00 8.00
SK Shane Komine 3.00 8.00
TT Taylor Teagarden 5.00 12.00

2007 Bowman Draft

This 54-card set, featuring 2007 rookies, was released in December, 2007. The set was issued in seven-card packs, which included two Bowman Chrome Draft cards, which came 24 packs to a box and 10 boxes per case.

COMMON RC (1-54) .15 .40
SEE 07 BOWMAN FOR BONDS PRICING
OVERALL PLATE ODDS 1:1294 HOBBY
PLATE PRINT RUN 1 SET PER COLOR
BLACK-CYAN-MAGENTA-YELLOW ISSUED
NO PLATE PRICING DUE TO SCARCITY
BDP1 Travis Buck (RC) .15 .40
BDP2 Matt Chico (RC) .15 .40
BDP3 Justin Upton RC .50 1.25
BDP4 Chase Wright RC .40 1.00
BDP5 Kevin Kouzmanoff (RC) .15 .40
BDP6 John Danks RC .25 .60
BDP7 Alejandro De Aza RC .25 .60
BDP8 Jamie Vermilyea RC .15 .40
BDP9 Jesus Flores RC .15 .40
BDP10 Glen Perkins (RC) .15 .40
BDP11 Tim Lincecum RC .75 2.00
BDP12 Cameron Maybin RC .25 .60
BDP13 Brandon Morrow RC .75 2.00
BDP14 Mike Rabelo RC .15 .40
BDP15 Alex Gordon RC .50 1.25
BDP16 Zack Segovia (RC) .15 .40
BDP17 Jon Knott (RC) .15 .40
BDP18 Joba Chamberlain RC .25 .60
BDP19 Danny Putnam (RC) .15 .40
BDP20 Matt DeSalvo (RC) .15 .40
BDP21 Fred Lewis (RC) .25 .60
BDP22 Sean Gallagher (RC) .15 .40
BDP23 Brandon Wood (RC) .15 .40
BDP24 Dennis Dove (RC) .15 .40
BDP25 Hunter Pence (RC) .50 1.25
BDP26 Jarrod Saltalamacchia (RC) .25 .60
BDP27 Ben Francisco (RC) .15 .40
BDP28 Doug Slaten RC .15 .40
BDP29 Tony Abreu RC .40 1.00
BDP30 Billy Butler (RC) .25 .60
BDP31 Jesse Litsch RC .25 .60
BDP32 Nate Schierholtz (RC) .15 .40
BDP33 Jared Burton RC .15 .40
BDP34 Matt Brown (RC) .15 .40
BDP35 Dallas Braden RC 1.00 2.50
BDP36 Carlos Gomez RC .30 .75
BDP37 Brian Stokes (RC) .15 .40
BDP38 Kory Casto (RC) .15 .40
BDP39 Mark McLemore (RC) .15 .40
BDP40 Andy LaRoche (RC) .15 .40
BDP41 Tyler Clippard (RC) .25 .60
BDP42 Curtis Thigpen (RC) .15 .40
BDP43 Yunel Escobar (RC) .15 .40
BDP44 Andy Sonnanstine RC .15 .40
BDP45 Felix Pie (RC) .15 .40
BDP46 Homer Bailey (RC) .25 .60
BDP47 Kyle Kendrick RC .40 1.00
BDP48 Angel Sanchez RC .15 .40
BDP49 Phil Hughes (RC) .40 1.00
BDP50 Ryan Braun (RC) .75 2.00
BDP51 Kevin Slowey (RC) .40 1.00
BDP52 Brendan Ryan (RC) .15 .40
BDP53 Yovani Gallardo (RC) .40 1.00
BDP54 Mark Reynolds RC .50 1.25

2007 Bowman Draft Blue

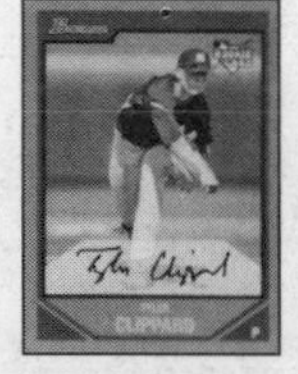

*BLUE: 1.2X TO 3X BASIC
STATED ODDS 1:29 HOBBY,1:84 RETAIL
STATED PRINT RUN 399 SER.#'d SETS

2007 Bowman Draft Gold

*GOLD: .6X TO 1.5X BASIC
APPX.GOLD ODDS ONE PER PACK

2007 Bowman Draft Red

STATED ODDS 1:10,377 HOBBY
STATED PRINT RUN ONE SER.#'d SET
NO PRICING DUE TO SCARCITY

2007 Bowman Draft Draft Picks

OVERALL PLATE ODDS 1:1294 HOBBY
PLATE PRINT RUN 1 SET PER COLOR
BLACK-CYAN-MAGENTA-YELLOW ISSUED
NO PLATE PRICING DUE TO SCARCITY
BDPP1 Cody Crowell .15 .40
BDPP2 Karl Bolt .25 .60
BDPP3 Corey Brown .25 .60
BDPP4 Tyler Mach .25 .60
BDPP5 Trevor Pippin .25 .60
BDPP6 Ed Easley .15 .40
BDPP7 Cory Luebke .15 .40
BDPP8 Darin Mastroianni .15 .40

BDPP9 Ryan Zink .25 .60
BDPP10 Brandon Hamilton .15 .40
BDPP11 Kyle Lotzkar .25 .60
BDPP12 Freddie Freeman 2.50 6.00
BDPP13 Nicholas Barnese .25 .60
BDPP14 Travis d'Arnaud .25 .60
BDPP15 Eric Eiland .15 .40
BDPP16 John Ely .15 .40
BDPP17 Oliver Marmol .15 .40
BDPP18 Eric Sogard .15 .40
BDPP19 Lars Davis .15 .40
BDPP20 Sam Runion .15 .40
BDPP21 Austin Gallagher .25 .60
BDPP22 Matt West .25 .60
BDPP23 Derek Norris .40 1.00
BDPP24 Taylor Holiday .25 .60
BDPP25 Dustin Biell .15 .40
BDPP26 Julio Borbon .25 .60
BDPP27 Brant Rustich .25 .60
BDPP28 Andrew Lambo .25 .60
BDPP29 Cory Kluber .75 2.00
BDPP30 Justin Jackson .25 .60
BDPP31 Scott Carroll .15 .40
BDPP32 Danny Rams .15 .40
BDPP33 Thomas Eager .15 .40
BDPP34 Matt Dominguez .40 1.00
BDPP35 Steven Souza .50 1.25
BDPP36 Craig Heyer .15 .40
BDPP37 Michael Taylor .60 1.50
BDPP38 Drew Bowman .15 .40
BDPP39 Frank Gailey .15 .40
BDPP40 Jeremy Hefner .15 .40
BDPP41 Reynaldo Navarro .25 .60
BDPP42 Daniel Descalso .25 .60
BDPP43 Leroy Hunt .15 .40
BDPP44 Jason Kiley .15 .40
BDPP45 Ryan Pope .40 1.00
BDPP46 Josh Horton .15 .40
BDPP47 Jason Monti .15 .40
BDPP48 Richard Lucas .15 .40
BDPP49 Jonathan Lucroy .40 1.00
BDPP50 Sean Doolittle .15 .40
BDPP51 Mike McDade .25 .60
BDPP52 Charlie Culberson .25 .60
BDPP53 Michael Moustakas .40 1.00
BDPP54 Jason Heyward 1.00 2.50
BDPP55 David Price .50 1.25
BDPP56 Brad Mills .15 .40
BDPP57 John Tolisano .50 1.25
BDPP58 Jarrod Parker .40 1.00
BDPP59 Wendell Fairley .25 .60
BDPP60 Gary Gaffis .15 .40
BDPP61 Madison Bumgarner 3.00 8.00
BDPP62 Danny Payne .15 .40
BDPP63 Jake Smolinski .50 1.25
BDPP64 Matt LaPorta .50 1.25
BDPP65 Jackson Williams .15 .40

2007 Bowman Draft Draft Picks Blue

*BLUE: 2X TO 5X BASIC
STATED ODDS 1:29 HOBBY,1:84 RETAIL
STATED PRINT RUN 399 SER.#'d SETS
BDPP61 Madison Bumgarner 10.00 25.00

2007 Bowman Draft Draft Picks Gold

*GOLD: .75X TO 2X BASIC
APPX.GOLD ODDS ONE PER PACK
BDPP61 Madison Bumgarner 5.00 12.00

2007 Bowman Draft Draft Picks Red

STATED ODDS 1:10,377 HOBBY
STATED PRINT RUN ONE SER.#'d SET
NO PRICING DUE TO SCARCITY

2007 Bowman Draft Future's Game Prospects

COMPLETE SET (45) 8.00 20.00
OVERALL PLATE ODDS 1:1294 HOBBY
PLATE PRINT RUN 1 SET PER COLOR
BLACK-CYAN-MAGENTA-YELLOW ISSUED
NO PLATE PRICING DUE TO SCARCITY
BDPP66 Pedro Beato .12 .30
BDPP67 Collin Balester .12 .30
BDPP68 Carlos Carrasco .20 .50
BDPP69 Clay Buchholz .40 1.00
BDPP70 Emiliano Fruto .12 .30
BDPP71 Joba Chamberlain .20 .50
BDPP72 Deolis Guerra .25 .60
BDPP73 Kevin Mulvey .30 .75
BDPP74 Franklin Morales .12 .30
BDPP75 Luke Hochevar .40 1.00
BDPP76 Henry Sosa .20 .50
BDPP77 Clayton Kershaw 2.50 6.00
BDPP78 Rich Thompson .12 .30
BDPP79 Chuck Lofgren .30 .75
BDPP80 Rick VandenHurk .12 .30
BDPP81 Michael Madsen .12 .30
BDPP82 Robinzon Diaz .12 .30
BDPP83 Jeff Niemann .20 .50
BDPP84 Max Ramirez .12 .30
BDPP85 Geovany Soto .50 1.25
BDPP86 Elvis Andrus .30 .75
BDPP87 Bryan Anderson .12 .30
BDPP88 German Duran .50 1.25
BDPP89 J.R. Towles .40 1.00
BDPP90 Alcides Escobar .30 .75
BDPP91 Brian Bocock .12 .30
BDPP92 Chin-Lung Hu .12 .30
BDPP93 Adrian Cardenas .12 .30
BDPP94 Freddy Sandoval .12 .30
BDPP95 Chris Coghlan .40 1.00
BDPP96 Craig Stansberry .12 .30
BDPP97 Brent Lillibridge .12 .30
BDPP98 Joey Votto .75 2.00
BDPP99 Evan Longoria 1.25 3.00
BDPP100 Wladimir Balentien .12 .30
BDPP101 Johnny Whittleman .12 .30
BDPP102 Gorkys Hernandez .30 .75
BDPP103 Jay Bruce .75 2.00
BDPP104 Matt Tolbert .12 .30
BDPP105 Jacoby Ellsbury .75 2.00
BDPP106 Michael Saunders .40 1.00
BDPP107 Cameron Maybin .20 .50
BDPP108 Carlos Gonzalez .30 .75
BDPP109 Colby Rasmus .30 .75
BDPP110 Justin Upton .40 1.00

2007 Bowman Draft Future's Game Prospects Blue

*BLUE: 1.2X TO 3X BASIC
STATED ODDS 1:29 HOBBY,1:84 RETAIL
STATED PRINT RUN 399 SER.#'d SETS

2007 Bowman Draft Future's Game Prospects Gold

*GOLD: .6X TO 1.5X BASIC
APPX.GOLD ODDS ONE PER PACK

2007 Bowman Draft Future's Game Prospects Red

STATED ODDS 1:10,377 HOBBY
STATED PRINT RUN ONE SER.#'d SET
NO PRICING DUE TO SCARCITY

2007 Bowman Draft Future's Game Prospects Jerseys

STATED ODDS 1:24 RETAIL
BDPP68 Carlos Carrasco 3.00 8.00
BDPP69 Clay Buchholz 5.00 12.00
BDPP71 Joba Chamberlain 10.00 25.00
BDPP73 Kevin Mulvey 3.00 8.00
BDPP74 Franklin Morales 3.00 8.00
BDPP75 Luke Hochevar 3.00 8.00
BDPP78 Rich Thompson 3.00 8.00
BDPP83 Jeff Niemann 3.00 8.00
BDPP84 Max Ramirez 3.00 8.00
BDPP89 J.R. Towles 3.00 8.00
BDPP95 Chris Coghlan 3.00 8.00
BDPP96 Craig Stansberry 3.00 8.00
BDPP97 Brent Lillibridge 3.00 8.00
BDPP98 Joey Votto 8.00 20.00
BDPP102 Gorkys Hernandez 3.00 8.00
BDPP105 Jacoby Ellsbury 8.00 20.00
BDPP106 Michael Saunders 3.00 8.00
BDPP107 Cameron Maybin 5.00 12.00
BDPP108 Carlos Gonzalez 4.00 10.00
BDPP110 Justin Upton 6.00 15.00

2007 Bowman Draft Future's Game Prospects Patches

STATED ODDS 1:384 HOBBY
STATED PRINT RUN 99 SER.#'d SETS
BDPP66 Pedro Beato 10.00 25.00
BDPP67 Collin Balester 10.00 25.00
BDPP68 Carlos Carrasco 12.50 30.00
BDPP69 Clay Buchholz 15.00 40.00
BDPP70 Emiliano Fruto 4.00 10.00
BDPP71 Joba Chamberlain 20.00 50.00
BDPP72 Deolis Guerra 12.50 30.00
BDPP73 Kevin Mulvey 6.00 15.00
BDPP74 Franklin Morales 6.00 15.00
BDPP75 Luke Hochevar 10.00 25.00
BDPP76 Henry Sosa 6.00 15.00
BDPP77 Clayton Kershaw 10.00 25.00
BDPP78 Rich Thompson 6.00 15.00
BDPP79 Chuck Lofgren 6.00 15.00
BDPP80 Rick VandenHurk 6.00 15.00
BDPP81 Michael Madsen 4.00 10.00
BDPP82 Robinzon Diaz 4.00 10.00
BDPP83 Jeff Niemann 6.00 15.00
BDPP84 Max Ramirez 10.00 25.00
BDPP85 Geovany Soto 15.00 40.00
BDPP86 Elvis Andrus 10.00 25.00
BDPP87 Bryan Anderson 10.00 25.00
BDPP88 German Duran 6.00 15.00
BDPP89 J.R. Towles 6.00 15.00
BDPP90 Alcides Escobar 6.00 15.00
BDPP91 Brian Bocock 6.00 15.00
BDPP92 Chin-Lung Hu 20.00 50.00
BDPP93 Adrian Cardenas 15.00 40.00
BDPP94 Freddy Sandoval 6.00 15.00
BDPP95 Chris Coghlan 6.00 15.00
BDPP96 Craig Stansberry 4.00 10.00
BDPP97 Brent Lillibridge 6.00 15.00
BDPP98 Joey Votto 10.00 25.00
BDPP99 Evan Longoria 10.00 25.00
BDPP100 Wladimir Balentien 6.00 15.00
BDPP101 Johnny Whittleman 6.00 15.00
BDPP102 Gorkys Hernandez 10.00 25.00
BDPP103 Jay Bruce 15.00 40.00
BDPP104 Matt Tolbert 15.00 40.00
BDPP105 Jacoby Ellsbury 15.00 40.00
BDPP106 Michael Saunders 10.00 25.00
BDPP107 Cameron Maybin 12.50 30.00
BDPP108 Carlos Gonzalez 10.00 25.00
BDPP109 Colby Rasmus 10.00 25.00
BDPP110 Justin Upton 15.00 40.00

2007 Bowman Draft Head of the Class Dual Autograph

STATED ODDS 1:4965 HOBBY
STATED PRINT RUN 174 SER.#'d SETS
EXCHANGE DEADLINE 12/31/2009
GH J.Gilmore/J.Heyward 12.50 30.00

2007 Bowman Draft Head of the Class Dual Autograph Refractors

*REF: .6X TO 1.5X BASIC
STATED ODDS 1:18,000 HOBBY
STATED PRINT RUN 50 SER.#'d SETS
EXCHANGE DEADLINE 12/31/2009
GH J.Gilmore/J.Heyward 40.00 80.00

2007 Bowman Draft Head of the Class Dual Autograph Gold Refractors

STATED ODDS 1:34,500 HOBBY
STATED PRINT RUN 25 SER.#'d SETS
NO PRICING DUE TO SCARCITY
EXCHANGE DEADLINE 12/31/2009

2007 Bowman Draft Signs of the Future

GROUP A ODDS 1:233 RETAIL
GROUP B ODDS 1:30 RETAIL
GROUP C ODDS 1:194 RETAIL
GROUP D ODDS 1:146 RETAIL
GROUP E ODDS 1:2945 RETAIL
AL Anthony Lerew 6.00 15.00
AM Adam Miller 5.00 12.00
BA Brandon Allen 4.00 10.00
CD Chris Dickerson 3.00 8.00
CM Casey McGehee 8.00 20.00
CMC Chris McConnell 4.00 10.00
CMM Carlos Marmol 6.00 15.00
CV Carlos Villanueva 3.00 8.00
FM Fernando Martinez 3.00 8.00
JGA Jaime Garcia 10.00 25.00
JK John Koronka 3.00 8.00
JR John Rheinecker 3.00 8.00
JV Jonathan Van Every 3.00 8.00
PH Philip Humber 4.00 10.00
RD Ryan Delaughter 3.00 8.00
SM Sergio Mitre 3.00 8.00
TC Trevor Crowe 3.00 8.00

2008 Bowman

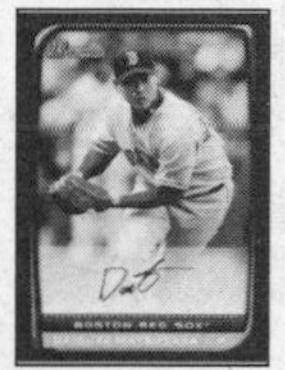

COMP.SET w/o AU's (220) 8.00 20.00
COMMON CARD (1-200) .12 .30
COMMON ROOKIE (201-220) .15 .40
COMMON AUTO (221-230) 4.00 10.00
AU RC ODDS 1:233 HOBBY
1-220 PLATE ODDS 1:732 HOBBY
221-231 AU PLATES 1:4700 HOBBY
PLATE PRINT RUN 1 SET PER COLOR
BLACK-CYAN-MAGENTA-YELLOW ISSUED
NO PLATE PRICING DUE TO SCARCITY
1 Ryan Braun .20 .50
2 David DeJesus .12 .30
3 Brandon Phillips .12 .30
4 Mark Teixeira .20 .50
5 Daisuke Matsuzaka .20 .50
6 Justin Upton .20 .50
7 Jered Weaver .20 .50
8 Todd Helton .20 .50
9 Cameron Maybin .12 .30
10 Erik Bedard .12 .30
11 Jason Bay .20 .50
12 Cole Hamels .25 .60
13 Bobby Abreu .12 .30
14 Carlos Zambrano .20 .50
15 Vladimir Guerrero .20 .50
16 Joe Blanton .12 .30
17 Bengie Molina .12 .30
18 Paul Maholm .12 .30
19 Adrian Gonzalez .20 .50
20 Brandon Webb .20 .50
21 Carl Crawford .20 .50
22 A.J. Burnett .12 .30
23 Dmitri Young .12 .30
24 Jeremy Hermida .12 .30
25 C.C. Sabathia .20 .50
26 Adam Dunn .20 .50
27 Matt Garza .12 .30
28 Adrian Beltre .30 .75
29 Kevin Millwood .12 .30
30 Manny Ramirez .30 .75
31 Javier Vazquez .12 .30
32 Carlos Delgado .12 .30
33 Jason Schmidt .12 .30
34 Torii Hunter .12 .30
35 Ivan Rodriguez .20 .50
36 Nick Markakis .25 .60
37 Gil Meche .12 .30
38 Garrett Atkins .12 .30
39 Fausto Carmona .12 .30
40 Joe Mauer .25 .60
41 Tom Glavine .20 .50
42 Hideki Matsui .30 .75
43 Scott Rolen .20 .50
44 Tim Lincecum .20 .50
45 Prince Fielder .20 .50
46 Ted Lilly .12 .30
47 Frank Thomas .30 .75
48 Tom Gorzelanny .12 .30
49 Lance Berkman .20 .50
50 David Ortiz .30 .75
51 Dontrelle Willis .12 .30
52 Travis Hafner .12 .30
53 Aaron Harang .12 .30
54 Chris Young .12 .30
55 Vernon Wells .12 .30
56 Francisco Liriano .12 .30
57 Eric Chavez .12 .30
58 Phil Hughes .12 .30
59 Melvin Mora .12 .30
60 Johan Santana .20 .50
61 Brian McCann .20 .50
62 Pat Burrell .12 .30
63 Chris Carpenter .20 .50
64 Brian Giles .12 .30
65 Jose Reyes .20 .50
66 Hanley Ramirez .20 .50
67 Ubaldo Jimenez .12 .30
68 Felix Pie .12 .30
69 Jeremy Bonderman .12 .30
70 Jimmy Rollins .20 .50
71 Miguel Tejada .20 .50
72 Derek Lowe .12 .30
73 Alex Gordon .20 .50
74 John Maine .12 .30
75 Alfonso Soriano .20 .50
76 Richie Sexson .12 .30
77 Ben Sheets .12 .30
78 Hunter Pence .20 .50
79 Magglio Ordonez .20 .50
80 Josh Beckett .12 .30
81 Victor Martinez .20 .50
82 Mark Buehrle .20 .50
83 Jason Varitek .30 .75
84 Chien-Ming Wang .20 .50
85 Ken Griffey Jr. .60 1.50
86 Billy Butler .12 .30
87 Brad Penny .12 .30
88 Carlos Beltran .20 .50
89 Curt Schilling .20 .50
90 Jorge Posada .20 .50
91 Andruw Jones .12 .30
92 Bobby Crosby .12 .30
93 Freddy Sanchez .12 .30
94 Barry Zito .20 .50
95 Miguel Cabrera .30 .75
96 B.J. Upton .20 .50
97 Matt Cain .20 .50
98 Lyle Overbay .12 .30
99 Austin Kearns .12 .30
100 Alex Rodriguez .40 1.00
101 Rich Harden .12 .30
102 Justin Morneau .20 .50
103 Oliver Perez .12 .30
104 Gary Matthews .12 .30
105 Matt Holliday .30 .75
106 Justin Verlander .30 .75
107 Orlando Cabrera .20 .50
108 Rich Hill .12 .30
109 Tim Hudson .20 .50
110 Ryan Zimmerman .20 .50
111 Roy Oswalt .20 .50
112 Nick Swisher .20 .50
113 Raul Ibanez .20 .50
114 Kelly Johnson .12 .30
115 Alex Rios .12 .30
116 John Lackey .20 .50
117 Robinson Cano .20 .50
118 Michael Young .12 .30
119 Jeff Francis .12 .30
120 Grady Sizemore .20 .50
121 Mike Lowell .12 .30
122 Aramis Ramirez .12 .30
123 Stephen Drew .12 .30
124 Yovani Gallardo .12 .30
125 Chase Utley .20 .50
126 Dan Haren .12 .30
127 Jose Vidro .12 .30
128 Ronnie Belliard .12 .30
129 Yunel Escobar .12 .30
130 Greg Maddux .40 1.00
131 Garret Anderson .12 .30
132 Aubrey Huff .12 .30
133 Paul Konerko .20 .50
134 Dan Uggla .12 .30
135 Roy Halladay .20 .50
136 Andre Ethier .20 .50
137 Orlando Hernandez .12 .30
138 Troy Tulowitzki .30 .75
139 Carlos Guillen .12 .30
140 Scott Kazmir .20 .50
141 Aaron Rowand .12 .30
142 Jim Edmonds .20 .50
143 Jermaine Dye .12 .30
144 Orlando Hudson .12 .30
145 Derrek Lee .12 .30
146 Travis Buck .12 .30
147 Zack Greinke .20 .50
148 Jeff Kent .12 .30
149 John Smoltz .30 .75
150 David Wright .20 .50
151 Joba Chamberlain .20 .50
152 Adam LaRoche .12 .30
153 Kevin Youkilis .12 .30
154 Troy Glaus .12 .30
155 Nick Johnson .12 .30
156 J.J. Hardy .12 .30
157 Felix Hernandez .20 .50
158 Khalil Greene .12 .30
159 Gary Sheffield .12 .30
160 Albert Pujols .40 1.00
161 Chuck James .12 .30
162 Rocco Baldelli .12 .30
163 Eric Byrnes .12 .30
164 Brad Hawpe .12 .30
165 Delmon Young .20 .50
166 Chris Young .12 .30
167 Brian Roberts .12 .30
168 Russell Martin .12 .30
169 Hank Blalock .12 .30
170 Yadier Molina .30 .75
171 Jeremy Guthrie .12 .30
172 Chipper Jones .30 .75
173 Johnny Damon .20 .50
174 Ryan Garko .12 .30
175 Jake Peavy .12 .30
176 Chone Figgins .12 .30
177 Edgar Renteria .12 .30
178 Jim Thome .20 .50
179 Carlos Pena .20 .50
180 Corey Patterson .12 .30
181 Dustin Pedroia .20 .50
182 Brett Myers .12 .30
183 Josh Hamilton .20 .50
184 Randy Johnson .30 .75
185 Ichiro Suzuki .40 1.00
186 Aaron Hill .12 .30
187 Jarrod Saltalamacchia .12 .30
188 Michael Cuddyer .12 .30
189 Jeff Francoeur .20 .50
190 Derek Jeter .75 2.00
191 Curtis Granderson .20 .50
192 James Loney .12 .30
193 Brian Bannister .12 .30
194 Carlos Lee .12 .30
195 Pedro Martinez .20 .50
196 Asdrubal Cabrera .20 .50
197 Kenji Johjima .12 .30
198 Bartolo Colon .12 .30
199 Jacoby Ellsbury .25 .60
200 Ryan Howard .20 .50
201 Radhames Liz RC .25 .60
202 Justin Ruggiano RC .25 .60
203 Lance Broadway (RC) .15 .40
204 Joey Votto (RC) .60 1.50
205 Billy Buckner (RC) .15 .40
206 Joe Koshansky (RC) .15 .40
207 Ross Detwiler RC .25 .60
208 Chin-Lung Hu (RC) .15 .40
209 Luke Hochevar RC .25 .60
210 Jeff Clement (RC) .25 .60
211 Troy Patton (RC) .15 .40
212 Hiroki Kuroda RC .40 1.00
213 Emilio Bonifacio RC .40 1.00
214 Armando Galarraga RC .25 .60
215 Josh Anderson (RC) .15 .40
216 Nick Blackburn RC .25 .60
217 Seth Smith (RC) .15 .40
218 Jonathan Meloan RC .25 .60
219 Alberto Gonzalez RC .25 .60
220 Josh Banks (RC) .15 .40
221 Clay Buchholz AU (RC) 5.00 12.00
222 Nyjer Morgan AU (RC) 4.00 10.00
223 Brandon Jones AU RC 4.00 10.00
224 Sam Fuld AU RC 5.00 12.00
225 Daric Barton AU (RC) 4.00 10.00
226 Chris Seddon AU (RC) 4.00 10.00
227 J.R. Towles AU RC 4.00 10.00
228 Steve Pearce AU RC 15.00 40.00
229 Ross Ohlendorf AU RC 4.00 10.00
230 Clint Sammons AU (RC) 4.00 10.00

2008 Bowman Blue

*BLUE 1-200: 2X TO 5X BASIC
*BLUE 201-220: 2X TO 5X BASIC
*BLUE AU 221-230: .4X TO 1X BASIC AU
1-220 ODDS 1:14 HOBBY,1:32 RETAIL
221-230 AU ODDS 1:620 HOBBY
STATED PRINT RUN 500 SERIAL #'d SETS

2008 Bowman Gold

*GOLD 1-200: 1.2X TO 3X BASIC
*GOLD 201-220: 1.2X TO 3X BASIC
OVERALL GOLD ODDS 1 PER PACK

2008 Bowman Orange

*ORANGE 1-200: 2.5X TO 6X BASIC
*ORANGE 201-220: 2.5X TO 6X BASIC
*ORANGE AU 221-230: .5X TO 1.2X BASIC AU
1-220 ODDS 1:26 HOBBY,1:65 RETAIL
221-230 AU ODDS 1:1160 HOBBY
STATED PRINT RUN 250 SERIAL #'d SETS

2008 Bowman Red

1-220 ODDS 1:4512 HOBBY
221-230 AU ODDS 1:243,648 HOBBY
STATED PRINT RUN 1 SER.#'d SET
NO PRICING DUE TO SCARCITY

2008 Bowman Prospects

COMPLETE SET (110) 12.50 30.00
PRINTING PLATE ODDS 1:732 HOBBY
PLATE PRINT RUN 1 SET PER COLOR
BLACK-CYAN-MAGENTA-YELLOW ISSUED
NO PLATE PRICING DUE TO SCARCITY
BP1 Max Sapp .15 .40
BP2 Jamie Richmond .15 .40
BP3 Darren Ford .15 .40
BP4 Sergio Romo .75 2.00
BP5 Jacob Butler .15 .40
BP6 Glenn Gibson .15 .40
BP7 Tom Hagan .15 .40
BP8 Michael McCormick .15 .40
BP9 Gregorio Petit .25 .60
BP10 Bobby Parnell .15 .40
BP11 Jeff Kindel .25 .60
BP12 Anthony Claggett .25 .60
BP13 Christopher Frey .15 .40
BP14 Jonah Nickerson .25 .60
BP15 Anthony Martinez .15 .40
BP16 Rusty Ryal .25 .60
BP17 Justin Berg .25 .60
BP18 Gerardo Parra .15 .40
BP19 Wesley Wright .15 .40
BP20 Stephen Chapman .15 .40
BP21 Chance Chapman .15 .40
BP22 Brett Pill .50 1.25
BP23 Zachary Phillips .25 .60
BP24 John Raynor .40 1.00
BP25 Danny Duffy .40 1.00
BP26 Brian Finegan .15 .40
BP27 Jonathan Venters .15 .40
BP28 Steve Tolleson .15 .40
BP29 Ben Jukich .25 .60
BP30 Matthew Weston .15 .40
BP31 Kyle Mura .15 .40
BP32 Luke Hetherington .15 .40
BP33 Michael Daniel .25 .60
BP34 Jake Renshaw .15 .40
BP35 Greg Halman .25 .60
BP36 Ryan Khoury .15 .40
BP37 Ryan Ouellette .15 .40
BP38 Mike Brantley .40 1.00
BP39 Eric Brown .15 .40
BP40 Jose Duarte .15 .40
BP41 Eli Tintor .15 .40
BP42 Kent Sakamoto .15 .40
BP43 Luke Montz .15 .40
BP44 Alex Cobb .15 .40
BP45 Michael McKenry .15 .40
BP46 Javier Castillo .15 .40
BP47 Jeffrey Stevens .15 .40
BP48 Greg Burns .15 .40
BP49 Blake Johnson .15 .40
BP50 Austin Jackson .75 2.00
BP51 Anthony Recker .15 .40
BP52 Luis Durango .15 .40
BP53 Engel Beltre .50 1.25
BP54 Seth Bynum .15 .40
BP55 Ryan Strieby .25 .60
BP56 Iggy Suarez .15 .40
BP57 Ryan Morris .25 .60
BP58 Scott Van Slyke .50 1.25
BP59 Tyler Kolodny .50 1.25
BP60 Joseph Martinez .15 .40
BP61 Aaron Mathews .15 .40
BP62 Phillip Cuadrado .15 .40
BP63 Alex Liddi .25 .60
BP64 Alex Burnett .25 .60
BP65 Brian Barton .25 .60
BP66 David Welch .15 .40
BP67 Kyle Reynolds .15 .40
BP68 Francisco Hernandez .15 .40
BP69 Logan Morrison .75 2.00
BP70 Ronald Ramirez .15 .40
BP71 Brad Miller .15 .40
BP72 Braedyn Pruitt .25 .60
BP73 Jason Fernandez .25 .60
BP74 Joseph Mahoney .15 .40
BP75 Quentin Davis .25 .60
BP76 P.J. Walters .15 .40
BP77 Jordan Czarniecki .15 .40
BP78 Jonathan Mota .15 .40
BP79 Michael Hernandez .15 .40
BP80 James Guerrero .15 .40
BP81 Chris Johnson .25 .60
BP82 Daniel Cortes .40 1.00
BP83 Sal Sanchez .25 .60
BP84 Sean Henry .15 .40
BP85 Caleb Gindl .15 .40
BP86 Tommy Everidge .15 .40
BP87 Matt Rizzotti .15 .40
BP88 Luis Munoz .15 .40
BP89 Matthew Klimas .15 .40
BP90 Angel Reyes .15 .40
BP91 Sean Danielson .15 .40
BP92 Omar Poveda .15 .40
BP93 Mario Lisson .15 .40
BP94 Brian Mathews .15 .40
BP95 Matthew Buschmann .15 .40
BP96 Greg Thomson .15 .40
BP97 Matt Inouye .15 .40
BP98 Aneury Rodriguez .25 .60
BP99 Brad Harman .25 .60

Card	Low	High
BP100 Aaron Bates	.40	1.00
BP101 Graham Taylor	.15	.40
BP102 Ken Holmberg	.15	.40
BP103 Greg Dowling	.15	.40
BP104 Ronnie Ray	.15	.40
BP105 Michael Wlodarczyk	.15	.40
BP106 Jose Martinez	.25	.60
BP107 Jason Stephens	.25	.60
BP108 Will Rhymes	.15	.40
BP109 Joey Side	.15	.40
BP110 Brandon Waring	.25	.60

2008 Bowman Prospects Blue

*BLUE 1-110: 1.2X TO 3X BASIC
1-110 ODDS 1:14 HOBBY,1:32 RETAIL
STATED PRINT RUN 500 SER.#'d SETS

2008 Bowman Prospects Gold

*GOLD 1-110: .75X TO 2X BASIC
OVERALL GOLD ODDS 1 PER PACK

2008 Bowman Prospects Orange

*ORANGE 1-110: 2X TO 5X BASIC
1-110 ODDS 1:26 HOBBY,1:65 RETAIL
STATED PRINT RUN 250 SER.#'d SETS

2008 Bowman Prospects Red

STATED ODDS 1:4512 HOBBY
STATED PRINT RUN 1 SER.#'d SET
NO PRICING DUE TO SCARCITY

2008 Bowman Scouts Autographs

GROUP A ODDS 1:176 HOB,1:410 RET
GROUP B ODDS 1:390 HOB,1:910 RET
EXCHANGE DEADLINE 5/31/2010

Card	Low	High
AS Alex Smith B	3.00	8.00
BB Bill Buck B	3.00	8.00
BE Bob Engle B	3.00	8.00
BF Bob Fontaine Jr. A	3.00	8.00
BS Bowman Scout A	3.00	8.00
CB Chris Bourjos A	3.00	8.00
DJ Dave Jennings B	3.00	8.00
DL Don Lyle B	3.00	8.00
DO Dan Ontiveros B	3.00	8.00
JC Jerome Cochran B EXCH	3.00	8.00
JD Jon Deeble A EXCH	3.00	8.00
JH Josue Herrera B	3.00	8.00
JL Jerry Lafferty A	3.00	8.00
JM Joe Mason B	3.00	8.00
LW Leon Wurth A	3.00	8.00
MR Mike Rizzo A	3.00	8.00
RA Ralph Avila A	3.00	8.00
TC Ty Coslow A	3.00	8.00
TCU Tom Couston A	3.00	8.00
TD Tony DeMacio A	3.00	8.00
TK Tim Kelly B	3.00	8.00

2008 Bowman Signs of the Future

GROUP A ODDS 1:26 RETAIL
GROUP B ODDS 1:305 RETAIL
EXCHANGE DEADLINE 5/31/2010
PLATE PRINT RUN 1 SET PER COLOR
BLACK-CYAN-MAGENTA-YELLOW ISSUED
NO PLATE PRICING DUE TO SCARCITY

Card	Low	High
AC Adam Carr	3.00	8.00
BK Brad Knox	3.00	8.00
BO Brian Omogrosso	3.00	8.00
BW Brian Wilson	10.00	25.00
CN Chris Nowak	4.00	10.00
CR Colby Rasmus	3.00	8.00
CT Clayton Tanner	3.00	8.00
CTI Chris Tillman	4.00	10.00
DS David Shafer	3.00	8.00
EJ Elliot Johnson	3.00	8.00
GM Garrett Mock	3.00	8.00
GP Gerardo Parra	8.00	20.00
GS Greg Smith	4.00	10.00
JE Jack Egbert	3.00	8.00
JG Jaime Garcia	6.00	15.00
JH Joel Hanrahan	5.00	12.00
JHI Jamar Hill	3.00	8.00
JHU Jon Huber	3.00	8.00
JJ Jason Jaramillo	3.00	8.00
JK Josh Kroeger	3.00	8.00
JL Jeff Locke	6.00	15.00
JM Jose Mijares EXCH	3.00	8.00
JV Jonathan Van Every	3.00	8.00
KB Kyle Bloom	3.00	8.00
LM Lou Marson	3.00	8.00
MC Mike Costanzo	3.00	8.00
ME Mitch Einertson	4.00	10.00
MP Matt Peterson	3.00	8.00
RK Ryan Kalish	6.00	15.00
RS Ryan Speier	3.00	8.00
SR Steven Register	3.00	8.00
TC Tyler Colvin	8.00	20.00
TM Tommy Manzella	3.00	8.00
TO Tim Olson	3.00	8.00
WI Will Inman	4.00	10.00

2008 Bowman Draft

This set was released on November 28, 2008. The base set consists of 55 cards.

Card	Low	High
COMPLETE SET (55)	10.00	25.00
COMMON CARD (1-55)	.20	.50

OVERALL PLATE ODDS 1:750 HOBBY
PLATE PRINT RUN 1 SET PER COLOR
BLACK-CYAN-MAGENTA-YELLOW ISSUED
NO PLATE PRICING DUE TO SCARCITY

Card	Low	High
BDP1 Nick Adenhart (RC)	.20	.50
BDP2 Michael Aubrey RC	.30	.75
BDP3 Mike Aviles RC	.30	.75
BDP4 Burke Badenhop RC	.30	.75
BDP5 Wladimir Balentien (RC)	.20	.50
BDP6 Collin Balester (RC)	.20	.50
BDP7 Josh Banks (RC)	.20	.50
BDP8 Wes Bankston (RC)	.20	.50
BDP9 Joey Votto (RC)	.75	2.00
BDP10 Mitch Boggs (RC)	.20	.50
BDP11 Jay Bruce (RC)	.60	1.50
BDP12 Chris Carter (RC)	.30	.75
BDP13 Justin Christian RC	.30	.75
BDP14 Chris Davis RC	.40	1.00
BDP15 Blake DeWitt (RC)	.30	.75
BDP16 Nick Evans RC	.20	.50
BDP17 Jaime Garcia RC	.75	2.00
BDP18 Brett Gardner (RC)	.50	1.25
BDP19 Carlos Gonzalez (RC)	.50	1.25
BDP20 Matt Harrison (RC)	.30	.75
BDP21 Micah Hoffpauir RC	.60	1.50
BDP22 Nick Hundley (RC)	.20	.50
BDP23 Eric Hurley (RC)	.20	.50
BDP24 Elliot Johnson (RC)	.20	.50
BDP25 Matt Joyce RC	.50	1.25
BDP26 Clayton Kershaw RC	3.00	8.00
BDP27 Evan Longoria RC	1.00	2.50
BDP28 Matt Macri (RC)	.20	.50
BDP29 Chris Perez RC	.30	.75
BDP30 Max Ramirez RC	.20	.50
BDP31 Greg Reynolds RC	.30	.75
BDP32 Brooks Conrad (RC)	.20	.50
BDP33 Max Scherzer RC	2.50	6.00
BDP34 Daryl Thompson (RC)	.20	.50
BDP35 Taylor Teagarden RC	.30	.75
BDP36 Rich Thompson RC	.30	.75
BDP37 Ryan Tucker (RC)	.20	.50
BDP38 Jonathan Van Every RC	.20	.50
BDP39 Chris Volstad (RC)	.20	.50
BDP40 Michael Hollimon RC	.20	.50
BDP41 Brad Ziegler RC	1.00	2.50
BDP42 Jamie D'Antona (RC)	.20	.50
BDP43 Clayton Richard (RC)	.20	.50
BDP44 Edgar Gonzalez (RC)	.20	.50
BDP45 Bryan LaHair RC	1.50	4.00
BDP46 Warner Madrigal (RC)	.20	.50
BDP47 Reid Brignac (RC)	.30	.75
BDP48 David Robertson RC	.50	1.25
BDP49 Nick Stavinoha RC	.20	.50
BDP50 Jai Miller (RC)	.20	.50
BDP51 Charlie Morton (RC)	.60	1.50
BDP52 Brandon Boggs (RC)	.30	.75
BDP53 Joe Mather RC	.30	.75
BDP54 Gregorio Petit RC	.30	.75
BDP55 Jeff Samardzija RC	.60	1.50

2008 Bowman Draft Blue

*BLUE: 1X TO 2.5X BASIC
STATED ODDS 1:19 HOBBY
STATED PRINT RUN 399 SER.#'d SETS

2008 Bowman Draft Gold

*GOLD: .6X TO 1.5X BASIC
APPX.GOLD ODDS ONE PER PACK

2008 Bowman Draft Red

STATED ODDS 1:6025 HOBBY
STATED PRINT RUN 1 SER.#'d SET
NO PRICING DUE TO SCARCITY

2008 Bowman Draft Prospects

Card	Low	High
COMPLETE SET (110)	12.50	30.00
COMMON CARD (1-65)	.20	.50

OVERALL PLATE ODDS 1:750 HOBBY
PLATE PRINT RUN 1 SET PER COLOR
BLACK-CYAN-MAGENTA-YELLOW ISSUED
NO PLATE PRICING DUE TO SCARCITY

Card	Low	High
BDPP1 Rick Porcello DP	.60	1.50
BDPP2 Braeden Schlehuber DP	.20	.50
BDPP3 Kenny Wilson DP	.20	.50
BDPP4 Jeff Lanning DP	.20	.50
BDPP5 Kevin Dubler DP	.20	.50
BDPP6 Eric Campbell DP	.30	.75
BDPP7 Tyler Chatwood DP	.30	.75
BDPP8 Tyreace House DP	.20	.50
BDPP9 Adrian Nieto DP	.20	.50
BDPP10 Robbie Grossman DP	.30	.75
BDPP11 Jordan Danks DP	.50	1.25
BDPP12 Jay Austin DP	.20	.50
BDPP13 Ryan Perry DP	.30	.75
BDPP14 Ryan Chaffee DP	.30	.75
BDPP15 Niko Vasquez DP	.50	1.25
BDPP16 Shane Dyer DP	.20	.50
BDPP17 Benji Gonzalez DP	.20	.50
BDPP18 Miles Reagan DP	.20	.50
BDPP19 Anthony Ferrara DP	.20	.50
BDPP20 Markus Brisker DP	.20	.50
BDPP21 Justin Bristow DP	.20	.50
BDPP22 Richard Bleier DP	.20	.50
BDPP23 Jeremy Beckham DP	.30	.75
BDPP24 Xavier Avery DP	.50	1.25
BDPP25 Christian Vazquez DP	.30	.75
BDPP26 Nick Romero DP	.20	.50
BDPP27 Trey Watten DP	.20	.50
BDPP28 Brett Jacobson DP	.20	.50
BDPP29 Tyler Sample DP	.20	.50
BDPP30 T.J. Steele DP	.30	.75
BDPP31 Christian Friedrich DP	.50	1.25
BDPP32 Graham Hicks DP	.30	.75
BDPP33 Shane Peterson DP	.30	.75
BDPP34 Brett Hunter DP	.20	.50
BDPP35 Tim Federowicz DP	.30	.75
BDPP36 Isaac Galloway DP	.30	.75
BDPP37 Logan Schafer DP	.20	.50
BDPP38 Paul Demny DP	.20	.50
BDPP39 Clayton Shunick DP	.20	.50
BDPP40 Andrew Liebel DP	.20	.50
BDPP41 Brandon Crawford DP	.50	1.25
BDPP42 Blake Tekotte DP	.30	.75
BDPP43 Jason Corder DP	.20	.50
BDPP44 Bryan Shaw DP	.20	.50
BDPP45 Edgar Olmos DP	.20	.50
BDPP46 Dusty Coleman DP	.20	.50
BDPP47 Johnny Giavotella DP	.60	1.50
BDPP48 Tyson Ross DP	.30	.75
BDPP49 Brent Morel DP	.30	.75
BDPP50 Dennis Raben DP	.30	.75
BDPP51 Jake Odorizzi DP	.60	1.50
BDPP52 Ryne White DP	.20	.50
BDPP53 Devaris Strange-Gordon DP	.60	1.50
BDPP54 Tim Murphy DP	.20	.50
BDPP55 Jake Jefferies DP	.20	.50
BDPP56 Anthony Capra DP	.20	.50
BDPP57 Kyle Weiland DP	.50	1.25
BDPP58 Anthony Bass DP	.30	.75
BDPP59 Scott Green DP	.20	.50
BDPP60 Zeke Spruill DP	.50	1.25
BDPP61 L.J. Hoes DP	.20	.50
BDPP62 Tyler Cline DP	.20	.50
BDPP63 Matt Cerda DP	.20	.50
BDPP64 Bobby Lanigan DP	.20	.50
BDPP65 Mike Sheridan DP	.20	.50
BDPP66 Carlos Carrasco FG	.30	.75
BDPP67 Nate Schierholtz FG	.30	.75
BDPP68 Jesus Delgado FG	.20	.50
BDPP70 Shairon Martis FG	.30	.75
BDPP71 Matt LaPorta FG	.30	.75
BDPP72 Eddie Morlan FG	.20	.50
BDPP73 Greg Golson FG	.20	.50
BDPP74 Julio Pimentel FG	.20	.50
BDPP75 Dexter Fowler FG	.30	.75
BDPP76 Henry Rodriguez FG	.20	.50
BDPP77 Cliff Pennington FG	.20	.50
BDPP78 Hector Rondon FG	.30	.75
BDPP79 Wes Hodges FG	.20	.50
BDPP80 Polin Trinidad FG	.20	.50
BDPP81 Chris Getz FG	.20	.50
BDPP82 Wellington Castillo FG	.20	.50
BDPP83 Mat Gamel FG	.50	1.25
BDPP84 Pablo Sandoval FG	.75	2.00
BDPP85 Jason Donald FG	.20	.50
BDPP86 Jesus Montero FG	.30	.75
BDPP87 Jamie D'Antona FG	.20	.50
BDPP88 Will Inman FG	.20	.50
BDPP89 Elvis Andrus FG	.50	1.25
BDPP90 Taylor Teagarden FG	.30	.75
BDPP91 Scott Campbell FG	.20	.50
BDPP92 Jake Arrieta FG	.50	1.25
BDPP93 Juan Francisco FG	.50	1.25
BDPP94 Lou Marson FG	.20	.50
BDPP95 Luke Hughes FG	.20	.50
BDPP96 Bryan Anderson FG	.20	.50
BDPP97 Ramiro Pena FG	.20	.50
BDPP98 Jesse Todd FG	.20	.50
BDPP99 Gorkys Hernandez FG	.20	.50
BDPP100 Casey Weathers FG	.20	.50
BDPP101 Fernando Martinez FG	.30	.75
BDPP102 Clayton Richard FG	.20	.50
BDPP103 Gerardo Parra FG	.20	.50
BDPP104 Kevin Pucetas FG	.30	.75
BDPP105 Wilkin Ramirez FG	.20	.50
BDPP106 Ryan Mattheus FG	.20	.50
BDPP107 Angel Villalona FG	.50	1.25
BDPP108 Brett Anderson FG	.30	.75
BDPP109 Chris Valaika FG	.20	.50
BDPP110 Trevor Cahill FG	.50	1.25

2008 Bowman Draft Prospects Blue

*BLUE: 1.5X TO 4X BASIC
STATED ODDS 1:19 HOBBY
STATED PRINT RUN 399 SER.#'d SETS

2008 Bowman Draft Prospects Gold

*GOLD: .75X TO 2X BASIC
APPX.GOLD ODDS ONE PER PACK

2008 Bowman Draft Prospects Red

STATED ODDS 1:6025 HOBBY
STATED PRINT RUN 1 SER.#'d SET
NO PRICING DUE TO SCARCITY

2008 Bowman Draft Prospects Jerseys

RANDOM INSERTS IN RETAIL PACKS
NO PRICING DUE TO LACK OF MARKET INFO

Card	Low	High
BDPP71 Matt LaPorta FG	3.00	8.00
BDPP75 Dexter Fowler FG	3.00	8.00

2008 Bowman Draft Signs of the Future

RANDOM INSERTS IN RETAIL PACKS

Card	Low	High
AC Adrain Cardenas	4.00	10.00
BP Billy Petrick	3.00	8.00
BS Brad Salmon	3.00	8.00
CW Corey Wimberly	6.00	15.00
DM Daniel Murphy	20.00	50.00
DS David Shafer	3.00	8.00
EM Evan MaClane	3.00	8.00
FG Freddy Galvis	3.00	8.00
GK George Kontos	3.00	8.00
JW Johnny Whittleman	3.00	8.00
KD Kyle Drabek	6.00	15.00
OP Omar Poveda	3.00	8.00
OS Oswaldo Sosa	3.00	8.00
TD Travis D'Arnaud	4.00	10.00
TS Travis Snider	5.00	12.00

2009 Bowman

Card	Low	High
COMP.SET w/o AU's (220)	12.50	30.00
COMMON CARD (1-190)	.12	.30
COMMON ROOKE (66/191-220)	.25	.60
COMMON AU RC (221-230)	4.00	10.00

PLATE PRINT RUN 1 SET PER COLOR
BLACK-CYAN-MAGENTA-YELLOW ISSUED
NO PLATE PRICING DUE TO SCARCITY

Card	Low	High
1 David Wright	.25	.60
2 Albert Pujols	.40	1.00
3 Alex Rodriguez	.40	1.00
4 Chase Utley	.20	.50
5 Chien-Ming Wang	.20	.50
6 Jimmy Rollins	.20	.50
7 Ken Griffey Jr.	.60	1.50
8 Manny Ramirez	.30	.75
9 Chipper Jones	.30	.75
10 Ichiro Suzuki	.40	1.00
11 Justin Morneau	.20	.50
12 Hanley Ramirez	.20	.50
13 Cliff Lee	.20	.50
14 Ryan Howard	.25	.60
15 Ian Kinsler	.20	.50
16 Jose Reyes	.20	.50
17 Ted Lilly	.12	.30
18 Miguel Cabrera	.30	.75
19 Nate McLouth	.12	.30
20 Josh Beckett	.12	.30
21 John Lackey	.20	.50
22 David Ortiz	.30	.75
23 Carlos Lee	.12	.30
24 Adam Dunn	.20	.50
25 B.J. Upton	.20	.50
26 Curtis Granderson	.25	.60
27 David DeJesus	.12	.30
28 CC Sabathia	.20	.50
29 Russell Martin	.20	.50
30 Torii Hunter	.12	.30
31 Rich Harden	.12	.30
32 Johnny Damon	.20	.50
33 Cristian Guzman	.12	.30
34 Grady Sizemore	.20	.50
35 Jorge Posada	.20	.50
36 Placido Polanco	.12	.30
37 Ryan Ludwick	.20	.50
38 Dustin Pedroia	.25	.60
39 Matt Garza	.12	.30
40 Prince Fielder	.20	.50
41 Rick Ankiel	.12	.30
42 Jonathan Sanchez	.12	.30
43 Erik Bedard	.12	.30
44 Ryan Braun	.20	.50
45 Ervin Santana	.12	.30
46 Brian Roberts	.12	.30
47 Mike Jacobs	.12	.30
48 Phil Hughes	.12	.30
49 Justin Masterson	.12	.30
50 Felix Hernandez	.20	.50
51 Stephen Drew	.12	.30
52 Bobby Abreu	.12	.30
53 Jay Bruce	.20	.50
54 Josh Hamilton	.20	.50
55 Garrett Atkins	.12	.30
56 Jacoby Ellsbury	.25	.60
57 Johan Santana	.20	.50
58 James Shields	.12	.30
59 Armando Galarraga	.12	.30
60 Carlos Pena	.20	.50
61 Matt Kemp	.25	.60
62 Joey Votto	.30	.75
63 Raul Ibanez	.20	.50
64 Casey Kotchman	.12	.30
65 Hunter Pence	.20	.50
66 Daniel Murphy RC	1.00	2.50
67 Carlos Beltran	.20	.50
68 Evan Longoria	.20	.50
69 Daisuke Matsuzaka	.20	.50
70 Cole Hamels	.25	.60
71 Robinson Cano	.20	.50
72 Clayton Kershaw	.60	1.50
73 Kenji Johjima	.20	.50
74 Kazuo Matsui	.12	.30
75 Jayson Werth	.20	.50
76 Brian McCann	.20	.50
77 Barry Zito	.20	.50
78 Glen Perkins	.12	.30
79 Jeff Francoeur	.20	.50
80 Derek Jeter	.75	2.00
81 Ryan Doumit	.12	.30
82 Dan Haren	.12	.30
83 Justin Duchscherer	.12	.30
84 Marlon Byrd	.12	.30
85 Derek Lowe	.12	.30
86 Pat Burrell	.12	.30
87 Jair Jurrjens	.12	.30
88 Zack Greinke	.20	.50
89 Jon Lester	.20	.50
90 Justin Verlander	.30	.75
91 Jorge Cantu	.12	.30
92 John Maine	.12	.30
93 Brad Hawpe	.12	.30
94 Mike Aviles	.12	.30
95 Victor Martinez	.20	.50
96 Ryan Dempster	.12	.30
97 Miguel Tejada	.20	.50
98 Joe Mauer	.25	.60
99 Scott Olsen	.12	.30
100 Tim Lincecum	.20	.50
101 Francisco Liriano	.12	.30
102 Chris Iannetta	.12	.30
103 Jamie Moyer	.12	.30
104 Milton Bradley	.12	.30
105 John Lannan	.12	.30
106 Yovani Gallardo	.12	.30
107 Xavier Nady	.12	.30
108 Jermaine Dye	.12	.30
109 Dioner Navarro	.12	.30
110 Joba Chamberlain	.12	.30
111 Nelson Cruz	.30	.75
112 Johnny Cueto	.12	.30
113 Adam LaRoche	.12	.30
114 Aaron Rowand	.12	.30
115 Jason Bay	.20	.50
116 Aaron Cook	.12	.30
117 Mark Teixeira	.20	.50
118 Gavin Floyd	.12	.30
119 Magglio Ordonez	.20	.50
120 Rafael Furcal	.12	.30
121 Mark Buehrle	.20	.50
122 Alexi Casilla	.12	.30
123 Scott Kazmir	.12	.30
124 Nick Swisher	.20	.50
125 Carlos Gomez	.12	.30
126 Javier Vazquez	.12	.30
127 Paul Konerko	.20	.50
128 Ronnie Belliard	.12	.30
129 Pat Neshek	.20	.50
130 Josh Johnson	.20	.50
131 Carlos Zambrano	.20	.50
132 Chris Davis	.20	.50
133 Bobby Crosby	.12	.30
134 Alex Gordon	.20	.50
135 Chris Young	.12	.30
136 Carlos Delgado	.12	.30
137 Adam Wainwright	.20	.50
138 Justin Upton	.20	.50
139 Tim Hudson	.20	.50
140 J.D. Drew	.12	.30
141 Adam Lind	.12	.30
142 Mike Lowell	.12	.30
143 Lance Berkman	.20	.50
144 J.J. Hardy	.12	.30
145 A.J. Burnett	.20	.50
146 Jake Peavy	.12	.30
147 Blake DeWitt	.12	.30
148 Matt Holliday	.30	.75
149 Carl Crawford	.20	.50
150 Andre Ethier	.20	.50
151 Howie Kendrick	.12	.30
152 Ryan Zimmerman	.20	.50
153 Troy Tulowitzki	.30	.75
154 Brett Myers	.12	.30
155 Chris Young	.12	.30
156 Jered Weaver	.20	.50
157 Jeff Clement	.12	.30
158 Alex Rios	.12	.30
159 Shane Victorino	.12	.30
160 Jeremy Hermida	.12	.30
161 James Loney	.12	.30
162 Michael Young	.12	.30
163 Aramis Ramirez	.12	.30
164 Geovany Soto	.20	.50
165 Aubrey Huff	.12	.30
166 Delmon Young	.20	.50
167 Vernon Wells	.12	.30
168 Chone Figgins	.12	.30
169 Carlos Quentin	.12	.30
170 Chad Billingsley	.20	.50
171 Matt Cain	.20	.50
172 Derrek Lee	.12	.30
173 A.J. Pierzynski	.12	.30
174 Collin Balester	.12	.30
175 Greg Smith	.12	.30
176 Alfonso Soriano	.20	.50
177 Adrian Gonzalez	.25	.60
178 George Sherrill	.12	.30
179 Nick Markakis	.25	.60
180 Brandon Webb	.20	.50
181 Vladimir Guerrero	.20	.50
182 Roy Oswalt	.20	.50
183 Adam Jones	.20	.50
184 Edinson Volquez	.12	.30
185 Yunel Escobar	.12	.30
186 Joe Saunders	.12	.30
187 Yadier Molina	.30	.75
188 Kevin Youkilis	.12	.30
189 Dan Uggla	.12	.30
190 Kosuke Fukudome	.20	.50
191 Matt Antonelli RC	.40	1.00
192 Jeff Baisley RC	.25	.60
193 Jason Bourgeois (RC)	.25	.60
194 Michael Bowden (RC)	.25	.60
195 Andrew Carpenter RC	.40	1.00
196 Phil Coke RC	.40	1.00
197 Aaron Cunningham RC	.25	.60
198 Alcides Escobar RC	.40	1.00
199 Dexter Fowler (RC)	.40	1.00
200 Mat Gamel RC	.60	1.50
201 Josh Geer (RC)	.25	.60
202 Greg Golson (RC)	.25	.60
203 John Jaso RC	.25	.60
204 Kila Ka'aihue (RC)	.40	1.00
205 George Kottaras (RC)	.25	.60
206 Lou Marson (RC)	.25	.60
207 Shairon Martis RC	.40	1.00
208 Juan Miranda RC	.40	1.00
209 Luke Montz RC	.25	.60
210 Jonathon Niese RC	.40	1.00
211 Bobby Parnell RC	.40	1.00
212 Fernando Perez (RC)	.25	.60
213 David Price RC	.50	1.25
214 Angel Salome (RC)	.25	.60
215 Gaby Sanchez RC	.40	1.00
216 Freddy Sandoval (RC)	.25	.60
217 Travis Snider RC	.40	1.00
218 Will Venable RC	.25	.60
219 Edwin Maysonet RC	.25	.60
220 Josh Outman RC	.40	1.00
221 Luke Montz AU	4.00	10.00
222 Kila Ka'aihue AU	4.00	10.00
223 Conor Gillaspie AU RC	4.00	10.00
224 Aaron Cunningham AU	4.00	10.00
225 Mat Gamel AU	6.00	15.00
226 Matt Antonelli AU	4.00	10.00
227 Robert Parnell AU	4.00	10.00
228 Jose Mijares AU RC	4.00	10.00
229 Josh Geer AU	4.00	10.00
230 Shairon Martis AU	6.00	15.00

2009 Bowman Blue

*BLUE 1-190: 2X TO 5X BASIC
*BLUE 66/191-220: 1.5X TO 4X BASIC
*BLUE AU 221-230: .4X TO 1X BASIC AU
1-220 ODDS 1:12 HOBBY
STATED PRINT RUN 500 SER.#'d SETS

2009 Bowman Gold

*GOLD 1-190: 1.2X TO 3X BASIC
*GOLD 66/191-220: 1X TO 2.5X BASIC
OVERALL GOLD ODDS 1 PER PACK

2009 Bowman Orange

*ORANGE 1-190: 2.5X TO 6X BASIC
*ORANGE 66/191-220: 2X TO 5X BASIC
*ORANGE AU 221-230: .5X TO 1.2X BASIC AU
1-220 ODDS 1:24 HOBBY
STATED PRINT RUN 250 SER.#'d SETS

2009 Bowman Checklists

RANDOM INSERTS IN PACKS

Card	Low	High
1 Checklist 1	.12	.30
2 Checklist 2	.12	.30
3 Checklist 3	.12	.30

2009 Bowman Major League Scout Autographs

Card	Low	High
SCBB Billy Blitzer	3.00	8.00
SCCJ Clarence Johns	3.00	8.00
SCDC Darrell Conner	3.00	8.00
SCFR Fred Repke	3.00	8.00
SCLP Larry Pardo	3.00	8.00
SCMW Mark Wilson	3.00	8.00
SCPC Paul Cogan	3.00	8.00
SCPD Pat Daugherty	3.00	8.00

2009 Bowman Prospects

Card	Low	High
COMPLETE SET (90)	15.00	40.00

PLATE PRINT RUN 1 SET PER COLOR
BLACK-CYAN-MAGENTA-YELLOW ISSUED
NO PLATE PRICING DUE TO SCARCITY

Card	Low	High
BP1 Neftali Feliz	.25	.60
BP2 Oscar Tejeda	.50	1.25
BP3 Greg Veloz	.15	.40
BP4 Julio Teheran	.50	1.25
BP5 Michael Almanzar	.25	.60
BP6 Stolmy Pimentel	.25	.60
BP7 Matthew Moore	1.25	3.00
BP8 Jericho Jones	.15	.40
BP9 Kelvin de la Cruz	.40	1.00
BP10 Jose Ceda	.15	.40
BP11 Jesse Darcy	.15	.40
BP12 Kenneth Gilbert	.15	.40
BP13 Will Smith	.25	.60
BP14 Samuel Freeman	.15	.40
BP15 Adam Reifer	.15	.40
BP16 Ehire Adrianza	.40	1.00
BP17 Michael Pineda	.40	1.00
BP18 Jordan Walden	.25	.60
BP19 Angel Morales	.25	.60
BP20 Neil Ramirez	.15	.40
BP21 Kyeong Kang	.25	.60
BP22 Luis Jimenez	.15	.40
BP23 Tyler Flowers	.40	1.00
BP24 Petey Paramore	.25	.60
BP25 Jeremy Hamilton	.15	.40
BP26 Tyler Yockey	.25	.60
BP27 Sawyer Carroll	.25	.60
BP28 Jeremy Farrell	.15	.40
BP29 Tyson Brummett	.15	.40
BP30 Alex Buchholz	.25	.60
BP31 Luis Sumoza	.25	.60
BP32 Jonathan Waltenbury	.25	.60
BP33 Edgar Osuna	.15	.40
BP34 Curt Smith	.15	.40
BP35 Evan Bigley	.25	.60
BP36 Miguel Fermin	.15	.40
BP37 Ben Lasater	.15	.40
BP38 David Freese	.50	1.25
BP39 Jon Kibler	.25	.60
BP40 Cristian Beltre	.25	.60
BP41 Alfredo Figaro	.15	.40
BP42 Marc Rzepczynski	.25	.60
BP43 Joshua Collmenter	.25	.60
BP44 Adam Mills	.15	.40
BP45 Wilson Ramos	.50	1.25
BP46 Esmil Rogers	.15	.40
BP47 Jon Mark Owings	.15	.40
BP48 Chris Johnson	.25	.60
BP49 Abraham Almonte	.15	.40
BP50 Patrick Ryan	.15	.40
BP51 Yefri Carvajal	.40	1.00
BP52 Ruben Tejada	.15	.40
BP53 Edilio Colina	.25	.60
BP54 Wilber Bucardo	.25	.60
BP55 Nelson Perez	.25	.60
BP56 Andrew Rundle	.25	.60
BP57 Anthony Ortega	.15	.40
BP58 Wilin Rosario	.25	.60
BP59 Parker Frazier	.15	.40
BP60 Kyle Farrell	.15	.40
BP61 Erik Komatsu	.25	.60
BP62 Michael Stutes	.15	.40
BP63 David Genao	.15	.40
BP64 Jack Cawley	.15	.40
BP65 Jacob Goldberg	.15	.40
BP66 Jarred Bogany	.15	.40
BP67 Jason McEachern	.15	.40
BP68 Matt Rigoli	.15	.40
BP69 Jose Duran	.25	.60
BP70 Justin Greene	.25	.60
BP71 Nino Leyja	.25	.60
BP72 Michael Swinson	.25	.60
BP73 Miguel Flores	.25	.60
BP74 Nick Buss	.25	.60
BP75 Brett Oberholtzer	.25	.60
BP76 Pat McAnaney	.25	.60
BP77 Sean Conner	.15	.40
BP78 Ryan Verdugo	.25	.60
BP79 Will Atwood	.15	.40

BP80 Tommy Johnson .40 1.00
BP81 Rene Garcia .25 .60
BP82 Robert Brooks .25 .60
BP83 Seth Garrison .15 .40
BP84 Steven Upchurch .15 .40
BP85 Zach Moore .15 .40
BP86 Derrick Phillips .15 .40
BP87 Dominic De La Osa .40 1.00
BP88 Jose Barajas .15 .40
BP89 Bryan Petersen .15 .40
BP90 Michael Cisco .25 .60

2009 Bowman Prospects Blue
*BLUE: 1.2X TO 3X BASIC
STATED ODDS 1:12 HOBBY
STATED PRINT RUN 500 SER.#'d SETS
BP17 Michael Pineda 10.00 25.00

2009 Bowman Prospects Gold
*GOLD: 1X TO 2.5X BASIC
OVERALL GOLD ODDS 1 PER PACK

2009 Bowman Prospects Orange
*ORANGE: 2X TO 5X BASIC
STATED ODDS 1:24 HOBBY
STATED PRINT RUN 250 SER.#'d SETS

2009 Bowman Prospects Autographs
BPAAH Anthony Hewitt 5.00 12.00
BPABH Brad Hand 5.00 12.00
BPADG Deolis Guerra 5.00 12.00
BPAGB Gordon Beckham 5.00 12.00
BPAGK George Kontos 5.00 12.00
BPAJK Jason Knapp 5.00 12.00
BPANG Nick Gorneault 5.00 12.00
BPABP Buster Posey 30.00 80.00
BPARK Ryan Kalish 5.00 12.00
BPATD Travis D'Arnaud 5.00 12.00

2009 Bowman WBC Prospects
COMPLETE SET (20) 6.00 15.00
PLATE PRINT RUN 1 SET PER COLOR
BLACK-CYAN-MAGENTA-YELLOW ISSUED
NO PLATE PRICING DUE TO SCARCITY
BW1 Yu Darvish 1.50 4.00
BW2 Phillippe Aumont .60 1.50
BW3 Concepcion Rodriguez .40 1.00
BW4 Michel Enriquez .40 1.00
BW5 Yulieski Gourriel 1.25 3.00
BW6 Shinnosuke Abe .60 1.50
BW7 Gift Ngoepe .40 1.00
BW8 Dylan Lindsay .60 1.50
BW9 Nick Weglarz .40 1.00
BW10 Mitch Dening .40 1.00
BW11 Justin Erasmus .40 1.00
BW12 Aroldis Chapman 2.00 5.00
BW13 Alex Liddi .60 1.50
BW14 Alexander Smit .40 1.00
BW15 Juan Carlos Sulbaran .40 1.00
BW16 Cheng-Min Peng .60 1.50
BW17 Chenhao Li .40 1.00
BW18 Tao Bu .40 1.00
BW19 Gregory Halman .60 1.50
BW20 Fu-Te Ni .60 1.50

2009 Bowman WBC Prospects Blue
*BLUE: 1.2X TO 3X BASIC
STATED ODDS 1:12 HOBBY
BW1 Yu Darvish 8.00 20.00

2009 Bowman WBC Prospects Gold
*GOLD: .75X TO 2X BASIC
OVERALL GOLD ODDS ONE PER PACK

2009 Bowman WBC Prospects Orange
*ORANGE: 1.5X TO 4X BASIC
STATED ODDS 1:24 HOBBY
BW1 Yu Darvish 15.00 40.00

2009 Bowman WBC Prospects Red
STATED ODDS 1:2720 HOBBY
STATED PRINT RUN 1 SER.#'d SETS
NO PRICING DUE TO SCARCITY

2009 Bowman Draft

COMPLETE SET (55) 6.00 15.00
COMMON CARD (1-55) .20 .50
OVERALL PLATE ODDS 1:1531 HOBBY
PLATE PRINT RUN 1 SET PER COLOR
BLACK-CYAN-MAGENTA-YELLOW ISSUED
NO PLATE PRICING DUE TO SCARCITY
BDP1 Tommy Hanson RC .50 1.25
BDP2 Jeff Manship RC .20 .50
BDP3 Trevor Bell (RC) .20 .50
BDP4 Trevor Cahill RC .50 1.25
BDP5 Trent Oeltjen (RC) .20 .50
BDP6 Wyatt Toregas RC .20 .50
BDP7 Kevin Mulvey RC .20 .50
BDP8 Rusty Ryal RC .20 .50
BDP9 Mike Carp (RC) .30 .75
BDP10 Jorge Padilla (RC) .20 .50
BDP11 J.D. Martin (RC) .20 .50
BDP12 Dusty Ryan RC .20 .50
BDP13 Alex Avila RC .60 1.50
BDP14 Brandon Allen (RC) .20 .50
BDP15 Tommy Everidge (RC) .30 .75
BDP16 Bud Norris RC .20 .50
BDP17 Neftali Feliz RC .30 .75
BDP18 Mat Latos RC .60 1.50
BDP19 Ryan Perry RC .50 1.25
BDP20 Craig Tatum (RC) .20 .50
BDP21 Chris Tillman RC .30 .75
BDP22 Jhoulys Chacin RC .30 .75
BDP23 Michael Saunders RC .50 1.25
BDP24 Jeff Stevens RC .20 .50
BDP25 Luis Valdez RC .20 .50
BDP26 Robert Manuel RC .20 .50
BDP27 Ryan Webb (RC) .20 .50
BDP28 Marc Rzepczynski RC .30 .75
BDP29 Travis Schlichting (RC) .30 .75
BDP30 Barbaro Canizares RC .20 .50
BDP31 Brad Mills RC .20 .50
BDP32 Dusty Brown (RC) .20 .50
BDP33 Tim Wood RC .20 .50
BDP34 Drew Sutton RC .30 .75
BDP35 Jarrett Hoffpauir (RC) .20 .50
BDP36 Jose Lobaton RC .20 .50
BDP37 Aaron Bates RC .20 .50
BDP38 Clayton Mortensen RC .20 .50
BDP39 Ryan Sadowski RC .20 .50
BDP40 Fu-Te Ni RC .30 .75
BDP41 Casey McGehee (RC) .20 .50
BDP42 Omir Santos RC .20 .50
BDP43 Brent Leach RC .30 .75
BDP44 Diory Hernandez RC .20 .50
BDP45 Wilkin Castillo RC .20 .50
BDP46 Trevor Crowe RC .20 .50
BDP47 Sean West (RC) .30 .75
BDP48 Clayton Richard (RC) .20 .50
BDP49 Julio Borbon RC .20 .50
BDP50 Kyle Blanks RC .30 .75
BDP51 Jeff Gray RC .20 .50
BDP52 Gio Gonzalez (RC) .30 .75
BDP53 Vin Mazzaro RC .20 .50
BDP54 Josh Reddick RC .30 .75
BDP55 Fernando Martinez RC .50 1.25

2009 Bowman Draft Blue
*BLUE: 1.5X TO 4X BASIC
STATED ODDS 1:12 HOBBY
STATED PRINT RUN 399 SER.#'d SETS

2009 Bowman Draft Gold
*GOLD: .75X TO 2X BASIC
APPX.GOLD ODDS ONE PER PACK

2009 Bowman Draft Prospect Autographs
RANDOM INSERTS IN RETAIL PACKS
AH Anthony Hewitt 5.00 12.00
BH Brad Hand 3.00 8.00
BP Buster Posey 60.00 120.00
JK Jason Knapp 3.00 8.00
LC Lonnie Chisenhall 3.00 8.00
LM Logan Morrison 5.00 12.00
MI Michael Inoa 3.00 8.00
MM Michael Moustakas 8.00 20.00
ZC Zach Collier 5.00 12.00

2009 Bowman Draft Prospects
COMPLETE SET (75) 8.00 20.00
OVERALL PLATE ODDS 1:1531 HOBBY
PLATE PRINT RUN 1 SET PER COLOR
BLACK-CYAN-MAGENTA-YELLOW ISSUED
NO PLATE PRICING DUE TO SCARCITY
BDPP1 Tanner Bushue .30 .75
BDPP2 Billy Hamilton .60 1.50
BDPP3 Enrique Hernandez .75 2.00
BDPP4 Virgil Hill .20 .50
BDPP5 Josh Hodges .30 .75
BDPP6 Christopher Lovett .20 .50
BDPP7 Michael Belfiore .20 .50
BDPP8 Jobduan Morales .20 .50
BDPP9 Anthony Morris .20 .50
BDPP10 Telvin Nash .60 1.50
BDPP11 Brooks Pounders .30 .75
BDPP12 Kyle Rose .20 .50
BDPP13 Seth Schwindenhammer .30 .75
BDPP14 Patrick Lehman .30 .75
BDPP15 Mathew Weaver .30 .75
BDPP16 Brian Dozier 1.00 2.50
BDPP17 Sequoyah Stonecipher .30 .75
BDPP18 Shannon Wilkerson .20 .50
BDPP19 Jerry Sullivan .20 .50
BDPP20 Jamie Johnson .20 .50
BDPP21 Kent Matthes .20 .50
BDPP22 Ben Paulsen .20 .50
BDPP23 Matthew Davidson .60 1.50
BDPP24 Benjamin Carlson .20 .50
BDPP25 Brock Holt .30 .75
BDPP26 Ben Orloff .20 .50
BDPP27 D.J. LeMahieu 3.00 8.00
BDPP28 Erik Castro .30 .75
BDPP29 James Jones .20 .50
BDPP30 Cory Burns .20 .50
BDPP31 Chris Wade .20 .50
BDPP32 Jaff Decker .30 .75
BDPP33 Naoya Washiya .20 .50
BDPP34 Brandt Walker .20 .50
BDPP35 Jordan Henry .30 .75
BDPP36 Austin Adams .20 .50
BDPP37 Andrew Bellatti .30 .75
BDPP38 Paul Applebee .30 .75
BDPP39 Robert Stock .30 .75
BDPP40 Michael Flacco .20 .50
BDPP41 Jonathan Meyer .20 .50
BDPP42 Cody Rogers .30 .75
BDPP43 Matt Heidenreich .20 .50
BDPP44 David Holmberg .50 1.25
BDPP45 Mycal Jones .20 .50
BDPP46 David Hale .50 1.25
BDPP47 Dusty Odenbach .20 .50
BDPP48 Robert Hefflinger .20 .50
BDPP49 Buddy Baumann .20 .50
BDPP50 Thomas Berryhill .20 .50
BDPP51 Darrell Ceciliani .20 .50
BDPP52 Derek McCallum .20 .50
BDPP53 Taylor Freeman .20 .50
BDPP54 Tyler Townsend .30 .75
BDPP55 Tobias Streich .30 .75
BDPP56 Ryan Jackson .20 .50
BDPP57 Chris Herrmann .30 .75
BDPP58 Robert Shields .20 .50
BDPP59 Devin Fuller .20 .50
BDPP60 Brad Stillings .20 .50
BDPP61 Ryan Goins .30 .75
BDPP62 Chase Austin .20 .50
BDPP63 Brett Nommensen .20 .50
BDPP64 Egan Smith .20 .50
BDPP65 Daniel Mahoney .20 .50
BDPP66 Darin Gorski .20 .50
BDPP67 Dustin Dickerson .30 .75
BDPP68 Victor Black .30 .75
BDPP69 Dallas Keuchel 1.50 4.00
BDPP70 Nate Baker .20 .50
BDPP71 David Nick .30 .75
BDPP72 Brian Moran .20 .50
BDPP73 Mark Fleury .20 .50
BDPP74 Brett Wallach .30 .75
BDPP75 Adam Buschini .20 .50

2009 Bowman Draft Prospects Blue
*BLUE: 1.5X TO 4X BASIC
STATED ODDS 1:12 HOBBY
STATED PRINT RUN 399 SER.#'d SETS

2009 Bowman Draft Prospects Gold
*GOLD: .75X TO 2X BASIC
APPX.GOLD ODDS ONE PER PACK

2009 Bowman Draft WBC Prospects
COMPLETE SET (35) 6.00 15.00
OVERALL PLATE ODDS 1:1531 HOBBY
PLATE PRINT RUN 1 SET PER COLOR
BLACK-CYAN-MAGENTA-YELLOW ISSUED
NO PLATE PRICING DUE TO SCARCITY
BDPW1 Ichiro Suzuki .60 1.50
BDPW2 Yu Darvish .75 2.00
BDPW3 Phillippe Aumont .30 .75
BDPW4 Derek Jeter 1.25 3.00
BDPW5 Dustin Pedroia .40 1.00
BDPW6 Earl Agnoly .20 .50
BDPW7 Jose Reyes .30 .75
BDPW8 Michel Enriquez .20 .50
BDPW9 David Ortiz .50 1.25
BDPW10 Chunhua Dong .30 .75
BDPW11 Munenori Kawasaki 1.00 2.50
BDPW12 Arquimedes Nieto .20 .50
BDPW13 Bernie Williams .30 .75
BDPW14 Pedro Lazo .20 .50
BDPW15 Jing-Chao Wang .30 .75
BDPW16 Chris Barnwell .20 .50
BDPW17 Elmer Dessens .20 .50
BDPW18 Russell Martin .20 .50
BDPW19 Luca Panerati .20 .50
BDPW20 Adam Dunn .30 .75
BDPW21 Andy Gonzalez .20 .50
BDPW22 Daisuke Matsuzaka .30 .75
BDPW23 Daniel Berg .20 .50
BDPW24 Aroldis Chapman 1.00 2.50
BDPW25 Justin Morneau .30 .75
BDPW26 Miguel Cabrera .50 1.25
BDPW27 Magglio Ordonez .30 .75
BDPW28 Shawn Bowman .20 .50
BDPW29 Robbie Cordemans .20 .50
BDPW30 Paolo Espino .20 .50
BDPW31 Chipper Jones .50 1.25
BDPW32 Frederich Cepeda .30 .75
BDPW33 Ubaldo Jimenez .20 .50
BDPW34 Seiichi Uchikawa .30 .75
BDPW35 Norichika Aoki .30 .75

2009 Bowman Draft WBC Prospects Blue
*BLUE: 1.5X TO 4X BASIC
STATED ODDS 1:12 HOBBY
STATED PRINT RUN 399 SER.#'d SETS
BDPW2 Yu Darvish 6.00 15.00

2009 Bowman Draft WBC Prospects Gold
*GOLD: .75X TO 2X BASIC
APPX.GOLD ODDS ONE PER PACK

2009 Bowman Draft WBC Prospects Red
STATED ODDS 1:4266 HOBBY
STATED PRINT RUN 1 SER.#'d SET
NO PRICING DUE TO SCARCITY

2010 Bowman

COMPLETE SET (220) 12.50 30.00
COMMON CARD (1-190) .12 .30
COMMON RC (191-220) .40 1.00
1 Ryan Braun .20 .50
2 Kevin Youkilis .12 .30
3 Jay Bruce .20 .50
4 Will Venable .12 .30
5 Zack Greinke .20 .50
6 Adrian Gonzalez .25 .60
7 Carl Crawford .20 .50
8 Scott Baker .12 .30
9 Matt Kemp .25 .60
10 Stephen Drew .12 .30
11 Jair Jurrjens .12 .30
12 Jose Reyes .20 .50
13 Josh Hamilton .20 .50
14 Carlos Pena .20 .50
15 Ubaldo Jimenez .12 .30
16 Jason Kubel .12 .30
17 Josh Beckett .12 .30
18 Martin Prado .12 .30
19 Jake Peavy .12 .30
20 Shin-Soo Choo .20 .50
21 Luke Hochevar .12 .30
22 Alcides Escobar .12 .30
23 Brandon Webb .20 .50
24 Raul Ibanez .20 .50
25 Ryan Zimmerman .20 .50
26 Jeff Niemann .12 .30
27 Adam Dunn .20 .50
28 Matt Cain .20 .50
29 Robinson Cano .20 .50
30 Andre Ethier .20 .50
31 Jhoulys Chacin .12 .30
32 Mark Buehrle .20 .50
33 Magglio Ordonez .20 .50
34 Michael Cuddyer .12 .30
35 Andrew Bailey .12 .30
36 Akinori Iwamura .12 .30
37 Brian Roberts .12 .30
38 Howie Kendrick .12 .30
39 Derek Holland .12 .30
40 Ken Griffey Jr. .60 1.50
41 A.J. Burnett .12 .30
42 Scott Rolen .20 .50
43 Kenshin Kawakami .20 .50
44 Carlos Lee .12 .30
45 Chris Carpenter .20 .50
46 Adam Lind .20 .50
47 Jered Weaver .20 .50
48 Chris Coghlan .12 .30
49 Clayton Kershaw .60 1.50
50 Prince Fielder .20 .50
51 Freddy Sanchez .12 .30
52 CC Sabathia .20 .50
53 Jayson Werth .20 .50
54 David Price .25 .60
55 Matt Holliday .30 .75
56 Brett Anderson .12 .30
57 Alexei Ramirez .20 .50
58 Johnny Cueto .20 .50
59 Bobby Abreu .12 .30
60 Ian Kinsler .20 .50
61 Ricky Romero .12 .30
62 Cristian Guzman .12 .30
63 Ryan Doumit .12 .30
64 Mat Latos .20 .50
65 Andrew McCutchen .30 .75
66 John Maine .12 .30
67 Kurt Suzuki .12 .30
68 Carlos Beltran .20 .50
69 Chad Billingsley .20 .50
70 Nick Markakis .25 .60
71 Yovani Gallardo .12 .30
72 Dexter Fowler .12 .30
73 David Ortiz .30 .75
74 Kosuke Fukudome .20 .50
75 Daisuke Matsuzaka .20 .50
76 Michael Young .12 .30
77 Rajai Davis .12 .30
78 Yadier Molina .30 .75
79 Francisco Liriano .12 .30
80 Evan Longoria .20 .50
81 Trevor Cahill .12 .30
82 Aramis Ramirez .12 .30
83 Jimmy Rollins .20 .50
84 Russell Martin .20 .50
85 Dan Haren .12 .30
86 Billy Butler .12 .30
87 James Shields .12 .30
88 Dan Uggla .12 .30
89 Wandy Rodriguez .12 .30
90 Chase Utley .20 .50
91 Ryan Dempster .12 .30
92 Ben Zobrist .20 .50
93 Jeff Francoeur .20 .50
94 Koji Uehara .12 .30
95 Victor Martinez .20 .50
96 Tim Hudson .20 .50
97 Carlos Gonzalez .20 .50
98 David DeJesus .12 .30
99 Brad Hawpe .12 .30
100 Justin Upton .20 .50
101 Jorge Posada .20 .50
102 Cole Hamels .25 .60
103 Elvis Andrus .20 .50
104 Adam Wainwright .20 .50
105 Alfonso Soriano .20 .50
106 James Loney .12 .30
107 Vernon Wells .12 .30
108 Lance Berkman .20 .50
109 Matt Garza .12 .30
110 Gordon Beckham .12 .30
111 Torii Hunter .12 .30
112 Brandon Phillips .12 .30
113 Nelson Cruz .30 .75
114 Chris Tillman .12 .30
115 Miguel Cabrera .30 .75
116 Kevin Slowey .12 .30
117 Shane Victorino .20 .50
118 Paul Maholm .12 .30
119 Kyle Blanks .12 .30
120 Johan Santana .20 .50
121 Nate McLouth .12 .30
122 Kazuo Matsui .12 .30
123 Troy Tulowitzki .30 .75
124 Jon Lester .20 .50
125 Chipper Jones .30 .75
126 Clay Buchholz .12 .30
127 Todd Helton .20 .50
128 Alex Gordon .20 .50
129 Derrek Lee .12 .30
130 Justin Morneau .20 .50
131 Michael Bourn .12 .30
132 B.J. Upton .20 .50
133 Jose Lopez .12 .30
134 Justin Verlander .30 .75
135 Hunter Pence .20 .50
136 Daniel Murphy .25 .60
137 Delmon Young .20 .50
138 Carlos Quentin .12 .30
139 Edinson Volquez .12 .30
140 Dustin Pedroia .25 .60
141 Justin Masterson .12 .30
142 Josh Willingham .20 .50
143 Miguel Montero .12 .30
144 Alex Rios .12 .30
145 David Wright .25 .60
146 Curtis Granderson .25 .60
147 Rich Harden .12 .30
148 Hideki Matsui .30 .75
149 Edwin Jackson .12 .30
150 Miguel Tejada .20 .50
151 John Lackey .20 .50
152 Vladimir Guerrero .20 .50
153 Max Scherzer .30 .75
154 Jason Bay .20 .50
155 Javier Vasquez .12 .30
156 Johnny Damon .20 .50
157 Cliff Lee .20 .50
158 Chone Figgins .12 .30
159 Kevin Millwood .12 .30
160 Roy Halladay .20 .50
161 Alex Rodriguez .40 1.00
162 Pablo Sandoval .20 .50
163 Ryan Howard .25 .60
164 Rick Porcello .20 .50
165 Hanley Ramirez .20 .50
166 Brian McCann .20 .50
167 Kendry Morales .12 .30
168 Josh Johnson .20 .50
169 Joe Mauer .25 .60
170 Grady Sizemore .20 .50
171 J.A. Happ .20 .50
172 Ichiro Suzuki .40 1.00
173 Aaron Hill .12 .30
174 Mark Teixeira .20 .50
175 Tim Lincecum .20 .50
176 Denard Span .12 .30
177 Roy Oswalt .20 .50
178 Manny Ramirez .30 .75
179 Jorge De La Rosa .12 .30
180 Joey Votto .30 .75
181 Neftali Feliz .12 .30
182 Yunel Escobar .12 .30
183 Carlos Zambrano .20 .50
184 Erick Aybar .12 .30
185 Albert Pujols .40 1.00
186 Felix Hernandez .20 .50
187 Adam Jones .20 .50
188 Jacoby Ellsbury .25 .60
189 Mark Reynolds .12 .30
190 Derek Jeter .75 2.00
191 John Raynor RC .40 1.00
192 Carlos Monasterios RC .60 1.50
193 Kanekoa Texeira RC .40 1.00
194 David Herndon RC .40 1.00
195 Ruben Tejada RC .60 1.50
196 Mike Leake RC 1.25 3.00
197 Jenrry Mejia RC .60 1.50
198 Austin Jackson RC .60 1.50
199 Scott Sizemore RC .60 1.50
200 Jason Heyward RC 1.50 4.00
201 Neil Walker (RC) .60 1.50
202 Tommy Manzella (RC) .40 1.00
203 Wade Davis (RC) .60 1.50
204 Eric Young Jr. (RC) .40 1.00
205 Luis Durango RC .40 1.00
206 Madison Bumgarner RC 3.00 8.00
207 Brent Dlugach (RC) .40 1.00
208 Buster Posey RC 3.00 8.00
209 Henry Rodriguez RC .40 1.00
210 Tyler Flowers RC .60 1.50
211 Michael Dunn RC .40 1.00
212 Drew Stubbs RC 1.00 2.50
213 Brandon Allen (RC) .40 1.00
214 Daniel McCutchen RC .60 1.50
215 Juan Francisco RC .60 1.50
216 Eric Hacker RC .60 1.50
217 Michael Brantley RC .60 1.50
218 Dustin Richardson RC .40 1.00
219 Josh Thole RC .60 1.50
220 Daniel Hudson RC .60 1.50

2010 Bowman Blue
*BLUE 1-190: 1.5X TO 4X BASIC
*BLUE: 191-220: .75X TO 2X BASIC
STATED ODDS 1:17 HOBBY
STATED PRINT RUN 520 SER.#'d SETS
200 Jason Heyward 8.00 20.00

2010 Bowman Gold
COMPLETE SET (220) 20.00 50.00
*GOLD 1-190: .75X TO 2X BASIC
*GOLD: 191-220: .6X TO 1.5X BASIC

2010 Bowman Orange
*ORANGE 1-190: 2.5X TO 6X BASIC
*ORAGE: 191-220: 1.2X TO 3X BASIC
STATED ODDS 1:35 HOBBY
STATED PRINT RUN 250 SER.#'d SETS

2010 Bowman 1992 Bowman Throwbacks

COMPLETE SET (110) 15.00 40.00
STATED ODDS 1:2 HOBBY
BT1 Jimmy Rollins .50 1.25
BT2 Ryan Zimmerman .50 1.25
BT3 Alex Rodriguez 1.00 2.50
BT4 Andrew McCutchen .75 2.00
BT5 Mark Reynolds .30 .75
BT6 Jason Bay .50 1.25
BT7 Hideki Matsui .75 2.00
BT8 Carlos Beltran .50 1.25
BT9 Justin Morneau .50 1.25
BT10 Matt Cain .50 1.25
BT11 Russell Martin .30 .75
BT12 Alfonso Soriano .50 1.25
BT13 Joe Mauer .60 1.50
BT14 Troy Tulowitzki .75 2.00
BT15 Miguel Tejada .50 1.25
BT16 Adrian Gonzalez .60 1.50
BT17 Carlos Zambrano .50 1.25
BT18 Hunter Pence .50 1.25
BT19 Torii Hunter .30 .75
BT20 Michael Young .30 .75
BT21 Pablo Sandoval .50 1.25
BT22 Manny Ramirez .75 2.00
BT23 Jose Reyes .50 1.25
BT24 Carl Crawford .50 1.25
BT25 CC Sabathia .50 1.25
BT26 Josh Beckett .30 .75
BT27 Dan Uggla .30 .75
BT28 Josh Johnson .50 1.25
BT29 Raul Ibanez .50 1.25
BT30 Grady Sizemore .50 1.25
BT31 Nate McLouth .30 .75
BT32 Robinson Cano .50 1.25
BT33 Carlos Lee .30 .75
BT34 Jorge Posada .50 1.25
BT35 B.J. Upton .50 1.25
BT36 Ubaldo Jimenez .30 .75
BT37 Ryan Braun .50 1.25
BT38 Aaron Hill .30 .75
BT39 Rick Porcello .50 1.25
BT40 Nick Markakis .60 1.50
BT41 Felix Hernandez .50 1.25
BT42 Matt Holliday .75 2.00
BT43 Prince Fielder .50 1.25
BT44 Yadier Molina .75 2.00
BT45 Justin Upton .50 1.25
BT46 Carlos Pena .50 1.25
BT47 Miguel Cabrera .75 2.00
BT48 Dan Haren .30 .75
BT49 Cliff Lee .50 1.25
BT50 Victor Martinez .50 1.25
BT51 Josh Hamilton .50 1.25
BT52 Evan Longoria .50 1.25
BT53 Johan Santana .50 1.25
BT54 Ryan Howard .60 1.50
BT55 Jon Lester .50 1.25
BT56 Mark Buehrle .50 1.25
BT57 Lance Berkman .50 1.25
BT58 Roy Oswalt .50 1.25
BT59 Dustin Pedroia .60 1.50
BT60 Daisuke Matsuzaka .50 1.25
BT61 Joey Votto .75 2.00
BT62 Ken Griffey Jr. 1.50 4.00
BT63 Jacoby Ellsbury .60 1.50
BT64 David Wright .60 1.50
BT65 Derek Jeter 2.00 5.00
BT66 Chase Utley .50 1.25
BT67 Mark Teixeira .50 1.25
BT68 Justin Verlander .75 2.00
BT69 Kendry Morales .30 .75
BT70 Adam Jones .50 1.25
BT71 Vladimir Guerrero .50 1.25
BT72 Albert Pujols 1.00 2.50
BT73 Roy Halladay .50 1.25
BT74 Matt Kemp .60 1.50
BT75 Kevin Youkilis .30 .75
BT76 Jake Peavy .30 .75
BT77 Hanley Ramirez .50 1.25
BT78 Ian Kinsler .50 1.25
BT79 Ichiro Suzuki 1.00 2.50
BT80 Curtis Granderson .60 1.50
BT81 Gordon Beckham .30 .75
BT82 Jayson Werth .50 1.25
BT83 Brandon Webb .50 1.25
BT84 Adam Dunn .50 1.25
BT85 David Ortiz .75 2.00
BT86 Cole Hamels .60 1.50
BT87 Brian McCann .50 1.25
BT88 Zack Greinke .50 1.25
BT89 Tim Lincecum .50 1.25
BT90 Andre Ethier .50 1.25
BT91 Matt Garza .30 .75
BT92 Billy Butler .30 .75
BT93 Yovani Gallardo .30 .75
BT94 Chone Figgins .30 .75
BT95 Yunel Escobar .30 .75
BT96 Alexei Ramirez .50 1.25
BT97 Clayton Kershaw 1.50 4.00
BT98 Chris Coghlan .30 .75
BT99 Denard Span .30 .75
BT100 A.J. Burnett .30 .75
BT101 Ivan Rodriguez .50 1.25
BT102 Chipper Jones .75 2.00
BT103 Carlos Delgado .30 .75
BT104 Gary Sheffield .30 .75
BT105 Garret Anderson .30 .75
BT106 Mariano Rivera 1.00 2.50
BT107 John Smoltz .75 2.00
BT108 Omar Vizquel .50 1.25
BT109 Jim Thome .50 1.25
BT110 Manny Ramirez .75 2.00

2010 Bowman Expectations
COMPLETE SET (50) 15.00 40.00
STATED ODDS 1:3 HOBBY
BE1 J.Posada/J.Montero .60 1.50
BE2 R.Howard/D.Brown 1.50 4.00
BE3 Ramirez/Stanton 3.00 8.00
BE4 C.Jones/F.Freeman 5.00 12.00
BE5 Lincecum/Strasburg 3.00 8.00
BE6 Jose Reyes/Wilmer Flores .60 1.50
BE7 D.Wright/I.Davis .75 2.00
BE8 A.Soriano/S.Castro 1.00 2.50
BE9 J.Bruce/T.Frazier 1.25 3.00
BE10 R.Braun/M.Gamel .60 1.50
BE11 Lester/Bumgarner 3.00 8.00
BE12 Ubaldo Jimenez/Tyler Matzek 1.00 2.50
BE13 J.Mauer/B.Posey 3.00 8.00
BE14 Carl Crawford/Desmond Jennings .60 1.50
BE15 E.Longoria/A.Liddi .60 1.50
BE16 A.McCutchen/J.Tabata 1.00 2.50
BE17 C.Jones/J.Heyward 1.50 4.00
BE18 Aramis Ramirez/Josh Vitters .40 1.00
BE19 Ryan Zimmerman/Ian Desmond .60 1.50
BE20 A.Gordon/M.Moustakas 1.00 2.50
BE21 Adam Dunn/Chris Marrero .60 1.50
BE22 Mike Napoli/Hank Conger .40 1.00
BE23 Pablo Sandoval/Thomas Neal .60 1.50
BE24 Carlos Quentin/Tyler Flowers .60 1.50
BE25 V.Martinez/C.Santana 1.25 3.00
BE26 Zambrano/Cashner .60 1.50
BE27 J.Lopez/D.Ackley 1.50 4.00
BE28 Rich Harden/Neftali Feliz .40 1.00
BE29 J.Damon/S.Heathcott 1.25 3.00
BE30 Kevin Youkilis/Lars Anderson .60 1.50
BE31 Dan Haren/Jarrod Parker 1.00 2.50
BE32 Matt Kemp/Jared Mitchell .75 2.00
BE33 W.Venable/D.Tate .40 1.00
BE34 Andre Ethier/Andrew Lambo .60 1.50
BE35 Brian McCann/Tony Sanchez 1.00 2.50
BE36 Josh Beckett/Chris Withrow .40 1.00
BE37 Matt Cain/Zack Wheeler 1.25 3.00
BE38 Johnny Cueto/Jenrry Mejia .60 1.50
BE39 David Price/Jake McGee .75 2.00
BE40 M.Garza/J.Hellickson 1.00 2.50
BE41 Nick Markakis/Josh Bell .75 2.00
BE42 Ivan Rodriguez/Derek Norris .60 1.50
BE43 Elvis Andrus/Jiovanni Mier .60 1.50
BE44 Mark Reynolds/Bobby Borchering .60 1.50
BE45 Prince Fielder/Chris Carter .60 1.50
BE46 Grady Sizemore/Jordan Brown .60 1.50
BE47 S.Drew/P.Ciriaco 1.25 3.00

BE48 Chad Billingsley/John Ely .60 1.50
BE49 Justin Morneau
Christopher Parmelee .60 1.50
BE50 R.Halladay/K.Drabek .60 1.50

2010 Bowman Futures Game Triple Relic

STATED ODDS 1:402 HOBBY
STATED PRINT RUN 99 SER.#'d SETS
AE Alcides Escobar 5.00 12.00
AL Alex Liddi 4.00 10.00
BC Barbaro Canizares 4.00 10.00
BL Brad Lincoln 4.00 10.00
CC Chris Carter 6.00 15.00
CH Chris Heisey 10.00 25.00
CS Carlos Santana 10.00 25.00
CT Chris Tillman 4.00 10.00
DD Danny Duffy 10.00 25.00
DJ Daryl Jones 4.00 10.00
DJE Desmond Jennings 8.00 20.00
DV Dayan Viciedo 4.00 10.00
EY Eric Young Jr. 4.00 10.00
FS Francisco Samuel 4.00 10.00
JC Jhoulys Chacin 4.00 10.00
JH Jason Heyward 12.50 30.00
JM Jesus Montero 10.00 25.00
JP Jarrod Parker 20.00 50.00
JV Josh Vitters 8.00 20.00
KD Kyle Drabek 5.00 12.00
KK Kyeong Kang 4.00 10.00
LD Luis Durango 5.00 12.00
LS Leyson Septimo 4.00 10.00
MB Madison Bumgarner 20.00 50.00
ML Mat Latos 12.50 30.00
MS Mike Stanton 15.00 40.00
NF Neftali Feliz 5.00 12.00
NW Nick Weglarz 8.00 20.00
PB Pedro Baez 4.00 10.00
RT Rene Tosoni 5.00 12.00
SC Starlin Castro 20.00 50.00
SS Scott Sizemore 5.00 12.00
TF Tyler Flowers 4.00 10.00
TG Tyson Gillies 6.00 15.00
TR Trevor Reckling 5.00 12.00
WF Wilmer Flores 5.00 12.00
YF Yohan Flande 8.00 20.00

2010 Bowman Prospects

COMP.SET w/o AU (110) 15.00 40.00
STRASBURG AU ODDS 1:2013 HOBBY
BP1a Stephen Strasburg 1.50 4.00
BP1b Stephen Strasburg AU 40.00 100.00
BP2 Melky Mesa .30 .75
BP3 Cole McCurry .20 .50
BP4 Tyler Henley .20 .50
BP5 Andrew Cashner .20 .50
BP6 Konrad Schmidt .20 .50
BP7 Jean Segura 1.00 2.50
BP8 Jon Gaston .30 .75
BP9 Nick Santomauro .20 .50
BP10 Aroldis Chapman .75 2.00
BP11 Logan Watkins .20 .50
BP12 Bo Bowman .20 .50
BP13 Jeff Antigua .20 .50
BP14 Matt Adams .60 1.50
BP15 Joseph Cruz .30 .75
BP16 Sebastian Valle .30 .75
BP17 Stefan Gartrell .20 .50
BP18 Pedro Ciriaco .60 1.50
BP19 Tyson Gillies .50 1.25
BP20 Casey Crosby .20 .50
BP21 Luis Exposito .20 .50
BP22 Welington Dotel .20 .50
BP23 Alexander Torres .20 .50
BP24 Byron Wiley .20 .50
BP25 Pedro Florimon .20 .50
BP26 Cody Satterwhite .30 .75
BP27 Craig Clark .75 2.00
BP28 Jason Christian .20 .50
BP29 Tommy Mendonca .20 .50
BP30 Ryan Dent .20 .50
BP31 Jhan Marinez .20 .50
BP32 Eric Niesen .20 .50
BP33 Gustavo Nunez .20 .50
BP34 Scott Shaw .20 .50
BP35 Welinton Ramirez .20 .50
BP36 Trevor May .75 2.00
BP37 Mitch Moreland .30 .75
BP38 Nick Czyz .20 .50
BP39 Edinson Rincon .20 .50
BP40 Domingo Santana .60 1.50
BP41 Carson Blair .20 .50
BP42 Rashun Dixon .20 .50
BP43 Alexander Colome .50 1.25
BP44 Allan Dykstra .20 .50
BP45 J.J. Hoover .20 .50
BP46 Abner Abreu .30 .75
BP47 Daniel Nava .20 .50
BP48 Simon Castro .20 .50
BP49 Brian Baisley .20 .50
BP50 Tony Delmonico .20 .50
BP51 Chase D'Arnaud .20 .50
BP52 Sheng-An Kuo .20 .50
BP53 Leandro Castro .20 .50
BP54 Charlie Leesman .20 .50
BP55 Caleb Joseph .20 .50
BP56 Rolando Gomez .20 .50
BP57 John Lamb .50 1.25
BP58 Adam Wilk .30 .75
BP59 Randall Delgado .30 .75
BP60 Neil Medchill .30 .75
BP61 Josh Donaldson 1.00 2.50
BP62 Zach Gentile .20 .50
BP63 Kiel Roling .20 .50
BP64 Wes Freeman .20 .50
BP65 Brian Pellegrini .30 .75
BP66 Kyle Jensen .20 .50
BP67 Evan Anundsen .20 .50
BP68 Hak-Ju Lee .30 .75
BP69 C.J. Retherford .20 .50
BP70 Dillon Gee .50 1.25
BP71 Bo Greenwell .20 .50
BP72 Matt Tucker .30 .75
BP73 Joe Serafin .20 .50
BP74 Matt Brown .20 .50
BP75 Alexis Oliveras .20 .50
BP76 James Beresford .20 .50
BP77 Steve Lombardozzi .30 .75
BP78 Curtis Petersen .20 .50
BP79 Eric Farris .20 .50
BP80 Yen-Wen Kuo .20 .50
BP81 Caleb Brewer .20 .50
BP82 Jacob Elmore .30 .75
BP83 Jared Clark .30 .75
BP84 Yowill Espinal .30 .75
BP85 Jae-Hoon Ha .20 .50
BP86 Michael Wing .20 .50
BP87 Wilmer Font .20 .50
BP88 Jake Kahaulelio .20 .50
BP89 Dustin Ackley .30 .75
BP90 Donavan Tate .20 .50
BP91 Nolan Arenado 3.00 8.00
BP92 Rex Brothers .20 .50
BP93 Brett Jackson .60 1.50
BP94 Chad Jenkins .20 .50
BP95 Slade Heathcott .60 1.50
BP96 J.R. Murphy .30 .75
BP97 Patrick Schuster .20 .50
BP98 Alexia Amarista .20 .50
BP99 Thomas Neal .30 .75
BP100 Starlin Castro .50 1.25
BP101 Anthony Rizzo 2.50 6.00
BP102 Felix Doubront .20 .50
BP103 Nick Franklin .50 1.25
BP104 Anthony Gose .30 .75
BP105 Julio Teheran .30 .75
BP106 Grant Green .20 .50
BP107 David Lough .20 .50
BP108 Jose Iglesias .60 1.50
BP109 Jaff Decker .50 1.25
BP110 D.J. LeMahieu 2.00 5.00

2010 Bowman Prospects Black

COMPLETE SET (110) 20.00 50.00
*BLACK: .75X TO 2X BASIC
ISSUED VIA WRAPPER REDEMPTION PROGRAM

2010 Bowman Prospects Blue

*BLUE: 1.2X TO 3X BASIC
STATED ODDS 1:17 HOBBY
STATED PRINT RUN 520 SER.#'d SETS
STRASBURG AU ODDS 1:5700 HOBBY
STRASBURG PRINT RUN 250 SER.#'d SETS
BP1b Stephen Strasburg AU 50.00 120.00

2010 Bowman Prospects Orange

*ORANGE: 2X TO 5X BASIC
STATED ODDS 1:35 HOBBY
STATED PRINT RUN 250 SER.#'d SETS
STRASBURG AU ODDS 1:56,500 HOBBY
STRASBURG PRINT RUN 25 SER.#'d SETS

2010 Bowman Prospect Autographs

BM Brent Morel 5.00 12.00
CV Cesar Valdez 3.00 8.00
DC Dusty Coleman 3.00 8.00
DH Darin Holcomb 3.00 8.00
DT Donavan Tate 6.00 15.00
EB Eric Berger 3.00 8.00
JB Justin Bristow 3.00 8.00
JF Jeremy Farrell 3.00 8.00
LF Logan Forsythe 3.00 8.00
MH Matt Hobgood 3.00 8.00
TS Tony Sanchez 3.00 8.00
ZS Zach Simons 3.00 8.00

2010 Bowman Topps 100 Prospects

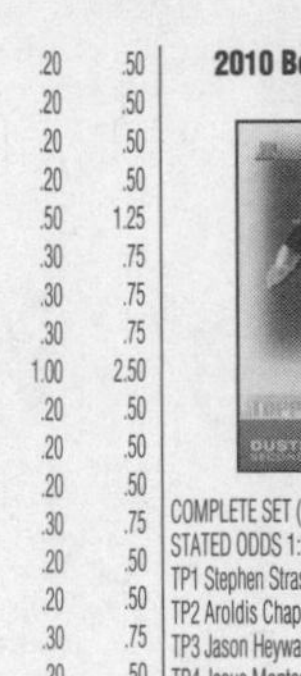

COMPLETE SET (100) 30.00 60.00
STATED ODDS 1:3 HOBBY
TP1 Stephen Strasburg 5.00 12.00
TP2 Aroldis Chapman 1.50 4.00
TP3 Jason Heyward 1.50 4.00
TP4 Jesus Montero .40 1.00
TP5 Mike Stanton 3.00 8.00
TP6 Mike Moustakas 1.00 2.50
TP7 Kyle Drabek .60 1.50
TP8 Tyler Matzek 1.00 2.50
TP9 Austin Jackson .60 1.50
TP10 Starlin Castro 1.00 2.50
TP11 Todd Frazier 1.25 3.00
TP12 Carlos Santana 1.25 3.00
TP13 Josh Vitters .40 1.00
TP14 Neftali Feliz .40 1.00
TP15 Tyler Flowers .60 1.50
TP16 Alcides Escobar .60 1.50
TP17 Ike Davis .75 2.00
TP18 Domonic Brown 1.50 4.00
TP19 Donavan Tate .40 1.00
TP20 Buster Posey 3.00 8.00
TP21 Dustin Ackley .60 1.50
TP22 Desmond Jennings .60 1.50
TP23 Brandon Allen .40 1.00
TP24 Freddie Freeman 5.00 12.00
TP25 Jake Arrieta 1.00 2.50
TP26 Bobby Borchering .60 1.50
TP27 Logan Morrison .60 1.50
TP28 Christian Friederich .60 1.50
TP29 Wilmer Flores .60 1.50
TP30 Austin Romine .60 1.50
TP31 Tony Sanchez 1.00 2.50
TP32 Madison Bumgarner 3.00 8.00
TP33 Mike Montgomery .60 1.50
TP34 Andrew Lambo .40 1.00
TP35 Derek Norris .60 1.50
TP36 Chris Withrow .40 1.00
TP37 Thomas Neal .60 1.50
TP38 Trevor Reckling .40 1.00
TP39 Andrew Cashner .40 1.00
TP40 Daniel Hudson .60 1.50
TP41 Jiovanni Mier .60 1.50
TP42 Grant Green .40 1.00
TP43 Jeremy Hellickson 1.00 2.50
TP44 Felix Doubront .40 1.00
TP45 Martin Perez 1.00 2.50
TP46 Jenrry Mejia .60 1.50
TP47 Adrian Cardenas .40 1.00
TP48 Ivan DeJesus Jr. .40 1.00
TP49 Nolan Arenado 6.00 15.00
TP50 Slade Heathcott 1.25 3.00
TP51 Ian Desmond .60 1.50
TP52 Michael Taylor .60 1.50
TP53 Jaime Garcia .60 1.50
TP54 Jose Tabata .60 1.50
TP55 Josh Bell .40 1.00
TP56 Jarrod Parker 1.00 2.50
TP57 Matt Dominguez 1.00 2.50
TP58 Koby Clemens .60 1.50
TP59 Angel Morales .40 1.00
TP60 Juan Francisco .60 1.50
TP61 John Ely .40 1.00
TP62 Brett Jackson 1.25 3.00
TP63 Chad Jenkins .40 1.00
TP64 Jose Iglesias 1.25 3.00
TP65 Logan Forsythe .40 1.00
TP66 Alex Liddi .60 1.50
TP67 Eric Arnett .40 1.00
TP68 Wilkin Ramirez .40 1.00
TP69 Lars Anderson .60 1.50
TP70 Jared Mitchell .60 1.50
TP71 Mike Leake 1.25 3.00
TP72 D.J. LeMahieu 4.00 10.00
TP73 Chris Marrero .40 1.00
TP74 Matt Moore 3.00 8.00
TP75 Jordan Brown .40 1.00
TP76 Christopher Parmelee .40 1.00
TP77 Ryan Kalish .60 1.50
TP78 A.J. Pollock 1.00 2.50
TP79 Alex White .60 1.50
TP80 Scott Sizemore .60 1.50
TP81 Jay Austin .40 1.00
TP82 Zach McAllister .60 1.50
TP83 Max Stassi .60 1.50
TP84 Robert Stock .40 1.00
TP85 Jake McGee .40 1.00
TP86 Zack Wheeler 1.25 3.00
TP87 Chase D'Arnaud .40 1.00
TP88 Danny Duffy .40 1.00
TP89 Josh Lindblom .40 1.00
TP90 Anthony Gose .60 1.50
TP91 Simon Castro .40 1.00
TP92 Chris Carter .60 1.50
TP93 Matt Hobgood 1.00 2.50
TP94 Ben Revere .60 1.50
TP95 Mat Gamel .40 1.00
TP96 Anthony Hewitt .40 1.00
TP97 Julio Teheran .60 1.50
TP98 Josh Reddick .40 1.00
TP99 Hank Conger .40 1.00
TP100 Jordan Walden .40 1.00

2010 Bowman Draft

COMPLETE SET (110) 8.00 20.00
COMMON CARD (1-110) .20 .50
BDP1 Stephen Strasburg RC 1.50 4.00
BDP2 Josh Bell (RC) .20 .50
BDP3 Ivan Nova RC 1.00 2.50
BDP4 Starlin Castro RC .50 1.25
BDP5 John Axford RC .20 .50
BDP6 Colin Curtis RC .20 .50
BDP7 Brennan Boesch RC .50 1.25
BDP8 Ike Davis RC .40 1.00
BDP9 Madison Bumgarner RC 1.50 4.00
BDP10 Austin Jackson RC .30 .75
BDP11 Andrew Cashner RC .20 .50
BDP12 Jose Tabata RC .30 .75
BDP13 Wade Davis (RC) .30 .75
BDP14 Ian Desmond (RC) .30 .75
BDP15 Felix Doubront RC .20 .50
BDP16 Danny Worth RC .20 .50
BDP17 John Ely RC .20 .50
BDP18 Jon Jay RC .30 .75
BDP19 Mike Leake RC .60 1.50
BDP20 Daniel Nava RC .20 .50
BDP21 Brad Lincoln RC .30 .75
BDP22 Jonathan Lucroy RC .50 1.25
BDP23 Brian Matusz RC .50 1.25
BDP24 Chris Nelson (RC) .30 .75
BDP25 Andy Oliver RC .20 .50
BDP26 Adam Ottavino RC .20 .50
BDP27 Trevor Plouffe (RC) .50 1.25
BDP28 Vance Worley RC .75 2.00
BDP29 Daniel McCutchen RC .30 .75
BDP30 Mike Stanton RC 1.50 4.00
BDP31 Drew Storen RC .30 .75
BDP32 Tyler Colvin RC .30 .75
BDP33 Travis Wood (RC) .30 .75
BDP34 Eric Young Jr. (RC) .20 .50
BDP35 Sam Demel RC .20 .50
BDP36 Wellington Castillo RC .20 .50
BDP37 Sam LeCure (RC) .20 .50
BDP38 Danny Valencia RC 1.25 3.00
BDP39 Fernando Salas RC .20 .50
BDP40 Jason Heyward RC .75 2.00
BDP41 Jake Arrieta RC .50 1.25
BDP42 Kevin Russo RC .20 .50
BDP43 Josh Donaldson RC 1.00 2.50
BDP44 Luis Atilano RC .20 .50
BDP45 Jason Donald RC .20 .50
BDP46 Jonny Venters RC .20 .50
BDP47 Bryan Anderson (RC) .20 .50
BDP48 Jay Sborz (RC) .20 .50
BDP49 Chris Heisey RC .30 .75
BDP50 Daniel Hudson RC .30 .75
BDP51 Ruben Tejada RC .30 .75
BDP52 Jeffrey Marquez RC .30 .75
BDP53 Brandon Hicks RC .30 .75
BDP54 Jeanmar Gomez RC .30 .75
BDP55 Erik Kratz RC .30 .75
BDP56 Lorenzo Cain RC .50 1.25
BDP57 Jhan Marinez RC .20 .50
BDP58 Omar Beltre (RC) .20 .50
BDP59 Drew Stubbs RC .50 1.25
BDP60 Alex Sanabia RC .20 .50
BDP61 Buster Posey RC 1.50 4.00
BDP62 Anthony Slama RC .20 .50
BDP63 Brad Davis RC .20 .50
BDP64 Logan Morrison RC .30 .75
BDP65 Luke Hughes (RC) .20 .50
BDP66 Thomas Diamond (RC) .20 .50
BDP67 Tommy Manzella (RC) .20 .50
BDP68 Jordan Smith RC .20 .50
BDP69 Carlos Santana RC .60 1.50
BDP70 Domonic Brown RC .75 2.00
BDP71 Scott Sizemore RC .30 .75
BDP72 Jordan Brown RC .20 .50
BDP73 Josh Thole RC .30 .75
BDP74 Jordan Norberto RC .20 .50
BDP75 Dayan Viciedo RC .30 .75
BDP76 Josh Tomlin RC .50 1.25
BDP77 Adam Moore RC .20 .50
BDP78 Kenley Jansen RC .60 1.50
BDP79 Juan Francisco RC .30 .75
BDP80 Blake Wood RC .20 .50
BDP81 John Hester RC .20 .50
BDP82 Lucas Harrell (RC) .20 .50
BDP83 Neil Walker (RC) .30 .75
BDP84 Cesar Valdez RC .20 .50
BDP85 Lance Zawadzki RC .20 .50
BDP86 Rommie Lewis RC .20 .50
BDP87 Steve Tolleson RC .20 .50
BDP88 Jeff Frazier (RC) .20 .50
BDP89 Drew Butera (RC) .20 .50
BDP90 Michael Brantley RC .30 .75
BDP91 Mitch Moreland RC .30 .75
BDP92 Alex Burnett RC .20 .50
BDP93 Allen Craig RC .50 1.25
BDP94 Sergio Santos (RC) .20 .50
BDP95 Matt Carson (RC) .20 .50
BDP96 Jenrry Mejia RC .30 .75
BDP97 Rhyne Hughes RC .20 .50
BDP98 Tyson Ross RC .20 .50
BDP99 Argenis Diaz RC .30 .75
BDP100 Hisanori Takahashi RC .30 .75
BDP101 Cole Gillespie RC .20 .50
BDP102 Ryan Kalish RC .30 .75
BDP103 J.P. Arencibia RC .40 1.00
BDP104 Peter Bourjos RC .30 .75
BDP105 Justin Turner RC 1.00 2.50
BDP106 Michael Dunn RC .20 .50
BDP107 Mike McCoy RC .20 .50
BDP108 Will Rhymes RC .20 .50
BDP109 Wilson Ramos RC .50 1.25
BDP110 Josh Butler RC .20 .50

2010 Bowman Draft Blue

*BLUE: 1.5X TO 4X BASIC
STATED PRINT RUN 399 SER.#'d SETS

2010 Bowman Draft Gold

*GOLD: 1X TO 2.5X BASIC

2010 Bowman Draft Red

STATED PRINT RUN 1 SER.#'d SET

2010 Bowman Draft Prospect Autographs

AL Andrew Liebel 3.00 8.00
AR Anthony Rizzo 15.00 40.00
BS Bryan Shaw 3.00 8.00
CG Conor Graham 3.00 8.00
DT Donavan Tate 6.00 15.00
EK Eddie Kunz 3.00 8.00
GH Graham Hicks 3.00 8.00
JJ Jake Jefferies 6.00 15.00
JM Jiovanni Mier 3.00 8.00
JP Jason Place 4.00 10.00
MH Matt Hobgood 3.00 8.00
MM Mike Montgomery 4.00 10.00
MY Michael Ynoa 3.00 8.00
NC Nick Carr 3.00 8.00
RC Ryan Chaffee 3.00 8.00
RG Randal Grichuk 10.00 25.00
RM Ryan Mattheus 3.00 8.00
SG Steve Garrison 3.00 8.00
SH Slade Heathcott 3.00 8.00
SP Shane Peterson 3.00 8.00
ZM Zach McAllister 3.00 8.00
JPI Julio Pimentel 3.00 8.00

2010 Bowman Draft Prospect Autographs Blue

*BLUE: .75X TO 2X BASIC
STATED PRINT RUN 199 SER.#'d SETS

2010 Bowman Draft Prospect Autographs Red

*RED: 1.2X TO 3X BASIC
STATED PRINT RUN 50 SER.#'d SETS

2010 Bowman Draft Prospects

BDPP1 Sam Tuivailala .25 .60
BDPP2 Alex Burgos .25 .60
BDPP3 Henry Ramos .40 1.00
BDPP4 Pat Dean .15 .40
BDPP5 Ryan Brett .25 .60
BDPP6 Jesse Biddle .25 .60
BDPP7 Leon Landry .40 1.00
BDPP8 Ryan LaMarre .25 .60
BDPP9 Josh Rutledge 1.00 2.50
BDPP10 Tyler Thornburg .40 1.00
BDPP11 Carter Jurica .15 .40
BDPP12 J.R. Bradley .15 .40
BDPP13 Devin Lohman .15 .40
BDPP14 Addison Reed .40 1.00
BDPP15 Micah Gibbs .25 .60
BDPP16 Derek Dietrich .40 1.00
BDPP18 Stephen Pryor .15 .40
BDPP19 Eddie Rosario 1.25 3.00
BDPP20 Blake Forsythe .15 .40
BDPP21 Rangel Ravelo .15 .40
BDPP22 Nick Longmire .25 .60
BDPP23 Andrelton Simmons .60 1.50
BDPP24 Chad Bettis .15 .40
BDPP25 Peter Tago .25 .60
BDPP26 Tyrell Jenkins .50 1.25
BDPP27 Marcus Knecht .15 .40
BDPP28 Seth Blair .25 .60
BDPP29 Brodie Greene .15 .40
BDPP30 Jason Martinson .15 .40
BDPP31 Bryan Morgado .25 .60
BDPP32 Eric Cantrell .15 .40
BDPP33 Niko Goodrum .50 1.25
BDPP34 Bobby Doran .15 .40
BDPP35 Cody Wheeler .15 .40
BDPP36 Cole Leonida .15 .40
BDPP37 Nate Roberts .15 .40
BDPP38 Dave Filak .15 .40
BDPP39 Taijuan Walker .40 1.00
BDPP40 Hayden Simpson .25 .60
BDPP41 Cameron Rupp .25 .60
BDPP42 Ben Heath .15 .40
BDPP43 Tyler Waldron .15 .40
BDPP44 Greg Garcia .15 .40
BDPP45 Vincent Velasquez .60 1.50
BDPP46 Jake Lemmerman .50 1.25
BDPP47 Russell Wilson 2.00 5.00
BDPP48 Cody Stanley .15 .40
BDPP49 Matt Suschak .15 .40
BDPP50 Logan Darnell .15 .40
BDPP51 Kevin Keyes .15 .40
BDPP52 Thomas Royse .15 .40
BDPP53 Scott Alexander .15 .40
BDPP54 Tony Thompson .15 .40
BDPP55 Seth Rosin .25 .60
BDPP56 Mickey Wiswall .15 .40
BDPP57 Albert Almora .50 1.25
BDPP58 Cole Billingsley .25 .60
BDPP58 Cody Hawn .25 .60
BDPP59 Drew Vettleson .25 .60
BDPP60 Matt Lipka .60 1.50
BDPP61 Michael Choice .25 .60
BDPP62 Zack Cox .50 1.25
BDPP63 Bryce Brentz .40 1.00
BDPP64 Chance Ruffin .15 .40
BDPP65 Mike Olt .50 1.25
BDPP66 Kellin Deglan .15 .40
BDPP67 Yasmani Grandal .25 .60
BDPP68 Kolbrin Vitek .40 1.00
BDPP69 Justin O'Conner .15 .40
BDPP70 Gary Brown .75 2.00
BDPP71 Mike Foltynewicz .40 1.00
BDPP72 Chevez Clarke .25 .60
BDPP73 Cito Culver .25 .60
BDPP74 Aaron Sanchez .60 1.50
BDPP75 Noah Syndergaard .60 1.50
BDPP76 Taylor Lindsey .25 .60
BDPP77 Josh Sale .50 1.25
BDPP78 Christian Yelich 3.00 8.00
BDPP79 Jameson Taillon .25 .60
BDPP80 Manny Machado 3.00 8.00
BDPP81 Christian Colon .25 .60
BDPP82 Drew Pomeranz .40 1.00
BDPP83 Delino DeShields .25 .60
BDPP84 Matt Harvey 1.00 2.50
BDPP85 Ryan Bolden .15 .40
BDPP86 Deck McGuire .25 .60
BDPP87 Zach Lee .40 1.00
BDPP88 Alex Wimmers .25 .60
BDPP89 Kaleb Cowart .25 .60
BDPP90 Mike Kvansnicka .15 .40
BDPP91 Jake Skole .25 .60
BDPP92 Chris Sale 2.00 5.00
BDPP93 Sean Brady .15 .40
BDPP94 Marc Brakeman .15 .40
BDPP95 Alex Bregman 2.00 5.00
BDPP96 Ryan Burr .40 1.00
BDPP97 Chris Chinea .25 .60
BDPP98 Troy Conyers .15 .40
BDPP99 Zach Green .15 .40
BDPP100 Carson Kelly .50 1.25
BDPP101 Timmy Lopes .15 .40
BDPP102 Adrian Marin .25 .60
BDPP103 Chris Okey .15 .40
BDPP104 Matt Olson 1.25 3.00
BDPP105 Ivan Pelaez .15 .40
BDPP106 Felipe Perez .15 .40
BDPP107 Nelson Rodriguez .25 .60
BDPP108 Corey Seager 4.00 10.00
BDPP109 Lucas Sims .40 1.00
BDPP110 Nick Travieso .25 .60

2010 Bowman Draft Prospects Blue

*BLUE: 2X TO 5X BASIC
STATED PRINT RUN 399 SER.#'d SETS

2010 Bowman Draft Prospects Gold

*GOLD: 1X TO 2.5X BASIC

2010 Bowman Draft USA Baseball Jerseys

STATED PRINT RUN 949 SER.#'d SETS
USAR1 Albert Almora 3.00 8.00
USAR2 Cole Billingsley 3.00 8.00
USAR3 Sean Brady 4.00 10.00
USAR4 Marc Brakeman 3.00 8.00
USAR5 Alex Bregman 4.00 10.00
USAR6 Ryan Burr 3.00 8.00
USAR7 Chris Chinea 4.00 10.00
USAR8 Troy Conyers 3.00 8.00
USAR9 Zach Green 3.00 8.00
USAR10 Carson Kelly 3.00 8.00
USAR11 Timmy Lopes 3.00 8.00
USAR12 Adrian Marin 3.00 8.00
USAR13 Chris Okey 3.00 8.00
USAR14 Matt Olson 6.00 15.00
USAR15 Ivan Pelaez 3.00 8.00
USAR16 Felipe Perez 3.00 8.00
USAR17 Nelson Rodriguez 3.00 8.00
USAR18 Corey Seager 4.00 10.00
USAR19 Lucas Sims 3.00 8.00
USAR20 Sheldon Neuse 3.00 8.00

2010 Bowman Draft USA Baseball Jerseys Blue

*BLUE: .5X TO 1.2X BASIC
STATED PRINT RUN 199 SER.#'d SETS

2010 Bowman Draft USA Baseball Jerseys Red

*RED: .6X TO 1.5X BASIC
STATED PRINT RUN 50 SER.#'d SETS

2011 Bowman

COMPLETE SET (220) 12.50 30.00
COMMON CARD (1-190) .12 .30
COMMON RC (191-220) .40 1.00
PLATE PRINT RUN 1 SET PER COLOR
BLACK-CYAN-MAGENTA-YELLOW ISSUED
NO PLATE PRICING DUE TO SCARCITY
1 Buster Posey .40 1.00
2 Alex Avila .20 .50
3 Edwin Jackson .12 .30
4 Miguel Montero .12 .30
5 Ryan Dempster .12 .30
6 Albert Pujols .40 1.00
7 Carlos Santana .30 .75
8 Ted Lilly .12 .30
9 Marlon Byrd .12 .30
10 Hanley Ramirez .20 .50
11 Josh Hamilton .20 .50
12 Orlando Hudson .12 .30
13 Matt Kemp .25 .60
14 Shane Victorino .20 .50
15 Domonic Brown .25 .60
16 Jeff Niemann .12 .30
17 Chipper Jones .30 .75
18 Joey Votto .30 .75
19 Brandon Phillips .12 .30
20 Michael Bourn .12 .30
21 Jason Heyward .25 .60
22 Curtis Granderson .25 .60
23 Brian McCann .20 .50
24 Mike Pelfrey .12 .30
25 Grady Sizemore .20 .50
26 Dustin Pedroia .25 .60
27 Chris Johnson .12 .30
28 Brian Matusz .12 .30
29 Jason Bay .20 .50
30 Mark Teixeira .20 .50
31 Carlos Quentin .12 .30
32 Miguel Tejada .20 .50
33 Ryan Howard .25 .60
34 Adrian Beltre .30 .75
35 Joe Mauer .25 .60
36 Johan Santana .20 .50
37 Logan Morrison .12 .30
38 C.J. Wilson .12 .30
39 Carlos Lee .12 .30
40 Ian Kinsler .20 .50
41 Shin-Soo Choo .20 .50
42 Adam Wainwright .20 .50
43 Derek Lowe .12 .30
44 Carlos Gonzalez .20 .50
45 Lance Berkman .20 .50
46 Jon Lester .20 .50
47 Miguel Cabrera .30 .75
48 Justin Verlander .30 .75
49 Tyler Colvin .12 .30
50 Matt Cain .20 .50
51 Brett Anderson .12 .30
52 Gordon Beckham .12 .30
53 David DeJesus .12 .30
54 Jonathan Sanchez .12 .30
55 Jorge Posada .20 .50
56 Neil Walker .20 .50
57 Jorge De La Rosa .12 .30
58 Torii Hunter .12 .30
59 Andrew McCutchen .30 .75
60 Mat Latos .20 .50
61 CC Sabathia .20 .50
62 Brett Myers .12 .30
63 Ryan Zimmerman .20 .50
64 Trevor Cahill .12 .30
65 Clayton Kershaw .60 1.50
66 Andre Ethier .20 .50
67 Kosuke Fukudome .20 .50
68 Justin Upton .20 .50
69 B.J. Upton .20 .50
70 J.P. Arencibia .12 .30
71 Phil Hughes .12 .30
72 Tim Hudson .20 .50
73 Francisco Liriano .12 .30
74 Ike Davis .12 .30
75 Delmon Young .20 .50
76 Paul Konerko .20 .50
77 Carlos Beltran .20 .50
78 Mike Stanton .30 .75
79 Adam Jones .20 .50
80 Jimmy Rollins .20 .50
81 Alex Rios .12 .30
82 Chad Billingsley .20 .50
83 Tommy Hanson .12 .30
84 Travis Wood .12 .30
85 Magglio Ordonez .20 .50
86 Jake Peavy .12 .30
87 Adrian Gonzalez .25 .60
88 Aaron Hill .12 .30
89 Kendry Morales .12 .30
90 Manny Ramirez .30 .75

91 Hunter Pence .20 .50
92 Josh Beckett .12 .30
93 Mark Reynolds .12 .30
94 Drew Stubbs .12 .30
95 Dan Haren .12 .30
96 Chris Carpenter .20 .50
97 Mitch Moreland .12 .30
98 Starlin Castro .20 .50
99 Roy Halladay .20 .50
100 Stephen Drew .12 .30
101 Aramis Ramirez .12 .30
102 Daniel Hudson .12 .30
103 Alexei Ramirez .20 .50
104 Rickie Weeks .12 .30
105 Will Venable .12 .30
106 David Price .25 .60
107 Dan Uggla .12 .30
108 Austin Jackson .12 .30
109 Evan Longoria .20 .50
110 Ryan Ludwick .12 .30
111 Chase Utley .20 .50
112 Johnny Cueto .20 .50
113 Billy Butler .12 .30
114 David Wright .25 .60
115 Jose Reyes .20 .50
116 Robinson Cano .20 .50
117 Josh Johnson .20 .50
118 Chris Coghlan .12 .30
119 David Ortiz .30 .75
120 Jay Bruce .20 .50
121 Jayson Werth .20 .50
122 Matt Holliday .30 .75
123 John Danks .12 .30
124 Franklin Gutierrez .12 .30
125 Zack Greinke .20 .50
126 Jacoby Ellsbury .25 .60
127 Madison Bumgarner .25 .60
128 Mike Leake .20 .50
129 Carl Crawford .20 .50
130 Clay Buchholz .12 .30
131 Gavin Floyd .12 .30
132 Mike Minor .12 .30
133 Jose Tabata .12 .30
134 Jason Castro .12 .30
135 Chris Young .12 .30
136 Jose Bautista .20 .50
137 Felix Hernandez .20 .50
138 Koji Uehara .12 .30
139 Dexter Fowler .20 .50
140 J.A. Happ .20 .50
141 Tim Lincecum .20 .50
142 Todd Helton .20 .50
143 Ubaldo Jimenez .12 .30
144 Yovani Gallardo .12 .30
145 Derek Jeter .75 2.00
146 Wade Davis .12 .30
147 Hiroki Kuroda .12 .30
148 Nelson Cruz .30 .75
149 Martin Prado .12 .30
150 Michael Cuddyer .12 .30
151 Mark Buehrle .12 .30
152 Danny Valencia .20 .50
153 Ichiro Suzuki .40 1.00
154 Brett Wallace .12 .30
155 Troy Tulowitzki .30 .75
156 Pedro Alvarez .75 2.00
157 Brandon Morrow .12 .30
158 Jered Weaver .20 .50
159 Michael Young .12 .30
160 Wandy Rodriguez .12 .30
161 Alfonso Soriano .20 .50
162 Kelly Johnson .12 .30
163 Roy Oswalt .20 .50
164 Brian Roberts .12 .30
165 Jaime Garcia .20 .50
166 Edinson Volquez .12 .30
167 Vladimir Guerrero .20 .50
168 Cliff Lee .20 .50
169 Johnny Damon .20 .50
170 Alex Rodriguez .40 1.00
171 Nick Markakis .25 .60
172 Cole Hamels .25 .60
173 Prince Fielder .20 .50
174 Kurt Suzuki .12 .30
175 Ryan Braun .20 .50
176 Justin Morneau .20 .50
177 Denard Span .12 .30
178 Elvis Andrus .20 .50
179 Stephen Strasburg .30 .75
180 Adam Lind .20 .50
181 Corey Hart .12 .30
182 Adam Dunn .20 .50
183 Bobby Abreu .12 .30
184 Gaby Sanchez .12 .30
185 Ian Kennedy .12 .30
186 Kevin Youkilis .12 .30
187 Vernon Wells .12 .30
188 Matt Garza .12 .30
189 Victor Martinez .20 .50
190 Casey McGehee .12 .30
191 Jake McGee (RC) .40 1.00
192 Lars Anderson RC .60 1.50
193 Mark Trumbo (RC) 1.00 2.50
194 Konrad Schmidt RC .40 1.00
195 Jeremy Jeffress RC .40 1.00
196 Brent Morel RC .40 1.00
197 Aroldis Chapman RC 1.25 3.00
198 Greg Halman RC .60 1.50
199 Jeremy Hellickson RC 1.00 2.50
200 Yunesky Maya RC .40 1.00
201 Kyle Drabek RC .60 1.50
202 Ben Revere RC .60 1.50
203 Desmond Jennings RC .60 1.50
204 Brandon Beachy RC 1.00 2.50
205 Freddie Freeman RC 6.00 15.00
206 Andrew Romine RC .40 1.00
207 John Lindsey RC .40 1.00
208 Mark Rogers (RC) .40 1.00
209 Brian Bogusevic (RC) .40 1.00
210 Yonder Alonso RC .60 1.50
211 Gregory Infante RC .40 1.00
212 Dillon Gee RC .60 1.50
213 Ozzie Martinez RC .40 1.00
214 Brandon Snyder (RC) .40 1.00
215 Daniel Descalso RC .40 1.00
216 Brett Sinkbeil RC .40 1.00
217 Lucas Duda RC 1.00 2.50
218 Cory Luebke RC .40 1.00
219 Hank Conger RC .60 1.50
220 Chris Sale RC 2.50 6.00

2011 Bowman Blue

*BLUE 1-190: 1.5X TO 4X BASIC
*BLUE: 191-220: .75X TO 2X BASIC
STATED PRINT RUN 500 SER.#'d SETS

2011 Bowman Gold

COMPLETE SET (220) 40.00 80.00
*GOLD 1-190: .75X TO 2X BASIC
*GOLD: 191-220: .5X TO 1.2X BASIC

2011 Bowman Green

*GREEN 1-190: 2X TO 5X BASIC
*GREEN: 191-220: .75X TO 2X BASIC
STATED PRINT RUN 450 SER.#'d SETS

2011 Bowman International

*INTER 1-190: 1.2X TO 3X BASIC
*INTER 191-220: .6X TO 1.5X BASIC
INT.PLATE PRINT RUN 1 SET PER COLOR
BLACK-CYAN-MAGENTA-YELLOW ISSUED
NO PLATE PRICING DUE TO SCARCITY

2011 Bowman Orange

*ORANGE 1-190: 2.5X TO 6X BASIC
*ORANGE 191-220: .75X TO 2X BASIC
STATED PRINT RUN 250 SER.#'d SETS

2011 Bowman Red

STATED PRINT RUN 1 SER.#'d SET
NO PRICING DUE TO SCARCITY

2011 Bowman Bowman's Best

COMPLETE SET (25) 8.00 20.00
*REF: 3X TO 8X BASIC
REF PRINT RUN 99 SER.#'d SETS
ATOMIC PRINT RUN 1 SER.#'d SET
NO ATOMIC PRICING AVAILABLE
XF PRINT RUN 25 SER.#'d SETS
NO XF PRICING DUE TO SCARCITY
BB1 Buster Posey 1.00 2.50
BB2 Roy Halladay .50 1.25
BB3 Miguel Cabrera .75 2.00
BB4 Mark Teixeira .50 1.25
BB5 Robinson Cano .50 1.25
BB6 Chase Utley .50 1.25
BB7 Ichiro Suzuki 1.00 2.50
BB8 Ryan Braun .50 1.25
BB9 Josh Hamilton .50 1.25
BB10 Mike Stanton .75 2.00
BB11 Derek Jeter 2.00 5.00
BB12 Joey Votto .75 2.00
BB13 Alex Rodriguez 1.00 2.50
BB14 Albert Pujols 1.00 2.50
BB15 Jason Heyward .60 1.50
BB16 Adrian Gonzalez .60 1.50
BB17 Troy Tulowitzki .75 2.00
BB18 Stephen Strasburg .75 2.00
BB19 Tim Lincecum .50 1.25
BB20 Felix Hernandez .50 1.25
BB21 Kevin Youkilis .30 .75
BB22 Joe Mauer .60 1.50
BB23 Ubaldo Jimenez .30 .75
BB24 Ryan Howard .60 1.50
BB25 Carl Crawford .50 1.25

2011 Bowman Bowman's Best Prospects

COMPLETE SET (50) 30.00 80.00
51-75 ODDS 1:8 HOBBY
51-75 REF.ODDS 1:256 HOBBY
REF PRINT RUN 99 SER.#'d SETS
51-75 ATOMIC ODDS 1:25,343 HOBBY
ATOMIC PRINT RUN 1 SER.#'d SET
NO ATOMIC PRICING AVAILABLE
51-75 XF ODDS 1:1013 HOBBY
XF PRINT RUN 25 SER.#'d SETS
NO XF PRICING DUE TO SCARCITY
BBP1 Bryce Harper 4.00 10.00
BBP2 Grant Green .30 .75
BBP3 Nick Franklin .50 1.25
BBP4 Simon Castro .30 .75
BBP5 Manny Machado 3.00 8.00
BBP6 Dustin Ackley .50 1.25
BBP7 Mike Moustakas .75 2.00
BBP8 Michael Pineda .75 2.00
BBP9 Mike Trout 75.00 200.00
BBP10 Jerry Sands .75 2.00
BBP11 Brett Jackson .75 2.00
BBP12 Jesus Montero .30 .75
BBP13 Jameson Taillon .50 1.25
BBP14 Julio Teheran .50 1.25
BBP15 Dee Gordon .50 1.25
BBP16 Shelby Miller 1.50 4.00
BBP17 Jacob Turner 1.25 3.00
BBP18 Brandon Belt .75 2.00
BBP19 Gary Sanchez 1.50 4.00
BBP20 Miguel Sano .60 1.50
BBP21 Devin Mesoraco .75 2.00
BBP22 Zach Britton .75 2.00
BBP23 Tyler Matzek .50 1.25
BBP24 Matt Dominguez .50 1.25
BBP25 Wil Myers .50 1.25
BBP51 Bryce Harper 4.00 10.00
BBP52 Shelby Miller 1.50 4.00
BBP53 Arodys Vizcaino .50 1.25
BBP54 Jonathan Singleton .50 1.25
BBP55 Manny Machado 3.00 8.00
BBP56 Matt Moore .75 2.00
BBP57 Devin Mesoraco .75 2.00
BBP58 Christian Colon .30 .75
BBP59 Chris Archer .60 1.50
BBP60 Martin Perez .75 2.00
BBP61 Aaron Hicks .50 1.25
BBP62 Jean Segura 1.25 3.00
BBP63 Delino DeShields Jr. .30 .75
BBP64 Wil Myers .50 1.25
BBP65 Jacob Turner 1.25 3.00
BBP66 Josh Sale .50 1.25
BBP67 Miguel Sano .60 1.50
BBP68 Jason Kipnis 1.00 2.50
BBP69 Luis Heredia .30 .75
BBP70 Anthony Ranaudo .75 2.00
BBP71 Stetson Allie .50 1.25
BBP72 Joe Benson .30 .75
BBP73 Nick Castellanos 1.50 4.00
BBP74 Billy Hamilton .60 1.50
BBP75 Manny Banuelos .75 2.00

2011 Bowman Bowman's Best Prospects Refractors

*REF: 3X TO 8X BASIC
51-75 STATED ODDS 1:256 HOBBY
STATED PRINT RUN 99 SER.#'d SETS
BBP1 Bryce Harper 20.00 50.00
BBP9 Mike Trout 600.00 1500.00
BBP51 Bryce Harper 20.00 50.00

2011 Bowman Bowman's Brightest

COMPLETE SET (25) 15.00 40.00
BBR1 Bryce Harper 4.00 10.00
BBR2 Mike Moustakas .75 2.00
BBR3 Mark Trumbo .75 2.00
BBR4 Paul Goldschmidt 3.00 8.00
BBR5 Rich Poythress .30 .75
BBR6 Mike Trout 30.00 80.00
BBR7 Dee Gordon .50 1.25
BBR8 Tyson Auer .30 .75
BBR9 Jay Austin .30 .75
BBR10 Eury Perez .30 .75
BBR11 Slade Heathcott .75 2.00
BBR12 Michael Taylor .30 .75
BBR13 Johermyn Chavez .30 .75
BBR14 Engel Beltre .30 .75
BBR15 Wilin Rosario .30 .75
BBR16 Freddie Freeman 5.00 12.00
BBR17 Wilmer Flores .50 1.25
BBR18 Domonic Brown .60 1.50
BBR19 Manny Machado 3.00 8.00
BBR20 Lonnie Chisenhall .50 1.25
BBR21 Jose Iglesias .50 1.25
BBR22 Desmond Jennings .50 1.25
BBR23 Jurickson Profar .75 2.00
BBR24 Tony Sanchez .50 1.25
BBR25 Jedd Gyorko .75 2.00

2011 Bowman Checklists

COMPLETE SET (5) .40 1.00
RED: 4X TO 10X BASIC
RED PRINT RUN 500 SER.#'d SETS

2011 Bowman Finest Futures

COMPLETE SET (25) 8.00 20.00
FF1 Jason Heyward .50 1.25
FF2 Buster Posey .75 2.00
FF3 Gordon Beckham .25 .60
FF4 Brian Matusz .25 .60
FF5 Mike Stanton .60 1.50
FF6 Starlin Castro .40 1.00
FF7 Carlos Santana .60 1.50
FF8 Aroldis Chapman .75 2.00
FF9 Pedro Alvarez .50 1.25
FF10 Freddie Freeman 4.00 10.00
FF11 Troy Tulowitzki .60 1.50
FF12 Domonic Brown .50 1.25
FF13 Chris Carter .25 .60
FF14 Ubaldo Jimenez .25 .60
FF15 Ike Davis .25 .60
FF16 Austin Jackson .25 .60
FF17 J.P. Arencibia .25 .60
FF18 Ryan Braun .40 1.00
FF19 Justin Upton .40 1.00
FF20 Mat Latos .40 1.00
FF21 Clayton Kershaw 1.25 3.00
FF22 Carlos Gonzalez .40 1.00
FF23 Stephen Strasburg .60 1.50
FF24 Andrew McCutchen .60 1.50
FF25 Madison Bumgarner .50 1.25

2011 Bowman Future's Game Triple Relics

STATED PRINT RUN 99 SER.#'d SETS
AL Alex Liddi 5.00 12.00
AR Austin Romine 5.00 12.00
AS Anthony Slama 4.00 10.00
AT Alex Torres 5.00 12.00
BJ Brett Jackson 10.00 25.00
BM Bryan Morris 5.00 12.00
BR Ben Revere 5.00 12.00
CC Chun-Hsiu Chen 10.00 25.00
CF Christian Friedrich 4.00 10.00
CP Carlos Peguero 4.00 10.00
DB Domonic Brown 12.50 30.00
DE Danny Espinosa 5.00 12.00
DG Dee Gordon 6.00 15.00
DJ Desmond Jennings 5.00 12.00
EP Eury Perez 4.00 10.00
ES Eduardo Sanchez 8.00 20.00
FP Francisco Peguero 4.00 10.00
GG Grant Green 4.00 10.00
GH Gorkys Hernandez 4.00 10.00
HA Henderson Alvarez 4.00 10.00
HC Hank Conger 4.00 10.00
HL Hak-Ju Lee 8.00 20.00
HN Hector Noesi 5.00 12.00
JF Jeurys Familia 4.00 10.00
JH Jeremy Hellickson 6.00 15.00
JT Julio Teheran 6.00 15.00
LC Lonnie Chisenhall 6.00 15.00
LJ Luis Jimenez 8.00 20.00
LM Logan Morrison 4.00 10.00
MM Mike Minor 6.00 15.00
MMO Mike Moustakas 4.00 10.00
MT Mike Trout 40.00 100.00
OM Ozzie Martinez 4.00 10.00
PB Pedro Baez 4.00 10.00
PC Pedro Ciriaco 6.00 15.00
PV Philippe Valiquette 8.00 20.00
SC Simon Castro 4.00 10.00
SM Shelby Miller 12.50 30.00
SP Stolmy Pimentel 4.00 10.00
TM Trystan Magnuson 4.00 10.00
WR Wilin Rosario 5.00 12.00
WRA Wilkin Ramirez 4.00 10.00
ZB Zach Britton 5.00 12.00
ZW Zack Wheeler 10.00 25.00

2011 Bowman Prospect Autographs

EXCHANGE DEADLINE 4/30/2014
BB Bryce Brentz 4.00 10.00
BBR Brett Brach 4.00 10.00
BC Bryce Brandon Crawford 8.00 20.00
CC Chevez Clarke 4.00 10.00
DD Daniel Descalso 4.00 10.00
DS Domingo Santana 10.00 25.00
JD Justin De Fratus 4.00 10.00
JG Joe Gardner 4.00 10.00
JO Justin O'Conner 4.00 10.00
JS Josh Sale 4.00 10.00
KC Kaleb Cowart 4.00 10.00
KV Kolbrin Vitek 4.00 10.00
MC Michael Choice 4.00 10.00
MM Manny Machado 40.00 100.00
MP Michael Pineda 6.00 15.00
TB Tim Beckham 8.00 20.00
YR Yorman Rodriguez 4.00 10.00
ZC Zack Cox 4.00 10.00
ZW Zack Wheeler 5.00 12.00

2011 Bowman Prospects

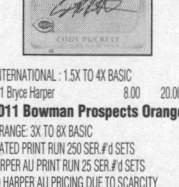

COMP.SET w/o AU (110) 20.00 50.00
PLATE PRINT RUN 1 SET PER COLOR
BLACK-CYAN-MAGENTA-YELLOW ISSUED
NO PLATE PRICING DUE TO SCARCITY
EXCHANGE DEADLINE 4/30/2014
BP1A Bryce Harper 6.00 15.00
BP1B Bryce Harper AU 75.00 200.00
BP2 Chris Dennis .15 .40
BP3 Jeremy Barfield .15 .40
BP4 Nate Freiman .15 .40
BP5 Tyler Moore .40 1.00
BP6 Anthony Carter .15 .40
BP7 Ryan Cavan .15 .40
BP8 Stephen Vogt .25 .60
BP9 Carlo Testa .15 .40
BP10 Erik Davis .15 .40
BP11 Jack Shuck .40 1.00
BP12 Charles Brewer .15 .40
BP13 Alex Castellanos .25 .60
BP14 Anthony Vasquez .15 .40
BP15 Michael Brenly .15 .40
BP16 Kody Hinze .25 .60
BP17 Hector Noesi .25 .60
BP18 Tyler Bortnick .15 .40
BP19 Thomas Layne .15 .40
BP20 Everett Teaford .15 .40
BP21 Jose Pirela .25 .60
BP22 Joel Carreno .15 .40
BP23 Vinnie Catricala .50 1.25
BP24 Tom Koehler .15 .40
BP25 Jonathan Schoop .25 .60
BP26 Chun-Hsiu Chen .40 1.00
BP27 Amaury Rivas .15 .40
BP28 Oswaldo Arcia .15 .40
BP29 Johermyn Chavez .15 .40
BP30 Michael Spina .15 .40
BP31 Kyle McPherson .25 .60
BP32 Albert Cartwright .15 .40
BP33 Joseph Wieland .40 1.00
BP34 Ben Paulsen .15 .40
BP35 Jason Hagerty .15 .40
BP36 Marcell Ozuna .60 1.50
BP37 Dave Sappelt .50 1.25
BP38 Eduardo Escobar .15 .40
BP39 Aaron Baker .15 .40
BP40 Deryk Hooker .15 .40
BP41 Ty Morrison .15 .40
BP42 Keon Broxton .15 .40
BP43 Corey Jones .15 .40
BP44 Manny Banuelos .40 1.00
BP45 Brandon Guyer .25 .60
BP46 Juan Nicasio .15 .40
BP47 Sean Ochinko .15 .40
BP48 Adam Warren .25 .60
BP49 Phillip Cerreto .15 .40
BP50 Mychal Givens .15 .40
BP51 James Fuller .15 .40
BP52 Ronnie Welty .15 .40
BP53 Dan Straily .75 2.00
BP54 Gabriel Jacobo .15 .40
BP55 David Rubinstein .15 .40
BP56 Kevin Mailloux .15 .40
BP57 Angel Castillo .15 .40
BP58 Adrian Salcedo .25 .60
BP59 Ronald Bermudez .15 .40
BP60 Jarek Cunningham .25 .60
BP61 Matt Magill .25 .60
BP62 Willie Cabrera .15 .40
BP63 Austin Hyatt .25 .60
BP64 Cody Puckett .25 .60
BP65 Jacob Goebbert .25 .60
BP66 Matt Carpenter 1.25 3.00
BP67 Dan Klein .25 .60
BP68 Sean Ratliff .15 .40
BP69 Elih Villanueva .15 .40
BP70 Wade Gaynor .15 .40
BP71 Evan Crawford .15 .40
BP72 Avisail Garcia .30 .75
BP73 Kevin Rivers .15 .40
BP74 Jim Gallagher .15 .40
BP75 Brian Broderick .15 .40
BP76 Tyson Auer .15 .40
BP77 Matt Klinker .15 .40
BP78 Cole Figueroa .15 .40
BP79 Rafael Ynoa .15 .40
BP80 Dee Gordon .25 .60
BP81 Blake Forsythe .15 .40
BP82 Jurickson Profar .40 1.00
BP83 Jedd Gyorko .40 1.00
BP84 Matt Hague .25 .60
BP85 Mason Williams .40 1.00
BP86 Stetson Allie .25 .60
BP87 Jarred Cosart .25 .60
BP88 Wagner Mateo .40 1.00
BP89 Allen Webster .25 .60
BP90 Adron Chambers .15 .40
BP91 Blake Smith .15 .40
BP92 J.D. Martinez 1.00 2.50
BP93 Brandon Belt .40 1.00
BP94 Drake Britton .15 .40
BP95 Addison Reed .15 .40
BP96 Adonis Cardona .25 .60
BP97 Yordy Cabrera .15 .40
BP98 Tony Wolters .15 .40
BP99 Paul Goldschmidt 1.50 4.00
BP100 Sean Coyle .25 .60
BP101 Rymer Liriano .40 1.00
BP102 Eric Thames .75 2.00
BP103 Brian Fletcher .15 .40
BP104 Ben Gamel .25 .60
BP105 Kyle Russell .25 .60
BP106 Sammy Solis .15 .40
BP107 Garin Cecchini .40 1.00
BP108 Carlos Perez .15 .40
BP109 Darin Mastroianni .15 .40
BP110 Jonathan Villar .40 1.00

2011 Bowman Prospects Blue

*BLUE: 1.5X TO 4X BASIC
STATED PRINT RUN 500 SER.#'d SETS
HARPER AU PRINT RUN 250 SER.#'d SETS
EXCHANGE DEADLINE 4/30/2014
BP1A Bryce Harper 15.00 40.00
BP1B Bryce Harper AU 125.00 300.00

2011 Bowman Prospects Green

*GREEN: 1.5X TO 4X BASIC
STATED PRINT RUN 450 SER.#'d SETS
BP1 Bryce Harper 12.00 30.00

2011 Bowman Prospects International

*INTERNATIONAL: 1.5X TO 4X BASIC
BP1 Bryce Harper 8.00 20.00

2011 Bowman Prospects Orange

*ORANGE: 3X TO 8X BASIC
STATED PRINT RUN 250 SER.#'d SETS
HARPER AU PRINT RUN 25 SER.#'d SETS
NO HARPER AU PRICING DUE TO SCARCITY
EXCHANGE DEADLINE 4/30/2014
BP1A Bryce Harper 25.00 60.00

2011 Bowman Prospects Purple

*PURPLE: 1.5X TO 4X BASIC
HARPER AU PRINT RUN 55 SER.#'d SETS
EXCHANGE DEADLINE 4/30/2014
BP1A Bryce Harper 20.00 50.00
BP1B Bryce Harper AU 400.00 800.00

2011 Bowman Prospects Red

STATED PRINT RUN 1 SER.#'d SET
NO PRICING DUE TO SCARCITY

2011 Bowman Topps 100

COMPLETE SET (100) 40.00 80.00
TP1 Bryce Harper 6.00 15.00
TP2 Jonathan Singleton .50 1.25
TP3 Tony Sanchez .50 1.25
TP4 Ryan Lavarnway 1.25 3.00
TP5 Rex Brothers .30 .75
TP6 Brandon Belt .75 2.00
TP7 Christian Colon .30 .75
TP8 Reymond Fuentes .30 .75
TP9 Alex Liddi .30 .75
TP10 Zack Cox .50 1.25
TP11 Derek Norris .30 .75
TP12 Hayden Simpson .30 .75
TP13 Alex Colome .30 .75
TP14 Lonnie Chisenhall .50 1.25
TP15 Mike Montgomery .50 1.25
TP16 Gary Sanchez 1.50 4.00
TP17 Shelby Miller 1.50 4.00
TP18 Matt Moore .75 2.00
TP19 Austin Romine .30 .75
TP20 Delino DeShields .30 .75
TP21 Drew Pomeranz .50 1.25
TP22 Michael Pineda .75 2.00
TP23 Thomas Neal .30 .75
TP24 Chun-Hsiu Chen .75 2.00
TP25 Arodys Vizcaino .50 1.25
TP26 Grant Green .30 .75
TP27 Eric Thames 1.50 4.00
TP28 Matt Davidson .50 1.25
TP29 Deck McGuire .30 .75
TP30 Adeiny Hechavarria .30 .75
TP31 Jean Segura 1.25 3.00
TP32 Paul Goldschmidt 3.00 8.00
TP33 Simon Castro .30 .75
TP34 Garin Cecchini .75 2.00
TP35 Julio Teheran .50 1.25
TP36 Hak-Ju Lee .30 .75
TP37 Randall Delgado .50 1.25
TP38 Sammy Solis .30 .75
TP39 Wil Myers .50 1.25
TP40 Miguel Sano .60 1.50
TP41 Michael Taylor .30 .75
TP42 Nolan Arenado 1.50 4.00
TP43 John Lamb .30 .75
TP44 Jurickson Profar .75 2.00
TP45 Jacob Turner 1.25 3.00
TP46 Anthony Rizzo 3.00 8.00
TP47 Slade Heathcott .75 2.00
TP48 Brody Colvin .30 .75
TP49 Yasmani Grandal .50 1.25
TP50 Dellin Betances .75 2.00
TP51 Charles Brewer .30 .75
TP52 Jared Mitchell .50 1.25
TP53 Nick Franklin .50 1.25
TP54 Manny Machado 3.00 8.00
TP55 Manny Banuelos .75 2.00
TP56 Allen Webster .50 1.25
TP57 Kolbrin Vitek .50 1.25
TP58 Jesus Montero .30 .75
TP59 Wilmer Flores .50 1.25
TP60 Jarrod Parker .75 2.00
TP61 Zach Lee .50 1.25
TP62 Alex Torres .30 .75
TP63 Adron Chambers .30 .75
TP64 Tyler Skaggs .75 2.00
TP65 Kyle Seager .75 2.00
TP66 Josh Vitters .50 1.25
TP67 Matt Harvey 2.00 5.00
TP68 Rudy Owens .30 .75
TP69 Donavan Tate .50 1.25
TP70 Jose Iglesias .50 1.25
TP71 Alex White .30 .75
TP72 Robbie Erlin .50 1.25
TP73 Johermyn Chavez .30 .75
TP74 Mauricio Robles .30 .75
TP75 Matt Dominguez .50 1.25
TP76 Jason Kipnis 1.00 2.50
TP77 Aaron Sanchez .50 1.25
TP78 Tyler Matzek .50 1.25
TP79 Chance Ruffin .30 .75
TP80 Jarred Cosart .50 1.25
TP81 Chris Withrow .30 .75
TP82 Drake Britton .30 .75
TP83 Michael Choice .50 1.25
TP84 Freddie Freeman 5.00 12.00
TP85 Jameson Taillon .50 1.25
TP86 Devin Mesoraco .75 2.00
TP87 Brandon Laird .50 1.25
TP88 Keon Broxton .30 .75
TP89 Mike Moustakas .75 2.00
TP90 Mike Trout 60.00 150.00
TP91 Danny Duffy .50 1.25
TP92 Brett Jackson .50 1.25
TP93 Dustin Ackley .50 1.25
TP94 Jerry Sands .75 2.00
TP95 Jake Skole .30 .75
TP96 Kyle Gibson .50 1.25
TP97 Martin Perez .75 2.00
TP98 Zach Britton .75 2.00
TP99 Xavier Avery .30 .75
TP100 Dee Gordon .50 1.25

2011 Bowman Topps of the Class

COMPLETE SET (25) 10.00 25.00
TC1 Jerry Sands .75 2.00
TC2 Mike Olt .50 1.25
TC3 Jared Clark .30 .75
TC4 Nick Franklin .50 1.25
TC5 Paul Goldschmidt 3.00 8.00
TC6 Mike Moustakas .75 2.00
TC7 Greg Halman .50 1.25
TC8 Chris Carter .30 .75
TC9 Rich Poythress .30 .75
TC10 Mark Trumbo .75 2.00

TC11 Johermyn Chavez .30 .75
TC12 Brandon Allen .30 .75
TC13 Brandon Laird .50 1.25
TC14 J.P. Arencibia .30 .75
TC15 Marcell Ozuna 1.25 3.00
TC16 Kevin Mailloux .30 .75
TC17 Clint Robinson .30 .75
TC18 Tyler Moore .75 2.00
TC19 Joe Benson .30 .75
TC20 Anthony Rizzo 3.00 8.00
TC21 Jesus Montero .30 .75
TC22 Tim Pahuta .30 .75
TC23 Grant Green .30 .75
TC24 Lucas Duda .75 2.00
TC25 Michael Spina .30 .75

2011 Bowman Draft

COMPLETE SET (110) 8.00 20.00
COMMON CARD (1-110) .20 .50
STATED PLATE ODDS 1:928 HOBBY
PLATE PRINT RUN 1 SET PER COLOR
BLACK-CYAN-MAGENTA-YELLOW ISSUED
NO PLATE PRICING DUE TO SCARCITY
1 Mike Moustakas RC .50 1.25
2 Ryan Adams RC .20 .50
3 Alexi Amarista RC .20 .50
4 Anthony Bass RC .20 .50
5 Pedro Beato RC .20 .50
6 Bruce Billings RC .20 .50
7 Charlie Blackmon RC 4.00 10.00
8 Brian Broderick RC .20 .50
9 Rex Brothers RC .20 .50
10 Tyler Chatwood RC .20 .50
11 Jose Altuve RC 2.00 5.00
12 Salvador Perez RC .75 2.00
13 Mark Hamburger RC .20 .50
14 Matt Carpenter RC 1.50 4.00
15 Ezequiel Carrera RC .20 .50
16 Jose Ceda RC .20 .50
17 Andrew Brown RC .30 .75
18 Maikel Cleto RC .20 .50
19 Steve Cishek RC .20 .50
20 Lonnie Chisenhall RC .30 .75
21 Henry Sosa RC .20 .50
22 Tim Collins RC .20 .50
23 Josh Collmenter RC .20 .50
24 David Cooper RC .20 .50
25 Brandon Crawford RC .30 .75
26 Brandon Laird RC .30 .75
27 Tony Cruz RC .50 1.25
28 Chase d'Arnaud RC .20 .50
29 Faultino De Los Santos RC .20 .50
30 Rubby De La Rosa RC .50 1.25
31 Andy Dirks RC .50 1.25
32 Jarrod Dyson RC .30 .75
33 Cody Eppley RC .20 .50
34 Logan Forsythe RC .20 .50
35 Todd Frazier RC .60 1.50
36 Eric Fryer RC .30 .75
37 Charlie Furbush RC .30 .75
38 Cory Gearrin RC .30 .75
39 Graham Godfrey RC .30 .75
40 Dee Gordon RC .30 .75
41 Brandon Gomes RC .20 .50
42 Bryan Shaw RC .20 .50
43 Brandon Guyer RC .30 .75
44 Mark Hamilton RC .30 .75
45 Brad Hand RC .20 .50
46 Anthony Recker RC .20 .50
47 Jeremy Horst RC .30 .75
48 Tommy Hottovy (RC) .30 .75
49 Jose Iglesias RC .30 .75
50 Craig Kimbrel RC .50 1.25
51 Josh Judy RC .20 .50
52 Cole Kimball RC .20 .50
53 Alan Johnson RC .20 .50
54 Brandon Kintzler RC .20 .50
55 Pete Kozma RC .50 1.25
56 D.J. LeMahieu RC 2.50 6.00
57 Duane Below RC .30 .75
58 Josh Lindblom RC .30 .75
59 Zack Cozart RC .50 1.25
60 Al Alburquerque RC .20 .50
61 Trystan Magnuson RC .20 .50
62 Michael Martinez RC .30 .75
63 Michael McKenry RC .30 .75
64 Daniel Moskos RC .20 .50
65 Lance Lynn RC .50 1.25
66 Juan Nicasio RC .30 .75
67 Joe Paterson RC .30 .75
68 Lance Pendleton RC .30 .75
69 Luis Perez RC .20 .50
70 Anthony Rizzo RC 2.00 5.00
71 Joel Carreno RC .20 .50
72 Alex Presley RC .30 .75
73 Vinnie Pestano RC .20 .50
74 Aneury Rodriguez RC .20 .50
75 Josh Rodriguez RC .20 .50
76 Eduardo Sanchez RC .30 .75
77 Matt Young RC .20 .50
78 Amauri Sanit RC .20 .50
79 Nathan Eovaldi RC .50 1.25
80 Javy Guerra (RC) .30 .75
81 Eric Sogard RC .20 .50
82 Henderson Alvarez RC .20 .50
83 Ryan Lavarnway RC .75 2.00
84 Michael Stutes RC .30 .75
85 Everett Teaford RC .30 .75
86 Blake Tekotte RC .20 .50
87 Eric Thames RC 1.00 2.50
88 Arodys Vizcaino RC .30 .75
89 Rene Tosoni RC .20 .50
90 Alex White RC .20 .50
91 Brayan Villarreal RC .20 .50
92 Tony Watson RC .30 .75
93 Johnny Giavotella RC .20 .50
94 Kevin Whelan (RC) .20 .50
95 Mike Nickeas (RC) .20 .50
96 Elih Villanueva RC .20 .50
97 Tom Wilhelmsen RC .20 .50
98 Adam Wilk RC .30 .75
99 Mike Wilson (RC) .20 .50
100 Jerry Sands RC .50 1.25
101 Mike Trout RC 75.00 200.00
102 Kyle Weiland RC .20 .50
103 Kyle Seager RC .50 1.25
104 Jason Kipnis RC .60 1.50
105 Chance Ruffin RC .20 .50
106 J.B. Shuck RC .50 1.25
107 Jacob Turner RC .75 2.00
108 Paul Goldschmidt RC 2.00 5.00
109 Justin Sellers RC .30 .75
110 Trayvon Robinson (RC) .30 .75

2011 Bowman Draft Blue

*BLUE: 1.5X TO 4X BASIC
STATED ODDS 1:17 HOBBY
STATED PRINT RUN 499 SER.#'d SETS
101 Mike Trout 250.00 600.00

2011 Bowman Draft Gold

*GOLD: 1X TO 2.5X BASIC
101 Mike Trout 150.00 400.00

2011 Bowman Draft Red

STATED ODDS 1:7410 HOBBY
STATED PRINT RUN 1 SER.#'d SET
NO PRICING DUE TO SCARCITY

2011 Bowman Draft Bryce Harper Green Border Autograph

STATED ODDS 1:6500 HOBBY
EXCHANGE DEADLINE 11/30/2014
BH Bryce Harper 200.00 400.00

2011 Bowman Draft Bryce Harper Relic Autographs

STATED BASE ODDS 1:23,660 HOBBY
STATED BLUE ODDS 1:32,500 HOBBY
STATED GOLD ODDS 1:65,000 HOBBY
STATED GREEN ODDS 1:312,000 HOBBY
STATED RED ODDS 1:1,560,000 HOBBY
BASE PRINT RUN 69 SER.#'d SETS
BLUE PRINT RUN 50 SER.#'d SETS
GOLD PRINT RUN 25 SER.#'d SETS
GREEN PRINT RUN 5 SER.#'d SETS
RED PRINT RUN 1 SER.#'d SET
NO PRICING ON QTY 25 OR LESS
BHAR1A Bryce Harper/69 150.00 300.00
BHAR1B Bryce Harper Blue/50 150.00 300.00

2011 Bowman Draft Future's Game Relics

AL Alex Liddi 3.00 8.00
AR Austin Romine 3.00 8.00
AS Alfredo Silverio 4.00 10.00
AV Arodys Vizcaino 3.00 8.00
BH Bryce Harper 12.50 30.00
BP Brad Peacock 3.00 8.00
DM Devin Mesoraco 4.00 10.00
DP Drew Pomeranz 4.00 10.00
DV Dayan Viciedo 4.00 10.00
GB Gary Brown 4.00 10.00
GG Grant Green 3.00 8.00
GI Gregory Infante 4.00 10.00
HA Henderson Alvarez 5.00 12.00
HL Hak-Ju Lee 3.00 8.00
JA Jose Altuve 5.00 12.00
JC Jarred Cosart 3.00 8.00
JD James Darnell 3.00 8.00
JK Jason Kipnis 6.00 15.00
JM Jhan Marinez 3.00 8.00
JMA Jefry Marte 3.00 8.00
JPR Jurickson Profar 10.00 25.00
JS Jonathan Schoop 5.00 12.00
JTU Jacob Turner 3.00 8.00
KG Kyle Gibson 5.00 12.00
KH Kelvin Herrera 4.00 10.00
LH Liam Hendriks 4.00 10.00
MH Matt Harvey 12.50 30.00
MM Manny Machado 8.00 20.00
MMO Matt Moore 5.00 12.00
MP Martin Perez 3.00 8.00
NA Nolan Arenado 5.00 12.00
PG Paul Goldschmidt 8.00 20.00
RF Reymond Fuentes 3.00 8.00
SM Starling Marte 4.00 10.00
SMI Shelby Miller 4.00 10.00
SV Sebastian Valle 3.00 8.00
TS Tyler Skaggs 3.00 8.00
TT Tyler Thornburg 4.00 10.00
WM Wil Myers 4.00 10.00
WMI Will Middlebrooks 6.00 15.00
WR Wilin Rosario 3.00 8.00
YA Yonder Alonso 4.00 10.00

2011 Bowman Draft Future's Game Relics Blue

*BLUE: .4X TO 1X BASIC
STATED PRINT RUN 199 SER.#'d SETS
NO PRICING DUE TO SCARCITY

2011 Bowman Draft Future's Game Relics Gold

*GOLD: .5X TO 1.2X BASIC
STATED PRINT RUN 50 SER.#'d SETS
NO PRICING DUE TO SCARCITY

2011 Bowman Draft Future's Game Relics Green

STATED PRINT RUN 25 SER.#'d SETS
NO PRICING DUE TO SCARCITY

2011 Bowman Draft Prospects

COMPLETE SET (110) 12.50 30.00
STATED PLATE ODDS 1:928 HOBBY
PLATE PRINT RUN 1 SET PER COLOR
BLACK-CYAN-MAGENTA-YELLOW ISSUED
NO PLATE PRICING DUE TO SCARCITY
BDPP1 John Hicks UER .25 .60
BDPP2 Cody Asche .40 1.00
BDPP3 Tyler Anderson .15 .40
BDPP4 Jack Armstrong .25 .60
BDPP5 Pratt Maynard .15 .40
BDPP6 Javier Baez 2.00 5.00
BDPP7 Kenneth Peoples-Walls .15 .40
BDPP8 Matt Barnes .25 .60
BDPP9 Trevor Bauer 1.50 4.00
BDPP10 Daniel Vogelbach .50 1.25
BDPP11 Mike Wright UER .15 .40
BDPP12 Dante Bichette .25 .60
BDPP13 Hudson Boyd .15 .40
BDPP14 Archie Bradley .50 1.25
BDPP15 Matthew Skole .25 .60
BDPP16 Jed Bradley .25 .60
BDPP17 Tyler Pill .15 .40
BDPP18 Dylan Bundy .50 1.25
BDPP19 Harold Martinez .25 .60
BDPP20 Will Lamb .15 .40
BDPP21 Harold Riggins .15 .40
BDPP22 Zach Cone .25 .60
BDPP23 Kyle Gaedele .15 .40
BDPP24 Kyle Crick .40 1.00
BDPP25 C.J. Cron .50 1.25
BDPP26 Nicholas Delmonico .15 .40
BDPP27 Alex Dickerson .25 .60
BDPP28 Tony Cingrani .75 2.00
BDPP29 Jose Fernandez .60 1.50
BDPP30 Michael Fulmer .40 1.00
BDPP31 Carl Thomore .15 .40
BDPP32 Sean Gilmartin .15 .40
BDPP33 Tyler Goeddel .15 .40
BDPP34 Drew Gagnon .15 .40
BDPP35 Sonny Gray .40 1.00
BDPP36 Larry Greene .25 .60
BDPP37 Nick Martini .15 .40
BDPP38 Taylor Guerrieri .15 .40
BDPP39 Jake Hager .15 .40
BDPP40 James Harris .15 .40
BDPP41 Travis Harrison .25 .60
BDPP42 Nick DeSantiago .25 .60
BDPP43 Chase Larsson .15 .40
BDPP44 Logan Moore .15 .40
BDPP45 Mason Hope .15 .40
BDPP46 Adrian Houser .25 .60
BDPP47 Sean Buckley .15 .40
BDPP48 Rick Anton .15 .40
BDPP49 Scott Woodward .25 .60
BDPP50 David Goforth .15 .40
BDPP51 Taylor Jungmann .25 .60
BDPP52 Blake Snell .60 1.50
BDPP53 Francisco Lindor 1.50 4.00
BDPP54 Mikie Mahtook .40 1.00
BDPP55 Brandon Martin .25 .60
BDPP56 Kevin Quackenbush .25 .60
BDPP57 Kevin Matthews .15 .40
BDPP58 C.J. McElroy .15 .40
BDPP59 Anthony Meo .15 .40
BDPP60 Justin James .25 .60
BDPP61 Levi Michael UER .25 .60
BDPP62 Joseph Musgrove .25 .60
BDPP63 Brandon Nimmo .75 2.00
BDPP64 Brandon Culbreth .15 .40
BDPP65 Javaris Reynolds .15 .40
BDPP66 Adam Ehrlich .15 .40
BDPP67 Henry Owens .25 .60
BDPP68 Joe Panik .40 1.00
BDPP69 Jace Peterson .25 .60
BDPP70 Lance Jeffries .15 .40
BDPP71 Matthew Budgell .15 .40
BDPP72 Dan Gamache .15 .40
BDPP73 Christopher Lee .15 .40
BDPP74 Kyle Kubitza .15 .40
BDPP75 Nick Ahmed .15 .40
BDPP76 Josh Parr .15 .40
BDPP77 Dwight Smith .15 .40
BDPP78 Steven Gruver .15 .40
BDPP79 Jeffrey Soptic .15 .40
BDPP80 Cory Spangenberg .25 .60
BDPP81 George Springer 1.00 2.50
BDPP82 Bubba Starling .25 .60
BDPP83 Robert Stephenson .30 .75
BDPP84 Trevor Story 2.00 5.00
BDPP85 Madison Boer .15 .40
BDPP86 Blake Swihart .25 .60
BDPP87 Kellen Moen .15 .40
BDPP88 Joe Tuschak .15 .40
BDPP89 Keenyn Walker .15 .40
BDPP91A William Abreu .25 .60
BDPP91B Kolten Wong .25 .60
BDPP92 Tyler Alamo .15 .40
BDPP93 Bryson Brigman .15 .40
BDPP94 Nick Ciuffo .15 .40
BDPP95 Trevor Clifton .15 .40
BDPP96 Zach Collins .25 .60
BDPP97 Joe DeMers .15 .40
BDPP98 Steven Farinaro .15 .40
BDPP99 Jake Jarvis .15 .40
BDPP100 Austin Meadows .60 1.50
BDPP101 Hunter Mercado-Hood .15 .40
BDPP102 Dom Nunez .15 .40
BDPP103 Arden Pabst .15 .40
BDPP104 Christian Pelaez .15 .40
BDPP105 Carson Sands .15 .40
BDPP106 Jordan Sheffield .15 .40
BDPP107 Keegan Thompson .15 .40
BDPP108 Dany Toussaint .25 .60
BDPP109 Riley Unroe .15 .40
BDPP110 Matt Vogel .15 .40

2011 Bowman Draft Prospects Blue

*BLUE: 1.5X TO 4X BASIC
STATED ODDS 1:17 HOBBY
STATED PRINT RUN 499 SER.#'d SETS

2011 Bowman Draft Prospects Gold

*GOLD: 1.2X TO 3X BASIC

2011 Bowman Draft Prospects Red

STATED ODDS 1:7410 HOBBY
STATED PRINT RUN 1 SER.#'d SET
NO PRICING DUE TO SCARCITY

2011 Bowman Draft Prospect Autographs

FOUND IN RETAIL PACKS
PLATE PRINT RUN 1 SET PER COLOR
BLACK-CYAN-MAGENTA-YELLOW ISSUED
NO PLATE PRICING DUE TO SCARCITY
AK Aaron Kurcz 3.00 8.00
AT Alex Torres 3.00 8.00
AW Alex Wimmers 3.00 8.00
CS Cody Scarpetta 3.00 8.00
EG Erik Goeddel 3.00 8.00
HA Henderson Alvarez 10.00 25.00
JC Jarek Cunningham 3.00 8.00
JK Jose Kelly 6.00 15.00
JW Jose Wieland 3.00 8.00
ML Matt Lollis 4.00 10.00
RP Rich Poythress 3.00 8.00
SV Sebastian Valle 4.00 10.00
TT Tyler Thornburg 6.00 15.00
BHO Bryan Holaday 4.00 10.00
CBM Chris Balcolm-Miller 3.00 8.00

2011 Bowman Draft Prospect Autographs Blue

*BLUE: .75X TO 2X BASIC
FOUND IN RETAIL PACKS
STATED PRINT RUN 199 SER.#'d SETS

2011 Bowman Draft Prospect Autographs Gold

*GOLD: 1.2X TO 3X BASIC
FOUND IN RETAIL PACKS
STATED PRINT RUN 50 SER.#'d SETS

2011 Bowman Draft Prospect Autographs Red

FOUND IN RETAIL PACKS
STATED PRINT RUN 25 SER.#'d SETS
NO PRICING DUE TO SCARCITY

2012 Bowman

COMP.SET w/o AU (220) 10.00 25.00
COMMON CARD (1-190) .12 .30
COMMON RC (191-220) .40 1.00
PLATE PRINT RUN 1 SET PER COLOR
BLACK-CYAN-MAGENTA-YELLOW ISSUED
NO PLATE PRICING DUE TO SCARCITY
1 Derek Jeter .75 2.00
2 Nick Swisher .25 .60
3 Jered Weaver .25 .60
4 Corey Hart .25 .60
5 Brennan Boesch .20 .50
6 Matt Garza .20 .50
7 Dan Uggla .25 .60
8 Paul Goldschmidt .30 .75
9 Cole Hamels .25 .60
10 Nelson Cruz .30 .75
11 Brett Gardner .25 .60
12 Matt Kemp .25 .60
13 Curtis Granderson .25 .60
14 Pablo Sandoval .25 .60
15 Brandon McCarthy .20 .50
16 Mark Teixeira .25 .60
17 J.J. Hardy .20 .50
18 Yadier Molina .30 .75
19 Daniel Hudson .20 .50
20 Jacoby Ellsbury .25 .60
21 Yunel Escobar .20 .50
22 Robinson Cano .25 .60
23 Colby Rasmus .25 .60
24 Neil Walker .25 .60
25 John Danks .20 .50
26 Brandon Morrow .20 .50
27 Brandon Beachy .20 .50
28 Mat Latos .25 .60
29 Jeremy Hellickson .20 .50
30 Anibal Sanchez .20 .50
31 Dexter Fowler .25 .60
32 Ryan Braun .20 .50
33 Chris Young .20 .50
34 Mike Trout 10.00 25.00
35 Aroldis Chapman .30 .75
36 Lance Berkman .25 .60
37 Dan Haren .20 .50
38 Paul Konerko .25 .60
39 Carl Crawford .25 .60
40 Melky Cabrera .20 .50
41 B.J. Upton .25 .60
42 Madison Bumgarner .25 .60
43 Casey Kotchman .20 .50
44 Michael Bourn .20 .50
45 Adam Jones .25 .60
46 Jon Lester .20 .50
47 Jaime Garcia .25 .60
48 Zack Greinke .25 .60
49 Albert Pujols .40 1.00
50 Jose Valverde .25 .60
51 Billy Butler .20 .50
52 Mark Reynolds .20 .50
53 Adam Lind .25 .60
54 Jordan Zimmermann .25 .60
55 Geovany Soto .25 .60
56 Ted Lilly .20 .50
57 Allen Craig .25 .60
58 Justin Masterson .20 .50
59 Adam Wainwright .25 .60
60 Jordan Walden .25 .60
61 Jemile Weeks RC .60 1.50
62 Justin Upton .25 .60
63 Alex Rodriguez .40 1.00
64 Josh Beckett .20 .50
65 Ben Revere .25 .60
66 Mariano Rivera .40 1.00
67 Hunter Pence .25 .60
68 Tommy Hanson .20 .50
69 Alexi Ogando .20 .50
70 Brian McCann .25 .60
71 Hanley Ramirez .25 .60
72 Tim Hudson .20 .50
73 Justin Morneau .25 .60
74 Derek Holland .20 .50
75 Roy Halladay .25 .60
76 Andrew McCutchen .30 .75
77 Justin Verlander .30 .75
78 Drew Storen .20 .50
79 Ryan Zimmerman .25 .60
80 Jimmy Rollins .25 .60
81 Eric Hosmer .25 .60
82 Joey Votto .30 .75
83 Shane Victorino .25 .60
84 Ian Kinsler .25 .60
85 Troy Tulowitzki .30 .75
86 David Wright .25 .60
87 Joe Mauer .25 .60
88 James Shields .20 .50
89 Brian Wilson .30 .75
90 Matt Cain .25 .60
91 Chipper Jones .30 .75
92 Miguel Montero .20 .50
93 Ervin Santana .20 .50
94 Shaun Marcum .20 .50
95 Adrian Beltre .30 .75
96 Jose Reyes .20 .50
97 Craig Kimbrel .25 .60
98 Nyjer Morgan .20 .50
99 Matt Holliday .30 .75
100 Chris Sale .30 .75
101 Miguel Cabrera .30 .75
102 Clay Buchholz .20 .50
103 Mike Moustakas .25 .60
104 Ike Davis .20 .50
105 Vance Worley .20 .50
106 Pedro Alvarez .20 .50
107 Ian Kennedy .20 .50
108 Torii Hunter .20 .50
109 Michael Cuddyer .20 .50
110 Dee Gordon .20 .50
111 Ricky Romero .20 .50
112 J.P. Arencibia .20 .50
113 Yovani Gallardo .20 .50
114 Adrian Gonzalez .25 .60
115 Ian Desmond .20 .50
116 Trevor Cahill .20 .50
117 Carlos Ruiz .20 .50
118 Alex Gordon .25 .60
119 Josh Johnson .25 .60
120 Cliff Lee .25 .60
121 Neftali Feliz .20 .50
122 Howie Kendrick .20 .50
123 Todd Helton .25 .60
124 Michael Pineda .20 .50
125 John Axford .20 .50
126 Carlos Santana .25 .60
127 Jose Bautista .25 .60
128 Doug Fister .20 .50
129 Ryan Howard .25 .60
130 Cory Luebke .20 .50
131 Nick Markakis .25 .60
132 Jason Motte .20 .50
133 Gio Gonzalez .25 .60
134 Alex Avila .20 .50
135 Josh Hamilton .25 .60
136 Desmond Jennings .25 .60
137 Roy Oswalt .25 .60
138 Heath Bell .20 .50
139 Tim Lincecum .25 .60
140 Michael Morse .25 .60
141 Dustin Pedroia .30 .75
142 Ryan Vogelsong .20 .50
143 Dustin Ackley .20 .50
144 Salvador Perez .25 .60
145 Brandon Phillips .20 .50
146 Martin Prado .20 .50
147 David Freese .20 .50
148 Rickie Weeks .20 .50
149 Evan Longoria .25 .60
150 Shin-Soo Choo .25 .60
151 Clayton Kershaw .60 1.50
152 Giancarlo Stanton .30 .75
153 Elvis Andrus .25 .60
154 Scott Rolen .25 .60
155 Ben Zobrist .25 .60
156 Mark Trumbo .20 .50
157 Chris Carpenter .25 .60
158 Mike Napoli .20 .50
159 David Ortiz .30 .75
160 R.A. Dickey .25 .60
161 Jason Heyward .25 .60
162 C.J. Wilson .20 .50
163 Buster Posey .40 1.00
164 Max Scherzer .30 .75
165 Ivan Nova .25 .60
166 Victor Martinez .25 .60
167 Asdrubal Cabrera .25 .60
168 Freddie Freeman .40 1.00
169 Stephen Strasburg .30 .75
170 Johnny Cueto .25 .60
171 Lucas Duda .25 .60
172 Bud Norris .20 .50
173 Matt Joyce .20 .50
174 Felix Hernandez .25 .60
175 Starlin Castro .25 .60
176 Ichiro Suzuki .40 1.00
177 Ubaldo Jimenez .20 .50
178 Jhonny Peralta .20 .50
179 Carlos Gonzalez .25 .60
180 Michael Young .20 .50
181 David Price .25 .60
182 Prince Fielder .25 .60
183 James Loney .20 .50
184 Chase Utley .25 .60
185 Jayson Werth .25 .60
186 Aramis Ramirez .20 .50
187 Kevin Youkilis .30 .75
188 Jay Bruce .25 .60
189 Delmon Young .25 .60
190 CC Sabathia .25 .60
191 Brett Lawrie RC .75 2.00
192 Alex Liddi RC .60 1.50
193 Yoenis Cespedes RC 1.50 4.00
194 James Darnell RC .60 1.50
195 Jordan Pacheco RC .60 1.50
196 Tom Milone RC .60 1.50
197 Michael Fiers RC .40 1.00
198 Brett Pill RC 1.00 2.50
199 Taylor Green RC .60 1.50
200 Eric Surkamp RC 1.00 2.50
201 Collin Cowgill RC .60 1.50
202 Tyler Pastornicky RC .60 1.50
203 Leonys Martin RC .60 1.50
204 Jeff Locke RC 1.00 2.50
205 Matt Dominguez RC .75 2.00
206 Michael Taylor RC .60 1.50
207 Adron Chambers RC 1.00 2.50
208 Liam Hendriks RC .60 1.50
209A Yu Darvish RC 1.50 4.00
209B Yu Darvish AU 100.00 200.00
210 Jesus Montero RC .60 1.50
211 Matt Moore RC 1.00 2.50
212 Drew Pomeranz RC .60 1.50
213 Jarrod Parker RC .75 2.00
214 Devin Mesoraco RC .60 1.50
215 Joe Benson RC .60 1.50
216 Brad Peacock RC .60 1.50
217 Dellin Betances RC 1.00 2.50
218 Wilin Rosario RC .60 1.50
219 Chris Parmelee RC .60 1.50
220 Addison Reed RC .60 1.50

2012 Bowman Blue

*BLUE 1-190: 1.5X TO 4X BASIC
*BLUE: 191-220: .6X TO 1.5X BASIC
STATED ODDS 1:16 HOBBY
STATED PRINT RUN 500 SER.#'d SETS

2012 Bowman Gold

*GOLD 1-190: .75X TO 2X BASIC
*GOLD: 191-220: .5X TO 1.2X BASIC

2012 Bowman International

*INT 1-190: 1.5X TO 4X BASIC
*INT 191-220: .6X TO 1.5X BASIC
STATED ODDS 1:8 HOBBY

2012 Bowman Orange

*ORANGE 1-190: 2.5X TO 6X BASIC
*ORANGE 191-220: 1X TO 2.5X BASIC
STATED ODDS 1:32 HOBBY
STATED PRINT RUN 250 SER.#'d SETS

2012 Bowman Red

STATED ODDS 1:4150 HOBBY
STATED PRINT RUN 1 SER.#'d SET
NO PRICING DUE TO SCARCITY

2012 Bowman Silver Ice

*SILVER ICE 1-190: 2X TO 5X BASIC
*SILVER ICE 191-220: .75X TO 2X BASIC
STATED ODDS 1:24 HOBBY

2012 Bowman Silver Ice Red

STATED ODDS 1:173 HOBBY
STATED PRINT RUN 25 SER.#'d SETS
NO PRICING DUE TO SCARCITY

2012 Bowman Bowman's Best

COMPLETE SET (25) 6.00 15.00
STATED ODDS 1:6 HOBBY
PLATE PRINT RUN 1 SET PER COLOR
BLACK-CYAN-MAGENTA-YELLOW ISSUED
NO PLATE PRICING DUE TO SCARCITY
BB1 CC Sabathia .40 1.00
BB2 Dellin Betances .50 1.25
BB3 Jesus Montero .30 .75
BB4 Matt Moore .50 1.25
BB5 Drew Pomeranz .30 .75
BB6 Jarrod Parker .40 1.00
BB7 Devin Mesoraco .30 .75
BB8 Matt Dominguez .40 1.00
BB9 Joe Benson .30 .75
BB10 Brad Peacock .30 .75
BB11 Miguel Cabrera .50 1.25
BB12 Evan Longoria .40 1.00
BB13 Jacob Turner .40 1.00
BB14 Jose Bautista .40 1.00
BB15 Troy Tulowitzki .50 1.25
BB16 Justin Verlander .50 1.25
BB17 Roy Halladay .40 1.00
BB18 Tim Lincecum .40 1.00
BB19 Matt Kemp .40 1.00
BB20 Clayton Kershaw 1.00 2.50
BB21 Ryan Braun .30 .75
BB22 Albert Pujols .60 1.50
BB23 Josh Hamilton .40 1.00
BB24 Robinson Cano .40 1.00
BB25 Jacoby Ellsbury .40 1.00

2012 Bowman Bowman's Best Die Cut Atomic Refractors

STATED ODDS 1:34,200 HOBBY
STATED PRINT RUN 1 SER.#'d SET
NO PRICING DUE TO SCARCITY

2012 Bowman Bowman's Best Die Cut Refractors

*REF: 1.5X TO 4X BASIC
STATED ODDS 1:496 HOBBY
STATED PRINT RUN 99 SER.#'d SETS

2012 Bowman Bowman's Best Die Cut X-Fractors

STATED ODDS 1:1975 HOBBY
STATED PRINT RUN 25 SER.#'d SETS
NO PRICING DUE TO SCARCITY

2012 Bowman Bowman's Best Prospects

COMPLETE SET (25) 8.00 20.00
STATED ODDS 1:6 HOBBY
PLATE PRINT RUN 1 SET PER COLOR
BLACK-CYAN-MAGENTA-YELLOW ISSUED
NO PLATE PRICING DUE TO SCARCITY
BBP1 Trevor Bauer 1.25 3.00
BBP2 Manny Machado 2.50 6.00
BBP3 Manny Banuelos .50 1.25
BBP4 Bryce Harper 6.00 15.00
BBP5 Shelby Miller .75 2.00
BBP6 Jonathan Singleton .50 1.25
BBP7 Brett Jackson .60 1.50
BBP8 Billy Hamilton .50 1.25
BBP9 Jurickson Profar .50 1.25
BBP10 Matt Harvey 2.50 6.00
BBP11 Travis d'Arnaud .50 1.25
BBP12 Miguel Sano .50 1.25
BBP13 Jameson Taillon .50 1.25
BBP14 Bubba Starling .50 1.25
BBP15 Gerrit Cole 2.50 6.00
BBP16 Wilmer Flores .50 1.25
BBP17 Gary Sanchez 1.25 3.00
BBP18 Zack Wheeler .75 2.00
BBP19 Rymer Liriano .40 1.00
BBP20 Anthony Gose .50 1.25
BBP21 Joe Panik .60 1.50
BBP22 Will Middlebrooks .50 1.25
BBP23 Starling Marte .50 1.25
BBP24 Tyler Skaggs .60 1.50
BBP25 Gary Brown .40 1.00

2012 Bowman Bowman's Best Prospects Die Cut Refractors

*REF: 1.5X TO 4X BASIC
STATED ODDS 1:496 HOBBY
STATED PRINT RUN 99 SER.#'d SETS

2012 Bowman Lucky Redemption Autographs

LUCKY 1 ODDS 1:48,000 HOBBY
LUCKY 2 ODDS 1:30,000 HOBBY
LUCKY 3 ODDS 1:24,000 HOBBY
ANNCD PRINT RUN OF 100
EXCHANGE DEADLINE 04/30/2013
L3YC Yoenis Cespedes 125.00 250.00
L3BH Bryce Harper 150.00 300.00
L3WM Will Middlebrooks 60.00 120.00

2012 Bowman Prospect Autographs

AW Allen Webster 3.00 8.00
BH Bryce Harper 100.00 200.00
CH Chad Huffman 3.00 8.00
CP Carlos Perez 3.00 8.00
DS Dwight Smith 3.00 8.00
JF Jose Fernandez 10.00 25.00
JG Jedd Gyorko 3.00 8.00
JK Joe Kelly 3.00 8.00
JV Jordany Valdespin 5.00 12.00
KK Kyle Kubitza 3.00 8.00
KW Kolten Wong 3.00 8.00
MA Matt Adams 3.00 8.00
ML Matt Lipka 3.00 8.00
MO Mike Olt 3.00 8.00
RG Robbie Grossman 3.00 8.00
SB Sean Buckley 3.00 8.00
SG Sonny Gray 5.00 12.00
TA Tyler Anderson 3.00 8.00
TG Taylor Guerrieri 3.00 8.00
TT Trayce Thompson 3.00 8.00

2012 Bowman Prospect Autographs Blue

*BLUE: .5X TO 1.2X BASIC
STATED PRINT RUN 500 SER.#'d SETS
BH Bryce Harper 200.00 300.00

2012 Bowman Prospect Autographs Orange

*ORANGE: .75X TO 2X BASIC
PRINT RUNS B/WN 15-250 COPIES PER
NO HARPER PRICING DUE TO SCARCITY

2012 Bowman Prospects

PLATE PRINT RUN 1 SET PER COLOR
BLACK-CYAN-MAGENTA-YELLOW ISSUED
NO PLATE PRICING DUE TO SCARCITY
BP1 Justin Nicolino .30 .75
BP2 Myrio Richard .25 .60
BP3 Francisco Lindor 1.50 4.00
BP4 Nathan Freiman .25 .60
BP5 A.J. Jimenez .25 .60
BP6 Noah Perio .25 .60
BP7 Adonys Cardona .25 .60
BP8 Nick Kingham .25 .60
BP9A Eddie Rosario .50 1.25
BP9B Paul Hoilman .25 .60
BP10 Bryce Harper 4.00 10.00
BP11 Philip Wunderlich .25 .60
BP12 Rafael Ortega .25 .60
BP13 Tyler Gagnon .25 .60
BP14 Brenny Paulino .25 .60
BP15 Jose Campos .30 .75
BP16 Jesus Galindo .25 .60
BP17 Tyler Austin .40 1.00
BP18 Brandon Drury .40 1.00
BP19 Richard Jones .25 .60
BP20A Robby Price .25 .60
BP20B Jeimer Candelario .30 .75
BP21 Jose Osuna .25 .60
BP22 Claudio Custodio .30 .75
BP23 Jake Marisnick .30 .75
BP24 J.R. Graham .25 .60
BP25 Raul Alcantara .25 .60
BP26 Joseph Staley .25 .60
BP27 Josh Bowman .25 .60
BP28 Josh Edgin .25 .60
BP29 Keith Couch .25 .60
BP30 Kyrell Hudson .25 .60
BP31 Nick Maronde .30 .75
BP32 Mario Yepez .25 .60
BP33 Matthew West .25 .60
BP34 Matthew Szczur .30 .75
BP35 Devon Ethier .25 .60
BP36 Michael Brady .25 .60
BP37 Michael Crouse .25 .60
BP38 Michael Gonzales .25 .60
BP39 Mike Murray .25 .60
BP41 Zach Walters .30 .75
BP42 Tim Crabbe .25 .60
BP43 Rookie Davis .25 .60
BP44 Adam Duvall 4.00 10.00
BP45 Angelys Nina .25 .60
BP46 Anthony Fernandez .25 .60
BP47 Ariel Pena .25 .60
BP48 Boone Whiting .25 .60
BP49 Brandon Brown .25 .60
BP50 Brennan Smith .25 .60
BP51 Brett Krill .30 .75
BP52 Dean Green .25 .60
BP53 Casey Haerther .25 .60
BP54 Casey Lawrence .25 .60
BP55 Jose Vinicio .30 .75
BP56 Kyle Simon .25 .60
BP57 Chris Rearick .25 .60
BP58 Cheslor Cuthbert .25 .60
BP59 Daniel Corcino .30 .75
BP60 Danny Barnes .25 .60
BP61 David Medina .25 .60
BP62A Kes Carter .25 .60
BP62B Dayan Diaz .30 .75
BP63 Todd McInnis .25 .60
BP64 Edwar Cabrera .25 .60
BP65 Emilio King .25 .60
BP66 Jackie Bradley .60 1.50
BP67 J.T. Wise .25 .60
BP68 Jeff Malm .25 .60
BP69 Jonathan Galvez .25 .60
BP70 Luis Heredia .25 .60
BP71 Jonathon Berti .25 .60
BP72 Jabari Blash .25 .60
BP73 Will Swanner .25 .60
BP74 Eric Arce .25 .60
BP75 Dillon Maples .25 .60
BP76 Ian Gac .25 .60
BP77 Clay Holmes .25 .60
BP78 Nick Castellanos .75 2.00
BP79 Josh Bell 1.00 2.50
BP80 Matt Purke .25 .60
BP81 Taylor Whitenton .25 .60
BP83 Jacob Anderson .30 .75
BP84 Bryan Brickhouse .30 .75
BP85 Levi Michael .25 .60
BP86 Gerrit Cole 1.50 4.00
BP87 Danny Hultzen .40 1.00
BP88 Anthony Rendon 1.25 3.00
BP89 Austin Hedges .25 .60
BP91 Dillon Howard .30 .75
BP92 Nick Delmonico .25 .60
BP93 Brandon Jacobs .30 .75
BP94 Charlie Tilson .25 .60
BP96 Greg Billo .25 .60
BP97 Andrew Susac .30 .75
BP98 Greg Bird .30 .75
BP99 Dante Bichette .30 .75
BP100 Tommy Joseph .50 1.25
BP101 Julio Rodriguez .25 .60
BP102 Oscar Taveras .40 1.00
BP103 Drew Hutchison .30 .75
BP104 Joc Pederson .40 1.00
BP105 Xander Bogaerts 1.00 2.50
BP106 Tyler Collins .30 .75
BP107 Joe Ross .25 .60
BP108A Carlos Martinez .40 1.00
BP108B Luis Angel .25 .60
BP109 Andrelton Simmons .40 1.00
BP110 Daniel Norris .30 .75

2012 Bowman Prospects Blue

*BLUE: 2X TO 5X BASIC
STATED ODDS 1:16 HOBBY
STATED PRINT RUN 500 SER.#'d SETS

2012 Bowman Prospects International

*INT: 1.25X TO 3X BASIC
STATED ODDS 1:8 HOBBY
BP10 Bryce Harper 8.00 20.00

2012 Bowman Prospects Orange

*ORANGE: 3X TO 8X BASIC
STATED ODDS 1:32 HOBBY
STATED PRINT RUN 250 SER.#'d SETS
BP10 Bryce Harper 15.00 40.00

2012 Bowman Prospects Purple

*PURPLE: 1.5X TO 4X BASIC

2012 Bowman Prospects Red

STATED ODDS 1:4150 HOBBY
STATED PRINT RUN 1 SER.#'d SET
NO PRICING DUE TO SCARCITY

2012 Bowman Prospects Silver Ice

*SILVER ICE: 2.5X TO 6X BASIC
STATED ODDS 1:24 HOBBY

2012 Bowman Draft

COMPLETE SET (55) 6.00 15.00
STATED PLATE ODDS 1:1600 HOBBY
PLATE PRINT RUN 1 SET PER COLOR
NO PLATE PRICING DUE TO SCARCITY
1 Trevor Bauer RC 1.00 2.50
2 Tyler Pastornicky RC .30 .75
3 A.J. Griffin RC .40 1.00
4 Yoenis Cespedes RC .75 2.00
5 Drew Smyly RC .30 .75
6 Jose Quintana RC .30 .75
7 Yasmani Grandal RC .30 .75
8 Tyler Thornburg RC .40 1.00
9 A.J. Pollock RC .50 1.25
10 Bryce Harper RC 5.00 12.00
11 Joe Kelly RC .50 1.25
12 Steve Clevenger RC .20 .50
13 Tanner Scheppers RC .20 .50
14 Casey Crosby RC .40 1.00
15 Wade Miley RC .40 1.00
16 Quintin Berry RC .50 1.25
17 Martin Perez RC .50 1.25
18 Addison Reed RC .30 .75
19 Liam Hendriks RC .30 .75
20 Matt Moore RC .50 1.25
21 Wilin Rosario RC .30 .75
22 Jarrod Parker RC .40 1.00
23 Matt Adams RC .40 1.00
24 Devin Mesoraco RC .30 .75
25 Jordan Pacheco RC .30 .75
26 Irving Falu RC .30 .75
27 Edwar Cabrera RC .30 .75
28 Stephen Pryor RC .20 .50
29 Norichika Aoki RC .40 1.00
30 Jesus Montero RC .30 .75
31 Drew Pomeranz RC .30 .75
32 Jordany Valdespin RC .40 1.00
33 Andrelton Simmons RC .50 1.25
34 Xavier Avery RC .30 .75
35 Chris Archer RC .30 .75
36 Drew Hutchison RC .40 1.00
37 Dallas Keuchel RC 1.50 4.00
38 Leonys Martin RC .30 .75
39 Brian Dozier RC 1.00 2.50
40 Will Middlebrooks RC .40 1.00
41 Kirk Nieuwenhuis RC .30 .75
42 Jeremy Hefner RC .30 .75
43 Derek Norris RC .30 .75
44 Tom Milone RC .30 .75
45 Wei-Yin Chen RC .75 2.00
46 Christian Friedrich RC .30 .75
47 Kole Calhoun RC .40 1.00
48 Wily Peralta RC .30 .75
49 Hisashi Iwakuma RC .60 1.50
50 Yu Darvish RC .75 2.00
51 Elian Herrera RC .50 1.25
52 Anthony Gose RC .40 1.00
53 Brett Jackson RC .50 1.25
54 Alex Liddi RC .30 .75
55 Matt Hague RC .30 .75

2012 Bowman Draft Blue

*BLUE: 1.2X TO 3X BASIC
STATED ODDS 1:13 HOBBY
STATED PRINT RUN 500 SER.#'d SETS
10 Bryce Harper 8.00 20.00

2012 Bowman Draft Orange

*ORANGE: 1.5X TO 4X BASIC
STATED ODDS 1:26 HOBBY
STATED PRINT RUN 250 SER.#'d SETS
10 Bryce Harper 10.00 25.00

2012 Bowman Draft Silver Ice

*SILVER: 2X TO 5X BASIC
10 Bryce Harper 12.50 30.00

2012 Bowman Draft Bowman's Best Die Cut Refractors

STATED ODDS 1:288 HOBBY
STATED PRINT RUN 99 SER.#'d SETS
BB1 Mike Zunino 6.00 15.00
BB2 Kevin Gausman 8.00 20.00
BB3 Max Fried 15.00 40.00
BB4 Kyle Zimmer 5.00 12.00
BB5 Andrew Heaney 5.00 12.00
BB6 David Dahl 12.00 30.00
BB7 Gavin Cecchini 5.00 12.00
BB8 Courtney Hawkins 4.00 10.00
BB9 Nick Travieso 5.00 12.00
BB10 Tyler Naquin 5.00 12.00
BB11 D.J. Davis 5.00 12.00
BB12 Michael Wacha 8.00 20.00
BB13 Lucas Sims 5.00 12.00
BB14 Marcus Stroman 6.00 15.00
BB15 James Ramsey 4.00 10.00
BB16 Richie Shaffer 5.00 12.00
BB17 Lewis Brinson 12.00 30.00
BB18 Ty Hensley 5.00 12.00
BB19 Brian Johnson 4.00 10.00
BB20 Joey Gallo 12.00 30.00
BB21 Keon Barnum 4.00 10.00
BB22 Anthony Alford 4.00 10.00
BB23 Austin Aune 5.00 12.00
BB24 Nick Williams 4.00 10.00
BB25 Stryker Trahan 4.00 10.00
BB26 Tyler Austin 6.00 15.00
BB27 Jackie Bradley Jr. 10.00 25.00
BB28 Cody Buckel 4.00 10.00
BB29 Nick Castellanos 12.00 30.00
BB30 Alen Hanson 5.00 12.00
BB31 George Springer 15.00 40.00
BB32 Oscar Taveras 6.00 15.00
BB33 Taijuan Walker 5.00 12.00
BB34 Miles Head 4.00 10.00
BB35 Archie Bradley 2.50 6.00
BB36 Jose Fernandez 10.00 25.00
BB37 Dylan Bundy 8.00 20.00
BB38 Daniel Vogelbach 6.00 15.00
BB39 Tony Cingrani 8.00 20.00
BB40 Matt Barnes 4.00 10.00
BB41 Christian Yelich 30.00 80.00
BB42 Mason Williams 6.00 15.00
BB43 Brad Miller 4.00 10.00
BB44 Eddie Rosario 8.00 20.00
BB45 Kolten Wong 4.00 10.00
BB46 Sean Nolin 4.00 10.00
BB47 Javier Baez 15.00 40.00
BB48 Nolan Arenado 12.00 30.00
BB49 Anthony Rendon 20.00 50.00
BB50 Danny Hultzen 6.00 15.00

2012 Bowman Draft Draft Picks

COMPLETE SET (165) 12.50 30.00
STATED PLATE ODDS 1:1600 HOBBY
PLATE PRINT RUN 1 SET PER COLOR
NO PLATE PRICING DUE TO SCARCITY
BDPP1 Lucas Sims .40 1.00
BDPP2 Kevin Gausman .60 1.50
BDPP3 Brian Johnson .30 .75
BDPP4 Pierce Johnson .40 1.00
BDPP5 Keon Barnum .30 .75
BDPP6 Paul Blackburn .30 .75
BDPP7 Nick Travieso .40 1.00
BDPP8 Jesse Winker .40 1.00
BDPP9 Tyler Naquin .40 1.00
BDPP10 Kyle Zimmer .40 1.00
BDPP11 Jesmuel Valentin .40 1.00
BDPP12 Andrew Heaney .40 1.00
BDPP13 Victor Roache .60 1.50
BDPP14 Mitch Haniger .75 2.00
BDPP15 Luke Bard .30 .75
BDPP16 Jose Berrios 1.00 2.50
BDPP17 Gavin Cecchini .40 1.00
BDPP18 Kevin Plawecki .40 1.00
BDPP19 Ty Hensley .40 1.00
BDPP20 Matt Olson .50 1.25
BDPP21 Mitch Gueller .30 .75
BDPP22 Shane Watson .40 1.00
BDPP23 Barrett Barnes .40 1.00
BDPP24 Travis Jankowski .40 1.00
BDPP25 Mike Zunino .50 1.25
BDPP26 Michael Wacha .60 1.50
BDPP27 James Ramsey .30 .75
BDPP28 Patrick Wisdom .30 .75
BDPP29 Steve Bean .40 1.00
BDPP30 Richie Shaffer .40 1.00
BDPP31 Lewis Brinson 1.00 2.50
BDPP32 Joey Gallo 1.00 2.50
BDPP33 D.J. Davis .40 1.00
BDPP34 Tyler Gonzalez .40 1.00
BDPP35 Marcus Stroman .50 1.25
BDPP36 Matt Smoral .30 .75
BDPP37 Branden Kline .30 .75
BDPP38 Jacob Thompson .40 1.00
BDPP39 Austin Aune .40 1.00
BDPP40 Peter O'Brien .50 1.25
BDPP41 Bruce Maxwell .30 .75
BDPP42 Dylan Cozens .50 1.25
BDPP43 Wyatt Mathisen .30 .75
BDPP44 Spencer Edwards .30 .75
BDPP45 Jamie Jarmon .30 .75
BDPP46 R.J. Alvarez .30 .75
BDPP47 Bryan De La Rosa .30 .75
BDPP48 Adrian Marin .30 .75
BDPP49 Austin Maddox .30 .75
BDPP50 Fernando Perez .30 .75
BDPP51 Austin Schotts .30 .75
BDPP52 Avery Romero .30 .75
BDPP53 Kolby Copeland .30 .75
BDPP54 Jonathan Sandfort .30 .75
BDPP55 Alex Yarbrough .30 .75
BDPP56 Justin Black .30 .75
BDPP57 Ty Buttrey .40 1.00
BDPP58 Austin Dean .30 .75
BDPP59 Andrew Pullin .40 1.00
BDPP60 Bralin Jackson .30 .75
BDPP61 Lex Rutledge .30 .75
BDPP62 Jordan John .30 .75
BDPP63 Andre Martinez .30 .75
BDPP64 Eric Wood .40 1.00
BDPP65 Derek Self .30 .75
BDPP66 Jacob Wilson .30 .75
BDPP67 Joe Bircher .30 .75
BDPP68 Matthew Price .30 .75
BDPP69 Hudson Randall .30 .75
BDPP70 Jorge Fernandez .30 .75
BDPP71 Nathan Minnich .30 .75
BDPP72 Yoenny Gonzalez .30 .75
BDPP73 Steven Schils .30 .75
BDPP74 Thomas Coyle .30 .75
BDPP75 Ron Miller .30 .75
BDPP76 Rowan Wick .30 .75
BDPP77 Mike Dodig .30 .75
BDPP78 John Kuchno .30 .75
BDPP79 Caleb Frare .40 1.00
BDPP80 William Carmona .30 .75
BDPP81 Clayton Henning .30 .75
BDPP82 Connor Lien .30 .75
BDPP83 Michael Meyers .30 .75
BDPP84 Julio Felix .30 .75
BDPP85 Alexander Muren .30 .75
BDPP86 Jacob Stallings .40 1.00
BDPP87 Max Foody .30 .75
BDPP88 Taylor Hawkins .30 .75
BDPP89 Jeffrey Wendelken .30 .75
BDPP90 Steven Golden .30 .75
BDPP91 Brett Wiley .30 .75
BDPP92 John Silviano .30 .75
BDPP93 Tyler Tewell .30 .75
BDPP94 Sean McAdams .40 1.00
BDPP95 Michael Vaughn .30 .75
BDPP96 Jake Proctor .30 .75
BDPP97 Richard Bielski .30 .75
BDPP98 Charles Gillies .30 .75
BDPP99 Erick Gonzalez .30 .75
BDPP100 Bennett Pickar .30 .75
BDPP101 Christopher Beck .30 .75
BDPP102 Brandon Brennan .30 .75
BDPP103 Eddie Butler .30 .75
BDPP104 David Dahl 1.00 2.50
BDPP105 Ryan Gibbard .30 .75
BDPP106 Hunter Scantling .30 .75
BDPP107 Zach Isler .30 .75
BDPP108 Joshua Turley .30 .75
BDPP109 Johendi Jiminian .30 .75
BDPP110 Jake Lamb .50 1.25
BDPP111 Mike Morin .30 .75
BDPP112 Parker Morin .30 .75
BDPP113 Scott Oberg .30 .75
BDPP114 Correlle Prime .30 .75
BDPP115 Mark Sappington .30 .75
BDPP116 Sam Selman .40 1.00
BDPP117 Paul Sewald .30 .75
BDPP118 Matt Wessinger .30 .75
BDPP119 Max White .30 .75
BDPP120 Adam Giacalone .40 1.00
BDPP121 Jeffrey Popick .30 .75
BDPP122 Alfredo Rodriguez .30 .75
BDPP123 Nick Routt .30 .75
BDPP124 Abe Ruiz .30 .75
BDPP125 Jason Stolz .30 .75
BDPP126 Ben Waldrip .30 .75
BDPP127 Eric Stamets .30 .75
BDPP128 Chris Cowell .30 .75
BDPP129 Fernelys Sanchez .30 .75
BDPP130 Kevin McKague .40 1.00
BDPP131 Rashad Brown .30 .75
BDPP132 Jorge Saez .30 .75
BDPP133 Shaun Valeriote .30 .75
BDPP134 Will Hurt .30 .75
BDPP135 Nicholas Grim .40 1.00
BDPP136 Patrick Merkling .30 .75
BDPP137 Jonathan Murphy .30 .75
BDPP138 Bryan Lippincott .30 .75
BDPP139 Austin Chubb .30 .75
BDPP140 Joseph Almaraz .30 .75
BDPP141 Robert Ravago .30 .75
BDPP142 Will Hudgins .30 .75
BDPP143 Tommy Richards .30 .75
BDPP144 Chad Carman .50 1.25
BDPP145 Joel Licon .30 .75
BDPP146 Jimmy Rider .30 .75
BDPP147 Jason Wilson .30 .75
BDPP148 Justin Jackson .30 .75
BDPP149 Casey McCarthy .30 .75
BDPP150 Hunter Bailey .30 .75
BDPP151 Jake Pintar .30 .75
BDPP152 David Cruz .30 .75
BDPP153 Mike Mudron .30 .75
BDPP154 Benjamin Kline .30 .75
BDPP155 Bryan Haar .30 .75
BDPP156 Patrick Claussen .30 .75
BDPP157 Derrick Bleeker .30 .75
BDPP158 Edward Sappelt .30 .75
BDPP159 Jeremy Lucas .30 .75
BDPP160 Josh Martin .30 .75
BDPP161 Robert Benincasa .30 .75
BDPP162 Craig Manuel .30 .75
BDPP163 Taylor Ard .30 .75
BDPP164 Dominic Leone .30 .75
BDPP165 Kevin Brady .30 .75

2012 Bowman Draft Draft Picks Blue

*BLUE: 1.5X TO 4X BASIC
STATED ODDS 1:13 HOBBY
STATED PRINT RUN 500 SER.#'d SETS

2012 Bowman Draft Draft Picks Orange

*ORANGE: 2X TO 5X BASIC
STATED ODDS 1:26 HOBBY
STATED PRINT RUN 250 SER.#'d SETS

2012 Bowman Draft Draft Picks Silver Ice

*SILVER: 2.5X TO 6X BASIC

2012 Bowman Draft Dual Top 10 Picks

COMPLETE SET (15)
STATED ODDS 1:6 HOBBY
BC Gavin Cecchini/Jay Bruce .50 1.25
BG D.Bundy/K.Gausman .75 2.00
BS R.Braun/B.Starling .50 1.25
CT M.Cain/M.Trout 20.00 50.00
ER James Ramsey/Jacoby Ellsbury .50 1.25
FL M.Fried/C.Kershaw 1.50 4.00
FT Prince Fielder/Troy Tulowitzki .60 1.50
HH J.Hamilton/B.Harper 6.00 15.00
JA A.Almora/D.Jeter 1.50 4.00
KH Courtney Hawkins/Paul Konerko .40 1.00
LZ E.Longoria/M.Zunino .60 1.50
MS A.McCutchen/G.Springer 1.50 4.00
PH Andrew Heaney/Jarrod Parker .50 1.25
UN Tyler Naquin/Chase Utley .50 1.25
VH J.Verlander/D.Hultzen .60 1.50

2012 Bowman Draft Future's Game Relics

STATED ODDS 1:345 HOBBY
STATED PRINT RUN 199 SER.#'d SETS
AG Anthony Gose 4.00 10.00
AM Alfredo Marte 3.00 8.00
AP Ariel Pena 3.00 8.00
AS Ali Solis 4.00 10.00
BH Billy Hamilton 10.00 25.00
BR Bruce Rondon 5.00 12.00
CB Christian Bethancourt 4.00 10.00
CY Christian Yelich 4.00 10.00
DB Dylan Bundy 12.50 30.00
DH Danny Hultzen 5.00 12.00
ER Enny Romero 3.00 8.00
FL Francisco Lindor 4.00 10.00
FR Felipe Rivero 6.00 15.00
GC Gerrit Cole 5.00 12.00
JF Jose Fernandez 10.00 25.00
JH Jae-Hoon Ha 3.00 8.00
JO Jake Odorizzi 5.00 12.00
JP Jurickson Profar 8.00 20.00
JR Julio Rodriguez 4.00 10.00
JS Jonathan Singleton 5.00 12.00
JSE Jean Segura 3.00 8.00
JT Jameson Taillon 4.00 10.00
KL Kyle Lotzkar 4.00 10.00
KW Kolten Wong 6.00 15.00
MB Matt Barnes 4.00 10.00
MC Michael Choice 3.00 8.00
MM Manny Machado 10.00 25.00
MO Mike Olt 4.00 10.00
NA Nolan Arenado 4.00 10.00
NC Nick Castellanos 6.00 15.00
OA Oswaldo Arcia 4.00 10.00
OT Oscar Taveras 12.50 30.00
RB Rob Brantly 6.00 15.00
RL Rymer Liriano 4.00 10.00
SG Scooter Gennett 6.00 15.00
TJ Tommy Joseph 4.00 10.00
TS Tyler Skaggs 3.00 8.00
TW Taijuan Walker 4.00 10.00
WF Wilmer Flores 3.00 8.00
WM Wil Myers 8.00 20.00
XB Xander Bogaerts 20.00 50.00
ZW Zack Wheeler 4.00 10.00

2013 Bowman

COMPLETE SET (220) 10.00 25.00
PRINTING PLATE ODDS 1:1881
PLATE PRINT RUN 1 SET PER COLOR
BLACK-CYAN-MAGENTA-YELLOW ISSUED
NO PLATE PRICING DUE TO SCARCITY
1 Adam Jones .25 .60
2 Jon Niese .20 .50
3 Aroldis Chapman .30 .75
4 Brett Jackson .20 .50
5 CC Sabathia .25 .60
6 David Freese .20 .50
7 Dustin Pedroia .25 .60
8 Hanley Ramirez .25 .60
9 Jered Weaver .25 .60
10 Johnny Cueto .25 .60
11 Justin Upton .25 .60
12 Mark Trumbo .20 .50
13 Melky Cabrera .20 .50
14 Allen Craig .20 .50
15 Torii Hunter .20 .50
16 Ryan Vogelsong .20 .50
17 Starlin Castro .20 .50
18 Trevor Bauer .30 .75
19 Will Middlebrooks .20 .50
20 Yonder Alonso .20 .50
21 A.J. Pierzynski .20 .50
22 Marco Scutaro .25 .60
23 Justin Morneau .25 .60
24 Jose Reyes .25 .60
25 Dan Uggla .20 .50
26 Darwin Barney .20 .50
27 Jeff Samardzija .20 .50
28 Josh Johnson .25 .60
29 Coco Crisp .20 .50
30 Ian Kennedy .20 .50
31 Michael Young .20 .50
32 Craig Kimbrel .25 .60
33 Brandon Morrow .20 .50
34 Ben Revere .20 .50
35 Tim Lincecum .25 .60
36 Alex Rios .25 .60
37 Curtis Granderson .25 .60
38 Gio Gonzalez .25 .60
39 Dylan Bundy RC 1.00 2.50
40 Adam Eaton RC .60 1.50
41 Casey Kelly RC .50 1.25
42 A.J. Ramos RC .50 1.25
43 Ryan Wheeler RC .40 1.00
44 Henry Rodriguez RC .40 1.00
45 Alex Rodriguez .40 1.00
46 Wei-Yin Chen .20 .50
47 Brian McCann .20 .50
48 Chris Sale .30 .75
49 David Price .25 .60
50 Albert Pujols .40 1.00
51 Evan Longoria .25 .60
52 Jacoby Ellsbury .25 .60
53 Jesus Montero .25 .60
54 Jon Jay .20 .50
55 Lance Lynn .20 .50
56 Matt Cain .20 .50
57 Michael Bourn .20 .50
58 Nelson Cruz .30 .75
59 Robinson Cano .25 .60
60 Ryan Zimmerman .25 .60
61 Starling Marte .25 .60
62 Raul Ibanez .25 .60
63 Austin Jackson .20 .50
64 Yovani Gallardo .20 .50
65 Chris Davis .25 .60
66 Chase Headley .20 .50
67 Alfonso Soriano .25 .60
68 Zack Cozart .20 .50
69 Kevin Youkilis .20 .50
70 Jake Peavy .20 .50
71 C.J. Wilson .20 .50
72 Ike Davis .20 .50
73 Angel Pagan .20 .50
74 Derek Holland .20 .50
75 Doug Fister .20 .50
76 Tim Hudson .25 .60
77 Jaime Garcia .25 .60
78 Miguel Cabrera .30 .75
79 Troy Tulowitzki .30 .75
80 Elvis Andrus .25 .60
81 Cliff Lee .25 .60
82 Kris Medlen .25 .60
83 Jurickson Profar RC .50 1.25
84 Avisail Garcia RC .50 1.25
85 Trevor Rosenthal (RC) .75 2.00
86 Jeurys Familia RC .60 1.50
87 Rob Brantly RC .40 1.00
88 Didi Gregorius RC 1.50 4.00
89 Joe Nathan .20 .50
90 Billy Butler .20 .50
91 Clayton Kershaw .60 1.50
92 David Wright .25 .60
93 Felix Hernandez .25 .60
94 Jason Heyward .25 .60
95 Joe Mauer .25 .60
96 Jordan Zimmermann .25 .60
97 Madison Bumgarner .25 .60
98 Matt Holliday .30 .75
99 Miguel Montero .20 .50
100 Andrew McCutchen .30 .75
101 Paul Goldschmidt .30 .75
102 Roy Halladay .25 .60
103 Salvador Perez .25 .60
104 Stephen Strasburg .30 .75
105 Cody Ross .20 .50
106 Yadier Molina .30 .75
107 David Murphy .20 .50
108 Jose Altuve .25 .60
109 Brandon Phillips .20 .50
110 Dayan Viciedo .20 .50
111 Desmond Jennings .25 .60
112 Mark Reynolds .20 .50
113 Mat Latos .25 .60
114 Homer Bailey .20 .50
115 Corey Hart .20 .50
116 B.J. Upton .25 .60
117 Mike Minor .20 .50
118 Tommy Milone .20 .50
119 Barry Zito .20 .50
120 Josh Beckett .20 .50
121 Mike Trout 2.50 6.00
122 Yu Darvish .30 .75
123 Edwin Encarnacion .30 .75
124 James Shields .20 .50
125 Adam Wainwright .25 .60
126 Shelby Miller RC 1.00 2.50
127 Jake Odorizzi RC .50 1.25
128 L.J. Hoes RC .50 1.25
129 Nick Maronde RC .50 1.25
130 Tyler Cloyd RC .50 1.25
131 Adeiny Hechavarria (RC) .50 1.25
132 Adrian Beltre .30 .75
133 Anthony Gose .20 .50
134 Brandon Beachy .20 .50
135 Cole Hamels .25 .60
136 Derek Jeter .75 2.00
137 Freddie Freeman .40 1.00
138 Jayson Werth .25 .60
139 Joey Votto .30 .75
140 Jose Bautista .25 .60
141 Mariano Rivera .40 1.00
142 Matt Kemp .25 .60
143 Mike Morse .20 .50
144 Pedro Alvarez .20 .50
145 Jason Motte .20 .50
146 Shaun Marcum .20 .50
147 David Ortiz .30 .75
148 Wade Miley .20 .50
149 Yasmani Grandal .20 .50
150 Bryce Harper .50 1.25
151 Carlos Santana .25 .60
152 Shin-Soo Choo .25 .60
153 Carlos Beltran .25 .60
154 Hunter Pence .25 .60
155 Mike Moustakas .25 .60
156 Colby Rasmus .25 .60
157 Jason Kipnis .25 .60
158 Jon Lester .25 .60
159 Ben Zobrist .25 .60
160 Asdrubal Cabrera .25 .60
161 Kyle Lohse .20 .50
162 Bronson Arroyo .20 .50
163 Vance Worley .25 .60
164 Fernando Rodney .20 .50
165 R.A. Dickey .25 .60
166 Alcides Escobar .25 .60
167 Adam Dunn .25 .60
168 Ian Kinsler .25 .60
169 Josh Reddick .20 .50
170 Mike Olt RC .50 1.25
171 Paco Rodriguez RC .60 1.50
172 Darin Ruf RC .75 2.00
173 Tony Cingrani RC .75 2.00
174 Kyuji Fujikawa RC .60 1.50
175 Ali Solis RC .40 1.00
176 Adrian Gonzalez .25 .60
177 Anthony Rizzo .50 1.25
178 Brandon Belt .25 .60
179 Carlos Gonzalez .25 .60
180 Josh Willingham .25 .60
181 Dexter Fowler .25 .60
182 Giancarlo Stanton .30 .75
183 Jean Segura .25 .60
184 Johan Santana .25 .60
185 Josh Hamilton .25 .60
186 Mark Teixeira .25 .60
187 Matt Moore .25 .60
188 Howard Kendrick .20 .50
189 Prince Fielder .25 .60
190 Ryan Howard .25 .60
191 Alex Gordon .25 .60
192 Todd Frazier .25 .60
193 Wilin Rosario .20 .50
194 Yoenis Cespedes .30 .75
195 Aaron Hill .20 .50
196 Ian Desmond .25 .60
197 Delmon Young .25 .60
198 Jay Bruce .25 .60
199 Rickie Weeks .20 .50
200 Buster Posey .40 1.00
201 Neil Walker .25 .60
202 A.J. Burnett .20 .50
203 Hiroki Kuroda .20 .50
204 Kendrys Morales .20 .50
205 Brett Lawrie .25 .60
206 Dan Haren .20 .50
207 Eric Hosmer .25 .60
208 Hisashi Iwakuma .20 .50
209 Jim Johnson .20 .50
210 Ryan Braun .25 .60
211 Carlos Ruiz .20 .50
212 Nick Swisher .25 .60
213 Andre Ethier .25 .60
214 Matt Harrison .20 .50
215 Manny Machado RC 2.50 6.00
216 Tyler Skaggs RC .60 1.50
217 Brock Holt RC .50 1.25
218 Hyun-Jin Ryu RC 1.00 2.50
219 Eury Perez RC .50 1.25
220 Melky Mesa RC .50 1.25
MB Marcel Bilak SP 6.00 15.00

2013 Bowman Blue

*BLUE VET: 1.5X TO 4X BASIC
*BLUE RC: .75X TO 2X BASIC
STATED ODDS 1:34 HOBBY
STATED PRINT RUN 500 SER.#'d SETS

2013 Bowman Gold

*GOLD VET: 1.5X TO 4X BASIC
*GOLD RC: .75X TO 2X BASIC

2013 Bowman Hometown

*HOME.VET: 2X TO 5X BASIC
*HOM.RC: 1X TO 2.5X BASIC
STATED ODDS 1:8 HOBBY

2013 Bowman Orange

*ORANGE VET: 4X TO 10X BASIC
*ORANGE RC: 2X TO 5X BASIC
STATED ODDS 1:67 HOBBY
STATED PRINT RUN 250 SER.#'d SETS

2013 Bowman Silver Ice

*SILVER.VET: 3X TO 8X BASIC
*SILVER.RC: 1.5X TO 4X BASIC
STATED ODDS 1:24 HOBBY

2013 Bowman Lucky Redemption Autographs

STATED ODDS 1:35,745 HOBBY
EXCHANGE DEADLINE 3/31/2016
1 Hyun-Jin Ryu 125.00 250.00
2 Jurickson Profar 20.00 50.00
3 Kevin Gausman 20.00 50.00
4 Yasiel Puig 300.00 600.00
5 Wil Myers 20.00 50.00

2013 Bowman Prospect Autographs

EXCHANGE DEADLINE 5/31/2016
AM Anthony Meo 3.00 8.00
AW Aaron West 3.00 8.00
BB Byron Buxton 15.00 40.00
BL Barret Loux 3.00 8.00
BR Ben Rowen 3.00 8.00
CC Carlos Correa 50.00 120.00
CK Carson Kelly 3.00 8.00
CW Collin Wiles 4.00 10.00

DP Dane Phillips 3.00 8.00
DS Danny Salazar 3.00 8.00
JB Josh Bowman 3.00 8.00
JC Ji-Man Choi 5.00 12.00
JCA Jamie Callahan 4.00 10.00
JG Jeff Gelalich 4.00 10.00
JH Jesse Hahn 3.00 8.00
KD Khris Davis 8.00 20.00
KM Kurtis Muller 5.00 12.00
LL Lenny Linsky 3.00 8.00
MM Matt Magill 3.00 8.00
MMQ Mike McQuillan 3.00 8.00
MW Max White 3.00 8.00
OC Orlando Calixte 3.00 8.00
TG Tyler Gonzales 3.00 8.00
TR Tanner Rahier 5.00 12.00
TS Tayler Scott 3.00 8.00

2013 Bowman Prospect Autographs Blue

*BLUE: .5X TO 1.2X BASIC
PRINT RUNS B/WN 25-500 COPIES PER
NO PRICING ON QTY 25 OR LESS
EXCHANGE DEADLINE 5/31/2016

2013 Bowman Prospect Autographs Orange

*ORANGE: .75X TO 2X BASIC
PRINT RUNS B/WN 10-250 COPIES PER
NO PRICING DUE TO SCARCITY
EXCHANGE DEADLINE 5/31/2016

2013 Bowman Prospects

COMPLETE SET (110) 10.00 25.00
PRINTING PLATE ODDS 1:1881
PLATE PRINT RUN 1 SET PER COLOR
BLACK-CYAN-MAGENTA-YELLOW ISSUED
NO PLATE PRICING DUE TO SCARCITY
BP1 Byron Buxton .40 1.00
BP2 Jonathan Griffin .15 .40
BP3 Mark Montgomery .25 .60
BP4 Gioskar Amaya .15 .40
BP5 Lucas Giolito .25 .60
BP6 Danny Salazar .30 .75
BP7 Jesse Hahn .15 .40
BP8 Tayler Scott .15 .40
BP9 Ji-Man Choi .20 .50
BP10 Tony Renda .15 .40
BP11 Jamie Callahan .15 .40
BP12 Collin Wiles .15 .40
BP13 Tanner Rahier .20 .50
BP14 Max White .15 .40
BP15 Jeff Gelalich .15 .40
BP16 Tyler Gonzales .15 .40
BP17 Mitch Nay .15 .40
BP18 Dane Phillips .15 .40
BP19 Carson Kelly .20 .50
BP20 Darwin Rivera .15 .40
BP21 Arismendy Alcantara .25 .60
BP22 Brandon Maurer .20 .50
BP23 Jin-De Jhang .15 .40
BP24 Bruce Rondon .15 .40
BP25 Jonathan Schoop .15 .40
BP26 Cory Hall .15 .40
BP27 Cory Vaughn .15 .40
BP28 Danny Muno .15 .40
BP29 Edwin Diaz .30 .75
BP30 Williams Astudillo .15 .40
BP31 Hansel Robles .15 .40
BP32 Harold Castro .15 .40
BP33 Ismael Guillon .15 .40
BP34 Jeremy Moore .15 .40
BP35 Jose Cisnero .15 .40
BP36 Jose Peraza .15 .40
BP37 Jose Ramirez .20 .50
BP38 Christian Villanueva .15 .40
BP39 Brett Gerritse .15 .40
BP40 Kris Hall .15 .40
BP41 Matt Stites .15 .40
BP42 Matt Wisler .15 .40
BP43 Matthew Koch .15 .40
BP44 Micah Johnson .20 .50
BP45 Michael Reed .15 .40
BP46 Michael Snyder .15 .40
BP47 Michael Taylor .15 .40
BP48 Nolan Sanburn .15 .40
BP49 Patrick Leonard .15 .40
BP50 Rafael Montero .25 .60
BP51 Ronnie Freeman .15 .40
BP52 Stephen Piscotty .30 .75
BP53 Steven Moya .25 .60
BP54 Chris McFarland .15 .40
BP55 Todd Kibby .15 .40
BP56 Tyler Heineman .15 .40
BP57 Wade Hinkle .15 .40
BP58 Wilfredo Rodriguez .15 .40
BP59 William Cuevas .15 .40
BP60 Yordano Ventura .20 .50
BP61 Zach Bird .15 .40
BP62 Socrates Brito .25 .60
BP63 Ben Rowen .15 .40
BP64 Seth Maness .15 .40
BP65 Corey Dickerson .20 .50
BP66 Travis Witherspoon .15 .40
BP67 Travis Shaw .15 .40
BP68 Lenny Linsky .15 .40
BP69 Anderson Feliz .15 .40
BP70 Casey Stevenson .15 .40
BP71 Pedro Ruiz .15 .40
BP72 Christian Bethancourt .25 .60
BP73 Pedro Guerra .15 .40
BP74 Ronald Guzman .25 .60
BP75 Jake Thompson .15 .40
BP76 Brian Goodwin .20 .50
BP77 Jorge Bonifacio .20 .50
BP78 Dilson Herrera .50 1.25
BP79 Gregory Polanco .30 .75
BP80 Alex Meyer .15 .40
BP81 Gabriel Encinas .15 .40
BP82 Yeicok Calderon .15 .40
BP83 Rio Ruiz .15 .40
BP84 Luis Sardinas .15 .40
BP85 Fu-Lin Kuo .20 .50
BP86 Kelvin De Leon .15 .40
BP87 Wyatt Mathisen .15 .40
BP88 Dorssys Paulino .20 .50
BP89 William Oliver .15 .40
BP90 Rony Bautista .15 .40
BP91 Gabriel Guerrero .20 .50
BP92 Patrick Kivlehan .15 .40
BP93 Ericson Leonora .15 .40
BP94 Mikeson Oliberto .15 .40
BP95 Roman Quinn .25 .60
BP96 Shane Broyles .15 .40
BP97 Cody Buckel .15 .40
BP98 Clayton Blackburn .25 .60
BP99 Evan Rutckyj .15 .40
BP100 Carlos Correa 1.50 4.00
BP101 Ronny Rodriguez .15 .40
BP102 Jayson Aquino .15 .40
BP103 Adalberto Mondesi .50 1.25
BP104 Victor Sanchez .20 .50
BP105 Jairo Beras .25 .60
BP106 Stefen Romero .15 .40
BP107 Alfredo Escalera-Maldonado .20 .50
BP108 Kevin Medrano .15 .40
BP109 Carlos Sanchez .15 .40
BP110 Sam Selman .15 .40

2013 Bowman Prospects Blue

*BLUE: 2X TO 5X BASIC
STATED ODDS 1:67 HOBBY
STATED PRINT RUN 500 SER.#'d SETS

2013 Bowman Prospects Hometown

*HOMETOWN: 1.5X TO 4X BASIC
STATED ODDS 1:8 HOBBY

2013 Bowman Prospects Orange

*ORANGE: 2.5X TO 6X BASIC
STATED ODDS 1:134 HOBBY
STATED PRINT RUN 250 SER.#'d SETS

2013 Bowman Prospects Purple

*PURPLE: 1.2X TO 3X BASIC

2013 Bowman Prospects Silver Ice

*SILVER: 2X TO 5X BASIC
BP1 Byron Buxton 10.00 25.00

2013 Bowman Top 100 Prospects

STATED ODDS 1:12 HOBBY
BTP1 Dylan Bundy .60 1.50
BTP2 Jurickson Profar .30 .75
BTP3 Oscar Taveras .30 .75
BTP4 Travis d'Arnaud .30 .75
BTP5 Jose Fernandez .60 1.50
BTP6 Gerrit Cole 1.50 4.00
BTP7 Zack Wheeler .50 1.25
BTP8 Wil Myers .30 .75
BTP9 Miguel Sano .30 .75
BTP10 Trevor Bauer .40 1.00
BTP11 Xander Bogaerts .75 2.00
BTP12 Tyler Skaggs .40 1.00
BTP13 Billy Hamilton .30 .75
BTP14 Javier Baez 1.00 2.50
BTP15 Mike Zunino .40 1.00
BTP16 Christian Yelich 2.00 5.00
BTP17 Taijuan Walker .30 .75
BTP18 Shelby Miller .60 1.50
BTP19 Jameson Taillon .30 .75
BTP20 Nick Castellanos .75 2.00
BTP21 Archie Bradley .25 .60
BTP22 Danny Hultzen .30 .75
BTP23 Taylor Guerrieri .25 .60
BTP24 Byron Buxton .60 1.50
BTP25 David Dahl .30 .75
BTP26 Francisco Lindor 1.50 4.00
BTP27 Bubba Starling .30 .75
BTP28 Carlos Correa 2.50 6.00
BTP29 Mike Olt .30 .75
BTP30 Jonathan Singleton .30 .75
BTP31 Anthony Rendon 1.25 3.00
BTP32 Gregory Polanco .50 1.25
BTP33 Carlos Martinez .40 1.00
BTP34 Jorge Soler .50 1.25
BTP35 Matt Barnes .30 .75
BTP36 Kevin Gausman .40 1.00
BTP37 Albert Almora .50 1.25
BTP38 Alen Hanson .30 .75
BTP39 Addison Russell .40 1.00
BTP40 Jedd Gyorko .30 .75
BTP41 Gary Sanchez .75 2.00
BTP42 Noah Syndergaard .30 .75
BTP43 Jackie Bradley .60 1.50
BTP44 Mason Williams .30 .75
BTP45 George Springer 1.00 2.50
BTP46 Aaron Sanchez .30 .75
BTP47 Nolan Arenado 1.25 3.00
BTP48 Corey Seager 1.00 2.50
BTP49 Kyle Zimmer .30 .75
BTP50 Tyler Austin .40 1.00
BTP51 Kyle Crick .40 1.00
BTP52 Robert Stephenson .25 .60
BTP53 Joc Pederson .40 1.00
BTP54 Julio Teheran .30 .75
BTP55 Brian Goodwin .30 .75
BTP56 Kaleb Cowart .30 .75
BTP57 Tony Cingrani .50 1.25
BTP58 Yasiel Puig 10.00 25.00
BTP59 Oswaldo Arcia .25 .60
BTP60 Trevor Rosenthal .50 1.25
BTP61 Alex Meyer .25 .60
BTP62 Jake Odorizzi .30 .75
BTP63 Jake Marisnick .30 .75
BTP64 Adam Eaton .40 1.00
BTP65 Rymer Liriano .25 .60
BTP66 Brad Miller .30 .75
BTP67 Max Fried 1.00 2.50
BTP68 Eddie Rosario .50 1.25
BTP69 Justin Nicolino .25 .60
BTP70 Cody Buckel .25 .60
BTP71 Jesse Biddle .30 .75
BTP72 James Paxton .30 .75
BTP73 Allen Webster .30 .75
BTP74 Kyle Gibson .40 1.00
BTP75 Nick Franklin .30 .75
BTP76 Dorssys Paulino .30 .75
BTP77 Hyun-Jin Ryu .60 1.50
BTP78 Courtney Hawkins .25 .60
BTP79 Delino DeShields .25 .60
BTP80 Joey Gallo .75 2.00
BTP81 Hak-Ju Lee .25 .60
BTP82 Kolten Wong .25 .60
BTP83 Aaron Hicks .40 1.00
BTP84 Michael Choice .25 .60
BTP85 Luis Heredia .30 .75
BTP86 C.J. Cron .30 .75
BTP87 Lucas Giolito .40 1.00
BTP88 Daniel Vogelbach .40 1.00
BTP89 Austin Hedges .30 .75
BTP90 Matt Davidson .30 .75
BTP91 Gary Brown .25 .60
BTP92 Daniel Corcino .25 .60
BTP93 Adalberto Mondesi .75 2.00
BTP94 Victor Sanchez .30 .75
BTP95 A.J. Cole .30 .75
BTP96 Joe Panik .40 1.00
BTP97 J.O. Berrios .40 1.00
BTP98 Trevor Story 1.00 2.50
BTP99 Stefen Romero .25 .60
BTP100 Andrew Heaney .30 .75

2013 Bowman Top 100 Prospects Die Cut Refractors

*REF: 5X TO 12X BASIC
STATED ODDS 1:372 HOBBY
STATED PRINT RUN 99 SER.#'d SETS

2013 Bowman Draft

STATED PLATE ODDS 1:2320 HOBBY
PLATE PRINT RUN 1 SET PER COLOR
BLACK-CYAN-MAGENTA-YELLOW ISSUED
NO PLATE PRICING DUE TO SCARCITY
1 Yasiel Puig RC 1.25 3.00
2 Tyler Skaggs RC .50 1.25
3 Nathan Karns RC .30 .75
4 Manny Machado RC 2.00 5.00
5 Anthony Rendon RC 1.50 4.00
6 Gerrit Cole RC 2.00 5.00
7 Sonny Gray RC .50 1.25
8 Henry Urrutia RC .40 1.00
9 Zoilo Almonte RC .40 1.00
10 Jose Fernandez RC .75 2.00
11 Danny Salazar RC .60 1.50
12 Nick Franklin RC .40 1.00
13 Mike Kickham RC .30 .75
14 Alex Colome RC .30 .75
15 Josh Phegley RC .30 .75
16 Drake Britton RC .40 1.00
17 Marcell Ozuna RC .75 2.00
18 Oswaldo Arcia RC .30 .75
19 Didi Gregorius RC 1.25 3.00
20 Zack Wheeler RC .60 1.50
21 Michael Wacha RC .40 1.00
22 Kyle Gibson RC .50 1.25
23 Johnny Hellweg RC .30 .75
24 Dylan Bundy RC .75 2.00
25 Tony Cingrani RC .60 1.50
26 Jurickson Profar RC .40 1.00
27 Scooter Gennett RC .50 1.25
28 Grant Green RC .50 1.25
29 Brad Miller RC .40 1.00
30 Hyun-Jin Ryu RC .75 2.00
31 Jedd Gyorko RC .40 1.00
32 Shelby Miller RC .75 2.00
33 Sean Nolin RC .40 1.00
34 Allen Webster RC .40 1.00
35 Corey Dickerson RC .40 1.00
36 Jarred Cosart RC .40 1.00
37 Evan Gattis RC .60 1.50
38 Kevin Gausman RC .50 1.25
39 Alex Wood RC .40 1.00
40 Christian Yelich RC 2.50 6.00
41 Nolan Arenado RC 1.50 4.00
42 Matt Magill RC .30 .75
43 Jackie Bradley Jr. RC .75 2.00
44 Mike Zunino RC .50 1.25
45 Wil Myers RC .40 1.00

2013 Bowman Draft Blue

*BLUE: 1X TO 2.5X BASIC
STATED ODDS 1:19 HOBBY
STATED PRINT RUN 500 SER.#'d SETS

2013 Bowman Draft Orange

*ORANGE: 1.2X TO 3X BASIC
STATED ODDS 1:37 HOBBY
STATED PRINT RUN 250 SER.#'d SETS

2013 Bowman Draft Red Ice

*RED ICE: 6X TO 15X BASIC
STATED ODDS 1:372 HOBBY
STATED PRINT RUN 25 SER.#'d SETS
1 Yasiel Puig 75.00 150.00

2013 Bowman Draft Silver Ice

*SILVER ICE: 1.2X TO 3X BASIC
STATED ODDS 1:24 HOBBY
1 Yasiel Puig 10.00 25.00

2013 Bowman Draft Draft Picks

BDPP1 Dominic Smith .50 1.25
BDPP2 Kohl Stewart .40 1.00
BDPP3 Josh Hart .30 .75
BDPP4 Nick Ciuffo .30 .75
BDPP5 Austin Meadows .60 1.50
BDPP6 Marco Gonzales .50 1.25
BDPP7 Jonathon Crawford .30 .75
BDPP8 D.J. Peterson .30 .75
BDPP9 Aaron Blair .30 .75
BDPP10 Dustin Peterson .30 .75
BDPP11 Billy Mckinney .40 1.00
BDPP12 Braden Shipley .30 .75
BDPP13 Tim Anderson 1.25 3.00
BDPP14 Chris Anderson .40 1.00
BDPP15 Clint Frazier 1.50 4.00
BDPP16 Hunter Renfroe .50 1.25
BDPP17 Andrew Knapp .30 .75
BDPP18 Corey Knebel .30 .75
BDPP19 Aaron Judge 8.00 20.00
BDPP20 Colin Moran .40 1.00
BDPP21 Ian Clarkin .30 .75
BDPP22 Teddy Stankiewicz .40 1.00
BDPP23 Blake Taylor .30 .75
BDPP24 Hunter Green .30 .75
BDPP25 Kevin Franklin .30 .75
BDPP26 Jonathan Gray .40 1.00
BDPP27 Reese McGuire .40 1.00
BDPP28 Travis Demeritte .40 1.00
BDPP29 Kevin Ziomek .30 .75
BDPP30 Tom Windle .30 .75
BDPP31 Ryan McMahon .40 1.00
BDPP32 J.P. Crawford .50 1.25
BDPP33 Hunter Harvey .40 1.00
BDPP34 Chance Sisco .60 1.50
BDPP35 Riley Unroe .30 .75
BDPP36 Oscar Mercado .50 1.25
BDPP37 Gosuke Katoh .40 1.00
BDPP38 Andrew Church .30 .75
BDPP39 Casey Meisner .30 .75
BDPP40 Ivan Wilson .30 .75
BDPP41 Drew Ward .40 1.00
BDPP42 Thomas Milone .30 .75
BDPP43 Jon Denney .40 1.00
BDPP44 Jan Hernandez .30 .75
BDPP45 Cord Sandberg .40 1.00
BDPP46 Jake Sweaney .30 .75
BDPP47 Patrick Murphy .30 .75
BDPP48 Carlos Salazar .30 .75
BDPP49 Stephen Gonsalves .30 .75
BDPP50 Jonah Heim .30 .75
BDPP51 Kean Wong .30 .75
BDPP52 Tyler Wade .50 1.25
BDPP53 Austin Kubitza .30 .75
BDPP54 Trevor Williams .30 .75
BDPP55 Trae Arbet .30 .75
BDPP56 Ian Mckinney .30 .75
BDPP57 Robert Kaminsky .40 1.00
BDPP58 Brian Navarreto .30 .75
BDPP59 Alex Murphy .30 .75
BDPP60 Jordon Austin .40 1.00
BDPP61 Jacob Nottingham .30 .75
BDPP62 Chris Rivera .30 .75
BDPP63 Trey Williams .50 1.25
BDPP64 Conner Greene .30 .75
BDPP65 Ian Stiffler .30 .75
BDPP66 Phil Ervin .30 .75
BDPP67 Roel Ramirez .30 .75
BDPP68 Michael Lorenzen .40 1.00
BDPP69 Jason Martin .30 .75
BDPP70 Aaron Blanton .30 .75
BDPP71 Dylan Manwaring .30 .75
BDPP72 Luis Guillorme .40 1.00
BDPP73 Brennan Middleton .30 .75
BDPP74 Austin Nicely .30 .75
BDPP75 Ian Hagenmiller .30 .75
BDPP76 Nelson Molina .30 .75
BDPP77 Denton Keys .40 1.00
BDPP78 Kendall Coleman .30 .75
BDPP79 Alec Grosser .30 .75
BDPP80 Ricardo Bautista .30 .75
BDPP81 John Costa .30 .75
BDPP82 Joseph Odom .30 .75
BDPP83 Elier Rodriguez .30 .75
BDPP84 Miles Williams .30 .75
BDPP85 Derrick Penilla .30 .75
BDPP86 Bryan Hudson .30 .75
BDPP87 Jordan Barnes .30 .75
BDPP88 Tyler Kinley .30 .75
BDPP89 Randolph Gassaway .30 .75
BDPP90 Blake Higgins .40 1.00
BDPP91 Caleb Kellogg .30 .75
BDPP92 Joseph Monge .30 .75
BDPP93 Steven Negron .30 .75
BDPP94 Justin Williams .40 1.00
BDPP95 William White .30 .75
BDPP96 Jared Wilson .30 .75
BDPP97 Niko Spezial .30 .75
BDPP98 Gabe Speier .30 .75
BDPP99 Juan Avila .30 .75
BDPP100 Jason Kanzler .30 .75
BDPP101 Tyler Brosius .30 .75
BDPP102 Tyler Vail .30 .75
BDPP103 Adam Landecker .30 .75
BDPP104 Ethan Carnes .30 .75
BDPP105 Austin Wilson .40 1.00
BDPP106 Jon Keller .30 .75
BDPP107 Gaither Bumgardner .30 .75
BDPP108 Garrett Gordon .30 .75
BDPP109 Connor Oliver .30 .75
BDPP110 Cody Harris .30 .75
BDPP111 Brandon Easton .30 .75
BDPP112 Matt Derosier .30 .75
BDPP113 Jeremy Hadley .30 .75
BDPP114 Will Morris .30 .75
BDPP115 Sean Hurley .30 .75
BDPP116 Orrin Sears .30 .75
BDPP117 Sean Townsley .30 .75
BDPP118 Chad Christensen .30 .75
BDPP119 Travis Ott .30 .75
BDPP120 Justin Maffei .30 .75
BDPP121 Reed Harper .30 .75
BDPP122 Adam Westmoreland .30 .75
BDPP123 Adrian Castano .30 .75
BDPP124 Hyrum Formo .30 .75
BDPP125 Jake Stone .40 1.00
BDPP126 Joel Effertz .30 .75
BDPP127 Matt Southard .30 .75
BDPP128 Jorge Perez .30 .75
BDPP129 Willie Medina .30 .75
BDPP130 Ty Afenir .30 .75

2013 Bowman Draft Draft Picks Blu

*BLUE: 1X TO 2.5X BASIC
STATED ODDS 1:19 HOBBY
STATED PRINT RUN 500 SER.#'d SETS
BDPP19 Aaron Judge 30.00 80.00

2013 Bowman Draft Draft Picks Orange

*ORANGE: 1.2X TO 3X BASIC INSERTS
STATED ODDS 1:37 HOBBY
STATED PRINT RUN 250 SER.#'d SETS
BDPP19 Aaron Judge 40.00 100.00

2013 Bowman Draft Draft Picks Red Ice

*RED ICE: 1.5X TO 4X BASIC
STATED PRINT RUN 25 SER.#'d SETS
BDPP5 Austin Meadows 40.00 100.00
BDPP15 Clint Frazier 40.00 100.00
BDPP19 Aaron Judge 150.00 400.00
BDPP26 Jonathan Gray 25.00 60.00

2013 Bowman Draft Draft Picks Silver Ice

*SILVER ICE: 1.2X TO 3X BASIC
STATED ODDS 1:24 HOBBY
BDPP19 Aaron Judge 40.00 100.00

2013 Bowman Draft Dual Draftee

COMPLETE SET (10) 5.00 12.00
STATED ODDS 1:18 HOBBY
AG M.Appel/J.Gray .30 .75
BD T.Ball/J.Denney .30 .75
BM K.Bryant/C.Moran 1.00 2.50
CJ I.Clarkin/E.Jagielo .25 .60
CS R.Stanek/N.Ciuffo .40 1.00
FM A.Meadows/C.Frazier 1.00 2.50
GK M.Gonzales/R.Kaminsky .30 .75
JC A.Judge/I.Clarkin 2.00 5.00
JJ E.Jagielo/A.Judge 2.00 5.00
MM A.Meadows/R.McGuire .40 1.00

2013 Bowman Draft Dual Draftee Autographs

STATED ODDS 1:11,700 HOBBY
STATED PRINT RUN 25 SER.#'d SETS
EXCHANGE DEADLINE 11/30/2016
AG Appel/Gray EXCH 20.00 50.00
BD Ball/Denney EXCH 15.00 40.00
BM K.Bryant/C.Moran 150.00 250.00
CJ I.Clarkin/E.Jagielo 40.00 80.00
FM Meadows/Frazier EXCH 200.00 400.00
GK M.Gonzales/R.Kaminsky 30.00 60.00
JC A.Judge/I.Clarkin 60.00 150.00
JJ E.Jagielo/A.Judge 60.00 150.00
MM Meadows/McGuire EXCH 125.00 250.00

2013 Bowman Draft Future of the Franchise

COMPLETE SET (30) 12.50 30.00
STATED ODDS 1:18 HOBBY
AR Addison Russell .40 1.00
AS Aaron Sanchez .30 .75
BB Byron Buxton .60 1.50
BH Billy Hamilton .30 .75
BHA Bryce Harper .60 1.50
CC Carlos Correa 2.50 6.00
CH Courtney Hawkins .25 .60
CY Christian Yelich 2.00 5.00
FL Francisco Lindor 1.50 4.00
GC Gerrit Cole 1.50 4.00
GS Gary Sanchez .75 2.00
HD Hunter Dozier .25 .60
JB Javier Baez 1.00 2.50
JC J.P. Crawford .40 1.00
JG Jonathan Gray .30 .75
JGY Jedd Gyorko .30 .75
JP Jurickson Profar .30 .75
JS Jean Segura .30 .75
JT Julio Teheran .30 .75
KC Kyle Crick .40 1.00
MH Matt Harvey .30 .75
MM Manny Machado 1.50 4.00
MT Mike Trout 3.00 8.00
MZ Mike Zunino .40 1.00
NC Nick Castellanos .75 2.00
OT Oscar Taveras .30 .75
PG Paul Goldschmidt .40 1.00
WM Wil Myers .30 .75
XB Xander Bogaerts .75 2.00
YP Yasiel Puig 1.00 2.50

2013 Bowman Draft Future of the Franchise Blue

*BLUE: 1.5X TO 4X BASIC
STATED ODDS 1:272 HOBBY
STATED PRINT RUN 250 SER.#'d SETS
YP Yasiel Puig 12.50 30.00

2013 Bowman Draft Future's Game Relics

STATED ODDS 1:589 HOBBY
STATED PRINT RUN 99 SER.#'d SETS
AA Arismendy Alcantara 4.00 10.00
AC A.J. Cole 6.00 15.00
AH Austin Hedges 4.00 10.00
AJ A.J. Jimenez 5.00 12.00
AR Andre Rienzo 4.00 10.00
ARA Anthony Ranaudo 4.00 10.00
ARU Addison Russell 4.00 10.00
BN Brandon Nimmo 8.00 20.00
CB Christian Bethancourt 5.00 12.00
CC C.J. Cron 5.00 12.00
CCO Carlos Contreras 10.00 25.00
CO Chris Owings 4.00 10.00
CR C.J. Riefenhauser 4.00 10.00
DD Delino DeShields 4.00 10.00
DH Dilson Herrera 5.00 12.00
EB Eddie Butler 4.00 10.00
ER Eduardo Rodriguez 5.00 12.00
ERO Enny Romero 4.00 10.00
FL Francisco Lindor 8.00 20.00
JB Jesse Biddle 5.00 12.00
JC Ji-Man Choi 4.00 10.00
JGA Jesus Galindo 4.00 10.00
JL Jordan Lennerton 5.00 12.00
JM James McCann 5.00 12.00
KC Kyle Crick 4.00 10.00
KW Kolten Wong 5.00 12.00
MA Miguel Almonte 5.00 12.00
MD Matt Davidson 5.00 12.00
MF Maikel Franco 10.00 25.00
MY Michael Ynoa 4.00 10.00
RD Rafael De Paula 4.00 10.00
RF Reymond Fuentes 4.00 10.00
RM Rafael Montero 5.00 12.00
YA Yeison Asencio 4.00 10.00
YV Yordano Ventura 4.00 10.00

2013 Bowman Draft Scout Autographs

STATED ODDS 1:27,081 HOBBY
STATED PRINT RUN 25 SER.#'d SETS
FB Freddy Berowski 12.50 30.00
JK Jeff Katofsky 20.00 50.00
JS J.P. Schwartz 20.00 50.00

2013 Bowman Draft Scout Breakouts

COMPLETE SET (50) 15.00 40.00
STATED ODDS 1:18 HOBBY
AA Andrew Aplin .40 1.00
AAL Aaron Altherr .40 1.00
AB Andy Burns .40 1.00
AR Alexis Rivera .40 1.00
AT Andrew Toles .40 1.00
AW Adam Walker .50 1.25
BB B.J. Boyd .40 1.00
BBR Bryan Brickhouse .40 1.00
BD Brandon Drury .40 1.00
CB Christian Binford .40 1.00
CBO Chris Bostick .40 1.00
CE C.J. Edwards .60 1.50
CT Chris Taylor .60 1.50
DW Daniel Winkler .40 1.00
GC Garin Cecchini .40 1.00
GE Gabriel Encinas .40 1.00
JH Josh Hader .75 2.00
JL Jake Lamb .60 1.50
JP Jeffrey Popick .40 1.00
JPO Jorge Polanco .40 1.00
JT Jake Thompson .40 1.00
JW Jacob Wilson .40 1.00
KF Kendry Flores .75 2.00
KP Kevin Plawecki .40 1.00
LJ Luke Jackson .40 1.00
MJ Micah Johnson .50 1.25
MS Mark Sappington .40 1.00
MW Mac Williamson .60 1.50
NF Nolan Fontana .50 1.25
NK Nick Kingham .40 1.00
NW Nick Williams .50 1.25
OC Orlando Castro .40 1.00
PJ Pierce Johnson .50 1.25
PK Patrick Kivlehan .40 1.00
PO Peter O'Brien .50 1.25
PT Preston Tucker .60 1.50
RA R.J. Alvarez .40 1.00
RC Ryan Casteel .50 1.25
RD Rafael De Paula .40 1.00
RM Raul Mondesi 1.25 3.00
RMO Rafael Montero .60 1.50
RS Rock Shoulders .40 1.00
SA Stetson Allie .60 1.50
SS Sam Selman .40 1.00
TD Taylor Dugas .50 1.25
TH Tyler Heineman .40 1.00
TM Tom Murphy .40 1.00
TP Tyler Pike .40 1.00
WR Wilfredo Rodriguez .40 1.00
YP Yasiel Puig 1.50 4.00

2013 Bowman Draft Scout Breakouts Die-Cuts

*DIE CUT: 1.2X TO 3X BASIC

2013 Bowman Draft Scout Breakouts Die-Cuts X-Fractors

*X-FRACTOR: 2X TO 5X BASIC
STATED ODDS 1:349 HOBBY
STATED PRINT RUN 99 SER.#'d SETS

2013 Bowman Draft Scout Breakouts Autographs

STATED ODDS 1:12,220 HOBBY
STATED PRINT RUN 24 SER.#'d SETS
EXCHANGE DEADLINE 11/30/2016
AA Andrew Aplin 15.00 40.00
AW Adam Walker 20.00 50.00
JT Jake Thompson EXCH 12.50 30.00
MW Mac Williamson EXCH 40.00 80.00
NW Nick Williams EXCH 15.00 40.00
PK Patrick Kivlehan 12.50 30.00
TM Tom Murphy EXCH 6.00 15.00
TP Tyler Pike 20.00 50.00

2013 Bowman Draft Top Prospects

STATED PLATE ODDS 1:2320 HOBBY
PLATE PRINT RUN 1 SET PER COLOR
BLACK-CYAN-MAGENTA-YELLOW ISSUED
NO PLATE PRICING DUE TO SCARCITY
TP1 Byron Buxton .40 1.00
TP2 Tyler Austin .25 .60
TP3 Mason Williams .20 .50
TP4 Albert Almora .30 .75
TP5 Joey Gallo .50 1.25
TP6 Jesse Biddle .20 .50
TP7 David Dahl .20 .50
TP8 Kevin Gausman .25 .60
TP9 Jorge Soler .30 .75
TP10 Carlos Correa 1.50 4.00
TP11 Preston Tucker .25 .60
TP12 Jameson Taillon .20 .50
TP13 Joc Pederson .25 .60
TP14 Max Fried .60 1.50
TP15 Taijuan Walker .20 .50
TP16 Chris Bostick .15 .40
TP17 Francisco Lindor 1.00 2.50
TP18 Daniel Vogelbach .25 .60
TP19 Kaleb Cowart .25 .60
TP20 George Springer .60 1.50
TP21 Yordano Ventura .20 .50
TP22 Noah Syndergaard .20 .50
TP23 Ty Hensley .20 .50
TP24 C.J. Cron .20 .50
TP25 Addison Russell .25 .60
TP26 Kyle Crick .25 .60
TP27 Javier Baez .60 1.50
TP28 Kolten Wong .15 .40
TP29 Taylor Guerrieri .15 .40
TP30 Archie Bradley .15 .40
TP31 Gary Sanchez .50 1.25
TP32 Billy Hamilton .20 .50
TP33 Alen Hanson .20 .50
TP34 Jonathan Singleton .20 .50
TP35 Mark Montgomery .25 .60
TP36 Nick Castellanos .50 1.25
TP37 Courtney Hawkins .15 .40
TP38 Gregory Polanco .30 .75
TP39 Matt Barnes .20 .50
TP40 Xander Bogaerts .50 1.25
TP41 Dorssys Paulino .20 .50
TP42 Corey Seager .60 1.50
TP43 Alex Meyer .15 .40
TP44 Aaron Sanchez .20 .50
TP45 Miguel Sano .20 .50

2013 Bowman Draft Top Prospects Blue

*BLUE: 1.5X TO 4X BASIC
STATED ODDS 1:19 HOBBY
STATED PRINT RUN 500 SER.#'d SETS

2013 Bowman Draft Top Prospects Orange

*ORANGE: 2X TO 5X BASIC
STATED ODDS 1:37 HOBBY
STATED PRINT RUN 250 SER.#'d SETS

2013 Bowman Draft Top Prospects Red Ice

*RED ICE: 12X TO 30X BASIC
STATED ODDS 1:372 HOBBY
STATED PRINT RUN 25 SER.#'d SETS

2013 Bowman Draft Top Prospects Silver Ice

*SILVER ICE: 2X TO 5X BASIC
STATED ODDS 1:24 HOBBY

2014 Bowman

COMPLETE SET (220) 10.00 25.00
PLATE PRINT RUN 1 SET PER COLOR
BLACK-CYAN-MAGENTA-YELLOW ISSUED
NO PLATE PRICING DUE TO SCARCITY
1 Derek Jeter .60 1.50
2 Gerrit Cole .25 .60
3 Derek Holland .15 .40
4 Brandon Beachy .15 .40
5 Jay Bruce .20 .50
6 Oswaldo Arcia .15 .40
7 Ian Kennedy .15 .40
8 Joe Nathan .15 .40
9 Chris Johnson .15 .40
10 Mike Leake .15 .40
11 Andrelton Simmons .15 .40
12 Trevor Rosenthal .20 .50
13 Evan Gattis .15 .40
14 Starling Marte .20 .50
15 Coco Crisp .15 .40
16 Starlin Castro .15 .40
17 Desmond Jennings .20 .50
18 Austin Jackson .15 .40

19 Giancarlo Stanton .25 .60
20 Nolan Arenado .30 .75
21 Jordan Zimmermann .20 .50
22 Johnny Cueto .20 .50
23 R.A. Dickey .20 .50
24 Bartolo Colon .15 .40
25 Carlos Gomez .15 .40
26 Jason Grilli .15 .40
27 Craig Kimbrel .20 .50
28 Salvador Perez .20 .50
29 Matt Cain .20 .50
30 Yu Darvish .25 .60
31 Adrian Beltre .25 .60
32 Sonny Gray .20 .50
33 Zack Wheeler .20 .50
34 Paul Goldschmidt .25 .60
35 Ivan Nova .20 .50
36 Matt Harvey .20 .50
37 Will Middlebrooks .15 .40
38 Torii Hunter .15 .40
39 Andrew Lambo RC .25 .60
40 Marcus Semien RC .25 .60
41 Wilmer Flores RC .30 .75
42 Kolten Wong RC .30 .75
43 James Paxton RC .40 1.00
44 Abraham Almonte RC .25 .60
45 Avisail Garcia .20 .50
46 Francisco Liriano .15 .40
47 Jayson Werth .20 .50
48 James Shields .15 .40
49 Josh Reddick .15 .40
50 Miguel Cabrera .25 .60
51 CC Sabathia .20 .50
52 Tony Cingrani .20 .50
53 Edwin Encarnacion .25 .60
54 Chase Headley .15 .40
55 Ian Desmond .15 .40
56 Carlos Gonzalez .20 .50
57 Mat Latos .20 .50
58 Curtis Granderson .20 .50
59 Alex Gordon .20 .50
60 Anibal Sanchez .15 .40
61 Ubaldo Jimenez .15 .40
62 Aroldis Chapman .25 .60
63 Jean Segura .20 .50
64 Yovani Gallardo .15 .40
65 Domonic Brown .20 .50
66 Dustin Pedroia .25 .60
67 Cole Hamels .20 .50
68 Jarrod Parker .15 .40
69 John Lackey .20 .50
70 Hiroki Kuroda .15 .40
71 Kendrys Morales .15 .40
72 Anthony Rizzo .40 1.00
73 Tim Lincecum .20 .50
74 David Freese .15 .40
75 Hanley Ramirez .20 .50
76 Albert Pujols .30 .75
77 Carlos Beltran .20 .50
78 Evan Longoria .20 .50
79 Jose Fernandez .25 .60
80 Matt Moore .20 .50
81 Jarred Cosart .15 .40
82 Hunter Pence .20 .50
83 Kevin Pillar RC .25 .60
84 Xander Bogaerts RC .75 2.00
85 Yordano Ventura RC .30 .75
86 Taijuan Walker RC .25 .60
87 Jake Marisnick RC .25 .60
88 Masahiro Tanaka RC .75 2.00
89 Alex Rios .20 .50
90 Jose Reyes .20 .50
91 Jeff Samardzija .15 .40
92 Jed Lowrie .15 .40
93 Adam Wainwright .20 .50
94 Max Scherzer .25 .60
95 Daniel Nava .15 .40
96 Anthony Rendon .25 .60
97 Adam Lind .20 .50
98 Jon Lester .20 .50
99 Adrian Gonzalez .20 .50
100 Clayton Kershaw .50 1.25
101 Matt Holliday .25 .60
102 Felix Hernandez .20 .50
103 Hisashi Iwakuma .20 .50
104 J.J. Hardy .15 .40
105 Yoenis Cespedes .25 .60
106 Christian Yelich .30 .75
107 Robinson Cano .20 .50
108 Alex Cobb .15 .40
109 Aaron Hill .15 .40
110 Manny Machado .25 .60
111 Wei-Yin Chen .15 .40
112 Allen Craig .20 .50
113 Joe Kelly .15 .40
114 Joey Votto .25 .60
115 Troy Tulowitzki .25 .60
116 Billy Butler .15 .40
117 Brian McCann .20 .50
118 Koji Uehara .15 .40
119 Jorge De La Rosa .15 .40
120 Alfonso Soriano .20 .50
121 Chris Sale .25 .60
122 Michael Cuddyer .15 .40
123 Josh Hamilton .20 .50
124 Mike Napoli .15 .40
125 Jose Bautista .20 .50
126 Josh Donaldson .20 .50
127 Nick Castellanos RC .75 2.00
128 Jonathan Schoop RC .25 .60
129 Jimmy Nelson RC .25 .60
130 Matt Davidson RC .30 .75
131 Andre Rienzo RC .25 .60
132 Billy Hamilton RC .30 .75
133 Homer Bailey .15 .40
134 Yadier Molina .25 .60
135 Michael Wacha .20 .50
136 Prince Fielder .20 .50
137 Mike Minor .15 .40
138 Wade Miley .15 .40
139 Carl Crawford .20 .50
140 Chris Davis .15 .40
141 Gio Gonzalez .20 .50
142 Brandon Moss .15 .40
143 Jonny Gomes .15 .40
144 Elvis Andrus .20 .50
145 Buster Posey .30 .75
146 Justin Verlander .25 .60
147 C.J. Wilson .15 .40
148 Pablo Sandoval .20 .50
149 Asdrubal Cabrera .20 .50
150 Andrew McCutchen .25 .60
151 Andre Ethier .20 .50
152 Kris Medlen .20 .50
153 Freddie Freeman .30 .75
154 Martin Prado .15 .40
155 A.J. Burnett .15 .40
156 Nick Swisher .20 .50
157 Brad Ziegler .15 .40
158 Mike Zunino .15 .40
159 Wil Myers .15 .40
160 Jason Kipnis .20 .50
161 Jered Weaver .20 .50
162 Trevor Bauer .25 .60
163 Zack Greinke .20 .50
164 David Wright .20 .50
165 Cliff Lee .20 .50
166 Matt Carpenter .25 .60
167 Justin Upton .20 .50
168 Mike Trout 1.25 3.00
169 Shelby Miller .20 .50
170 Jurickson Profar .20 .50
171 Christian Bethancourt RC .25 .60
172 J.R. Murphy RC .25 .60
173 Josmil Pinto RC .25 .60
174 Michael Choice RC .25 .60
175 Erik Johnson RC .25 .60
176 Jose Ramirez RC 2.00 5.00
177 Adam Jones .20 .50
178 Brett Lawrie .20 .50
179 Kevin Gausman .25 .60
180 Roy Halladay .20 .50
181 Ian Kinsler .20 .50
182 Andrew Cashner .15 .40
183 Chase Utley .20 .50
184 Patrick Corbin .20 .50
185 Marco Scutaro .20 .50
186 Ryan Zimmerman .20 .50
187 Jose Iglesias .20 .50
188 Eric Hosmer .20 .50
189 Joe Mauer .20 .50
190 Jedd Gyorko .15 .40
191 Mark Trumbo .15 .40
192 Tim Hudson .20 .50
193 Pedro Alvarez .15 .40
194 Tyler Skaggs .15 .40
195 Nick Franklin .15 .40
196 Chris Archer .15 .40
197 Carlos Santana .20 .50
198 Julio Teheran .20 .50
199 Fernando Rodney .15 .40
200 Bryce Harper .40 1.00
201 Matt Kemp .20 .50
202 Jason Heyward .20 .50
203 Brandon Phillips .15 .40
204 Carlos Ruiz .15 .40
205 Shane Victorino .20 .50
206 Jonathan Lucroy .20 .50
207 Hyun-Jin Ryu .20 .50
208 David Ortiz .25 .60
209 David Price .20 .50
210 Jacoby Ellsbury .20 .50
211 Madison Bumgarner .20 .50
212 Wilin Rosario .15 .40
213 Stephen Strasburg .25 .60
214 Yasiel Puig .25 .60
215 Tim Beckham RC .40 1.00
216 Travis d'Arnaud RC .30 .75
217 Enny Romero RC .25 .60
218 David Holmberg RC .25 .60
219 Chris Owings RC .25 .60
220 Onelki Garcia RC .25 .60

2014 Bowman Black

*BLK VET: 10X TO 25X BASIC VET
*BLK RC: 15X TO 40X BASIC RC
STATED ODDS 1:547 HOBBY
STATED PRINT RUN 25 SER.#'d SETS
1 Derek Jeter 60.00 120.00

2014 Bowman Blue

*BLUE VET: 2X TO 5X BASIC VET
*BLUE RC: 1.2X TO 3X BASIC RC
STATED ODDS 1:27 HOBBY
STATED PRINT RUN 500 SER.#'d SETS

2014 Bowman Gold

*GOLD VET: 6X TO 15X BASIC VET
*GOLD RC: 4X TO 10X BASIC RC
STATED ODDS 1:273 HOBBY
STATED PRINT RUN 50 SER.#'d SETS
1 Derek Jeter 40.00 80.00
168 Mike Trout 30.00 60.00

2014 Bowman Green

*GREEN VET: 4X TO 10X BASIC VET
*GREEN RC: 2.5X TO 6X BASIC RC
STATED ODDS 1:91 HOBBY
STATED PRINT RUN 150 SER.#'d SETS

2014 Bowman Hometown

*HOMETOWN VET: 1.5X TO 4X BASIC VET
*HOMETOWN RC: 1X TO 2.5X BASIC RC
STATED ODDS 1:8 HOBBY

2014 Bowman Orange

*ORANGE VET: 3X TO 8X BASIC VET
*ORANGE RC: 2X TO 5X BASIC RC
STATED ODDS 1:55 HOBBY
STATED PRINT RUN 250 SER.#'d SETS

2014 Bowman Red Ice

*RED ICE VET: 10X TO 25X BASIC VET
*RED ICE RC: 10X TO 25X BASIC RC
STATED ODDS 1:275 HOBBY
STATED PRINT RUN 25 SER.#'d SETS
1 Derek Jeter 60.00 120.00

2014 Bowman Silver

*SILVER VET: 6X TO 15X BASIC VET
*SILVER RC: 4X TO 10X BASIC RC
STATED ODDS 1:182 HOBBY
STATED PRINT RUN 75 SER.#'d SETS

2014 Bowman Silver Ice

*SILVER ICE VET: 2X TO 5X BASIC VET
*SILVER ICE RC: 1.2X TO 3X BASIC RC
STATED ODDS 1:24 HOBBY

2014 Bowman Yellow

*YEL VET: 6X TO 15X BASIC VET
*YEL RC: 4X TO 10X BASIC RC
STATED ODDS 1:138 HOBBY
STATED PRINT RUN 99 SER.#'d SETS

2014 Bowman '89 Bowman is Back Silver Diamond Refractors

COMPLETE SET (145)
BOWMAN ODDS 1:24 HOBBY
STERLING ODDS 1:6 HOBBY
89BIBAC A.J. Cole BS .60 1.50
89BIBAJ Alex Jackson BD .50 1.25
89BIBAJ Adam Jones BI 1.25 3.00
89BIBAM Andrew McCutchen BP 1.25 3.00
89BIBAM Austin Meadows BD .60 1.50
89BIBAM Alex Meyer BS .60 1.50
89BIBAN Aaron Nola BD 2.50 6.00
89BIBAR Addison Russell BS 1.00 2.50
89BIBAS Aaron Sanchez BS .60 1.50
89BIBBB Byron Buxton B .50 1.25
89BIBBH Billy Hamilton B .50 1.25
89BIBBH Bryce Harper BI 2.50 6.00
89BIBBJ Bo Jackson B .60 1.50
89BIBBL Ben Lively BD .40 1.00
89BIBBP Buster Posey BS 1.25 3.00
89BIBBS Braden Shipley BD .40 1.00
89BIBCB Christian Binford BD .40 1.00
89BIBCB Craig Biggio B .50 1.25
89BIBCC Carlos Correa BP 4.00 10.00
89BIBCD Chris Davis BP .75 2.00
89BIBCE C.J. Edwards BS .75 2.00
89BIBCF Clint Frazier BI 4.00 10.00
89BIBCFI Carlton Fisk BI 1.25 3.00
89BIBCK Clayton Kershaw BI 3.00 8.00
89BIBCM Colin Moran BI 1.00 2.50
89BIBCR Cal Ripken B 2.00 5.00
89BIBCS Corey Seager BD 1.50 4.00
89BIBDD David Dahl BD .50 1.25
89BIBDE Dennis Eckersley BI 1.25 3.00
89BIBDJ Derek Jeter B 1.50 4.00
89BIBDO David Ortiz BI 1.50 4.00
89BIBDP Dustin Pedroia BP 1.25 3.00
89BIBDR Daniel Robertson BP 1.00 2.50
89BIBDS Deion Sanders BI 1.25 3.00
89BIBDS Dominic Smith BS .60 1.50
89BIBDT Devon Travis BP .75 2.00
89BIBDW David Wright B .50 1.25
89BIBEB Eddie Butler BI 1.00 2.50
89BIBEL Evan Longoria BP 1.00 2.50
89BIBER Eddie Rosario BS 1.25 3.00
89BIBFF Freddie Freeman BS 1.25 3.00
89BIBFH Felix Hernandez BI 1.25 3.00
89BIBFL Francisco Lindor B 2.50 6.00
89BIBGB George Brett B 1.25 3.00
89BIBGM Greg Maddux B .75 2.00
89BIBGP Gregory Polanco BI 1.50 4.00
89BIBGS Gary Sanchez BI 3.00 8.00
89BIBGS Giancarlo Stanton BP 1.25 3.00
89BIBHH Hunter Harvey BD .40 1.00
89BIBHJR Hyun-Jin Ryu BP 1.00 2.50
89BIBHO Henry Owens BS .75 2.00
89BIBHR Hunter Renfroe BP 1.00 2.50
89BIBJA Jose Abreu BP 6.00 15.00
89BIBJA Jorge Alfaro BS .75 2.00
89BIBJB Josh Bell BD .75 2.00
89BIBJB Javier Baez BP 3.00 8.00
89BIBJB Jesse Biddle BI 1.25 3.00
89BIBJE Jacoby Ellsbury B .50 1.25
89BIBJG Jonathan Gray BP 1.00 2.50
89BIBJG Joey Gallo BS 1.25 3.00
89BIBJH Jeff Hoffman BD .60 1.50
89BIBJP Joc Pederson BS 1.00 2.50
89BIBJS Jorge Soler BI 2.00 5.00
89BIBJSM John Smoltz BI 1.50 4.00
89BIBJT Julio Teheran BS .75 2.00
89BIBJT Jameson Taillon BD .50 1.25
89BIBJU Julio Urias BD 2.00 5.00
89BIBJV Joey Votto BS 1.00 2.50
89BIBJV Justin Verlander BP 1.25 3.00
89BIBKB Kris Bryant B 3.00 8.00
89BIBKF Kyle Freeland BD .75 2.00
89BIBKG Ken Griffey Jr. B 1.25 3.00
89BIBKM Kodi Medeiros BD .40 1.00
89BIBKS Kyle Schwarber BS 2.50 6.00
89BIBKS Kohl Stewart BP .75 2.00
89BIBLG Lucas Giolito BD .60 1.50
89BIBLS Luis Severino BD .60 1.50
89BIBMA Mark Appel B .50 1.25
89BIBMB Mookie Betts BS 12.00 30.00
89BIBMC Michael Conforto BD .75 2.00
89BIBMC Matt Carpenter BP 1.25 3.00
89BIBMF Maikel Franco B .50 1.25
89BIBMM Mark McGwire BP 2.50 6.00
89BIBMM Manny Machado BI 1.50 4.00
89BIBMP Max Pentecost BD .40 1.00
89BIBMS Max Scherzer BS 1.00 2.50
89BIBMS Miguel Sano BI 1.25 3.00
89BIBMT Mike Trout BP 6.00 15.00
89BIBMTA Masahiro Tanaka BP 2.50 6.00
89BIBMW Michael Wacha BI 1.25 3.00
89BIBNC Nick Castellanos BI 3.00 8.00
89BIBNG Nick Gordon BS .75 2.00
89BIBNS Noah Syndergaard BS .75 2.00
89BIBOS Ozzie Smith BP 1.50 4.00
89BIBOT Oscar Taveras B .50 1.25
89BIBPG Paul Goldschmidt BI 1.50 4.00
89BIBPM Paul Molitor B .60 1.50
89BIBPS Pablo Sandoval BP 1.00 2.50
89BIBRB Ryan Braun BS .75 2.00
89BIBRC Robinson Cano BS .75 2.00
89BIBRH Rosell Herrera BP 1.25 3.00
89BIBRM Raul Mondesi BI 3.00 8.00
89BIBRS Robert Stephenson BI 1.00 2.50
89BIBRY Robin Yount BP 1.25 3.00
89BIBTB Tyler Beede BD .60 1.50
89BIBTD Travis d'Arnaud B .50 1.25
89BIBTG Tom Glavine B .50 1.25
89BIBTG Tony Gwynn BP 1.25 3.00
89BIBTG Tyler Glasnow BS 1.00 2.50
89BIBTK Tyler Kolek BS .60 1.50
89BIBTK Trea Turner BD 1.25 3.00
89BIBTT Troy Tulowitzki B .60 1.50
89BIBTW Taijuan Walker BI 1.00 2.50
89BIBWB Wade Boggs BP 1.00 2.50
89BIBWF Wilmer Flores B .50 1.25
89BIBWM Wil Myers B .40 1.00
89BIBXB Xander Bogaerts B 1.25 3.00
89BIBYD Yu Darvish BI 1.50 4.00
89BIBYM Yadier Molina B .60 1.50
89BIBYP Yasiel Puig B .60 1.50
BIB89AG Alexander Guerrero BC .50 1.25
BIB89BH Bryce Harper BC 1.00 2.50
BIB89CS Chris Sale BC .60 1.50
BIB89DP David Price BC .50 1.25
BIB89FT Frank Thomas BC .60 1.50
BIB89GC Gary Carter BC .50 1.25
BIB89GK Gosuke Katoh BC .60 1.50
BIB89JF Jose Fernandez BC .60 1.50
BIB89JK Jason Kipnis BC .50 1.25
BIB89JS Jean Segura BC .50 1.25
BIB89KC Kyle Crick BC .40 1.00
BIB89MC Miguel Cabrera BC .60 1.50
BIB89MP Mike Piazza BC .60 1.50
BIB89MR Mariano Rivera BC .75 2.00
BIB89MT Masahiro Tanaka BC 1.25 3.00
BIB89RT Rowdy Tellez BC .40 1.00
BIB89SG Sonny Gray BC .50 1.25
BIB89SS Shae Simmons BC .40 1.00
BIB89YC Yoenis Cespedes BC .60 1.50
89BIBBLI Brandon Nimmo BD .60 1.50
89BIBBSW Blake Swihart BD .50 1.25
89BIBJBE Jose Berrios BD .60 1.50
89BIBJHA Josh Hader BD 1.00 2.50
89BIBMBU Madison Bumgarner BS .75 2.00
89BIBSST Stephen Strasburg BC .60 1.50

2014 Bowman '89 Bowman is Back Autographs Black Refractors

STATED ODDS 1:16,200 HOBBY
STERLING ODDS 1:302 HOBBY
PRINT RUNS B/WN 15-25 COPIES PER
EXCHANGE DEADLINE 4/30/2017
STERLING EXCHANGE 12/31/2017
89BIBCC Carlos Correa/25 150.00 300.00
89BIBDP Dustin Pedroia/25 30.00 80.00
89BIBDR Daniel Robertson/25 40.00 100.00
89BIBEL Evan Longoria/25 30.00 80.00
89BIBJA Jose Abreu/25 300.00 500.00
89BIBJG Jonathan Gray/25 30.00 80.00
89BIBMT Mike Trout/25 300.00 500.00
89BIBOS Ozzie Smith/25 40.00 100.00
89BIBWB Wade Boggs/25 30.00 60.00
89BIBACB Craig Biggio/25 50.00 100.00
89BIBACR Ripken Jr. EXCH 75.00 200.00
89BIBAJT Julio Teheran/25 15.00 40.00
89BIBAKB Kris Bryant/25 900.00 1200.00
89BIBAKG Griffey Jr. 250.00 350.00
89BIBAMA Mark Appel/25 75.00 200.00
89BIBANG Nick Gordon/25 50.00 100.00
89BIBAPM Paul Molitor EXCH/25 20.00 50.00
89BIBARB Ryan Braun/25 12.00 30.00
89BIBARC Robinson Cano/25 25.00 60.00
89BIBATG Glavine EXCH 75.00 150.00
89BIBATT Tulowitzki EXCH 50.00 100.00
89BIBAWM Wil Myers/25 75.00 150.00
89BIBAXB Xander Bogaerts/25 75.00 150.00

2014 Bowman Black Collection Autographs

BOWMAN ODDS 1:6500 HOBBY
BOW.CHROME ODDS 1:3667 HOBBY
BOW.DRAFT ODDS 1:7350 HOBBY
STERLING ODDS 1:226 HOBBY
STATED PRINT RUN 25 SER.#'d SETS
BOWMAN EXCH DEADLINE 4/30/2017
INCEPTION EXCH DEADLINE 6/30/2017
PLATINUM EXCH DEADLINE 7/31/2017
BOW.CHR.EXCH DEADLINE 9/30/2017
BOW.DRAFT EXCH DEADLINE 11/30/2017
STERLING EXCH DEADLINE 12/31/2017
BBAB Akeem Bostick BP 12.00 30.00
BBBB Byron Buxton 75.00 150.00
BBCF Chris Flexen BP 10.00 25.00
BBCS Cord Sandberg BP 12.00 30.00
BBCV Cory Vaughn BP 10.00 25.00
BBDR Daniel Robertson BP 12.00 30.00
BBDT Devon Travis BP 12.00 30.00
BBJA Jose Abreu BP 200.00 300.00
BBJB Javier Baez BP 25.00 200.00
BBJBA Jake Barrett BP 25.00 60.00
BBKB Kris Bryant BP 300.00 500.00
BBLT Lewis Thorpe BP 10.00 25.00
BBMA Mark Appel BP 60.00 120.00
BBOT Oscar Taveras BP 50.00 100.00
BBRH Rosell Herrera BP 6.00 15.00
BBRT Raimel Tapia BP 20.00 50.00
BBSS Shae Simmons BP 40.00 80.00
BBWR Wendell Rijo BP 15.00 40.00
BBYG Yimi Garcia BP 10.00 25.00
BBZB Zach Borenstein BP 10.00 25.00
BBCAA Arismendy Alcantara BI 20.00 50.00
BBCAB Archie Bradley BI 12.00 30.00
BBCAB Akeem Bostick BC 10.00 25.00
BBCAB Alex Blandino BD 15.00 40.00
BBCABU Andy Burns BC EXCH 20.00 50.00
BBCAG Alexander Guerrero BI 30.00 80.00
BBCAJ Alex Jackson BD 75.00 150.00
BBCAM Adalberto Mejia BI 12.00 30.00
BBCAN Aaron Nola BD 60.00 150.00
BBCAS Aaron Sanchez BS EXCH 12.00 30.00
BBCAT Alberto Tirado BC EXCH 20.00 50.00
BBCAT Andrew Toles 10.00 25.00
BBCAW Adam Walker BI 12.00 30.00
BBCBAN Blake Anderson BD 10.00 25.00
BBCBD Braxton Davidson BD 25.00 60.00
BBCBL Ben Lively BC 10.00 25.00
BBCBT Brandon Trinkwon EXCH 10.00 25.00
BBCBZ Bradley Zimmer BS 20.00 50.00
BBCCA Cody Anderson BC 10.00 25.00
BBCCB Chris Bostick 10.00 25.00
BBCCBI Christian Binford 15.00 40.00
BBCCC Carlos Contreras BC 10.00 25.00
BBCCJ Connor Joe BD 10.00 25.00
BBCCM Casey Meisner 10.00 25.00
BBCCP Cesar Puello 20.00 50.00
BBCCT Chris Taylor 12.00 30.00
BBCDH Derek Hill BD 10.00 25.00
BBCDM Daniel McGrath 30.00 60.00
BBCDP Daniel Palka BI 6.00 15.00
BBCDW Daniel Winkler BC 10.00 25.00
BBCDW Kean Wong BC 10.00 25.00
BBCEE Edwin Escobar BI 10.00 25.00
BBCEF Erick Fedde BD 25.00 60.00
BBCFB Franklin Barreto BC EXCH 50.00 100.00
BBCFC Franchy Cordero 15.00 40.00
BBCFG Foster Griffin BD 10.00 25.00
BBCFL-Francisco Lindor BI 20.00 50.00
BBCFR Franmil Reyes BC 12.00 30.00
BBCFW Forrest Wall BD 10.00 25.00
BBCGE Gabriel Encinas EXCH 10.00 25.00
BBCGH Grant Holmes BS 40.00 100.00
BBCGS Gary Sanchez BI 15.00 40.00
BBCIK Isiah Kiner-Falefa BC 20.00 50.00
BBCJF Jack Flaherty BD 15.00 40.00
BBCJG Jonathan Gray BI 12.00 30.00
BBCJG Joan Gregorio 10.00 25.00
BBCJGA Jacob Gatewood BS EXCH 20.00 50.00
BBCJH Jeff Hoffman BD 25.00 60.00
BBCJH Jason Hursh 20.00 50.00
BBCJHA Josh Hader 10.00 25.00
BBCJL Jake Lamb BI EXCH 25.00 60.00
BBCJR Jose Rondon BC 6.00 15.00
BBCJS Jonathan Schoop BI 15.00 40.00
BBCJS Justus Sheffield BD 10.00 25.00
BBCJU Julio Urias BI EXCH 50.00 100.00
BBCJU Jose Urena BC 10.00 25.00
BBCJW Jamie Westbrook BC 10.00 25.00
BBCJWI Jacob Wilson BC EXCH 15.00 40.00
BBCKD Kelly Dugan BC 20.00 50.00
BBCKF Kendry Flores EXCH 10.00 25.00
BBCKG Kevin Garcia EXCH 15.00 40.00
BBCKS Kyle Schwarber BD 60.00 150.00
BBCLR Luigi Rodriguez BC 10.00 25.00
BBCLW LeVon Washington BC 10.00 25.00
BBCLW Luke Weaver BD 20.00 50.00
BBCMA Mark Appel BI EXCH 30.00 60.00
BBCMCH Matt Chapman BD 10.00 25.00
BBCMF Maikel Franco 50.00 100.00
BBCMJ Micah Johnson EXCH 10.00 25.00
BBCMM Mike Mayers EXCH 10.00 25.00
BBCMP Max Pentecost BD 15.00 40.00
BBCMS Marcus Semien BI 10.00 25.00
BBCMSA Miguel Sano BI 30.00 60.00
BBCNG Nick Gordon BD 60.00 120.00
BBCNH Nick Howard BD 20.00 50.00
BBCNS Noah Syndergaard BI 20.00 50.00
BBCNT Nick Travieso 20.00 50.00
BBCPT Preston Tucker 6.00 15.00
BBCRB Rony Bautista 10.00 25.00
BBCRM Rafael Montero BI 12.00 30.00
BBCRO Roberto Osuna BI EXCH 20.00 50.00
BBCRS Robert Stephenson BS 60.00 150.00
BBCRU Richard Urena BC 10.00 25.00
BBCSG Severino Gonzalez 10.00 25.00
BBCSS Shae Simmons BC EXCH 30.00 60.00
BBCTB Tyler Beede BS EXCH 20.00 50.00
BBCTK Tyler Kolek BD 12.00 30.00
BBCTT Trea Turner BD 30.00 80.00
BBCTW Tyler Wade 10.00 25.00
BBCTW Taijuan Walker BI 12.00 30.00
BBCWG Willy Garcia BC 15.00 40.00
BBCZL Zech Lemond BD 10.00 25.00

2014 Bowman Future's Game Relics

STATED ODDS 1:3700 HOBBY
STATED PRINT RUN 25 SER.#'d SETS
FGRAA Arismendy Alcantara 6.00 15.00
FGRAB Archie Bradley 10.00 25.00
FGRAC A.J. Cole 15.00 40.00
FGRAH Austin Hedges 6.00 15.00
FGRAR Addison Russell 12.00 30.00
FGRARA Anthony Ranaudo 8.00 20.00
FGRBB Byron Buxton 100.00 200.00
FGRBN Brandon Nimmo 8.00 20.00
FGRCC C.J. Cron 8.00 20.00
FGRDD Delino DeShields 4.00 10.00
FGRDH Dilson Herrera 4.00 10.00
FGREB Eddie Butler 15.00 40.00
FGRER Eduardo Rodriguez 4.00 10.00
FGRFL Francisco Lindor 12.00 30.00
FGRGP Gregory Polanco 100.00 200.00
FGRJB Jesse Biddle 10.00 25.00
FGRJG Joey Gallo 15.00 40.00
FGRJP Joc Pederson 12.00 30.00
FGRKC Kyle Crick 6.00 15.00
FGRMA Miguel Almonte 12.00 30.00
FGRMF Maikel Franco 15.00 40.00
FGRMY Michael Ynoa 4.00 10.00
FGRNS Noah Syndergaard 4.00 80.00
FGRRM Rafael Montero 15.00 40.00

2014 Bowman Golden Debut Contract Winner

BGCAF Adriano Fieramosca 5.00 12.00

2014 Bowman Lucky Redemption Autographs

EXCH 1 ODDS 1:24,300 HOBBY
EXCH 2 ODDS 1:24,300 HOBBY
EXCH 3 ODDS 1:24,300 HOBBY
EXCH 4 ODDS 1:24,300 HOBBY
EXCH 5 ODDS 1:24,300 HOBBY
EXCHANGE DEADLINE 4/30/2017
1 Kris Bryant EXCH 300.00 600.00
2 Kris Bryant EXCH 300.00 600.00
3 Kris Bryant EXCH 300.00 600.00
4 Kris Bryant EXCH 300.00 600.00
5 Kris Bryant EXCH 300.00 600.00

2014 Bowman Oversized Purple Ice Autographs

STATED PRINT RUN 25 SER.#'d SETS
EXCHANGE DEADLINE 4/30/2017
OIBM Billy McKinney EXCH 15.00 40.00
OICF Clint Frazier EXCH 50.00 100.00
OIDT Devon Travis 30.00 60.00
OIJA Jose Abreu 75.00 200.00
OIJU Julio Urias EXCH 60.00 120.00
OIMA Mark Appel 60.00 120.00
OIMF Maikel Franco 30.00 60.00
OIMJ Micah Johnson EXCH 20.00 50.00
OIOT Oscar Taveras 60.00 120.00

2014 Bowman Oversized Silver Ice

STATED PRINT RUN 99 SER.#'d SETS
OIAR Anthony Ranaudo 4.00 10.00
OIBM Billy McKinney 5.00 12.00
OICF Clint Frazier 15.00 40.00
OIDT Devon Travis 4.00 10.00
OIJA Jose Abreu 20.00 50.00
OIJU Julio Urias 20.00 50.00
OIMF Maikel Franco 5.00 12.00
OIMJ Micah Johnson 4.00 10.00
OIOT Oscar Taveras 5.00 12.00

2014 Bowman Prospect Autographs

EXCHANGE DEADLINE 4/30/2017
PAAR Alex Reyes 15.00 40.00
PAGS Gus Schlosser 3.00 8.00
PAIK Isiah Kiner-Faleta 3.00 8.00
PAJW Jamie Westbrook 3.00 8.00
PAKB Kris Bryant 50.00 120.00
PAKW Kyle Waldrop 3.00 8.00
PALV Logan Vick 3.00 8.00
PALW Levon Washington 3.00 8.00
PAMA Mark Appel 8.00 20.00
PAMF Michael Feliz 3.00 8.00
PAMT Michael Taylor 4.00 10.00
PANK Nick Kingham 3.00 8.00
PARH Robert Hefflinger 3.00 8.00
PASM Sam Moll 3.00 8.00
PASP Shawn Pleffner 3.00 8.00
PATC Tim Cooney 3.00 8.00
PATCO Thomas Coyle 3.00 8.00
PATG Trevor Gretzky 3.00 8.00
PATK Tommy Kahnle 3.00 8.00
PATM Tommy Murphy 3.00 8.00
PAWM Wyatt Mathisen 3.00 8.00
PAZP Zach Petrick 3.00 8.00

2014 Bowman Prospect Autographs Blue

*BLUE: .5X TO 1.2X BASIC
STATED PRINT RUN 500 SER.#'d SETS
EXCHANGE DEADLINE 4/30/2017

2014 Bowman Prospect Autographs Gold

*GOLD: 1X TO 2.5X BASIC
STATED PRINT RUN 50 SER.#'d SETS
EXCHANGE DEADLINE 4/30/2017

2014 Bowman Prospect Autographs Green

*GREEN: .75X TO 2X BASIC
STATED PRINT RUN 100 SER.#'d SETS
EXCHANGE DEADLINE 4/30/2017

2014 Bowman Prospect Autographs Orange

*ORANGE: .6X TO 1.5X BASIC
STATED PRINT RUN 250 SER.#'d SETS
EXCHANGE DEADLINE 4/30/2017

2014 Bowman Prospect Autographs Silver

*SILVER: 1X TO 2.5X BASIC
STATED PRINT RUN 35 SER.#'d SETS
EXCHANGE DEADLINE 4/30/2017
PAKB Kris Bryant 125.00 300.00

2014 Bowman Prospects

COMPLETE SET (111) 10.00 25.00
R.WILSON ODDS 1:9300 HOBBY
PLATE PRINT RUN 1 SET PER COLOR
BLACK-CYAN-MAGENTA-YELLOW ISSUED
NO PLATE PRICING DUE TO SCARCITY
BP1 Jason Hursh .15 .40
BP2 Trey Ball .15 .40
BP3 Jacob May .20 .50
BP4 Rosell Herrera .25 .60
BP5 Mark Appel .20 .50
BP6 Julio Urias .75 2.00
BP7 Devin Williams .40 1.00
BP8 Ryan Eades .15 .40
BP9 Eric Jagielo .15 .40
BP10 Zach Borenstein .20 .50
BP11 Jake Barrett .20 .50
BP12 Wendell Rijo .15 .40
BP13 Armando Rivero .15 .40
BP14 Chris Taylor .75 2.00
BP15 Edwin Diaz .30 .75
BP16 Dylan Floro .20 .50
BP17 Jose Abreu 1.25 3.00
BP18 Luke Jackson .15 .40
BP19 Billy Burns .15 .40
BP20 Leonardo Molina .15 .40
BP21 Billy McKinney .20 .50
BP22 Chris Flexen .20 .50
BP23 Kyle Parker .20 .50
BP24 Pierce Johnson .20 .50
BP25 Kris Bryant 1.25 3.00
BP26 Micah Johnson .15 .40
BP27 Raimel Tapia .20 .50
BP28 Preston Tucker .25 .60
BP29 Christian Binford .15 .40
BP30 Ty Buttrey .15 .40
BP31 Brandon Trinkwon .20 .50
BP32 Lewis Thorpe .15 .40
BP33 Devon Travis .15 .40
BP34 Cesar Puello .15 .40
BP35 Tyler Wade .25 .60
BP36 Daniel Robertson .20 .50
BP37 Maikel Franco .20 .50
BP38 Cody Reed .15 .40
BP39 Sam Moll .15 .40
BP40 Logan Vick .15 .40
BP41 Gus Schlosser .15 .40
BP42 Levon Washington .15 .40
BP43 Chris Beck .15 .40
BP44 Tim Cooney .15 .40
BP45 Michael Feliz .20 .50
BP46 Jamie Westbrook .15 .40
BP47 Alex Reyes .25 .60
BP48 Trevor Gretzky .15 .40
BP49 Isiah Kiner-Falefa .25 .60
BP50 Shawn Pleffner .15 .40
BP51 Hunter Dozier .15 .40
BP52 Hunter Renfroe .20 .50
BP53 Ryder Jones .15 .40
BP54 Tyler Danish .15 .40
BP55 Matt McPherson .15 .40
BP56 Gosuke Katoh .25 .60
BP57 Andrew Thurman .15 .40
BP58 Jordan Paroubeck .15 .40
BP59 Tucker Neuhaus .15 .40
BP60 Dillon Overton .15 .40
BP61 Ryon Healy .25 .60
BP62 Chase Anderson .15 .40
BP63 Daniel Palka .15 .40
BP64 Duane Underwood .15 .40
BP65 Carlos Contreras .15 .40
BP66 Ben Lively .15 .40
BP67 Anthony Santander .20 .50
BP68 Melvin Mercedes .15 .40
BP69 Josh Hader .40 1.00
BP70 Yimi Garcia .15 .40
BP71 Orlando Arcia .25 .60
BP72 Matthew Bowman .15 .40
BP73 Jacob deGrom 1.00 2.50
BP74 John Gant .15 .40
BP75 Robert Gsellman .20 .50
BP76 Gabriel Ynoa .20 .50
BP77 Anthony Aliotti .15 .40
BP78 Chris Bostick .20 .50
BP79 Drew Granier .15 .40
BP80 Austin Wright .15 .40
BP81 Brandon Cumpton .15 .40
BP82 Kendry Flores .15 .40
BP83 Jason Rogers .15 .40
BP84 Ryne Stanek .15 .40
BP85 Nomar Mazara .40 1.00
BP86 Victor Payano .15 .40
BP87 Franklin Barreto .20 .50
BP88 Santiago Nessy .15 .40
BP89 Michael Ratterree .15 .40
BP90 Manuel Margot .25 .60
BP91 Gabriel Rosa .15 .40
BP92 Nelson Rodriguez .20 .50
BP93 Yency Almonte .15 .40
BP94 Bobby Coyle .15 .40
BP95 Pat Stover .15 .40

BP96 Wuilmer Becerra .15 .40
BP97 Miller Diaz .15 .40
BP98 Akeel Morris .15 .40
BP99 Kenny Giles .20 .50
BP100 Brian Ragira .15 .40
BP101 Victor De Leon .15 .40
BP102 Steven Ramos .15 .40
BP103 Chris Kohler .15 .40
BP104 Seth Mejias-Brean .15 .40
BP105 Miguel Alfredo Gonzalez .15 .40
BP106 Alexander Guerrero .20 .50
BP107 Jose Herrera .15 .40
BP108 Tyler Marlette .15 .40
BP109 Mookie Betts 3.00 8.00
BP110 Joe Wendle .15 .40
BPRW Russell Wilson SP 60.00 120.00

2014 Bowman Prospects Black

*BLACK: 6X TO 15X BASIC
STATED PRINT RUN 99 SER.#'d SETS

2014 Bowman Prospects Blue

*BLUE: 1.5X TO 4X BASIC
STATED ODDS 1:79 HOBBY
STATED PRINT RUN 500 SER.#'d SETS

2014 Bowman Prospects Green

*GREEN: 3X TO 8X BASIC
STATED PRINT RUN 199 SER.#'d SETS

2014 Bowman Prospects Hometown

*HOMETOWN: 1.2X TO 3X BASIC
STATED ODDS 1:8 HOBBY

2014 Bowman Prospects Orange

*ORANGE: 2.5X TO 6X BASIC
STATED ODDS 1:150 HOBBY
STATED PRINT RUN 250 SER.#'d SETS

2014 Bowman Prospects Purple

*PURPLE: 1X TO 2.5X BASIC

2014 Bowman Prospects Red Ice

*RED ICE: 15X TO 40X BASIC
STATED ODDS 1:24 HOBBY
STATED PRINT RUN 25 SER.#'d SETS
BP6 Julio Urias 25.00 60.00
BP17 Jose Abreu 80.00 200.00
BP25 Kris Bryant 100.00 200.00
BP37 Maikel Franco 15.00 40.00
BP47 Alex Reyes 15.00 40.00
BP90 Manuel Margot 20.00 50.00
BP106 Alexander Guerrero 15.00 40.00
BP109 Mookie Betts 20.00 50.00

2014 Bowman Prospects Silver Ice

*SILVER ICE: 1.5X TO 4X BASIC
STATED ODDS 1:24 HOBBY
BP17 Jose Abreu 10.00 25.00

2014 Bowman Draft

STATED PLATE ODDS 1:5225 HOBBY
PLATE PRINT RUN 1 SET PER COLOR
BLACK-CYAN-MAGENTA-YELLOW ISSUED
NO PLATE PRICING DUE TO SCARCITY
DP1 Tyler Kolek .20 .50
DP2 Kyle Schwarber .75 2.00
DP3 Alex Jackson .25 .60
DP4 Aaron Nola 1.25 3.00
DP5 Kyle Freeland .40 1.00
DP6 Jeff Hoffman .30 .75
DP7 Michael Conforto .40 1.00
DP8 Max Pentecost .20 .50
DP9 Kodi Medeiros .20 .50
DP10 Trea Turner .60 1.50
DP11 Tyler Beede .30 .75
DP12 Sean Newcomb .30 .75
DP14 Erick Fedde .20 .50
DP15 Nick Howard .20 .50
DP16 Casey Gillaspie .30 .75
DP17 Bradley Zimmer .30 .75
DP18 Grant Holmes .20 .50
DP19 Derek Hill .20 .50
DP20 Cole Tucker .20 .50
DP21 Matt Chapman 1.00 2.50
DP22 Michael Chavis 1.00 2.50
DP23 Luke Weaver .60 1.50
DP24 Foster Griffin .20 .50
DP25 Alex Blandino .20 .50
DP26 Luis Ortiz .20 .50
DP27 Justus Sheffield .40 1.00
DP28 Braxton Davidson .20 .50
DP29 Michael Kopech .50 1.25
DP30 Jack Flaherty .75 2.00
DP32 Ryan Ripken .25 .60
DP33 Forrest Wall .30 .75
DP34 Blake Anderson .20 .50
DP35 Derek Fisher .30 .75
DP36 Mike Papi .20 .50
DP37 Connor Joe .20 .50
DP38 Chase Vallot .20 .50
DP39 Jacob Gatewood .20 .50
DP40 A.J. Reed .40 1.00
DP41 Justin Twine .20 .50
DP42 Spencer Adams .25 .60
DP43 Jake Stinnett .20 .50
DP44 Nick Burdi .20 .50
DP45 Matt Imhof .20 .50
DP46 Ryan Castellani .20 .50
DP47 Sean Reid-Foley .20 .50
DP48 Monte Harrison .30 .75
DP49 Michael Gettys .25 .60
DP50 Aramis Garcia .20 .50
DP51 Joe Gatto .20 .50
DP52 Cody Reed .20 .50
DP53 Jacob Lindgren .25 .60
DP54 Scott Blewett .20 .50
DP55 Taylor Sparks .20 .50
DP56 Ti'Quan Forbes .20 .50
DP57 Cameron Varga .20 .50
DP58 Grant Hockin .20 .50
DP59 Alex Verdugo .40 1.00
DP60 Austin DeCarr .20 .50
DP61 Sam Travis .40 1.00
DP62 Trey Supak .20 .50
DP63 Marcus Wilson .20 .50
DP64 Zech Lemond .20 .50
DP65 Jakson Reetz .20 .50
DP66 Jeff Brigham .20 .50
DP67 Chris Ellis .20 .50
DP68 Gareth Morgan .20 .50
DP69 Mitch Keller .30 .75
DP70 Spencer Turnbull .20 .50
DP71 Daniel Gossett .20 .50
DP72 Garrett Fulenchek .20 .50
DP73 Brett Graves .20 .50
DP74 Ronnie Williams .20 .50
DP75 Isan Diaz .50 1.25
DP76 Andrew Morales .20 .50
DP77 Brent Honeywell .30 .75
DP78 Carson Sands .20 .50
DP79 Dylan Cease .50 1.25
DP80 Jace Fry .20 .50
DP81 J.D. Davis .30 .75
DP82 Austin Cousino .20 .50
DP83 Aaron Brown .20 .50
DP84 Milton Ramos .20 .50
DP85 Brian Gonzalez .20 .50
DP86 Bobby Bradley .25 .60
DP87 Chad Sobotka .20 .50
DP88 Jonathan Holder .20 .50
DP89 Nick Wells .20 .50
DP90 Josh Morgan .20 .50
DP91 Brian Anderson .20 .50
DP92 Mark Zagunis .20 .50
DP93 Michael Cederoth .25 .60
DP94 Dylan Davis .20 .50
DP95 Matt Railey .20 .50
DP96 Eric Skoglund .20 .50
DP97 Wyatt Strahan .20 .50
DP98 John Richy .20 .50
DP99 Grayson Greiner .20 .50
DP100 Jordan Luplow .20 .50
DP101 Jake Cosart .25 .60
DP102 Michael Mader .20 .50
DP103 Brian Schales .20 .50
DP104 Brett Austin .20 .50
DP105 Ryan Yarbrough .30 .75
DP106 Chris Oliver .20 .50
DP107 Matt Morgan .20 .50
DP108 Trace Loehr .20 .50
DP109 Austin Gomber .25 .60
DP110 Casey Soltis .20 .50
DP111 Troy Stokes .20 .50
DP112 Nick Torres .20 .50
DP113 Jeremy Rhoades .20 .50
DP114 Jordan Montgomery .40 1.00
DP115 Gavin LaValley .20 .50
DP116 Brett Martin .20 .50
DP117 Sam Hentges .20 .50
DP118 Taylor Gushue .20 .50
DP119 Jordan Schwartz .20 .50
DP120 Justin Steele .20 .50
DP121 Jake Reed .20 .50
DP122 Rhys Hoskins 3.00 8.00
DP123 Kevin Padlo .20 .50
DP124 Lane Thomas .20 .50
DP125 Dustin DeMuth .20 .50
DP126 Nick Gordon .25 .60
DP127 Auston Bousfield .20 .50
DP128 Jordan Foley .20 .50
DP129 Corey Ray .20 .50
DP130 Jared Walker .20 .50
DP131 Tejay Antone .20 .50
DP132 Shane Zeile .20 .50

2014 Bowman Draft Blue

*BLUE: 1.2X TO 3X BASIC
STATED ODDS 1:52 HOBBY
STATED PRINT RUN 399 SER.#'d SETS

2014 Bowman Draft Green

*GREEN: 5X TO 12X BASIC
RANDOM INSERTS IN PACKS
STATED PRINT RUN 75 SER.#'d SETS

2014 Bowman Draft Orange Ice

*ORANGE ICE: 8X TO 20X BASIC
RANDOM INSERTS IN PACKS
STATED PRINT RUN 25 SER.#'d SETS

2014 Bowman Draft Purple Ice

*PURPLE ICE: 5X TO 12X BASIC
STATED ODDS 1:211 HOBBY
STATED PRINT RUN 99 SER.#'d SETS

2014 Bowman Draft Red Ice

*RED ICE: 4X TO 10X BASIC
STATED ODDS 1:137 HOBBY
STATED PRINT RUN 150 SER.#'d SETS

2014 Bowman Draft Silver Ice

*SILVER ICE: 1.2X TO 3X BASIC
STATED ODDS 1:12 HOBBY

2014 Bowman Draft Draft Night

COMPLETE SET (7) 3.00 8.00
STATED ODDS 1:12 HOBBY
DNDH Derek Hill .25 .60
DNGH Grant Holmes .25 .60
DNJG Jacob Gatewood .25 .60
DNKM Kodi Medeiros .25 .60
DNMC Michael Chavis 1.25 3.00
DNMH Monte Harrison .40 1.00
DNNG Nick Gordon .30 .75

2014 Bowman Draft Dual Draftees

COMPLETE SET (10) 3.00 8.00
STATED ODDS 1:18 HOBBY
DDCK Chavis/Kopech 1.25 3.00
DDHB Nick Howard .25 .60
Alex Blandino
DDHP Jeff Hoffman .40 1.00
Max Pentecost
DDJC A.Jackson/M.Conforto .50 1.25
DDKA Blake Anderson .25 .60
Tyler Kolek
DDKN A.Nola/T.Kolek 1.50 4.00
DDNH Grant Holmes .40 1.00
Sean Newcomb
DDSG K.Schwarber/N.Gordon 1.00 2.50
DDSS J.Stinnett/K.Schwarber 1.00 2.50
DDWF Flaherty/Luke Weaver 1.00 2.50

2014 Bowman Draft Dual Draftees Autographs

STATED ODDS 1:23,000 HOBBY
STATED PRINT RUN 25 SER.#'d SETS
EXCHANGE DEADLINE 11/30/2017
DDHB Nick Howard 10.00 25.00
Alex Blandino EXCH
DDHP Hoffman/Pentecost 50.00 100.00
DDKA Anderson/Kolek EXCH 50.00 100.00
DDKN Nola/Kolek EXCH 15.00 40.00
DDSG Schwarber/Gordon EXCH 100.00 200.00
DDSS Stinnett/Schwarber EXCH 75.00 150.00
DDWF Flaherty/Weaver EXCH 20.00 50.00

2014 Bowman Draft Future's Game Relics

RANDOM INSERTS IN PACKS
STATED PRINT RUN 50 SER.#'d SETS
FGRBS Braden Shipley 4.00 10.00
FGRCB Christian Binford 4.00 10.00
FGRCS Corey Seager 25.00 60.00
FGRHH Hunter Harvey 4.00 10.00
FGRHO Henry Owens 5.00 12.00
FGRJA Jorge Alfaro 5.00 12.00
FGRJB Josh Bell 8.00 20.00
FGRJBE Jose Berrios 6.00 15.00
FGRJC J.P. Crawford 4.00 10.00
FGRJP Jose Peraza 10.00 25.00
FGRJT Jake Thompson 4.00 10.00
FGRJW Jesse Winker 5.00 12.00
FGRLG Lucas Giolito 6.00 15.00
FGRLS Luis Severino 6.00 15.00
FGRMF Michael Feliz 5.00 12.00
FGRPO Peter O'Brien 5.00 12.00
FGRRH Rosell Herrera 6.00 15.00
FGRRN Renato Nunez 8.00 20.00

2014 Bowman Draft Initiation

STATED 1:552 HOBBY
STATED PRINT RUN 99 SER.#'d SETS
BIAB Alex Blandino 2.00 5.00
BIAJ Alex Jackson 2.50 6.00
BIAN Aaron Nola 12.00 30.00
BIBD Braxton Davidson 2.00 5.00
BIBZ Bradley Zimmer 3.00 8.00
BICG Casey Gillaspie 3.00 8.00
BICT Cole Tucker 2.00 5.00
BIDH Derek Hill 2.00 5.00
BIEF Erick Fedde 2.00 5.00
BIFG Foster Griffin 2.00 5.00
BIFW Forrest Wall 3.00 8.00
BIGH Grant Holmes 2.00 5.00
BIJF Jack Flaherty 8.00 20.00
BIJG Jacob Gatewood 2.00 5.00
BIJH Jeff Hoffman 3.00 8.00
BIJL Jacob Lindgren 2.50 6.00
BIJS Justus Sheffield 4.00 10.00
BIKF Kyle Freeland 4.00 10.00
BIKM Kodi Medeiros 2.00 5.00
BIKS Kyle Schwarber 8.00 20.00
BILO Luis Ortiz 2.00 5.00
BILW Luke Weaver 6.00 15.00
BIMC Michael Conforto 4.00 10.00
BIMCH Matt Chapman 10.00 25.00
BIMCHA Michael Chavis 10.00 25.00
BIMK Michael Kopech 5.00 12.00
BIMP Max Pentecost 2.00 5.00
BING Nick Gordon 2.50 6.00
BINH Nick Howard 2.00 5.00
BISN Sean Newcomb 3.00 8.00
BITB Tyler Beede 3.00 8.00
BITK Tyler Kolek 2.00 5.00
BITS Trey Supak 2.00 5.00
BITT Trea Turner 6.00 15.00
BIZL Zech Lemond 2.00 5.00

2014 Bowman Draft Scouts Breakout

COMPLETE SET (35) 10.00 25.00
STATED ODDS 1:18 HOBBY
BSBAB Aaron Blair .40 1.00
BSBAJ Aaron Judge 6.00 15.00
BSBAR Alex Reyes .60 1.50
BSBBJ Brian Johnson .40 1.00
BSBBL Ben Lively .40 1.00
BSBBP Brett Phillips .50 1.25
BSBCP Chad Pinder .40 1.00
BSBCS Chance Sisco .75 2.00
BSBCW Chad Wallach .60 1.50
BSBDR Daniel Robertson .50 1.25
BSBES Edmundo Sosa .40 1.00
BSBFM Francellis Montas .40 1.00
BSBGG Gabriel Guerrero .40 1.00
BSBJB Jake Bauers .60 1.50
BSBJD Jose De Leon .60 1.50
BSBJH Jabari Henry .75 2.00
BSBJJ JaCoby Jones .60 1.50
BSBJL Jordy Lara .40 1.00
BSBJP Jose Peraza .40 1.00
BSBJW Justin Williams .50 1.25
BSBKW Kyle Waldrop .40 1.00
BSBKZ Kevin Ziomek .40 1.00
BSBLS Luis Severino .60 1.50
BSBLW LeVon Washington .40 1.00
BSBMM Marcos Molina .50 1.25
BSBMO Matt Olson .60 1.50
BSBNL Nick Longhi .60 1.50
BSBNM Nomar Mazara 1.00 2.50
BSBRM Ryan McMahon .40 1.00
BSBRN Renato Nunez .75 2.00
BSBSC Sean Coyle .40 1.00
BSBSM Steven Matz .75 2.00
BSBTD Tyler Danish .40 1.00
BSBTG Tayron Guerrero .40 1.00
BSBWL Will Locante .40 1.00

2014 Bowman Draft Top Prospects

STATED PLATE ODDS 1:5225 HOBBY
PLATE PRINT RUN 1 SET PER COLOR
BLACK-CYAN-MAGENTA-YELLOW ISSUED
NO PLATE PRICING DUE TO SCARCITY
TP1 Kohl Stewart .20 .50
TP2 Miguel Sano .25 .60
TP3 Carlos Correa 1.00 2.50
TP4 Mark Appel .25 .60
TP5 Jameson Taillon .25 .60
TP6 Raul Mondesi .60 1.50
TP7 Jorge Alfaro .25 .60
TP8 Max Fried .75 2.00
TP9 Lucas Giolito .30 .75
TP10 Austin Meadows .30 .75
TP11 Clint Frazier .75 2.00
TP12 Colin Moran .20 .50
TP13 Lucas Sims .20 .50
TP14 Julio Urias 1.00 2.50
TP15 David Dahl .25 .60
TP16 Josh Bell .40 1.00
TP17 Braden Shipley .20 .50
TP18 D.J. Peterson .20 .50
TP19 Jose Berrios .30 .75
TP20 Trey Ball .20 .50
TP21 Rosell Herrera .30 .75
TP22 J.P. Crawford .20 .50
TP23 Reese McGuire .20 .50
TP24 Phil Ervin .20 .50
TP25 Jesse Winker .25 .60
TP26 Dominic Smith .20 .50
TP27 Hunter Harvey .20 .50
TP28 Vincent Velasquez .30 .75
TP29 Gabriel Guerrero .20 .50
TP30 Brandon Nimmo .30 .75
TP31 Jose Peraza .20 .50
TP32 Hunter Renfroe .25 .60
TP33 Eloy Jimenez 2.50 6.00
TP34 Alen Hanson .20 .50
TP35 Albert Almora .30 .75
TP36 Lance McCullers .20 .50
TP37 Rafael Devers 2.00 5.00
TP38 Luis Severino .30 .75
TP39 Aaron Judge 3.00 8.00
TP40 Peter O'Brien .25 .60
TP41 Corey Seager .75 2.00
TP42 Aaron Blair .20 .50
TP43 Ben Lively .25 .60
TP44 Daniel Robertson .20 .50
TP45 Josh Hader .50 1.25
TP46 Hunter Dozier .20 .50
TP47 Tim Anderson .40 1.00
TP48 Tyler Danish .20 .50
TP49 Alex Jackson .30 .75
TP50 JaCoby Jones .30 .75
TP51 Eric Jagielo .20 .50
TP52 Rob Kaminsky .20 .50
TP53 Lewis Brinson .30 .75
TP54 Travis Demeritte .25 .60
TP55 Luis Torrens .20 .50
TP56 Ian Clarkin .20 .50
TP57 Josh Hart .20 .50
TP58 Michael Lorenzen .20 .50
TP59 Robert Stephenson .20 .50
TP60 Ryan McMahon .20 .50
TP61 Tyler Glasnow .30 .75
TP62 Kris Bryant 1.50 4.00
TP63 Kyle Crick .20 .50
TP64 Mason Williams .20 .50
TP65 Christian Binford .20 .50
TP66 Jake Thompson .20 .50
TP67 Sean Coyle .20 .50
TP68 James Ramsey .20 .50
TP69 Byron Buxton .25 .60
TP70 Nick Williams .25 .60
TP71 Miguel Almonte .20 .50
TP72 C.J. Edwards .25 .60
TP73 Delino DeShields .20 .50
TP74 Trevor Story .75 2.00
TP75 Raimel Tapia .25 .60
TP76 Michael Feliz .25 .60
TP77 Brandon Drury .25 .60
TP78 Franklin Barreto .30 .75
TP79 Chris Stratton .20 .50
TP80 Joey Gallo .40 1.00
TP81 Christian Arroyo 1.25 3.00
TP82 Mac Williamson .25 .60
TP83 Clayton Blackburn .30 .75
TP84 Blake Swihart .25 .60
TP85 Gosuke Katoh .30 .75
TP86 Roberto Osuna .20 .50
TP87 Courtney Hawkins .20 .50
TP88 Tyler Naquin .25 .60
TP89 Devon Travis .20 .50
TP90 Nomar Mazara .50 1.25

2014 Bowman Draft Top Prospects Blue

*BLUE: 1X TO 2.5X BASIC
STATED ODDS 1:52 HOBBY
STATED PRINT RUN 399 SER.#'d SETS

2014 Bowman Draft Top Prospects Green

*GREEN: 4X TO 10X BASIC
RANDOM INSERTS IN PACKS
STATED PRINT RUN 75 SER.#'d SETS

2014 Bowman Draft Top Prospects Orange Ice

*ORANGE ICE: 5X TO 12X BASIC
RANDOM INSERTS IN PACKS
STATED PRINT RUN 25 SER.#'d SETS

2014 Bowman Draft Top Prospects Purple Ice

*PURPLE ICE: 4X TO 10X BASIC
STATED ODDS 1:211 HOBBY
STATED PRINT RUN 99 SER.#'d SETS

2014 Bowman Draft Top Prospects Red Ice

*RED ICE: 3X TO 8X BASIC
STATED ODDS 1:137 HOBBY
STATED PRINT RUN 150 SER.#'d SETS

2014 Bowman Draft Top Prospects Silver Ice

*SILVER ICE: 1X TO 2.5X BASIC
STATED ODDS 1:12 HOBBY

2015 Bowman

COMPLETE SET (150) 8.00 20.00
PRINTING PLATES RANDOMLY INSERTS
PLATE PRINT RUN 1 SET PER COLOR
BLACK-CYAN-MAGENTA-YELLOW ISSUED
NO PLATE PRICING DUE TO SCARCITY
1 Clayton Kershaw .50 1.25
2 Eric Hosmer .20 .50
3 Alex Gordon .20 .50
4 Jay Bruce .20 .50
5 Anthony Rizzo .40 1.00
6 Brad Ziegler .15 .40
7 Ken Giles .15 .40
8 Shin-Soo Choo .20 .50
9 Brandon Crawford .20 .50
10 Danny Salazar .20 .50
11 Ian Desmond .15 .40
12 Adam Eaton .15 .40
13 Jonathan Lucroy .20 .50
14 Zack Wheeler .20 .50
15 Zack Greinke .20 .50
16 Matt Holliday .25 .60
17 Jose Reyes .20 .50
18 Jarrod Saltalamacchia .15 .40
19 Manny Machado .25 .60
20 Paul Goldschmidt .25 .60
21 Garrett Richards .20 .50
22 Christian Yelich .30 .75
23 Josh Harrison .15 .40
24 Alex Cobb .15 .40
25 Yasiel Puig .25 .60
26 Anthony Rendon .25 .60
27 Mookie Betts .40 1.00
28 Craig Kimbrel .20 .50
29 Ian Kinsler .20 .50
30 Jose Altuve .20 .50
31 Charlie Blackmon .25 .60
32 Michael Pineda .15 .40
33 Kyle Seager .15 .40
34 Kennys Vargas .15 .40
35 Joaquin Benoit .15 .40
36 Mike Zunino .15 .40
37 Josh Reddick .15 .40
38 Jason Kipnis .20 .50
39 Chris Sale .25 .60
40 Oswaldo Arcia .15 .40
41 Matt Shoemaker .20 .50
42 J.J. Hardy .15 .40
43 Matt Carpenter .25 .60
44 Dellin Betances .20 .50
45 Joey Votto .25 .60
46 Ben Revere .15 .40
47 Tanner Roark .15 .40
48 Justin Morneau .20 .50
49 Jake Arrieta .20 .50
50 Mike Trout 1.25 3.00
51 Chris Owings .15 .40
52 David Wright .20 .50
53 Kevin Kiermaier .20 .50
54 Domonic Brown .20 .50
55 Justin Turner .20 .50
56 Mark Trumbo .15 .40
57 Carlos Gomez .15 .40
58 Hisashi Iwakuma .20 .50
59 Gregor Blanco .15 .40
60 Adeiny Hechavarria .15 .40
61 Starlin Castro .15 .40
62 Josh Hamilton .25 .60
63 Chase Headley .15 .40
64 Edwin Encarnacion .25 .60
65 Coco Crisp .15 .40
66 Jon Singleton .20 .50
67 Troy Tulowitzki .25 .60
68 Andre Ethier .20 .50
69 Victor Martinez .20 .50
70 Austin Jackson .15 .40
71 Evan Gattis .15 .40
72 Kole Calhoun .15 .40
73 Adrian Gonzalez .20 .50
74 Corey Dickerson .15 .40
75 Jacob deGrom .25 .60
76 David Ortiz .25 .60
77 Evan Longoria .20 .50
78 R.A. Dickey .20 .50
79 Chris Davis .15 .40
80 Corey Kluber .20 .50
81 Xander Bogaerts .25 .60
82 Jose Quintana .15 .40
83 Lorenzo Cain .15 .40
84 Henderson Alvarez .15 .40
85 Kurt Suzuki .15 .40
86 Cliff Lee .20 .50
87 Jedd Gyorko .15 .40
88 Yusmeiro Petit .15 .40
89 Matt Garza .15 .40
90 Nick Castellanos .25 .60
91 Marcell Ozuna .25 .60
92 Phil Hughes .15 .40
93 CC Sabathia .20 .50
94 Jhonny Peralta .15 .40
95 Bryce Harper .40 1.00
96 Devin Mesoraco .15 .40
97 Alcides Escobar .20 .50
98 Travis d'Arnaud .20 .50
99 Ian Kennedy .15 .40
100 Madison Bumgarner .20 .50
101 Greg Holland .15 .40
102 Johnny Cueto .20 .50
103 Dexter Fowler .20 .50
104 Billy Hamilton .20 .50
105 Lonnie Chisenhall .15 .40
106 Sonny Gray .20 .50
107 David Price .20 .50
108 Aramis Ramirez .15 .40
109 Doug Fister .15 .40
110 Elvis Andrus .20 .50
111 Adam Wainwright .20 .50
112 Yu Darvish .25 .60
113 Aaron Sanchez .25 .60
114 Brandon Belt .20 .50
115 Andrew McCutchen .25 .60
116 Jake McGee .15 .40
117 Mike Napoli .15 .40
118 Yan Gomes .15 .40
119 Andrelton Simmons .15 .40
120 Jose Abreu .25 .60
121 Jorge Soler RC .40 1.00
122 Anthony Ranaudo RC .25 .60
123 Rymer Liriano RC .25 .60
124 Daniel Corcino RC .25 .60
125 Rusney Castillo RC .30 .75
126 Bryce Brentz RC .25 .60
127 Bryan Mitchell RC .25 .60
128 Cory Spangenberg RC .25 .60
129 Dilson Herrera RC .30 .75
130 Joc Pederson RC .50 1.25
131 Brandon Finnegan RC .25 .60
132 Yimi Garcia RC .25 .60
133 Edwin Escobar RC .25 .60
134 Mike Foltynewicz RC .25 .60
135 Jason Rogers RC .25 .60
136 R.J. Alvarez RC .25 .60
137 Maikel Franco RC .30 .75
138 Buck Farmer RC .25 .60
139 Michael Taylor RC .25 .60
140 Trevor May RC .25 .60
141 Nick Tropeano RC .25 .60
142 Gary Brown RC .25 .60
143 Matt Barnes RC .25 .60
144 Christian Walker RC .50 1.25
145 Xavier Scruggs RC .25 .60
146 Daniel Norris RC .25 .60
147 Dalton Pompey RC .30 .75
148 Steven Moya RC .30 .75
149 Jake Lamb RC .40 1.00
150 Javier Baez RC 2.00 5.00

2015 Bowman Blue

*BLUE: 2.5X TO 6X BASIC
*BLUE RC: 1.5X TO 4X BASIC RC
STATED ODDS 1:175 HOBBY
STATED PRINT RUN 150 SER.#'d SETS

2015 Bowman Gold

*GOLD: 8X TO 20X BASIC
*GOLD RC: 5X TO 12X BASIC RC
STATED ODDS 1:525 HOBBY
STATED PRINT RUN 50 SER.#'d SETS

2015 Bowman Green

*GREEN: 4X TO 10X BASIC
*GREEN RC: 2.5X TO 6X BASIC RC
STATED ODDS 1:47 RETAIL
STATED PRINT RUN 99 SER.#'d SETS

2015 Bowman Orange

*ORANGE: 10X TO 25X BASIC
*ORANGE RC: 6X TO 15X BASIC RC
STATED ODDS 1:243 HOBBY
STATED PRINT RUN 25 SER.#'d SETS

2015 Bowman Purple

*PURPLE: 2X TO 5X BASIC
*PURPLE RC: 1.2X TO 3X BASIC RC
STATED ODDS 1:105 HOBBY
STATED PRINT RUN 250 SER.#'d SETS

2015 Bowman Purple Ice

*PURPLE ICE: 8X TO 20X BASIC
*PURPLE ICE RC: 5X TO 12X BASIC RC
STATED ODDS 1:525 HOBBY
STATED PRINT RUN 50 SER.#'d SETS

2015 Bowman Silver

*SILVER: 1.5X TO 4X BASIC
*SILVER RC: 1X TO 2.5X BASIC RC
STATED ODDS 1:53 HOBBY
STATED PRINT RUN 499 SER.#'d SETS

2015 Bowman Silver Ice

*SILVER ICE: 1.2X TO 3X BASIC
*SILVER ICE RC: .75X TO 2X BASIC
STATED ODDS 1:24 HOBBY

2015 Bowman Black Collection Autographs

BOW.ODDS 1:6153 HOBBY
BI.ODDS 1:75 HOBBY
BB ODDS 1:313 MINI BOX
STATED PRINT RUN 25 SER.#'d SETS
BOW.EXCH DEADLINE 4/30/2018
BI EXCH.DEADLINE 6/30/2018
BB EXCH.DEADLINE 12/21/2017
BBCAB Andrew Benintendi BB 150.00 250.00
BBCAJ Aaron Judge BI 100.00 250.00
BBCAK Austin Kubitza BC 6.00 15.00
BBCAR Adrian Rondon BC 10.00 25.00
BBCARO Avery Romero BC 6.00 15.00
BBCBF Brandon Finnegan BC 10.00 25.00
BBCBL Ben Lively BI 20.00 50.00
BBCBP Brett Phillips BC 50.00 100.00
BBCBS Blake Swihart BI 20.00 50.00
BBCCF Carson Fulmer BD 15.00 40.00
BBCCG Casey Gillaspie BC 12.00 30.00
BBCCR Carlos Rodon BC 25.00 60.00
BBCDG Domingo German BC 30.00 80.00
BBCDG Dermis Garcia BC 20.00 50.00
BBCDH Dilson Herrera BI 15.00 40.00
BBCDT Dillon Tate BB 8.00 20.00
BBCDW Drew Ward BC 15.00 40.00
BBCEJ Eric Jagielo BI 6.00 15.00
BBCFM Francellis Montas BC 8.00 20.00
BBCGG Gabby Guerrero BI 60.00 150.00
BBCGG Grayson Greiner BC 6.00 15.00
BBCGT Gleyber Torres BC 60.00 150.00
BBCGW Garrett Whitley BD 15.00 40.00
BBCHR Harold Ramirez BC 15.00 40.00
BBCJC Jake Cave BC 15.00 40.00
BBCJH Josh Hader BI 6.00 15.00
BBCJHK Jung Ho Kang BC 60.00 150.00
BBCJK James Kaprielian BB 20.00 50.00
BBCJN Josh Naylor BB 8.00 20.00
BBCJW Jesse Winker BI 25.00 60.00
BBCKM Keury Mella BC 6.00 15.00
BBCKT Kyle Tucker BD 40.00 100.00
BBCLM Logan Moon BC 10.00 25.00
BBCLS Luis Severino BC 30.00 80.00
BBCMF Michael Feliz BI 6.00 15.00
BBCMH Monte Harrison BI 10.00 25.00
BBCMM Manuel Margot BI 20.00 50.00
BBCMO Matt Olson BI 40.00 100.00
BBCNS Nolan Sanburn BC 6.00 15.00
BBCOA Orlando Arcia BC 30.00 80.00
BBCPB Phil Bickford BD 6.00 15.00
BBCPS Pedro Severino BC 15.00 40.00
BBCRC Rusney Castillo BC 8.00 20.00
BBCRD Rafael Devers BC 125.00 300.00
BBCRI Raisel Iglesias BC 30.00 80.00
BBCRM Ryan Merritt BC 10.00 25.00
BBCRM Richie Martin BB 12.00 30.00
BBCRR Robert Refsnyder BC 25.00 60.00
BBCSC Sean Coyle BI 6.00 15.00
BBCTC Trent Clark BD 6.00 15.00
BBCTH Teoscar Hernandez BC 20.00 50.00
BBCTJ Tyler Jay BB 6.00 15.00
BBCTS Tyler Stephenson BB 12.00 30.00
BBCTT Touki Toussaint BC 25.00 60.00
BBCVC Victor Caratini BC 10.00 25.00
BBCYT Yasmany Tomas BI 15.00 40.00

2015 Bowman Dual Autographs

STATED ODDS 1:3872 HOBBY
STATED PRINT RUN 99 SER.#'d SETS
EXCHANGE DEADLINE 4/30/2018
*ORANGE/25: .5X TO 1.2X BASIC
BDABS Schwarber/Bryant 100.00 250.00
BDAGA Gallo/Alfaro 20.00 50.00
BDAGB Gordon/Buxton 40.00 100.00
BDAGF K.Freeland/J.Gray 8.00 20.00
BDAJP Jackson/Peterson 40.00 100.00
BDARK Kolek/Rodon 30.00 80.00
BDASO Owens/Swihart EXCH 25.00 60.00
BDASS Severino/Sanchez 40.00 100.00
BDATS Toussaint/Shipley 8.00 20.00

2015 Bowman Future's Game Relics

STATED ODDS 1:3595 RETAIL
STATED PRINT RUN 25 SER.#'d SETS
FGRAM Alex Meyer 10.00 25.00
FGRBS Braden Shipley 15.00 40.00
FGRCS Corey Seager 30.00 80.00
FGRFL Francisco Lindor 60.00 150.00
FGRHO Henry Owens 10.00 25.00
FGRJC J.P. Crawford 50.00 120.00
FGRJW Jesse Winker 15.00 40.00
FGRKB Kris Bryant 150.00 300.00
FGRSM Steven Moya 12.00 30.00
FGRJBE Josh Bell 20.00 50.00

2015 Bowman Golden Debut Contract Winner

STATED ODDS 1:7544 HOBBY
BGCJB Jim Boyle SP 4.00 10.00

2015 Bowman Prospects

COMPLETE SET (150) 10.00 25.00
PRINTING PLATES RANDOMLY INSERTED
PLATE PRINT RUN 1 SET PER COLOR
NO PLATE PRICING DUE TO SCARCITY
BP1 Tyler Kolek .15 .40
BP2 Jose Queliz .15 .40

BP3 Kevin Plawecki .15 .40
BP4 Jen-Ho Tseng .15 .40
BP5 Dixon Machado .20 .50
BP6 Pedro Severino .15 .40
BP7 Roman Quinn .25 .60
BP8 A.J. Cole .15 .40
BP9 Fernando Perez .15 .40
BP10 Logan Moon .15 .40
BP11 Giovanny Urshela 1.00 2.50
BP12 Emerson Jimenez .15 .40
BP13 Dermis Garcia .25 .60
BP14 Marco Gonzales .25 .60
BP15 Jeremy Rhoades .15 .40
BP16 Joe Ross .15 .40
BP17 Trevor Gott .15 .40
BP18 Forrest Wall .15 .40
BP19 David Dahl .20 .50
BP20 Adrian Sampson .15 .40
BP21 Alex Verdugo .25 .60
BP22 Williams Perez .20 .50
BP23 Alex Reyes .20 .50
BP24 Ty Blach .20 .50
BP25 Yasmany Tomas .20 .50
BP26 Hunter Harvey .15 .40
BP27 Touki Toussaint .20 .50
BP28 Austin Voth .15 .40
BP29 Luis Lugo .15 .40
BP30 Teoscar Hernandez .50 1.25
BP31 Jimmy Reed .15 .40
BP32 Austin Kubitza .15 .40
BP33 Miguel Sano .20 .50
BP34 Rafael Devers 1.00 2.50
BP35 Harold Ramirez .20 .50
BP36 Alex Meyer .15 .40
BP37 Archie Bradley .15 .40
BP38 Tim Cooney .15 .40
BP39 Jorge Lopez .15 .40
BP40 Ryan Merritt .25 .60
BP41 Carlos Correa .75 2.00
BP42 Rafael Bautista .15 .40
BP43 Francisco Mejia .40 1.00
BP44 Robert Stephenson .15 .40
BP45 James Dykstra .15 .40
BP46 Tyler DeLoach .15 .40
BP47 Kyle Lloyd .15 .40
BP48 Erik Gonzalez .15 .40
BP49 Sal Romano .15 .40
BP50 Julio Urias .50 1.25
BP51 Juan Herrera .15 .40
BP52 Jon Gray .15 .40
BP53 Corey Littrell .15 .40
BP54 Chris Stratton .15 .40
BP55 Conrad Gregor .15 .40
BP56 Hunter Dozier .15 .40
BP57 Jantzen Witte .25 .60
BP58 Kyle Schwarber .60 1.50
BP59 Champ Stuart .15 .40
BP60 James Needy .15 .40
BP61 Willy Adames .25 .60
BP62 Jose De Leon .25 .60
BP63 Buddy Borden .15 .40
BP64 Jordan Betts .15 .40
BP65 Gabriel Quintana .15 .40
BP66 Gareth Morgan .15 .40
BP67 Matt Andriese .15 .40
BP68 Raimel Tapia .25 .60
BP69 Drew Ward .15 .40
BP70 Carlos Asuaje .15 .40
BP71 Ozhaino Albies 1.50 4.00
BP72 Josh Bell .30 .75
BP73 Kyle Zimmer .15 .40
BP74 Greg Bird .20 .50
BP75 Nick Gordon .20 .50
BP76 Aaron Blair .15 .40
BP77 T.J. Chism .15 .40
BP78 Marcos Molina .15 .40
BP79 Avery Romero .15 .40
BP80 Jose Peraza .15 .40
BP81 Tim Anderson .30 .75
BP82 Nick Travieso .15 .40
BP83 Matt Wisler .15 .40
BP84 Nick Petree .15 .40
BP85 Mark Appel .15 .40
BP86 Frank Schwindel .20 .50
BP87 Jorge Mateo .50 1.25
BP88 Reese McGuire .15 .40
BP89 Tyler Naquin .20 .50
BP90 Nate Smith .15 .40
BP91 Jose Berrios .25 .60
BP92 Henry Owens .15 .40
BP93 Justin Nicolino .15 .40
BP94 Jairo Labourt .15 .40
BP95 Edmundo Sosa .20 .50
BP96 Seth Streich .15 .40
BP97 Victor Reyes .15 .40
BP98 Jhoan Urena .15 .40
BP99 Adam Engel .15 .40
BP100 Kris Bryant 1.00 2.50
BP101 Rio Ruiz .15 .40
BP102 Wes Parsons .15 .40
BP103 Raisel Iglesias .20 .50
BP104 Robert Refsnyder .20 .50
BP105 Aaron Slegers .15 .40
BP106 Tim Berry .15 .40
BP107 Nick Williams .20 .50
BP108 Jack Reinheimer .20 .50
BP109 Domingo Santana .20 .50
BP110 Chad Pinder .20 .50
BP111 Andre Wheeler .15 .40
BP112 Chih-Wei Hu .25 .60
BP113 Gary Sanchez .50 1.25
BP114 Ryan McMahon .15 .40
BP115 Taylor Williams .15 .40
BP116 Nelson Gomez .20 .50
BP117 Addison Russell .50 1.25
BP118 Domingo German .25 .60
BP119 Scott Schebler .25 .60
BP120 Joe Jackson .15 .40
BP121 Gilbert Lara .20 .50
BP122 Hunter Renfroe .25 .60
BP123 Rob Kaminsky .15 .40
BP124 Steven Matz .25 .60
BP125 Luis Severino .25 .60
BP126 Austin Meadows .25 .60
BP127 Luis Heredia .15 .40
BP128 Victor Alcantara .15 .40
BP129 Trevor Frank .15 .40
BP130 Jake Johansen .15 .40
BP131 JaCoby Jones .20 .50
BP132 Jake Bauers .25 .60
BP133 Trey Ball .15 .40
BP134 Aaron Nola .25 .60
BP135 Orlando Arcia .25 .60
BP136 Keury Mella .15 .40
BP137 Brett Phillips .15 .40
BP138 Mike Yastrzemski 2.00 5.00
BP139 Jose Valdez .15 .40
BP140 Eric Haase .15 .40
BP141 Jaycob Brugman .20 .50
BP142 Albert Almora .20 .50
BP143 Tyler Wagner .15 .40
BP144 Francellis Montas .20 .50
BP145 Dariel Alvarez .15 .40
BP146 Raul Alcantara .15 .40
BP147 Ricardo Sanchez .15 .40
BP148 Jarlin Garcia .20 .50
BP149 Colin Moran .15 .40
BP150 Carlos Rodon .25 .60

2015 Bowman Prospects Blue

*BLUE: 2X TO 5X BASIC
STATED ODDS 1:175 HOBBY
STATED PRINT RUN 150 SER.#'d SETS

2015 Bowman Prospects Gold

*GOLD: 5X TO 12X BASIC
STATED ODDS 1:525 HOBBY
STATED PRINT RUN 50 SER.#'d SETS

2015 Bowman Prospects Green

*GREEN: 2.5X TO 6X BASIC
STATED ODDS 1:47 RETAIL
STATED PRINT RUN 99 SER.#'d SETS

2015 Bowman Prospects Orange

*ORANGE: 8X TO 20X BASIC
STATED ODDS 1:243 HOBBY
STATED PRINT RUN 25 SER.#'d SETS

2015 Bowman Prospects Purple

*PURPLE: 1.5X TO 4X BASIC
STATED ODDS 1:105 HOBBY
STATED PRINT RUN 250 SER.#'d SETS

2015 Bowman Prospects Purple Ice

*PURPLE ICE: 5X TO 12X BASIC
STATED ODDS 1:525 HOBBY
STATED PRINT RUN 50 SER.#'d SETS

2015 Bowman Prospects Silver

*SILVER: 1.2X TO 3X BASIC
STATED ODDS 1:53 HOBBY
STATED PRINT RUN 499 SER.#'d SETS

2015 Bowman Prospects Silver Ice

*SILVER ICE: 1X TO 2.5X BASIC
STATED ODDS 1:24 HOBBY

2015 Bowman Prospects Yellow

*YELLOW: 1.2X TO 3X BASIC
RANDOM INSERTS IN PACKS

2015 Bowman Prospects Autographs

STATED ODDS 1:18 RETAIL
EXCHANGE DEADLINE 4/30/2018
PAAB Alex Balog 2.50 6.00
PAABA Anthony Banda 3.00 8.00
PAAP Adam Plutko 2.50 6.00
PAAT Andrew Triggs 2.50 6.00
PAAW Adam Walker 2.50 6.00
PABA Beau Amaral 3.00 8.00
PABB Bobby Bundy 2.50 6.00
PACH Connor Harrell 2.50 6.00
PACJ Chris Jensen 2.50 6.00
PACR Carlos Rodon 12.00 30.00
PAFM Francisco Mejia 8.00 20.00
PAJC Jason Coats 2.50 6.00
PAJH Josh Hader 2.50 6.00
PAJU Jose Urena 2.50 6.00
PAJW Jason Wheeler 2.50 6.00
PALG Luis Guillorme 2.50 6.00
PAMO Mike O'Neill 3.00 8.00
PANL Nick Longhi 3.00 8.00
PARS Rob Segedin 2.50 6.00
PASF Steven Farinaro 2.50 6.00
PATD Taylor Dugas 2.50 6.00
PATF Taylor Featherston 2.50 6.00
PAWL Will Locante 2.50 6.00
PAZJ Zack Jones 2.50 6.00

2015 Bowman Prospects Autographs Blue

*BLUE: .6X TO 1.5X BASIC
STATED ODDS 1:376 RETAIL
STATED PRINT RUN 150 SER.#'d SETS
EXCHANGE DEADLINE 4/30/2018

2015 Bowman Prospects Autographs Gold

*GOLD: 1X TO 2.5X BASIC
STATED ODDS 1:572 RETAIL
STATED PRINT RUN 50 SER.#'d SETS
EXCHANGE DEADLINE 3/31/2018

2015 Bowman Prospects Autographs Green

*GREEN: .75X TO 2X BASIC
STATED ODDS 1:572 RETAIL
STATED PRINT RUN 99 SER.#'d SETS
EXCHANGE DEADLINE 4/30/2018

2015 Bowman Prospects Autographs Orange

*ORANGE: 1.2X TO 3X BASIC
STATED ODDS 1:2288 RETAIL
STATED PRINT RUN 25 SER.#'d SETS
EXCHANGE DEADLINE 4/30/2018

2015 Bowman Prospects Autographs Purple

*PURPLE: .5X TO 1.2X BASIC
STATED ODDS 1:227 RETAIL
STATED PRINT RUN 250 SER.#'d SETS
EXCHANGE DEADLINE 4/30/2018

2015 Bowman Prospects Autographs Silver

*SILVER: .5X TO 1.2X BASIC
STATED ODDS 1:114 RETAIL
STATED PRINT RUN 499 SER.#'d SETS
EXCHANGE DEADLINE 4/30/2018

2015 Bowman Sophomore Standouts Autographs

STATED ODDS 1:3872 HOBBY
STATED PRINT RUN 99 SER.#'d SETS
EXCHANGE DEADLINE 4/30/2018
*GOLD/50: .6X TO 1.5X BASIC
SSAAA Arismendy Alcantara 4.00 10.00
SSAAS Aaron Sanchez 6.00 15.00
SSACC C.J. Cron 4.00 10.00
SSAGP Gregory Polanco 5.00 12.00
SSAGS George Springer 15.00 40.00
SSAJA Jose Abreu 10.00 25.00
SSAJD Jacob deGrom 25.00 60.00
SSAJP Joe Panik 15.00 40.00
SSAJS Jon Singleton 5.00 12.00
SSAKV Kennys Vargas 6.00 15.00
SSANC Nick Castellanos 6.00 15.00
SSARM Rafael Montero 4.00 10.00
SSATL Tommy La Stella 4.00 10.00
SSAYV Yordano Ventura 8.00 20.00

2015 Bowman Draft

COMPLETE SET (200) 12.00 30.00
STATED PLATE ODDS 1:5000 HOBBY
PLATE PRINT RUN 1 SET PER COLOR
NO PLATE PRICING DUE TO SCARCITY
1 Dansby Swanson 1.00 2.50
2 Yoan Lopez .15 .40
3 Bailey Falter .15 .40
4 Casey Gillaspie .25 .60
5 Demi Orimoloye .20 .50
6 Steven Duggar .15 .40
7 Tyler Alexander .15 .40
8 Courtney Hawkins .15 .40
9 Casey Hughston .15 .40
10 Kolby Allard .15 .40
11 Austin Meadows .25 .60
12 Joe McCarthy .15 .40
13 Tyler Stephenson .20 .50
14 Ashe Russell .15 .40
15 Dylan Moore .15 .40
16 Donnie Dewees .25 .60
17 Beau Burrows .20 .50
18 Greg Pickett .15 .40
19 Parker French .15 .40
20 Cam Gibson .20 .50
21 Braden Bishop .15 .40
22 Ryan Kellogg .15 .40
23 Monte Harrison .25 .60
24 Zack Erwin .15 .40
25 J.P. Crawford .15 .40
26 Ryan McMahon .15 .40
27 Kyle Holder .20 .50
28 Ian Happ .60 1.50
29 Anthony Hermelyn .15 .40
30 Jimmy Herget .15 .40
31 Mike Nikorak .15 .40
32 Alex Young .15 .40
33 Tyler Mark .15 .40
34 Trent Clark .15 .40
35 Benton Moss .15 .40
36 Matt Withrow .15 .40
37 Chris Shaw .30 .75
38 Manuel Margot .15 .40
39 Lucas Giolito .30 .75
40 Chase Ingram .15 .40
41 Lucas Herbert .15 .40
42 Trey Supak .15 .40
43 Blake Trahan .15 .40
44 Jeff Degano .20 .50
45 Desmond Lindsay .25 .60
46 Walker Buehler 1.00 2.50
47 Cody Ponce .15 .40
48 Adam Brett Walker .15 .40
49 Tyler Danish .15 .40
50 Dillon Tate .20 .50
51 Thomas Szapucki .15 .40
52 Spencer Adams .15 .40
53 Kevin Duchene .15 .40
54 Blake Perkins .15 .40
55 Thomas Eshelman .15 .40
56 Lucas Williams .15 .40
57 David Fletcher 1.50 4.00
58 James Kaprielian .25 .60
59 Preston Morrison .15 .40
60 Ryan Burr .15 .40
61 Brett Lilek .15 .40
62 Trevor Megill .15 .40
63 Jordy Lara .15 .40
64 Kevin Newman .25 .60
65 Luis Ortiz .15 .40
66 Cornelius Randolph .15 .40
67 Domingo Leyba .15 .40
68 Sean Reid-Foley .20 .50
69 Josh Naylor .20 .50
70 Michael Matuella .20 .50
71 Cole Tucker .15 .40
72 Kyle Wilcox .15 .40
73 Forrest Wall .15 .40
74 Alex Jackson .20 .50
75 Kyle Tucker 1.00 2.50
76 Hunter Harvey .15 .40
77 Brandon Waddell .15 .40
78 Travis Neubeck .15 .40
79 Ronnie Jebavy .15 .40
80 Ryan Mountcastle .60 1.50
81 Kyle Zimmer .15 .40
82 A.J. Reed .20 .50
83 Alex Reyes .20 .50
84 Garrett Whitley .25 .60
85 Derek Hill .20 .50
86 Ryan Clark .15 .40
87 Andrew Sopko .15 .40
88 Breckin Williams .15 .40
89 Tate Matheny .15 .40
90 Kyle Crick .20 .50
91 Andrew Moore .20 .50
92 Hutton Moyer .15 .40
93 Jordan Ramsey .15 .40
94 Javier Medina .15 .40
95 Jack Wynkoop .15 .40
96 Triston McKenzie .15 .40
97 Jose De Leon .25 .60
98 Justin Cohen .15 .40
99 Mark Mathias .20 .50
100 Julio Urias .50 1.25
101 Jared Foster .15 .40
102 Roman Quinn .25 .60
103 Max Wotell .15 .40
104 Jake Gatewood .15 .40
105 Willy Adames .25 .60
106 Rafael Devers 1.00 2.50
107 Blake Snell .20 .50
108 Cody Poteet .15 .40
109 Bryce Denton .25 .60
110 Nolan Watson .15 .40
111 Tyler Nevin .25 .60
112 Antonio Santillan .20 .50
113 Mac Marshall .15 .40
114 Mariano Rivera .25 .60
115 Grant Hockin .15 .40
116 Raul Mondesi
117 Richie Martin .15 .40
118 Carson Fulmer .15 .40
119 Mikey White .20 .50
120 Lucas Sims .15 .40
121 Peter Lambert .15 .40
122 Roman Collins .15 .40
123 Austin Allen .20 .50
124 David Thompson .20 .50
125 Ka'ai Tom .15 .40
126 Renato Nunez .30 .75
127 Zech Lemond .15 .40
128 Nick Gordon .20 .50
129 Phil Bickford .15 .40
130 Taylor Ward .25 .60
131 Corey Taylor .15 .40
132 Chris Ellis .15 .40
133 Michael Chavis .40 1.00
134 Cody Jones .15 .40
135 Tyrone Taylor .15 .40
136 Tyler Jay .15 .40
137 Ke'Bryan Hayes .25 .60
138 Scott Kingery .25 .60
139 Carl Wise .20 .50
140 Juan Hillman .15 .40
141 Bowdien Derby .15 .40
142 D.J. Peterson .15 .40
143 Jacob Nix .15 .40
144 Josh Staumont .15 .40
145 Nathan Kirby .15 .40
146 D.J. Stewart .15 .40
147 Matt Hall .15 .40
148 Kohl Stewart .15 .40
149 Drew Jackson .20 .50
150 Aaron Judge 2.50 6.00
151 Nick Plummer .20 .50
152 David Dahl .20 .50
153 Brian Mundell .15 .40
154 Bradley Zimmer .25 .60
155 Tanner Rainey .15 .40
156 JC Cardenas .15 .40
157 Austin Riley 2.00 5.00
158 Kevin Kramer .20 .50
159 Hunter Renfroe .25 .60
160 Grant Holmes .20 .50
161 Isaiah White .20 .50
162 Justin Jacome .15 .40
163 Amed Rosario .25 .60
164 Josh Bell .30 .75
165 Eric Jenkins .15 .40
166 Reese McGuire .15 .40
167 Sean Newcomb .20 .50
168 Reynaldo Lopez .20 .50
169 Conor Biggio .15 .40
170 Andrew Suarez .20 .50
171 Trey Ball .15 .40
172 Austin Rei .20 .50
173 Drew Finley .15 .40
174 Skye Bolt .20 .50
175 Daniel Robertson .15 .40
176 Avery Romero .15 .40
177 Jon Harris .20 .50
178 Christin Stewart .20 .50
179 Nelson Rodriguez .20 .50
180 Austin Smith .15 .40
181 Michael Soroka 1.00 2.50
182 Andrew Benintendi .75 2.00
183 Matt Crownover .15 .40
184 Franklin Barreto .20 .50
185 Willie Calhoun .50 1.25
186 Braxton Davidson .15 .40
187 Jake Woodford .15 .40
188 Ryan McKenna .15 .40
189 Ryan Helsley .20 .50
190 Carson Sands .15 .40
191 Tyler Beede .20 .50
192 Jeff Hendrix .20 .50
193 Nick Howard .25 .60
194 Chris Betts .20 .50
195 Jagger Rusconi .15 .40
196 Matt Olson .20 .50
197 Jake Cronenworth 2.00 5.00
198 Alex Robinson .15 .40
199 Albert Almora .20 .50
200 Brendan Rodgers .60 1.50

2015 Bowman Draft Blue

*BLUE: 2X TO 5X BASIC
STATED ODDS 1:134 HOBBY
STATED PRINT RUN 150 SER.#'d SETS
1 Dansby Swanson 5.00 12.00
182 Andrew Benintendi 12.00 30.00

2015 Bowman Draft Gold

*GOLD: 4X TO 10X BASIC
STATED ODDS 1:401 HOBBY
STATED PRINT RUN 50 SER.#'d SETS
1 Dansby Swanson 10.00 25.00
182 Andrew Benintendi 25.00 60.00

2015 Bowman Draft Green

*GREEN: 2.5X TO 6X BASIC
STATED ODDS 1:203 HOBBY
STATED PRINT RUN 99 SER.#'d SETS
1 Dansby Swanson 6.00 15.00
182 Andrew Benintendi 15.00 40.00

2015 Bowman Draft Orange

*ORANGE: 5X TO 12X BASIC
STATED ODDS 1:283 HOBBY
STATED PRINT RUN 25 SER.#'d SETS
1 Dansby Swanson 12.00 30.00
182 Andrew Benintendi 30.00 80.00

2015 Bowman Draft Silver

*SILVER: 1.2X TO 3X BASIC
STATED ODDS 1:41 HOBBY
STATED PRINT RUN 499 SER.#'d SETS
182 Andrew Benintendi 8.00 20.00

2015 Bowman Draft Draft Dividends

STATED ODDS 1:12 HOBBY
DDAB Andrew Benintendi 2.50 6.00
DDBZ Bradley Zimmer .60 1.50
DDCA Chris Anderson .40 1.00
DDDS Dansby Swanson 2.50 6.00
DDEF Erick Fedde .40 1.00
DDEJ Eric Jagielo .40 1.00
DDHR Hunter Renfroe .60 1.50
DDJH Jon Harris .50 1.25
DDJK James Kaprielian .60 1.50
DDLW Luke Weaver .60 1.50
DDMP Mike Papi .40 1.00
DDRM Richie Martin .40 1.00
DDTW Taylor Ward .60 1.50
DDABL Alex Blandino .40 1.00
DDDST D.J. Stewart .40 1.00

2015 Bowman Draft Draft Dividends Autographs

STATED ODDS 1:5649 HOBBY
*ORANGE/25: .6X TO 1.5X BASIC
DDAB Andrew Benintendi 60.00 150.00
DDBZ Bradley Zimmer 12.00 30.00
DDDS Dansby Swanson 30.00 80.00
DDJK James Kaprielian 12.00 30.00
DDLW Luke Weaver 12.00 30.00
DDRM Richie Martin 8.00 20.00
DDTW Taylor Ward 12.00 30.00
DDDST D.J. Stewart 8.00 20.00

2015 Bowman Draft Draft Night

STATED ODDS 1:12 HOBBY
*ORANGE/25: 1.5X TO 4X BASIC
DN1 Brendan Rodgers 1.50 4.00
DN2 Mike Nikorak .40 1.00
DN3 Ashe Russell .40 1.00
DN4 Garrett Whitley .60 1.50

2015 Bowman Draft Initiation

STATED ODDS 1:288 HOBBY
*GOLD/25: .6X TO 1.5X BASIC
BI1 Dansby Swanson 6.00 15.00
BI2 Brendan Rodgers 5.00 12.00
BI3 Dillon Tate 2.00 5.00
BI4 Kyle Tucker 10.00 25.00
BI5 Tyler Jay 1.50 4.00
BI6 Andrew Benintendi 6.00 15.00
BI7 Carson Fulmer 1.50 4.00
BI8 Ian Happ 4.00 10.00
BI9 Cornelius Randolph 1.50 4.00
BI10 Tyler Stephenson 2.00 5.00
BI11 Josh Naylor 2.00 5.00
BI12 Garrett Whitley 2.50 6.00
BI13 Kolby Allard 1.50 4.00
BI14 Trent Clark 1.50 4.00
BI15 James Kaprielian 2.50 6.00
BI16 Phil Bickford 1.50 4.00
BI17 Kevin Newman 2.50 6.00
BI18 Richie Martin 1.50 4.00
BI19 Ashe Russell 1.50 4.00
BI20 Beau Burrows 2.00 5.00

2016 Bowman

PRINTING PLATE ODDS 1:5355 HOBBY
PLATE PRINT RUN 1 SET PER COLOR
BLACK-CYAN-MAGENTA-YELLOW ISSUED
NO PLATE PRICING DUE TO SCARCITY
1 Mike Trout 1.25 3.00
2 Josh Donaldson .20 .50
3 Albert Pujols .30 .75
4 A.J. Pollock .15 .40
5 Paul Goldschmidt .25 .60
6 Yasmany Tomas .15 .40
7 Freddie Freeman .30 .75
8 Andrelton Simmons .15 .40
9 Shelby Miller .20 .50
10 David Ortiz .25 .60
11 Manny Machado .25 .60
12 Chris Davis .15 .40
13 Mookie Betts .40 1.00
14 Adam Jones .20 .50
15 Dustin Pedroia .25 .60
16 Xander Bogaerts .25 .60
17 Jon Lester .20 .50
18 Jake Arrieta .20 .50
19 Jorge Soler .20 .50
20 Kris Bryant .30 .75
21 Anthony Rizzo .40 1.00
22 Jose Abreu .25 .60
23 Chris Sale .25 .60
24 Carlos Rodon .25 .60
25 Aroldis Chapman .25 .60
26 Brandon Phillips .15 .40
27 Joey Votto .25 .60
28 Francisco Lindor .25 .60
29 Corey Kluber .20 .50
30 Carlos Correa .25 .60
31 Charlie Blackmon .25 .60
32 Nolan Arenado .30 .75
33 Miguel Cabrera .25 .60
34 Ian Kinsler .20 .50
35 Justin Verlander .25 .60
36 George Springer .20 .50
37 Carlos Santana .20 .50
38 Dallas Keuchel .20 .50
39 Jose Altuve .20 .50
40 Clayton Kershaw .50 1.25
41 Lorenzo Cain .15 .40
42 Salvador Perez .20 .50
43 Eric Hosmer .20 .50
44 Evan Gattis .15 .40
45 Zack Greinke .25 .60
46 Adrian Gonzalez .20 .50
47 Yasiel Puig .25 .60
48 Giancarlo Stanton .25 .60
49 Jose Fernandez .25 .60
50 Ichiro Suzuki .30 .75
51 Ryan Braun .20 .50
52 Byron Buxton .20 .50
53 Brian Dozier .20 .50
54 Joe Mauer .20 .50
55 Yoenis Cespedes .25 .60
56 Matt Harvey .20 .50
57 Jacob deGrom .25 .60
58 Noah Syndergaard .20 .50
59 Dellin Betances .20 .50
60 Masahiro Tanaka .20 .50
61 Alex Rodriguez .30 .75
62 Sonny Gray .20 .50
63 Billy Butler .15 .40
64 Stephen Vogt .20 .50
65 Maikel Franco .20 .50
66 Ryan Howard .20 .50
67 Odubel Herrera .20 .50
68 Andrew McCutchen .25 .60
69 Josh Harrison .15 .40
70 Buster Posey .30 .75
71 Gregory Polanco .20 .50
72 Justin Upton .20 .50
73 Tyson Ross .15 .40
74 James Shields .15 .40
75 Jung Ho Kang .15 .40
76 Madison Bumgarner .20 .50
77 Brandon Crawford .20 .50
78 Brandon Belt .20 .50
79 Robinson Cano .20 .50
80 Felix Hernandez .20 .50
81 Nelson Cruz .25 .60
82 Jason Heyward .20 .50
83 Yadier Molina .25 .60
84 Evan Longoria .20 .50
85 Chris Archer .15 .40
86 Kevin Kiermaier .20 .50
87 Prince Fielder .20 .50
88 Cole Hamels .20 .50
89 Adrian Beltre .25 .60
90 Yu Darvish .25 .60
91 Jose Bautista .20 .50
92 David Price .20 .50
93 Edwin Encarnacion .25 .60
94 Wei-Yin Chen .15 .40
95 Max Scherzer .25 .60
96 Stephen Strasburg .25 .60
97 Garrett Richards .25 .60
98 David Peralta .15 .40
99 Julio Teheran .20 .50
100 Bryce Harper .40 1.00
101 Adam Eaton .15 .40
102 Todd Frazier .20 .50
103 Jay Bruce .20 .50
104 Carlos Gonzalez .20 .50
105 J.D. Martinez .25 .60
106 Andrew Miller .20 .50
107 Brian McCann .20 .50
108 Jacoby Ellsbury .20 .50
109 Josh Reddick .15 .40
110 Matt Kemp .20 .50
111 Craig Kimbrel .20 .50
112 Kyle Seager .15 .40
113 Marcus Stroman .20 .50
114 Mark Melancon .15 .40
115 Trevor Rosenthal .20 .50
116 Hunter Pence .20 .50
117 Michael Brantley .20 .50
118 Adam Wainwright .20 .50
119 Wade Davis .15 .40
120 Troy Tulowitzki .25 .60
121 Matt Reynolds RC .25 .60
122 Kyle Schwarber RC .75 2.00
123 Stephen Piscotty RC .40 1.00
124 Carl Edwards Jr. RC .30 .75
125 Aaron Nola RC .50 1.25
126 Hector Olivera RC .30 .75
127 Rob Refsnyder RC .30 .75
128 Jose Peraza RC .30 .75
129 Henry Owens RC .30 .75
130 Trea Turner RC .75 2.00
131 Michael Conforto RC .30 .75
132 Greg Bird RC .30 .75
133 Richie Shaffer RC .25 .60
134 Jon Gray RC .25 .60
135 Luis Severino RC .30 .75
136 Miguel Almonte RC .25 .60
137 Brandon Drury RC .40 1.00
138 Zach Lee RC .25 .60
139 Kyle Waldrop RC .30 .75
140 Miguel Sano RC .40 1.00
141 Peter O'Brien RC .25 .60
142 Frankie Montas RC .30 .75
143 Gary Sanchez RC .75 2.00
144 Ketel Marte RC .50 1.25
145 Trayce Thompson RC .40 1.00
146 Jorge Lopez RC .25 .60
147 Max Kepler RC .40 1.00
148 Tom Murphy RC .25 .60
149 Raul Mondesi RC .30 .75
150 Corey Seager RC 2.00 5.00

2016 Bowman Blue

*BLUE: 2.5X TO 6X BASIC
*BLUE RC: 1.5X TO 4X BASIC RC
STATED ODDS 1:143 HOBBY
STATED PRINT RUN 150 SER.#'d SETS

2016 Bowman Gold

*GOLD: 6X TO 15X BASIC
*GOLD RC: 4X TO 10X BASIC RC
STATED ODDS 1:429 HOBBY
STATED PRINT RUN 50 SER.#'d SETS

2016 Bowman Green

*GREEN: 4X TO 10X BASIC
*GREEN RC: 2.5X TO 6X BASIC RC
RANDOM INSERTS IN PACKS
STATED PRINT RUN 99 SER.#'d SETS

2016 Bowman Orange

*ORANGE: 8X TO 20X BASIC
*ORANGE RC: 5X TO 12X BASIC RC
STATED ODDS 1:165 HOBBY
STATED PRINT RUN 25 SER.#'d SETS
143 Gary Sanchez 25.00 60.00

2016 Bowman Purple

*PURPLE: 2X TO 5X BASIC
*PURPLE RC: 1.2X TO 3X BASIC RC
STATED ODDS 1:86 HOBBY
STATED PRINT RUN 250 SER.#'d SETS

2016 Bowman Silver

*SILVER: 1.5X TO 4X BASIC
*SILVER RC: 1X TO 2.5X BASIC RC
STATED ODDS 1:43 HOBBY

2016 Bowman Family Tree

COMPLETE SET (7) 2.00 5.00
STATED ODDS 1:24 HOBBY
*BLUE/150: 2X TO 5X BASIC
*GREEN/99: 2.5X TO 6X BASIC
*ORANGE/25: 5X TO 12X BASIC
FTB C.Biggio/C.Biggio .40 1.00
FTH K.Hayes/C.Hayes .30 .75
FTM T.Matheny/M.Matheny .40 1.00
FTN P.Nevin/T.Nevin .50 1.25
FTR M.Rivera/M.Rivera .60 1.50
FTT Tatis Jr./Tatis 5.00 12.00
FTGU Guerrero/Guerrero Jr. 2.50 6.00

2016 Bowman Family Tree Autographs

STATED ODDS 1:20,311 HOBBY
STATED PRINT RUN 25 SER.#'d SETS
EXCHANGE DEADLINE 3/31/2018
FTB C.Biggio/C.Biggio 20.00 50.00
FTH K.Hayes/C.Hayes 20.00 50.00
FTN P.Nevin/T.Nevin 20.00 50.00
FTR M.Rivera/M.Rivera 100.00 250.00

2016 Bowman International Ink

COMPLETE SET (9) 2.00 5.00
STATED ODDS 1:12 HOBBY
*BLUE/150: 1.2X TO 3X BASIC
*GREEN/99: 1.5X TO 4X BASIC
*ORANGE/25: 4X TO 10X BASIC
IICV Carlos Vargas .40 1.00
IIFR Franklin Reyes .30 .75
IIFT Fernando Tatis Jr. 6.00 15.00

IIJG Jeison Guzman .30 .75
IIJS Juan Soto 6.00 15.00
IILT Leody Taveras 1.00 2.50
IIOC Oneal Cruz 2.00 5.00
IIRO Raffy Ozuna .30 .75
IIWJ Wander Javier .50 1.25

2016 Bowman International Ink Autographs Gold

STATED ODDS 1:3202 HOBBY
STATED PRINT RUN 25 SER.#'d SETS
EXCHANGE DEADLINE 3/31/2018
IIFR Franklin Reyes EXCH 20.00 50.00
IIFT Fernando Tatis Jr. 150.00 400.00
IIJG Jeison Guzman 20.00 50.00
IIJS Juan Soto 400.00 800.00
IIWJ Wander Javier EXCH 30.00 80.00

2016 Bowman Lucky Redemption Autograph

STATED ODDS 1:25,609 HOBBY
EXCHANGE DEADLINE 3/31/2018
NNO Exchange Card EXCH 250.00 400.00

2016 Bowman Prospects

COMPLETE SET (150) 12.00 30.00
PRINTING PLATE ODDS 1:5355 HOBBY
PLATE PRINT RUN 1 SET PER COLOR
BLACK-CYAN-MAGENTA-YELLOW ISSUED
NO PLATE PRICING DUE TO SCARCITY
BP1 Daz Cameron .15 .40
BP2 Orlando Arcia .20 .50
BP3 Domingo Leyba .15 .40
BP4 Alex Bregman 1.00 2.50
BP5 Yadier Alvarez .25 .60
BP6 Touki Toussaint .20 .50
BP7 Brady Aiken .40 1.00
BP8 Billy McKinney .20 .50
BP9 Stone Garrett .15 .40
BP10 Victor Robles .60 1.50
BP11 Wei-Chieh Huang .15 .40
BP12 Jomar Reyes .25 .60
BP13 Lucius Fox .25 .60
BP14 Samuel Coonrod .15 .40
BP15 Seuly Matias .50 1.25
BP16 Willson Contreras 1.00 2.50
BP17 Fernando Tatis Jr. 15.00 40.00
BP18 Starling Heredia .30 .75
BP19 Drew Jackson .15 .40
BP20 Ruddy Giron .15 .40
BP21 Anfernee Seymour .15 .40
BP22 Iolana Akau .25 .60
BP23 Kevin Padlo .15 .40
BP24 Brady Lail .15 .40
BP25 Dillon Tate .20 .50
BP26 Jharel Cotton .15 .40
BP27 John Norwood .15 .40
BP28 Manny Sanchez .20 .50
BP29 Juan Yepez .15 .40
BP30 David Denson .15 .40
BP31 Jhailyn Ortiz .30 .75
BP32 Wander Javier .25 .60
BP33 Sal Romano .15 .40
BP34 Francis Martes .20 .50
BP35 Domingo Acevedo .25 .60
BP36 Mark Zagunis .15 .40
BP37 Franklyn Kilome .20 .50
BP38 Trey Mancini .50 1.25
BP39 Corey Black .15 .40
BP40 Anderson Espinoza .15 .40
BP41 Jordan Guerrero .15 .40
BP42 Mauricio Dubon .20 .50
BP43 Paul DeJong 1.00 2.50
BP44 Mikey White .15 .40
BP45 Andrew Suarez .20 .50
BP46 Kevin Kramer .20 .50
BP47 Nate Smith .15 .40
BP48 Ariel Jurado .15 .40
BP49 Rafael Bautista .15 .40
BP50 Dansby Swanson .50 1.25
BP51 Anthony Banda .15 .40
BP52 Mike Clevinger .30 .75
BP53 Daniel Poncedeleon .20 .50
BP54 Ian Kahaloa .15 .40
BP55 Vladimir Guerrero Jr. 6.00 15.00
BP56 Logan Allen .15 .40
BP57 Kyle Survance Jr. .15 .40
BP58 Omar Carrizales .15 .40
BP59 Anthony Alford .15 .40
BP60 Kyle Tucker .60 1.50
BP61 Tyler Jay .15 .40
BP62 Andrew Benintendi .50 1.25
BP63 Carson Fulmer .15 .40
BP64 Ian Happ .30 .75
BP65 Sean Newcomb .20 .50
BP66 Tyler Stephenson .15 .40
BP67 Josh Naylor .20 .50
BP68 Garrett Whitley .20 .50
BP69 Kolby Allard .15 .40
BP70 Trent Clark .15 .40
BP71 James Kaprielian .20 .50
BP72 Phil Bickford .15 .40
BP73 Kevin Newman .25 .60
BP74 Richie Martin .15 .40
BP75 Ashe Russell .15 .40
BP76 Beau Burrows .15 .40
BP77 Nick Plummer .20 .50
BP78 Walker Buehler .40 1.00
BP79 D.J. Stewart .15 .40
BP80 Taylor Ward .20 .50
BP81 Mike Nikorak .15 .40
BP82 Michael Soroka .50 1.25
BP83 Kyle Holder .20 .50
BP84 Chris Shaw .25 .60
BP85 Ke'Bryan Hayes .15 .40
BP86 Nolan Watson .15 .40
BP87 Christin Stewart .20 .50
BP88 Ryan Mountcastle .25 .60
BP89 Jack Flaherty .25 .60
BP90 Raimel Tapia .20 .50
BP91 Michael Fulmer .25 .60
BP92 A.J. Reed .15 .40
BP93 Gavin Cecchini .15 .40
BP94 Jorge Mateo .20 .50
BP95 Amed Rosario .25 .60
BP96 Daniel Robertson .15 .40
BP97 Nick Gordon .15 .40
BP98 Rob Kaminsky .15 .40
BP99 Amir Garrett .15 .40
BP100 Brendan Rodgers .25 .60
BP101 Duane Underwood .15 .40
BP102 Alen Hanson .20 .50
BP103 Jorge Alfaro .25 .60
BP104 Grant Holmes .20 .50
BP105 Nick Williams .20 .50
BP106 Tyler Wade .25 .60
BP107 Jake Thompson .15 .40
BP108 Alex Reyes .20 .50
BP109 Rafael Devers .50 1.25
BP110 Ozzie Albies .60 1.50
BP111 Alex Young .20 .50
BP112 Tyrell Jenkins .15 .40
BP113 Max Fried .25 .60
BP114 Chance Sisco .30 .75
BP115 Michael Kopech .40 1.00
BP116 Pierce Johnson .15 .40
BP117 Tyler Danish .15 .40
BP118 Keury Mella .15 .40
BP119 Alex Blandino .15 .40
BP120 Justus Sheffield .30 .75
BP121 Jeff Hoffman .20 .50
BP122 Ryan McMahon .15 .40
BP123 JaCoby Jones .20 .50
BP124 Colin Moran .15 .40
BP125 Derek Fisher .15 .40
BP126 Scott Blewett .15 .40
BP127 Jeimer Candelario .20 .50
BP128 Fernando Perez .15 .40
BP129 Andrew Knapp .15 .40
BP130 Sean Manaea .15 .40
BP131 Jake Bauers .25 .60
BP132 Rowdy Tellez .25 .60
BP133 Gabby Guerrero .15 .40
BP134 Christian Arroyo .50 1.25
BP135 Adam Brett Walker II .15 .40
BP136 Brett Phillips .15 .40
BP137 Lewis Brinson .25 .60
BP138 Bubba Starling .20 .50
BP139 Chad Pinder .15 .40
BP140 Chris Bostick .15 .40
BP141 Luke Weaver .25 .60
BP142 Kenta Maeda .30 .75
BP143 Luiz Gohara .15 .40
BP144 Yoan Lopez .15 .40
BP145 Courtney Hawkins .15 .40
BP146 Austin Dean .15 .40
BP147 Matt Chapman .25 .60
BP148 Yoan Moncada .40 1.00
BP149 Nick Travieso .15 .40
BP150 Lucas Giolito .25 .60

2016 Bowman Prospects Blue

*BLUE: 2X TO 5X BASIC
STATED ODDS 1:143 HOBBY
STATED PRINT RUN 150 SER.#'d SETS

2016 Bowman Prospects Gold

*GOLD: 5X TO 12X BASIC
STATED ODDS 1:429 HOBBY
STATED PRINT RUN 50 SER.#'d SETS

2016 Bowman Prospects Green

*GREEN: 2.5X TO 6X BASIC
INSERTED IN RETAIL PACKS
STATED PRINT RUN 99 SER.#'d SETS

2016 Bowman Prospects Orange

*ORANGE: 8X TO 20X BASIC
STATED ODDS 1:165 HOBBY
STATED PRINT RUN 25 SER.#'d SETS

2016 Bowman Prospects Purple

*PURPLE: 1.5X TO 4X BASIC
STATED ODDS 1:86 HOBBY
STATED PRINT RUN 250 SER.#'d SETS

2016 Bowman Prospects Silver

*SILVER: 1.2X TO 3X BASIC
STATED ODDS 1:43 HOBBY

2016 Bowman Prospects Yellow

*YELLOW: 1.2X TO 3X BASIC
INSERTED IN RETAIL PACKS

2016 Bowman Prospects Autographs

INSERTED IN RETAIL PACKS
EXCHANGE DEADLINE 3/31/2018
PAAN Aaron Northcraft 2.50 6.00
PAAR Adam Ravenelle 3.00 8.00
PABA Blake Anderson 2.50 6.00
PABB B.J. Boyd 2.50 6.00
PABD Brady Dragmire 2.50 6.00
PACG Conner Greene 2.50 6.00
PACM Casey Meisner 2.50 6.00
PACS Connor Sadzeck 2.50 6.00
PADM Daniel Mengden 10.00 25.00
PADS Dansby Swanson 40.00 100.00
PADW Drew Weeks 2.50 6.00
PAEW Erich Weiss 4.00 10.00
PAFM Francisco Mejia 4.00 10.00
PAIK Ian Kahaloa 2.50 6.00
PAJO John Omahen 2.50 6.00
PAJS Joe Sclafani 2.50 6.00
PALS Lucas Sims 2.50 6.00
PAMG Mike Gerber 2.50 6.00
PANG Nick Gordon 2.50 6.00
PAOA Orlando Arcia 3.00 8.00
PAPB Phil Bickford 2.50 6.00
PAPR Pierce Romero 4.00 10.00
PARM Reese McGuire 2.50 6.00
PARP Ricardo Pinto 3.00 8.00
PARW Ryan Williams 5.00 12.00
PATM Thomas Milone 2.50 6.00
PATT Touki Toussaint 4.00 10.00
PAYG Yeudy Garcia 2.50 6.00
PAJST Josh Staumont 3.00 8.00

2016 Bowman Prospects Autographs Gold

*GOLD: 1X TO 2.5X BASIC
INSERTED IN RETAIL PACKS
STATED PRINT RUN 50 SER.#'d SETS
EXCHANGE DEADLINE 3/31/2018
PADT Dillon Tate 8.00 20.00
PAIH Ian Happ 40.00 100.00

2016 Bowman Prospects Autographs Green

*GREEN: .75X TO 2X BASIC
INSERTED IN RETAIL PACKS
STATED PRINT RUN 99 SER.#'d SETS
EXCHANGE DEADLINE 3/31/2018
PADT Dillon Tate 6.00 15.00
PAIH Ian Happ 30.00 80.00

2016 Bowman Prospects Autographs Orange

*ORANGE: 1.2X TO 3X BASIC
INSERTED IN RETAIL PACKS
STATED PRINT RUN 25 SER.#'d SETS
EXCHANGE DEADLINE 3/31/2018
PADS Dansby Swanson 100.00 250.00
PADT Dillon Tate 10.00 25.00
PAIH Ian Happ 50.00 120.00

2016 Bowman Prospects Autographs Purple

*PURPLE: .5X TO 1.2X BASIC
INSERTED IN RETAIL PACKS
STATED PRINT RUN 250 SER.#'d SETS
EXCHANGE DEADLINE 3/31/2018
PADT Dillon Tate 4.00 10.00
PAIH Ian Happ 20.00 50.00

2016 Bowman Sophomore Standouts

COMPLETE SET (15) 4.00 10.00
STATED ODDS 1:8 HOBBY
*BLUE/150: 1.2X TO 3X BASIC
*GREEN/99: 1.5X TO 4X BASIC
*ORANGE/25: 4X TO 10X BASIC
SS1 Kris Bryant .60 1.50
SS2 Byron Buxton .40 1.00
SS3 Carlos Correa .50 1.25
SS4 Francisco Lindor .50 1.25
SS5 Blake Swihart .40 1.00
SS6 Jorge Soler .50 1.25
SS7 Steven Matz .40 1.00
SS8 Rusney Castillo .30 .75
SS9 Noah Syndergaard .40 1.00
SS10 Joc Pederson .40 1.00
SS11 Addison Russell .50 1.25
SS12 Yasmany Tomas .30 .75
SS13 Jung Ho Kang .30 .75
SS14 Daniel Norris .30 .75
SS15 Maikel Franco .40 1.00

2016 Bowman Draft

COMPLETE SET (200) 12.00 30.00
STATED PLATE ODDS 1:947 HOBBY
PLATE PRINT RUN 1 SET PER COLOR
NO PLATE PRICING DUE TO SCARCITY
BD1 Mickey Moniak .75 2.00
BD2 Thomas Jones .15 .40
BD3 Dylan Carlson 2.00 5.00
BD4 Cole Irvin .40 1.00
BD5 Kevin Gowdy .25 .60
BD6 Dakota Hudson .25 .60
BD7 Walker Robbins .15 .40
BD8 Khalil Lee .25 .60
BD9 Logan Ice .15 .40
BD10 Braxton Garrett .20 .50
BD11 Anfernee Grier .20 .50
BD12 Kyle Hart .15 .40
BD13 Taylor Trammell 1.25 3.00
BD14 Brian Serven .15 .40
BD15 Buddy Reed .15 .40
BD16 Carter Kieboom 1.00 2.50
BD17 Jimmy Lambert .15 .40
BD18 Nick Solak .50 1.25
BD19 Alexis Torres .20 .50
BD20 Cal Quantrill .15 .40
BD21 JaVon Shelby .15 .40
BD22 Kyle Funkhouser .20 .50
BD23 Dom Thompson-Williams .25 .60
BD24 Jeremy Martinez .40 1.00
BD25 A.J. Puk .25 .60
BD26 Brett Cumberland .25 .60
BD27 Mason Thompson .15 .40
BD28 Easton McGee .15 .40
BD29 Justin Dunn .15 .40
BD30 Matt Manning .25 .60
BD31 Delvin Perez .50 1.25
BD32 Nolan Jones .25 .60
BD33 Matt Krook .15 .40
BD34 Stephen Alemais .25 .60
BD35 Joey Wentz .25 .60
BD36 Ben Bowden .15 .40
BD37 Drew Harrington .15 .40
BD38 C.J. Chatham .20 .50
BD39 Will Craig .15 .40
BD40 Zack Collins .20 .50
BD41 Skylar Szynski .15 .40
BD42 Sheldon Neuse .20 .50
BD43 Nicholas Lopez .25 .60
BD44 Heath Quinn .30 .75
BD45 Alex Speas .20 .50
BD46 Cody Sedlock .25 .60
BD47 Blake Tiberi .20 .50
BD48 Mario Feliciano .20 .50
BD49 Brett Adcock .15 .40
BD50 Riley Pint .15 .40
BD51 Jacob Heyward .15 .40
BD52 Hudson Potts .20 .50
BD53 Ronnie Dawson .15 .40
BD54 Nick Hanson .15 .40
BD55 Forrest Whitley 1.25 3.00
BD56 Ryan Hendrix .15 .40
BD57 Eric Lauer .20 .50
BD58 Tyson Miller .25 .60
BD59 Jesus Luzardo 1.00 2.50
BD60 Kyle Lewis 3.00 8.00
BD61 Connor Justus .15 .40
BD62 Cole Stobbe .15 .40
BD63 Garrett Hampson .30 .75
BD64 Cole Ragans .20 .50
BD65 Kyle Muller .20 .50
BD66 Logan Shore .20 .50
BD67 Gavin Lux 1.50 4.00
BD68 Shane Bieber 2.00 5.00
BD69 T.J. Zeuch .20 .50
BD70 Joshua Lowe .15 .40
BD71 Justin Alleman .15 .40
BD72 Ryan Howard .15 .40
BD73 Jake Fraley .20 .50
BD74 Bo Bichette 4.00 10.00
BD75 D.J. Peters .75 2.00
BD76 Jake Rogers .75 2.00
BD77 Bryan Reynolds .50 1.25
BD78 Colton Welker .25 .60
BD79 Nick Banks .15 .40
BD80 Will Benson .25 .60
BD81 Cavan Biggio 1.50 4.00
BD82 Braden Webb .15 .40
BD83 Chris Okey .15 .40
BD84 Will Smith 1.25 3.00
BD85 A.J. Puckett .20 .50
BD86 Colby Woodmansee .20 .50
BD87 Andy Yerzy .15 .40
BD88 J.B. Woodman .25 .60
BD89 Corbin Burnes .25 .60
BD90 Alex Kirilloff 1.50 4.00
BD91 Robert Tyler .15 .40
BD92 Pete Alonso 3.00 8.00
BD93 Alec Hansen .20 .50
BD94 Daniel Johnson .15 .40
BD95 Mike Shawaryn .20 .50
BD96 Daulton Jefferies .20 .50
BD97 Jordan Sheffield .15 .40
BD98 Conner Capel .15 .40
BD99 Bobby Dalbec .60 1.50
BD100 Corey Ray .25 .60
BD101 Ben Rortvedt .20 .50
BD102 Tim Lynch .25 .60
BD103 Charles Leblanc .15 .40
BD104 Dane Dunning .20 .50
BD105 Bryson Brigman .15 .40
BD106 Nolan Martinez .20 .50
BD107 Connor Jones .20 .50
BD108 Alex Call .15 .40
BD109 Reggie Lawson .15 .40
BD110 Matt Thaiss .15 .40
BD111 Bryse Wilson .50 1.25
BD112 Zack Burdi .20 .50
BD113 Nolan Williams .15 .40
BD114 Mark Ecker .15 .40
BD115 Michael Paez .25 .60
BD116 Zach Jackson .15 .40
BD117 Joe Rizzo .15 .40
BD118 Ryan Boldt .20 .50
BD119 Mikey York .15 .40
BD120 Ian Anderson .40 1.00
BD121 Austin Meadows .25 .60
BD122 Nick Gordon .15 .40
BD123 Forrest Wall .15 .40
BD124 Antonio Senzatela .15 .40
BD125 Justus Sheffield .30 .75
BD126 Christian Arroyo .50 1.25
BD127 Dylan Cease .40 1.00
BD128 Scott Kingery .25 .60
BD129 Daniel Palka .15 .40
BD130 Bradley Zimmer .25 .60
BD131 Amir Garrett .15 .40
BD132 Dillon Tate .20 .50
BD133 Domingo Leyba .15 .40
BD134 Tyler Jay .15 .40
BD135 Sean Reid-Foley .20 .50
BD136 James Kaprielian .20 .50
BD137 Kyle Tucker .60 1.50
BD138 Derek Fisher .15 .40
BD139 Tyler O'Neill .20 .50
BD140 Anderson Espinoza .15 .40
BD141 Christin Stewart .20 .50
BD142 Grant Holmes .20 .50
BD143 Rafael Devers .50 1.25
BD144 Mitch Keller .20 .50
BD145 Francis Martes .20 .50
BD146 Nellie Rodriguez .15 .40
BD147 Chih-Wei Hu .20 .50
BD148 Anthony Banda .15 .40
BD149 Trent Clark .15 .40
BD150 Brendan Rodgers .25 .60
BD151 Ryan Cordell .15 .40
BD152 Daz Cameron .15 .40
BD153 Billy McKinney .20 .50
BD154 Jomar Reyes .25 .60
BD155 Jake Bauers .25 .60
BD156 Willy Adames .25 .60
BD157 Josh Hader .20 .50
BD158 Luis Ortiz .15 .40
BD159 Erick Fedde .15 .40
BD160 Gleyber Torres 2.50 6.00
BD161 Francisco Mejia .25 .60
BD162 Kolby Allard .15 .40
BD163 Ronnie Williams .15 .40
BD164 Matt Chapman .25 .60
BD165 Austin Riley .50 1.25
BD166 Austin Dean .15 .40
BD167 Ryan McMahon .15 .40
BD168 Anfernee Seymour .15 .40
BD169 Marcos Diplan .15 .40
BD170 Anthony Alford .15 .40
BD171 Nick Neidert .15 .40
BD172 Bobby Bradley .20 .50
BD173 Tyler Wade .25 .60
BD174 Chase De Jong .20 .50
BD175 Brett Phillips .15 .40
BD176 Dominic Smith .15 .40
BD177 Touki Toussaint .20 .50
BD178 Reese McGuire .15 .40
BD179 Franklin Barreto .15 .40
BD180 Ian Happ .30 .75
BD181 Javier Guerra .15 .40
BD182 Tyler Beede .20 .50
BD183 Drew Jackson .15 .40
BD184 Brent Honeywell .25 .60
BD185 Michael Gettys .15 .40
BD186 Rhys Hoskins .60 1.50
BD187 Dylan Cozens .15 .40
BD188 Jon Harris .20 .50
BD189 Phil Bickford .15 .40
BD190 Amed Rosario .25 .60
BD191 Eloy Jimenez .60 1.50
BD192 Jack Flaherty .25 .60
BD193 Alex Young .20 .50
BD194 Andrew Sopko .15 .40
BD195 Rafael Bautista .15 .40
BD196 Chris Shaw .25 .60
BD197 Mike Gerber .15 .40
BD198 Kevin Newman .25 .60
BD199 Ryan Mountcastle .25 .60
BD200 Lucius Fox .25 .60

2016 Bowman Draft Blue

*BLUE: 2X TO 5X BASIC
STATED ODDS 1:26 HOBBY
STATED PRINT RUN 150 SER.#'d SETS
BD160 Gleyber Torres 15.00 40.00

2016 Bowman Draft Gold

*GOLD: 4X TO 10X BASIC
STATED ODDS 1:76 HOBBY
STATED PRINT RUN 50 SER.#'d SETS
BD160 Gleyber Torres 30.00 80.00

2016 Bowman Draft Green

*GREEN: 2.5X TO 6X BASIC
STATED ODDS 1:39 HOBBY
STATED PRINT RUN 99 SER.#'d SETS
BD160 Gleyber Torres 20.00 50.00

2016 Bowman Draft Orange

*ORANGE: 5X TO 12X BASIC
STATED ODDS 1:152 HOBBY
STATED PRINT RUN 25 SER.#'d SETS
BD160 Gleyber Torres 40.00 100.00

2016 Bowman Draft Silver

*SILVER: 1X TO 2.5X BASIC
STATED ODDS 1:8 HOBBY
STATED PRINT RUN 499 SER.#'d SETS
BD160 Gleyber Torres 8.00 20.00

2016 Bowman Draft Golden Debut Contract Winner

STATED ODDS 1:1520 HOBBY
GDWFP Francis Pablo 6.00 15.00

2017 Bowman

COMPLETE SET (100) 6.00 15.00
PRINTING PLATE ODDS 1:8827 HOBBY
PLATE PRINT RUN 1 SET PER COLOR
BLACK-CYAN-MAGENTA-YELLOW ISSUED
NO PLATE PRICING DUE TO SCARCITY
1 Kris Bryant .30 .75
2 Kenta Maeda .20 .50
3 Bryce Harper .40 1.00
4 Jeff Hoffman RC .25 .60
5 Trevor Story .25 .60
6 Mookie Betts .40 1.00
7 Cole Hamels .20 .50
8 Matt Carpenter .25 .60
9 Carlos Correa .25 .60
10 Jose Bautista .20 .50
11 Ryan Braun .20 .50
12 Trea Turner .20 .50
13 Stephen Piscotty .20 .50
14 Stephen Strasburg .25 .60
15 Buster Posey .30 .75
16 Joey Votto .25 .60
17 Yoenis Cespedes .25 .60
18 Andrew McCutchen .20 .50
19 Jose Altuve .50 1.25
20 Manny Margot RC .20 .50
21 Giancarlo Stanton .25 .60
22 Carson Fulmer RC .20 .50
23 Andrew Benintendi RC .75 2.00
24 Craig Kimbrel .20 .50
25 Yoan Moncada RC .75 2.00
26 Teoscar Hernandez RC .75 2.00
27 Reynaldo Lopez RC .25 .60
28 Miguel Cabrera .25 .60
29 Yulieski Gurriel RC .40 1.00
30 Nomar Mazara .15 .40
31 Josh Donaldson .20 .50
32 Aaron Judge RC 3.00 8.00
33 Ichiro .30 .75
34 Robert Gsellman RC .25 .60
35 Ryon Healy RC .30 .75
36 Anthony Rizzo .40 1.00
37 Evan Longoria .20 .50
38 Andrew Miller .20 .50
39 Noah Syndergaard .20 .50
40 Manny Machado .25 .60
41 Orlando Arcia RC .40 1.00
42 Jose De Leon RC .25 .60
43 Max Scherzer .25 .60
44 Freddie Freeman .30 .75
45 Kyle Schwarber .25 .60
46 Willson Contreras .25 .60
47 Tim Anderson .25 .60
48 Gregory Polanco .20 .50
49 Nolan Arenado .30 .75
50 Corey Seager .25 .60
51 Troy Tulowitzki .25 .60
52 David Ortiz .25 .60
53 Odubel Herrera .20 .50
54 David Dahl RC .30 .75
55 Rob Segedin RC .25 .60
56 Tyler Glasnow RC .30 .75
57 Dansby Swanson RC .60 1.50
58 Francisco Lindor .25 .60
59 Nelson Cruz .25 .60
60 Jorge Alfaro RC .30 .75
61 Jameson Taillon .25 .60
62 Jake Thompson RC .25 .60
63 Hunter Dozier RC .25 .60
64 Matt Strahm RC .25 .60
65 Ben Zobrist .20 .50
66 Gavin Cecchini RC .25 .60
67 Aledmys Diaz .20 .50
68 Mark Trumbo .15 .40
69 Wil Myers .15 .40
70 Felix Hernandez .20 .50
71 Jake Lamb .20 .50
72 Dellin Betances .20 .50
73 Jacob deGrom .25 .60
74 Robinson Cano .20 .50
75 Alex Bregman RC 1.00 2.50
76 Xander Bogaerts .25 .60
77 Julio Urias .25 .60
78 Raimel Tapia RC .30 .75
79 Jon Lester .20 .50
80 Clayton Kershaw .50 1.25
81 Yu Darvish .25 .60
82 Jackie Bradley Jr. .25 .60
83 Braden Shipley RC .25 .60
84 Starling Marte .20 .50
85 Gary Sanchez .25 .60
86 Tyler Austin RC .40 1.00
87 George Springer .20 .50
88 Paul Goldschmidt .25 .60
89 Jharel Cotton RC .25 .60
90 Brandon Belt .20 .50
91 Chris Sale .25 .60
92 Joe Musgrove RC .25 .60
93 Danny Salazar .20 .50
94 Michael Fulmer .15 .40
95 Justin Bour .20 .50
96 Jake Arrieta .20 .50
97 Daniel Murphy .20 .50
98 Alex Reyes RC .30 .75
99 Hunter Renfroe RC .30 .75
100 Mike Trout 1.25 3.00

2017 Bowman Blue

*BLUE: 2.5X TO 6X BASIC
*BLUE RC: 1.5X TO 4X BASIC RC
STATED ODDS 1:235 HOBBY
STATED PRINT RUN 150 SER.#'d SETS

2017 Bowman Gold

*GOLD: 6X TO 15X BASIC
*GOLD RC: 4X TO 10X BASIC RC
STATED ODDS 1:703 HOBBY
STATED PRINT RUN 50 SER.#'d SETS

2017 Bowman Green

*GREEN: 4X TO 10X BASIC
*GREEN RC: 2.5X TO 6X BASIC RC
RANDOM INSERTS IN RETAIL PACKS
STATED PRINT RUN 99 SER.#'d SETS

2017 Bowman Orange

*ORANGE: 8X TO 20X BASIC
*ORANGE RC: 5X TO 12X BASIC RC
STATED ODDS 1:304 HOBBY
STATED PRINT RUN 25 SER.#'d SETS

2017 Bowman Purple

*PURPLE: 2X TO 5X BASIC
*PURPLE RC: 1.2X TO 3X BASIC RC
STATED ODDS 1:141 HOBBY
STATED PRINT RUN 250 SER.#'d SETS

2017 Bowman Silver

*SILVER: 1.5X TO 4X BASIC
*SILVER RC: 1X TO 2.5X BASIC RC
STATED ODDS 1:71 HOBBY
STATED PRINT RUN 499 SER.#'d SETS

2017 Bowman Buyback Autographs

STATED ODDS 1:14,772 HOBBY
STATED PRINT RUN 20 SER.#'d SETS
EXCHANGE DEADLINE 3/31/2019
20 Roberto Alomar EXCH 30.00 80.00
82 Pedro Martinez 75.00 200.00
148 Greg Maddux 75.00 200.00
197 Mark McGwire EXCH 60.00 150.00
253 Randy Johnson
266 John Smoltz EXCH 40.00 100.00
320 Frank Thomas 125.00 250.00
461 Mike Piazza 150.00 300.00
569 Chipper Jones 250.00 500.00

2017 Bowman Prospect Autographs

RANDOMLY INSERTED IN RETAIL PACKS
EXCHANGE DEADLINE 3/31/2019
PAAP A.J. Puk 4.00 10.00
PADE Dietrich Enns 3.00 8.00
PADL Dinelson Lamet 10.00 25.00
PADLU Dawel Lugo 2.50 6.00
PADW Devin Williams 8.00 20.00
PAEA Eddy Alvarez 3.00 8.00
PAER Edwin Rios 8.00 20.00
PAGA Greg Allen 4.00 10.00
PAIA Ian Anderson
PAIW Isaiah White 2.50 6.00
PAJDP Juan De Paula 3.00 8.00
PAJG Jason Groome 8.00 20.00
PAJM Jorge Mateo 8.00 20.00
PAJR Josh Rogers 3.00 8.00
PAJS Jackson Stephens 3.00 8.00
PAKG Kelvin Gutierrez 2.50 6.00
PAKL Kyle Lewis
PALT Leody Taveras 10.00 25.00
PAMM Mickey Moniak 12.00 30.00
PAMMA Matt Manning
PAMS Miguelangel Sierra 5.00 12.00
PAMW Mitchell White 4.00 10.00
PANN Nick Neidert 2.50 6.00
PANS Nick Senzel 40.00 100.00
PAPW Patrick Weigel 2.50 6.00
PARR Raudy Read 3.00 8.00
PASM Scott Moss 4.00 10.00
PASN Sean Newcomb 4.00 10.00
PATM Tyson Miller 3.00 8.00
PATS Tanner Scott 2.50 6.00
PAZR Zach Rice 3.00 8.00

2017 Bowman Prospect Autographs Gold

*GOLD: 1X TO 2.5X BASIC
INSERTED IN RETAIL PACKS
STATED PRINT RUN 50 SER.#'d SETS
EXCHANGE DEADLINE 3/31/2019

2017 Bowman Prospect Autographs Green

*GREEN: .75X TO 2X BASIC
INSERTED IN RETAIL PACKS
STATED PRINT RUN 99 SER.#'d SETS
EXCHANGE DEADLINE 3/31/2019

2017 Bowman Prospect Autographs Orange

*ORANGE: 1.2X TO 3X BASIC
INSERTED IN RETAIL PACKS
STATED PRINT RUN 25 SER.#'d SETS
EXCHANGE DEADLINE 3/31/2019

2017 Bowman Prospect Autographs Purple

*PURPLE: .5X TO 1.2X BASIC
INSERTED IN RETAIL PACKS
STATED PRINT RUN 250 SER.#'d SETS
EXCHANGE DEADLINE 3/31/2019

2017 Bowman Prospects

COMPLETE SET (150) 40.00 100.00
PRINTING PLATE ODDS 1:5838 HOBBY
PLATE PRINT RUN 1 SET PER COLOR
NO PLATE PRICING DUE TO SCARCITY
BP1 Nick Senzel .50 1.25
BP2 Gavin Lux 1.00 2.50
BP3 Ronald Guzman .20 .50
BP4 A.J. Puckett .15 .40
BP5 Mike Soroka .50 1.25
BP6 Roniel Raudes .15 .40
BP7 Lucas Erceg .20 .50
BP8 Luis Almanzar .15 .40
BP9 Beau Burrows .15 .40
BP10 Chase Vallot .15 .40
BP11 P.J. Conlon .15 .40
BP12 Erick Fedde .15 .40
BP13 Rookie Davis .15 .40
BP14 Chris Shaw .15 .40
BP15 Nick Burdi .15 .40
BP16 Clint Frazier .30 .75
BP17 Luiz Gohara .15 .40
BP18 Lourdes Gurriel Jr. .25 .60
BP19 Eric Jenkins .15 .40
BP20 Angel Perdomo .15 .40
BP21 Dustin May 1.00 2.50
BP22 Freddy Peralta .25 .60
BP23 Jarlin Garcia .15 .40
BP24 Tyler O'Neill .20 .50
BP25 Lazarito Armenteros .40 1.00
BP26 Paul DeJong .50 1.25
BP27 Antonio Senzatela .15 .40
BP28 Kyle Tucker .30 .75
BP29 Aramis Garcia .15 .40
BP30 Willie Calhoun .25 .60
BP31 Chance Adams .25 .60
BP32 Vladimir Guerrero Jr. 2.00 5.00
BP33 Braxton Garrett .15 .40
BP34 Yeudy Garcia .15 .40
BP35 Dane Dunning .15 .40
BP36 Andy Ibanez .15 .40
BP37 Francisco Rios .15 .40
BP38 Joe Jimenez .15 .40
BP39 Dylan Cozens .15 .40
BP40 Mauricio Dubon .20 .50
BP41 Franklyn Kilome .20 .50

BP42 Chance Sisco .30 .75
BP43 Sandy Alcantara .20 .50
BP44 Stephen Gonsalves .15 .40
BP45 Grant Holmes .15 .40
BP46 Dakota Chalmers .15 .40
BP47 Kolby Allard .15 .40
BP48 Tyler Alexander .15 .40
BP49 Phil Bickford .15 .40
BP50 Eloy Jimenez .60 1.50
BP51 Francisco Mejia .25 .60
BP52 Kohl Stewart .15 .40
BP53 Garrett Whitley .15 .40
BP54 Anderson Espinoza .15 .40
BP55 Cal Quantrill .15 .40
BP56 Tetsuto Yamada .30 .75
BP57 Tyler Beede .15 .40
BP58 Jake Bauers .20 .50
BP59 Ariel Jurado .15 .40
BP60 Austin Voth .15 .40
BP61 Tyler Stephenson .15 .40
BP62 Yoshitomo Tsutsugo .25 .60
BP63 Dominic Smith .15 .40
BP64 Matt Thaiss .15 .40
BP65 Austin Meadows .25 .60
BP66 Mitch Keller .20 .50
BP67 Jahmai Jones .15 .40
BP68 Alex Speas .15 .40
BP69 Nolan Jones .25 .60
BP70 Kevin Newman .25 .60
BP71 T.J. Friedl .15 .40
BP72 Oscar De La Cruz .15 .40
BP73 Victor Robles .40 1.00
BP74 Patrick Weigel .15 .40
BP75 Ryan Mountcastle .25 .60
BP76 Amed Rosario .25 .60
BP77 Nick Solak .40 1.00
BP78 Abrahan Gutierrez .25 .60
BP79 Yu-Cheng Chang .25 .60
BP80 Gleyber Torres 2.50 6.00
BP81 J.D. Davis .20 .50
BP82 Walker Buehler .40 1.00
BP83 Andrew Sopko .15 .40
BP84 Brent Honeywell .20 .50
BP85 Kyle Funkhouser .20 .50
BP86 Brian Mundell .15 .40
BP87 Brian Anderson .20 .50
BP88 Brendan Rodgers .20 .50
BP89 Josh Staumont .15 .40
BP90 Cody Sedlock .15 .40
BP91 D.J. Stewart .15 .40
BP92 Wuilmer Becerra .15 .40
BP93 Nate Smith .15 .40
BP94 Alfredo Rodriguez .20 .50
BP95 Daz Cameron .15 .40
BP96 Taylor Ward .20 .50
BP97 Takahiro Norimoto .15 .40
BP98 Tomoyuki Sugano .25 .60
BP99 Drew Jackson .15 .40
BP100 Kevin Maitan .40 1.00
BP101 Rafael Devers .30 .75
BP102 Alex Kirilloff .40 1.00
BP103 Jack Flaherty .25 .60
BP104 Adonis Medina .25 .60
BP105 Ke'Bryan Hayes .15 .40
BP106 Josh Hader .15 .40
BP107 Luis Urias .60 1.50
BP108 Donnie Dewees .15 .40
BP109 Kyle Freeland .20 .50
BP110 Matt Chapman .25 .60
BP111 Sam Coonrod .15 .40
BP112 Andrew Suarez .15 .40
BP113 David Fletcher .50 1.25
BP114 Tyler Jay .15 .40
BP115 Franklin Barreto .15 .40
BP116 Michael Kopech .30 .75
BP117 Rhys Hoskins .60 1.50
BP118 Triston McKenzie .15 .40
BP119 Luis Garcia .50 1.25
BP120 Harold Ramirez .20 .50
BP121 Blake Rutherford .25 .60
BP122 Matt Manning .25 .60
BP123 Josh Morgan .15 .40
BP124 Dylan Cease .40 1.00
BP125 Kyle Lewis .30 .75
BP126 Nick Neidert .15 .40
BP127 Ronald Acuna 10.00 25.00
BP128 Luis Ortiz .15 .40
BP129 Isael Soto .15 .40
BP130 Adrian Morejon .25 .60
BP131 Mark Zagunis .15 .40
BP132 Justus Sheffield .25 .60
BP133 Jaime Schultz .15 .40
BP134 Fernando Romero .15 .40
BP135 Mickey Moniak .40 1.00
BP136 Jorge Bonifacio .15 .40
BP137 Jomar Reyes .15 .40
BP138 Thomas Szapucki .20 .50
BP139 Sean Reid-Foley .15 .40
BP140 Willy Adames .20 .50
BP141 Yang Hyeon-Jong .20 .50
BP142 Bo Bichette .60 1.50
BP143 Harrison Bader .25 .60
BP144 Travis Demeritte .15 .40
BP145 Juan Hillman .15 .40
BP146 Francis Martes .15 .40
BP147 Wilkerman Garcia .20 .50
BP148 Christin Stewart .20 .50
BP149 Cody Bellinger 2.50 6.00
BP150 Jason Groome .30 .75

2017 Bowman Prospects 70th Red

*70TH RED: 1.5X TO 4X BASIC
STATED ODDS 1:94 HOBBY

2017 Bowman Prospects Blue

*BLUE: 2X TO 5X BASIC
STATED ODDS 1:157 HOBBY
STATED PRINT RUN 150 SER.#'d SETS
BP149 Cody Bellinger 25.00 60.00

2017 Bowman Prospects Gold

*GOLD: 5X TO 12X BASIC
STATED ODDS 1:469 HOBBY
STATED PRINT RUN 50 SER.#'d SETS
BP1 Nick Senzel 15.00 40.00
BP121 Blake Rutherford 15.00 40.00
BP149 Cody Bellinger 60.00 150.00

2017 Bowman Prospects Green

*GREEN: 2.5X TO 6X BASIC
RANDOMLY INSERTED IN RETAIL PACKS
STATED PRINT RUN 99 SER.#'d SETS
BP1 Nick Senzel 8.00 20.00
BP121 Blake Rutherford 8.00 20.00
BP149 Cody Bellinger 30.00 80.00

2017 Bowman Prospects Orange

*ORANGE: 8X TO 20X BASIC
STATED ODDS 1:203 HOBBY
STATED PRINT RUN 25 SER.#'d SETS
BP1 Nick Senzel 25.00 60.00
BP121 Blake Rutherford 25.00 60.00
BP149 Cody Bellinger 100.00 250.00

2017 Bowman Prospects Purple

*PURPLE: 1.5X TO 4X BASIC
STATED ODDS 1:94 HOBBY
STATED PRINT RUN 250 SER.#'d SETS
BP149 Cody Bellinger 20.00 50.00

2017 Bowman Prospects Silver

*SILVER: 1.2X TO 3X BASIC
STATED ODDS 1:47 HOBBY
STATED PRINT RUN 499 SER.#'d SETS

2017 Bowman Prospects Yellow

*YELLOW: 1.2X TO 3X BASIC
RANDOMLY INSERTED IN RETAIL PACKS

2017 Bowman Draft

COMPLETE SET (200) 12.00 30.00
STATED PLATE ODDS 1:1136 HOBBY
PLATE PRINT RUN 1 SET PER COLOR
BLACK-CYAN-MAGENTA-YELLOW ISSUED
NO PLATE PRICING DUE TO SCARCITY
BD1 Royce Lewis 1.25 3.00
BD2 Jacob Gonzalez .50 1.25
BD3 Seth Elledge .15 .40
BD4 Stuart Fairchild .20 .50
BD5 Franklin Perez .25 .60
BD6 Jeter Downs .30 .75
BD7 Yu-Cheng Chang .25 .60
BD8 T.J. Friedl .15 .40
BD9 Alex Scherff .25 .60
BD10 Nick Solak .40 1.00
BD11 Lincoln Henzman .15 .40
BD12 Heliot Ramos 1.25 3.00
BD13 Riley Adams .20 .50
BD14 Wyatt Mills .15 .40
BD15 Alex Faedo .25 .60
BD16 Marcos Diplan .15 .40
BD17 Daulton Varsho .20 .50
BD18 Jacob Heatherly .15 .40
BD19 Lourdes Gurriel Jr. .25 .60
BD20 Zach Kirtley .20 .50
BD21 Cal Quantrill .15 .40
BD22 Jacob Heyward .15 .40
BD23 Alec Hansen .15 .40
BD24 Quinn Brodey .15 .40
BD25 MacKenzie Gore 1.00 2.50
BD26 Mitch Keller .20 .50
BD27 Joey Morgan .20 .50
BD28 Juan Hillman .15 .40
BD29 Freddy Peralta .25 .60
BD30 Morgan Cooper .20 .50
BD31 Brett Netzer .30 .75
BD32 Alex Lange .25 .60
BD33 Hans Crouse .40 1.00
BD34 Michael Kopech .30 .75
BD35 Cole Ragans .15 .40
BD36 Kolby Allard .15 .40
BD37 Matt Manning .25 .60
BD38 Bo Bichette .60 1.50
BD39 Ronald Acuna 3.00 8.00
BD40 Cristian Pache .75 2.00
BD41 Ryan Vilade .25 .60
BD42 Tyler Freeman .15 .40
BD43 Cory Abbott .15 .40
BD44 Shane Baz .25 .60
BD45 Brian Miller .15 .40
BD46 Luis Campusano .20 .50
BD47 A.J. Puk .25 .60
BD48 Griffin Canning .25 .60
BD49 Justin Dunn .15 .40
BD50 Jorge Mateo .15 .40
BD51 Trevor Clifton .15 .40
BD52 Carter Kieboom .25 .60
BD53 Trevor Rogers .25 .60
BD54 Tommy Doyle .15 .40
BD55 Adam Hall .25 .60
BD56 Will Benson .15 .40
BD57 Ariel Jurado .15 .40
BD58 Forrest Whitley .50 1.25
BD59 Daniel Tillo .25 .60
BD60 Austin Beck .60 1.50
BD61 Jahmai Jones .15 .40
BD62 Adonis Medina .25 .60
BD63 Blayne Enlow .20 .50
BD64 Ryley Widell .25 .60
BD65 Tanner Houck .75 2.00
BD66 Caden Lemons .15 .40
BD67 Buddy Reed .15 .40
BD68 T.J. Zeuch .15 .40
BD69 Vladimir Gutierrez .15 .40
BD70 Anderson Espinoza .15 .40
BD71 Fernando Tatis Jr. 1.25 3.00
BD72 Eloy Jimenez .60 1.50
BD73 Jose Taveras .20 .50
BD74 Christopher Seise .25 .60
BD75 Keston Hiura 1.25 3.00
BD76 Charlie Barnes .15 .40
BD77 Connor Seabold .15 .40
BD78 David Peterson .20 .50
BD79 Seth Corry .15 .40
BD80 Blake Rutherford .25 .60
BD81 Conner Uselton .25 .60
BD82 D.L. Hall .20 .50
BD83 Peter Alonso 1.50 4.00
BD84 Glenn Otto .15 .40
BD85 Gavin Sheets .25 .60
BD86 Luis Gonzalez .20 .50
BD87 Taylor Walls .15 .40
BD88 Ernie Clement .20 .50
BD89 Dylan Carlson 1.00 2.50
BD90 Drew Waters 1.00 2.50
BD91 Christin Stewart .20 .50
BD92 Cal Mitchell .30 .75
BD93 Troy Bacon .25 .60
BD94 Zac Lowther .20 .50
BD95 Jo Adell 1.25 3.00
BD96 Francisco Rios .15 .40
BD97 Mason House .25 .60
BD98 Corey Ray .20 .50
BD99 Anfernee Grier .15 .40
BD100 Brendan McKay .60 1.50
BD101 Kacy Clemens .20 .50
BD102 Isan Diaz .40 1.00
BD103 Drew Strotman .15 .40
BD104 Will Gaddis .15 .40
BD105 Jacob Pearson .15 .40
BD106 Tyler Ivey .15 .40
BD107 Nick Allen .20 .50
BD108 Andy Ibanez .15 .40
BD109 J.J. Matijevic .20 .50
BD110 KJ Harrison .25 .60
BD111 Riley Pint .15 .40
BD112 Franklyn Kilome .20 .50
BD113 Peyton Remy .25 .60
BD114 Scott Kingery .25 .60
BD115 Adam Haseley .30 .75
BD116 Will Smith .40 1.00
BD117 Anderson Tejeda .15 .40
BD118 Quentin Holmes .20 .50
BD119 Nate Pearson .40 1.00
BD120 Kyle Wright .50 1.25
BD121 Matthew Whatley .15 .40
BD122 Brent Rooker .40 1.00
BD123 Daulton Jefferies .20 .50
BD124 Taylor Ward .20 .50
Missing card number
BD125 Triston McKenzie .15 .40
BD126 Scott Hurst .20 .50
BD127 Noah Bremer .15 .40
BD128 Angel Perdomo .15 .40
BD129 Touki Toussaint .20 .50
BD130 A.J. Puckett .15 .40
BD131 Lucas Erceg .20 .50
BD132 Riley Mahan .15 .40
BD133 Corbin Martin .15 .40
BD134 Jordan Sheffield .15 .40
BD135 Lazarito Armenteros .40 1.00
BD136 Dylan Cease .40 1.00
BD137 Kevin Newman .25 .60
BD138 Hagen Danner .20 .50
BD139 Mark Vientos .25 .60
BD140 Justus Sheffield .25 .60
BD141 Bubba Thompson .25 .60
BD142 Desmond Lindsay .15 .40
BD143 J.B. Bukauskas .25 .60
BD144 Freddy Tarnok .20 .50
BD145 Blake Hunt .15 .40
BD146 David Thompson .20 .50
BD147 Delvin Perez .25 .60
BD148 Peter Solomon .20 .50
BD149 Brendan Murphy .15 .40
BD150 Vladimir Guerrero Jr. 2.00 5.00
BD151 Yusniel Diaz .50 1.25
BD152 Dillon Tate .20 .50
BD153 Nonie Williams .25 .60
BD154 Kyle Lewis .30 .75
BD155 Bobby Dalbec .40 1.00
BD156 Ian Anderson .40 1.00
BD157 Brendan Rodgers .20 .50
BD158 Drew Ellis .25 .60
BD159 Joseph Dunand .30 .75
BD160 Kevin Maitan .40 1.00
BD161 Kramer Robertson .30 .75
BD162 Juan Soto 3.00 8.00
BD163 Chris Okey .15 .40
BD164 Tristen Lutz .25 .60
BD165 Wil Crowe .25 .60
BD166 Taylor Trammell .25 .60
BD167 Trevor Stephan .25 .60
BD168 Matt Tabor .15 .40
BD169 James Marinan .25 .60
BD170 Cody Sedlock .15 .40
BD171 Gavin Lux 1.00 2.50
BD172 MJ Melendez .25 .60
BD173 Kade McClure .15 .40
BD174 Dylan Busby .15 .40
BD175 Kevin Merrell .20 .50
BD176 Dawel Lugo .15 .40
BD177 Jake Burger .30 .75
BD178 Evan White .25 .60
BD179 Cal Stajduhar .15 .40
BD180 Connor Wong .25 .60
BD181 Canaan Smith .50 1.25
BD182 Nick Raquet .15 .40
BD183 Kyle Tucker .30 .75
BD184 Sam Carlson .20 .50
BD185 Wuilmer Becerra .15 .40
Missing card number
BD186 Dane Dunning .15 .40
BD187 Joe Perez .20 .50
BD188 Brendon Little .20 .50
BD189 Will Craig .15 .40
BD190 Ricardo De La Torre .15 .40
BD191 Nick Gordon .15 .40
BD192 Kevin Smith .15 .40
BD193 Cole Brannen .25 .60
BD194 Logan Warmoth .25 .60
BD195 Pavin Smith .50 1.25
BD196 Colton Hock .20 .50
BD197 Clarke Schmidt .25 .60
BD198 Cash Case .25 .60
BD199 Luis Ortiz .15 .40
BD200 Gleyber Torres 2.50 6.00

2017 Bowman Draft Blue

*BLUE: 2X TO 5X BASIC
STATED ODDS 1:31 HOBBY
STATED PRINT RUN 150 SER.#'d SETS

2017 Bowman Draft Gold

*GOLD: 4X TO 10X BASIC
STATED ODDS 1:91 HOBBY
STATED PRINT RUN 50 SER.#'d SETS
BD12 Heliot Ramos 15.00 40.00

2017 Bowman Draft Green

*GREEN: 2.5X TO 6X BASIC
STATED ODDS 1:46 HOBBY
STATED PRINT RUN 99 SER.#'d SETS

2017 Bowman Draft Orange

*ORANGE: 5X TO 12X BASIC
STATED ODDS 1:127 HOBBY
STATED PRINT RUN 25 SER.#'d SETS
BD12 Heliot Ramos 20.00 50.00

2017 Bowman Draft Purple

*PURPLE: 2X TO 5X BASIC
STATED ODDS 1:19 HOBBY
STATED PRINT RUN 250 SER.#'d SETS

2017 Bowman Draft Silver

*SILVER: 1X TO 2.5X BASIC
STATED ODDS 1:10 HOBBY
STATED PRINT RUN 499 SER.#'d SETS

2018 Bowman

COMPLETE SET (100) 10.00 25.00
PRINTING PLATE ODDS 1:11,757 HOBBY
PLATE PRINT RUN 1 SET PER COLOR
BLACK-CYAN-MAGENTA-YELLOW ISSUED
NO PLATE PRICING DUE TO SCARCITY
1 Mike Trout 1.25 3.00
2 Francisco Mejia RC .30 .75
3 Corey Kluber .20 .50
4 Zack Greinke .20 .50
5 Paul Goldschmidt .25 .60
6 Victor Robles RC .60 1.50
7 Keon Broxton .15 .40
8 Hunter Renfroe .15 .40
9 Zack Granite RC .25 .60
10 Rhys Hoskins RC 1.00 2.50
11 Jen-Ho Tseng RC .15 .40
12 Chance Sisco RC .30 .75
13 Maikel Franco .20 .50
14 George Springer .20 .50
15 Corey Knebel .15 .40
16 Matt Olson .15 .40
17 Nicholas Castellanos .25 .60
18 Salvador Perez .20 .50
19 Yoan Moncada .25 .60
20 Raudy Read RC .25 .60
21 Noah Syndergaard .25 .60
22 Albert Pujols .30 .75
23 Richard Urena RC .25 .60
24 Aaron Judge .60 1.50
25 Rafael Devers RC .75 2.00
26 Clint Frazier RC .50 1.25
27 Wil Myers .15 .40
28 Manny Machado .25 .60
29 Miguel Cabrera .25 .60
30 Stephen Strasburg .25 .60
31 Willie Calhoun RC .30 .75
32 Tyler Mahle RC .30 .75
33 Anthony Rizzo .40 1.00
34 Amed Rosario RC .30 .75
35 Erick Fedde RC .20 .50
36 Dustin Fowler RC .25 .60
37 Sandy Alcantara RC .25 .60
38 Andrew Benintendi .40 1.00
39 Jose Berrios .20 .50
40 Francisco Lindor .25 .60
41 Freddie Freeman .30 .75
42 Harrison Bader RC .40 1.00
43 Joey Votto .25 .60
44 Chris Archer .15 .40
45 Khris Davis .25 .60
46 Austin Hays RC .25 .60
47 Cody Bellinger .50 1.25
48 Jackson Stephens RC .25 .60
49 Shohei Ohtani RC 1.50 4.00
50 Carlos Correa .25 .60
51 Marcell Ozuna .25 .60
52 J.D. Davis RC .30 .75
53 Charlie Blackmon .25 .60
54 Byron Buxton .20 .50
55 Dominic Smith RC .20 .50
56 Nomar Mazara .15 .40
57 Anthony Banda RC .25 .60
58 Josh Donaldson .20 .50
59 Walker Buehler RC 1.25 3.00
60 Aaron Altherr .15 .40
61 Dansby Swanson .25 .60
62 Ozzie Albies RC .75 2.00
63 Robinson Cano .20 .50
64 Clayton Kershaw .50 1.25
65 Marcus Stroman .20 .50
66 Victor Arano RC .25 .60
67 Giancarlo Stanton .25 .60
68 Andrew McCutchen .25 .60
69 Bryce Harper .40 1.00
70 Parker Bridwell RC .25 .60
71 J.P. Crawford RC .25 .60
72 Alex Verdugo RC .40 1.00
73 Nick Williams RC .30 .75
74 Garrett Cooper RC .25 .60
75 Miguel Andujar RC 1.00 2.50
76 Tomas Nido RC .25 .60
77 Avisail Garcia .20 .50
78 Jack Flaherty RC .40 1.00
79 Buster Posey .30 .75
80 Evan Longoria .20 .50
81 Nolan Arenado .30 .75
82 Lucas Sims RC .25 .60
83 Nicky Delmonico RC .25 .60
84 Paul DeJong .25 .60
85 Andrew Stevenson RC .25 .60
86 Rougned Odor .20 .50
87 Tommy Pham .15 .40
88 Felix Hernandez .20 .50
89 Brandon Crawford .20 .50
90 Max Fried RC 1.00 2.50
91 Luiz Gohara RC .25 .60
92 Josh Bell .20 .50
93 Michael Conforto .20 .50
94 Chris Sale .25 .60
95 Jonathan Schoop .15 .40
96 Raisel Iglesias .20 .50
97 Gary Sanchez .25 .60
98 Whit Merrifield .25 .60
99 Ryan McMahon RC .30 .75
100 Kris Bryant .30 .75

2018 Bowman Blue

*BLUE: 3X TO 8X BASIC
*BLUE RC: 2X TO 5X BASIC
STATED ODDS 1:313 HOBBY
STATED PRINT RUN 150 SER.#'d SETS
49 Shohei Ohtani 40.00 100.00

2018 Bowman Gold

*GOLD: 6X TO 15X BASIC
*GOLD RC: 4X TO 10X BASIC
STATED ODDS 1:939 HOBBY
STATED PRINT RUN 50 SER.#'d SETS
49 Shohei Ohtani 75.00 200.00

2018 Bowman Green

*GREEN: 4X TO 10X BASIC
*GREEN RC: 2.5X TO 6X BASIC
STATED ODDS 1:XX RETAIL
STATED PRINT RUN 99 SER.#'d SETS
49 Shohei Ohtani 50.00 120.00

2018 Bowman Orange

*ORANGE: 10X TO 25X BASIC
*ORANGE RC: 6X TO 15X BASIC
STATED ODDS 1:438 HOBBY
STATED PRINT RUN 25 SER.#'d SETS
49 Shohei Ohtani 125.00 300.00

2018 Bowman Purple

*PURPLE: 2.5X TO 6X BASIC
*PURPLE RC: 1.5X TO 4X BASIC
STATED ODDS 1:188 HOBBY
STATED PRINT RUN 250 SER.#'d SETS
49 Shohei Ohtani 30.00 80.00

2018 Bowman Sky Blue

*SKY BLUE: 1.5X TO 4X BASIC
*SKY BLUE RC: 1X TO 2.5X BASIC
STATED ODDS 1:95 HOBBY
STATED PRINT RUN 499 SER.#'d SETS
49 Shohei Ohtani 20.00 50.00

2018 Bowman Big League Breakthrough Redemptions

RANDOM INSERTS IN PACKS
EXCHANGE DEADLINE 9/31/2018
BLAB Austin Beck 4.00 10.00
BLAG Andres Gimenez 4.00 10.00
BLAM Austin Meadows 20.00 50.00
BLAR Austin Riley 15.00 40.00
BLBH Brent Honeywell 5.00 12.00
BLBM Brendan McKay 5.00 12.00
BLCA Chance Adams 10.00 25.00
BLCB Casey Gillaspie 6.00 15.00
BLCR Corey Ray 6.00 15.00
BLDC Dylan Cozens 12.00 30.00
BLEJ Eloy Jimenez 30.00 80.00
BLGT Gleyber Torres 75.00 200.00
BLHG Hunter Greene 12.00 30.00
BLJB Jake Burger 10.00 25.00
BLJG Jay Groome 4.00 10.00
BLJS Justus Sheffield 12.00 30.00
BLKH Keston Hiura 15.00 40.00
BLKW Kyle Wright 8.00 20.00
BLLR Luis Robert 25.00 60.00
BLLT Leody Taveras 4.00 10.00
BLMC Michael Chavis 5.00 12.00
BLMG MacKenzie Gore 6.00 15.00
BLMK Michael Kopech 15.00 40.00
BLMM Mickey Moniak 8.00 20.00
BLNG Nick Gordon 12.00 30.00
BLNS Nick Senzel 10.00 25.00
BLPS Pavin Smith 3.00 8.00
BLRA Ronald Acuna 100.00 250.00
BLRL Royce Lewis 10.00 25.00
BLRM Ryan Mountcastle 10.00 25.00
BLSB Shane Baz 8.00 20.00
BLSK Scott Kingery 25.00 60.00
BLSS Sixto Sanchez 8.00 20.00
BLTO Tyler O'Neill 25.00 60.00
BLTT Taylor Trammell 8.00 20.00
BLWA Willy Adames 20.00 50.00
BLFTJ Fernando Tatis Jr. 20.00 50.00
BLJSA Jesus Sanchez 3.00 8.00
BLJSO Juan Soto 60.00 150.00
BLVGJ Vladimir Guerrero Jr. 50.00 120.00

2018 Bowman Prospect Autographs

RANDOMLY INSERTED IN RETAIL PACKS
EXCHANGE DEADLINE 3/31/2020
*PURPLE/250: .5X TO 1.2X BASE
*BLUE/150: .6X TO 1.5X BASE
*GREEN/99: .75X TO 2X BASE
*GOLD/50: 1X TO 2.5X BASE
*ORANGE/25: 1.2X TO 3X BASE
PAAK Aaron Knapp 2.50 6.00
PABB Brock Burke 2.50 6.00
PABK Brad Keller 2.50 6.00
PABM Brendan McKay 10.00 25.00
PABMU Brian Mundell 2.50 6.00
PACB Charcer Burks 2.50 6.00
PACC Carl Chester 2.50 6.00
PACF Colby Fitch 2.50 6.00
PADB David Bote 8.00 20.00
PADD Dean Deetz 2.50 6.00
PADM Dustin May 15.00 40.00
PADS Dennis Santana 4.00 10.00
PAEC Edgar Cabral 3.00 8.00
PAEU Erich Uelman 3.00 8.00
PAGT Gleyber Torres 30.00 80.00
PAHF Heath Fillmyer 2.50 6.00
PAHG Hunter Greene 60.00 150.00
PAJG Jose Gomez 2.50 6.00
PAJK Jeren Kendall 3.00 8.00
PAJR JoJo Romero 5.00 12.00
PAMB Matt Beaty 3.00 8.00
PAMD Matthias Dietz 2.50 6.00
PAMG Matt Givin 2.50 6.00
PAMK Mitch Keller 3.00 8.00
PANL Nicky Lopez 6.00 15.00
PANS Nick Solak 6.00 15.00
PAPA Peter Alonso 40.00 100.00
PARL Royce Lewis 12.00 30.00
PASH Sam Hilliard 3.00 8.00
PASS Shea Spitzbarth 3.00 8.00
PATB Trevor Bettencourt 3.00 8.00
PATE Thairo Estrada 15.00 40.00
PAWS Will Smith 20.00 50.00

2018 Bowman Prospects

PRINTING PLATE ODDS 1:7838 HOBBY
PLATE PRINT RUN 1 SET PER COLOR
BLACK-CYAN-MAGENTA-YELLOW ISSUED
NO PLATE PRICING DUE TO SCARCITY
BP1 Ronald Acuna 3.00 8.00
BP2 Bryan Mata .20 .50
BP3 Daniel Johnson .15 .40
BP4 Hunter Harvey .15 .40
BP5 Aaron Knapp .15 .40
BP6 Austin Beck .20 .50
BP7 Carter Kieboom .25 .60
BP8 Cole Ragans .15 .40
BP9 Alex Jackson .15 .40
BP10 Justin Williams .15 .40
BP11 Rowdy Tellez .15 .40
BP12 Thomas Hatch .20 .50
BP13 Sam Hilliard .40 1.00
BP14 Kyle Wright .40 1.00
BP15 Tyler O'Neill .25 .60
BP16 Michael Mercado .20 .50
BP17 Kevin Newman .25 .60
BP18 Eric Lauer .25 .60
BP19 Johan Mieses .25 .60
BP20 Will Smith .40 1.00
BP21 Luis Robert 12.00 30.00
BP22 Yadier Alvarez .20 .50
BP23 Jeren Kendall .20 .50
BP24 Bobby Bradley .20 .50
BP25 Drew Ellis .20 .50
BP26 Alfredo Rodriguez .15 .40
BP27 Jose Trevino .15 .40
BP28 Kolby Allard .15 .40
BP29 Taylor Ward .20 .50
BP30 Cornelius Randolph .15 .40
BP31 DJ Peters .40 1.00
BP32 Domingo Acevedo .15 .40
BP33 James Nelson .15 .40
BP34 Josh Ockimey .15 .40
BP35 Marcos Molina .15 .40
BP36 Dennis Santana .15 .40
BP37 Jake Burger .15 .40
BP38 Mitch Keller .20 .50
BP39 Colton Welker .15 .40
BP40 Pedro Avila .15 .40
BP41 Jason Martin .15 .40
BP42 Braxton Garrett .15 .40
BP43 Brendan Rodgers .20 .50
BP44 James Kaprielian .15 .40
BP45 Greg Deichmann .20 .50
BP46 Cristian Pache .75 2.00
BP47 Ibandel Isabel .25 .60
BP48 Hunter Greene .50 1.25
BP49 Nick Gordon .15 .40
BP50 Eloy Jimenez .60 1.50
BP51 Adonis Medina .25 .60
BP52 Juan Soto 3.00 8.00
BP53 Miguelangel Sierra .15 .40
BP54 Alex Lange .15 .40
BP55 Kyle Tucker .30 .75
BP56 TJ Zeuch .15 .40
BP57 Luis Urias .30 .75
BP58 Sean Murphy .25 .60
BP59 Oscar De La Cruz .15 .40
BP60 Brian Miller .15 .40
BP61 Matt Thaiss .15 .40
BP62 Kyle Cody .15 .40
BP63 Dylan Cozens .15 .40
BP64 MJ Melendez .15 .40
BP65 Scott Kingery .25 .60
BP66 Jordan Humphreys .15 .40
BP67 Michel Baez .15 .40
BP68 Brendan McKay .25 .60
BP69 Justus Sheffield .20 .50
BP70 Merandy Gonzalez .15 .40
BP71 Touki Toussaint .20 .50
BP72 Andres Gimenez .20 .50
BP73 Adrian Morejon .15 .40
BP74 Austin Voth .15 .40
BP75 Luis Garcia .25 .60
BP76 Isaac Paredes .75 2.00
BP77 Jake Kalish .15 .40
BP78 Shed Long .15 .40
BP79 Keibert Ruiz .50 1.25
BP80 Matt Hall .15 .40
BP81 Nick Pratto .20 .50
BP82 Justin Dunn .20 .50
BP83 Ian Anderson .40 1.00
BP84 Franklyn Kilome .20 .50
BP85 Dane Dunning .15 .40
BP86 Michael Kopech .30 .75
BP87 McKenzie Mills .15 .40
BP88 Quentin Holmes .15 .40
BP89 Mike Soroka .50 1.25
BP90 Stephen Gonsalves .15 .40
BP91 Spencer Howard .15 .40
BP92 Ryan Vilade .15 .40
BP93 Royce Lewis .60 1.50
BP94 Adam Haseley .25 .60
BP95 Jorge Mateo .15 .40
BP96 Junior Fernandez .25 .60
BP97 Corey Ray .20 .50
BP98 Evan White .25 .60
BP99 Logan Allen .15 .40
BP100 Gleyber Torres 1.50 4.00
BP101 Zack Littell .15 .40
BP102 Matt Sauer .15 .40
BP103 Mitchell White .15 .40
BP104 Nick Solak .40 1.00
BP105 Jorge Ona .15 .40
BP106 D.J. Stewart .15 .40
BP107 D.L. Hall .15 .40
BP108 Chris Rodriguez .15 .40
BP109 Sam Howard .15 .40
BP110 Eric Pardinho .30 .75
BP111 JoJo Romero .20 .50
BP112 Aramis Garcia .15 .40
BP113 Taylor Clarke .15 .40
BP114 Fernando Tatis Jr. 1.25 3.00
BP115 Cal Quantrill .15 .40
BP116 Khalil Lee .15 .40
BP117 C.J. Chatham .20 .50
BP118 Lazaro Armenteros .30 .75
BP119 Gavin LaValley .15 .40
BP120 Nick Senzel .50 1.25
BP121 Jose Adolis Garcia .20 .50
BP122 Ronald Guzman .15 .40
BP123 Jordan Hicks .30 .75
BP124 Alex Faedo .25 .60
BP125 J.B. Bukauskas .15 .40
BP126 Jesus Luzardo .25 .60
BP127 Josh Lowe .15 .40
BP128 Yu-Cheng Chang .20 .50
BP129 Kyle Young .20 .50
BP130 Christin Stewart .20 .50
BP131 MacKenzie Gore .30 .75
BP132 Corbin Burnes .25 .60
BP133 Tyler Stephenson .15 .40
BP134 Wander Javier .20 .50
BP135 Bryse Wilson .25 .60
BP136 Jo Adell .50 1.25
BP137 Pete Alonso 1.50 4.00
BP138 Delvin Perez .15 .40
BP139 Travis Lakins .15 .40
BP140 Blake Rutherford .20 .50
BP141 Blayne Enlow .15 .40
BP142 A.J. Puk .20 .50
BP143 Heliot Ramos .25 .60
BP144 Jahmai Jones .15 .40
BP145 Adbert Alzolay .20 .50
BP146 Will Craig .15 .40
BP147 Forrest Whitley .25 .60
BP148 Trevor Rogers .15 .40
BP149 Steven Duggar .15 .40
BP150 Vladimir Guerrero Jr. 1.50 4.00

2018 Bowman Prospects Blue

*BLUE: 1.5X TO 4X BASIC
STATED ODDS 1:209 HOBBY
STATED PRINT RUN 150 SER.#'d SETS

2018 Bowman Prospects Camo

*CAMO: .6X TO 1.5X BASIC
THREE PER RETAIL VALUE PACK

2018 Bowman Prospects Gold

*GOLD: 4X TO 10X BASIC
STATED ODDS 1:711 HOBBY
STATED PRINT RUN 50 SER.#'d SETS

2018 Bowman Prospects Green

GREEN: 2X TO 5X BASIC
STATED ODDS 1:150 RETAIL
STATED PRINT RUN 99 SER.#'d SETS

2018 Bowman Prospects Orange

*ORANGE: 8X TO 20X BASIC
STATED ODDS 1:292 HOBBY
STATED PRINT RUN 25 SER.#'d SETS

2018 Bowman Prospects Purple

*PURPLE: 1.5X TO 4X BASIC
STATED ODDS 1:126 HOBBY
STATED PRINT RUN 250 SER.#'d SETS

2018 Bowman Prospects Sky Blue

*SKY BLUE: 1.2X TO 3X BASIC
STATED ODDS 1:63 HOBBY
STATED PRINT RUN 499 SER.#'d SETS

2018 Bowman Draft

COMPLETE SET (200) 12.00 30.00
STATED PLATE ODDS 1:1198 HOBBY
PLATE PRINT RUN 1 SET PER COLOR
BLACK-CYAN-MAGENTA-YELLOW ISSUED
NO PLATE PRICING DUE TO SCARCITY
BD1 Casey Mize 1.25 3.00
BD2 Matt Vierling .30 .75
BD3 Brusdar Graterol .30 .75
BD4 Lawrence Butler .25 .60
BD5 Terrin Vavra .30 .75
BD6 Jarred Kelenic 1.50 4.00
BD7 Yusniel Diaz .50 1.25
BD8 Lenny Torres .20 .50
BD9 Shane McClanahan .25 .60
BD10 Blayne Enlow .15 .40
BD11 Brice Turang .50 1.25
BD12 Tim Cate .25 .60
BD13 Pedro Avila .15 .40
BD14 Kyle Isbel .40 1.00
BD15 Devin Mann .25 .60
BD16 Jazz Chisholm .40 1.00
BD17 Luis Medina .25 .60
BD18 Adrian Morejon .15 .40
BD19 Arbert Cipion .15 .40
BD20 Trevor Stephan .15 .40
BD21 Drew Ellis .20 .50
BD22 Taylor Trammell .25 .60
BD23 Jayson Schroeder .15 .40
BD24 Joe Jacques .15 .40
BD25 Alec Bohm .75 2.00
BD26 Beau Burrows .20 .50
BD27 Jonathan Stiever .15 .40
BD28 Parker Meadows .30 .75
BD29 Jonathan Ornelas .40 1.00
BD30 Matthew Liberatore .20 .50
BD31 Greyson Jenista .30 .75
BD32 Bo Bichette .60 1.50
BD33 Durbin Feltman .25 .60
BD34 Nick Sandlin .15 .40
BD35 Jahmai Jones .15 .40
BD36 Brandon Marsh .20 .50
BD37 Lency Delgado .30 .75
BD38 Nick Madrigal 1.00 2.50
BD39 Kris Bubic .25 .60
BD40 Oneil Cruz .25 .60
BD41 Alex Faedo .25 .60
BD42 Thomas Ponticelli .15 .40
BD43 Bryan Lavastida .15 .40
BD44 Nick Schnell .20 .50
BD45 Cal Mitchell .25 .60
BD46 Nick Solak .40 1.00
BD47 Brennen Davis 1.25 3.00
BD48 Ethan Hankins .20 .50
BD49 Keston Hiura .40 1.00
BD50 Ke'Bryan Hayes .15 .40
BD51 Jeremiah Jackson .25 .60
BD52 Lolo Sanchez .20 .50
BD53 Gregory Soto .15 .40
BD54 Nicky Lopez .15 .40
BD55 Jake Wong .15 .40
BD56 Jordan Groshans .75 2.00
BD57 Josh Breaux .20 .50
BD58 Hunter Greene .50 1.25
BD59 Dylan Cease .40 1.00
BD60 Carlos Cortes .20 .50
BD61 Korry Howell .15 .40
BD62 Joey Wentz .20 .50
BD63 Logan Gilbert .25 .60
BD64 Ryan Rolison .30 .75
BD65 Anthony Seigler .40 1.00
BD66 Jorge Guzman .15 .40
BD67 Mark Vientos .25 .60
BD68 Chris Paddack .40 1.00
BD69 Kole Cottam .20 .50
BD70 Trevor Larnach 1.00 2.50
BD71 Monte Harrison .15 .40
BD72 Aramis Ademan .25 .60
BD73 Grayson Rodriguez .30 .75
BD74 Nick Gordon .15 .40
BD75 Sixto Sanchez .40 1.00
BD76 Joe Gray .25 .60
BD77 Drevian Williams-Nelson .15 .40
BD78 Tanner Dodson .20 .50
BD79 Ryan Vilade .15 .40
BD80 Blake Rivera .15 .40
BD81 Adam Haseley .25 .60
BD82 Braydon Fisher .60 1.50
BD83 Kevon Jackson .15 .40
BD84 Ryder Green .30 .75
BD85 Jawuan Harris .15 .40
BD86 Mitch Keller .20 .50
BD87 Royce Lewis .60 1.50
BD88 Jordyn Adams 1.00 2.50
BD89 Korey Holland .15 .40
BD90 Thad Ward .15 .40
BD91 Sean Murphy .25 .60
BD92 Calvin Coker .15 .40
BD93 Carter Kieboom .25 .60
BD94 Jake McCarthy .25 .60
BD95 Braxton Ashcraft .25 .60
BD96 Colton Eastman .40 1.00
BD97 Mitchell White .15 .40
BD98 Nick Pratto .20 .50
BD99 Alex McKenna .20 .50
BD100 Brendan McKay .25 .60
BD101 Mike Shawaryn .15 .40
BD102 Levi Kelly .15 .40
BD103 Osiris Johnson .20 .50
BD104 Justin Jarvis .15 .40
BD105 Ford Proctor .20 .50
BD106 Ezequiel Pagan .20 .50
BD107 Jo Adell .50 1.25
BD108 Jon Duplantier .15 .40
BD109 Luken Baker .25 .60
BD110 Grant Little .15 .40
BD111 Micah Bello .25 .60
BD112 Jonathan India .25 .60
BD113 Will Banfield .15 .40
BD114 Keibert Ruiz .50 1.25
BD115 Grant Koch .15 .40
BD116 Jeren Kendall .20 .50
BD117 Nolan Gorman 1.00 2.50
BD118 Nate Pearson .40 1.00
BD119 Corbin Martin .15 .40
BD120 Shed Long .15 .40
BD121 Kody Clemens .30 .75
BD122 Josh Naylor .20 .50
BD123 Sheldon Neuse .15 .40
BD124 Nick Decker .30 .75
BD125 Cole Roederer .50 1.25
BD126 Albert Abreu .15 .40
BD127 Dallas Woolfolk .15 .40
BD128 Adonis Medina .25 .60
BD129 Tristan Pompey .25 .60
BD130 Michel Baez .15 .40
BD131 Pavin Smith .15 .40
BD132 Brian Miller .15 .40
BD133 Heliot Ramos .25 .60
BD134 Cadyn Grenier .20 .50
BD135 Brady Singer .30 .75
BD136 Andres Gimenez .20 .50
BD137 Griffin Roberts .15 .40
BD138 Greg Deichmann .20 .50
BD139 Sean Hjelle .20 .50
BD140 Kenen Irizarry .25 .60
BD141 Alfonso Rivas .15 .40
BD142 Daniel Lynch .20 .50
BD143 Matt Mercer .15 .40
BD144 Sean Guilbe .20 .50
BD145 Matt Manning .25 .60
BD146 Alec Hansen .15 .40
BD147 Jackson Goddard .15 .40
BD148 Jesus Luzardo .25 .60
BD149 Nick Dunn .50 1.25
BD150 MacKenzie Gore .30 .75
BD151 Jeter Downs .25 .60
BD152 Grant Witherspoon .20 .50
BD153 Griffin Conine .30 .75
BD154 Adam Hill .15 .40
BD155 Alek Thomas .60 1.50
BD156 Tyler Frank .15 .40
BD157 Sean Wymer .15 .40
BD158 Connor Scott .20 .50
BD159 Owen White .25 .60
BD160 Jameson Hannah .25 .60
BD161 Mike Siani .20 .50
BD162 Triston McKenzie .15 .40
BD163 Bobby Bradley .20 .50
BD164 Mason Denaburg .20 .50
BD165 Nico Hoerner .75 2.00
BD166 Matt Thaiss .15 .40
BD167 Ryan Mountcastle .25 .60
BD168 Eloy Jimenez .60 1.50
BD169 Logan Allen .15 .40
BD170 Dane Dunning .15 .40
BD171 Triston Casas 1.25 3.00
BD172 Bryan Mata .20 .50
BD173 Cole Winn .25 .60
BD174 Leury Tejada .15 .40
BD175 Sam Carlson .20 .50
BD176 Raynel Delgado .40 1.00
BD177 Leody Taveras .20 .50
BD178 Justin Dunn .20 .50
BD179 Jeremy Eierman .20 .50
BD180 Jesus Sanchez .15 .40
BD181 Simeon Woods-Richardson .20 .50
BD182 Ryan Weathers .20 .50
BD183 Ian Anderson .40 1.00
BD184 Matt Sauer .15 .40
BD185 Adam Wolf .20 .50
BD186 Grant Lavigne .75 2.00
BD187 Estevan Florial .25 .60
BD188 Luis Robert 3.00 8.00
BD189 J.B. Bukauskas .15 .40
BD190 Josh Stowers .40 1.00
BD191 Brent Rooker .20 .50
BD192 Ryan Jeffers .30 .75
BD193 Noah Naylor .25 .60
BD194 Cody Deason .15 .40
BD195 Cal Quantrill .15 .40
BD196 Jackson Kowar .15 .40
BD197 Griffin Canning .15 .40
BD198 Travis Swaggerty .50 1.25
BD199 Alex Kirilloff .25 .60
BD200 Lazaro Armenteros .30 .75

2018 Bowman Draft Blue

*BLUE: 2X TO 5X BASIC
STATED ODDS 1:32 HOBBY
STATED PRINT RUN 150 SER.#'d SETS
BD117 Nolan Gorman 15.00 40.00

2018 Bowman Draft Gold

*GOLD: 4X TO 10X BASIC
STATED ODDS 1:96 HOBBY
STATED PRINT RUN 50 SER.#'d SETS
BD117 Nolan Gorman 30.00 80.00

2018 Bowman Draft Green

*GREEN: 2.5X TO 6X BASIC
STATED ODDS 1:49 HOBBY
STATED PRINT RUN 99 SER.#'d SETS
BD117 Nolan Gorman 20.00 50.00

2018 Bowman Draft Orange

*ORANGE: 5X TO 12X BASIC
STATED ODDS 1:130 HOBBY
STATED PRINT RUN 25 SER.#'d SETS
BD117 Nolan Gorman 40.00 100.00

2018 Bowman Draft Purple

*PURPLE: 2X TO 5X BASIC
STATED ODDS 1:20 HOBBY
STATED PRINT RUN 250 SER.#'d SETS
BD117 Nolan Gorman 12.00 30.00

2018 Bowman Draft Sky Blue

*SKY BLUE: 1X TO 2.5X BASIC
STATED ODDS 1:10 HOBBY
STATED PRINT RUN 499 SER.#'d SETS
BD117 Nolan Gorman 8.00 20.00

2019 Bowman

COMP.SET w/o SP (100) 10.00 25.00
PRINTING PLATE ODDS 1:13,380 HOBBY
PLATE PRINT RUN 1 SET PER COLOR
BLACK-CYAN-MAGENTA-YELLOW ISSUED
NO PLATE PRICING DUE TO SCARCITY
1 Mike Trout 1.25 3.00
2 Cody Bellinger .50 1.25
3A Joey Wendle .15 .40
3B Bryce Harper SP 12.00 30.00
4 Cedric Mullins RC .40 1.00
5 Kyle Freeland .20 .50
6 Brad Keller RC .25 .60
7 Jonathan Loaisiga RC .30 .75
8 Scooter Gennett .20 .50
9 Khris Davis .25 .60
10 Willy Adames .15 .40
11 Matt Chapman .25 .60
12 Justus Sheffield RC .40 1.00
13 Aaron Nola .20 .50
14 Christian Yelich .30 .75
15 Clayton Kershaw .50 1.25
16 Aaron Judge .60 1.50
17 Trey Mancini .20 .50
18 Anthony Rizzo .40 1.00
19 Touki Toussaint RC .30 .75
20 Bryse Wilson RC .30 .75
21 Miguel Cabrera .25 .60
22 Nolan Arenado .30 .75
23 Salvador Perez .20 .50
24 Willians Astudillo RC .25 .60
25 Luis Urias RC .40 1.00
26 Edwin Diaz .20 .50
27 Yoan Moncada .25 .60
28 Rowdy Tellez RC .40 1.00
29 Taylor Ward RC .25 .60
30 Steven Duggar RC .30 .75
31 Francisco Arcia RC .40 1.00
32 Eugenio Suarez .20 .50
33 Christin Stewart RC .30 .75
34 Shohei Ohtani .30 .75
35 J.D. Martinez .25 .60
36 Yadier Molina .25 .60
37 Jose Berrios .20 .50
38 Ramon Laureano RC .50 1.25
39 Luis Guillorme RC .25 .60
40 Marcus Stroman .20 .50
41 Zack Greinke .20 .50
42 Chris Shaw RC .40 1.00
43 Giancarlo Stanton .25 .60
44 Ryan Borucki RC .25 .60
45 Whit Merrifield .25 .60
46 Chris Archer .15 .40
47 Maikel Franco .20 .50
48 Danny Jansen RC .25 .60
49 David Fletcher RC .75 2.00
50 Mookie Betts .40 1.00
51 Kris Bryant .30 .75
52 Kyle Wright RC .40 1.00
53 Aramis Garcia RC .25 .60
54 Kevin Newman RC .40 1.00
55 Jose Abreu .25 .60
56 Mychal Givens .15 .40
57 Brandon Crawford .20 .50
58 Sean Reid-Foley RC .25 .60
59 Evan Longoria .20 .50
60 Kevin Kramer RC .30 .75
61 Jake Cave RC .30 .75
62 Jose Altuve .20 .50
63 Eddie Rosario .20 .50
64 Justin Verlander .25 .60
65 Corbin Burnes RC .40 1.00
66 Jose Ramirez .20 .50
67 DJ Stewart RC .30 .75
68 Starling Marte .20 .50
69 Chance Adams RC .25 .60
70 Enyel De Los Santos RC .25 .60
71 Max Scherzer .25 .60
72 Kolby Allard RC .40 1.00
73 Dakota Hudson RC .30 .75
74 Matt Carpenter .25 .60
75 Michael Kopech RC .50 1.25
76 Jake Bauers RC .40 1.00
77 Rougned Odor .20 .50
78 Ronald Acuna Jr. 1.25 3.00
79 J.T. Realmuto .25 .60
80 Mitch Haniger .20 .50
81 Nicholas Castellanos .25 .60
82 Dawel Lugo RC .40 1.00
83 Amed Rosario .20 .50
84 Adolis Garcia RC .25 .60
85 Paul Goldschmidt .25 .60
86 Eric Hosmer .20 .50
87 Josh James RC .40 1.00
88 Ronald Guzman .15 .40
89 Francisco Lindor .25 .60
90 Jeff McNeil RC .60 1.50
91 Brian Anderson .15 .40
92 Juan Soto .75 2.00
93 Ryan O'Hearn RC .25 .60
94 Kyle Tucker RC .50 1.25
95 Kevin Pillar .15 .40
96 Ozzie Albies .25 .60
97 Josh Hader .15 .40
98 Brandon Lowe RC .40 1.00
99 Wil Myers .15 .40
100 Jacob deGrom .25 .60

2019 Bowman Gold

*GOLD: 6X TO 15X BASIC
*GOLD RC: 4X TO 10X BASIC
STATED ODDS 1:1067 HOBBY
STATED PRINT RUN 50 SER.#'d SETS
3B Bryce Harper 60.00 150.00

2019 Bowman Green

*GREEN: 4X TO 10X BASIC
*GREEN RC: 2.5X TO 6X BASIC
STATED ODDS 1:212 BLASTER
STATED PRINT RUN 99 SER.#'d SETS
3B Bryce Harper 40.00 100.00

2019 Bowman Orange

*ORANGE: 10X TO 25X BASIC
*ORANGE RC: 6X TO 15X BASIC
STATED ODDS 1:493 HOBBY
STATED PRINT RUN 25 SER.#'d SETS
3B Bryce Harper 100.00 250.00

2019 Bowman Purple

*PURPLE: 2.5X TO 6X BASIC
*PURPLE RC: 1.5X TO 4X BASIC
STATED ODDS 1:214 HOBBY
STATED PRINT RUN 250 SER.#'d SETS
3B Bryce Harper 25.00 60.00

2019 Bowman Sky Blue

*SKY BLUE: 1.5X TO 4X BASIC
*SKY BLUE RC: 1X TO 2.5X BASIC
STATED ODDS 1:107 HOBBY
STATED PRINT RUN 499 SER.#'d SETS
3B Bryce Harper 15.00 40.00

2019 Bowman '89 Bowman Buyback Autographs

STATED ODDS 1:3,299 HOBBY
EXCHANGE DEADLINE 3/31/2021
9 Cal Ripken Jr. 60.00 150.00
26 Roger Clemens 30.00 80.00
41 Bert Blyleven 10.00 25.00
62 Carlton Fisk 25.00 60.00
190 Dennis Eckersley 15.00 40.00
197 Mark McGwire 40.00 100.00
211 Tino Martinez 20.00 50.00
216 Edgar Martinez 50.00 120.00
220 Ken Griffey Jr. 500.00 1000.00
266 John Smoltz 25.00 60.00
276 Dale Murphy 40.00 100.00
290 Ryne Sandberg 20.00 50.00
298 Andre Dawson 25.00 60.00

2019 Bowman Prospect Autographs

STATED ODDS 1:67 BLASTER
EXCHANGE DEADLINE 3/31/2021
*PURPLE/250: .5X TO 1.2X BASE
*BLUE/150: .6X TO 1.5X BASE
*GREEN/99: .75X TO 2X BASE
*GOLD/50: 1X TO 2.5X BASE
*ORANGE/25: 1.2X TO 3X BASE
PAAI Andrew Istler 2.50 6.00
PAAM Alex McKenna 4.00 10.00
PAAR Alex Royalty 2.50 6.00
PAAW Adam Wolf 4.00 10.00
PABB Braden Bishop 3.00 8.00
PABD Brett Daniels 2.50 6.00
PABH Brigham Hill 3.00 8.00
PABT Bo Takahashi 2.50 6.00
PACM Casey Mize 12.00 30.00
PAEJ Eduardo Jimenez 3.00 8.00
PAJB Joey Bart 40.00 100.00
PAJK Jarred Kelenic 30.00 80.00
PAJM James Marvel 4.00 10.00
PAJO James Outman 2.50 6.00
PAJS Jesus Sanchez 2.50 6.00
PAJYC Jing-Yu Chang 6.00 15.00
PALJC Li-Jen Chu 3.00 8.00
PAMK Matt Krook 2.50 6.00
PANA Nick Allen 2.50 6.00
PANH Nolan Hoffman 2.50 6.00
PANM Nick Meyer 2.50 6.00
PAOM Owen Miller 3.00 8.00
PAPO Pablo Olivares 4.00 10.00
PASE Santiago Espinal 4.00 10.00
PASL Shed Long 4.00 10.00
PASS Sterling Sharp 4.00 10.00
PATM Tobias Myers 2.50 6.00
PAYA Yadier Alvarez 2.50 6.00

2019 Bowman Prospects

PRINTING PLATE ODDS 1:8920 HOBBY
PLATE PRINT RUN 1 SET PER COLOR
BLACK-CYAN-MAGENTA-YELLOW ISSUED
NO PLATE PRICING DUE TO SCARCITY
BP1 Vladimir Guerrero Jr. 1.00 2.50
BP2 Alec Bohm .60 1.50
BP3 Justin Dunn .15 .40
BP4 Jo Adell .50 1.25
BP5 Victor Victor Mesa .30 .75
BP6 Brusdar Graterol .20 .50
BP7 Tirso Ornelas .15 .40
BP8 Nick Neidert .15 .40
BP9 Taylor Widener .15 .40
BP10 Adrian Morejon .15 .40
BP11 Derian Cruz .15 .40
BP12 Corey Ray .15 .40
BP13 Jarred Kelenic .60 1.50
BP14 Seth Beer 1.00 2.50
BP15 Ethan Hankins .20 .50
BP16 Cole Tucker .25 .60
BP17 A.J. Puk .20 .50
BP18 Leody Taveras .15 .40
BP19 Logan Allen .15 .40
BP20 Blake Rutherford .15 .40
BP21 Freudis Nova .25 .60
BP22 Daniel Johnson .15 .40
BP23 Rylan Bannon .20 .50
BP24 Taylor Trammell .20 .50
BP25 Fernando Tatis Jr. 1.50 4.00
BP26 Beau Burrows .15 .40
BP27 Jay Groome .15 .40
BP28 Adam Haseley .25 .60
BP29 Adonis Medina .25 .60
BP30 Julio Pablo Martinez .15 .40
BP31 Evan White .25 .60
BP32 Cristian Javier .20 .50
BP33 Julio Rodriguez 3.00 8.00
BP34 Domingo Acevedo .15 .40
BP35 Miguel Amaya .25 .60
BP36 Ryan Vilade .15 .40
BP37 JoJo Romero .15 .40
BP38 Sandro Fabian .15 .40
BP39 Franklyn Kilome .15 .40
BP40 Triston McKenzie .15 .40
BP41 Ryan Mountcastle .20 .50
BP42 Jordyn Adams .20 .50
BP43 Nick Senzel .50 1.25
BP44 Luis Robert 1.50 4.00
BP45 Brent Rooker .20 .50
BP46 Anthony Seigler .25 .60
BP47 Ian Anderson .40 1.00
BP48 Griffin Canning .25 .60
BP49 Casey Mize .40 1.00
BP50 Joey Bart .50 1.25
BP51 Hunter Greene .25 .60
BP52 Forrest Whitley .25 .60
BP53 Blaze Alexander .15 .40
BP54 Keston Hiura .50 1.25
BP55 Chris Paddack .30 .75
BP56 Franklin Perez .15 .40
BP57 Joey Wentz .15 .40
BP58 Kevin Smith .15 .40
BP59 Nico Hoerner .50 1.25
BP60 Nolan Gorman .50 1.25
BP61 Jazz Chisholm .40 1.00
BP62 Cristian Pache .40 1.00
BP63 Nick Madrigal .50 1.25
BP64 Luis Garcia .20 .50
BP65 Colton Welker .15 .40
BP66 Ryan Weathers .15 .40
BP67 Jonathan Duplantier .15 .40
BP68 Reggie Lawson .15 .40
BP69 Orelvis Martinez 1.25 3.00
BP70 Sixto Sanchez .20 .50
BP71 Ke'Bryan Hayes .15 .40
BP72 Brewer Hicklen .25 .60
BP73 MacKenzie Gore .30 .75
BP74 Estevan Florial .25 .60
BP75 Cole Winn .15 .40
BP76 Zack Collins .20 .50
BP77 Andres Gimenez .20 .50
BP78 Alex Faedo .20 .50
BP79 Logan Webb .25 .60
BP80 Dustin May .50 1.25
BP81 Ryan McKenna .15 .40
BP82 Marco Luciano 1.50 4.00
BP83 Heliot Ramos .25 .60
BP84 Aramis Ademan .15 .40
BP85 Matt Manning .25 .60
BP86 Daz Cameron .15 .40
BP87 Chad Spanberger .15 .40
BP88 Brent Honeywell .20 .50
BP89 Esteury Ruiz .20 .50
BP90 Keegan Thompson .15 .40
BP91 Will Smith .40 1.00
BP92 Michael Chavis .25 .60
BP93 Travis Swaggerty .25 .60
BP94 Dane Dunning .15 .40
BP95 Lyon Richardson .20 .50
BP96 Jesus Luzardo .25 .60
BP97 Noelvi Marte 1.50 4.00
BP98 Carter Kieboom .25 .60
BP99 Nate Pearson .40 1.00
BP100 Wander Franco 5.00 12.00
BP101 Ryan Costello .20 .50
BP102 Jonathan India .20 .50
BP103 Royce Lewis .30 .75
BP104 Victor Mesa Jr. .40 1.00
BP105 Brendan McKay .25 .60
BP106 Michel Baez .15 .40
BP107 Ronny Mauricio 1.50 4.00
BP108 Anthony Kay .15 .40
BP109 Yusniel Diaz .25 .60
BP110 Brady Singer .30 .75
BP111 Bo Bichette .50 1.25
BP112 Matthew Liberatore .15 .40
BP113 Dylan Cease .40 1.00
BP114 Edward Cabrera .25 .60
BP115 Jeter Downs .25 .60
BP116 Luken Baker .20 .50
BP117 Shane Baz .15 .40
BP118 Keibert Ruiz .40 1.00
BP119 Jonathan Hernandez .15 .40
BP120 Matt Mercer .15 .40
BP121 Ryan Helsley .20 .50
BP122 Cole Ragans .15 .40
BP123 Yordan Alvarez 1.00 2.50
BP124 DJ Peters .25 .60
BP125 Cal Quantrill .15 .40
BP126 Drew Waters .50 1.25
BP127 Peter Alonso 1.25 3.00
BP128 MJ Melendez .25 .60
BP129 Austin Riley .75 2.00
BP130 Gavin Lux .50 1.25
BP131 Brandon Marsh .15 .40
BP132 Andrew Knizner .25 .60
BP133 Mitch Keller .20 .50
BP134 Cristian Santana .60 1.50
BP135 Jesus Sanchez .15 .40
BP136 Peter Lambert .25 .60
BP137 Brock Burke .15 .40
BP138 Alex Kirilloff .25 .60
BP139 DL Hall .15 .40
BP140 Bryan Mata .15 .40
BP141 Austin Beck .15 .40
BP142 Genesis Cabrera .25 .60
BP143 Brendan Rodgers .25 .60
BP144 Sean Murphy .20 .50
BP145 Roberto Ramos .20 .50
BP146 Ronaldo Hernandez .15 .40
BP147 Albert Abreu .15 .40
BP148 William Contreras .20 .50
BP149 Jose de la Cruz .50 1.25
BP150 Eloy Jimenez .60 1.50

2019 Bowman Prospects Blue

*BLUE: 1.5X TO 4X BASIC
STATED ODDS 1:238 HOBBY
STATED PRINT RUN 150 SER.#'d SETS

2019 Bowman Prospects Camo

*CAMO: .6X TO 1.5X BASIC
THREE PER RETAIL VALUE PACK

2019 Bowman Prospects Gold

*GOLD: 4X TO 10X BASIC
STATED ODDS 1:626 HOBBY
STATED PRINT RUN 50 SER.#'d SETS
BP1 Vladimir Guerrero Jr. 30.00 80.00
BP50 Joey Bart 50.00 120.00
BP100 Wander Franco 75.00 200.00

2019 Bowman Prospects Green

*GREEN: 2X TO 5X BASIC
STATED ODDS 1:141 BLASTER
STATED PRINT RUN 99 SER.#'d SETS
BP1 Vladimir Guerrero Jr. 15.00 40.00

2019 Bowman Prospects Orange

*ORANGE: 8X TO 20X BASIC
STATED ODDS 1:329 HOBBY
STATED PRINT RUN 25 SER.#'d SETS
BP1 Vladimir Guerrero Jr. 60.00 150.00
BP50 Joey Bart 100.00 250.00
BP100 Wander Franco 150.00 400.00

2019 Bowman Prospects Purple

*PURPLE: 1.5X TO 4X BASIC
STATED ODDS 1:143 HOBBY
STATED PRINT RUN 250 SER.#'d SETS

2019 Bowman Prospects Sky Blue

*SKY BLUE: 1.2X TO 3X BASIC
STATED ODDS 1:72 HOBBY
STATED PRINT RUN 499 SER.#'d SETS

2019 Bowman Draft

COMPLETE SET (200) 12.00 30.00
STATED PLATE ODDS 1:1241 HOBBY
PLATE PRINT RUN 1 SET PER COLOR
BLACK-CYAN-MAGENTA-YELLOW ISSUED
NO PLATE PRICING DUE TO SCARCITY
BD1 Adley Rutschman 3.00 8.00
BD2 Jarred Kelenic .60 1.50
BD3 Alek Manoah .30 .75
BD4 Grant McCray .25 .60
BD5 Brock Deatherage .15 .40
BD6 Matt Wallner .30 .75
BD7 Josh Jung 1.50 4.00
BD8 Andres Gimenez .20 .50
BD9 Jackson Kowar .15 .40
BD10 Logan Davidson .15 .40
BD11 Isaiah Campbell .30 .75
BD12 Blake Walston .25 .60
BD13 Izzy Wilson .15 .40
BD14 Yordys Valdes .30 .75
BD15 Alec Marsh .20 .50
BD16 Ryan Zeferjahn .20 .50
BD17 Brady McConnell .25 .60
BD18 Jordan Groshans .30 .75
BD19 Sammy Siani .20 .50
BD20 Kristian Robinson .40 1.00
BD21 Eric Pardinho .20 .50
BD22 Gunnar Henderson .30 .75
BD23 Joseph Ortiz .20 .50
BD24 Justin Slaten .15 .40
BD25 Drew Waters .50 1.25
BD26 Cal Mitchell .25 .60
BD27 Daniel Espino .20 .50
BD28 Ethan Small .20 .50
BD29 Logan Wyatt .25 .60
BD30 Estevan Florial .25 .60
BD31 Hunter Bishop 1.50 4.00
BD32 Thomas Dillard .30 .75
BD33 DL Hall .15 .40
BD34 T.J. Sikkema .25 .60
BD35 Dominic Fletcher .15 .40
BD36 Antoine Kelly .30 .75
BD37 Albert Abreu .15 .40
BD38 Mateo Gil .20 .50
BD39 Brett Baty 1.25 3.00
BD40 Brandon Lewis .25 .60
BD41 Jamari Baylor 1.00 2.50
BD42 Nolan Gorman .50 1.25
BD43 Jack Little .25 .60
BD44 Quinn Priester .25 .60
BD45 Freudis Nova .25 .60
BD46 Royce Lewis .30 .75
BD47 Tyler Callihan .20 .50
BD48 Matthew Allan 1.25 3.00
BD49 Will Stewart .15 .40
BD50 Riley Greene 2.00 5.00
BD51 Ethan Hankins .20 .50
BD52 Derian Cruz .15 .40
BD53 Andre Pallante .20 .50
BD54 Dane Dunning .15 .40
BD55 Matt Mercer .15 .40
BD56 Chris Murphy .15 .40
BD57 Michael Busch .50 1.25
BD58 James Beard .50 1.25
BD59 Braden Shewmake .50 1.25
BD60 Julio Rodriguez 1.25 3.00
BD61 JJ Goss .20 .50
BD62 Ronny Mauricio .40 1.00
BD63 Dasan Brown .40 1.00
BD64 Michael Toglia .75 2.00
BD65 Keoni Cavaco .40 1.00
BD66 Greg Jones .75 2.00
BD67 Shea Langeliers 1.00 2.50
BD68 Evan Fitterer .40 1.00
BD69 Hudson Head .75 2.00
BD70 Tony Locey .20 .50
BD71 Julio Pablo Martinez .15 .40
BD72 Jake Agnos .25 .60
BD73 Matt Gorski .25 .60
BD74 Peyton Burdick .60 1.50
BD75 Brewer Hicklen .25 .60
BD76 Kyle Stowers .25 .60
BD77 Erik Rivera .30 .75
BD78 Leonardo Jimenez .25 .60
BD79 Bryson Stott 1.50 4.00
BD80 Cristian Santana .25 .60
BD81 Davis Wendzel .20 .50
BD82 Jake Sanford .30 .75
BD83 Casey Golden .25 .60
BD84 Tirso Ornelas .15 .40
BD85 CJ Abrams 2.00 5.00
BD86 Josh Smith .30 .75
BD87 Triston Casas .60 1.50
BD88 Victor Victor Mesa .30 .75
BD89 Sixto Sanchez .20 .50
BD90 Seth Johnson .15 .40
BD91 Ryan Jensen .25 .60
BD92 Tim Tebow .75 2.00
BD93 Wander Franco 2.50 6.00
BD94 Matthew Thompson .20 .50
BD95 Jake Mangum .60 1.50
BD96 Jake Guenther .20 .50
BD97 Jonathan India .20 .50
BD98 Jack Kochanowicz .20 .50
BD99 Noah Song .50 1.25
BD100 Andrew Vaughn 2.50 6.0
BD101 Anthony Prato .15 .4
BD102 Domingo Acevedo .15 .4
BD103 MacKenzie Gore .30 .7
BD104 Zack Thompson .25 .6
BD105 Nick Quintana .30 .7
BD106 Kyle Isbel .20 .5
BD107 Ryan Weathers .15 .4
BD108 Andre Lipcius .40 1.0
BD109 Tyler Baum .20 .5
BD110 Conner Capel .20 .5
BD111 Michael Massey .20 .5
BD112 Diosbel Arias .15 .4
BD113 Brandon Williamson .25 .6
BD114 Jeter Downs .25 .6
BD115 George Kirby .25 .6
BD116 Graeme Stinson .15 .4
BD117 Brent Rooker .20 .5
BD118 Eric Yang .20 .5
BD119 Josh Wolf .20 .5
BD120 Andrew Schultz .15 .4
BD121 Grayson Rodriguez .30 .7
BD122 MJ Melendez .25 .6
BD123 Bryant Packard .25 .6
BD124 Aramis Ademan .15 .4
BD125 Corbin Carroll 1.25 3.0
BD126 Kyle McCann .20 .5
BD127 Matthew Liberatore .15 .4
BD128 Beau Philip .25 .6
BD129 Aaron Schunk .30 .7
BD130 Brice Turang .20 .5
BD131 Rece Hinds 1.00 2.5
BD132 Jimmy Lewis .15 .4
BD133 Will Robertson .25 .6
BD134 Joey Bart .50 1.2
BD135 Miguel Amaya .25 .6
BD136 Jonathan Ornelas .20 .5
BD137 Vince Fernandez .20 .5
BD138 Grant Gambrell .20 .5

139 Matthew Lugo .25 .60
140 Korey Lee .30 .75
141 Nasim Nunez .15 .40
142 Denyi Reyes .20 .50
143 Moises Gomez .25 .60
144 John Rave .15 .40
145 Grae Kessinger .25 .60
146 Isiah Gilliam .20 .50
147 Ryne Nelson .20 .50
148 Ryan Garcia .15 .40
149 Matt Canterino .20 .50
150 J.J. Bleday 2.00 5.00
151 Ryan Costello .20 .50
152 Tyler Fitzgerald .20 .50
153 Spencer Steer .15 .40
154 Jose Devers .25 .60
155 Blaze Alexander .15 .40
156 John Doxakis .20 .50
157 Armani Smith .50 1.25
158 Jordyn Adams .20 .50
159 Sean Hjelle .20 .50
160 Cristian Javier .20 .50
161 Jared Triolo .25 .60
162 Alec Bohm 1.00 2.50
163 Jahmai Jones .15 .40
164 Deivi Garcia .75 2.00
165 Brennan Malone .15 .40
166 Cameron Cannon .30 .75
167 Glenallen Hill Jr. .25 .60
168 Evan Edwards .15 .40
169 Shervyen Newton .25 .60
170 Travis Swaggerty .25 .60
171 Anthony Seigler .25 .60
172 Evan White .25 .60
173 Luken Baker .20 .50
174 Trejyn Fletcher .25 .60
175 Spencer Brickhouse .40 1.00
176 Daulton Varsho .15 .40
177 Hayden Wesneski .20 .50
178 Chase Strumpf .75 2.00
179 Logan Gilbert .25 .60
180 Joshua Mears .75 2.00
181 Matt Vierling .25 .60
182 Will Wilson .75 2.00
183 Logan Driscoll .25 .60
184 Tyler Freeman .15 .40
185 Ian Anderson .40 1.00
186 Owen Miller .20 .50
187 Kody Hoese 1.00 2.50
188 Grant Lavigne .20 .50
189 Nick Lodolo .30 .75
190 Clarke Schmidt .25 .60
191 Erik Miller .40 1.00
192 Seth Beer .40 1.00
193 Alejandro Kirk .25 .60
194 Drey Jameson .15 .40
195 Christian Cairo .25 .60
196 Kameron Misner .40 1.00
197 Tommy Henry .20 .50
198 Lazaro Armenteros .20 .50
199 Kendall Williams .25 .60
200 Cooper Johnson .25 .60

2019 Bowman Draft Blue

UE: 2X TO 5X BASIC
TED ODDS 1:34 HOBBY
TED PRINT RUN 150 SER.#'d SETS

2019 Bowman Draft Gold

LD: 4X TO 10X BASIC
TED ODDS 1:100 HOBBY
TED PRINT RUN 50 SER.#'d SETS

2019 Bowman Draft Green

REEN: 2.5X TO 6X BASIC
TED ODDS 1:51 HOBBY
TED PRINT RUN 99 SER.#'d SETS

2019 Bowman Draft Orange

RANGE: 5X TO 12X BASIC
TED ODDS 1:134 HOBBY
TED PRINT RUN 25 SER.#'d SETS

2019 Bowman Draft Purple

RPLE: 2X TO 5X BASIC
TED ODDS 1:20 HOBBY
TED PRINT RUN 250 SER.#'d SETS

2019 Bowman Draft Sky Blue

Y BLUE: 1X TO 2.5X BASIC
TED ODDS 1:10 HOBBY
TED PRINT RUN 499 SER.#'d SETS

2020 Bowman

MPLETE SET (100) 10.00 25.00
NTING PLATE ODDS 1:17,308 HOBBY
TE PRINT RUN 1 SET PER COLOR
CK-CYAN-MAGENTA-YELLOW ISSUED
PLATE PRICING DUE TO SCARCITY
ike Trout 1.25 3.00
ron Judge .60 1.50
etel Marte .20 .50
ancisco Lindor .25 .60
an Diaz RC .40 1.00
rdan Yamamoto RC .30 .75
ike Soroka .25 .60
avan Biggio .30 .75
ax Muncy .20 .50
uan Soto .75 2.00
ean Murphy RC .40 1.00
hys Hoskins .30 .75
hane Bieber .25 .60
Villie Calhoun .15 .40
ustin Dunn RC .30 .75
ravis Demeritte RC .30 .75
nthony Kay RC .25 .60
uis Robert RC 2.50 6.00
dbert Alzolay RC .30 .75
20 Bobby Bradley RC .30 .75
21 Ramon Laureano .25 .60
22 Kris Bryant .30 .75
23 Abraham Toro RC .30 .75
24 Randy Arozarena RC 2.00 5.00
25 Yordan Alvarez RC 1.25 3.00
26 Shohei Ohtani .30 .75
27 Ronald Acuna Jr. 1.00 2.50
28 Lorenzo Cain .15 .40
29 Eduardo Escobar .15 .40
30 Matthew Boyd .15 .40
31 Bryan Reynolds .20 .50
32 Jose Berrios .20 .50
33 Nolan Arenado .30 .75
34 John Means .15 .40
35 Logan Allen RC .25 .60
36 Robel Garcia RC .25 .60
37 Whit Merrifield .25 .60
38 Dustin May RC 1.00 2.50
39 Junior Fernandez RC .25 .60
40 Aaron Civale RC .40 1.00
41 George Springer .20 .50
42 Michel Baez RC .20 .50
43 Joey Votto .25 .60
44 Seth Brown RC .25 .60
45 Mookie Betts .50 1.25
46 Austin Nola RC .40 1.00
47 Fernando Tatis Jr. 1.00 2.50
48 Zack Collins RC .30 .75
49 Eddie Rosario .20 .50
50 Vladimir Guerrero Jr. .50 1.25
51 Dan Vogelbach .15 .40
52 Bo Bichette RC 2.00 5.00
53 Max Scherzer .25 .60
54 Bryce Harper .40 1.00
55 Paul DeJong .25 .60
56 Luis Castillo .20 .50
57 Francisco Mejia .20 .50
58 Dylan Cease RC .50 1.25
59 Lucas Giolito .20 .50
60 Jose Urena .15 .40
61 Jesus Luzardo RC .50 1.25
62 Kevin Newman .20 .50
63 Tony Gonsolin RC 1.00 2.50
64 A.J. Puk RC .50 1.25
65 Adrian Morejon RC .25 .60
66 Yu Chang RC .40 1.00
67 Sheldon Neuse RC .30 .75
68 Blake Snell .20 .50
69 Alex Young RC .25 .60
70 Nomar Mazara .15 .40
71 Gavin Lux RC 1.50 4.00
72 Nico Hoerner RC 1.00 2.50
73 Matt Chapman .25 .60
74 Gleyber Torres .50 1.25
75 Zac Gallen RC .60 1.50
76 Mauricio Dubon RC .30 .75
77 Jeff McNeil .25 .60
78 Kyle Lewis RC 2.00 5.00
79 Aristides Aquino RC .50 1.25
80 Yusei Kikuchi .20 .50
81 Willy Adames .15 .40
82 Trevor Story .25 .60
83 Trent Grisham RC 1.00 2.50
84 Starlin Castro .15 .40
85 Cody Bellinger .50 1.25
86 Buster Posey .30 .75
87 Hanser Alberto .15 .40
88 Jose Altuve .20 .50
89 Brusdar Graterol RC .40 1.00
90 Andres Munoz RC .30 .75
91 Hunter Dozier .15 .40
92 Mike Yastrzemski .40 1.00
93 Miguel Cabrera .25 .60
94 Jack Flaherty .20 .50
95 Xander Bogaerts .25 .60
96 Nick Solak RC .40 1.00
97 Tim Anderson .25 .60
98 Pete Alonso .60 1.50
99 Javier Baez .30 .75
100 Christian Yelich .30 .75

2020 Bowman '90 Bowman Buyback Autographs

STATED ODDS 1:3499 HOBBY
PRINT RUNS B/WN 20-50 COPIES PER
EXCHANGE DEADLINE 3/31/2022
268 Roger Clemens/20 30.00 80.00
320 Frank Thomas/50 75.00 200.00
404 Robin Yount/50 25.00 60.00

2020 Bowman 1st Edition

BFE1 Wander Franco 2.00 5.00
BFE2 Drew Waters .50 1.25
BFE3 Jacob Amaya .75 2.00
BFE4 Kody Hoese .60 1.50
BFE5 Cristian Pache .60 1.50
BFE6 Zack Thompson .20 .50
BFE7 Briam Campusano .20 .50
BFE8 Jasson Dominguez 50.00 120.00
BFE9 Aaron Shortridge .20 .50
BFE10 Xavier Edwards .75 2.00
BFE11 Jesus Sanchez .20 .50
BFE12 Ronaldo Hernandez .20 .50
BFE13 Blake Rutherford .20 .50
BFE14 Ulrich Bojarski .20 .50
BFE15 Jordyn Adams .25 .60
BFE16 Austin Beck .25 .60
BFE17 Niko Hulsizer .50 1.25
BFE18 Triston Casas .50 1.25
BFE19 Julio Rodriguez 1.25 3.00
BFE20 Shane Baz .25 .60
BFE21 Shea Langeliers .40 1.00
BFE22 Grayson Rodriguez .30 .75
BFE23 Ruben Cardenas .25 .60
BFE24 Mason Denaburg .20 .50
BFE25 Bobby Witt Jr. 10.00 25.00
BFE26 Andrew Vaughn .75 2.00
BFE27 Kristian Robinson .60 1.50
BFE28 Ronny Mauricio .50 1.25
BFE29 Alec Bohm 1.25 3.00
BFE30 Jhon Diaz 2.00 5.00
BFE31 Estevan Florial .30 .75
BFE32 Elehuris Montero .25 .60
BFE33 Sam Huff .40 1.00
BFE34 Zack Brown .20 .50
BFE35 Brice Turang .20 .50
BFE36 Ryan Mountcastle .30 .75
BFE37 Wilfred Astudillo .15 .40
BFE38 Gus Varland .20 .50
BFE39 Nick Lodolo .30 .75
BFE40 Tyler Freeman .25 .60
BFE41 Rece Hinds .25 .60
BFE42 Brady Singer .25 .60
BFE43 Cal Mitchell .20 .50
BFE44 Ethan Hankins .20 .50
BFE45 Daz Cameron .20 .50
BFE46 Sherten Apostel 1.00 2.50
BFE47 Hunter Greene .30 .75
BFE48 Josiah Gray .30 .75
BFE49 Brailyn Marquez .50 1.25
BFE50 Adley Rutschman 1.25 3.00
BFE51 Everson Pereira .50 1.25
BFE52 Bayron Lora 5.00 12.00
BFE53 Clarke Schmidt .30 .75
BFE54 Brady McConnell .25 .60
BFE55 Spencer Howard .75 2.00
BFE56 Cristian Javier .20 .50
BFE57 Aaron Ashby .20 .50
BFE58 Logan Gilbert .25 .60
BFE59 Glenallen Hill Jr. .30 .75
BFE60 Alvaro Seijas .20 .50
BFE61 Jeremy Pena .50 1.25
BFE62 CJ Abrams .75 2.00
BFE63 Franklin Perez .20 .50
BFE64 Tanner Houck .50 1.25
BFE65 Damon Jones .25 .60
BFE66 Nolan Gorman .40 1.00
BFE67 Ke'Bryan Hayes .50 1.25
BFE68 Bryson Stott .50 1.25
BFE69 Canaan Smith .30 .75
BFE70 Forrest Whitley .25 .60
BFE71 Drew Mendoza .50 1.25
BFE72 Jazz Chisholm .50 1.25
BFE73 Jonathan India .25 .60
BFE74 MacKenzie Gore .40 1.00
BFE75 Seth Beer .40 1.00
BFE76 Joey Cantillo .20 .50
BFE77 Evan White .20 .50
BFE78 Chris Vallimont .20 .50
BFE79 Sixto Sanchez .30 .75
BFE80 Alex Kirilloff .40 1.00
BFE81 Tristen Lutz .25 .60
BFE82 Freudis Nova .20 .50
BFE83 Tim Cate .20 .50
BFE84 Daniel Lynch .20 .50
BFE85 Antonio Cabello .60 1.50
BFE86 Bobby Dalbec .50 1.25
BFE87 Colton Welker .20 .50
BFE88 Logan Davidson .25 .60
BFE89 Matthew Liberatore .25 .60
BFE90 Adam Hall .25 .60
BFE91 Jackson Rutledge .30 .75
BFE92 Dane Dunning .20 .50
BFE93 Royce Lewis .50 1.25
BFE94 Jarred Kelenic 1.25 3.00
BFE95 Nolan Jones .30 .75
BFE96 Jerar Encarnacion .60 1.50
BFE97 Ian Anderson .50 1.25
BFE98 Alek Thomas .25 .60
BFE99 Matt Manning .25 .60
BFE100 Jo Adell .75 2.00
BFE101 Nick Madrigal .60 1.50
BFE102 Owen Miller .20 .50
BFE103 Marco Luciano .75 2.00
BFE104 Jordan Groshans .40 1.00
BFE105 Nick Allen .20 .50
BFE106 Dylan Carlson .75 2.00
BFE107 Cole Winn .20 .50
BFE108 Tarik Skubal 1.00 2.50
BFE109 Oscar Gonzalez .50 1.25
BFE110 Aramis Ademan .20 .50
BFE111 Oneil Cruz .25 .60
BFE112 Joey Bart .60 1.50
BFE113 Josh Jung .50 1.25
BFE114 Luis Garcia .30 .75
BFE115 Jasseel De La Cruz .50 1.25
BFE116 J.J. Bleday .60 1.50
BFE117 Joe Ryan .20 .50
BFE118 Keoni Cavaco .20 .50
BFE119 Hans Crouse .20 .50
BFE120 Isaac Paredes .30 .75
BFE121 Grant Lavigne .20 .50
BFE122 Riley Greene .75 2.00
BFE123 Jordan Balazovic .40 1.00
BFE124 Nate Pearson .40 1.00
BFE125 Deivi Garcia .75 2.00
BFE126 Luis Garcia .75 2.00
BFE127 Leody Taveras .20 .50
BFE128 Bryan Mata .20 .50
BFE129 Hunter Bishop .40 1.00
BFE130 Taylor Trammell .20 .50
BFE131 Miguel Vargas .50 1.25
BFE132 Luis Gil .30 .75
BFE133 Grant Little .20 .50
BFE134 Gunnar Henderson .25 .60
BFE135 Eric Pardinho .20 .50
BFE136 Miguel Amaya .25 .60
BFE137 Ryan Rolison .20 .50
BFE138 Jorge Mateo .20 .50
BFE139 Anthony Volpe .75 2.00
BFE140 Nick Bennett .20 .50
BFE141 Brennen Davis .40 1.00
BFE142 Casey Mize .60 1.50
BFE143 Keibert Ruiz .50 1.25
BFE144 Jarren Duran .75 2.00
BFE145 Robert Puason 6.00 15.00
BFE146 Travis Swaggerty .25 .60
BFE147 Will Wilson .25 .60
BFE148 Heliot Ramos .30 .75
BFE149 Alek Manoah .25 .60
BFE150 Luis Robert 2.00 5.00

2020 Bowman 1st Edition Blue Foil

*BLUE FOIL: 3X TO 8X BASIC
STATED ODDS 1:10 PACKS
STATED PRINT RUN 150 SER.#'d SETS
BFE8 Jasson Dominguez 150.00 400.00
BFE25 Bobby Witt Jr. 100.00 250.00
BFE52 Bayron Lora 50.00 120.00

2020 Bowman 1st Edition Gold Foil

*GOLD FOIL: X TO X BASIC
STATED ODDS 1:28 PACKS
STATED PRINT RUN 50 SER.#'d SETS
BFE8 Jasson Dominguez 600.00 1500.00
BFE25 Bobby Witt Jr. 200.00 500.00
BFE52 Bayron Lora 100.00 250.00

2020 Bowman 1st Edition Orange Foil

*ORANGE FOIL: X TO X BASIC
STATED ODDS 1:56 PACKS
STATED PRINT RUN 25 SER.#'d SETS
BFE8 Jasson Dominguez 1250.00 3000.00
BFE25 Bobby Witt Jr. 400.00 1000.00
BFE52 Bayron Lora 125.00 300.00

2020 Bowman 1st Edition Sky Blue Foil

*SKY BLUE FOIL: X TO X BASIC
STATED ODDS 1:2 PACKS
BFE8 Jasson Dominguez 15.00 300.00
BFE25 Bobby Witt Jr. 50.00 120.00
BFE52 Bayron Lora 25.00 60.00

2020 Bowman 1st Edition Yellow Foil

*YELLOW FOIL: X TO X BASIC
STATED ODDS 1:19 PACKS
STATED PRINT RUN 75 SER.#'d SETS
BFE8 Jasson Dominguez 300.00 800.00
BFE25 Bobby Witt Jr. 150.00 400.00
BFE52 Bayron Lora 60.00 150.00

2020 Bowman Blue

*BLUE: 3X TO 8X BASIC
*BLUE RC: 2X TO 5X BASIC
STATED ODDS 1:460 HOBBY
STATED PRINT RUN 150 SER.#'d SETS
1 Mike Trout 12.00 30.00
18 Luis Robert 20.00 50.00
25 Yordan Alvarez 15.00 40.00
52 Bo Bichette 20.00 50.00

2020 Bowman Gold

*GOLD: 6X TO 15X BASIC
*GOLD RC: 4X TO 10X BASIC
STATED ODDS 1:1378 HOBBY
STATED PRINT RUN 50 SER.#'d SETS
1 Mike Trout 25.00 60.00
18 Luis Robert 40.00 100.00
25 Yordan Alvarez 30.00 80.00
52 Bo Bichette 40.00 100.00

2020 Bowman Green

*GREEN: 4X TO 10X BASIC
*GREEN RC: 2.5X TO 6X BASIC
STATED ODDS 1:326 BLASTER
STATED PRINT RUN 99 SER.#'d SETS
1 Mike Trout 15.00 40.00
18 Luis Robert 25.00 60.00
25 Yordan Alvarez 20.00 50.00
52 Bo Bichette 25.00 60.00

2020 Bowman Orange

*ORANGE: 10X TO 25X BASIC
*ORANGE RC: 6X TO 15X BASIC
STATED ODDS 1:551 HOBBY
STATED PRINT RUN 25 SER.#'d SETS
1 Mike Trout 40.00 100.00
18 Luis Robert 60.00 150.00
25 Yordan Alvarez 50.00 120.00
52 Bo Bichette 60.00 150.00

2020 Bowman Purple

*PURPLE: 2.5X TO 6X BASIC
*PURPLE RC: 1.5X TO 4X BASIC
STATED ODDS 1:276 HOBBY
STATED PRINT RUN 250 SER.#'d SETS
1 Mike Trout 10.00 25.00
18 Luis Robert 15.00 40.00
25 Yordan Alvarez 12.00 30.00
52 Bo Bichette 15.00 40.00

2020 Bowman Sky Blue

*SKY BLUE: 1.5X TO 4X BASIC
*SKY BLUE RC: 1X TO 2.5X BASIC
STATED ODDS 1:138 HOBBY
STATED PRINT RUN 499 SER.#'d SETS
1 Mike Trout 6.00 15.00
18 Luis Robert 10.00 25.00
25 Yordan Alvarez 8.00 20.00
52 Bo Bichette 10.00 25.00

2020 Bowman Yellow

*YELLOW: 5X TO 12X BASIC
*YELLOW RC: 3X TO 8X BASIC
STATED ODDS 1:326 BLASTER
STATED PRINT RUN 99 SER.#'d SETS
1 Mike Trout 20.00 50.00
18 Luis Robert 30.00 80.00
25 Yordan Alvarez 25.00 60.00
52 Bo Bichette 30.00 80.00

2020 Bowman Prospect Autographs

STATED ODDS 1:62 BLASTER
EXCHANGE DEADLINE 3/31/2022
*PURPLE/250: .5X TO 1.2X BASE
*BLUE/150: .6X TO 1.5X BASE
*GREEN/99: .75X TO 2X BASE
*GOLD/50: 1X TO 2.5X BASE
*ORANGE/25: 1.2X TO 3X BASE
PAAB Andrew Bechtold 2.50 6.00
PAAR Adley Rutschman 25.00 60.00
PAASH Avery Short 2.50 6.00
PABC Briam Campusano 2.50 6.00
PABWJ Bobby Witt Jr. 50.00 120.00
PACB Colin Barber 8.00 20.00
PACM Casey Mize 12.00 30.00
PACS Cole Stobbe 2.50 6.00
PAEW Eli White 3.00 8.00
PAIM Ian McKinney 2.50 6.00
PAJC Joey Cantillo 5.00 12.00
PAJCB Jacob Condra-Bogan 2.50 6.00
PAJD Jhoan Duran 4.00 10.00
PAJJ Joe Jacques 2.50 6.00
PAJR John Rave 2.50 6.00
PAKB Kris Bubic 4.00 10.00
PAKH Kody Hoese 8.00 20.00
PAKP Konnor Pilkington 2.50 6.00
PAKR Kristian Robinson 10.00 25.00
PAKW Ken Waldichuk 3.00 8.00
PALI Logan Ice 2.50 6.00
PALJ Liam Jenkins 2.50 6.00
PAMIM Michael Mercado 3.00 8.00
PAMM Matt Manning 3.00 8.00
PAMME MJ Melendez 2.50 6.00
PAMS Mitch Stallings 2.50 6.00
PANP Nick Pratto 2.50 6.00
PAOM Orelvis Martinez 6.00 15.00
PAPC Pedro Castellanos 3.00 8.00
PARH Rece Hinds 3.00 8.00
PARK Ryan Kreidler 3.00 8.00
PASC Sam Carlson 2.50 6.00
PASH Spencer Howard 10.00 25.00
PASHE Sam Hentges 2.50 6.00
PATB Tyler Baum 2.50 6.00
PATF Tyler Fitzgerald 3.00 8.00
PATM Trevor McDonald 2.50 6.00
PAWF Wander Franco 50.00 120.00
PAWS Will Stewart 2.50 6.00
PAWT Will Toffey 2.50 6.00
PAZB Zack Brown 2.50 6.00

2020 Bowman Prospects

PRINTING PLATE ODDS 1:11,389 HOBBY
PLATE PRINT RUN 1 SET PER COLOR
BLACK-CYAN-MAGENTA-YELLOW ISSUED
NO PLATE PRICING DUE TO SCARCITY
BP1 Wander Franco 1.50 4.00
BP2 Drew Waters .40 1.00
BP3 Jacob Amaya .60 1.50
BP4 Kody Hoese .50 1.25
BP5 Cristian Pache .50 1.25
BP6 Zack Thompson .15 .40
BP7 Briam Campusano .15 .40
BP8 Jasson Dominguez 8.00 20.00
BP9 Aaron Shortridge .15 .40
BP10 Xavier Edwards .60 1.50
BP11 Jesus Sanchez .15 .40
BP12 Ronaldo Hernandez .15 .40
BP13 Blake Rutherford .15 .40
BP14 Ulrich Bojarski .15 .40
BP15 Jordyn Adams .20 .50
BP16 Austin Beck .20 .50
BP17 Niko Hulsizer .40 1.00
BP18 Triston Casas .40 1.00
BP19 Julio Rodriguez 1.00 2.50
BP20 Shane Baz .15 .40
BP21 Shea Langeliers .30 .75
BP22 Grayson Rodriguez .25 .60
BP23 Ruben Cardenas .20 .50
BP24 Mason Denaburg .15 .40
BP25 Bobby Witt Jr. 4.00 10.00
BP26 Andrew Vaughn .60 1.50
BP27 Kristian Robinson .50 1.25
BP28 Ronny Mauricio .40 1.00
BP29 Alec Bohm 1.00 2.50
BP30 Jhon Diaz 1.50 4.00
BP31 Estevan Florial .25 .60
BP32 Elehuris Montero .20 .50
BP33 Sam Huff .30 .75
BP34 Zack Brown .15 .40
BP35 Brice Turang .15 .40
BP36 Ryan Mountcastle .25 .60
BP37 Wilfred Astudillo .15 .40
BP38 Gus Varland .15 .40
BP39 Nick Lodolo .25 .60
BP40 Tyler Freeman .20 .50
BP41 Rece Hinds .20 .50
BP42 Brady Singer .20 .50
BP43 Cal Mitchell .15 .40
BP44 Ethan Hankins .20 .50
BP45 Daz Cameron .15 .40
BP46 Sherten Apostel .75 2.00
BP47 Hunter Greene .25 .60
BP48 Josiah Gray .25 .60
BP49 Brailyn Marquez .40 1.00
BP50 Adley Rutschman 1.00 2.50
BP51 Everson Pereira .40 1.00
BP52 Bayron Lora 2.50 6.00
BP53 Clarke Schmidt .25 .60
BP54 Brady McConnell .20 .50
BP55 Spencer Howard .60 1.50
BP56 Cristian Javier .15 .40
BP57 Aaron Ashby .15 .40
BP58 Logan Gilbert .20 .50
BP59 Glenallen Hill Jr. .60 1.50
BP60 Alvaro Seijas .15 .40
BP61 Jeremy Pena .40 1.00
BP62 CJ Abrams .60 1.50
BP63 Franklin Perez .15 .40
BP64 Tanner Houck .40 1.00
BP65 Damon Jones .20 .50
BP66 Nolan Gorman .30 .75
BP67 Ke'Bryan Hayes .15 .40
BP68 Bryson Stott .40 1.00
BP69 Canaan Smith .25 .60
BP70 Forrest Whitley .15 .40
BP71 Drew Mendoza .40 1.00
BP72 Jazz Chisholm .40 1.00
BP73 Jonathan India .20 .50
BP74 MacKenzie Gore .30 .75
BP75 Seth Beer .30 .75
BP76 Joey Cantillo .15 .40
BP77 Evan White .15 .40
BP78 Chris Vallimont .15 .40
BP79 Sixto Sanchez .25 .60
BP80 Alex Kirilloff .30 .75
BP81 Tristen Lutz .20 .50
BP82 Freudis Nova .15 .40
BP83 Tim Cate .15 .40
BP84 Daniel Lynch .15 .40
BP85 Antonio Cabello .50 1.25
BP86 Bobby Dalbec .40 1.00
BP87 Colton Welker .15 .40
BP88 Logan Davidson .20 .50
BP89 Matthew Liberatore .20 .50
BP90 Adam Hall .20 .50
BP91 Jackson Rutledge .25 .60
BP92 Dane Dunning .15 .40
BP93 Royce Lewis .40 1.00
BP94 Jarred Kelenic 1.00 2.50
BP95 Nolan Jones .25 .60
BP96 Jerar Encarnacion 2.00 5.00
BP97 Ian Anderson .40 1.00
BP98 Alek Thomas .20 .50
BP99 Matt Manning .20 .50
BP100 Jo Adell .60 1.50
BP101 Nick Madrigal .50 1.25
BP102 Owen Miller .15 .40
BP103 Marco Luciano .60 1.50
BP104 Jordan Groshans .30 .75
BP105 Nick Allen .15 .40
BP106 Dylan Carlson .60 1.50
BP107 Cole Winn .15 .40
BP108 Tarik Skubal .75 2.00
BP109 Oscar Gonzalez .40 1.00
BP110 Aramis Ademan .15 .40
BP111 Oneil Cruz .20 .50
BP112 Joey Bart .50 1.25
BP113 Josh Jung .40 1.00
BP114 Luis Garcia .25 .60
BP115 Jasseel De La Cruz .25 .60
BP116 J.J. Bleday .50 1.25
BP117 Joe Ryan .15 .40
BP118 Keoni Cavaco .15 .40
BP119 Hans Crouse .15 .40
BP120 Isaac Paredes .25 .60
BP121 Grant Lavigne .15 .40
BP122 Riley Greene .60 1.50
BP123 Jordan Balazovic .30 .75
BP124 Nate Pearson .30 .75
BP125 Deivi Garcia .60 1.50
BP126 Luis Garcia .60 1.50
BP127 Leody Taveras .15 .40
BP128 Bryan Mata .15 .40
BP129 Hunter Bishop .30 .75
BP130 Taylor Trammell .20 .50
BP131 Miguel Vargas .40 1.00
BP132 Luis Gil .25 .60
BP133 Grant Little .15 .40
BP134 Gunnar Henderson .20 .50
BP135 Eric Pardinho .15 .40
BP136 Miguel Amaya .20 .50
BP137 Ryan Rolison .15 .40
BP138 Jorge Mateo .15 .40
BP139 Anthony Volpe 1.50 4.00
BP140 Nick Bennett .15 .40
BP141 Brennen Davis .30 .75
BP142 Casey Mize .50 1.25
BP143 Keibert Ruiz .40 1.00
BP144 Jarren Duran .60 1.50
BP145 Robert Puason 3.00 8.00
BP146 Travis Swaggerty .20 .50
BP147 Will Wilson .20 .50
BP148 Heliot Ramos .25 .60
BP149 Alek Manoah .20 .50
BP150 Luis Robert 1.50 4.00

2020 Bowman Prospects Blue

*BLUE: 1.5X TO 4X BASIC
STATED ODDS 1:307 HOBBY
STATED PRINT RUN 150 SER.#'d SETS
BP8 Jasson Dominguez 60.00 150.00
BP25 Bobby Witt Jr. 25.00 60.00
BP145 Robert Puason 12.00 30.00

2020 Bowman Prospects Camo

*CAMO: .6X TO 1.5X BASIC
FIVE PER RETAIL VALUE PACK
BP145 Robert Puason 5.00 12.00

2020 Bowman Prospects Gold

*GOLD: 4X TO 10X BASIC
STATED ODDS 1:919 HOBBY
STATED PRINT RUN 50 SER.#'d SETS
BP8 Jasson Dominguez 150.00 400.00
BP25 Bobby Witt Jr. 60.00 150.00
BP145 Robert Puason 30.00 80.00

2020 Bowman Prospects Green

*GREEN: 2X TO 5X BASIC
STATED ODDS 1:218 BLASTER
STATED PRINT RUN 99 SER.#'d SETS
BP8 Jasson Dominguez 75.00 200.00
BP25 Bobby Witt Jr. 30.00 80.00
BP145 Robert Puason 15.00 40.00

2020 Bowman Prospects Orange

*ORANGE: 8X TO 20X BASIC
STATED ODDS 1:367 HOBBY
STATED PRINT RUN 25 SER.#'d SETS
BP8 Jasson Dominguez 300.00 800.00
BP25 Bobby Witt Jr. 125.00 300.00
BP145 Robert Puason 60.00 150.00

2020 Bowman Prospects Purple

*PURPLE: 1.5X TO 4X BASIC
STATED ODDS 1:185 HOBBY
STATED PRINT RUN 250 SER.#'d SETS
BP8 Jasson Dominguez 60.00 150.00
BP25 Bobby Witt Jr. 25.00 60.00
BP145 Robert Puason 12.00 30.00

2020 Bowman Prospects Sky Blue

2019 Bowman Prospects Sky Blue
2019 Bowman Prospects Sky Blue
2019 Bowman Prospects Sky Blue
BP8 Jasson Dominguez 50.00 120.00
BP25 Bobby Witt Jr. 20.00 50.00
BP145 Robert Puason 10.00 25.00

2020 Bowman Prospects Yellow

*YELLOW: 2.5X TO 6X BASIC
STATED ODDS 1:613 HOBBY
STATED PRINT RUN 75 SER.#'d SETS
BP8 Jasson Dominguez 100.00 250.00
BP25 Bobby Witt Jr. 40.00 100.00
BP145 Robert Puason 20.00 50.00

2020 Bowman Draft

STATED PLATE ODDS 1:XXX HOBBY
PLATE PRINT RUN 1 SET PER COLOR
BLACK-CYAN-MAGENTA-YELLOW ISSUED
NO PLATE PRICING DUE TO SCARCITY
BD1 Niko Hulsizer .40 1.00
BD2 Jackson Kowar .15 .40
BD3 Korey Lee .20 .50
BD4 Milan Tolentino .25 .60
BD5 Jeter Downs .25 .60
BD6 Hans Crouse .15 .40
BD7 Mike Siani .15 .40
BD8 Dane Acker .20 .50
BD9 Ryan Jensen .20 .50
BD10 Shane Baz .15 .40
BD11 Trei Cruz .60 1.50
BD12 Emerson Hancock .60 1.50
BD13 Joey Cantillo .15 .40
BD14 Nick Loftin .25 .60
BD15 Rece Hinds .20 .50
BD16 Jared Shuster .30 .75
BD17 Jesse Franklin V .60 1.50
BD18 Kaden Polcovich .25 .60
BD19 Ben Hernandez .25 .60
BD20 Spencer Strider .25 .60
BD21 Tyler Brown .25 .60
BD22 Keoni Cavaco .15 .40
BD23 Case Williams .20 .50
BD24 Cade Cavalli .30 .75
BD25 Burl Carraway .40 1.00
BD26 Daniel Espino .20 .50
BD27 Oswald Peraza .40 1.00
BD28 Zach DeLoach .60 1.50
BD29 Nick Yorke .75 2.00
BD30 Clayton Beeter .40 1.00
BD31 Joe Ryan .15 .40
BD32 Jordan Groshans .30 .75
BD33 Gage Workman .75 2.00
BD34 Austin Hendrick 1.50 4.00
BD35 Jimmy Glowenke .40 1.00
BD36 Ryan Rolison .15 .40
BD37 Logan Gilbert .20 .50
BD38 Bobby Miller .60 1.50
BD39 Robert Hassell 1.25 3.00
BD40 JJ Goss .15 .40
BD41 Reid Detmers .40 1.00
BD42 Michael Busch .40 1.00
BD43 Chris McMahon .20 .50
BD44 Xavier Edwards .60 1.50
BD45 Alec Burleson .25 .60
BD46 Freddy Zamora .25 .60
BD47 Travis Swaggerty .20 .50
BD48 Sammy Infante .60 1.50
BD49 Owen Caissie .60 1.50
BD50 Max Meyer .60 1.50
BD51 Logan Allen .15 .40
BD52 Landon Knack .50 1.25
BD53 Quinn Priester .25 .60
BD54 Colt Keith .75 2.00
BD55 Jarren Duran .60 1.50
BD56 Austin Wells 1.50 4.00
BD57 Jordan Walker 2.00 5.00
BD58 Jordan Balazovic .30 .75
BD59 Masyn Winn .60 1.50
BD60 Carson Tucker 1.25 3.00
BD61 Nick Bitsko 1.00 2.50
BD62 Daniel Cabrera .60 1.50
BD63 Marco Raya .30 .75

BD64 Kyle Nicolas .20 .50
BD65 Oneil Cruz .20 .50
BD66 Hunter Barnhart .25 .60
BD67 Cole Henry .20 .50
BD68 Tristen Lutz .20 .50
BD69 Petey Halpin .40 1.00
BD70 Jared Jones .25 .60
BD71 Connor Phillips .25 .60
BD72 Pete Crow-Armstrong 2.00 5.00
BD73 Casey Martin 1.50 4.00
BD74 Bryce Bonnin .25 .60
BD75 Daniel Lynch .15 .40
BD76 Tekoah Roby .15 .40
BD77 Isaiah Greene .60 1.50
BD78 Tyler Freeman .20 .50
BD79 Heliot Ramos .25 .60
BD80 Miguel Amaya .20 .50
BD81 Nick Gonzales 2.50 6.00
BD82 DL Hall .15 .40
BD83 Triston Casas .40 1.00
BD84 Christian Chamberlain .25 .60
BD85 Slade Cecconi .20 .50
BD86 Tink Hence .25 .60
BD87 Adisyn Coffey .20 .50
BD88 Asa Lacy 1.00 2.50
BD89 Geraldo Perdomo .15 .40
BD90 Nick Garcia .25 .60
BD91 Nick Swiney .30 .75
BD92 Matthew Dyer .25 .60
BD93 CJ Van Eyk .25 .60
BD94 Alerick Soularie .25 .60
BD95 Garrett Crochet 1.50 4.00
BD96 Ian Seymour .15 .40
BD97 Zavier Warren .15 .40
BD98 Ed Howard 3.00 8.00
BD99 Justin Lange .15 .40
BD100 Ian Bedell .25 .60
BD101 Aaron Shortridge .15 .40
BD102 Trevor Larnach .30 .75
BD103 David Calabrese .40 1.00
BD104 Quin Cotton .15 .40
BD105 Luke Little .25 .60
BD106 Drew Romo .40 1.00
BD107 Zac Veen 2.00 5.00
BD108 Brady McConnell .20 .50
BD109 Sam Weatherly .15 .40
BD110 Jordan Nwogu .60 1.50
BD111 Jordan Westburg .40 1.00
BD112 Zach McCambley .15 .40
BD113 Trevor Hauver .25 .60
BD114 Corbin Carroll .25 .60
BD115 Tanner Burns .25 .60
BD116 Jackson Miller .40 1.00
BD117 Carter Baumler .25 .60
BD118 Garrett Mitchell 1.25 3.00
BD119 Tyler Soderstrom .60 1.50
BD120 Holden Powell .15 .40
BD121 Spencer Torkelson 5.00 12.00
BD122 Heston Kjerstad 2.50 6.00
BD123 Alexander Canario .15 .40
BD124 Justin Foscue .60 1.50
BD125 Levi Prater .20 .50
BD126 Evan Carter .75 2.00
BD127 Bryce Jarvis .15 .40
BD128 Werner Blakely .20 .50
BD129 Casey Schmitt .50 1.25
BD130 Hudson Haskin .60 1.50
BD131 Daxton Fulton .30 .75
BD132 Luis Gil .25 .60
BD133 Zach Daniels .25 .60
BD134 Jeff Criswell .25 .60
BD135 Shane McClanahan .20 .50
BD136 Alika Williams .20 .50
BD137 Gilberto Jimenez .75 2.00
BD138 Trent Palmer .20 .50
BD139 Alex Santos .40 1.00
BD140 Bryson Stott .40 1.00
BD141 Ethan Hankins .20 .50
BD142 Kody Hoese .50 1.25
BD143 Francisco Alvarez .50 1.25
BD144 Dillon Dingler .50 1.25
BD145 Carson Ragsdale .20 .50
BD146 Patrick Bailey .50 1.25
BD147 Liam Norris .15 .40
BD148 RJ Dabovich .15 .40
BD149 Carmen Mlodzinski .15 .40
BD150 AJ Vukovich 1.00 2.50
BD151 Jasson Dominguez 4.00 10.00
BD152 Bobby Witt Jr. .75 2.00
BD153 Andrew Vaughn .60 1.50
BD154 Adley Rutschman 1.00 2.50
BD155 Robert Puason .50 1.25
BD156 Jay Groome .15 .40
BD157 Will Klein .20 .50
BD158 Zach Britton .20 .50
BD159 Owen Miller .15 .40
BD160 Logan Hofmann .15 .40
BD161 Ronaldo Hernandez .15 .40
BD162 Jack Blomgren .25 .60
BD163 Adam Seminaris .20 .50
BD164 Bailey Horn .20 .50
BD165 Joe Boyle .25 .60
BD166 Ryan Murphy .15 .40
BD167 Thomas Saggese .15 .40
BD168 George Kirby .25 .60
BD169 Jeremiah Jackson .15 .40
BD170 Shane Drohan .20 .50
BD171 Brandon Pfaadt .15 .40
BD172 Blake Rutherford .15 .40
BD173 Hayden Cantrelle .15 .40
BD174 Mark Vientos .15 .40
BD175 Michael Toglia .15 .40
BD176 Mitchell Parker .15 .40
BD177 Jackson Rutledge .25 .60
BD178 Anthony Volpe .60 1.50
BD179 Nick Lodolo .25 .60
BD180 Riley Greene .60 1.50
BD181 JJ Bleday .50 1.25
BD182 Kyle Isbel .15 .40
BD183 Shea Langeliers .30 .75
BD184 Brett Baty .50 1.25
BD185 Jerar Encarnacion .50 1.25
BD186 Aaron Ashby .15 .40
BD187 Brennen Davis .30 .75
BD188 Julio Rodriguez 1.00 2.50
BD189 CJ Abrams .60 1.50
BD190 Marco Luciano .60 1.50
BD191 Grayson Rodriguez .25 .60
BD192 Kristian Robinson .50 1.25
BD193 Jordyn Adams .20 .50
BD194 Nolan Gorman .30 .75
BD195 Alek Thomas .20 .50
BD196 Hunter Greene .25 .60
BD197 Josh Jung .40 1.00
BD198 Matthew Liberatore .20 .50
BD199 Ronny Mauricio .40 1.00
BD200 Hunter Bishop .30 .75

2020 Bowman Draft Blue

*BLUE: 2X TO 5X BASIC
STATED ODDS 1:XXX HOBBY
STATED PRINT RUN 150 SER.#'d SETS
BD62 Daniel Cabrera 8.00 20.00
BD72 Pete Crow-Armstrong 10.00 25.00

2020 Bowman Draft Gold

*GOLD: 4X TO 10X BASIC
STATED ODDS 1:XXX HOBBY
STATED PRINT RUN 50 SER.#'d SETS
BD62 Daniel Cabrera 15.00 40.00
BD72 Pete Crow-Armstrong 20.00 50.00

2020 Bowman Draft Green

*GREEN: 2.5X TO 6X BASIC
STATED ODDS 1:XXX HOBBY
STATED PRINT RUN 99 SER.#'d SETS
BD62 Daniel Cabrera 10.00 25.00
BD72 Pete Crow-Armstrong 12.00 30.00

2020 Bowman Draft Orange

*ORANGE: 5X TO 12X BASIC
STATED ODDS 1:XXX HOBBY
STATED PRINT RUN 25 SER.#'d SETS
BD62 Daniel Cabrera 20.00 50.00
BD72 Pete Crow-Armstrong 25.00 60.00

2020 Bowman Draft Purple

*PURPLE: 2X TO 5X BASIC
STATED ODDS 1:XXX HOBBY
STATED PRINT RUN 250 SER.#'d SETS
BD62 Daniel Cabrera 6.00 15.00
BD72 Pete Crow-Armstrong 8.00 20.00

2020 Bowman Draft Sky Blue

*SKY BLUE: 1X TO 2.5X BASIC
STATED ODDS 1:XXX HOBBY
STATED PRINT RUN 499 SER.#'d SETS
BD62 Daniel Cabrera 4.00 10.00
BD72 Pete Crow-Armstrong 5.00 12.00

2020 Bowman Draft 1st Edition

BD1 Niko Hulsizer .50 1.25
BD2 Jackson Kowar .20 .50
BD3 Korey Lee .25 .60
BD4 Milan Tolentino .30 .75
BD5 Jeter Downs .30 .75
BD6 Hans Crouse .20 .50
BD7 Mike Siani .20 .50
BD8 Dane Acker .25 .60
BD9 Ryan Jensen .25 .60
BD10 Shane Baz .20 .50
BD11 Trei Cruz .75 2.00
BD12 Emerson Hancock .75 2.00
BD13 Joey Cantillo .20 .50
BD14 Nick Loftin .30 .75
BD15 Rece Hinds .25 .60
BD16 Jared Shuster .40 1.00
BD17 Jesse Franklin V .75 2.00
BD18 Kaden Polcovich .30 .75
BD19 Ben Hernandez .30 .75
BD20 Spencer Strider .30 .75
BD21 Tyler Brown .30 .75
BD22 Keoni Cavaco .20 .50
BD23 Case Williams .25 .60
BD24 Cade Cavalli .40 1.00
BD25 Burl Carraway .50 1.25
BD26 Daniel Espino .25 .60
BD27 Oswald Peraza .50 1.25
BD28 Zach DeLoach .75 2.00
BD29 Nick Yorke 1.00 2.50
BD30 Clayton Beeter .50 1.25
BD31 Joe Ryan .20 .50
BD32 Jordan Groshans .40 1.00
BD33 Gage Workman 1.00 2.50
BD34 Austin Hendrick 2.00 5.00
BD35 Jimmy Glowenke .50 1.25
BD36 Ryan Rolison .20 .50
BD37 Logan Gilbert .25 .60
BD38 Bobby Miller .75 2.00
BD39 Robert Hassell 4.00 10.00
BD40 JJ Goss .20 .50
BD41 Reid Detmers .50 1.25
BD42 Michael Busch .50 1.25
BD43 Chris McMahon .25 .60
BD44 Xavier Edwards .75 2.00
BD45 Alec Burleson .30 .75
BD46 Freddy Zamora .30 .75
BD47 Travis Swaggerty .25 .60
BD48 Sammy Infante .75 2.00
BD49 Owen Caissie .75 2.00
BD50 Max Meyer .75 2.00
BD51 Logan Allen .20 .50
BD52 Landon Knack .60 1.50
BD53 Quinn Priester .30 .75
BD54 Colt Keith 1.00 2.50
BD55 Jarren Duran .75 2.00
BD56 Austin Wells 2.00 5.00
BD57 Jordan Walker 2.50 6.00
BD58 Jordan Balazovic .40 1.00
BD59 Masyn Winn .75 2.00
BD60 Carson Tucker 1.50 4.00
BD61 Nick Bitsko 1.25 3.00
BD62 Daniel Cabrera .75 2.00
BD63 Marco Raya .40 1.00
BD64 Kyle Nicolas .25 .60
BD65 Oneil Cruz .25 .60
BD66 Hunter Barnhart .30 .75
BD67 Cole Henry .25 .60
BD68 Tristen Lutz .25 .60
BD69 Petey Halpin .50 1.25
BD70 Jared Jones .30 .75
BD71 Connor Phillips .30 .75
BD72 Pete Crow-Armstrong 2.50 6.00
BD73 Casey Martin 2.00 5.00
BD74 Bryce Bonnin .30 .75
BD75 Daniel Lynch .20 .50
BD76 Tekoah Roby .20 .50
BD77 Isaiah Greene 1.00 2.50
BD78 Tyler Freeman .25 .60
BD79 Heliot Ramos .30 .75
BD80 Miguel Amaya .25 .60
BD81 Nick Gonzales 4.00 10.00
BD82 DL Hall .20 .50
BD83 Triston Casas .50 1.25
BD84 Christian Chamberlain .30 .75
BD85 Slade Cecconi .25 .60
BD86 Tink Hence .30 .75
BD87 Adisyn Coffey .25 .60
BD88 Asa Lacy 3.00 8.00
BD89 Geraldo Perdomo .20 .50
BD90 Nick Garcia .30 .75
BD91 Nick Swiney .40 1.00
BD92 Matthew Dyer .30 .75
BD93 CJ Van Eyk .30 .75
BD94 Alerick Soularie .30 .75
BD95 Garrett Crochet 4.00 10.00
BD96 Ian Seymour .20 .50
BD97 Zavier Warren .20 .50
BD98 Ed Howard 6.00 15.00
BD99 Justin Lange .20 .50
BD100 Ian Bedell .30 .75
BD101 Aaron Shortridge .20 .50
BD102 Trevor Larnach .40 1.00
BD103 David Calabrese .50 1.25
BD104 Quin Cotton .20 .50
BD105 Luke Little .30 .75
BD106 Drew Romo .50 1.25
BD107 Zac Veen 5.00 12.00
BD108 Brady McConnell .25 .60
BD109 Sam Weatherly .20 .50
BD110 Jordan Nwogu .75 2.00
BD111 Jordan Westburg .50 1.25
BD112 Zach McCambley .20 .50
BD113 Trevor Hauver .30 .75
BD114 Corbin Carroll .30 .75
BD115 Tanner Burns .30 .75
BD116 Jackson Miller .50 1.25
BD117 Carter Baumler .30 .75
BD118 Garrett Mitchell 2.50 6.00
BD119 Tyler Soderstrom 2.50 6.00
BD120 Holden Powell .20 .50
BD121 Spencer Torkelson 30.00 80.00
BD122 Heston Kjerstad 6.00 15.00
BD123 Alexander Canario .20 .50
BD124 Justin Foscue .75 2.00
BD125 Levi Prater .25 .60
BD126 Evan Carter 1.00 2.50
BD127 Bryce Jarvis .20 .50
BD128 Werner Blakely .25 .60
BD129 Casey Schmitt .60 1.50
BD130 Hudson Haskin .75 2.00
BD131 Daxton Fulton .40 1.00
BD132 Luis Gil .30 .75
BD133 Zach Daniels .30 .75
BD134 Jeff Criswell .30 .75
BD135 Shane McClanahan .25 .60
BD136 Alika Williams .25 .60
BD137 Gilberto Jimenez 1.00 2.50
BD138 Trent Palmer .25 .60
BD139 Alex Santos .50 1.25
BD140 Bryson Stott .50 1.25
BD141 Ethan Hankins .25 .60
BD142 Kody Hoese .60 1.50
BD143 Francisco Alvarez .60 1.50
BD144 Dillon Dingler 1.00 2.50
BD145 Carson Ragsdale .30 .75
BD146 Patrick Bailey 2.00 5.00
BD147 Liam Norris .20 .50
BD148 RJ Dabovich .20 .50
BD149 Carmen Mlodzinski .20 .50
BD150 AJ Vukovich 1.25 3.00
BD151 Jasson Dominguez 5.00 12.00
BD152 Bobby Witt Jr. 1.00 2.50
BD153 Andrew Vaughn .75 2.00
BD154 Adley Rutschman 1.25 3.00
BD155 Robert Puason .60 1.50
BD156 Jay Groome .20 .50
BD157 Will Klein .25 .60
BD158 Zach Britton .25 .60
BD159 Owen Miller .20 .50
BD160 Logan Hofmann .20 .50
BD161 Ronaldo Hernandez .20 .50
BD162 Jack Blomgren .30 .75
BD163 Adam Seminaris .25 .60
BD164 Bailey Horn .25 .60
BD165 Joe Boyle .30 .75
BD166 Ryan Murphy .20 .50
BD167 Thomas Saggese .20 .50
BD168 George Kirby .30 .75
BD169 Jeremiah Jackson .20 .50
BD170 Shane Drohan .25 .60
BD171 Brandon Pfaadt .20 .50
BD172 Blake Rutherford .20 .50
BD173 Hayden Cantrelle .20 .50
BD174 Mark Vientos .20 .50
BD175 Michael Toglia .20 .50
BD176 Mitchell Parker .20 .50
BD177 Jackson Rutledge .30 .75
BD178 Anthony Volpe .75 2.00
BD179 Nick Lodolo .30 .75
BD180 Riley Greene .75 2.00
BD181 JJ Bleday .60 1.50
BD182 Kyle Isbel .20 .50
BD183 Shea Langeliers .40 1.00
BD184 Brett Baty .60 1.50
BD185 Jerar Encarnacion .60 1.50
BD186 Aaron Ashby .20 .50
BD187 Brennen Davis .40 1.00
BD188 Julio Rodriguez 1.25 3.00
BD189 CJ Abrams .75 2.00
BD190 Marco Luciano .75 2.00
BD191 Grayson Rodriguez .30 .75
BD192 Kristian Robinson .60 1.50
BD193 Jordyn Adams .25 .60
BD194 Nolan Gorman .40 1.00
BD195 Alek Thomas .25 .60
BD196 Hunter Greene .30 .75
BD197 Josh Jung .50 1.25
BD198 Matthew Liberatore .25 .60
BD199 Ronny Mauricio .50 1.25
BD200 Hunter Bishop .40 1.00

2020 Bowman Draft 1st Edition Blue Foil

*BLUE FOIL: 3X TO 8X BASIC
STATED ODDS 1:XXX HOBBY
STATED PRINT RUN 150 SER.#'d SETS
BD39 Robert Hassell 30.00 80.00
BD57 Jordan Walker 30.00 80.00
BD59 Masyn Winn 12.00 30.00
BD62 Daniel Cabrera 15.00 40.00
BD72 Pete Crow-Armstrong 25.00 60.00
BD88 Asa Lacy 25.00 60.00
BD121 Spencer Torkelson 150.00 400.00

2020 Bowman Draft 1st Edition Gold Foil

*GOLD FOIL: 10X TO 25X BASIC
STATED ODDS 1:XXX HOBBY
STATED PRINT RUN 50 SER.#'d SETS
BD39 Robert Hassell 100.00 250.00
BD57 Jordan Walker 100.00 250.00
BD59 Masyn Winn 40.00 100.00
BD62 Daniel Cabrera 50.00 120.00
BD72 Pete Crow-Armstrong 75.00 200.00
BD88 Asa Lacy 75.00 200.00
BD121 Spencer Torkelson 400.00 1000.00

2020 Bowman Draft 1st Edition Orange Foil

*ORANGE FOIL: 12X TO 30X BASIC
STATED ODDS 1:XXX HOBBY
STATED PRINT RUN 25 SER.#'d SETS
BD39 Robert Hassell 125.00 300.00
BD57 Jordan Walker 125.00 300.00
BD59 Masyn Winn 50.00 120.00
BD62 Daniel Cabrera 60.00 150.00
BD72 Pete Crow-Armstrong 100.00 250.00
BD88 Asa Lacy 100.00 250.00
BD121 Spencer Torkelson 500.00 1200.00

2020 Bowman Draft 1st Edition Sky Blue Foil

*SKY BLUE FOIL: 1X TO 2.5X BASIC
STATED ODDS 1:XXX HOBBY
BD39 Robert Hassell 12.00 30.00
BD62 Daniel Cabrera 6.00 15.00
BD72 Pete Crow-Armstrong 10.00 25.00
BD88 Asa Lacy 10.00 25.00

2020 Bowman Draft 1st Edition Yellow Foil

*YELLOW FOIL: 6X TO 15X BASIC
STATED ODDS 1:XXX HOBBY
STATED PRINT RUN 75 SER.#'d SETS
BD39 Robert Hassell 60.00 150.00
BD57 Jordan Walker 60.00 150.00
BD59 Masyn Winn 25.00 60.00
BD62 Daniel Cabrera 30.00 80.00
BD72 Pete Crow-Armstrong 50.00 120.00
BD88 Asa Lacy 50.00 120.00
BD121 Spencer Torkelson 250.00 600.00

1997 Bowman Chrome

The 1997 Bowman Chrome set was issued in one series totalling 300 cards and was distributed in four-card packs with a suggested retail price of $3.00. The cards parallel the 1997 Bowman brand and the 300 card set represents a selection of top cards taken from the 441-card 1997 Bowman set. The product was released in the Winter, after the end of the 1997 season. The fronts feature color action player photos printed on dazzling chromium stock. The backs carry player information. Rookie Cards in this set include Adrian Beltre, Kris Benson, Lance Berkman, Kris Benson, Eric Chavez, Jose Cruz Jr., Travis Lee, Aramis Ramirez, Miguel Tejada, Vernon Wells and Kerry Wood.

COMPLETE SET (300) 40.00 80.00
1 Derek Jeter 1.25 3.00
2 Chipper Jones .50 1.25
3 Hideo Nomo .50 1.25
4 Tim Salmon .30 .75
5 Robin Ventura .20 .50
6 Tony Clark .20 .50
7 Barry Larkin .30 .75
8 Paul Molitor .20 .50
9 Andy Benes .20 .50
10 Ryan Klesko .20 .50
11 Mark McGwire 1.25 3.00
12 Ken Griffey Jr. 1.00 2.50
13 Robb Nen .20 .50
14 Cal Ripken 1.50 4.00
15 John Valentin .20 .50
16 Ricky Bottalico .20 .50
17 Mike Lansing .20 .50
18 Ryne Sandberg .75 2.00
19 Carlos Delgado .20 .50
20 Craig Biggio .30 .75
21 Eric Karros .20 .50
22 Kevin Appier .20 .50
23 Mariano Rivera .50 1.25
24 Vinny Castilla .20 .50
25 Juan Gonzalez .20 .50
26 Al Martin .20 .50
27 Jeff Cirillo .20 .50
28 Ray Lankford .20 .50
29 Manny Ramirez .30 .75
30 Roberto Alomar .30 .75
31 Will Clark .30 .75
32 Chuck Knoblauch .20 .50
33 Harold Baines .20 .50
34 Edgar Martinez .30 .75
35 Mike Mussina .30 .75
36 Kevin Brown .20 .50
37 Dennis Eckersley .20 .50
38 Tino Martinez .30 .75
39 Raul Mondesi .20 .50
40 Sammy Sosa .50 1.25
41 John Smoltz .30 .75
42 Billy Wagner .20 .50
43 Ken Caminiti .20 .50
44 Wade Boggs .30 .75
45 Andres Galarraga .20 .50
46 Roger Clemens 1.00 2.50
47 Matt Williams .20 .50
48 Albert Belle .20 .50
49 Jeff King .20 .50
50 John Wetteland .20 .50
51 Deion Sanders .30 .75
52 Ellis Burks .20 .50
53 Pedro Martinez .30 .75
54 Kenny Lofton .20 .50
55 Randy Johnson .50 1.25
56 Bernie Williams .30 .75
57 Marquis Grissom .20 .50
58 Gary Sheffield .20 .50
59 Curt Schilling .20 .50
60 Reggie Sanders .20 .50
61 Bobby Higginson .20 .50
62 Moises Alou .20 .50
63 Tom Glavine .30 .75
64 Mark Grace .30 .75
65 Rafael Palmeiro .30 .75
66 John Olerud .20 .50
67 Dante Bichette .20 .50
68 Jeff Bagwell .30 .75
69 Barry Bonds 1.25 3.00
70 Pat Hentgen .20 .50
71 Jim Thome .30 .75
72 Andy Pettitte .30 .75
73 Jay Bell .20 .50
74 Jim Edmonds .20 .50
75 Ron Gant .20 .50
76 David Cone .20 .50
77 Jose Canseco .30 .75
78 Jay Buhner .20 .50
79 Greg Maddux .75 2.00
80 Lance Johnson .20 .50
81 Travis Fryman .20 .50
82 Paul O'Neill .30 .75
83 Ivan Rodriguez .30 .75
84 Fred McGriff .30 .75
85 Mike Piazza .75 2.00
86 Brady Anderson .20 .50
87 Marty Cordova .20 .50
88 Joe Carter .20 .50
89 Brian Jordan .20 .50
90 David Justice .20 .50
91 Tony Gwynn .60 1.50
92 Larry Walker .20 .50
93 Mo Vaughn .20 .50
94 Sandy Alomar Jr. .20 .50
95 Rusty Greer .20 .50
96 Roberto Hernandez .20 .50
97 Hal Morris .20 .50
98 Todd Hundley .20 .50
99 Rondell White .20 .50
100 Frank Thomas .50 1.25
101 Bubba Trammell RC .60 1.50
102 Sidney Ponson RC 1.00 2.50
103 Ricky Ledee RC .60 1.50
104 Brett Tomko .20 .50
105 Braden Looper RC .40 1.00
106 Jason Dickson .20 .50
107 Chad Green RC .40 1.00
108 R.A. Dickey RC 4.00 10.00
109 Jeff Liefer .20 .50
110 Richard Hidalgo .20 .50
111 Chad Hermansen RC .40 1.00
112 Felix Martinez .20 .50
113 J.J. Johnson .20 .50
114 Todd Dunwoody .20 .50
115 Katsuhiro Maeda .20 .50
116 Darin Erstad .20 .50
117 Elieser Marrero .20 .50
118 Bartolo Colon .20 .50
119 Ugueth Urbina .20 .50
120 Jaime Bluma .20 .50
121 Seth Greisinger RC .40 1.00
122 Jose Cruz Jr. RC .60 1.50
123 Todd Dunn .20 .50
124 Justin Towle RC .40 1.00
125 Brian Rose .20 .50
126 Jose Guillen .20 .50
127 Andruw Jones .30 .75
128 Mark Kotsay RC 1.50 4.00
129 Wilton Guerrero .20 .50
130 Jacob Cruz .20 .50
131 Mike Sweeney .20 .50
132 Matt Morris .20 .50
133 John Thomson .20 .50
134 Javier Valentin .20 .50
135 Mike Drumright RC .40 1.00
136 Michael Barrett .20 .50
137 Tony Saunders RC .40 1.00
138 Kevin Brown .20 .50
139 Anthony Sanders RC .40 1.00
140 Jeff Abbott .20 .50
141 Eugene Kingsale .20 .50
142 Paul Konerko .30 .75
143 Randall Simon RC .60 1.50
144 Freddy Adrian Garcia .20 .50
145 Karim Garcia .20 .50
146 Carlos Guillen .20 .50
147 Aaron Boone .20 .50
148 Donnie Sadler .20 .50
149 Brooks Kieschnick .20 .50
150 Scott Spiezio .20 .50
151 Kevin Orie .20 .50
152 Russ Johnson .20 .50
153 Livan Hernandez .20 .50
154 Vladimir Nunez RC .40 1.00
155 Pokey Reese .20 .50
156 Chris Carpenter .20 .50
157 Eric Milton RC .60 1.50
158 Richie Sexson .20 .50
159 Carl Pavano .20 .50
160 Pat Cline .20 .50
161 Ron Wright .20 .50
162 Dante Powell .20 .50
163 Mark Bellhorn .20 .50
164 George Lombard .20 .50
165 Paul Wilder RC .40 1.00
166 Brad Fullmer .20 .50
167 Kris Benson RC 1.00 2.50
168 Torii Hunter .20 .50
169 D.T. Cromer RC .40 1.00
170 Nelson Figueroa RC .40 1.00
171 Hiram Bocachica RC .40 1.00
172 Shane Monahan .20 .50
173 Juan Melo .20 .50
174 Calvin Pickering RC .40 1.00
175 Reggie Taylor .20 .50
176 Geoff Jenkins .20 .50
177 Steve Rain RC .40 1.00
178 Nerio Rodriguez RC .40 1.00
179 Derrick Gibson .20 .50
180 Darin Blood .20 .50
181 Ben Davis .20 .50
182 Adrian Beltre RC 15.00 40.00
183 Kerry Wood RC 3.00 8.00
184 Nate Rolison RC .40 1.00
185 Fernando Tatis RC .40 1.00
186 Jake Westbrook RC 1.00 2.50
187 Edwin Diaz .20 .50
188 Joe Fontenot RC .40 1.00
189 Matt Halloran RC .40 1.00
190 Matt Clement RC 1.00 2.50
191 Todd Greene .20 .50
192 Eric Chavez RC 4.00 10.00
193 Edgard Velazquez .20 .50
194 Bruce Chen RC 1.00 2.50
195 Jason Brester .20 .50
196 Chris Reitsma RC .60 1.50
197 Neifi Perez .20 .50
198 Hideki Irabu RC .60 1.50
199 Don Denbow RC .40 1.00
200 Derrek Lee .30 .75
201 Todd Walker .20 .50
202 Scott Rolen .30 .75
203 Wes Helms .20 .50
204 Bob Abreu .30 .75
205 John Patterson RC 1.50 4.00
206 Alex Gonzalez RC 1.00 2.50
207 Grant Roberts RC .40 1.00
208 Jeff Suppan .20 .50
209 Luke Wilcox .20 .50
210 Marlon Anderson .20 .50
211 Mike Caruso RC .40 1.00
212 Roy Halladay RC 12.00 30.00
213 Jeremi Gonzalez RC .40 1.00
214 Aramis Ramirez RC 4.00 10.00
215 Dee Brown RC .40 1.00
216 Justin Thompson .20 .50
217 Danny Clyburn .20 .50
218 Bruce Aven .20 .5(
219 Keith Foulke RC 1.50 4.0
220 Shannon Stewart .20 .5
221 Larry Barnes RC .40 1.0
222 Mark Johnson RC .40 1.0
223 Randy Winn .20 .5
224 Nomar Garciaparra .75 2.0
225 Jacque Jones RC 1.50 4.0
226 Chris Clemons .20 .5
227 Todd Helton .50 1.2
228 Ryan Brannan RC .40 1.0
229 Alex Sanchez RC .60 1.5
230 Russell Branyan .20 .5
231 Daryle Ward .40 1.0
232 Kevin Witt .20 .5
233 Gabby Martinez .20 .5
234 Preston Wilson .20 .5
235 Donzell McDonald RC .40 1.0
236 Orlando Cabrera RC 1.50 4.0
237 Brian Banks .20 .5
238 Robbie Bell .40 1.0
239 Brad Rigby .20 .5
240 Scott Elarton .20 .5
241 Donny Leon RC .40 1.0
242 Abraham Nunez RC .40 1.0
243 Adam Eaton RC 1.00 2.5
244 Octavio Dotel RC .60 1.5
245 Sean Casey 1.00 2.5
246 Joe Lawrence RC .40 1.0
247 Adam Johnson RC .40 1.0
248 Ronnie Belliard RC 1.25 3.0
249 Bobby Estalella .20 .5
250 Corey Lee RC .40 1.0
251 Mike Cameron .20 .5
252 Kerry Robinson RC .40 1.0
253 A.J. Zapp RC .40 1.0
254 Jarrod Washburn .20 .5
255 Ben Grieve .20 .5
256 Javier Vazquez RC 1.50 4.0
257 Travis Lee RC .60 1.5
258 Dennis Reyes RC .40 1.0
259 Danny Buxbaum .20 .5
260 Kelvim Escobar RC 1.00 2.5
261 Danny Klassen .20 .5
262 Ken Cloude RC .40 1.0
263 Gabe Alvarez .20 .5
264 Clayton Bruner RC .40 1.0
265 Jason Marquis RC 1.50 4.0
266 Jamey Wright .20 .5
267 Matt Snyder RC .40 1.0
268 Josh Garrett RC .40 1.0
269 Juan Encarnacion .20 .5
270 Heath Murray .20 .5
271 Brent Butler RC .40 1.0
272 Danny Peoples RC .40 1.0
273 Miguel Tejada RC 4.00 10.0
274 Jim Pittsley .20 .5
275 Dmitri Young .20 .5
276 Vladimir Guerrero .50 1.2
277 Cole Liniak RC .40 1.0
278 Ramon Hernandez .20 .5
279 Cliff Politte RC .40 1.0
280 Mel Rosario RC .40 1.0
281 Jorge Carrion RC .40 1.0
282 John Barnes RC .40 1.0
283 Chris Stowe RC .40 1.0
284 Vernon Wells RC 3.00 8.0
285 Brett Caradonna RC .40 1.0
286 Scott Hodges RC .40 1.0
287 Jon Garland RC 2.50 6.
288 Nathan Haynes RC .40 1.
289 Geoff Goetz RC .40 1.
290 Adam Kennedy RC 1.00 2.5
291 T.J. Tucker RC .40 1.0
292 Aaron Akin RC .40 1.0
293 Jayson Werth RC 3.00 8.
294 Glenn Davis RC .40 1.
295 Mark Mangum RC .40 1.
296 Troy Cameron RC .40 1.
297 J.J. Davis RC .40 1.
298 Lance Berkman RC 4.00 10.
299 Jason Standridge RC .40 1.
300 Jason Dellaero RC .40 1.

1997 Bowman Chrome International

*STARS: 1.25X TO 3X BASIC CARDS
*ROOKIES: .4X TO 1X BASIC CARDS
STATED ODDS 1:4
108 R.A. Dickey 8.00 20.

1997 Bowman Chrome International Refractors

*STARS: 6X TO 15X BASIC CARDS
*ROOKIES: 2X TO 5X BASIC CARDS
STATED ODDS 1:24
108 R.A. Dickey 15.00 40.
182 Adrian Beltre 100.00 250.
212 Roy Halladay 100.00 250.
273 Miguel Tejada 20.00 50.
284 Vernon Wells 15.00 40.
293 Jayson Werth 30.00 60.

1997 Bowman Chrome Refractors

STARS: 3X TO 8X BASIC CARDS
ROOKIES: 1.5X TO 4X BASIC CARDS
TATED ODDS 1:12
NT'L REF.STATED ODDS 1:24

Card	Low	High
12 Roy Halladay	60.00	150.00
73 Miguel Tejada	15.00	40.00
84 Vernon Wells	12.50	30.00

1997 Bowman Chrome 1998 ROY Favorites

andomly inserted in packs at the rate of one in 24, ards from this 15-card set features color action hotos of 1998 Rookie of the Year prospective andidates printed on chromium cards.

Card	Low	High
OMPLETE SET (15)	10.00	25.00
TATED ODDS 1:24		
REFRACTORS: .75X TO 2X BASIC ROY		
EFRACTOR STATED ODDS 1:72		
OY1 Jeff Abbott	.60	1.50
OY2 Karim Garcia	.60	1.50
OY3 Todd Helton	1.50	4.00
OY4 Richard Hidalgo	.60	1.50
OY5 Geoff Jenkins	.60	1.50
OY6 Russ Johnson	.60	1.50
OY7 Paul Konerko	1.00	2.50
OY8 Mark Kotsay	1.00	2.50
OY9 Ricky Ledee	.40	1.00
OY10 Travis Lee	.40	1.00
OY11 Derrek Lee	1.00	2.50
OY12 Eliesar Marrero	.60	1.50
OY13 Juan Melo	.60	1.50
OY14 Brian Rose	.60	1.50
OY15 Fernando Tatis	.25	.60

1997 Bowman Chrome Scout's Honor Roll

andomly inserted in packs at a rate of one in 12, is 15-card set features color photos of top rospects and rookies printed on chromium cards. he backs carry player information.

Card	Low	High
OMPLETE SET (15)	12.50	30.00
TATED ODDS 1:12		
REF: .75X TO 2X BASIC CHR.HONOR		
EFRACTOR STATED ODDS 1:36		
HR1 Dmitri Young	.50	1.25
HR2 Bob Abreu	.75	2.00
HR3 Vladimir Guerrero	1.25	3.00
HR4 Paul Konerko	.75	2.00
HR5 Kevin Orie	.50	1.25
HR6 Todd Walker	.50	1.25
HR7 Ben Grieve	.50	1.25
HR8 Darin Erstad	.50	1.25
HR9 Derrek Lee	.75	2.00
HR10 Jose Cruz Jr.	.50	1.25
HR11 Scott Rolen	.75	2.00
HR12 Travis Lee	.50	1.25
HR13 Andruw Jones	.75	2.00
HR14 Wilton Guerrero	.50	1.25
HR15 Nomar Garciaparra	2.00	5.00

1998 Bowman Chrome

e 1998 Bowman Chrome set was issued in two parate series with a total of 441 cards. The four-rd packs retailed for $3.00 each. These cards are rallel to the regular Bowman set but with a emium Chrome finish. Unlike the 1997 brand, the 98 issue parallels the entire Bowman brand. ookie Cards include Ryan Anderson, Jack Cust, oy Glaus, Orlando Hernandez, Gabe Kapler, Carlos e, Ted Lilly, Ruben Mateo, Kevin Millwood, agglio Ordonez and Jimmy Rollins.

Card	Low	High
OMPLETE SET (441)	20.00	50.00
OMPLETE SERIES 1 (221)	10.00	25.00
OMPLETE SERIES 2 (220)	10.00	25.00
Nomar Garciaparra	.75	2.00
Scott Rolen	.30	.75
Andy Pettitte	.30	.75
van Rodriguez	.30	.75
Mark McGwire	1.25	3.00
6 Jason Dickson	.20	.50
7 Jose Cruz Jr.	.20	.50
8 Jeff Kent	.20	.50
9 Mike Mussina	.30	.75
10 Jason Kendall	.20	.50
11 Brett Tomko	.20	.50
12 Jeff King	.20	.50
13 Brad Radke	.20	.50
14 Robin Ventura	.20	.50
15 Jeff Bagwell	.30	.75
16 Greg Maddux	.75	2.00
17 John Jaha	.20	.50
18 Mike Piazza	.75	2.00
19 Edgar Martinez	.30	.75
20 David Justice	.20	.50
21 Todd Hundley	.20	.50
22 Tony Gwynn	.60	1.50
23 Larry Walker	.20	.50
24 Bernie Williams	.30	.75
25 Edgar Renteria	.20	.50
26 Rafael Palmeiro	.30	.75
27 Tim Salmon	.30	.75
28 Matt Morris	.20	.50
29 Shawn Estes	.20	.50
30 Vladimir Guerrero	.50	1.25
31 Fernando Tatis	.20	.50
32 Justin Thompson	.20	.50
33 Ken Griffey Jr.	1.00	2.50
34 Edgardo Alfonzo	.20	.50
35 Mo Vaughn	.20	.50
36 Marty Cordova	.20	.50
37 Craig Biggio	.30	.75
38 Roger Clemens	1.00	2.50
39 Mark Grace	.30	.75
40 Ken Caminiti	.20	.50
41 Tony Womack	.20	.50
42 Albert Belle	.20	.50
43 Tino Martinez	.30	.75
44 Sandy Alomar Jr.	.20	.50
45 Jeff Cirillo	.20	.50
46 Jason Giambi	.20	.50
47 Darin Erstad	.20	.50
48 Livan Hernandez	.20	.50
49 Mark Grudzielanek	.20	.50
50 Sammy Sosa	.50	1.25
51 Curt Schilling	.20	.50
52 Brian Hunter	.20	.50
53 Neifi Perez	.20	.50
54 Todd Walker	.20	.50
55 Jose Guillen	.20	.50
56 Jim Thome	.30	.75
57 Tom Glavine	.30	.75
58 Todd Greene	.20	.50
59 Rondell White	.20	.50
60 Roberto Alomar	.30	.75
61 Tony Clark	.20	.50
62 Vinny Castilla	.20	.50
63 Barry Larkin	.30	.75
64 Hideki Irabu	.20	.50
65 Johnny Damon	.30	.75
66 Juan Gonzalez	.20	.50
67 John Olerud	.20	.50
68 Gary Sheffield	.20	.50
69 Raul Mondesi	.20	.50
70 Chipper Jones	.50	1.25
71 David Ortiz	2.50	6.00
72 Warren Morris RC	.40	1.00
73 Alex Gonzalez	.20	.50
74 Nick Bierbrodt	.20	.50
75 Roy Halladay	1.00	2.50
76 Danny Buxbaum	.20	.50
77 Adam Kennedy	.20	.50
78 Jared Sandberg	.20	.50
79 Michael Barrett	.20	.50
80 Gil Meche	.60	1.50
81 Jayson Werth	.20	.50
82 Abraham Nunez	.20	.50
83 Ben Petrick	.20	.50
84 Brett Caradonna	.20	.50
85 Mike Lowell RC	2.50	6.00
86 Clay Bruner	.20	.50
87 John Curtice RC	.60	1.50
88 Bobby Estalella	.20	.50
89 Juan Melo	.20	.50
90 Arnold Gooch	.20	.50
91 Kevin Millwood RC	1.50	4.00
92 Richie Sexson	.20	.50
93 Orlando Cabrera	.20	.50
94 Pat Cline	.20	.50
95 Anthony Sanders	.20	.50
96 Russ Johnson	.20	.50
97 Ben Grieve	.20	.50
98 Kevin McGlinchy	.20	.50
99 Paul Wilder	.20	.50
100 Russ Ortiz	.20	.50
101 Ryan Jackson RC	.40	1.00
102 Heath Murray	.20	.50
103 Brian Rose	.20	.50
104 Ryan Radmanovich RC	.40	1.00
105 Ricky Ledee	.20	.50
106 Jeff Wallace RC	.40	1.00
107 Ryan Minor RC	.40	1.00
108 Dennis Reyes	.20	.50
109 James Manias	.20	.50
110 Chris Carpenter	.20	.50
111 Daryle Ward	.20	.50
112 Vernon Wells	.20	.50
113 Chad Green	.20	.50
114 Mike Stoner RC	.40	1.00
115 Brad Fullmer	.20	.50
116 Adam Eaton	.20	.50
117 Jeff Liefer	.20	.50
118 Corey Koskie RC	1.00	2.50
119 Todd Helton	.30	.75
120 Jaime Jones RC	.40	1.00
121 Mel Rosario	.20	.50
122 Geoff Goetz	.20	.50
123 Adrian Beltre	.20	.50
124 Jason Dellaero	.20	.50
125 Gabe Kapler RC	1.00	2.50
126 Scott Schoeneweis	.20	.50
127 Ryan Brannan	.20	.50
128 Aaron Akin	.20	.50
129 Ryan Anderson RC	.40	1.00
130 Brad Penny	.20	.50
131 Bruce Chen	.20	.50
132 Eli Marrero	.20	.50
133 Eric Chavez	.20	.50
134 Troy Glaus RC	3.00	8.00
135 Troy Cameron	.20	.50
136 Brian Sikorski RC	.40	1.00
137 Mike Kinkade RC	.40	1.00
138 Braden Looper	.20	.50
139 Mark Mangum	.20	.50
140 Danny Peoples	.20	.50
141 J.J. Davis	.20	.50
142 Ben Davis	.20	.50
143 Jacque Jones	.20	.50
144 Derrick Gibson	.20	.50
145 Bronson Arroyo	1.50	4.00
146 Luis De Los Santos RC	.40	1.00
147 Jeff Abbott	.20	.50
148 Mike Cuddyer RC	1.50	4.00
149 Jason Romano	.20	.50
150 Shane Monahan	.20	.50
151 Ntema Ndungidi RC	.40	1.00
152 Alex Sanchez	.20	.50
153 Jack Cust RC	3.00	8.00
154 Brent Butler	.20	.50
155 Ramon Hernandez	.20	.50
156 Norm Hutchins	.20	.50
157 Jason Marquis	.20	.50
158 Jacob Cruz	.20	.50
159 Rob Burger RC	.40	1.00
160 Dave Coggin	.20	.50
161 Preston Wilson	.20	.50
162 Jason Fitzgerald RC	.40	1.00
163 Dan Serafini	.20	.50
164 Pete Munro	.20	.50
165 Trot Nixon	.20	.50
166 Homer Bush	.20	.50
167 Dermal Brown	.20	.50
168 Chad Hermansen	.20	.50
169 Julio Moreno RC	.40	1.00
170 John Roskos RC	.40	1.00
171 Grant Roberts	.20	.50
172 Ken Cloude	.20	.50
173 Jason Brester	.20	.50
174 Jason Conti	.20	.50
175 Jon Garland	.20	.50
176 Robbie Bell	.20	.50
177 Nathan Haynes	.20	.50
178 Ramon Ortiz RC	.60	1.50
179 Shannon Stewart	.20	.50
180 Pablo Ortega	.20	.50
181 Jimmy Rollins RC	4.00	10.00
182 Sean Casey	.20	.50
183 Ted Lilly RC	1.00	2.50
184 Chris Enochs RC	.40	1.00
185 Magglio Ordonez UER RC	4.00	10.00
186 Mike Drumright	.20	.50
187 Aaron Boone	.20	.50
188 Matt Clement	.20	.50
189 Todd Dunwoody	.20	.50
190 Larry Rodriguez	.20	.50
191 Todd Noel	.20	.50
192 Geoff Jenkins	.20	.50
193 George Lombard	.20	.50
194 Lance Berkman	.20	.50
195 Marcus McCain	.20	.50
196 Ryan McGuire	.20	.50
197 Jhensy Sandoval	.20	.50
198 Corey Lee	.20	.50
199 Mario Valdez	.20	.50
200 Robert Fick RC	.60	1.50
201 Donnie Sadler	.20	.50
202 Marc Kroon	.20	.50
203 David Miller	.20	.50
204 Jarrod Washburn	.20	.50
205 Miguel Tejada	.50	1.25
206 Raul Ibanez	.20	.50
207 John Patterson	.20	.50
208 Calvin Pickering	.20	.50
209 Felix Martinez	.20	.50
210 Mark Redman	.20	.50
211 Scott Elarton	.20	.50
212 Jose Amado RC	.40	1.00
213 Kerry Wood	.20	.50
214 Dante Powell	.20	.50
215 Aramis Ramirez	.20	.50
216 A.J. Hinch	.20	.50
217 Dustin Carr RC	.40	1.00
218 Mark Kotsay	.20	.50
219 Jason Standridge	.20	.50
220 Luis Ordaz	.20	.50
221 Orlando Hernandez RC	2.00	5.00
222 Cal Ripken	1.50	4.00
223 Paul Molitor	.20	.50
224 Derek Jeter	1.25	3.00
225 Barry Bonds	1.25	3.00
226 Jim Edmonds	.20	.50
227 John Smoltz	.30	.75
228 Eric Karros	.20	.50
229 Ray Lankford	.20	.50
230 Rey Ordonez	.20	.50
231 Kenny Lofton	.20	.50
232 Alex Rodriguez	.75	2.00
233 Dante Bichette	.20	.50
234 Pedro Martinez	.30	.75
235 Carlos Delgado	.20	.50
236 Rod Beck	.20	.50
237 Matt Williams	.20	.50
238 Charles Johnson	.20	.50
239 Rico Brogna	.20	.50
240 Frank Thomas	.50	1.25
241 Paul O'Neill	.30	.75
242 Jaret Wright	.20	.50
243 Brant Brown	.20	.50
244 Ryan Klesko	.20	.50
245 Chuck Finley	.20	.50
246 Derek Bell	.20	.50
247 Delino DeShields	.20	.50
248 Chan Ho Park	.20	.50
249 Wade Boggs	.30	.75
250 Jay Buhner	.20	.50
251 Butch Huskey	.20	.50
252 Steve Finley	.20	.50
253 Will Clark	.30	.75
254 John Valentin	.20	.50
255 Bobby Higginson	.20	.50
256 Darryl Strawberry	.20	.50
257 Randy Johnson	.50	1.25
258 Al Martin	.20	.50
259 Travis Fryman	.20	.50
260 Fred McGriff	.30	.75
261 Jose Valentin	.20	.50
262 Andruw Jones	.30	.75
263 Kenny Rogers	.20	.50
264 Moises Alou	.20	.50
265 Denny Neagle	.20	.50
266 Ugueth Urbina	.20	.50
267 Derrek Lee	.30	.75
268 Ellis Burks	.20	.50
269 Mariano Rivera	.50	1.25
270 Dean Palmer	.20	.50
271 Eddie Taubensee	.20	.50
272 Brady Anderson	.20	.50
273 Brian Giles	.20	.50
274 Quinton McCracken	.20	.50
275 Henry Rodriguez	.20	.50
276 Andres Galarraga	.20	.50
277 Jose Canseco	.30	.75
278 David Segui	.20	.50
279 Bret Saberhagen	.20	.50
280 Kevin Brown	.30	.75
281 Chuck Knoblauch	.20	.50
282 Jeromy Burnitz	.20	.50
283 Jay Bell	.20	.50
284 Manny Ramirez	.30	.75
285 Rick Helling	.20	.50
286 Francisco Cordova	.20	.50
287 Bob Abreu	.20	.50
288 J.T. Snow	.20	.50
289 Hideo Nomo	.50	1.25
290 Brian Jordan	.20	.50
291 Javy Lopez	.20	.50
292 Travis Lee	.20	.50
293 Russell Branyan	.20	.50
294 Paul Konerko	.20	.50
295 Masato Yoshii RC	.60	1.50
296 Kris Benson	.20	.50
297 Juan Encarnacion	.20	.50
298 Eric Milton	.20	.50
299 Mike Caruso	.20	.50
300 Ricardo Aramboles RC	.40	1.00
301 Bobby Smith	.20	.50
302 Billy Koch	.20	.50
303 Richard Hidalgo	.20	.50
304 Justin Baughman RC	.40	1.00
305 Chris Gissell	.20	.50
306 Donnie Bridges RC	.40	1.00
307 Nelson Lara RC	.40	1.00
308 Randy Wolf RC	.60	1.50
309A Jason LaRue COR RC Reds logo	.60	1.50
309B Jason LaRue ERR RC Red Sox logo	.60	1.50
310 Jason Gooding RC	.40	1.00
311 Edgard Clemente	.20	.50
312 Andrew Vessel	.20	.50
313 Chris Reitsma	.20	.50
314 Jesus Sanchez RC	.40	1.00
315 Buddy Carlyle RC	.40	1.00
316 Randy Winn	.20	.50
317 Luis Rivera RC	.40	1.00
318 Marcus Thames RC	2.50	6.00
319 A.J. Pierzynski	.20	.50
320 Scott Randall	.20	.50
321 Damian Sapp	.20	.50
322 Ed Yarnall RC	.40	1.00
323 Luke Allen RC	.40	1.00
324 J.D. Smart	.20	.50
325 Willie Martinez	.20	.50
326 Alex Ramirez	.20	.50
327 Eric DuBose RC	.40	1.00
328 Kevin Witt	.20	.50
329 Dan McKinley RC	.40	1.00
330 Cliff Politte	.20	.50
331 Vladimir Nunez	.20	.50
332 John Halama RC	.40	1.00
333 Nerio Rodriguez	.20	.50
334 Desi Relaford	.20	.50
335 Robinson Checo	.20	.50
336 John Nicholson	.30	.75
337 Tom LaRosa RC	.40	1.00
338 Kevin Nicholson RC	.40	1.00
339 Javier Vazquez	.20	.50
340 A.J. Zapp	.20	.50
341 Tom Evans	.20	.50
342 Kerry Robinson	.20	.50
343 Gabe Gonzalez RC	.40	1.00
344 Ralph Milliard	.20	.50
345 Enrique Wilson	.20	.50
346 Elvin Hernandez	.20	.50
347 Mike Lincoln RC	.40	1.00
348 Cesar King RC	.40	1.00
349 Cristian Guzman RC	.60	1.50
350 Donzell McDonald	.20	.50
351 Jim Parque RC	.40	1.00
352 Mike Saipe RC	.40	1.00
353 Carlos Febles RC	.60	1.50
354 Dernell Stenson RC	.40	1.00
355 Mark Osborne RC	.40	1.00
356 Odalis Perez RC	1.50	4.00
357 Jason Dewey RC	.40	1.00
358 Joe Fontenot	.20	.50
359 Jason Grilli RC	.40	1.00
360 Kevin Haverbusch RC	.40	1.00
361 Jay Yennaco RC	.40	1.00
362 Brian Buchanan	.20	.50
363 John Barnes	.20	.50
364 Chris Fussell	.20	.50
365 Kevin Gibbs RC	.40	1.00
366 Joe Lawrence	.20	.50
367 DaRond Stovall	.20	.50
368 Brian Fuentes RC	.40	1.00
369 Jimmy Anderson	.20	.50
370 Lariel Gonzalez RC	.40	1.00
371 Scott Williamson RC	.40	1.00
372 Milton Bradley	.20	.50
373 Jason Halper RC	.40	1.00
374 Brent Billingsley RC	.40	1.00
375 Joe DePastino RC	.40	1.00
376 Jake Westbrook	.20	.50
377 Octavio Dotel	.20	.50
378 Jason Williams RC	.40	1.00
379 Julio Ramirez RC	.40	1.00
380 Seth Greisinger	.20	.50
381 Mike Judd RC	.40	1.00
382 Ben Ford RC	.40	1.00
383 Tom Bennett RC	.40	1.00
384 Adam Butler RC	.40	1.00
385 Wade Miller RC	1.00	2.50
386 Kyle Peterson RC	.40	1.00
387 Tommy Peterman RC	.40	1.00
388 Onan Masaoka	.20	.50
389 Jason Rakers RC	.40	1.00
390 Rafael Medina	.20	.50
391 Luis Lopez RC	.40	1.00
392 Jeff Yoder	.20	.50
393 Vance Wilson RC	.40	1.00
394 Fernando Seguignol RC	.40	1.00
395 Ron Wright	.20	.50
396 Ruben Mateo RC	.40	1.00
397 Steve Lomasney RC	.60	1.50
398 Damian Jackson	.20	.50
399 Mike Jerzembeck RC	.40	1.00
400 Luis Rivas RC	1.00	2.50
401 Kevin Burford RC	.40	1.00
402 Glenn Davis	.20	.50
403 Robert Luce RC	.40	1.00
404 Cole Liniak	.20	.50
405 Matt LeCroy RC	.60	1.50
406 Jeremy Giambi RC	.60	1.50
407 Shawn Chacon	.20	.50
408 Dewayne Wise RC	.40	1.00
409 Steve Woodard	.20	.50
410 Francisco Cordero RC	1.00	2.50
411 Damon Minor RC	.40	1.00
412 Lou Collier	.20	.50
413 Justin Towle	.20	.50
414 Juan LeBron	.20	.50
415 Michael Coleman	.20	.50
416 Felix Rodriguez	.20	.50
417 Paul Ah Yat RC	.40	1.00
418 Kevin Barker RC	.40	1.00
419 Brian Meadows	.20	.50
420 Darnell McDonald RC	.40	1.00
421 Matt Kinney RC	.40	1.00
422 Mike Vavrek RC	.40	1.00
423 Courtney Duncan RC	.40	1.00
424 Kevin Millar RC	1.50	4.00
425 Ruben Rivera	.20	.50
426 Steve Shoemaker RC	.40	1.00
427 Dan Reichert RC	.40	1.00
428 Carlos Lee RC	2.50	6.00
429 Rod Barajas	1.00	2.50
430 Pablo Ozuna RC	.60	1.50
431 Todd Belitz RC	.40	1.00
432 Sidney Ponson	.20	.50
433 Steve Carver RC	.40	1.00
434 Esteban Yan RC	.60	1.50
435 Cedrick Bowers	.20	.50
436 Marlon Anderson	.20	.50
437 Carl Pavano	.20	.50
438 Jae Weong Seo RC	.60	1.50
439 Jose Taveras RC	.40	1.00
440 Matt Anderson RC	.40	1.00
441 Darron Ingram RC	.40	1.00

1998 Bowman Chrome Golden Anniversary

*STARS: 6X TO 15X BASIC CARDS
*ROOKIES: 3X TO 8X BASIC CARDS
SER.1 STATED ODDS 1:164
SER.2 STATED ODDS 1:133
STATED PRINT RUN 50 SERIAL #'d SETS

1998 Bowman Chrome Golden Anniversary Refractors

SER.1 STATED ODDS 1:1279
SER.2 STATED ODDS 1:1022
STATED PRINT RUN 5 SERIAL #'d SETS
NO PRICING DUE TO SCARCITY

1998 Bowman Chrome International

*STARS: 1.5X TO 4X BASIC CARDS
*ROOKIES: .4X TO 1X BASIC
STATED ODDS 1:4

1998 Bowman Chrome International Refractors

Card	Low	High
COMPLETE SET (441)	2500.00	5000.00

*STARS: 5X TO 12X BASIC CARDS
*ROOKIES: 2X TO 5X BASIC CARDS
STATED ODDS 1:24

1998 Bowman Chrome Refractors

Card	Low	High
COMPLETE SET (441)	1500.00	2500.00

*STARS: 3X TO 8X BASIC CARDS
*ROOKIES: 1.5X TO 4X BASIC CARDS
STATED ODDS 1:12

1998 Bowman Chrome Reprints

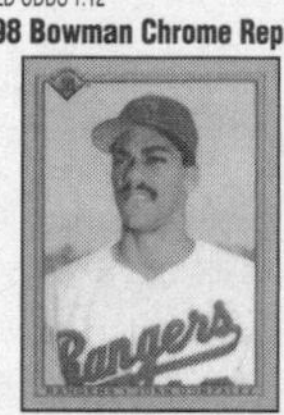

Randomly inserted in first and second packs at a rate of one in 12, these cards are replicas of classic Bowman Rookie Cards from 1948-1955 and 1989-present. Odd numbered cards (1, 3, 5 etc) were distributed in first series packs and even numbered cards in second series packs. The upgraded Chrome silver-colored stock gives them a striking appearance and makes them easy to differentiate from the originals.

Card	Low	High
COMPLETE SET (50)	75.00	150.00
COMPLETE SERIES 1 (25)	30.00	80.00
COMPLETE SERIES 2 (25)	30.00	80.00
STATED ODDS 1:12		
*REFRACTORS: 1X TO 2.5X BASIC REPRINTS		
REFRACTOR STATED ODDS 1:36		
ODD NUMBER CARDS DIST.IN SER.1		
EVEN NUMBER CARDS DIST.IN SER.2		
1 Yogi Berra	1.50	4.00
2 Jackie Robinson	1.50	4.00
3 Don Newcombe	.60	1.50
4 Satchell Paige	1.50	4.00
5 Willie Mays	4.00	10.00
6 Gil McDougald	.60	1.50
7 Don Larsen	.60	1.50
8 Elston Howard	1.00	2.50
9 Robin Ventura	.60	1.50
10 Brady Anderson	.60	1.50
11 Gary Sheffield	.60	1.50
12 Tino Martinez	1.00	2.50
13 Ken Griffey Jr.	3.00	8.00
14 John Smoltz	1.00	2.50
15 Sandy Alomar Jr.	.40	1.00
16 Larry Walker	.60	1.50
17 Todd Hundley	.40	1.00
18 Mo Vaughn	.60	1.50
19 Sammy Sosa	1.50	4.00
20 Frank Thomas	1.50	4.00
21 Chuck Knoblauch	.60	1.50
22 Bernie Williams	1.00	2.50
23 Juan Gonzalez	.60	1.50
24 Mike Mussina	1.00	2.50
25 Jeff Bagwell	1.00	2.50
26 Tim Salmon	1.00	2.50
27 Ivan Rodriguez	1.00	2.50
28 Kenny Lofton	.60	1.50
29 Chipper Jones	1.50	4.00
30 Javy Lopez	.60	1.50
31 Ryan Klesko	.60	1.50
32 Raul Mondesi	.60	1.50
33 Jim Thome	1.00	2.50
34 Carlos Delgado	.60	1.50
35 Mike Piazza	2.50	6.00
36 Manny Ramirez	1.00	2.50
37 Andy Pettitte	1.00	2.50
38 Derek Jeter	4.00	10.00
39 Brad Fullmer	.40	1.00
40 Richard Hidalgo	.40	1.00
41 Tony Clark	.40	1.00
42 Andruw Jones	1.00	2.50
43 Vladimir Guerrero	1.50	4.00
44 Nomar Garciaparra	2.50	6.00
45 Paul Konerko	.60	1.50
46 Ben Grieve	.40	1.00
47 Hideo Nomo	1.50	4.00
48 Scott Rolen	1.00	2.50
49 Jose Guillen	.60	1.50
50 Livan Hernandez	.60	1.50

1999 Bowman Chrome

The 1999 Bowman Chrome set was issued in two distinct series and were distributed in four card packs with a suggested retail price of $3.00. The set contains 440 regular cards printed on brilliant chromium 18-pt. Stock. Within the set are 300 top prospects that are designated with silver and blue foil. Each player's facsimile rookie signature are featured on these cards. There are also 140 vereran stars designated with a red and silver foil stamp. The backs contain information on each player's rookie and most recent season, career statistics and a scouting report from early league days. Rookie Cards include Pat Burrell, Carl Crawford, Adam Dunn, Rafael Furcal, Freddy Garcia, Tim Hudson, Nick Johnson, Austin Kearns, Willy Mo Pena, Adam Piatt, Corey Patterson and Alfonso Soriano.

Card	Low	High
COMPLETE SET (440)	60.00	120.00
COMPLETE SERIES 1 (220)	20.00	50.00
COMPLETE SERIES 2 (220)	30.00	80.00
COMMON CARD (1-440)	.20	.50
COMMON RC	.40	1.00
1 Ben Grieve	.20	.50
2 Kerry Wood	.20	.50
3 Ruben Rivera	.20	.50
4 Sandy Alomar Jr.	.20	.50
5 Cal Ripken	1.50	4.00
6 Mark McGwire	.75	2.00
7 Vladimir Guerrero	.30	.75
8 Moises Alou	.20	.50
9 Jim Edmonds	.30	.75
10 Greg Maddux	.60	1.50
11 Gary Sheffield	.20	.50
12 John Valentin	.20	.50
13 Chuck Knoblauch	.20	.50
14 Tony Clark	.20	.50
15 Rusty Greer	.20	.50
16 Al Leiter	.20	.50
17 Travis Lee	.20	.50
18 Jose Cruz Jr.	.20	.50
19 Pedro Martinez	.30	.75
20 Paul O'Neill	.30	.75
21 Todd Walker	.20	.50
22 Vinny Castilla	.20	.50
23 Barry Larkin	.30	.75
24 Curt Schilling	.20	.50
25 Jason Kendall	.20	.50
26 Scott Erickson	.20	.50
27 Andres Galarraga	.30	.75
28 Jeff Shaw	.20	.50
29 John Olerud	.20	.50
30 Orlando Hernandez	.20	.50
31 Larry Walker	.30	.75
32 Andruw Jones	.20	.50
33 Jeff Cirillo	.20	.50
34 Barry Bonds	.75	2.00
35 Manny Ramirez	.50	1.25
36 Mark Kotsay	.20	.50
37 Ivan Rodriguez	.30	.75
38 Jeff King	.20	.50
39 Brian Hunter	.20	.50
40 Ray Durham	.20	.50
41 Bernie Williams	.30	.75
42 Darin Erstad	.20	.50
43 Chipper Jones	.50	1.25
44 Pat Hentgen	.20	.50
45 Eric Young	.20	.50
46 Jaret Wright	.20	.50
47 Juan Guzman	.20	.50
48 Jorge Posada	.30	.75
49 Bobby Higginson	.20	.50
50 Jose Guillen	.20	.50
51 Trevor Hoffman	.30	.75
52 Ken Griffey Jr.	1.00	2.50
53 David Justice	.20	.50
54 Matt Williams	.20	.50
55 Eric Karros	.20	.50
56 Derek Bell	.20	.50
57 Ray Lankford	.20	.50
58 Mariano Rivera	.60	1.50
59 Brett Tomko	.20	.50
60 Mike Mussina	.30	.75
61 Kenny Lofton	.20	.50
62 Chuck Finley	.20	.50
63 Alex Gonzalez	.20	.50
64 Mark Grace	.30	.75
65 Raul Mondesi	.20	.50
66 David Cone	.20	.50
67 Brad Fullmer	.20	.50
68 Andy Benes	.20	.50
69 John Smoltz	.30	.75
70 Shane Reynolds	.20	.50
71 Bruce Chen	.20	.50
72 Adam Kennedy	.20	.50
73 Jack Cust	.20	.50
74 Matt Clement	.20	.50
75 Derrick Gibson	.20	.50
76 Darnell McDonald	.20	.50
77 Adam Everett RC	.60	1.50
78 Ricardo Aramboles	.20	.50
79 Mark Quinn RC	.40	1.00
80 Jason Rakers	.20	.50
81 Seth Etherton RC	.40	1.00
82 Jeff Urban RC	.40	1.00
83 Manny Aybar	.20	.50
84 Mike Nannini RC	.40	1.00
85 Onan Masaoka	.20	.50
86 Rod Barajas	.20	.50
87 Mike Frank	.20	.50
88 Scott Randall	.20	.50
89 Justin Bowles RC	.40	1.00
90 Chris Haas	.20	.50
91 Arturo McDowell RC	.40	1.00
92 Matt Belisle RC	.40	1.00
93 Scott Elarton	.20	.50
94 Vernon Wells	.20	.50
95 Pat Cline	.20	.50
96 Ryan Anderson	.20	.50
97 Kevin Barker	.20	.50
98 Ruben Mateo	.20	.50
99 Robert Fick	.20	.50
100 Corey Koskie	.20	.50
101 Ricky Ledee	.20	.50
102 Rick Elder RC	.40	1.00
103 Jack Cressend RC	.40	1.00
104 Joe Lawrence	.20	.50

105 Mike Lincoln .20 .50
106 Kit Pellow RC .40 1.00
107 Matt Burch RC .40 1.00
108 Cole Liniak .20 .50
109 Jason Dewey .20 .50
110 Cesar King .20 .50
111 Julio Ramirez .20 .50
112 Jake Westbrook .20 .50
113 Eric Valent RC .40 1.00
114 Roosevelt Brown RC .40 1.00
115 Choo Freeman RC .40 1.00
116 Juan Melo .20 .50
117 Jason Grilli .20 .50
118 Jared Sandberg .20 .50
119 Glenn Davis .20 .50
120 David Riske RC .40 1.00
121 Jacque Jones .20 .50
122 Corey Lee .20 .50
123 Michael Barrett .20 .50
124 Lariel Gonzalez .20 .50
125 Mitch Meluskey .20 .50
126 F.Adrian Garcia .20 .50
127 Tony Torcato RC .40 1.00
128 Jeff Liefer .20 .50
129 Ntema Ndungidi .20 .50
130 Andy Brown RC .40 1.00
131 Ryan Mills RC .40 1.00
132 Andy Abad RC .40 1.00
133 Carlos Febles .20 .50
134 Jason Tyner RC .40 1.00
135 Mark Osborne .20 .50
136 Phil Norton RC .40 1.00
137 Nathan Haynes .20 .50
138 Roy Halladay .30 .75
139 Juan Encarnacion .20 .50
140 Brad Penny .20 .50
141 Grant Roberts .20 .50
142 Aramis Ramirez .20 .50
143 Cristian Guzman .20 .50
144 Mamon Tucker RC .40 1.00
145 Ryan Bradley .20 .50
146 Brian Simmons .20 .50
147 Dan Reichert .20 .50
148 Russell Branyan .20 .50
149 Victor Valencia RC .40 1.00
150 Scott Schoeneweis .20 .50
151 Sean Spencer RC .40 1.00
152 Odalis Perez .20 .50
153 Joe Fontenot .20 .50
154 Milton Bradley .20 .50
155 Josh McKinley RC .40 1.00
156 Terrence Long .20 .50
157 Danny Klassen .20 .50
158 Paul Hoover RC .40 1.00
159 Ron Belliard .20 .50
160 Armando Rios .20 .50
161 Ramon Hernandez .20 .50
162 Jason Conti .20 .50
163 Chad Hermansen .20 .50
164 Jason Standridge .20 .50
165 Jason Dellaero .20 .50
166 John Curtice .20 .50
167 Clayton Andrews RC .40 1.00
168 Jeremy Giambi .20 .50
169 Alex Ramirez .20 .50
170 Gabe Molina RC .40 1.00
171 Mario Encarnacion RC .40 1.00
172 Mike Zywica RC .40 1.00
173 Chip Ambres RC .40 1.00
174 Trot Nixon .20 .50
175 Pat Burrell RC 1.50 4.00
176 Jeff Yoder .20 .50
177 Chris Jones RC .40 1.00
178 Kevin Witt .20 .50
179 Keith Luuloa RC .40 1.00
180 Billy Koch .20 .50
181 Damaso Marte RC .40 1.00
182 Ryan Glynn RC .40 1.00
183 Calvin Pickering .20 .50
184 Michael Cuddyer .20 .50
185 Nick Johnson RC 1.00 2.50
186 Doug Mientkiewicz RC .60 1.50
187 Nate Cornejo RC .40 1.00
188 Octavio Dotel .20 .50
189 Wes Helms .20 .50
190 Nelson Lara .20 .50
191 Chuck Abbott RC .40 1.00
192 Tony Armas Jr. .20 .50
193 Gil Meche .20 .50
194 Ben Petrick .20 .50
195 Chris George RC .40 1.00
196 Scott Hunter RC .40 1.00
197 Ryan Brannan .20 .50
198 Amaury Garcia RC .40 1.00
199 Chris Gissell .20 .50
200 Austin Kearns RC 1.50 4.00
201 Alex Gonzalez .20 .50
202 Wade Miller .20 .50
203 Scott Williamson .20 .50
204 Chris Enochs .20 .50
205 Fernando Seguignol .20 .50
206 Marlon Anderson .20 .50
207 Todd Sears RC .40 1.00
208 Nate Bump RC .40 1.00
209 J.M. Gold RC .40 1.00
210 Matt LeCroy .20 .50
211 Alex Hernandez .20 .50
212 Luis Rivera .20 .50
213 Troy Cameron .20 .50
214 Alex Escobar RC .40 1.00
215 Jason LaRue .20 .50
216 Kyle Peterson .20 .50
217 Brent Butler .20 .50
218 Dernell Stenson .20 .50
219 Adrian Beltre .50 1.25
220 Daryle Ward .20 .50
221 Jim Thome .30 .75
222 Cliff Floyd .20 .50
223 Rickey Henderson .50 1.25
224 Garret Anderson .20 .50
225 Ken Caminiti .20 .50
226 Bret Boone .20 .50
227 Jeromy Burnitz .20 .50
228 Steve Finley .20 .50
229 Miguel Tejada .30 .75
230 Greg Vaughn .20 .50
231 Jose Offerman .20 .50
232 Andy Ashby .20 .50
233 Albert Belle .20 .50
234 Fernando Tatis .20 .50
235 Todd Helton .30 .75
236 Sean Casey .20 .50
237 Brian Giles .20 .50
238 Andy Pettitte .30 .75
239 Fred McGriff .30 .75
240 Roberto Alomar .30 .75
241 Edgar Martinez .30 .75
242 Lee Stevens .20 .50
243 Shawn Green .20 .50
244 Ryan Klesko .20 .50
245 Sammy Sosa .50 1.25
246 Todd Hundley .20 .50
247 Shannon Stewart .20 .50
248 Randy Johnson .50 1.25
249 Rondell White .20 .50
250 Mike Piazza .50 1.25
251 Craig Biggio .30 .75
252 David Wells .20 .50
253 Brian Jordan .20 .50
254 Edgar Renteria .20 .50
255 Bartolo Colon .20 .50
256 Frank Thomas .50 1.25
257 Will Clark .30 .75
258 Dean Palmer .20 .50
259 Dmitri Young .20 .50
260 Scott Rolen .30 .75
261 Jeff Kent .20 .50
262 Dante Bichette .20 .50
263 Nomar Garciaparra .30 .75
264 Tony Gwynn .50 1.25
265 Alex Rodriguez .60 1.50
266 Jose Canseco .30 .75
267 Jason Giambi .20 .50
268 Jeff Bagwell .30 .75
269 Carlos Delgado .20 .50
270 Tom Glavine .30 .75
271 Eric Davis .20 .50
272 Edgardo Alfonzo .20 .50
273 Tim Salmon .20 .50
274 Johnny Damon .30 .75
275 Rafael Palmeiro .30 .75
276 Denny Neagle .20 .50
277 Neifi Perez .20 .50
278 Roger Clemens .60 1.50
279 Brant Brown .20 .50
280 Kevin Brown .20 .50
281 Jay Bell .20 .50
282 Jay Buhner .20 .50
283 Matt Lawton .20 .50
284 Robin Ventura .20 .50
285 Juan Gonzalez .20 .50
286 Mo Vaughn .20 .50
287 Kevin Millwood .20 .50
288 Tino Martinez .20 .50
289 Justin Thompson .20 .50
290 Derek Jeter 1.25 3.00
291 Ben Davis .20 .50
292 Mike Lowell .20 .50
293 Calvin Murray .20 .50
294 Micah Bowie RC .40 1.00
295 Lance Berkman .30 .75
296 Jason Marquis .20 .50
297 Chad Green .20 .50
298 Dee Brown .20 .50
299 Jerry Hairston Jr. .20 .50
300 Gabe Kapler .20 .50
301 Brent Stentz RC .40 1.00
302 Scott Mullen RC .40 1.00
303 Brandon Reed .20 .50
304 Shea Hillenbrand RC .60 1.50
305 J.D. Closser RC .40 1.00
306 Gary Matthews Jr. .20 .50
307 Toby Hall RC .40 1.00
308 Jason Phillips RC .40 1.00
309 Jose Macias RC .40 1.00
310 Jung Bong RC .40 1.00
311 Ramon Soler RC .40 1.00
312 Kelly Dransfeldt RC .40 1.00
313 Carlos E. Hernandez RC .40 1.00
314 Kevin Haverbusch .20 .50
315 Aaron Myette RC .40 1.00
316 Chad Harville RC .40 1.00
317 Kyle Farnsworth RC .40 1.00
318 Gookie Dawkins RC .40 1.00
319 Willie Martinez .20 .50
320 Carlos Lee .20 .50
321 Carlos Pena RC 1.25 3.00
322 Peter Bergeron RC .40 1.00
323 A.J. Burnett RC .60 1.50
324 Bucky Jacobsen RC .40 1.00
325 Mo Bruce RC .40 1.00
326 Reggie Taylor .20 .50
327 Jackie Rexrode .20 .50
328 Alvin Morrow RC .40 1.00
329 Carlos Beltran .30 .75
330 Eric Chavez .20 .50
331 John Patterson .20 .50
332 Jayson Werth .30 .75
333 Richie Sexson .20 .50
334 Randy Wolf .20 .50
335 Eli Marrero .20 .50
336 Paul LoDuca .20 .50
337 J.D Smart .20 .50
338 Ryan Minor .20 .50
339 Kris Benson .20 .50
340 George Lombard .20 .50
341 Troy Glaus .20 .50
342 Eddie Yarnall .20 .50
343 Kip Wells RC .40 1.00
344 C.C. Sabathia RC 3.00 8.00
345 Sean Burroughs RC .40 1.00
346 Felipe Lopez RC .60 1.50
347 Ryan Rupe RC .40 1.00
348 Orber Moreno RC .40 1.00
349 Rafael Roque RC .40 1.00
350 Alfonso Soriano RC 4.00 10.00
351 Pablo Ozuna .20 .50
352 Corey Patterson RC 1.00 2.50
353 Braden Looper .20 .50
354 Robbie Bell .20 .50
355 Mark Mulder RC 1.25 3.00
356 Angel Pena .20 .50
357 Kevin McGlinchy .20 .50
358 Michael Restovich RC .40 1.00
359 Eric DuBose .20 .50
360 Geoff Jenkins .20 .50
361 Mark Harriger RC .40 1.00
362 Junior Herndon RC .40 1.00
363 Tim Raines Jr. RC .40 1.00
364 Rafael Furcal RC 1.25 3.00
365 Marcus Giles RC 1.00 2.50
366 Ted Lilly .20 .50
367 Jorge Toca RC .40 1.00
368 David Kelton RC .40 1.00
369 Adam Dunn RC 1.50 4.00
370 Guillermo Mota RC .40 1.00
371 Brett Laxton RC .40 1.00
372 Travis Harper RC .40 1.00
373 Tom Davey RC .40 1.00
374 Darren Blakely RC .40 1.00
375 Tim Hudson RC 1.50 4.00
376 Jason Romano .20 .50
377 Dan Reichert .20 .50
378 Julio Lugo RC .60 1.50
379 Jose Garcia RC .40 1.00
380 Erubiel Durazo RC .40 1.00
381 Jose Jimenez .20 .50
382 Chris Fussell .20 .50
383 Steve Lomasney .20 .50
384 Juan Pena RC .40 1.00
385 Allen Levrault RC .40 1.00
386 Juan Rivera RC 1.00 2.50
387 Steve Colyer RC .40 1.00
388 Joe Nathan RC 1.00 2.50
389 Ron Walker RC .40 1.00
390 Nick Bierbrodt .20 .50
391 Luke Prokopec RC .40 1.00
392 Dave Roberts RC 1.00 2.50
393 Mike Darr .20 .50
394 Abraham Nunez RC .40 1.00
395 Giuseppe Chiaramonte RC .40 1.00
396 Jermaine Van Buren RC .40 1.00
397 Mike Kusiewicz .20 .50
398 Matt Wise RC .40 1.00
399 Joe McEwing RC .40 1.00
400 Matt Holliday RC 2.00 5.00
401 Willi Mo Pena RC 1.25 3.00
402 Ruben Quevedo RC .40 1.00
403 Rob Ryan RC .40 1.00
404 Freddy Garcia RC 1.00 2.50
405 Kevin Eberwein RC .40 1.00
406 Jesus Colome RC .40 1.00
407 Chris Singleton .20 .50
408 Bubba Crosby RC .40 1.00
409 Jesus Cordero RC .40 1.00
410 Donny Leon .20 .50
411 Goefrey Tomlinson RC .40 1.00
412 Jeff Winchester RC .40 1.00
413 Adam Piatt RC .40 1.00
414 Robert Stratton .20 .50
415 T.J. Tucker .20 .50
416 Ryan Langerhans RC .60 1.50
417 Anthony Shumaker RC .40 1.00
418 Matt Miller RC .40 1.00
419 Doug Clark RC .40 1.00
420 Kory DeHaan RC .40 1.00
421 David Eckstein RC 1.25 3.00
422 Brian Cooper RC .40 1.00
423 Brady Clark RC .40 1.00
424 Chris Magruder RC .40 1.00
425 Bobby Seay RC .40 1.00
426 Aubrey Huff RC 1.00 2.50
427 Mike Jerzembeck .20 .50
428 Matt Blank RC .40 1.00
429 Benny Agbayani RC .40 1.00
430 Kevin Beirne RC .40 1.00
431 Josh Hamilton RC 3.00 8.00
432 Josh Girdley RC .40 1.00
433 Kyle Snyder RC .40 1.00
434 Mike Paradis RC .40 1.00
435 Jason Jennings RC .60 1.50
436 David Walling RC .40 1.00
437 Omar Ortiz RC .40 1.00
438 Jay Gehrke RC .40 1.00
439 Casey Burns RC .30 .75
440 Carl Crawford RC 2.00 5.00

1999 Bowman Chrome Gold

*GOLD: 2.5X TO 6X BASIC
*GOLD RC: 1.25X TO 3X BASIC RC
SER.1 STATED ODDS 1:12
SER.2 STATED ODDS 1:24

1999 Bowman Chrome Gold Refractors

*GOLD REF: 20X TO 50X BASIC
SER.1 STATED ODDS 1:305
SER.2 STATED ODDS 1:200
STATED PRINT RUN 25 SERIAL #'d SETS
NO RC PRICING DUE TO SCARCITY

1999 Bowman Chrome International

*INT: 1.25X TO 3X BASIC
*INT.RC: .6X TO 1.5X BASIC
SER.1 STATED ODDS 1:4
SER.2 STATED ODDS 1:12

1999 Bowman Chrome International Refractors

*INT REF: 6X TO 15X BASIC
*INT RC: 4X TO 8X BASIC RC
SER.1 STATED ODDS 1:76
SER.2 STATED ODDS 1:50
STATED PRINT RUN 100 SERIAL #'d SETS
369 Adam Dunn 75.00 150.00

1999 Bowman Chrome Refractors

*REF: 4X TO 10X BASIC
*REF RC: 2X TO 5X BASIC RC
SER.1 AND SER.2 STATED ODDS 1:12

1999 Bowman Chrome 2000 ROY Favorites

Randomly inserted in second series packs at a rate of one in 20, this 10-card insert set features borderless, double-etched foil cards and feature players that had potential to win Rookie of the Year honors for the 2000 seasons.

COMPLETE SET (10) 5.00 12.00
SER.2 STATED ODDS 1:20
*REF: .75X TO 2X BASIC CHR.2000 ROY
REFRACTOR SER.2 STATED ODDS 1:100
ROY1 Ryan Anderson .40 1.00
ROY2 Pat Burrell 1.50 4.00
ROY3 A.J. Burnett .60 1.50
ROY4 Ruben Mateo .40 1.00
ROY5 Alex Escobar .40 1.00
ROY6 Pablo Ozuna .40 1.00
ROY7 Mark Mulder 1.25 3.00
ROY8 Corey Patterson 1.00 2.50
ROY9 George Lombard .40 1.00
ROY10 Nick Johnson 1.00 2.50

1999 Bowman Chrome Diamond Aces

Randomly inserted in first series packs at the rate of one in 21, this 18-card set features nine emerging stars such as Pat Burrell and Troy Glaus as well as nine proven veterans including Derek Jeter and Ken Griffey Jr.

COMPLETE SET (18) 12.50 30.00
SER.1 STATED ODDS 1:21
*REF: .75X TO 2X BASIC CHR.ACES
REFRACTOR SER.1 ODDS 1:84
DA1 Troy Glaus .40 1.00
DA2 Eric Chavez .40 1.00
DA3 Fernando Seguignol .40 1.00
DA4 Ryan Anderson .40 1.00
DA5 Ruben Mateo .40 1.00
DA6 Carlos Beltran .60 1.50
DA7 Adrian Beltre 1.00 2.50
DA8 Bruce Chen .40 1.00
DA9 Pat Burrell 1.50 4.00
DA10 Mike Piazza 1.00 2.50
DA11 Ken Griffey Jr. 2.00 5.00
DA12 Chipper Jones 1.00 2.50
DA13 Derek Jeter 2.50 6.00
DA14 Mark McGwire 1.50 4.00
DA15 Nomar Garciaparra .60 1.50
DA16 Sammy Sosa 1.00 2.50
DA17 Juan Gonzalez .40 1.00
DA18 Alex Rodriguez 1.25 3.00

1999 Bowman Chrome Impact

Randomly inserted in second series packs at the rate of one in 15, this 15-card insert set features 20 players separated into three distinct categories; Early Impact, Initial Impact and Lasting Impact.

COMPLETE SET (20) 15.00 40.00
SER.2 STATED ODDS 1:15
*REF.: .75X TO 2X BASIC IMPACT
REFRACTOR SER.2 STATED ODDS 1:75
I1 Alfonso Soriano 4.00 10.00
I2 Pat Burrell 1.50 4.00
I3 Ruben Mateo .40 1.00
I4 A.J. Burnett .60 1.50
I5 Corey Patterson 1.00 2.50
I6 Daryle Ward .40 1.00
I7 Eric Chavez .40 1.00
I8 Troy Glaus .40 1.00
I9 Sean Casey .40 1.00
I10 Joe McEwing .40 1.00
I11 Gabe Kapler .40 1.00
I12 Michael Barrett .40 1.00
I13 Sammy Sosa 1.00 2.50
I14 Alex Rodriguez 1.25 3.00
I15 Mark McGwire 1.50 4.00
I16 Derek Jeter 2.50 6.00
I17 Nomar Garciaparra .60 1.50
I18 Mike Piazza 1.00 2.50
I19 Chipper Jones 1.00 2.50
I20 Ken Griffey Jr. 2.00 5.00

1999 Bowman Chrome Scout's Choice

Randomly inserted in first series packs at the rate of one in twelve, this 21-card insert set features borderless, double-etched foil cards showcase a selection of the game's top young prospects.

COMPLETE SET (21) 10.00 25.00
SER.1 STATED ODDS 1:12
*REF: .75X TO 2X BASIC
REFRACTOR SER.1 ODDS 1:48
SC1 Ruben Mateo .40 1.00
SC2 Ryan Anderson .40 1.00
SC3 Pat Burrell 1.50 4.00
SC4 Troy Glaus .40 1.00
SC5 Eric Chavez .40 1.00
SC6 Adrian Beltre 1.00 2.50
SC7 Bruce Chen .40 1.00
SC8 Carlos Beltran .60 1.50
SC9 Alex Gonzalez .40 1.00
SC10 Carlos Lee .40 1.00
SC11 George Lombard .40 1.00
SC12 Matt Clement .40 1.00
SC13 Calvin Pickering .40 1.00
SC14 Marlon Anderson .40 1.00
SC15 Chad Hermansen .40 1.00
SC16 Russell Branyan .40 1.00
SC17 Jeremy Giambi .40 1.00
SC18 Ricky Ledee .40 1.00
SC19 John Patterson .40 1.00
SC20 Roy Halladay .60 1.50
SC21 Michael Barrett .40 1.00

2000 Bowman Chrome

The 2000 Bowman Chrome product was released in late July, 2000 as a 440-card set that featured 140 veteran players (1-140), and 300 rookies and prospects (141-440). Each pack contained four cards, and carried a suggested retail price of $3.00. Rookie Cards include Rick Asadoorian, Bobby Bradley, Kevin Mench, Ben Sheets and Barry Zito. In addition, Topps designated five prospects as Bowman Chrome "exclusives" whereby their only appearance in a Topps brand for the year 2000 would be in this set. Jason Hart and Chin-Hui Tsao highlight this selection of Bowman Chrome exclusive Rookie Cards.

COMPLETE SET (440) 40.00 80.00
COMMON CARD (1-440) .20 .50
COMMON RC .20 .50
1 Vladimir Guerrero .30 .75
2 Chipper Jones .50 1.25
3 Todd Walker .20 .50
4 Barry Larkin .30 .75
5 Bernie Williams .30 .75
6 Todd Helton .30 .75
7 Jermaine Dye .20 .50
8 Brian Giles .20 .50
9 Freddy Garcia .20 .50
10 Greg Vaughn .20 .50
11 Alex Gonzalez .20 .50
12 Luis Gonzalez .20 .50
13 Ron Belliard .20 .50
14 Ben Grieve .20 .50
15 Carlos Delgado .20 .50
16 Brian Jordan .20 .50
17 Fernando Tatis .20 .50
18 Ryan Rupe .20 .50
19 Miguel Tejada .30 .75
20 Mark Grace .30 .75
21 Kenny Lofton .20 .50
22 Eric Karros .20 .50
23 Cliff Floyd .20 .50
24 John Halama .20 .50
25 Cristian Guzman .20 .50
26 Scott Williamson .20 .50
27 Mike Lieberthal .20 .50
28 Tim Hudson .30 .75
29 Warren Morris .20 .50
30 Pedro Martinez .30 .75
31 John Smoltz .50 1.25
32 Ray Durham .20 .50
33 Chad Allen .20 .50
34 Tony Clark .20 .50
35 Tino Martinez .20 .50
36 J.T. Snow .20 .50
37 Kevin Brown .20 .50
38 Bartolo Colon .20 .50
39 Rey Ordonez .20 .50
40 Jeff Bagwell .30 .75
41 Ivan Rodriguez .30 .75
42 Eric Chavez .20 .50
43 Eric Milton .20 .50
44 Jose Canseco .30 .75
45 Shawn Green .20 .50
46 Rich Aurilia .20 .50
47 Roberto Alomar .30 .75
48 Brian Daubach .20 .50
49 Magglio Ordonez .30 .75
50 Derek Jeter 1.25 3.00
51 Kris Benson .20 .50
52 Albert Belle .20 .50
53 Rondell White .20 .50
54 Justin Thompson .20 .50
55 Nomar Garciaparra .30 .75
56 Chuck Finley .20 .50
57 Omar Vizquel .30 .75
58 Luis Castillo .20 .50
59 Richard Hidalgo .20 .50
60 Barry Bonds .75 2.00
61 Craig Biggio .30 .75
62 Doug Glanville .20 .50
63 Gabe Kapler .20 .50
64 Johnny Damon .30 .75
65 Pokey Reese .20 .50
66 Andy Pettitte .30 .75
67 B.J. Surhoff .20 .50
68 Richie Sexson .20 .50
69 Javy Lopez .20 .50
70 Raul Mondesi .20 .50
71 Darin Erstad .20 .50
72 Kevin Millwood .20 .50
73 Ricky Ledee .20 .50
74 John Olerud .20 .50
75 Sean Casey .20 .50
76 Carlos Febles .20 .50
77 Paul O'Neill .30 .75
78 Bob Abreu .20 .50
79 Neifi Perez .20 .50
80 Tony Gwynn .50 1.25
81 Russ Ortiz .20 .50
82 Matt Williams .20 .50
83 Chris Carpenter .30 .75
84 Roger Cedeno .20 .50
85 Tim Salmon .20 .50
86 Billy Koch .20 .50
87 Jeromy Burnitz .20 .50
88 Edgardo Alfonzo .20 .50
89 Jay Bell .20 .50
90 Manny Ramirez .50 1.25
91 Frank Thomas .50 1.25
92 Mike Mussina .30 .75
93 J.D. Drew .20 .50
94 Adrian Beltre .50 1.25
95 Alex Rodriguez .60 1.50
96 Larry Walker .30 .75
97 Juan Encarnacion .20 .50
98 Mike Sweeney .20 .50
99 Rusty Greer .20 .50
100 Randy Johnson .50 1.25
101 Jose Vidro .20 .50
102 Preston Wilson .20 .50
103 Greg Maddux .60 1.50
104 Jason Giambi .20 .50
105 Cal Ripken 1.50 4.00
106 Carlos Beltran .30 .75
107 Vinny Castilla .20 .50
108 Mariano Rivera .60 1.50
109 Mo Vaughn .20 .50
110 Rafael Palmeiro .30 .75
111 Shannon Stewart .20 .50
112 Mike Hampton .20 .50
113 Joe Nathan .20 .50
114 Ben Davis .20 .50
115 Andruw Jones .20 .50
116 Robin Ventura .20 .50
117 Damion Easley .20 .50
118 Jeff Cirillo .20 .50
119 Kerry Wood .20 .50
120 Scott Rolen .30 .75
121 Sammy Sosa .50 1.25
122 Ken Griffey Jr. 1.00 2.50
123 Shane Reynolds .20 .50
124 Troy Glaus .20 .50
125 Tom Glavine .30 .75
126 Michael Barrett .20 .5
127 Al Leiter .20 .5
128 Jason Kendall .20 .5
129 Roger Clemens .60 1.5
130 Juan Gonzalez .20 .5
131 Corey Koskie .20 .5
132 Curt Schilling .30 .7
133 Mike Piazza .50 1.2
134 Gary Sheffield .20 .5
135 Jim Thome .30 .7
136 Orlando Hernandez .20 .5
137 Ray Lankford .20 .5
138 Geoff Jenkins .20 .5
139 Jose Lima .20 .5
140 Mark McGwire .75 2.0
141 Adam Piatt .20 .5
142 Pat Manning RC .20 .5
143 Marcos Castillo RC .20 .5
144 Lesli Brea RC .20 .5
145 Humberto Cota RC .20 .5
146 Ben Petrick .20 .5
147 Kip Wells .20 .5
148 Wily Pena .20 .5
149 Chris Wakeland RC .20 .5
150 Brad Baker RC .20 .5
151 Robbie Morrison RC .20 .5
152 Reggie Taylor .20 .5
153 Matt Ginter RC .20 .5
154 Peter Bergeron .20 .5
155 Roosevelt Brown .20 .5
156 Matt Cepicky RC .20 .5
157 Ramon Castro .20 .5
158 Brad Baisley RC .20 .5
159 Jason Hart RC .20 .5
160 Mitch Meluskey .20 .5
161 Chad Harville .20 .5
162 Brian Cooper .20 .5
163 Marcus Giles .20 .5
164 Jim Morris 2.50 6.0
165 Geoff Goetz .20 .5
166 Bobby Bradley RC .20 .5
167 Rob Bell .20 .5
168 Joe Crede .20 .5
169 Michael Restovich .20 .5
170 Quincy Foster RC .20 .5
171 Enrique Cruz RC .20 .5
172 Mark Quinn .20 .5
173 Nick Johnson .20 .5
174 Jeff Liefer .20 .5
175 Kevin Mench RC .50 1.2
176 Steve Lomasney .20 .5
177 Jayson Werth .30 .7
178 Tim Drew .20
179 Chip Ambres .20 .5
180 Ryan Anderson .20 .5
181 Matt Blank .20 .5
182 Giuseppe Chiaramonte .20 .5
183 Corey Myers RC .20
184 Jeff Yoder .20 .5
185 Craig Dingman RC .20
186 Jon Hamilton RC .20
187 Toby Hall .20
188 Russell Branyan .20 .5
189 Brian Falkenborg RC .20 .5
190 Aaron Harang RC 1.25 3.0
191 Juan Pena .20
192 Chin-Hui Tsao RC .50 1.2
193 Alfonso Soriano .50 1.2
194 Alejandro Diaz RC .20
195 Carlos Pena .30
196 Kevin Nicholson .20 .5
197 Mo Bruce .20

98 C.C. Sabathia .30 .75
99 Carl Crawford .30 .75
00 Rafael Furcal .30 .75
01 Andrew Beinbrink RC .20 .50
02 Jimmy Osting .20 .50
03 Aaron McNeal RC .20 .50
04 Brett Laxton .20 .50
05 Chris George .20 .50
06 Felipe Lopez .20 .50
07 Ben Sheets RC .50 1.25
08 Mike Meyers RC .30 .75
09 Jason Conti .20 .50
10 Milton Bradley .20 .50
11 Chris Mears RC .20 .50
12 Carlos Hernandez RC .20 .50
13 Jason Romano .20 .50
14 Geofrey Tomlinson .20 .50
15 Jimmy Rollins .30 .75
16 Pablo Ozuna .20 .50
17 Steve Cox .20 .50
18 Terrence Long .20 .50
19 Jeff DaVanon RC .20 .50
20 Rick Ankiel .30 .75
21 Jason Standridge .20 .50
22 Tony Armas Jr. .20 .50
23 Jason Tyner .20 .50
24 Ramon Ortiz .20 .50
25 Daryle Ward .20 .50
26 Enger Veras RC .20 .50
27 Chris Jones .20 .50
28 Eric Cammack RC .20 .50
29 Ruben Mateo .20 .50
30 Ken Harvey RC .20 .50
31 Jake Westbrook .20 .50
32 Rob Purvis RC .20 .50
33 Choo Freeman .20 .50
34 Aramis Ramirez .20 .50
35 A.J. Burnett .20 .50
36 Kevin Barker .20 .50
37 Chance Caple RC .20 .50
38 Jarrod Washburn .20 .50
39 Lance Berkman .30 .75
40 Michael Wenner RC .20 .50
41 Alex Sanchez .20 .50
42 Pat Daneker .20 .50
43 Grant Roberts .20 .50
44 Mark Ellis RC .30 .75
45 Donny Leon .20 .50
46 David Eckstein .20 .50
47 Dicky Gonzalez RC .20 .50
48 John Patterson .20 .50
49 Chad Green .20 .50
50 Scot Shields RC .20 .50
51 Troy Cameron .20 .50
52 Jose Molina .20 .50
53 Rob Pugmire RC .20 .50
54 Rick Elder .20 .50
55 Sean Burroughs .20 .50
56 Josh Kalinowski RC .20 .50
57 Matt LeCroy .20 .50
58 Alex Graman RC .20 .50
59 Juan Silvestre RC .20 .50
60 Brady Clark .20 .50
61 Rico Washington RC .20 .50
62 Gary Matthews Jr. .20 .50
63 Matt Wise .20 .50
64 Keith Reed RC .20 .50
65 Santiago Ramirez RC .20 .50
66 Ben Broussard RC .30 .75
67 Ryan Langerhans .20 .50
68 Juan Rivera .20 .50
69 Shawn Gallagher .20 .50
70 Jorge Toca .20 .50
71 Brad Lidge .20 .50
72 Leoncio Estrella RC .20 .50
73 Ruben Quevedo .20 .50
74 Jack Cust .20 .50
75 T.J. Tucker .20 .50
76 Mike Colangelo .20 .50
77 Brian Schneider .20 .50
78 Calvin Murray .20 .50
79 Josh Girdley .20 .50
80 Mike Paradis .20 .50
81 Chad Hermansen .20 .50
82 Ty Howington RC .20 .50
83 Aaron Myette .20 .50
84 D'Angelo Jimenez .20 .50
85 Dernell Stenson .20 .50
86 Jerry Hairston Jr. .20 .50
87 Gary Majewski RC .20 .50
88 Derrin Ebert .20 .50
89 Steve Fish RC .20 .50
90 Carlos E. Hernandez .20 .50
91 Allen Levrault .20 .50
92 Sean McNally RC .20 .50
93 Randey Dorame RC .20 .50
94 Wes Anderson RC .20 .50
95 B.J. Ryan .20 .50
96 Alan Webb RC .20 .50
97 Brandon Inge RC 1.25 3.00
98 David Walling .20 .50
99 Sun Woo Kim RC .20 .50
00 Pat Burrell .20 .50
01 Rick Guttormson RC .20 .50
2 Gil Meche .20 .50
3 Carlos Zambrano RC 1.25 3.00
04 Eric Byrnes UER RC .20 .50
05 Robb Quinlan RC .20 .50
06 Jackie Rexrode .20 .50
07 Nate Bump .20 .50
08 Sean DePaula RC .20 .50
9 Matt Riley .20 .50
0 Ryan Minor .20 .50
311 J.J. Davis .20 .50
312 Randy Wolf .20 .50
313 Jason Jennings .20 .50
314 Scott Seabol RC .20 .50
315 Doug Davis .20 .50
316 Todd Moser RC .20 .50
317 Rob Ryan .20 .50
318 Bubba Crosby .20 .50
319 Lyle Overbay RC .30 .75
320 Mario Encarnacion .20 .50
321 Francisco Rodriguez RC 1.25 3.00
322 Michael Cuddyer .20 .50
323 Ed Yarnall .20 .50
324 Cesar Saba RC .20 .50
325 Gookie Dawkins .20 .50
326 Alex Escobar .20 .50
327 Julio Zuleta RC .20 .50
328 Josh Hamilton .60 1.50
329 Carlos Urquiola RC .20 .50
330 Matt Belisle .20 .50
331 Kurt Ainsworth RC .20 .50
332 Tim Raines Jr. .20 .50
333 Eric Munson .20 .50
334 Donzell McDonald .20 .50
335 Larry Bigbie RC .20 .50
336 Matt Watson RC .20 .50
337 Aubrey Huff .20 .50
338 Julio Ramirez .20 .50
339 Jason Grabowski RC .20 .50
340 Jon Garland .20 .50
341 Austin Kearns .20 .50
342 Josh Pressley RC .20 .50
343 Miguel Olivo RC .30 .75
344 Julio Lugo .20 .50
345 Roberto Vaz .20 .50
346 Ramon Soler .20 .50
347 Brandon Phillips RC .75 2.00
348 Vince Faison RC .20 .50
349 Mike Venafro .20 .50
350 Rick Asadoorian RC .20 .50
351 B.J. Garbe RC .20 .50
352 Dan Reichert .20 .50
353 Jason Stumm RC .20 .50
354 Ruben Salazar RC .20 .50
355 Francisco Cordero .20 .50
356 Juan Guzman RC .20 .50
357 Mike Bacsik RC .20 .50
358 Jared Sandberg .20 .50
359 Rod Barajas .20 .50
360 Junior Brignac RC .20 .50
361 J.M. Gold .20 .50
362 Octavio Dotel .20 .50
363 David Kelton .20 .50
364 Scott Morgan .20 .50
365 Wascar Serrano RC .20 .50
366 Wilton Veras .20 .50
367 Eugene Kingsale .20 .50
368 Ted Lilly .20 .50
369 George Lombard .20 .50
370 Chris Haas .20 .50
371 Wilton Pena RC .20 .50
372 Vernon Wells .20 .50
373 Keith Ginter RC .20 .50
374 Jeff Heaverlo RC .20 .50
375 Calvin Pickering .20 .50
376 Mike Lamb RC .20 .50
377 Kyle Snyder .20 .50
378 Javier Cardona RC .20 .50
379 Aaron Rowand RC 1.00 2.50
380 Dee Brown .20 .50
381 Brett Myers RC .60 1.50
382 Abraham Nunez .20 .50
383 Eric Valent .20 .50
384 Jody Gerut RC .20 .50
385 Adam Dunn .30 .75
386 Jay Gehrke .20 .50
387 Omar Ortiz .20 .50
388 Darnell McDonald .20 .50
389 Tony Schrager RC .20 .50
390 J.D. Closser .20 .50
391 Ben Christensen RC .20 .50
392 Adam Kennedy .20 .50
393 Nick Green RC .20 .50
394 Ramon Hernandez .20 .50
395 Roy Oswalt RC 3.00 8.00
396 Andy Tracy RC .20 .50
397 Eric Gagne .20 .50
398 Michael Tejera RC .20 .50
399 Adam Everett .20 .50
400 Corey Patterson .20 .50
401 Gary Knotts RC .20 .50
402 Ryan Christianson RC .20 .50
403 Eric Ireland RC .20 .50
404 Andrew Good RC .20 .50
405 Brad Penny .20 .50
406 Jason LaRue .20 .50
407 Kit Pellow .20 .50
408 Kevin Beirne .20 .50
409 Kelly Dransfeldt .20 .50
410 Jason Grilli .20 .50
411 Scott Downs RC .20 .50
412 Jesus Colome .20 .50
413 John Sneed RC .20 .50
414 Tony McKnight .20 .50
415 Luis Rivera .20 .50
416 Adam Eaton .20 .50
417 Mike MacDougal RC .30 .75
418 Mike Nannini .20 .50
419 Barry Zito RC 1.50 4.00
420 DeWayne Wise .20 .50
421 Jason Dellaero .20 .50
422 Chad Moeller .20 .50
423 Jason Marquis .20 .50
424 Tim Redding RC .30 .75
425 Mark Mulder .20 .50
426 Josh Paul .20 .50
427 Chris Enochs .20 .50
428 Wilfredo Rodriguez RC .20 .50
429 Kevin Witt .20 .50
430 Scott Sobkowiak RC .20 .50
431 McKay Christensen .20 .50
432 Jung Bong .20 .50
433 Keith Evans RC .20 .50
434 Garry Maddox Jr. RC .20 .50
435 Ramon Santiago RC .20 .50
436 Alex Cora .30 .75
437 Carlos Lee .20 .50
438 Jason Repko RC .20 .50
439 Matt Burch .20 .50
440 Shawn Sonnier RC .20 .50

2000 Bowman Chrome Oversize

Inserted into hobby boxes as a chip-topper at one per box, this eight-card oversized set features some of the Major Leagues most promising young players.

COMPLETE SET (8) 2.50 6.00
ONE PER HOBBY BOX CHIP-TOPPER
1 Pat Burrell .40 1.00
2 Josh Hamilton 1.25 3.00
3 Rafael Furcal .60 1.50
4 Corey Patterson .40 1.00
5 A.J. Burnett .40 1.00
6 Eric Munson .40 1.00
7 Nick Johnson .40 1.00
8 Alfonso Soriano 1.00 2.50

2000 Bowman Chrome Refractors

*STARS: 3X TO 8X BASIC CARDS
*ROOKIES: 3X TO 8X BASIC CARDS
STATED ODDS 1:12

2000 Bowman Chrome Retro/Future

*RETRO: 1.5X TO 4X BASIC
STATED ODDS 1:6

2000 Bowman Chrome Retro/Future Refractors

*RETRO REF.: 6X TO 15X BASIC CARDS
STATED ODDS 1:60

2000 Bowman Chrome Bidding for the Call

Randomly inserted into packs at one in 16, this 15-card insert features players that are looking to break into the Major Leagues during the 2000 season. Card backs carry a "BC" prefix. It's worth noting that top prospect Chin-Feng Chen's very first MLB-licensed card was included in this set.

COMPLETE SET (15) 5.00 12.00
STATED ODDS 1:16
*REFRACTORS: 1.25X TO 3X BASIC BID
REFRACTOR STATED ODDS 1:160
BC1 Adam Piatt .40 1.00
BC2 Pat Burrell .40 1.00
BC3 Mark Mulder .40 1.00
BC4 Nick Johnson .40 1.00
BC5 Alfonso Soriano 1.00 2.50
BC6 Chin-Feng Chen 1.25 3.00
BC7 Scott Sobkowiak .40 1.00
BC8 Corey Patterson .40 1.00
BC9 Jack Cust .40 1.00
BC10 Sean Burroughs .40 1.00
BC11 Josh Hamilton 1.25 3.00
BC12 Corey Myers .40 1.00
BC13 Eric Munson .40 1.00
BC14 Wes Anderson .40 1.00
BC15 Lyle Overbay .60 1.50

2000 Bowman Chrome Meteoric Rise

Randomly inserted into packs at one in 24, this 10-card insert features players that have risen to the occasion during their careers. Card backs carry a "MR" prefix.

COMPLETE SET (10) 10.00 25.00
STATED ODDS 1:24
*REF: 1.25X TO 3X BASIC METEORIC
REFRACTOR STATED ODDS 1:240
MR1 Nomar Garciaparra .60 1.50
MR2 Mark McGwire 1.50 4.00
MR3 Ken Griffey Jr. 2.00 5.00
MR4 Chipper Jones 1.00 2.50
MR5 Manny Ramirez 1.00 2.50
MR6 Mike Piazza 1.00 2.50
MR7 Cal Ripken 3.00 8.00
MR8 Ivan Rodriguez .60 1.50
MR9 Greg Maddux 1.25 3.00
MR10 Randy Johnson 1.00 2.50

2000 Bowman Chrome Rookie Class 2000

Randomly inserted into packs at one in 24, this 10-card insert features players that made their Major League debuts in 2000. Card backs carry a "RC" prefix.

COMPLETE SET (10) 2.50 6.00
STATED ODDS 1:24
*REF: 1.25X TO 3X BASIC ROOKIE CLASS
REFRACTOR STATED ODDS 1:240
RC1 Pat Burrell .40 1.00
RC2 Rick Ankiel .60 1.50
RC3 Ruben Mateo .40 1.00
RC4 Vernon Wells .40 1.00
RC5 Mark Mulder .40 1.00
RC6 A.J. Burnett .40 1.00
RC7 Chad Hermansen .40 1.00
RC8 Corey Patterson .40 1.00
RC9 Rafael Furcal .60 1.50
RC10 Mike Lamb .40 1.00

2000 Bowman Chrome Teen Idols

Randomly inserted into packs at one in 16, this 15-card insert set features Major League players that either made it to the majors as teenagers or are top current prospects who are still in their teens in 2000. Card backs carry a "TI" prefix.

COMPLETE SET (15) 8.00 20.00
*SINGLES: 1X TO 2.5X BASIC CARDS
STATED ODDS 1:16
*REFRACTORS: 1.25X TO 3X BASIC TEEN
REFRACTOR STATED ODDS 1:160
TI1 Alex Rodriguez 1.25 3.00
TI2 Andruw Jones .40 1.00
TI3 Juan Gonzalez .40 1.00
TI4 Ivan Rodriguez .60 1.50
TI5 Ken Griffey Jr. 2.00 5.00
TI6 Bobby Bradley .40 1.00
TI7 Brett Myers 1.25 3.00
TI8 C.C. Sabathia .60 1.50
TI9 Ty Howington .40 1.00
TI10 Brandon Phillips 1.50 4.00
TI11 Rick Asadoorian .40 1.00
TI12 Wily Mo Pena .40 1.00
TI13 Sean Burroughs .40 1.00
TI14 Josh Hamilton 1.25 3.00
TI15 Rafael Furcal .60 1.50

2000 Bowman Chrome Draft

The 2000 Bowman Chrome Draft Picks and Prospects set was released in December, 2000 as a 110-card parallel of the 2000 Bowman Draft Picks set. This product was distributed only in factory set form. Each set features Topps' Chrome technology. A limited selection of prospects were switched out from the Bowman checklist and are featured exclusively in this Bowman Chrome set. The most notable of these players include Timo Perez and Jon Rauch. Other notable Rookie Cards include Chin-Feng Chen and Adrian Gonzalez.

COMP.FACT.SET (110) 15.00 40.00
COMMON CARD (1-110) .20 .50
COMMON RC .20 .50
1 Pat Burrell .20 .50
2 Rafael Furcal .30 .75
3 Grant Roberts .20 .50
4 Barry Zito 1.50 4.00
5 Julio Zuleta .20 .50
6 Mark Mulder .20 .50
7 Rob Bell .20 .50
8 Adam Piatt .20 .50
9 Mike Lamb .20 .50
10 Pablo Ozuna .20 .50
11 Jason Tyner .20 .50
12 Jason Marquis .20 .50
13 Eric Munson .20 .50
14 Seth Etherton .20 .50
15 Milton Bradley .20 .50
16 Nick Green .20 .50
17 Chin-Feng Chen RC .60 1.50
18 Matt Boone RC .20 .50
19 Kevin Gregg RC .20 .50
20 Eddy Garabito RC .20 .50
21 Aaron Capista RC .20 .50
22 Esteban German RC .20 .50
23 Derek Thompson RC .20 .50
24 Phil Merrell RC .20 .50
25 Brian O'Connor RC .20 .50
26 Yamid Haad .20 .50
27 Hector Mercado RC .20 .50
28 Jason Woolf RC .20 .50
29 Eddy Furniss RC .20 .50
30 Cha Sueng Baek RC .20 .50
31 Colby Lewis RC .50 1.25
32 Pasqual Coco RC .20 .50
33 Jorge Cantu RC .30 .75
34 Erasmo Ramirez RC .20 .50
35 Bobby Kielty RC .20 .50
36 Joaquin Benoit RC .20 .50
37 Brian Esposito RC .20 .50
38 Michael Wenner .20 .50
39 Juan Rincon RC .20 .50
40 Yorvit Torrealba RC .30 .75
41 Chad Durham RC .20 .50
42 Jim Mann RC .20 .50
43 Shane Loux RC .20 .50
44 Luis Rivas .20 .50
45 Ken Chenard RC .20 .50
46 Mike Lockwood RC .20 .50
47 Yovanny Lara RC .20 .50
48 Bubba Carpenter RC .20 .50
49 Ryan Dittfurth RC .20 .50
50 John Stephens RC .20 .50
51 Pedro Feliz RC .50 1.25
52 Kenny Kelly RC .20 .50
53 Neil Jenkins RC .20 .50
54 Mike Glendenning RC .20 .50
55 Bo Porter .20 .50
56 Eric Byrnes .20 .50
57 Tony Alvarez RC .20 .50
58 Kazuhiro Sasaki RC .50 1.25
59 Chad Durbin RC .20 .50
60 Mike Bynum RC .20 .50
61 Travis Wilson RC .20 .50
62 Jose Leon RC .20 .50
63 Ryan Vogelsong RC 2.00 5.00
64 Geraldo Guzman RC .20 .50
65 Craig Anderson RC .20 .50
66 Carlos Silva RC .20 .50
67 Brad Thomas RC .20 .50
68 Chin-Hui Tsao .50 1.25
69 Mark Buehrle RC 3.00 8.00
70 Juan Salas RC .20 .50
71 Denny Abreu RC .20 .50
72 Keith McDonald RC .20 .50
73 Chris Richard RC .20 .50
74 Tomas De la Rosa RC .20 .50
75 Vicente Padilla RC .50 1.25
76 Justin Brunette RC .20 .50
77 Scott Linebrink RC .20 .50
78 Jeff Sparks RC .20 .50
79 Tike Redman RC .20 .50
80 John Lackey RC 1.25 3.00
81 Joe Strong RC .20 .50
82 Brian Tollberg RC .20 .50
83 Steve Sisco RC .20 .50
84 Chris Clapinski RC .20 .50
85 Augie Ojeda RC .20 .50
86 Adrian Gonzalez RC 6.00 15.00
87 Mike Stodolka RC .20 .50
88 Adam Johnson RC .20 .50
89 Matt Wheatland RC .20 .50
90 Corey Smith RC .20 .50
91 Rocco Baldelli RC .50 1.25
92 Keith Bucktrot RC .20 .50
93 Adam Wainwright RC 2.00 5.00
94 Blaine Boyer RC .20 .50
95 Aaron Herr RC .30 .75
96 Scott Thorman RC .30 .75
97 Bryan Digby RC .20 .50
98 Josh Shortslef RC .20 .50
99 Sean Smith RC .20 .50
100 Alex Cruz RC .20 .50
101 Marc Love RC .20 .50
102 Kevin Lee RC .20 .50
103 Timo Perez RC .30 .75
104 Alex Cabrera RC .20 .50
105 Shane Heams RC .20 .50
106 Tripper Johnson RC .20 .50
107 Brent Abernathy RC .20 .50
108 John Cotton RC .20 .50
109 Brad Wilkerson RC .50 1.25
110 Jon Rauch RC .20 .50

2001 Bowman Chrome

The 2001 Bowman Chrome set was distributed in four-card packs with a suggested retail price of $3.99. This 352-card set consists of 110 leading hitters and pitchers (1-110), 110 rising young stars (201-310), 110 top rookies including 20 not found in the regular Bowman set (111-200, 311-330), 20 autographed rookie refractor cards (331-350) each serial numbered to 500 copies and two Ichiro Suzuki Rookie Cards (351) in available in English and Japanese text variations. Both Ichiro cards were only available via mail redemption whereby exchange cards were seeded into packs. In addition, an exchange card was seeded into packs for the Albert Pujols signed Rookie Card. The deadline to send these cards in was June 30th, 2003.

COMP.SET w/o SP's (220) 30.00 80.00
COMMON (1-110/201-310) .20 .50
COM.REF (111-200/311-330) 2.00 5.00
111-200/311-330 STATED ODDS 1:4
COMMON AU REF (331-350) 6.00 15.00
331-350 STATED ODDS 1:147
331-350 PRINT RUN 500 SERIAL #'d SETS
CARDS 111-200/311-350 ARE REFRACTORS
ICHIRO EXCH ODDS SAME AS OTHER REF.
ICHIRO PRINT RUN: 50% ENGL.-50% JAPAN
EXCHANGE DEADLINE 06/30/03
1 Jason Giambi .20 .50
2 Rafael Furcal .20 .50
3 Bernie Williams .30 .75
4 Kenny Lofton .20 .50
5 Al Leiter .20 .50
6 Albert Belle .20 .50
7 Craig Biggio .30 .75
8 Mark Mulder .20 .50
9 Carlos Delgado .20 .50
10 Darin Erstad .20 .50
11 Richie Sexson .20 .50
12 Randy Johnson .50 1.25
13 Greg Maddux .75 2.00
14 Orlando Hernandez .20 .50
15 Javier Vazquez .20 .50
16 Jeff Kent .20 .50
17 Jim Thome .30 .75
18 John Olerud .20 .50
19 Jason Kendall .20 .50
20 Scott Rolen .30 .75
21 Tony Gwynn .60 1.50
22 Edgardo Alfonzo .20 .50
23 Pokey Reese .20 .50
24 Todd Helton .30 .75
25 Mark Quinn .20 .50
26 Dean Palmer .20 .50
27 Ray Durham .20 .50
28 Rafael Palmeiro .30 .75
29 Carl Everett .20 .50
30 Vladimir Guerrero .50 1.25
31 Livan Hernandez .20 .50
32 Preston Wilson .20 .50
33 Jose Vidro .20 .50
34 Fred McGriff .30 .75
35 Kevin Brown .20 .50
36 Miguel Tejada .20 .50
37 Chipper Jones .50 1.25
38 Edgar Martinez .30 .75
39 Tony Batista .20 .50
40 Jorge Posada .30 .75
41 Sammy Sosa .50 1.25
42 Gary Sheffield .20 .50
43 Bartolo Colon .20 .50
44 Pat Burrell .20 .50
45 Jay Payton .20 .50
46 Mike Mussina .30 .75
47 Nomar Garciaparra .75 2.00
48 Darren Dreifort .20 .50
49 Richard Hidalgo .20 .50
50 Troy Glaus .20 .50
51 Ben Grieve .20 .50
52 Jim Edmonds .20 .50
53 Raul Mondesi .20 .50
54 Andruw Jones .30 .75
55 Mike Sweeney .20 .50
56 Derek Jeter 1.25 3.00
57 Ruben Mateo .20 .50
58 Cristian Guzman .20 .50
59 Mike Hampton .20 .50
60 J.D. Drew .20 .50
61 Matt Lawton .20 .50
62 Moises Alou .20 .50
63 Terrence Long .20 .50
64 Geoff Jenkins .20 .50
65 Manny Ramirez Sox .30 .75
66 Johnny Damon .30 .75
67 Pedro Martinez .30 .75
68 Juan Gonzalez .20 .50
69 Roger Clemens 1.00 2.50
70 Carlos Beltran .20 .50
71 Roberto Alomar .30 .75
72 Barry Bonds 1.25 3.00
73 Tim Hudson .20 .50
74 Tom Glavine .30 .75
75 Jeromy Burnitz .20 .50
76 Adrian Beltre .20 .50
77 Mike Piazza .75 2.00
78 Kerry Wood .20 .50
79 Steve Finley .20 .50
80 Bob Abreu .20 .50
81 Neifi Perez .20 .50
82 Mark Redman .20 .50
83 Paul Konerko .20 .50
84 Jermaine Dye .20 .50
85 Brian Giles .20 .50
86 Ivan Rodriguez .30 .75
87 Adam Kennedy .20 .50
88 Eric Chavez .20 .50
89 Billy Koch .20 .50
90 Shawn Green .20 .50
91 Matt Williams .20 .50
92 Greg Vaughn .20 .50
93 Jeff Cirillo .20 .50
94 Frank Thomas .50 1.25
95 David Justice .20 .50
96 Cal Ripken 1.50 4.00
97 Curt Schilling .20 .50
98 Barry Zito .30 .75
99 Brian Jordan .20 .50
100 Chan Ho Park .20 .50
101 J.T. Snow .20 .50
102 Kazuhiro Sasaki .20 .50
103 Alex Rodriguez .60 1.50
104 Mariano Rivera .50 1.25
105 Eric Milton .20 .50
106 Andy Pettitte .30 .75
107 Ken Griffey Jr. 1.00 2.50
108 Bengie Molina .20 .50
109 Jeff Bagwell .30 .75
110 Mark McGwire 1.25 3.00
111 Dan Tosca RC 2.00 5.00
112 Sergio Contreras RC 3.00 8.00
113 Mitch Jones RC 3.00 8.00
114 Ramon Carvajal RC 3.00 8.00
115 Ryan Madson RC 4.00 10.00
116 Hank Blalock RC 6.00 15.00
117 Ben Washburn RC 2.00 5.00
118 Erick Almonte RC 2.00 5.00
119 Shawn Fagan RC 3.00 8.00
120 Gary Johnson RC 2.00 5.00
121 Brett Evert RC 2.00 5.00
122 Joe Hamer RC 3.00 8.00
123 Yhency Brazoban RC 4.00 10.00
124 Domingo Guante RC 2.00 5.00
125 Deivi Mendez RC 2.00 5.00
126 Adrian Hernandez RC 2.00 5.00
127 Reggie Abercrombie RC 4.00 10.00
128 Steve Bennett RC 2.00 5.00
129 Matt White RC 3.00 8.00
130 Brian Hitchcox RC 2.00 5.00
131 Deivis Santos RC 2.00 5.00
132 Luis Montanez RC 4.00 10.00
133 Eric Reynolds RC 2.00 5.00
134 Denny Bautista RC 4.00 10.00
135 Hector Garcia RC 2.00 5.00
136 Joe Thurston RC 3.00 8.00
137 Tsuyoshi Shinjo RC 4.00 10.00
138 Elpidio Guzman RC 2.00 5.00
139 Brian Bass RC 2.00 5.00
140 Mark Burnett RC 3.00 8.00
141 Russ Jacobson UER 2.00 5.00
142 Travis Hafner RC 5.00 12.00
143 Wilson Betemit RC 6.00 15.00
144 Luke Lockwood RC 3.00 8.00
145 Noel Devarez RC 3.00 8.00
146 Doug Gredvig RC 2.00 5.00
147 Seung Song RC 3.00 8.00
148 Andy Van Hekken RC 2.00 5.00
149 Ryan Kohlmeier 2.00 5.00
150 Dee Haynes RC 2.00 5.00
151 Jim Journell RC 3.00 8.00
152 Chad Petty RC 2.00 5.00
153 Danny Borrell RC 2.00 5.00
154 Dave Krynzel 2.00 5.00
155 Octavio Martinez RC 3.00 8.00
156 David Parrish RC 2.00 5.00
157 Jason Miller RC 2.00 5.00
158 Corey Spencer RC 2.00 5.00
159 Maxim St. Pierre RC 3.00 8.00
160 Pat Magness RC 3.00 8.00
161 Ranier Olmedo RC 3.00 8.00
162 Brandon Mims RC 2.00 5.00
163 Phil Wilson RC 3.00 8.00
164 Jose Reyes RC 12.00 30.00
165 Matt Butler RC 3.00 8.00
166 Joel Pineiro 3.00 8.00
167 Ken Chenard 2.00 5.00
168 Alexis Gomez RC 2.00 5.00
169 Justin Morneau RC 6.00 15.00
170 Josh Fogg RC 3.00 8.00
171 Charles Frazier RC 2.00 5.00
172 Ryan Ludwick RC 3.00 8.00
173 Seth McClung RC 3.00 8.00
174 Justin Wayne RC 3.00 8.00
175 Rafael Soriano RC 4.00 10.00
176 Jared Abruzzo RC 2.00 5.00
177 Jason Richardson RC 2.00 5.00
178 Darwin Cubillan RC 2.00 5.00
179 Blake Williams RC 2.00 5.00
180 Valentino Pascucci RC 3.00 8.00
181 Ryan Hannaman RC 3.00 8.00
182 Steve Smyth RC 3.00 8.00
183 Jake Peavy RC 5.00 12.00
184 Onix Mercado RC 3.00 8.00
185 Luis Torres RC 3.00 8.00
186 Casey Fossum RC 2.00 5.00
187 Eduardo Figueroa RC 2.00 5.00

188 Bryan Barnowski RC 2.00 5.00
189 Jason Standridge 2.00 5.00
190 Marvin Seale RC 3.00 8.00
191 Steve Smitherman RC 3.00 8.00
192 Rafael Boitel RC 2.00 5.00
193 Dany Morban RC 2.00 5.00
194 Justin Woodrow RC 3.00 8.00
195 Ed Rogers RC 2.00 5.00
196 Ben Hendrickson RC 2.00 5.00
197 Thomas Mitchell 2.00 5.00
198 Adam Pettyjohn RC 2.00 5.00
199 Doug Nickle RC 2.00 5.00
200 Jason Jones RC 2.00 5.00
201 Larry Barnes .20 .50
202 Ben Diggins .20 .50
203 Dee Brown .20 .50
204 Rocco Baldelli .20 .50
205 Luis Terrero .20 .50
206 Milton Bradley .20 .50
207 Kurt Ainsworth .20 .50
208 Sean Burroughs .20 .50
209 Rick Asadoorian .20 .50
210 Ramon Castro .20 .50
211 Nick Neugebauer .20 .50
212 Aaron Myette .20 .50
213 Luis Matos .20 .50
214 Donnie Bridges .20 .50
215 Alex Cintron .20 .50
216 Bobby Kielty .20 .50
217 Matt Belisle .20 .50
218 Adam Everett .20 .50
219 John Lackey .20 .50
220 Adam Wainwright .75 2.00
221 Jerry Hairston Jr. .20 .50
222 Mike Bynum .20 .50
223 Ryan Christianson .20 .50
224 J.J. Davis .20 .50
225 Alex Graman .20 .50
226 Abraham Nunez .20 .50
227 Sun Woo Kim .20 .50
228 Jimmy Rollins .20 .50
229 Ruben Salazar .20 .50
230 Josh Girdley .20 .50
231 Carl Crawford .20 .50
232 Ben Davis .20 .50
233 Jason Grabowski .20 .50
234 Chris George .20 .50
235 Roy Oswalt .50 1.25
236 Brian Cole .20 .50
237 Corey Patterson .20 .50
238 Vernon Wells .20 .50
239 Brad Baker .20 .50
240 Gookie Dawkins .20 .50
241 Michael Cuddyer .20 .50
242 Ricardo Aramboles .20 .50
243 Ben Sheets .30 .75
244 Toby Hall .20 .50
245 Jack Cust .20 .50
246 Pedro Feliz .20 .50
247 Josh Beckett .30 .75
248 Alex Escobar .20 .50
249 Marcus Giles .20 .50
250 Jon Rauch .20 .50
251 Kevin Mench .20 .50
252 Shawn Sonnier .20 .50
253 Aaron Rowand .20 .50
254 C.C. Sabathia .20 .50
255 Bubba Crosby .20 .50
256 Josh Hamilton .40 1.00
257 Carlos Hernandez .20 .50
258 Carlos Pena .20 .50
259 Miguel Cabrera UER 4.00 10.00
260 Brandon Phillips .20 .50
261 Tony Pena Jr. .20 .50
262 Cristian Guerrero .20 .50
263 Jin Ho Cho .20 .50
264 Aaron Herr .20 .50
265 Keith Ginter .20 .50
266 Felipe Lopez .20 .50
267 Travis Harper .20 .50
268 Joe Torres .20 .50
269 Eric Byrnes .20 .50
270 Ben Christensen .20 .50
271 Aubrey Huff .20 .50
272 Lyle Overbay .20 .50
273 Vince Faison .20 .50
274 Bobby Bradley .20 .50
275 Joe Crede .50 1.25
276 Matt Wheatland .20 .50
277 Grady Sizemore .75 2.00
278 Adrian Gonzalez .60 1.50
279 Tim Raines Jr. .20 .50
280 Phil Dumatrait .20 .50
281 Jason Hart .20 .50
282 David Kelton .20 .50
283 David Walling .20 .50
284 J.R. House .20 .50
285 Kenny Kelly .20 .50
286 Aaron McNeal .20 .50
287 Nick Johnson .20 .50
288 Scott Heard .20 .50
289 Brad Wilkerson .20 .50
290 Allen Levrault .20 .50
291 Chris Richard .20 .50
292 Jared Sandberg .20 .50
293 Tike Redman .20 .50
294 Adam Dunn .30 .75
295 Josh Pressley .20 .50
296 Jose Ortiz .20 .50
297 Jason Romano .20 .50
298 Tim Redding .20 .50
299 Alex Gordon .20 .50
300 Ben Petrick .20 .50
301 Eric Munson .20 .50
302 Luis Rivas .20 .50
303 Matt Ginter .20 .50
304 Alfonso Soriano .30 .75
305 Wilfredo Rodriguez .20 .50
306 Brett Myers .20 .50
307 Scott Seabol .20 .50
308 Tony Alvarez .20 .50
309 Donzell McDonald .20 .50
310 Austin Kearns .20 .50
311 Will Ohman RC 3.00 8.00
312 Ryan Soules RC 2.00 5.00
313 Cody Ross RC 6.00 15.00
314 Bill Whitecotton RC 2.00 5.00
315 Mike Burns RC 3.00 8.00
316 Manuel Acosta RC 2.00 5.00
317 Lance Niekro RC 4.00 10.00
318 Travis Thompson RC 3.00 8.00
319 Zach Sorensen RC 3.00 8.00
320 Austin Evans RC 2.00 5.00
321 Brad Stiles RC 2.00 5.00
322 Joe Kennedy RC 4.00 10.00
323 Luke Martin RC 3.00 8.00
324 Juan Diaz RC 3.00 8.00
325 Pat Hallmark RC 2.00 5.00
326 Christian Parker RC 2.00 5.00
327 Ronny Corona RC 3.00 8.00
328 Jermaine Clark RC 2.00 5.00
329 Scott Dunn RC 3.00 8.00
330 Scott Chiasson RC 3.00 8.00
331 Greg Nash AU RC 6.00 15.00
332 Brad Cresse AU 6.00 15.00
333 John Buck AU RC 6.00 15.00
334 Freddie Bynum AU RC 6.00 15.00
335 Felix Diaz AU RC 6.00 15.00
336 Jason Belcher AU RC 6.00 15.00
337 Troy Farnsworth AU RC 6.00 15.00
338 Roberto Miniel AU RC 6.00 15.00
339 Esix Snead AU RC 6.00 15.00
340 Albert Pujols AU RC 2000.00 4000.00
341 Jeff Andra AU RC 6.00 15.00
342 Victor Hall AU RC 6.00 15.00
343 Pedro Liriano AU RC 6.00 15.00
344 Andy Beal AU RC 6.00 15.00
345 Bob Keppel AU RC 6.00 15.00
346 Brian Schmitt AU RC 6.00 15.00
347 Ron Davenport AU RC 6.00 15.00
348 Tony Blanco AU RC 6.00 15.00
349 Reggie Griggs AU RC 6.00 15.00
350 Derrick Van Dusen AU RC 6.00 15.00
351A Ichiro Suzuki English RC 75.00 200.00
351B Ichiro Suzuki Japan RC 75.00 200.00

2001 Bowman Chrome Gold Refractors

*STARS: 8X TO 20X BASIC CARDS
*ROOKIES: 1.5X TO 4X BASIC CARDS
STATED ODDS 1:47
STATED PRINT RUN 99 SERIAL #'d SETS
ICHIRO ENGLISH PRINT RUN 50 #'d CARDS
ICHIRO JAPAN PRINT RUN 49 #'d CARDS
ICHIRO ENGLISH ARE EVEN SERIAL #'d
ICHIRO ENGLISH ARE ODD SERIAL #'d
ICHIRO EXCHANGE DEADLINE 06/30/03
56 Derek Jeter 40.00 80.00
NNOA Ichiro English/50 400.00 800.00
NNOB Ichiro Japan/49 400.00 800.00

2001 Bowman Chrome X-Fractors

*STARS: 4X TO 10X BASIC CARDS
*ROOKIES: .75X TO 2X BASIC CARDS
STATED ODDS 1:23
ICHIRO PRINT RUN: 50% ENGL.-50% JAPAN
EXCHANGE DEADLINE 06/30/03

2001 Bowman Chrome Futures Game Relics

Randomly inserted in packs at the rate of one in 460, this 30-card set features color photos of players who participated in the 2000 Futures Game in Atlanta with pieces of game-worn uniform numbers and letters embedded in the cards.

STATED ODDS 1:460
FGRAE Alex Escobar 3.00 8.00
FGRAM Aaron Myette 3.00 8.00
FGRBB Bobby Bradley 3.00 8.00
FGRBP Ben Petrick 3.00 8.00
FGRBS Ben Sheets 6.00 15.00
FGRBW Brad Wilkerson 3.00 8.00
FGRBZ Barry Zito 6.00 15.00
FGRCA Craig Anderson 3.00 8.00
FGRCC Chin-Feng Chen 30.00 60.00
FGRCG Chris George 3.00 8.00
FGRCH Carlos Hernandez 4.00 10.00
FGRCP Carlos Pena 10.00 25.00
FGRCT Chin-Hui Tsao 40.00 80.00
FGREM Eric Munson 3.00 8.00
FGRFL Felipe Lopez 4.00 10.00
FGRJC Jack Cust 3.00 8.00
FGRJH Josh Hamilton 6.00 15.00
FGRJR Jason Romano 3.00 8.00
FGRJZ Julio Zuleta 3.00 8.00
FGRKA Kurt Ainsworth 3.00 8.00
FGRMB Mike Bynum 3.00 8.00
FGRMG Marcus Giles 4.00 10.00
FGRNN Ntema Ndungidi 3.00 8.00
FGRRA Ryan Anderson 3.00 8.00
FGRRC Ramon Castro 3.00 8.00
FGRRD Randey Dorame 3.00 8.00
FGRSK Sun Woo Kim 3.00 8.00
FGRTO Tomo Ohka 3.00 8.00
FGRTW Travis Wilson 3.00 8.00
FGRDCP Corey Patterson 3.00 8.00

2001 Bowman Chrome Rookie Reprints

Randomly inserted in packs at the rate of one in 12, this 25-card set features reprints of classic 1948-1955 Bowman rookies printed on polished Chrome finishes.

COMPLETE SET (25) 20.00 50.00
STATED ODDS 1:12
*REFRACTORS: .75X TO 2X BASIC REPRINT
REFRACTOR STATED ODDS 1:203
REF.PRINT RUN 299 SERIAL #'d SETS
1 Yogi Berra 3.00 8.00
2 Ralph Kiner 1.50 4.00
3 Stan Musial 5.00 12.00
4 Warren Spahn 1.50 4.00
5 Roy Campanella 3.00 8.00
6 Bob Lemon 1.50 4.00
7 Robin Roberts 1.50 4.00
8 Duke Snider 1.50 4.00
9 Early Wynn 1.50 4.00
10 Richie Ashburn 1.50 4.00
11 Gil Hodges 2.50 6.00
12 Hank Bauer 1.50 4.00
13 Don Newcombe 1.50 4.00
14 Al Rosen 1.50 4.00
15 Willie Mays 6.00 15.00
16 Joe Garagiola 1.50 4.00
17 Whitey Ford 1.50 4.00
18 Lew Burdette 1.50 4.00
19 Gil McDougald 1.50 4.00
20 Minnie Minoso 1.50 4.00
21 Eddie Mathews 2.50 6.00
22 Harvey Kuenn 1.50 4.00
23 Don Larsen 1.50 4.00
24 Elston Howard 1.50 4.00
25 Don Zimmer 1.50 4.00

2001 Bowman Chrome Rookie Reprints Relics

This six-card insert set features color player photos with pieces of their Rookie Season game-worn jerseys or game-used bats embedded in the cards. The insertion rate for the Mike Piazza Bat card is one in 3674 and one in 244 for the jersey cards. Three cards are Bowman Rookie card reprints and three cards are re-created "cards that never were."

STATED BAT ODDS 1:3674
STATED JSY ODDS 1:244
1 David Justice Jsy 4.00 10.00
2 Richie Sexson Jsy 4.00 10.00
3 Sean Casey Jsy 4.00 10.00
4 Mike Piazza Bat 15.00 40.00
5 Carlos Delgado Jsy 4.00 10.00
6 Chipper Jones Jsy 6.00 15.00

2002 Bowman Chrome

This 405 card set was issued in July, 2002. It was issued in four card packs with an SRP of $4 which were packed 18 packs to a box and 12 boxes to a case. The first 110 card of the set featured veteran players. The next grouping of cards (111-383) featured a mix of rookies and prospect cards. The then final grouping (384-405) featured signed rookie cards. Both So Taguchi and Kazuhisa Ishii were also printed without autographs on their cards. An exchange was inserted into packs for Jake Mauer's autographed RC. The exchange card was intended to be card number 388 in the checklist but the actual Mauer autograph mailed out to collectors was card number 324. Thus, this set actually has two cards numbered 324 (the Jake Mauer autograph and a basic-issue Ben Broussard card) and no number 388.

COMP.RED SET (110) 15.00 40.00
COMP.BLUE w/o SP's (110) 15.00 40.00
SP STATED ODDS 1:3
324B/384-405 GROUP A AUTO ODDS 1:28
403-404 GROUP B AUTO ODDS 1:1290
324B/384-405 OVERALL AUTO ODDS 1:27
FULL SET INCLUDES ISHII/TAGUCHI RC'S
FULL SET EXCLUDES ISHII/TAGUCHI AU'S
BROUSSARD/MAUER ARE BOTH CARD 324
CARD 388 DOES NOT EXIST
1 Adam Dunn .30 .75
2 Derek Jeter 1.25 3.00
3 Alex Rodriguez .60 1.50
4 Miguel Tejada .30 .75
5 Nomar Garciaparra .30 .75
6 Toby Hall .20 .50
7 Brandon Duckworth .20 .50
8 Paul LoDuca .20 .50
9 Brian Giles .20 .50
10 C.C. Sabathia .30 .75
11 Curt Schilling .30 .75
12 Tsuyoshi Shinjo .20 .50
13 Ramon Hernandez .20 .50
14 Jose Cruz Jr. .20 .50
15 Albert Pujols 1.00 2.50
16 Joe Mays .20 .50
17 Javy Lopez .20 .50
18 J.T. Snow .20 .50
19 David Segui .20 .50
20 Jorge Posada .30 .75
21 Doug Mientkiewicz .20 .50
22 Jerry Hairston Jr. .20 .50
23 Bernie Williams .30 .75
24 Mike Sweeney .20 .50
25 Jason Giambi .20 .50
26 Ryan Dempster .20 .50
27 Ryan Klesko .20 .50
28 Mark Quinn .20 .50
29 Jeff Kent .20 .50
30 Eric Chavez .20 .50
31 Adrian Beltre .50 1.25
32 Andruw Jones .20 .50
33 Alfonso Soriano .30 .75
34 Aramis Ramirez .20 .50
35 Greg Maddux .75 2.00
36 Andy Pettitte .30 .75
37 Bartolo Colon .20 .50
38 Ben Sheets .20 .50
39 Bobby Higginson .20 .50
40 Ivan Rodriguez .30 .75
41 Brad Penny .20 .50
42 Carlos Lee .20 .50
43 Damion Easley .20 .50
44 Preston Wilson .20 .50
45 Jeff Bagwell .30 .75
46 Eric Milton .20 .50
47 Rafael Palmeiro .30 .75
48 Gary Sheffield .20 .50
49 J.D. Drew .20 .50
50 Jim Thome .30 .75
51 Ichiro Suzuki .60 1.50
52 Bud Smith .20 .50
53 Chan Ho Park .30 .75
54 D'Angelo Jimenez .20 .50
55 Ken Griffey Jr. 1.00 2.50
56 Wade Miller .20 .50
57 Vladimir Guerrero .30 .75
58 Troy Glaus .20 .50
59 Shawn Green .20 .50
60 Kerry Wood .20 .50
61 Jack Wilson .20 .50
62 Kevin Brown .20 .50
63 Marcus Giles .20 .50
64 Pat Burrell .20 .50
65 Larry Walker .30 .75
66 Sammy Sosa .50 1.25
67 Raul Mondesi .20 .50
68 Tim Hudson .30 .75
69 Lance Berkman .30 .75
70 Mike Mussina .30 .75
71 Barry Zito .20 .50
72 Jimmy Rollins .30 .75
73 Barry Bonds .75 2.00
74 Craig Biggio .30 .75
75 Todd Helton .30 .75
76 Roger Clemens .60 1.50
77 Frank Catalanotto .20 .50
78 Josh Towers .20 .50
79 Roy Oswalt .30 .75
80 Chipper Jones .50 1.25
81 Cristian Guzman .20 .50
82 Darin Erstad .20 .50
83 Freddy Garcia .20 .50
84 Jason Tyner .20 .50
85 Carlos Delgado .20 .50
86 Jon Lieber .20 .50
87 Juan Pierre .20 .50
88 Matt Morris .20 .50
89 Phil Nevin .20 .50
90 Jim Edmonds .30 .75
91 Magglio Ordonez .30 .75
92 Mike Hampton .20 .50
93 Rafael Furcal .20 .50
94 Richie Sexson .20 .50
95 Luis Gonzalez .20 .50
96 Scott Rolen .30 .75
97 Tim Redding .20 .50
98 Moises Alou .20 .50
99 Jose Vidro .20 .50
100 Mike Piazza .50 1.25
101 Pedro Martinez .30 .75
102 Geoff Jenkins .20 .50
103 Johnny Damon Sox .30 .75
104 Mike Cameron .20 .50
105 Randy Johnson .50 1.25
106 David Eckstein .20 .50
107 Javier Vazquez .20 .50
108 Mark Mulder .20 .50
109 Robert Fick .20 .50
110 Roberto Alomar .30 .75
111 Wilson Betemit .30 .75
112 Chris Tritle SP RC 1.25 3.00
113 Ed Rogers .30 .75
114 Juan Pena .30 .75
115 Josh Beckett .30 .75
116 Juan Cruz .30 .75
117 Noochie Varner SP RC 1.25 3.00
118 Blake Williams .30 .75
119 Mike Rivera .30 .75
120 Hank Blalock .30 .75
121 Hansel Izquierdo SP RC 1.25 3.00
122 Orlando Hudson .30 .75
123 Bill Hall SP 1.25 3.00
124 Jose Reyes .75 2.00
125 Juan Rivera .30 .75
126 Eric Valent .30 .75
127 Scotty Layfield SP RC 1.25 3.00
128 Austin Kearns .30 .75
129 Nic Jackson SP RC 1.25 3.00
130 Scott Chiasson .30 .75
131 Chad Qualls SP RC 2.00 5.00
132 Marcus Thames .30 .75
133 Nathan Haynes .30 .75
134 Joe Borchard .30 .75
135 Josh Hamilton .50 1.25
136 Corey Patterson .30 .75
137 Travis Wilson .30 .75
138 Alex Escobar .30 .75
139 Alexis Gomez .30 .75
140 Nick Johnson .30 .75
141 Marlon Byrd .30 .75
142 Kory DeHaan .30 .75
143 Carlos Hernandez .30 .75
144 Sean Burroughs .30 .75
145 Angel Berroa .30 .75
146 Aubrey Huff .30 .75
147 Travis Hafner .30 .75
148 Brandon Berger .30 .75
149 J.R. House .30 .75
150 Dewon Brazelton .30 .75
151 Jayson Werth .50 1.25
152 Larry Barnes .30 .75
153 Ruben Gotay SP RC 1.25 3.00
154 Tommy Marx SP RC 1.25 3.00
155 John Suomi SP RC 1.25 3.00
156 Javier Colina SP 1.25 3.00
157 Greg Sain SP RC 1.25 3.00
158 Robert Cosby SP RC 1.25 3.00
159 Angel Pagan SP RC 3.00 8.00
160 Ralph Santana RC .30 .75
161 Joe Orloski RC .30 .75
162 Shayne Wright SP RC 1.25 3.00
163 Jay Caligiuri SP RC 1.25 3.00
164 Greg Montalbano SP RC 1.25 3.00
165 Rich Harden SP RC 4.00 10.00
166 Rich Thompson SP RC 1.25 3.00
167 Fred Bastardo SP RC 1.25 3.00
168 Alejandro Giron SP RC 1.25 3.00
169 Jesus Medrano SP RC 1.25 3.00
170 Kevin Deaton SP RC 1.25 3.00
171 Mike Rosamond RC .30 .75
172 Jon Guzman SP RC 1.25 3.00
173 Gerard Oakes SP RC 1.25 3.00
174 Francisco Liriano SP RC 6.00 15.00
175 Matt Allegra SP RC 1.25 3.00
176 Mike Snyder SP RC 1.25 3.00
177 James Shanks SP RC 1.25 3.00
178 Anderson Hernandez SP RC 1.25 3.00
179 Dan Trumble SP RC 1.25 3.00
180 Luis DePaula SP RC 1.25 3.00
181 Randall Shelley SP RC 1.25 3.00
182 Richard Lane SP RC 1.25 3.00
183 Antwon Rollins SP RC 1.25 3.00
184 Ryan Bukvich SP RC 1.25 3.00
185 Derrick Lewis SP 1.25 3.00
186 Eric Miller SP RC 1.25 3.00
187 Justin Schuda SP RC 1.25 3.00
188 Brian West SP RC 1.25 3.00
189 Brad Wilkerson .30 .75
190 Neal Frendling SP RC 1.25 3.00
191 Jeremy Hill SP RC 1.25 3.00
192 James Barrett SP RC 1.25 3.00
193 Brett Kay SP RC 1.25 3.00
194 Ryan Mottl SP RC 1.25 3.00
195 Brad Nelson SP RC 1.25 3.00
196 Juan M. Gonzalez SP RC 1.25 3.00
197 Curtis Legendre SP RC 1.25 3.00
198 Ronald Acuna SP RC 1.25 3.00
199 Chris Flinn SP RC 1.25 3.00
200 Nick Alvarez SP RC 1.25 3.00
201 Jason Ellison SP RC 1.25 3.00
202 Blake McGinley SP RC 1.25 3.00
203 Dan Phillips SP RC 1.25 3.00
204 Demetrius Heath SP RC 1.25 3.00
205 Eric Bruntlett SP RC 1.25 3.00
206 Joe Jiannetti SP RC 1.25 3.00
207 Mike Hill SP RC 1.25 3.00
208 Ricardo Cordova SP RC 1.25 3.00
209 Mark Hamilton SP RC 1.25 3.00
210 David Mattox SP RC 1.25 3.00
211 Jose Morban SP RC 1.25 3.00
212 Scott Wiggins SP RC 1.25 3.00
213 Steve Green .30 .75
214 Brian Rogers SP 1.25 3.00
215 Kenny Baugh .30 .75
216 Anastacio Martinez SP RC 1.25 3.00
217 Richard Lewis .30 .75
218 Tim Kalita SP RC 1.25 3.00
219 Edwin Almonte SP RC 1.25 3.00
220 Hee Seop Choi .30 .75
221 Ty Howington .30 .75
222 Victor Alvarez SP RC 1.25 3.00
223 Morgan Ensberg .30 .75
224 Jeff Austin SP RC 1.25 3.00
225 Clint Weibl SP RC 1.25 3.00
226 Eric Cyr .30 .75
227 Marlyn Tisdale SP RC 1.25 3.00
228 John VanBenschoten .30 .75
229 David Krynzel .30 .75
230 Raul Chavez SP RC 1.25 3.00
231 Brett Evert .30 .75
232 Joe Rogers SP RC 1.25 3.00
233 Adam Wainwright .50 1.25
234 Matt Herges RC .30 .75
235 Matt Childers SP RC 1.25 3.00
236 Nick Neugebauer .30 .75
237 Carl Crawford .50 1.25
238 Seung Song .30 .75
239 Randy Flores .30 .75
240 Jason Lane .30 .75
241 Chase Utley 1.25 3.00
242 Ben Howard SP RC 1.25 3.00
243 Eric Glaser SP RC 1.25 3.00
244 Josh Wilson RC .30 .75
245 Jose Valverde SP RC 2.00 5.00
246 Chris Smith .30 .75
247 Mark Prior .50 1.25
248 Brian Mallette SP RC 1.25 3.00
249 Chone Figgins SP RC 2.00 5.00
250 Jimmy Alvarez SP RC 1.25 3.00
251 Luis Terrero .30 .75
252 Josh Bonifay SP RC 1.25 3.00
253 Garrett Guzman SP RC 1.25 3.00
254 Jeff Verplancke SP RC 1.25 3.00
255 Nate Espy SP RC 1.25 3.00
256 Jeff Lincoln SP RC 1.25 3.00
257 Ryan Snare SP RC 1.25 3.00
258 Jose Ortiz .30 .75
259 Denny Bautista .30 .75
260 Willy Aybar .30 .75
261 Kelly Johnson .75 2.00
262 Shawn Fagan .30 .75
263 Yurendell DeCaster SP RC 1.25 3.00
264 Mike Peeples SP RC 1.25 3.00
265 Joel Guzman .30 .75
266 Ryan Vogelsong 1.50 4.00
267 Jorge Padilla SP RC 1.25 3.00
268 Joe Jester SP RC 1.25 3.00
269 Ryan Church SP RC 1.25 3.00
270 Mitch Jones .30 .75
271 Travis Foley SP RC 1.25 3.00
272 Bobby Crosby .75 2.00
273 Adrian Gonzalez .75 2.00
274 Ronnie Merrill .30 .75
275 Joel Pineiro .30 .75
276 John-Ford Griffin .30 .75
277 Brian Forystek SP RC 1.25 3.00
278 Sean Douglass .30 .75
279 Manny Delcarmen SP RC 1.25 3.00
280 Jim Kavourias SP RC 1.25 3.00
281 Gabe Gross .30 .75
282 Bill Ortega .30 .75
283 Joey Hammond SP RC 1.25 3.00
284 Brett Myers .30 .75
285 Carlos Pena .50 1.25
286 Ezequiel Astacio SP RC 1.25 3.00
287 Edwin Yan SP RC 1.25 3.00
288 Chris Duffy SP RC 1.25 3.00
289 Jason Kinchen .30 .75
290 Rafael Soriano .30 .75
291 Colin Young RC .30 .75
292 Eric Byrnes .30 .75
293 Chris Narveson SP RC 1.25 3.00
294 John Rheinecker .30 .75
295 Mike Wilson SP RC 1.25 3.00
296 Justin Sherrod SP RC 1.25 3.00
297 Deivi Mendez .30 .75
298 Wily Mo Pena .30 .75
299 Brett Roneberg SP RC 1.25 3.00
300 Trey Lunsford SP RC 1.25 3.00
301 Christian Parker .30 .75
302 Brent Butler .30 .75
303 Aaron Heilman .30 .75
304 Wilkin Ruan .30 .75
305 Kenny Kelly .30 .75
306 Cody Ransom .30 .75
307 Koyie Hill SP 1.25 3.00
308 Tony Fontana SP RC 1.25 3.00
309 Mark Teixeira .50 1.25
310 Doug Sessions SP RC 1.25 3.00
311 Josh Cisneros SP RC 1.25 3.00
312 Carlos Brackley SP RC 1.25 3.00
313 Tim Raines Jr. .30 .75
314 Ross Peeples SP RC 1.25 3.00
315 Alex Requena SP RC 1.25 3.00
316 Chin-Hui Tsao .30 .75
317 Tony Alvarez .30 .75
318 Craig Kuzmic SP RC 1.25 3.00
319 Pete Zamora SP RC 1.25 3.00
320 Matt Parker SP RC 1.25 3.00
321 Keith Ginter .30 .75
322 Gary Cates Jr. SP RC 1.25 3.00
323 Matt Belisle .30 .75
324A Ben Broussard .30 .75
324B Jake Mauer AU A RC 4.00 10.00
325 Dennis Tankersley .30 .75
326 Juan Silvestre .30 .75
327 Henry Pichardo SP RC 1.25 3.00
328 Michael Floyd SP RC 1.25 3.00
329 Clint Nageotte SP RC 1.25 3.00
330 Raymond Cabrera SP RC 1.25 3.00
331 Mauricio Lara SP RC 1.25 3.00
332 Alejandro Cadena SP RC 1.25 3.00
333 Jonny Gomes SP RC 4.00 10.00
334 Jason Bulger SP RC 1.25 3.00
335 Nate Teut .30 .75
336 David Gil SP RC 1.25 3.00
337 Joel Crump SP RC 1.25 3.00
338 Brandon Phillips .30 .75
339 Macay McBride .30 .75
340 Brandon Claussen .30 .75
341 Josh Phelps .30 .75
342 Freddie Money SP RC 1.25 3.00
343 Cliff Bartosh SP RC 1.25 3.00
344 Terrance Hill SP RC 1.25 3.00
345 John Rodriguez SP RC 1.25 3.00
346 Chris Latham SP RC 1.25 3.00
347 Carlos Cabrera SP RC 1.25 3.00
348 Jose Bautista SP RC 10.00 25.00
349 Kevin Frederick SP RC 1.25 3.00
350 Jerome Williams .30 .75
351 Napoleon Calzado SP RC 1.25 3.00
352 Benito Baez SP 1.25 3.00
353 Xavier Nady .30 .75
354 Jason Botts SP RC 1.25 3.00
355 Steve Bechler SP RC 1.25 3.00
356 Reed Johnson SP RC 2.00 5.00
357 Mark Outlaw SP RC 1.25 3.00
358 Jake Peavy .30 .75
359 Josh Shaffer SP RC 1.25 3.00
360 Dan Wright SP 1.25 3.00
361 Ryan Gripp SP RC 1.25 3.00
362 Nelson Castro SP RC 1.25 3.00
363 Jason Bay SP RC 6.00 15.00
364 Franklyn German SP RC 1.25 3.00
365 Corwin Malone SP RC 1.25 3.00
366 Kelly Ramos SP RC 1.25 3.00
367 John Ennis SP RC 1.25 3.00
368 George Perez SP 1.25 3.00
369 Rene Reyes SP RC 1.25 3.00
370 Rolando Viera SP RC 1.25 3.00
371 Earl Snyder SP RC 1.25 3.00
372 Kyle Kane SP RC 1.25 3.00
373 Mario Ramos SP RC 1.25 3.00
374 Tyler Yates SP RC 1.25 3.00
375 Jason Young SP RC 1.25 3.00
376 Chris Bootcheck SP RC 1.25 3.00
377 Jesus Cota SP RC 1.25 3.00
378 Corky Miller SP 1.25 3.00
379 Matt Erickson SP RC 1.25 3.00
380 Justin Huber SP RC 1.25 3.00
381 Felix Escalona SP RC 1.25 3.00
382 Kevin Cash SP RC 1.25 3.00
383 J.J. Putz SP RC 2.00 5.00
384 Chris Snelling AU A RC 4.00 10.00
385 David Wright AU A RC 30.00 80.00
386 Brian Wolfe AU A RC 4.00 10.00
387 Justin Reid AU A RC 4.00 10.00
389 Ryan Raburn AU A RC 4.00 10.00
390 Josh Barfield AU A RC 4.00 10.00
391 Joe Mauer AU A RC 60.00 150.00
392 Bobby Jenks AU A RC 4.00 10.00
393 Rob Henkel AU A RC 4.00 10.00
394 Jimmy Gobble AU A RC 4.00 10.00
395 Jesse Foppert AU A RC 4.00 10.00
396 Gavin Floyd AU A RC 4.00 10.00
397 Nate Field AU A RC 4.00 10.00
398 Ryan Doumit AU A RC 4.00 10.00
399 Ron Calloway AU A RC 4.00 10.00
400 Taylor Buchholz AU A RC 4.00 10.00
401 Adam Roller AU A RC 4.00 10.00
402 Cole Barthel AU A RC 4.00 10.00
403 Kazuhisa Ishii SP RC 2.00 5.00
403A Kazuhisa Ishii AU B 30.00 50.00
404 So Taguchi SP RC 2.00 5.00
404A So Taguchi AU B 30.00 50.00
405 Chris Baker AU A RC 4.00 10.00

2002 Bowman Chrome Facsimile Autograph Variations

118 Taylor Buchholz 4.00 10.00
130 Chris Baker 4.00 10.00
189 Adam Roller 4.00 10.00
229 Ryan Raburn 6.00 15.00
231 Chris Snelling 4.00 10.00
233 Nate Field 4.00 10.00
237 Ron Calloway 4.00 10.00
239 Cole Barthel 4.00 10.00
244 Rob Henkel 4.00 10.00
251 Gavin Floyd 10.00 25.00
301 Jimmy Gobble 4.00 10.00
305 Brian Wolfe 4.00 10.00
313 Jesse Foppert 4.00 10.00
316 Joe Mauer 80.00 200.00
317 David Wright 60.00 150.00
323 Justin Reid 4.00 10.00
324 Jake Mauer 4.00 10.00
326 Josh Barfield 6.00 15.00

335 Bobby Jenks 6.00 15.00
338 Ryan Doumit 6.00 15.00

2002 Bowman Chrome Uncirculated

ONE EXCHANGE CARD PER BOX
AU EXCHANGE CARDS ARE HOBBY-ONLY
STATED PRINT RUN 350 SETS
AU STATED PRINT RUN 10 SETS
EXCHANGE DEADLINE 12/31/02
112 Chris Tritle 1.00 2.50
117 Noochie Varner 1.00 2.50
121 Hansel Izquierdo 1.00 2.50
123 Bill Hall 1.00 2.50
127 Scotty Layfield 1.00 2.50
129 Nic Jackson 1.00 2.50
131 Chad Qualls 1.50 4.00
153 Ruben Gotay 1.00 2.50
154 Tommy Marx 1.00 2.50
155 John Suomi 1.00 2.50
156 Javier Colina 1.00 2.50
157 Greg Sain 1.00 2.50
158 Robert Crosby 1.00 2.50
159 Angel Pagan 2.50 6.00
162 Shayne Wright 1.00 2.50
163 Jay Caliguiri 1.00 2.50
164 Greg Montalbano 1.00 2.50
165 Rich Harden 3.00 8.00
166 Rich Thompson 1.00 2.50
167 Fred Bastardo 1.00 2.50
168 Alejandro Giron 1.00 2.50
169 Jesus Medrano 1.00 2.50
170 Kevin Deaton 1.00 2.50
172 Jon Guzman 1.00 2.50
173 Gerard Oakes 1.00 2.50
174 Francisco Liriano 5.00 12.00
175 Matt Allegra 1.00 2.50
176 Mike Snyder 1.00 2.50
178 Anderson Hernandez 1.00 2.50
179 Dan Trumble 1.00 2.50
180 Luis DePaula 1.00 2.50
181 Randall Shelley 1.00 2.50
182 Richard Lane 1.00 2.50
183 Antwon Rollins 1.00 2.50
184 Ryan Bukvich 1.00 2.50
185 Derrick Lewis 1.00 2.50
186 Eric Miller 1.00 2.50
187 Justin Schuda 1.00 2.50
188 Brian West 1.00 2.50
190 Neal Frendling 1.00 2.50
191 Jeremy Hill 1.00 2.50
192 James Barrett 1.00 2.50
193 Brett Kay 1.00 2.50
194 Ryan Mottl 1.00 2.50
195 Brad Nelson 1.00 2.50
196 Juan M. Gonzalez 1.00 2.50
197 Curtis Legendre 1.00 2.50
198 Ronald Acuna 1.00 2.50
199 Chris Flinn 1.00 2.50
200 Nick Alvarez 1.00 2.50
201 Jason Ellison 1.00 2.50
202 Blake McGinley 1.00 2.50
203 Dan Phillips 1.00 2.50
204 Demetrius Heath 1.00 2.50
205 Eric Bruntlett 1.00 2.50
206 Joe Jiannetti 1.00 2.50
207 Mike Hill 1.00 2.50
208 Ricardo Cordova 1.00 2.50
209 Mark Hamilton 1.00 2.50
210 David Mattox 1.00 2.50
211 Jose Morban 1.00 2.50
212 Scott Wiggins 1.00 2.50
214 Brian Rogers 1.00 2.50
216 Anastacio Martinez 1.00 2.50
218 Tim Kalita 1.00 2.50
219 Edwin Almonte 1.00 2.50
222 Victor Alvarez 1.00 2.50
224 Jeff Austin 1.00 2.50
225 Clint Weibl 1.00 2.50
227 Marlyn Tisdale 1.00 2.50
230 Raul Chavez 1.00 2.50
232 Joe Rogers 1.00 2.50
235 Matt Childers 1.00 2.50
242 Ben Howard 1.00 2.50
243 Eric Glaser 1.00 2.50
245 Jose Valverde 1.50 4.00
248 Brian Mallette 1.00 2.50
249 Chone Figgins 1.50 4.00
250 Jimmy Alvarez 1.00 2.50
252 Josh Bonifay 1.00 2.50
253 Garrett Guzman 1.00 2.50
254 Jeff Verplancke 1.00 2.50
255 Nate Espy 1.00 2.50
256 Jeff Lincoln 1.00 2.50
257 Ryan Snare 1.00 2.50
263 Yurendell DeCaster 1.00 2.50
264 Mike Peeples 1.00 2.50
267 Jorge Padilla 1.00 2.50
268 Joe Jester 1.00 2.50
269 Ryan Church 1.00 2.50
271 Travis Foley 1.00 2.50
277 Brian Forystek 1.00 2.50
279 Manny Delcarmen 1.00 2.50
280 Jim Kavourias 1.00 2.50
283 Joey Hammond 1.00 2.50
286 Ezequiel Astacio 1.00 2.50
287 Edwin Yan 1.00 2.50
288 Chris Duffy 1.00 2.50
293 Chris Narveson 1.00 2.50
295 Mike Wilson 1.00 2.50
296 Justin Sherrod 1.00 2.50
299 Brett Roneberg 1.00 2.50
300 Trey Lunsford 1.00 2.50
307 Koyie Hill 1.00 2.50
308 Tony Fontana 1.00 2.50
310 Doug Sessions 1.00 2.50
311 Josh Cisneros 1.00 2.50
312 Carlos Brackley 1.00 2.50
314 Ross Peeples 1.00 2.50
315 Alex Requena 1.00 2.50
318 Craig Kuzmic 1.00 2.50
319 Pete Zamora 1.00 2.50
320 Matt Parker 1.00 2.50
322 Gary Cates Jr. 1.00 2.50
327 Henry Pichardo 1.00 2.50
328 Michael Floyd 1.00 2.50
329 Clint Nageotte 1.00 2.50
330 Raymond Cabrera 1.00 2.50
331 Mauricio Lara 1.00 2.50
332 Alejandro Cadena 1.00 2.50
333 Jonny Gomes 3.00 8.00
334 Jason Bulger 1.00 2.50
336 David Gil 1.00 2.50
337 Joel Crump 1.00 2.50
342 Freddie Money 1.00 2.50
343 Cliff Bartosh 1.00 2.50
344 Terrance Hill 1.00 2.50
345 John Rodriguez 1.00 2.50
346 Chris Latham 1.00 2.50
347 Carlos Cabrera 1.00 2.50
348 Jose Bautista 8.00 20.00
349 Kevin Frederick 1.00 2.50
351 Napolean Calzado 1.00 2.50
352 Benito Baez 1.00 2.50
354 Jason Botts 1.00 2.50
355 Steve Bechler 1.00 2.50
356 Reed Johnson 1.50 4.00
357 Mark Outlaw 1.00 2.50
359 Josh Shaffer 1.00 2.50
360 Dan Wright 1.00 2.50
361 Ryan Gripp 1.00 2.50
362 Nelson Castro 1.00 2.50
363 Jason Bay 5.00 12.00
364 Franklyn German 1.00 2.50
365 Corwin Malone 1.00 2.50
366 Kelly Ramos 1.00 2.50
367 John Ennis 1.00 2.50
368 George Perez 1.00 2.50
369 Rene Reyes 1.00 2.50
370 Rolando Viera 1.00 2.50
371 Earl Snyder 1.00 2.50
372 Kyle Kane 1.00 2.50
373 Mario Ramos 1.00 2.50
374 Tyler Yates 1.00 2.50
375 Jason Young 1.00 2.50
376 Chris Bootcheck 1.00 2.50
377 Jesus Cota 1.00 2.50
378 Corky Miller 1.00 2.50
379 Matt Erickson 1.00 2.50
380 Justin Huber 1.00 2.50
381 Felix Escalona 1.00 2.50
382 Kevin Cash 1.00 2.50
383 J.J. Putz 1.50 4.00
403 Kazuhisa Ishii 1.50 4.00
404 So Taguchi 1.50 4.00

2002 Bowman Chrome Refractors

*REF RED: 1.5X TO 4X BASIC
*REF BLUE: 2.5X TO 6X BASIC
*REF BLUE SP: .6X TO 1.5X BASIC
*REF AU: .5X TO 1.2X BASIC AU'S
1-383/403-404 ODDS 1:6
324B/384-405 GROUP A AUTO ODDS 1:88
403-404 GROUP B AUTO ODDS 1:4392
324B/384-405 OVERALL AUTO ODDS 1:86
1-383/403-404 PRINT 500 SERIAL #'d SETS
324B/384-405 GROUP A PRINT RUN 500 SETS
403-404 GROUP B PRINT RUN 100 SETS
403 Kazuhisa Ishii AU B 40.00 80.00
404 So Taguchi AU B 30.00 60.00

2002 Bowman Chrome Gold Refractors

*GOLD REF RED: 5X TO 12X BASIC
*GOLD REF BLUE: 5X TO 12X BASIC
*GOLD REF BLUE SP: 1.2X TO 3X BASIC
*GOLD REF AU: 1.5X TO 4X BASIC
1-383/403-404 ODDS 1:56
384-405 GROUP A AUTO ODDS 1:879
403-404 GROUP B AUTO ODDS 1:59,616
324B/384-405 OVERALL AUTO ODDS 1:866
1-383/403-404 PRINT 50 SERIAL #'d SETS
324B/384-405 GROUP A AU PRINT 50 SETS
403-404 GROUP B AU PRINT RUN 10 SETS
NO GROUP B AU PRICING DUE TO SCARCITY
174 Francisco Liriano 100.00 200.00
241 Chase Utley 60.00 120.00
348 Jose Bautista 100.00 200.00
363 Jason Bay 100.00 200.00
391 Joe Mauer AU A 600.00 800.00

2002 Bowman Chrome X-Fractors

*XFRACT RED: 3X TO 8X BASIC
*XFRACT BLUE: 3X TO 8X BASIC
*XFRACT BLUE SP: .75X TO 2X BASIC
*XFRACT AU: .75X TO 2X BASIC
1-383/403-404 ODDS 1:10
324B/384-405 GROUP A AUTO ODDS 1:176
403-404 GROUP B AUTO ODDS 1:9072
324B/384-405 OVERALL AUTO ODDS 1:173
1-383/403-404 PRINT RUN 250 SERIAL #'d SETS
324B/384-405 GROUP A PRINT RUN 250 SETS
403-404 GROUP B PRINT RUN 50 SETS
403 Kazuhisa Ishii AU B 60.00 100.00
404 So Taguchi AU B 60.00 100.00

2002 Bowman Chrome Reprints

Isssued at stated odds of one in six, these 20 cards feature reprint cards of players who have made their debut since Bowman was reintroduced as a major brand in 1989.

COMPLETE SET (20) 10.00 25.00
STATED ODDS 1:6
*BLACK REF: .6X TO 1.5X BASIC REPRINTS
BLACK REFRACTOR ODDS 1:18
BCRAJ Andruw Jones 95 .75 2.00
BCRBC Bartolo Colon 95 .75 2.00
BCRBW Bernie Williams 90 .75 2.00
BCRCD Carlos Delgado 92 .75 2.00
BCRCJ Chipper Jones 91 1.00 2.50
BCRDJ Derek Jeter 93 3.00 8.00
BCRFT Frank Thomas 90 1.00 2.50
BCRGS Gary Sheffield 89 .75 2.00
BCRIR Ivan Rodriguez 91 .75 2.00
BCRJB Jeff Bagwell 91 .75 2.00
BCRJG Juan Gonzalez 90 .75 2.00
BCRJK Jason Kendall 93 .75 2.00
BCRJP Jorge Posada 94 .75 2.00
BCRKG Ken Griffey Jr. 89 2.50 6.00
BCRLG Luis Gonzalez 91 .75 2.00
BCRLW Larry Walker 90 .75 2.00
BCRMP Mike Piazza 92 2.00 5.00
BCRMS Mike Sweeney 96 .75 2.00
BCRSR Scott Rolen 95 .75 2.00
BCRVG Vladimir Guerrero 95 1.00 2.50

2002 Bowman Chrome Draft

Inserted two per Bowman Draft pack, this is a parallel to the Bowman Draft Pick set. Each of these cards uses the Topps "Chrome" technology and these cards were inserted two per bowman draft pack. Cards numbered 166 through 175 are not parallels to the regular Bowman cards and they feature autographs of the players. Those ten cards were issued at a stated rate of one in 45 Bowman Draft packs.

COMPLETE SET (175) 125.00 300.00
COMP.SET w/o AU'S (165) 40.00 100.00
1-165 TWO PER BOWMAN DRAFT PACK
166-175 AU ODDS 1:45 BOWMAN DRAFT
1 Clint Everts RC .40 1.00
2 Fred Lewis RC .40 1.00
3 Jon Broxton RC 1.00 2.50
4 Jason Anderson RC .40 1.00
5 Mike Eusebio RC .40 1.00
6 Zack Greinke RC 6.00 15.00
7 Joe Blanton RC .60 1.50
8 Sergio Santos RC .40 1.00
9 Jason Cooper RC .40 1.00
10 Delwyn Young RC .40 1.00
11 Jeremy Hermida RC .60 1.50
12 Dan Ortmeier RC .40 1.00
13 Kevin Jepsen RC .40 1.00
14 Russ Adams RC .40 1.00
15 Mike Nixon RC .40 1.00
16 Nick Swisher RC 2.50 6.00
17 Cole Hamels RC 5.00 12.00
18 Brian Dopirak RC .40 1.00
19 James Loney RC 1.00 2.50
20 Denard Span RC .60 1.50
21 Billy Petrick RC .40 1.00
22 Jared Doyle RC .40 1.00
23 Jeff Francoeur RC 2.50 6.00
24 Nick Bourgeois RC .40 1.00
25 Matt Cain RC 2.50 6.00
26 John McCurdy RC .40 1.00
27 Mark Kiger RC .40 1.00
28 Bill Murphy RC .40 1.00
29 Matt Craig RC .40 1.00
30 Mike Megrew RC .40 1.00
31 Ben Crockett RC .40 1.00
32 Luke Hagerty RC .40 1.00
33 Matt Whitney RC .40 1.00
34 Dan Meyer RC .40 1.00
35 Jeremy Brown RC .40 1.00
36 Doug Johnson RC .40 1.00
37 Steve Obenchain RC .40 1.00
38 Matt Clanton RC .40 1.00
39 Mark Teahen RC .40 1.00
40 Tom Carrow RC .40 1.00
41 Micah Schilling RC .40 1.00
42 Blair Johnson RC .40 1.00
43 Jason Pridie RC .40 1.00
44 Joey Votto RC 25.00 60.00
45 Taber Lee RC .40 1.00
46 Adam Peterson RC .40 1.00
47 Adam Donachie RC .40 1.00
48 Josh Murray RC .40 1.00
49 Brent Clevlen RC .40 1.00
50 Chad Pleiness RC .40 1.00
51 Zach Hammes RC .40 1.00
52 Chris Snyder RC .40 1.00
53 Chris Smith RC .40 1.00
54 Justin Maureau RC .40 1.00
55 David Bush RC .40 1.00
56 Tim Gilhooly RC .40 1.00
57 Blair Barbier RC .40 1.00
58 Zach Segovia RC .40 1.00
59 Jeremy Reed RC .40 1.00
60 Matt Pender RC .40 1.00
61 Eric Thomas RC .40 1.00
62 Justin Jones RC .40 1.00
63 Brian Slocum RC .40 1.00
64 Larry Broadway RC .40 1.00
65 Bo Flowers RC .40 1.00
66 Scott White RC .40 1.00
67 Steve Stanley RC .40 1.00
68 Alex Merricks RC .40 1.00
69 Josh Womack RC .40 1.00
70 Dave Jensen RC .40 1.00
71 Curtis Granderson RC 5.00 12.00
72 Pat Osborn RC .40 1.00
73 Nic Carter RC .40 1.00
74 Mitch Talbot RC .40 1.00
75 Don Murphy RC .40 1.00
76 Val Majewski RC .40 1.00
77 Javy Rodriguez RC .40 1.00
78 Fernando Pacheco RC .40 1.00
79 Steve Russell RC .40 1.00
80 Jon Slack RC .40 1.00
81 John Baker RC .40 1.00
82 Aaron Coonrod RC .40 1.00
83 Josh Johnson RC 2.50 6.00
84 Jake Blalock RC .40 1.00
85 Alex Hart RC .40 1.00
86 Wes Bankston RC .40 1.00
87 Josh Rupe RC .40 1.00
88 Dan Cevette RC .40 1.00
89 Kiel Fisher RC .40 1.00
90 Alan Rick RC .40 1.00
91 Charlie Morton RC 3.00 8.00
92 Chad Spann RC .40 1.00
93 Kyle Boyer RC .40 1.00
94 Bob Malek RC .40 1.00
95 Ryan Rodriguez RC .40 1.00
96 Jordan Renz RC .40 1.00
97 Randy Frye RC .40 1.00
98 Rich Hill RC 1.00 2.50
99 B.J. Upton RC 2.00 5.00
100 Dan Christensen RC .40 1.00
101 Casey Kotchman RC .60 1.50
102 Eric Good RC .40 1.00
103 Mike Fontenot RC .40 1.00
104 John Webb RC .40 1.00
105 Jason Dubois RC .40 1.00
106 Ryan Kibler RC .40 1.00
107 Jhonny Peralta RC .60 1.50
108 Kirk Saarloos RC .40 1.00
109 Rhett Parrott RC .40 1.00
110 Jason Grove RC .40 1.00
111 Colt Griffin RC .40 1.00
112 Dallas McPherson RC .40 1.00
113 Oliver Perez RC 1.00 2.50
114 Marshall McDougall RC .40 1.00
115 Mike Wood RC .40 1.00
116 Scott Hairston RC .40 1.00
117 Jason Simontacchi RC .40 1.00
118 Taggert Bozied RC .40 1.00
119 Shelley Duncan RC 1.00 2.50
120 Dontrelle Willis RC 1.00 2.50
121 Sean Burnett .15 .40
122 Aaron Cook .15 .40
123 Brett Evert .15 .40
124 Jimmy Journell .15 .40
125 Brett Myers .15 .40
126 Brad Baker .15 .40
127 Billy Traber RC .40 1.00
128 Adam Wainwright .25 .60
129 Jason Young .15 .40
130 John Buck .40 1.00
131 Kevin Cash .15 .40
132 Jason Stokes RC .40 1.00
133 Drew Henson .15 .40
134 Chad Tracy RC .60 1.50
135 Orlando Hudson .15 .40
136 Brandon Phillips .15 .40
137 Joe Borchard .15 .40
138 Marlon Byrd .15 .40
139 Carl Crawford .25 .60
140 Michael Restovich .15 .40
141 Corey Hart RC 2.00 5.00
142 Edwin Almonte .15 .40
143 Francis Beltran RC .40 1.00
144 Jorge De La Rosa RC .40 1.00
145 Gerardo Garcia RC .40 1.00
146 Franklyn German RC .40 1.00
147 Francisco Liriano .75 2.00
148 Francisco Rodriguez .25 .60
149 Ricardo Rodriguez .15 .40
150 Seung Song .15 .40
151 John Stephens .15 .40
152 Justin Huber RC .40 1.00
153 Victor Martinez .25 .60
154 Hee Seop Choi .15 .40
155 Justin Morneau .40 1.00
156 Miguel Cabrera 4.00 10.00
157 Victor Diaz RC .40 1.00
158 Jose Reyes .40 1.00
159 Omar Infante .40 1.00
160 Angel Berroa .15 .40
161 Tony Alvarez .15 .40
162 Shin Soo Choo RC 3.00 8.00
163 Wily Mo Pena .15 .40
164 Andres Torres .15 .40
165 Jose Lopez RC .60 1.50
166 Scott Moore AU RC 4.00 10.00
167 Chris Gruler AU RC 4.00 10.00
168 Joe Saunders AU RC 4.00 10.00
169 Jeff Francis AU RC 4.00 10.00
170 Royce Ring AU RC 4.00 10.00
171 Greg Miller AU RC 4.00 10.00
172 Brandon Weeden AU RC 6.00 15.00
173 Drew Meyer AU RC 4.00 10.00
174 Khalil Greene AU RC 4.00 10.00
175 Mark Schramek AU RC 4.00 10.00

2002 Bowman Chrome Draft Refractors

*REFRACTOR 1-165: 4X TO 10X BASIC
*REFRACTOR RC 1-165: 1.5X TO 4X BASIC
*REFRACTOR 166-175: .5X TO 1.2X BASIC
1-165 ODDS 1:11 BOWMAN DRAFT
166-175 AU ODDS 1:154 BOWMAN DRAFT
1-165 PRINT RUN 300 SERIAL #'d SETS
166-175 ARE NOT SERIAL NUMBERED

2002 Bowman Chrome Draft Gold Refractors

*GOLD REF 1-165: 10X TO 25X BASIC
*GOLD REF RC 1-165: 4X TO 10X BASIC
1-165 ODDS 1:67 BOWMAN DRAFT
166-175 AU ODDS 1:1546 BOWMAN DRAFT
1-165 PRINT RUN 50 SERIAL #'d SETS
166-175 ARE NOT SERIAL-NUMBERED
166-175 NO PRICING DUE TO SCARCITY
23 Jeff Francoeur 75.00 150.00
25 Matt Cain 250.00 500.00
44 Joey Votto 800.00 1200.00
156 Miguel Cabrera 50.00 125.00

2002 Bowman Chrome Draft X-Fractors

*X-FRACTOR 1-165: 6X TO 15X BASIC
*X-FRACTOR RC 1-165: 3X TO 6X BASIC
*X-FRACTOR 166-175: .75X TO 1.5X BASIC
1-165 ODDS 1:22 BOWMAN DRAFT
166-175 AU ODDS 1:309 BOWMAN DRAFT
1-165 PRINT RUN 150 SERIAL #'d SETS
166-175 ARE NOT SERIAL-NUMBERED
156 Miguel Cabrera 30.00 80.00

2003 Bowman Chrome

This 351 card set was released in July, 2003. The set was issued in four-card packs with an $4 SRP which came 18 to a box and 12 boxes to a case. Cards numbered 1 through 165 feature veteran players while cards 166 through 330 feature rookie players. Cards numbered 331 through 350 feature autograph cards of Rookie Cards. Each of those cards, with the exception of Jose Contreras (number 332) was issued to a stated print run of 1700 sets and were seeded at a stated rate of one in 26. The Contreras card was issued to a stated print run of 340 cards and was issued at a stated rate of one in 3,3351 packs. The final card of the set features baseball legend Willie Mays. That card was issued as a box-loader and an authentic autograph on that card was also randomly inserted into packs. The autograph card was inserted at a stated rate of one in 384 box loader packs and was issued to a stated print run of 150 sets. Bryan Bullington did not return his cards in time for pack out and those cards could be redeemed until July 31st, 2005.

COMPLETE SET (351) 300.00 500.00
COMP.SET w/o AU's (331) 75.00 150.00
COMMON CARD (1-165) .20 .50
COMMON CARD (166-330) .20 .50
COMMON RC (156-330) .40 1.00
331/333-350 AU A STATED ODDS 1:26
331/333-350 AU A PRINT RUN 1700 SETS
AU A CARDS ARE NOT SERIAL-NUMBERED
AU A EXCH.DEADLINE 07/31/05
332 AU B STATED ODDS 1:3351
332 AU B PRINT RUN 340 CARDS
AU B IS NOT SERIAL-NUMBERED
COMP.SET w/o AU'S INCLUDES 351 MAYS
MAYS ODDS ONE PER BOX LOADER PACK
MAYS AU ODDS 1:384 BOX LOADER PACKS
MAYS AU PRINT RUN 150 CARDS
MAYS AU IS NOT-SERIAL-NUMBERED
MAYS AU IS NOT PART OF 351-CARD SET
1 Garret Anderson .20 .50
2 Derek Jeter 1.25 3.00
3 Gary Sheffield .20 .50
4 Matt Morris .20 .50
5 Derek Lowe .20 .50
6 Andy Van Hekken .20 .50
7 Sammy Sosa .50 1.25
8 Ken Griffey Jr. 1.00 2.50
9 Omar Vizquel .30 .75
10 Jorge Posada .30 .75
11 Lance Berkman .30 .75
12 Mike Sweeney .20 .50
13 Adrian Beltre .50 1.25
14 Richie Sexson .20 .50
15 A.J. Pierzynski .20 .50
16 Bartolo Colon .20 .50
17 Mike Mussina .30 .75
18 Paul Byrd .20 .50
19 Bobby Abreu .20 .50
20 Miguel Tejada .30 .75
21 Aramis Ramirez .20 .50
22 Edgardo Alfonzo .20 .50
23 Edgar Martinez .30 .75
24 Albert Pujols .60 1.50
25 Carl Crawford .30 .75
26 Eric Hinske .20 .50
27 Tim Salmon .20 .50
28 Luis Gonzalez .20 .50
29 Jay Gibbons .20 .50
30 John Smoltz .50 1.25
31 Tim Wakefield .30 .75
32 Mark Prior .30 .75
33 Magglio Ordonez .30 .75
34 Adam Dunn .30 .75
35 Larry Walker .30 .75
36 Luis Castillo .20 .50
37 Wade Miller .20 .50
38 Carlos Beltran .30 .75
39 Odalis Perez .20 .50
40 Alex Sanchez .20 .50
41 Torii Hunter .20 .50
42 Cliff Floyd .20 .50
43 Andy Pettitte .30 .75
44 Francisco Rodriguez .30 .75
45 Eric Chavez .20 .50
46 Kevin Millwood .20 .50
47 Dennis Tankersley .20 .50
48 Hideo Nomo .50 1.25
49 Freddy Garcia .20 .50
50 Randy Johnson .50 1.25
51 Aubrey Huff .20 .50
52 Carlos Delgado .20 .50
53 Troy Glaus .20 .50
54 Junior Spivey .20 .50
55 Mike Hampton .20 .50
56 Sidney Ponson .20 .50
57 Aaron Boone .20 .50
58 Kerry Wood .20 .50
59 Willie Harris .20 .50
60 Nomar Garciaparra .30 .75
61 Todd Helton .30 .75
62 Mike Lowell .20 .50
63 Roy Oswalt .30 .75
64 Raul Ibanez .30 .75
65 Brian Jordan .20 .50
66 Geoff Jenkins .20 .50
67 Jermaine Dye .20 .50
68 Tom Glavine .30 .75
69 Bernie Williams .30 .75
70 Vladimir Guerrero .30 .75
71 Mark Mulder .20 .50
72 Jimmy Rollins .30 .75
73 Oliver Perez .20 .50
74 Rich Aurilia .20 .50
75 Joel Pineiro .20 .50
76 J.D. Drew .20 .50
77 Ivan Rodriguez .30 .75
78 Josh Phelps .20 .50
79 Darin Erstad .20 .50
80 Curt Schilling .30 .75
81 Paul Lo Duca .20 .50
82 Marty Cordova .20 .50
83 Manny Ramirez .50 1.25
84 Bobby Hill .20 .50
85 Paul Konerko .30 .75
86 Austin Kearns .20 .50
87 Jason Jennings .20 .50
88 Brad Penny .20 .50
89 Jeff Bagwell .30 .75
90 Shawn Green .20 .50
91 Jason Schmidt .20 .50
92 Doug Mientkiewicz .20 .50
93 Jose Vidro .20 .50
94 Bret Boone .20 .50
95 Jason Giambi .20 .50
96 Barry Zito .30 .75
97 Roy Halladay .30 .75
98 Pat Burrell .20 .50
99 Sean Burroughs .20 .50
100 Barry Bonds .75 2.00
101 Kazuhiro Sasaki .20 .50
102 Fernando Vina .20 .50
103 Chan Ho Park .30 .75
104 Andruw Jones .20 .50
105 Adam Kennedy .20 .50
106 Shea Hillenbrand .20 .50
107 Greg Maddux .60 1.50
108 Jim Edmonds .30 .75
109 Pedro Martinez .30 .75
110 Moises Alou .20 .50
111 Jeff Weaver .20 .50
112 C.C. Sabathia .30 .75
113 Robert Fick .20 .50
114 A.J. Burnett .20 .50
115 Jeff Kent .20 .50
116 Kevin Brown .20 .50
117 Rafael Furcal .20 .50
118 Cristian Guzman .20 .50
119 Brad Wilkerson .20 .50
120 Mike Piazza .50 1.25
121 Alfonso Soriano .30 .75
122 Mark Ellis .20 .50
123 Vicente Padilla .20 .50
124 Eric Gagne .20 .50
125 Ryan Klesko .20 .50
126 Ichiro Suzuki .60 1.50
127 Tony Batista .20 .50
128 Roberto Alomar .30 .75
129 Alex Rodriguez .60 1.50
130 Jim Thome .30 .75
131 Jarrod Washburn .20 .50
132 Orlando Hudson .20 .50
133 Chipper Jones .50 1.25
134 Rodrigo Lopez .20 .50
135 Johnny Damon .30 .75
136 Matt Clement .20 .50
137 Frank Thomas .50 1.25
138 Ellis Burks .20 .50
139 Carlos Pena .30 .75
140 Josh Beckett .20 .50
141 Joe Randa .20 .50
142 Brian Giles .20 .50
143 Kazuhisa Ishii .20 .50
144 Corey Koskie .20 .50
145 Orlando Cabrera .20 .50
146 Mark Buehrle .30 .75
147 Roger Clemens .60 1.50
148 Tim Hudson .30 .75
149 Randy Wolf .20 .50
150 Josh Fogg .20 .50
151 Phil Nevin .20 .50
152 John Olerud .20 .50
153 Scott Rolen .30 .75
154 Joe Kennedy .20 .50
155 Rafael Palmeiro .30 .75
156 Chad Hutchinson .20 .50
157 Quincy Carter XRC .40 1.00
158 Hee Seop Choi .20 .50
159 Joe Borchard .20 .50
160 Brandon Phillips .20 .50
161 Wily Mo Pena .20 .50
162 Victor Martinez .30 .75
163 Jason Stokes .20 .50
164 Ken Harvey .20 .50
165 Juan Rivera .20 .50
166 Joe Valentine RC .40 1.00
167 Dan Haren RC 2.00 5.00
168 Michel Hernandez RC .40 1.00
169 Eider Torres RC .40 1.00
170 Chris De La Cruz RC .40 1.00
171 Ramon Nivar-Martinez RC .40 1.00
172 Mike Adams RC .60 1.50
173 Justin Arneson RC .40 1.00
174 Jamie Athas RC .40 1.00

175 Dwaine Bacon RC .40 1.00
176 Clint Barmes RC 1.00 2.50
177 B.J. Barns RC .40 1.00
178 Tyler Johnson RC .40 1.00
179 Brandon Webb RC 1.25 3.00
180 T.J. Bohn RC .40 1.00
181 Ozzie Chavez RC .40 1.00
182 Brandon Bowe RC .40 1.00
183 Craig Brazell RC .40 1.00
184 Dusty Brown RC .40 1.00
185 Brian Bruney RC .40 1.00
186 Greg Bruso RC .40 1.00
187 Jaime Bubela RC .40 1.00
188 Matt Diaz RC .60 1.50
189 Brian Burgamy RC .40 1.00
190 Eny Cabreja RC 1.50 4.00
191 Daniel Cabrera RC .60 1.50
192 Ryan Cameron RC .40 1.00
193 Lance Caracciolí RC .40 1.00
194 David Cash RC .40 1.00
195 Bernie Castro RC .40 1.00
196 Ismael Castro RC .40 1.00
197 Cory Doyne RC .40 1.00
198 Jeff Clark RC .40 1.00
199 Chris Colton RC .40 1.00
200 Dexter Cooper RC .40 1.00
201 Callix Crabbe RC .40 1.00
202 Chien-Ming Wang RC 1.50 4.00
203 Eric Crozier RC .40 1.00
204 Nook Logan RC .40 1.00
205 David DeJesus RC 1.00 2.50
206 Matt DeMarco RC .40 1.00
207 Chris Duncan RC 1.25 3.00
208 Eric Eckenstahler .20 .50
209 Willie Eyre RC .40 1.00
210 Evel Bastida-Martinez RC .40 1.00
211 Chris Fallon RC .40 1.00
212 Mike Flannery RC .40 1.00
213 Mike O'Keefe RC .40 1.00
214 Lew Ford RC .40 1.00
215 Kason Gabbard RC .40 1.00
216 Mike Gallo RC .40 1.00
217 Jairo Garcia RC .40 1.00
218 Angel Garcia RC .40 1.00
219 Michael Garciaparra RC .40 1.00
220 Jeremy Griffiths RC .40 1.00
221 Dusty Gomon RC .40 1.00
222 Bryan Grace RC .40 1.00
223 Tyson Graham RC .40 1.00
224 Henry Guerrero RC .40 1.00
225 Franklin Gutierrez RC 1.00 2.50
226 Carlos Guzman RC .40 1.00
227 Matthew Hagen RC .40 1.00
228 Josh Hall RC .40 1.00
229 Rob Hammock RC .40 1.00
230 Brendan Harris RC .40 1.00
231 Gary Harris RC .40 1.00
232 Clay Hensley RC .40 1.00
233 Michael Hinckley RC .40 1.00
234 Luis Hodge RC .40 1.00
235 Donnie Hood RC .40 1.00
236 Matt Hensley RC .40 1.00
237 Edwin Jackson RC .60 1.50
238 Ardley Jansen RC .40 1.00
239 Ferenc Jongejan RC .40 1.00
240 Matt Kata RC .40 1.00
241 Kazuhiro Takeoka RC .40 1.00
242 Charlie Manning RC .40 1.00
243 Il Kim RC .40 1.00
244 Brennan King RC .40 1.00
245 Chris Kroski RC .40 1.00
246 David Martinez RC .40 1.00
247 Pete LaForest RC .40 1.00
248 Wil Ledezma RC .40 1.00
249 Jeremy Bonderman RC 1.50 4.00
250 Gonzalo Lopez RC .40 1.00
251 Brian Luderer RC .40 1.00
252 Ruddy Lugo RC .40 1.00
253 Wayne Lydon RC .40 1.00
254 Mark Malaska RC .40 1.00
255 Andy Marte RC .40 1.00
256 Tyler Martin RC .40 1.00
257 Branden Florence RC .40 1.00
258 Aneudis Mateo RC .40 1.00
259 Derell McCall RC .40 1.00
260 Elizardo Ramirez RC .40 1.00
261 Mike McNutt RC .40 1.00
262 Jacobo Meque RC .40 1.00
263 Derek Michaelis RC .40 1.00
264 Aaron Miles RC .40 1.00
265 Jose Morales RC .40 1.00
266 Dustin Moseley RC .40 1.00
267 Adrian Myers RC .40 1.00
268 Dan Neil RC .40 1.00
269 Jon Nelson RC .40 1.00
270 Mike Neu RC .40 1.00
271 Leigh Neuage RC .40 1.00
272 Wes O'Brien RC .40 1.00
273 Trent Oeltjen RC .40 1.00
274 Tim Olson RC .40 1.00
275 David Pahucki RC .40 1.00
276 Nathan Panther RC .40 1.00
277 Arnie Munoz RC .40 1.00
278 Dave Pember RC .40 1.00
279 Jason Perry RC .40 1.00
280 Matthew Peterson RC .40 1.00
281 Greg Aquino RC .40 1.00
282 Jorge Piedra RC .40 1.00
283 Simon Pond RC .40 1.00
284 Aaron Rakers RC .40 1.00
285 Felix Sanchez RC .40 1.00
286 Manuel Ramirez RC .40 1.00
287 Kevin Randel RC .40 1.00
288 Kelly Shoppach RC .60 1.50
289 Prentice Redman RC .40 1.00
290 Eric Reed RC .40 1.00
291 Wilton Reynolds RC .40 1.00
292 Eric Riggs RC .40 1.00
293 Carlos Rijo RC .40 1.00
294 Tyler Adamczyk RC .40 1.00
295 Jon-Mark Sprowl RC .40 1.00
296 Arturo Rivas RC .40 1.00
297 Kyle Roat RC .40 1.00
298 Bubba Nelson RC .40 1.00
299 Levi Robinson RC .40 1.00
300 Ray Sadler RC .40 1.00
301 Rylan Reed RC .40 1.00
302 Jon Schuerholz RC .40 1.00
303 Nobuaki Yoshida RC .40 1.00
304 Brian Shackelford RC .40 1.00
305 Bill Simon RC .40 1.00
306 Haj Turay RC .40 1.00
307 Sean Smith RC .40 1.00
308 Ryan Spataro RC .40 1.00
309 Jemel Spearman RC .40 1.00
310 Keith Stamler RC .40 1.00
311 Luke Steidlmayer RC .40 1.00
312 Adam Stern RC .40 1.00
313 Jay Sitzman RC .40 1.00
314 Mike Wodnicki RC .40 1.00
315 Terry Tiffee RC .40 1.00
316 Nick Trzesniak RC .40 1.00
317 Denny Tussen RC .40 1.00
318 Scott Tyler RC .40 1.00
319 Shane Victorino RC 1.25 3.00
320 Doug Waechter RC .40 1.00
321 Brandon Watson RC .40 1.00
322 Todd Wellemeyer RC .40 1.00
323 Eli Whiteside RC .40 1.00
324 Josh Willingham RC 1.25 3.00
325 Travis Wong RC .40 1.00
326 Brian Wright RC .40 1.00
327 Felix Pie RC .60 1.50
328 Andy Sisco RC .40 1.00
329 Dustin Yount RC .40 1.00
330 Andrew Dominique RC .40 1.00
331 Brian McCann AU A RC 8.00 20.00
332 Jose Contreras AU B RC 12.50 30.00
333 Corey Shafer AU A RC 4.00 10.00
334 Hanley Ramirez AU A RC 10.00 25.00
335 Ryan Shealy AU A RC 4.00 10.00
336 Kevin Youkilis AU A RC 6.00 15.00
337 Jason Kubel AU A RC 4.00 10.00
338 Aron Weston AU A RC 4.00 10.00
339 J.D. Durbin AU A RC 4.00 10.00
340 Gary Schneidmiller AU A RC 4.00 10.00
341 Travis Ishikawa AU A RC 4.00 10.00
342 Ben Francisco AU A RC 4.00 10.00
343 Bobby Basham AU A RC 4.00 10.00
344 Joey Gomes AU A RC 4.00 10.00
345 Beau Kemp AU A RC 4.00 10.00
346 T.Story-Harden AU A RC 4.00 10.00
347 Daryl Clark AU A RC 4.00 10.00
348 Bryan Bullington AU A RC 4.00 10.00
349 Rajai Davis AU A RC 4.00 10.00
350 Darrell Rasner AU A RC 4.00 10.00
351 Willie Mays 1.00 2.50
351AU Willie Mays AU 150.00 300.00

2003 Bowman Chrome Refractors

*REF 1-155: 1.5X TO 4X BASIC
*REF 156-330: 1.5X TO 4X BASIC
*REF 156-330 RC'S: 1.5X TO 4X BASIC
1-330 STATED ODDS 1:4 HOBBY
*REF AU A 331/333-350: .5X TO 1.2X BASIC
AU A ODDS 1:92 HOBBY
AU A STATED PRINT RUN 500 SETS
AU A CARDS ARE NOT SERIAL-NUMBERED
AU A EXCH.DEADLINE 07/31/05
AU B ODDS 1:11,479 HOBBY
AU B STATED PRINT RUN 100 CARDS
AU B CARDS ARE NOT SERIAL-NUMBERED
*REF.MAYS: 2X TO 5X BASIC
REF.MAYS ODDS 1:12 BOX LOADER PACKS
332 Jose Contreras AU B 30.00 60.00

2003 Bowman Chrome Blue Refractors

*BLUE: 1.5X TO 4X BASIC
ONE EXCH.CARD PER BOX LOADER PACK
ONE BOX LOADER PACK PER HOBBY BOX
EXCHANGE DEADLINE 11/30/05
SEE WWW.THEPIT.COM FOR PRICING

2003 Bowman Chrome Gold Refractors

*GOLD REF 1-155: 3X TO 8X BASIC
*GOLD REF 156-330: 3X TO 8X BASIC
*GOLD REF RC'S 156-330: 3X TO 8X BASIC
1-330 ODDS ONE PER BOX LOADER PACK
1-330 PRINT RUN 170 SERIAL #'d SETS
AU A ODDS 1:1202 HOBBY
AU A STATED PRINT RUN 50 SETS
AU A CARDS ARE NOT SERIAL-NUMBERED
AU A EXCH.DEADLINE 07/31/05
AU B ODDS 1:177,606 HOBBY
AU B PRINT RUN 10 CARDS
AU B CARD IS NOT SERIAL-NUMBERED
NO AU B PRICING DUE TO SCARCITY
*GOLD MAYS: 6X TO 15X BASIC
GOLD MAYS ODDS 1:116 BOX LDR PACKS
SET EXCH.CARDS ODDS 1:78,936 HOBBY
SET EXCH.CARD PRINT RUN 10 CARDS
SET EXCHANGE CARD DEADLINE 11/30/05
331 Brian McCann AU A 100.00 250.00
333 Corey Shafer AU A 30.00 60.00
334 Hanley Ramirez AU A 100.00 250.00
335 Ryan Shealy AU A 30.00 60.00
337 Jason Kubel AU A 30.00 60.00
338 Aron Weston AU A 30.00 60.00
339 J.D. Durbin AU A 30.00 60.00
340 Gary Schneidmiller AU A 30.00 60.00
341 Travis Ishikawa AU A 30.00 60.00
342 Ben Francisco AU A 30.00 60.00
343 Bobby Basham AU A 30.00 60.00
344 Joey Gomes AU A 30.00 60.00
345 Beau Kemp AU A 30.00 60.00
346 Thomari Story-Harden AU A 30.00 60.00
347 Daryl Clark AU A 30.00 60.00
348 Bryan Bullington AU A 30.00 60.00
349 Rajai Davis AU A 30.00 60.00
350 Darrell Rasner AU A 30.00 60.00

2003 Bowman Chrome X-Fractors

*X-FR 1-155: 2.5X TO 6X BASIC
*X-FR 156-330: 2.5X TO 6X BASIC
*X-FR RC'S 156-330: 1.25X TO 3X BASIC
1-330 STATED ODDS 1:9 HOBBY
*X-FR AU A 331/333-350: .6X TO 1.5X BASIC
AU A ODDS 1:199 HOBBY
AU A STATED PRINT RUN 250 SETS
AU A CARDS ARE NOT SERIAL-NUMBERED
AU A EXCH.DEADLINE 07/31/05
AU B ODDS 1:22,959 HOBBY
AU B STATED PRINT RUN 50 CARDS
AU B CARD IS NOT SERIAL-NUMBERED
*X-FR MAYS: 4X TO 10X BASIC
X-FR MAYS ODDS 1:58 BOX LOADER PACKS
332 Jose Contreras AU B 40.00 80.00

2003 Bowman Chrome Draft

This 176-card set was inserted as part of the 2003 Bowman Draft Packs. Each pack contained 2 Bowman Chrome Cards numbered between 1-165. In addition, cards numbered 166 through 176 were inserted at a stated rate of one in 41 packs. Each of those cards can be easily idenitifed as they were autographed. Please note that these cards were issued as a mix of live and exchange cards with a deadline for redeeming the exchange cards of November 30, 2005.

COMPLETE SET (176) 400.00 550.00
COMP.SET w/o AU's (165) 30.00 60.00
COMMON CARD (1-165) .20 .50
COMMON RC .40 1.00
COMMON RC YR .20 .50
1-165 TWO PER BOWMAN DRAFT PACK
COMMON CARD (166-176) 4.00 10.00
166-176 STATED ODDS 1:41 H/R
168-176 ARE ALL PARTIAL LIVE/EXCH DIST.
168-176 EXCH.DEADLINE 11/30/05
LUBANSKI IS AN SP BY 1000 COPIES
1 Dontrelle Willis .20 .50
2 Freddy Sanchez .20 .50
3 Miguel Cabrera 2.50 6.00
4 Ryan Ludwick .20 .50
5 Ty Wigginton .20 .50
6 Mark Teixeira .30 .75
7 Trey Hodges .20 .50
8 Laynce Nix .20 .50
9 Antonio Perez .20 .50
10 Jody Gerut .20 .50
11 Jae Weong Seo .20 .50
12 Erick Almonte .20 .50
13 Lyle Overbay .20 .50
14 Billy Traber .20 .50
15 Andres Torres .20 .50
16 Jose Valverde .20 .50
17 Aaron Heilman .20 .50
18 Brandon Larson .20 .50
19 Jung Bong .20 .50
20 Jesse Foppert .20 .50
21 Angel Berroa .20 .50
22 Jeff DaVanon .20 .50
23 Kurt Ainsworth .20 .50
24 Brandon Claussen .20 .50
25 Xavier Nady .20 .50
26 Travis Hafner .20 .50
27 Jerome Williams .20 .50
28 Jose Reyes .50 1.25
29 Sergio Mitre RC .40 1.00
30 Bo Hart RC .40 1.00
31 Adam Miller RC 1.50 4.00
32 Brian Finch RC .40 1.00
33 Taylor Mattingly RC .40 1.00
34 Daric Barton RC .60 1.50
35 Chris Ray RC .60 1.50
36 Jarrod Saltalamacchia RC 2.00 5.00
37 Dennis Dove RC .40 1.00
38 James Houser RC .40 1.00
39 Clint King RC .40 1.00
40 Lou Palmisano RC .40 1.00
41 Dan Moore RC .40 1.00
42 Craig Stansberry RC .40 1.00
43 Jo Jo Reyes RC .40 1.00
44 Jake Stevens RC .40 1.00
45 Tom Gorzelanny RC .60 1.50
46 Brian Marshall RC .40 1.00
47 Scott Beerer RC .40 1.00
48 Javi Herrera RC .40 1.00
49 Steve LeRud RC .40 1.00
50 Josh Banks RC .40 1.00
51 Jon Papelbon RC 4.00 10.00
52 Juan Valdes RC .40 1.00
53 Beau Vaughan RC .40 1.00
54 Matt Chico RC .40 1.00
55 Todd Jennings RC .40 1.00
56 Anthony Gwynn RC .40 1.00
57 Matt Harrison RC 1.50 4.00
58 Aaron Marsden RC .40 1.00
59 Casey Abrams RC .40 1.00
60 Cory Stuart RC .40 1.00
61 Mike Wagner RC .40 1.00
62 Jordan Pratt RC .40 1.00
63 Andre Randolph RC .40 1.00
64 Blake Balkcom RC .40 1.00
65 Josh Muecke RC .40 1.00
66 Jamie D'Antona RC .40 1.00
67 Cole Seifrig RC .40 1.00
68 Josh Anderson RC .40 1.00
69 Matt Lorenzo RC .40 1.00
70 Nate Spears RC .40 1.00
71 Chris Goodman RC .40 1.00
72 Brian McFall RC .40 1.00
73 Billy Hogan RC .40 1.00
74 Jamie Romak RC .40 1.00
75 Jeff Cook RC .40 1.00
76 Brooks McNiven RC .40 1.00
77 Xavier Paul RC .40 1.00
78 Bob Zimmerman RC .40 1.00
79 Mickey Hall RC .40 1.00
80 Shaun Marcum RC .40 1.00
81 Matt Nachreiner RC .40 1.00
82 Chris Kinsey RC .40 1.00
83 Jonathan Fulton RC .40 1.00
84 Edgardo Baez RC .40 1.00
85 Robert Valido RC .40 1.00
86 Kenny Lewis RC .40 1.00
87 Trent Peterson RC .40 1.00
88 Johnny Woodard RC .40 1.00
89 Wes Littleton RC .40 1.00
90 Sean Rodriguez RC .60 1.50
91 Kyle Pearson RC .40 1.00
92 Josh Rainwater RC .40 1.00
93 Travis Schlichting RC .40 1.00
94 Tim Battle RC .40 1.00
95 Aaron Hill RC 1.25 3.00
96 Bob McCrory RC .40 1.00
97 Rick Guarno RC .40 1.00
98 Brandon Yarbrough RC .40 1.00
99 Peter Stonard RC .40 1.00
100 Darin Downs RC .40 1.00
101 Matt Bruback RC .40 1.00
102 Danny Garcia RC .40 1.00
103 Cory Stewart RC .40 1.00
104 Ferdin Tejeda RC .40 1.00
105 Kade Johnson RC .40 1.00
106 Andrew Brown RC .40 1.00
107 Aquilino Lopez RC .40 1.00
108 Stephen Randolph RC .40 1.00
109 Dave Matranga RC .40 1.00
110 Dustin McGowan RC .40 1.00
111 Juan Camacho RC .40 1.00
112 Cliff Lee 1.25 3.00
113 Jeff Duncan RC .40 1.00
114 C.J. Wilson 1.50 4.00
115 Brandon Roberson RC .40 1.00
116 David Corrente RC .40 1.00
117 Kevin Beavers RC .40 1.00
118 Anthony Webster RC .40 1.00
119 Oscar Villarreal RC .40 1.00
120 Hong-Chih Kuo RC 2.00 5.00
121 Josh Barfield .20 .50
122 Denny Bautista .20 .50
123 Chris Burke RC .40 1.00
124 Robinson Cano RC 6.00 15.00
125 Jose Castillo .20 .50
126 Neal Cotts .20 .50
127 Jorge De La Rosa .20 .50
128 J.D. Durbin .20 .50
129 Edwin Encarnacion 1.50 4.00
130 Gavin Floyd .20 .50
131 Alexis Gomez .20 .50
132 Edgar Gonzalez RC .40 1.00
133 Khalil Greene .30 .75
134 Zack Greinke .50 1.25
135 Franklin Gutierrez .50 1.25
136 Rich Harden .30 .75
137 J.J. Hardy RC 3.00 8.00
138 Ryan Howard RC 3.00 8.00
139 Justin Huber .20 .50
140 David Kelton .20 .50
141 Dave Krynzel .20 .50
142 Pete LaForest .20 .50
143 Adam LaRoche .20 .50
144 Preston Larrison RC .40 1.00
145 John Maine RC .60 1.50
146 Andy Marte .20 .50
147 Jeff Mathis .20 .50
148 Joe Mauer .50 1.25
149 Clint Nageotte .20 .50
150 Chris Narveson .20 .50
151 Ramon Nivar .20 .50
152 Felix Pie .30 .75
153 Guillermo Quiroz RC .40 1.00
154 Rene Reyes .20 .50
155 Royce Ring .20 .50
156 Alexis Rios .20 .50
157 Grady Sizemore .30 .75
158 Stephen Smitherman .20 .50
159 Seung Song .20 .50
160 Scott Thorman .20 .50
161 Chad Tracy .20 .50
162 Chin-Hui Tsao .20 .50
163 John VanBenschoten .20 .50
164 Kevin Youkilis 1.25 3.00
165 Chien-Ming Wang .75 2.00
166 Chris Lubanski AU SP RC 4.00 10.00
167 Ryan Harvey AU RC 4.00 10.00
168 Matt Murton AU RC 4.00 10.00
169 Jay Sborz AU RC 4.00 10.00
170 Brandon Wood AU RC 5.00 12.00
171 Nick Markakis AU RC 25.00 60.00
172 Rickie Weeks AU RC 4.00 10.00
173 Eric Duncan AU RC 4.00 10.00
174 Chad Billingsley AU RC 4.00 10.00
175 Ryan Wagner AU RC 4.00 10.00
176 Delmon Young AU RC 4.00 10.00

2003 Bowman Chrome Draft Refractors

*REFRACTOR 1-165: 1.25X TO 3X BASIC
*REFRACTOR RC 1-165: .6X TO 1.5X BASIC
*REFRACTOR RC YR 1-165: .6X TO 1.5X BASIC
*REFRACTOR AU 166-176: .6X TO 1.5X BASIC
1-165 ODDS 1:11 BOWMAN DRAFT H/R
166-176 AU ODDS 1:196 BOW.DRAFT HOBBY
166-176 AU ODDS 1:197 BOW.DRAFT RETAIL
166-176 AU PRINT RUN 500 SETS
166-176 AU PRINT RUN PROVIDED BY TOPPS
166-176 AU'S ARE NOT SERIAL-NUMBERED
51 Jon Papelbon 15.00 40.00

2003 Bowman Chrome Draft Gold Refractors

*GOLD REF 1-165: 6X TO 15X BASIC
*GOLD REF RC 1-165: 3X TO 8X BASIC
*GOLD REF RC YR 1-165: 3X TO 8X BASIC
1-165 ODDS 1:98 BOWMAN DRAFT HOBBY
166-176 AU ODDS 1:1479 BOW.DRAFT HOBBY
1-165 PRINT RUN 50 SERIAL #'d SETS
166-176 AU PRINT RUN 50 SETS
166-176 AU PRINT RUN PROVIDED BY TOPPS
166-176 AU'S ARE NOT SERIAL-NUMBERED
GOLD.REF ARE HOBBY-ONLY DISTRIBUTION
51 Jon Papelbon 125.00 250.00
124 Robinson Cano 75.00 200.00
138 Ryan Howard 100.00 200.00

2003 Bowman Chrome Draft X-Fractors

*X-FRACTOR 1-165: 2.5X TO 6X BASIC
*X-FRACTOR RC 1-165: 1.25X TO 3X BASIC
*X-FRACTOR RC YR 1-165: 1.25X TO 3X BASIC
*X-FRACTOR AU 166-176: .75X TO 2X BASIC
1-165 ODDS 1:50 BOWMAN DRAFT HOBBY
1-165 ODDS 1:52 BOWMAN DRAFT RETAIL
166-176 AU ODDS 1:393 BOW.DRAFT HOBBY
166-176 AU ODDS 1:394 BOW.DRAFT RETAIL
1-165 PRINT RUN 130 SERIAL #'d SETS
166-176 AU PRINT RUN 250 SETS
166-176 AU PRINT RUN PROVIDED BY TOPPS
166-176 AU'S ARE NOT SERIAL-NUMBERED

2004 Bowman Chrome

This 350-card set was released in August, 2004. The set was issued in four card packs with an $4 SRP which came 18 packs and 12 boxes to a case. The first 144 cards feature veterans while cards numbered 145 through 165 feature leading prospects. Cards numbered 166 through 350 are all Rookie Cards with the last 20 cards of the set being autographed. The Autographed cards (331-350) were inserted at a stated rate of one in 25 with a stated print run of 2000 sets. The Bobby Brownlie cards were issued as exchange cards with a stated expiry date of August 31, 2006.

COMPLETE SET (350) 150.00 300.00
COMP.SET w/o AU's (330) 30.00 60.00
COMMON CARD (1-150) .20 .50
COMMON CARD (151-165) .20 .50
COMMON CARD (166-330) .40 1.00
COMMON AUTO (331-350) 4.00 10.00
331-350 AU STATED ODDS 1:25
331-350 AU PRINT RUN 2000 SETS
331-350 AU'S ARE NOT SERIAL-NUMBERED
331-350 PRINT RUN PROVIDED BY TOPPS
EXCHANGE DEADLINE 08/31/06
1 Garret Anderson .20 .50
2 Larry Walker .30 .75
3 Derek Jeter 1.25 3.00
4 Curt Schilling .30 .75
5 Carlos Zambrano .30 .75
6 Shawn Green .20 .50
7 Manny Ramirez .50 1.25
8 Randy Johnson .50 1.25
9 Jeremy Bonderman .20 .50
10 Alfonso Soriano .30 .75
11 Scott Rolen .30 .75
12 Kerry Wood .20 .50
13 Eric Gagne .20 .50
14 Ryan Klesko .20 .50
15 Kevin Millar .20 .50
16 Ty Wigginton .20 .50
17 David Ortiz .50 1.25
18 Luis Castillo .20 .50
19 Bernie Williams .30 .75
20 Edgar Renteria .20 .50
21 Matt Kata .20 .50
22 Bartolo Colon .20 .50
23 Derrek Lee .20 .50
24 Gary Sheffield .20 .50
25 Nomar Garciaparra .30 .75
26 Kevin Millwood .20 .50
27 Corey Patterson .20 .50
28 Carlos Beltran .30 .75
29 Mike Lieberthal .20 .50
30 Troy Glaus .20 .50
31 Preston Wilson .20 .50
32 Jorge Posada .30 .75
33 Bo Hart .20 .50
34 Mark Prior .30 .75
35 Hideo Nomo .50 1.25
36 Jason Kendall .20 .50
37 Roger Clemens .60 1.50
38 Dmitri Young .20 .50
39 Jason Giambi .20 .50
40 Jim Edmonds .30 .75
41 Ryan Ludwick .20 .50
42 Brandon Webb .20 .50
43 Todd Helton .30 .75
44 Jacque Jones .20 .50
45 Jamie Moyer .20 .50
46 Tim Salmon .20 .50
47 Kelvim Escobar .20 .50
48 Tony Batista .20 .50
49 Nick Johnson .20 .50
50 Jim Thome .30 .75
51 Casey Blake .20 .50
52 Trot Nixon .20 .50
53 Luis Gonzalez .20 .50
54 Dontrelle Willis .20 .50
55 Mike Mussina .30 .75
56 Carl Crawford .30 .75
57 Mark Buehrle .30 .75
58 Scott Podsednik .20 .50
59 Brian Giles .20 .50
60 Rafael Furcal .20 .50
61 Miguel Cabrera .50 1.25
62 Rich Harden .20 .50
63 Mark Teixeira .30 .75
64 Frank Thomas .50 1.25
65 Johan Santana .30 .75
66 Jason Schmidt .20 .50
67 Aramis Ramirez .20 .50
68 Jose Reyes .30 .75
69 Magglio Ordonez .30 .75
70 Mike Sweeney .20 .50
71 Eric Chavez .20 .50
72 Rocco Baldelli .20 .50
73 Sammy Sosa .50 1.25
74 Javy Lopez .20 .50
75 Roy Oswalt .30 .75
76 Raul Ibanez .30 .75
77 Ivan Rodriguez .30 .75
78 Jerome Williams .20 .50
79 Carlos Lee .20 .50
80 Geoff Jenkins .20 .50
81 Sean Burroughs .20 .50
82 Marcus Giles .20 .50
83 Mike Lowell .20 .50
84 Barry Zito .30 .75
85 Aubrey Huff .20 .50
86 Esteban Loaiza .20 .50
87 Torii Hunter .20 .50
88 Phil Nevin .20 .50
89 Andruw Jones .20 .50
90 Josh Beckett .20 .50
91 Mark Mulder .20 .50
92 Hank Blalock .20 .50
93 Jason Phillips .20 .50
94 Russ Ortiz .20 .50
95 Juan Pierre .20 .50
96 Tom Glavine .30 .75
97 Gil Meche .20 .50
98 Ramon Ortiz .20 .50
99 Richie Sexson .20 .50
100 Albert Pujols .60 1.50
101 Javier Vazquez .20 .50
102 Johnny Damon .30 .75
103 Alex Rodriguez .60 1.50
104 Omar Vizquel .30 .75
105 Chipper Jones .50 1.25
106 Lance Berkman .30 .75
107 Tim Hudson .30 .75
108 Carlos Delgado .20 .50
109 Austin Kearns .20 .50
110 Orlando Cabrera .20 .50
111 Edgar Martinez .30 .75
112 Melvin Mora .20 .50
113 Jeff Bagwell .30 .75
114 Marlon Byrd .20 .50
115 Vernon Wells .20 .50
116 C.C. Sabathia .30 .75
117 Cliff Floyd .20 .50
118 Ichiro Suzuki .60 1.50
119 Miguel Olivo .20 .50
120 Mike Piazza .50 1.25
121 Adam Dunn .30 .75
122 Paul Lo Duca .20 .50
123 Brett Myers .20 .50
124 Michael Young .20 .50
125 Sidney Ponson .20 .50
126 Greg Maddux .60 1.50
127 Vladimir Guerrero .30 .75
128 Miguel Tejada .30 .75
129 Andy Pettitte .30 .75
130 Rafael Palmeiro .30 .75
131 Ken Griffey Jr. 1.00 2.50
132 Shannon Stewart .20 .50
133 Joel Pineiro .20 .50
134 Luis Matos .20 .50
135 Jeff Kent .20 .50
136 Randy Wolf .20 .50
137 Chris Woodward .20 .50
138 Jody Gerut .20 .50
139 Jose Vidro .20 .50
140 Bret Boone .20 .50
141 Bill Mueller .20 .50
142 Angel Berroa .20 .50
143 Bobby Abreu .20 .50
144 Roy Halladay .30 .75
145 Delmon Young .30 .75
146 Jonny Gomes .20 .50
147 Rickie Weeks .20 .50
148 Edwin Jackson .20 .50
149 Neal Cotts .20 .50
150 Jason Bay .30 .75
151 Khalil Greene .30 .75
152 Joe Mauer .40 1.00
153 Bobby Jenks .20 .50
154 Chin-Feng Chen .20 .50
155 Chien-Ming Wang .75 2.00
156 Mickey Hall .20 .50
157 James Houser .20 .50
158 Jay Sborz .20 .50
159 Jonathan Fulton .20 .50
160 Steven Lerud .20 .50
161 Grady Sizemore .30 .75
162 Felix Pie .20 .50
163 Dustin McGowan .20 .50
164 Chris Lubanski .20 .50
165 Tom Gorzelanny .20 .50
166 Rudy Guillen RC .40 1.00
167 Aarom Baldiris RC .40 1.00
168 Conor Jackson RC 1.25 3.00
169 Matt Moses RC .60 1.50
170 Ervin Santana RC 1.00 2.50
171 Merkin Valdez RC .40 1.00
172 Erick Aybar RC 1.00 2.50
173 Brad Sullivan RC .40 1.00
174 Joey Gathright RC .40 1.00
175 Brad Snyder RC .40 1.00
176 Alberto Callaspo RC 1.00 2.50
177 Brandon Medders RC .40 1.00
178 Zach Miner RC .60 1.50
179 Charlie Zink RC .40 1.00
180 Adam Greenberg RC 2.00 5.00
181 Kevin Howard RC .40 1.00
182 Wanell Severino RC .40 1.00
183 Chin-Lung Hu RC .40 1.00
184 Joel Zumaya RC 1.50 4.00
185 Skip Schumaker RC .60 1.50
186 Nic Ungs RC .40 1.00
187 Todd Self RC .40 1.00
188 Brian Steffek RC .40 1.00
189 Brock Peterson RC .40 1.00
190 Greg Thissen RC .40 1.00

191 Frank Brooks RC .40 1.00
192 Scott Olsen RC .40 1.00
193 Chris Mabeus RC .40 1.00
194 Dan Giese RC .40 1.00
195 Jared Wells RC .40 1.00
196 Carlos Sosa RC .40 1.00
197 Bobby Madritsch .40 1.00
198 Calvin Hayes RC .40 1.00
199 Omar Quintanilla RC .40 1.00
200 Chris O'Riordan RC .40 1.00
201 Tim Hutting RC .40 1.00
202 Carlos Quentin RC 1.50 4.00
203 Brayan Pena RC .40 1.00
204 Jeff Salazar RC .40 1.00
205 David Murphy RC .60 1.50
206 Alberto Garcia RC .40 1.00
207 Ramon Ramirez RC .40 1.00
208 Luis Bolivar RC .40 1.00
209 Rodney Choy Foo RC .40 1.00
210 Fausto Carmona RC .60 1.50
211 Anthony Acevedo RC .40 1.00
212 Chad Santos RC .40 1.00
213 Jason Frasor RC .40 1.00
214 Jesse Roman RC .40 1.00
215 James Tomlin RC .40 1.00
216 Josh Labandeira RC .40 1.00
217 Ryan Meaux RC .40 1.00
218 Don Sutton RC .40 1.00
219 Danny Gonzalez RC .40 1.00
220 Javier Guzman RC .40 1.00
221 Anthony Lerew RC .40 1.00
222 Jon Connolly RC .40 1.00
223 Jesse English RC .40 1.00
224 Hector Made RC .40 1.00
225 Travis Hanson RC .40 1.00
226 Jesse Floyd RC .40 1.00
227 Nick Gorneault RC .40 1.00
228 Craig Ansman RC .40 1.00
229 Paul McAnulty RC .40 1.00
230 Carl Loadenthal RC .40 1.00
231 Dave Crouthers RC .40 1.00
232 Harvey Garcia RC .40 1.00
233 Casey Kopitzke RC .40 1.00
234 Ricky Nolasco RC .60 1.50
235 Miguel Perez RC .40 1.00
236 Ryan Mulhern RC .40 1.00
237 Chris Aguila RC .40 1.00
238 Brooks Conrad RC .40 1.00
239 Damaso Espino RC .40 1.00
240 Jereme Milons RC .40 1.00
241 Luke Hughes RC 1.00 2.50
242 Kory Casto RC .40 1.00
243 Jose Valdez RC .40 1.00
244 J.T. Stotts RC .40 1.00
245 Lee Gwaltney RC .40 1.00
246 Yoann Torrealba RC .40 1.00
247 Omar Falcon RC .40 1.00
248 Jon Coutlangus RC .40 1.00
249 George Sherrill RC .40 1.00
250 John Santor RC .40 1.00
251 Tony Richie RC .40 1.00
252 Kevin Richardson RC .40 1.00
253 Tim Bittner RC .40 1.00
254 Chris Saenz RC .40 1.00
255 Jose Capellan RC .40 1.00
256 Donald Levinski RC .40 1.00
257 Jerome Gamble RC .40 1.00
258 Jeff Keppinger RC .60 1.50
259 Jason Szuminski RC .40 1.00
260 Akinori Otsuka RC .40 1.00
261 Ryan Budde RC .40 1.00
262 Marland Williams RC .40 1.00
263 Jeff Allison RC .40 1.00
264 Hector Gimenez RC .40 1.00
265 Tim Frend RC .40 1.00
266 Tom Farmer RC .40 1.00
267 Shawn Hill RC .40 1.00
268 Mike Huggins RC .40 1.00
269 Scott Proctor RC .40 1.00
270 Jorge Mejia RC .40 1.00
271 Terry Jones RC .40 1.00
272 Zach Duke RC .60 1.50
273 Jesse Crain RC .60 1.50
274 Luke Anderson RC .40 1.00
275 Hunter Brown RC .40 1.00
276 Matt Lemanczyk RC .40 1.00
277 Fernando Cortez RC .40 1.00
278 Vince Perkins RC .40 1.00
279 Tommy Murphy RC .40 1.00
280 Mike Gosling RC .40 1.00
281 Paul Bacot RC .40 1.00
282 Matt Capps RC .40 1.00
283 Juan Gutierrez RC .40 1.00
284 Teodoro Encarnacion RC .40 1.00
285 Chad Bentz RC .40 1.00
286 Kazuo Matsui RC .60 1.50
287 Ryan Hankins RC .40 1.00
288 Leo Nunez RC .40 1.00
289 Dave Wallace RC .40 1.00
290 Rob Tejeda RC .40 1.00
291 Paul Maholm RC .60 1.50
292 Casey Daigle RC .40 1.00
293 Tydus Meadows RC .40 1.00
294 Khalid Ballouli RC .40 1.00
295 Benji DeQuin RC .40 1.00
296 Tyler Davidson RC .40 1.00
297 Brant Colamarino RC .40 1.00
298 Marcus McBeth RC .40 1.00
299 Brad Eldred RC .40 1.00
300 David Pauley RC .60 1.50
301 Yadier Molina RC 15.00 40.00
302 Chris Shelton RC .40 1.00
303 Nyjer Morgan RC .40 1.00
304 Jon DeVries RC .40 1.00
305 Sheldon Fulse RC .40 1.00
306 Vito Chiaravalloti RC .40 1.00
307 Warner Madrigal RC .40 1.00
308 Reid Gorecki RC .40 1.00
309 Sung Jung RC .40 1.00
310 Pete Shier RC .40 1.00
311 Michael Mooney RC .40 1.00
312 Kenny Perez RC .40 1.00
313 Michael Mallory RC .40 1.00
314 Ben Himes RC .40 1.00
315 Ivan Ochoa RC .40 1.00
316 Donald Kelly RC .60 1.50
317 Tom Mastny RC .40 1.00
318 Kevin Davidson RC .40 1.00
319 Brian Pilkington RC .40 1.00
320 Alex Romero RC .40 1.00
321 Chad Chop RC .40 1.00
322 Kody Kirkland RC .40 1.00
323 Casey Myers RC .40 1.00
324 Mike Rouse RC .40 1.00
325 Sergio Silva RC .40 1.00
326 J.J. Furmaniak RC .40 1.00
327 Brad Vericker RC .40 1.00
328 Blake Hawksworth RC .40 1.00
329 Brock Jacobsen RC .40 1.00
330 Alec Zumwalt RC .40 1.00
331 Wardell Starling AU RC 4.00 10.00
332 Estee Harris AU RC 4.00 10.00
333 Kyle Sleeth AU RC 4.00 10.00
334 Dioner Navarro AU RC 4.00 10.00
335 Logan Kensing AU RC 4.00 10.00
336 Travis Blackley AU RC 4.00 10.00
337 Lincoln Holdzkom AU RC 4.00 10.00
338 Jason Hirsh AU RC 4.00 10.00
339 Juan Cedeno AU RC 4.00 10.00
340 Matt Creighton AU RC 4.00 10.00
341 Tim Stauffer AU RC 4.00 10.00
342 Shingo Takatsu AU RC 4.00 10.00
343 Lastings Milledge AU RC 4.00 10.00
344 Dustin Nippert AU RC 4.00 10.00
345 Felix Hernandez AU RC 25.00 60.00
346 Joaquin Arias AU RC 4.00 10.00
347 Kevin Kouzmanoff AU RC 4.00 10.00
348 Bobby Brownlie AU RC 4.00 10.00
349 David Aardsma AU RC 4.00 10.00
350 Jon Knott AU RC 6.00 15.00

2004 Bowman Chrome Refractors

*REF 1-150: 1.5X TO 4X BASIC
*REF 151-165: 2X TO 5X BASIC
*REF 166-330: 1X TO 2.5X BASIC
1-330 STATED ODDS 1:4 HOBBY
*REF AU 331-350: .5X TO 1.2X BASIC
331-350 AU ODDS 1:100 HOBBY
331-350 AU PRINT RUN 500 SETS
331-350 AU'S ARE NOT SERIAL-NUMBERED
331-350 PRINT RUN PROVIDED BY TOPPS
EXCHANGE DEADLINE 08/31/06

2004 Bowman Chrome Blue Refractors

*BLUE REF 166-330: 1.25X TO 3X BASIC
EXCH.CARDS AVAIL.VIA PIT.COM WEBSITE
ONE EXCH.CARD PER BOX-LOADER PACK
ONE BOX-LOADER PACK PER HOBBY BOX
STATED PRINT RUN 290 SETS
EXCHANGE DEADLINE 12/31/04
301 Yadier Molina 75.00 200.00
NNO Exchange Card

2004 Bowman Chrome Gold Refractors

*GOLD REF 1-150: 5X TO 12X BASIC
*GOLD REF 151-165: 8X TO 20X BASIC
*GOLD REF 166-330: 6X TO 15X BASIC
1-330 STATED ODDS 1:60 HOBBY
1-330 PRINT RUN 50 SERIAL #'d SETS
*GOLD REF 331-350: 2X TO 4X BASIC
331-350 AU ODDS 1:1003 HOBBY
331-350 AU STATED PRINT RUN 50 SETS
331-350 AU'S ARE NOT SERIAL-NUMBERED
331-350 PRINT RUN PROVIDED BY TOPPS
EXCHANGE DEADLINE 08/31/06

2004 Bowman Chrome X-Fractors

*X-FR 1-150: 3X TO 8X BASIC
*X-FR 151-165: 4X TO 10X BASIC
*X-FR 166-330: 2X TO 5X BASIC
1-330 ODDS ONE PER BOX LOADER PACK
ONE BOX LOADER PACK PER HOBY BOX
INSTANT WIN 1-330 ODDS 1:103,968 H
1-330 PRINT RUN 172 SERIAL #'d SETS
SETS 1-10 AVAIL.VIA INSTANT WIN CARD
SETS 11-172 ISSUED IN BOX-LOADER PACKS
*X-FR AU 331-350: .6X TO 1.5X BASIC
331-350 AU ODDS 1:200 HOBBY
331-350 AU STATED PRINT RUN 250 SETS
331-350 AU'S ARE NOT SERIAL-NUMBERED
331-350 PRINT RUNS PROVIDED BY TOPPS
EXCHANGE DEADLINE 08/31/06
NNO Complete 1-330 Instant Win/10

2004 Bowman Chrome Stars of the Future

STATED ODDS 1:600 HOBBY
STATED PRINT RUN 500 SETS
CARDS ARE NOT SERIAL-NUMBERED
PRINT RUN INFO PROVIDED BY TOPPS
REFRACTORS RANDOM INSERTS IN PACKS
NO REFRACTOR PRICING DUE TO SCARCITY
EXCHANGE DEADLINE 08/31/06
LHC Luban/Harvey/Cord 10.00 25.00
MHD Markakis/Hill/Duncan 10.00 25.00
YSS Delmon/Sleeth/Stauffer 10.00 25.00

2004 Bowman Chrome Draft

This 175-card set was issued as part of the Bowman Draft release. The first 165 cards were issued at a stated rate of two per Bowman Draft pack while the final 10 cards, all of which were autographed, were issued at a stated rate of one in 60 hobby and retail packs and were issued to a stated print run of 1695 sets.

COMPLETE SET (175) 175.00 300.00
COMP.SET w/o SP's (165) 50.00 100.00
COMMON CARD (1-165) .15 .40
COMMON RC .40 1.00
COMMON RC YR .15 .40
1-165 TWO PER BOWMAN DRAFT PACK
COMMON CARD (166-175) 4.00 10.00
166-175 ODDS 1:60 BOWMAN DRAFT HOBBY
166-175 ODDS 1:60 BOWMAN DRAFT RETAIL
166-175 STATED PRINT RUN 1695 SETS
166-175 ARE NOT SERIAL-NUMBERED
166-175 PRINT RUN PROVIDED BY TOPPS
PLATES 1-165 ODDS 1:559 HOBBY
PLATES 166-175 ODDS 1:18,354 HOBBY
PLATES PRINT RUN 1 SERIAL #'d SET
BLACK-CYAN-MAGENTA-YELLOW EXIST
NO PLATES PRICING DUE TO SCARCITY
1 Lyle Overbay .15 .40
2 David Newhan .15 .40
3 J.R. House .15 .40
4 Chad Tracy .15 .40
5 Humberto Quintero .15 .40
6 Dave Bush .15 .40
7 Scott Hairston .15 .40
8 Mike Wood .15 .40
9 Alexis Rios .15 .40
10 Sean Burnett .15 .40
11 Wilson Valdez .15 .40
12 Lew Ford .15 .40
13 Freddy Thon RC .40 1.00
14 Zack Greinke .40 1.00
15 Bucky Jacobsen .15 .40
16 Kevin Youkilis .15 .40
17 Grady Sizemore .25 .60
18 Denny Bautista .15 .40
19 David DeJesus .15 .40
20 Casey Kotchman .15 .40
21 David Kelton .15 .40
22 Charles Thomas RC .40 1.00
23 Kazuhito Tadano RC .40 1.00
24 Justin Leone RC .40 1.00
25 Eduardo Villacis RC .40 1.00
26 Brian Dallimore RC .40 1.00
27 Nick Green .15 .40
28 Sam McConnell RC .40 1.00
29 Brad Halsey RC .40 1.00
30 Roman Colon RC .40 1.00
31 Josh Fields RC .60 1.50
32 Cody Bunkelman RC .40 1.00
33 Jay Rainville RC .40 1.00
34 Richie Robnett RC .40 1.00
35 Jon Poterson RC .40 1.00
36 Huston Street RC .60 1.50
37 Erick San Pedro RC .40 1.00
38 Cory Dunlap RC .40 1.00
39 Kurt Suzuki RC .60 1.50
40 Anthony Swarzak RC .60 1.50
41 Ian Desmond RC .60 1.50
42 Chris Covington RC .40 1.00
43 Christian Garcia RC .60 1.50
44 Gaby Hernandez RC .60 1.50
45 Steven Register RC .40 1.00
46 Eduardo Morlan RC .60 1.50
47 Collin Balester RC .40 1.00
48 Nathan Phillips RC .40 1.00
49 Dan Schwartzbauer RC .40 1.00
50 Rafael Gonzalez RC .40 1.00
51 K.C. Herren RC .40 1.00
52 William Susdorf RC .40 1.00
53 Rob Johnson RC .40 1.00
54 Louis Marson RC .60 1.50
55 Joe Koshansky RC .60 1.50
56 Jamar Walton RC .40 1.00
57 Mark Lowe RC .60 1.50
58 Matt Macri RC .60 1.50
59 Donny Lucy RC .40 1.00
60 Mike Ferris RC .40 1.00
61 Mike Nickeas RC .40 1.00
62 Eric Hurley RC .60 1.50
63 Scott Elbert RC .40 1.00
64 Blake DeWitt RC .60 1.50
65 Danny Putnam RC .40 1.00
66 J.P. Howell RC .40 1.00
67 John Wiggins RC .40 1.00
68 Justin Orenduff RC .60 1.50
69 Ray Liotta RC .40 1.00
70 Billy Buckner RC .40 1.00
71 Eric Campbell RC .40 1.00
72 Olin Wick RC .40 1.00
73 Sean Gamble RC .40 1.00
74 Seth Smith RC .60 1.50
75 Wade Davis RC 1.00 2.50
76 Joe Jacobitz RC .40 1.00
77 J.A. Happ RC 1.00 2.50
78 Eric Ridener RC .40 1.00
79 Matt Tuiasosopo RC 1.00 2.50
80 Brad Bergesen RC .40 1.00
81 Javy Guerra RC 1.00 2.50
82 Buck Shaw RC .40 1.00
83 Paul Janish RC .60 1.50
84 Sean Kazmar RC .40 1.00
85 Josh Johnson RC .40 1.00
86 Angel Salome RC .40 1.00
87 Jordan Parraz RC .60 1.50
88 Kelvin Vazquez RC .40 1.00
89 Grant Hansen RC .40 1.00
90 Matt Fox RC .40 1.00
91 Trevor Plouffe RC 1.00 2.50
92 Wes Whisler RC .40 1.00
93 Curtis Thigpen RC .40 1.00
94 Donnie Smith RC .40 1.00
95 Luis Rivera RC .40 1.00
96 Jesse Hoover RC .40 1.00
97 Jason Vargas RC .60 1.50
98 Clary Carlsen RC .40 1.00
99 Mark Robinson RC .40 1.00
100 J.C. Holt RC .40 1.00
101 Chad Blackwell RC .40 1.00
102 Daryl Jones RC .40 1.00
103 Jonathan Tierce RC .40 1.00
104 Patrick Bryant RC .40 1.00
105 Eddie Prasch RC .40 1.00
106 Mitch Einertson RC .40 1.00
107 Kyle Waldrop RC .40 1.00
108 Jeff Marquez RC .40 1.00
109 Zach Jackson RC .40 1.00
110 Josh Wahpepah RC .40 1.00
111 Adam Lind RC .60 1.50
112 Kyle Bloom RC .40 1.00
113 Ben Harrison RC .40 1.00
114 Taylor Tankersley RC .40 1.00
115 Steven Jackson RC .40 1.00
116 David Purcey RC .60 1.50
117 Jacob McGee RC .60 1.50
118 Lucas Harrell RC .40 1.00
119 Brandon Allen RC .40 1.00
120 Van Pope RC .40 1.00
121 Jeff Francis .15 .40
122 Joe Blanton .15 .40
123 Wil Ledezma .15 .40
124 Bryan Bullington .15 .40
125 Jairo Garcia .15 .40
126 Matt Cain 1.00 2.50
127 Arnie Munoz .15 .40
128 Clint Everts .15 .40
129 Jesus Cota .15 .40
130 Gavin Floyd .15 .40
131 Edwin Encarnacion .40 1.00
132 Koyie Hill .15 .40
133 Ruben Gotay .15 .40
134 Jeff Mathis .15 .40
135 Andy Marte .15 .40
136 Dallas McPherson .15 .40
137 Justin Morneau .25 .60
138 Rickie Weeks .15 .40
139 Joel Guzman .15 .40
140 Shin Soo Choo .25 .60
141 Yusmeiro Petit RC 1.00 2.50
142 Jorge Cortes RC .40 1.00
143 Val Majewski .15 .40
144 Felix Pie .15 .40
145 Aaron Hill .15 .40
146 Jose Capellan .15 .40
147 Dioner Navarro .25 .60
148 Fausto Carmona .25 .60
149 Robinzon Diaz RC .40 1.00
150 Felix Hernandez 2.50 6.00
151 Andres Blanco RC .40 1.00
152 Jason Kubel .15 .40
153 Willy Taveras RC 1.00 2.50
154 Merkin Valdez .15 .40
155 Robinson Cano .50 1.25
156 Bill Murphy .15 .40
157 Chris Burke .15 .40
158 Kyle Sleeth .15 .40
159 B.J. Upton .25 .60
160 Tim Stauffer .25 .60
161 David Wright .30 .75
162 Conor Jackson .50 1.25
163 Brad Thompson RC .60 1.50
164 Delmon Young .25 .60
165 Jeremy Reed .15 .40
166 Matt Bush AU RC 6.00 15.00
167 Mark Rogers AU RC 4.00 10.00
168 Thomas Diamond AU RC 4.00 10.00
169 Greg Golson AU RC 4.00 10.00
170 Homer Bailey AU RC 5.00 12.00
171 Chris Lambert AU RC 4.00 10.00
172 Neil Walker AU RC 6.00 15.00
173 Bill Bray AU RC 4.00 10.00
174 Philip Hughes AU RC 5.00 12.00
175 Gio Gonzalez AU RC 4.00 10.00

2004 Bowman Chrome Draft Refractors

*REF 1-165: 1.5X TO 4X BASIC
*REF RC 1-165: 1.25X TO 3X BASIC
*REF RC YR 1-165: 1.5X TO 4X BASIC
1-165 ODDS 1:11 BOWMAN DRAFT HOBBY
1-165 ODDS 1:11 BOWMAN DRAFT RETAIL
*REF AU 166-175: .6X TO 1.5X BASIC
166-175 AU ODDS BOW.DRAFT 1:204 HOB
166-175 AU ODDS BOW.DRAFT 1:204 RET
166-175 STATED PRINT RUN 500 SETS
166-175 ARE NOT SERIAL-NUMBERED
166-175 PRINT RUN PROVIDED BY TOPPS

2004 Bowman Chrome Draft Gold Refractors

*GOLD REF 1-165: 8X TO 20X BASIC
*GOLD REF RC 1-165: 8X TO 20X BASIC
*GOLD REF RC YR 1-165: 6X TO 15X BASIC
1-165 ODDS 1:119 BOWMAN DRAFT HOBBY
1-165 ODDS 1:205 BOWMAN DRAFT RETAIL
1-165 PRINT RUN 50 SERIAL #'d SETS
*GOLD REF 166-175: 4X TO 8X BASIC
166-175 AU ODDS 1:2045 BOW.DRAFT HOB
166-175 AU ODDS 1:2055 BOW.DRAFT RET
166-175 STATED PRINT RUN 50 SETS
166-175 ARE NOT SERIAL-NUMBERED
166-175 PRINT RUN PROVIDED BY TOPPS

2004 Bowman Chrome Draft X-Fractors

*XF 1-165: 3X TO 8X BASIC
*XF RC 1-165: 2.5X TO 6X BASIC
*XF RC YR 1-165: 2.5X TO 6X BASIC
1-165 ODDS 1:48 BOWMAN DRAFT HOBBY
1-165 ODDS 1:80 BOWMAN DRAFT RETAIL
1-165 PRINT RUN 125 SERIAL #'d SETS
*XF AU 166-175: .75X TO 2X BASIC
166-175 AU ODDS 1:407 BOW.DRAFT HOB
166-175 AU ODDS 1:407 BOW.DRAFT RET
166-175 STATED PRINT RUN 250 SETS
166-175 ARE NOT SERIAL-NUMBERED
166-175 PRINT RUN PROVIDED BY TOPPS

2004 Bowman Chrome Draft AFLAC

COMP.FACT.SET (12) 12.50 30.00
ONE SET VIA MAIL PER AFLAC EXCH.CARD
ONE EXCH.PER '04 BOW.DRAFT HOBBY BOX
EXCH.CARD DEADLINE WAS 11/30/05
SETS ACTUALLY SENT OUT JANUARY, 2006
RED REF PRINT RUN 1 SERIAL #'d SET
NO RED REF PRICING DUE TO SCARCITY
1 C.J. Henry .60 1.50
2 John Drennen .60 1.50
3 Beau Jones .60 1.50
4 Jeff Lyman .60 1.50
5 Andrew McCutchen 10.00 25.00
6 Chris Volstad 1.00 2.50
7 Jonathan Egan .60 1.50
8 P.J. Phillips .60 1.50
9 Steve Johnson .60 1.50
10 Ryan Tucker .60 1.50
11 Cameron Maybin 2.00 5.00
12 Shane Funk .60 1.50

2004 Bowman Chrome Draft AFLAC Refractors

COMP.FACT.SET (12) 40.00 80.00
*REF: 1.5X TO 4X BASIC
ONE SET VIA MAIL PER AFLAC EXCH.CARD
ONE EXCH.PER '04 BOW.DRAFT HOBBY BOX
STATED PRINT RUN 550 SERIAL #'d SETS
EXCH.CARD DEADLINE WAS 11/30/05
SETS ACTUALLY SENT OUT JANUARY, 2006

2004 Bowman Chrome Draft AFLAC Gold Refractors

COMP.FACT.SET (12) 200.00 400.00
*GOLD REF: X TO X BASIC
ONE SET VIA MAIL PER AFLAC EXCH.CARD
ONE EXCH.PER '04 BOW.DRAFT HOBBY BOX
STATED PRINT RUN 50 SERIAL #'d SETS
EXCH.CARD DEADLINE WAS 11/30/05
SETS ACTUALLY SENT OUT JANUARY, 2006

2004 Bowman Chrome Draft AFLAC X-Fractors

COMP.FACT.SET (12) 100.00 200.00
*X-FRAC: 4X TO 10X BASIC
ONE SET VIA MAIL PER AFLAC EXCH.CARD
ONE EXCH.PER '04 BOW.DRAFT HOBBY BOX
STATED PRINT RUN 125 SERIAL #'d SETS
EXCH.CARD DEADLINE WAS 11/30/05
SETS ACTUALLY SENT OUT JANUARY, 2006

2004 Bowman Chrome Draft AFLAC Autograph Refractors

ONE SET VIA MAIL PER GOLD EXCH.CARD
STATED PRINT RUN 125 SERIAL #'d SETS
SETS ACTUALLY SENT OUT JUNE, 2006
AM Andrew McCutchen 40.00 100.00
CH C.J. Henry 15.00 40.00
CM Cameron Maybin 25.00 60.00
JU Justin Upton 100.00 250.00

2005 Bowman Chrome

This 353-card set was released in August, 2005. The set was issued in four card packs with an $4 SRP which came 18 packs to a box and 12 boxes to a case. Cards 1-140 feature active veterans while cards 141-165 feature leading prospects and cards 166-330 feature Rookies. Cards 331-353 are signed Rookie Cards which were inserted into boxes at a stated rate of one in 28 packs.

COMP.SET w/o AU's (330) 20.00 50.00
COMMON CARD (1-140) .20 .50
COMMON CARD (141-165) .20 .50
COMMON CARD (166-330) .40 1.00
COMMON AUTO (331-353) 4.00 10.00
331-353 AU ODDS 1:28 HOBBY, 1:83 RETAIL
1-330 PLATE ODDS 1:779 HOBBY
331-353 AU PLATE ODDS 1:10,996 HOBBY
PLATE PRINT RUN 1 SET PER COLOR
BLACK-CYAN-MAGENTA-YELLOW ISSUED
NO PLATE PRICING DUE TO SCARCITY
1 Gavin Floyd .20 .50
2 Eric Chavez .20 .50
3 Miguel Tejada .30 .75
4 Dmitri Young .20 .50
5 Hank Blalock .20 .50
6 Kerry Wood .20 .50
7 Andy Pettitte .30 .75
8 Pat Burrell .20 .50
9 Johnny Estrada .20 .50
10 Frank Thomas .50 1.25
11 Juan Pierre .20 .50
12 Tom Glavine .30 .75
13 Lyle Overbay .20 .50
14 Jim Edmonds .30 .75
15 Steve Finley .20 .50
16 Jermaine Dye .20 .50
17 Omar Vizquel .30 .75
18 Nick Johnson .20 .50
19 Brian Giles .20 .50
20 Justin Morneau .30 .75
21 Preston Wilson .20 .50
22 Wily Mo Pena .20 .50
23 Rafael Palmeiro .30 .75
24 Scott Kazmir .50 1.25
25 Derek Jeter 1.25 3.00
26 Barry Zito .30 .75
27 Mike Lowell .20 .50
28 Jason Bay .20 .50
29 Ken Harvey .20 .50
30 Nomar Garciaparra .30 .75
31 Roy Halladay .30 .75
32 Todd Helton .30 .75
33 Mark Kotsay .20 .50
34 Jake Peavy .20 .50
35 David Wright .40 1.00
36 Dontrelle Willis .20 .50
37 Marcus Giles .20 .50
38 Chone Figgins .20 .50
39 Sidney Ponson .20 .50
40 Randy Johnson .50 1.25
41 John Smoltz .50 1.25
42 Kevin Millar .20 .50
43 Mark Teixeira .30 .75
44 Alex Rios .20 .50
45 Mike Piazza .50 1.25
46 Victor Martinez .20 .50
47 Jeff Bagwell .30 .75
48 Shawn Green .20 .50
49 Ivan Rodriguez .30 .75
50 Alex Rodriguez .60 1.50
51 Kazuo Matsui .20 .50
52 Mark Mulder .20 .50
53 Michael Young .20 .50
54 Javy Lopez .20 .50
55 Johnny Damon .30 .75
56 Jeff Francis .20 .50
57 Rich Harden .20 .50
58 Bobby Abreu .20 .50
59 Mark Loretta .20 .50
60 Gary Sheffield .20 .50
61 Jamie Moyer .20 .50
62 Garret Anderson .20 .50
63 Vernon Wells .20 .50
64 Orlando Cabrera .20 .50
65 Magglio Ordonez .30 .75
66 Ronnie Belliard .20 .50
67 Carlos Lee .20 .50
68 Carl Pavano .20 .50
69 Jon Lieber .20 .50
70 Aubrey Huff .20 .50
71 Rocco Baldelli .20 .50
72 Jason Schmidt .20 .50
73 Bernie Williams .30 .75
74 Hideki Matsui .75 2.00
75 Ken Griffey Jr. 1.00 2.50
76 Josh Beckett .20 .50
77 Mark Buehrle .30 .75
78 David Ortiz .50 1.25
79 Luis Gonzalez .20 .50
80 Scott Rolen .30 .75
81 Joe Mauer .40 1.00
82 Jose Reyes .30 .75
83 Adam Dunn .30 .75
84 Greg Maddux .60 1.50
85 Bartolo Colon .20 .50
86 Bret Boone .20 .50
87 Mike Mussina .30 .75
88 Ben Sheets .20 .50
89 Lance Berkman .30 .75
90 Miguel Cabrera .50 1.25
91 C.C. Sabathia .30 .75
92 Mike Maroth .20 .50
93 Andruw Jones .20 .50
94 Jack Wilson .20 .50
95 Ichiro Suzuki .60 1.50
96 Geoff Jenkins .20 .50
97 Zack Greinke .50 1.25
98 Jorge Posada .30 .75
99 Travis Hafner .20 .50
100 Barry Bonds .75 2.00
101 Aaron Rowand .20 .50
102 Aramis Ramirez .20 .50
103 Curt Schilling .30 .75
104 Melvin Mora .20 .50
105 Albert Pujols .60 1.50
106 Austin Kearns .20 .50
107 Shannon Stewart .20 .50
108 Carl Crawford .30 .75
109 Carlos Zambrano .30 .75
110 Roger Clemens .60 1.50
111 Javier Vazquez .20 .50
112 Randy Wolf .20 .50
113 Chipper Jones .50 1.25
114 Larry Walker .30 .75
115 Alfonso Soriano .30 .75
116 Brad Wilkerson .20 .50
117 Bobby Crosby .20 .50
118 Jim Thome .30 .75
119 Oliver Perez .20 .50
120 Vladimir Guerrero .30 .75
121 Roy Oswalt .30 .75
122 Torii Hunter .20 .50
123 Rafael Furcal .20 .50
124 Luis Castillo .20 .50
125 Carlos Beltran .30 .75
126 Mike Sweeney .20 .50
127 Johan Santana .30 .75
128 Tim Hudson .30 .75
129 Troy Glaus .20 .50
130 Manny Ramirez .50 1.25
131 Jeff Kent .20 .50
132 Jose Vidro .20 .50
133 Edgar Renteria .20 .50
134 Russ Ortiz .20 .50
135 Sammy Sosa .50 1.25

136 Carlos Delgado .20 .50
137 Richie Sexson .20 .50
138 Pedro Martinez .30 .75
139 Adrian Beltre .50 1.25
140 Mark Prior .30 .75
141 Omar Quintanilla .20 .50
142 Carlos Quentin .30 .75
143 Dan Johnson .20 .50
144 Jake Stevens .20 .50
145 Nate Schierholtz .20 .50
146 Neil Walker .30 .75
147 Bill Bray .20 .50
148 Taylor Tankersley .20 .50
149 Trevor Plouffe .50 1.25
150 Felix Hernandez .60 1.50
151 Philip Hughes .50 1.25
152 James Houser .20 .50
153 David Murphy .30 .75
154 Ervin Santana .20 .50
155 Anthony Whittington .20 .50
156 Chris Lambert .20 .50
157 Jeremy Sowers .20 .50
158 Giovanny Gonzalez .30 .75
159 Blake DeWitt .30 .75
160 Thomas Diamond .20 .50
161 Greg Golson .20 .50
162 David Aardsma .20 .50
163 Paul Maholm .20 .50
164 Mark Rogers .20 .50
165 Homer Bailey .20 .50
166 Elvin Puello RC .40 1.00
167 Tony Giarratano RC .40 1.00
168 Darren Fenster RC .40 1.00
169 Elvys Quezada RC .40 1.00
170 Glen Perkins RC .40 1.00
171 Ian Kinsler RC 2.00 5.00
172 Adam Bostick RC .40 1.00
173 Jeremy West RC .40 1.00
174 Brett Harper RC .40 1.00
175 Kevin West RC .40 1.00
176 Luis Hernandez RC .40 1.00
177 Matt Campbell RC .40 1.00
178 Nate McLouth RC .60 1.50
179 Ryan Goleski RC .40 1.00
180 Matthew Lindstrom RC .40 1.00
181 Matt DeSalvo RC .40 1.00
182 Kole Strayhorn RC .40 1.00
183 Jose Vaquedano RC .40 1.00
184 James Jurries RC .40 1.00
185 Ian Bladergroen RC .40 1.00
186 Kila Kaaihue RC 1.00 2.50
187 Luke Scott RC 1.00 2.50
188 Chris Denorfia RC .40 1.00
189 Jai Miller RC .40 1.00
190 Melky Cabrera RC 1.25 3.00
191 Ryan Sweeney RC .60 1.50
192 Sean Marshall RC 1.00 2.50
193 Erick Abreu RC .40 1.00
194 Tyler Pelland RC .40 1.00
195 Cole Armstrong RC .40 1.00
196 John Hudgins RC .40 1.00
197 Wade Robinson RC .40 1.00
198 Dan Santin RC .40 1.00
199 Steve Doetsch RC .40 1.00
200 Shane Costa RC .40 1.00
201 Scott Mathieson RC .40 1.00
202 Ben Jones RC .40 1.00
203 Michael Rogers RC .40 1.00
204 Matt Rogelstad RC .40 1.00
205 Luis Ramirez RC .40 1.00
206 Landon Powell RC .40 1.00
207 Erik Cordier RC .40 1.00
208 Chris Seddon RC .40 1.00
209 Chris Roberson RC .40 1.00
210 Thomas Oldham RC .40 1.00
211 Dana Eveland RC .40 1.00
212 Cody Haerther RC .40 1.00
213 Danny Core RC .40 1.00
214 Craig Tatum RC .40 1.00
215 Elliot Johnson RC .40 1.00
216 Ender Chavez RC .40 1.00
217 Errol Simonitsch RC .40 1.00
218 Matt Van Der Bosch RC .40 1.00
219 Eulogio de la Cruz RC .40 1.00
220 Drew Toussaint RC .40 1.00
221 Adam Boeve RC .40 1.00
222 Adam Harben RC .40 1.00
223 Baltazar Lopez RC .40 1.00
224 Russ Martin RC 1.25 3.00
225 Brian Bannister RC .60 1.50
226 Chris Walker RC .40 1.00
227 Casey McGehee RC .60 1.50
228 Humberto Sanchez RC .60 1.50
229 Javon Moran RC .40 1.00
230 Brandon McCarthy RC .60 1.50
231 Danny Zell RC .40 1.00
232 Kevin Barry RC .40 1.00
233 Juan Tejeda RC .40 1.00
234 Keith Ramsey RC .40 1.00
235 Lorenzo Scott RC .40 1.00
236 Jon Barratt RC .40 1.00
237 Martin Prado RC 2.50 6.00
238 Matt Albers RC .40 1.00
239 Brian Schweiger RC .40 1.00
240 Raul Tablado RC .40 1.00
241 Pat Misch RC .40 1.00
242 Pat Osborn .40 1.00
243 Ryan Feierabend RC .40 1.00
244 Shaun Marcum 1.00 2.50
245 Kevin Collins RC .40 1.00
246 Stuart Pomeranz RC .40 1.00
247 Tetsu Yofu RC .40 1.00
248 Hernan Iribarren RC .40 1.00
249 Mike Spidale RC .40 1.00
250 Tony Arnerich RC .40 1.00
251 Manny Parra RC 1.00 2.50
252 Drew Anderson RC .40 1.00
253 T.J. Beam RC .40 1.00
254 Claudio Arias RC .40 1.00
255 Andy Sides RC .40 1.00
256 Bear Bay RC .40 1.00
257 Bill McCarthy RC .40 1.00
258 Daniel Haigwood RC .40 1.00
259 Brian Sprout RC .40 1.00
260 Bryan Triplett RC .40 1.00
261 Steven Bondurant RC .40 1.00
262 Darwinson Salazar RC .40 1.00
263 David Shepard RC .40 1.00
264 Johan Silva RC .40 1.00
265 J.B. Thurmond RC .40 1.00
266 Brandon Moorhead RC .40 1.00
267 Kyle Nichols RC .40 1.00
268 Jonathan Sanchez RC 1.50 4.00
269 Mike Esposito RC .40 1.00
270 Erik Schindewolf RC .40 1.00
271 Peeter Ramos RC .40 1.00
272 Juan Senreiso RC .40 1.00
273 Travis Chick RC .40 1.00
274 Vinny Rottino RC .40 1.00
275 Micah Furtado RC .40 1.00
276 George Kottaras RC .60 1.50
277 Abel Gomez RC .40 1.00
278 Buck Coats RC .40 1.00
279 Kenny Durost RC .40 1.00
280 Nick Touchstone RC .40 1.00
281 Jerry Owens RC .40 1.00
282 Stefan Bailie RC .40 1.00
283 Jesse Gutierrez RC .40 1.00
284 Chuck Tiffany RC 1.00 2.50
285 Brendan Ryan RC .40 1.00
286 Julio Pimentel RC .40 1.00
287 Shawn Bowman RC .40 1.00
288 Alexander Smit RC .40 1.00
289 Micah Schnurstein RC .40 1.00
290 Jared Gothreaux RC .40 1.00
291 Jair Jurrjens RC 2.00 5.00
292 Bobby Livingston RC .40 1.00
293 Ryan Speier RC .40 1.00
294 Zach Parker RC .40 1.00
295 Christian Colonel RC .40 1.00
296 Scott Mitchinson RC .40 1.00
297 Neil Wilson RC .40 1.00
298 Chuck James RC 1.00 2.50
299 Heath Totten RC .40 1.00
300 Sean Tracey RC .40 1.00
301 Tadahito Iguchi RC .60 1.50
302 Matt Brown RC .40 1.00
303 Franklin Morales RC .60 1.50
304 Brandon Sing RC .40 1.00
305 D.J. Houlton RC .40 1.00
306 Jayce Tingler RC .40 1.00
307 Mitchell Arnold RC .40 1.00
308 Jim Burt RC .40 1.00
309 Jason Motte RC .60 1.50
310 David Gassner RC .40 1.00
311 Andy Santana RC .40 1.00
312 Kelvin Pichardo RC .40 1.00
313 Carlos Carrasco RC 1.00 2.50
314 Willy Mota RC .40 1.00
315 Frank Mata RC .40 1.00
316 Carlos Gonzalez RC 3.00 8.00
317 Jesse Floyd .40 1.00
318 Chris B.Young RC 1.25 3.00
319 Billy Sadler RC .40 1.00
320 Ricky Barrett RC .40 1.00
321 Ben Harrison .40 1.00
322 Steve Nelson RC .40 1.00
323 Daryl Thompson RC .40 1.00
324 Davis Romero RC .40 1.00
325 Jeremy Harts RC .40 1.00
326 Nick Masset RC .40 1.00
327 Thomas Pauly RC .40 1.00
328 Mike Garber RC .40 1.00
329 Kennard Bibbs RC .40 1.00
330 Collier Bean RC .40 1.00
331 Justin Verlander AU RC 125.00 300.00
332 Chip Cannon AU RC 4.00 10.00
333 Kevin Melillo AU RC 4.00 10.00
334 Jake Postlewait AU RC 4.00 10.00
335 Wes Swackhamer AU RC 4.00 10.00
336 Mike Rodriguez AU RC 4.00 10.00
337 Philip Humber AU RC 4.00 10.00
338 Jeff Niemann AU RC 4.00 10.00
339 Brian Miller AU RC 4.00 10.00
340 Chris Vines AU RC 4.00 10.00
341 Andy LaRoche AU RC 4.00 10.00
342 Mike Bourn AU RC 4.00 10.00
343 Eric Nielsen AU RC 4.00 10.00
344 Wladimir Balentien AU RC 4.00 10.00
345 Ismael Ramirez AU RC 4.00 10.00
346 Pedro Lopez AU RC 4.00 10.00
347 Shawn Bowman AU 4.00 10.00
348 Hayden Penn AU RC 4.00 10.00
349 Matthew Kemp AU RC 25.00 60.00
350 Brian Stavisky AU RC 4.00 10.00
351 C.J. Smith AU RC 4.00 10.00
352 Mike Morse AU RC 4.00 10.00
353 Billy Butler AU RC 5.00 12.00

2005 Bowman Chrome Refractors

*REF 1-165: 1.5X TO 4X BASIC
*REF 166-330: .75X TO 2X BASIC
1-330 ODDS 1:4 HOBBY, 1:6 RETAIL
*REF AU 331-353: .5X TO 1.2X BASIC AU
331-353 AU ODDS 1:88 HOB, 1:259 RET
331-353 PRINT RUN 500 SERIAL #'d SETS

2005 Bowman Chrome Blue Refractors

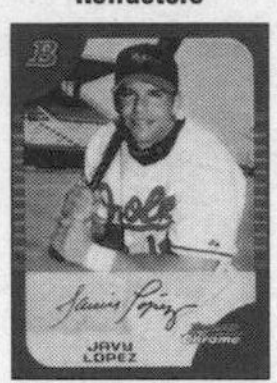

*BLUE REF 1-165: 2.5X TO 6X BASIC
*BLUE REF 166-330: 1.2X TO 3X BASIC
1-330 ODDS 1:20 HOBBY, 1:69 RETAIL
*BLUE REF AU 331-353: 1.25X TO 2.5X BASIC
331-353 AU ODDS 1:294 HOB, 1:866 RET
STATED PRINT RUN 150 SERIAL #'d SETS
331 Justin Verlander AU 600.00 1200.00

2005 Bowman Chrome Gold Refractors

*GOLD REF 1-165: 4X TO 10X BASIC
*GOLD REF 166-330: 2X TO 5X BASIC
1-330 ODDS 1:61 HOBBY, 1:206 RETAIL
*GOLD REF AU 331-353: 1.5X TO 4X BASIC
331-353 AU ODDS 1:880 HOB, 1:2612 RET
STATED PRINT RUN 50 SERIAL #'d SETS
331 Justin Verlander AU 2000.00 4000.00
349 Matthew Kemp AU 150.00 400.00

2005 Bowman Chrome Green Refractors

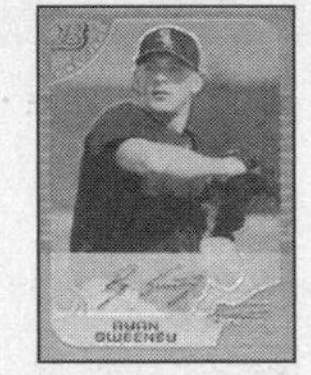

*GREEN: 1.5X TO 4X BASIC
ISSUED VIA THE PIT.COM
STATED PRINT RUN 225 SERIAL #'d SETS

2005 Bowman Chrome Super-Fractors

1-330 STATED ODDS 1:3117 H
331-353 AU STATED ODDS 1:47,238 H
STATED PRINT RUN 1 SERIAL #'d SET
NO PRICING DUE TO SCARCITY

2005 Bowman Chrome X-Fractors

*X-FRACTOR 1-165: 2X TO 5X BASIC
*X-FRACTOR 166-330: 1X TO 2.5X BASIC
1-330 ODDS 1:13 HOBBY, 1:61 RETAIL
*X-FRACT AU 331-353: .6X TO 1.5X BASIC AU
331-353 AU ODDS 1:196 HOB, 1:573 RET
STATED PRINT RUN 225 SERIAL #'d SETS

2005 Bowman Chrome A-Rod Throwback

COMPLETE SET (4) 4.00 10.00
COMMON CARD (94-97) 1.25 3.00
STATED ODDS 1:9 HOBBY, 1:12 RETAIL
*REF: 1X TO 2.5X BASIC
REFRACTOR ODDS 1:445 HOBBY
REFRACTOR PRINT RUN 499 #'d SETS
SUPER-FRACTOR ODDS 1:226,044 HOBBY
SUPER-FRACTOR PRINT RUN 1 #'d SET
NO SUPER-FRACTOR PRICING AVAILABLE
*X-FRACTOR: 1.5X TO 4X BASIC
X-FRACTOR ODDS 1:2241 HOBBY
X-FRACTOR PRINT RUN 99 #'d SETS
94AR Alex Rodriguez 1994 1.00 2.50
95AR Alex Rodriguez 1995 1.00 2.50
96AR Alex Rodriguez 1996 1.00 2.50
97AR Alex Rodriguez 1997 1.00 2.50

2005 Bowman Chrome A-Rod Throwback Autographs

1994 CARD STATED ODDS 1:614,088 H
1995 CARD STATED ODDS 1:36,122 H
1996 CARD STATED ODDS 1:18,061 H
1997 CARD STATED ODDS 1:9042 H
1994 CARD PRINT RUN 1 #'d CARD
1995 CARD PRINT RUN 25 #'d CARDS
1996 CARD PRINT RUN 50 #'d CARDS
1997 CARD PRINT RUN 99 #'d CARDS
NO PRICING ON 1994 CARD AVAILABLE
96AR A.Rodriguez 1996 RF/50 100.00 175.00
97AR A.Rodriguez 1997 CH/99 60.00 120.00

2005 Bowman Chrome Two of a Kind Autographs

STATED ODDS 1:76,761 HOBBY
STATED PRINT RUN 13 SERIAL #'d CARDS
NO PRICING DUE TO SCARCITY

2005 Bowman Chrome Draft

These cards were issued two per Bowman Draft Pack. Cards numbered 166 through 180, which were not issued as regular Bowman cards feature signed cards of some leading prospects. Those cards were issued at different odds depending on the player who signed the cards.

COMP.SET w/o SP's (165) 15.00 40.00
COMMON CARD (1-165) .15 .40
COMMON RC .40 1.00
COMMON RC YR .15 .40
1-165 TWO PER BOWMAN DRAFT PACK
166-180 GROUP A ODDS 1:671 H, 1:643 R
166-180 GROUP B ODDS 1:69 H, 1:69 R
1-165 PLATE ODDS 1:826 HOBBY
166-180 AU PLATE ODDS 1:18,411 HOBBY
PLATE PRINT RUN 1 SET PER COLOR
BLACK-CYAN-MAGENTA-YELLOW ISSUED
NO PLATE PRICING DUE TO SCARCITY
1 Rickie Weeks .15 .40
2 Kyle Davies .15 .40
3 Garrett Atkins .15 .40
4 Chien-Ming Wang .60 1.50
5 Dallas McPherson .15 .40
6 Dan Johnson .15 .40
7 Andy Sisco .15 .40
8 Ryan Doumit .15 .40
9 J.P. Howell .15 .40
10 Tim Stauffer .15 .40
11 Willy Taveras .15 .40
12 Aaron Hill .25 .60
13 Victor Diaz .15 .40
14 Wilson Betemit .15 .40
15 Ervin Santana .15 .40
16 Mike Morse .50 1.25
17 Yadier Molina .40 1.00
18 Kelly Johnson .15 .40
19 Clint Barmes .15 .40
20 Robinson Cano .50 1.25
21 Brad Thompson .15 .40
22 Jorge Cantu .15 .40
23 Brad Halsey .15 .40
24 Lance Niekro .15 .40
25 D.J. Houlton .15 .40
26 Ryan Church .15 .40
27 Hayden Penn .15 .40
28 Chris Young .25 .60
29 Chad Orvella RC .40 1.00
30 Mark Teahen .15 .40
31 Mark McCormick FY RC .40 1.00
32 Jay Bruce FY RC 3.00 8.00
33 Beau Jones FY RC 1.00 2.50
34 Tyler Greene FY RC .40 1.00
35 Zach Ward FY RC .40 1.00
36 Josh Bell FY RC .60 1.50
37 Josh Wall FY RC .60 1.50
38 Nick Webber FY RC .40 1.00
39 Travis Buck FY RC .40 1.00
40 Kyle Winters FY RC .40 1.00
41 Mitch Boggs FY RC .40 1.00
42 Tommy Mendoza FY RC .40 1.00
43 Brad Corley FY RC .40 1.00
44 Drew Butera FY RC .40 1.00
45 Ryan Mount FY RC .40 1.00
46 Tyler Herron FY RC .40 1.00
47 Nick Weglarz FY RC .40 1.00
48 Brandon Erbe FY RC 1.25 3.00
49 Cody Allen FY RC .40 1.00
50 Eric Fowler FY RC .40 1.00
51 James Boone FY RC .40 1.00
52 Josh Flores FY RC .40 1.00
53 Brandon Monk FY RC .40 1.00
54 Kieron Pope FY RC .40 1.00
55 Kyle Cofield FY RC .40 1.00
56 Brent Lillibridge FY RC .40 1.00
57 Daryl Jones FY RC .40 1.00
58 Eli Iorg FY RC .40 1.00
59 Brett Hayes FY RC .40 1.00
60 Mike Durant FY RC .40 1.00
61 Michael Bowden FY RC .60 1.50
62 Paul Kelly FY RC .40 1.00
63 Andrew McCutchen FY RC 5.00 12.00
64 Travis Wood FY RC 1.00 2.50
65 Cesar Ramos FY RC .40 1.00
66 Chaz Roe FY RC .40 1.00
67 Matt Torra FY RC .40 1.00
68 Kevin Slowey FY RC 2.00 5.00
69 Trayvon Robinson FY RC 1.00 2.50
70 Reid Engel FY RC .40 1.00
71 Kris Harvey FY RC .40 1.00
72 Craig Italiano FY RC .40 1.00
73 Matt Maloney FY RC .40 1.00
74 Sean West FY RC .60 1.50
75 Henry Sanchez FY RC .60 1.50
76 Scott Blue FY RC .40 1.00
77 Jordan Schafer FY RC 2.00 5.00
78 Chris Robinson FY RC .40 1.00
79 Chris Hobdy FY RC .40 1.00
80 Brandon Durden FY RC .40 1.00
81 Clay Buchholz FY RC 2.00 5.00
82 Josh Geer FY RC .40 1.00
83 Sam LeCure FY RC .40 1.00
84 Justin Thomas FY RC .40 1.00
85 Brett Gardner FY RC 1.25 3.00
86 Tommy Manzella FY RC .40 1.00
87 Matt Green FY RC .40 1.00
88 Yunel Escobar FY RC 1.50 4.00
89 Mike Costanzo FY RC .40 1.00
90 Nick Hundley FY RC .40 1.00
91 Zach Simons FY RC .40 1.00
92 Jacob Marceaux FY RC .40 1.00
93 Jed Lowrie FY RC .40 1.00
94 Brandon Snyder FY RC 1.00 2.50
95 Matt Goyen FY RC .40 1.00
96 Jon Egan FY RC .40 1.00
97 Drew Thompson FY RC .40 1.00
98 Bryan Anderson FY RC .40 1.00
99 Clayton Richard FY RC .40 1.00
100 Jimmy Shull FY RC .40 1.00
101 Mark Pawelek FY RC .40 1.00
102 P.J. Phillips FY RC .40 1.00
103 John Drennen FY RC .40 1.00
104 Nolan Reimold FY RC 1.50 4.00
105 Troy Tulowitzki FY RC 4.00 10.00
106 Kevin Whelan FY RC .40 1.00
107 Wade Townsend FY RC .40 1.00
108 Micah Owings FY RC .40 1.00
109 Ryan Tucker FY RC .40 1.00
110 Jeff Clement FY RC .40 1.00
111 Josh Sullivan FY RC .40 1.00
112 Jeff Lyman FY RC .40 1.00
113 Brian Bogusevic FY RC .40 1.00
114 Trevor Bell FY RC .40 1.00
115 Brent Cox FY RC .40 1.00
116 Michael Billek FY RC .40 1.00
117 Garrett Olson FY RC .40 1.00
118 Steven Johnson FY RC .40 1.00
119 Chase Headley FY RC .60 1.50
120 Daniel Carte FY RC .40 1.00
121 Francisco Liriano PROS .40 1.00
122 Fausto Carmona PROS .15 .40
123 Zach Jackson PROS .15 .40
124 Adam Loewen PROS .15 .40
125 Chris Lambert PROS .15 .40
126 Scott Mathieson FY .15 .40
127 Paul Maholm PROS .15 .40
128 Fernando Nieve PROS .15 .40
129 Justin Verlander FY 15.00 40.00
130 Yusmeiro Petit PROS .15 .40
131 Joel Zumaya PROS .40 1.00
132 Merkin Valdez PROS .15 .40
133 Ryan Garko FY RC .40 1.00
134 Edison Volquez FY RC 1.25 3.00
135 Russ Martin FY .50 1.25
136 Conor Jackson PROS .25 .60
137 Miguel Montero FY RC 1.25 3.00
138 Josh Barfield PROS .25 .60
139 Delmon Young PROS .40 1.00
140 Andy LaRoche FY .15 .40
141 William Bergolla PROS .15 .40
142 B.J. Upton PROS .25 .60
143 Hernan Iribarren FY .15 .40
144 Brandon Wood PROS .25 .60
145 Jose Bautista PROS .60 1.50
146 Edwin Encarnacion PROS .40 1.00
147 Javier Herrera FY RC .40 1.00
148 Jeremy Hermida PROS .25 .60
149 Frank Diaz PROS RC .40 1.00
150 Chris B.Young FY .50 1.25
151 Shin-Soo Choo PROS .25 .60
152 Kevin Thompson PROS RC .40 1.00
153 Hanley Ramirez PROS .25 .60
154 Lastings Milledge PROS .15 .40
155 Luis Montanez PROS .15 .40
156 Justin Huber PROS .15 .40
157 Zach Duke PROS .15 .40
158 Jeff Francoeur PROS .40 1.00
159 Melky Cabrera FY .50 1.25
160 Bobby Jenks PROS .15 .40
161 Ian Snell PROS .15 .40
162 Fernando Cabrera PROS .15 .40
163 Troy Patton PROS .15 .40
164 Anthony Lerew PROS .15 .40
165 Nelson Cruz FY RC 3.00 8.00
166 Stephen Drew AU A RC 4.00 10.00
167 Jered Weaver AU A RC 10.00 25.00
168 Ryan Braun AU B RC 20.00 50.00
169 John Mayberry Jr. AU B RC 4.00 10.00
170 Aaron Thompson AU B RC 4.00 10.00
171 Cesar Carrillo AU B RC 4.00 10.00
172 Jacoby Ellsbury AU B RC 8.00 20.00
173 Matt Garza AU B RC 5.00 12.00
174 Cliff Pennington AU B RC 4.00 10.00
175 Colby Rasmus AU B RC 5.00 12.00
176 Chris Volstad AU B RC 4.00 10.00
177 Ricky Romero AU B RC 4.00 10.00
178 Ryan Zimmerman AU B RC 20.00 50.00
179 C.J. Henry AU B RC 4.00 10.00
180 Eddy Martinez AU B RC 4.00 10.00

2005 Bowman Chrome Draft Refractors

*REF 1-165: 2X TO 5X BASIC
*REF 1-165: .75X TO 2X BASIC RC
1-165 ODDS 1:11 BOWMAN DRAFT HOBBY
1-165 ODDS 1:11 BOWMAN DRAFT RETAIL
*REF AU 166-180: .6X TO 1.5X BASIC
166-180 AU ODDS 1:186 BOW.DRAFT HOB
166-180 AU ODDS 1:186 BOW.DRAFT RET
166-180 PRINT RUN 500 SERIAL #'d SETS
129 Justin Verlander FY 50.00 120.00

2005 Bowman Chrome Draft Blue Refractors

*BLUE 1-165: 4X TO 10X BASIC
*BLUE 1-165: 3X TO 8X BASIC RC
1-165 ODDS 1:52 BOWMAN DRAFT HOBBY
1-165 ODDS 1:107 BOWMAN DRAFT RETAIL
*BLUE AU 166-180: 1.25X TO 2.5X BASIC
166-180 AU ODDS 1:619 BOW.DRAFT HOB
166-180 AU ODDS 1:619 BOW.DRAFT RET
STATED PRINT RUN 150 SERIAL #'d SETS
129 Justin Verlander FY 200.00 500.00

2005 Bowman Chrome Draft Gold Refractors

*GOLD REF 1-165: 10X TO 25X BASIC
*GOLD REF 1-165: 12.5X TO 25X BASIC RC
*GOLD REF 1-165: 12.5X TO 30X BASIC RC YR
1-165 ODDS 1:155 BOWMAN DRAFT HOBBY
1-165 ODDS 1:323 BOWMAN DRAFT HOBBY
*GOLD REF AU 166-180: 4X TO 8X BASIC
166-180 AU ODDS 1:1857 BOW.DRAFT HOB
166-180 AU ODDS 1:1856 BOW.DRAFT RET
STATED PRINT RUN 50 SERIAL #'d SETS
20 Robinson Cano 40.00 80.00
129 Justin Verlander FY 250.00 600.00

2005 Bowman Chrome Draft X-Fractors

*XF 1-165: 2.5X TO 6X BASIC
*XF 1-165: 1X TO 2.5X BASIC RC
1-165 ODDS 1:31 BOWMAN DRAFT HOBBY
1-165 ODDS 1:64 BOWMAN DRAFT RETAIL
*XF AU 166-180: 1X TO 2.5X BASIC
166-180 AU ODDS 1:372 BOW.DRAFT HOB
166-180 AU ODDS 1:371 BOW.DRAFT RET
STATED PRINT RUN 250 SERIAL #'d SETS
129 Justin Verlander FY 60.00 150.00

2005 Bowman Chrome Draft AFLAC Exchange Cards

BASIC ODDS 1:109 BOW.DRAFT H
REFRACTOR ODDS 1:2184 BOW.DRAFT H
X-FRACTOR ODDS 1:4369 BOW.DRAFT H
BLUE REF ODDS 1:7261 BOW.DRAFT H
GOLD REF ODDS 1:21,937 BOW.DRAFT H
RED REF ODDS 1:1,031,040 BOW.DRAFT H
SUP-FRAC ODDS 1:1,031,040 BOW.DRAFT H
REFRACTOR PRINT RUN 500 CARDS
X-FRACTOR PRINT RUN 250 CARDS
BLUE REF PRINT RUN 150 CARDS
GOLD REF PRINT RUN 50 CARDS
RED REF PRINT RUN 1 CARD
SUPER-FRACTOR PRINT RUN 1 CARD
PLATES PRINT RUN 1 SET PER COLOR
NO RED/SUPER PRICING DUE TO SCARCITY
NO PLATES PRICING DUE TO SCARCITY
EXCHANGE DEADLINE 12/26/06
1 Basic Set 15.00 30.00
3 Refractor Set/500 90.00 150.00
4 Blue Refractor Set/150 250.00 400.00
5 Gold Refractor Set/50 700.00 1000.00
8 X-Fractor Set/250 175.00 300.00

2005 Bowman Chrome Draft AFLAC

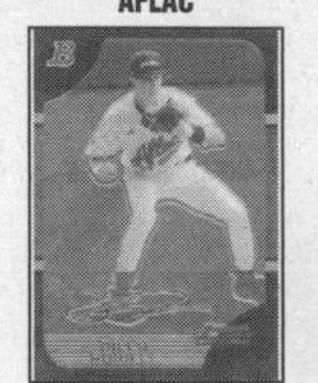

COMP.FACT.SET (14) 8.00 20.00
ONE SET VIA MAIL PER AFLAC EXCH.CARD
BASIC ODDS 1:109 '05 BOW.DRAFT HOB.
SETS ACTUALLY SENT OUT JANUARY, 2007
EXCHANGE DEADLINE 12/26/06
REFRACTOR ODDS 1:2184 BOW.DRAFT H
REF PRINT RUN 500 SER.#'d SETS
X-FRACTOR ODDS 1:4369 BOW.DRAFT H
BLUE REF ODDS 1:7261 BOW.DRAFT H
BLUE REF PRINT RUN 150 SER.#'d SETS
GOLD REF ODDS 1:21,937 BOW.DRAFT H
GOLD REF PRINT RUN 50 SER.#'d SETS
RED REF ODDS 1:1,031,040 BOW.DRAFT H
RED REF PRINT RUN 1 SER.#'d SET
NO RED PRICING DUE TO SCARCITY
SUPER ODDS 1:1,031,040 BOW.DRAFT H
SUPER-FRAC PRINT RUN 1 SER.#'d SET
NO SUPER PRICING DUE TO SCARCITY
PLATE PRINT RUN 1 SET PER COLOR
BLACK-CYAN-MAGENTA-YELLOW ISSUED
NO PLATE PRICING DUE TO SCARCITY
1 Billy Rowell 1.50 4.00
2 Kasey Kiker 1.00 2.50
3 Chris Marrero 2.00 5.00
4 Jeremy Jeffress .60 1.50
5 Kyle Drabek 1.00 2.50
6 Chris Parmelee 1.00 2.50
7 Colton Willems .60 1.50
8 Cody Johnson .60 1.50
9 Hank Conger 1.00 2.50
10 Cory Rasmus .60 1.50
11 David Christensen .60 1.50
12 Chris Tillman 1.00 2.50
13 Torre Langley .60 1.50
14 Robby Alcombrack .60 1.50

2005 Bowman Chrome Draft AFLAC Refractors

COMP.FACT.SET (14) 50.00 100.00
*REF: 1.2X TO 3X BASIC
ONE SET VIA MAIL PER EXCH.CARD
STATED ODDS 1:2184 BOW.DRAFT H
STATED PRINT RUN 500 SER.#'d SETS
EXCHANGE DEADLINE 12/26/06
SETS ACTUALLY SENT OUT JANUARY, 2007

2005 Bowman Chrome Draft AFLAC Blue Refractors

COMP.FACT.SET (14) 150.00 300.00
*BLUE REF: 4X TO 10X BASIC
ONE SET VIA MAIL PER EXCH.CARD
STATED ODDS 1:7261 BOW.DRAFT H

STATED PRINT RUN 150 SER.#'d SETS
EXCHANGE DEADLINE 12/26/06
SETS ACTUALLY SENT OUT JANUARY, 2007

2005 Bowman Chrome Draft AFLAC Gold Refractors

*GOLD REF: 12X TO 30X BASIC
ONE SET VIA MAIL PER EXCH.CARD
STATED ODDS 1:21,937 BOW.DRAFT H
STATED PRINT RUN 50 SER.#'d SETS
EXCHANGE DEADLINE 12/26/06
SETS ACTUALLY SENT OUT JANUARY, 2007

2005 Bowman Chrome Draft AFLAC X-Fractors

COMP.FACT.SET (14) 100.00 200.00
*X-FRAC: 2.5X TO 6X BASIC
STATED ODDS 1:4369 BOW.DRAFT H
ONE SET VIA MAIL PER EXCH.CARD
STATED PRINT RUN 250 SER.#'d SETS
EXCHANGE DEADLINE 12/26/06
SETS ACTUALLY SENT OUT JANUARY, 2007

2006 Bowman Chrome

This 224-card set was released in August, 2006. The set was issued in four card hobby packs with an $3 SRP which came 18 packs to a box and 12 boxes to a case. Card number 219, Kenji Johjima was available in both a regular and an autographed version. Cards numbered 221 through 224 were only available in a signed form. The first 200-cards of this set feature veterans while the rest of this set feature players who qualified for the Rookie Card designation under the new Rookie Card rules which began in 2006.

COMP.SET w/o AU's (220) 30.00 60.00
COMMON CARD (1-200) .20 .50
COMMON ROOKIE (201-220) .25 .60
219 AU ODDS 1:2734 HOBBY, 1:6617 RETAIL
221-224 AU ODDS 1:27 HOBBY, 1:65 RETAIL
1-220 PLATE ODDS 1:836 HOBBY
219 AU PLATE ODDS 1:292,536 HOBBY
221-224 AU PLATES ODDS 1:9,000 HOBBY
PLATE PRINT RUN 1 SET PER COLOR
BLACK-CYAN-MAGENTA-YELLOW ISSUED
NO PLATE PRICING DUE TO SCARCITY
1 Nick Swisher .30 .75
2 Ted Lilly .20 .50
3 John Smoltz .50 1.25
4 Lyle Overbay .20 .50
5 Alfonso Soriano .30 .75
6 Javier Vazquez .20 .50
7 Ronnie Belliard .20 .50
8 Jose Reyes .30 .75
9 Brian Roberts .20 .50
10 Curt Schilling .30 .75
11 Adam Dunn .30 .75
12 Zack Greinke .30 .75
13 Carlos Guillen .20 .50
14 Jon Garland .20 .50
15 Robinson Cano .30 .75
16 Chris Burke .20 .50
17 Barry Zito .30 .75
18 Russ Adams .20 .50
19 Chris Capuano .20 .50
20 Scott Rolen .30 .75
21 Kerry Wood .20 .50
22 Scott Kazmir .30 .75
23 Brandon Webb .30 .75
24 Jeff Kent .20 .50
25 Albert Pujols .60 1.50
26 C.C. Sabathia .30 .75
27 Adrian Beltre .50 1.25
28 Brad Wilkerson .20 .50
29 Randy Wolf .20 .50
30 Jason Bay .20 .50
31 Austin Kearns .20 .50
32 Clint Barmes .20 .50
33 Mike Sweeney .20 .50
34 Kevin Youkilis .20 .50
35 Justin Morneau .30 .75
36 Scott Podsednik .20 .50
37 Jason Giambi .20 .50
38 Steve Finley .20 .50
39 Morgan Ensberg .20 .50
40 Eric Chavez .20 .50
41 Roy Halladay .30 .75
42 Horacio Ramirez .20 .50
43 Ben Sheets .20 .50
44 Chris Carpenter .30 .75
45 Andruw Jones .20 .50
46 Carlos Zambrano .30 .75
47 Jonny Gomes .20 .50
48 Shawn Green .20 .50
49 Moises Alou .20 .50
50 Ichiro Suzuki .60 1.50
51 Juan Pierre .20 .50
52 Grady Sizemore .30 .75
53 Kazuo Matsui .20 .50
54 Jose Vidro .20 .50
55 Jake Peavy .20 .50
56 Dallas McPherson .20 .50
57 Ryan Howard .40 1.00
58 Zach Duke .20 .50
59 Michael Young .20 .50
60 Todd Helton .30 .75
61 David DeJesus .20 .50
62 Ivan Rodriguez .30 .75
63 Johan Santana .30 .75
64 Danny Haren .20 .50
65 Derek Jeter 1.25 3.00
66 Greg Maddux .60 1.50
67 Jorge Cantu .20 .50
68 J.J. Hardy .20 .50
69 Victor Martinez .30 .75
70 David Wright .40 1.00
71 Ryan Church .20 .50
72 Khalil Greene .20 .50
73 Jimmy Rollins .30 .75
74 Hank Blalock .20 .50
75 Pedro Martinez .30 .75
76 Chris Shelton .20 .50
77 Felipe Lopez .20 .50
78 Jeff Francis .20 .50
79 Andy Sisco .20 .50
80 Hideki Matsui .50 1.25
81 Ken Griffey Jr. 1.00 2.50
82 Nomar Garciaparra .30 .75
83 Kevin Millwood .20 .50
84 Paul Konerko .30 .75
85 A.J. Burnett .20 .50
86 Mike Piazza .50 1.25
87 Brian Giles .20 .50
88 Johnny Damon .30 .75
89 Jim Thome .30 .75
90 Roger Clemens .60 1.50
91 Aaron Rowand .20 .50
92 Rafael Furcal .20 .50
93 Gary Sheffield .20 .50
94 Mike Cameron .20 .50
95 Carlos Delgado .20 .50
96 Jorge Posada .30 .75
97 Denny Bautista .20 .50
98 Mike Maroth .20 .50
99 Brad Radke .20 .50
100 Alex Rodriguez .60 1.50
101 Freddy Garcia .20 .50
102 Oliver Perez .20 .50
103 Jon Lieber .20 .50
104 Melvin Mora .20 .50
105 Travis Hafner .20 .50
106 Alex Rios .20 .50
107 Derek Lowe .20 .50
108 Luis Castillo .20 .50
109 Livan Hernandez .20 .50
110 Tadahito Iguchi .20 .50
111 Shawn Chacon .20 .50
112 Frank Thomas .50 1.25
113 Josh Beckett .20 .50
114 Aubrey Huff .20 .50
115 Derrek Lee .20 .50
116 Chien-Ming Wang .30 .75
117 Joe Crede .20 .50
118 Torii Hunter .20 .50
119 J.D. Drew .20 .50
120 Troy Glaus .20 .50
121 Sean Casey .20 .50
122 Edgar Renteria .20 .50
123 Craig Wilson .20 .50
124 Adam Eaton .20 .50
125 Jeff Francoeur .50 1.25
126 Bruce Chen .20 .50
127 Cliff Floyd .20 .50
128 Jeremy Reed .20 .50
129 Jake Westbrook .20 .50
130 Wily Mo Pena .20 .50
131 Toby Hall .20 .50
132 David Ortiz .50 1.25
133 David Eckstein .20 .50
134 Brady Clark .20 .50
135 Marcus Giles .20 .50
136 Aaron Hill .20 .50
137 Mark Kotsay .20 .50
138 Carlos Lee .20 .50
139 Roy Oswalt .30 .75
140 Chone Figgins .20 .50
141 Mike Mussina .30 .75
142 Orlando Hernandez .20 .50
143 Magglio Ordonez .30 .75
144 Jim Edmonds .30 .75
145 Bobby Abreu .20 .50
146 Nick Johnson .20 .50
147 Carlos Beltran .30 .75
148 Jhonny Peralta .20 .50
149 Pedro Feliz .20 .50
150 Miguel Tejada .30 .75
151 Luis Gonzalez .20 .50
152 Carl Crawford .30 .75
153 Yadier Molina .50 1.25
154 Rich Harden .20 .50
155 Tim Wakefield .30 .75
156 Rickie Weeks .20 .50
157 Johnny Estrada .20 .50
158 Gustavo Chacin .20 .50
159 Dan Johnson .20 .50
160 Willy Taveras .20 .50
161 Garret Anderson .20 .50
162 Randy Johnson .50 1.25
163 Jermaine Dye .20 .50
164 Joe Mauer .30 .75
165 Ervin Santana .20 .50
166 Jeremy Bonderman .20 .50
167 Garrett Atkins .20 .50
168 Manny Ramirez .50 1.25
169 Brad Eldred .20 .50
170 Chase Utley .30 .75
171 Mark Loretta .20 .50
172 John Patterson .20 .50
173 Tom Glavine .30 .75
174 Dontrelle Willis .20 .50
175 Mark Teixeira .30 .75
176 Felix Hernandez .30 .75
177 Cliff Lee .30 .75
178 Jason Schmidt .20 .50
179 Chad Tracy .20 .50
180 Rocco Baldelli .20 .50
181 Aramis Ramirez .20 .50
182 Andy Pettitte .30 .75
183 Mark Mulder .20 .50
184 Geoff Jenkins .20 .50
185 Chipper Jones .50 1.25
186 Vernon Wells .20 .50
187 Bobby Crosby .20 .50
188 Lance Berkman .30 .75
189 Vladimir Guerrero .30 .75
190 Coco Crisp .20 .50
191 Brad Penny .20 .50
192 Jose Guillen .20 .50
193 Brett Myers .20 .50
194 Miguel Cabrera .50 1.25
195 Bartolo Colon .20 .50
196 Craig Biggio .30 .75
197 Tim Hudson .30 .75
198 Mark Prior .30 .75
199 Mark Buehrle .30 .75
200 Barry Bonds .75 2.00
201 Anderson Hernandez (RC) .25 .60
202 Jose Capellan (RC) .25 .60
203 Jeremy Accardo RC .25 .60
204 Hanley Ramirez (RC) .40 1.00
205 Matt Capps (RC) .25 .60
206 Jonathan Papelbon (RC) 1.25 3.00
207 Chuck James (RC) .25 .60
208 Matt Cain (RC) 1.50 4.00
209 Cole Hamels (RC) .75 2.00
210 Jason Botts (RC) .25 .60
211 Lastings Milledge (RC) .25 .60
212 Conor Jackson (RC) .40 1.00
213 Yusmeiro Petit (RC) .25 .60
214 Alay Soler RC .25 .60
215 Willy Aybar (RC) .25 .60
216 Adam Loewen (RC) .25 .60
217 Justin Verlander (RC) 2.00 5.00
218 Francisco Liriano (RC) .60 1.50
219 Kenji Johjima RC .60 1.50
219A Kenji Johjima AU 6.00 15.00
220 Craig Hansen RC .60 1.50
221 Prince Fielder AU (RC) 8.00 20.00
222 Josh Barfield AU (RC) 6.00 15.00
223 Fausto Carmona AU (RC) 6.00 15.00
224 James Loney AU (RC) 6.00 15.00

2006 Bowman Chrome Refractors

*REF 1-200: 1.5X TO 4X BASIC
*REF 201-220: 1X TO 2.5X BASIC
1-220 ODDS 1:4 HOB, 1:6 RET
219 AU ODDS 1:5100 HOB, 1:12,432 RET
219 AU PRINT RUN 250 SERIAL #'d CARDS
*REF AU 221-224: .5X TO 1.2X BASIC
221-224 AU ODDS 1:82 HOB, 1:200 RET
221-224 AU PRINT RUN 500 SER.#'d SETS
219A Kenji Johjima AU/250 10.00 25.00

2006 Bowman Chrome Blue Refractors

*BLUE REF 1-200: 4X TO 10X BASIC
*BLUE REF 201-220: 4X TO 10X BASIC
1-220 ODDS 1:25 HOB, 1:73 RET
219 AU ODDS 1:16,877 HOB, 1:61,760 RET
219 AU PRINT RUN 75 SERIAL #'d CARDS
*BLUE REF AU 221-224: .75X TO 2X BASIC
221-224 AU ODDS 1:266 HOB, 1:890 RET
STATED PRINT RUN 150 SERIAL #'d SETS
219A Kenji Johjima AU/75 15.00 40.00

2006 Bowman Chrome Gold Refractors

*GOLD REF 1-200: 6X TO 15X BASIC
*GOLD REF 201-220: 5X TO 12X BASIC
1-220 ODDS 1:74 HOB, 1:247 RET
219 AU ODDS 1:26,000 HOB, 1:52,937 RET
*GOLD REF AU 221-224: 2X TO 5X BASIC
221-224 AU ODDS 1:820 HOB, 1:1910 RET
STATED PRINT RUN 50 SERIAL #'d SETS
219A Kenji Johjima AU 20.00 50.00
224 James Loney AU 50.00 100.00

2006 Bowman Chrome Orange Refractors

*ORANGE REF 1-200: 15X TO 40X BASIC
1-220 ODDS 1:181 HOB, 1:182 RET
219 AU ODDS 1:62,686 HOB, 1:62,607 RET
221-224 AU ODDS 1:1640 HOB, 1:3820 RET
STATED PRINT RUN 25 SERIAL #'d SETS
NO RC/AU PRICING DUE TO SCARCITY

2006 Bowman Chrome X-Fractors

*X-FRACTOR 1-200: 3X TO 8X BASIC
*X-FRACTOR 201-220: 2.5X TO 6X BASIC
1-220 ODDS 1:15 HOB, 1:44 RET
1-220 PRINT RUN 250 SERIAL #'d SETS
219 AU ODDS 1:10,205 HOB 1:28,500 RET
219 AU PRINT RUN 125 SERIAL #'d CARDS
*X-FRAC AU 221-224: .6X TO 1.5X BASIC
221-224 AU ODDS 1:182 HOB, 1:478 RET
221-224 AU PRINT RUN 225 SERIAL #'d SETS
219A Kenji Johjima AU/125 12.50 30.00

2006 Bowman Chrome Prospects

COMP.SET w/o AU's (220) 75.00 150.00
COMP.SERIES 1 SET (110) 30.00 60.00
COMP.SERIES 2 SET (110) 40.00 80.00
1-110 TWO PER HOBBY PACK
1-110 FOUR PER HTA PACK
111-220 TWO PER HOB/RET PACKS
221-247 AU ODDS 1:27 HOB, 1:65 RET
1-110 PLATE ODDS 1:588 HOB,1:575 HTA
111-220 PLATE ODDS 1:636 HOBBY
221-247 AU PLATES 1: 9000 HOBBY
PLATE PRINT RUN 1 PER COLOR
BLACK-CYAN-MAGENTA-YELLOW ISSUED
NO PLATE PRICING DUE TO SCARCITY
1-110 ISSUED IN BOWMAN PACKS
111-247 ISSUED IN BOW.CHROME PACKS
EXCHANGE DEADLINE 8/31/08
BC1 Alex Gordon 1.25 3.00
BC2 Jonathan George .40 1.00
BC3 Scott Walter .40 1.00
BC4 Brian Holliday .40 1.00
BC5 Ben Copeland .40 1.00
BC6 Bobby Wilson .40 1.00
BC7 Mayker Sandoval .40 1.00
BC8 Alejandro de Aza .60 1.50
BC9 David Munoz .40 1.00
BC10 Josh LeBlanc .40 1.00
BC11 Philippe Valiquette .40 1.00
BC12 Edwin Bellorin .40 1.00
BC13 Jason Quarles .40 1.00
BC14 Mark Trumbo 1.00 2.50
BC15 Steve Kelly .40 1.00
BC16 Jamie Hoffman .40 1.00
BC17 Joe Bauserman .40 1.00
BC18 Nick Adenhart .40 1.00
BC19 Mike Butia .40 1.00
BC20 Jon Weber .40 1.00
BC21 Luis Valdez .40 1.00
BC22 Rafael Rodriguez .40 1.00
BC23 Wyatt Toregas .40 1.00
BC24 John Vanden Berg .40 1.00
BC25 Mike Connolly .40 1.00
BC26 Mike O'Connor .40 1.00
BC27 Garrett Mock .40 1.00
BC28 Bill Layman .40 1.00
BC29 Luis Pena .40 1.00
BC30 Billy Killian .40 1.00
BC31 Ross Ohlendorf .40 1.00
BC32 Mark Kaiser .40 1.00
BC33 Ryan Costello .40 1.00
BC34 Dale Thayer .40 1.00
BC35 Steve Garrabrants .40 1.00
BC36 Samuel Deduno .40 1.00
BC37 Juan Portes .40 1.00
BC38 Javier Martinez .40 1.00
BC39 Clint Sammons .40 1.00
BC40 Andrew Kown .40 1.00
BC41 Matt Tolbert .40 1.00
BC42 Michael Ekstrom .40 1.00
BC43 Shawn Norris .40 1.00
BC44 Diory Hernandez .40 1.00
BC45 Chris Maples .40 1.00
BC46 Aaron Hathaway .40 1.00
BC47 Steven Baker .40 1.00
BC48 Greg Creek .40 1.00
BC49 Collin Mahoney .40 1.00
BC50 Corey Ragsdale .40 1.00
BC51 Ariel Nunez .40 1.00
BC52 Max Ramirez .60 1.50
BC53 Eric Rodland .40 1.00
BC54 Dante Brinkley .40 1.00
BC55 Casey Craig .40 1.00
BC56 Ryan Spilborghs .40 1.00
BC57 Fredy Deza .40 1.00
BC58 Jeff Frazier .40 1.00
BC59 Vince Cordova .40 1.00
BC60 Oswaldo Navarro .40 1.00
BC61 Jarod Rine .40 1.00
BC62 Jordan Tata .40 1.00
BC63 Ben Julianel .40 1.00
BC64 Yung-Chi Chen .60 1.50
BC65 Carlos Torres .40 1.00
BC66 Juan Francia .40 1.00
BC67 Brett Smith .40 1.00
BC68 Francisco Leandro .40 1.00
BC69 Chris Turner .40 1.00
BC70 Matt Joyce 2.00 5.00
BC71 Jason Jones .40 1.00
BC72 Jose Diaz .40 1.00
BC73 Kevin Ool .40 1.00
BC74 Nate Bumstead .40 1.00
BC75 Omir Santos .40 1.00
BC76 Shawn Riggans .40 1.00
BC77 Ofilio Castro .40 1.00
BC78 Mike Rozier .40 1.00
BC79 Wilkin Ramirez .60 1.50
BC80 Yobal Duenas .40 1.00
BC81 Adam Bourassa .40 1.00
BC82 Tony Granadillo .40 1.00
BC83 Brad McCann .40 1.00
BC84 Dustin Majewski .40 1.00
BC85 Kelvin Jimenez .40 1.00
BC86 Mark Reed .40 1.00
BC87 Asdrubal Cabrera 2.00 5.00
BC88 James Barthmaier .40 1.00
BC89 Brandon Boggs .40 1.00
BC90 Raul Valdez .40 1.00
BC91 Jose Campusano .40 1.00
BC92 Henry Owens .40 1.00
BC93 Tug Hulett .40 1.00
BC94 Nate Gold .40 1.00
BC95 Lee Mitchell .40 1.00
BC96 John Hardy .40 1.00
BC97 Aaron Wideman .40 1.00
BC98 Brandon Roberts .40 1.00
BC99 Lou Santangelo .40 1.00
BC100 Kyle Kendrick 1.00 2.50
BC101 Michael Collins .40 1.00
BC102 Camilo Vazquez .40 1.00
BC103 Mark McLemore .40 1.00
BC104 Alexander Peralta .40 1.00
BC105 Josh Whitesell .40 1.00
BC106 Carlos Guevara .40 1.00
BC107 Michael Aubrey .60 1.50
BC108 Brandon Chaves .40 1.00
BC109 Leonard Davis .40 1.00
BC110 Kendry Morales 1.00 2.50
BC111 Koby Clemens .60 1.50
BC112 Lance Broadway .40 1.00
BC113 Cameron Maybin 1.25 3.00
BC114 Mike Aviles .60 1.50
BC115 Kyle Blanks 1.50 4.00
BC116 Chris Dickerson .60 1.50
BC117 Sean Gallagher .40 1.00
BC118 Jamar Hill .40 1.00
BC119 Garrett Mock .40 1.00
BC120 Russ Rohlicek .40 1.00
BC121 Clete Thomas .40 1.00
BC122 Elvis Andrus 1.25 3.00
BC123 Brandon Moss .40 1.00
BC124 Mark Holliman .40 1.00
BC125 Jose Tabata .60 1.50
BC126 Corey Wimberly .40 1.00
BC127 Bobby Wilson .40 1.00
BC128 Edward Mujica .40 1.00
BC129 Hunter Pence 1.50 4.00
BC130 Adam Heether .40 1.00
BC131 Andy Wilson .40 1.00
BC132 Radhames Liz .40 1.00
BC133 Garrett Patterson .40 1.00
BC134 Carlos Gomez .75 2.00
BC135 Jared Lansford .40 1.00
BC136 Jose Arredondo .40 1.00
BC137 Renee Cortez .40 1.00
BC138 Francisco Rosario .40 1.00
BC139 Brian Stokes .40 1.00
BC140 Will Thompson .40 1.00
BC141 Ernesto Frieri .40 1.00
BC142 Jose Mijares .40 1.00
BC143 Jeremy Slayden .40 1.00
BC144 Brandon Fahey .40 1.00
BC145 Jason Windsor .40 1.00
BC146 Shawn Nottingham .40 1.00
BC147 Dallas Trahern .40 1.00
BC148 Jon Niese 1.00 2.50
BC149 A.J. Shappi .40 1.00
BC150 Jordan Pals .40 1.00
BC151 Tim Moss .40 1.00
BC152 Stephen Marek .40 1.00
BC153 Mat Gamel 1.00 2.50
BC154 Sean Henn .40 1.00
BC155 Matt Guillory .40 1.00
BC156 Brandon Jones .40 1.00
BC157 Gary Galvez .40 1.00
BC158 Shane Lindsay 1.00 2.50
BC159 Jesus Reina .40 1.00
BC160 Lorenzo Cain 2.00 5.00
BC161 Chris Britton .40 1.00
BC162 Yovani Gallardo 1.25 3.00
BC163 Matt Walker .40 1.00
BC164 Shaun Cumberland .40 1.00
BC165 Ryan Patterson .40 1.00
BC166 Michael Hollimon .40 1.00
BC167 Eude Brito .40 1.00
BC168 John Bowker .40 1.00
BC169 James Avery .40 1.00
BC170 John Bannister .40 1.00
BC171 Juan Ciriaco .40 1.00
BC172 Manuel Corpas .40 1.00
BC173 Leo Rosales .40 1.00
BC174 Tim Kennelly .40 1.00
BC175 Adam Russell .40 1.00
BC176 Jeremy Hellickson 1.25 3.00
BC177 Ryan Klosterman .40 1.00
BC178 Evan Meek .40 1.00
BC179 Steve Murphy .40 1.00
BC180 Scott Feldman .40 1.00
BC181 Pablo Sandoval 1.50 4.00
BC182 Dexter Fowler 1.25 3.00
BC183 Jairo Cuevas .40 1.00
BC184 Andrew Pinckney .40 1.00
BC185 Marino Salas .40 1.00
BC186 Justin Christian .40 1.00
BC187 Ching-Lung Lo .40 1.00
BC188 Randy Roth .40 1.00
BC189 Andy Sonnanstine .40 1.00
BC190 Josh Outman .40 1.00
BC191 Yuber Rodriguez .40 1.00
BC192 Hainley Statia .40 1.00
BC193 Kevin Estrada .40 1.00
BC194 Jeff Karstens .40 1.00
BC195 Corey Coles .40 1.00
BC196 Gustavo Espinoza .40 1.00
BC197 Brian Horwitz .40 1.00
BC198 Landon Jacobsen .40 1.00
BC199 Ben Krosschell .40 1.00
BC200 Jason Jaramillo .40 1.00
BC201 Josh Wilson .40 1.00
BC202 Jason Ray .40 1.00
BC203 Brent Dlugach .40 1.00
BC204 Cesar Jimenez .40 1.00
BC205 Eric Haberer .40 1.00
BC206 Felipe Paulino .40 1.00
BC207 Alcides Escobar 1.50 4.00
BC208 Jose Ascanio .40 1.00
BC209 Yoel Hernandez .40 1.00
BC210 Geoff Vandel .40 1.00
BC211 Travis Denker .40 1.00
BC212 Ramon Alvarado .40 1.00
BC213 Welinson Baez .40 1.00
BC214 Chris Kolkhorst .40 1.00
BC215 Emiliano Fruto .40 1.00
BC216 Luis Cota .40 1.00
BC217 Mark Worrell .40 1.00
BC218 Cla Meredith .40 1.00
BC219 Emmanuel Garcia .40 1.00
BC220 B.J. Szymanski .40 1.00
BC221 Alex Gordon AU 12.00 30.00
BC223 Justin Upton AU 15.00 40.00
BC224 Sean West AU 4.00 10.00
BC225 Tyler Greene AU 4.00 10.00
BC226 Josh Kinney AU 4.00 10.00
BC227 Pedro Lopez AU 4.00 10.00
BC228 Troy Patton AU 4.00 10.00
BC229 Chris Iannetta AU 4.00 10.00
BC230 Jared Wells AU 4.00 10.00
BC231 Brandon Wood AU 4.00 10.00
BC232 Josh Geer AU 4.00 10.00
BC233 Cesar Carrillo AU 4.00 10.00
BC234 Franklin Gutierrez AU 4.00 10.00
BC235 Matt Garza AU 4.00 10.00
BC236 Eli Iorg AU 4.00 10.00
BC237 Trevor Bell AU 4.00 10.00
BC238 Jeff Lyman AU 4.00 10.00
BC239 Jon Lester AU 25.00 60.00
BC240 Kendry Morales AU 5.00 12.00
BC241 J. Brent Cox AU 4.00 10.00
BC242 Jose Bautista AU 10.00 25.00
BC243 Josh Sullivan AU 4.00 10.00
BC244 Brandon Snyder AU 4.00 10.00
BC245 Elvin Puello AU 4.00 10.00
BC247 Jacob Marceaux AU 4.00 10.00

2006 Bowman Chrome Prospects Refractors

*REF 1-110: 1.25X TO 3X BASIC
*REF 111-220: 1.25X TO 3X BASIC
1-110 ODDS 1:36 HOBBY, 1:12 HTA
111-220 ODDS 1:22 HOBBY, 1:81 RETAIL
*REF AU 221-247: .5X TO 1.2X BASIC
221-247 AU ODDS 1:82 HOB, 1:200 RET
STATED PRINT RUN 500 SERIAL #'d SETS
1-110 ISSUED IN BOWMAN PACKS
111-247 ISSUED IN BOW.CHROME PACKS
EXCHANGE DEADLINE 8/31/08

2006 Bowman Chrome Prospects Blue Refractors

*BLUE REF 1-220: 2.5X TO 6X BASIC
1-110 ODDS 1:118 HOBBY, 1:39 HTA
111-220 ODDS 1:25 HOBBY
*BLUE AU 221-247: .75X TO 2X BASIC
221-247 AU ODDS 1:266 HOB, 1:890 RET
STATED PRINT RUN 150 SERIAL #'d SETS
1-110 ISSUED IN BOWMAN PACKS
111-247 ISSUED IN BOW.CHROME PACKS
EXCHANGE DEADLINE 8/31/08

2006 Bowman Chrome Prospects Gold Refractors

*GOLD REF 1-110: 3X TO 8X BASIC
*GOLD REF 111-220: 3X TO 8X BASIC
1-110 ODDS 1:355 HOBBY, 1:116 HTA
111-220 ODDS: 1:74 HOBBY
COMMON AUTO (221-247) 15.00 40.00
221-247 AU ODDS 1:820 HOB, 1:1910 RET
STATED PRINT RUN 50 SERIAL #'d SETS
1-110 ISSUED IN BOWMAN PACKS
111-247 ISSUED IN BOW.CHROME PACKS
EXCHANGE DEADLINE 8/31/08
BC221 Alex Gordon AU 100.00 200.00

2006 Bowman Chrome Prospects Orange Refractors

1-110 ODDS 1:710 HOBBY, 1:233 HTA
111-220 ODDS 1:181 HOBBY
221-247 AU ODDS 1:1640 HOB, 1:3820 RET
STATED PRINT RUN 25 SERIAL #'d SETS
1-110 ISSUED IN BOWMAN PACKS
111-247 ISSUED IN BOW.CHROME PACKS
NO PRICING DUE TO SCARCITY
EXCHANGE DEADLINE 8/31/08

2006 Bowman Chrome Prospects X-Fractors

*X-F 1-220: 1.5X TO 4X BASIC
1-110 ODDS 1:72 HOBBY, 1:23 HTA
111-220 ODDS 1:15 HOBBY
1-220 PRINT RUN 250 SERIAL #'d SETS
*X-F AU 221-247: .6X TO 1.5X BASIC
221-247 AU ODDS 1:182 HOB, 1:478 RET
221-247 AU PRINT RUN 225 SERIAL #'d SETS
1-110 ISSUED IN BOWMAN PACKS
111-247 ISSUED IN BOW.CHROME PACKS
EXCHANGE DEADLINE 8/31/08

2006 Bowman Chrome Draft

This 55-card set was issued at a stated rate of one card in every other pack of Bowman Draft Picks. All fifty-five cards in this set feature players who made their major league debut in 2006.

COMPLETE SET (55) 15.00 40.00
COMMON RC (1-55) .40 1.00
APPX. ODDS 1:2 HOBBY, 1:2 RETAIL
ODDS INFO PROVIDED BY BECKETT
OVERALL PLATE ODDS 1:990 HOBBY
PLATE PRINT RUN 1 SET PER COLOR
BLACK-CYAN-MAGENTA-YELLOW ISSUED
NO PLATE PRICING DUE TO SCARCITY
1 Matt Kemp (RC) 1.00 2.50
2 Taylor Tankersley (RC) .40 1.00
3 Mike Napoli RC .60 1.50
4 Brian Bannister (RC) .40 1.00
5 Melky Cabrera (RC) .60 1.50
6 Bill Bray (RC) .40 1.00
7 Brian Anderson (RC) .40 1.00
8 Jered Weaver (RC) 1.25 3.00
9 Chris Duncan (RC) .60 1.50
10 Boof Bonser (RC) .60 1.50
11 Mike Rouse (RC) .40 1.00
12 David Pauley (RC) .40 1.00
13 Russ Martin (RC) .60 1.50
14 Jeremy Sowers (RC) .40 1.00
15 Kevin Reese (RC) .40 1.00
16 John Rheinecker (RC) .40 1.00
17 Tommy Murphy (RC) .40 1.00
18 Sean Marshall (RC) .40 1.00
19 Jason Kubel (RC) .40 1.00

20 Chad Billingsley (RC) .60 1.50
21 Kendry Morales (RC) 1.00 2.50
22 Jon Lester RC 1.50 4.00
23 Brandon Fahey RC .40 1.00
24 Josh Johnson (RC) 1.00 2.50
25 Kevin Frandsen (RC) .40 1.00
26 Casey Janssen RC .40 1.00
27 Scott Thorman (RC) .40 1.00
28 Scott Mathieson (RC) .40 1.00
29 Jeremy Hermida (RC) .40 1.00
30 Dustin Nippert (RC) .40 1.00
31 Kevin Thompson (RC) .40 1.00
32 Bobby Livingston (RC) .40 1.00
33 Travis Ishikawa (RC) .60 1.50
34 Jeff Mathis (RC) .40 1.00
35 Charlie Haeger RC .60 1.50
36 Josh Willingham (RC) .60 1.50
37 Taylor Buchholz (RC) .40 1.00
38 Joel Guzman (RC) .40 1.00
39 Zach Jackson (RC) .40 1.00
40 Howie Kendrick (RC) .75 2.00
41 T.J. Beam (RC) .40 1.00
42 Ty Taubenheim RC .60 1.50
43 Erick Aybar (RC) .40 1.00
44 Anibal Sanchez (RC) .40 1.00
45 Michael Pelfrey RC 1.00 2.50
46 Shawn Hill (RC) .40 1.00
47 Chris Roberson (RC) .40 1.00
48 Carlos Villanueva RC .40 1.00
49 Andre Ethier (RC) 1.25 3.00
50 Anthony Reyes (RC) .40 1.00
51 Franklin Gutierrez (RC) .40 1.00
52 Angel Guzman (RC) .40 1.00
53 Michael O'Connor RC .40 1.00
54 James Shields RC 1.25 3.00
55 Nate McLouth (RC) .40 1.00

2006 Bowman Chrome Draft Refractors

*REF: 1.25X TO 3X BASIC
STATED ODDS 1:11 HOBBY, 1:11 RETAIL

2006 Bowman Chrome Draft Blue Refractors

*BLUE REF: 3X TO 8X BASIC
STATED ODDS 1:50 HOBBY, 1:94 RETAIL
STATED PRINT RUN 199 SER.#'d SETS

2006 Bowman Chrome Draft Gold Refractors

*GOLD REF: 5X TO 12X BASIC
STATED ODDS 1:197 H, 1:388 R
STATED PRINT RUN 50 SER.#'d SETS

2006 Bowman Chrome Draft Orange Refractors

STATED ODDS 1:395 HOBBY, 1:770 RETAIL
STATED PRINT RUN 25 SERIAL #'d SETS
NO PRICING DUE TO SCARCITY

2006 Bowman Chrome Draft X-Fractors

*X-F: 2X TO 5X BASIC
STATED ODDS 1:32 H, 1:74 R
STATED PRINT RUN 299 SER.#'d SETS

2006 Bowman Chrome Draft Draft Picks

APPX. ODDS 1:1 HOBBY, 1:1 RETAIL
ODDS INFO PROVIDED BY BECKETT
66-90 AU ODDS 1:50 HOB.,1:51 RET.
1-65 PLATE ODDS 1:990 HOBBY
66-90 AU PLATE ODDS 1:13,200 HOBBY
PLATE PRINT RUN 1 SET PER COLOR
BLACK-CYAN-MAGENTA-YELLOW ISSUED
NO PLATE PRICING DUE TO SCARCITY
1 Tyler Colvin .60 1.50
2 Chris Marrero .60 1.50
3 Hank Conger .60 1.50
4 Chris Parmelee .60 1.50
5 Jason Place .40 1.00
6 Billy Rowell 1.00 2.50
7 Travis Snider 1.25 3.00
8 Colton Willems .40 1.00
9 Chase Fontaine .40 1.00
10 Jon Jay .60 1.50
11 Wade Leblanc .60 1.50
12 Justin Masterson .60 1.50
13 Gary Daley .40 1.00
14 Justin Edwards .40 1.00
15 Charlie Yarbrough .40 1.00
16 Cyle Hankerd .40 1.00
17 Zach McAllister .40 1.00
18 Tyler Robertson .40 1.00
19 Joe Smith .40 1.00
20 Nate Culp .40 1.00
21 John Holdzkom .40 1.00
22 Patrick Bresnehan .40 1.00
23 Chad Lee .40 1.00
24 Ryan Morris .40 1.00
25 D'Arby Myers .40 1.00
26 Garrett Olson .40 1.00
27 Jon Still .40 1.00
28 Brandon Rice .40 1.00
29 Chris Davis .75 2.00
30 Zack Daeges .40 1.00
31 Bobby Henson .40 1.00
32 George Kontos .40 1.00
33 Jermaine Mitchell .40 1.00
34 Adam Coe .40 1.00
35 Dustin Richardson .40 1.00
36 Allen Craig 1.00 2.50
37 Austin McClune .40 1.00
38 Doug Fister .60 1.50
39 Corey Madden .40 1.00
40 Justin Jacobs .40 1.00
41 Jim Negrych .40 1.00
42 Tyler Norrick .40 1.00
43 Adam Davis .40 1.00
44 Brett Logan .40 1.00
45 Brian Omogrosso .40 1.00
46 Kyle Drabek .60 1.50
47 Jamie Ortiz .40 1.00
48 Alex Presley .60 1.50
49 Terrance Warren .40 1.00
50 David Christensen .40 1.00
51 Helder Velazquez .40 1.00
52 Matt McBride .40 1.00
53 Quintin Berry 1.00 2.50
54 Michael Eisenberg .40 1.00
55 Dan Garcia .40 1.00
56 Scott Cousins .40 1.00
57 Sean Land .40 1.00
58 Kristopher Medlen 2.00 5.00
59 Tyler Reves .40 1.00
60 John Shelby .40 1.00
61 Jordan Newton .40 1.00
62 Ricky Orta .40 1.00
63 Jason Donald .40 1.00
64 David Huff .40 1.00
65 Brett Sinkbeil .40 1.00
66 Evan Longoria AU 20.00 50.00
67 Cody Johnson AU 4.00 10.00
68 Kris Johnson AU 4.00 10.00
69 Kasey Kiker AU 4.00 10.00
70 Ronnie Bourquin AU 4.00 10.00
71 Adrian Cardenas AU 4.00 10.00
72 Matt Antonelli AU 4.00 10.00
73 Brooks Brown AU 4.00 10.00
74 Steven Evarts AU 4.00 10.00
75 Joshua Butler AU 4.00 10.00
76 Chad Huffman AU 4.00 10.00
77 Steven Wright AU 4.00 10.00
78 Cory Rasmus AU 4.00 10.00
79 Brad Furnish AU 4.00 10.00
80 Andrew Carpenter AU 4.00 10.00
81 Dustin Evans AU 4.00 10.00
82 Tommy Hickman AU 4.00 10.00
83 Matt Long AU 4.00 10.00
84 Clayton Kershaw AU 300.00 800.00
85 Kyle McCulloch AU 4.00 10.00
86 Pedro Beato AU 4.00 10.00
87 Kyler Burke AU 4.00 10.00
88 Stephen Englund AU 4.00 10.00
89 Michael Felix AU 4.00 10.00
90 Sean Watson AU 4.00 10.00

2006 Bowman Chrome Draft Draft Picks Refractors

*REF 1-65: 1.25X TO 3X BASIC
1-65 ODDS 1:11 HOBBY, 1:11 RETAIL
*REF AU 66-90: .5X TO 1.2X BASIC AU
AU 66-90 ODDS 1:156 HOB, 1:157 RET
66-90 AU PRINT RUN 500 SER.#'d SETS
84 Clayton Kershaw AU 600.00 1500.00

2006 Bowman Chrome Draft Draft Picks Blue Refractors

*BLUE REF 1-65: 5X TO 12X BASIC
1-65 STATED ODDS 1:50 H, 1:94 R
1-65 PRINT RUN 199 SER.#'d SETS
*BLUE AU 66-90: 1.25X TO 3X BASIC AU
66-90 STATED ODDS 1:535 H, 1:535 R
66-90 PRINT RUN 150 SER.#'d SETS
84 Clayton Kershaw AU 1250.00 3000.00

2006 Bowman Chrome Draft Draft Picks Gold Refractors

*GOLD REF 1-65: 10X TO 25X BASIC
1-65 STATED ODDS 1:197 H, 1:388 R
66-90 AU ODDS 1:1575 H, 1:1600 R
STATED PRINT RUN 50 SER.#'d SETS
66 Evan Longoria AU 200.00 400.00
67 Cody Johnson AU 20.00 50.00
68 Kris Johnson AU 20.00 50.00
70 Ronnie Bourquin AU 20.00 50.00
73 Brooks Brown AU 20.00 50.00
74 Steven Evarts AU 20.00 50.00
75 Joshua Butler AU 20.00 50.00
77 Steven Wright AU 20.00 50.00
78 Cory Rasmus AU 20.00 50.00
79 Brad Furnish AU 20.00 50.00
80 Andrew Carpenter AU 20.00 50.00
81 Dustin Evans AU 20.00 50.00
82 Tommy Hickman AU 20.00 50.00
83 Matt Long AU 20.00 50.00
84 Clayton Kershaw AU 2500.00 6000.00
85 Kyle McCulloch AU 20.00 50.00
86 Pedro Beato AU 20.00 50.00
87 Kyler Burke AU 20.00 50.00
88 Stephen Englund AU 20.00 50.00
89 Michael Felix AU 20.00 50.00
90 Sean Watson AU 20.00 50.00

2006 Bowman Chrome Draft Draft Picks Orange Refractors

1-65 STATD ODDS 1:395 HOB.,1:770 RET.
66-90 AU ODDS 1:3232 HOB.,1:3232 RET.
STATED PRINT RUN 25 SER.#'d SETS
NO PRICING DUE TO SCARCITY

2006 Bowman Chrome Draft Draft Picks X-Fractors

*X-F 1-65: 2X TO 5X BASIC
1-65 STATED ODDS 1:32 H, 1:74 R
1-65 PRINT RUN 299 SER.#'d SETS
*X-F AU 66-90: .75X TO 2X BASIC
66-90 AU STATED ODDS 1:351 H, 1:353 R
66-90 AU PRINT RUN 225 SER.#'d SETS
84 Clayton Kershaw AU 750.00 2000.00

2006 Bowman Chrome Draft Future's Game Prospects

COMPLETE SET (45) 10.00 25.00
APPX. ODDS 1:2 HOBBY, 1:2 RETAIL
ODDS INFO PROVIDED BY BECKETT
OVERALL PLATE ODDS 1:990 HOBBY
PLATE PRINT RUN 1 SET PER COLOR
BLACK-CYAN-MAGENTA-YELLOW ISSUED
NO PLATE PRICING DUE TO SCARCITY
1 Nick Adenhart .40 1.00
2 Joel Guzman .40 1.00
3 Ryan Braun 2.00 5.00
4 Carlos Carrasco .60 1.50
5 Neil Walker .60 1.50
6 Pablo Sandoval 1.50 4.00
7 Gio Gonzalez .60 1.50
8 Joey Votto 2.50 6.00
9 Luis Cruz .40 1.00
10 Nolan Reimold .60 1.50
11 Juan Salas .40 1.00
12 Josh Fields .40 1.00
13 Yovani Gallardo 1.25 3.00
14 Radhames Liz .40 1.00
15 Eric Patterson .40 1.00
16 Cameron Maybin 1.25 3.00
17 Edgar Martinez .40 1.00
18 Hunter Pence 1.50 4.00
19 Philip Hughes 1.00 2.50
20 Trent Oeltjen .40 1.00
21 Nick Pereira .40 1.00
22 Wladimir Balentien .40 1.00
23 Stephen Drew .75 2.00
24 Davis Romero .40 1.00
25 Joe Koshansky .40 1.00
26 Chin Lung Hu .40 1.00
27 Jason Hirsh .40 1.00
28 Jose Tabata .60 1.50
29 Eric Hurley .40 1.00
30 Yung Chi Chen .60 1.50
31 Howie Kendrick .75 2.00
32 Humberto Sanchez .40 1.00
33 Alex Gordon 1.25 3.00
34 Yunel Escobar .40 1.00
35 Travis Buck .40 1.00
36 Billy Butler 1.00 2.50
37 Homer Bailey 1.00 2.50
38 George Kottaras .40 1.00
39 Kurt Suzuki .40 1.00
40 Joaquin Arias .40 1.00
41 Matt Lindstrom .40 1.00
42 Sean Smith .40 1.00
43 Carlos Gonzalez 1.00 2.50
44 Jaime Garcia 2.00 5.00
45 Jose Garcia .40 1.00

2006 Bowman Chrome Draft Future's Game Prospects Refractors

*REF: .75X TO 2X BASIC
STATED ODDS 1:11 HOBBY, 1:11 RETAIL

2006 Bowman Chrome Draft Future's Game Prospects Blue Refractors

*BLUE REF: 1.5X TO 4X BASIC
STATED ODDS 1:50 HOBBY, 1:94 RETAIL
STATED PRINT RUN 199 SER.#'d SETS

2006 Bowman Chrome Draft Future's Game Prospects Gold Refractors

*GOLD REF: 4X TO 10X BASIC
STATED ODDS 1:197 H, 1:388 R
STATED PRINT RUN 50 SER.#'d SETS
6 Pablo Sandoval 100.00 200.00

2006 Bowman Chrome Draft Future's Game Prospects Orange Refractors

STATED ODDS 1:395 HOBBY, 1:770 RETAIL
STATED PRINT RUN 25 SERIAL #'d SETS
NO PRICING DUE TO SCARCITY

2006 Bowman Chrome Draft Future's Game Prospects X-Fractors

*X-F: 1.25X TO 3X BASIC
STATED ODDS 1:32 H, 1:74 R
STATED PRINT RUN 299 SER.#'d SETS

2007 Bowman Chrome

This 220-card set was released in August, 2007. The set was issued through both hobby and retail channels. The hobby version was issued on in standard (no HTA) packs and those four-card packs with an $4 SRP were issued 18 packs per box and 12 boxes per case. Cards numbered 1-190 feature veterans while cards 191-220 honored 2007 rookies.

COMPLETE SET (220) 30.00 60.00
COMMON CARD (1-190) .20 .50
COMMON ROOKIE (191-220) .30 .75
1-220 PLATE ODDS 1:1054 HOBBY
PLATE PRINT RUN 1 SET PER COLOR
BLACK-CYAN-MAGENTA-YELLOW ISSUED
NO PLATE PRICING DUE TO SCARCITY
1 Hanley Ramirez .30 .75
2 Justin Verlander .50 1.25
3 Ryan Zimmerman .30 .75
4 Jered Weaver .30 .75
5 Stephen Drew .20 .50
6 Jonathan Papelbon .50 1.25
7 Melky Cabrera .20 .50
8 Francisco Liriano .20 .50
9 Prince Fielder .30 .75
10 Dan Uggla .20 .50
11 Jeremy Sowers .20 .50
12 Carlos Quentin .20 .50
13 Chuck James .20 .50
14 Andre Ethier .30 .75
15 Cole Hamels .40 1.00
16 Kenji Johjima .50 1.25
17 Chad Billingsley .30 .75
18 Ian Kinsler .30 .75
19 Jason Hirsh .20 .50
20 Nick Markakis .40 1.00
21 Jeremy Hermida .20 .50
22 Ryan Shealy .20 .50
23 Scott Olsen .20 .50
24 Russell Martin .20 .50
25 Conor Jackson .20 .50
26 Erik Bedard .20 .50
27 Brian McCann .20 .50
28 Michael Barrett .20 .50
29 Brandon Phillips .20 .50
30 Garrett Atkins .20 .50
31 Freddy Garcia .20 .50
32 Mark Loretta .20 .50
33 Craig Biggio .30 .75
34 Jeremy Bonderman .20 .50
35 Johan Santana .30 .75
36 Jorge Posada .30 .75
37 Victor Martinez .30 .75
38 Carlos Delgado .20 .50
39 Gary Matthews Jr. .20 .50
40 Mike Cameron .20 .50
41 Adrian Beltre .50 1.25
42 Freddy Sanchez .20 .50
43 Austin Kearns .20 .50
44 Mark Buehrle .30 .75
45 Miguel Cabrera .50 1.25
46 Josh Beckett .20 .50
47 Chone Figgins .20 .50
48 Edgar Renteria .20 .50
49 Derek Lowe .20 .50
50 Ryan Howard .40 1.00
51 Shawn Green .20 .50
52 Jason Giambi .20 .50
53 Ervin Santana .20 .50
54 Aaron Hill .20 .50
55 Roy Oswalt .30 .75
56 Dan Haren .20 .50
57 Jose Vidro .20 .50
58 Kevin Millwood .20 .50
59 Jim Edmonds .30 .75
60 Carl Crawford .30 .75
61 Randy Wolf .20 .50
62 Paul LoDuca .20 .50
63 Johnny Estrada .20 .50
64 Brian Roberts .20 .50
65 Manny Ramirez .50 1.25
66 Jose Contreras .20 .50
67 Josh Barfield .20 .50
68 Juan Pierre .20 .50
69 David DeJesus .20 .50
70 Gary Sheffield .20 .50
71 Michael Young .20 .50
72 Randy Johnson .50 1.25
73 Rickie Weeks .20 .50
74 Brian Giles .20 .50
75 Ichiro Suzuki .60 1.50
76 Nick Swisher .30 .75
77 Justin Morneau .30 .75
78 Scott Kazmir .30 .75
79 Lyle Overbay .20 .50
80 Alfonso Soriano .30 .75
81 Brandon Webb .30 .75
82 Joe Crede .20 .50
83 Corey Patterson .20 .50
84 Kenny Rogers .20 .50
85 Ken Griffey Jr. 1.00 2.50
86 Cliff Lee .30 .75
87 Mike Lowell .20 .50
88 Marcus Giles .20 .50
89 Orlando Cabrera .20 .50
90 Derek Jeter 1.25 3.00
91 Ramon Hernandez .20 .50
92 Carlos Guillen .20 .50
93 Bill Hall .20 .50
94 Michael Cuddyer .20 .50
95 Miguel Tejada .30 .75
96 Todd Helton .30 .75
97 C.C. Sabathia .30 .75
98 Tadahito Iguchi .20 .50
99 Jose Reyes .30 .75
100 David Wright .40 1.00
101 Barry Zito .30 .75
102 Jake Peavy .20 .50
103 Richie Sexson .20 .50
104 A.J. Burnett .20 .50
105 Eric Chavez .20 .50
106 Vernon Wells .20 .50
107 Grady Sizemore .30 .75
108 Bronson Arroyo .20 .50
109 Mike Mussina .30 .75
110 Magglio Ordonez .30 .75
111 Anibal Sanchez .20 .50
112 Jeff Francoeur .50 1.25
113 Kevin Youkilis .20 .50
114 Aubrey Huff .20 .50
115 Carlos Zambrano .30 .75
116 Mark Teahen .20 .50
117 Mark Mulder .20 .50
118 Pedro Martinez .30 .75
119 Hideki Matsui .50 1.25
120 Mike Piazza .50 1.25
121 Jason Schmidt .20 .50
122 Greg Maddux .60 1.50
123 Joe Blanton .20 .50
124 Chris Carpenter .30 .75
125 David Ortiz .50 1.25
126 Alex Rios .20 .50
127 Nick Johnson .20 .50
128 Carlos Lee .20 .50
129 Pat Burrell .20 .50
130 Ben Sheets .20 .50
131 Derrek Lee .20 .50
132 Adam Dunn .30 .75
133 Jermaine Dye .20 .50
134 Curt Schilling .30 .75
135 Chad Tracy .20 .50
136 Vladimir Guerrero .30 .75
137 Melvin Mora .20 .50
138 John Smoltz .50 1.25
139 Craig Monroe .20 .50
140 Dontrelle Willis .20 .50
141 Jeff Francis .20 .50
142 Chipper Jones .50 1.25
143 Frank Thomas .50 1.25
144 Brett Myers .20 .50
145 Tom Glavine .30 .75
146 Robinson Cano .30 .75
147 Jeff Kent .20 .50
148 Scott Rolen .30 .75
149 Roy Halladay .30 .75
150 Joe Mauer .40 1.00
151 Bobby Abreu .20 .50
152 Matt Cain .30 .75
153 Hank Blalock .20 .50
154 Chris Young .20 .50
155 Jake Westbrook .20 .50
156 Javier Vazquez .20 .50
157 Garret Anderson .20 .50
158 Aramis Ramirez .20 .50
159 Mark Kotsay .20 .50
160 Matt Kemp .40 1.00
161 Adrian Gonzalez .40 1.00
162 Felix Hernandez .30 .75
163 David Eckstein .20 .50
164 Curtis Granderson .40 1.00
165 Paul Konerko .30 .75
166 Alex Rodriguez .60 1.50
167 Tim Hudson .30 .75
168 J.D. Drew .20 .50
169 Chien-Ming Wang .30 .75
170 Jimmy Rollins .30 .75
171 Matt Morris .20 .50
172 Raul Ibanez .30 .75
173 Mark Teixeira .30 .75
174 Ted Lilly .20 .50
175 Albert Pujols .60 1.50
176 Carlos Beltran .30 .75
177 Lance Berkman .30 .75
178 Ivan Rodriguez .30 .75
179 Torii Hunter .20 .50
180 Johnny Damon .30 .75
181 Chase Utley .30 .75
182 Jason Bay .30 .75
183 Jeff Weaver .20 .50
184 Troy Glaus .20 .50
185 Rocco Baldelli .20 .50
186 Rafael Furcal .20 .50
187 Jim Thome .30 .75
188 Travis Hafner .20 .50
189 Matt Holliday .50 1.25
190 Andruw Jones .20 .50
191 Andrew Miller RC 1.25 3.00
192 Ryan Braun RC .30 .75
193 Oswaldo Navarro RC .30 .75
194 Mike Rabelo RC .30 .75
195 Delwyn Young (RC) .30 .75
196 Miguel Montero (RC) .30 .75
197 Matt Lindstrom (RC) .30 .75
198 Josh Hamilton (RC) 1.00 2.50
199 Elijah Dukes RC .50 1.25
200 Sean Henn (RC) .30 .75
201 Delmon Young (RC) .50 1.25
202 Alexi Casilla RC .50 1.25
203 Hunter Pence (RC) 1.00 2.50
204 Jeff Baker (RC) .30 .75
205 Hector Gimenez (RC) .30 .75
206 Ubaldo Jimenez (RC) 1.00 2.50
207 Adam Lind (RC) .30 .75
208 Joaquin Arias (RC) .30 .75
209 David Murphy (RC) .30 .75
210 Daisuke Matsuzaka RC 1.25 3.00
211 Jerry Owens (RC) .30 .75
212 Ryan Sweeney (RC) .30 .75
213 Kei Igawa RC .75 2.00
214 Mitch Maier RC .30 .75
215 Philip Humber (RC) .30 .75
216 Troy Tulowitzki (RC) 1.00 2.50
217 Tim Lincecum RC 1.50 4.00
218 Michael Bourn (RC) .50 1.25
219 Hideki Okajima RC 1.50 4.00
220 Josh Fields (RC) .30 .75

2007 Bowman Chrome Refractors

*REF 1-190: 1.25X TO 3X BASIC
*REF 191-220: .75X TO 2X BASIC
1-220 ODDS 1:4 HOBBY, 1:6 RETAIL

2007 Bowman Chrome Blue Refractors

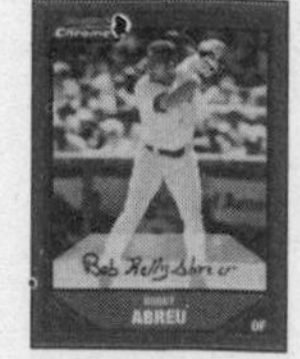

*BLUE REF 1-190: 3X TO 8X BASIC
*BLUE REF 191-220: 2X TO 5X BASIC
1-220 ODDS 1:30 HOBBY, 1:205 RETAIL
STATED PRINT RUN 150 SERIAL #'d SETS

2007 Bowman Chrome Gold Refractors

*GOLD REF 1-190: 8X TO 20X BASIC
*GOLD REF 191-220: 5X TO 12X BASIC
1-220 ODDS 1:88 HOBBY, 1:615 RETAIL
STATED PRINT RUN 50 SERIAL #'d SETS

2007 Bowman Chrome Orange Refractors

*ORANGE REF 1-190: 8X TO 20X BASIC
1-220 ODDS 1:176 HOBBY, 1:1220 RETAIL
STATED PRINT RUN 25 SERIAL #'d SETS
NO RC 191-220 PRICING DUE TO SCARCITY
75 Ichiro Suzuki 40.00 80.00
85 Ken Griffey Jr. 40.00 100.00
169 Chien-Ming Wang 60.00 120.00

2007 Bowman Chrome X-Fractors

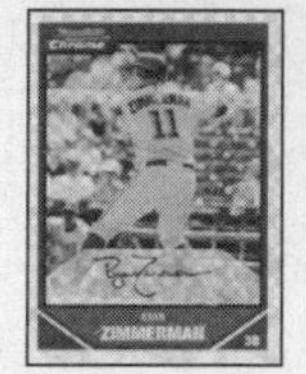

*X-FRACTOR 1-190: 2.5X TO 6X BASIC
*X-FRACTOR 191-220: 1.5X TO 4X BASIC
1-220 ODDS 1:18 HOBBY, 1:123 RETAIL
STATED PRINT RUN 250 SER.#'d SETS

2007 Bowman Chrome Prospects

COMP.SET w/o AU's (220) 40.00 100.00
COMP.SERIES 1 SET (110) 20.00 50.00
COMP.SERIES 2 SET (110) 20.00 50.00
221-256 AU ODDS 1:29 HOB, 1:59 RET
1-110 PLATE ODDS 1:1468 H, 1:212 HTA
111-220 PLATE ODDS 1:1054 HOBBY
221-256 AU PLATE ODDS 1:9668 HOBBY
PLATE PRINT RUN 1 SET PER COLOR
BLACK-CYAN-MAGENTA-YELLOW ISSUED
NO PLATE PRICING DUE TO SCARCITY
1-110 ISSUED IN BOWMAN PACKS
111-256 ISSUED IN BOW.CHROME PACKS
EXCHANGE DEADLINE 8/31/2009
BC1 Cooper Brannon .30 .75
BC2 Jason Taylor .30 .75
BC3 Shawn O'Malley .30 .75
BC4 Robert Alcombrack .30 .75
BC5 Dellin Betances 1.00 2.50
BC6 Jeremy Papelbon .30 .75
BC7 Adam Carr .30 .75
BC8 Matthew Clarkson .30 .75
BC9 Darin McDonald .30 .75
BC10 Brandon Rice .30 .75
BC11 Matthew Sweeney 1.00 2.50
BC12 Scott Deal .30 .75
BC13 Brennan Boesch .50 1.25
BC14 Scott Taylor .30 .75

BC15 Michael Brantley .75 2.00
BC16 Yahmed Yema .30 .75
BC17 Brandon Morrow 1.50 4.00
BC18 Cole Gamer .30 .75
BC19 Erik Lis .50 1.25
BC20 Lucas French .30 .75
BC21 Aaron Cunningham .50 1.25
BC22 Ryan Schreppel .30 .75
BC23 Kevin Russo .30 .75
BC24 Yohan Pino .50 1.25
BC25 Michael Sullivan .30 .75
BC26 Trey Shields .30 .75
BC27 Daniel Matienzo .30 .75
BC28 Chuck Lofgren .75 2.00
BC29 Gerrit Simpson .30 .75
BC30 David Haehnel .30 .75
BC31 Marvin Lowrance .30 .75
BC32 Kevin Ardoin .30 .75
BC33 Edwin Maysonet .30 .75
BC34 Derek Griffith .30 .75
BC35 Sam Fuld 1.00 2.50
BC36 Chase Wright .75 2.00
BC37 Brandon Roberts .30 .75
BC38 Kyle Aselton .30 .75
BC39 Steven Sollmann .30 .75
BC40 Mike Devaney .30 .75
BC41 Charlie Fermaint .30 .75
BC42 Jesse Litsch .50 1.25
BC43 Bryan Hansen .30 .75
BC44 Ramon Garcia .30 .75
BC45 John Otness .30 .75
BC46 Trey Hearne .30 .75
BC47 Habelito Hernandez .30 .75
BC48 Edgar Garcia .30 .75
BC49 Seth Fortenberry .30 .75
BC50 Reid Brignac .50 1.25
BC51 Derek Rodriguez .30 .75
BC52 Ervin Alcantara .30 .75
BC53 Thomas Hottovy .30 .75
BC54 Jesus Flores .30 .75
BC55 Matt Palmer .30 .75
BC56 Brian Henderson .30 .75
BC57 John Gragg .30 .75
BC58 Jay Garthwaite .30 .75
BC59 Esmerling Vasquez .30 .75
BC60 Gilberto Mejia .30 .75
BC61 Aaron Jensen .30 .75
BC62 Cedric Brooks .30 .75
BC63 Brandon Mann .30 .75
BC64 Myron Leslie .30 .75
BC65 Ray Aguilar .30 .75
BC66 Jesus Guzman .50 1.25
BC67 Sean Thompson .30 .75
BC68 Jarrett Hoffpauir .30 .75
BC69 Matt Goodson .30 .75
BC70 Neal Musser .30 .75
BC71 Tony Abreu .75 2.00
BC72 Tony Peguero .30 .75
BC73 Michael Bertram .30 .75
BC74 Randy Wells .75 2.00
BC75 Bradley Davis .30 .75
BC76 Jay Sawatski .30 .75
BC77 Vic Butler .30 .75
BC78 Jose Oyervidez .30 .75
BC79 Doug Deeds .30 .75
BC80 Dan Dement .30 .75
BC81 Spike Lundberg .30 .75
BC82 Ricardo Nanita .30 .75
BC83 Brad Knox .30 .75
BC84 Will Venable .50 1.25
BC85 Greg Smith .50 1.25
BC86 Pedro Powell .30 .75
BC87 Gabriel Medina .30 .75
BC88 Duke Sardinha .30 .75
BC89 Mike Madsen .30 .75
BC90 Rayner Bautista .30 .75
BC91 T.J. Nall .30 .75
BC92 Neil Sellers .30 .75
BC93 Andrew Dobies .30 .75
BC94 Leo Daigle .30 .75
BC95 Brian Duensing .50 1.25
BC96 Vincent Blue .30 .75
BC97 Fernando Rodriguez .30 .75
BC98 Derin McMains .30 .75
BC99 Adam Bass .30 .75
BC100 Justin Ruggiano .50 1.25
BC101 Jared Burton .30 .75
BC102 Mike Parisi .30 .75
BC103 Aaron Peel .30 .75
BC104 Evan Englebrook .30 .75
BC105 Sendy Vasquez .30 .75
BC106 Desmond Jennings 1.25 3.00
BC107 Clay Harris .30 .75
BC108 Cody Strait .30 .75
BC109 Ryan Mullins .30 .75
BC110 Ryan Webb .30 .75
BC111 Mike Carp 1.00 2.50
BC112 Gregory Porter .30 .75
BC113 Joe Ness .30 .75
BC114 Matt Camp .30 .75
BC115 Carlos Fisher .30 .75
BC116 Bryan Bass .30 .75
BC117 Jeff Baisley .50 1.25
BC118 Burke Badenhop .50 1.25
BC119 Grant Psomas .30 .75
BC120 Eric Young Jr. .50 1.25
BC121 Henry Rodriguez .30 .75
BC122 Carlos Fernandez-Oliva .50 1.25
BC123 Chris Errecart .50 1.25
BC124 Brandon Hynick .75 2.00
BC125 Jose Constanza .75 2.00
BC126 Steve Delabar .30 .75
BC127 Raul Barron .30 .75
BC128 Nick DeBarr .30 .75
BC129 Reegie Corona .50 1.25
BC130 Thomas Fairchild .30 .75
BC131 Bryan Byrne .30 .75
BC132 Kurt Mertins .30 .75
BC133 Erik Averill .30 .75
BC134 Matt Young .30 .75
BC135 Ryan Rogowski .30 .75
BC136 Andrew Bailey 1.25 3.00
BC137 Jonathan Van Every .30 .75
BC138 Scott Shoemaker .30 .75
BC139 Steve Singleton .30 .75
BC140 Mitch Atkins .30 .75
BC141 Robert Rohrbaugh .50 1.25
BC142 Ole Sheldon .30 .75
BC143 Adam Ricks .30 .75
BC144 Daniel Mayora .75 2.00
BC145 Johnny Cueto 1.00 2.50
BC146 Jim Fasano .30 .75
BC147 Jared Goedert .75 2.00
BC148 Jonathan Ash .30 .75
BC149 Derek Miller .50 1.25
BC150 Juan Miranda .50 1.25
BC151 J.R. Mathes .30 .75
BC152 Craig Cooper .50 1.25
BC153 Drew Locke .30 .75
BC154 Michael MacDonald .30 .75
BC155 Ryan Norwood .30 .75
BC156 Tony Butler .75 2.00
BC157 Pat Dobson .30 .75
BC158 Cody Ehlers .30 .75
BC159 Dan Fournier .30 .75
BC160 Joe Gaetti .30 .75
BC161 Mark Wagner .50 1.25
BC162 Tommy Hanson 1.00 2.50
BC163 Sharlon Schoop .30 .75
BC164 Woods Fines .30 .75
BC165 Chad Boyd .30 .75
BC166 Kala Kaaihue .50 1.25
BC167 Chris Salamida .30 .75
BC168 Brendan Katin .30 .75
BC169 Terrance Blunt .30 .75
BC170 Tobi Stoner .30 .75
BC171 Phil Coke .50 1.25
BC172 O.D. Gonzalez .30 .75
BC173 Christopher Cody .30 .75
BC174 Cedric Hunter .75 2.00
BC175 Whit Robbins .30 .75
BC176 Chris Begg .30 .75
BC177 Nathan Southard .30 .75
BC178 Dan Brauer .30 .75
BC179 Jared Keel .30 .75
BC180 Chance Douglass .30 .75
BC181 Daniel Murphy 1.50 4.00
BC182 Anthony Hatch .30 .75
BC183 Justin Byler .30 .75
BC184 Scott Lewis .75 2.00
BC185 Andrew Fie .30 .75
BC186 Chorye Spoone .50 1.25
BC187 Cole Bruce .30 .75
BC188 Adam Cowart .75 2.00
BC189 Chris Nowak .30 .75
BC190 Gorkys Hernandez .75 2.00
BC191 Devin Ivany .30 .75
BC192 Jordan Smith .30 .75
BC193 Philip Britton .30 .75
BC194 Cole Gillespie .50 1.25
BC195 Brett Anderson .75 2.00
BC196 Joe Mather .30 .75
BC197 Eddie Degerman .30 .75
BC198 Ronald Prettyman .30 .75
BC199 Patrick Reilly .30 .75
BC200 Tyler Clippard .50 1.25
BC201 Nick Van Stratten .30 .75
BC202 Todd Redmond .30 .75
BC203 Michael Martinez .30 .75
BC204 Alberto Bastardo .30 .75
BC205 Vasili Spanos .30 .75
BC206 Shane Benson .30 .75
BC207 Brent Johnson .30 .75
BC208 Brett Campbell .30 .75
BC209 Dustin Martin .30 .75
BC210 Chris Carter 1.00 2.50
BC211 Alfred Joseph .30 .75
BC212 Carlos Leon .30 .75
BC213 Gabriel Sanchez .50 1.25
BC214 Carlos Corporan .30 .75
BC215 Emerson Frostad .30 .75
BC216 Karl Gelinas .30 .75
BC217 Ryan Finan .30 .75
BC218 Noe Rodriguez .30 .75
BC219 Archie Gilbert .30 .75
BC220 Jeff Locke .75 2.00
BC221 Fernando Martinez AU 6.00 15.00
BC222 Jeremy Papelbon AU 3.00 8.00
BC223 Ryan Adams AU 3.00 8.00
BC224 Chris Perez AU 4.00 10.00
BC225 J.R. Towles AU 3.00 8.00
BC226 Tommy Mendoza AU 3.00 8.00
BC227 Jeff Samardzija AU 5.00 12.00
BC228 Sergio Perez AU 3.00 8.00
BC229 Justin Reed AU 3.00 8.00
BC230 Luke Hochevar AU 3.00 8.00
BC231 Ivan De Jesus Jr. AU 3.00 8.00
BC232 Kevin Mulvey AU 3.00 8.00
BC233 Chris Coghlan AU 4.00 10.00
BC234 Trevor Cahill AU 3.00 8.00
BC235 Peter Bourjos AU 3.00 8.00
BC236 Joba Chamberlain AU 3.00 8.00
BC237 Josh Rodriguez AU 3.00 8.00
BC238 Tim Lincecum AU 20.00 50.00
BC239 Josh Papelbon AU 3.00 8.00
BC240 Greg Reynolds AU 3.00 8.00
BC241 Wes Hodges AU 3.00 8.00
BC242 Chad Reineke AU 3.00 8.00
BC243 Emmanuel Burriss AU 4.00 10.00
BC244 Henry Sosa AU 3.00 8.00
BC245 Cesar Nicolas AU 3.00 8.00
BC246 Young Il Jung AU 3.00 8.00
BC247 Eric Patterson AU 3.00 8.00
BC248 Hunter Pence AU 8.00 20.00
BC249 Dellin Betances AU 10.00 25.00
BC250 Will Venable AU 3.00 8.00
BC251 Zach McAllister AU 3.00 8.00
BC252 Mark Hamilton AU 3.00 8.00
BC253 Paul Estrada AU 3.00 8.00
BC254 Brad Lincoln AU 3.00 8.00
BC255 Cedric Hunter AU 3.00 8.00
BC256 Chad Rodgers AU 3.00 8.00

2007 Bowman Chrome Prospects Refractors

*REF 1-110: 2X TO 5X BASIC CHROME
*REF 111-220: 2X TO 5X BASIC CHROME
1-110 ODDS 1:48 H, 1:8 HTA, 1:142 R
111-220 ODDS 1:27 HOB, 1:186 RET
*REF AU 221-256: .5X TO 1.2X BASIC
221-256 AU ODDS 1:89 HOB, 1:197 RET
STATED PRINT RUN 500 SERIAL #'d SETS
1-110 ISSUED IN BOWMAN PACKS
111-256 ISSUED IN BOW.CHROME PACKS
EXCHANGE DEADLINE 8/31/2009

2007 Bowman Chrome Prospects Blue Refractors

*BLUE 1-110: 4X TO 10X BASIC CHROME
*BLUE 111 220: 4X TO 10X BASIC CHROME
1-110 ODDS 1:481 H, 1:80 HTA, 1:1375 R
111-220 ODDS 1:30 H, 1:205 R
*BLUE AU 221-256: 1X TO 2.5X BASIC
221-256 AU ODDS 1:296 HOB, 1:825 RET
STATED PRINT RUN 150 SER.#'d SETS
1-110 ISSUED IN BOWMAN PACKS
111-256 ISSUED IN BOW.CHROME PACKS
EXCHANGE DEADLINE 8/31/2009

2007 Bowman Chrome Prospects Gold Refractors

*GOLD 1-110: 12X TO 30X BASIC CHROME
*GOLD 111-220: 12X TO 30X BASIC CHROME
1-110 ODDS 1:481 H, 1:80 HTA, 1:1375 R
111-220 ODDS 1:88 HOB, 1:615 RET
221-256 AU ODDS 1:889 HOB, 1:8500 RET
STATED PRINT RUN 50 SER.#'d SETS
1-110 ISSUED IN BOWMAN PACKS
111-256 ISSUED IN BOW.CHROME PACKS
EXCHANGE DEADLINE 8/31/2009
BC221 Fernando Martinez AU 50.00 100.00
BC222 Jeremy Papelbon AU 10.00 25.00
BC223 Ryan Adams AU 10.00 25.00
BC224 Chris Perez AU 40.00 80.00
BC225 J.R. Towles AU 10.00 25.00
BC226 Tommy Mendoza AU 10.00 25.00
BC227 Jeff Samardzija AU 15.00 40.00
BC228 Sergio Perez AU 10.00 25.00
BC229 Justin Reed AU 10.00 25.00
BC230 Luke Hochevar AU 10.00 25.00
BC231 Ivan De Jesus Jr. AU 10.00 25.00
BC232 Kevin Mulvey AU 10.00 25.00
BC233 Chris Coghlan AU 40.00 80.00
BC234 Trevor Cahill AU 10.00 25.00
BC235 Peter Bourjos AU 10.00 25.00
BC236 Joba Chamberlain AU 10.00 25.00
BC237 Josh Rodriguez AU 10.00 25.00
BC238 Tim Lincecum AU 100.00 250.00
BC239 Josh Papelbon AU 10.00 60.00
BC240 Greg Reynolds AU 10.00 60.00
BC241 Wes Hodges AU 10.00 60.00
BC242 Chad Reineke AU 10.00 60.00
BC243 Emmanuel Burriss AU 10.00 60.00
BC244 Henry Sosa AU 10.00 60.00
BC245 Cesar Nicolas AU 10.00 60.00
BC246 Young Il Jung AU 10.00 60.00
BC247 Eric Patterson AU 10.00 25.00
BC249 Dellin Betances AU 50.00 120.00
BC250 Will Venable AU 10.00 25.00
BC251 Zach McAllister AU 10.00 25.00
BC252 Mark Hamilton AU 10.00 25.00
BC253 Paul Estrada AU 10.00 25.00
BC254 Brad Lincoln AU 10.00 25.00
BC255 Cedric Hunter AU 10.00 25.00
BC256 Chad Rodgers AU 10.00 25.00

2007 Bowman Chrome Prospects Orange Refractors

1-110 ODDS 1:961 H, 1:160 HTA, 1:2800 R
111-220 ODDS 1:176 HOB, 1:1220 RET
221-256 AU ODDS 1:1780 HOB, 1:3650 RET
STATED PRINT RUN 25 SER.#'d SETS
1-110 ISSUED IN BOWMAN PACKS
111-220 ISSUED IN BOW.CHROME PACKS
NO PRICING DUE TO SCARCITY
EXCHANGE DEADLINE 8/31/2009

2007 Bowman Chrome Prospects X-Fractors

*X-F 1-110: 2.5X TO 6X BASIC CHROME
*X-F 111-220: 2.5X TO 6X BASIC CHROME
1-110 ODDS 1:87 H, 1:15 HTA, 1:260 R
111-220 ODDS 1:18 H, 1:123 R
1-110 PRINT RUN 275 SER.#'d SETS
111-220 PRINT RUN 250 SER.#'d SETS
*X-F AU 221-256: .6X TO 1.5X BASIC
221-256 AU ODDS 1:198 HOB, 1:480 RET
211-256 PRINT RUN 225 SERIAL #'d SETS
1-110 ISSUED IN BOWMAN PACKS
111-256 ISSUED IN BOW.CHROME PACKS
EXCHANGE DEADLINE 8/31/2009

2007 Bowman Chrome Draft

This 55-card set, was inserted at a stated rate of two per Bowman Draft pack. This set was also released in December, 2007. In addition to the same 54 players from the basic Bowman Draft set, card #237 featuring Barry Bonds was also included in this set.

COMPLETE SET (55) 15.00 40.00
COMMON RC (1-55) .25 .60
OVERALL PLATE ODDS 1:1204 HOBBY
PLATE PRINT RUN 1 SET PER COLOR
BLACK-CYAN-MAGENTA-YELLOW ISSUED
NO PLATE PRICING DUE TO SCARCITY
BDP1 Travis Buck (RC) .25 .60
BDP2 Matt Chico (RC) .25 .60
BDP3 Justin Upton RC .75 2.00
BDP4 Chase Wright RC .60 1.50
BDP5 Kevin Kouzmanoff (RC) .25 .60
BDP6 John Danks RC .40 1.00
BDP7 Alejandro De Aza RC .40 1.00
BDP8 Jamie Vermilyea RC .25 .60
BDP9 Jesus Flores RC .25 .60
BDP10 Glen Perkins (RC) .25 .60
BDP11 Tim Lincecum RC 1.25 3.00
BDP12 Cameron Maybin RC .40 1.00
BDP13 Brandon Morrow RC 1.25 3.00
BDP14 Mike Rabelo RC .25 .60
BDP15 Alex Gordon RC .75 2.00
BDP16 Zack Segovia (RC) .25 .60
BDP17 Jon Knott (RC) .25 .60
BDP18 Joba Chamberlain RC .40 1.00
BDP19 Danny Putnam (RC) .25 .60
BDP20 Matt DeSalvo (RC) .25 .60
BDP21 Fred Lewis (RC) .40 1.00
BDP22 Sean Gallagher (RC) .25 .60
BDP23 Brandon Wood (RC) .25 .60
BDP24 Dennis Dove (RC) .25 .60
BDP25 Hunter Pence (RC) .75 2.00
BDP26 Jarrod Saltalamacchia (RC) .40 1.00
BDP27 Ben Francisco (RC) .25 .60
BDP28 Doug Slaten RC .25 .60
BDP29 Tony Abreu RC .60 1.50
BDP30 Billy Butler (RC) .40 1.00
BDP31 Jesse Litsch RC .40 1.00
BDP32 Nate Schierholtz (RC) .25 .60
BDP33 Jared Burton RC .25 .60
BDP34 Matt Brown (RC) .25 .60
BDP35 Dallas Braden RC 1.50 4.00
BDP36 Carlos Gomez RC .50 1.25
BDP37 Brian Stokes (RC) .25 .60
BDP38 Kory Casto (RC) .25 .60
BDP39 Mark McLemore (RC) .25 .60
BDP40 Andy LaRoche (RC) .25 .60
BDP41 Tyler Clippard (RC) .40 1.00
BDP42 Curtis Thigpen (RC) .25 .60
BDP43 Yunel Escobar (RC) .25 .60
BDP44 Andy Sonnanstine RC .25 .60
BDP45 Felix Pie (RC) .25 .60
BDP46 Homer Bailey (RC) .40 1.00
BDP47 Kyle Kendrick RC .60 1.50
BDP48 Angel Sanchez RC .25 .60
BDP49 Phil Hughes (RC) .60 1.50
BDP50 Ryan Braun (RC) 1.25 3.00
BDP51 Kevin Slowey (RC) .60 1.50
BDP52 Brendan Ryan (RC) .25 .60
BDP53 Yovani Gallardo (RC) .60 1.50
BDP54 Mark Reynolds RC .75 2.00
237 Barry Bonds 1.00 2.50

2007 Bowman Chrome Draft Refractors

*REF: 1X TO 2.5X BASIC
STATED ODDS 1:11 HOBBY,1:11 RETAIL

2007 Bowman Chrome Draft Blue Refractors

*BLUE REF: 2X TO 5X BASIC
STATED ODDS 1:58 HOBBY,1:171 RETAIL
STATED PRINT RUN 199 SER.#'d SETS

2007 Bowman Chrome Draft Gold Refractors

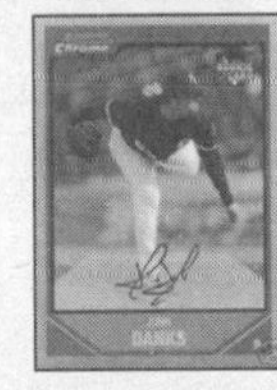

*GOLD REF: 5X TO 12X BASIC
STATED ODDS 1:232 H, 1:659 R
STATED PRINT RUN 50 SER.#'d SETS

2007 Bowman Chrome Draft Orange Refractors

STATED ODDS 1:463 H, 1:1349 R
STATED PRINT RUN 25 SER.#'d SETS
NO PRICING DUE TO SCARCITY

2007 Bowman Chrome Draft X-Fractors

*X-F: 1.5X TO 4X BASIC
STATED ODDS 1:39 HOBBY,1:106 RETAIL
STATED PRINT RUN 299 SER.#'d SETS

2007 Bowman Chrome Draft Draft Picks

66-95 AU ODDS 1:38 HOBBY,1:575 RETAIL
1-65 PLATE ODDS 1:1294 HOBBY
66-95 AU PLATE ODDS 1:14,255 HOBBY
PLATE PRINT RUN 1 SET PER COLOR
BLACK-CYAN-MAGENTA-YELLOW ISSUED
NO PLATE PRICING DUE TO SCARCITY
BDPP1 Cody Crowell .30 .75
BDPP2 Karl Bolt .50 1.25
BDPP3 Corey Brown .50 1.25
BDPP4 Tyler Mach .50 1.25
BDPP5 Trevor Pippin .50 1.25
BDPP6 Ed Easley .30 .75
BDPP7 Cory Luebke .30 .75
BDPP8 Darin Mastroianni .30 .75
BDPP9 Ryan Zink .50 1.25
BDPP10 Brandon Hamilton .30 .75
BDPP11 Kyle Lotzkar .50 1.25
BDPP12 Freddie Freeman 5.00 12.00
BDPP13 Nicholas Barnese .50 1.25
BDPP14 Travis d'Arnaud .50 1.25
BDPP15 Eric Eiland .30 .75
BDPP16 John Ely .30 .75
BDPP17 Oliver Marmol .30 .75
BDPP18 Eric Sogard .30 .75
BDPP19 Lars Davis .30 .75
BDPP20 Sam Runion .30 .75
BDPP21 Austin Gallagher .50 1.25
BDPP22 Matt West .50 1.25
BDPP23 Derek Norris .75 2.00
BDPP24 Taylor Holiday .50 1.25
BDPP25 Dustin Biell .30 .75
BDPP26 Julio Borbon .50 1.25
BDPP27 Brant Rustich .50 1.25
BDPP28 Andrew Lambo .50 1.25
BDPP29 Cory Kluber 1.50 4.00
BDPP30 Justin Jackson .50 1.25
BDPP31 Scott Carroll .30 .75
BDPP32 Danny Rams .30 .75
BDPP33 Thomas Eager .30 .75
BDPP34 Matt Dominguez .75 2.00
BDPP35 Steven Souza 1.00 2.50
BDPP36 Craig Heyer .30 .75
BDPP37 Michael Taylor 1.25 3.00
BDPP38 Drew Bowman .30 .75
BDPP39 Frank Gailey .30 .75
BDPP40 Jeremy Hefner .30 .75
BDPP41 Reynaldo Navarro .50 1.25
BDPP42 Daniel Descalso .50 1.25
BDPP43 Leroy Hunt .30 .75
BDPP44 Jason Kiley .30 .75
BDPP45 Ryan Pope .75 2.00
BDPP46 Josh Horton .30 .75
BDPP47 Jason Monti .30 .75
BDPP48 Richard Lucas .30 .75
BDPP49 Jonathan Lucroy .75 2.00
BDPP50 Sean Doolittle .30 .75
BDPP51 Mike McDade .50 1.25
BDPP52 Charlie Culberson .50 1.25
BDPP53 Michael Moustakas .75 2.00
BDPP54 Jason Heyward 2.00 5.00
BDPP55 David Price 1.00 2.50
BDPP56 Brad Mills .30 .75
BDPP57 John Tolisano 1.00 2.50
BDPP58 Jarrod Parker .75 2.00
BDPP59 Wendell Fairley .50 1.25
BDPP60 Gary Gattis .30 .75
BDPP61 Madison Bumgarner 2.00 5.00
BDPP62 Danny Payne .30 .75
BDPP63 Jake Smolinski 1.00 2.50
BDPP64 Matt LaPorta 1.00 2.50
BDPP65 Jackson Williams .30 .75
BDPP111 Daniel Moskos AU 3.00 8.00
BDPP112 Ross Detwiler AU 3.00 8.00
BDPP113 Tim Alderson AU 3.00 8.00
BDPP114 Beau Mills AU 3.00 8.00
BDPP115 Devin Mesoraco AU 6.00 15.00
BDPP116 Kyle Lotzkar AU 3.00 8.00
BDPP117 Blake Beavan AU 3.00 8.00
BDPP118 Peter Kozma AU 3.00 8.00
BDPP119 Chris Withrow AU 3.00 8.00
BDPP120 Cory Luebke AU 3.00 8.00
BDPP121 Nick Schmidt AU 3.00 8.00
BDPP122 Michael Main AU 3.00 8.00
BDPP123 Aaron Poreda AU 3.00 8.00
BDPP124 James Simmons AU 3.00 8.00
BDPP125 Ben Revere AU 3.00 8.00
BDPP126 Joe Savery AU 3.00 8.00
BDPP127 Jonathan Gilmore AU 3.00 8.00
BDPP128 Todd Frazier AU 6.00 15.00
BDPP129 Matt Mangini AU 3.00 8.00
BDPP130 Casey Weathers AU 3.00 8.00
BDPP131 Nick Noonan AU 3.00 8.00
BDPP132 Kellen Kulbacki AU 3.00 8.00
BDPP133 Michael Burgess AU 3.00 8.00
BDPP134 Nick Hagadone AU 3.00 8.00
BDPP135 Clayton Mortensen AU 3.00 8.00
BDPP136 Justin Jackson AU 3.00 8.00
BDPP137 Ed Easley AU 3.00 8.00
BDPP138 Corey Brown AU 3.00 8.00
BDPP139 Danny Payne AU 3.00 8.00
BDPP140 Travis d'Arnaud AU 8.00 20.00

2007 Bowman Chrome Draft Draft Picks Refractors

*REF 1-65: 1.5X TO 4X BASIC
1-65 ODDS 1:11 HOBBY, 1:11 RETAIL
*REF AU 66-95: .5X TO 1.2X BASIC AU
AU 66-95 ODDS 1:118 H, 1:1700 R
66-95 AU PRINT RUN 500 SER.#'d SETS

2007 Bowman Chrome Draft Draft Picks Blue Refractors

*BLUE REF 1-65: 4X TO 10X BASIC
1-65 ODDS 1:58 HOBBY, 1:171 HOBBY
1-65 PRINT RUN 199 SER.#'d SETS
*BLUE REF AU 66-95: 1X TO 2.5X BASIC AU
AU 66-95 ODDS 1:400 H, 1:12,000 R
66-95 AU PRINT RUN 150 SER.#'d SETS

2007 Bowman Chrome Draft Draft Picks Gold Refractors

*GOLD REF 1-65: 8X TO 20X BASIC
1-65 ODDS 1:232 H, 1:659 R
1-65 PRINT RUN 50 SER.#'d SETS
COMMON AUTO (66-95) 30.00 60.00
AU 66-95 ODDS 1:1270 H, 1:9440 R
66-95 AU PRINT RUN 50 SER.#'d SETS
BDPP111 Daniel Moskos AU 12.50 30.00
BDPP112 Ross Detwiler AU 12.50 30.00
BDPP113 Tim Alderson AU 12.50 30.00
BDPP114 Beau Mills AU 12.50 30.00
BDPP115 Devin Mesoraco AU 40.00 100.00
BDPP116 Kyle Lotzkar AU 12.50 30.00
BDPP117 Blake Beavan AU 12.50 30.00
BDPP118 Peter Kozma AU 12.50 30.00
BDPP119 Chris Withrow AU 12.50 30.00
BDPP120 Cory Luebke AU 12.50 30.00
BDPP121 Nick Schmidt AU 12.50 30.00
BDPP122 Michael Main AU 12.50 30.00
BDPP123 Aaron Poreda AU 12.50 30.00
BDPP124 James Simmons AU 12.50 30.00
BDPP125 Ben Revere AU 12.00 30.00
BDPP126 Joe Savery AU 12.00 30.00
BDPP127 Jonathan Gilmore AU 12.00 30.00
BDPP129 Matt Mangini AU 12.50 30.00
BDPP130 Casey Weathers AU 12.50 30.00
BDPP131 Nick Noonan AU 12.50 30.00
BDPP132 Kellen Kulbacki AU 12.50 30.00
BDPP133 Michael Burgess AU 12.50 30.00
BDPP134 Nick Hagadone AU 12.50 30.00
BDPP135 Clayton Mortensen AU 12.50 30.00
BDPP136 Justin Jackson AU 12.50 30.00
BDPP137 Ed Easley AU 12.50 30.00
BDPP138 Corey Brown AU 12.50 30.00
BDPP139 Danny Payne AU 12.50 30.00
BDPP140 Travis d'Arnaud AU 75.00 150.00

2007 Bowman Chrome Draft Draft Picks Orange Refractors

1-65 STATED ODDS 1:463 H, 1:1349 R
66-95 AU ODDS 1:2345 H, 1:28,320 R
STATED PRINT RUN 25 SERIAL #'d SETS
NO PRICING DUE TO SCARCITY

2007 Bowman Chrome Draft Draft Picks X-Fractors

*X-F 1-65: 2.5X TO 6X BASIC
1-65 STATED ODDS 1:39 H, 1:106 R
1-65 PRINT RUN 299 SER.#'d SETS
*X-F AU 66-95: .6X TO 1.5X BASIC
66-95 AU STATED ODDS 1:262 H, 1:14,000 R
66-95 AU PRINT RUN 225 SER.#'d SETS

2007 Bowman Chrome Draft Future's Game Prospects

COMPLETE SET (45) 12.50 30.00
OVERALL PLATE ODDS 1:1294 HOBBY
PLATE PRINT RUN 1 SET PER COLOR
BLACK-CYAN-MAGENTA-YELLOW ISSUED
NO PLATE PRICING DUE TO SCARCITY
BDPP66 Pedro Beato .20 .50
BDPP67 Collin Balester .20 .50
BDPP68 Carlos Carrasco .30 .75
BDPP69 Clay Buchholz .60 1.50
BDPP70 Emiliano Fruto .20 .50
BDPP71 Joba Chamberlain .30 .75
BDPP72 Deolis Guerra .40 1.00
BDPP73 Kevin Mulvey .50 1.25
BDPP74 Franklin Morales .30 .75
BDPP75 Luke Hochevar .60 1.50
BDPP76 Henry Sosa .30 .75
BDPP77 Clayton Kershaw 4.00 10.00
BDPP78 Rich Thompson .20 .50
BDPP79 Chuck Lofgren .50 1.25
BDPP80 Rick VandenHurk .20 .50
BDPP81 Michael Madsen .20 .50
BDPP82 Robinzon Diaz .20 .50
BDPP83 Jeff Niemann .30 .75
BDPP84 Max Ramirez .20 .50
BDPP85 Geovany Soto .75 2.00
BDPP86 Elvis Andrus .50 1.25
BDPP87 Bryan Anderson .20 .50
BDPP88 German Duran .75 2.00
BDPP89 J.R. Towles .60 1.50
BDPP90 Alcides Escobar .50 1.25
BDPP91 Brian Bocock .20 .50
BDPP92 Chin-Lung Hu .20 .50
BDPP93 Adrian Cardenas .20 .50
BDPP94 Freddy Sandoval .20 .50
BDPP95 Chris Coghlan .60 1.50
BDPP96 Craig Stansberry .20 .50
BDPP97 Brent Lillibridge .20 .50
BDPP98 Joey Votto 1.25 3.00
BDPP99 Evan Longoria 2.00 5.00
BDPP100 Wladimir Balentien .20 .50
BDPP101 Johnny Whittleman .20 .50
BDPP102 Gorkys Hernandez .50 1.25
BDPP103 Jay Bruce 1.25 3.00
BDPP104 Matt Tolbert .20 .50
BDPP105 Jacoby Ellsbury 1.25 3.00
BDPP106 Michael Saunders .60 1.50
BDPP107 Cameron Maybin .30 .75
BDPP108 Carlos Gonzalez .50 1.25
BDPP109 Colby Rasmus .50 1.25
BDPP110 Justin Upton .60 1.50

2007 Bowman Chrome Draft Future's Game Prospects Refractors

*REF: 1X TO 2.5X BASIC
STATED ODDS 1:11 HOBBY,1:11 RETAIL

2007 Bowman Chrome Draft Future's Game Prospects Blue Refractors

*BLUE REF: 2X TO 5X BASIC
STATED ODDS 1:58 HOBBY,1:171 RETAIL
STATED PRINT RUN 199 SER.#'d SETS

2007 Bowman Chrome Draft Future's Game Prospects Gold Refractors

*GOLD REF: 5X TO 12X BASIC
STATED ODDS 1:232 H, 1:659 R
STATED PRINT RUN 50 SER.#'d SETS

2007 Bowman Chrome Draft Future's Game Prospects Orange Refractors

STATED ODDS 1:463 H, 1:1349 R
STATED PRINT RUN 25 SER.#'d SETS
NO PRICING DUE TO SCARCITY

2007 Bowman Chrome Draft Future's Game Prospects X-Fractors

*X-F: 1.5X TO 4X BASIC
STATED ODDS 1:39 HOBBY,1:106 RETAIL
STATED PRINT RUN 299 SER.#'d SETS

2007 Bowman Chrome Draft Future's Game Prospects Bases

STATED ODDS 1:633 HOBBY
STATED PRINT RUN 135 SER.#'d SETS
BDPP86 Elvis Andrus 4.00 10.00
BDPP87 Bryan Anderson 3.00 8.00
BDPP88 German Duran 3.00 8.00
BDPP89 J.R. Towles 3.00 8.00
BDPP91 Brian Bocock 3.00 8.00
BDPP92 Chin-Lung Hu 10.00 25.00
BDPP93 Adrian Cardenas 3.00 8.00
BDPP94 Freddy Sandoval 3.00 8.00
BDPP95 Chris Coghlan 3.00 8.00
BDPP97 Brent Lillibridge 4.00 10.00
BDPP98 Joey Votto 5.00 12.00
BDPP99 Evan Longoria 12.50 30.00
BDPP101 Johnny Whittleman 3.00 8.00
BDPP102 Gorkys Hernandez 4.00 10.00
BDPP103 Jay Bruce 6.00 15.00
BDPP105 Jacoby Ellsbury 6.00 15.00
BDPP106 Michael Saunders 4.00 10.00
BDPP108 Carlos Gonzalez 4.00 10.00
BDPP109 Colby Rasmus 6.00 15.00
BDPP110 Justin Upton 10.00 25.00

2008 Bowman Chrome

COMPLETE SET (220) 15.00 40.00
COMMON CARD (1-190) .20 .50
COMMON ROOKIE (1-220) .60 1.50
1-220 PLATE ODDS 1:1382 HOBBY
PLATE PRINT RUN 1 SET PER COLOR
BLACK-CYAN-MAGENTA-YELLOW ISSUED
NO PLATE PRICING DUE TO SCARCITY
1 Ryan Braun .30 .75
2 David DeJesus .20 .50
3 Brandon Phillips .20 .50
4 Mark Teixeira .30 .75
5 Daisuke Matsuzaka .30 .75
6 Justin Upton .30 .75
7 Jered Weaver .30 .75
8 Todd Helton .30 .75
9 Adam Jones .30 .75
10 Erik Bedard .20 .50
11 Jason Bay .20 .50
12 Cole Hamels .40 1.00
13 Bobby Abreu .20 .50
14 Carlos Zambrano .30 .75
15 Vladimir Guerrero .30 .75
16 Joe Blanton .20 .50
17 Paul Maholm .20 .50
18 Adrian Gonzalez .30 .75
19 Brandon Webb .30 .75
20 Carl Crawford .30 .75
21 A.J. Burnett .20 .50
22 Dmitri Young .20 .50
23 Jeremy Hermida .20 .50
24 C.C. Sabathia .30 .75
25 Adam Dunn .30 .75
26 Matt Garza .20 .50
27 Adrian Beltre .50 1.25
28 Kevin Millwood .20 .50
29 Manny Ramirez .50 1.25
30 Javier Vazquez .20 .50
31 Carlos Delgado .20 .50
32 Torii Hunter .20 .50
33 Ivan Rodriguez .30 .75
34 Nick Markakis .40 1.00
35 Gil Meche .20 .50
36 Garrett Atkins .20 .50
37 Fausto Carmona .20 .50
38 Joe Mauer .40 1.00
39 Tom Glavine .30 .75
40 Hideki Matsui .50 1.25
41 Scott Rolen .30 .75
42 Tim Lincecum .30 .75
43 Prince Fielder .30 .75
44 Kazuo Matsui .20 .50
45 Tom Gorzelanny .20 .50
46 Lance Berkman .30 .75
47 David Ortiz .50 1.25
48 Dontrelle Willis .20 .50
49 Travis Hafner .20 .50
50 Aaron Harang .20 .50
51 Chris Young .20 .50
52 Vernon Wells .20 .50
53 Francisco Liriano .20 .50
54 Eric Chavez .20 .50
55 Phil Hughes .20 .50
56 Melvin Mora .20 .50
57 Johan Santana .30 .75
58 Brian McCann .30 .75
59 Pat Burrell .20 .50
60 Chris Carpenter .30 .75
61 Brian Giles .20 .50
62 Jose Reyes .30 .75
63 Hanley Ramirez .30 .75
64 Ubaldo Jimenez .20 .50
65 Felix Pie .20 .50
66 Jeremy Bonderman .20 .50
67 Jimmy Rollins .30 .75
68 Miguel Tejada .30 .75
69 Derek Lowe .20 .50
70 Alex Gordon .30 .75
71 John Maine .20 .50
72 Alfonso Soriano .30 .75
73 Ben Sheets .20 .50
74 Hunter Pence .30 .75
75 Magglio Ordonez .30 .75
76 Josh Beckett .20 .50
77 Victor Martinez .30 .75
78 Mark Buehrle .30 .75
79 Jason Varitek .50 1.25
80 Chien-Ming Wang .30 .75
81 Ken Griffey Jr. 1.00 2.50
82 Billy Butler .20 .50
83 Brad Penny .20 .50
84 Carlos Beltran .30 .75
85 Curt Schilling .30 .75
86 Jorge Posada .30 .75
87 Andruw Jones .20 .50
88 Bobby Crosby .20 .50
89 Freddy Sanchez .20 .50
90 Barry Zito .30 .75
91 Miguel Cabrera .50 1.25
92 B.J. Upton .20 .50
93 Matt Cain .30 .75
94 Lyle Overbay .20 .50
95 Austin Kearns .20 .50
96 Alex Rodriguez .60 1.50
97 Rich Harden .20 .50
98 Justin Morneau .30 .75
99 Oliver Perez .20 .50
100 Gary Matthews .20 .50
101 Matt Holliday .50 1.25
102 Justin Verlander .50 1.25
103 Orlando Cabrera .30 .75
104 Rich Hill .20 .50
105 Tim Hudson .30 .75
106 Ryan Zimmerman .30 .75
107 Roy Oswalt .30 .75
108 Nick Swisher .30 .75
109 Raul Ibanez .30 .75
110 Kelly Johnson .20 .50
111 Alex Rios .20 .50
112 John Lackey .30 .75
113 Robinson Cano .30 .75
114 Michael Young .20 .50
115 Jeff Francis .20 .50
116 Grady Sizemore .30 .75
117 Mike Lowell .20 .50
118 Aramis Ramirez .20 .50
119 Stephen Drew .20 .50
120 Yovani Gallardo .20 .50
121 Chase Utley .30 .75
122 Dan Haren .20 .50
123 Yunel Escobar .20 .50
124 Greg Maddux .60 1.50
125 Garret Anderson .20 .50
126 Aubrey Huff .20 .50
127 Paul Konerko .30 .75
128 Dan Uggla .20 .50
129 Roy Halladay .30 .75
130 Andre Ethier .30 .75
131 Orlando Hernandez .20 .50
132 Troy Tulowitzki .50 1.25
133 Carlos Guillen .20 .50
134 Scott Kazmir .30 .75
135 Aaron Rowand .20 .50
136 Jim Edmonds .30 .75
137 Jermaine Dye .20 .50
138 Orlando Hudson .20 .50
139 Derrek Lee .20 .50
140 Travis Buck .30 .75
141 Zack Greinke .30 .75
142 Jeff Kent .20 .50
143 John Smoltz .50 1.25
144 David Wright .30 .75
145 Joba Chamberlain .20 .50
146 Adam LaRoche .20 .50
147 Kevin Youkilis .20 .50
148 Troy Glaus .30 .75
149 Nick Johnson .20 .50
150 J.J. Hardy .20 .50
151 Felix Hernandez .30 .75
152 Gary Sheffield .20 .50
153 Albert Pujols .60 1.50
154 Chuck James .20 .50
155 Kosuke Fukudome RC 4.00 10.00
155b Kosuke Fukudome Japan 4.00 10.00
155c Fukudome No Sig/1600 * 10.00 25.00
156 Eric Byrnes .20 .50
157 Brad Hawpe .20 .50
158 Delmon Young .30 .75
159 Brian Roberts .20 .50
160 Russ Martin .20 .50
161 Hank Blalock .20 .50
162 Yadier Molina .50 1.25
163 Jeremy Guthrie .20 .50
164 Chipper Jones .50 1.25
165 Johnny Damon .30 .75
166 Ryan Garko .20 .50
167 Jake Peavy .20 .50
168 Chone Figgins .20 .50
169 Edgar Renteria .20 .50
170 Jim Thome .30 .75
171 Carlos Pena .30 .75
172 Dustin Pedroia .30 .75
173 Brett Myers .20 .50
174 Josh Hamilton .30 .75
175 Randy Johnson .50 1.25
176 Ichiro Suzuki .60 1.50
177 Aaron Hill .20 .50
178 Corey Hart .20 .50
179 Jarrod Saltalamacchia .20 .50
180 Jeff Francoeur .30 .75
181 Derek Jeter 1.25 3.00
182 Curtis Granderson .30 .75
183 James Loney .20 .50
184 Brian Bannister .20 .50
185 Carlos Lee .20 .50
186 Pedro Martinez .30 .75
187 Asdrubal Cabrera .30 .75
188 Kenji Johjima .20 .50
189 Jacoby Ellsbury .40 1.00
190 Ryan Howard .30 .75
191 Sean Rodriguez (RC) .60 1.50
192 Justin Ruggiano RC 1.00 2.50
193 Jed Lowrie (RC) .60 1.50
194 Joey Votto (RC) 2.50 6.00
195 Denard Span (RC) 1.00 2.50
196 Brad Harman RC 1.00 2.50
197 Jeff Niemann (RC) .60 1.50
198 Chin-Lung Hu (RC) .60 1.50
199 Luke Hochevar RC 1.00 2.50
200 German Duran RC 1.00 2.50
201 Troy Patton (RC) .60 1.50
202 Hiroki Kuroda RC 1.50 4.00
203 David Purcey (RC) .60 1.50
204 Armando Galarraga RC 1.00 2.50
205 John Bowker (RC) .60 1.50
206 Nick Blackburn RC 1.00 2.50
207 Hernan Iribarren (RC) 1.00 2.50
208 Greg Smith RC .60 1.50
209 Alberto Gonzalez RC 1.00 2.50
210 Justin Masterson RC 1.50 4.00
211 Brian Barton RC 1.00 2.50
212 Robinzon Diaz (RC) .60 1.50
213 Clete Thomas RC 1.00 2.50
214 Kazuo Fukumori RC 1.00 2.50
215 Jayson Nix (RC) .60 1.50
216 Evan Longoria RC 3.00 8.00
217 Johnny Cueto RC 1.50 4.00
218 Matt Tolbert RC 1.00 2.50
219 Masahide Kobayashi RC 1.00 2.50
220 Callix Crabbe (RC) .60 1.50

2008 Bowman Chrome Refractors

*REF 1-190: 1X TO 2.5X BASIC
*REF 1-221: .6X TO 1.5X BASIC
1-221 ODDS

2008 Bowman Chrome Blue Refractors

*BLUE REF 1-190: 2.5X TO 6X BASIC
*BLUE REF 1-221: 1.2X TO 3X BASIC
1-221 ODDS 1:66 HOBBY
STATED PRINT RUN 150 SERIAL #'d SETS
198 Chin-Lung Hu 10.00 25.00
204 Armando Galarraga 10.00 25.00

2008 Bowman Chrome Gold Refractors

*GOLD REF 1-190: 4X TO 10X BASIC
*GOLD REF 1-221: 2X TO 5X BASIC
1-221 ODDS 1:197 HOBBY
STATED PRINT RUN 50 SERIAL #'d SETS
42 Tim Lincecum 15.00 40.00
80 Chien-Ming Wang 60.00 120.00
96 Alex Rodriguez 20.00 50.00
176 Ichiro Suzuki 20.00 50.00
181 Derek Jeter 30.00 60.00
189 Jacoby Ellsbury 15.00 40.00
198 Chin-Lung Hu 30.00 60.00
204 Armando Galarraga 30.00 60.00
210 Justin Masterson 20.00 50.00

2008 Bowman Chrome Orange Refractors

STATED ODDS 1:393 HOBBY
STATED PRINT RUN 25 SER.#'d SETS
NO PRICING DUE TO SCARCITY

2008 Bowman Chrome X-Fractors

*X-FRACTOR 1-190: 2X TO 5X BASIC
*X-FRACTOR 1-221: 1X TO 2.5X BASIC
1-221 ODDS 1:40 HOBBY
STATED PRINT RUN 250 SER.#'d SETS
155 Kosuke Fukudome 10.00 25.00
155b Kosuke Fukudome Japan 10.00 25.00
198 Chin-Lung Hu 5.00 12.00
204 Armando Galarraga 8.00 20.00

2008 Bowman Chrome Head of the Class Dual Autograph

STATED ODDS 1:1773 HOBBY
STATED PRINT RUN 350 SER.#'d SETS
CH Joba/P.Hughes 4.00 10.00
FL Prince Fielder/Matt LaPorta 8.00 20.00
LP E.Logoria/D.Price 12.00 30.00

2008 Bowman Chrome Head of the Class Dual Autograph X-Fractors

*X-F: .6X TO 1.5X BASIC
STATED ODDS 1:12,823 HOBBY
STATED PRINT RUN 50 SER.#'d SETS

2008 Bowman Chrome Head of the Class Dual Autograph Refractors

*REF: .5X TO 1.2X BASIC
STATED ODDS 1:6298 HOBBY
STATED PRINT RUN 99 SER.#'d SETS

2008 Bowman Chrome Prospects

COMP.SET w/o AU's (220) 30.00 60.00
COMP.SET w/o AU's (1-110) 12.50 30.00
COMP.SET w/o AU's (131-240) 12.50 30.00
111-130 AU ODDS 1:37 HOBBY
241-285 AU ODDS 1:31 HOBBY
1-110 PLATE ODDS 1:732 HOBBY
111-130 AU PLATE ODDS 1:4700 HOBBY
131-240 PLATE ODDS 1:1132 HOBBY
241-285 AU PLATES 1:10,471 HOBBY
PLATE PRINT RUN 1 SET PER COLOR
BLACK-CYAN-MAGENTA-YELLOW ISSUED
NO PLATE PRICING DUE TO SCARCITY
BCP1 Max Sapp .20 .50
BCP2 Jamie Richmond .20 .50
BCP3 Darren Ford .20 .50
BCP4 Sergio Romo 1.00 2.50
BCP5 Jacob Butler .20 .50
BCP6 Glenn Gibson .20 .50
BCP7 Tom Hagan .20 .50
BCP8 Michael McCormick .20 .50
BCP9 Gregorio Petit .30 .75
BCP10 Bobby Parnell .20 .50
BCP11 Jeff Kindel .30 .75
BCP12 Anthony Claggett .20 .50
BCP13 Christopher Frey .20 .50
BCP14 Jonah Nickerson .30 .75
BCP15 Anthony Martinez .20 .50
BCP16 Rusty Ryal .30 .75
BCP17 Justin Berg .30 .75
BCP18 Gerardo Parra .20 .50
BCP19 Wesley Wright .20 .50
BCP20 Stephen Chapman .20 .50
BCP21 Chance Chapman .20 .50
BCP22 Brett Pill .60 1.50
BCP23 Zachary Phillips .20 .50
BCP24 John Raynor .50 1.25
BCP25 Danny Duffy .50 1.25
BCP26 Brian Finegan .20 .50
BCP27 Jonathan Venters .20 .50
BCP28 Steve Tolleson .20 .50
BCP29 Ben Jukich .30 .75
BCP30 Matthew Weston .20 .50
BCP31 Kyle Mura .20 .50
BCP32 Luke Hetherington .20 .50
BCP33 Michael Daniel .30 .75
BCP34 Jake Renshaw .20 .50
BCP35 Greg Halman .30 .75
BCP36 Ryan Khoury .20 .50
BCP37 Ryan Ouellette .20 .50
BCP38 Mike Brantley .50 1.25
BCP39 Eric Brown .20 .50
BCP40 Jose Duarte .20 .50
BCP41 Eli Tintor .20 .50
BCP42 Kent Sakamoto .20 .50
BCP43 Luke Montz .20 .50
BCP44 Alex Cobb .20 .50
BCP45 Michael McKenry .20 .50
BCP46 Javier Castillo .20 .50
BCP47 Jeffrey Stevens .20 .50
BCP48 Greg Burns .20 .50
BCP49 Blake Johnson .20 .50
BCP50 Austin Jackson 1.00 2.50
BCP51 Anthony Recker .20 .50
BCP52 Luis Durango .20 .50
BCP53 Engel Beltre .60 1.50
BCP54 Seth Bynum .20 .50
BCP55 Ryan Strieby .30 .75
BCP56 Iggy Suarez .20 .50
BCP57 Ryan Morris .30 .75
BCP58 Scott Van Slyke .60 1.50
BCP59 Tyler Kolodny .60 1.50
BCP60 Joseph Martinez .20 .50
BCP61 Aaron Mathews .20 .50
BCP62 Phillip Cuadrado .20 .50
BCP63 Alex Liddi .30 .75
BCP64 Alex Burnett .30 .75
BCP65 Brian Barton .30 .75
BCP66 David Welch .20 .50
BCP67 Kyle Reynolds .20 .50
BCP68 Francisco Hernandez .20 .50
BCP69 Logan Morrison 1.00 2.50
BCP70 Ronald Ramirez .20 .50
BCP71 Brad Miller .20 .50
BCP72 Braedyn Pruitt .30 .75
BCP73 Jason Fernandez .30 .75
BCP74 Joseph Mahoney .20 .50
BCP75 Quentin Davis .30 .75
BCP76 P.J. Walters .20 .50
BCP77 Jordan Czarniecki .20 .50
BCP78 Jonathan Mota .20 .50
BCP79 Michael Hernandez .20 .50
BCP80 James Guerrero .20 .50
BCP81 Chris Johnson .30 .75
BCP82 Daniel Cortes .50 1.25
BCP83 Sal Sanchez .30 .75
BCP84 Sean Henry .20 .50
BCP85 Caleb Gindl .20 .50
BCP86 Tommy Everidge .20 .50
BCP87 Matt Rizzotti .20 .50
BCP88 Luis Munoz .20 .50
BCP89 Matthew Klimas .20 .50
BCP90 Angel Reyes .20 .50
BCP91 Sean Danielson .20 .50
BCP92 Omar Poveda .20 .50
BCP93 Mario Lisson .20 .50
BCP94 Brian Mathews .20 .50
BCP95 Matthew Buschmann .20 .50
BCP96 Greg Thomson .20 .50
BCP97 Matt Inouye .20 .50
BCP98 Aneury Rodriguez .30 .75
BCP99 Brad Harman .20 .50
BCP100 Aaron Bates .50 1.25
BCP101 Graham Taylor .20 .50
BCP102 Ken Holmberg .20 .50
BCP103 Greg Dowling .20 .50
BCP104 Ronnie Ray .20 .50
BCP105 Michael Wlodarczyk .20 .50
BCP106 Jose Martinez .30 .75
BCP107 Jason Stephens .30 .75
BCP108 Will Rhymes .20 .50
BCP109 Joey Side .20 .50
BCP110 Brandon Waring .30 .75
BCP111 David Price AU 12.00 30.00
BCP112 Michael Moustakas AU 5.00 12.00
BCP113 Matt LaPorta AU 3.00 8.00
BCP114 Wendell Fairley AU 3.00 8.00
BCP115 Josh Vitters AU 3.00 8.00
BCP116 Jonathan Bachanov AU 3.00 8.00
BCP117 Edward Kunz AU 3.00 8.00
BCP118 Matt Dominguez AU 3.00 8.00
BCP119 Kyle Lotzkar AU 3.00 8.00
BCP120 M.Bumgarner AU 40.00 100.00
BCP121 Jason Heyward AU 8.00 20.00
BCP122 Julio Borbon AU 3.00 8.00
BCP123 Josh Smoker AU 3.00 8.00
BCP124 Jarrod Parker AU 3.00 8.00
BCP125 Kevin Ahrens AU 3.00 8.00
BCP126 J.P. Arencibia AU 3.00 8.00
BCP127 Josh Bell AU 3.00 8.00
BCP128 Scott Cousins AU 3.00 8.00
BCP129 Brandon Hynick AU 3.00 8.00
BCP130 Alan Johnson AU 3.00 8.00
BCP131 Zhenwang Zhang .30 .75
BCP132 Chris Nash .20 .50
BCP133 Sergio Morales .20 .50
BCP134 Carlos Santana .60 1.50
BCP135 Carlos Monasterios .20 .50
BCP136 Quincy Latimore .20 .50
BCP137 Yamaico Navarro .60 1.50
BCP138 Ryan Mullins .20 .50
BCP139 Collin DeLome .30 .75
BCP140 Hector Correa .20 .50
BCP141 Mitch Canham .20 .50
BCP142 Robert Fish .20 .50
BCP143 Ryan Royster .20 .50
BCP144 Eric Barrett .20 .50
BCP145 Deibinson Romero .30 .75
BCP146 Jeff Gerbe .20 .50
BCP147 Lucas Duda .60 1.50
BCP148 Bryan Morris .30 .75
BCP149 Andrew Romine .20 .50
BCP150 Glenn Gibson .20 .50
BCP151 Danny Brezeale .20 .50
BCP152 Shairon Martis .30 .75
BCP153 Helder Velazquez .20 .50
BCP154 Alan Farina .20 .50
BCP155 Brandon Barnes .20 .50
BCP156 Waldis Joaquin .20 .50
BCP157 Luis De La Cruz .20 .50
BCP158 Yunesky Sanchez .20 .50
BCP159 Mitch Hilligross .20 .50
BCP160 Vin Mazzaro .60 1.50
BCP161 Marcus Davis .20 .50
BCP162 Tony Barnette .20 .50
BCP163 Joe Benson .50 1.25
BCP164 Jake Arrieta .50 1.25
BCP165 Alfredo Silverio .50 1.25
BCP166 Duane Below .20 .50
BCP167 Kai Liu .30 .75
BCP168 Zach Britton .60 1.50
BCP169 Jamie Pedroza .30 .75
BCP170 Frank Herrmann .20 .50
BCP171 Justin Turner 1.00 2.50
BCP172 Jeff Manship .20 .50
BCP173 Paul Winterling .20 .50
BCP174 Nathan Vineyard .30 .75
BCP175 Jason Delaney .20 .50
BCP176 Ivan Nova 1.25 3.00
BCP177 Esmailyn Gonzalez .60 1.50
BCP178 Brett Cecil .30 .75
BCP179 Jose Martinez .20 .50
BCP180 Brad Peacock .60 1.50
BCP181 Justin Snyder .30 .75
BCP182 Steve Garrison .20 .50
BCP183 Joe Mahoney .20 .50

BCP184 Graham Godfrey .20 .50
BCP185 Larry Williams .20 .50
BCP186 Jeremy Haynes .20 .50
BCP187 Brent Brewer .50 1.25
BCP188 Jhoulys Chacin .30 .75
BCP189 Nevin Ashley .30 .75
BCP190 Justin Cassel .20 .50
BCP191 Jon Jay .30 .75
BCP192 Chris Huseby .20 .50
BCP193 D.J. Jones .30 .75
BCP194 David Bromberg .30 .75
BCP195 Juan Francisco .50 1.25
BCP196 Zach Jevne .20 .50
BCP197 Darwin Barney 1.00 2.50
BCP198 Jose Ortegano .30 .75
BCP199 Dominic Brown 1.25 3.00
BCP200 Kyle Ginley .20 .50
BCP201 David Wood .20 .50
BCP202 Jhonny Nunez .20 .50
BCP203 Carlos Rivero .50 1.25
BCP204 Anthony Varvaro .20 .50
BCP205 Christian Lopez .20 .50
BCP206 Travis Banwart .20 .50
BCP207 Rhyne Hughes .20 .50
BCP208 Heath Rollins .30 .75
BCP209 Zack Cozart .60 1.50
BCP210 Mike Dunn .20 .50
BCP211 Chris Pettit .20 .50
BCP212 Dan Berlind .20 .50
BCP213 Ernesto Mejia .30 .75
BCP214 Hector Rondon .30 .75
BCP215 Jose Vallejo .30 .75
BCP216 Kyle Schmidt .20 .50
BCP217 Bubba Bell .50 1.25
BCP218 Charlie Furbush .20 .50
BCP219 Pedro Baez .50 1.25
BCP220 Brandon MaGee .20 .50
BCP221 Clint Robinson .20 .50
BCP222 Fabio Castillo .30 .75
BCP223 Brad Emaus .30 .75
BCP224 Mike DeJesus .20 .50
BCP225 Brandon Laird .30 .75
BCP226 R.J. Seidel .20 .50
BCP227 Agustin Murillo .20 .50
BCP228 Trevor Reckling .60 1.50
BCP229 Hector Gomez .50 1.25
BCP230 Jordan Norberto .20 .50
BCP231 Steve Hill .20 .50
BCP232 Hassan Pena .20 .50
BCP233 Justin Henry .30 .75
BCP234 Chase Lirette .20 .50
BCP235 Christian Marrero .30 .75
BCP236 Will Kline .20 .50
BCP237 Johan Limonta .20 .50
BCP238 Duke Welker .20 .50
BCP239 Jeudy Valdez .30 .75
BCP240 Elvin Ramirez .20 .50
BCP241 Josh Kreuzer AU 3.00 8.00
BCP242 Ryan Zink AU 3.00 8.00
BCP243 Matt Harrison AU 3.00 8.00
BCP244 Dustin Richardson AU 3.00 8.00
BCP245 Fautino De Los Santos AU 3.00 8.00
BCP246 Austin Jackson AU 3.00 8.00
BCP247 Jordan Schafer AU 3.00 8.00
BCP248 Daryl Thompson AU 3.00 8.00
BCP249 Lars Anderson AU 3.00 8.00
BCP250 Tim Bascom AU 3.00 8.00
BCP251 Brandon Hicks AU 3.00 8.00
BCP252 David Kopp AU 3.00 8.00
BCP253 Danny Lehmann AU 3.00 8.00
BCP254 Zimmerman AU UER 3.00 8.00
BCP255 Cale Iorg AU 3.00 8.00
BCP256 Austin Romine AU 3.00 8.00
BCP257 Chaz Roe AU 3.00 8.00
BCP258 Danny Rams AU 3.00 8.00
BCP259 Daniel Bard AU 3.00 8.00
BCP260 Engel Beltre AU 3.00 8.00
BCP261 Michael Watt AU 3.00 8.00
BCP262 Brennan Boesch AU 3.00 8.00
BCP263 Matt Latos AU 4.00 10.00
BCP264 John Jaso AU 3.00 8.00
BCP265 Adrian Alaniz AU 3.00 8.00
BCP266 Matt Green AU 3.00 8.00
BCP267 Andrew Lambo AU 3.00 8.00
BCP268 Michael McCardell AU 3.00 8.00
BCP269 Chris Valaika AU 3.00 8.00
BCP270 Cole Rohrbough AU 3.00 8.00
BCP271 Andrew Brackman AU 3.00 8.00
BCP272 Bud Norris AU 3.00 8.00
BCP273 Ryan Kalish AU 3.00 8.00
BCP274 Jake McGee AU 3.00 8.00
BCP275 Aaron Cunningham AU 3.00 8.00
BCP276 Mitch Boggs AU 3.00 8.00
BCP277 Bradley Suttle AU 3.00 8.00
BCP278 Henry Rodriguez AU 3.00 8.00
BCP279 Mario Lisson AU 3.00 8.00
BCP280 Ludovicus Van Mil AU 3.00 8.00
BCP281 Angel Villalona AU 3.00 8.00
BCP282 Mark Melancon AU 3.00 8.00
BCP283 Brian Dinkelman AU 3.00 8.00
BCP284 Daniel McCutchen AU 3.00 8.00
BCP285 Rene Tosoni AU 3.00 8.00

2008 Bowman Chrome Prospects Refractors

*REF 1-110: 2.5X TO 6X BASIC
*REF 131-240: 2.5X TO 6X BASIC
1-110 ODDS 1:34 HOBBY,1:88 RETAIL
131-240 ODDS 1:40 HOBBY
1-110 PRINT RUN 599 SER.#'d SETS
131-240 PRINT RUN 500 SER.#'d SETS
*REF AU 111-130: .5X TO 1.2X BASIC
*REF AU 241-285: .5X TO 1.2X BASIC
111-130 AU ODDS 1:113 HOBBY
241-285 AU ODDS 1:88 HOBBY
111-130 AU PRINT RUN 500 SER.#'d SETS
241-285 AU PRINT RUN 500 SER.#'d SETS

2008 Bowman Chrome Prospects Blue Refractors

*BLUE 1-110: 5X TO 12X BASIC
*BLUE 131-240: 5X TO 12X BASIC
1-110 ODDS 1:126 HOBBY,1:350 RETAIL
131-240 ODDS 1:131 HOBBY
1-110 PRINT RUN 150 SER.#'d SETS
131-240 PRINT RUN 150 SER.#'d SETS
*BLUE AU 111-130: 1.2X TO 3X BASIC
*BLUE AU 241-285: 1.2X TO 3X BASIC
111-130 AU ODDS 1:372 HOBBY
241-285 AU ODDS 1:295 HOBBY
111-130 AU PRINT RUN 150 SER.#'d SETS
241-285 AU PRINT RUN 150 SER.#'d SETS
BCP120 M.Bumgarner AU 150.00 400.00

2008 Bowman Chrome Prospects Gold Refractors

*GOLD 1-110: 12X TO 30X BASIC
*GOLD 131-240: 12X TO 30X BASIC
1-110 ODDS 1:380 HOB, 1:1040 RET
131-240 ODDS 1:393 HOBBY
1-110 PRINT RUN 50 SER.#'d SETS
131-240 PRINT RUN 50 SER.#'d SETS
111-130 AU ODDS 1:1155 HOBBY
241-285 AU ODDS 1:953 HOBBY
111-130 AU PRINT RUN 50 SER.#'d SETS
241-285 AU PRINT RUN 50 SER.#'d SETS
BCP111 David Price AU 75.00 200.00
BCP120 M.Bumgarner AU 500.00 1000.00

2008 Bowman Chrome Prospects Orange Refractors

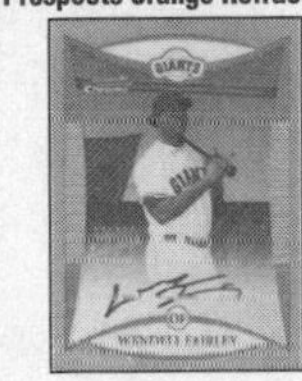

1-110 ODDS 1:750 HOB, 1:2075 RET
111-130 AU ODDS 1:2495 HOBBY
131-240 ODDS 1:785 HOBBY
241-285 AU ODDS 1:1784 HOBBY
STATED PRINT RUN 25 SER.#'d SETS
NO PRICING DUE TO SCARCITY

2008 Bowman Chrome Prospects X-Fractors

*X-F 1-110: 3X TO 8X BASIC
*X-F 131-240: 3X TO 8X BASIC
1-110 ODDS 1:65 HOBBY,1:188 RETAIL
131-240 ODDS 1:79 HOBBY
1-110 PRINT RUN 275 SER.#'d SETS
131-240 PRINT RUN 250 SER.#'d SETS
*X-F AU 111-130: .6X TO 1.5X BASIC
*X-F AU 241-285: .6X TO 1.5X BASIC
111-130 X-F AU ODDS 1:226 HOBBY
241-285 X-F AU ODDS 1:175 HOBBY
111-130 AU PRINT RUN 275 SER.#'d SETS
241-285 AU PRINT RUN 250 SER.#'d SETS

2008 Bowman Chrome Draft

This set was released on November 28, 2008. The base set consists of 60 cards.

COMP.SET w/o AU's (55) 12.50 30.00
COMMON CARD (1-60) .25 .60
COMMON AUTO 4.00 10.00
AU ODDS 1:627 HOBBY
OVERALL PLATE ODDS 1:750 HOBBY
AUTO PLATE ODDS 1:49,870 HOBBY
PLATE PRINT RUN 1 SET PER COLOR
BLACK-CYAN-MAGENTA-YELLOW ISSUED
NO PLATE PRICING DUE TO SCARCITY

BDP1 Nick Adenhart (RC) .25 .60
BDP2 Michael Aubrey RC .40 1.00
BDP3 Mike Aviles RC .40 1.00
BDP4 Burke Badenhop RC .40 1.00
BDP5 Wladimir Balentien (RC) .25 .60
BDP6a Collin Balester (RC) .25 .60
BDP6b Collin Balester AU 4.00 10.00
BDP7 Josh Banks (RC) .25 .60
BDP8 Wes Bankston (RC) .25 .60
BDP9 Joey Votto (RC) 1.00 2.50
BDP10 Mitch Boggs (RC) .25 .60
BDP11 Jay Bruce (RC) .75 2.00
BDP12 Chris Carter (RC) .40 1.00
BDP13 Justin Christian RC .40 1.00
BDP14 Chris Davis RC .50 1.25
BDP15a Blake DeWitt (RC) .40 1.00
BDP15b Blake DeWitt AU 8.00 20.00
BDP16 Nick Evans RC .25 .60
BDP17 Jaime Garcia RC 1.00 2.50
BDP18 Brett Gardner (RC) .60 1.50
BDP19 Carlos Gonzalez (RC) .60 1.50
BDP20 Matt Harrison (RC) .40 1.00
BDP21 Micah Hoffpauir RC .75 2.00
BDP22 Nick Hundley (RC) .25 .60
BDP23 Eric Hurley (RC) .25 .60
BDP24 Elliot Johnson (RC) .25 .60
BDP25 Matt Joyce RC .60 1.50
BDP26a Clayton Kershaw RC 8.00 20.00
BDP26b Clayton Kershaw AU 200.00 500.00
BDP27a Evan Longoria RC 1.25 3.00
BDP27b Evan Longoria AU 20.00 50.00
BDP28 Matt Macri (RC) .25 .60
BDP29 Chris Perez RC .40 1.00
BDP30 Max Ramirez RC .25 .60
BDP31 Greg Reynolds RC .40 1.00
BDP32 Brooks Conrad (RC) .25 .60
BDP33 Max Scherzer RC 6.00 15.00
BDP34 Daryl Thompson (RC) .25 .60
BDP35 Taylor Teagarden RC .40 1.00
BDP36 Rich Thompson RC .40 1.00
BDP37 Ryan Tucker (RC) .25 .60
BDP38 Jonathan Van Every RC .25 .60
BDP39a Chris Volstad (RC) .25 .60
BDP39b Chris Volstad AU 4.00 10.00
BDP40 Michael Hollimon RC .25 .60
BDP41 Brad Ziegler RC 1.25 3.00
BDP42 Jamie D'Antona (RC) .25 .60
BDP43 Clayton Richard (RC) .25 .60
BDP44 Edgar Gonzalez (RC) .25 .60
BDP45 Bryan LaHair RC 2.00 5.00
BDP46 Warner Madrigal (RC) .25 .60
BDP47 Reid Brignac (RC) .40 1.00
BDP48 David Robertson RC .60 1.50
BDP49 Nick Stavinoha RC .40 1.00
BDP50 Jai Miller (RC) .25 .60
BDP51 Charlie Morton (RC) .75 2.00
BDP52 Brandon Boggs (RC) .40 1.00
BDP53 Joe Mather RC .40 1.00
BDP54 Gregorio Petit RC .40 1.00
BDP55 Jeff Samardzija RC .75 2.00

2008 Bowman Chrome Draft Refractors

*REF: 1X TO 2.5X BASIC
RANDOM INSERTS IN PACKS
*REF AU: .5X TO 1.2X BASIC AU
REF AUTO ODDS 1:2,000 PACKS
REF AUTO PRINT RUN 99 SER.#'d SETS

2008 Bowman Chrome Draft Blue Refractors

*BLUE REF: 2.5X TO 6X BASIC
STATED ODDS 1:76 HOBBY
STATED PRINT RUN 99 SER.#'d SETS
BDP26 Clayton Kershaw 75.00 200.00

2008 Bowman Chrome Draft Gold Refractors

*GOLD REF: 5X TO 12X BASIC
STATED ODDS 1:150 HOBBY
STATED PRINT RUN 50 SER.#'d SETS
*GODL REF AU: 1.2X TO 3X BASIC AU
GLD.REF AUTO ODDS 1:3965 PACKS
GLD.REF AU PRINT RUN 50 SER.#'d SETS
BDP26a Clayton Kershaw 150.00 400.00

2008 Bowman Chrome Draft Orange Refractors

STATED ODDS 1:301 HOBBY
AUTO ODDS 1:7962 HOBBY
STATED PRINT RUN 25 SER.#'d SETS
NO PRICING DUE TO SCARCITY
BDP26a Clayton Kershaw

2008 Bowman Chrome Draft X-Fractors

*X-F: 1.2X TO 3X BASIC
STATED ODDS 1:38 HOBBY
STATED PRINT RUN 199 SER.#'d SETS
BDP26 Clayton Kershaw 40.00 100.00

2008 Bowman Chrome Draft Prospects

COMP.SET w/o AU's (110) 20.00 50.00
STATED AUTO ODDS 1:38 HOBBY
OVERALL PLATE ODDS 1:750 HOBBY
AUTO PLATE ODDS 1:13,732 HOBBY
PLATE PRINT RUN 1 SET PER COLOR
BLACK-CYAN-MAGENTA-YELLOW ISSUED
NO PLATE PRICING DUE TO SCARCITY
EXCHANGE DEADLINE 11/30/2010

BDPP1 Rick Porcello DP 1.00 2.50
BDPP2 Braeden Schlehuber DP .30 .75
BDPP3 Kenny Wilson DP .30 .75
BDPP4 Jeff Lanning DP .30 .75
BDPP5 Kevin Dubler DP .30 .75
BDPP6 Eric Campbell DP .50 1.25
BDPP7 Tyler Chatwood DP .50 1.25
BDPP8 Tyreace House DP .30 .75
BDPP9 Adrian Nieto DP .30 .75
BDPP10 Bobbie Grossman DP .50 1.25
BDPP11 Jordan Danks DP .75 2.00
BDPP12 Jay Austin DP .30 .75
BDPP13 Ryan Perry DP .50 1.25
BDPP14 Ryan Chaffee DP .50 1.25
BDPP15 Niko Vasquez DP .75 2.00
BDPP16 Shane Dyer DP .30 .75
BDPP17 Benji Gonzalez DP .30 .75
BDPP18 Miles Reagan DP .30 .75
BDPP19 Anthony Ferrara DP .30 .75
BDPP20 Markus Brisker DP .30 .75
BDPP21 Justin Bristow DP .30 .75
BDPP22 Richard Bleier DP .50 1.25
BDPP23 Jeremy Beckham DP .50 1.25
BDPP24 Xavier Avery DP .75 2.00
BDPP25 Christian Vazquez DP .50 1.25
BDPP26 Nick Romero DP .30 .75
BDPP27 Trey Watten DP .30 .75
BDPP28 Brett Jacobson DP .30 .75
BDPP29 Tyler Sample DP .30 .75
BDPP30 T.J. Steele DP .50 1.25
BDPP31 Christian Friedrich DP .75 2.00
BDPP32 Graham Hicks DP .50 1.25
BDPP33 Shane Peterson DP .50 1.25
BDPP34 Brett Hunter DP .30 .75
BDPP35 Tim Federowicz DP .50 1.25
BDPP36 Isaac Galloway DP .50 1.25
BDPP37 Logan Schafer DP .30 .75
BDPP38 Paul Demny DP .30 .75
BDPP39 Clayton Shunick DP .30 .75
BDPP40 Andrew Liebel DP .30 .75
BDPP41 Brandon Crawford DP .75 2.00
BDPP42 Blake Tekotte DP .50 1.25
BDPP43 Jason Corder DP .30 .75
BDPP44 Bryan Shaw DP .30 .75
BDPP45 Edgar Olmos DP .30 .75
BDPP46 Dusty Coleman DP .30 .75
BDPP47 Johnny Giavotella DP 1.00 2.50
BDPP48 Tyson Ross DP .50 1.25
BDPP49 Brent Morel DP .50 1.25
BDPP50 Dennis Raben DP .50 1.25
BDPP51 Jake Odorizzi DP 1.00 2.50
BDPP52 Ryne White DP .50 1.25
BDPP53 Devaris Strange-Gordon DP 1.00 2.50
BDPP54 Tim Murphy DP .30 .75
BDPP55 Jake Jefferies DP .30 .75
BDPP56 Anthony Capra DP .30 .75
BDPP57 Kyle Weiland DP .75 2.00
BDPP58 Anthony Bass DP .50 1.25
BDPP59 Scott Green DP .30 .75
BDPP60 Zeke Spruill DP .75 2.00
BDPP61 L.J. Hoes DP .30 .75
BDPP62 Tyler Cline DP .30 .75
BDPP63 Matt Cerda DP .30 .75
BDPP64 Bobby Lanigan DP .30 .75
BDPP65 Mike Sheridan DP .30 .75
BDPP66 Carlos Carrasco FG .50 1.25
BDPP67 Nate Schierholtz FG .30 .75
BDPP68 Jesus Delgado FG .30 .75
BDPP70 Shairon Martis FG .50 1.25
BDPP71 Matt LaPorta FG .50 1.25
BDPP72 Eddie Morlan FG .30 .75
BDPP73 Greg Golson FG .30 .75
BDPP74 Julio Pimentel FG .30 .75
BDPP75 Dexter Fowler FG .50 1.25
BDPP76 Henry Rodriguez FG .30 .75
BDPP77 Cliff Pennington FG .30 .75
BDPP78 Hector Rondon FG .50 1.25
BDPP79 Wes Hodges FG .30 .75
BDPP80 Polin Trinidad FG .30 .75
BDPP81 Chris Getz FG .30 .75
BDPP82 Wellington Castillo FG .30 .75
BDPP83 Mat Gamel FG .75 2.00
BDPP84 Pablo Sandoval FG 1.25 3.00
BDPP85 Jason Donald FG .30 .75
BDPP86 Jesus Montero FG .50 1.25
BDPP87 Jamie D'Antona FG .30 .75
BDPP88 Will Inman FG .30 .75
BDPP89 Elvis Andrus FG .75 2.00
BDPP90 Taylor Teagarden FG .50 1.25
BDPP91 Scott Campbell FG .30 .75
BDPP92 Jake Arrieta FG .75 2.00
BDPP93 Juan Francisco FG .75 2.00
BDPP94 Lou Marson FG .30 .75
BDPP95 Luke Hughes FG .30 .75
BDPP96 Bryan Anderson FG .30 .75
BDPP97 Ramiro Pena FG .30 .75
BDPP98 Jesse Todd FG .30 .75
BDPP99 Gorkys Hernandez FG .30 .75
BDPP100 Casey Weathers FG .30 .75
BDPP101 Fernando Martinez FG .50 1.25
BDPP102 Clayton Richard FG .30 .75
BDPP103 Gerardo Parra FG .30 .75
BDPP104 Kevin Pucetas FG .50 1.25
BDPP105 Wilkin Ramirez FG .30 .75
BDPP106 Ryan Mattheus FG .30 .75
BDPP107 Angel Villalona FG .75 2.00
BDPP108 Brett Anderson FG .50 1.25
BDPP109 Chris Valaika FG .30 .75
BDPP110 Trevor Cahill FG .75 2.00
BDPP111 Wilmer Flores AU 4.00 10.00
BDPP112 Lonnie Chisenhall AU 4.00 10.00
BDPP113 Carlos Gutierrez AU 4.00 10.00
BDPP114 Derek Holland AU 5.00 12.00
BDPP115 Michael Stanton AU 150.00 400.00
BDPP116 Ike Davis AU 4.00 10.00
BDPP117 Anthony Hewitt AU 4.00 10.00
BDPP118 Gordon Beckham AU 4.00 10.00
BDPP119 Daniel Schlereth AU 4.00 10.00
BDPP120 Zach Collier AU 4.00 10.00
BDPP121 Evan Frederickson AU 4.00 10.00
BDPP122 Mike Montgomery AU 4.00 10.00
BDPP123 Cody Adams AU 4.00 10.00
BDPP124 Brad Hand AU 4.00 10.00
BDPP125 Josh Reddick AU 4.00 10.00
BDPP127 Jesus Montero AU 4.00 10.00
BDPP128 Buster Posey AU 75.00 200.00
BDPP142 Michael Inoa AU 4.00 10.00

2008 Bowman Chrome Draft Prospects Refractors

*REF: 1.5X TO 4X BASIC
RANDOM INSERTS IN PACKS
*REF AU: .5X TO 1.2X BASIC
REF.AU ODDS 1:118 HOBBY
REF.AU PRINT RUN 500 SER.#'d SETS
EXCHANGE DEADLINE 11/30/2010
BDPP115 Michael Stanton AU 400.00 800.00
BDPP128 Buster Posey AU 150.00 300.00

2008 Bowman Chrome Draft Prospects Blue Refractors

*BLUE REF: 4X TO 10X BASIC
STATED ODDS 1:76 HOBBY
STATED PRINT RUN 99 SER.#'d SETS
*BLUE REF AU: 1X TO 2.5X BASIC
BLUE REF.AU ODDS 1:396 HOBBY
BLUE REF.AU PRINT RUN 150 SER.#'d SETS
EXCHANGE DEADLINE 11/30/2010
BDPP36 Isaac Galloway DP 15.00 40.00
BDPP115 Michael Stanton AU 800.00 1200.00
BDPP128 Buster Posey AU 300.00 600.00

2008 Bowman Chrome Draft Prospects Gold Refractors

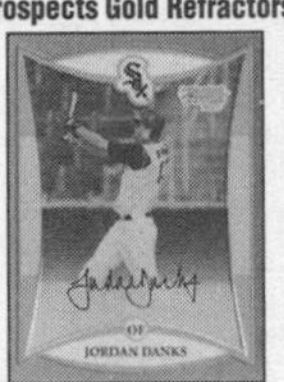

*GOLD REF: 12.5X TO 30X BASIC
STATED ODDS 1:150 HOBBY
STATED PRINT RUN 50 SER.#'d SETS
*GOLD REF AU: 1X TO 2.5X BASIC
GOLD REF.AU ODDS 1:1258 HOBBY
GOLD AU PRINT RUN 50 SER.#'d SETS
EXCHANGE DEADLINE 11/30/2010
BDPP9 Adrian Nieto DP 20.00 50.00
BDPP36 Isaac Galloway DP 30.00 60.00
BDPP51 Jake Odorizzi DP 30.00 60.00
BDPP57 Kyle Weiland DP 30.00 60.00
BDPP114 Derek Holland AU 50.00 100.00
BDPP115 Michael Stanton AU 1500.00 2000.00
BDPP128 Buster Posey AU 800.00 1200.00

2008 Bowman Chrome Draft Prospects Orange Refractors

STATED ODDS 1:301 HOBBY
AUTO ODDS 1:2700 HOBBY
STATED PRINT RUN 25 SER.#'d SETS
NO PRICING DUE TO SCARCITY

2008 Bowman Chrome Draft Prospects X-Fractors

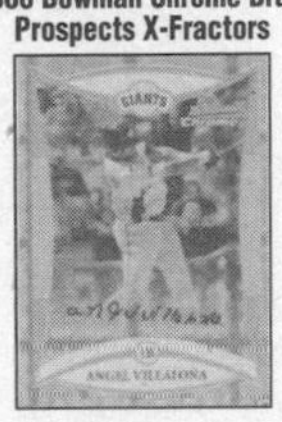

*X-F: 2.5X TO 6X BASIC
STATED ODDS 1:38 HOBBY
STATED PRINT RUN 199 SER.#'d SETS
*X-F AU: .6X TO 1.5X BASIC
X-F AU ODDS 1:270 HOBBY
X-F AU PRINT RUN 225 SER.#'d SETS
EXCHANGE DEADLINE 11/30/2010
BDPP115 Michael Stanton AU 500.00 800.00
BDPP128 Buster Posey AU 250.00 400.00

2009 Bowman Chrome

COMPLETE SET (220) 75.00 150.00
COMMON CARD (1-190) .20 .50
COMMON ROOKIE .60 1.50
PRINTING PLATE ODDS 1:538 HOBBY
PLATE PRINT RUN 1 SET PER COLOR
BLACK-CYAN-MAGENTA-YELLOW ISSUED
NO PLATE PRICING DUE TO SCARCITY

1 David Wright .40 1.00
2 Albert Pujols .60 1.50
3 Alex Rodriguez .60 1.50
4 Chase Utley .30 .75
5 Chien-Ming Wang .30 .75
6 Jimmy Rollins .30 .75
7 Ken Griffey Jr. 1.00 2.50
8 Manny Ramirez .50 1.25
9 Chipper Jones .50 1.25
10 Ichiro Suzuki .60 1.50
11 Justin Morneau .30 .75
12 Hanley Ramirez .30 .75
13 Cliff Lee .30 .75
14 Ryan Howard .40 1.00
15 Ian Kinsler .30 .75
16 Jose Reyes .30 .75
17 Ted Lilly .20 .50
18 Miguel Cabrera .50 1.25
19 Nate McLouth .20 .50
20 Josh Beckett .20 .50
21 John Lackey .20 .50
22 David Ortiz .50 1.25
23 Carlos Lee .20 .50
24 Adam Dunn .30 .75
25 B.J. Upton .30 .75
26 Curtis Granderson .40 1.00
27 David DeJesus .20 .50
28 CC Sabathia .30 .75
29 Russell Martin .20 .50
30 Torii Hunter .20 .50
31 Rich Harden .20 .50
32 Johnny Damon .30 .75
33 Cristian Guzman .20 .50
34 Grady Sizemore .30 .75
35 Jorge Posada .30 .75
36 Placido Polanco .20 .50
37 Ryan Ludwick .30 .75
38 Dustin Pedroia .40 1.00
39 Matt Garza .20 .50
40 Prince Fielder .30 .75
41 Rick Ankiel .20 .50
42 David Huff RC .60 1.50
43 Erik Bedard .20 .50
44 Ryan Braun .30 .75
45 Ervin Santana .20 .50
46 Brian Roberts .20 .50
47 Mike Jacobs .20 .50
48 Phil Hughes .20 .50
49 Justin Masterson .20 .50
50 Felix Hernandez .30 .75
51 Stephen Drew .20 .50
52 Bobby Abreu .20 .50
53 Jay Bruce .30 .75
54 Josh Hamilton .30 .75
55 Garrett Atkins .20 .50
56 Jacoby Ellsbury .40 1.00
57 Johan Santana .30 .75
58 James Shields .20 .50
59 Sergio Escalona RC 1.00 2.50
60 Carlos Pena .30 .75
61 Matt Kemp .40 1.00
62 Joey Votto .50 1.25
63 Raul Ibanez .30 .75
64 Casey Kotchman .20 .50
65 Hunter Pence .30 .75
66 Daniel Murphy RC 2.50 6.00
67 Carlos Beltran .30 .75
68 Evan Longoria .30 .75
69 Daisuke Matsuzaka .30 .75
70 Cole Hamels .40 1.00
71 Robinson Cano .30 .75
72 Clayton Kershaw 1.00 2.50
73 Kenji Johjima .30 .75
74 Kazuo Matsui .20 .50
75 Jayson Werth .30 .75
76 Brian McCann .30 .75
77 Barry Zito .30 .75
78 Glen Perkins .20 .50
79 Jeff Francoeur .30 .75
80 Derek Jeter 1.25 3.00
81 Ryan Doumit .20 .50
82 Dan Haren .20 .50
83 Justin Duchscherer .20 .50
84 Marlon Byrd .20 .50
85 Derek Lowe .20 .50
86 Pat Burrell .20 .50
87 Jair Jurrjens .20 .50
88 Zack Greinke .30 .75
89 Jon Lester .30 .75
90 Justin Verlander .50 1.25
91 Jorge Cantu .20 .50
92 John Maine .20 .50
93 Brad Hawpe .20 .50
94 Mike Aviles .20 .50
95 Victor Martinez .30 .75
96 Ryan Dempster .20 .50
97 Miguel Tejada .30 .75
98 Joe Mauer .40 1.00
99 Scott Olsen .20 .50
100 Tim Lincecum .30 .75
101 Francisco Liriano .20 .50
102 Chris Iannetta .20 .50
103 Greg Burke RC 1.00 2.50
104 Milton Bradley .20 .50
105 John Lannan .20 .50
106 Yovani Gallardo .20 .50
107 Luke French (RC) .60 1.50
108 Jermaine Dye .20 .50
109 Dioner Navarro .20 .50
110 Joba Chamberlain .20 .50
111 Nelson Cruz .50 1.25
112 Johnny Cueto .30 .75
113 Adam LaRoche .20 .50
114 Aaron Rowand .20 .50
115 Jason Bay .30 .75
116 Roy Halladay .30 .75
117 Mark Teixeira .30 .75
118 Gavin Floyd .20 .50
119 Magglio Ordonez .30 .75
120 Rafael Furcal .20 .50
121 Mark Buehrle .30 .75
122 Alexi Casilla .20 .50
123 Scott Kazmir .20 .50
124 Nick Swisher .30 .75
125 Carlos Gomez .20 .50
126 Javier Vazquez .20 .50
127 Paul Konerko .30 .75
128 Nolan Reimold (RC) .60 1.50
129 Gerardo Parra RC 1.00 2.50
130 Josh Johnson .30 .75
131 Carlos Zambrano .30 .75
132 Chris Davis .20 .50
133 Bobby Crosby .20 .50
134 Alex Gordon .30 .75
135 Chris Young .20 .50
136 Carlos Delgado .20 .50
137 Adam Wainwright .30 .75
138 Justin Upton .30 .75
139 Chris Coghlan RC 1.50 4.00
140 J.D. Drew .20 .50
141 Adam Lind .20 .50
142 Mike Lowell .20 .50
143 Lance Berkman .30 .75
144 J.J. Hardy .20 .50
145 A.J. Burnett .20 .50
146 Jake Peavy .20 .50
147 Xavier Paul (RC) .60 1.50
148 Matt Holliday .50 1.25
149 Carl Crawford .30 .75
150 Andre Ethier .30 .75

151 Howie Kendrick .20 .50
152 Ryan Zimmerman .30 .75
153 Troy Tulowitzki .50 1.25
154 Brett Myers .20 .50
155 Chris Young .20 .50
156 Jered Weaver .30 .75
157 Jeff Clement .20 .50
158 Alex Rios .20 .50
159 Shane Victorino .20 .50
160 Jeremy Hermida .20 .50
161 James Loney .20 .50
162 Michael Young .20 .50
163 Aramis Ramirez .20 .50
164 Geovany Soto .30 .75
165 Aubrey Huff .20 .50
166 Rick Porcello RC 2.00 5.00
167 Vernon Wells .20 .50
168 Chone Figgins .20 .50
169 Carlos Quentin .20 .50
170 Chad Billingsley .30 .75
171 Matt Cain .30 .75
172 Derrek Lee .20 .50
173 A.J. Pierzynski .20 .50
174 Daniel Bard RC .60 1.50
175 Bobby Scales RC 1.00 2.50
176 Alfonso Soriano .30 .75
177 Adrian Gonzalez .40 1.00
178 Andrew McCutchen (RC) 3.00 8.00
179 Nick Markakis .40 1.00
180 Brandon Webb .30 .75
181 Vladimir Guerrero .30 .75
182 Roy Oswalt .30 .75
183 Adam Jones .30 .75
184 Edinson Volquez .20 .50
185 Gordon Beckham RC 1.00 2.50
186 Joe Saunders .20 .50
187 Yadier Molina .50 1.25
188 Kevin Youkilis .20 .50
189 Dan Uggla .20 .50
190 Kosuke Fukudome .30 .75
191 Matt LaPorta RC 1.00 2.50
192 Trevor Cahill RC 1.50 4.00
193 Derek Holland RC 1.00 2.50
194 Michael Bowden (RC) .60 1.50
195 Andrew Carpenter RC 1.00 2.50
196 Phil Coke RC 1.00 2.50
197 Graham Taylor RC 1.00 2.50
198 Alcides Escobar RC 1.00 2.50
199 Dexter Fowler (RC) 1.00 2.50
200 Mat Gamel RC 1.50 4.00
201 Jordan Zimmermann RC 1.50 4.00
202 Greg Golson (RC) .60 1.50
203 Andrew Bailey RC 1.50 4.00
204 David Hernandez RC .60 1.50
205 George Kottaras (RC) .60 1.50
206 Lou Marson (RC) .60 1.50
207 Shairon Martis RC 1.00 2.50
208 Juan Miranda RC 1.00 2.50
209 Tyler Greene (RC) .60 1.50
210 Jonathon Niese RC 1.00 2.50
211 Bobby Parnell RC 1.00 2.50
212 Colby Rasmus (RC) 1.00 2.50
213 David Price RC 1.25 3.00
214 Angel Salome (RC) .60 1.50
215 Gaby Sanchez RC 1.00 2.50
216 Freddy Sandoval (RC) .60 1.50
217 Travis Snider RC 1.00 2.50
218 Will Venable RC .60 1.50
219 Brett Anderson RC 1.00 2.50
220 Josh Outman RC 1.00 2.50

2009 Bowman Chrome Refractors

*REF VET: 1X TO 2.5X BASIC
*REF RC: .6X TO 1.5X BASIC RC
STATED ODDS 1:4 HOBBY

2009 Bowman Chrome Blue Refractors

*BLUE VET: 2X TO 6X BASIC
*BLUE RC: 1.2X TO 3X BASIC RC
STATED ODDS 1:17 HOBBY
STATED PRINT RUN 150 SER.#'d SETS

2009 Bowman Chrome Gold Refractors

*GOLD VET: 5X TO 12X BASIC
*GOLD RC: 2X TO 5X BASIC RC
STATED ODDS 1:50 HOBBY
STATED PRINT RUN 50 SER.#'d SETS

2009 Bowman Chrome X-Fractors

*XF VET: 1.5X TO 4X BASIC
*XF RC: 1X TO 2.5X BASIC RC
STATED ODDS 1:10 HOBBY
STATED PRINT RUN 250 SER.#'d SETS

2009 Bowman Chrome Prospects

COMP.SET w/o AU's (160) 30.00 60.00
BOWMAN AU ODDS 1:47 HOBBY
BOW.CHR AU ODDS 1:34 HOBBY
PRINTING PLATE ODDS 1:538 HOBBY
AU PRINT.PLATE ODDS 1:7400 HOBBY
PLATE PRINT RUN 1 SET PER COLOR
BLACK-CYAN-MAGENTA-YELLOW ISSUED
NO PLATE PRICING DUE TO SCARCITY
BCP1 Neftali Feliz .30 .75
BCP2 Oscar Tejada .20 .50
BCP3 Greg Veloz .20 .50
BCP4 Julio Teheran .60 1.50
BCP5 Michael Almanzar .30 .75
BCP6 Stolmy Pimentel .30 .75
BCP7 Matthew Moore 1.50 4.00
BCP8 Jericho Jones .20 .50
BCP9 Kelvin de la Cruz .50 1.25
BCP10 Jose Ceda .20 .50
BCP11 Jesse Darcy .20 .50
BCP12 Kenneth Gilbert .20 .50
BCP13 Will Smith .30 .75
BCP14 Samuel Freeman .20 .50
BCP15 Adam Reifer .20 .50
BCP16 Ehire Adrianza .50 1.25
BCP17 Michael Pineda .50 1.25
BCP18 Jordan Walden .30 .75
BCP19 Angel Morales .30 .75
BCP20 Neil Ramirez .20 .50
BCP21 Kyeong Kang .30 .75
BCP22 Luis Jimenez .20 .50
BCP23 Tyler Flowers .50 1.25
BCP24 Petey Paramore .20 .50
BCP25 Jeremy Hamilton .20 .50
BCP26 Tyler Yockey .30 .75
BCP27 Sawyer Carroll .30 .75
BCP28 Jeremy Farrell .20 .50
BCP29 Tyson Brummett .20 .50
BCP30 Alex Buchholz .30 .75
BCP31 Luis Sumoza .20 .50
BCP32 Jonathan Waltenbury .30 .75
BCP33 Edgar Osuna .30 .75
BCP34 Curt Smith .30 .75
BCP35 Evan Bigley .30 .75
BCP36 Miguel Fermin .20 .50
BCP37 Ben Lasater .20 .50
BCP38 David Freese .60 1.50
BCP39 Jon Kibler .30 .75
BCP40 Cristian Beltre .30 .75
BCP41 Alfredo Figaro .20 .50
BCP42 Marc Rzepczynski .30 .75
BCP43 Joshua Collmenter .30 .75
BCP44 Adam Mills .20 .50
BCP45 Wilson Ramos .60 1.50
BCP46 Esmil Rogers .20 .50
BCP47 Jon Mark Owings .20 .50
BCP48 Chris Johnson .30 .75
BCP49 Abraham Almonte .20 .50
BCP50 Patrick Ryan .20 .50
BCP51 Yefri Carvajal .50 1.25
BCP52 Ruben Tejada .20 .50
BCP53 Edilio Colina .30 .75
BCP54 Wilber Bucardo .30 .75
BCP55 Nelson Perez .30 .75
BCP56 Andrew Rundle .30 .75
BCP57 Anthony Ortega .20 .50
BCP58 Wilin Rosario .30 .75
BCP59 Parker Frazier .20 .50
BCP60 Kyle Farrell .20 .50
BCP61 Erik Komatsu .30 .75
BCP62 Michael Stutes .20 .50
BCP63 David Genao .30 .75
BCP64 Jack Cawley .20 .50
BCP65 Jacob Goldberg .20 .50
BCP66 Jarred Bogany .20 .50
BCP67 Jason McEachern .20 .50
BCP68 Matt Rigoli .20 .50
BCP69 Jose Duran .30 .75
BCP70 Justin Greene .30 .75
BCP71 Nino Leyja .30 .75
BCP72 Michael Swinson .30 .75
BCP73 Miguel Flores .30 .75
BCP74 Nick Buss .20 .50
BCP75 Brett Oberholtzer .30 .75
BCP76 Pat McAnaney .30 .75
BCP77 Sean Conner .20 .50
BCP78 Ryan Verdugo .30 .75
BCP79 Will Atwood .20 .50
BCP80 Tommy Johnson .50 1.25
BCP81 Rene Garcia .30 .75
BCP82 Robert Brooks .20 .50
BCP83 Seth Garrison .20 .50
BCP84 Steven Upchurch .20 .50
BCP85 Zach Moore .20 .50
BCP86 Derrick Phillips .20 .50
BCP87 Dominic De La Osa .50 1.25
BCP88 Jose Barajas .20 .50
BCP89 Bryan Petersen .20 .50
BCP90 Michael Cisco .30 .75
BCP91 Rinku Singh AU 6.00 15.00
BCP92 Dinesh Kumar Patel AU 3.00 8.00
BCP93 Matt Miller AU 3.00 8.00
BCP94 Pat Venditte AU 3.00 8.00
BCP95 Zach Putnam AU 3.00 8.00
BCP96 Robbie Grossman AU 3.00 8.00
BCP97 Tommy Hanson AU 3.00 8.00
BCP98 Graham Hicks AU 3.00 8.00
BCP99 Matt Mitchell AU 3.00 8.00
BCP100 Christopher Marrero AU 3.00 8.00
BCP101 Freddie Freeman AU 125.00 300.00
BCP102 Chris Johnson AU 3.00 8.00
BCP103 Edgar Olmos AU 3.00 8.00
BCP104 Argenis Diaz AU 3.00 8.00
BCP105 Brett Anderson AU 3.00 8.00
BCP106 Juancarlos Sulbaran AU 3.00 8.00
BCP107 Cody Scarpetta AU 3.00 8.00
BCP108 Carlos Santana AU 12.00 30.00
BCP109 Brad Emaus AU 3.00 8.00
BCP110 Dayan Viciedo AU 3.00 8.00
BCP111b Tim Federowicz AU 3.00 8.00
BCP111a Bearner Weems AU 3.00 8.00
BCP112a Logan Morrison AU 6.00 15.00
BCP112b Allen Craig AU 3.00 8.00
BCP113b Kyle Weiland AU 3.00 8.00
BCP113a Greg Halman AU 3.00 8.00
BCP114a Logan Forsythe AU 3.00 8.00
BCP114b Connor Graham AU 3.00 8.00
BCP115 Lance Lynn AU 3.00 8.00
BCP116 Javier Rodriguez AU 3.00 8.00
BCP117 Josh Lindblom AU 3.00 8.00
BCP118 Blake Tekotte AU 3.00 8.00
BCP119 Johnny Giavotella AU 3.00 8.00
BCP120 Jason Knapp AU 3.00 8.00
BCP121 Charlie Blackmon AU 50.00 120.00
BCP122 David Hernandez AU 3.00 8.00
BCP123 Adam Moore AU 3.00 8.00
BCP124 Bobby Lanigan AU 3.00 8.00
BCP125 Jay Austin AU 3.00 8.00
BCP126 Quinton Miller AU 3.00 8.00
BCP127 Eric Sogard AU 3.00 8.00
BCP128 Efrain Nieves .30 .75
BCP129 Kam Mickolio .20 .50
BCP130 Terrell Alliman .20 .50
BCP131 J.R. Higley .30 .75
BCP132 Rashun Dixon .50 1.25
BCP133 Brian Baisley .20 .50
BCP134 Tim Collins .30 .75
BCP135 Kyle Greenwalt .50 1.25
BCP136 C.J. Lee .20 .50
BCP137 Hector Correa .20 .50
BCP138 Wily Peralta .30 .75
BCP139 Bryan Price .20 .50
BCP140 Jarrod Holloway .20 .50
BCP141 Alfredo Silverio .20 .50
BCP142 Brad Dydalewicz .30 .75
BCP143 Alexander Torres .20 .50
BCP144 Chris Hicks .20 .50
BCP145 Andy Parrino .20 .50
BCP146 Christopher Schwinden .20 .50
BCP147 Matt Mitchell .20 .50
BCP148 Mathew Kennelly .30 .75
BCP149 Freddy Galvis .30 .75
BCP150 Mauricio Robles .50 1.25
BCP151 Kevin Eichhorn .20 .50
BCP152 Dan Hudson .30 .75
BCP153 Carlos Martinez .30 .75
BCP154 Danny Carroll .20 .50
BCP155 Maikel Cleto .20 .50
BCP156 Michael Affronti .20 .50
BCP157 Mike Pontius .30 .75
BCP158 Richard Castillo .30 .75
BCP159 Jon Redding .20 .50
BCP160 Aaron King .20 .50
BCP161 Mark Hallberg .20 .50
BCP162 Chris Luck .50 1.25
BCP163 Wilmer Font .20 .50
BCP164 Chad Lundahl .20 .50
BCP165 Isaias Asencio .20 .50
BCP166 Denny Almonte .30 .75
BCP167 Carmen Angelini .20 .50
BCP168 Paul Clemens .20 .50
BCP169 Federico Hernandez .20 .50
BCP170 Mario Martinez .30 .75
BCP171 Bryan Shaw .20 .50
BCP172 Bryan Augenstein .20 .50
BCP173 Santos Rodriguez .30 .75
BCP174 Delvi Cid .20 .50
BCP175 Todd Doolittle .20 .50
BCP176 Rossmel Perez .20 .50
BCP177 Philippe-Alexandre Valiquette .20 .50
BCP178 Julian Sampson .30 .75
BCP179 Eric Farris .20 .50
BCP180 Taylor Harbin .20 .50
BCP181 Clayton Cook .30 .75
BCP182 Jovan Rosa .20 .50
BCP183 Starlin Castro 1.00 2.50
BCP184 Brock Huntzinger .20 .50
BCP185 Jack McGeary .20 .50
BCP186 Moises Sierra .50 1.25
BCP187 Luis Exposito .50 1.25
BCP188 Danny Farquhar .20 .50
BCP189 Layton Hiller .20 .50
BCP190 Michael Harrington .20 .50
BCP191 Nate Tenbrink .20 .50
BCP192 Jason Rook .20 .50
BCP193 Ryan Kulik .20 .50
BCP194 Kennil Gomez .20 .50
BCP195 Brad James .20 .50
BCP196 John Anderson .20 .50
BCP197 Pernell Halliman .20 .50

2009 Bowman Chrome Prospects Refractors

*REF 1-197: 2.5X TO 6X BASIC
1-90 ODDS 1:22 HOBBY
128-197 ODDS 1:15 HOBBY
NON-AU PRINT RUN 599 SER.#'d SETS
*REF AU: .5X TO 1.2X BASIC
BOW.REF.AU ODDS 1:95 HOBBY
BOW.CHR. AU ODDS 1:70 HOBBY
AUTO PRINT RUN 500 SER.#'d SETS

2009 Bowman Chrome Prospects Blue Refractors

*BLUE REF: 5X TO 12X BASIC
BLUE 1-90 ODDS 1:90 HOBBY
BLUE 128-197 ODDS 1:17 HOBBY
BLUE NON-AU PRT RUN 150 SER.#'d SETS
*BLUE REF AU: .75X TO 2X BASIC
BOW.BLU.REF AU ODDS 1:314 HOBBY
BOW.CHR.BLU.REF ODDS 1:246 HOBBY
BLUE REF AU PRINT RUN 150 SER.#'d SETS

2009 Bowman Chrome Prospects Gold Refractors

*GOLD REF: 10X TO 25X BASIC
GOLD 1-90 ODDS 1:271 HOBBY
GOLD 128-197 ODDS 1:50 HOBBY
GOLD PRINT RUN 50 SER.#'d SETS
*GOLD REF AU: 2X TO 5X BASIC
BOW.GLD.REF AU ODDS 1:943 HOBBY
BOW.CHR.GLD.REF AU ODDS 1:715 HOBBY
GOLD REF AU PRINT RUN 50 SER.#'d SETS

2009 Bowman Chrome Prospects Orange Refractors

1-90 STATED ODDS 1:542 HOBBY
91-110 STATED ODDS 1:1500 HOBBY
111-127 STATED ODDS 1:1882 HOBBY
128-197 STATED ODDS 1:100 HOBBY
STATED PRINT RUN 25 SER.#'d SETS
NO PRICING DUE TO SCARCITY

2009 Bowman Chrome Prospects X-Fractors

*X-FRAC: 4X TO 10X BASIC
X-FRAC 1-90 ODDS 1:45 HOBBY
X-FRAC 128-197 ODDS 1:10 HOBBY
1-90 X-F PRINT RUN 299 SER.#'d SETS
128-197 X-F PRINT RUN 250 SER.#'d SETS
*X-F AU: .6X TO 1.5X BASIC
BOW.X-F AU ODDS 1:198 HOBBY
BOW.CHR.X-F AU ODDS 1:144 HOBBY
X-F AU PRINT RUN 250 SER.#'d SETS

2009 Bowman Chrome WBC Prospects

21-60 PRINTING PLATE ODDS 1:538 HOBBY
PLATE PRINT RUN 1 SET PER COLOR
BLACK-CYAN-MAGENTA-YELLOW ISSUED
NO PLATE PRICING DUE TO SCARCITY
BCW1 Yu Darvish 1.50 4.00
BCW2 Phillippe Aumont .60 1.50
BCW3 Concepcion Rodriguez .40 1.00
BCW4 Michel Enriquez .40 1.00
BCW5 Yulieski Gourriel 1.25 3.00
BCW6 Shinnosuke Abe .60 1.50
BCW7 Gift Ngoepe .40 1.00
BCW8 Dylan Lindsay .60 1.50
BCW9 Nick Weglarz .40 1.00
BCW10 Mitch Dening .40 1.00
BCW11 Justin Erasmus .40 1.00
BCW12 Aroldis Chapman 2.00 5.00
BCW13 Alex Liddi .60 1.50
BCW14 Alexander Smit .40 1.00
BCW15 Juan Carlos Sulbaran .40 1.00
BCW16 Cheng-Min Peng .60 1.50
BCW17 Chenhao Li .40 1.00
BCW18 Tao Bu .40 1.00
BCW19 Gregory Halman .60 1.50
BCW20 Fu-Te Ni .60 1.50
BCW21 Norichika Aoki .60 1.50
BCW22 Hisashi Iwakuma 1.25 3.00
BCW23 Tae Kyun Kim .40 1.00
BCW24 Dae Ho Lee .40 1.00
BCW25 Wang Chao .40 1.00
BCW26 Yi-Chuan Lin .60 1.50
BCW27 James Beresford .40 1.00
BCW28 Shuichi Murata .60 1.50
BCW29 Hung-Wen Chen .40 1.00
BCW30 Masahiro Tanaka 2.00 5.00
BCW31 Kao Kuo-Ching .40 1.00
BCW32 Po Yu Lin .40 1.00
BCW33 Yolexis Ulacia .40 1.00
BCW34 Kwang-Hyun Kim .60 1.50
BCW35 Kenley Jansen 1.25 3.00
BCW36 Luis Durango .40 1.00
BCW37 Ray Chang .40 1.00
BCW38 Hein Robb .40 1.00
BCW39 Kyuji Fujikawa 1.00 2.50
BCW40 Ruben Tejada .40 1.00
BCW41 Hector Olivera 1.25 3.00
BCW42 Bryan Engelhardt .40 1.00
BCW43 Dennis Neuman .40 1.00
BCW44 Vladimir Garcia .40 1.00
BCW45 Michihiro Ogasawara .60 1.50
BCW46 Yen-Wen Kuo .40 1.00
BCW47 Takahiro Mahara .40 1.00
BCW48 Hiroyuki Nakajima .60 1.50
BCW49 Yoennis Cespedes 1.50 4.00
BCW50 Alfredo Despaigne 1.00 2.50
BCW51 Suk Min-Yoon .40 1.00
BCW52 Chih-Hsien Chiang 1.00 2.50
BCW53 Hyun-Soo Kim .40 1.00
BCW54 Chih-Kang Kao .40 1.00
BCW55 Frederich Cepeda .60 1.50
BCW56 Yi-Feng Kuo .40 1.00
BCW57 Toshiya Sugiuchi .40 1.00
BCW58 Shunsuke Watanabe .60 1.50
BCW59 Max Ramirez .40 1.00
BCW60 Brad Harman .40 1.00

2009 Bowman Chrome WBC Prospects Refractors

*REF: 2X TO 5X BASIC
1-20 ODDS 1:22 HOBBY
21-60 ODDS 1:15 HOBBY
1-20 PRINT RUN 599 SER.#'d SETS
21-60 PRINT RUN 500 SER.#'d SETS

2009 Bowman Chrome WBC Prospects Blue Refractors

*BLUE REF: 3X TO 8X BASIC
1-20 ODDS 1:90 HOBBY
21-60 ODDS 1:17 HOBBY
STATED PRINT RUN 150 SER.#'d SETS

2009 Bowman Chrome WBC Prospects Gold Refractors

*GOLD REF: 6X TO 15X BASIC
1-20 ODDS 1:271 HOBBY
21-60 ODDS 1:50 HOBBY
STATED PRINT RUN 50 SER.#'d SETS

2009 Bowman Chrome WBC Prospects X-Fractors

*X-F: 2.5X TO 6X BASIC
1-20 ODDS 1:45 HOBBY
21-60 ODDS 1:10 HOBBY
1-20 PRINT RUN 299 SER.#'d SETS
21-60 PRINT RUN 250 SER.#'d SETS

2009 Bowman Chrome Draft

COMPLETE SET (55) 10.00 25.00
COMMON CARD (1-55) .30 .75
OVERALL PLATE ODDS 1:1531 HOBBY
PLATE PRINT RUN 1 SET PER COLOR
BLACK-CYAN-MAGENTA-YELLOW ISSUED
NO PLATE PRICING DUE TO SCARCITY
BDP1 Tommy Hanson RC .75 2.00
BDP2 Jeff Manship RC .30 .75
BDP3 Trevor Bell (RC) .30 .75
BDP4 Trevor Cahill RC .75 2.00
BDP5 Trent Oeltjen (RC) .30 .75
BDP6 Wyatt Toregas RC .30 .75
BDP7 Kevin Mulvey RC .30 .75
BDP8 Rusty Ryal RC .30 .75
BDP9 Mike Carp (RC) .50 1.25
BDP10 Jorge Padilla (RC) .30 .75
BDP11 J.D. Martin (RC) .30 .75
BDP12 Dusty Ryan RC .30 .75
BDP13 Alex Avila RC 1.00 2.50
BDP14 Brandon Allen (RC) .30 .75
BDP15 Tommy Everidge (RC) .50 1.25
BDP16 Bud Norris RC .30 .75
BDP17 Neftali Feliz RC .50 1.25
BDP18 Mat Latos RC 1.00 2.50
BDP19 Ryan Perry RC .75 2.00
BDP20 Craig Tatum (RC) .30 .75
BDP21 Chris Tillman RC .50 1.25
BDP22 Jhoulys Chacin RC .50 1.25
BDP23 Michael Saunders RC .75 2.00
BDP24 Jeff Stevens RC .30 .75
BDP25 Luis Valdez RC .30 .75
BDP26 Robert Manuel RC .30 .75
BDP27 Ryan Webb (RC) .30 .75
BDP28 Marc Rzepczynski RC .50 1.25
BDP29 Travis Schlichting (RC) .50 1.25
BDP30 Barbaro Canizares RC .30 .75
BDP31 Brad Mills RC .30 .75
BDP32 Dusty Brown (RC) .30 .75
BDP33 Tim Wood RC .30 .75
BDP34 Drew Sutton RC .50 1.25
BDP35 Jarrett Hoffpauir (RC) .30 .75
BDP36 Jose Lobaton RC .30 .75
BDP37 Aaron Bates RC .30 .75
BDP38 Clayton Mortensen RC .30 .75
BDP39 Ryan Sadowski RC .30 .75
BDP40 Fu-Te Ni RC .50 1.25
BDP41 Casey McGehee (RC) .30 .75
BDP42 Omir Santos RC .30 .75
BDP43 Brent Leach RC .50 1.25
BDP44 Diory Hernandez RC .30 .75
BDP45 Wilkin Castillo RC .30 .75
BDP46 Trevor Crowe RC .30 .75
BDP47 Sean West (RC) .50 1.25
BDP48 Clayton Richard (RC) .30 .75
BDP49 Julio Borbon RC .30 .75
BDP50 Kyle Blanks RC .50 1.25
BDP51 Jeff Gray RC .30 .75
BDP52 Gio Gonzalez (RC) .50 1.25
BDP53 Vin Mazzaro RC .30 .75
BDP54 Josh Reddick RC .50 1.25
BDP55 Fernando Martinez RC .75 2.00

2009 Bowman Chrome Draft Refractors

*REF: 1X TO 2.5X BASIC
STATED ODDS 1:11 HOBBY

2009 Bowman Chrome Draft Blue Refractors

*BLUE REF: 2.5X TO 6X BASIC
STATED ODDS 1:49 HOBBY
STATED PRINT RUN 99 SER.#'d SETS
BDP40 Fu-Te Ni 15.00 40.00

2009 Bowman Chrome Draft Gold Refractors

*GOLD: 4X TO 10X BASIC
STATED ODDS 1:96 HOBBY
STATED PRINT RUN 50 SER.#'d SETS
BDP40 Fu-Te Ni 30.00 80.00

2009 Bowman Chrome Draft Purple Refractors

*PURPLE: 2X TO 5X BASIC
RANDOM INSERTS IN RETAIL PACKS

2009 Bowman Chrome Draft X-Fractors

*X-F: 1.5X TO 4X BASIC
STATED ODDS 1:24 HOBBY
STATED PRINT RUN 199 SER.#'d SETS
BDP40 Fu-Te Ni 6.00 15.00

2009 Bowman Chrome Draft Prospects

COMP.SET w/o AU's (75) 12.50 30.00
STATED AU ODDS 1:24 HOBBY
OVERALL PLATE ODDS 1:1531 HOBBY
OVERALL AUTO PLATE ODDS 1:7973 HOBBY
PLATE PRINT RUN 1 SET PER COLOR
BLACK-CYAN-MAGENTA-YELLOW ISSUED
NO PLATE PRICING DUE TO SCARCITY
BDPP1 Tanner Bushue .50 1.25
BDPP2 Billy Hamilton 1.00 2.50
BDPP3 Enrique Hernandez 1.25 3.00
BDPP4 Virgil Hill .30 .75
BDPP5 Josh Hodges .50 1.25
BDPP6 Christopher Lovett .30 .75
BDPP7 Michael Belfiore .30 .75
BDPP8 Jobduan Morales .30 .75
BDPP9 Anthony Morris .30 .75
BDPP10 Telvin Nash 1.00 2.50
BDPP11 Brooks Pounders .50 1.25
BDPP12 Kyle Rose .30 .75
BDPP13 Seth Schwindenhammer .50 1.25
BDPP14 Patrick Lehman .50 1.25
BDPP15 Mathew Weaver .50 1.25
BDPP16 Brian Dozier 1.50 4.00
BDPP17 Sequoyah Stonecipher .50 1.25
BDPP18 Shannon Wilkerson .30 .75
BDPP19 Jerry Sullivan .30 .75
BDPP20 Jamie Johnson .30 .75
BDPP21 Kent Matthes .30 .75
BDPP22 Ben Paulsen .30 .75
BDPP23 Matthew Davidson 1.00 2.50
BDPP24 Benjamin Carlson .30 .75
BDPP25 Brock Holt .50 1.25
BDPP26 Ben Orloff .30 .75
BDPP27 D.J. LeMahieu 5.00 12.00
BDPP28 Erik Castro .50 1.25
BDPP29 James Jones .30 .75
BDPP30 Cory Burns .30 .75
BDPP31 Chris Wade .30 .75
BDPP32 Jaff Decker .50 1.25
BDPP33 Naoya Washiya .30 .75
BDPP34 Brandt Walker .30 .75
BDPP35 Jordan Henry .50 1.25
BDPP36 Austin Adams .30 .75
BDPP37 Andrew Bellatti .50 1.25
BDPP38 Paul Applebee .50 1.25
BDPP39 Robert Stock .50 1.25
BDPP40 Michael Flacco .30 .75
BDPP41 Jonathan Meyer .30 .75
BDPP42 Cody Rogers .50 1.25
BDPP43 Matt Heidenreich .30 .75
BDPP44 David Holmberg .75 2.00
BDPP45 Mycal Jones .30 .75
BDPP46 David Hale .75 2.00
BDPP47 Dusty Odenbach .30 .75
BDPP48 Robert Hefflinger .30 .75
BDPP49 Buddy Baumann .30 .75
BDPP50 Thomas Berryhill .30 .75
BDPP51 Darrell Ceciliani .30 .75
BDPP52 Derek McCallum .30 .75
BDPP53 Taylor Freeman .30 .75
BDPP54 Tyler Townsend .50 1.25
BDPP55 Tobias Streich .50 1.25
BDPP56 Ryan Jackson .30 .75
BDPP57 Chris Herrmann .50 1.25
BDPP58 Robert Shields .30 .75
BDPP59 Devin Fuller .30 .75
BDPP60 Brad Stillings .30 .75
BDPP61 Ryan Goins .50 1.25
BDPP62 Chase Austin .30 .75
BDPP63 Brett Nommensen .30 .75
BDPP64 Egan Smith .30 .75
BDPP65 Daniel Mahoney .30 .75
BDPP66 Darin Gorski .30 .75
BDPP67 Dustin Dickerson .50 1.25
BDPP68 Victor Black .50 1.25
BDPP69 Dallas Keuchel 2.50 6.00
BDPP70 Nate Baker .30 .75
BDPP71 David Nick .50 1.25
BDPP72 Brian Moran .30 .75
BDPP73 Mark Fleury .30 .75
BDPP74 Brett Wallach .50 1.25
BDPP75 Adam Buschini .30 .75
BDPP76 Tony Sanchez AU 3.00 8.00
BDPP77 Eric Arnett AU 3.00 8.00
BDPP78 Tim Wheeler AU 3.00 8.00
BDPP79 Matt Hobgood AU 3.00 8.00
BDPP80 Matt Bashore AU 3.00 8.00
BDPP81 Randal Grichuk AU 8.00 20.00
BDPP82 A.J. Pollock AU 8.00 20.00
BDPP83 Reymond Fuentes AU 3.00 8.00
BDPP84 Jiovanni Mier AU 3.00 8.00
BDPP85 Steve Matz AU 20.00 50.00
BDPP86 Zack Wheeler AU 8.00 20.00
BDPP87 Mike Minor AU 3.00 8.00
BDPP88 Jared Mitchell AU 5.00 12.00
BDPP89 Mike Trout AU 5000.00 10000.00
BDPP90 Alex White AU 3.00 8.00
BDPP91 Bobby Borchering AU 3.00 8.00
BDPP92 Chad James AU 3.00 8.00
BDPP93 Tyler Matzek AU 3.00 8.00
BDPP94 Max Stassi AU 3.00 8.00
BDPP95 Drew Storen AU 5.00 12.00
BDPP96 Brad Boxberger AU 3.00 8.00
BDPP97 Mike Leake AU 3.00 8.00

2009 Bowman Chrome Draft Prospects Refractors

*REF: 1.5X TO 4X BASIC
STATED ODDS 1:11 HOBBY
*REF AU: .5X TO 1.2X BASIC AU
STATED AUTO ODDS 1:71 HOBBY
AUTO PRINT RUN 500 SER.#'d SETS
BDPP89 Mike Trout AU 8000.00 12000.00

2009 Bowman Chrome Draft Prospects Blue Refractors

*BLUE REF: 4X TO 10X BASIC
STATED ODDS 1:49 HOBBY
STATED PRINT RUN 99 SER.#'d SETS
*BLUE REF AU: 1X TO 2.5X BASIC AU
STATED AUTO ODDS 1:241 HOBBY
AUTO PRINT RUN 150 SER.#'d SETS
BDPP89 Mike Trout AU 15000.00 20000.00

2009 Bowman Chrome Draft Prospects Gold Refractors

*GOLD REF: 8X TO 20X BASIC
STATED ODDS 1:96 HOBBY
STATED PRINT RUN 50 SER.#'d SETS
*GOLD REF AU: 2X TO 5X BASIC AU
STATED AUTO ODDS 1:736 HOBBY
AUTO PRINT RUN 50 SER.#'d SETS
BDPP2 Billy Hamilton 150.00 250.00
BDPP89 Mike Trout AU 25000.00 30000.00

2009 Bowman Chrome Draft Prospects Orange Refractors

STATED ODDS 1:192 HOBBY
STATED AUTO ODDS 1:1545 HOBBY
STATED PRINT RUN 25 SER.#'d SETS
NO PRICING DUE TO SCARCITY

2009 Bowman Chrome Draft Prospects Purple Refractors

*PURPLE: 2X TO 5X BASIC
RANDOM INSERTS IN RETAIL PACKS

2009 Bowman Chrome Draft Prospects X-Fractors

*X-F: 2.5X TO 6X BASIC
STATED ODDS 1:24 HOBBY
STATED PRINT RUN 199 SER.#'d SETS
*X-F AU: .6X TO 1.5X BASIC AU
STATED AUTO ODDS 1:159 HOBBY
AUTO PRINT RUN 225 SER.#'d SETS
BDPP89 Mike Trout AU 10000.00 15000.00

2009 Bowman Chrome Draft WBC Prospects

COMPLETE SET (35) 8.00 20.00
OVERALL PLATE ODDS 1:1531 HOBBY
PLATE PRINT RUN 1 SET PER COLOR
BLACK-CYAN-MAGENTA-YELLOW ISSUED
NO PLATE PRICING DUE TO SCARCITY
BDPW1 Ichiro Suzuki 1.00 2.50
BDPW2 Yu Darvish 1.25 3.00
BDPW3 Phillippe Aumont .50 1.25
BDPW4 Derek Jeter 2.00 5.00
BDPW5 Dustin Pedroia .60 1.50
BDPW6 Earl Agnoly .30 .75
BDPW7 Jose Reyes .50 1.25
BDPW8 Michel Enriquez .30 .75
BDPW9 David Ortiz .75 2.00
BDPW10 Chunhua Dong .50 1.25
BDPW11 Munenori Kawasaki 1.50 4.00
BDPW12 Arquimedes Nieto .30 .75
BDPW13 Bernie Williams .50 1.25
BDPW14 Pedro Lazo .30 .75
BDPW15 Jing-Chao Wang .50 1.25
BDPW16 Chris Barnwell .30 .75
BDPW17 Elmer Dessens .30 .75
BDPW18 Russell Martin .30 .75
BDPW19 Luca Panerati .30 .75
BDPW20 Adam Dunn .50 1.25
BDPW21 Andy Gonzalez .30 .75
BDPW22 Daisuke Matsuzaka .50 1.25
BDPW23 Daniel Berg .30 .75
BDPW24 Aroldis Chapman 1.50 4.00
BDPW25 Justin Morneau .50 1.25
BDPW26 Miguel Cabrera .75 2.00
BDPW27 Magglio Ordonez .50 1.25
BDPW28 Shawn Bowman .30 .75
BDPW29 Robbie Cordemans .30 .75
BDPW30 Paolo Espino .30 .75
BDPW31 Chipper Jones .75 2.00

BDPW32 Frederich Cepeda .50 1.25
BDPW33 Ubaldo Jimenez .30 .75
BDPW34 Seiichi Uchikawa .50 1.25
BDPW35 Norichika Aoki .50 1.25

2009 Bowman Chrome Draft WBC Prospects Refractors

*REF: 1X TO 2.5X BASIC
STATED ODDS 1:11 HOBBY

2009 Bowman Chrome Draft WBC Prospects Blue Refractors

*BLUE REF: 2.5X TO 6X BASIC
STATED ODDS 1:49 HOBBY
STATED PRINT RUN 99 SER.#'d SETS

2009 Bowman Chrome Draft WBC Prospects Gold Refractors

*GOLD: 4X TO 10X BASIC
STATED ODDS 1:96 HOBBY
STATED PRINT RUN 50 SER.#'d SETS

2009 Bowman Chrome Draft WBC Prospects Orange Refractors

STATED ODDS 1:192 HOBBY
STATED PRINT RUN 25 SER.#'d SETS
NO PRICING DUE TO SCARCITY

2009 Bowman Chrome Draft WBC Prospects Purple Refractors

*PURPLE: 1.2X TO 3X BASIC
RANDOM INSERTS IN RETAIL PACKS

2009 Bowman Chrome Draft WBC Prospects X-Fractors

*X-F: 1.5X TO 4X BASIC
STATED ODDS 1:24 HOBBY
STATED PRINT RUN 199 SER.#'d SETS

2010 Bowman Chrome

COMP.SET w/o AU's (220) 40.00 80.00
COMMON CARD (1-180) .20 .50
COMMON RC (181-220) .60 1.50
COMMON AU 3.00 8.00
BOW.STATED AU ODDS 1:113 HOBBY
STRASBURG AU ODDS 1:3810 HOBBY
BOW.CHR.PLATE ODDS 1:1405 HOBBY
STRASBURG AU PLATE ODDS 1:12,000 HOBBY
EXCHANGE DEADLINE 9/30/2013
1 Ryan Braun .30 .75
2 Will Venable .20 .50
3 Zack Greinke .30 .75
4 Matt Kemp .40 1.00
5 Jair Jurrjens .20 .50
6 Josh Hamilton .30 .75
7 Josh Beckett .20 .50
8 Jake Peavy .20 .50
9 Luke Hochevar .20 .50
10 Ryan Zimmerman .30 .75
11 Robinson Cano .30 .75
12 Magglio Ordonez .30 .75
13 Brian Roberts .20 .50
14 A.J. Burnett .20 .50
15 Chris Carpenter .30 .75
16 Clayton Kershaw 1.00 2.50
17 Jayson Werth .30 .75
18 Alexei Ramirez .30 .75
19 Ricky Romero .20 .50
20 Andrew McCutchen .50 1.25
21 Chad Billingsley .30 .75
22 David Ortiz .50 1.25
23 Rajai Davis .20 .50
24 Trevor Cahill .20 .50
25 Dan Haren .20 .50
26 Dan Uggla .20 .50
27 Ryan Dempster .20 .50
28 Koji Uehara .20 .50
29 Carlos Gonzalez .30 .75
30 Justin Upton .30 .75
31 Elvis Andrus .30 .75
32 James Loney .20 .50
33 Matt Garza .20 .50
34 Brandon Phillips .20 .50
35 Miguel Cabrera .50 1.25
36 Shane Victorino .30 .75
37 Kyle Blanks .20 .50
38 Troy Tulowitzki .50 1.25
39 Chipper Jones .50 1.25
40 Todd Helton .30 .75
41 Derrek Lee .20 .50
42 Michael Bourn .20 .50
43 Jose Lopez .20 .50
44 Hunter Pence .30 .75
45 Edinson Volquez .20 .50
46 Miguel Montero .20 .50
47 Kevin Youkilis .20 .50
48 Adrian Gonzalez .40 1.00
49 Carl Crawford .30 .75
50 Stephen Drew .20 .50
51 Carlos Pena .30 .75
52 Ubaldo Jimenez .30 .75
53 Martin Prado .20 .50
54 Alcides Escobar .30 .75
55 Jeff Niemann .20 .50
56 Andre Ethier .30 .75
57 Michael Cuddyer .20 .50
58 Howard Kendrick .20 .50
59 Scott Rolen .30 .75
60 Adam Lind .30 .75
61 Prince Fielder .30 .75
62 David Price .40 1.00
63 Johnny Cueto .30 .75
64 John Maine .20 .50
65 Nick Markakis .40 1.00
66 Kosuke Fukudome .30 .75
67 Yadier Molina .50 1.25
68 Aramis Ramirez .20 .50
69 Billy Butler .20 .50
70 Wandy Rodriguez .20 .50
71 Ben Zobrist .30 .75
72 Victor Martinez .30 .75
73 Jorge Posada .30 .75
74 Adam Wainwright .30 .75
75 Vernon Wells .20 .50
76 Gordon Beckham .20 .50
77 Nelson Cruz .50 1.25
78 Kevin Slowey .20 .50
79 Paul Maholm .20 .50
80 Johan Santana .30 .75
81 Kazuo Matsui .20 .50
82 Jon Lester .30 .75
83 Clay Buchholz .20 .50
84 Alex Gordon .30 .75
85 Justin Morneau .30 .75
86 B.J. Upton .30 .75
87 Justin Verlander .50 1.25
88 Carlos Quentin .20 .50
89 Dustin Pedroia .40 1.00
90 Josh Willingham .30 .75
91 Alex Rios .20 .50
92 David Wright .40 1.00
93 Adam Dunn .30 .75
94 Jhoulys Chacin .20 .50
95 Andrew Bailey .20 .50
96 Derek Holland .20 .50
97 Kenshin Kawakami .30 .75
98 Jered Weaver .30 .75
99 Freddy Sanchez .20 .50
100 Matt Holliday .50 1.25
101 Bobby Abreu .20 .50
102 Ryan Doumit .20 .50
103 Kurt Suzuki .20 .50
104 Yovani Gallardo .20 .50
105 Daisuke Matsuzaka .30 .75
106 Francisco Liriano .20 .50
107 Jimmy Rollins .30 .75
108 James Shields .20 .50
109 Chase Utley .30 .75
110 Jeff Francoeur .30 .75
111 Tim Hudson .30 .75
112 Brad Hawpe .20 .50
113 Cole Hamels .40 1.00
114 Alfonso Soriano .30 .75
115 Lance Berkman .30 .75
116 Torii Hunter .20 .50
117 Chris Tillman .20 .50
118 Alex Rodriguez .60 1.50
119 Pablo Sandoval .30 .75
120 Ryan Howard .40 1.00
121 Rick Porcello .30 .75
122 Hanley Ramirez .30 .75
123 Brian McCann .30 .75
124 Kendry Morales .20 .50
125 Josh Johnson .30 .75
126 Joe Mauer .40 1.00
127 Grady Sizemore .30 .75
128 J.A. Happ .30 .75
129 Ichiro .60 1.50
130 Aaron Hill .20 .50
131 Mark Teixeira .30 .75
132 Tim Lincecum .30 .75
133 Denard Span .20 .50
134 Roy Oswalt .30 .75
135 Manny Ramirez .50 1.25
136 Jorge De La Rosa .20 .50
137 Joey Votto .50 1.25
138 Neftali Feliz .20 .50
139 Yunel Escobar .20 .50
140 Carlos Zambrano .30 .75
141 Erick Aybar .20 .50
142 Albert Pujols .60 1.50
143 Felix Hernandez .30 .75
144 Adam Jones .30 .75
145 Jacoby Ellsbury .40 1.00
146 Mark Reynolds .20 .50
147 Derek Jeter 1.25 3.00
148 Scott Baker .20 .50
149 Jose Reyes .30 .75
150 Jason Kubel .20 .50
151 Shin-Soo Choo .30 .75
152 Raul Ibanez .30 .75
153 Matt Cain .30 .75
154 Mark Buehrle .30 .75
155 Ken Griffey Jr. 1.00 2.50
156 Carlos Lee .20 .50
157 Chris Coghlan .20 .50
158 CC Sabathia .30 .75
159 Brett Anderson .20 .50
160 Ian Kinsler .30 .75
161 Mat Latos .30 .75
162 Carlos Beltran .30 .75
163 Dexter Fowler .30 .75
164 Michael Young .20 .50
165 Evan Longoria .30 .75
166 Curtis Granderson .40 1.00
167 Rich Harden .20 .50
168 Hideki Matsui .50 1.25
169 Edwin Jackson .20 .50
170 Miguel Tejada .30 .75
171 John Lackey .30 .75
172 Vladimir Guerrero .30 .75
173 Max Scherzer .50 1.25
174 Jason Bay .30 .75
175 Javier Vazquez .20 .50
176 Johnny Damon .30 .75
177 Cliff Lee .30 .75
178 Chone Figgins .20 .50
179 Kevin Millwood .20 .50
180 Roy Halladay .30 .75
181 Drew Butera (RC) .60 1.50
182 Matt Carson (RC) .60 1.50
183 Ian Desmond (RC) 1.00 2.50
184 Kila Ka'aihue (RC) 1.00 2.50
185 Brian Matusz RC 1.50 4.00
186 Mike Leake RC 2.00 5.00
187 Jenrry Mejia RC 1.00 2.50
188 Austin Jackson RC 1.00 2.50
189 Scott Sizemore RC 1.00 2.50
190 Jason Heyward RC 2.50 6.00
191 Travis Wood (RC) 1.00 2.50
192 Josh Donaldson RC 3.00 8.00
193 John Ely RC .60 1.50
194 Eric Young Jr. (RC) .60 1.50
195 Jason Donald RC .60 1.50
196 Andrew Cashner RC .60 1.50
197 Kevin Russo RC .60 1.50
198A Austin Jackson AU 4.00 10.00
198B Mike Stanton RC 5.00 12.00
199A Scott Sizemore AU 5.00 12.00
199B Drew Storen RC 1.00 2.50
200A Jason Heyward AU 6.00 15.00
200B Jonathan Lucroy RC 1.50 4.00
201 Wade Davis (RC) 1.00 2.50
202 Jon Jay RC 1.00 2.50
203 Ike Davis RC 1.25 3.00
204 Michael Brantley RC 1.00 2.50
205A Stephen Strasburg RC 5.00 12.00
205B Stephen Strasburg AU 25.00 60.00
206 Drew Stubbs RC 1.50 4.00
207 Daniel McCutchen RC 1.00 2.50
208 Brennan Boesch RC 1.50 4.00
209A Henry Rodriguez AU 3.00 8.00
209B Wilson Ramos RC 1.50 4.00
210 Chris Heisey RC 1.00 2.50
211A Michael Dunn AU 3.00 8.00
211B Starlin Castro RC 1.50 4.00
212A Drew Stubbs AU 3.00 8.00
212B Trevor Plouffe (RC) 1.50 4.00
213A Brandon Allen AU 3.00 8.00
213B Luis Atilano RC .60 1.50
214A Daniel McCutchen AU 3.00 8.00
214B Carlos Santana RC 2.00 5.00
215A Juan Francisco AU 3.00 8.00
215B Allen Craig RC 1.50 4.00
216A Eric Hacker AU 3.00 8.00
216B Ruben Tejada RC 1.00 2.50
217A Michael Brantley AU 10.00 25.00
217B Andy Oliver RC .60 1.50
218A Dustin Richardson AU 3.00 8.00
218B Tyler Colvin RC 1.00 2.50
219A Josh Thole AU 4.00 10.00
219B Cesar Valdez RC .60 1.50
220A Daniel Hudson AU 3.00 8.00
220B Lance Zawadzki RC .60 1.50

2010 Bowman Chrome Refractors

*REF VET: 1X TO 2.5X BASIC
*REF RC: .6X TO 1.5X BASIC RC
REF ODDS 1:4 HOBBY
*REF AU: .6X TO 1.5X BASIC
REF AU ODDS 1:277 HOBBY
STRASBURG AU ODDS 1:105 HOBBY
REF AU PRINT RUN 500 SER.#'d SETS
EXCHANGE DEADLINE 9/30/2013

2010 Bowman Chrome Blue Refractors

*BLUE VET: 2.5X TO 6X BASIC
*BLUE RC: 1.2X TO 3X BASIC
BLUE REF ODDS 1:48 HOBBY
STATED PRINT RUN 150 SER.#'d SETS
*BLUE AU: .75X TO 2X BASIC
BLUE AU ODDS 1:545 HOBBY
BLUE STRASBURG AU ODDS 1:352 HOBBY
BLUE AU PRINT RUN 250 SER.#'d SETS
EXCHANGE DEADLINE 9/30/2013

2010 Bowman Chrome Gold Refractors

*GOLD VET: 5X TO 12X BASIC
*GOLD RC: 2X TO 5X BASIC
GOLD REF ODDS 1:142 HOBBY
STATED PRINT RUN 50 SER.#'d SETS
*GOLD AU: 1.2X TO 3X BASIC
GOLD AU ODDS 1:2733 HOBBY
GOLD STRASBURG AU ODDS 1:1073 HOBBY
GOLD AU PRINT RUN 50 SER.#'d SETS
EXCHANGE DEADLINE 9/30/2013
200A Jason Heyward AU 20.00 50.00
205B Stephen Strasburg AU 300.00 500.00
213A Brandon Allen AU 20.00 50.00

2010 Bowman Chrome 18U USA Baseball

COMPLETE SET (20) 15.00 40.00
STATED ODDS 1:4 HOBBY
18BC1 Cody Buckel 1.50 4.00
18BC2 Nick Castellanos 3.00 8.00
18BC3 Garin Cecchini 2.00 5.00
18BC4 Sean Coyle .60 1.50
18BC5 Nicky Delmonico 1.00 2.50
18BC6 Kevin Gausman 2.00 5.00
18BC7 Cory Hahn .60 1.50
18BC8 Bryce Harper 12.00 30.00
18BC9 Kavin Keyes .60 1.50
18BC10 Manny Machado 8.00 20.00
18BC11 Connor Mason .60 1.50
18BC12 Ladson Montgomery .60 1.50
18BC13 Phillip Pfeifer .60 1.50
18BC14 Brian Ragira .60 1.50
18BC15 Robbie Ray .60 1.50
18BC16 Kyle Ryan .60 1.50
18BC17 Jameson Taillon 1.00 2.50
18BC18 A.J. Vanegas 1.00 2.50
18BC19 Karsten Whitson 1.00 2.50
18BC20 Tony Wolters 1.00 2.50

2010 Bowman Chrome 18U USA Baseball Refractors

*REF: .75X TO 2X BASIC
STATED ODDS 1:16 HOBBY
STATED PRINT RUN 777 SER.#'d SETS

2010 Bowman Chrome 18U USA Baseball Blue Refractors

*BLUE REF: 2X TO 5X BASIC
STATED ODDS 1:46 HOBBY
STATED PRINT RUN 250 SER.#'d SETS

2010 Bowman Chrome 18U USA Baseball Gold Refractors

*GOLD REF: 3X TO 8X BASIC
STATED ODDS 1:228 HOBBY
STATED PRINT RUN 50 SER.#'d SETS

2010 Bowman Chrome 18U USA Baseball Orange Refractors

STATED ODDS 1:463 HOBBY
STATED PRINT RUN 25 SER.#'d SETS

2010 Bowman Chrome 18U USA Baseball Autographs

STATED ODDS 1:207 HOBBY
PRINTING PLATE ODDS 1:24,605 HOBBY
AA Albert Almora 5.00 12.00
AV A.J. Vanegas 3.00 8.00
BR Brian Ragira 4.00 10.00
BS Bubba Starling 4.00 10.00
CL Christian Lopes 3.00 8.00
CM Christian Montgomery 3.00 8.00
DC Daniel Camarena 3.00 8.00
DM Dillon Maples 3.00 8.00
ES Elvin Soto 3.00 8.00
FL Francisco Lindor 50.00 120.00
HO Henry Owens 5.00 12.00
JH John Hochstatter 3.00 8.00
JS John Simms 3.00 8.00
LM Lance McCullers 5.00 12.00
ML Marcus Littlewood 3.00 8.00
ND Nicky Delmonico 3.00 8.00
PP Phillip Pfeifer III 3.00 8.00
TW Tony Wolters 3.00 8.00
BSW Blake Swihart 6.00 15.00
MIL Michael Lorenzen 4.00 10.00

2010 Bowman Chrome 18U USA Baseball Autographs Refractors

*REF: .6X TO 1.5X BASIC
STATED ODDS 1:646 HOBBY
STATED PRINT RUN 199 SER.#'d SETS

2010 Bowman Chrome 18U USA Baseball Autographs Blue Refractors

*BLUE REF: 1X TO 2.5X BASIC
STATED ODDS 1:1310 HOBBY
STATED PRINT RUN 99 SER.#'d SETS

2010 Bowman Chrome 18U USA Baseball Autographs Gold Refractors

*GOLD REF: 1.5X TO 4X BASIC
STATED ODDS 1:2630 HOBBY
STATED PRINT RUN 50 SER.#'d SETS

2010 Bowman Chrome 18U USA Baseball Autographs Orange Refractors

STATED ODDS 1:5410 HOBBY
STATED PRINT RUN 25 SER.#'d SETS

2010 Bowman Chrome Prospects

COMP.SET w/o AU's (220) 60.00 120.00
BOW.STATED AU ODDS 1:38 HOBBY
BOW.CHR.STATED AU ODDS 1:24 HOBBY
PLATE ODDS 1:1405 HOBBY
PLATE AU ODDS 1:12,000 HOBBY
BCP1 Stephen Strasburg 2.00 5.00
BCP2 Melky Mesa .50 1.25
BCP3 Cole McCurry .30 .75
BCP4 Tyler Henley .30 .75
BCP5 Andrew Cashner .30 .75
BCP6 Konrad Schmidt .30 .75
BCP7 Jean Segura 1.50 4.00
BCP8 Jon Gaston .50 1.25
BCP9 Nick Santomauro .30 .75
BCP10 Aroldis Chapman 1.25 3.00
BCP11 Logan Watkins .30 .75
BCP12 Bo Bowman .30 .75
BCP13 Jeff Antigua .30 .75
BCP14 Matt Adams 1.00 2.50
BCP15 Joseph Cruz .50 1.25
BCP16 Sebastian Valle .50 1.25
BCP17 Stefan Gartrell .30 .75
BCP18 Pedro Ciriaco 1.00 2.50
BCP19 Tyson Gillies .75 2.00
BCP20 Casey Crosby .30 .75
BCP21 Luis Exposito .30 .75
BCP22 Wellington Dotel .30 .75
BCP23 Alexander Torres .30 .75
BCP24 Byron Wiley .30 .75
BCP25 Pedro Florimon .30 .75
BCP26 Cody Satterwhite .50 1.25
BCP27 Craig Clark 1.25 3.00
BCP28 Jason Christian .30 .75
BCP29 Tommy Mendonca .30 .75
BCP30 Ryan Dent .30 .75
BCP31 Jhan Marinez .30 .75
BCP32 Eric Niesen .30 .75
BCP33 Gustavo Nunez .30 .75
BCP34 Scott Shaw .30 .75
BCP35 Welinton Ramirez .30 .75
BCP36 Trevor May 1.25 3.00
BCP37 Mitch Moreland .50 1.25
BCP38 Nick Czyz .30 .75
BCP39 Edinson Rincon .30 .75
BCP40 Domingo Santana 1.00 2.50
BCP41 Carson Blair .30 .75
BCP42 Rashun Dixon .30 .75
BCP43 Alexander Colome .75 2.00
BCP44 Allan Dykstra .30 .75
BCP45 J.J. Hoover .30 .75
BCP46 Abner Abreu .50 1.25
BCP47 Daniel Nava .30 .75
BCP48 Simon Castro .30 .75
BCP49 Brian Dalsley .30 .75
BCP50 Tony Delmonico .30 .75
BCP51 Chase D'Arnaud .30 .75
BCP52 Sheng-An Kuo .30 .75
BCP53 Leandro Castro .30 .75
BCP54 Charlie Lossman .30 .75
BCP55 Caleb Joseph .30 .75
BCP56 Ronaldo Gomez .30 .75
BCP57 John Lamb .75 2.00
BCP58 Adam Wilk .50 1.25
BCP59 Randall Delgado .50 1.25
BCP60 Neil Medchill .50 1.25
BCP61 Josh Donaldson 1.50 4.00
BCP62 Zach Gentile .30 .75
BCP63 Kiel Roling .30 .75
BCP64 Wes Freeman .30 .75
BCP65 Brian Pellegrini .50 1.25
BCP66 Kyle Jensen .30 .75
BCP67 Evan Anundsen .30 .75
BCP68 Hak-Ju Lee .50 1.25
BCP69 C.J. Retherford .30 .75
BCP70 Dillon Gee .75 2.00
BCP71 Bo Greenwell .30 .75
BCP72 Matt Tucker .50 1.25
BCP73 Joe Serafin .30 .75
BCP74 Matt Brown .30 .75
BCP75 Alexis Oliveras .30 .75
BCP76 James Beresford .30 .75
BCP77 Steve Lombardozzi .50 1.25
BCP78 Curtis Petersen .30 .75
BCP79 Eric Farris .30 .75
BCP80 Yen-Wen Kuo .30 .75
BCP81 Caleb Brewer .30 .75
BCP82 Jacob Elmore .50 1.25
BCP83 Jared Clark .50 1.25
BCP84 Yowill Espinal .50 1.25
BCP85 Jae-Hoon Ha .30 .75
BCP86 Michael Wing .30 .75
BCP87 Wilmer Font .30 .75
BCP88 Jake Kahaulelio .30 .75
BCP89A Dustin Ackley .50 1.25
BCP89B Dustin Ackley AU 4.00 10.00
BCP90A Donavan Tate .30 .75
BCP90B Donavan Tate AU 3.00 8.00
BCP91A Nolan Arenado 5.00 12.00
BCP91B Nolan Arenado AU 150.00 400.00
BCP92A Rex Brothers .30 .75
BCP92B Rex Brothers AU 3.00 8.00
BCP93A Brett Jackson 1.00 2.50
BCP93B Brett Jackson AU 3.00 8.00
BCP94A Chad Jenkins .30 .75
BCP94B Chad Jenkins AU 3.00 8.00
BCP95A Slade Heathcott 1.00 2.50
BCP95B Slade Heathcott AU 4.00 10.00
BCP96A J.R. Murphy .50 1.25
BCP96B J.R. Murphy AU 3.00 8.00
BCP97A Patrick Schuster .30 .75
BCP97B Patrick Schuster AU 3.00 8.00
BCP98A Alexia Amarista .30 .75
BCP98B Alexia Amarista AU 3.00 8.00
BCP99A Thomas Neal .50 1.25
BCP99B Thomas Neal AU 3.00 8.00
BCP100A Starlin Castro .75 2.00
BCP100B Starlin Castro AU 8.00 20.00
BCP101A Anthony Rizzo 4.00 10.00
BCP101B Anthony Rizzo AU 75.00 200.00
BCP102A Felix Doubront .30 .75
BCP102B Felix Doubront AU 3.00 8.00
BCP103A Nick Franklin .75 2.00
BCP103B Nick Franklin AU 3.00 8.00
BCP104A Anthony Gose .50 1.25
BCP104B Anthony Gose AU 3.00 8.00
BCP105A Julio Teheran .50 1.25
BCP105B Julio Teheran AU 6.00 15.00
BCP106A Grant Green .30 .75
BCP106B Grant Green AU 3.00 8.00
BCP107A David Lough .30 .75
BCP107B David Lough AU 3.00 8.00
BCP108A Jose Iglesias 1.00 2.50
BCP108B Jose Iglesias AU 5.00 12.00
BCP109A Jaff Decker .75 2.00
BCP109B Jaff Decker AU 3.00 8.00
BCP110A D.J. LeMahieu 3.00 8.00
BCP110B D.J. LeMahieu AU 50.00 120.00
BCP111A Craig Clark 1.25 3.00
BCP111B Craig Clark AU 3.00 8.00
BCP112A Jefry Marte .30 .75
BCP112B Jefry Marte AU 3.00 8.00
BCP113A Josh Donaldson 1.50 4.00
BCP113B Josh Donaldson AU 12.00 30.00
BCP114A Steven Hensley .30 .75
BCP114B Steven Hensley AU 3.00 8.00
BCP115A James Darnell .50 1.25
BCP115B James Darnell AU 3.00 8.00
BCP116A Kirk Nieuwenhuis .30 .75
BCP116B Kirk Nieuwenhuis AU 3.00 8.00
BCP117A Wil Myers .50 1.25
BCP117B Wil Myers AU 12.00 30.00
BCP118A Bryan Mitchell .30 .75
BCP118B Bryan Mitchell AU 3.00 8.00
BCP119A Martin Perez .75 2.00
BCP119B Martin Perez AU 4.00 10.00
BCP120 Taylor Sinclair .30 .75
BCP121 Max Walla .30 .75
BCP122 Darin Ruf 1.25 3.00
BCP123 Nicholas Hernandez .75 2.00
BCP124 Salvador Perez 1.50 4.00
BCP125 Yan Gomes .50 1.25
BCP126 Rlaan Spanjer-Furstenburg .30 .75
BCP127 Andrei Lobanov .30 .75
BCP128 Eliezer Mesa .30 .75
BCP129 Scott Barnes .30 .75
BCP130 Jerry Sands .75 2.00
BCP131 Chris Masters .30 .75
BCP132 Brandon Short .30 .75
BCP133 Rafael Dolis .30 .75
BCP134 Kevin Coddington .30 .75
BCP135 Jordan Pacheco .75 2.00
BCP136 Mike Zuanich .30 .75
BCP137 Jose Altuve 5.00 12.00
BCP138 Jimmy Paredes .75 2.00
BCP139 Yohan Flande .30 .75
BCP140 Drew Cumberland .30 .75
BCP141 Jose Yepez .30 .75
BCP142 Joe Gardner .30 .75
BCP143 Michael Kirkman .30 .75
BCP144 Thomas Di Benedetto .30 .75
BCP145 Blake Lalli .30 .75
BCP146 Avery Barnes .30 .75
BCP147 Brayan Villareal .30 .75
BCP148 Zoilo Almonte 2.50 6.00
BCP149 Tommy Pham .50 1.25
BCP150 Vince Belnome .30 .75
BCP151 Carlos Pimentel .30 .75
BCP152 Jeremy Barnes .30 .75
BCP153 Josh Stinson .30 .75
BCP154 Brady Shoemaker .30 .75
BCP155 Rudy Owens .50 1.25
BCP156 Kevin Mahoney .30 .75
BCP157 Luke Putkonen .30 .75
BCP158 Taylor Green .30 .75
BCP159 Anderson Hidalgo .30 .75
BCP160 Jonathan Villar .75 2.00
BCP161 Justin Bour .75 2.00
BCP162 Evan Bronson .30 .75
BCP163 Rossmel Perez .30 .75
BCP164 Jacob Cowan .30 .75
BCP165 J.D. Martinez 3.00 8.00
BCP166 Chris Schwinden .30 .75
BCP167 Rawley Bishop .30 .75
BCP168 Tim Pahuta .30 .75
BCP169 Buck Afenir .30 .75
BCP170 Eduardo Nunez .75 2.00
BCP171 Ethan Hollingsworth .30 .75
BCP172 Brad Correll .30 .75
BCP173 Armando Rodriguez .30 .75
BCP174 Ryan Wiegand .30 .75
BCP175 Terry Doyle .30 .75
BCP176 Grant Hogue .50 1.25
BCP177 Stephen Parker .30 .75
BCP178 Nathan Adcock .50 1.25
BCP179 Will Middlebrooks .50 1.25
BCP180 Chris Archer 1.00 2.50
BCP181A T.J. McFarland .30 .75
BCP181B T.J. McFarland AU 3.00 8.00
BCP182A Alex Liddi .50 1.25
BCP182B Alex Liddi AU 3.00 8.00
BCP183A Liam Hendriks .75 2.00
BCP183B Liam Hendriks AU 3.00 8.00
BCP184A Ozzie Martinez .30 .75
BCP184B Ozzie Martinez AU 3.00 8.00
BCP185A Eury Perez .30 .75
BCP185B Eury Perez AU 3.00 8.00
BCP186A Jhan Marinez .30 .75
BCP186B Jhan Marinez AU 3.00 8.00
BCP187A Carlos Peguero .50 1.25
BCP187B Carlos Peguero AU 3.00 8.00
BCP188A Tyler Chatwood .30 .75
BCP188B Tyler Chatwood AU 3.00 8.00
BCP189A Francisco Peguero .30 .75
BCP189B Francisco Peguero AU 4.00 10.00
BCP190A Pedro Baez .30 .75
BCP190B Pedro Baez AU 3.00 8.00
BCP191A Wilkin Ramirez .30 .75
BCP191B Wilkin Ramirez AU 3.00 8.00
BCP192A Wilin Rosario .30 .75
BCP192B Wilin Rosario AU 3.00 8.00
BCP193A Dan Tuttle .30 .75
BCP193B Dan Tuttle AU 3.00 8.00
BCP194A Trevor Reckling .30 .75
BCP194B Trevor Reckling AU 3.00 8.00
BCP195A Kyle Seager .75 2.00
BCP195B Kyle Seager AU 6.00 15.00
BCP196A Jason Kipnis 1.25 3.00
BCP196B Jason Kipnis AU 5.00 12.00
BCP197A Jeurys Familia .75 2.00
BCP197B Jeurys Familia AU 3.00 8.00
BCP198A Adeinis Hechavarria .30 .75
BCP198B Adeinis Hechavarria AU 3.00 8.00
BCP199A Aroldis Chapman 1.25 3.00
BCP199B Aroldis Chapman AU 12.00 30.00
BCP200A Everett Williams .30 .75
BCP200B Everett Williams AU 3.00 8.00
BCP201A Ehire Adrianza .30 .75
BCP201B Ehire Adrianza AU 3.00 8.00
BCP202A Kyle Gibson 1.25 3.00
BCP202B Kyle Gibson AU 3.00 8.00
BCP203A Max Kepler 1.00 2.50
BCP203B Max Kepler AU 6.00 15.00
BCP204A Shelby Miller 1.50 4.00
BCP204B Shelby Miller AU 4.00 10.00
BCP205A Miguel Sano 2.00 5.00
BCP205B Miguel Sano AU 15.00 40.00
BCP206A Scooter Gennett .60 1.50
BCP206B Scooter Gennett AU 5.00 12.00
BCP207A Gary Sanchez 3.00 8.00
BCP207B Gary Sanchez AU 40.00 100.00
BCP208A Graham Stoneburner .50 1.25
BCP208B Graham Stoneburner AU 3.00 8.00
BCP209 Josh Satin .50 1.25
BCP210A Matt Davidson 1.00 2.50
BCP210B Matt Davidson AU 3.00 8.00
BCP211A Arodys Vizcaino .75 2.00
BCP211B Arodys Vizcaino AU 3.00 8.00
BCP212A Anthony Bass .30 .75
BCP212B Anthony Bass AU 3.00 8.00
BCP213A Robinson Chirinos .30 .75
BCP213B Robinson Chirinos AU 3.00 8.00
BCP214A Trayce Thompson .75 2.00
BCP214B Trayce Thompson AU 3.00 8.00
BCP215A Simon Castro .30 .75
BCP215B Simon Castro AU 3.00 8.00
BCP216A Corban Joseph .30 .75
BCP216B Corban Joseph AU 3.00 8.00
BCP217 Noel Arguelles .50 1.25
BCP218A Daniel Fields .30 .75
BCP218B Daniel Fields AU 3.00 8.00
BCP219A Robbie Erlin .75 2.00
BCP219B Robbie Erlin AU 4.00 10.00
BCP220A Juan Urbina .50 1.25
BCP220B Juan Urbina AU 3.00 8.00
BCP221 Marc Krauss AU 4.00 10.00
BCP222 Ryan Wheeler AU 4.00 10.00

2010 Bowman Chrome Prospects Refractors

*1-110 REF: 1.5X TO 4X BASIC
*111-220 REF: 1.5X TO 4X BASIC
BOW.ODDS 1:16 HOBBY
BOW.CHR.ODDS 1:39 HOBBY
1-110 PRINT RUN 777 SER.#'d SETS
111-220 PRINT RUN 500 SER.#'d SETS
*REF AU: .5X TO 1.2X BASIC
BOW.REF AU ODDS 1:96 HOBBY
BOW.CHR.REF AU ODDS 1:105 HOBBY
REF AU PRINT RUN 500 SER.#'d SETS
BCP110B D.J. LeMahieu AU 75.00 200.00
BCP137 Jose Altuve 75.00 200.00

2010 Bowman Chrome Prospects Blue Refractors

*BLUE REF: 3X TO 8X BASIC
BOW.ODDS 1:46 HOBBY
BOW.CHR.ODDS 1:48 HOBBY
1-110 PRINT RUN 250 SER.#'d SETS
111-220 PRINT RUN 150 SER.#'d SETS
*BLUE REF AU: 1.2X TO 3X BASIC
BOW.BLUE AU ODDS 1:139 HOBBY
BOW.CHR.BLUE AU ODDS 1:352 HOBBY
REF AU PRINT RUN 150 SER.#'d SETS
BCP91B Nolan Arenado AU 500.00 1000.00
BCP110B D.J. LeMahieu AU 125.00 300.00
BCP137 Jose Altuve 300.00 600.00

2010 Bowman Chrome Prospects Gold Refractors

*GOLD REF: 8X TO 20X BASIC
BOW.ODDS 1:228 HOBBY
BOW.CHR.ODDS 1:142 HOBBY
STATED PRINT RUN 50 SER.#'d SETS
*GOLD REF AU: 2.5X TO 6X BASIC
BOW.GOLD AU ODDS 1:957 HOBBY
BOW.CHR.GOLD AU ODDS 1:1073 HOBBY
GOLD AU PRINT RUN 50 SER.#'d SETS
BCP91B Nolan Arenado AU 1200.00 1500.00
BCP93A Brett Jackson 30.00 60.00
BCP100A Starlin Castro 40.00 80.00
BCP110B D.J. LeMahieu AU 400.00 800.00
BCP113B Josh Donaldson AU 125.00 250.00
BCP137 Jose Altuve 800.00 1200.00

2010 Bowman Chrome Prospects Green X-Fractors

*X-F: 1.2X TO 3X BASIC
RANDOM INSERTS IN RETAIL PACKS

2010 Bowman Chrome Prospects Orange Refractors

BOW.STATED ODDS 1:463 HOBBY
BOW.STATED AU ODDS 1:1917 HOBBY
BOW.CHR.ODDS 1:284 HOBBY
BOW.CHR.AU ODDS 1:2200 HOBBY
STATED PRINT RUN 25 SER.#'d SETS

2010 Bowman Chrome Prospects Purple Refractors

*REF: 1X TO 2.5X BASIC
1-110 PRINT RUN 999 SER.#'d SETS
111-220 PRINT RUN 899 SER.#'d SETS
BCP1 Stephen Strasburg 12.00 30.00
BCP137 Jose Altuve 40.00 100.00

2010 Bowman Chrome Topps 100 Prospects

STATED ODDS 1:28 HOBBY
STATED PRINT RUN 999 SER.#'d SETS
*REF: .5X TO 1.2X BASIC
REFRACTOR ODDS 1:55 HOBBY
REFRACTOR PRINT RUN 499 SER.#'d SETS
*GOLD REF: 2X TO 5X BASIC
GOLD REF ODDS 1:610 HOBBY
GOLD REF PRINT RUN 50 SER.#'d SETS
SUPERFRACTOR ODDS 1:19,684 HOBBY
SUPERFRACTOR PRINT RUN 1 SER.#'d SET
TPC1 Stephen Strasburg 4.00 10.00
TPC2 Aroldis Chapman 2.00 5.00
TPC3 Jason Heyward 2.00 5.00
TPC4 Jesus Montero .50 1.25
TPC5 Mike Stanton 4.00 10.00
TPC6 Mike Moustakas 1.25 3.00
TPC7 Kyle Drabek .75 2.00
TPC8 Tyler Matzek 1.25 3.00
TPC9 Austin Jackson .75 2.00
TPC10 Starlin Castro 1.25 3.00
TPC11 Todd Frazier 1.50 4.00
TPC12 Carlos Santana 1.50 4.00
TPC13 Josh Vitters .50 1.25
TPC14 Neftali Feliz .50 1.25
TPC15 Tyler Flowers .75 2.00
TPC16 Alcides Escobar .50 1.25
TPC17 Ike Davis 1.00 2.50
TPC18 Domonic Brown 2.00 5.00
TPC19 Donavan Tate .50 1.25
TPC20 Buster Posey 4.00 10.00
TPC21 Dustin Ackley .75 2.00
TPC22 Desmond Jennings .75 2.00
TPC23 Brandon Allen .50 1.25
TPC24 Freddie Freeman 6.00 15.00
TPC25 Jake Arrieta 1.25 3.00
TPC26 Bobby Borchering .75 2.00
TPC27 Logan Morrison .75 2.00
TPC28 Christian Friedrich .75 2.00
TPC29 Wilmer Flores .75 2.00
TPC30 Austin Romine .75 2.00
TPC31 Tony Sanchez 1.25 3.00
TPC32 Madison Bumgarner 4.00 10.00
TPC33 Mike Montgomery .75 2.00
TPC34 Andrew Lambo .50 1.25
TPC35 Derek Norris .75 2.00
TPC36 Chris Withrow .50 1.25
TPC37 Thomas Neal .75 2.00
TPC38 Trevor Reckling .50 1.25
TPC39 Andrew Cashner .50 1.25
TPC40 Daniel Hudson .75 2.00
TPC41 Jiovanni Mier .75 2.00
TPC42 Grant Green .50 1.25
TPC43 Jeremy Hellickson 1.25 3.00
TPC44 Felix Doubront .50 1.25
TPC45 Martin Perez 1.25 3.00
TPC46 Jenrry Mejia .75 2.00
TPC47 Adrian Cardenas .50 1.25
TPC48 Ivan DeJesus Jr. .50 1.25
TPC49 Nolan Arenado 8.00 20.00
TPC50 Slade Heathcott 1.50 4.00
TPC51 Ian Desmond .75 2.00
TPC52 Michael Taylor .75 2.00
TPC53 Jaime Garcia .75 2.00
TPC54 Jose Tabata .75 2.00
TPC55 Josh Bell .50 1.25
TPC56 Jarrod Parker 1.25 3.00
TPC57 Matt Dominguez 1.25 3.00
TPC58 Koby Clemens .75 2.00
TPC59 Angel Morales .50 1.25
TPC60 Juan Francisco .75 2.00
TPC61 John Ely .50 1.25
TPC62 Brett Jackson 1.50 4.00
TPC63 Chad Jenkins .50 1.25
TPC64 Jose Iglesias 1.50 4.00
TPC65 Logan Forsythe .50 1.25
TPC66 Alex Liddi .75 2.00
TPC67 Eric Arnett .50 1.25
TPC68 Wilkin Ramirez .50 1.25
TPC69 Lars Anderson .50 1.25
TPC70 Jared Mitchell .75 2.00
TPC71 Mike Leake 1.50 4.00
TPC72 D.J. LeMahieu 5.00 12.00
TPC73 Chris Marrero .50 1.25
TPC74 Matt Moore 4.00 10.00
TPC75 Jordan Brown .50 1.25
TPC76 Christopher Parmelee .50 1.25
TPC77 Ryan Kalish .75 2.00
TPC78 A.J. Pollock 1.25 3.00
TPC79 Alex White .75 2.00
TPC80 Scott Sizemore .75 2.00
TPC81 Jay Austin .50 1.25
TPC82 Zach McAllister .75 2.00
TPC83 Max Stassi .75 2.00
TPC84 Robert Stock .50 1.25
TPC85 Jake McGee .50 1.25
TPC86 Zack Wheeler 1.50 4.00
TPC87 Chase D'Arnaud .50 1.25
TPC88 Danny Duffy .75 2.00
TPC89 Josh Lindblom .50 1.25
TPC90 Anthony Gose .75 2.00
TPC91 Simon Castro .50 1.25
TPC92 Chris Carter .75 2.00
TPC93 Matt Hobgood 1.25 3.00
TPC94 Ben Revere .75 2.00
TPC95 Mat Gamel .50 1.25
TPC96 Anthony Hewitt .50 1.25
TPC97 Julio Teheran .75 2.00
TPC98 Josh Reddick .50 1.25
TPC99 Hank Conger .50 1.25
TPC100 Jordan Walden .50 1.25

2010 Bowman Chrome USA Baseball

COMPLETE SET (22) 10.00 25.00
STATED ODDS 1:4 HOBBY
BC1 Trevor Bauer 3.00 8.00
BC2 Chad Bettis .60 1.50
BC3 Bryce Brentz 1.50 4.00
BC4 Michael Choice 1.00 2.50
BC5 Gerrit Cole 6.00 15.00
BC6 Christian Colon 1.00 2.50
BC7 Blake Forsythe .60 1.50
BC8 Yasmani Grandal 1.00 2.50
BC9 Sonny Gray 1.50 4.00
BC10 Rick Hague .60 1.50
BC11 Tyler Holt .60 1.50
BC12 Casey McGrew .60 1.50
BC13 Brad Miller 1.50 4.00
BC14 Matt Newman .60 1.50
BC15 Nick Pepitone .60 1.50
BC16 Drew Pomeranz 1.50 4.00
BC17 T.J. Walz .60 1.50
BC18 Cody Wheeler .60 1.50
BC19 Andy Wilkins .60 1.50
BC20 Asher Wojciechowski 1.50 4.00
BC21 Kolten Wong 1.00 2.50
BC22 Tony Zych .60 1.50

2010 Bowman Chrome USA Baseball Refractors

*REF: .75X TO 2X BASIC
STATED ODDS 1:16 HOBBY
STATED PRINT RUN 777 SER.#'d SETS

2010 Bowman Chrome USA Baseball Blue Refractors

*BLUE REF: 2X TO 5X BASIC
STATED ODDS 1:46 HOBBY
STATED PRINT RUN 250 SER.#'d SETS

2010 Bowman Chrome USA Baseball Gold Refractors

*GOLD REF: 4X TO 10X BASIC
STATED ODDS 1:228 HOBBY
STATED PRINT RUN 50 SER.#'d SETS

2010 Bowman Chrome USA Baseball Orange Refractors

STATED ODDS 1:463 HOBBY
STATED PRINT RUN 25 SER.#'d SETS

2010 Bowman Chrome USA Baseball Dual Autographs

STATED ODDS 1:1393 HOBBY
STATED PRINT RUN 500 SER.#'d SETS
USAD1 B.Starling/L.McCullers 8.00 20.00
USAD2 Elvin Soto 6.00 15.00
Blake Swihart
USAD3 Nicky Delmonico 6.00 15.00
Tony Wolters
USAD4 Henry Owens 6.00 15.00
Phillip Pfeifer III
USAD5 Christian Montgomery 6.00 15.00
John Simms
USAD6 Albert Almora 10.00 25.00
Brian Ragira
USAD7 Marcus Littlewood 6.00 15.00
Christian Lopes
USAD8 Dillon Maples 6.00 15.00
A.J. Vanegas
USAD9 Daniel Camarena 6.00 15.00
John Hochstatter
USAD10 F.Lindor/M.Lorenzen 20.00 50.00

2010 Bowman Chrome USA Baseball Buyback Autographs

ISSUED VIA WRAPPER REDEMPTION PROGRAM
STATED PRINT RUN 100 SER.#'d SETS
BC3 Bryce Brentz 20.00 50.00
BC4 Michael Choice 20.00 50.00
BC6 Christian Colon 12.50 30.00
BC8 Yasmani Grandal 12.50 30.00
BC16 Drew Pomeranz 10.00 25.00
18BC8 Bryce Harper 1000.00 1500.00
18BC10 Manny Machado 250.00 500.00
18BC17 Jameson Taillon 20.00 50.00

2010 Bowman Chrome USA Baseball Wrapper Redemption Autographs

ISSUED VIA WRAPPER REDEMPTION PROGRAM
STATED PRINT RUN 99 SER.#'d SETS
WR3 Kyle Winkler 6.00 15.00
WR6 AJ Vanegas 6.00 15.00
WR7 Albert Almora 20.00 50.00
WR8 Blake Swihart 30.00 60.00
WR9 Brian Ragira 6.00 15.00
WR10 Bubba Starling 15.00 40.00
WR11 Christian Lopes 6.00 15.00
WR12 Daniel Camarena 6.00 15.00
WR13 Dillon Maples 12.50 30.00
WR14 Elvin Soto 10.00 25.00
WR15 Francisco Lindor 30.00 60.00
WR16 Henry Owens 20.00 50.00
WR17 John Simms 6.00 15.00
WR18 Lance McCullers 6.00 15.00
WR19 Marcus Littlewood 10.00 25.00
WR20 Michael Lorenzen 6.00 15.00
WR21 Phillip Pfeifer 10.00 25.00
WR22 Alex Dickerson 6.00 15.00
WR23 Andrew Maggi 6.00 15.00
WR24 Brad Miller 50.00 100.00
WR25 Brett Mooneyham 10.00 25.00
WR26 Brian Johnson 12.50 30.00
WR27 George Springer 125.00 300.00
WR28 Gerrit Cole 100.00 200.00
WR29 Jackie Bradley Jr. 75.00 200.00
WR30 Jason Esposito 10.00 25.00
WR32 Matt Barnes 20.00 50.00
WR33 Mikie Mahtook 10.00 25.00
WR34 Nick Ramirez 15.00 40.00
WR35 Noe Ramirez 6.00 15.00
WR36 Nolan Fontana 10.00 25.00
WR37 Peter O'Brien 20.00 50.00
WR38 Ryan Wright 6.00 15.00
WR39 Scott McGough 6.00 15.00
WR40 Sean Gilmartin 15.00 40.00
WR41 Steve Rodriguez 6.00 15.00
WR42 Tyler Anderson 6.00 15.00

2010 Bowman Chrome USA Baseball Wrapper Redemption Autographs Black

ISSUED VIA WRAPPER REDEMPTION PROGRAM
STATED PRINT RUN 25 SER.#'d SETS

2010 Bowman Chrome USA Stars

COMPLETE SET (20) 6.00 15.00
USA1 Albert Almora 2.00 5.00
USA2 Daniel Camarena .60 1.50
USA3 Nicky Delmonico 1.00 2.50
USA4 John Hochstatter .60 1.50
USA5 Francisco Lindor 5.00 12.00
USA6 Marcus Littlewood 1.00 2.50
USA7 Christian Lopes 1.00 2.50
USA8 Michael Lorenzen .60 1.50
USA9 Dillon Maples .60 1.50
USA10 Lance McCullers 1.00 2.50
USA11 Christian Montgomery .60 1.50
USA12 Henry Owens 1.00 2.50
USA13 Phillip Pfeifer III .60 1.50
USA14 Brian Ragira .60 1.50
USA15 John Simms 1.00 2.50
USA16 Elvin Soto .60 1.50
USA17 Bubba Starling 1.00 2.50
USA18 Blake Swihart 1.50 4.00
USA19 A.J. Vanegas 1.00 2.50
USA20 Tony Wolters 1.00 2.50

2010 Bowman Chrome USA Stars Refractors

*REF: 1X TO 2.5X BASIC
STATED ODDS 1:39 HOBBY
STATED PRINT RUN 500 SER.#'d SETS

2010 Bowman Chrome USA Stars Blue Refractors

*BLUE REF: 2X TO 5X BASIC
STATED ODDS 1:48 HOBBY
STATED PRINT RUN 150 SER.#'d SETS

2010 Bowman Chrome USA Stars Gold Refractors

*GOLD REF: 5X TO 12X BASIC
STATED ODDS 1:142 HOBBY
STATED PRINT RUN 50 SER.#'d SETS

2010 Bowman Chrome USA Stars Orange Refractors

STATED ODDS 1:284 HOBBY
STATED PRINT RUN 25 SER.#'d SETS

2010 Bowman Chrome Wrapper Redemption Autographs

ISSUED VIA WRAPPER REDEMPTION PROGRAM
STATED PRINT RUN 100 SER.#'d SETS
WR1 Buster Posey 125.00 250.00
WR2 Mike Stanton 125.00 250.00
WR3 Mike Moustakas 40.00 80.00
WR4 Miguel Sano 200.00 300.00
WR5 Dustin Ackley 40.00 80.00

2010 Bowman Chrome Draft

COMP.SET w/o AU (110) 15.00 40.00
BDP1A Stephen Strasburg RC 2.50 6.00
BDP1B Stephen Strasburg AU 125.00 250.00
BDP2 Josh Bell (RC) .30 .75
BDP3 Ivan Nova RC 1.50 4.00
BDP4 Starlin Castro RC .75 2.00
BDP5 John Axford RC .30 .75
BDP6 Colin Curtis RC .30 .75
BDP7 Brennan Boesch RC .75 2.00
BDP8 Ike Davis RC .60 1.50
BDP9 Madison Bumgarner RC 2.50 6.00
BDP10 Austin Jackson RC .50 1.25
BDP11 Andrew Cashner RC .30 .75
BDP12 Jose Tabata RC .50 1.25
BDP13 Wade Davis (RC) .50 1.25
BDP14 Ian Desmond (RC) .50 1.25
BDP15 Felix Doubront RC .30 .75
BDP16 Danny Worth RC .30 .75
BDP17 John Ely RC .30 .75
BDP18 Jon Jay RC .50 1.25
BDP19 Mike Leake RC 1.00 2.50
BDP20 Daniel Nava RC .30 .75
BDP21 Brad Lincoln RC .50 1.25
BDP22 Jonathan Lucroy RC .75 2.00
BDP23 Brian Matusz RC .75 2.00
BDP24 Chris Nelson (RC) .50 1.25
BDP25 Andy Oliver RC .30 .75
BDP26 Adam Ottavino RC .30 .75
BDP27 Trevor Plouffe (RC) .75 2.00
BDP28 Vance Worley RC 1.25 3.00
BDP29 Daniel McCutchen RC .50 1.25
BDP30 Mike Stanton RC 2.50 6.00
BDP31 Drew Storen RC .50 1.25
BDP32 Tyler Colvin RC .50 1.25
BDP33 Travis Wood (RC) .50 1.25
BDP34 Eric Young Jr. (RC) .30 .75
BDP35 Sam Demel RC .30 .75
BDP36 Wellington Castillo RC .30 .75
BDP37 Sam LeCure (RC) .30 .75
BDP38 Danny Valencia RC 2.00 5.00
BDP39 Fernando Salas RC .30 .75
BDP40 Jason Heyward RC 1.25 3.00
BDP41 Jake Arrieta RC .75 2.00
BDP42 Kevin Russo RC .30 .75
BDP43 Josh Donaldson RC 1.50 4.00
BDP44 Luis Atilano RC .30 .75
BDP45 Jason Donald RC .30 .75
BDP46 Jonny Venters RC .30 .75
BDP47 Bryan Anderson (RC) .30 .75
BDP48 Jay Sborz (RC) .30 .75
BDP49 Chris Heisey RC .50 1.25
BDP50 Daniel Hudson RC .50 1.25
BDP51 Ruben Tejada RC .50 1.25
BDP52 Jeffrey Marquez RC .50 1.25
BDP53 Brandon Hicks RC .50 1.25
BDP54 Jeanmar Gomez RC .50 1.25
BDP55 Erik Kratz RC .50 1.25
BDP56 Lorenzo Cain RC .75 2.00
BDP57 Jhan Marinez RC .30 .75
BDP58 Omar Beltre (RC) .30 .75
BDP59 Drew Stubbs RC .75 2.00
BDP60 Alex Sanabia RC .30 .75
BDP61 Buster Posey RC 2.50 6.00
BDP62 Anthony Slama RC .30 .75
BDP63 Brad Davis RC .30 .75
BDP64 Logan Morrison RC .50 1.25
BDP65 Luke Hughes (RC) .30 .75
BDP66 Thomas Diamond (RC) .30 .75
BDP67 Tommy Manzella (RC) .30 .75
BDP68 Jordan Smith RC .30 .75
BDP69 Carlos Santana RC 1.00 2.50
BDP70 Dominic Brown RC 1.25 3.00
BDP71 Scott Sizemore RC .50 1.25
BDP72 Jordan Brown RC .30 .75
BDP73 Josh Thole RC .50 1.25
BDP74 Jordan Norberto RC .30 .75
BDP75 Dayan Viciedo RC .50 1.25
BDP76 Josh Tomlin RC .75 2.00
BDP77 Adam Moore RC .30 .75
BDP78 Kenley Jansen RC 1.00 2.50
BDP79 Juan Francisco RC .50 1.25
BDP80 Blake Wood RC .30 .75
BDP81 John Hester RC .30 .75
BDP82 Lucas Harrell (RC) .30 .75
BDP83 Neil Walker (RC) .50 1.25
BDP84 Cesar Valdez RC .30 .75
BDP85 Lance Zawadzki RC .30 .75
BDP86 Rommie Lewis RC .30 .75
BDP87 Steve Tolleson RC .30 .75
BDP88 Jeff Frazier (RC) .30 .75
BDP89 Drew Butera (RC) .30 .75
BDP90 Michael Brantley RC .50 1.25
BDP91 Mitch Moreland RC .50 1.25
BDP92 Alex Burnett RC .30 .75
BDP93 Allen Craig RC .75 2.00
BDP94 Sergio Santos (RC) .30 .75
BDP95 Matt Carson (RC) .30 .75
BDP96 Jenrry Mejia RC .50 1.25
BDP97 Rhyne Hughes RC .30 .75
BDP98 Tyson Ross RC .30 .75
BDP99 Argenis Diaz RC .50 1.25
BDP100 Hisanori Takahashi RC .50 1.25
BDP101 Cole Gillespie RC .30 .75
BDP102 Ryan Kalish RC .50 1.25
BDP103 J.P. Arencibia RC .60 1.50
BDP104 Peter Bourjos RC .50 1.25
BDP105 Justin Turner RC 1.50 4.00
BDP106 Michael Dunn RC .30 .75
BDP107 Mike McCoy RC .30 .75
BDP108 Will Rhymes RC .30 .75
BDP109 Wilson Ramos RC .75 2.00
BDP110 Josh Butler RC .30 .75

2010 Bowman Chrome Draft Refractors

*REF: .75X TO 2X BASIC

2010 Bowman Chrome Draft Blue Refractors

*BLUE REF: 2X TO 5X BASIC
STATED PRINT RUN 199 SER.#'d SETS

2010 Bowman Chrome Draft Gold Refractors

*GOLD REF: 3X TO 8X BASIC
STATED PRINT RUN 50 SER.#'d SETS
BDP1 Stephen Strasburg 30.00 80.00
BDP30 Mike Stanton 20.00 50.00
BDP61 Buster Posey 50.00 100.00

2010 Bowman Chrome Draft Orange Refractors

STATED PRINT RUN 25 SER.#'d SETS

2010 Bowman Chrome Draft Purple Refractors

*PURPLE REF: .75X TO 2X BASIC

2010 Bowman Chrome Draft Prospect Autographs

BDPP61 Michael Choice 3.00 8.00
BDPP62 Zack Cox 3.00 8.00
BDPP63 Bryce Brentz 3.00 8.00
BDPP64 Chance Ruffin 3.00 8.00
BDPP65 Mike Olt 4.00 10.00
BDPP66 Kellin Deglan 3.00 8.00
BDPP67 Yasmani Grandal 4.00 10.00
BDPP68 Kolbrin Vitek 3.00 8.00
BDPP69 Justin O'Conner 3.00 8.00
BDPP70 Gary Brown 4.00 10.00
BDPP71 Mike Foltynewicz 8.00 20.00
BDPP72 Chevez Clarke 3.00 8.00
BDPP73 Cito Culver 3.00 8.00
BDPP74 Aaron Sanchez 6.00 15.00
BDPP75 Noah Syndergaard 40.00 100.00
BDPP76 Taylor Lindsey 3.00 8.00
BDPP77 Josh Sale 3.00 8.00
BDPP78 Christian Yelich 200.00 500.00
BDPP79 Jameson Taillon 6.00 15.00
BDPP80 Manny Machado 75.00 200.00
BDPP81 Christian Colon 3.00 8.00
BDPP82 Drew Pomeranz 6.00 15.00
BDPP83 Delino DeShields 4.00 10.00
BDPP84 Matt Harvey 12.00 30.00
BDPP85 Ryan Bolden 3.00 8.00
BDPP86 Deck McGuire 3.00 8.00
BDPP87 Zach Lee 3.00 8.00
BDPP88 Alex Wimmers 3.00 8.00
BDPP89 Kaleb Cowart 3.00 8.00
BDPP90 Mike Kvasnicka 3.00 8.00
BDPP91 Jake Skole 3.00 8.00
BDPP92 Chris Sale 60.00 150.00

2010 Bowman Chrome Draft Prospect Autographs Refractors

*REF: .5X TO 1.2X BASIC
STATED PRINT RUN 500 SER.#'d SETS
BDPP78 Christian Yelich 300.00 600.00
BDPP80 Manny Machado 150.00 400.00

2010 Bowman Chrome Draft Prospect Autographs Blue Refractors

*BLUE REF: 1.2X TO 3X BASIC
STATED PRINT RUN 150 SER.#'d SETS
BDPP75 Noah Syndergaard 100.00 250.00
BDPP78 Christian Yelich 1000.00 2000.00
BDPP80 Manny Machado 400.00 800.00

2010 Bowman Chrome Draft Prospect Autographs Gold Refractors

*GOLD REF: 2X TO 5X BASIC
STATED PRINT RUN 50 SER.#'d SETS
BDPP75 Noah Syndergaard 150.00 400.00
BDPP78 Christian Yelich 2000.00 3000.00
BDPP80 Manny Machado 900.00 1200.00

2010 Bowman Chrome Draft Prospect Autographs Orange Refractors

STATED PRINT RUN 25 SER.#'d SETS

2010 Bowman Chrome Draft Prospects

BDPP1 Sam Tuivailala .30 .75
BDPP2 Alex Burgos .30 .75
BDPP3 Henry Ramos .50 1.25
BDPP4 Pat Dean .20 .50
BDPP5 Ryan Brett .30 .75
BDPP6 Jesse Biddle .30 .75
BDPP7 Leon Landry .50 1.25
BDPP8 Ryan LaMarre .30 .75
BDPP9 Josh Rutledge 1.25 3.00
BDPP10 Tyler Thornburg .50 1.25
BDPP11 Carter Jurica .20 .50
BDPP12 J.R. Bradley .20 .50
BDPP13 Devin Lohman .20 .50
BDPP14 Addison Reed .50 1.25
BDPP15 Micah Gibbs .20 .50
BDPP16 Derek Dietrich .50 1.25
BDPP18 Stephen Pryor .20 .50
BDPP19 Eddie Rosario 1.50 4.00
BDPP20 Blake Forsythe .20 .50
BDPP21 Rangel Ravelo .20 .50
BDPP22 Nick Longmire .30 .75
BDPP23 Andrelton Simmons .75 2.00
BDPP24 Chad Bettis .20 .50
BDPP25 Peter Tago .30 .75
BDPP26 Tyrell Jenkins .60 1.50
BDPP27 Marcus Knecht .20 .50
BDPP28 Seth Blair .30 .75
BDPP29 Brodie Greene .20 .50
BDPP30 Jason Martinson .20 .50
BDPP31 Bryan Morgado .30 .75
BDPP32 Eric Cantrell .20 .50
BDPP33 Niko Goodrum .60 1.50
BDPP34 Bobby Doran .20 .50
BDPP35 Cody Wheeler .20 .50
BDPP36 Cole Leonida .20 .50
BDPP37 Nate Roberts .20 .50
BDPP38 Dave Filak .20 .50
BDPP39 Taijuan Walker .50 1.25
BDPP40 Hayden Simpson .30 .75
BDPP41 Cameron Rupp .30 .75
BDPP42 Ben Heath .20 .50
BDPP43 Tyler Waldron .20 .50
BDPP44 Greg Garcia .20 .50
BDPP45 Vincent Velasquez .75 2.00
BDPP46 Jake Lemmerman .60 1.50
BDPP47 Russell Wilson 2.00 5.00
BDPP48 Cody Stanley .20 .50
BDPP49 Matt Suschak .20 .50
BDPP50 Logan Darnell .20 .50
BDPP51 Kevin Keyes .20 .50
BDPP52 Thomas Royse .20 .50
BDPP53 Scott Alexander .20 .50
BDPP54 Tony Thompson .20 .50
BDPP55 Seth Rosin .30 .75
BDPP56 Mickey Wiswall .20 .50
BDPP57 Albert Almora .60 1.50
BDPP58 Cole Billingsley .20 .50
BDPP58 Cody Hawn .30 .75
BDPP59 Drew Vettleson .30 .75
BDPP60 Matt Lipka .75 2.00
BDPP61 Michael Choice .30 .75
BDPP62 Zack Cox .60 1.50
BDPP63 Bryce Brentz .50 1.25
BDPP64 Chance Ruffin .20 .50
BDPP65 Mike Olt .60 1.50
BDPP66 Kellin Deglan .20 .50
BDPP67 Yasmani Grandal .30 .75
BDPP68 Kolbrin Vitek .50 1.25
BDPP69 Justin O'Conner .20 .50
BDPP70 Gary Brown 1.00 2.50
BDPP71 Mike Foltynewicz .50 1.25
BDPP72 Chevez Clarke .30 .75
BDPP73 Cito Culver .30 .75
BDPP74 Aaron Sanchez .75 2.00
BDPP75 Noah Syndergaard .75 2.00
BDPP76 Taylor Lindsey .30 .75
BDPP77 Josh Sale .60 1.50
BDPP78 Christian Yelich 15.00 40.00
BDPP79 Jameson Taillon .30 .75
BDPP80 Manny Machado 4.00 10.00
BDPP81 Christian Colon .30 .75
BDPP82 Drew Pomeranz .50 1.25
BDPP83 Delino DeShields .30 .75
BDPP84 Matt Harvey 1.25 3.00
BDPP85 Ryan Bolden .20 .50
BDPP86 Deck McGuire .30 .75
BDPP87 Zach Lee .50 1.25
BDPP88 Alex Wimmers .30 .75
BDPP89 Kaleb Cowart .30 .75
BDPP90 Mike Kvasnicka .20 .50
BDPP91 Jake Skole .30 .75
BDPP92 Chris Sale 2.50 6.00
BDPP93 Sean Brady .20 .50
BDPP94 Marc Brakeman .20 .50
BDPP95 Alex Bregman 2.50 6.00
BDPP96 Ryan Burr .50 1.25
BDPP97 Chris Chinea .30 .75
BDPP98 Troy Conyers .20 .50
BDPP99 Zach Green .20 .50
BDPP100 Carson Kelly .60 1.50
BDPP101 Timmy Lopes .20 .50
BDPP102 Adrian Marin .30 .75
BDPP103 Chris Okey .20 .50
BDPP104 Matt Olson 1.50 4.00
BDPP105 Ivan Pelaez .20 .50
BDPP106 Felipe Perez .20 .50
BDPP107 Nelson Rodriguez .30 .75
BDPP108 Corey Seager 6.00 15.00
BDPP109 Lucas Sims .50 1.25
BDPP110 Nick Travieso .30 .75

2010 Bowman Chrome Draft Prospects Refractors

*REF: 2X TO 5X BASIC
BDPP78 Christian Yelich 40.00 100.00

2010 Bowman Chrome Draft Prospects Blue Refractors

*BLUE REF: 4X TO 10X BASIC
STATED PRINT RUN 199 SER.#'d SETS
BDPP78 Christian Yelich 75.00 200.00

2010 Bowman Chrome Draft Prospects Gold Refractors

*GOLD REF: 8X TO 20X BASIC
STATED PRINT RUN 50 SER.#'d SETS
BDPP78 Christian Yelich 150.00 400.00

2010 Bowman Chrome Draft Prospects Orange Refractors

STATED PRINT RUN 25 SER.#'d SETS

2010 Bowman Chrome Draft Prospects Purple Refractors

*PURPLE REF: 1.2X TO 3X BASIC

2010 Bowman Chrome Draft USA Baseball Autographs

USAA1 Albert Almora 10.00 25.00
USAA2 Cole Billingsley 4.00 10.00
USAA3 Sean Brady 4.00 10.00
USAA4 Marc Brakeman 4.00 10.00
USAA5 Alex Bregman 30.00 80.00
USAA6 Ryan Burr 4.00 10.00
USAA7 Chris Chinea 4.00 10.00
USAA8 Troy Conyers 4.00 10.00
USAA9 Zach Green 4.00 10.00
USAA10 Carson Kelly 6.00 15.00
USAA11 Timmy Lopes 4.00 10.00
USAA12 Adrian Marin 4.00 10.00
USAA13 Chris Okey 8.00 20.00
USAA14 Matt Olson 20.00 50.00
USAA15 Ivan Pelaez 4.00 10.00
USAA16 Felipe Perez 4.00 10.00
USAA17 Nelson Rodriguez 5.00 12.00
USAA18 Corey Seager 75.00 200.00
USAA19 Lucas Sims 10.00 25.00
USAA20 Sheldon Neuse 4.00 10.00

2010 Bowman Chrome Draft USA Baseball Autographs Refractors

*REF: .5X TO 1.2X BASIC
STATED PRINT RUN 199 SER.#'d SETS

2010 Bowman Chrome Draft USA Baseball Autographs Blue Refractors

*BLUE REF: .75X TO 2X BASIC
STATED PRINT RUN 99 SER.#'d SETS

2010 Bowman Chrome Draft USA Baseball Autographs Gold Refractors

*GOLD REF: 1.25X TO 3X BASIC
STATED PRINT RUN 50 SER.#'d SETS

2010 Bowman Chrome Draft USA Baseball Autographs Orange Refractors

STATED PRINT RUN 25 SER.#'d SETS

2011 Bowman Chrome

COMP.SET w/o AU's (220) 20.00 50.00
COMMON RC (171-220) .40 1.00
STATED PLATE ODDS 1:960 HOBBY
PLATE PRINT RUN 1 SET PER COLOR
BLACK-CYAN-MAGENTA-YELLOW ISSUED
NO PLATE PRICING DUE TO SCARCITY
EXCHANGE DEADLINE 9/30/2014
1 Buster Posey .60 1.50
2 Alex Avila .30 .75
3 Edwin Jackson .20 .50
4 Miguel Montero .20 .50

Albert Pujols .60 1.50
Carlos Santana .50 1.25
Marlon Byrd .20 .50
Hanley Ramirez .30 .75
Josh Hamilton .30 .75
Matt Kemp .40 1.00
Shane Victorino .30 .75
2 Domonic Brown .40 1.00
3 Chipper Jones .50 1.25
4 Joey Votto .50 1.25
5 Brandon Phillips .20 .50
6 Jason Heyward .40 1.00
7 Curtis Granderson .40 1.00
8 Brian McCann .30 .75
9 Dustin Pedroia .40 1.00
0 Chris Johnson .20 .50
1 Brian Matusz .20 .50
2 Mark Teixeira .30 .75
3 Miguel Tejada .30 .75
4 Ryan Howard .40 1.00
5 Adrian Beltre .50 1.25
6 Joe Mauer .40 1.00
7 Logan Morrison .20 .50
8 Brian Wilson .50 1.25
9 Carlos Lee .20 .50
0 Ian Kinsler .30 .75
1 Shin-Soo Choo .30 .75
2 Adam Wainwright .30 .75
3 Carlos Gonzalez .30 .75
4 Lance Berkman .30 .75
5 Jon Lester .30 .75
6 Miguel Cabrera .50 1.25
7 Justin Verlander .50 1.25
8 Tyler Colvin .20 .50
9 Matt Cain .30 .75
0 Brett Anderson .20 .50
1 Gordon Beckham .20 .50
2 David DeJesus .20 .50
3 Jonathan Sanchez .20 .50
4 Jorge De La Rosa .20 .50
5 Torii Hunter .20 .50
6 Andrew McCutchen .50 1.25
47 Mat Latos .30 .75
48 CC Sabathia .30 .75
49 Brett Myers .20 .50
50 Ryan Zimmerman .30 .75
51 Trevor Cahill .20 .50
52 Clayton Kershaw 1.00 2.50
53 Andre Ethier .30 .75
54 Justin Upton .30 .75
55 B.J. Upton .30 .75
56 J.P. Arencibia .20 .50
57 Phil Hughes .20 .50
58 Tim Hudson .30 .75
59 Francisco Liriano .20 .50
60 Ike Davis .20 .50
61 Delmon Young .30 .75
62 Paul Konerko .30 .75
63 Carlos Beltran .30 .75
64 Mike Stanton .50 1.25
65 Adam Jones .30 .75
66 Jimmy Rollins .30 .75
67 Alex Rios .20 .50
68 Chad Billingsley .30 .75
69 Tommy Hanson .20 .50
70 Travis Wood .20 .50
71 Magglio Ordonez .30 .75
72 Jake Peavy .20 .50
73 Adrian Gonzalez .40 1.00
74 Aaron Hill .20 .50
75 Kendrys Morales .20 .50
76 Ryan Dempster .20 .50
77 Hunter Pence .30 .75
78 Josh Beckett .20 .50
79 Mark Reynolds .20 .50
80 Drew Stubbs .20 .50
81 Dan Haren .20 .50
82 Chris Carpenter .30 .75
83 Mitch Moreland .20 .50
84 Starlin Castro .30 .75
85 Roy Halladay .30 .75
86 Stephen Drew .20 .50
87 Aramis Ramirez .20 .50
88 Daniel Hudson .20 .50
89 Alexei Ramirez .30 .75
90 Rickie Weeks .20 .50
91 Will Venable .20 .50
92 David Price .40 1.00
93 Dan Uggla .20 .50
94 Austin Jackson .20 .50
95 Evan Longoria .30 .75
96 Ryan Ludwick .20 .50
97 Chase Utley .30 .75
98 Johnny Cueto .30 .75
99 Billy Butler .20 .50
100 David Wright .40 1.00
101 Jose Reyes .30 .75
102 Robinson Cano .30 .75
103 Josh Johnson .30 .75
104 Chris Coghlan .20 .50
105 David Ortiz .50 1.25
106 Jay Bruce .30 .75
107 Jayson Werth .30 .75
108 Matt Holliday .50 1.25
109 John Danks .20 .50
110 Franklin Gutierrez .20 .50
111 Zack Greinke .30 .75
112 Jacoby Ellsbury .40 1.00
113 Madison Bumgarner .40 1.00
114 Mike Leake .30 .75
115 Carl Crawford .30 .75
116 Clay Buchholz .20 .50
117 Gavin Floyd .20 .50
118 Mike Minor .20 .50
119 Jose Tabata .20 .50
120 Jason Castro .20 .50
121 Chris Young .20 .50
122 Jose Bautista .30 .75
123 Felix Hernandez .30 .75
124 Dexter Fowler .30 .75
125 Tim Lincecum .30 .75
126 Todd Helton .30 .75
127 Ubaldo Jimenez .20 .50
128 Yovani Gallardo .20 .50
129 Derek Jeter 1.25 3.00
130 Wade Davis .20 .50
131 Nelson Cruz .50 1.25
132 Michael Cuddyer .20 .50
133 Mark Buehrle .30 .75
134 Danny Valencia .30 .75
135 Ichiro Suzuki .60 1.50
136 Brett Wallace .20 .50
137 Troy Tulowitzki .50 1.25
138 Pedro Alvarez .40 1.00
139 Brandon Morrow .20 .50
140 Jered Weaver .30 .75
141 Michael Young .20 .50
142 Wandy Rodriguez .20 .50
143 Alfonso Soriano .30 .75
144 Roy Oswalt .30 .75
145 Brian Roberts .20 .50
146 Jaime Garcia .30 .75
147 Edinson Volquez .20 .50
148 Vladimir Guerrero .30 .75
149 Cliff Lee .30 .75
150 Johnny Damon .30 .75
151 Alex Rodriguez .60 1.50
152 Nick Markakis .40 1.00
153 Cole Hamels .40 1.00
154 Prince Fielder .30 .75
155 Kurt Suzuki .20 .50
156 Ryan Braun .30 .75
157 Justin Morneau .30 .75
158 Elvis Andrus .30 .75
159 Stephen Strasburg .50 1.25
160 Adam Lind .30 .75
161 Corey Hart .20 .50
162 Adam Dunn .30 .75
163 Bobby Abreu .20 .50
164 Gaby Sanchez .20 .50
165 Ian Kennedy .20 .50
166 Kevin Youkilis .20 .50
167 Vernon Wells .20 .50
168 Matt Garza .20 .50
169 Victor Martinez .30 .75
170 Casey McGehee .20 .50
171 Jake McGee (RC) .40 1.00
172 Lars Anderson RC .60 1.50
173 Mark Trumbo (RC) 1.00 2.50
174 Konrad Schmidt RC .40 1.00
175 Mike Trout RC 200.00 500.00
176 Brent Morel RC .40 1.00
177 Aroldis Chapman RC 1.25 3.00
178 Greg Halman RC .60 1.50
179 Jeremy Hellickson RC 1.00 2.50
180 Yunesky Maya RC .40 1.00
181 Kyle Drabek RC .60 1.50
182 Ben Revere RC .60 1.50
183 Desmond Jennings RC .60 1.50
184 Brandon Beachy RC 1.00 2.50
185 Freddie Freeman RC 6.00 15.00
186 Randall Delgado RC .60 1.50
187 John Lindsey RC .40 1.00
188 Mark Rogers (RC) .40 1.00
189 Brian Bogusevic (RC) .40 1.00
190 Yonder Alonso RC .60 1.50
191 Gregory Infante RC .40 1.00
192 Dillon Gee RC .60 1.50
193 Ozzie Martinez RC .40 1.00
194 Brandon Snyder (RC) .40 1.00
195 Daniel Descalso RC .40 1.00
196A Eric Hosmer RC 2.50 6.00
196B Eric Hosmer AU EXCH 75.00 150.00
197 Lucas Duda RC 1.00 2.50
198 Cory Luebke RC .40 1.00
199 Hank Conger RC .60 1.50
200 Chris Sale RC 2.50 6.00
201 Julio Teheran RC .60 1.50
202 Danny Duffy RC .60 1.50
203 Brandon Belt RC 1.00 2.50
204 Ivan Nova (RC) .60 1.50
205 Danny Espinosa RC .40 1.00
206 Alexi Ogando RC 1.00 2.50
207 Darwin Barney RC 1.25 3.00
208 Jordan Walden RC .40 1.00
209 Tsuyoshi Nishioka RC 1.25 3.00
210 Zach Britton RC 1.00 2.50
211 Andrew Cashner (RC) .40 1.00
212A Dustin Ackley RC .60 1.50
212B Dustin Ackley AU 8.00 20.00
213 Carlos Peguero RC .60 1.50
214 Hector Noesi RC .60 1.50
215 Eduardo Nunez RC 1.00 2.50
216 Michael Pineda RC 1.00 2.50
217 Alex Cobb RC .40 1.00
218 Ivan DeJesus Jr. RC .40 1.00
219 Scott Cousins RC .40 1.00
220 Aaron Crow RC .60 1.50

2011 Bowman Chrome Refractors

*REF: 1X TO 2.5X BASIC
*REF RC: .5X TO 1.2X BASIC RC
STATED ODDS 1:4 HOBBY
175 Mike Trout 300.00 800.00

2011 Bowman Chrome Blue Refractors

*BLUE REF: 2X TO 5X BASIC
*BLUE REF RC: 2X TO 5X BASIC RC
STATED ODDS 1:31 HOBBY
STATED PRINT RUN 150 SER.#'d SETS
175 Mike Trout 1000.00 2000.00

2011 Bowman Chrome Gold Canary Diamond

STATED ODDS 1:3840 HOBBY
STATED PRINT RUN 1 SER.#'d SET
NO PRICING DUE TO SCARCITY

2011 Bowman Chrome Gold Refractors

*GOLD REF: 6X TO 15X BASIC
*GOLD REF RC: 3X TO 8X BASIC RC
STATED ODDS 1:94 HOBBY
STATED PRINT RUN 50 SER.#'d SETS
EXCHANGE DEADLINE 9/30/2014
175 Mike Trout 4000.00 6000.00
196B Eric Hosmer AU EXCH 250.00 400.00
212B Dustin Ackley AU 40.00 80.00

2011 Bowman Chrome Orange Refractors

STATED ODDS 1:198 HOBBY
STATED PRINT RUN 25 SER.#'d SETS
NO PRICING DUE TO SCARCITY
EXCHANGE DEADLINE 9/30/2014

2011 Bowman Chrome Red Refractors

STATED ODDS 1:900 HOBBY
STATED PRINT RUN 5 SER.#'d SETS
NO PRICING DUE TO SCARCITY

2011 Bowman Chrome 18U USA National Team Refractors

STATED ODDS 1:2063 HOBBY
STATED PLATE ODDS 1:365,000 HOBBY
PLATE PRINT RUN 1 SET PER COLOR
BLACK-CYAN-MAGENTA-YELLOW ISSUED
NO PLATE PRICING DUE TO SCARCITY
EXCHANGE DEADLINE 10/26/2012
18U1 Albert Almora 2.50 6.00
18U2 Alex Bregman 10.00 25.00
18U3 Gavin Cecchini 2.50 6.00
18U4 Troy Conyers 1.50 4.00
18U6 Chase DeJong 3.00 8.00
18U8 Carson Fulmer 3.00 8.00
18U13 Cole Irvin 2.50 6.00
18U15 Jeremy Martinez 1.50 4.00
18U17 Chris Okey 1.50 4.00
18U18 Cody Poteet 1.50 4.00
18U19 Nelson Rodriguez 2.50 6.00
18U21 Addison Russell 5.00 12.00
18U22 Clate Schmidt 1.50 4.00
18U24 Hunter Virant 1.50 4.00
18U25 Walker Weickel 1.50 4.00
18U26 Mikey White 1.50 4.00
18U28 Jesse Winker 1.50 4.00

2011 Bowman Chrome 18U USA National Team Blue Refractors

*BLUE: 1.2X TO 3X BASIC
STATED ODDS 1:13,205 HOBBY
STATED PRINT RUN 99 SER.#'d SETS
EXCHANGE DEADLINE 10/26/2012

2011 Bowman Chrome 18U USA National Team Gold Refractors

*GOLD REF: 1.5X TO 4X BASIC
STATED ODDS 1:27,000 HOBBY
STATED PRINT RUN 50 SER.#'d SETS
EXCHANGE DEADLINE 10/26/2012

2011 Bowman Chrome 18U USA National Team Orange Refractors

STATED ODDS 1:50,685 HOBBY
STATED PRINT RUN 25 SER.#'d SETS
NO PRICING DUE TO SCARCITY
EXCHANGE DEADLINE 10/26/2012

2011 Bowman Chrome 18U USA National Team Red Refractors

STATED ODDS 1:253,424 HOBBY
STATED PRINT RUN 5 SER.#'d SETS
NO PRICING DUE TO SCARCITY
EXCHANGE DEADLINE 10/26/2012

2011 Bowman Chrome 18U USA National Team X-Fractors

*XFRACTOR: .6X TO 1.5X BASIC
STATED ODDS 1:4281 HOBBY
STATED PRINT RUN 299 SER.#'d SETS
EXCHANGE DEADLINE 10/26/2012

2011 Bowman Chrome 18U USA National Team Autographs Refractors

STATED ODDS 1:192 HOBBY
STATED PRINT RUN 417 SER.#'d SETS
STATED PLATE ODDS 1:15,839 HOBBY
PLATE PRINT RUN 1 SET PER COLOR
BLACK-CYAN-MAGENTA-YELLOW ISSUED
NO PLATE PRICING DUE TO SCARCITY
18U1 Albert Almora 12.00 30.00
18U2 Alex Bregman 30.00 80.00
18U3 Gavin Cecchini 4.00 10.00
18U4 Troy Conyers 4.00 10.00
18U6 Chase DeJong 4.00 10.00
18U8 Carson Fulmer 8.00 20.00
18U13 Cole Irvin 4.00 10.00
18U15 Jeremy Martinez 4.00 10.00
18U15 Clate Schmidt 4.00 10.00
18U17 Chris Okey 3.00 8.00
18U18 Cody Poteet 4.00 10.00
18U19 Nelson Rodriguez 4.00 10.00
18U21 Addison Russell 12.00 30.00
18U24 Hunter Virant 4.00 10.00
18U25 Walker Weickel 4.00 10.00
18U26 Mikey White 4.00 10.00
18U28 Jesse Winker 12.00 30.00

2011 Bowman Chrome 18U USA National Team Autographs Blue Refractors

*BLUE REF: .75X TO 2X BASIC
STATED ODDS 1:829 HOBBY
STATED PRINT RUN 99 SER.#'d SETS

2011 Bowman Chrome 18U USA National Team Autographs Gold Refractors

*GOLD REF: 1.5X TO 4X BASIC
STATED ODDS 1:1695 HOBBY
STATED PRINT RUN 50 SER.#'d SETS

2011 Bowman Chrome 18U USA National Team Autographs Orange Refractors

STATED ODDS 1:3625 HOBBY
STATED PRINT RUN 25 SER.#'d SETS
NO PRICING DUE TO SCARCITY

2011 Bowman Chrome 18U USA National Team Autographs Red Refractors

STATED ODDS 1:15,919 HOBBY
STATED PRINT RUN 5 SER.#'d SETS
NO PRICING DUE TO SCARCITY

2011 Bowman Chrome 18U USA National Team Autographs Superfractors

STATED ODDS 1:63,356 HOBBY
STATED PRINT RUN 1 SER.#'d SET
NO PRICING DUE TO SCARCITY

2011 Bowman Chrome 18U USA National Team Autographs X-Fractors

*X-FRACTOR: .5X TO 1.2X BASIC
STATED ODDS 1:268 HOBBY
STATED PRINT RUN 299 SER.#'d SETS

2011 Bowman Chrome Bryce Harper Retail Exclusive

INSERTED IN RETAIL VALUE BOXES
BCE1G Bryce Harper Gold 8.00 20.00
BCE1R Bryce Harper Red 4.00 10.00
BCE1S Bryce Harper Silver 4.00 10.00

2011 Bowman Chrome Futures

COMPLETE SET (25) 12.50 30.00
STATED ODDS 1:9 HOBBY
MICRO-FRAC. ODDS 1:2035 HOBBY
MICRO-FRAC. PRINT RUN 25 SER.#'d SETS
NO MICRO-FRAC.PRICING AVAILABLE
1 Bryce Harper 8.00 20.00
2 Manny Machado 4.00 10.00
3 Jameson Taillon .60 1.50
4 Delino DeShields Jr. .40 1.00
5 Grant Green .40 1.00
6 Devin Mesoraco 1.00 2.50
7 Anthony Ranaudo 1.00 2.50
8 Stetson Allie .60 1.50
9 Shelby Miller 2.00 5.00
10 Arodys Vizcaino .60 1.50
11 Manny Banuelos 1.00 2.50
12 Jonathan Singleton .60 1.50
13 Tyler Matzek .60 1.50
14 Gary Sanchez 2.00 5.00
15 Jean Segura 1.50 4.00
16 Peter Tago .40 1.00
17 Matt Dominguez .60 1.50
18 Miguel Sano .75 2.00
19 Jesus Montero .40 1.00
20 Josh Sale .60 1.50
21 Brett Jackson .60 1.50
22 Mike Montgomery .60 1.50
23 Chris Archer .75 2.00
24 Jacob Turner 1.50 4.00
25 Wil Myers .60 1.50

2011 Bowman Chrome Futures Refractors

*REF: .5X TO 1.2X BASIC

2011 Bowman Chrome Futures Fusion-Fractors 99

*FUSION: 2X TO 5X BASIC
STATED ODDS 1:512 HOBBY
STATED PRINT RUN 99 SER.#'d SETS
1 Bryce Harper 30.00 60.00

2011 Bowman Chrome Futures Future-Fractors

*FUTURE: .6X TO 1.5X BASIC

2011 Bowman Chrome Prospect Autographs

Bryce Harper #BCP111B BGS 10 (Pristine) sold for $1335 (eBay;
111-220 PLATE ODDS 1:9051 HOBBY
PLATE PRINT RUN 1 SET PER COLOR
BLACK-CYAN-MAGENTA-YELLOW ISSUED
NO PLATE PRICING DUE TO SCARCITY
EXCHANGE DEADLINE 4/30/2014
BCP80 Dee Gordon 3.00 8.00
BCP81 Blake Forsythe 3.00 8.00
BCP82 Jurickson Profar 6.00 15.00
BCP83 Jedd Gyorko 3.00 8.00
BCP84 Matt Hague 3.00 8.00
BCP85 Mason Williams 3.00 8.00
BCP86 Stetson Allie 3.00 8.00
BCP87 Jarred Cosart 3.00 8.00
BCP88 Wagner Mateo 3.00 8.00
BCP89 Allen Webster 3.00 8.00
BCP90 Adron Chambers 3.00 8.00
BCP91 Blake Smith 3.00 8.00
BCP92 J.D. Martinez 25.00 60.00
BCP93 Brandon Belt 10.00 25.00
BCP94 Drake Britton 3.00 8.00
BCP95 Addison Reed 3.00 8.00
BCP96 Adonis Cardona 3.00 8.00
BCP97 Yordy Cabrera 3.00 8.00
BCP98 Tony Wolters 3.00 8.00
BCP99 Paul Goldschmidt 40.00 100.00
BCP100 Sean Coyle 3.00 8.00
BCP101 Rymer Liriano 3.00 8.00
BCP102 Eric Thames 3.00 8.00
BCP103 Brian Fletcher 3.00 8.00
BCP104 Ben Gamel 6.00 15.00
BCP105 Kyle Russell 3.00 8.00
BCP106 Sammy Solis 3.00 8.00
BCP107 Garin Cecchini 3.00 8.00
BCP108 Carlos Perez 3.00 8.00
BCP110 Jonathan Villar 3.00 8.00
BCP111A Adam Warren 3.00 8.00
BCP111B Bryce Harper 250.00 600.00
BCP112 Rick Hague 3.00 8.00
BCP113 Carlos Perez 3.00 8.00
BCP130 Hunter Morris 3.00 8.00
BCP131 Jean Segura 3.00 8.00
BCP132 Melky Mesa 3.00 8.00
BCP133 Manny Banuelos 3.00 8.00
BCP134 Chris Archer 3.00 8.00
BCP157 Danny Brewer 3.00 8.00
BCP158 David Bromberg 3.00 8.00
BCP160 A.J. Cole 3.00 8.00
BCP161 Alex Colome 3.00 8.00
BCP162 Brody Colvin 3.00 8.00
BCP163 Khris Davis 4.00 10.00
BCP164 Cutter Dykstra 3.00 8.00
BCP165 Nathan Eovaldi 4.00 10.00
BCP167 Garrett Gould 3.00 8.00
BCP168 Brandon Guyer 3.00 8.00
BCP169 Shaeffer Hall 3.00 8.00
BCP170 Reese Havens 3.00 8.00
BCP171 Luis Heredia 3.00 8.00
BCP172 Aaron Hicks 6.00 15.00
BCP173 Bryan Holaday 3.00 8.00
BCP174 Brad Holt 3.00 8.00
BCP175 Brett Lawrie 4.00 10.00
BCP176 Matt Lollis 3.00 8.00
BCP178 Starling Marte 8.00 20.00
BCP179 Ethan Martin 3.00 8.00
BCP180 Trey McNutt 3.00 8.00
BCP182 Keyvius Sampson 3.00 8.00
BCP183 Jordan Swagerty 3.00 8.00
BCP184 Dickie Joe Thon 3.00 8.00
BCP185 Jacob Turner 3.00 8.00
BCP186 Christopher Wallace 3.00 8.00
BCP189 Kendrick Perkins 3.00 8.00
BCP192 Enny Romero 3.00 8.00
BCP212 Brock Holt 3.00 8.00
BCP214 Brandon Laird 3.00 8.00
BCP220 Matt Moore 4.00 10.00

2011 Bowman Chrome Prospect Autographs Refractors

*REF: .6X TO 1.5X BASIC
111-220 STATED ODDS 1:88 HOBBY
STATED PRINT RUN 500 SER.#'d SETS
EXCHANGE DEADLINE 4/30/2014

2011 Bowman Chrome Prospect Autographs Blue Refractors

*BLUE REF: 1.2X TO 3X BASIC
111-220 STATED ODDS 1:295 HOBBY
STATED PRINT RUN 150 SER.#'d SETS
EXCHANGE DEADLINE 4/30/2014

2011 Bowman Chrome Prospect Autographs Gold Refractors

*GOLD REF: 1.5X TO 4X BASIC
111-220 STATED ODDS 1:916 HOBBY
STATED PRINT RUN 50 SER.#'d SETS
EXCHANGE DEADLINE 4/30/2014

2011 Bowman Chrome Prospect Autographs Orange Refractors

111-220 STATED ODDS 1:1936 HOBBY
STATED PRINT RUN 25 SER.#'d SETS
NO PRICING DUE TO SCARCITY
EXCHANGE DEADLINE 4/30/2014

2011 Bowman Chrome Prospect Autographs Red Refractors

111-220 STATED ODDS 1:8675 HOBBY
STATED PRINT RUN 5 SER.#'d SETS
NO PRICING DUE TO SCARCITY
EXCHANGE DEADLINE 4/30/2014

2011 Bowman Chrome Prospects

COMPLETE SET (221) 40.00 80.00
1-110 ISSUED IN BOWMAN
111-220 ISSUED IN BOWMAN CHROME
STATED PLATE ODDS 1:960 HOBBY
PLATE PRINT RUN 1 SET PER COLOR
BLACK-CYAN-MAGENTA-YELLOW ISSUED
NO PLATE PRICING DUE TO SCARCITY
BCP1 Bryce Harper 6.00 15.00
BCP2 Chris Dennis .25 .60
BCP3 Jeremy Barfield .25 .60
BCP4 Nate Freiman .25 .60
BCP5 Tyler Moore .60 1.50
BCP6 Anthony Carter .25 .60
BCP7 Ryan Cavan .25 .60
BCP8 Stephen Vogt .40 1.00
BCP9 Carlo Testa .25 .60
BCP10 Erik Davis .25 .60
BCP11 Jack Shuck .60 1.50
BCP12 Charles Brewer .25 .60
BCP13 Alex Castellanos .40 1.00
BCP14 Anthony Vasquez .25 .60
BCP15 Michael Brenly .25 .60
BCP16 Kody Hinze .40 1.00
BCP17 Hector Noesi .40 1.00
BCP18 Tyler Bortnick .25 .60
BCP19 Thomas Layne .25 .60
BCP20 Everett Teaford .25 .60
BCP21 Jose Pirela .40 1.00
BCP22 Joel Carreno .25 .60
BCP23 Vinnie Catricala .75 2.00
BCP24 Tom Koehler .25 .60
BCP25 Jonathan Schoop .40 1.00
BCP26 Chun-Hsiu Chen .60 1.50
BCP27 Amaury Rivas .25 .60
BCP28 Oswaldo Arcia .25 .60
BCP29 Johermyn Chavez .25 .60
BCP30 Michael Spina .25 .60
BCP31 Kyle McPherson .40 1.00
BCP32 Albert Cartwright .25 .60
BCP33 Joseph Wieland .60 1.50
BCP34 Ben Paulsen .25 .60
BCP35 Jason Hagerty .25 .60
BCP36 Marcell Ozuna 1.00 2.50
BCP37 Dave Sappelt .75 2.00
BCP38 Eduardo Escobar .25 .60
BCP39 Aaron Baker .25 .60
BCP40 Deryk Hooker .25 .60
BCP41 Ty Morrison .25 .60
BCP42 Keon Broxton .25 .60
BCP43 Corey Jones .25 .60
BCP44 Manny Banuelos .60 1.50
BCP45 Brandon Guyer .40 1.00
BCP46 Juan Nicasio .25 .60
BCP47 Sean Ochinko .25 .60
BCP48 Adam Warren .40 1.00
BCP49 Phillip Cerreto .25 .60
BCP50 Mychal Givens .25 .60
BCP51 James Fuller .25 .60
BCP52 Ronnie Welty .25 .60
BCP53 Dan Straily 1.25 3.00
BCP54 Gabriel Jacobo .25 .60
BCP55 David Rubinstein .25 .60
BCP56 Kevin Mailloux .25 .60
BCP57 Angel Castillo .25 .60
BCP58 Adrian Salcedo .40 1.00
BCP59 Ronald Bermudez .25 .60
BCP60 Jarek Cunningham .40 1.00
BCP61 Matt Magill .40 1.00
BCP62 Willie Cabrera .25 .60
BCP63 Austin Hyatt .40 1.00
BCP64 Cody Puckett .40 1.00
BCP65 Jacob Goebbert .40 1.00
BCP66 Matt Carpenter 2.00 5.00
BCP67 Dan Klein .40 1.00
BCP68 Sean Ratliff .25 .60
BCP69 Elih Villanueva .25 .60
BCP70 Wade Gaynor .25 .60
BCP71 Evan Crawford .25 .60
BCP72 Avisail Garcia .40 1.00
BCP73 Kevin Rivers .25 .60
BCP74 Jim Gallagher .25 .60
BCP75 Brian Broderick .25 .60
BCP76 Tyson Auer .25 .60
BCP77 Matt Klinker .25 .60
BCP78 Cole Figueroa .25 .60
BCP79 Rafael Ynoa .25 .60
BCP80 Dee Gordon .40 1.00
BCP81 Blake Forsythe .25 .60
BCP82 Jurickson Profar .60 1.50
BCP83 Jedd Gyorko .60 1.50
BCP84 Matt Hague .40 1.00
BCP85 Mason Williams .60 1.50
BCP86 Stetson Allie .40 1.00
BCP87 Jarred Cosart .40 1.00
BCP88 Wagner Mateo .60 1.50
BCP89 Allen Webster .40 1.00
BCP90 Adron Chambers .25 .60
BCP91 Blake Smith .25 .60
BCP92 J.D. Martinez 1.50 4.00
BCP93 Brandon Belt .60 1.50
BCP94 Drake Britton .25 .60
BCP95 Addison Reed .25 .60
BCP96 Adonis Cardona .40 1.00
BCP97 Yordy Cabrera .25 .60
BCP98 Tony Wolters .25 .60
BCP99 Paul Goldschmidt 2.50 6.00
BCP100 Sean Coyle .40 1.00
BCP101 Rymer Liriano .60 1.50
BCP102 Eric Thames 1.25 3.00
BCP103 Brian Fletcher .25 .60
BCP104 Ben Gamel .40 1.00
BCP105 Kyle Russell .40 1.00
BCP106 Sammy Solis .25 .60
BCP107 Garin Cecchini .60 1.50
BCP108 Carlos Perez .25 .60
BCP109 Darin Mastroianni .25 .60
BCP110 Jonathan Villar .60 1.50
BCP111 Bryce Harper 6.00 15.00
BCP112 Aaron Altherr .25 .60
BCP113 Oswaldo Arcia .25 .60
BCP114 Kyle Blair .25 .60
BCP115 Nick Bucci .25 .60
BCP116 Jose Casilla .25 .60
BCP117 Zach Cates .25 .60
BCP118 Dimaster Delgado .25 .60
BCP119 Jose DePaula .25 .60
BCP120 Zack Dodson .25 .60
BCP121 John Gast .25 .60
BCP122 Cesar Hernandez .25 .60
BCP123 Kyle Higashioka .25 .60
BCP124 Luke Jackson .40 1.00
BCP125 Jiwan James .25 .60
BCP126 Jonathan Joseph .25 .60
BCP127A Gustavo Pierre .25 .60
BCP127B Ryan Tatusko .40 1.00
BCP128 Jeff Kobernus .25 .60
BCP129 Tom Koehler .25 .60
BCP130 Hunter Morris .25 .60
BCP131 Jean Segura 1.00 2.50
BCP132 Melky Mesa .25 .60
BCP133 Manny Banuelos .60 1.50
BCP134 Chris Archer .50 1.25
BCP135 Ian Krol .25 .60
BCP136 Trystan Magnuson .25 .60
BCP137 Roman Mendez .25 .60
BCP138 Tyler Moore .60 1.50
BCP139 Ramon Morla .25 .60
BCP140 Ty Morrison .25 .60
BCP141 Tyler Pastornicky .40 1.00
BCP142 Jon Pettibone .25 .60
BCP143 Zach Quate .25 .60
BCP144 J.C. Ramirez .25 .60
BCP145 Elmer Reyes .25 .60
BCP146 Aderlin Rodriguez .25 .60
BCP147 Conner Crumbliss .40 1.00
BCP148 David Rohm .25 .60
BCP149 Adrian Sanchez .25 .60
BCP150 Tommy Shirley .25 .60
BCP151 Matt Packer .25 .60
BCP152 Jake Thompson .25 .60
BCP153 Miguel Velazquez .25 .60
BCP154 Dakota Watts .25 .60
BCP155 Chase Whitley 1.25 3.00
BCP156 Cameron Bedrosian .25 .60
BCP157 Daniel Brewer .25 .60
BCP158 Dave Bromberg .25 .60
BCP159 Jorge Polanco .25 .60
BCP160 A.J. Cole .40 1.00
BCP161 Alex Colome .25 .60
BCP162 Brody Colvin .25 .60
BCP163 Khris Davis 1.25 3.00
BCP164 Cutter Dykstra .25 .60
BCP165 Nathan Eovaldi .60 1.50
BCP166 Ramon Flores .60 1.50
BCP167 Garrett Gould .25 .60
BCP168 Brandon Guyer .40 1.00
BCP169 Shaeffer Hall .40 1.00
BCP170 Reese Havens .25 .60
BCP171 Luis Heredia .25 .60
BCP172 Aaron Hicks .40 1.00
BCP173 Bryan Holaday .25 .60
BCP174 Brad Holt .25 .60
BCP175 Brett Lawrie 1.00 2.50
BCP176 Matt Lollis .40 1.00
BCP177 Cesar Puello .40 1.00
BCP178 Starling Marte .60 1.50
BCP179 Ethan Martin .25 .60
BCP180 Trey McNutt .25 .60
BCP181 Anthony Ranaudo .60 1.50
BCP182 Keyvius Sampson .25 .60
BCP183 Jordan Swagerty .40 1.00
BCP184 Dickie Joe Thon .40 1.00
BCP185 Jacob Turner 1.00 2.50
BCP186 Rob Brantly .60 1.50
BCP187 Arquimedes Caminero .25 .60
BCP188 Miles Head .40 1.00
BCP189 Erasmo Ramirez .25 .60
BCP190 Ryan Pressly .40 1.00
BCP191 Colton Cain .25 .60
BCP192 Enny Romero .25 .60
BCP193 Zack Von Rosenberg .25 .60
BCP194 Tyler Skaggs .60 1.50
BCP195 Michael Blanke .25 .60
BCP196 Juan Duran .40 1.00
BCP197 Kyle Parker .40 1.00
BCP198 Jake Marisnick .40 1.00
BCP199 Manuel Soliman .25 .60
BCP200 Jordany Valdespin .25 .60
BCP201 Brock Holt .25 .60
BCP202 Chris Owings .25 .60
BCP203 Cameron Garfield .25 .60
BCP204 Rob Scahill .25 .60
BCP205 Ronnie Welty .25 .60
BCP206 Scott Maine .25 .60
BCP207 Kyle Smit .25 .60
BCP208 Spencer Arroyo .25 .60
BCP209 Mariekson Gregorious 6.00 15.00
BCP210 Neftali Soto .40 1.00
BCP211 Wade Gaynor .25 .60
BCP212 Chris Carpenter .25 .60
BCP213 Josh Judy .25 .60
BCP214 Brandon Laird .40 1.00
BCP215 Peter Tago .25 .60
BCP216 Andy Dirks .60 1.50
BCP217 Steve Cishek ERR NNO .25 .60
BCP218 Cory Riordan .25 .60
BCP219 Fernando Abad .25 .60
BCP220 Matt Moore .60 1.50

2011 Bowman Chrome Prospects Refractors

*REF: 2X TO 5X BASIC
111-220 STATED ODDS 1:28 HOBBY
1-110 PRINT RUN 799 SER.#'d SETS
111-220 PRINT RUN 500 SER.#'d SETS
BCP1 Bryce Harper 40.00 100.00
BCP111 Bryce Harper 40.00 100.00

2011 Bowman Chrome Prospects Blue Refractors

*BLUE REF: 4X TO 10X BASIC
111-220 STATED ODDS 1:31 HOBBY
1-110 PRINT RUN 250 SER.#'d SETS
111-220 PRINT RUN 150 SER.#'d SETS
BCP1 Bryce Harper 50.00 120.00
BCP111 Bryce Harper 50.00 120.00

2011 Bowman Chrome Prospects Gold Canary Diamond

STATED ODDS 1:3840 HOBBY
STATED PRINT RUN 1 SER.#'d SET
NO PRICING DUE TO SCARCITY

2011 Bowman Chrome Prospects Gold Refractors

*GOLD REF: 10X TO 25X BASIC
111-220 STATED ODDS 1:94 HOBBY
STATED PRINT RUN 50 SER.#'d SETS
BCP1 Bryce Harper 250.00 500.00
BCP111 Bryce Harper 250.00 500.00

2011 Bowman Chrome Prospects Green X-Fractors

*GREEN XF: 1.5X TO 4X BASIC
RETAIL ONLY PARALLEL
BCP111 Bryce Harper 12.00 30.00
BCP220 Matt Moore 6.00 15.00

2011 Bowman Chrome Prospects Orange Refractors

111-220 STATED ODDS 1:198 HOBBY
STATED PRINT RUN 25 SER.#'d SETS
NO PRICING DUE TO SCARCITY

2011 Bowman Chrome Prospects Purple Refractors

*PURPLE REF: 2.5X TO 6X BASIC
1-110 PRINT RUN 700 SER.#'d SETS
111-220 PRINT RUN 799 SER.#'d SETS
BCP1 Bryce Harper 25.00 60.00
BCP111 Bryce Harper 25.00 60.00

2011 Bowman Chrome Prospects Red Refractors

111-220 STATED ODDS 1:900 HOBBY
STATED PRINT RUN 5 SER.#'d SETS
NO PRICING DUE TO SCARCITY

2011 Bowman Chrome Rookie Autographs

PLATE PRINT RUN 1 SET PER COLOR
BLACK-CYAN-MAGENTA-YELLOW ISSUED
NO PLATE PRICING DUE TO SCARCITY
EXCHANGE DEADLINE 4/30/2014
191 Jake McGee 4.00 10.00
192 Lars Anderson 4.00 10.00
195 Jeremy Jeffress 4.00 10.00
196 Brent Morel 4.00 10.00
197 Aroldis Chapman 10.00 25.00
198 Greg Halman 4.00 10.00
199 Jeremy Hellickson 4.00 10.00
200 Yunesky Maya 4.00 10.00
201 Kyle Drabek 4.00 10.00
203 Desmond Jennings 4.00 10.00
205 Freddie Freeman 60.00 150.00
209 Brian Bogusevic 4.00 10.00
210 Yonder Alonso 3.00 8.00
212 Dillon Gee 4.00 10.00
220 Chris Sale 12.00 30.00

2011 Bowman Chrome Rookie Autographs Refractors

*REF: .5X TO 1.2X BASIC
STATED PRINT RUN 500 SER.#'d SETS
EXCHANGE DEADLINE 4/30/2014

2011 Bowman Chrome Rookie Autographs Blue Refractors

*BLUE REF: .6X TO 1.5X BASIC
STATED PRINT RUN 250 SER.#'d SETS
EXCHANGE DEADLINE 4/30/2014

2011 Bowman Chrome Rookie Autographs Gold Refractors

*GOLD REF: 1X TO 2.5X BASIC
STATED PRINT RUN 50 SER.#'d SETS
EXCHANGE DEADLINE 4/30/2014

2011 Bowman Chrome Throwbacks

COMPLETE SET (25) 10.00 25.00
STATED ODDS 1:8 HOBBY
ATOMIC ODDS 1:25,353 HOBBY
ATOMIC PRINT RUN 1 SER.#'d SET
NO ATOMIC PRICING DUE TO SCARCITY
X-FRACTOR ODDS 1:1013 HOBBY
X-FRACTOR PRINT RUN 25 SER.#'d SETS
NO X-FRACTOR PRICING AVAILABLE
37 Chipper Jones 1.00 2.50
103 Alex Rodriguez 1.25 3.00
340 Albert Pujols 6.00 15.00
351A Ichiro Suzuki English 1.25 3.00
351B Ichiro Suzuki Japanese 1.25 3.00
BCT1 Tony Sanchez .60 1.50
BCT2 Dee Gordon .60 1.50
BCT3 Anthony Rizzo 4.00 10.00
BCT4 Nick Franklin .60 1.50
BCT5 Jameson Taillon .60 1.50
BCT6 Wil Myers .60 1.50
BCT7 Grant Green .40 1.00
BCT8 Jacob Turner 1.50 4.00
BCT9 Tyler Matzek .60 1.50
BCT10 Bryce Harper 4.00 10.00
BCT11 Manny Banuelos 1.00 2.50
BCT12 Brett Lawrie 1.50 4.00
BCT13 Devin Mesoraco 1.00 2.50
BCT14 Shelby Miller 2.00 5.00
BCT15 Delino DeShields Jr. .40 1.00
BCT16 Dustin Ackley .60 1.50
BCT17 Manny Machado 4.00 10.00
BCT18 Lonnie Chisenhall .60 1.50
BCT19 Arodys Vizcaino .60 1.50
BCT20 Stetson Allie .60 1.50

2011 Bowman Chrome Throwbacks Refractors

*REF: 2.5X TO 6X BASIC
STATED ODDS 1:256 HOBBY
STATED PRINT RUN 99 SER.#'d SETS

2011 Bowman Chrome Draft

COMPLETE SET (110) 12.50 30.00
COMMON CARD (1-110) .30 .75
STATED PLATE ODDS 1:928 HOBBY
PLATE PRINT RUN 1 SET PER COLOR
BLACK-CYAN-MAGENTA-YELLOW ISSUED
NO PLATE PRICING DUE TO SCARCITY
1 Mike Moustakas RC .75 2.00
2 Ryan Adams RC .30 .75
3 Alexi Amarista RC .30 .75
4 Anthony Bass RC .30 .75
5 Pedro Beato RC .30 .75
6 Bruce Billings RC .30 .75
7 Charlie Blackmon RC 6.00 15.00
8 Brian Broderick RC .30 .75
9 Rex Brothers RC .30 .75
10 Tyler Chatwood RC .30 .75
11 Jose Altuve RC 3.00 8.00
12 Salvador Perez RC 1.25 3.00
13 Mark Hamburger RC .30 .75
14 Matt Carpenter RC 2.50 6.00
15 Ezequiel Carrera RC .30 .75
16 Jose Ceda RC .30 .75
17 Andrew Brown RC .50 1.25
18 Maikel Cleto RC .30 .75
19 Steve Cishek RC .30 .75
20 Lonnie Chisenhall RC .50 1.25
21 Henry Sosa RC .30 .75
22 Tim Collins RC .30 .75
23 Josh Collmenter RC .30 .75
24 David Cooper RC .30 .75
25 Brandon Crawford RC .50 1.25
26 Brandon Laird RC .50 1.25
27 Tony Cruz RC .75 2.00
28 Chase d'Arnaud RC .30 .75
29 Faustino De Los Santos RC .30 .75
30 Rubby De La Rosa RC .75 2.00
31 Andy Dirks RC .75 2.00
32 Jarrod Dyson RC .50 1.25
33 Cody Eppley RC .30 .75
34 Logan Forsythe RC .30 .75
35 Todd Frazier RC 1.00 2.50
36 Eric Fryer RC .50 1.25
37 Charlie Furbush RC .30 .75
38 Cory Gearrin RC .30 .75
39 Graham Godfrey RC .30 .75
40 Dee Gordon RC .50 1.25
41 Brandon Gomes RC .30 .75
42 Bryan Shaw RC .30 .75
43 Brandon Guyer RC .50 1.25
44 Mark Hamilton RC .50 1.25
45 Brad Hand RC .30 .75
46 Anthony Recker RC .30 .75
47 Jeremy Horst RC .50 1.25
48 Tommy Hottovy (RC) .50 1.25
49 Jose Iglesias RC .50 1.25
50 Craig Kimbrel RC .75 2.00
51 Josh Judy RC .30 .75
52 Cole Kimball RC .30 .75
53 Alan Johnson RC .30 .75
54 Brandon Kintzler RC .30 .75
55 Pete Kozma RC .75 2.00
56 D.J. LeMahieu RC 4.00 10.00
57 Duane Below RC .50 1.25
58 Josh Lindblom RC .50 1.25
59 Zack Cozart RC .75 2.00
60 Al Alburquerque RC .30 .75
61 Trystan Magnuson RC .30 .75
62 Michael Martinez RC .50 1.25
63 Michael McKenry RC .50 1.25
64 Daniel Moskos RC .30 .75
65 Lance Lynn RC .75 2.00
66 Juan Nicasio RC .30 .75
67 Joe Paterson RC .50 1.25
68 Lance Pendleton RC .30 .75
69 Luis Perez RC .30 .75
70 Anthony Rizzo RC 3.00 8.00
71 Joel Carreno RC .30 .75
72 Alex Presley RC .50 1.25
73 Vinnie Pestano RC .30 .75
74 Aneury Rodriguez RC .30 .75
75 Josh Rodriguez RC .30 .75
76 Eduardo Sanchez RC .50 1.25
77 Matt Young RC .30 .75
78 Amauri Sanit RC .30 .75
79 Nathan Eovaldi RC .75 2.00
80 Javy Guerra (RC) .50 1.25
81 Eric Sogard RC .30 .75
82 Henderson Alvarez RC .30 .75
83 Ryan Lavarnway RC 1.25 3.00
84 Michael Stutes RC .50 1.25
85 Everett Teaford RC .30 .75
86 Blake Tekotte RC .30 .75
87 Eric Thames RC 1.50 4.00
88 Arodys Vizcaino RC .50 1.25
89 Rene Tosoni RC .30 .75
90 Alex White RC .30 .75
91 Brayan Villarreal RC .30 .75
92 Tony Watson RC .30 .75
93 Johnny Giavotella RC .30 .75
94 Kevin Whelan (RC) .30 .75
95 Mike Nickeas (RC) .30 .75
96 Elih Villanueva RC .30 .75
97 Tom Wilhelmsen RC .30 .75
98 Adam Wilk RC .50 1.25
99 Mike Wilson (RC) .30 .75
100 Jerry Sands RC .75 2.00
101 Mike Trout RC 200.00 500.00
102 Kyle Weiland RC .30 .75
103 Kyle Seager RC .75 2.00
104 Jason Kipnis RC 1.00 2.50
105 Chance Ruffin RC .30 .75
106 J.B. Shuck RC .75 2.00
107 Jacob Turner RC 1.25 3.00
108 Paul Goldschmidt RC 3.00 8.00
109 Justin Sellers RC .50 1.25
110 Trayvon Robinson (RC) .50 1.25

2011 Bowman Chrome Draft Refractors

*REF: .75X TO 2X BASIC
STATED ODDS 1:4 HOBBY

2011 Bowman Chrome Draft Blue Refractors

*BLUE REF: 2X TO 5X BASIC
STATED ODDS 1:41 HOBBY
STATED PRINT RUN 199 SER.#'d SETS
101 Mike Trout 2500.00 5000.00

2011 Bowman Chrome Draft Gold Canary Diamond

STATED ODDS 1:7410 HOBBY
STATED PRINT RUN 1 SER.#'d SET
NO PRICING DUE TO SCARCITY

2011 Bowman Chrome Draft Gold Refractors

*GOLD REF: 3X TO 8X BASIC
STATED ODDS 1:162 HOBBY
STATED PRINT RUN 50 SER.#'d SETS
101 Mike Trout 4000.00 8000.00

2011 Bowman Chrome Draft Orange Refractors

STATED ODDS 1:324 HOBBY
STATED PRINT RUN 25 SER.#'d SETS
NO PRICING DUE TO SCARCITY

2011 Bowman Chrome Draft Purple Refractors

*PURPLE REF: .75X TO 2X BASIC

2011 Bowman Chrome Draft Red Refractors

STATED ODDS 1:1620 HOBBY
STATED PRINT RUN 5 SER.#'d SETS
NO PRICING DUE TO SCARCITY

2011 Bowman Chrome Draft 16U USA National Team Autographs

STATED ODDS 1:763 HOBBY
STATED PLATE ODDS 1:20,280 HOBBY
PLATE PRINT RUN 1 SET PER COLOR
BLACK-CYAN-MAGENTA-YELLOW ISSUED
NO PLATE PRICING DUE TO SCARCITY
AM Austin Meadows 20.00 50.00
AP Arden Pabst 4.00 10.00
BB Bryson Brigman 4.00 10.00
CP Christian Pelaez 4.00 10.00
CS Carson Sands 4.00 10.00
DN Dom Nunez 4.00 10.00
DT Dany Toussaint 8.00 20.00
HM Hunter Mercado-Hood 4.00 10.00
JD Joe DeMers 4.00 10.00
JJ Jake Jarvis 4.00 10.00
JS Jordan Sheffield 5.00 12.00
KT Keegan Thompson 4.00 10.00
MV Matt Vogel 4.00 10.00
NC Nick Ciuffo 5.00 12.00
RU Riley Unroe 4.00 10.00
SF Steven Farinaro 4.00 10.00
TA Tyler Alamo 4.00 10.00
TC Trevor Clifton 4.00 10.00
WA William Abreu 5.00 12.00
ZC Zach Collins 4.00 10.00

2011 Bowman Chrome Draft 16U USA National Team Autographs Refractors

*REF: .6X TO 1.5X BASIC
STATED ODDS 1:410 HOBBY
STATED PRINT RUN 199 SER.#'d SETS

2011 Bowman Chrome Draft 16U USA National Team Autographs Blue Refractors

*BLUE REF: .75X TO 2X BASIC
STATED ODDS 1:825 HOBBY
STATED PRINT RUN 99 SER.#'d SETS

2011 Bowman Chrome Draft 16U USA National Team Autographs Gold Refractors

*GOLD REF: 1.2X TO 3X BASIC
STATED ODDS 1:1635 HOBBY
STATED PRINT RUN 50 SER.#'d SETS

2011 Bowman Chrome Draft 16U USA National Team Autographs Orange Refractors

STATED ODDS 1:3273 HOBBY
STATED PRINT RUN 25 SER.#'d SETS
NO PRICING DUE TO SCARCITY

2011 Bowman Chrome Draft 16U USA National Team Autographs Purple Refractors

STATED ODDS 1:8176 HOBBY
STATED PRINT RUN 10 SER.#'d SETS
NO PRICING DUE TO SCARCITY

2011 Bowman Chrome Draft 16U USA National Team Autographs Red Refractors

STATED ODDS 1:16,348 HOBBY
STATED PRINT RUN 5 SER.#'d SETS
NO PRICING DUE TO SCARCITY

2011 Bowman Chrome Draft Prospects

COMPLETE SET (110) 20.00 50.00
STATED PLATE ODDS 1:928 HOBBY
PLATE PRINT RUN 1 SET PER COLOR
BLACK-CYAN-MAGENTA-YELLOW ISSUED
NO PLATE PRICING DUE TO SCARCITY
BDPP1 John Hicks UER .40 1.00
BDPP2 Cody Asche .60 1.50
BDPP3 Tyler Anderson .25 .60
BDPP4 Jack Armstrong .40 1.00
BDPP5 Pratt Maynard .25 .60
BDPP6 Javier Baez 3.00 8.00
BDPP7 Kenneth Peoples-Walls .25 .60
BDPP8 Matt Barnes .40 1.00
BDPP9 Trevor Bauer 2.50 6.00
BDPP10 Daniel Vogelbach .75 2.00
BDPP11 Mike Wright UER .25 .60
BDPP12 Dante Bichette .40 1.00
BDPP13 Hudson Boyd .25 .60
BDPP14 Archie Bradley .75 2.00
BDPP15 Matthew Skole .40 1.00
BDPP16 Jed Bradley .40 1.00
BDPP17 Tyler Pill .25 .60
BDPP18 Dylan Bundy .75 2.00
BDPP19 Harold Martinez .40 1.00
BDPP20 Will Lamb .25 .60
BDPP21 Harold Riggins .25 .60
BDPP22 Zach Cone .40 1.00
BDPP23 Kyle Gaedele .25 .60
BDPP24 Kyle Crick .60 1.50
BDPP25 C.J. Cron .75 2.00
BDPP26 Nicholas Delmonico .25 .60
BDPP27 Alex Dickerson .40 1.00
BDPP28 Tony Cingrani 1.25 3.00
BDPP29 Jose Fernandez 1.00 2.50
BDPP30 Michael Fulmer .60 1.50
BDPP31 Carl Thomore .25 .60
BDPP32 Sean Gilmartin .25 .60
BDPP33 Tyler Goeddel .25 .60
BDPP34 Drew Gagnon .25 .60
BDPP35 Sonny Gray .60 1.50
BDPP36 Larry Greene .40 1.00
BDPP37 Nick Martini .25 .60
BDPP38 Taylor Guerrieri .25 .60
BDPP39 Jake Hager .25 .60
BDPP40 James Harris .25 .60
BDPP41 Travis Harrison .40 1.00
BDPP42 Nick DeSantiago .40 1.00
BDPP43 Chase Larsson .25 .60
BDPP44 Logan Moore .25 .60
BDPP45 Mason Hope .25 .60
BDPP46 Adrian Houser .40 1.00
BDPP47 Sean Buckley .25 .60
BDPP48 Rick Anton .25 .60
BDPP49 Scott Woodward .40 1.00
BDPP50 David Goforth .25 .60
BDPP51 Taylor Jungmann .40 1.00
BDPP52 Blake Snell 1.00 2.50
BDPP53 Francisco Lindor 2.50 6.00
BDPP54 Mikie Mahtook .60 1.50
BDPP55 Brandon Martin .40 1.00
BDPP56 Kevin Quackenbush .40 1.00
BDPP57 Kevin Matthews .25 .60
BDPP58 C.J. McElroy .25 .60
BDPP59 Anthony Meo .25 .60
BDPP60 Justin James .40 1.00
BDPP61 Levi Michael UER .40 1.00
BDPP62 Joseph Musgrove .40 1.00
BDPP63 Brandon Nimmo 1.25 3.00
BDPP64 Brandon Culbreth .25 .60
BDPP65 Javaris Reynolds .25 .60
BDPP66 Adam Ehrlich .25 .60
BDPP67 Henry Owens .40 1.00
BDPP68 Joe Panik .60 1.50
BDPP69 Jace Peterson .25 .60
BDPP70 Lance Jeffries .25 .60
BDPP71 Matthew Budgell .25 .60
BDPP72 Dan Gamache .25 .60
BDPP73 Christopher Lee .25 .60
BDPP74 Kyle Kubitza .25 .60
BDPP75 Nick Ahmed .25 .60
BDPP76 Josh Parr .25 .60
BDPP77 Dwight Smith .25 .60
BDPP78 Steven Gruver .25 .60
BDPP79 Jeffrey Soptic .25 .60
BDPP80 Cory Spangenberg .40 1.00
BDPP81 George Springer 1.50 4.00
BDPP82 Bubba Starling .40 1.00
BDPP83 Robert Stephenson .50 1.25
BDPP84 Trevor Story 3.00 8.00
BDPP85 Madison Boer .25 .60
BDPP86 Blake Swihart .40 1.00
BDPP87 Kellen Moen .25 .60
BDPP88 Joe Tuschak .25 .60
BDPP89 Keenyn Walker .25 .60
BDPP90 Kolten Wong .40 1.00
BDPP91 William Abreu .40 1.00
BDPP92 Tyler Alamo .25 .60
BDPP93 Bryson Brigman .25 .60
BDPP94 Nick Ciuffo .25 .60
BDPP95 Trevor Clifton .25 .60
BDPP96 Zach Collins .40 1.00
BDPP97 Joe DeMers .25 .60
BDPP98 Steven Farinaro .25 .60
BDPP99 Jake Jarvis .25 .60
BDPP100 Austin Meadows 1.00 2.50
BDPP101 Hunter Mercado-Hood .25 .60
BDPP102 Dom Nunez .25 .60
BDPP103 Arden Pabst .25 .60
BDPP104 Christian Pelaez .25 .60
BDPP105 Carson Sands .25 .60
BDPP106 Jordan Sheffield .25 .60
BDPP107 Keegan Thompson .25 .60
BDPP108 Dany Toussaint .40 1.00
BDPP109 Riley Unroe .25 .60
BDPP110 Matt Vogel .25 .60

2011 Bowman Chrome Draft Prospects Refractors

*REF: 1.5X TO 4X BASIC
STATED ODDS 1:4 HOBBY

2011 Bowman Chrome Draft Prospects Blue Refractors

*BLUE REF: 4X TO 10X BASIC
STAED ODDS 1:41 HOBBY
STATED PRINT RUN 199 SER.#'d SETS

2011 Bowman Chrome Draft Prospects Gold Canary Diamond

STATED ODDS 1:7410 HOBBY
STATED PRINT RUN 1 SER.#'d SET
NO PRICING DUE TO SCARCITY

2011 Bowman Chrome Draft Prospects Gold Refractors

*GOLD REF: 10X TO 25X BASIC
STAED ODDS 1:162 HOBBY
STATED PRINT RUN 50 SER.#'d SETS

2011 Bowman Chrome Draft Prospects Orange Refractors

STATED ODDS 1:324 HOBBY
STATED PRINT RUN 25 SER.#'d SETS
NO PRICING DUE TO SCARCITY

2011 Bowman Chrome Draft Prospects Purple Refractors

*PURPLE REF: 2X TO 5X BASIC

2011 Bowman Chrome Draft Prospects Red Refractors

STATED ODDS 1:1620 HOBBY
STATED PRINT RUN 5 SER.#'d SETS
NO PRICING DUE TO SCARCITY

2011 Bowman Chrome Draft Prospect Autographs

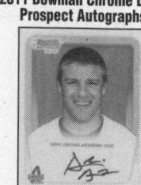

STATED ODDS 1:37 HOBBY
STATED PLATE ODDS 1:120,000 HOBBY
PLATE PRINT RUN 1 SET PER COLOR
BLACK-CYAN-MAGENTA-YELLOW ISSUED
NO PLATE PRICING DUE TO SCARCITY
EXCHANGE DEADLINE 11/30/2014
AB Archie Bradley 5.00 12.00
BM Brandon Martin 3.00 8.00
BN Brandon Nimmo 10.00 25.00
BS Bubba Starling 6.00 15.00
BSN Blake Snell 25.00 60.00
BSW Blake Swihart 5.00 12.00
CC C.J. Cron 4.00 10.00
CS Cory Spangenberg 3.00 8.00
DB Dylan Bundy 12.00 30.00
DV Daniel Vogelbach 8.00 20.00
FL Francisco Lindor 150.00 400.00
GS George Springer 60.00 150.00
JB Jed Bradley 3.00 8.00
JBA Javier Baez 150.00 400.00
JF Jose Fernandez 10.00 25.00
JH James Harris 3.00 8.00
JHA Jake Hager 3.00 8.00
JP Joe Panik 6.00 15.00
KCR Kyle Crick 3.00 8.00
KM Kevin Matthews 3.00 8.00
KW Kolten Wong 8.00 20.00
KWA Keenyn Walker 3.00 8.00
LG Larry Greene 3.00 8.00
MB Matt Barnes 3.00 8.00
MF Michael Fulmer 6.00 15.00
RS Robert Stephenson 8.00 20.00
SGR Sonny Gray 15.00 40.00
TA Tyler Anderson 3.00 8.00
TB Trevor Bauer 20.00 50.00
TG Tyler Goeddel 3.00 8.00
TGU Taylor Guerrieri 3.00 8.00
TH Travis Harrison 3.00 8.00
TJ Taylor Jungmann 4.00 10.00
TS Trevor Story 60.00 150.00

2011 Bowman Chrome Draft Prospect Autographs Refractors

*REF: .6X TO 1.5X BASIC
STATED ODDS 1:101 HOBBY
STATED PRINT RUN 500 SER.#'d SETS
EXCHANGE DEADLINE 11/30/2014
FL Francisco Lindor 250.00 500.00

2011 Bowman Chrome Draft Prospect Autographs Blue Refractors

*BLUE REF: 1.2X TO 3X BASIC
STATED ODDS 1:337 HOBBY
STATED PRINT RUN 150 SER.#'d SETS
EXCHANGE DEADLINE 11/30/2014
FL Francisco Lindor 400.00 800.00

2011 Bowman Chrome Draft Prospect Autographs Gold Refractors

*GOLD REF: 2.5X TO 6X BASIC
STATED ODDS 1:1004 HOBBY
STATED PRINT RUN 50 SER.#'d SETS
EXCHANGE DEADLINE 11/30/2014
FL Francisco Lindor 800.00 1200.00

2011 Bowman Chrome Draft Prospect Autographs Orange Refractors

STATED ODDS 1:2008 HOBBY
STATED PRINT RUN 25 SER.#'d SETS
NO PRICING DUE TO SCARCITY
EXCHANGE DEADLINE 11/30/2014

2011 Bowman Chrome Draft Prospect Autographs Purple Refractors

STATED ODDS 1:5050 HOBBY
STATED PRINT RUN 10 SER.#'d SETS
NO PRICING DUE TO SCARCITY
EXCHANGE DEADLINE 11/30/2014

2011 Bowman Chrome Draft Prospect Autographs Red Refractors

STATED ODDS 1:10,150 HOBBY
STATED PRINT RUN 5 SER.#'d SETS
NO PRICING DUE TO SCARCITY
EXCHANGE DEADLINE 11/30/2014

2012 Bowman Chrome

COMPLETE SET (220) 20.00 50.00
STATED PLATE ODDS 1:986 HOBBY
PLATE PRINT RUN 1 SET PER COLOR
BLACK-CYAN-MAGENTA-YELLOW ISSUED
NO PLATE PRICING DUE TO SCARCITY
1 Roy Halladay .25 .60
2 Josh Johnson .25 .60
3 Buster Posey .40 1.00
4 Jeremy Hellickson .20 .50
5 Giancarlo Stanton .30 .75
6 Alex Liddi RC .30 .75
7 Mat Latos .25 .60
8 Anibal Sanchez .20 .50
9 Hanley Ramirez .25 .60
10 Derek Jeter .75 2.00
11 Derek Norris RC .30 .75
12 Daniel Hudson .20 .50
13 Brandon Morrow .20 .50
14 Pablo Sandoval .25 .60
15 Josh Beckett .20 .50
16 David Price .25 .60
17 Tim Hudson .25 .60
18 Joe Benson RC .30 .75
19 Doug Fister .20 .50
20 Nick Markakis .25 .60
21 Brad Peacock RC .30 .75
22 Adam Jones .25 .60
23 Billy Butler .20 .50
24 Kirk Nieuwenhuis RC .30 .75
25 Jordan Danks RC .30 .75
26 CC Sabathia .25 .60
27 Zack Greinke .25 .60
28 Mark Reynolds .20 .50
29 Jose Bautista .25 .60
30 Brett Lawrie RC .40 1.0
31 Cole Hamels .25 .6
32 Jayson Werth .25 .6
33 Carl Crawford .25 .6
34 Chipper Jones .30 .7
35 Ervin Santana .20 .5
36 Miguel Cabrera .30 .7
37 Michael Pineda .20 .5
38 Brandon Beachy .20 .5
39 Liam Hendriks RC .30 .7
40 Alex Gordon .25 .6
41 Martin Prado .20 .5
42 Tim Lincecum .25 .6
43 Vance Worley .25 .6
44 Yoenis Cespedes RC .75 2.0
45 Clayton Kershaw .60 1.5
46 Devin Mesoraco RC .30 .75
47 Andrelton Simmons RC .50 1.25
48 B.J. Upton .25 .60
49 Ivan Nova .25 .60
50 Nyjer Morgan .20 .50
51 Carlos Santana .25 .60
52 Norichika Aoki RC .40 1.00
53 David Wright .25 .60
54 Joey Votto .30 .75
55 Felix Hernandez .25 .60
56 Troy Tulowitzki .30 .75
57 Dellin Betances RC .50 1.25
58 Evan Longoria .25 .60
59 Addison Reed RC .30 .75
60 Derek Holland .20 .50
61 Gio Gonzalez .25 .60
62 Shin-Soo Choo .25 .60
63 Jose Reyes .20 .50
64 Ian Kinsler .25 .60
65 Jimmy Rollins .25 .60
66 Alex Rodriguez .40 1.00
67 Cory Luebke .20 .50
68 J.D. Martinez .30 .75
69 Carlos Gonzalez .25 .60
70 Chris Archer RC .30 .75
71 Yovani Gallardo .25 .60
72 Kevin Youkilis .30 .75
73 Neftali Feliz .20 .50
74 Xavier Avery RC .30 .75
75 Jemile Weeks RC .20 .50
76 Matt Hague RC .30 .75
77 Drew Smyly RC .30 .75
78 Yadier Molina .30 .75
79 Yunel Escobar .20 .50
80 Jason Motte .20 .50
81 Drew Hutchison RC .40 1.00
82 Jordany Valdespin RC .40 1.00
83 Justin Masterson .20 .50
84 Yu Darvish RC .75 2.00
85 Alex Avila .20 .50
86 Nick Swisher .25 .60
87 Mark Teixeira .25 .60
88 Dan Haren .20 .50
89 Jaime Garcia .25 .60
90 Melky Cabrera .20 .50
91 Brian Dozier RC 1.00 2.50
92 Matt Garza .20 .50
93 Hunter Pence .25 .60
94 Brandon Phillips .20 .50
95 Ubaldo Jimenez .20 .50
96 Prince Fielder .25 .60
97 Matt Kemp .25 .60
98 Freddie Freeman .40 1.00
99 Jarrod Parker RC .40 1.00
100 Daniel Bard .20 .50
101 Corey Hart .20 .50
102 Ike Davis .20 .50
103 Curtis Granderson .25 .60
104 Eric Hosmer .25 .60
105 Madison Bumgarner .25 .60
106 Michael Bourn .20 .50
107 Albert Pujols .40 1.00
108 Matt Moore RC .50 1.25
109 Matt Holliday .30 .75
110 Tyler Pastornicky RC .50 1.25
111 Colby Rasmus .25 .60
112 Nelson Cruz .30 .75
113 Craig Kimbrel .25 .60
114 Desmond Jennings .25 .60
115 Irving Falu RC .30 .75
116 Jon Lester .20 .50
117 John Axford .20 .50
118 Wilin Rosario RC .50 1.25
119 Todd Helton .25 .60
120 Ryan Zimmerman .25 .60
121 Josh Hamilton .25 .60
122 Paul Konerko .25 .60
123 Dee Gordon .20 .50
124 J.P. Arencibia .20 .50
125 J.J. Hardy .20 .50
126 David Ortiz .30 .75
127 Shane Victorino .20 .50
128 James Shields .20 .50
129 Mariano Rivera .40 1.00
130 Jon Niese .20 .50
131 Paul Goldschmidt .30 .75
132 Aramis Ramirez .20 .50
133 Emilio Bonifacio .20 .50
134 Salvador Perez .25 .60
135 C.J. Wilson .20 .50
136 Jhonny Peralta .20 .50
137 Chris Parmelee RC .50 1.25
138 Ryan Howard .25 .60
139 Mark Trumbo .20 .50
140 Asdrubal Cabrera .25 .60
141 Lucas Duda .25 .60
142 Dan Uggla .25 .60

143 Rickie Weeks .20 .50
144 Johnny Cueto .25 .60
145 Shaun Marcum .20 .50
146 Elvis Andrus .25 .60
147 Michael Young .20 .50
148 Donovan Solano RC 2.50 6.00
149 Adrian Beltre .30 .75
150 Drew Pomeranz RC .30 .75
151 Lance Berkman .25 .60
152 Heath Bell .20 .50
153 Dustin Ackley .20 .50
154 Stephen Strasburg .30 .75
155 Ichiro Suzuki .40 1.00
156 Michael Cuddyer .20 .50
157 Mike Trout 20.00 50.00
158 Brett Gardner .25 .60
159 Wade Miley RC .40 1.00
160 Chris Young .20 .50
161 Jordan Zimmermann .25 .60
162 Matt Dominguez RC .40 1.00
163 Jay Bruce .25 .60
164 Max Scherzer .30 .75
165 Ricky Romero .20 .50
166 Brandon McCarthy .20 .50
167 Brian McCann .25 .60
168 Jordan Pacheco RC .30 .75
169 Chris Carpenter .25 .60
170 Joe Mauer .25 .60
171 Carlos Ruiz .20 .50
172 Jacoby Ellsbury .25 .60
173 Trevor Bauer RC 1.00 2.50
174 Ryan Braun .20 .50
175 Torii Hunter .25 .60
176 Tommy Hanson .20 .50
177 Elian Herrera RC .50 1.25
178 Quintin Berry RC .50 1.25
179 Adam Lind .25 .60
180 Andrew McCutchen .30 .75
181 Adrian Gonzalez .25 .60
182 Jose Valverde .25 .60
183 Justin Upton .25 .60
184 Hisashi Iwakuma RC .60 1.50
185 Wei-Yin Chen RC .75 2.00
186 Ted Lilly .20 .50
187 Jeremy Hefner RC .30 .75
188 Kole Calhoun RC .40 1.00
189 Will Middlebrooks RC .40 1.00
190 Starlin Castro .25 .60
191 Adam Wainwright .25 .60
192 Ian Kennedy .20 .50
193 Michael Morse .20 .50
194 Mike Moustakas .25 .60
195 Matt Cain .25 .60
196 Tom Milone RC .30 .75
197 Chase Utley .25 .60
198 Ryan Vogelsong .20 .50
199 Wily Peralta RC .30 .75
200 Jered Weaver .25 .60
201 Cliff Lee .25 .60
202 Jason Heyward .25 .60
203 Jesus Montero RC .30 .75
204 Clay Buchholz .20 .50
205 David Freese .20 .50
206 Justin Morneau .25 .60
207 Christian Friedrich RC .30 .75
208 Mike Napoli .25 .60
209 Robinson Cano .25 .60
210 Aroldis Chapman .30 .75
211 Alexi Ogando .20 .50
212 Brennan Boesch .20 .50
213 R.A. Dickey .25 .60
214 Bryce Harper RC 10.00 25.00
215 Matt Adams RC .40 1.00
216 Jamie Moyer .20 .50
217 Dustin Pedroia .25 .60
218 Justin Verlander .30 .75
219 Miguel Montero .20 .50
220 Ben Zobrist .25 .60

2012 Bowman Chrome Refractors

*REF: 1X TO 2.5X BASIC
*REF RC: .6X TO 1.5X BASIC RC
STATED ODDS 1:4 HOBBY
214 Bryce Harper 30.00 80.00

2012 Bowman Chrome Blue Refractors

*BLUE REF: 1.5X TO 4X BASIC
*BLUE REF RC: 1.5X TO 4X BASIC RC
STATED ODDS 1:19 HOBBY
STATED PRINT RUN 250 SER.#'d SETS
157 Mike Trout 125.00 300.00
214 Bryce Harper 75.00 200.00

2012 Bowman Chrome Gold Refractors

*GOLD REF: 6X TO 15X BASIC
*GOLD REF RC: 4X TO 10X BASIC RC
STATED ODDS 1:96 HOBBY
STATED PRINT RUN 50 SER.#'d SETS
44 Yoenis Cespedes 15.00 40.00
70 Chris Archer 8.00 20.00
155 Ichiro Suzuki 20.00 50.00
214 Bryce Harper 125.00 300.00

2012 Bowman Chrome Green Refractors

*GREEN REF: 1.2X TO 3X BASIC
*GREEN REF RC: .75X TO 2X BASIC RC
214 Bryce Harper 40.00 100.00

2012 Bowman Chrome Purple Refractors

*PURPLE REF: 1.5X TO 4X BASIC
*PURPLE REF RC: 1.5X TO 4X BASIC RC
STATED ODDS 1:24 HOBBY
STATED PRINT RUN 199 SER.#'d SETS
214 Bryce Harper 75.00 200.00

2012 Bowman Chrome X-Fractors

*X-FRAC: 1X TO 2.5X BASIC
*X-FRAC RC: .6X TO 1.5X BASIC RC
214 Bryce Harper 30.00 80.00

2012 Bowman Chrome Franchise All-Stars

COMPLETE SET (20) 12.50 30.00
STATED ODDS 1:12 HOBBY
AP J.Profar/E.Andrus .60 1.50
BG Ryan Braun/Scooter Gennett .75 2.00
BGO Anthony Gose/Jose Bautista .60 1.50
BM W.Myers/B.Butler .60 1.50
BT C.Beltran/O.Taveras .75 2.00
CA Robinson Cano/Tyler Austin .75 2.00
CC M.Cabrera/N.Castellanos 1.50 4.00
CL A.Cabrera/F.Lindor 3.00 8.00
GA Arenado/Gonzalez 1.50 4.00
HH Felix Hernandez/Danny Hultzen .75 2.00
HO Mike Olt/Josh Hamilton .60 1.50
JB D.Bundy/A.Jones 1.00 2.50
MC G.Cole/A.McCutchen 3.00 8.00
OB X.Bogaerts/D.Ortiz 2.00 5.00
PJ T.Joseph/B.Posey 1.00 2.50
SF Fernandez/Stanton 1.25 3.00
TS J.Segura/M.Trout 5.00 12.00
VH B.Hamilton/J.Votto .75 2.00
VR B.Rondon/J.Verlander .75 2.00
WW Zack Wheeler/David Wright 1.00 2.50

2012 Bowman Chrome Futures Game

STATED ODDS 1:12 HOBBY
AG Anthony Gose .60 1.50
AM Alfredo Marte .30 .75
AP Ariel Pena .50 1.25
AS Ali Solis 1.25 3.00
BH Billy Hamilton .60 1.50
BR Bruce Rondon .30 .75
CB Christian Bethancourt .50 1.25
CY Christian Yelich 4.00 10.00
DB Dylan Bundy 1.00 2.50
DH Danny Hultzen .75 2.00
ER Enny Romero .30 .75
FL Francisco Lindor 3.00 8.00
FR Felipe Rivero .75 2.00
GC Gerrit Cole 3.00 8.00
JA Jesus Aguilar 1.50 4.00
JF Jose Fernandez 1.25 3.00
JH Jae-Hoon Ha .30 .75
JO Jake Odorizzi .60 1.50
JP Jurickson Profar .60 1.50
JR Julio Rodriguez .50 1.25
JS Jonathan Singleton .60 1.50
JSE Jean Segura .75 2.00
JT Jameson Taillon .60 1.50
KL Kyle Lotzkar .30 .75
KW Kolten Wong .50 1.25
MB Matt Barnes .50 1.25
MC Michael Choice .50 1.25
MM Manny Machado 3.00 8.00
MO Mike Olt .60 1.50
NA Nolan Arenado 1.50 4.00
NC Nick Castellanos 1.50 4.00
OA Oswaldo Arcia .30 .75
OT Oscar Taveras .75 2.00
RB Rob Brantly .75 2.00
RL Rymer Liriano .50 1.25
SG Scooter Gennett .75 2.00
TA Tyler Austin .75 2.00
TJ Tommy Joseph 1.00 2.50
TS Tyler Skaggs .75 2.00
TW Taijuan Walker .60 1.50
WF Wilmer Flores .60 1.50
WM Wil Myers .60 1.50
XB Xander Bogaerts 2.00 5.00
YV Yordano Ventura .50 1.25
ZW Zack Wheeler 1.00 2.50

2012 Bowman Chrome Legends In The Making Die Cuts

STATED ODDS 1:24 HOBBY
AC Aroldis Chapman 1.00 2.50
AP Albert Pujols 1.25 3.00
BH Bryce Harper 5.00 12.00
BL Brett Lawrie .75 2.00
BP Buster Posey 1.25 3.00
CG Carlos Gonzalez .75 2.00
CK Clayton Kershaw 2.00 5.00
DB Dylan Bundy 1.25 3.00
DF David Freese .60 1.50
DP Dustin Pedroia .75 2.00
FH Felix Hernandez .75 2.00
JE Jacoby Ellsbury .75 2.00
JV Justin Verlander 1.00 2.50
JW Jered Weaver .75 2.00
MC Miguel Cabrera 1.00 2.50
MK Matt Kemp .75 2.00
MM Matt Moore 1.00 2.50
PF Prince Fielder .75 2.00
RB Ryan Braun .60 1.50
RC Robinson Cano 1.00 2.50
SS Stephen Strasburg 1.00 2.50
TB Trevor Bauer 2.00 5.00
TT Troy Tulowitzki 1.00 2.50
YC Yoenis Cespedes 1.50 4.00
YD Yu Darvish 1.50 4.00

2012 Bowman Chrome Prospect Autographs

BOWMAN GRP A ODDS 1:42 HOB
BOWMAN GRP B ODDS 1:1118 HOB
BOWMAN GRP C ODDS 1:1289 HOB
BOWMAN GRP D ODDS 1:1672 HOB
BOW.CHR. ODDS 1:19 HOBBY
BOW.CHR.PLATE ODDS 1:8125 HOB
PLATE PRINT RUN 1 SET PER COLOR
BLACK-CYAN-MAGENTA-YELLOW ISSUED
NO PLATE PRICING DUE TO SCARCITY
EXCHANGE DEADLINE 04/30/2015
AC Adam Conley 3.00 8.00
AG Avisail Garcia 10.00 25.00
BC Bobby Crocker 3.00 8.00
BH Billy Hamilton 4.00 10.00
BM Boss Moanaroa 3.00 8.00
CD Chase Davidson 3.00 8.00
CV Christian Villanueva 3.00 8.00
FH Frazier Hall 3.00 8.00
FR Felipe Rivero 4.00 10.00
FS Felix Sterling 3.00 8.00
JC Jose Campos 3.00 8.00
JG Jonathan Griffin 3.00 8.00
JH John Hellweg 3.00 8.00
JM Jake Marisnick 4.00 10.00
JP James Paxton 10.00 25.00
JR Josh Rutledge 3.00 8.00
JS Jonathan Singleton 3.00 8.00
KS Kevan Smith 3.00 8.00
MH Miles Head 3.00 8.00
MO Marcell Ozuna 25.00 60.00
MS Matt Szczur 5.00 12.00
NC Nick Castellanos 25.00 60.00
NM Nomar Mazara 15.00 40.00
PM Pratt Maynard 3.00 8.00
RG Ronald Guzman 8.00 20.00
RO Rougned Odor 8.00 20.00
RS Ravel Santana 3.00 8.00
SD Shawon Dunston Jr. 3.00 8.00
SG Scooter Gennett 6.00 15.00
SN Sean Nolin 3.00 8.00
TA Tyler Austin 8.00 20.00
TC Tony Cingrani 3.00 8.00
TM Trevor May 3.00 8.00
TS Tyler Skaggs 6.00 15.00
WJ Williams Jerez 3.00 8.00
ZD Zeke DeVoss 3.00 8.00
ACH Andrew Chafin 3.00 8.00
BMI Brad Miller 3.00 8.00
CBU Cody Buckel 3.00 8.00
JRG J.R. Graham 3.00 8.00
JSO Jorge Soler 15.00 40.00
BCP9 Eddie Rosario 10.00 25.00
BCP18 Brandon Drury 15.00 40.00
BCP20 Jeimer Candelario 8.00 20.00
BCP31 Nick Maronde 3.00 8.00
BCP43 Rookie Davis 3.00 8.00
BCP52 Dean Green 3.00 8.00
BCP58 Cheslor Cuthbert 3.00 8.00
BCP62 Kes Carter 3.00 8.00
BCP66 Jackie Bradley Jr. 10.00 25.00
BCP74 Eric Arce 3.00 8.00
BCP75 Dillon Maples 3.00 8.00
BCP77 Clay Holmes 3.00 8.00
BCP79 Josh Bell 40.00 100.00
BCP80 Matt Purke 3.00 8.00
BCP83 Jacob Anderson 3.00 8.00
BCP84 Bryan Brickhouse 3.00 8.00
BCP86 Gerrit Cole 75.00 200.00
BCP87 Danny Hultzen 3.00 8.00
BCP88 Anthony Rendon 50.00 120.00
BCP89 Austin Hedges 4.00 10.00
BCP91 Dillon Howard 3.00 8.00
BCP92 Nick Delmonico 8.00 20.00
BCP93 Brandon Jacobs 3.00 8.00
BCP94 Charlie Tilson 3.00 8.00
BCP97 Andrew Susac 3.00 8.00
BCP98 Greg Bird 6.00 15.00
BCP99 Dante Bichette 3.00 8.00
BCP100 Tommy Joseph 3.00 8.00
BCP101 Julio Rodriguez 3.00 8.00
BCP102 Oscar Taveras 4.00 10.00
BCP103 Drew Hutchison 3.00 8.00
BCP104 Joc Pederson 15.00 40.00
BCP105 Xander Bogaerts 60.00 150.00
BCP106 Tyler Collins 3.00 8.00
BCP107 Joe Ross 4.00 10.00
BCP108 Carlos Martinez 10.00 25.00
BCP109 Andrelton Simmons 8.00 20.00
BCP110 Daniel Norris 3.00 8.00

2012 Bowman Chrome Prospect Autographs Blue Refractors

*BLUE REF: 1.5X TO 4X BASIC
BOWMAN ODDS 1:429 HOBBY
BOW.CHR.ODDS 1:252 HOBBY
STATED PRINT RUN 150 SER.#'d SETS
BOW.EXCH DEADLINE 04/30/2015
BC EXCH DEADLINE 09/30/2015

2012 Bowman Chrome Prospect Autographs Blue Wave Refractors

STATED PRINT RUN 50 SER.#'d SETS
AC Adam Conley 6.00 15.00
AG Avisail Garcia 20.00 50.00
BC Bobby Crocker 6.00 15.00
BH Billy Hamilton 15.00 40.00
BM Boss Moanaroa 6.00 15.00
CD Chase Davidson 6.00 15.00
CV Christian Villanueva 6.00 15.00
FH Frazier Hall 6.00 15.00
FR Felipe Rivero 6.00 15.00
FS Felix Sterling 6.00 15.00
JC Jose Campos 6.00 15.00
JG Jonathan Griffin 6.00 15.00
JH John Hellweg 6.00 15.00
JM Jake Marisnick 8.00 20.00
JP James Paxton 50.00 120.00
JR Josh Rutledge 6.00 15.00
JS Jonathan Singleton 6.00 15.00
KS Kevan Smith 6.00 15.00
MH Miles Head 6.00 15.00
MO Marcell Ozuna 50.00 120.00
MS Matt Szczur 10.00 25.00
NC Nick Castellanos 50.00 120.00
NM Nomar Mazara 30.00 80.00
PM Pratt Maynard 6.00 15.00
RG Ronald Guzman 25.00 60.00
RO Rougned Odor 25.00 60.00
RS Ravel Santana 6.00 15.00
SD Shawon Dunston Jr. 6.00 15.00
SG Scooter Gennett 30.00 80.00
SN Sean Nolin 6.00 15.00
TA Tyler Austin 15.00 40.00
TC Tony Cingrani 6.00 15.00
TM Trevor May 6.00 15.00
TS Tyler Skaggs 12.00 30.00
WJ Williams Jerez 6.00 15.00
ZD Zeke DeVoss 6.00 15.00
ACH Andrew Chafin 6.00 15.00
BMI Brad Miller 6.00 15.00
CBU Cody Buckel 6.00 15.00
JRG J.R. Graham 6.00 15.00
BCP9 Eddie Rosario 20.00 50.00
BCP18 Brandon Drury 30.00 80.00
BCP20 Jeimer Candelario 15.00 40.00
BCP31 Nick Maronde 6.00 15.00
BCP43 Rookie Davis 6.00 15.00
BCP52 Dean Green 6.00 15.00
BCP58 Cheslor Cuthbert 6.00 15.00
BCP62 Kes Carter 6.00 15.00
BCP66 Jackie Bradley Jr. 20.00 50.00
BCP74 Eric Arce 6.00 15.00
BCP75 Dillon Maples 6.00 15.00
BCP77 Clay Holmes 6.00 15.00
BCP79 Josh Bell 500.00 1000.00
BCP80 Matt Purke 6.00 15.00
BCP83 Jacob Anderson 6.00 15.00
BCP84 Bryan Brickhouse 6.00 15.00
BCP86 Gerrit Cole 500.00 1000.00
BCP87 Danny Hultzen 6.00 15.00
BCP88 Anthony Rendon 100.00 250.00
BCP89 Austin Hedges 8.00 20.00
BCP91 Dillon Howard 6.00 15.00
BCP92 Nick Delmonico 15.00 40.00
BCP93 Brandon Jacobs 6.00 15.00
BCP94 Charlie Tilson 6.00 15.00
BCP97 Andrew Susac 6.00 15.00
BCP98 Greg Bird 12.00 30.00
BCP99 Dante Bichette 6.00 15.00
BCP100 Tommy Joseph 6.00 15.00
BCP101 Julio Rodriguez 6.00 15.00
BCP102 Oscar Taveras 8.00 20.00
BCP103 Drew Hutchison 6.00 15.00
BCP104 Joc Pederson 40.00 100.00
BCP105 Xander Bogaerts 125.00 300.00
BCP106 Tyler Collins 6.00 15.00
BCP107 Joe Ross 8.00 20.00
BCP108 Carlos Martinez 20.00 50.00
BCP109 Andrelton Simmons 15.00 40.00
BCP110 Daniel Norris 6.00 15.00

2012 Bowman Chrome Prospect Autographs Gold Refractors

*GOLD REF: 2X TO 5X BASIC
BOWMAN ODDS 1:1300 HOBBY
BOW.CHR.ODDS 1:755 HOBBY
STATED PRINT RUN 50 SER.#'d SETS
BOW.EXCH DEADLINE 04/30/2015
BC EXCH DEADLINE 09/30/2015
BCP79 Josh Bell 500.00 1000.00
BCP86 Gerrit Cole 500.00 1000.00

2012 Bowman Chrome Prospect Autographs Refractors

*REF: .6X TO 1.5X BASIC
BOW.ODDS 1:132 HOBBY
BOW.CHR.ODDS 1:75 HOBBY
STATED PRINT RUN 500 SER.#'d SETS
BOW.EXCH DEADLINE 04/30/2015
BC EXCH DEADLINE 09/30/2015

2012 Bowman Chrome Prospects

COMP.BOW.SET (1-110) 12.50 30.00
COMP.BC SET W/O VAR (111-220) 12.50 30.00
BOW.CHR.ODDS 1:986 HOBBY
PLATE PRINT RUN 1 SET PER COLOR
BLACK-CYAN-MAGENTA-YELLOW ISSUED
NO PLATE PRICING DUE TO SCARCITY
BCP1 Justin Nicolino .30 .75
BCP2 Myrio Richard .25 .60
BCP3 Francisco Lindor 1.50 4.00
BCP4 Nathan Freiman .25 .60
BCP5 A.J. Jimenez .25 .60
BCP6 Noah Perio .25 .60
BCP7 Adonys Cardona .25 .60
BCP8 Nick Kingham .25 .60
BCP9 Eddie Rosario .50 1.25
BCP10 Bryce Harper 6.00 15.00
BCP11 Philip Wunderlich .25 .60
BCP12 Rafael Ortega .25 .60
BCP13 Tyler Gagnon .25 .60
BCP14 Brenny Paulino .25 .60
BCP15 Jose Campos .30 .75
BCP16 Jesus Galindo .25 .60
BCP17 Tyler Austin .40 1.00
BCP18 Brandon Drury .40 1.00
BCP19 Richard Jones .25 .60
BCP20 Jeimer Candelario .30 .75
BCP21 Jose Osuna .25 .60
BCP22 Claudio Custodio .30 .75
BCP23 Jake Marisnick .30 .75
BCP24 J.R. Graham .25 .60
BCP25 Raul Alcantara .25 .60
BCP26 Joseph Staley .25 .60
BCP27 Josh Bowman .25 .60
BCP28 Josh Edgin .25 .60
BCP29 Keith Couch .25 .60
BCP30 Kyrell Hudson .25 .60
BCP31 Nick Maronde .30 .75
BCP32 Mario Yepez .25 .60
BCP33 Matthew West .25 .60
BCP34 Matthew Szczur .30 .75
BCP35 Devon Ethier .25 .60
BCP36 Michael Brady .25 .60
BCP37 Michael Crouse .25 .60
BCP38 Michael Gonzales .25 .60
BCP39 Mike Murray .25 .60
BCP40 Paul Hoilman .25 .60
BCP41 Zach Walters .30 .75
BCP42 Tim Crabbe .25 .60
BCP43 Rookie Davis .25 .60
BCP44 Adam Duvall 4.00 10.00
BCP45 Angelys Nina .25 .60
BCP46 Anthony Fernandez .25 .60
BCP47 Ariel Pena .25 .60
BCP48 Boone Whiting .25 .60
BCP49 Brandon Brown .25 .60
BCP50 Brennan Smith .25 .60
BCP51 Brett Krill .30 .75
BCP52 Dean Green .25 .60
BCP53 Casey Haerther .25 .60
BCP54 Casey Lawrence .25 .60
BCP55 Jose Vinicio .30 .75
BCP56 Kyle Simon .25 .60
BCP57 Chris Rearick .25 .60
BCP58 Cheslor Cuthbert .25 .60
BCP59 Daniel Corcino .30 .75
BCP60 Danny Barnes .25 .60
BCP61 David Medina .25 .60
BCP62 Kes Carter .25 .60
BCP63 Todd McInnis .25 .60
BCP64 Edwar Cabrera .25 .60
BCP65 Emilio King .25 .60
BCP66 Jackie Bradley .60 1.50
BCP67 J.T. Wise .25 .60
BCP68 Jeff Malm .25 .60
BCP69 Jonathan Galvez .25 .60
BCP70 Luis Heredia .25 .60
BCP71 Jonathon Berti .25 .60
BCP72 Jabari Blash .25 .60
BCP73 Will Swanner .25 .60
BCP74 Eric Arce .25 .60
BCP75 Dillon Maples .25 .60
BCP76 Ian Gac .25 .60
BCP77 Clay Holmes .25 .60
BCP78 Nick Castellanos .75 2.00
BCP79 Josh Bell 1.00 2.50
BCP80 Matt Purke .25 .60
BCP81 Taylor Whitenton .25 .60
BCP82 Dayan Diaz .30 .75
BCP83 Jacob Anderson .25 .60
BCP84 Bryan Brickhouse .25 .60
BCP85 Levi Michael .25 .60
BCP86 Gerrit Cole 1.50 4.00
BCP87 Danny Hultzen .40 1.00
BCP88 Anthony Rendon 1.25 3.00
BCP89 Austin Hedges .25 .60
BCP90 Robby Price .25 .60
BCP91 Dillon Howard .30 .75
BCP92 Nick Delmonico .25 .60
BCP93 Brandon Jacobs .30 .75
BCP94 Charlie Tilson .25 .60
BCP95 Luis Angel .25 .60
BCP96 Greg Billo .25 .60
BCP97 Andrew Susac .30 .75
BCP98 Greg Bird .30 .75
BCP99 Dante Bichette .30 .75
BCP100 Tommy Joseph .50 1.25
BCP101 Julio Rodriguez .25 .60
BCP102 Oscar Taveras .40 1.00
BCP103 Drew Hutchison .30 .75
BCP104 Joc Pederson .40 1.00
BCP105 Xander Bogaerts 1.00 2.50
BCP106 Tyler Collins .30 .75
BCP107 Joe Ross .30 .75
BCP108 Carlos Martinez .40 1.00
BCP109 Andrelton Simmons .40 1.00
BCP110 Daniel Norris .30 .75
BCP111 Rob Rasmussen .25 .60
BCP112A Maikel Franco .60 1.50
BCP112B M.Franco Fld SP 15.00 40.00
BCP113 Granden Goetzman .25 .60
BCP114A Will Lamb .25 .60
BCP114B W.Lamb Follow thr.SP 12.50 30.00
BCP115 Sam Stafford .25 .60
BCP116 Boss Moanaroa .25 .60
BCP117 Shawon Dunston Jr. .30 .75
BCP118A Matt Dean .25 .60
BCP118B M.Dean w/Glove SP 12.50 30.00
BCP119A Kevin Pillar .30 .75
BCP119B K.Pillar Throw SP 10.00 25.00
BCP120 Jorge Soler 1.00 2.50
BCP121 Ravel Santana .25 .60
BCP122 Felipe Rivero .40 1.00
BCP123 Drew Leachman .30 .75
BCP124 Julio Morban .30 .75
BCP125 Donald Lutz .40 1.00
BCP126 Christian Bergman .25 .60
BCP127 Michael Earley .25 .60
BCP128A Jeremy Nowak .25 .60
BCP128B J.Nowak Bat down SP 12.50 30.00
BCP129 Tyler Kelly .25 .60
BCP130A Kyle Hendricks 1.50 4.00
BCP130B Hendricks Red Jsy SP 20.00 50.00
BCP131 Mike O'Neill .30 .75
BCP132 Garrett Wittels .30 .75
BCP133 Jon Talley .30 .75
BCP134 Daniel Santana .30 .75
BCP135 Starlin Rodriguez .25 .60
BCP136 Gregory Hopkins .25 .60
BCP137A Colin Walsh .30 .75
BCP137B C.Walsh Fld SP 10.00 25.00
BCP138A Chris Hawkins .30 .75
BCP138B C.Hawkins Batting SP 12.50 30.00
BCP139 Lane Adams .25 .60
BCP140 Brent Keys .25 .60
BCP141 Hanser Alberto .30 .75
BCP142 Tyler Massey .25 .60
BCP143 Alen Hanson .30 .75
BCP144A Blair Walters .25 .60
BCP144B Walt Hand together SP 12.50 30.00
BCP145A Jordan Scott .30 .75
BCP145B Jordan Scott Running SP 6.00 15.00
BCP146 Jamal Austin .25 .60
BCP147 Joel Caminero .25 .60
BCP148 JaDamion Williams .25 .60
BCP149 Mike Gallic .25 .60
BCP150 Kenny Vargas .50 1.25
BCP151 Camden Maron .25 .60
BCP152 Roberto De La Cruz .25 .60
BCP153 Luis Mateo .25 .60
BCP154 William Beckwith .30 .75
BCP155 Art Charles .25 .60
BCP156 Guillermo Pimentel .25 .60
BCP157 Cameron Seitzer .25 .60
BCP158 Anthony Garcia .25 .60
BCP159 Tyler Rahmatulla .25 .60
BCP160 Gary Apelian .25 .60
BCP161 Derek Christensen .25 .60
BCP162 Tim Shibuya .25 .60
BCP163 Wilsen Palacios .25 .60
BCP164 Brandon Eckerle .25 .60
BCP165 Carlos Valenzuela .30 .75
BCP166 Wander Ramos .25 .60
BCP167 Juaner Aguasvivas .25 .60
BCP168 Willy Garcia .30 .75
BCP169A Brian Pointer .30 .75
BCP169B B.Pointer Swing SP 10.00 25.00
BCP170 Austin Brice .25 .60
BCP171 Matthew Summers .25 .60
BCP172 O'Koyea Dickson .30 .75
BCP173 David Kandilas .25 .60
BCP174 Francisco Arcia .30 .75
BCP175 Taylor Siemens .25 .60
BCP176 Aaron Brooks .25 .60
BCP177 Yeison Hernandez .25 .60
BCP178 Jesus Solorzano .25 .60
BCP179 Narciso Mesa .25 .60
BCP180 Brian Humphries .25 .60
BCP181 Estarlin Martinez .25 .60
BCP182 Gregory Polanco .50 1.25
BCP183 Garrett Buechele .30 .75
BCP184 Austin Barnes .40 1.00
BCP185 Logan Pevny .25 .60
BCP186 Frank Lafreniere .25 .60
BCP187A Joshua Magee .25 .60
BCP187B J.Magee Fld SP 10.00 25.00
BCP188A Michael Antonio .25 .60
BCP188B M.Antonio Throw SP 10.00 25.00
BCP189A Julio Concepcion .25 .60
BCP189B Julio Concepcion Throwing SP 6.00 15.00
BCP190 Daniel Paolini .25 .60
BCP191 Danny Winkler .25 .60
BCP192 Felix Munoz .25 .60
BCP193 Evan Marshall .25 .60
BCP194 Manuel Hernandez .25 .60
BCP195 Ben Alsup .25 .60
BCP196 Montreal Robertson .25 .60
BCP197 Miguel Chalas .25 .60
BCP198A Bobby Bundy .25 .60
BCP198B B.Bundy Glv up SP 12.50 30.00
BCP199 Gabriel Lino .30 .75
BCP200A Eduardo Rodriguez .75 2.00
BCP200B Rodriguez Leg up SP 10.00 25.00
BCP201 Matt Benedict .25 .60
BCP202 Nate Jones .25 .60
BCP203 Marcos Camarena .30 .75
BCP204 Matt Hoffman .25 .60
BCP205A Kenny Faulk .25 .60
BCP205B Kenny Faulk Arm down SP 6.00 15.00
BCP206 Jordan Shipers .25 .60
BCP207 Forrest Snow .40 1.00
BCP208 Theo Bowe .30 .75
BCP209 David Freitas .25 .60
BCP210 Carlos Alonso .30 .75
BCP211A Domingo Tapia .30 .75
BCP211B D.Tapia White jsy SP 8.00 20.00
BCP212 Juan Lagares .50 1.25
BCP213A Junior Lake .25 .60
BCP213B J.Lake Fld SP 6.00 15.00
BCP214 Kevin Chapman .25 .60
BCP215A Jake Buchanan .30 .75
BCP215B Buch Grey jsy SP 12.50 30.00
BCP216 Wilfredo Tovar .30 .75
BCP217 Manny Machado 1.50 4.00
BCP218 John Hellweg .25 .60
BCP219 Matthew Neil .25 .60
BCP220 Ruben Alaniz .25 .60

2012 Bowman Chrome Prospects Blue Refractors

*BLUE REF: 3X TO 8X BASIC
BOWMAN ODDS 1:108 HOBBY
BOW.CHR.ODDS 1:19 HOBBY
STATED PRINT RUN 250 SER.#'d SETS

2012 Bowman Chrome Prospects Blue Wave Refractors

*BLUE WAVE: 2.5X TO 6X BASIC

2012 Bowman Chrome Prospects Gold Refractors

*GOLD REF: 8X TO 20X BASIC
BOWMAN ODDS 1:544 HOBBY
BOW.CHR.ODDS 1:96 HOBBY
STATED PRINT RUN 50 SER.#'d SETS
BCP117 Shawon Dunston Jr. 10.00 25.00

2012 Bowman Chrome Prospects Green Refractors

*GREEN REF: 1.5X TO 4X BASIC

2012 Bowman Chrome Prospects Purple Refractors

*PURPLE REF: 3X TO 8X BASIC
BOW.CHR.ODDS 1:24 HOBBY
STATED PRINT RUN 199 SER.#'d SETS

2012 Bowman Chrome Prospects Refractors

*1-110 REF: 2X TO 5X BASIC
*111-220 REF: 1.2X TO 3X BASIC
BOW.ODDS 1:54 HOBBY
BOW.CHR.ODDS 1:4 HOBBY
1-110 PRINT RUN 500 SER.#'d SETS

2012 Bowman Chrome Prospects X-Fractors

*X-FRAC: 2X TO 5X BASIC

2012 Bowman Chrome Rookie Autographs

GROUP A ODDS 1:2275 HOBBY
GROUP B ODDS 1:556 HOBBY
PLATE PRINT RUN 1 SET PER COLOR
BLACK-CYAN-MAGENTA-YELLOW ISSUED
NO PLATE PRICING DUE TO SCARCITY
EXCHANGE DEADLINE 04/30/2015
BH Bryce Harper 150.00 300.00
TB Trevor Bauer 6.00 15.00
WM Will Middlebrooks 5.00 12.00
YD Yu Darvish 100.00 200.00
204 Jeff Locke 6.00 15.00
209 Yu Darvish 100.00 200.00
210 Jesus Montero 8.00 20.00
211 Matt Moore 10.00 25.00
212 Drew Pomeranz 5.00 12.00
213 Jarrod Parker 5.00 12.00
214 Devin Mesoraco 5.00 12.00
215 Joe Benson 3.00 8.00
216 Brad Peacock 3.00 8.00
217 Dellin Betances 3.00 8.00
218 Wilin Rosario 5.00 12.00
220 Addison Reed 4.00 10.00

2012 Bowman Chrome Rookie Autographs Blue Refractors

*BLUE REF: .75X TO 2X BASIC
BOW.ODDS 1:1940 HOBBY
BOW.CHR.ODDS 1:3810 HOBBY
STATED PRINT RUN 250 SER.#'d SETS
BOW.EXCH DEADLINE 04/30/2015
BC EXCH DEADLINE 09/30/2015
BH Bryce Harper/99 200.00 400.00
YD Yu Darvish/99 200.00 400.00
209 Yu Darvish/250 200.00 400.00

2012 Bowman Chrome Rookie Autographs Gold Refractors

*GOLD REF: 1.5X TO 4X BASIC
BOW.ODDS 1:7050 HOBBY
BOW.CHR.ODDS 1:7515 HOBBY
STATED PRINT RUN 50 SER.#'d SETS
BOW.EXCH DEADLINE 04/30/2015
BC EXCH DEADLINE 09/30/2015
BH Bryce Harper 400.00 600.00
YD Yu Darvish EXCH 500.00 800.00
209 Yu Darvish 400.00 600.00

2012 Bowman Chrome Rookie Autographs Refractors

*REF: .5X TO 1.2X BASIC
STATED ODDS 1:990 HOBBY
STATED PRINT RUN 500 SER.#'d SETS
EXCHANGE DEADLINE 04/30/2015

2012 Bowman Chrome Draft

COMPLETE SET (55) 8.00 20.00
STATED PLATE ODDS 1:1600 HOBBY
PLATE PRINT RUN 1 SET PER COLOR
NO PLATE PRICING DUE TO SCARCITY
1 Trevor Bauer RC 1.50 4.00
2 Tyler Pastornicky RC .50 1.25
3 A.J. Griffin RC .60 1.50
4 Yoenis Cespedes RC 1.25 3.00
5 Drew Smyly RC .50 1.25
6 Jose Quintana RC .50 1.25
7 Yasmani Grandal RC .50 1.25
8 Tyler Thornburg RC .60 1.50
9 A.J. Pollock RC .75 2.00
10 Bryce Harper RC 8.00 20.00
11 Joe Kelly RC .75 2.00
12 Steve Clevenger RC .30 .75
13 Tanner Scheppers RC .30 .75
14 Casey Crosby RC .60 1.50
15 Wade Miley RC .60 1.50
16 Quintin Berry RC .75 2.00
17 Martin Perez RC .75 2.00
18 Addison Reed RC .50 1.25
19 Liam Hendriks RC .50 1.25
20 Matt Moore RC .75 2.00
21 Wilin Rosario RC .50 1.25
22 Jarrod Parker RC .60 1.50
23 Matt Adams RC .60 1.50
24 Devin Mesoraco RC .50 1.25
25 Jordan Pacheco RC .50 1.25

26 Irving Falu RC .50 1.25
27 Edwar Cabrera RC .50 1.25
28 Stephen Pryor RC .30 .75
29 Norichika Aoki RC .60 1.50
30 Jesus Montero RC .50 1.25
31 Drew Pomeranz RC .50 1.25
32 Jordany Valdespin RC .60 1.50
33 Andrelton Simmons RC .75 2.00
34 Xavier Avery RC .50 1.25
35 Chris Archer RC .50 1.25
36 Drew Hutchison RC .60 1.50
37 Dallas Keuchel RC 2.50 6.00
38 Leonys Martin RC .50 1.25
39 Brian Dozier RC 1.50 4.00
40 Will Middlebrooks RC .60 1.50
41 Kirk Nieuwenhuis RC .50 1.25
42 Jeremy Hefner RC .50 1.25
43 Derek Norris RC .50 1.25
44 Tom Milone RC .50 1.25
45 Wei-Yin Chen RC 1.25 3.00
46 Christian Friedrich RC .50 1.25
47 Kole Calhoun RC .60 1.50
48 Wily Peralta RC .50 1.25
49 Hisashi Iwakuma RC 1.00 2.50
50 Yu Darvish RC 1.25 3.00
51 Elian Herrera RC .75 2.00
52 Anthony Gose RC .60 1.50
53 Brett Jackson RC .75 2.00
54 Alex Liddi RC .50 1.25
55 Matt Hague RC .50 1.25

2012 Bowman Chrome Draft Refractors
*REF: 1.2X TO 3X BASIC
STATED PRINT RUN 300 SER.#'d SETS
STATED PRINT RUN 1:4 HOBBY
10 Bryce Harper 20.00 50.00

2012 Bowman Chrome Draft Blue Refractors
*BLUE REF: 1.2X TO 3X BASIC
STATED PRINT RUN 250 SER.#'d SETS
STATED PRINT RUN 1:26 HOBBY
10 Bryce Harper 30.00 80.00

2012 Bowman Chrome Draft Gold Refractors
*GOLD REF: 3X TO 8X BASIC
STATED PRINT RUN 50 SER.#'d SETS
STATED PRINT RUN 1:128 HOBBY
4 Yoenis Cespedes 30.00 60.00
10 Bryce Harper 60.00 120.00
50 Yu Darvish 40.00 80.00

2012 Bowman Chrome Draft Draft Pick Autographs
STATED ODDS 1:41 HOBBY
STATED PLATE ODDS 1:11,250 HOBBY
PLATE PRINT RUN 1 SET PER COLOR
NO PLATE PRICING DUE TO SCARCITY
EXCHANGE DEADLINE 11/30/2015
AA Albert Almora 15.00 40.00
AAU Austin Aune 4.00 10.00
AH Andrew Heaney 5.00 12.00
AR Addison Russell 25.00 60.00
BJ Brian Johnson 8.00 20.00
BM Bruce Maxwell 4.00 10.00
CH Courtney Hawkins 4.00 10.00
CS Corey Seager 100.00 250.00
CST Chris Stratton 4.00 10.00
DD David Dahl 20.00 50.00
DDA D.J. Davis 4.00 10.00
DM Deven Marrero 4.00 10.00
GC Gavin Cecchini 6.00 15.00
JG Joey Gallo 25.00 60.00
JR James Ramsey 4.00 10.00
KB Keon Barnum 4.00 10.00
KG Kevin Gausman 6.00 15.00
KP Kevin Plawecki 4.00 10.00
KZ Kyle Zimmer 3.00 8.00
LB Lewis Brinson 15.00 40.00
LS Lucas Sims 8.00 20.00
MF Max Fried 30.00 80.00
MH Mitch Haniger 15.00 30.00
MN Mitch Nay 4.00 10.00
MS Marcus Stroman 20.00 50.00
MSM Matthew Smoral 4.00 10.00
MW Michael Wacha 10.00 25.00
MZ Mike Zunino 10.00 25.00
NF Nolan Fontana 4.00 10.00
NT Nick Travieso 4.00 10.00
NW Nick Williams 8.00 20.00
PB Paul Blackburn 4.00 10.00
PL Pat Light 4.00 10.00
RS Richie Shaffer 4.00 10.00
SB Steve Bean 4.00 10.00
ST Stryker Trahan 4.00 10.00
SW Shane Watson 4.00 10.00
TH Ty Hensley 4.00 10.00
TN Tyler Naquin 4.00 10.00
TT Tyrone Taylor 5.00 12.00

2012 Bowman Chrome Draft Draft Pick Autographs Refractors
*REF: .5X TO 1.2X BASIC
STATED PRINT RUN 1:90 HOBBY
EXCHANGE DEADLINE 11/30/2015

2012 Bowman Chrome Draft Draft Pick Autographs Blue Refractors
*BLUE REF: 1.2X TO 3X BASIC
STATED PRINT RUN 150 SER.#'d SETS
STATED PRINT RUN 1:299 HOBBY
EXCHANGE DEADLINE 11/30/2015
CS Corey Seager 600.00 1000.00

2012 Bowman Chrome Draft Draft Pick Autographs Blue Wave Refractors
*BLUE WAVE: .6X TO 1.5X BASIC
STATED PRINT RUN 50 SER.#'d SETS

2012 Bowman Chrome Draft Draft Pick Autographs Gold Refractors
*GOLD REF: 2X TO 5X BASIC
STATED PRINT RUN 50 SER.#'d SETS
STATED PRINT RUN 1:893 HOBBY
EXCHANGE DEADLINE 11/30/2015
CS Corey Seager 1000.00 1500.00
DD David Dahl 200.00 400.00
JG Joey Gallo 200.00 500.00

2012 Bowman Chrome Draft Draft Picks
COMPLETE SET (165) 15.00 40.00
STATED PLATE ODDS 1:1600 HOBBY
PLATE PRINT RUN 1 SET PER COLOR
NO PLATE PRICING DUE TO SCARCITY
BDPP1 Lucas Sims .30 .75
BDPP2 Kevin Gausman .50 1.25
BDPP3 Brian Johnson .25 .60
BDPP4 Pierce Johnson .30 .75
BDPP5 Keon Barnum .25 .60
BDPP6 Paul Blackburn .25 .60
BDPP7 Nick Travieso .30 .75
BDPP8 Jesse Winker .30 .75
BDPP9 Tyler Naquin .30 .75
BDPP10 Kyle Zimmer .30 .75
BDPP11 Jesmuel Valentin .30 .75
BDPP12 Andrew Heaney .30 .75
BDPP13 Victor Roache .50 1.25
BDPP14 Mitch Haniger .60 1.50
BDPP15 Luke Bard .25 .60
BDPP16 Jose Berrios .75 2.00
BDPP17 Gavin Cecchini .30 .75
BDPP18 Kevin Plawecki .30 .75
BDPP19 Ty Hensley .30 .75
BDPP20 Matt Olson .40 1.00
BDPP21 Mitch Gueller .25 .60
BDPP22 Shane Watson .30 .75
BDPP23 Barrett Barnes .30 .75
BDPP24 Travis Jankowski .30 .75
BDPP25 Mike Zunino .40 1.00
BDPP26 Michael Wacha .50 1.25
BDPP27 James Ramsey .25 .60
BDPP28 Patrick Wisdom .25 .60
BDPP29 Steve Bean .25 .60
BDPP30 Richie Shaffer .30 .75
BDPP31 Lewis Brinson .75 2.00
BDPP32 Joey Gallo .75 2.00
BDPP33 D.J. Davis .30 .75
BDPP34 Tyler Gonzalez .30 .75
BDPP35 Marcus Stroman .40 1.00
BDPP36 Matt Smoral .25 .60
BDPP37 Branden Kline .25 .60
BDPP38 Jacob Thompson .30 .75
BDPP39 Austin Aune .30 .75
BDPP40 Peter O'Brien .40 1.00
BDPP41 Bruce Maxwell .25 .60
BDPP42 Dylan Cozens .40 1.00
BDPP43 Wyatt Mathisen .25 .60
BDPP44 Spencer Edwards .25 .60
BDPP45 Jamie Jarmon .25 .60
BDPP46 R.J. Alvarez .25 .60
BDPP47 Bryan De La Rosa .25 .60
BDPP48 Adrian Marin .25 .60
BDPP49 Austin Maddox .25 .60
BDPP50 Fernando Perez .25 .60
BDPP51 Austin Schotts .25 .60
BDPP52 Avery Romero .25 .60
BDPP53 Kolby Copeland .25 .60
BDPP54 Jonathan Sandfort .25 .60
BDPP55 Alex Yarbrough .25 .60
BDPP56 Justin Black .25 .60
BDPP57 Ty Buttrey .30 .75
BDPP58 Austin Dean .25 .60
BDPP59 Andrew Pullin .30 .75
BDPP60 Bralin Jackson .25 .60
BDPP61 Lex Rutledge .25 .60
BDPP62 Jordan John .25 .60
BDPP63 Andre Martinez .25 .60
BDPP64 Eric Wood .30 .75
BDPP65 Derek Self .25 .60
BDPP66 Jacob Wilson .25 .60
BDPP67 Joe Bircher .25 .60
BDPP68 Matthew Price .25 .60
BDPP69 Hudson Randall .25 .60
BDPP70 Jorge Fernandez .25 .60
BDPP71 Nathan Minnich .25 .60
BDPP72 Yoenny Gonzalez .25 .60
BDPP73 Steven Schils .25 .60
BDPP74 Thomas Coyle .25 .60
BDPP75 Ron Miller .25 .60
BDPP76 Rowan Wick .25 .60
BDPP77 Mike Dodig .25 .60
BDPP78 John Kuchno .25 .60
BDPP79 Caleb Frare .30 .75
BDPP80 William Carmona .25 .60
BDPP81 Clayton Henning .25 .60
BDPP82 Connor Lien .25 .60
BDPP83 Michael Meyers .25 .60
BDPP84 Julio Felix .25 .60
BDPP85 Alexander Muren .25 .60
BDPP86 Jacob Stallings .30 .75
BDPP87 Max Foody .25 .60
BDPP88 Taylor Hawkins .25 .60
BDPP89 Jeffrey Wendelken .25 .60
BDPP90 Steven Golden .25 .60
BDPP91 Brett Wiley .25 .60
BDPP92 John Silviano .25 .60
BDPP93 Tyler Tewell .25 .60
BDPP94 Sean McAdams .30 .75
BDPP95 Michael Vaughn .25 .60
BDPP96 Jake Proctor .25 .60
BDPP97 Richard Bielski .25 .60
BDPP98 Charles Gillies .25 .60
BDPP99 Erick Gonzalez .25 .60
BDPP100 Bennett Pickar .25 .60
BDPP101 Christopher Beck .25 .60
BDPP102 Brandon Brennan .25 .60
BDPP103 Eddie Butler .25 .60
BDPP104 David Dahl .75 2.00
BDPP105 Ryan Gibbard .25 .60
BDPP106 Hunter Scantling .25 .60
BDPP107 Zach Isler .25 .60
BDPP108 Joshua Turley .25 .60
BDPP109 Johendi Jiminian .25 .60
BDPP110 Jake Lamb .40 1.00
BDPP111 Mike Morin .25 .60
BDPP112 Parker Morin .25 .60
BDPP113 Scott Oberg .25 .60
BDPP114 Correlle Prime .25 .60
BDPP115 Mark Sappington .25 .60
BDPP116 Sam Selman .30 .75
BDPP117 Paul Sewald .25 .60
BDPP118 Matt Wessinger .25 .60
BDPP119 Max White .25 .60
BDPP120 Adam Giacalone .30 .75
BDPP121 Jeffrey Popick .25 .60
BDPP122 Alfredo Rodriguez .25 .60
BDPP123 Nick Routt .25 .60
BDPP124 Abe Ruiz .25 .60
BDPP125 Jason Stolz .25 .60
BDPP126 Ben Waldrip .25 .60
BDPP127 Eric Stamets .25 .60
BDPP128 Chris Cowell .25 .60
BDPP129 Fernelys Sanchez .25 .60
BDPP130 Kevin McKague .30 .75
BDPP131 Rashad Brown .25 .60
BDPP132 Jorge Saez .25 .60
BDPP133 Shaun Valeriote .25 .60
BDPP134 Will Hurt .25 .60
BDPP135 Nicholas Grim .30 .75
BDPP136 Patrick Merkling .25 .60
BDPP137 Jonathan Murphy .25 .60
BDPP138 Bryan Lippincott .25 .60
BDPP139 Austin Chubb .25 .60
BDPP140 Joseph Almaraz .25 .60
BDPP141 Robert Ravago .25 .60
BDPP142 Will Hudgins .25 .60
BDPP143 Tommy Richards .25 .60
BDPP144 Chad Carman .40 1.00
BDPP145 Joel Licon .25 .60
BDPP146 Jimmy Rider .25 .60
BDPP147 Jason Wilson .25 .60
BDPP148 Justin Jackson .25 .60
BDPP149 Casey McCarthy .25 .60
BDPP150 Hunter Bailey .25 .60
BDPP151 Jake Pintar .25 .60
BDPP152 David Cruz .25 .60
BDPP153 Mike Mudron .25 .60
BDPP154 Benjamin Kline .25 .60
BDPP155 Bryan Haar .25 .60
BDPP156 Patrick Claussen .25 .60
BDPP157 Derrick Bleeker .25 .60
BDPP158 Edward Sappelt .25 .60
BDPP159 Jeremy Lucas .25 .60
BDPP160 Josh Martin .25 .60
BDPP161 Robert Benincasa .25 .60
BDPP162 Craig Manuel .25 .60
BDPP163 Taylor Ard .25 .60
BDPP164 Dominic Leone .25 .60
BDPP165 Kevin Brady .25 .60

2012 Bowman Chrome Draft Draft Picks Refractors
*REF: 1.2X TO 3X BASIC
STATED PRINT RUN 1:4 HOBBY

2012 Bowman Chrome Draft Draft Picks Blue Refractors
*BLUE REF: 3X TO 8X BASIC
STATED PRINT RUN 250 SER.#'d SETS
STATED PRINT RUN 1:26 HOBBY

2012 Bowman Chrome Draft Draft Picks Blue Wave Refractors
*BLUE WAVE: 2.5X TO 6X BASIC

2012 Bowman Chrome Draft Draft Picks Gold Refractors
*GOLD REF: 10X TO 25X BASIC
STATED PRINT RUN 50 SER.#'d SETS
STATED PRINT RUN 1:128 HOBBY

2012 Bowman Chrome Draft Rookie Autographs
STATED ODDS 1:6700 HOBBY
EXCHANGE DEADLINE 11/30/2015
BH Bryce Harper 150.00 300.00
YD Yu Darvish EXCH 100.00 200.00

2013 Bowman Chrome
COMPLETE SET (220) 30.00 60.00
STATED PLATE ODDS 1:1015 HOBBY
PLATE PRINT RUN 1 SET PER COLOR
BLACK-CYAN-MAGENTA-YELLOW ISSUED
NO PLATE PRICING DUE TO SCARCITY
1 Bryce Harper .50 1.25
2 Wil Myers RC .50 1.25
3 Jose Reyes .25 .60
4 Rob Brantly RC .40 1.00
5 Elvis Andrus .25 .60
6 Matt Moore .25 .60
7 Starling Marte .25 .60
8 Kyuji Fujikawa RC .60 1.50
9 Aaron Hicks RC .60 1.50
10 Brandon Maurer RC .50 1.25
11 Casey Kelly RC .50 1.25
12 Jeurys Familia RC .60 1.50
13 Mike Minor .20 .50
14 Alex Wood RC .50 1.25
15 Joey Votto .30 .75
16 Curtis Granderson .25 .60
17 Ben Revere .20 .50
18 Giancarlo Stanton .30 .75
19 Mariano Rivera .40 1.00
20 Tim Lincecum .25 .60
21 Billy Butler .20 .50
22 Yonder Alonso .20 .50
23 Adeiny Hechavarria RC .50 1.25
24 Nolan Arenado RC 2.00 5.00
25 Felix Hernandez .25 .60
26 C.J. Wilson .20 .50
27 Tommy Milone .20 .50
28 Kyle Gibson RC .60 1.50
29 Carlos Ruiz .20 .50
30 Gerrit Cole RC 2.50 6.00
31 Avisail Garcia RC .50 1.25
32 Ike Davis .20 .50
33 Jordan Zimmermann .25 .60
34 Yoenis Cespedes .30 .75
35 Carlos Beltran .25 .60
36 Troy Tulowitzki .30 .75
37 Wei-Yin Chen .20 .50
38 Adam Wainwright .25 .60
39 Oswaldo Arcia RC .40 1.00
40 Alex Gordon .25 .60
41 Marco Scutaro .25 .60
42 Jon Lester .25 .60
43 Mike Morse .20 .50
44 Jedd Gyorko RC .50 1.25
45 Nelson Cruz .30 .75
46 Yu Darvish .30 .75
47 Josh Beckett .20 .50
48 Kevin Youkilis .20 .50
49 Zack Wheeler RC .75 2.00
50 Mike Trout 2.50 6.00
51 Fernando Rodney .20 .50
52 Jason Kipnis .25 .60
53 Tim Hudson .25 .60
54 Alex Colome RC .40 1.00
55 Alfredo Marte RC .40 1.00
56 Jason Heyward .25 .60
57 Jurickson Profar RC .50 1.25
58 Craig Kimbrel .25 .60
59 Adam Dunn .25 .60
60 Hanley Ramirez .25 .60
61 Jacoby Ellsbury .25 .60
62 Jonathan Pettibone RC .60 1.50
63 Jered Weaver .25 .60
64 Eury Perez RC .50 1.25
65 Jeff Samardzija .20 .50
66 Matt Kemp .25 .60
67 Carlos Santana .25 .60
68 Brett Marshall RC .50 1.25
69 Ryan Vogelsong .20 .50
70 Edwin Encarnacion .30 .75
71 Mike Zunino RC .60 1.50
72 Buster Posey .40 1.00
73 Ben Zobrist .25 .60
74 Madison Bumgarner .25 .60
75 Robinson Cano .25 .60
76 Jake Odorizzi RC .50 1.25
77 Eric Hosmer .25 .60
78 Yasiel Puig RC 1.50 4.00
79 Hisashi Iwakuma .25 .60
80 Ryan Zimmerman .25 .60
81 Adam Warren RC .40 1.00
82 Jake Peavy .20 .50
83 Mike Olt RC .50 1.25
84 Homer Bailey .20 .50
85 Barry Zito .20 .50
86 Wade Miley .20 .50
87 Nick Swisher .25 .60
88 Roy Halladay .25 .60
89 Jackie Bradley Jr. RC 1.00 2.50
90 Jose Bautista .25 .60
91 Will Middlebrooks .20 .50
92 Yasmani Grandal .20 .50
93 Allen Craig .20 .50
94 Brandon Phillips .20 .50
95 Lance Lynn .20 .50
96 Justin Upton .25 .60
97 Anthony Rendon RC 2.00 5.00
98 Ian Desmond .20 .50
99 Matt Harrison .20 .50
100 Justin Verlander .30 .75
101 Adrian Gonzalez .25 .60
102 Chris Davis .25 .60
103 Jose Fernandez RC 1.00 2.50
104 Dexter Fowler .25 .60
105 A.J. Burnett .20 .50
106 Derek Holland .20 .50
107 Cole Hamels .25 .60
108 Marcell Ozuna RC 1.00 2.50
109 James Shields .20 .50
110 Josh Hamilton .25 .60
111 Desmond Jennings .25 .60
112 Jaime Garcia .25 .60
113 Shin-Soo Choo .25 .60
114 Freddie Freeman .40 1.00
115 Nate Karns RC .40 1.00
116 Shelby Miller RC 1.00 2.50
117 Johnny Cueto .25 .60
118 Jay Bruce .25 .60
119 Chris Sale .30 .75
120 Alex Rios .25 .60
121 Michael Wacha RC .50 1.25
122 Mike Moustakas .25 .60
123 Adam Eaton RC .60 1.50
124 Joe Nathan .20 .50
125 Mark Trumbo .20 .50
126 David Freese .20 .50
127 Todd Frazier .25 .60
128 Austin Jackson .20 .50
129 Anthony Rizzo .50 1.25
130 Nick Maronde RC .50 1.25
131 Mat Latos .25 .60
132 Salvador Perez .25 .60
133 Albert Pujols .40 1.00
134 Dylan Bundy RC 1.00 2.50
135 Allen Webster RC .50 1.25
136 Andrew McCutchen .30 .75
137 Jason Motte .20 .50
138 Joe Mauer .25 .60
139 Trevor Rosenthal RC .75 2.00
140 Nick Franklin RC .50 1.25
141 Asdrubal Cabrera .25 .60
142 B.J. Upton .25 .60
143 Aaron Hill .20 .50
144 Jean Segura .25 .60
145 Josh Willingham .25 .60
146 Michael Bourn .20 .50
147 Didi Gregorius RC 1.50 4.00
148 Jon Jay .20 .50
149 Evan Longoria .25 .60
150 Matt Cain .25 .60
151 Yovani Gallardo .20 .50
152 Paul Goldschmidt .30 .75
153 Brett Lawrie .25 .60
154 Hyun-Jin Ryu RC 1.00 2.50
155 Jayson Werth .25 .60
156 R.A. Dickey .25 .60
157 Adrian Beltre .30 .75
158 Hunter Pence .25 .60
159 Adam Jones .25 .60
160 Brandon Morrow .20 .50
161 Coco Crisp .20 .50
162 Dustin Pedroia .30 .75
163 Ian Kennedy .20 .50
164 Stephen Strasburg .30 .75
165 Jon Niese .20 .50
166 Vidal Nuno RC .40 1.00
167 Matt Holliday .30 .75
168 Carter Capps RC .40 1.00
169 Ryan Howard .25 .60
170 David Ortiz .30 .75
171 Alex Rodriguez .40 1.00
172 CC Sabathia .25 .60
173 David Wright .25 .60
174 Wilin Rosario .20 .50
175 Ryan Braun .25 .60
176 Angel Pagan .20 .50
177 Josh Reddick .20 .50
178 Miguel Montero .20 .50
179 Corey Hart .20 .50
180 Cliff Lee .25 .60
181 Kevin Gausman RC .60 1.50
182 Melky Cabrera .20 .50
183 Jesus Montero .20 .50
184 Doug Fister .20 .50
185 Jim Johnson .20 .50
186 Carlos Gonzalez .25 .60
187 Starlin Castro .20 .50
188 Tyler Skaggs RC .60 1.50
189 Tony Cingrani RC .75 2.00
190 Matt Magill RC .40 1.00
191 Mark Reynolds .20 .50
192 Bruce Rondon RC .40 1.00
193 Prince Fielder .25 .60
194 Jose Altuve .25 .60
195 Chase Headley .20 .50
196 Andre Ethier .25 .60
197 Hiroki Kuroda .20 .50
198 Gio Gonzalez .25 .60
199 Mark Teixeira .25 .60
200 Miguel Cabrera .30 .75
201 Aroldis Chapman .30 .75
202 Nate Freiman RC .40 1.00
203 Ian Kinsler .25 .60
204 Trevor Bauer .30 .75
205 Manny Machado RC 2.50 6.00
206 Josh Johnson .25 .60
207 Melky Mesa RC .50 1.25
208 Michael Young .20 .50
209 Evan Gattis RC .75 2.00
210 Yadier Molina .30 .75
211 Kris Medlen .25 .60
212 Sean Doolittle RC .40 1.00
213 Torii Hunter .20 .50
214 Brian McCann .25 .60
215 Derek Jeter .75 2.00
216 Mike Kickham RC .40 1.00
217 Carlos Martinez RC .60 1.50
218 Paco Rodriguez RC .60 1.50
219 David Price .25 .60
220 Clayton Kershaw .60 1.50

2013 Bowman Chrome Blue Refractors
*BLUE REF: 2.5X TO 6X BASIC
*BLUE REF RC: 1.2X TO 3X BASIC RC
STATED ODDS 1:21 HOBBY
STATED PRINT RUN 250 SER.#'d SETS
2 Wil Myers 8.00 20.00
205 Manny Machado 8.00 20.00
209 Evan Gattis 6.00 15.00

2013 Bowman Chrome Gold Refractors
*GOLD REF: 8X TO 20X BASIC
*GOLD REF RC: 4X TO 10X BASIC RC
STATED ODDS 1:105 HOBBY
STATED PRINT RUN 50 SER.#'d SETS
1 Bryce Harper 20.00 50.00
49 Zack Wheeler 8.00 20.00
50 Mike Trout 25.00 60.00
71 Mike Zunino 15.00 40.00
78 Yasiel Puig 100.00 200.00
200 Miguel Cabrera 20.00 50.00
205 Manny Machado 40.00 80.00
215 Derek Jeter 30.00 60.00

2013 Bowman Chrome Green Refractors
*GREEN REF: 2X TO 5X BASIC
*GREEN REF RC: 1X TO 2.5X BASIC RC
78 Yasiel Puig 15.00 40.00

2013 Bowman Chrome Magenta Refractors
*MAGENTA REF: 12X TO 30X BASIC
*MAGENTA REF RC: 6X TO 15X BASIC RC
STATED ODDS 1:101 HOBBY
STATED PRINT RUN 35 SER.#'d SETS
215 Derek Jeter 40.00 100.00

2013 Bowman Chrome Orange Refractors
*ORANGE REF: 12X TO 30X BASIC
*ORANGE REF RC: 6X TO 15X BASIC RC
STATED ODDS 1:210 HOBBY
STATED PRINT RUN 25 SER.#'d SETS
1 Bryce Harper 30.00 80.00
30 Gerrit Cole 30.00 80.00
49 Zack Wheeler 12.00 30.00
50 Mike Trout 40.00 100.00
72 Buster Posey 30.00 80.00
78 Yasiel Puig 200.00 300.00
100 Justin Verlander 25.00 60.00
103 Jose Fernandez 30.00 80.00
134 Dylan Bundy 25.00 60.00
197 Hiroki Kuroda 15.00 40.00
205 Manny Machado 60.00 120.00
209 Evan Gattis 25.00 60.00
210 Yadier Molina 15.00 40.00
215 Derek Jeter 60.00 150.00

2013 Bowman Chrome Purple Refractors
*PURPLE REF: 2.5X TO 6X BASIC
*PURPLE REF RC: 1.2X TO 3X BASIC RC
STATED ODDS 1:26 HOBBY
STATED PRINT RUN 199 SER.#'d SETS
205 Manny Machado 8.00 20.00
209 Evan Gattis 6.00 15.00

2013 Bowman Chrome Refractors
*REF: 1.5X TO 4X BASIC
*REF RC: .75X TO 2X BASIC RC
STATED ODDS 1:4 HOBBY

2013 Bowman Chrome X-Fractors
*XFRACTOR: 1X TO 2.5X BASIC
*XFRACTOR RC: .6X TO 1.5X BASIC RC
78 Yasiel Puig 10.00 25.00

2013 Bowman Chrome Fit the Bill
STATED ODDS 1:630 HOBBY
STATED PRINT RUN 99 SER.#'d SETS
AC Aroldis Chapman 5.00 12.00
AM Andrew McCutchen 5.00 12.00
AR Anthony Rizzo 8.00 20.00
BH Bryce Harper 10.00 25.00
BP Buster Posey 15.00 40.00
CG Carlos Gonzalez 4.00 10.00
CK Clayton Kershaw 10.00 25.00
CKR Craig Kimbrel 4.00 10.00
CS Chris Sale 5.00 12.00
DP David Price 4.00 10.00
DW David Wright 4.00 10.00
EL Evan Longoria 4.00 10.00
FH Felix Hernandez 4.00 10.00
GS Giancarlo Stanton 5.00 12.00
JH Jason Heyward 4.00 10.00
JU Justin Upton 8.00 20.00
MH Matt Harvey 4.00 10.00
MM Manny Machado 12.00 30.00
MMO Matt Moore 4.00 10.00
MT Mike Trout 12.00 30.00
PG Paul Goldschmidt 10.00 25.00
SS Stephen Strasburg 5.00 12.00
YC Yoenis Cespedes 5.00 12.00
YD Yu Darvish 5.00 12.00
YP Yasiel Puig 15.00 40.00

2013 Bowman Chrome Fit the Bill X-Fractors
*X-FRACTORS: 1X TO 2.5X BASIC
STATED ODDS 1:1943 HOBBY
STATED PRINT RUN 24 SER.#'d SETS

2013 Bowman Chrome Rising Through the Ranks Mini
COMPLETE SET (30) 15.00 40.00
STATED ODDS 1:18 HOBBY
AA Albert Almora 1.00 2.50
AB Archie Bradley .50 1.25
AH Alen Hanson .60 1.50
AM Alex Meyer .50 1.25
AR Addison Russell .75 2.00
CC C.J. Cron .60 1.50
CCO Carlos Correa 5.00 12.00
CS Corey Seager 2.00 5.00
DD David Dahl .60 1.50
DP Dorssys Paulino .60 1.50
DV Dan Vogelbach .75 2.00
FL Francisco Lindor 3.00 8.00
GP Gregory Polanco 1.00 2.50
GS Gary Sanchez 1.50 4.00
JG Joey Gallo 1.50 4.00
JP Joc Pederson .75 2.00
JS Jorge Soler 1.00 2.50
KC Kyle Crick .75 2.00
KCO Kaleb Cowart .60 1.50
KZ Kyle Zimmer .60 1.50
MB Matt Barnes .60 1.50
MF Michael Fulmer .75 2.00
MFR Max Fried 2.00 5.00
MW Mason Williams .60 1.50
RQ Roman Quinn .75 2.00
RS Robert Stephenson .50 1.25
TA Tyler Anderson .50 1.25
TAU Tyler Austin .75 2.00
TG Taylor Guerrieri .50 1.25
XB Xander Bogaerts 1.50 4.00

2013 Bowman Chrome Rising Through the Ranks Mini Blue Refractor
*BLUE REF: 1.2X TO 3X BASIC
STATED ODDS 1:231 HOBBY
STATED PRINT RUN 250 SER.#'d SETS

2013 Bowman Chrome Rising Through the Ranks Mini Autographs
STATED ODDS 1:14,860 HOBBY
STATED PRINT RUN 25 SER.#'d SETS
EXCHANGE DEADLINE 9/30/2016
DD David Dahl 4.00 10.00
DV Dan Vogelbach 6.00 15.00
JS Jorge Soler 6.00 15.00
MF Michael Fulmer 10.00 25.00

2013 Bowman Chrome Cream of the Crop Mini Refractors
STATED ODDS 1:6 HOBBY
A1 Kaleb Cowart .30 .75
A2 C.J. Cron .30 .75
A3 Nick Maronde .30 .75
A4 Taylor Lindsey .25 .60
A5 R.J. Alvarez .25 .60
AB1 Julio Teheran .30 .75
AB2 Christian Bethancourt .40 1.00
AB3 Lucas Sims .30 .75
AB4 J.R. Graham .25 .60
AB5 Sean Gilmartin .25 .60
AD1 Tyler Skaggs .40 1.00
AD2 Archie Bradley .25 .60
AD3 Matt Davidson .30 .75
AD4 Adam Eaton .40 1.00
AD5 Stryker Trahan .25 .60
BO1 Dylan Bundy .60 1.50
BO2 Kevin Gausman .40 1.00
BO3 Jonathan Schoop .25 .60
BO4 L.J. Hoes .30 .75
BO5 Nick Delmonico .30 .75
CC1 Javier Baez 1.00 2.50
CC2 Jorge Soler .50 1.25
CC3 Albert Almora .50 1.25
CC4 Dan Vogelbach .40 1.00
CC5 Jeimer Candelario .30 .75
CI1 Trevor Bauer .40 1.00
CI2 Francisco Lindor 1.50 4.00
CI3 Dorssys Paulino .30 .75
CI4 Tyler Naquin .30 .75
CI5 Ronny Rodriguez .25 .60
CR1 Billy Hamilton .30 .75
CR2 Robert Stephenson .25 .60
CR3 Tony Cingrani .50 1.25
CR4 Daniel Corcino .25 .60
CR5 Nick Travieso .30 .75
DT1 Nick Castellanos .75 2.00
DT2 Bruce Rondon .25 .60
DT3 Avisail Garcia .30 .75
DT4 Jake Thompson .25 .60
DT5 Danry Vasquez .25 .60
HA1 Carlos Correa 2.50 6.00
HA2 Jonathan Singleton .30 .75
HA3 George Springer 1.00 2.50
HA4 Delino DeShields .25 .60
HA5 Jarred Cosart .30 .75
MB1 Wily Peralta .25 .60
MB2 Tyler Thornburg .30 .75
MB3 Hunter Morris .30 .75
MB4 Taylor Jungmann .25 .60
MB5 Johnny Hellweg .25 .60
MM1 Jose Fernandez .60 1.50
MM2 Christian Yelich 2.00 5.00
MM3 Jake Marisnick .30 .75
MM4 Justin Nicolino .25 .60
MM5 Andrew Heaney .30 .75
MT1 Miguel Sano .30 .75
MT2 Byron Buxton .60 1.50
MT3 Oswaldo Arcia .25 .60
MT4 Alex Meyer .25 .60
MT5 Eddie Rosario .50 1.25
OA1 Addison Russell .40 1.00
OA2 Michael Choice .25 .60
OA3 Miles Head .30 .75
OA4 Sonny Gray .40 1.00
OA5 Grant Green .40 1.00
PP1 Jesse Biddle .30 .75
PP2 Tommy Joseph .50 1.25
PP3 Ethan Martin .25 .60
PP4 Roman Quinn .40 1.00
PP5 Adam Morgan .25 .60
SM1 Mike Zunino .40 1.00
SM2 Taijuan Walker .30 .75
SM3 Danny Hultzen .30 .75
SM4 Brad Miller .30 .75
SM5 James Paxton .30 .75

TR1 Jurickson Profar .30 .75
TR2 Mike Olt .30 .75
TR3 Cody Buckel .25 .60
TR4 Joey Gallo .75 2.00
TR5 Jairo Beras .40 1.00
WN1 Anthony Rendon 1.25 3.00
WN2 Brian Goodwin .30 .75
WN3 Lucas Giolito .40 1.00
WN4 A.J. Cole .30 .75
WN5 Matt Skole .30 .75
BRS1 Xander Bogaerts .75 2.00
BRS2 Matt Barnes .30 .75
BRS3 Jackie Bradley .60 1.50
BRS4 Allen Webster .30 .75
BRS5 Bryce Brentz .25 .60
CRO1 David Dahl .30 .75
CRO2 Nolan Arenado 1.25 3.00
CRO3 Trevor Story 1.00 2.50
CRO4 Jayson Aquino .25 .60
CRO5 Kyle Parker .25 .60
CWS1 Courtney Hawkins .25 .60
CWS2 Trayce Thompson .40 1.00
CWS3 Keon Barnum .25 .60
CWS4 Carlos Sanchez .25 .60
CWS5 Erik Johnson .25 .60
KCR1 Bubba Starling .30 .75
KCR2 Kyle Zimmer .30 .75
KCR3 Adalberto Mondesi .75 2.00
KCR4 Jorge Bonifacio .30 .75
KCR5 Orlando Calixte .30 .75
LAD1 Corey Seager 1.00 2.50
LAD2 Joc Pederson .40 1.00
LAD3 Yasiel Puig 1.00 2.50
LAD4 Hyun-Jin Ryu .60 1.50
LAD5 Zach Lee .30 .75
NYM1 Travis d'Arnaud .30 .75
NYM2 Zack Wheeler .50 1.25
NYM3 Noah Syndergaard .30 .75
NYM4 Michael Fulmer .40 1.00
NYM5 Wilmer Flores .30 .75
NYY1 Gary Sanchez .75 2.00
NYY2 Mason Williams .30 .75
NYY3 Tyler Austin .40 1.00
NYY4 Mark Montgomery .40 1.00
NYY5 Ty Hensley .30 .75
PPI1 Gerrit Cole 1.50 4.00
PPI2 Jameson Taillon .30 .75
PPI3 Gregory Polanco .50 1.25
PPI4 Alen Hanson .30 .75
PPI5 Luis Heredia .30 .75
SDP1 Jedd Gyorko .30 .75
SDP2 Rymer Liriano .25 .60
SDP3 Max Fried 1.00 2.50
SDP4 Austin Hedges .30 .75
SDP5 Casey Kelly .30 .75
SFG1 Kyle Crick .40 1.00
SFG2 Gary Brown .25 .60
SFG3 Joe Panik .40 1.00
SFG4 Clayton Blackburn .40 1.00
SFG5 Chris Stratton .25 .60
STL1 Oscar Taveras .30 .75
STL2 Shelby Miller .60 1.50
STL3 Carlos Martinez .40 1.00
STL4 Trevor Rosenthal .50 1.25
STL5 Kolten Wong .25 .60
TBJ1 Aaron Sanchez .30 .75
TBJ2 D.J. Davis .30 .75
TBJ3 Sean Nolin .30 .75
TBJ4 Marcus Stroman .40 1.00
TBJ5 Daniel Norris .30 .75
TBR1 Wil Myers .30 .75
TBR2 Taylor Guerrieri .25 .60
TBR3 Jake Odorizzi .30 .75
TBR4 Hak-Ju Lee .25 .60
TBR5 Blake Snell .30 .75

2013 Bowman Chrome Cream of the Crop Mini Blue Wave Refractors

*REF: 2.5X TO 6X BASIC
STATED ODDS 1:98 HOBBY
STATED PRINT RUN 250 SER.#'d SETS

2013 Bowman Chrome Prospect Autographs

BOW. ODDS 1:38 HOBBY
BOW.CHROME ODDS 1:20 HOBBY
PLATE PRINT RUN 1 SET PER COLOR
BLACK-CYAN-MAGENTA-YELLOW ISSUED
NO PLATE PRICING DUE TO SCARCITY
BOW.EXCH DEADLINE 5/31/2016
BOW.CHR EXCH DEADLINE 9/30/2016
AA Andrew Aplin 3.00 8.00
AAL Arismendy Alcantara 3.00 8.00
AH Alen Hanson 4.00 10.00
AM Alex Meyer 3.00 8.00
AM Adalberto Mejia 3.00 8.00
AMO Adalberto Mondesi 30.00 80.00
AP Adys Portillo 3.00 8.00
AR Andre Rienzo 3.00 8.00
AS Austin Schotts 3.00 8.00
AW Adam Walker 3.00 8.00
BB Byron Buxton 30.00 80.00
BG Brian Goodwin 3.00 8.00
CA Cody Asche 3.00 8.00
CB Christian Bethancourt 3.00 8.00
CBL Clayton Blackburn 3.00 8.00
CC Carlos Correa 60.00 150.00
CE C.J. Edwards 3.00 8.00
CG Cameron Gallagher 3.00 8.00
CT Carlos Tocci 5.00 12.00
DC Dylan Cozens 4.00 10.00
DC Daniel Corcino 3.00 8.00
DG Deivi Grullon 3.00 8.00
DH Dilson Herrera 5.00 12.00
DL Dan Langfield 3.00 8.00
DP Dorssys Paulino 3.00 8.00
DV Danry Vasquez 3.00 8.00
EB Eddie Butler 3.00 8.00
EE Edwin Escobar 3.00 8.00
EJ Erik Johnson 3.00 8.00
ER Eduardo Rodriguez 5.00 12.00
GA Gioskar Amaya 3.00 8.00
GG Gabriel Guerrero 3.00 8.00
GP Gregory Polanco 6.00 15.00
HC Harold Castro 3.00 8.00
HL Hak-Ju Lee 3.00 8.00
HO Henry Owens 3.00 8.00
JA Jorge Alfaro 5.00 12.00
JA Jayson Aquino 3.00 8.00
JB Jorge Bonifacio 5.00 12.00
JB Jose Berrios 10.00 25.00
JBA Jeremy Baltz 3.00 8.00
JBE Jairo Beras 3.00 8.00
JBI Jesse Biddle 3.00 8.00
JC J.T. Chargois 3.00 8.00
JL Jake Lamb 4.00 10.00
JM Julio Morban 3.00 8.00
JN Justin Nicolino 3.00 8.00
JN Jimmy Nelson 3.00 8.00
JP Jose Peraza 4.00 10.00
JPO Jorge Polanco 4.00 10.00
JT Jake Thompson 3.00 8.00
KD Keury de la Cruz 3.00 8.00
KP Kevin Pillar 4.00 10.00
KS Kyle Smith 3.00 8.00
LG Lucas Giolito 20.00 50.00
LM Lance McCullers 10.00 25.00
LMA Luis Mateo 3.00 8.00
LME Luis Merejo 3.00 8.00
LS Luis Sardinas 3.00 8.00
LT Luis Torrens 3.00 8.00
MA Miguel Almonte 3.00 8.00
MAJ Miguel Andujar 40.00 100.00
MC Mauricio Cabrera 4.00 10.00
MK Mike Kickham 3.00 8.00
MM Mark Montgomery 3.00 8.00
MO Matt Olson 20.00 50.00
MR Matt Reynolds 3.00 8.00
MS Matthew Skole 3.00 8.00
MW Mac Williamson 4.00 10.00
MWI Matt Wisler 3.00 8.00
NT Nik Turley 3.00 8.00
NTR Nick Tropeano 3.00 8.00
OA Oswaldo Arcia 4.00 10.00
OG Onelki Garcia 3.00 8.00
PK Patrick Kivlehan 3.00 8.00
PL Patrick Leonard 4.00 10.00
PW Patrick Wisdom 3.00 8.00
RD Rafael De Paula 3.00 8.00
RM Rafael Montero 3.00 8.00
RN Renato Nunez 6.00 15.00
RO Roberto Osuna 4.00 10.00
RQ Roman Quinn 3.00 8.00
RR Rio Ruiz 3.00 8.00
RRO Ronny Rodriguez 3.00 8.00
SP Stephen Piscotty 5.00 12.00
SR Stefen Romero 3.00 8.00
SS Sam Selman 3.00 8.00
TG Tyler Glasnow 6.00 15.00
TH Tyler Heineman 3.00 8.00
TM Tom Murphy 5.00 12.00
TP Tyler Pike 3.00 8.00
TW Taijuan Walker 3.00 8.00
VR Victor Roache 4.00 10.00
VS Victor Sanchez 3.00 8.00
WF Wilfredo Rodriguez 3.00 8.00
WM Wyatt Mathisen 3.00 8.00
YA Yeison Asencio 3.00 8.00
YP Yasiel Puig 60.00 150.00
YV Yordano Ventura 6.00 15.00

2013 Bowman Chrome Prospect Autographs Blue Refractors

*BLUE REF: 1.2X TO 3X BASIC
BOW.ODDS 1:578 HOBBY
BOW.CHROME ODDS 1:227 HOBBY
STATED PRINT RUN 150 SER.#'d SETS
BOW.EXCH DEADLINE 5/31/2016
BOW.CHR EXCH DEADLINE 9/30/2016
CC Carlos Correa 500.00 1000.00
JB Jose Berrios 50.00 120.00
MAJ Miguel Andujar 125.00 300.00

2013 Bowman Chrome Prospect Autographs Blue Wave Refractors

STATED PRINT RUN 50 SER.#'d SETS
AA Andrew Aplin 10.00 25.00
AAL Arismendy Alcantara 10.00 25.00
AH Alen Hanson 12.00 30.00
AM Alex Meyer 10.00 25.00
AM Adalberto Mejia 10.00 25.00
AP Adys Portillo 6.00 15.00
AR Andre Rienzo 10.00 25.00
AS Austin Schotts 10.00 25.00
AW Adam Walker 10.00 25.00
BB Byron Buxton 300.00 600.00
BG Brian Goodwin 20.00 50.00
CA Cody Asche 8.00 20.00
CB Christian Bethancourt 12.00 30.00
CC Carlos Correa 600.00 1200.00
CE C.J. Edwards 20.00 50.00
CG Cameron Gallagher 6.00 15.00
CT Carlos Tocci 20.00 50.00
DC Dylan Cozens 40.00 100.00
DC Daniel Corcino 12.00 30.00
DG Deivi Grullon 30.00 60.00
DH Dilson Herrera 20.00 50.00
DL Dan Langfield 12.00 30.00
DP Dorssys Paulino 12.00 30.00
DV Danry Vasquez 12.50 30.00
EB Eddie Butler 25.00 60.00
EE Edwin Escobar 20.00 50.00
EJ Erik Johnson 6.00 15.00
ER Eduardo Rodriguez 60.00 150.00
GA Gioskar Amaya 20.00 50.00
GG Gabriel Guerrero 6.00 15.00
HC Harold Castro 8.00 20.00
HL Hak-Ju Lee 10.00 25.00
HO Henry Owens 10.00 25.00
JA Jayson Aquino 8.00 20.00
JB Jorge Bonifacio 20.00 50.00
JB Jose Berrios 75.00 200.00
JBA Jeremy Baltz 10.00 25.00
JBE Jairo Beras 10.00 25.00
JBI Jesse Biddle 6.00 15.00
JC J.T. Chargois 6.00 15.00
JL Jake Lamb 8.00 20.00
JM Julio Morban 6.00 15.00
JN Justin Nicolino 12.50 30.00
JN Jimmy Nelson 12.50 30.00
JP Jose Peraza 40.00 100.00
JPO Jorge Polanco 20.00 50.00
JT Jake Thompson 8.00 20.00
KD Keury de la Cruz 8.00 20.00
KP Kevin Pillar 20.00 50.00
KS Kyle Smith 8.00 20.00
LG Lucas Giolito 100.00 250.00
LM Lance McCullers
LMA Luis Mateo 8.00 20.00
LME Luis Merejo 15.00 40.00
LS Luis Sardinas 6.00 15.00
LT Luis Torrens 30.00 80.00
MA Miguel Almonte 12.00 30.00
MAJ Miguel Andujar 150.00 400.00
MC Mauricio Cabrera 15.00 40.00
MK Mike Kickham 6.00 15.00
MM Mark Montgomery 6.00 15.00
MR Matt Reynolds 15.00 40.00
MS Matthew Skole 15.00 40.00
MW Mac Williamson 20.00 50.00
MWI Matt Wisler 10.00 25.00
NT Nik Turley 10.00 25.00
NTR Nick Tropeano 10.00 25.00
OA Oswaldo Arcia 15.00 40.00
OG Onelki Garcia 12.50 30.00
PK Patrick Kivlehan 15.00 40.00
PL Patrick Leonard
PW Patrick Wisdom 15.00 40.00
RD Rafael De Paula 15.00 40.00
RM Rafael Montero 6.00 15.00
RN Renato Nunez 25.00 60.00
RO Roberto Osuna
RQ Roman Quinn 6.00 15.00
RR Rio Ruiz
RRO Ronny Rodriguez 15.00 40.00
SP Stephen Piscotty 10.00 25.00
SR Stefen Romero 10.00 25.00
SS Sam Selman 15.00 40.00
TG Tyler Glasnow 20.00 50.00
TH Tyler Heineman 10.00 25.00
TM Tom Murphy 12.00 30.00
TP Tyler Pike 10.00 25.00
TW Taijuan Walker 25.00 60.00
VR Victor Roache 12.00 30.00
VS Victor Sanchez 12.00 30.00
WF Wilfredo Rodriguez 6.00 15.00
WM Wyatt Mathisen 6.00 15.00
YA Yeison Asencio 6.00 15.00
YP Yasiel Puig 125.00 300.00
YV Yordano Ventura 25.00 60.00

2013 Bowman Chrome Prospect Autographs Gold Refractors

*GOLD REF: 2.5X TO 6X BASIC
BOW.STATED ODDS 1:1734 HOBBY
BOW.CHROME ODDS 1:682 HOBBY
STATED PRINT RUN 50 SER.#'d SETS
BOW.EXCH DEADLINE 5/31/2016
BOW.CHR EXCH DEADLINE 9/30/2016
BB Byron Buxton 400.00 800.00
CC Carlos Correa 600.00 1200.00
JB Jose Berrios 75.00 200.00
LS Luis Sardinas 30.00 60.00
MAJ Miguel Andujar 150.00 400.00
YP Yasiel Puig 400.00 800.00

2013 Bowman Chrome Prospect Autographs Refractors

*REF: .5X TO 1.2X BASIC
BOW.STATED ODDS 1:174 HOBBY
BOW.CHROME ODDS 1:68 HOBBY
STATED PRINT RUN 500 SER.#'d SETS
BOW.EXCH DEADLINE 5/31/2016
BOW.CHROME DEADLINE 9/30/2016
JB Jose Berrios 20.00 50.00

2013 Bowman Chrome Prospects

BOWMAN PRINTING PLATE ODDS 1:1881
PLATE PRINT RUN 1 SET PER COLOR
BLACK-CYAN-MAGENTA-YELLOW ISSUED
NO PLATE PRICING DUE TO SCARCITY
BCP1 Byron Buxton .60 1.50
BCP2 Jonathan Griffin .25 .60
BCP3 Mark Montgomery .40 1.00
BCP4 Gioskar Amaya .25 .60
BCP5 Lucas Giolito .40 1.00
BCP6 Danny Salazar .50 1.25
BCP7 Jesse Hahn .25 .60
BCP8 Tayler Scott .25 .60
BCP9 Ji-Man Choi .30 .75
BCP10 Tony Renda .25 .60
BCP11 Jamie Callahan .25 .60
BCP12 Collin Wiles .25 .60
BCP13 Tanner Rahier .30 .75
BCP14 Max White .25 .60
BCP15 Jeff Gelalich .25 .60
BCP16 Tyler Gonzales .25 .60
BCP17 Mitch Nay .25 .60
BCP18 Dane Phillips .25 .60
BCP19 Carson Kelly .30 .75
BCP20 Darwin Rivera .25 .60
BCP21 Arismendy Alcantara .40 1.00
BCP22 Brandon Maurer .30 .75
BCP23 Jin-De Jhang .25 .60
BCP24 Bruce Rondon .25 .60
BCP25 Jonathan Schoop .25 .60
BCP26 Cory Hall .25 .60
BCP27 Cory Vaughn .25 .60
BCP28 Danny Muno .25 .60
BCP29 Edwin Diaz .50 1.25
BCP30 Willians Astudillo .25 .60
BCP31 Hansel Robles .25 .60
BCP32 Harold Castro .25 .60
BCP33 Ismael Guillon .25 .60
BCP34 Jeremy Moore .25 .60
BCP35 Jose Cisnero .25 .60
BCP36 Jose Peraza .25 .60
BCP37 Jose Ramirez .30 .75
BCP38 Christian Villanueva .25 .60
BCP39 Brett Gerritse .25 .60
BCP40 Kris Hall .25 .60
BCP41 Matt Stites .25 .60
BCP42 Matt Wisler .25 .60
BCP43 Matthew Koch .25 .60
BCP44 Micah Johnson .30 .75
BCP45 Michael Reed .25 .60
BCP46 Michael Snyder .25 .60
BCP47 Michael Taylor .25 .60
BCP48 Nolan Sanburn .25 .60
BCP49 Patrick Leonard .25 .60
BCP50 Rafael Montero .40 1.00
BCP51 Ronnie Freeman .25 .60
BCP52 Stephen Piscotty .50 1.25
BCP53 Steven Moya .40 1.00
BCP54 Chris McFarland .25 .60
BCP55 Todd Kibby .25 .60
BCP56 Tyler Heineman .25 .60
BCP57 Wade Hinkle .25 .60
BCP58 Wilfredo Rodriguez .25 .60
BCP59 William Cuevas .25 .60
BCP60 Yordano Ventura .30 .75
BCP61 Zach Bird .25 .60
BCP62 Socrates Brito .40 1.00
BCP63 Ben Rowen .25 .60
BCP64 Seth Maness .25 .60
BCP65 Corey Dickerson .30 .75
BCP66 Travis Witherspoon .25 .60
BCP67 Travis Shaw .25 .60
BCP68 Lenny Linsky .25 .60
BCP69 Anderson Feliz .25 .60
BCP70 Casey Stevenson .25 .60
BCP71 Pedro Ruiz .25 .60
BCP72 Christian Bethancourt .40 1.00
BCP73 Pedro Guerra .25 .60
BCP74 Ronald Guzman .40 1.00
BCP75 Jake Thompson .25 .60
BCP76 Brian Goodwin .30 .75
BCP77 Jorge Bonifacio .30 .75
BCP78 Dilson Herrera .75 2.00
BCP79 Gregory Polanco .50 1.25
BCP80 Alex Meyer .25 .60
BCP81 Gabriel Encinas .25 .60
BCP82 Yeicok Calderon .25 .60
BCP83 Rio Ruiz .25 .60
BCP84 Luis Sardinas .25 .60
BCP85 Fu-Lin Kuo .30 .75
BCP86 Kelvin De Leon .25 .60
BCP87 Wyatt Mathisen .25 .60
BCP88 Dorssys Paulino .30 .75
BCP89 William Oliver .25 .60
BCP90 Rony Bautista .25 .60
BCP91 Gabriel Guerrero .30 .75
BCP92 Patrick Kivlehan .25 .60
BCP93 Ericson Leonora .25 .60
BCP94 Mikeson Oliberto .25 .60
BCP95 Roman Quinn .40 1.00
BCP96 Shane Broyles .25 .60
BCP97 Cody Buckel .25 .60
BCP98 Clayton Blackburn .40 1.00
BCP99 Evan Rutckyj .25 .60
BCP100 Carlos Correa 2.50 6.00
BCP101 Ronny Rodriguez .25 .60
BCP102 Jayson Aquino .25 .60
BCP103 Adalberto Mondesi .75 2.00
BCP104 Victor Sanchez .30 .75
BCP105 Jairo Beras .40 1.00
BCP106 Stefen Romero .25 .60
BCP107 Alfredo Escalera-Maldonado .30 .75
BCP108 Kevin Medrano .25 .60
BCP109 Carlos Sanchez .25 .60
BCP110 Sam Selman .25 .60
BCP111 Daniel Watts .25 .60
BCP112A Nolan Fontana .30 .75
BCP112B N.Fontana SP VAR 10.00 25.00
BCP113A Addison Russell .40 1.00
BCP113B A.Russell SP VAR 15.00 40.00
BCP114 Mauricio Cabrera .25 .60
BCP115 Marco Hernandez .25 .60
BCP116 Jack Leathersich .25 .60
BCP117 Edwin Escobar .30 .75
BCP118 Onelki Garcia .25 .60
BCP119 Arismendy Alcantara .40 1.00
BCP120A Deven Marrero .25 .60
BCP120B D.Marrero SP VAR 15.00 40.00
BCP121 Adam Walker .30 .75
BCP122 Erik Johnson .25 .60
BCP123A Stryker Trahan .25 .60
BCP123B S.Trahan SP VAR 6.00 15.00
BCP124 Dan Langfield .25 .60
BCP125A Corey Seager 1.00 2.50
BCP125B C.Seager SP VAR 15.00 40.00
BCP126 Harold Castro .25 .60
BCP127A Victor Roache .30 .75
BCP127B V.Roache SP VAR 10.00 25.00
BCP128 Deivi Grullon .25 .60
BCP129 Francellis Montas .25 .60
BCP130 Mike Piazza .25 .60
BCP131 Miguel Almonte .25 .60
BCP132 Renato Nunez .50 1.25
BCP133 Tzu-Wei Lin .30 .75
BCP134 Tyler Glasnow .40 1.00
BCP135 Zach Eflin .30 .75
BCP136 Gustavo Cabrera .60 1.50
BCP137 J.T. Chargois .25 .60
BCP138A Max Fried 1.00 2.50
BCP139 Ty Buttrey .25 .60
BCP140 Jimmy Nelson .25 .60
BCP141 Alexis Rivera .25 .60
BCP142 Jeremy Rathjen .25 .60
BCP143 Ismael Guillon .25 .60
BCP144 C.J. Edwards .40 1.00
BCP145 Jorge Martinez .25 .60
BCP146 Nik Turley .25 .60
BCP147 Jeremy Baltz .25 .60
BCP148 Wilfredo Rodriguez .25 .60
BCP149 Matt Wisler .25 .60
BCP150A Henry Owens .30 .75
BCP150B H.Owens SP VAR 10.00 25.00
BCP151 Luis Merejo .25 .60
BCP152A Pat Light .25 .60
BCP152B P.Light SP VAR 6.00 15.00
BCP153 Rainy Lara .25 .60
BCP154A Chris Stratton .25 .60
BCP154B C.Stratton SP VAR 15.00 40.00
BCP155 Taylor Dugas .30 .75
BCP156 Andrew Toles .25 .60
BCP157 Matt Reynolds .30 .75
BCP158A Tyrone Taylor .25 .60
BCP158B T.Taylor SP VAR 10.00 25.00
BCP159 Andry Ubiera .30 .75
BCP160 Miguel Andujar 2.00 5.00
BCP161 Jake Lamb .40 1.00
BCP162 Parker Bridwell .25 .60
BCP163 Matt Curry .25 .60
BCP164 Viosergy Rosa .25 .60
BCP165 Carlos Tocci .25 .60
BCP166 Ryan Court .25 .60
BCP167 Breyvic Valera .30 .75
BCP168 David Holmberg .25 .60
BCP169 Derek Jones .25 .60
BCP170 R.J. Alvarez .25 .60
BCP171 Adalberto Mejia .25 .60
BCP172 Saxon Butler .25 .60
BCP173 Nestor Molina .25 .60
BCP174 Rafael De Paula .25 .60
BCP175 Adys Portillo .25 .60
BCP176 Yohander Mendez .25 .60
BCP177 Cameron Gallagher .25 .60
BCP178A Rock Shoulders .25 .60
BCP178B R.Shoulders SP VAR 10.00 25.00
BCP179 Nick Tropeano .25 .60
BCP180 Tyler Heineman .25 .60
BCP181 Wade Hinkle .25 .60
BCP182 Roberto Osuna .25 .60
BCP183 Drew Steckenrider .25 .60
BCP184 Austin Schotts .30 .75
BCP185 Joan Gregorio .30 .75
BCP186 Dylan Cozens .25 .60
BCP187 Jose Peraza .30 .75
BCP188 Mitch Brown .25 .60
BCP189 Yeison Asencio .25 .60
BCP190A Danry Vasquez .25 .60
BCP191 Jose Berrios .40 1.00
BCP192 Cody Asche .40 1.00
BCP193 Julian Yan .25 .60
BCP194A Tyler Pike .25 .60
BCP194B T.Pike SP VAR 6.00 15.00
BCP195 Gabriel Encinas .25 .60
BCP196 Luis Mateo .25 .60
BCP197 Michael Perez .25 .60
BCP198 Hanser Alberto .25 .60
BCP199 Andrew Aplin .25 .60
BCP200A Lance McCullers .25 .60
BCP200B L.McCullers SP VAR 10.00 25.00
BCP201 Tom Murphy .25 .60
BCP202 Patrick Leonard .25 .60
BCP203 B.J. Boyd .25 .60
BCP204A Rafael Montero .40 1.00
BCP204B R.Montero SP VAR 15.00 40.00
BCP205 Kyle Smith .25 .60
BCP206A Albert Almora .50 1.25
BCP206B A.Almora SP VAR 15.00 40.00
BCP207A Eduardo Rodriguez .75 2.00
BCP207B E.Rodriguez SP VAR 12.50 30.00
BCP208 Anthony Alford .25 .60
BCP209 Dustin Geiger .25 .60
BCP210 Andre Rienzo .25 .60
BCP211 Jin-De Jhang .25 .60
BCP212 Jorge Polanco .25 .60
BCP213A Jorge Alfaro .50 1.25
BCP213B J.Alfaro SP VAR 10.00 25.00
BCP214 Luis Torrens .25 .60
BCP215 Luiz Gohara .30 .75
BCP216 Luigi Rodriguez .25 .60
BCP217A Courtney Hawkins .25 .60
BCP217B C.Hawkins SP VAR 10.00 25.00
BCP218 Tommy Kahnle .25 .60
BCP219 Keury de la Cruz .25 .60
BCP220 Mac Williamson .40 1.00

2013 Bowman Chrome Prospects Refractors

*REF 1-110: 2.5X TO 6X BASIC
*REF 111-220: 2X TO 5X BASIC
BOWMAN ODDS 1:67 HOBBY
1-110 PRINT RUN 500 SER.#'d SETS
111-220 ARE NOT SERIAL NUMBERED

2013 Bowman Chrome Prospects Black Refractors

*BLK 1-110 REF: 6X TO 15X BASIC
BOWMAN ODDS 1:217 HOBBY
1-110 PRINT RUN 99 SER.#'d SETS
111-220 PRINT RUN 15 SER.#'d SETS
NO PRICING ON QTY 15

2013 Bowman Chrome Prospects Blue Refractors

*BLUE REF: 5X TO 12X BASIC
BOWMAN ODDS 1:134 HOBBY
STATED PRINT RUN 250 SER.#'d SETS

2013 Bowman Chrome Prospects Blue Wave Refractors

*BLUE WAVE REF: 4X TO 10X BASIC

2013 Bowman Chrome Prospects Gold Refractors

*GOLD REF: 10X TO 25X BASIC
BOWMAN ODDS 1:670 HOBBY
STATED PRINT RUN 50 SER.#'d SETS

2013 Bowman Chrome Prospects Green Refractors

*GREEN REF: 2.5X TO 6X BASIC

2013 Bowman Chrome Prospects Magenta Refractors

*MAGENTA REF: 12X TO 30X BASIC
STATED PRINT RUN 35 SER.#'d SETS

2013 Bowman Chrome Prospects Purple Refractors

*PURPLE REF: 5X TO 12X BASIC
STATED PRINT RUN 199 SER.#'d SETS

2013 Bowman Chrome Prospects X-Fractors

*X-FRACTORS: 3X TO 8X BASIC

2013 Bowman Chrome Rookie Autographs

BOW.ODDS 1:316 HOBBY
BOW.CHROME ODDS 1:2444 HOBBY
PLATE PRINT RUN 1 SET PER COLOR
BLACK-CYAN-MAGENTA-YELLOW ISSUED
NO PLATE PRICING DUE TO SCARCITY
BOW.EXCH DEADLINE 5/31/2016
BOW.CHR.EXCH DEADLINE 9/30/2016
AE Adam Eaton 3.00 8.00
AG Avisail Garcia 3.00 8.00
BM Brandon Maurer 4.00 10.00
BR Bruce Rondon 10.00 25.00
CK Casey Kelly 3.00 8.00
DB Dylan Bundy 10.00 25.00
DR Darin Ruf 3.00 8.00
EG Evan Gattis 20.00 50.00
HJR Hyun-Jin Ryu 50.00 120.00
JF Jeurys Familia 3.00 8.00
JO Jake Odorizzi 5.00 12.00
JP J.Profar Field 15.00 40.00
JP J.Profar Throw 12.00 30.00
MM Manny Machado 25.00 60.00
MO Mike Olt 6.00 15.00
NM Nick Maronde 3.00 8.00
PR Paco Rodriguez 4.00 10.00
SM Shelby Miller 5.00 12.00
TS Tyler Skaggs 3.00 8.00
WM Wil Myers 20.00 50.00

2013 Bowman Chrome Rookie Autographs Refractors

*REF: .5X TO 1.2X BASIC
STATED ODDS 1:729 HOBBY
STATED PRINT RUN 500 SER.#'d SETS
BOW.EXCH DEADLINE 05/31/2016

2013 Bowman Chrome Rookie Autographs Blue Refractors

*BLUE REF: .75X TO 2X BASIC
*BLUE REF/99: .75X TO 2X BASIC
STATED ODDS 1:1121 HOBBY
BOW.CHROME ODDS 1:6297 HOBBY
STATED PRINT RUN 250 SER.#'d SETS
BOW.CHR. PRINT RUN 99 SER.#'d SETS
EXCHANGE DEADLINE 05/31/2016
BOW.CHR.EXCH DEADLINE 9/30/2016
EG Evan Gattis 40.00 100.00
HJR Hyun-Jin Ryu 100.00 250.00

2013 Bowman Chrome Rookie Autographs Gold Refractors

*GOLD REF: 1.2X TO 3X BASIC
BOWMAN ODDS 1:5602 HOBBY
BOW.CHROME ODDS 1:12,522 HOBBY
STATED PRINT RUN 50 SER.#'d SETS
BOW.EXCH DEADLINE 05/31/2016
BOW.CHR.EXCH DEADLINE 9/30/2016
DB Dylan Bundy 40.00 100.00
HJR Hyun-Jin Ryu 125.00 300.00

2013 Bowman Rookie Reprint Blue Sapphire Refractors

COMPLETE SET (64) 40.00 100.00
BOWMAN ODDS 1:24 HOBBY
BOW.PLATINUM ODDS 1:20 HOBBY
BOW.CHROME ODDS 1:18 HOBBY
68 Jim Thome .40 1.00
71 David Ortiz .60 1.50
78 Yasiel Puig 12.50 30.00
AB Adrian Beltre .60 1.50
AG Adrian Gonzalez .50 1.25
AJ Andruw Jones .40 1.00
AK Al Kaline .60 1.50
AM Andrew McCutchen .60 1.50
AP Andy Pettitte .50 1.25
264 Albert Pujols .75 2.00
AR Alex Rodriguez .75 2.00
350 Alfonso Soriano .50 1.25
BF Bob Feller .50 1.25
BH Bryce Harper 1.00 2.50
BP Buster Posey .75 2.00
CB Carlos Beltran .50 1.25
CG Curtis Granderson .50 1.25
CK Clayton Kershaw 1.25 3.00
CS CC Sabathia .50 1.25
CU Chase Utley .50 1.25
15 Derek Jeter 6.00 15.00
DS Duke Snider .50 1.25
DW David Wright .50 1.25
EL Evan Longoria .50 1.25
EM Eddie Mathews .60 1.50
FH Felix Hernandez .50 1.25
FT Frank Thomas .60 1.50
BCP86 Gerrit Cole 2.50 6.00
HA Hank Aaron 1.25 3.00
JH Josh Hamilton .50 1.25
JR Jose Reyes .50 1.25
JR Jackie Robinson .60 1.50
JV Joey Votto .60 1.50
174 Justin Verlander .60 1.50
MC Matt Cain .50 1.25
MH Matt Holliday .60 1.50
MK Matthew Kemp .50 1.25
MR Mariano Rivera .75 2.00
MS Michael Stanton .60 1.50
MT Mark Teixeira .50 1.25
MT Mike Trout 10.00 25.00
PF Prince Fielder .50 1.25
PK Paul Konerko .50 1.25
PR Phil Rizzuto .50 1.25
RB Ryan Braun .50 1.25
BDP124 Robinson Cano .50 1.25
RH Roy Halladay .50 1.25
SM Stan Musial 1.00 2.50
SS Stephen Strasburg .60 1.50
378 Todd Helton .50 1.25
TH Torii Hunter .40 1.00
TL Tim Lincecum .50 1.25
98 Ted Williams 1.25 3.00
WF Whitey Ford .50 1.25
WM Willie Mays 1.25 3.00
WS Warren Spahn .50 1.25
YD Yu Darvish .60 1.50
181 Jimmy Rollins .60 1.50
220 Ken Griffey Jr. 1.25 3.00
242 Ernie Banks .60 1.50
266 John Smoltz .60 1.50
379 Joe Mauer .50 1.25
421 Jose Bautista .50 1.25
BDP138 Ryan Howard .50 1.25

2013 Bowman Chrome Draft

STATED PLATE ODDS 1:2230 HOBBY
PLATE PRINT RUN 1 SET PER COLOR
BLACK-CYAN-MAGENTA-YELLOW ISSUED
NO PLATE PRICING DUE TO SCARCITY
1 Yasiel Puig RC 1.25 3.00
2 Tyler Skaggs RC .50 1.25
3 Nathan Karns RC .30 .75
4 Manny Machado RC 2.00 5.00
5 Anthony Rendon RC 1.50 4.00
6 Gerrit Cole RC 2.00 5.00
7 Sonny Gray RC .50 1.25
8 Henry Urrutia RC .40 1.00
9 Zoilo Almonte RC .40 1.00
10 Jose Fernandez RC .75 2.00
11 Danny Salazar RC .60 1.50
12 Nick Franklin RC .40 1.00
13 Mike Kickham RC .30 .75
14 Alex Colome RC .40 1.00
15 Josh Phegley RC .30 .75
16 Drake Britton RC .40 1.00
17 Marcell Ozuna RC .75 2.00
18 Oswaldo Arcia RC .30 .75
19 Didi Gregorius RC 1.25 3.00
20 Zack Wheeler RC .60 1.50
21 Michael Wacha RC .40 1.00
22 Kyle Gibson RC .50 1.25
23 Johnny Hellweg RC .30 .75
24 Dylan Bundy RC .75 2.00
25 Tony Cingrani RC .60 1.50
26 Jurickson Profar RC .40 1.00
27 Scooter Gennett RC .50 1.25
28 Grant Green RC .50 1.25
29 Brad Miller RC .40 1.00
30 Hyun-Jin Ryu RC .75 2.00
31 Jedd Gyorko RC .40 1.00
32 Shelby Miller RC .75 2.00
33 Sean Nolin RC .40 1.00
34 Allen Webster RC .40 1.00
35 Corey Dickerson RC .40 1.00
36 Jarred Cosart RC .40 1.00
37 Evan Gattis RC .60 1.50
38 Kevin Gausman RC .50 1.25
39 Alex Wood RC .40 1.00
40 Christian Yelich RC 2.50 6.00
41 Nolan Arenado RC 1.50 4.00
42 Matt Magill RC .30 .75
43 Jackie Bradley Jr. RC .75 2.00
44 Mike Zunino RC .50 1.25
45 Wil Myers RC .40 1.00

2013 Bowman Chrome Draft Black Refractors
*BLACK REF: 5X TO 12X BASIC
STATED ODDS 1:224 HOBBY
STATED PRINT RUN 35 SER.#'d SETS
10 Jose Fernandez 10.00 25.00

2013 Bowman Chrome Draft Black Wave Refractors
*BLACK WAVE: 2X TO 5X BASIC

2013 Bowman Chrome Draft Blue Refractors
*BLUE REF: 2X TO 5X BASIC
STATED ODDS 1:93 HOBBY
STATED PRINT RUN 99 SER.#'d SETS

2013 Bowman Chrome Draft Blue Wave Refractors
*BLUE WAVE: 1.5X TO 4X BASIC

2013 Bowman Chrome Draft Gold Refractors
*GOLD REF: 5X TO 12X BASIC
STATED ODDS 1:185 HOBBY
STATED PRINT RUN 50 SER.#'d SETS
4 Manny Machado 30.00 60.00

2013 Bowman Chrome Draft Green Refractors
*GREEN REF: 2.5X TO 6X BASIC
STATED ODDS 1:124 HOBBY
STATED PRINT RUN 75 SER.#'d SETS

2013 Bowman Chrome Draft Orange Refractors
*ORANGE REF: 6X TO 15X BASIC
STATED PRINT RUN 25 SER.#'d SETS
4 Manny Machado 40.00 80.00

2013 Bowman Chrome Draft Red Wave Refractors
*RED WAVE: 6X TO 15X BASIC
STATED PRINT RUN 25 SER.#'d SETS
4 Manny Machado 40.00 80.00
10 Jose Fernandez 30.00 60.00

2013 Bowman Chrome Draft Silver Wave Refractors
*SILVER WAVE: 6X TO 15X BASIC
STATED PRINT RUN 25 SER.#'d SETS
10 Jose Fernandez 30.00 60.00

2013 Bowman Chrome Draft Draft Pick Autographs
STATED ODDS 1:35 HOBBY
K.BRYANT ISSUED IN 14 BOW.INCEPTION
EXCHANGE DEADLINE 11/30/2016
AB Aaron Blair 3.00 8.00
AC Andrew Church 3.00 8.00
AJ Aaron Judge 300.00 800.00
AK Andrew Knapp 3.00 8.00
AM Austin Meadows 25.00 60.00
BS Braden Shipley 3.00 8.00
BT Blake Taylor 3.00 8.00
CA Chris Anderson 3.00 8.00
CF Clint Frazier 40.00 100.00
CM Colin Moran 3.00 8.00
CS Chance Sisco 6.00 15.00
CSA Cord Sandberg 8.00 20.00
DP D.J. Peterson 3.00 8.00
DPE Dustin Peterson 3.00 8.00
DS Dominic Smith 15.00 40.00
EJ Eric Jagielo 3.00 8.00
HD Hunter Dozier 3.00 8.00
HG Hunter Green 3.00 8.00
HH Hunter Harvey 3.00 8.00
HR Hunter Renfroe 3.00 8.00
IC Ian Clarkin 3.00 8.00
JC J.P. Crawford 3.00 8.00
JCR Jonathon Crawford 3.00 8.00
JD Jon Denney 3.00 8.00
JG Jonathan Gray 3.00 8.00
JH Josh Hart 3.00 8.00
JW Justin Williams 6.00 15.00
KB K.Brynt Issued in 2014 150.00 400.00
KF Kevin Franklin 3.00 8.00
KS Kohl Stewart 3.00 8.00
KZ Kevin Ziomek 3.00 8.00
MG Marco Gonzales 8.00 20.00
ML Michael Lorenzen 3.00 8.00
NC Nick Ciuffo 3.00 8.00
OM Oscar Mercado 8.00 20.00
PE Phil Ervin 3.00 8.00
RE Ryan Eades 3.00 8.00
RJ Ryder Jones 3.00 8.00
RK Robert Kaminsky 3.00 8.00
RM Reese McGuire 4.00 10.00
RMC Ryan McMahon 6.00 15.00
RU Riley Unroe 3.00 8.00
TA Tim Anderson 50.00 120.00
TB Trey Ball 3.00 8.00
TD Travis Demeritte 3.00 8.00
TDA Tyler Danish 3.00 8.00
TW Trevor Williams 3.00 8.00
TWI Tom Windle 3.00 8.00

2013 Bowman Chrome Draft Draft Pick Autographs Black Refractors
*BLACK REF: 2.5X TO 6X BASIC
STATED ODDS 1:1097 HOBBY
STATED PRINT RUN 35 SER.#'d SETS
EXCHANGE DEADLINE 11/30/2016

2013 Bowman Chrome Draft Draft Pick Autographs Black Wave Refractors
*BLACK WAVE: 1.5X TO 4X BASIC
STATED PRINT RUN 50 SER.#'d SETS
EXCHANGE DEADLINE 11/30/2016

2013 Bowman Chrome Draft Draft Pick Autographs Blue Refractors
*BLUE REF: 1.5X TO 4X BASIC
STATED ODDS 1:659 HOBBY
STATED PRINT RUN 99 SER.#'d SETS
EXCHANGE DEADLINE 11/30/2016

2013 Bowman Chrome Draft Draft Pick Autographs Blue Wave Refractors
*BLUE WAVE: 1.5X TO 4X BASIC
STATED PRINT RUN 50 SER.#'d SETS
EXCHANGE DEADLINE 11/30/2016

2013 Bowman Chrome Draft Draft Pick Autographs Gold Refractors
*GOLD: 2.5X TO 6X BASIC
STATED ODDS 1:1309 HOBBY
STATED PRINT RUN 50 SER.#'d SETS
EXCHANGE DEADLINE 11/30/2016

2013 Bowman Chrome Draft Draft Pick Autographs Green Refractors
*GREEN REF: 1.5X TO 4X BASIC
STATED ODDS 1:872 HOBBY
STATED PRINT RUN 75 SER.#'d SETS
EXCHANGE DEADLINE 11/30/2016

2013 Bowman Chrome Draft Draft Pick Autographs Refractors
*REFRACTORS: .5X TO 1.2X BASIC
STATED ODDS 1:132 HOBBY
EXCHANGE DEADLINE 11/30/2016

2013 Bowman Chrome Draft Draft Picks
STATED PLATE ODDS 1:2230 HOBBY
PLATE PRINT RUN 1 SET PER COLOR
BLACK-CYAN-MAGENTA-YELLOW ISSUED
NO PLATE PRICING DUE TO SCARCITY
BDPP1 Dominic Smith .40 1.00
BDPP2 Kohl Stewart .30 .75
BDPP3 Josh Hart .25 .60
BDPP4 Nick Ciuffo .25 .60
BDPP5 Austin Meadows .50 1.25
BDPP6 Marco Gonzales .40 1.00
BDPP7 Jonathon Crawford .25 .60
BDPP8 D.J. Peterson .25 .60
BDPP9 Aaron Blair .25 .60
BDPP10 Dustin Peterson .25 .60
BDPP11 Billy Mckinney .30 .75
BDPP12 Braden Shipley .25 .60
BDPP13 Tim Anderson 1.00 2.50
BDPP14 Chris Anderson .30 .75
BDPP15 Clint Frazier 1.25 3.00
BDPP16 Hunter Renfroe .40 1.00
BDPP17 Andrew Knapp .25 .60
BDPP18 Corey Knebel .25 .60
BDPP19 Aaron Judge 12.00 30.00
BDPP20 Colin Moran .30 .75
BDPP21 Ian Clarkin .25 .60
BDPP22 Teddy Stankiewicz .30 .75
BDPP23 Blake Taylor .25 .60
BDPP24 Hunter Green .25 .60
BDPP25 Kevin Franklin .25 .60
BDPP26 Jonathan Gray .30 .75
BDPP27 Reese McGuire .30 .75
BDPP28 Travis Demeritte .30 .75
BDPP29 Kevin Ziomek .25 .60
BDPP30 Tom Windle .25 .60
BDPP31 Ryan McMahon .30 .75
BDPP32 J.P. Crawford .60 1.50
BDPP33 Hunter Harvey .30 .75
BDPP34 Chance Sisco .50 1.25
BDPP35 Riley Unroe .25 .60
BDPP36 Oscar Mercado .40 1.00
BDPP37 Gosuke Katoh .30 .75
BDPP38 Andrew Church .25 .60
BDPP39 Casey Meisner .25 .60
BDPP40 Ivan Wilson .25 .60
BDPP41 Drew Ward .30 .75
BDPP42 Thomas Milone .25 .60
BDPP43 Jon Denney .30 .75
BDPP44 Jan Hernandez .25 .60
BDPP45 Cord Sandberg .30 .75
BDPP46 Jake Sweaney .25 .60
BDPP47 Patrick Murphy .25 .60
BDPP48 Carlos Salazar .25 .60
BDPP49 Stephen Gonsalves .25 .60
BDPP50 Jonah Heim .25 .60
BDPP51 Kean Wong .25 .60
BDPP52 Tyler Wade .40 1.00
BDPP53 Austin Kubitza .25 .60
BDPP54 Trevor Williams .25 .60
BDPP55 Trae Arbet .25 .60
BDPP56 Ian McKinney .25 .60
BDPP57 Robert Kaminsky .30 .75
BDPP58 Brian Navarreto .25 .60
BDPP59 Alex Murphy .25 .60
BDPP60 Jordon Austin .30 .75
BDPP61 Jacob Nottingham .25 .60
BDPP62 Chris Rivera .25 .60
BDPP63 Trey Williams .40 1.00
BDPP64 Conner Greene .25 .60
BDPP65 Ian Stiffler .25 .60
BDPP66 Phil Ervin .25 .60
BDPP67 Roel Ramirez .25 .60
BDPP68 Michael Lorenzen .30 .75
BDPP69 Jason Martin .25 .60
BDPP70 Aaron Blanton .25 .60
BDPP71 Dylan Manwaring .25 .60
BDPP72 Luis Guillorme .30 .75
BDPP73 Brennan Middleton .25 .60
BDPP74 Austin Nicely .25 .60
BDPP75 Ian Hagenmiller .25 .60
BDPP76 Nelson Molina .25 .60
BDPP77 Denton Keys .30 .75
BDPP78 Kendall Coleman .25 .60
BDPP79 Alec Grosser .25 .60
BDPP80 Ricardo Bautista .25 .60
BDPP81 John Costa .25 .60
BDPP82 Joseph Odom .25 .60
BDPP83 Elier Rodriguez .25 .60
BDPP84 Miles Williams .25 .60
BDPP85 Derrick Penilla .25 .60
BDPP86 Bryan Hudson .25 .60
BDPP87 Jordan Barnes .25 .60
BDPP88 Tyler Kinley .25 .60
BDPP89 Randolph Gassaway .25 .60
BDPP90 Blake Higgins .30 .75
BDPP91 Caleb Kellogg .25 .60
BDPP92 Joseph Monge .25 .60
BDPP93 Steven Negron .25 .60
BDPP94 Justin Williams .30 .75
BDPP95 William White .25 .60
BDPP96 Jared Wilson .25 .60
BDPP97 Niko Spezial .25 .60
BDPP98 Gabe Speier .25 .60
BDPP99 Juan Avila .25 .60
BDPP100 Jason Kanzler .25 .60
BDPP101 Tyler Brosius .25 .60
BDPP102 Tyler Vail .25 .60
BDPP103 Adam Landecker .25 .60
BDPP104 Ethan Carnes .25 .60
BDPP105 Austin Wilson .30 .75
BDPP106 Jon Keller .25 .60
BDPP107 Galther Bumgardner .25 .60
BDPP108 Garrett Gordon .25 .60
BDPP109 Connor Oliver .25 .60
BDPP110 Cody Harris .25 .60
BDPP111 Brandon Easton .25 .60
BDPP112 Matt Derosier .25 .60
BDPP113 Jeremy Hadley .25 .60
BDPP114 Will Morris .25 .60
BDPP115 Sean Hurley .25 .60
BDPP116 Orrin Sears .25 .60
BDPP117 Sean Townsley .25 .60
BDPP118 Chad Christensen .25 .60
BDPP119 Travis Ott .25 .60
BDPP120 Justin Maffei .25 .60
BDPP121 Reed Harper .25 .60
BDPP122 Adam Westmoreland .25 .60
BDPP123 Adrian Castano .25 .60
BDPP124 Hyrum Formo .25 .60
BDPP125 Jake Stone .30 .75
BDPP126 Joel Effertz .25 .60
BDPP127 Matt Southard .25 .60
BDPP128 Jorge Perez .25 .60
BDPP129 Willie Medina .25 .60
BDPP130 Ty Afenir .25 .60

2013 Bowman Chrome Draft Draft Picks Black Refractors
*BLACK REF: 15X TO 40X BASIC
STATED ODDS 1:224 HOBBY
STATED PRINT RUN 35 SER.#'d SETS
BDPP19 Aaron Judge 250.00 600.00

2013 Bowman Chrome Draft Draft Picks Black Wave Refractors
*BLACK WAVE: 4X TO 10X BASIC
BDPP19 Aaron Judge 125.00 300.00

2013 Bowman Chrome Draft Draft Picks Blue Refractors
*BLUE REF: 6X TO 15X BASIC
STATED ODDS 1:93 HOBBY
STATED PRINT RUN 99 SER.#'d SETS
BDPP19 Aaron Judge 200.00 500.00

2013 Bowman Chrome Draft Draft Picks Blue Wave Refractors
*BLUE WAVE: 3X TO 8X BASIC
BDPP19 Aaron Judge 100.00 250.00

2013 Bowman Chrome Draft Draft Picks Gold Refractors
*GOLD REF: 15X TO 40X BASIC
STATED ODDS 1:185 HOBBY
STATED PRINT RUN 50 SER.#'d SETS
BDPP19 Aaron Judge 250.00 600.00

2013 Bowman Chrome Draft Draft Picks Green Refractors
*GREEN REF: 6X TO 15X BASIC
STATED ODDS 1:124 HOBBY
STATED PRINT RUN 75 SER.#'d SETS
BDPP5 Austin Meadows 20.00 50.00
BDPP19 Aaron Judge 200.00 500.00

2013 Bowman Chrome Draft Draft Picks Orange Refractors
*ORANGE REF: 20X TO 50X BASIC
STATED ODDS 1:372 HOBBY
STATED PRINT RUN 25 SER.#'d SETS
BDPP19 Aaron Judge 300.00 800.00

2013 Bowman Chrome Draft Draft Picks Red Wave Refractors
*RED WAVE: 20X TO 50X BASIC
STATED PRINT RUN 25 SER.#'d SETS
BDPP19 Aaron Judge 300.00 800.00

2013 Bowman Chrome Draft Draft Picks Refractors
*REF: 2X TO 5X BASIC
STATED ODDS 1:3 HOBBY
BDPP19 Aaron Judge 40.00 100.00

2013 Bowman Chrome Draft Draft Picks Silver Wave Refractors
*SILVER WAVE: 20X TO 50X BASIC
STATED PRINT RUN 25 SER.#'d SETS
BDPP19 Aaron Judge 300.00 800.00

2013 Bowman Chrome Draft Refractors
*REF: 1.2X TO 3X BASIC CARDS
STATED ODDS 1:3 HOBBY

2013 Bowman Chrome Draft Rookie Autographs
STATED ODDS 1:38,000 HOBBY
EXCHANGE DEADLINE 11/30/2016
YP Yasiel Puig 125.00 250.00

2013 Bowman Chrome Draft Top Prospects
STATED PLATE ODDS 1:2230 HOBBY
PLATE PRINT RUN 1 SET PER COLOR
BLACK-CYAN-MAGENTA-YELLOW ISSUED
NO PLATE PRICING DUE TO SCARCITY
TP1 Byron Buxton .50 1.25
TP2 Tyler Austin .30 .75
TP3 Mason Williams .25 .60
TP4 Albert Almora .40 1.00
TP5 Joey Gallo .60 1.50
TP6 Jesse Biddle .25 .60
TP7 David Dahl .25 .60
TP8 Kevin Gausman .30 .75
TP9 Jorge Soler .40 1.00
TP10 Carlos Correa 2.00 5.00
TP11 Preston Tucker .30 .75
TP12 Jameson Taillon .25 .60
TP13 Joc Pederson .30 .75
TP14 Max Fried .75 2.00
TP15 Taijuan Walker .25 .60
TP16 Chris Bostick .20 .50
TP17 Francisco Lindor 1.25 3.00
TP18 Daniel Vogelbach .30 .75
TP19 Kaleb Cowart .25 .60
TP20 George Springer .75 2.00
TP21 Yordano Ventura .25 .60
TP22 Noah Syndergaard .25 .60
TP23 Ty Hensley .25 .60
TP24 C.J. Cron .25 .60
TP25 Addison Russell .30 .75
TP26 Kyle Crick .30 .75
TP27 Javier Baez .75 2.00
TP28 Kolten Wong .20 .50
TP29 Taylor Guerrieri .20 .50
TP30 Archie Bradley .20 .50
TP31 Gary Sanchez .60 1.50
TP32 Billy Hamilton .25 .60
TP33 Alen Hanson .25 .60
TP34 Jonathan Singleton .25 .60
TP35 Mark Montgomery .30 .75
TP36 Nick Castellanos .60 1.50
TP37 Courtney Hawkins .20 .50
TP38 Gregory Polanco .40 1.00
TP39 Matt Barnes .25 .60
TP40 Xander Bogaerts .60 1.50
TP41 Dorssys Paulino .25 .60
TP42 Corey Seager .75 2.00
TP43 Alex Meyer .20 .50
TP44 Aaron Sanchez .25 .60
TP45 Miguel Sano .25 .60

2013 Bowman Chrome Draft Top Prospects Black Refractors
*BLACK REF:8X TO 20X BASIC
STATED ODDS 1:224 HOBBY
STATED PRINT RUN 35 SER.#'d SETS

2013 Bowman Chrome Draft Top Prospects Black Wave Refractors
*BLACK WAVE: 2X TO 5X BASIC

2013 Bowman Chrome Draft Top Prospects Blue Refractors
*BLUE REF: 3X TO 8X BASIC
STATED ODDS 1:93 HOBBY
STATED PRINT RUN 99 SER.#'d SETS

2013 Bowman Chrome Draft Top Prospects Blue Wave Refractors
*BLUE WAVE REF: 1.5X TO 4X BASIC

2013 Bowman Chrome Draft Top Prospects Gold Refractors
*GOLD REF: 8X TO 20X BASIC
STATED ODDS 1:185 HOBBY
STATED PRINT RUN 50 SER.#'d SETS

2013 Bowman Chrome Draft Top Prospects Green Refractors
*GREEN REF: 4X TO 10X BASIC
STATED ODDS 1:124 HOBBY
STATED PRINT RUN 75 SER.#'d SETS

2013 Bowman Chrome Draft Top Prospects Orange Refractors
*ORANGE REF: 20X TO 50X BASIC
STATED ODDS 1:372 HOBBY
STATED PRINT RUN 25 SER.#'d SETS

2013 Bowman Chrome Draft Top Prospects Red Wave Refractors
*RED WAVE: 12X TO 30X BASIC
STATED PRINT RUN 25 SER.#'d SETS
TP10 Carlos Correa 25.00 60.00

2013 Bowman Chrome Draft Top Prospects Refractors
*REF: 1.2X TO 3X BASIC
STATED ODDS 1:3 HOBBY

2013 Bowman Chrome Draft Top Prospects Silver Wave Refractors
*SILVER WAVE: 10X TO 25X BASIC
STATED PRINT RUN 25 SER.#'d SETS
TP10 Carlos Correa 20.00 50.00

2014 Bowman Chrome
COMP.SET w/o SP's (220) 20.00 50.00
STATED PLATE ODDS 1:1740 HOBBY
PLATE PRINT RUN 1 SET PER COLOR
BLACK-CYAN-MAGENTA-YELLOW ISSUED
NO PLATE PRICING DUE TO SCARCITY
1A Xander Bogaerts RC 1.00 2.50
1B Xander Bogaerts/99 12.00 30.00
2A Nick Castellanos RC 1.00 2.50
2B Nick Castellanos/99 20.00 50.00
3 Erisbel Arruebarrena RC .30 .75
4 Jeff Kobernus RC .30 .75
5A Jose Abreu RC 2.50 6.00
5B Jose Abreu/99 20.00 50.00
6 Yangervis Solarte RC .30 .75
7 Jonathan Schoop RC .30 .75
8 John Ryan Murphy RC .30 .75
9 Travis d'Arnaud RC .40 1.00
10 Marcus Semien RC .30 .75
11 Luis Sardinas RC .30 .75
12 Oscar Taveras RC .40 1.00
13 Josmil Pinto RC .30 .75
14 Gregory Polanco RC .50 1.25
15 Wilmer Flores RC .40 1.00
16A Yordano Ventura RC .40 1.00
16B Yordano Ventura/99 8.00 20.00
17 Matt Davidson RC .40 1.00
18 Michael Choice RC .30 .75
19A Alex Guerrero RC .40 1.00
20 Kolten Wong RC .40 1.00
21A Taijuan Walker RC .30 .75
21B Taijuan Walker/99 8.00 20.00
22 Jon Singleton RC .40 1.00
23 Rougned Odor RC .60 1.50
24 Chris Owings RC .30 .75
25A James Paxton RC .50 1.25
25B James Paxton/99 10.00 25.00
26 Garin Cecchini RC .30 .75
27A Billy Hamilton RC .40 1.00
27B Billy Hamilton/99 8.00 20.00
28 Roenis Elias RC .30 .75
29A George Springer RC 1.25 3.00
30A Masahiro Tanaka RC 1.00 2.50
30B Masahiro Tanaka/99 20.00 50.00
31 Mike Trout 1.50 4.00
32 Salvador Perez .25 .60
33 Carlos Gomez .20 .50
34 Chris Sale .30 .75
35 Stephen Strasburg .30 .75
36 Max Scherzer .30 .75
37 Carlos Gonzalez .25 .60
38 Buster Posey .40 1.00
39 Jayson Werth .25 .60
40 Jose Fernandez .30 .75
41 Madison Bumgarner .25 .60
42 Adam Wainwright .25 .60
43 Freddie Freeman .40 1.00
44 Paul Goldschmidt .30 .75
45 Jose Bautista .25 .60
46 Anthony Rendon .30 .75
47 Pedro Alvarez .20 .50
48 Chris Archer .20 .50
49 Felix Hernandez .25 .60
50 David Price .25 .60
51 Gio Gonzalez .25 .60
52 Michael Wacha .25 .60
53 Evan Longoria .25 .60
54 Troy Tulowitzki .30 .75
55 Hanley Ramirez .25 .60
56 Brandon Belt .25 .60
57 Tony Cingrani .25 .60
58 Yovani Gallardo .20 .50
59 Justin Verlander .30 .75
60 Yadier Molina .30 .75
61 Starlin Castro .20 .50
62 Giancarlo Stanton .30 .75
63 Shin-Soo Choo .25 .60
64 Hyun-Jin Ryu .25 .60
65 John Lackey .25 .60
66 Andrew Cashner .20 .50
67 Sonny Gray .25 .60
68 Matt Carpenter .30 .75
69 Ryan Braun .25 .60
70 Starling Marte .25 .60
71 Adam Jones .25 .60
72 Jacoby Ellsbury .25 .60
73 Mark Trumbo .20 .50
74 Austin Jackson .20 .50
75 Anthony Rizzo .50 1.25
76 Matt Garza .20 .50
77 Anibal Sanchez .20 .50
78 James Shields .20 .50
79 Ben Zobrist .25 .60
80 Juan Lagares .20 .50
81 David Wright .25 .60
82 Matt Adams .20 .50
83 Albert Pujols .40 1.00
84 Jeff Samardzija .20 .50
85 Johnny Cueto .25 .60
86 Garrett Richards .25 .60
87 Justin Masterson .20 .50
88 Gerrit Cole .30 .75
89 Derek Jeter .75 2.00
90 Adeiny Hechavarria .20 .50
91 Andrew McCutchen .30 .75
92 Ryan Zimmerman .25 .60
93 Nelson Cruz .30 .75
94 Alex Rios .25 .60
95 Chris Tillman .20 .50
96 Francisco Liriano .20 .50
97 Bartolo Colon .20 .50
98 Zack Wheeler .25 .60
99 Brett Gardner .25 .60
100 Curtis Granderson .25 .60
101 Adrian Beltre .30 .75
102 Daniel Murphy .25 .60
103 Ian Kinsler .25 .60
104 Prince Fielder .25 .60
105 Alex Cobb .20 .50
106 Julio Teheran .25 .60
107 Alex Wood .20 .50
108 Dan Straily .20 .50
109 CC Sabathia .25 .60
110 Hiroki Kuroda .20 .50
111 A.J. Burnett .20 .50
112 Cliff Lee .25 .60
113 Carlos Santana .25 .60
114 Todd Frazier .25 .60
115 Jason Kipnis .25 .60
116 Robinson Cano .25 .60
117 Christian Yelich .40 1.00
118 Justin Upton .25 .60
119 Khris Davis .30 .75
120 Jean Segura .25 .60
121 Domonic Brown .25 .60
122 Ryan Howard .25 .60
123 Chase Utley .25 .60
124 Jimmy Rollins .25 .60
125 Jay Bruce .25 .60
126 Joey Votto .30 .75
127 Chris Davis .20 .50
128 Manny Machado .30 .75
129 Ubaldo Jimenez .20 .50
130 Jon Lester .25 .60
131 Clay Buchholz .20 .50
132 Jake Peavy .20 .50
133 Jason Castro .20 .50
134 Joe Mauer .25 .60
135 Josh Hamilton .25 .60
136 Jered Weaver .25 .60
137 Eric Hosmer .25 .60
138 Alex Gordon .25 .60
139 Billy Butler .20 .50
140 David Ortiz .30 .75
141 Brian McCann .25 .60
142 Carlos Beltran .25 .60
143 Yoenis Cespedes .30 .75
144 Hisashi Iwakuma .25 .60
145 Wil Myers .20 .50
146 Yu Darvish .30 .75
147 Edwin Encarnacion .30 .75
148 Jose Reyes .25 .60
149 Andrelton Simmons .20 .50
150 Ervin Santana .20 .50
151 Craig Kimbrel .25 .60
152 Mat Latos .25 .60
153 Wilin Rosario .20 .50
154 Aroldis Chapman .30 .75
155 Kenley Jansen .25 .60
156 Matt Kemp .25 .60
157 Adrian Gonzalez .25 .60
158 Clayton Kershaw .60 1.50
159 Yasiel Puig .30 .75
160 Zack Greinke .30 .75
161 Jonathon Niese .20 .50
162 Marlon Byrd .20 .50
163 Cole Hamels .25 .60
164 Tyson Ross .20 .50
165 Chase Headley .20 .50
166 Everth Cabrera .20 .50
167 Ian Kennedy .20 .50
168 Pablo Sandoval .25 .60
169 Matt Cain .25 .60
170 Tim Hudson .25 .60
171 Hunter Pence .25 .60
172 Jhonny Peralta .20 .50
173 Shelby Miller .25 .60
174 Matt Holliday .30 .75
175 Bryce Harper .50 1.25
176 Jordan Zimmermann .25 .60
177 Angel Pagan .20 .50
178 Doug Fister .20 .50
179 Wilson Ramos .20 .50
180 Edinson Volquez .20 .50
181 Dan Haren .20 .50
182 Homer Bailey .20 .50
183 Jonathan Papelbon .25 .60
184 Huston Street .20 .50
185 Greg Holland .20 .50
186 Joe Nathan .20 .50
187 Trevor Rosenthal .20 .50
188 Addison Reed .20 .50
189 David Robertson .20 .50
190 Fernando Rodney .20 .50
191 Shane Victorino .25 .60
192 Mike Minor .20 .50
193 Ian Desmond .20 .50
194 Dustin Pedroia .30 .75
195 Josh Donaldson .25 .60
196 Jonathan Lucroy .25 .60
197 Mike Napoli .20 .50
198 Jose Altuve .25 .60
199 Jason Heyward .25 .60
200 Alexei Ramirez .25 .60
201 Kyle Seager .20 .50
202 Michael Brantley .25 .60
203 Brian Dozier .25 .60
204 Brandon Moss .20 .50
205 Dee Gordon .20 .50
206 Victor Martinez .25 .60
207 Alcides Escobar .25 .60
208 Phil Hughes .20 .50
209 Corey Kluber .25 .60
210 Jose Quintana .20 .50
211 Dallas Keuchel .25 .60
212 Jason Hammel .25 .60
213 Henderson Alvarez .20 .50
214 Scott Kazmir .20 .50
215 Jesse Chavez .20 .50
216 Drew Pomeranz .25 .60
217 Drew Hutchison .20 .50
218 Aaron Harang .20 .50
219 Jarred Cosart .20 .50
220 Josh Beckett .20 .50

2014 Bowman Chrome Black Static Refractors
*STATIC REF RC: 5X TO 12X BASIC
*STATIC REF VET: 8X TO 20X BASIC
STATED ODDS 1:205 HOBBY
STATED PRINT RUN 35 SER.#'d SETS
31 Mike Trout 40.00 100.00
89 Derek Jeter 50.00 120.00

2014 Bowman Chrome Blue Refractors
*BLUE REF RC: 2X TO 5X BASIC
*BLUE REF VET: 3X TO 8X BASIC
STATED ODDS 1:29 HOBBY
STATED PRINT RUN 250 SER.#'d SETS

2014 Bowman Chrome Bubble Refractors
*BUB REF RC: 3X TO 8X BASIC
*BUB REF VET: 5X TO 12X BASIC
STATED ODDS 1:68 HOBBY
STATED PRINT RUN 99 SER.#'d SETS
89 Derek Jeter 25.00 60.00

2014 Bowman Chrome Gold Refractors
*GOLD REF RC: 3X TO 8X BASIC
*GOLD REF VET: 5X TO 12X BASIC
STATED ODDS 1:138 HOBBY
STATED PRINT RUN 50 SER.#'d SETS
31 Mike Trout 30.00 80.00
89 Derek Jeter 40.00 100.00

2014 Bowman Chrome Green Refractors
*GREEN REF RC: 3X TO 8X BASIC
*GREEN REF VET: 5X TO 12X BASIC
STATED ODDS 1:90 HOBBY
STATED PRINT RUN 75 SER.#'d SETS

2014 Bowman Chrome Orange Refractors
*ORANGE REF RC: 5X TO 12X BASIC
*ORANGE REF VET: 8X TO 20X BASIC
STATED ODDS 1:276 HOBBY
STATED PRINT RUN 25 SER.#'d SETS
31 Mike Trout 50.00 120.00
89 Derek Jeter 60.00 150.00
158 Clayton Kershaw 40.00 80.00

2014 Bowman Chrome Purple Refractors
*PURP REF RC: 2X TO 5X BASIC
*PURP REF VET: 3X TO 8X BASIC
STATED ODDS 1:47 HOBBY
STATED PRINT RUN 150 SER.#'d SETS
31 Mike Trout 10.00 25.00
89 Derek Jeter 12.00 30.00

2014 Bowman Chrome Refractors
*REF RC: 1.2X TO 3X BASIC
*REF VET: 2X TO 5X BASIC
STATED ODDS 1:15 HOBBY
STATED PRINT RUN 500 SER.#'d SETS

2014 Bowman Chrome Bowman Scout Top 5 Mini Refractors
STATED ODDS 1:6 HOBBY
BMA1 C.J. Cron .50 1.25
BMA2 Zach Borenstein .60 1.50
BMA3 Kaleb Cowart .50 1.25
BMA4 Hunter Green .50 1.25
BMA5 Alex Yarbrough .50 1.25
BMAB1 Lucas Sims .50 1.25
BMAB2 Christian Bethancourt .50 1.25
BMAB3 Jason Hursh .50 1.25
BMAB4 J.R. Graham .50 1.25
BMAB5 Jose Peraza .50 1.25
BMAD1 Archie Bradley .50 1.25
BMAD2 Matt Davidson .60 1.50
BMAD3 Chris Owings .50 1.25
BMAD4 Daniel Palka .50 1.25
BMAD5 Brandon Drury .50 1.25
BMBO1 Dylan Bundy .60 1.50
BMBO2 Eduardo Rodriguez .60 1.50
BMBO3 Hunter Harvey .50 1.25
BMBO4 Jonathan Schoop .50 1.25
BMBO5 Michael Ohlman .50 1.25
BMCC1 Javier Baez 2.00 5.00
BMCC2 Kris Bryant 4.00 10.00
BMCC3 C.J. Edwards .60 1.50
BMCC4 Jorge Soler 1.00 2.50
BMCC5 Albert Almora .75 2.00
BMCI1 Francisco Lindor 3.00 8.00
BMCI2 Clint Frazier 2.00 5.00
BMCI3 Tyler Naquin .60 1.50
BMCI4 Dorssys Paulino .50 1.25
BMCI5 Trevor Bauer .75 2.00
BMCR1 Billy Hamilton .60 1.50
BMCR2 Robert Stephenson .50 1.25
BMCR3 Phil Ervin .50 1.25
BMCR4 Seth Mejias-Brean .50 1.25
BMCR5 Nick Travieso .50 1.25

BMDT1 Nick Castellanos 1.50 4.00
BMDT2 Devon Travis .50 1.25
BMDT3 Jonathon Crawford .50 1.25
BMDT4 Jake Thompson .50 1.25
BMDT5 Corey Knebel .50 1.25
BMHA1 Carlos Correa 2.50 6.00
BMHA2 Mark Appel .60 1.50
BMHA3 George Springer 2.00 5.00
BMHA4 Lance McCullers .50 1.25
BMHA5 Delino DeShields .50 1.25
BMMB1 Jimmy Nelson .50 1.25
BMMB2 Tyrone Taylor .50 1.25
BMMB3 Devin Williams 1.25 3.00
BMMB4 Victor Roache .50 1.25
BMMB5 Taylor Jungmann .50 1.25
BMMM1 Andrew Heaney .50 1.25
BMMM2 Colin Moran .50 1.25
BMMM3 Justin Nicolino .50 1.25
BMMM4 Jake Marisnick .50 1.25
BMMM5 Trevor Williams .50 1.25
BMMT1 Byron Buxton .60 1.50
BMMT2 Miguel Sano .60 1.50
BMMT3 Alex Meyer .50 1.25
BMMT4 Kohl Stewart .50 1.25
BMMT5 Eddie Rosario 1.00 2.50
BMOA1 Addison Russell .75 2.00
BMOA2 Michael Ynoa .50 1.25
BMOA3 Billy McKinney .60 1.50
BMOA4 Renato Nunez 1.00 2.50
BMOA5 B.J. Boyd .50 1.25
BMPP1 Maikel Franco .60 1.50
BMPP2 Jesse Biddle .60 1.50
BMPP3 J.P. Crawford .50 1.25
BMPP4 Miguel Alfredo Gonzalez .50 1.25
BMPP5 Roman Quinn .75 2.00
BMSM1 Taijuan Walker .50 1.25
BMSM2 D.J. Peterson .50 1.25
BMSM3 Danny Hultzen .50 1.25
BMSM4 Victor Sanchez .50 1.25
BMSM5 Chris Taylor 2.50 6.00
BMTR1 Joey Gallo 1.00 2.50
BMTR2 Jorge Alfaro .60 1.50
BMTR3 Rougned Odor 1.00 2.50
BMTR4 Michael Choice .50 1.25
BMTR5 Luis Sardinas .50 1.25
BMWN1 Lucas Giolito .75 2.00
BMWN2 A.J. Cole .50 1.25
BMWN3 Brian Goodwin .50 1.25
BMWN4 Nathan Karns .50 1.25
BMWN5 Jake Johansen .60 1.50
BMBRS1 Xander Bogaerts 1.50 4.00
BMBRS2 Henry Owens .60 1.50
BMBRS3 Garin Cecchini .50 1.25
BMBRS4 Mookie Betts 10.00 25.00
BMBRS5 Anthony Ranaudo .50 1.25
BMCRO1 Jonathan Gray .60 1.50
BMCRO2 Eddie Butler .50 1.25
BMCRO3 David Dahl .60 1.50
BMCRO4 Rosell Herrera .75 2.00
BMCRO5 Raimel Tapia .60 1.50
BMCWS1 Jose Abreu 4.00 10.00
BMCWS2 Erik Johnson .50 1.25
BMCWS3 Micah Johnson .50 1.25
BMCWS4 Tim Anderson 1.00 2.50
BMCWS5 Courtney Hawkins .50 1.25
BMKCR1 Yordano Ventura .60 1.50
BMKCR2 Kyle Zimmer .50 1.25
BMKCR3 Raul Mondesi 1.50 4.00
BMKCR4 Bubba Starling .60 1.50
BMKCR5 Hunter Dozier .50 1.25
BMLAD1 Joc Pederson .75 2.00
BMLAD2 Julio Urias 2.50 6.00
BMLAD3 Corey Seager 2.00 5.00
BMLAD4 Chris Anderson .50 1.25
BMLAD5 Zach Lee .50 1.25
BMNYM1 Noah Syndergaard .60 1.50
BMNYM2 Travis d'Arnaud .60 1.50
BMNYM3 Rafael Montero .50 1.25
BMNYM4 Kevin Plawecki .50 1.25
BMNYM5 Wilmer Flores .60 1.50
BMNYY1 Gary Sanchez 1.50 4.00
BMNYY2 Masahiro Tanaka 1.50 4.00
BMNYY3 Tyler Austin .50 1.25
BMNYY4 Rafael De Paula .50 1.25
BMNYY5 Mason Williams .50 1.25
BMPPI1 Gregory Polanco .75 2.00
BMPPI2 Tyler Glasnow .75 2.00
BMPPI3 Alen Hanson .50 1.25
BMPPI4 Jameson Taillon .60 1.50
BMPPI5 Austin Meadows .75 2.00
BMSDP1 Austin Hedges .50 1.25
BMSDP2 Max Fried 2.00 5.00
BMSDP3 Rymer Liriano .50 1.25
BMSDP4 Matt Wisler .50 1.25
BMSDP5 Jace Peterson .50 1.25
BMSFG1 Kyle Crick .50 1.25
BMSFG2 Clayton Blackburn .75 2.00
BMSFG3 Edwin Escobar .50 1.25
BMSFG4 Martin Agosta .50 1.25
BMSFG5 Mac Williamson .60 1.50
BMSTL1 Oscar Taveras .60 1.50
BMSTL2 Kolten Wong .60 1.50
BMSTL3 Carlos Martinez .60 1.50
BMSTL4 Stephen Piscotty .60 1.50
BMSTL5 James Ramsey .50 1.25
BMTBJ1 Aaron Sanchez .50 1.25
BMTBJ2 Marcus Stroman .75 2.00
BMTBJ3 Roberto Osuna .50 1.25
BMTBJ4 D.J. Davis .50 1.25
BMTBJ5 Daniel Norris .60 1.50
BMTBR1 Taylor Guerrieri .50 1.25
BMTBR2 Hak-Ju Lee .50 1.25
BMTBR3 Andrew Toles .60 1.50
BMTBR4 Dylan Floro .60 1.50
BMTBR5 Jeff Ames .50 1.25

2014 Bowman Chrome Bowman Scout Top 5 Mini Blue Refractors

*BLUE REF: 1X TO 2.5X BASIC
STATED ODDS 1:65 HOBBY
STATED PRINT RUN 250 SER.#'d SETS

2014 Bowman Chrome Bowman Scout Top 5 Mini Gold Refractors

*GOLD REF: 3X TO 8X BASIC
STATED ODDS 1:540 HOBBY
STATED PRINT RUN 25 SER.#'d SETS
BMCC2 Kris Bryant 60.00 120.00
BMLAD2 Julio Urias 20.00 50.00

2014 Bowman Chrome Bowman Scout Top 5 Mini Orange Refractors

*ORANGE REF: 2.5X TO 6X BASIC
STATED ODDS 1:326 HOBBY
STATED PRINT RUN 50 SER.#'d SETS
BMCC2 Kris Bryant 30.00 80.00

2014 Bowman Chrome Bowman Scout Top 5 Mini Purple Refractors

*PURPLE REF: 1.5X TO 4X BASIC
STATED PRINT RUN 99 SER.#'d SETS
BMCC2 Kris Bryant 25.00 60.00
BMMT1 Byron Buxton 12.00 30.00

2014 Bowman Chrome Dualing Die-Cut Refractors

COMPLETE SET (25) 15.00 40.00
STATED ODDS 1:18 HOBBY
DDCAG J.Gray/M.Appel .60 1.50
DDCAS R.Stephenson/A.Almora .75 2.00
DDCASO J.Abreu/J.Soler 2.50 6.00
DDCAV Velasquez/Alfaro .75 2.00
DDCBC C.Correa/B.Buxton 2.50 6.00
DDCBR J.Baez/A.Russell 2.00 5.00
DDCBS A.Sanchez/M.Betts 10.00 25.00
DDCCC G.Cecchini/G.Cecchini .50 1.25
DDCDB D.Dahl/A.Bradley .60 1.50
DDCGN L.Giolito/B.Nimmo .75 2.00
DDCHS A.Heaney/N.Syndergaard .60 1.50
DDCLM R.Mondesi/F.Lindor 3.00 8.00
DDCMB C.Moran/K.Bryant 2.50 6.00
DDCMC K.Crick/B.McKinney .60 1.50
DDCMF C.Frazier/A.Meadows 2.00 5.00
DDCMFR R.Montero/M.Franco .60 1.50
DDCOS G.Sanchez/H.Owens 1.50 4.00
DDCPE C.Edwards/S.Piscotty .60 1.50
DDCSB E.Butler/C.Seager 2.00 5.00
DDCSW T.Walker/G.Springer 2.00 5.00
DDCTP Polanco/Taveras .75 2.00
DDCUR J.Urias/H.Renfroe 2.50 6.00
DDCVC N.Castellanos/Y.Ventura 1.50 4.00
DDCWP J.Pederson/M.Wisler .75 2.00
DDCZM K.Zimmer/A.Meyer .50 1.25

2014 Bowman Chrome Dualing Die-Cut Atomic Refractors

*ATOMIC REF: .75X TO 2X BASIC
STATED ODDS 1:924 HOBBY
STATED PRINT RUN 99 SER.#'d SETS

2014 Bowman Chrome Dualing Die-Cut Shimmer Refractors

*SHIMMER REF: 1.5X TO 4X BASIC
STATED ODDS 1:1835 HOBBY
STATED PRINT RUN 50 SER.#'d SETS

2014 Bowman Chrome Dualing Die-Cut X-Fractors

*X-FRACTOR: 2.5X TO 6X BASIC
STATED ODDS 1:3660 HOBBY
STATED PRINT RUN 25 SER.#'d SETS

2014 Bowman Chrome Fire Die-Cut Refractors

STATED ODDS 1:18 HOBBY
FDCAB Archie Bradley .50 1.25
FDCAH Andrew Heaney .50 1.25
FDCAHE Austin Hedges .50 1.25
FDCAR Addison Russell .75 2.00
FDCAT Taijuan Walker .50 1.25
FDCBB Byron Buxton .60 1.50
FDCBH Bryce Harper 1.25 3.00
FDCBHA Billy Hamilton .60 1.50
FDCCC Carlos Correa 2.50 6.00
FDCCO Chris Owings .50 1.25
FDCFL Francisco Lindor 3.00 8.00
FDCGP Gregory Polanco .75 2.00
FDCGS George Springer 2.00 5.00
FDCJA Jose Abreu 4.00 10.00
FDCJB Javier Baez 2.00 5.00
FDCJG Jonathan Gray .60 1.50
FDCKB Kris Bryant 4.00 10.00
FDCKW Kolten Wong .60 1.50
FDCMA Mark Appel .60 1.50
FDCMD Matt Davidson .60 1.50
FDCMF Maikel Franco .60 1.50
FDCMS Miguel Sano .60 1.50
FDCMT Masahiro Tanaka 1.50 4.00
FDCMTR Mike Trout 4.00 10.00
FDCNC Nick Castellanos 1.50 4.00
FDCNS Noah Syndergaard .60 1.50
FDCOT Oscar Taveras .60 1.50
FDCTD Travis d'Arnaud .60 1.50
FDCTW Taijuan Walker .50 1.25
FDCXB Xander Bogaerts 1.50 4.00
FDCYV Yordano Ventura .60 1.50

2014 Bowman Chrome Fire Die-Cut Atomic Refractors

*DC ATOMIC: 1X TO 2.5X BASIC
STATED ODDS 1:770 HOBBY
STATED PRINT RUN 99 SER.#'d SETS
FDCJA Jose Abreu 10.00 25.00
FDCKB Kris Bryant 10.00 25.00
FDCMTR Mike Trout 12.00 30.00

2014 Bowman Chrome Fire Die-Cut X-Fractors

*X-FRACTORS: 1.5X TO 4X BASIC
STATED ODDS 1:3070 HOBBY
STATED PRINT RUN 25 SER.#'d SETS
FDCJA Jose Abreu 20.00 50.00
FDCKB Kris Bryant 25.00 60.00
FDCMTR Mike Trout 20.00 50.00

2014 Bowman Chrome Fire Die-Cut Refractor Autographs

STATED ODDS 1:9250 HOBBY
STATED PRINT RUN 25 SER.#'d SETS
EXCHANGE DEADLIN 9/30/2017
FDAAB Archie Bradley EXCH 20.00 50.00
FDABH Bryce Harper EXCH 100.00 200.00
FDABHA Billy Hamilton EXCH 25.00 60.00
FDAJB Javier Baez EXCH 30.00 80.00
FDAKB Kris Bryant 300.00 600.00
FDAMS Miguel Sano EXCH 60.00 150.00
FDAMTR Mike Trout 300.00 500.00
FDAOT Oscar Taveras 25.00 60.00
FDATW Taijuan Walker 20.00 50.00

2014 Bowman Chrome Franchise Dual Autograph Refractors

STATED ODDS 1:9800 HOBBY
STATED PRINT RUN 25 SER.#'d SETS
EXCHANGE DEADLINE 4/30/2017
DFAAC Correa/Appel EXCH 60.00 120.00
DFABA Bryant/Alcantara 300.00 400.00
DFABB M.Barnes/M.Betts 40.00 100.00
DFABJ B.Johnson/M.Barnes 10.00 25.00
DFAHS J.Hursh/L.Sims 30.00 80.00
DFAJM D.Maples/P.Johnson 15.00 40.00
DFAMB D.Marrero/M.Betts 40.00 100.00
DFAOB M.Barnes/H.Owens 30.00 80.00
DFAWB T.Wade/G.Bird 40.00 100.00

2014 Bowman Chrome Mini

STATED ODDS 1:18 HOBBY
MCAB Archie Bradley .40 1.00
MCAG Alex Guerrero .50 1.25
MCAH Andrew Heaney .40 1.00
MCAM Austin Meadows .60 1.50
MCAMC Andrew McCutchen .60 1.50
MCAP Albert Pujols .75 2.00
MCAR Addison Russell .60 1.50
MCBB Byron Buxton .50 1.25
MCBH Bryce Harper 1.00 2.50
MCBHA Billy Hamilton .50 1.25
MCCC Carlos Correa 2.00 5.00
MCCE C.J. Edwards .50 1.25
MCCF Clint Frazier 1.50 4.00
MCCK Clayton Kershaw 1.25 3.00
MCCS Chris Sale .60 1.50
MCCY Christian Yelich .75 2.00
MCFF Freddie Freeman .75 2.00
MCFL Francisco Lindor 2.50 6.00
MCGC Gerrit Cole .60 1.50
MCGP Gregory Polanco .60 1.50
MCGS George Springer 1.50 4.00
MCGST Giancarlo Stanton .60 1.50
MCHR Hyun-Jin Ryu .50 1.25
MCJA Jose Abreu 3.00 8.00
MCJB Javier Baez 1.50 4.00
MCJF Jose Fernandez .60 1.50
MCJG Jonathan Gray .60 1.50
MCJS Jorge Soler .75 2.00
MCJU Julio Urias 2.00 5.00
MCKB Kris Bryant 6.00 15.00
MCKZ Kyle Zimmer .40 1.00
MCMA Mark Appel .50 1.25
MCMB Madison Bumgarner .50 1.25
MCMC Miguel Cabrera .60 1.50
MCMF Maikel Franco .50 1.25
MCMS Miguel Sano .50 1.25
MCMT Mike Trout 3.00 8.00
MCMTA Masahiro Tanaka 1.25 3.00
MCMW Michael Wacha .50 1.25
MCNC Nick Castellanos 1.25 3.00
MCNS Noah Syndergaard .60 1.50
MCOT Oscar Taveras .50 1.25
MCPG Paul Goldschmidt .60 1.50
MCSS Stephen Strasburg .60 1.50
MCWM Wil Myers .40 1.00
MCXB Xander Bogaerts 1.25 3.00
MCYC Yoenis Cespedes .60 1.50
MCYD Yu Darvish .60 1.50
MCYP Yasiel Puig .60 1.50
MCYV Yordano Ventura .50 1.25

2014 Bowman Chrome Mini Die-Cut Black Wave Refractors

*BLACK WAVE: 3X TO 8X BASIC
RANDOM INSERTS IN PACKS
STATED PRINT RUN 25 SER.#'d SETS
MCMT Mike Trout 40.00 100.00

2014 Bowman Chrome Mini Die-Cut Blue Wave Refractors

*DC BLUE WAVE: 1X TO 2.5X BASIC
STATED ODDS 1:465 HOBBY
STATED PRINT RUN 99 SER.#'d SETS
MCMT Mike Trout 12.00 30.00

2014 Bowman Chrome Mini Die-Cut Gold Refractors

*GOLD REF: 2.5X TO 6X BASIC
STATED ODDS 1:915 HOBBY
STATED PRINT RUN 50 SER.#'d SETS
MCMT Mike Trout 30.00 80.00

2014 Bowman Chrome Mini Die-Cut Refractors

*DC REF: .75X TO 2X BASIC
STATED ODDS 1:18 HOBBY
STATED PRINT RUN 150 SER.#'d SETS
MCMT Mike Trout 10.00 25.00

2014 Bowman Chrome Mini Autograph Gold Refractors

*GOLD REF: .75X TO 2X BASIC
STATED ODDS 1:3465 HOBBY
STATED PRINT RUN 25 SER.#'d SETS
EXCHANGE DEADLINE 4/30/2017

2014 Bowman Chrome Mini Autograph Purple Refractors

STATED PRINT RUN 50 SER.#'d SETS
EXCHANGE DEADLINE 4/30/2017
CMACF Clint Frazier 20.00 50.00
CMAGS George Springer 30.00 80.00
CMAJA Jeff Ames EXCH 5.00 12.00
CMAJU Julio Urias 60.00 150.00
CMAMA Mark Appel 25.00 60.00
CMAMD Matt Davidson EXCH 10.00 25.00
CMAMF Maikel Franco 30.00 80.00
CMAMJ Micah Johnson EXCH 20.00 50.00
CMAOT Oscar Taveras 20.00 50.00
CMATD Travis d'Arnaud EXCH 12.00 30.00

2014 Bowman Chrome Prospect Autographs

BOW.STATED ODDS 1:42 HOBBY
BOW.CHR.ODDS 1:13 HOBBY
PLATE PRINT RUN 1 SET PER COLOR
BLACK-CYAN-MAGENTA-YELLOW ISSUED
NO PLATE PRICING DUE TO SCARCITY
BOW.EXCH DEADLINE 4/30/2017
BOW.CHR.EXCH 6/30/2017
BCAPAA Aristides Aquino 40.00 100.00
BCAPAAV Abiatal Avelino 3.00 8.00
BCAPAB Akeem Bostick 3.00 8.00
BCAPABR Aaron Brooks 5.00 12.00
BCAPAM Adam Morgan 3.00 8.00
BCAPAMA Adrian Marin 3.00 8.00
BCAPAN Austin Nola 6.00 15.00
BCAPAR Anthony Ranaudo 3.00 8.00
BCAPARI Armando Rivero 3.00 8.00
BCAPAS Anthony Santander 4.00 10.00
BCAPAT Andrew Toles 4.00 10.00
BCAPATH Andrew Thurman 3.00 8.00
BCAPAW Austin Wilson 3.00 8.00
BCAPAY Alex Yarbrough 3.00 8.00
BCAPBB Billy Burns 3.00 8.00
BCAPBD Brandon Dixon 3.00 8.00
BCAPBL Ben Lively 3.00 8.00
BCAPBT Brandon Trinkwon 4.00 10.00
BCAPBV Breyvic Valera 3.00 8.00
BCAPCA Cody Anderson 3.00 8.00
BCAPCB Christian Binford 3.00 8.00
BCAPCBO Chris Bostick 4.00 10.00
BCAPCC Carlos Contreras 3.00 8.00
BCAPCD Chase DeJong 3.00 8.00
BCAPCF Chris Flexen 4.00 10.00
BCAPCK Chris Kohler 3.00 8.00
BCAPCKN Corey Knebel 3.00 8.00
BCAPCM Casey Meisner 3.00 8.00
BCAPCP Cesar Puello 3.00 8.00
BCAPCR Cody Reed 3.00 8.00
BCAPCT Chris Taylor 6.00 20.00
BCAPDF Dylan Floro 4.00 10.00
BCAPDH David Holmberg 3.00 8.00
BCAPDM Daniel McGrath 4.00 10.00
BCAPDN Dom Nunez 3.00 8.00
BCAPDP Daniel Palka 3.00 8.00
BCAPDR Daniel Robertson 4.00 10.00
BCAPDT Devon Travis 3.00 8.00
BCAPDU Duane Underwood 3.00 8.00
BCAPDUN Dylan Unsworth 3.00 8.00
BCAPDW Daniel Winkler 3.00 8.00
BCAPDWI Devin Williams 12.00 30.00
BCAPED Edwin Diaz 6.00 15.00
BCAPEM Edwin Moreno 3.00 8.00
BCAPFB Franklin Barreto 5.00 12.00
BCAPFC Franchy Cordero 12.00 30.00
BCAPFL Fred Lewis 3.00 8.00
BCAPFR Franmil Reyes 10.00 25.00
BCAPGE Gabriel Encinas 4.00 10.00
BCAPGK Gosuke Katoh 10.00 25.00
BCAPGR Gabriel Rosa 3.00 8.00
BCAPGY Gabriel Ynoa 4.00 10.00
BCAPIK Isiah Kiner-Falefa 5.00 12.00
BCAPJAB Jose Abreu 60.00 150.00
BCAPJB Jake Barrett 4.00 10.00
BCAPJBE Javier Betancourt 4.00 10.00
BCAPJF Johnny Field 3.00 8.00
BCAPJG Joan Gregorio 3.00 8.00
BCAPJH Jose Herrera 3.00 8.00
BCAPJHA Josh Hader 8.00 20.00
BCAPJHU Jason Hursh 3.00 8.00
BCAPJJ JaCoby Jones 5.00 12.00
BCAPJJO Jacob Johansen 4.00 10.00
BCAPJM Jacob May 4.00 10.00
BCAPJMA Jason Martin 5.00 12.00
BCAPJMC Jeff McNeil 25.00 60.00
BCAPJN Jacob Nottingham 4.00 10.00
BCAPJR Jose Ramirez 3.00 8.00
BCAPJRE Jonathan Reynoso 3.00 8.00
BCAPJRO Jose Rondon 3.00 8.00
BCAPJS Jacob Scavuzzo 5.00 12.00
BCAPJSI Juan Silva 3.00 8.00
BCAPJSW Jake Sweaney 3.00 8.00
BCAPJU Julio Urias 20.00 50.00
BCAPJUR Jose Urena 4.00 10.00
BCAPJW Jesse Winker 4.00 10.00
BCAPJWE Jamie Westbrook 3.00 8.00
BCAPKB Kris Bryant 75.00 200.00
BCAPKD Kelly Dugan 3.00 8.00
BCAPKF Kendry Flores 3.00 8.00
BCAPKM Ketel Marte 30.00 80.00
BCAPKP Kyle Parker 4.00 10.00
BCAPKW Kean Wong 3.00 8.00
BCAPLJ Luke Jackson 3.00 8.00
BCAPLM Leonardo Molina 3.00 8.00
BCAPLR Luigi Rodriguez 3.00 8.00
BCAPLT Lewis Thorpe 3.00 8.00
BCAPLW LeVon Washington 3.00 8.00
BCAPMA Mark Appel 4.00 10.00
BCAPMB Mookie Betts 300.00 800.00
BCAPMF Maikel Franco 4.00 10.00
BCAPMFE Michael Feliz 4.00 10.00
BCAPMJ Micah Johnson 3.00 8.00
BCAPMM Mike Mayers 3.00 8.00
BCAPMMA Manuel Margot 5.00 12.00
BCAPMMC Matt McPhearson 3.00 8.00
BCAPMO Michael O'Neill 3.00 8.00
BCAPMTA Michael Taylor 4.00 10.00
BCAPMW Matt Whitehouse 3.00 8.00
BCAPNK Nick Kingham 4.00 10.00
BCAPNM Nathan Mikolas 3.00 8.00
BCAPPJ Pierce Johnson 4.00 10.00
BCAPPT Preston Tucker 6.00 15.00
BCAPRB Rony Bautista 3.00 8.00
BCAPRC Ryan Casteel 3.00 8.00
BCAPRG Robert Gsellman 4.00 10.00
BCAPRH Rosell Herrera 5.00 12.00
BCAPRHE Ryon Healy 5.00 12.00
BCAPRHA Ryan Hafner 3.00 8.00
BCAPRMC Ryan McNeil 3.00 8.00
BCAPRT Raimel Tapia 4.00 10.00
BCAPRU Richard Urena 4.00 10.00
BCAPSG Severino Gonzalez 3.00 8.00
BCAPSMB Seth Mejias-Brean 3.00 8.00
BCAPTA Trae Arbet 3.00 8.00
BCAPTB Ty Buttrey 3.00 8.00
BCAPTC Tim Cooney 3.00 8.00
BCAPTMA Tyler Mahle 3.00 8.00
BCAPTN Tucker Neuhaus 3.00 8.00
BCAPTS Teddy Stankiewicz 3.00 8.00
BCAPTW Tyler Wade 6.00 15.00
BCAPWG Willy Garcia 3.00 8.00
BCAPWR Wendell Rijo 3.00 8.00
BCAPYA Yency Almonte 3.00 8.00
BCAPYG Yimi Garcia 3.00 8.00
BCAPYM Yohander Mendez 3.00 8.00
BCAPZB Zach Borenstein 4.00 10.00

2014 Bowman Chrome Prospect Autographs Black Refractors

*BLACK REF: .75X TO 2X BASIC
BOW.ODDS 1:775 HOBBY
STATED PRINT RUN 99 SER.#'d SETS
BOW.EXCH DEADLINE 4/30/2017
BOW.CHR.EXCH DEADLINE 9/30/2017
BCAPFR Franmil Reyes 60.00 150.00
BCAPKB Kris Bryant 200.00 500.00

2014 Bowman Chrome Prospect Autographs Black Wave Refractors

*BLACK WAVE REF: 1.2X TO 3X BASIC
STATED PRINT RUN 50 SER.#'d SETS
BOW.EXCH DEADLINE 4/30/2017
BOW.CHR.EXCH DEADLINE 6/30/2017
BCAPABR Aaron Brooks 15.00 40.00
BCAPARI Armando Rivero 15.00 40.00
BCAPFR Franmil Reyes 100.00 250.00
BCAPKB Kris Bryant 300.00 800.00
BCAPMB Mookie Betts 1500.00 4000.00

2014 Bowman Chrome Prospect Autographs Blue Refractors

*BLUE REF: 1X TO 2.5X BASIC
BOW.ODDS 1:515 HOBBY
BOW.CHR.ODDS 1:207 HOBBY
STATED PRINT RUN 150 SER.#'d SETS
BOW.EXCH DEADLINE 4/30/2017
BOW.CHR.EXCH DEADLINE 9/30/2017
BCAPFR Franmil Reyes 60.00 150.00
BCAPKB Kris Bryant 200.00 500.00
BCAPMB Mookie Betts 1000.00 2500.00

2014 Bowman Chrome Prospect Autographs Blue Wave Refractors

*BLUE WAVE REF: 1.2X TO 3X BASIC
STATED PRINT RUN 50 SER.#'d SETS
BOW.EXCH DEADLINE 4/30/2017
BOW.CHR.EXCH DEADLINE 6/30/2017
BCAPABR Aaron Brooks 15.00 40.00
BCAPAT Andrew Toles 12.00 30.00
BCAPFR Franmil Reyes 100.00 250.00
BCAPKB Kris Bryant 300.00 800.00
BCAPMB Mookie Betts 1500.00 4000.00

2014 Bowman Chrome Prospect Autographs Bubble Refractors

*BUBBLE REF: .75X TO 2X BASIC
STATED ODDS 1:340 HOBBY
STATED PRINT RUN 99 SER.#'d SET
EXCHANGE DEADLINE 9/30/2017
BCAPFR Franmil Reyes 60.00 150.00

2014 Bowman Chrome Prospect Autographs Gold Refractors

*GOLD REF: 2X TO 5X BASIC
BOW.ODDS 1:1555 HOBBY
BOW.CHR.ODDS 1:614 HOBBY
STATED PRINT RUN 50 SER.#'d SETS
BOW.EXCH DEADLINE 4/30/2017
BOW.CHR.EXCH DEADLINE 6/30/2017
BCAPABR Aaron Brooks 30.00 80.00
BCAPARI Armando Rivero 25.00 60.00
BCAPFR Franmil Reyes 150.00 400.00
BCAPKB Kris Bryant 400.00 1000.00
BCAPMB Mookie Betts 2500.00 6000.00

2014 Bowman Chrome Prospect Autographs Green Refractors

*GREEN REF: .75X TO 2X BASIC
BOW.ODDS 1:1035 HOBBY
BOW.CHR.ODDS 1:410 HOBBY
STATED PRINT RUN 150 SER.#'d SETS
BOW.EXCH DEADLINE 4/30/2017
BOW.CHR.EXCH DEADLINE 6/30/2017
BCAPFR Franmil Reyes 60.00 150.00
BCAPKB Kris Bryant 200.00 500.00

2014 Bowman Chrome Prospect Autographs Refractors

*REF: .5X TO 1.2X BASIC
BOW.STATED ODDS 1:155 HOBBY
BOW.CHR ODDS 1:82 HOBBY
STATED PRINT RUN 500 SER.#'d SETS
BOW.EXCH DEADLINE 4/30/2017
BOW.CHR.EXCH 9/30/2017
BCAPFR Franmil Reyes 30.00 80.00

2014 Bowman Chrome Prospects

COMPLETE SET (110) 15.00 40.00
PLATE PRINT RUN 1 SET PER COLOR
BLACK-CYAN-MAGENTA-YELLOW ISSUED
NO PLATE PRICING DUE TO SCARCITY
BCP1 Jason Hursh .25 .60
BCP2 Trey Ball .25 .60
BCP3 Jacob May .30 .75
BCP4 Rosell Herrera .40 1.00
BCP5 Mark Appel .30 .75
BCP6 Julio Urias 1.25 3.00
BCP7 Devin Williams .60 1.50
BCP8 Ryan Eades .25 .60
BCP9 Eric Jagielo .25 .60
BCP10 Zach Borenstein .30 .75
BCP11 Jake Barrett .30 .75
BCP12 Wendell Rijo .25 .60
BCP13 Armando Rivero .25 .60
BCP14 Chris Taylor 1.25 3.00
BCP15 Edwin Diaz .50 1.25
BCP16 Dylan Floro .30 .75
BCP17 Jose Abreu 3.00 8.00
BCP18 Luke Jackson .25 .60
BCP19 Billy Burns .25 .60
BCP20 Leonardo Molina .25 .60
BCP21 Billy McKinney .30 .75
BCP22 Chris Flexen .30 .75
BCP23 Kyle Parker .30 .75
BCP24 Pierce Johnson .30 .75
BCP25 Kris Bryant 8.00 20.00
BCP26 Micah Johnson .25 .60
BCP27 Raimel Tapia .30 .75
BCP28 Preston Tucker .40 1.00
BCP29 Christian Binford .25 .60
BCP30 Ty Buttrey .25 .60
BCP31 Brandon Trinkwon .30 .75
BCP32 Lewis Thorpe .25 .60
BCP33 Devon Travis .25 .60
BCP34 Cesar Puello .25 .60
BCP35 Tyler Wade .40 1.00
BCP36 Daniel Robertson .30 .75
BCP37 Maikel Franco .30 .75
BCP38 Cody Reed .25 .60
BCP39 Sam Moll .25 .60
BCP40 Logan Vick .25 .60
BCP41 Gus Schlosser .25 .60
BCP42 Levon Washington .25 .60
BCP43 Chris Beck .25 .60
BCP44 Tim Cooney .25 .60
BCP45 Michael Feliz .30 .75
BCP46 Jamie Westbrook .25 .60
BCP47 Alex Reyes .40 1.00
BCP48 Trevor Gretzky .25 .60
BCP49 Isiah Kiner-Falefa .40 1.00
BCP50 Shawn Pleffner .25 .60
BCP51 Hunter Dozier .25 .60
BCP52 Hunter Renfroe .30 .75
BCP53 Ryder Jones .25 .60
BCP54 Tyler Danish .25 .60
BCP55 Matt McPhearson .25 .60
BCP56 Gosuke Katoh .40 1.00
BCP57 Andrew Thurman .25 .60
BCP58 Jordan Paroubeck .25 .60
BCP59 Tucker Neuhaus .25 .60
BCP60 Dillon Overton .25 .60
BCP61 Ryon Healy .40 1.00
BCP62 Chase Anderson .25 .60
BCP63 Daniel Palka .25 .60
BCP64 Duane Underwood .25 .60
BCP65 Carlos Contreras .25 .60
BCP66 Ben Lively .25 .60
BCP67 Anthony Santander .30 .75
BCP68 Melvin Mercedes .25 .60
BCP69 Josh Hader .60 1.50
BCP70 Yimi Garcia .25 .60
BCP71 Orlando Arcia .40 1.00
BCP72 Matthew Bowman .25 .60
BCP73 Jacob deGrom 1.50 4.00
BCP74 John Gant .25 .60
BCP75 Robert Gsellman .30 .75
BCP76 Gabriel Ynoa .30 .75
BCP77 Anthony Aliotti .25 .60
BCP78 Chris Bostick .30 .75
BCP79 Drew Granier .25 .60
BCP80 Austin Wright .25 .60
BCP81 Brandon Cumpton .25 .60
BCP82 Kendry Flores .25 .60
BCP83 Jason Rogers .25 .60
BCP84 Ryne Stanek .25 .60
BCP85 Nomar Mazara .60 1.50
BCP86 Victor Payano .25 .60
BCP87 Franklin Barreto .30 .75
BCP88 Santiago Nessy .25 .60
BCP89 Michael Ratterree .25 .60
BCP90 Manuel Margot .40 1.00
BCP91 Gabriel Rosa .25 .60
BCP92 Nelson Rodriguez .30 .75
BCP93 Yency Almonte .25 .60
BCP94 Bobby Coyle .25 .60
BCP95 Pat Stover .25 .60
BCP96 Wuilmer Becerra .25 .60
BCP97 Miller Diaz .25 .60
BCP98 Akeel Morris .25 .60
BCP99 Kenny Giles .30 .75
BCP100 Brian Ragira .25 .60
BCP101 Victor De Leon .25 .60
BCP102 Steven Ramos .25 .60
BCP103 Chris Kohler .25 .60
BCP104 Seth Mejias-Brean .25 .60
BCP105 Miguel Alfredo Gonzalez .25 .60
BCP106 Alexander Guerrero .30 .75
BCP107 Jose Herrera .25 .60
BCP108 Tyler Marlette .25 .60
BCP109 Mookie Betts 30.00 80.00
BCP110 Joe Wendle .25 .60

2014 Bowman Chrome Prospects Black Refractors

*BLACK REF: 5X TO 12X BASIC
STATED ODDS 1:229 HOBBY
STATED PRINT RUN 99 SER.#'d SETS

2014 Bowman Chrome Prospects Black Wave Refractors

*BLACK WAVE: 3X TO 8X BASIC

2014 Bowman Chrome Prospects Blue Refractors

*BLUE REF: 3X TO 8X BASIC
STATED ODDS 1:91 HOBBY
STATED PRINT RUN 250 SER.#'d SETS

2014 Bowman Chrome Prospects Blue Wave Refractors

*BLUE WAVE: 2X TO 5X BASIC

2014 Bowman Chrome Prospects Gold Refractors

*GOLD REF: 8X TO 20X BASIC
STATED ODDS 1:453 HOBBY
STATED PRINT RUN 50 SER.#'d SETS
BCP6 Julio Urias 25.00 60.00
BCP17 Jose Abreu 60.00 150.00

2014 Bowman Chrome Prospects Green Refractors

*GREEN REF: 6X TO 15X BASIC
STATED ODDS 1:303 HOBBY
STATED PRINT RUN 75 SER.#'d SETS

2014 Bowman Chrome Prospects Green Wave Refractors

*GREEN WAVE: 10X TO 25X BASIC
STATED PRINT RUN 25 SER.#'d SETS
BCP6 Julio Urias 25.00 60.00

2014 Bowman Chrome Prospects Orange Refractors

*ORANGE REF: 10X TO 25X BASIC
STATED ODDS 1:908 HOBBY
STATED PRINT RUN 25 SER.#'d SETS

2014 Bowman Chrome Prospects Orange Wave Refractors

*ORANGE WAVE: 4X TO 10X BASIC

2014 Bowman Chrome Prospects Purple Refractors

*PURPLE REF: 4X TO 10X BASIC
STATED PRINT RUN 199 SER.#'d SETS

2014 Bowman Chrome Prospects Red Wave Refractors

*RED WAVE: 10X TO 25X BASIC
STATED PRINT RUN 25 SER.#'d SETS
BCP6 Julio Urias 25.00 60.00

2014 Bowman Chrome Prospects Refractors

*REF: 2X TO 5X BASIC
STATED ODDS 1:45 HOBBY
STATED PRINT RUN 500 SER.#'d SETS

2014 Bowman Chrome Prospects Silver Wave Refractors

*SILVER WAVE: 10X TO 25X BASIC
STATED PRINT RUN 25 SER.#'d SETS
BCP6 Julio Urias 25.00 60.00

2014 Bowman Chrome Prospects Series 2

PRINTING PLATE ODDS 1:1740 HOBBY
PLATE PRINT RUN 1 SET PER COLOR
BLACK-CYAN-MAGENTA-YELLOW ISSUED
NO PLATE PRICING DUE TO SCARCITY
BCP1 Shae Simmons .25 .60
BCP2 Kean Wong .25 .60
BCP3 Gosuke Katoh .40 1.00
BCP4 Franklin Barreto .40 1.00
BCP5 Ryan Casteel .25 .60
BCP6 Akeem Bostick .25 .60
BCP7 Carlos Contreras .25 .60
BCP8 Alberto Tirado .25 .60
BCP9 Willy Garcia .25 .60
BCP10 Richard Urena .30 .75
BCP11 Isiah Kiner-Falefa .40 1.00
BCP12 Jamie Westbrook .25 .60
BCP13 Franmil Reyes .75 2.00
BCP14 Kelly Dugan .25 .60

BCP15 Jose Rondon .25 .60
BCP16 Ben Lively .25 .60
BCP17 LeVon Washington .25 .60
BCP18 Luigi Rodriguez .25 .60
BCP19 Jordan Patterson .25 .60
BCP20 Cody Anderson .25 .60
BCP21 R.J. Alvarez .25 .60
BCP22 Andy Burns .25 .60
BCP23 Daniel Winkler .25 .60
BCP24 Vincent Velasquez .40 1.00
BCP25 Teddy Stankiewicz .25 .60
BCP26 Dillon Overton .25 .60
BCP27 Nick Kingham .30 .75
BCP28 Austin Wilson .25 .60
BCP29 Manuel Margot .40 1.00
BCP30 Dom Nunez .25 .60
BCP31 Jacob Nottingham .30 .75
BCP32 Michael Feliz .30 .75
BCP33 Adrian Marin .25 .60
BCP34 Trevor Gretzky .25 .60
BCP35 Nick Ramirez .25 .60
BCP36 Juan Silva .25 .60
BCP37 Jonathan Reynoso .25 .60
BCP38 Daniel Palka .25 .60
BCP39 Raul Mondesi .75 2.00
BCP40 Michael Taylor .30 .75
BCP41 Joe Wendle .25 .60
BCP42 Tim Cooney .25 .60
BCP43 Yimi Garcia .25 .60
BCP44 Cody Reed .25 .60
BCP45 Jose Urena .30 .75
BCP46 Andrew Thurman .25 .60
BCP47 Corey Knebel .25 .60
BCP48 Michael O'Neill .25 .60
BCP49 Devin Williams .60 1.50
BCP50 Tyler Marlette .25 .60
BCP51 Gabriel Ynoa .30 .75
BCP52 Tyler Mahle .25 .60
BCP53 Jason Martin .40 1.00
BCP54 Spencer Patton .25 .60
BCP55 Aaron Brooks .40 1.00
BCP56 Jeff McNeil 1.50 4.00
BCP57 Johnny Field .25 .60
BCP58 Nathan Mikolas .25 .60
BCP59 Ryan McNeil .25 .60
BCP60 Trae Arbet .25 .60
BCP61 Austin Nola .30 .75
BCP62 Brandon Dixon .25 .60
BCP63 Ryan Hafner .25 .60
BCP64 Matt Whitehouse .25 .60
BCP65 Fred Lewis .25 .60
BCP66 Dylan Unsworth .25 .60
BCP67 Ryan Kussmaul .30 .75
BCP68 JaCoby Jones .40 1.00
BCP69 Breyvic Valera .25 .60
BCP70 Jose Ramirez .25 .60
BCP71 Michael Ohlman .25 .60
BCP72 Sebastian Vader .25 .60
BCP73 Robert Whalen .25 .60
BCP74 Tim Berry .25 .60
BCP75 Chris Heston .25 .60
BCP76 Jeff Ames .25 .60
BCP77 Harold Ramirez .40 1.00
BCP78 Luis Severino .40 1.00
BCP79 Bobby Wahl .25 .60
BCP80 Thairo Estrada 1.00 2.50
BCP81 Logan Bawcom .25 .60
BCP82 Rafael Medina .25 .60
BCP83 Elvis Araujo .25 .60
BCP84 Stuart Turner .25 .60
BCP85 Chad Pinder .25 .60
BCP86 Cam Perkins .25 .60
BCP87 Jose Pujols .25 .60
BCP88 Jake Sanchez .25 .60
BCP89 Dawel Lugo .25 .60
BCP90 Victor Caratini .75 2.00
BCP91 Dalton Pompey .40 1.00
BCP92 L.J. Mazzilli .25 .60
BCP93 Buck Farmer .25 .60
BCP94 Kevin Encarnacion .25 .60
BCP95 Taylor Cole .25 .60
BCP96 Felix Jorge .25 .60
BCP97 Ariel Soriano .25 .60
BCP98 Amaurys Minier .25 .60
BCP99 Wilmer Oberto .25 .60
BCP100 Yonathan Mejia .25 .60

2014 Bowman Chrome Prospects Series 2 Error Card Variations

STATED ODDS 1:928 HOBBY
PECAB Andy Burns 4.00 10.00
PECABO Aaron Books 6.00 15.00
PECAT Andrew Thurboy 4.00 10.00
PECAW Austin Wilson 4.00 10.00
PECBL Ben Lively 4.00 10.00
PECBV Valera Breyvic 4.00 10.00
PECEK Evel Knebel 4.00 10.00
PECCR Cody Write 4.00 10.00
PECDW Daniel Winkler 4.00 10.00
PECGK Gosuke Katoh 6.00 15.00
PECJR Jose Ramirez 4.00 10.00
PECJW Joe Wendle 4.00 10.00
PECKW Kean Wrong 4.00 10.00
PECMM Manuel Margot 5.00 12.00
PECMO Michael Ohlboy 4.00 10.00
PECMR Mario Rodriguez 4.00 10.00
PECMT Taylor Michael 5.00 12.00
PECNK Nick Princeham 5.00 12.00
PECRA P.J. Alvarez 4.00 10.00
PECRM Raul Mondesi III 12.00 30.00
PECSS Shea Simmons 4.00 10.00
PECTM Tyler Earthlette 4.00 10.00
PECTS Teddy Stankiewich 4.00 10.00
PECVV Vincent Velazquez 6.00 15.00
PECYG Yimi Garcia 4.00 10.00

2014 Bowman Chrome Prospects Series 2 Short Prints

STATED ODDS 1:288 HOBBY
PSAT Andrew Thurman 2.50 6.00
PSAW Austin Wilson 2.50 6.00
PSFB Franklin Barreto 4.00 10.00
PSGK Gosuke Katoh 4.00 10.00
PSKW Kean Wong 2.50 6.00
PSMM Manuel Margot 4.00 10.00
PSNK Nick Kingham 3.00 8.00
PSSS Shae Simmons 2.50 6.00
PSVV Vincent Velasquez 4.00 10.00
PSYG Yimi Garcia 2.50 6.00

2014 Bowman Chrome Prospects Series 2 Black Static Refractors

*BLACK STATIC: 8X TO 20X BASIC
STATED ODDS 1:205 HOBBY
STATED PRINT RUN 35 SER.#'d SETS
BCP78 Luis Severino 25.00 60.00
BCP91 Dalton Pompey 25.00 60.00

2014 Bowman Chrome Prospects Series 2 Black Wave Refractors

*BLACK WAVE: 3X TO 8X BASIC
RANDOM INSERTS IN PACKS

2014 Bowman Chrome Prospects Series 2 Blue Refractors

*BLUE REF: 3X TO 8X BASIC
STATED ODDS 1:29 HOBBY
STATED PRINT RUN 250 SER.#'d SETS

2014 Bowman Chrome Prospects Series 2 Blue Wave Refractors

*BLUE WAVE: 2X TO 5X BASIC
RANDOM INSERTS IN PACKS

2014 Bowman Chrome Prospects Series 2 Bubble Refractors

*BUBBLE REF: 5X TO 12X BASIC
STATED ODDS 1:63 HOBBY
STATED PRINT RUN 99 SER.#'d SETS

2014 Bowman Chrome Prospects Series 2 Gold Refractors

*GOLD: 8X TO 20X BASIC
STATED ODDS 1:138 HOBBY
STATED PRINT RUN 50 SER.#'d SETS
BCP78 Luis Severino 25.00 60.00

2014 Bowman Chrome Prospects Series 2 Green Refractors

*GREEN REF: 6X TO 15X BASIC
STATED ODDS 1:90 HOBBY
STATED PRINT RUN 75 SER.#'d SETS

2014 Bowman Chrome Prospects Series 2 Orange Refractors

*ORANGE REF: 10X TO 25X BASIC
STATED ODDS 1:276 HOBBY
STATED PRINT RUN 25 SER.#'d SETS
BCP78 Luis Severino 30.00 80.00
BCP91 Dalton Pompey 30.00 80.00

2014 Bowman Chrome Prospects Series 2 Pink Wave Refractors

*PINK WAVE: 6X TO 15X BASIC
STATED ODDS 1:35,000 HOBBY
STATED PRINT RUN 65 SER.#'d SETS

2014 Bowman Chrome Prospects Series 2 Purple Refractors

*PURPLE REF: 4X TO 10X BASIC
STATED ODDS 1:47 HOBBY
STATED PRINT RUN 150 SER.#'d SETS

2014 Bowman Chrome Prospects Series 2 Red Wave Refractors

*RED WAVE: 8X TO 20X BASIC
RANDOM INSERTS IN PACKS
STATED PRINT RUN 25 SER.#'d SETS
BCP78 Luis Severino 25.00 60.00
BCP91 Dalton Pompey 25.00 60.00

2014 Bowman Chrome Prospects Series 2 Refractors

*REF: 2X TO 5X BASIC
STATED ODDS 1:15 HOBBY
STATED PRINT RUN 500 SER.#'d SETS

2014 Bowman Chrome Prospects Series 2 Silver Wave Refractors

*SILVER WAVE: 8X TO 20X BASIC
RANDOM INSERTS IN PACKS
STATED PRINT RUN 25 SER.#'d SETS

2014 Bowman Chrome Rookie Autographs

BOW.ODDS 1:960 HOBBY
BOW.CHR.ODDS 1:1835 HOBBY
BOW.CHR.PLATE ODDS 1:116,000 HOBBY
PLATE PRINT RUN 1 SET PER COLOR
BLACK-CYAN-MAGENTA-YELLOW ISSUED
NO PLATE PRICING DUE TO SCARCITY
BOW.EXCH DEADLINE 4/30/2017
BOW.CHR.EXCH DEADLINE 9/30/2017
BCARAG Alex Guerrero 8.00 20.00
BCARBH Billy Hamilton 8.00 20.00
BCARCO Chris Owings 3.00 8.00
BCARER Enny Romero 3.00 8.00
BCARJA Jose Abreu 40.00 100.00
BCARJK Jeff Kobernus 3.00 8.00
BCARJM Jake Marisnick 3.00 8.00
BCARJN Jimmy Nelson 3.00 8.00
BCARJR J.R. Murphy 3.00 8.00
BCARJS Jonathan Schoop 12.00 30.00
BCARKW Kolten Wong 4.00 10.00
BCARMC Michael Choice 3.00 8.00
BCARMD Matt Davidson 4.00 10.00
BCARNC Nick Castellanos 12.00 30.00
BCAROT Oscar Taveras 4.00 10.00
BCARTD Travis d'Arnaud 4.00 10.00
BCARTW Taijuan Walker 6.00 15.00
BCARWF Wilmer Flores 4.00 10.00
BCARYS Yangervis Solarte 3.00 8.00
BCARYV Yordano Ventura 8.00 20.00

2014 Bowman Chrome Rookie Autographs Black Refractors

*BLACK REF: 1.5X TO 4X BASIC
STATED ODDS 1:1452 HOBBY
STATED PRINT RUN 35 SER.#'d SETS
EXCHANGE DEADLINE 4/30/2017

2014 Bowman Chrome Rookie Autographs Blue Refractors

*BLUE REF: .6X TO 1.5X BASIC
BOW.ODDS 1:938 HOBBY
BOW.CHR.ODDS 1:3060 HOBBY
BOWMAN PRINT RUN 250 SER.#'d SETS
BOW.CHR. PRINT RUN 150 SER.#'d SETS
BOW.EXCH DEADLINE 4/30/2017
BOW.CHR.EXCH DEADLINE 9/30/2017

2014 Bowman Chrome Rookie Autographs Bubble Refractors

*BUBBLE REF: .75X TO 2X BASIC
STATED ODDS 1:4620 HOBBY
STATED PRINT RUN 99 SER.#'d SETS
EXCHANGE DEADLINE 9/30/2017

2014 Bowman Chrome Rookie Autographs Gold Refractors

*GOLD REF: 1X TO 2.5X BASIC
BOW.ODDS 1:4700 HOBBY
BOW.CHR.ODDS 1:9250 HOBBY
STATED PRINT RUN 50 SER.#'d SETS
BOW.EXCH DEADLINE 4/30/2017
BOW.CHR.EXCH DEADLINE 9/30/2017
BCARBH Billy Hamilton 20.00 50.00
BCARJS Jonathan Schoop 60.00 150.00

2014 Bowman Chrome Rookie Autographs Green Refractors

*GREEN REF/75: .75X TO 2X BASIC
BOWMAN PRINT RUN 20 SER.#'d SETS
BOW.CHR PRINT RUN 75 SER.#'d SETS
NO BOWMAN PRICING DUE TO SCARCITY
BOW.EXCH DEADLINE 4/30/2017
BOW.CHR.EXCH DEADLINE 9/30/2017

2014 Bowman Chrome Rookie Autographs Orange Refractors

*ORANGE: 1.5X TO 4X BASIC
BOW.ODDS 1:9400 HOBBY
BOW.CHR.ODDS 1:13,000 HOBBY
STATED PRINT RUN 25 SER.#'d SETS
BOW.EXCH DEADLINE 4/30/2017
BOW.CHR.EXCH DEADLINE 9/30/2017
BCARAG Alex Guerrero 40.00 100.00
BCARXB Xander Bogaerts 150.00 250.00

2014 Bowman Chrome Rookie Autographs Orange Wave Refractors

*ORANGE WAVE: 1.5X TO 4X BASIC
PRINT RUNS B/WN 25-35 COPIES PER
EXCHANGE DEADLINE 4/30/2017
BCARXB Xander Bogaerts/25 150.00 250.00

2014 Bowman Chrome Rookie Autographs Refractors

*REF: .5X TO 1.2X BASIC
STATED ODDS 1:1005 HOBBY
STATED PRINT RUN 500 SER.#'d SETS
EXCHANGE DEADLINE 4/30/2017

2014 Bowman Chrome Top 100 Prospects

STATED ODDS 1:12 HOBBY
BTP1 Byron Buxton .60 1.50
BTP2 Oscar Taveras .60 1.50
BTP3 Miguel Sano .60 1.50
BTP4 Xander Bogaerts 1.50 4.00
BTP5 Carlos Correa 2.50 6.00
BTP6 Javier Baez 2.00 5.00
BTP7 Taijuan Walker .50 1.25
BTP8 Kris Bryant 4.00 10.00
BTP9 Archie Bradley .50 1.25
BTP10 Billy Hamilton .60 1.50
BTP11 Mark Appel .60 1.50
BTP12 Francisco Lindor 3.00 8.00
BTP13 Dylan Bundy .60 1.50
BTP14 Gregory Polanco .75 2.00
BTP15 Travis d'Arnaud .60 1.50
BTP16 Tyler Glasnow .75 2.00
BTP17 Jonathan Gray .60 1.50
BTP18 Kyle Crick .50 1.25
BTP19 George Springer 2.00 5.00
BTP20 Robert Stephenson .50 1.25
BTP21 C.J. Edwards .60 1.50
BTP22 Lucas Giolito .75 2.00
BTP23 Lance McCullers .50 1.25
BTP24 Alex Meyer .50 1.25
BTP25 Eddie Butler .50 1.25
BTP26 Andrew Heaney .50 1.25
BTP27 Nick Castellanos 1.50 4.00
BTP28 Clint Frazier 2.00 5.00
BTP29 Maikel Franco .60 1.50
BTP30 Jameson Taillon .60 1.50
BTP31 Noah Syndergaard .60 1.50
BTP32 Masahiro Tanaka 1.50 4.00
BTP33 Addison Russell .75 2.00
BTP34 Jose Abreu 4.00 10.00
BTP35 Austin Meadows .75 2.00
BTP36 Alen Hanson .50 1.25
BTP37 D.J. Peterson .50 1.25
BTP38 Kevin Gausman .60 1.50
BTP39 Carlos Martinez .60 1.50
BTP40 Joc Pederson .75 2.00
BTP41 Jorge Soler 1.00 2.50
BTP42 Gary Sanchez 1.50 4.00
BTP43 Albert Almora .75 2.00
BTP44 Julio Urias 2.50 6.00
BTP45 Aaron Sanchez .50 1.25
BTP46 Yordano Ventura .60 1.50
BTP47 David Dahl .60 1.50
BTP48 Phil Ervin .50 1.25
BTP49 Kyle Zimmer .50 1.25
BTP50 Erik Johnson .50 1.25
BTP51 Henry Owens .60 1.50
BTP52 Danny Hultzen .50 1.25
BTP53 Colin Moran .50 1.25
BTP54 Kohl Stewart .50 1.25
BTP55 C.J. Cron .50 1.25
BTP56 Austin Hedges .50 1.25
BTP57 Corey Seager 2.00 5.00
BTP58 Lucas Sims .50 1.25
BTP59 Victor Sanchez .50 1.25
BTP60 Garin Cecchini .50 1.25
BTP61 Chris Anderson .50 1.25
BTP62 Raul Mondesi 1.50 4.00
BTP63 Delino DeShields .50 1.25
BTP64 Tyler Austin .50 1.25
BTP65 Bubba Starling .60 1.50
BTP66 Mookie Betts 10.00 25.00
BTP67 Chris Owings .50 1.25
BTP68 Jesse Biddle .60 1.50
BTP69 Kolten Wong .60 1.50
BTP70 Jonathan Singleton .60 1.50
BTP71 Micah Johnson .50 1.25
BTP72 Taylor Guerrieri .50 1.25
BTP73 Mike Foltynewicz .50 1.25
BTP74 Jorge Alfaro .60 1.50
BTP75 Joey Gallo 1.00 2.50
BTP76 Rafael De Paula .50 1.25
BTP77 Rougned Odor 1.00 2.50
BTP78 Mason Williams .50 1.25
BTP79 Chris Taylor 2.50 6.00
BTP80 Rafael Montero .50 1.25
BTP81 Michael Choice .50 1.25
BTP82 Eddie Rosario 1.00 2.50
BTP83 Max Fried 2.00 5.00
BTP84 Anthony Ranaudo .50 1.25
BTP85 A.J. Cole .50 1.25
BTP86 Matt Davidson .60 1.50
BTP87 Devon Travis .50 1.25
BTP88 Jackie Bradley Jr. .75 2.00
BTP89 Rosell Herrera .75 2.00
BTP90 Lewis Thorpe .50 1.25
BTP91 Luis Heredia .50 1.25
BTP92 Hak-Ju Lee .50 1.25
BTP93 Marcus Stroman .75 2.00
BTP94 Jose Berrios .75 2.00
BTP95 Christian Bethancourt .50 1.25
BTP96 Miguel Andujar 1.50 4.00
BTP97 Edwin Diaz 1.00 2.50
BTP98 Dan Vogelbach .75 2.00
BTP99 Preston Tucker .75 2.00
BTP100 Josh Bell 1.00 2.50

2014 Bowman Chrome Top 100 Prospects Die Cut Refractors

*REF: 2.5X TO 6X BASIC
STATED ODDS 1:247 HOBBY
STATED PRINT RUN 99 SER.#'d SETS

2014 Bowman Chrome Top 100 Prospects Die Cut X-Fractor Autographs

STATED ODDS 1:10,203 HOBBY
STATED PRINT RUN 24 SER.#'d SETS
BTP1 Byron Buxton 250.00 350.00
BTP11 Mark Appel 100.00 200.00
BTP12 Francisco Lindor 30.00 80.00
BTP15 Travis d'Arnaud 15.00 40.00
BTP19 George Springer 60.00 150.00
BTP29 Maikel Franco 60.00 150.00
BTP34 Jose Abreu 300.00 500.00
BTP64 Tyler Austin 12.00 30.00

2014 Bowman Chrome Draft

STATED PLATE ODDS 1:5200 HOBBY
PLATE PRINT RUN 1 SET PER COLOR
BLACK-CYAN-MAGENTA-YELLOW ISSUED
NO PLATE PRICING DUE TO SCARCITY
CDP1 Tyler Kolek .30 .75
CDP2 Kyle Schwarber 1.25 3.00
CDP3 Alex Jackson .40 1.00
CDP4 Aaron Nola 2.00 5.00
CDP5 Kyle Freeland .60 1.50
CDP6 Jeff Hoffman .50 1.25
CDP7 Michael Conforto .60 1.50
CDP8 Max Pentecost .30 .75
CDP9 Kodi Medeiros .30 .75
CDP10 Trea Turner 1.00 2.50
CDP11 Tyler Beede .50 1.25
CDP12 Sean Newcomb .50 1.25
CDP14 Erick Fedde .30 .75
CDP15 Nick Howard .30 .75
CDP16 Casey Gillaspie .50 1.25
CDP17 Bradley Zimmer .50 1.25
CDP18 Grant Holmes .30 .75
CDP19 Derek Hill .30 .75
CDP20 Cole Tucker .30 .75
CDP21 Matt Chapman 1.50 4.00
CDP22 Michael Chavis 1.50 4.00
CDP23 Luke Weaver 1.00 2.50
CDP24 Foster Griffin .30 .75
CDP25 Alex Blandino .30 .75
CDP26 Luis Ortiz .30 .75
CDP27 Justus Sheffield .60 1.50
CDP28 Braxton Davidson .30 .75
CDP29 Michael Kopech .75 2.00
CDP30 Jack Flaherty 1.25 3.00
CDP32 Ryan Ripken .40 1.00
CDP33 Forrest Wall .50 1.25
CDP34 Blake Anderson .30 .75
CDP35 Derek Fisher .50 1.25
CDP36 Mike Papi .30 .75
CDP37 Connor Joe .30 .75
CDP38 Chase Vallot .30 .75
CDP39 Jacob Gatewood .30 .75
CDP40 A.J. Reed .60 1.50
CDP41 Justin Twine .30 .75
CDP42 Spencer Adams .40 1.00
CDP43 Jake Stinnett .30 .75
CDP44 Nick Burdi .30 .75
CDP45 Matt Imhof .30 .75
CDP46 Ryan Castellani .30 .75
CDP47 Sean Reid-Foley .30 .75
CDP48 Monte Harrison .50 1.25
CDP49 Michael Gettys .40 1.00
CDP50 Aramis Garcia .30 .75
CDP51 Joe Gatto .30 .75
CDP52 Cody Reed .30 .75
CDP53 Jacob Lindgren .40 1.00
CDP54 Scott Blewett .30 .75
CDP55 Taylor Sparks .30 .75
CDP56 Ti'Quan Forbes .30 .75
CDP57 Cameron Varga .30 .75
CDP58 Grant Hockin .30 .75
CDP59 Alex Verdugo .60 1.50
CDP60 Austin DeCarr .30 .75
CDP61 Sam Travis .60 1.50
CDP62 Trey Supak .30 .75
CDP63 Marcus Wilson .30 .75
CDP64 Zech Lemond .30 .75
CDP65 Jakson Reetz .30 .75
CDP66 Jeff Brigham .30 .75
CDP67 Chris Ellis .30 .75
CDP68 Gareth Morgan .30 .75
CDP69 Mitch Keller .50 1.25
CDP70 Spencer Turnbull .30 .75
CDP71 Daniel Gossett .30 .75
CDP72 Garrett Fulenchek .30 .75
CDP73 Brett Graves .30 .75
CDP74 Ronnie Williams .30 .75
CDP75 Isan Diaz .75 2.00
CDP76 Andrew Morales .30 .75
CDP77 Brent Honeywell .50 1.25
CDP78 Carson Sands .30 .75
CDP79 Dylan Cease .75 2.00
CDP80 Jace Fry .30 .75
CDP81 J.D. Davis .50 1.25
CDP82 Austin Cousino .30 .75
CDP83 Aaron Brown .30 .75
CDP84 Milton Ramos .30 .75
CDP85 Brian Gonzalez .30 .75
CDP86 Bobby Bradley .40 1.00
CDP87 Chad Sobotka .30 .75
CDP88 Jonathan Holder .30 .75
CDP89 Nick Wells .30 .75
CDP90 Josh Morgan .30 .75
CDP91 Brian Anderson .30 .75
CDP92 Mark Zagunis .30 .75
CDP93 Michael Cederoth .40 1.00
CDP94 Dylan Davis .40 1.00
CDP95 Matt Railey .30 .75
CDP96 Eric Skoglund .30 .75
CDP97 Wyatt Strahan .30 .75
CDP98 John Richy .30 .75
CDP99 Grayson Greiner .30 .75
CDP100 Jordan Luplow .30 .75
CDP101 Jake Cosart .40 1.00
CDP102 Michael Mader .30 .75
CDP103 Brian Schales .30 .75
CDP104 Brett Austin .30 .75
CDP105 Ryan Yarbrough .50 1.25
CDP106 Chris Oliver .30 .75
CDP107 Matt Morgan .30 .75
CDP108 Trace Loehr .30 .75
CDP109 Austin Gomber .40 1.00
CDP110 Casey Soltis .30 .75
CDP111 Troy Stokes .30 .75
CDP112 Nick Torres .30 .75
CDP113 Jeremy Rhoades .30 .75
CDP114 Jordan Montgomery .60 1.50
CDP115 Gavin LaValley .30 .75
CDP116 Brett Martin .30 .75
CDP117 Sam Hentges .30 .75
CDP118 Taylor Gushue .30 .75
CDP119 Jordan Schwartz .30 .75
CDP120 Justin Steele .30 .75
CDP121 Jake Reed .30 .75
CDP122 Rhys Hoskins 5.00 12.00
CDP123 Kevin Padlo .30 .75
CDP124 Lane Thomas .30 .75
CDP125 Dustin DeMuth .30 .75
CDP126 Nick Gordon .40 1.00
CDP127 Austin Bousfield .30 .75
CDP128 Jordan Foley .30 .75
CDP129 Corey Ray .30 .75
CDP130 Jared Walker .30 .75
CDP131 Tejay Antone .30 .75
CDP132 Shane Zeile .30 .75

2014 Bowman Chrome Draft Black Refractors

*BLACK REF: 3X TO 8X BASIC
STATED ODDS 1:116 HOBBY
STATED PRINT RUN 75 SER.#'d SETS

2014 Bowman Chrome Draft Blue Refractors

*BLUE REF: 2X TO 5X BASIC
STATED ODDS 1:37 HOBBY
STATED PRINT RUN 399 SER.#'d SETS

2014 Bowman Chrome Draft Blue Wave Refractors

*BLUE WAVE: 2X TO 5X BASIC
STATED ODDS 1:524 HOBBY

2014 Bowman Chrome Draft Gold Refractors

*GOLD REF: 6X TO 15X BASIC
STATED ODDS 1:418 HOBBY
STATED PRINT RUN 50 SER.#'d SETS
CDP2 Kyle Schwarber 50.00 100.00
CDP7 Michael Conforto 50.00 100.00
CDP122 Rhys Hoskins 200.00 400.00

2014 Bowman Chrome Draft Green Refractors

*GREEN REF: 2.5X TO 6X BASIC
STATED ODDS 1:133 HOBBY
STATED PRINT RUN 150 SER.#'d SETS

2014 Bowman Chrome Draft Orange Refractors

*ORANGE REF: 8X TO 20X BASIC
STATED ODDS 1:834 HOBBY
STATED PRINT RUN 25 SER.#'d SETS
CDP2 Kyle Schwarber 50.00 120.00
CDP7 Michael Conforto 50.00 120.00
CDP122 Rhys Hoskins 250.00 500.00

2014 Bowman Chrome Draft Purple Ice Refractors

*PURPLE ICE: X TO X BASIC
RANDOM INSERTS IN PACKS
STATED PRINT RUN 99 SER.#'d SETS

2014 Bowman Chrome Draft Red Ice Refractors

*RED ICE: X TO X BASIC
RANDOM INSERTS IN PACKS
STATED PRINT RUN 150 SER.#'d SETS

2014 Bowman Chrome Draft Red Wave Refractors

*RED WAVE REF: 8X TO 20X BASIC
RANDOM INSERTS IN PACKS
STATED PRINT RUN 25 SER.#'d SETS
CDP2 Kyle Schwarber 50.00 120.00
CDP7 Michael Conforto 50.00 120.00
CDP122 Rhys Hoskins 250.00 500.00

2014 Bowman Chrome Draft Refractors

*REFRACTOR: .75X TO 2X BASIC
STATED ODDS 1:3 HOBBY
STATED MANZIEL ODDS 1:19,000 HOBBY
CDP31 Johnny Manziel 3.00 8.00

2014 Bowman Chrome Draft Silver Wave Refractors

*SILVER WAVE REF: 8X TO 20X BASIC
RANDOM INSERTS IN PACKS
STATED PRINT RUN 25 SER.#'d SETS
CDP2 Kyle Schwarber 50.00 120.00
CDP7 Michael Conforto 50.00 120.00
CDP122 Rhys Hoskins 250.00 500.00

2014 Bowman Chrome Draft Draft Pick Autographs

STATED ODDS 1:37 HOBBY
STATED PLATE ODDS 1:16,300 HOBBY
PLATE PRINT RUN 1 SET PER COLOR
BLACK-CYAN-MAGENTA-YELLOW ISSUED
NO PLATE PRICING DUE TO SCARCITY
EXCHANGE DEADLINE 11/30/2017
BCAAB Alex Blandino 3.00 8.00
BCAAD Austin DeCarr 3.00 8.00
BCAAG Aramis Garcia 3.00 8.00
BCAAJ Alex Jackson 4.00 10.00
BCAAN Aaron Nola 20.00 50.00
BCAAR A.J. Reed 3.00 8.00
BCAAV Alex Verdugo 20.00 50.00
BCABAN Blake Anderson 3.00 8.00
BCABD Braxton Davidson 3.00 8.00
BCABGO Brian Gonzalez 3.00 8.00
BCABZ Bradley Zimmer 12.00 30.00
BCACE Chris Ellis 3.00 8.00
BCACJ Connor Joe 3.00 8.00
BCACS Carson Sands 3.00 8.00
BCACSO Chad Sobotka 3.00 8.00
BCACT Cole Tucker 3.00 8.00
BCACV Chase Vallot 3.00 8.00
BCACVA Cameron Varga 3.00 8.00
BCADC Dylan Cease 15.00 40.00
BCADF Derek Fisher 4.00 10.00
BCADH Derek Hill 3.00 8.00
BCADPO Dillon Overton 3.00 8.00
BCAEF Erick Fedde 3.00 8.00
BCAFG Foster Griffin 3.00 8.00
BCAFW Forrest Wall 5.00 12.00
BCAGF Garrett Fulenchek 3.00 8.00
BCAGH Grant Holmes 3.00 8.00
BCAGHO Grant Hockin 3.00 8.00
BCAGM Gareth Morgan 3.00 8.00
BCAJB Jeff Brigham 3.00 8.00
BCAJF Jack Flaherty 20.00 50.00
BCAJG Jacob Gatewood 3.00 8.00
BCAJGA Joe Gatto 3.00 8.00
BCAJH Jeff Hoffman 5.00 12.00
BCAJL Jacob Lindgren 4.00 10.00
BCAJR Jakson Reetz 3.00 8.00
BCAJS Justus Sheffield 8.00 20.00
BCAJST Jake Stinnett 3.00 8.00
BCAJT Justin Twine 3.00 8.00
BCAKF Kyle Freeland 10.00 25.00
BCAKM Kodi Medeiros 3.00 8.00
BCAKS Kyle Schwarber 20.00 50.00
BCALO Luis Ortiz 3.00 8.00
BCALW Luke Weaver 3.00 8.00
BCAMCH Matt Chapman 30.00 80.00
BCAMG Michael Gettys 4.00 10.00
BCAMH Monte Harrison 15.00 40.00
BCAMI Matt Imhof 3.00 8.00
BCAMIC Michael Chavis 12.00 30.00
BCAMK Michael Kopech 20.00 50.00
BCAMP Max Pentecost 3.00 8.00
BCAMPA Mike Papi 3.00 8.00
BCAMW Marcus Wilson 3.00 8.00
BCANB Nick Burdi 3.00 8.00
BCANG Nick Gordon 4.00 10.00
BCANH Nick Howard 3.00 8.00
BCANW Nick Wells 3.00 8.00
BCAMC Conforto Issued in '15 BC 30.00 80.00
BCARC Ryan Castellani 3.00 8.00
BCARR Ryan Ripken 4.00 10.00
BCARW R.Williams Issued in '15 BC 3.00 8.00
BCASA Spencer Adams 4.00 10.00
BCASB Scott Blewett 3.00 8.00
BCASN Sean Newcomb 5.00 12.00
BCASRF Sean Reid-Foley 3.00 8.00
BCATB Tyler Beede 5.00 12.00
BCATF Ti'Quan Forbes 3.00 8.00
BCATK Tyler Kolek 3.00 8.00
BCATS Taylor Sparks 3.00 8.00
BCATSU Trey Supak 3.00 8.00
BCATT Trea Turner 40.00 100.00
BCAZL Zech Lemond 3.00 8.00

2014 Bowman Chrome Draft Draft Pick Autographs Black Refractors

*BLACK REF: 2X TO 5X BASIC
STATED ODDS 1:781 HOBBY
STATED PRINT RUN 35 SER.#'d SETS
EXCHANGE DEADLINE 11/30/2017
BCABD Braxton Davidson 60.00 150.00
BCAMIC Michael Chavis 150.00 400.00

2014 Bowman Chrome Draft Draft Pick Autographs Blue Refractors

*BLUE REF: 1.2X TO 3X BASIC
STATED ODDS 1:436 HOBBY
STATED PRINT RUN 150 SER.#'d SETS
EXCHANGE DEADLINE 11/30/2017

2014 Bowman Chrome Draft Draft Pick Autographs Gold Refractors

*GOLD REF: 1.2X TO 3X BASIC
STATED ODDS 1:1310 HOBBY
STATED PRINT RUN 50 SER.#'d SETS
EXCHANGE DEADLINE 11/30/2017
BCABD Braxton Davidson 60.00 150.00
BCAMIC Michael Chavis 150.00 400.00

2014 Bowman Chrome Draft Draft Pick Autographs Green Refractors

*GREEN REF: 1X TO 2.5X BASIC
STATED ODDS 1:664 HOBBY
STATED PRINT RUN 99 SER.#'d SETS
EXCHANGE DEADLINE 11/30/2017

2014 Bowman Chrome Draft Draft Pick Autographs Refractors

*REF: .5X TO 1.2X BASIC
STATED ODDS 1:131 HOBBY
EXCHANGE DEADLINE 11/30/2017
BCAJM Johnny Manziel 15.00 40.00

2014 Bowman Chrome Draft Future of the Franchise Mini

STATED ODDS 1:12 HOBBY
*BLUE/99: 1X TO 2.5X BASIC
FFAJ Alex Jackson .50 1.25
FFBS Braden Shipley .40 1.00
FFBSW Blake Swihart .50 1.25
FFCC Carlos Correa 2.00 5.00
FFCCO Clint Coulter .40 1.00
FFCE C.J. Edwards .50 1.25
FFCF Clint Frazier 1.50 4.00
FFCG Casey Gillaspie .60 1.50
FFDD David Dahl .50 1.25
FFDH Derek Hill .40 1.00
FFDR Daniel Robertson .50 1.25
FFDS Dominic Smith .40 1.00
FFHH Hunter Harvey .40 1.00
FFHR Hunter Renfroe .50 1.25
FFJA Jorge Alfaro .50 1.25
FFJC J.P. Crawford .40 1.00
FFJH Jeff Hoffman .60 1.50
FFJU Julio Urias 2.00 5.00
FFJW Jesse Winker .50 1.25
FFKZ Kyle Zimmer .40 1.00
FFLG Lucas Giolito .60 1.50
FFLS Lucas Sims .40 1.00
FFLSE Luis Severino .60 1.50
FFMS Miguel Sano .50 1.25
FFRK Rob Kaminsky .40 1.00
FFSN Sean Newcomb .60 1.50
FFTA Tim Anderson .75 2.00
FFTB Tyler Beede .60 1.50
FFTG Tyler Glasnow .60 1.50
FFTK Tyler Kolek .40 1.00

2014 Bowman Chrome Draft Scouts Breakout Die-Cut Refractors

STATED ODDS 1:96 HOBBY
*X-FRACTOR/99: .5X TO 1.2X BASIC
BSBAB Aaron Blair .75 2.00
BSBAJ Aaron Judge 12.00 30.00
BSBAR Alex Reyes 1.25 3.00
BSBBJ Brian Johnson .75 2.00
BSBBL Ben Lively .75 2.00
BSBBP Brett Phillips 1.00 2.50
BSBCP Chad Pinder .75 2.00
BSBCS Chance Sisco 1.50 4.00
BSBCW Chad Wallach 1.25 3.00
BSBDR Daniel Robertson 1.00 2.50
BSBES Edmundo Sosa .75 2.00
BSBFM Francellis Montas .75 2.00
BSBGG Gabriel Guerrero .75 2.00
BSBJB Jake Bauers 1.25 3.00
BSBJD Jose De Leon 1.25 3.00
BSBJH Jabari Henry 1.50 4.00
BSBJJ JaCoby Jones 1.25 3.00
BSBJL Jordy Lara .75 2.00
BSBJP Jose Peraza .75 2.00
BSBJW Justin Williams 1.00 2.50
BSBKW Kyle Waldrop .75 2.00
BSBKZ Kevin Ziomek .75 2.00
BSBLS Luis Severino 1.25 3.00
BSBLW LeVon Washington .75 2.00
BSBMM Marcos Molina 1.00 2.50
BSBMO Matt Olson 1.25 3.00
BSBNL Nick Longhi 1.25 3.00
BSBNM Nomar Mazara 2.00 5.00
BSBRM Ryan McMahon .75 2.00
BSBRN Renato Nunez 1.50 4.00
BSBSC Sean Coyle .75 2.00
BSBSM Steven Matz 1.50 4.00
BSBTD Tyler Danish .75 2.00
BSBTG Tayron Guerrero .75 2.00
BSBWL Will Locante .75 2.00

2014 Bowman Chrome Draft Scouts Breakout Die-Cut Autographs

STATED ODDS 1:4640 HOBBY
STATED PRINT RUN 99 SER.#'d SETS
EXCHANGE DEADLINE 11/30/2017
BSAAR Alex Reyes 20.00 50.00
BSAES Edmundo Sosa 12.00 30.00
BSAKW Kyle Waldrop 6.00 15.00
BSALS Luis Severino 40.00 100.00
BSALW LeVon Washington 6.00 15.00
BSAMO Matt Olson 15.00 40.00
BSANL Nick Longhi 10.00 25.00
BSATD Tyler Danish 6.00 15.00
BSATG Tayron Guerrero EXCH 6.00 15.00

2014 Bowman Chrome Draft Top Prospects

STATED PLATE ODDS 1:5200 HOBBY
PLATE PRINT RUN 1 SET PER COLOR
BLACK-CYAN-MAGENTA-YELLOW ISSUED
NO PLATE PRICING DUE TO SCARCITY
CTP1 Kohl Stewart .30 .75
CTP2 Miguel Sano .40 1.00
CTP3 Carlos Correa 1.50 4.00
CTP4 Mark Appel .40 1.00
CTP5 Jameson Taillon .40 1.00
CTP6 Raul Mondesi 1.00 2.50
CTP7 Jorge Alfaro .40 1.00
CTP8 Max Fried 1.25 3.00
CTP9 Lucas Giolito .50 1.25
CTP10 Austin Meadows .50 1.25
CTP11 Clint Frazier 1.25 3.00
CTP12 Colin Moran .30 .75
CTP13 Lucas Sims .30 .75
CTP14 Julio Urias 1.50 4.00
CTP15 David Dahl .40 1.00
CTP16 Josh Bell .60 1.50
CTP17 Braden Shipley .30 .75
CTP18 D.J. Peterson .30 .75
CTP19 Jose Berrios .50 1.25
CTP20 Trey Ball .30 .75
CTP21 Rosell Herrera .50 1.25
CTP22 J.P. Crawford .30 .75
CTP23 Reese McGuire .30 .75
CTP24 Phil Ervin .30 .75
CTP25 Jesse Winker .40 1.00
CTP26 Dominic Smith .30 .75
CTP27 Hunter Harvey .30 .75
CTP28 Vincent Velasquez .50 1.25
CTP29 Gabriel Guerrero .30 .75
CTP30 Brandon Nimmo .50 1.25
CTP31 Jose Peraza .30 .75
CTP32 Hunter Renfroe .40 1.00
CTP33 Eloy Jimenez 4.00 10.00
CTP34 Alen Hanson .30 .75
CTP35 Albert Almora .50 1.25
CTP36 Lance McCullers .30 .75
CTP37 Rafael Devers 3.00 8.00
CTP38 Luis Severino .50 1.25
CTP39 Aaron Judge 5.00 12.00
CTP40 Peter O'Brien .40 1.00
CTP41 Corey Seager 1.25 3.00
CTP42 Aaron Blair .30 .75
CTP43 Ben Lively .30 .75
CTP44 Daniel Robertson .40 1.00
CTP45 Josh Hader .75 2.00
CTP46 Hunter Dozier .30 .75
CTP47 Tim Anderson .60 1.50
CTP48 Tyler Danish .30 .75
CTP49 Alex Gonzalez .50 1.25
CTP50 JaCoby Jones .50 1.25
CTP51 Eric Jagielo .30 .75
CTP52 Rob Kaminsky .30 .75
CTP53 Lewis Brinson .50 1.25
CTP54 Travis Demeritte .40 1.00
CTP55 Luis Torrens .30 .75
CTP56 Ian Clarkin .30 .75
CTP57 Josh Hart .30 .75
CTP58 Michael Lorenzen .30 .75
CTP59 Robert Stephenson .30 .75
CTP60 Ryan McMahon .30 .75
CTP61 Tyler Glasnow .50 1.25
CTP62 Kris Bryant 2.50 6.00
CTP63 Kyle Crick .30 .75
CTP64 Mason Williams .30 .75
CTP65 Christian Binford .30 .75
CTP66 Jake Thompson .30 .75
CTP67 Sean Coyle .30 .75
CTP68 James Ramsey .30 .75
CTP69 Byron Buxton .40 1.00
CTP70 Nick Williams .40 1.00
CTP71 Miguel Almonte .30 .75
CTP72 C.J. Edwards .40 1.00
CTP73 Delino DeShields .30 .75
CTP74 Trevor Story 1.25 3.00
CTP75 Raimel Tapia .40 1.00
CTP76 Michael Feliz .40 1.00
CTP77 Brandon Drury .30 .75
CTP78 Franklin Barreto .50 1.25
CTP79 Chris Stratton .30 .75
CTP80 Joey Gallo .60 1.50
CTP81 Christian Arroyo 2.00 5.00
CTP82 Mac Williamson .40 1.00
CTP83 Clayton Blackburn .50 1.25
CTP84 Blake Swihart .40 1.00
CTP85 Gosuke Katoh .50 1.25
CTP86 Roberto Osuna .30 .75
CTP87 Courtney Hawkins .30 .75
CTP88 Tyler Naquin .40 1.00
CTP89 Devon Travis .30 .75
CTP90 Nomar Mazara .75 2.00

2014 Bowman Chrome Draft Top Prospects Black Refractors

*BLACK REF: 2.5X TO 6X BASIC
STATED ODDS 1:116 HOBBY
STATED PRINT RUN 75 SER.#'d SETS
CTP39 Aaron Judge 50.00 120.00

2014 Bowman Chrome Draft Top Prospects Blue Refractors

*BLUE REF: 1.5X TO 4X BASIC
STATED ODDS 1:37 HOBBY
STATED PRINT RUN 399 SER.#'d SETS
CTP39 Aaron Judge 30.00 80.00

2014 Bowman Chrome Draft Top Prospects Blue Wave Refractors

*BLUE WAVE: 1.5X TO 4X BASIC
STATED ODDS 1:524 HOBBY
CTP39 Aaron Judge 30.00 80.00

2014 Bowman Chrome Draft Top Prospects Gold Refractors

*GOLD REF: 5X TO 12X BASIC
STATED ODDS 1:418 HOBBY
STATED PRINT RUN 50 SER.#'d SETS
CTP39 Aaron Judge 100.00 250.00

2014 Bowman Chrome Draft Top Prospects Green Refractors

*GREEN REF: 2X TO 5X BASIC
STATED ODDS 1:133 HOBBY
STATED PRINT RUN 150 SER.#'d SETS
CTP39 Aaron Judge 40.00 100.00

2014 Bowman Chrome Draft Top Prospects Orange Refractors

*ORANGE REF: 6X TO 15X BASIC
STATED ODDS 1:834 HOBBY
STATED PRINT RUN 25 SER.#'d SETS
CTP39 Aaron Judge 125.00 300.00

2014 Bowman Chrome Draft Top Prospects Purple Ice Refractors

*PURPLE ICE: X TO X BASIC
RANDOM INSERTS IN PACKS
STATED PRINT RUN 99 SER.#'d SETS

2014 Bowman Chrome Draft Top Prospects Red Ice Refractors

*RED ICE: X TO X BASIC
RANDOM INSERTS IN PACKS
STATED PRINT RUN 25 SER.#'d SETS

2014 Bowman Chrome Draft Top Prospects Red Wave Refractors

*RED WAVE REF: 6X TO 15X BASIC
RANDOM INSERTS IN PACKS
STATED PRINT RUN 25 SER.#'d SETS
CTP39 Aaron Judge 125.00 300.00

2014 Bowman Chrome Draft Top Prospects Refractors

*REFRACTOR: .6X TO 1.5X BASIC
STATED ODDS 1:3 HOBBY

2014 Bowman Chrome Draft Top Prospects Silver Wave Refractors

*SILVER WAVE REF: 6X TO 15X BASIC
RANDOM INSERTS IN PACKS
STATED PRINT RUN 25 SER.#'d SETS
CTP39 Aaron Judge 125.00 300.00

2015 Bowman Chrome

COMPLETE SET (200) 25.00 60.00
STATED PLATE ODDS 1:5068 HOBBY
PLATE PRINT RUN 1 SET PER COLOR
BLACK-CYAN-MAGENTA-YELLOW ISSUED
NO PLATE PRICING DUE TO SCARCITY
1 Miguel Cabrera .30 .75
2 Michael Brantley .25 .60
3 Yasmani Grandal .20 .50
4 Byron Buxton RC .60 1.50
5 Daniel Murphy .25 .60
6 Clay Buchholz .20 .50
7 James Loney .20 .50
8 Dee Gordon .20 .50
9 Khris Davis .30 .75
10 Trevor Rosenthal .20 .50
11 Jered Weaver .25 .60
12 Lucas Duda .25 .60
13 James Shields .20 .50
14 Jacob Lindgren RC .50 1.25
15 Michael Bourn .20 .50
16 Yunel Escobar .20 .50
17 George Springer .25 .60
18 Ryan Howard .25 .60
19 Justin Upton .25 .60
20 Zach Britton .25 .60
21 Santiago Casilla .20 .50
22 Max Scherzer .30 .75
23 Carlos Carrasco .20 .50
24 Angel Pagan .20 .50
25 Wade Miley .20 .50
26 Ryan Braun .25 .60
27 Carlos Gonzalez .25 .60
28 Chase Utley .25 .60
29 Brandon Moss .20 .50
30 Juan Lagares .20 .50
31 David Robertson .20 .50
32 Carlos Santana .25 .60
33 Ender Inciarte RC .40 1.00
34 Jimmy Rollins .25 .60
35 J.D. Martinez .30 .75
36 Yadier Molina .30 .75
37 Ryan Zimmerman .25 .60
38 Stephen Strasburg .30 .75
39 Torii Hunter .20 .50
40 Anibal Sanchez .20 .50
41 Michael Cuddyer .20 .50
42 Jorge De La Rosa .20 .50
43 Shane Greene .20 .50
44 John Lackey .25 .60
45 Hyun-Jin Ryu .25 .60
46 Lance Lynn .25 .60
47 David Freese .20 .50
48 Russell Martin .20 .50
49 Jose Iglesias .25 .60
50 Pablo Sandoval .25 .60
51 Will Middlebrooks .20 .50
52 Joe Mauer .25 .60
53 Chris Archer .20 .50
54 Starling Marte .25 .60
55 Jason Heyward .25 .60
56 Taijuan Walker .20 .50
57 Pedro Alvarez .20 .50
58 Jose Fernandez .30 .75
59 Marlon Byrd .20 .50
60 Neil Walker .20 .50
61 Mike Moustakas .25 .60
62 Trevor Bauer .30 .75
63 Steven Souza Jr. .25 .60
64 Michael Saunders .25 .60
65 Andrew Miller .25 .60
66 Melky Cabrera .20 .50
67 Denard Span .20 .50
68 Yovani Gallardo .20 .50
69 Wade Davis .20 .50
70 Nelson Cruz .30 .75
71 Chris Carter .20 .50
72 Alex Avila .25 .60
73 Mark Melancon .20 .50
74 Zack Cozart .20 .50
75 Jeff Samardzija .20 .50
76 Jake Marisnick .20 .50
77 Kolten Wong .25 .60
78 Josh Collmenter .20 .50
79 Alex Rios .25 .60
80 Dustin Ackley .20 .50
81 Felix Hernandez .25 .60
82 Curtis Granderson .25 .60
83 Jean Segura .25 .60
84 Adam LaRoche .20 .50
85 Hunter Pence .25 .60
86 Francisco Liriano .20 .50
87 Josh Donaldson .25 .60
88 Kendrys Morales .20 .50
89 Francisco Lindor RC 8.00 20.00
90 Freddie Freeman .40 1.00
91 Rick Porcello .25 .60
92 Tyson Ross .20 .50
93 Billy Butler .20 .50
94 Scott Kazmir .20 .50
95 Martin Prado .20 .50
96 Pat Neshek .20 .50
97 Travis Wood .20 .50
98 Brandon Phillips .20 .50
99 Jayson Werth .25 .60
100 Buster Posey .40 1.00
101 Norichika Aoki .20 .50
102 Prince Fielder .25 .60
103 Brett Lawrie .25 .60
104 Cole Hamels .25 .60
105 Jon Lester .25 .60
106 Aaron Hill .20 .50
107 Wei-Yin Chen .20 .50
108 Joe Panik .25 .60
109 DJ LeMahieu .30 .75
110 Carlos Correa RC 4.00 10.00
111 Robinson Cano .25 .60
112 Neftali Feliz .20 .50
113 Adam Jones .25 .60
114 Asdrubal Cabrera .25 .60
115 Wil Myers .20 .50
116 Matt Kemp .25 .60
117 Fernando Rodney .20 .50
118 Addison Reed .20 .50
119 Aroldis Chapman .30 .75
120 Brian Dozier .25 .60
121 Edinson Volquez .20 .50
122 Chris Tillman .20 .50
123 Huston Street .20 .50
124 Todd Frazier .25 .60
125 Miguel Montero .20 .50
126 Francisco Rodriguez .25 .60
127 Avisail Garcia .25 .60
128 Yoenis Cespedes .25 .60
129 Nick Swisher .25 .60
130 Jason Grilli .20 .50
131 Giancarlo Stanton .30 .75
132 Yordano Ventura .25 .60
133 Jordan Zimmermann .25 .60
134 Stephen Vogt .25 .60
135 Anthony DeSclafani .20 .50
136 Dustin Pedroia .30 .75
137 Steve Pearce .30 .75
138 Koji Uehara .20 .50
139 Mitch Moreland .20 .50
140 Albert Pujols .40 1.00
141 Jacoby Ellsbury .25 .60
142 Matt Adams .20 .50
143 Alex Wood .20 .50
144 Adrian Beltre .30 .75
145 Julio Teheran .25 .60
146 Nick Markakis .25 .60
147 Alexei Ramirez .25 .60
148 Salvador Perez .25 .60
149 Gerrit Cole .30 .75
150 Matt Harvey .25 .60
151 Gregory Polanco .25 .60
152 Glen Perkins .20 .50
153 Ichiro Suzuki .40 1.00
154 Dallas Keuchel .25 .60
155 Hanley Ramirez .25 .60
156 Alex Rodriguez .40 1.00
157 Brett Gardner .25 .60
158 Howie Kendrick .20 .50
159 Danny Santana .20 .50
160 Nolan Arenado .40 1.00
161 Addison Russell RC 1.25 3.00
162 Delino DeShields Jr. RC .40 1.00
163 Kevin Plawecki RC .40 1.00
164 Michael Lorenzen RC .40 1.00
165 Brandon Finnegan RC .40 1.00
166 A.J. Cole RC .40 1.00
167 Joc Pederson RC .75 2.00
168 Jake Lamb RC .60 1.50
169 Chi Chi Gonzalez RC .60 1.50
170 Keone Kela RC .50 1.25
171 Jorge Soler RC .60 1.50
172 Yasmany Tomas RC .50 1.25
173 Roberto Osuna RC .40 1.00
174 Rusney Castillo RC .50 1.25
175 Carlos Rodon RC .60 1.50
176 Eddie Rosario RC .75 2.00
177 Tim Cooney RC .40 1.00
178 Javier Baez RC 3.00 8.00
179 Dalton Pompey RC .50 1.25
180 Blake Swihart RC .50 1.25
181 Daniel Norris RC .40 1.00
182 Devon Travis RC .40 1.00
183 Raisel Iglesias RC .50 1.25
184 Preston Tucker RC .40 1.00
185 Joey Gallo RC .75 2.00
186 Miguel Castro RC .40 1.00
187 Michael Taylor RC .40 1.00
188 Austin Hedges RC .40 1.00
189 Jung Ho Kang RC .60 1.50
190 Archie Bradley RC .40 1.00
191 James McCann RC .60 1.50
192 Noah Syndergaard RC .75 2.00
193 Mark Canha RC .60 1.50
194 Paulo Orlando RC .60 1.50
195 Kendall Graveman RC .40 1.00
196 Eduardo Rodriguez RC .60 1.50
197 Anthony Ranaudo RC .40 1.00
198 Maikel Franco RC .50 1.25
199 Odubel Herrera RC .60 1.50
200 Kris Bryant RC 2.50 6.00

2015 Bowman Chrome Blue Refractors

*BLUE REF VET: 4X TO 10X BASIC
*BLUE REF RC: 2X TO 5X BASIC
STATED ODDS 1:68 HOBBY
STATED PRINT RUN 150 SER.#'d SETS
200 Kris Bryant 25.00 60.00

2015 Bowman Chrome Gold Refractors

*GOLD REF VET: 8X TO 20X BASIC
*GOLD REF RC: 4X TO 10X BASIC
STATED ODDS 1:204 HOBBY
STATED PRINT RUN 50 SER.#'d SETS
4 Byron Buxton 10.00 25.00
108 Joe Panik 8.00 20.00
110 Carlos Correa 75.00 200.00
153 Ichiro Suzuki 10.00 25.00
189 Jung Ho Kang 25.00 60.00
200 Kris Bryant 75.00 200.00

2015 Bowman Chrome Green Refractors

*GREEN REF VET: 6X TO 15X BASIC
*GREEN REF RC: 3X TO 8X BASIC
STATED ODDS 1:103 HOBBY
STATED PRINT RUN 99 SER.#'d SETS
4 Byron Buxton 8.00 20.00
110 Carlos Correa 40.00 100.00
200 Kris Bryant 30.00 80.00

2015 Bowman Chrome Orange Refractors

*ORANGE REF VET: 8X TO 20X BASIC
*ORANGE REF RC: 4X TO 10X BASIC
STATED ODDS 1:151 HOBBY
STATED PRINT RUN 25 SER.#'d SETS
4 Byron Buxton 12.00 30.00
108 Joe Panik 10.00 25.00
110 Carlos Correa 100.00 250.00
189 Jung Ho Kang 30.00 80.00
200 Kris Bryant 100.00 250.00

2015 Bowman Chrome Purple Refractors

*PURPLE REF VET: 3X TO 8X BASIC
*PURPLE REF RC: 1.5X TO 4X BASIC
STATED ODDS 1:41 HOBBY
STATED PRINT RUN 250 SER.#'d SETS
200 Kris Bryant 15.00 40.00

2015 Bowman Chrome Refractors

*REF VET: 2X TO 5X BASIC
*REF RC: 1X TO 2.5X BASIC
STATED ODDS 1:21 HOBBY
STATED PRINT RUN 499 SER.#'d SETS
4 Byron Buxton 3.00 8.00
108 Joe Panik 2.50 6.00
110 Carlos Correa 15.00 40.00
200 Kris Bryant 12.00 30.00

2015 Bowman Chrome Bowman Scouts Top 100

COMPLETE SET (100) 75.00 150.00
STATED ODDS 1:8 HOBBY
*DIECUT/99: 2X TO 5X BASIC
BTP1 Byron Buxton .60 1.50
BTP2 Kris Bryant 2.50 6.00
BTP3 Carlos Correa 2.00 5.00
BTP4 Addison Russell 1.25 3.00
BTP5 Daniel Norris .40 1.00
BTP6 Jorge Soler .60 1.50
BTP7 Joey Gallo .75 2.00
BTP8 Miguel Sano .50 1.25
BTP9 Noah Syndergaard .75 2.00
BTP10 Lucas Giolito .75 2.00
BTP11 Julio Urias 1.25 3.00
BTP12 Francisco Lindor 2.50 6.00
BTP13 Carlos Rodon .60 1.50
BTP14 Tyler Glasnow .50 1.25
BTP15 Corey Seager 1.50 4.00
BTP16 J.P. Crawford .40 1.00
BTP17 Archie Bradley .40 1.00
BTP18 Kyle Schwarber 1.50 4.00
BTP19 Jon Gray .40 1.00
BTP20 Tyler Kolek .40 1.00
BTP21 Dylan Bundy .50 1.25
BTP22 Alex Jackson .50 1.25
BTP23 Luis Severino .50 1.25
BTP24 Hunter Harvey .40 1.00
BTP25 Henry Owens .40 1.00
BTP26 Nick Gordon .50 1.25
BTP27 Braden Shipley .40 1.00
BTP28 Jameson Taillon .40 1.00
BTP29 Michael Conforto .50 1.25
BTP30 Robert Stephenson .40 1.00
BTP31 Kyle Zimmer .40 1.00
BTP32 Blake Swihart .50 1.25
BTP33 Joc Pederson .75 2.00
BTP34 Andrew Heaney .40 1.00
BTP35 Jose Peraza .40 1.00
BTP36 Josh Bell .75 2.00
BTP37 Aaron Nola .60 1.50
BTP38 Dalton Pompey .50 1.25
BTP39 Raul Mondesi
BTP40 Austin Meadows .60 1.50
BTP41 Kevin Plawecki .40 1.00
BTP42 Jeff Hoffman .50 1.25
BTP43 Michael Taylor .40 1.00
BTP44 Mark Appel .40 1.00
BTP45 Rusney Castillo .50 1.25
BTP46 Brandon Finnegan .40 1.00
BTP47 Marco Gonzales .60 1.50
BTP48 Kohl Stewart .40 1.00
BTP49 Eduardo Rodriguez .60 1.50
BTP50 C.J. Edwards .60 1.50
BTP51 Jose Berrios .60 1.50
BTP52 Austin Hedges .40 1.00
BTP53 Aaron Judge 8.00 20.00
BTP54 D.J. Peterson .40 1.00
BTP55 Dilson Herrera .50 1.25
BTP56 Aaron Blair .40 1.00
BTP57 Clint Frazier 1.50 4.00
BTP58 Maikel Franco .50 1.25
BTP59 Trea Turner 1.25 3.00
BTP60 Manuel Margot .40 1.00
BTP61 Alex Reyes .50 1.25
BTP62 David Dahl .50 1.25
BTP63 Reynaldo Lopez .50 1.25
BTP64 Daniel Robertson .40 1.00
BTP65 Nick Kingham .40 1.00
BTP66 Aaron Sanchez .50 1.25
BTP67 Tim Anderson .75 2.00
BTP68 Eddie Butler .40 1.00
BTP69 Rafael Montero .40 1.00
BTP70 Jorge Alfaro .60 1.50
BTP71 Matt Olson .60 1.50
BTP72 Gary Sanchez 1.25 3.00
BTP73 Ozhaino Albies 4.00 10.00
BTP74 Garin Cecchini .40 1.00
BTP75 Mike Foltynewicz .40 1.00
BTP76 Grant Holmes .50 1.25
BTP77 Sean Manaea .40 1.00
BTP78 Touki Toussaint .50 1.25
BTP79 Tyrone Taylor .40 1.00
BTP80 Kyle Crick .50 1.25
BTP81 Max Pentecost .40 1.00
BTP82 Alex Meyer .40 1.00
BTP83 Steven Matz .60 1.50
BTP84 Franklin Barreto .50 1.25
BTP85 Casey Gillaspie .60 1.50
BTP86 Albert Almora .50 1.25
BTP87 Lucas Sims .40 1.00
BTP88 Willy Adames .60 1.50
BTP89 Derek Hill .50 1.25
BTP90 Tyler Beede .50 1.25
BTP91 Bradley Zimmer .60 1.50
BTP92 Stephen Piscotty .50 1.25
BTP93 Sean Newcomb .50 1.25
BTP94 Rafael Devers 2.50 6.00
BTP95 Kyle Freeland .50 1.25
BTP96 Robbie Ray .40 1.00
BTP97 Lance McCullers .40 1.00
BTP98 Matt Wisler .40 1.00
BTP99 Luis Ortiz .40 1.00
BTP100 Max Fried 1.50 4.00

2015 Bowman Chrome Bowman Scouts Top 100 Autographs Die Cut Orange

STATED ODDS 1:2424 HOBBY
STATED PRINT RUN 25 SER.#'d SETS
EXCHANGE DEADLINE 4/30/2018
BTP1 Byron Buxton 75.00 150.00
BTP2 Kris Bryant 300.00 500.00
BTP5 Daniel Norris 20.00 50.00
BTP6 Jorge Soler 75.00 150.00
BTP7 Joey Gallo EXCH 125.00 250.00
BTP9 Noah Syndergaard 40.00 100.00
BTP10 Lucas Giolito 40.00 100.00
BTP12 Francisco Lindor 40.00 100.00
BTP13 Carlos Rodon 100.00 200.00
BTP14 Tyler Glasnow 25.00 60.00
BTP16 J.P. Crawford 40.00 100.00
BTP17 Archie Bradley 25.00 60.00
BTP18 Kyle Schwarber 100.00 200.00
BTP21 Dylan Bundy 20.00 50.00
BTP22 Alex Jackson 12.00 30.00
BTP24 Hunter Harvey 25.00 60.00
BTP26 Nick Gordon 20.00 50.00
BTP28 Jameson Taillon 20.00 50.00
BTP32 Blake Swihart 30.00 80.00
BTP33 Joc Pederson 150.00 250.00
BTP36 Josh Bell 30.00 80.00
BTP42 Jeff Hoffman 12.00 30.00
BTP45 Rusney Castillo 12.00 30.00
BTP52 Austin Hedges 20.00 50.00
BTP53 Aaron Judge 75.00 200.00
BTP57 Clint Frazier 25.00 60.00
BTP59 Trea Turner 20.00 50.00
BTP61 Alex Reyes 20.00 50.00
BTP62 David Dahl 12.00 30.00
BTP65 Nick Kingham 10.00 25.00
BTP66 Aaron Sanchez 12.00 30.00
BTP72 Gary Sanchez 60.00 150.00
BTP76 Grant Holmes 25.00 60.00
BTP78 Touki Toussaint 25.00 60.00
BTP80 Kyle Crick 12.00 30.00
BTP81 Max Pentecost 30.00 80.00
BTP89 Derek Hill 30.00 80.00
BTP91 Bradley Zimmer 125.00 250.00
BTP93 Sean Newcomb 20.00 50.00
BTP94 Rafael Devers 125.00 300.00
BTP96 Robbie Ray 10.00 25.00
BTP97 Lance McCullers 20.00 50.00
BTP98 Matt Wisler 20.00 50.00

2015 Bowman Chrome Bowman Scouts Update

COMPLETE SET (25) 10.00 25.00
STATED ODDS 1:6 HOBBY
*DIECUT/99: 2X TO 5X BASIC
BSUAC A.J. Cole .40 1.00
BSUAG Alex Gonzalez .60 1.50
BSUAH Alen Hanson .40 1.00
BSUAR Amed Rosario .60 1.50
BSUBN Brandon Nimmo .60 1.50
BSUCM Colin Moran .40 1.00
BSUDS Dominic Smith .40 1.00
BSUEF Erick Fedde .40 1.00
BSUFW Forrest Wall .40 1.00
BSUGB Greg Bird .50 1.25
BSUHD Hunter Dozier .40 1.00
BSUHR Hunter Renfroe .60 1.50
BSUJW Jesse Winker .40 1.00
BSULJ Luke Jackson .40 1.00
BSUMF Michael Feliz .40 1.00
BSUMH Monte Harrison .60 1.50
BSUNM Nomar Mazara .60 1.50
BSUNW Nick Williams .50 1.25
BSUOA Orlando Arcia .50 1.25
BSURK Rob Kaminsky .40 1.00
BSURM Reese McGuire .40 1.00
BSURR Rob Refsnyder .40 1.00
BSURT Raimel Tapia .60 1.50
BSUSA Spencer Adams .40 1.00
BSUYT Yasmany Tomas .50 1.25

2015 Bowman Chrome Bowman Scouts Update Die Cut Autographs

STATED ODDS 1:1276 HOBBY
EXCHANGE DEADLINE 8/31/2017
*ORANGE/25: .6X TO 1.5X BASIC
BSUAC A.J. Cole 4.00 10.00
BSUCM Colin Moran 4.00 10.00
BSUDS Dominic Smith 4.00 10.00
BSUEF Erick Fedde 4.00 10.00
BSUFW Forrest Wall 4.00 10.00
BSUMF Michael Feliz 4.00 10.00
BSURM Reese McGuire 4.00 10.00
BSUSA Spencer Adams 4.00 10.00

2015 Bowman Chrome Dual Autographs

STATED ODDS 1:8466 HOBBY
STATED PRINT RUN 25 SER.#'d SETS
EXCHANGE DEADLINE 8/31/2017
BDAAR Adames/Rondon 40.00 100.00
BDABS J.Baez/J.Soler 25.00 60.00
BDABSA B.Buxton/M.Sano 40.00 100.00
BDADG C.Gonzalez/D.Dahl 20.00 50.00
BDADN A.Sanchez/D.Norris 25.00 60.00
BDADS deGrom/Syndergaard 150.00 300.00
BDAGS Scherzer/Giolito EXCH 30.00 80.00
BDAJC R.Cano/A.Jackson 20.00 50.00
BDAKF T.Kolek/J.Fernandez 20.00 50.00
BDAOP Porcello/Owens EXCH 10.00 25.00
BDARA C.Rodon/J.Abreu 25.00 60.00
BDASJ Judge/Severino 125.00 250.00
BDATG Tomas/Goldschmidt 20.00 50.00

2015 Bowman Chrome Farm's Finest Minis

COMPLETE SET (150) 75.00 150.00
STATED ODDS 1:6 HOBBY
*PURPLE/250: .6X TO 1.5X BASIC
*BLUE/150: .75X TO 2X BASIC
*GREEN/99: 1X TO 2.5X BASIC
*GOLD/50: 1.5X TO 4X BASIC
*ORANGE/25: 3X TO 8X BASIC
FFMAB Archie Bradley .40 1.00
FFMABL Aaron Blair .40 1.00
FFMAC A.J. Cole .40 1.00
FFMADR Adrian Rondon .50 1.25
FFMAG Alex Gonzalez .60 1.50
FFMAH Andrew Heaney .40 1.00
FFMAHE Austin Hedges .40 1.00
FFMAJ Aaron Judge 6.00 15.00
FFMAJA Alex Jackson .50 1.25
FFMAK Austin Kubitza .40 1.00
FFMALB Alex Blandino .40 1.00
FFMAM Austin Meadows .60 1.50
FFMAN Aaron Nola .60 1.50
FFMAR Addison Russell 1.25 3.00
FFMARE Alex Reyes .50 1.25
FFMARO Avery Romero .40 1.00
FFMAS Aaron Sanchez .50 1.25
FFMAV Alex Verdugo .60 1.50
FFMAVE Andrew Velazquez .40 1.00
FFMAW Austin Wilson .40 1.00
FFMBB Byron Buxton .60 1.50
FFMBD Brandon Drury .40 1.00
FFMBDA Braxton Davidson .40 1.00
FFMBF Buck Farmer .40 1.00
FFMBFI Brandon Finnegan .40 1.00
FFMBL Ben Lively .40 1.00
FFMBN Brandon Nimmo .60 1.50
FFMBS Braden Shipley .40 1.00
FFMBSW Blake Swihart .50 1.25
FFMBZ Bradley Zimmer .60 1.50
FFMCA Christian Arroyo 1.25 3.00
FFMCB Christian Binford .40 1.00
FFMCBL Clayton Blackburn .60 1.50
FFMCC Carlos Correa 2.00 5.00
FFMCE C.J. Edwards .60 1.50
FFMCEL Chris Ellis .40 1.00
FFMCF Clint Frazier 1.50 4.00
FFMCG Casey Gillaspie .60 1.50
FFMCH Courtney Hawkins .40 1.00
FFMCM Colin Moran .40 1.00
FFMCR Carlos Rodon .60 1.50
FFMCS Chance Sisco .75 2.00
FFMCSE Corey Seager 1.50 4.00
FFMCW Christian Walker .75 2.00
FFMDA Dariel Alvarez .40 1.00
FFMDB Dylan Bundy .50 1.25
FFMDD David Dahl .50 1.25
FFMDH Derek Hill .50 1.25
FFMDN Daniel Norris .40 1.00
FFMDO Dillon Overton .40 1.00
FFMDP D.J. Peterson .40 1.00
FFMDPO Dalton Pompey .50 1.25
FFMDR Daniel Robertson .40 1.00
FFMEB Eddie Butler .40 1.00
FFMEF Erick Fedde .40 1.00
FFMEJ Eric Jagielo .40 1.00
FFMFB Franklin Barreto .50 1.25
FFMFL Francisco Lindor 2.50 6.00
FFMFM Francellis Montas .50 1.25
FFMGB Greg Bird .50 1.25
FFMGG Gabby Guerrero .40 1.00
FFMGH Grant Holmes .50 1.25
FFMGS Gary Sanchez 1.25 3.00
FFMHH Hunter Harvey .40 1.00
FFMHO Henry Owens .40 1.00
FFMHR Hunter Renfroe .60 1.50
FFMJA Jorge Alfaro .60 1.50
FFMJAG Jacob Gatewood .40 1.00
FFMJB Jose Berrios .60 1.50
FFMJBE Josh Bell .75 2.00
FFMJC J.P. Crawford .40 1.00
FFMJG Jon Gray .40 1.00
FFMJGA Joe Gatto .40 1.00
FFMJH Josh Hader .40 1.00
FFMJHO Jeff Hoffman .50 1.25
FFMJJ JaCoby Jones .50 1.25
FFMJN Justin Nicolino .40 1.00
FFMJOG Joey Gallo .75 2.00
FFMJOU Jose Urena .40 1.00
FFMJP Jose Peraza .40 1.00
FFMJPE Joc Pederson .75 2.00
FFMJR James Ramsey .40 1.00
FFMJRO Jose Rondon .40 1.00

FFMJS Jorge Soler .60 1.50
FFMJT Jameson Taillon .50 1.25
FFMJU Julio Urias 1.25 3.00
FFMJW Jesse Winker .40 1.00
FFMJWI Justin Williams .40 1.00
FFMKB Kris Bryant 2.50 6.00
FFMKC Kyle Crick .50 1.25
FFMKF Kyle Freeland .50 1.25
FFMKM Kodi Medeiros .40 1.00
FFMKME Keury Mella .40 1.00
FFMKP Kevin Plawecki .40 1.00
FFMKS Kyle Schwarber 1.50 4.00
FFMKST Kohl Stewart .40 1.00
FFMKZ Kevin Ziomek .40 1.00
FFMKZI Kyle Zimmer .40 1.00
FFMLG Lucas Giolito .75 2.00
FFMLO Luis Ortiz .40 1.00
FFMLS Lucas Sims .40 1.00
FFMLSE Luis Severino .50 1.25
FFMMA Mark Appel .40 1.00
FFMMC Michael Conforto .50 1.25
FFMMF Max Fried 1.50 4.00
FFMMFO Mike Foltynewicz .40 1.00
FFMMFR Maikel Franco .50 1.25
FFMMG Marco Gonzales .60 1.50
FFMMH Monte Harrison .60 1.50
FFMMJ Micah Johnson .40 1.00
FFMML Michael Lorenzen .40 1.00
FFMMM Manuel Margot .40 1.00
FFMMO Matt Olson .50 1.25
FFMMP Max Pentecost .40 1.00
FFMMS Miguel Sano .50 1.25
FFMMT Michael Taylor .40 1.00
FFMMW Matt Wisler .40 1.00
FFMNG Nick Gordon .50 1.25
FFMNM Nomar Mazara .60 1.50
FFMNS Noah Syndergaard .75 2.00
FFMNT Nick Tropeano .40 1.00
FFMOA Ozhaino Albies 4.00 10.00
FFMOAR Orlando Arcia .50 1.25
FFMPE Phil Ervin .40 1.00
FFMPK Patrick Kivlehan .40 1.00
FFMRC Rusney Castillo .50 1.25
FFMRD Rafael Devers 2.50 6.00
FFMRK Rob Kaminsky .40 1.00
FFMRL Reynaldo Lopez .50 1.25
FFMRM Raul Mondesi
FFMRN Renato Nunez .75 2.00
FFMRQ Roman Quinn .60 1.50
FFMRS Robert Stephenson .40 1.00
FFMRT Raimel Tapia .60 1.50
FFMSM Steven Moya .50 1.25
FFMSMA Sean Manaea .40 1.00
FFMSN Sean Newcomb .50 1.25
FFMSP Stephen Piscotty .50 1.25
FFMSTM Steven Matz .60 1.50
FFMTA Tim Anderson .75 2.00
FFMTB Tyler Beede .50 1.25
FFMTC Tim Cooney .40 1.00
FFMTG Tyler Glasnow .50 1.25
FFMTK Tyler Kolek .40 1.00
FFMTN Tyler Naquin .50 1.25
FFMTT Touki Toussaint .50 1.25
FFMTTA Tyrone Taylor .40 1.00
FFMTTU Trea Turner 1.25 3.00
FFMTW Trevor Williams .40 1.00
FFMWA Willy Adames .60 1.50

2015 Bowman Chrome Farm's Finest Minis Autographs

STATED ODDS 1:775 HOBBY
EXCHANGE DEADLINE 4/30/2018
*GOLD/50: .6X TO 1.5X BASIC
*ORANGE/25: .75X TO 2X BASIC
FFMAB Archie Bradley 4.00 10.00
FFMABL Aaron Blair 4.00 10.00
FFMAJ Aaron Judge 60.00 150.00
FFMAJA Alex Jackson 5.00 12.00
FFMAM Austin Meadows 6.00 15.00
FFMARE Alex Reyes 8.00 20.00
FFMARO Avery Romero 4.00 10.00
FFMAS Aaron Sanchez 5.00 12.00
FFMBF Buck Farmer 4.00 10.00
FFMBS Braden Shipley 4.00 10.00
FFMBSW Blake Swihart 5.00 12.00
FFMCE C.J. Edwards 6.00 15.00
FFMCF Clint Frazier 8.00 20.00
FFMCR Carlos Rodon 6.00 15.00
FFMDB Dylan Bundy 5.00 12.00
FFMDD David Dahl 10.00 25.00
FFMDH Derek Hill 5.00 12.00
FFMDP D.J. Peterson 4.00 10.00
FFMFL Francisco Lindor 8.00 20.00
FFMGH Grant Holmes 5.00 12.00
FFMGS Gary Sanchez 30.00 80.00
FFMHH Hunter Harvey 6.00 15.00
FFMHO Henry Owens EXCH 4.00 10.00
FFMJA Jorge Alfaro 6.00 15.00
FFMJC J.P. Crawford EXCH 4.00 10.00
FFMJHO Jeff Hoffman 5.00 12.00
FFMJN Justin Nicolino 4.00 10.00
FFMJP Jose Peraza 6.00 15.00
FFMJS Jorge Soler 15.00 40.00
FFMKB Kris Bryant 60.00 150.00
FFMKF Kyle Freeland 5.00 12.00
FFMKS Kyle Schwarber 15.00 40.00
FFMKST Kohl Stewart 4.00 10.00
FFMLG Lucas Giolito 12.00 30.00
FFMLSE Luis Severino 20.00 50.00
FFMMC Michael Conforto 25.00 60.00
FFMMF Max Fried 6.00 15.00
FFMMJ Micah Johnson 4.00 10.00
FFMMO Matt Olson 12.00 30.00
FFMMS Miguel Sano 8.00 20.00
FFMMT Michael Taylor 4.00 10.00
FFMNG Nick Gordon 12.00 30.00
FFMNS Noah Syndergaard 25.00 60.00
FFMRC Rusney Castillo 5.00 12.00
FFMRD Rafael Devers 50.00 120.00
FFMRS Robert Stephenson 10.00 25.00
FFMSM Steven Moya 5.00 12.00
FFMSN Sean Newcomb 5.00 12.00
FFMTB Tyler Beede 5.00 12.00
FFMTG Tyler Glasnow 5.00 12.00
FFMTK Tyler Kolek 8.00 20.00
FFMTT Touki Toussaint 5.00 12.00
FFMTTU Trea Turner 15.00 40.00

2015 Bowman Chrome Farm's Finest Minis Autographs Gold Refractors

*GOLD REF: .6X TO 1.5X BASIC
RANDOM INSERTS IN PACKS
STATED PRINT RUN 50 SER.#'d SETS
EXCHANGE DEADLINE 4/30/2018

2015 Bowman Chrome Farm's Finest Minis Autographs Orange Refractors

*ORANGE REF: .75X TO 2X BASIC
STATED ODDS 1:727 HOBBY
STATED PRINT RUN 25 SER.#'d SETS
EXCHANGE DEADLINE 4/30/2018

2015 Bowman Chrome Lucky Redemption Autographs

EXCH 1 ODDS 1:38,390 HOBBY
EXCH 2 ODDS 1:38,390 HOBBY
EXCH 3 ODDS 1:38,390 HOBBY
EXCH 4 ODDS 1:38,390 HOBBY
EXCH 5 ODDS 1:38,390 HOBBY
EXCHANGE DEADLINE 4/30/2018
1 Kyle Schwarber EXCH 150.00 250.00
LRKS Kyle Schwarber 150.00 250.00

2015 Bowman Chrome Prime Position Autographs

STATED ODDS 1:581 HOBBY
EXCHANGE DEADLINE 8/31/2017
*GREEN: .75X TO 2X BASIC
*GOLD/50: 1X TO 2.5X BASIC
*ORANGE/25: 1.2X TO 3X BASIC
PPAAJ Alex Jackson 4.00 10.00
PPAAM Austin Meadows 5.00 12.00
PPABB Byron Buxton 8.00 20.00
PPABS Blake Swihart 4.00 10.00
PPACF Clint Frazier 15.00 40.00
PPADP D.J. Peterson 3.00 8.00
PPADS Dominic Smith 3.00 8.00
PPAFL Francisco Lindor 15.00 40.00
PPAKS Kyle Schwarber 20.00 50.00
PPALG Lucas Giolito 6.00 15.00
PPAMO Matt Olson 8.00 20.00
PPARS Robert Stephenson 3.00 8.00
PPATG Tyler Glasnow 6.00 15.00

2015 Bowman Chrome Prospect Autographs

BOW.STATED ODDS 1:86 HOBBY
BOW.CHR.ODDS 1:13 HOBBY
BOW.PLATE ODDS 1:16,064 HOBBY
BOW.CHR.PLATE ODDS 1:12,406 HOBBY
PLATE PRINT RUN 1 SET PER COLOR
NO PLATE PRICING DUE TO SCARCITY
BOW.EXCH.DEADLINE 4/30/2018
BOW.CHR.EXCH. 8/31/2017
BCAPABR Aaron Brown 3.00 8.00
BCAPAC Austin Cousino 3.00 8.00
BCAPAD Austin Dean 3.00 8.00
BCAPAG Arquimedes Gamboa 4.00 10.00
BCAPAGA Amir Garrett 3.00 8.00
BCAPAK Austin Kubitza 3.00 8.00
BCAPAM Amaurys Minier 3.00 8.00
BCAPAMO Akeel Morris 3.00 8.00
BCAPAMR Amed Rosario 12.00 30.00
BCAPAR Alex Reyes 4.00 10.00
BCAPARO Adrian Rondon 4.00 10.00
BCAPAS Antonio Senzatela 4.00 10.00
BCAPASA Adrian Sampson 3.00 8.00
BCAPAV Austin Voth 3.00 8.00
BCAPAVR Avery Romero 3.00 8.00
BCAPBB Bobby Bradley 10.00 25.00
BCAPBG Brett Graves 3.00 8.00
BCAPBH Brent Honeywell 8.00 20.00
BCAPBP Brett Phillips 3.00 8.00
BCAPBW Bobby Wahl 3.00 8.00
BCAPCA Carlos Asuaje 3.00 8.00
BCAPCBE Cody Bellinger 250.00 500.00
BCAPCG Casey Gillaspie 5.00 12.00
BCAPCP Corelle Prime 3.00 8.00
BCAPCP Chad Pinder 4.00 10.00
BCAPCR Carlos Rodon 5.00 12.00
BCAPCR Cody Reed 4.00 10.00
BCAPCS Casey Soltis 3.00 8.00
BCAPCSI Carson Smith 3.00 8.00
BCAPDA Daniel Alvarez 3.00 8.00
BCAPDC Daniel Carbonell 4.00 10.00
BCAPDD Drew Dosch 3.00 8.00
BCAPDG Dermis Garcia 5.00 12.00
BCAPDGE Domingo German 25.00 60.00
BCAPDM Dixon Machado 4.00 10.00
BCAPDS Darnell Sweeney 3.00 8.00
BCAPDW Drew Ward 3.00 8.00
BCAPEB Endrys Briceno 3.00 8.00
BCAPEG Erik Gonzalez 3.00 8.00
BCAPEH Eric Haase 3.00 8.00
BCAPES Edmundo Sosa 4.00 10.00
BCAPFM Francellis Montas 4.00 10.00
BCAPFP Fernando Perez 3.00 8.00
BCAPGG Grayson Greiner 3.00 8.00
BCAPGL Gilbert Lara 4.00 10.00
BCAPGT Gleyber Torres 300.00 800.00
BCAPGU Giovanny Urshela 15.00 40.00
BCAPHO Hector Olivera 4.00 10.00
BCAPHR Harold Ramirez 4.00 10.00
BCAPIS Isael Soto 3.00 8.00
BCAPJB Jake Bauers 5.00 12.00
BCAPJBE Jordan Betts 3.00 8.00
BCAPJC Jake Cave 3.00 8.00
BCAPJD J.D. Davis 10.00 25.00
BCAPJDE Jose De Leon 5.00 12.00
BCAPJG Jarlin Garcia 4.00 10.00
BCAPJH Juan Herrera 3.00 8.00
BCAPJL Jorge Lopez 3.00 8.00
BCAPJL Jairo Labourt 3.00 8.00
BCAPJLU Jordan Luplow 3.00 8.00
BCAPJM Jorge Mateo 8.00 20.00
BCAPJM Juan Meza 3.00 8.00
BCAPJMO Jon Moscot 3.00 8.00
BCAPJOM Josh Morgan 3.00 8.00
BCAPJR Jefry Rodriguez 3.00 8.00
BCAPJS Justin Steele 3.00 8.00
BCAPJU Jhoan Urena 3.00 8.00
BCAPJUL Julian Leon 3.00 8.00
BCAPJW Joe Wendle 4.00 10.00
BCAPKM Keury Mella 3.00 8.00
BCAPLG Luiz Gohara 3.00 8.00
BCAPLM Logan Moon 3.00 8.00
BCAPLS Luis Severino 20.00 50.00
BCAPLY Luis Ysla 3.00 8.00
BCAPMC Miguel Castro 3.00 8.00
BCAPMD Marcos Diplan 3.00 8.00
BCAPMDL Michael De Leon 3.00 8.00
BCAPMM Marcos Molina 3.00 8.00
BCAPMRA Milton Ramos 3.00 8.00
BCAPMS Mallex Smith 5.00 12.00
BCAPMY Mike Yastrzemski 60.00 150.00
BCAPNP Nick Pivetta 3.00 8.00
BCAPNS Nolan Sanburn 3.00 8.00
BCAPOA Orlando Arcia 4.00 10.00
BCAPOAL Ozhaino Albies 75.00 200.00
BCAPPO Peter O'Brien 5.00 12.00
BCAPPS Pedro Severino 3.00 8.00
BCAPRD Rafael Devers 100.00 250.00
BCAPRI Raisel Iglesias 4.00 10.00
BCAPRL Reynaldo Lopez 4.00 10.00
BCAPRM Ryan Merritt 5.00 12.00
BCAPRR Robert Refsnyder 4.00 10.00
BCAPRT Rowdy Tellez 5.00 12.00
BCAPSA Sergio Alcantara 3.00 8.00
BCAPSB Stephen Bruno 3.00 8.00
BCAPSG Stephen Gonsalves 3.00 8.00
BCAPSK Spencer Kieboom 3.00 8.00
BCAPSM Simon Mercedes 3.00 8.00
BCAPSO Steven Okert 3.00 8.00
BCAPSST Seth Streich 3.00 8.00
BCAPSTU Spencer Turnbull 3.00 8.00
BCAPTB Tim Berry 3.00 8.00
BCAPTBL Ty Blach 4.00 10.00
BCAPTGO Trevor Gott 3.00 8.00
BCAPTH Teoscar Hernandez 20.00 50.00
BCAPTL Trace Loehr 3.00 8.00
BCAPTM Trey Michalczewski 3.00 8.00
BCAPTT Touki Toussaint 3.00 8.00
BCAPTW Tyler Wagner 3.00 8.00
BCAPVA Victor Arano 3.00 8.00
BCAPVC Victor Caratini 5.00 12.00
BCAPVR Victor Reyes 3.00 8.00
BCAPWA Willy Adames 10.00 25.00
BCAPWD Wilmer Difo 3.00 8.00
BCAPWG Wilkerman Garcia 6.00 15.00
BCAPWP Wes Parsons 3.00 8.00
BCAPYL Yoan Lopez 3.00 8.00
BCAPYT Yasmany Tomas 4.00 10.00
BCAPZB Zach Bird 3.00 8.00
BCAPZR Zac Reininger 3.00 8.00

2015 Bowman Chrome Prospect Autographs Blue Refractors

*BLUE REF: .75X TO 2X BASIC
BOW.ODDS 1:427 HOBBY
BOW.CHR.ODDS 1:328 HOBBY
STATED PRINT RUN 150 SER.#'d SETS
BOW.EXCH DEADLINE 4/30/2018
BOW.CHR.EXCH 8/31/2017
BCAPCBE Cody Bellinger 1000.00 2000.00
BCAPGT Gleyber Torres 800.00 1500.00
BCAPKS Kyle Schwarber 25.00 60.00
BCAPLS Luis Severino 50.00 120.00
BCAPNG Nick Gordon 8.00 20.00
BCAPTK Tyler Kolek 6.00 15.00

2015 Bowman Chrome Prospect Autographs Gold Refractors

*GOLD REF: 1.2X TO 3X BASIC
BOW.STATED ODDS 1:1278 HOBBY
BOW.CHR.ODDS 1:982 HOBBY
STATED PRINT RUN 50 SER.#'d SETS
BOW.EXCH.DEADLINE 4/30/2018
BOW.CHR.EXCH 5/31/2017
BCAPCBE Cody Bellinger 2000.00 4000.00
BCAPGT Gleyber Torres 2500.00 5000.00
BCAPKS Kyle Schwarber 40.00 100.00
BCAPLS Luis Severino 125.00 300.00
BCAPNG Nick Gordon 12.00 30.00
BCAPTK Tyler Kolek 10.00 25.00

2015 Bowman Chrome Prospect Autographs Green Refractors

*GREEN REF: 1X TO 2.5X BASIC
BOW.STATED ODDS 1:191 RETAIL
BOW.CHR.ODDS 1:496 HOBBY
STATED PRINT RUN 99 SER.#'d SETS
BOW.EXCH.DEADLINE 4/30/2018
BOW.CHR.EXCH. 8/31/2017
BCAPCBE Cody Bellinger 1500.00 2500.00
BCAPGT Gleyber Torres 1000.00 2000.00
BCAPKS Kyle Schwarber 30.00 80.00
BCAPLS Luis Severino 75.00 200.00
BCAPNG Nick Gordon 10.00 25.00
BCAPTK Tyler Kolek 8.00 20.00

2015 Bowman Chrome Prospect Autographs Orange Refractors

*ORANGE REF: 1.5X TO 4X BASIC
BOW.STATED ODDS 1:606 HOBBY
BOW.CHR.ODDS 1:452 HOBBY
STATED PRINT RUN 25 SER.#'d SETS
BOW.EXCH DEADLINE 4/30/2018
BOW.CHR.EXCH 8/31/2017
BCAPCBE Cody Bellinger 4000.00 8000.00
BCAPGT Gleyber Torres 3000.00 6000.00
BCAPKS Kyle Schwarber 50.00 120.00
BCAPLS Luis Severino 150.00 400.00
BCAPNG Nick Gordon 15.00 40.00
BCAPTK Tyler Kolek 12.00 30.00

2015 Bowman Chrome Prospect Autographs Purple Refractors

*PURPLE REF: .6X TO 1.5X BASIC
BOW.STATED ODDS 1:256 HOBBY
BOW.STATED ODDS 1:197 HOBBY
STATED PRINT RUN 250 SER.#'d SETS
BOW.EXCH DEADLINE 4/30/2018
BOW.CHR.EXCH 8/31/2017
BCAPCBE Cody Bellinger 600.00 1200.00
BCAPGT Gleyber Torres 600.00 1200.00
BCAPKS Kyle Schwarber 20.00 50.00
BCAPLS Luis Severino 40.00 100.00
BCAPNG Nick Gordon 6.00 15.00
BCAPTK Tyler Kolek 5.00 12.00

2015 Bowman Chrome Prospect Autographs Refractors

*REF: .5X TO 1.2X BASIC
BOW.ODDS 1:129 HOBBY
BOW.CHR.ODDS 1:99 HOBBY
STATED PRINT RUN 499 SER.#'d SETS
BOW.EXCH DEADLINE 4/30/2018
BOW.CHR.EXCH 8/31/2017
BCAPCBE Cody Bellinger 500.00 1000.00
BCAPGT Gleyber Torres 500.00 1000.00
BCAPLS Luis Severino 30.00 80.00

2015 Bowman Chrome Prospect Profiles Minis

COMPLETE SET (25) 10.00 25.00
STATED ODDS 1:6 HOBBY
*GREEN/99: 1.2X TO 3X BASIC
PP1 Byron Buxton .60 1.50
PP2 Carlos Correa 2.00 5.00
PP3 Corey Seager 1.50 4.00
PP4 Joey Gallo .75 2.00
PP5 Lucas Giolito .75 2.00
PP6 Francisco Lindor 2.50 6.00
PP7 Julio Urias 1.25 3.00
PP8 Miguel Sano .50 1.25
PP9 Tyler Glasnow .50 1.25
PP10 Kyle Schwarber 1.50 4.00
PP11 Alex Jackson .50 1.25
PP12 Robert Stephenson .40 1.00
PP13 Braden Shipley .40 1.00
PP14 Jameson Taillon .50 1.25
PP15 Mark Appel .40 1.00
PP16 Steven Matz .60 1.50
PP17 Raul Mondesi
PP18 Luis Severino .50 1.25
PP19 Jose Berrios .60 1.50
PP20 Tyler Kolek .40 1.00
PP21 Aaron Judge 6.00 15.00
PP22 Hunter Harvey .40 1.00
PP23 Jose Peraza .40 1.00
PP24 Henry Owens .40 1.00
PP25 Nick Gordon .50 1.25

2015 Bowman Chrome Prospect Profiles Minis Gold Refractors

*GOLD: 2X TO 5X BASIC
STATED ODDS 1:1628 HOBBY
STATED PRINT RUN 50 SER.#'d SETS
PP2 Carlos Correa 20.00 50.00

2015 Bowman Chrome Prospect Profiles Minis Orange Refractors

*ORANGE: 2.5X TO 6X BASIC
STATED ODDS 1:1204 HOBBY
STATED PRINT RUN 25 SER.#'d SETS
PP2 Carlos Correa 25.00 60.00

2015 Bowman Chrome Prospects

COMPLETE SET (250) 25.00 60.00
BOW.PLATE ODDS 1:6523 HOBBY
BOW.CHR.PLATE ODDS 1:5068 HOBBY
PLATE PRINT RUN 1 SET PER COLOR
NO PLATE PRICING DUE TO SCARCITY
BCP1 Tyler Kolek .25 .60
BCP2 Jose Queliz .25 .60
BCP3 Kevin Plawecki .25 .60
BCP4 Jen-Ho Tseng .25 .60
BCP5 Dixon Machado .30 .75
BCP6 Pedro Severino .25 .60
BCP7 Roman Quinn .40 1.00
BCP8 A.J. Cole .25 .60
BCP9 Fernando Perez .25 .60
BCP10 Logan Moon .25 .60
BCP11 Giovanny Urshela 1.50 4.00
BCP12 Emerson Jimenez .25 .60
BCP13 Dermis Garcia .40 1.00
BCP14 Marco Gonzales .40 1.00
BCP15 Jeremy Rhoades .25 .60
BCP16 Joe Ross .25 .60
BCP17 Trevor Gott .25 .60
BCP18 Forrest Wall .25 .60
BCP19 David Dahl .30 .75
BCP20 Adrian Sampson .25 .60
BCP21 Alex Verdugo .40 1.00
BCP22 Williams Perez .30 .75
BCP23 Alex Reyes .30 .75
BCP24 Ty Blach .30 .75
BCP25 Yasmany Tomas .30 .75
BCP26 Hunter Harvey .25 .60
BCP27 Touki Toussaint .30 .75
BCP28 Austin Voth .25 .60
BCP29 Luis Lugo .25 .60
BCP30 Teoscar Hernandez .75 2.00
BCP31 Jimmy Reed .25 .60
BCP32 Austin Kubitza .25 .60
BCP33 Miguel Sano .30 .75
BCP34 Rafael Devers 1.50 4.00
BCP35 Harold Ramirez .30 .75
BCP36 Alex Meyer .25 .60
BCP37 Archie Bradley .25 .60
BCP38 Tim Cooney .25 .60
BCP39 Jorge Lopez .25 .60
BCP40 Ryan Merritt .40 1.00
BCP41 Carlos Correa 1.25 3.00
BCP42 Rafael Bautista .25 .60
BCP43 Francisco Mejia .60 1.50
BCP44 Robert Stephenson .25 .60
BCP45 James Dykstra .25 .60
BCP46 Tyler DeLoach .25 .60
BCP47 Kyle Lloyd .25 .60
BCP48 Erik Gonzalez .25 .60
BCP49 Sal Romano .25 .60
BCP50 Julio Urias .75 2.00
BCP51 Juan Herrera .25 .60
BCP52 Jon Gray .25 .60
BCP53 Corey Littrell .25 .60
BCP54 Chris Stratton .25 .60
BCP55 Conrad Gregor .25 .60
BCP56 Hunter Dozier .25 .60
BCP57 Jantzen Witte .40 1.00
BCP58 Kyle Schwarber 1.00 2.50
BCP59 Champ Stuart .25 .60
BCP60 James Needy .25 .60
BCP61 Willy Adames .40 1.00
BCP62 Jose De Leon .40 1.00
BCP63 Buddy Borden .25 .60
BCP64 Jordan Betts .25 .60
BCP65 Gabriel Quintana .25 .60
BCP66 Gareth Morgan .25 .60
BCP67 Matt Andriese .25 .60
BCP68 Raimel Tapia .40 1.00
BCP69 Drew Ward .25 .60
BCP70 Carlos Asuaje .25 .60
BCP71 Ozhaino Albies 6.00 15.00
BCP72 Josh Bell .50 1.25
BCP73 Kyle Zimmer .25 .60
BCP74 Greg Bird .30 .75
BCP75 Nick Gordon .30 .75
BCP76 Aaron Blair .25 .60
BCP77 T.J. Chism .25 .60
BCP78 Marcos Molina .25 .60
BCP79 Avery Romero .25 .60
BCP80 Jose Peraza .25 .60
BCP81 Tim Anderson .50 1.25
BCP82 Nick Travieso .25 .60
BCP83 Matt Wisler .25 .60
BCP84 Nick Petree .25 .60
BCP85 Mark Appel .25 .60
BCP86 Frank Schwindel .30 .75
BCP87 Jorge Mateo .75 2.00
BCP88 Reese McGuire .25 .60
BCP89 Tyler Naquin .30 .75
BCP90 Nate Smith .25 .60
BCP91 Jose Berrios .40 1.00
BCP92 Henry Owens .25 .60
BCP93 Justin Nicolino .25 .60
BCP94 Jairo Labourt .25 .60
BCP95 Edmundo Sosa .30 .75
BCP96 Seth Streich .25 .60
BCP97 Victor Reyes .25 .60
BCP98 Jhoan Urena .25 .60
BCP99 Adam Engel .25 .60
BCP100 Kris Bryant 1.50 4.00
BCP101 Rio Ruiz .25 .60
BCP102 Wes Parsons .25 .60
BCP103 Raisel Iglesias .30 .75
BCP104 Robert Refsnyder .25 .60
BCP105 Aaron Slegers .25 .60
BCP106 Tim Berry .25 .60
BCP107 Nick Williams .30 .75
BCP108 Jack Reinheimer .25 .60
BCP109 Domingo Santana .30 .75
BCP110 Chad Pinder .30 .75
BCP111 Andre Wheeler .25 .60
BCP112 Chih-Wei Hu .40 1.00
BCP113 Gary Sanchez .75 2.00
BCP114 Ryan McMahon .25 .60
BCP115 Taylor Williams .25 .60
BCP116 Nelson Gomez .30 .75
BCP117 Addison Russell .75 2.00
BCP118 Domingo German .40 1.00
BCP119 Scott Schebler .40 1.00
BCP120 Joe Jackson .25 .60
BCP121 Gilbert Lara .30 .75
BCP122 Hunter Renfroe .40 1.00
BCP123 Rob Kaminsky .25 .60
BCP124 Steven Matz .40 1.00
BCP125 Luis Severino .30 .75
BCP126 Austin Meadows .40 1.00
BCP127 Luis Heredia .25 .60
BCP128 Victor Alcantara .25 .60
BCP129 Trevor Frank .25 .60
BCP130 Jake Johansen .25 .60
BCP131 JaCoby Jones .30 .75
BCP132 Jake Bauers .40 1.00
BCP133 Trey Ball .25 .60
BCP134 Aaron Nola .40 1.00
BCP135 Orlando Arcia .30 .75
BCP136 Keury Mella .25 .60
BCP137 Brett Phillips .25 .60
BCP138 Mike Yastrzemski 3.00 8.00
BCP139 Jose Valdez .25 .60
BCP140 Eric Haase .25 .60
BCP141 Jaycob Brugman .30 .75
BCP142 Albert Almora .25 .60
BCP143 Tyler Wagner .25 .60
BCP144 Francellis Montas .30 .75
BCP145 Daniel Alvarez .25 .60
BCP146 Raul Alcantara .25 .60
BCP147 Ricardo Sanchez .25 .60
BCP148 Jarlin Garcia .30 .75
BCP149 Colin Moran .25 .60
BCP150 Carlos Rodon .40 1.00
BCP151 Kyle Lloyd .25 .60
BCP152 Matt Olson .30 .75
BCP153 J.P. Crawford .25 .60
BCP154 Tony Kemp .25 .60
BCP155 Alen Hanson .25 .60
BCP156 C.J. Edwards .40 1.00
BCP157 Christian Arroyo .75 2.00
BCP158 Amir Garrett .25 .60
BCP159 Justin Steele .25 .60
BCP160 D.J. Peterson .25 .60
BCP161 Edwin Diaz .50 1.25
BCP162 Max Pentecost .25 .60
BCP163 Jon Moscot .25 .60
BCP164 Carson Smith .25 .60
BCP165 Luiz Gohara .25 .60
BCP166 Nick Wells .25 .60
BCP167 Trace Loehr .25 .60
BCP168 Kodi Medeiros .25 .60
BCP169 Stephen Piscotty .30 .75
BCP170 Jorge Alfaro .40 1.00
BCP171 Dan Vogelbach .40 1.00
BCP172 Bobby Wahl .25 .60
BCP173 Parker Bridwell .25 .60
BCP174 Joe Wendle .30 .75
BCP175 Rowan Wick .25 .60
BCP176 Pierce Johnson .25 .60
BCP177 Nolan Sanburn .25 .60
BCP178 Mitch Keller .30 .75
BCP179 Tyrell Jenkins .30 .75
BCP180 Brandon Nimmo .40 1.00
BCP181 Bobby Bradley .30 .75
BCP182 Sean Newcomb .30 .75
BCP183 Antonio Senzatela .30 .75
BCP184 Dawel Lugo .25 .60
BCP185 Endrys Briceno .25 .60
BCP186 Eloy Jimenez .75 2.00
BCP187 Kyle Freeland .30 .75
BCP188 Max Fried 1.00 2.50
BCP189 Daniel Carbonell .30 .75
BCP190 Chance Sisco .50 1.25
BCP191 Amaurys Minier .25 .60
BCP192 Jake Thompson .25 .60
BCP193 Justin O'Conner .25 .60
BCP194 Andrew Velazquez .25 .60
BCP195 Derek Hill .30 .75
BCP196 Brandon Drury .25 .60
BCP197 Kohl Stewart .25 .60
BCP198 Luis Ysla .25 .60
BCP199 Mallex Smith .40 1.00
BCP200 Lucas Giolito .50 1.25
BCP201 Luke Jackson .25 .60
BCP202 Nick Kingham .30 .75
BCP203 Tyler Glasnow .30 .75
BCP204 Jake Cave .25 .60
BCP205 Jefry Rodriguez .25 .60
BCP206 Monte Harrison .40 1.00
BCP207 Jesse Winker .25 .60
BCP208 Alex Jackson .30 .75
BCP209 Eric Jagielo .25 .60
BCP210 Correlle Prime .25 .60
BCP211 Lucas Sims .25 .60
BCP212 Ian Clarkin .25 .60
BCP213 Austin Brice .25 .60
BCP214 J.D. Davis .40 1.00
BCP215 Simon Mercedes .25 .60
BCP216 Casey Gillaspie .40 1.00
BCP217 Spencer Kieboom .25 .60
BCP218 Michael Conforto .30 .75
BCP219 Stephen Bruno .25 .60
BCP220 Victor Caratini .75 2.00
BCP221 Spencer Turnbull .25 .60
BCP222 Tyler Danish .25 .60
BCP223 Bradley Zimmer .40 1.00
BCP224 Dominic Smith .25 .60
BCP225 Matt Chapman .40 1.00
BCP226 Miguel Almonte .25 .60
BCP227 Franklin Barreto .30 .75
BCP228 Braden Shipley .25 .60
BCP229 Luis Ortiz .25 .60
BCP230 Manuel Margot .25 .60
BCP231 Amed Rosario .40 1.00
BCP232 Felix Jorge .25 .60
BCP233 Cody Reed .30 .75
BCP234 Raul Mondesi
BCP235 Kyle Crick .30 .75
BCP236 Jeff Hoffman .30 .75
BCP237 Grant Holmes .30 .75
BCP238 Billy McKinney .30 .75
BCP239 Jake Gatewood .30 .75
BCP240 Clint Frazier 1.00 2.50
BCP241 Wilmer Difo .25 .60
BCP242 Alex Blandino .25 .60
BCP243 Zac Reininger .25 .60
BCP244 Austin Cousino .25 .60
BCP245 Grayson Greiner .25 .60
BCP246 Reynaldo Lopez .30 .75
BCP247 Jameson Taillon .30 .75
BCP248 Daniel Robertson .25 .60
BCP249 Michael De Leon .25 .60
BCP250 Corey Seager 1.00 2.50

2015 Bowman Chrome Prospects Black Asia Refractors

*BLACK REF: 1.5X TO 4X BASIC
DISTRIBUTED IN ASIA

2015 Bowman Chrome Prospects Black Wave Asia Refractors

*BLACK WAVE REF: 1.5X TO 4X BASIC
DISTRIBUTED IN ASIA

2015 Bowman Chrome Prospects Blue Refractors

*BLUE REF: 2X TO 5X BASIC
BOW.ODDS 1:175 HOBBY
BOW.CHR.ODDS 1:136 HOBBY
STATED PRINT RUN 150 SER.#'d SETS

2015 Bowman Chrome Prospects Blue Wave Refractors

*BLUE WAVE REF: 1.5X TO 4X BASIC
RANDOM INSERTS IN PACKS

2015 Bowman Chrome Prospects Gold Refractors

*GOLD REF: 5X TO 12X BASIC
BOW.ODDS 1:525 HOBBY
BOW.CHR.ODDS 1:407 HOBBY
STATED PRINT RUN 50 SER.#'d SETS

2015 Bowman Chrome Prospects Green Refractors

*GREEN REF: 2.5X TO 6X BASIC
BOW.ODDS 1:44 RETAIL
BOW.CHR.ODDS 1:206 HOBBY
STATED PRINT RUN 99 SER.#'d SETS

2015 Bowman Chrome Prospects Orange Refractors

*ORANGE REF: 6X TO 15X BASIC
BOW.ODDS 1:243 HOBBY
BOW.CHR.ODDS 1:302 HOBBY
STATED PRINT RUN 25 SER.#'d SETS

2015 Bowman Chrome Prospects Orange Wave Refractors

*ORANGE WAVE REF: 4X TO 8X BASIC
RANDOM INSERTS IN PACKS

2015 Bowman Chrome Prospects Purple Refractors

*PURPLE REF: 1.5X TO 4X BASIC
BOW.ODDS 1:105 HOBBY
BOW.CHR.ODDS 1:82 HOBBY
STATED PRINT RUN 250 SER.#'d SETS

2015 Bowman Chrome Prospects Refractors

*REF: 1.5X TO 4X BASIC
BOW.STATED ODDS 1:53 HOBBY
BOW.CHR.STATED ODDS 1:41 HOBBY
STATED PRINT RUN 499 SER.#'d SETS

2015 Bowman Chrome Rookie Autographs

BOW.STATED ODDS 1:295 HOBBY
BOW.CHR. ODDS 1:355 HOBBY
BOW.EXCH DEADLINE 4/30/2018
BOW.CHR.EXCH. 8/31/2017
BCARAB Archie Bradley 3.00 8.00
BCARAR Anthony Ranaudo 3.00 8.00
BCARBB Byron Buxton 12.00 30.00
BCARBBR Bryce Brentz 3.00 8.00
BCARBF Brandon Finnegan 3.00 8.00
BCARBFA Buck Farmer 3.00 8.00
BCARCR Carlos Rodon 5.00 12.00
BCARCS Cory Spangenberg 3.00 8.00
BCARCW Christian Walker 10.00 25.00
BCARDC Daniel Corcino 3.00 8.00
BCARDH Dilson Herrera 4.00 10.00
BCARDN Daniel Norris 3.00 8.00
BCARDP Dalton Pompey 4.00 10.00
BCARDT Devon Travis 3.00 8.00
BCARFL Francisco Lindor 25.00 60.00
BCARJB Javier Baez 30.00 80.00
BCARJHK Jung Ho Kang 3.00 8.00
BCARJL Jake Lamb 5.00 12.00
BCARJM James McCann 5.00 12.00
BCARJP J.Pederson Gray jsy 10.00 25.00
BCARJPE J.Pederson White jsy 10.00 25.00
BCARJR Jason Rogers 3.00 8.00
BCARJS J.Soler Face Rt 10.00 25.00
BCARJSO J.Soler Face Left 10.00 25.00
BCARKB Kris Bryant 60.00 150.00
BCARKG Kendall Graveman 3.00 8.00
BCARMB Matt Barnes 3.00 8.00
BCARMFO Mike Foltynewicz 3.00 8.00
BCARMT Michael Taylor 3.00 8.00
BCARNS Noah Syndergaard 20.00 50.00
BCARRC Rusney Castillo 4.00 10.00
BCARRI Raisel Iglesias 4.00 10.00
BCARRL Rymer Liriano 3.00 8.00
BCARSM Steven Moya 4.00 10.00
BCARTM Trevor May 3.00 8.00
BCARYT Yasmany Tomas 4.00 10.00

2015 Bowman Chrome Rookie Autographs Blue Refractors

*BLUE REF: .6X TO 1.5X BASIC
BOW.STATED ODDS 1:1278 HOBBY
BOW.CHR. ODDS 1:2729 HOBBY

STATED PRINT RUN 150 SER.#'d SETS
BOW.EXCH DEADLINE 4/30/2018
BOW.CHR.EXCH. 8/31/2017
BCARDP Dalton Pompey 10.00 25.00
BCARKB Kris Bryant 250.00 500.00
BCARMF Maikel Franco 6.00 15.00
BCARNS Noah Syndergaard 40.00 100.00

2015 Bowman Chrome Rookie Autographs Gold Refractors

*GOLD REF: 1X TO 2.5X BASIC
BOW.STATED ODDS 1:3839 HOBBY
BOW.CHR. ODDS 1:6368 HOBBY
STATED PRINT RUN 50 SER.#'d SETS
BOW.EXCH DEADLINE 4/30/2018
BOW.CHR.EXCH. 8/31/2017
BCARBB Byron Buxton 60.00 150.00
BCARCW Christian Walker 50.00 120.00
BCARDP Dalton Pompey 30.00 80.00
BCARJP J.Pederson Gray jsy 50.00 120.00
BCARJPE J.Pederson White jsy 50.00 120.00
BCARJS J.Soler Face Rt 50.00 120.00
BCARJSO J.Soler Face Left 50.00 120.00
BCARKB Kris Bryant 400.00 800.00
BCARKG Kendall Graveman 12.00 30.00
BCARMF Maikel Franco 10.00 25.00
BCARNS Noah Syndergaard 175.00 350.00
BCARSM Steven Moya 12.00 30.00
BCARYT Yasmany Tomas 20.00 50.00

2015 Bowman Chrome Rookie Autographs Green Refractors

*GREEN REF: .75X TO 2X BASIC
BOW.STATED ODDS 1:572 RETAIL
BOW.CHR. ODDS 1:3227 HOBBY
STATED PRINT RUN 99 SER.#'d SETS
BOW.EXCH DEADLINE 4/30/2018
BOW.CHR.EXCH. 8/31/2017
BCARCW Christian Walker 30.00 80.00
BCARDP Dalton Pompey 12.00 30.00
BCARKB Kris Bryant 300.00 600.00
BCARMF Maikel Franco 8.00 20.00
BCARNS Noah Syndergaard 50.00 120.00

2015 Bowman Chrome Rookie Autographs Orange Refractors

*ORANGE REF: 2X TO 5X BASIC
BOW.STATED ODDS 1:1819 HOBBY
BOW.CHR. ODDS 1:2949 HOBBY
STATED PRINT RUN 25 SER.#'d SETS
BOW.EXCH DEADLINE 4/30/2018
BOW.CHR.EXCH. 8/31/2017
BCARAB Archie Bradley 12.00 30.00
BCARBB Byron Buxton 75.00 200.00
BCARBBR Bryce Brentz 10.00 25.00
BCARCW Christian Walker 75.00 200.00
BCARDP Dalton Pompey 60.00 150.00
BCARDT Devon Travis 12.00 30.00
BCARJP J.Pederson Gray jsy 60.00 150.00
BCARJPE J.Pederson White jsy 60.00 150.00
BCARJS J.Soler Face Rt 60.00 150.00
BCARJSO J.Soler Face Left 60.00 150.00
BCARKG Kendall Graveman 25.00 60.00
BCARMF Maikel Franco 20.00 50.00
BCARSM Steven Moya 25.00 60.00
BCARYT Yasmany Tomas 40.00 100.00

2015 Bowman Chrome Rookie Autographs Refractors

*REF: .5X TO 1.2X BASIC
BOW.STATED ODDS 1:385 HOBBY
BOW.CHR. ODDS 1:640 HOBBY
STATED PRINT RUN 499 SER.#'d SETS
BOW.EXCH DEADLINE 4/30/2018
BOW.CHR.EXCH. 8/31/2017
BCARMF Maikel Franco 5.00 12.00

2015 Bowman Chrome Rookie Recollections

COMPLETE SET (7) 3.00 8.00
STATED ODDS 1:24 HOBBY
RRIBW Bernie Williams .50 1.25
RRICB Carlos Baerga .40 1.00
RRIFT Frank Thomas .60 1.50
RRIJG Juan Gonzalez .40 1.00
RRIJO John Olerud .40 1.00
RRIMA Moises Alou .40 1.00
RRIMG Marquis Grissom .40 1.00

2015 Bowman Chrome Rookie Recollections Autographs

STATED ODDS 1:2560 HOBBY
EXCHANGE DEADLINE 4/30/2018
*REF/99: .5X TO 1.2X BASIC
*GOLD REF/50: 1X TO 2.5X BASIC
RRBW Bernie Williams 30.00 80.00
RRCB Carlos Baerga 4.00 10.00
RRFT Frank Thomas 50.00 120.00
RRJG Juan Gonzalez 4.00 10.00
RRJO John Olerud 8.00 20.00
RRMA Moises Alou 8.00 20.00
RRMG Marquis Grissom 8.00 20.00

2015 Bowman Chrome Series Next Die Cuts

COMPLETE SET (35) 15.00 40.00
STATED ODDS 1:9 HOBBY
*GREEN/99: 1X TO 2.5X BASIC
*PURPLE/25: 2.5X TO 6X BASIC
SNAB Archie Bradley .40 1.00
SNAR Addison Russell 1.25 3.00
SNBF Brandon Finnegan .40 1.00
SNBH Billy Hamilton .50 1.25
SNBHA Bryce Harper 1.00 2.50
SNBS Blake Swihart .50 1.25
SNCR Carlos Rodon .60 1.50
SNCY Christian Yelich .75 2.00
SNDB Dellin Betances .50 1.25
SNDN Daniel Norris .40 1.00
SNDT Devon Travis .40 1.00
SNGC Gerrit Cole .60 1.50
SNGP Gregory Polanco .50 1.25
SNGS George Springer .50 1.25
SNJA Jose Abreu .60 1.50
SNJB Javier Baez 3.00 8.00
SNJD Jacob deGrom .60 1.50
SNJF Jose Fernandez .60 1.50
SNJP Joc Pederson .75 2.00
SNJPA Joe Panik .50 1.25
SNJS Jorge Soler .60 1.50
SNJT Julio Teheran .50 1.25
SNKB Kris Bryant 2.50 6.00
SNKP Kevin Plawecki .40 1.00
SNKV Kennys Vargas .40 1.00
SNKW Kolten Wong .50 1.25
SNMAT Masahiro Tanaka .50 1.25
SNMBE Mookie Betts 1.00 2.50
SNMF Maikel Franco .50 1.25
SNMT Mike Trout 3.00 8.00
SNRC Rusney Castillo .50 1.25
SNSG Sonny Gray .50 1.25
SNTW Taijuan Walker .40 1.00
SNXB Xander Bogaerts .60 1.50
SNYP Yasiel Puig .60 1.50

2015 Bowman Chrome Series Next Die Cuts Autographs Green Haze Refractors

STATED ODDS 1:3227 HOBBY
PRINT RUNS B/WN 10-99 COPIES PER
NO PRICING ON QTY 10
EXCHANGE DEADLINE 8/31/2017
*PURPLE/25: .75X TO 2X BASIC
SNAB Archie Bradley/99 10.00 25.00
SNAR Addison Russell/99 15.00 40.00
SNBF Brandon Finnegan/99 4.00 10.00
SNBS Blake Swihart/99 10.00 25.00
SNDN Daniel Norris/99 10.00 25.00
SNGP Gregory Polanco/99 8.00 20.00
SNJB Javier Baez/99 10.00 25.00
SNJD Jacob deGrom/99 25.00 60.00
SNJF Jose Fernandez/99 25.00 60.00
SNKP Kevin Plawecki/99 6.00 15.00
SNKV Kennys Vargas/99 10.00 25.00
SNRC Rusney Castillo/99 5.00 12.00
SNSG Sonny Gray/99 5.00 12.00

2015 Bowman Chrome Draft

COMPLETE SET (200) 20.00 50.00
STATED PLATE ODDS 1:500 HOBBY
PLATE PRINT RUN 1 SET PER COLOR
NO PLATE PRICING DUE TO SCARCITY
1 Dansby Swanson 1.50 4.00
2 Yoan Lopez .25 .60
3 Bailey Falter .25 .60
4 Casey Gillaspie .40 1.00
5 Demi Orimoloye .30 .75
6 Steven Duggar .25 .60
7 Tyler Alexander .25 .60
8 Courtney Hawkins .25 .60
9 Casey Hughston .25 .60
10 Kolby Allard .25 .60
11 Austin Meadows .40 1.00
12 Joe McCarthy .25 .60
13 Tyler Stephenson .30 .75
14 Ashe Russell .25 .60
15 Dylan Moore .25 .60
16 Donnie Dewees .40 1.00
17 Beau Burrows .30 .75
18 Greg Pickett .25 .60
19 Parker French .25 .60
20 Cam Gibson .30 .75
21 Braden Bishop .25 .60
22 Ryan Kellogg .25 .60
23 Monte Harrison .40 1.00
24 Zack Erwin .25 .60
25 J.P. Crawford .25 .60
26 Ryan McMahon .25 .60
27 Kyle Holder .30 .75
28 Ian Happ 1.00 2.50
29 Anthony Hermelyn .25 .60
30 Jimmy Herget .25 .60
31 Mike Nikorak .25 .60
32 Alex Young .25 .60
33 Tyler Mark .25 .60
34 Trent Clark .25 .60
35 Benton Moss .25 .60
36 Matt Withrow .25 .60
37 Chris Shaw .50 1.25
38 Manuel Margot .25 .60
39 Lucas Giolito .50 1.25
40 Chase Ingram .25 .60
41 Lucas Herbert .25 .60
42 Trey Supak .25 .60
43 Blake Trahan .25 .60
44 Jeff Degano .30 .75
45 Desmond Lindsay .40 1.00
46 Walker Buehler 1.50 4.00
47 Cody Ponce .25 .60
48 Adam Brett Walker .25 .60
49 Tyler Danish .25 .60
50 Dillon Tate .30 .75
51 Thomas Szapucki .25 .60
52 Spencer Adams .25 .60
53 Kevin Duchene .25 .60
54 Blake Perkins .25 .60
55 Thomas Eshelman .25 .60
56 Lucas Williams .25 .60
57 David Fletcher 2.50 6.00
58 James Kaprielian .40 1.00
59 Preston Morrison .25 .60
60 Ryan Burr .25 .60
61 Brett Lilek .25 .60
62 Trevor Megill .25 .60
63 Jordy Lara .25 .60
64 Kevin Newman .40 1.00
65 Luis Ortiz .25 .60
66 Cornelius Randolph .25 .60
67 Domingo Leyba .25 .60
68 Sean Reid-Foley .30 .75
69 Josh Naylor .30 .75
70 Michael Matuella .30 .75
71 Cole Tucker .25 .60
72 Kyle Wilcox .25 .60
73 Forrest Wall .25 .60
74 Alex Jackson .30 .75
75 Kyle Tucker 1.50 4.00
76 Hunter Harvey .25 .60
77 Brandon Waddell .25 .60
78 Travis Neubeck .25 .60
79 Ronnie Jebavy .25 .60
80 Ryan Mountcastle 1.00 2.50
81 Kyle Zimmer .25 .60
82 A.J. Reed .30 .75
83 Alex Reyes .30 .75
84 Garrett Whitley .40 1.00
85 Derek Hill .30 .75
86 Ryan Clark .25 .60
87 Andrew Sopko .25 .60
88 Breckin Williams .25 .60
89 Tate Matheny .25 .60
90 Kyle Crick .30 .75
91 Andrew Moore .30 .75
92 Hutton Moyer .25 .60
93 Jordan Ramsey .25 .60
94 Javier Medina .25 .60
95 Jack Wynkoop .25 .60
96 Triston McKenzie .25 .60
97 Jose De Leon .40 1.00
98 Justin Cohen .25 .60
99 Mark Mathias .30 .75
100 Julio Urias .75 2.00
101 Jared Foster .25 .60
102 Roman Quinn .40 1.00
103 Max Wotell .25 .60
104 Jake Gatewood .25 .60
105 Willy Adames .40 1.00
106 Rafael Devers 1.50 4.00
107 Blake Snell .30 .75
108 Cody Poteet .25 .60
109 Bryce Denton .40 1.00
110 Nolan Watson .25 .60
111 Tyler Nevin .40 1.00
112 Antonio Santillan .30 .75
113 Mac Marshall .25 .60
114 Mariano Rivera .40 1.00
115 Grant Hockin .25 .60
116 Raul Mondesi
117 Richie Martin .25 .60
118 Carson Fulmer .25 .60
119 Mikey White .30 .75
120 Lucas Sims .25 .60
121 Peter Lambert .25 .60
122 Roman Collins .25 .60
123 Austin Allen .30 .75
124 David Thompson .30 .75
125 Ka'ai Tom .25 .60
126 Renato Nunez .50 1.25
127 Zech Lemond .25 .60
128 Nick Gordon .30 .75
129 Phil Bickford .25 .60
130 Taylor Ward .40 1.00
131 Corey Taylor .25 .60
132 Chris Ellis .25 .60
133 Michael Chavis .60 1.50
134 Cody Jones .25 .60
135 Tyrone Taylor .25 .60
136 Tyler Jay .25 .60
137 Ke'Bryan Hayes .40 1.00
138 Scott Kingery .40 1.00
139 Carl Wise .30 .75
140 Juan Hillman .25 .60
141 Bowdien Derby .25 .60
142 D.J. Peterson .25 .60
143 Jacob Nix .25 .60
144 Josh Staumont .30 .75
145 Nathan Kirby .30 .75
146 D.J. Stewart .25 .60
147 Matt Hall .25 .60
148 Kohl Stewart .25 .60
149 Drew Jackson .30 .75
150 Aaron Judge 4.00 10.00
151 Nick Plummer .30 .75
152 David Dahl .30 .75
153 Brian Mundell .25 .60
154 Bradley Zimmer .40 1.00
155 Tanner Rainey .25 .60
156 JC Cardenas .25 .60
157 Austin Riley 3.00 8.00
158 Kevin Kramer .30 .75
159 Hunter Renfroe .40 1.00
160 Grant Holmes .30 .75
161 Isaiah White .30 .75
162 Justin Jacome .25 .60
163 Amed Rosario .40 1.00
164 Josh Bell .50 1.25
165 Eric Jenkins .25 .60
166 Reese McGuire .25 .60
167 Sean Newcomb .30 .75
168 Reynaldo Lopez .30 .75
169 Conor Biggio .25 .60
170 Andrew Suarez .30 .75
171 Trey Ball .25 .60
172 Austin Rei .30 .75
173 Drew Finley .25 .60
174 Skye Bolt .30 .75
175 Daniel Robertson .25 .60
176 Avery Romero .25 .60
177 Jon Harris .30 .75
178 Christin Stewart .30 .75
179 Nelson Rodriguez .30 .75
180 Austin Smith .25 .60
181 Michael Soroka 1.50 4.00
182 Andrew Benintendi 4.00 10.00
183 Matt Crownover .25 .60
184 Franklin Barreto .30 .75
185 Willie Calhoun .75 2.00
186 Braxton Davidson .25 .60
187 Jake Woodford .25 .60
188 Ryan McKenna .25 .60
189 Ryan Helsley .30 .75
190 Carson Sands .25 .60
191 Tyler Beede .30 .75
192 Jeff Hendrix .30 .75
193 Nick Howard .40 1.00
194 Chris Betts .30 .75
195 Jagger Rusconi .25 .60
196 Matt Olson .30 .75
197 Jake Cronenworth 3.00 8.00
198 Alex Robinson .25 .60
199 Albert Almora .30 .75
200 Brendan Rodgers 1.00 2.50

2015 Bowman Chrome Draft Blue Refractors

*BLUE REF: 2X TO 5X BASIC
STATED ODDS 1:134 HOBBY
STATED PRINT RUN 150 SER.#'d SETS
1 Dansby Swanson 15.00 40.00
182 Andrew Benintendi 30.00 80.00

2015 Bowman Chrome Draft Gold Refractors

*GOLD REF: 6X TO 15X BASIC
STATED ODDS 1:401 HOBBY
STATED PRINT RUN 50 SER.#'d SETS
1 Dansby Swanson 50.00 120.00
182 Andrew Benintendi 100.00 250.00

2015 Bowman Chrome Draft Green Refractors

*GREEN REF: 2.5X TO 6X BASIC
STATED ODDS 1:203 HOBBY
STATED PRINT RUN 99 SER.#'d SETS
1 Dansby Swanson 20.00 50.00
182 Andrew Benintendi 40.00 100.00

2015 Bowman Chrome Draft Orange Refractors

*ORANGE REF: 8X TO 20X BASIC
STATED ODDS 1:283 HOBBY
STATED PRINT RUN 25 SER.#'d SETS
1 Dansby Swanson 30.00 80.00
182 Andrew Benintendi 125.00 300.00

2015 Bowman Chrome Draft Refractors

*REF: .75X TO 2X BASIC
STATED ODDS 1:3 HOBBY
182 Andrew Benintendi 8.00 20.00

2015 Bowman Chrome Draft Sky Blue Refractors

*SKY BLUE: 1X TO 2.5X BASIC
STATED ODDS 1:12 HOBBY

2015 Bowman Chrome Draft Draft Pick Autographs

STATED ODDS 1:39 HOBBY
PLATE ODDS 1:16,666 HOBBY
PLATE PRINT RUN 1 SET PER COLOR
NO PLATE PRICING DUE TO SCARCITY
BCAAB Andrew Benintendi 30.00 80.00
BCAAR Ashe Russell 5.00 12.00
BCAARI Austin Riley 50.00 120.00
BCAASM Austin Smith 3.00 8.00
BCAASU Andrew Suarez 4.00 10.00
BCAAY Alex Young 3.00 8.00
BCABB Beau Burrows 4.00 10.00
BCABL Brett Lilek 3.00 8.00
BCABR Brendan Rodgers 40.00 100.00
BCACB Chris Betts 4.00 10.00
BCACBI Conor Biggio 3.00 8.00
BCACF Carson Fulmer 3.00 8.00
BCACG Cam Gibson 4.00 10.00
BCACP Cody Ponce 3.00 8.00
BCACS Chris Shaw 6.00 15.00
BCACST Christin Stewart 4.00 10.00
BCADD Donnie Dewees 5.00 12.00
BCADF Drew Finley 3.00 8.00
BCADL Desmond Lindsay 5.00 12.00
BCADS Dansby Swanson 20.00 50.00
BCADST D.J. Stewart 3.00 8.00
BCADT Dillon Tate 4.00 10.00
BCAEJ Eric Jenkins 3.00 8.00
BCAGW Garrett Whitley 5.00 12.00
BCAIH Ian Happ 12.00 30.00
BCAJD Jeff Degano 4.00 10.00
BCAJHI Juan Hillman 3.00 8.00
BCAJK James Kaprielian 5.00 12.00
BCAJN Josh Naylor 15.00 40.00
BCAJNI Jacob Nix 3.00 8.00
BCAJW Jake Woodford 3.00 8.00
BCAKA Kolby Allard 5.00 12.00
BCAKH Kyle Holder 4.00 10.00
BCAKHA Ke'Bryan Hayes 40.00 100.00
BCAKN Kevin Newman 5.00 12.00
BCAKT Kyle Tucker 40.00 100.00
BCALH Lucas Herbert 3.00 8.00
BCAMM Michael Matuella 4.00 10.00
BCAMR Mariano Rivera 5.00 12.00
BCAMS Michael Soroka 20.00 50.00
BCAMW Mike Nikorak 3.00 8.00
BCAMWO Max Wotell 3.00 8.00
BCANK Nathan Kirby 4.00 10.00
BCANN Nick Neidert 3.00 8.00
BCANP Nick Plummer 4.00 10.00
BCANW Nolan Watson 3.00 8.00
BCAPB Phil Bickford 3.00 8.00
BCAPL Peter Lambert 3.00 8.00
BCARM Richie Martin 3.00 8.00
BCARMO Ryan Mountcastle 40.00 100.00
BCASK Scott Kingery 8.00 20.00
BCATC Trent Clark 20.00 50.00
BCATE Thomas Eshelman 3.00 8.00
BCATJ Tyler Jay 3.00 8.00
BCATMA Tate Matheny 3.00 8.00
BCATN Tyler Nevin 5.00 12.00
BCATR Tanner Rainey 3.00 8.00
BCATS Tyler Stephenson 4.00 10.00
BCATW Taylor Ward 5.00 12.00
BCAWB Walker Buehler 75.00 200.00

2015 Bowman Chrome Draft Draft Pick Autographs Black Refractors

*BLACK REF: 1.2X TO 3X BASIC
RANDOM INSERTS IN PACKS
STATED PRINT RUN 35 SER.#'d SETS
BCAAB Andrew Benintendi 200.00 500.00
BCABR Brendan Rodgers 400.00 800.00
BCADS Dansby Swanson 200.00 500.00
BCAKHA Ke'Bryan Hayes 150.00 400.00
BCAKT Kyle Tucker 300.00 600.00
BCAWB Walker Buehler 300.00 800.00

2015 Bowman Chrome Draft Draft Pick Autographs Gold Refractors

*GOLD REF: 1.2X TO 3X BASIC
STATED ODDS 1:1324 HOBBY
STATED PRINT RUN 50 SER.#'d SETS
BCAAB Andrew Benintendi 200.00 500.00
BCABR Brendan Rodgers 400.00 800.00
BCADS Dansby Swanson 200.00 500.00
BCAKHA Ke'Bryan Hayes 150.00 400.00
BCAKT Kyle Tucker 300.00 600.00
BCAWB Walker Buehler/50 300.00 800.00

2015 Bowman Chrome Draft Draft Pick Autographs Green Refractors

*GREEN REF: 1X TO 2.5X BASIC
STATED ODDS 1:669 HOBBY
STATED PRINT RUN 99 SER.#'d SETS

2015 Bowman Chrome Draft Draft Pick Autographs Orange Refractors

*ORANGE REF: 1.5X TO 4X BASIC
STATED ODDS 1:935 HOBBY
STATED PRINT RUN 25 SER.#'d SETS
BCAAB Andrew Benintendi 250.00 600.00
BCABR Brendan Rodgers 800.00 1500.00
BCADS Dansby Swanson 250.00 600.00
BCAKHA Ke'Bryan Hayes 200.00 500.00
BCAKT Kyle Tucker 400.00 800.00
BCAWB Walker Buehler 400.00 1000.00

2015 Bowman Chrome Draft Draft Pick Autographs Purple Refractors

*PURPLE REF: .6X TO 1.5X BASIC
STATED ODDS 1:265 HOBBY
STATED PRINT RUN 250 SER.#'d SETS

2015 Bowman Chrome Draft Draft Pick Autographs Refractors

*REF: .5X TO 1.2X BASIC
STATED ODDS 1:133 HOBBY

2015 Bowman Chrome Draft Prime Pairings Autographs

STATED ODDS 1:10,384 HOBBY
STATED PRINT RUN 25 SER.#'d SETS
PPASO M.Soroka/K.Allard 15.00 40.00
PPABB T.Beede/P.Bickford 12.00 30.00
PPAFA S.Adams/C.Fulmer 50.00 120.00
PPAKC I.Clarkin/J.Kaprielian 60.00 150.00
PPASR B.Rodgers/D.Swanson 300.00 500.00
PPAWR G.Whitley/D.Robertson 12.00 30.00

2015 Bowman Chrome Draft Scouts Fantasy Impacts

STATED ODDS 1:12 HOBBY
*GOLD/50: 1.5X TO 4X BASIC
*ORANGE/25: 2X TO 5X BASIC
BSIAB Andrew Benintendi 2.00 5.00
BSICF Carson Fulmer .40 1.00
BSIDS Dansby Swanson 2.50 6.00
BSIDT Dillon Tate .50 1.25
BSIIH Ian Happ 1.50 4.00
BSIJA Jorge Alfaro .60 1.50
BSIJC J.P. Crawford .40 1.00
BSIJK James Kaprielian .60 1.50
BSIKC Kyle Crick .50 1.25
BSIKF Kyle Freeland .50 1.25
BSIKN Kevin Newman .60 1.50
BSIKZ Kyle Zimmer .40 1.00
BSILG Lucas Giolito .75 2.00
BSIMO Matt Olson .50 1.25
BSITA Tim Anderson .75 2.00
BSITE Thomas Eshelman .40 1.00
BSITG Tyler Glasnow .50 1.25
BSITJ Tyler Jay .40 1.00
BSIWB Walker Buehler 2.50 6.00
BSIYL Yoan Lopez .40 1.00

2015 Bowman Chrome Draft Teams of Tomorrow Die Cuts

STATED ODDS 1:24 HOBBY
PRINTING PLATES RANDOMLY INSERTED
PLATE PRINT RUN 1 SET PER COLOR
NO PLATE PRICING DUE TO SCARCITY
*GOLD/50: 1X TO 2.5X BASIC
*ORANGE/25: 1.5X TO 4X BASIC
TDC1 T.Ball/A.Benintendi 2.00 5.00
TDC2 D.Swanson/D.Leyba 2.50 6.00
TDC3 B.Rodgers/K.Freeland 1.50 4.00
TDC4 L.Ortiz/D.Tate .50 1.25
TDC5 K.Tucker/T.Hernandez 2.50 6.00
TDC6 Tyler Jay .50 1.25
Nick Gordon
TDC7 C.Fulmer/T.Danish .40 1.00
TDC8 I.Happ/B.McKinney 1.50 4.00
TDC9 C.Randolph/R.Quinn .60 1.50
TDC10 Tyler Stephenson .50 1.25
Jesse Winker
TDC11 Josh Naylor .50 1.25
Avery Romero
TDC12 Garrett Whitley .60 1.50
Casey Gillaspie
TDC13 K.Allard/B.Davidson .40 1.00
TDC14 Trent Clark .60 1.50
Monte Harrison
TDC15 J.Kaprielian/J.Mateo 1.25 3.00
TDC16 Tyler Beede .50 1.25
Phil Bickford
TDC17 Kevin Newman .60 1.50
Austin Meadows
TDC18 R.Martin/M.Olson .50 1.25
TDC19 Kyle Zimmer .40 1.00
Ashe Russell
TDC20 Derek Hill .50 1.25
Beau Burrows

2015 Bowman Chrome Draft Top of the Class

STATED ODDS 1:118 HOBBY BOXES
*ORANGE/25: 1.5X TO 4X BASIC
TOCAB Andrew Benintendi 8.00 20.00
TOCBR Brendan Rodgers 6.00 15.00
TOCCF Carson Fulmer 1.50 4.00
TOCCR Cornelius Randolph 1.50 4.00
TOCDS Dansby Swanson 10.00 25.00
TOCDT Dillon Tate 2.00 5.00
TOCIH Ian Happ 6.00 15.00
TOCKT Kyle Tucker 10.00 25.00
TOCTJ Tyler Jay 1.50 4.00
TOCTS Tyler Stephenson 2.00 5.00

2015 Bowman Chrome Draft Top of the Class Autographs

STATED ODDS 1:458 HOBBY BOXES
STATED PRINT RUN 25 SER.#'d SETS
TOCAB Andrew Benintendi 300.00 500.00
TOCBR Brendan Rodgers 150.00 300.00
TOCCF Carson Fulmer 125.00 250.00
TOCDS Dansby Swanson 800.00 1000.00
TOCIH Ian Happ 150.00 300.00
TOCKT Kyle Tucker 250.00 500.00

2016 Bowman Chrome

COMPLETE SET (100) 25.00 60.00
STATED PLATE ODDS 1:1239 HOBBY
PLATE PRINT RUN 1 SET PER COLOR
BLACK-CYAN-MAGENTA-YELLOW ISSUED
NO PLATE PRICING DUE TO SCARCITY
1 Mike Trout 1.50 4.00
2 David Ortiz .30 .75
3 Albert Pujols .40 1.00
4 Jacob deGrom .30 .75
5 Maikel Franco .25 .60
6 Josh Reddick .20 .50
7 Byung-Ho Park RC .50 1.25
8 Manny Machado .30 .75
9 Jose Fernandez .30 .75
10 Nomar Mazara RC .60 1.50
11 Freddie Freeman .40 1.00
12 Hunter Pence .25 .60
13 Wade Davis .20 .50
14 Jameson Taillon RC .50 1.25
15 Seung-Hwan Oh RC 1.00 2.50
16 Tyler White RC .40 1.00
17 Felix Hernandez .25 .60
18 Noah Syndergaard .25 .60
19 Josh Donaldson .25 .60
20 Aledmys Diaz RC .60 1.50
21 Troy Tulowitzki .30 .75
22 Mookie Betts .50 1.25
23 Paul Goldschmidt .30 .75
24 Dustin Pedroia .30 .75
25 Kenta Maeda RC .75 2.00
26 Zack Greinke .25 .60
27 Miguel Sano RC .60 1.50
28 Andrew McCutchen .30 .75
29 Jon Gray RC .40 1.00
30 Aaron Nola RC .75 2.00
31 Kyle Schwarber RC 1.25 3.00
32 Francisco Lindor .30 .75
33 Jose Abreu .30 .75
34 Robinson Cano .25 .60
35 Evan Longoria .25 .60
36 Mallex Smith RC .40 1.00
37 Ichiro Suzuki .40 1.00
38 Dallas Keuchel .25 .60
39 Carlos Correa .30 .75
40 Corey Seager RC 3.00 8.00
41 Michael Fulmer RC .60 1.50
42 Tyson Ross .20 .50
43 Adam Jones .25 .60
44 Jason Heyward .25 .60
45 Anthony Rizzo .50 1.25
46 Carl Edwards Jr. RC .50 1.25
47 Yu Darvish .30 .75
48 Stephen Piscotty RC .60 1.50
49 David Price .25 .60
50 Clayton Kershaw .60 1.50
51 Trea Turner RC 1.25 3.00
52 Nelson Cruz .30 .75
53 Chris Sale .30 .75
54 Buster Posey .40 1.00
55 Jose Berrios RC .50 1.25
56 Salvador Perez .25 .60
57 Trevor Story RC 1.50 4.00
58 Madison Bumgarner .25 .60
59 Evan Gattis .20 .50
60 Julio Urias RC 1.25 3.00
61 Todd Frazier .25 .60
62 Yadier Molina .30 .75
63 Dellin Betances .25 .60
64 J.D. Martinez .30 .75
65 Chris Archer .20 .50
66 Adam Wainwright .25 .60
67 Luis Severino RC .50 1.25
68 Henry Owens RC .50 1.25
69 Aroldis Chapman .30 .75
70 Kris Bryant .40 1.00
71 Sean Manaea RC .40 1.00
72 Yoenis Cespedes .30 .75
73 Ryan Braun .25 .60
74 Eric Hosmer .25 .60
75 Jacoby Ellsbury .25 .60
76 Adrian Gonzalez .25 .60
77 Edwin Encarnacion .30 .75
78 Adrian Beltre .30 .75
79 Max Scherzer .30 .75
80 Joey Votto .30 .75
81 Masahiro Tanaka .25 .60
82 Michael Conforto RC .50 1.25
83 Albert Almora RC .50 1.25
84 A.J. Pollock .20 .50
85 Sonny Gray .25 .60
86 Miguel Cabrera .30 .75
87 Jose Bautista .25 .60
88 James Shields .20 .50
89 Jake Arrieta .25 .60
90 Gary Sanchez RC 1.25 3.00
91 Giancarlo Stanton .30 .75
92 Hector Olivera RC .50 1.25
93 Aaron Blair RC .40 1.00
94 Byron Buxton .25 .60
95 Justin Upton .25 .60
96 Nolan Arenado .40 1.00
97 Craig Kimbrel .25 .60
98 Blake Snell RC .50 1.25
99 Robert Stephenson RC .40 1.00
100 Bryce Harper .50 1.25

2016 Bowman Chrome Blue Refractors

*BLUE REF VET: 4X TO 10X BASIC
*BLUE REF RC: 2X TO 5X BASIC
STATED ODDS 1:34 HOBBY
STATED PRINT RUN 150 SER.#'d SETS

2016 Bowman Chrome Gold Refractors

*GOLD REF VET: 8X TO 20X BASIC
*GOLD REF RC: 4X TO 10X BASIC
STATED ODDS 1:100 HOBBY
STATED PRINT RUN 50 SER.#'d SETS

2016 Bowman Chrome Green Refractors

*GREEN REF VET: 4X TO 10X BASIC
*GREEN REF RC: 2X TO 5X BASIC
STATED ODDS 1:51 HOBBY
STATED PRINT RUN 99 SER.#'d SETS

2016 Bowman Chrome Orange Refractors

*ORANGE REF VET: 10X TO 25X BASIC
*ORANGE REF RC: 5X TO 12X BASIC
STATED ODDS 1:199 HOBBY
STATED PRINT RUN 25 SER.#'d SETS

2016 Bowman Chrome Purple Refractors

*PURPLE REF VET: 2X TO 5X BASIC
*PURPLE REF RC: 1X TO 2.5X BASIC
C
STATED PRINT RUN 250 SER.#'d SETS

2016 Bowman Chrome Refractors

*REF VET: 1.5X TO 4X BASIC
*REF RC: .75X TO 2X BASIC
STATED ODDS 1:10 HOBBY
STATED PRINT RUN 499 SER.#'d SETS

2016 Bowman Chrome Vending '16 Bowman

COMPLETE SET (100) 12.00 30.00
FOUND IN VENDING BOXES
1 Mike Trout 2.00 5.00
2 Josh Donaldson .30 .75
3 Albert Pujols .50 1.25
5 Paul Goldschmidt .40 1.00
6 Yasmany Tomas .25 .60
7 Freddie Freeman .50 1.25
10 David Ortiz .40 1.00
11 Manny Machado .40 1.00
12 Chris Davis .25 .60
13 Mookie Betts .60 1.50
14 Adam Jones .30 .75
16 Xander Bogaerts .40 1.00
17 Jon Lester .30 .75
18 Jake Arrieta .30 .75
20 Kris Bryant .50 1.25
23 Chris Sale .40 1.00
27 Joey Votto .40 1.00
28 Francisco Lindor .40 1.00
30 Carlos Correa .40 1.00
33 Miguel Cabrera .40 1.00

34 Ian Kinsler .30 .75
38 Dallas Keuchel .30 .75
39 Jose Altuve .30 .75
40 Clayton Kershaw .75 2.00
41 Lorenzo Cain .25 .60
43 Eric Hosmer .30 .75
45 Zack Greinke .30 .75
47 Yasiel Puig .40 1.00
48 Giancarlo Stanton .40 1.00
49 Jose Fernandez .40 1.00
50 Ichiro Suzuki .50 1.25
51 Ryan Braun .30 .75
52 Byron Buxton .30 .75
53 Brian Dozier .30 .75
55 Yoenis Cespedes .40 1.00
56 Matt Harvey .30 .75
57 Jacob deGrom .40 1.00
58 Noah Syndergaard .30 .75
59 Dellin Betances .30 .75
60 Masahiro Tanaka .30 .75
61 Alex Rodriguez .50 1.25
62 Sonny Gray .25 .60
64 Stephen Vogt .30 .75
67 Odubel Herrera .30 .75
68 Andrew McCutchen .40 1.00
70 Buster Posey .50 1.25
73 Tyson Ross .25 .60
75 Jung Ho Kang .25 .60
76 Madison Bumgarner .30 .75
78 Brandon Belt .30 .75
80 Felix Hernandez .30 .75
85 Chris Archer .25 .60
86 Kevin Kiermaier .30 .75
87 Prince Fielder .30 .75
91 Jose Bautista .30 .75
92 David Price .30 .75
94 Wei-Yin Chen .25 .60
96 Stephen Strasburg .40 1.00
97 Garrett Richards .30 .75
98 David Peralta .25 .60
99 Julio Teheran .30 .75
100 Bryce Harper .60 1.50
101 Adam Eaton .25 .60
103 Jay Bruce .30 .75
104 Carlos Gonzalez .30 .75
110 Matt Kemp .30 .75
112 Kyle Seager .25 .60
113 Marcus Stroman .30 .75
115 Trevor Rosenthal .30 .75
117 Michael Brantley .30 .75
118 Adam Wainwright .30 .75
119 Wade Davis .25 .60
122 Kyle Schwarber .75 2.00
123 Stephen Piscotty .40 1.00
124 Carl Edwards Jr. .30 .75
125 Aaron Nola .50 1.25
126 Hector Olivera .30 .75
127 Rob Refsnyder .30 .75
128 Jose Peraza .30 .75
129 Henry Owens .30 .75
130 Trea Turner .75 2.00
131 Michael Conforto .30 .75
132 Greg Bird .30 .75
133 Richie Shaffer .25 .60
134 Jon Gray .25 .60
135 Luis Severino .30 .75
136 Miguel Almonte .25 .60
137 Brandon Drury .40 1.00
138 Zach Lee .25 .60
139 Kyle Waldrop .30 .75
140 Miguel Sano .40 1.00
142 Frankie Montas .30 .75
143 Gary Sanchez .75 2.00
144 Ketel Marte .50 1.25
145 Trayce Thompson .40 1.00
146 Jorge Lopez .25 .60
147 Max Kepler .40 1.00
148 Tom Murphy .25 .60
149 Raul Mondesi .30 .75
150 Corey Seager 2.00 5.00

2016 Bowman Chrome AFL Fall Stars

COMP.SET w/o SP (20) 8.00 20.00
STATED ODDS 1:6 HOBBY
SP ODDS 1:1981 HOBBY
SP PRINT RUN 250 SER.#'d SETS
*BLUE/150: .75X TO 2X BASIC
*GOLD/50: 2X TO 5X BASIC
*ORANGE/25: 2.5X TO 6X BASIC
AFLAB Alex Blandino .40 1.00
AFLABW Adam Brett Walker .40 1.00
AFLAD Austin Dean .40 1.00
AFLAE Adam Engel .40 1.00
AFLAM Austin Meadows .60 1.50
AFLCA Christian Arroyo 1.25 3.00
AFLCF Clint Frazier 1.50 4.00
AFLCP Chad Pinder .40 1.00
AFLDF Derek Fisher .40 1.00
AFLDP D.J. Peterson .40 1.00
AFLJB Jake Bauers .60 1.50
AFLJP Jurickson Profar .50 1.25
AFLKF Kyle Freeland .50 1.25
AFLLS Lucas Sims .40 1.00
AFLNB Renato Nunez .75 2.00
AFLRM Reese McGuire .40 1.00
AFLRT Raimel Tapia .50 1.25
AFLSGS Sanchez MVP SP/250 15.00 40.00
AFLSM Sean Manaea .40 1.00
AFLST Sam Travis .75 2.00
AFLWC Willson Contreras 1.00 2.50

2016 Bowman Chrome AFL Fall Stars Autographs

STATED ODDS 1:416 HOBBY
STATED SP ODDS 1:9659 HOBBY
STATED PRINT RUN 25 SER.#'d SETS
NO PRICING ON QTY 17 OR LESS
BOW.CHR.EXCH.DEADLINE 8/31/2018
*GOLD/50: .6X TO 1.5X BASIC
AFLABW Adam Brett Walker/199 3.00 8.00
AFLAGS Gary Sanchez MVP SP/50 75.00 200.00
AFLCP Chad Pinder/22 3.00 8.00
AFLDP D.J. Peterson
AFLJB Jake Bauers/50 6.00 15.00
AFLJP Jurickson Profar/75 10.00 25.00
AFLLS Lucas Sims/199 4.00 10.00
AFLWC Willson Contreras/199 10.00 25.00

2016 Bowman Chrome AFL Fall Stars Relic Autographs

STATED ODDS 1:2752 HOBBY
STATED PRINT RUN 25 SER.#'d SETS
BOW.CHR.EXCH.DEADLINE 8/31/2018
AFLRAB Alex Blandino 30.00 80.00
AFLRAE Adam Engel 8.00 20.00
AFLRDF Derek Fisher 12.00 30.00
AFLRGS Gary Sanchez 150.00 250.00
AFLRJC Jeimer Candelario 20.00 50.00
AFLRJP Jurickson Profar 10.00 25.00
AFLRRM Reese McGuire 8.00 20.00

2016 Bowman Chrome AFL Fall Stars Relics

STATED ODDS 1:626 HOBBY
STATED PRINT RUN 99 SER.#'d SETS
*ORANGE/25: .75X TO 2X BASIC
AFLRABW Adam Brett Walker 3.00 8.00
AFLRAD Austin Dean 3.00 8.00
AFLRAK Andrew Knapp 3.00 8.00
AFLRAM Austin Meadows 5.00 12.00
AFLRCA Christian Arroyo 8.00 20.00
AFLRCF Clint Frazier 12.00 30.00
AFLRCP Chad Pinder 3.00 8.00
AFLRDP D.J. Peterson 3.00 8.00
AFLRGS Gary Sanchez 25.00 60.00
AFLRJB Jake Bauers 5.00 12.00
AFLRJP Jurickson Profar 8.00 20.00
AFLRKF Kyle Freeland 4.00 10.00
AFLRLS Lucas Sims 3.00 8.00
AFLRRN Renato Nunez 6.00 15.00
AFLRRT Rowdy Tellez 5.00 12.00
AFLRRTA Raimel Tapia 4.00 10.00
AFLRSM Sean Manaea 8.00 20.00
AFLRST Sam Travis 6.00 15.00

2016 Bowman Chrome Bowman Scouts Top 100

STATED ODDS 1:8 HOBBY
*GREEN/99: .75X TO 2X BASIC
*GOLD/50: 2X TO 5X BASIC
*ORANGE/25: 3X TO 8X BASIC
BTP1 Corey Seager 3.00 8.00
BTP2 Byron Buxton .50 1.25
BTP3 Lucas Giolito .60 1.50
BTP4 J.P. Crawford .40 1.00
BTP5 Alex Reyes .50 1.25
BTP6 Orlando Arcia .50 1.25
BTP7 Julio Urias 1.25 3.00
BTP8 Tyler Glasnow .50 1.25
BTP9 Anderson Espinoza .40 1.00
BTP10 Brendan Rodgers .60 1.50
BTP11 Blake Snell .60 1.50
BTP12 Jose Berrios .50 1.25
BTP13 Steven Matz .50 1.25
BTP14 Trea Turner 1.25 3.00
BTP15 Gleyber Torres 6.00 15.00
BTP16 Dansby Swanson 1.25 3.00
BTP17 Alex Bregman 2.50 6.00
BTP18 Manuel Margot .40 1.00
BTP19 Ozzie Albies 1.50 4.00
BTP20 Jose De Leon .40 1.00
BTP21 Andrew Benintendi 1.25 3.00
BTP22 Nomar Mazara .60 1.50
BTP23 Victor Robles 1.50 4.00
BTP24 A.J. Reed .40 1.00
BTP25 Joey Gallo .50 1.25
BTP26 Sean Newcomb .50 1.25
BTP27 Jorge Lopez .40 1.00
BTP28 Aaron Blair .40 1.00
BTP29 Max Kepler .60 1.50
BTP30 Rafael Devers 1.25 3.00
BTP31 Aaron Judge 3.00 8.00
BTP32 Archie Bradley .40 1.00
BTP33 Bradley Zimmer .60 1.50
BTP34 Jorge Mateo .60 1.50
BTP35 Carson Fulmer .40 1.00
BTP36 Brett Phillips .40 1.00
BTP37 Kolby Allard .40 1.00
BTP38 Raul Mondesi .50 1.25
BTP39 Lewis Brinson .60 1.50
BTP40 Jeff Hoffman .50 1.25
BTP41 Anthony Alford .40 1.00
BTP42 Brady Aiken 1.00 2.50
BTP43 Jon Gray .40 1.00
BTP44 Robert Stephenson .40 1.00
BTP45 Mark Appel .40 1.00
BTP46 Dillon Tate .50 1.25
BTP47 Austin Meadows .60 1.50
BTP48 Willy Adames .60 1.50
BTP49 Ian Happ .75 2.00
BTP50 Clint Frazier 1.50 4.00
BTP51 Francis Martes .50 1.25
BTP52 Jake Thompson .40 1.00
BTP53 David Dahl .50 1.25
BTP54 Dylan Bundy .50 1.25
BTP55 Kyle Tucker 1.50 4.00
BTP56 Franklin Barreto .40 1.00
BTP57 Josh Bell .75 2.00
BTP58 Brent Honeywell .60 1.50
BTP59 Tyler Stephenson .40 1.00
BTP60 Jesse Winker .40 1.00
BTP61 Jose Peraza .50 1.25
BTP62 Trent Clark .40 1.00
BTP63 Brian Johnson .40 1.00
BTP64 Jameson Taillon .50 1.25
BTP65 Miguel Almonte .40 1.00
BTP66 Sean Manaea .40 1.00
BTP67 Jon Harris .50 1.25
BTP68 Willson Contreras 2.50 6.00
BTP69 Dominic Smith .40 1.00
BTP70 James Kaprielian .50 1.25
BTP71 Marco Gonzales .50 1.25
BTP72 Amir Garrett .40 1.00
BTP73 Gary Sanchez 1.25 3.00
BTP74 Hector Olivera .50 1.25
BTP75 Michael Fulmer .60 1.50
BTP76 Phil Bickford .40 1.00
BTP77 Hunter Renfroe .50 1.25
BTP78 Nick Gordon .40 1.00
BTP79 Nick Williams .50 1.25
BTP80 Cody Reed .40 1.00
BTP81 Grant Holmes .50 1.25
BTP82 Tyler Jay .40 1.00
BTP83 Tyler Kolek .50 1.25
BTP84 Bobby Bradley .50 1.25
BTP85 Alex Jackson .50 1.25
BTP86 Gavin Cecchini .40 1.00
BTP87 Tim Anderson 1.50 4.00
BTP88 Christian Arroyo 1.25 3.00
BTP89 Hunter Harvey .40 1.00
BTP90 Franklyn Kilome .50 1.25
BTP91 Cornelius Randolph .40 1.00
BTP92 Sean Reid-Foley .50 1.25
BTP93 Rob Kaminsky .40 1.00
BTP94 Jake Bauers .60 1.50
BTP95 Mac Williamson .40 1.00
BTP96 Ke'Bryan Hayes .40 1.00
BTP97 Beau Burrows .40 1.00
BTP98 Josh Naylor .50 1.25
BTP99 Edwin Diaz .75 2.00
BTP100 Brandon Nimmo .60 1.50

2016 Bowman Chrome Bowman Scouts Top 100 Autographs Gold

STATED ODDS 1:3386 HOBBY
EXCHANGE DEADLINE 3/31/2018
BTP2 Byron Buxton 15.00 40.00
BTP3 Lucas Giolito 30.00 80.00
BTP5 Alex Reyes 10.00 25.00
BTP10 Brendan Rodgers 20.00 50.00
BTP11 Blake Snell 20.00 50.00
BTP12 Jose Berrios 15.00 40.00
BTP14 Trea Turner 30.00 80.00
BTP16 Dansby Swanson 40.00 100.00
BTP17 Alex Bregman 80.00 200.00
BTP21 Andrew Benintendi 40.00 100.00
BTP31 Aaron Judge 75.00 200.00
BTP35 Carson Fulmer 12.00 30.00
BTP46 Dillon Tate 15.00 40.00
BTP47 Austin Meadows 20.00 50.00
BTP48 Willy Adames 20.00 50.00

2016 Bowman Chrome Bowman Scouts Updates

COMPLETE SET (25) 5.00 12.00
STATED ODDS 1:3 HOBBY
*BLUE/150: .75X TO 2X BASIC
*GOLD/50: 2X TO 5X BASIC
*ORANGE/25: 2.5X TO 6X BASIC
BSUAJ Ariel Jurado .40 1.00
BSUAR Austin Riley 1.25 3.00
BSUAS Antonio Senzatela .40 1.00
BSUAV Alex Verdugo .60 1.50
BSUCB Cody Bellinger 6.00 15.00
BSUCE Chris Ellis .40 1.00
BSUCS Connor Sadzeck .40 1.00
BSUDJ Drew Jackson .40 1.00
BSUDU Duane Underwood .40 1.00
BSUJC Jharel Cotton .40 1.00
BSUJF Jack Flaherty .60 1.50
BSUJG Jarlin Garcia .40 1.00
BSUJM Joe Musgrove .40 1.00
BSUJN Jacob Nottingham .40 1.00
BSUJO Jhailyn Ortiz .75 2.00
BSUKN Kevin Newman .60 1.50
BSUMC Mike Clevinger .75 2.00
BSUMS Michael Soroka 1.25 3.00
BSUNP Nick Plummer .50 1.25
BSURG Ruddy Giron .40 1.00
BSURL Reynaldo Lopez .40 1.00
BSUTM Trey Mancini 1.25 3.00
BSUTO Tyler O'Neill .50 1.25
BSUTW Taylor Ward .50 1.25
BSUYA Yadier Alvarez .60 1.50

2016 Bowman Chrome Bowman Scouts Updates Autographs

STATED ODDS 1:543 HOBBY
STATED PRINT RUN 199 SER.#'d SETS
BOW.CHR.EXCH.DEADLINE 8/31/2018
*GOLD REF: .75X TO 2X BASIC
BSUAJ Ariel Jurado 3.00 8.00
BSUAR Austin Riley 60.00 150.00
BSUCS Connor Sadzeck 3.00 8.00
BSUDJ Drew Jackson 3.00 8.00
BSUJC Jharel Cotton 3.00 8.00
BSUJO Jhailyn Ortiz 6.00 15.00
BSUKN Kevin Newman 5.00 12.00
BSUMC Mike Clevinger 6.00 15.00
BSUMS Michael Soroka 10.00 25.00
BSUNP Nick Plummer 4.00 10.00
BSUTM Trey Mancini 10.00 25.00
BSUTO Tyler O'Neill 4.00 10.00
BSUTW Taylor Ward 4.00 10.00
BSUYA Yadier Alvarez 10.00 25.00

2016 Bowman Chrome Out of the Gate

COMPLETE SET (10) 8.00 20.00
STATED ODDS 1:12 HOBBY
*BLUE/150: 1.2X TO 3X BASIC
*GOLD/50: 2X TO 5X BASIC
*ORANGE/25: 2.5X TO 6X BASIC
OOG1 Trevor Story 1.50 4.00
OOG2 Tyler White .40 1.00
OOG3 Aledmys Diaz .60 1.50
OOG4 Kenta Maeda .75 2.00
OOG5 Michael Conforto .50 1.25
OOG6 Nomar Mazara .60 1.50
OOG7 Aaron Nola .75 2.00
OOG8 Byung-ho Park .50 1.25
OOG9 Stephen Piscotty .60 1.50
OOG10 Blake Snell .50 1.25

2016 Bowman Chrome Prime Position Autographs

STATED ODDS 1:432 HOBBY
STATED PRINT RUN 250 SER.#'d SETS
BOW.CHR.EXCH.DEADLINE 8/31/2018
*GREEN/99: .6X TO 1.5X BASIC
*GOLD/50: .75X TO 2X BASIC
*ORANGE/25: 1X TO 2.5X BASIC
PPAAB Andrew Benintendi 25.00 60.00
PPAAJ Aaron Judge 60.00 150.00
PPAAR A.J. Reed 4.00 10.00
PPAARE Alex Reyes 10.00 25.00
PPACS Corey Seager 20.00 50.00
PPADS Dansby Swanson 15.00 40.00
PPAJB Jose Berrios 6.00 15.00
PPAKS Kyle Schwarber 12.00 30.00
PPAMS Miguel Sano 8.00 20.00
PPANM Nomar Mazara 8.00 20.00
PPAOA Orlando Arcia 5.00 12.00
PPARD Rafael Devers 20.00 50.00
PPATS Tyler Stephenson 4.00 10.00
PPAYM Yoan Moncada 40.00 100.00

2016 Bowman Chrome Prospect Autographs

BOW.ODDS 1:56 HOBBY
BOW.CHR.ODDS 1:11 HOBBY
BOW.PLATE ODDS 1:17,849 HOBBY
BOW.CHR.PLATE ODDS 1:5568 HOBBY
PLATE PRINT RUN 1 SET PER COLOR
NO PLATE PRICING DUE TO SCARCITY
BOW.EXCH.DEADLINE 3/31/2018
BOW.CHR.EXCH.DEADLINE 8/31/2018
BCAPAG Austin Gomber 3.00 8.00
BCAPASA Antonio Santillan EXCH 3.00 8.00
BCAPCG Conner Greene 3.00 8.00
BCAPCK Chad Kuhl 3.00 8.00
BCAPCR Cornelius Randolph 3.00 8.00
BCAPCS Connor Sadzeck 3.00 8.00
BCAPCZ Corey Zangari 3.00 8.00
BCAPDFO Dustin Fowler 4.00 10.00
BCAPDP David Paulino 4.00 10.00
BCAPEJM Eddy Julio Martinez 4.00 10.00
BCAPFR Franklin Reyes 3.00 8.00
BCAPHJP Hoy-Jun Park 4.00 10.00
BCAPID Isan Diaz 8.00 20.00
BCAPJA Jonah Arenado 4.00 10.00
BCAPJF Junior Fernandez 5.00 12.00
BCAPJFA Jacob Faria 3.00 8.00
BCAPJG Jeison Guzman 3.00 8.00
BCAPJGU Javier Guerra 3.00 8.00
BCAPJJ Jahmai Jones 6.00 15.00
BCAPJOS Jordan Stephens 3.00 8.00
BCAPJP Jermaine Palacios 4.00 10.00
BCAPJS Jaime Schultz 3.00 8.00
BCAPMG Mike Gerber 3.00 8.00
BCAPOC Oneal Cruz 25.00 60.00
BCAPRO Rafty Ozuna 3.00 8.00
BCAPRW Ryan Williams 3.00 8.00
BCAPSH Sam Howard 3.00 8.00
BCAPSTR Sam Travis 4.00 10.00
BCAPTA Tyler Alexander 3.00 8.00
BCAPTJ Tyrell Jenkins 3.00 8.00
BCAPVA Victor Alcantara 3.00 8.00
BCAPWC Willie Calhoun 6.00 15.00
BCAPYG Yeudy Garcia 3.00 8.00
CPAAA Anthony Alford 8.00 20.00
CPAAB Alex Bregman 100.00 250.00
CPAABA Anthony Banda 3.00 8.00
CPAAE Anderson Espinoza 6.00 15.00
CPAAEN Adam Engel 3.00 8.00
CPAAJ Ariel Jurado 3.00 8.00
CPAAS Anfernee Seymour 3.00 8.00
CPABL Brady Lail 3.00 8.00
CPABM Billy McKinney 4.00 10.00
CPABR Brendan Rodgers 25.00 60.00
CPACB Corey Black 3.00 8.00
CPADA Domingo Acevedo 5.00 12.00
CPADAS Dansby Swanson 20.00 50.00
CPADC Daz Cameron 10.00 25.00
CPADD David Denson 3.00 8.00
CPADH David Hess 3.00 8.00
CPADJ Drew Jackson 3.00 8.00
CPADL Domingo Leyba 3.00 8.00
CPADP Daniel Poncedeleon 4.00 10.00
CPAFK Franklyn Kilome 4.00 10.00
CPAFM Francis Martes 5.00 12.00
CPAFT Fernando Tatis Jr. 750.00 2000.00
CPAHB Harrison Bader 10.00 25.00
CPAIA Iolana Akau 5.00 12.00
CPAJC Jharel Cotton 3.00 8.00
CPAJGU Jordan Guerrero 3.00 8.00
CPAJMU Joe Musgrove 3.00 8.00
CPAJN John Norwood 3.00 8.00
CPAJO Jhailyn Ortiz 6.00 15.00
CPAJP Jordan Patterson 3.00 8.00
CPAJS Juan Soto 1000.00 2000.00
CPAJT Jesus Tinoco 3.00 8.00
CPAJY Juan Yepez 3.00 8.00
CPAKK Kevin Kramer 4.00 10.00
CPAKM Kenta Maeda 15.00 40.00
CPALF Lucius Fox 5.00 12.00
CPAMC Mike Clevinger 10.00 25.00
CPAMD Mauricio Dubon 10.00 25.00
CPAMW Mikey White 3.00 8.00
CPAMZ Mark Zagunis 3.00 8.00
CPANS Nate Smith 3.00 8.00
CPAOD Oscar De La Cruz 4.00 10.00
CPAPD Paul DeJong 12.00 30.00
CPARB Rafael Bautista 3.00 8.00
CPARG Ruddy Giron 3.00 8.00
CPARS Ricardo Sanchez 3.00 8.00
CPASC Samuel Coonrod 3.00 8.00
CPASG Stone Garrett 3.00 8.00
CPASR Sal Romano 3.00 8.00
CPATM Trey Mancini 15.00 40.00
CPATO Tyler O'Neill 6.00 15.00
CPATW Tyler White 3.00 8.00
CPAVG Vladimir Guerrero Jr. 300.00 600.00
CPAVR Victor Robles 25.00 60.00
CPAWC Willson Contreras 30.00 80.00
CPAWH Wei-Chieh Huang 3.00 8.00
CPAYA Yadier Alvarez 5.00 12.00
CPAYM Yoan Moncada 100.00 250.00
CPAYMU Yairo Munoz 8.00 20.00

2016 Bowman Chrome Prospect Autographs Blue Refractors

*BLUE REF: 1X TO 2.5X BASIC
BOW.ODDS 1:483 HOBBY
BOW.CHR.ODDS 1:139 HOBBY
STATED PRINT RUN 150 SER.#'D SETS
BOW.EXCH.DEADLINE 3/31/2018
BOW.CHR.EXCH.DEADLINE 8/31/2018
BCAPJA Jonah Arenado 25.00 60.00
CPAAB Alex Bregman 300.00 600.00
CPAFT Fernando Tatis Jr. 4000.00 10000.00
CPAJS Juan Soto 2000.00 4000.00
CPAPD Paul DeJong 50.00 120.00
CPATO Tyler O'Neill 60.00 150.00
CPAVG Vladimir Guerrero Jr. 2000.00 3000.00
CPAVR Victor Robles 200.00 500.00

2016 Bowman Chrome Prospect Autographs Green Refractors

*GREEN REF: 1.2X TO 3X BASIC
INSERTED IN RETAIL PACKS
BOW.CHR.ODDS 1:208 HOBBY
STATED PRINT RUN 99 SER.#'D SETS
BOW.EXCH.DEADLINE 3/31/2018
BOW.CHR.EXCH.DEADLINE 8/31/2018
BCAPJA Jonah Arenado 30.00 80.00
BCAPRO Rafty Ozuna 20.00 50.00
CPAAB Alex Bregman 400.00 800.00
CPAFT Fernando Tatis Jr. 5000.00 12000.00
CPAJS Juan Soto 2500.00 5000.00
CPAPD Paul DeJong 60.00 150.00
CPATO Tyler O'Neill 75.00 200.00
CPAVG Vladimir Guerrero Jr. 2000.00 3000.00
CPAVR Victor Robles 250.00 600.00

2016 Bowman Chrome Prospect Autographs Gold Refractors

*GOLD REF: 1.5X TO 4X BASIC
BOW.STATED ODDS 1:1448 HOBBY
STATED PRINT RUN 50 SER.#'d SETS
BOW.EXCH.DEADLINE 3/31/2018
BOW.CHR.EXCH.DEADLINE 8/31/2018
BCAPJA Jonah Arenado 60.00 150.00
BCAPJGU Javier Guerra 30.00 80.00
BCAPOC Oneal Cruz 300.00 600.00
BCAPRO Rafty Ozuna 25.00 60.00
CPAAA Anthony Alford 125.00 300.00
CPAAB Alex Bregman 500.00 1000.00
CPAAE Anderson Espinoza 50.00 120.00
CPAFK Franklyn Kilome 25.00 60.00
CPAFM Francis Martes 40.00 100.00
CPAFT Fernando Tatis Jr. 6000.00 15000.00
CPAJMU Joe Musgrove 25.00 60.00
CPAJS Juan Soto 3000.00 6000.00
CPAJY Juan Yepez 50.00 120.00
CPALF Lucius Fox 40.00 100.00
CPAMZ Mark Zagunis 20.00 50.00
CPAOD Oscar De La Cruz 30.00 80.00
CPAPD Paul DeJong 75.00 200.00
CPARB Rafael Bautista 30.00 80.00
CPARG Ruddy Giron 25.00 60.00
CPASG Stone Garrett 50.00 120.00
CPATO Tyler O'Neill 200.00 500.00
CPATW Tyler White 20.00 50.00
CPAVG Vladimir Guerrero Jr. 4000.00 8000.00
CPAVR Victor Robles 600.00 1200.00
CPAYA Yadier Alvarez 50.00 120.00

2016 Bowman Chrome Prospect Autographs Orange Refractors

*ORANGE REF: 3X TO 8X BASIC
BOW.STATED ODDS 1:687 HOBBY
BOW.CHR.ODDS 1:372 HOBBY
STATED PRINT RUN 25 SER.#'d SETS
BOW.EXCH.DEADLINE 3/31/2018
BOW.CHR.EXCH.DEADLINE 8/31/2018
BCAPJA Jonah Arenado 125.00 300.00
BCAPJGU Javier Guerra 60.00 150.00
BCAPOC Oneal Cruz 600.00 1200.00
BCAPRO Rafty Ozuna 50.00 120.00
CPAAA Anthony Alford 150.00 400.00
CPAAB Alex Bregman 800.00 1200.00
CPAAE Anderson Espinoza 100.00 250.00
CPAFK Franklyn Kilome 30.00 80.00
CPAFM Francis Martes 50.00 120.00
CPAFT Fernando Tatis Jr. 10000.00 25000.00
CPAJMU Joe Musgrove 50.00 120.00
CPAJS Juan Soto 6000.00 12000.00
CPAJY Juan Yepez 60.00 150.00
CPALF Lucius Fox 75.00 200.00
CPAMZ Mark Zagunis 25.00 60.00
CPAOD Oscar De La Cruz 60.00 150.00
CPAPD Paul DeJong 200.00 500.00
CPARB Rafael Bautista 40.00 100.00
CPARG Ruddy Giron 30.00 80.00
CPASG Stone Garrett 100.00 250.00
CPATO Tyler O'Neill 300.00 600.00
CPATW Tyler White 40.00 100.00
CPAVG Vladimir Guerrero Jr. 10000.00 15000.00
CPAVR Victor Robles 1000.00 2000.00
CPAYA Yadier Alvarez 60.00 150.00

2016 Bowman Chrome Prospect Autographs Purple Refractors

*PURPLE REF: .6X TO 1.5X BASIC
BOW.STATED ODDS 1:290 HOBBY
BOW.CHR.ODDS 1:83 HOBBY
STATED PRINT RUN 250 SER.#'d SETS
BOW.EXCH.DEADLINE 3/31/2018
BOW.CHR.EXCH.DEADLINE 8/31/2018
CPAAB Alex Bregman 200.00 500.00
CPAFT Fernando Tatis Jr. 2000.00 5000.00
CPAJS Juan Soto 2000.00 4000.00
CPATO Tyler O'Neill 25.00 60.00
CPAVG Vladimir Guerrero Jr. 600.00 1200.00

2016 Bowman Chrome Prospect Autographs Refractors

*REF: .5X TO 1.2X BASIC
BOW.ODDS 1:145 HOBBY
BOW.CHR.ODDS 1:42 HOBBY
STATED PRINT RUN 499 SER.#'D SETS
BOW.EXCH.DEADLINE 3/31/2018
BOW.CHR.EXCH.DEADLINE 8/31/2018
CPAFT Fernando Tatis Jr. 1500.00 4000.00
CPAJS Juan Soto 1200.00 2500.00
CPATO Tyler O'Neill 20.00 50.00
CPAVG Vladimir Guerrero Jr. 500.00 1000.00

2016 Bowman Chrome Prospects

COMPLETE SET (250) 20.00 50.00
BOW.PLATE ODDS 1:4119 HOBBY
BOW.CHR.PLATE ODDS 1:4116 HOBBY
PLATE PRINT RUN 1 SET PER COLOR
NO PLATE PRICING DUE TO SCARCITY
BCP1 Daz Cameron .25 .60
BCP2 Orlando Arcia .30 .75
BCP3 Domingo Leyba .25 .60
BCP4 Alex Bregman 1.50 4.00
BCP5 Yadier Alvarez .40 1.00
BCP6 Touki Toussaint .30 .75
BCP7 Brady Aiken .60 1.50
BCP8 Billy McKinney .30 .75
BCP9 Stone Garrett .25 .60
BCP10 Victor Robles 1.00 2.50
BCP11 Wei-Chieh Huang .25 .60
BCP12 Jomar Reyes .40 1.00
BCP13 Lucius Fox .40 1.00
BCP14 Samuel Coonrod .25 .60
BCP15 Seuly Matias .75 2.00
BCP16 Willson Contreras 1.50 4.00
BCP17 Fernando Tatis Jr. 75.00 200.00
BCP18 Starling Heredia .50 1.25
BCP19 Drew Jackson .25 .60
BCP20 Ruddy Giron .25 .60
BCP21 Anfernee Seymour .25 .60
BCP22 Iolana Akau .40 1.00
BCP23 Kevin Padlo .25 .60
BCP24 Brady Lail .25 .60
BCP25 Dillon Tate .30 .75
BCP26 Jharel Cotton .25 .60
BCP27 John Norwood .25 .60
BCP28 Manny Sanchez .30 .75
BCP29 Juan Yepez .25 .60
BCP30 David Denson .25 .60
BCP31 Jhailyn Ortiz .50 1.25
BCP32 Wander Javier .40 1.00
BCP33 Sal Romano .25 .60
BCP34 Francis Martes .30 .75
BCP35 Domingo Acevedo .40 1.00
BCP36 Mark Zagunis .25 .60
BCP37 Franklyn Kilome .30 .75
BCP38 Trey Mancini .75 2.00
BCP39 Corey Black .25 .60
BCP40 Anderson Espinoza .25 .60
BCP41 Jordan Guerrero .25 .60
BCP42 Mauricio Dubon .30 .75
BCP43 Paul DeJong 1.50 4.00
BCP44 Mikey White .25 .60
BCP45 Andrew Suarez .30 .75
BCP46 Kevin Kramer .30 .75
BCP47 Nate Smith .25 .60
BCP48 Ariel Jurado .25 .60
BCP49 Rafael Bautista .25 .60
BCP50 Dansby Swanson .75 2.00
BCP51 Anthony Banda .25 .60
BCP52 Mike Clevinger .50 1.25
BCP53 Daniel Poncedeleon .30 .75
BCP54 Ian Kahaloa .25 .60
BCP55 Vladimir Guerrero Jr. 15.00 40.00
BCP56 Logan Allen .25 .60
BCP57 Kyle Survance Jr. .25 .60
BCP58 Omar Carrizales .25 .60
BCP59 Anthony Alford .25 .60
BCP60 Kyle Tucker 1.00 2.50
BCP61 Tyler Jay .25 .60
BCP62 Andrew Benintendi .75 2.00
BCP63 Carson Fulmer .25 .60
BCP64 Ian Happ .50 1.25
BCP65 Sean Newcomb .30 .75
BCP66 Tyler Stephenson .25 .60
BCP67 Josh Naylor .30 .75
BCP68 Garrett Whitley .30 .75
BCP69 Kolby Allard .25 .60
BCP70 Trent Clark .25 .60
BCP71 James Kaprielian .30 .75
BCP72 Phil Bickford .25 .60
BCP73 Kevin Newman .40 1.00
BCP74 Richie Martin .25 .60
BCP75 Ashe Russell .25 .60
BCP76 Beau Burrows .25 .60
BCP77 Nick Plummer .30 .75
BCP78 Walker Buehler .60 1.50
BCP79 D.J. Stewart .25 .60
BCP80 Taylor Ward .30 .75
BCP81 Mike Nikorak .25 .60
BCP82 Michael Soroka .75 2.00
BCP83 Kyle Holder .30 .75
BCP84 Chris Shaw .40 1.00
BCP85 Ke'Bryan Hayes .25 .60
BCP86 Nolan Watson .25 .60
BCP87 Christin Stewart .30 .75
BCP88 Ryan Mountcastle .40 1.00
BCP89 Jack Flaherty .40 1.00
BCP90 Raimel Tapia .30 .75
BCP91 Michael Fulmer .40 1.00
BCP92 A.J. Reed .25 .60
BCP93 Gavin Cecchini .25 .60
BCP94 Jorge Mateo .30 .75
BCP95 Amed Rosario .40 1.00
BCP96 Daniel Robertson .25 .60
BCP97 Nick Gordon .25 .60
BCP98 Rob Kaminsky .25 .60
BCP99 Amir Garrett .25 .60
BCP100 Brendan Rodgers .40 1.00
BCP101 Duane Underwood .25 .60
BCP102 Alen Hanson .30 .75
BCP103 Jorge Alfaro .40 1.00
BCP104 Grant Holmes .30 .75
BCP105 Nick Williams .30 .75
BCP106 Tyler Wade .40 1.00
BCP107 Jake Thompson .25 .60
BCP108 Alex Reyes .30 .75
BCP109 Rafael Devers .75 2.00
BCP110 Ozzie Albies 1.00 2.50
BCP111 Alex Young .30 .75
BCP112 Tyrell Jenkins .25 .60
BCP113 Max Fried .40 1.00
BCP114 Chance Sisco .50 1.25
BCP115 Michael Kopech .60 1.50
BCP116 Pierce Johnson .25 .60
BCP117 Tyler Danish .25 .60
BCP118 Keury Mella .25 .60
BCP119 Alex Blandino .25 .60
BCP120 Justus Sheffield .50 1.25
BCP121 Jeff Hoffman .30 .75
BCP122 Ryan McMahon .25 .60
BCP123 JaCoby Jones .30 .75
BCP124 Colin Moran .25 .60
BCP125 Derek Fisher .25 .60
BCP126 Scott Blewett .25 .60
BCP127 Jeimer Candelario .30 .75
BCP128 Fernando Perez .25 .60
BCP129 Andrew Knapp .25 .60
BCP130 Sean Manaea .25 .60
BCP131 Jake Bauers .40 1.00
BCP132 Rowdy Tellez .40 1.00
BCP133 Gabby Guerrero .25 .60
BCP134 Christian Arroyo .75 2.00
BCP135 Adam Brett Walker II .25 .60
BCP136 Brett Phillips .25 .60
BCP137 Lewis Brinson .40 1.00
BCP138 Bubba Starling .30 .75
BCP139 Chad Pinder .25 .60
BCP140 Chris Bostick .25 .60
BCP141 Luke Weaver .40 1.00
BCP142 Kenta Maeda .50 1.25
BCP143 Luiz Gohara .25 .60
BCP144 Yoan Lopez .25 .60
BCP145 Courtney Hawkins .25 .60
BCP146 Austin Dean .25 .60
BCP147 Matt Chapman .40 1.00
BCP148 Yoan Moncada .60 1.50
BCP149 Nick Travieso .25 .60
BCP150 Lucas Giolito .40 1.00
BCP151 Jose De Leon .25 .60
BCP152 Willy Adames .40 1.00
BCP153 Dustin Fowler .30 .75
BCP154 Chad Kuhl .25 .60
BCP155 Roman Quinn .40 1.00
BCP156 Yeudy Garcia .25 .60
BCP157 Cody Reed .25 .60
BCP158 Sam Howard .25 .60
BCP159 Josh Staumont .30 .75
BCP160 Franklin Barreto .30 .75
BCP161 Shane Dawson .25 .60
BCP162 Austin Gomber .25 .60
BCP163 Blake Trahan .25 .60
BCP164 Wilkerman Garcia .30 .75
BCP165 Austin Rei .25 .60
BCP166 Todd Hankins .25 .60
BCP167 Ben Lively .25 .60
BCP168 Victor Alcantara .25 .60
BCP169 Willie Calhoun .75 2.00
BCP170 D.J. Wilson .30 .75
BCP171 Dylan Cease .60 1.50
BCP172 Connor Sadzeck .25 .60
BCP173 Donny Sands .30 .75
BCP174 Kyle Freeland .30 .75

BCP175 David Dahl .30 .75
BCP176 Junior Fernandez .40 1.00
BCP177 Antonio Santillan .25 .60
BCP178 Jahmai Jones .30 .75
BCP179 Forrest Wall .25 .60
BCP180 Andrew Stevenson .25 .60
BCP181 Clayton Blackburn .25 .60
BCP182 Cody Bellinger 6.00 15.00
BCP183 Raffy Ozuna .25 .60
BCP184 Anderson Miller .25 .60
BCP185 Travis Blankenhorn 1.25 3.00
BCP186 Jacob Faria .25 .60
BCP187 George Iskenderian .25 .60
BCP188 Alex Verdugo .40 1.00
BCP189 Brent Honeywell .40 1.00
BCP190 Spencer Adams .25 .60
BCP191 Ryan McKenna .25 .60
BCP192 Chance Adams .40 1.00
BCP193 Jaime Schultz .25 .60
BCP194 Michael Soroka .75 2.00
BCP195 Helmis Rodriguez .25 .60
BCP196 Juan Hillman .25 .60
BCP197 Jermaine Palacios .30 .75
BCP198 Reese McGuire .25 .60
BCP199 Yohander Mendez .25 .60
BCP200 Eloy Jimenez 1.00 2.50
BCP201 Hoy-Jun Park .30 .75
BCP202 Austin Riley .75 2.00
BCP203 Isaiah White .25 .60
BCP204 Oneal Cruz 1.50 4.00
BCP205 Mac Marshall .25 .60
BCP206 Jalen Miller .25 .60
BCP207 Mitch Keller .30 .75
BCP208 Franklin Reyes .25 .60
BCP209 Josh Sborz .40 1.00
BCP210 Manuel Margot .25 .60
BCP211 Tyler Beede .30 .75
BCP212 Magneuris Sierra .75 2.00
BCP213 David Paulino .30 .75
BCP214 Bradley Zimmer .40 1.00
BCP215 Ray Black .25 .60
BCP216 Josh Hader .30 .75
BCP217 Zach Eflin .30 .75
BCP218 Ali Sanchez .25 .60
BCP219 Yadir Drake .30 .75
BCP220 Jose Adames .25 .60
BCP221 Ryan Williams .25 .60
BCP222 Conner Greene .25 .60
BCP223 Zack Erwin .25 .60
BCP224 Sean Reid-Foley .30 .75
BCP225 Joe Jimenez .30 .75
BCP226 Nick Burdi .25 .60
BCP227 Jairo Beras .25 .60
BCP228 Blake Perkins .25 .60
BCP229 Sam Travis .50 1.25
BCP230 Stephen Gonsalves .25 .60
BCP231 Dakota Chalmers .25 .60
BCP232 Isan Diaz .60 1.50
BCP233 Taylor Guerrieri .25 .60
BCP234 Andrew Moore .30 .75
BCP235 Tyler Alexander .25 .60
BCP236 Gleyber Torres 4.00 10.00
BCP237 Kohl Stewart .25 .60
BCP238 Demi Orimoloye .25 .60
BCP239 Hunter Renfroe .30 .75
BCP240 Jonah Arenado .30 .75
BCP241 Mike Gerber .25 .60
BCP242 Nellie Rodriguez .30 .75
BCP243 Braden Bishop .25 .60
BCP244 Jacob Nottingham .25 .60
BCP245 Bryce Denton .40 1.00
BCP246 Harold Ramirez .30 .75
BCP247 Luis Ortiz .25 .60
BCP248 Ricardo Pinto .30 .75
BCP249 Triston McKenzie .30 .75
BCP250 Austin Meadows .40 1.00

2016 Bowman Chrome Prospects Black and Gold Refractors

*BLACK/GLD.REF: .6X TO 1.5X BASIC
INSERTED IN VENDING BOXES

2016 Bowman Chrome Prospects Blue Refractors

*BLUE REF: 2X TO 5X BASIC
BOW.ODDS 1:110 HOBBY
BOW.CHR.ODDS 1:111 HOBBY
STATED PRINT RUN 150 SER.#'d SETS
BCP55 Vladimir Guerrero Jr. 125.00 300.00
BCP148 Yoan Moncada 12.00 30.00
BCP185 Travis Blankenhorn 10.00 25.00

2016 Bowman Chrome Prospects Blue Shimmer Refractors

*BLUE SHIMMER: 2X TO 5X BASIC
RANDOM INSERTS IN PACKS
BCP185 Travis Blankenhorn 10.00 25.00

2016 Bowman Chrome Prospects Gold Refractors

*GOLD REF: 5X TO 12X BASIC
BOW.ODDS 1:329 HOBBY
BOW.CHR.ODDS 1:331 HOBBY
STATED PRINT RUN 50 SER.#'d SETS
BCP55 Vladimir Guerrero Jr. 400.00 800.00
BCP148 Yoan Moncada 30.00 80.00
BCP185 Travis Blankenhorn 25.00 60.00

2016 Bowman Chrome Prospects Green Refractors

*GREEN REF: 2.5X TO 6X BASIC
BOW.INSERTED IN RETAIL PACKS
BOW.CHR.ODDS 1:51 HOBBY
STATED PRINT RUN 99 SER.#'d SETS
BCP55 Vladimir Guerrero Jr. 150.00 400.00
BCP148 Yoan Moncada 15.00 40.00
BCP185 Travis Blankenhorn 12.00 30.00

2016 Bowman Chrome Prospects Green Shimmer Refractors

*GRN SHIM REF: 2.5X TO 6X BASIC
STATED ODDS 1:167 HOBBY
STATED PRINT RUN 99 SER.#'d SETS
BCP55 Vladimir Guerrero Jr. 150.00 400.00
BCP148 Yoan Moncada 15.00 40.00

2016 Bowman Chrome Prospects Orange Refractors

*ORANGE REF: 8X TO 20X BASIC
BOW.ODDS 1:165 HOBBY
BOW.CHR.ODDS 1:199 HOBBY
STATED PRINT RUN 25 SER.#'d SETS
BCP55 Vladimir Guerrero Jr. 600.00 1200.00
BCP148 Yoan Moncada 50.00 120.00
BCP185 Travis Blankenhorn 40.00 100.00

2016 Bowman Chrome Prospects Orange Shimmer Refractors

*ORNG SHIM REF/25: 8X TO 20X BASIC
*ORNG SHIM REF: 2.5X TO 6X BASIC
BOW.ODDS 1:658 HOBBY
BOW.CHR.RANDOMLY INSERTED
1-150 PRINT RUN 25 SER.#'d SETS
151-250 ARE NOT SERIAL NUMBERED
BCP55 Vladimir Guerrero Jr. 600.00 1200.00
BCP148 Yoan Moncada 50.00 120.00
BCP185 Travis Blankenhorn 40.00 100.00

2016 Bowman Chrome Prospects Purple Refractors

*PURPLE REF: 1.5X TO 4X BASIC
BOW.ODDS 1:66 HOBBY
BOW.CHR.ODDS 1:67 HOBBY
STATED PRINT RUN 250 SER.#'d SETS
BCP148 Yoan Moncada 10.00 25.00
BCP185 Travis Blankenhorn 8.00 20.00

2016 Bowman Chrome Prospects Refractors

*REF: 1.5X TO 4X BASIC
BOW.ODDS 1:33 HOBBY
BOW.CHR.ODDS 1:34 HOBBY
STATED PRINT RUN 499 SER.#'d SETS
BCP148 Yoan Moncada 10.00 25.00

2016 Bowman Chrome Refractors That Never Were

STATED ODDS 1:331 HOBBY
STATED PRINT RUN 499 SER.#'d SETS
*ORANGE/25: 2.5X TO 6X BASIC
RTNWAK Al Kaline 1.25 3.00
RTNWCD Carlos Delgado .75 2.00
RTNWCJ Chipper Jones 1.25 3.00
RTNWJG Juan Gonzalez .75 2.00
RTNWJR Jackie Robinson 1.25 3.00
RTNWJS John Smoltz 1.25 3.00
RTNWMP Mike Piazza 1.25 3.00
RTNWPM Pedro Martinez 1.00 2.50
RTNWVG Vladimir Guerrero 1.00 2.50
RTNWWM Willie Mays 2.50 6.00

2016 Bowman Chrome Refractors That Never Were Autographs

STATED ODDS 1:2181 HOBBY
STATED PRINT RUN 99 SER.#'d SETS
BOW.CHR.EXCH.DEADLINE 8/31/2018
RTNWAK Al Kaline 40.00 100.00
RTNWCD Carlos Delgado 8.00 20.00
RTNWCJ Chipper Jones 40.00 100.00
RTNWJG Juan Gonzalez 8.00 20.00
RTNWJS John Smoltz 20.00 50.00
RTNWMP Mike Piazza 60.00 150.00

2016 Bowman Chrome Rookie Autographs

BOW.ODDS 1:339 HOBBY
BOW.CHR.ODDS 1:174 HOBBY
BOW.PLATE ODDS 1:65,446 HOBBY
BOW.CHR.PLATE ODDS 1:18,202 HOBBY
PLATE PRINT RUN 1 SET PER COLOR
NO PLATE PRICING DUE TO SCARCITY
BOW.EXCH.DEADLINE 3/31/2018
BOW.CHR.EXCH.DEADLINE 8/31/2018
CRAAN Aaron Nola 15.00 40.00
CRACE Carl Edwards Jr. 4.00 10.00
CRAGB Greg Bird 4.00 10.00
CRAHO Hector Olivera 4.00 10.00
CRAHOW Henry Owens 4.00 10.00
CRALS Luis Severino 4.00 10.00
CRAMS Sano Wht jrsy 10.00 25.00
CRARR Rob Refsnyder 4.00 10.00
CRASP Stephen Piscotty 5.00 12.00
CRATT Trea Turner 25.00 60.00
BCARAR A.J. Reed 3.00 8.00
BCARBP Byung-Ho Park 4.00 10.00
BCARBS Blake Snell 10.00 25.00
BCARFM Frankie Montas 4.00 10.00
BCARJBE Jose Berrios 10.00 25.00
BCARJP Jose Peraza 4.00 10.00
BCARLS Luis Severino 4.00 10.00
BCARMR Matt Reynolds 3.00 8.00
BCARTT Trayce Thompson 5.00 12.00

2016 Bowman Chrome Rookie Autographs Blue Refractors

*BLUE REF: 1X TO 2.5X BASIC
BOW.ODDS 1:1693 HOBBY
BOW.CHR.ODDS 1:480 HOBBY
STATED PRINT RUN 150 SER.#'d SETS
BOW.EXCH.DEADLINE 3/31/2018
BOW.CHR.EXCH.DEADLINE 8/31/2018
CRACS C.Seager Bttng 100.00 250.00
CRAJG Jon Gray 8.00 20.00
CRAKS Schwarber Wht jrsy 40.00 100.00
CRAMC Michael Conforto 30.00 80.00
BCARAA Albert Almora 20.00 50.00
BCARCS C.Seager Fldng 100.00 250.00
BCARHO Henry Owens 10.00 25.00
BCARJU Julio Urias 25.00 60.00
BCARKEM Kenta Maeda 10.00 25.00
BCARKS Schwarber Blue jrsy 30.00 80.00
BCARLG Lucas Giolito 12.00 30.00
BCARMS Sano Blue jrsy 15.00 40.00
BCARRM Raul Mondesi 30.00 80.00

2016 Bowman Chrome Rookie Autographs Gold Refractors

*GOLD REF: 1.5X TO 4X BASIC
BOW.ODDS 1:5078 HOBBY
BOW.CHR.ODDS 1:1439 HOBBY
STATED PRINT RUN 50 SER.#'d SETS
BOW.EXCH.DEADLINE 3/31/2018
BOW.CHR.EXCH.DEADLINE 8/31/2018
CRACS C.Seager Bttng 150.00 400.00
CRAJG Jon Gray 12.00 30.00
CRAKS Schwarber Wht jrsy 60.00 150.00
CRAMC Michael Conforto 75.00 200.00
BCARAA Albert Almora 30.00 80.00
BCARBP Byung-Ho Park 40.00 100.00
BCARCS C.Seager Fldng 150.00 400.00
BCARHO Henry Owens 15.00 40.00
BCARJU Julio Urias 40.00 100.00
BCARKEM Kenta Maeda 15.00 40.00
BCARKS Schwarber Blue jrsy 50.00 120.00
BCARLG Lucas Giolito 20.00 50.00
BCARMS Sano Blue jrsy 25.00 60.00
BCARRM Raul Mondesi 50.00 120.00

2016 Bowman Chrome Rookie Autographs Green Refractors

*GREEN REF: 1.2X TO 3X BASIC
INSERTED IN RETAIL PACKS
BOW.CHR.ODDS 1:727 HOBBY
STATED PRINT RUN 99 SER.#'d SETS
BOW.EXCH.DEADLINE 3/31/2018
BOW.CHR.EXCH.DEADLINE 8/31/2018
CRACS C.Seager Bttng 125.00 300.00
CRAJG Jon Gray 10.00 25.00
CRAKS Schwarber Wht jrsy 50.00 120.00
CRAMC Michael Conforto 40.00 100.00
BCARAA Albert Almora 25.00 60.00
BCARCS C.Seager Fldng 125.00 300.00
BCARHO Henry Owens 12.00 30.00
BCARJU Julio Urias 30.00 80.00
BCARKEM Kenta Maeda 12.00 30.00
BCARKS Schwarber Blue jrsy 40.00 100.00
BCARLG Lucas Giolito 15.00 40.00
BCARMS Sano Blue jrsy 20.00 50.00
BCARRM Raul Mondesi 40.00 100.00

2016 Bowman Chrome Rookie Autographs Orange Refractors

*ORANGE REF: 3X TO 8X BASIC
BOW.ODDS 1:2414 HOBBY
BOW.CHR.ODDS 1:1294 HOBBY
STATED PRINT RUN 25 SER.#'d SETS
BOW.EXCH.DEADLINE 3/31/2018
BOW.CHR.EXCH.DEADLINE 8/31/2018
CRACS C.Seager Bttng 300.00 600.00
CRAJG Jon Gray 25.00 60.00
CRAKS Schwarber Wht jrsy 100.00 250.00
CRAMC Michael Conforto 150.00 400.00
BCARAA Albert Almora 60.00 150.00
BCARBP Byung-Ho Park 75.00 200.00
BCARCS C.Seager Fldng 300.00 600.00
BCARHO Henry Owens 30.00 80.00
BCARJU Julio Urias 80.00 200.00
BCARKEM Kenta Maeda 30.00 80.00
BCARKS Schwarber Blue jrsy 100.00 250.00
BCARLG Lucas Giolito 40.00 100.00
BCARMS Sano Blue jrsy 50.00 120.00
BCARRM Raul Mondesi 60.00 150.00

2016 Bowman Chrome Rookie Autographs Refractors

*REF: .5X TO 1.2X BASIC
BOW.ODDS 1:509 HOBBY
BOW.CHR.ODDS 1:155 HOBBY
STATED PRINT RUN 499 SER.#'d SETS
BOW.EXCH.DEADLINE 3/31/2018
BOW.CHR.EXCH.DEADLINE 8/31/2018
CRACS C.Seager Bttng 60.00 150.00
CRAJG Jon Gray 4.00 10.00
CRAKS Schwarber Wht jrsy 30.00 80.00
BCARCS C.Seager Fldng 60.00 150.00
BCARHO Henry Owens 5.00 12.00
BCARJU Julio Urias 12.00 30.00
BCARKEM Kenta Maeda 5.00 12.00
BCARLG Lucas Giolito 6.00 15.00
BCARMS Sano Blue jrsy 8.00 20.00
BCARRM Raul Mondesi 15.00 40.00

2016 Bowman Chrome Rookie Recollections

COMPLETE SET (7) 4.00 10.00
STATED ODDS 1:24 HOBBY
*GOLD/99: 2.5X TO 6X BASIC
*GOLD/50: 4X TO 10X BASIC
*ORANGE/25: 5X TO 12X BASIC
RRBB Bret Boone .40 1.00
RRCJ Chipper Jones .60 1.50
RRIR Ivan Rodriguez .50 1.25
RRJB Jeff Bagwell .50 1.25
RRJC Jeff Conine .40 1.00
RRLG Luis Gonzalez .50 1.25
RRRK Ryan Klesko .40 1.00

2016 Bowman Chrome Rookie Recollections Autographs

STATED ODDS 1:2414 HOBBY
PRINT RUNS B/WN 75-200 COPIES PER
EXCHANGE DEADLINE 3/31/2018
*GOLD/50: .6X TO 1.5X BASIC
RRABB Bret Boone/200 5.00 12.00
RRAGE Carl Everett/150 5.00 12.00
RRACJ Chipper Jones/75 50.00 120.00
RRAIR Ivan Rodriguez/150 20.00 50.00
RRAJB Jeff Bagwell/75 25.00 60.00
RRAJC Jeff Conine/150 5.00 12.00
RRALG Luis Gonzalez/200 6.00 15.00
RRAPH Pat Hentgen EXCH 5.00 12.00
RRARK Ryan Klesko/200 5.00 12.00

2016 Bowman Chrome Sophomore Standouts Autographs

STATED ODDS 1:2561 HOBBY
EXCHANGE DEADLINE 3/31/2018
*GOLD/50: .6X TO 1.5X BASIC
SSABS Blake Swihart 5.00 12.00
SSACC Carlos Correa 75.00 200.00
SSAFL Francisco Lindor 15.00 40.00
SSAJP Joc Pederson 6.00 15.00
SSAJS Jorge Soler 6.00 15.00
SSAKB Kris Bryant 75.00 200.00
SSANS Noah Syndergaard 15.00 40.00
SSARC Rusney Castillo 4.00 10.00
SSASM Steven Matz 5.00 12.00

2016 Bowman Chrome Turn Two

STATED ODDS 1:24 HOBBY
*GREEN/99: 1X TO 2.5X BASIC
*GOLD/50: 1.2X TO 3X BASIC
*ORANGE/25: 3X TO 8X BASIC
TTAP A.Alford/M.Pentecost .30 .75
TTBB T.Beede/P.Bickford .40 1.00
TTBC Bregman/Cameron 2.00 5.00
TTBJ T.Jay/J.Berrios .40 1.00
TTBO F.Barreto/M.Olson .50 1.25
TTCT J.Crawford/J.Thompson .30 .75
TTDM Devers/Benintendi 1.00 2.50
TTFA T.Anderson/C.Fulmer 1.25 3.00
TTFH D.Hill/M.Fulmer .50 1.25
TTGL R.Lopez/L.Giolito .50 1.25
TTGM T.Glasnow/A.Meadows .50 1.25
TTHS H.Harvey/D.Stewart .30 .75
TTJG A.Jackson/L.Gohara .40 1.00
TTJM Judge/Mateo 2.50 6.00
TTKN J.Naylor/T.Kolek .40 1.00
TTMR A.Russell/R.Mondesi .40 1.00
TTNE V.Alcantara/J.Gatto .30 .75
TTNR A.Rosario/B.Nimmo .50 1.25
TTPC T.Clark/B.Phillips .30 .75
TTRD Rodgers/Dahl .50 1.25
TTRF J.Flaherty/A.Reyes .50 1.25
TTRR H.Renfroe/M.Margot .40 1.00
TTSL B.Shipley/Y.Lopez .30 .75
TTSN Newcomb/Swanson 1.00 2.50
TTSS T.Stephenson/R.Stephenson .30 .75
TTTD D.Tate/L.Brinson .50 1.25
TTTM Torres/McKinney 5.00 12.00
TTUD Urias/De Leon 1.00 2.50
TTWA W.Adames/G.Whitley .50 1.25
TTZF B.Zimmer/C.Frazier 1.25 3.00

2016 Bowman Chrome Turn Two Autographs Gold

STATED ODDS 1:3386 HOBBY
EXCHANGE DEADLINE 3/31/2018
TTBC Bregman/Cameron 75.00 200.00
TTBJ Jay/Berrios 15.00 40.00
TTFH Hill/Fulmer 25.00 60.00
TTGM Glasnow/Meadows 40.00 100.00
TTJM Judge/Mateo 75.00 200.00
TTKN Naylor/Kolek 15.00 40.00
TTPC Clark/Phillips 40.00 100.00
TTRD Rodgers/Dahl 50.00 120.00
TTSN Sean Newcomb 75.00 200.00
Dansby Swanson
TTSS Stephenson/Stephenson 30.00 80.00
TTTB Tate/Brinson 30.00 80.00
TTWA Adames/Whitley 20.00 50.00

2016 Bowman Chrome Draft

COMPLETE SET (200) 20.00 50.00
STATED PLATE ODDS 1:947 HOBBY
PLATE PRINT RUN 1 SET PER COLOR
NO PLATE PRICING DUE TO SCARCITY
BDC1 Mickey Moniak 1.25 3.00
BDC2 Thomas Jones .25 .60
BDC3 Dylan Carlson 6.00 15.00
BDC4 Cole Irvin .60 1.50
BDC5 Kevin Gowdy .40 1.00
BDC6 Dakota Hudson .40 1.00
BDC7 Walker Robbins .25 .60
BDC8 Khalil Lee .40 1.00
BDC9 Logan Ice .25 .60
BDC10 Braxton Garrett .30 .75
BDC11 Anfernee Grier .30 .75
BDC12 Kyle Hart .25 .60
BDC13 Taylor Trammell 2.00 5.00
BDC14 Brian Serven .25 .60
BDC15 Buddy Reed .25 .60
BDC16 Carter Kieboom 1.50 4.00
BDC17 Jimmy Lambert .25 .60
BDC18 Nick Solak .75 2.00
BDC19 Alexis Torres .30 .75
BDC20 Cal Quantrill .25 .60
BDC21 JaVon Shelby .25 .60
BDC22 Kyle Funkhouser .30 .75
BDC23 Dom Thompson-Williams .40 1.00
BDC24 Jeremy Martinez .60 1.50
BDC25 A.J. Puk .40 1.00
BDC26 Brett Cumberland .40 1.00
BDC27 Mason Thompson .25 .60
BDC28 Easton McGee .25 .60
BDC29 Justin Dunn .25 .60
BDC30 Matt Manning .40 1.00
BDC31 Delvin Perez .75 2.00
BDC32 Nolan Jones .40 1.00
BDC33 Matt Krook .25 .60
BDC34 Stephen Alemais .40 1.00
BDC35 Joey Wentz .40 1.00
BDC36 Ben Bowden .25 .60
BDC37 Drew Harrington .25 .60
BDC38 C.J. Chatham .30 .75
BDC39 Will Craig .25 .60
BDC40 Zack Collins .30 .75
BDC41 Skylar Szynski .25 .60
BDC42 Sheldon Neuse .30 .75
BDC43 Nicholas Lopez .40 1.00
BDC44 Heath Quinn .50 1.25
BDC45 Alex Speas .30 .75
BDC46 Cody Sedlock .40 1.00
BDC47 Blake Tiberi .30 .75
BDC48 Mario Feliciano .30 .75
BDC49 Brett Adcock .25 .60
BDC50 Riley Pint .25 .60
BDC51 Jacob Heyward .25 .60
BDC52 Hudson Potts .30 .75
BDC53 Ronnie Dawson .25 .60
BDC54 Nick Hanson .30 .75
BDC55 Forrest Whitley 2.00 5.00
BDC56 Ryan Hendrix .25 .60
BDC57 Eric Lauer .25 .60
BDC58 Tyson Miller .40 1.00
BDC59 Jesus Luzardo 1.50 4.00
BDC60 Kyle Lewis 10.00 25.00
BDC61 Connor Justus .25 .60
BDC62 Cole Stobbe .25 .60
BDC63 Garrett Hampson .50 1.25
BDC64 Cole Ragans .30 .75
BDC65 Kyle Muller .30 .75
BDC66 Logan Shore .30 .75
BDC67 Gavin Lux 6.00 15.00
BDC68 Shane Bieber 5.00 12.00
BDC69 T.J. Zeuch .30 .75
BDC70 Joshua Lowe .25 .60
BDC71 Justin Alleman .25 .60
BDC72 Ryan Howard .25 .60
BDC73 Jake Fraley .30 .75
BDC74 Bo Bichette 12.00 30.00
BDC75 DJ Peters 1.25 3.00
BDC76 Jake Rogers 1.25 3.00
BDC77 Bryan Reynolds .75 2.00
BDC78 Colton Welker .40 1.00
BDC79 Nick Banks .25 .60
BDC80 Will Benson .40 1.00
BDC81 Cavan Biggio 2.50 6.00
BDC82 Braden Webb .25 .60
BDC83 Chris Okey .25 .60
BDC84 Will Smith 2.00 5.00
BDC85 A.J. Puckett .30 .75
BDC86 Colby Woodmansee .30 .75
BDC87 Andy Yerzy .25 .60
BDC88 J.B. Woodman .40 1.00
BDC89 Corbin Burnes .40 1.00
BDC90 Alex Kirilloff 5.00 12.00
BDC91 Robert Tyler .25 .60
BDC92 Pete Alonso 8.00 20.00
BDC93 Alec Hansen .30 .75
BDC94 Daniel Johnson .25 .60
BDC95 Mike Shawaryn .30 .75
BDC96 Daulton Jefferies .30 .75
BDC97 Jordan Sheffield .25 .60
BDC98 Conner Capel .25 .60
BDC99 Bobby Dalbec 1.00 2.50
BDC100 Corey Ray .40 1.00
BDC101 Ben Rortvedt .30 .75
BDC102 Tim Lynch .40 1.00
BDC103 Charles Leblanc .25 .60
BDC104 Dane Dunning .30 .75
BDC105 Bryson Brigman .25 .60
BDC106 Nolan Martinez .30 .75
BDC107 Connor Jones .30 .75
BDC108 Alex Call .25 .60
BDC109 Reggie Lawson .25 .60
BDC110 Matt Thaiss .25 .60
BDC111 Bryse Wilson .75 2.00
BDC112 Zack Burdi .30 .75
BDC113 Nolan Williams .25 .60
BDC114 Mark Ecker .25 .60
BDC115 Michael Paez .40 1.00
BDC116 Zach Jackson .25 .60
BDC117 Joe Rizzo .25 .60
BDC118 Ryan Boldt .30 .75
BDC119 Mikey York .30 .75
BDC120 Ian Anderson .60 1.50
BDC121 Austin Meadows .40 1.00
BDC122 Nick Gordon .25 .60
BDC123 Forrest Wall .25 .60
BDC124 Antonio Senzatela .25 .60
BDC125 Justus Sheffield .50 1.25
BDC126 Christian Arroyo .75 2.00
BDC127 Dylan Cease .60 1.50
BDC128 Scott Kingery .40 1.00
BDC129 Daniel Palka .25 .60
BDC130 Bradley Zimmer .40 1.00
BDC131 Amir Garrett .25 .60
BDC132 Dillon Tate .30 .75
BDC133 Domingo Leyba .25 .60
BDC134 Tyler Jay .25 .60
BDC135 Sean Reid-Foley .30 .75
BDC136 James Kaprielian .30 .75
BDC137 Kyle Tucker 1.00 2.50
BDC138 Derek Fisher .25 .60
BDC139 Tyler O'Neill .30 .75
BDC140 Anderson Espinoza .25 .60
BDC141 Christin Stewart .30 .75
BDC142 Grant Holmes .30 .75
BDC143 Gleyber Torres 6.00 15.00
BDC144 Mitch Keller .30 .75
BDC145 Francis Martes .30 .75
BDC146 Nellie Rodriguez .25 .60
BDC147 Chih-Wei Hu .30 .75
BDC148 Anthony Banda .25 .60
BDC149 Trent Clark .25 .60
BDC150 Brendan Rodgers .40 1.00
BDC151 Ryan Cordell .25 .60
BDC152 Daz Cameron .25 .60
BDC153 Billy McKinney .30 .75
BDC154 Jomar Reyes .40 1.00
BDC155 Jake Bauers .40 1.00
BDC156 Willy Adames .40 1.00
BDC157 Josh Hader .30 .75
BDC158 Luis Ortiz .25 .60
BDC159 Erick Fedde .25 .60
BDC160 Rafael Devers .75 2.00
BDC161 Francisco Mejia .40 1.00
BDC162 Kolby Allard .25 .60
BDC163 Ronnie Williams .25 .60
BDC164 Matt Chapman .40 1.00
BDC165 Austin Riley .75 2.00
BDC166 Austin Dean .25 .60
BDC167 Ryan McMahon .30 .75
BDC168 Anfernee Seymour .25 .60
BDC169 Marcos Diplan .25 .60
BDC170 Anthony Alford .25 .60
BDC171 Nick Neidert .25 .60
BDC172 Bobby Bradley .30 .75
BDC173 Tyler Wade .40 1.00
BDC174 Chase De Jong .30 .75
BDC175 Brett Phillips .30 .75
BDC176 Dominic Smith .25 .60
BDC177 Touki Toussaint .30 .75
BDC178 Reese McGuire .25 .60
BDC179 Franklin Barreto .25 .60
BDC180 Ian Happ .50 1.25
BDC181 Javier Guerra .25 .60
BDC182 Tyler Beede .30 .75
BDC183 Drew Jackson .25 .60
BDC184 Brent Honeywell .40 1.00
BDC185 Michael Gettys .25 .60
BDC186 Rhys Hoskins 1.00 2.50
BDC187 Dylan Cozens .25 .60
BDC188 Jon Harris .30 .75
BDC189 Phil Bickford .25 .60
BDC190 Amed Rosario .40 1.00
BDC191 Eloy Jimenez 1.00 2.50
BDC192 Jack Flaherty .40 1.00
BDC193 Alex Young .30 .75
BDC194 Andrew Sopko .25 .60
BDC195 Rafael Bautista .25 .60
BDC196 Chris Shaw .40 1.00
BDC197 Mike Gerber .25 .60
BDC198 Kevin Newman .40 1.00
BDC199 Ryan Mountcastle .40 1.00
BDC200 Lucius Fox .40 1.00

2016 Bowman Chrome Draft Blue Refractors

*BLUE REF: 2X TO 5X BASIC
STATED ODDS 1:26 HOBBY
STATED PRINT RUN 150 SER.#'d SETS

2016 Bowman Chrome Draft Gold Refractors

*GOLD REF: 5X TO 12X BASIC
STATED ODDS 1:76 HOBBY
STATED PRINT RUN 50 SER.#'d SETS

2016 Bowman Chrome Draft Green Refractors

*GREEN REF: 2.5X TO 6X BASIC
STATED ODDS 1:39 HOBBY
STATED PRINT RUN 99 SER.#'d SETS

2016 Bowman Chrome Draft Orange Refractors

*ORANGE REF: 8X TO 20X BASIC
STATED ODDS 1:152 HOBBY
STATED PRINT RUN 25 SER.#'d SETS

2016 Bowman Chrome Draft Purple Refractors

*PURPLE REF: 1.5X TO 4X BASIC
STATED ODDS 1:16 HOBBY
STATED PRINT RUN 250 SER.#'d SETS

2016 Bowman Chrome Draft Refractors

*REFRACTORS: .75X TO 2X BASIC
RANDOM INSERTS IN PACKS

2016 Bowman Chrome Draft Sky Blue Refractors

*SKY BLUE: 1X TO 2.5X BASIC
STATED ODDS 1:8 HOBBY

2016 Bowman Chrome Draft Draft Dividends

COMPLETE SET (15) 6.00 15.00
STATED ODDS 1:4 HOBBY
*GOLD/50: 1.2X TO 3X BASIC
DDAP A.J. Puk .60 1.50
DDAY Alex Young .50 1.25
DDBL Brett Lilek .40 1.00
DDCQ Cal Quantrill .40 1.00
DDCR Corey Ray .60 1.50
DDDD Dane Dunning .50 1.25
DDDH Dakota Hudson .60 1.50
DDDJ Daulton Jefferies .50 1.25
DDEL Eric Lauer .50 1.25
DDJD Justin Dunn .40 1.00
DDJS Jordan Sheffield .40 1.00
DDMT Matt Thaiss .40 1.00
DDTZ T.J. Zeuch .50 1.25
DDWC Will Craig .40 1.00
DDZC Zack Collins .50 1.25

2016 Bowman Chrome Draft Dividends Autographs

STATED ODDS 1:750 HOBBY
STATED PRINT RUN 50 SER.#'d SETS
EXCHANGE DEADLINE 11/30/2018
*GOLD/50: .5X TO 1.2X BASIC
DDAP A.J. Puk 8.00 20.00
DDCQ Cal Quantrill 5.00 12.00
DDCR Corey Ray 8.00 20.00
DDEL Eric Lauer 6.00 15.00
DDJD Justin Dunn 5.00 12.00
DDMT Matt Thaiss 5.00 12.00
DDTZ T.J. Zeuch 6.00 15.00
DDWC Will Craig 10.00 25.00
DDZC Zack Collins 10.00 25.00

2016 Bowman Chrome Draft Draft Night Autographs

STATED ODDS 1:3733 HOBBY
STATED PRINT RUN 99 SER.#'d SETS
EXCHANGE DEADLINE 11/30/2018
*GOLD/50: .5X TO 1.2X BASIC
DNAIA Ian Anderson 15.00 40.00
DNAWB Will Benson 20.00 50.00

2016 Bowman Chrome Draft Pick Autographs

STATED ODDS 1:7 HOBBY
PRINTING PLATE ODDS 1:3389 HOBBY
PLATE PRINT RUN 1 SET PER COLOR
NO PLATE PRICING DUE TO SCARCITY
EXCHANGE DEADLINE 11/30/2018
CDAAG Anfernee Grier 4.00 10.00
CDAAH Alec Hansen 4.00 10.00
CDAAK Alex Kirilloff 50.00 120.00
CDAAP A.J. Puk 12.00 30.00
CDAAY Andy Yerzy 3.00 8.00
CDABB Ben Bowden 3.00 8.00
CDABD Bobby Dalbec 30.00 80.00
CDABG Braxton Garrett 4.00 10.00
CDABOB Bo Bichette 125.00 300.00
CDABRE Buddy Reed 3.00 8.00
CDABRR Bryan Reynolds 10.00 25.00
CDABW Bryse Wilson 20.00 50.00
CDACB Cavan Biggio 20.00 50.00
CDACC C.J. Chatham 4.00 10.00
CDACJ Connor Jones 4.00 10.00
CDACO Chris Okey 3.00 8.00
CDACQ Cal Quantrill 3.00 8.00
CDACR Corey Ray 5.00 12.00
CDACRA Cole Ragans 4.00 10.00
CDACS Cody Sedlock 3.00 8.00
CDADC Dylan Carlson 60.00 150.00
CDADD Dane Dunning 4.00 10.00
CDADH Dakota Hudson 6.00 15.00
CDADJ Daulton Jefferies 4.00 10.00
CDADP Delvin Perez 4.00 10.00
CDAEL Eric Lauer 4.00 10.00
CDAFW Forrest Whitley 20.00 50.00
CDAGH Garrett Hampson 6.00 15.00
CDAGL Gavin Lux 100.00 250.00
CDAHS Hudson Potts 6.00 15.00
CDAIA Ian Anderson 40.00 100.00
CDAJD Justin Dunn 5.00 12.00
CDAJF Jake Fraley 4.00 10.00
CDAJL Joshua Lowe 6.00 15.00
CDAJLU Jesus Luzardo 25.00 60.00
CDAJR Joe Rizzo 3.00 8.00
CDAJS Jordan Sheffield 3.00 8.00
CDAKL Kyle Lewis 100.00 250.00
CDAKM Kyle Muller 4.00 10.00
CDAMM Matt Manning 20.00 50.00
CDAMM Mickey Moniak 15.00 40.00
CDAMT Matt Thaiss 3.00 8.00
CDANJ Nolan Jones 25.00 60.00
CDANM Nolan Martinez 4.00 10.00
CDAPA Pete Alonso 150.00 400.00
CDARD Ronnie Dawson 3.00 8.00
CDARP Riley Pint 3.00 8.00
CDART Robert Tyler 3.00 8.00
CDATL Tim Lynch 5.00 12.00
CDATT Taylor Trammell 20.00 50.00
CDATZ T.J. Zeuch 4.00 10.00
CDAWB Will Benson 5.00 12.00
CDAWC Will Craig 3.00 8.00
CDAWS Will Smith 30.00 80.00
CDAZB Zack Burdi 4.00 10.00
CDAZC Zack Collins 4.00 10.00

2016 Bowman Chrome Draft Pick Autographs Black Refractors

*BLACK REF: 1.5X TO 4X BASIC
RANDOM INSERTS IN PACKS
STATED PRINT RUN 75 SER.#'d SETS
EXCHANGE DEADLINE 11/30/2018
CDAGL Gavin Lux 600.00 1200.00

2016 Bowman Chrome Draft Pick Autographs Blue Refractors

*BLUE REF: 1X TO 2.5X BASIC
STATED ODDS 1:91 HOBBY
STATED PRINT RUN 150 SER.#'d SETS
EXCHANGE DEADLINE 11/30/2018

2016 Bowman Chrome Draft Pick Autographs Blue Wave Refractors

*BLUE WAVE REF: 1X TO 2.5X BASIC
STATED ODDS 1:91 HOBBY
STATED PRINT RUN 150 SER.#'d SETS
EXCHANGE DEADLINE 11/30/2018

2016 Bowman Chrome Draft Draft Pick Autographs Gold Refractors

*GOLD REF: 2.5X TO 6X BASIC
STATED ODDS 1:271 HOBBY
STATED PRINT RUN 50 SER.#'d SETS
EXCHANGE DEADLINE 11/30/2018
CDAGL Gavin Lux 800.00 1500.00
CDAWC Will Craig 20.00 50.00

2016 Bowman Chrome Draft Draft Pick Autographs Gold Wave Refractors

*GOLD WAVE REF: 2.5X TO 6X BASIC
STATED ODDS 1:271 HOBBY
STATED PRINT RUN 50 SER.#'d SETS
EXCHANGE DEADLINE 11/30/2018
CDAGL Gavin Lux 800.00 1500.00
CDAWC Will Craig 20.00 50.00

2016 Bowman Chrome Draft Draft Pick Autographs Green Refractors

*GREEN REF: 1.2X TO 3X BASIC
STATED ODDS 1:137 HOBBY
STATED PRINT RUN 99 SER.#'d SETS
EXCHANGE DEADLINE 11/30/2018

2016 Bowman Chrome Draft Draft Pick Autographs Orange Refractors

*ORANGE REF: 3X TO 8X BASIC
STATED ODDS 1:540 HOBBY
STATED PRINT RUN 25 SER.#'d SETS
EXCHANGE DEADLINE 11/30/2018
CDAGL Gavin Lux 1000.00 2000.00
CDANJ Nolan Jones 600.00 1000.00
CDAWC Will Craig 25.00 60.00

2016 Bowman Chrome Draft Draft Pick Autographs Purple Refractors

*PURPLE REF: .6X TO 1.5X BASIC
STATED ODDS 1:54 HOBBY
STATED PRINT RUN 250 SER.#'d SETS
EXCHANGE DEADLINE 11/30/2018

2016 Bowman Chrome Draft Draft Pick Autographs Refractors

*REF: .5X TO 1.2X BASIC
STATED ODDS 1:28 HOBBY
STATED PRINT RUN 499 SER.#'d SETS
EXCHANGE DEADLINE 11/30/2018

2016 Bowman Chrome Draft MLB Draft History

COMPLETE SET (15) 6.00 15.00
STATED ODDS 1:6 HOBBY
*GOLD/50: 4X TO 10X BASIC
MLBDBJ Bo Jackson .60 1.50
MLBDCB Craig Biggio .50 1.25
MLBDCJ Chipper Jones .60 1.50
MLBDCR Cal Ripken Jr. 2.00 5.00
MLBDFT Frank Thomas .60 1.50
MLBDGM Greg Maddux .75 2.00
MLBDJB Johnny Bench .60 1.50
MLBDKGJ Ken Griffey Jr. 1.25 3.00
MLBDMP Mike Piazza .60 1.50
MLBDNG Nomar Garciaparra .50 1.25
MLBDNR Nolan Ryan 2.00 5.00
MLBDOS Ozzie Smith .75 2.00
MLBDRC Roger Clemens .75 2.00
MLBDRJ Reggie Jackson .50 1.25
MLBDTG Tom Glavine .50 1.25

2016 Bowman Chrome Draft MLB Draft History Autographs

STATED ODDS 1:750 HOBBY
STATED PRINT RUN 99 SER.#'d SETS
EXCHANGE DEADLINE 11/30/2018
MLBDABJ Bo Jackson 40.00 100.00
MLBDACJ Chipper Jones 40.00 100.00
MLBDACR Cal Ripken Jr. 50.00 120.00
MLBDAFT Frank Thomas 40.00 100.00
MLBDAGM Greg Maddux 40.00 100.00
MLBDAJB Johnny Bench 40.00 100.00
MLBDAKGJ Ken Griffey Jr. 250.00 500.00
MLBDAMP Mike Piazza 50.00 120.00
MLBDANR Nolan Ryan 75.00 200.00
MLBDARC Roger Clemens 30.00 80.00

2016 Bowman Chrome Draft Scouts Fantasy Impacts

COMPLETE SET (20) 6.00 15.00
STATED ODDS 1:3 HOBBY
*GOLD/50: 1.5X TO 4X BASIC
BSIAM Austin Meadows .60 1.50
BSIAP A.J. Puk .60 1.50
BSIBM Billy McKinney .50 1.25
BSIBZ Bradley Zimmer .60 1.50
BSICA Christian Arroyo 1.25 3.00
BSICD Chase De Jong .50 1.25
BSICQ Cal Quantrill .40 1.00
BSICR Corey Ray .60 1.50
BSIDC Dylan Cozens .40 1.00
BSIDS Dominic Smith .40 1.00
BSIFB Franklin Barreto .40 1.00
BSIFM Francis Martes .50 1.25
BSIJD Justin Dunn .40 1.00
BSIKL Kyle Lewis 4.00 10.00
BSIMT Matt Thaiss .40 1.00
BSITB Tyler Beede .50 1.25
BSITZ T.J. Zeuch .50 1.25
BSIWC Will Craig .40 1.00
BSIZB Zack Burdi .50 1.25
BSIZC Zack Collins .50 1.25

2016 Bowman Chrome Draft Scouts Fantasy Impacts Autographs

STATED ODDS 1:1484 HOBBY
STATED PRINT RUN 50 SER.#'d SETS
EXCHANGE DEADLINE 11/30/2018
BSIAP A.J. Puk 12.00 30.00
BSIBM Billy McKinney 8.00 20.00
BSICD Chase De Jong
BSICQ Cal Quantrill 6.00 15.00
BSICR Corey Ray 10.00 25.00
BSIDS Dominic Smith
BSIJD Justin Dunn 12.00 30.00
BSITB Tyler Beede 12.00 30.00
BSIZB Zack Burdi 8.00 20.00
BSIZC Zack Collins 8.00 20.00

2016 Bowman Chrome Draft Top of the Class Box Topper

*GOLD/50: .5X TO 1.2X BASIC
TOCAP A.J. Puk 2.50 6.00
TOCBG Braxton Garrett 2.00 5.00
TOCCQ Cal Quantrill 1.50 4.00
TOCCR Corey Ray 2.50 6.00
TOCFW Forrest Whitley 12.00 30.00
TOCIA Ian Anderson 4.00 10.00
TOCJL Joshua Lowe 1.50 4.00
TOCKL Kyle Lewis 30.00 80.00
TOCMM Matt Manning 2.50 6.00
TOCMM Mickey Moniak 12.00 30.00
TOCNS Nick Senzel 30.00 80.00
TOCRP Riley Pint 1.50 4.00
TOCWB Will Benson 2.50 6.00
TOCZC Zack Collins 2.00 5.00

2016 Bowman Chrome Draft Top of the Class Box Topper Autographs Orange

STATED ODDS 1:140 HOBBY BOXES
STATED PRINT RUN 35 SER.#'d SETS
EXCHANGE DEADLINE 11/30/2018
TOCAP A.J. Puk 30.00 80.00
TOCBG Braxton Garrett 30.00 80.00
TOCCQ Cal Quantrill
TOCCR Corey Ray 100.00 250.00
TOCFW Forrest Whitley 30.00 80.00
TOCIA Ian Anderson 40.00 100.00
TOCMM Mickey Moniak 125.00 300.00
TOCMM Matt Manning 40.00 100.00
TOCRP Riley Pint 10.00 25.00
TOCZC Zack Collins 50.00 120.00

2017 Bowman Chrome

SP ODDS 1:119 HOBBY
PLATE PRINT RUN 1 SET PER COLOR
BLACK-CYAN-MAGENTA-YELLOW ISSUED
NO PLATE PRICING DUE TO SCARCITY
1 Kris Bryant .40 1.00
2 Jesse Winker RC .40 1.00
3 Paul Goldschmidt .30 .75
4 Zack Greinke .25 .60
5 Albert Pujols .40 1.00
6A Alex Reyes RC .50 1.25
6B Reyes SP Pntng up 5.00 12.00
7 Byron Buxton .25 .60
8 Ichiro .40 1.00
9 Miguel Cabrera .30 .75
10 Sonny Gray .25 .60
11 Wil Myers .20 .50
12A Alex Bregman RC 1.50 4.00
12B Bregman SP On bench 8.00 20.00
13 David Ortiz .30 .75
14 Robinson Cano .25 .60
15 Chris Sale .30 .75
16 Stephen Piscotty .25 .60
17 Masahiro Tanaka .25 .60
18 Joe Jimenez RC .40 1.00
19 Justin Verlander .30 .75
20 Andrew Miller .25 .60
21 Kyle Schwarber .30 .75
22A Jharel Cotton RC .40 1.00
22B Cotton SP Grn jrsy 4.00 10.00
23 Francisco Lindor .30 .75
24 Cole Hamels .25 .60
25 Corey Seager .30 .75
26 Xander Bogaerts .30 .75
27 Cody Bellinger RC 5.00 12.00
28 Ryan Braun .25 .60
29 Christian Arroyo RC .60 1.50
30 Ryon Healy RC .50 1.25
31A David Dahl RC .50 1.25
31B Dahl SP Prple jrsy 5.00 12.00
32 Jose Quintana .20 .50
33 Jacob deGrom .30 .75
34 Salvador Perez .25 .60
35 Manny Machado .30 .75
36 Yoenis Cespedes .30 .75
37 Maikel Franco .25 .60
38 Adam Duvall .30 .75
39 Jose Bautista .25 .60
40 Mark Melancon .20 .50
41 Corey Kluber .25 .60
42 Mitch Haniger RC .60 1.50
43 Carson Fulmer RC .40 1.00
44 Jordan Montgomery RC .60 1.50
45 Joe Musgrove RC .40 1.00
46 Felix Hernandez .25 .60
47 Zach Britton .25 .60
48 Anthony Rizzo .50 1.25
49 Rougned Odor .25 .60
50A Yoan Moncada RC 1.25 3.00
50B Moncada SP Blck jrsy 8.00 20.00
51 Josh Donaldson .25 .60
52 Trea Turner .25 .60
53 Manny Margot RC .40 1.00
54 Brian Dozier .30 .75
55 Trevor Story .30 .75
56A Aaron Judge RC 5.00 12.00
56B Judge SP In dugout 50.00 125.00
57A Yulieski Gurriel RC .60 1.50
57B Gurriel SP Blue jrsy 6.00 15.00
58 Michael Fulmer .20 .50
59 Braden Shipley RC .40 1.00
60 Odubel Herrera .25 .60
61 Jeff Hoffman RC .40 1.00
62 Joey Votto .30 .75
63 Mookie Betts .50 1.25
64 Gary Sanchez .30 .75
65 Aroldis Chapman .30 .75
66 Giancarlo Stanton .30 .75
67 Noah Syndergaard .25 .60
68A Andrew Benintendi RC 1.25 3.00
68B Benintendi SP Gatorade 12.00 30.00
69 Chris Archer .20 .50
70 Josh Bell RC 1.00 2.50
71 Aledmys Diaz .25 .60
72 Nolan Arenado .40 1.00
73 Evan Longoria .25 .60
74 Ryan Schimpf .20 .50
75A Jose De Leon RC .40 1.00
75B De Leon SP Thrwng rght 4.00 10.00
76 Max Scherzer .30 .75
77A Orlando Arcia RC .60 1.50
77B Arcia SP Sit w/bat 6.00 15.00
78 Jose Abreu .30 .75
79 Jonathan Villar .20 .50
80A Tyler Glasnow RC .50 1.25
80B Glasnow SP Whte jrsy 5.00 12.00
81A Robert Gsellman RC .40 1.00
81B Gsellman SP Bckwrds hat 4.00 10.00
82 Carlos Correa .30 .75
83 Khris Davis .30 .75
84A Jorge Alfaro RC .50 1.25
84B Alfaro SP At bat 5.00 12.00
85 Raimel Tapia RC .50 1.25
86A Dansby Swanson RC 1.00 2.50
86B Swanson SP Blue jrsy 10.00 25.00
87 Jose Altuve .25 .60
88A Hunter Renfroe RC .50 1.25
88B Renfroe SP Blue jrsy 5.00 12.00
89 Freddie Freeman .40 1.00
90 Gregory Polanco .25 .60
91 Buster Posey .40 1.00
92 Gerrit Cole .30 .75
93 Clayton Kershaw .60 1.50
94 Danny Duffy .20 .50
95 Amir Garrett RC .40 1.00
96 Bryce Harper .50 1.25
97 Adrian Beltre .30 .75
98 Eric Hosmer .25 .60
99 Matt Kemp .25 .60
100 Mike Trout 1.50 4.00

2017 Bowman Chrome Blue Refractors

*BLUE REF VET: 4X TO 10X BASIC
*BLUE REF RC: 2X TO 5X BASIC
STATED ODDS 1:60 HOBBY
STATED PRINT RUN 150 SER.#'d SETS
56 Aaron Judge 50.00 120.00
100 Mike Trout 12.00 30.00

2017 Bowman Chrome Gold Refractors

*GOLD REF VET: 8X TO 20X BASIC
*GOLD REF RC: 4X TO 10X BASIC
STATED ODDS 1:178 HOBBY
STATED PRINT RUN 50 SER.#'d SETS
1 Kris Bryant 30.00 80.00
13 David Ortiz 10.00 25.00
56 Aaron Judge 125.00 300.00
84 Jorge Alfaro 15.00 40.00
100 Mike Trout 40.00 100.00

2017 Bowman Chrome Green Refractors

*GREEN REF VET: 4X TO 10X BASIC
*GREEN REF RC: 2X TO 5X BASIC
STATED ODDS 1:90 HOBBY
STATED PRINT RUN 99 SER.#'d SETS
56 Aaron Judge 50.00 120.00
100 Mike Trout 12.00 30.00

2017 Bowman Chrome Orange Refractors

*ORANGE REF VET: 10X TO 25X BASIC
*ORANGE REF RC: 5X TO 12X BASIC
STATED ODDS 1:356 HOBBY
STATED PRINT RUN 25 SER.#'d SETS
1 Kris Bryant 40.00 100.00
13 David Ortiz 12.00 30.00
56 Aaron Judge 150.00 400.00
84 Jorge Alfaro 20.00 50.00
100 Mike Trout 50.00 120.00

2017 Bowman Chrome Purple Refractors

*PURPLE REF VET: 2X TO 5X BASIC
*PURPLE REF RC: 1X TO 2.5X BASIC
STATED ODDS 1:36 HOBBY
STATED PRINT RUN 250 SER.#'d SETS
56 Aaron Judge 30.00 80.00
100 Mike Trout 8.00 20.00

2017 Bowman Chrome Refractors

*REF VET: 1.5X TO 4X BASIC
*REF RC: .75X TO 2X BASIC
STATED ODDS 1:18 HOBBY
STATED PRINT RUN 499 SER.#'d SETS
56 Aaron Judge 20.00 50.00

2017 Bowman Chrome '16 AFL Fall Stars

COMP.SET w/o SP (20) 12.00 30.00
STATED ODDS 1:6 HOBBY
SP ODDS 1:3569 HOBBY
SP PRINT RUN 250 SER.#'d SETS
*ORANGE/25: 2X TO 5X BASIC
AFLAA Anthony Alford .40 1.00
AFLAV Alex Verdugo .60 1.50
AFLBA Brian Anderson .50 1.25
AFLBP Brett Phillips .50 1.25
AFLBZ Bradley Zimmer .50 1.25
AFLCB Cody Bellinger 3.00 8.00
AFLCK Carson Kelly .50 1.25
AFLDL Dawel Lugo .40 1.00
AFLDS D.J. Stewart .40 1.00
AFLDT Dillon Tate .40 1.00
AFLEJ Eloy Jimenez 1.50 4.00
AFLFB Franklin Barreto .40 1.00
AFLGB Greg Bird .50 1.25
AFLGT Gleyber Torres 6.00 15.00
AFLIH Ian Happ .75 2.00
AFLNG Nick Gordon .40 1.00
AFLPDJ Paul DeJong 1.25 3.00
AFLTO Tyler O'Neill .50 1.25
AFLWC Willie Calhoun .60 1.50
AFLSWC Calhoun MVP/250 10.00 20.00
AFLYM Yoan Moncada 1.25 3.00

2017 Bowman Chrome '16 AFL Fall Stars Autograph Relics

STATED ODDS 1:1334 HOBBY
STATED PRINT RUN 50 SER.#'d SETS
EXCHANGE DEADLINE 8/31/2019
AFLRBP Brett Phillips 20.00 50.00
AFLRDL Dawel Lugo 25.00 60.00
AFLREJ Eloy Jimenez 75.00 200.00
AFLRFB Franklin Barreto 25.00 60.00
AFLRGT Gleyber Torres 75.00 300.00
AFLRRO Ryan O'Hearn 30.00 80.00
AFLRWC Willie Calhoun EXCH 25.00 60.00

2017 Bowman Chrome '16 AFL Fall Stars Relics

STATED ODDS 1:450 HOBBY
STATED PRINT RUN 99 SER.#'d SETS
*ORANGE/25: .6X TO 1.5X BASIC
AFLRAA Anthony Alford 3.00 8.00
AFLRBA Brian Anderson 4.00 10.00
AFLRBH Brent Honeywell 10.00 25.00
AFLRBP Brett Phillips 4.00 10.00
AFLRBZ Bradley Zimmer 4.00 10.00
AFLRCB Cody Bellinger 20.00 50.00
AFLRDL Dawel Lugo 3.00 8.00
AFLRDP David Paulino 4.00 10.00
AFLRDS D.J. Stewart 3.00 8.00
AFLREJ Eloy Jimenez 8.00 20.00
AFLRFB Franklin Barreto 3.00 8.00
AFLRFM Francis Martes 3.00 8.00
AFLRGT Gleyber Torres 8.00 20.00
AFLRHB Harrison Bader 3.00 8.00
AFLRNG Nick Gordon 3.00 8.00
AFLRPD Paul DeJong 4.00 10.00
AFLRRM Ryan McMahon 3.00 8.00
AFLRRO Ryan O'Hearn 6.00 15.00
AFLRTO Tyler O'Neill 8.00 20.00
AFLRTW Taylor Ward 8.00 20.00
AFLRWC Willie Calhoun 5.00 12.00

2017 Bowman Chrome '48 Bowman Autographs

STATED ODDS 1:38,095 HOBBY
STATED PRINT RUN 25 SER.#'d SETS
EXCHANGE DEADLINE 3/31/2019
48BHA Hank Aaron 250.00 500.00
48BKB Kris Bryant 250.00 500.00
48BSK Sandy Koufax 400.00 800.00

2017 Bowman Chrome '48 Bowman Refractors

COMPLETE SET (10) 6.00 15.00
STATED ODDS 1:24 HOBBY
*GREEN/99: 2.5X TO 6X BASIC
*GOLD/50: 4X TO 10X BASIC
*ORANGE/25: 5X TO 12X BASIC
48BAB Alex Bregman 1.50 4.00
48BGS Giancarlo Stanton .60 1.50
48BHA Hank Aaron 1.25 3.00
48BJC J.P. Crawford .40 1.00
48BKB Kris Bryant .75 2.00
48BMT Mike Trout 3.00 8.00
48BPR Phil Rizzuto .50 1.25
48BSK Sandy Koufax 1.25 3.00
48BWS Warren Spahn .50 1.25
48BYM Yoan Moncada 1.25 3.00

2017 Bowman Chrome '51 Bowman Refractors

COMPLETE SET (19) 20.00 50.00
STATED ODDS 1:24 HOBBY
*GREEN/99: 2.5X TO 6X BASIC
*GOLD/50: 4X TO 10X BASIC
*ORANGE/25: 5X TO 12X BASIC
1 Whitey Ford .50 1.25
2 Ted Williams 1.25 3.00
3 Monte Irvin .50 1.25
4 Phil Rizzuto .50 1.25
5 Duke Snider .50 1.25
6 Bob Feller .50 1.25
7 Alex Bregman 1.50 4.00
8 Kris Bryant .75 2.00
9 Mike Trout 3.00 8.00
10 Bryce Harper 1.00 2.50
11 Carlos Correa .60 1.50
12 Xander Bogaerts .60 1.50
13 Clayton Kershaw 1.25 3.00
15 Corey Seager .60 1.50
16 Yoan Moncada 1.25 3.00
17 J.P. Crawford .40 1.00
18 Dansby Swanson 1.00 2.50
19 Austin Meadows .60 1.50
20 Brendan Rodgers .50 1.25

2017 Bowman Chrome '92 Bowman Autographs

STATED ODDS 1:14,772 HOBBY
STATED PRINT RUN 25 SER.#'d SETS
EXCHANGE DEADLINE 3/31/2019
92BAB Alex Bregman 75.00 200.00
92BAR Anthony Rizzo EXCH 60.00 150.00
92BCJ Chipper Jones 100.00 250.00
92BGM Greg Maddux 100.00 250.00
92BJM Jorge Mateo EXCH 60.00 150.00
92BMM Mark McGwire 60.00 150.00
92BMP Mike Piazza 150.00 300.00
92BSN Sean Newcomb 50.00 120.00

2017 Bowman Chrome '92 Bowman Refractors

COMPLETE SET (20) 6.00 15.00
STATED ODDS 1:12 HOBBY
*GREEN/99: 2X TO 5X BASIC
*GOLD/50: 3X TO 8X BASIC
*ORANGE/25: 4X TO 10X BASIC
92BAB Alex Bregman 1.50 4.00
92BAR Anthony Rizzo 1.00 2.50
92BBH Bryce Harper 1.00 2.50
92BCJ Chipper Jones .60 1.50
92BDS Darryl Strawberry .40 1.00
92BDSW Dansby Swanson 1.00 2.50
92BGM Greg Maddux .75 2.00
92BIR Ivan Rodriguez .50 1.25
92BJM Jorge Mateo .40 1.00
92BKB Kris Bryant .75 2.00
92BKGJ Ken Griffey Jr. 1.25 3.00
92BMM Mark McGwire 1.00 2.50
92BMP Mike Piazza .60 1.50
92BNA Nolan Arenado .75 2.00
92BNS Noah Syndergaard .50 1.25
92BOA Orlando Arcia .60 1.50
92BRD Rafael Devers .75 2.00
92BSN Sean Newcomb .50 1.25
92BXB Xander Bogaerts .60 1.50
92BYC Yoenis Cespedes .60 1.50

2017 Bowman Chrome Ascent Autographs

STATED ODDS 1:19671 HOBBY
STATED PRINT RUN 150 SER.#'d SETS
EXCHANGE DEADLINE 3/31/2019
*ORANGE/25: .75X TO 2X BASIC
BAAD Aledmys Diaz 6.00 15.00
BAAR Anthony Rizzo 30.00 80.00
BAARU Addison Russell EXCH 15.00 40.00
BABH Bryce Harper 100.00 250.00
BACC Carlos Correa 30.00 80.00
BACS Corey Seager
Inserted in '18 Transcendent VIP Packs
BAFL Francisco Lindor 30.00 80.00
BAJA Jose Altuve 20.00 50.00
BAKB Kris Bryant EXCH 75.00 200.00
BAMT Mike Trout 200.00 400.00
BANM Nomar Mazara 20.00 50.00
BANS Noah Syndergaard 15.00 40.00
BASM Steven Matz 6.00 15.00
BASP Stephen Piscotty 6.00 15.00
BATS Trevor Story 8.00 20.00
BAWC Willson Contreras 15.00 40.00

2017 Bowman Chrome Autograph Relics

STATED ODDS 1:263 HOBBY
STATED PRINT RUN 150 SER.#'d SETS
EXCHANGE DEADLINE 8/31/2019
CARAR Amed Rosario 15.00 40.00
CARAV Alex Verdugo 25.00 60.00
CARCWH Chih-Wei Hu 15.00 40.00
CARDC Dylan Cozens 6.00 15.00
CARDL Dawel Lugo 6.00 15.00
CAREJ Eloy Jimenez 30.00 80.00
CARFB Franklin Barreto 4.00 10.00
CARFR Francisco Rios 4.00 10.00
CARGB Greg Bird 5.00 12.00
CARGT Gleyber Torres 60.00 150.00
CARJJ Joe Jimenez 4.00 10.00
CARPD Paul DeJong 10.00 25.00
CARSN Sean Newcomb 5.00 12.00
CARTO Tyler O'Neill 5.00 12.00
CARWC Willie Calhoun 8.00 20.00

2017 Bowman Chrome Autograph Relics Gold Refractors

*GOLD REF: .5X TO 1.2X BASIC
STATED ODDS 1:1020 HOBBY
STATED PRINT RUN 50 SER.#'d SETS
EXCHANGE DEADLINE 8/31/2019
CARCWH Chih-Wei Hu 60.00 150.00
CAREJ Eloy Jimenez 60.00 150.00

2017 Bowman Chrome Autograph Relics Orange Refractors

*ORANGE REF: .75X TO 2X BASIC
STATED ODDS 1:1734 HOBBY
STATED PRINT RUN 25 SER.#'d SETS
EXCHANGE DEADLINE 8/31/2019
CARCWH Chih-Wei Hu 100.00 250.00
CARDL Dawel Lugo 40.00 100.00
CAREJ Eloy Jimenez 150.00 400.00

2017 Bowman Chrome Lucky Autograph Redemptions

STATED ODDS 1:28,952 HOBBY
EXCHANGE DEADLINE 3/31/2019
LARIH Ian Happ 10.00 25.00

2017 Bowman Chrome Prime Chrome Inscription Autographs

STATED ODDS 1:1039 HOBBY
STATED PRINT RUN 75 SER.#'d SETS
EXCHANGE DEADLINE 8/31/2019
BIAAE Anderson Espinoza 5.00 12.00
BIAAP A.J. Puk 12.00 30.00
BIABR Blake Rutherford 8.00 20.00
BIACK Carter Kieboom 40.00 100.00
BIACR Corey Ray 8.00 20.00
BIAGT Gleyber Torres 50.00 120.00
BIAIA Ian Anderson 40.00 100.00
BIAJG Jason Groome 10.00 25.00
BIAJM Jorge Mateo 12.00 30.00
BIAKL Kyle Lewis 40.00 100.00
BIAKM Kevin Maitan 40.00 100.00
BIALAB Luis Alexander Basabe 8.00 20.00
BIALG Lourdes Gurriel Jr. 20.00 50.00
BIALT Leody Taveras 25.00 60.00
BIAMK Mitch Keller 10.00 25.00
BIAMM Mickey Moniak 25.00 60.00
BIANS Nick Senzel
BIASN Sean Newcomb 6.00 15.00
BIATC Trevor Clifton EXCH 5.00 12.00
BIATH Torii Hunter Jr. 12.00 30.00
BIAWC Willie Calhoun

2017 Bowman Chrome Prime Chrome Inscription Autographs Orange Refractors

*ORANGE REF: .6X TO 1.5X BASIC
RANDOM INSERTS IN PACKS
STATED PRINT RUN 25 SER.#'d SETS
EXCHANGE DEADLINE 8/31/2019
BIABR Blake Rutherford 125.00 300.00
BIACK Carter Kieboom 100.00 250.00
BIAGT Gleyber Torres 150.00 400.00
BIAKM Kevin Maitan 60.00 150.00
BIALAB Luis Alexander Basabe 15.00 40.00
BIALT Leody Taveras 40.00 100.00
BIATH Torii Hunter Jr. 20.00 50.00
BIAWC Willie Calhoun 50.00 120.00

2017 Bowman Chrome Prospect Autographs

BOW.STATED ODDS 1:68 HOBBY
BOW.CHR.STATED ODDS 1:11 HOBBY
BOW.PLATE ODDS 1:18,095 HOBBY
PLATE PRINT RUN 1 SET PER COLOR
BLACK-CYAN-MAGENTA-YELLOW ISSUED
NO PLATE PRICING DUE TO SCARCITY
BOW.EXCH.DEADLINE 3/31/2019
BOW.CHR.EXCH.DEADLINE 8/31/2019
CPAAA Albert Abreu 8.00 20.00
CPAACA Andrew Calica 3.00 8.00
CPAAE Anderson Espinoza 3.00 8.00
CPAAG Abrahan Gutierrez 5.00 12.00
CPAAH Austin Hays 8.00 20.00
CPAAI Andy Ibanez 3.00 8.00
CPAAK Anthony Kay 6.00 15.00
CPAAM Adrian Morejon 5.00 12.00
CPAAME Adonis Medina 5.00 12.00
CPAAP Angel Perdomo 3.00 8.00
CPAAPU A.J. Puckett 3.00 8.00
CPAAR Alfredo Rodriguez 4.00 10.00
CPAAS Andrew Sopko 3.00 8.00
CPAAST Andrew Stevenson 4.00 10.00
CPAAT Anderson Tejeda 3.00 8.00
CPAATI Alberto Tirado 3.00 8.00
CPABB Bryson Brigman 3.00 8.00
CPABBI Braden Bishop 5.00 12.00
CPABM Brian Mundell 3.00 8.00
CPABR Blake Rutherford 8.00 20.00
CPACAD Chance Adams 6.00 15.00
CPACF Clint Frazier 10.00 25.00
CPACH C.J. Hinojosa 3.00 8.00
CPACHR Christian Arroyo 10.00 25.00
CPACP Chris Paddack 15.00 40.00
CPACS Cole Stobbe 3.00 8.00
CPACWH Chih-Wei Hu 8.00 20.00
CPADF David Fletcher 8.00 20.00
CPADG Daniel Gossett 3.00 8.00
CPADL Dawel Lugo 3.00 8.00
CPADLA Dinelson Lamet 12.00 30.00
CPADT David Thompson 4.00 10.00
CPAEG Elniery Garcia 3.00 8.00
CPAEJ Eloy Jimenez 150.00 400.00
CPAFJ Felix Jorge 3.00 8.00
CPAFM Francisco Mejia 6.00 15.00
CPAFP Freddy Peralta 10.00 25.00
CPAFR Francisco Rios 3.00 8.00
CPAFRO Fernando Romero 3.00 8.00
CPAGH Gage Hinsz 3.00 8.00
CPAGJ Griffin Jax 3.00 8.00
CPAGL Grayson Long 3.00 8.00
CPAGT Gleyber Torres 50.00 120.00
CPAHQ Heath Quinn 4.00 10.00
CPAIW Isaiah White 3.00 8.00
CPAJAZ Jose Azocar 3.00 8.00
CPAJC Jazz Chisholm 20.00 50.00
CPAJD Jon Duplantier 5.00 12.00
CPAJF Jameson Fisher 3.00 8.00
CPAJG Jason Groome 15.00 40.00
CPAJHE Jacob Heyward 3.00 8.00
CPAJJ Joe Jimenez 3.00 8.00
CPAJM Justin Maese 3.00 8.00
CPAJMI Jalen Miller 3.00 8.00
CPAJO Josh Ockimey 8.00 20.00
CPAJO Jorge Ona 4.00 10.00
CPAJP Jose Pujols 4.00 10.00
CPAJS Jesus Sanchez 15.00 40.00
CPAJSB Josh Sborz 3.00 8.00
CPAJT Jose Trevino 3.00 8.00
CPAJT Jose Taveras 4.00 10.00
CPAKA Keegan Akin 4.00 10.00
CPAKF Kyle Funkhouser 4.00 10.00
CPAKL Khalil Lee 10.00 25.00
CPAKM Kevin Maitan 20.00 50.00
CPALA Luis Arraez 15.00 40.00
CPALA Lazarito Armenteros 15.00 40.00
CPALAB Luis Alexander Basabe 5.00 12.00
CPALAL Luis Almanzar 3.00 8.00
CPALB Lewis Brinson 5.00 12.00
CPALCA Luis Carpio 3.00 8.00
CPALE Lucas Erceg 6.00 15.00
CPALGU Lourdes Gurriel Jr. 15.00 40.00
CPALI Logan Ice 3.00 8.00
CPALT Leody Taveras 10.00 25.00
CPAMG Miguel Gomez 3.00 8.00
CPAMK Michael Kopech 10.00 25.00
CPAMK Mitch Keller 12.00 30.00
CPAMM Mickey Moniak 8.00 20.00
CPAMS Magneuris Sierra 10.00 25.00
CPAMSC Max Schrock 6.00 15.00
CPAMV Meibrys Viloria 3.00 8.00
CPAMW Mitchell White 5.00 12.00
CPANB Nick Banks 3.00 8.00
CPANS Nick Senzel 75.00 200.00
CPANSO Nick Solak 8.00 20.00
CPAOP Ofelky Peralta 3.00 8.00
CPAPC P.J. Conlon 3.00 8.00
CPAPW Patrick Weigel 3.00 8.00
CPARA Ronald Acuna 800.00 1500.00
CPARH Ryan Howard 4.00 10.00
CPAROH Ryan O'Hearn 4.00 10.00
CPARR Roniel Raudes 3.00 8.00
CPASA Sandy Alcantara 8.00 20.00
CPASD Steven Duggar 3.00 8.00
CPASH Starling Heredia 6.00 15.00
CPASS Sixto Sanchez 30.00 80.00
CPATC Trevor Clifton 3.00 8.00
CPATC Taylor Clarke 3.00 8.00
CPATF T.J. Friedl 4.00 10.00
CPATH Torii Hunter Jr. 3.00 8.00
CPATM Triston McKenzie 12.00 30.00
CPATN Tomas Nido 3.00 8.00
CPATS Thomas Szapucki 4.00 10.00
CPAVG Vladimir Gutierrez 3.00 8.00
CPAWB Wuilmer Becerra 3.00 8.00
CPAWJ Wander Javier 3.00 8.00
CPAYCC Yu-Cheng Chang 8.00 20.00
CPAYD Yusniel Diaz 6.00 15.00

2017 Bowman Chrome Prospect Autographs 70th Blue Refractors

*70TH BLUE: 1.2X TO 3X BASIC
BOW.STATED ODDS 1:1463 HOBBY
BOW.EXCH.DEADLINE 3/31/2019
BOW.CHR.EXCH.DEADLINE 8/31/2019
CPAAE Anderson Espinoza 20.00 50.00
CPAAME Adonis Medina 40.00 100.00
CPAEG Elniery Garcia 20.00 50.00
CPAEJ Eloy Jimenez 500.00 1000.00
CPAKM Kevin Maitan 100.00 250.00
CPANS Nick Senzel 300.00 600.00
CPARA Ronald Acuna 2500.00 5000.00
CPAYCC Yu-Cheng Chang 30.00 80.00

2017 Bowman Chrome Prospect Autographs Blue Refractors

*BLUE REF: 1X TO 2.5X BASIC
BOW.STATED ODDS 1:488 HOBBY
BOW.CHR.STATED ODDS 1:196 HOBBY
STATED PRINT RUN 150 SER.#'D SETS
BOW.EXCH.DEADLINE 3/31/2019
BOW.CHR.EXCH.DEADLINE 8/31/2019
CPAEJ Eloy Jimenez 300.00 800.00
CPAJS Jesus Sanchez 60.00 150.00
CPAKM Kevin Maitan 75.00 200.00
CPALA Lazarito Armenteros 50.00 120.00
CPANS Nick Senzel 250.00 500.00
CPARA Ronald Acuna 2000.00 4000.00
CPAYCC Yu-Cheng Chang 25.00 60.00

2017 Bowman Chrome Prospect Autographs Blue Mega Refractors

*BLUE REF: 1X TO 2.5X BASIC
STATED PRINT RUN 150 SER.#'D SETS
EXCHANGE DEADLINE 8/31/2019
CPAJS Jesus Sanchez 60.00 150.00
CPALA Lazarito Armenteros 50.00 120.00

2017 Bowman Chrome Prospect Autographs Gold Refractors

*GOLD: 1.5X TO 4X BASIC
BOW.ODDS 1:1463 HOBBY
BOW.CHR.ODDS 1:588 HOBBY
STATED PRINT RUN 50 SER.#'d SETS
EXCHANGE DEADLINE 3/31/2019
BOW.CHR.EXCH.DEADLINE 8/31/2019
CPAACA Andrew Calica 25.00 60.00
CPAAE Anderson Espinoza 25.00 60.00
CPAAME Adonis Medina 50.00 120.00
CPACS Cole Stobbe 20.00 50.00
CPAEG Elniery Garcia 25.00 60.00
CPAEJ Eloy Jimenez 600.00 1200.00
CPAJG Jason Groome 100.00 250.00
CPAJP Jose Pujols 30.00 80.00
CPAJS Jesus Sanchez 200.00 500.00
CPAKM Kevin Maitan 125.00 300.00
CPALA Lazarito Armenteros 75.00 200.00
CPALAL Luis Almanzar 50.00 120.00
CPALCA Luis Carpio 20.00 50.00
CPALT Leody Taveras 150.00 300.00
CPANS Nick Senzel 400.00 800.00
CPAPW Patrick Weigel 25.00 60.00

CPARA Ronald Acuna 3000.00 6000.00
CPATF T.J. Friedl 40.00 100.00
CPATS Thomas Szapucki 50.00 120.00
CPAYCC Yu-Cheng Chang 60.00 150.00
CPAYD Yusniel Diaz 50.00 120.00

2017 Bowman Chrome Prospect Autographs Gold Shimmer Refractors

*GOLD SHIMMER: 1.5X TO 4X BASIC
BOW.STATED ODDS 1:1463 HOBBY
STATED PRINT RUN 50 SER.#'d SETS
BOW.EXCH.DEADLINE 3/31/2019
BOW.CHR.EXCH.DEADLINE 8/31/2019
CPAACA Andrew Calica 25.00 60.00
CPAAE Anderson Espinoza 25.00 60.00
CPAAME Adonis Medina 50.00 120.00
CPACS Cole Stobbe 20.00 50.00
CPAEG Elniery Garcia 25.00 60.00
CPAEJ Eloy Jimenez 600.00 1200.00
CPAJG Jason Groome 100.00 250.00
CPAJP Jose Pujols 30.00 80.00
CPAJS Jesus Sanchez 200.00 500.00
CPAKM Kevin Maitan 125.00 300.00
CPALA Lazarito Armenteros 75.00 200.00
CPALAL Luis Almanzar 50.00 120.00
CPALCA Luis Carpio 20.00 50.00
CPALT Leody Taveras 150.00 300.00
CPANS Nick Senzel 400.00 800.00
CPAPW Patrick Weigel 25.00 60.00
CPARA Ronald Acuna 3000.00 6000.00
CPATF T.J. Friedl 40.00 100.00
CPATS Thomas Szapucki 50.00 120.00
CPAYCC Yu-Cheng Chang 60.00 150.00
CPAYD Yusniel Diaz 50.00 120.00

2017 Bowman Chrome Prospect Autographs Green Refractors

*GREEN REF: 1.2X TO 3X BASIC
RANDOM INSERTS IN BOW.RET PACKS
BOW.CHR.STATED ODDS 1:297
STATED PRINT RUN 99 SER.#'D SETS
BOW.EXCH.DEADLINE 3/31/2019
BOW.CHR.EXCH.DEADLINE 8/31/2019
CPAEJ Eloy Jimenez 500.00 1000.00
CPAJS Jesus Sanchez 75.00 200.00
CPAKM Kevin Maitan 100.00 250.00
CPALA Lazarito Armenteros 60.00 150.00
CPANS Nick Senzel 300.00 600.00
CPARA Ronald Acuna 2000.00 5000.00
CPAYCC Yu-Cheng Chang 30.00 80.00
CPAYD Yusniel Diaz 25.00 60.00

2017 Bowman Chrome Prospect Autographs Green Shimmer Refractors

*GREEN REF: 1.2X TO 3X BASIC
RANDOMLY INSERTED IN RETAIL PACKS
STATED PRINT RUN 99 SER.#'D SETS
BOW.EXCH.DEADLINE 3/31/2019
BOW.CHR.EXCH.DEADLINE 8/31/2019
CPAEJ Eloy Jimenez 500.00 1000.00
CPAJS Jesus Sanchez 75.00 200.00
CPAKM Kevin Maitan 100.00 250.00
CPALA Lazarito Armenteros 60.00 150.00
CPANS Nick Senzel 300.00 600.00
CPARA Ronald Acuna 2000.00 5000.00
CPAYCC Yu-Cheng Chang 30.00 80.00
CPAYD Yusniel Diaz 25.00 60.00

2017 Bowman Chrome Prospect Autographs Orange Refractors

*ORANGE REF: 3X TO 8X BASIC
STATED ODDS 1:744 HOBBY
BOW.CHR.STATED ODDS 1:655 HOBBY
STATED PRINT RUN 25 SER.#'d SETS
BOW.EXCH.DEADLINE 3/31/2019
BOW.CHR.EXCH.DEADLINE 8/31/2019
CPAACA Andrew Calica 50.00 120.00
CPAAE Anderson Espinoza 30.00 80.00
CPAAME Adonis Medina 100.00 250.00
CPACS Cole Stobbe 40.00 100.00
CPAEG Elniery Garcia 50.00 120.00
CPAEJ Eloy Jimenez 1500.00 2000.00
CPAJG Jason Groome 250.00 500.00
CPAJP Jose Pujols 40.00 100.00
CPAJS Jesus Sanchez 300.00 800.00
CPAKM Kevin Maitan 250.00 600.00
CPALA Lazarito Armenteros 150.00 400.00
CPALAL Luis Almanzar 100.00 250.00
CPALCA Luis Carpio 40.00 100.00
CPALT Leody Taveras 300.00 600.00
CPANS Nick Senzel 500.00 1000.00
CPAPW Patrick Weigel 50.00 120.00
CPARA Ronald Acuna 4000.00 8000.00
CPATF T.J. Friedl 60.00 150.00
CPATS Thomas Szapucki 60.00 150.00
CPAYCC Yu-Cheng Chang 75.00 200.00
CPAYD Yusniel Diaz 200.00 500.00

2017 Bowman Chrome Prospect Autographs Orange Shimmer Refractors

*ORANGE SHIMMER: 3X TO 8X BASIC
BOW.STATED ODDS 1:744 HOBBY
STATED PRINT RUN 25 SER.#'d SETS
BOW.EXCH.DEADLINE 3/31/2019
BOW.CHR.EXCH.DEADLINE 8/31/2019
CPAACA Andrew Calica 50.00 120.00
CPAAE Anderson Espinoza 30.00 80.00
CPAAME Adonis Medina 100.00 250.00
CPACS Cole Stobbe 40.00 100.00
CPAEG Elniery Garcia 50.00 120.00
CPAEJ Eloy Jimenez 1500.00 2000.00
CPAJG Jason Groome 250.00 500.00
CPAJP Jose Pujols 40.00 100.00
CPAJS Jesus Sanchez 300.00 800.00
CPAKM Kevin Maitan 250.00 600.00
CPALA Lazarito Armenteros 150.00 400.00
CPALAL Luis Almanzar 100.00 250.00
CPALCA Luis Carpio 40.00 100.00
CPALT Leody Taveras 300.00 600.00
CPANS Nick Senzel 500.00 1000.00
CPAPW Patrick Weigel 50.00 120.00
CPARA Ronald Acuna 4000.00 8000.00
CPATF T.J. Friedl 60.00 150.00
CPATS Thomas Szapucki 60.00 150.00
CPAYCC Yu-Cheng Chang 75.00 200.00
CPAYD Yusniel Diaz 200.00 500.00

2017 Bowman Chrome Prospect Autographs Orange Wave Refractors

*ORANGE WAVE REF: 3X TO 8X BASIC
STATED PRINT RUN 25 SER.#'d SETS
BOW.CHR.EXCH.DEADLINE 8/31/2019
CPAACA Andrew Calica 50.00 120.00
CPACS Cole Stobbe 40.00 100.00
CPAJS Jesus Sanchez 300.00 800.00
CPALA Lazarito Armenteros 150.00 400.00
CPALT Leody Taveras 300.00 600.00
CPAYD Yusniel Diaz 200.00 500.00

2017 Bowman Chrome Prospect Autographs Purple Refractors

*PURPLE REF: .6X TO 1.5X BASIC
BOW.CHR.STATED ODDS 1:118 HOBBY
BOW.STATED ODDS 1:293 HOBBY
STATED PRINT RUN 250 SER.#'d SETS
BOW.EXCH.DEADLINE 3/31/2019
BOW.CHR.EXCH.DEADLINE 8/31/2019
CPAEJ Eloy Jimenez 250.00 600.00
CPAJS Jesus Sanchez 40.00 100.00
CPAKM Kevin Maitan 50.00 120.00
CPALA Lazarito Armenteros 30.00 80.00

2017 Bowman Chrome Prospect Autographs Refractors

*REF: .5X TO 1.2X BASIC
BOW.STATED ODDS 1:147 HOBBY
BOW.CHR.ODDS 1:59 HOBBY
STATED PRINT RUN 499 SER.#'D SETS
BOW.EXCH.DEADLINE 3/31/2019
BOW.CHR.EXCH.DEADLINE 8/31/2019
CPALA Lazarito Armenteros 25.00 60.00

2017 Bowman Chrome Prospects

COMPLETE SET (250) 100.00 250.00
BOW.PLATE ODDS 1:5838 HOBBY
BOW.CHR.PLATE ODDS 1:4116 HOBBY
PLATE PRINT RUN 1 SET PER COLOR
NO PLATE PRICING DUE TO SCARCITY
BCP1 Nick Senzel .75 2.00
BCP2 Gavin Lux 1.50 4.00
BCP3 Ronald Guzman .30 .75
BCP4 A.J. Puckett .25 .60
BCP5 Mike Soroka .75 2.00
BCP6 Roniel Raudes .25 .60
BCP7 Lucas Erceg .30 .75
BCP8 Luis Almanzar .25 .60
BCP9 Beau Burrows .25 .60
BCP10 Chase Vallot .25 .60
BCP11 P.J. Conlon .25 .60
BCP12 Erick Fedde .25 .60
BCP13 Rookie Davis .25 .60
BCP14 Chris Shaw .25 .60
BCP15 Nick Burdi .25 .60
BCP16 Clint Frazier .50 1.25
BCP17 Luiz Gohara .25 .60
BCP18 Lourdes Gurriel Jr. .40 1.00
BCP19 Eric Jenkins .25 .60
BCP20 Angel Perdomo .25 .60
BCP21 Dustin May 1.50 4.00
BCP22 Freddy Peralta .40 1.00
BCP23 Jarlin Garcia .25 .60
BCP24 Tyler O'Neill .30 .75
BCP25 Lazarito Armenteros .60 1.50
BCP26 Paul DeJong .75 2.00
BCP27 Antonio Senzatela .25 .60
BCP28 Kyle Tucker .50 1.25
BCP29 Aramis Garcia .25 .60
BCP30 Willie Calhoun .40 1.00
BCP31 Chance Adams .40 1.00
BCP32 Vladimir Guerrero Jr. 3.00 8.00
BCP33 Braxton Garrett .25 .60
BCP34 Yeudy Garcia .25 .60
BCP35 Dane Dunning .25 .60
BCP36 Andy Ibanez .25 .60
BCP37 Francisco Rios .25 .60
BCP38 Joe Jimenez .25 .60
BCP39 Dylan Cozens .25 .60
BCP40 Mauricio Dubon .30 .75
BCP41 Franklyn Kilome .30 .75
BCP42 Chance Sisco .50 1.25
BCP43 Sandy Alcantara .30 .75
BCP44 Stephen Gonsalves .25 .60
BCP45 Grant Holmes .25 .60
BCP46 Dakota Chalmers .25 .60
BCP47 Kolby Allard .25 .60
BCP48 Tyler Alexander .25 .60
BCP49 Phil Bickford .25 .60
BCP50 Eloy Jimenez 1.00 2.50
BCP51 Francisco Mejia .40 1.00
BCP52 Kohl Stewart .25 .60
BCP53 Garrett Whitley .25 .60
BCP54 Anderson Espinoza .25 .60
BCP55 Cal Quantrill .25 .60
BCP56 Tetsuto Yamada .50 1.25
BCP57 Tyler Beede .25 .60
BCP58 Jake Bauers .30 .75
BCP59 Ariel Jurado .25 .60
BCP60 Austin Voth .25 .60
BCP61 Tyler Stephenson .25 .60
BCP62 Yoshitomo Tsutsugo .40 1.00
BCP63 Dominic Smith .25 .60
BCP64 Matt Thaiss .25 .60
BCP65 Austin Meadows .40 1.00
BCP66 Mitch Keller .30 .75
BCP67 Jahmai Jones .25 .60
BCP68 Alex Speas .25 .60
BCP69 Nolan Jones .40 1.00
BCP70 Kevin Newman .40 1.00
BCP71 T.J. Friedl .25 .60
BCP72 Oscar De La Cruz .25 .60
BCP73 Victor Robles .60 1.50
BCP74 Patrick Weigel .25 .60
BCP75 Ryan Mountcastle .40 1.00
BCP76 Amed Rosario .40 1.00
BCP77 Nick Solak .60 1.50
BCP78 Abrahan Gutierrez .40 1.00
BCP79 Yu-Cheng Chang .40 1.00
BCP80 Gleyber Torres 4.00 10.00
BCP81 J.D. Davis .30 .75
BCP82 Walker Buehler .60 1.50
BCP83 Andrew Sopko .25 .60
BCP84 Brent Honeywell .30 .75
BCP85 Kyle Funkhouser .30 .75
BCP86 Brian Mundell .25 .60
BCP87 Brian Anderson .30 .75
BCP88 Brendan Rodgers .30 .75
BCP89 Josh Staumont .25 .60
BCP90 Cody Sedlock .25 .60
BCP91 D.J. Stewart .25 .60
BCP92 Wuilmer Becerra .25 .60
BCP93 Nate Smith .25 .60
BCP94 Alfredo Rodriguez .30 .75
BCP95 Daz Cameron .25 .60
BCP96 Taylor Ward .30 .75
BCP97 Takahiro Norimoto .25 .60
BCP98 Tomoyuki Sugano .40 1.00
BCP99 Drew Jackson .25 .60
BCP100 Kevin Maitan .60 1.50
BCP101 Rafael Devers .50 1.25
BCP102 Alex Kirilloff .60 1.50
BCP103 Jack Flaherty .40 1.00
BCP104 Adonis Medina .40 1.00
BCP105 Ke'Bryan Hayes .25 .60
BCP106 Josh Hader .25 .60
BCP107 Luis Urias 1.00 2.50
BCP108 Donnie Dewees .25 .60
BCP109 Kyle Freeland .30 .75
BCP110 Matt Chapman .40 1.00
BCP111 Sam Coonrod .25 .60
BCP112 Andrew Suarez .25 .60
BCP113 David Fletcher .75 2.00
BCP114 Tyler Jay .25 .60
BCP115 Franklin Barreto .25 .60
BCP116 Michael Kopech .50 1.25
BCP117 Rhys Hoskins 1.00 2.50
BCP118 Triston McKenzie .75 2.00
BCP119 Luis Garcia .75 2.00
BCP120 Harold Ramirez .30 .75
BCP121 Blake Rutherford .40 1.00
BCP122 Matt Manning .40 1.00
BCP123 Josh Morgan .25 .60
BCP124 Dylan Cease .60 1.50
BCP125 Kyle Lewis .50 1.25
BCP126 Nick Neidort .25 .60
BCP127 Ronald Acuna 40.00 100.00
BCP128 Luis Ortiz .25 .60
BCP129 Isael Soto .25 .60
BCP130 Adrian Morejon .40 1.00
BCP131 Mark Zagunis .25 .60
BCP132 Justus Sheffield .40 1.00
BCP133 Jaime Schultz .25 .60
BCP134 Fernando Romero .25 .60
BCP135 Mickey Moniak .60 1.50
BCP136 Jorge Bonifacio .25 .60
BCP137 Jomar Reyes .25 .60
BCP138 Thomas Szapucki .30 .75
BCP139 Sean Reid-Foley .25 .60
BCP140 Willy Adames .30 .75
BCP141 Yang Hyeon-Jong .30 .75
BCP142 Bo Bichette 1.00 2.50
BCP143 Harrison Bader .40 1.00
BCP144 Travis Demeritte .25 .60
BCP145 Juan Hillman .25 .60
BCP146 Francis Martes .30 .75
BCP147 Wilkerman Garcia .30 .75
BCP148 Christin Stewart .30 .75
BCP149 Cody Bellinger 4.00 10.00
BCP150 Jason Groome .50 1.25
BCP151 Amed Rosario .40 1.00
BCP152 Andrew Moore .30 .75
BCP153 Albert Abreu .30 .75
BCP154 Max Schrock .40 1.00
BCP155 Jonathan Arauz .30 .75
BCP156 Max Fried 1.00 2.50
BCP157 Bobby Bradley .30 .75
BCP158 Leody Taveras .75 2.00
BCP159 Jacob Nottingham .25 .60
BCP160 Fernando Tatis Jr. 2.00 5.00
BCP161 Austin Riley .75 2.00
BCP162 Trevor Clifton .25 .60
BCP163 Anthony Banda .25 .60
BCP164 Richard Urena .40 1.00
BCP165 Reggie Lawson .25 .60
BCP166 Felix Jorge .25 .60
BCP167 Clint Frazier .50 1.25
BCP168 Jorge Ona .30 .75
BCP169 Brandon Woodruff .30 .75
BCP170 Sam Travis .25 .60
BCP171 Derek Fisher .30 .75
BCP172 Touki Toussaint .30 .75
BCP173 Forrest Whitley .75 2.00
BCP174 Scott Kingery .40 1.00
BCP175 Jorge Mateo .25 .60
BCP176 Joshua Lowe .25 .60
BCP177 Rowdy Tellez .25 .60
BCP178 Kevin Kramer .25 .60
BCP179 Desmond Lindsay .25 .60
BCP180 Juan Soto 10.00 25.00
BCP181 Isan Diaz .60 1.50
BCP182 Rob Kaminsky .25 .60
BCP183 Domingo Acevedo .25 .60
BCP184 Brian Anderson .30 .75
BCP185 Andy Yerzy .25 .60
BCP186 Brent Honeywell .30 .75
BCP187 Tirso Ornelas .30 .75
BCP188 Rafael Devers .50 1.25
BCP189 Adam Ravenelle .25 .60
BCP190 Mitchell White .40 1.00
BCP191 Dawel Lugo .25 .60
BCP192 Vladimir Gutierrez .25 .60
BCP193 Max Povse .25 .60
BCP194 Delvin Perez .40 1.00
BCP195 Jacob Nix .25 .60
BCP196 Josh Sborz .25 .60
BCP197 Torii Hunter Jr. .60 1.50
BCP198 Jaime Schultz .25 .60
BCP199 Yasel Antuna 1.25 3.00
BCP200 Jason Groome .50 1.25
BCP201 Nick Gordon .25 .60
BCP202 Brett Phillips .30 .75
BCP203 Yairo Munoz .25 .60
BCP204 Bryan Reynolds .40 1.00
BCP205 Dakota Hudson .40 1.00
BCP206 Miguelangel Sierra .50 1.25
BCP207 Jazz Chisholm 1.00 2.50
BCP208 DJ Peters .60 1.50
BCP209 Jacob Faria .25 .60
BCP210 Sixto Sanchez .60 1.50
BCP211 Braden Bishop .40 1.00
BCP212 Ryan O'Hearn .50 1.25
BCP213 Garrett Stubbs .25 .60
BCP214 Paul DeJong .75 2.00
BCP215 Trent Clark .25 .60
BCP216 Jose Albertos .60 1.50
BCP217 Ryan McMahon .25 .60
BCP218 Khalil Lee .40 1.00
BCP219 Victor Robles .60 1.50
BCP220 Steven Duggar .25 .60
BCP221 Franklin Perez .40 1.00
BCP222 Tomas Nido .25 .60
BCP223 Justin Dunn .25 .60
BCP224 Austin Hays .60 1.50
BCP225 Nick Senzel .75 2.00
BCP226 Starling Heredia .50 1.25
BCP227 Bryson Brigman .25 .60
BCP228 Jesus Sanchez 1.25 3.00
BCP229 Yusniel Diaz .75 2.00
BCP230 Eloy Jimenez 1.00 2.50
BCP231 Brendan Rodgers .30 .75
BCP232 Ian Anderson .60 1.50
BCP233 Mark Zagunis .25 .60
BCP234 Jameson Fisher .25 .60
BCP235 Michael Kopech .50 1.25
BCP236 Keegan Akin .30 .75
BCP237 James Kaprielian .25 .60
BCP238 Jeisson Rosario .30 .75
BCP239 Carter Kieboom .40 1.00
BCP240 Nick Williams .30 .75
BCP241 Brandon Marsh .60 1.50
BCP242 Wander Javier .25 .60
BCP243 Chris Paddack .60 1.50
BCP244 Luis Alexander Basabe .40 1.00
BCP245 Zack Burdi .25 .60
BCP246 Anthony Kay .25 .60
BCP247 Anderson Tejeda .25 .60
BCP248 Daniel Gossett .25 .60
BCP249 Heath Quinn .30 .75
BCP250 Gleyber Torres 4.00 10.00

2017 Bowman Chrome Prospects 70th Blue Refractors

*70TH BLUE REF: 1.5X TO 4X BASIC
BOW.ODDS 1:94 HOBBY
BOW.CHR.ODDS 1:45 HOBBY
BCP1 Nick Senzel 5.00 12.00
BCP127 Ronald Acuna 150.00 400.00

2017 Bowman Chrome Prospects Blue Refractors

*BLUE REF: 2X TO 5X BASIC
BOW.ODDS 1:157 HOBBY
BOW.CHR.ODDS 1:60 HOBBY
STATED PRINT RUN 150 SER.#'d SETS
BCP1 Nick Senzel 12.00 30.00
BCP127 Ronald Acuna 200.00 500.00

2017 Bowman Chrome Prospects Blue Shimmer Refractors

*BLUE SHIMMER: 2X TO 5X BASIC
BOW.ODDS 1:157 HOBBY
BOW.CHR.ODDS 1:60 HOBBY
BCP151-BCP250 PRINT RUN 150 SER.#'d SETS
BCP1 Nick Senzel 6.00 15.00
BCP127 Ronald Acuna 200.00 500.00

2017 Bowman Chrome Prospects Gold Refractors

*GOLD REF: 5X TO 12X BASIC
BOW.ODDS 1:469 HOBBY
BOW.CHR.ODDS 1:178 HOBBY
STATED PRINT RUN 50 SER.#'d SETS
BCP1 Nick Senzel 40.00 100.00
BCP127 Ronald Acuna 500.00 1200.00
BCP226 Starling Heredia 20.00 50.00

2017 Bowman Chrome Prospects Gold Shimmer Refractors

*GOLD REF: 5X TO 12X BASIC
BOW.ODDS 1:469 HOBBY
BOW.CHR.ODDS 1:178 HOBBY
BCP1 Nick Senzel 40.00 100.00
BCP127 Ronald Acuna 500.00 1200.00
BCP226 Starling Heredia 20.00 50.00

2017 Bowman Chrome Prospects Green Refractors

*GREEN REF: 2.5X TO 6X BASIC
RANDOMLY INSERTED IN RETAIL PACKS
BOW.CHR.ODDS 1:90 HOBBY
STATED PRINT RUN 99 SER.#'d SETS
BCP1 Nick Senzel 20.00 50.00
BCP127 Ronald Acuna 250.00 600.00

2017 Bowman Chrome Prospects Green Shimmer Refractors

*GRN SHIM REF: 2.5X TO 6X BASIC
RANDOMLY INSERTED IN RETAIL PACKS
BOW.CHR.ODDS 1:90 HOBBY
STATED PRINT RUN 99 SER.#'d SETS
BCP1 Nick Senzel 20.00 50.00
BCP127 Ronald Acuna 250.00 600.00

2017 Bowman Chrome Prospects Orange Refractors

*ORANGE REF: 8X TO 20X BASIC
BOW.ODDS 1:203 HOBBY
BOW.CHR.ODDS 1:356 HOBBY
STATED PRINT RUN 25 SER.#'d SETS
BCP1 Nick Senzel 50.00 120.00
BCP127 Ronald Acuna 800.00 2000.00

2017 Bowman Chrome Prospects Orange Shimmer Refractors

*ORNG SHIM REF/25: 8X TO 20X BASIC
BOW.ODDS 1:203 HOBBY
BOW.CHR.ODDS 1:356 HOBBY
STATED PRINT RUN 25 SER.#'d SETS
BCP1 Nick Senzel 50.00 120.00
BCP127 Ronald Acuna 800.00 2000.00

2017 Bowman Chrome Prospects Purple Refractors

*PURPLE REF: 2X TO 5X BASIC
BOW.ODDS 1:94 HOBBY
BOW.CHR.ODDS 1:36 HOBBY
STATED PRINT RUN 250 SER.#'d SETS
BCP1 Nick Senzel 6.00 15.00
BCP127 Ronald Acuna 200.00 500.00

2017 Bowman Chrome Prospects Purple Shimmer Refractors

*PRPLE SHIMMER: 2X TO 5X BASIC
STATED ODDS 1:36 HOBBY

2017 Bowman Chrome Prospects Refractors

*REF: 1.5X TO 4X BASIC
BOW.ODDS 1:47 HOBBY
BOW.CHR.ODDS 1:18 HOBBY
STATED PRINT RUN 499 SER.#'d SETS
BCP1 Nick Senzel 5.00 12.00
BCP127 Ronald Acuna 150.00 400.00

2017 Bowman Chrome Refractors That Never Were

STATED ODDS 1:179 HOBBY
STATED PRINT RUN 499 SER.#'d SETS
RTNWAP Andy Pettitte 2.00 5.00
RTNWBW Bernie Williams 2.00 5.00
RTNWCS Curt Schilling 2.00 5.00
RTNWDJ Derek Jeter 6.00 15.00
RTNWIR Ivan Rodriguez 2.00 5.00
RTNWMI Monte Irvin 2.00 5.00
RTNWRK Ralph Kiner 2.00 5.00
RTNWRR Robin Roberts 2.00 5.00
RTNWRS Red Schoendienst 2.00 5.00
RTNWWS Warren Spahn 2.00 5.00

2017 Bowman Chrome Refractors That Never Were Orange Refractors

*ORANGE REF: 1X TO 2.5X BASIC
STATED ODDS 1:3569 HOBBY
STATED PRINT RUN 25 SER.#'d SETS
RTNWDJ Derek Jeter 25.00 60.00

2017 Bowman Chrome Refractors That Never Were Autographs

STATED ODDS 1:3134 HOBBY
PRINT RUNS B/WN 30-99 COPIES PER
EXCHANGE DEADLINE 8/31/2019
RTNWAP Andy Pettitte/99 20.00 50.00
RTNWBW Bernie Williams/99
RTNWDJ Derek Jeter/30 400.00 800.00
RTNWIR Ivan Rodriguez/99 15.00 40.00

2017 Bowman Chrome Rookie Autographs

BOW.STATED ODDS 1:260 HOBBY
2017 Bowman Chrome Prospect Autographs Orange Refractors
BOW.PLATE ODDS 1:48,253 HOBBY
PLATE PRINT RUN 1 SET PER COLOR
BLACK-CYAN-MAGENTA-YELLOW ISSUED
NO PLATE PRICING DUE TO SCARCITY
BOW.EXCH.DEADLINE 3/31/2019
2017 Bowman Chrome Prospect Autographs Orange Refractors
BCARAB A.Bregman Htting 20.00 50.00
BCARAG Amir Garrett 3.00 8.00
BCARBZ Bradley Zimmer 4.00 10.00
BCARCA Christian Arroyo 5.00 12.00
BCARCB Cody Bellinger 125.00 300.00
BCARGC Gavin Cecchini 3.00 8.00
BCARHD Hunter Dozier 6.00 15.00
BCARJDL De Leon TB jrsy 3.00 8.00
BCARJH Jeff Hoffman 3.00 8.00
BCARJHA Josh Hader 3.00 8.00
BCARJT Jake Thompson 3.00 8.00
BCARMM Manny Margot 3.00 8.00
BCARRG Robert Gsellman 3.00 8.00
BCARRL Reynaldo Lopez 3.00 8.00
BCARTM Trey Mancini 8.00 20.00
BCARYG Gurriel Ornge jrsy 12.00 30.00
BCARYM Moncada CHI jrsy 25.00 60.00
CRAAB Bregman Trwng 20.00 50.00
CRAABE Andrew Benintendi 15.00 40.00
CRAAJ Aaron Judge 125.00 300.00
CRAAR Alex Reyes 4.00 10.00
CRACF Carson Fulmer 3.00 8.00
CRADD David Dahl 4.00 10.00
CRADS Dansby Swanson 20.00 50.00
CRAHR Hunter Renfroe 4.00 10.00
CRAJA Jorge Alfaro 4.00 10.00
CRAJCO Jharel Cotton 3.00 8.00
CRAJDL De Leon LAD jrsy 3.00 8.00
CRAJMU Joe Musgrove 3.00 8.00
CRART Raimel Tapia 4.00 10.00
CRATA Tyler Austin 5.00 12.00
CRATG Tyler Glasnow 6.00 15.00
CRAYG Gurriel Blue jrsy 12.00 30.00
CRAYM Moncada CHI jrsy 40.00 100.00

2017 Bowman Chrome Rookie Autographs Blue Refractors

*BLUE REF: .6X TO 1.5X BASIC
BOW.STATED ODDS 1:1300 HOBBY
BOW.CHR.STATED ODDS 1:519 HOBBY
PRINT RUNS B/WN 125-150 COPIES PER1
BOW.EXCH.DEADLINE 3/31/2019
BOW.CHR.EXCH.DEADLINE 8/31/2019
CRAAB Bregman Trwng 30.00 80.00
CRAABE Andrew Benintendi 40.00 100.00
CRAAJ Aaron Judge 300.00 600.00

2017 Bowman Chrome Rookie Autographs Gold Refractors

*GOLD REF: 1.2X TO 3X BASIC
BOW.STATED ODDS 1:3892 HOBBY
BOW.CHR.STATED ODDS 1:1559 HOBBY
STATED PRINT RUN 50 SER.#'d SETS
BOW.EXCH.DEADLINE 3/31/2019
BOW.CHR.EXCH.DEADLINE 8/31/2019
BCARCB Cody Bellinger 400.00 800.00
CRAAB Bregman Trwng 60.00 150.00
CRAABE Andrew Benintendi 75.00 200.00
CRAAJ Aaron Judge 400.00 800.00
CRAYM Moncada CHI jrsy 150.00 400.00

2017 Bowman Chrome Rookie Autographs Green Refractors

*GREEN REF: .6X TO 1.5X BASIC
RANDOM INSERTS IN BOW.RETAIL PACKS
BOW.CHR.STATED ODDS 1:786 HOBBY
STATED PRINT RUN 99 SER.#'d SETS
BOW.EXCH.DEADLINE 3/31/2019
BOW.CHR.EXCH.DEADLINE 8/31/2019
CRAAB Bregman Trwng 30.00 80.00
CRAABE Andrew Benintendi 40.00 100.00
CRAAJ Aaron Judge 300.00 600.00
CRAYM Moncada CHI jrsy 75.00 200.00

2017 Bowman Chrome Rookie Autographs Orange Refractors

*ORANGE REF: 2.5X TO 6X BASIC
BOW.STATED ODDS 1:1983 HOBBY
BOW.CHR.STATED ODDS 1:1734 HOBBY
STATED PRINT RUN 25 SER.#'d SETS
BOW.EXCH.DEADLINE 3/31/2019
BOW.CHR.EXCH.DEADLINE 8/31/2019
BCARCB Cody Bellinger 1000.00 1500.00
CRAAB Bregman Trwng 125.00 300.00
CRAABE Andrew Benintendi 150.00 400.00
CRAAJ Aaron Judge 500.00 1000.00
CRAYM Moncada CHI jrsy 200.00 500.00

2017 Bowman Chrome Rookie Autographs Refractors

*REF: .5X TO 1.2X BASIC
BOW.STATED ODDS 1:391 HOBBY
BOW.CHR.STATED ODDS 1:156 HOBBY
STATED PRINT RUN 499 SER.#'d SETS
BOW.EXCH.DEADLINE 3/31/2019
BOW.CHR.EXCH.DEADLINE 8/31/2019

2017 Bowman Chrome Rookie of the Year Favorites Autographs

STATED ODDS 1:1951 HOBBY
STATED PRINT RUN 150 SER.#'d SETS
EXCHANGE DEADLINE 3/31/2019
*ORANGE/25: .75X TO 2X BASIC
ROYFAB Alex Bregman 20.00 50.00
ROYFABE Andrew Benintendi 50.00 120.00
ROYFAJ Aaron Judge 100.00 250.00
ROYFDD David Dahl 6.00 15.00
ROYFDS Dansby Swanson 15.00 40.00
ROYFHR Hunter Renfroe 8.00 20.00
ROYFJDL Jose De Leon 5.00 12.00
ROYFTG Tyler Glasnow 6.00 15.00
ROYFYG Yulieski Gurriel 8.00 20.00
ROYFYM Yoan Moncada 50.00 120.00

2017 Bowman Chrome Rookie of the Year Favorites Refractors

COMPLETE SET (15) 6.00 15.00
STATED ODDS 1:8 HOBBY
*GREEN/99: 1.5X TO 4X BASIC
*GOLD/50: 3X TO 8X BASIC
*ORANGE/25: 4X TO 10X BASIC
ROYF1 Yoan Moncada 1.25 3.00
ROYF2 Dansby Swanson 1.00 2.50
ROYF3 Alex Bregman 1.50 4.00
ROYF4 Yulieski Gurriel .60 1.50
ROYF5 Andrew Benintendi 1.25 3.00
ROYF6 Jose De Leon .40 1.00
ROYF7 Tyler Glasnow .50 1.25
ROYF8 David Dahl .50 1.25
ROYF9 Aaron Judge 3.00 8.00
ROYF10 Orlando Arcia .60 1.50
ROYF11 Hunter Renfroe .50 1.25
ROYF12 Josh Bell 1.00 2.50
ROYF13 Carson Fulmer .40 1.00
ROYF14 Alex Reyes .50 1.25
ROYF15 Jharel Cotton .40 1.00

2017 Bowman Chrome Scouts Top 100 Autographs

STATED ODDS 1:1668 HOBBY
PRINT RUNS B/WN 50-150 COPIES PER
EXCHANGE DEADLINE 3/31/2019
BTP1 Yoan Moncada 50.00 120.00
BTP2 Alex Reyes 10.00 25.00
BTP3 Dansby Swanson 30.00 80.00
BTP4 Andrew Benintendi 75.00 200.00
BTP5 Lucas Giolito 12.00 30.00
BTP12 Brendan Rodgers 15.00 40.00
BTP13 Nick Senzel 60.00 150.00
BTP24 Jason Groome 50.00 120.00
BTP25 Riley Pint 20.00 50.00
BTP26 Corey Ray 6.00 15.00
BTP29 A.J. Puk 8.00 20.00
BTP31 Ian Anderson 30.00 80.00
BTP35 A.J. Reed 5.00 12.00
BTP39 Jorge Mateo 15.00 40.00
BTP40 Francisco Mejia 25.00 60.00
BTP43 Francis Martes 5.00 12.00
BTP44 Brent Honeywell 8.00 20.00
BTP45 Aaron Judge 100.00 250.00
BTP46 Ian Happ 30.00 80.00
BTP50 Luke Weaver 6.00 15.00
BTP54 Forrest Whitley 8.00 20.00
BTP55 Cody Reed 8.00 20.00
BTP56 Sean Newcomb 6.00 15.00
BTP57 Cal Quantrill 5.00 12.00
BTP59 Leody Taveras 30.00 80.00
BTP60 Juan Soto 125.00 300.00
BTP65 Trent Clark 5.00 12.00
BTP70 Cody Sedlock 8.00 20.00
BTP74 Kyle Tucker 25.00 60.00
BTP79 Delvin Perez 30.00 80.00
BTP82 Bradley Zimmer 15.00 40.00
BTP83 Matt Thaiss 10.00 25.00
BTP84 Gavin Lux 8.00 20.00
BTP90 James Kaprielian 12.00 30.00
BTP91 Phil Bickford 5.00 12.00

2017 Bowman Chrome Scouts Top 100 Refractors

STATED ODDS 1:8 HOBBY
*GREEN/99: .1X TO 2.5X BASIC
*GOLD/50: 2X TO 5X BASIC
*ORANGE/25: 3X TO 8X BASIC
BTP1 Yoan Moncada 1.25 3.00
BTP2 Alex Reyes .50 1.25
BTP3 Dansby Swanson 1.00 2.50
BTP4 Andrew Benintendi 1.25 3.00
BTP5 Lucas Giolito .50 1.25
BTP6 Tyler Glasnow .50 1.25
BTP7 Amed Rosario .60 1.50
BTP8 Eloy Jimenez 1.50 4.00
BTP9 J.P. Crawford .40 1.00
BTP10 Victor Robles 1.00 2.50
BTP11 Austin Meadows .60 1.50
BTP12 Brendan Rodgers .50 1.25
BTP13 Nick Senzel 1.25 3.00
BTP14 Rafael Devers .75 2.00
BTP15 Ozzie Albies 1.50 4.00
BTP16 Clint Frazier .75 2.00
BTP17 Cody Bellinger 6.00 15.00
BTP18 Jose De Leon .40 1.00
BTP19 Gleyber Torres 6.00 15.00
BTP20 Anderson Espinoza .40 1.00
BTP21 Mitch Keller .50 1.25
BTP22 Manny Margot .40 1.00
BTP23 Kolby Allard .40 1.00
BTP24 Jason Groome .75 2.00
BTP25 Riley Pint .40 1.00
BTP26 Corey Ray .50 1.25
BTP27 Mickey Moniak 1.00 2.50
BTP28 Lewis Brinson .60 1.50
BTP29 A.J. Puk .60 1.50
BTP30 Willy Adames .50 1.25
BTP31 Ian Anderson 1.00 2.50
BTP32 Michael Kopech .75 2.00
BTP33 Jeff Hoffman .40 1.00
BTP34 Kyle Lewis .75 2.00
BTP35 A.J. Reed .40 1.00
BTP36 Luis Ortiz .40 1.00
BTP37 Dominic Smith .40 1.00
BTP38 Josh Hader .40 1.00
BTP39 Jorge Mateo .40 1.00
BTP40 Francisco Mejia .60 1.50
BTP41 Josh Bell 1.00 2.50
BTP42 Tyler O'Neill .50 1.25
BTP43 Francis Martes .40 1.00
BTP44 Brent Honeywell .50 1.25
BTP45 Aaron Judge 5.00 12.00
BTP46 Ian Happ .75 2.00
BTP47 Zack Collins .50 1.25
BTP48 Nick Gordon .40 1.00
BTP49 Braxton Garrett .40 1.00
BTP50 Luke Weaver .50 1.25
BTP51 Anthony Alford .40 1.00
BTP52 Reynaldo Lopez .40 1.00

BTP53 Amir Garrett .40 1.00
BTP54 Forrest Whitley 1.25 3.00
BTP55 Cody Reed .40 1.00
BTP56 Sean Newcomb .50 1.25
BTP57 Kevin Newman .60 1.50
BTP58 Cal Quantrill .40 1.00
BTP59 Leody Taveras 1.25 3.00
BTP60 Juan Soto 8.00 20.00
BTP61 Brady Aiken 1.00 2.50
BTP62 Alex Verdugo .60 1.50
BTP63 Dylan Cease 1.00 2.50
BTP64 Yadier Alvarez .60 1.50
BTP65 Trent Clark .40 1.00
BTP66 Franklin Barreto .40 1.00
BTP67 Hunter Renfroe .50 1.25
BTP68 Jack Flaherty .60 1.50
BTP69 Matt Manning .60 1.50
BTP70 Cody Sedlock .40 1.00
BTP71 Carson Fulmer .40 1.00
BTP72 Trevor Clifton .40 1.00
BTP73 Robert Stephenson .40 1.00
BTP74 Kyle Tucker .75 2.00
BTP75 Jahmai Jones .40 1.00
BTP76 Franklyn Kilome .50 1.25
BTP77 Isan Diaz 1.00 2.50
BTP78 Justin Dunn .40 1.00
BTP79 Delvin Perez .60 1.50
BTP80 Erick Fedde .40 1.00
BTP81 Justus Sheffield .60 1.50
BTP82 Bradley Zimmer .50 1.25
BTP83 Matt Thaiss .40 1.00
BTP84 Gavin Lux 2.50 6.00
BTP85 Triston McKenzie .40 1.00
BTP86 Tyler Beede .40 1.00
BTP87 Sean Reid-Foley .40 1.00
BTP88 Blake Rutherford .60 1.50
BTP89 Chance Sisco .75 2.00
BTP90 James Kaprielian .40 1.00
BTP91 Phil Bickford .40 1.00
BTP92 Kevin Maitan 1.00 2.50
BTP93 Albert Almora .40 1.00
BTP94 Raimel Tapia .50 1.25
BTP95 Luis Urias 1.50 4.00
BTP96 Yohander Mendez .40 1.00
BTP97 Vladimir Guerrero Jr. 5.00 12.00
BTP98 Alex Kirilloff 1.00 2.50
BTP99 Matt Chapman .60 1.50
BTP100 Hunter Dozier .40 1.00

2017 Bowman Chrome Scouts Top 100 Update

STATED ODDS 1:3 HOBBY
*ORANGE/25: 2X TO 5X BASIC
BSUAH Alec Hansen .40 1.00
BSUAM Adonis Medina .60 1.50
BSUAR Adrian Rondon .50 1.25
BSUBB Bo Bichette 1.50 4.00
BSUCA Chance Adams .60 1.50
BSUCK Carson Kelly .50 1.25
BSUDC Dylan Cozens .40 1.00
BSUDD Dane Dunning .40 1.00
BSUDF Dustin Fowler .50 1.25
BSUFR Fernando Romero .40 1.00
BSUGH Garrett Hampson .60 1.50
BSUID Isan Diaz 1.00 2.50
BSUJJ Joe Jimenez .40 1.00
BSULC Luis Castillo 1.25 3.00
BSULE Lucas Erceg .50 1.25
BSULG Luiz Gohara .40 1.00
BSUMM Michael Matuella .50 1.25
BSUMS Mike Soroka 1.25 3.00
BSUPDJ Paul DeJong 1.25 3.00
BSURA Ronald Acuna 3.00 8.00
BSURR Roniel Raudes .40 1.00
BSUSG Stephen Gonsalves .40 1.00
BSUTS Thomas Szapucki .50 1.25
BSUTT Taylor Trammell .60 1.50
BSUWB Walker Buehler 1.00 2.50

2017 Bowman Chrome Scouts Top 100 Update Autographs

STATED ODDS 1:1039 HOBBY
STATED PRINT RUN 150 SER.#'d SETS
EXCHANGE DEADLINE 8/31/2019
BSUAH Alec Hansen 8.00 20.00
BSUAR Adrian Rondon 5.00 12.00
BSUBB Bo Bichette 25.00 60.00
BSUCK Carson Kelly 5.00 12.00
BSUDC Dylan Cozens 4.00 10.00
BSUDD Dane Dunning 4.00 10.00
BSUDF Dustin Fowler 5.00 12.00
BSUGH Garrett Hampson 6.00 15.00
BSUJJ Joe Jimenez 4.00 10.00
BSULE Lucas Erceg 8.00 20.00
BSUMM Michael Matuella 5.00 12.00
BSUPDJ Paul DeJong 8.00 20.00
BSURA Ronald Acuna 125.00 300.00
BSURR Roniel Raudes 4.00 10.00
BSUTS Thomas Szapucki 8.00 20.00
BSUTT Taylor Trammell 12.00 30.00
BSUWB Walker Buehler 15.00 40.00

2017 Bowman Chrome Sensation Autographs

STATED ODDS 1:786 HOBBY
STATED PRINT RUN 99 SER.#'d SETS
EXCHANGE DEADLINE 8/31/2019
CSAAA Albert Abreu 8.00 20.00
CSAAE Anderson Espinoza 5.00 12.00
CSABR Blake Rutherford 8.00 20.00
CSACR Corey Ray 6.00 15.00
CSAGT Gleyber Torres 40.00 100.00
CSAIA Ian Anderson 6.00 15.00
CSAJG Jason Groome 10.00 25.00
CSAJM Jorge Mateo 6.00 15.00
CSAKL Kyle Lewis 10.00 25.00
CSAKM Kevin Maitan 15.00 40.00
CSALA Lazarito Armenteros 12.00 30.00
CSALG Lourdes Gurriel Jr. 10.00 25.00
CSALT Leody Taveras 30.00 80.00
CSAMK Mitch Keller 6.00 15.00
CSAMM Mickey Moniak 12.00 30.00
CSANS Nick Senzel 30.00 80.00
CSASH Starling Heredia 10.00 25.00
CSASN Sean Newcomb 6.00 15.00
CSATC Trevor Clifton EXCH 5.00 12.00
CSATH Torii Hunter Jr. 12.00 30.00
CSAWC Willie Calhoun 15.00 40.00

2017 Bowman Chrome Sensation Autographs Gold Refractors

*GOLD REF: .6X TO 1.5X BASIC
STATED ODDS 1:1559 HOBBY
STATED PRINT RUN 50 SER.#'d SETS
EXCHANGE DEADLINE 8/31/2019
CSABR Blake Rutherford 10.00 25.00
CSAMM Mickey Moniak 15.00 40.00
CSANS Nick Senzel 40.00 100.00
CSASH Starling Heredia 50.00 120.00

2017 Bowman Chrome Sensation Autographs Orange Refractors

*ORANGE REF: .6X TO 1.5X BASIC
STATED ODDS 1:1734 HOBBY
STATED PRINT RUN 25 SER.#'d SETS
EXCHANGE DEADLINE 8/31/2019
CSAAA Albert Abreu 25.00 60.00
CSABR Blake Rutherford
CSAMM Mickey Moniak 20.00 50.00
CSANS Nick Senzel 50.00 120.00
CSASH Starling Heredia 60.00 150.00

2017 Bowman Chrome Talent Pipeline Refractors

COMPLETE SET (30) 20.00 50.00
STATED ODDS 1:12 HOBBY
*GREEN/99: .6X TO 1.5X BASIC
*GOLD/50: 1.2X TO 3X BASIC
*ORANGE/25: 2.5X TO 6X BASIC
TPARI Alex Young .40 1.00
Taylor Clarke
Anthony Banda
TPATL Allard/Albies/Ellis 1.50 4.00
TPBAL Sedlock/Lee/Sisco .75 2.00
TPBOS Devers/Tavarez/Travis .75 2.00
TPCHI Jimenez/Happ/Zagunis 1.50 4.00
TPCHW Zack Collins .50 1.25
Spencer Adams
Zack Burdi
TPCIN Senzel/Mahle/Garrett 1.25 3.00
TPCLE Francisco Mejia .60 1.50
Nellie Rodriguez
Bradley Zimmer
TPCOL Brendan Rodgers .50 1.25
Ryan McMahon
Kyle Freeland
TPDET Manning/Stewart/Jimenez .60 1.50
TPHOU Tuc/Mar/Fis .75 2.00
TPKCR Vallot/O'Hearn/Bonifacio .75 2.00
TPLAA Matt Thaiss 1.25 3.00
David Fletcher
Nate Smith
TPLAD Alvarez/Calhoun/Bellinger 6.00 15.00
TPMIA Stone Garrett .40 1.00
Austin Dean
J.T. Riddle
TPMIL Ray/Phillips/Brinson .60 1.50
TPMIN Nick Gordon .40 1.00
Tyler Jay
Jake Reed
TPNYM Dunn/Rosario/Nimmo .60 1.50
TPNYY Trrs/Shffld/Frzr 6.00 15.00
TPOAK Puk/Munoz/Barreto .60 1.50
TPPHI Moniak/Cozens/Crawford 1.00 2.50
TPPIT Mitch Keller .60 1.50
Kevin Newman
Austin Meadows
TPSDP Anderson Espinoza .50 1.25
Austin Allen
Dinelson Lamet
TPSEA Lewis/O'Neill/Peterson .75 2.00
TPSFG Reynolds/Arroyo/Blackburn .60 1.50
TPSTL Flaherty/Bader/Valera .60 1.50
TPTBR Joshua Lowe .50 1.25
Willy Adames
Jacob Faria
TPTEX Tvrs/Ibnz/Gzmn 1.25 3.00
TPTOR Sean Reid-Foley .60 1.50
Richard Urena
A.J. Jimenez
TPWAS Robles/Fedde/Voth 1.00 2.50

2017 Bowman Chrome Draft

COMPLETE SET (200) 20.00 50.00
STATED PLATE ODDS 1:1136 HOBBY
PLATE PRINT RUN 1 SET PER COLOR
BLACK-CYAN-MAGENTA-YELLOW ISSUED
NO PLATE PRICING DUE TO SCARCITY
BDC1 Royce Lewis 5.00 12.00
BDC2 Jacob Gonzalez .75 2.00
BDC3 Seth Elledge .25 .60
BDC4 Stuart Fairchild .30 .75
BDC5 Franklin Perez .40 1.00
BDC6 Jeter Downs .50 1.25
BDC7 Yu-Cheng Chang .40 1.00
BDC8 T.J. Friedl .25 .60
BDC9 Alex Scherff .40 1.00
BDC10 Nick Solak .60 1.50
BDC11 Lincoln Henzman .25 .60
BDC12 Heliot Ramos 3.00 8.00
BDC13 Riley Adams .30 .75
BDC14 Wyatt Mills .25 .60
BDC15 Alex Faedo .40 1.00
BDC16 Marcos Diplan .25 .60
BDC17 Daulton Varsho .30 .75
BDC18 Jacob Heatherly .25 .60
BDC19 Lourdes Gurriel Jr. .40 1.00
BDC20 Zach Kirtley .30 .75
BDC21 Cal Quantrill .25 .60
BDC22 Jacob Heyward .25 .60
BDC23 Alec Hansen .25 .60
BDC24 Quinn Brodey .25 .60
BDC25 MacKenzie Gore 4.00 10.00
BDC26 Mitch Keller .30 .75
BDC27 Joey Morgan .30 .75
BDC28 Juan Hillman .25 .60
BDC29 Freddy Peralta .40 1.00
BDC30 Morgan Cooper .30 .75
BDC31 Brett Netzer .50 1.25
BDC32 Alex Lange .40 1.00
BDC33 Hans Crouse .60 1.50
BDC34 Michael Kopech .50 1.25
BDC35 Cole Ragans .25 .60
BDC36 Kolby Allard .25 .60
BDC37 Matt Manning .40 1.00
BDC38 Bo Bichette 1.00 2.50
BDC39 Ronald Acuna 6.00 15.00
BDC40 Cristian Pache 1.25 3.00
BDC41 Ryan Vilade .40 1.00
BDC42 Tyler Freeman .25 .60
BDC43 Cory Abbott .25 .60
BDC44 Shane Baz .40 1.00
BDC45 Brian Miller .30 .75
BDC46 Luis Campusano .30 .75
BDC47 A.J. Puk .40 1.00
BDC48 Griffin Canning .40 1.00
BDC49 Justin Dunn .25 .60
BDC50 Jorge Mateo .25 .60
BDC51 Trevor Clifton .25 .60
BDC52 Carter Kieboom .40 1.00
BDC53 Trevor Rogers .40 1.00
BDC54 Tommy Doyle .25 .60
BDC55 Adam Hall .40 1.00
BDC56 Will Benson .25 .60
BDC57 Ariel Jurado .25 .60
BDC58 Forrest Whitley .75 2.00
BDC59 Daniel Tillo .40 1.00
BDC60 Austin Beck 1.00 2.50
BDC61 Jahmai Jones .25 .60
BDC62 Adonis Medina .40 1.00
BDC63 Blayne Enlow .30 .75
BDC64 Ryley Widell .40 1.00
BDC65 Tanner Houck 1.25 3.00
BDC66 Caden Lemons .25 .60
BDC67 Buddy Reed .25 .60
BDC68 T.J. Zeuch .25 .60
BDC69 Vladimir Gutierrez .25 .60
BDC70 Anderson Espinoza .25 .60
BDC71 Fernando Tatis Jr. 5.00 12.00
BDC72 Eloy Jimenez 1.00 2.50
BDC73 Jose Taveras .30 .75
BDC74 Christopher Seise .40 1.00
BDC75 Keston Hiura 2.00 5.00
BDC76 Charlie Barnes .25 .60
BDC77 Connor Seabold .25 .60
BDC78 David Peterson .30 .75
BDC79 Seth Corry .25 .60
BDC80 Blake Rutherford .40 1.00
BDC81 Conner Uselton .40 1.00
BDC82 D.L. Hall .30 .75
BDC83 Peter Alonso 2.50 6.00
BDC84 Glenn Otto .25 .60
BDC85 Gavin Sheets .40 1.00
BDC86 Luis Gonzalez .30 .75
BDC87 Taylor Walls .25 .60
BDC88 Ernie Clement .30 .75
BDC89 Dylan Carlson 1.50 4.00
BDC90 Drew Waters 1.50 4.00
BDC91 Christin Stewart .30 .75
BDC92 Cal Mitchell .50 1.25
BDC93 Troy Bacon .40 1.00
BDC94 Zac Lowther .30 .75
BDC95 Jo Adell 2.00 5.00
BDC96 Francisco Rios .25 .60
BDC97 Mason House .40 1.00
BDC98 Corey Ray .30 .75
BDC99 Anfernee Grier .25 .60
BDC100 Brendan McKay 1.00 2.50
BDC101 Kacy Clemens .30 .75
BDC102 Isan Diaz .60 1.50
BDC103 Drew Strotman .25 .60
BDC104 Will Gaddis .25 .60
BDC105 Jacob Pearson .25 .60
BDC106 Tyler Ivey .25 .60
BDC107 Nick Allen .30 .75
BDC108 Andy Ibanez .25 .60
BDC109 J.J. Matijevic .30 .75
BDC110 KJ Harrison .40 1.00
BDC111 Riley Pint .25 .60
BDC112 Franklyn Kilome .30 .75
BDC113 Peyton Remy .40 1.00
BDC114 Scott Kingery .40 1.00
BDC115 Adam Haseley .50 1.25
BDC116 Will Smith .60 1.50
BDC117 Anderson Tejeda .25 .60
BDC118 Quentin Holmes .30 .75
BDC119 Nate Pearson .60 1.50
BDC120 Kyle Wright .75 2.00
BDC121 Matthew Whatley .25 .60
BDC122 Brent Rooker .60 1.50
BDC123 Daulton Jefferies .30 .75
BDC124 Taylor Ward .30 .75
Missing card number
BDC125 Triston McKenzie .25 .60
BDC126 Scott Hurst .30 .75
BDC127 Noah Bremer .25 .60
BDC128 Angel Perdomo .25 .60
BDC129 Touki Toussaint .30 .75
BDC130 A.J. Puckett .25 .60
BDC131 Lucas Erceg .30 .75
BDC132 Riley Mahan .25 .60
BDC133 Corbin Martin .25 .60
BDC134 Jordan Sheffield .25 .60
BDC135 Lazarito Armenteros .60 1.50
BDC136 Dylan Cease .60 1.50
BDC137 Kevin Newman .40 1.00
BDC138 Hagen Danner .30 .75
BDC139 Mark Vientos .40 1.00
BDC140 Justus Sheffield .40 1.00
BDC141 Bubba Thompson .40 1.00
BDC142 Desmond Lindsay .25 .60
BDC143 J.B. Bukauskas .40 1.00
BDC144 Freddy Tarnok .30 .75
BDC145 Blake Hunt .25 .60
BDC146 David Thompson .30 .75
BDC147 Delvin Perez .40 1.00
BDC148 Peter Solomon .30 .75
BDC149 Brendan Murphy .25 .60
BDC150 Vladimir Guerrero Jr. 3.00 8.00
BDC151 Yusniel Diaz .75 2.00
BDC152 Dillon Tate .25 .60
BDC153 Nonie Williams .25 .60
BDC154 Kyle Lewis .50 1.25
BDC155 Bobby Dalbec .60 1.50
BDC156 Ian Anderson .60 1.50
BDC157 Brendan Rodgers .30 .75
BDC158 Drew Ellis .40 1.00
BDC159 Joseph Dunand .50 1.25
BDC160 Kevin Maitan .60 1.50
BDC161 Kramer Robertson .50 1.25
BDC162 Juan Soto 6.00 15.00
BDC163 Chris Okey .25 .60
BDC164 Tristen Lutz .40 1.00
BDC165 Wil Crowe .40 1.00
BDC166 Taylor Trammell .40 1.00
BDC167 Trevor Stephan .40 1.00
BDC168 Matt Tabor .25 .60
BDC169 James Marinan .40 1.00
BDC170 Cody Sedlock .25 .60
BDC171 Gavin Lux 1.50 4.00
BDC172 MJ Melendez .40 1.00
BDC173 Kade McClure .25 .60
BDC174 Dylan Busby .25 .60
BDC175 Kevin Merrell .30 .75
BDC176 Dawel Lugo .25 .60
BDC177 Jake Burger .50 1.25
BDC178 Evan White .40 1.00
BDC179 Carl Stajduhar .25 .60
BDC180 Connor Wong .40 1.00
BDC181 Canaan Smith .75 2.00
BDC182 Nick Raquet .25 .60
BDC183 Kyle Tucker .50 1.25
BDC184 Sam Carlson .30 .75
BDC185 Wuilmer Becerra .25 .60
Missing card number
BDC186 Dane Dunning .25 .60
BDC187 Joe Perez .30 .75
BDC188 Brendon Little .30 .75
BDC189 Will Craig .25 .60
BDC190 Ricardo De La Torre .25 .60
BDC191 Nick Gordon .25 .60
BDC192 Kevin Smith .25 .60
BDC193 Cole Brannen .40 1.00
BDC194 Logan Warmoth .40 1.00
BDC195 Pavin Smith .75 2.00
BDC196 Colton Hock .30 .75
BDC197 Clarke Schmidt .40 1.00
BDC198 Cash Case .40 1.00
BDC199 Luis Ortiz .25 .60
BDC200 Gleyber Torres 4.00 10.00

2017 Bowman Chrome Draft 70th Blue Refractors

*70TH BLUE REF: 2X TO 5X BASIC
STATED ODDS 1:23 HOBBY
STATED PRINT RUN 200 SER.#'d SETS
BDC1 Royce Lewis 30.00 80.00

2017 Bowman Chrome Draft Blue Refractors

*BLUE REF: 2X TO 5X BASIC
STATED ODDS 1:31 HOBBY
STATED PRINT RUN 150 SER.#'d SETS
BDC1 Royce Lewis 30.00 80.00

2017 Bowman Chrome Draft Facsimile Variations

STATED ODDS 1:173 HOBBY
BD1 Royce Lewis 12.00 30.00
BD25 MacKenzie Gore 6.00 15.00
BD60 Austin Beck 4.00 10.00
BD70 Anderson Espinoza 1.00 2.50
BD80 Blake Rutherford 8.00 20.00
BD95 Jo Adell 30.00 80.00
BD100 Brendan McKay 5.00 12.00
BD115 Adam Haseley 2.00 5.00
BD120 Kyle Wright 3.00 8.00
BD135 Lazarito Armenteros 4.00 10.00
BD140 Justus Sheffield 1.50 4.00
BD150 Vladimir Guerrero Jr. 12.00 30.00
BD160 Kevin Maitan 2.50 6.00
BD195 Pavin Smith 8.00 20.00

2017 Bowman Chrome Draft Gold Refractors

*GOLD REF: 5X TO 12X BASIC
STATED ODDS 1:91 HOBBY
STATED PRINT RUN 50 SER.#'d SETS
BDC1 Royce Lewis 75.00 200.00
BDC95 Jo Adell 40.00 100.00

2017 Bowman Chrome Draft Green Refractors

*GREEN REF: 2.5X TO 6X BASIC
STATED ODDS 1:46 HOBBY
STATED PRINT RUN 99 SER.#'d SETS
BDC1 Royce Lewis 40.00 100.00

2017 Bowman Chrome Draft Image Variation Autographs

STATED ODDS 1:898 HOBBY
STATED PRINT RUN 99 SER.#'d SETS
EXCHANGE DEADLINE 11/30/2019
BD1 Royce Lewis 150.00 300.00
BD25 MacKenzie Gore 75.00 200.00
BD60 Austin Beck 100.00 250.00
BD95 Jo Adell 250.00 500.00
BD100 Brendan McKay 150.00 400.00
BD115 Adam Haseley 60.00 150.00
BD120 Kyle Wright 50.00 120.00
BD160 Kevin Maitan 50.00 120.00

2017 Bowman Chrome Draft Orange Refractors

*ORANGE REF: 8X TO 20X BASIC
STATED ODDS 1:182 HOBBY
STATED PRINT RUN 25 SER.#'d SETS
BDC1 Royce Lewis 125.00 300.00
BDC95 Jo Adell 50.00 120.00

2017 Bowman Chrome Draft Purple Refractors

*PURPLE REF: 1.5X TO 4X BASIC
STATED ODDS 1:19 HOBBY
STATED PRINT RUN 250 SER.#'d SETS
BDC1 Royce Lewis 25.00 60.00

2017 Bowman Chrome Draft Refractors

*REFRACTORS: .75X TO 2X BASIC
RANDOM INSERTS IN PACKS

2017 Bowman Chrome Draft Sky Blue Refractors

*SKY BLUE REF: 1X TO 2.5X BASIC
STATED ODDS 1:8 HOBBY
STATED PRINT RUN 399 SER.#'d SETS
BDC1 Royce Lewis 15.00 40.00

2017 Bowman Chrome Draft Autographs

STATED ODDS 1:8 HOBBY
PRINTING PLATE ODDS 1:3917 HOBBY
PLATE PRINT RUN 1 SET PER COLOR
BLACK-CYAN-MAGENTA-YELLOW ISSUED
NO PLATE PRICING DUE TO SCARCITY
EXCHANGE DEADLINE 11/30/2019
CDAAB Austin Beck 10.00 25.00
CDAAF Alex Faedo 5.00 12.00
CDAAH Adam Haseley 8.00 20.00
CDABE Blayne Enlow 4.00 10.00
CDABH Blake Hunt 3.00 8.00
CDABM Brendan McKay 25.00 60.00
CDABMI Brian Miller 4.00 10.00
CDABMU Brendan Murphy 3.00 8.00
CDABN Brett Netzer 3.00 8.00
CDABR Brent Rooker 12.00 30.00
CDABT Bubba Thompson 8.00 20.00
CDACA Cory Abbott 3.00 8.00
CDACB Cole Brannen 5.00 12.00
CDACBA Charlie Barnes 3.00 8.00
CDACC Cash Case 5.00 12.00
CDACH Colton Hock 4.00 10.00
CDACL Caden Lemons 3.00 8.00
CDACMA Corbin Martin 3.00 8.00
CDACS Clarke Schmidt 10.00 25.00
CDACSE Christopher Seise 5.00 12.00
CDACW Connor Wong 5.00 12.00
CDADB Dylan Busby 3.00 8.00
CDADE Drew Ellis 5.00 12.00
CDADH D.L. Hall 8.00 20.00
CDADP David Peterson 4.00 10.00
CDADW Drew Waters 40.00 100.00
CDAEC Ernie Clement 4.00 10.00
CDAEW Evan White 30.00 80.00
CDAGC Griffin Canning 5.00 12.00
CDAGS Gavin Sheets 5.00 12.00
CDAHC Hans Crouse 5.00 12.00
CDAHD Hagen Danner 4.00 10.00
CDAHR Heliot Ramos 30.00 80.00
CDAJA Jo Adell 400.00 800.00
CDAJB Jake Burger 10.00 25.00
CDAJD Jeter Downs 30.00 80.00
CDAJJM J.J. Matijevic 6.00 15.00
CDAJM Joey Morgan 4.00 10.00
CDAJP Joe Perez 4.00 10.00
CDAJPE Jacob Pearson 3.00 8.00
CDAKC Kacy Clemens 4.00 10.00
CDAKH Keston Hiura 100.00 250.00
CDAKM Kevin Merrell 4.00 10.00
CDAKMC Kade McClure 3.00 8.00
CDAKS Kevin Smith 10.00 25.00
CDAKW Kyle Wright 12.00 30.00
CDALC Luis Campusano 20.00 50.00
CDALG Luis Gonzalez 4.00 10.00
CDALH Lincoln Henzman 3.00 8.00
CDALW Logan Warmoth 5.00 12.00
CDAMC Morgan Cooper 4.00 10.00
CDAMG MacKenzie Gore 50.00 120.00
CDAMJM MJ Melendez 5.00 12.00
CDAMT Matt Tabor 3.00 8.00
CDAMV Mark Vientos 25.00 60.00
CDANP Nick Pratto 5.00 12.00
CDANPE Nate Pearson 25.00 60.00
CDAPS Pavin Smith 5.00 12.00
CDAPSO Peter Solomon 4.00 10.00
CDAQB Quinn Brodey 3.00 8.00
CDAQH Quentin Holmes 6.00 15.00
CDARL Royce Lewis 60.00 150.00
CDARM Riley Mahan 3.00 8.00
CDARV Ryan Vilade 8.00 20.00
CDASB Shane Baz 12.00 30.00
CDASC Sam Carlson 4.00 10.00
CDASCO Seth Corry 10.00 25.00
CDASF Stuart Fairchild 4.00 10.00
CDATD Tommy Doyle 3.00 8.00
CDATH Tanner Houck 20.00 50.00
CDATL Tristen Lutz 5.00 12.00
CDATR Trevor Rogers 8.00 20.00
CDATW Taylor Walls 3.00 8.00
CDAWG Will Gaddis 3.00 8.00
CDAZK Zach Kirtley 4.00 10.00
CDAZL Zac Lowther 4.00 10.00

2017 Bowman Chrome Draft Autographs 70th Blue Refractors

*70TH BLUE REF: 1.5X TO 4X BASIC
STATED ODDS 1:223 HOBBY
STATED PRINT RUN 70 SER.#'d SETS
EXCHANGE DEADLINE 11/30/2019
CDADE Drew Ellis 30.00 80.00
CDALW Logan Warmoth 40.00 100.00
CDAPS Pavin Smith 50.00 120.00
CDARL Royce Lewis 400.00 1000.00
CDARV Ryan Vilade 50.00 125.00

2017 Bowman Chrome Draft Autographs Black Refractors

*BLACK REF: 1.5X TO 4X BASIC
STATED ODDS 1:124 HOBBY
STATED PRINT RUN 75 SER.#'d SETS
EXCHANGE DEADLINE 11/30/2019
CDADE Drew Ellis 30.00 80.00
CDALW Logan Warmoth 40.00 100.00
CDAPS Pavin Smith 50.00 120.00
CDARL Royce Lewis 400.00 1000.00
CDARV Ryan Vilade 50.00 125.00

2017 Bowman Chrome Draft Autographs Blue Refractors

*BLUE REF: 1X TO 2.5X BASIC
STATED ODDS 1:105 HOBBY
STATED PRINT RUN 150 SER.#'d SETS
EXCHANGE DEADLINE 11/30/2019
CDADE Drew Ellis 20.00 50.00
CDALW Logan Warmoth 25.00 60.00
CDAPS Pavin Smith 30.00 80.00
CDARL Royce Lewis 250.00 600.00
CDARV Ryan Vilade 30.00 80.00

2017 Bowman Chrome Draft Autographs Blue Wave Refractors

*BLUE WAVE REF: 1X TO 2.5X BASIC
STATED ODDS 1:105 HOBBY
STATED PRINT RUN 150 SER.#'d SETS
EXCHANGE DEADLINE 11/30/2019
CDADE Drew Ellis 20.00 50.00
CDALW Logan Warmoth 25.00 60.00
CDAPS Pavin Smith 30.00 80.00
CDARL Royce Lewis 250.00 600.00
CDARV Ryan Vilade 30.00 80.00

2017 Bowman Chrome Draft Autographs Gold Refractors

*GOLD REF: 2.5X TO 6X BASIC
STATED ODDS 1:313 HOBBY
STATED PRINT RUN 50 SER.#'d SETS
EXCHANGE DEADLINE 11/30/2019
CDADE Drew Ellis 50.00 120.00
CDAJA Jo Adell 1000.00 2000.00
CDALW Logan Warmoth 60.00 150.00
CDAPS Pavin Smith 75.00 200.00
CDARL Royce Lewis 600.00 1200.00
CDARV Ryan Vilade 75.00 200.00

2017 Bowman Chrome Draft Autographs Gold Wave Refractors

*GOLD WAVE REF: 2.5X TO 6X BASIC
STATED ODDS 1:313 HOBBY
STATED PRINT RUN 50 SER.#'d SETS
EXCHANGE DEADLINE 11/30/2019
CDADE Drew Ellis 50.00 120.00
CDAJA Jo Adell 1000.00 2000.00
CDALW Logan Warmoth 60.00 150.00
CDAPS Pavin Smith 75.00 200.00
CDARL Royce Lewis 600.00 1200.00
CDARV Ryan Vilade 75.00 200.00

2017 Bowman Chrome Draft Autographs Green Refractors

*GREEN REF: 1.2X TO 3X BASIC
STATED ODDS 1:158 HOBBY
STATED PRINT RUN 99 SER.#'d SETS
EXCHANGE DEADLINE 11/30/2019
CDADE Drew Ellis 25.00 60.00
CDALW Logan Warmoth 30.00 80.00
CDAPS Pavin Smith 40.00 100.00
CDARL Royce Lewis 300.00 800.00
CDARV Ryan Vilade 40.00 100.00

2017 Bowman Chrome Draft Autographs Orange Refractors

*ORANGE REF: 3X TO 8X BASIC
STATED ODDS 1:435 HOBBY
STATED PRINT RUN 25 SER.#'d SETS
EXCHANGE DEADLINE 11/30/2019
CDADE Drew Ellis 60.00 150.00
CDAJA Jo Adell 2000.00 3000.00
CDALW Logan Warmoth 75.00 200.00
CDAPS Pavin Smith 100.00 250.00
CDARL Royce Lewis 1200.00 1500.00
CDARV Ryan Vilade 100.00 250.00

2017 Bowman Chrome Draft Autographs Purple Refractors

*PURPLE REF: .6X TO 1.5X BASIC
STATED ODDS 1:63 HOBBY
STATED PRINT RUN 250 SER.#'d SETS
EXCHANGE DEADLINE 11/30/2019
CDAPS Pavin Smith 20.00 50.00
CDARL Royce Lewis 200.00 500.00
CDARV Ryan Vilade 20.00 50.00

2017 Bowman Chrome Draft Autographs Refractors

*REF: .5X TO 1.2X BASIC
STATED ODDS 1:32 HOBBY
STATED PRINT RUN 499 SER.#'d SETS
EXCHANGE DEADLINE 11/30/2019
CDARL Royce Lewis 150.00 400.00

2017 Bowman Chrome Draft Class of '17 Autographs

STATED ODDS 1:119 HOBBY
STATED PRINT RUN 250 SER.#'d SETS
EXCHANGE DEADLINE 11/30/2019
*GOLD/50: .75X TO 2X BASIC
C17AAB Austin Beck 10.00 25.00
C17AAF Alex Faedo 8.00 20.00
C17AAH Adam Haseley 12.00 30.00
C17ABM Brendan McKay 10.00 25.00
C17ABMC Brendan McKay 10.00 25.00
C17ABMI Brian Miller 6.00 15.00
C17ABR Brent Rooker 12.00 30.00
C17ACS Clarke Schmidt 8.00 20.00
C17ACSE Christopher Seise 8.00 20.00
C17ADP David Peterson 6.00 15.00
C17AEW Evan White 8.00 20.00
C17AJA Jo Adell 30.00 80.00
C17AJB Jake Burger 12.00 30.00
C17AJD Jeter Downs 10.00 25.00
C17AKH Keston Hiura 15.00 40.00
C17AKM Kevin Merrell 6.00 15.00
C17AKW Kyle Wright 10.00 25.00
C17ALW Logan Warmoth 8.00 20.00
C17AMG MacKenzie Gore 20.00 50.00
C17AMV Mark Vientos 12.00 30.00
C17ANPE Nate Pearson 12.00 30.00
C17APS Pavin Smith 15.00 40.00
C17AQH Quentin Holmes 20.00 50.00
C17ARL Royce Lewis 40.00 100.00
C17ARV Ryan Vilade 8.00 20.00
C17ASB Shane Baz 8.00 20.00
C17ATH Tanner Houck 25.00 60.00
C17ATL Tristen Lutz 8.00 20.00
C17ATR Trevor Rogers 8.00 20.00

2017 Bowman Chrome Draft Defining Moments

COMPLETE SET (21) 8.00 20.00
STATED ODDS 1:3 HOBBY
*REF/250: .5X TO 1.2X BASIC
*GOLD REF/50: 1.2X TO 3X BASIC
BDMAB Austin Beck 1.00 2.50
BDMAH Adam Haseley .50 1.25
BDMBM Brendan McKay 1.00 2.50
BDMBMC Brendan McKay 1.00 2.50
BDMCS Clarke Schmidt .40 1.00
BDMEJ Eloy Jimenez 1.00 2.50
BDMFT Fernando Tatis Jr. 2.00 5.00
BDMGT Gleyber Torres 4.00 10.00
BDMJA Jo Adell 2.00 5.00
BDMJB Jake Burger .50 1.25
BDMJM Jorge Mateo .25 .60
BDMKH Keston Hiura 1.25 3.00
BDMKM Kevin Maitan .60 1.50
BDMKW Kyle Wright .75 2.00
BDMMG MacKenzie Gore 1.50 4.00
BDMMM Mickey Moniak .60 1.50
BDMNS Nick Senzel .75 2.00
BDMPS Pavin Smith .75 2.00
BDMRA Ronald Acuna 4.00 10.00
BDMRL Royce Lewis 2.00 5.00

2017 Bowman Chrome Draft Defining Moments Autographs Refractors

STATED ODDS 1:600 HOBBY
STATED PRINT RUN 99 SER.#'d SETS
EXCHANGE DEADLINE 11/30/2019
*GOLD/50: .5X TO 1.2X BASIC
BDMAAB Austin Beck 25.00 60.00
BDMAAH Adam Haseley 15.00 40.00
BDMABM Brendan McKay 25.00 60.00
BDMABMC Brendan McKay 25.00 60.00
BDMACS Clarke Schmidt 6.00 15.00
BDMAGT Gleyber Torres 40.00 100.00
BDMAJA Jo Adell 30.00 80.00
BDMAKH Keston Hiura 25.00 60.00
BDMAKM Kevin Maitan 20.00 50.00
BDMAKW Kyle Wright
BDMAMG MacKenzie Gore 25.00 60.00
BDMAMM Mickey Moniak 15.00 40.00
BDMAPS Pavin Smith 12.00 30.00
BDMARL Royce Lewis

2017 Bowman Chrome Draft Draft Night Autographs

STATED ODDS 1:1796 HOBBY
STATED PRINT RUN 99 SER.#'d SETS
EXCHANGE DEADLINE 11/30/2019
DNAJA Jo Adell 125.00 300.00
DNATR Trevor Rogers 15.00 40.00

2017 Bowman Chrome Draft Draft Night Autographs Gold Refractors

*GOLD: .5X TO 1.2X BASIC
STATED ODDS 1:3570 HOBBY
STATED PRINT RUN 50 SER.#'d SETS

EXCHANGE DEADLINE 11/30/2019
ONAJA Jo Adell 150.00 400.00

2017 Bowman Chrome Draft MLB Draft History
COMPLETE SET (10) 4.00 10.00
STATED ODDS 1:6 HOBBY
*REF/250: 1.2X TO 3X BASIC
*GOLD REF/50: 3X TO 8X BASIC
MLBDAP Andy Pettitte .50 1.25
MLBDBL Barry Larkin .50 1.25
MLBDCF Carlton Fisk .50 1.25
MLBDDJ Derek Jeter 1.50 4.00
MLBDJT Jim Thome .50 1.25
MLBDRH Rickey Henderson .60 1.50
MLBDRHA Roy Halladay .50 1.25
MLBDRJ Randy Johnson .60 1.50
MLBDRS Ryne Sandberg 1.25 3.00
MLBDWB Wade Boggs .50 1.25

2017 Bowman Chrome Draft MLB Draft History Autographs Refractors
STATED ODDS 1:1795 HOBBY
STATED PRINT RUN 99 SER.#'d SETS
EXCHANGE DEADLINE 11/30/2019
MLBDAAP Andy Pettitte 8.00 20.00
MLBDADJ Derek Jeter 200.00 500.00
MLBDARH Rickey Henderson 30.00 80.00
MLBDARJ Randy Johnson 25.00 60.00
MLBDARS Ryne Sandberg 25.00 60.00

2017 Bowman Chrome Draft Recommended Viewing
COMPLETE SET (15) 4.00 10.00
STATED ODDS 1:3 HOBBY
*REF/250: .5X TO 1.2X BASIC
*GOLD REF/50: 1.2X TO 3X BASIC
RVARI Smith/Ellis .75 2.00
RVATL Waters/Wright 1.50 4.00
RVCWS Burger/Sheets .50 1.25
RVHOU Martin/Bukauskas .40 1.00
RVLAA Adell/Canning 2.00 5.00
RVMIL Hiura/Lutz 1.25 3.00
RVMIN Lewis/Rooker 2.00 5.00
RVNYY Sauer/Schmidt .40 1.00
RVOAK Merrell/Beck 1.00 2.50
RVPHI Haseley/Howard .50 1.25
RVPIT Jennings/Baz .40 1.00
RVSDP Campusano/Gore 1.50 4.00
RVSEA White/Carlson .40 1.00
RVSFG Ramos/Gonzalez 2.00 5.00
RVTAM Walls/McKay 1.00 2.50

2017 Bowman Chrome Draft Top of The Class Box Topper
STATED ODDS 1:36 HOBBY BOXES
STATED PRINT RUN 99 SER.#'d SETS
*GOLD/50: .5X TO 1.2X BASIC
TOCAB Austin Beck 8.00 20.00
TOCAH Adam Haseley 3.00 8.00
TOCBM Brendan McKay 8.00 20.00
TOCBMC Brendan McKay 8.00 20.00
TOCCS Clarke Schmidt 2.50 6.00
TOCJA Jo Adell 12.00 30.00
TOCJB Jake Burger 12.00 30.00
TOCJBU J.B. Bukauskas 2.50 6.00
TOCKH Keston Hiura 8.00 20.00
TOCKW Kyle Wright 8.00 20.00
TOCMG MacKenzie Gore 10.00 25.00
TOCPS Pavin Smith 12.00 30.00
TOCRL Royce Lewis 12.00 30.00
TOCSB Shane Baz 2.50 6.00
TOCTR Trevor Rogers 2.50 6.00

2017 Bowman Chrome Draft Top of The Class Box Topper Autographs Refractors
STATED ODDS 1:1769 HOBBY BOXES
STATED PRINT RUN 35 SER.#'d SETS
EXCHANGE DEADLINE 11/30/2019
TOCAB Austin Beck
TOCAH Adam Haseley 12.00 30.00
TOCBM Brendan McKay 75.00 200.00
TOCBMC Brendan McKay 75.00 200.00
TOCCS Clarke Schmidt
TOCJA Jo Adell 60.00 150.00
TOCJB Jake Burger
TOCJBU J.B. Bukauskas
TOCKH Keston Hiura 40.00 100.00
TOCKW Kyle Wright 30.00 80.00
TOCMG MacKenzie Gore 50.00 120.00
TOCPS Pavin Smith 20.00 50.00
TOCRL Royce Lewis 75.00 200.00
TOCSB Shane Baz
TOCTR Trevor Rogers 20.00 50.00

2017 Bowman Chrome Mega Box Autograph Refractors
STATED ODDS 1:18 RETAIL
*GREEN/99: .6X TO 1.5X BASIC
*ORANGE/25: 1.2X TO 3X BASIC
MAAE Anderson Espinoza 6.00 15.00
MAAI Andy Ibanez 6.00 15.00
MABD Bobby Dalbec 10.00 25.00
MADA Domingo Acevedo 6.00 15.00
MADC Dylan Cozens 12.00 30.00
MAFM Francisco Mejia 25.00 60.00
MAJG Jason Groome 12.00 30.00
MAJJ Jahmai Jones 6.00 15.00
MAJM Jorge Mateo 20.00 50.00
MAJS Justus Sheffield 10.00 25.00
MAKM Kevin Maitan 200.00 400.00
MALC Luis Castillo 20.00 50.00
MALGJ Lourdes Gurriel Jr. 10.00 25.00
MAMK Mitch Keller 20.00 50.00
MAMM Mickey Moniak 50.00 120.00
BMANS Nick Senzel 150.00 300.00
BMARR Roniel Raudes 10.00 25.00
BMASN Sean Newcomb 10.00 25.00
BMATS Thomas Szapucki 8.00 20.00
BMAWB Wuilmer Becerra 6.00 15.00
BMAZC Zack Collins 12.00 30.00

2017 Bowman Chrome Mega Box Prospects Refractors
*PURPLE/250: .5X TO 1.2X BASIC
*GREEN/99: .6X TO 1.5X BASIC
BCP1 Nick Senzel 3.00 8.00
BCP3 Ronald Guzman 1.25 3.00
BCP4 A.J. Puckett 1.00 2.50
BCP6 Roniel Raudes 1.00 2.50
BCP7 Lucas Erceg 1.25 3.00
BCP8 Luis Almanzar 1.00 2.50
BCP9 Beau Burrows 1.00 2.50
BCP10 Chase Vallot 1.00 2.50
BCP11 P.J. Conlon 1.00 2.50
BCP12 Erick Fedde 1.00 2.50
BCP13 Rookie Davis 1.00 2.50
BCP14 Chris Shaw 1.00 2.50
BCP16 Clint Frazier 2.00 5.00
BCP18 Lourdes Gurriel Jr. 1.50 4.00
BCP20 Angel Perdomo 1.00 2.50
BCP22 Freddy Peralta 1.50 4.00
BCP23 Jarlin Garcia 1.00 2.50
BCP24 Tyler O'Neill 1.25 3.00
BCP25 Lazarito Armenteros 2.50 6.00
BCP27 Antonio Senzatela 1.00 2.50
BCP28 Kyle Tucker 2.00 5.00
BCP30 Willie Calhoun 1.50 4.00
BCP31 Shohei Otani UER 80.00 200.00
Ohtani
BCP32 Vladimir Guerrero Jr. 5.00 12.00
BCP33 Braxton Garrett 1.00 2.50
BCP36 Andy Ibanez 1.00 2.50
BCP37 Francisco Rios 1.00 2.50
BCP39 Dylan Cozens 1.00 2.50
BCP40 Mauricio Dubon 1.25 3.00
BCP41 Franklyn Kilome 1.25 3.00
BCP42 Chance Sisco 2.00 5.00
BCP43 Sandy Alcantara 1.25 3.00
BCP44 Stephen Gonsalves 1.00 2.50
BCP45 Grant Holmes 1.00 2.50
BCP47 Kolby Allard 1.00 2.50
BCP50 Eloy Jimenez 4.00 10.00
BCP51 Francisco Mejia 1.50 4.00
BCP54 Anderson Espinoza 1.00 2.50
BCP55 Cal Quantrill 1.00 2.50
BCP57 Tyler Beede 1.00 2.50
BCP59 Ariel Jurado 1.00 2.50
BCP61 Tyler Stephenson 1.00 2.50
BCP63 Dominic Smith 1.00 2.50
BCP65 Austin Meadows 1.50 4.00
BCP66 Mitch Keller 1.25 3.00
BCP67 Jahmai Jones 1.00 2.50
BCP68 Alex Speas 1.00 2.50
BCP69 Nolan Jones 1.50 4.00
BCP70 Kevin Newman 1.50 4.00
BCP71 T.J. Friedl 1.00 2.50
BCP72 Oscar De La Cruz 1.00 2.50
BCP73 Victor Robles 2.50 6.00
BCP74 Patrick Weigel 1.00 2.50
BCP76 Amed Rosario 1.50 4.00
BCP77 Nick Solak 2.50 6.00
BCP78 Abrahan Gutierrez 1.50 4.00
BCP79 Yu-Cheng Chang 1.50 4.00
BCP80 Gleyber Torres 15.00 40.00
BCP83 Andrew Sopko 1.00 2.50
BCP84 Brent Honeywell 1.25 3.00
BCP85 Kyle Funkhouser 1.25 3.00
BCP88 Brendan Rodgers 1.25 3.00
BCP89 Josh Staumont 1.00 2.50
BCP92 Wuilmer Becerra 1.00 2.50
BCP94 Alfredo Rodriguez 1.25 3.00
BCP95 Daz Cameron 1.00 2.50
BCP99 Drew Jackson 1.00 2.50
BCP100 Kevin Maitan 2.50 6.00
BCP101 Rafael Devers 2.00 5.00
BCP103 Jack Flaherty 1.50 4.00
BCP104 Adonis Medina 1.50 4.00
BCP106 Josh Hader 1.00 2.50
BCP107 Luis Urias 4.00 10.00
BCP109 Kyle Freeland 1.25 3.00
BCP110 Matt Chapman 1.50 4.00
BCP113 David Fletcher 3.00 8.00
BCP114 Tyler Jay 1.00 2.50
BCP115 Franklin Barreto 1.00 2.50
BCP116 Michael Kopech 2.00 5.00
BCP117 Rhys Hoskins 4.00 10.00
BCP118 Triston McKenzie 1.00 2.50
BCP119 Luis Garcia 3.00 8.00
BCP121 Blake Rutherford 1.50 4.00
BCP124 Dylan Cease 2.50 6.00
BCP127 Ronald Acuna 75.00 200.00
BCP128 Luis Ortiz 1.00 2.50
BCP130 Adrian Morejon 1.50 4.00
BCP132 Justus Sheffield 1.50 4.00
BCP134 Fernando Romero 1.00 2.50
BCP135 Mickey Moniak 2.50 6.00
BCP137 Jomar Reyes 1.00 2.50
BCP138 Thomas Szapucki 1.25 3.00
BCP140 Willy Adames 1.25 3.00
BCP141 Yang Hyeon-Jong 1.25 3.00
BCP142 Bo Bichette 4.00 10.00
BCP143 Harrison Bader 1.50 4.00
BCP145 Juan Hillman 1.00 2.50
BCP148 Christin Stewart 1.25 3.00
BCP149 Cody Bellinger 15.00 40.00
BCP150 Jason Groome 2.00 5.00

2017 Bowman Chrome Mega Box Prospects Orange Refractors
*ORANGE: 1.5X TO 4X BASIC
STATED ODDS 1:56 RETAIL
STATED PRINT RUN 25 SER.#'d SETS
BCP1 Nick Senzel 40.00 100.00
BCP31 Shohei Otani UER 1200.00 2500.00
Ohtani
BCP100 Kevin Maitan 125.00 300.00

2017 Bowman Chrome Mega Box Rookie of the Year Favorites Autographs Refractors
STATED ODDS 1:122 RETAIL
STATED PRINT RUN 75 SER.#'d SETS
*ORANGE/25: .75X TO 2X BASIC
ROYFAAB Alex Bregman 30.00 80.00
ROYFAABE Andrew Benintendi 75.00 200.00
ROYFAAJ Aaron Judge 200.00 400.00
ROYFAAR Alex Reyes 10.00 25.00
ROYFACF Carson Fulmer 5.00 12.00
ROYFADD David Dahl 10.00 25.00
ROYFADS Dansby Swanson 25.00 60.00
ROYFAHR Hunter Renfroe 12.00 30.00
ROYFAJA Jorge Alfaro 20.00 50.00
ROYFAJC Jharel Cotton
ROYFAJDL Jose De Leon 10.00 25.00
ROYFAOA Orlando Arcia 20.00 50.00
ROYFAYG Yulieski Gurriel 10.00 25.00
ROYFAYM Yoan Moncada 75.00 200.00

2017 Bowman Chrome Mega Box Rookie of the Year Favorites Refractors
STATED ODDS 1:4 RETAIL
*PURPLE/250: .6X TO 1.5X BASIC
*GREEN/99: 1.2X TO 3X BASIC
*ORANGE/25: 2X TO 5X BASIC
ROYFIAB Alex Bregman 2.50 6.00
ROYFIABE Andrew Benintendi 2.00 5.00
ROYFIAJ Aaron Judge 50.00 120.00
ROYFIAR Alex Reyes .75 2.00
ROYFICF Carson Fulmer .60 1.50
ROYFIDD David Dahl .75 2.00
ROYFIDS Dansby Swanson 1.50 4.00
ROYFIHR Hunter Renfroe .75 2.00
ROYFIJA Jorge Alfaro .75 2.00
ROYFIJC Jharel Cotton .60 1.50
ROYFIJDL Jose De Leon .60 1.50
ROYFILW Luke Weaver .75 2.00
ROYFIMM Manny Margot .60 1.50
ROYFIOA Orlando Arcia 1.00 2.50
ROYFIRH Ryan Healy .75 2.00
ROYFIRL Reynaldo Lopez .60 1.50
ROYFITA Tyler Austin 1.00 2.50
ROYFITG Tyler Glasnow .75 2.00
ROYFIYG Yulieski Gurriel .60 1.50
ROYFIYM Yoan Moncada 2.00 5.00

2017 Bowman Chrome Mega Box Talent Pipeline Refractors
STATED ODDS 1:2 RETAIL
*PURPLE/250: .5X TO 1.2X BASIC
*GREEN/99: 1X TO 2.5X BASIC
*ORANGE/25: 1.5X TO 4X BASIC
TPARI Alex Young .40 1.00
Taylor Clarke
Anthony Banda
TPATL Allard/Albies/Ellis 1.50 4.00
TPBAL Sdlck/Lee/Ssco .75 2.00
TPBOS Dvrs/Tvrz/Trvs .75 2.00
TPCHI Jmnz/Happ/Zgns 1.50 4.00
TPCHW Zack Collins .50 1.25
Spencer Adams
Zack Burdi
TPCIN Srzl/Mhle/Grll 1.25 3.00
TPCLE Francisco Mejia .60 1.50
Nellie Rodriguez
Bradley Zimmer
TPCOL Brendan Rodgers .50 1.25
Ryan McMahon
Kyle Freeland
TPDET Mnnng/Strwt/Jmnz .60 1.50
TPHOU Tckr/Mrts/Fshr .75 2.00
TPKCR Vallot/O'Hearn/Bonifacio .75 2.00
TPLAA Matt Thaiss 1.25 3.00
David Fletcher
Nate Smith
TPLAD Alvrz/Clhn/Bllngr 6.00 15.00
TPMIA Stone Garrett .40 1.00
Austin Dean
J.T. Riddle
TPMIL Ray/Phllps/Brnsn .60 1.50
TPMIN Nick Gordon .40 1.00
Tyler Jay
Jake Reed
TPNYM Dunn/Rsro/Nmmo .60 1.50
TPNYY Trrs/Shflld/Frzr 6.00 15.00
TPOAK Puk/Mnz/Brrto .60 1.50
TPPHI Mnk/Crns/Crwfrd 1.00 2.50
TPPIT Mitch Keller .60 1.50
Kevin Newman
Austin Meadows
TPSDP Anderson Espinoza .50 1.25
Austin Allen
Dinelson Lamet
TPSEA Lewis/O'Neill/Peterson .75 2.00
TPSFG Rynlds/Arryo/Blckbrn .60 1.50
TPSTL Flhrty/Bdr/Vlra .60 1.50
TPTBR Joshua Lowe .50 1.25
Willy Adames
Jacob Faria
TPTEX Trvs/Ibnz/Gzmn 1.25 3.00
TPTOR Sean Reid-Foley .60 1.50
Richard Urena
A.J. Jimenez
TPWAS Rbls/Fdde/Vth 1.00 2.50

2018 Bowman Chrome
COMPLETE SET (100)
1 Shohei Ohtani RC 8.00 20.00
2 Byron Buxton .25 .60
3 Scott Kingery RC .60 1.50
4 Michael Fulmer .20 .50
5 Starlin Castro .20 .50
6 Anthony Rizzo .50 1.25
7 Mookie Betts .50 1.25
8 Rafael Devers RC 1.25 3.00
9 Nelson Cruz .30 .75
10 Gary Sanchez .30 .75
11 Amed Rosario RC .50 1.25
12 Tyler O'Neill RC .60 1.50
13 Christian Yelich .40 1.00
14 Yoan Moncada .30 .75
15 Justin Verlander .30 .75
16 Jordan Hicks RC .75 2.00
17 Joey Lucchesi RC .40 1.00
18 Lucas Giolito .25 .60
19 Sandy Alcantara RC .40 1.00
20 Ender Inciarte .20 .50
21 Clint Frazier RC .75 2.00
22 Aaron Nola .25 .60
23 Alex Gordon .25 .60
24 Salvador Perez .25 .60
25 Rhys Hoskins RC 1.50 4.00
26 Cole Hamels .25 .60
27 Yoenis Cespedes .30 .75
28 Odubel Herrera .25 .60
29 Albert Pujols .40 1.00
30 Yu Darvish .30 .75
31 Francisco Lindor .30 .75
32 Joey Votto .30 .75
33 Francisco Mejia RC .50 1.25
34 Walker Buehler RC 2.00 5.00
35 Nick Williams RC .50 1.25
36 Ryan McMahon RC .50 1.25
37 Mike Trout 1.50 4.00
38 Adrian Beltre .30 .75
39 Billy Hamilton .25 .60
40 Ronald Acuna Jr. RC 8.00 20.00
41 Tyler Mahle RC .50 1.25
42 Matt Chapman .30 .75
43 Johnny Cueto .25 .60
44 Dominic Smith RC .40 1.00
45 Carlos Correa .30 .75
46 Josh Harrison .20 .50
47 Alex Verdugo RC .60 1.50
48 Yadier Molina .30 .75
49 Josh Bell .25 .60
50 Kris Bryant .40 1.00
51 Willie Calhoun RC .50 1.25
52 Victor Robles RC 1.00 2.50
53 Andrew Benintendi .30 .75
54 Garrett Cooper RC .40 1.00
55 Matt Olson .20 .50
56 Andrew Stevenson RC .40 1.00
57 Corey Seager .30 .75
58 J.D. Martinez .30 .75
59 Buster Posey .40 1.00
60 Justin Upton .25 .60
61 Miguel Cabrera .30 .75
62 Roberto Osuna .20 .50
63 Chris Archer .20 .50
64 Mike Soroka RC 1.25 3.00
65 J.P. Crawford RC .40 1.00
66 Paul Goldschmidt .30 .75
67 Ichiro .40 1.00
68 Harrison Bader RC .60 1.50
69 Miguel Andujar RC 1.50 4.00
70 Nolan Arenado .40 1.00
71 Giancarlo Stanton .30 .75
72 Jack Flaherty RC .60 1.50
73 Kevin Kiermaier .25 .60
74 Tim Beckham .25 .60
75 Justin Bour .20 .50
76 Tomas Nido RC .40 1.00
77 Chance Sisco RC .50 1.25
78 Todd Frazier .25 .60
79 Charlie Blackmon .30 .75
80 Dustin Fowler RC .40 1.00
81 Zack Granite RC .40 1.00
82 Eric Hosmer .25 .60
83 Gleyber Torres RC 4.00 10.00
84 Bryce Harper .50 1.25
85 Manny Machado .30 .75
86 Hunter Renfroe .20 .50
87 Austin Hays RC .60 1.50
88 Cody Bellinger .60 1.50
89 Lorenzo Cain .20 .50
90 Brian Dozier .25 .60
91 Troy Tulowitzki .30 .75
92 Ozzie Albies RC 1.25 3.00
93 Paul DeJong .30 .75
94 Max Scherzer .30 .75
95 Jose Ramirez .25 .60
96 Freddie Freeman .40 1.00
97 Jake Lamb .25 .60
98 Clayton Kershaw .60 1.50
99 Luiz Gohara RC .40 1.00
100 Aaron Judge .75 2.00

2018 Bowman Chrome Blue Refractors
*BLUE REF VET: 4X TO 10X BASIC
*BLUE REF RC: 2X TO 5X BASIC
STATED ODDS 1:XX HOBBY
STATED PRINT RUN 150 SER.#'d SETS
1 Shohei Ohtani 60.00 150.00
37 Mike Trout 15.00 40.00
40 Ronald Acuna Jr. 150.00 400.00

2018 Bowman Chrome Gold Refractors
*GOLD REF VET: 8X TO 20X BASIC
*GOLD REF RC: 4X TO 10X BASIC
STATED ODDS 1:XX HOBBY
STATED PRINT RUN 50 SER.#'d SETS
1 Shohei Ohtani 125.00 300.00
37 Mike Trout 60.00 150.00
40 Ronald Acuna Jr. 250.00 600.00
69 Miguel Andujar 30.00 80.00
83 Gleyber Torres 30.00 80.00

2018 Bowman Chrome Green Refractors
*GREEN REF VET: 5X TO 12X BASIC
*GREEN REF RC: 2.5X TO 6X BASIC
STATED ODDS 1:XX HOBBY
STATED PRINT RUN 99 SER.#'d SETS
1 Shohei Ohtani 75.00 200.00
37 Mike Trout 20.00 50.00
40 Ronald Acuna Jr. 200.00 500.00

2018 Bowman Chrome Orange Refractors
*ORANGE REF VET: 10X TO 25X BASIC
*ORANGE REF RC: 5X TO 12X BASIC
STATED ODDS 1:421 HOBBY
STATED PRINT RUN 25 SER.#'d SETS
1 Shohei Ohtani 150.00 400.00
3 Scott Kingery 20.00 50.00
37 Mike Trout 75.00 200.00
40 Ronald Acuna Jr. 300.00 800.00
69 Miguel Andujar 40.00 100.00
72 Jack Flaherty 20.00 50.00
83 Gleyber Torres 40.00 100.00

2018 Bowman Chrome Purple Refractors
*PURPLE REF VET: 2X TO 5X BASIC
*PURPLE REF RC: 1X TO 2.5X BASIC
STATED ODDS 1:XX HOBBY
STATED PRINT RUN 250 SER.#'d SETS
1 Shohei Ohtani 30.00 80.00
37 Mike Trout 8.00 20.00
40 Ronald Acuna Jr. 40.00 100.00

2018 Bowman Chrome Refractors
*REF VET: 1.5X TO 4X BASIC
*REF RC: .75X TO 2X BASIC
STATED ODDS 1:XX HOBBY
STATED PRINT RUN 499 SER.#'d SETS
1 Shohei Ohtani 25.00 60.00
37 Mike Trout 6.00 15.00
40 Ronald Acuna Jr. 30.00 80.00

2018 Bowman Chrome Rookie Image Varitations
STATED ODDS 1:XX HOBBY
1 Ohtani Crmg bag 30.00 80.00
8 Devers Swgng bat 8.00 20.00
11 Amed Rosario 3.00 8.00
Blue sleeve
21 Frazier Warm-ups 5.00 12.00
25 Hoskins Pullover 3.00 8.00
33 Francisco Mejia 3.00 8.00
Wearing gear
35 Nick Williams 3.00 8.00
Gray jersey
44 Dominic Smith 2.50 6.00
Wearing pullover
47 Alex Verdugo 4.00 10.00
Front of jersey showing
52 Robles T-Shirt 6.00 15.00
65 J.P. Crawford 2.50 6.00
White jersey
68 Bader White jrsy 4.00 10.00
72 Jack Flaherty 4.00 10.00
Batting
87 Austin Hays 4.00 10.00
No helmet
92 Albies Pullover 8.00 20.00

2018 Bowman Chrome Rookie Image Variation Autographs
STATED ODDS 1:XX HOBBY
STATED PRINT RUN 25 SER.#'d SETS
EXCHANGE DEADLINE 8/31/2020
1 Shohei Ohtani 1500.00 2500.00
8 Rafael Devers 150.00 400.00
11 Amed Rosario EXCH 20.00 50.00
21 Clint Frazier 30.00 80.00
25 Rhys Hoskins 250.00 500.00
33 Francisco Mejia
44 Dominic Smith
52 Victor Robles 200.00 400.00
65 J.P. Crawford 15.00 40.00
68 Harrison Bader 25.00 60.00
72 Jack Flaherty 25.00 60.00
87 Austin Hays 60.00 150.00
92 Ozzie Albies 50.00 125.00

2018 Bowman Chrome '17 AFL Fall Stars Refractors
STATED ODDS 1:XX HOBBY
*ATOMIC/150: 1.2X TO 3X BASE
*ORANGE/25: 4X TO 10X BASE
AFLAA Adbert Alzolay .50 1.25
AFLCR Corey Ray .50 1.25
AFLDB David Bote 1.00 2.50
AFLEF Estevan Florial .60 1.50
AFLJS Justus Sheffield .50 1.25
AFLKT Kyle Tucker .75 2.00
AFLLU Luis Urias .75 2.00
AFLMB Matt Beaty .50 1.25
AFLMF Matt Festa .40 1.00
AFLMK Mitch Keller .50 1.25
AFLMT Matt Thaiss .40 1.00
AFLRA Ronald Acuna 8.00 20.00
AFLSA Sandy Alcantara .40 1.00
AFLSN Sheldon Neuse .40 1.00
AFLTJ Tyler Jay .40 1.00
AFLTN Tomas Nido .40 1.00
AFLTS Tanner Scott .40 1.00
AFLTT Touki Toussaint .50 1.25
AFLTZ T.J. Zeuch .40 1.00
AFLVR Victor Robles 1.00 2.50
AFLSVR Victor Robles MVP SP 1.25 3.00

2018 Bowman Chrome '17 AFL Fall Stars Autographs
STATED ODDS 1:XXX HOBBY
PRINT RUNS B/WN 40-150 COPIES PER
EXCHANGE DEADLINE 8/31/2020
AFLAA Adbert Alzolay/150 5.00 12.00
AFLCR Corey Ray/45 6.00 15.00
AFLDB David Bote/90 20.00 50.00
AFLEF Estevan Florial/150 20.00 50.00
AFLJS Justus Sheffield
AFLMB Matt Beaty/105 5.00 12.00
AFLMF Matt Festa/150 4.00 10.00
AFLMK Mitch Keller/150 6.00 15.00
AFLMT Matt Thaiss/100 10.00 25.00
AFLRA Ronald Acuna/150 100.00 250.00
AFLSA Sandy Alcantara/150 4.00 10.00
AFLSN Sheldon Neuse/150 4.00 10.00
AFLTJ Tyler Jay/80 4.00 10.00
AFLTN Tomas Nido/150 4.00 10.00
AFLTS Tanner Scott/40 6.00 15.00
AFLTT Touki Toussaint/75 15.00 40.00
AFLTZ T.J. Zeuch/150 4.00 10.00
AFLVR Victor Robles/150 10.00 25.00
AFLSVR Victor Robles MVP/100 10.00 25.00

2018 Bowman Chrome '17 AFL Fall Stars Autograph Relics
STATED ODDS 1:XXX HOBBY
STATED PRINT RUN 50 SER.#'d SETS
EXCHANGE DEADLINE 8/31/2020
AFLRAA Adbert Alzolay 10.00 25.00
AFLRDB David Bote 30.00 80.00
AFLRFM Francisco Mejia EXCH 12.00 30.00
AFLRLU Luis Urias
AFLRMB Matt Beaty 12.00 30.00
AFLRMF Matt Festa 8.00 20.00
AFLRSA Sandy Alcantara 8.00 20.00
AFLRSN Sheldon Neuse 8.00 20.00
AFLRTE Thairo Estrada 60.00 150.00
AFLRTN Tomas Nido 8.00 20.00

2018 Bowman Chrome '17 AFL Fall Stars Relics
STATED ODDS 1:XXX HOBBY
STATED PRINT RUN 99 SER.#'d SETS
AFLRAA Adbert Alzolay 4.00 10.00
AFLRAR Austin Riley 10.00 25.00
AFLRBB Braden Bishop 10.00 25.00
AFLRCR Corey Ray 4.00 10.00
AFLRDB David Bote 12.00 30.00
AFLRFM Francisco Mejia 4.00 10.00
AFLRJH Jordan Hicks 6.00 15.00
AFLRJS Justus Sheffield 4.00 10.00
AFLRKT Kyle Tucker 6.00 15.00
AFLRLU Luis Urias 6.00 15.00
AFLRMB Matt Beaty 4.00 10.00
AFLRMF Matt Festa 3.00 8.00
AFLRMK Mitch Keller 4.00 10.00
AFLRRA Ronald Acuna 25.00 60.00
AFLRRM Ryan Mountcastle 5.00 12.00
AFLRSA Sandy Alcantara 3.00 8.00
AFLRSN Sheldon Neuse 3.00 8.00
AFLRTE Thairo Estrada 8.00 20.00
AFLRTN Tomas Nido 3.00 8.00
AFLRTT Touki Toussaint 5.00 12.00

2018 Bowman Chrome '17 AFL Fall Stars Relics Orange Refractors
*ORANGE: .6X TO 1.5X BASIC
STATED ODDS 1:XXX HOBBY
STATED PRINT RUN 25 SER.#'d SETS
AFLRRA Ronald Acuna 125.00 300.00

2018 Bowman Chrome Autograph Relics
STATED ODDS 1:XXX HOBBY
STATED PRINT RUN 150 SER.#'d SETS
EXCHANGE DEADLINE 8/31/2020
BCARAA Adbert Alzolay/150 8.00 20.00
BCARAR Amed Rosario/150 6.00 15.00
BCARCF Clint Frazier/150 12.00 30.00
BCARCS Chance Sisco/150 5.00 12.00
BCARDS Dominic Smith/125 4.00 10.00
BCARFM Francisco Mejia EXCH 8.00 20.00
BCARGT Gleyber Torres/150 50.00 120.00
BCARJC J.P. Crawford/150 6.00 15.00
BCARJF Jack Flaherty/150 25.00 60.00
BCARKB Kris Bryant/75 50.00 120.00
BCARLE Luis Escobar/150 4.00 10.00
BCARLSE Luis Severino/150 5.00 12.00
BCARLU Luis Urias/150 20.00 50.00
BCARMT Mike Trout/30
BCARNS Noah Syndergaard/75 10.00 25.00
BCARPD Paul DeJong
BCARRD Rafael Devers/150 12.00 30.00
BCARSN Sheldon Neuse/150 5.00 12.00
BCARTE Thairo Estrada/150 8.00 20.00
BCARVR Victor Robles/150 10.00 25.00
BCARWM Whit Merrifield/150 10.00 25.00

2018 Bowman Chrome Autograph Relics Gold Refractors
*GOLD REF: .6X TO 1.5X BASIC
STATED ODDS 1:XXX HOBBY
STATED PRINT RUN 50 SER.#'d SETS
EXCHANGE DEADLINE 8/31/2020

2018 Bowman Chrome Autograph Relics Orange Refractors
*ORANGE REF: 1X TO 2.5X BASIC
STATED ODDS 1:XXX HOBBY
STATED PRINT RUN 25 SER.#'d SETS
EXCHANGE DEADLINE 8/31/2020
BCARCS Chance Sisco 50.00 120.00
BCARFM Francisco Mejia EXCH 40.00 100.00
BCARMT Mike Trout 250.00 500.00
BCARPD Paul DeJong 25.00 60.00

2018 Bowman Chrome Bowman Birthdays Refractors
STATED ODDS 1:8 HOBBY
*ATOMIC REF/150: 1.2X TO 3X BASE
*GREEN REF/99: 1.5X TO 4X BASE
*ORANGE REF/25: 5X TO 12X BASE
BBBB Byron Buxton .30 .75
BBFL Francisco Lindor .40 1.00
BBJG Joey Gallo .30 .75
BBKS Kyle Schwarber .40 1.00
BBLM Lance McCullers Jr. .25 .60
BBLW Luke Weaver .30 .75
BBMC Michael Conforto .30 .75
BBMCH Matt Chapman .40 1.00
BBMF Michael Fulmer .25 .60
BBMK Max Kepler .30 .75
BBNW Nick Williams .30 .75
BBPD Paul DeJong .40 1.00
BBRH Rhys Hoskins 1.00 2.50
BBTG Tyler Glasnow .25 .60
BBTT Trea Turner .30 .75

2018 Bowman Chrome Dual Prospect Autographs Refractors
RANDOM INSERTS IN PACKS
STATED PRINT RUN 25 SER.#'d SETS
EXCHANGE DEADLINE 3/31/2020
DBAGM Greene/McKay 250.00 500.00
DBAKI Isabel/Kendall
DBALG Gore/Lewis 60.00 150.00
DBALL Littell/Lewis 60.00 150.00
DBASL Siri/Long 200.00 400.00

2018 Bowman Chrome Hashtag Bowman Trending Refractors
STATED ODDS 1:6 HOBBY
*ATOMIC REF/150: 1X TO 2.5X BASE
*GREEN REF/99: 1.2X TO 3X BASE
*ORANGE REF/25: 3X TO 8X BASE
AP A.J. Puk .30 .75
BB Bo Bichette 1.00 2.50
CA Chance Adams .40 1.00
CQ Cal Quantrill .25 .60
FP Franklin Perez .25 .60
FR Fernando Romero .25 .60
FT Fernando Tatis Jr. 2.00 5.00
JS Jesus Sanchez .25 .60
LT Leody Taveras .30 .75
LU Luis Urias .50 1.25
MC Michael Chavis .40 1.00
NG Nick Gordon .25 .60
RA Ronald Acuna 5.00 12.00
SG Stephen Gonsalves .25 .60
SK Scott Kingery .40 1.00
SS Sixto Sanchez .60 1.50
TM Triston McKenzie .25 .60
TT Taylor Trammell .40 1.00
VG Vladimir Guerrero Jr. 2.50 6.00
YD Yusniel Diaz .75 2.00

2018 Bowman Chrome Peaks of Potential Refractors
STATED ODDS 1:XX HOBBY
*ATOMIC/150: .75X TO 2X BASE
*ORANGE/25: 2X TO 5X BASE
PPAA Aramis Ademan .60 1.50
PPAAL Adbert Alzolay .50 1.25
PPAG Andres Gimenez .50 1.25
PPBB Bo Bichette 1.50 4.00
PPBM Brandon Marsh .50 1.25
PPBMC Brendan McKay .60 1.50
PPCB Corbin Burnes .60 1.50
PPCP Cristian Pache 2.00 5.00
PPCW Colton Welker .40 1.00
PPEF Estevan Florial .60 1.50
PPFP Franklin Perez .40 1.00
PPFT Fernando Tatis Jr. 3.00 8.00
PPGT Gleyber Torres 4.00 10.00
PPHG Hunter Greene 1.25 3.00
PPHR Heliot Ramos .60 1.50
PPJA Jo Adell 1.25 3.00
PPJB Jake Burger .40 1.00
PPJG Jorge Guzman .40 1.00
PPJH Jordan Hicks .75 2.00
PPJS Jesus Sanchez .40 1.00
PPKR Keibert Ruiz 1.25 3.00
PPLR Luis Robert 8.00 20.00
PPLU Luis Urias .75 2.00
PPMG MacKenzie Gore .75 2.00
PPMW Mitchell White .40 1.00
PPRL Royce Lewis 1.50 4.00
PPSM Sean Murphy .60 1.50
PPSN Sheldon Neuse .40 1.00
PPSS Sixto Sanchez 1.00 2.50
PPYA Yordan Alvarez 3.00 8.00

2018 Bowman Chrome Peaks of Potential Autographs

STATED ODDS 1:XXX HOBBY
STATED PRINT RUN 99 SER.#'d SETS
EXCHANGE DEADLINE 8/31/2020
*ORNGE REF/25: .6X TO 1.5X BASE
PPAAA Aramis Ademan 5.00 12.00
PPAAAL Adbert Alzolay 6.00 15.00
PPAAG Andres Gimenez 4.00 10.00
PPABM Brandon Marsh 12.00 30.00
PPABMC Brendan McKay 10.00 25.00
PPACB Corbin Burnes 6.00 15.00
PPACP Cristian Pache 12.00 30.00
PPACW Colton Welker 3.00 8.00
PPAEF Estevan Florial 50.00 120.00
PPAFP Franklin Perez 10.00 25.00
PPAGT Gleyber Torres EXCH 40.00 100.00
PPAHG Hunter Greene 20.00 50.00
PPAHR Heliot Ramos 12.00 30.00
PPAJA Jo Adell 40.00 100.00
PPAJB Jake Burger 6.00 15.00
PPAJG Jorge Guzman 6.00 15.00
PPAKR Keibert Ruiz 10.00 25.00
PPALR Luis Robert 50.00 120.00
PPALU Luis Urias EXCH 20.00 50.00
PPAMG MacKenzie Gore 6.00 15.00
PPAMW Mitchell White 6.00 15.00
PPARL Royce Lewis 20.00 50.00
PPASN Sheldon Neuse 3.00 8.00
PPASS Sixto Sanchez 15.00 40.00
PPAZL Zack Littell 6.00 15.00

2018 Bowman Chrome Prospect Autographs

OVERALL AUTO ODDS 1:24 HOBBY
STATED PLATE ODDS 1:18,041 HOBBY
PLATE PRINT RUN 1 SET PER COLOR
BLACK-CYAN-MAGENTA-YELLOW ISSUED
NO PLATE PRICING DUE TO SCARCITY
BOW.EXCH.DEADLINE 3/31/2020
BOW.CHR.EXCH 8/31/2020
BCPAAA Aramis Ademan 6.00 15.00
BCPAAAL Austin Allen 4.00 10.00
BCPAAB Akil Baddoo 8.00 20.00
CPAAA Adbert Alzolay 6.00 15.00
CPAAG Andres Gimenez 20.00 50.00
CPABC Brett Cumberland 3.00 8.00
CPABHE Brayan Hernandez 3.00 8.00
CPABMC Brendan McKay 8.00 20.00
CPABW Jose Adolis Garcia 4.00 10.00
CPACB Corbin Burnes 6.00 15.00
CPACD Chris DeVito 3.00 8.00
CPACM Cedric Mullins 5.00 12.00
CPACP Cristian Pache 60.00 150.00
CPACR Chris Rodriguez 3.00 8.00
CPACRI Carlos Rincon 4.00 10.00
CPACW Colton Welker 10.00 25.00
CPADG Daniel Gonzalez 3.00 8.00
CPADH Darick Hall 3.00 8.00
CPADJ Daniel Johnson 6.00 15.00
CPADP DJ Peters 12.00 30.00
CPADS Dennis Santana 3.00 8.00
CPAEF Estevan Florial 25.00 60.00
CPAEO Edward Olivares 4.00 10.00
CPAEPA Eric Pardinho 10.00 25.00
CPAGD Greg Deichmann 4.00 10.00
CPAGL

Gavin LaValley

3.00

2018 Bowman Chrome Prospect Autographs

CPAHF Heath Fillmyer 3.00 8.00
CPAHG Hunter Greene 25.00 60.00
CPAII Ibandel Isabel 8.00 20.00
CPAJB Jaime Barria 4.00 10.00
CPAJBU J.B. Bukauskas 3.00 8.00
CPAJG Jose Gomez 3.00 8.00
CPAJH Jordan Humphreys 3.00 8.00
CPAJHI Jordan Hicks 6.00 15.00
CPAJJR JoJo Romero 4.00 10.00
CPAJK Jeren Kendall 4.00 10.00
CPAJN James Nelson 3.00 8.00
CPAJRI Jake Ring 3.00 8.00
CPAJRO Jake Rogers 4.00 10.00
CPAJS Jose Siri 3.00 8.00
CPAJW Joey Wentz 4.00 10.00
CPAKC Kyle Cody 3.00 8.00
CPAKR Keibert Ruiz 30.00 80.00
CPAKY Kyle Young 4.00 10.00
CPALA Logan Allen 3.00 8.00
CPALE Luis Escobar 3.00 8.00
CPALR Luis Robert 500.00 1200.00
CPAMA Micker Adolfo 8.00 20.00
CPAMB Michel Baez 3.00 8.00
CPAMD Matthias Dietz 3.00 8.00
CPAMGO MacKenzie Gore 10.00 25.00
CPAMH Matt Hall 3.00 8.00
CPAMM Michael Mercado 4.00 10.00
CPAMMI McKenzie Mills 3.00 8.00
CPAMS Mike Shawaryn 3.00 8.00
CPAMSA Matt Sauer 3.00 8.00
CPANF Nick Fanti 3.00 8.00
CPAPA Pedro Avila 3.00 8.00
CPARH Ryan Helsley 4.00 10.00
CPARL Royce Lewis 50.00 120.00
CPARS Ranger Suarez 3.00 8.00
CPASCC Shao-Ching Chiang 4.00 10.00
CPASF Sandro Fabian 3.00 8.00
CPASH Spencer Howard 20.00 50.00
CPASHI Sam Hilliard 10.00 25.00
CPASL Shed Long 5.00 12.00
CPASMU Sean Murphy 15.00 40.00
CPASR Seth Romero 3.00 8.00
CPATH Thomas Hatch 6.00 15.00
CPATL Travis Lakins 3.00 8.00
CPAWA Willie Abreu 3.00 8.00
CPAYA Yordan Alvarez 200.00 500.00
CPAZL Zack Littell 3.00 8.00
BCPAAF Antoni Flores 8.00 20.00
BCPAAW Alex Wells 3.00 8.00
BCPABG Brusdar Graterol 12.00 30.00
BCPABL Brendon Little 3.00 8.00
BCPABM Brandon Marsh 12.00 30.00
BCPACB Charcer Burks 3.00 8.00
BCPACC Conner Capel 3.00 8.00
BCPACF Cole Freeman 4.00 10.00
BCPACK Carter Kieboom 15.00 40.00
BCPACP Chase Pinder 4.00 10.00
BCPACS Connor Seabold 3.00 8.00
BCPACT Chris Torres 3.00 8.00
BCPADH Darwinzon Hernandez 4.00 10.00
BCPADM Dustin May 15.00 40.00
BCPADV Daulton Varsho 12.00 30.00
BCPAED Eduardo Diaz 4.00 10.00
BCPAEDL Enyel De Los Santos 4.00 10.00
BCPAER Edwin Rios 20.00 50.00
BCPAES Evan Steele 4.00 10.00
BCPAFP Franklin Perez 6.00 15.00
BCPAGSO Gregory Soto 3.00 8.00
BCPAJAL Jose Albertos 3.00 8.00
BCPAJD Joe Dunand 4.00 10.00
BCPAJG Jorge Guzman 3.00 8.00
BCPAJL Joey Lucchesi 5.00 12.00
BCPAJLO Jonathan Loaisiga 12.00 30.00
BCPAJS Jairo Solis 6.00 15.00
BCPAKM Kevin Maitan 6.00 15.00
BCPAKR Kristian Robinson 75.00 200.00
BCPALG Luis Guillorme 3.00 8.00
BCPALGA Luis Garcia 25.00 60.00
BCPALM Luis Medina 10.00 25.00
BCPALR Leonardo Rivas 3.00 8.00
BCPALS Logan Shore 3.00 8.00
BCPALSA LoLo Sanchez 6.00 15.00
BCPALU Luis Urias 15.00 40.00
BCPALW LaMonte Wade 3.00 8.00
BCPAMB Mike Baumann 5.00 12.00
BCPANA Nick Allen 3.00 8.00
BCPANL Nicky Lopez 3.00 8.00
BCPARAD Riley Adams 4.00 10.00
BCPARAR Rogelio Armenteros 3.00 8.00
BCPARW Russell Wilson 100.00 250.00
BCPASB Shane Bieber 50.00 120.00
BCPASN Sheldon Neuse 5.00 12.00
BCPATF Tyler Freeman 15.00 40.00
BCPATO Trevor Oaks 3.00 8.00
BCPATS Trevor Stephan 3.00 8.00
BCPAWCO William Contreras 12.00 30.00

2018 Bowman Chrome Prospect Autographs Atomic Refractors

*ATMOIC REF: 1.2X TO 3X BASIC
STATED ODDS 1:XX HOBBY
STATED PRINT RUN 100 SER.#'D SETS
EXCHANGE DEADLINE 3/31/2020
CPABMC Brendan McKay 30.00 80.00

2018 Bowman Chrome Prospect Autographs Blue Refractors

*BLUE REF: 1.2X TO 3X BASIC
STATED ODDS 1:XX HOBBY
STATED PRINT RUN 150 SER.#'D SETS
BOW.EXCH.DEADLINE 3/31/2020
BOW.CHR.EXCH 8/31/2020
CPABMC Brendan McKay 30.00 80.00
BCPACK Carter Kieboom 75.00 200.00
BCPAYA Yasel Antuna 60.00 150.00

2018 Bowman Chrome Prospect Autographs Gold Refractors

*GOLD REF: 1.5X TO 4X BASIC
STATED ODDS 1:XX HOBBY
STATED PRINT RUN 50 SER.#'d SETS
BOW.EXCH.DEADLINE 3/31/2020
BOW.CHR.EXCH 8/31/2020
BCPAAA Aramis Ademan 60.00 150.00
BCPAAB Akil Baddoo 40.00 100.00
CPABMC Brendan McKay 40.00 100.00
CPAEF Estevan Florial 300.00 600.00
CPAJN James Nelson 40.00 100.00
CPAMA Micker Adolfo 50.00 120.00
CPARS Ranger Suarez 20.00 50.00
CPASCC Shao-Ching Chiang 30.00 80.00
CPAWA Willie Abreu 25.00 60.00
CPAYA Yordan Alvarez 1000.00 2500.00
BCPACB Charcer Burks 25.00 60.00
BCPACK Carter Kieboom 250.00 600.00
BCPACT Chris Torres 25.00 60.00
BCPAEDL Enyel De Los Santos 25.00 60.00
BCPAFP Franklin Perez 25.00 60.00
BCPALR Leonardo Rivas 20.00 50.00
BCPANA Nick Allen 25.00 60.00
BCPANL Nicky Lopez 30.00 80.00
BCPATS Trevor Stephan 25.00 60.00
BCPAYA Yasel Antuna 75.00 200.00

2018 Bowman Chrome Prospect Autographs Gold Shimmer Refractors

*GOLD SHMR REF: 1.5X TO 4X BASIC
STATED ODDS 1:XX HOBBY
STATED PRINT RUN 50 SER.#'d SETS
BOW.EXCH.DEADLINE 3/31/2020
BOW.CHR.EXCH 8/31/2020
BCPAAA Aramis Ademan 60.00 150.00
BCPAAB Akil Baddoo 40.00 100.00
CPABMC Brendan McKay 40.00 100.00
CPAEF Estevan Florial 300.00 600.00
CPAJN James Nelson 40.00 100.00
CPAMA Micker Adolfo 50.00 120.00
CPARS Ranger Suarez 20.00 50.00
CPASCC Shao-Ching Chiang 30.00 80.00
CPAWA Willie Abreu 25.00 60.00
CPAYA Yordan Alvarez 1000.00 2500.00
BCPACB Charcer Burks 25.00 60.00
BCPACK Carter Kieboom 250.00 600.00
BCPACT Chris Torres 25.00 60.00
BCPAEDL Enyel De Los Santos 25.00 60.00
BCPAFP Franklin Perez 25.00 60.00
BCPALR Leonardo Rivas 20.00 50.00
BCPANA Nick Allen 25.00 60.00
BCPANL Nicky Lopez 30.00 80.00
BCPATS Trevor Stephan 25.00 60.00
BCPAYA Yasel Antuna 75.00 200.00

2018 Bowman Chrome Prospect Autographs Green Refractors

*GREEN REF: 1.2X TO 3X BASIC
STATED ODDS 1:XX HOBBY
STATED PRINT RUN 99 SER.#'d SETS
BOW.EXCH.DEADLINE 3/31/2020
BOW.CHR.EXCH 8/31/2020
CPABMC Brendan McKay 30.00 80.00
BCPACK Carter Kieboom 75.00 200.00
BCPAYA Yasel Antuna 60.00 150.00

2018 Bowman Chrome Prospect Autographs Green Atomic Refractors

*GRN ATOMIC REF: 1.2X TO 3X BASIC
STATED ODDS 1:XX HOBBY
STATED PRINT RUN 99 SER.#'D SETS
BOW.EXCH.DEADLINE 3/31/2020
BOW.CHR.EXCH 8/31/2020
BCPACK Carter Kieboom 75.00 200.00
BCPAYA Yasel Antuna 60.00 150.00

2018 Bowman Chrome Prospect Autographs Green Shimmer Refractors

*GRN SHMMR REF: 1.2X TO 3X BASIC
STATED ODDS 1:XX HOBBY
STATED PRINT RUN 99 SER.#'D SETS
BOW.EXCH.DEADLINE 3/31/2020
BOW.CHR.EXCH 8/31/2020
CPABMC Brendan McKay 30.00 80.00

2018 Bowman Chrome Prospect Autographs Orange Refractors

*ORANGE REF: 3X TO 8X BASIC
STATED ODDS 1:XX HOBBY
STATED PRINT RUN 25 SER.#'D SETS
BOW.EXCH.DEADLINE 3/31/2020
BOW.CHR.EXCH 8/31/2020
BCPAAA Aramis Ademan 125.00 300.00
BCPAAB Akil Baddoo 75.00 200.00
CPABMC Brendan McKay 75.00 200.00
CPAEF Estevan Florial 500.00 1000.00
CPAJN James Nelson 75.00 200.00
CPAMA Micker Adolfo 100.00 250.00
CPARS Ranger Suarez 40.00 100.00
CPASCC Shao-Ching Chiang 60.00 150.00
CPAWA Willie Abreu 50.00 120.00
CPAYA Yordan Alvarez 2000.00 5000.00
BCPACB Charcer Burks 50.00 120.00
BCPACK Carter Kieboom 500.00 1200.00
BCPACT Chris Torres 50.00 120.00
BCPAEDL Enyel De Los Santos 50.00 120.00
BCPAFP Franklin Perez 50.00 120.00
BCPALR Leonardo Rivas 40.00 100.00
BCPANA Nick Allen 50.00 120.00
BCPANL Nicky Lopez 60.00 150.00
BCPATS Trevor Stephan 50.00 120.00
BCPAYA Yasel Antuna 150.00 400.00

2018 Bowman Chrome Prospect Autographs Orange Shimmer Refractors

*ORNGE SHMMR REF: 3X TO 8X BASIC
STATED ODDS 1:XX HOBBY
STATED PRINT RUN 25 SER.#'D SETS
BOW.EXCH.DEADLINE 3/31/2020
BOW.CHR.EXCH 8/31/2020
CPABMC Brendan McKay 75.00 200.00
CPAEF Estevan Florial 500.00 1000.00
CPASCC Shao-Ching Chiang 60.00 150.00
CPAYA Yordan Alvarez 2000.00 5000.00

2018 Bowman Chrome Prospect Autographs Orange Wave Refractors

*ORNGE WAVE REF: 3X TO 8X BASIC
STATED ODDS 1:XX HOBBY
STATED PRINT RUN 25 SER.#'D SETS
BOW.EXCH.DEADLINE 3/31/2020
BOW.CHR.EXCH 8/31/2020
BCPAAA Aramis Ademan 125.00 300.00
BCPAAB Akil Baddoo 75.00 200.00
CPAEF Estevan Florial 500.00 1000.00
CPAJN James Nelson 75.00 200.00
CPAMA Micker Adolfo 100.00 250.00
CPARS Ranger Suarez 40.00 100.00
CPASCC Shao-Ching Chiang 60.00 150.00
CPAWA Willie Abreu 50.00 120.00
CPAYA Yordan Alvarez 2000.00 5000.00
BCPACB Charcer Burks 50.00 120.00
BCPACK Carter Kieboom 500.00 1200.00
BCPACT Chris Torres 50.00 120.00
BCPAEDL Enyel De Los Santos 50.00 120.00
BCPAFP Franklin Perez 50.00 120.00
BCPALR Leonardo Rivas 40.00 100.00
BCPANA Nick Allen 50.00 120.00
BCPANL Nicky Lopez 60.00 150.00
BCPATS Trevor Stephan 50.00 120.00
BCPAYA Yasel Antuna 150.00 400.00

2018 Bowman Chrome Prospect Autographs Purple Refractors

*PURPLE REF: .75X TO 2X BASIC
STATED ODDS 1:53 HOBBY JUMBO
STATED PRINT RUN 250 SER.#'D SETS
BOW.EXCH.DEADLINE 3/31/2020
BOW.CHR.EXCH 8/31/2020
BCPACK Carter Kieboom 40.00 100.00

2018 Bowman Chrome Prospect Autographs Refractors

*REF: .5X TO 1.2X BASIC
STATED ODDS 1:27 HOBBY JUMBO
STATED PRINT RUN 499 SER.#'D SETS
BOW.EXCH.DEADLINE 3/31/2020
BOW.CHR.EXCH 8/31/2020
BCPALG Luis Guillorme 4.00 10.00

2018 Bowman Chrome Prospects

PRINTING PLATE ODDS 1:7838 HOBBY
PLATE PRINT RUN 1 SET PER COLOR
BLACK-CYAN-MAGENTA-YELLOW ISSUED
NO PLATE PRICING DUE TO SCARCITY
BCP1 Ronald Acuna 4.00 10.00
BCP2 Bryan Mata .25 .60
BCP3 Daniel Johnson .20 .50
BCP4 Hunter Harvey .20 .50
BCP5 Aaron Knapp .20 .50
BCP6 Austin Beck .25 .60
BCP7 Carter Kieboom .30 .75
BCP8 Cole Ragans .20 .50
BCP9 Alex Jackson .20 .50
BCP10 Justin Williams .20 .50
BCP11 Rowdy Tellez .20 .50
BCP12 Thomas Hatch .25 .60
BCP13 Sam Hilliard .50 1.25
BCP14 Kyle Wright .50 1.25
BCP15 Tyler O'Neill .30 .75
BCP16 Michael Mercado .25 .60
BCP17 Kevin Newman .30 .75
BCP18 Eric Lauer .25 .60
BCP19 Johan Mieses .30 .75
BCP20 Will Smith .50 1.25
BCP21 Luis Robert 40.00 100.00
BCP22 Yadier Alvarez .25 .60
BCP23 Jeren Kendall .25 .60
BCP24 Bobby Bradley .25 .60
BCP25 Drew Ellis .25 .60
BCP26 Alfredro Rodriguez .20 .50
BCP27 Jose Trevino .20 .50
BCP28 Kolby Allard .25 .60
BCP29 Taylor Ward .25 .60
BCP30 Cornelius Randolph .20 .50
BCP31 DJ Peters .50 1.25
BCP32 Domingo Acevedo .20 .50
BCP33 James Nelson .20 .50
BCP34 Josh Ockimey .20 .50
BCP35 Marcos Molina .20 .50
BCP36 Dennis Santana .20 .50
BCP37 Jake Burger .20 .50
BCP38 Mitch Keller .25 .60
BCP39 Colton Welker .20 .50
BCP40 Pedro Avila .20 .50
BCP41 Jason Martin .20 .50
BCP42 Braxton Garrett .20 .50
BCP43 Brendan Rodgers .25 .60
BCP44 James Kaprielian .20 .50
BCP45 Greg Deichmann .25 .60
BCP46 Cristian Pache 1.00 2.50
BCP47 Ibandel Isabel .30 .75
BCP48 Hunter Greene 1.25 3.00
BCP49 Nick Gordon .20 .50
BCP50 Eloy Jimenez .75 2.00
BCP51 Adonis Medina .30 .75
BCP52 Juan Soto 4.00 10.00
BCP53 Miguelangel Sierra .20 .50
BCP54 Alex Lange .20 .50
BCP55 Kyle Tucker .40 1.00
BCP56 TJ Zeuch .20 .50
BCP57 Luis Urias .40 1.00
BCP58 Sean Murphy .30 .75
BCP59 Oscar De La Cruz .20 .50
BCP60 Brian Miller .20 .50
BCP61 Matt Thaiss .20 .50
BCP62 Kyle Cody .20 .50
BCP63 Dylan Cozens .20 .50
BCP64 MJ Melendez .20 .50
BCP65 Scott Kingery .30 .75
BCP66 Jordan Humphreys .20 .50
BCP67 Michel Baez .20 .50
BCP68 Brendan McKay .30 .75
BCP69 Justus Sheffield .25 .60
BCP70 Merandy Gonzalez .20 .50
BCP71 Touki Toussaint .25 .60
BCP72 Andres Gimenez .25 .60
BCP73 Adrian Morejon .20 .50
BCP74 Austin Voth .20 .50
BCP75 Luis Garcia .30 .75
BCP76 Isaac Paredes 1.00 2.50
BCP77 Jake Kalish .20 .50
BCP78 Shed Long .20 .50
BCP79 Keibert Ruiz .60 1.50
BCP80 Matt Hall .20 .50
BCP81 Nick Pratto .25 .60
BCP82 Justin Dunn .25 .60
BCP83 Ian Anderson .50 1.25
BCP84 Franklyn Kilome .25 .60
BCP85 Dane Dunning .20 .50
BCP86 Michael Kopech .40 1.00
BCP87 McKenzie Mills .20 .50
BCP88 Quentin Holmes .20 .50
BCP89 Mike Soroka .60 1.50
BCP90 Stephen Gonsalves .20 .50
BCP91 Spencer Howard .20 .50
BCP92 Ryan Vilade .20 .50
BCP93 Royce Lewis .75 2.00
BCP94 Adam Haseley .30 .75
BCP95 Jorge Mateo .20 .50
BCP96 Junior Fernandez .30 .75
BCP97 Corey Ray .25 .60
BCP98 Evan White .30 .75
BCP99 Logan Allen .20 .50
BCP100 Gleyber Torres 2.00 5.00
BCP101 Zack Littell .20 .50
BCP102 Matt Sauer .20 .50
BCP103 Mitchell White .20 .50
BCP104 Nick Solak .50 1.25
BCP105 Jorge Ona .20 .50
BCP106 D.J. Stewart .20 .50
BCP107 D.L. Hall .20 .50
BCP108 Chris Rodriguez .20 .50
BCP109 Sam Howard .20 .50
BCP110 Eric Pardinho .40 1.00
BCP111 JoJo Romero .25 .60
BCP112 Aramis Garcia .20 .50
BCP113 Taylor Clarke .20 .50
BCP114 Fernando Tatis Jr. 1.50 4.00
BCP115 Cal Quantrill .20 .50
BCP116 Khalil Lee .20 .50
BCP117 C.J. Chatham .25 .60
BCP118 Lazaro Armenteros .40 1.00
BCP119 Gavin LaValley .20 .50
BCP120 Nick Senzel .60 1.50
BCP121 Jose Adolis Garcia .25 .60
BCP122 Ronald Guzman .20 .50
BCP123 Jordan Hicks .40 1.00
BCP124 Alex Faedo .30 .75
BCP125 J.B. Bukauskas .20 .50
BCP126 Jesus Lugardo .30 .75
BCP127 Josh Lowe .20 .50
BCP128 Yu-Cheng Chang .25 .60
BCP129 Kyle Young .25 .60
BCP130 Christin Stewart .25 .60
BCP131 MacKenzie Gore .40 1.00
BCP132 Corbin Burnes .30 .75
BCP133 Tyler Stephenson .20 .50
BCP134 Wander Javier .25 .60
BCP135 Bryse Wilson .30 .75
BCP136 Jo Adell .60 1.50
BCP137 Pete Alonso 2.00 5.00
BCP138 Delvin Perez .20 .50
BCP139 Travis Lakins .20 .50
BCP140 Blake Rutherford .25 .60
BCP141 Blayne Enlow .20 .50
BCP142 A.J. Puk .25 .60
BCP143 Heliot Ramos .30 .75
BCP144 Jahmai Jones .20 .50
BCP145 Adbert Alzolay .25 .60
BCP146 Will Craig .20 .50
BCP147 Forrest Whitley .30 .75
BCP148 Trevor Rogers .20 .50
BCP149 Steven Duggar .20 .50
BCP150 Vladimir Guerrero Jr. 2.00 5.00
BCP151 Russell Wilson 1.00 2.50
BCP152 Luis Garcia .40 1.00
BCP153 Enyel De Los Santos .25 .60
BCP154 Cole Brannen .25 .60
BCP155 Austin Riley .60 1.50
BCP156 Taylor Trammell .30 .75
BCP157 Luis Ortiz .20 .50
BCP158 Nick Allen .20 .50
BCP159 LaMonte Wade .20 .50
BCP160 Kyle Tucker .40 1.00
BCP161 Luis Medina .30 .75
BCP162 Brian Mundell .20 .50
BCP163 Tanner Houck .50 1.25
BCP164 Connor Seabold .20 .50
BCP165 Sheldon Neuse .20 .50
BCP166 Brent Rooker .25 .60
BCP167 Ryan Mountcastle .30 .75
BCP168 Trevor Stephan .20 .50
BCP169 Bryse Wilson .30 .75
BCP170 Charcer Burks .20 .50
BCP171 Jeter Downs .30 .75
BCP172 Tyler Freeman .20 .50
BCP173 Yasel Antuna .40 1.00
BCP174 Keston Hiura .50 1.25
BCP175 Dylan Cease .50 1.25
BCP176 Dakota Hudson .30 .75
BCP177 Alec Hansen .20 .50
BCP178 Sixto Sanchez .50 1.25
BCP179 Peter Lambert .20 .50
BCP180 Jorge Guzman .20 .50
BCP181 Joe Perez .25 .60
BCP182 Brandon Marsh .25 .60
BCP183 Triston McKenzie .20 .50
BCP184 Rogelio Armenteros .20 .50
BCP185 Franklin Perez .20 .50
BCP186 Kristian Robinson 10.00 25.00
BCP187 Kyle Funkhouser .25 .60
BCP188 Jon Duplantier .20 .50
BCP189 Nolan Jones .30 .75
BCP190 Patrick Weigel .20 .50
BCP191 Aramis Ademan .30 .75
BCP192 Carter Kieboom .30 .75
BCP193 D.J. Daniels .20 .50
BCP194 Fernando Romero .25 .60
BCP195 Nicky Lopez .20 .50
BCP196 Darwinzon Hernandez .50 1.25
BCP197 Jake Bauers .25 .60
BCP198 Daulton Varsho .25 .60
BCP199 Bo Bichette .75 2.00
BCP200 Willy Adames .25 .60
BCP201 Shane Baz .25 .60
BCP202 Logan Shore .20 .50
BCP203 Austin Allen .25 .60
BCP204 Isan Diaz .50 1.25
BCP205 David Peterson .25 .60
BCP206 Tony Santillan .20 .50
BCP207 Chris Torres .20 .50
BCP208 Chance Adams .30 .75
BCP209 Matt Manning .30 .75
BCP210 Mickey Moniak .50 1.25
BCP211 Cody Sedlock .20 .50
BCP212 Jay Groome .25 .60
BCP213 Shane Bieber 2.50 6.00
BCP214 Pavin Smith .20 .50
BCP215 Luis Urias .40 1.00
BCP216 Beau Burrows .25 .60
BCP217 Mike Baumann .20 .50
BCP218 Brusdar Graterol .40 1.00
BCP219 Riley Pint .20 .50
BCP220 Anderson Espinoza .20 .50
BCP221 Freddy Peralta .20 .50
BCP222 Chase Pinder .25 .60
BCP223 Michael Chavis .30 .75
BCP224 Zack Burdi .20 .50
BCP225 Eduardo Diaz .25 .60
BCP226 Daz Cameron .20 .50
BCP227 Justin Meadows .30 .75
BCP228 Will Benson .20 .50
BCP229 Jose Albertos .20 .50
BCP230 Zack Collins .25 .60
BCP231 Justin Williams .20 .50
BCP232 Jairo Solis .50 1.25
BCP233 Brendon Little .20 .50
BCP234 Albert Abreu .20 .50
BCP235 Dillon Tate .20 .50
BCP236 Garrett Hampson .30 .75
BCP237 Kevin Maitan .25 .60
BCP238 Monte Harrison .20 .50
BCP239 Gregory Soto .20 .50
BCP240 Leody Taveras .25 .60
BCP241 Riley Adams .25 .60
BCP242 Bobby Dalbec .50 1.25
BCP243 Gavin Sheets .25 .60
BCP244 Kyle Lewis .40 1.00
BCP245 Evan Steele .25 .60
BCP247 LoLo Sanchez .25 .60
BCP248 Luis Guillorme .20 .50
BCP249 Nate Pearson .50 1.25
BCP250 Nick Senzel .60 1.50

2018 Bowman Chrome Prospects Aqua Refractors

*AQUA REF: 2.5X TO 6X BASIC
STATED ODDS 1:132 HOBBY
STATED PRINT RUN 125 SER.#'d SETS

2018 Bowman Chrome Prospects Aqua Shimmer Refractors

*AQUA SHIM REF: 2.5X TO 6X BASIC
STATED ODDS 1:132 HOBBY
STATED PRINT RUN 125 SER.#'d SETS

2018 Bowman Chrome Prospects Atomic Refractors

*ATOMIC REF: 1.5X TO 4X BASIC
STATED ODDS 1:24 HOBBY

2018 Bowman Chrome Prospects Blue Refractors

*BLUE REF: 2X TO 5X BASIC
STATED ODDS 1:209 HOBBY
STATED PRINT RUN 150 SER.#'d SETS

2018 Bowman Chrome Prospects Blue Shimmer Refractors

*BLUE SHIM REF: 2X TO 5X BASIC
STATED ODDS 1:209 HOBBY
STATED PRINT RUN 150 SER.#'d SETS

2018 Bowman Chrome Prospects Canary Yellow Refractors

*CANARY YELLOW REF: 4X TO 10X BASIC
STATED ODDS 1:417 HOBBY
STATED PRINT RUN 75 SER.#'d SETS

2018 Bowman Chrome Prospects Gold Refractors

*GOLD REF: 6X TO 15X BASIC
STATED ODDS 1:626 HOBBY
STATED PRINT RUN 50 SER.#'d SETS

2018 Bowman Chrome Prospects Gold Shimmer Refractors

*GOLD SHIM REF: 6X TO 15X BASIC
STATED ODDS 1:626 HOBBY
STATED PRINT RUN 50 SER.#'d SETS

2018 Bowman Chrome Prospects Green Refractors

*GREEN REF: 3X TO 8X BASIC
STATED ODDS 1:150 RETAIL
STATED PRINT RUN 99 SER.#'d SETS

2018 Bowman Chrome Prospects Green Shimmer Refractors

*GREEN SHIM REF: 3X TO 8X BASIC
STATED ODDS 1:150 RETAIL
STATED PRINT RUN 99 SER.#'d SETS

2018 Bowman Chrome Prospects Orange Refractors

*ORANGE REF: 10X TO 25X BASIC
STATED ODDS 1:292 HOBBY
STATED PRINT RUN 25 SER.#'d SETS

2018 Bowman Chrome Prospects Orange Shimmer Refractors

*ORANGE SHIM REF: 10X TO 25X BASIC
STATED ODDS 1:292 HOBBY
STATED PRINT RUN 25 SER.#'d SETS

2018 Bowman Chrome Prospects Purple Refractors

*PURPLE REF: 1.5X TO 4X BASIC
STATED ODDS 1:126 HOBBY
STATED PRINT RUN 250 SER.#'d SETS

2018 Bowman Chrome Prospects Purple Shimmer Refractors

*PRPL SHMMR REF: 1X TO 2.5X BASIC
STATED ODDS 1:XX HOBBY
STATED PRINT RUN 665 SER.#'d SETS

2018 Bowman Chrome Prospects Refractors

*REF: 1.2X TO 3X BASIC
STATED ODDS 1:63 HOBBY
STATED PRINT RUN 499 SER.#'d SETS

2018 Bowman Chrome Prime Chrome Signatures

STATED ODDS 1:XXX HOBBY
STATED PRINT RUN 50 SER.#'d SETS
EXCHANGE DEADLINE 8/31/2020
PCSAA Aramis Ademan 12.00 30.00
PCSAAL Adbert Alzolay 12.00 30.00
PCSAB Austin Beck 10.00 25.00
PCSBL Brendon Little
PCSBM Brandon Marsh 30.00 80.00
PCSBMC Brendan McKay 30.00 80.00
PCSCB Corbin Burnes 8.00 20.00
PCSCP Cristian Pache 40.00 100.00
PCSEDL Enyel De Los Santos 20.00 50.00
PCSEF Estevan Florial 100.00 250.00
PCSFP Franklin Perez 6.00 15.00
PCSGS Gregory Soto 6.00 15.00
PCSHG Hunter Greene 40.00 100.00
PCSJA Jo Adell EXCH 40.00 100.00
PCSJB Jake Burger 6.00 15.00
PCSJG Jorge Guzman 6.00 15.00
PCSKH Keston Hiura 15.00 40.00
PCSKM Kevin Maitan
PCSKR Keibert Ruiz 20.00 50.0
PCSLR Luis Robert 30.00 80.0
PCSLU Luis Urias 40.00 100.0
PCSMG MacKenzie Gore 12.00 30.0
PCSMW Mitchell White 4.00 10.0
PCSNL Nicky Lopez 15.00 40.0
PCSRL Royce Lewis 25.00 60.0
PCSSB Shane Bieber 20.00 50.0
PCSSN Sheldon Neuse 10.00 25.0

2018 Bowman Chrome Prime Chrome Signatures Orange Refractors

*ORANGE REF: .5X TO 1.2X BASIC
STATED ODDS 1:XXX HOBBY
STATED PRINT RUN 25 SER.#'d SETS
EXCHANGE DEADLINE 8/31/2020
PCSBL Brendon Little 15.00 40.0
PCSBM Brandon Marsh 150.00 400.0
PCSCP Cristian Pache 100.00 250.0
PCSFP Franklin Perez 20.00 50.0
PCSKH Keston Hiura 40.00 100.0

2018 Bowman Chrome Rookie Autographs

STATED ODDS 1:XXX
PRINTING PLATES RANDOMLY INSERTED
PLATE PRINT RUN 1 SET PER COLOR
BLACK-CYAN-MAGENTA-YELLOW ISSUED
NO PLATE PRICING DUE TO SCARCITY
BOW.EXCH.DEADLINE 3/31/2020
BOW.CHR.EXCH. 8/31/2020
BCRAAR Amed Rosario 5.00 12.0
BCRAAS Andrew Stevenson 3.00 8.0
BCRAAV Alex Verdugo 6.00 15.0
BCRACF Clint Frazier 8.00 20.0
BCRAFM Francisco Mejia 8.00 20.0
BCRAGA Greg Allen 3.00 8.0
BCRAGC Garrett Cooper 3.00 8.0
BCRAGT Gleyber Torres 50.00 120.0
BCRAJD J.D. Davis 4.00 10.0
BCRAJF Jack Flaherty 5.00 12.0
BCRALS Lucas Sims 3.00 8.0
BCRAOA Ozzie Albies 30.00 80.0
BCRARA Ronald Acuna 150.00 400.0
BCRARD Rafael Devers 25.00 60.0
BCRARU Richard Urena 3.00 8.0
BCRASA Sandy Alcantara 3.00 8.0
BCRASO S.Ohtani Bttng 300.00 600.0
BCRATN Tomas Nido 3.00 8.0
BCRAVR Victor Robles 25.00 60.0
BCRAWA Willy Adames 4.00 10.0
CRAAB Anthony Banda 3.00 8.0
CRAAH Austin Hays 5.00 12.0
CRAAR Amed Rosario 5.00 12.0
CRAAV Alex Verdugo 6.00 15.0
CRACF Clint Frazier 8.00 20.0
CRACS Chance Sisco 4.00 10.0
CRADS Dominic Smith 6.00 15.0
CRAHB Harrison Bader 5.00 12.0
CRAJF Jack Flaherty 5.00 12.0
CRAMA Miguel Andujar 15.00 40.0
CRAND Nicky Delmonico 3.00 8.0
CRARD Rafael Devers 25.00 60.0
CRARH Rhys Hoskins 75.00 200.0
CRARM Ryan McMahon 4.00 10.0
CRASO S.Ohtani Ptchng 400.00 800.0
CRATM Tyler Mahle 4.00 10.0
CRAVR Victor Robles 25.00 60.0
CRAWB Walker Buehler 25.00 60.0

2018 Bowman Chrome Rookie Autographs Atomic Refractors

*ATOMIC REF: .75X TO 2X BASIC
STATED ODDS 1:733 HOBBY

STATED PRINT RUN 100 SER.#'d SETS
EXCHANGE DEADLINE 3/31/2020
CRAAV Alex Verdugo 40.00 100.00
CRACF Clint Frazier 40.00 100.00
CRARD Rafael Devers 125.00 300.00
CRASO S.Ohtani Ptchng 800.00 1200.00
CRATM Tyler Mahle 8.00 20.00
CRAVR Victor Robles 75.00 200.00

2018 Bowman Chrome Rookie Autographs Blue Refractors

*BLUE REF: .75X TO 2X BASIC
STATED ODDS 1:84 JUMBO
STATED PRINT RUN 150 SER.#'d SETS
BOW.EXCH.DEADLINE 3/31/2020
BOW.CHR.EXCH. 8/31/2020
CRASO Ohtani Ptchng Knji
CRASO S.Ohtani Ptchng 800.00 1200.00

2018 Bowman Chrome Rookie Autographs Gold Refractors

*GOLD REF: 1.2X TO 3X BASIC
STATED ODDS 1:1438 HOBBY
STATED PRINT RUN 50 SER.#'d SETS
BOW.EXCH.DEADLINE 3/31/2020
BOW.CHR.EXCH. 8/31/2020
BCRAAR Amed Rosario 25.00 60.00
BCRACF Clint Frazier 30.00 80.00
BCRARA Ronald Acuna 800.00 1500.00
BCRASO S.Ohtani Bttng 1500.00 3000.00
BCRAVR Victor Robles 125.00 300.00
CRAAR Amed Rosario 25.00 60.00
CRACF Clint Frazier 30.00 80.00
CRARD Rafael Devers 100.00 250.00
CRARH Rhys Hoskins 400.00 1000.00
CRASO S.Ohtani Ptchng 3000.00 5000.00
CRATM Tyler Mahle 12.00 30.00
CRAVR Victor Robles 125.00 300.00

2018 Bowman Chrome Rookie Autographs Green Refractors

*GREEN REF: .75X TO 2X BASIC
STATED ODDS 1:397 RETAIL
STATED PRINT RUN 99 SER.#'d SETS
BOW.EXCH.DEADLINE 3/31/2020
BOW.CHR.EXCH. 8/31/2020
BCRASO S.Ohtani Bttng 600.00 1000.00
CRASO S.Ohtani Ptchng 800.00 1200.00

2018 Bowman Chrome Rookie Autographs Orange Refractors

*ORANGE REF: 2.5X TO 6X BASIC
STATED ODDS 1:858 HOBBY
STATED PRINT RUN 25 SER.#'d SETS
BOW.EXCH.DEADLINE 3/31/2020
BOW.CHR.EXCH. 8/31/2020
BCRAAR Amed Rosario 50.00 120.00
BCRAAV Alex Verdugo 75.00 200.00
BCRACF Clint Frazier 60.00 150.00
BCRARA Ronald Acuna 2000.00 4000.00
BCRARD Rafael Devers 200.00 500.00
BCRASO S.Ohtani Bttng 5000.00 8000.00
BCRAVR Victor Robles 150.00 400.00
CRAAR Amed Rosario 50.00 120.00
CRAAV Alex Verdugo 75.00 200.00
CRACF Clint Frazier 60.00 150.00
CRARD Rafael Devers 200.00 500.00
CRARH Rhys Hoskins 800.00 2000.00
CRASO S.Ohtani Ptchng 8000.00 12000.00
CRATM Tyler Mahle 25.00 60.00
CRAVR Victor Robles 150.00 400.00

2018 Bowman Chrome Rookie Autographs Refractors

*REF: .6X TO 1.2X BASIC
STATED ODDS 1:XXX HOBBY JUMBO
STATED PRINT RUN 499 SER.#'D SETS
BOW.EXCH.DEADLINE 3/31/2020
BOW.CHR.EXCH. 8/31/2020

2018 Bowman Chrome Rookie of the Year Favorites Refractors

STATED ODDS 1:8 HOBBY
*ATOMIC REF: 1X TO 2.5X BASIC
*GREEN REF/99: 2.5X TO 6X BASIC
*ORNGE REF/25: 8X TO 20X BASIC
ROYFAB Anthony Banda .25 .60
ROYFAR Amed Rosario .30 .75
ROYFAV Alex Verdugo .40 1.00
ROYFCF Clint Frazier .50 1.25
ROYFDS Dominic Smith .25 .60
ROYFFM Francisco Mejia .30 .75
ROYFHB Harrison Bader .40 1.00
ROYFJC J.P. Crawford .25 .60
ROYFJF Jack Flaherty .40 1.00
ROYFNW Nick Williams .30 .75
ROYFOA Ozzie Albies .75 2.00
ROYFRD Rafael Devers .75 2.00
ROYFRH Rhys Hoskins 1.00 2.50
ROYFVR Victor Robles .60 1.50
ROYFWC Willie Calhoun .30 .75

2018 Bowman Chrome Rookie of the Year Favorites Autographs Refractors

STATED ODDS 1:2176 HOBBY
STATED PRINT RUN 150 SER.#'d SETS
EXCHANGE DEADLINE 3/31/2020
GOLD REF/50: .6X TO 1.5X BASE
ROYFAAB Anthony Banda 5.00 12.00
ROYFAAR Amed Rosario 20.00 50.00
ROYFAAV Alex Verdugo 8.00 20.00
ROYFACF Clint Frazier 20.00 50.00
ROYFAHB Harrison Bader 8.00 20.00
ROYFAJF Jack Flaherty 8.00 20.00
ROYFARD Rafael Devers 25.00 60.00
ROYFAVR Victor Robles 25.00 60.00

2018 Bowman Chrome Rookie of the Year Favorites Autographs Orange Refractors

*ORANGE/25: .75X TO 2X BASIC
STATED ODDS 1:3876 HOBBY
STATED PRINT RUN 25 SER.#'d SETS
EXCHANGE DEADLINE 3/31/2020
ROYFAVR Victor Robles 125.00 300.00

2018 Bowman Chrome Scouts Top 100

STATED ODDS 1:4 HOBBY
*ATOMIC REF/150: 1.5X TO 4X BASIC
*GREEN REF/99: 1.5X TO 4X BASIC
*GOLD REF/50: 3X TO 8X BASIC
*ORNGE REF/25: 5X TO 12X BASIC
BTP1 Vladimir Guerrero Jr. 2.50 6.00
BTP2 Ronald Acuna 5.00 12.00
BTP3 Victor Robles .60 1.50
BTP4 Gleyber Torres 2.50 6.00
BTP5 Eloy Jimenez 1.00 2.50
BTP6 Walker Buehler 1.25 3.00
BTP7 Alex Reyes .30 .75
BTP8 Michael Kopech .50 1.25
BTP9 Mitch Keller .30 .75
BTP10 Fernando Tatis Jr. 2.00 5.00
BTP11 Hunter Greene .75 2.00
BTP12 Bo Bichette 1.00 2.50
BTP13 MacKenzie Gore .50 1.25
BTP14 Brendan Rodgers .30 .75
BTP15 Francisco Mejia .30 .75
BTP16 Nick Senzel .75 2.00
BTP17 Kyle Tucker .50 1.25
BTP18 Nick Gordon .25 .60
BTP19 A.J. Puk .30 .75
BTP20 Royce Lewis 1.00 2.50
BTP21 Luiz Gohara .25 .60
BTP22 Brent Honeywell .40 1.00
BTP23 Forrest Whitley .40 1.00
BTP24 Triston McKenzie .25 .60
BTP25 Mike Soroka .75 2.00
BTP26 Austin Hays .40 1.00
BTP27 Willy Adames .30 .75
BTP28 Alex Verdugo .40 1.00
BTP29 Luis Robert 5.00 12.00
BTP30 Sixto Sanchez .60 1.50
BTP31 Scott Kingery .40 1.00
BTP32 Michael Chavis .40 1.00
BTP33 Franklin Perez .25 .60
BTP34 Alec Hansen .25 .60
BTP35 Ian Anderson .60 1.50
BTP36 Chance Sisco .30 .75
BTP37 J.P. Crawford .25 .60
BTP38 Pavin Smith .25 .60
BTP39 Jo Adell .75 2.00
BTP40 Lewis Brinson .25 .60
BTP41 Brendan McKay .40 1.00
BTP42 Jack Flaherty .40 1.00
BTP43 Kyle Lewis .50 1.25
BTP44 Juan Soto 5.00 12.00
BTP45 Estevan Florial .40 1.00
BTP46 Keston Hiura .60 1.50
BTP47 Cal Quantrill .25 .60
BTP48 Shane Baz .30 .75
BTP49 Carson Kelly .25 .60
BTP50 Justus Sheffield .30 .75
BTP51 Leody Taveras .30 .75
BTP52 Kevin Newman .40 1.00
BTP53 Nate Pearson .60 1.50
BTP54 Heliot Ramos .40 1.00
BTP55 Yordan Alvarez 2.00 5.00
BTP56 Michel Baez .25 .60
BTP57 Jon Duplantier .25 .60
BTP58 Jahmai Jones .25 .60
BTP59 Jay Groome .30 .75
BTP60 Luis Urias .50 1.25
BTP61 Dylan Cease .60 1.50
BTP62 Bobby Bradley .30 .75
BTP63 Ryan McMahon .30 .75
BTP64 Nick Pratto .30 .75
BTP65 Keibert Ruiz .75 2.00
BTP66 Trevor Rogers .25 .60
BTP67 Chance Adams .40 1.00
BTP68 Jesus Luzardo .40 1.00
BTP69 Chris Shaw .25 .60
BTP70 Adam Haseley .40 1.00
BTP71 Jesus Sanchez .25 .60
BTP72 Corbin Burnes .40 1.00
BTP73 Cole Ragans .25 .60
BTP74 Anthony Alford .25 .60
BTP75 Austin Meadows .40 1.00
BTP76 Kolby Allard .25 .60
BTP77 Carter Kieboom .40 1.00
BTP78 D.L. Hall .25 .60
BTP79 Sam Travis .25 .60
BTP80 David Peterson .30 .75
BTP81 Tyler Mahle .30 .75
BTP82 Bryse Wilson .40 1.00
BTP83 Victor Caratini .30 .75
BTP84 Taylor Trammell .40 1.00
BTP85 Dane Dunning .25 .60
BTP86 Adbert Alzolay .30 .75
BTP87 Riley Pint .25 .60
BTP88 J.B. Bukauskas .25 .60
BTP89 Matt Manning .40 1.00
BTP90 Brandon Marsh .30 .75
BTP91 Andres Gimenez .30 .75
BTP92 Monte Harrison .25 .60
BTP93 Jeren Kendall .30 .75
BTP94 Stephen Gonsalves .25 .60
BTP95 Albert Abreu .25 .60
BTP96 Franklin Barreto .25 .60
BTP97 Jorge Mateo .25 .60
BTP98 Christian Arroyo .25 .60
BTP99 Willie Calhoun .30 .75
BTP100 Austin Riley .75 2.00

2018 Bowman Chrome Scouts Top 100 Autographs Refractors

STATED ODDS 1:1383 HOBBY
STATED PRINT RUN 50 SER. #'d SETS
EXCHANGE DEADLINE 3/31/2020
BTP2 Ronald Acuna 300.00 600.00
BTP3 Victor Robles 30.00 80.00
BTP4 Gleyber Torres 125.00 300.00
BTP6 Walker Buehler 50.00 120.00
BTP7 Alex Reyes
BTP8 Michael Kopech 12.00 30.00
BTP9 Mitch Keller 8.00 20.00
BTP11 Hunter Greene 100.00 250.00
BTP14 Brendan Rodgers 15.00 40.00
BTP19 A.J. Puk 8.00 20.00
BTP20 Royce Lewis 40.00 100.00
BTP26 Austin Hays 10.00 25.00
BTP28 Alex Verdugo 25.00 60.00
BTP32 Michael Chavis 10.00 25.00
BTP35 Ian Anderson 15.00 40.00
BTP36 Chance Sisco 25.00 60.00
BTP37 J.P. Crawford 6.00 15.00
BTP38 Pavin Smith 6.00 15.00
BTP40 Lewis Brinson 6.00 15.00
BTP41 Brendan McKay 40.00 100.00
BTP42 Jack Flaherty 10.00 25.00
BTP46 Keston Hiura 20.00 50.00
BTP47 Cal Quantrill 6.00 15.00
BTP48 Shane Baz 8.00 20.00
BTP50 Justus Sheffield 25.00 60.00
BTP53 Nate Pearson 20.00 50.00
BTP54 Heliot Ramos 25.00 60.00
BTP56 Michel Baez 30.00 80.00
BTP57 Jon Duplantier 6.00 15.00
BTP58 Jahmai Jones 6.00 15.00
BTP59 Jay Groome 8.00 20.00
BTP63 Ryan McMahon 8.00 20.00
BTP64 Nick Pratto 25.00 60.00
BTP65 Keibert Ruiz 20.00 50.00
BTP66 Trevor Rogers
BTP68 Jesus Luzardo
BTP69 Chris Shaw 15.00 40.00
BTP70 Adam Haseley 10.00 25.00
BTP72 Corbin Burnes 10.00 25.00
BTP77 Carter Kieboom 25.00 60.00
BTP79 Sam Travis 6.00 15.00
BTP80 David Peterson 12.00 30.00
BTP81 Tyler Mahle 8.00 20.00
BTP86 Adbert Alzolay
BTP87 Riley Pint 6.00 15.00
BTP88 J.B. Bukauskas 6.00 15.00
BTP91 Andres Gimenez 8.00 20.00
BTP93 Jeren Kendall 25.00 60.00
BTP95 Albert Abreu 12.00 30.00
BTP96 Franklin Barreto 6.00 15.00
BTP97 Jorge Mateo 10.00 25.00
BTP98 Christian Arroyo 6.00 15.00

2018 Bowman Chrome Talent Pipeline Refractors

STATED ODDS 1:12 HOBBY
*ATOMIC REF/150: .75X TO 2X BASIC
*GREEN REF/99: 1X TO 2.5X BASIC
*ORANGE REF/25: 2X TO 5X BASIC
TPARI Jon Duplantier .30 .75
Anthony Banda
Alex Young
TPATL Braves 4.00 10.00
TPBAL Chance Sisco .50 1.25
Ryan Mountcastle
Alex Wells
TPBOS Tzu-Wei Lin .50 1.25
Michael Chavis
Jay Groome
TPCHI Cubs .40 1.00
TPCHW White Sox 1.25 3.00
TPCIN Reds 1.00 2.50
TPCLE Nellie Rodriguez .40 1.00
Triston McKenzie
Bobby Bradley
TPCOL Brendan Rodgers .40 1.00
Sam Howard
Riley Pint
TPDET Tigers .50 1.25
TPHOU Forrest Whitley .50 1.25
Rogelio Armenteros
Yordan Alvarez
TPKCR Josh Staumont .30 .75
Foster Griffin
Khalil Lee
TPLAA Fletcher/Thaiss/Jones 1.00 2.50
TPLAD Dodgers 1.00 2.50
TPMIA John Norwood .30 .75
Victor Payano
Braxton Garrett
TPMIL Dubon/Ortiz/Hiura .75 2.00
TPMIN Twins 1.25 3.00
TPNYM Mets .40 1.00
TPNYY Yankees 3.00 8.00
TPOAK Paul Blackburn .50 1.25
A.J. Puk
Jesus Luzardo
TPPHI Phillies .75 2.00
TPPIT Austin Meadows .50 1.25
Mitch Keller
Will Craig
TPSDP Padres 2.50 6.00
TPSEA Max Povse .60 1.50
Kyle Lewis
Braden Bishop
TPSFG Chris Shaw .30 .75
C.J. Hinojosa
Ryan Howard
TPSTL Cardinals .60 1.50
TPTBR Ryas .50 1.25
TPTEX Rangers .40 1.00
TPTOR Jays 3.00 8.00
TPWAS Nationals 6.00 15.00

2018 Bowman Chrome Draft

COMPLETE SET (200) 20.00 50.00
STATED PLATE ODDS 1:1198 HOBBY
PLATE PRINT RUN 1 SET PER COLOR
BLACK-CYAN-MAGENTA-YELLOW ISSUED
NO PLATE PRICING DUE TO SCARCITY
BDC1 Casey Mize 2.00 5.00
BDC2 Matt Vierling .50 1.25
BDC3 Brusdar Graterol .50 1.25
BDC4 Lawrence Butler .40 1.00
BDC5 Terrin Vavra .50 1.25
BDC6 Jarred Kelenic 12.00 30.00
BDC7 Yusniel Diaz .75 2.00
BDC8 Lenny Torres .30 .75
BDC9 Shane McClanahan .40 1.00
BDC10 Blayne Enlow .25 .60
BDC11 Brice Turang .75 2.00
BDC12 Tim Cate .40 1.00
BDC13 Pedro Avila .25 .60
BDC14 Kyle Isbel .60 1.50
BDC15 Devin Mann .40 1.00
BDC16 Jazz Chisholm .60 1.50
BDC17 Luis Medina .40 1.00
BDC18 Adrian Morejon .25 .60
BDC19 Arbert Cipion .25 .60
BDC20 Trevor Stephan .25 .60
BDC21 Drew Ellis .30 .75
BDC22 Taylor Trammell .40 1.00
BDC23 Jayson Schroeder .25 .60
BDC24 Joe Jacques .25 .60
BDC25 Alec Bohm 1.25 3.00
BDC26 Beau Burrows .30 .75
BDC27 Jonathan Stiever .25 .60
BDC28 Parker Meadows .50 1.25
BDC29 Jonathan Ornelas .60 1.50
BDC30 Matthew Liberatore .30 .75
BDC31 Greyson Jenista .50 1.25
BDC32 Bo Bichette 1.00 2.50
BDC33 Durbin Feltman .40 1.00
BDC34 Nick Sandlin .25 .60
BDC35 Jahmai Jones .25 .60
BDC36 Brandon Marsh .30 .75
BDC37 Lency Delgado .50 1.25
BDC38 Nick Madrigal 1.50 4.00
BDC39 Kris Bubic .40 1.00
BDC40 Oneil Cruz .40 1.00
BDC41 Alex Faedo .40 1.00
BDC42 Thomas Ponticelli .25 .60
BDC43 Bryan Lavastida .25 .60
BDC44 Nick Schnell .30 .75
BDC45 Cal Mitchell .40 1.00
BDC46 Nick Solak .60 1.50
BDC47 Brennen Davis 2.00 5.00
BDC48 Ethan Hankins .30 .75
BDC49 Keston Hiura .60 1.50
BDC50 Ko'Bryan Hayes .25 .60
BDC51 Jeremiah Jackson .40 1.00
BDC52 Lolo Sanchez .30 .75
BDC53 Gregory Soto .25 .60
BDC54 Nicky Lopez .25 .60
BDC55 Jake Wong .25 .60
BDC56 Jordan Groshans 1.25 3.00
BDC57 Josh Breaux .30 .75
BDC58 Hunter Greene .75 2.00
BDC59 Dylan Cease .60 1.50
BDC60 Carlos Cortes .30 .75
BDC61 Korry Howell .25 .60
BDC62 Joey Wentz .30 .75
BDC63 Logan Gilbert .40 1.00
BDC64 Ryan Rolison .50 1.25
BDC65 Anthony Seigler .60 1.50
BDC66 Jorge Guzman .25 .60
BDC67 Mark Vientos .40 1.00
BDC68 Chris Paddack .60 1.50
BDC69 Kole Cottam .30 .75
BDC70 Trevor Larnach 1.50 4.00
BDC71 Monte Harrison .25 .60
BDC72 Aramis Ademan .40 1.00
BDC73 Grayson Rodriguez .50 1.25
BDC74 Nick Gordon .25 .60
BDC75 Sixto Sanchez .60 1.50
BDC76 Joe Gray .40 1.00
BDC77 Drevian Williams-Nelson .25 .60
BDC78 Tanner Dodson .30 .75
BDC79 Ryan Vilade .25 .60
BDC80 Blake Rivera .25 .60
BDC81 Adam Haseley .40 1.00
BDC82 Braydon Fisher 1.00 2.50
BDC83 Kevon Jackson .25 .60
BDC84 Ryder Green .50 1.25
BDC85 Jawuan Harris .25 .60
BDC86 Mitch Keller .30 .75
BDC87 Royce Lewis 1.00 2.50
BDC88 Jordyn Adams 1.50 4.00
BDC89 Korey Holland .25 .60
BDC90 Thad Ward .25 .60
BDC91 Sean Murphy .40 1.00
BDC92 Calvin Coker .25 .60
BDC93 Carter Kieboom .40 1.00
BDC94 Jake McCarthy .40 1.00
BDC95 Braxton Ashcraft .40 1.00
BDC96 Colton Eastman .60 1.50
BDC97 Mitchell White .25 .60
BDC98 Nick Pratto .30 .75
BDC99 Alex McKenna .30 .75
BDC100 Brendan McKay .40 1.00
BDC101 Mike Shawaryn .25 .60
BDC102 Levi Kelly .25 .60
BDC103 Osiris Johnson .30 .75
BDC104 Justin Jarvis .25 .60
BDC105 Ford Proctor .30 .75
BDC106 Ezequiel Pagan .30 .75
BDC107 Jo Adell .75 2.00
BDC108 Jon Duplantier .25 .60
BDC109 Luken Baker .40 1.00
BDC110 Grant Little .25 .60
BDC111 Micah Bello .40 1.00
BDC112 Jonathan India .40 1.00
BDC113 Will Banfield .25 .60
BDC114 Keibert Ruiz .75 2.00
BDC115 Grant Koch .25 .60
BDC116 Jeren Kendall .30 .75
BDC117 Nolan Gorman 1.50 4.00
BDC118 Nate Pearson .60 1.50
BDC119 Corbin Martin .25 .60
BDC120 Shed Long .25 .60
BDC121 Kody Clemens .50 1.25
BDC122 Josh Naylor .30 .75
BDC123 Sheldon Neuse .25 .60
BDC124 Nick Decker .50 1.25
BDC125 Cole Roederer .75 2.00
BDC126 Albert Abreu .25 .60
BDC127 Dallas Woolfolk .25 .60
BDC128 Adonis Medina .40 1.00
BDC129 Tristan Pompey .40 1.00
BDC130 Michel Baez .25 .60
BDC131 Pavin Smith .25 .60
BDC132 Brian Miller .25 .60
BDC133 Heliot Ramos .40 1.00
BDC134 Cadyn Grenier .30 .75
BDC135 Brady Singer .50 1.25
BDC136 Andres Gimenez .30 .75
BDC137 Griffin Roberts .25 .60
BDC138 Greg Deichmann .30 .75
BDC139 Sean Hjelle .30 .75
BDC140 Kenen Irizarry .40 1.00
BDC141 Alfonso Rivas .25 .60
BDC142 Daniel Lynch .30 .75
BDC143 Matt Mercer .25 .60
BDC144 Sean Guilbe .30 .75
BDC145 Matt Manning .40 1.00
BDC146 Alec Hansen .25 .60
BDC147 Jackson Goddard .25 .60
BDC148 Jesus Luzardo .40 1.00
BDC149 Nick Dunn .75 2.00
BDC150 MacKenzie Gore .50 1.25
BDC151 Jeter Downs .40 1.00
BDC152 Grant Witherspoon .30 .75
BDC153 Griffin Conine .50 1.25
BDC154 Adam Hill .25 .60
BDC155 Alek Thomas 1.00 2.50
BDC156 Tyler Frank .25 .60
BDC157 Sean Wymer .25 .60
BDC158 Connor Scott .30 .75
BDC159 Owen White .40 1.00
BDC160 Jameson Hannah .40 1.00
BDC161 Mike Siani .30 .75
BDC162 Triston McKenzie .25 .60
BDC163 Bobby Bradley .30 .75
BDC164 Mason Denaburg .30 .75
BDC165 Nico Hoerner 1.25 3.00
BDC166 Matt Thaiss .25 .60
BDC167 Ryan Mountcastle .40 1.00
BDC168 Eloy Jimenez 1.00 2.50
BDC169 Logan Allen .25 .60
BDC170 Dane Dunning .25 .60
BDC171 Triston Casas 2.00 5.00
BDC172 Bryan Mata .30 .75
BDC173 Cole Winn .40 1.00
BDC174 Leury Tejada .25 .60
BDC175 Sam Carlson .30 .75
BDC176 Raynel Delgado .60 1.50
BDC177 Leody Taveras .30 .75
BDC178 Justin Dunn .30 .75
BDC179 Jeremy Eierman .30 .75
BDC180 Jesus Sanchez .25 .60
BDC181 Simeon Woods-Richardson .30 .75
BDC182 Ryan Weathers .30 .75
BDC183 Ian Anderson .60 1.50
BDC184 Matt Sauer .25 .60
BDC185 Adam Wolf .30 .75
BDC186 Grant Lavigne 1.25 3.00
BDC187 Estevan Florial .40 1.00
BDC188 Luis Robert 8.00 20.00
BDC189 J.B. Bukauskas .25 .60
BDC190 Josh Stowers .60 1.50
BDC191 Brent Rooker .30 .75
BDC192 Ryan Jeffers .50 1.25
BDC193 Noah Naylor .40 1.00
BDC194 Cody Deason .25 .60
BDC195 Cal Quantrill .25 .60
BDC196 Jackson Kowar .25 .60
BDC197 Griffin Canning .25 .60
BDC198 Travis Swaggerty .75 2.00
BDC199 Alex Kirilloff .40 1.00
BDC200 Lazaro Armenteros .50 1.25

2018 Bowman Chrome Draft Blue Refractors

*BLUE REF: 2X TO 5X BASIC
STATED ODDS 1:32 HOBBY
STATED PRINT RUN 150 SER.#'d SETS
BDC117 Nolan Gorman 50.00 120.00
BDC165 Nico Hoerner 15.00 40.00
BDC188 Luis Robert 60.00 150.00

2018 Bowman Chrome Draft Gold Refractors

*GOLD REF: 5X TO 12X BASIC
STATED ODDS 1:96 HOBBY
STATED PRINT RUN 50 SER.#'d SETS
BDC2 Matt Vierling 15.00 40.00
BDC25 Alec Bohm 40.00 100.00
BDC81 Adam Haseley 15.00 40.00
BDC117 Nolan Gorman 125.00 300.00
BDC165 Nico Hoerner 40.00 100.00
BDC188 Luis Robert 100.00 250.00
BDC193 Noah Naylor 10.00 25.00

2018 Bowman Chrome Draft Green Refractors

*GREEN REF: 2.5X TO 6X BASIC
STATED ODDS 1:49 HOBBY
STATED PRINT RUN 99 SER.#'d SETS
BDC117 Nolan Gorman 60.00 150.00
BDC165 Nico Hoerner 20.00 50.00
BDC188 Luis Robert 75.00 200.00

2018 Bowman Chrome Draft Purple Refractors

*PURPLE REF: 1.5X TO 4X BASIC
STATED ODDS 1:20 HOBBY
STATED PRINT RUN 250 SER.#'d SETS
BDC117 Nolan Gorman 15.00 40.00
BDC165 Nico Hoerner 12.00 30.00
BDC188 Luis Robert 50.00 120.00

2018 Bowman Chrome Draft Refractors

*REF: .75X TO 2X BASIC
RANDOM INSERTS IN PACKS
BDC188 Luis Robert 20.00 50.00

2018 Bowman Chrome Draft Sky Blue Refractors

*SKY BLUE REF: 1X TO 2.5X BASIC
RANDOM INSERTS IN PACKS
STATED PRINT RUN 402 SER.#'d SETS
BDC117 Nolan Gorman 15.00 40.00
BDC165 Nico Hoerner 8.00 20.00
BDC188 Luis Robert 25.00 60.00

2018 Bowman Chrome Draft Sparkle Refractors

*SPARKLE REF: 1.5X TO 4X BASIC
STATED ODDS 1:24 HOBBY
BDC117 Nolan Gorman 15.00 40.00
BDC165 Nico Hoerner 12.00 30.00
BDC188 Luis Robert 50.00 120.00

2018 Bowman Chrome Draft Image Variation Refractors

STATED ODDS 1:196 HOBBY
BDC1 Casey Mize
White Jersey
BDC3 Brusdar Graterol
Gray Pants
BDC6 Jarred Kelenic
Gray Jersey
BDC20 Trevor Stephan
New York visable on jersey
BDC25 Alec Bohm
Red Jersey
BDC32 Bo Bichette
Fielding
BDC38 Nick Madrigal
Fielding
BDC72 Aramis Ademan
Ball visable
BDC87 Royce Lewis
Hand on bat barrel
BDC93 Carter Kieboom
No hat
BDC112 Jonathan India
Running
BDC182 Ryan Weathers
White Jersey
BDC198 Travis Swaggerty
Tipping helmet

2018 Bowman Chrome Draft Image Variation Autographs Refractors

STATED ODDS 1:948 HOBBY
STATED PRINT RUN 99 SER.#'d SETS
EXCHANGE DEADLINE 11/30/2020
BDC1 Casey Mize 100.00 250.00
BDC6 Jarred Kelenic 200.00 500.00
BDC25 Alec Bohm 100.00 250.00
BDC38 Nick Madrigal 125.00 300.00
BDC93 Carter Kieboom 75.00 200.00
BDC112 Jonathan India 75.00 200.00
BDC182 Ryan Weathers 25.00 60.00

2018 Bowman Chrome Draft Orange Refractors

*ORANGE REF: 8X TO 20X BASIC
STATED ODDS 1:130 HOBBY
STATED PRINT RUN 25 SER.#'d SETS
BDC2 Matt Vierling 25.00 60.00
BDC25 Alec Bohm 60.00 150.00
BDC81 Adam Haseley 25.00 60.00
BDC112 Jonathan India 60.00 150.00
BDC117 Nolan Gorman 200.00 500.00
BDC165 Nico Hoerner 60.00 150.00
BDC188 Luis Robert 250.00 600.00
BDC193 Noah Naylor 15.00 40.00

2018 Bowman Chrome Draft '98 Bowman

STATED ODDS 1:6 HOBBY
*REF/250: .5X TO 1.2X BASE
*GOLD REF/50: 2.5X TO 6X BASE
98BAB Alec Bohm 1.25 3.00
98BBS Brady Singer .50 1.25
98BCM Casey Mize 2.00 5.00
98BGR Grayson Rodriguez .50 1.25
98BJI Jonathan India .40 1.00
98BJK Jarred Kelenic 2.50 6.00
98BNM Nick Madrigal 1.50 4.00
98BRW Ryan Weathers .30 .75
98BTC Triston Casas 2.00 5.00
98BTS Travis Swaggerty .75 2.00

2018 Bowman Chrome Draft '98 Bowman Autographs

STATED ODDS 1:948 HOBBY
STATED PRINT RUN 99 SER.#'d SETS
EXCHANGE DEADLINE 11/30/2020
98BAAB Alec Bohm 30.00 80.00
98BACM Casey Mize 50.00 125.00
98BAJI Jonathan India 10.00 25.00
98BAJK Jarred Kelenic 50.00 120.00
98BANM Nick Madrigal 25.00 60.00
98BARW Ryan Weathers 20.00 50.00
98BATS Travis Swaggerty 20.00 50.00

2018 Bowman Chrome Draft Autographs

OVERALL AUTO ODDS 1:8 HOBBY
STATED PLATE ODDS 1:3987 HOBBY
PLATE PRINT RUN 1 SET PER COLOR
BLACK-CYAN-MAGENTA-YELLOW ISSUED
NO PLATE PRICING DUE TO SCARCITY
EXCHANGE DEADLINE 11/30/2020
CDAAB Alec Bohm 100.00 250.00
CDAAS Anthony Seigler 8.00 20.00
CDAAT Alek Thomas 30.00 80.00
CDABA Braxton Ashcraft 5.00 12.00
CDABS Brady Singer 20.00 50.00
CDABT Brice Turang 15.00 40.00
CDACC Carlos Cortes 5.00 12.00
CDACG Cadyn Grenier 5.00 12.00
CDACM Casey Mize 50.00 120.00
CDACR Cole Roederer 6.00 15.00
CDACSC Connor Scott 6.00 15.00
CDACW Cole Winn 5.00 12.00
CDADL Daniel Lynch 8.00 20.00
CDAEH Ethan Hankins 8.00 20.00
CDAGC Griffin Conine 10.00 25.00
CDAGJ Greyson Jenista 6.00 15.00
CDAGL Grant Lavigne 10.00 25.00
CDAGR Grayson Rodriguez 20.00 50.00
CDAGRO Griffin Roberts 4.00 10.00
CDAJA Jordyn Adams 20.00 50.00
CDAJBR Josh Breaux 8.00 20.00
CDAJE Jeremy Eierman 5.00 12.00
CDAJG Jordan Groshans 25.00 60.00
CDAJGR Joe Gray 5.00 12.00
CDAJI Jonathan India 15.00 40.00
CDAJJ Jeremiah Jackson 12.00 30.00
CDAJK Jarred Kelenic 100.00 250.00
CDAJKO Jackson Kowar 8.00 20.00
CDAJM Jake McCarthy 5.00 12.00
CDAJOG Josiah Gray 15.00 40.00
CDAJS Josh Stowers 6.00 15.00
CDAJSC Jayson Schroeder 4.00 10.00
CDAJW Jake Wong 3.00 8.00
CDAKB Kris Bubic 8.00 20.00
CDAKC Kody Clemens 6.00 15.00
CDALB Luken Baker 5.00 12.00
CDALG Logan Gilbert 15.00 40.00
CDALT Lenny Torres 4.00 10.00
CDAMD Mason Denaburg 6.00 15.00
CDAML Matthew Liberatore 15.00 40.00
CDANG Nolan Gorman 60.00 150.00
CDANH Nico Hoerner 15.00 40.00
CDANM Nick Madrigal 40.00 100.00
CDANN Noah Naylor 10.00 25.00
CDANS Nick Schnell 6.00 15.00
CDAOJ Osiris Johnson 4.00 10.00
CDAOW Owen White 5.00 12.00
CDAPM Parker Meadows 6.00 15.00
CDARG Ryder Green 6.00 15.00
CDARJ Ryan Jeffers 6.00 15.00
CDARR Ryan Rolison 5.00 12.00
CDARW Ryan Weathers 4.00 10.00
CDASM Shane McClanahan 10.00 25.00
CDASWR Simeon Woods-Richardson 4.00 10.00
CDATC Triston Casas 40.00 100.00
CDATCA Tim Cate 5.00 12.00
CDATD Tanner Dodson 4.00 10.00
CDATF Tyler Frank 5.00 12.00
CDATL Trevor Larnach 25.00 60.00
CDATP Tristan Pompey 6.00 15.00
CDATS Travis Swaggerty 12.00 30.00
CDAWB Will Banfield 5.00 12.00

2018 Bowman Chrome Draft Autographs Black Refractors

*BLACK REF: 1.5X TO 4X BASIC
STATED ODDS 1:144 HOBBY
STATED PRINT RUN 75 SER.#'d SETS
EXCHANGE DEADLINE 11/30/2020
CDAAB Alec Bohm/75 400.00 1000.00
CDABT Brice Turang/75 100.00 250.00
CDAGL Grant Lavigne/75 75.00 200.00
CDAJBR Josh Breaux/75 50.00 120.00
CDAJS Josh Stowers/75 40.00 100.00
CDANN Noah Naylor/75 50.00 120.00
CDATC Triston Casas/75 200.00 500.00
CDATS Travis Swaggerty/75 50.00 120.00

2018 Bowman Chrome Draft Autographs Blue Refractors

*BLUE REF: 1X TO 2.5X BASIC
STATED ODDS 1:107 HOBBY
STATED PRINT RUN 150 SER.#'d SETS
EXCHANGE DEADLINE 11/30/2020
CDAAB Alec Bohm/150 250.00 600.00
CDABT Brice Turang/150 60.00 150.00
CDAGC Griffin Conine/150 30.00 80.00

CDAGL Grant Lavigne/150 50.00 120.00
CDAJBR Josh Breaux/150 30.00 80.00
CDAJS Josh Stowers/150 25.00 60.00
CDANN Noah Naylor/150 30.00 80.00
CDATC Triston Casas/150 125.00 300.00
CDATS Travis Swaggerty/150 30.00 80.00

2018 Bowman Chrome Draft Autographs Blue Wave Refractors

*BLUE WAVE REF: 1X TO 2.5X BASIC
STATED ODDS 1:107 HOBBY
STATED PRINT RUN 150 SER.#'d SETS
EXCHANGE DEADLINE 11/30/2020
CDAAB Alec Bohm 250.00 600.00
CDABT Brice Turang 60.00 150.00
CDAGC Griffin Conine 30.00 80.00
CDAGL Grant Lavigne 50.00 120.00
CDAJBR Josh Breaux 30.00 80.00
CDAJS Josh Stowers 25.00 60.00
CDANN Noah Naylor 30.00 80.00
CDATC Triston Casas 125.00 300.00
CDATS Travis Swaggerty 30.00 80.00

2018 Bowman Chrome Draft Autographs Gold Refractors

*GOLD REF: 2.5X TO 6X BASIC
STATED ODDS 1:319 HOBBY
STATED PRINT RUN 50 SER.#'d SETS
EXCHANGE DEADLINE 11/30/2020
CDAAB Alec Bohm/50 600.00 1500.00
CDAAT Alek Thomas/50 300.00 800.00
CDABT Brice Turang/50 150.00 400.00
CDAGC Griffin Conine/50 75.00 200.00
CDAGL Grant Lavigne/50 125.00 300.00
CDAJBR Josh Breaux/50 75.00 200.00
CDAJS Josh Stowers/50 75.00 200.00
CDANN Noah Naylor/50 75.00 200.00
CDATC Triston Casas/50 250.00 600.00
CDATS Travis Swaggerty/50 75.00 200.00

2018 Bowman Chrome Draft Autographs Gold Wave Refractors

*GOLD WAVE REF: 2.5X TO 6X BASIC
STATED ODDS 1:319 HOBBY
STATED PRINT RUN 50 SER.#'d SETS
EXCHANGE DEADLINE 11/30/2020
CDAAB Alec Bohm 600.00 1500.00
CDAAT Alek Thomas 300.00 800.00
CDABT Brice Turang 150.00 400.00
CDAGC Griffin Conine 75.00 200.00
CDAGL Grant Lavigne 125.00 300.00
CDAJBR Josh Breaux 75.00 200.00
CDAJS Josh Stowers 75.00 200.00
CDANN Noah Naylor 75.00 200.00
CDATC Triston Casas 250.00 600.00
CDATS Travis Swaggerty 75.00 200.00

2018 Bowman Chrome Draft Autographs Green Refractors

*GREEN REF: 1.2X TO 3X BASIC
STATED ODDS 1:161 HOBBY
STATED PRINT RUN 99 SER.#'d SETS
EXCHANGE DEADLINE 11/30/2020
CDAAB Alec Bohm/99 300.00 800.00
CDABT Brice Turang/99 75.00 200.00
CDAGC Griffin Conine/99 40.00 100.00
CDAGL Grant Lavigne/99 60.00 150.00
CDAJBR Josh Breaux/99 40.00 100.00
CDAJS Josh Stowers/99 30.00 80.00
CDANN Noah Naylor/99 40.00 100.00
CDATC Triston Casas/99 150.00 400.00
CDATS Travis Swaggerty/99 40.00 100.00

2018 Bowman Chrome Draft Autographs Orange Refractors

*ORANGE REF: 3X TO 8X BASIC
STATED ODDS 1:430 HOBBY
STATED PRINT RUN 25 SER.#'d SETS
EXCHANGE DEADLINE 11/30/2020
CDAAB Alec Bohm/25 750.00 2000.00
CDAAT Alek Thomas/25 1000.00 2000.00
CDABT Brice Turang/25 200.00 500.00
CDACR Cole Roederer/25 300.00 600.00
CDACW Cole Winn/25 125.00 300.00
CDAGC Griffin Conine/25 300.00 600.00
CDAGL Grant Lavigne/25 300.00 600.00
CDAGR Grayson Rodriguez/25 150.00 400.00
CDAJBR Josh Breaux/25 100.00 250.00
CDAJGR Joe Gray/25 40.00 100.00
CDAJI Jonathan India/25 300.00 800.00
CDAJK Jarred Kelenic/25 1000.00 2000.00
CDAJS Josh Stowers/25 100.00 250.00
CDAKC Kody Clemens/25 125.00 300.00
CDAML Matthew Liberatore/25 200.00 500.00
CDANG Nolan Gorman/25 1500.00 2500.00
CDANN Noah Naylor/25 100.00 250.00
CDARG Ryder Green/25 50.00 125.00
CDATC Triston Casas/25 500.00 1200.00
CDATS Travis Swaggerty/25 125.00 300.00

2018 Bowman Chrome Draft Autographs Purple Refractors

*PURPLE REF: .6X TO 1.5X BASIC
STATED ODDS 1:64 HOBBY
STATED PRINT RUN 250 SER.#'d SETS
EXCHANGE DEADLINE 11/30/2020
CDAAB Alec Bohm/250 150.00 400.00
CDABT Brice Turang/250 40.00 100.00
CDAGL Grant Lavigne/250 30.00 80.00
CDAJBR Josh Breaux/250 15.00 40.00
CDATC Triston Casas/250 75.00 200.00

2018 Bowman Chrome Draft Autographs Refractors

*REF: .5X TO 1.2X BASIC
STATED ODDS 1:32 HOBBY
PRINT RUNS B/WN 485-499 COPIES PER
EXCHANGE DEADLINE 11/30/2020
CDAAB Alec Bohm/499 125.00 300.00
CDABT Brice Turang/499 30.00 80.00
CDAGL Grant Lavigne/499 25.00 60.00
CDATC Triston Casas/499 60.00 150.00

2018 Bowman Chrome Draft Autographs Sparkle Refractors

*SPARKEL REF: 1.5X TO 4X BASIC
STATED ODDS 1:225 HOBBY
STATED PRINT RUN 71 SER.#'d SETS
EXCHANGE DEADLINE 11/30/2020
CDAAB Alec Bohm 400.00 1000.00
CDABT Brice Turang 100.00 250.00
CDAGC Griffin Conine 50.00 120.00
CDAGL Grant Lavigne 75.00 200.00
CDAJBR Josh Breaux 50.00 120.00
CDAJS Josh Stowers 40.00 100.00
CDANN Noah Naylor 50.00 120.00
CDATC Triston Casas 200.00 500.00
CDATS Travis Swaggerty 50.00 120.00

2018 Bowman Chrome Draft Class of '18 Autographs

STATED ODDS 1:114 HOBBY
STATED PRINT RUN 250 SER.#'d SETS
EXCHANGE DEADLINE 11/30/2020
*GOLD/50: 1X TO 2.5X BASIC
C18AAB Alec Bohm 25.00 60.00
C18AAS Anthony Seigler 10.00 25.00
C18ABS Brady Singer 8.00 20.00
C18ABT Brice Turang 6.00 15.00
C18ACG Cadyn Grenier 5.00 12.00
C18ACM Casey Mize 30.00 80.00
C18ACSC Connor Scott 5.00 12.00
C18ACW Cole Winn 6.00 15.00
C18AGR Grayson Rodriguez EXCH 10.00 25.00
C18AJA Jordyn Adams 15.00 40.00
C18AJG Jordan Groshans 12.00 30.00
C18AJI Jonathan India 20.00 50.00
C18AJK Jarred Kelenic 40.00 100.00
C18AJKO Jackson Kowar 4.00 10.00
C18AJM Jake McCarthy 6.00 15.00
C18AKB Kris Bubic 6.00 15.00
C18ALG Logan Gilbert 10.00 25.00
C18AMD Mason Denaburg EXCH 5.00 12.00
C18AML Matthew Liberatore 10.00 25.00
C18ANG Nolan Gorman 50.00 120.00
C18ANH Nico Hoerner 40.00 100.00
C18ANM Nick Madrigal 15.00 40.00
C18ANN Noah Naylor 6.00 15.00
C18ANS Nick Schnell 8.00 20.00
C18ARR Ryan Rolison 8.00 20.00
C18ARW Ryan Weathers 12.00 30.00
C18ASM Shane McClanahan 6.00 15.00
C18ATC Triston Casas 15.00 40.00
C18ATL Trevor Larnach 12.00 30.00
C18ATS Travis Swaggerty 8.00 20.00

2018 Bowman Chrome Draft Draft Night Autographs

STATED ODDS 1:1896 HOBBY
STATED PRINT RUN 99 SER.#'d SETS
EXCHANGE DEADLINE 11/30/2020
*GOLD/50: .5X TO 1.2X BASIC
DNAAB Alec Bohm 25.00 60.00
DNAAS Anthony Seigler 25.00 60.00
DNATC Triston Casas 15.00 40.00
DNATS Travis Swaggerty 20.00 50.00

2018 Bowman Chrome Draft Franchise Futures

STATED ODDS 1:3 HOBBY
*REF/250: .5X TO 1.2X BASE
*GOLD REF/50: 1.2X TO 3X BASE
FFARI McCarthy/Thomas 1.00 2.50
FFBAL Grenier/Rodriguez .50 1.25
FFCIN Siani/India .40 1.00
FFCWS Pilkington/Madrigal 1.50 4.00
FFDET Clemens/Mize 2.00 5.00
FFKCR Kowar/Singer .50 1.25
FFNYM Cortes/Kelenic 2.50 6.00
FFNYY Seigler/Breaux .60 1.50
FFSDP Xavier Edwards .40 1.00
Ryan Weathers
FFSEA Stowers/Gilbert .60 1.50

2018 Bowman Chrome Draft Recommended Viewing

STATED ODDS 1:3 HOBBY
*REF/250: .5X TO 1.2X BASE
*GOLD REF/50: 1.2X TO 3X BASE
RVBT Kris Bubic .40 1.00
Lenny Torres
RVCS Stowers/Conine .60 1.50
RVGC Casas/Gorman 2.00 5.00
RVGE Xavier Edwards .40 1.00
Cadyn Grenier
RVGT Thomas/Gray 1.00 2.50
RVKH Ethan Hankins .30 .75
Jackson Kowar
RVLJ Jenista/Lavigne 1.25 3.00
RVMG Groshans/Madrigal 1.50 4.00
RVMI Madrigal/India 1.50 4.00
RVMS Mize/Singer 2.00 5.00
RVSM Jake McCarthy .40 1.00
Nick Schnell
RVSN Naylor/Seigler .60 1.50
RVWC Tim Cate .40 1.00
Owen White
RVWL Liberatore/Winn .40 1.00
RVWRA Simeon Woods-Richardson .40 1.00
Braxton Ashcraft

2018 Bowman Chrome Draft Recommended Viewing Dual Autographs

STATED ODDS 1:633 HOBBY
STATED PRINT RUN 99 SER.#'d SETS
EXCHANGE DEADLINE 11/30/2020
*GOLD/50: .5X TO 1.2X BASIC
RVACS Conine/Stowers EXCH 15.00 40.00
RVAGC Gorman/Casas 100.00 250.00
RVAJB Breaux/Jeffers 10.00 25.00
RVAKH Kowar/Hankins EXCH 10.00 25.00
RVALJ Lavigne/Jenista EXCH 25.00 60.00
RVAMG Groshans/Madrigal 40.00 100.00
RVAMI India/Madrigal 60.00 150.00
RVAMS Singer/Mize 40.00 100.00
RVASN Seigler/Naylor EXCH 12.00 30.00
RVAWC Cate/White EXCH 8.00 20.00
RVAWL Winn/Liberatore EXCH 20.00 50.00

2018 Bowman Chrome Draft Top of the Class Box Topper

STATED ODDS 1:46 HOBBY BOXES
STATED PRINT RUN 99 SER.#'d SETS
*GOLD/50: .5X TO 1.2X BASIC
TOCAB Alec Bohm 8.00 20.00
TOCCM Casey Mize 12.00 30.00
TOCGR Grayson Rodriguez 3.00 8.00
TOCJA Jordyn Adams 10.00 25.00
TOCJB Joey Bart 25.00 60.00
TOCJG Jordan Groshans 5.00 12.00
TOCJI Jonathan India 2.50 6.00
TOCJK Jarred Kelenic 15.00 40.00
TOCML Matthew Liberatore 2.00 5.00
TOCNM Nick Madrigal 10.00 25.00
TOCRW Ryan Weathers 2.00 5.00
TOCTS Travis Swaggerty 5.00 12.00

2018 Bowman Chrome Draft Top of the Class Box Topper Autographs

STATED ODDS 1:2184 HOBBY BOXES
STATED PRINT RUN 35 SER.#'d SETS
EXCHANGE DEADLINE 11/30/2020
TOCAB Alec Bohm 25.00 60.00
TOCCM Casey Mize 40.00 100.00
TOCGR Grayson Rodriguez
TOCJA Jordyn Adams
TOCJG Jordan Groshans 15.00 40.00
TOCJI Jonathan India 75.00 200.00
TOCJK Jarred Kelenic
TOCML Matthew Liberatore
TOCNM Nick Madrigal 30.00 80.00
TOCRW Ryan Weathers
TOCTS Travis Swaggerty 15.00 40.00

2019 Bowman Chrome

1 Ronald Acuna Jr. 1.50 4.00
2 Chris Davis .20 .50
3 Jake Bauers RC .60 1.50
4 Yasiel Puig .30 .75
5 Jake Cave RC .50 1.25
6 Corey Kluber .25 .60
7 Christin Stewart RC .50 1.25
8 David Peralta .20 .50
9 DJ Stewart RC .50 1.25
10 Brandon Lowe RC .60 1.50
11 Kolby Allard RC .60 1.50
12 Jonathan Loaisiga RC .50 1.25
13 Francisco Lindor .30 .75
14 Dansby Swanson .30 .75
15 Blake Snell .25 .60
16 Chance Adams RC .40 1.00
17 Brandon Belt .25 .60
18 Eddie Rosario .25 .60
19 Ian Kinsler .25 .60
20 Starling Marte .25 .60
21 Yoan Moncada .30 .75
22 Whit Merrifield .30 .75
23 Miguel Cabrera .30 .75
24 Dakota Hudson RC .50 1.25
25 Kyle Tucker RC .75 2.00
26 Fernando Tatis Jr. RC 15.00 40.00
27 Nolan Arenado .40 1.00
28 Rowdy Tellez RC .60 1.50
29 Cedric Mullins RC .60 1.50
30 Lourdes Gurriel Jr. .25 .60
31 Manny Machado .30 .75
32 Corbin Burnes RC .60 1.50
33 Josh Hader .20 .50
34 Taylor Ward RC .40 1.00
35 Mark Trumbo .20 .50
36 Enyel De Los Santos RC .40 1.00
37 Ryan Borucki RC .40 1.00
38 Giancarlo Stanton .30 .75
39 Joey Votto .30 .75
40 Willians Astudillo RC .40 1.00
41 Billy Hamilton .25 .60
42 Keston Hiura RC 1.25 3.00
43 Josh James RC .60 1.50
44 Juan Soto 1.00 2.50
45 Griffin Canning RC .60 1.50
46 Khris Davis .30 .75
47 Cal Quantrill RC .40 1.00
48 Pete Alonso RC 4.00 10.00
49 Jacob deGrom .30 .75
50 Shohei Ohtani 1.50 4.00
51 Josh Bell .25 .60
52 Charlie Blackmon .30 .75
53 Luis Urias RC .60 1.50
54 Brad Keller .20 .50
55 Bryce Harper .50 1.25
56 Anthony Rizzo .50 1.25
57 Zack Greinke .25 .60
58 Justus Sheffield RC .60 1.50
59 Jon Duplantier RC .40 1.00
60 Alex Bregman .30 .75
61 Rhys Hoskins .40 1.00
62 Bryse Wilson RC .50 1.25
63 Christian Yelich .40 1.00
64 Clayton Kershaw .60 1.50
65 Lewis Brinson .20 .50
66 Robinson Cano .25 .60
67 Ramon Laureano RC .75 2.00
68 Joey Gallo .25 .60
69 Jose Abreu .30 .75
70 Nelson Cruz .30 .75
71 Edwin Encarnacion .30 .75
72 Buster Posey .40 1.00
73 Vladimir Guerrero Jr. RC 5.00 12.00
74 Carter Kieboom RC .60 1.50
75 Mookie Betts .50 1.25
76 Kyle Wright RC .60 1.50
77 Brian Anderson .20 .50
78 Blake Treinen .20 .50
79 Willy Adames .20 .50
80 Nicholas Castellanos .30 .75
81 Eloy Jimenez RC 1.50 4.00
82 Michael Kopech RC .75 2.00
83 Jose Altuve .25 .60
84 Austin Riley RC 2.00 5.00
85 Chris Sale .30 .75
86 Kris Bryant .40 1.00
87 Marcus Stroman .25 .60
88 Danny Jansen RC .40 1.00
89 Touki Toussaint RC .50 1.25
90 Aaron Judge .75 2.00
91 Yusei Kikuchi RC .60 1.50
92 Ryan O'Hearn RC .40 1.00
93 Paul DeJong .30 .75
94 Miles Mikolas .30 .75
95 Ronald Guzman .20 .50
96 Mitch Haniger .25 .60
97 Victor Robles .40 1.00
98 Nick Senzel RC 1.25 3.00
99 Justin Turner .25 .60
100 Mike Trout 1.50 4.00

2019 Bowman Chrome Blue Refractors

*BLUE REF VET: 4X TO 10X BASIC
*BLUE REF RC: 2X TO 5X BASIC
STATED ODDS 1:71 HOBBY
STATED PRINT RUN 150 SER.#'d SETS
26 Fernando Tatis Jr. 150.00 400.00
42 Keston Hiura 10.00 25.00
48 Pete Alonso 30.00 80.00
73 Vladimir Guerrero Jr. 25.00 60.00
81 Eloy Jimenez 12.00 30.00
100 Mike Trout 25.00 60.00

2019 Bowman Chrome Gold Refractors

*GOLD REF VET: 8X TO 20X BASIC
*GOLD REF RC: 4X TO 10X BASIC
STATED ODDS 1:211 HOBBY
STATED PRINT RUN 50 SER.#'d SETS
1 Ronald Acuna Jr. 50.00 120.00
26 Fernando Tatis Jr. 300.00 800.00
42 Keston Hiura 20.00 50.00
48 Pete Alonso 60.00 150.00
55 Bryce Harper 30.00 80.00
73 Vladimir Guerrero Jr. 50.00 120.00
81 Eloy Jimenez 25.00 60.00
100 Mike Trout 100.00 250.00

2019 Bowman Chrome Green Refractors

*GREEN REF VET: 5X TO 12X BASIC
*GREEN REF RC: 2.5X TO 6X BASIC
STATED ODDS 1:107 HOBBY
STATED PRINT RUN 99 SER.#'d SETS
26 Fernando Tatis Jr. 200.00 500.00
42 Keston Hiura 12.00 30.00
48 Pete Alonso 40.00 100.00
73 Vladimir Guerrero Jr. 30.00 80.00
81 Eloy Jimenez 15.00 40.00
100 Mike Trout 30.00 80.00

2019 Bowman Chrome Orange Refractors

*ORANGE REF VET: 10X TO 25X BASIC
*ORANGE REF RC: 5X TO 12X BASIC
STATED ODDS 1:XXX HOBBY
STATED PRINT RUN 25 SER.#'d SETS
1 Ronald Acuna Jr. 60.00 150.00
26 Fernando Tatis Jr. 400.00 1000.00
42 Keston Hiura 25.00 60.00
48 Pete Alonso 75.00 200.00
55 Bryce Harper 40.00 100.00
73 Vladimir Guerrero Jr. 60.00 150.00
81 Eloy Jimenez 30.00 80.00
100 Mike Trout 125.00 300.00

2019 Bowman Chrome Purple Refractors

*PURPLE REF VET: 2X TO 5X BASIC
*PURPLE REF RC: 1X TO 2.5X BASIC
STATED ODDS 1:43 HOBBY
STATED PRINT RUN 250 SER.#'d SETS
1 Ronald Acuna Jr. 8.00 20.00
26 Fernando Tatis Jr. 75.00 200.00
42 Keston Hiura 5.00 12.00
48 Pete Alonso 25.00 60.00
73 Vladimir Guerrero Jr. 15.00 40.00
81 Eloy Jimenez 6.00 15.00
100 Mike Trout 12.00 30.00

2019 Bowman Chrome Refractors

*REF VET: 1.5X TO 4X BASIC
*REF RC: .75X TO 2X BASIC
STATED ODDS 1:21 HOBBY
STATED PRINT RUN 499 SER.#'d SETS
1 Ronald Acuna Jr. 6.00 15.00
26 Fernando Tatis Jr. 50.00 120.00
42 Keston Hiura 4.00 10.00
48 Pete Alonso 20.00 50.00
73 Vladimir Guerrero Jr. 12.00 30.00
81 Eloy Jimenez 5.00 12.00
100 Mike Trout 10.00 25.00

2019 Bowman Chrome Rookie Image Variations

STATED ODDS 1:141 HOBBY
3 Jake Bauers 5.00 12.00
7 Christin Stewart 4.00 10.00
11 Kolby Allard 5.00 12.00
16 Chance Adams 3.00 8.00
25 Kyle Tucker 6.00 15.00
29 Cedric Mullins 5.00 12.00
32 Corbin Burnes 5.00 12.00
37 Ryan Borucki 3.00 8.00
42 Chris Shaw 5.00 12.00
53 Luis Urias 5.00 12.00
58 Justus Sheffield 5.00 12.00
76 Kyle Wright 5.00 12.00
82 Michael Kopech 6.00 15.00
88 Danny Jansen 2.50 6.00
92 Ryan O'Hearn 3.00 8.00

2019 Bowman Chrome Rookie Image Variation Autographs

STATED ODDS 1:7728 HOBBY
STATED PRINT RUN 25 SER.#'d SETS
EXCHANGE DEADLINE 8/31/2021
11 Kolby Allard 30.00 80.00
16 Chance Adams 15.00 40.00
58 Justus Sheffield 25.00 60.00
76 Kyle Wright 25.00 60.00

2019 Bowman Chrome '18 AFL Fall Stars

STATED ODDS 1:6 HOBBY
STATED MVP SP ODDS 1:4186 HOBBY
*ATOMIC/150: 1.2X TO 3X BASE
*ORANGE/25: 4X TO 10X BASE
AFLAG Andres Gimenez .50 1.25
AFLBD Bobby Dalbec 1.00 2.50
AFLBR Buddy Reed .40 1.00
AFLSBR Buddy Reed MVP/250 8.00 20.00
AFLCB Cavan Biggio 2.00 5.00
AFLCK Carter Kieboom .60 1.50
AFLCP Cristian Pache 1.00 2.50
AFLDC Daz Cameron .40 1.00
AFLDH Darwinzon Hernandez .40 1.00
AFLDJ Daniel Johnson .40 1.00
AFLDV Daulton Varsho .40 1.00
AFLEF Estevan Florial .60 1.50
AFLEW Evan White .60 1.50
AFLFW Forrest Whitley .60 1.50
AFLGS Gregory Soto .40 1.00
AFLJD Jon Duplantier .40 1.00
AFLJPM Julio Pablo Martinez .40 1.00
AFLJR Jake Rogers .50 1.25
AFLJY Jordan Yamamoto .40 1.00
AFLKH Keston Hiura 1.25 3.00
AFLKR Keibert Ruiz 1.00 2.50
AFLLJC Li-Jen Chu .50 1.25
AFLLR Luis Robert 4.00 10.00
AFLNH Nico Hoerner 1.25 3.00
AFLNP Nate Pearson 1.00 2.50
AFLPA Pete Alonso 3.00 8.00
AFLRH Ronaldo Hernandez .40 1.00
AFLRM Ryan McKenna .40 1.00
AFLSL Shed Long .60 1.50
AFLVGJ Vladimir Guerrero Jr. 2.50 6.00
AFLZB Zack Burdi .40 1.00

2019 Bowman Chrome '18 AFL Fall Stars Autograph Relics

STATED ODDS 1:4275 HOBBY
STATED PRINT RUN 50 SER.#'d SETS
EXCHANGE DEADLINE 8/31/2021
AFLRBD Bobby Dalbec 15.00 40.00
AFLRDH Darwinzon Hernandez 20.00 50.00
AFLRKH Keston Hiura 25.00 60.00
AFLRKR Keibert Ruiz 20.00 50.00
AFLRNH Nico Hoerner 50.00 120.00
AFLRPA Peter Alonso 125.00 300.00
AFLRRM Ryan McKenna 8.00 20.00

2019 Bowman Chrome '18 AFL Fall Stars Autographs

STATED ODDS 1:727 HOBBY
STATED MVP ODDS 1:18,955 HOBBY
PRINT RUNS B/WN 50-150 COPIES PER
EXCHANGE DEADLINE 8/31/2021
AFLBR Buddy Reed/50 6.00 15.00
AFLSBR Buddy Reed MVP/100 5.00 12.00
AFLCK Carter Kieboom/75 10.00 25.00
AFLDC Daz Cameron/110 4.00 10.00
AFLDJ Daniel Johnson/150 4.00 10.00
AFLDV Daulton Varsho/150 8.00 20.00
AFLEW Evan White/150 12.00 30.00
AFLGS Gregory Soto/150 4.00 10.00
AFLJPM Julio Pablo Martinez/150 4.00 10.00
AFLJR Jake Rogers/150 8.00 20.00
AFLJY Jordan Yamamoto/150 8.00 20.00
AFLKH Keston Hiura/150 20.00 50.00
AFLLJC Li-Jen Chu/150 5.00 12.00
AFLLR Luis Robert/110 60.00 150.00
AFLNH Nico Hoerner/150 8.00 20.00
AFLNP Nate Pearson/50 15.00 40.00
AFLPA Pete Alonso/75 60.00 150.00
AFLRH Ronaldo Hernandez/150 6.00 15.00
AFLRM Ryan McKenna/150 4.00 10.00
AFLSL Shed Long/150 6.00 15.00
AFLZB Zack Burdi/150 4.00 10.00

2019 Bowman Chrome '18 AFL Fall Stars Relics

STATED ODDS 1:483 HOBBY
STATED PRINT RUN 99 SER.#'d SETS
*ORANGE/25: .6X TO 1.5X BASIC
AFLRAG Andres Gimenez 4.00 10.00
AFLRBD Bobby Dalbec 8.00 20.00
AFLRCB Cavan Biggio 10.00 25.00
AFLRCK Carter Kieboom 5.00 12.00
AFLRCP Cristian Pache 8.00 20.00
AFLRCT Cole Tucker 5.00 12.00
AFLRDH Darwinzon Hernandez 3.00 8.00
AFLREF Estevan Florial 8.00 20.00
AFLREW Evan White 5.00 12.00
AFLRFW Forrest Whitley 5.00 12.00
AFLRJD Jon Duplantier 3.00 8.00
AFLRJJ Jahmai Jones 3.00 8.00
AFLRKH Keston Hiura 8.00 20.00
AFLRKL Khalil Lee 3.00 8.00
AFLRKR Keibert Ruiz 8.00 20.00
AFLRLR Luis Robert 12.00 30.00
AFLRNH Nico Hoerner 10.00 25.00
AFLRNP Nate Pearson 8.00 20.00
AFLRPA Peter Alonso 10.00 25.00
AFLRRM Ryan McKenna 3.00 8.00
AFLRSL Shed Long 8.00 20.00
AFLRVGJ Vladimir Guerrero Jr. 20.00 50.00

2019 Bowman Chrome 30th Anniversary

STATED ODDS 1:8 HOBBY
*ATOMIC REF/150: 2.5X TO 6X BASE
*GREEN REF/99: 2.5X TO 6X BASE
*GOLD REF/50: 4X TO 10X BASIC
*ORANGE REF/25: 8X TO 20X BASE
B30AJ Aaron Judge 1.00 2.50
B30AK Alex Kirilloff .40 1.00
B30AN Aaron Nola .30 .75
B30AR Anthony Rizzo .60 1.50
B30BB Bo Bichette .75 2.00
B30BM Brendan McKay .40 1.00
B30BR Brendan Rodgers .40 1.00
B30BS Blake Snell .30 .75
B30CK Carter Kieboom .40 1.00
B30CKE Clayton Kershaw .75 2.00
B30CM Casey Mize .60 1.50
B30CP Cristian Pache .60 1.50
B30DC Dylan Cease .60 1.50
B30EF Estevan Florial .40 1.00
B30EJ Eloy Jimenez 1.00 2.50
B30FL Francisco Lindor .40 1.00
B30FTJ Fernando Tatis Jr. 2.50 6.00
B30FW Forrest Whitley .40 1.00
B30GT Gleyber Torres .75 2.00
B30HG Hunter Greene .40 1.00
B30IA Ian Anderson .60 1.50
B30JA Jo Adell .75 2.00
B30JAL Jose Altuve .30 .75
B30JB Joey Bart .75 2.00
B30JD Jacob deGrom .40 1.00
B30JL Jesus Luzardo .40 1.00
B30JPM Julio Pablo Martinez .25 .60
B30JS Justus Sheffield .40 1.00
B30JSO Juan Soto 1.25 3.00
B30KB Kris Bryant .50 1.25
B30KR Keibert Ruiz .60 1.50
B30KT Kyle Tucker .50 1.25
B30LU Luis Urias .40 1.00
B30MA Miguel Amaya .40 1.00
B30MB Mookie Betts .60 1.50
B30MG MacKenzie Gore .50 1.25
B30MK Michael Kopech .50 1.25
B30MKE Mitch Keller .30 .75
B30MT Mike Trout 3.00 8.00
B30NG Nolan Gorman .75 2.00
B30NM Nick Madrigal .75 2.00
B30NS Nick Senzel .75 2.00
B30RAJ Ronald Acuna Jr. 2.00 5.00
B30RLE Royce Lewis .50 1.25
B30SB Seth Beer .60 1.50
B30SO Shohei Ohtani .50 1.25
B30SS Sixto Sanchez .30 .75
B30VGJ Vladimir Guerrero Jr. 1.50 4.00
B30WF Wander Franco 4.00 10.00
B30YA Yordan Alvarez 1.50 4.00

2019 Bowman Chrome 30th Anniversary Autographs

STATED ODDS 1:5887 HOBBY
PRINT RUNS B/WN 10-30 COPIES PER
NO PRICING ON QTY 10
EXCHANGE DEADLINE 3/31/2021
B30AR Anthony Rizzo/30 30.00 80.00
B30BS Blake Snell/30 12.00 30.00
B30CM Casey Mize/30 30.00 80.00
B30CP Cristian Pache/30 75.00 200.00
B30FL Francisco Lindor/30 40.00 100.00
B30FTJ Fernando Tatis Jr./30 150.00 400.00
B30HG Hunter Greene/30 15.00 40.00
B30JA Jo Adell/30 40.00 100.00
B30JAL Jose Altuve/30 12.00 30.00
B30JB Joey Bart/30 100.00 250.00
B30JD Jacob deGrom/30 25.00 60.00
B30JS Justus Sheffield/30 30.00 80.00
B30JSO Juan Soto/30 40.00 100.00
B30KB Kris Bryant/20 50.00 120.00
B30KR Keibert Ruiz/30 20.00 50.00
B30KT Kyle Tucker/30 40.00 100.00
B30LU Luis Urias/30 15.00 40.00
B30MA Miguel Amaya/30 20.00 50.00
B30MG MacKenzie Gore/30 40.00 100.00
B30MK Michael Kopech/30 10.00 25.00
B30MKE Mitch Keller/30 12.00 30.00
B30NM Nick Madrigal/30 30.00 80.00
B30RAJ Ronald Acuna Jr./30 100.00 250.00
B30SB Seth Beer/30 50.00 120.00
B30SS Sixto Sanchez/30 12.00 30.00
B30WF Wander Franco/30 400.00 800.00

2019 Bowman Chrome AFL Alumni

STATED ODDS 1:144 HOBBY
*ORANGE REF/25: 1.2X TO 3X BASE
AFLAAJ Aaron Judge 8.00 20.00
AFLAAP Albert Pujols 4.00 10.00
AFLABB Byron Buxton 2.50 6.00
AFLABH Bryce Harper 5.00 12.00
AFLABP Buster Posey 4.00 10.00
AFLACB Cody Bellinger 6.00 15.00
AFLACK Craig Kimbrel 2.50 6.00
AFLACS Corey Seager 3.00 8.00
AFLADG Didi Gregorius 2.50 6.00
AFLADJ Derek Jeter 10.00 25.00
AFLAFL Francisco Lindor 3.00 8.00
AFLAGB Greg Bird 2.50 6.00
AFLAGS Gary Sanchez 3.00 8.00
AFLAGT Gleyber Torres 6.00 15.00
AFLAHB Harrison Bader 2.50 6.00
AFLAIH Ian Happ 2.50 6.00
AFLAKB Kris Bryant 4.00 10.00
AFLAKD Khris Davis 3.00 8.00
AFLAMB Mookie Betts 5.00 12.00
AFLAMP Mike Piazza 3.00 8.00
AFLAMT Mike Trout 12.00 30.00
AFLANA Nolan Arenado 4.00 10.00
AFLARB Ryan Braun 2.50 6.00
AFLARAJ Ronald Acuna Jr. 15.00 40.00

2019 Bowman Chrome AFL Alumni Autographs

STATED ODDS 1:3806 HOBBY
PRINT RUNS B/WN 14-75 COPIES PER
NO PRICING ON QTY 14 OR LESS
EXCHANGE DEADLINE 8/31/2021
AFLABP Buster Posey/30 25.00 60.00
AFLADG Didi Gregorius/75 12.00 30.00
AFLAFL Francisco Lindor/60 25.00 60.00
AFLAIH Ian Happ/75 8.00 20.00
AFLAKB Kris Bryant/40 30.00 80.00
AFLAMT Mike Trout/25 250.00 500.00
AFLARAJ Ronald Acuna Jr./60 60.00 150.00

2019 Bowman Chrome Autograph Relics

STATED ODDS 1:490 HOBBY
PRINT RUNS B/WN 30-150 COPIES PER
EXCHANGE DEADLINE 8/31/2021
*GOLD/50: .6X TO 1.5X BASIC
BCARAK Andrew Knizner/150 6.00 15.00
BCARAR Anthony Rizzo/75 20.00 50.00
BCARBD Bobby Dalbec/150 10.00 25.00
BCARCR Corey Ray/150 4.00 10.00
BCARDH Darwinzon Hernandez/150 4.00 10.00
BCARDJ Danny Jansen/150 4.00 10.00
BCARFTJ Fernando Tatis Jr. EXCH 200.00 500.00
BCARJSO Juan Soto/75 50.00 120.00
BCARKB Kris Bryant/75 50.00 120.00
BCARKH Keston Hiura/150 25.00 60.00
BCARKR Keibert Ruiz/150 10.00 25.00
BCARLU Luis Urias/150 15.00 40.00
BCARMA Miguel Amaya/150 6.00 15.00
BCARMAN Miguel Andujar/75 15.00 40.00
BCARMM Miles Mikolas/150 6.00 15.00
BCARMT Mike Trout/30 300.00 600.00
BCARNH Nico Hoerner/150 15.00 40.00
BCARNL Nate Lowe/150 8.00 20.00
BCARPA Peter Alonso/150 125.00 300.00
BCARPD Paul DeJong/150 8.00 20.00
BCARSM Seuly Matias 8.00 20.00

2019 Bowman Chrome Autograph Relics Orange Refractors

*ORANGE REF: 1X TO 2.5X BASIC
STATED ODDS 1:1523 HOBBY
STATED PRINT RUN 25 SER.#'d SETS
EXCHANGE DEADLINE 8/31/2021
BCARMT Mike Trout 400.00 800.00

2019 Bowman Chrome Bowman Sterling Continuity

STATED ODDS 1:24 HOBBY
*ATOMIC REF/150: 2X TO 5X BASE
*GOLD REF/50: 3X TO 8X BASIC
*ORANGE REF/25: 5X TO 12X BASE
BS1 Shohei Ohtani .60 1.50
BS2 Joey Bart 2.50 6.00
BS3 Brusdar Graterol .40 1.00
BS4 Seuly Matias .40 1.00
BS5 Casey Mize .75 2.00
BS6 Aramis Ademan .30 .75
BS7 Kris Bryant .60 1.50
BS8 Alec Bohm 1.25 3.00
BS9 Estevan Florial .50 1.25
BS10 Wander Franco 5.00 12.00
BS11 Jonathan India .40 1.00
BS12 Luis Urias .50 1.25
BS13 Ronaldo Hernandez .30 .75
BS14 Jarred Kelenic 1.25 3.00
BS15 Yordan Alvarez 4.00 10.00
BS16 Kyle Tucker .60 1.50
BS17 Genesis Cabrera .50 1.25
BS18 Nick Madrigal 1.00 2.50
BS19 Julio Pablo Martinez .30 .75
BS20 Mike Trout 3.00 8.00

2019 Bowman Chrome Bowman Sterling Continuity Autographs

STATED ODDS 1:3226 HOBBY
STATED PRINT RUN 99 SER.#'d SETS
EXCHANGE DEADLINE 3/31/2021

BSAAB Alec Bohm 15.00 40.00
BSABG Brusdar Graterol 12.00 30.00
BSACM Casey Mize 30.00 80.00
BSAGC Genesis Cabrera 8.00 20.00
BSAJB Joey Bart 30.00 80.00
BSAJK Jarred Kelenic 25.00 60.00
BSAJPM Julio Pablo Martinez 15.00 40.00
BSAKT Kyle Tucker 15.00 40.00
BSALU Luis Urias 12.00 30.00
BSANM Nick Madrigal 15.00 40.00
BSARH Ronaldo Hernandez 5.00 12.00
BSASM Seuly Matias 6.00 15.00
BSAWF Wander Franco 125.00 300.00

2019 Bowman Chrome Bowman Sterling Continuity Autographs Orange Refractors

*ORANGE REF: .75X TO 2X BASIC
STATED ODDS 1:5226 HOBBY
STATED PRINT RUN 25 SER.#'d SETS
EXCHANGE DEADLINE 3/31/2021
BSAKB Kris Bryant 125.00 300.00
BSAMT Mike Trout 400.00 800.00

2019 Bowman Chrome Dual Prospect Autographs

STATED ODDS 1:20,656 HOBBY
STATED PRINT RUN 25 SER.#'d SETS
EXCHANGE DEADLINE 3/31/2021
DPACW Cruz/Wilson 30.00 80.00
DPAHPM Martinez/Hernandez 10.00 25.00
DPAKM Knizner/Montero 75.00 200.00
DPALH Lowe/Hernandez 20.00 50.00
DPAMB McKenna/Bannon 40.00 100.00
DPAMS Mize/Singer
DPARM Rodriguez/Marte

2019 Bowman Chrome Elite Farmhands

STATED ODDS 1:12 HOBBY
*ATOMIC REF/150: 1X TO 2.5X BASE
*ORANGE REF/25: 3X TO 8X BASE
EFBB Bo Bichette 1.00 2.50
EFCM Casey Mize .75 2.00
EFJA Jordyn Adams .40 1.00
EFJB Joey Bart 1.00 2.50
EFJI Jonathan India .40 1.00
EFJK Jarred Kelenic 1.25 3.00
EFJPM Julio Pablo Martinez .30 .75
EFMA Miguel Amaya .50 1.25
EFNG Nolan Gorman 1.00 2.50
EFRL Royce Lewis .60 1.50
EFSM Seuly Matias .40 1.00
EFTS Travis Swaggerty .50 1.25
EFVMJ Victor Mesa Jr. .75 2.00
EFVVM Victor Victor Mesa .60 1.50
EFWF Wander Franco 5.00 12.00

2019 Bowman Chrome Elite Farmhands Autographs

STATED ODDS 1:2133 HOBBY
STATED PRINT RUN 75 SER.#'d SETS
EXCHANGE DEADLINE 8/31/2021
*ORANGE/25: .6X TO 1.5X BASIC
EFACM Casey Mize 12.00 30.00
EFAFTJ Fernando Tatis Jr. EXCH 100.00 250.00
EFAJA Jordyn Adams 4.00 10.00
EFAJB Joey Bart 30.00 80.00
EFAJK Jarred Kelenic 40.00 100.00
EFASM Seuly Matias 4.00 10.00
EFAVMJ Victor Mesa Jr. 8.00 20.00
EFAVVM Victor Victor Mesa 6.00 15.00
EFAWF Wander Franco 100.00 250.00

2019 Bowman Chrome Prime Chrome Signatures

STATED ODDS 1:1282 HOBBY
STATED PRINT RUN 50 SER.#'d SETS
EXCHANGE DEADLINE 8/31/2021
*ORANGE/25: .5X TO 1.2X BASIC
PCSAB Alec Bohm 30.00 80.00
PCSAK Andrew Knizner 5.00 12.00
PCSCM Casey Mize 20.00 50.00
PCSDC Diego Cartaya 20.00 50.00
PCSEJ Eloy Jimenez 20.00 50.00
PCSEM Elehuris Montero 20.00 50.00
PCSFTJ Fernando Tatis Jr. EXCH 125.00 300.00
PCSGC Genesis Cabrera 6.00 15.00
PCSJA Jordyn Adams 8.00 20.00
PCSJB Joey Bart 40.00 100.00
PCSJI Jonathan India 12.00 30.00
PCSJK Jarred Kelenic 100.00 250.00
PCSJPM Julio Pablo Martinez 25.00 60.00
PCSJR Julio Rodriguez 60.00 150.00
PCSLG Luis Garcia 25.00 60.00
PCSMA Miguel Amaya 15.00 40.00
PCSNH Nico Hoerner 25.00 60.00
PCSNM Nick Madrigal 25.00 60.00
PCSRH Ronaldo Hernandez 3.00 8.00
PCSRM Ronny Mauricio 20.00 50.00
PCSSB Seth Beer 8.00 20.00
PCSSM Seuly Matias 12.00 30.00
PCSTW Travis Swaggerty 10.00 25.00
PCSVGJ Vladimir Guerrero Jr. 200.00 500.00
PCSVMJ Victor Mesa Jr. 10.00 25.00
PCSVVM Victor Victor Mesa 6.00 15.00
PCSWF Wander Franco 100.00 250.00

2019 Bowman Chrome Prospect Autographs

BOW.STATED ODDS 1:69 HOBBY
BOW.CHR.STATED ODDS 1:9 HOBBY
BOW.PRINTING PLATE ODDS 1:17,064 HOBBY
PLATE PRINT RUN 1 SET PER COLOR
BLACK-CYAN-MAGENTA-YELLOW ISSUED
NO PLATE PRICING DUE TO SCARCITY
BOW.EXCH.DEADLINE 3/31/2021
BOW.CHR.EXCH.DEADLINE 8/31/2021
CPAAB Alec Bohm 30.00 80.00
CPAABE Andrew Bechtold 3.00 8.00
CPAAC Aaron Civale 5.00 12.00
CPAAC Alexander Canario 25.00 60.00
CPAAK Andrew Knizner 6.00 15.00
CPAAK Alejandro Kirk 20.00 50.00
CPAAKL Adam Kloffenstein 12.00 30.00
CPAAT Abraham Toro 6.00 15.00
CPAAW Austin Warner 3.00 8.00
CPABA Blaze Alexander 8.00 20.00
CPABA Bryan Abreu 5.00 12.00
CPABB Brandon Bielak 5.00 12.00
CPABBU Brock Burke 3.00 8.00
CPABD Brock Deatherage 3.00 8.00
CPABH Brewer Hicklen 5.00 12.00
CPABK Blaine Knight 4.00 10.00
CPABM Brailyn Marquez 15.00 40.00
CPABR Brayan Rocchio 12.00 30.00
CPABS Brady Singer 6.00 15.00
CPACC Conner Capel 4.00 10.00
CPACG Casey Golden 8.00 20.00
CPACH Carlos Hernandez 3.00 8.00
CPACI Cole Irvin 3.00 8.00
CPACJ Cristian Javier 15.00 40.00
CPACM Casey Mize 25.00 60.00
CPACMI Cal Mitchell 12.00 30.00
CPACR Cal Raleigh 12.00 30.00
CPACR Cam Roegner 3.00 8.00
CPACS Chad Spanberger 8.00 20.00
CPACSA Cristian Santana 10.00 25.00
CPADC Derian Cruz 3.00 8.00
CPADCA Diego Cartaya 30.00 80.00
CPADD Danny Diaz 5.00 12.00
CPADF Durbin Feltman 3.00 8.00
CPADG Deivi Garcia 40.00 100.00
CPADK Dean Kremer 4.00 10.00
CPADTW Dom Thompson-Williams 4.00 10.00
CPAEC Edward Cabrera 8.00 20.00
CPAEJ Eloy Jimenez 20.00 50.00
CPAEM Elehuris Montero 8.00 20.00
CPAEMO Eli Morgan 3.00 8.00
CPAER Esteury Ruiz 8.00 20.00
CPAEU Edwin Uceta 4.00 10.00
CPAEW Eli White 4.00 10.00
CPAFM Francisco Morales 4.00 10.00
CPAFN Freudis Nova 15.00 40.00
CPAGC Gabriel Cancel 5.00 12.00
CPAGCA Genesis Cabrera 5.00 12.00
CPAGG Gregory Guerrero 5.00 12.00
CPAGP Geraldo Perdomo 20.00 50.00
CPAGW Garrett Whitlock 3.00 8.00
CPAIG Isiah Gilliam 4.00 10.00
CPAIP Israel Pineda 5.00 12.00
CPAIW Israel Wilson 4.00 10.00
CPAJA Jorge Alcala 3.00 8.00
CPAJB James Bourque 3.00 8.00
CPAJB Joey Bart 100.00 250.00
CPAJD Jose Devers 10.00 25.00
CPAJDU Jhoan Duran 5.00 12.00
CPAJH Jonathan Hernandez 3.00 8.00
CPAJHA Jameson Hannah 4.00 10.00
CPAJM Jonatan Machado 6.00 15.00
CPAJO Jared Oliva 6.00 15.00
CPAJOR Jonathan Ornelas 4.00 10.00
CPAJPM Julio Pablo Martinez 8.00 20.00
CPAJRO Julio Rodriguez 125.00 300.00
CPAJS Jose Suarez 3.00 8.00
CPAJY Jordan Yamamoto 5.00 12.00
CPAKP Konnor Pilkington 3.00 8.00
CPAKT Keegan Thompson 3.00 8.00
CPALG Luis Garcia 12.00 30.00
CPALGI Luis Gil 6.00 15.00
CPALJ Leonardo Jimenez 6.00 15.00
CPALR Lyon Richardson 4.00 10.00
CPALS Livan Soto 4.00 10.00
CPALW Logan Webb 5.00 12.00
CPAMA Melvin Adon 5.00 12.00
CPAMAM Miguel Amaya 15.00 40.00
CPAME Mason Englert 3.00 8.00
CPAMG Moises Gomez 5.00 12.00
CPAMG Mateo Gil 4.00 10.00
CPAMH Miguel Hiraldo 10.00 25.00
CPAMK Michael King 6.00 15.00
CPAML Marco Luciano 150.00 400.00
CPAMM Matt Mercer 3.00 8.00
CPAMMA Mason Martin 20.00 50.00
CPAMS Mike Siani 5.00 12.00
CPAMV Matt Vierling 5.00 12.00
CPANG Nick Green 4.00 10.00
CPANL Nate Lowe 10.00 25.00
CPANM Nick Madrigal 20.00 50.00
CPANM Noelvi Marte 125.00 300.00
CPAOM Orelvis Martinez 40.00 100.00
CPAOM Owen Miller 6.00 15.00
CPAPH Payton Henry 3.00 8.00
CPAPS Patrick Sandoval 3.00 8.00
CPAQTC Quintin Torres-Costa 3.00 8.00
CPARB Rylan Bannon 10.00 25.00
CPARC Ryan Costello 4.00 10.00
CPARF Ryan Feltner 3.00 8.00
CPARG Richard Gallardo 4.00 10.00
CPARH Ronaldo Hernandez 6.00 15.00
CPARL Reggie Lawson 3.00 8.00
CPARM Ronny Mauricio 50.00 120.00
CPARM Ryan McKenna 3.00 8.00
CPARMC Ryan McKenna 3.00 8.00
CPARO Robinson Ortiz 3.00 8.00
CPARR Roberto Ramos 4.00 10.00
CPASB Seth Beer 12.00 30.00
CPASH Sean Hjelle 4.00 10.00
CPASHE Sam Hentges 3.00 8.00
CPASM Seuly Matias 4.00 10.00
CPASN Shervyen Newton 6.00 15.00
CPASW Steele Walker 10.00 25.00
CPATA Telmito Agustin 4.00 10.00
CPATA Telmito Agustin 4.00 10.00
CPATO Tirso Ornelas 6.00 15.00
CPATP Tyler Phillips 3.00 8.00
CPATR Tommy Romero 4.00 10.00
CPATV Terrin Vavra 6.00 15.00
CPATW Taylor Widener 3.00 8.00
CPAVF Vince Fernandez 4.00 10.00
CPAVGJ Vladimir Guerrero Jr. 75.00 200.00
CPAVMJ Victor Mesa Jr. 25.00 60.00
CPAVVM Victor Victor Mesa 30.00 80.00
CPAWF Wander Franco 300.00 800.00
CPAWP Wenceel Perez 5.00 12.00
CPAWS Will Stewart 3.00 8.00
CPAYDR Yefri Del Rosario 3.00 8.00
CPAZB Zack Brown 3.00 8.00

2019 Bowman Chrome Prospect Autographs Atomic Refractors

*ATMOIC REF: .75X TO 2X BASIC
STATED ODDS 1:725 HOBBY
STATED PRINT RUN 100 SER.#'D SETS
EXCHANGE DEADLINE 3/31/2021
CPABA Blaze Alexander 25.00 60.00
CPACSA Cristian Santana 40.00 100.00
CPARH Ronaldo Hernandez 25.00 60.00
CPAWF Wander Franco 1200.00 2500.00

2019 Bowman Chrome Prospect Autographs Blue Refractors

*BLUE REF: .75X TO 2X BASIC
BOW.STATED ODDS 1:483 HOBBY
BOW.CHR.STATED ODDS 1:201 HOBBY
STATED PRINT RUN 150 SER.#'D SETS
BOW.EXCH.DEADLINE 3/31/2021
BOW.CHR.EXCH.DEADLINE 8/31/2021
CPABA Blaze Alexander 25.00 60.00
CPACSA Cristian Santana 40.00 100.00
CPAEU Edwin Uceta 15.00 40.00
CPAJO Jared Oliva 30.00 80.00
CPAOM Orelvis Martinez 200.00 500.00
CPARH Ronaldo Hernandez 25.00 60.00
CPASB Seth Beer 50.00 120.00
CPASHE Sam Hentges 6.00 15.00
CPASN Shervyen Newton 30.00 80.00
CPAWF Wander Franco 1200.00 2500.00

2019 Bowman Chrome Prospect Autographs Gold Refractors

*GOLD REF: 1.5X TO 4X BASIC
BOW.STATED ODDS 1:1399 HOBBY
BOW.CHR.STATED ODDS 1:592 HOBBY
BOW.STATED PRINT RUN 50 SER.#'D SETS
EXCHANGE DEADLINE 3/31/2021
BOW.CHR.EXCH.DEADLINE 8/31/2021
CPABA Bryan Abreu 20.00 50.00
CPABA Blaze Alexander 50.00 120.00
CPABM Brailyn Marquez 75.00 200.00
CPACSA Cristian Santana 50.00 120.00
CPAEU Edwin Uceta 30.00 80.00
CPAFM Francisco Morales 25.00 60.00
CPAGG Gregory Guerrero 30.00 80.00
CPAGP Geraldo Perdomo 150.00 400.00
CPAJO Jared Oliva 60.00 150.00
CPAJRO Julio Rodriguez 800.00 1500.00
CPALG Luis Garcia 125.00 300.00
CPALS Livan Soto 30.00 80.00
CPAMG Mateo Gil 25.00 60.00
CPAMH Miguel Hiraldo 60.00 150.00
CPAML Marco Luciano 1000.00 2000.00
CPANL Nate Lowe 50.00 120.00
CPAOM Orelvis Martinez 400.00 1000.00
CPAOM Owen Miller 50.00 120.00
CPARH Ronaldo Hernandez 50.00 120.00
CPASB Seth Beer 150.00 400.00
CPASHE Sam Hentges 12.00 30.00
CPASN Shervyen Newton 75.00 200.00
CPATO Tirso Ornelas 50.00 120.00
CPAVMJ Victor Mesa Jr. 150.00 400.00
CPAWF Wander Franco 2500.00 5000.00

2019 Bowman Chrome Prospect Autographs Gold Shimmer Refractors

*GOLD SHMR REF: 1.5X TO 4X BASIC
BOW.STATED ODDS 1:1399 HOBBY
STATED PRINT RUN 50 SER.#'D SETS
BOW.EXCH.DEADLINE 3/31/2021
BOW.CHR.EXCH.DEADLINE 8/31/2021
CPABA Bryan Abreu 20.00 50.00
CPABA Blaze Alexander 50.00 120.00
CPABM Brailyn Marquez 75.00 200.00
CPACSA Cristian Santana 50.00 120.00
CPAEU Edwin Uceta 30.00 80.00
CPAFM Francisco Morales 25.00 60.00
CPAGG Gregory Guerrero 30.00 80.00
CPAGP Geraldo Perdomo 150.00 400.00
CPAJO Jared Oliva 60.00 150.00
CPAJRO Julio Rodriguez 800.00 1500.00
CPALG Luis Garcia 125.00 300.00
CPALS Livan Soto 30.00 80.00
CPAMG Mateo Gil 25.00 60.00
CPAMH Miguel Hiraldo 60.00 150.00
CPAML Marco Luciano 1000.00 2000.00
CPANL Nate Lowe 50.00 120.00
CPAOM Orelvis Martinez 400.00 1000.00
CPAOM Owen Miller 50.00 120.00
CPARH Ronaldo Hernandez 50.00 120.00
CPASB Seth Beer 150.00 400.00
CPASHE Sam Hentges 12.00 30.00
CPASN Shervyen Newton 75.00 200.00
CPATO Tirso Ornelas 50.00 120.00
CPAVMJ Victor Mesa Jr. 150.00 400.00
CPAWF Wander Franco 2500.00 5000.00

2019 Bowman Chrome Prospect Autographs Green Refractors

*GREEN REF: .75X TO 2X BASIC
BOW.STATED ODDS 1:366 BLASTER
BOW.CHR.STATED ODDS 1:304 HOBBY
STATED PRINT RUN 99 SER.#'D SETS
BOW.EXCH.DEADLINE 3/31/2021
BOW.CHR.EXCH.DEADLINE 8/31/2021
CPABA Blaze Alexander 25.00 60.00
CPACSA Cristian Santana 40.00 100.00
CPAEU Edwin Uceta 15.00 40.00
CPAJO Jared Oliva 30.00 80.00
CPAOM Orelvis Martinez 200.00 500.00
CPARH Ronaldo Hernandez 25.00 60.00
CPASB Seth Beer 50.00 120.00
CPASHE Sam Hentges 6.00 15.00
CPASN Shervyen Newton 30.00 80.00
CPAWF Wander Franco 1200.00 2500.00

2019 Bowman Chrome Prospect Autographs Green Atomic Refractors

*GREEN ATMOIC REF: .75X TO 2X BASIC
RANDOM INSERTS IN PACKS
STATED PRINT RUN 99 SER.#'D SETS
BOW.CHR.EXCH.DEADLINE 8/31/2021
CPAEU Edwin Uceta 15.00 40.00
CPAJO Jared Oliva 30.00 80.00
CPAOM Orelvis Martinez 200.00 500.00
CPASB Seth Beer 50.00 120.00
CPASHE Sam Hentges 6.00 15.00
CPASN Shervyen Newton 30.00 80.00

2019 Bowman Chrome Prospect Autographs Green Shimmer Refractors

*GRN SHMMR REF: .75X TO 2X BASIC
STATED ODDS 1:366 BLASTER
STATED PRINT RUN 99 SER.#'D SETS
BOW.EXCH.DEADLINE 3/31/2021
CPABA Blaze Alexander 25.00 60.00
CPACSA Cristian Santana 40.00 100.00
CPARH Ronaldo Hernandez 25.00 60.00
CPAWF Wander Franco 1200.00 2500.00

2019 Bowman Chrome Prospect Autographs HTA Choice Refractors

CPAEU Edwin Uceta 15.00 40.00
CPAJO Jared Oliva 30.00 80.00
CPAOM Orelvis Martinez 200.00 500.00
CPASB Seth Beer 50.00 120.00
CPASHE Sam Hentges 6.00 15.00
CPASN Shervyen Newton 30.00 80.00

2019 Bowman Chrome Prospect Autographs Orange Refractors

*ORNGE REF: 3X TO 8X BASIC
BOW.STATED ODDS 1:793 HOBBY
BOW.CHR.STATED ODDS 1:636 HOBBY
STATED PRINT RUN 25 SER.#'D SETS
BOW.EXCH.DEADLINE 3/31/2021
BOW.CHR.EXCH.DEADLINE 8/31/2021
CPABA Bryan Abreu 40.00 100.00
CPABA Blaze Alexander 100.00 250.00
CPABM Brailyn Marquez 150.00 400.00
CPACG Casey Golden 100.00 250.00
CPACR Cal Raleigh 125.00 300.00
CPACSA Cristian Santana 100.00 250.00
CPAEU Edwin Uceta 60.00 150.00
CPAFM Francisco Morales 50.00 120.00
CPAGG Gregory Guerrero 60.00 150.00
CPAGP Geraldo Perdomo 300.00 800.00
CPAJO Jared Oliva 125.00 300.00
CPAJRO Julio Rodriguez 1500.00 3000.00
CPALG Luis Garcia 250.00 600.00
CPALS Livan Soto 60.00 150.00
CPAMG Mateo Gil 50.00 120.00
CPAMH Miguel Hiraldo 125.00 300.00
CPAML Marco Luciano 1500.00 3000.00
CPANL Nate Lowe 100.00 250.00
CPANM Noelvi Marte 1200.00 2500.00
CPAOM Orelvis Martinez 800.00 2000.00
CPAOM Owen Miller 100.00 250.00
CPARH Ronaldo Hernandez 100.00 250.00
CPASB Seth Beer 300.00 800.00
CPASHE Sam Hentges 25.00 60.00
CPASN Shervyen Newton 150.00 400.00
CPATO Tirso Ornelas 100.00 250.00
CPAVMJ Victor Mesa Jr. 300.00 800.00
CPAWF Wander Franco 5000.00 10000.00

2019 Bowman Chrome Prospect Autographs Orange Shimmer Refractors

*ORNGE SHMMR REF: 3X TO 8X BASIC
STATED ODDS 1:793 HOBBY
STATED PRINT RUN 25 SER.#'D SETS
BOW.EXCH.DEADLINE 3/31/2021
CPABA Blaze Alexander 100.00 250.00
CPACG Casey Golden 100.00 250.00
CPACSA Cristian Santana 100.00 250.00
CPAJRO Julio Rodriguez 1500.00 3000.00
CPAMG Mateo Gil 50.00 120.00
CPAML Marco Luciano 1500.00 3000.00
CPANL Nate Lowe 100.00 250.00
CPARH Ronaldo Hernandez 100.00 250.00
CPATO Tirso Ornelas 100.00 250.00
CPAVMJ Victor Mesa Jr. 300.00 800.00
CPAWF Wander Franco 5000.00 10000.00

2019 Bowman Chrome Prospect Autographs Orange Wave Refractors

*ORNGE WAVE REF: 3X TO 8X BASIC
RANDOM INSERTS IN PACKS
STATED PRINT RUN 25 SER.#'D SETS
BOW.CHR.EXCH.DEADLINE 8/31/2021
CPABA Bryan Abreu 40.00 100.00
CPABM Brailyn Marquez 150.00 400.00
CPACR Cal Raleigh 125.00 300.00
CPAEU Edwin Uceta 60.00 150.00
CPAFM Francisco Morales 50.00 120.00
CPAGG Gregory Guerrero 60.00 150.00
CPAGP Geraldo Perdomo 300.00 800.00
CPAJO Jared Oliva 125.00 300.00
CPALG Luis Garcia 250.00 600.00
CPALS Livan Soto 60.00 150.00
CPAMH Miguel Hiraldo 125.00 300.00
CPANM Noelvi Marte 1200.00 2500.00
CPAOM Orelvis Martinez 800.00 2000.00
CPAOM Owen Miller 100.00 250.00
CPASB Seth Beer 300.00 800.00
CPASHE Sam Hentges 25.00 60.00
CPASN Shervyen Newton 150.00 400.00

2019 Bowman Chrome Prospect Autographs Purple Refractors

*PURPLE REF: .6X TO 1.5X BASIC
BOW.STATED ODDS 1:312 HOBBY
BOW.CHR.STATED ODDS 1:120 HOBBY
STATED PRINT RUN 250 SER.#'D SETS
BOW.EXCH.DEADLINE 3/31/2021
BOW.CHR.EXCH.DEADLINE 8/31/2021
CPAJO Jared Oliva 20.00 50.00
CPARH Ronaldo Hernandez 15.00 40.00
CPASHE Sam Hentges 5.00 12.00
CPASN Shervyen Newton 20.00 50.00
CPAWF Wander Franco 800.00 1500.00

2019 Bowman Chrome Prospect Autographs Refractors

*REF: .5X TO 1.2X BASIC
BOW.STATED ODDS 1:151 HOBBY
BOW.CHR.STATED ODDS 1:61 HOBBY
STATED PRINT RUN 499 SER.#'D SETS
BOW.EXCH.DEADLINE 3/31/2021
BOW.CHR.EXCH.DEADLINE 8/31/2021
CPASHE Sam Hentges 4.00 10.00
CPAWF Wander Franco 500.00 1200.00

2019 Bowman Chrome Prospect Autographs Speckle Refractors

*SPECKLE REF: .6X TO 1.5X BASIC
STATED ODDS 1:261 HOBBY
STATED PRINT RUN 299 SER.#'D SETS
EXCHANGE DEADLINE 3/31/2021
CPARH Ronaldo Hernandez 15.00 40.00
CPAWF Wander Franco 800.00 1500.00

2019 Bowman Chrome Prospects

BOW.PLATE ODDS 1:8920 HOBBY
PLATE PRINT RUN 1 SET PER COLOR
BLACK-CYAN-MAGENTA-YELLOW ISSUED
NO PLATE PRICING DUE TO SCARCITY
BCP1 Vladimir Guerrero Jr. 1.25 3.00
BCP2 Alec Bohm .75 2.00
BCP3 Justin Dunn .20 .50
BCP4 Jo Adell .60 1.50
BCP5 Victor Victor Mesa .40 1.00
BCP6 Brusdar Graterol .25 .60
BCP7 Tirso Ornelas .20 .50
BCP8 Nick Neidert .20 .50
BCP9 Taylor Widener .20 .50
BCP10 Adrian Morejon .20 .50
BCP11 Derian Cruz .20 .50
BCP12 Corey Ray .20 .50
BCP13 Jarred Kelenic .75 2.00
BCP14 Seth Beer .50 1.25
BCP15 Ethan Hankins .25 .60
BCP16 Cole Tucker .30 .75
BCP17 A.J. Puk .25 .60
BCP18 Leody Taveras .20 .50
BCP19 Logan Allen .20 .50
BCP20 Blake Rutherford .20 .50
BCP21 Freudis Nova .30 .75
BCP22 Daniel Johnson .20 .50
BCP23 Rylan Bannon .25 .60
BCP24 Taylor Trammell .25 .60
BCP25 Fernando Tatis Jr. 3.00 8.00
BCP26 Beau Burrows .20 .50
BCP27 Jay Groome .20 .50
BCP28 Adam Haseley .30 .75
BCP29 Adonis Medina .30 .75
BCP30 Julio Pablo Martinez .20 .50
BCP31 Evan White .30 .75
BCP32 Cristian Javier .20 .50
BCP33 Julio Rodriguez 6.00 15.00
BCP34 Domingo Acevedo .20 .50
BCP35 Miguel Amaya .30 .75
BCP36 Ryan Vilade .20 .50
BCP37 JoJo Romero .20 .50
BCP38 Sandro Fabian .20 .50
BCP39 Franklyn Kilome .20 .50
BCP40 Triston McKenzie .20 .50
BCP41 Ryan Mountcastle .25 .60
BCP42 Jordyn Adams .25 .60
BCP43 Nick Senzel .60 1.50
BCP44 Luis Robert 3.00 8.00
BCP45 Brent Rooker .25 .60
BCP46 Anthony Seigler .30 .75
BCP47 Ian Anderson .50 1.25
BCP48 Griffin Canning .30 .75
BCP49 Casey Mize .50 1.25
BCP50 Joey Bart 3.00 8.00
BCP51 Hunter Greene .30 .75
BCP52 Forrest Whitley .30 .75
BCP53 Blaze Alexander .20 .50
BCP54 Keston Hiura .60 1.50
BCP55 Chris Paddack .40 1.00
BCP56 Franklin Perez .20 .50
BCP57 Joey Wentz .20 .50
BCP58 Kevin Smith .20 .50
BCP59 Nico Hoerner .60 1.50
BCP60 Nolan Gorman .60 1.50
BCP61 Jazz Chisholm .50 1.25
BCP62 Cristian Pache .50 1.25
BCP63 Nick Madrigal .60 1.50
BCP64 Luis Garcia .25 .60
BCP65 Colton Welker .20 .50
BCP66 Ryan Weathers .20 .50
BCP67 Jonathan Duplantier .20 .50
BCP68 Reggie Lawson .20 .50
BCP69 Orelvis Martinez 1.50 4.00
BCP70 Sixto Sanchez .25 .60
BCP71 Ke'Bryan Hayes .20 .50
BCP72 Brewer Hicklen .30 .75
BCP73 MacKenzie Gore .40 1.00
BCP74 Estevan Florial .30 .75
BCP75 Cole Winn .20 .50
BCP76 Zack Collins .25 .60
BCP77 Andres Gimenez .25 .60
BCP78 Alex Faedo .25 .60
BCP79 Logan Webb .30 .75
BCP80 Dustin May .60 1.50
BCP81 Ryan McKenna .20 .50
BCP82 Marco Luciano 10.00 25.00
BCP83 Heliot Ramos .30 .75
BCP84 Aramis Ademan .20 .50
BCP85 Matt Manning .30 .75
BCP86 Daz Cameron .20 .50
BCP87 Chad Spanberger .20 .50
BCP88 Brent Honeywell .25 .60
BCP89 Esteury Ruiz .25 .60
BCP90 Keegan Thompson .20 .50
BCP91 Will Smith .50 1.25
BCP92 Michael Chavis .30 .75
BCP93 Travis Swaggerty .30 .75
BCP94 Dane Dunning .20 .50
BCP95 Lyon Richardson .25 .60
BCP96 Jesus Luzardo .30 .75
BCP97 Noelvi Marte 6.00 15.00
BCP98 Carter Kieboom .30 .75
BCP99 Nate Pearson .50 1.25
BCP100 Wander Franco 30.00 80.00
BCP101 Ryan Costello .25 .60
BCP102 Jonathan India .25 .60
BCP103 Royce Lewis .40 1.00
BCP104 Victor Mesa Jr. 2.00 5.00
BCP105 Brendan McKay .30 .75
BCP106 Michel Baez .20 .50
BCP107 Ronny Mauricio .50 1.25
BCP108 Anthony Kay .20 .50
BCP109 Yusniel Diaz .30 .75
BCP110 Brady Singer .40 1.00
BCP111 Bo Bichette .60 1.50
BCP112 Matthew Liberatore .20 .50
BCP113 Dylan Cease .50 1.25
BCP114 Edward Cabrera .30 .75
BCP115 Jeter Downs .30 .75
BCP116 Luken Baker .25 .60
BCP117 Shane Baz .20 .50
BCP118 Keibert Ruiz .50 1.25
BCP119 Jonathan Hernandez .20 .50
BCP120 Matt Mercer .20 .50
BCP121 Ryan Helsley .25 .60
BCP122 Cole Ragans .20 .50
BCP123 Yordan Alvarez 3.00 8.00
BCP124 DJ Peters .30 .75
BCP125 Cal Quantrill .20 .50
BCP126 Drew Waters .60 1.50
BCP127 Peter Alonso 2.00 5.00
BCP128 MJ Melendez .30 .75
BCP129 Austin Riley 1.00 2.50
BCP130 Gavin Lux .60 1.50
BCP131 Brandon Marsh .30 .75
BCP132 Andrew Knizner .30 .75
BCP133 Mitch Keller .25 .60
BCP134 Cristian Santana .30 .75
BCP135 Jesus Sanchez .20 .50
BCP136 Peter Lambert .20 .50
BCP137 Brock Burke .20 .50
BCP138 Alex Kirilloff .30 .75
BCP139 DL Hall .20 .50
BCP140 Bryan Mata .20 .50
BCP141 Austin Beck .20 .50
BCP142 Genesis Cabrera .30 .75
BCP143 Brendan Rodgers .30 .75
BCP144 Sean Murphy .25 .60
BCP145 Roberto Ramos .25 .60
BCP146 Ronaldo Hernandez .20 .50
BCP147 Albert Abreu .20 .50
BCP148 William Contreras .25 .60
BCP149 Jose de la Cruz .60 1.50
BCP150 Eloy Jimenez .75 2.00
BCP151 Royce Lewis .40 1.00
BCP152 Zack Brown .20 .50
BCP153 Robinson Ortiz .20 .50
BCP154 Bobby Dalbec .50 1.25
BCP155 Nolan Jones .30 .75
BCP156 Tim Tebow 1.50 4.00
BCP157 Bryan Abreu .30 .75
BCP158 Taylor Trammell .25 .60
BCP159 Adbert Alzolay .20 .50
BCP160 Roansy Contreras .50 1.25
BCP161 Spencer Howard .20 .50
BCP162 Michael King .25 .60
BCP163 Alec Bohm .75 2.00
BCP164 Micker Adolfo .20 .50
BCP165 Kristian Robinson .50 1.25
BCP166 Eric Pardinho .25 .60
BCP167 Jarred Kelenic .75 2.00
BCP168 Eli White .75 2.00
BCP169 Nick Green .25 .60
BCP170 Owen Miller .25 .60
BCP171 Brice Turang .25 .60
BCP172 Mitchell White .20 .50
BCP173 Nick Madrigal .60 1.50
BCP174 Joey Bart .60 1.50
BCP175 Parker Meadows .25 .60
BCP176 Jose Devers .30 .75
BCP177 Austin Warner .20 .50
BCP178 Jahmai Jones .20 .50
BCP179 Daulton Varsho .20 .50
BCP180 Leonardo Jimenez .30 .75
BCP181 Grayson Rodriguez .40 1.00
BCP182 Estevan Florial .30 .75
BCP183 Sean Hjelle .25 .60
BCP184 Miguel Hiraldo .60 1.50
BCP185 Jesus Sanchez .20 .50
BCP186 Alex Kirilloff .30 .75
BCP187 Genesis Cabrera .30 .75
BCP188 Richard Gallardo .25 .60
BCP189 Kyle Funkhouser .20 .50
BCP190 Nick Pratto .20 .50
BCP191 Geraldo Perdomo 4.00 10.00
BCP192 Logan Gilbert .30 .75
BCP193 Anderson Tejeda .25 .60
BCP194 Bo Naylor .20 .50
BCP195 Kyle Muller .20 .50
BCP196 Ryan Rolison .20 .50
BCP197 Hansel Moreno .20 .50
BCP198 Jameson Hannah .25 .60
BCP199 Tony Santillan .20 .50
BCP200 Victor Victor Mesa .40 1.00
BCP201 Briam Campusano .20 .50
BCP202 Alejandro Kirk .30 .75
BCP203 Jordan Yamamoto .30 .75
BCP204 Isiah Gilliam .25 .60
BCP205 Sixto Sanchez .25 .60
BCP206 Wander Javier .20 .50
BCP207 Corey Ray .20 .50
BCP208 Aramis Ademan .20 .50
BCP209 Brayan Rocchio .75 2.00
BCP210 Hans Crouse .20 .50
BCP211 Shaun Anderson .20 .50
BCP212 Lazaro Armenteros .25 .60
BCP213 Triston Casas .75 2.00
BCP214 Deon Stafford .25 .60
BCP215 Khalil Lee .20 .50
BCP216 Wenceel Perez .30 .75
BCP217 Jorge Mateo .20 .50
BCP218 Luis Gil .30 .75
BCP219 Mason Englert .20 .50
BCP220 Konnor Pilkington .20 .50
BCP221 Nolan Gorman .60 1.50
BCP222 Garrett Whitlock .20 .50
BCP223 Mason Denaburg .25 .60
BCP224 Joe Jacques .20 .50
BCP225 Jhoan Duran .30 .75
BCP226 Grant Lavigne .25 .60
BCP227 Corbin Martin .30 .75
BCP228 Mike Siani .30 .75
BCP229 Ryan Feltner .20 .50
BCP230 Hudson Potts .20 .50
BCP231 Ryan McKenna .20 .50
BCP232 Tommy Wilson .30 .75
BCP233 J.B. Bukauskas .20 .50
BCP234 Bo Bichette .60 1.50
BCP235 Keibert Ruiz .50 1.25
BCP236 Patrick Sandoval .20 .50
BCP237 Luis Garcia .75 2.00
BCP238 Cam Roegner .20 .50
BCP239 Brendan McKay .30 .75
BCP240 Casey Mize .50 1.25
BCP241 Deivi Garcia 1.00 2.50
BCP242 Quintin Torres-Costa .20 .50
BCP243 Yefri Del Rosario .20 .50
BCP244 Francisco Morales .25 .60
BCP245 MacKenzie Gore .40 1.00
BCP246 Sam Hentges .20 .50
BCP247 Israel Pineda .30 .75
BCP248 Shervyen Newton .30 .75
BCP249 Clarke Schmidt .30 .75
BCP250 Jo Adell .60 1.50

2019 Bowman Chrome Prospects Aqua Refractors

*AQUA REF: 2.5X TO 6X BASIC
STATED ODDS 1:151 HOBBY
STATED PRINT RUN 125 SER.#'d SETS
BCP100 Wander Franco 200.00 500.00

2019 Bowman Chrome Prospects Aqua Shimmer Refractors

*AQUA SHIM REF: 2.5X TO 6X BASIC
STATED ODDS 1:151 HOBBY
STATED PRINT RUN 125 SER.#'d SETS
BCP100 Wander Franco 200.00 500.00

2019 Bowman Chrome Prospects Atomic Refractors

*ATOMIC REF: 1.5X TO 4X BASIC
STATED ODDS 1:24 HOBBY
BCP100 Wander Franco 125.00 300.00

2019 Bowman Chrome Prospects Blue Refractors

*BLUE REF: 2X TO 5X BASIC
BOW.STATED ODDS 1:238 HOBBY
BOW.CHR.ODDS 1:71 HOBBY
STATED PRINT RUN 150 SER.#'d SETS
BCP100 Wander Franco 150.00 400.00

2019 Bowman Chrome Prospects Blue Shimmer Refractors
*BLUE SHIM REF: 2X TO 5X BASIC
STATED ODDS 1:238 HOBBY
STATED PRINT RUN 150 SER.#'d SETS
BCP100 Wander Franco 150.00 400.00

2019 Bowman Chrome Prospects Gold Refractors
*GOLD REF: 6X TO 15X BASIC
BOW.STATED ODDS 1:711 HOBBY
BOW.CHR.ODDS 1:211 HOBBY
STATED PRINT RUN 50 SER.#'d SETS
BCP100 Wander Franco 500.00 1200.00

2019 Bowman Chrome Prospects Gold Shimmer Refractors
*GOLD SHIM REF: 6X TO 15X BASIC
BOW.STATED ODDS 1:711 HOBBY
BOW.CHR.ODDS 1:211 HOBBY
STATED PRINT RUN 50 SER.#'d SETS
BCP100 Wander Franco 500.00 1200.00

2019 Bowman Chrome Prospects Green Refractors
*GREEN REF: 3X TO 8X BASIC
BOW.STATED ODDS 1:141 RETAIL
BOW.CHR.ODDS 1:107 HOBBY
STATED PRINT RUN 99 SER.#'d SETS
BCP100 Wander Franco 250.00 600.00

2019 Bowman Chrome Prospects Green Shimmer Refractors
*GREEN SHIM REF: 3X TO 8X BASIC
BOW.STATED ODDS 1:141 RETAIL
BOW.CHR.ODDS 1:107 HOBBY
STATED PRINT RUN 99 SER.#'d SETS
BCP100 Wander Franco 250.00 600.00

2019 Bowman Chrome Prospects Orange Refractors
*ORANGE REF: 10X TO 25X BASIC
BOW.STATED ODDS 1:329 HOBBY
BOW.CHR.ODDS 1:421 HOBBY
STATED PRINT RUN 25 SER.#'d SETS
BCP100 Wander Franco 750.00 2000.00

2019 Bowman Chrome Prospects Orange Shimmer Refractors
*ORANGE SHIM REF: 10X TO 25X BASIC
BOW.CHR.ODDS 1:421 HOBBY
BOW.STATED ODDS 1:329 HOBBY
STATED PRINT RUN 25 SER.#'d SETS
BCP100 Wander Franco 750.00 2000.00

2019 Bowman Chrome Prospects Purple Refractors
*PURPLE REF: 1.5X TO 4X BASIC
BOW.STATED ODDS 1:143 HOBBY
BOW.CHR.ODDS 1:43 HOBBY
STATED PRINT RUN 250 SER.#'d SETS
BCP100 Wander Franco 125.00 300.00

2019 Bowman Chrome Prospects Purple Shimmer Refractors
*PURPLE SHIM REF: 1.2X TO 3X BASIC
BOW.CHR.ODDS 1:15 HOBBY

2019 Bowman Chrome Prospects Refractors
*REF: 1.2X TO 3X BASIC
BOW.STATED ODDS 1:72 HOBBY
BOW.CHR.ODDS 1:21 HOBBY
STATED PRINT RUN 499 SER.#'d SETS
BCP100 Wander Franco 100.00 250.00

2019 Bowman Chrome Prospects Speckle Refractors
*SPECKLE REF: 1.5X TO 4X BASIC
STATED ODDS 1:119 HOBBY
STATED PRINT RUN 299 SER.#'d SETS
BCP100 Wander Franco 125.00 300.00

2019 Bowman Chrome Prospects Yellow Refractors
*YELLOW REF: 4X TO 10X BASIC
STATED ODDS 1:474 HOBBY
STATED PRINT RUN 75 SER.#'d SETS
BCP100 Wander Franco 300.00 800.00

2019 Bowman Chrome Ready for the Show
STATED ODDS 1:6 HOBBY
*ATOMIC REF/150: 2.5X TO 6X BASE
*GREEN REF/99: 2.5X TO 6X BASE
*GOLD REF/50: 4X TO 10X BASIC
*ORANGE REF/25: 8X TO 20X BASE
RFTS1 Vladimir Guerrero Jr. 1.50 4.00
RFTS2 Bo Bichette .75 2.00
RFTS3 Triston McKenzie .25 .60
RFTS4 Mitch Keller .30 .75
RFTS5 Will Smith .60 1.50
RFTS6 Jon Duplantier .25 .60
RFTS7 Austin Riley 1.25 3.00
RFTS8 Ryan Mountcastle .30 .75
RFTS9 Nick Senzel .75 2.00
RFTS10 Fernando Tatis Jr. 2.50 6.00
RFTS11 Peter Alonso 2.00 5.00
RFTS12 Forrest Whitley .40 1.00
RFTS13 Yusniel Diaz .40 1.00
RFTS14 Brendan McKay .40 1.00
RFTS15 Jesus Luzardo .40 1.00
RFTS16 Brendan Rodgers .40 1.00
RFTS17 Yordan Alvarez 1.50 4.00
RFTS18 Keston Hiura .75 2.00
RFTS19 Brent Honeywell .30 .75
RFTS20 Eloy Jimenez 1.00 2.50

2019 Bowman Chrome Rookie Autographs
BOW.STATED ODDS 1:551 HOBBY
BOW.CHR.STATED ODDS 1:482 HOBBY
BOW.PRINTING PLATE ODDS 1:69,259 HOBBY
PLATE PRINT RUN 1 SET PER COLOR
BLACK-CYAN-MAGENTA-YELLOW ISSUED
NO PLATE PRICING DUE TO SCARCITY
BOW.EXCH.DEADLINE 3/31/2021
BOW.CHR.EXCH.8/31/2021
CRACA C.Adams Blue jrsy 3.00 8.00
CRACA C.Adams Gry jrsy 3.00 8.00
CRACB C.Burns Arm back 5.00 12.00
CRACB C.Burns Leg Up 5.00 12.00
CRACM Cedric Mullins 5.00 12.00
CRACST Chris Shaw 5.00 12.00
CRADJ Danny Jansen Batting 5.00 12.00
CRADJ Danny Jansen Catching 5.00 12.00
CRADS DJ Stewart 4.00 10.00
CRAFTJ Fernando Tatis Jr. 150.00 400.00
CRAJB Jake Bauers 5.00 12.00
CRAJC Jake Cave 4.00 10.00
CRAJS J.Sheffield M's 5.00 12.00
CRAJS J.Sheffield Yanks 5.00 12.00
CRAKA Kolby Allard 5.00 12.00
CRAKT Kyle Tucker 15.00 40.00
CRAKW K.Wright Face forward 4.00 10.00
CRAKW K.Wright Face right 4.00 10.00
CRALU Luis Urias 5.00 12.00
CRAMK Michael Kopech 12.00 30.00
CRARB Ryan Borucki 3.00 8.00
CRARB Ryan Borucki 3.00 8.00
CRAROG Ryan O'Hearn 3.00 8.00
CRAWA Willians Astudillo 3.00 8.00
CRAYK Y.Kikuchi EXCH 10.00 25.00
CRAYK Y.Kikuchi Drk blue jrsy 10.00 25.00

2019 Bowman Chrome Rookie Autographs Atomic Refractors
*ATOMIC REF: .6X TO 1.5X BASIC
STATED ODDS 1:2751 HOBBY
STATED PRINT RUN 100 SER.#'d SETS
EXCHANGE DEADLINE 3/31/2021

2019 Bowman Chrome Rookie Autographs Blue Refractors
*BLUE REF: .6X TO 1.5X BASIC
BOW.STATED ODDS 1:1834 JUMBO
BOW.CHR.STATED ODDS 1:2133
STATED PRINT RUN 150 SER.#'d SETS
BOW.EXCH.DEADLINE 3/31/2021
BOW.CHR.EXCH.DEADLINE 8/31/2021
CRAKH Keston Hiura 50.00 120.00

2019 Bowman Chrome Rookie Autographs Gold Refractors
*GOLD REF: 1.2X TO 3X BASIC
BOW.STATED ODDS 1:5502 HOBBY
BOW.CHR.STATED ODDS 1:2404 HOBBY
STATED PRINT RUN 50 SER.#'d SETS
BOW.EXCH.DEADLINE 3/31/2021
BOW.CHR.EXCH.DEADLINE 8/31/2021
CRAFTJ Fernando Tatis Jr. 600.00 1500.00
CRAKH Keston Hiura 100.00 250.00
CRAPA Pete Alonso 500.00 1000.00
CRAVGJ Vladimir Guerrero Jr. 400.00 800.00

2019 Bowman Chrome Rookie Autographs Green Refractors
*GREEN REF: .6X TO 1.5X BASIC
BOW.STATED ODDS 1:1442 RETAIL
BOW.CHR.STATED ODDS 1:3231 HOBBY
STATED PRINT RUN 99 SER.#'d SETS
BOW.EXCH.DEADLINE 3/31/2021
BOW.CHR.EXCH.DEADLINE 8/31/2021
CRAFTJ Fernando Tatis Jr. 300.00 800.00
CRAKH Keston Hiura 50.00 120.00
CRAPA Pete Alonso 250.00 500.00
CRAVGJ Vladimir Guerrero Jr. 200.00 400.00

2019 Bowman Chrome Rookie Autographs Orange Refractors
*ORANGE REF: 2X TO 5X BASIC
BOW.STATED ODDS 1:3226 HOBBY
BOW.CHR.STATED ODDS 1:2570 HOBBY
STATED PRINT RUN 25 SER.#'d SETS
BOW.EXCH.DEADLINE 3/31/2021
BOW.CHR.EXCH.DEADLINE 8/31/2021
CRAFTJ Fernando Tatis Jr. 1000.00 2500.00
CRAKH Keston Hiura 150.00 400.00
CRAPA Pete Alonso 800.00 1500.00
CRAVGJ Vladimir Guerrero Jr. 600.00 1200.00

2019 Bowman Chrome Rookie Autographs Refractors
*REF: .6X TO 1.2X BASIC
BOW.STATED ODDS 1:552 HOBBY
BOW.CHR.STATED ODDS 1:642 HOBBY
STATED PRINT RUN 499 SER.#'D SETS
BOW.EXCH.DEADLINE 3/31/2021
BOW.CHR.EXCH 8/31/2021
CRAKH Keston Hiura 40.00 100.00

2019 Bowman Chrome Rookie of the Year Favorites
STATED ODDS 1:11 HOBBY
*ATOMIC REF/150: 2.5X TO 6X BASE
*GREEN REF/99: 2.5X TO 6X BASE
*GOLD REF/50: 4X TO 10X BASIC
*ORANGE REF/25: 8X TO 20X BASE
ROYF1 Kyle Tucker .50 1.25
ROYF2 Brandon Lowe .40 1.00
ROYF3 Dawel Lugo .40 1.00
ROYF4 Luis Urias .40 1.00
ROYF5 Chance Adams .25 .60
ROYF6 Danny Jansen .25 .60
ROYF7 Kyle Wright .40 1.00
ROYF8 Chris Shaw .40 1.00
ROYF9 Kolby Allard .40 1.00
ROYF10 Christin Stewart .30 .75
ROYF11 Justus Sheffield .40 1.00

2019 Bowman Chrome Rookie of the Year Favorites Autographs
STATED ODDS 1:2500 HOBBY
STATED PRINT RUN 150 SER.#'d SETS
EXCHANGE DEADLINE 3/31/2021
*GOLD REF/50: .6X TO 1.5X BASIC
*ORANGE REF/25: 1X TO 2.5X BASIC
ROYFCM Cedric Mullins 6.00 15.00
ROYFKW Kyle Wright 6.00 15.00
ROYFACB Corbin Burnes 6.00 15.00
ROYFADJ Danny Jansen 4.00 10.00
ROYFAJB Jake Bauers 6.00 15.00
ROYFAJS Justus Sheffield 6.00 15.00
ROYFAKA Kolby Allard 6.00 15.00
ROYFAKT Kyle Tucker 8.00 20.00
ROYFALU Luis Urias 10.00 25.00
ROYFAMK Michael Kopech 10.00 25.00
ROYFROH Ryan O'Hearn 4.00 10.00

2019 Bowman Chrome Scouts Top 100
STATED ODDS 1:4 HOBBY
*ATOMIC REF/150: 2.5X TO 6X BASE
*GREEN REF/99: 2.5X TO 6X BASE
*GOLD REF/50: 4X TO 10X BASIC
*ORANGE REF/25: 6X TO 15X BASE
BTP1 Vladimir Guerrero Jr. 1.50 4.00
BTP2 Eloy Jimenez 1.00 2.50
BTP3 Fernando Tatis Jr. 2.50 6.00
BTP4 Wander Franco 2.50 6.00
BTP5 Forrest Whitley .40 1.00
BTP6 Victor Robles .50 1.25
BTP7 Bo Bichette .75 2.00
BTP8 Michael Kopech .50 1.25
BTP9 Jo Adell .75 2.00
BTP10 Royce Lewis .50 1.25
BTP11 Nick Senzel .75 2.00
BTP12 Casey Mize .60 1.50
BTP13 Alex Kirilloff .40 1.00
BTP14 MacKenzie Gore .50 1.25
BTP15 Kyle Tucker .50 1.25
BTP16 Brendan Rodgers .40 1.00
BTP17 Jesus Luzardo .40 1.00
BTP18 Sixto Sanchez .30 .75
BTP19 Dylan Cease .60 1.50
BTP20 Justus Sheffield .40 1.00
BTP21 Mitch Keller .30 .75
BTP22 Mike Soroka .40 1.00
BTP23 Nick Madrigal .75 2.00
BTP24 Keibert Ruiz .60 1.50
BTP25 Ian Anderson .60 1.50
BTP26 Taylor Trammell .30 .75
BTP27 Keston Hiura .75 2.00
BTP28 Touki Toussaint .30 .75
BTP29 Brent Honeywell .30 .75
BTP30 Adrian Morejon .25 .60
BTP31 Cristian Pache .60 1.50
BTP32 Ke'Bryan Hayes .25 .60
BTP33 Joey Bart 2.50 6.00
BTP34 Griffin Canning .40 1.00
BTP35 Francisco Mejia .30 .75
BTP36 Andres Gimenez .30 .75
BTP37 Brendan McKay .40 1.00
BTP38 Brady Singer .50 1.25
BTP39 Jarred Kelenic 1.00 2.50
BTP40 Luis Urias .40 1.00
BTP41 Austin Riley 1.25 3.00
BTP42 Alex Reyes .30 .75
BTP43 A.J. Puk .30 .75
BTP44 Carter Kieboom .40 1.00
BTP45 Hunter Greene .40 1.00
BTP46 Yordan Alvarez 1.25 3.00
BTP47 Luis Robert 2.50 6.00
BTP48 Kyle Wright .40 1.00
BTP49 Corbin Burnes .40 1.00
BTP50 Sean Murphy .30 .75
BTP51 Jon Duplantier .25 .60
BTP52 Peter Alonso 3.00 8.00
BTP53 Alex Verdugo .30 .75
BTP54 Luis Garcia .30 .75
BTP55 Nolan Gorman .75 2.00
BTP56 Jonathan Loaisiga .30 .75
BTP57 Jesus Sanchez .25 .60
BTP58 Bryse Wilson .30 .75
BTP59 Luiz Gohara .25 .60
BTP60 Dakota Hudson .30 .75
BTP61 Chris Paddack .50 1.25
BTP62 Triston McKenzie .25 .60
BTP63 Jazz Chisholm .60 1.50
BTP64 Jason Groome .25 .60
BTP65 Adonis Medina .40 1.00
BTP66 Dustin May .75 2.00
BTP67 Yusniel Diaz .40 1.00
BTP68 Jonathan India .30 .75
BTP69 D.L. Hall .25 .60
BTP70 Oneil Cruz .40 1.00
BTP71 Estevan Florial .40 1.00
BTP72 Sandy Alcantara .25 .60
BTP73 Travis Swaggerty .40 1.00
BTP74 Nate Pearson .60 1.50
BTP75 Leody Taveras .25 .60
BTP76 Ronny Mauricio .60 1.50
BTP77 Matthew Liberatore .25 .60
BTP78 Brandon Marsh .25 .60
BTP79 Khalil Lee .25 .60
BTP80 Alex Scherff .40 1.00
BTP81 Miguel Amaya .40 1.00
BTP82 Brice Turang .30 .75
BTP83 Jackson Kowar .25 .60
BTP84 Daz Cameron .25 .60
BTP85 Nolan Jones .40 1.00
BTP86 Franklin Perez .25 .60
BTP87 Cole Winn .25 .60
BTP88 Kyle Lewis .50 1.25
BTP89 Brusdar Graterol .30 .75
BTP90 Logan Allen .25 .60
BTP91 Taylor Widener .25 .60
BTP92 Grayson Rodriguez .50 1.25
BTP93 Michel Baez .25 .60
BTP94 Corey Ray .30 .75
BTP95 Evan White .40 1.00
BTP96 Peter Lambert .40 1.00
BTP97 George Valera .50 1.25
BTP98 Matt Manning .40 1.00
BTP99 Luis Patino .40 1.00
BTP100 Julio Pablo Martinez .25 .60

2019 Bowman Chrome Scouts Top 100 Autographs
STATED ODDS 1:1832 HOBBY
PRINT RUNS B/WN 20-50 COPIES PER
EXCHANGE DEADLINE 3/31/2021
BTP3 Fernando Tatis Jr./50 125.00 300.00
BTP4 Wander Franco/50 125.00 300.00
BTP8 Michael Kopech/50 10.00 25.00
BTP9 Jo Adell/50 30.00 80.00
BTP10 Royce Lewis/50 15.00 40.00
BTP12 Casey Mize/50 30.00 80.00
BTP14 MacKenzie Gore/50 10.00 25.00
BTP15 Kyle Tucker/50 40.00 100.00
BTP18 Sixto Sanchez/50 20.00 50.00
BTP20 Justus Sheffield/50 8.00 20.00
BTP21 Mitch Keller/50 6.00 15.00
BTP23 Nick Madrigal/50 30.00 80.00
BTP24 Keibert Ruiz/50 20.00 50.00
BTP27 Keston Hiura/35 20.00 50.00
BTP28 Touki Toussaint/50 6.00 15.00
BTP31 Cristian Pache/50 40.00 100.00
BTP33 Joey Bart/50 60.00 150.00
BTP34 Griffin Canning/50 10.00 25.00
BTP38 Brady Singer/50 15.00 40.00
BTP39 Jarred Kelenic/50 30.00 80.00
BTP43 A.J. Puk/20 40.00 100.00
BTP44 Carter Kieboom/50 8.00 20.00
BTP45 Hunter Greene/50 15.00 40.00
BTP47 Luis Robert/35 50.00 120.00
BTP48 Kyle Wright/50 8.00 20.00
BTP49 Corbin Burnes/50 12.00 30.00
BTP50 Sean Murphy/50 6.00 15.00
BTP51 Jon Duplantier/50 5.00 12.00
BTP55 Nolan Gorman/50 25.00 60.00
BTP56 Jonathan Loaisiga/50 6.00 15.00
BTP57 Jesus Sanchez/50 5.00 12.00
BTP58 Bryse Wilson/50 6.00 15.00
BTP60 Dakota Hudson/50 6.00 15.00
BTP66 Dustin May/50 20.00 50.00
BTP67 Yusniel Diaz/50 8.00 20.00
BTP68 Jonathan India/50 6.00 15.00
BTP72 Sandy Alcantara/50 5.00 12.00
BTP73 Travis Swaggerty/50 8.00 20.00
BTP74 Nate Pearson/50 8.00 20.00
BTP76 Ronny Mauricio/50 12.00 30.00
BTP77 Matthew Liberatore/50 5.00 12.00
BTP78 Brandon Marsh/50 8.00 20.00
BTP81 Miguel Amaya/50 8.00 20.00
BTP82 Brice Turang/50 6.00 15.00
BTP83 Jackson Kowar/50 10.00 25.00
BTP84 Daz Cameron/50 8.00 20.00
BTP86 Franklin Perez/50 5.00 12.00
BTP87 Cole Winn/50 8.00 20.00
BTP91 Taylor Widener/50 5.00 12.00
BTP93 Michel Baez/50 5.00 12.00
BTP94 Corey Ray/50 15.00 40.00
BTP95 Evan White/50 12.00 30.00
BTP96 Peter Lambert/50 8.00 20.00
BTP100 Julio Pablo Martinez/50 30.00 80.00

2019 Bowman Chrome Stat Tracker
STATED ODDS 1:3 HOBBY
*ATOMIC REF/150: 1X TO 2.5X BASE
*ORANGE REF/25: 3X TO 8X BASE
STAB Alec Bohm 1.00 2.50
STAK Andrew Knizner .40 1.00
STAM Adonis Medina .40 1.00
STBD Brock Deatherage .25 .60
STBS Brady Singer .50 1.25
STBT Brice Turang .30 .75
STCM Casey Mize .60 1.50
STCS Connor Scott .30 .75
STDW Drew Waters .75 2.00
STEM Elehuris Montero .40 1.00
STGC Genesis Cabrera .40 1.00
STHC Hans Crouse .25 .60
STJA Jordyn Adams .30 .75
STJB Joey Bart .75 2.00
STJG Jordan Groshans .50 1.25
STJI Jonathan India .30 .75
STJK Jarred Kelenic 1.00 2.50
STJPM Julio Pablo Martinez .25 .60
STMA Miguel Amaya .40 1.00
STNG Nolan Gorman .75 2.00
STNH Nico Hoerner .75 2.00
STNM Nick Madrigal .75 2.00
STRH Ronaldo Hernandez .25 .60
STRM Ronny Mauricio .60 1.50
STRW Ryan Weathers .25 .60
STSB Seth Beer .60 1.50
STSM Seuly Matias .30 .75
STTS Travis Swaggerty .40 1.00
STVB Vidal Brujan 1.50 4.00
STWF Wander Franco 4.00 10.00

2019 Bowman Chrome Stat Tracker Autographs
STATED ODDS 1:777 HOBBY
STATED PRINT RUN 75 SER.#'d SETS
EXCHANGE DEADLINE 8/31/2021
*ORANGE/25: .6X TO 1.5X BASIC
STAAK Andrew Knizner 8.00 20.00
STABS Brady Singer 6.00 15.00
STABT Brice Turang 8.00 20.00
STACM Casey Mize 8.00 20.00
STACS Connor Scott 12.00 30.00
STAEM Elehuris Montero 6.00 15.00
STAFTJ Fernando Tatis Jr. EXCH 125.00 300.00
STAGC Genesis Cabrera 5.00 12.00
STAJA Jordyn Adams 4.00 10.00
STAJB Joey Bart 25.00 60.00
STAJG Jordan Groshans 6.00 15.00
STAJI Jonathan India 10.00 25.00
STAMA Miguel Amaya 10.00 25.00
STANH Nico Hoerner 20.00 50.00
STANM Nick Madrigal 10.00 25.00
STARH Ronaldo Hernandez 3.00 8.00
STARM Ronny Mauricio 8.00 20.00
STASB Seth Beer 12.00 30.00
STASM Seuly Matias 8.00 20.00
STAWF Wander Franco 75.00 200.00

2019 Bowman Chrome Talent Pipeline
STATED ODDS 1:12 HOBBY
*ATOMIC REF/150: 2X TO 5X BASE
*GREEN REF/99: 2X TO 5X BASE
*GOLD REF/50: 3X TO 8X BASIC
*ORANGE REF/25: 5X TO 12X BASE
TPARI Jazz Chisholm .75 2.00
Taylor Clarke
Taylor Widener
TPATL Riley/Anderson/Contreras 1.50 4.00
TPBAL DJ Stewart .40 1.00
Ryan Mountcastle
DL Hall
TPBOS Josh Ockimey .75 2.00
Bryan Mata
Bobby Dalbec
TPCHI Alzolay/Hatch/Hoerner 1.00 2.50
TPCIN Long/Greene/Senzel 1.00 2.50
TPCLE Yu Chang .50 1.25
Triston McKenzie
Nolan Jones
TPCOL Brendan Rodgers .50 1.25
Colton Welker
Roberto Ramos
TPCWS Collins/Jimenez/Rutherford 1.25 3.00
TPDET Hall/Mize/Rogers .75 2.00
TPHOU Alvarez/Whitley/Beer 2.00 5.00
TPKCR Lopez/Lee/Matias .50 1.25
TPLAA Thaiss/Adell/Marsh 1.00 2.50
TPLAD Smith/White/Kendall .75 2.00
TPMIA Nick Neidert .40 1.00
Austin Dean
Tristan Pompey
TPMIL Burnes/Hiura/Lutz 1.00 2.50
TPMIN Nick Gordon .50 1.25
Brent Rooker
Alex Kirilloff
TPNYM Alonso/Gimenez/Kay 2.50 6.00
TPNYY Adams/Stephan/Florial .50 1.25
TPOAK Jesus Luzardo .50 1.25
Skye Bolt
Austin Beck
TPPHI Ranger Suarez .50 1.25
Darick Hall
Adam Haseley
TPPIT Mitch Keller .40 1.00
Ke'Bryan Hayes
Luis Escobar
TPSDP Urias/Gore/Naylor .60 1.50
TPSEA Ian Miller .50 1.25
Evan White
Braden Bishop
TPSFG Shaw/Anderson/Bart 1.00 2.50
TPSTL Knizner/Montero/Cabrera .50 1.25
TPTBR Honeywell/Hernandez/Solak 1.00 2.50
TPTEX Andy Ibanez .30 .75
Jonathan Hernandez
Leody Taveras
TPTOR Vlad Jr/Pearson/Bichette 2.00 5.00
TPWAS Ward/Garcia/Kieboom .50 1.25

2019 Bowman Chrome Draft
COMPLETE SET (200) 30.00 80.00
STATED PLATE ODDS 1:1241 HOBBY
PLATE PRINT RUN 1 SET PER COLOR
BLACK-CYAN-MAGENTA-YELLOW ISSUED
NO PLATE PRICING DUE TO SCARCITY
BDC1 Adley Rutschman 15.00 40.00
BDC2 Jarred Kelenic 1.00 2.50
BDC3 Alek Manoah .50 1.25
BDC4 Grant McCray .40 1.00
BDC5 Brock Deatherage .25 .60
BDC6 Matt Wallner .50 1.25
BDC7 Josh Jung 2.50 6.00
BDC8 Andres Gimenez .30 .75
BDC9 Jackson Kowar .25 .60
BDC10 Logan Davidson .25 .60
BDC11 Isaiah Campbell .50 1.25
BDC12 Blake Walston .40 1.00
BDC13 Izzy Wilson .25 .60
BDC14 Yordys Valdes .50 1.25
BDC15 Alec Marsh .30 .75
BDC16 Ryan Zeferjahn .30 .75
BDC17 Brady McConnell .40 1.00
BDC18 Jordan Groshans .50 1.25
BDC19 Sammy Siani .30 .75
BDC20 Kristian Robinson .60 1.50
BDC21 Eric Pardinho .30 .75
BDC22 Gunnar Henderson .50 1.25
BDC23 Joseph Ortiz .30 .75
BDC24 Justin Slaten .25 .60
BDC25 Drew Waters .75 2.00
BDC26 Cal Mitchell .40 1.00
BDC27 Daniel Espino .30 .75
BDC28 Ethan Small .30 .75
BDC29 Logan Wyatt .40 1.00
BDC30 Estevan Florial .40 1.00
BDC31 Hunter Bishop 2.50 6.00
BDC32 Thomas Dillard .50 1.25
BDC33 DL Hall .25 .60
BDC34 T.J. Sikkema .40 1.00
BDC35 Dominic Fletcher .25 .60
BDC36 Antoine Kelly .50 1.25
BDC37 Albert Abreu .25 .60
BDC38 Mateo Gil .30 .75
BDC39 Brett Baty 3.00 8.00
BDC40 Brandon Lewis .40 1.00
BDC41 Jamari Baylor 1.50 4.00
BDC42 Nolan Gorman .75 2.00
BDC43 Jack Little .40 1.00
BDC44 Quinn Priester .40 1.00
BDC45 Freudis Nova .40 1.00
BDC46 Royce Lewis .50 1.25
BDC47 Tyler Callihan .30 .75
BDC48 Matthew Allan 2.00 5.00
BDC49 Will Stewart .25 .60
BDC50 Riley Greene 5.00 12.00
BDC51 Ethan Hankins .30 .75
BDC52 Derian Cruz .25 .60
BDC53 Andre Pallante .30 .75
BDC54 Dane Dunning .25 .60
BDC55 Matt Mercer .25 .60
BDC56 Chris Murphy .25 .60
BDC57 Michael Busch .75 2.00
BDC58 James Beard .75 2.00
BDC59 Braden Shewmake .75 2.00
BDC60 Julio Rodriguez 2.00 5.00
BDC61 JJ Goss .30 .75
BDC62 Ronny Mauricio .60 1.50
BDC63 Dasan Brown .60 1.50
BDC64 Michael Toglia 1.25 3.00
BDC65 Keoni Cavaco 1.25 3.00
BDC66 Greg Jones 1.25 3.00
BDC67 Shea Langeliers 1.50 4.00
BDC68 Evan Fitterer .60 1.50
BDC69 Hudson Head 1.25 3.00
BDC70 Tony Locey .30 .75
BDC71 Julio Pablo Martinez .25 .60
BDC72 Jake Agnos .40 1.00
BDC73 Matt Gorski .40 1.00
BDC74 Peyton Burdick 1.00 2.50
BDC75 Brewer Hicklen .40 1.00
BDC76 Kyle Stowers .40 1.00
BDC77 Erik Rivera .50 1.25
BDC78 Leonardo Jimenez .40 1.00
BDC79 Bryson Stott 5.00 12.00
BDC80 Cristian Santana .40 1.00
BDC81 Davis Wendzel .30 .75
BDC82 Jake Sanford .50 1.25
BDC83 Casey Golden .40 1.00
BDC84 Tirso Ornelas .25 .60
BDC85 CJ Abrams 5.00 12.00
BDC86 Josh Smith .50 1.25
BDC87 Triston Casas 1.00 2.50
BDC88 Victor Victor Mesa .50 1.25
BDC89 Sixto Sanchez .30 .75
BDC90 Seth Johnson .25 .60
BDC91 Ryan Jensen .40 1.00
BDC92 Tim Tebow 1.25 3.00
BDC93 Wander Franco 4.00 10.00
BDC94 Matthew Thompson .30 .75
BDC95 Jake Mangum 1.00 2.50
BDC96 Jake Guenther .30 .75
BDC97 Jonathan India .30 .75
BDC98 Jack Kochanowicz .30 .75
BDC99 Noah Song .75 2.00
BDC100 Andrew Vaughn 8.00 20.00
BDC101 Anthony Prato .25 .60
BDC102 Domingo Acevedo .25 .60
BDC103 MacKenzie Gore .50 1.25
BDC104 Zack Thompson .40 1.00
BDC105 Nick Quintana .50 1.25
BDC106 Kyle Isbel .30 .75
BDC107 Ryan Weathers .25 .60
BDC108 Andre Lipcius .60 1.50
BDC109 Tyler Baum .30 .75
BDC110 Conner Capel .30 .75
BDC111 Michael Massey .30 .75
BDC112 Diosbel Arias .25 .60
BDC113 Brandon Williamson .40 1.00
BDC114 Jeter Downs .40 1.00
BDC115 George Kirby .40 1.00
BDC116 Graeme Stinson .25 .60
BDC117 Brent Rooker .30 .75
BDC118 Eric Yang .30 .75
BDC119 Josh Wolf .30 .75
BDC120 Andrew Schultz .25 .60
BDC121 Grayson Rodriguez .50 1.25
BDC122 MJ Melendez .40 1.00
BDC123 Bryant Packard .40 1.00
BDC124 Aramis Ademan .25 .60
BDC125 Corbin Carroll 2.00 5.00
BDC126 Kyle McCann .30 .75
BDC127 Matthew Liberatore .25 .60
BDC128 Beau Philip .40 1.00
BDC129 Aaron Schunk .50 1.25
BDC130 Brice Turang .30 .75
BDC131 Rece Hinds 1.50 4.00
BDC132 Jimmy Lewis .25 .60
BDC133 Will Robertson .40 1.00
BDC134 Joey Bart .75 2.00
BDC135 Miguel Amaya .40 1.00
BDC136 Jonathan Ornelas .30 .75
BDC137 Vince Fernandez .30 .75
BDC138 Grant Gambrell .30 .75
BDC139 Matthew Lugo .75 2.00
BDC140 Korey Lee .50 1.25
BDC141 Nasim Nunez .25 .60
BDC142 Denyi Reyes .30 .75
BDC143 Moises Gomez .40 1.00
BDC144 John Rave .25 .60
BDC145 Grae Kessinger .40 1.00
BDC146 Isiah Gilliam .30 .75
BDC147 Ryne Nelson .30 .75
BDC148 Ryan Garcia .25 .60
BDC149 Matt Canterino .30 .75
BDC150 J.J. Bleday 5.00 12.00
BDC151 Ryan Costello .30 .75
BDC152 Tyler Fitzgerald .30 .75
BDC153 Spencer Steer .25 .60
BDC154 Jose Devers .40 1.00
BDC155 Blaze Alexander .25 .60
BDC156 John Doxakis .40 1.00
BDC157 Armani Smith .75 2.00
BDC158 Jordyn Adams .30 .75
BDC159 Sean Hjelle .30 .75
BDC160 Cristian Javier .30 .75
BDC161 Jared Triolo .40 1.00
BDC162 Alec Bohm 1.50 4.00
BDC163 Jahmai Jones .25 .60
BDC164 Deivi Garcia 1.25 3.00
BDC165 Brennan Malone .25 .60
BDC166 Cameron Cannon .50 1.25
BDC167 Glenallen Hill Jr. .40 1.00
BDC168 Evan Edwards .25 .60
BDC169 Shervyen Newton .40 1.00
BDC170 Travis Swaggerty .40 1.00
BDC171 Anthony Seigler .40 1.00
BDC172 Evan White .40 1.00
BDC173 Luken Baker .30 .75
BDC174 Trejyn Fletcher .40 1.00
BDC175 Spencer Brickhouse .60 1.50
BDC176 Daulton Varsho .25 .60
BDC177 Hayden Wesneski .30 .75
BDC178 Chase Strumpf 1.25 3.00
BDC179 Logan Gilbert .40 1.00
BDC180 Joshua Mears 1.25 3.00
BDC181 Matt Vierling .40 1.00
BDC182 Will Wilson 1.25 3.00
BDC183 Logan Driscoll .40 1.00
BDC184 Tyler Freeman .25 .60
BDC185 Ian Anderson .60 1.50
BDC186 Owen Miller .30 .75
BDC187 Kody Hoese 1.50 4.00
BDC188 Grant Lavigne .30 .75
BDC189 Nick Lodolo .50 1.25
BDC190 Clarke Schmidt .40 1.00
BDC191 Erik Miller .60 1.50
BDC192 Seth Beer .60 1.50
BDC193 Alejandro Kirk .40 1.00
BDC194 Drey Jameson .25 .60
BDC195 Christian Cairo .40 1.00
BDC196 Kameron Misner .60 1.50
BDC197 Tommy Henry .30 .75
BDC198 Lazaro Armenteros .30 .75
BDC199 Kendall Williams .40 1.00
BDC200 Cooper Johnson .40 1.00

2019 Bowman Chrome Draft Blue Refractors
*BLUE REF: 2X TO 5X BASIC
STATED ODDS 1:34 HOBBY
STATED PRINT RUN 150 SER.#'d SETS

2019 Bowman Chrome Draft Gold Refractors
*GOLD REF: 5X TO 12X BASIC
STATED ODDS 1:100 HOBBY
STATED PRINT RUN 50 SER.#'d SETS

2019 Bowman Chrome Draft Green Refractors
*GREEN REF: 2.5X TO 6X BASIC
STATED ODDS 1:51 HOBBY
STATED PRINT RUN 99 SER.#'d SETS

2019 Bowman Chrome Draft Orange Refractors
*ORANGE REF: 8X TO 20X BASIC
STATED ODDS 1:134 HOBBY
STATED PRINT RUN 25 SER.#'d SETS

2019 Bowman Chrome Draft Purple Refractors
*PURPLE REF: 1.5X TO 4X BASIC
STATED ODDS 1:20 HOBBY
STATED PRINT RUN 250 SER.#'d SETS

2019 Bowman Chrome Draft Refractors
*REF: .75X TO 2X BASIC
RANDOM INSERTS IN PACKS

2019 Bowman Chrome Draft Sky Blue Refractors
*SKY BLUE REF: 1X TO 2.5X BASIC
STATED ODDS 1:8 HOBBY

2019 Bowman Chrome Draft Sparkle Refractors
*SPARKLE REF: 1.5X TO 4X BASIC
STATED ODDS 1:24 HOBBY

2019 Bowman Chrome Draft Image Variations
STATED ODDS 1:203 HOBBY
BDC1 Adley Rutschman 30.00 80.00
BDC3 Alek Manoah 8.00 20.00
BDC7 Josh Jung 12.00 30.00

BDC31 Hunter Bishop 12.00 30.00
BDC50 Riley Greene 15.00 40.00
BDC67 Shea Langeliers 8.00 20.00
BDC85 CJ Abrams 15.00 40.00
BDC88 Victor Victor Mesa 8.00 20.00
BDC93 Wander Franco 30.00 80.00
BDC100 Andrew Vaughn 12.00 30.00
BDC134 Joey Bart 12.00 30.00
BDC150 J.J. Bleday 20.00 50.00
BDC189 Nick Lodolo 8.00 20.00
BDC192 Seth Beer 10.00 25.00

2019 Bowman Chrome Draft Image Variation Autographs

STATED ODDS 1:691 HOBBY
STATED PRINT RUN 99 SER.#'d SETS
EXCHANGE DEADLINE 11/30/2021
BDC1 Adley Rutschman 400.00 800.00
BDC7 Josh Jung 250.00 500.00
BDC50 Riley Greene 250.00 500.00
BDC67 Shea Langeliers 150.00 300.00
BDC85 CJ Abrams 200.00 400.00
BDC88 Victor Victor Mesa 40.00 100.00
BDC93 Wander Franco 300.00 600.00
BDC100 Andrew Vaughn 250.00 500.00
BDC134 Joey Bart 125.00 300.00
BDC150 J.J. Bleday 200.00 400.00
BDC189 Nick Lodolo 50.00 120.00
BDC192 Seth Beer 50.00 120.00

2019 Bowman Chrome Draft Autographs

STATED ODDS 1:9 HOBBY
PRINTING PLATE ODDS 1:3201 HOBBY
PLATE PRINT RUN 1 SET PER COLOR
BLACK-CYAN-MAGENTA-YELLOW ISSUED
NO PLATE PRICING DUE TO SCARCITY
EXCHANGE DEADLINE 11/30/2021
CDAAK Antoine Kelly 6.00 15.00
CDAAL Andre Lipcius 8.00 20.00
CDAAM Alek Manoah 12.00 30.00
CDAAMA Alec Marsh 4.00 10.00
CDAAR Adley Rutschman 125.00 300.00
CDAAS Aaron Schunk 8.00 20.00
CDAAV Andrew Vaughn 125.00 300.00
CDABB Brett Baty 25.00 60.00
CDABM Brennan Malone 3.00 8.00
CDABMC Brady McConnell 5.00 12.00
CDABP Beau Philip 8.00 20.00
CDABS Bryson Stott 25.00 60.00
CDABSH Braden Shewmake 20.00 50.00
CDABW Blake Walston 6.00 15.00
CDABWI Brandon Williamson 12.00 30.00
CDACA CJ Abrams 100.00 250.00
CDACC Corbin Carroll 30.00 80.00
CDACCA Cameron Cannon 6.00 15.00
CDACS Chase Strumpf 8.00 20.00
CDADB Dasan Brown 8.00 20.00
CDADE Daniel Espino 12.00 30.00
CDADF Dominic Fletcher 8.00 20.00
CDADJ Drey Jameson 3.00 8.00
CDADW Davis Wendzel 4.00 10.00
CDAES Ethan Small 6.00 15.00
CDAGH Gunnar Henderson 15.00 40.00
CDAGJ Greg Jones 12.00 30.00
CDAGK George Kirby 12.00 30.00
CDAGM Grant McCray 5.00 12.00
CDAHB Hunter Bishop 40.00 100.00
CDAIC Isaiah Campbell 4.00 10.00
CDAJB Jamari Baylor 8.00 20.00
CDAJD John Doxakis 5.00 12.00
CDAJJ Josh Jung 40.00 100.00
CDAJJB J.J. Bleday 60.00 150.00
CDAJJG JJ Goss 6.00 15.00
CDAJK Jack Kochanowicz 5.00 12.00
CDAJL Jimmy Lewis 6.00 15.00
CDAJM Joshua Mears 10.00 25.00
CDAJS Josh Smith 12.00 30.00
CDAJSA Jake Sanford 10.00 25.00
CDAJT Jared Triolo 5.00 12.00
CDAJW Josh Wolf 4.00 10.00
CDAKC Keoni Cavaco 40.00 100.00
CDAKH Kody Hoese 25.00 60.00
CDAKM Kameron Misner 25.00 60.00
CDAKP Kyren Paris 12.00 30.00
CDAKS Kyle Stowers 8.00 20.00
CDAKW Kendall Williams 5.00 12.00
CDALD Logan Davidson 5.00 12.00
CDALDR Logan Driscoll 5.00 12.00
CDALW Logan Wyatt 6.00 15.00
CDAMB Michael Busch 15.00 40.00
CDAMC Matt Canterino 4.00 10.00
CDAMG Matt Gorski 5.00 12.00
CDAML Matthew Lugo
CDAMT Michael Toglia 15.00 40.00
CDAMTH Matthew Thompson 15.00 40.00
CDAMW Matt Wallner 10.00 25.00
CDANL Nick Lodolo 15.00 40.00
CDANN Nasim Nunez 6.00 15.00
CDANQ Nick Quintana 6.00 15.00
CDANS Noah Song 8.00 20.00
CDAPB Peyton Burdick 30.00 80.00
CDAQP Quinn Priester. 10.00 25.00
CDARG Riley Greene 125.00 300.00
CDARGA Ryan Garcia 3.00 8.00
CDARH Rece Hinds 15.00 40.00
CDARJ Ryan Jensen 5.00 12.00
CDARN Ryne Nelson 4.00 10.00
CDARZ Ryan Zeferjahn 4.00 10.00
CDASJ Seth Johnson 3.00 8.00
CDASL Shea Langeliers 40.00 100.00
CDASS Sammy Siani 4.00 10.00
CDASST Spencer Steer 3.00 8.00
CDATB Tyler Baum 4.00 10.00
CDATC Tyler Callihan 12.00 30.00
CDATH Tommy Henry 4.00 10.00
CDATJS T.J. Sikkema 5.00 12.00
CDAWW Will Wilson 15.00 40.00
CDAZT Zack Thompson 6.00 15.00

2019 Bowman Chrome Draft Autographs Black Refractors

*BLACK REF: 1X TO 2.5X BASIC
STATED ODDS 1:117 HOBBY
STATED PRINT RUN 75 SER.#'D SETS
EXCHANGE DEADLINE 11/30/2021
CDAAR Adley Rutschman 400.00 1000.00
CDACC Corbin Carroll 150.00 400.00
CDAJJ Josh Jung 200.00 500.00
CDAKM Kameron Misner 50.00 120.00
CDAML Matthew Lugo 40.00 100.00
CDAWW Will Wilson 50.00 120.00

2019 Bowman Chrome Draft Autographs Blue Refractors

*BLUE REF: .75X TO 2X BASIC
STATED ODDS 1:86 HOBBY
STATED PRINT RUN 150 SER.#'D SETS
EXCHANGE DEADLINE 11/30/2021
CDAAR Adley Rutschman 300.00 800.00
CDACC Corbin Carroll 125.00 300.00
CDAJJ Josh Jung 150.00 400.00
CDAKM Kameron Misner 40.00 100.00
CDAML Matthew Lugo 30.00 80.00

2019 Bowman Chrome Draft Autographs Blue Wave Refractors

*BLUE WAVE REF: .75X TO 2X BASIC
STATED ODDS 1:86 HOBBY
STATED PRINT RUN 150 SER.#'D SETS
EXCHANGE DEADLINE 11/30/2021
CDAAR Adley Rutschman 300.00 800.00
CDACC Corbin Carroll 125.00 300.00
CDAJJ Josh Jung 150.00 400.00
CDAKM Kameron Misner 40.00 100.00
CDAML Matthew Lugo 30.00 80.00

2019 Bowman Chrome Draft Autographs Gold Refractors

*GOLD REF: 1.5X TO 4X BASIC
STATED ODDS 1:256 HOBBY
STATED PRINT RUN 50 SER.#'D SETS
EXCHANGE DEADLINE 11/30/2021
CDAAM Alek Manoah 125.00 300.00
CDAAR Adley Rutschman 800.00 1500.00
CDAAS Aaron Schunk 75.00 200.00
CDAAV Andrew Vaughn 1000.00 2000.00
CDACA CJ Abrams 500.00 1200.00
CDACC Corbin Carroll 250.00 600.00
CDACCA Cameron Cannon 40.00 100.00
CDACS Chase Strumpf 50.00 120.00
CDADB Dasan Brown 75.00 200.00
CDADF Dominic Fletcher 75.00 200.00
CDAGH Gunnar Henderson 100.00 250.00
CDAJJ Josh Jung 300.00 800.00
CDAKH Kody Hoese 200.00 500.00
CDAKM Kameron Misner 75.00 200.00
CDAMB Michael Busch 125.00 300.00
CDAML Matthew Lugo 60.00 150.00
CDAMT Michael Toglia 100.00 250.00
CDAMW Matt Wallner 75.00 200.00
CDAWW Will Wilson 125.00 300.00

2019 Bowman Chrome Draft Autographs Gold Wave Refractors

*GOLD WAVE REF: 1.5X TO 4X BASIC
STATED ODDS 1:256 HOBBY
STATED PRINT RUN 50 SER.#'D SETS
EXCHANGE DEADLINE 11/30/2021
CDAAM Alek Manoah 125.00 300.00
CDAAR Adley Rutschman 800.00 1500.00
CDAAS Aaron Schunk 75.00 200.00
CDAAV Andrew Vaughn 1000.00 2000.00
CDACA CJ Abrams 500.00 1200.00
CDACC Corbin Carroll 250.00 600.00
CDACCA Cameron Cannon 40.00 100.00
CDACS Chase Strumpf 50.00 120.00
CDADB Dasan Brown 75.00 200.00
CDADF Dominic Fletcher 75.00 200.00
CDAGH Gunnar Henderson 100.00 250.00
CDAJJ Josh Jung 300.00 800.00
CDAKH Kody Hoese 200.00 500.00
CDAKM Kameron Misner 75.00 200.00
CDAMB Michael Busch 125.00 300.00
CDAML Matthew Lugo 60.00 150.00
CDAMT Michael Toglia 100.00 250.00
CDAMW Matt Wallner 75.00 200.00
CDAWW Will Wilson 125.00 300.00

2019 Bowman Chrome Draft Autographs Green Refractors

*GREEN REF: .75X TO 2X BASIC
STATED ODDS 1:130 HOBBY
STATED PRINT RUN 99 SER.#'D SETS
EXCHANGE DEADLINE 11/30/2021
CDAAR Adley Rutschman 300.00 800.00
CDACC Corbin Carroll 125.00 300.00
CDAJJ Josh Jung 150.00 400.00
CDAKM Kameron Misner 40.00 100.00
CDAML Matthew Lugo 30.00 80.00

2019 Bowman Chrome Draft Autographs Orange Refractors

*ORANGE REF: 3X TO 8X BASIC
STATED ODDS 1:350 HOBBY
STATED PRINT RUN 25 SER.#'D SETS
EXCHANGE DEADLINE 11/30/2021
CDAAM Alek Manoah 250.00 600.00
CDAAR Adley Rutschman 1500.00 3000.00
CDAAS Aaron Schunk 150.00 400.00
CDAAV Andrew Vaughn 2000.00 4000.00
CDACA CJ Abrams 1000.00 2500.00
CDACC Corbin Carroll 500.00 1200.00
CDACCA Cameron Cannon 75.00 200.00
CDACS Chase Strumpf 100.00 250.00
CDADB Dasan Brown 150.00 400.00
CDADF Dominic Fletcher 150.00 400.00
CDAGH Gunnar Henderson 200.00 500.00
CDAJJ Josh Jung 1500.00 2500.00
CDAKH Kody Hoese 400.00 1000.00
CDAKM Kameron Misner 150.00 400.00
CDAMB Michael Busch 250.00 600.00
CDAML Matthew Lugo 125.00 300.00
CDAMT Michael Toglia 200.00 500.00
CDAMW Matt Wallner 150.00 400.00
CDAPB Peyton Burdick 300.00 800.00
CDAWW Will Wilson 250.00 600.00

2019 Bowman Chrome Draft Autographs Purple Refractors

*PURPLE REF: .6X TO 1.5X BASIC
STATED ODDS 1:52 HOBBY
STATED PRINT RUN 250 SER.#'D SETS
EXCHANGE DEADLINE 11/30/2021
CDAKM Kameron Misner 30.00 80.00
CDAML Matthew Lugo 25.00 60.00

2019 Bowman Chrome Draft Autographs Refractors

*REF: .5X TO 1.2X BASIC
STATED ODDS 1:26 HOBBY
STATED PRINT RUN 499 SER.#'D SETS
EXCHANGE DEADLINE 11/30/2021
CDAAR Adley Rutschman 200.00 500.00
CDAJJ Josh Jung 60.00 150.00
CDAML Matthew Lugo 20.00 50.00

2019 Bowman Chrome Draft Autographs Sparkle Refractors

*SPARKLE REF: 1X TO 2.5X BASIC
STATED ODDS 1:180 HOBBY
STATED PRINT RUN 71 SER.#'D SETS
EXCHANGE DEADLINE 11/30/2021
CDAAR Adley Rutschman 400.00 1000.00
CDACC Corbin Carroll 150.00 400.00
CDAJJ Josh Jung 200.00 500.00
CDAKM Kameron Misner 50.00 120.00
CDAML Matthew Lugo 40.00 100.00
CDAWW Will Wilson 50.00 120.00

2019 Bowman Chrome Draft Bowman 30th Anniversary

STATED ODDS 1:12 HOBBY
*ATOMIC REF/150: 2X TO 5X BASE
*ORANGE REF/25: 6X TO 15X BASE
B30AR Adley Rutschman 2.00 5.00
B30AV Andrew Vaughn 1.00 2.50
B30CJA CJ Abrams 1.50 4.00
B30JB Joey Bart 1.00 2.50
B30JJ Josh Jung 1.00 2.50
B30JJB J.J. Bleday 1.50 4.00
B30RG Riley Greene 1.25 3.00
B30SB Seth Beer .75 2.00
B30VVM Victor Victor Mesa .60 1.50
B30WF Wander Franco 2.00 5.00

2019 Bowman Chrome Draft Bowman 30th Anniversary Autographs

STATED ODDS 1:967 HOBBY
STATED PRINT RUN 99 SER.#'d SETS
EXCHANGE DEADLINE 11/30/2021
*ORANGE/25: .6X TO 1.5X BASIC
B30AAR Adley Rutschman 100.00 250.00
B30AAV Andrew Vaughn 40.00 100.00
B30ACJA CJ Abrams 50.00 120.00
B30AJB Joey Bart 40.00 100.00
B30AJJB J.J. Bleday 50.00 120.00
B30ANL Nick Lodolo 10.00 25.00
B30ARG Riley Greene 40.00 100.00
B30ASB Seth Beer 12.00 30.00
B30AVVM Victor Victor Mesa 12.00 30.00
B30AWF Wander Franco 100.00 250.00

2019 Bowman Chrome Draft Class of '19 Autographs

STATED ODDS 1:116 HOBBY
STATED PRINT RUN 99 SER.#'d SETS
EXCHANGE DEADLINE 11/30/2021
C19AAM Alek Manoah 10.00 25.00
C19AAR Adley Rutschman 50.00 120.00
C19AAV Andrew Vaughn 40.00 100.00
C19ABB Brett Baty 15.00 40.00
C19ABM Brennan Malone 5.00 12.00
C19ABS Bryson Stott 10.00 25.00
C19ABSH Braden Shewmake 10.00 25.00
C19ABW Blake Walston 5.00 12.00
C19ACC Corbin Carroll 12.00 30.00
C19ACJA CJ Abrams 25.00 60.00
C19ADE Daniel Espino 8.00 20.00
C19AES Ethan Small 4.00 10.00
C19AGJ Greg Jones 8.00 20.00
C19AGK George Kirby 5.00 12.00
C19AHB Hunter Bishop 15.00 40.00
C19AJJ Josh Jung 15.00 40.00
C19AJJB J.J. Bleday 20.00 50.00
C19AKC Keoni Cavaco 10.00 25.00
C19AKH Kody Hoese 15.00 40.00
C19AKL Korey Lee 15.00 40.00
C19ALD Logan Davidson 8.00 20.00
C19AMB Michael Busch 10.00 25.00
C19AMT Michael Toglia 12.00 30.00
C19ANL Nick Lodolo 12.00 30.00
C19AQP Quinn Priester 6.00 15.00
C19ARG Riley Greene 30.00 80.00
C19ARJ Ryan Jensen 5.00 12.00
C19ASL Shea Langeliers 15.00 40.00
C19ASS Sammy Siani 8.00 20.00
C19AWW Will Wilson 10.00 25.00
C19AZT Zack Thompson 5.00 12.00

2019 Bowman Chrome Draft Class of '19 Autographs Gold Refractors

*GOLD REF: .6X TO 1.5X BASIC
STATED ODDS 1:670 HOBBY
STATED PRINT RUN 50 SER.#'d SETS
EXCHANGE DEADLINE 11/30/2021

2019 Bowman Chrome Draft Draft Night Autographs

STATED ODDS 1:3233 HOBBY
STATED PRINT RUN 99 SER.#'d SETS
EXCHANGE DEADLINE 11/30/2021
*GOLD/50: .5X TO 1.2X BASIC
*ORANGE/25: .6X TO 1.5X BASIC
DNABB Brett Baty 30.00 80.00
DNABM Brennan Malone 10.00 25.00
DNADE Daniel Espino 12.00 30.00

2019 Bowman Chrome Draft Draft Pick Breakdown

STATED ODDS 1:6 HOBBY
*REF/250: .6X TO 1.5X BASE
*GREEN REF/99: .75X TO 2X BASE
*GOLD REF/50: 1.5X TO 4X BASE
BSBAM Alek Manoah .50 1.25
BSBAR Adley Rutschman 1.50 4.00
BSBAV Andrew Vaughn .75 2.00
BSBCA CJ Abrams 1.25 3.00
BSBHB Hunter Bishop .75 2.00
BSBJJ Josh Jung .75 2.00
BSBJJB J.J. Bleday 1.25 3.00
BSBNL Nick Lodolo .50 1.25
BSBRG Riley Greene 1.00 2.50
BSBSL Shea Langeliers .50 1.25

2019 Bowman Chrome Draft Draft Pick Breakdown Autographs

STATED ODDS 1:967 HOBBY
STATED PRINT RUN 99 SER.#'d SETS
EXCHANGE DEADLINE 11/30/2021
BSBAAM Alek Manoah 10.00 25.00
BSBAAR Adley Rutschman 60.00 150.00
BSBAAV Andrew Vaughn 30.00 80.00
BSBACA CJ Abrams 20.00 50.00
BSBAJJ Josh Jung 25.00 60.00
BSBAJJB J.J. Bleday 25.00 60.00
BSBANL Nick Lodolo 12.00 30.00
BSBARG Riley Greene 25.00 60.00
BSBASL Shea Langeliers 20.00 50.00

2019 Bowman Chrome Draft Draft Progression

STATED ODDS 1:3 HOBBY
*REF/250: .6X TO 1.5X BASE
*GREEN REF/250: .75X TO 2X BASE
*GOLD REF/50: 1.5X TO 4X BASE
DPRARI Smith/Carroll/McCarthy .40 1.00
DPRATL Waters/Jenista/Langeliers .75 2.00
DPRBAL Rutschman/Rodriguez/Hall 1.50 4.00
DPRCIN Lodolo/Greene/India .50 1.25
DPRCWS Vaughn/Burger/Madrigal .75 2.00
DPRDET Greene/Faedo/Mize 1.00 2.50
DPRMIA Scott/Bleday/Rogers 1.25 3.00
DPRNYM Cortes/Baty/Peterson .50 1.25
DPRPIT Priester/Mitchell/Swaggerty .40 1.00
DPRSDP Abrams/Gore/Weathers 1.25 3.00
DPRSFG Bishop/Bart/Ramos .75 2.00
DPRSTL Thompson/Kirtley/Gorman .75 2.00
DPRTEX Seise/Jung/Winn .75 2.00
DPRTOR Pearson/Groshans/Manoah .60 1.50

2019 Bowman Chrome Draft Franchise Futures

STATED ODDS 1:3 HOBBY
*REF/250: .6X TO 1.5X BASE
*GREEN REF/250: .75X TO 2X BASE
*GOLD REF/50: 1.5X TO 4X BASE
FFAM C.Abrams/J.Mears 1.25 3.00
FFBM J.Bleday/K.Misner 1.25 3.00
FFCW M.Wallner/K.Cavaco .60 1.50
FFGQ N.Quintana/R.Greene 1.00 2.50
FFHB M.Busch/K.Hoese .75 2.00
FFLS S.Langeliers/B.Shewmake .75 2.00
FFPS S.Siani/Q.Priester .40 1.00
FFRH A.Rutschman/G.Henderson 1.50 4.00
FFVT A.Vaughn/M.Thompson .75 2.00
FFWMA B.Walston/B.Malone .40 1.00

2019 Bowman Chrome Draft Franchise Futures Autographs

STATED ODDS 1:745 HOBBY
STATED PRINT RUN 99 SER.#'d SETS
EXCHANGE DEADLINE 11/30/2021
*GOLD/50: .5X TO 1.2X BASIC
*ORANGE/25: .6X TO 1.5X BASIC
FFAAM C.Abrams/J.Mears 25.00 60.00
FFABM J.Bleday/K.Misner 30.00 80.00
FFACW M.Wallner/K.Cavaco 20.00 50.00
FFAGQ N.Quintana/R.Greene 30.00 80.00
FFAHB Busch/Hoese EXCH 30.00 80.00
FFAJG J.Goss/G.Jones 10.00 25.00
FFALS S.Langeliers/B.Shewmake 30.00 80.00
FFAMW K.Williams/A.Manoah 10.00 25.00
FFAPS S.Siani/Q.Priester 8.00 20.00
FFARH Rtschmn/Hndrsn EXCH 75.00 200.00
FFAWMA B.Walston/B.Malone 8.00 20.00

2019 Bowman Chrome Draft Top of the Class Box Toppers

RANDOM INSERTS IN HOBBY BOXES
STATED PRINT RUN 99 SER.#'d SETS
*GOLD/50: .5X TO 1.2X BASIC
TOCAM Alek Manoah 4.00 10.00
TOCAR Adley Rutschman 12.00 30.00
TOCAV Andrew Vaughn 6.00 15.00
TOCBB Brett Baty 4.00 10.00
TOCCJA CJ Abrams 10.00 25.00
TOCHB Hunter Bishop 6.00 15.00
TOCJJ Josh Jung 6.00 15.00
TOCJJB J.J. Bleday 10.00 25.00
TOCKC Keoni Cavaco 5.00 12.00
TOCNL Nick Lodolo 4.00 10.00
TOCRG Riley Greene 8.00 20.00
TOCSL Shea Langeliers 4.00 10.00

2019 Bowman Chrome Draft Top of the Class Box Toppers Autographs

STATED ODDS 1:2278 HOBBY BOXES
STATED PRINT RUN 35 SER.#'d SETS
EXCHANGE DEADLINE 11/30/2021
TOCAM Alek Manoah 12.00 30.00
TOCAR Adley Rutschman 100.00 250.00
TOCAV Andrew Vaughn 40.00 100.00
TOCBB Brett Baty 60.00 150.00
TOCCJA CJ Abrams 50.00 120.00
TOCJJ Josh Jung 50.00 120.00
TOCJJB J.J. Bleday 30.00 80.00
TOCKC Keoni Cavaco 40.00 100.00
TOCNL Nick Lodolo 25.00 60.00
TOCRG Riley Greene 60.00 150.00
TOCSL Shea Langeliers 25.00 60.00

2020 Bowman Chrome

1 Mike Trout 1.50 4.00
2 Manny Machado .30 .75
3 Francisco Lindor .30 .75
4 Paul Goldschmidt .30 .75
5 Brusdar Graterol RC .60 1.50
6 Whit Merrifield .30 .75
7 Andres Munoz RC .50 1.25
8 Luis Robert RC 4.00 10.00
9 Zack Collins RC .50 1.25
10 Jose Berrios .25 .60
11 Randy Arozarena RC 6.00 15.00
12 John Means .20 .50
13 Aaron Judge .75 2.00
14 Yadier Molina .30 .75
15 Logan Allen RC .40 1.00
16 Anthony Kay RC .40 1.00
17 J.D. Martinez .30 .75
18 Kris Bryant .40 1.00
19 Willie Calhoun .20 .50
20 Justin Dunn RC .50 1.25
21 Buster Posey .40 1.00
22 Freddie Freeman .40 1.00
23 Keston Hiura .40 1.00
24 Jordan Yamamoto RC .50 1.25
25 Yordan Alvarez RC 4.00 10.00
26 Rhys Hoskins .40 1.00
27 Jacob deGrom .30 .75
28 Ronald Acuna Jr. 1.50 4.00
29 Stephen Strasburg .30 .75
30 Sheldon Neuse RC .50 1.25
31 Mookie Betts 1.00 2.50
32 Gleyber Torres .60 1.50
33 Eugenio Suarez .25 .60
34 A.J. Puk RC .75 2.00
35 Bryce Harper .50 1.25
36 Aaron Civale RC .60 1.50
37 Yoshi Tsutsugo RC .50 1.25
38 Mauricio Dubon RC .50 1.25
39 Yusei Kikuchi .25 .60
40 Jorge Alfaro .25 .60
41 Blake Snell .25 .60
42 Evan Longoria .25 .60
43 Matt Chapman .30 .75
44 Nico Hoerner RC 1.50 4.00
45 Josh Bell .25 .60
46 Charlie Blackmon .30 .75
47 Bobby Bradley RC .50 1.25
48 Adrian Morejon RC .40 1.00
49 Yu Chang RC .60 1.50
50 Bo Bichette RC 3.00 8.00
51 Michel Baez RC .40 1.00
52 Eddie Rosario .25 .60
53 Matthew Boyd .20 .50
54 Juan Soto 1.00 2.50
55 Gerrit Cole .50 1.25
56 Alex Bregman .30 .75
57 Adbert Alzolay RC .50 1.25
58 Shohei Ohtani .40 1.00
59 Salvador Perez .25 .60
60 Austin Meadows .25 .60
61 Nolan Arenado .40 1.00
62 Jesus Luzardo RC .75 2.00
63 Seth Brown RC .40 1.00
64 Trent Grisham RC 1.50 4.00
65 Pete Alonso .75 2.00
66 Alex Young RC .40 1.00
67 Corey Kluber .25 .60
68 Justin Verlander .30 .75
69 Hyun-jin Ryu .25 .60
70 Mike Clevinger .25 .60
71 Shogo Akiyama RC .60 1.50
72 Dylan Cease RC .75 2.00
73 Ketel Marte .25 .60
74 Tony Gonsolin RC 1.50 4.00
75 Marcus Semien .20 .50
76 Christian Yelich .40 1.00
77 Xander Bogaerts .30 .75
78 Vladimir Guerrero Jr. .60 1.50
79 Aristides Aquino RC .75 2.00
80 Brendan McKay RC .60 1.50
81 Zac Gallen RC 1.00 2.50
82 Fernando Tatis Jr. 1.25 3.00
83 Gavin Lux RC 3.00 8.00
84 Bryan Reynolds .25 .60
85 Tim Anderson .30 .75
86 Miguel Cabrera .30 .75
87 Sean Murphy RC .60 1.50
88 Trey Mancini .30 .75
89 Joey Votto .30 .75
90 Kyle Lewis RC 3.00 8.00
91 Abraham Toro RC .50 1.25
92 Anthony Rizzo .50 1.25
93 Anthony Rendon .30 .75
94 Dan Vogelbach .20 .50
95 Eduardo Escobar .20 .50
96 Dustin May RC 1.50 4.00
97 Isan Diaz RC .60 1.50
98 Nick Solak RC .60 1.50
99 Jose Abreu .30 .75
100 Cody Bellinger .60 1.50

2020 Bowman Chrome Blue Refractors

*BLUE REF VET: 4X TO 10X BASIC
*BLUE REF RC: 2X TO 5X BASIC
STATED ODDS 1:XX HOBBY
STATED PRINT RUN 150 SER.#'d SETS
1 Mike Trout 20.00 50.00
8 Luis Robert 60.00 150.00
11 Randy Arozarena 125.00 300.00
31 Mookie Betts 20.00 50.00
50 Bo Bichette 50.00 120.00
82 Fernando Tatis Jr. 25.00 60.00
90 Kyle Lewis 25.00 60.00

2020 Bowman Chrome Gold Refractors

*GOLD REF VET: 8X TO 20X BASIC
*GOLD REF RC: 4X TO 10X BASIC
STATED ODDS 1:XXX HOBBY
STATED PRINT RUN 50 SER.#'d SETS
1 Mike Trout 125.00 300.00
8 Luis Robert 125.00 300.00
11 Randy Arozarena 250.00 600.00
31 Mookie Betts 50.00 120.00
50 Bo Bichette 100.00 250.00
82 Fernando Tatis Jr. 50.00 120.00
90 Kyle Lewis 50.00 120.00

2020 Bowman Chrome Green Refractors

*GREEN REF VET: 5X TO 12X BASIC
*GREEN REF RC: 2.5X TO 6X BASIC
STATED ODDS 1:XXX HOBBY
STATED PRINT RUN 99 SER.#'d SETS
1 Mike Trout 25.00 60.00
8 Luis Robert 75.00 200.00
11 Randy Arozarena 150.00 400.00
31 Mookie Betts 25.00 60.00
50 Bo Bichette 60.00 150.00
82 Fernando Tatis Jr. 30.00 80.00
90 Kyle Lewis 30.00 80.00

2020 Bowman Chrome Orange Refractors

*ORANGE REF VET: 10X TO 25X BASIC
*ORANGE REF RC: 5X TO 12X BASIC
STATED ODDS 1:XXX HOBBY
STATED PRINT RUN 25 SER.#'d SETS
1 Mike Trout 150.00 400.00
8 Luis Robert 150.00 400.00
11 Randy Arozarena 300.00 800.00
31 Mookie Betts 60.00 150.00
50 Bo Bichette 125.00 300.00
82 Fernando Tatis Jr. 60.00 150.00
90 Kyle Lewis 60.00 150.00

2020 Bowman Chrome Purple Refractors

*PURPLE REF VET: 2X TO 5X BASIC
*PURPLE REF RC: 1X TO 2.5X BASIC
STATED ODDS 1:XX HOBBY
STATED PRINT RUN 250 SER.#'d SETS
1 Mike Trout 10.00 25.00
8 Luis Robert 30.00 80.00
11 Randy Arozarena 60.00 150.00
31 Mookie Betts 10.00 25.00
50 Bo Bichette 25.00 60.00
82 Fernando Tatis Jr. 12.00 30.00
90 Kyle Lewis 12.00 30.00

2020 Bowman Chrome Refractors

*REF VET: 1.5X TO 4X BASIC
*REF RC: .75X TO 2X BASIC
STATED ODDS 1:XX HOBBY
STATED PRINT RUN 499 SER.#'d SETS
1 Mike Trout 8.00 20.00
8 Luis Robert 25.00 60.00
11 Randy Arozarena 50.00 120.00
31 Mookie Betts 8.00 20.00
50 Bo Bichette 20.00 50.00
82 Fernando Tatis Jr. 10.00 25.00
90 Kyle Lewis 10.00 25.00

2020 Bowman Chrome Rookie Image Variations

STATED ODDS 1:XXX HOBBY
5 Brusdar Graterol 4.00 10.00
25 Yordan Alvarez 15.00 40.00
30 Sheldon Neuse 3.00 8.00
34 A.J. Puk 5.00 12.00
44 Nico Hoerner 6.00 15.00
50 Bo Bichette 40.00 100.00
51 Michel Baez 2.50 6.00
62 Jesus Luzardo 6.00 15.00
72 Dylan Cease 5.00 12.00
79 Aristides Aquino 5.00 12.00
80 Brendan McKay 4.00 10.00
83 Gavin Lux 15.00 40.00
87 Sean Murphy 4.00 10.00
90 Kyle Lewis 20.00 50.00
96 Dustin May 8.00 20.00

2020 Bowman Chrome Rookie Image Variation Autographs

STATED ODDS 1:XXX HOBBY
STATED PRINT RUN 25 SER.#'d SETS
EXCHANGE DEADLINE 8/31/2022
44 Nico Hoerner
79 Aristides Aquino 40.00 100.00
80 Brendan McKay
90 Kyle Lewis 200.00 500.00
96 Dustin May 200.00 500.00

2020 Bowman Chrome '19 AFL MVP

STATED ODDS 1:XX HOBBY
STATED PRINT RUN 250 SER.#'d SETS
AFLSRL Royce Lewis 4.00 10.00

2020 Bowman Chrome '19 AFL MVP Autographs

STATED ODDS 1:XXX HOBBY
STATED PRINT RUN 100 SER.#'d SETS
AFLSRL Royce Lewis 25.00 60.00

2020 Bowman Chrome '19 Fall Stars

STATED ODDS 1:XX HOBBY
*ATOMIC/150: 1.2X TO 3X BASE
*ORANGE/25: 2.5X TO 6X BASE
AFLAB Alec Bohm 2.00 5.00
AFLAG Andres Gimenez .40 1.00
AFLBM Brandon Marsh .30 .75
AFLCJC C.J. Chatham .40 1.00
AFLDK Dean Kremer .40 1.00
AFLDL Daniel Lynch .30 .75
AFLFW Forrest Whitley .30 .75
AFLGD Greg Deichmann .40 1.00
AFLGP Geraldo Perdomo .30 .75
AFLHR Heliot Ramos .50 1.25
AFLIH Ivan Herrera .50 1.25
AFLJA Jo Adell 1.25 3.00
AFLJB Joey Bart 1.00 2.50
AFLJD Jarren Duran 1.25 3.00
AFLJJM JJ Matijevic .40 1.00
AFLJL Josh Lowe .30 .75
AFLJR Julio Rodriguez 2.00 5.00
AFLKI Kyle Isbel .30 .75
AFLLG Luis Garcia .50 1.25
AFLMA Miguel Amaya .40 1.00
AFLNJ Nolan Jones .50 1.25
AFLNN Nick Neidert .30 .75
AFLOC Oneil Cruz .40 1.00
AFLSB Seth Beer .60 1.50
AFLSBA Shane Baz .30 .75
AFLSH Spencer Howard 1.25 3.00
AFLTH Trey Harris .40 1.00
AFLTS Tyler Stephenson .30 .75
AFLVB Vidal Brujan 1.00 2.50
AFLVVM Victor Victor Mesa .50 1.25

2020 Bowman Chrome '19 Fall Stars Autograph Relics

STATED ODDS 1:XXX HOBBY
STATED PRINT RUN 50 SER.#'d SETS
EXCHANGE DEADLINE 8/31/2022
AFLRAB Alec Bohm
AFLRIH Ivan Herrera 40.00 100.00
AFLRJA Jo Adell EXCH 50.00 120.00
AFLRJD Jarren Duran 40.00 100.00
AFLRSB Seth Beer
AFLRTH Trey Harris 25.00 60.00
AFLRVVM Victor Victor Mesa

2020 Bowman Chrome '19 Fall Stars Autographs

STATED ODDS 1:XXX HOBBY
EXCHANGE DEADLINE 8/31/2022
AFLAB Alec Bohm 25.00 60.00
AFLBM Brandon Marsh 4.00 10.00
AFLDK Dean Kremer 6.00 15.00
AFLDL Daniel Lynch 4.00 10.00
AFLGP Geraldo Perdomo 6.00 15.00
AFLHR Heliot Ramos 6.00 15.00
AFLJB Joey Bart 20.00 50.00
AFLJD Jarren Duran 15.00 40.00
AFLJJM JJ Matijevic 5.00 12.00
AFLLG Luis Garcia 10.00 25.00
AFLMA Miguel Amaya 6.00 15.00
AFLSB Seth Beer 8.00 20.00
AFLSH Spencer Howard 12.00 30.00
AFLVVM Victor Victor Mesa 6.00 15.00

2020 Bowman Chrome '19 Fall Stars Relics

STATED ODDS 1:XXX HOBBY
STATED PRINT RUN 99 SER.#'d SETS
*ORANGE/25: .6X TO 1.5X BASIC
AFLRTS Tyler Stephenson 3.00 8.00
AFLRAB Alec Bohm 12.00 30.00
AFLRAG Andres Gimenez 4.00 10.00
AFLRBM Brandon Marsh 3.00 8.00
AFLRCJC C.J. Chatham 4.00 10.00
AFLRDK Dean Kremer 8.00 20.00
AFLRDL Daniel Lynch 3.00 8.00
AFLRGD Greg Deichmann 4.00 10.00
AFLRIH Ivan Herrera 10.00 25.00
AFLRJA Jo Adell 8.00 20.00
AFLRJD Jarren Duran 6.00 15.00
AFLRJJM JJ Matijevic 4.00 10.00
AFLRJR Julio Rodriguez 10.00 25.00
AFLRLG Luis Garcia 5.00 12.00
AFLRMA Miguel Amaya 4.00 10.00
AFLRNN Nick Neidert 3.00 8.00
AFLRRL Royce Lewis 6.00 15.00
AFLRSB Seth Beer 6.00 15.00

AFLRTH Trey Harris 4.00 10.00
AFLRVVM Victor Victor Mesa 5.00 12.00

2020 Bowman Chrome '90 Bowman

STATED ODDS 1:8 HOBBY
*ATOMIC REF/150: 2.5X TO 6X BASE
*GREEN REF/99: 2.5X TO 6X BASE
*GOLD REF/50: 4X TO 10X BASIC
*ORANGE REF/25: 8X TO 20X BASE
90BAA Aristides Aquino .50 1.25
90BAB Alec Bohm 1.50 4.00
90BAK Alex Kirilloff .50 1.25
90BAP A.J. Puk .50 1.25
90BAR Adley Rutschman 1.50 4.00
90BAV Andrew Vaughn 1.00 2.50
90BBB Bo Bichette 2.00 5.00
90BBH Bryce Harper .60 1.50
90BBWJ Bobby Witt Jr. 1.25 3.00
90BCA CJ Abrams 1.00 2.50
90BCK Clayton Kershaw .75 2.00
90BCM Casey Mize .75 2.00
90BCP Cristian Pache .75 2.00
90BCY Christian Yelich .50 1.25
90BDC Dylan Carlson 1.00 2.50
90BDCE Dylan Cease .50 1.25
90BDH DL Hall .25 .60
90BDW Drew Waters .60 1.50
90BFW Forrest Whitley .25 .60
90BGL Gavin Lux 1.50 4.00
90BGT Gleyber Torres .75 2.00
90BIA Ian Anderson .60 1.50
90BJA Jo Adell 1.00 2.50
90BJB Joey Bart .75 2.00
90BJJB JJ Bleday .75 2.00
90BJK Jarred Kelenic 1.50 4.00
90BJL Jesus Luzardo .50 1.25
90BJR Julio Rodriguez 1.50 4.00
90BJS Juan Soto 1.25 3.00
90BKL Kyle Lewis 2.00 5.00
90BLR Luis Robert 2.50 6.00
90BMG MacKenzie Gore .50 1.25
90BML Matthew Liberatore .30 .75
90BMM Matt Manning .30 .75
90BMS Max Scherzer .40 1.00
90BMT Mike Trout 2.00 5.00
90BNG Nolan Gorman .50 1.25
90BNH Nico Hoerner 1.00 2.50
90BNP Nate Pearson .50 1.25
90BPA Pete Alonso 1.00 2.50
90BRAJ Ronald Acuna Jr. 1.50 4.00
90BRG Riley Greene 1.00 2.50
90BRL Royce Lewis .60 1.50
90BSH Spencer Howard 1.00 2.50
90BSM Sean Murphy .40 1.00
90BSS Sixto Sanchez .40 1.00
90BTT Taylor Trammell .30 .75
90BWF Wander Franco 2.50 6.00
90BXB Xander Bogaerts .40 1.00
90BYA Yordan Alvarez 1.25 3.00

2020 Bowman Chrome '90 Bowman Autographs

BOW.STATED ODDS 1:4,400 HOBBY
BOW.CHR.ODDS 1:XXX HOBBY
STATED PRINT RUN 30 SER.#'d SETS
BOW.CHR.EXCH.DEADLINE 8/31/2022
90BAA Aristides Aquino 12.00 30.00
90BAP A.J. Puk 12.00 30.00
90BAR Adley Rutschman 75.00 200.00
90BAV Andrew Vaughn 25.00 60.00
90BBB Bo Bichette 100.00 250.00
90BBWJ Bobby Witt Jr. 75.00 200.00
90BCA C.J. Abrams 50.00 120.00
90BCM Casey Mize 30.00 80.00
90BDC Dylan Carlson 60.00 150.00
90BDCE Dylan Cease 12.00 30.00
90BGL Gavin Lux 75.00 200.00
90BGT Gleyber Torres 50.00 120.00
90BJA Jo Adell 100.00 250.00
90BJB Joey Bart 30.00 80.00
90BJK Jarred Kelenic 60.00 150.00
90BJL Jesus Luzardo 30.00 80.00
90BJR Julio Rodriguez 60.00 150.00
90BKL Kyle Lewis 75.00 200.00
90BMG MacKenzie Gore 30.00 80.00
90BML Matthew Liberatore 50.00 12.00
90BMM Matt Manning 50.00 120.00
90BMS Max Scherzer 50.00 12.00
90BMT Mike Trout 500.00 1000.00
90BNG Nolan Gorman
90BNH Nico Hoerner 50.00 120.00
90BRAJ Ronald Acuna Jr. 150.00 400.00
90BRG Riley Greene 75.00 200.00
90BRL Royce Lewis 30.00 80.00
90BSH Spencer Howard 40.00 100.00
90BSM Sean Murphy 25.00 60.00
90BSS Sixto Sanchez 40.00 100.00
90BWF Wander Franco 125.00 300.00
90BYA Yordan Alvarez 125.00 300.00

2020 Bowman Chrome Autograph Relics

STATED ODDS 1:XXX HOBBY
PRINT RUNS B/WN 30-75 COPIES PER
EXCHANGE DEADLINE 8/31/2022
*GOLD/50: .4X TO 1X BASIC
*GOLD/25: .75X TO 2X BASIC
BCARAA Aristides Aquino/75 15.00 40.00
BCARAR Austin Riley/75 20.00 50.00
BCARBH Bryce Harper/40 125.00 300.00
BCARBR Brendan Rodgers/75 6.00 15.00
BCARGS George Springer/75 15.00 40.00
BCARJA Jose Altuve/50 12.00 30.00
BCARJR Jake Rogers/75 6.00 15.00
BCARJS Jorge Soler/75 8.00 20.00
BCARKN Kevin Newman/75 6.00 15.00
BCARMC Michael Chavis/75 8.00 20.00
BCARMT Mike Trout/30 400.00 1000.00
BCARPA Pete Alonso/75 30.00 80.00
BCARRAJ Ronald Acuna Jr./75 75.00 200.00

2020 Bowman Chrome Dawn of Glory

DG1 Sherten Apostel 1.50 4.00
DG2 Gus Varland .30 .75
DG3 Jasseel De La Cruz .50 1.25
DG4 Nick Lodolo .50 1.25
DG5 Jarren Duran 1.25 3.00
DG6 Isaac Paredes .50 1.25
DG7 Dylan File .30 .75
DG8 Joe Ryan .30 .75
DG9 Ruben Cardenas .40 1.00
DG10 Sam Huff .60 1.50
DG11 Lewin Diaz .30 .75
DG12 Andrew Vaughn 1.25 3.00
DG13 Adley Rutschman 2.00 5.00
DG14 Jordan Balazovic .60 1.50
DG15 Kevin Smith .30 .75

2020 Bowman Chrome Dawn of Glory Autographs

STATED ODDS 1:XXX HOBBY
STATED PRINT RUN 99 SER.#'d SETS
EXCHANGE DEADLINE 8/31/2022
*ORANGE/25: .5X TO 1.2X BASIC
DGAAR Adley Rutschman 30.00 80.00
DGAAV Andrew Vaughn 12.00 30.00
DGAJB Jordan Balazovic EXCH 10.00 25.00
DGAJD Jarren Duran 15.00 40.00
DGAJR Joe Ryan 6.00 15.00
DGAKS Kevin Smith 6.00 15.00
DGANL Nick Lodolo 8.00 20.00
DGARC Ruben Cardenas 8.00 20.00
DGASA Sherten Apostel 12.00 30.00
DGASH Sam Huff 12.00 30.00

2020 Bowman Chrome Dual Prospect Autographs

STATED ODDS 1:17,538 HOBBY
STATED PRINT RUN 25 SER.#'d SETS
EXCHANGE DEADLINE 3/31/2022
DPABE Bleday/Encarnacion 200.00 500.00
DPACP Patino/Cantillo 125.00 300.00
DPAHA Arias/Huff 75.00 200.00
DPARH Hall/Rutschman 200.00 500.00
DPAVA Amaya/Vargas 50.00 120.00
DPAVP Pereira/Volpe 125.00 300.00

2020 Bowman Chrome Farm to Fame

STATED ODDS 1:XXX HOBBY
*ORANGE/25: .75X TO 2X BASIC
FTFBL Barry Larkin 3.00 8.00
FTFCF Carlton Fisk 3.00 8.00
FTFCJ Chipper Jones 4.00 10.00
FTFCY Carl Yastrzemski 6.00 15.00
FTFEM Edgar Martinez 3.00 8.00
FTFFT Frank Thomas 4.00 10.00
FTFGB George Brett 10.00 25.00
FTFHA Hank Aaron 8.00 20.00
FTFIR Ivan Rodriguez 3.00 8.00
FTFJB Johnny Bench 4.00 10.00
FTFMR Mariano Rivera 5.00 12.00
FTFNR Nolan Ryan 12.00 30.00
FTFOS Ozzie Smith 5.00 12.00
FTFPM Pedro Martinez 3.00 8.00
FTFRC Rod Carew 3.00 8.00
FTFRF Rollie Fingers 3.00 8.00
FTFRH Rickey Henderson 15.00 4.00
FTFRJ Reggie Jackson 3.00 8.00
FTFRY Robin Yount 4.00 10.00
FTFSC Steve Carlton 3.00 8.00
FTFTP Tony Perez 3.00 8.00
FTFWB Wade Boggs 3.00 8.00
FTFWM Willie Mays 8.00 20.00
FTFCRJ Cal Ripken Jr. 12.00 30.00

2020 Bowman Chrome Farm to Fame Autographs

RANDOM INSERTS IN PACKS
EXCHANGE DEADLINE 8/31/2022
FTFBL Barry Larkin 75.00 200.00
FTFCF Carlton Fisk 20.00 50.00
FTFCJ Chipper Jones 100.00 250.00
FTFCY Carl Yastrzemski 75.00 200.00
FTFFT Frank Thomas 40.00 100.00
FTFHA Hank Aaron 400.00 1000.00
FTFIR Ivan Rodriguez 25.00 60.00
FTFJB Johnny Bench 40.00 100.00
FTFMR Mariano Rivera 100.00 250.00
FTFNR Nolan Ryan 200.00 500.00
FTFOS Ozzie Smith 25.00 60.00
FTFPM Pedro Martinez 50.00 120.00
FTFRF Rollie Fingers 30.00 80.00
FTFSC Steve Carlton 15.00 40.00
FTFTP Tony Perez 15.00 40.00
FTFWB Wade Boggs 30.00 80.00
FTFCRJ Cal Ripken Jr. 75.00 200.00

2020 Bowman Chrome Hidden Finds

STATED ODDS 1:24 HOBBY
*ATOMIC REF/150: 2.5X TO 6X BASE
*GOLD REF/50: 4X TO 10X BASIC
*ORANGE REF/25: 8X TO 20X BASE
HFCM Cedric Mullins .40 1.00
HFCP Chris Paddack .40 1.00
HFDJ Danny Jansen .25 .60
HFGV Gus Varland .25 .60
HFIG Isiah Gilliam .30 .75
HFJB Jordan Balazovic .50 1.25
HFJC Joey Cantillo .25 .60
HFJCA Jake Cave .30 .75
HFJD Jarren Duran 1.00 2.50
HFJDM J.D. Martinez .40 1.00
HFJM Jeff McNeil .30 .75
HFJY Jordan Yamamoto .30 .75
HFLA Logan Allen .25 .60
HFMK Mike King .40 1.00
HFMM Max Muncy .30 .75
HFPG Paul Goldschmidt .40 1.00
HFRB Ryan Borucki .25 .60
HFRH Rhys Hoskins .50 1.25
HFRT Rowdy Tellez .30 .75
HFSH Sam Huff .50 1.25

2020 Bowman Chrome Hidden Finds Autographs

BOW.STATED ODDS 1:XXX HOBBY
BOW.CHR.STATED ODDS 1:XXX HOBBY
STATED PRINT RUN 99 SER.#'d SETS
BOW.EXCH.DEADLINE 3/31/2022
BOW.CHR.EXCHANGE DEADLINE 8/31/2022
HFCP Chris Paddack 6.00 15.00
HFGV Gus Varland 4.00 10.00
HFIG Isiah Gilliam 5.00 12.00
HFJC Joey Cantillo 4.00 10.00
HFJDM J.D. Martinez
HFJM Jeff McNeil 8.00 20.00
HFJY Jordan Yamamoto 5.00 12.00
HFLA Logan Allen 4.00 10.00
HFMM Max Muncy 5.00 12.00
HFPG Paul Goldschmidt
HFRH Rhys Hoskins
HFSH Sam Huff 20.00 50.00

2020 Bowman Chrome Hidden Finds Autographs Orange Refractors

*ORANGE REF: .75X TO 2X BASIC
BOW.STATED ODDS 1:3835 HOBBY
BOW.CHR.STATED ODDS 1:XXX HOBBY
STATED PRINT RUN 25 SER.#'d SETS
BOW.EXCH.DEADLINE 3/31/2022
BOW.CHR.EXCHANGE DEADLINE 8/31/2022
HFJDM J.D. Martinez 20.00 50.00
HFPG Paul Goldschmidt 25.00 60.00
HFRH Rhys Hoskins 15.00 40.00

2020 Bowman Chrome Prime Chrome Signatures

STATED ODDS 1:XXX HOBBY
STATED PRINT RUN 50 SER.#'d SETS
EXCHANGE DEADLINE 8/31/2022
*ORANGE/25: .5X TO 1.2X BASIC
PCSAR Adley Rutschman 40.00 100.00
PCSASP Alex Speas 6.00 15.00
PCSAV Andrew Vaughn 20.00 50.00
PCSAVO Anthony Volpe 25.00 60.00
PCSBB Brett Baty 15.00 40.00
PCSBD Brenton Doyle 20.00 50.00
PCSBWJ Bobby Witt Jr. 50.00 120.00
PCSED Ezequiel Duran 10.00 25.00
PCSGJ Gilberto Jimenez 15.00 40.00
PCSGM Gabriel Moreno 5.00 12.00
PCSJA Jacob Amaya 12.00 30.00
PCSJB Jordan Balazovic EXCH 6.00 15.00
PCSJDU Jarren Duran 15.00 40.00
PCSJR Jackson Rutledge 12.00 30.00
PCSKC Keoni Cavaco 6.00 15.00
PCSKS Kevin Smith 3.00 8.00
PCSLD Lewin Diaz 8.00 20.00
PCSML Max Lazar
PCSNH Niko Hulsizer 25.00 60.00
PCSNL Nick Lodolo 6.00 15.00
PCSRC Ruben Cardenas 20.00 50.00
PCSRG Riley Greene 25.00 60.00
PCSSA Sherten Apostel 25.00 60.00
PCSSH Sam Huff 15.00 40.00
PCSWW Will Wilson 8.00 20.00
PCSXE Xavier Edwards 15.00 40.00

2020 Bowman Chrome Prospect Autographs

RANDOM INSERTS IN PACKS
BOW.PLATE ODDS 1:11,389 HOBBY
BOW.CHR.PLATE ODDS 1:XXX HOBBY
PLATE PRINT RUN 1 SET PER COLOR
BLACK-CYAN-MAGENTA-YELLOW ISSUED
NO PLATE PRICING DUE TO SCARCITY
BOW.EXCH.DEADLINE 3/31/2022
BOW.CHR.EXCH.DEADLINE 8/31/2022
CPAAA Aaron Ashby 3.00 8.00
CPAAC Antonio Cabello 6.00 15.00
CPAAD Andrew Dalquist 3.00 8.00
CPAAG Anthony Garcia 15.00 40.00
CPAAH Austin Hansen 4.00 10.00
CPAAH Adam Hall 4.00 10.00
CPAAHI Adam Hill 3.00 8.00
CPAAP Andy Pages 30.00 80.00
CPAAR Adley Rutschman 30.00 80.00
CPAAS Alvaro Seijas 3.00 8.00
CPAAS Alex Speas 3.00 8.00
CPAASH Austin Shenton 12.00 30.00
CPAASH Aaron Shortridge 3.00 8.00
CPAAV Anthony Volpe 25.00 60.00
CPAAV Alex Vesia 3.00 8.00
CPAAVA Andrew Vaughn 15.00 40.00
CPABB Ben Braymer 3.00 8.00
CPABBA Bryce Ball 40.00 100.00
CPABD Brennen Davis 50.00 120.00
CPABD Brenton Doyle 15.00 40.00
CPABH Brandon Howlett 5.00 12.00
CPABL Brandon Lewis 5.00 12.00
CPABL Bayron Lora 100.00 250.00
CPABP Bryant Packard 4.00 10.00
CPABW Brady Whalen 5.00 12.00
CPABWJ Bobby Witt Jr. 125.00 300.00
CPACB Cody Bolton 4.00 10.00
CPACBA Colin Barber 10.00 25.00
CPACC Connor Cannon 12.00 30.00
CPACG Chris Gittens 5.00 12.00
CPACJ Cooper Johnson 3.00 8.00
CPACK Christian Koss 10.00 25.00
CPACR Chandler Redmond 6.00 15.00
CPACS Canaan Smith 6.00 15.00
CPACT Curtis Terry 6.00 15.00
CPACV Chris Vallimont 3.00 8.00
CPADA Diosbel Arias 4.00 10.00
CPADA Drew Avans 4.00 10.00
CPADF Dylan File 3.00 8.00
CPADJ Damon Jones 4.00 10.00
CPADM Drew Millas 4.00 10.00
CPADMA Devin Mann 6.00 15.00
CPAED Ezequiel Duran 12.00 30.00
CPAEL Ethan Lindow 4.00 10.00
CPAEM Erik Miller 3.00 8.00
CPAEP Everson Pereira 12.00 30.00
CPAEPE Erick Pena 60.00 150.00
CPAERI Erik Rivera 3.00 8.00
CPAFA Francisco Alvarez 50.00 120.00
CPAFP Ford Proctor 3.00 8.00
CPAGHJ Glenallen Hill Jr. 6.00 15.00
CPAGJ Gilberto Jimenez 30.00 80.00
CPAGL Grant Little 3.00 8.00
CPAGM Gabriel Moreno 8.00 20.00
CPAGMA Gunner Mayer 3.00 8.00
CPAGST Graeme Stinson 3.00 8.00
CPAGV Gus Varland 3.00 8.00
CPAHH Hogan Harris 3.00 8.00
CPAHY Hector Yan 4.00 10.00
CPAIH Ivan Herrera 20.00 50.00
CPAIP Isaac Paredes EXCH 12.00 30.00
CPAJA Jacob Amaya 8.00 20.00
CPAJBE James Beard 5.00 12.00
CPAJBR Jordan Brewer 10.00 25.00
CPAJC Joey Cantillo 3.00 8.00
CPAJD Jarren Duran 30.00 80.00
CPAJDC Jasseel De La Cruz 5.00 12.00
CPAJDI Jhon Diaz 30.00 80.00
CPAJDO Jasson Dominguez 400.00 1000.00
CPAJE Jerar Encarnacion 10.00 25.00
CPAJG Joe Genord 4.00 10.00
CPAJJB J.J. Bleday 20.00 50.00
CPAJMA Joan Martinez 4.00 10.00
CPAJP Jeremy Pena 6.00 15.00
CPAJR Jackson Rutledge 10.00 25.00
CPAJRY Joe Ryan 3.00 8.00
CPAJS Junior Santos 6.00 15.00
CPAJS Jonathan Stiever 3.00 8.00
CPAJT Jhon Torres 20.00 50.00
CPAKK Karl Kauffmann 3.00 8.00
CPAKS Kevin Smith 3.00 8.00
CPAKSI Kendall Simmons 8.00 20.00
CPALA Luisangel Acuna 100.00 250.00
CPALD Lewin Diaz 8.00 20.00
CPALD Lency Delgado 3.00 8.00
CPALK Levi Kelly 3.00 8.00
CPALM Luis Matos 50.00 120.00
CPALOH Logan O'Hoppe 5.00 12.00
CPALP Luis Patino 20.00 50.00
CPALV Leonel Valera 5.00 12.00
CPAMB Micah Bello 4.00 10.00
CPAMF Mario Feliciano 5.00 12.00
CPAMH Michael Harris 25.00 60.00
CPAML Max Lazar 4.00 10.00
CPAMM Michael Massey 4.00 10.00
CPAMV Miguel Vargas 15.00 40.00
CPANH Niko Hulsizer 8.00 20.00
CPANK Nick Kahle 4.00 10.00
CPAOE Omar Estevez 6.00 15.00
CPAOG Oscar Gonzalez 6.00 15.00
CPAOP Oswald Peraza 25.00 60.00
CPAOR Osiel Rodriguez 5.00 12.00
CPAPC Philip Clarke 3.00 8.00
CPAPN Packy Naughton 3.00 8.00
CPAPP Pedro Pages 3.00 8.00
CPAPR Paul Richan 3.00 8.00
CPAQC Quin Cotton 8.00 20.00
CPARC Ruben Cardenas 4.00 10.00
CPARF Randy Florentino 4.00 10.00
CPARG Riley Greene 20.00 50.00
CPARP Robert Puason 75.00 200.00
CPARPE Ryan Pepiot 5.00 12.00
CPARS Raimfer Salinas 12.00 30.00
CPARV Ricky Vanasco 5.00 12.00
CPASA Sherten Apostel 25.00 60.00
CPASG Seth Gray 5.00 12.00
CPASH Sam Huff 30.00 80.00
CPASP Stephen Paolini 10.00 25.00
CPATD Tony Dibrell 3.00 8.00
CPATDI Thomas Dillard 3.00 8.00
CPATDY Tyler Dyson 3.00 8.00
CPATH Trey Harris 10.00 25.00
CPATI Tyler Ivey 4.00 10.00
CPATJ Taylor Jones 3.00 8.00
CPATM Tucupita Marcano 8.00 20.00
CPATS Tarik Skubal 12.00 30.00
CPATT Tahnaj Thomas 6.00 15.00
CPATW Thad Ward 5.00 12.00
CPAUB Ulrich Bojarski 3.00 8.00
CPAVB Vidal Brujan 30.00 80.00
CPAVG Vaughn Grissom 12.00 30.00
CPAWH Will Holland 5.00 12.00
CPAWP Wilderd Patino 15.00 40.00
CPAXE Xavier Edwards 15.00 40.00
CPAYG Yoendrys Gomez 8.00 20.00
CPAZH Zack Hess 4.00 10.00
CPAZW Zach Watson 4.00 10.00

2020 Bowman Chrome Prospect Autographs Atomic Refractors

*ATOMIC REF: .75X TO 2X BASIC
STATED ODDS 1:742 HOBBY
STATED PRINT RUN 100 SER.#'D SETS
EXCHANGE DEADLINE 3/31/2022
CPAXE Xavier Edwards 50.00 120.00

2020 Bowman Chrome Prospect Autographs Blue Refractors

*BLUE REF: .75X TO 2X BASIC
BOW.STATED ODDS 1:495 HOBBY
BOW.CHR.STATED ODDS 1:XXX HOBBY
STATED PRINT RUN 150 SER.#'D SETS
BOW.EXCH.DEADLINE 3/31/2022
BOW.CHR.EXCH.DEADLINE 8/31/2022
CPAAC Antonio Cabello 30.00 80.00
CPABL Bayron Lora 250.00 600.00
CPACBA Colin Barber 30.00 80.00
CPAEPE Erick Pena 150.00 400.00
CPAGJ Gilberto Jimenez 60.00 150.00
CPAIH Ivan Herrera 60.00 150.00
CPAWP Wilderd Patino 50.00 120.00
CPAXE Xavier Edwards 50.00 120.00

2020 Bowman Chrome Prospect Autographs Gold Refractors

*GOLD REF: 1.5X TO 4X BASIC
BOW.STATED ODDS 1:1483 HOBBY
BOW.CHR.STATED ODDS 1:XXX BLASTER
STATED PRINT RUN 50 SER.#'D SETS
BOW.EXCH.DEADLINE 3/31/2022
BOW.CHR.EXCH.DEADLINE 8/31/2022
CPAAC Antonio Cabello 60.00 150.00
CPAAV Anthony Volpe 200.00 500.00
CPABL Bayron Lora 600.00 1500.00
CPACBA Colin Barber 60.00 150.00
CPAEPE Erick Pena 300.00 800.00
CPAGJ Gilberto Jimenez 125.00 300.00
CPAIH Ivan Herrera 125.00 300.00
CPALA Luisangel Acuna 600.00 1500.00
CPALM Luis Matos 300.00 800.00
CPALOH Logan O'Hoppe 30.00 80.00
CPAOP Oswald Peraza 125.00 300.00
CPATM Tucupita Marcano 50.00 120.00
CPAWP Wilderd Patino 100.00 250.00
CPAXE Xavier Edwards 100.00 250.00
CPAYG Yoendrys Gomez 30.00 80.00

2020 Bowman Chrome Prospect Autographs Gold Shimmer Refractors

*GOLD SHIM REF: 1.5X TO 4X BASIC
BOW.STATED ODDS 1:1483 HOBBY
BOW.CHR.STATED ODDS 1:XXX BLASTER
STATED PRINT RUN 50 SER.#'D SETS
BOW.EXCH.DEADLINE 3/31/2022
BOW.CHR.EXCH.DEADLINE 8/31/2022
CPAAC Antonio Cabello 60.00 150.00
CPAAV Anthony Volpe 200.00 500.00
CPABL Bayron Lora 600.00 1500.00
CPACBA Colin Barber 60.00 150.00
CPAEPE Erick Pena 300.00 800.00
CPAGJ Gilberto Jimenez 125.00 300.00
CPAIH Ivan Herrera 125.00 300.00
CPALA Luisangel Acuna 600.00 1500.00
CPALM Luis Matos 300.00 800.00
CPALOH Logan O'Hoppe 30.00 80.00
CPAOP Oswald Peraza 125.00 300.00
CPATM Tucupita Marcano 50.00 120.00
CPAWP Wilderd Patino 100.00 250.00
CPAXE Xavier Edwards 100.00 250.00
CPAYG Yoendrys Gomez 30.00 80.00

2020 Bowman Chrome Prospect Autographs Green Refractors

*GREEN REF: .75X TO 2X BASIC
BOW.STATED ODDS 1:576 BLASTER
BOW.CHR.STATED ODDS 1:XXX BLASTER
STATED PRINT RUN 99 SER.#'D SETS
BOW.EXCH.DEADLINE 3/31/2022
BOW.CHR.EXCH.DEADLINE 8/31/2022
CPAAC Antonio Cabello 30.00 80.00
CPABL Bayron Lora 250.00 600.00
CPACBA Colin Barber 30.00 80.00
CPAEPE Erick Pena 150.00 400.00
CPAGJ Gilberto Jimenez 60.00 150.00
CPAIH Ivan Herrera 60.00 150.00
CPAWP Wilderd Patino 50.00 120.00
CPAXE Xavier Edwards 50.00 120.00

2020 Bowman Chrome Prospect Autographs Green Atomic Refractors

*GREEN ATOMIC REF: .75X TO 2X BASIC
BOW.CHR.STATED ODDS 1:XXX BLASTER
STATED PRINT RUN 99 SER.#'D SETS
BOW.CHR.EXCH.DEADLINE 8/31/2022
CPAAC Antonio Cabello 30.00 80.00
CPABL Bayron Lora 250.00 600.00
CPACBA Colin Barber 30.00 80.00
CPAEPE Erick Pena 150.00 400.00
CPAGJ Gilberto Jimenez 60.00 150.00
CPAIH Ivan Herrera 60.00 150.00
CPAWP Wilderd Patino 50.00 120.00

2020 Bowman Chrome Prospect Autographs Green Shimmer Refractors

*GREEN SHIM REF: .75X TO 2X BASIC
STATED ODDS 1:576 BLASTER
STATED PRINT RUN 99 SER.#'D SETS
EXCHANGE DEADLINE 3/31/2022
CPAXE Xavier Edwards 50.00 120.00

2020 Bowman Chrome Prospect Autographs HTA Choice Refractors

*HTA CHOICE REF: .75X TO 2X BASIC
BOW.CHR.STATED ODDS 1:XXX HOBBY
STATED PRINT RUN 150 SER.#'D SETS
BOW.CHR.EXCH.DEADLINE 8/31/2022
CPAAC Antonio Cabello 30.00 80.00
CPABL Bayron Lora 250.00 600.00
CPACBA Colin Barber 30.00 80.00
CPAEPE Erick Pena 150.00 400.00
CPAGJ Gilberto Jimenez 60.00 150.00
CPAIH Ivan Herrera 60.00 150.00
CPAWP Wilderd Patino 50.00 120.00

2020 Bowman Chrome Prospect Autographs Orange Refractors

*ORANGE REF: 3X TO 8X BASIC
BOW.STATED ODDS 1:914 HOBBY
BOW.CHR.STATED ODDS 1:XXX HOBBY
STATED PRINT RUN 25 SER.#'D SETS
BOW.EXCH.DEADLINE 3/31/2022
BOW.CHR.EXCH.DEADLINE 8/31/2022
CPAAC Antonio Cabello 125.00 300.00
CPAAV Anthony Volpe 250.00 600.00
CPABL Bayron Lora 1250.00 3000.00
CPACBA Colin Barber 125.00 300.00
CPAEPE Erick Pena 600.00 1500.00
CPAGJ Gilberto Jimenez 250.00 600.00
CPAIH Ivan Herrera 250.00 600.00
CPALA Luisangel Acuna 1250.00 3000.00
CPALM Luis Matos 600.00 1500.00
CPALOH Logan O'Hoppe 60.00 150.00
CPAOP Oswald Peraza 250.00 600.00
CPATM Tucupita Marcano 100.00 250.00
CPAWP Wilderd Patino 200.00 500.00
CPAXE Xavier Edwards 200.00 500.00
CPAYG Yoendrys Gomez 60.00 150.00

2020 Bowman Chrome Prospect Autographs Orange Shimmer Refractors

*ORANGE SHIM REF: 3X TO 8X BASIC
STATED ODDS 1:914 HOBBY
STATED PRINT RUN 25 SER.#'D SETS
EXCHANGE DEADLINE 3/31/2022
CPAAV Anthony Volpe 250.00 600.00
CPAXE Xavier Edwards 200.00 500.00

2020 Bowman Chrome Prospect Autographs Orange Wave Refractors

*ORANGE WAVE REF: 3X TO 8X BASIC
BOW.CHR.STATED ODDS 1:XXX HOBBY
STATED PRINT RUN 25 SER.#'D SETS
EXCHANGE DEADLINE 8/31/2022
CPAAC Antonio Cabello 125.00 300.00
CPABL Bayron Lora 1250.00 3000.00
CPACBA Colin Barber 125.00 300.00
CPAEPE Erick Pena 600.00 1500.00
CPAGJ Gilberto Jimenez 250.00 600.00
CPAIH Ivan Herrera 250.00 600.00
CPALA Luisangel Acuna 1250.00 3000.00
CPALM Luis Matos 600.00 1500.00
CPALOH Logan O'Hoppe 60.00 150.00
CPAOP Oswald Peraza 250.00 600.00
CPATM Tucupita Marcano 100.00 250.00
CPAWP Wilderd Patino 200.00 500.00
CPAYG Yoendrys Gomez 60.00 150.00

2020 Bowman Chrome Prospect Autographs Purple Refractors

*PURPLE REF: .6X TO 1.5X BASIC
BOW.STATED ODDS 1:319 HOBBY
BOW.CHR.STATED ODDS 1:XXX HOBBY
STATED PRINT RUN 250 SER.#'D SETS
BOW.EXCH.DEADLINE 3/31/2022
BOW.CHR.EXCH.DEADLINE 8/31/2022
CPABL Bayron Lora 200.00 500.00

2020 Bowman Chrome Prospect Autographs Refractors

*REF: .5X TO 1.2X BASIC
BOW.STATED ODDS 1:160 HOBBY
BOW.CHR.STATED ODDS 1:XXX HOBBY
STATED PRINT RUN 499 SER.#'D SETS
BOW.EXCH.DEADLINE 3/31/2022
BOW.CHR.EXCH.DEADLINE 8/31/2022
CPABL Bayron Lora 150.00 400.00

2020 Bowman Chrome Prospect Autographs Speckle Refractors

*SPECKLE REF: .6X TO 1.5X BASIC
STATED ODDS 1:267 HOBBY
STATED PRINT RUN 299 SER.#'D SETS
EXCHANGE DEADLINE 3/31/2022

2020 Bowman Chrome Prospect Autographs Yellow Refractors

*YELLOW REF: .75X TO 2X BASIC
STATED ODDS 1:5221 BLASTER
STATED PRINT RUN 75 SER.#'D SETS
EXCHANGE DEADLINE 3/31/2022
CPAAV Anthony Volpe 100.00 250.00
CPAXE Xavier Edwards 50.00 120.00

2020 Bowman Chrome Prospects

BOW.PLATE ODDS 1:11,389 HOBBY
PLATE PRINT RUN 1 SET PER COLOR
BLACK-CYAN-MAGENTA-YELLOW ISSUED
NO PLATE PRICING DUE TO SCARCITY
BCP1 Wander Franco 2.00 5.00
BCP2 Drew Waters .50 1.25
BCP3 Jacob Amaya .75 2.00
BCP4 Kody Hoese .60 1.50
BCP5 Cristian Pache .60 1.50
BCP6 Zack Thompson .20 .50
BCP7 Briam Campusano .20 .50
BCP8 Jasson Dominguez 20.00 50.00
BCP9 Aaron Shortridge .20 .50
BCP10 Xavier Edwards .75 2.00
BCP11 Jesus Sanchez .20 .50
BCP12 Ronaldo Hernandez .20 .50
BCP13 Blake Rutherford .20 .50
BCP14 Ulrich Bojarski .20 .50
BCP15 Jordyn Adams .25 .60
BCP16 Austin Beck .25 .60
BCP17 Niko Hulsizer .50 1.25
BCP18 Triston Casas .50 1.25
BCP19 Julio Rodriguez 1.25 3.00
BCP20 Shane Baz .20 .50
BCP21 Shea Langeliers .40 1.00
BCP22 Grayson Rodriguez .30 .75
BCP23 Ruben Cardenas .25 .60
BCP24 Mason Denaburg .20 .50
BCP25 Bobby Witt Jr. 5.00 12.00
BCP26 Andrew Vaughn .75 2.00
BCP27 Kristian Robinson .60 1.50
BCP28 Ronny Mauricio .50 1.25
BCP29 Alec Bohm 1.25 3.00
BCP30 Jhon Diaz 2.00 5.00
BCP31 Estevan Florial .30 .75
BCP32 Elehuris Montero .25 .60
BCP33 Sam Huff .40 1.00
BCP34 Zack Brown .20 .50
BCP35 Brice Turang .20 .50
BCP36 Ryan Mountcastle .30 .75
BCP37 Wilfred Astudillo .25 .60
BCP38 Gus Varland .20 .50
BCP39 Nick Lodolo .30 .75
BCP40 Tyler Freeman .25 .60
BCP41 Rece Hinds .25 .60
BCP42 Brady Singer .25 .60
BCP43 Cal Mitchell .20 .50
BCP44 Ethan Hankins .25 .60
BCP45 Daz Cameron .20 .50
BCP46 Sherten Apostel 1.00 2.50
BCP47 Hunter Greene .30 .75
BCP48 Josiah Gray .30 .75
BCP49 Brailyn Marquez .50 1.25
BCP50 Adley Rutschman 1.25 3.00
BCP51 Everson Pereira .50 1.25
BCP52 Bayron Lora 3.00 8.00
BCP53 Clarke Schmidt .30 .75
BCP54 Brady McConnell .25 .60
BCP55 Spencer Howard .75 2.00
BCP56 Cristian Javier .20 .50
BCP57 Aaron Ashby .20 .50
BCP58 Logan Gilbert .25 .60
BCP59 Glenallen Hill Jr. .30 .75
BCP60 Alvaro Seijas .20 .50
BCP61 Jeremy Pena .50 1.25
BCP62 CJ Abrams .75 2.00
BCP63 Franklin Perez .20 .50
BCP64 Tanner Houck .50 1.25
BCP65 Damon Jones .20 .50
BCP66 Nolan Gorman .40 1.00
BCP67 Ke'Bryan Hayes .20 .50
BCP68 Bryson Stott .50 1.25
BCP69 Canaan Smith .30 .75
BCP70 Forrest Whitley .20 .50
BCP71 Drew Mendoza .50 1.25
BCP72 Jazz Chisholm .50 1.25
BCP73 Jonathan India .25 .60
BCP74 MacKenzie Gore .40 1.00
BCP75 Seth Beer .40 1.00
BCP76 Joey Cantillo .20 .50
BCP77 Evan White .20 .50
BCP78 Chris Vallimont .20 .50
BCP79 Sixto Sanchez .30 .75
BCP80 Alex Kirilloff .40 1.00
BCP81 Tristen Lutz .25 .60
BCP82 Freudis Nova .20 .50
BCP83 Tim Cate .20 .50
BCP84 Daniel Lynch .20 .50
BCP85 Antonio Cabello .60 1.50
BCP86 Bobby Dalbec .50 1.25
BCP87 Colton Welker .20 .50
BCP88 Logan Davidson .25 .60
BCP89 Matthew Liberatore .25 .60
BCP90 Adam Hall .25 .60
BCP91 Jackson Rutledge .30 .75
BCP92 Dane Dunning .20 .50
BCP93 Royce Lewis .50 1.25
BCP94 Jarred Kelenic 1.25 3.00
BCP95 Nolan Jones .30 .75
BCP96 Jerar Encarnacion .60 1.50
BCP97 Ian Anderson .50 1.25
BCP98 Alek Thomas .25 .60
BCP99 Matt Manning .25 .60
BCP100 Jo Adell .75 2.00
BCP101 Nick Madrigal .60 1.50
BCP102 Owen Miller .20 .50
BCP103 Marco Luciano .75 2.00
BCP104 Jordan Groshans .40 1.00
BCP105 Nick Allen .20 .50
BCP106 Dylan Carlson .75 2.00
BCP107 Cole Winn .20 .50
BCP108 Tarik Skubal 1.00 2.50
BCP109 Oscar Gonzalez .50 1.25
BCP110 Aramis Ademan .20 .50
BCP111 Oneil Cruz .25 .60
BCP112 Joey Bart .60 1.50
BCP113 Josh Jung .50 1.25
BCP114 Luis Garcia .30 .75
BCP115 Jasseel De La Cruz .30 .75
BCP116 J.J. Bleday .60 1.50
BCP117 Joe Ryan .20 .50
BCP118 Keoni Cavaco .20 .50
BCP119 Hans Crouse .20 .50
BCP120 Isaac Paredes .30 .75

BCP121 Grant Lavigne .20 .50
BCP122 Riley Greene .75 2.00
BCP123 Jordan Balazovic .40 1.00
BCP124 Nate Pearson .40 1.00
BCP125 Deivi Garcia .75 2.00
BCP126 Luis Garcia .75 2.00
BCP127 Leody Taveras .20 .50
BCP128 Bryan Mata .20 .50
BCP129 Hunter Bishop .40 1.00
BCP130 Taylor Trammell .25 .60
BCP131 Miguel Vargas .50 1.25
BCP132 Luis Gil .30 .75
BCP133 Grant Little .20 .50
BCP134 Gunnar Henderson .25 .60
BCP135 Eric Pardinho .20 .50
BCP136 Miguel Amaya .25 .60
BCP137 Ryan Rolison .20 .50
BCP138 Jorge Mateo .20 .50
BCP139 Anthony Volpe 2.50 6.00
BCP140 Nick Bennett .20 .50
BCP141 Brennen Davis .40 1.00
BCP142 Casey Mize .60 1.50
BCP143 Keibert Ruiz .50 1.25
BCP144 Jarren Duran .75 2.00
BCP145 Robert Puason 8.00 20.00
BCP146 Travis Swaggerty .25 .60
BCP147 Will Wilson .25 .60
BCP148 Heliot Ramos .30 .75
BCP149 Alek Manoah .25 .60
BCP150 Luis Robert 4.00 10.00
BCP151 Alex Kirilloff .40 1.00
BCP152 Michael Busch .50 1.25
BCP153 Daulton Jefferies .20 .50
BCP154 Mark Vientos .20 .50
BCP155 Diego Cartaya .40 1.00
BCP156 Monte Harrison .20 .50
BCP157 Nolan Jones .30 .75
BCP158 Alex Faedo .25 .60
BCP159 Bayron Lora 3.00 8.00
BCP160 Bobby Witt Jr. 5.00 12.00
BCP161 Noah Song .25 .60
BCP162 Nolan Gorman .40 1.00
BCP163 Wander Franco 2.00 5.00
BCP164 Tanner Houck .50 1.25
BCP165 Kyle Isbel .20 .50
BCP166 Brandon Marsh .20 .50
BCP167 Mickey Moniak .50 1.25
BCP168 Brice Turang .20 .50
BCP169 Noelvi Marte .75 2.00
BCP170 Yusniel Diaz .30 .75
BCP171 Elehuris Montero .25 .60
BCP172 Sixto Sanchez .30 .75
BCP173 Robert Puason 2.50 6.00
BCP174 Jackson Kowar .20 .50
BCP175 Julio Rodriguez 1.25 3.00
BCP176 Steele Walker .30 .75
BCP177 Tony Santillan .20 .50
BCP178 Mike Siani .20 .50
BCP179 Shane McCarthy .20 .50
BCP180 Keoni Cavaco .20 .50
BCP181 Daulton Varsho .20 .50
BCP182 Ryan Castellani .20 .50
BCP183 Adonis Medina .30 .75
BCP184 MacKenzie Gore .40 1.00
BCP185 Jay Groome .20 .50
BCP186 Andres Gimenez .25 .60
BCP187 Tristen Lutz .25 .60
BCP188 Leody Taveras .20 .50
BCP189 Triston McKenzie .30 .75
BCP190 Simeon Woods Richardson .30 .75
BCP191 Kyle Muller .20 .50
BCP192 Forrest Whitley .20 .50
BCP193 Korey Lee .25 .60
BCP194 Freudis Nova .20 .50
BCP195 Royce Lewis .50 1.25
BCP196 Keegan Akin .20 .50
BCP197 Quinn Priester .30 .75
BCP198 Francisco Alvarez .60 1.50
BCP199 Luis Garcia .75 2.00
BCP200 Brennan Malone .20 .50
BCP201 Cristian Pache .60 1.50
BCP202 Geraldo Perdomo .20 .50
BCP203 Ethan Hearn .30 .75
BCP204 Jesus Sanchez .20 .50
BCP205 Tim Cate .20 .50
BCP206 Cole Roederer .40 1.00
BCP207 Jorge Mateo .20 .50
BCP208 Triston Casas .50 1.25
BCP209 Matthew Liberatore .25 .60
BCP210 Keibert Ruiz .50 1.25
BCP211 Blake Rutherford .20 .50
BCP212 Jarred Kelenic 1.25 3.00
BCP213 Marco Luciano .75 2.00
BCP214 Deivi Garcia .75 2.00
BCP215 Sean Hjelle .30 .75
BCP216 Clarke Schmidt .30 .75
BCP217 Mason Denaburg .20 .50
BCP218 Luis Campusano .30 .75
BCP219 Braden Shewmake .30 .75
BCP220 Ke'Bryan Hayes .20 .50
BCP221 Shane Baz .20 .50
BCP222 Corbin Carroll .30 .75
BCP223 Estevan Florial .30 .75
BCP224 Isaac Paredes .30 .75
BCP225 Michael Toglia .20 .50
BCP226 Alejandro Kirk .75 2.00
BCP227 Jeter Downs .30 .75
BCP228 Tyler Stephenson .30 .75
BCP229 Matt Manning .25 .60
BCP230 Luis Garcia .30 .75
BCP231 Ryan Jensen .25 .60
BCP232 Dane Dunning .20 .50
BCP233 William Contreras .25 .60
BCP234 Bo Naylor .25 .60
BCP235 Luis Patino .30 .75
BCP236 Dylan Carlson .75 2.00
BCP237 Sam Huff .40 1.00
BCP238 D.L. Hall .20 .50
BCP239 Jackson Rutledge .30 .75
BCP240 Ryan Vilade .20 .50
BCP241 Vidal Brujan .60 1.50
BCP242 Seth Corry .20 .50
BCP243 Jasson Dominguez 6.00 15.00
BCP244 Jeremiah Jackson .20 .50
BCP245 Orelvis Martinez .50 1.25
BCP246 Kyren Paris .20 .50
BCP247 Brett Baty .60 1.50
BCP248 Corey Ray .20 .50
BCP249 Trevor Larnach .40 1.00
BCP250 Casey Mize .60 1.50

2020 Bowman Chrome Prospects Aqua Refractors

*AQUA REF: 2X TO 5X BASIC
STATED ODDS 1:162 HOBBY
STATED PRINT RUN 125 SER.#'d SETS
BCP8 Jasson Dominguez 150.00 400.00
BCP52 Bayron Lora 25.00 60.00

2020 Bowman Chrome Prospects Aqua Shimmer Refractors

*AQUA SHIM REF: 2X TO 5X BASIC
STATED ODDS 1:162 HOBBY
STATED PRINT RUN 125 SER.#'d SETS
BCP8 Jasson Dominguez 150.00 400.00
BCP52 Bayron Lora 25.00 60.00

2020 Bowman Chrome Prospects Atomic Refractors

*ATOMIC REF: 1.5X TO 4X BASIC
STATED ODDS 1:24 HOBBY
BCP8 Jasson Dominguez 125.00 300.00
BCP52 Bayron Lora 20.00 50.00

2020 Bowman Chrome Prospects Blue Refractors

*BLUE REF: 2X TO 5X BASIC
BOW.STATED ODDS 1:307 HOBBY
BOW.CHR.STATED ODDS 1:XXX HOBBY
STATED PRINT RUN 150 SER.#'d SETS
BCP8 Jasson Dominguez 150.00 400.00
BCP52 Bayron Lora 25.00 60.00
BCP159 Bayron Lora 25.00 60.00

2020 Bowman Chrome Prospects Blue Shimmer Refractors

*BLUE SHIM REF: 2X TO 5X BASIC
STATED ODDS 1:307 HOBBY
STATED PRINT RUN 150 SER.#'d SETS
BCP8 Jasson Dominguez 150.00 400.00
BCP52 Bayron Lora 25.00 60.00

2020 Bowman Chrome Prospects Gold Refractors

*GOLD REF: 6X TO 15X BASIC
BOW.STATED ODDS 1:919 HOBBY
BOW.CHR.STATED ODDS 1:XXX HOBBY
STATED PRINT RUN 50 SER.#'d SETS
BCP8 Jasson Dominguez 500.00 1200.00
BCP52 Bayron Lora 75.00 200.00
DCP159 Bayron Lora 75.00 200.00

2020 Bowman Chrome Prospects Gold Shimmer Refractors

*GOLD SHIM REF: 6X TO 15X BASIC
BOW.STATED ODDS 1:919 HOBBY
BOW.CHR.STATED ODDS 1:XX HOBBY
STATED PRINT RUN 50 SER.#'d SETS
BCP8 Jasson Dominguez 500.00 1200.00
BCP52 Bayron Lora 75.00 200.00
BCP159 Bayron Lora 75.00 200.00

2020 Bowman Chrome Prospects Green Refractors

*GREEN REF: 3X TO 8X BASIC
BOW.STATED ODDS 1:218 RETAIL
BOW.CHR.STATED ODDS 1:XXX RETAIL
STATED PRINT RUN 99 SER.#'d SETS
BCP8 Jasson Dominguez 250.00 600.00
BCP52 Bayron Lora 40.00 100.00
BCP159 Bayron Lora 40.00 100.00

2020 Bowman Chrome Prospects Green Shimmer Refractors

*GREEN SHIM REF: 3X TO 8X BASIC
BOW.STATED ODDS 1:218 RETAIL
BOW.CHR.STATED ODDS 1:XXX RETAIL
STATED PRINT RUN 99 SER.#'d SETS
BCP8 Jasson Dominguez 250.00 600.00
BCP52 Bayron Lora 40.00 100.00
BCP159 Bayron Lora 40.00 100.00

2020 Bowman Chrome Prospects Orange Refractors

*ORANGE REF: 10X TO 25X BASIC
BOW.STATED ODDS 1:367 HOBBY
BOW.CHR.STATED ODDS 1:367 HOBBY
STATED PRINT RUN 25 SER.#'d SETS
BCP8 Jasson Dominguez 750.00 2000.00
BCP52 Bayron Lora 100.00 250.00
BCP159 Bayron Lora 100.00 250.00

2020 Bowman Chrome Prospects Orange Shimmer Refractors

*ORANGE SHIM REF: 10X TO 25X BASIC
BOW.STATED ODDS 1:367 HOBBY
BOW.CHR.STATED ODDS 1:XXX HOBBY
STATED PRINT RUN 25 SER.#'d SETS
BCP8 Jasson Dominguez 750.00 2000.00
BCP52 Bayron Lora 100.00 250.00
BCP159 Bayron Lora 100.00 250.00

2020 Bowman Chrome Prospects Purple Refractors

*PURPLE REF: 1.5X TO 4X BASIC
BOW.STATED ODDS 1:185 HOBBY
BOW.CHR.STATED ODDS 1:XXX HOBBY
STATED PRINT RUN 250 SER.#'d SETS
BCP8 Jasson Dominguez 125.00 300.00
BCP52 Bayron Lora 20.00 50.00
BCP159 Bayron Lora 20.00 50.00

2020 Bowman Chrome Prospects Purple Shimmer Refractors

*PURPLE SHIM REF: 1X TO 2.5X BASIC
STATED ODDS 1:XXX HOBBY
BCP159 Bayron Lora 12.00 30.00

2020 Bowman Chrome Prospects Refractors

*REF: 1.2X TO 3X BASIC
BOW.STATED ODDS 1:93 HOBBY
BOW.CHR.STATED ODDS 1:XX HOBBY
STATED PRINT RUN 499 SER.#'d SETS
BCP8 Jasson Dominguez 100.00 250.00
BCP52 Bayron Lora 15.00 40.00
BCP159 Bayron Lora 15.00 40.00

2020 Bowman Chrome Prospects Speckle Refractors

*SPECKLE REF: 1.5X TO 4X BASIC
STATED ODDS 1:155 HOBBY
STATED PRINT RUN 299 SER.#'d SETS
BCP8 Jasson Dominguez 125.00 300.00
BCP52 Bayron Lora 20.00 50.00

2020 Bowman Chrome Prospects Yellow Refractors

*YELLOW REF: 4X TO 10X BASIC
STATED ODDS 1:613 HOBBY
STATED PRINT RUN 75 SER.#'d SETS
BCP8 Jasson Dominguez 300.00 800.00
BCP52 Bayron Lora 50.00 120.00

2020 Bowman Chrome Rookie Autographs

BOW.STATED ODDS 1:667 HOBBY
BOW.CHR.STATED ODDS 1:XXX HOBBY
BOW.PLATE ODDS 1:18,527 HOBBY
PLATE PRINT RUN 1 SET PER COLOR
BLACK-CYAN-MAGENTA-YELLOW ISSUED
NO PLATE PRICING DUE TO SCARCITY
BOW.EXCH.DEADLINE 3/31/2022
BOW.CHR.EXCH.DEADLINE 8/31/2022
CRAAA Aristides Aquino 15.00 40.00
CRAAK Anthony Kay 3.00 8.00
CRAAM Andres Munoz 4.00 10.00
CRAAP A.J. Puk 8.00 20.00
CRABB Bobby Bradley 4.00 10.00
CRABG Brusdar Graterol 20.00 50.00
CRABM McKay Arm Frwrd 10.00 25.00
CRADC Dylan Cease 10.00 25.00
CRADM Dustin May 20.00 50.00
CRAGL Gavin Lux 40.00 100.00
CRAID Isan Diaz 5.00 12.00
CRAJD Justin Dunn 4.00 10.00
CRAJF Jake Fraley 4.00 10.00
CRAJL Jesus Luzardo 15.00 40.00
CRAJY Jordan Yamamoto 4.00 10.00
CRAKL Kyle Lewis 50.00 120.00
CRALA Logan Allen 3.00 8.00
CRALR L.Robert Face Lft 200.00 500.00
CRALR L.Robert Face Rght 200.00 500.00
CRAMD Mauricio Dubon 4.00 10.00
CRANH Nico Hoerner 20.00 50.00
CRANS Nick Solak 5.00 12.00
CRASB Seth Brown 3.00 8.00
CRATG Trent Grisham 12.00 30.00
CRAYA Yordan Alvarez 50.00 120.00
CRAYT Yoshi Tsutsugo 40.00 100.00
CRAZC Zack Collins 4.00 10.00

2020 Bowman Chrome Rookie Autographs Atomic Refractors

*ATOMIC REF: .75X TO 2X BASIC
STATED ODDS 1:2917 HOBBY
STATED PRINT RUN 100 SER.#'d SETS
EXCHANGE DEADLINE 3/31/2022
CRAAAQ Aristides Aquino 25.00 60.00
CRAYC Yu Chang 12.00 30.00

2020 Bowman Chrome Rookie Autographs Blue Refractors

*BLUE REF: .6X TO 1.5X BASIC
BOW.STATED ODDS 1:1946 HOBBY
BOW.CHR.STATED ODDS 1:XXX HOBBY
STATED PRINT RUN 150 SER.#'d SETS
BOW.EXCH.DEADLINE 3/31/2022
BOW.CHR.EXCH.DEADLINE 8/31/2022
CRAAAQ Aristides Aquino 20.00 50.00
CRADL Domingo Leyba 6.00 15.00
CRAYC Yu Chang 10.00 25.00

2020 Bowman Chrome Rookie Autographs Gold Refractors

*GOLD REF: 1.2X TO 3X BASIC
BOW.STATED ODDS 1:5847 HOBBY
BOW.CHR.STATED ODDS 1:XXX HOBBY
STATED PRINT RUN 50 SER.#'d SETS
BOW.EXCH.DEADLINE 3/31/2022
BOW.CHR.EXCH.DEADLINE 8/31/2022
CRAAAQ Aristides Aquino 40.00 100.00
CRABBI Bo Bichette 300.00 800.00
CRABM McKay Arm Back 30.00 80.00
CRADL Domingo Leyba 12.00 30.00
CRAKL Kyle Lewis 250.00 600.00
CRAYC Yu Chang 20.00 50.00
CRAYT Yoshi Tsutsugo 60.00 150.00

2020 Bowman Chrome Rookie Autographs Green Refractors

*GREEN REF: .75X TO 2X BASIC
BOW.STATED ODDS 1:2264 BLASTER
BOW.CHR.STATED ODDS 1:XXX HOBBY
STATED PRINT RUN 99 SER.#'d SETS
BOW.EXCH.DEADLINE 3/31/2022
BOW.CHR.EXCH.DEADLINE 8/31/2022
CRAAAQ Aristides Aquino 25.00 60.00
CRADL Domingo Leyba 8.00 20.00
CRAKL Kyle Lewis 150.00 400.00
CRAYC Yu Chang 12.00 30.00
CRAYT Yoshi Tsutsugo 50.00 120.00

2020 Bowman Chrome Rookie Autographs Orange Refractors

*ORANGE REF: 2X TO 5X BASIC
BOW.STATED ODDS 1:3575 HOBBY
BOW.CHR.STATED ODDS 1:XXX HOBBY
STATED PRINT RUN 25 SER.#'d SETS
BOW.EXCH.DEADLINE 3/31/2022
BOW.CHR.EXCH.DEADLINE 8/31/2022
CRAAAQ Aristides Aquino 60.00 150.00
CRABBI Bo Bichette 500.00 1200.00
CRABM McKay Arm Back 50.00 120.00
CRADL Domingo Leyba 20.00 50.00
CRAKL Kyle Lewis 400.00 1000.00
CRAYC Yu Chang 30.00 80.00
CRAYT Yoshi Tsutsugo 100.00 250.00

2020 Bowman Chrome Rookie Autographs Refractors

*REF: .5X TO 1.2X BASIC
BOW.STATED ODDS 1:798 HOBBY
BOW.CHR.STATED ODDS 1:XXX HOBBY
STATED PRINT RUN 499 SER.#'d SETS
BOW.EXCH.DEADLINE 3/31/2022
BOW.CHR.EXCH.DEADLINE 8/31/2022
CRADL Domingo Leyba 5.00 12.00

2020 Bowman Chrome Rookie Autographs Yellow Refractors

*YELLOW REF: .75X TO 2X BASIC
STATED ODDS 1:5139 HOBBY
STATED PRINT RUN 75 SER.#'d SETS
EXCHANGE DEADLINE 3/31/2022
CRAAAQ Aristides Aquino 25.00 60.00
CRABBI Bo Bichette 200.00 500.00
CRABM McKay Arm Back 10.00 25.00
CRAYC Yu Chang 12.00 30.00

2020 Bowman Chrome Rookie of the Year Favorites

STATED ODDS 1:8 HOBBY
*ATOMIC REF/150: 2.5X TO 6X BASE
*GREEN REF/99: 2.5X TO 6X BASE
*GOLD REF/50: 4X TO 10X BASIC
*ORANGE REF/25: 8X TO 20X BASE
ROYFAA Adbert Alzolay .30 .75
ROYFAAQ Aristides Aquino .50 1.25
ROYFAC Aaron Civale .40 1.00
ROYFAP A.J. Puk .50 1.25
ROYFBB Bo Bichette 2.00 5.00
ROYFBM Brendan McKay .40 1.00
ROYFDC Dylan Cease .50 1.25
ROYFDM Dustin May 1.00 2.50
ROYFGL Gavin Lux 1.50 4.00
ROYFJL Jesus Luzardo .50 1.25
ROYFJY Jordan Yamamoto .30 .75
ROYFKL Kyle Lewis 2.00 5.00
ROYFNH Nico Hoerner 1.00 2.50
ROYFSM Sean Murphy .40 1.00
ROYFYA Yordan Alvarez 1.25 3.00

2020 Bowman Chrome Rookie of the Year Favorites Autographs

STATED ODDS 1:2653 HOBBY
STATED PRINT RUN 150 SER.#'d SETS
EXCHANGE DEADLINE 3/31/2022
*GOLD REF/50: .5X TO 1.2X
*ORANGE REF/25: .6X TO 1.5X
ROYFAAQ Aristides Aquino 20.00 50.00
ROYFAAP A.J. Puk 6.00 15.00
ROYFABB Bobby Bradley 4.00 10.00
ROYFABM Brendan McKay 10.00 25.00
ROYFADC Dylan Cease 10.00 25.00
ROYFAGL Gavin Lux 50.00 120.00
ROYFAJL Jesus Luzardo 6.00 15.00
ROYFAJY Jordan Yamamoto 4.00 10.00
ROYFANH Nico Hoerner
ROYFAYA Yordan Alvarez 40.00 100.00
ROYFAZC Zack Collins 4.00 10.00

2020 Bowman Chrome Scouts Top 100

STATED ODDS 1:4 HOBBY
*ATOMIC REF/150: 2.5X TO 6X BASE
*GREEN REF/99: 2.5X TO 6X BASE
*GOLD REF/50: 4X TO 10X BASE
*GARY VEE/55: 4X TO 10X BASE
*ORANGE REF/25: 8X TO 20X BASE
BTP1 Wander Franco 2.50 6.00
BTP2 Luis Robert 2.50 6.00
BTP3 Jo Adell 1.00 2.50
BTP4 MacKenzie Gore .50 1.25
BTP5 Gavin Lux 1.50 4.00
BTP6 Jesus Luzardo .50 1.25
BTP7 Adley Rutschman 1.50 4.00
BTP8 Forrest Whitley .25 .60
BTP9 Joey Bart .75 2.00
BTP10 Nate Pearson .50 1.25
BTP11 Casey Mize .75 2.00
BTP12 Jarred Kelenic 1.50 4.00
BTP13 Cristian Pache .75 2.00
BTP14 Brendan McKay .40 1.00
BTP15 Dylan Carlson 1.00 2.50
BTP16 Julio Rodriguez 1.50 4.00
BTP17 Matt Manning .30 .75
BTP18 Alex Kirilloff .50 1.25
BTP19 Carter Kieboom .30 .75
BTP20 Dustin May 1.00 2.50
BTP21 Royce Lewis .60 1.50
BTP22 Brendan Rodgers .40 1.00
BTP23 Sixto Sanchez .40 1.00
BTP24 Ian Anderson .60 1.50
BTP25 Bobby Witt Jr. 1.25 3.00
BTP26 Luis Patino .40 1.00
BTP27 A.J. Puk .50 1.25
BTP28 Andrew Vaughn 1.00 2.50
BTP29 Alec Bohm 1.50 4.00
BTP30 Drew Waters .60 1.50
BTP31 Michael Kopech .50 1.25
BTP32 DL Hall .25 .60
BTP33 Nico Hoerner 1.00 2.50
BTP34 Taylor Trammell .30 .75
BTP35 Riley Greene 1.00 2.50
BTP36 Spencer Howard 1.00 2.50
BTP37 Matthew Liberatore .30 .75
BTP38 Mitch Keller .40 1.00
BTP39 Tarik Skubal 1.25 3.00
BTP40 CJ Abrams 1.00 2.50
BTP41 Brusdar Graterol .40 1.00
BTP42 Nick Madrigal .75 2.00
BTP43 Nolan Gorman .50 1.25
BTP44 Ke'Bryan Hayes .25 .60
BTP45 Daniel Lynch .25 .60
BTP46 Logan Gilbert .30 .75
BTP47 Jordan Groshans .50 1.25
BTP48 Jesus Sanchez .25 .60
BTP49 Grayson Rodriguez .40 1.00
BTP50 Nolan Jones .40 1.00
BTP51 Hunter Greene .40 1.00
BTP52 Triston Casas .60 1.50
BTP53 Jasson Dominguez 6.00 15.00
BTP54 Adrian Morejon .25 .60
BTP55 Kyle Wright .40 1.00
BTP56 JJ Bleday .75 2.00
BTP57 Marco Luciano 1.00 2.50
BTP58 Evan White .25 .60
BTP59 Bobby Dalbec .60 1.50
BTP60 Jeter Downs .40 1.00
BTP61 Alek Thomas .30 .75
BTP62 Brady Singer .30 .75
BTP63 Kristian Robinson .75 2.00
BTP64 Justin Dunn .30 .75
BTP65 Keibert Ruiz .60 1.50
BTP66 Jonathan India .30 .75
BTP67 Ronny Mauricio .60 1.50
BTP68 Kyle Muller .25 .60
BTP69 Oneil Cruz .30 .75
BTP70 Deivi Garcia 1.00 2.50
BTP71 Bryse Wilson .30 .75
BTP72 Justus Sheffield .40 1.00
BTP73 Andres Gimenez .30 .75
BTP74 Bryan Mata .25 .60
BTP75 Daulton Varsho .25 .60
BTP76 Nick Lodolo .40 1.00
BTP77 Francisco Alvarez .75 2.00
BTP78 Josiah Gray .40 1.00
BTP79 Sean Murphy .40 1.00
BTP80 Heliot Ramos .40 1.00
BTP81 Jackson Kowar .25 .60
BTP82 Vidal Brujan .75 2.00
BTP83 Shane Baz .25 .60
BTP84 Yusniel Diaz .40 1.00
BTP85 Triston McKenzie .40 1.00
BTP86 George Valera .50 1.25
BTP87 Hunter Bishop .50 1.25
BTP88 Ryan Mountcastle .40 1.00
BTP89 Trevor Larnach .50 1.25
BTP90 Corbin Carroll .40 1.00
BTP91 Tyler Freeman .30 .75
BTP92 Hans Crouse .25 .60
BTP93 Shane McClanahan .30 .75
BTP94 Edward Cabrera .40 1.00
BTP95 Luis Garcia .40 1.00
BTP96 Luis Campusano .40 1.00
BTP97 Brailyn Marquez .60 1.50
BTP98 Tony Gonsolin 1.00 2.50
BTP99 Elehuris Montero .30 .75
BTP100 Ronaldo Hernandez .25 .60

2020 Bowman Chrome Scouts Top 100 Autographs

STATED ODDS 1:1300 HOBBY
STATED PRINT RUN 50 SER.#'d SETS
EXCHANGE DEADLINE 3/31/2022
BTP1 Wander Franco 125.00 300.00
BTP3 Jo Adell 60.00 150.00
BTP4 MacKenzie Gore 25.00 60.00
BTP5 Gavin Lux 50.00 120.00
BTP6 Jesus Luzardo 10.00 25.00
BTP7 Adley Rutschman 75.00 200.00
BTP9 Joey Bart 30.00 80.00
BTP11 Casey Mize 30.00 80.00
BTP12 Jarred Kelenic 40.00 100.00
BTP14 Brendan McKay 15.00 40.00
BTP15 Dylan Carlson 40.00 100.00
BTP16 Julio Rodriguez 50.00 120.00
BTP17 Matt Manning 40.00 100.00
BTP19 Carter Kieboom 6.00 15.00
BTP21 Royce Lewis 25.00 60.00
BTP22 Brendan Rodgers 12.00 30.00
BTP23 Sixto Sanchez 20.00 50.00
BTP25 Bobby Witt Jr. 125.00 300.00
BTP27 A.J. Puk 10.00 25.00
BTP28 Andrew Vaughn 20.00 50.00
BTP31 Michael Kopech 10.00 25.00
BTP33 Nico Hoerner 20.00 50.00
BTP35 Riley Greene 40.00 100.00
BTP36 Spencer Howard 40.00 100.00
BTP37 Matthew Liberatore 15.00 40.00
BTP38 Mitch Keller 8.00 20.00
BTP39 Tarik Skubal 25.00 60.00
BTP40 C.J. Abrams 40.00 100.00
BTP41 Brusdar Graterol 8.00 20.00
BTP42 Nick Madrigal 12.00 30.00
BTP43 Nolan Gorman 10.00 25.00
BTP46 Logan Gilbert 6.00 15.00
BTP47 Jordan Groshans 10.00 25.00
BTP49 Grayson Rodriguez 15.00 40.00
BTP51 Hunter Greene 15.00 40.00
BTP52 Triston Casas 30.00 80.00
BTP53 Jasson Dominguez 300.00 800.00
BTP55 Kyle Wright 12.00 30.00
BTP58 Evan White 30.00 80.00
BTP59 Bobby Dalbec 15.00 40.00
BTP60 Jeter Downs 15.00 40.00
BTP61 Alek Thomas 15.00 40.00
BTP62 Brady Singer 15.00 40.00
BTP63 Kristian Robinson 20.00 50.00
BTP65 Keibert Ruiz 12.00 30.00
BTP66 Jonathan India 12.00 30.00
BTP67 Ronny Mauricio 20.00 50.00
BTP68 Kyle Muller 10.00 25.00
BTP70 Deivi Garcia 20.00 50.00
BTP71 Bryse Wilson 6.00 15.00
BTP72 Justus Sheffield 8.00 20.00
BTP75 Daulton Varsho 30.00 80.00
BTP76 Nick Lodolo 10.00 25.00
BTP78 Josiah Gray 10.00 25.00
BTP79 Sean Murphy
BTP80 Heliot Ramos 12.00 30.00
BTP81 Jackson Kowar 5.00 12.00
BTP88 Ryan Mountcastle 25.00 60.00
BTP89 Trevor Larnach 10.00 25.00
BTP90 Corbin Carroll 8.00 20.00
BTP91 Tylor Freeman 10.00 25.00
BTP93 Shane McClanahan 12.00 30.00
BTP95 Luis Garcia 15.00 40.00
BTP97 Brailyn Marquez 20.00 50.00
BTP99 Elehuris Montero 6.00 15.00
BTP100 Ronaldo Hernandez 5.00 12.00

2020 Bowman Chrome Spanning the Globe

STATED ODDS 1:6 HOBBY
*ATOMIC REF/150: 2.5X TO 6X BASE
*GREEN REF/99: 2.5X TO 6X BASE
*GOLD REF/50: 4X TO 10X BASIC
*ORANGE REF/25: 8X TO 20X BASE
STGAA Adbert Alzolay .30 .75
STGAM Andres Munoz .30 .75
STGCM Casey Mize .75 2.00
STGDB Dasan Brown .60 1.50
STGEP Eric Pardinho .25 .60
STGHR Heliot Ramos .40 1.00
STGIP Isaac Paredes .40 1.00
STGJA Jo Adell 1.00 2.50
STGJB Jordan Balazovic .50 1.25
STGJD Jasson Dominguez 6.00 15.00
STGJL Jesus Luzardo .50 1.25
STGLP Luis Patino .40 1.00
STGLR Luis Robert 2.50 6.00
STGMA Miguel Amaya .30 .75
STGML Matthew Lugo .40 1.00
STGRH Ronaldo Hernandez .25 .60
STGUB Ulrich Bojarski .25 .60
STGVVM Victor Victor Mesa .40 1.00
STGWF Wander Franco 2.50 6.00
STGYC Yu Chang .40 1.00

2020 Bowman Chrome Stat Track

STATED ODDS 1:XX HOBBY
*ATOMIC/150: 1.2X TO 3X BASE
*ORANGE/25: 2.5X TO 6X BASE
ST1 Jordan Balazovic .60 1.50
ST2 Sam Huff .60 1.50
ST3 Niko Hulsizer .75 2.00
ST4 Riley Greene 1.25 3.00
ST5 Max Lazar .40 1.00
ST6 Cristian Pache 1.00 2.50
ST7 Glenallen Hill Jr. .50 1.25
ST8 Bayron Lora 1.00 2.50
ST9 Jarren Duran 1.25 3.00
ST10 Alek Manoah .40 1.00
ST11 Bobby Witt Jr. 1.50 4.00
ST12 Ulrich Bojarski .30 .75
ST13 Antonio Cabello 1.00 2.50
ST14 Brenton Doyle 1.50 4.00
ST15 Daniel Espino .40 1.00
ST16 Anthony Volpe 1.25 3.00
ST17 Will Wilson .40 1.00
ST18 Adley Rutschman 2.00 5.00
ST19 Everson Pereira .75 2.00
ST20 Joe Ryan .30 .75
ST21 Isaac Paredes .50 1.25
ST22 Ethan Lindow .40 1.00
ST23 Alvaro Seijas .30 .75
ST24 Lewin Diaz .30 .75
ST25 Andrew Vaughn 1.25 3.00
ST26 Braden Shewmake .50 1.25
ST27 George Kirby .50 1.25
ST28 Ezequiel Duran .60 1.50
ST29 Xavier Edwards 1.25 3.00
ST30 Canaan Smith .50 1.25

2020 Bowman Chrome Stat Track Autographs

STATED ODDS 1:XXX HOBBY
STATED PRINT RUN 99 SER.#'d SETS
EXCHANGE DEADLINE 8/31/2022
*ORANGE/25: .5X TO 1.2X BASIC
STAAM Alek Manoah 4.00 10.00
STAAR Adley Rutschman 25.00 60.00
STAAS Alvaro Seijas 6.00 15.00
STAAV Andrew Vaughn 12.00 30.00
STAAVO Anthony Volpe 12.00 30.00
STABD Brenton Doyle 20.00 50.00
STABWJ Bobby Witt Jr. 50.00 120.00
STACS Canaan Smith 8.00 20.00
STAED Ezequiel Duran 10.00 25.00
STAEL Ethan Lindow 6.00 15.00
STAEP Everson Pereira 12.00 30.00
STAGHJ Glenallen Hill Jr. 5.00 12.00
STAJB Jordan Balazovic EXCH 10.00 25.00
STAJD Jarren Duran 15.00 40.00
STAJR Joe Ryan 6.00 15.00
STALD Lewin Diaz 6.00 15.00
STAML Max Lazar 4.00 10.00
STANH Niko Hulsizer 8.00 20.00
STARG Riley Greene 15.00 40.00
STASH Sam Huff 12.00 30.00
STAXE Xavier Edwards 8.00 20.00

2020 Bowman Chrome Talent Pipeline

STATED ODDS 1:12 HOBBY
*ATOMIC REF/150: 1.2X TO 3X BASE
*GREEN REF/99: 1.2X TO 3X BASE
*GOLD REF/50: 4X TO 10X BASIC
*ORANGE REF/25: 5X TO 12X BASE
TPARI Rbnsn/Wdnr/Beer .75 2.00
TPATL Andrsn/Shwmke/Lnglrs .60 1.50
TPBAL Mntcstle/Diaz/Rtschmn 1.50 4.00
TPBOS Dlbc/Css/Drn 1.00 2.50
TPCHI Clftn/Thmpsn/Rdrr .50 1.25
TPCIN Inda/Grne/Rdrgz .40 1.00
TPCLE Daniel Johnson .40 1.00
Nolan Jones
Bo Naylor
TPCOL Roberto Ramos .25 .60
Grant Lavigne
Colton Welker
TPCWS Adlfo/Rbrt/Vghn 2.00 5.00
TPDET Cmrn/Grne/Mize 1.00 2.50
TPHOU Forrest Whitley .30 .75
J.J. Matijevic
Freudis Nova
TPKCR Foster Griffin .40 1.00
Khalil Lee
Kris Bubic
TPLAA Adll/Jns/Adms 1.00 2.50
TPLAD Ptrs/Dwns/Hse .75 2.00
TPMIA Chshlm/Snchz/Bldy .75 2.00
TPMIL Corey Ray .25 .60
Jake Gatewood
Brice Turang
TPMIN Rkr/Lws/Blzvc .60 1.50
TPNYM Ali Sanchez .75 2.00
Andres Gimenez
Brett Baty
TPNYY Grca/Schmdt/Flrl 1.00 2.50
TPOAK Alfonso Rivas .30 .75
Greg Deichmann
Lazaro Armenteros
TPPHI Jns/Bohm/Grca 1.50 4.00
TPPIT Ke'Bryan Hayes .30 .75
Oneil Cruz
Cal Mitchell
TPSDP Gtlys/Abrms/Trmmll 1.00 2.50
TPSEA Klnic/RdrgzKnpp 1.50 4.00
TPSFG Bshp/Bart/Mllr .75 2.00
TPSTL Crlsn/Mntro/Grmn 1.00 2.50
TPTBR Brjn/Frnco/Pdlo 2.50 6.00
TPTEX Huff/Tvrs/Ibnz .50 1.25
TPTOR Smth/Prsn/Prdnho .50 1.25
TPWAS Wil Crowe .40 1.00
Luis Garcia
Jackson Rutledge

2020 Bowman Chrome Draft

STATED PLATE ODDS 1:XXX HOBBY
PLATE PRINT RUN 1 SET PER COLOR
BLACK-CYAN-MAGENTA-YELLOW ISSUED
NO PLATE PRICING DUE TO SCARCITY
BD1 Niko Hulsizer .60 1.50
BD2 Jackson Kowar .25 .60
BD3 Korey Lee .30 .75
BD4 Milan Tolentino .40 1.00
BD5 Jeter Downs .40 1.00
BD6 Hans Crouse .25 .60
BD7 Mike Siani .25 .60
BD8 Dane Acker .30 .75
BD9 Ryan Jensen .30 .75
BD10 Shane Baz .25 .60
BD11 Trei Cruz 1.00 2.50
BD12 Emerson Hancock 1.00 2.50
BD13 Joey Cantillo .25 .60
BD14 Nick Loftin .40 1.00
BD15 Rece Hinds .30 .75
BD16 Jared Shuster .50 1.25
BD17 Jesse Franklin V 1.00 2.50
BD18 Kaden Polcovich .40 1.00
BD19 Ben Hernandez .40 1.00
BD20 Spencer Strider .40 1.00
BD21 Tyler Brown .40 1.00
BD22 Keoni Cavaco .25 .60
BD23 Case Williams .30 .75
BD24 Cade Cavalli .50 1.25
BD25 Burl Carraway .60 1.50
BD26 Daniel Espino .30 .75
BD27 Oswald Peraza .60 1.50
BD28 Zach DeLoach 1.00 2.50
BD29 Nick Yorke 1.25 3.00
BD30 Clayton Beeter .60 1.50

BD31 Joe Ryan .25 .60
BD32 Jordan Groshans .50 1.25
BD33 Gage Workman 1.25 3.00
BD34 Austin Hendrick 2.50 6.00
BD35 Jimmy Glowenke .60 1.50
BD36 Ryan Rolison .25 .60
BD37 Logan Gilbert .30 .75
BD38 Bobby Miller 1.00 2.50
BD39 Robert Hassell 3.00 8.00
BD40 JJ Goss .25 .60
BD41 Reid Detmers .60 1.50
BD42 Michael Busch .60 1.50
BD43 Chris McMahon .30 .75
BD44 Xavier Edwards 1.00 2.50
BD45 Alec Burleson .40 1.00
BD46 Freddy Zamora .40 1.00
BD47 Travis Swaggerty .30 .75
BD48 Sammy Infante 1.00 2.50
BD49 Owen Caissie 1.00 2.50
BD50 Max Meyer 1.00 2.50
BD51 Logan Allen .25 .60
BD52 Landon Knack .75 2.00
BD53 Quinn Priester .40 1.00
BD54 Colt Keith 1.25 3.00
BD55 Jarren Duran 1.00 2.50
BD56 Austin Wells 2.50 6.00
BD57 Jordan Walker 3.00 8.00
BD58 Jordan Balazovic .50 1.25
BD59 Masyn Winn 2.00 5.00
BD60 Carson Tucker 2.00 5.00
BD61 Nick Bitsko .75 2.00
BD62 Daniel Cabrera 1.00 2.50
BD63 Marco Raya .50 1.25
BD64 Kyle Nicolas .30 .75
BD65 Oneil Cruz .30 .75
BD66 Hunter Barnhart .40 1.00
BD67 Cole Henry .30 .75
BD68 Tristen Lutz .30 .75
BD69 Petey Halpin .60 1.50
BD70 Jared Jones .40 1.00
BD71 Connor Phillips .40 1.00
BD72 Pete Crow-Armstrong 3.00 8.00
BD73 Casey Martin .75 2.00
BD74 Bryce Bonnin .40 1.00
BD75 Daniel Lynch .25 .60
BD76 Tekoah Roby .25 .60
BD77 Isaiah Greene 1.00 2.50
BD78 Tyler Freeman .30 .75
BD79 Heliot Ramos .40 1.00
BD80 Miguel Amaya .30 .75
BD81 Nick Gonzales 4.00 10.00
BD82 DL Hall .25 .60
BD83 Triston Casas .60 1.50
BD84 Christian Chamberlain .40 1.00
BD85 Slade Cecconi .30 .75
BD86 Tink Hence .40 1.00
BD87 Adisyn Coffey .30 .75
BD88 Asa Lacy 3.00 8.00
BD89 Geraldo Perdomo .25 .60
BD90 Nick Garcia .40 1.00
BD91 Nick Swiney .50 1.25
BD92 Matthew Dyer .40 1.00
BD93 CJ Van Eyk .40 1.00
BD94 Alerick Soularie .40 1.00
BD95 Garrett Crochet 4.00 10.00
BD96 Ian Seymour .25 .60
BD97 Zavier Warren .25 .60
BD98 Ed Howard 6.00 15.00
BD99 Justin Lange .25 .60
BD100 Ian Bedell .40 1.00
BD101 Aaron Shortridge .25 .60
BD102 Trevor Larnach .50 1.25
BD103 David Calabrese .60 1.50
BD104 Quin Cotton .25 .60
BD105 Luke Little .40 1.00
BD106 Drew Romo .60 1.50
BD107 Zac Veen 6.00 15.00
BD108 Brady McConnell .30 .75
BD109 Sam Weatherly .25 .60
BD110 Jordan Nwogu 1.00 2.50
BD111 Jordan Westburg .60 1.50
BD112 Zach McCambley .25 .60
BD113 Trevor Hauver .40 1.00
BD114 Corbin Carroll .40 1.00
BD115 Tanner Burns .40 1.00
BD116 Jackson Miller .60 1.50
BD117 Carter Baumler .40 1.00
BD118 Garrett Mitchell 4.00 10.00
BD119 Tyler Soderstrom 3.00 8.00
BD120 Holden Powell .25 .60
BD121 Spencer Torkelson 20.00 50.00
BD122 Heston Kjerstad 6.00 15.00
BD123 Alexander Canario .25 .60
BD124 Justin Foscue 1.00 2.50
BD125 Levi Prater .30 .75
BD126 Evan Carter 1.25 3.00
BD127 Bryce Jarvis .25 .60
BD128 Werner Blakely .30 .75
BD129 Casey Schmitt .75 2.00
BD130 Hudson Haskin 1.00 2.50
BD131 Daxton Fulton .50 1.25
BD132 Luis Gil .40 1.00
BD133 Zach Daniels .40 1.00
BD134 Jeff Criswell .40 1.00
BD135 Shane McClanahan .30 .75
BD136 Alika Williams .30 .75
BD137 Gilberto Jimenez 1.25 3.00
BD138 Trent Palmer .30 .75
BD139 Alex Santos .60 1.50
BD140 Bryson Stott .60 1.50
BD141 Ethan Hankins .30 .75
BD142 Kody Hoese .75 2.00
BD143 Francisco Alvarez .75 2.00
BD144 Dillon Dingler 1.25 3.00
BD145 Carson Ragsdale .40 1.00
BD146 Patrick Bailey 2.50 6.00
BD147 Liam Norris .25 .60
BD148 RJ Dabovich .25 .60
BD149 Carmen Mlodzinski .25 .60
BD150 AJ Vukovich 2.50 6.00
BD151 Jasson Dominguez 6.00 15.00
BD152 Bobby Witt Jr. 1.25 3.00
BD153 Andrew Vaughn 1.00 2.50
BD154 Adley Rutschman 1.50 4.00
BD155 Robert Puason .75 2.00
BD156 Jay Groome .25 .60
BD157 Will Klein .30 .75
BD158 Zach Britton .30 .75
BD159 Owen Miller .25 .60
BD160 Logan Hofmann .25 .60
BD161 Ronaldo Hernandez .25 .60
BD162 Jack Blomgren .40 1.00
BD163 Adam Seminaris .30 .75
BD164 Bailey Horn .30 .75
BD165 Joe Boyle .40 1.00
BD166 Ryan Murphy .25 .60
BD167 Thomas Saggese .25 .60
BD168 George Kirby .40 1.00
BD169 Jeremiah Jackson .25 .60
BD170 Shane Drohan .30 .75
BD171 Brandon Pfaadt .25 .60
BD172 Blake Rutherford .25 .60
BD173 Hayden Cantrelle .25 .60
BD174 Mark Vientos .25 .60
BD175 Michael Toglia .25 .60
BD176 Mitchell Parker .25 .60
BD177 Jackson Rutledge .40 1.00
BD178 Anthony Volpe 1.00 2.50
BD179 Nick Lodolo .40 1.00
BD180 Riley Greene 1.00 2.50
BD181 JJ Bleday .75 2.00
BD182 Kyle Isbel .25 .60
BD183 Shea Langeliers .50 1.25
BD184 Brett Baty .75 2.00
BD185 Jerar Encarnacion .75 2.00
BD186 Aaron Ashby .25 .60
BD187 Brennen Davis .50 1.25
BD188 Julio Rodriguez 1.50 4.00
BD189 CJ Abrams 1.00 2.50
BD190 Marco Luciano 1.00 2.50
BD191 Grayson Rodriguez .40 1.00
BD192 Kristian Robinson .75 2.00
BD193 Jordyn Adams .30 .75
BD194 Nolan Gorman .50 1.25
BD195 Alek Thomas .30 .75
BD196 Hunter Greene .40 1.00
BD197 Josh Jung .60 1.50
BD198 Matthew Liberatore .30 .75
BD199 Ronny Mauricio .60 1.50
BD200 Hunter Bishop .50 1.25

2020 Bowman Chrome Draft Blue Refractors

*BLUE REF: 2X TO 5X BASIC
STATED ODDS 1:XXX HOBBY
STATED PRINT RUN 150 SER.#'d SETS
BD34 Austin Hendrick 25.00 60.00
BD39 Robert Hassell 30.00 80.00
BD49 Owen Caissie 12.00 30.00
BD57 Jordan Walker 30.00 80.00
BD62 Daniel Cabrera 15.00 40.00
BD72 Pete Crow-Armstrong 25.00 60.00
BD77 Isaiah Greene 12.00 30.00
BD81 Nick Gonzales 30.00 80.00
BD88 Asa Lacy 15.00 40.00

2020 Bowman Chrome Draft Gold Refractors

*GOLD REF: 5X TO 12X BASIC
STATED ODDS 1:XXX HOBBY
STATED PRINT RUN 50 SER.#'d SETS
BD34 Austin Hendrick 60.00 150.00
BD39 Robert Hassell 75.00 200.00
BD49 Owen Caissie 30.00 80.00
BD57 Jordan Walker 75.00 200.00
BD62 Daniel Cabrera 40.00 100.00
BD72 Pete Crow-Armstrong 60.00 150.00
BD77 Isaiah Greene 30.00 80.00
BD81 Nick Gonzales 75.00 200.00
BD88 Asa Lacy 40.00 100.00

2020 Bowman Chrome Draft Green Refractors

*GREEN REF: 2.5X TO 6X BASIC
STATED ODDS 1:XXX HOBBY
STATED PRINT RUN 99 SER.#'d SETS
BD34 Austin Hendrick 30.00 80.00
BD39 Robert Hassell 40.00 100.00
BD49 Owen Caissie 15.00 40.00
BD57 Jordan Walker 40.00 100.00
BD62 Daniel Cabrera 20.00 50.00
BD72 Pete Crow-Armstrong 30.00 80.00
BD77 Isaiah Greene 15.00 40.00
BD81 Nick Gonzales 40.00 100.00
BD88 Asa Lacy 20.00 50.00

2020 Bowman Chrome Draft Orange Refractors

*ORANGE REF: 8X TO 20X BASIC
STATED ODDS 1:XXX HOBBY
STATED PRINT RUN 25 SER.#'d SETS
BD34 Austin Hendrick 100.00 250.00
BD39 Robert Hassell 125.00 300.00
BD49 Owen Caissie 50.00 120.00
BD57 Jordan Walker 125.00 300.00
BD62 Daniel Cabrera 60.00 150.00
BD72 Pete Crow-Armstrong 100.00 250.00
BD77 Isaiah Greene 50.00 120.00
BD81 Nick Gonzales 125.00 300.00
BD88 Asa Lacy 60.00 150.00

2020 Bowman Chrome Draft Purple Refractors

*PURPLE REF: 1.5X TO 4X BASIC
STATED ODDS 1:XXX HOBBY
STATED PRINT RUN 250 SER.#'d SETS
BD34 Austin Hendrick 20.00 50.00
BD39 Robert Hassell 25.00 60.00
BD49 Owen Caissie 10.00 25.00
BD57 Jordan Walker 25.00 60.00
BD62 Daniel Cabrera 12.00 30.00
BD72 Pete Crow-Armstrong 20.00 50.00
BD77 Isaiah Greene 10.00 25.00
BD81 Nick Gonzales 25.00 60.00
BD88 Asa Lacy 12.00 30.00

2020 Bowman Chrome Draft Refractors

*REF: .75X TO 2X BASIC
RANDOM INSERTS IN PACKS

2020 Bowman Chrome Draft Sky Blue Refractors

*SKY BLUE REF: 1X TO 2.5X BASIC
STATED ODDS 1:XXX HOBBY
BD72 Pete Crow-Armstrong 12.00 30.00
BD77 Isaiah Greene 6.00 15.00
BD81 Nick Gonzales 15.00 40.00
BD88 Asa Lacy 8.00 20.00

2020 Bowman Chrome Draft Sparkle Refractors

*SPARKLE REF: 1.5X TO 4X BASIC
STATED ODDS 1:XXX HOBBY
BD39 Robert Hassell 20.00 50.00
BD72 Pete Crow-Armstrong 15.00 40.00
BD77 Isaiah Greene 8.00 20.00
BD81 Nick Gonzales 20.00 50.00
BD88 Asa Lacy 10.00 25.00

2020 Bowman Chrome Draft Image Variations

STATED ODDS 1:XXX HOBBY
BD12 Emerson Hancock 8.00 20.00
BD34 Austin Hendrick 40.00 100.00
BD39 Robert Hassell 25.00 60.00
BD41 Reid Detmers 12.00 30.00
BD81 Nick Gonzales 50.00 120.00
BD88 Asa Lacy 20.00 50.00
BD107 Zac Veen 30.00 80.00
BD121 Spencer Torkelson 75.00 200.00
BD122 Heston Kjerstad 30.00 80.00
BD146 Patrick Bailey 20.00 50.00
BD151 Jasson Dominguez 50.00 120.00
BD152 Bobby Witt Jr. 25.00 60.00
BD153 Andrew Vaughn 8.00 20.00
BD154 Adley Rutschman 20.00 50.00
BD155 Robert Puason 12.00 30.00

2020 Bowman Chrome Draft Image Variation Autographs

STATED ODDS 1:XXX HOBBY BOXES
STATED PRINT RUN 99 SER.#'d SETS
EXCHANGE DEADLINE 11/30/2022
BD151 Jasson Dominguez 400.00 1000.00
BD154 Adley Rutschman 100.00 250.00
BD155 Robert Puason 75.00 200.00
BDC12 Emerson Hancock 75.00 200.00
BDC39 Robert Hassell 250.00 600.00
BDC50 Max Meyer 75.00 200.00
BDC81 Nick Gonzales 150.00 400.00
BDC88 Asa Lacy 100.00 250.00
BDC121 Spencer Torkelson 600.00 1500.00
BDC122 Heston Kjerstad 150.00 400.00

2020 Bowman Chrome Draft 1st Edition Autographs

STATED ODDS 1:XXX HOBBY
STATED PRINT RUN 30 SER.#'d SETS
EXCHANGE DEADLINE 11/30/2022
*BLUE/20: .4X TO 1X BASIC
CDAAL Asa Lacy 200.00 500.00
CDABJA Bryce Jarvis 60.00 150.00
CDACCA Cade Cavalli
CDACS Casey Schmitt 80.00 200.00
CDACT Carson Tucker
CDAJC Jeff Criswell 40.00 100.00
CDAJF Justin Foscue
CDAJS Jared Shuster 50.00 125.00
CDAMM Max Meyer 100.00 250.00
CDANB Nick Bitsko 125.00 300.00
CDAPB Patrick Bailey 250.00 600.00
CDARD Reid Detmers
CDARHA Robert Hassell 250.00 600.00
CDAST Spencer Torkelson 1250.00 3000.00
CDAZD Zach DeLoach
CDAZV Zac Veen 750.00 2000.00

2020 Bowman Chrome Draft 20 in '20

STATED ODDS 1:XXX HOBBY
*REF/250: .6X TO 1.5.X BASE
*GREEN REF/99: .75X TO 2X BASE
*GOLD REF/50: 1.5X TO 4X BASE
20IN20AH Austin Hendrick 2.50 6.00
20IN20AL Asa Lacy 1.50 4.00
20IN20BJ Bryce Jarvis .25 .60
20IN20CC Cade Cavalli .50 1.25
20IN20CT Carson Tucker .75 2.00
20IN20EH Ed Howard 2.00 5.00
20IN20EHA Emerson Hancock 1.00 2.50
20IN20GC Garrett Crochet .60 1.50
20IN20HK Heston Kjerstad 1.25 3.00
20IN20JF Justin Foscue 1.00 2.50
20IN20MM Max Meyer 1.00 2.50
20IN20NB Nick Bitsko .75 2.00
20IN20NG Nick Gonzales 1.25 3.00
20IN20NY Nick Yorke 1.25 3.00
20IN20PB Patrick Bailey .75 2.00
20IN20PC Pete Crow-Armstrong .75 2.00
20IN20RD Reid Detmers .60 1.50
20IN20RH Robert Hassell 2.00 5.00
20IN20ST Spencer Torkelson 2.50 6.00
20IN20ZV Zac Veen 1.25 3.00

2020 Bowman Chrome Draft 20 in '20 Autographs

STATED ODDS 1:XXX HOBBY
STATED PRINT RUN 99 SER.#'d SETS
EXCHANGE DEADLINE 11/30/2022
20IN20AAH Austin Hendrick EXCH 60.00 150.00
20IN20AAL Asa Lacy 40.00 100.00
20IN20ACT Carson Tucker 20.00 50.00
20IN20AEHA Emerson Hancock 25.00 60.00
20IN20ANG Nick Gonzales 50.00 120.00
20IN20ARD Reid Detmers 15.00 40.00
20IN20ARHA Robert Hassell 50.00 125.00
20IN20AST Spencer Torkelson 150.00 400.00
20IN20AZV Zac Veen 50.00 120.00

2020 Bowman Chrome Draft Applied Pressure

STATED ODDS 1:XXX HOBBY
*ATOMIC REF/150: 2.5X TO 6X BASIC
*ORANGE REF/25: 8X TO 20X BASIC
APAA Aaron Ashby .25 .60
APAS Aaron Shortridge .25 .60
APBC Burl Carraway .60 1.50
APBD Brennen Davis .50 1.25
APJB Jordan Balazovic .50 1.25
APJC Joey Cantillo .25 .60
APJD Jarren Duran 1.00 2.50
APJR Joe Ryan .25 .60
APKI Kyle Isbel .25 .60
APMS Mike Siani .25 .60

2020 Bowman Chrome Draft Applied Pressure Autographs

STATED ODDS 1:XXX HOBBY
STATED PRINT RUN 99 SER.#'d SETS
EXCHANGE DEADLINE 11/30/2022
*ORANGE/25: .6X TO 1.5X BASIC
APDCAAA Aaron Ashby 8.00 20.00
APDCAAS Aaron Shortridge 4.00 10.00
APDCABB Bryce Ball 40.00 100.00
APDCABC Burl Carraway 10.00 25.00
APDCABD Brennen Davis 30.00 80.00
APDCAJD Jarren Duran 25.00 60.00
APDCAJR Joe Ryan 10.00 25.00
APDCAMS Mike Siani 10.00 25.00
APDCANH Niko Hulsizer EXCH 10.00 25.00
APDCAQC Quin Cotton EXCH 8.00 20.00

2020 Bowman Chrome Draft Autographs

STATED ODDS 1:XXX HOBBY
PRINTING PLATE ODDS 1:XXX HOBBY
PLATE PRINT RUN 1 SET PER COLOR
BLACK-CYAN-MAGENTA-YELLOW ISSUED
NO PLATE PRICING DUE TO SCARCITY
EXCHANGE DEADLINE 11/30/2022
CDAAB Alec Burleson 8.00 20.00
CDAAC Adisyn Coffey 4.00 10.00
CDAAH Austin Hendrick EXCH 100.00 250.00
CDAAL Asa Lacy 50.00 120.00
CDAASAN Alex Santos 8.00 20.00
CDAASE Adam Seminaris 4.00 10.00
CDAASO Alerick Soularie 10.00 25.00
CDAAV AJ Vukovich 25.00 60.00
CDAAW Alika Williams 12.00 30.00
CDAAWE Austin Wells 30.00 80.00
CDABB Bryce Bonnin 5.00 12.00
CDABBE Bradlee Beesley 12.00 30.00
CDABC Burl Carraway 8.00 20.00
CDABE Bryce Elder 8.00 20.00
CDABHO Bailey Horn 4.00 10.00
CDABJA Bryce Jarvis 6.00 15.00
CDABM Bobby Miller 25.00 60.00
CDABP Brandon Pfaadt 3.00 8.00
CDACB Carter Baumler 6.00 15.00
CDACBE Clayton Beeter 10.00 25.00
CDACC Christian Chamberlain 5.00 12.00
CDACHE Cole Henry 4.00 10.00
CDACM Casey Martin 20.00 50.00
CDACML Carmen Mlodzinski 6.00 15.00
CDACMM Chris McMahon 4.00 10.00
CDACRA Carson Ragsdale 5.00 12.00
CDACS Casey Schmitt 10.00 25.00
CDACT Carson Tucker 30.00 80.00
CDACV CJ Van Eyk 6.00 15.00
CDACWI Case Williams 4.00 10.00
CDADA Dane Acker 4.00 10.00
CDADC David Calabrese 12.00 30.00
CDADCA Daniel Cabrera 20.00 50.00
CDADCR Trent Palmer 4.00 10.00
CDADD Dillon Dingler 15.00 40.00
CDADF Daxton Fulton 6.00 15.00
CDAEC Evan Carter 15.00 40.00
CDAEH Ed Howard 125.00 300.00
CDAEHA Emerson Hancock 25.00 60.00
CDAEO Eric Orze 6.00 15.00
CDAFZ Freddy Zamora 10.00 25.00
CDAGC Garrett Crochet 50.00 120.00
CDAGM Garrett Mitchell 60.00 150.00
CDAGW Gage Workman 15.00 40.00
CDAHB Hunter Barnhart 6.00 15.00
CDAHCA Hayden Cantrelle 8.00 20.00
CDAHK Heston Kjerstad 100.00 250.00
CDAHP Holden Powell 3.00 8.00
CDAIB Ian Bedell 5.00 12.00
CDAIG Isaiah Greene 25.00 60.00
CDAIS Ian Seymour 3.00 8.00
CDAJB Jack Blomgren 6.00 15.00
CDAJBO Joe Boyle 5.00 12.00
CDAJC Jeff Criswell 5.00 12.00
CDAJF Justin Foscue 30.00 80.00
CDAJFR Jesse Franklin V 15.00 40.00
CDAJGL Jimmy Glowenke 8.00 20.00
CDAJH Jeff Hakanson 3.00 8.00
CDAJL Justin Lange 6.00 15.00
CDAJM Jackson Miller 10.00 25.00
CDAJN Jordan Nwogu 25.00 60.00
CDAJW Jordan Walker EXCH 100.00 250.00
CDAKC Keith Colt 12.00 30.00
CDAKNI Kyle Nicolas 4.00 10.00
CDAKR Kala'i Rosario 15.00 40.00
CDALH Logan Hofmann 3.00 8.00
CDALK Landon Knack 10.00 25.00
CDALL Luke Little 8.00 20.00
CDALP Levi Prater 4.00 10.00
CDAMD Matthew Dyer 8.00 20.00
CDAMH Tink Hence 6.00 15.00
CDAMM Max Meyer 25.00 60.00
CDAMR Marco Raya 6.00 15.00
CDAMT Milan Tolentino 10.00 25.00
CDANB Nick Bitsko 10.00 25.00
CDANG Nick Garcia 5.00 12.00
CDANGO Nick Gonzales 75.00 200.00
CDANL Nick Loftin 10.00 25.00
CDANS Nick Swiney 6.00 15.00
CDANY Nick Yorke 40.00 100.00
CDAOC Owen Caissie 25.00 60.00
CDAPB Patrick Bailey 25.00 60.00
CDAPC Pete Crow-Armstrong 75.00 200.00
CDAPH Petey Halpin 10.00 25.00
CDARD Reid Detmers 20.00 50.00
CDARDA RJ Dabovich 3.00 8.00
CDARH Kaden Polcovich 6.00 15.00
CDARHA Robert Hassell 60.00 150.00
CDARM Ryan Murphy 3.00 8.00
CDASD Shane Drohan 4.00 10.00
CDASG Saul Garza 6.00 15.00
CDASI Sammy Infante 12.00 30.00
CDASS Spencer Strider 5.00 12.00
CDAST Spencer Torkelson 300.00 800.00
CDATB Tanner Burns 8.00 20.00
CDATBR Tyler Brown 5.00 12.00
CDATC Trei Cruz 12.00 30.00
CDATH Trevor Hauver 15.00 40.00
CDATR Tekoah Roby 5.00 12.00
CDATS Tyler Soderstrom 50.00 120.00
CDATSA Thomas Saggese 10.00 25.00
CDAWB Werner Blakely 10.00 25.00
CDAWK Will Klein 4.00 10.00
CDAZB Zach Britton 10.00 25.00
CDAZD Zach DeLoach 12.00 30.00
CDAZDA Zach Daniels 10.00 25.00
CDAZM Zach McCambley 3.00 8.00
CDAZV Zac Veen 100.00 250.00
CDAZW Zavier Warren 8.00 20.00

2020 Bowman Chrome Draft Autographs Black Refractors

*BLACK REF: 1.2X TO 3X BASIC
STATED ODDS 1:XXX HOBBY
STATED PRINT RUN 75 SER.#'D SETS
EXCHANGE DEADLINE 11/30/2022
CDABH Ben Hernandez 15.00 40.00
CDACCA Cade Cavalli 30.00 80.00
CDACP Connor Phillips 20.00 50.00
CDADR Drew Romo 50.00 120.00
CDAHH Hudson Haskin 40.00 100.00
CDAJJ Jared Jones 30.00 80.00
CDAJS Jared Shuster 40.00 100.00
CDAJW Jordan Walker EXCH 250.00 600.00
CDAJWE Jordan Westburg 60.00 150.00
CDASC Slade Cecconi EXCH 25.00 60.00

2020 Bowman Chrome Draft Autographs Blue Refractors

*BLUE REF: .75X TO 2X BASIC
STATED ODDS 1:XXX HOBBY
STATED PRINT RUN 150 SER.#'D SETS
EXCHANGE DEADLINE 11/30/2022
CDABH Ben Hernandez 10.00 25.00
CDACCA Cade Cavalli 20.00 50.00
CDACP Connor Phillips 12.00 30.00
CDADR Drew Romo 30.00 80.00
CDAHH Hudson Haskin 25.00 60.00
CDAJJ Jared Jones 20.00 50.00
CDAJS Jared Shuster 25.00 60.00
CDAJW Jordan Walker EXCH 150.00 400.00
CDAJWE Jordan Westburg 40.00 100.00
CDASC Slade Cecconi EXCH 15.00 40.00

2020 Bowman Chrome Draft Autographs Blue Wave Refractors

*BLUE WAVE REF: .75X TO 2X BASIC
STATED ODDS 1:XXX HOBBY
STATED PRINT RUN 150 SER.#'D SETS
EXCHANGE DEADLINE 11/30/2022
CDABH Ben Hernandez 10.00 25.00
CDACCA Cade Cavalli 20.00 50.00
CDACP Connor Phillips 12.00 30.00
CDADR Drew Romo 30.00 80.00
CDAHH Hudson Haskin 25.00 60.00
CDAJJ Jared Jones 20.00 50.00
CDAJS Jared Shuster 25.00 60.00
CDAJW Jordan Walker EXCH 150.00 400.00
CDAJWE Jordan Westburg 40.00 100.00
CDASC Slade Cecconi EXCH 15.00 40.00

2020 Bowman Chrome Draft Autographs Gold Refractors

*GOLD REF: 1.5X TO 4X BASIC
STATED ODDS 1:XXX HOBBY
STATED PRINT RUN 50 SER.#'D SETS
EXCHANGE DEADLINE 11/30/2022
CDAAB Alec Burleson 50.00 120.00
CDABH Ben Hernandez 20.00 50.00
CDACBE Clayton Beeter 75.00 200.00
CDACCA Cade Cavalli 40.00 100.00
CDACM Casey Martin 125.00 300.00
CDACP Connor Phillips 25.00 60.00
CDACT Carson Tucker 200.00 500.00
CDADR Drew Romo 60.00 150.00
CDAEHA Emerson Hancock 125.00 300.00
CDAHH Hudson Haskin 50.00 125.00
CDAHK Heston Kjerstad 600.00 1500.00
CDAJJ Jared Jones 40.00 100.00
CDAJS Jared Shuster 50.00 120.00
CDAJW Jordan Walker EXCH 300.00 800.00
CDAJWE Jordan Westburg 75.00 200.00
CDAPC Pete Crow-Armstrong 400.00 1000.00
CDAPH Petey Halpin 75.00 200.00
CDARHA Robert Hassell 400.00 1000.00
CDASC Slade Cecconi EXCH 30.00 80.00
CDASI Sammy Infante 75.00 200.00
CDAST Spencer Torkelson 2000.00 4000.00
CDAWB Werner Blakely 60.00 150.00

2020 Bowman Chrome Draft Autographs Gold Wave Refractors

*GRN WAVE REF: 1X TO 2.5X BASIC
STATED ODDS 1:XXX HOBBY
STATED PRINT RUN 99 SER.#'D SETS
EXCHANGE DEADLINE 11/30/2022
CDAAB Alec Burleson 50.00 120.00
CDABH Ben Hernandez 20.00 50.00
CDACBE Clayton Beeter 75.00 200.00
CDACCA Cade Cavalli 40.00 100.00
CDACM Casey Martin 125.00 300.00
CDACP Connor Phillips 25.00 60.00
CDACT Carson Tucker 200.00 500.00
CDADR Drew Romo 60.00 150.00
CDAEHA Emerson Hancock 125.00 300.00
CDAHH Hudson Haskin 50.00 125.00
CDAHK Heston Kjerstad 600.00 1500.00
CDAJJ Jared Jones 40.00 100.00
CDAJS Jared Shuster 50.00 120.00
CDAJW Jordan Walker EXCH 300.00 800.00
CDAJWE Jordan Westburg 75.00 200.00
CDAPC Pete Crow-Armstrong 400.00 1000.00
CDAPH Petey Halpin 75.00 200.00
CDARHA Robert Hassell 400.00 1000.00
CDASC Slade Cecconi EXCH 30.00 80.00
CDASI Sammy Infante 75.00 200.00
CDAST Spencer Torkelson 2000.00 4000.00
CDAWB Werner Blakely 60.00 150.00

2020 Bowman Chrome Draft Autographs Green Refractors

*GREEN REF: 1X TO 2.5X BASIC
STATED ODDS 1:XXX HOBBY
STATED PRINT RUN 99 SER.#'D SETS
EXCHANGE DEADLINE 11/30/2022
CDABH Ben Hernandez 12.00 30.00
CDACCA Cade Cavalli 25.00 60.00
CDACP Connor Phillips 15.00 40.00
CDADR Drew Romo 40.00 100.00
CDAHH Hudson Haskin 30.00 80.00
CDAJJ Jared Jones 25.00 60.00
CDAJS Jared Shuster 30.00 80.00
CDAJW Jordan Walker EXCH 200.00 500.00
CDAJWE Jordan Westburg 50.00 120.00
CDASC Slade Cecconi EXCH 20.00 50.00

2020 Bowman Chrome Draft Autographs Orange Refractors

*ORANGE REF: 3X TO 8X BASIC
STATED ODDS 1:XXX HOBBY
STATED PRINT RUN 25 SER.#'D SETS
EXCHANGE DEADLINE 11/30/2022
CDAAB Alec Burleson 100.00 250.00
CDABH Ben Hernandez 40.00 100.00
CDACBE Clayton Beeter 150.00 400.00
CDACCA Cade Cavalli 75.00 200.00
CDACM Casey Martin 250.00 600.00
CDACP Connor Phillips 50.00 120.00
CDACT Carson Tucker 400.00 1000.00
CDADR Drew Romo 125.00 300.00
CDAEHA Emerson Hancock 250.00 600.00
CDAHH Hudson Haskin 100.00 250.00
CDAHK Heston Kjerstad 1250.00 3000.00
CDAJJ Jared Jones 75.00 200.00
CDAJS Jared Shuster 100.00 250.00
CDAJW Jordan Walker EXCH 600.00 1500.00
CDAJWE Jordan Westburg 150.00 400.00
CDAPC Pete Crow-Armstrong 750.00 2000.00
CDAPH Petey Halpin 150.00 400.00
CDARHA Robert Hassell 750.00 2000.00
CDASC Slade Cecconi EXCH 60.00 150.00
CDASI Sammy Infante 150.00 400.00
CDAST Spencer Torkelson 4000.00 8000.00
CDAWB Werner Blakely 125.00 300.00

2020 Bowman Chrome Draft Autographs Purple Refractors

*PURPLE REF: .6X TO 1.5X BASIC
STATED ODDS 1:XXX HOBBY
STATED PRINT RUN 250 SER.#'D SETS
EXCHANGE DEADLINE 11/30/2022
CDABH Ben Hernandez 8.00 20.00
CDACCA Cade Cavalli 15.00 40.00
CDACP Connor Phillips 10.00 25.00
CDADR Drew Romo 25.00 60.00
CDAHH Hudson Haskin 20.00 50.00
CDAJJ Jared Jones 15.00 40.00
CDAJS Jared Shuster 20.00 50.00
CDAJW Jordan Walker EXCH 125.00 300.00
CDAJWE Jordan Westburg 30.00 80.00
CDASC Slade Cecconi EXCH 12.00 30.00

2020 Bowman Chrome Draft Autographs Refractors

*REF: .5X TO 1.2X BASIC
STATED ODDS 1:XXX HOBBY
STATED PRINT RUN 499 SER.#'D SETS
EXCHANGE DEADLINE 11/30/2022
CDABH Ben Hernandez 6.00 15.00
CDACCA Cade Cavalli 12.00 30.00
CDACP Connor Phillips 8.00 20.00
CDADR Drew Romo 20.00 50.00
CDAHH Hudson Haskin 15.00 40.00
CDAJJ Jared Jones 12.00 30.00
CDAJS Jared Shuster 15.00 40.00
CDAJWE Jordan Westburg 25.00 60.00
CDASC Slade Cecconi EXCH 10.00 25.00

2020 Bowman Chrome Draft Autographs Sparkle Refractors

*SPARKLE REF: 1.2X TO 3X BASIC
STATED ODDS 1:XXX HOBBY
STATED PRINT RUN 71 SER.#'D SETS
EXCHANGE DEADLINE 11/30/2022
CDABH Ben Hernandez 12.00 30.00
CDACCA Cade Cavalli 225.00 60.00
CDACP Connor Phillips 15.00 40.00
CDADR Drew Romo 40.00 100.00
CDAHH Hudson Haskin 30.00 80.00
CDAJJ Jared Jones 25.00 60.00
CDAJS Jared Shuster 30.00 80.00
CDAJW Jordan Walker EXCH 200.00 500.00
CDAJWE Jordan Westburg 50.00 120.00
CDASC Slade Cecconi EXCH 20.00 50.00

2020 Bowman Chrome Draft Franchise Futures

STATED ODDS 1:XXX HOBBY
*REF/250: 1.2X TO 3X BASE
*GREEN REF/99: 1.5X TO 4X BASE
*GOLD REF/50: 3X TO 8X BASE
FFAN Lacy/Loftin 1.50 4.00
FFCE DeLoach/Hancock 1.00 2.50
FFDR Detmers/Calabrese .60 1.50
FFEB Howard/Carraway 2.00 5.00
FFHJ Kjerstad/Westburg 1.25 3.00
FFJZ Romo/Veen 1.25 3.00
FFMD Meyer/Fulton 1.00 2.50
FFNC Mlodzinski/Gonzales 1.25 3.00
FFRJ Lange/Hassel 2.00 5.00
FFSD Dingler/Torkelson 2.50 6.00

2020 Bowman Chrome Draft Glimpses of Greatness

STATED ODDS 1:XXX HOBBY
*REF/250: .6X TO 1.5X BASE
*GREEN REF/99: .75X TO 2X BASE
*GOLD REF/50: 1.5X TO 4X BASE
GOGAL Asa Lacy 1.50 4.00
GOGAR Adley Rutschman 1.50 4.00
GOGAV Andrew Vaughn 1.00 2.50
GOGBW Bobby Witt Jr. 1.25 3.00
GOGCA CJ Abrams 1.00 2.50
GOGEH Emerson Hancock 1.00 2.50
GOGHK Heston Kjerstad 1.25 3.00
GOGJB JJ Bleday .75 2.00
GOGJD Jasson Dominguez 2.50 6.00
GOGML Marco Luciano 1.00 2.50
GOGMM Max Meyer 1.00 2.50
GOGNG Nick Gonzales 1.25 3.00
GOGRG Riley Greene 1.00 2.50
GOGST Spencer Torkelson 2.50 6.00
GOGZV Zac Veen 1.25 3.00

2020 Bowman Chrome Draft Top of the Class Box Topper

RANDOM INSERTS IN HOBBY BOXES
STATED PRINT RUN 99 SER.#'d SETS
*GOLD/50: .5X TO 1.2X BASIC
TOCAL Asa Lacy 12.00 30.00
TOCEHA Emerson Hancock 10.00 25.00
TOCGM Reid Detmers 12.00 30.00
TOCHK Heston Kjerstad
TOCJK Robert Hassell 12.00 30.00
TOCMA Austin Hendrick 12.00 30.00
TOCMM Max Meyer 8.00 20.00
TOCNG Nick Gonzales 12.00 30.00
TOCPB Patrick Bailey
TOCRD Garrett Crochet 12.00 30.00
TOCST Spencer Torkelson 25.00 60.00
TOCZV Zac Veen 12.00 30.00

2020 Bowman Chrome Draft Top of the Class Box Topper Autographs

STATED ODDS 1:XXX HOBBY BOXES
STATED PRINT RUN 35 SER.#'d SETS
EXCHANGE DEADLINE 11/30/2022
TOCAL Asa Lacy 30.00 80.00
TOCEHA Emerson Hancock 30.00 80.00
TOCHK Heston Kjerstad
TOCMM Max Meyer 30.00 80.00
TOCNG Nick Gonzales
TOCRD Reid Detmers 40.00 100.00
TOCRH Robert Hassell 50.00 120.00
TOCST Spencer Torkelson 125.00 300.00
TOCZV Zac Veen 100.00 250.00

2018 Bowman Chrome Mega Box Prospects Refractors

BCP1 Ronald Acuna 6.00 15.00
BCP2 Bryan Mata .40 1.00
BCP3 Daniel Johnson .30 .75
BCP5 Aaron Knapp .30 .75
BCP6 Austin Beck .40 1.00
BCP7 Carter Kieboom .50 1.25
BCP8 Cole Ragans .30 .75
BCP10 Justin Williams .30 .75
BCP12 Thomas Hatch .40 1.00

BCP13 Sam Hilliard .75 2.00
BCP14 Kyle Wright .75 2.00
BCP16 Michael Mercado .40 1.00
BCP17 Kevin Newman .50 1.25
BCP19 Johan Mieses .50 1.25
BCP21 Luis Robert 30.00 80.00
BCP22 Yadier Alvarez .40 1.00
BCP23 Jeren Kendall .40 1.00
BCP24 Bobby Bradley .40 1.00
BCP25 Drew Ellis .40 1.00
BCP28 Kolby Allard .30 .75
BCP31 DJ Peters .75 2.00
BCP32 Domingo Acevedo .30 .75
BCP36 Dennis Santana .30 .75
BCP37 Jake Burger .30 .75
BCP38 Mitch Keller .40 1.00
BCP39 Colton Welker .30 .75
BCP40 Pedro Avila .30 .75
BCP43 Brendan Rodgers .40 1.00
BCP44 James Kaprielian .30 .75
BCP45 Greg Deichmann .40 1.00
BCP46 Cristian Pache 1.50 4.00
BCP47 Ibandel Isabel .50 1.25
BCP48 Hunter Greene 2.50 6.00
BCP49 Nick Gordon .30 .75
BCP50 Eloy Jimenez 1.25 3.00
BCP52 Juan Soto 6.00 15.00
BCP55 Kyle Tucker .60 1.50
BCP57 Luis Urias .60 1.50
BCP58 Sean Murphy .50 1.25
BCP62 Kyle Cody .30 .75
BCP63 Dylan Cozens .30 .75
BCP65 Scott Kingery .50 1.25
BCP66 Jordan Humphreys .30 .75
BCP67 Michel Baez .30 .75
BCP68 Brendan McKay
BCP69 Justus Sheffield .40 1.00
BCP70 Merandy Gonzalez .30 .75
BCP71 Touki Toussaint .40 1.00
BCP72 Andres Gimenez .40 1.00
BCP77 Jake Kalish .30 .75
BCP78 Shed Long .30 .75
BCP79 Keibert Ruiz 1.00 2.50
BCP80 Matt Hall .30 .75
BCP83 Ian Anderson .75 2.00
BCP85 Dane Dunning .30 .75
BCP86 Michael Kopech .60 1.50
BCP87 McKenzie Mills .30 .75
BCP88 Quentin Holmes .30 .75
BCP89 Mike Soroka 1.00 2.50
BCP90 Stephen Gonsalves .30 .75
BCP91 Spencer Howard .30 .75
BCP92 Ryan Vilade .30 .75
BCP93 Royce Lewis 1.25 3.00
BCP94 Adam Haseley .50 1.25
BCP95 Jorge Mateo .30 .75
BCP97 Corey Ray .40 1.00
BCP99 Logan Allen .30 .75
BCP100 Gleyber Torres 3.00 8.00
BCP101 Zack Littell .30 .75
BCP102 Matt Sauer .30 .75
BCP103 Mitchell White .30 .75
BCP104 Nick Solak .75 2.00
BCP107 D.L. Hall .30 .75
BCP108 Chris Rodriguez .30 .75
BCP110 Eric Pardinho .60 1.50
BCP111 JoJo Romero .40 1.00
BCP113 Taylor Clarke .30 .75
BCP114 Fernando Tatis Jr. 2.50 6.00
BCP115 Cal Quantrill .30 .75
BCP116 Khalil Lee .30 .75
BCP118 Lazaro Armenteros .60 1.50
BCP120 Nick Senzel 1.00 2.50
BCP121 Jose Adolis Garcia .40 1.00
BCP123 Jordan Hicks .60 1.50
BCP125 J.B. Bukauskas .30 .75
BCP126 Jesus Luzardo .50 1.25
BCP131 MacKenzie Gore .60 1.50
BCP132 Corbin Burnes .50 1.25
BCP135 Bryse Wilson .50 1.25
BCP136 Jo Adell 1.00 2.50
BCP137 Pete Alonso 3.00 8.00
BCP139 Travis Lakins .30 .75
BCP141 Blayne Enlow .30 .75
BCP142 A.J. Puk .40 1.00
BCP143 Heliot Ramos .50 1.25
BCP144 Jahmai Jones .30 .75
BCP145 Adbert Alzolay .40 1.00
BCP147 Forrest Whitley .50 1.25
BCP148 Trevor Rogers .30 .75
BCP150 Vladimir Guerrero Jr. 3.00 8.00

2018 Bowman Chrome Mega Box Prospects Gold Refractors

*GOLD REF: 4X TO 10X BASIC
STATED ODDS 1:31 PACKS
STATED PRINT RUN 50 SER.#'d SETS
BCP1 Ronald Acuna 60.00 150.00
BCP100 Gleyber Torres 40.00 100.00

2018 Bowman Chrome Mega Box Prospects Green Refractors

*GREEN REF: 2X TO 5X BASIC
STATED ODDS 1:16 PACKS
STATED PRINT RUN 99 SER.#'d SETS
BCP1 Ronald Acuna 30.00 80.00
BCP100 Gleyber Torres 20.00 50.00

2018 Bowman Chrome Mega Box Prospects Orange Refractors

*ORANGE REF: 6X TO 15X BASIC
STATED ODDS 1:62 PACKS
STATED PRINT RUN 25 SER.#'d SETS
BCP1 Ronald Acuna 100.00 250.00
BCP100 Gleyber Torres 60.00 150.00

2018 Bowman Chrome Mega Box Prospects Purple Refractors

*PURPLE REF: 1X TO 2.5X BASIC
STATED ODDS 1:7 PACKS
STATED PRINT RUN 250 SER.#'d SETS
BCP1 Ronald Acuna 15.00 40.00
BCP100 Gleyber Torres 10.00 25.00

2018 Bowman Chrome Mega Box Prospects Image Variaton Refractors

STATED ODDS 1:69 PACKS
BCP1 Ronald Acuna 60.00 150.00
BCP7 Carter Kieboom 20.00 50.00
BCP14 Kyle Wright 12.00 30.00
BCP38 Mitch Keller 10.00 25.00
BCP50 Eloy Jimenez 30.00 80.00
BCP61 Brendan McKay 20.00 50.00
BCP68 Brendan McKay 20.00 50.00
BCP93 Royce Lewis 20.00 50.00
BCP100 Gleyber Torres 50.00 125.00

2018 Bowman Chrome Mega Box Prospects Image Variaton Autograph Refractors

STATED ODDS 1:853 PACKS
STATED PRINT RUN 25 SER.#'d SETS
EXCHANGE DEADLINE 4/30/2020
BCP1 Ronald Acuna 600.00 1200.00
BCP7 Carter Kieboom 100.00 250.00
BCP14 Kyle Wright 60.00 150.00
BCP38 Mitch Keller 30.00 80.00
BCP61 Brendan McKay 75.00 200.00
BCP68 Brendan McKay 75.00 200.00
BCP93 Royce Lewis 100.00 250.00
BCP100 Gleyber Torres 300.00 600.00

2018 Bowman Chrome Mega Box Autograph Refractors

STATED ODDS 1:19 PACKS
EXCHANGE DEADLINE 4/30/2020
*GREEN/99: .75X TO 2X BASIC
BMAAA Adbert Alzolay 8.00 20.00
BMABE Blayne Enlow 4.00 10.00
BMABM Brendan McKay 30.00 80.00
BMAEF Estevan Florial 60.00 150.00
BMAHC Hans Crouse 10.00 25.00
BMAHG Hunter Greene 75.00 200.00
BMAII Ibandel Isabel 12.00 30.00
BMAJH Jordan Hicks 12.00 30.00
BMAJHU Jordan Humphreys 4.00 10.00
BMAJMI Johan Mieses 10.00 25.00
BMAJS Jose Siri 8.00 20.00
BMAKR Keibert Ruiz 40.00 100.00
BMAMB Michel Baez 12.00 30.00
BMAMG Merandy Gonzalez 4.00 10.00
BMAMS Mike Shawaryn 4.00 10.00
BMAQH Quentin Holmes 4.00 10.00
BMARV Ryan Vilade 5.00 12.00
BMASH Spencer Howard 4.00 10.00
BMASL Shed Long 4.00 10.00
BMATH Thomas Hatch 5.00 12.00
BMAWA Willie Abreu 4.00 10.00
BMAZL Zack Littell 4.00 10.00

2018 Bowman Chrome Mega Box Autograph Orange Refractors

*ORANGE REF: 2X TO 5X BASIC
STATED ODDS 1:300 PACKS
STATED PRINT RUN 25 SER.#'d SETS
EXCHANGE DEADLINE 4/30/2020
BMAHG Hunter Greene 300.00 600.00
BMAII Ibandel Isabel 40.00 100.00
BMAJH Jordan Hicks 100.00 250.00

2018 Bowman Chrome Mega Box Hashtag Trending Refractors

STATED ODDS 1:4 PACKS
*PURPLE/250: .6X TO 1.5X BASIC
*GREEN/99: 1X TO 2.5X BASIC
*ORANGE/25: 4X TO 10X BASIC
AP A.J. Puk .40 1.00
BB Bo Bichette 1.25 3.00
CA Chance Adams .50 1.25
CQ Cal Quantrill .30 .75
FP Franklin Perez .30 .75
FR Fernando Romero .30 .75
FT Fernando Tatis Jr. 2.50 6.00
JS Jesus Sanchez .30 .75
LT Leody Taveras .40 1.00
LU Luis Urias .60 1.50
MC Michael Chavis .50 1.25
NG Nick Gordon .30 .75
RA Ronald Acuna 6.00 15.00
SG Stephen Gonsalves .30 .75
SK Scott Kingery .50 1.25
SS Sixto Sanchez .75 2.00
TM Triston McKenzie .30 .75
TT Taylor Trammell .50 1.25
VG Vladimir Guerrero Jr. 3.00 8.00
YD Yusniel Diaz 1.00 2.50

2018 Bowman Chrome Mega Box Ohtani Bowman Chrome Rookie Autograph Redemption

RANDOM INSERTS IN PACKS
EXCHANGE DEADLINE 4/30/2020
CRASO Shohei Ohtani 1000.00 1500.00

2018 Bowman Chrome Mega Box Rookie of the Year Favorites Refractors

STATED ODDS 1:2 PACKS
ROYFAB Anthony Banda .30 .75
ROYFAH Austin Hays .50 1.25
ROYFAR Amed Rosario .40 1.00
ROYFAV Alex Verdugo .50 1.25
ROYFCF Clint Frazier .60 1.50
ROYFDF Dustin Fowler .30 .75
ROYFDS Dominic Smith .30 .75
ROYFFM Francisco Mejia .40 1.00
ROYFHB Harrison Bader .50 1.25
ROYFJC J.P. Crawford .30 .75
ROYFJF Jack Flaherty .50 1.25
ROYFND Nicky Delmonico .30 .75
ROYFNW Nick Williams .40 1.00
ROYFOA Ozzie Albies 1.00 2.50
ROYFRD Rafael Devers 1.00 2.50
ROYFRH Rhys Hoskins 1.25 3.00
ROYFSO Shohei Ohtani 20.00 50.00
ROYFVR Victor Robles .75 2.00
ROYFWB Walker Buehler 1.50 4.00
ROYFWC Willie Calhoun .40 1.00

2018 Bowman Chrome Mega Box Rookie of the Year Favorites Green Refractors

*GREEN REF: 1X TO 2.5X BASIC
STATED ODDS 1:78 PACKS
STATED PRINT RUN 99 SER.#'d SETS
ROYFOA Ozzie Albies 15.00 40.00
ROYFSO Shohei Ohtani 150.00 400.00

2018 Bowman Chrome Mega Box Rookie of the Year Favorites Orange Refractors

*ORANGE REF: 5X TO 12X BASIC
STATED ODDS 1:307 PACKS
STATED PRINT RUN 25 SER.#'d SETS
ROYFOA Ozzie Albies 30.00 80.00
ROYFSO Shohei Ohtani 300.00 600.00

2018 Bowman Chrome Mega Box Rookie of the Year Favorites Purple Refractors

*PURPLE REF: .6X TO 1.5X BASIC
STATED ODDS 1:31 PACKS
STATED PRINT RUN 250 SER.#'d SETS
ROYFOA Ozzie Albies 10.00 25.00
ROYFSO Shohei Ohtani 75.00 200.00

2018 Bowman Chrome Mega Box Rookie of the Year Favorites Autographs Refractors

STATED ODDS 1:102 PACKS
STATED PRINT RUN 99 SER.#'d SETS
EXCHANGE DEADLINE 4/30/2020
*ORANGE/25: 1.2X TO 3X BASIC
ROYFAAB Anthony Banda 8.00 20.00
ROYFAAR Amed Rosario 10.00 25.00
ROYFAAV Alex Verdugo 12.00 30.00
ROYFACF Clint Frazier 25.00 60.00
ROYFACS Chance Sisco 15.00 40.00
ROYFADS Dominic Smith 8.00 20.00
ROYFAFM Francisco Mejia 20.00 50.00
ROYFAHB Harrison Bader 12.00 30.00
ROYFAJC J.P. Crawford 8.00 20.00
ROYFAJF Jack Flaherty 12.00 30.00
ROYFAMA Miguel Andujar 75.00 200.00
ROYFAOA Ozzie Albies 100.00 250.00
ROYFARD Rafael Devers 25.00 60.00
ROYFATM Tyler Mahle 10.00 25.00
ROYFAVR Victor Robles 25.00 60.00

2019 Bowman Chrome Mega Box Prospects Refractors

BCP1 Vladimir Guerrero Jr. 2.00 5.00
BCP2 Alec Bohm 1.25 3.00
BCP4 Jo Adell 1.00 2.50
BCP5 Victor Victor Mesa .60 1.50
BCP7 Tirso Ornelas .30 .75
BCP10 Adrian Morejon .30 .75
BCP11 Derian Cruz .30 .75
BCP13 Jarred Kelenic 1.25 3.00
BCP14 Seth Beer .75 2.00
BCP17 A.J. Puk .40 1.00
BCP18 Leody Taveras .30 .75
BCP19 Logan Allen .30 .75
BCP20 Blake Rutherford .30 .75
BCP21 Freudis Nova 1.00 2.50
BCP23 Rylan Bannon .40 1.00
BCP24 Taylor Trammell .40 1.00
BCP25 Fernando Tatis Jr. 3.00 8.00
BCP30 Julio Pablo Martinez .30 .75
BCP32 Cristian Javier .40 1.00
BCP33 Julio Rodriguez 6.00 15.00
BCP35 Miguel Amaya .50 1.25
BCP40 Triston McKenzie .30 .75
BCP41 Ryan Mountcastle .40 1.00
BCP43 Nick Senzel 1.00 2.50
BCP44 Luis Robert 15.00 40.00
BCP47 Ian Anderson .75 2.00
BCP48 Griffin Canning .50 1.25
BCP49 Casey Mize .75 2.00
BCP50 Joey Bart 4.00 10.00
BCP51 Hunter Greene .50 1.25
BCP52 Forrest Whitley .50 1.25
BCP53 Blaze Alexander .30 .75
BCP54 Keston Hiura 1.00 2.50
BCP55 Chris Paddack .60 1.50
BCP56 Franklin Perez .30 .75
BCP60 Nolan Gorman 1.00 2.50
BCP62 Cristian Pache .75 2.00
BCP63 Nick Madrigal 1.00 2.50
BCP64 Luis Garcia .40 1.00
BCP66 Ryan Weathers .30 .75
BCP67 Jon Duplantier .30 .75
BCP68 Reggie Lawson .30 .75
BCP69 Orelvis Martinez 2.50 6.00
BCP70 Sixto Sanchez .40 1.00
BCP71 Ke'Bryan Hayes .30 .75
BCP72 Brewer Hicklen .50 1.25
BCP73 MacKenzie Gore .60 1.50
BCP74 Estevan Florial .50 1.25
BCP77 Andres Gimenez .40 1.00
BCP78 Alex Faedo .40 1.00
BCP79 Logan Webb .50 1.25
BCP80 Dustin May 1.00 2.50
BCP81 Ryan McKenna .30 .75
BCP82 Marco Luciano 6.00 15.00
BCP83 Heliot Ramos .50 1.25
BCP85 Matt Manning .50 1.25
BCP87 Chad Spanberger .30 .75
BCP88 Brent Honeywell .40 1.00
BCP89 Esteury Ruiz .40 1.00
BCP90 Keegan Thompson .30 .75
BCP92 Michael Chavis .50 1.25
BCP93 Travis Swaggerty .50 1.25
BCP94 Dane Dunning .30 .75
BCP95 Lyon Richardson .40 1.00
BCP96 Jesus Luzardo .50 1.25
BCP97 Noelvi Marte 3.00 8.00
BCP98 Carter Kieboom .50 1.25
BCP100 Wander Franco 25.00 60.00
BCP101 Ryan Costello .40 1.00
BCP102 Jonathan India .40 1.00
BCP103 Royce Lewis .60 1.50
BCP104 Victor Mesa Jr. 2.00 5.00
BCP105 Brendan McKay .50 1.25
BCP107 Ronny Mauricio .75 2.00
BCP109 Yusniel Diaz .40 1.00
BCP110 Brady Singer .60 1.50
BCP111 Bo Bichette 1.00 2.50
BCP112 Matthew Liberatore .30 .75
BCP113 Dylan Cease .75 2.00
BCP114 Edward Cabrera .50 1.25
BCP118 Keibert Ruiz .75 2.00
BCP119 Jonathan Hernandez .30 .75
BCP120 Matt Mercer .30 .75
BCP123 Yordan Alvarez 5.00 12.00
BCP127 Peter Alonso 4.00 10.00
BCP129 Austin Riley 1.50 4.00
BCP130 Gavin Lux 1.00 2.50
BCP132 Andrew Knizner .50 1.25
BCP133 Mitch Keller .40 1.00
BCP134 Cristian Santana .50 1.25
BCP135 Jesus Sanchez .30 .75
BCP137 Brock Burke .30 .75
BCP138 Alex Kirilloff .50 1.25
BCP142 Genesis Cabrera .50 1.25
BCP143 Brendan Rodgers .50 1.25
BCP144 Sean Murphy .40 1.00
BCP145 Roberto Ramos .40 1.00
BCP146 Ronaldo Hernandez .30 .75
BCP149 Jose de la Cruz 1.00 2.50
BCP150 Eloy Jimenez 1.25 3.00

2019 Bowman Chrome Mega Box Prospects Gold Refractors

*GOLD REF: 4X TO 10X BASIC
STATED ODDS 1:62 PACKS
STATED PRINT RUN 50 SER.#'d SETS

2019 Bowman Chrome Mega Box Prospects Green Refractors

*GREEN REF: 2X TO 5X BASIC
STATED ODDS 1:32 PACKS
STATED PRINT RUN 99 SER.#'d SETS

2019 Bowman Chrome Mega Box Prospects Orange Refractors

*ORANGE REF: 6X TO 15X BASIC
STATED ODDS 1:126 PACKS
STATED PRINT RUN 25 SER.#'d SETS

2019 Bowman Chrome Mega Box Prospects Purple Refractors

*PURPLE REF: 1X TO 2.5X BASIC
STATED ODDS 1:13 PACKS
STATED PRINT RUN 250 SER.#'d SETS

2019 Bowman Chrome Mega Box Prospects Image Variation Refractors

STATED ODDS 1:140 PACKS
BCP1 Vladimir Guerrero Jr. 50.00 120.00
BCP4 Jo Adell 30.00 80.00
BCP25 Fernando Tatis Jr. 30.00 80.00
BCP43 Nick Senzel 20.00 50.00
BCP49 Casey Mize 40.00 100.00
BCP50 Joey Bart 75.00 200.00
BCP60 Nolan Gorman 30.00 80.00
BCP100 Wander Franco 150.00 400.00
BCP107 Ronny Mauricio 40.00 100.00
BCP150 Eloy Jimenez 20.00 50.00

2019 Bowman Chrome Mega Box Prospects Image Variation Autograph Refractors

STATED ODDS 1:1531 PACKS
STATED PRINT RUN 25 SER.#'d SETS
BCP1 Vladimir Guerrero Jr. 800.00 1200.00
BCP25 Fernando Tatis Jr. 150.00 400.00
BCP49 Casey Mize 200.00 500.00
BCP50 Joey Bart 400.00 800.00
BCP60 Nolan Gorman 200.00 500.00
BCP100 Wander Franco 1500.00 2000.00
BCP107 Ronny Mauricio 200.00 500.00
BCP150 Eloy Jimenez 150.00 400.00

2019 Bowman Chrome Mega Box Autographs Refractors

STATED ODDS 1:16 PACKS
*GREEN REF/99: .75X TO 2X
BMAAB Alec Bohm 15.00 40.00
BMAAK Andrew Knizner 10.00 25.00
BMAAT Alek Thomas 8.00 20.00
BMABA Blaze Alexander 4.00 10.00
BMABB Brock Burke 4.00 10.00
BMABD Bobby Dalbec 8.00 20.00
BMACM Casey Mize 40.00 100.00
BMACS Cristian Santana 6.00 15.00
BMACSP Chad Spanberger 4.00 10.00
BMAEJ Eloy Jimenez 40.00 100.00
BMAFN Freudis Nova 20.00 50.00
BMAGJ Greyson Jenista 5.00 12.00
BMAJA Jordyn Adams 5.00 12.00
BMAJB Joey Bart 60.00 150.00
BMAJG Joe Gray 5.00 12.00
BMAJJ Jeremiah Jackson 6.00 15.00
BMAJPM Julio Pablo Martinez 4.00 10.00
BMAKC Kody Clemens 5.00 12.00
BMAKT Keegan Thompson 4.00 10.00
BMALB Luken Baker 5.00 12.00
BMANH Nico Hoerner 12.00 30.00
BMARB Rylan Bannon 5.00 12.00
BMASB Seth Beer 15.00 40.00
BMAVGJ Vladimir Guerrero Jr. 100.00 250.00
BMAWB Will Banfield 4.00 10.00
BMAWF Wander Franco 250.00 500.00

2019 Bowman Chrome Mega Box Autographs Orange Refractors

*ORANGE REF: 1.5X TO 4X BASIC
STATED ODDS 1:300 PACKS
STATED PRINT RUN 25 SER.#'d SETS
BMAAK Andrew Knizner 75.00 200.00
BMAJA Jordyn Adams 75.00 200.00
BMAJPM Julio Pablo Martinez 15.00 40.00
BMARB Rylan Bannon 60.00 150.00

2019 Bowman Chrome Mega Box Ready for the Show Refractors

STATED ODDS 1:4 PACKS
*PURPLE/250: .6X TO 1.5X BASIC
*GREEN/99: 1X TO 2.5X BASIC
*GOLD/50: 2X TO 5X BASIC
*ORANGE/25: 4X TO 10X BASIC
RFTS1 Vladimir Guerrero Jr. 1.50 4.00
RFTS2 Bo Bichette .75 2.00
RFTS3 Triston McKenzie .25 .60
RFTS4 Mitch Keller .30 .75
RFTS5 Will Smith .60 1.50
RFTS6 Jon Duplantier .25 .60
RFTS7 Austin Riley 1.25 3.00
RFTS8 Ryan Mountcastle .30 .75
RFTS9 Nick Senzel .75 2.00
RFTS10 Fernando Tatis Jr. 2.50 6.00
RFTS11 Peter Alonso 2.00 5.00
RFTS12 Forrest Whitley .40 1.00
RFTS13 Yusniel Diaz .40 1.00
RFTS14 Brendan McKay .40 1.00
RFTS15 Jesus Luzardo .40 1.00
RFTS16 Brendan Rodgers .40 1.00
RFTS17 Yordan Alvarez 2.00 5.00
RFTS18 Keston Hiura .75 2.00
RFTS19 Brent Honeywell .30 .75
RFTS20 Eloy Jimenez 1.00 2.50

2019 Bowman Chrome Mega Box Rookie of the Year Favorites Autograph Refractors

STATED ODDS 1:207 PACKS
STATED PRINT RUN 99 SER.#'d SETS
*ORANGE/25: .75X TO 2X BASIC
ROYFACA Chance Adams 3.00 8.00
ROYFACB Corbin Burnes 5.00 12.00
ROYFACM Cedric Mullins 5.00 12.00
ROYFACST Chris Shaw 10.00 25.00
ROYFADJ Danny Jansen 8.00 20.00
ROYFADL Dawel Lugo 5.00 12.00
ROYFAJB Jake Bauers 5.00 12.00
ROYFAKA Kolby Allard 5.00 12.00
ROYFAKT Kyle Tucker 12.00 30.00
ROYFAKW Kyle Wright 8.00 20.00
ROYFALU Luis Urias 10.00 25.00
ROYFAMK Michael Kopech 10.00 25.00
ROYFARB Ryan Borucki 3.00 8.00
ROYFAROH Ryan O'Hearn 3.00 8.00
ROYFASD Steven Duggar 15.00 40.00

2019 Bowman Chrome Mega Box Rookie of the Year Favorites Refractors

STATED ODDS 1:2 PACKS
*PURPLE/250: .6X TO 1.5X BASIC
*GREEN/99: 1X TO 2.5X BASIC
*ORANGE/25: 4X TO 10X BASIC
ROYF1 Kyle Tucker .50 1.25
ROYF2 Dakota Hudson .30 .75
ROYF3 Dawel Lugo .40 1.00
ROYF4 Kevin Newman .40 1.00
ROYF5 Chance Adams .25 .60
ROYF6 Danny Jansen .25 .60
ROYF7 Kyle Wright .40 1.00
ROYF8 Chris Shaw .40 1.00
ROYF9 Kolby Allard .40 1.00
ROYF10 Christin Stewart .30 .75
ROYF11 Rowdy Tellez .40 1.00
ROYF12 Kohl Stewart .30 .75
ROYF13 Brandon Lowe .40 1.00
ROYF14 Luis Urias .40 1.00
ROYF15 Justus Sheffield .40 1.00
ROYF16 Touki Toussaint .30 .75
ROYF17 Josh James .40 1.00
ROYF18 Jacob Nix .30 .75
ROYF19 Jonathan Loaisiga .30 .75
ROYF20 Williams Astudillo .25 .60

2020 Bowman Chrome Mega Box Prospects Refractors

BCP1 Wander Franco 5.00 12.00
BCP2 Drew Waters .75 2.00
BCP3 Jacob Amaya 1.25 3.00
BCP4 Kody Hoese 1.00 2.50
BCP5 Cristian Pache 2.00 5.00
BCP8 Jasson Dominguez 30.00 80.00
BCP9 Aaron Shortridge .30 .75
BCP10 Xavier Edwards 1.25 3.00
BCP11 Jesus Sanchez .30 .75
BCP14 Ulrich Bojarski .30 .75
BCP15 Jordyn Adams .40 1.00
BCP16 Austin Beck .40 1.00
BCP17 Niko Hulsizer .75 2.00
BCP18 Triston Casas .75 2.00
BCP19 Julio Rodriguez 3.00 8.00
BCP23 Ruben Cardenas .40 1.00
BCP25 Bobby Witt Jr. 12.00 30.00
BCP26 Andrew Vaughn 1.25 3.00
BCP27 Kristian Robinson 1.00 2.50
BCP28 Ronny Mauricio .75 2.00
BCP29 Alec Bohm 2.00 5.00
BCP30 Jhon Diaz 3.00 8.00
BCP31 Estevan Florial .50 1.25
BCP33 Sam Huff .60 1.50
BCP34 Zack Brown .30 .75
BCP35 Brice Turang .30 .75
BCP36 Ryan Mountcastle .50 1.25
BCP37 Wilfred Astudillo .40 1.00
BCP38 Gus Varland .30 .75
BCP39 Nick Lodolo .50 1.25
BCP42 Brady Singer .40 1.00
BCP44 Ethan Hankins .40 1.00
BCP46 Sherten Apostel 1.50 4.00
BCP47 Hunter Greene .50 1.25
BCP50 Adley Rutschman 4.00 10.00
BCP51 Everson Pereira .75 2.00
BCP53 Clarke Schmidt .50 1.25
BCP54 Brady McConnell .40 1.00
BCP55 Spencer Howard 1.25 3.00
BCP56 Cristian Javier .30 .75
BCP57 Aaron Ashby .30 .75
BCP59 Glenallen Hill Jr. .50 1.25
BCP60 Alvaro Seijas .30 .75
BCP61 Jeremy Pena .75 2.00
BCP62 CJ Abrams 1.25 3.00
BCP63 Franklin Perez .30 .75
BCP65 Damon Jones .40 1.00
BCP66 Nolan Gorman .60 1.50
BCP67 Ke'Bryan Hayes .30 .75
BCP70 Forrest Whitley .30 .75
BCP72 Jazz Chisholm .75 2.00
BCP76 Joey Cantillo .30 .75
BCP78 Chris Vallimont .30 .75
BCP80 Alex Kirilloff .60 1.50
BCP82 Freudis Nova .30 .75
BCP83 Tim Cate .30 .75
BCP85 Antonio Cabello 1.00 2.50
BCP87 Colton Welker .30 .75
BCP88 Logan Davidson .40 1.00
BCP89 Matthew Liberatore .40 1.00
BCP91 Jackson Rutledge .50 1.25
BCP92 Dane Dunning .30 .75
BCP93 Royce Lewis .75 2.00
BCP94 Jarred Kelenic 2.00 5.00
BCP95 Nolan Jones .50 1.25
BCP96 Jerar Encarnacion 1.00 2.50
BCP98 Alek Thomas .40 1.00
BCP99 Matt Manning .40 1.00
BCP100 Jo Adell 1.25 3.00
BCP101 Nick Madrigal 1.00 2.50
BCP106 Dylan Carlson 1.25 3.00
BCP108 Tarik Skubal 1.50 4.00
BCP109 Oscar Gonzalez .75 2.00
BCP110 Aramis Ademan .30 .75
BCP111 Oneil Cruz .40 1.00
BCP112 Joey Bart 1.00 2.50
BCP113 Josh Jung .75 2.00
BCP114 Luis Garcia .50 1.25
BCP115 Jasseel De La Cruz .50 1.25
BCP116 J.J. Bleday 1.00 2.50
BCP117 Joe Ryan .30 .75
BCP119 Hans Crouse .30 .75
BCP121 Grant Lavigne .30 .75
BCP122 Riley Greene 1.25 3.00
BCP123 Jordan Balazovic .60 1.50
BCP124 Nate Pearson .60 1.50
BCP125 Deivi Garcia 1.25 3.00
BCP128 Bryan Mata .30 .75
BCP130 Taylor Trammell .40 1.00
BCP131 Miguel Vargas .75 2.00
BCP134 Gunnar Henderson .40 1.00
BCP136 Miguel Amaya .40 1.00
BCP139 Anthony Volpe 5.00 12.00
BCP140 Nick Bennett .30 .75
BCP142 Casey Mize 1.00 2.50
BCP143 Keibert Ruiz .75 2.00
BCP144 Jarren Duran 3.00 8.00
BCP145 Robert Puason 10.00 25.00
BCP149 Alek Manoah .40 1.00
BCP150 Luis Robert 10.00 25.00
BCP151 Alex Kirilloff .60 1.50
BCP152 Michael Busch .75 2.00
BCP153 Daulton Jefferies .30 .75
BCP154 Mark Vientos .30 .75
BCP155 Diego Cartaya .60 1.50
BCP156 Monte Harrison .30 .75
BCP157 Nolan Jones .50 1.25
BCP158 Alex Faedo .40 1.00
BCP159 Bayron Lora 1.25 3.00
BCP160 Bobby Witt Jr. 6.00 15.00
BCP161 Noah Song .40 1.00
BCP162 Nolan Gorman .60 1.50
BCP163 Wander Franco 5.00 12.00
BCP164 Tanner Houck .75 2.00
BCP165 Kyle Isbel .30 .75
BCP166 Brandon Marsh .30 .75
BCP167 Mickey Moniak .75 2.00
BCP168 Brice Turang .30 .75
BCP169 Noelvi Marte 1.25 3.00
BCP170 Yusniel Diaz .50 1.25
BCP171 Elehuris Montero .40 1.00
BCP172 Sixto Sanchez .50 1.25
BCP173 Robert Puason 3.00 8.00
BCP174 Jackson Kowar .30 .75
BCP175 Julio Rodriguez 3.00 8.00
BCP176 Steele Walker .50 1.25
BCP177 Tony Santillan .30 .75
BCP178 Mike Siani .30 .75
BCP179 Shane McCarthy .30 .75
BCP180 Keoni Cavaco .30 .75
BCP181 Daulton Varsho .30 .75
BCP182 Ryan Castellani .30 .75
BCP183 Adonis Medina .50 1.25
BCP184 MacKenzie Gore .60 1.50
BCP185 Jay Groome .30 .75
BCP186 Andres Gimenez .40 1.00
BCP187 Tristen Lutz .40 1.00
BCP188 Leody Taveras .30 .75
BCP189 Triston McKenzie .50 1.25
BCP190 Simeon Woods Richardson .50 1.25
BCP191 Kyle Muller .30 .75
BCP192 Forrest Whitley .30 .75
BCP193 Korey Lee .40 1.00
BCP194 Freudis Nova .30 .75
BCP195 Royce Lewis .75 2.00
BCP196 Keegan Akin .30 .75
BCP197 Quinn Priester .50 1.25
BCP198 Francisco Alvarez 3.00 8.00
BCP199 Luis Garcia 1.25 3.00
BCP200 Brennan Malone .30 .75
BCP201 Cristian Pache 2.00 5.00
BCP202 Geraldo Perdomo .30 .75
BCP203 Ethan Hearn .50 1.25
BCP204 Jesus Sanchez .30 .75
BCP205 Tim Cate .30 .75
BCP206 Cole Roederer .60 1.50
BCP207 Jorge Mateo .30 .75
BCP208 Triston Casas .75 2.00
BCP209 Matthew Liberatore .40 1.00
BCP210 Keibert Ruiz .75 2.00
BCP211 Blake Rutherford .30 .75
BCP212 Jarred Kelenic 2.00 5.00
BCP213 Marco Luciano 1.25 3.00
BCP214 Deivi Garcia 1.25 3.00
BCP215 Sean Hjelle .50 1.25
BCP216 Clarke Schmidt .50 1.25
BCP217 Mason Denaburg .30 .75
BCP218 Luis Campusano .50 1.25
BCP219 Braden Shewmake .50 1.25
BCP220 Ke'Bryan Hayes .30 .75
BCP221 Shane Baz .30 .75
BCP222 Corbin Carroll .50 1.25
BCP223 Estevan Florial .50 1.25
BCP224 Isaac Paredes .50 1.25
BCP225 Michael Toglia .30 .75
BCP226 Alejandro Kirk 1.25 3.00
BCP227 Jeter Downs .50 1.25
BCP228 Tyler Stephenson .30 .75
BCP229 Matt Manning .40 1.00
BCP230 Luis Garcia .50 1.25
BCP231 Ryan Jensen .40 1.00
BCP232 Dane Dunning .30 .75
BCP233 William Contreras .40 1.00
BCP234 Bo Naylor .40 1.00
BCP235 Luis Patino .50 1.25
BCP236 Dylan Carlson 1.25 3.00
BCP237 Sam Huff .60 1.50
BCP238 D.L. Hall .30 .75
BCP239 Jackson Rutledge .50 1.25
BCP240 Ryan Vilade .30 .75
BCP241 Vidal Brujan 1.00 2.50
BCP242 Seth Corry .30 .75
BCP243 Jasson Dominguez 15.00 40.00
BCP244 Jeremiah Jackson .30 .75
BCP245 Orelvis Martinez .75 2.00
BCP246 Kyren Paris .30 .75
BCP247 Brett Baty 1.00 2.50
BCP248 Corey Ray .30 .75
BCP249 Trevor Larnach .60 1.50
BCP250 Casey Mize 1.00 2.50

2020 Bowman Chrome Mega Box Prospects Blue Refractors

*BLUE REF: 1.2X TO 3X BASIC
BOW.MEGA ODDS 1:32 HOBBY
BOW.CHR.MEGA ODDS 1:19 HOBBY
STATED PRINT RUN 150 SER.#'d SETS
BCP5 Cristian Pache 8.00 20.00
BCP8 Jasson Dominguez 150.00 400.00
BCP145 Robert Puason 50.00 120.00
BCP173 Robert Puason 12.00 30.00
BCP201 Cristian Pache 8.00 20.00
BCP243 Jasson Dominguez 60.00 150.00

2020 Bowman Chrome Mega Box Prospects Gold Refractors

*GOLD REF: 4X TO 10X BASIC
BOW.MEGA ODDS 1:95 HOBBY
BOW.CHR.MEGA ODDS 1:56 HOBBY
STATED PRINT RUN 50 SER.#'d SETS
BCP5 Cristian Pache 20.00 50.00
BCP8 Jasson Dominguez 500.00 1000.00
BCP29 Alec Bohm 30.00 80.00
BCP46 Sherten Apostel 30.00 80.00

BCP94 Jarred Kelenic 25.00 60.00
BCP112 Joey Bart 40.00 100.00
BCP145 Robert Puason 150.00 400.00
BCP173 Robert Puason 40.00 100.00
BCP198 Francisco Alvarez 25.00 60.00
BCP201 Cristian Pache 20.00 50.00
BCP212 Jarred Kelenic 25.00 60.00
BCP243 Jasson Dominguez 200.00 500.00

2020 Bowman Chrome Mega Box Prospects Green Refractors

*GREEN REF: 1.5X TO 4X BASIC
BOW.MEGA ODDS 1:48 HOBBY
BOW.CHR.MEGA ODDS 1:29 HOBBY
STATED PRINT RUN 99 SER.#'d SETS
BCP5 Cristian Pache 10.00 25.00
BCP8 Jasson Dominguez 200.00 500.00
BCP29 Alec Bohm 12.00 30.00
BCP94 Jarred Kelenic 10.00 25.00
BCP112 Joey Bart 15.00 40.00
BCP145 Robert Puason 60.00 150.00
BCP173 Robert Puason 15.00 40.00
BCP201 Cristian Pache 10.00 25.00
BCP212 Jarred Kelenic 10.00 25.00
BCP243 Jasson Dominguez 75.00 200.00

2020 Bowman Chrome Mega Box Prospects Orange Refractors

*ORANGE REF: 6X TO 15X BASIC
BOW.MEGA ODDS 1:189 HOBBY
BOW.CHR.MEGA ODDS 1:112 HOBBY
STATED PRINT RUN 25 SER.#'d SETS
BCP5 Cristian Pache 30.00 80.00
BCP8 Jasson Dominguez 600.00 1500.00
BCP29 Alec Bohm 50.00 120.00
BCP46 Sherten Apostel 50.00 120.00
BCP94 Jarred Kelenic 40.00 100.00
BCP112 Joey Bart 60.00 150.00
BCP145 Robert Puason 250.00 600.00
BCP173 Robert Puason 60.00 150.00
BCP198 Francisco Alvarez 40.00 100.00
BCP201 Cristian Pache 30.00 80.00
BCP212 Jarred Kelenic 40.00 100.00
BCP243 Jasson Dominguez 300.00 800.00

2020 Bowman Chrome Mega Box Prospects Pink Refractors

*PINK REF: 1.2X TO 3X BASIC
BOW.MEGA ODDS 1:24 HOBBY
BOW.CHR.MEGA ODDS 1:15 HOBBY
STATED PRINT RUN 199 SER.#'d SETS
BCP5 Cristian Pache 8.00 20.00
BCP145 Robert Puason 50.00 120.00
BCP201 Cristian Pache 8.00 20.00
BCP243 Jasson Dominguez 60.00 150.00

2020 Bowman Chrome Mega Box Prospects Purple Refractors

*PURPLE REF: 1X TO 2.5X BASIC
BOW.MEGA ODDS 1:19 HOBBY
BOW.CHR.MEGA ODDS 1:12 HOBBY
STATED PRINT RUN 250 SER.#'d SETS
BCP145 Robert Puason 40.00 100.00

2020 Bowman Chrome Mega Box Prospects Image Variation Refractors

BOW.MEGA ODDS 1:210 HOBBY
BOW.CHR.MEGA ODDS 1:125 HOBBY
BCP25 Bobby Witt Jr. 40.00 100.00
BCP26 Andrew Vaughn 15.00 40.00
BCP50 Adley Rutschman 25.00 60.00
BCP91 Jackson Rutledge 6.00 15.00
BCP94 Jarred Kelenic 25.00 60.00
BCP139 Anthony Volpe 25.00 60.00
BCP142 Casey Mize 12.00 30.00
BCP144 Jarren Duran 15.00 40.00
BCP145 Robert Puason 40.00 100.00
BCP150 Luis Robert 60.00 150.00
BCP151 Alex Kirilloff 8.00 20.00
BCP159 Bayron Lora 40.00 100.00
BCP162 Nolan Gorman 8.00 20.00
BCP192 Forrest Whitley 4.00 10.00
BCP195 Royce Lewis 10.00 25.00
BCP218 Luis Campusano 10.00 25.00
BCP220 Ke'Bryan Hayes 4.00 10.00
BCP241 Vidal Brujan 12.00 30.00
BCP243 Jasson Dominguez 60.00 150.00

2020 Bowman Chrome Mega Box Prospects Image Variation Autograph Refractors

BOW.MEGA ODDS 1:2037 HOBBY
BOW.CHR.MEGA ODDS 1:1570 HOBBY
STATED PRINT RUN 25 SER.#'d SETS
BCP25 Bobby Witt Jr. 500.00 1200.00
BCP26 Andrew Vaughn
BCP50 Adley Rutschman
BCP91 Jackson Rutledge 40.00 100.00
BCP94 Jarred Kelenic
BCP139 Anthony Volpe 125.00 300.00
BCP142 Casey Mize
BCP144 Jarren Duran 100.00 250.00
BCP145 Robert Puason 300.00 800.00
BCP150 Luis Robert 1000.00 2000.00
BCP151 Alex Kirilloff
BCP159 Bayron Lora
BCP162 Nolan Gorman 60.00 150.00
BCP192 Forrest Whitley
BCP195 Royce Lewis 30.00 80.00
BCP218 Luis Campusano
BCP220 Ke'Bryan Hayes 75.00 200.00
BCP241 Vidal Brujan
BCP243 Jasson Dominguez 800.00 1500.00

2020 Bowman Chrome Mega Box Dawn of Glory Autograph Refractors

STATED ODDS 1:186 HOBBY
STATED PRINT RUN 99 SER.#'d SETS
DGAAR Adley Rutschman 30.00 80.00
DGAAV Andrew Vaughn 15.00 40.00
DGAGV Gus Varland 4.00 10.00
DGAJD Jarren Duran 15.00 40.00
DGAJR Joe Ryan 4.00 10.00
DGAKS Kevin Smith 4.00 10.00
DGALD Lewin Diaz 4.00 10.00
DGANL Nick Lodolo 6.00 15.00
DGASA Sherten Apostel 12.00 30.00
DGASH Sam Huff 12.00 30.00
DGAJDL Jasseel De La Cruz 6.00 15.00

2020 Bowman Chrome Mega Box Dawn of Glory Autograph Orange Refractors

*ORANGE/25: .6X TO 1.5X
STATED ODDS 1:733 HOBBY
STATED PRINT RUN 25 SER.#'d SETS
DGAAV Andrew Vaughn 30.00 80.00

2020 Bowman Chrome Mega Box Dawn of Glory Refractors

STATED ODDS 1:2 HOBBY
*BLUE/150: .6X TO 1.5X
*GREEN/99: 1X TO 2.5X
DG1 Sherten Apostel 2.00 5.00
DG2 Gus Varland .40 1.00
DG3 Jasseel De La Cruz .60 1.50
DG4 Nick Lodolo .60 1.50
DG5 Jarren Duran 1.50 4.00
DG6 Isaac Paredes .60 1.50
DG7 Dylan File .40 1.00
DG8 Joe Ryan .40 1.00
DG9 Ruben Cardenas .50 1.25
DG10 Sam Huff .75 2.00
DG11 Lewin Diaz .40 1.00
DG12 Andrew Vaughn 1.50 4.00
DG13 Adley Rutschman 2.50 6.00
DG14 Jordan Balazovic .75 2.00
DG15 Kevin Smith .40 1.00
DG16 Jo Adell 1.50 4.00
DG17 Casey Mize 1.25 3.00
DG18 Joey Bart 1.25 3.00
DG19 MacKenzie Gore .75 2.00
DG20 Wander Franco 4.00 10.00

2020 Bowman Chrome Mega Box Dawn of Glory Gold Refractors

*GOLD/50: 1.2X TO 3X
STATED ODDS 1:280 HOBBY
STATED PRINT RUN 50 SER.#'d SETS
DG20 Wander Franco 40.00 100.00

2020 Bowman Chrome Mega Box Dawn of Glory Orange Refractors

*ORANGE/25: 2.5X TO 6X
STATED ODDS 1:560 HOBBY
STATED PRINT RUN 25 SER.#'d SETS
DG20 Wander Franco 75.00 200.00

2020 Bowman Chrome Mega Box Farm to Fame Refractors

STATED ODDS 1:80 HOBBY
FTFBL Barry Larkin 2.00 5.00
FTFCF Carlton Fisk 8.00 20.00
FTFCJ Chipper Jones 10.00 25.00
FTFCY Carl Yastrzemski 8.00 20.00
FTFEM Edgar Martinez 8.00 20.00
FTFFT Frank Thomas 15.00 40.00
FTFGB George Brett 5.00 12.00
FTFHA Hank Aaron 10.00 25.00
FTFIR Ivan Rodriguez 2.00 5.00
FTFJB Johnny Bench 10.00 25.00
FTFMR Mariano Rivera 8.00 20.00
FTFNR Nolan Ryan 15.00 40.00
FTFOS Ozzie Smith 10.00 25.00
FTFPM Pedro Martinez 3.00 8.00
FTFRC Rod Carew 5.00 12.00
FTFRF Rollie Fingers 6.00 15.00
FTFRH Rickey Henderson 20.00 50.00
FTFRJ Reggie Jackson 6.00 15.00
FTFRY Robin Yount 5.00 12.00
FTFSC Steve Carlton 2.00 5.00
FTFTP Tony Perez 2.00 5.00
FTFWB Wade Boggs 6.00 15.00
FTFWM Willie Mays 8.00 20.00
FTFCRJ Cal Ripken Jr. 12.00 30.00

2020 Bowman Chrome Mega Box Farm to Fame Orange Refractors

*ORANGE/25: .6X TO 1.5X
STATED ODDS 1:560 HOBBY
STATED PRINT RUN 25 SER.#'d SETS
FTFEM Edgar Martinez 15.00 40.00
FTFNR Nolan Ryan 40.00 100.00
FTFPM Pedro Martinez 20.00 50.00
FTFCRJ Cal Ripken Jr. 40.00 100.00

2020 Bowman Chrome Mega Box Prospect Autograph Refractors

BOW.MEGA ODDS 1:16 HOBBY
BOW.CHR.MEGA ODDS 1:9 HOBBY
*BLUE REF/150: .6X TO 1.5X
BMAAA Aaron Ashby 4.00 10.00
BMAAR Adley Rutschman 40.00 100.00
BMAAS Aaron Shortridge 4.00 10.00
BMAAV Andrew Vaughn 15.00 40.00
BMAAVO Anthony Volpe 40.00 100.00
BMABM Brady McConnell 5.00 12.00
BMABS Braden Shewmake 6.00 15.00
BMABWJ Bobby Witt Jr. 100.00 250.00
BMACJA CJ Abrams 20.00 50.00
BMAGH Gunnar Henderson 5.00 12.00
BMAGHJ Glenallen Hill Jr. 6.00 15.00
BMAJA Jacob Amaya 8.00 20.00
BMAJC Joey Cantillo 4.00 10.00
BMAJD Jasson Dominguez 300.00 800.00
BMAJDU Jarren Duran 15.00 40.00
BMAJE Jerar Encarnacion 8.00 20.00
BMAJJG JJ Goss 4.00 10.00
BMAJR Joe Ryan 4.00 10.00
BMAJS Jake Sanford 6.00 15.00
BMAKS Kyle Stowers 4.00 10.00
BMANH Niko Hulsizer 10.00 25.00
BMARG Riley Greene 20.00 50.00
BMARH Rece Hinds 5.00 12.00
BMASL Shea Langeliers 8.00 20.00
BMASS Sammy Siani 4.00 10.00
BMATS Tarik Skubal 8.00 20.00
BMATSI T.J. Sikkema 4.00 10.00
BMAUB Ulrich Bojarski 4.00 10.00
BCMAAH Austin Hansen 5.00 12.00
BCMAAP Andy Pages 10.00 25.00
BCMAAR Adley Rutschman 40.00 100.00
BCMAAS Alex Speas 4.00 10.00
BCMAAV Andrew Vaughn 15.00 40.00
BCMACS Canaan Smith 6.00 15.00
BCMADE Daniel Espino 5.00 12.00
BCMAEL Ethan Lindow 5.00 12.00
BCMAGM Gabriel Moreno 6.00 15.00
BCMAHB Hunter Bishop 10.00 25.00
BCMAJD Jasson Dominguez 300.00 600.00
BCMAJE Jerar Encarnacion 8.00 20.00
BCMAKS Kevin Smith 4.00 10.00
BCMALD Lewin Diaz 6.00 15.00
BCMALM Luis Matos 20.00 50.00
BCMAML Max Lazar 5.00 12.00
BCMANL Nick Lodolo 6.00 15.00
BCMARG Riley Greene 20.00 50.00
BCMARP Robert Puason 30.00 80.00
BCMATS Tarik Skubal 8.00 20.00
BCMAJDU Jarren Duran 15.00 40.00
BCMAMLU Matthew Lugo 6.00 15.00

2020 Bowman Chrome Mega Box Prospect Autograph Green Refractors

*GREEN REF: .75X TO 2X BASIC
BOW.MEGA ODDS 1:195 HOBBY
BOW.CHR.MEGA ODDS 1:121 HOBBY
STATED PRINT RUN 99 SER.#'d SETS
BMAJE Jerar Encarnacion 25.00 60.00
BCMAJE Jerar Encarnacion 25.00 60.00
BCMARP Robert Puason 75.00 200.00

2020 Bowman Chrome Mega Box Prospect Autograph Orange Refractors

*ORANGE REF: 1.5X TO 4X BASIC
BOW.MEGA ODDS 1:767 HOBBY
BOW.CHR.MEGA ODDS 1:478 HOBBY
STATED PRINT RUN 25 SER.#'d SETS
BMAJA Jacob Amaya 60.00 150.00
BMAJD Jasson Dominguez 2000.00 4000.00
BMAJE Jerar Encarnacion 50.00 120.00
BMARG Riley Greene 100.00 250.00
BMATS Tarik Skubal 40.00 100.00
BCMAAP Andy Pages 100.00 250.00
BCMAJD Jasson Dominguez 2000.00 4000.00
BCMAJE Jerar Encarnacion 50.00 120.00
BCMARG Riley Greene 100.00 250.00
BCMARP Robert Puason 150.00 400.00
BCMATS Tarik Skubal 40.00 100.00

2020 Bowman Chrome Mega Box Rookie of the Year Favorites Autograph Refractors

STATED ODDS 1:311 HOBBY
STATED PRINT RUN 99 SER.#'d SETS
*ORANGE/25: .6X TO 1.5X BASIC
ROYFAAJP A.J. Puk 12.00 30.00
ROYFABB Bobby Bradley 4.00 10.00
ROYFABM Brendan McKay 12.00 30.00
ROYFADC Dylan Cease 6.00 15.00
ROYFAGL Gavin Lux 60.00 150.00
ROYFAJY Jordan Yamamoto 6.00 15.00
ROYFASB Seth Brown 10.00 25.00
ROYFAYA Yordan Alvarez 60.00 150.00

2020 Bowman Chrome Mega Box Rookie of the Year Favorites Refractors

STATED ODDS 1:2 HOBBY
*PURPLE/250: .6X TO 1.5X BASIC
*PINK/199: .6X TO 1.5X BASIC
*BLUE/150: .75X TO 2X BASIC
*GREEN/99: 1X TO 2.5X BASIC
*ORANGE/25: 2.5X TO 6X BASIC
ROYFAA Adbert Alzolay .50 1.25
ROYFAAQ Aristides Aquino .75 2.00
ROYFAC Aaron Civale .60 1.50
ROYFAP A.J. Puk .75 2.00
ROYFAT Abraham Toro .50 1.25
ROYFBB Bo Bichette 3.00 8.00
ROYFBM Brendan McKay .60 1.50
ROYFBR Brusdar Graterol .60 1.50
ROYFDC Dylan Cease .75 2.00
ROYFDM Dustin May 1.50 4.00
ROYFGL Gavin Lux 2.50 6.00
ROYFJD Justin Dunn .50 1.25
ROYFJL Jesus Luzardo .75 2.00
ROYFJY Jordan Yamamoto .50 1.25
ROYFKL Kyle Lewis 3.00 8.00
ROYFNH Nico Hoerner 1.50 4.00
ROYFSB Seth Brown .40 1.00
ROYFSH Sam Hilliard .60 1.50
ROYFSM Sean Murphy .60 1.50
ROYFYA Yordan Alvarez 2.00 5.00

2020 Bowman Chrome Mega Box Spanning the Globe Refractors

STATED ODDS 1:4 HOBBY
STGAA Adbert Alzolay .50 1.25
STGAM Andres Munoz .50 1.25
STGCM Casey Mize 1.25 3.00
STGDB Dasan Brown 1.00 2.50
STGEP Eric Pardinho .40 1.00
STGHR Heliot Ramos .60 1.50
STGIP Isaac Paredes .60 1.50
STGJA Jo Adell 1.50 4.00
STGJB Jordan Balazovic .75 2.00
STGJD Jasson Dominguez 10.00 25.00
STGJL Jesus Luzardo .75 2.00
STGLP Luis Patino .60 1.50
STGLR Luis Robert 6.00 15.00
STGMA Miguel Amaya .50 1.25
STGML Matthew Lugo .60 1.50
STGRH Ronaldo Hernandez .40 1.00
STGUB Ulrich Bojarski .40 1.00
STGVVM Victor Victor Mesa .60 1.50
STGWF Wander Franco 4.00 10.00
STGYC Yu Chang .60 1.50

2020 Bowman Chrome Mega Box Spanning the Globe Blue Refractors

*BLUE: .75X TO 2X BASIC
STATED ODDS 1:157 HOBBY
STATED PRINT RUN 150 SER.#'d SETS
STGJD Jasson Dominguez 50.00 120.00

2020 Bowman Chrome Mega Box Spanning the Globe Green Refractors

*GREEN: 1X TO 2.5X BASIC
STATED ODDS 1:238 HOBBY
STATED PRINT RUN 99 SER.#'d SETS
STGJD Jasson Dominguez 60.00 150.00

2020 Bowman Chrome Mega Box Spanning the Globe Orange Refractors

*ORANGE: 2.5X TO 6X BASIC
STATED ODDS 1:940 HOBBY
STATED PRINT RUN 25 SER.#'d SETS
STGJD Jasson Dominguez 150.00 400.00

2020 Bowman Chrome Mega Box Spanning the Globe Pink Refractors

*PINK: .6X TO 1.5X BASIC
STATED ODDS 1:119 HOBBY
STATED PRINT RUN 199 SER.#'d SETS
STGJD Jasson Dominguez 40.00 100.00

2020 Bowman Chrome Mega Box Spanning the Globe Purple Refractors

*PURPLE: .6X TO 1.5X BASIC
STATED ODDS 1:95 HOBBY
STATED PRINT RUN 250 SER.#'d SETS
STGJD Jasson Dominguez 40.00 100.00

2013 Bowman Chrome Mini

COMPLETE SET (330) 15.00 40.00
PLATE PRINT RUN 1 SET PER COLOR
BLACK-CYAN-MAGENTA-YELLOW ISSUED
NO PLATE PRICING DUE TO SCARCITY
1 Byron Buxton .75 2.00
2 Stefen Romero .30 .75
3 Justin Williams .40 1.00
4 Jacob Nottingham .30 .75
5 Justin Maffei .30 .75
6 Jeremy Moore .30 .75
7 Tzu-Wei Lin .40 1.00
8 Jonathon Crawford .30 .75
9 Edwin Escobar .40 1.00
10 Gregory Polanco .60 1.50
11 Riley Unroe .30 .75
12 Carlos Tocci .30 .75
13 Luis Guillorme .40 1.00
14 Tayler Scott .30 .75
15 Victor Roache .40 1.00
16 Francellis Montas .40 1.00
17 Kean Wong .30 .75
18 Andrew Aplin .30 .75
19 Jose Ramirez .40 1.00
20 Courtney Hawkins .30 .75
21 Aaron Blair .30 .75
22 Keury de la Cruz .30 .75
23 Chris Stratton .30 .75
24 R.J. Alvarez .30 .75
25 Jimmy Nelson .30 .75
26 Danry Vasquez .30 .75
27 Steven Moya .50 1.25
28 Nik Turley .30 .75
29 Cody Asche .50 1.25
30 Carlos Correa 3.00 8.00
31 Steven Negron .30 .75
32 Gabe Speier .30 .75
33 Collin Wiles .30 .75
34 Michael Taylor .30 .75
35 Ben Rowen .30 .75
36 Roel Ramirez .30 .75
37 Ivan Wilson .30 .75
38 Ian Hagenmiller .30 .75
39 Mike Piazza .30 .75
40 Austin Meadows .60 1.50
41 Denton Keys .40 1.00
42 Ericson Leonora .30 .75
43 Ian Clarkin .30 .75
44 Danny Muno .30 .75
45 Brennan Middleton .30 .75
46 Jan Hernandez .30 .75
47 Mac Williamson .50 1.25
48 Christian Bethancourt .50 1.25
49 Kevin Medrano .30 .75
50 Braden Shipley .30 .75
51 Michael Perez .30 .75
52 Cory Hall .30 .75
53 Todd Kibby .30 .75
54 Jordon Austin .40 1.00
55 Jeff Gelalich .30 .75
56 Joan Gregorio .40 1.00
57 Brian Navarreto .30 .75
58 Pedro Guerra .30 .75
59 Matthew Koch .30 .75
60 Henry Owens .40 1.00
61 Michael Lorenzen .40 1.00
62 Cord Sandberg .40 1.00
63 Andrew Toles .30 .75
64 Luis Torrens .30 .75
65 Tim Anderson 1.25 3.00
66 Derrick Penilla .30 .75
67 Orrin Sears .30 .75
68 Jayson Aquino .30 .75
69 Drew Ward .40 1.00
70 Hunter Renfroe .50 1.25
71 Rainy Lara .30 .75
72 Jonathan Griffin .30 .75
73 Joseph Monge .30 .75
74 Cory Vaughn .30 .75
75 Tyler Wade .50 1.25
76 Matt Derosier .30 .75
77 Jorge Bonifacio .40 1.00
78 Jesse Hahn .30 .75
79 Ricardo Bautista .30 .75
80 Eduardo Rodriguez 1.00 2.50
81 Casey Stevenson .30 .75
82 Zach Bird .30 .75
83 Ji-Man Choi .40 1.00
84 Anthony Alford .30 .75
85 Evan Rutckyj .30 .75
86 Nolan Fontana .40 1.00
87 Travis Witherspoon .30 .75
88 Breyvic Valera .40 1.00
89 Socrates Brito .50 1.25
90 Billy Mckinney .40 1.00
91 Parker Bridwell .30 .75
92 Tony Renda .30 .75
93 Danny Salazar .60 1.50
94 Randolph Gassaway .30 .75
95 Gioskar Amaya .30 .75
96 Ty Afenir .30 .75
97 Deivi Grullon .30 .75
98 Wyatt Mathisen .30 .75
99 Jamie Callahan .30 .75
100 Adalberto Mondesi 1.00 2.50
101 Yordano Ventura .40 1.00
102 Jonah Heim .30 .75
103 Tyler Vail .30 .75
104 Ronnie Freeman .30 .75
105 Kevin Ziomek .30 .75
106 Elier Rodriguez .30 .75
107 Stephen Gonsalves .30 .75
108 Jake Sweaney .30 .75
109 Marco Hernandez .30 .75
110 Jose Berrios .50 1.25
111 Victor Sanchez .40 1.00
112 Tyrone Taylor .30 .75
113 Ty Buttrey .30 .75
114 Stryker Trahan .30 .75
115 Travis Shaw .30 .75
116 Jordan Barnes .30 .75
117 Roman Quinn .50 1.25
118 Shane Broyles .30 .75
119 Luis Merejo .30 .75
120 Luis Sardinas .30 .75
121 B.J. Boyd .30 .75
122 Jake Stone .40 1.00
123 Zach Eflin .40 1.00
124 Patrick Kivlehan .30 .75
125 Alex Murphy .30 .75
126 Andre Rienzo .30 .75
127 Adam Landecker .30 .75
128 Tyler Kinley .30 .75
129 Dan Langfield .30 .75
130 D.J. Peterson .30 .75
131 Jeremy Baltz .30 .75
132 Viosergy Rosa .30 .75
133 Tom Windle .30 .75
134 Mikeson Oliberto .30 .75
135 Drew Steckenrider .30 .75
136 Sean Hurley .30 .75
137 Corey Dickerson .40 1.00
138 Andrew Church .30 .75
139 Will Morris .30 .75
140 Lucas Giolito .50 1.25
141 Andry Ubiera .40 1.00
142 Oscar Mercado .50 1.25
143 Blake Higgins .40 1.00
144 Carlos Sanchez .30 .75
145 Tom Murphy .30 .75
146 Brandon Maurer .40 1.00
147 Hanser Alberto .30 .75
148 Gaither Bumgardner .30 .75
149 Jon Keller .30 .75
150 Addison Russell .50 1.25
151 Jason Kanzler .30 .75
152 Casey Meisner .30 .75
153 Mark Montgomery .50 1.25
154 David Holmberg .30 .75
155 Aaron Blanton .30 .75
156 Ryan McMahon .40 1.00
157 Luiz Gohara .40 1.00
158 Hunter Green .30 .75
159 Tommy Kahnle .30 .75
160 Tyler Glasnow .50 1.25
161 Yeison Asencio .30 .75
162 Daniel Watts .30 .75
163 Robert Kaminsky .40 1.00
164 Anderson Feliz .30 .75
165 Jake Thompson .30 .75
166 Luigi Rodriguez .30 .75
167 Ronny Rodriguez .30 .75
168 J.T. Chargois .30 .75
169 Matt Stites .30 .75
170 Marco Gonzales .50 1.25
171 Matt Reynolds .40 1.00
172 Adam Westmoreland .30 .75
173 Alexis Rivera .30 .75
174 Andrew Knapp .30 .75
175 Dylan Manwaring .30 .75
176 Tyler Pike .30 .75
177 Darwin Rivera .30 .75
178 Kyle Smith .30 .75
179 Miles Williams .30 .75
180 Max Fried 1.25 3.00
181 Ian McKinney .30 .75
182 Jorge Martinez .30 .75
183 Alec Grosser .30 .75
184 Jason Martin .30 .75
185 Pat Light .30 .75
186 Christian Villanueva .30 .75
187 Chris Rivera .30 .75
188 Micah Johnson .40 1.00
189 Dustin Geiger .30 .75
190 Clayton Blackburn .50 1.25
191 Gosuke Katoh .40 1.00
192 Reed Harper .30 .75
193 William Oliver .30 .75
194 Michael Snyder .30 .75
195 Miguel Andujar 2.50 6.00
196 Ryan Court .30 .75
197 Jorge Perez .30 .75
198 Renato Nunez .60 1.50
199 Jose Cisnero .30 .75
200 Albert Almora .60 1.50
201 Lenny Linsky .30 .75
202 Max White .30 .75
203 Cody Buckel .30 .75
204 Dorssys Paulino .40 1.00
205 Willians Astudillo .30 .75
206 Niko Spezial .30 .75
207 Mauricio Cabrera .30 .75
208 Jon Denney .40 1.00
209 Dylan Cozens .30 .75
210 Dominic Smith .50 1.25
211 Trevor Williams .30 .75
212 Rio Ruiz .30 .75
213 Chris McFarland .30 .75
214 Kris Hall .30 .75
215 Teddy Stankiewicz .40 1.00
216 Julian Yan .30 .75
217 Adys Portillo .30 .75
218 Nick Tropeano .30 .75
219 Austin Wilson .40 1.00
220 Colin Moran .40 1.00
221 Caleb Kellogg .30 .75
222 Nolan Sanburn .30 .75
223 Carson Kelly .40 1.00
224 Mitch Brown .30 .75
225 Hansel Robles .30 .75
226 Matt Curry .30 .75
227 Kendall Coleman .30 .75
228 Alfredo Escalera-Maldonado .40 1.00
229 Luis Mateo .40 1.00
230 Jonathan Schoop .30 .75
231 Corey Knebel .30 .75
232 Tyler Gonzales .30 .75
233 Deven Marrero .30 .75
234 Taylor Dugas .40 1.00
235 Michael Reed .30 .75
236 Cameron Gallagher .30 .75
237 Erik Johnson .30 .75
238 Edwin Diaz .60 1.50
239 Stephen Piscotty .60 1.50
240 Rafael DePaula .30 .75
241 Adam Walker .40 1.00
242 Pedro Ruiz .30 .75
243 Seth Maness .30 .75
244 Alex Meyer .30 .75
245 Phil Ervin .30 .75
246 Ian Stiffler .30 .75
247 Gabriel Guerrero .40 1.00
248 Connor Oliver .30 .75
249 Nestor Molina .30 .75
250 C.J. Edwards .50 1.25
251 Travis Ott .30 .75
252 Kelvin De Leon .30 .75
253 Trey Williams .50 1.25
254 Josh Hart .30 .75
255 Brett Gerritse .30 .75
256 Ronald Guzman .50 1.25
257 Kevin Franklin .30 .75
258 Jairo Beras .50 1.25
259 Joseph Odom .30 .75
260 Lance McCullers .30 .75
261 Matt Southard .30 .75
262 Nick Ciuffo .30 .75
263 Trae Arbet .30 .75
264 Jake Lamb .50 1.25
265 Sam Selman .30 .75
266 Onelki Garcia .40 1.00
267 Austin Kubitza .30 .75
268 Brian Goodwin .40 1.00
269 Austin Schotts .40 1.00
270 J.P. Crawford .50 1.25
271 Derek Jones .30 .75
272 Blake Taylor .30 .75
273 Patrick Murphy .30 .75
274 Roberto Osuna .30 .75
275 Tanner Rahier .40 1.00
276 William White .30 .75
277 William Cuevas .30 .75
278 Rock Shoulders .30 .75
279 Rony Bautista .30 .75
280 Kohl Stewart .40 1.00
281 Nelson Molina .30 .75
282 Chris Anderson .40 1.00
283 Garrett Gordon .30 .75
284 Ethan Carnes .30 .75
285 Willie Medina .30 .75
286 Dustin Peterson .30 .75
287 Travis Demeritte .40 1.00
288 Carlos Salazar .30 .75
289 Dane Phillips .30 .75
290 Corey Seager 1.25 3.00
291 Sean Townsley .30 .75
292 Adalberto Mejia .30 .75
293 Jorge Polanco .30 .75
294 Tyler Brosius .30 .75
295 Thomas Milone .30 .75
296 Chance Sisco .60 1.50
297 Reese McGuire .40 1.00
298 Yeicok Calderon .30 .75
299 Austin Nicely .30 .75
300 Jorge Alfaro .60 1.50
301 Jack Leathersich .30 .75
302 Miguel Almonte .30 .75
303 Bruce Rondon .30 .75
304 Fu-Lin Kuo .40 1.00
305 Gustavo Cabrera .75 2.00
306 Jeremy Rathjen .30 .75
307 Bryan Hudson .30 .75
308 Yohander Mendez .30 .75
309 Saxon Butler .30 .75
310 Jonathan Gray .40 1.00
311 Aaron Judge 15.00 40.00
312 Dilson Herrera 1.00 2.50
313 Mitch Nay .30 .75
314 Hunter Harvey .40 1.00
315 Clint Frazier 1.50 4.00
316 Gerrit Cole 2.00 5.00
317 Anthony Rendon 1.50 4.00
318 Christian Yelich 2.50 6.00
319 Evan Gattis .60 1.50
320 Henry Urrutia .40 1.00
321 Hyun-Jin Ryu .75 2.00
322 Jose Fernandez .75 2.00
323 Jurickson Profar .40 1.00
324 Manny Machado 2.00 5.00
325 Michael Wacha .40 1.00
326 Shelby Miller .75 2.00
327 Sonny Gray .50 1.25
328 Wil Myers .40 1.00
329 Zack Wheeler .60 1.50
330 Yasiel Puig 1.25 3.00

2013 Bowman Chrome Mini Black Refractors

*BLACK REF: 5X TO 12X BASIC
STATED PRINT RUN 25 SER.#'d SETS
311 Aaron Judge 200.00 500.0

2013 Bowman Chrome Mini Blu Refractors

*BLUE REF: 2X TO 5X BASIC
STATED PRINT RUN 99 SER.#'d SETS
311 Aaron Judge 100.00 250.0

2013 Bowman Chrome Mini Gol Refractors

*GOLD REF: 3X TO 3X BASIC
STATED PRINT RUN 50 SER.#'d SETS
311 Aaron Judge 150.00 400.0

2013 Bowman Chrome Mini Green Refractors

*GREEN REF: 2.5X TO 6X BASIC
STATED PRINT RUN 75 SER.#'d SETS
311 Aaron Judge 125.00 300.0

2013 Bowman Chrome Mini Refractors

*REFRACTORS: 1X TO 2.5X BASIC
STATED PRINT RUN 125 SER.#'d SETS
311 Aaron Judge 40.00 100.0

2013 Bowman Chrome Mini X-fractors

*X-FRACTORS: 2X TO 5X BASIC
STATED PRINT RUN 100 SER.#'d SETS
311 Aaron Judge 100.00 250.

2014 Bowman Chrome Mini Factory Set

PRINTING PLATE RANDOMLY INSERTED
PLATE PRINT RUN 1 SET PER COLOR
BLACK-CYAN-MAGENTA-YELLOW ISSUED
NO PLATE PRICING DUE TO SCARCITY
1 Kris Bryant 1.50 4.
2 Julio Urias 1.00 2.
3 Travis d'Arnaud .25
4 R.J. Alvarez .20
5 Akeem Bostick .20
6 Kelly Dugan .20
7 Ryan Hafner .20
8 Ryan Kussmaul .25
9 Ryan McNeil .20
10 Dom Nunez .20
11 Cam Perkins .20
12 Franmil Reyes .60 1
13 Dylan Unsworth .20
14 Robert Whalen .20
15 Spencer Adams .25

6 Bobby Bradley .25 .60
7 Michael Chavis 1.00 2.50
8 Dustin DeMuth .20 .50
9 Ti'Quan Forbes .20 .50
0 Taylor Gushue .20 .50
1 Brent Honeywell .30 .75
2 Michael Kopech .50 1.25
3 Brett Martin .20 .50
4 Corey Ray .20 .50
5 Ryan Ripken .25 .60
6 Casey Soltis .20 .50
7 Nick Torres .20 .50
8 Alex Verdugo .40 1.00
9 Mark Zagunis .20 .50
0 Franklin Barreto .30 .75
1 Billy Burns .20 .50
2 Victor De Leon .20 .50
3 Dylan Floro .25 .60
4 Alexander Guerrero .25 .60
5 Isiah Kiner-Falefa .30 .75
6 Seth Mejias-Brean .20 .50
7 Dillon Overton .20 .50
8 Cody Reed .20 .50
9 Gabriel Rosa .20 .50
0 Chris Taylor 1.00 2.50
1 Taijuan Walker .20 .50
2 Jeff Ames .20 .50
3 Aaron Brooks .30 .75
4 Fred Lewis .20 .50
5 Rafael Medina .20 .50
6 Michael O'Neill .20 .50
7 Chad Pinder .20 .50
8 Jonathan Reynoso .20 .50
9 Ariel Soriano .20 .50
0 Jose Urena .25 .60
1 Matt Whitehouse .20 .50
2 Blake Anderson .20 .50
3 Jeff Brigham .20 .50
4 Isan Diaz .50 1.25
5 Austin Gomber .25 .60
6 Monte Harrison .30 .75
7 Rhys Hoskins 3.00 8.00
8 Gavin LaValley .20 .50
9 Chris Oliver .20 .50
0 A.J. Reed .40 1.00
1 Carson Sands .20 .50
2 Taylor Sparks .20 .50
3 Sam Travis .40 1.00
4 Jared Walker .20 .50
5 Jake Barrett .25 .60
6 Jacob deGrom 1.25 3.00
7 Maikel Franco .25 .60
8 Josh Hader .50 1.25
9 Chris Kohler .20 .50
0 Melvin Mercedes .20 .50
1 Daniel Palka .20 .50
2 Alex Reyes .30 .75
3 Anthony Santander .25 .60
4 Lewis Thorpe .20 .50
5 Levon Washington .20 .50
6 Cody Anderson .20 .50
7 Andy Burns .20 .50
8 Kevin Encarnacion .20 .50
9 Chris Heston .20 .50
0 Dawel Lugo .20 .50
1 Yonathan Mejia .20 .50
2 Wilmer Oberto .20 .50
3 Luigi Rodriguez .20 .50
4 Richard Urena .25 .60
5 Austin Wilson .20 .50
6 Brian Anderson .20 .50
7 Aaron Brown .20 .50
8 Jake Cosart .25 .60
9 Chris Ellis .20 .50
0 Jace Fry .20 .50
1 Brian Gonzalez .20 .50
2 Sam Hentges .20 .50
3 Zech Lemond .20 .50
4 Jordan Montgomery .40 1.00
5 Luis Ortiz .20 .50
6 Cody Reed .20 .50
7 Brian Schales .20 .50
8 Miguel Sano .25 .60
9 Forrest Wall .30 .75
00 Anthony Aliotti .20 .50
01 Wuilmer Becerra .20 .50
02 Michael Choice .20 .50
03 Miller Diaz .20 .50
04 John Gant .20 .50
05 Ryon Healy .30 .75
06 Ben Lively .20 .50
07 Leonardo Molina .20 .50
08 Jordan Paroubeck .20 .50
09 D.J. Peterson .20 .50
10 Gus Schlosser .20 .50
11 Andrew Thurman .20 .50
12 Joe Wendle .20 .50
13 Elvis Araujo .20 .50
14 Victor Caratini .60 1.50
15 Thairo Estrada .75 2.00
16 JaCoby Jones .30 .75
17 Tyler Mahle .20 .50
18 Nathan Mikolas .20 .50
19 Dalton Pompey .30 .75
20 Jose Rondon .20 .50
21 Teddy Stankiewicz .20 .50
22 Sebastian Vader .20 .50
23 Daniel Winkler .20 .50
24 Brett Austin .20 .50
25 Nick Burdi .20 .50
26 Austin Cousino .20 .50
27 Garrett Fulenchek .20 .50
28 Nick Gordon .25 .60
129 Carlos Correa 1.00 2.50
130 Jacob Lindgren .25 .60
131 Andrew Morales .20 .50
132 Kevin Padlo .20 .50
133 Jake Reed .20 .50
134 Jake Stinnett .20 .50
135 Spencer Turnbull .20 .50
136 Luke Weaver .60 1.50
137 Yency Almonte .20 .50
138 Mookie Betts 4.00 10.00
139 Carlos Contreras .20 .50
140 Yimi Garcia .20 .50
141 Jose Herrera .20 .50
142 Manuel Margot .30 .75
143 Sam Moll .20 .50
144 Victor Payano .20 .50
145 Wendell Rijo .20 .50
146 Jonathan Schoop .20 .50
147 Devon Travis .20 .50
148 Devin Williams .50 1.25
149 Trae Arbet .20 .50
150 Ryan Casteel .20 .50
151 Buck Farmer .20 .50
152 Felix Jorge .20 .50
153 Adrian Marin .20 .50
154 Amaurys Minier .20 .50
155 Michael Ohlman .20 .50
156 Jose Pujols .20 .50
157 Jake Sanchez .20 .50
158 Breyvic Valera .20 .50
159 Kean Wong .20 .50
160 Ryan Castellani .20 .50
161 Braxton Davidson .20 .50
162 Raul Mondesi .60 1.50
163 Aramis Garcia .20 .50
164 Daniel Gossett .20 .50
165 Grant Hockin .20 .50
166 Trace Loehr .20 .50
167 Gareth Morgan .20 .50
168 Miko Papi .20 .50
169 Jakson Reetz .20 .50
170 Lucas Giolito .30 .75
171 Troy Stokes .20 .50
172 Chase Anderson .20 .50
173 Christian Binford .20 .50
174 Tim Cooney .20 .50
175 Michael Feliz .25 .60
176 Kenny Giles .25 .60
177 Rosell Herrera .30 .75
178 Tyler Marlette .20 .50
179 Akeel Morris .20 .50
180 Shawn Pleffner .20 .50
181 Armando Rivero .20 .50
182 Ryne Stanek .20 .50
183 Brandon Trinkwon .25 .60
184 Austin Wright .20 .50
185 Erisbel Arruebarrena .20 .50
186 Johnny Field .20 .50
187 Clint Frazier .75 2.00
188 Raul Mondesi .60 1.50
189 Jordan Patterson .20 .50
190 Harold Ramirez .30 .75
191 Roenis Elias .20 .50
192 Vincent Velasquez .30 .75
193 Kolten Wong .25 .60
194 Alex Blandino .20 .50
195 Dylan Cease .50 1.25
196 Dylan Davis .25 .60
197 Derek Fisher .30 .75
198 Jacob Gatewood .20 .50
199 Brett Graves .20 .50
200 Jeff Hoffman .30 .75
201 Connor Joe .20 .50
202 Jordan Luplow .20 .50
203 Josh Morgan .20 .50
204 Sean Reid-Foley .20 .50
205 Justus Sheffield .40 1.00
206 Wyatt Strahan .20 .50
207 Braden Shipley .20 .50
208 Justin Twine .20 .50
209 Ronnie Williams .20 .50
210 Tim Anderson .40 1.00
211 Miguel Alfredo Gonzalez .20 .50
212 Jason Hursh .20 .50
213 Jacob May .25 .60
214 Jorge Alfaro .25 .60
215 C.J. Edwards .25 .60
216 Daniel Robertson .25 .60
217 Blake Swihart .25 .60
218 Joey Gallo .40 1.00
219 Gabriel Ynoa .25 .60
220 Logan Bawcom .20 .50
221 Taylor Cole .20 .50
222 Willy Garcia .20 .50
223 Nick Kingham .25 .60
224 L.J. Mazzilli .20 .50
225 Austin Nola .25 .60
226 Spencer Patton .20 .50
227 Jose Ramirez .20 .50
228 Juan Silva .20 .50
229 Alberto Tirado .20 .50
230 Bobby Wahl .20 .50
231 Chris Owings .20 .50
232 Scott Blewett .20 .50
233 Michael Cederoth .25 .60
234 J.D. Davis .30 .75
235 Jack Flaherty .75 2.00
236 Joe Gatto .20 .50
237 Grayson Greiner .20 .50
238 Jonathan Holder .20 .50
239 Mitch Keller .30 .75
240 Michael Mader .20 .50
241 Michael Taylor .25 .60
242 Matt Railey .20 .50
243 Dominic Smith .20 .50
244 Trey Supak .20 .50
245 Chase Vallot .20 .50
246 Rougned Odor .40 1.00
247 Orlando Arcia .30 .75
248 Zach Borenstein .25 .60
249 Brandon Cumpton .20 .50
250 Kendry Flores .20 .50
251 Drew Granier .20 .50
252 Luke Jackson .20 .50
253 Santiago Nessy .20 .50
254 Steven Ramos .20 .50
255 Nelson Rodriguez .25 .60
256 Tim Berry .20 .50
257 Brandon Dixon .20 .50
258 Trevor Gretzky .20 .50
259 Corey Knebel .20 .50
260 Jeff McNeil 1.25 3.00
261 Kohl Stewart .20 .50
262 James Paxton .30 .75
263 Nick Ramirez .20 .50
264 Shae Simmons .20 .50
265 Stuart Turner .20 .50
266 Jamie Westbrook .20 .50
267 Luis Sardinas .20 .50
268 Albert Almora .30 .75
269 Matt Chapman 1.00 2.50
270 Austin DeCarr .20 .50
271 Jordan Foley .20 .50
272 Michael Gettys .25 .60
273 Foster Griffin .20 .50
274 Grant Holmes .20 .50
275 Johnny Manziel
276 Milton Ramos .20 .50
277 John Richy .20 .50
278 Corey Seager .75 2.00
279 Lane Thomas .20 .50
280 Cameron Varga .20 .50
281 Ryan Yarbrough .30 .75
282 Trey Ball .20 .50
283 Matthew Bowman .20 .50
284 Wilmer Flores .25 .60
285 Robert Gsellman .25 .60
286 Eric Jagielo .20 .50
287 Matt McPhearson .20 .50
288 Tucker Neuhaus .20 .50
289 Michael Ratterree .20 .50
290 Jason Rogers .20 .50
291 Raimel Tapia .25 .60
292 Logan Vick .20 .50
293 Casey Gillaspie .30 .75
294 Aaron Nola 1.25 3.00
295 Michael Conforto .40 1.00
296 Kyle Freeland .40 1.00
297 Bradley Zimmer .30 .75
298 Nick Howard .20 .50
299 Erick Fedde .20 .50
300 Trea Turner .60 1.50
301 Kodi Medeiros .20 .50
302 Kyle Schwarber .75 2.00
303 Tyler Beede .30 .75
304 Alex Jackson .25 .60
305 Max Pentecost .20 .50
306 Nomar Mazara .50 1.25
307 Tyler Kolek .20 .50
308 Sean Newcomb .30 .75
309 Luis Severino .30 .75
310 Hunter Harvey .20 .50
311 Hunter Dozier .20 .50
312 Jose Berrios .30 .75
313 Cole Tucker .20 .50
314 Derek Hill .20 .50
315 Austin Meadows .30 .75
316 Gosuke Katoh .30 .75
317 Mark Appel .25 .60
318 Tyler Glasnow .30 .75
319 J.P. Crawford .20 .50
320 Masahiro Tanaka .60 1.50
321 Jose Abreu 1.50 4.00
322 Gregory Polanco .30 .75
323 George Springer .75 2.00
324 Oscar Taveras .25 .60
325 Billy Hamilton .25 .60
326 Nick Castellanos .60 1.50
327 Garin Cecchini .20 .50
328 Xander Bogaerts .60 1.50
329 Yordano Ventura .25 .60
330 Jon Singleton .25 .60

2014 Bowman Chrome Mini Factory Set Black Shimmer Refractors

*BLACK SHIMMER: 3X TO 8X BASIC
OVERALL 30 REF.PER FACTORY SET

2014 Bowman Chrome Mini Factory Set Blue Refractors

*BLUE REF: 4X TO 10X BASIC
OVERALL 30 REF.PER FACTORY SET
STATED PRINT RUN 20 SER.#'d SETS
1 Kris Bryant 40.00 100.00

2014 Bowman Chrome Mini Factory Set Refractors

*REF:1.5X TO 4X BASIC
OVERALL 30 REF.PER FACTORY SET

2014 Bowman Chrome Mini Factory Set Yellow Refractors

*YELLOW REF: 5X TO 12X BASIC
OVERALL 30 REF.PER FACTORY SET
STATED PRINT RUN 25 SER.#'d SETS
1 Kris Bryant 40.00 100.00

2017 Bowman Chrome Mini

OVERALL 30 PARALLELS PER SET
PLATE PRINT RUN 1 SET PER COLOR
BLACK-CYAN-MAGENTA-YELLOW ISSUED
NO PLATE PRICING DUE TO SCARCITY
2 Jesse Winker .40 1.00
4 Jeff Hoffman .40 1.00
18 Joe Jimenez .40 1.00
20 Manny Margot .40 1.00
22 Carson Fulmer .40 1.00
23 Andrew Benintendi 1.25 3.00
25 Yoan Moncada 1.25 3.00
26 Teoscar Hernandez 1.25 3.00
27 Reynaldo Lopez .40 1.00
27 Cody Bellinger 6.00 15.00
29 Yulieski Gurriel .60 1.50
29 Christian Arroyo .60 1.50
32 Aaron Judge 5.00 12.00
34 Robert Gsellman .40 1.00
35 Ryon Healy .50 1.25
41 Orlando Arcia .60 1.50
42 Jose De Leon .40 1.00
42 Mitch Haniger .60 1.50
44 Jordan Montgomery .60 1.50
54 David Dahl .50 1.25
55 Rob Segedin .40 1.00
56 Tyler Glasnow .50 1.25
57 Dansby Swanson 1.00 2.50
60 Jorge Alfaro .50 1.25
62 Jake Thompson .40 1.00
63 Hunter Dozier .40 1.00
64 Matt Strahm .40 1.00
66 Gavin Cecchini .40 1.00
70 Josh Bell 1.00 2.50
75 Alex Bregman 1.50 4.00
78 Raimel Tapia .50 1.25
83 Braden Shipley .40 1.00
86 Tyler Austin .60 1.50
89 Jharel Cotton .40 1.00
92 Joe Musgrove .40 1.00
95 Amir Garrett .40 1.00
98 Alex Reyes .50 1.25
99 Hunter Renfroe .50 1.25

2017 Bowman Chrome Mini 70th Blue Refractors

*70TH BLUE REF: 2X TO 5X BASIC
OVERALL 30 PARALLELS PER SET
STATED PRINT RUN 70 SER.#'d SETS

2017 Bowman Chrome Mini Black Shimmer Refractors

*BLACK SHIMMER REF: 2X TO 5X BASIC
OVERALL 30 PARALLELS PER SET
STATED PRINT RUN 100 SER.#'d SETS

2017 Bowman Chrome Mini Blue Shimmer Refractors

*BLUE SHIMMER REF: 1.5X TO 4X BASIC
OVERALL 30 PARALLELS PER SET
STATED PRINT RUN 150 SER.#'d SETS

2017 Bowman Chrome Mini Gold Refractors

*GOLD REF: 2.5X TO 6X BASIC
OVERALL 30 PARALLELS PER SET
STATED PRINT RUN 50 SER.#'d SETS

2017 Bowman Chrome Mini Green Refractors

*GREEN REF: 2X TO 5X BASIC
OVERALL 30 PARALLELS PER SET
STATED PRINT RUN 99 SER.#'d SETS

2017 Bowman Chrome Mini Orange Refractors

*ORANGE REF: 5X TO 12X BASIC
OVERALL 30 PARALLELS PER SET
STATED PRINT RUN 25 SER.#'d SETS

2017 Bowman Chrome Mini Refractors

*REF: .75X TO 2X BASIC
OVERALL 30 PARALLELS PER SET

2017 Bowman Chrome Mini Prospects

OVERALL 30 PARALLELS PER SET
PLATE PRINT RUN 1 SET PER COLOR
BLACK-CYAN-MAGENTA-YELLOW ISSUED
NO PLATE PRICING DUE TO SCARCITY
BCP1 Nick Senzel .75 2.00
BCP2 Gavin Lux 1.50 4.00
BCP3 Ronald Guzman .30 .75
BCP4 A.J. Puckett .25 .60
BCP5 Mike Soroka .75 2.00
BCP6 Roniel Raudes .25 .60
BCP7 Lucas Erceg .30 .75
BCP8 Luis Almanzar .25 .60
BCP9 Beau Burrows .25 .60
BCP10 Chase Vallot .25 .60
BCP11 P.J. Conlon .25 .60
BCP12 Erick Fedde .25 .60
BCP13 Rookie Davis .25 .60
BCP14 Chris Shaw .25 .60
BCP15 Nick Burdi .25 .60
BCP16 Clint Frazier .50 1.25
BCP17 Luiz Gohara .25 .60
BCP18 Lourdes Gurriel Jr. .40 1.00
BCP19 Eric Jenkins .25 .60
BCP20 Angel Perdomo .25 .60
BCP21 Dustin May 1.50 4.00
BCP22 Freddy Peralta .40 1.00
BCP23 Jarlin Garcia .25 .60
BCP24 Tyler O'Neill .30 .75
BCP25 Lazarito Armenteros .60 1.50
BCP26 Paul De Jong .75 2.00
BCP27 Antonio Senzatela .25 .60
BCP28 Kyle Tucker .50 1.25
BCP29 Aramis Garcia .25 .60
BCP30 Willie Calhoun .40 1.00
BCP31 Chance Adams .40 1.00
BCP32 Vladimir Guerrero Jr. 3.00 8.00
BCP33 Braxton Garrett .25 .60
BCP34 Yeudy Garcia .25 .60
BCP35 Dane Dunning .25 .60
BCP36 Andy Ibanez .25 .60
BCP37 Francisco Rios .25 .60
BCP38 Joe Jimenez .25 .60
BCP39 Dylan Cozens .25 .60
BCP40 Mauricio Dubon .30 .75
BCP41 Franklyn Kilome .30 .75
BCP42 Chance Sisco .50 1.25
BCP43 Sandy Alcantara .30 .75
BCP44 Stephen Gonsalves .25 .60
BCP45 Grant Holmes .25 .60
BCP46 Dakota Chalmers .25 .60
BCP47 Kolby Allard .25 .60
BCP48 Tyler Alexander .25 .60
BCP49 Phil Bickford .25 .60
BCP50 Eloy Jimenez 1.00 2.50
BCP51 Francisco Mejia .40 1.00
BCP52 Kohl Stewart .25 .60
BCP53 Garrett Whitley .25 .60
BCP54 Anderson Espinoza .25 .60
BCP55 Cal Quantrill .25 .60
BCP56 Tetsuto Yamada .50 1.25
BCP57 Tyler Beede .25 .60
BCP58 Jake Bauers .30 .75
BCP59 Ariel Jurado .25 .60
BCP60 Austin Voth .25 .60
BCP61 Tyler Stephenson .25 .60
BCP62 Yoshitomo Tsutsugo .40 1.00
BCP63 Dominic Smith .25 .60
BCP64 Matt Thaiss .25 .60
BCP65 Austin Meadows .40 1.00
BCP66 Mitch Keller .30 .75
BCP67 Jahmai Jones .25 .60
BCP68 Alex Speas .25 .60
BCP69 Nolan Jones .40 1.00
BCP70 Kevin Newman .40 1.00
BCP71 T.J. Friedl .25 .60
BCP72 Oscar De La Cruz .25 .60
BCP73 Victor Robles .60 1.50
BCP74 Patrick Weigel .25 .60
BCP75 Ryan Mountcastle .40 1.00
BCP76 Amed Rosario .40 1.00
BCP77 Nick Solak .60 1.50
BCP78 Abrahan Gutierrez .40 1.00
BCP79 Yu-Cheng Chang .40 1.00
BCP80 Gleyber Torres 4.00 10.00
BCP81 J.D. Davis .30 .75
BCP82 Walker Buehler .60 1.50
BCP83 Andrew Sopko .25 .60
BCP84 Brent Honeywell .30 .75
BCP85 Kyle Funkhouser .30 .75
BCP86 Brian Mundell .25 .60
BCP87 Brian Anderson .30 .75
BCP88 Brendan Rodgers .30 .75
BCP89 Josh Staumont .25 .60
BCP90 Cody Sedlock .25 .60
BCP91 D.J. Stewart .25 .60
BCP92 Wuilmer Becerra .25 .60
BCP93 Nate Smith .25 .60
BCP94 Alfredo Rodriguez .30 .75
BCP95 Daz Cameron .25 .60
BCP96 Taylor Ward .30 .75
BCP97 Takahiro Norimoto .25 .60
BCP98 Tomoyuki Sugano .40 1.00
BCP99 Drew Jackson .25 .60
BCP100 Kevin Maitan .60 1.50
BCP101 Rafael Devers .50 1.25
BCP102 Alex Kirilloff .60 1.50
BCP103 Jack Flaherty .40 1.00
BCP104 Adonis Medina .40 1.00
BCP105 Ke'Bryan Hayes .25 .60
BCP106 Josh Hader .25 .60
BCP107 Luis Urias 1.00 2.50
BCP108 Donnie Dewees .25 .60
BCP109 Kyle Freeland .30 .75
BCP110 Matt Chapman .40 1.00
BCP111 Sam Coonrod .25 .60
BCP112 Andrew Suarez .25 .60
BCP113 David Fletcher .75 2.00
BCP114 Tyler Jay .25 .60
BCP115 Franklin Barreto .25 .60
BCP116 Michael Kopech .50 1.25
BCP117 Rhys Hoskins 1.00 2.50
BCP118 Triston McKenzie .25 .60
BCP119 Luis Garcia .75 2.00
BCP120 Harold Ramirez .30 .75
BCP121 Blake Rutherford .40 1.00
BCP122 Matt Manning .40 1.00
BCP123 Josh Morgan .25 .60
BCP124 Dylan Cease .60 1.50
BCP125 Kyle Lewis .50 1.25
BCP126 Nick Neidert .25 .60
BCP127 Ronald Acuna 30.00 80.00
BCP128 Luis Ortiz .25 .60
BCP129 Isael Soto .25 .60
BCP130 Adrian Morejon .40 1.00
BCP131 Mark Zagunis .25 .60
BCP132 Justus Sheffield .40 1.00
BCP133 Jaime Schultz .25 .60
BCP134 Fernando Romero .25 .60
BCP135 Mickey Moniak .60 1.50
BCP136 Jorge Bonifacio .25 .60
BCP137 Jomar Reyes .25 .60
BCP138 Thomas Szapucki .30 .75
BCP139 Sean Reid-Foley .25 .60
BCP140 Willy Adames .30 .75
BCP141 Yang Hyeon-Jong .30 .75
BCP142 Bo Bichette 1.00 2.50
BCP143 Harrison Bader .40 1.00
BCP144 Travis Demeritte .25 .60
BCP145 Juan Hillman .25 .60
BCP146 Francis Martes .25 .60
BCP147 Wilkerman Garcia .30 .75
BCP148 Christin Stewart .30 .75
BCP149 Cody Bellinger 4.00 10.00
BCP150 Jason Groome .50 1.25
BCP152 Andrew Moore .30 .75
BCP153 Albert Abreu .30 .75
BCP154 Max Schrock .40 1.00
BCP155 Jonathan Arauz .30 .75
BCP156 Max Fried 1.00 2.50
BCP157 Bobby Bradley .30 .75
BCP158 Leody Taveras .75 2.00
BCP159 Jacob Nottingham .25 .60
BCP160 Fernando Tatis Jr. 2.00 5.00
BCP161 Austin Riley .75 2.00
BCP162 Trevor Clifton .25 .60
BCP163 Anthony Banda .25 .60
BCP164 Richard Urena .40 1.00
BCP165 Reggie Lawson .25 .60
BCP166 Felix Jorge .25 .60
BCP168 Jorge Ona .30 .75
BCP169 Brandon Woodruff .25 .60
BCP170 Sam Travis .25 .60
BCP171 Derek Fisher .30 .75
BCP172 Touki Toussaint .30 .75
BCP173 Forrest Whitley .75 2.00
BCP174 Scott Kingery .40 1.00
BCP175 Jorge Mateo .25 .60
BCP176 Joshua Lowe .25 .60
BCP177 Rowdy Tellez .25 .60
BCP178 Kevin Kramer .25 .60
BCP179 Desmond Lindsay .25 .60
BCP180 Juan Soto 6.00 15.00
BCP181 Isan Diaz .60 1.50
BCP182 Rob Kaminsky .25 .60
BCP183 Domingo Acevedo .25 .60
BCP185 Andy Yerzy .25 .60
BCP187 Tirso Ornelas .30 .75
BCP189 Adam Ravenelle .25 .60
BCP190 Mitchell White .40 1.00
BCP191 Dawel Lugo .25 .60
BCP192 Vladimir Gutierrez .25 .60
BCP193 Max Povse .25 .60
BCP194 Delvin Perez .40 1.00
BCP195 Jacob Nix .25 .60
BCP196 Josh Sborz .25 .60
BCP197 Torii Hunter Jr. .60 1.50
BCP199 Yasel Antuna 1.25 3.00
BCP201 Nick Gordon .25 .60
BCP202 Brett Phillips .30 .75
BCP203 Yairo Munoz .25 .60
BCP204 Bryan Reynolds .40 1.00
BCP205 Dakota Hudson .40 1.00
BCP206 Miguelangel Sierra .50 1.25
BCP207 Jazz Chisholm 1.00 2.50
BCP208 DJ Peters .60 1.50
BCP209 Jacob Faria .25 .60
BCP210 Sixto Sanchez .60 1.50
BCP211 Braden Bishop .40 1.00
BCP212 Ryan O'Hearn .50 1.25
BCP213 Garrett Stubbs .25 .60
BCP215 Trent Clark .25 .60
BCP216 Jose Albertos .60 1.50
BCP217 Ryan McMahon .25 .60
BCP218 Khalil Lee .40 1.00
BCP220 Steven Duggar .25 .60
BCP221 Franklin Perez .40 1.00
BCP222 Tomas Nido .25 .60
BCP223 Justin Dunn .25 .60
BCP224 Austin Hays .60 1.50
BCP226 Starling Heredia .50 1.25
BCP227 Bryson Brigman .25 .60
BCP228 Jesus Sanchez 1.25 3.00
BCP229 Yusniel Diaz .75 2.00
BCP232 Ian Anderson .60 1.50
BCP234 Jameson Fisher .25 .60
BCP236 Keegan Akin .30 .75
BCP237 James Kaprielian .25 .60
BCP238 Jeisson Rosario .30 .75
BCP239 Carter Kieboom .40 1.00
BCP240 Nick Williams .30 .75
BCP241 Brandon Marsh .60 1.50
BCP242 Wander Javier .25 .60
BCP243 Chris Paddack .60 1.50
BCP244 Luis Alexander Basabe .40 1.00
BCP245 Zack Burdi .25 .60
BCP246 Anthony Kay .25 .60
BCP247 Anderson Tejeda .25 .60
BCP248 Daniel Gossett .25 .60
BCP249 Heath Quinn .30 .75

2017 Bowman Chrome Mini Prospects 70th Blue Refractors

*70TH BLUE REF: 2.5X TO 6X BASIC
OVERALL 30 PARALLELS PER SET
STATED PRINT RUN 70 SER.#'d SETS
BCP127 Ronald Acuna 125.00 300.00

2017 Bowman Chrome Mini Prospects Black Shimmer Refractors

*BLACK SHIMMER: 2X TO 5X BASIC
OVERALL 30 PARALLELS PER SET
STATED PRINT RUN 100 SER.#'d SETS
BCP127 Ronald Acuna 100.00 250.00

2017 Bowman Chrome Mini Prospects Blue Shimmer Refractors

*BLUE SHIMMER REF: 1.5X TO 4X BASIC
OVERALL 30 PARALLELS PER SET
STATED PRINT RUN 150 SER.#'d SETS
BCP127 Ronald Acuna 75.00 200.00

2017 Bowman Chrome Mini Prospects Gold Refractors

*GOLD REF: 3X TO 8X BASIC
OVERALL 50 PARALLELS PER SET
STATED PRINT RUN 50 SER.#'d SETS
BCP127 Ronald Acuna 150.00 400.00

2017 Bowman Chrome Mini Prospects Green Refractors

*GREEN REF: 2X TO 5X BASIC
OVERALL 30 PARALLELS PER SET
STATED PRINT RUN 99 SER.#'d SETS
BCP127 Ronald Acuna 100.00 250.00

2017 Bowman Chrome Mini Prospects Orange Refractors

*ORANGE REF: 4X TO 10X BASIC
OVERALL 30 PARALLELS PER SET
STATED PRINT RUN 25 SER.#'d SETS
BCP127 Ronald Acuna 200.00 500.00

2017 Bowman Chrome Mini Prospects Refractors

*REF: 1.2X TO 3X BASIC
OVERALL 30 PARALLELS PER SET
BCP127 Ronald Acuna 40.00 100.00

2019 Bowman Heritage

COMPLETE SET (118) 25.00 60.00
53VR1 Mike Trout 1.50 4.00
53VR2 Justin Verlander .30 .75
53VR3 Chris Archer .20 .50
53VR4 Carter Kieboom RC .60 1.50
53VR5 Whit Merrifield .30 .75
53VR6 Josh Hader .20 .50
53VR7 Chance Adams RC .40 1.00
53VR8 Yoan Moncada .30 .75
53VR9 Zack Greinke .25 .60
53VR10 Juan Soto 1.00 2.50
53VR11 Willy Adames .20 .50
53VR12 Ronald Acuna Jr. 1.50 4.00
53VR13 David Fletcher RC 1.25 3.00
53VR14 Josh James RC .60 1.50
53VR15 Evan Longoria .25 .60
53VR16 Joey Wendle .20 .50
53VR17 Michael Chavis RC .60 1.50
53VR18 Ryan Helsley RC .50 1.25
53VR19 Jake Cave RC .50 1.25
53VR20 Kyle Freeland .25 .60
53VR21 Jacob deGrom .30 .75
53VR22 Scooter Gennett .25 .60
53VR23 Aaron Judge .75 2.00
53VR24 Rowdy Tellez RC .60 1.50
53VR25 Kolby Allard RC .60 1.50
53VR26 Vladimir Guerrero Jr. RC 2.50 6.00
53VR27 DJ Stewart RC .50 1.25
53VR28 Ryan O'Hearn RC .40 1.00
53VR29 Taylor Ward RC .40 1.00
53VR30 Fernando Tatis Jr. RC 6.00 15.00
53VR31 Mookie Betts .50 1.25
53VR32 Keston Hiura RC 1.25 3.00
53VR33 Jon Duplantier RC .40 1.00
53VR34 Brandon Crawford .25 .60
53VR35 Aramis Garcia RC .40 1.00
53VR36 Danny Jansen RC .40 1.00
53VR37 Michael Kopech RC .75 2.00
53VR38 Eddie Rosario .25 .60
53VR39 Maikel Franco .25 .60
53VR40 Cedric Mullins RC .60 1.50
53VR41 Willians Astudillo RC .40 1.00
53VR42 Brian Anderson .20 .50
53VR43 Kevin Newman RC .60 1.50
53VR44 Jose Altuve .25 .60
53VR45 Ramon Laureano RC .75 2.00
53VR46 Chris Shaw RC .60 1.50
53VR47 Nick Senzel RC 1.25 3.00
53VR48 Kyle Tucker RC .75 2.00
53VR49 Trey Mancini .25 .60
53VR50 Bryce Harper .50 1.25
53VR51 Steven Duggar RC .50 1.25
53VR52 Nicholas Castellanos .30 .75
53VR53 Dakota Hudson RC .50 1.25
53VR54 Salvador Perez .25 .60
53VR55 Mitch Keller RC .50 1.25
53VR56 Jose Abreu .30 .75
53VR57 Paul Goldschmidt .30 .75
53VR58 Edwin Diaz .25 .60
53VR59 Cal Quantrill RC .40 1.00
53VR60 Clayton Kershaw .60 1.50
53VR61 Kevin Pillar .20 .50
53VR62 Ronald Guzman .20 .50
53VR63 Amed Rosario .25 .60
53VR64 Mychal Givens .20 .50
53VR65 Marcus Stroman .25 .60
53VR66 Ryan Borucki RC .40 1.00
53VR67 J.T. Realmuto .30 .75
53VR68 Rougned Odor .25 .60
53VR69 Francisco Arcia RC .60 1.50
53VR70 Eric Hosmer .25 .60
53VR71 J.D. Martinez .30 .75
53VR72 Dawel Lugo RC .60 1.50
53VR73 Christin Stewart RC .50 1.25
53VR74 Starling Marte .25 .60
53VR75 Max Scherzer .30 .75
53VR76 Peter Lambert RC .60 1.50
53VR77 Griffin Canning RC .60 1.50
53VR78 Luis Urias RC .60 1.50
53VR79 Brad Keller RC .40 1.00
53VR80 Ozzie Albies .30 .75
53VR81 Sean Reid-Foley RC .40 1.00
53VR82 Justus Sheffield RC .60 1.50
53VR83 Bryse Wilson RC .50 1.25
53VR84 Luis Guillorme RC .40 1.00
53VR85 Matt Chapman .30 .75
53VR86 Enyel De Los Santos RC .40 1.00
53VR87 Matt Carpenter .30 .75

53VR88 Touki Toussaint RC .50 1.25
53VR89 Jose Ramirez .25 .60
53VR90 Jeff McNeil RC 1.00 2.50
53VR91 Andrew Knizner RC .60 1.50
53VR92 Shohei Ohtani .40 1.00
53VR93 Anthony Rizzo .50 1.25
53VR94 Eloy Jimenez RC 1.50 4.00
53VR95 Mitch Haniger .25 .60
53VR96 Adolis Garcia RC .40 1.00
53VR97 Giancarlo Stanton .30 .75
53VR98 Khris Davis .30 .75
53VR99 Miguel Cabrera .30 .75
53VR100 Christian Yelich .40 1.00
53VR101 Cody Bellinger .60 1.50
53VR102 Brandon Lowe RC .60 1.50
53VR103 Kevin Kramer RC .50 1.25
53VR104 Jose Berrios .25 .60
53VR105 Jake Bauers RC .60 1.50
53VR106 Francisco Lindor .30 .75
53VR107 Will Smith RC 1.00 2.50
53VR108 Corbin Burnes RC .60 1.50
53VR109 Kyle Wright RC .60 1.50
53VR110 Chris Paddack RC .75 2.00
53VR111 Wil Myers .20 .50
53VR112 Nolan Arenado .40 1.00
53VR113 Jonathan Loaisiga RC .50 1.25
53VR114 Eugenio Suarez .25 .60
53VR115 Yadier Molina .30 .75
53VR116 Kris Bryant .40 1.00
53VR117 Aaron Nola .25 .60
53VR118 Pete Alonso RC 3.00 8.00

2019 Bowman Heritage Black and White

*BW: 1.2X TO 3X BASIC
*BW RC: .6X TO 1.5X BASIC RC
RANDOM INSERTS IN PACKS
53VR26 Vladimir Guerrero Jr. 15.00 40.00
53VR30 Fernando Tatis Jr. 20.00 50.00
53VR118 Pete Alonso 10.00 25.00

2019 Bowman Heritage Chrome Prospect Autographs

RANDOM INSERTS IN PACKS
PRINTING PLATES RANDOMLY INSERTED
PLATE PRINT RUN 1 SET PER COLOR
BLACK-CYAN-MAGENTA-YELLOW ISSUED
NO PLATE PRICING DUE TO SCARCITY
53PAAB Alec Bohm 15.00 40.00
53PABD Brock Deatherage 3.00 8.00
53PACC Conner Capel 4.00 10.00
53PACM Casey Mize 20.00 50.00
53PACMI Cal Mitchell 5.00 12.00
53PACS Cristian Santana 5.00 12.00
53PACSP Chad Spanberger 3.00 8.00
53PADK Dean Kremer 4.00 10.00
53PAGC Gabriel Cancel 5.00 12.00
53PAJB Joey Bart 30.00 80.00
53PAJPM Julio Pablo Martinez 3.00 8.00
53PAJR Julio Rodriguez 50.00 120.00
53PAMG Mateo Gil 4.00 10.00
53PAML Marco Luciano 40.00 100.00
53PAMM Mason Martin 10.00 25.00
53PANM Nick Madrigal 12.00 30.00
53PARB Rylan Bannon 4.00 10.00
53PARC Ryan Costello 4.00 10.00
53PARR Roberto Ramos 4.00 10.00
53PASW Steele Walker
53PAVF Vince Fernandez 4.00 10.00
53PAVMJ Victor Mesa Jr. 8.00 20.00
53PAVVM Victor Victor Mesa 6.00 15.00
53PAWF Wander Franco 100.00 250.00

2019 Bowman Heritage Chrome Prospect Autographs Gold Refractors

*GOLD REF: 1X TO 2.5X BASIC
RANDOM INSERTS IN PACKS
STATED PRINT RUN 50 SER.#'d SETS
53PASW Steele Walker 10.00 25.00
53PAWF Wander Franco 400.00 1000.00

2019 Bowman Heritage Chrome Prospect Autographs Orange Refractors

*ORANGE REF: 1.2X TO 3X BASIC
RANDOM INSERTS IN PACKS
STATED PRINT RUN 25 SER.#'d SETS
53PASW Steele Walker 12.00 30.00
53PAWF Wander Franco 500.00 1200.00

2019 Bowman Heritage Chrome Prospects

RANDOM INSERTS IN PACKS
*REF/199: 2X TO 5X BASIC
*BLUE REF/99: 4X TO 10X BASIC
*YLLW REF/75: 5X TO 12X BASIC
*GOLD REF/50: 6X TO 15X BASIC
*ORNGE REF/25: 10X TO 25X BASIC
53CP1 Wander Franco 3.00 8.00
53CP2 Blake Rutherford .20 .50
53CP3 Heliot Ramos .30 .75
53CP4 Beau Burrows .20 .50
53CP5 Ronny Mauricio .50 1.25
53CP6 Drew Waters .60 1.50
53CP7 Matt Mercer .20 .50
53CP8 Brewer Hicklen .30 .75
53CP9 Ryan Vilade .20 .50
53CP10 Chad Spanberger .20 .50
53CP11 Dylan Cease .50 1.25
53CP12 Edward Cabrera .30 .75
53CP13 Jordyn Adams .25 .60
53CP14 Austin Beck .20 .50
53CP15 Alex Faedo .25 .60
53CP16 Domingo Acevedo .20 .50
53CP17 Matt Manning .30 .75
53CP18 Julio Rodriguez 1.50 4.00
53CP19 Reggie Lawson .20 .50
53CP20 Anthony Seigler .30 .75
53CP21 Jose de la Cruz .60 1.50
53CP22 MJ Melendez .30 .75
53CP23 Alex Kirilloff .30 .75
53CP24 Adonis Medina .30 .75
53CP25 Victor Mesa Jr. .50 1.25
53CP26 Sixto Sanchez .25 .60
53CP27 William Contreras .25 .60
53CP28 Hunter Greene .30 .75
53CP29 Noelvi Marte .75 2.00
53CP30 Orelvis Martinez .50 1.25
53CP31 Adam Haseley .30 .75
53CP32 Travis Swaggerty .30 .75
53CP33 Seth Beer .50 1.25
53CP34 Brendan Rodgers .30 .75
53CP35 Jarred Kelenic .75 2.00
53CP36 Nick Madrigal .60 1.50
53CP37 Julio Pablo Martinez .20 .50
53CP38 Kevin Smith .20 .50
53CP39 Taylor Trammell .25 .60
53CP40 Taylor Widener .20 .50
53CP41 Ryan McKenna .20 .50
53CP42 Brandon Marsh .20 .50
53CP43 Franklyn Kilome .20 .50
53CP44 Lyon Richardson .25 .60
53CP45 DJ Peters .30 .75
53CP46 Royce Lewis .40 1.00
53CP47 Gavin Lux .60 1.50
53CP48 Colton Welker .20 .50
53CP49 Alec Bohm .75 2.00
53CP50 Luis Robert 2.00 5.00
53CP51 Ryan Mountcastle .25 .60
53CP52 Brent Rooker .25 .60
53CP53 Brent Honeywell .25 .60
53CP54 Nick Neidert .20 .50
53CP55 Daniel Johnson .20 .50
53CP56 Derian Cruz .20 .50
53CP57 Aramis Ademan .20 .50
53CP58 Joey Wentz .20 .50
53CP59 Anthony Kay .20 .50
53CP60 Nate Pearson .50 1.25
53CP61 Ian Anderson .50 1.25
53CP62 Forrest Whitley .30 .75
53CP63 Cole Ragans .20 .50
53CP64 Ronaldo Hernandez .20 .50
53CP65 Jeter Downs .30 .75
53CP66 Sandro Fabian .20 .50
53CP67 Cristian Santana .30 .75
53CP68 Keibert Ruiz .50 1.25
53CP69 Ke'Bryan Hayes .20 .50
53CP70 Cristian Pache .50 1.25
53CP71 Joey Bart .60 1.50
53CP72 Cole Winn .20 .50
53CP73 Jonathan India .25 .60
53CP74 Ryan Weathers .25 .60
53CP75 Luken Baker .25 .60
53CP76 Justin Dunn .20 .50
53CP77 Nolan Gorman .60 1.50
53CP78 Bo Bichette .60 1.50
53CP79 Esteury Ruiz .25 .60
53CP80 Genesis Cabrera .30 .75
53CP81 Sean Murphy .25 .60
53CP82 Ryan Costello .25 .60
53CP83 Freudis Nova .30 .75
53CP84 Albert Abreu .20 .50
53CP85 Jazz Chisholm .50 1.25
53CP86 Logan Webb .30 .75
53CP87 Shane Baz .20 .50
53CP88 Marco Luciano 1.25 3.00
53CP89 Nico Hoerner .60 1.50
53CP90 A.J. Puk .25 .60
53CP91 Jesus Sanchez .20 .50
53CP92 Cole Tucker .20 .50
53CP93 Blaze Alexander .20 .50
53CP94 Triston McKenzie .20 .50
53CP95 Franklin Perez .20 .50
53CP96 Jonathan Hernandez .20 .50
53CP97 Rylan Bannon .20 .50
53CP98 Andres Gimenez .25 .60
53CP99 Keegan Thompson .20 .50
53CP100 Jo Adell .60 1.50
53CP101 Evan White .30 .75
53CP102 Dustin May .60 1.50
53CP103 Daz Cameron .20 .50
53CP104 Brady Singer .40 1.00
53CP105 Victor Victor Mesa .40 1.00
53CP106 Ethan Hankins .25 .60
53CP107 Yusniel Diaz .30 .75
53CP108 Brock Burke .20 .50
53CP109 Bryan Mata .20 .50
53CP110 Luis Garcia .25 .60
53CP111 Matthew Liberatore .20 .50
53CP112 Adrian Morejon .20 .50
53CP113 DL Hall .20 .50
53CP114 Cristian Javier .25 .60
53CP115 Michel Baez .20 .50
53CP116 Roberto Ramos .25 .60
53CP117 Dane Dunning .20 .50
53CP118 Jesus Luzardo .30 .75
53CP119 MacKenzie Gore .40 1.00
53CP120 Brendan McKay .30 .75
53CP121 Leody Taveras .20 .50
53CP122 JoJo Romero .20 .50
53CP123 Tirso Ornelas .20 .50
53CP124 Jay Groome .20 .50
53CP125 Estevan Florial .30 .75
53CP126 Brusdar Graterol .25 .60
53CP127 Miguel Amaya .30 .75
53CP128 Corey Ray .20 .50
53CP129 Casey Mize .50 1.25

2019 Bowman Heritage Chrome Rookie Autographs

RANDOM INSERTS IN PACKS
PRINTING PLATES RANDOMLY INSERTED
PLATE PRINT RUN 1 SET PER COLOR
BLACK-CYAN-MAGENTA-YELLOW ISSUED
NO PLATE PRICING DUE TO SCARCITY
53RACB Corbin Burnes
53RAEJ Eloy Jimenez 40.00 100.00
53RAKW Kyle Wright 5.00 12.00
53RAVGJ Vladimir Guerrero Jr. 75.00 200.00

2019 Bowman Heritage Chrome Rookie Autographs Gold Refractors

53RACB Corbin Burnes 8.00 20.00

2019 Bowman Heritage Chrome Rookie Autographs Orange Refractors

53RACB Corbin Burnes 12.00 30.00

2019 Bowman Heritage Prospects

53P1 Wander Franco 3.00 8.00
53P2 Blake Rutherford .20 .50
53P3 Heliot Ramos .30 .75
53P4 Beau Burrows .20 .50
53P5 Ronny Mauricio .50 1.25
53P6 Drew Waters .60 1.50
53P7 Matt Mercer .20 .50
53P8 Brewer Hicklen .30 .75
53P9 Ryan Vilade .20 .50
53P10 Chad Spanberger .20 .50
53P11 Dylan Cease .50 1.25
53P12 Edward Cabrera .30 .75
53P13 Jordyn Adams .25 .60
53P14 Austin Beck .20 .50
53P15 Alex Faedo .25 .60
53P16 Domingo Acevedo .20 .50
53P17 Matt Manning .30 .75
53P18 Julio Rodriguez 1.50 4.00
53P19 Reggie Lawson .20 .50
53P20 Anthony Seigler .30 .75
53P21 Jose de la Cruz .60 1.50
53P22 MJ Melendez .30 .75
53P23 Alex Kirilloff .30 .75
53P24 Adonis Medina .30 .75
53P25 Victor Mesa Jr. .50 1.25
53P26 Sixto Sanchez .25 .60
53P27 William Contreras .25 .60
53P28 Hunter Greene .30 .75
53P29 Noelvi Marte .75 2.00
53P30 Orelvis Martinez .50 1.25
53P31 Adam Haseley .30 .75
53P32 Travis Swaggerty .30 .75
53P33 Seth Beer .50 1.25
53P34 Brendan Rodgers .30 .75
53P35 Jarred Kelenic .75 2.00
53P36 Nick Madrigal .60 1.50
53P37 Julio Pablo Martinez .20 .50
53P38 Kevin Smith .20 .50
53P39 Taylor Trammell .25 .60
53P40 Taylor Widener .20 .50
53P41 Ryan McKenna .20 .50
53P42 Brandon Marsh .20 .50
53P43 Franklyn Kilome .20 .50
53P44 Lyon Richardson .25 .60
53P45 DJ Peters .30 .75
53P46 Royce Lewis .40 1.00
53P47 Gavin Lux .60 1.50
53P48 Colton Welker .20 .50
53P49 Alec Bohm .75 2.00
53P50 Luis Robert 2.00 5.00
53P51 Ryan Mountcastle .25 .60
53P52 Brent Rooker .25 .60
53P53 Brent Honeywell .25 .60
53P54 Nick Neidert .20 .50
53P55 Daniel Johnson .20 .50
53P56 Derian Cruz .20 .50
53P57 Aramis Ademan .20 .50
53P58 Joey Wentz .20 .50
53P59 Anthony Kay .20 .50
53P60 Nate Pearson .50 1.25
53P61 Ian Anderson .50 1.25
53P62 Forrest Whitley .30 .75
53P63 Cole Ragans .20 .50
53P64 Ronaldo Hernandez .20 .50
53P65 Jeter Downs .30 .75
53P66 Sandro Fabian .20 .50
53P67 Cristian Santana .30 .75
53P68 Keibert Ruiz .50 1.25
53P69 Ke'Bryan Hayes .20 .50
53P70 Cristian Pache .50 1.25
53P71 Joey Bart .60 1.50
53P72 Cole Winn .20 .50
53P73 Jonathan India .25 .60
53P74 Ryan Weathers .25 .60
53P75 Luken Baker .25 .60
53P76 Justin Dunn .20 .50
53P77 Nolan Gorman .60 1.50
53P78 Bo Bichette .60 1.50
53P79 Esteury Ruiz .25 .60
53P80 Genesis Cabrera .30 .75
53P81 Sean Murphy .25 .60
53P82 Ryan Costello .25 .60
53P83 Freudis Nova .30 .75
53P84 Albert Abreu .20 .50
53P85 Jazz Chisholm .50 1.25
53P86 Logan Webb .30 .75
53P87 Shane Baz .20 .50
53P88 Marco Luciano 1.25 3.00
53P89 Nico Hoerner .60 1.50
53P90 A.J. Puk .25 .60
53P91 Jesus Sanchez .20 .50
53P92 Cole Tucker .30 .75
53P93 Blaze Alexander .20 .50
53P94 Triston McKenzie .20 .50
53P95 Franklin Perez .20 .50
53P96 Jonathan Hernandez .20 .50
53P97 Rylan Bannon .25 .60
53P98 Andres Gimenez .25 .60
53P99 Keegan Thompson .20 .50
53P100 Jo Adell .60 1.50
53P101 Evan White .30 .75
53P102 Dustin May .60 1.50
53P103 Daz Cameron .20 .50
53P104 Brady Singer .40 1.00
53P105 Victor Victor Mesa .40 1.00
53P106 Ethan Hankins .25 .60
53P107 Yusniel Diaz .30 .75
53P108 Brock Burke .20 .50
53P109 Bryan Mata .20 .50
53P110 Luis Garcia .25 .60
53P111 Matthew Liberatore .20 .50
53P112 Adrian Morejon .20 .50
53P113 DL Hall .20 .50
53P114 Cristian Javier .25 .60
53P115 Michel Baez .20 .50
53P116 Roberto Ramos .25 .60
53P117 Dane Dunning .20 .50
53P118 Jesus Luzardo .30 .75
53P119 MacKenzie Gore .40 1.00
53P120 Brendan McKay .30 .75
53P121 Leody Taveras .20 .50
53P122 JoJo Romero .20 .50
53P123 Tirso Ornelas .20 .50
53P124 Jay Groome .20 .50
53P125 Estevan Florial .30 .75
53P126 Brusdar Graterol .25 .60
53P127 Miguel Amaya .30 .75
53P128 Corey Ray .20 .50
53P129 Casey Mize .50 1.25
53P130 Yordan Alvarez 1.25 3.00
53P131 Logan Allen .20 .50
53P132 Zack Collins .25 .60

2019 Bowman Heritage Prospects Black and White

*BW: 1.2X TO 3X BASIC
RANDOM INSERTS IN PACKS
53P18 Julio Rodriguez 10.00 25.00

2017 Bowman High Tek

BHTAE Anderson Espinoza .40 1.00
BHTAI Andy Ibanez .40 1.00
BHTAK Alex Kiriloff 1.00 2.50
BHTAM Adrian Morejon .60 1.50
BHTAME Austin Meadows .60 1.50
BHTAP A.J. Puk .60 1.50
BHTAR Amed Rosario .60 1.50
BHTARO Alfredo Rodriguez .50 1.25
BHTBB Bo Bichette 1.50 4.00
BHTBG Braxton Garrett .40 1.00
BHTBR Brendan Rodgers .50 1.25
BHTCB Cody Bellinger 4.00 10.00
BHTCF Clint Frazier .75 2.00
BHTCR Corey Ray .50 1.25
BHTCS Cody Sedlock .40 1.00
BHTDC Dylan Cozens .40 1.00
BHTEJ Eloy Jimenez 1.50 4.00
BHTFM Francisco Mejia .60 1.50
BHTFR Fernando Romero .40 1.00
BHTFW Forrest Whitley 1.25 3.00
BHTGT Gleyber Torres 6.00 15.00
BHTIA Ian Anderson 1.00 2.50
BHTID Isan Diaz 1.00 2.50
BHTIH Ian Happ .75 2.00
BHTJC J.P. Crawford .40 1.00
BHTJD Justin Dunn .40 1.00
BHTJF Junior Fernandez .40 1.00
BHTJG Jason Groome .75 2.00
BHTJM Jorge Mateo .40 1.00
BHTJO Jhailyn Ortiz .75 2.00
BHTJS Justus Sheffield .60 1.50
BHTKL Kyle Lewis .75 2.00
BHTKM Kevin Maitan 1.00 2.50
BHTLA Lazarito Armenteros 1.00 2.50
BHTLB Lewis Brinson .60 1.50
BHTLC Luis Castillo 1.25 3.00
BHTLF Lucius Fox .40 1.00
BHTLGJ Lourdes Gurriel Jr. .60 1.50
BHTMK Mitch Keller .50 1.25
BHTMM Mickey Moniak 1.00 2.50
BHTMMA Matt Manning .60 1.50
BHTNS Nick Senzel 1.25 3.00
BHTOA Ozzie Albies 1.50 4.00
BHTPC P.J. Conlon .40 1.00
BHTPW Patrick Weigel .40 1.00
BHTRD Rafael Devers .75 2.00
BHTRH Rhys Hoskins 1.50 4.00
BHTRR Roniel Raudes .40 1.00
BHTSN Sean Newcomb .50 1.25
BHTTO Tyler O'Neill .50 1.25
BHTTS Thomas Szapucki .50 1.25
BHTVR Victor Robles 1.00 2.50
BHTWB Wuilmer Becerra .40 1.00
BHTWC Willie Calhoun .60 1.50
BHTYA Yadier Alvarez .60 1.50
BHTZC Zack Collins .50 1.25

2017 Bowman High Tek Circuit Board

*CIRCUIT: .6X TO 1.5X BASIC
STATED ODDS 1:3 HOBBY

2017 Bowman High Tek Diamond Dots

*DIAMOND DOTS: 1.5X TO 4X BASIC
STATED ODDS 1:18 HOBBY

2017 Bowman High Tek Gold Rainbow

*GOLD RAINBOW: 1.5X TO 4X BASIC
RANDOM INSERTS IN PACKS
STATED PRINT RUN 50 SER.#'d SETS
BHTCB Cody Bellinger 25.00 60.00

2017 Bowman High Tek Green Rainbow

*GREEN RAINBOW: 1X TO 2.5X BASIC
RANDOM INSERTS IN PACKS
STATED PRINT RUN 99 SER.#'d SETS
BHTCB Cody Bellinger 15.00 40.00

2017 Bowman High Tek Hexagon

*HEXAGON: .75X TO 2X BASIC
STATED ODDS 1:6 HOBBY

2017 Bowman High Tek Orange Magma Diffractors

*ORANGE MAGMA: 2.5X TO 6X BASIC
RANDOM INSERTS IN PACKS
STATED PRINT RUN 25 SER.#'d SETS
BHTCB Cody Bellinger 40.00 100.00

2017 Bowman High Tek Pinwheel

*PINWHEEL: .5X TO 1.2X BASIC
RANDOM INSERTS IN PACKS

2017 Bowman High Tek Shatter

*SHATTER: .75X TO 2X BASIC
STATED ODDS 1:4 HOBBY

2017 Bowman High Tek Squiggles and Dots

*SQUIG DOTS: 1.2X TO 3X BASIC
STATED ODDS 1:12 HOBBY

2017 Bowman High Tek Stripes and Arrows

*STRIPE ARROW: .5X TO 1.2X BASIC
RANDOM INSERTS IN PACKS

2017 Bowman High Tek Tidal Diffractors

*TIDAL DIFF: .75X TO 2X BASIC
RANDOM INSERTS IN PACKS
STATED PRINT RUN 199 SER.#'d SETS
BHTCB Cody Bellinger 12.00 30.00

2017 Bowman High Tek '17 Bowman Rookie Autographs

RANDOM INSERTS IN PACKS
STATED PRINT RUN 50 SER.#'d SETS
EXCHANGE DEADLINE 9/30/2019
17BTAB Alex Bregman 30.00 80.00
17BTAJ Aaron Judge 250.00 500.00
17BTDD David Dahl 20.00 50.00
17BTYG Yulieski Gurriel 12.00 30.00
17BTABE Andrew Benintendi 40.00 100.00

2017 Bowman High Tek '17 Bowman Rookies

RANDOM INSERTS IN PACKS
STATED PRINT RUN 75 SER.#'d SETS
17BTAB Alex Bregman 10.00 25.00
17BTABE Andrew Benintendi 8.00 20.00
17BTAJ Aaron Judge 60.00 150.00
17BTAR Alex Reyes 3.00 8.00
17BTDD David Dahl 3.00 8.00
17BTDS Dansby Swanson 6.00 15.00
17BTJDL Jose De Leon 2.50 6.00
17BTTG Tyler Glasnow 3.00 8.00
17BTYG Yulieski Gurriel 4.00 10.00
17BTYM Yoan Moncada 8.00 20.00

2017 Bowman High Tek '92 Bowman

RANDOM INSERTS IN PACKS
STATED PRINT RUN 75 SER.#'d SETS
92BAR Amed Rosario 8.00 20.00
92BBR Brendan Rodgers 2.50 6.00
92BCR Corey Ray 2.50 6.00
92BEJ Eloy Jimenez 5.00 12.00
92BIA Ian Anderson 5.00 12.00
92BJC J.P. Crawford 6.00 15.00
92BJG Jason Groome 4.00 10.00
92BJM Jorge Mateo 2.00 5.00
92BKM Kevin Maitan 6.00 15.00
92BLA Lazarito Armenteros 5.00 12.00
92BLGJ Lourdes Gurriel Jr. 3.00 8.00
92BMM Mickey Moniak 5.00 12.00
92BNS Nick Senzel 6.00 15.00
92BVR Victor Robles 5.00 12.00
92BYA Yadier Alvarez 3.00 8.00

2017 Bowman High Tek '92 Bowman Autographs

RANDOM INSERTS IN PACKS
STATED PRINT RUN 35 SER.#'d SETS
EXCHANGE DEADLINE 9/30/2019
92BAR Amed Rosario 10.00 25.00
92BBR Brendan Rodgers 15.00 40.00
92BCR Corey Ray 8.00 20.00
92BEJ Eloy Jimenez 100.00 250.00
92BIA Ian Anderson 15.00 40.00
92BJG Jason Groome 12.00 30.00
92BJM Jorge Mateo 6.00 15.00
92BKM Kevin Maitan 8.00 20.00
92BLA Lazarito Armenteros 15.00 40.00
92BLGJ Lourdes Gurriel Jr. 25.00 60.00
92BMM Mickey Moniak 15.00 40.00
92BNS Nick Senzel 40.00 100.00
92BYA Yadier Alvarez 10.00 25.00

2017 Bowman High Tek Autographs

RANDOM INSERTS IN PACKS
EXCHANGE DEADLINE 9/30/2019
BHTAE Anderson Espinoza 2.50 6.00
BHTAK Alex Kiriloff 10.00 25.00
BHTAM Adrian Morejon 3.00 8.00
BHTAP A.J. Puk 5.00 12.00
BHTAR Amed Rosario 4.00 10.00
BHTARO Alfredo Rodriguez 3.00 8.00
BHTBB Bo Bichette 30.00 80.00
BHTBG Braxton Garrett 2.50 6.00
BHTBR Brendan Rodgers 6.00 15.00
BHTCR Corey Ray 3.00 8.00
BHTCS Cody Sedlock 2.50 6.00
BHTDC Dylan Cozens 2.50 6.00
BHTEJ Eloy Jimenez
BHTFM Francisco Mejia 5.00 12.00
BHTFW Forrest Whitley 10.00 25.00
BHTGT Gleyber Torres 25.00 60.00
BHTIA Ian Anderson 12.00 30.00
BHTID Isan Diaz 6.00 15.00
BHTJD Justin Dunn 2.50 6.00
BHTJF Junior Fernandez 4.00 10.00
BHTJG Jason Groome 5.00 12.00
BHTJM Jorge Mateo
BHTJS Justus Sheffield 4.00 10.00
BHTKL Kyle Lewis 30.00 80.00
BHTKM Kevin Maitan 4.00 10.00
BHTLA Lazarito Armenteros 6.00 15.00
BHTLC Luis Castillo 8.00 20.00
BHTLF Lucius Fox 2.50 6.00
BHTLGJ Lourdes Gurriel Jr. 6.00 15.00
BHTMK Mitch Keller 4.00 10.00
BHTMM Mickey Moniak 6.00 15.00
BHTMMA Matt Manning 4.00 10.00
BHTNS Nick Senzel 8.00 20.00
BHTPC P.J. Conlon 2.50 6.00
BHTPW Patrick Weigel 2.50 6.00
BHTRH Rhys Hoskins 10.00 25.00
BHTRR Roniel Raudes 2.50 6.00
BHTSN Sean Newcomb 3.00 8.00
BHTTS Thomas Szapucki 3.00 8.00
BHTWB Wuilmer Becerra 2.50 6.00
BHTWC Willie Calhoun 6.00 15.00
BHTYA Yadier Alvarez 4.00 10.00
BHTZC Zack Collins 3.00 8.00

2017 Bowman High Tek Autographs Gold Rainbow

*GOLD RAINBOW: .75X TO 2X BASIC
RANDOM INSERTS IN PACKS
STATED PRINT RUN 50 SER.#'d SETS
EXCHANGE DEADLINE 9/30/2019
BHTFM Francisco Mejia 10.00 25.00
BHTJM Jorge Mateo 5.00 12.00
BHTMK Mitch Keller 20.00 50.00

2017 Bowman High Tek Autographs Green Rainbow

*GREEN RAINBOW: .5X TO 1.2X BASIC
RANDOM INSERTS IN PACKS
STATED PRINT RUN 99 SER.#'d SETS
EXCHANGE DEADLINE 9/30/2019
BHTJM Jorge Mateo 3.00 8.00

2017 Bowman High Tek Autographs Orange Magma Diffractors

*ORANGE MAGMA: 1X TO 2.5X BASIC
RANDOM INSERTS IN PACKS
STATED PRINT RUN 25 SER.#'d SETS
EXCHANGE DEADLINE 9/30/2019
BHTAK Alex Kiriloff 30.00 80.00
BHTBR Brendan Rodgers 12.00 30.00
BHTEJ Eloy Jimenez 75.00 200.00
BHTFM Francisco Mejia 12.00 30.00
BHTMK Mitch Keller 25.00 60.00
BHTNS Nick Senzel 20.00 50.00

2017 Bowman High Tek Autographs Rush Diffractors

*RUSH DIF: .5X TO 1.2X BASIC
RANDOM INSERTS IN PACKS
EXCHANGE DEADLINE 9/30/2019
BHTJM Jorge Mateo 3.00 8.00

2017 Bowman High Tek Autographs Tidal Diffractors

*TIDAL DIF: .5X TO 1.2X BASIC
RANDOM INSERTS IN PACKS
STATED PRINT RUN 199 SER.#'d SETS
EXCHANGE DEADLINE 9/30/2019
BHTJM Jorge Mateo 3.00 8.00

2017 Bowman High Tek Bashers

RANDOM INSERTS IN PACKS
STATED PRINT RUN 75 SER.#'d SETS
BBH Bryce Harper 5.00 12.00
BCB Cody Bellinger 30.00 80.00
BDC Dylan Cozens 2.00 5.00
BJO Jhailyn Ortiz 4.00 10.00
BKB Kris Bryant 4.00 10.00
BKL Kyle Lewis 4.00 10.00
BMC Miguel Cabrera 8.00 20.00
BMT Mike Trout 30.00 80.00
BNA Nolan Arenado 4.00 10.00
BNS Nick Senzel 6.00 15.00
BRC Robinson Cano 2.50 6.00
BRH Rhys Hoskins 8.00 20.00
BTO Tyler O'Neill 2.50 6.00
BWC Willie Calhoun 3.00 8.00
BZC Zack Collins 2.50 6.00

2017 Bowman High Tek Bashers Autographs

RANDOM INSERTS IN PACKS
STATED PRINT RUN 50 SER.#'d SETS
EXCHANGE DEADLINE 9/30/2019
BBH Bryce Harper 50.00 120.00
BDC Dylan Cozens 12.00 30.00
BKB Kris Bryant 100.00 250.00
BKL Kyle Lewis 8.00 20.00
BMT Mike Trout 200.00 400.00
BNS Nick Senzel 30.00 80.00
BRH Rhys Hoskins 75.00 200.00
BZC Zack Collins

2017 Bowman High Tek Foundations of the Franchise

RANDOM INSERTS IN PACKS
STATED PRINT RUN 50 SER.#'d SETS
FFAR Nolan Arenado 4.00 10.00
Brendan Rodgers
FFARA Orlando Arcia 3.00 8.00
Corey Ray
FFBD Devers/Betts 12.00 30.00
FFBJ Bryant/Jimenez 12.00 30.00
FFCL Cano/Lewis 4.00 10.00
FFCT Castro/Torres 30.00 80.00
FFDG Nick Gordon 3.00 8.00
Brian Dozier
FFDP Diaz/Perez 3.00 8.00
FFFC Maikel Franco 2.50 6.00
J.P. Crawford
FFHR Harper/Robles 12.00 30.00
FFKB Kershaw/Bellinger 15.00 40.00
FFLM Mejia/Lindor 3.00 8.00
FFMM Austin Meadows 3.00 8.00
Starling Marte
FFSA Swanson/Albies 8.00 20.00
FFSD Justin Dunn 2.50 6.00
Noah Syndergaard

2018 Bowman High Tek

RHTAR Amed Rosario .50 1.25
RHTAV Alex Verdugo .60 1.50
RHTCF Clint Frazier .75 2.00
RHTFM Francisco Mejia .50 1.25
RHTJC J.P. Crawford .40 1.00
RHTNW Nick Williams .50 1.25
RHTOA Ozzie Albies 1.25 3.00
RHTRD Rafael Devers 1.25 3.00
RHTRH Rhys Hoskins 1.50 4.00
RHTSO Shohei Ohtani 2.50 6.00
RHTVR Victor Robles 1.00 2.50

2018 Bowman High Tek Circle Gear

*CIRCLE GEAR: 1.5X TO 4X BASIC
STATED ODDS 1:XXX

2018 Bowman High Tek Circuit Board

*CIRCUIT BOARD: 1.2X TO 3X BASIC
STATED ODDS 1:XXX

2018 Bowman High Tek Dots Bow Tie

*DOTS BOW TIE: .6X TO 1.5X BASIC
STATED ODDS 1:XXX

2018 Bowman High Tek Gold Rainbow

*GOLD RAINBOW: 2X TO 5X BASIC
STATED ODDS 1:XXX
STATED PRINT RUN 50 SER.#'d SETS
RHTSO Shohei Ohtani 30.00 80.00

2018 Bowman High Tek Green Rainbow

*GREEN RAINBOW: 1X TO 2.5X BASIC
STATED ODDS 1:XXX
STATED PRINT RUN 99 SER.#'d SETS
RHTSO Shohei Ohtani 15.00 40.00

2018 Bowman High Tek Lightning Tree

*LIGHTNING TREE: 1.2X TO 3X BASIC
STATED ODDS 1:XXX

2018 Bowman High Tek Ocean Blue Tidal

*OCEAN BLUE: 1.5X TO 4X BASIC
STATED ODDS 1:XXX
STATED PRINT RUN 75 SER.#'d SETS
RHTSO Shohei Ohtani 25.00 60.00

2018 Bowman High Tek Orange Magma Diffractors

*ORANGE MAGMA: 3X TO 8X BASIC
STATED ODDS 1:XXX
STATED PRINT RUN 25 SER.#'d SETS
RHTSO Shohei Ohtani 50.00 120.00

2018 Bowman High Tek Purple Rainbow

*PURPLE RAINBOW: .75X TO 2X BASIC
STATED ODDS 1:XXX
STATED PRINT RUN 191 SER.#'d SETS
RHTSO Shohei Ohtani 12.00 30.00

2018 Bowman High Tek Shatter

*SHATTER: 1.5X TO 4X BASIC
STATED ODDS 1:XXX

2018 Bowman High Tek Stripes

*STRIPES: .5X TO 1.2X BASIC
STATED ODDS 1:XXX

2018 Bowman High Tek Zig Zag

*ZIG ZAG: .6X TO 1.5X BASIC
STATED ODDS 1:XXX

2018 Bowman High Tek First Bowman TEK

STATED ODDS 1:XX HOBBY
STATED PRINT RUN 99 SER.#'d SETS
*BLUE/25: .6X TO 1.5X BASIC
FBTAA Adbert Alzolay 1.25 3.00
FBTAG Andres Gimenez 1.25 3.00
FBTBM Bryan Mata 1.25 3.00
FBTHG Hunter Greene 3.00 8.00
FBTJH Jordan Hicks 2.00 5.00
FBTJK Jeren Kendall 1.25 3.00
FBTKR Keibert Ruiz 3.00 8.00
FBTLR Luis Robert 20.00 50.00
FBTMB Michel Baez 1.00 2.50

2019 Bowman Heritage Black and White

BTRM Ronny Mauricio	2.50	6.00
BTZL Zack Littell	1.00	2.50

2018 Bowman High Tek First Bowman TEK Autographs

TATED ODDS 1:XX HOBBY
TATED PRINT RUN 99 SER.#'d SETS
XCHANGE DEADLINE 8/31/2020
BLUE/25: .6X TO 1.5X BASIC

BTAA Adbert Alzolay	5.00	12.00
BTAG Andres Gimenez	5.00	12.00
BTBM Bryan Mata	8.00	20.00
BTHG Hunter Greene	12.00	30.00
BTJH Jordan Hicks	10.00	25.00
BTJK Jeren Kendall	5.00	12.00
BTKR Keibert Ruiz	12.00	30.00
BTLR Luis Robert	40.00	100.00
BTMB Michel Baez	4.00	10.00
BTZL Zack Littell	4.00	10.00

2018 Bowman High Tek Prospect Autographs

TATED ODDS 1:XX HOBBY
XCHANGE DEADLINE 8/31/2020
PURPLE/150: .5X TO 1.2X
GREEN/99: .6X TO 1.5X
BLUE/75: .75X TO 2X
GOLD/50: 1X TO 2.5X
ORANGE/25: 1.2X TO 3X

HTAA Adbert Alzolay	3.00	8.00
HTAB Austin Beck	3.00	8.00
HTAF Alex Faedo	4.00	10.00
HTAG Andres Gimenez	8.00	20.00
HTAH Adam Haseley	3.00	8.00
HTBM Brendan McKay	8.00	20.00
HTBR Brent Rooker	3.00	8.00
HTCB Corbin Burnes	4.00	10.00
HTCP Cristian Pache	20.00	50.00
HTCW Colton Welker	2.50	6.00
HTDH D.L. Hall	2.50	6.00
HTDJ Daniel Johnson	2.50	6.00
HTEW Evan White	6.00	15.00
HTFP Franklin Perez	2.50	6.00
HTGT Gleyber Torres	30.00	80.00
HTHG Hunter Greene	8.00	20.00
HTHR Heliot Ramos	4.00	10.00
HTII Ibandel Isabel	6.00	15.00
HTJA Jo Adell	25.00	60.00
HTJB Jake Burger	2.50	6.00
HTJD Jeter Downs	4.00	10.00
HTJG Jorge Guzman	2.50	6.00
HTJK Jeren Kendall	3.00	8.00
HTJS Jesus Sanchez	4.00	10.00
HTKH Keston Hiura	8.00	20.00
HTKR Keibert Ruiz	6.00	15.00
HTKW Kyle Wright	8.00	20.00
HTLR Luis Robert	60.00	150.00
HTMB Michel Baez	2.50	6.00
HTMG MacKenzie Gore	12.00	30.00
HTMW Mitchell White	2.50	6.00
HTNP Nick Pratto	3.00	8.00
HTPS Pavin Smith	2.50	6.00
HTRA Ronald Acuna	75.00	200.00
PHTRL Royce Lewis	12.00	30.00
PHTRV Ryan Vilade	2.50	6.00
PHTSB Shane Baz	3.00	8.00
PHTSL Shed Long	2.50	6.00
PHTSS Sixto Sanchez	8.00	20.00
PHTTL Tristen Lutz	3.00	8.00

2018 Bowman High Tek Prospects

PHTAA Adbert Alzolay	.40	1.00
PHTAB Austin Beck	.40	1.00
PHTAF Alex Faedo	.50	1.25
PHTAG Andres Gimenez	.40	1.00
PHTAH Adam Haseley	.50	1.25
PHTBM Brendan McKay	.50	1.25
PHTBR Brent Rooker	.40	1.00
PHTBRO Brendan Rodgers	.40	1.00
PHTCB Corbin Burnes	.50	1.25
PHTCP Cristian Pache	1.50	4.00
PHTCW Colton Welker	.30	.75
PHTDH D.L. Hall	.30	.75
PHTDJ Daniel Johnson	.30	.75
PHTEW Evan White	.50	1.25
PHTFP Franklin Perez	.30	.75
PHTGT Gleyber Torres	3.00	8.00
PHTHG Hunter Greene	1.00	2.50
PHTHR Heliot Ramos	.50	1.25
PHTII Ibandel Isabel	.50	1.25
PHTJA Jo Adell	1.00	2.50
PHTJB Jake Burger	.30	.75
PHTJD Jeter Downs	.50	1.25
PHTJG Jorge Guzman	.30	.75
PHTJH Jordan Hicks	.60	1.50
PHTJK Jeren Kendall	.40	1.00
PHTJM Jorge Mateo	.30	.75
PHTJS Jesus Sanchez	.30	.75
PHTKH Keston Hiura	.75	2.00
PHTKR Keibert Ruiz	1.00	2.50
PHTKW Kyle Wright	.75	2.00
PHTLR Luis Robert	6.00	15.00
PHTMB Michel Baez	.30	.75
PHTMG MacKenzie Gore	.60	1.50
PHTMW Mitchell White	.30	.75
PHTNP Nick Pratto	.40	1.00
PHTPS Pavin Smith	.30	.75
PHTRA Ronald Acuna	6.00	15.00
PHTRL Royce Lewis	1.25	3.00
PHTRM Ronny Mauricio	.75	2.00
PHTRV Ryan Vilade	.30	.75
PHTSB Shane Baz	.40	1.00
PHTSL Shed Long	.30	.75
PHTSM Sean Murphy	.50	1.25
PHTSS Sixto Sanchez	.75	2.00
PHTTL Tristen Lutz	.40	1.00

2018 Bowman High Tek Prospects Circle Gear

*CIRCLE GEAR: 1.5X TO 4X BASIC
STATED ODDS 1:XXX

2018 Bowman High Tek Prospects Circuit Board

*CIRCUIT BOARD: 1.2X TO 3X BASIC
STATED ODDS 1:XXX

2018 Bowman High Tek Prospects Dots Bow Tie

*DOTS BOW TIE: .6X TO 1.5X BASIC
STATED ODDS 1:XXX

2018 Bowman High Tek Prospects Gold Rainbow

*GOLD RAINBOW: 2X TO 5X BASIC
STATED ODDS 1:XXX
STATED PRINT RUN 50 SER.#'d SETS

2018 Bowman High Tek Prospects Green Rainbow

*GREEN RAINBOW: 1X TO 2.5X BASIC
STATED ODDS 1:XXX
STATED PRINT RUN 99 SER.#'d SETS

2018 Bowman High Tek Prospects Lightning Tree

*LIGHTNING TREE: 1.2X TO 3X BASIC
STATED ODDS 1:XXX

2018 Bowman High Tek Prospects Ocean Blue Tidal

*OCEAN BLUE: 1.5X TO 4X BASIC
STATED ODDS 1:XXX
STATED PRINT RUN 75 SER.#'d SETS

2018 Bowman High Tek Prospects Orange Magma Diffractors

*ORANGE MAGMA: 2.5X TO 6X BASIC
STATED ODDS 1:XXX
STATED PRINT RUN 25 SER.#'d SETS

2018 Bowman High Tek Prospects Purple Rainbow

*PURPLE RAINBOW: .75X TO 2X BASIC
STATED ODDS 1:XXX
STATED PRINT RUN 191 SER.#'d SETS

2018 Bowman High Tek Prospects Shatter

*SHATTER: 1.5X TO 4X BASIC
STATED ODDS 1:XXX

2018 Bowman High Tek Prospects Stripes

*STRIPES: .5X TO 1.2X BASIC
STATED ODDS 1:XXX

2018 Bowman High Tek Prospects Zig Zag

*ZIG ZAG: .6X TO 1.5X BASIC
STATED ODDS 1:XXX

2018 Bowman High Tek PyroTEKnics

STATED ODDS 1:XXX HOBBY
STATED PRINT RUN 99 SER.#'d SETS
*BLUE/25: .6X TO 1.5X BASIC

PYAR Amed Rosario	1.25	3.00
PYBM Brendan McKay	1.50	4.00
PYBR Brendan Rodgers	1.25	3.00
PYCF Clint Frazier	2.00	5.00
PYGT Gleyber Torres	10.00	25.00
PYHG Hunter Greene	3.00	8.00
PYJB Jake Burger	1.00	2.50
PYLR Luis Robert	20.00	50.00
PYRA Ronald Acuna	20.00	50.00
PYRD Rafael Devers	3.00	8.00
PYRH Rhys Hoskins	4.00	10.00
PYRL Royce Lewis	4.00	10.00
PYSO Shohei Ohtani	20.00	50.00
PYVR Victor Robles	2.50	6.00
PYVGJ Vladimir Guerrero Jr.	15.00	40.00

2018 Bowman High Tek PyroTEKnics Autographs

STATED ODDS 1:XX HOBBY
PRINT RUNS B/WN 50-75 COPIES PER
EXCHANGE DEADLINE 8/31/2020
*BLUE/25: .6X TO 1.5X BASIC

PYAR Amed Rosario/50	5.00	12.00
PYBM Brendan McKay/75	10.00	25.00
PYGT Gleyber Torres/75	30.00	80.00
PYHG Hunter Greene EXCH	12.00	30.00
PYJB Jake Burger/75	4.00	10.00
PYLR Luis Robert/75	80.00	200.00
PYRA Ronald Acuna/75	75.00	200.00
PYRD Rafael Devers/50	15.00	40.00
PYRH Rhys Hoskins/50	20.00	50.00
PYRL Royce Lewis/50	20.00	50.00
PYVR Victor Robles/50	10.00	25.00

2018 Bowman High Tek Rookie Autographs

STATED ODDS 1:XX HOBBY
EXCHANGE DEADLINE 8/31/2020
*PURPLE/150: .5X TO 1.2X
*GREEN/99: .6X TO 1.5X
*BLUE/75: .75X TO 2X
*GOLD/50: 1X TO 2.5X
*ORANGE/25: 1.2X TO 3X

RHTAR Amed Rosario	3.00	8.00
RHTOA Ozzie Albies	12.00	30.00
RHTRD Rafael Devers	20.00	50.00
RHTRH Rhys Hoskins	12.00	30.00
RHTSO Shohei Ohtani EXCH	150.00	300.00
RHTVR Victor Robles	10.00	25.00

2018 Bowman High Tek Tides of Youth

STATED ODDS 1:XXX HOBBY
STATED PRINT RUN 99 SER.#'d SETS
*BLUE/25: .6X TO 1.5X BASIC

TYAB Austin Beck	1.25	3.00
TYAF Alex Faedo	1.50	4.00
TYAH Adam Haseley	1.50	4.00
TYAR Amed Rosario	1.25	3.00
TYAV Alex Verdugo	1.50	4.00
TYBM Brendan McKay	1.50	4.00
TYCF Clint Frazier	2.00	5.00
TYCP Cristian Pache	5.00	12.00
TYFM Francisco Mejia	1.25	3.00
TYGT Gleyber Torres	10.00	25.00
TYHG Hunter Greene	3.00	8.00
TYHR Heliot Ramos	1.50	4.00
TYJA Jo Adell	3.00	8.00
TYJB Jake Burger	1.00	2.50
TYJC J.P. Crawford	1.00	2.50
TYJK Jeren Kendall	1.25	3.00
TYJM Jorge Mateo	1.00	2.50
TYJS Jesus Sanchez	1.00	2.50
TYKR Keibert Ruiz	3.00	8.00
TYLR Luis Robert	20.00	50.00
TYMG MacKenzie Gore	2.00	5.00
TYNW Nick Williams	1.25	3.00
TYOA Ozzie Albies	3.00	8.00
TYRA Ronald Acuna	12.00	30.00
TYRD Rafael Devers	3.00	8.00
TYRH Rhys Hoskins	4.00	10.00
TYRL Royce Lewis	4.00	10.00
TYSO Shohei Ohtani	20.00	50.00
TYVR Victor Robles	2.50	6.00
TYWB Walker Buehler	5.00	12.00

2018 Bowman High Tek Tides of Youth Autographs

STATED ODDS 1:XX HOBBY
STATED PRINT RUN 75 COPIES PER
EXCHANGE DEADLINE 8/31/2020

TYAB Austin Beck/75	5.00	12.00
TYAF Alex Faedo/75	6.00	15.00
TYAH Adam Haseley/75	4.00	10.00
TYAV Alex Verdugo/75	8.00	20.00
TYBM Brendan McKay/75	10.00	25.00
TYFM Francisco Mejia/75	8.00	20.00
TYGT Gleyber Torres/75	30.00	80.00
TYHG Hunter Greene/75	12.00	30.00
TYHR Heliot Ramos/75	6.00	15.00
TYJA Jo Adell/75	25.00	60.00
TYJB Jake Burger/75	4.00	10.00
TYKR Keibert Ruiz/75	12.00	30.00
TYLR Luis Robert/75	80.00	200.00
TYMG MacKenzie Gore/75	8.00	20.00
TYOA Ozzie Albies/75	20.00	50.00
TYRA Ronald Acuna/75	75.00	200.00
TYRD Rafael Devers/75	15.00	40.00
TYRH Rhys Hoskins/75	20.00	50.00
TYRL Royce Lewis/75	20.00	50.00
TYVR Victor Robles/75	10.00	25.00

2018 Bowman High Tek Tides of Youth Autographs Blue

*BLUE: .6X TO 1.5X BASIC
STATED ODDS 1:XX HOBBY
STATED PRINT RUN 25 SER.#'d SETS
EXCHANGE DEADLINE 8/31/2020

TYAR Amed Rosario	8.00	20.00

2010 Bowman Platinum

COMMON CARD (1-100)	.15	.40
COMMON RC (1-100)	.40	1.00
1 Stephen Strasburg RC	3.00	8.00
2 Derek Jeter	1.00	2.50
3 Felix Doubront RC	.40	1.00
4 Miguel Cabrera	.40	1.00
5 Albert Pujols	.50	1.25
6 Domonic Brown RC	1.50	4.00
7 Ryan Braun	.25	.60
8 Justin Upton	.25	.60
9 Dustin Pedroia	.30	.75
10 Shin-Soo Choo	.25	.60
11 Jake Arrieta RC	1.00	2.50
12 Hanley Ramirez	.25	.60
13 Matt Kemp	.30	.75
14 Joe Mauer	.30	.75
15 Joey Votto	.40	1.00
16 Andrew Cashner RC	.40	1.00
17 Josh Hamilton	.25	.60
18 Buster Posey RC	3.00	8.00
19 Ubaldo Jimenez	.15	.40
20 Peter Bourjos RC	.60	1.50
21 CC Sabathia	.25	.60
22 Alfonso Soriano	.25	.60
23 Carlos Santana RC	1.25	3.00
24 Kevin Youkilis	.15	.40
25 Brian McCann	.25	.60
26 Troy Tulowitzki	.40	1.00
27 Hunter Pence	.25	.60
28 Jay Sborz (RC)	.40	1.00
29 Andre Ethier	.25	.60
30 Kendry Morales	.15	.40
31 Brian Matusz RC	1.00	2.50
32 Vladimir Guerrero	.25	.60
33 Prince Fielder	.25	.60
34 J.P. Arencibia RC	.75	2.00
35 Roy Halladay	.25	.60
36 Mark Teixeira	.25	.60
37 Ryan Kalish RC	.60	1.50
38 Tim Lincecum	.25	.60
39 Andrew McCutchen	.40	1.00
40 Johan Santana	.25	.60
41 Josh Bell (RC)	.40	1.00
42 Daniel Nava RC	.40	1.00
43 Manny Ramirez	.40	1.00
44 Ichiro Suzuki	.50	1.25
45 Pablo Sandoval	.25	.60
46 Chris Coghlan	.15	.40
47 Mike Leake RC	1.25	3.00
48 Adrian Gonzalez	.30	.75
49 Torii Hunter	.15	.40
50 Brennan Boesch RC	1.00	2.50
51 Justin Verlander	.40	1.00
52 Matt Holliday	.40	1.00
53 Evan Longoria	.25	.60
54 Adam Jones	.25	.60
55 Wade Davis (RC)	.60	1.50
56 Jose Reyes	.25	.60
57 Martin Prado	.15	.40
58 Brad Lincoln RC	.60	1.50
59 Billy Butler	.15	.40
60 Mat Latos	.25	.60
61 Logan Morrison RC	.60	1.50
62 Ryan Howard	.30	.75
63 Cliff Lee	.25	.60
64 Adam Dunn	.25	.60
65 David Ortiz	.40	1.00
66 Ike Davis RC	.75	2.00
67 Victor Martinez	.25	.60
68 Josh Johnson	.25	.60
69 Dayan Viciedo RC	.60	1.50
70 Jimmy Rollins	.25	.60
71 Jered Weaver	.25	.60
72 Robinson Cano	.25	.60
73 Madison Bumgarner RC	3.00	8.00
74 Clayton Kershaw	.75	2.00
75 Tommy Hanson	.15	.40
76 Carl Crawford	.25	.60
77 Trevor Plouffe (RC)	1.00	2.50
78 Ruy Oswalt	.25	.60
79 Austin Jackson RC	.60	1.50
80 Dan Haren	.15	.40
81 Gordon Beckham	.15	.40
82 Zack Greinke	.25	.60
83 Neil Walker (RC)	.60	1.50
84 Vernon Wells	.15	.40
85 Lance Berkman	.25	.60
86 Mike Stanton RC	3.00	8.00
87 Ryan Zimmerman	.25	.60
88 Nick Markakis	.30	.75
89 Jose Tabata RC	.60	1.50
90 Chipper Jones	.40	1.00
91 Jason Heyward RC	1.50	4.00
92 Alex Rodriguez	.50	1.25
93 Matt Cain	.25	.60
94 Justin Morneau	.25	.60
95 Jon Lester	.25	.60
96 Starlin Castro RC	1.00	2.50
97 Chase Utley	.25	.60
98 Felix Hernandez	.25	.60
99 Wilson Ramos RC	1.00	2.50
100 David Wright	.30	.75

2010 Bowman Platinum Refractors

*REF VET: 2X TO 5X BASIC
*REF RC: .6X TO 1.5X BASIC
STATED PRINT RUN 999 SER.#'d SETS

2010 Bowman Platinum Gold Refractors

*GOLD VET: 2.5X TO 6X BASIC
*GOLD RC: 1X TO 2.5X RC
STATED PRINT RUN 539 SER.#'d SETS

2010 Bowman Platinum Dual Relic Autographs Refractors

STATED PRINT RUN 99 SER.#'d SETS

AJ T.Anderson/B.Johnson	6.00	15.00
BM M.Barnes/S.McGough	8.00	20.00
BS J.Bradley Jr./G.Springer	30.00	80.00
DM A.Dickerson/A.Maggi	6.00	15.00
ER J.Esposito/S.Rodriguez	6.00	15.00
FM N.Fontana/M.Mahtook	6.00	15.00
GC S.Gray/G.Cole	20.00	50.00
MW B.Miller/R.Wright	6.00	15.00
RW N.Ramirez/K.Winkler	6.00	15.00
SH S.Strasburg/J.Heyward	125.00	250.00

2010 Bowman Platinum Hexagraph Autographs

STATED PRINT RUN 6 SER.#'d SETS

2010 Bowman Platinum Prospect Autographs Refractors

AC Alexander Colome	5.00	12.00
ACH Aroldis Chapman	10.00	25.00
AH Adeiny Hechavarria	2.00	5.00
AW Alex Wilson	2.00	5.00
AWE Allen Webster	3.00	8.00
CA Chris Archer	6.00	15.00
CD Chase D'Arnaud	2.00	5.00
CO Chris Owings	2.00	5.00
DM Dan Merklinger	2.00	5.00
ET Eric Thames	5.00	12.00
FF Freddie Freeman	30.00	80.00
FM Fabio Martinez	2.00	5.00
GH Gorkys Hernandez	2.00	5.00
IK Ian Krol	2.00	5.00
JDM J.D. Martinez	20.00	50.00
JH Jordan Henry	2.00	5.00
JJ Jake Jefferies	2.00	5.00
JK Joe Kelly	2.00	5.00
JL Josh Lindblom	2.00	5.00
JM Jesus Montero	2.00	5.00
JMA Justin Marks	2.00	5.00
JMC Jake McGee	2.00	5.00
JMI Jiovanni Mier	3.00	8.00
JP Jarrod Parker	5.00	12.00
JR Javier Rodriguez	2.00	5.00
JS Jerry Sands	5.00	12.00
JS Jonathan Singleton	5.00	12.00
KSA Keyvius Sampson	5.00	12.00
LC Lonnie Chisenhall	3.00	8.00
LS Logan Schafer	2.00	5.00
MR Matt Rizzotti	2.00	5.00
MRO Mauricio Robles	2.00	5.00
MS Miguel Sano	5.00	12.00
MT Mike Trout	400.00	800.00
NB Nick Barnese	2.00	5.00
NN Nick Noonan	2.00	5.00
NT Nate Tenbrink	2.00	5.00
PC Pat Corbin	6.00	15.00
PG Paul Goldschmidt	20.00	50.00
RC Ryan Chaffee	2.00	5.00
RP Rich Poythress	2.00	5.00
RU Rudy Owens	3.00	8.00
SG Steve Garrison	2.00	5.00
SH Steven Hensley	2.00	5.00
TS Tony Sanchez	5.00	12.00

2010 Bowman Platinum Prospect Autographs Blue Refractors

*BLUE: .75X TO 2X BASIC
STATED PRINT RUN 99 SER.#'d SETS

MT Mike Trout	1500.00	2000.00

2010 Bowman Platinum Prospect Autographs Green Refractors

*GREEN: .6X TO 1.5X BASIC
STATED PRINT RUN 199 SER.#'d SETS

MT Mike Trout	600.00	1200.00

2010 Bowman Platinum Prospect Autographs Red Refractors

STATED PRINT RUN 10 SER.#'d SETS

2010 Bowman Platinum Prospect Dual Autographs Refractors

STATED PRINT RUN 99 SER.#'d SETS

BD J.Bradley Jr./A.Dickerson	15.00	40.00
CB G.Cole/M.Barnes	12.50	30.00
GE S.Gray/J.Esposito	8.00	20.00
GW S.Gilmartin/K.Winkler	8.00	20.00
JM B.Jackson/J.Mitchell	8.00	20.00
JM B.Johnson/B.Mooneyham	8.00	20.00
MF M.Mahtook/N.Fontana	8.00	20.00
MS B.Miller/G.Springer	15.00	40.00
OR P.O'Brien/S.Rodriguez	8.00	20.00
RR N.Ramirez/N.Ramirez	8.00	20.00
WM R.Wright/A.Maggi	8.00	20.00

2010 Bowman Platinum Prospects

PP1 Jerry Sands	1.00	2.50
PP2 Desmond Jennings	.60	1.50
PP3 Jeremy Hellickson	1.00	2.50
PP4 Jesus Montero	.40	1.00
PP5 Mike Trout	40.00	100.00
PP6 Dustin Ackley	.60	1.50
PP7 Zach Britton	1.25	3.00
PP8 Adeiny Hechavarria	.40	1.00
PP9 Mike Moustakas	1.00	2.50
PP10 Aroldis Chapman	1.50	4.00
PP11 Lonnie Chisenhall	.60	1.50
PP12 Mike Montgomery	.60	1.50
PP13 Freddie Freeman	5.00	12.00
PP14 Kyle Drabek	.60	1.50
PP15 Grant Green	.40	1.00
PP16 Brett Jackson	1.25	3.00
PP17 Slade Heathcott	1.25	3.00
PP18 Mike Minor	.60	1.50
PP19 Austin Romine	.60	1.50
PP20 Kyle Gibson	1.50	4.00
PP21 Chris Withrow	.40	1.00
PP22 John Lamb	1.00	2.50
PP23 J.D. Martinez	4.00	10.00
PP24 Donavan Tate	.40	1.00
PP25 Shelby Miller	2.00	5.00
PP26 Jose Iglesias	1.25	3.00
PP27 Hak-Ju Lee	.60	1.50
PP28 Miguel Sano	2.50	6.00
PP29 Tyler Anderson	.60	1.50
PP30 Matt Barnes	1.00	2.50
PP31 Jackie Bradley Jr.	1.50	4.00
PP32 Gerrit Cole	4.00	10.00
PP33 Alex Dickerson	.40	1.00
PP34 Jason Esposito	1.00	2.50
PP35 Nolan Fontana	.60	1.50
PP36 Sean Gilmartin	.60	1.50
PP37 Sonny Gray	1.00	2.50
PP38 Brian Johnson	.40	1.00
PP39 Andrew Maggi	.40	1.00
PP40 Mikie Mahtook	1.00	2.50
PP41 Scott McGough	1.00	2.50
PP42 Brad Miller	1.00	2.50
PP43 Brett Mooneyham	1.00	2.50
PP44 Peter O'Brien	1.00	2.50
PP45 Nick Ramirez	.60	1.50
PP46 Noe Ramirez	.60	1.50
PP47 Steve Rodriguez	.60	1.50
PP48 George Springer	2.50	6.00
PP49 Kyle Winkler	1.00	2.50
PP50 Ryan Wright	.40	1.00

2010 Bowman Platinum Prospects Refractors Thick Stock

*REF: .75X TO 2X BASIC
STATED PRINT RUN 999 SER.#'d SETS

PP5 Mike Trout	125.00	300.00

2010 Bowman Platinum Prospects Refractors Thin Stock

*REF: .75X TO 2X BASIC
STATED PRINT RUN 999 SER.#'d SETS

PP5 Mike Trout	125.00	300.00

2010 Bowman Platinum Prospects Blue Refractors

*BLUE REF: 1.5X TO 4X BASIC
STATED PRINT RUN 99 SER.#'d SETS

PP5 Mike Trout	400.00	800.00

2010 Bowman Platinum Prospects Gold Refractors Thick Stock

*GOLD REF: 1X TO 2.5X BASIC
STATED PRINT RUN 539 SER.#'d SETS

PP5 Mike Trout	150.00	400.00

2010 Bowman Platinum Prospects Gold Refractors Thin Stock

*GOLD REF: 1X TO 2.5X BASIC
STATED PRINT RUN 539 SER.#'d SETS

PP5 Mike Trout	150.00	400.00

2010 Bowman Platinum Prospects Green Refractors

*GREEN REF: 1X TO 2.5X BASIC
STATED PRINT RUN 499 SER.#'d SETS

PP5 Mike Trout	150.00	400.00

2010 Bowman Platinum Prospects Purple Refractors

*PURPLE REF: .6X TO 1.5X BASIC

PP5 Mike Trout	100.00	250.00

2010 Bowman Platinum Prospects Red Refractors

STATED PRINT RUN 25 SER.#'d SETS

2010 Bowman Platinum Relic Autographs Refractors

STATED PRINT RUN 740 SER.#'d SETS
STRASBURG PRINT RUN 240 SER.#'d SETS

AC Andrew Cashner	5.00	12.00
AD Alex Dickerson	5.00	12.00
AM Andrew Maggi	6.00	15.00
AMC Andrew McCutchen	15.00	40.00
BC Brett Cecil	5.00	12.00
BJ Brian Johnson	5.00	12.00
BL Brad Lincoln	5.00	12.00
BM Brad Miller	6.00	15.00
BMO Brett Mooneyham	5.00	12.00
CJ Chris Johnson	5.00	12.00
CP Carlos Pena	5.00	12.00
GC Gerrit Cole	20.00	50.00
GS George Springer	15.00	40.00
JB Jackie Bradley Jr.	10.00	25.00
JBA Jose Bautista	6.00	15.00
JE Jason Esposito	5.00	12.00
JH Jason Heyward	5.00	12.00
JJ Josh Johnson	5.00	12.00
JT Jose Tabata	5.00	12.00
KW Kyle Winkler	5.00	12.00
MB Matt Barnes	8.00	20.00
MM Mikie Mahtook	5.00	12.00
NC Nelson Cruz	5.00	12.00
NF Nolan Fontana	5.00	12.00
NR Nick Ramirez	5.00	12.00
NRA Noe Ramirez	5.00	12.00
PF Prince Fielder	6.00	15.00
PO Peter O'Brien	5.00	12.00
PS Pablo Sandoval	6.00	15.00
RC Robinson Cano	8.00	20.00
RH Ryan Howard	12.00	30.00
RW Ryan Wright	5.00	12.00
SC Starlin Castro	5.00	12.00
SG Sean Gilmartin	5.00	12.00
SGR Sonny Gray	5.00	12.00
SM Scott McGough	10.00	25.00
SR Steve Rodriguez	5.00	12.00
SS Stephen Strasburg/240	40.00	100.00
TA Tyler Anderson	5.00	12.00

2010 Bowman Platinum Relic Autographs Blue Refractors

*BLUE: .75X TO 2X BASIC
STATED PRINT RUN 50 SER.#'d SETS

2010 Bowman Platinum Relic Autographs Green Refractors

*GREEN: .6X TO 1.5X BASIC
STATED PRINT RUN 199 SER.#'d SETS

2010 Bowman Platinum Relic Autographs Red Refractors

STATED PRINT RUN 10 SER.#'d SETS

2010 Bowman Platinum Triple Autographs

STATED PRINT RUN 89 SER.#'d SETS

AJM And/Johnson/Moon	10.00	25.00
CBG Cole/Barnes/Gray	25.00	60.00
CVM Wright/Vitters/Moustakas	15.00	40.00
MMF Maggi/Mahtook/Fontana	10.00	25.00
MOW Miller/O'Brien/Wright	12.00	30.00
REG Ramirez/Esposito/Gilmartin	10.00	25.00
RWM Ramirez/Winkler/McGough	12.00	30.00
SBD Springer/Bradley/Dickerson	12.00	40.00
SPM Santana/Posey/Montero	40.00	80.00
TRU Tillman/Reimold/Uehara	10.00	25.00

2011 Bowman Platinum

COMPLETE SET (100)	10.00	25.00
COMMON CARD (1-100)	.12	.30
COMMON RC (1-100)	.30	.75
1 Ryan Howard	.25	.60
2 Josh Rodriguez RC	.30	.75
3 Adam Jones	.20	.50
4 Jon Lester	.20	.50
5 Brad Emaus RC	.30	.75
6 Miguel Cabrera	.30	.75
7 Hank Conger RC	.50	1.25
8 Hanley Ramirez	.20	.50
9 Derek Jeter	.75	2.00
10 Austin Jackson	.12	.30
11 Justin Upton	.20	.50
12 Jimmy Rollins	.20	.50
13 Carlos Santana	.30	.75
14 Jeremy Hellickson RC	.75	2.00
15 Roy Oswalt	.20	.50
16 Carl Crawford	.20	.50
17 Ryan Braun	.20	.50
18 Adam Dunn	.20	.50
19 Carlos Gonzalez	.20	.50
20 Pedro Alvarez RC	.60	1.50
21 Mark Trumbo (RC)	.75	2.00
22 Daniel Descalso RC	.30	.75
23 Mike Stanton	.30	.75
24 Andre Ethier	.20	.50
25 Brandon Beachy RC	.75	2.00
26 Robinson Cano	.20	.50
27 Jake McGee (RC)	.30	.75
28 Buster Posey	.40	1.00
29 Brent Morel RC	.30	.75
30 Felix Hernandez	.20	.50
31 Adrian Gonzalez	.25	.60
32 Jason Heyward	.25	.60
33 Madison Bumgarner	.25	.60
34 Nick Markakis	.25	.60
35 Chris Sale RC	2.00	5.00
36 Johan Santana	.20	.50
37 Josh Johnson	.20	.50
38 Manny Ramirez	.30	.75
39 Brian McCann	.20	.50
40 Clay Buchholz	.12	.30
41 Gordon Beckham	.12	.30
42 Ubaldo Jimenez	.12	.30
43 Joey Votto	.30	.75
44 Jeremy Jeffress RC	.30	.75
45 Torii Hunter	.12	.30
46 Kendry Morales	.12	.30
47 Cory Luebke RC	.30	.75
48 Mark Teixeira	.20	.50
49 Joe Mauer	.25	.60
50 Mat Latos	.20	.50
51 Jose Bautista	.20	.50
52 Brandon Belt RC	.75	2.00
53 David Ortiz	.30	.75
54 Matt Cain	.20	.50
55 Michael Pineda RC	.75	2.00
56 Jered Weaver	.20	.50
57 Freddie Freeman RC	5.00	12.00
58 Clayton Kershaw	.60	1.50
59 Justin Morneau	.20	.50
60 CC Sabathia	.20	.50
61 Jayson Werth	.20	.50
62 David Wright	.25	.60
63 Prince Fielder	.20	.50
64 Hunter Pence	.20	.50
65 Albert Pujols	.40	1.00
66 Dustin Pedroia	.25	.60
67 Victor Martinez	.20	.50
68 Stephen Strasburg	.30	.75
69 Jose Reyes	.20	.50
70 Zack Greinke	.20	.50
71 Dan Haren	.12	.30
72 Tim Lincecum	.20	.50
73 Ryan Zimmerman	.20	.50
74 Starlin Castro	.20	.50
75 Josh Hamilton	.20	.50

76 Yonder Alonso RC .50 1.25
77 Dan Uggla .12 .30
78 Jonathan Sanchez .12 .30
79 Andrew McCutchen .30 .75
80 Billy Butler .12 .30
81 Carlos Pena .20 .50
82 Justin Verlander .30 .75
83 Cole Hamels .25 .60
84 Ike Davis .12 .30
85 Jacoby Ellsbury .25 .60
86 Chipper Jones .30 .75
87 Cliff Lee .20 .50
88 Vernon Wells .12 .30
89 Shin-Soo Choo .20 .50
90 Alex Rodriguez .40 1.00
91 Troy Tulowitzki .30 .75
92 Kevin Youkilis .12 .30
93 Aroldis Chapman RC 1.00 2.50
94 Chase Utley .20 .50
95 Kyle Drabek RC .50 1.25
96 Matt Kemp .25 .60
97 Evan Longoria .20 .50
98 Matt Holliday .30 .75
99 Roy Halladay .20 .50
100 Ichiro Suzuki .40 1.00

2011 Bowman Platinum Emerald

*EMERALD: 2X TO 5X BASIC
*EMERALD RC: .75X TO 2X BASIC RC

2011 Bowman Platinum Gold

*GOLD: 1.5X TO 4X BASIC
*GOLD RC: .6X TO 1.5X BASIC RC

2011 Bowman Platinum Ruby

*RUBY: 3X TO 8X BASIC
*RUBY RC: 1.2X TO 3X BASIC RC

2011 Bowman Platinum Dual Autographs

STATED PRINT RUN 89 SER.#'d SETS
RED PRINT RUN 10 SER.#'d SETS
NO RED PRICING DUE TO SCARCITY
SUPERFRACTOR PRINT RUN 1 SER.#'d SET
NO SUPERFRACTOR PRICING AVAILABLE
EXCHANGE DEADLINE 7/31/2014
CM L.Chisenhall/M.Moustakas 8.00 20.00
DT Jaff Decker/Donavan Tate 5.00 12.00
GC G.Green/M.Choice 5.00 12.00
GL D.Gordon/L.Landry 5.00 12.00
HT B.Harper/J.Taillon 100.00 250.00
MC M.Machado/C.Colon 20.00 50.00
MM M.Montgomery/M.Moustakas 8.00 20.00
NW Hector Noesi/Adam Warren 5.00 12.00
SD Jake Skole/Kellin Deglan EXCH 3.00 8.00
SM G.Sanchez/J.Montero 30.00 80.00

2011 Bowman Platinum Dual Autographs Red Refractors

STATED PRINT RUN 10 SER.#'d SETS
NO PRICING DUE TO SCARCITY
EXCHANGE DEADLINE 7/31/2014

2011 Bowman Platinum Dual Relic Autographs

STATED PRINT RUN 89 SER.#'d SETS
RED PRINT RUN 10 SER.#'d SETS
NO RED PRICING DUE TO SCARCITY
SUPERFRACTOR PRINT RUN 1 SER.#'d SET
NO SUPERFRACTOR PRICING AVAILABLE
EXCHANGE DEADLINE 7/31/2014
CB S.Castro/M.Byrd 10.00 25.00
CP J.Chamberlain/R.Perry 10.00 25.00
DP I.Davis/A.Pagan 12.50 30.00
GC A.Gonzalez/C.Crawford 20.00 50.00
HK D.Haren/S.Kazmir 10.00 25.00
IV R.Ibanez/S.Victorino 10.00 25.00
JS J.Johnson/M.Stanton 30.00 60.00
JU A.Jones/J.Upton 15.00 40.00
JW C.Johnson/B.Wallace EXCH 10.00 25.00
KB I.Kinsler/G.Beckham 10.00 25.00
SB D.Span/B.Boesch 10.00 25.00
SM P.Sandoval/C.McGehee 10.00 25.00

2011 Bowman Platinum Dual Relic Autographs Red Refractors

STATED PRINT RUN 10 SER.#'d SETS
NO PRICING DUE TO SCARCITY
EXCHANGE DEADLINE 7/31/2014

2011 Bowman Platinum Hexagraph Patches

STATED PRINT RUN 10 SER.#'d SETS
NO PRICING DUE TO SCARCITY

2011 Bowman Platinum Hexagraphs

STATED PRINT RUN 10 SER.#'d SETS
NO PRICING DUE TO SCARCITY

2011 Bowman Platinum Prospect Autograph Refractors

PLATE PRINT RUN 1 SET PER COLOR
BLACK-CYAN-MAGENTA-YELLOW ISSUED
NO PLATE PRICING DUE TO SCARCITY
EXCHANGE DEADLINE 7/31/2014
AF Anderson Feliz 3.00 8.00
AW Alex Wimmers 3.00 8.00
AWA Adam Warren 3.00 8.00
BE Brett Eibner 4.00 10.00
BG Brandon Guyer 3.00 8.00
BH Bryce Harper 100.00 250.00
BHO Brad Holt 3.00 8.00
CD Cutter Dykstra 3.00 8.00
CR Clint Robinson 3.00 8.00
CS Cody Scarpetta 3.00 8.00
DD Delino DeShields 3.00 8.00
DJ Dickie Joe Thon 3.00 8.00
DM Deck McGuire 3.00 8.00
DS Domingo Santana 6.00 15.00
GR Garrett Richards 4.00 10.00
HN Hector Noesi 3.00 8.00
HS Hayden Simpson 3.00 8.00
JB Joe Benson 3.00 8.00
JJ Jiwan James 3.00 8.00
JP Jimmy Paredes 4.00 10.00
JPA Jordan Pacheco 4.00 10.00
JSE Jean Segura 3.00 8.00
JSW Jordan Swagerty 3.00 8.00
JT Jameson Taillon 4.00 10.00
KP Kyle Parker 6.00 15.00
KS Kyle Seager 6.00 15.00
LL Leon Landry 3.00 8.00
MC Michael Choice 4.00 10.00
MD Miguel De Los Santos 3.00 8.00
MF Mike Foltynewicz 3.00 8.00
MH Matt Harvey 6.00 15.00
MM Manny Machado EXCH 15.00 40.00
RD Rashun Dixon 3.00 8.00
RDE Randall Delgado 3.00 8.00
SH Shaeffer Hall 3.00 8.00
SM Shelby Miller 3.00 8.00
TS Tyler Skaggs 4.00 10.00
NNO Mystery EXCH 10.00 25.00

2011 Bowman Platinum Prospect Autograph Blue Refractors

*BLUE: .75X TO 2X BASIC
STATED PRINT RUN 99 SER.#'d SETS
EXCHANGE DEADLINE 7/31/2014
BH Bryce Harper 150.00 400.00

2011 Bowman Platinum Prospect Autograph Gold Refractors

*GOLD : 1.2X TO 3X BASIC
STATED PRINT RUN 50 SER.#'d SETS
EXCHANGE DEADLINE 7/31/2014
BH Bryce Harper 300.00 600.00
DM Deck McGuire 15.00 40.00

2011 Bowman Platinum Prospect Autograph Green Refractors

*GREEN : .5X TO 1.2X BASIC
STATED PRINT RUN 399 SER.#'d SETS
EXCHANGE DEADLINE 7/31/2014
BH Bryce Harper 125.00 300.00

2011 Bowman Platinum Prospect Autograph Red Refractors

STATED PRINT RUN 10 SER.#'d SETS
NO PRICING DUE TO SCARCITY
EXCHANGE DEADLINE 7/31/2014

2011 Bowman Platinum Prospects

COMPLETE SET (100) 40.00 80.00
PLATE PRINT RUN 1 SET PER COLOR
BLACK-CYAN-MAGENTA-YELLOW ISSUED
NO PLATE PRICING DUE TO SCARCITY
BPP1 Bryce Harper 8.00 20.00
BPP2 Dee Gordon .60 1.50
BPP3 Jesus Montero .40 1.00
BPP4 Daniel Fields .40 1.00
BPP5 Deck McGuire .40 1.00
BPP6 Zach Lee .60 1.50
BPP7 Travis D'Arnaud .60 1.50
BPP8 Anderson Feliz .40 1.00
BPP9 Blake Smith .40 1.00
BPP10 Jonathan Singleton .60 1.50
BPP11 Kyle Seager 1.00 2.50
BPP12 Avisail Garcia .60 1.50
BPP13 Miguel De Los Santos .40 1.00
BPP14 Ronnie Welty .40 1.00
BPP15 Ryan Lavarnway 1.50 4.00
BPP16 Yasmani Grandal .60 1.50
BPP17 Kolbrin Vitek .60 1.50
BPP18 Zack Cox .60 1.50
BPP19 Jimmy Paredes 1.00 2.50
BPP20 Joe Benson .40 1.00
BPP21 Austin Hyatt .60 1.50
BPP22 Corban Joseph .40 1.00
BPP23 Josh Zeid .40 1.00
BPP24 Oswaldo Arcia .40 1.00
BPP25 Jacob Turner 1.50 4.00
BPP26 Jose Iglesias .60 1.50
BPP27 Jarred Cosart .60 1.50
BPP28 Shaeffer Hall .60 1.50
BPP29 Manny Banuelos 1.00 2.50
BPP30 Tyler Skaggs 1.00 2.50
BPP31 Domingo Santana 1.00 2.50
BPP32 Dustin Ackley .60 1.50
BPP33 Dickie Joe Thon .60 1.50
BPP34 Jurickson Profar 1.00 2.50
BPP35 Tony Wolters .40 1.00
BPP36 Aderlin Rodriguez .40 1.00
BPP37 Cito Culver 1.50 4.00
BPP38 Billy Hamilton .75 2.00
BPP39 Yorman Rodriguez .60 1.50
BPP40 Matt Dominguez .60 1.50
BPP41 Delino DeShields .40 1.00
BPP42 Brandon Short .60 1.50
BPP43 Michael Choice .60 1.50
BPP44 Wilmer Flores .60 1.50
BPP45 Jake Marisnick .60 1.50
BPP46 Leon Landry .60 1.50
BPP47 Derek Norris .40 1.00
BPP48 Mike Foltynewicz .40 1.00
BPP49 Rashun Dixon .40 1.00
BPP50 Drew Pomeranz .60 1.50
BPP51 Alex Wimmers .40 1.00
BPP52 Cody Scarpetta .40 1.00
BPP53 Eduardo Escobar .40 1.00
BPP54 Jake Skole .40 1.00
BPP55 David Cooper .40 1.00
BPP56 Jarrod Parker 1.00 2.50
BPP57 Jacob Goebbert .60 1.50
BPP58 Carlos Perez .40 1.00
BPP59 Kevin Mailloux .40 1.00
BPP60 Drew Vettleson .40 1.00
BPP61 Hayden Simpson .40 1.00
BPP62 Hector Noesi .60 1.50
BPP63 Jonathan Schoop .60 1.50
BPP64 Nick Franklin .60 1.50
BPP65 Jameson Taillon .60 1.50
BPP66 Matt Harvey 2.50 6.00
BPP67 Keon Broxton .40 1.00
BPP68 Allen Webster .60 1.50
BPP69 Kyle Parker .60 1.50
BPP70 Brad Brach .40 1.00
BPP71 Johermyn Chavez .40 1.00
BPP72 Shelby Miller 2.00 5.00
BPP73 Julio Teheran .60 1.50
BPP74 Jordan Swagerty .60 1.50
BPP75 Sean Coyle .60 1.50
BPP76 Kyle Russell .60 1.50
BPP77 Cutter Dykstra .40 1.00
BPP78 Brad Holt .40 1.00
PP79 Chun-Hsiu Chen 1.00 2.50
BPP80 Brandon Guyer .60 1.50
BPP81 Cesar Puello .60 1.50
BPP82 Garrett Richards 1.00 2.50
BPP83 Manny Machado 4.00 10.00
BPP84 Jared Mitchell .60 1.50
BPP85 Brody Colvin .40 1.00
BPP86 Tim Beckham 1.00 2.50
BPP87 Adron Chambers .40 1.00
BPP88 Marcell Ozuna 1.50 4.00
BPP89 Sammy Solis .40 1.00
BPP90 Gary Brown 1.00 2.50
BPP91 Kaleb Cowart .60 1.50
BPP92 Trey McNutt .40 1.00
BPP93 Jordan Pacheco .40 1.00
BPP94 Adam Warren .60 1.50
BPP95 Matt Lipka .60 1.50
BPP96 Christian Colon .40 1.00
BPP97 Carlos Perez .40 1.00
BPP98 Matt Moore 1.00 2.50
BPP99 Chris Archer .75 2.00
BPP100 Jaff Decker .40 1.00

2011 Bowman Platinum Prospects Refractors

*REF: .5X TO 1.2X BASIC
BPP1 Bryce Harper 10.00 25.00

2011 Bowman Platinum Prospects Blue Refractors

*BLUE: 1.2X TO 3X BASIC
STATED PRINT RUN 199 SER.#'d SETS
BPP1 Bryce Harper 30.00 80.00

2011 Bowman Platinum Prospects Gold Canary Diamond Refractors

STATED PRINT RUN 1 SER.#'d SET
NO PRICING DUE TO SCARCITY

2011 Bowman Platinum Prospects Gold Refractors

*GOLD: 3X TO 8X BASIC
STATED PRINT RUN 50 SER.#'d SETS
BPP1 Bryce Harper 125.00 250.00

2011 Bowman Platinum Prospects Green Refractors

*GREEN: .75X TO 2X BASIC
STATED PRINT RUN 599 SER.#'d SETS
BPP1 Bryce Harper 15.00 40.00

2011 Bowman Platinum Prospects Purple Refractors

*PURPLE: .6X TO 1.5X BASIC
BPP1 Bryce Harper 8.00 20.00

2011 Bowman Platinum Prospects Red Refractors

STATED PRINT RUN 25 SER.#'d SETS
NO PRICING DUE TO SCARCITY

2011 Bowman Platinum Prospects X-Fractors

*X-FRACTOR: .5X TO 1.2X BASIC

2011 Bowman Platinum Relic Autograph Refractors

PRINT RUN B/WN 115-1166 COPIES PER
2011 Bowman Platinum Relic Autograph Blue Refractors
AJ Austin Jackson/115 6.00 15.00
AR Adam Rosales/1166 4.00 10.00
BC Brett Cecil EXCH 4.00 10.00
CM Cristhian Martinez/1166 4.00 10.00
EB Emilio Bonifacio/1166 4.00 10.00
EE Edwin Encarnacion/1166 4.00 10.00
EM Evan Meek/1166 4.00 10.00
FF Freddie Freeman/115 20.00 50.00
FM Franklin Morales/1166 4.00 10.00
JA J.P. Arencibia/666 5.00 12.00
JC Jesse Crain/1166 4.00 10.00
JF Juan Francisco/1166 4.00 10.00
JM Jake McGee/1166 4.00 10.00
JM Jhan Marinez/1166 4.00 10.00
JM John McDonald/1166 4.00 10.00
JM Juan Miranda/1166 4.00 10.00
LN Leo Nunez/1166 4.00 10.00
MR Max Ramirez/1166 4.00 10.00
OM Ozzie Martinez/1166 4.00 10.00
RT Robinson Tejeda/1166 4.00 10.00
SC Starlin Castro/666 8.00 20.00
TB Trevor Bell EXCH 4.00 10.00
YN Yamacio Navarro/1166 4.00 10.00
JHL Jeremy Hellickson/115 6.00 15.00

2011 Bowman Platinum Relic Autograph Blue Refractors

*BLUE: .6X TO 1.5X BASIC pr/666-1166
*BLUE: .4X TO 1X BASIC pr/115
STATED PRINT RUN 99 SER.#'d SETS
EXCHANGE DEADLINE 7/31/2014

2011 Bowman Platinum Relic Autograph Gold Refractors

STATED PRINT RUN 25 SER.#'d SETS
NO PRICING DUE TO SCARCITY
EXCHANGE DEADLINE 7/31/2014

2011 Bowman Platinum Relic Autograph Green Refractors

*GREEN: .5X TO 1.2X BASIC
STATED PRINT RUN 199 SER.#'d SETS
EXCHANGE DEADLINE 7/31/2014

2011 Bowman Platinum Relic Autograph Red Refractors

STATED PRINT RUN 10 SER.#'d SETS
NO PRICING DUE TO SCARCITY
EXCHANGE DEADLINE 7/31/2014

2011 Bowman Platinum Team USA National Team Autographs

EXCHANGE DEADLINE 12/31/2012
BR Brady Rodgers 3.00 8.00
CE Chris Elder 4.00 10.00
DF Dominic Ficociello 5.00 12.00
DL David Lyon 3.00 8.00
DM Deven Marrero 3.00 8.00
EW Erich Weiss 4.00 10.00
HM Hoby Milner 4.00 10.00
KG Kevin Gausman 8.00 20.00
MA Mark Appel 6.00 15.00
ML Michael Lorenzen 3.00 8.00
MR Matt Reynolds 4.00 10.00
MS Marcus Stroman 6.00 15.00
NNO Mystery EXCH 10.00 25.00

2011 Bowman Platinum Triple Autographs Red Refractors

STATED PRINT RUN 10 SER.#'d SETS
NO PRICING DUE TO SCARCITY
EXCHANGE DEADLINE 7/31/2014

2011 Bowman Platinum Triple Autographs

STATED PRINT RUN 89 SER.#'d SETS
RED PRINT RUN 10 SER.#'d SETS
NO RED PRICING DUE TO SCARCITY
SUPERFRACTOR PRINT RUN 1 SER.#'d SET
NO SUPERFRACTOR PRICING AVAILABLE
EXCHANGE DEADLINE 7/31/2014
CWJ Castro/Wall/John 15.00 40.00
FHD Free/How/Davis 40.00 100.00
HKW Har/Kaz/Wald 8.00 20.00
HSB Hey/Stan/D.Brow 75.00 150.00
MAC Mon/Ack/Chis EXCH 15.00 40.00
PMM Pos/Mauer/Mon EXCH 30.00 80.00
SPG Soto/Pena/Garza 10.00 25.00

2012 Bowman Platinum

COMPLETE SET (100) 15.00 40.00
STATED PLATE ODDS 1:1118 HOBBY
PLATE PRINT RUN 1 SET PER COLOR
BLACK-CYAN-MAGENTA-YELLOW ISSUED
NO PLATE PRICING DUE TO SCARCITY
1 Michael Pineda .20 .50
2 Joe Mauer .25 .60
3 Liam Hendriks RC .50 1.25
4 Adrian Beltre .30 .75
5 Josh Johnson .25 .60
6 Miguel Cabrera .30 .75
7 Matt Kemp .25 .60
8 Ichiro Suzuki .40 1.00
9 Yu Darvish RC 1.25 3.00
10 Carlos Gonzalez .25 .60
11 Jose Reyes .20 .50
12 Eric Hosmer .25 .60
13 Jay Bruce .25 .60
14 Derek Jeter .75 2.00
15 Lance Berkman .25 .60
16 Mike Trout 10.00 25.00
17 Tyler Pastornicky RC .50 1.25
18 Tommy Hanson .20 .50
19 Dustin Pedroia .25 .60
20 Prince Fielder .25 .60
21 Yoenis Cespedes RC 1.25 3.00
22 Jose Bautista .25 .60
23 Ian Kennedy .20 .50
24 Chipper Jones .30 .75
25 Jeremy Hellickson .20 .50
26 James Shields .20 .50
27 Brian McCann .25 .60
28 David Price .25 .60
29 Mike Napoli .20 .50
30 Adrian Gonzalez .25 .60
31 Andre Ethier .25 .60
32 Giancarlo Stanton .30 .75
33 Adam Jones .25 .60
34 Ryan Braun .20 .50
35 Joey Votto .30 .75
36 Alex Rodriguez .40 1.00
37 Justin Verlander .30 .75
38 Ian Kinsler .25 .60
39 Justin Upton .25 .60
40 Ubaldo Jimenez .20 .50
41 Carlos Santana .25 .60
42 Rickie Weeks .20 .50
43 Mark Teixeira .25 .60
44 Leonys Martin RC .50 1.25
45 Mariano Rivera .40 1.00
46 Andrew McCutchen .30 .75
47 Ryan Howard .25 .60
48 Kirk Nieuwenhuis RC .50 1.25
49 Robinson Cano .25 .60
50 Josh Beckett .20 .50
51 Troy Tulowitzki .30 .75
52 Addison Reed RC .50 1.25
53 Desmond Jennings .25 .60
54 Evan Longoria .25 .60
55 Clayton Kershaw .60 1.50
56 Bryce Harper RC 8.00 20.00
57 Buster Posey .40 1.00
58 Paul Konerko .20 .50
59 Josh Hamilton .25 .60
60 Brad Peacock RC .50 1.25
61 C.J. Wilson .20 .50
62 Alex Gordon .25 .60
63 Dan Uggla .25 .60
64 David Ortiz .30 .75
65 Jesus Montero .20 .50
66 Michael Morse .20 .50
67 Cole Hamels .25 .60
68 Albert Pujols .40 1.00
69 Drew Pomeranz RC .50 1.25
70 Jon Lester .20 .50
71 Tim Hudson .25 .60
72 Curtis Granderson .25 .60
73 Madison Bumgarner .25 .60
74 Nelson Cruz .30 .75
75 Kevin Youkilis .30 .75
76 Tim Lincecum .25 .60
77 Pablo Sandoval .25 .60
78 Jered Weaver .25 .60
79 Starlin Castro .25 .60
80 Stephen Strasburg .30 .75
81 Hisashi Iwakuma RC 1.00 2.50
82 David Freese .20 .50
83 Devin Mesoraco RC .50 1.25
84 Justin Morneau .25 .60
85 Felix Hernandez .25 .60
86 Ryan Zimmerman .25 .60
87 Zack Greinke .25 .60
88 CC Sabathia .25 .60
89 Hanley Ramirez .25 .60
90 David Wright .25 .60
91 Cliff Lee .25 .60
92 Wilin Rosario RC .50 1.25
93 Roy Halladay .25 .60
94 Mat Latos .25 .60
95 Asdrubal Cabrera .25 .60
96 Jarrod Parker RC .60 1.50
97 Matt Holliday .30 .75
98 Freddie Freeman .40 1.00
99 Matt Moore RC .75 2.00
100 Jacoby Ellsbury .25 .60

2012 Bowman Platinum Emerald

*EMERALD: 2X TO 5X BASIC
*EMERALD RC: .75X TO 2X BASIC RC
STATED ODDS 1:10 HOBBY

2012 Bowman Platinum Gold

*GOLD: 1.5X TO 4X BASIC
*GOLD RC: .6X TO 1.5X BASIC RC
STATED ODDS 1:5 HOBBY

2012 Bowman Platinum Ruby

*RUBY: 3X TO 8X BASIC
*RUBY RC: 1.2X TO 3X BASIC RC
STATED ODDS 1:20 HOBBY

2012 Bowman Platinum Blue National Promo

ISSUED AT 2012 NATIONAL CONVENTION
STATED PRINT RUN 499 SER.#'d SETS
9 Yu Darvish 4.00 10.00
21 Yoenis Cespedes 4.00 10.00
44 Leonys Martin 1.50 4.00
52 Addison Reed 1.50 4.00
56 Bryce Harper 25.00 60.00
60 Brad Peacock 1.50 4.00
65 Jesus Montero 1.50 4.00
69 Drew Pomeranz 1.50 4.00
81 Norichika Aoki 2.00 5.00
83 Devin Mesoraco 1.50 4.00
92 Wilin Rosario 1.50 4.00
96 Jarrod Parker 2.00 5.00
99 Matt Moore 2.50 6.00

2012 Bowman Platinum Cutting Edge Stars

STATED ODDS 1:10 HOBBY
I Ichiro Suzuki 1.25 3.00
AC Allen Craig .75 2.00
AG Adrian Gonzalez .75 2.00
AM Andrew McCutchen 1.00 2.50
AP Albert Pujols 1.25 3.00
BH Bryce Harper 6.00 15.00
BL Brett Lawrie .75 2.00
BM Brian McCann .75 2.00
BP Buster Posey 1.25 3.00
CG Carlos Gonzalez .75 2.00
CJ Chipper Jones 1.00 2.50
DA Dustin Ackley .60 1.50
DF David Freese .60 1.50
DH Daniel Hudson .60 1.50
DJ Derek Jeter 2.50 6.00
DO David Ortiz 1.00 2.50
DU Dan Uggla .75 2.00
DW David Wright .75 2.00
EH Eric Hosmer .75 2.00
EL Evan Longoria .75 2.00
FF Freddie Freeman 1.25 3.00
HB Heath Bell .60 1.50
HR Hanley Ramirez .75 2.00
IK Ian Kinsler .75 2.00
IN Ivan Nova .75 2.00
JB Jose Bautista .75 2.00
JM Jason Motte .60 1.50
JS James Shields .60 1.50
JU Justin Upton .75 2.00
JV Justin Verlander 1.00 2.50
MC Miguel Cabrera 1.00 2.50
MM Matt Moore 1.00 2.50
MP Michael Pineda .60 1.50
MT Mark Trumbo .60 1.50
NC Nelson Cruz 1.00 2.50
PF Prince Fielder .75 2.00
PG Paul Goldschmidt 1.00 2.50
RB Ryan Braun .60 1.50
RC Robinson Cano .75 2.00
RR Ricky Romero .60 1.50
SC Starlin Castro .75 2.00
TT Troy Tulowitzki 1.00 2.50
YA Yonder Alonso .60 1.50
YD Yu Darvish 1.50 4.00
YG Yovani Gallardo .75 2.00
ZG Zack Greinke .75 2.00
IKE Ian Kennedy .60 1.50
JDM J.D. Martinez 1.00 2.50
JMO Jesus Montero .60 1.50
MMS Michael Morse .60 1.50

2012 Bowman Platinum Cutting Edge Stars Relics

STATED ODDS 1:490 HOBBY
STATED PRINT RUN 50 SER.#'d SETS
AG Adrian Gonzalez 8.00 20.00
AM Andrew McCutchen 12.50 30.00
AP Albert Pujols 8.00 20.00
BM Brian McCann 8.00 20.00
BP Buster Posey 12.50 30.00
CJ Chipper Jones 12.50 30.00
DJ Derek Jeter 12.50 30.00
DO David Ortiz 8.00 20.00
DU Dan Uggla 4.00 10.00
DW David Wright 8.00 20.00
EH Eric Hosmer 6.00 15.00
EL Evan Longoria 8.00 20.00
FF Freddie Freeman 8.00 20.00
HR Hanley Ramirez 6.00 15.00
IK Ian Kinsler 4.00 10.00
JS James Shields 5.00 12.00
JU Justin Upton 6.00 15.00
JV Justin Verlander 12.50 30.00
NC Nelson Cruz 4.00 10.00
RB Ryan Braun 8.00 20.00
RR Ricky Romero 4.00 10.00
TT Troy Tulowitzki 6.00 15.00
YG Yovani Gallardo 4.00 10.00
ZG Zack Greinke 4.00 10.00
JBA Jose Bautista 5.00 12.00

2012 Bowman Platinum Dual Autographs

STATED ODDS 1:1066 HOBBY
STATED PRINT RUN 50 SER.#'d SETS
EXCHANGE DEADLINE 06/30/2015
BJ T.Jungmann/J.Bradley 15.00 40.00
BS Blake Swihart/Matt Barnes 15.00 40.00
CT J.Taillon/G.Cole 50.00 100.00
HM Brandon Martin/Jake Hager 15.00 40.00
HP Paxton/Hultzen EXCH 20.00 50.00
JP J.Panik/T.Joseph 15.00 40.00
LB J.Baez/F.Lindor 40.00 80.00
SB J.Bell/B.Starling EXCH 40.00 80.00
ST Terdoslavich/Simmons EXCH 40.00 80.00
TT O.Taveras/C.Tilson 60.00 120.00

2012 Bowman Platinum Jumbo Relic Autograph Refractors

STATED ODDS 1:180 HOBBY
PRINTING PLATE ODDS 1:11,186 HOBBY
PLATE PRINT RUN 1 SET PER COLOR
BLACK-CYAN-MAGENTA-YELLOW ISSUED
NO PLATE PRICING DUE TO SCARCITY
EXCHANGE DEADLINE 06/30/2015
AG Anthony Gose EXCH 5.00 12.00
BH Bryce Harper 100.00 200.00
DH Danny Hultzen 6.00 15.00
GC Gerrit Cole 15.00 40.00
JP Joe Panik 12.50 30.00
JS Jean Segura 5.00 12.00
MA Matt Adams 8.00 20.00
MC Michael Choice 5.00 12.00
NA Nolan Arenado 40.00 100.00

2012 Bowman Platinum Jumbo Relic Autograph Blue Refractors

*BLUE: .6X TO 1.5X BASIC
STATED ODDS 1:258 HOBBY
STATED PRINT RUN 199 SER.#'d SETS
EXCHANGE DEADLINE 06/30/2015

2012 Bowman Platinum Jumbo Relic Autograph Gold Refractors

*GOLD: 1.2X TO 3X BASIC
STATED ODDS 1:1025 HOBBY
STATED PRINT RUN 50 SER.#'d SETS
EXCHANGE DEADLINE 06/30/2015
BH Bryce Harper 150.00 300.00

2012 Bowman Platinum Prospect Autographs

STATED ODDS 1:14 HOBBY
PRINTING PLATE ODDS 1:2728 HOBBY
PLATE PRINT RUN 1 SET PER COLOR
BLACK-CYAN-MAGENTA-YELLOW ISSUED
NO PLATE PRICING DUE TO SCARCITY
EXCHANGE DEADLINE 06/30/2015
AR Anthony Rendon 25.00 60.00
ASU Andrew Susac 3.00 8.00
BB Bryan Brickhouse 3.00 8.00
BJ Brandon Jacobs 4.00 10.00
BS Bubba Starling EXCH 4.00 10.00
CC Carter Capps 3.00 8.00
CH Clay Holmes 3.00 8.00
CT Charlie Tilson 3.00 8.00
DB Dylan Bundy 10.00 25.00
DBU David Buchanan 3.00 8.00
DC Daniel Corcino 3.00 8.00
DH Danny Hultzen 3.00 8.00
DM Dillon Maples 3.00 8.00
DN Daniel Norris 4.00 10.00
DNO Derek Norris EXCH 3.00 8.00
EA Eric Arce 3.00 8.00
GB Greg Bird 15.00 40.00
GC Gerrit Cole 10.00 25.00
GP Guillermo Pimentel EXCH 3.00 8.00
JB Josh Bell 8.00 20.00
JG Jonathan Galvez 3.00 8.00
JM Jermaine Mitchell 3.00 8.00
JR Joe Ross 3.00 8.00
JT Joe Terdoslavich 3.00 8.00
KC Kole Calhoun 3.00 8.00
LM Levi Michael 3.00 8.00
MM Mikie Mahtook 3.00 8.00
MP Matt Purke 6.00 15.00
MW Mike Wright 3.00 8.00
OA Oswaldo Arcia 3.00 8.00
RR Robbie Ray 6.00 15.00
TB Trevor Bauer 4.00 10.00
TBK Tyler Bortnick 3.00 8.00
TC Tyler Collins 3.00 8.00
TJ Tyrell Jenkins EXCH 3.00 8.00
TN Telvin Nash 4.00 10.00
TW Taijuan Walker 3.00 8.00
VC Vinnie Catricala 4.00 10.00
YA Yazy Arbelo 3.00 8.00
YC Yoenis Cespedes 12.50 30.00
YD Yu Darvish 30.00 80.00

2012 Bowman Platinum Prospect Autographs Blue Refractors

*BLUE: .6X TO 1.5X BASIC
STATED ODDS 1:145 HOBBY
STATED PRINT RUN 199 SER.#'d SETS
EXCHANGE DEADLINE 06/30/2015

2012 Bowman Platinum Prospect Autographs Gold Refractors

*GOLD: 1X TO 2.5X BASIC
STATED ODDS 1:450 HOBBY
STATED PRINT RUN 50 SER.#'d SETS
EXCHANGE DEADLINE 06/30/2015
DB Dylan Bundy 15.00 40.00
TB Trevor Bauer 20.00 50.00

2012 Bowman Platinum Prospect Autographs Green Refractors

*GREEN: .5X TO 1.2X BASIC
STATED ODDS 1:74 HOBBY
STATED PRINT RUN 399 SER.#'d SETS
EXCHANGE DEADLINE 06/30/2015

2012 Bowman Platinum Prospects

COMPLETE SET (100) 50.00 100.00
PRINTING PLATE ODDS 1:1118 HOBBY
PLATE PRINT RUN 1 SET PER COLOR
BLACK-CYAN-MAGENTA-YELLOW ISSUED
NO PLATE PRICING DUE TO SCARCITY
BPP1 Matt Adams .75 2.00
BPP2 Nolan Arenado 2.00 5.00
BPP3 Manny Banuelos .75 2.00
BPP4 Trevor Bauer 2.00 5.00
BPP5 Chad Bettis .60 1.50
BPP6 Gary Brown .60 1.50
BPP7 Garin Cecchini .75 2.00
BPP8 Michael Choice .60 1.50
BPP9 Travis d'Arnaud .75 2.00
BPP10 Brandon Drury 1.00 2.50
BPP11 Robbie Erlin .75 2.00
BPP12 Wilmer Flores .75 2.00
BPP13 Anthony Gose .75 2.00
BPP14 Robbie Grossman .60 1.50
BPP15 Jedd Gyorko .75 2.00
BPP16 Billy Hamilton .75 2.00
BPP17 Joe Terdoslavich .75 2.00
BPP18 Matt Harvey 4.00 10.00
BPP19 Brett Jackson 1.00 2.50
BPP20 Hak-Ju Lee .60 1.50
BPP21 Taylor Lindsey .60 1.50
BPP22 Rymer Liriano .60 1.50
BPP23 Manny Machado 4.00 10.00
BPP24 Starling Marte .75 2.00
BPP25 Trevor May .60 1.50
BPP26 Will Middlebrooks .75 2.00
BPP27 Shelby Miller 1.25 3.00
BPP28 Mike Montgomery .60 1.50
BPP29 Jake Odorizzi .75 2.00
BPP30 Mike Olt .75 2.00
BPP31 Marcell Ozuna 1.50 4.00
BPP32 Joe Panik 1.00 2.50
BPP33 Wily Peralta .60 1.50
BPP34 Martin Perez 1.00 2.50
BPP35 Jurickson Profar .75 2.00
BPP36 Eddie Rosario 1.25 3.00
BPP37 Keenyn Walker .60 1.50
BPP38 Gary Sanchez 2.00 5.00
BPP39 Miguel Sano .75 2.00
BPP40 Jonathan Schoop .60 1.50
BPP41 Jonathan Singleton .75 2.00
BPP42 Tyler Skaggs 1.00 2.50
BPP43 Alexi Amarista .60 1.50
BPP44 Noah Syndergaard .75 2.00
BPP45 Jameson Taillon .75 2.00
BPP46 Taijuan Walker .75 2.00
BPP47 Allen Webster .75 2.00

PP48 Zack Wheeler 1.25 3.00
PP49 Christian Yelich 5.00 12.00
PP50 Drew Hutchison .75 2.00
PP51 Oscar Taveras 1.00 2.50
PP52 A.J. Cole .75 2.00
PP53 Jake Marisnick .75 2.00
PP54 Nick Franklin .75 2.00
PP55 Nestor Molina .60 1.50
PP56 Jeurys Familia 1.00 2.50
PP57 Tim Wheeler .75 2.00
PP58 Jonathan Galvez .60 1.50
PP59 Vincent Catricala .60 1.50
PP60 Keyvius Sampson .60 1.50
PP61 Archie Bradley .40 1.00
PP62 Brian Dozier 2.00 5.00
PP63 John Lamb .60 1.50
PP64 Dylan Bundy 1.25 3.00
PP65 Jean Segura 1.00 2.50
PP66 Daniel Corcino .75 2.00
PP67 Tyler Thornburg .75 2.00
PP68 Yorman Rodriguez .40 1.00
PP69 Gerrit Cole 4.00 10.00
PP70 Tyler Pastornicky .60 1.50
PP71 Zach Cone .75 2.00
PP72 Brandon Jacobs .75 2.00
PP73 Kevin Matthews .60 1.50
PP74 Jake Hager .60 1.50
PP75 Sean Buckley .60 1.50
PP76 Andrelton Simmons 1.00 2.50
PP77 Julio Rodriguez .60 1.50
PP78 Sonny Gray 1.00 2.50
PP79 Jabari Blash .60 1.50
PP80 Wil Myers .75 2.00
PP81 Jarred Cosart .60 1.50
PP82 Chris Archer .60 1.50
PP83 Guillermo Pimentel .60 1.50
PP84 Tyler Matzek .40 1.00
PP85 Javier Baez 2.50 6.00
PP86 Cory Spangenberg .60 1.50
PP87 John Hellweg .60 1.50
PP88 Chad James .60 1.50
PP89 Telvin Nash .60 1.50
PP90 Mason Williams 1.00 2.50
PP91 Heath Hembree .75 2.00
PP92 Bryce Brentz .60 1.50
PP93 Anthony Ranaudo .75 2.00
PP94 Tommy Joseph 1.25 3.00
PP95 Trey McNutt .60 1.50
PP96 Matt Davidson .75 2.00
PP97 Nick Castellanos 2.00 5.00
PP98 Jordan Swagerty .60 1.50
PP99 Sebastian Valle .60 1.50
PP100 Bubba Starling .75 2.00

2012 Bowman Platinum Prospects Refractors
*REF: .5X TO 1.2X BASIC
STATED ODDS 1:4 HOBBY

2012 Bowman Platinum Prospects Blue Refractors
*BLUE: 1.2X TO 3X BASIC
STATED ODDS 1:31 HOBBY
STATED PRINT RUN 199 SER.#'d SETS

2012 Bowman Platinum Prospects Gold Refractors
*GOLD: 2.5X TO 6X BASIC
STATED ODDS 1:123 HOBBY
STATED PRINT RUN 50 SER.#'d SETS
BPP51 Oscar Taveras 30.00 60.00

2012 Bowman Platinum Prospects Green Refractors
*GREEN: .6X TO 1.5X BASIC
STATED ODDS 1:16 HOBBY
STATED PRINT RUN 399 SER.#'d SETS

2012 Bowman Platinum Prospects Purple Refractors
*REF: .5X TO 1.2X BASIC

2012 Bowman Platinum Prospects X-Fractors
*X-FRACTORS: .6X TO 1.5X BASIC
STATED ODDS 1:20 HOBBY

2012 Bowman Platinum Prospects Blue National Promo
ISSUED AT 2012 NATIONAL CONVENTION
STATED PRINT RUN 499 SER.#'d SETS
BPP4 Trevor Bauer 5.00 12.00
BPP23 Manny Machado 10.00 25.00
BPP27 Shelby Miller 3.00 8.00
BPP35 Jurickson Profar 2.00 5.00
BPP39 Miguel Sano 2.00 5.00
BPP42 Tyler Skaggs 2.50 6.00
BPP45 Jameson Taillon 2.00 5.00
BPP52 A.J. Cole 2.00 5.00
BPP64 Dylan Bundy 3.00 8.00
BPP69 Gerrit Cole 10.00 25.00
BPP70 Tyler Pastornicky 1.50 4.00
BPP100 Bubba Starling 2.00 5.00

2012 Bowman Platinum Relic Autographs
STATE ODDS 1:43 HOBBY
PRINTING PLATE ODDS 1:3608 HOBBY
PLATE PRINT RUN 1 SET PER COLOR
BLACK-CYAN-MAGENTA-YELLOW ISSUED
NO PLATE PRICING DUE TO SCARCITY
EXCHANGE DEADLINE 06/30/2015
AE Andre Ethier EXCH 6.00 15.00
AG Adrian Gonzalez 8.00 20.00
AR Anthony Rizzo 20.00 50.00
BL Brett Lawrie 4.00 10.00
CG Carlos Gonzalez 8.00 20.00
CM Carlos Martinez 6.00 15.00
DH Daniel Hudson 4.00 10.00
DM Devin Mesoraco 4.00 10.00
DP Dustin Pedroia 20.00 50.00
DU Dan Uggla 5.00 12.00
EH Eric Hosmer 15.00 40.00
FH Felix Hernandez 12.50 30.00
FM Francisco Martinez 6.00 15.00
JB Jay Bruce 8.00 20.00
JD Jaff Decker 4.00 10.00
JJ Jon Jay 4.00 10.00
JM J.D. Martinez 12.00 30.00
JMO Jesus Montero 8.00 20.00
JPX James Paxton 12.00 30.00
JW Jered Weaver EXCH 12.50 30.00
MD Matt Dominguez 4.00 10.00
MM Matt Moore 5.00 12.00
MMS Mike Morse 5.00 12.00
MO Mike Olt 8.00 20.00
MS Matt Szczur 4.00 10.00
MT Mike Trout 200.00 500.00
NC Nelson Cruz 8.00 20.00
PG Paul Goldschmidt 25.00 60.00
RZ Ryan Zimmerman 10.00 25.00
SM Starling Marte 5.00 12.00
TT Tyler Thornburg 5.00 12.00
YD Yu Darvish 125.00 250.00

2012 Bowman Platinum Relic Autographs Blue Refractors
*BLUE: .5X TO 1.2X BASIC
STATED ODDS 1:101 HOBBY
STATED PRINT RUN 199 SER.#'d SETS
EXCHANGE DEADLINE 06/30/2015
MT Mike Trout 250.00 600.00
YD Yu Darvish 150.00 300.00

2012 Bowman Platinum Relic Autographs Gold Refractors
*GOLD: .75X TO 2X BASIC
STATED ODDS 1:297 HOBBY
STATED PRINT RUN 50 SER.#'d SETS
EXCHANGE DEADLINE 06/30/2015
AG Adrian Gonzalez 10.00 25.00
DP Dustin Pedroia 30.00 60.00
MT Mike Trout 400.00 1000.00
SC Starlin Castro 20.00 50.00
YD Yu Darvish 250.00 350.00

2012 Bowman Platinum Top Prospects
STATED ODDS 1:5 HOBBY
AG Anthony Gose .75 2.00
BB Bryce Brentz .60 1.50
BD Brian Dozier 2.00 5.00
BH Billy Hamilton .75 2.00
BJ Brett Jackson 1.00 2.50
BS Bubba Starling .75 2.00
CS Cory Spangenberg .60 1.50
CY Christian Yelich 5.00 12.00
ER Eddie Rosario 1.25 3.00
GB Gary Brown .60 1.50
GC Gerrit Cole 4.00 10.00
JG Jedd Gyorko .75 2.00
JL John Lamb .60 1.50
JM Jake Marisnick .75 2.00
JP Jurickson Profar .75 2.00
JR Julio Rodriguez .60 1.50
JS Jean Segura 1.00 2.50
JT Jameson Taillon .75 2.00
KS Keyvius Sampson .60 1.50
MA Matt Adams .75 2.00
MB Manny Banuelos .75 2.00
MC Michael Choice .60 1.50
MH Matt Harvey 4.00 10.00
MM Manny Machado 4.00 10.00
MS Miguel Sano .75 2.00
MW Mason Williams 1.00 2.50
NA Nolan Arenado 2.00 5.00
NC Nick Castellanos 2.00 5.00
NS Noah Syndergaard .75 2.00
OT Oscar Taveras 1.00 2.50
RE Robbie Erlin .75 2.00
RL Rymer Liriano .60 1.50
SM Shelby Miller 1.25 3.00
TB Trevor Bauer 2.00 5.00
Td Travis d'Arnaud .75 2.00
TL Taylor Lindsey .60 1.50
TM Trevor May .60 1.50
TS Tyler Skaggs 1.00 2.50
TT Tyler Thornburg .75 2.00
TW Tim Wheeler .75 2.00
VC Vincent Catricala .60 1.50
WM Wil Myers .75 2.00
ZW Zack Wheeler 1.25 3.00
JGZ Jonathan Galvez .60 1.50
JPK Joe Panik 1.00 2.50
JSN Jonathan Singleton .75 2.00
JSW Jordan Swagerty .60 1.50
SME Starling Marte .75 2.00
TJW Taijuan Walker .75 2.00
WMK Will Middlebrooks .75 2.00

2013 Bowman Platinum
COMPLETE SET (100) 15.00 40.00
STATED PLATE ODDS 1:1490 HOBBY
PLATE PRINT RUN 1 SET PER COLOR
BLACK-CYAN-MAGENTA-YELLOW ISSUED
NO PLATE PRICING DUE TO SCARCITY
1 Albert Pujols .30 .75
2 Mike Trout 2.00 5.00
3 Jered Weaver .20 .50
4 Norichika Aoki .15 .40
5 Jacoby Ellsbury .20 .50
6 Jose Bautista .20 .50
7 Adam Wainwright .30 .75
8 David Freese .15 .40
9 Ryan Braun .20 .50
10 Yoenis Cespedes .25 .60
11 Paul Goldschmidt .40 1.00
12 Evan Gattis RC .60 1.50
13 Mark Trumbo .25 .60
14 Yadier Molina .25 .60
15 Carl Crawford .20 .50
16 Starlin Castro .15 .40
17 Ryan Howard .30 .75
18 Anthony Rizzo .40 1.00
19 Justin Upton .30 .75
20 Matt Kemp .20 .50
21 Aaron Hicks RC .50 1.25
22 Adrian Gonzalez .30 .75
23 Clayton Kershaw .50 1.25
24 Alfredo Marte RC .30 .75
25 Chase Utley .30 .75
26 Edwin Encarnacion .40 1.00
27 Matt Cain .20 .50
28 Buster Posey .50 1.25
29 Mariano Rivera .50 1.25
30 Brandon Maurer RC .40 1.00
31 Felix Hernandez .20 .50
32 Oswaldo Arcia RC .30 .75
33 Josh Reddick .15 .40
34 Jose Reyes .20 .50
35 Giancarlo Stanton .25 .60
36 David Wright .20 .50
37 R.A. Dickey .20 .50
38 Michael Young .15 .40
39 Bryce Harper .40 1.00
40 Stephen Strasburg .25 .60
41 Gio Gonzalez .20 .50
42 Manny Machado RC 2.00 5.00
43 Adam Jones .20 .50
44 Jarrod Parker .15 .40
45 Cliff Lee .20 .50
46 Chase Headley .15 .40
47 Carlos Ruiz .15 .40
48 Cole Hamels .20 .50
49 Mike Olt RC .60 1.50
50 Rob Brantly RC .30 .75
51 Andrew McCutchen .25 .60
52 Kris Medlen .20 .50
53 Freddie Freeman .30 .75
54 Josh Hamilton .20 .50
55 Adrian Beltre .25 .60
56 Yu Darvish .25 .60
57 Adam Eaton RC .50 1.25
58 David Price .20 .50
59 Evan Longoria .20 .50
60 Will Middlebrooks .15 .40
61 Dustin Pedroia .25 .60
62 Tony Cingrani RC .60 1.50
63 Jason Heyward .20 .50
64 Joey Votto .25 .60
65 Shelby Miller RC 1.25 3.00
66 Salvador Perez .20 .50
67 Aroldis Chapman .25 .60
68 Johnny Cueto .20 .50
69 Troy Tulowitzki .25 .60
70 Carlos Gonzalez .20 .50
71 Tim Lincecum .20 .50
72 Billy Butler .15 .40
73 Justin Verlander .25 .60
74 Jake Odorizzi RC .60 1.50
75 Prince Fielder .20 .50
76 Miguel Cabrera .25 .60
77 Joe Mauer .25 .60
78 Robinson Cano .20 .50
79 Tyler Skaggs RC .50 1.25
80 Adeiny Hechavarria RC .60 1.50
81 Derek Jeter .60 1.50
82 Alex Rodriguez .30 .75
83 CC Sabathia .20 .50
84 Jackie Bradley Jr. RC .75 2.00
85 Jose Fernandez RC 1.25 3.00
86 Jeurys Familia RC .50 1.25
87 Trevor Rosenthal RC 1.00 2.50
88 Didi Gregorius RC 1.25 3.00
89 Kevin Youkilis .15 .40
90 Jedd Gyorko RC .60 1.50
91 Darin Ruf RC 1.00 2.50
92 Paul Konerko .20 .50
93 Pablo Sandoval .20 .50
94 Paco Rodriguez RC .50 1.25
95 Carlos Beltran .20 .50
96 Hyun-Jin Ryu RC 1.25 3.00
97 Chris Sale .25 .60
98 Avisail Garcia RC .60 1.50
99 Dylan Bundy RC .75 2.00
100 Jurickson Profar RC .60 1.50

2013 Bowman Platinum Gold
*GOLD: 1.5X TO 4X BASIC
*GOLD RC: .75X TO 2X BASIC RC
STATED ODDS 1:5 HOBBY

2013 Bowman Platinum Ruby
*RUBY: 2.5X TO 6X BASIC
*RUBY RC: 1.2X TO 3X BASIC RC
STATED ODDS 1:20 HOBBY

2013 Bowman Platinum Sapphire
*SAPPHIRE: 2X TO 5X BASIC
*SAPPHIRE RC: 1X TO 2.5X BASIC RC
STATED ODDS 1:10 HOBBY

2013 Bowman Platinum Cutting Edge Stars
STATED ODDS 1:10 HOBBY
AD Raul Mondesi 1.25 3.00
AJ Adam Jones .50 1.25
AM Andrew McCutchen .60 1.50
AP Albert Pujols .75 2.00
AR Anthony Rendon 2.00 5.00
BH Bryce Harper 1.00 2.50
BP Buster Posey .75 2.00
CC C.J. Cron .50 1.25
CG Carlos Gonzalez .50 1.25
CK Clayton Kershaw 1.25 3.00
CSA Chris Sale .60 1.50
DB Dylan Bundy 1.00 2.50
DD David Dahl .50 1.25
DJ Derek Jeter 1.50 4.00
DW David Wright .50 1.25
EL Evan Longoria .50 1.25
FH Felix Hernandez .50 1.25
FL Francisco Lindor 2.50 6.00
GG Gio Gonzalez .50 1.25
GS George Springer 1.50 4.00
GST Giancarlo Stanton .60 1.50
HR Hanley Ramirez .50 1.25
JB Jose Bautista .50 1.25
JH Jeremy Hellickson .40 1.00
JK Jason Kipnis .50 1.25
JM Joe Mauer .50 1.25
JP Jurickson Profar .50 1.25
JS James Shields .40 1.00
JT Julio Teheran .50 1.25
JV Joey Votto .60 1.50
JVE Justin Verlander .60 1.50
JW Jered Weaver .50 1.25
KZ Kyle Zimmer .50 1.25
MB Matt Barnes .50 1.25
MC Miguel Cabrera .60 1.50
MK Matt Kemp .50 1.25
MM Manny Machado 2.50 6.00
MR Mariano Rivera .75 2.00
MT Mark Trumbo .40 1.00
MTR Mike Trout 5.00 12.00
MZ Mike Zunino .60 1.50
NC Nick Castellanos 1.25 3.00
PF Prince Fielder .50 1.25
RB Ryan Braun .50 1.25
RC Robinson Cano .60 1.50
SS Stephen Strasburg .60 1.50
YC Yoenis Cespedes .60 1.50
YD Yu Darvish .60 1.50
YG Yovani Gallardo .40 1.00
YP Yasiel Puig 1.50 4.00

2013 Bowman Platinum Cutting Edge Stars Relics
STATED ODDS 1:626 HOBBY
STATED PRINT RUN 50 SER.#'d SETS
AJ Adam Jones 8.00 20.00
AM Andrew McCutchen 8.00 20.00
AR Anthony Rendon 10.00 25.00
BH Bryce Harper 15.00 40.00
BP Buster Posey 12.50 30.00
CS Chris Sale 6.00 15.00
DB Dylan Bundy 6.00 15.00
DJ Derek Jeter 15.00 40.00
FH Felix Hernandez 4.00 10.00
GG Gio Gonzalez 4.00 10.00
GS Giancarlo Stanton 8.00 20.00
JB Jose Bautista 10.00 25.00
JV Justin Verlander 8.00 20.00
JVO Joey Votto 6.00 15.00
JW Jered Weaver 4.00 10.00
MC Miguel Cabrera 12.50 30.00
MK Matt Kemp 6.00 15.00
MR Mariano Rivera 8.00 20.00
MT Mike Trout 20.00 50.00
PF Prince Fielder 10.00 25.00
RB Ryan Braun 4.00 10.00
RC Robinson Cano 10.00 25.00
SS Stephen Strasburg 10.00 25.00
YC Yoenis Cespedes 6.00 15.00
YD Yu Darvish 6.00 15.00

2013 Bowman Platinum Diamonds in the Rough
STATED ODDS 1:20 HOBBY
AA Arismendy Alcantara .60 1.50
BV Breyvic Valera .50 1.25
CE C.J. Edwards .60 1.50
CT Carlos Tocci .40 1.00
DH Dilson Herrera 1.25 3.00
HA Hanser Alberto .40 1.00
HR Hansel Robles .40 1.00
IG Ismael Guillon .40 1.00
JJ Jin-De Jhang .40 1.00
JP Jorge Polanco .40 1.00
LM Luis Merejo .40 1.00
MH Marco Hernandez .40 1.00
MS Michael Snyder .40 1.00
WH Wade Hinkle .40 1.00
WR Wilfredo Rodriguez .40 1.00

2013 Bowman Platinum Diamonds in the Rough Autographs
STATED ODDS 1:2095 HOBBY
STATED PRINT RUN 50 SER.#'d SETS
EXCHANGE DEADLINE 07/31/2016
CE C.J. Edwards 20.00 50.00
CT Carlos Tocci EXCH 30.00 60.00
DH Dilson Herrera 20.00 50.00
IG Ismael Guillon EXCH 30.00 60.00
JJ Jin-De Jhang EXCH 40.00 80.00
JP Jorge Polanco 30.00 60.00
LM Luis Merejo EXCH 15.00 40.00

2013 Bowman Platinum Jumbo Relic Autographs Blue Refractors
*BLUE REF: .5X TO 1.2X BASIC
STATED ODDS 1:388 HOBBY
STATED PRINT RUN 199 SER.#'d SETS
EXCHANGE DEADLINE 07/31/2016

2013 Bowman Platinum Jumbo Relic Autographs Gold Refractors
*GOLD REF: 1.2X TO 3X BASIC
STATED ODDS 1:1775 HOBBY
STATED PRINT RUN 50 SER.#'d SETS
PRICING FOR BASIC PATCHES
PREMIUM PATCHES MAY SELL FOR MORE
EXCHANGE DEADLINE 07/31/2016

2013 Bowman Platinum Jumbo Relic Autographs Refractors
STATED ODDS 1:243 HOBBY
STATED PLATE ODDS 1:21,282 HOBBY
PLATE PRINT RUN 1 SET PER COLOR
BLACK-CYAN-MAGENTA-YELLOW ISSUED
NO PLATE PRICING DUE TO SCARCITY
EXCHANGE DEADLINE 07/31/2016
AG Avisail Garcia 6.00 15.00
AR Anthony Rendon 12.00 30.00
GS George Springer 10.00 25.00
HL Hak-Ju Lee 4.00 10.00
JS Jonathan Singleton 5.00 12.00
MD Matt Davidson 5.00 12.00
PL Patrick Leonard 4.00 10.00
TC Tyler Collins 4.00 10.00

2013 Bowman Platinum Prospect Autographs
STATED ODDS 1:14 HOBBY
STATED PLATE ODDS 1:4026 HOBBY
PLATE PRINT RUN 1 SET PER COLOR
BLACK-CYAN-MAGENTA-YELLOW ISSUED
NO PLATE PRICING DUE TO SCARCITY
EXCHANGE DEADLINE 07/31/2016
AC Adam Conley 3.00 8.00
AM Anthony Meo 3.00 8.00
AR Addison Russell 10.00 25.00
BB Byron Buxton 12.00 30.00
BL Barret Loux 3.00 8.00
BT Beau Taylor 3.00 8.00
CC Carlos Correa 25.00 60.00
CM Carlos Martinez 6.00 15.00
DD David Dahl 5.00 12.00
DP Dorssys Paulino 3.00 8.00
DS Danny Salazar 3.00 8.00
JA Jorge Alfaro 4.00 10.00
JAM Jeff Ames 3.00 8.00
JB Jose Berrios 6.00 15.00
JBI Jesse Biddle 3.00 8.00
JG J.R. Graham 3.00 8.00
JH John Hellweg 3.00 8.00
KD Keury de la Cruz 3.00 8.00
LM Luis Mateo 3.00 8.00
LMC Lance McCullers 3.00 8.00
MF Maikel Franco 5.00 10.00
MK Max Kepler 4.00 10.00
MKI Michael Kickham 3.00 8.00
MM Matt Magill 3.00 8.00
MO Marcell Ozuna 3.00 8.00
MON Mike O'Neill 3.00 8.00
MS Miguel Sano 3.00 8.00
MZ Mike Zunino 3.00 8.00
NA Nick Ahmed 3.00 8.00
NR Nate Roberts 3.00 8.00
OC Orlando Calixte 3.00 8.00
PO Peter O'Brien 5.00 12.00
RO Rougned Odor 6.00 15.00
SD Shawon Dunston Jr. 3.00 8.00
TM Trevor May 3.00 8.00
TS Tayler Scott 3.00 8.00
WS Will Swanner 3.00 8.00

2013 Bowman Platinum Prospect Autographs Blue Refractors
*BLUE REF: .6X TO 1.5X BASIC
STATED ODDS 1:142 HOBBY
STATED PRINT RUN 199 SER.#'d SETS
EXCHANGE DEADLINE 07/31/2016

2013 Bowman Platinum Prospect Autographs Gold Refractors
*GOLD REF: .75X TO 2X BASIC
STATED ODDS 1:565 HOBBY
STATED PRINT RUN 50 SER.#'d SETS
EXCHANGE DEADLINE 07/31/2016
JA Jorge Alfaro 8.00 20.00
JBI Jesse Biddle 15.00 40.00

2013 Bowman Platinum Prospect Autographs Green Refractors
*GREEN REF: .5X TO 1.2X BASIC
STATED ODDS 1:69 HOBBY
STATED PRINT RUN 399 SER.#'d SETS
EXCHANGE DEADLINE 07/31/2016

2013 Bowman Platinum Prospects
STATED PLATE ODDS 1:1490 HOBBY
PLATE PRINT RUN 1 SET PER COLOR
BLACK-CYAN-MAGENTA-YELLOW ISSUED
NO PLATE PRICING DUE TO SCARCITY
EXCHANGE DEADLINE 07/31/2016
BPP1 Oscar Taveras .30 .75
BPP2 Travis d'Arnaud .30 .75
BPP3 Lewis Brinson .30 .75
BPP4 Gerrit Cole 1.50 4.00
BPP5 Zack Wheeler .50 1.25
BPP6 Wil Myers .30 .75
BPP7 Miguel Sano .30 .75
BPP8 Xander Bogaerts .75 2.00
BPP9 Billy Hamilton .30 .75
BPP10 Javier Baez 1.00 2.50
BPP11 Mike Zunino .40 1.00
BPP12 Christian Yelich 2.00 5.00
BPP13 Taijuan Walker .30 .75
BPP14 Jameson Taillon .30 .75
BPP15 Nick Castellanos .75 2.00
BPP16 Archie Bradley .25 .60
BPP17 Danny Hultzen .30 .75
BPP18 Taylor Guerrieri .25 .60
BPP19 Byron Buxton .60 1.50
BPP20 David Dahl .30 .75
BPP21 Francisco Lindor 1.50 4.00
BPP22 Bubba Starling .30 .75
BPP23 Carlos Correa 2.50 6.00
BPP24 Jonathan Singleton .30 .75
BPP25 Anthony Rendon 1.25 3.00
BPP26 Gregory Polanco .50 1.25
BPP27 Carlos Martinez .40 1.00
BPP28 Jorge Soler .50 1.25
BPP29 Matt Barnes .30 .75
BPP30 Kevin Gausman .40 1.00
BPP31 Albert Almora .50 1.25
BPP32 Alen Hanson .30 .75
BPP33 Addison Russell .40 1.00
BPP34 Gary Sanchez .75 2.00
BPP35 Noah Syndergaard .30 .75
BPP36 Victor Roache .30 .75
BPP37 Mason Williams .30 .75
BPP38 George Springer 1.00 2.50
BPP39 Aaron Sanchez .30 .75
BPP40 Nolan Arenado 1.25 3.00
BPP41 Corey Seager 1.00 2.50
BPP42 Kyle Zimmer .30 .75
BPP43 Tyler Austin .40 1.00
BPP44 Kyle Crick .40 1.00
BPP45 Robert Stephenson .25 .60
BPP46 Joc Pederson .40 1.00
BPP47 Brian Goodwin .30 .75
BPP48 Kaleb Cowart .30 .75
BPP49A Yasiel Puig 1.00 2.50
NCA49 Yasiel Puig AU 250.00 500.00
BPP50 Mike Piazza .25 .60
BPP51 Alex Meyer .25 .60
BPP52 Jake Marisnick .30 .75
BPP53 Lucas Sims .30 .75
BPP54 Brad Miller .30 .75
BPP55 Max Fried 1.00 2.50
BPP56 Eddie Rosario .50 1.25
BPP57 Justin Nicolino .25 .60
BPP58 Cody Buckel .25 .60
BPP59 Jesse Biddle .30 .75
BPP60 James Paxton .30 .75
BPP61 Allen Webster .30 .75
BPP62 Kyle Gibson .40 1.00
BPP63 Nick Franklin .30 .75
BPP64 Dorssys Paulino .30 .75
BPP65 Courtney Hawkins .25 .60
BPP66 Delino DeShields .25 .60
BPP67 Joey Gallo .75 2.00
BPP68 Hak-Ju Lee .25 .60
BPP69 Kolten Wong .25 .60
BPP70 Renato Nunez .50 1.25
BPP71 Michael Choice .25 .60
BPP72 Luis Heredia .30 .75
BPP73 C.J. Cron .30 .75
BPP74 Lucas Giolito .40 1.00
BPP75 Daniel Vogelbach .40 1.00
BPP76 Austin Hedges .30 .75
BPP77 Matt Davidson .30 .75
BPP78 Gary Brown .25 .60
BPP79 Daniel Corcino .25 .60
BPP80 D.J. Davis .30 .75
BPP81 Victor Sanchez .30 .75
BPP82 Joe Ross .25 .60
BPP83 Joe Panik .40 1.00
BPP84 Jose Berrios .40 1.00
BPP85 Trevor Story 1.00 2.50
BPP86 Stefen Romero .25 .60
BPP87 Andrew Heaney .30 .75
BPP88 Mark Montgomery .40 1.00
BPP89 Deven Marrero .25 .60
BPP90 Marcell Ozuna .60 1.50
BPP91 Michael Wacha .30 .75
BPP92 Gavin Cecchini .30 .75
BPP93 Richie Shaffer .25 .60
BPP94 Ty Hensley .30 .75
BPP95 Nick Williams .30 .75
BPP96 Tyrone Taylor .25 .60
BPP97 Christian Bethancourt .40 1.00
BPP98 Roman Quinn .40 1.00
BPP99 Luis Sardinas .25 .60
BPP100 Jonathan Schoop .25 .60

2013 Bowman Platinum Chrome Prospects Refractors
*REFRACTORS: .75X TO 2X BASIC
STATED ODDS 1:4 HOBBY

2013 Bowman Platinum Chrome Prospects Blue Refractors
*BLUE REF: 2.5X TO 6X BASIC
STATED ODDS 1:39 HOBBY
STATED PRINT RUN 199 SER.#'d SETS

2013 Bowman Platinum Chrome Prospects Gold Refractors
*GOLD REF: 8X TO 20X BASIC
STATED ODDS 1:157 HOBBY
STATED PRINT RUN 50 SER.#'d SETS
BPCP19 Byron Buxton 40.00 80.00

2013 Bowman Platinum Chrome Prospects Green Refractors
*GREEN REF: 2X TO 5X BASIC
STATED ODDS 1:20 HOBBY
STATED PRINT RUN 399 SER.#'d SETS

2013 Bowman Platinum Chrome Prospects Purple Refractors
*PURPLE REF: 1X TO 2.5X BASIC

2013 Bowman Platinum Chrome Prospects X-Fractors
*X-FRACTOR: 1.2X TO 3X BASIC
STATED ODDS 1:20 HOBBY

2013 Bowman Platinum Relic Autographs
STATED ODDS 1:43 HOBBY
STATED PLATE ODDS 1:3464 HOBBY
PLATE PRINT RUN 1 SET PER COLOR
BLACK-CYAN-MAGENTA-YELLOW ISSUED
NO PLATE PRICING DUE TO SCARCITY
EXCHANGE DEADLINE 07/31/2016
AG Anthony Gose 4.00 10.00
BH Billy Hamilton 4.00 10.00
BHA Bryce Harper 200.00 300.00
BM Brad Miller 5.00 12.00
CB Christian Bethancourt 6.00 15.00
CO Chris Owings 4.00 10.00
CS Cory Spangenberg 4.00 10.00
CY Christian Yelich 6.00 150.00
DB Dylan Bundy 10.00 25.00
DHU Danny Hultzen 4.00 10.00
GB Gary Brown 4.00 10.00
GC Gerrit Cole 5.00 12.00
HR Hyun-Jin Ryu EXCH 20.00 50.00
JC Jarred Cosart 4.00 10.00
JF Jeurys Familia 4.00 10.00
JM Jake Marisnick 4.00 10.00
JMO Julio Morban 4.00 10.00
JP Joe Panik 12.00 30.00
JPA James Paxton 4.00 10.00
JPR Jurickson Profar 6.00 15.00
KW Kolten Wong 4.00 10.00
MB Matt Barnes 4.00 10.00
MC Michael Choice 4.00 10.00
MD Matt Davidson 4.00 10.00
MM Manny Machado EXCH 15.00 40.00
MO Mike Olt 4.00 10.00
MS Matt Skole 4.00 10.00
MZ Mike Zunino 4.00 10.00
NA Nolan Arenado 40.00 100.00
NC Nick Castellanos 10.00 25.00
NF Nick Franklin EXCH 5.00 12.00
OA Oswaldo Arcia 4.00 10.00
OT Oscar Taveras 5.00 12.00
RS Richie Shaffer 4.00 10.00
SH Slade Heathcott 6.00 15.00
TB Trevor Bauer 4.00 10.00
TC Tony Cingrani 8.00 20.00
WM Will Middlebrooks 6.00 15.00
WMY Wil Myers 20.00 50.00
YD Yu Darvish 60.00 120.00
YV Yordano Ventura 6.00 15.00
ZW Zack Wheeler 4.00 10.00

2013 Bowman Platinum Relic Autographs Blue Refractors
*BLUE REF: .5X TO 1.2X BASIC
STATED ODDS 1:77 HOBBY
STATED PRINT RUN 199 SER.#'d SETS
EXCHANGE DEADLINE 07/31/2016

2013 Bowman Platinum Relic Autographs Gold Refractors
*GOLD REF: 1X TO 2.5X BASIC
STATED ODDS 1:306 HOBBY
STATED PRINT RUN 50 SER.#'d SETS
EXCHANGE DEADLINE 07/31/2016
BM Brad Miller 25.00 60.00
CB Christian Bethancourt 25.00 60.00
MD Matt Davidson 20.00 50.00
MM Manny Machado EXCH 30.00 80.00
NC Nick Castellanos 20.00 50.00
NF Nick Franklin EXCH 20.00 50.00
WMY Wil Myers 40.00 80.00

2013 Bowman Platinum Top Prospects
STATED ODDS 1:5 HOBBY
AA Albert Almora .60 1.50
AB Archie Bradley .30 .75
AH Alen Hanson .40 1.00
AM Alex Meyer .30 .75
AR Anthony Rendon 1.50 4.00
ARU Addison Russell .50 1.25
BB Byron Buxton .75 2.00
BG Brian Goodwin .40 1.00
BH Billy Hamilton .40 1.00
BS Bubba Starling .40 1.00
CB Cody Buckel .30 .75
CC Carlos Correa 3.00 8.00
CH Courtney Hawkins .30 .75
CS Corey Seager 1.25 3.00
CY Christian Yelich 2.50 6.00
DD David Dahl .40 1.00
DP Dorssys Paulino .40 1.00
DV Daniel Vogelbach .50 1.25
FL Francisco Lindor 2.00 5.00
GC Gerrit Cole 2.00 5.00
GP Gregory Polanco .60 1.50
GS Gary Sanchez 1.00 2.50
GSP George Springer 1.25 3.00
JB Javier Baez 1.25 3.00
JF Jose Fernandez .75 2.00
JG Joey Gallo 1.00 2.50
JP Joc Pederson .50 1.25
JS Jonathan Singleton .40 1.00
JSO Jorge Soler .60 1.50
JT Jameson Taillon .40 1.00
KC Kaleb Cowart .40 1.00
KG Kevin Gausman .50 1.25

KW Kolten Wong .30 .75
MB Matt Barnes .40 1.00
MS Miguel Sano .40 1.00
MW Mason Williams .40 1.00
MZ Mike Zunino .50 1.25
NA Nolan Arenado 1.50 4.00
NC Nick Castellanos 1.00 2.50
NS Noah Syndergaard .40 1.00
OA Oswaldo Arcia .30 .75
OT Oscar Taveras .40 1.00
TA Tyler Austin .50 1.25
TD Travis d'Arnaud .40 1.00
TG Taylor Guerrieri .30 .75
TW Taijuan Walker .40 1.00
WM Wil Myers .40 1.00
XB Xander Bogaerts 1.00 2.50
YP Yasiel Puig 1.25 3.00
ZW Zack Wheeler .60 1.50

2013 Bowman Platinum Orange National Convention

COMPLETE SET (100) 150.00 400.00
ISSUED AT THE 2013 NSCC IN CHICAGO
STATED PRINT RUN 125 SER.#'d SETS
NC1 Oscar Taveras 1.25 3.00
NC2 Travis d'Arnaud 1.25 3.00
NC3 Lewis Brinson 1.25 3.00
NC4 Gerrit Cole 6.00 15.00
NC5 Zack Wheeler 2.00 5.00
NC6 Wil Myers 1.25 3.00
NC7 Miguel Sano 1.25 3.00
NC8 Xander Bogaerts 3.00 8.00
NC9 Billy Hamilton 1.25 3.00
NC10 Javier Baez 4.00 10.00
NC11 Mike Zunino 1.50 4.00
NC12 Christian Yelich 8.00 20.00
NC13 Taijuan Walker 1.25 3.00
NC14 Jameson Taillon 1.25 3.00
NC15 Nick Castellanos 3.00 8.00
NC16 Archie Bradley 1.00 2.50
NC17 Danny Hultzen 1.25 3.00
NC18 Taylor Guerrieri 1.00 2.50
NC19 Byron Buxton 12.50 30.00
NC20 David Dahl 1.25 3.00
NC21 Francisco Lindor 6.00 15.00
NC22 Bubba Starling 1.25 3.00
NC23 Carlos Correa 12.50 30.00
NC24 Jonathan Singleton 1.25 3.00
NC25 Anthony Rendon 5.00 12.00
NC26 Gregory Polanco 2.00 5.00
NC27 Carlos Martinez 1.50 4.00
NC28 Jorge Soler 2.00 5.00
NC29 Matt Barnes 1.25 3.00
NC30 Kevin Gausman 1.50 4.00
NC31 Albert Almora 2.00 5.00
NC32 Alen Hanson 1.25 3.00
NC33 Addison Russell 1.50 4.00
NC34 Gary Sanchez 3.00 8.00
NC35 Noah Syndergaard 1.25 3.00
NC36 Victor Roache 1.25 3.00
NC37 Mason Williams 1.25 3.00
NC38 George Springer 4.00 10.00
NC39 Aaron Sanchez 1.25 3.00
NC40 Nolan Arenado 5.00 12.00
NC41 Corey Seager 4.00 10.00
NC42 Kyle Zimmer 1.25 3.00
NC43 Tyler Austin 1.50 4.00
NC44 Kyle Crick 1.50 4.00
NC45 Robert Stephenson 1.00 2.50
NC46 Joc Pederson 1.50 4.00
NC47 Brian Goodwin 1.25 3.00
NC48 Kaleb Cowart 1.25 3.00
NC49 Yasiel Puig 60.00 120.00
NC50 Mike Piazza 1.00 2.50
NC51 Alex Meyer 1.00 2.50
NC52 Jake Marisnick 1.25 3.00
NC53 Lucas Sims 1.25 3.00
NC54 Brad Miller 1.25 3.00
NC55 Max Fried 4.00 10.00
NC56 Eddie Rosario 2.00 5.00
NC57 Justin Nicolino 1.00 2.50
NC58 Cody Buckel 1.00 2.50
NC59 Jesse Biddle 1.25 3.00
NC60 James Paxton 1.25 3.00
NC61 Allen Webster 1.25 3.00
NC62 Kyle Gibson 1.50 4.00
NC63 Nick Franklin 1.25 3.00
NC64 Dorssys Paulino 1.00 2.50
NC65 Courtney Hawkins 1.00 2.50
NC66 Delino DeShields 1.00 2.50
NC67 Joey Gallo 3.00 8.00
NC68 Hak-Ju Lee 1.00 2.50
NC69 Kolten Wong 1.00 2.50
NC70 Renato Nunez 2.00 5.00
NC71 Michael Choice 1.00 2.50
NC72 Luis Heredia 1.25 3.00
NC73 C.J. Cron 1.25 3.00
NC74 Lucas Giolito 1.50 4.00
NC75 Daniel Vogelbach 1.50 4.00
NC76 Austin Hedges 1.25 3.00
NC77 Matt Davidson 1.25 3.00
NC78 Gary Brown 1.00 2.50
NC79 Daniel Corcino 1.00 2.50
NC80 D.J. Davis 1.25 3.00
NC81 Victor Sanchez 1.25 3.00
NC82 Joe Ross 1.00 2.50
NC83 Joe Panik 1.50 4.00
NC84 Jose Berrios 1.50 4.00
NC85 Trevor Story 4.00 10.00
NC86 Stefen Romero 1.00 2.50
NC87 Andrew Heaney 1.25 3.00
NC88 Mark Montgomery 1.50 4.00
NC89 Deven Marrero 1.00 2.50
NC90 Marcell Ozuna 2.50 6.00
NC91 Michael Wacha 1.25 3.00
NC92 Gavin Cecchini 1.25 3.00
NC93 Richie Shaffer 1.00 2.50
NC94 Ty Hensley 1.25 3.00
NC95 Nick Williams 1.25 3.00
NC96 Tyrone Taylor 1.00 2.50
NC97 Christian Bethancourt 1.50 4.00
NC98 Roman Quinn 1.50 4.00
NC99 Luis Sardinas 1.00 2.50
NC100 Jonathan Schoop 1.00 2.50

2014 Bowman Platinum

COMPLETE SET (100) 15.00 40.00
PLATE PRINT RUN 1 SET PER COLOR
BLACK-CYAN-MAGENTA-YELLOW ISSUED
NO PLATE PRICING DUE TO SCARCITY
1 Taijuan Walker .15 .40
2 Mike Trout 1.25 3.00
3 Andrew McCutchen .25 .60
4 Josh Donaldson .20 .50
5 Carlos Gomez .15 .40
6 Miguel Cabrera .25 .60
7 Matt Carpenter .25 .60
8 Evan Longoria .20 .50
9 Chris Davis .15 .40
10 Paul Goldschmidt .25 .60
11 Manny Machado .25 .60
12 Clayton Kershaw .50 1.25
13 Max Scherzer .25 .60
14 Anibal Sanchez .15 .40
15 Adam Wainwright .20 .50
16 Matt Harvey .20 .50
17 Felix Hernandez .20 .50
18 Cliff Lee .20 .50
19 Chris Sale .25 .60
20 Yu Darvish .25 .60
21 Joey Votto .25 .60
22 Robinson Cano .20 .50
23 David Wright .20 .50
24 Troy Tulowitzki .25 .60
25 David Price .20 .50
26 Stephen Strasburg .25 .60
27 James Shields .15 .40
28 Buster Posey .30 .75
29 Carlos Santana .20 .50
30 Jason Heyward .20 .50
31 Giancarlo Stanton .25 .60
32 Pablo Sandoval .20 .50
33 Jose Bautista .20 .50
34 CC Sabathia .20 .50
35 Hisashi Iwakuma .20 .50
36 Jose Fernandez .25 .60
37 Yasiel Puig .25 .60
38 Adrian Beltre .25 .60
39 Carlos Gonzalez .20 .50
40 Bryce Harper .40 1.00
41 Madison Bumgarner .20 .50
42 Cole Hamels .20 .50
43 Jon Lester .20 .50
44 Matt Moore .20 .50
45 Hanley Ramirez .20 .50
46 Dustin Pedroia .25 .60
47 Ryan Braun .20 .50
48 Yadier Molina .25 .60
49 Freddie Freeman .30 .75
50 Danny Salazar .20 .50
51 Tony Cingrani .20 .50
52 Gio Gonzalez .20 .50
53 Jacoby Ellsbury .20 .50
54 Salvador Perez .20 .50
55 Jason Kipnis .20 .50
56 Jean Segura .20 .50
57 Zack Greinke .20 .50
58 Francisco Liriano .15 .40
59 Zack Wheeler .20 .50
60 Matt Cain .20 .50
61 Mat Latos .20 .50
62 Craig Kimbrel .20 .50
63 Aroldis Chapman .25 .60
64 Jose Reyes .20 .50
65 Edwin Encarnacion .25 .60
66 Anthony Rizzo .40 1.00
67 Pedro Alvarez .15 .40
68 Jay Bruce .20 .50
69 Prince Fielder .20 .50
70 Justin Upton .20 .50
71 David Ortiz .25 .60
72 Matt Holliday .25 .60
73 Shelby Miller .20 .50
74 Jered Weaver .20 .50
75 Xander Bogaerts RC 1.00 2.50
76 Jose Abreu RC 2.50 6.00
77 Masahiro Tanaka RC 1.00 2.50
78 Billy Hamilton RC .40 1.00
79 Travis d'Arnaud RC .40 1.00
80 James Paxton RC .50 1.25
81 Nick Castellanos RC 1.00 2.50
82 Wilmer Flores RC .40 1.00
83 Jake Marisnick RC .30 .75
84 Yordano Ventura RC .40 1.00
85 Matt Davidson RC .40 1.00
86 Kevin Gausman RC .40 1.00
87 Kolten Wong RC .40 1.00
88 Jimmy Nelson RC .30 .75
89 Marcus Semien RC .30 .75
90 Chris Owings RC .30 .75
91 Michael Choice RC .30 .75
92 Jonathan Schoop RC .30 .75
93 Erik Johnson RC .30 .75
94 Christian Bethancourt RC .30 .75
95 Tony Sanchez RC .30 .75
96 Oscar Taveras RC .40 1.00
97 Jon Singleton RC .40 1.00
98 J.R. Murphy RC .30 .75
99 Enny Romero RC .30 .75
100 Alex Guerrero RC .40 1.00

2014 Bowman Platinum Gold

*GOLD: 1X TO 2.5X BASIC
*GOLD RC: .5X TO 1.2X BASIC RC

2014 Bowman Platinum Ruby

*RUBY: 1.5X TO 4X BASIC
*RUBY RC: .75X TO 2X BASIC RC

2014 Bowman Platinum Sapphire

*SAPPHIRE: 1.2X TO 3X BASIC
*SAPPHIRE RC: .6X TO 1.5X BASIC RC

2014 Bowman Platinum Chrome Prospects Refractors

*REFRACTORS: .5X TO 1.2X BASIC

2014 Bowman Platinum Chrome Prospects Blue Refractors

*BLUE REF: 1.5X TO 4X BASIC
STATED PRINT RUN 199 SER.#'d SETS

2014 Bowman Platinum Chrome Prospects Gold Refractors

*GOLD REF: 5X TO 12X BASIC
STATED PRINT RUN 50 SER.#'d SETS

2014 Bowman Platinum Chrome Prospects Green Refractors

*GREEN REF: 1.2X TO 3X BASIC
STATED PRINT RUN 399 SER.#'d SETS

2014 Bowman Platinum Chrome Prospects Japan Fractors

*JAPAN REF: 5X TO 12X BASIC
STATED PRINT RUN 35 SER.#'d SETS

2014 Bowman Platinum Chrome Prospects Red Refractors

*RED REF: 6X TO 15X BASIC
STATED PRINT RUN 25 SER.#'d SETS

2014 Bowman Platinum Chrome Prospects X-Fractors

*X-FRACTOR: .75X TO 2X BASIC

2014 Bowman Platinum Cutting Edge Stars

CESAM Andrew McCutchen .75 2.00
CESBB Byron Buxton .60 1.50
CESBH Bryce Harper 1.25 3.00
CESBHA Billy Hamilton .60 1.50
CESBP Buster Posey 1.00 2.50
CESCC Carlos Correa 2.50 6.00
CESDJ Derek Jeter 2.00 5.00
CESDO David Ortiz .75 2.00
CESHI Hisashi Iwakuma .60 1.50
CESJA Jose Abreu 4.00 10.00
CESJB Javier Baez 2.00 5.00
CESJF Jose Fernandez .75 2.00
CESMC Miguel Cabrera .75 2.00
CESMT Masahiro Tanaka 1.50 4.00
CESMTR Mike Trout 4.00 10.00
CESTW Taijuan Walker .50 1.25
CESWM Wil Myers .50 1.25
CESXB Xander Bogaerts 1.50 4.00
CESYD Yu Darvish .75 2.00
CESYP Yasiel Puig .75 2.00

2014 Bowman Platinum Cutting Edge Stars Blue Refractors

*BLUE REF: 1.5X TO 4X BASIC
STATED PRINT RUN 49 SER.#'d SETS
CESDJ Derek Jeter 12.00 30.00
CESMTR Mike Trout 20.00 50.00

2014 Bowman Platinum Cutting Edge Stars Autographs

STATED PRINT RUN 25 SER.#'d SETS
EXCHANGE DEADLINE 7/31/2017
CEBP Buster Posey EXCH 40.00 100.00
CECC Carlos Correa 40.00 100.00
CEJA Jose Abreu 250.00 400.00
CEJB Javier Baez 50.00 120.00
CEMC Miguel Cabrera 60.00 150.00
CEMTR Mike Trout 250.00 400.00
CETW Taijuan Walker 8.00 20.00

2014 Bowman Platinum Cutting Edge Stars Relics

STATED PRINT RUN 49 SER.#'d SETS
CESDAM Andrew McCutchen 5.00 12.00
CESDBB Byron Buxton 4.00 10.00
CESDBH Bryce Harper 8.00 20.00
CESDBP Buster Posey 6.00 15.00
CESDCC Carlos Correa 30.00 80.00
CESDDJ Derek Jeter 20.00 50.00
CESDDO David Ortiz 5.00 12.00
CESDHI Hisashi Iwakuma 4.00 10.00
CESDMC Miguel Cabrera 5.00 12.00
CESDMT Mike Trout 20.00 50.00
CESDWM Wil Myers 3.00 8.00
CESDXB Xander Bogaerts 10.00 25.00
CESDYD Yu Darvish 5.00 12.00
CESDYP Yasiel Puig 5.00 12.00
CESDMTA Masahiro Tanaka 10.00 25.00

2014 Bowman Platinum Dual Autographs

STATED PRINT RUN 25 SER.#'d SETS
EXCHANGE DEADLINE 7/31/2017
DAAM L.McCullers/M.Appel 100.00 200.00
DAAT A.Almora/O.Taveras 20.00 50.00
DAAV A.Almora/D.Vogelbach 20.00 50.00
DABA A.Almora/J.Baez 60.00 150.00
DABJ B.Johnson/M.Barnes 12.00 30.00
DABS B.Buxton/M.Sano 100.00 200.00
DACC G.Cecchini/G.Cecchini 12.00 30.00
DAGH A.Heaney/L.Giolito 40.00 80.00
DANH A.Heaney/J.Nicolino 20.00 50.00
DASO R.Odor/L.Sardinas 25.00 60.00

2014 Bowman Platinum Five Tool Die Cuts

5TDCAA Albert Almora 3.00 8.00
5TDCAJ Adam Jones 2.50 6.00
5TDCAM Andrew McCutchen 3.00 8.00
5TDCAME Austin Meadows 3.00 8.00
5TDCBB Byron Buxton 2.50 6.00
5TDCBH Bryce Harper 5.00 12.00
5TDCBS Bubba Starling 2.50 6.00
5TDCCF Clint Frazier 8.00 20.00
5TDCCG Carlos Gonzalez 2.50 6.00
5TDCDW David Wright 2.50 6.00
5TDCGP Gregory Polanco 3.00 8.00
5TDCGS George Springer 8.00 20.00
5TDCJE Jacoby Ellsbury 2.50 6.00
5TDCMT Mike Trout 15.00 40.00
5TDCYP Yasiel Puig 3.00 8.00

2014 Bowman Platinum Jumbo Relic Autographs Refractors

EXCHANGE DEADLINE 7/31/2017
AJRAA Albert Almora 8.00 20.00
AJRBB Byron Buxton 5.00 12.00
AJRCM Colin Moran 4.00 10.00
AJRDD Delino DeShields 4.00 10.00
AJRGC Garin Cecchini 4.00 10.00

2014 Bowman Platinum Jumbo Relic Autographs Blue Refractors

*BLUE REF: .4X TO 1X BASIC
STATED PRINT RUN 199 SER.#'d SETS
EXCHANGE DEADLINE 7/31/2017

2014 Bowman Platinum Jumbo Relic Autographs Gold Refractors

*GOLD REF: .75X TO 2X BASIC
STATED PRINT RUN 50 SER.#'d SETS
EXCHANGE DEADLINE 7/31/2017

2014 Bowman Platinum Jumbo Relic Autographs Red Refractors

*RED REF: 1X TO 2.5X BASIC
STATED PRINT RUN 25 SER.#'d SETS
EXCHANGE DEADLINE 7/31/2017

2014 Bowman Platinum Platinum Cut Relic Autographs

STATED PRINT RUN 49 SER.#'d SETS
EXCHANGE DEADLINE 7/31/2017
APCAA Albert Almora 15.00 40.00
APCAB Archie Bradley 8.00 20.00
APCBB Byron Buxton 10.00 25.00
APCBH Bryce Harper EXCH 125.00 250.00
APCCC Carlos Correa 50.00 100.00
APCCM Colin Moran 8.00 20.00
APCCO Chris Owings 8.00 20.00
APCDD Delino DeShields 8.00 20.00
APCFL Francisco Lindor 50.00 125.00
APCGC Garin Cecchini 8.00 20.00
APCGS George Springer 30.00 80.00
APCMC Miguel Cabrera 60.00 150.00
APCMS Miguel Sano 10.00 25.00
APCMT Mike Trout 150.00 250.00
APCNC Nick Castellanos 25.00 60.00
APCTW Taijuan Walker 8.00 20.00
APCYV Yordano Ventura 10.00 25.00
APCZW Zack Wheeler 10.00 25.00

2014 Bowman Platinum Prospect Autographs

PLATE PRINT RUN 1 SET PER COLOR
BLACK-CYAN-MAGENTA-YELLOW ISSUED
NO PLATE PRICING DUE TO SCARCITY
EXCHANGE DEADLINE 07/31/2017
APAG Alexander Guerrero 8.00 20.00
APAK Akeem Bostick 3.00 8.00
APAT Andrew Thurman 3.00 8.00
APBB Bryce Bandilla 3.00 8.00
APBBU Byron Buxton 5.00 12.00
APBS Braden Shipley 3.00 8.00
APCB Christian Binford 3.00 8.00
APCC Curt Casali 3.00 8.00
APCCO Carlos Correa 15.00 40.00
APCF Chris Flexen 4.00 10.00
APCFR Clint Frazier 12.00 30.00
APCS Cord Sandberg 3.00 8.00
APCT Chris Taylor 12.00 30.00
APCV Cory Vaughn 3.00 8.00
APDR Daniel Robertson 4.00 10.00
APDT Devon Travis 3.00 8.00
APER Eduardo Rodriguez 4.00 10.00
APGY Gabriel Ynoa 4.00 10.00
APHR Hunter Renfroe 6.00 15.00
APJA Jose Abreu 15.00 40.00
APJB Jake Barrett 4.00 10.00
APJBA Javier Baez 25.00 60.00
APJC Jose Campos 3.00 8.00
APJG Joan Gregorio 3.00 8.00
APJS Jake Sweaney 3.00 8.00
APKB Kris Bryant 175.00 350.00
APLT Lewis Thorpe 3.00 8.00
APMA Miguel Almonte 3.00 8.00
APMAP Mark Appel 4.00 10.00
APMR Michael Ratterree 3.00 8.00
APMS Miguel Sano 3.00 8.00
APOT Oscar Taveras 4.00 10.00
APRH Rosell Herrera 5.00 12.00
APRHE Ryon Healy 5.00 12.00
APRT Raimel Tapia 4.00 10.00
APSG Sean Gilmartin 3.00 8.00
APSS Shae Simmons 3.00 8.00
APSSC Scott Schebler 8.00 20.00
APTD Tyler Danish 3.00 8.00
APWR Wendell Rijo 3.00 8.00
APYG Yimi Garcia 3.00 8.00
APZB Zach Borenstein 4.00 10.00

2014 Bowman Platinum Prospect Autographs Blue Refractors

*BLUE REF: .6X TO 1.5X BASIC
STATED PRINT RUN 199 SER.#'d SETS
EXCHANGE DEADLINE 07/31/2017

2014 Bowman Platinum Prospect Autographs Camo Refractors

*CAMO REF: 1X TO 2.5X BASIC
STATED PRINT RUN 35 SER.#'d SETS
EXCHANGE DEADLINE 07/31/2017
APAG Alexander Guerrero 30.00 80.00
APCCO Carlos Correa 60.00 150.00
APKB Kris Bryant 300.00 600.00

2014 Bowman Platinum Prospect Autographs Gold Refractors

*GOLD REF: .75X TO 2X BASIC
STATED PRINT RUN 50 SER.#'d SETS
EXCHANGE DEADLINE 07/31/2017
APCCO Carlos Correa 50.00 120.00

2014 Bowman Platinum Prospect Autographs Green Refractors

*GREEN REF: .5X TO 1.2X BASIC
STATED PRINT RUN 399 SER.#'d SETS
EXCHANGE DEADLINE 07/31/2017

2014 Bowman Platinum Prospect Autographs Red Refractors

*RED REF: 1X TO 2.5X BASIC
STATED PRINT RUN 25 SER.#'d SETS
EXCHANGE DEADLINE 07/31/2017
APCCO Carlos Correa 60.00 150.00
APKB Kris Bryant 300.00 600.00

2014 Bowman Platinum Prospects

PLATE PRINT RUN 1 SET PER COLOR
BLACK-CYAN-MAGENTA-YELLOW ISSUED
NO PLATE PRICING DUE TO SCARCITY
EXCHANGE DEADLINE 07/31/2017
BPP1 Francisco Lindor 1.50 4.00
BPP2 Jorge Soler .50 1.25
BPP3 Andrew Susac .30 .75
BPP4 Braden Shipley .25 .60
BPP5 Jose Berrios .40 1.00
BPP6 Gary Sanchez .75 2.00
BPP7 Kyle Zimmer .25 .60
BPP8 Taylor Guerrieri .25 .60
BPP9 Max Fried 1.00 2.50
BPP10 Byron Buxton .30 .75
BPP11 Alex Meyer .25 .60
BPP12 Jonathan Gray .30 .75
BPP13 Austin Hedges .25 .60
BPP14 Mason Williams .25 .60
BPP15 Alen Hanson .25 .60
BPP16 Bubba Starling .30 .75
BPP17 Jesse Biddle .30 .75
BPP18 Kyle Crick .25 .60
BPP19 Joc Pederson .40 1.00
BPP20 Carlos Correa 1.25 3.00
BPP21 Raul Mondesi .75 2.00
BPP22 Corey Seager 1.00 2.50
BPP23 Andrew Heaney .25 .60
BPP24 Clint Frazier 1.00 2.50
BPP25 Henry Owens .30 .75
BPP26 Roberto Osuna .25 .60
BPP27 Arismendy Alcantara .25 .60
BPP28 Matt Barnes .25 .60
BPP29 David Dahl .30 .75
BPP30 Addison Russell .40 1.00
BPP31 Zach Lee .25 .60
BPP32 Justin Nicolino .25 .60
BPP33 Lance McCullers .25 .60
BPP34 Kohl Stewart .25 .60
BPP35 Mike Foltynewicz .25 .60
BPP36 Eddie Rosario .50 1.25
BPP37 Tyler Austin .25 .60
BPP38 Lucas Giolito .40 1.00
BPP39 Austin Meadows .40 1.00
BPP40 Kris Bryant 2.50 6.00
BPP41 Daniel Robertson .30 .75
BPP42 Colin Moran .25 .60
BPP43 A.J. Cole .25 .60
BPP44 Garin Cecchini .25 .60
BPP45 Eddie Butler .25 .60
BPP46 Julio Urias 1.25 3.00
BPP47 Marcus Stroman .40 1.00
BPP48 Lucas Sims .25 .60
BPP49 Clayton Blackburn .40 1.00
BPP50 Javier Baez 1.00 2.50
BPP51 Rougned Odor .50 1.25
BPP52 Tyler Glasnow .40 1.00
BPP53 Rosell Herrera .40 1.00
BPP54 Eduardo Rodriguez .30 .75
BPP55 Devon Travis .25 .60
BPP56 Hunter Dozier .25 .60
BPP57 Delino DeShields .25 .60
BPP58 Domingo Santana .40 1.00
BPP59 Michael Ynoa .25 .60
BPP60 Aaron Sanchez .25 .60
BPP61 Billy McKinney .30 .75
BPP62 D.J. Peterson .25 .60
BPP63 Chris Taylor 1.25 3.00
BPP64 Joey Gallo .50 1.25
BPP65 Dominic Smith .25 .60
BPP66 Brandon Nimmo .40 1.00
BPP67 J.P. Crawford .25 .60
BPP68 Maikel Franco .30 .75
BPP69 Brian Goodwin .25 .60
BPP70 Mark Appel .30 .75
BPP71 Dan Vogelbach .40 1.00
BPP72 C.J. Edwards .30 .75
BPP73 Luis Heredia .25 .60
BPP74 Josh Bell .50 1.25
BPP75 Reese McGuire .25 .60
BPP76 Nick Kingham .30 .75
BPP77 Marco Gonzales .40 1.00
BPP78 Stephen Piscotty .30 .75
BPP79 Rob Kaminsky .25 .60
BPP80 Jorge Alfaro .30 .75
BPP81 Jake Barrett .30 .75
BPP82 Stryker Trahan .25 .60
BPP83 Trevor Story 1.00 2.50
BPP84 Chris Anderson .25 .60
BPP85 Rymer Liriano .25 .60
BPP86 Hunter Renfroe .30 .75
BPP87 Chris Stratton .25 .60
BPP88 Joe Panik .40 1.00
BPP89 Christian Arroyo 1.50 4.00
BPP90 Albert Almora .40 1.00
BPP91 Luis Sardinas .25 .60
BPP92 Jairo Beras .25 .60
BPP93 Hak-Ju Lee .25 .60
BPP94 Arodys Vizcaino .25 .60
BPP95 Dorssys Paulino .25 .60
BPP96 Slade Heathcott .30 .75
BPP97 Courtney Hawkins .25 .60
BPP98 Tim Anderson .50 1.25
BPP99 Nick Travieso .25 .60
BPP100 Robert Stephenson .25 .60

2014 Bowman Platinum Relic Autographs

PLATE PRINT RUN 1 SET PER COLOR
BLACK-CYAN-MAGENTA-YELLOW ISSUED
NO PLATE PRICING DUE TO SCARCITY
EXCHANGE DEADLINE 07/31/2017
ARAC A.J. Cole 3.00 8.00
ARARI Andre Rienzo 3.00 8.00
ARAS Andrew Susac 4.00 10.00
ARASA Aaron Sanchez 4.00 10.00
ARCCO Carlos Contreras 3.00 8.00
ARCK Corey Knebel 3.00 8.00
ARCY Christian Yelich 30.00 80.00
ARDG David Goforth 3.00 8.00
ARDH Dilson Herrera 15.00 40.00
ARDT Devon Travis 3.00 8.00
AREB Eddie Butler 3.00 8.00
AREG Evan Gattis 3.00 8.00
ARER Eduardo Rodriguez 4.00 10.00
ARGP Gregory Polanco 5.00 12.00
ARJB Jake Barrett 4.00 10.00
ARJBI Jesse Biddle 4.00 10.00
ARJM James McCann 8.00 20.00
ARJP Joc Pederson 5.00 12.00
ARJS Jorge Soler 10.00 25.00
ARKC Kyle Crick 3.00 8.00
ARKP Kyle Parker 4.00 10.00
ARKS Keyvius Sampson 3.00 8.00
ARMB Mookie Betts 100.00 250.00
ARMM Mike Montgomery 3.00 8.00
ARMST Marcus Stroman 5.00 12.00
ARMSTI Matt Stites 3.00 8.00
ARMW Mason Williams 3.00 8.00
ARMY Michael Ynoa 3.00 8.00
ARNS Noah Syndergaard 15.00 40.00
ARPO Peter O'Brien EXCH 4.00 10.00
ARSP Stephen Piscotty 8.00 20.00
ARSR Stefen Romero 3.00 8.00
ARTA Tyler Austin 3.00 8.00
ARTL Taylor Lindsey 3.00 8.00
ARTN Tyler Naquin 4.00 10.00
ARYA Yeison Asencio 3.00 8.00

2014 Bowman Platinum Relic Autographs Blue Refractors

*BLUE REF: .5X TO 1.2X BASIC
STATED PRINT RUN 199 SER.#'d SETS
EXCHANGE DEADLINE 07/31/2017
ARAB Archie Bradley 8.00 20.00
ARMS Miguel Sano 10.00 25.00
ARWM Wil Myers 4.00 10.00
ARZW Zack Wheeler 5.00 12.00
AJRBM B.Nimmo Retail Excl 6.00 15.00
AJRCB Bethancourt Retail Excl 8.00 20.00
AJRCCR C.Cron Retail Excl 8.00 20.00

2014 Bowman Platinum Relic Autographs Gold Refractors

*GOLD REF: .75X TO 2X BASIC
STATED PRINT RUN 50 SER.#'d SETS
EXCHANGE DEADLINE 07/31/2017
ARAB Archie Bradley 10.00 25.00
ARCC Carlos Correa 25.00 60.00
ARMS Miguel Sano 12.00 30.00
ARWM Wil Myers 6.00 15.00
ARZW Zack Wheeler 8.00 20.00

2014 Bowman Platinum Relic Autographs Red Refractors

*RED REF: 1X TO 2.5X BASIC
STATED PRINT RUN 25 SER.#'d SETS
EXCHANGE DEADLINE 07/31/2017
ARAB Archie Bradley 12.00 30.00
ARBH Billy Hamilton EXCH 40.00 100.00
ARCC Carlos Correa 30.00 80.00
ARGS George Springer 30.00 80.00
ARMS Miguel Sano 15.00 40.00
ARMTR Mike Trout 200.00 400.00
ARWM Wil Myers 8.00 20.00
ARZW Zack Wheeler 10.00 25.00

2014 Bowman Platinum Toolsy Die Cuts

TDCAA Albert Almora .60 1.50
TDCAH Austin Hedges .40 1.00
TDCAHA Alen Hanson .40 1.00
TDCAHE Austin Hedges .40 1.00
TDCAM Austin Meadows .60 1.50
TDCAR Addison Russell .60 1.50
TDCBB Byron Buxton .50 1.25
TDCBG Brian Goodwin .40 1.00
TDCBH Billy Hamilton .50 1.25
TDCCB Christian Bethancourt .40 1.00
TDCCC C.J. Cron .40 1.00
TDCCCO Carlos Correa 2.00 5.00
TDCCH Courtney Hawkins .40 1.00
TDCCM Colin Moran .40 1.00
TDCCS Corey Seager 1.50 4.00
TDCDD Delino DeShields .40 1.00
TDCDDA David Dahl .50 1.25
TDCDP D.J. Peterson .40 1.00
TDCDS Dominic Smith .40 1.00
TDCDV Dan Vogelbach .60 1.50
TDCFL Francisco Lindor 2.50 6.00
TDCGC Garin Cecchini .40 1.00
TDCGP Gregory Polanco .60 1.50
TDCGS George Springer 1.50 4.00
TDCGSA Gary Sanchez 1.25 3.00
TDCHL Hak-Ju Lee .40 1.00
TDCJA Jose Abreu 3.00 8.00
TDCJAL Jorge Alfaro .50 1.25
TDCJB Javier Baez 1.50 4.00
TDCJC J.P. Crawford .40 1.00
TDCJCR J.P. Crawford .40 1.00
TDCJG Joey Gallo .75 2.00
TDCJP Joc Pederson .60 1.50
TDCJS Jorge Soler .75 2.00
TDCJSI Jonathan Singleton .50 1.25
TDCKB Kris Bryant 3.00 8.00
TDCKW Kolten Wong .50 1.25
TDCLS Luis Sardinas .40 1.00
TDCMB Mookie Betts 8.00 20.00
TDCMF Maikel Franco .50 1.25
TDCMJ Micah Johnson .40 1.00
TDCMS Miguel Sano .50 1.25
TDCMW Mason Williams .40 1.00
TDCNC Nick Castellanos 1.25 3.00
TDCOT Oscar Taveras .50 1.25
TDCRM Raul Mondesi 1.25 3.00
TDCRMC Reese McGuire .40 1.00
TDCRW Russell Wilson 5.00 12.00
TDCTA Tyler Austin .40 1.00
TDCXB Xander Bogaerts 1.25 3.00

2014 Bowman Platinum Top Prospects Die Cuts

TPAA Albert Almora .50 1.25
TPAB Archie Bradley .30 .75
TPAH Alen Hanson .30 .75
TPAHE Andrew Heaney .30 .75
TPAM Austin Meadows .50 1.25
TPAR Addison Russell .50 1.25
TPAS Aaron Sanchez .30 .75
TPBB Byron Buxton .40 1.00
TPCC C.J. Cron .30 .75
TPCE C.J. Edwards .40 1.00
TPCF Clint Frazier 1.25 3.00
TPDD David Dahl .40 1.00
TPEB Eddie Butler .30 .75
TPFL Francisco Lindor 2.00 5.00
TPGP Gregory Polanco .50 1.25
TPGS Gary Sanchez 1.00 2.50
TPGSP George Springer 1.25 3.00
TPJA Jose Abreu 2.50 6.00
TPJB Javier Baez 1.25 3.00
TPJS Jorge Soler .60 1.50
TPKB Kris Bryant 2.50 6.00
TPLG Lucas Giolito .50 1.25
TPLM Lance McCullers .30 .75
TPMA Mark Appel .40 1.00
TPMF Maikel Franco .40 1.00
TPMS Miguel Sano .40 1.00
TPMT Masahiro Tanaka 1.00 2.50
TPOT Oscar Taveras .40 1.00
TPPE Phil Ervin .30 .75
TPTG Tyler Glasnow .50 1.25

2014 Bowman Platinum Top Prospects Die Cuts Refractors

*REF: 2X TO 5X BASIC
STATED PRINT RUN 25 SER.#'d SETS

2014 Bowman Platinum Top Prospects Die Cuts Blue Refractors

*BLUE REF: 1.5X TO 4X BASIC
STATED PRINT RUN 49 SER.#'d SETS

2016 Bowman Platinum

COMPLETE SET (100) 20.00 50.00
PRINTING PLATE ODDS 1:742 RETAIL
PLATE PRINT RUN 1 SET PER COLOR
BLACK-CYAN-MAGENTA-YELLOW ISSUED
NO PLATE PRICING DUE TO SCARCITY
1 Mike Trout 2.50 6.00
2 Gary Sanchez RC 1.50 4.00
3 Miguel Cabrera .50 1.25
4 Carl Edwards Jr. RC .60 1.50
5 Kris Bryant .60 1.50
6 Gerrit Cole .50 1.25
7 Dustin Pedroia .50 1.25
8 Paul Goldschmidt .50 1.25
9 Jose Abreu .50 1.25
10 Carlos Rodon .50 1.25
11 Michael Fulmer RC .75 2.00
12 Brian McCann .40 1.00
13 Francisco Lindor .50 1.25

4 Evan Longoria .40 1.00
5 Stephen Piscotty RC .75 2.00
6 Chris Sale .50 1.25
7 Jeurys Familia .40 1.00
18 Ryan Braun .40 1.00
19 Aaron Blair RC .50 1.25
20 Troy Tulowitzki .50 1.25
21 Nolan Arenado .60 1.50
22 Byung-Ho Park RC .60 1.50
23 Yoenis Cespedes .50 1.25
24 Hector Olivera RC .60 1.50
25 Kyle Seager .30 .75
26 Julio Urias RC 1.50 4.00
27 Aroldis Chapman .50 1.25
28 Henry Owens RC .60 1.50
29 Jose Fernandez .50 1.25
30 Jose Peraza RC .60 1.50
31 Cole Hamels .40 1.00
32 Kyle Schwarber RC 1.50 4.00
33 Giancarlo Stanton .50 1.25
34 Anthony Rizzo .75 2.00
35 Albert Almora RC .60 1.50
36 Buster Posey .60 1.50
37 Jose Berrios RC .60 1.50
38 Jon Lester .40 1.00
39 Mookie Betts .75 2.00
40 Corey Seager RC 4.00 10.00
41 Matt Harvey .40 1.00
42 Seung-hwan Oh RC 1.25 3.00
43 Zack Greinke .40 1.00
44 Wade Davis .30 .75
45 Yu Darvish .50 1.25
46 Tyler Naquin RC .60 1.50
47 Jorge Soler .50 1.25
48 Matt Carpenter .50 1.25
49 Jake Arrieta .40 1.00
50 Bryce Harper .75 2.00
51 Raul Mondesi RC .60 1.50
52 David Wright .40 1.00
53 Felix Hernandez .40 1.00
54 Wil Myers .30 .75
55 Andrew McCutchen .50 1.25
56 Jameson Taillon RC .60 1.50
57 Prince Fielder .40 1.00
58 Joey Votto .50 1.25
59 Blake Snell RC .60 1.50
60 Joey Gallo .40 1.00
61 Freddie Freeman .60 1.50
62 Eric Hosmer .40 1.00
63 Kenta Maeda RC 1.00 2.50
64 Luis Severino RC .60 1.50
65 Nomar Mazara RC .75 2.00
66 Max Scherzer .50 1.25
67 Dee Gordon .30 .75
68 Craig Kimbrel .40 1.00
69 Michael Conforto RC .60 1.50
70 Sonny Gray .40 1.00
71 Brian Dozier .40 1.00
72 Noah Syndergaard .40 1.00
73 Edwin Encarnacion .50 1.25
74 Rob Refsnyder RC .60 1.50
75 Dallas Keuchel .40 1.00
76 Ichiro Suzuki .60 1.50
77 David Ortiz .50 1.25
78 Trea Turner RC 1.50 4.00
79 Josh Donaldson .40 1.00
80 Jose Altuve .40 1.00
81 Eddie Rosario .40 1.00
82 A.J. Pollock .30 .75
83 Salvador Perez .40 1.00
84 Miguel Sano RC .75 2.00
85 Adam Jones .40 1.00
86 Joc Pederson .40 1.00
87 Tyson Ross .30 .75
88 Robert Stephenson RC .50 1.25
89 J.D. Martinez .50 1.25
90 Tyler White RC .50 1.25
91 Sean Manaea RC .50 1.25
92 Madison Bumgarner .40 1.00
93 Byron Buxton .40 1.00
94 Jacob deGrom .50 1.25
95 Jon Gray RC .50 1.25
96 David Price .40 1.00
97 Carlos Correa .50 1.25
98 Trevor Story RC 2.00 5.00
99 Aaron Nola RC 1.00 2.50
100 Clayton Kershaw 1.00 2.50

2016 Bowman Platinum Green

*GREEN: 2.5X TO 6X BASIC
*GREEN RC: 1.5X TO 4X BASIC RC
STATED ODDS 1:31 RETAIL
STATED PRINT RUN 99 SER.#'d SETS
5 Kris Bryant 10.00 25.00

2016 Bowman Platinum Ice

*ICE: 1.2X TO 3X BASIC
*ICE RC: .75X TO 2X BASIC RC
RANDOM INSERTS IN PACKS
5 Kris Bryant 5.00 12.00

2016 Bowman Platinum Orange

*ORANGE: 3X TO 8X BASIC
*ORANGE RC: 2X TO 5X BASIC RC
STATED ODDS 1:119 RETAIL
STATED PRINT RUN 25 SER.#'d SETS
50 Bryce Harper 12.00 30.00

2016 Bowman Platinum Purple

*PURPLE: 1.5X TO 4X BASIC
*PURPLE RC: 1X TO 2.5X BASIC RC
STATED ODDS 1:12 RETAIL
STATED PRINT RUN 250 SER.#'d SETS
5 Kris Bryant 6.00 15.00

2016 Bowman Platinum Autographs

STATED ODDS 1:635 RETAIL
PAAN Aaron Nola 6.00 15.00
PAAP A.J. Pollock 3.00 8.00
PABB Byron Buxton 8.00 20.00
PABHP Byung-Ho Park 4.00 10.00
PABS Blake Snell 4.00 10.00
PACC Carlos Correa 25.00 60.00
PACR Carlos Rodon
PACS Corey Seager
PAER Eddie Rosario 4.00 10.00
PAFM Frankie Montas 4.00 10.00
PAJB Jose Berrios 4.00 10.00
PAJF Jeurys Familia 4.00 10.00
PAJG Joey Gallo
PAJU Julio Urias 15.00 40.00
PAKB Kris Bryant 75.00 200.00
PAKM Kenta Maeda
PAKS Kyle Schwarber
PALS Luis Severino 6.00 15.00
PAMF Michael Fulmer 12.00 30.00
PAMS Max Scherzer 15.00 40.00
PAMSA Miguel Sano 5.00 12.00
PAMT Mike Trout 125.00 250.00
PARS Robert Stephenson 3.00 8.00
PATS Trevor Story 12.00 30.00

2016 Bowman Platinum Autographs Green

*GREEN: .6X TO 1.5X BASIC
STATED ODDS 1:1091 RETAIL
STATED PRINT RUN 75 SER.#'d SETS
PACR Carlos Rodon 6.00 15.00
PACS Corey Seager 100.00 250.00
PAJG Joey Gallo
PAKB Kris Bryant
PAKM Kenta Maeda 40.00 100.00
PAKS Kyle Schwarber 30.00 80.00
PAMT Mike Trout

2016 Bowman Platinum Autographs Orange

*ORANGE: .75X TO 2X BASIC
STATED ODDS 1:2775 RETAIL
STATED PRINT RUN 25 SER.#'d SETS
PACR Carlos Rodon 10.00 25.00
PACS Corey Seager 150.00 400.00
PAJG Joey Gallo 8.00 20.00
PAKB Kris Bryant
PAKM Kenta Maeda 60.00 150.00
PAKS Kyle Schwarber 50.00 120.00
PAMT Mike Trout

2016 Bowman Platinum Next Generation

STATED ODDS 1:2 RETAIL
*PURPLE/250: 1.5X TO 4X BASIC
*GREEN/99: 2X TO 6X BASIC
*ORANGE/25: 3X TO 8X BASIC
NG1 Kaleb Cowart .40 1.00
NG2 Brandon Drury .60 1.50
NG3 Hector Olivera .50 1.25
NG4 Dylan Bundy .50 1.25
NG5 Henry Owens .50 1.25
NG6 Kris Bryant .75 2.00
NG7 Carlos Rodon .60 1.50
NG8 Jose Peraza .50 1.25
NG9 Francisco Lindor .60 1.50
NG10 Trevor Story 1.50 4.00
NG11 Daniel Norris .40 1.00
NG12 Carlos Correa .60 1.50
NG13 Raul Mondesi .50 1.25
NG14 Kenta Maeda .75 2.00
NG15 Justin Bour .50 1.25
NG16 Jorge Lopez .40 1.00
NG17 Miguel Sano .60 1.50
NG18 Jacob deGrom .60 1.50
NG19 Luis Severino .50 1.25
NG20 Sean Manaea .40 1.00
NG21 Odubel Herrera .50 1.25
NG22 Gregory Polanco .50 1.25
NG23 Colin Rea .40 1.00
NG24 Chris Heston .40 1.00
NG25 Ketel Marte .75 2.00
NG26 Randal Grichuk .40 1.00
NG27 Blake Snell .50 1.25
NG28 Nomar Mazara .60 1.50
NG29 Roberto Osuna .40 1.00
NG30 Trea Turner 1.25 3.00

2016 Bowman Platinum Next Generation Prospects

STATED ODDS 1:2 RETAIL
*PURPLE/250: 1X TO 2.5X BASIC
*GREEN/99: 1.2X TO 3X BASIC
*ORANGE/25: 2X TO 5X BASIC
NGP1 Taylor Ward .50 1.25
NGP2 Braden Shipley .40 1.00
NGP3 Dansby Swanson 1.25 3.00
NGP4 Hunter Harvey .40 1.00
NGP5 Yoan Moncada 1.00 2.50
NGP6 Gleyber Torres 6.00 15.00
NGP7 Carson Fulmer .40 1.00
NGP8 Jesse Winker .40 1.00
NGP9 Bradley Zimmer .60 1.50
NGP10 Brendan Rodgers .60 1.50
NGP11 Beau Burrows .40 1.00
NGP12 Alex Bregman 2.50 6.00
NGP13 Kyle Zimmer .40 1.00
NGP14 Jose De Leon .40 1.00
NGP15 Tyler Kolek .50 1.25
NGP16 Orlando Arcia .50 1.25
NGP17 Tyler Jay .40 1.00
NGP18 Dominic Smith .40 1.00
NGP19 Jorge Mateo .50 1.25
NGP20 Franklin Barreto .40 1.00
NGP21 J.P. Crawford .40 1.00
NGP22 Tyler Glasnow .50 1.25
NGP23 Manuel Margot .40 1.00
NGP24 Christian Arroyo 1.25 3.00
NGP25 Alex Jackson .50 1.25
NGP26 Alex Reyes .50 1.25
NGP27 Brent Honeywell .60 1.50
NGP28 Lewis Brinson .60 1.50
NGP29 Anthony Alford .40 1.00
NGP30 Lucas Giolito .60 1.50

2016 Bowman Platinum Platinum Cut Autographs

STATED ODDS 1:2258 RETAIL
STATED PRINT RUN 25 SER.#'d SETS
PCAAA Anthony Alford
PCAAB Alex Bregman 75.00 200.00
PCAABE Andrew Benintendi 60.00 150.00
PCAAE Anderson Espinoza
PCAAJ Aaron Judge 125.00 300.00
PCAAR A.J. Reed 8.00 20.00
PCAARE Alex Reyes 40.00 100.00
PCABR Brendan Rodgers
PCABZ Bradley Zimmer
PCACF Carson Fulmer 8.00 20.00
PCADD David Dahl 50.00 120.00
PCADS Dansby Swanson 75.00 200.00
PCADT Dillon Tate
PCAIH Ian Happ
PCAJB Josh Bell 25.00 60.00
PCAJG Javier Guerra 12.00 30.00
PCAJM Jorge Mateo 10.00 25.00
PCAKA Kolby Allard 20.00 50.00
PCAKT Kyle Tucker
PCALF Lucius Fox
PCALG Lucas Giolito
PCALS Lucas Sims 8.00 20.00
PCAOA Orlando Arcia
PCARD Rafael Devers 75.00 200.00
PCASN Sean Newcomb 10.00 25.00
PCAVG Vladimir Guerrero Jr. 300.00 600.00
PCAVR Victor Robles
PCAWC Willson Contreras
PCAYM Yoan Moncada

2016 Bowman Platinum Platinum Presence

STATED ODDS 1:4 RETAIL
*GREEN/99: 1X TO 2.5X BASIC
*ORANGE/25: X TO X BASIC
PP1 Yoan Moncada 1.00 2.50
PP2 Dansby Swanson 1.25 3.00
PP3 Vladimir Guerrero Jr. 8.00 20.00
PP4 Alex Bregman 2.50 6.00
PP5 Brendan Rodgers .60 1.50
PP6 Daz Cameron .40 1.00
PP7 Lucius Fox .60 1.50
PP8 Andrew Benintendi 1.25 3.00
PP9 Ian Happ .75 2.00
PP10 Lucas Giolito .60 1.50
PP11 David Dahl .50 1.25
PP12 Jose De Leon .40 1.00
PP13 Alex Reyes .50 1.25
PP14 Kolby Allard .40 1.00
PP15 Orlando Arcia .50 1.25
PP16 Francis Martes .50 1.25
PP17 Anderson Espinoza .40 1.00
PP18 Domingo Acevedo .60 1.50
PP19 Javier Guerra .40 1.00
PP20 Rafael Devers 1.25 3.00
PP21 Josh Bell .75 2.00
PP22 Austin Meadows .60 1.50
PP23 J.P. Crawford .40 1.00
PP24 Anthony Alford .40 1.00
PP25 Aaron Judge 10.00 25.00
PP26 Sean Newcomb .50 1.25
PP27 Tyler Glasnow .50 1.25
PP28 Franklin Barreto .40 1.00
PP29 Jorge Mateo .50 1.25
PP30 Victor Robles 1.50 4.00

2016 Bowman Platinum Platinum Presence Autographs

STATED ODDS 1:1518 RETAIL
STATED PRINT RUN 99 SER.#'d SETS
PPAAB Alex Bregman
PPAABE Andrew Benintendi
PPAAE Anderson Espinoza 6.00 15.00
PPAAR Alex Reyes 10.00 25.00
PPABR Brendan Rodgers
PPADA Domingo Acevedo 10.00 25.00
PPADC Daz Cameron
PPADD David Dahl 8.00 20.00
PPADS Dansby Swanson
PPAFM Francis Martes 4.00 10.00
PPAIH Ian Happ 6.00 15.00
PPAJG Javier Guerra 3.00 8.00
PPAKA Kolby Allard 6.00 15.00
PPALF Lucius Fox
PPALG Lucas Giolito 5.00 12.00
PPAOA Orlando Arcia 6.00 15.00
PPARD Rafael Devers 20.00 50.00
PPAVGJ Vladimir Guerrero Jr.
PPAWC Willson Contreras
PPAYM Yoan Moncada

2016 Bowman Platinum Platinum Presence Autographs Green

*GREEN: .5X TO 1.2X BASIC
STATED ODDS 1:1091 RETAIL
STATED PRINT RUN 75 SER.#'d SETS
PPAAB Alex Bregman 40.00 100.00
PPAABE Andrew Benintendi 40.00 100.00
PPABR Brendan Rodgers 6.00 15.00
PPADC Daz Cameron 4.00 10.00
PPADS Dansby Swanson 40.00 100.00
PPALF Lucius Fox 8.00 20.00
PPAVGJ Vladimir Guerrero Jr. 125.00 300.00
PPAWC Willson Contreras 25.00 60.00
PPAYM Yoan Moncada 40.00 100.00

2016 Bowman Platinum Platinum Presence Autographs Orange

*ORANGE: .6X TO 1.5X BASIC
STATED ODDS 1:3237 RETAIL
STATED PRINT RUN 25 SER.#'d SETS
PPAAB Alex Bregman 60.00 150.00
PPAABE Andrew Benintendi 60.00 150.00
PPABR Brendan Rodgers 10.00 25.00
PPADC Daz Cameron 6.00 15.00
PPADS Dansby Swanson 60.00 150.00
PPALF Lucius Fox 12.00 30.00
PPAVGJ Vladimir Guerrero Jr. 200.00 500.00
PPAWC Willson Contreras 40.00 100.00
PPAYM Yoan Moncada 60.00 150.00

2016 Bowman Platinum Top Prospects

SP ODDS 1:100 RETAIL
PRINTING PLATE ODDS 1:742 RETAIL
PLATE PRINT RUN 1 SET PER COLOR
BLACK-CYAN-MAGENTA-YELLOW ISSUED
NO PLATE PRICING DUE TO SCARCITY
*ICE: .6X TO 1.5X BASIC
*PURPLE/250: .75X TO 2X BASIC
*GREEN/99: 1X TO 2.5X BASIC
TPAA Anthony Alford .30 .75
TPAB Alex Bregman 2.00 5.00
TPABE Andrew Benintendi 1.00 2.50
TPABW Adam Brett Walker II .30 .75
TPAE Anderson Espinoza .30 .75
TPAEN Adam Engel .30 .75
TPAG Amir Garrett .30 .75
TPAJ Judge SP Rnnng 40.00 100.00
TPAJU Ariel Jurado .30 .75
TPAR A.J. Reed .30 .75
TPARE Alex Reyes .40 1.00
TPARO Amed Rosario .50 1.25
TPAS Antonio Santillan .30 .75
TPASE Antonio Senzatela .30 .75
TPAV Alex Verdugo .50 1.25
TPBA Brady Aiken .75 2.00
TPBD Braxton Davidson .30 .75
TPBH Brent Honeywell .50 1.25
TPBM Billy McKinney .40 1.00
TPBP Brett Phillips .30 .75
TPBR Brendan Rodgers .50 1.25
TPBZ Zimmer SP Bttng 40.00 100.00
TPCA Arroyo SP Fldng 20.00 50.00
TPCB Cody Bellinger 5.00 12.00
TPCF Clint Frazier SP 40.00 100.00
TPCFU Carson Fulmer SP 20.00 50.00
TPCG Conner Greene .30 .75
TPCR Cornelius Randolph .30 .75
TPCRE Cody Reed .30 .75
TPDA Domingo Acevedo .50 1.25
TPDC Daz Cameron .30 .75
TPDD David Dahl .40 1.00
TPDDE David Denson .30 .75
TPDSM Dominic Smith .30 .75
TPDJ Drew Jackson .30 .75
TPDP David Paulino .40 1.00
TPDS Dansby Swanson 1.00 2.50
TPDT Dillon Tate .30 .75
TPFB Franklin Barreto .30 .75
TPFM Francis Martes .40 1.00
TPFT Fernando Tatis Jr. 15.00 40.00
TPGH Grant Holmes .40 1.00
TPGT Gleyber Torres 5.00 12.00
TPGW Garrett Whitley .40 1.00
TPHR Harold Ramirez .40 1.00
TPHR Hunter Renfroe SP
TPIH Ian Happ .60 1.50
TPJC Jharel Cotton .30 .75
TPJC Crwfrd SP Rnnng 10.00 25.00
TPJDL Jose De Leon SP 20.00 50.00
TPJF Jacob Faria .30 .75
TPJG Javier Guerra .30 .75
TPJGU Jordan Guerrero .30 .75
TPJH Jeff Hoffman .40 1.00
TPJM Jorge Mateo .40 1.00
TPJMU Joe Musgrove .30 .75
TPJN Josh Naylor .40 1.00
TPJO Jhailyn Ortiz .60 1.50
TPJR Jomar Reyes .50 1.25
TPJS Justus Sheffield .60 1.50
TPJT Jake Thompson .30 .75
TPJUF Junior Fernandez .50 1.25
TPJW Jesse Winker .30 .75
TPKA Kolby Allard .30 .75
TPKK Kevin Kramer .40 1.00
TPKP Kevin Padlo .40 1.00
TPKT Kyle Tucker 1.25 3.00
TPKZ Kyle Zimmer .30 .75
TPLB Lewis Brinson SP 12.00 30.00
TPLF Lucius Fox .50 1.25
TPLG Lucas Giolito .50 1.25
TPLO Luis Ortiz .40 1.00
TPLW Luke Weaver .50 1.25
TPMD Mauricio Dubon .40 1.00
TPMM Manuel Margot .30 .75
TPNG Nick Gordon .30 .75
TPNS Nate Smith .30 .75
TPNW Nick Williams .40 1.00
TPOA Orlando Arcia .40 1.00
TPOAL Ozzie Albies 1.25 3.00
TPRB Rafael Bautista .30 .75
TPRD Rafael Devers 1.00 2.50
TPRG Ruddy Giron .30 .75
TPRM Reese McGuire .30 .75
TPRMC Ryan McMahon .30 .75
TPRR Rio Ruiz .30 .75
TPRRA Roniel Raudes .50 1.25
TPSG Stone Garrett .30 .75
TPSK Scott Kingery .50 1.25
TPSN Sean Newcomb .40 1.00
TPTA Tim Anderson 1.25 3.00
TPTC Trent Clark .30 .75
TPTG Tyler Glasnow .40 1.00
TPTJ Tyler Jay .30 .75
TPTM Trey Mancini 1.00 2.50
TPTO Tyler O'Neill .40 1.00
TPTS Tyler Stephenson .30 .75
TPTT Touki Toussaint .40 1.00
TPTW Taylor Ward .40 1.00
TPVG Vladimir Guerrero Jr. 5.00 12.00
TPVR Victor Robles 1.25 3.00
TPWA Willy Adames .50 1.25
TPWC1 Willson Contreras 2.00 5.00
TPWC2 Cntrrs SP Bttng 25.00 60.00
TPWCH Wei-Chieh Huang .30 .75
TPWG Wilkerman Garcia .40 1.00
TPWJ Wander Javier .50 1.25
TPYG Yeudy Garcia .30 .75
TPYL Yoan Lopez .30 .75
TPYM Yoan Moncada .75 2.00

2016 Bowman Platinum Top Prospects Orange

*ORANGE: 2X TO 5X BASIC
STATED ODDS 1:119 RETAIL
STATED PRINT RUN 25 SER.#'d SETS
TPABE Andrew Benintendi 20.00 50.00

2016 Bowman Platinum Top Prospects Autographs

STATED ODDS 1:105 RETAIL
TPAAA Anthony Alford 2.50 6.00
TPAAB Alex Bregman
TPAABE Andrew Benintendi 25.00 60.00
TPAABW Adam Brett Walker II 2.50 6.00
TPAAE Anderson Espinoza 4.00 10.00
TPAAJU Ariel Jurado 2.50 6.00
TPAAR A.J. Reed 2.50 6.00
TPAARE Alex Reyes 5.00 12.00
TPABD Braxton Davidson 2.50 6.00
TPABM Billy McKinney
TPABR Brendan Rodgers
TPACR Cornelius Randolph 2.50 6.00
TPADA Domingo Acevedo 4.00 10.00
TPADC Daz Cameron
TPADD David Dahl 3.00 8.00
TPADJ Drew Jackson 2.50 6.00
TPADS Dansby Swanson
TPADT Dillon Tate 3.00 8.00
TPAFM Francis Martes 3.00 8.00
TPAGH Grant Holmes 3.00 8.00
TPAGW Garrett Whitley 3.00 8.00
TPAIH Ian Happ 15.00 40.00
TPAJG Javier Guerra 2.50 6.00
TPAJM Jorge Mateo 3.00 8.00
TPAKA Kolby Allard 2.50 6.00
TPAKP Kevin Padlo 2.50 6.00
TPALF Lucius Fox
TPALG Lucas Giolito 4.00 10.00
TPALW Luke Weaver 4.00 10.00
TPAMM Manuel Margot 2.50 6.00
TPANG Nick Gordon 2.50 6.00
TPAOA Orlando Arcia 3.00 8.00
TPARD Rafael Devers 8.00 20.00
TPARM Reese McGuire 2.50 6.00
TPARR Rio Ruiz 2.50 6.00
TPASN Sean Newcomb 3.00 8.00
TPATT Touki Toussaint 3.00 8.00
TPAVGJ Vladimir Guerrero Jr.
TPAVR Victor Robles 12.00 30.00
TPAWA Willy Adames 4.00 10.00
TPAWC Willson Contreras 10.00 25.00
TPAYM Yoan Moncada 50.00 120.00

2016 Bowman Platinum Top Prospects Autographs Green

*GREEN: .6X TO 1.5X BASIC
STATED ODDS 1:562 RETAIL
STATED PRINT RUN 75 SER.#'d SETS
TPAAB Alex Bregman 50.00 120.00
TPABM Billy McKinney 5.00 12.00
TPABR Brendan Rodgers 6.00 15.00
TPADC Daz Cameron 4.00 10.00
TPADS Dansby Swanson 40.00 100.00
TPALF Lucius Fox 10.00 25.00
TPAVGJ Vladimir Guerrero Jr. 125.00 300.00
TPAYM Yoan Moncada

2016 Bowman Platinum Top Prospects Autographs Orange

*ORANGE: 1X TO 2.5X BASIC
STATED ODDS 1:1646 RETAIL
STATED PRINT RUN 25 SER.#'d SETS
TPAAB Alex Bregman 75.00 200.00
TPABM Billy McKinney 8.00 20.00
TPABR Brendan Rodgers 10.00 25.00
TPADC Daz Cameron 6.00 15.00
TPADS Dansby Swanson 60.00 150.00
TPALF Lucius Fox 15.00 40.00
TPAVGJ Vladimir Guerrero Jr. 200.00 500.00
TPAYM Yoan Moncada 100.00 250.00

2016 Bowman Platinum Top Prospects Autographs Purple

*PURPLE: .5X TO 1.2X BASIC
STATED ODDS 1:289 RETAIL
STATED PRINT RUN 150 SER.#'d SETS
TPAAB Alex Bregman 40.00 100.00
TPABM Billy McKinney 4.00 10.00
TPABR Brendan Rodgers 5.00 12.00
TPADC Daz Cameron 3.00 8.00
TPADS Dansby Swanson 30.00 80.00
TPALF Lucius Fox 8.00 20.00
TPAVGJ Vladimir Guerrero Jr. 100.00 250.00
TPAYM Yoan Moncada

2017 Bowman Platinum

COMP.SET w/o SP's (100) 25.00 60.00
STATED SP ODDS 1:165 RETAIL
1A Kris Bryant .50 1.25
1B Bryant SP w/Bat 5.00 12.00
2 Bryce Harper .60 1.50
3 Daniel Murphy .30 .75
4 Dellin Betances .30 .75
5 Nomar Mazara .25 .60
6 Cole Hamels .30 .75
7 Matt Carpenter .40 1.00
8 Joey Votto .40 1.00
9 Stephen Strasburg .40 1.00
10 Aledmys Diaz .30 .75
11 Jake Thompson RC .40 1.00
12 Carson Fulmer RC .40 1.00
13A Andrew Benintendi RC 1.25 3.00
13B Bnntndi SP Dugout 12.00 30.00
14 David Ortiz .40 1.00
15 Gregory Polanco .30 .75
16 Starling Marte .30 .75
17 Jharel Cotton RC .40 1.00
18 Gavin Cecchini RC .40 1.00
19 Jackie Bradley Jr. .40 1.00
20 Anthony Rizzo .60 1.50
21 Francisco Lindor .40 1.00
22 Robert Gsellman RC .40 1.00
23 Max Scherzer .40 1.00
24 Trevor Story .40 1.00
25A Yoan Moncada RC 1.25 3.00
25B Mncda SP Glasses 8.00 20.00
26 Paul Goldschmidt .40 1.00
27 Amir Garrett RC .40 1.00
28 Tyler Glasnow RC .50 1.25
29 Nelson Cruz .40 1.00
30 Brandon Belt .30 .75
31 Tim Anderson .40 1.00
32 A.J. Pollock .25 .60
33 Evan Longoria .30 .75
34 Manny Machado .40 1.00
35 David Dahl RC .50 1.25
36 Jameson Taillon .30 .75
37 Danny Salazar .30 .75
38 Yoenis Cespedes .40 1.00
39 Braden Shipley RC .40 1.00
40 Jon Lester .30 .75
41 Andrew McCutchen .40 1.00
42 Robinson Cano .30 .75
43 Ryon Healy RC .50 1.25
44 Mark Trumbo .25 .60
45 Carlos Correa .40 1.00
46 Antonio Senzatela RC .40 1.00
47 Raimel Tapia RC .50 1.25
48 Freddie Freeman .50 1.25
49 Giancarlo Stanton .40 1.00
50 Corey Seager .40 1.00
51 Matt Strahm RC .40 1.00
52 Julio Urias .40 1.00
53 Nolan Arenado .60 1.50
54 Stephen Piscotty .30 .75
55 Joe Musgrove RC .40 1.00
56 Josh Donaldson .30 .75
57 Jose Altuve .40 1.00
58 Yulieski Gurriel RC .60 1.50
59 Odubel Herrera .30 .75
60 Kenta Maeda .30 .75
61 Jorge Alfaro RC .50 1.25
62 Reynaldo Lopez RC .40 1.00
63A Mookie Betts .60 1.50
63B Betts SP Red jrsy 6.00 15.00
64 Ryan Braun .30 .75
65 Gary Sanchez .40 1.00
66 Craig Kimbrel .30 .75
67 Yu Darvish .40 1.00
68 Michael Fulmer .25 .60
69 Jose De Leon RC .40 1.00
70 Jose Bautista .30 .75
71 Chris Sale .40 1.00
72 Alex Reyes RC .50 1.25
73 Troy Tulowitzki .40 1.00
74 Andrew Miller .30 .75
75A Alex Bregman RC 1.50 4.00
75B Bregman SP Thrwng 10.00 25.00
76 Cody Bellinger RC 6.00 15.00
77 George Springer .30 .75
78A Dansby Swanson RC 1.00 2.50
78B Swanson SP w/Bat 6.00 15.00
79 Tyler Austin RC .60 1.50
80 Felix Hernandez .30 .75
81 Jacob deGrom .40 1.00
82 Clayton Kershaw .75 2.00
83 Ben Zobrist .30 .75
84 Ichiro .50 1.25
85 Noah Syndergaard .30 .75
86 Willson Contreras .40 1.00
87 Kyle Schwarber .40 1.00
88 Hunter Renfroe RC .50 1.25
89 Manny Margot RC .40 1.00
90 Jake Lamb .30 .75
91 Aaron Judge RC 5.00 12.00
92 Orlando Arcia RC .60 1.50
93 Jeff Hoffman RC .40 1.00
94 Wil Myers .25 .60
95 Jake Arrieta .30 .75
96 Buster Posey .50 1.25
97 Xander Bogaerts .40 1.00
98 Miguel Cabrera .40 1.00
99 Trea Turner .30 .75
100A Mike Trout 2.00 5.00
100B Trout SP No hat 20.00 50.00

2017 Bowman Platinum Green

*GREEN: 1.5X TO 4X BASIC
*GREEN RC: 1X TO 2.5X BASIC RC
STATED ODDS 1:84 RETAIL
STATED PRINT RUN 99 SER.#'d SETS

2017 Bowman Platinum Ice

*ICE: .6X TO 1.5X BASIC
*ICE RC: .6X TO 1.5X BASIC RC
RANDOM INSERTS IN PACKS

2017 Bowman Platinum Orange

*ORANGE: 5X TO 12X BASIC
*ORANGE RC: 3X TO 8X BASIC RC
STATED ODDS 1:329 RETAIL
STATED PRINT RUN 25 SER.#'d SETS

2017 Bowman Platinum Purple

*PURPLE: 1.2X TO 3X BASIC
*PURPLE RC: .75X TO 2X BASIC RC
STATED ODDS 1:33 RETAIL
STATED PRINT RUN 250 SER.#'d SETS

2017 Bowman Platinum MLB Autographs

STATED ODDS 1:390 RETAIL
PRINT RUNS B/WN 60-250 COPIES PER
EXCHANGE DEADLINE 6/30/2019
*GREEN/75: .5X TO 1.2X BASIC
MLBAAB Alex Bregman/60 20.00 50.00
MLBAABE Andrew Benintendi/100 30.00 80.00
MLBAAR Alex Reyes/80 8.00 20.00
MLBADB Dellin Betances/60 4.00 10.00
MLBADS Dansby Swanson
MLBAJD Jacob deGrom
MLBAJU Julio Urias
MLBAKB Kris Bryant
MLDALG Lucas Giolito/70 20.00 50.00
MLBARH Ryon Healy/250 5.00 12.00
MLBAYG Yulieski Gurriel/70 10.00 25.00

2017 Bowman Platinum MLB Autographs Orange

*ORANGE: .75X TO 2X BASIC
STATED ODDS 1:1186 RETAIL
STATED PRINT RUN 25 SER.#'d SETS
EXCHANGE DEADLINE 6/30/2019
MLBADS Dansby Swanson 40.00 100.00
MLBAJD Jacob deGrom 20.00 50.00

2017 Bowman Platinum Next Generation

STATED ODDS 1:5 RETAIL
*PURPLE/250: 1X TO 2.5X BASIC
*GREEN/99: 1.5X TO 4X BASIC
*ORANGE/25: 2X TO 5X BASIC
BNGAA Anthony Alford .25 .60
BNGAB Anthony Banda .25 .60
BNGAE Anderson Espinoza .25 .60
BNGAM Austin Meadows .40 1.00
BNGAR Amed Rosario .40 1.00
BNGBG Braxton Garrett .25 .60
BNGBR Brendan Rodgers .30 .75
BNGCA Christian Arroyo .40 1.00
BNGCB Cody Bellinger 4.00 10.00
BNGCS Cody Sedlock .25 .60
BNGEJ Eloy Jimenez 1.00 2.50
BNGFB Franklin Barreto .25 .60
BNGFM Francisco Mejia .40 1.00
BNGFMA Francis Martes .25 .60
BNGGT Gleyber Torres 4.00 10.00
BNGHB Harrison Bader .60 1.50
BNGJC J.P. Crawford .25 .60
BNGJJ Jahmai Jones .25 .60
BNGJS Josh Staumont .25 .60
BNGKL Kyle Lewis .50 1.25
BNGLB Lewis Brinson .40 1.00
BNGLT Leody Taveras .75 2.00
BNGMM Matt Manning .40 1.00
BNGNG Nick Gordon .25 .60
BNGNS Nick Senzel .75 2.00
BNGOA Ozzie Albies 1.00 2.50
BNGRD Rafael Devers .50 1.25
BNGVR Victor Robles .60 1.50
BNGWA Willy Adames .30 .75
BNGZC Zack Collins .30 .75

2017 Bowman Platinum Platinum Cut Autographs

STATED ODDS 1:553 RETAIL
STATED PRINT RUN 25 SER.#'d SETS
EXCHANGE DEADLINE 6/30/2019
PCAAA Anthony Alford
PCAAE Anderson Espinoza
PCAAK Alex Kirilloff
PCAAR Amed Rosario 60.00 150.00
PCAAV Alex Verdugo 40.00 100.00
PCABD Bobby Dalbec 15.00 40.00
PCABR Blake Rutherford EXCH 40.00 100.00
PCACB Cody Bellinger EXCH 150.00 400.00
PCACR Corey Ray 6.00 15.00
PCADC Dylan Cozens 5.00 12.00
PCAEJ Eloy Jimenez 60.00 150.00
PCAFB Franklin Barreto
PCAFM Francisco Mejia 40.00 100.00
PCAGL Gavin Lux 60.00 150.00
PCAGT Gleyber Torres 60.00 150.00
PCAIA Ian Anderson 20.00 50.00
PCAJG Jason Groome 30.00 80.00
PCAJM Jorge Mateo 25.00 60.00
PCAKL Kyle Lewis 20.00 50.00
PCAKM Kevin Maitan 75.00 200.00
PCAMK Mitch Keller 10.00 25.00

PCAMM Mickey Moniak 20.00 50.00
PCANS Nick Senzel 50.00 120.00
PCASN Sean Newcomb
PCATC Trevor Clifton
PCAWC Willie Calhoun 20.00 50.00
PCAZC Zack Collins

2017 Bowman Platinum Platinum Presence

STATED ODDS 1:10 RETAIL
*ORANGE/25: 2X TO 5X BASIC
PPAB Alex Bregman 1.25 3.00
PPABE Andrew Benintendi 1.00 2.50
PPAE Anderson Espinoza .30 .75
PPAJ Aaron Judge 8.00 20.00
PPAR Anthony Rizzo .75 2.00
PPARE Alex Reyes .40 1.00
PPARO Amed Rosario .50 1.25
PPBH Bryce Harper .75 2.00
PPCC Carlos Correa .50 1.25
PPCF Clint Frazier .60 1.50
PPCR Corey Ray .40 1.00
PPCS Corey Seager .50 1.25
PPDP Dustin Pedroia .50 1.25
PPDS Dansby Swanson .75 2.00
PPGT Gleyber Torres 5.00 12.00
PPJC J.P. Crawford .30 .75
PPJD Josh Donaldson .40 1.00
PPJG Jason Groome .60 1.50
PPKB Kris Bryant .60 1.50
PPKL Kyle Lewis .60 1.50
PPMM Mickey Moniak .75 2.00
PPMMA Manny Machado .50 1.25
PPMT Mike Trout 2.50 6.00
PPNS Nick Senzel 1.00 2.50
PPOA Orlando Arcia .50 1.25
PPPG Paul Goldschmidt .50 1.25
PPTG Tyler Glasnow .40 1.00
PPTS Trevor Story .50 1.25
PPVR Victor Robles .75 2.00
PPYM Yoan Moncada 1.00 2.50

2017 Bowman Platinum Platinum Presence Green

*GREEN: 1.2X TO 3X BASIC
STATED ODDS 1:277 RETAIL
STATED PRINT RUN 99 SER.#'d SETS
PPAJ Aaron Judge 40.00 100.00

2017 Bowman Platinum Platinum Presence Orange

*ORANGE: 2.5X TO 6X BASIC
STATED ODDS 1:1100 RETAIL
STATED PRINT RUN 25 SER.#'d SETS
PPAJ Aaron Judge 125.00 300.00
PPKB Kris Bryant 20.00 50.00
PPMT Mike Trout 20.00 50.00

2017 Bowman Platinum Platinum Presence Autographs

STATED ODDS 1:415 RETAIL
STATED PRINT RUN 50 SER.#'d SETS
EXCHANGE DEADLINE 6/30/2019
PPAB Alex Bregman 15.00 40.00
PPABE Andrew Benintendi 40.00 100.00
PPAJ Aaron Judge 200.00 400.00
PPAR Anthony Rizzo 20.00 50.00
PPARE Alex Reyes 8.00 20.00
PPARO Amed Rosario 25.00 60.00
PPCC Carlos Correa 15.00 40.00
PPCR Corey Ray 6.00 15.00
PPGT Gleyber Torres 40.00 100.00
PPJG Jason Groome 8.00 20.00
PPKB Kris Bryant 30.00 80.00
PPKL Kyle Lewis 15.00 40.00
PPMM Mickey Moniak 25.00 60.00
PPNS Nick Senzel 12.00 30.00
PPYM Yoan Moncada 30.00 80.00

2017 Bowman Platinum Rookie Radar

STATED ODDS 1:5 RETAIL
RRAB Alex Bregman 1.25 3.00
RRABE Andrew Benintendi 1.00 2.50
RRAJ Aaron Judge 6.00 15.00
RRAR Alex Reyes .40 1.00
RRCA Christian Arroyo .50 1.25
RRCB Cody Bellinger 5.00 12.00
RRDD David Dahl .40 1.00
RRDS Dansby Swanson .75 2.00
RRHR Hunter Renfroe .40 1.00
RRJA Jorge Alfaro .40 1.00
RRJC Jharel Cotton .30 .75
RRJDL Jose De Leon .30 .75
RRLW Luke Weaver .40 1.00
RRMM Manny Margot .30 .75
RROA Orlando Arcia .50 1.25
RRRT Raimel Tapia .40 1.00
RRTA Tyler Austin .50 1.25
RRTG Tyler Glasnow .40 1.00
RRYG Yulieski Gurriel .50 1.25
RRYM Yoan Moncada 1.00 2.50

2017 Bowman Platinum Rookie Radar Green

*GREEN: 1.2X TO 3X BASIC
STATED ODDS 1:416 RETAIL
STATED PRINT RUN 99 SER.#'d SETS
RRAJ Aaron Judge 40.00 100.00
RRCB Cody Bellinger 30.00 80.00

2017 Bowman Platinum Rookie Radar Orange

*ORANGE: 2.5X TO 6X BASIC
STATED ODDS 1:1643 RETAIL
STATED PRINT RUN 25 SER.#'d SETS
RRAJ Aaron Judge 75.00 200.00
RRCB Cody Bellinger 60.00 150.00

2017 Bowman Platinum Rookie Radar Purple

*PURPLE: .75X TO 2X BASIC
STATED ODDS 1:165 RETAIL
STATED PRINT RUN 250 SER.#'d SETS
RRAJ Aaron Judge 25.00 60.00
RRCB Cody Bellinger 20.00 50.00

2017 Bowman Platinum Rookie Radar Autographs

STATED ODDS 1:553 RETAIL
STATED PRINT RUN 50 SER.#'d SETS
EXCHANGE DEADLINE 6/30/2019
RRAB Alex Bregman 15.00 40.00
RRABE Andrew Benintendi 40.00 100.00
RRAJ Aaron Judge 200.00 400.00
RRAR Alex Reyes 8.00 20.00
RRDD David Dahl 8.00 20.00
RRDS Dansby Swanson 40.00 100.00
RRHR Hunter Renfroe 10.00 25.00
RRJA Jorge Alfaro 15.00 40.00
RRJDL Jose De Leon 10.00 25.00
RRLW Luke Weaver 8.00 20.00
RRMM Manny Margot 6.00 15.00
RRTA Tyler Austin 8.00 20.00
RRYG Yulieski Gurriel 12.00 30.00
RRYM Yoan Moncada 30.00 80.00

2017 Bowman Platinum Tools of the Craft Autographs Hitting

HITTING ODDS 1:587 RETAIL
PRINT RUNS B/WN 7-35 COPIES PER
NO PRICING ON QTY 10 OR LESS
EXCHANGE DEADLINE 6/30/2019
*SPEED: .4X TO 1X HITTING
*ARM: .4X TO 1X HITTING
*POWER: .4X TO 1X HITTING
*GLOVE: .4X TO 1X HITTING
TOCAAA Anthony Alford/35 4.00 10.00
TOCAAB Alex Bregman/35 20.00 50.00
TOCAABE Andrew Benintendi/35 30.00 80.00
TOCAAI Andy Ibanez/35 10.00 25.00
TOCAAV Alex Verdugo/35 20.00 50.00
TOCABP Brett Phillips/35 10.00 25.00
TOCABR Blake Rutherford/35 50.00 120.00
TOCACB Cody Bellinger/35 75.00 200.00
TOCACS Corey Seager/35 25.00 60.00
TOCAFB Franklin Barreto/35 10.00 25.00
TOCAGT Gleyber Torres/35 40.00 100.00
TOCAJA Jose Altuve/35 25.00 60.00
TOCAJM Jorge Mateo/35 20.00 50.00
TOCAKL Kyle Lewis/35 10.00 25.00
TOCAMM Mickey Moniak/35 25.00 60.00
TOCANS Nick Senzel/35 30.00 80.00
TOCAWC Willie Calhoun/35 10.00 25.00

2017 Bowman Platinum Top Prospects

COMP.SET w/o SP's (100) 25.00 60.00
STATED SP ODDS 1:146 RETAIL
TPAA Anthony Alford .25 .60
TPAE Anderson Espinoza .25 .60
TPAI Andy Ibanez .25 .60
TPAK Alex Kirilloff .60 1.50
TPAM Austin Meadows SP 8.00 20.00
TPAMO Adrian Morejon SP 10.00 25.00
TPAP A.J. Puk .50 1.25
TPAR Amed Rosario .40 1.00
TPARO Alfredo Rodriguez .30 .75
TPAS Andrew Sopko .25 .60
TPAV Alex Verdugo .40 1.00
TPBA Brady Aiken .60 1.50
TPBB Bo Bichette SP 20.00 50.00
TPBD Bobby Dalbec .60 1.50
TPBH Brent Honeywell .30 .75
TPBM Brandon Marsh .60 1.50
TPBP Brett Phillips .30 .75
TPBR Blake Rutherford .40 1.00
TPBRO Brendan Rodgers .30 .75
TPBW Brandon Woodruff .25 .60
TPBX Braxton Garrett .25 .60
TPBZ Bradley Zimmer SP 6.00 15.00
TPCA Chance Adams .40 1.00
TPCF Clint Frazier .50 1.25
TPCK Carter Kieboom .40 1.00
TPCQ Cal Quantrill .25 .60
TPCR Corey Ray .30 .75
TPCR Ray SP Running 10.00 25.00
TPCS Cody Sedlock SP 5.00 12.00
TPDC Dylan Cozens .25 .60
TPDCE Dylan Cease .60 1.50
TPDL Dawel Lugo .25 .60
TPDLA Dinelson Lamet .25 .60
TPDS Dominic Smith SP 10.00 25.00
TPEJ Eloy Jimenez 1.00 2.50
TPFB Franklin Barreto .25 .60
TPFM Francisco Mejia .40 1.00
TPFR Fernando Romero .25 .60
TPFRI Francisco Rios .25 .60
TPFW Forrest Whitley .75 2.00
TPGL Gavin Lux 1.50 4.00
TPGT Gleyber Torres 4.00 10.00
TPIA Ian Anderson .60 1.50
TPID Isan Diaz SP 12.00 30.00
TPIH Ian Happ .50 1.25
TPJC J.P. Crawford .25 .60
TPJD Justin Dunn .25 .60
TPJF Junior Fernandez .40 1.00
TPJG Jason Groome .50 1.25
TPJG Jason Groome SP Hand at knee 6.00 15.00
TPJH Josh Hader .25 .60
TPJJ Joe Jimenez .25 .60
TPJJO Jahmai Jones .25 .60
TPJK James Kaprielian .25 .60
TPJM Jorge Mateo .25 .60
TPJO Jhailyn Ortiz .50 1.25
TPJS Juan Soto 5.00 12.00
TPJSH Justus Sheffield SP 12.00 30.00
TPKA Kolby Allard .25 .60
TPKF Kyle Funkhouser .30 .75
TPKL Kyle Lewis .50 1.25
TPKM Kevin Maitan .60 1.50
TPKN Kevin Newman .40 1.00
TPKT Kyle Tucker .50 1.25
TPLA Lazarito Armenteros .60 1.50
TPLAB Luis Alexander Basabe .40 1.00
TPLB Lewis Brinson .40 1.00
TPLC Luis Castillo .75 2.00
TPLF Lucius Fox .25 .60
TPLGJ Lourdes Gurriel Jr. .40 1.00
TPLO Luis Ortiz .25 .60
TPLT Leody Taveras .75 2.00
TPLU Luis Urias 1.00 2.50
TPMC Matt Chapman .40 1.00
TPMF Max Fried 1.00 2.50
TPMK Mitch Keller .30 .75
TPMKO Michael Kopech .50 1.25
TPMM Mickey Moniak .60 1.50
TPMM Mickey Moniak SP Throwing 8.00 20.00
TPMMA Matt Manning SP 8.00 20.00
TPNG Nick Gordon .25 .60
TPNJ Nolan Jones .40 1.00
TPNS Nick Senzel .75 2.00
TPNW Nick Williams .30 .75
TPOA Ozzie Albies SP 20.00 50.00
TPOD Oscar de la Cruz .25 .60
TPPC P.J. Conlon .25 .60
TPPW Patrick Weigel .25 .60
TPRD Rafael Devers .50 1.25
TPRH Rhys Hoskins 1.00 2.50
TPRP Riley Pint .25 .60
TPRR Raudy Read .30 .75
TPRRA Roniel Raudes .25 .60
TPSN Sean Newcomb .30 .75
TPSS Sixto Sanchez .60 1.50
TPTAC Taylor Clarke .25 .60
TPTC Trevor Clifton .25 .60
TPTCL Trent Clark .25 .60
TPTF T.J. Friedl .25 .60
TPTJ Thomas Jones .25 .60
TPTM Triston McKenzie .25 .60
TPTO Tyler O'Neill .30 .75
TPTS Thomas Szapucki .30 .75
TPTT Taylor Trammell .40 1.00
TPVR Victor Robles .60 1.50
TPWA Willy Adames .30 .75
TPWB Will Benson .25 .60
TPWBE Wuilmer Becerra .25 .60
TPWC Willie Calhoun .40 1.00
TPWCR Will Craig .25 .60
TPYA Yadier Alvarez .40 1.00
TPYCC Yu-Cheng Chang .40 1.00
TPZC Zack Collins .30 .75

2017 Bowman Platinum Top Prospects Blue Ice

*BLUE ICE: .75X TO 2X BASIC
RANDOM INSERTS IN PACKS

2017 Bowman Platinum Top Prospects Green

*GREEN: 1.2X TO 3X BASIC
STATED ODDS 1:84 RETAIL
STATED PRINT RUN 99 SER.#'d SETS
TPSS Sixto Sanchez 15.00 40.00

2017 Bowman Platinum Top Prospects Orange

*ORANGE: 3X TO 8X BASIC
STATED ODDS 1:287 RETAIL
STATED PRINT RUN 25 SER.#'d SETS

2017 Bowman Platinum Top Prospects Purple

*PURPLE: 1X TO 2.5X BASIC
STATED ODDS 1:121 RETAIL
STATED PRINT RUN 250 SER.#'d SETS

2017 Bowman Platinum Top Prospects White Ice

*WHITE ICE: .75X TO 2X BASIC
RANDOM INSERTS IN PACKS

2017 Bowman Platinum Top Prospects Autographs

STATED ODDS 1:19 RETAIL
EXCHANGE DEADLINE 6/30/2019
TPAA Anthony Alford 3.00 8.00
TPAE Anderson Espinoza 3.00 8.00
TPAI Andy Ibanez 3.00 8.00
TPAK Alex Kirilloff 8.00 20.00
TPAR Amed Rosario 15.00 40.00
TPAS Andrew Sopko 3.00 8.00
TPAV Alex Verdugo 5.00 12.00
TPBD Bobby Dalbec 8.00 20.00
TPBP Brett Phillips 4.00 10.00
TPBR Blake Rutherford 5.00 12.00
TPCK Carter Kieboom 8.00 20.00
TPCR Corey Ray 6.00 15.00
TPDC Dylan Cozens 6.00 15.00
TPDLA Dinelson Lamet 3.00 8.00
TPEJ Eloy Jimenez 30.00 80.00
TPFB Franklin Barreto 3.00 8.00
TPFM Francisco Mejia 6.00 15.00
TPFRI Francisco Rios 3.00 8.00
TPFW Forrest Whitley 6.00 15.00
TPGT Gleyber Torres 30.00 80.00
TPIA Ian Anderson 25.00 60.00
TPIH Ian Happ 15.00 40.00
TPJG Jason Groome 10.00 25.00
TPJJ Joe Jimenez 3.00 8.00
TPJJO Jahmai Jones 3.00 8.00
TPJM Jorge Mateo 3.00 8.00
TPJS Juan Soto 125.00 300.00
TPKL Kyle Lewis 6.00 15.00
TPKM Kevin Maitan 5.00 12.00
TPLA Lazarito Armenteros 8.00 20.00
TPLAB Luis Alexander Basabe 5.00 12.00
TPLGJ Lourdes Gurriel Jr. 5.00 12.00
TPMK Mitch Keller 4.00 10.00
TPMM Mickey Moniak 10.00 25.00
TPNS Nick Senzel 25.00 60.00
TPPC P.J. Conlon 3.00 8.00
TPRR Raudy Read 4.00 10.00
TPRRA Roniel Raudes 3.00 8.00
TPSN Sean Newcomb 4.00 10.00
TPTC Trevor Clifton 3.00 8.00
TPTM Triston McKenzie 6.00 15.00
TPWB Will Benson 3.00 8.00
TPWC Willie Calhoun 8.00 20.00
TPWCR Will Craig 3.00 8.00
TPZC Zack Collins 4.00 10.00

2017 Bowman Platinum Top Prospects Autographs Blue

*BLUE: .75X TO 2X BASIC
RANDOM INSERTS IN PACKS
STATED PRINT RUN 20 SER.#'d SETS
EXCHANGE DEADLINE 6/30/2019
TPLA Lazarito Armenteros 30.00 80.00

2017 Bowman Platinum Top Prospects Autographs Green

*GREEN: .6X TO 1.5X BASIC
STATED ODDS 1:158 RETAIL
STATED PRINT RUN 75 SER.#'d SETS
EXCHANGE DEADLINE 6/30/2019

2017 Bowman Platinum Top Prospects Autographs Orange

*ORANGE: .75X TO 2X BASIC
STATED ODDS 1:320 RETAIL
STATED PRINT RUN 25 SER.#'d SETS
EXCHANGE DEADLINE 6/30/2019
TPLA Lazarito Armenteros 30.00 80.00

2017 Bowman Platinum Top Prospects Autographs Purple

*PURPLE: .5X TO 1.2X BASIC
STATED ODDS 1:79 RETAIL
STATED PRINT RUN 150 SER.#'d SETS
EXCHANGE DEADLINE 6/30/2019

2018 Bowman Platinum

1 Kris Bryant .40 1.00
2 Rafael Devers RC 1.00 2.50
3 Jon Lester .25 .60
4 Paul DeJong .30 .75
5 Lorenzo Cain .20 .50
6 Freddie Freeman .40 1.00
7 Max Scherzer .30 .75
8 Nick Williams RC .40 1.00
9 Corey Kluber .25 .60
10 Jake Lamb .25 .60
11 Carlos Correa .30 .75
12 Daniel Murphy .25 .60
13 Victor Robles RC .75 2.00
14 Francisco Mejia RC .40 1.00
15 Joey Votto .30 .75
16 Robinson Cano .25 .60
17 Andrew McCutchen .30 .75
18 Joe Mauer .25 .60
19 Jonathan Schoop .20 .50
20 Justin Smoak .20 .50
21 Josh Bell .25 .60
22 Yoan Moncada .30 .75
23 Clayton Kershaw .60 1.50
24 Matt Carpenter .30 .75
25 Christian Yelich .40 1.00
26 Luiz Gohara RC .30 .75
27 Javier Baez .40 1.00
28 Manny Machado .30 .75
29 Austin Hays RC .50 1.25
30 George Springer .25 .60
31 Marcell Ozuna .30 .75
32 Cody Bellinger .60 1.50
33 Byron Buxton .25 .60
34 Shohei Ohtani RC 2.00 5.00
35 Dominic Smith RC .30 .75
36 Carlos Santana .25 .60
37 Alex Bregman .30 .75
38 Ender Inciarte .20 .50
39 Miguel Cabrera .30 .75
40 Andrew Benintendi .30 .75
41 Ozzie Albies RC 1.00 2.50
42 Corey Seager .30 .75
43 Willie Calhoun RC .40 1.00
44 Tyler Mahle RC .40 1.00
45 Hunter Renfroe .20 .50
46 Kevin Kiermaier .25 .60
47 Alcides Escobar .25 .60
48 Josh Donaldson .25 .60
49 Mike Trout 1.50 4.00
50 Joey Gallo .25 .60
51 Wil Myers .20 .50
52 Eric Thames .25 .60
53 Rhys Hoskins RC 1.25 3.00
54 Jose Altuve .25 .60
55 Khris Davis .30 .75
56 Gregory Polanco .25 .60
57 Yoenis Cespedes .30 .75
58 Michael Fulmer .20 .50
59 Chance Sisco RC .40 1.00
60 Jose Abreu .30 .75
61 Josh Harrison .20 .50
62 Chris Sale .30 .75
63 Anthony Rizzo .50 1.25
64 Alex Verdugo RC .50 1.25
65 Charlie Blackmon .30 .75
66 Albert Pujols .40 1.00
67 Harrison Bader RC .50 1.25
68 Buster Posey .40 1.00
69 Adrian Beltre .30 .75
70 Paul Goldschmidt .30 .75
71 Felix Hernandez .25 .60
72 Giancarlo Stanton .30 .75
73 Luis Severino .25 .60
74 Ryan McMahon RC .40 1.00
75 Noah Syndergaard .25 .60
76 Nolan Arenado .40 1.00
77 Mookie Betts .50 1.25
78 Starlin Castro .20 .50
79 Clint Frazier RC .60 1.50
80 Francisco Lindor .30 .75
81 Stephen Piscotty .20 .50
82 Amed Rosario RC .40 1.00
83 Gary Sanchez .30 .75
84 Dee Gordon .20 .50
85 Cole Hamels .25 .60
86 Aaron Judge .75 2.00
87 Adam Jones .25 .60
88 Chris Archer .20 .50
89 Marcus Stroman .25 .60
90 Dansby Swanson .30 .75
91 Evan Longoria .25 .60
92 Zack Greinke .25 .60
93 Billy Hamilton .25 .60
94 Jack Flaherty RC .50 1.25
95 Justin Verlander .30 .75
96 Gerrit Cole .30 .75
97 Walker Buehler RC 1.50 4.00
98 Salvador Perez .25 .60
99 Justin Bour .20 .50
100 Bryce Harper .50 1.25

2018 Bowman Platinum Blue

*BLUE: 1.2X TO 3X BASIC
*BLUE RC: .75X TO 2X BASIC
STATED ODDS 1:78 RETAIL
STATED PRINT RUN 150 SER.#'d SETS
34 Shohei Ohtani 12.00 30.00
49 Mike Trout 6.00 15.00

2018 Bowman Platinum Green

*GREEN: 1.5X TO 4X BASIC
*GREEN RC: 1X TO 2.5X BASIC
STATED ODDS 1:119 RETAIL
STATED PRINT RUN 99 SER.#'d SETS
34 Shohei Ohtani 15.00 40.00
49 Mike Trout 8.00 20.00

2018 Bowman Platinum Ice

*ICE: .75X TO 2X BASIC
*ICE RC: .5X TO 1.2X BASIC
FOUR PER VALUE BOX
49 Mike Trout 4.00 10.00

2018 Bowman Platinum Orange

*ORANGE: 5X TO 12X BASIC
*ORANGE RC: 3X TO 8X BASIC
STATED ODDS 1:191 RETAIL
STATED PRINT RUN 25 SER.#'d SETS
34 Shohei Ohtani 50.00 120.00
49 Mike Trout 25.00 60.00

2018 Bowman Platinum Purple

*PURPLE: 1X TO 2.5X BASIC
*PURPLE RC: .6X TO 1.5X BASIC
STATED ODDS 1:47 RETAIL
STATED PRINT RUN 250 SER.#'d SETS
49 Mike Trout 5.00 12.00

2018 Bowman Platinum Sky Blue

*SKY BLUE: 1X TO 2.5X BASIC
*SKY BLUE RC: .6X TO 1.5X BASIC
INSERTED IN FAT PACKS
49 Mike Trout 5.00 12.00

2018 Bowman Platinum Base Set Photo Variations

STATED ODDS 1:391 RETAIL
1 Bryant Gray jrsy 3.00 8.00
2 Devers Snglsss 5.00 12.00
23 Krshw Blue shirt 8.00 20.00
32 Bllngr Ctchng 4.00 10.00
34 Ohtani w/Bag 12.00 30.00
49 Trout Snglsss 20.00 50.00
54 Altuve w/Glove 6.00 15.00
80 Lindor T-shirt 6.00 15.00
86 Judge Bat on shldr 10.00 25.00
100 Harper Knee up 4.00 10.00

2018 Bowman Platinum 80 Grade Prospect Autographs

STATED ODDS 1:556 RETAIL
STATED PRINT RUN 80 SER.#'d SETS
EXCHANGE DEADLINE 6/30/2020
80GAAA Albert Abreu 5.00 12.00
80GAAP A.J. Puk
80GABM Brendan McKay 8.00 20.00
80GAGT Gleyber Torres 50.00 125.00
80GAHG Hunter Greene 15.00 40.00
80GAHR Heliot Ramos 8.00 20.00
80GAIA Ian Anderson
80GAJA Jo Adell 40.00 100.00
80GAJB Jake Burger 10.00 25.00
80GAJG Jay Groome 8.00 20.00
80GAKH Keston Hiura 15.00 40.00
80GAKM Kevin Maitan 6.00 15.00
80GAKR Keibert Ruiz 8.00 20.00
80GALR Luis Robert 75.00 200.00
80GAMB Michel Baez 5.00 12.00
80GAMK Michael Kopech 20.00 50.00
80GARL Royce Lewis 10.00 25.00

2018 Bowman Platinum Die Cut Autographs

STATED ODDS 1:617 RETAIL
PRINT RUNS B/WN 25-50 COPIES PER
EXCHANGE DEADLINE 6/30/2020
PCAABR Alex Bregman/25 20.00 50.00
PCAAG Andres Gimenez/50 15.00 40.00
PCAAH Austin Hays/50 25.00 60.00
PCAAJ Aaron Judge
PCAAR Amed Rosario 10.00 25.00
PCAAV Alex Verdugo/25 12.00 30.00
PCACK Carter Kieboom/50 12.00 30.00
PCACP Cristian Pache/25 25.00 60.00
PCACS Chris Shaw/50 12.00 30.00
PCAFM Francisco Mejia/50 6.00 15.00
PCAGT Gleyber Torres
PCAHC Hans Crouse/50 8.00 20.00
PCAHR Heliot Ramos/50 25.00 60.00
PCAJH Jordan Hicks/50 10.00 25.00
PCAJK James Kaprielian/50 10.00 25.00
PCAKM Kevin Maitan/25 6.00 15.00
PCAKR Keibert Ruiz/25 20.00 50.00
PCAMB Michel Baez/50 10.00 25.00
PCAMK Mitch Keller/25 12.00 30.00
PCAMKO Michael Kopech/25 20.00 50.00
PCAMT Mike Trout
PCANS Nick Senzel/25 25.00 60.00
PCAOA Ozzie Albies EXCH 30.00 80.00
PCAPD Paul DeJong/25 8.00 20.00
PCARA Ronald Acuna Jr./50 75.00 200.00
PCARL Royce Lewis 15.00 40.00
PCARM Ryan Mountcastle/50 8.00 20.00
PCASA Sandy Alcantara
PCASB Shane Baz
PCATL Tristen Lutz/50 8.00 20.00
PCATR Trevor Rogers
PCAVR Victor Robles/25 30.00 80.00

2018 Bowman Platinum Hunter Greene Short Print Autographs

STATED ODDS 1:6615 RETAIL
STATED PRINT RUN 10 SER.#'d SETS
EXCHANGE DEADLINE 6/30/2020
HG1 Hunter Greene 75.00 200.00
HG2 Hunter Greene 75.00 200.00
HG3 Hunter Greene 75.00 200.00
HG4 Hunter Greene 75.00 200.00
HG5 Hunter Greene 75.00 200.00
HG6 Hunter Greene 75.00 200.00
HG7 Hunter Greene 75.00 200.00
HG8 Hunter Greene 75.00 200.00
HG9 Hunter Greene 75.00 200.00
HG10 Hunter Greene 75.00 200.00

2018 Bowman Platinum Hunter Greene Short Prints

STATED ODDS 1:234 RETAIL
HG1 Hunter Greene 2.50 6.00
HG2 Hunter Greene 2.50 6.00
HG3 Hunter Greene 2.50 6.00
HG4 Hunter Greene 2.50 6.00
HG5 Hunter Greene 2.50 6.00
HG6 Hunter Greene 2.50 6.00
HG7 Hunter Greene 2.50 6.00
HG8 Hunter Greene 2.50 6.00
HG9 Hunter Greene 2.50 6.00
HG10 Hunter Greene 2.50 6.00

2018 Bowman Platinum Platinum Presence

STATED ODDS 1:10 RETAIL
*PURPLE/250: 1.2X TO 3X BASIC
*GREEN/99: 1.5X TO 4X BASIC
*ORANGE/25: 6X TO 15X BASIC
PP1 Nick Senzel .75 2.00
PP2 Jo Adell .75 2.00
PP3 Keston Hiura .60 1.50
PP4 Michel Baez .25 .60
PP5 Austin Hays .40 1.00
PP6 Heliot Ramos .40 1.00
PP7 Alex Verdugo .40 1.00
PP8 Albert Abreu .25 .60
PP9 Michael Kopech .50 1.25
PP10 Kris Bryant .50 1.25
PP11 Luis Robert .60 1.50
PP12 Amed Rosario .30 .75
PP13 Brendan McKay .40 1.00
PP14 Colton Welker .25 .60
PP15 Mitch Keller .30 .75
PP16 Mike Trout 2.00 5.00
PP17 Clayton Kershaw .75 2.00
PP18 Francisco Lindor .40 1.00
PP19 Jose Altuve .30 .75
PP20 Nolan Arenado .50 1.25

2018 Bowman Platinum Platinum Presence Autographs

STATED ODDS 1:892 RETAIL
STATED PRINT RUN 50 SER.#'d SETS
EXCHANGE DEADLINE 6/30/2020
PPAAA Albert Abreu 8.00 20.00
PPAAH Austin Hays 8.00 20.00
PPAAR Amed Rosario 10.00 25.00
PPAAV Alex Verdugo 8.00 20.00
PPABM Brendan McKay 8.00 20.00
PPACW Colton Welker 6.00 15.00
PPAHR Heliot Ramos 15.00 40.00
PPAJA Jo Adell 40.00 100.00
PPAKB Kris Bryant
PPAKH Keston Hiura 10.00 25.00
PPALR Luis Robert 50.00 120.00
PPAMB Michel Baez 5.00 12.00
PPAMK Mitch Keller 6.00 15.00
PPAMKO Michael Kopech 15.00 40.00
PPANS Nick Senzel 15.00 40.00

2018 Bowman Platinum Prismatic Prodigies

STATED ODDS 1:5 RETAIL
*PURPLE/250: 1.5X TO 4X BASIC
*GREEN/99: 2X TO 5X BASIC
*ORANGE/25: 6X TO 15X BASIC
PPP1 Eloy Jimenez 1.00 2.50
PPP2 D.L. Hall .25 .60
PPP3 Tanner Houck .60 1.50
PPP4 Jake Burger .25 .60
PPP5 Colton Welker .25 .60
PPP6 Franklin Perez .25 .60
PPP7 Forrest Whitley .40 1.00
PPP8 Nick Pratto .30 .75
PPP9 Jay Groome .30 .75
PPP10 Royce Lewis 1.00 2.50
PPP11 Gleyber Torres 2.00 5.00
PPP12 Lazarito Armenteros .50 1.25
PPP13 Evan White .40 1.00
PPP14 Brendan McKay .40 1.00
PPP15 Bubba Thompson .40 1.00
PPP16 Eric Pardinho .50 1.25
PPP17 Jon Duplantier .25 .60
PPP18 Cristian Pache 1.25 3.00
PPP19 Adbert Alzolay .30 .75
PPP20 Tony Santillan .25 .60
PPP21 Brendan Rodgers .30 .75
PPP22 Jeren Kendall .30 .75
PPP23 Trevor Rogers .25 .60
PPP24 Corbin Burnes .40 1.00
PPP25 Peter Alonso 2.50 6.00
PPP26 Adam Haseley .40 1.00
PPP27 Mitch Keller .30 .75
PPP28 MacKenzie Gore .50 1.25
PPP29 Heliot Ramos .40 1.00
PPP30 Jordan Hicks .50 1.25
PPP31 Seth Romero .25 .60
PPP32 Ryan Mountcastle .40 1.00
PPP33 Steven Duggar .25 .60
PPP34 Fernando Tatis Jr. 2.00 5.00
PPP35 Andres Gimenez .30 .75
PPP36 Alex Faedo .40 1.00
PPP37 Kyle Wright .60 1.50
PPP38 Keston Hiura .60 1.50
PPP39 Brandon Marsh .30 .75
PPP40 Carter Kieboom .40 1.00

2018 Bowman Platinum Prismatic Prodigies Autographs

STATED ODDS 1:498 RETAIL
STATED PRINT RUN 50 SER.#'d SETS
EXCHANGE DEADLINE 6/30/2020
PPPAAA Adbert Alzolay 6.00 15.00
PPPAAF Alex Faedo 8.00 20.00
PPPABMC Brendan McKay 8.00 20.00
PPPABR Brendan Rodgers 10.00 25.00
PPPABT Bubba Thompson 8.00 20.00
PPPACB Corbin Burnes 8.00 20.00
PPPACP Cristian Pache 12.00 30.00
PPPACW Colton Welker 6.00 15.00
PPPAEP Eric Pardinho 10.00 25.00
PPPAEW Evan White
PPPAGT Gleyber Torres 60.00 150.00
PPPAHR Heliot Ramos 15.00 40.00
PPPAJB Jake Burger
PPPAJD Jon Duplantier 5.00 12.00
PPPAJG Jay Groome
PPPAJH Jordan Hicks 10.00 25.00
PPPAJK Jeren Kendall 6.00 15.00
PPPAKW Kyle Wright
PPPALA Lazarito Armenteros
PPPAMK Mitch Keller 6.00 15.00
PPPANP Nick Pratto 6.00 15.00
PPPAPA Peter Alonso 40.00 100.00
PPPARL Royce Lewis EXCH 20.00 50.00
PPPATH Tanner Houck 12.00 30.00
PPPATR Trevor Rogers 5.00 12.00

2018 Bowman Platinum Rookie Autograph Pieces

STATED ODDS 1:374 RETAIL
STATED PRINT RUN 99 SER.#'d SETS
EXCHANGE DEADLINE 6/30/2020
*ORANGE/25: .6X TO 1.5X BASIC
PRAPAH Austin Hays 5.00 12.00
PRAPAR Amed Rosario 8.00 20.00
PRAPAS Andrew Stevenson 3.00 8.00
PRAPAV Alex Verdugo 5.00 12.00
PRAPBW Brandon Woodruff 4.00 10.00
PRAPCF Clint Frazier
PRAPDS Dominic Smith 3.00 8.00
PRAPFM Francisco Mejia 8.00 20.00
PRAPHB Harrison Bader 5.00 12.00
PRAPJF Jack Flaherty 5.00 12.00
PRAPLS Lucas Sims 3.00 8.00
PRAPMG Miguel Gomez 3.00 8.00
PRAPND Nicky Delmonico 3.00 8.00
PRAPRD Rafael Devers EXCH 15.00 40.00
PRAPRM Ryan McMahon 6.00 15.00
PRAPSO Shohei Ohtani
PRAPTM Tyler Mahle 4.00 10.00
PRAPTN Tomas Nido 4.00 10.00
PRAPVR Victor Robles 10.00 25.00
PRAPZG Zack Granite

2018 Bowman Platinum Rookie Revelations

STATED ODDS 1:5 RETAIL
*PURPLE/250: 1.5X TO 4X BASIC
*GREEN/99: 2X TO 5X BASIC
*ORANGE/25: 6X TO 15X BASIC
RR1 Rhys Hoskins 1.00 2.50
RR2 Victor Robles .60 1.50
RR3 Francisco Mejia .30 .75
RR4 Miguel Andujar 1.00 2.50

RR5 Brandon Woodruff .30 .75
RR6 Max Fried 1.00 2.50
RR7 Ozzie Albies .75 2.00
RR8 J.P. Crawford .25 .60
RR9 Shohei Ohtani 1.50 4.00
RR10 Tyler Mahle .30 .75
RR11 Andrew Stevenson .25 .60
RR12 Nicky Delmonico .25 .60
RR13 Rafael Devers .75 2.00
RR14 Amed Rosario .30 .75
RR15 Clint Frazier .50 1.25
RR16 Alex Verdugo .40 1.00
RR17 Nick Williams .30 .75
RR18 Willie Calhoun .30 .75
RR19 Walker Buehler 1.25 3.00
RR20 Harrison Bader .40 1.00

2018 Bowman Platinum Rookie Revelations Autographs

STATED ODDS 1:707 RETAIL
STATED PRINT RUN 50 SER.#'d SETS
EXCHANGE DEADLINE 6/30/2020
RRAAR Amed Rosario/50 10.00 25.00
RRAAS Andrew Stevenson/99
RRAAV Alex Verdugo/50 8.00 20.00
RRAFM Francisco Mejia/50 6.00 15.00
RRAMA Miguel Andujar/99
RRAMF Max Fried/99
RRAND Nicky Delmonico/99
RRAOA Ozzie Albies/50
RRARD Rafael Devers/50
RRARH Rhys Hoskins/50 40.00 100.00
RRASO Shohei Ohtani/50 300.00 600.00
RRATM Tyler Mahle/99
RRAVR Victor Robles/99 8.00 20.00

2018 Bowman Platinum Top Prospect Autographs

STATED ODDS 1:15 RETAIL
EXCHANGE DEADLINE 6/30/2020
*BLUE/150: .5X TO 1.2X BASE
*GREEN/99: .5X TO 1.2X BASE
*ORANGE/25: 1X TO 2.5X BASE
TOP1 Brendan McKay 8.00 20.00
TOP2 Ronald Acuna 75.00 200.00
TOP3 Gleyber Torres 40.00 100.00
TOP4 Hunter Greene 15.00 40.00
TOP5 Royce Lewis 20.00 50.00
TOP6 MacKenzie Gore 8.00 20.00
TOP8 Luis Robert 60.00 150.00
TOP10 Kevin Maitan 3.00 8.00
TOP11 Jo Adell 30.00 80.00
TOP12 Mitch Keller 3.00 8.00
TOP13 Keston Hiura 15.00 40.00
TOP14 Michael Kopech 6.00 15.00
TOP15 Peter Alonso 40.00 100.00
TOP17 Jay Groome 3.00 8.00
TOP18 Keibert Ruiz 4.00 10.00
TOP19 Adbert Alzolay 3.00 8.00
TOP20 Joey Wentz 3.00 8.00
TOP21 Cristian Pache 15.00 40.00
TOP22 Gavin Lux 25.00 60.00
TOP23 McKenzie Mills 2.50 6.00
TOP24 Michel Baez 2.50 6.00
TOP25 Albert Abreu 4.00 10.00
TOP26 P.J. Conlon 2.50 6.00
TOP27 Dennis Santana 2.50 6.00
TOP29 Heliot Ramos 4.00 10.00
TOP31 Dawel Lugo 2.50 6.00
TOP32 Andres Gimenez 4.00 10.00
TOP33 Sean Murphy 4.00 10.00
TOP34 Tyler Freeman 2.50 6.00
TOP35 Kelvin Gutierrez 2.50 6.00
TOP36 Hans Crouse 4.00 10.00
TOP37 Matt Festa 2.50 6.00
TOP38 MJ Melendez 2.50 6.00
TOP40 Drew Ellis 3.00 8.00
TOP41 Corbin Martin 2.50 6.00
TOP42 Kacy Clemens 3.00 8.00
TOP43 CJ Chatham 3.00 8.00
TOP44 Kevin Kramer 2.50 6.00
TOP45 Jose Adolis Garcia 3.00 8.00
TOP46 Enyel De Los Santos 3.00 8.00
TOP47 Carter Kieboom 8.00 20.00
TOP48 Brian Mundell 2.50 6.00
TOP53 Quentin Holmes 2.50 6.00
TOP54 Johan Mieses 4.00 10.00
TOP55 Keegan Akin 3.00 8.00
TOP71 Daniel Johnson 2.50 6.00
TOP73 Brayan Hernandez 2.50 6.00
TOP80 Shane Bieber 15.00 40.00
TOP81 Trevor Stephan 2.50 6.00
TOP82 Nick Allen 2.50 6.00
TOP93 Evan White 4.00 10.00
TOP95 Eric Pardinho 5.00 12.00
TOP97 Jordan Hicks 4.00 10.00
TOP99 Jeren Kendall 4.00 10.00

2018 Bowman Platinum Top Prospect Autographs Ice

*ICE: .6X TO 1.5X BASIC
STATED ODDS 1:247 RETAIL
STATED PRINT RUN 50 SER.#'d SETS
EXCHANGE DEADLINE 6/30/2020
TOP2 Ronald Acuna 125.00 300.00

2018 Bowman Platinum Top Prospects

TOP1 Brendan McKay .40 1.00
TOP2 Ronald Acuna Jr. 5.00 12.00
TOP3 Gleyber Torres 2.50 6.00
TOP4 Hunter Greene .75 2.00
TOP5 Royce Lewis 1.00 2.50
TOP6 MacKenzie Gore .50 1.25
TOP7 A.J. Puk .30 .75
TOP8 Luis Robert 5.00 12.00
TOP9 Jake Burger .25 .60
TOP10 Kevin Maitan .30 .75
TOP11 Jo Adell .75 2.00
TOP12 Mitch Keller .30 .75
TOP13 Keston Hiura .60 1.50
TOP14 Michael Kopech .50 1.25
TOP15 Peter Alonso 2.50 6.00
TOP16 Kyle Tucker .50 1.25
TOP17 Jay Groome .30 .75
TOP18 Keibert Ruiz .75 2.00
TOP19 Adbert Alzolay .30 .75
TOP20 Joey Wentz .30 .75
TOP21 Cristian Pache 1.25 3.00
TOP22 Gavin Lux .75 2.00
TOP23 McKenzie Mills .25 .60
TOP24 Michel Baez .25 .60
TOP25 Albert Abreu .25 .60
TOP26 P.J. Conlon .25 .60
TOP27 Dennis Santana .25 .60
TOP28 Zack Littell .25 .60
TOP29 Heliot Ramos .40 1.00
TOP30 Hudson Potts .30 .75
TOP31 Dawel Lugo .25 .60
TOP32 Andres Gimenez .25 .60
TOP33 Sean Murphy .40 1.00
TOP34 Tyler Freeman .25 .60
TOP35 Kelvin Gutierrez .25 .60
TOP36 Hans Crouse .40 1.00
TOP37 Matt Festa .25 .60
TOP38 MJ Melendez .25 .60
TOP39 Jacob Gonzalez .50 1.25
TOP40 Drew Ellis .30 .75
TOP41 Corbin Martin .25 .60
TOP42 Kacy Clemens .30 .75
TOP43 C.J. Chatham .30 .75
TOP44 Kevin Kramer .25 .60
TOP45 Jose Adonis Garcia .30 .75
TOP46 Enyel De Los Santos .30 .75
TOP47 Carter Kieboom .40 1.00
TOP48 Brian Mundell .25 .60
TOP49 Jorge Guzman .25 .60
TOP50 Merandy Gonzalez .25 .60
TOP51 Jordan Humphreys .25 .60
TOP52 Matt Beaty .30 .75
TOP53 Quentin Holmes .25 .60
TOP54 Johan Mieses .40 1.00
TOP55 Keegan Akin .30 .75
TOP56 Vladimir Guerrero Jr. 2.50 6.00
TOP57 Estevan Florial .40 1.00
TOP58 Alex Faedo .40 1.00
TOP59 Zack Burdi .25 .60
TOP60 Eloy Jimenez 1.00 2.50
TOP61 Mickey Moniak .60 1.50
TOP62 Bo Bichette 1.00 2.50
TOP63 Riley Pint .25 .60
TOP64 Cole Brannen .30 .75
TOP65 J.B. Bukauskas .25 .60
TOP66 Seth Romero .25 .60
TOP67 Shed Long .25 .60
TOP68 Pedro Avila .25 .60
TOP69 Thomas Hatch .30 .75
TOP70 Isaac Paredes 1.25 3.00
TOP71 Daniel Johnson .25 .60
TOP72 Greg Deichmann .30 .75
TOP73 Brayan Hernandez .25 .60
TOP74 Gregory Soto .25 .60
TOP75 Franklin Perez .25 .60
TOP76 Nicky Lopez .25 .60
TOP77 LoLo Sanchez .30 .75
TOP78 Nick Senzel .75 2.00
TOP79 Sheldon Neuse .25 .60
TOP80 Shane Bieber 3.00 8.00
TOP81 Trevor Stephan .25 .60
TOP82 Nick Allen .25 .60
TOP83 Ryan Mountcastle .40 1.00
TOP84 Colton Welker .25 .60
TOP85 Shane Baz .30 .75
TOP86 Tristen Lutz .30 .75
TOP87 Chris Shaw .25 .60
TOP88 Corbin Burnes .40 1.00
TOP89 D.L. Hall .25 .60
TOP90 Tanner Houck .60 1.50
TOP91 Nick Pratto .30 .75
TOP92 Lazarito Armenteros .50 1.25
TOP93 Evan White .40 1.00
TOP94 Bubba Thompson .40 1.00
TOP95 Eric Pardinho .50 1.25
TOP96 Jon Duplantier .25 .60
TOP97 Jordan Hicks .50 1.25
TOP98 Brendan Rodgers .30 .75
TOP99 Jeren Kendall .30 .75
TOP100 Trevor Rogers .25 .60

2018 Bowman Platinum Top Prospects Blue

*BLUE: 1X TO 2.5X BASIC
STATED ODDS 1:78 RETAIL
STATED PRINT RUN 150 SER.#'d SETS

2018 Bowman Platinum Top Prospects Green

*GREEN: 1.2X TO 3X BASIC
STATED ODDS 1:119 RETAIL
STATED PRINT RUN 99 SER.#'d SETS

2018 Bowman Platinum Top Prospects Ice

*ICE: .6X TO 1.5X BASIC
FOUR PER VALUE BOX

2018 Bowman Platinum Top Prospects Orange

*ORANGE: 4X TO 10X BASIC
STATED ODDS 1:191 RETAIL
STATED PRINT RUN 25 SER.#'d SETS

2018 Bowman Platinum Top Prospects Purple

*PURPLE: .75X TO 2X BASIC
STATED ODDS 1:47 RETAIL
STATED PRINT RUN 250 SER.#'d SETS

2018 Bowman Platinum Top Prospects Sky Blue

*SKY BLUE: .75X TO 2X BASIC
INSERTED IN FAT PACKS

2019 Bowman Platinum

COMPLETE SET (100) 12.00 30.00
1 Mike Trout 1.50 4.00
2 Shohei Ohtani .40 1.00
3 Taylor Ward RC .30 .75
4 Albert Pujols .40 1.00
5 Jose Altuve .25 .60
6 Kyle Tucker RC .60 1.50
7 Josh James RC .50 1.25
8 Carlos Correa .30 .75
9 Alex Bregman .30 .75
10 Justin Verlander .30 .75
11 Khris Davis .30 .75
12 Ramon Laureano .40 1.00
13 Matt Chapman .30 .75
14 Danny Jansen RC .30 .75
15 Lourdes Gurriel Jr. .25 .60
16 Rowdy Tellez RC .50 1.25
17 Ryan Borucki RC .30 .75
18 Ronald Acuna Jr. 1.50 4.00
19 Touki Toussaint RC .40 1.00
20 Kolby Allard RC .50 1.25
21 Ozzie Albies .30 .75
22 Christian Yelich .40 1.00
23 Josh Hader .20 .50
24 Corbin Burnes RC .50 1.25
25 Paul Goldschmidt .30 .75
26 Harrison Bader .25 .60
27 Dakota Hudson RC .40 1.00
28 Yadier Molina .30 .75
29 Kris Bryant .40 1.00
30 Anthony Rizzo .50 1.25
31 Javier Baez .40 1.00
32 Zack Greinke .25 .60
33 Jake Lamb .25 .60
34 Clayton Kershaw .60 1.50
35 Walker Buehler .40 1.00
36 A.J. Pollock .20 .50
37 Cody Bellinger .60 1.50
38 Corey Seager .30 .75
39 Max Muncy .25 .60
40 Buster Posey .40 1.00
41 Brandon Crawford .25 .60
42 Steven Duggar RC .40 1.00
43 Dereck Rodriguez .20 .50
44 Francisco Lindor .30 .75
45 Jose Ramirez .25 .60
46 Corey Kluber .25 .60
47 Justus Sheffield RC .50 1.25
48 Yusei Kikuchi RC .50 1.25
49 Mitch Haniger .25 .60
50 Austin Dean RC .30 .75
51 Brian Anderson .20 .50
52 Jacob deGrom .30 .75
53 Noah Syndergaard .25 .60
54 Edwin Diaz .25 .60
55 Robinson Cano .25 .60
56 Juan Soto 1.00 2.50
57 Max Scherzer .30 .75
58 Victor Robles .40 1.00
59 Cedric Mullins RC .50 1.25
60 Trey Mancini .25 .60
61 Luis Urias RC .50 1.25
62 Eric Hosmer .25 .60
63 Rhys Hoskins .40 1.00
64 Andrew McCutchen .30 .75
65 Aaron Nola .25 .60
66 Chris Archer .20 .50
67 Kevin Newman RC .50 1.25
68 Starling Marte .25 .60
69 Joey Gallo .25 .60
70 Nomar Mazara .20 .50
71 Blake Snell .25 .60
72 Willy Adames .20 .50
73 Austin Meadows .25 .60
74 Mookie Betts .50 1.25
75 Andrew Benintendi .30 .75
76 Rafael Devers .40 1.00
77 J.D. Martinez .30 .75
78 Chris Sale .30 .75
79 David Price .25 .60
80 Joey Votto .30 .75
81 Yasiel Puig .30 .75
82 Scooter Gennett .25 .60
83 Nolan Arenado .40 1.00
84 Trevor Story .30 .75
85 Charlie Blackmon .30 .75
86 Whit Merrifield .30 .75
87 Ryan O'Hearn RC .30 .75
88 Salvador Perez .25 .60
89 Miguel Cabrera .30 .75
90 Christin Stewart RC .40 1.00
91 Willians Astudillo RC .30 .75
92 Eddie Rosario .25 .60
93 Jose Berrios .25 .60
94 Jose Abreu .30 .75
95 Michael Kopech RC .60 1.50
96 Chance Adams RC .30 .75
97 Gleyber Torres .60 1.50
98 Aaron Judge .75 2.00
99 Miguel Andujar .30 .75
100 Giancarlo Stanton .30 .75

2019 Bowman Platinum Blue

*BLUE: 1.2X TO 3X BASIC
*BLUE RC: .75X TO 2X BASIC
STATED ODDS 1:132 MEGA
STATED PRINT RUN 150 SER.#'d SETS
1 Mike Trout 6.00 15.00

2019 Bowman Platinum Gold

*GOLD: 4X TO 10X BASIC
*GOLD RC: 2.5X TO 6X BASIC
STATED ODDS 1:396 MEGA
STATED PRINT RUN 50 SER.#'d SETS
1 Mike Trout 20.00 50.00

2019 Bowman Platinum Green

*GREEN: 1.5X TO 4X BASIC
*GREEN RC: 1X TO 2.5X BASIC
STATED ODDS 1:200 MEGA
STATED PRINT RUN 99 SER.#'d SETS
1 Mike Trout 8.00 20.00

2019 Bowman Platinum Ice

*ICE: .75X TO 2X BASIC
*ICE RC: .5X TO 1.2X BASIC
STATED ODDS 1:2 BLASTER
1 Mike Trout 4.00 10.00

2019 Bowman Platinum Orange

*ORANGE: 5X TO 12X BASIC
*ORANGE RC: 3X TO 8X BASIC
STATED ODDS 1:287 MEGA
STATED PRINT RUN 25 SER.#'d SETS
1 Mike Trout 25.00 60.00

2019 Bowman Platinum Purple

*PURPLE: 1X TO 2.5X BASIC
*PURPLE RC: .6X TO 1.5X BASIC
STATED ODDS 1:80 MEGA
STATED PRINT RUN 250 SER.#'d SETS
1 Mike Trout 5.00 12.00

2019 Bowman Platinum Sky Blue

*SKY BLUE: 1X TO 2.5X BASIC
*SKY BLUE RC: .6X TO 1.5X BASIC
RANDOM INSERTS IN PACKS
1 Mike Trout 5.00 12.00

2019 Bowman Platinum Base Set Variations

STATED ODDS 1:275 JUMBO
*ICE: .5X TO 1.2X BASIC
*PURPLE/250: 1.2X TO 3X BASIC
*BLUE/150: 1.2X TO 3X BASIC
*GREEN/99: 1.5X TO 4X BASIC
*GOLD/50: 2.5X TO 6X BASIC
*ORANGE/25: 3X TO 8X BASIC
1 Mike Trout 25.00 60.00
2 Shohei Ohtani 15.00 40.00
9 Alex Bregman 6.00 15.00
18 Ronald Acuna Jr. 15.00 40.00
20 Pete Alonso 5.00 12.00
22 Christian Yelich 8.00 20.00
23 Fernando Tatis Jr. 6.00 15.00
27 Vladimir Guerrero Jr. 4.00 10.00
48 Yusei Kikuchi 6.00 15.00
56 Juan Soto 10.00 25.00
63 Rhys Hoskins 8.00 20.00
74 Mookie Betts 8.00 20.00
74 Eloy Jimenez 2.50 6.00
97 Gleyber Torres 8.00 20.00

2019 Bowman Platinum Die Cut Autographs

STATED ODDS 1:1582 JUMBO
PRINT RUNS B/WN 25-50 COPIES PER
EXCHANGE DEADLINE 5/31/2021
PCABB Brock Burke/50 8.00 20.00
PCABD Bobby Dalbec/50 10.00 25.00
PCACMI Casey Mize/25 20.00 50.00
PCACS Chad Spanberger/50 4.00 10.00
PCADH Dakota Hudson
PCADR Dereck Rodriguez/50 15.00 40.00
PCAEJ Eloy Jimenez/25 40.00 100.00
PCAEW Evan White/50
PCAJA Jordyn Adams
PCAJI Jonathan India/25 6.00 15.00
PCAJL Jesus Luzardo/50 15.00 40.00
PCAJS Justus Sheffield/25
PCAJSO Juan Soto/25 40.00 100.00
PCAKA Kolby Allard EXCH 12.00 30.00
PCAKB Kris Bryant/25
PCAKH Keston Hiura/50 20.00 50.00
PCAKT Kyle Tucker/25
PCALU Luis Urias/25 15.00 40.00
PCAMM Max Muncy/50 15.00 40.00
PCAMN Nick Madrigal/25
PCAPA Pete Alonso/50 75.00 200.00
PCARA Ronald Acuna Jr./25 50.00 120.00
PCASB Seth Beer/50 50.00 120.00
PCASO Shohei Ohtani
PCAVG Vladimir Guerrero Jr./25 100.00 250.00
PCAWA Willy Adames/50 10.00 25.00
PCAWF Wander Franco/50 125.00 300.00

2019 Bowman Platinum Platinum Pieces Autograph Relics

STATED ODDS 1:1049 JUMBO
PRINT RUNS B/WN 30-99 COPIES PER
EXCHANGE DEADLINE 5/31/2021
PPARAG Adolis Garcia/99 4.00 10.00
PPARBN Brandon Nimmo/99 5.00 12.00
PPARDC Dylan Cozens/99 4.00 10.00
PPARDJ Danny Jansen/99 6.00 15.00
PPARJF Jack Flaherty/99 5.00 12.00
PPARJH Josh Hader/99 6.00 15.00
PPARJM Jeff McNeil/99 15.00 40.00
PPARJN Jacob Nix/99 5.00 12.00
PPARKA Kolby Allard/99 6.00 15.00
PPARKB Kris Bryant/30 30.00 80.00
PPARKN Kevin Newman/99 10.00 25.00
PPARKS Kohl Stewart 5.00 12.00
PPARKT Kyle Tucker 10.00 25.00
PPARKW Kyle Wright 6.00 15.00
PPARRA Ronald Acuna Jr./50 40.00 100.00
PPARRB Ryan Borucki 4.00 10.00
PPARRD Rafael Devers/50 20.00 50.00
PPARRO Ryan O'Hearn 4.00 10.00
PPARSK Scott Kingery 5.00 12.00
PPARVR Victor Robles 8.00 20.00

2019 Bowman Platinum Platinum Pieces Autograph Relics Orange

*ORANGE: .6X TO 1.5X p/r 99
*ORANGE: .5X TO 1.2X p/r 30-50
STATED ODDS 1:1400 MEGA
STATED PRINT RUN 25 SER.#'d SETS
EXCHANGE DEADLINE 5/31/2021
PPARSK Scott Kingery 20.00 50.00

2019 Bowman Platinum Platinum Presence

STATED ODDS 1:4 JUMBO
*PURPLE/250: .75X TO 2X BASIC
*GREEN/99: 1X TO 2.5X BASIC
*ORANGE/25: 4X TO 10X BASIC
PP1 Yusei Kikuchi .40 1.00
PP2 Vladimir Guerrero Jr. 1.50 4.00
PP3 Eloy Jimenez 1.00 2.50
PP4 Matt Chapman .40 1.00
PP5 Seth Beer .60 1.50
PP6 Joey Bart .75 2.00
PP7 Wander Franco 4.00 10.00
PP8 Gleyber Torres .75 2.00
PP9 Juan Soto 1.25 3.00
PP10 Victor Victor Mesa .50 1.25
PP11 Jacob deGrom .40 1.00
PP12 Miguel Andujar .40 1.00
PP13 Keibert Ruiz .60 1.50
PP14 Rafael Devers .50 1.25
PP15 Victor Robles .50 1.25
PP16 Rhys Hoskins .50 1.25
PP17 Christian Yelich .50 1.25
PP18 Jose Ramirez .30 .75
PP19 Aaron Judge 1.00 2.50
PP20 Ronald Acuna Jr. 2.00 5.00

2019 Bowman Platinum Platinum Presence Autographs

STATED ODDS 1:12540 JUMBO
STATED PRINT RUN 50 SER.#'d SETS
EXCHANGE DEADLINE 5/31/2021
PPAEJ Eloy Jimenez 15.00 40.00
PPAJB Joey Bart 25.00 60.00
PPAJD Jacob deGrom 20.00 50.00
PPAJR Jose Ramirez 8.00 20.00
PPAJS Juan Soto 40.00 100.00
PPAKR Keibert Ruiz 12.00 30.00
PPAMA Miguel Andujar 10.00 25.00
PPARD Rafael Devers 15.00 40.00
PPARH Rhys Hoskins 20.00 50.00
PPASB Seth Beer 20.00 50.00
PPAVG Vladimir Guerrero Jr. 125.00 300.00
PPAVM Victor Victor Mesa 12.00 30.00
PPAVR Victor Robles 8.00 20.00
PPAWF Wander Franco 125.00 300.00
PPAYK Yusei Kikuchi 12.00 30.00

2019 Bowman Platinum Prismatic Prodigies

STATED ODDS 1:2 JUMBO
*PURPLE/250: .75X TO 2X BASIC
*GREEN/99: 1X TO 2.5X BASIC
*ORANGE/25: 4X TO 10X BASIC
PPP1 Jo Adell .75 2.00
PPP2 Victor Victor Mesa .50 1.25
PPP3 Jonathan India .30 .75
PPP4 Jordan Groshans .50 1.25
PPP5 Jarred Kelenic 1.00 2.50
PPP6 Triston Casas 1.00 2.50
PPP7 Brady Singer .50 1.25
PPP8 Nolan Gorman .75 2.00
PPP9 Jesus Luzardo .40 1.00
PPP10 Estevan Florial .40 1.00
PPP11 William Contreras .30 .75
PPP12 Mark Vientos .40 1.00
PPP13 Alec Bohm 1.00 2.50
PPP14 Carter Kieboom .40 1.00
PPP15 Miguel Amaya .40 1.00
PPP16 Corey Ray .25 .60
PPP17 Travis Swaggerty .40 1.00
PPP18 Taylor Widener .25 .60
PPP19 Grant Lavigne .30 .75
PPP20 Keibert Ruiz .60 1.50
PPP21 Bobby Dalbec .60 1.50
PPP22 Joey Bart .75 2.00
PPP23 Yusniel Diaz .40 1.00
PPP24 Wander Franco 4.00 10.00
PPP25 Luis Robert 2.50 6.00
PPP26 Ethan Hankins .30 .75
PPP27 Casey Mize .60 1.50
PPP28 Brusdar Graterol .40 1.00
PPP29 Seth Beer .60 1.50
PPP30 Cole Winn .25 .60
PPP31 Anthony Seigler .40 1.00
PPP32 Vladimir Guerrero Jr. 1.50 4.00
PPP33 Nick Solak .75 2.00
PPP34 Alex Kirilloff .40 1.00
PPP35 Bo Bichette .75 2.00
PPP36 Hunter Greene .40 1.00
PPP37 Nico Hoerner .75 2.00
PPP38 Garrett Whitlock .25 .60
PPP39 Nick Madrigal .75 2.00
PPP40 Matthew Liberatore .25 .60

2019 Bowman Platinum Prismatic Prodigies Autographs

STATED ODDS 1:1270 JUMBO
STATED PRINT RUN 50 SER.#'d SETS
EXCHANGE DEADLINE 5/31/2021
PPPAAB Alec Bohm 10.00 25.00
PPPAAS Anthony Seigler 6.00 15.00
PPPABG Brusdar Graterol
PPPABS Brady Singer 8.00 20.00
PPPACK Carter Kieboom 6.00 15.00
PPPACM Casey Mize 25.00 60.00
PPPACR Corey Ray 4.00 10.00
PPPACW Cole Winn 4.00 10.00
PPPAEF Estevan Florial 15.00 40.00
PPPAEH Ethan Hankins 5.00 12.00
PPPAGL Grant Lavigne 5.00 12.00
PPPAJA Jo Adell 20.00 50.00
PPPAJB Joey Bart 40.00 100.00
PPPAJG Jordan Groshans
PPPAJI Jonathan India 5.00 12.00
PPPAJK Jarred Kelenic 20.00 50.00
PPPAJL Jesus Luzardo
PPPAKR Keibert Ruiz 12.00 30.00
PPPALR Luis Robert 50.00 120.00
PPPAMA Miguel Amaya 6.00 15.00
PPPANG Nolan Gorman 20.00 50.00
PPPANM Nick Madrigal 12.00 30.00
PPPASB Seth Beer 20.00 50.00
PPPATC Triston Casas 15.00 40.00
PPPATS Travis Swaggerty 6.00 15.00
PPPATW Taylor Widener 4.00 10.00
PPPAVM Victor Victor Mesa 12.00 30.00
PPPAWC William Contreras
PPPAWF Wander Franco 125.00 300.00
PPPAYD Yusniel Diaz 6.00 15.00

2019 Bowman Platinum Prolific Power

STATED ODDS 1:165 JUMBO
POW1 Jo Adell 3.00 8.00
POW2 Ronaldo Hernandez 1.00 2.50
POW3 Keibert Ruiz 2.50 6.00
POW4 Carter Kieboom 1.50 4.00
POW5 Nolan Gorman 3.00 8.00
POW6 Wander Franco 15.00 40.00
POW7 Joey Bart 3.00 8.00
POW8 Vladimir Guerrero Jr. 6.00 15.00
POW9 Ibandel Isabel 1.50 4.00
POW10 Corey Ray 1.00 2.50

2019 Bowman Platinum Refined Autographs

STATED ODDS 1:960 JUMBO
PRINT RUNS B/WN 15-99 COPIES PER
NO PRICING ON QTY 15
EXCHANGE DEADLINE 5/31/2021
RAAK Andrew Knizner/99 8.00 20.00
RABB Brock Burke/99 3.00 8.00
RACK Carter Kieboom/99 12.00 30.00
RACR Corey Ray/99 3.00 8.00
RADH Darwinzon Hernandez/99 3.00 8.00
RADM Dustin May/99 10.00 25.00
RAEJ Eloy Jimenez/20 40.00 100.00
RAJL Jesus Luzardo/99 5.00 12.00
RAKR Keibert Ruiz/99 8.00 20.00
RAMS Brandon Marsh/99 6.00 15.00
RANL Nicky Lopez/99 6.00 15.00
RANS Nick Solak/99 10.00 25.00
RARL Royce Lewis/30
RARM Ryan McKenna/99 3.00 8.00
RARMO Ryan Mountcastle/99 10.00 25.00
RARR Roberto Ramos/99 4.00 10.00
RASL Fernando Tatis Jr./40 125.00 300.00
RASN Sheldon Neuse/99 3.00 8.00
RATW Taylor Widener/99 3.00 8.00
RAWF Wander Franco/99 100.00 250.00

2019 Bowman Platinum Renowned Rookies

STATED ODDS 1:2 JUMBO
*PURPLE/250: .75X TO 2X BASIC
*GREEN/99: 1X TO 2.5X BASIC
*ORANGE/25: 4X TO 10X BASIC
RR1 Yusei Kikuchi .40 1.00
RR2 Willians Astudillo .25 .60
RR3 Ramon Laureano .50 1.25
RR4 Jeff McNeil .60 1.50
RR5 Justus Sheffield .40 1.00
RR6 Dakota Hudson .30 .75
RR7 Josh James .40 1.00
RR8 Chance Adams .25 .60
RR9 Luis Urias .40 1.00
RR10 Rowdy Tellez .40 1.00
RR11 Danny Jansen .25 .60
RR12 Ryan O'Hearn .25 .60
RR13 Michael Kopech .50 1.25
RR14 Corbin Burnes .40 1.00
RR15 Kolby Allard .40 1.00
RR16 Cionel Perez .25 .60
RR17 Touki Toussaint .30 .75
RR18 Brad Keller .25 .60
RR19 Christin Stewart .30 .75
RR20 Kevin Newman .40 1.00

2019 Bowman Platinum Renowned Rookies Autographs

STATED ODDS 1:2540 JUMBO
STATED PRINT RUN 50 SER.#'d SETS
EXCHANGE DEADLINE 5/31/2021
RRACA Chance Adams 4.00 10.00
RRACB Corbin Burnes 6.00 15.00
RRADH Dakota Hudson 12.00 30.00
RRADJ Danny Jansen
RRAJJ Josh James
RRAJM Jeff McNeil 25.00 60.00
RRAJS Justus Sheffield
RRAKA Kolby Allard
RRALU Luis Urias 12.00 30.00
RRAMK Michael Kopech 8.00 20.00
RRARL Ramon Laureano 20.00 50.00
RRARO Ryan O'Hearn 4.00 10.00
RRART Rowdy Tellez 6.00 15.00
RRAWA Willians Astudillo 4.00 10.00
RRAYK Yusei Kikuchi 12.00 30.00

2019 Bowman Platinum Top Prospect Autographs

STATED ODDS 1:24 JUMBO
EXCHANGE DEADLINE 5/31/2021
*BLUE/150: .5X TO 1.2X BASE
*GREEN/99: .5X TO 1.2X BASE
*ICE/50: .6X TO 1.5X BASE
*ORANGE/25: .75X TO 2X BASE
TOP1 Vladimir Guerrero Jr. 60.00 150.00
TOP2 Shervyen Newton 4.00 10.00
TOP3 Casey Mize 6.00 15.00
TOP4 Joey Bart 20.00 50.00
TOP5 Nick Madrigal 8.00 20.00
TOP6 Alec Bohm 25.00 60.00
TOP7 Jonathan India 3.00 8.00
TOP8 Jarred Kelenic 10.00 25.00
TOP9 Wander Franco 75.00 200.00
TOP10 Estevan Florial 10.00 25.00
TOP11 Victor Victor Mesa 8.00 20.00
TOP12 Seuly Matias 3.00 8.00
TOP13 Jordan Groshans 6.00 15.00
TOP14 Victor Mesa Jr. 6.00 15.00
TOP15 Jordyn Adams 3.00 8.00
TOP16 Nick Solak 8.00 20.00
TOP18 Logan Gilbert 4.00 10.00
TOP19 Brady Singer 8.00 20.00
TOP20 Nolan Gorman 12.00 30.00
TOP21 Luis Garcia 3.00 8.00
TOP22 Elehuris Montero 4.00 10.00
TOP23 Yusniel Diaz 4.00 10.00
TOP24 Keegan Thompson 2.50 6.00
TOP25 Anthony Seigler 4.00 10.00
TOP26 Luis Arraez 8.00 20.00
TOP27 Nico Hoerner 12.00 30.00
TOP28 Seth Beer 6.00 15.00
TOP29 Jose Azocar 2.50 6.00
TOP30 Logan Webb 4.00 10.00
TOP31 Bobby Dalbec 6.00 15.00
TOP32 Nicky Lopez 4.00 10.00
TOP33 Miguel Amaya 4.00 10.00
TOP34 Ethan Hankins 3.00 8.00
TOP35 Shane McClanahan 3.00 8.00
TOP36 Taylor Widener 2.50 6.00
TOP37 Dauris Valdez 2.50 6.00
TOP38 Pablo Olivares 4.00 10.00
TOP39 Chad Spanberger 2.50 6.00
TOP40 Tristan Pompey 3.00 8.00
TOP41 Alex Royalty 2.50 6.00
TOP42 Griffin Conine 4.00 10.00
TOP43 Owen White 2.50 6.00
TOP44 Josiah Gray 8.00 20.00
TOP45 Luken Baker 3.00 8.00
TOP46 Brewer Hicklen 4.00 10.00
TOP47 Cash Case 3.00 8.00
TOP48 Connor Wong 3.00 8.00
TOP49 Griffin Canning 4.00 10.00
TOP50 Liam Jenkins 2.50 6.00
TOP51 Adam Wolf 4.00 10.00
TOP52 Ronaldo Hernandez 2.50 6.00
TOP53 Tommy Romero 3.00 8.00
TOP54 Blaze Alexander 2.50 6.00
TOP55 Owen Miller 3.00 8.00
TOP56 Matt Mercer 2.50 6.00
TOP57 Ronny Mauricio 10.00 25.00
TOP59 Andrew Knizner 4.00 10.00
TOP60 Freudis Nova 6.00 15.00
TOP62 Tirso Ornelas 5.00 12.00

2019 Bowman Platinum Top Prospects

TOP1 Vladimir Guerrero Jr. 1.50 4.00
TOP2 Shervyen Newton .40 1.00
TOP3 Casey Mize .60 1.50
TOP4 Joey Bart .75 2.00
TOP5 Nick Madrigal .75 2.00
TOP6 Alec Bohm 1.00 2.50
TOP7 Jonathan India .30 .75
TOP8 Jarred Kelenic 1.00 2.50
TOP9 Wander Franco 4.00 10.00
TOP10 Estevan Florial .40 1.00
TOP11 Victor Victor Mesa .50 1.25
TOP12 Seuly Matias .30 .75
TOP13 Jordan Groshans .50 1.25
TOP14 Victor Mesa Jr. .60 1.50
TOP15 Jordyn Adams .30 .75
TOP16 Nick Solak .75 2.00
TOP17 Matthew Liberatore .25 .60
TOP18 Logan Gilbert .40 1.00
TOP19 Brady Singer .50 1.25
TOP20 Nolan Gorman .75 2.00
TOP21 Luis Garcia .30 .75
TOP22 Elehuris Montero .40 1.00
TOP23 Yusniel Diaz .40 1.00
TOP24 Keegan Thompson .25 .60
TOP25 Anthony Seigler .40 1.00
TOP26 Luis Arraez 1.00 2.50
TOP27 Nico Hoerner .75 2.00
TOP28 Seth Beer .60 1.50
TOP29 Jose Azocar .25 .60
TOP30 Logan Webb .40 1.00
TOP31 Bobby Dalbec .60 1.50
TOP32 Nicky Lopez .40 1.00
TOP33 Miguel Amaya .40 1.00

TOP34 Ethan Hankins .30 .75
TOP35 Shane McClanahan .30 .75
TOP36 Taylor Widener .25 .60
TOP37 Dauris Valdez .25 .60
TOP38 Pablo Olivares .40 1.00
TOP39 Chad Spanberger .25 .60
TOP40 Tristan Pompey .30 .75
TOP41 Alex Royalty .25 .60
TOP42 Griffin Conine .40 1.00
TOP43 Owen White .25 .60
TOP44 Josiah Gray .40 1.00
TOP45 Luken Baker .30 .75
TOP46 Brewer Hicklen .40 1.00
TOP47 Cash Case .30 .75
TOP48 Connor Wong .30 .75
TOP49 Griffin Canning .40 1.00
TOP50 Liam Jenkins .25 .60
TOP51 Adam Wolf .40 1.00
TOP52 Ronaldo Hernandez .25 .60
TOP53 Tommy Romero .30 .75
TOP54 Blaze Alexander .25 .60
TOP55 Owen Miller .30 .75
TOP56 Matt Mercer .25 .60
TOP57 Ronny Mauricio .60 1.50
TOP58 Diego Cartaya .50 1.25
TOP59 Andrew Knizner .40 1.00
TOP60 Freudis Nova .40 1.00
TOP61 Brice Turang .30 .75
TOP62 Tirso Ornelas .25 .60
TOP63 Julio Rodriguez 2.00 5.00
TOP64 Sheldon Neuse .25 .60
TOP65 Will Smith .60 1.50
TOP66 Cristian Javier .30 .75
TOP67 Noelvi Marte 1.00 2.50
TOP68 Rylan Bannon .30 .75
TOP69 Josh Breaux .30 .75
TOP70 Deivi Garcia 10.00 25.00
TOP71 Alex Kirilloff .40 1.00
TOP72 Jo Adell .75 2.00
TOP73 Brendan Rodgers .40 1.00
TOP74 Carter Kieboom .40 1.00
TOP75 Brock Deatherage .25 .60
TOP76 James Marvel .40 1.00
TOP77 Jose de la Cruz .75 2.00
TOP78 Carlos Cortes .25 .60
TOP79 Eli Morgan .25 .60
TOP80 Matt Vierling .40 1.00
TOP81 Royce Lewis .50 1.25
TOP82 Bo Bichette .75 2.00
TOP83 Mackenzie Gore .50 1.25
TOP84 Hunter Greene .40 1.00
TOP85 Brendan McKay .40 1.00
TOP86 Keston Hiura .75 2.00
TOP87 Pedro Castellanos .25 .60
TOP88 Luis Robert 4.00 10.00
TOP89 Andres Munoz .40 1.00
TOP90 Sean Murphy .30 .75
TOP91 Cristian Pache .60 1.50
TOP92 Heliot Ramos .40 1.00
TOP93 Jon Duplantier .25 .60
TOP94 Nate Pearson .60 1.50
TOP95 Ryan Weathers .25 .60
TOP96 Alek Thomas .40 1.00
TOP97 Triston Casas 1.00 2.50
TOP98 Cole Roederer .75 2.00
TOP99 Triston McKenzie .25 .60
TOP100 Yordan Alvarez 4.00 10.00

2019 Bowman Platinum Top Prospects Blue

*BLUE: 1X TO 2.5X BASIC
STATED ODDS 1:55 JUMBO
STATED PRINT RUN 150 SER.#'d SETS

2019 Bowman Platinum Top Prospects Gold

*GOLD: 3X TO 8X BASIC
STATED ODDS 1:165 JUMBO
STATED PRINT RUN 50 SER.#'d SETS

2019 Bowman Platinum Top Prospects Green

*GREEN: 1.2X TO 3X BASIC
STATED ODDS 1:84 JUMBO
STATED PRINT RUN 99 SER.#'d SETS

2019 Bowman Platinum Top Prospects Ice

*ICE: .6X TO 1.5X BASIC
STATED ODDS 1:4 BLASTER

2019 Bowman Platinum Top Prospects Orange

*ORANGE: 4X TO 10X BASIC
STATED ODDS 1:287 MEGA
STATED PRINT RUN 25 SER.#'d SETS

2019 Bowman Platinum Top Prospects Purple

*PURPLE: .75X TO 2X BASIC
STATED ODDS 1:33 JUMBO
STATED PRINT RUN 250 SER.#'d SETS

2019 Bowman Platinum Top Prospects Sky Blue

*SKY BLUE: .75X TO 2X BASIC
STATED ODDS 1:2 JUMBO

2020 Bowman Platinum

1 Mookie Betts .60 1.50
2 Max Scherzer .30 .75
3 DJ LeMahieu .30 .75
4 John Means .20 .50
5 Shohei Ohtani .40 1.00
6 Gleyber Torres .60 1.50
7 J.D. Martinez .30 .75
8 Nick Solak RC .50 1.25
9 Isan Diaz RC .50 1.25
10 Paul DeJong .30 .75
11 Ozzie Albies .30 .75
12 Gavin Lux RC 2.00 5.00
13 Bryce Harper .50 1.25
14 Justin Dunn RC .40 1.00
15 Manny Machado .30 .75
16 Freddie Freeman .40 1.00
17 Chris Paddack .30 .75
18 Nico Hoerner RC 1.25 3.00
19 Brendan McKay RC .50 1.25
20 Trey Mancini .30 .75
21 Corey Kluber .25 .60
22 J.T. Realmuto .30 .75
23 Anthony Rizzo .50 1.25
24 Vladimir Guerrero Jr. .60 1.50
25 Clayton Kershaw .60 1.50
26 Francisco Lindor .30 .75
27 Whit Merrifield .30 .75
28 Giancarlo Stanton .30 .75
29 Luis Robert RC 3.00 8.00
30 Josh Bell .25 .60
31 Nolan Arenado .40 1.00
32 Ketel Marte .25 .60
33 Didi Gregorius .25 .60
34 Elvis Andrus .25 .60
35 Andrew Benintendi .30 .75
36 Kris Bryant .40 1.00
37 Keston Hiura .40 1.00
38 Nick Senzel .30 .75
39 Miguel Cabrera .30 .75
40 Alex Bregman .30 .75
41 Starling Marte .25 .60
42 Stephen Strasburg .30 .75
43 Matt Chapman .30 .75
44 Rafael Devers .40 1.00
45 A.J. Puk RC .60 1.50
46 Jose Altuve .25 .60
47 Zack Greinke .25 .60
48 Eloy Jimenez .60 1.50
49 Pete Alonso .75 2.00
50 Kyle Lewis RC 2.50 6.00
51 Jesus Luzardo RC .60 1.50
52 Eugenio Suarez .25 .60
53 Jeff McNeil .25 .60
54 Nick Castellanos .30 .75
55 Trevor Story .30 .75
56 Chris Sale .30 .75
57 Cavan Biggio .40 1.00
58 Jorge Soler .30 .75
59 Aristides Aquino RC .60 1.50
60 Justin Verlander .30 .75
61 Blake Snell .25 .60
62 Ronald Acuna Jr. 1.25 3.00
63 Buster Posey .40 1.00
64 Anthony Rendon .30 .75
65 Mike Trout 1.50 4.00
66 Austin Meadows .25 .60
67 Shane Bieber .30 .75
68 Aaron Judge .75 2.00
69 George Springer .25 .60
70 Aaron Nola .30 .75
71 Jack Flaherty .25 .60
72 Javier Baez .40 1.00
73 Rhys Hoskins .40 1.00
74 Christian Yelich .40 1.00
75 Jordan Yamamoto RC .40 1.00
76 Paul Goldschmidt .30 .75
77 Walker Buehler .40 1.00
78 Bo Bichette RC 2.50 6.00
79 Jacob deGrom .30 .75
80 Mike Soroka .30 .75
81 Fernando Tatis Jr. 1.25 3.00
82 Cody Bellinger .60 1.50
83 Juan Soto 1.00 2.50
84 Noah Syndergaard .25 .60
85 Yadier Molina .30 .75
86 Bryan Reynolds .25 .60
87 Josh Hader .20 .50
88 Zac Gallen RC .75 2.00
89 Josh Donaldson .25 .60
90 Joey Votto .30 .75
91 Carlos Correa .30 .75
92 Mike Yastrzemski- .50 1.25
93 Jose Ramirez .25 .60
94 Nelson Cruz .30 .75
95 Tim Anderson .30 .75
96 Albert Pujols .40 1.00
97 Xander Bogaerts .30 .75
98 Hyun-Jin Ryu .25 .60
99 Gerrit Cole .50 1.25
100 Yordan Alvarez RC 1.50 4.00

2020 Bowman Platinum Blue

*BLUE: 1.2X TO 3X BASIC
*BLUE RC: .8X TO 2X BASIC RC
RANDOM INSERTS IN PACKS
STATED PRINT RUN 150 SER.#'d SETS
29 Luis Robert 10.00 25.00

2020 Bowman Platinum Gold

*GOLD: 3X TO 8X BASIC
*GOLD RC: 2X TO 5X BASIC RC
RANDOM INSERTS IN PACKS
STATED PRINT RUN 50 SER.#'d SETS
29 Luis Robert 25.00 60.00
50 Kyle Lewis 20.00 50.00
78 Bo Bichette 20.00 50.00

2020 Bowman Platinum Green

*GREEN: 1.5X TO 4X BASIC
*GREEN RC: 1X TO 2.5X BASIC RC
RANDOM INSERTS IN PACKS
STATED PRINT RUN 99 SER.#'d SETS
29 Luis Robert 12.00 30.00
50 Kyle Lewis 10.00 25.00
78 Bo Bichette 10.00 25.00

2020 Bowman Platinum Orange

*ORANGE: 5X TO 12X BASIC
*ORANGE RC: 3X TO 8X BASIC RC
RANDOM INSERTS IN PACKS
STATED PRINT RUN 25 SER.#'d SETS
29 Luis Robert 50.00 120.00
50 Kyle Lewis 30.00 80.00
65 Mike Trout 30.00 80.00
78 Bo Bichette 30.00 80.00

2020 Bowman Platinum Pink

*PINK: 1.2X TO 3X BASIC
*PINK RC: .8X TO 2X BASIC RC
RANDOM INSERTS IN PACKS
STATED PRINT RUN 199 SER.#'d SETS
29 Luis Robert 10.00 25.00

2020 Bowman Platinum Purple

*PURPLE: 1X TO 2.5X BASIC
*PURPLE RC: .6X TO 1.5X BASIC RC
RANDOM INSERTS IN PACKS
STATED PRINT RUN 250 SER.#'d SETS
29 Luis Robert 8.00 20.00

2020 Bowman Platinum Teal

*TEAL: 1X TO 2.5X BASIC
*TEAL RC: .6X TO 1.5X BASIC RC
RANDOM INSERTS IN PACKS
STATED PRINT RUN 299 SER.#'d SETS
29 Luis Robert 6.00 15.00

2020 Bowman Platinum Cut Autographs

RANDOM INSERTS IN PACKS
PRINT RUNS B/WN 25-50 COPIES PER
EXCHANGE DEADLINE XX/XX/XX
PCAAA Aristides Aquino/50 8.00 20.00
PCAAB Alec Bohm/25 50.00 120.00
PCAAM Andres Munoz/50 5.00 12.00
PCAAR Adley Rutschman/25 40.00 100.00
PCAAT Alek Thomas/50 5.00 12.00
PCABH Bryce Harper
PCABM Brendan McKay/25 8.00 20.00
PCABW Bobby Witt Jr./25 60.00 150.00
PCACA CJ Abrams/50 15.00 40.00
PCACB Cavan Biggio/50 25.00 60.00
PCAGC Gerrit Cole/25 30.00 80.00
PCAGR Grayson Rodriguez/50 6.00 15.00
PCAJB Joey Bart/25 20.00 50.00
PCAJK Jarred Kelenic/50 40.00 100.00
PCAJR Julio Rodriguez
PCAKH Keston Hiura
PCAKL Kyle Lewis/50 30.00 80.00
PCALA Luis Arraez/50 8.00 20.00
PCAMY Mike Yastrzemski/50 25.00 60.00
PCANH Nico Hoerner
PCAPA Pete Alonso/25 30.00 80.00
PCARA Ronald Acuna Jr./25 60.00 150.00
PCARG Riley Greene/25 20.00 50.00
PCASB Seth Beer
PCATA Tim Anderson/50 8.00 20.00
PCATL Trevor Larnach/50 8.00 20.00
PCAVG Vladimir Guerrero Jr./25 30.00 80.00
PCAWB Walker Buehler/25 15.00 40.00
PCAYA Yordan Alvarez/25 25.00 60.00

2020 Bowman Platinum Platinum Pieces Autograph Relics

RANDOM INSERTS IN PACKS
PRINT RUNS B/WN 35-99 COPIES PER
EXCHANGE DEADLINE XX/XX/XX
PPARAA Adbert Alzolay/99 4.00 10.00
PPARAC Aaron Civale/99 5.00 12.00
PPARAM Andres Munoz/99 4.00 10.00
PPARAT Abraham Toro/99 4.00 10.00
PPARBB Bobby Bradley/99 4.00 10.00
PPARBH Bryce Harper
PPARGL Gavin Lux/75 20.00 50.00
PPARID Isan Diaz/99 5.00 12.00
PPARJC Johan Camargo/99 3.00 8.00
PPARJM Jeff McNeil/99 8.00 20.00
PPARJY Jordan Yamamoto/99 4.00 10.00
PPARMK Mike King/99 5.00 12.00
PPARMT Matt Thaiss/99 4.00 10.00
PPARNS Noah Syndergaard/35
PPARRM Ryan McMahon/99 3.00 8.00
PPARRY Ryan Yarbrough/99 3.00 8.00
PPARSB Seth Brown/99 3.00 8.00
PPARSM Sean Murphy/99 5.00 12.00
PPARTZ T.J. Zeuch/99 3.00 8.00
PPARYA Yordan Alvarez/45 20.00 50.00
PPARAAQ Aristides Aquino/99 6.00 15.00
PPARJLU Jesus Luzardo/99 6.00 15.00

2020 Bowman Platinum Platinum Pieces Autograph Relics Orange

*ORANGE: .5X TO 1.2X p/r 75-99
*ORANGE: .6X TO 1.5X p/r 35-45
RANDOM INSERTS IN PACKS
STATED PRINT RUN 25 SER.#'d SETS
EXCHANGE DEADLINE XX/XX/XX
PPARBH Bryce Harper 100.00 250.00

2020 Bowman Platinum Polished Gems

RANDOM INSERTS IN PACKS
PG1 Mike Trout 2.00 5.00
PG2 Ketel Marte .30 .75
PG3 Ronald Acuna Jr. 1.50 4.00
PG4 Dansby Swanson .40 1.00
PG5 Eloy Jimenez .75 2.00
PG6 Lucas Giolito .30 .75
PG7 Mike Clevinger .30 .75
PG8 Jorge Soler .40 1.00
PG9 Walker Buehler .50 1.25
PG10 Will Smith .50 1.25
PG11 Josh Hader .25 .60
PG12 Keston Hiura .50 1.25
PG13 Pete Alonso 1.00 2.50
PG14 Gio Urshela .40 1.00
PG15 Gleyber Torres .75 2.00
PG16 DJ LeMahieu .40 1.00
PG17 Chris Paddack .40 1.00
PG18 Jack Flaherty .30 .75
PG19 Austin Meadows .30 .75
PG20 Victor Robles .50 1.25

2020 Bowman Platinum Polished Gems Green

*GREEN: 1.2X TO 3X BASIC
RANDOM INSERTS IN PACKS
STATED PRINT RUN 99 SER.#'d SETS
PG1 Mike Trout 10.00 25.00

2020 Bowman Platinum Polished Gems Orange

*ORANGE: 4X TO 10X BASIC
RANDOM INSERTS IN PACKS
STATED PRINT RUN 25 SER.#'d SETS
PG1 Mike Trout 30.00 80.00
PG3 Ronald Acuna Jr. 40.00 100.00

2020 Bowman Platinum Polished Gems Purple

*PURPLE: .8X TO 2X BASIC
RANDOM INSERTS IN PACKS
STATED PRINT RUN 250 SER.#'d SETS
PG1 Mike Trout 6.00 15.00

2020 Bowman Platinum Polished Gems Autographs

RANDOM INSERTS IN PACKS
PRINT RUNS B/WN 25-50 COPIES PER
EXCHANGE DEADLINE XX/XX/XX
PGAAM Austin Meadows/50 5.00 12.00
PGACP Chris Paddack/50 6.00 15.00
PGADS Dansby Swanson/50 8.00 20.00
PGAEJ Eloy Jimenez/50 12.00 30.00
PGAGT Gleyber Torres/25 25.00 60.00
PGAJF Jack Flaherty/50 15.00 40.00
PGAJH Josh Hader/50 4.00 10.00
PGAJS Jorge Soler/50 6.00 15.00
PGAKH Keston Hiura/50 8.00 20.00
PGAKM Ketel Marte
PGAMT Mike Trout
PGAPA Pete Alonso/50 25.00 60.00
PGARA Ronald Acuna Jr./25 60.00 150.00
PGAVR Victor Robles/50 8.00 20.00
PGAWB Walker Buehler/50 12.00 30.00
PGAWS Will Smith/41 10.00 25.00

2020 Bowman Platinum Precious Elements

RANDOM INSERTS IN PACKS
PE1 Jo Adell 1.00 2.50
PE2 Alek Thomas .30 .75
PE3 Cristian Pache .75 2.00
PE4 Adley Rutschman 1.50 4.00
PE5 Bobby Dalbec .60 1.50
PE6 Miguel Amaya .30 .75
PE7 Andrew Vaughn 1.00 2.50
PE8 Nick Lodolo .40 1.00
PE9 Nolan Jones .40 1.00
PE10 Colton Welker .25 .60
PE11 Casey Mize .75 2.00
PE12 J.J. Matijevic .30 .75
PE13 Bobby Witt Jr. 1.25 3.00
PE14 Keibert Ruiz .60 1.50
PE15 Jesus Sanchez .25 .60
PE16 Antoine Kelly .50 1.25
PE17 Royce Lewis .60 1.50
PE18 Brett Baty .75 2.00
PE19 Jasson Dominguez 4.00 10.00
PE20 Jorge Mateo .25 .60
PE21 Alec Bohm 1.50 4.00
PE22 Travis Swaggerty .30 .75
PE23 MacKenzie Gore .50 1.25
PE24 Joey Bart .75 2.00
PE25 Jarred Kelenic 1.50 4.00
PE26 Nolan Gorman .50 1.25
PE27 Wander Franco 2.50 6.00
PE28 Josh Jung .60 1.50
PE29 Jordan Groshans .50 1.25
PE30 Tim Cate .25 .60

2020 Bowman Platinum Precious Elements Green

*GREEN: 1.2X TO 3X BASIC
RANDOM INSERTS IN PACKS
STATED PRINT RUN 99 SER.#'d SETS
PE19 Jasson Dominguez 40.00 100.00

2020 Bowman Platinum Precious Elements Orange

*ORANGE: 4X TO 10X BASIC
RANDOM INSERTS IN PACKS
STATED PRINT RUN 25 SER.#'d SETS
PE19 Jasson Dominguez 75.00 200.00

2020 Bowman Platinum Precious Elements Purple

*PURPLE: .8X TO 2X BASIC
RANDOM INSERTS IN PACKS
STATED PRINT RUN 250 SER.#'d SETS
PE19 Jasson Dominguez 25.00 60.00

2020 Bowman Platinum Precious Elements Autographs

RANDOM INSERTS IN PACKS
STATED PRINT RUN 25 SER.#'d SETS
EXCHANGE DEADLINE XX/XX/XX
PEAAB Alec Bohm 30.00 80.00
PEAAK Antoine Kelly 8.00 20.00
PEAAR Adley Rutschman 30.00 80.00
PEAAT Alek Thomas 5.00 12.00
PEAAV Andrew Vaughn 15.00 40.00
PEABB Brett Baty 12.00 30.00
PEABD Bobby Dalbec 10.00 25.00
PEABW Bobby Witt Jr. 50.00 120.00
PEACM Casey Mize 20.00 50.00
PEACW Colton Welker 4.00 10.00
PEAJA Jo Adell 25.00 60.00
PEAJB Joey Bart 15.00 40.00
PEAJD Jasson Dominguez 100.00 250.00
PEAJG Jordan Groshans 8.00 20.00
PEAJJ Josh Jung 10.00 25.00
PEAJK Jarred Kelenic 40.00 100.00
PEAKR Keibert Ruiz 10.00 25.00
PEAMA Miguel Amaya 5.00 12.00
PEAMG MacKenzie Gore 8.00 20.00
PEANG Nolan Gorman 15.00 40.00
PEANL Nick Lodolo 6.00 15.00
PEARL Royce Lewis 10.00 25.00
PEATC Tim Cate 4.00 10.00
PEATS Travis Swaggerty 10.00 25.00
PEAWF Wander Franco 50.00 120.00

2020 Bowman Platinum Precision Autographs

RANDOM INSERTS IN PACKS
STATED PRINT RUN 25 SER.#'d SETS
EXCHANGE DEADLINE XX/XX/XX
PP1 Mike Soroka 8.00 20.00
PP2 Casey Mize 25.00 60.00
PP3 Matt Manning 6.00 15.00
PP6 Brady Singer 6.00 15.00
PP7 Clayton Kershaw 40.00 100.00
PP10 Gerrit Cole 30.00 80.00
PP11 Jesus Luzardo 10.00 25.00
PP12 A.J. Puk 10.00 25.00
PP13 Chris Paddack 8.00 20.00
PP14 Max Scherzer 25.00 60.00

2020 Bowman Platinum Refined Autographs

RANDOM INSERTS IN PACKS
PRINT RUNS B/WN 25-99 COPIES PER
EXCHANGE DEADLINE XX/XX/XX
RABD Bobby Dalbec/99 8.00 20.00
RACJ Cristian Javier/99 3.00 8.00
RACM Casey Mize/25 25.00 60.00
RACP Cristian Pache/45 20.00 50.00
RADG Deivi Garcia/99 15.00 40.00
RAJA Jo Adell/99 20.00 50.00
RAJB Joey Bart/25 20.00 50.00
RAJD Jarren Duran/99 10.00 25.00
RAJG Josiah Gray/99 5.00 12.00
RAJI Jonathan India/50 5.00 12.00
RAJK Jarred Kelenic/50 40.00 100.00
RAMM Matt Manning/99 4.00 10.00
RANM Nick Madrigal/40 15.00 40.00
RASB Seth Beer/99 6.00 15.00
RAWC William Contreras/99 4.00 10.00
RAWF Wander Franco/99 50.00 120.00

2020 Bowman Platinum Renowned Rookies

RANDOM INSERTS IN PACKS
RR1 Brendan McKay .40 1.00
RR2 Yordan Alvarez 1.25 3.00
RR3 Luis Robert 2.50 6.00
RR4 Bo Bichette 2.00 5.00
RR5 Gavin Lux 1.50 4.00
RR6 Nico Hoerner 1.00 2.50
RR7 Aristides Aquino .50 1.25
RR8 A.J. Puk .50 1.25
RR9 Jesus Luzardo .50 1.25
RR10 Kyle Lewis 2.00 5.00
RR11 Adbert Alzolay .30 .75
RR12 Justin Dunn .30 .75
RR13 Nick Solak .40 1.00
RR14 Anthony Kay .25 .60
RR15 Seth Brown .25 .60
RR16 Jose Urquidy .30 .75
RR17 Sean Murphy .40 1.00
RR18 Shun Yamaguchi .30 .75
RR19 Shogo Akiyama .40 1.00
RR20 Jordan Yamamoto .30 .75

2020 Bowman Platinum Renowned Rookies Green

*GREEN: 1.2X TO 3X BASIC
RANDOM INSERTS IN PACKS
STATED PRINT RUN 99 SER.#'d SETS
RR3 Luis Robert 12.00 30.00

2020 Bowman Platinum Renowned Rookies Orange

*ORANGE: 4X TO 10X BASIC
RANDOM INSERTS IN PACKS
STATED PRINT RUN 25 SER.#'d SETS
RR3 Luis Robert 40.00 100.00

2020 Bowman Platinum Renowned Rookies Purple

*PURPLE: .8X TO 2X BASIC
RANDOM INSERTS IN PACKS
STATED PRINT RUN 250 SER.#'d SETS
RR3 Luis Robert 8.00 20.00

2020 Bowman Platinum Renowned Rookies Autographs

RANDOM INSERTS IN PACKS
STATED PRINT RUN 25 SER.#'d SETS
EXCHANGE DEADLINE XX/XX/XX
RRAAA Adbert Alzolay 5.00 12.00
RRAAK Anthony Kay 4.00 10.00
RRAAP A.J. Puk 8.00 20.00
RRABM Brendan McKay 6.00 15.00
RRAGL Gavin Lux 25.00 60.00
RRAJD Justin Dunn 5.00 12.00
RRAJL Jesus Luzardo 8.00 20.00
RRAKL Kyle Lewis 30.00 80.00
RRALR Luis Robert 75.00 200.00
RRANH Nico Hoerner 15.00 40.00
RRANS Nick Solak 6.00 15.00
RRASB Seth Brown 4.00 10.00
RRAYA Yordan Alvarez 20.00 50.00
RRAAAQ Aristides Aquino 8.00 20.00

2020 Bowman Platinum Top Prospect Autographs

RANDOM INSERTS IN PACKS
EXCHANGE DEADLINE XX/XX/XX
*PURPLE/199: .5X TO 1.2X BASIC
*BLUE/150: .5X TO 1.2X BASIC
*GREEN/99: .5X TO 1.2X BASIC
*ICE/50: .6X TO 1.5X BASIC
*ORANGE/25: .8X TO 2X BASIC
TOP1 Casey Golden 4.00 10.00
TOP5 Jacob Amaya 5.00 12.00
TOP6 Quinn Priester 4.00 10.00
TOP7 Peyton Burdick 10.00 25.00
TOP10 CJ Abrams 10.00 25.00
TOP11 Grayson Rodriguez 4.00 10.00
TOP13 Rece Hinds 3.00 8.00
TOP15 Adley Rutschman 20.00 50.00
TOP18 Josh Smith 5.00 12.00
TOP20 Xavier Edwards 6.00 15.00
TOP22 Alek Manoah 3.00 8.00
TOP23 Jackson Rutledge 4.00 10.00
TOP24 Davis Wendzel 3.00 8.00
TOP25 Bobby Witt Jr. 30.00 80.00
TOP26 JJ Bleday 8.00 20.00
TOP30 Edwin Uceta 3.00 8.00
TOP31 Bo Naylor 3.00 8.00
TOP33 Blake Walston 4.00 10.00
TOP34 Kody Hoese 8.00 20.00
TOP35 Adam Kloffenstein 4.00 10.00
TOP37 Logan Davidson 3.00 8.00
TOP41 Logan Wyatt 4.00 10.00
TOP43 Kris Bubic 4.00 10.00
TOP44 Canaan Smith 4.00 10.00
TOP45 Antoine Kelly 5.00 12.00
TOP46 Brett Baty 8.00 20.00
TOP47 Hogan Harris 2.50 6.00
TOP48 Ryne Nelson 3.00 8.00
TOP49 Kendall Williams 4.00 10.00
TOP50 Joe Ryan 2.50 6.00
TOP51 Tim Cate 2.50 6.00
TOP52 Jeremy Pena 6.00 15.00
TOP53 Greg Jones 3.00 8.00
TOP54 Korey Lee 3.00 8.00
TOP55 Andrew Vaughn 10.00 25.00
TOP56 Ryan Jeffers 5.00 12.00
TOP59 Joey Cantillo 2.50 6.00
TOP60 Ryan Jensen 3.00 8.00
TOP62 Ryan Zeferjahn 3.00 8.00
TOP64 Riley Greene 10.00 25.00
TOP66 Aaron Schunk 5.00 12.00
TOP68 Terrin Vavra 5.00 12.00
TOP69 Zack Thompson 2.50 6.00
TOP70 Gunnar Henderson 3.00 8.00
TOP71 Dominic Fletcher 2.50 6.00
TOP75 Logan Driscoll 4.00 10.00
TOP78 Jake Latz 2.50 6.00
TOP79 Corbin Carroll 4.00 10.00
TOP81 Devin Mann 4.00 10.00
TOP82 Bryce Ball 10.00 25.00
TOP83 Michael Toglia 2.50 6.00
TOP84 Joey Bart 10.00 25.00
TOP86 Kameron Misner 4.00 10.00
TOP89 Sam Huff 5.00 12.00
TOP91 Ethan Small 3.00 8.00
TOP92 Nick Lodolo 4.00 10.00
TOP95 Andy Pages 3.00 8.00
TOP96 Marshall Kasowski 4.00 10.00
TOP97 Josh Jung 6.00 15.00
TOP98 Jarren Duran 8.00 20.00
TOP100 Matt Wallner 5.00 12.00

2020 Bowman Platinum Top Prospects

RANDOM INSERTS IN PACKS
*CHARTREUSE: .6X TO 1.5X BASIC
*ICE: .6X TO 1.5X BASIC
TOP1 Casey Golden .40 1.00
TOP2 William Contreras .30 .75
TOP3 Evan White .25 .60
TOP4 Jordan Balazovic .50 1.25
TOP5 Jacob Amaya 1.00 2.50
TOP6 Quinn Priester .40 1.00
TOP7 Peyton Burdick 1.00 2.50
TOP8 Jo Adell 1.00 2.50
TOP9 Will Wilson .30 .75
TOP10 CJ Abrams 1.00 2.50
TOP11 Grayson Rodriguez .40 1.00
TOP12 Ryan Garcia .25 .60
TOP13 Rece Hinds .30 .75
TOP14 Hunter Bishop .50 1.25
TOP15 Adley Rutschman 1.50 4.00
TOP16 Gilberto Jimenez 1.25 3.00
TOP17 Jonathan India .30 .75
TOP18 Josh Smith .50 1.25
TOP19 Keoni Cavaco .25 .60
TOP20 Xavier Edwards 1.00 2.50
TOP21 Braden Shewmake .40 1.00
TOP22 Alek Manoah .30 .75
TOP23 Jackson Rutledge .40 1.00
TOP24 Davis Wendzel .30 .75
TOP25 Bobby Witt Jr. 1.25 3.00
TOP26 JJ Bleday .75 2.00
TOP27 Alex Faedo .30 .75
TOP28 Casey Mize .75 2.00
TOP29 Anthony Volpe 1.00 2.50
TOP30 Edwin Uceta .30 .75
TOP31 Bo Naylor .30 .75
TOP32 Alec Bohm 1.50 4.00
TOP33 Blake Walston .40 1.00
TOP34 Kody Hoese .75 2.00
TOP35 Adam Kloffenstein .40 1.00
TOP36 Seth Beer .50 1.25
TOP37 Logan Davidson .30 .75
TOP38 JJ Goss .25 .60
TOP39 Matt Canterino .30 .75
TOP40 Noelvi Marte 1.00 2.50
TOP41 Logan Wyatt .40 1.00
TOP42 Trevor Larnach .50 1.25
TOP43 Kris Bubic .40 1.00
TOP44 Canaan Smith .40 1.00
TOP45 Antoine Kelly .50 1.25
TOP46 Brett Baty .75 2.00
TOP47 Hogan Harris .25 .60
TOP48 Ryne Nelson .30 .75
TOP49 Kendall Williams .40 1.00
TOP50 Joe Ryan .25 .60
TOP51 Tim Cate .25 .60
TOP52 Jeremy Pena .60 1.50
TOP53 Greg Jones .30 .75
TOP54 Korey Lee .30 .75
TOP55 Andrew Vaughn 1.00 2.50
TOP56 Ryan Jeffers .50 1.25
TOP57 Deivi Garcia 1.00 2.50
TOP58 Tyler Nevin .40 1.00
TOP59 Joey Cantillo .25 .60
TOP60 Ryan Jensen .30 .75
TOP61 T.J. Sikkema .25 .60
TOP62 Ryan Zeferjahn .30 .75
TOP63 Brandon Bielak .25 .60
TOP64 Riley Greene 1.00 2.50
TOP65 Daniel Lynch .25 .60
TOP66 Aaron Schunk .50 1.25
TOP67 Luis Gil .40 1.00
TOP68 Terrin Vavra .50 1.25
TOP69 Zack Thompson .25 .60
TOP70 Gunnar Henderson .30 .75
TOP71 Dominic Fletcher .25 .60
TOP72 Shea Langeliers .50 1.25
TOP73 Joshua Mears .50 1.25
TOP74 Mason Martin .50 1.25
TOP75 Logan Driscoll .40 1.00
TOP76 Ezequiel Duran .50 1.25
TOP77 Keibert Ruiz .60 1.50
TOP78 Jake Latz .25 .60
TOP79 Corbin Carroll .40 1.00
TOP80 Ford Proctor .25 .60
TOP81 Devin Mann .40 1.00
TOP82 Bryce Ball 1.25 3.00
TOP83 Michael Toglia .25 .60
TOP84 Joey Bart .75 2.00
TOP85 Kyle Stowers .25 .60
TOP86 Kameron Misner .40 1.00
TOP87 Seth Corry .25 .60
TOP88 Alexander Canario .25 .60
TOP89 Sam Huff .50 1.25
TOP90 Jarred Kelenic 1.50 4.00
TOP91 Ethan Small .30 .75
TOP92 Nick Lodolo .40 1.00
TOP93 Josiah Gray .40 1.00
TOP94 Julio Rodriguez 1.50 4.00
TOP95 Andy Pages .30 .75
TOP96 Marshall Kasowski .40 1.00
TOP97 Josh Jung .60 1.50
TOP98 Jarren Duran 1.00 2.50
TOP99 Matt Manning .30 .75
TOP100 Matt Wallner .50 1.25
TOP101 Jasson Dominguez 4.00 10.00
TOP102 Robert Puason .75 2.00

2020 Bowman Platinum Top Prospects Blue

*BLUE: 1X TO 2.5X BASIC
RANDOM INSERTS IN PACKS
STATED PRINT RUN 150 SER.#'d SETS
TOP101 Jasson Dominguez 30.00 80.00

2020 Bowman Platinum Top Prospects Gold

*GOLD: 2.5X TO 6X BASIC
RANDOM INSERTS IN PACKS
STATED PRINT RUN 50 SER.#'d SETS
TOP32 Alec Bohm 12.00 30.00
TOP101 Jasson Dominguez 75.00 200.00

2020 Bowman Platinum Top Prospects Green

*GREEN: 1.2X TO 3X BASIC
RANDOM INSERTS IN PACKS
STATED PRINT RUN 99 SER.#'d SETS
TOP101 Jasson Dominguez 40.00 100.00

2020 Bowman Platinum Top Prospects Orange

*ORANGE: 4X TO 10X BASIC
RANDOM INSERTS IN PACKS
STATED PRINT RUN 25 SER.#'d SETS
TOP32 Alec Bohm 20.00 50.00
TOP101 Jasson Dominguez 125.00 300.00

2020 Bowman Platinum Top Prospects Pink

*PINK: 1X TO 2.5X BASIC
RANDOM INSERTS IN PACKS
STATED PRINT RUN 199 SER.#'d SETS
TOP101 Jasson Dominguez 30.00 80.00

2020 Bowman Platinum Top Prospects Purple

*PURPLE: .8X TO 2X BASIC
RANDOM INSERTS IN PACKS
STATED PRINT RUN 250 SER.#'d SETS
TOP101 Jasson Dominguez 25.00 60.00

2020 Bowman Platinum Top Prospects Teal

*TEAL: .8X TO 2X BASIC

RANDOM INSERTS IN PACKS
STATED PRINT RUN 299 SER.#'d SETS
TOP101 Jasson Dominguez 25.00 60.00

2004 Bowman Sterling

This 138-card set was released in December, 2004. The set was issued in five-card packs with a $50 SRP and they came six packs to a box and four boxes to a case. Just about every basic card is a "hit" as the cards are either memorabilia cards of veterans, or rookie cards with the possibility of them being either autographed or with a jersey swatch on it. Despite the high price point for the packs, this product did extremely well in the secondary market.

COMMON FY .75 2.00
FY ODDS APPX.TWO PER HOBBY PACK
COMMON FY AU 3.00 8.00
FY AU ODDS APPX.ONE PER HOBBY PACK
COMMON AU-GU 4.00 10.00
AU-GU ODDS APPX.ONE PER HOBBY PACK
AU-GU 1:2 WRAPPER ODDS IS AN ERROR
COMMON AU-GU RC 4.00 10.00
COMMON GU 2.00 5.00
GU ODDS APPX. 1.5 PER HOBBY PACK
GU 1:2 WRAPPER ODDS IS AN ERROR
AB Angel Berroa Bat 2.00 5.00
ABA Aarom Baldiris FY RC .40 1.00
AC Alberto Callaspo FY AU RC 4.00 10.00
AD Adam Dunn Bat 2.00 5.00
AER Alex Rodriguez Bat 6.00 15.00
AJ Andruw Jones Jsy 3.00 8.00
AK Austin Kearns Jsy 2.00 5.00
ANR Aramis Ramirez Bat 2.00 5.00
AP Albert Pujols Jsy 8.00 20.00
AR Alex Romero FY AU RC 3.00 8.00
AW Adam Wainwright AU Jsy 6.00 15.00
AWH A.Whittington FY RC .40 1.00
AZ Alec Zumwalt FY AU RC 3.00 8.00
BB Brian Bixler AU Jsy RC 4.00 10.00
BBR Bill Bray FY RC .40 1.00
BDU Billy Buckner FY RC .40 1.00
BC2 Bobby Crosby Jsy 2.00 5.00
BD Blake DeWitt AU Jsy RC 6.00 15.00
BE Brad Eldred FY RC .40 1.00
BH B.Hawksworth FY AU RC 4.00 10.00
BT Brad Thompson FY RC .60 1.50
BU B.J. Upton AU Bat 4.00 10.00
BW Bernie Williams Jsy 3.00 8.00
CA Chris Aguila FY AU RC 3.00 8.00
CB Craig Biggio Jsy 3.00 8.00
CC Chad Cordero AU Jsy 6.00 15.00
CG Christian Garcia AU Jsy RC 6.00 15.00
CH Chin-Lung Hu FY RC .40 1.00
CIB Carlos Beltran Bat 2.00 5.00
CJ Conor Jackson FY RC 1.25 3.00
CL Chris Lubanski AU Bat 4.00 10.00
CLA Chris Lambert FY RC .40 1.00
CN Chris Nelson FY RC .40 1.00
CQ Carlos Quentin FY AU RC 4.00 10.00
CT Curtis Thigpen FY RC .40 1.00
DD David DeJesus AU Jsy 6.00 15.00
DP Danny Putnam AU Jsy RC 4.00 10.00
DPU David Purcey FY RC .60 1.50
DW David Wright AU Jsy 10.00 25.00
DWW Dontrelle Willis Jsy 3.00 8.00
DY Delmon Young AU Bat 5.00 12.00
EG Eric Gagne Jsy 2.00 5.00
EH Eric Hurley FY RC .40 1.00
ESP Erick San Pedro FY RC .40 1.00
FC Fausto Carmona FY RC .60 1.50
FG Freddy Guzman FY RC .40 1.00
FH Felix Hernandez FY RC 6.00 15.00
FP Felix Pie AU Jsy 10.00 25.00
FT Frank Thomas Bat 3.00 8.00
GG Greg Golson FY RC .40 1.00
GH Gaby Hernandez FY RC .60 1.50
GIG Glo Gonzalez FY RC .60 1.50
GS Gary Sheffield Bat 2.00 5.00
HB Homer Bailey AU Jsy RC 3.00 8.00
HC Hee Seop Choi Bat 2.00 5.00
HG Hector Gimenez FY AU RC 3.00 8.00
HJB Hank Blalock Bat 2.00 5.00
HM Hector Made FY RC .40 1.00
HS Huston Street AU Jsy RC 5.00 12.00
IR Ivan Rodriguez Bat 3.00 8.00
JB Jeff Bagwell Jsy 3.00 8.00
JC Jose Capellan FY RC .40 1.00
JCR Jesse Crain FY RC .60 1.50
JD Johnny Damon Bat 3.00 8.00
JE Johnny Estrada Bat 2.00 5.00
JFI Josh Fields FY RC .60 1.50
JG Joey Gathright FY RC .40 1.00
JH Jesse Hoover FY RC .40 1.00
JK Jason Kendall Bat 2.00 5.00
JM Jeff Marquez AU Jsy RC 4.00 10.00
JO Justin Orenduff FY RC .60 1.50
JP Juan Pierre Bat 2.00 5.00
JPH J.P. Howell FY RC .40 1.00
JR Jay Rainville FY AU RC 5.00 12.00
JS Jeremy Sowers FY AU RC 3.00 8.00
JZ Jon Zeringue FY RC .40 1.00
KCH K.C. Herren FY RC .40 1.00
KS Kurt Suzuki FY RC .60 1.50
KT Kazuhito Tadano FY RC .40 1.00
KW Kerry Wood Jsy 2.00 5.00
KWA Kyle Waldrop AU Jsy RC 4.00 10.00
LB Lance Berkman Jsy 2.00 5.00
LC Luis Castillo Jsy 2.00 5.00
LH Linc Holdzkom FY AU RC 3.00 8.00
LN Laynce Nix Bat 2.00 5.00
MA Moises Alou Bat 2.00 5.00
MAM Mark Mulder Jsy 2.00 5.00
MAR Manny Ramirez Bat 3.00 8.00
MB Matt Bush AU Jsy RC 3.00 8.00
MC Miguel Cabrera Bat 3.00 8.00
MCT Mark Teixeira Bat 3.00 8.00
ME Mitch Einertson FY RC .40 1.00
MF Mike Ferris FY RC .40 1.00
MFO Matt Fox FY RC .40 1.00
MJP Mike Piazza Bat 3.00 8.00
MM Matt Moses FY AU RC 6.00 15.00
MMC Matt Macri FY RC .60 1.50
MP Mark Prior Jsy 3.00 8.00
MR Mike Rouse FY AU RC 3.00 8.00
MRO Mark Rogers FY RC .60 1.50
MT M.Tuiasosopo AU Bat RC 6.00 15.00
MT1 Miguel Tejada Bat 2.00 5.00
MT2 Miguel Tejada Jsy 2.00 5.00
MW Marland Williams FY RC .40 1.00
MY Michael Young Bat 2.00 5.00
NJ Nick Johnson Bat 2.00 5.00
NM Nyjer Morgan FY RC .40 1.00
NS Nate Schierholtz FY RC .40 1.00
NW Neil Walker FY RC 2.00 5.00
OQ Omar Quintanilla FY RC .40 1.00
PGM Paul Maholm FY RC .60 1.50
PH Philip Hughes FY RC 1.00 2.50
PL Paul LoDuca Bat 2.00 5.00
PR Pokey Reese Bat 2.00 5.00
RB Rocco Baldelli Bat 2.00 5.00
RBR Reid Brignac FY RC 1.00 2.50
RC Robinson Cano AU Jsy 10.00 25.00
RH Ryan Harvey AU Bat 6.00 15.00
RJH Richard Hidalgo Bat 2.00 5.00
RM Ryan Meaux FY AU RC 3.00 8.00
RO Russ Ortiz Jsy 2.00 5.00
RP Rafael Palmeiro Bat 3.00 8.00
SK Scott Kazmir AU Jsy RC 3.00 8.00
SO Scott Olsen AU Jsy RC 4.00 10.00
SS Sammy Sosa Jsy 3.00 8.00
SSM Seth Smith FY RC .60 1.50
TD Thomas Diamond FY RC .40 1.00
TG Troy Glaus Bat 2.00 5.00
TLH Todd Helton Bat 3.00 8.00
TM Tino Martinez Bat 3.00 8.00
TMG Tom Glavine Jsy 3.00 8.00
TP Trevor Plouffe AU Jsy RC 4.00 10.00
TT T.Tankersley AU Jsy RC 4.00 10.00
VG Vladimir Guerrero Bat 3.00 8.00
VP Vince Perkins FY AU RC 4.00 10.00
YP Yusmeiro Petit FY RC 1.00 2.50
ZD Zach Duke FY RC .60 1.50
ZJ Zach Jackson FY RC .40 1.00

2004 Bowman Sterling Refractors

*REF.FY: 1.25X TO 3X BASIC
FY ODDS 1:4 HOBBY
*REF.FY AU: 1X TO 2.5X BASIC FY AU
FY AU ODDS 1:8 HOBBY
*REF.AU-GU: .6X TO 1.5X BASIC AU-GU
AU-GU ODDS 1:9 HOBBY
*REF.GU: .6X TO 1.5X BASIC GU
GU ODDS 1:5 HOBBY
STATED PRINT RUN 199 SERIAL #'d SETS
BD Blake DeWitt AU Jsy 8.00 20.00
FP Felix Pie AU Jsy 12.50 30.00

2004 Bowman Sterling Original Autographs

GROUP A ODDS 1:221 HOBBY
GROUP B ODDS 1:25 HOBBY
GROUP A = A.ROD/BONDS
GROUP B = CHAVEZ/REYES/SORIANO
PRINT RUNS B/WN 1-106 COPIES PER
NO PRICING ON QTY OF 25 OR LESS
ISSUED IN HOBBY BOX LOADER PACKS
AR11 Alex Rodriguez 03BC/28 60.00 120.00
AS7 Alfonso Soriano 02B/54 4.00 10.00
AS8 Alfonso Soriano 02BC/33 10.00 25.00
AS9 Alfonso Soriano 03B/102 8.00 20.00
AS10 Alfonso Soriano 03BC/49 8.00 20.00
AS11 Alfonso Soriano 04B/26 10.00 25.00
EC10 Eric Chavez 02B/68 10.00 25.00
EC11 Eric Chavez 02BC/21 12.50 30.00
EC12 Eric Chavez 03B/106 10.00 25.00
EC13 Eric Chavez 03BC/22 12.50 30.00
JR1 Jose Reyes 02B/52 10.00 25.00
JR2 Jose Reyes 02BD/22 20.00 50.00
JR3 Jose Reyes 02BD/34 20.00 50.00
JR4 Jose Reyes 02BC/31 20.00 50.00
JR5 Jose Reyes 02BCD/41 10.00 25.00
JR6 Jose Reyes 03BD/92 10.00 25.00

2005 Bowman Sterling

COMMON CARD .60 1.50
BASIC CARDS APPX.TWO PER HOBBY PACK
BASIC CARDS APPX.TWO PER RETAIL PACK
AU GROUP A ODDS 1:2 HOBBY
AU GROUP B ODDS 1:3 HOBBY
AU-GU GROUP A ODDS 1:2 H, 1:2 R
AU-GU GROUP B ODDS 1:37 H, 1:37 R
AU-GU GROUP C ODDS 1:11 H, 1:11 R
AU-GU GROUP D ODDS 1:10 H, 1:10 R
AU-GU GROUP E ODDS 1:27 H, 1:27 R
AU-GU GROUP F ODDS 1:13 H, 1:13 R
GU GROUP A ODDS 1:3 H, 1:3 R
GU GROUP B ODDS 1:5 H, 1:5 R
GU GROUP C ODDS 1:6 H, 1:6 R
ACL Andy LaRoche RC .60 1.50
AL Adam Lind AU Bat B 4.00 10.00
AM A.McCutchen AU Jsy D RC 15.00 40.00
AP Albert Pujols Jsy B 6.00 15.00
AR Alex Rodriguez Jsy B UER 6.00 15.00
ARA Aramis Ramirez Bat A 2.00 5.00
AS Alfonso Soriano Bat A 2.00 5.00
AT Aaron Thompson AU A RC 4.00 10.00
BA Brian Anderson RC 1.00 2.50
BB Billy Buckner AU Jsy A 4.00 10.00
BBU Billy Butler RC 3.00 8.00
BC Brent Cox AU Jsy D RC 6.00 15.00
BCR Brad Corley RC .60 1.50
BE Brad Eldred AU Jsy C 4.00 10.00
BH Brett Hayes RC .60 1.50
BJ Beau Jones AU Jsy A RC 8.00 20.00
BL B.Livingston AU Jsy A RC 4.00 10.00
BLB Barry Bonds Jsy C 6.00 15.00
BM B.McCarthy AU Jsy A RC 4.00 10.00
BMU Bill Mueller Jsy C 2.00 5.00
BRB Brian Bogusevic RC .60 1.50
BS Brandon Sing AU A RC 4.00 8.00
BSN Brandon Snyder RC 1.50 4.00
BZ Barry Zito Uni A 2.00 5.00
CB Carlos Beltran Bat A 2.00 5.00
CBU Clay Buchholz RC 3.00 8.00
CC Cesar Carrillo RC 1.00 2.50
CD Carlos Delgado Jsy A 2.00 5.00
CH C.J. Henry AU B RC 3.00 8.00
CHE Chase Headley RC 1.00 2.50
CI Craig Italiano RC .60 1.50
CJ Chuck James RC 1.50 4.00
CLT Chuck Tiffany RC 1.50 4.00
CN Chris Nelson AU Jsy A 4.00 10.00
CP Cliff Pennington AU B RC 4.00 10.00
CPP C.Pignatiello AU Jsy A RC 4.00 10.00
CR Colby Rasmus AU Jsy A RC 4.00 10.00
CRA Cesar Ramos RC .60 1.50
CRO Chaz Roe AU Jsy A RC 4.00 10.00
CS C.J. Smith AU Jsy A RC 4.00 10.00
CSU Curt Schilling Jsy C 3.00 8.00
CT Curtis Thigpen AU Jsy A 4.00 10.00
CV Chris Volstad AU B RC 3.00 8.00
DC Dan Carte RC .60 1.50
DL Derrek Lee Bat A 3.00 8.00
DO David Ortiz Bat A 3.00 8.00
DP Dustin Pedroia AU Jsy A 30.00 80.00
DT Drew Thompson RC .60 1.50
DW Dontrelle Willis Jsy C 2.00 5.00
EC Eric Chavez Uni B 2.00 5.00
EI Eli Iorg AU Jsy C RC 3.00 8.00
EM Eddy Martinez AU A RC 4.00 10.00
GK George Kottaras AU A RC 3.00 8.00
GM Greg Maddux Jsy C 4.00 10.00
GO Garrett Olson AU A RC 3.00 8.00
GS Gary Sheffield Bat A 2.00 5.00
HAS Henry Sanchez RC 1.00 2.50
HB Hank Blalock Bat A 2.00 5.00
HI Hernan Iribarren RC .60 1.50
HM Hideki Matsui AS Jsy C 6.00 15.00
HS Hum Sanchez AU A RC 8.00 20.00
IR Ivan Rodriguez Bat A 3.00 8.00
JB Jay Bruce AU Jsy D RC 6.00 15.00
JBE Josh Beckett Uni A 2.00 5.00
JC Jeff Clement RC .60 1.50
JCN John Nelson AU Uni A RC 4.00 10.00
JD Johnny Damon Bat A 3.00 8.00
JDR John Drennen RC .60 1.50
JE J.Ellsbury AU Jsy E RC 5.00 12.00
JEG Jon Egan RC .60 1.50
JF Josh Fields AU Jsy A 4.00 10.00
JG Josh Geer AU Jsy A RC 4.00 10.00
JGI Josh Gibson Seat C 8.00 20.00
JL Jed Lowrie AU Jsy F RC 4.00 10.00
JLY Jeff Lyman RC .60 1.50
JM John Mayberry Jr. AU A RC 8.00 20.00
JMA Jacob Marceaux RC .60 1.50
JN Jeff Niemann AU Jsy A RC 4.00 10.00
JO Justin Olson AU Jsy A RC 4.00 10.00
JP Jorge Posada Bat A 3.00 8.00
JPE Jim Edmonds Jsy B 2.00 5.00
JS John Smoltz Jsy A 3.00 8.00
JV J.Verlander AU Jsy A RC 60.00 150.00
JW Josh Wall RC .60 1.50
JWE Jered Weaver RC 3.00 8.00
KG Khalil Greene Jsy B 3.00 8.00
KM Kevin Millar Bat A 2.00 5.00
KS Kevin Slowey RC 3.00 8.00
KW Kevin Whelan RC .60 1.50
LWJ Chipper Jones Bat A 3.00 8.00
MA Matt Albers AU A RC 4.00 10.00
MAM Matt Maloney RC .60 1.50
MB M.Bowden AU Jsy A RC 4.00 10.00
MC Mike Conroy AU Jsy A RC 4.00 10.00
MCA Miguel Cabrera Jsy A 3.00 8.00
MCO Mike Costanzo RC .60 1.50
MG Matt Green AU A RC 3.00 8.00
MGA Matt Garza RC 1.00 2.50
MGI Marcus Gilles AS Jsy B 2.00 5.00
MM Mark Mulder Uni B 2.00 5.00
MMC Matt McCormick RC .60 1.50
MP Mike Piazza Bat A 3.00 8.00
MPR Mark Prior Jsy B 3.00 8.00
MR Manny Ramirez Bat A 3.00 8.00
MT Miguel Tejada Uni A 2.00 5.00
MTE Mark Teixeira Bat A 3.00 8.00
MTO Matt Torra RC .60 1.50
MY Michael Young Bat A 2.00 5.00
NH Nick Hundley RC .60 1.50
NR Nolan Reimold RC 2.50 6.00
NW Nick Webber RC .60 1.50
PH Philip Humber AU Jsy A RC 4.00 10.00
PK Paul Kelly RC .60 1.50
PL Paul Lo Duca Bat A 2.00 5.00
PM Pedro Martinez Jsy A 3.00 8.00
PP P.J. Phillips RC .60 1.50
RB Ryan Braun AU A RC 10.00 25.00
RBE Ronnie Belliard Bat A 2.00 5.00
RF Rafael Furcal Jsy A 2.00 5.00
RM Russ Martin AU Jsy F RC 5.00 12.00
RMO Ryan Mount RC .60 1.50
RR Ricky Romero RC 1.00 2.50
RT Raul Tablado AU Jsy A RC 4.00 10.00
RZ Ryan Zimmerman RC 3.00 8.00
SD Stephen Drew RC 2.00 5.00
SE Scott Elbert AU Jsy A 4.00 10.00
SM Steve Marek AU Jsy A RC 4.00 10.00
SR Scott Rolen Jsy B 3.00 8.00
SS Sammy Sosa Bat A 3.00 8.00
SW Steven White AU B RC 3.00 8.00
TB Trevor Bell AU Jsy C RC 4.00 10.00
TBU Travis Buck RC .60 1.50
TC Travis Chick AU A RC 3.00 8.00
TG Tyler Greene RC .60 1.50
TH Torii Hunter Bat A 2.00 5.00
THE Tyler Herron RC .60 1.50
THU Tim Hudson Uni A 2.00 5.00
TI Tadahito Iguchi RC 1.00 2.50
TLH Todd Helton Jsy B 3.00 8.00
TM Tyler Minges AU Jsy A RC 4.00 10.00
TM Tino Martinez Bat A 3.00 8.00
TN Trot Nixon Bat A 2.00 5.00
TT Troy Tulowitzki RC 6.00 15.00
TW Travis Wood RC 1.50 4.00
VG Vladimir Guerrero Bat A 3.00 8.00
VM Victor Martinez Bat A 2.00 5.00
WT Wade Townsend RC .60 1.50
YE Yunel Escobar RC 2.50 6.00
ZS Zach Simons RC .60 1.50

2005 Bowman Sterling Refractors

*RFF: 1.25X TO 3X BASIC
BASIC ODDS 1:6 H, 1:6 R
*REF AU: 1X TO 2.5X BASIC AU
AU ODDS 1:13 HOBBY
*REF AU-GU: .6X TO 1.5X BASIC AU-GU
AU-GU ODDS 1:9 H, 1:9 R
*REF GU: .6X TO 1.5X BASIC GU
GU ODDS 1:6 H, 1: R
STATED PRINT RUN 199 SERIAL #'d SETS
BE Brad Eldred AU Jsy 12.50 30.00

2005 Bowman Sterling Black Refractors

BASIC ODDS 1:5 BOX-LOADER
NO BASIC PRICING DUE TO SCARCITY
AU ODDS 1:17 BOX-LOADER
NO AU PRICING DUE TO SCARCITY
AU-GU ODDS 1:8 BOX-LOADER
NO AU-GU PRICING DUE TO SCARCITY
*BLACK GU: 2X TO 5X BASIC GU
GU ODDS 1:5 BOX-LOADER
ONE BOX-LOADER PACK PER HOBBY BOX
STATED PRINT RUN 25 SERIAL #'d SETS
BLB Barry Bonds Jsy 60.00 120.00

2005 Bowman Sterling MLB Logo Patch Autograph

STATED ODDS 1:665 BOX-LOADER
ONE BOX-LOADER PACK PER HOBBY BOX
STATED PRINT RUN 1 SERIAL #'d SET
NO PRICING DUE TO SCARCITY

2005 Bowman Sterling Original Autographs

GROUP A ODDS 1:665 BOX-LOADER
GROUP B ODDS 1:250 BOX-LOADER
GROUP C ODDS 1:63 BOX-LOADER
GROUP D ODDS 1:50 BOX-LOADER
GROUP E ODDS 1:42 BOX-LOADER
GROUP F ODDS 1:28 BOX-LOADER
GROUP G ODDS 1:25 BOX-LOADER
GROUP H ODDS 1:21 BOX-LOADER
GROUP I ODDS 1:6 BOX-LOADER
ONE BOX-LOADER PACK PER HOBBY BOX
PRINT RUNS B/WN 1-160 COPIES PER
NO PRICING ON QTY OF 13 OR LESS
AJ1 Andruw Jones 98 B/18 20.00 50.00
AJ2 Andruw Jones 99 B/18 20.00 50.00
AJ6 Andruw Jones 02 B/122 6.00 15.00
AJ8 Andruw Jones 03 B/112 6.00 15.00
AJ9 Andruw Jones 03 BC/18 20.00 50.00
AJ10 Andruw Jones 04 B/71 6.00 15.00
DL1 Derrek Lee 95 B/17 10.00 25.00
DL2 Derrek Lee 96 B/29 10.00 25.00
DL3 Derrek Lee 96 BB/15 12.50 30.00
DL4 Derrek Lee 97 BC/16 12.50 30.00
DL5 Derrek Lee 98 B/22 10.00 25.00
DL6 Derrek Lee 04 B/92 6.00 15.00
DW1 David Wright 04 BD/98 6.00 15.00
DW3 David Wright 05 B/139 6.00 15.00
GA3 Garret Anderson 03 B/33 6.00 15.00
GA4 Garret Anderson 04 B/33 6.00 15.00
GA5 Garret Anderson 04 BC/36 6.00 15.00
GA6 Garret Anderson 05 B/48 5.00 12.00
JR1 Jeremy Reed 04 BD/82 4.00 10.00
JR2 Jeremy Reed 04 BCD/48 5.00 12.00
MC2 M.Cabrera 02 BD/26 100.00 200.00
MC4 M.Cabrera 03 BD/27 100.00 200.00
MC5 M.Cabrera 03 BCD/25 100.00 200.00
MC6 M.Cabrera 04 B/127 20.00 50.00
MC7 M.Cabrera 04 BC/25 100.00 200.00
MC8 M.Cabrera 05 B/154 20.00 50.00
MC9 M.Cabrera 05 BC/25 100.00 200.00
MK1 Mark Kotsay 97 B/18 20.00 50.00
MK3 Mark Kotsay 98 B/56 8.00 20.00
MK4 Mark Kotsay 98 BC/23 10.00 25.00
MK5 Mark Kotsay 99 B/75 6.00 15.00
MK6 Mark Kotsay 99 BC/23 10.00 25.00
MK7 Mark Kotsay 05 B/160 6.00 15.00
MK8 Mark Kotsay 05 BC/46 8.00 20.00
MY1 Michael Young 04 B/148 6.00 15.00
MY2 Michael Young 04 BC/64 8.00 20.00
MY3 Michael Young 05 B/92 6.00 15.00

2006 Bowman Sterling

This 117-card set was released in January, 2007. This set was issued in five-card packs with an $50 SRP which came six packs per box and eight boxes per case. The set is a mix of game-used relics from veteran playerts and players who were rookies in 2006. Some of the rookies either signed some of the cards or signed some of the cards and had a game-used relic included as well as their signature.

COMMON ROOKIE .75 2.00
COMMON AUTO RC 3.00 8.00
AU RC AUTO ODDS 1:4 HOBBY
COMMON AU-GU RC 4.00 10.00
AU-GU RC ODDS 1:4 HOBBY
COMMON GU VET 2.50 6.00
GU VET ODDS 1:4 HOBBY
OVERALL PLATE ODDS 1:23 BOXES
PLATE PRINT RUN 1 SET PER COLOR
BLACK-CYAN-MAGENTA-YELLOW ISSUED
NO PLATE PRICING DUE TO SCARCITY
EXCHANGE DEADLINE 12/31/08
AD Adam Dunn Jsy 2.50 6.00
AE Andre Ethier AU (RC) 3.00 8.00
AER Alex Rodriguez Bat 10.00 25.00
AJ Andruw Jones Jsy 3.00 8.00
ALR A.Reyes Jsy AU (RC) EXCH 4.00 10.00
ALS Alay Soler RC .75 2.00
AP Albert Pujols Jsy 8.00 20.00
AP2 Albert Pujols Bat 8.00 20.00
APS Alfonso Soriano Bat 4.00 10.00
AR Aramis Ramirez Bat UER 3.00 8.00
AS Anibal Sanchez (RC) .75 2.00
BA Brian Anderson (RC) .75 2.00
BB Brian Bannister (RC) .75 2.00
BL B.Livingston Jsy AU (RC) 4.00 10.00
BLB Barry Bonds Bat 6.00 15.00
BON Boof Bonser (RC) 1.25 3.00
BR Brian Roberts Jsy 2.50 6.00
BZ Ben Zobrist (RC) 1.25 3.00
CB Carlos Beltran Jsy 2.50 6.00
CB2 Carlos Beltran Bat 2.50 6.00
CC Chris Carpenter Jsy 4.00 10.00
CH Cole Hamels Jsy AU (RC) 10.00 25.00
CHJ Chuck James (RC) .75 2.00
CI Chris Iannetta Jsy AU RC 4.00 10.00
CJ Conor Jackson (RC) 1.25 3.00
CJJ Casey Janssen RC .75 2.00
CQ Carlos Quentin (RC) 1.25 3.00
CRB Chad Billingsley (RC) 1.25 3.00
CRH Craig Hansen RC 2.00 5.00
CS Curt Schilling Jsy 3.00 8.00
DG David Gassner (RC) .75 2.00
DO David Ortiz Bat 4.00 10.00
DP David Pauley (RC) .75 2.00
DU Dan Uggla (RC) 1.25 3.00
DW David Wright Jsy 6.00 15.00
DWW Dontrelle Willis Jsy 2.50 6.00
EC Eric Chavez Pants 2.50 6.00
EG Enrique Gonzalez (RC) .75 2.00
FG Franklin Gutierrez (RC) .75 2.00
FL Francisco Liriano (RC) 2.00 5.00
GS Grady Sizemore Jsy 4.00 10.00
HB Hank Blalock Jsy 2.50 6.00
HK1 Howie Kendrick (RC) 1.50 4.00
HK2 Howie Kendrick Jsy AU 6.00 15.00
HM Hideki Matsui Bat 6.00 15.00
HP Hayden Penn (RC) .75 2.00
HR Hanley Ramirez (RC) 1.25 3.00
IK Ian Kinsler AU (RC) 4.00 10.00
IR Ivan Rodriguez Jsy 3.00 8.00
IS Ichiro Suzuki Jsy 10.00 25.00
JAS Johan Santana Jsy 4.00 10.00
JB J.Bulger Jsy AU (RC) EXCH 3.00 8.00
JBS Jeremy Sowers (RC) .75 2.00
JCB Jason Botts AU (RC) 3.00 8.00
JD Joey Devine RC .75 2.00
JDD Johnny Damon Bat 4.00 10.00
JHT Jim Thome Bat 4.00 10.00
JI Joe Inglett AU RC 5.00 12.00
JJ Josh Johnson (RC) 2.00 5.00
JK Jeff Karstens RC .75 2.00
JL James Loney (RC) 1.25 3.00
JLB Josh Barfield AU (RC) 3.00 8.00
JM Jeff Mathis (RC) .75 2.00
JP Jonathan Papelbon (RC) 4.00 10.00
JRH Rich Harden Jsy 2.50 6.00
JS James Shields RC 2.50 6.00
JT Jack Taschner Jsy AU (RC) 4.00 10.00
JTA Jordan Tata RC .75 2.00
JTL Jon Lester Jsy AU RC 15.00 40.00
JV Justin Verlander (RC) 6.00 15.00
JW Jered Weaver (RC) 2.50 6.00
JZ Joel Zumaya (RC) 2.00 5.00
KF Kevin Frandsen (RC) .75 2.00
KJ Kenji Johjima RC 2.00 5.00
KM Kendry Morales (RC) 2.00 5.00
LB Lance Berkman Jsy 3.00 8.00
LM Lastings Milledge AU (RC) 8.00 20.00
LWJ Chipper Jones Jsy 4.00 10.00
MC Miguel Cabrera Jsy 3.00 8.00
MC2 Miguel Cabrera Bat 3.00 8.00
MCC Melky Cabrera (RC) 1.25 3.00
MCM Mickey Mantle Bat 30.00 60.00
MCT Mark Teixeira Bat 3.00 8.00
ME Morgan Ensberg Jsy 2.50 6.00
MJP Mike Piazza Bat 4.00 10.00
MK Matt Kemp (RC) 2.00 5.00
MM Mark Mulder Pants 2.50 6.00
MN Mike Napoli Jsy AU RC 4.00 10.00
MP Martin Prado Jsy AU (RC) 5.00 12.00
MPP Mike Pelfrey RC 2.00 5.00
MR Manny Ramirez Jsy 4.00 10.00
MR2 Manny Ramirez Bat 4.00 10.00
MS Matt Smith (RC) 1.25 3.00
MT Miguel Tejada Pants 2.50 6.00
NM Nick Markakis (RC) 1.50 4.00
PF Prince Fielder Jsy AU (RC) 6.00 15.00
PK Paul Konerko Bat 3.00 8.00
PM Pedro Martinez Pants 3.00 8.00
RC Robinson Cano Bat 5.00 12.00
RH Ryan Howard Jsy 8.00 20.00
RK Ryan Garko (RC) .75 2.00
RM Russ Martin (RC) 1.25 3.00
RN Ricky Nolasco AU (RC) 3.00 8.00
RP Ronny Paulino Jsy AU (RC) 6.00 15.00
RZ Ryan Zimmerman (RC) 2.50 6.00
SD Stephen Drew (RC) 1.50 4.00
SM Scott Mathieson (RC) .75 2.00
SO Scott Olsen (RC) .75 2.00
SR Scott Rolen Pants 3.00 8.00
TGJ Tony Gwynn Jr (RC) .75 2.00
TH Todd Helton Jsy 3.00 8.00
TT Taylor Tankersley (RC) .75 2.00
VG Vladimir Guerrero Jsy 3.00 8.00
WA Willy Aybar (RC) .75 2.00
YP Yusmeiro Petit Jsy AU (RC) 4.00 10.00
ZM Zach Miner AU (RC) 3.00 8.00

2006 Bowman Sterling Refractors

*REF RC: .6X TO 1.5X BASIC
RC ODDS 1:6 HOBBY
*REF AU RC: .6X TO 1.5X BASIC AU
AU RC ODDS 1:5 HOBBY
*REF AU-GU RC: .5X TO 1.2X BASIC AU-GU
AU-GU RC ODDS 1:20 HOBBY
*REF GU VET: .5X TO 1.2X BASIC GU
GU VET ODDS 1:7 HOBBY
STATED PRINT RUN 199 SERIAL #'d SETS
EXCHANGE DEADLINE 12/31/08
BLB Barry Bonds Bat 12.50 30.00
HK2 Howie Kendrick Jsy AU 10.00 25.00
HM Hideki Matsui Bat 12.50 30.00
MCM Mickey Mantle Bat 40.00 80.00

2006 Bowman Sterling Gold Refractors

STATED GOLD RC ODDS 1:18 BOXES
STATED PRINT RUN 10 SERIAL #'d SETS
NO PRICING DUE TO SCARCITY

2006 Bowman Sterling Original Autographs

GROUP A ODDS 1:356 BOXES
GROUP B ODDS 1:90 BOXES
GROUP C ODDS 1:45 BOXES
GROUP D ODDS 1:8 BOXES
PRINT RUNS B/WN 1-233 COPIES PER
NO PRICING ON QTY OF 25 OR LESS
EXCHANGE DEADLINE 12/31/08
JD5 J.Damon 02 B/47 C 6.00 15.00
JM1 J.Morneau 02 B/199 D 10.00 25.00
JM2 J.Morneau 06 B/48 D 12.50 30.00
JP1 J.Papelbon 03 BD/71 D 30.00 60.00
JP2 J.Papelbon 06 B/225 D 15.00 40.00
JV1 J.Verlander 05 BD/233 D 30.00 60.00
JV3 J.Verlander 06 B/59 D 40.00 80.00

2006 Bowman Sterling Prospects

COMMON CARD .60 1.50
GROUP A AUTO ODDS 1:2 HOBBY
GROUP B AUTO ODDS 1:2 HOBBY
OVERALL PLATE ODDS 1:23 BOXES
PLATE PRINT RUN 1 SET PER COLOR
BLACK-CYAN-MAGENTA-YELLOW ISSUED
NO PLATE PRICING DUE TO SCARCITY
EXCHANGE DEADLINE 12/31/08
AC Adrian Cardenas AU A 4.00 10.00
ADC Adam Coe .60 1.50
AG Alex Gordon AU B 8.00 20.00
AJC Asdrubal Cabrera 3.00 8.00
AO Adam Ottovino AU A 5.00 12.00
AP Andrew Pinckney .50 1.25
AS A.J. Shappi .60 1.50
BA Brandon Allen AU B 4.00 10.00
BB Brooks Brown AU A 3.00 8.00
BC Ben Copeland .60 1.50
BD Brent Dlugach .60 1.50
BF Brad Furnish AU A 3.00 8.00
BH Brett Hayes AU B 3.00 8.00
BJ Brandon Jones .60 1.50
BJS B.J. Szymanski .60 1.50
BM Brandon Moss AU A 3.00 8.00
BS Brandon Snyder AU B 3.00 8.00
BSI Brett Sinkbeil AU B 6.00 15.00
BW Brandon Wood AU B 6.00 15.00
BWM Brad McCann .60 1.50
CD Chris Dickerson AU A 4.00 10.00
CD Chris Dickerson 1.00 2.50
CH Chase Headley AU B 8.00 20.00
CHH Chad Huffman AU B 3.00 8.00
CJ Cody Johnson AU B 3.00 8.00
CK Clayton Kershaw AU A 125.00 300.00
CM Cameron Maybin AU A 8.00 20.00
CMT Matt Tolbert .60 1.50
CP Chris Parmelee AU B 3.00 8.00
CR Cory Rasmus AU A 5.00 12.00
CT Chad Tracy AU A 3.00 8.00
CW Colton Willems AU B 3.00 8.00
CW Corey Wimberly .60 1.50
DE Dustin Evans AU A 3.00 8.00
DF Dexter Fowler 2.00 5.00
DH Daniel Halgwood AU B 3.00 8.00
DHU David Huff AU B 3.00 8.00
DIH Diory Hernandez .60 1.50
DM Dustin Majewski .60 1.50
DT Dallas Trahern .60 1.50
EA Elvis Andrus 2.00 5.00
EL Evan Longoria AU B 10.00 25.00
EM Evan MacLane .60 1.50
EP Elvin Puello AU A 3.00 8.00
GLM Garrett Mock .60 1.50
GM Garrett Mock AU B 3.00 8.00
HC Hank Conger AU B 5.00 12.00
HP Hunter Pence 2.50 6.00
JAC Jose Campusano .60 1.50
JBU Joshua Butler AU A 3.00 8.00
JC Jeff Clement AU B 3.00 8.00
JF Juan Francia .60 1.50
JJ Jeremy Jeffress AU B 4.00 10.00
JJ Jason Jaramillo .60 1.50
JKF Jeff Frazier .60 1.50
JN Jason Neighborgall AU B 3.00 8.00
JR Joshua Rodriguez AU A 3.00 8.00
JRB Jimmy Barthmaier .60 1.50
JS Jarrod Saltalamacchia AU A 3.00 8.00
JT Jose Tabata 1.00 2.50
JTL Jared Lansford .60 1.50
JU Justin Upton AU B 6.00 15.00
JW Johnny Whittleman AU B 8.00 20.00
KB Kyler Burke AU A 3.00 8.00
KC Koby Clemens AU A 4.00 10.00
KD Kyle Drabek AU B 3.00 8.00
KJ Kris Johnson AU A 3.00 8.00
KK Kasey Kiker AU B 3.00 8.00
KM Kyle McCulloch AU B 3.00 8.00
LH Luke Hochevar AU A 3.00 8.00
MA Mike Aviles AU B 4.00 10.00
MAA Matt Antonelli AU B 4.00 10.00
MC Michael Collins .60 1.50
MF Michael Felix AU A 3.00 8.00
MG Mat Gamel 1.50 4.00
MH Michael Hollimon .60 1.50
MM Mark McCormick AU B 3.00 8.00
MO Micah Owings AU B 6.00 15.00
MR Mark Reed .60 1.50
MRA Michael Aubrey 1.00 2.50
MRR Max Ramirez 1.00 2.50
MSM Mark McLemore .60 1.50
MT Mark Trumbo 1.50 4.00
NA Nick Adenhart .60 1.50
ON Oswaldo Navarro .60 1.50
OS Omir Santos .60 1.50
PB Pedro Beato AU A 3.00 8.00
PL Pedro Lopez AU A 3.00 8.00
RB Ronny Bourquin AU B 3.00 8.00
RK Ryan Klosterman .60 1.50
RL Radhames Liz .60 1.50
RP Ryan Patterson .60 1.50
SC Shaun Cumberland .60 1.50
SE Steven Evarts AU A 3.00 8.00
SGG Steve Garrabrants .60 1.50
SM Stephen Marek .60 1.50
SMM Steve Murphy .60 1.50
SR Shawn Riggans .60 1.50
SW Steven Wright AU A 3.00 8.00
SWA Sean Watson AU B 3.00 8.00
TB Travis Buck AU B 6.00 15.00
TC Trevor Crowe AU A 3.00 8.00
TC Tyler Colvin AU B 4.00 10.00
TP Troy Patton AU A 3.00 8.00
WR Wilkin Ramirez 1.00 2.50
WT Wade Townsend AU B 3.00 8.00
WV Will Venable .60 1.50
YC Yung-Chi Chen 1.00 2.50
YG Yovani Gallardo 2.00 5.00

2006 Bowman Sterling Prospects Refractors

*REF: .75X TO 2X BASIC
REF ODDS 1:6 HOBBY
*REF AU: .75X TO 2X BASIC AU
AU ODDS 1:5 HOBBY
STATED PRINT RUN 199 SERIAL #'d SETS
EXCHANGE DEADLINE 12/31/08
HC Hank Conger AU 10.00 25.00
JW Johnny Whittleman AU 15.00 40.00

KB Kyler Burke AU 10.00 25.00
MO Micah Owings AU 12.50 30.00
TB Travis Buck AU 10.00 25.00

2006 Bowman Sterling Prospects Gold Refractors

STATED GOLD ODDS 1:18 BOXES
STATED PRINT RUN 10 SERIAL #'d SETS
NO PRICING DUE TO SCARCITY

2007 Bowman Sterling

This 117-card set was released in January, 2008. The set was issued in five-card mini-boxes, with an $50 SRP, which came six mini-boxes per display box, four display boxes per carton and two cartons per case.

COMMON ROOKIE .40 1.00
COMMON AUTO RC 3.00 8.00
AU RC SEMIS 4.00 10.00
AU RC UNLISTED 5.00 12.00
AU RC AUTO ODDS 1:2 PACKS
COMMON GU VET 2.50 6.00
GU VET GROUP A ODDS 1:5 PACKS
GU VET GROUP B ODDS 1:3 PACKS
GU VET GROUP C ODDS 1:253 PACKS
PRINTING PLATE ODDS 1:29 BOXES
PRINTING PLATE AU ODDS 1:41 BOXES
PLATE PRINT RUN 1 SET PER COLOR
BLACK-CYAN-MAGENTA-YELLOW ISSUED
NO PLATE PRICING DUE TO SCARCITY
AAL Adam Lind (RC) .40 1.00
AER Alex Rodriguez Bat A 6.00 15.00
AG Alex Gordon RC 1.25 3.00
AI Akinori Iwamura RC 1.00 2.50
AJ Andruw Jones Bat B 2.50 6.00
AL Andy LaRoche (RC) .40 1.00
AM Andrew Miller RC 1.50 4.00
AP Albert Pujols Jsy A 5.00 12.00
AR Alex Rios Jsy B 2.50 6.00
AS Alfonso Soriano Bat B 2.50 6.00
ASS Andy Sonnanstine RC .40 1.00
BB Billy Butler (RC) .60 1.50
BF Ben Francisco (RC) .40 1.00
BLB Barry Bonds Pants A 4.00 10.00
BP Brad Penny Jsy B 2.50 6.00
BR Brian Roberts Jsy A 2.50 6.00
BS Brian Stokes (RC) .40 1.00
BU B.J. Upton Bat B 2.50 6.00
BW Brandon Webb Jsy B 2.50 6.00
BW Brandon Wood (RC) .40 1.00
CAB Craig Biggio Jsy B 3.00 8.00
CAG Carlos Guillen Jsy B 2.50 6.00
CG Carlos Gomez RC .75 2.00
CH Cole Hamels Jsy A 3.00 8.00
CH Chase Headley AU (RC) 3.00 8.00
CL Carlos Lee Jsy B 2.50 6.00
CM Cameron Maybin AU RC 4.00 10.00
CMS Curt Schilling Jsy B 2.50 6.00
CT Curtis Thigpen (RC) .40 1.00
DDY Dmitri Young Jsy B 2.50 6.00
DM Daisuke Matsuzaka RC 1.50 4.00
DMM David Murphy (RC) .40 1.00
DO David Ortiz Bat B 3.00 8.00
DP Danny Putnam (RC) .40 1.00
DW David Wright Bat B 4.00 10.00
DWW Dontrelle Willis Jsy B 2.50 6.00
DY Delmon Young (RC) .60 1.50
EC Eric Chavez Pants B 2.50 6.00
FL Fred Lewis (RC) .60 1.50
FP Felix Pie AU (RC) 3.00 8.00
GO Garrett Olson (RC) .40 1.00
GP Glen Perkins AU (RC) 4.00 10.00
HB Homer Bailey AU (RC) 3.00 8.00
HG Hector Gimenez (RC) .40 1.00
HO Hideki Okajima RC 2.00 5.00
HP Hunter Pence (RC) 1.25 3.00
IS Ichiro Suzuki Bat B 5.00 12.00
JAV Jason Varitek Jsy B 3.00 8.00
JB Jeff Baker (RC) .40 1.00
JBR Jose Reyes Jsy A 3.00 8.00
JC1 Joba Chamberlain RC .60 1.50
JC2 Joba Chamberlain AU 5.00 12.00
JD John Danks AU RC 3.00 8.00
JDF Josh Fields (RC) .40 1.00
JE Jim Edmonds Jsy B 3.00 8.00
JE Jacoby Ellsbury (RC) 2.00 5.00
JF Jesus Flores RC .40 1.00
JH Josh Hamilton AU (RC) 6.00 15.00
JL Jesse Litsch AU RC 3.00 8.00
JQF Jake Fox RC .40 1.00
JR Jo-Jo Reyes (RC) .40 1.00
JS Johan Santana Jsy A 3.00 8.00
JS J.Salty AU (RC) 3.00 8.00
JU Justin Upton RC 1.25 3.00
JV Justin Verlander Jsy B 5.00 12.00
KI Kei Igawa RC 1.00 2.50
KK Kevin Kouzmanoff (RC) .40 1.00
KKS Kurt Suzuki AU (RC) 3.00 8.00
KRK Kyle Kendrick AU RC 3.00 8.00
KS Kevin Slowey AU (RC) 6.00 15.00
LB Lance Berkman Jsy B 2.50 6.00
MAR Manny Ramirez Bat B 2.50 6.00
MB Michael Bourn (RC) .60 1.50
MC Melky Cabrera Bat B 2.50 6.00
MC Matt Chico AU (RC) 3.00 8.00
MCT Mark Teixeira Bat A 2.50 6.00
MF Mike Fontenot (RC) .40 1.00
MH Matt Holliday Jsy B 3.00 8.00
MJO Magglio Ordonez Bat B 2.50 6.00
MK Masumi Kuwata RC .40 1.00
MM Mickey Mantle Jsy C 30.00 60.00
MM Miguel Montero (RC) .40 1.00
MO Micah Owings (RC) .40 1.00
MP Manny Parra (RC) .40 1.00
MR Mark Reynolds RC 1.25 3.00
MSM Mark McLemore (RC) .40 1.00
MT Miguel Tejada Pants B 2.50 6.00
MY Michael Young Jsy B 2.50 6.00
NG Nick Gorneault AU (RC) 3.00 8.00
NS Nate Schierholtz AU (RC) 3.00 8.00
OC Orlando Cabrera Jsy 2.50 6.00
PF Prince Fielder Jsy A 3.00 8.00
PH Phil Hughes (RC) 1.00 2.50
PH Phil Hughes AU (RC) 3.00 8.00
RB Rocco Baldelli Jsy B 2.50 6.00
RB Ryan Braun AU (RC) 5.00 12.00
RC Roger Clemens Jsy B 4.00 10.00
RJC Robinson Cano Bat B 3.00 8.00
RJH Ryan Howard Bat A 4.00 10.00
RS Ryan Sweeney (RC) .40 1.00
RV Rick Vanden Hurk RC .40 1.00
RZ Ryan Zimmerman Bat B 3.00 8.00
SD Shelley Duncan (RC) 1.00 2.50
SG Sean Gallagher (RC) .40 1.00
SK Scott Kazmir Jsy B 2.50 6.00
TA Tony Abreu RC 1.00 2.50
TB Travis Buck (RC) .40 1.00
TC Tyler Clippard (RC) .60 1.50
TH Tim Hudson Jsy B 2.50 6.00
TL Tim Lincecum AU RC 12.00 30.00
TLH Todd Helton Bat A 2.50 6.00
TM Travis Metcalf RC .60 1.50
TW Tim Wakefield Jsy B 2.50 6.00
UJ Ubaldo Jimenez (RC) 1.25 3.00
VG Vladimir Guerrero Jsy A 2.50 6.00
YE Yunel Escobar (RC) .40 1.00
YG Yovani Gallardo AU (RC) 3.00 8.00

2007 Bowman Sterling Refractors

*REF RC: 1X TO 2.5X BASIC
RC ODDS 1:7 PACKS
*REF AU RC: .5X TO 1.2X BASIC AU
AU RC ODDS 1:5 PACKS
*REF GU VET: .5X TO 1.2X BASIC GU
GU VET ODDS 1:8 PACKS
STATED PRINT RUN 199 SERIAL #'d SETS
JH Josh Hamilton AU 8.00 20.00
JU Justin Upton 20.00 50.00
KS Kevin Slowey AU 10.00 25.00

2007 Bowman Sterling Dual Autographs

STATED ODDS 1:5 BOXES
STATED PRINT RUN 275 SER.#'d SETS
BV J.Bruce/J.Votto 15.00 40.00
CH S.Choo/C.Hu 6.00 15.00
GM D.Guerra/F.Martinez 5.00 12.00
HC P.Hughes/J.Chamberlain 10.00 25.00
HP L.Hochevar/D.Price 8.00 20.00
LC E.Longoria/C.Crawford 6.00 15.00
MM J.Maine/L.Milledge 4.00 10.00
PB H.Pence/R.Braun 12.50 30.00
PP J.Papelbon/J.Papelbon 4.00 10.00
PS F.Pie/J.Samardzija 10.00 25.00

2007 Bowman Sterling Dual Autographs Refractors

*REF: .4X TO 1X BASIC
STATED ODDS 1:6 BOXES
STATED PRINT RUN 199 SER.#'d SETS

2007 Bowman Sterling Prospects

COMMON CARD .50 1.25
COMMON AUTO 3.00 8.00
STATED AU ODDS 1:1 PACKS
COMMON AU-GU 3.00 8.00
AU-GU ODDS 1:5 PACKS
PRINTING PLATE ODDS 1:29 BOXES
PRINTING PLATE AU ODDS 1:41 BOXES
PLATE PRINT RUN 1 SET PER COLOR
BLACK-CYAN-MAGENTA-YELLOW ISSUED
NO PLATE PRICING DUE TO SCARCITY
AC Adrian Cardenas Jsy AU 4.00 10.00
AF Andrew Fie .50 1.25
ALC Aaron Cunningham .75 2.00
AP Aaron Poreda AU 3.00 8.00
BB Brian Bocock Jsy AU 3.00 8.00
BB Blake Beavan AU 3.00 8.00
BEL Brad Lincoln .50 1.25
BH Brandon Hamilton .50 1.25
BHB Burke Badenhop .75 2.00
BL Bryan LaHair AU 3.00 8.00
BM Brandon MaGee AU 3.00 8.00
BMI Beau Mills AU 3.00 8.00
BR Ben Revere AU 6.00 15.00
BWH Brandon Hynick 1.25 3.00
CB Collin Balester Jsy AU 3.00 8.00
CC Chris Carter 1.50 4.00
CD Chance Douglass .50 1.25
CG Cole Gillespie AU 3.00 8.00
CH Chin-Lung Hu Jsy AU 4.00 10.00
CH Cedric Hunter 1.25 3.00
CK Clayton Kershaw Jsy AU 75.00 200.00
CL Chuck Lofgren Jsy AU 4.00 10.00
CM Clayton Mortensen AU 3.00 8.00
CN Chris Nowak .50 1.25
CR Colby Rasmus Jsy AU 3.00 8.00
CS Cody Strait .50 1.25
CW Chris Withrow AU 4.00 10.00
CWW Casey Weathers AU 3.00 8.00
DB Daniel Bard AU 3.00 8.00
DBE Dellin Betances 1.50 4.00
DG Deolis Guerra Jsy AU 4.00 10.00
DI Devin Ivany .50 1.25
DJ Desmond Jennings 2.00 5.00
DL Drew Locke .50 1.25
DM Daniel Moskos AU 3.00 8.00
DME Devin Mesoraco AU 4.00 10.00
DMM Derek Miller .75 2.00
DPP David Price AU 12.00 30.00
DS James Simmons AU 3.00 8.00
EE Ed Easley .50 1.25
EL Evan Longoria Jsy AU 6.00 15.00
EL Erik Lis AU 3.00 8.00
EM Emerson Frostad .50 1.25
EY Eric Young Jr. .75 2.00
FF Freddie Freeman 8.00 20.00
GD German Duran Jsy AU 3.00 8.00
GH Gorkys Hernandez 1.25 3.00
GP Gregory Porter .50 1.25
GR Greg Reynolds 1.25 3.00
GS Greg Smith .75 2.00
HS Henry Sosa Jsy AU 4.00 10.00
ID Ivan De Jesus Jr. .75 2.00
IS Ian Stewart Jsy AU 5.00 12.00
JA J.P. Arencibia AU 3.00 8.00
JAA James Avery AU 3.00 8.00
JB Jay Bruce Jsy AU 6.00 15.00
JB Joe Benson AU 5.00 12.00
JBO Julio Borbon AU 6.00 15.00
JG Jonathan Gilmore AU 3.00 8.00
JGA Joe Gaetti .50 1.25
JGO Jared Goedert 1.25 3.00
JH Jason Heyward AU 4.00 10.00
JJ Justin Jackson .75 2.00
JL Jeff Locke 1.25 3.00
JM Joe Mather .50 1.25
JO Josh Outman AU 3.00 8.00
JP Jason Place .75 2.00
JPA Jeremy Papelbon .50 1.25
JPP Josh Papelbon .50 1.25
JS Joe Savery AU 3.00 8.00
JS Jeff Samardzija 2.00 5.00
JSM Jake Smolinski 1.50 4.00
JT J.R. Towles 1.50 4.00
JV Joey Votto Jsy AU 15.00 40.00
JV Josh Vitters AU 3.00 8.00
JVE Jonathan Van Every .50 1.25
JW Johnny Whittleman Jsy AU 3.00 8.00
KA Kevin Ahrens AU 3.00 8.00
KK Kellen Kulbacki AU 3.00 8.00
KK Kala Kaaihue .75 2.00
MB Michael Burgess AU 3.00 8.00
MBB Madison Bumgarner AU 30.00 80.00
MC Mike Carp 1.50 4.00
MCA Mitch Canham AU 3.00 8.00
MD Mike Daniel AU 3.00 8.00
MDE Mike Devaney .50 1.25
MDO Matt Dominguez AU 4.00 10.00
MH Mark Hamilton .50 1.25
MIM Michael Main AU 3.00 8.00
MLP Matt LaPorta AU 3.00 8.00
MM Michael Madsen Jsy AU 3.00 8.00
MM Matt McBride AU 3.00 8.00
MMG Matt Mangini AU 3.00 8.00
MP Mike Parisi AU 3.00 8.00
MS Michael Saunders 1.50 4.00
MY Matt Young .50 1.25
NH Nick Hagadone AU 4.00 10.00
NN Nick Noonan AU 5.00 12.00
NS Nick Schmidt AU 3.00 8.00
OS Ole Sheldon .50 1.25
PB Pedro Beato Jsy AU 3.00 8.00
PK Peter Kozma AU 3.00 8.00
RD Ross Detwiler AU 3.00 8.00
RM Ryan Mount AU 3.00 8.00
RT Rich Thompson .50 1.25
SF Sam Fuld 1.50 4.00
SP Steve Pearce Jsy AU 6.00 15.00
TA Tim Alderson AU 3.00 8.00
TF Todd Frazier AU 6.00 15.00
TF Thomas Fairchild .50 1.25
TM Thomas Manzella AU 3.00 8.00
TS Travis Snider AU 4.00 10.00
TW Ty Weeden AU 3.00 8.00
VB Vic Buttler .50 1.25
VS Vasili Spanos .50 1.25
WF Wendell Fairley AU 3.00 8.00
WT Wade Townsend AU 3.00 8.00
ZM Zach McAllister .75 2.00

2007 Bowman Sterling Prospects Refractors

*REF: 1.2X TO 3X BASIC
REF ODDS 1:7 PACKS
*REF AU: .75X TO 2X BASIC AU
REF AU ODDS 1:5 PACKS
*REF AU-GU RC: .5X TO 1.2X BASIC AU-GU
REF AU-GU ODDS 1:20 PACKS
STATED PRINT RUN 199 SERIAL #'d SETS

2008 Bowman Sterling

This set was released on December 29, 2008.

COMMON GU VET 2.50 6.00
EXCHANGE DEADLINE 11/30/2010
COMMON RC 1.00 2.50
COMMON RC VAR 1.25 3.00
RC VAR ODDS 1:2 BOXES
RC VAR PRINT RUN 399 SER.#'d SETS
COMMON AU RC 3.00 8.00
AU RC ODDS 1:3 PACKS
PRINTING PLATE ODDS 1:93 PACKS
PRINTING PLATE AU ODDS 1:238 PACKS
PLATE PRINT RUN 1 SET PER COLOR
BLACK-CYAN-MAGENTA-YELLOW ISSUED
NO PLATE PRICING DUE TO SCARCITY
AAG Armando Galarraga AU RC 3.00 8.00
AP Albert Pujols Jsy 5.00 12.00
AR Alex Rodriguez Jsy 5.00 12.00
ARA Aramis Ramirez Mem 2.50 6.00
ARU Adam Russell AU (RC) 3.00 8.00
BG Brett Gardner (RC) 2.50 6.00
BH Brian Horwitz RC 1.00 2.50
BJ Brandon Jones RC 2.50 6.00
BJB Brian Bixler AU (RC) 3.00 8.00
BM Brian McCann Bat 2.50 6.00
BZ Brad Ziegler RC 5.00 12.00
CC Carl Crawford Jsy 2.50 6.00
CD Chris Davis RC 2.00 5.00
CDB Clay Buchholz (RC) 1.50 4.00
CEGa Carlos Gonzalez (RC) 2.50 6.00
CEGb Carlos Gonzalez VAR SP 3.00 8.00
CG Chris Getz AU RC 3.00 8.00
CG Curtis Granderson Mem 3.00 8.00
CH Cole Hamels Jsy 3.00 8.00
CJ Chipper Jones Jsy 3.00 8.00
CKa Clayton Kershaw RC 30.00 80.00
CKb Clayton Kershaw VAR SP 25.00 60.00
CLH Chin-Lung Hu (RC) 1.00 2.50
CM Charlie Morton (RC) 3.00 8.00
CMT Matt Tolbert RC 1.50 4.00
CP Chris Perez AU RC 3.00 8.00
CR Clayton Richard (RC) 1.00 2.50
CRPa Cliff Pennington (RC) 1.00 2.50
CRPb Cliff Pennington VAR SP 1.25 3.00
CU Chase Utley Jsy 4.00 10.00
CW Chien-Ming Wang Jsy 4.00 10.00
DB Daric Barton (RC) 1.00 2.50
DM Daisuke Matsuzaka Jsy 4.00 10.00
DO David Ortiz Jsy 3.00 8.00
DP David Purcey (RC) 1.00 2.50
DW David Wright Bat 4.00 10.00
DY Delmon Young Jsy 2.50 6.00
EH Eric Hurley (RC) 1.00 2.50
EL Evan Longoria AU RC 10.00 25.00
EV Edinson Volquez Jsy 2.50 6.00
FC Fausto Carmona Mem 3.00 8.00
GB Gregor Blanco (RC) 1.00 2.50
GD German Duran RC 1.50 4.00
GR Greg Reynolds RC 1.50 4.00
GS Geovany Soto Jsy 3.00 8.00
GTS Greg Smith AU RC 3.00 8.00
HI Hernan Iribarren (RC) 1.50 4.00
HKa Hiroki Kuroda RC 2.50 6.00
HKb Hiroki Kuroda VAR SP 3.00 8.00
HP Hunter Pence Jsy 3.00 8.00
HR Hanley Ramirez Jsy 2.50 6.00
IS Ichiro Suzuki Jsy 6.00 15.00
JABa Jay Bruce (RC) 3.00 8.00
JABb Jay Bruce VAR SP 4.00 10.00
JB Josh Banks (RC) 1.00 2.50
JBC Jeff Clement (RC) 1.50 4.00
JBR Jose Reyes Jsy 3.00 8.00
JC Joba Chamberlain Jsy 5.00 12.00
JCH Justin Christian RC 1.50 4.00
JCO Johnny Cueto RC 2.50 6.00
JE Jacoby Ellsbury Jsy 4.00 10.00
JH Josh Hamilton Jsy 5.00 12.00
JLa Jed Lowrie (RC) 1.00 2.50
JLb Jed Lowrie VAR SP 1.25 3.00
JMR Justin Ruggiano AU RC 3.00 8.00
JN Jeff Niemann (RC) 1.00 2.50
JR Jimmy Rollins Jsy 3.00 8.00
JSa Jeff Samardzija RC 3.00 8.00
JSb Jeff Samardzija VAR SP 4.00 10.00
JT J.R. Towles RC 1.50 4.00
JU Justin Upton Bat 2.50 6.00
JVa Joey Votto (RC) 4.00 10.00
JVb Joey Votto VAR SP 5.00 12.00
KFa Kosuke Fukudome RC 3.00 8.00
KFb Kosuke Fukudome VAR SP 4.00 10.00
LHb Luke Hochevar RC 1.50 4.00
MA Michael Aubrey RC 1.50 4.00
MC Miguel Cabrera Bat 3.00 8.00
MH Matt Holliday Bat 2.50 6.00
MJ Matt Joyce RC 2.50 6.00
MK Masahide Kobayashi RC 1.50 4.00
MM Mickey Mantle Jsy 30.00 60.00
MR Manny Ramirez Jsy 4.00 10.00
MRRa Max Ramirez RC 1.00 2.50
MRRb Max Ramirez VAR SP 1.25 3.00
MT Mark Teixeira Bat 3.00 8.00
MTA Miguel Tejada Mem 2.50 6.00
MTH Michael Holliman RC 1.00 2.50
NA Nick Adenhart (RC) 1.00 2.50
NB Nick Blackburn RC 1.50 4.00
NE Nick Evans RC 1.00 2.50
NH Nick Hundley (RC) 1.00 2.50
NLS Nick Stavinoha RC 1.50 4.00
NM Nick Markakis Jsy 4.00 10.00
PF Prince Fielder Jsy 3.00 8.00
RB Ryan Braun Jsy 4.00 10.00
RB Reid Brignac (RC) 1.50 4.00
RH Ryan Howard Jsy 4.00 10.00
RJM Jai Miller (RC) 1.00 2.50
RL Radhames Liz RC 1.50 4.00
RM Russ Martin Bat 3.00 8.00
RT Ryan Tucker (RC) 1.00 2.50
SR Sean Rodriguez (RC) 1.00 2.50
SS Seth Smith AU (RC) 3.00 8.00
TL Tim Lincecum Jsy 6.00 15.00
TT Taylor Teagarden AU RC 5.00 12.00
VG Vladimir Guerrero Jsy 2.50 6.00
VM Victor Martinez Jsy 2.50 6.00
WB Wladimir Balentien (RC) 1.00 2.50
WCC Chris Carter (RC) 1.50 4.00

2008 Bowman Sterling Refractors

*GU VET REF: .5X TO 1.2X BASIC
GU VET REF ODDS 1:5 PACKS
GU VET REF PRINT RUN 199 SER.#'d SETS
*RC REF: .5X TO 1.2X BASIC
RC REF ODDS 1:4 PACKS
RC REF PRINT RUN 199 SER.#'d SETS
*RC VAR REF: .4X TO 1X BASIC
RC VAR REF ODDS 1:5 BOXES
RC VAR REF PRINT RUN 149 SER.#'d SETS
*RC AU REF: .5X TO 1.2X BASIC
RC AU REF ODDS 1:5 PACKS
RC AU REF PRINT RUN 199 SER.#'d SETS

2008 Bowman Sterling Gold Refractors

*GU VET GLD: .75X TO 2X BASIC
GU VET GLD ODDS 1:19 PACKS
GU VET GLD PRINT RUN 50 SER.#'d SETS
*RC GLD: 1X TO 2.5X BASIC
RC GLD ODDS 1:15 PACKS
RC GLD PRINT RUN 50 SER.#'d SETS
*RC VAR GLD: .75X TO 2X BASIC
RC VAR GLD ODDS 1:13 BOXES
RC VAR GLD PRINT RUN 50 SER.#'d SETS
*RC AU GLD: .75X TO 2X BASIC
RC AU GLD ODDS 1:21 PACKS
RC AU GLD PRINT RUN 50 SER.#'d SETS
AP Albert Pujols Jsy 12.50 30.00
AR Alex Rodriguez Jsy 12.50 30.00
BZ Brad Ziegler 25.00 60.00
CLH Chin-Lung Hu 4.00 10.00
CW Chien-Ming Wang Jsy 20.00 50.00
DM Daisuke Matsuzaka Jsy 10.00 25.00
HKa Hiroki Kuroda 12.00 30.00
HKb Hiroki Kuroda VAR 12.00 30.00
IS Ichiro Suzuki Jsy 15.00 40.00
JE Jacoby Ellsbury Jsy 15.00 40.00
TT Taylor Teagarden AU 20.00 50.00

2008 Bowman Sterling Dual Autographs

STATED ODDS 1:29 PACKS
STATED PRINT RUN 325 SER.#'d SETS
LS E.Longoria/G.Soto 6.00 15.00
MM J.Montero/M.Melancon 8.00 20.00
PB B.Posey/G.Beckham 20.00 50.00
RS A.Rios/T.Snider 6.00 15.00

2008 Bowman Sterling Dual Autographs Refractors

*REF: .5X TO 1.2X BASIC
STATED ODDS 1:93 PACKS
STATED PRINT RUN 99 SER.#'d SETS

2008 Bowman Sterling Dual Autographs Gold Refractors

*GLD REF: .6X TO 1.5X BASIC
STATED ODDS 1:185 PACKS
STATED PRINT RUN 50 SER.#'d SETS

2008 Bowman Sterling Prospects

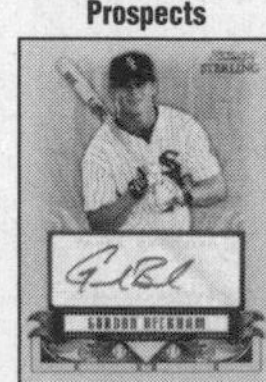

COMMON CARD .40 1.00
COMMON AU 3.00 8.00
STATED AUTO ODDS 1:3 PACKS
COMMON JSY AU 5.00 12.00
STATED JSY AU ODDS 1:4 PACKS
PRINTING PLATE ODDS 1:93 PACKS
PRINTING PLATE AU ODDS 1:238 PACKS
PLATE PRINT RUN 1 SET PER COLOR
BLACK-CYAN-MAGENTA-YELLOW ISSUED
NO PLATE PRICING DUE TO SCARCITY
AA Adrian Alaniz .40 1.00
AB Andrew Brackman .60 1.50
AC Alex Cobb .40 1.00
AC Andrew Cashner AU 3.00 8.00
AH Anthony Hewitt AU 4.00 10.00
AJ Austin Jackson 2.00 5.00
AM Aaron Mathews .40 1.00
AMO Adam Moore AU 3.00 8.00
AR Aneury Rodriguez .60 1.50
BB Bubba Bell 1.00 2.50
BC Brett Cecil .60 1.50
BH Brandon Hicks .40 1.00
BHA Brad Hand AU 3.00 8.00
BP Buster Posey AU 40.00 100.00
BS Braeden Schlehuber .40 1.00
BW Brandon Waring .60 1.50
CB Charlie Blackmon AU 25.00 60.00
CC Carlos Carrasco Jsy AU 3.00 8.00
CGU Carlos Gutierrez AU 3.00 8.00
CI Cale Iorg .40 1.00
CJ Chris Johnson .60 1.50
CSA Carlos Santana AU 4.00 10.00
CT Chris Tillman AU 3.00 8.00
CV Chris Valaika .40 1.00
DC Daniel Cortes 1.00 2.50
DD Danny Duffy 1.00 2.50
DH David Hernandez AU 3.00 8.00
DS Daniel Schlereth AU 3.00 8.00
EA Elvis Andrus Jsy AU 4.00 10.00
EB Engel Beltre 1.25 3.00
EH Eric Hacker AU 3.00 8.00
EK Edward Kunz .60 1.50
FM Fernando Martinez Jsy AU 6.00 15.00
FS Fautino de los Santos .40 1.00
GB Gordon Beckham AU 4.00 10.00
GGH Gorkys Hernandez Jsy AU 5.00 12.00
GH Greg Halman AU 6.00 15.00
GP Gerardo Parra .40 1.00
GT Graham Taylor .40 1.00
IDA Ike Davis AU 5.00 12.00
JA Jake Arrieta Jsy AU 12.00 30.00
JB Jonathan Bachanov .40 1.00
JC Jhoulys Chacin .60 1.50
JD Jason Donald Jsy AU 5.00 12.00
JJ Jon Jay .60 1.50
JK Jason Knapp AU 3.00 8.00
JL Jeff Locke AU 3.00 8.00
JLC Jordan Czarniecki .40 1.00
JLI Josh Lindblom AU 3.00 8.00
JM Jake McGee .40 1.00
JM Jesus Montero Jsy AU 5.00 12.00
JR Javier Rodriguez AU 3.00 8.00
JS Justin Snyder .60 1.50
JSM Josh Smoker .40 1.00
JZ Jordan Zimmermann 1.00 2.50
KK Kala Kaaihue AU 3.00 8.00
KW Kenny Wilson .40 1.00
LA Lars Anderson AU 4.00 10.00
LC Lonnie Chisenhall AU 4.00 10.00
LL Lance Lynn AU 5.00 12.00
LM Logan Morrison 2.00 5.00
MB Mike Brantley 1.00 2.50
MC Mitch Canham .40 1.00
MD Michael Daniel .60 1.50
MI Matt Inouye .40 1.00
MM Mark Melancon AU 3.00 8.00
MR Matt Rizzotti .40 1.00
MW Michael Watt .40 1.00
NR Nick Romero .40 1.00
NV Niko Vasquez 1.00 2.50
PT Polin Trinidad AU 3.00 8.00
QM Quinton Miller AU 3.00 8.00
RK Ryan Kalish 1.00 2.50
RM Ryan Morris .60 1.50
RP Rick Porcello 1.25 3.00
RR Rusty Ryal .60 1.50
RT Rene Tosoni .40 1.00
SM Shairon Martis .60 1.50
ST Steve Tolleson .40 1.00
TF Tim Fedroff AU 3.00 8.00
TH Tom Hagan .40 1.00
VM Vin Mazzaro AU 3.00 8.00
XA Xavier Avery 1.00 2.50
YS Yunesky Sanchez .40 1.00
ZB Zach Britton 1.25 3.00

2008 Bowman Sterling Prospects Refractors

*PROS REF: 1X TO 2.5X BASIC
PROS REF ODDS 1:4 PACKS
*PROS AU REF: .75X TO 2X BASIC
PROS AU REF ODDS 1:5 PACKS
*PROS JSY AU REF: .75X TO 2X BASIC
PROS JSY AU REF ODDS 1:28 PACKS
REFRACTOR PRINT RUN 199 SER.#'d SETS
BP Buster Posey AU 75.00 150.00
RP Rick Porcello 15.00 40.00

2008 Bowman Sterling Prospects Gold Refractors

*PROS GLD: 3X TO 8X BASIC
RC GLD ODDS 1:15 PACKS
*PROS AU GLD: 2X TO 5X BASIC
PROS AU GLD ODDS 1:21 PACKS
*PROS JSY AU GLD: 1.5X TO 4X BASIC
PROS JSY AU GLD ODDS 1:113 PACKS
GOLD REF PRINT RUN 50 SER.#'d SETS
BP Buster Posey AU 175.00 350.00

2008 Bowman Sterling WBC Patch

STATED ODDS 1:24 PACKS
EXCHANGE DEADLIN 12/31/2009
1 Yu Darvish 125.00 250.00
2 Ichiro Suzuki 60.00 120.00
8 Chenhao Li 6.00 15.00
9 Xiaolian Zhang 10.00 25.00
10 Po Hsuan Keng 6.00 15.00
12 Yoennis Cespedes 150.00 300.00
16 Masahiro Tanaka 300.00 500.00
17 Gift Ngoepe• 6.00 15.00
18 Juan Carlos Sulbaran 6.00 15.00
22 Alexander Mayeta 6.00 15.00
NNO EXCH Card 50.00 100.00

2009 Bowman Sterling

COMMON CARD 1.00 2.50
COMMON AU 4.00 10.00
OVERALL AUTO ODDS TWO PER PACK
PRINTING PLATE ODDS 1:91 HOBBY
AU PRINTING PLATE ODDS 1:245 HOBBY
PLATE PRINT RUN 1 SET PER COLOR
BLACK-CYAN-MAGENTA-YELLOW ISSUED
NO PLATE PRICING DUE TO SCARCITY
AA Alex Avila RC 3.00 8.00
AB Antonio Bastardo AU RC 4.00 10.00
AB Andrew Bailey RC 2.50 6.00
AC Andrew Carpenter RC 1.50 4.00
AM Andrew McCutchen (RC) 5.00 12.00
BD Brian Duensing RC 1.50 4.00
BN Brad Nelson (RC) 1.00 2.50
BS Bobby Scales RC 1.50 4.00
CC Chris Coghlan RC 2.50 6.00
CM C.McGehee AU (RC) 1.00 2.50
CR Colby Rasmus (RC) 1.50 4.00
CT Chris Tillman AU RC 3.00 8.00
DB Daniel Bard RC 1.00 2.50
DF Dexter Fowler (RC) 1.50 4.00
DH David Hernandez RC 1.00 2.50
DP David Price RC 2.00 5.00
DS Daniel Schlereth AU RC 4.00 10.00
EC Everth Cabrera RC 1.50 4.00
EY Eric Young Jr. RC 1.00 2.50
FC Francisco Cervelli RC 2.50 6.00
FM Fernando Martinez RC 2.50 6.00
FN Fu-Te Ni RC 1.00 2.50
GB Gordon Beckham AU RC 4.00 10.00
GG Greg Golson (RC) 1.00 2.50
GK George Kottaras (RC) 1.00 2.50
GP Gerardo Parra RC 1.50 4.00
JB Julio Borbon RC 1.00 2.50
JC Jhoulys Chacin RC 1.50 4.00
JH Jarrett Hoffpauir (RC) 1.00 2.50
JM Justin Masterson AU (RC) 3.00 8.00
JM Juan Miranda RC 1.50 4.00
JS Jordan Schafer (RC) 1.50 4.00
JZ Jordan Zimmermann RC 2.50 6.00
KB Kyle Blanks RC 1.50 4.00
KK Kenshin Kawakami RC 1.50 4.00
KU Koji Uehara RC 2.50 6.00
MG Mat Gamel RC 2.50 6.00
ML Mat Latos RC 3.00 8.00
MM Mark Melancon RC 1.00 2.50
MS Michael Saunders RC 2.50 6.00
MT Matt Tuiasosopo (RC) 1.00 2.50
NR Nolan Reimold AU 6.00 15.00
NR Nolan Reimold (RC) 1.00 2.50
RP Ryan Perry AU RC 4.00 10.00
RP Rick Porcello RC 3.00 8.00
SR Shane Robinson RC 1.00 2.50
TC Trevor Crowe RC 1.00 2.50
TG Tyler Greene (RC) 1.00 2.50
TH Tommy Hanson AU RC 6.00 15.00
TS Travis Snider RC 1.50 4.00
WR Wilkin Ramirez RC 1.00 2.50
WV Will Venable RC 1.00 2.50
ABB Aaron Bates RC 1.00 2.50
CTT Carlos Torres RC 1.00 2.50
DFR David Freese RC 3.00 8.00
DHE Diory Hernandez RC 1.00 2.50
DHO Derek Holland RC 1.50 4.00
JHO Jamie Hoffmann RC 1.00 2.50
JMA John Mayberry Jr. (RC) 1.50 4.00

2009 Bowman Sterling Refractors

*REF: .5X TO 1.2X BASIC
REF ODDS 1:4 HOBBY
*REF AUTO: .5X TO 1.2X BASIC AUTO
REF AUTO ODDS 1:5 HOBBY
STATED PRINT RUN 199 SER.#'d SETS
CM Casey McGehee AU 4.00 10.00

2009 Bowman Sterling Gold Refractors
*GOLD REF: 1X TO 2.5X BASIC
GOLD REF ODDS 1:15 HOBBY
*GOLD REF AU: .75X TO 2X BASIC AU
GOLD REF AU ODDS 1:21 HOBBY
STATED PRINT RUN 50 SER.#'d SETS
CM Casey McGehee AU 5.00 12.00

2009 Bowman Sterling Dual Autographs
STATED ODDS 1:8 HOBBY
*REF: .5X TO 1.2 BASIC
REF.ODDS 1:27 HOBBY
REF. PRINT RUN 199 SER.#'d SETS
BLK REF ODDS 1:238 HOBBY
BLK REF PRINT RUN 25 SER.#'d SETS
NO BLACK PRICING DUE TO SCARCITY
*GLD REF: .75X TO 2X BASIC
GLD REF ODDS 1:111 HOBBY
GLD REF PRINT RUN 50 SER.#'d SETS
RED REF ODDS 1:4968 HOBBY
RED REF PRINT RUN 1 SER.#'d SETS
NO RED PRICING DUE TO SCARCITY
BPFC B.Posey/F.Cervelli 20.00 50.00
BPGB B.Posey/G.Beckham 20.00 50.00
CTDH C.Tillman/D.Hernandez 5.00 12.00
JKZC Jason Knapp/Zach Collier 5.00 12.00
JMFD J.Mejia/F.Doubront 5.00 12.00
NRJR N.Reimold/J.Reddick 6.00 15.00
RPCI Ryan Perry/Cale Iorg 5.00 12.00

2009 Bowman Sterling Prospects
OVERALL AUTO ODDS TWO PER PACK
PRINTING PLATE ODDS 1:91 HOBBY
AU PRINTING PLATE ODDS 1:245 HOBBY
PLATE PRINT RUN 1 SET PER COLOR
BLACK-CYAN-MAGENTA-YELLOW ISSUED
NO PLATE PRICING DUE TO SCARCITY
AA Abraham Almonte .75 2.00
AB Alex Buchholz 1.25 3.00
AF Alfredo Figaro .75 2.00
AM Adam Mills .75 2.00
AO Anthony Ortega .75 2.00
AP A.J. Pollock AU 6.00 15.00
AR Andrew Rundle 1.25 3.00
AS Alfredo Silverio .75 2.00
AW Alex White AU 3.00 8.00
BB Bobby Borchering AU 5.00 12.00
BB Brian Baisley .75 2.00
BO Brett Oberholtzer 1.25 3.00
BP Bryan Petersen .75 2.00
CA Carmen Angelini .75 2.00
CH Chris Heisey AU 6.00 15.00
CJ Chad Jenkins AU 3.00 8.00
CL C.J. Lee .75 2.00
CM Carlos Martinez 1.25 3.00
DA Denny Almonte 1.25 3.00
DH Daniel Hudson AU 4.00 10.00
DP Dinesh Patel AU 6.00 15.00
DS Drew Storen AU 3.00 8.00
DV Dayan Viciedo AU 3.00 8.00
EA Eric Arnett AU 3.00 8.00
EA Ehire Adrianza 2.00 5.00
EC Edilio Colina 1.25 3.00
EK Erik Komatsu 1.25 3.00
FG Freddy Galvis 1.25 3.00
GV Greg Veloz .75 2.00
JC Jose Ceda .75 2.00
JG Justin Greene 1.25 3.00
JM Jared Mitchell AU 4.00 10.00
JR Jovan Rosa .75 2.00
JT Julio Teheran 2.50 6.00
JW Jordan Walden 1.25 3.00
KK Kyeong Kang 1.25 3.00
LE Luis Exposito 2.00 5.00
LJ Luis Jimenez .75 2.00
LS Luis Sumoza 1.25 3.00
MA Michael Almanzar 1.25 3.00
MC Michael Cisco 1.25 3.00
MH Matt Hobgood AU 8.00 20.00
ML Mike Leake AU 6.00 15.00
MM Matthew Moore 6.00 15.00
MM Mike Minor AU 3.00 8.00
MP Michael Pineda 2.00 5.00
MS Michael Swinson 1.25 3.00
MT Mike Trout AU 2000.00 4000.00
NB Nick Buss .75 2.00
NP Nelson Perez 1.25 3.00
NR Neil Ramirez .75 2.00
OT Oscar Tejeda 2.50 6.00
PP Petey Paramore 1.25 3.00
PV Pat Venditte AU 3.00 8.00
RD Rashun Dixon 2.00 5.00
RF Reymond Fuentes AU 3.00 8.00
RG Robbie Grossman AU 3.00 8.00
RS Rinku Singh AU 6.00 15.00
RT Ruben Tejada .75 2.00
SC Scott Campbell AU 3.00 8.00
SP Stolmy Pimentel 1.25 3.00
SW Christopher Schwinden .75 2.00
TF Tyler Flowers 2.00 5.00
TM Tyler Matzek AU 3.00 8.00
TS Tony Sanchez AU 5.00 12.00
TW Tim Wheeler AU 3.00 8.00
TY Tyler Yockey 1.25 3.00
WF Wilmer Font .75 2.00
WR Wilin Rosario 1.25 3.00
WS Will Smith 1.25 3.00
ZW Zack Wheeler AU 4.00 10.00
CJA Chad James AU 4.00 10.00
CLU Chad Lundahl .75 2.00
JMM Jiovanni Mier AU 5.00 12.00
JMO Jon Mark Owings .75 2.00
MAF Michael Affronti .75 2.00
RGR Randal Grichuk AU 6.00 15.00
TME Tommy Mendonca AU 5.00 12.00

2009 Bowman Sterling Prospects Refractors
*REF: .5X TO 1.2X BASIC
REF ODDS 1:4 HOBBY
*REF AUTO: .5X TO 1.2X BASIC AUTO
REF AUTO ODDS 1:5 HOBBY
STATED PRINT RUN 199 SER.#'d SETS
MT Mike Trout AU 2000.00 3000.00

2009 Bowman Sterling Prospects Gold Refractors
*GOLD REF: 1.5X TO 4X BASIC
GOLD REF ODDS 1:15 HOBBY
*GOLD REF AU: .6X TO 1.5X BASIC AU
GOLD REF AU ODDS 1:21 HOBBY
STATED PRINT RUN 50 SER.#'d SETS
MT Mike Trout AU 6000.00 8000.00

2009 Bowman Sterling WBC Relics
STATED ODDS ONE PER PACK
AC Aroldis Chapman 10.00 25.00
AM Alexander Mayeta 3.00 8.00
AO Adam Ottavino 3.00 8.00
AS Alexander Smit 3.00 8.00
BW Bernie Williams 3.00 8.00
CL Chenhao Li 3.00 8.00
CR Concepcion Rodriguez 3.00 8.00
DL Dae Ho Lee 4.00 10.00
DN Drew Naylor 3.00 8.00
EG Edgar Gonzalez 3.00 8.00
FC Frederich Cepeda 3.00 8.00
FF Fei Feng 3.00 8.00
FN Fu-Te Ni 5.00 12.00
GH Greg Halman 3.00 8.00
HC Hung-Wen Chen 3.00 8.00
HO Hein Robb 3.00 8.00
HR Hanley Ramirez 3.00 8.00
IS Ichiro Suzuki 10.00 25.00
JC Johnny Cueto 3.00 8.00
JE Justin Erasmus 3.00 8.00
JL Jae Woo Lee 3.00 8.00
JS Juancarlos Sulbaran 3.00 8.00
KF Kosuke Fukudome 5.00 12.00
KK Kwang-Hyun Kim 4.00 10.00
KL Kai Liu 3.00 8.00
LH Luke Hughes 3.00 8.00
LR Luis Rodriguez 3.00 8.00
MC Miguel Cabrera 3.00 8.00
MD Mitchell Dening 3.00 8.00
ME Michel Enriquez 3.00 8.00
MT Miguel Tejada 3.00 8.00
NA Norichika Aoki 6.00 15.00
NP Nick Punto 3.00 8.00
NW Nick Weglarz 3.00 8.00
PA Phillippe Aumont 5.00 12.00
PK Po-Hsuan Keng 3.00 8.00
PM Pedro Martinez 3.00 8.00
RM Russell Martin 3.00 8.00
SA Shinnosuke Abe 5.00 12.00
SC Shin-Soo Choo 5.00 12.00
TK Tae Kyun Kim 4.00 10.00
XZ Xiaotian Zhang 3.00 8.00
YC Yoennis Cespedes 10.00 25.00
YD Yu Darvish 10.00 25.00
YG Yulieski Gourriel 3.00 8.00
HRR Hyun-Jin Ryu 8.00 20.00
JCC Jorge Cantu 3.00 8.00
JLL Jin Young Lee 4.00 10.00
LHH Liam Hendriks 3.00 8.00

2009 Bowman Sterling WBC Relics Refractors
*REF: .5X TO 1.2X BASIC
REF ODDS 1:5 HOBBY
REF PRINT RUN 199 SER.#'d SETS

2009 Bowman Sterling WBC Relics Blue Refractors
*BLUE REF: .5X TO 1.2X BASIC
BLUE REF ODDS ONE PER BOX LOADER
BLUE PRINT RUN 125 SER.#'d SETS
FN Fu-Te Ni 12.50 30.00

2009 Bowman Sterling WBC Relics Gold Refractors
*GOLD REF: .75X TO 2X BASIC
GOLD REF ODDS 1:21 HOBBY
GOLD REF PRINT RUN 50 SER.#'d SETS
FN Fu-Te Ni 30.00 60.00

2010 Bowman Sterling

COMMON CARD .60 1.50
PRINTING PLATE ODDS 1:105 HOBBY
1 Stephen Strasburg RC 5.00 12.00
2 Josh Bell (RC) .60 1.50
3 Starlin Castro RC 1.50 4.00
4 J.P. Arencibia RC 1.25 3.00
5 Brennan Boesch RC 1.50 4.00
6 Ike Davis RC 1.25 3.00
7 Madison Bumgarner RC 5.00 12.00
8 Austin Jackson RC 1.00 2.50
9 Andrew Cashner RC .60 1.50
10 Jose Tabata RC 1.00 2.50
11 Wade Davis (RC) 1.00 2.50
12 Felix Doubront RC .60 1.50
13 Mike Leake RC 2.00 5.00
14 Logan Morrison RC 1.00 2.50
15 Brian Matusz RC 1.50 4.00
16 Trevor Plouffe (RC) 1.50 4.00
17 Mike Stanton RC 5.00 12.00
18 Drew Storen RC 1.00 2.50
19 Tyler Colvin RC 1.00 2.50
20 Jason Heyward RC 2.50 6.00
21 Jake Arrieta RC 1.50 4.00
22 Daniel Hudson RC 1.00 2.50
23 Buster Posey RC 5.00 12.00
24 Neil Walker (RC) 1.00 2.50
25 Carlos Santana RC 2.00 5.00
26 Josh Thole RC 1.00 2.50
27 Dayan Viciedo RC 1.00 2.50
28 Wilson Ramos RC 1.50 4.00
29 Ian Desmond (RC) 1.00 2.50
30 John Ely RC .60 1.50
31 Daniel Nava RC .60 1.50
32 Chris Nelson (RC) 1.00 2.50
33 Andy Oliver RC .60 1.50
34 Danny Valencia RC 4.00 10.00
35 Brad Lincoln RC 1.00 2.50
36 Domonic Brown RC 2.50 6.00
37 Jay Sborz (RC) .60 1.50
38 Daniel McCutchen RC 1.00 2.50
39 Eric Young Jr. (RC) .60 1.50
40 Peter Bourjos RC 1.00 2.50
41 Drew Stubbs RC 1.50 4.00
42 Chris Heisey RC 1.00 2.50
43 Jason Castro RC 1.50 4.00
44 Jason Donald RC .60 1.50
45 Ruben Tejada RC 1.00 2.50
46 Jon Jay RC 1.00 2.50
47 Travis Wood (RC) 1.00 2.50
48 Ryan Kalish RC 1.00 2.50
49 Mike Minor RC 1.00 2.50
50 Brett Wallace RC 1.50 4.00

2010 Bowman Sterling Refractors

*REF: 1.2X TO 3X BASIC
STATED ODDS 1:5 HOBBY
STATED PRINT RUN 199 SER.#'d SETS

2010 Bowman Sterling Gold Refractors
*GOLD REF: 2X TO 5X BASIC
STATED ODDS 1:17 HOBBY
STATED PRINT RUN 50 SER.#'d SETS

2010 Bowman Sterling Dual Relics
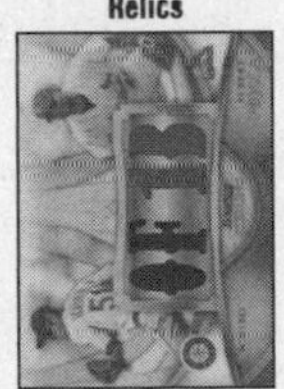

STATED PRINT RUN 199 SER.#'d SETS
BL1 A.Pujols/M.Cabrera 6.00 15.00
BL2 D.Jeter/H.Ramirez 8.00 20.00
BL3 Joe Mauer/Brian McCann 4.00 10.00
BL4 A.Rodriguez/E.Longoria 8.00 20.00
BL5 R.Braun/J.Upton 5.00 12.00
BL6 Prince Fielder/Pablo Sandoval 4.00 10.00
BL7 R.Halladay/C.Lee 8.00 20.00
BL8 Josh Hamilton/Nelson Cruz 4.00 10.00
BL9 J.Heyward/M.Stanton 6.00 15.00
BL10 I.Suzuki/A.Pujols 10.00 25.00
BL11 Adrian Gonzalez/Justin Morneau 4.00 10.00
BL12 D.Pedroia/K.Youkilis 5.00 12.00
BL13 Mark Teixeira/Chipper Jones 4.00 10.00
BL14 C.Utley/R.Cano 5.00 12.00
BL15 D.Wright/R.Zimmerman 5.00 12.00
BL16 Jimmy Rollins/Ryan Howard 4.00 10.00
BL17 S.Strasburg/J.Heyward 4.00 10.00
BL18 T.Tulowitzki/C.Gonzalez 5.00 12.00
BL19 D.Jeter/A.Rodriguez 10.00 25.00

2010 Bowman Sterling Dual Relics Refractors
*REF: .5X TO 1.2X BASIC
STATED ODDS 1:4 BOXES
STATED PRINT RUN 99 SER.#'d SETS

2010 Bowman Sterling Dual Relics Gold Refractors
*GOLD REF: .6X TO 1.5X BASIC
STATED ODDS 1:8 BOXES
STATED PRINT RUN 50 SER.#'d SETS

2010 Bowman Sterling Prospect Autographs
RANDOM INSERTS IN PACKS
PRINTING PLATE ODDS 1:250 HOBBY
AC Aroldis Chapman 8.00 20.00
AM Aaron Miller 4.00 10.00
AW Alex Wimmers 3.00 8.00
CB Chad Bettis 3.00 8.00
CR Chance Ruffin 3.00 8.00
CS Chris Sale 10.00 25.00
CY Christian Yelich 60.00 150.00
DD Delino DeShields 4.00 10.00
DM Deck McGuire 3.00 8.00
DP Drew Pomeranz 3.00 8.00
GB Gary Brown 5.00 12.00
HS Hayden Simpson 4.00 10.00
JB Jesse Biddle 6.00 15.00
JS John Singleton 4.00 10.00
JS Jake Skole 4.00 10.00
JT Jameson Taillon 6.00 15.00
JW Justin Wilson 3.00 8.00
KD Kellin Deglan 3.00 8.00
MF Mike Foltynewicz 3.00 8.00
ML Matt Lipka 6.00 15.00
MO Mike Olt 3.00 8.00
PT Peter Tago 3.00 8.00
RL Ryan Lavarnway 3.00 8.00
SB Seth Blair 3.00 8.00
TB Tim Beckham 6.00 15.00
TJ Tyrell Jenkins 3.00 8.00
TL Taylor Lindsey 3.00 8.00
YG Yasmani Grandal 4.00 10.00
ZL Zach Lee 5.00 12.00
CCO Christian Colon 3.00 8.00
CPU Cesar Puello 3.00 8.00
RBO Ryan Bolden 3.00 8.00
TWA Taijuan Walker 3.00 8.00

2010 Bowman Sterling Prospect Autographs Refractors
*REF: .75X TO 2X BASIC
STATED ODDS 1:6 HOBBY
STATED PRINT RUN 199 SER.#'d SETS

2010 Bowman Sterling Prospect Autographs Gold Refractors
*GOLD REF: 1.2X TO 3X BASIC
STATED ODDS 1:21 HOBBY
STATED PRINT RUN 50 SER.#'d SETS

2010 Bowman Sterling Prospects

PRINTING PLATE ODDS 1:105 HOBBY
AA Alexia Amarista .50 1.25
AC Aroldis Chapman 2.00 5.00
AD Allan Dykstra .50 1.25
AH Adeinis Hechavarria .50 1.25
AR Anthony Rizzo 6.00 15.00
AV Arodys Vizcaino 1.25 3.00
BJ Brett Jackson 1.50 4.00
BM Bryan Mitchell .50 1.25
BO Brett Oberholtzer .50 1.25
BS Brandon Short .50 1.25
CA Chris Archer 1.50 4.00
CJ Corban Joseph .50 1.25
CM Chris Masters .50 1.25
CP Carlos Peguero .75 2.00
DA Dustin Ackley .75 2.00
DC Drew Cumberland .50 1.25
DF Daniel Fields .50 1.25
DT Donavan Tate .50 1.25
GG Grant Green .50 1.25
GS Gary Sanchez 15.00 40.00
HL Hak-Ju Lee .75 2.00
JH J.J. Hoover .50 1.25
JI Jose Iglesias .50 1.25
JL John Lamb 1.25 3.00
JM J.D. Martinez 5.00 12.00
JS John Singleton 1.25 3.00
KG Kyle Gibson 2.00 5.00
KS Konrad Schmidt .50 1.25
MD Matt Davidson 1.50 4.00
MP Martin Perez 1.25 3.00
MS Miguel Sano 3.00 8.00
NA Nolan Arenado 10.00 25.00
RB Rex Brothers .50 1.25
RE Robbie Erlin 1.25 3.00
SH Steven Hensley .50 1.25
SM Shelby Miller 2.50 6.00
SV Sebastian Valle .75 2.00
TB Tim Beckham 2.00 5.00
TC Tyler Chatwood .50 1.25
TN Thomas Neal .75 2.00
WM Wil Myers .75 2.00
YA Yonder Alonso 1.25 3.00
CPU Cesar Puello .50 1.25
FPE Francisco Peguero .50 1.25
JOS Josh Satin .75 2.00
JRM J.R. Murphy .75 2.00
JSA Jerry Sands 1.25 3.00
JSE Jean Segura 2.50 6.00
MKE Max Kepler 1.50 4.00
WMI Will Middlebrooks .75 2.00

2010 Bowman Sterling Prospects Refractors

*REF: 1X TO 2.5X BASIC
STATED ODDS 1:5 HOBBY
STATED PRINT RUN 199 SER.#'d SETS

2010 Bowman Sterling Prospects Gold Refractors
*GOLD REF: 1.5X TO 4X BASIC
STATED ODDS 1:17 HOBBY
STATED PRINT RUN 50 SER.#'d SETS
SM Shelby Miller 15.00 40.00

2010 Bowman Sterling Rookie Autographs

STATED ODDS 1:
STRASBURG ODDS 1:25 HOBBY
EXCHANGE DEADLINE 12/31/2013
PRINTING PLATE ODDS 1:250 HOBBY
STRASBURG PLATE ODDS 1:10,014 HOBBY
1 Stephen Strasburg 30.00 80.00
10 Jose Tabata 4.00 10.00
20 Jason Heyward 6.00 15.00
22 Daniel Hudson 4.00 10.00
25 Carlos Santana 4.00 10.00
34 Danny Valencia 4.00 10.00
36 Domonic Brown 4.00 10.00
43 Josh Tomlin 4.00 10.00
46 Jon Jay 4.00 10.00
47 Travis Wood 4.00 10.00

2010 Bowman Sterling Rookie Autographs Refractors
*REF: .5X TO 1.2X BASIC
STATED ODDS 1:6 HOBBY
STRASBURG ODDS 1:212 HOBBY
STATED PRINT RUN 199 SER.#'d SETS
EXCHANGE DEADLINE 12/31/2013

2010 Bowman Sterling Rookie Autographs Gold Refractors
*GOLD: 1.2X TO 3X BASIC
STATED ODDS 1:21 HOBBY
STRASBURG ODDS 1:852 HOBBY
STATED PRINT RUN 50 SER.#'d SETS
EXCHANGE DEADLINE 12/31/2013

2010 Bowman Sterling USA Baseball Autograph Relics Red
STATED ODDS 1:976 HOBBY
STATED PRINT RUN 1 SER.#'d SET

2010 Bowman Sterling USA Baseball Dual Autographs
NATIONAL TEAM ODDS 1:27 HOBBY
18U TEAM ODDS 1:18 HOBBY
PRINTING PLATE ODDS 1:494 HOBBY
BSDA1 Tony Wolters/Nicky Delmonico 4.00 10.00
BSDA2 P.Pfeifer/H.Owens 8.00 20.00
BSDA3 C.Lopes/F.Lindor 6.00 15.00
BSDA4 B.Starling/L.McCullers 4.00 10.00
BSDA5 B.Swihart/D.Camarena 10.00 25.00
BSDA6 Dillon Maples/A.J. Vanegas 4.00 10.00
BSDA7 M.Lorenzen/C.Montgomery 4.00 10.00
BSDA8 A.Almora/M.Littlewood 4.00 10.00
BSDA9 John Hochstatter/Brian Ragira 4.00 10.00
BSDA10 John Simms/Elvin Soto 4.00 10.00
BSDA11 M.Barnes/B.Miller 6.00 15.00
BSDA12 G.Cole/J.Bradley Jr. 12.00 30.00
BSDA13 S.Gray/G.Springer 12.00 30.00
BSDA14 Ryan Wright/Nolan Fontana 4.00 10.00
BSDA15 Andrew Maggi/Kyle Winkler 4.00 10.00
BSDA16 P.O'Brien/A.Dickerson 10.00 25.00
BSDA17 Jason Esposito/Sean Gilmartin 4.00 10.00
BSDA18 Nick Ramirez/Steve Rodriguez 4.00 10.00
BSDA19 T.Anderson/S.McGough 4.00 10.00
BSDA20 Noe Ramirez/Brett Mooneyham 4.00 10.00
BSDA21 M.Mahtook/B.Johnson 6.00 15.00

2010 Bowman Sterling USA Baseball Dual Autographs Refractors
*REF: .5X TO 1.2X BASIC
STATED ODDS 1:21 HOBBY
STATED PRINT RUN 99 SER.#'d SETS

2010 Bowman Sterling USA Baseball Dual Autographs Gold Refractors
*GOLD REF: .75X TO 2X BASIC
STATED ODDS 1:42 HOBBY
STATED PRINT RUN 50 SER.#'d SETS

2010 Bowman Sterling USA Baseball Relics

RANDOM INSERTS IN PACKS
USAR1 Albert Almora 2.50 6.00
USAR2 Daniel Camarena 2.50 6.00
USAR3 Nicky Delmonico 2.50 6.00
USAR4 John Hochstatter 2.50 6.00
USAR5 Francisco Lindor 4.00 10.00
USAR6 Marcus Littlewood 2.50 6.00
USAR7 Christian Lopes 2.50 6.00
USAR8 Michael Lorenzen 2.50 6.00
USAR9 Dillon Maples 2.50 6.00
USAR10 Lance McCullers 2.50 6.00
USAR11 Ricardo Jacquez 2.50 6.00
USAR12 Henry Owens 2.50 6.00
USAR13 Phillip Pfeifer 2.50 6.00
USAR14 Brian Ragira 2.50 6.00
USAR15 John Simms 2.50 6.00
USAR16 Elvin Soto 2.50 6.00
USAR17 Bubba Starling 3.00 8.00
USAR18 Blake Swihart 2.50 6.00
USAR19 A.J. Vanegas 2.50 6.00
USAR20 Tony Wolters 2.50 6.00
USAR21 Tyler Anderson 2.50 6.00
USAR22 Matt Barnes 3.00 8.00
USAR23 Jackie Bradley Jr. 3.00 8.00
USAR24 Gerrit Cole 4.00 10.00
USAR25 Alex Dickerson 2.50 6.00
USAR26 Jason Esposito 2.50 6.00
USAR27 Nolan Fontana 2.50 6.00
USAR28 Sean Gilmartin 2.50 6.00
USAR29 Sonny Gray 2.50 6.00
USAR30 Brian Johnson 2.50 6.00
USAR31 Andrew Maggi 2.50 6.00
USAR32 Mikie Mahtook 2.50 6.00
USAR33 Scott McGough 2.50 6.00
USAR34 Brad Miller 2.50 6.00
USAR35 Brett Mooneyham 2.50 6.00
USAR36 Peter O'Brien 2.50 6.00
USAR37 Nick Ramirez 2.50 6.00
USAR38 Noe Ramirez 2.50 6.00
USAR39 Steve Rodriguez 2.50 6.00
USAR40 George Springer 6.00 15.00
USAR41 Kyle Winkler 2.50 6.00
USAR42 Ryan Wright 2.50 6.00

2010 Bowman Sterling USA Baseball Relics Refractors

*REF: .5X TO 1.2X BASIC
STATED ODDS 1:6 HOBBY
STATED PRINT RUN 99 SER.#'d SETS

2010 Bowman Sterling USA Baseball Relics Gold Refractors
*GOLD REF: .6X TO 1.5X BASIC
STATED ODDS 1:22 HOBBY
STATED PRINT RUN 50 SER.#'d SETS

2011 Bowman Sterling

COMMON CARD .60 1.50
PRINTING PLATES RANDOMLY INSERTED
PLATE PRINT RUN 1 SET PER COLOR
BLACK-CYAN-MAGENTA-YELLOW ISSUED
NO PLATE PRICING DUE TO SCARCITY
1 Freddie Freeman RC 10.00 25.00
2 Al Alburquerque RC .60 1.50
3 Salvador Perez RC 2.50 6.00
4 Ryan Lavarnway RC 2.50 6.00
5 Jason Kipnis RC 2.00 5.00
6 Arodys Vizcaino RC 1.00 2.50
7 Chance Ruffin RC .60 1.50
8 Dee Gordon RC 1.00 2.50
9 Mike Moustakas RC 1.50 4.00
10 Johnny Giavotella RC .60 1.50
11 Dustin Ackley RC 1.00 2.50
12 Chase d'Arnaud RC .60 1.50
13 Jimmy Paredes RC 1.50 4.00
14 Fautino De Los Santos RC .60 1.50
15 Jose Altuve RC 20.00 50.00
16 Brandon Beachy RC 1.50 4.00
17 Trayvon Robinson (RC) 1.00 2.50
18 Mark Trumbo (RC) 1.50 4.00
19 Jacob Turner RC 2.50 6.00
20 Anthony Rizzo RC 6.00 15.00
21 Kyle Weiland RC .60 1.50
22 Mike Trout RC 400.00 800.00
23 Ben Revere RC 1.00 2.50
24 Hector Noesi RC 1.00 2.50
25 Danny Duffy RC 1.00 2.50
26 Juan Nicasio RC .60 1.50
27 Paul Goldschmidt RC 20.00 50.00
28 Tyler Chatwood RC .60 1.50
29 Eric Thames RC 3.00 8.00
30 Yonder Alonso RC 1.00 2.50
31 Todd Frazier RC 2.00 5.00
32 Andy Dirks RC 1.50 4.00
33 Javy Guerra (RC) 1.00 2.50
34 Michael Stutes RC 1.00 2.50
35 Michael Pineda RC 1.50 4.00
36 Aaron Crow RC 1.00 2.50
37 Alexi Ogando RC 1.50 4.00
38 Alex Cobb RC .60 1.50
39 Brandon Belt RC 1.50 4.00
40 Lonnie Chisenhall RC 1.00 2.50
41 Zach Britton RC 1.50 4.00
42 Jordan Walden RC .60 1.50
43 Jose Iglesias RC 1.00 2.50
44 Julio Teheran RC 1.00 2.50
45 Desmond Jennings RC 1.00 2.50
46 Blake Beavan RC 1.00 2.50
47 Craig Kimbrel RC 1.50 4.00
48 Eric Hosmer RC 4.00 10.00
49 Jerry Sands RC 1.50 4.00
50 Kyle Seager RC 1.50 4.00

2011 Bowman Sterling Refractors
*REF: .75X TO 2X BASIC
STATED ODDS 1:8
STATED PRINT RUN 199 SER.#'d SETS
22 Mike Trout 500.00 1000.00

2011 Bowman Sterling Gold Refractors
*GOLD REF: 2.5X TO 6X BASIC
STATED ODDS 1:31
STATED PRINT RUN 50 SER.#'d SETS
22 Mike Trout 600.00 1200.00

2011 Bowman Sterling Dual Autographs
STATED ODDS 1:10
PRINT RUNS B/WN 225-299 COPIES PER
PRINTING PLATE ODDS 1:703
PLATE PRINT RUN 1 SET PER COLOR
BLACK-CYAN-MAGENTA-YELLOW ISSUED
NO PLATE PRICING DUE TO SCARCITY
EXCHANGE DEADLINE 12/31/2014
AB M.Appel/D.Baxendale 6.00 15.00
AW A.Almora/M.White 8.00 20.00
BC A.Bregman/G.Cecchini 15.00 40.00
DC D.Duffy/A.Crow 4.00 10.00
DW D.Dahl/J.Winker 6.00 15.00
EL Chris Elder
Michael Lorenzen 4.00 10.00
EN J.Elander/T.Naquin 6.00 15.00
FF Dominic Ficociello
Nolan Fontana 4.00 10.00
GJ K.Gausman/B.Johnson 6.00 15.00
ID Cole Irvin
Chase DeJong 4.00 10.00
KG C.Kelly/J.Gallo 6.00 15.00
KK Branden Kline
Corey Knebel 4.00 10.00
LM David Lyon
Tom Murphy 4.00 10.00
MM Hoby Milner
Andrew Mitchell 4.00 10.00
MR D.Marrero/M.Reynolds 4.00 10.00
OC Chris Okey
Troy Conyers 4.00 10.00
OH A.Ogando/M.Hamburger 4.00 10.00
RH B.Revere/L.Hendriks 5.00 12.00
RM N.Rodriguez/J.Martinez 6.00 15.00
RW B.Rodgers/M.Wacha 4.00 10.00
SD J.Sands/R.De La Rosa 6.00 15.00
SP Clate Schmidt
Cody Poteet 4.00 10.00
SW M.Stroman/E.Weiss 4.00 10.00
TB M.Trumbo/B.Belt 6.00 15.00
TBE J.Teheran/B.Beachy 10.00 25.00
TR E.Thames/B.Revere 20.00 50.00
VW H.Virant/W.Weickel 4.00 10.00

2011 Bowman Sterling Dual Autographs Refractors
*REF: .5X TO 1.2X BASIC
STATED ODDS 1:29
STATED PRINT RUN 99 SER.#'d SETS
EXCHANGE DEADLINE 12/31/2014

2011 Bowman Sterling Dual Autographs Black Refractors
STATED ODDS 1:112
STATED PRINT RUN 25 SER.#'d SETS
NO PRICING DUE TO SCARCITY
EXCHANGE DEADLINE 12/31/2014

2011 Bowman Sterling Dual Autographs Gold Refractors
*GOLD REF: .6X TO 1.5X BASIC
STATED ODDS 1:57
STATED PRINT RUN 50 SER.#'d SETS
EXCHANGE DEADLINE 12/31/2014

2011 Bowman Sterling Dual Relics
STATED ODDS 1:1 BOXES
PRINT RUNS B/WN 54-246 PER

AE Dustin Ackley/Danny Espinosa 4.00 10.00
BD Zach Britton/Danny Duffy 4.00 10.00
BF Ryan Braun/Prince Fielder 5.00 12.00
BH Brandon Beachy/Tommy Hanson 6.00 15.00
BJ Zach Britton/Adam Jones 5.00 12.00
CB Starlin Castro/Darwin Barney 6.00 15.00
CD Aaron Crow/Danny Duffy 4.00 10.00
FH F.Freeman/J.Heyward 6.00 15.00
GC C.Granderson/R.Cano 5.00 12.00
GG Curtis Granderson
Carlos Gonzalez/246 4.00 10.00
GJ Curtis Granderson/Adam Jones 4.00 10.00
GK D.Gordon/M.Kemp 6.00 15.00
GS Carlos Gonzalez/Mike Stanton 5.00 12.00
HM E.Hsmer/M.Mustakas 8.00 20.00
HP F.Hernandez/M.Pineda 5.00 12.00
JN D.Jeter/E.Nunez/54 10.00 25.00
MC Mike Moustakas/Lonnie Chisenhall 4.00 10.00
OF Alexi Ogando/Neftali Feliz 4.00 10.00
PB B.Posey/B.Belt 6.00 15.00
PBR Michael Pineda/Zach Britton 4.00 10.00
PH David Price/Jeremy Hellickson 5.00 12.00
PH David Price/Felix Hernandez 4.00 10.00
PHO A.Pujols/M.Holliday 5.00 12.00
PJ David Price/Desmond Jennings 4.00 10.00
SC Carlos Santana/Lonnie Chisenhall 4.00 10.00
SR Mike Stanton/Hanley Ramirez 4.00 10.00
SS Chris Sale/Sergio Santos 4.00 10.00
TC Mark Trumbo/Hank Conger 6.00 15.00
TG Troy Tulowitzki/Carlos Gonzalez 6.00 15.00
VH J.Verlander/R.Halladay 5.00 12.00
WC Jered Weaver/Tyler Chatwood 4.00 10.00
WK Jordan Walden/Craig Kimbrel 4.00 10.00
WW Rickie Weeks/Jemile Weeks 4.00 10.00
ZE Ryan Zimmerman/Danny Espinosa 4.00 10.00

2011 Bowman Sterling Dual Relics Refractors

*REF: .5X TO 1.2X BASIC
STATED PRINT RUNS B/WN 25-99
STATED ODDS 1:4 BOXES
NO PRICING ON QTY 25

2011 Bowman Sterling Dual Relics Gold Refractors

*GOLD REF: .6X TO 1.5X BASIC
STATED PRINT RUN 50 SER.#'d SETS
STATED ODDS 1:8 BOXES
JN Derek Jeter 10.00 25.00
Eduardo Nunez

2011 Bowman Sterling Prospect Autographs

STATED ODDS 1:20
PRINTING PLATE ODDS 1:260
PLATE PRINT RUN 1 SET PER COLOR
BLACK-CYAN-MAGENTA-YELLOW ISSUED
NO PLATE PRICING DUE TO SCARCITY
EXCHANGE DEADLINE 12/31/2014
AB Archie Bradley 3.00 8.00
AH Aaron Hicks 5.00 12.00
BB Bryce Brentz 3.00 *8.00
BHO Bryan Holaday 3.00 8.00
BM Brandon Martin 3.00 8.00
BN Brandon Nimmo 4.00 10.00
BS Blake Snell 10.00 25.00
BST Bubba Starling 5.00 12.00
BSW Blake Swihart 4.00 10.00
CB Charles Brewer 3.00 8.00
CC Collin Cowgill 3.00 8.00
CCR C.J. Cron 3.00 8.00
CS Cory Spangenberg 3.00 8.00
CW Christopher Wallace 3.00 8.00
DBU Dylan Bundy 4.00 10.00
DV Dan Vogelbach 5.00 12.00
FL Francisco Lindor 20.00 50.00
GG Garrett Gould 3.00 8.00
GS George Springer 15.00 40.00
JB Javier Baez 30.00 80.00
JB Jed Bradley 3.00 8.00
JF Jose Fernandez 6.00 15.00
JH Jake Hager 3.00 8.00
JHA James Harris 3.00 8.00
JK Jake Skole 3.00 8.00
JP Joe Panik 5.00 12.00
KC Kyle Crick 3.00 8.00
KM Kevin Matthews 3.00 8.00
KW Kolten Wong 4.00 10.00
KWA Keenyn Walker 3.00 8.00
LG Larry Greene 3.00 8.00
MB Manny Banuelos 4.00 10.00
MBA Matt Barnes 3.00 8.00
MF Michael Fulmer 5.00 12.00
MG Mychal Givens 3.00 8.00
MMO Matt Moore 4.00 10.00
RS Robert Stephenson 3.00 8.00
SG Sonny Gray 4.00 10.00
SGI Sean Gilmartin 4.00 10.00
SM Starling Marte 4.00 10.00
TA Tyler Anderson 3.00 8.00
TB Trevor Bauer 10.00 25.00
TG Tyler Goeddel 3.00 8.00
TGU Taylor Guerrieri 3.00 8.00
TH Travis Harrison 3.00 8.00
TJ Taylor Jungmann 4.00 10.00
TS Trevor Story 40.00 100.00
ZC Zach Cone 3.00 8.00
ZL Zach Lee 3.00 8.00

2011 Bowman Sterling Prospect Autographs Refractors

*REF: .5X TO 1.5X BASIC
STATED ODDS 1:6
STATED PRINT RUN 199 SER.#'d SETS
HARPER PRINT RUN 109 SER.#'d SETS
EXCHANGE DEADLINE 12/31/2014
BH Bryce Harper/109 300.00 500.00

2011 Bowman Sterling Prospect Autographs Gold Refractors

*GOLD REF: 1.5X TO 4X BASIC
STATED ODDS 1:21
STATED PRINT RUN 50 SER.#'d SETS
EXCHANGE DEADLINE 12/31/2014
BH Bryce Harper 500.00 700.00

2011 Bowman Sterling Prospects

PRINTING PLATES RANDOMLY INSERTED
PLATE PRINT RUN 1 SET PER COLOR
BLACK-CYAN-MAGENTA-YELLOW ISSUED
NO PLATE PRICING DUE TO SCARCITY
1 Bryce Harper 25.00 60.00
2 Shelby Miller 3.00 8.00
3 Jesus Montero .60 1.50
4 Manny Banuelos 1.50 4.00
5 Wil Myers 1.00 2.50
6 Aaron Hicks 1.00 2.50
7 Matt Moore 1.50 4.00
8 Jameson Taillon 1.00 2.50
9 Manny Machado 6.00 15.00
10 Jonathan Singleton 1.00 2.50
11 Devin Mesoraco 1.50 4.00
12 John Lamb .60 1.50
13 Blake Snell 2.50 6.00
14 Gary Sanchez 3.00 8.00
15 Brett Jackson 1.00 2.50
16 Zack Wheeler 2.00 5.00
17 Jean Segura 2.50 6.00
18 Wilmer Flores 1.00 2.50
19 Miguel Sano 1.25 3.00
20 Larry Greene 1.00 2.50
21 Chris Archer 1.25 3.00
22 Travis d'Arnaud 1.00 2.50
23 George Springer 4.00 10.00
24 Trevor Story 8.00 20.00
25 Jarrod Parker 1.50 4.00
26 Christian Colon .60 1.50
27 Dellin Betances 1.50 4.00
28 Tony Sanchez 1.00 2.50
29 Billy Hamilton 1.25 3.00
30 Tyler Goeddel .60 1.50
31 Dante Bichette 1.00 2.50
32 Trevor Bauer 6.00 15.00
33 Cory Spangenberg 1.00 2.50
34 Javier Baez 8.00 20.00
35 C.J. Cron 2.00 5.00
36 Sonny Gray 1.50 4.00
37 Jake Hager .60 1.50
38 James Harris .60 1.50
39 Brandon Martin 1.00 2.50
40 Joe Panik 1.50 4.00
41 Robert Stephenson 1.25 3.00
42 Jose Fernandez 2.50 6.00
43 Kolten Wong 1.00 2.50
44 Taylor Jungmann 1.00 2.50
45 Francisco Lindor 6.00 15.00
46 Matt Barnes 1.00 2.50
47 Brandon Nimmo 3.00 8.00
48 Bubba Starling 1.00 2.50
49 Dan Vogelbach 2.00 5.00
50 Kevin Matthews .60 1.50

2011 Bowman Sterling Prospects Refractors

*REF: .75X TO 2X BASIC
STATED ODDS 1:8
STATED PRINT RUN 199 SER.#'d SETS

2011 Bowman Sterling Prospects Gold Refractors

*GOLD REF: 2X TO 5X BASIC
STATED ODDS 1:31
STATED PRINT RUN 50 SER.#'d SETS

2011 Bowman Sterling Rookie Autographs

GROUP A STATED ODDS 1:18
GROUP B STATED ODDS 1:10
GROUP C STATED ODDS 1:4
PRINTING PLATE ODDS 1:260
PLATE PRINT RUN 1 SET PER COLOR
BLACK-CYAN-MAGENTA-YELLOW ISSUED
NO PLATE PRICING DUE TO SCARCITY
EXCHANGE DEADLINE 12/31/2014
1 Michael Pineda 3.00 8.00
2 Hector Noesi 3.00 8.00
3 Jerry Sands 3.00 8.00
4 Anthony Rizzo 20.00 50.00
5 Julio Teheran 4.00 10.00
6 Eric Hosmer 20.00 50.00
7 Freddie Freeman 25.00 60.00
8 Dustin Ackley 3.00 8.00
9 Kyle Seager 5.00 12.00
10 Danny Duffy 3.00 8.00
11 Aaron Crow 3.00 8.00
12 Nathan Eovaldi 3.00 8.00
13 Mike Moustakas 12.00 30.00
14 Alex Cobb 3.00 8.00
15 Dee Gordon 4.00 10.00
16 Rubby De La Rosa 3.00 8.00
17 Ben Revere 3.00 8.00
18 Alex White 3.00 8.00
20 Maikel Cleto 3.00 8.00
21 Jemile Weeks 3.00 8.00
22 Brandon Beachy 3.00 8.00
23 Eric Thames 4.00 10.00

2011 Bowman Sterling Rookie Autographs Refractors

*REF: .6X TO 1.5X BASIC
STATED ODDS 1:6
STRASBURG ODDS 1:3018
STATED PRINT RUN 199 SER.#'d SETS
TROUT PRINT RUN 109 SER.#'d SETS
STRASBURG PRINT RUN 25 SER.#'d SETS
NO STRASBURG PRICING AVAILABLE
EXCHANGE DEADLINE 12/31/2014
19 Mike Trout/109 350.00 500.00

2011 Bowman Sterling Rookie Autographs Gold Refractors

*GOLD REF: 1.5X TO 4X BASIC
STATED ODDS 1:21
STATED PRINT RUN 50 SER.#'d SETS
EXCHANGE DEADLINE 12/31/2014
19 Mike Trout 350.00 500.00

2011 Bowman Sterling Rookie Dual Relic X-Fractors

STATED ODDS 1:126
PRINT RUNS B/WN 25-199 COPIES PER
NO PRICING ON QTY 25
AC Aaron Crow 3.00 8.00
AO Alexi Ogando 5.00 12.00
AR Anthony Rizzo 20.00 50.00
BB Brandon Belt 5.00 12.00
BB Brandon Beachy 5.00 12.00
BR Ben Revere 3.00 8.00
CK Craig Kimbrel 5.00 12.00
DA Dustin Ackley 3.00 8.00
DE Danny Espinosa 2.00 5.00
EH Eric Hosmer/25 12.00 30.00
FF Freddie Freeman 30.00 80.00
JW Jordan Walden 2.00 5.00
LC Lonnie Chisenhall 3.00 8.00
MM Mike Moustakas/25 5.00 12.00
MP Michael Pineda 5.00 12.00
MT Mark Trumbo 5.00 12.00
ZB Zach Britton 5.00 12.00

2011 Bowman Sterling Rookie Relics

STATED ODDS 1:18
AC Aaron Crow 3.00 8.00
AO Alexi Ogando 3.00 8.00
AR Anthony Rizzo 6.00 15.00
AW Alex White 3.00 8.00
BB Brandon Belt 4.00 10.00
BB Brandon Beachy 3.00 8.00
BR Ben Revere 3.00 8.00
CK Craig Kimbrel 4.00 10.00
CL Cory Luebke 3.00 8.00
CS Chris Sale 6.00 15.00
DA Dustin Ackley 3.00 8.00
DB Darwin Barney 3.00 8.00
DD Danny Duffy 3.00 8.00
DE Danny Espinosa 3.00 8.00
DJ Desmond Jennings 3.00 8.00
EH Eric Hosmer 4.00 10.00
FF Freddie Freeman 4.00 10.00
JH Jeremy Hellickson 4.00 10.00
JT Justin Turner 3.00 8.00
JW Jordan Walden 3.00 8.00
LC Lonnie Chisenhall 3.00 8.00
MM Mike Moustakas 4.00 10.00
MP Michael Pineda 4.00 10.00
MT Mark Trumbo 5.00 12.00
TC Tyler Chatwood 3.00 8.00
ZB Zach Britton 3.00 8.00
ACO Alex Cobb 3.00 8.00
JWE Jemile Weeks 4.00 10.00
MMI Mike Minor 3.00 8.00

2011 Bowman Sterling Rookie Triple Relic Gold Refractors

STATED ODDS 1:126
PRINT RUNS B/WN 10-50 COPIES PER
NO PRICING ON QTY 10
AC Aaron Crow 4.00 10.00
AO Alexi Ogando 5.00 12.00
AR Anthony Rizzo 10.00 25.00
BB Brandon Belt 10.00 25.00
CK Craig Kimbrel 8.00 20.00
CS Chris Sale 8.00 20.00
DA Dustin Ackley 20.00 50.00
DD Danny Duffy 5.00 12.00
FF Freddie Freeman 15.00 40.00
JW Jordan Walden 4.00 10.00
LC Lonnie Chisenhall 8.00 20.00
MP Michael Pineda/30 8.00 20.00
MT Mark Trumbo 12.50 30.00
ZB Zach Britton 4.00 10.00

2011 Bowman Sterling USA Baseball Dual Relic X-Fractors

COMMON CARD 3.00 8.00
STATED ODDS 1:18 3.00 8.00
STATED PRINT RUN 199 SER.#'d SETS
AM Andrew Mitchell 3.00 8.00
BJ Brian Johnson 3.00 8.00
BK Branden Kline 3.00 8.00
BR Brady Rodgers 3.00 8.00
CE Chris Elder 3.00 8.00
CK Corey Knebel 3.00 8.00
DB DJ Baxendale 4.00 10.00
DF Dominic Ficociello 3.00 8.00
DL David Lyon 3.00 8.00
DM Deven Marrero 4.00 10.00
EW Erich Weiss 3.00 8.00
HM Hoby Milner 3.00 8.00
JE Josh Elander 3.00 8.00
KG Kevin Gausman 3.00 8.00
MA Mark Appel 5.00 12.00
ML Michael Lorenzen 3.00 8.00
MR Matt Reynolds 3.00 8.00
MS Marcus Stroman 4.00 10.00
MW Michael Wacha 5.00 12.00
NF Nolan Fontana 3.00 8.00
TM Tom Murphy 3.00 8.00
TN Tyler Naquin 3.00 8.00

2011 Bowman Sterling USA Baseball Relics

RANDOM INSERTS IN PACKS
AM Andrew Mitchell 3.00 8.00
BJ Brian Johnson 3.00 8.00
BK Branden Kline 3.00 8.00
BR Brady Rodgers 3.00 8.00
CE Chris Elder 3.00 8.00
CK Corey Knebel 3.00 8.00
DB DJ Baxendale 4.00 10.00
DF Dominic Ficociello 3.00 8.00
DL David Lyon 3.00 8.00
DM Deven Marrero 3.00 8.00
EW Erich Weiss 3.00 8.00
HM Hoby Milner 3.00 8.00
JE Josh Elander 3.00 8.00
KG Kevin Gausman 3.00 8.00
MA Mark Appel 4.00 10.00
ML Michael Lorenzen 3.00 8.00
MR Matt Reynolds 3.00 8.00
MS Marcus Stroman 3.00 8.00
MW Michael Wacha 3.00 8.00
NF Nolan Fontana 3.00 8.00
TM Tom Murphy 3.00 8.00
TN Tyler Naquin 3.00 8.00

2011 Bowman Sterling USA Baseball Triple Relic Gold Refractors

STATED ODDS 1:69
STATED PRINT RUN 50 SER.#'d SETS
AM Andrew Mitchell 5.00 12.00
BJ Brian Johnson 5.00 12.00
BK Branden Kline 5.00 12.00
BR Brady Rodgers 5.00 12.00
CE Chris Elder 5.00 12.00
CK Corey Knebel 5.00 12.00
DB DJ Baxendale 6.00 15.00
DF Dominic Ficociello 5.00 12.00
DL David Lyon 5.00 12.00
DM Deven Marrero 6.00 15.00
EW Erich Weiss 5.00 12.00
HM Hoby Milner 5.00 12.00
JE Josh Elander 5.00 12.00
KG Kevin Gausman 5.00 12.00
MA Mark Appel 6.00 15.00
ML Michael Lorenzen 5.00 12.00
MR Matt Reynolds 5.00 12.00
MS Marcus Stroman 5.00 12.00
MW Michael Wacha 8.00 20.00
NF Nolan Fontana 5.00 12.00
TM Tom Murphy 5.00 12.00
TN Tyler Naquin 5.00 12.00

2012 Bowman Sterling

PRINTING PLATE ODDS 1:150 HOBBY
PLATE PRINT RUN 1 SET PER COLOR
NO PLATE PRICING DUE TO SCARCITY
1 Bryce Harper RC 40.00 100.00
2 Wade Miley RC 1.25 3.00
3 Brian Dozier RC 3.00 8.00
4 Brett Jackson RC 1.50 4.00
5 Edwar Cabrera RC 1.00 2.50
6 A.J. Griffin RC 1.25 3.00
7 Leonys Martin RC 1.00 2.50
8 Casey Crosby RC 1.25 3.00
9 Anthony Gose RC 1.25 3.00
10 Yu Darvish RC 2.50 6.00
11 Jarrod Parker RC 1.25 3.00
12 Yasmani Grandal RC 1.00 2.50
13 Addison Reed RC 1.00 2.50
14 Matt Moore RC 1.50 4.00
15 Tyler Thornburg RC 1.25 3.00
16 Jordany Valdespin RC 1.25 3.00
17 Jordan Danks RC 1.00 2.50
18 Martin Perez RC 1.50 4.00
19 Steve Clevenger RC .60 1.50
20 Trevor Bauer RC 3.00 8.00
21 Derek Norris RC 1.00 2.50
22 Tommy Milone RC 1.00 2.50
23 Quintin Berry RC 1.50 4.00
24 Wilin Rosario RC 1.00 2.50
25 Kole Calhoun RC 1.25 3.00
26 Wily Peralta RC 1.00 2.50
27 A.J. Pollock RC 1.50 4.00
28 Wei-Yin Chen RC 2.50 6.00
29 Jeremy Hefner RC 1.00 2.50
30 Yoenis Cespedes RC 2.50 6.00
31 Drew Smyly RC 1.00 2.50
32 Drew Pomeranz RC 1.00 2.50
33 Kirk Nieuwenhuis RC 1.00 2.50
34 Jose Quintana RC 1.00 2.50
35 Stephen Pryor RC .60 1.50
36 Drew Hutchison RC 1.25 3.00
37 Joe Kelly RC 1.50 4.00
38 Andrelton Simmons RC 1.50 4.00
39 Norichika Aoki RC 1.25 3.00
40 Jesus Montero RC 1.00 2.50
41 Matt Adams RC 1.25 3.00
42 Xavier Avery RC 1.00 2.50
43 Chris Archer RC 1.00 2.50
44 Jean Segura RC 2.50 6.00
45 Devin Mesoraco RC 1.00 2.50
46 Liam Hendriks RC 1.00 2.50
47 Jordan Pacheco RC 1.00 2.50
48 Starling Marte RC 1.25 3.00
49 Matt Harvey RC 6.00 15.00
50 Will Middlebrooks RC 1.25 3.00

2012 Bowman Sterling Refractors

*REF: .75X TO 2X BASIC
STATED ODDS 1:6 HOBBY
STATED PRINT RUN 199 SER.#'d SETS
1 Bryce Harper 60.00 150.00
44 Jean Segura 5.00 12.00

2012 Bowman Sterling Gold Refractors

*GOLD REF: 2.5X TO 6X BASIC
STATED ODDS 1:24 HOBBY
STATED PRINT RUN 50 SER.#'d SETS
1 Bryce Harper 100.00 200.00

2012 Bowman Sterling Box Topper Triple Autographs

RANDOM INSERT IN BOXES
EXCHANGE DEADLINE 12/31/2015
ADH Hawkins/Almora/Dahl 100.00 200.00
BHC Bundy/Cole/Hultzen 100.00 175.00
DBA Moore/Yu/Bauer 150.00 250.00
THM Harper/Middle/Trout 500.00 1000.00

2012 Bowman Sterling Dual Autographs Refractors

STATED ODDS 1:69 HOBBY
PRINT RUNS B/WN 38-99 COPIES PER
PRINTING PLATE ODDS 1:1284 HOBBY
PLATE PRINT RUN 1 SET PER COLOR
NO PLATE PRICING DUE TO SCARCITY
EXCHANGE DEADLINE 12/31/2015
AB J.Baez/A.Almora 40.00 80.00
AD A.Almora/D.Dahl 20.00 50.00
BB J.Bradley/X.Bogaerts 75.00 200.00
CT G.Cole/J.Taillon/38 40.00 80.00
GB D.Bundy/K.Gausman 30.00 80.00
HB K.Barnum/C.Hawkins 12.00 30.00
HF Andrew Heaney/Jose Fernandez 30.00 60.00
JL J.Gallo/L.Brinson EXCH 15.00 40.00
OA Austin Aune/Peter O'Brien 12.00 30.00
PC Gavin Cecchini/Kevin Plawecki 12.00 30.00
SV J.Valentin/C.Seager 20.00 50.00

2012 Bowman Sterling Dual Autographs Gold Refractors

*GOLD REF: .75X TO 2X BASIC
STATED ODDS 1:146 HOBBY
STATED PRINT RUN 50 SER.#'d SETS
EXCHANGE DEADLINE 12/31/2015

2012 Bowman Sterling Ichiro Yankees Commemorative Logo Patch

RANDOM INSERTS IN PACKS
STATED PRINT RUN 100 SER.#'d SETS
MPR1 Ichiro Suzuki 40.00 80.00

2012 Bowman Sterling Japanese Player Autographs

EXCHANGE DEADLINE 12/31/2015
HI Hisashi Iwakuma 40.00 80.00
TW Tsuyoshi Wada EXCH 30.00 60.00
YD Yu Darvish/75 125.00 250.00

2012 Bowman Sterling Next In Line

COMPLETE SET (10) 12.50 30.00
STATED ODDS 1:6 HOBBY
NIL1 Tyler Skaggs/Trevor Bauer 2.00 5.00
NIL2 M.Zunino/J.Montero 1.00 2.50
NIL3 A.Rendon/B.Harper 10.00 25.00
NIL4 Bradley/Middlebrooks 1.50 4.00
NIL5 J.Segura/M.Trout 30.00 80.00
NIL6 O.Taveras/M.Adams 1.00 2.50
NIL7 C.Buckel/Y.Darvish 1.50 4.00
NIL8 J.Baez/A.Rizzo 2.50 6.00
NIL9 B.Lawrie/T.d'Arnaud .75 2.00
NIL10 Rymer Liriano/Yasmani Grandal .60 1.50

2012 Bowman Sterling Prospect Autographs

PRINTING PLATE ODDS 1:246 HOBBY
PLATE PRINT RUN 1 SET PER COLOR
NO PLATE PRICING DUE TO SCARCITY
EXCHANGE DEADLINE 12/31/2015
AA Albert Almora 5.00 12.00
AAU Austin Aune 3.00 8.00
AH Andrew Heaney 5.00 12.00
AR Addison Russell 6.00 15.00
BB Barrett Barnes 3.00 8.00
BH Billy Hamilton 5.00 12.00
BJ Brian Johnson 3.00 8.00
BM Bruce Maxwell 3.00 8.00
BS Bubba Starling 3.00 8.00
CH Courtney Hawkins 3.00 8.00
CHE Chris Heston 3.00 8.00
CK Carson Kelly 3.00 8.00
CO Chris Owings 3.00 8.00
CS Corey Seager 25.00 60.00
DB Dylan Bundy 5.00 12.00
DD David Dahl 5.00 12.00
DDA D.J. Davis 3.00 8.00
DM Deven Marrero 3.00 8.00
DS Daniel Straily 5.00 12.00
DV David Vidal 3.00 8.00
EB Eddie Butler 3.00 8.00
FL Francisco Lindor 15.00 40.00
GC Gavin Cecchini 3.00 8.00
GCO Gerrit Cole 6.00 15.00
JC Jamie Callahan 3.00 8.00
JGA Joey Gallo 6.00 15.00
JJ Jamie Jarmon 3.00 8.00
JR James Ramsey 3.00 8.00
JS Jonathan Singleton 3.00 8.00
JSC Jonathan Schoop 4.00 10.00
JV Jesmuel Valentin 4.00 10.00
JWI Jesse Winker 5.00 12.00
KB Keon Barnum 3.00 8.00
KG Kevin Gausman 3.00 8.00
KP Kevin Plawecki 3.00 8.00
KZ Kyle Zimmer 3.00 8.00
LB Lewis Brinson 4.00 10.00
LBA Luke Bard 3.00 8.00
LS Lucas Sims 3.00 8.00
MF Max Fried 12.00 30.00
MH Mitch Haniger 3.00 8.00
MN Mitch Nay 3.00 8.00
MO Matthew Olson 5.00 12.00
MS Marcus Stroman 3.00 8.00
MSM Matthew Smoral 3.00 8.00
MZ Mike Zunino 4.00 10.00
NC Nick Castellanos 6.00 15.00
NF Nolan Fontana 3.00 8.00
NT Nicholas Travieso 3.00 8.00
PB Paul Blackburn 3.00 8.00
PJ Pierce Johnson 3.00 8.00
PL Pat Light 3.00 8.00
PO Peter O'Brien 3.00 8.00
PW Patrick Wisdom 3.00 8.00
RL Rymer Liriano 3.00 8.00
RS Richard Shaffer 3.00 8.00
SB Steve Bean 3.00 8.00
SN Sean Nolin 3.00 8.00
SP Stephen Piscotty 5.00 12.00
ST Stryker Trahan 3.00 8.00
TH Ty Hensley 3.00 8.00
TJ Travis Jankowski 3.00 8.00
TN Tyler Naquin 3.00 8.00
TRE Tony Renda 3.00 8.00
TS Tyler Skaggs -3.00 8.00
TT Tyrone Taylor 4.00 10.00
TW Taijuan Walker 3.00 8.00
VR Victor Roache 3.00 8.00

2012 Bowman Sterling Prospect Autographs Refractors

*REF: .6X TO 1.5X BASIC
STATED ODDS 1:5 HOBBY
STATED PRINT RUN 199 SER.#'d SETS
EXCHANGE DEADLINE 12/31/2015

2012 Bowman Sterling Prospect Autographs Gold Refractors

*GOLD REF: 1.5X TO 4X BASIC
STATED ODDS 1:20 HOBBY
STATED PRINT RUN 50 SER.#'d SETS
EXCHANGE DEADLINE 12/31/2015

2012 Bowman Sterling Prospects

PRINTING PLATE ODDS 1:150 HOBBY
PLATE PRINT RUN 1 SET PER COLOR
NO PLATE PRICING DUE TO SCARCITY
BSP1 Nolan Arenado 4.00 10.00
BSP2 Tyler Austin 2.00 5.00
BSP3 Matt Barnes 1.25 3.00
BSP4 Dante Bichette Jr. 1.50 4.00
BSP5 Xander Bogaerts 5.00 12.00
BSP6 Archie Bradley .75 2.00
BSP7 Jackie Bradley Jr. 3.00 8.00
BSP8 Gary Brown 1.25 3.00
BSP9 Cody Buckel 1.25 3.00
BSP10 Dylan Bundy 2.50 6.00
BSP11 Jose Campos 1.50 4.00
BSP12 Nick Castellanos 4.00 10.00
BSP13 Tony Cingrani 2.50 6.00
BSP14 Gerrit Cole 8.00 20.00
BSP15 Travis d'Arnaud 1.50 4.00
BSP16 Matt Davidson 1.50 4.00
BSP17 Corey Dickerson 1.25 3.00
BSP18 Jose Fernandez 3.00 8.00
BSP19 Nick Franklin 1.50 4.00
BSP20 Billy Hamilton 1.50 4.00
BSP21 Miles Head 1.25 3.00
BSP22 Danny Hultzen 2.00 5.00
BSP23 Francisco Lindor 8.00 20.00
BSP24 Rymer Liriano 1.25 3.00
BSP25 Austin Barnes 2.00 5.00
BSP26 Shelby Miller 2.50 6.00
BSP27 Brad Miller 1.25 3.00
BSP28 Sean Nolin 1.25 3.00
BSP29 Jonathan Galvez 1.25 3.00
BSP30 Chris Owings .75 2.00
BSP31 Marcell Ozuna 3.00 8.00
BSP32 James Paxton 2.00 5.00
BSP33 Alen Hanson 1.50 4.00
BSP34 Jurickson Profar 1.50 4.00
BSP35 Eddie Rosario 2.50 6.00
BSP36 Miguel Sano 1.50 4.00
BSP37 Daniel Vogelbach 2.00 5.00
BSP38 Travis Shaw 1.50 4.00
BSP39 Jonathan Singleton 1.50 4.00
BSP40 Tyler Skaggs 2.00 5.00
BSP41 George Springer 5.00 12.00
BSP42 Bubba Starling 1.50 4.00
BSP43 Jameson Taillon 1.50 4.00
BSP44 Oscar Taveras 2.00 5.00
BSP45 Keury de la Cruz 1.25 3.00
BSP46 Taijuan Walker 1.50 4.00
BSP47 Zack Wheeler 2.50 6.00
BSP48 Mason Williams 2.00 5.00
BSP49 Kolten Wong 1.25 3.00
BSP50 Christian Yelich 10.00 25.00

2012 Bowman Sterling Prospects Refractors

*REF: .6X TO 1.5X BASIC
STATED ODDS 1:6 HOBBY
STATED PRINT RUN 199 SER.#'d SETS

2012 Bowman Sterling Prospects Gold Refractors

*GOLD REF: 2X TO 5X BASIC
STATED ODDS 1:24 HOBBY
STATED PRINT RUN 50 SER.#'d SETS

2012 Bowman Sterling Rookie Autographs

STATED ODDS 1:6 HOBBY
PRINTING PLATE ODDS 1:777 HOBBY
PLATE PRINT RUN 1 SET PER COLOR
NO PLATE PRICING DUE TO SCARCITY
EXCHANGE DEADLINE 12/31/2015
AG Anthony Gose 4.00 10.00
BH Bryce Harper 75.00 150.00
BJ Brett Jackson 3.00 8.00
CA Chris Archer 6.00 15.00
DN Derek Norris 4.00 10.00
JM Jesus Montero 5.00 12.00
JP Jarrod Parker 5.00 12.00
JS Jean Segura 3.00 8.00
KN Kirk Nieuwenhuis 3.00 8.00
MA Matt Adams 5.00 12.00
MM Matt Moore 4.00 10.00
MT Mike Trout 400.00 1000.00
SC Steve Clevenger 3.00 8.00
SM Starling Marte 6.00 15.00
TB Trevor Bauer 6.00 15.00
WM Will Middlebrooks 3.00 8.00
WMI Wade Miley 3.00 8.00
WR Wilin Rosario 3.00 8.00
YC Yoenis Cespedes 15.00 40.00
YD Yu Darvish 90.00 150.00

2012 Bowman Sterling Rookie Autographs Refractors

*REF: .5X TO 1.2X BASIC
STATED ODDS 1:18 HOBBY
STATED PRINT RUN 199 SER.#'d SETS
EXCHANGE DEADLINE 12/31/2015

2012 Bowman Sterling Rookie Autographs Gold Refractors

*GOLD REF: 1.2X TO 3X BASIC
STATED ODDS 1:63 HOBBY
STATED PRINT RUN 50 SER.#'d SETS
EXCHANGE DEADLINE 12/31/2015
BH Bryce Harper 125.00 300.00
YD Yu Darvish 150.00 300.00

2013 Bowman Sterling

PLATE PRINT RUN 1 SET PER COLOR
BLACK-CYAN-MAGENTA-YELLOW ISSUED
NO PLATE PRICING DUE TO SCARCITY
1 Tyler Skaggs RC 1.00 2.50
2 Tony Cingrani RC 1.25 3.00
3 Shelby Miller RC 1.50 4.00
4 Oswaldo Arcia RC .60 1.50
5 Nolan Arenado RC 8.00 20.00
6 Nate Freiman RC .60 1.50
7 Mike Olt RC .75 2.00
8 Matt Magill RC .60 1.50
9 Marcell Ozuna RC 1.50 4.00
10 Manny Machado RC 8.00 20.00
11 Kyuji Fujikawa RC 1.00 2.50
12 Jurickson Profar RC .75 2.00
13 Jose Fernandez RC 1.50 4.00
14 Jedd Gyorko RC .75 2.00
15 Jake Odorizzi RC .75 2.00
16 Jackie Bradley Jr. RC 1.50 4.00
17 Hyun-Jin Ryu RC 1.50 4.00
18 Evan Gattis RC 1.25 3.00
19 Dylan Bundy RC 1.50 4.00
20 Didi Gregorius RC 2.50 6.00
21 Carlos Martinez RC 1.00 2.50
22 Bruce Rondon RC .60 1.50
23 Anthony Rendon RC 3.00 8.00
24 Allen Webster RC .75 2.00
25 Adeiny Hechavarria RC .75 2.00
26 Adam Eaton RC 1.00 2.50
27 Aaron Hicks RC 1.00 2.50
28 Michael Wacha RC .75 2.00
29 Michael Kickham RC .60 1.50
30 Jonathan Pettibone RC 1.00 2.50
31 Nick Franklin RC .75 2.00
32 Yasiel Puig RC 2.50 6.00
33 Gerrit Cole RC 4.00 10.00
34 Zack Wheeler RC 1.25 3.00
35 Wil Myers RC .75 2.00
36 Mike Zunino RC 1.00 2.50
37 Alex Wood RC .75 2.00
38 Christian Yelich RC 10.00 25.00
39 Jarred Cosart RC .75 2.00
40 Henry Urrutia RC .75 2.00
41 Sonny Gray RC 1.00 2.50
42 Grant Green RC 1.00 2.50
43 Cody Asche RC 1.00 2.50
44 Kyle Gibson RC 1.00 2.50
45 Josh Phegley RC .60 1.50
46 Brad Miller RC .75 2.00
47 Zoilo Almonte RC .75 2.00
48 Johnny Hellweg RC .60 1.50
49 Drake Britton RC .75 2.00
50 Jonathan Villar RC 1.00 2.50

2013 Bowman Sterling Blue Refractors

*BLUE REF: 2.5X TO 6X BASIC
STATED PRINT RUN 25 SER.#'d SETS

2013 Bowman Sterling Gold Refractors
GOLD REF: 2X TO 5X BASIC
STATED PRINT RUN 50 SER.#'d SETS

2013 Bowman Sterling Refractors
*REF: 1X TO 2.5X BASIC
STATED PRINT RUN 199 SER.#'d SETS

2013 Bowman Sterling Blue Sapphire Signings
STATED PRINT RUN 25 SER.#'d SETS
EXCHANGE DEADLINE 12/31/2016
BB Byron Buxton 75.00 150.00
HR Hyun-Jin Ryu 25.00 60.00
JP Jurickson Profar 20.00 50.00
MM Manny Machado 50.00 100.00
MS Miguel Sano 12.00 30.00
MT Mike Trout 100.00 200.00
OT Oscar Taveras 20.00 50.00
SM Shelby Miller 40.00 80.00
TD Travis d'Arnaud 5.00 12.00
WM Wil Myers 12.00 30.00

2013 Bowman Sterling Blue Sapphire Signings Ruby
*RUBY: .5X TO 1.2X BASIC
STATED PRINT RUN 25 SER.#'d SETS
EXCHANGE DEADLINE 12/31/2016

2013 Bowman Sterling Dual Autographs Refractors
STATED PRINT RUN 35 SER.#'d SETS
EXCHANGE DEADLINE 12/31/2016
BL F.Lindor/J.Baez 50.00 100.00
CN G.Cecchini/B.Nimmo 12.50 30.00
CS G.Springer/C.Correa 100.00 200.00
DS T.d'Arnaud/N.Syndergaard 60.00 120.00
HM T.Hensley/M.Montgomery 12.50 30.00
LC F.Lindor/C.Correa 90.00 150.00
HD H.Jin Ryu/Y.Darvish 90.00 150.00
RT T.Taylor/V.Roache
RV D.Vogelbach/A.Rizzo 12.50 30.00
ZW M.Zunino/T.Walker 30.00 60.00

2013 Bowman Sterling Asia Exclusive Autographs
HI Hisashi Iwakuma
JT Junichi Tazawa 50.00 100.00
KF Kyuji Fujikawa EXCH
TW Tsuyoshi Wada EXCH
YD Yu Darvish
HR Hyun-Jin Ryu 60.00 120.00

2013 Bowman Sterling Prospect Autographs
PLATE PRINT RUN 1 SET PER COLOR
BLACK-CYAN-MAGENTA-YELLOW ISSUED
NO PLATE PRICING DUE TO SCARCITY
EXCHANGE DEADLINE 12/31/2016
AB Archie Bradley 3.00 8.00
ABL Aaron Blair 3.00 8.00
AC Andrew Church 3.00 8.00
AH Alen Hanson 3.00 8.00
AJ Aaron Judge 75.00 200.00
AK Andrew Knapp 4.00 10.00
AM Austin Meadows 6.00 15.00
AT Andrew Thurman 3.00 8.00
AW Austin Wilson 3.00 8.00
BB Byron Buxton 4.00 10.00
BM Billy McKinney 4.00 10.00
BMI Brad Miller 3.00 8.00
BS Braden Shipley 3.00 8.00
BT Blake Taylor 3.00 8.00
CA Chris Anderson 3.00 8.00
CC Carlos Correa 15.00 40.00
CE C.J. Edwards 3.00 8.00
CF Clint Frazier 6.00 15.00
CH Courtney Hawkins 3.00 8.00
CK Corey Knebel 3.00 8.00
CM Colin Moran 3.00 8.00
CS Chance Sisco 3.00 8.00
CSA Cord Sandberg 3.00 8.00
DO Dillon Overton 3.00 8.00
DP D.J. Peterson 6.00 15.00
DPL Daniel Palka 3.00 8.00
DS Dominic Smith 6.00 15.00
DW Devin Williams 8.00 20.00
EJ Eric Jagielo 3.00 8.00
ER Eduardo Rodriguez 3.00 8.00
GK Gosuke Katoh 3.00 8.00
GP Gregory Polanco 4.00 10.00
HD Hunter Dozier 3.00 8.00
HG Hunter Green 3.00 8.00
HH Hunter Harvey 3.00 8.00
HR Hunter Renfroe 5.00 12.00
IC Ian Clarkin 3.00 8.00
JC J.P. Crawford 6.00 15.00
JCA Jamie Callahan 3.00 8.00
JCR Jonathon Crawford 3.00 8.00
JD Jon Denney 3.00 8.00
JG Jonathan Gray 3.00 8.00
JH Josh Hart 3.00 8.00
JMA Jacob May 3.00 8.00
JMO Julio Morban 3.00 8.00
JP Joc Pederson 6.00 15.00
JS Jorge Soler 5.00 12.00
JSW Jake Sweaney 3.00 8.00
JU Julio Urias 15.00 40.00
JW Justin Williams 3.00 8.00
KF Kevin Franklin 3.00 8.00
KS Kohl Stewart 3.00 8.00
KZ Kevin Ziomek 3.00 8.00
LM L.J. Mazzilli 3.00 8.00
ML Michael Lorenzen 3.00 8.00
MM Matt McPhearson 3.00 8.00
MMO Mark Montgomery 3.00 8.00
MO Michael O'Neill 3.00 8.00
MS Miguel Sano 5.00 12.00
NC Nick Ciuffo 4.00 10.00
NK Nick Kingham 3.00 8.00
NS Noah Syndergaard 10.00 25.00
NTU Nik Turley 3.00 8.00
OM Oscar Mercado 4.00 10.00
OT Oscar Taveras 3.00 8.00
PE Phil Ervin 3.00 8.00
PK Patrick Kivlehan 3.00 8.00
RD Rafael DePaula 3.00 8.00
RE Ryan Eades 3.00 8.00
RH Ryon Healy 5.00 12.00
RJ Ryder Jones 3.00 8.00
RK Robert Kaminsky 3.00 8.00
RM Raul Mondesi 6.00 15.00
RMC Reese McGuire 5.00 12.00
RMM Ryan McMahon 5.00 12.00
RQ Roman Quinn 3.00 8.00
RU Riley Unroe 3.00 8.00
TA Tim Anderson 15.00 40.00
TAU Tyler Austin 3.00 8.00
TB Trey Ball 3.00 8.00
TDA Tyler Danish 3.00 8.00
TN Tucker Neuhaus 3.00 8.00
TW Taijuan Walker 3.00 8.00
TWI Trevor Williams 3.00 8.00
TWN Tom Windle 3.00 8.00
VS Victor Sanchez 3.00 8.00
XB Xander Bogaerts
YV Yordano Ventura 5.00 12.00

2013 Bowman Sterling Prospect Autographs Blue Refractors
*BLUE REF: 1.2X TO 3X BASIC
STATED PRINT RUN 25 SER.#'d SETS
EXCHANGE DEADLINE 12/31/2016

2013 Bowman Sterling Prospect Autographs Gold Refractors
*ORANGE REF: .75X TO 2X BASIC
STATED PRINT RUN 50 SER.#'d SETS
EXCHANGE DEADLINE 12/31/2016

2013 Bowman Sterling Prospect Autographs Green Refractors
*GREEN REF: .5X TO 1.2X BASIC
STATED PRINT RUN 125 SER.#'d SETS
EXCHANGE DEADLINE 12/31/2016

2013 Bowman Sterling Prospect Autographs Orange Refractors
*ORANGE REF: .6X TO 1.5X BASIC
STATED PRINT RUN 75 SER.#'d SETS
EXCHANGE DEADLINE 12/31/2016

2013 Bowman Sterling Prospect Autographs Refractors
*REF: .5X TO 1.2X BASIC
STATED PRINT RUN 150 SER.#'d SETS
EXCHANGE DEADLINE 12/31/2016

2013 Bowman Sterling Prospect Autographs Ruby Refractors
*RUBY REF: .5X TO 1.2X BASIC
STATED PRINT RUN 99 SER.#'d SETS
EXCHANGE DEADLINE 12/31/2016

2013 Bowman Sterling Prospects
PLATE PRINT RUN 1 SET PER COLOR
BLACK-CYAN-MAGENTA-YELLOW ISSUED
NO PLATE PRICING DUE TO SCARCITY
1 Mark Appel 1.00 2.50
2 Xander Bogaerts 2.00 5.00
3 Tyler Austin 1.00 2.50
4 Clint Frazier 3.00 8.00
5 Taylor Guerrieri .60 1.50
6 Taijuan Walker .75 2.00
7 Rafael De Paula .60 1.50
8 Noah Syndergaard .75 2.00
9 Nick Castellanos 2.00 5.00
10 Miguel Sano .75 2.00
11 Kris Bryant 20.00 50.00
12 Pierce Johnson .75 2.00
13 Max Fried 2.50 6.00
14 Matt Barnes .75 2.00
15 Mason Williams .75 2.00
16 Mark Montgomery 1.00 2.50
17 Kolten Wong .60 1.50
18 Dominic Smith 1.00 2.50
19 Austin Meadows 1.25 3.00
20 Jorge Soler 1.25 3.00
21 Jonathan Singleton .75 2.00
22 Joey Gallo 2.00 5.00
23 Joc Pederson 1.00 2.50
24 Jesse Biddle .75 2.00
25 Javier Baez 2.50 6.00
26 Jameson Taillon .75 2.00
27 Gregory Polanco 1.25 3.00
28 George Springer 2.50 6.00
29 Gary Sanchez 2.00 5.00
30 Francisco Lindor 4.00 10.00
31 Dorssys Paulino .75 2.00
32 David Dahl .75 2.00
33 Colin Moran .75 2.00
34 Raul Mondesi 2.00 5.00
35 Courtney Hawkins .60 1.50
36 Kohl Stewart .75 2.00
37 Carlos Correa 20.00 50.00
38 C.J. Cron .75 2.00
39 Byron Buxton 1.50 4.00
40 Bubba Starling .75 2.00
41 Billy Hamilton .75 2.00
42 Archie Bradley .60 1.50
43 Alex Meyer .60 1.50
44 Alen Hanson .75 2.00
45 Addison Russell 1.00 2.50
46 Adam Walker .75 2.00
47 Oscar Taveras .75 2.00
48 Dan Vogelbach 1.00 2.50
49 Trey Ball 1.00 2.50
50 Jonathan Gray .75 2.00

2013 Bowman Sterling Prospects Blue Refractors
*BLUE REF: 2.5X TO 6X BASIC
STATED PRINT RUN 25 SER.#'d SETS
4 Clint Frazier 20.00 50.00
19 Austin Meadows 20.00 50.00

2013 Bowman Sterling Prospects Gold Refractors
*GOLD REF: 2X TO 5X BASIC
STATED PRINT RUN 50 SER.#'d SETS
4 Clint Frazier 15.00 40.00

2013 Bowman Sterling Prospects Refractors
*REF: .75X TO 2X BASIC
STATED PRINT RUN 199 SER.#'d SETS

2013 Bowman Sterling Rookie Autographs
PLATE PRINT RUN 1 SET PER COLOR
BLACK-CYAN-MAGENTA-YELLOW ISSUED
NO PLATE PRICING DUE TO SCARCITY
EXCHANGE DEADLINE 12/31/2016
AE Adam Eaton 3.00 8.00
AW Allen Webster 3.00 8.00
AWO Alex Wood 3.00 8.00
CM Carlos Martinez 6.00 15.00
DB Dylan Bundy 5.00 12.00
DG Didi Gregorius 5.00 12.00
EG Evan Gattis 4.00 10.00
JF Jose Fernandez 20.00 50.00
JG Jedd Gyorko 3.00 8.00
JP Jonathan Pettibone 3.00 8.00
MW Michael Wacha 5.00 12.00
NA Nolan Arenado 40.00 100.00
SM Shelby Miller 3.00 8.00
TC Tony Cingrani 3.00 8.00
TS Tyler Skaggs 3.00 8.00
WM Wil Myers 6.00 15.00
YP Yasiel Puig 60.00 150.00
ZW Zack Wheeler 5.00 12.00

2013 Bowman Sterling Rookie Autographs Gold Refractors
*GOLD REF: .75X TO 2X BASIC
STATED PRINT RUN 50 SER.#'d SETS
EXCHANGE DEADLINE 12/31/2016
AE Adam Eaton 8.00 20.00

2013 Bowman Sterling Rookie Autographs Green Refractors
*GREEN REF: .5X TO 1.2X BASIC
STATED PRINT RUN 125 SER.#'d SETS
EXCHANGE DEADLINE 12/31/2016

2013 Bowman Sterling Rookie Autographs Orange Refractors
*ORANGE REF: .6X TO 1.5X BASIC
STATED PRINT RUN 75 SER.#'d SETS
EXCHANGE DEADLINE 12/31/2016

2013 Bowman Sterling Rookie Autographs Refractors
*REF: .5X TO 1.2X BASIC
STATED PRINT RUN 150 SER.#'d SETS
EXCHANGE DEADLINE 12/31/2016

2013 Bowman Sterling Rookie Autographs Ruby Refractors
*RUBY REF: .5X TO 1.2X BASIC
STATED PRINT RUN 99 SER.#'d SETS
EXCHANGE DEADLINE 12/31/2016

2013 Bowman Sterling Showcase Autographs
STATED PRINT RUN 25 SER.#'d SETS
EXCHANGE DEADLINE 12/31/2016
BB Byron Buxton 150.00 250.00
BH Bryce Harper 150.00 300.00
JP Jurickson Profar 12.00 30.00
MC Miguel Cabrera EXCH 100.00 200.00
MM Manny Machado 75.00 150.00
MT Mike Trout 200.00 350.00
OT Oscar Taveras 10.00 25.00
SM Shelby Miller 50.00 100.00
YD Yu Darvish
YP Yasiel Puig 50.00 120.00

2013 Bowman Sterling The Duel
BA T.Austin/M.Barnes .50 1.25
BJ A.Judge/T.Ball 5.00 12.00
BP J.Pederson/C.Blackburn .50 1.25
CS D.Smith/I.Clarkin .50 1.25
DT M.Trout/Y.Darvish 4.00 10.00
GB T.Guerrieri/X.Bogaerts 1.00 2.50
HH B.Harper/M.Harvey .75 2.00
HM D.Marrero/T.Hensley .40 1.00
JH C.Hawkins/P.Johnson .40 1.00
MB J.Baez/S.Miller 1.25 3.00

2014 Bowman Sterling
PRINTING PLATE ODDS 1:424 HOBBY
PLATE PRINT RUN 1 SET PER COLOR
BLACK-CYAN-MAGENTA-YELLOW ISSUED
NO PLATE PRICING DUE TO SCARCITY
1 Jose Abreu RC 6.00 15.00
2 Alex Guerrero RC 1.00 2.50
3 Andrew Heaney RC .75 2.00
4 Eddie Butler RC .75 2.00
5 Joe Panik RC 1.25 3.00
6 Luis Sardinas RC .75 2.00
7 Taijuan Walker RC .75 2.00
8 Yordano Ventura RC 1.00 2.50
9 Andrew Susac RC 1.00 2.50
10 Billy Hamilton RC 1.00 2.50
11 Chase Anderson RC .75 2.00
12 Jesse Hahn RC 1.00 2.50
13 Arismendy Alcantara RC .75 2.00
14 Cam Bedrosian RC .75 2.00
15 Erisbel Arruebarrena RC .75 2.00
16 Rougned Odor RC 1.50 4.00
17 Mookie Betts RC 20.00 50.00
18 Xander Bogaerts RC 2.50 6.00
19 Michael Choice RC .75 2.00
20 George Springer RC 3.00 8.00
21 Jonathan Schoop RC .75 2.00
22 Rafael Montero RC .75 2.00
23 Tommy La Stella RC .75 2.00
24 Jacob deGrom RC 5.00 12.00
25 Masahiro Tanaka RC 2.50 6.00
26 Nick Castellanos RC 2.50 6.00
27 James Paxton RC 1.25 3.00
28 Kennys Vargas RC .75 2.00
29 Travis d'Arnaud RC 1.00 2.50
30 Oscar Taveras RC 1.00 2.50
31 Danny Santana RC 1.00 2.50
32 Kolten Wong RC 1.00 2.50
33 Aaron Sanchez RC .75 2.00
34 Matt Davidson RC 1.00 2.50
35 Jimmy Nelson RC .75 2.00
36 Chris Owings RC .75 2.00
37 Kyle Parker RC 1.00 2.50
38 Josmil Pinto RC .75 2.00
39 Stefen Romero RC .75 2.00
40 Jon Singleton RC 1.00 2.50
41 C.J. Cron RC .75 2.00
42 Marcus Stroman RC 1.25 3.00
43 Yangervis Solarte RC .75 2.00
44 Zach Walters RC .75 2.00
45 Jake Marisnick RC .75 2.00
46 Ken Giles RC 1.00 2.50
47 Christian Bethancourt RC .75 2.00
48 Roenis Elias RC .75 2.00
49 Garin Cecchini RC .75 2.00
50 Gregory Polanco RC 1.25 3.00

2014 Bowman Sterling Blue Refractors
*BLUE REF: 1.2X TO 3X BASIC
STATED ODDS 1:68 HOBBY
STATED PRINT RUN 25 SER.#'d SETS

2014 Bowman Sterling Japan Fractors
*JAPAN REF: 1.2X TO 3X BASIC
RELEASED EXCLUSIVELY IN ASIA
STATED PRINT RUN 25 SER.#'d SETS

2014 Bowman Sterling Purple Refractors
*PURPLE REF: 1X TO 2.5X BASIC
STATED ODDS 1:34 HOBBY
STATED PRINT RUN 50 SER.#'d SETS

2014 Bowman Sterling Refractors
*REF: .6X TO 1.5X BASIC
STATED ODDS 1:9 HOBBY
STATED PRINT RUN 199 SER.#'d SETS

2014 Bowman Sterling Box Topper Purple Wave Refractors
STATED ODDS 1:15 HOBBY BOXES
STATED PRINT RUN 50 SER.#'d SETS
*BLACK/35: .5X TO 1.2X BASIC
BBTAB Archie Bradley 2.00 5.00
BBTAJ Alex Jackson 2.50 6.00
BBTAR Addison Russell 3.00 8.00
BBTBB Byron Buxton 2.50 6.00
BBTCC Carlos Correa 10.00 25.00
BBTFL Francisco Lindor 12.00 30.00
BBTGP Gregory Polanco 10.00 25.00
BBTGS George Springer 8.00 20.00
BBTHH Hunter Harvey 2.00 5.00
BBTJA Jose Abreu 15.00 40.00
BBTJB Javier Baez 8.00 20.00
BBTJG Jon Gray 2.50 6.00
BBTJS Jorge Soler 4.00 10.00
BBTKB Kris Bryant 15.00 40.00
BBTKS Kyle Schwarber 8.00 20.00
BBTLG Lucas Giolito 3.00 8.00
BBTMT Masahiro Tanaka 6.00 15.00
BBTNG Nick Gordon 2.50 6.00
BBTOT Oscar Taveras 2.50 6.00
BBTTK Tyler Kolek 2.00 5.00

2014 Bowman Sterling Die Cut Autographs Refractors
STATED ODDS 1:85 HOBBY
STATED PRINT RUN 50 SER.#'d SETS
EXCHANGE DEADLINE 12/31/2017
*BLUE/30: .5X TO 1.2X BASIC
SAAB Archie Bradley EXCH 6.00 15.00
SAAJ Alex Jackson 8.00 20.00
SAAN Aaron Nola 40.00 100.00
SABB Byron Buxton 30.00 80.00
SACC Carlos Correa 75.00 200.00
SACF Clint Frazier 15.00 40.00
SAFL Francisco Lindor 40.00 100.00
SAGP Gregory Polanco 15.00 40.00
SAGS George Springer 25.00 60.00
SAJA Jose Abreu 25.00 60.00
SAJB Javier Baez 25.00 60.00
SAJSO Jorge Soler EXCH 12.00 30.00
SAKS Kyle Schwarber EXCH 75.00 200.00
SALG Lucas Giolito 20.00 50.00
SAMB Mookie Betts 40.00 100.00
SAMS Miguel Sano 20.00 50.00
SANG Nick Gordon 25.00 60.00
SANS Noah Syndergaard 15.00 40.00
SATK Tyler Kolek 25.00 60.00

2014 Bowman Sterling Die Cut Autographs Blue Refractors
*BLUE REF: .5X TO 1.2X BASIC
STATED ODDS 1:142 HOBBY
STATED PRINT RUN 30 SER.#'d SETS
EXCHANGE DEADLINE 12/31/2017

2014 Bowman Sterling Dual Autographs Refractors
STATED ODDS 1:242 HOBBY
STATED PRINT RUN 35 SER.#'d SETS
*BLUE/25: .5X TO 1.2X BASIC
PRINTING PLATE ODDS 1:2118 HOBBY
PLATE PRINT RUN 1 SET PER COLOR
BLACK-CYAN-MAGENTA-YELLOW ISSUED
NO PLATE PRICING DUE TO SCARCITY
EXCHANGE DEADLINE 12/31/2017
BDAAC Abreu/Cabrera 60.00 150.00
BDABT Buxton/Taveras EXCH 25.00 60.00
BDAGS M.Sano/N.Gordon 30.00 80.00
BDAKH Heaney/Kolek EXCH 6.00 15.00
BDASC G.Springer/C.Correa 60.00 150.00
BDASP Puig/Soler EXCH 30.00 80.00

2014 Bowman Sterling Japan Darvish Die Cut Refractors
INSERTED IN BOW.STERLING ASIAN PACKS
STATED PRINT RUN 25 SER.#'d SETS
YD1 Yu Darvish 5.00 12.00
YD2 Yu Darvish 5.00 12.00
YD3 Yu Darvish 5.00 12.00
YD4 Yu Darvish 5.00 12.00
YD5 Yu Darvish 5.00 12.00

2014 Bowman Sterling Japan Darvish Jersey Die Cut
INSERTED IN BOW.STERLING ASIAN PACKS
STATED PRINT RUN 10 SER.#'d SETS
YD1 Yu Darvish 10.00 25.00
YD2 Yu Darvish 10.00 25.00
YD3 Yu Darvish 10.00 25.00
YD4 Yu Darvish 10.00 25.00
YD5 Yu Darvish 10.00 25.00

2014 Bowman Sterling Japan Tanaka Die Cut Refractors
INSERTED IN BOW.STERLING ASIAN PACKS
STATED PRINT RUN 25 SER.#'d SETS
MT1 Masahiro Tanaka 3.00 8.00
MT2 Masahiro Tanaka 3.00 8.00
MT3 Masahiro Tanaka 3.00 8.00
MT4 Masahiro Tanaka 3.00 8.00
MT5 Masahiro Tanaka 3.00 8.00

2014 Bowman Sterling Japan Tanaka Jersey Die Cut
INSERTED IN BOW.STERLING ASIAN PACKS
STATED PRINT RUN 10 SER.#'d SETS
MT1 Masahiro Tanaka 8.00 20.00
MT2 Masahiro Tanaka 8.00 20.00
MT3 Masahiro Tanaka 8.00 20.00
MT4 Masahiro Tanaka 8.00 20.00
MT5 Masahiro Tanaka 8.00 20.00

2014 Bowman Sterling Prospect Autographs
PRINTING PLATE ODDS 1:326 HOBBY
PLATE PRINT RUN 1 SET PER COLOR
BLACK-CYAN-MAGENTA-YELLOW ISSUED
NO PLATE PRICING DUE TO SCARCITY
EXCHANGE DEADLINE 12/31/2017
BSPAAA Albert Almora 5.00 12.00
BSPAABL Alex Blandino 3.00 8.00
BSPAAC A.J. Cole 3.00 8.00
BSPAAH Alen Hanson 3.00 8.00
BSPAAJ Alex Jackson 4.00 10.00
BSPAAME Austin Meadows 5.00 12.00
BSPAAN Aaron Northcraft 3.00 8.00
BSPAANO Aaron Nola 8.00 20.00
BSPABD Braxton Davidson 3.00 8.00
BSPABF Brandon Finnegan 3.00 8.00
BSPABS Blake Swihart 4.00 10.00
BSPABZ Bradley Zimmer 5.00 12.00
BSPACC Carlos Correa 12.00 30.00
BSPACE C.J. Edwards 4.00 10.00
BSPACF Clint Frazier 8.00 20.00
BSPACM Colin Moran 3.00 8.00
BSPACT Cole Tucker 3.00 8.00
BSPACV Chase Vallot 3.00 8.00
BSPADDE Delino DeShields Jr. 3.00 8.00
BSPADF Derek Fisher 5.00 12.00
BSPADH Derek Hill 3.00 8.00
BSPADS Dominic Smith 3.00 8.00
BSPAEF Erick Fedde 3.00 8.00
BSPAER Eduardo Rodriguez 4.00 10.00
BSPAERO Eddie Rosario 6.00 15.00
BSPAFG Foster Griffin 3.00 8.00
BSPAFL Francisco Lindor 20.00 50.00
BSPAGCE Gavin Cecchini 3.00 8.00
BSPAGH Grant Holmes 3.00 8.00
BSPAGM Gareth Morgan 3.00 8.00
BSPAGS Gary Sanchez 15.00 40.00
BSPAHH Hunter Harvey 3.00 8.00
BSPAHO Henry Owens 4.00 10.00
BSPAJA Jorge Alfaro 4.00 10.00
BSPAJAG Jacob Gatewood 3.00 8.00
BSPAJB Jorge Bonifacio 3.00 8.00
BSPAJBA Javier Baez 20.00 50.00
BSPAJC J.P. Crawford 3.00 8.00
BSPAJF Jack Flaherty 12.00 30.00
BSPAJGA Joey Gallo 6.00 15.00
BSPAJH Jason Hursh 3.00 8.00
BSPAJHO Jeff Hoffman 5.00 12.00
BSPAJN Justin Nicolino 3.00 8.00
BSPAJPE Jose Peraza 3.00 8.00
BSPAJS Justus Sheffield 4.00 10.00
BSPAKC Kyle Crick 3.00 8.00
BSPAKF Kyle Freeland 3.00 8.00
BSPAKSC Kyle Schwarber 6.00 15.00
BSPAKV Kennys Vargas 3.00 8.00
BSPALG Lucas Giolito 5.00 12.00
BSPALO Luis Ortiz 3.00 8.00
BSPALS Luis Severino 10.00 25.00
BSPALSI Lucas Sims 3.00 8.00
BSPALW Luke Weaver 5.00 12.00
BSPAMBA Matt Barnes 3.00 8.00
BSPAMC Michael Conforto 12.00 30.00
BSPAMF Michael Foltynewicz 3.00 8.00
BSPAMG Mitch Gueller 3.00 8.00
BSPAMIC Michael Chavis 6.00 15.00
BSPAMJ Micah Johnson 3.00 8.00
BSPAMK Michael Kopech 5.00 12.00
BSPAMP Max Pentecost 3.00 8.00
BSPAMPA Mike Papi 3.00 8.00
BSPAMS Miguel Sano 4.00 10.00
BSPANG Nick Gordon 4.00 10.00
BSPANH Nick Howard 3.00 8.00
BSPANS Noah Syndergaard 8.00 20.00
BSPARA Raul Alcantara 3.00 8.00
BSPARS Robert Stephenson 3.00 8.00
BSPASC Sean Coyle 3.00 8.00
BSPASN Sean Newcomb 5.00 12.00
BSPASP Stephen Piscotty 4.00 10.00
BSPATB Tyler Beede 5.00 12.00
BSPATG Tyler Glasnow 5.00 12.00
BSPATK Tyler Kolek 3.00 8.00
BSPATM Tom Murphy 3.00 8.00

2014 Bowman Sterling Prospect Autographs Blue Refractors
*BLUE REF: 1X TO 2.5X BASIC
STATED ODDS 1:53 HOBBY
STATED PRINT RUN 25 SER.#'d SETS
EXCHANGE DEADLINE 12/31/2017
BSPAAB Archie Bradley 8.00 20.00
BSPABB Byron Buxton 15.00 40.00

2014 Bowman Sterling Prospect Autographs Green Refractors
*GREEN REF: .5X TO 1.2X BASIC
STATED ODDS 1:11 HOBBY
STATED PRINT RUN 125 SER.#'d SETS
EXCHANGE DEADLINE 12/31/2017
BSPAAB Archie Bradley 4.00 10.00
BSPABB Byron Buxton 8.00 20.00

2014 Bowman Sterling Prospect Autographs Magenta Refractors
*MAGENTA REF: .6X TO 1.5X BASIC
STATED ODDS 1:14 HOBBY
STATED PRINT RUN 99 SER.#'d SETS
EXCHANGE DEADLINE 12/31/2017
BSPAAB Archie Bradley 5.00 12.00
BSPABB Byron Buxton 10.00 25.00

2014 Bowman Sterling Prospect Autographs Orange Refractors
*ORANGE REF: .6X TO 1.5X BASIC
STATED ODDS 1:18 HOBBY
STATED PRINT RUN 75 SER.#'d SETS
EXCHANGE DEADLINE 12/31/2017
BSPAAB Archie Bradley 5.00 12.00
BSPABB Byron Buxton 10.00 25.00

2014 Bowman Sterling Prospect Autographs Purple Refractors
*PURPLE REF: .75X TO 2X BASIC
STATED ODDS 1:27 HOBBY
STATED PRINT RUN 50 SER.#'d SETS
EXCHANGE DEADLINE 12/31/2017
BSPAAB Archie Bradley 6.00 15.00
BSPABB Byron Buxton 12.00 30.00

2014 Bowman Sterling Prospect Autographs Refractors
*REF: .5X TO 1.2X BASIC
STATED ODDS 1:9 HOBBY
STATED PRINT RUN 150 SER.#'d SETS
EXCHANGE DEADLINE 12/31/2017
BSPAAB Archie Bradley 4.00 10.00
BSPABB Byron Buxton 8.00 20.00

2014 Bowman Sterling Prospects
PRINTING PLATE ODDS 1:424 HOBBY
PLATE PRINT RUN 1 SET PER COLOR
BLACK-CYAN-MAGENTA-YELLOW ISSUED
NO PLATE PRICING DUE TO SCARCITY
BSP1 Kris Bryant 25.00 60.00
BSP2 Francisco Lindor 4.00 10.00
BSP3 Aaron Nola 4.00 10.00
BSP4 J.P. Crawford .60 1.50
BSP5 Miguel Sano .75 2.00
BSP6 Alex Meyer .60 1.50
BSP7 Nick Howard .60 1.50
BSP8 Kodi Medeiros .60 1.50
BSP9 Jon Gray .75 2.00
BSP10 Joey Gallo 1.25 3.00
BSP11 Braden Shipley .60 1.50
BSP12 Robert Stephenson .60 1.50
BSP13 Luis Severino 1.00 2.50
BSP14 Alex Jackson .75 2.00
BSP15 Hunter Harvey .60 1.50
BSP16 Sean Newcomb 1.00 2.50
BSP17 Nick Gordon .75 2.00
BSP18 Colin Moran .60 1.50
BSP19 Mark Appel .75 2.00
BSP20 Carlos Correa 3.00 8.00
BSP21 Jorge Soler 1.25 3.00
BSP22 Michael Conforto 1.25 3.00
BSP23 Tyler Glasnow 1.00 2.50
BSP24 Jorge Alfaro .75 2.00
BSP25 Jeff Hoffman 1.00 2.50
BSP26 Joc Pederson 1.00 2.50
BSP27 Clint Frazier 2.50 6.00
BSP28 David Dahl .75 2.00
BSP29 Tyler Kolek .60 1.50
BSP30 Addison Russell 1.00 2.50
BSP31 Henry Owens .75 2.00
BSP32 Julio Urias 3.00 8.00
BSP33 Maikel Franco .75 2.00
BSP34 Blake Swihart .75 2.00
BSP35 Tyler Beede 1.00 2.50
BSP36 Trea Turner 2.00 5.00
BSP37 Erick Fedde .60 1.50
BSP38 Kohl Stewart .60 1.50
BSP39 Austin Meadows 1.00 2.50
BSP40 Kyle Schwarber 6.00 15.00
BSP41 Kyle Zimmer .60 1.50
BSP42 Max Pentecost .60 1.50
BSP43 Brandon Finnegan .60 1.50
BSP44 Javier Baez 2.50 6.00
BSP45 Noah Syndergaard .75 2.00
BSP46 Archie Bradley .60 1.50
BSP47 Dominic Smith .60 1.50
BSP48 Lucas Giolito 1.00 2.50
BSP49 Kyle Freeland 1.25 3.00
BSP50 Byron Buxton .75 2.00

2014 Bowman Sterling Prospects Blue Refractors
*BLUE REF: 1.2X TO 3X BASIC
STATED ODDS 1:68 HOBBY
STATED PRINT RUN 25 SER.#'d SETS

2014 Bowman Sterling Prospects Japan Fractors
*JAPAN REF: 1.2X TO 3X BASIC
RELEASED EXCLUSIVELY IN ASIA
STATED PRINT RUN 25 SER.#'d SETS

2014 Bowman Sterling Prospects Purple Refractors
*PURPLE REF: 1X TO 2.5X BASIC
STATED ODDS 1:34 HOBBY
STATED PRINT RUN 50 SER.#'d SETS

2014 Bowman Sterling Prospects Refractors
*REF: .6X TO 1.5X BASIC
STATED ODDS 1:9 HOBBY
STATED PRINT RUN 199 SER.#'d SETS

2014 Bowman Sterling Rookie Autographs
STATED ODDS 1:5 HOBBY
PRINTING PLATE ODDS 1:1065 HOBBY
PLATE PRINT RUN 1 SET PER COLOR
BLACK-CYAN-MAGENTA-YELLOW ISSUED
NO PLATE PRICING DUE TO SCARCITY
EXCHANGE DEADLINE 12/31/2017
BSRAAA Arismendy Alcantara 3.00 8.00
BSRAAH Andrew Heaney 3.00 8.00
BSRAASU Andrew Susac 4.00 10.00
BSRABH Billy Hamilton 4.00 10.00
BSRACB Cam Bedrosian 3.00 8.00
BSRACC C.J. Cron 3.00 8.00
BSRACO Chris Owings 3.00 8.00
BSRAGC Garin Cecchini 3.00 8.00
BSRAGP Gregory Polanco 5.00 12.00
BSRAGS George Springer 12.00 30.00
BSRAJAG Jesus Aguilar 5.00 12.00
BSRAJN Jimmy Nelson 3.00 8.00
BSRAMB Mookie Betts 100.00 250.00
BSRANC Nick Castellanos 10.00 25.00
BSRAOT Oscar Taveras 4.00 10.00
BSRARE Roenis Elias 3.00 8.00
BSRARO Rougned Odor 6.00 15.00
BSRATL Tommy La Stella 3.00 8.00
BSRAYS Yangervis Solarte 3.00 8.00
BSRAYV Yordano Ventura 4.00 10.00

2014 Bowman Sterling Rookie Autographs Blue Refractors
*BLUE REF: 1X TO 2.5X BASIC
STATED ODDS 1:170 HOBBY
STATED PRINT RUN 25 SER.#'d SETS
EXCHANGE DEADLINE 12/31/2017
BSRAJA Jose Abreu 100.00 250.00
BSRAJPA Joe Panik 20.00 50.00

2014 Bowman Sterling Rookie Autographs Green Refractors
*GREEN REF: .5X TO 1.2X BASIC
STATED ODDS 1:34 HOBBY
STATED PRINT RUN 125 SER.#'d SETS
EXCHANGE DEADLINE 12/31/2017
BSRAJPA Joe Panik 10.00 25.00

2014 Bowman Sterling Rookie Autographs Magenta Refractors
*MAGENTA REF: .6X TO 1.5X BASIC
STATED ODDS 1:43 HOBBY
STATED PRINT RUN 99 SER.#'d SETS
EXCHANGE DEADLINE 12/31/2017
BSRAJPA Joe Panik 12.00 30.00

2014 Bowman Sterling Rookie Autographs Orange Refractors
*ORANGE REF: .6X TO 1.5X BASIC
STATED ODDS 1:57 HOBBY
STATED PRINT RUN 75 SER.#'d SETS
EXCHANGE DEADLINE 12/31/2017
BSRAJA Jose Abreu 60.00 150.00
BSRAJPA Joe Panik 12.00 30.00

2014 Bowman Sterling Rookie Autographs Purple Refractors
*PURPLE REF: .75X TO 2X BASIC
STATED ODDS 1:85 HOBBY
STATED PRINT RUN 50 SER.#'d SETS
EXCHANGE DEADLINE 12/31/2017
BSRAJA Jose Abreu 75.00 200.00
BSRAJPA Joe Panik 15.00 40.00

2014 Bowman Sterling Rookie Autographs Refractors
*REF: .5X TO 1.2X BASIC
STATED ODDS 1:29 HOBBY
STATED PRINT RUN 150 SER.#'d SETS
EXCHANGE DEADLINE 12/31/2017
BSRAJPA Joe Panik 10.00 25.00

2014 Bowman Sterling Showcase Autographs
STATED ODDS 1:340 HOBBY
STATED PRINT RUN 25 SER.#'d SETS
EXCHANGE DEADLINE 12/31/2017
SASBB Byron Buxton 15.00 40.00
SASCC Carlos Correa 100.00 200.00
SASGP Gregory Polanco EXCH 25.00 60.00
SASJA Jose Abreu 40.00 100.00
SASJB Javier Baez 30.00 80.00
SASNG Nick Gordon 10.00 25.00
SASTK Tyler Kolek 10.00 25.00
SASYP Yasiel Puig 60.00 150.00

2018 Bowman Sterling Refractors
BOW.STATED ODDS 1:24 HOBBY
BOW.DFT.ODDS 1:12 HOBBY
BSAB Alec Bohm BD 1.50 4.00
BSAG Andres Gimenez .40 1.00
BSAH Adam Haseley .50 1.25
BSAJ Aaron Judge 1.25 3.00
BSAR Amed Rosario .40 1.00
BSBH Bryce Harper .75 2.00
BSBM Brendan McKay .50 1.25
BSBS Brady Singer BD .60 1.50
BSCC Carlos Correa .50 1.25
BSCF Clint Frazier .60 1.50
BSCM Casey Mize BD 2.50 6.00
BSEF Estevan Florial .50 1.25
BSEJ Eloy Jimenez 1.25 3.00
BSFM Francisco Mejia .40 1.00
BSFP Franklin Perez .30 .75
BSGR Grayson Rodriguez BD .60 1.50
BSGT Gleyber Torres 3.00 8.00
BSHG Hunter Greene 1.00 2.50
BSHR Heliot Ramos .50 1.25
BSJI Jonathan India BD .50 1.25
BSJK Jarred Kelenic BD 3.00 8.00
BSJK Jeren Kendall .40 1.00
BSJM Jorge Mateo .30 .75
BSKB Kris Bryant .60 1.50
BSKH Keston Hiura .75 2.00
BSLR Luis Robert 10.00 25.00
BSMB Michel Baez .30 .75
BSMG MacKenzie Gore .60 1.50
BSMK Michael Kopech .60 1.50
BSMM Mickey Moniak .75 2.00
BSMT Mike Trout 2.50 6.00
BSNM Nick Madrigal BD 2.00 5.00
BSNP Nick Pratto .40 1.00
BSNW Nick Williams .40 1.00
BSOA Ozzie Albies 1.00 2.50
BSRA Ronald Acuna 6.00 15.00
BSRD Rafael Devers 1.00 2.50
BSRH Rhys Hoskins 1.25 3.00
BSRL Royce Lewis 1.25 3.00
BSRW Ryan Weathers BD .40 1.00
BSSO Shohei Ohtani 2.00 5.00
BSTC Triston Casas BD 2.50 6.00
BSTS Travis Swaggerty BD 1.00 2.50
BSVR Victor Robles .75 2.00
BSVGJ Vladimir Guerrero Jr. 3.00 8.00

2018 Bowman Sterling Atomic Refractors
*ATOMIC: 1.2X TO 3X BASIC
BOW.ODDS 1:823 HOBBY
BOW.DFT.ODDS 1:640 HOBBY
STATED PRINT RUN 150 SER. #'d SETS

2018 Bowman Sterling Orange Refractors
*ORANGE: 4X TO 10X BASIC
BOW.ODDS 1:2185 HOBBY
BOW.DFT.ODDS 1:2575 HOBBY
STATED PRINT RUN 25 SER. #'d SETS

2018 Bowman Sterling Autographs Refractors
BOW.ODDS 1:2791 HOBBY
BOW.DFT.ODDS 1:791 HOBBY
PRINT RUNS B/WN 15-99 COPIES PER
NO PRICING ON QTY 15
BOW.EXCH.DEADLINE 3/31/2020
BOW.CHR.EXCH. 8/31/2020
BOW.DFT.EXCH. 11/30/2020
BSAAB Alec Bohm/99 40.00 100.00
BSAAG Andres Gimenez/99 20.00 50.00
BSAAH Adam Haseley/99 8.00 20.00
BSAAR Amed Rosario/99 6.00 15.00
BSABM Brendan McKay/99 8.00 20.00
BSABS Brady Singer/99 10.00 25.00
BSACF Clint Frazier/99 10.00 25.00
BSACM Casey Mize/99 20.00 50.00
BSAEF Estevan Florial/99 15.00 40.00
BSAFP Franklin Perez/99 5.00 12.00
BSAGT Gleyber Torres/99 50.00 125.00
BSAHG Hunter Greene/99 20.00 50.00
BSAJI Jonathan India/99 8.00 20.00
BSAJK Jarred Kelenic/99
BSAJK Jeren Kendall/99 6.00 15.00
BSAKH Keston Hiura/99 15.00 40.00
BSALR Luis Robert/99 75.00 200.00
BSANM Nick Madrigal/99 30.00 80.00
BSANP Nick Pratto/99 6.00 15.00
BSARD Rafael Devers/99 15.00 40.00
BSARL Royce Lewis/99 20.00 50.00
BSARW Ryan Weathers/99 6.00 15.00
BSASO Shohei Ohtani/30 400.00 800.00
BSATC Triston Casas/99 40.00 100.00
BSATS Travis Swaggerty/99 20.00 50.00
BSAVR Victor Robles/99 20.00 50.00

2018 Bowman Sterling Autographs Orange Refractors
*ORANGE: .75X TO 2X BASIC
BOW.ODDS 1:2677 HOBBY
BOW.DFT.ODDS 1:2102 HOBBY
STATED PRINT RUN 25 SER. #'d SETS
BOW.EXCH.DEADLINE 3/31/2020
BOW.CHR.EXCH. 8/31/2020
BOW.DFT.EXCH. 11/30/2020
BSACM Casey Mize 100.00 250.00
BSAKB Kris Bryant 75.00 200.00
BSASO Shohei Ohtani EXCH 600.00 1000.00

2019 Bowman Sterling Die Cut Autographs
STATED ODDS 1:67 HOBBY
PRINT RUNS B/WN 15-50 COPIES PER
NO PRICING ON QTY 15
EXCHANGE DEADLINE 7/31/2021
*BLUE/25: .4X TO 1X p/r 30
*BLUE/25: .5X TO 1.2X p/r 40-99
SDCAAB Alec Bohm/40 40.00 100.00
SDCACK Carter Kieboom/75 8.00 20.00
SDCACM Casey Mize/30 30.00 80.00
SDCAEM Elehuris Montero/99 8.00 20.00
SDCAJA Jordyn Adams/99 6.00 15.00
SDCAJB Joey Bart/40 50.00 120.00
SDCAJI Jonathan India/50 6.00 15.00
SDCAJK Jarred Kelenic/55 25.00 60.00
SDCAJR Julio Rodriguez/75 60.00 150.00
SDCAJS Justus Sheffield/50 8.00 20.00
SDCALU Luis Urias/55 8.00 20.00
SDCAMA Miguel Amaya/99 8.00 20.00
SDCANM Nick Madrigal/40 20.00 50.00
SDCARH Ronaldo Hernandez/75 8.00 20.00
SDCARM Ronny Mauricio/99 20.00 50.00
SDCASM Seuly Matias/75 6.00 15.00
SDCAWF Wander Franco/65 75.00 200.00
SDCAJPM Julio Pablo Martinez/65 5.00 12.00
SDCAVGJ Vladimir Guerrero Jr/30 150.00 400.00
SDCAVMJ Victor Mesa Jr./75 12.00 30.00
SDCAVVM Victor Victor Mesa/65 15.00 40.00

2019 Bowman Sterling Dual Autographs Refractors
STATED ODDS 1:407 HOBBY
STATED PRINT RUN 25 SER.#'d SETS
EXCHANGE DEADLINE 7/31/2021
DRAFH Hernandez/Franco 150.00 400.00
DRAGJ Guerrero Jr./Jimenez 150.00 400.00
DRAGT Guerrero Jr./Tatis Jr. 400.00 1000.00
DRAKS Kikuchi/Sheffield 20.00 50.00
DRAMM Mesa Jr./Mesa 50.00 120.00
DRAMMA Maitan/Marsh 12.00 30.00
DRAMN Newton/Mauricio 100.00 250.00
DRAMP Mize/Perez 30.00 80.00
DRARF Florial/Robert 100.00 250.00
DRATG Tatis Jr./Gore 200.00 500.00

2019 Bowman Sterling Prospect Autographs
OVERALL AUTO ODDS 1:1 HOBBY
EXCHANGE DEADLINE 7/31/2021
BSPAAB Akil Baddoo 3.00 8.00
BSPAABO Alec Bohm 20.00 50.00
BSPAAK Andrew Knizner 4.00 10.00
BSPAAS Anthony Seigler 6.00 15.00
BSPABA Blaze Alexander 5.00 12.00
BSPABB Brock Burke 2.50 6.00
BSPABD Brock Deatherage 2.50 6.00
BSPABM Brandon Marsh 4.00 10.00
BSPABN Bo Naylor 2.50 6.00
BSPABS Brady Singer 5.00 12.00
BSPABSI Luken Baker 3.00 8.00
BSPABT Brice Turang 3.00 8.00
BSPACK Carter Kieboom 6.00 15.00
BSPACM Casey Mize 30.00 80.00
BSPACS Connor Scott 3.00 8.00
BSPACSA Cristian Santana 4.00 10.00
BSPACSP Chad Spanberger 2.50 6.00
BSPACW Cole Winn 2.50 6.00
BSPADK Dean Kremer 5.00 12.00
BSPADM Dustin May 15.00 40.00
BSPAEM Elehuris Montero 4.00 10.00
BSPAFN Freudis Nova 4.00 10.00
BSPAFP Franklin Perez 3.00 8.00
BSPAGR Grayson Rodriguez 5.00 12.00
BSPAIW Isranel Wilson 3.00 8.00
BSPAJA Jordyn Adams 3.00 8.00
BSPAJB Joey Bart 15.00 40.00
BSPAJG Jordan Groshans 5.00 12.00
BSPAJH Jonathan Hernandez 2.50 6.00
BSPAJI Jonathan India 8.00 20.00
BSPAJPM Julio Pablo Martinez 2.50 6.00
BSPAJR Julio Rodriguez 50.00 120.00
BSPAJW Jackson Kowar 5.00 12.00
BSPAKC Kody Clemens 3.00 8.00
BSPAKM Kevin Maitan 3.00 8.00
BSPAKR Keibert Ruiz 6.00 15.00
BSPAMA Miguel Amaya 4.00 10.00
BSPAML Matthew Liberatore 8.00 20.00
BSPAMLU Marco Luciano 50.00 120.00
BSPAMM Matt Mercer 2.50 6.00
BSPANH Nico Hoerner 15.00 40.00
BSPANM Nick Madrigal 10.00 25.00
BSPANMA Noelvi Marte 20.00 50.00
BSPANS Nick Schnell 2.50 6.00
BSPAOM Orelvis Martinez 8.00 20.00
BSPARB Rylan Bannon 5.00 12.00
BSPARH Ronaldo Hernandez 2.50 6.00
BSPARM Ronny Mauricio 10.00 25.00
BSPARR Roberto Ramos 3.00 8.00
BSPASM Seuly Matias 3.00 8.00
BSPASN Sheldon Neuse 2.50 6.00
BSPATL Trevor Larnach 6.00 15.00
BSPATO Tirso Ornelas 2.50 6.00
BSPATS Travis Swaggerty 4.00 10.00
BSPAVF Vince Fernandez 3.00 8.00
BSPAVMJ Victor Mesa Jr. 6.00 15.00
BSPAVVM Victor Victor Mesa 5.00 12.00
BSPAWF Wander Franco EXCH 75.00 200.00

2019 Bowman Sterling Prospect Autographs Blue Refractors
*BLUE REF: 1.5X TO 4X BASIC
STATED ODDS 1:76 HOBBY
STATED PRINT RUN 25 SER.#'d SETS
EXCHANGE DEADLINE 7/31/2021
BSPAEM Elehuris Montero 25.00 60.00
BSPAJK Jarred Kelenic 75.00 200.00
BSPALG Logan Gilbert 20.00 50.00
BSPAMLU Marco Luciano 250.00 600.00
BSPANM Nick Madrigal 50.00 120.00
BSPARM Ronny Mauricio 75.00 200.00

2019 Bowman Sterling Prospect Autographs Gold Refractors
*GOLD REF: 1.2X TO 3X BASIC
STATED ODDS 1:38 HOBBY
STATED PRINT RUN 50 SER.#'d SETS
EXCHANGE DEADLINE 7/31/2021
BSPAEM Elehuris Montero 20.00 50.00
BSPAJK Jarred Kelenic 60.00 150.00
BSPALG Logan Gilbert 15.00 40.00
BSPAMLU Marco Luciano 200.00 500.00
BSPANM Nick Madrigal 40.00 100.00
BSPARM Ronny Mauricio 60.00 150.00

2019 Bowman Sterling Prospect Autographs Orange Refractors
*ORANGE REF: .75X TO 2X BASIC
STATED ODDS 1:26 HOBBY
STATED PRINT RUN 75 SER.#'d SETS
EXCHANGE DEADLINE 7/31/2021
BSPAJK Jarred Kelenic 40.00 100.00
BSPALG Logan Gilbert 10.00 25.00
BSPANM Nick Madrigal 25.00 60.00
BSPARM Ronny Mauricio 40.00 100.00

2019 Bowman Sterling Prospect Autographs Refractors
*REF: .5X TO 1.2X BASIC
STATED ODDS 1:13 HOBBY
STATED PRINT RUN 150 SER.#'d SETS
EXCHANGE DEADLINE 7/31/2021
BSPALG Logan Gilbert 6.00 15.00
BSPANM Nick Madrigal 15.00 40.00

2019 Bowman Sterling Prospect Autographs Speckle Refractors
*SPECKLE REF: .6X TO 1.5X BASIC
STATED ODDS 1:20 HOBBY
STATED PRINT RUN 99 SER.#'d SETS
EXCHANGE DEADLINE 7/31/2021
BSPAJK Jarred Kelenic 30.00 80.00
BSPALG Logan Gilbert 8.00 20.00
BSPANM Nick Madrigal 20.00 50.00

2019 Bowman Sterling Prospect Autographs Wave Refractors
*WAVE REF: .5X TO 1.2X BASIC
STATED ODDS 1:16 HOBBY
STATED PRINT RUN 125 SER.#'d SETS
EXCHANGE DEADLINE 7/31/2021
BSPALG Logan Gilbert 6.00 15.00
BSPANM Nick Madrigal 15.00 40.00

2019 Bowman Sterling Prospects
PRINTING PLATE ODDS 1:260 HOBBY
PLATE PRINT RUN 1 SET PER COLOR
BLACK-CYAN-MAGENTA-YELLOW ISSUED
NO PLATE PRICING DUE TO SCARCITY
BPR1 Royce Lewis 1.25 3.00
BPR2 Nolan Jones 1.00 2.50
BPR3 Seth Beer 1.50 4.00
BPR4 Jarred Kelenic 2.50 6.00
BPR5 Triston McKenzie .60 1.50
BPR6 Jazz Chisholm 1.50 4.00
BPR7 MacKenzie Gore 1.25 3.00
BPR8 Jesus Luzardo 1.00 2.50
BPR9 Jesus Sanchez .60 1.50
BPR10 Ryan Mountcastle .75 2.00
BPR11 Luis Robert 6.00 15.00
BPR12 Alex Kirilloff 1.00 2.50
BPR13 Nick Madrigal 2.00 5.00
BPR14 Travis Swaggerty 1.00 2.50
BPR15 Adonis Medina 1.00 2.50
BPR16 Cristian Pache 1.50 4.00
BPR17 Ronaldo Hernandez .60 1.50
BPR18 Victor Mesa Jr. 1.50 4.00
BPR19 Hunter Greene 1.00 2.50
BPR20 Adrian Morejon .60 1.50
BPR21 Joey Bart 2.50 6.00
BPR22 Yordan Alvarez 4.00 10.00
BPR23 Yusniel Diaz 1.00 2.50
BPR24 Jonathan India .75 2.00
BPR25 Bo Bichette 3.00 8.00
BPR26 Mitch Keller .75 2.00
BPR27 Ian Anderson 1.50 4.00
BPR28 Brock Deatherage .60 1.50
BPR29 Dylan Cease 1.50 4.00
BPR30 Taylor Trammell .75 2.00
BPR31 Wander Franco 10.00 25.00
BPR32 Gavin Lux 2.00 5.00
BPR33 Nolan Gorman 2.00 5.00
BPR34 Casey Mize 1.50 4.00
BPR35 Seuly Matias .75 2.00
BPR36 Ke'Bryan Hayes .60 1.50
BPR37 Alec Bohm 2.50 6.00
BPR38 Estevan Florial 1.00 2.50
BPR39 Julio Pablo Martinez .60 1.50
BPR40 Sixto Sanchez .75 2.00
BPR41 Jo Adell 2.00 5.00
BPR42 Andres Gimenez .75 2.00
BPR43 Matthew Liberatore .75 2.00
BPR44 Dustin May 2.00 5.00
BPR45 Brendan McKay 1.00 2.50
BPR46 Keibert Ruiz 1.50 4.00
BPR47 Drew Waters 2.00 5.00
BPR48 Brady Singer 1.25 3.00
BPR49 Forrest Whitley 1.00 2.50
BPR50 Victor Victor Mesa 1.25 3.00

2019 Bowman Sterling Prospects Blue Refractors
*BLUE REF: 2X TO 5X BASIC
STATED ODDS 1:42 HOBBY
STATED PRINT RUN 25 SER.#'d SETS
BPR22 Yordan Alvarez 50.00 120.00
BPR25 Bo Bichette 25.00 60.00
BPR31 Wander Franco 60.00 150.00

2019 Bowman Sterling Prospects Gold Refractors
*GOLD REF: 1.2X TO 3X BASIC
STATED ODDS 1:21 HOBBY
STATED PRINT RUN 50 SER.#'d SETS
BPR22 Yordan Alvarez 30.00 80.00
BPR25 Bo Bichette 15.00 40.00
BPR31 Wander Franco 40.00 100.00

2019 Bowman Sterling Prospects Refractors
*REF: .6X TO 1.5X BASIC
STATED ODDS 1:6 HOBBY
STATED PRINT RUN 199 SER.#'d SETS
BPR22 Yordan Alvarez 12.00 30.00
BPR23 Yusniel Diaz 1.50 4.00
BPR25 Bo Bichette 8.00 20.00
BPR31 Wander Franco 20.00 50.00

2019 Bowman Sterling Prospects Speckle Refractors
*SPEC REF: .75X TO 2X BASIC
STATED ODDS 1:11 HOBBY
STATED PRINT RUN 99 SER.#'d SETS
BPR22 Yordan Alvarez 15.00 40.00
BPR25 Bo Bichette 10.00 25.00
BPR31 Wander Franco 25.00 60.00

2019 Bowman Sterling Retrospect
STATED ODDS 1:43 HOBBY
STATED PRINT RUN 99 SER.#'d SETS
*GOLD/50: .6X TO 1.5X BASIC
*BLUE/25: .75X TO 2X BASIC
SRAJ Aaron Judge 6.00 15.00
SRAN Aaron Nola 2.00 5.00
SRAR Anthony Rizzo 4.00 10.00
SRBH Bryce Harper 4.00 10.00
SRCY Christian Yelich 3.00 8.00
SRFF Freddie Freeman 3.00 8.00
SRFL Francisco Lindor 2.50 6.00
SRGS George Springer 2.00 5.00
SRJA Jose Altuve 2.00 5.00
SRJD Jacob deGrom 2.50 6.00
SRJR Jose Ramirez 2.00 5.00
SRJS Juan Soto 8.00 20.00
SRJV Joey Votto 2.50 6.00
SRKB Kris Bryant 3.00 8.00
SRLS Luis Severino 2.00 5.00
SRMA Miguel Andujar 2.50 6.00
SRMC Matt Chapman 2.50 6.00
SRMT Mike Trout 20.00 50.00
SRNS Noah Syndergaard 2.00 5.00
SROA Ozzie Albies 2.50 6.00
SRRAJ Ronald Acuna Jr. 12.00 30.00
SRRH Rhys Hoskins 3.00 8.00
SRSO Shohei Ohtani 3.00 8.00
SRSP Salvador Perez 2.00 5.00
SRYM Yadier Molina 2.50 6.00

2019 Bowman Sterling Retrospect Autographs
STATED ODDS 1:108 HOBBY
PRINT RUNS B/WN 15-50 COPIES PER
NO PRICING ON QTY 15
EXCHANGE DEADLINE 7/31/2021
*BLUE/25: .4X TO 1X p/r 25-35
*BLUE/25: .5X TO 1.2X p/r 45-50
SRAAJ Aaron Judge/25 75.00 200.00
SRAAN Aaron Nola/50 10.00 25.00
SRAAR Anthony Rizzo/45 20.00 50.00
SRACK Corey Kluber/50 8.00 20.00
SRACS Chris Sale/50 10.00 25.00
SRAFF Freddie Freeman/30 30.00 80.00
SRAGS George Springer/30 6.00 15.00
SRAJA Jose Altuve/30 20.00 50.00
SRAJR Jose Ramirez/50 10.00 25.00
SRAJS Juan Soto/35 50.00 120.00
SRAJV Joey Votto/45 15.00 40.00
SRAKB Kris Bryant/45 60.00 150.00
SRALS Luis Severino/35 12.00 30.00
SRAMA Miguel Andujar/30 12.00 30.00
SRANS Noah Syndergaard/30 12.00 30.00
SRARAJ Ronald Acuna Jr./25 125.00 300.00
SRARH Rhys Hoskins/35 15.00 40.00
SRASP Salvador Perez/35 12.00 30.00
SRAWM Whit Merrifield/50 10.00 25.00

2019 Bowman Sterling Rookie Autographs
STATED ODDS 1:36 HOBBY
EXCHANGE DEADLINE 7/31/2021
BSRABL Brandon Lowe 10.00 25.00
BSRABW Bryse Wilson 4.00 10.00
BSRACA Chance Adams 2.50 6.00
BSRACB Corbin Burnes 4.00 10.00
BSRACM Cedric Mullins 4.00 10.00
BSRADL Dawel Lugo 4.00 10.00
BSRAJS Justus Sheffield 4.00 10.00
BSRAKA Kolby Allard 4.00 10.00
BSRAKW Kyle Wright 4.00 10.00
BSRALU Luis Urias 4.00 10.00
BSRARB Ryan Borucki 2.50 6.00

2019 Bowman Sterling Rookie Autographs Blue Refractors
*BLUE REF: 1X TO 2.5X BASIC
STATED ODDS 1:215 HOBBY
STATED PRINT RUN 25 SER.#'d SETS
EXCHANGE DEADLINE 7/31/2021
BSRAMK Michael Kopech 20.00 50.00
BSRAPA Peter Alonso 200.00 500.00
BSRAVGJ Vladimir Guerrero Jr. 200.00 500.00

2019 Bowman Sterling Rookie Autographs Gold Refractors
*GOLD REF: .75X TO 2X BASIC
STATED ODDS 1:108 HOBBY
STATED PRINT RUN 50 SER.#'d SETS
EXCHANGE DEADLINE 7/31/2021
BSRAMK Michael Kopech 15.00 40.00
BSRAPA Peter Alonso 150.00 400.00
BSRAVGJ Vladimir Guerrero Jr. 75.00 200.00

2019 Bowman Sterling Rookie Autographs Orange Refractors
*ORANGE REF: .6X TO 1.5X BASIC
STATED ODDS 1:72 HOBBY
STATED PRINT RUN 75 SER.#'d SETS
EXCHANGE DEADLINE 7/31/2021
BSRAMK Michael Kopech 12.00 30.00
BSRAPA Peter Alonso 125.00 300.00
BSRAVGJ Vladimir Guerrero Jr. 60.00 150.00

2019 Bowman Sterling Rookie Autographs Refractors
*REF: .5X TO 1.2X BASIC
STATED ODDS 1:36 HOBBY
STATED PRINT RUN 150 SER.#'d SETS
EXCHANGE DEADLINE 7/31/2021
BSRAMK Michael Kopech 10.00 25.00

2019 Bowman Sterling Rookie Autographs Speckle Refractors
*SPECKLE REF: .5X TO 1.2X BASIC
STATED ODDS 1:55 HOBBY
STATED PRINT RUN 99 SER.#'d SETS
EXCHANGE DEADLINE 7/31/2021
BSRAMK Michael Kopech 10.00 25.00

2019 Bowman Sterling Rookie Autographs Wave Refractors
*WAVE REF: .5X TO 1.2X BASIC
STATED ODDS 1:43 HOBBY
STATED PRINT RUN 125 SER.#'d SETS
EXCHANGE DEADLINE 7/31/2021
BSRAMK Michael Kopech 10.00 25.00

2019 Bowman Sterling Rookies
PRINTING PLATE ODDS 1:260 HOBBY
PLATE PRINT RUN 1 SET PER COLOR
BLACK-CYAN-MAGENTA-YELLOW ISSUED
NO PLATE PRICING DUE TO SCARCITY
BSR51 Kyle Tucker 1.25 3.00
BSR52 Keston Hiura 2.00 5.00
BSR53 Enyel De Los Santos .60 1.50
BSR54 Jake Bauers 1.00 2.50
BSR55 Brandon Lowe 1.00 2.50
BSR56 Christin Stewart .75 2.00
BSR57 Willians Astudillo .60 1.50
BSR58 Brad Keller .60 1.50
BSR59 Ryan Borucki .60 1.50
BSR60 Kyle Wright 1.00 2.50
BSR61 Pete Alonso 6.00 15.00
BSR62 Rowdy Tellez 1.00 2.50
BSR63 Josh James 1.00 2.50
BSR64 Jonathan Loaisiga .75 2.00
BSR65 Jake Cave .75 2.00
BSR66 Chance Adams .60 1.50
BSR67 Cedric Mullins 1.00 2.50
BSR68 Ryan O'Hearn .60 1.50
BSR69 Austin Riley 3.00 8.00
BSR70 Eloy Jimenez 2.50 6.00
BSR71 Dawel Lugo 1.00 2.50
BSR72 Bryse Wilson .75 2.00
BSR73 Fernando Tatis Jr. 10.00 25.00
BSR74 Reese McGuire 1.00 2.50
BSR75 Justus Sheffield 1.00 2.50
BSR76 Kevin Newman 1.00 2.50
BSR77 Taylor Ward .60 1.50
BSR78 Brendan Rodgers 1.00 2.50
BSR79 Chris Shaw .60 1.50
BSR80 Heath Fillmyer .60 1.50
BSR81 Touki Toussaint .75 2.00
BSR82 Garrett Hampson .60 1.50
BSR83 Kolby Allard 1.00 2.50
BSR84 Corbin Burnes 1.00 2.50
BSR85 Luis Urias 1.00 2.50
BSR86 Ramon Laureano 1.25 3.00
BSR87 Steven Duggar .75 2.00
BSR88 Michael Kopech 1.25 3.00
BSR89 Vladimir Guerrero Jr. 4.00 10.00
BSR90 Cionel Perez .60 1.50
BSR91 Jeff McNeil 1.50 4.00
BSR92 Dean Deetz .60 1.50
BSR93 Dakota Hudson .75 2.00
BSR94 Nick Senzel 2.00 5.00
BSR95 Danny Jansen .60 1.50
BSR96 Sean Reid-Foley .60 1.50
BSR97 David Fletcher 2.00 5.00
BSR98 Kevin Kramer .75 2.00
BSR99 Carter Kieboom 1.00 2.50
BSR100 Yusei Kikuchi 1.00 2.50

2019 Bowman Sterling Rookies Blue Refractors
*BLUE REF: 2X TO 5X BASIC
STATED ODDS 1:42 HOBBY
STATED PRINT RUN 25 SER.#'d SETS
BSR61 Pete Alonso 50.00 120.00
BSR89 Vladimir Guerrero Jr. 50.00 210.00

2019 Bowman Sterling Rookies Gold Refractors
*GOLD REF: 1.2X TO 3X BASIC
STATED ODDS 1:21 HOBBY
STATED PRINT RUN 50 SER.#'d SETS
BSR61 Pete Alonso 30.00 80.00
BSR89 Vladimir Guerrero Jr. 30.00 80.00

2019 Bowman Sterling Rookies Refractors
*REF: .6X TO 1.5X BASIC
STATED ODDS 1:6 HOBBY
STATED PRINT RUN 199 SER.#'d SETS
BSR61 Pete Alonso 15.00 40.00
BSR89 Vladimir Guerrero Jr. 15.00 40.00

2019 Bowman Sterling Rookies Speckle Refractors
*SPEC REF: .75X TO 2X BASIC
STATED ODDS 1:11 HOBBY
STATED PRINT RUN 99 SER.#'d SETS
BSR61 Pete Alonso 20.00 50.00
BSR89 Vladimir Guerrero Jr. 20.00 50.00

2019 Bowman Sterling Triple Autographs Refractors
STATED ODDS 1:809 HOBBY
STATED PRINT RUN 25 SER.#'d SETS
EXCHANGE DEADLINE 7/31/2021
TRAGTJ Jimenez/Tatis Jr/Vladdy Jr 400.00 1000.00
TRAKKS Kikuchi/Sheffield/Kopech 25.00 60.00
TRAMBB Bart/Mize/Bohm 100.00 250.00
TRAMMP Perez/Manning/Mize 75.00 200.00
TRAMNA Alonso/Mauricio/Newton

2020 Bowman Sterling Rookies
BSR51 Bobby Bradley .75 2.00
BSR52 Jaylin Davis 1.00 2.50
BSR53 Abraham Toro .75 2.00
BSR54 Nick Solak 1.00 2.50
BSR55 Brusdar Graterol 1.00 2.50
BSR56 Bo Bichette 5.00 12.00
BSR57 Nico Hoerner 2.50 6.00
BSR58 A.J. Puk 1.25 3.00
BSR59 Jesus Luzardo 1.25 3.00
BSR60 Jordan Yamamoto .75 2.00
BSR61 James Karinchak 6.00 15.00
BSR62 Brendan McKay 1.00 2.50
BSR63 Tony Gonsolin 2.50 6.00
BSR64 Hunter Harvey 1.00 2.50
BSR65 Sean Murphy 1.00 2.50
BSR66 Sam Hilliard 1.00 2.50
BSR67 Isan Diaz 1.00 2.50
BSR68 Kwang-Hyun Kim 2.00 5.00
BSR69 Junior Fernandez .60 1.50
BSR70 Brock Burke .60 1.50
BSR71 Randy Arozarena 5.00 12.00
BSR72 Seth Brown .60 1.50
BSR73 Yu Chang 1.00 2.50
BSR74 Aaron Civale 1.00 2.50
BSR75 Shun Yamaguchi .75 2.00
BSR76 Sheldon Neuse .75 2.00
BSR77 Justin Dunn .75 2.00
BSR78 Travis Demeritte .75 2.00
BSR79 Trent Grisham 2.50 6.00
BSR80 Luis Robert 6.00 15.00
BSR81 Kyle Lewis 6.00 15.00
BSR82 Adbert Alzolay .75 2.00
BSR83 Gavin Lux 4.00 10.00
BSR84 Mauricio Dubon .75 2.00
BSR85 Shogo Akiyama 3.00 8.00
BSR86 Andres Munoz .75 2.00
BSR87 Dustin May 3.00 8.00
BSR88 Zack Collins .75 2.00
BSR89 Alex Young .60 1.50
BSR90 Adrian Morejon .60 1.50
BSR91 Zac Gallen 1.50 4.00
BSR92 Logan Allen .60 1.50
BSR93 Aristides Aquino 4.00 10.00
BSR94 Jake Rogers .60 1.50
BSR95 Yordan Alvarez 5.00 12.00
BSR96 Anthony Kay .60 1.50
BSR97 Michel Baez .60 1.50
BSR98 Dylan Cease 1.25 3.00
BSR99 Robel Garcia .60 1.50
BSR100 Jose Urquidy .75 2.00

2020 Bowman Sterling Rookies Blue Refractors
*BLUE REF: 2X TO 5X BASIC
STATED ODDS 1:XX HOBBY
STATED PRINT RUN 25 SER.#'d SETS
BSR56 Bo Bichette 50.00 120.00
BSR61 James Karinchak 60.00 150.00
BSR80 Luis Robert 50.00 120.00
BSR81 Kyle Lewis 40.00 100.00

2020 Bowman Sterling Rookies Gold Refractors
*GOLD REF: 1.2X TO 3X BASIC
STATED ODDS 1:XX HOBBY
STATED PRINT RUN 50 SER.#'d SETS
BSR56 Bo Bichette 30.00 80.00
BSR61 James Karinchak 40.00 100.00
BSR80 Luis Robert 30.00 80.00
BSR81 Kyle Lewis 25.00 60.00

2020 Bowman Sterling Rookies Magenta Refractors
*MAGENTA REF: 1X TO 2.5X BASIC
STATED ODDS 1:XX HOBBY
STATED PRINT RUN 75 SER.#'d SETS
BSR56 Bo Bichette 25.00 60.00
BSR61 James Karinchak 30.00 80.00
BSR80 Luis Robert 25.00 60.00
BSR81 Kyle Lewis 20.00 50.00

2020 Bowman Sterling Rookies Refractors
*REF: .6X TO 1.5X BASIC
STATED ODDS 1:XX HOBBY
STATED PRINT RUN 199 SER.#'d SETS
BSR56 Bo Bichette 15.00 40.00
BSR61 James Karinchak 20.00 50.00
BSR81 Kyle Lewis 10.00 25.00

2020 Bowman Sterling Rookies Speckle Refractors
*SPEC REF: .75X TO 2X BASIC
STATED ODDS 1:XX HOBBY
STATED PRINT RUN 99 SER.#'d SETS
BSR56 Bo Bichette 20.00 50.00
BSR61 James Karinchak 25.00 60.00
BSR80 Luis Robert 20.00 50.00
BSR81 Kyle Lewis 15.00 40.00

2020 Bowman Sterling Bowman Die Cut Autographs
STATED ODDS 1:XX HOBBY
PRINT RUNS B/WN 75-99 COPIES PER
EXCHANGE DEADLINE 7/31/22
BDCAAA Aristides Aquino/99 15.00 40.00
BDCAAR Adley Rutschman/75 25.00 60.00
BDCAAV Andrew Vaughn/99 15.00 40.00
BDCABM Brendan McKay 20.00
BDCAJJ Josh Jung/99 20.00 50.00
BDCAJL Jesus Luzardo/99 15.00 40.00
BDCAJR Jackson Rutledge/99 6.00 15.00
BDCALP Luis Patino/99 12.00 30.00
BDCANH Nico Hoerner/99 10.00 25.00
BDCANL Nick Lodolo/99 6.00 15.00
BDCARP Robert Puason/99 20.00 50.00
BDCASH Sam Huff/99 12.00 30.00
BDCASL Shea Langeliers/99 12.00 30.00
BDCATS Tarik Skubal/99 20.00 50.00
BDCAXE Xavier Edwards/99 15.00 40.00
BDCAYA Yordan Alvarez/75 40.00 100.00
BDCAAVO Anthony Volpe/99 20.00 50.00
BDCABBA Brett Baty/99 15.00 40.00
BDCABWJ Bobby Witt Jr./99 75.00 200.00
BDCAJJB JJ Bleday/75 15.00 40.00

2020 Bowman Sterling Bowman Die Cut Autographs Blue Refractors
*BLUE REF: .6X TO 1.5X BASIC
STATED ODDS 1:XX HOBBY
STATED PRINT RUN 25 SER.#'d SETS
EXCHANGE DEADLINE 7/31/22
BDCABM Brendan McKay 10.00 25.00
BDCAAVO Anthony Volpe 40.00 100.00

2020 Bowman Sterling Dual Autographs Refractors
STATED ODDS 1:XX HOBBY
STATED PRINT RUN 25 SER.#'d SETS
BDAAB B.Bichette/Y.Alvarez 125.00 300.00
BDABR H.Ramos/J.Bart 50.00 120.00
BDACD B.Dalbec/T.Casas 50.00 120.00
BDACG D.Carlson/N.Gorman 125.00 300.00
BDADG D.Garcia/J.Dominguez 400.00 800.00
BDAFH W.Franco/R.Hernandez 75.00 200.00
BDAGA M.Gore/C.Abrams 100.00 250.00
BDALL T.Larnach/R.Lewis 50.00 120.00
BDALP A.Puk/J.Luzardo 25.00 60.00
BDAMG C.Mize/R.Greene 100.00 250.00
BDARM R.Mountcastle/A.Rutschman 100.00 250.00
BDARW E.White/J.Rodriguez
BDATR K.Robinson/A.Thomas 50.00 120.00
BDAVM N.Madrigal/A.Vaughn 75.00 200.00
BDAWS B.Singer/B.Witt Jr. 100.00 250.00

2020 Bowman Sterling Prospects
BPR1 Wander Franco 6.00 15.00
BPR2 Brandon Marsh .60 1.50
BPR3 Taylor Trammell .75 2.00
BPR4 Alex Kirilloff 1.25 3.00
BPR5 Ronny Mauricio 1.50 4.00
BPR6 Nolan Jones 1.00 2.50
BPR7 Luis Patino 1.00 2.50
BPR8 Royce Lewis 1.50 4.00
BPR9 Oneil Cruz .75 2.00
BPR10 Nick Lodolo 1.00 2.50
BPR11 Jazz Chisholm 1.50 4.00
BPR12 Jarred Kelenic 4.00 10.00
BPR13 Sixto Sanchez 1.00 2.50
BPR14 Josh Jung 1.50 4.00
BPR15 Jasson Dominguez 10.00 25.00
BPR16 Ke'Bryan Hayes .60 1.50
BPR17 Alek Thomas .75 2.00
BPR18 Julio Rodriguez 4.00 10.00
BPR19 Vidal Brujan 2.00 5.00
BPR20 Drew Waters 1.50 4.00
BPR21 MacKenzie Gore 1.25 3.00
BPR22 Andrew Vaughn 2.50 6.00
BPR23 Jeter Downs 2.50 6.00
BPR24 Alec Bohm 4.00 10.00
BPR25 Matt Manning .75 2.00
BPR26 CJ Abrams 2.50 6.00
BPR27 Kristian Robinson 2.00 5.00
BPR28 Matthew Liberatore .75 2.00
BPR29 Bobby Witt Jr. 5.00 12.00
BPR30 Cristian Pache 4.00 10.00

BPR31 Forrest Whitley .60 1.50
BPR32 Nolan Gorman 1.25 3.00
BPR33 Adley Rutschman 4.00 10.00
BPR34 Jo Adell 4.00 10.00
BPR35 Luis Campusano 3.00 8.00
BPR36 Dylan Carlson 2.50 6.00
BPR37 Nick Madrigal 2.50 6.00
BPR38 Ian Anderson 1.50 4.00
BPR39 Hunter Greene 1.00 2.50
BPR40 Marco Luciano 2.50 6.00
BPR41 Casey Mize 5.00 12.00
BPR42 Logan Gilbert .75 2.00
BPR43 JJ Bleday 2.00 5.00
BPR44 Tarik Skubal 3.00 8.00
BPR45 Spencer Howard 2.50 6.00
BPR46 Grayson Rodriguez 1.00 2.50
BPR47 Evan White .60 1.50
BPR48 Riley Greene 2.50 6.00
BPR49 Joey Bart 3.00 8.00
BPR50 Nate Pearson 4.00 10.00

2020 Bowman Sterling Prospects Blue Refractors
*BLUE REF: 2X TO 5X BASIC
STATED ODDS 1:XX HOBBY
STATED PRINT RUN 25 SER.#'d SETS
BPR1 Wander Franco 60.00 150.00
BPR5 Ronny Mauricio 12.00 30.00
BPR15 Jasson Dominguez 75.00 200.00
BPR18 Julio Rodriguez 30.00 80.00
BPR29 Bobby Witt Jr. 60.00 150.00
BPR30 Cristian Pache 30.00 80.00

2020 Bowman Sterling Prospects Gold Refractors
*GOLD REF: 1.2X TO 3X BASIC
STATED ODDS 1:XX HOBBY
STATED PRINT RUN 50 SER.#'d SETS
BPR1 Wander Franco 40.00 100.00
BPR5 Ronny Mauricio 8.00 20.00
BPR15 Jasson Dominguez 50.00 120.00
BPR18 Julio Rodriguez 20.00 50.00
BPR29 Bobby Witt Jr. 40.00 100.00
BPR30 Cristian Pache 20.00 50.00

2020 Bowman Sterling Prospects Magenta Refractors
*MAGENTA REF: 1X TO 2.5X BASIC
STATED ODDS 1:XX HOBBY
STATED PRINT RUN 75 SER.#'d SETS
BPR1 Wander Franco 25.00 60.00
BPR5 Ronny Mauricio 6.00 15.00
BPR15 Jasson Dominguez 40.00 100.00
BPR29 Bobby Witt Jr. 20.00 50.00
BPR30 Cristian Pache 15.00 40.00

2020 Bowman Sterling Prospects Refractors
*REF: .6X TO 1.5X BASIC
STATED ODDS 1:XX HOBBY
STATED PRINT RUN 199 SER.#'d SETS
BPR5 Ronny Mauricio 4.00 10.00
BPR15 Jasson Dominguez 25.00 60.00
BPR29 Bobby Witt Jr. 12.00 30.00
BPR30 Cristian Pache 10.00 25.00

2020 Bowman Sterling Prospects Speckle Refractors
*SPEC REF: .75X TO 2X BASIC
STATED ODDS 1:XX HOBBY
STATED PRINT RUN 99 SER.#'d SETS
BPR1 Wander Franco 20.00 50.00
BPR5 Ronny Mauricio 5.00 12.00
BPR15 Jasson Dominguez 30.00 80.00
BPR29 Bobby Witt Jr. 15.00 40.00
BPR30 Cristian Pache 12.00 30.00

2020 Bowman Sterling Prospect Autographs
STATED ODDS 1:XX HOBBY
EXCHANGE DEADLINE 7/31/22
BSPAAA Aaron Ashby 2.50 6.00
BSPAAM Alek Manoah 3.00 8.00
BSPAAP Andy Pages 6.00 15.00
BSPAAR Adley Rutschman 25.00 60.00
BSPAAV Anthony Volpe 10.00 25.00
BSPAAVA Andrew Vaughn 12.00 30.00
BSPABB Brett Baty 8.00 20.00
BSPABD Brennen Davis 8.00 20.00
BSPABM Brady McConnell 3.00 8.00
BSPABMA Brennan Malone 4.00 10.00
BSPABS Bryson Stott 6.00 15.00
BSPABSH Braden Shewmake 4.00 10.00
BSPABWJ Bobby Witt Jr. 30.00 80.00
BSPACC Corbin Carroll 4.00 10.00
BSPACS Canaan Smith 5.00 12.00
BSPADE Daniel Espino 3.00 8.00
BSPADJ Drey Jameson 2.50 6.00
BSPAGG Grant Gambrell 3.00 8.00
BSPAGHJ Glenallen Hill Jr. 4.00 10.00
BSPAGJ Greg Jones 3.00 8.00
BSPAGV Gus Varland 2.50 6.00
BSPAHB Hunter Bishop 8.00 20.00
BSPAJA Jacob Amaya 4.00 10.00
BSPAJC Joey Cantillo 2.50 6.00
BSPAJD Jasson Dominguez 125.00 300.00
BSPAJDU Jarren Duran 10.00 25.00
BSPAJJB JJ Bleday 12.00 30.00
BSPAJJG JJ Goss 2.50 6.00
BSPAJJU Josh Jung 8.00 20.00
BSPAJP Jeremy Pena 4.00 10.00
BSPAJR Jackson Rutledge 4.00 10.00
BSPAJRY Joe Ryan 2.50 6.00
BSPAJS Jake Sanford 4.00 10.00
BSPAKC Keoni Cavaco 2.50 6.00
BSPAKP Kyren Paris 4.00 10.00
BSPALD Logan Davidson 3.00 8.00
BSPALP Luis Patino 5.00 12.00
BSPAMB Michael Busch 5.00 12.00
BSPAML Matthew Lugo 4.00 10.00
BSPAMT Matthew Thompson 3.00 8.00
BSPAMTO Michael Toglia 2.50 6.00
BSPAMV Miguel Vargas 6.00 15.00
BSPAMW Matt Wallner 5.00 12.00
BSPANL Nick Lodolo 4.00 10.00
BSPAQP Quinn Priester 4.00 10.00
BSPARC Ruben Cardenas 3.00 8.00
BSPARG Riley Greene 15.00 40.00
BSPARH Rece Hinds 3.00 8.00
BSPARP Robert Puason 20.00 50.00
BSPASA Sherten Apostel 5.00 12.00
BSPASH Sam Huff 8.00 20.00
BSPASL Shea Langeliers 6.00 15.00
BSPASS Sammy Siani 2.50 6.00
BSPATS Tarik Skubal 8.00 20.00
BSPAWW Will Wilson 3.00 8.00
BSPAXE Xavier Edwards 5.00 12.00

2020 Bowman Sterling Prospect Autographs Blue Refractors
*BLUE REF: 1X TO 2.5X BASIC
STATED ODDS 1:XX HOBBY
STATED PRINT RUN 25 SER.#'d SETS
EXCHANGE DEADLINE 7/31/22
BSPARP Robert Puason 75.00 200.00

2020 Bowman Sterling Prospect Autographs Gold Refractors
*GOLD REF: .75X TO 2X BASIC
STATED ODDS 1:XX HOBBY
STATED PRINT RUN 50 SER.#'d SETS
EXCHANGE DEADLINE 7/31/22
BSPARP Robert Puason 60.00 150.00

2020 Bowman Sterling Prospect Autographs Orange Refractors
*ORANGE REF: .6X TO 1.5X BASIC
STATED ODDS 1:XX HOBBY
STATED PRINT RUN 75 SER.#'d SETS
EXCHANGE DEADLINE 7/31/22
BSPARP Robert Puason 50.00 120.00

2020 Bowman Sterling Prospect Autographs Refractors
*REF: .5X TO 1.2X BASIC
STATED ODDS 1:XX HOBBY
STATED PRINT RUN 150 SER.#'d SETS
EXCHANGE DEADLINE 7/31/22
BSPARP Robert Puason 40.00 100.00

2020 Bowman Sterling Prospect Autographs Speckle Refractors
*SPEC REF: .5X TO 1.2X BASIC
STATED ODDS 1:XX HOBBY
STATED PRINT RUN 99 SER.#'d SETS
EXCHANGE DEADLINE 7/31/22
BSPARP Robert Puason 40.00 100.00

2020 Bowman Sterling Prospect Autographs Wave Refractors
*WAVE REF: .5X TO 1.2X BASIC
STATED ODDS 1:XX HOBBY
STATED PRINT RUN 125 SER.#'d SETS
EXCHANGE DEADLINE 7/31/22
BSPARP Robert Puason 40.00 100.00

2020 Bowman Sterling Rookie Autographs Blue Refractors
*BLUE REF: 1X TO 2.5X BASIC
STATED ODDS 1:XX HOBBY
STATED PRINT RUN 25 SER.#'d SETS
EXCHANGE DEADLINE 7/31/22
BSRADM Dustin May 60.00 150.00
BSRANS Nick Solak 25.00 60.00
BSRAYA Yordan Alvarez 75.00 200.00

2020 Bowman Sterling Rookie Autographs Gold Refractors
*GOLD REF: .75X TO 2X BASIC
STATED ODDS 1:XX HOBBY
STATED PRINT RUN 50 SER.#'d SETS
EXCHANGE DEADLINE 7/31/22
BSRADM Dustin May 50.00 120.00
BSRANS Nick Solak 20.00 50.00
BSRAYA Yordan Alvarez 60.00 150.00

2020 Bowman Sterling Rookie Autographs Orange Refractors
*ORANGE REF: .6X TO 1.5X BASIC
STATED ODDS 1:XX HOBBY
STATED PRINT RUN 75 SER.#'d SETS
EXCHANGE DEADLINE 7/31/22
BSRADM Dustin May 40.00 100.00

2020 Bowman Sterling Rookie Autographs Refractors
*REF: .5X TO 1.2X BASIC
STATED ODDS 1:XX HOBBY
STATED PRINT RUN 150 SER.#'d SETS
EXCHANGE DEADLINE 7/31/22

2020 Bowman Sterling Rookie Autographs Speckle Refractors
*SPEC REF: .5X TO 1.2X BASIC
STATED ODDS 1:XX HOBBY
STATED PRINT RUN 99 SER.#'d SETS
EXCHANGE DEADLINE 7/31/22
BSRADM Dustin May 25.00 60.00

2020 Bowman Sterling Rookie Autographs Wave Refractors
*WAVE REF: .5X TO 1.2X BASIC
STATED ODDS 1:XX HOBBY
STATED PRINT RUN 125 SER.#'d SETS
EXCHANGE DEADLINE 7/31/22
BSRADM Dustin May 25.00 60.00

2020 Bowman Sterling Sterling First Signs
STATED ODDS 1:XX HOBBY
STATED PRINT RUN 25 SER.#'d SETS
SFSAJ Aaron Judge 6.00 15.00
SFSAR Austin Riley 4.00 10.00
SFSBB Bo Bichette 15.00 40.00
SFSBH Bryce Harper 4.00 10.00
SFSCB Cavan Biggio 3.00 8.00
SFSCK Clayton Kershaw 5.00 12.00
SFSCY Christian Yelich 3.00 8.00
SFSEJ Eloy Jimenez 5.00 12.00
SFSFL Francisco Lindor 2.50 6.00
SFSGS George Springer 2.00 5.00
SFSGT Gleyber Torres 5.00 12.00
SFSJA Jose Altuve 2.00 5.00
SFSKB Kris Bryant 3.00 8.00
SFSKH Keston Hiura 3.00 8.00
SFSMT Mike Trout 25.00 60.00
SFSNA Nolan Arenado 3.00 8.00
SFSOA Ozzie Albies 2.50 6.00
SFSPA Pete Alonso 6.00 15.00
SFSPD Paul DeJong 2.50 6.00
SFSRH Rhys Hoskins 3.00 8.00
SFSXB Xander Bogaerts 2.50 6.00
SFSARI Anthony Rizzo 4.00 10.00
SFSFTJ Fernando Tatis Jr. 20.00 50.00
SFSRAJ Ronald Acuna Jr. 10.00 25.00
SFSVGJ Vladimir Guerrero Jr. 5.00 12.00

2020 Bowman Sterling Sterling First Signs Blue Refractors
*BLUE REF: .8X TO 2X BASIC
STATED ODDS 1:XX HOBBY
STATED PRINT RUN 25 SER.#'d SETS
SFSBB Bo Bichette 50.00 120.00
SFSMT Mike Trout 75.00 200.00

2020 Bowman Sterling Sterling First Signs Gold Refractors
*GOLD REF: .6X TO 1.5X BASIC
STATED ODDS 1:XX HOBBY
STATED PRINT RUN 50 SER.#'d SETS
SFSBB Bo Bichette 40.00 100.00
SFSMT Mike Trout 50.00 120.00

2020 Bowman Sterling Sterling First Signs Autographs
STATED ODDS 1:XX HOBBY
PRINT RUNS B/WN 30-50 COPIES PER
EXCHANGE DEADLINE 7/31/22
SFSABH Bryce Harper
SFSAEJ Eloy Jimenez 30.00 80.00
SFSAGT Gleyber Torres 40.00 100.00
SFSAJA Jose Altuve 12.00 30.00
SFSAMT Mike Trout
SFSARH Rhys Hoskins 20.00 50.00
SFSAXB Xander Bogaerts 20.00 50.00
SFSARAJ Ronald Acuna Jr. 60.00 150.00

2020 Bowman Sterling Sterling First Signs Autographs Blue Refractors
*BLUE REF: .5X TO 1.2X BASIC
STATED ODDS 1:XX HOBBY
STATED PRINT RUN 25 SER.#'d SETS
EXCHANGE DEADLINE 7/31/22
SFSABH Bryce Harper 125.00 300.00
SFSAMT Mike Trout 500.00 1000.00
SFSARAJ Ronald Acuna Jr. 125.00 300.00

2020 Bowman Sterling Triple Autographs Refractors
STATED ODDS 1:XX HOBBY
STATED PRINT RUN 25 SER.#'d SETS
BTACGM Gorman/Carlson/Montero 150.00 400.00
BTADRG Downs/Ruiz/Gray 40.00 100.00
BTAFMH Franco/Hernandez/McKay 150.00 400.00
BTAGIL India/Lodolo/Greene 60.00 150.00
BTAKRW Kelenic/Rodriguez/White 150.00 400.00
BTALPM Murphy/Puk/Luzardo 30.00 80.00
BTAMMG Manning/Greene/Mize 150.00 400.00
BTARRM Rutschman/Rodriguez/Mountcastle 100.00
250.00
BTATRV Robinson/Thomas/Varsho 100.00 250.00
BTAWSK Kowar/Witt Jr./Singer 125.00 300.00

2017 Bowman Topps Holiday
THAB Andrew Benintendi .75 2.00
THABR Alex Bregman 1.00 2.50
THAJ Aaron Judge 3.00 8.00
THAM Austin Meadows .40 1.00
THAR Amed Rosario .40 1.00
THARE Alex Reyes .30 .75
THARI Anthony Rizzo .60 1.50
THAS Andrew Sopko .25 .60
THAV Alex Verdugo .40 1.00
THAY Andy Yerzy .25 .60
THBB Bo Bichette 1.00 2.50
THBD Bobby Dalbec .60 1.50
THBH Brent Honeywell .30 .75
THBHA Bryce Harper .60 1.50
THBR Bryan Reynolds .30 .75
THBRO Brendan Rodgers .30 .75
THBRU Blake Rutherford .40 1.00
THBZ Bradley Zimmer .30 .75
THCA Christian Arroyo .40 1.00
THCB Cody Bellinger 4.00 10.00
THCBL Charlie Blackmon .40 1.00
THCC Carlos Correa .40 1.00
THCF Clint Frazier .50 1.25
THCK Clayton Kershaw .75 2.00
THCS Christin Stewart .30 .75
THCSA Chris Sale .40 1.00
THCSE Corey Seager .40 1.00
THCW Colton Welker .25 .60
THDC Dylan Cease .60 1.50
THDD David Dahl .40 1.00
THDS Dansby Swanson .60 1.50
THEJ Eloy Jimenez 1.00 2.50
THFB Franklin Barreto .25 .60
THFL Francisco Lindor .40 1.00
THFM Francisco Mejia .40 1.00
THFR Francisco Rios .25 .60
THFW Forrest Whitley .75 2.00
THGL Gavin Lux 1.50 4.00
THGS Giancarlo Stanton .40 1.00
THGT Gleyber Torres 4.00 10.00
THHR Hunter Renfroe .30 .75
THIH Ian Happ .50 1.25
THJA Jorge Alfaro .30 .75
THJAB Jose Abreu .40 1.00
THJAL Jose Altuve .30 .75
THJC Jake Cave .25 .60
THJG Jay Groome .50 1.25
THJL Jesus Luzardo .40 1.00
THJS Justus Sheffield .40 1.00
THJSO Juan Soto 5.00 12.00
THKB Kris Bryant .50 1.25
THKH Kyle Holder .30 .75
THKM Kevin Maitan .60 1.50
THKT Kyle Tucker .50 1.25
THLA Lazarito Armenteros .60 1.50
THLB Lewis Brinson .40 1.00
THLE Lucas Erceg .30 .75
THLT Leody Taveras .75 2.00
THMB Mookie Betts .60 1.50
THMC Michael Conforto .30 .75
THMCA Miguel Cabrera .40 1.00
THMF Michael Fulmer .25 .60
THMG Mike Gerber .25 .60
THMK Mitch Keller .30 .75
THMKO Michael Kopech .50 1.25
THMM Mickey Moniak .60 1.50
THMM Manny Machado .40 1.00
THMS Max Scherzer .40 1.00
THMT Mike Trout 2.00 5.00
THNA Nolan Arenado .50 1.25
THNS Nick Senzel .75 2.00
THNSY Noah Syndergaard .30 .75
THOA Ozzie Albies 1.00 2.50
THPC P.J. Conlon .25 .60
THPG Paul Goldschmidt .40 1.00
THPW Patrick Weigel .25 .60
THRA Ronald Acuna 6.00 15.00
THRD Rafael Devers .50 1.25
THRH Rhys Hoskins 1.00 2.50
THRHE Ryon Healy .30 .75
THRM Ryan Mountcastle .40 1.00
THRT Raimel Tapia .30 .75
THR Rudolph .20 .50
THSC Santa Claus .20 .50
THSK Scott Kingery .40 1.00
THSN Sean Newcomb .30 .75
THS Snowman .20 .50
THTE Thairo Estrada .50 1.25
THTL Tim Lynch .30 .75
THTM Triston McKenzie .25 .60
THTMA Trey Mancini .50 1.25
THTS Tyler Stephenson .25 .60
THTT Taylor Trammell .40 1.00
THVGJ Vladimir Guerrero Jr. 3.00 8.00
THVR Victor Robles .60 1.50
THWB Wuilmer Becerra .25 .60
THWBU Walker Buehler .60 1.50
THWC Willie Calhoun .40 1.00
THYG Yulieski Gurriel .40 1.00
THYM Yoan Moncada .75 2.00

2017 Bowman Topps Holiday Ugly Sweater Green
*UGLY GREEN: 2.5X TO 6X
STATED PRINT RUN 99 SER.#'d SETS

2017 Bowman Topps Holiday Autographs
THAR Amed Rosario/85 6.00 15.00
THARI Anthony Rizzo
THAS Andrew Sopko/35 4.00 10.00
THAY Andy Yerzy/99 4.00 10.00
THBD Bobby Dalbec/99 10.00 25.00
THBH Brent Honeywell/5
THBR Bryan Reynolds/99 6.00 15.00
THCBL Charlie Blackmon/85 6.00 15.00
THCS Christin Stewart/99 5.00 12.00
THDD David Dahl/99 5.00 12.00
THFR Francisco Rios/35 4.00 10.00
THGL Gavin Lux/99 25.00 60.00
THGT Gleyber Torres/65 60.00 150.00
THIH Ian Happ/50 8.00 20.00
THJA Jorge Alfaro/99 5.00 12.00
THJC Jake Cave/99 4.00 10.00
THJG Jay Groome/99 8.00 20.00
THJL Jesus Luzardo/99 6.00 15.00
THJS Justus Sheffield/99 6.00 15.00
THKH Kyle Holder/99 5.00 12.00
THKM Kevin Maitan/99 10.00 25.00
THLE Lucas Erceg/99 5.00 12.00
THMC Michael Conforto/5
THMF Michael Fulmer/50 4.00 10.00
THMG Mike Gerber/99 4.00 10.00
THMK Mitch Keller/99 5.00 12.00
THMM Manny Machado/10
THPW Patrick Weigel/99 4.00 10.00
THRA Ronald Acuna
THRD Rafael Devers/99 8.00 20.00
THRM Ryan Mountcastle/99 6.00 15.00
THRT Raimel Tapia/65 5.00 12.00
THSK Scott Kingery/40 6.00 15.00
THTE Thairo Estrada/99 30.00 80.00
THTL Tim Lynch/99 5.00 12.00
THTM Triston McKenzie/99 4.00 10.00
THTMA Trey Mancini/50 8.00 20.00
THTS Tyler Stephenson/80 4.00 10.00
THTT Taylor Trammell/82 6.00 15.00
THWB Wuilmer Becerra/99 4.00 10.00
THWBU Walker Buehler/10
THYG Yulieski Gurriel

2020 Bowman Transcendent
ONE COMPLETE SET PER BOX
STATED PRINT RUN 100 SER.#'d SETS
1 Wander Franco 60.00 150.00
2 Luis Robert 150.00 400.00
3 Justin Dunn 12.00 30.00
4 Cristian Pache 15.00 40.00
5 Matt Manning 10.00 25.00
6 Bobby Bradley 12.00 30.00
7 Casey Mize 12.00 30.00
8 Yoshi Tsutsugo 8.00 20.00
9 Dylan Carlson 15.00 40.00
10 Sixto Sanchez 8.00 20.00
11 JJ Bleday 30.00 80.00
12 Aaron Civale 6.00 15.00
13 Alec Bohm 25.00 60.00
14 Jasson Dominguez 150.00 400.00
15 Trent Grisham 15.00 40.00
16 Dustin May 20.00 50.00
17 Nick Madrigal 12.00 30.00
18 Royce Lewis 10.00 25.00
19 Jo Adell 50.00 120.00
20 A.J. Puk 8.00 20.00
21 Nico Hoerner 15.00 40.00
22 MacKenzie Gore 10.00 25.00
23 Sean Murphy 12.00 30.00
24 Yordan Alvarez 60.00 150.00
25 Jordan Yamamoto 5.00 12.00
26 Julio Rodriguez 50.00 120.00
27 Adley Rutschman 25.00 60.00
28 Nate Pearson 8.00 20.00
29 Michel Baez 4.00 10.00
30 CJ Abrams 15.00 40.00
31 Shun Yamaguchi 5.00 12.00
32 Nolan Gorman 8.00 20.00
33 Anthony Kay 4.00 10.00
34 Jarred Kelenic 60.00 150.00
35 Brusdar Graterol 12.00 30.00
36 Bo Bichette 75.00 200.00
37 Forrest Whitley 8.00 20.00
38 Marco Luciano 15.00 40.00
39 Bobby Witt Jr. 60.00 150.00
40 Dylan Cease 8.00 20.00
41 Jesus Luzardo 8.00 20.00
42 Shogo Akiyama 6.00 15.00
43 Brendan McKay 12.00 30.00
44 Andrew Vaughn 30.00 80.00
45 Aristides Aquino 8.00 20.00
46 Joey Bart 12.00 30.00
47 Adbert Alzolay 5.00 12.00
48 Kyle Lewis 75.00 200.00
49 Gavin Lux 50.00 120.00
50 Riley Greene 20.00 50.00

2020 Bowman Transcendent Autographs
OVERALL TWENTY EIGHT AUTOS PER BOX
STATED PRINT RUN 25 SER.#'d SETS
*VARIATION/25: .4X TO 1X BASIC
*BLUE/10: .5X TO 1.2X BASIC
*VAR BLUE/10: .5X TO 1.2X BASIC
BTAAR Adley Rutschman 80.00 200.00
BTAAT Alek Thomas 25.00 60.00
BTAAV Andrew Vaughn 50.00 120.00
BTABB Brett Baty 40.00 100.00
BTABBI Bo Bichette 150.00 400.00
BTABL Bayron Lora 200.00 500.00
BTABWJ Bobby Witt Jr. 150.00 400.00
BTACA CJ Abrams 50.00 125.00
BTACM Casey Mize 40.00 100.00
BTACP Cristian Pache 60.00 150.00
BTADG Deivi Garcia 100.00 250.00
BTADL Daniel Lynch 12.00 30.00
BTAEW Evan White 30.00 80.00
BTAGL Gavin Lux 80.00 200.00
BTAHB Hunter Bishop 50.00 120.00
BTAJA Jo Adell 75.00 200.00
BTAJB Joey Bart 40.00 100.00
BTAJD Jasson Dominguez 600.00 1500.00
BTAJG Jordan Groshans 25.00 60.00
BTAJJ Josh Jung 30.00 80.00
BTAJJB JJ Bleday 40.00 100.00
BTAJK Jarred Kelenic 125.00 300.00
BTAJR Julio Rodriguez 80.00 200.00
BTAKH Ke'Bryan Hayes 50.00 120.00
BTAKL Aristides Aquino 25.00 60.00
BTALR Luis Robert 200.00 500.00
BTANG Nolan Gorman 25.00 60.00
BTANH Nico Hoerner 50.00 120.00
BTANL Nick Lodolo 20.00 50.00
BTANP Nate Pearson 25.00 60.00
BTARG Riley Greene 50.00 125.00
BTASH Sam Huff 30.00 80.00
BTATS Tarik Skubal 40.00 100.00
BTATT Taylor Trammell 25.00 60.00
BTAWF Wander Franco 120.00 300.00
BTAYA Yordan Alvarez 75.00 200.00

1994 Bowman's Best
This 200-card standard-size set (produced by Topps) consists of 90 veteran stars, 90 rookies and prospects and 20 Mirror Image cards. The veteran cards have red fronts and are designated 1R-90R. The rookies and prospects cards have blue fronts and are designated 1B-90B. The Mirror Image cards feature a veteran star and a prospect matched by position in a horizontal design. These cards are numbered 91-110. Subsets featured are Super Vet (1R-6R), Super Rookie (82R-90R), and Blue Chip (1B-11B). Rookie Cards include Edgardo Alfonzo, Tony Clark, Brad Fullmer, Chan Ho Park, Jorge Posada and Edgar Renteria.

COMPLETE SET (200) 15.00 40.00
B1 Chipper Jones .50 1.25
B2 Derek Jeter 2.00 5.00
B3 Bill Pulsipher .20 .50
B4 James Baldwin .08 .25
B5 Brooks Kieschnick RC .20 .50
B6 Justin Thompson .08 .25
B7 Midre Cummings .08 .25
B8 Joey Hamilton .08 .25
B9 Pokey Reese .08 .25
B10 Brian Barber .08 .25
B11 John Burke .08 .25
B12 DeShawn Warren .08 .25
B13 Edgardo Alfonzo RC .40 1.00
B14 Eddie Pearson RC .20 .50
B15 Jimmy Haynes .08 .25
B16 Danny Bautista .08 .25
B17 Roger Cedeno .08 .25
B18 Jon Lieber .20 .50
B19 Billy Wagner RC 2.00 5.00
B20 Tate Seefried RC .20 .50
B21 Chad Mottola .08 .25
B22 Jose Malave .08 .25
B23 Terrell Wade RC .20 .50
B24 Shane Andrews .08 .25
B25 Chan Ho Park RC .60 1.50
B26 Kirk Presley RC .20 .50
B27 Robbie Beckett .08 .25
B28 Orlando Miller .08 .25
B29 Jorge Posada RC 4.00 10.00
B30 Frankie Rodriguez .08 .25
B31 Brian L. Hunter .08 .25
B32 Billy Ashley .08 .25
B33 Rondell White .20 .50
B34 John Roper .08 .25
B35 Marc Valdes .08 .25
B36 Scott Ruffcorn .08 .25
B37 Rod Henderson .08 .25
B38 Curtis Goodwin RC .20 .50
B39 Russ Davis .08 .25
B40 Rick Gorecki .08 .25
B41 Johnny Damon .50 1.25
B42 Roberto Petagine .08 .25
B43 Chris Snopek .08 .25
B44 Mark Acre RC .08 .25
B45 Todd Hollandsworth .08 .25
B46 Shawn Green .50 1.25
B47 John Carter RC .20 .50
B48 Jim Pittsley RC .20 .50
B49 John Wasdin RC .20 .50
B50 D.J. Boston RC .20 .50
B51 Tim Clark .08 .25
B52 Alex Ochoa .08 .25
B53 Chad Roper .08 .25
B54 Mike Kelly .08 .25
B55 Brad Fullmer RC .40 1.00
B56 Carl Everett .20 .50
B57 Tim Belk RC .20 .50
B58 Jimmy Hurst RC .20 .50
B59 Mac Suzuki RC .40 1.00
B60 Mike Moore .08 .25
B61 Alan Benes RC .20 .50
B62 Tony Clark RC .60 1.50
B63 Edgar Renteria RC 2.50 6.00
B64 Trey Beamon .08 .25
B65 LaTroy Hawkins RC .40 1.00
B66 Wayne Gomes RC .40 1.00
B67 Ray McDavid .08 .25
B68 John Dettmer .08 .25
B69 Willie Greene .08 .25
B70 Dave Stevens .08 .25
B71 Kevin Orie RC .20 .50
B72 Chad Ogea .08 .25
B73 Ben Van Ryn RC .20 .50
B74 Kym Ashworth RC .20 .50
B75 Dmitri Young .20 .50
B76 Herbert Perry RC .20 .50
B77 Joey Eischen .08 .25
B78 Arquimedez Pozo RC .20 .50
B79 Ugueth Urbina .08 .25
B80 Keith Williams RC .20 .50
B81 John Frascatore RC .20 .50
B82 Garey Ingram RC .20 .50
B83 Aaron Small .20 .50
B84 Olmedo Saenz RC .20 .50
B85 Jesus Tavarez RC .20 .50
B86 Jose Silva RC .40 1.00
B87 Jay Witasick RC .20 .50
B88 Jay Maldonado RC .20 .50
B89 Keith Heberling RC .20 .50
B90 Rusty Greer RC .60 1.50
R1 Paul Molitor .20 .50
R2 Eddie Murray .50 1.25
R3 Ozzie Smith .75 2.00
R4 Rickey Henderson .50 1.25
R5 Lee Smith .20 .50
R6 Dave Winfield .20 .50
R7 Roberto Alomar .30 .75
R8 Matt Williams .20 .50
R9 Mark Grace .30 .75
R10 Lance Johnson .08 .25
R11 Darren Daulton .20 .50
R12 Tom Glavine .30 .75
R13 Gary Sheffield .20 .50
R14 Rod Beck .08 .25
R15 Fred McGriff .30 .75
R16 Joe Carter .20 .50
R17 Dante Bichette .08 .25
R18 Danny Tartabull .08 .25
R19 Juan Gonzalez .20 .50
R20 Steve Avery .08 .25
R21 John Wetteland .20 .50
R22 Ben McDonald .08 .25
R23 Jack McDowell .08 .25
R24 Jose Canseco .30 .75
R25 Tim Salmon .30 .75
R26 Wilson Alvarez .08 .25
R27 Gregg Jefferies .08 .25
R28 John Burkett .08 .25
R29 Greg Vaughn .08 .25
R30 Robin Ventura .20 .50
R31 Paul O'Neill .30 .75
R32 Cecil Fielder .20 .50
R33 Kevin Mitchell .08 .25
R34 Jeff Conine .20 .50
R35 Carlos Baerga .08 .25
R36 Greg Maddux .75 2.00
R37 Roger Clemens 1.00 2.50
R38 Deion Sanders .30 .75
R39 Delino DeShields .08 .25
R40 Ken Griffey Jr. 1.00 2.50
R41 Albert Belle .20 .50
R42 Wade Boggs .30 .75
R43 Andres Galarraga .20 .50
R44 Aaron Sele .08 .25
R45 Don Mattingly 1.25 3.00
R46 David Cone .20 .50
R47 Len Dykstra .20 .50
R48 Brett Butler .20 .50
R49 Bill Swift .08 .25
R50 Bobby Bonilla .20 .50
R51 Rafael Palmeiro .30 .75
R52 Moises Alou .20 .50
R53 Jeff Bagwell .30 .75
R54 Mike Mussina .30 .75
R55 Frank Thomas .50 1.25
R56 Jose Rijo .08 .25
R57 Ruben Sierra .20 .50
R58 Randy Myers .08 .25
R59 Barry Bonds 1.25 3.00
R60 Jimmy Key .20 .50
R61 Travis Fryman .20 .50
R62 John Olerud .20 .50
R63 David Justice .20 .50
R64 Ray Lankford .20 .50
R65 Bob Tewksbury .08 .25
R66 Chuck Carr .08 .25
R67 Jay Buhner .20 .50
R68 Kenny Lofton .20 .50
R69 Marquis Grissom .20 .50
R70 Sammy Sosa .50 1.25
R71 Cal Ripken 1.50 4.00
R72 Ellis Burks .20 .50
R73 Jeff Montgomery .08 .25
R74 Julio Franco .20 .50
R75 Kirby Puckett .50 1.25
R76 Larry Walker .20 .50
R77 Andy Van Slyke .30 .75
R78 Tony Gwynn .60 1.50
R79 Will Clark .30 .75
R80 Mo Vaughn .20 .50
R81 Mike Piazza 1.00 2.50
R82 James Mouton .08 .25
R83 Carlos Delgado .30 .75
R84 Ryan Klesko .20 .50
R85 Javier Lopez .20 .50
R86 Raul Mondesi .20 .50
R87 Cliff Floyd .20 .50
R88 Manny Ramirez .50 1.25
R89 Hector Carrasco .08 .25
R90 Jeff Granger .08 .25
X91 F.Thomas / D.Young .30 .75
X92 F.McGriff / B.Kieschnick .20 .50
X93 M.Williams / S.Andrews .08 .25
X94 C.Ripken / K.Orie .75 2.00
X95 D.Jeter / B.Larkin .75 2.00
X96 K.Griffey Jr. / J.Damon .50 1.25
X97 B.Bonds / R.White .60 1.50
X98 A.Belle / J.Hurst .20 .50
X99 R.Rivera RC / R.Mondesi .20 .50
X100 R.Clemens / S.Ruffcorn .50 1.25
X101 G.Maddux / J.Wasdin .50 1.25
X102 T.Salmon / C.Mottola .30 .75
X103 C.Baerga / A.Pozo .08 .25
X104 M.Piazza / B.Hughes .50 1.25
X105 C.Delgado / M.Nieves .30 .75
X106 J.Posada / J.Lopez 1.00 2.50
X107 M.Ramirez / J.Malave .50 1.25
X108 C.Jones / T.Fryman .30 .75
X109 S.Avery / B.Pulsipher .08 .25
X110 J.Olerud / S.Green .50 1.25

1994 Bowman's Best Refractors

COMPLETE SET (200)	500.00	1000.00
*RED STARS: 4X TO 10X BASIC CARDS		
*BLUE STARS: 4X TO 10X BASIC CARDS		
*BLUE ROOKIES: 1.5X TO 4X BASIC		
*MIRROR IMAGE: 2X TO 5X BASIC		
STATED ODDS 1:9		
B2 Derek Jeter	75.00	200.00
B63 Edgar Renteria	10.00	25.00

1995 Bowman's Best

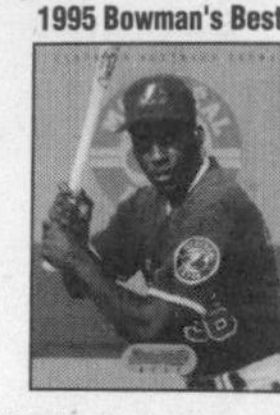

This 195 card standard-size set (produced by Topps) consists of 90 veteran stars, 90 rookies and prospects and 15 dual player Mirror Image cards. The packs contain seven cards and the suggested retail price was $5. The veteran cards have red fronts and are designated R1-R90. Cards of rookies and prospects have blue fronts and are designated B1-B90. The Mirror Image cards feature a veteran star and a prospect matched by position in a horizontal design. These cards are numbered X1-X15. Rookie Cards include Bob Abreu, Bartolo Colon, Scott Elarton, Juan Encarnacion, Vladimir Guerrero, Andruw Jones, Hideo Nomo, Rey Ordonez, Scott Rolen and Richie Sexson.

COMPLETE SET (195)	50.00	100.00
COMMON CARD (B1-R90)	.20	.50
COMMON CARD (X1-X15)	.20	.50
B1 Derek Jeter	1.00	2.50
B2 Vladimir Guerrero RC	15.00	40.00
B3 Bob Abreu RC	3.00	8.00
B4 Chan Ho Park	.20	.50
B5 Paul Wilson	.20	.50
B6 Chad Ogea	.20	.50
B7 Andruw Jones RC	5.00	12.00
B8 Brian Barber	.20	.50
B9 Andy Larkin	.20	.50
B10 Richie Sexson RC	4.00	10.00
B11 Everett Stull	.20	.50
B12 Brooks Kieschnick	.20	.50
B13 Matt Murray	.20	.50
B14 John Wasdin	.20	.50
B15 Shannon Stewart	.20	.50
B16 Luis Ortiz	.20	.50
B17 Marc Kroon	.20	.50
B18 Todd Greene	.20	.50
B19 Juan Acevedo RC	.40	1.00
B20 Tony Clark	.20	.50
B21 Jermaine Dye	.20	.50
B22 Derrek Lee	.50	1.25
B23 Pat Watkins	.20	.50
B24 Pokey Reese	.20	.50
B25 Ben Grieve	.20	.50
B26 Julio Santana RC	.20	.50
B27 Felix Rodriguez RC	.40	1.00
B28 Paul Konerko	3.00	8.00
B29 Nomar Garciaparra	2.00	5.00
B30 Pat Ahearne RC	.20	.50
B31 Jason Schmidt	.50	1.25
B32 Billy Wagner	.30	.75
B33 Rey Ordonez RC	1.25	3.00
B34 Curtis Goodwin	.20	.50
B35 Sergio Nunez RC	.40	1.00
B36 Tim Belk	.20	.50
B37 Scott Elarton RC	.75	2.00
B38 Jason Isringhausen	.20	.50
B39 Trot Nixon	.20	.50
B40 Sid Roberson RC	.40	1.00
B41 Ron Villone	.20	.50
B42 Ruben Rivera	.20	.50
B43 Rick Huisman	.20	.50
B44 Todd Hollandsworth	.20	.50
B45 Johnny Damon	.30	.75
B46 Garret Anderson	.20	.50
B47 Jeff D'Amico	.20	.50
B48 Dustin Hermanson	.20	.50
B49 Juan Encarnacion RC	1.25	3.00
B50 Andy Pettitte	.30	.75
B51 Chris Stynes	.20	.50
B52 Troy Percival	.20	.50
B53 LaTroy Hawkins	.20	.50
B54 Roger Cedeno	.20	.50
B55 Alan Benes	.20	.50
B56 Karim Garcia RC	.40	1.00
B57 Andrew Lorraine	.20	.50
B58 Gary Rath RC	.40	1.00
B59 Bret Wagner	.20	.50
B60 Jeff Suppan	.20	.50
B61 Bill Pulsipher	.20	.50
B62 Jay Payton RC	1.25	3.00
B63 Alex Ochoa	.20	.50
B64 Ugueth Urbina	.20	.50
B65 Armando Benitez	.20	.50
B66 George Arias	.20	.50
B67 Raul Casanova RC	.40	1.00
B68 Matt Drews	.20	.50
B69 Jimmy Haynes	.20	.50
B70 Jimmy Hurst	.20	.50
B71 C.J. Nitkowski	.20	.50
B72 Tommy Davis RC	.40	1.00
B73 Bartolo Colon RC	2.50	6.00
B74 Chris Carpenter RC	3.00	8.00
B75 Trey Beamon	.20	.50
B76 Bryan Rekar	.20	.50
B77 James Baldwin	.20	.50
B78 Marc Valdes	.20	.50
B79 Tom Fordham RC	.40	1.00
B80 Marc Newfield	.20	.50
B81 Angel Martinez	.20	.50
B82 Brian L. Hunter	.20	.50
B83 Jose Herrera	.20	.50
B84 Glenn Dishman RC	.40	1.00
B85 Jacob Cruz RC	.75	2.00
B86 Paul Shuey	.20	.50
B87 Scott Rolen RC	4.00	10.00
B88 Doug Million	.20	.50
B89 Desi Relaford	.20	.50
B90 Michael Tucker	.20	.50
R1 Randy Johnson	.50	1.25
R2 Joe Carter	.20	.50
R3 Chili Davis	.20	.50
R4 Moises Alou	.20	.50
R5 Gary Sheffield	.20	.50
R6 Kevin Appier	.20	.50
R7 Denny Neagle	.20	.50
R8 Ruben Sierra	.20	.50
R9 Darren Daulton	.20	.50
R10 Cal Ripken	1.50	4.00
R11 Bobby Bonilla	.20	.50
R12 Manny Ramirez	.30	.75
R13 Barry Bonds	1.25	3.00
R14 Eric Karros	.20	.50
R15 Greg Maddux	.75	2.00
R16 Jeff Bagwell	.30	.75
R17 Paul Molitor	.20	.50
R18 Ray Lankford	.20	.50
R19 Mark Grace	.30	.75
R20 Kenny Lofton	.20	.50
R21 Tony Gwynn	.60	1.50
R22 Will Clark	.30	.75
R23 Roger Clemens	1.00	2.50
R24 Dante Bichette	.20	.50
R25 Barry Larkin	.30	.75
R26 Wade Boggs	.30	.75
R27 Kirby Puckett	.50	1.25
R28 Cecil Fielder	.20	.50
R29 Jose Canseco	.30	.75
R30 Juan Gonzalez	.20	.50
R31 David Cone	.20	.50
R32 Craig Biggio	.30	.75
R33 Tim Salmon	.30	.75
R34 David Justice	.20	.50
R35 Sammy Sosa	.50	1.25
R36 Mike Piazza	.75	2.00
R37 Carlos Baerga	.20	.50
R38 Jeff Conine	.20	.50
R39 Rafael Palmeiro	.30	.75
R40 Bret Saberhagen	.20	.50
R41 Len Dykstra	.20	.50
R42 Mo Vaughn	.20	.50
R43 Wally Joyner	.20	.50
R44 Chuck Knoblauch	.20	.50
R45 Robin Ventura	.20	.50
R46 Don Mattingly	1.25	3.00
R47 Dave Hollins	.20	.50
R48 Andy Benes	.20	.50
R49 Ken Griffey Jr.	1.00	2.50
R50 Albert Belle	.20	.50
R51 Matt Williams	.20	.50
R52 Rondell White	.20	.50
R53 Raul Mondesi	.20	.50
R54 Brian Jordan	.20	.50
R55 Greg Vaughn	.20	.50
R56 Fred McGriff	.30	.75
R57 Roberto Alomar	.30	.75
R58 Dennis Eckersley	.20	.50
R59 Lee Smith	.20	.50
R60 Eddie Murray	.50	1.25
R61 Kenny Rogers	.20	.50
R62 Ron Gant	.20	.50
R63 Larry Walker	.20	.50
R64 Chad Curtis	.20	.50
R65 Frank Thomas	.50	1.25
R66 Paul O'Neill	.30	.75
R67 Kevin Seitzer	.20	.50
R68 Marquis Grissom	.20	.50
R69 Mark McGwire	1.50	4.00
R70 Travis Fryman	.20	.50
R71 Andres Galarraga	.20	.50
R72 Carlos Perez RC	.75	2.00
R73 Tyler Green	.20	.50
R74 Marty Cordova	.20	.50
R75 Shawn Green	.20	.50
R76 Vaughn Eshelman	.20	.50
R77 John Mabry	.20	.50
R78 Jason Bates	.20	.50
R79 Jon Nunnally	.20	.50
R80 Ray Durham	.20	.50
R81 Edgardo Alfonzo	.20	.50
R82 Esteban Loaiza	.20	.50
R83 Hideo Nomo RC	3.00	8.00
R84 Orlando Miller	.20	.50
R85 Alex Gonzalez	.20	.50
R86 Mark Grudzielanek RC	1.25	3.00
R87 Julian Tavarez	.20	.50
R88 Benji Gil	.20	.50
R89 Quilvio Veras	.20	.50
R90 Ricky Bottalico	.20	.50
X1 B.Davis RC	.60	1.50
I.Rodriguez		
X2 M.Redman RC	.60	1.50
M.Ramirez		
X3 R.Taylor RC	.60	1.50
D.Sanders		
X4 R.Jaroncyk RC	.20	.50
S.Green		
X5 C.Beltran UER	1.50	4.00
J.Gonz		
X6 T.McKnight RC	.20	.50
C.Biggio		
X7 M.Barrett RC	.60	1.50
T.Fryman		
X8 C.Jenkins RC	.20	.50
M.Vaughn		
X9 R.Rivera	.50	1.25
F.Thomas		
X10 C.Goodwin	.20	.50
K.Lofton		
X11 B.Hunter	.30	.75
T.Gwynn		
X12 T.Greene	.60	1.50
K.Griffey Jr.		
X13 K.Garcia	.20	.50
M.Williams		
X14 B.Wagner	.30	.75
R.Johnson		
X15 P.Watkins	.30	.75
J.Bagwell		

1995 Bowman's Best Refractors

*STARS: 4X TO 10X BASIC CARDS		
*ROOKIES: 1.5X TO 4X BASIC CARDS		
*MIRROR IMAGE: 1.25X TO 3X BASIC		
RED/BLUE REF.STATED ODDS 1:6		
MIRROR IMAGE REF.STATED ODDS 1:12		
B1 Derek Jeter	60.00	120.00
B2 Vladimir Guerrero	125.00	300.00
B3 Bob Abreu	20.00	50.00
B10 Richie Sexson	8.00	20.00
B73 Bartolo Colon	12.00	30.00

1995 Bowman's Best Jumbo Refractors

COMPLETE SET (10)	50.00	120.00
COMMON CARD (1-10)	2.00	5.00
COMMON DP	1.50	4.00
1 Albert Belle DP	1.50	4.00
2 Ken Griffey Jr	8.00	20.00
3 Tony Gwynn	6.00	15.00
4 Greg Maddux	3.00	8.00
5 Hideo Nomo	6.00	15.00
6 Mike Piazza	6.00	15.00
7 Cal Ripken	12.50	30.00
8 Sammy Sosa	5.00	12.00
9 Frank Thomas	4.00	10.00
10 Cal Ripken	12.50	30.00

1996 Bowman's Best Previews

Printed with Finest technology, this 30-card set features the hottest 15 top prospects and 15 veterans and was randomly inserted in 1996 Bowman packs at the rate of one in 12. The fronts display a color action player photo. The backs carry player information.

COMPLETE SET (30)	25.00	60.00
STATED ODDS 1:12		
*REFRACTORS: .5X TO 1.2X BASIC PREVIEWS		
REFRACTOR STATED ODDS 1:24		
*ATOMIC: 1X TO 2.5X BASIC PREVIEWS		
ATOMIC STATED ODDS 1:48		
BBP1 Chipper Jones	1.00	2.50
BBP2 Alan Benes	.40	1.00
BBP3 Brooks Kieschnick	.40	1.00
BBP4 Barry Bonds	2.50	6.00
BBP5 Rey Ordonez	.40	1.00
BBP6 Tim Salmon	.60	1.50
BBP7 Mike Piazza	1.50	4.00
BBP8 Billy Wagner	.40	1.00
BBP9 Andruw Jones	1.50	4.00
BBP10 Tony Gwynn	1.25	3.00
BBP11 Paul Wilson	.40	1.00
BBP12 Pokey Reese	.40	1.00
BBP13 Frank Thomas	1.00	2.50
BBP14 Greg Maddux	1.50	4.00
BBP15 Derek Jeter	5.00	12.00
BBP16 Jeff Bagwell	.60	1.50
BBP17 Barry Larkin	.60	1.50
BBP18 Todd Greene	.40	1.00
BBP19 Ruben Rivera	.40	1.00
BBP20 Richard Hidalgo	.40	1.00
BBP21 Larry Walker	.40	1.00
BBP22 Carlos Baerga	.40	1.00
BBP23 Derrick Gibson	.40	1.00
BBP24 Richie Sexson	.60	1.50
BBP25 Mo Vaughn	.40	1.00
BBP26 Hideo Nomo	1.00	2.50
BBP27 Nomar Garciaparra	2.00	5.00
BBP28 Cal Ripken	3.00	8.00
BBP29 Karim Garcia	.40	1.00
BBP30 Ken Griffey Jr.	2.00	5.00

1996 Bowman's Best

This 180-card set was (produced by Topps) issued in packs of six cards at the cost of $4.99 per pack. The fronts feature a color action player cutout of 90 outstanding veteran players on a chromium gold background design and 90 up and coming prospects and rookies on a silver design. The backs carry a color player portrait, player information and statistics. Card number 33 was never actually issued. Instead, both Roger Clemens and Rafael Palmeiro are erroneously numbered 32. A chrome reprint of the 1952 Bowman Mickey Mantle was inserted at the rate of one in 24 packs. A Refractor version of the Mantle was seeded at 1:96 packs and an Atomic Refractor version was seeded at 1:192. Notable Rookie Cards include Geoff Jenkins and Mike Sweeney.

COMPLETE SET (180)	15.00	40.00
NUMBER 33 NEVER ISSUED		
CLEMENS AND PALMEIRO NUMBERED 32		
MANTLE CHROME ODDS 1:24 HOB, 1:20 RET		
MANTLE REF.ODDS 1:96 HOB, 1:160 RET		
MANTLE ATOMIC ODDS 1:192 HOB,1:320 RET		
1 Hideo Nomo	.40	1.00
2 Edgar Martinez	.25	.60
3 Cal Ripken	1.25	3.00
4 Wade Boggs	.25	.60
5 Cecil Fielder	.15	.40
6 Albert Belle	.15	.40
7 Chipper Jones	.40	1.00
8 Ryne Sandberg	.60	1.50
9 Tim Salmon	.25	.60
10 Barry Bonds	1.00	2.50
11 Ken Caminiti	.15	.40
12 Ron Gant	.15	.40
13 Frank Thomas	.40	1.00
14 Dante Bichette	.15	.40
15 Jason Kendall	.15	.40
16 Mo Vaughn	.15	.40
17 Rey Ordonez	.15	.40
18 Henry Rodriguez	.15	.40
19 Ryan Klesko	.15	.40
20 Jeff Bagwell	.25	.60
21 Randy Johnson	.40	1.00
22 Jim Edmonds	.15	.40
23 Kenny Lofton	.15	.40
24 Andy Pettitte	.25	.60
25 Brady Anderson	.15	.40
26 Mike Piazza	.60	1.50
27 Greg Vaughn	.15	.40
28 Joe Carter	.15	.40
29 Jason Giambi	.15	.40
30 Ivan Rodriguez	.25	.60
31 Jeff Conine	.15	.40
32 Rafael Palmeiro	.25	.60
33 Roger Clemens UER	.75	2.00
34 Chuck Knoblauch	.15	.40
35 Reggie Sanders	.15	.40
36 Andres Galarraga	.15	.40
37 Paul O'Neill	.25	.60
38 Tony Gwynn	.50	1.25
39 Paul Wilson	.15	.40
40 Garret Anderson	.15	.40
41 David Justice	.15	.40
42 Eddie Murray	.40	1.00
43 Mike Grace RC	.20	.50
44 Marty Cordova	.15	.40
45 Kevin Appier	.15	.40
46 Raul Mondesi	.15	.40
47 Jim Thome	.25	.60
48 Sammy Sosa	.40	1.00
49 Craig Biggio	.25	.60
50 Marquis Grissom	.15	.40
51 Alan Benes	.15	.40
52 Manny Ramirez	.25	.60
53 Gary Sheffield	.15	.40
54 Mike Mussina	.25	.60
55 Robin Ventura	.15	.40
56 Johnny Damon	.25	.60
57 Jose Canseco	.25	.60
58 Juan Gonzalez	.15	.40
59 Tino Martinez	.25	.60
60 Brian Hunter	.15	.40
61 Fred McGriff	.25	.60
62 Jay Buhner	.15	.40
63 Carlos Delgado	.15	.40
64 Moises Alou	.15	.40
65 Roberto Alomar	.25	.60
66 Barry Larkin	.25	.60
67 Vinny Castilla	.15	.40
68 Ray Durham	.15	.40
69 Travis Fryman	.15	.40
70 Jason Isringhausen	.15	.40
71 Ken Griffey Jr.	.75	2.00
72 John Smoltz	.25	.60
73 Matt Williams	.15	.40
74 Chan Ho Park	.15	.40
75 Mark McGwire	1.25	3.00
76 Jeffrey Hammonds	.15	.40
77 Will Clark	.25	.60
78 Kirby Puckett	.40	1.00
79 Derek Jeter	1.25	3.00
80 Derek Bell	.15	.40
81 Eric Karros	.15	.40
82 Len Dykstra	.15	.40
83 Larry Walker	.15	.40
84 Mark Grudzielanek	.15	.40
85 Greg Maddux	.60	1.50
86 Carlos Baerga	.15	.40
87 Paul Molitor	.15	.40
88 John Valentin	.15	.40
89 Mark Grace	.25	.60
90 Ray Lankford	.15	.40
91 Andruw Jones	.60	1.50
92 Nomar Garciaparra	.75	2.00
93 Alex Ochoa	.15	.40
94 Derrick Gibson	.15	.40
95 Jeff D'Amico	.15	.40
96 Ruben Rivera	.15	.40
97 Vladimir Guerrero	.75	2.00
98 Pokey Reese	.15	.40
99 Richard Hidalgo	.15	.40
100 Bartolo Colon	.40	1.00
101 Karim Garcia	.15	.40
102 Ben Davis	.15	.40
103 Jay Powell	.15	.40
104 Chris Snopek	.15	.40
105 Glendon Rusch RC	.40	1.00
106 Enrique Wilson	.15	.40
107 Antonio Alfonseca RC	.40	1.00
108 Wilton Guerrero RC	.20	.50
109 Jose Guillen RC	1.50	4.00
110 Miguel Mejia RC	.20	.50
111 Jay Payton	.15	.40
112 Scott Elarton	.15	.40
113 Brooks Kieschnick	.15	.40
114 Dustin Hermanson	.15	.40
115 Roger Cedeno	.15	.40
116 Matt Wagner	.15	.40
117 Lee Daniels	.15	.40
118 Ben Grieve	.15	.40
119 Ugueth Urbina	.15	.40
120 Danny Graves	.15	.40
121 Dan Donato RC	.20	.50
122 Matt Ruebel RC	.20	.50
123 Mark Sievert RC	.20	.50
124 Chris Stynes	.15	.40
125 Jeff Abbott	.15	.40
126 Rocky Coppinger RC	.20	.50
127 Jermaine Dye	.15	.40
128 Todd Greene	.15	.40
129 Chris Carpenter	.25	.60
130 Edgar Renteria	.15	.40
131 Matt Drews	.15	.40
132 Edgard Velazquez RC	.20	.50
133 Casey Whitten	.15	.40
134 Ryan Jones RC	.20	.50
135 Todd Walker	.15	.40
136 Geoff Jenkins RC	.75	2.00
137 Matt Morris RC	1.50	4.00
138 Richie Sexson	.25	.60
139 Todd Dunwoody RC	.20	.50
140 Gabe Alvarez RC	.20	.50
141 J.J. Johnson	.15	.40
142 Shannon Stewart	.15	.40
143 Brad Fullmer	.15	.40
144 Julio Santana	.15	.40
145 Scott Rolen	.40	1.00
146 Amaury Telemaco	.15	.40
147 Trey Beamon	.15	.40
148 Billy Wagner	.15	.40
149 Todd Hollandsworth	.15	.40
150 Doug Million	.15	.40
151 Javier Valentin RC	.20	.50
152 Wes Helms RC	.40	1.00
153 Jeff Suppan	.15	.40
154 Luis Castillo RC	.60	1.50
155 Bob Abreu	.40	1.00
156 Paul Konerko	.40	1.00
157 Jamey Wright	.15	.40
158 Eddie Pearson	.15	.40
159 Jimmy Haynes	.15	.40
160 Derrek Lee	.25	.60
161 Damian Moss	.15	.40
162 Carlos Guillen RC	1.00	2.50
163 Chris Fussell RC	.20	.50
164 Mike Sweeney RC	1.00	2.50
165 Donnie Sadler	.15	.40
166 Desi Relaford	.15	.40
167 Steve Gibralter	.15	.40
168 Neifi Perez	.15	.40
169 Antone Williamson	.15	.40
170 Marty Janzen RC	.20	.50
171 Todd Helton	.75	2.00
172 Raul Ibanez RC	1.50	4.00
173 Bill Selby	.15	.40
174 Shane Monahan RC	.20	.50
175 Robin Jennings	.15	.40
176 Bobby Chouinard	.15	.40
177 Einar Diaz	.15	.40
178 Jason Thompson RC	.15	.40
179 Rafael Medina RC	.20	.50
180 Kevin Orie	.15	.40
NNO 1952 Mantle Atomic Ref.	4.00	10.00
NNO 1952 Mantle Refractor	2.00	5.00
NNO 1952 Mantle Chrome	1.00	2.50

1996 Bowman's Best Atomic Refractors

*GOLD STARS: 6X TO 15X BASIC CARDS
*SILVER STARS: 6X TO 15X BASIC CARDS
*ROOKIES: 4X TO 10X BASIC CARDS
STATED ODDS 1:48 HOB, 1:80 RET

1996 Bowman's Best Refractors

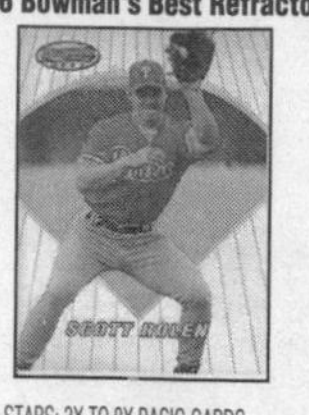

*GOLD STARS: 3X TO 8X BASIC CARDS
*SILVER STARS: 3X TO 8X BASIC CARDS
*ROOKIES: 2X TO 5X BASIC CARDS
STATED ODDS 1:12 HOB, 1:20 RET

1996 Bowman's Best Cuts

Randomly inserted in hobby packs at a rate of one in 24 and retail packs at a rate on one in 40, this chromium card die-cut set features 15 top hobby stars.

COMPLETE SET (15)	30.00	80.00
STATED ODDS 1:24 HOB, 1:40 RET		
*REFRACTORS: .6X TO 1.5X BASIC CUTS		
REF.STATED ODDS 1:48 HOB, 1:80 RET		
*ATOMIC: 1X TO 2.5X BASIC CUTS		
ATOMIC STATED ODDS 1:96 HOB, 1:160 RET		
1 Ken Griffey Jr.	3.00	8.00
2 Jason Isringhausen	.60	1.50
3 Derek Jeter	4.00	10.00
4 Andruw Jones	2.50	6.00
5 Chipper Jones	1.50	4.00
6 Ryan Klesko	.60	1.50
7 Raul Mondesi	.60	1.50
8 Hideo Nomo	1.50	4.00
9 Mike Piazza	2.50	6.00
10 Manny Ramirez	1.00	2.50
11 Cal Ripken	5.00	12.00
12 Ruben Rivera	.60	1.50
13 Tim Salmon	1.00	2.50
14 Frank Thomas	1.50	4.00
15 Jim Thome	1.00	2.50

1996 Bowman's Best Mirror Image

Randomly inserted in hobby packs at a rate of one in 48 and retail packs at a rate of one in 80, this 10-card set features four top players on a single card at one of ten different positions. The fronts display a color photo of an AL veteran with a semicircle containing a color portrait of a prospect who plays the same position. The backs carry a color photo of an NL veteran with a semicircle color portrait of a prospect.

COMPLETE SET (10)	15.00	40.00
STATED ODDS 1:48 HOB, 1:80 RET		
*REFRACTORS: .6X TO 1.5X BASIC MI		
REFRACTOR ODDS 1:96 HOB, 1:160 RET		
*ATOMIC REF: .75X TO 2X BASIC MI		
ATOMIC ODDS 1:192 HOB, 1:320 RET		
1 F.Thom	2.50	6.00
Helton		
Bagw		
Sexson		
2 R.Alom	1.00	2.50
Biggio		
L.Cast		
Rela		
3 C.Jones	1.50	4.00
Rolen		
Boggs		
4 Ripken	5.00	12.00
Larkin		
Bellhorn		
5 A.Belle	1.00	2.50
L.Walker		
K.Garcia		
6 A.Jones	2.50	6.00
Bonds		
Lofton		
7 K.Griff	3.00	8.00
Gwynn		
Grieve		
Vlad		
8 M.Piazza	1.50	4.00
I.Rod		
B.Davis		
9 G.Maddux	2.50	6.00
Mussina		
B.Colon		
10 J.Washburn	1.50	4.00
R.John		
Glav		

1997 Bowman's Best Preview

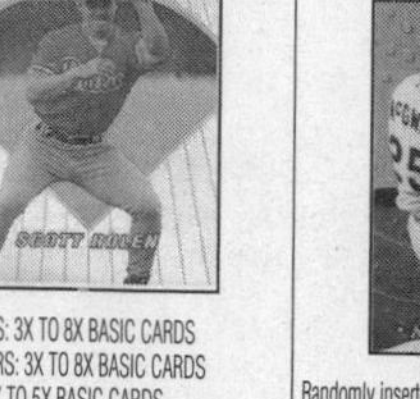

Randomly inserted in 1997 Bowman Series 1 packs at a rate of one in 12, this 20-card set features color photos of 10 rookies and 10 veterans that would be appearing in the 1997 Bowman's Best set. The background of each card features a flag of the featured player's homeland.

COMPLETE SET (20)	30.00	80.00
STATED ODDS 1:12		
*REF: .75X TO 2X BASIC PREVIEWS		
REFRACTOR STATED ODDS 1:48		
*ATOMIC REF: 1.5X TO 4X BASIC PREVIEWS		
ATOMIC STATED ODDS 1:96		
DISTRIBUTED IN 1997 BOWMAN SER.1 PACKS		
1 Frank Thomas	1.50	4.00
2 Ken Griffey Jr.	3.00	8.00
3 Barry Bonds	4.00	10.00
4 Derek Jeter	4.00	10.00
5 Chipper Jones	1.50	4.00
6 Mark McGwire	5.00	12.00
7 Cal Ripken	5.00	12.00
8 Kenny Lofton	.60	1.50
9 Gary Sheffield	.60	1.50
10 Jeff Bagwell	1.00	2.50
11 Wilton Guerrero	.60	1.50
12 Scott Rolen	1.00	2.50
13 Todd Walker	.60	1.50
14 Ruben Rivera	.60	1.50
15 Andruw Jones	1.00	2.50
16 Nomar Garciaparra	2.50	6.00
17 Vladimir Guerrero	1.50	4.00
18 Miguel Tejada	1.50	4.00
19 Bartolo Colon	.60	1.50
20 Katsuhiro Maeda	.60	1.50

1997 Bowman's Best

The 1997 Bowman's Best set (produced by Topps) was issued in one series totalling 200 cards and was distributed in six-card packs (SRP $4.99). The fronts feature borderless color player photos printed on chromium card stock. The cards of the 100 current veteran stars display a classic gold design while the cards of the 100 top prospects carry a sleek silver design. Rookie Cards include Adrian Beltre, Kris Benson, Jose Cruz Jr., Travis Lee, Fernando Tatis, Miguel Tejada and Kerry Wood.

COMPLETE SET (200)	15.00	40.00
1 Ken Griffey Jr.	.75	2.00
2 Cecil Fielder	.15	.40
3 Albert Belle	.15	.40
4 Todd Hundley	.15	.40
5 Mike Piazza	.60	1.50
6 Matt Williams	.15	.40
7 Mo Vaughn	.15	.40
8 Ryne Sandberg	.60	1.50
9 Chipper Jones	.40	1.00
10 Edgar Martinez	.25	.60
11 Kenny Lofton	.15	.40
12 Ron Gant	.15	.40
13 Moises Alou	.15	.40
14 Pat Hentgen	.15	.40
15 Steve Finley	.15	.40
16 Mark Grace	.25	.60
17 Jay Buhner	.15	.40
18 Jeff Conine	.15	.40
19 Jim Edmonds	.15	.40
20 Todd Hollandsworth	.15	.40
21 Andy Pettitte	.25	.60
22 Jim Thome	.25	.60
23 Eric Young	.15	.40
24 Ray Lankford	.15	.40
25 Marquis Grissom	.15	.40
26 Tony Clark	.15	.40
27 Jermaine Allensworth	.15	.40
28 Ellis Burks	.15	.40
29 Tony Gwynn	.50	1.25
30 Barry Larkin	.25	.60
31 John Olerud	.15	.40
32 Mariano Rivera	.40	1.00
33 Paul Molitor	.15	.40
34 Ken Caminiti	.15	.40
35 Gary Sheffield	.15	.40
36 Al Martin	.15	.40

7 John Valentin .15 .40
8 Frank Thomas .40 1.00
9 John Jaha .15 .40
0 Greg Maddux .60 1.50
1 Alex Fernandez .15 .40
2 Dean Palmer .15 .40
3 Bernie Williams .25 .60
4 Deion Sanders .25 .60
5 Mark McGwire 1.25 3.00
6 Brian Jordan .15 .40
7 Bernard Gilkey .15 .40
8 Will Clark .25 .60
9 Kevin Appier .15 .40
0 Tom Glavine .25 .60
1 Chuck Knoblauch .15 .40
2 Rondell White .15 .40
3 Greg Vaughn .15 .40
4 Mike Mussina .25 .60
5 Brian McRae .15 .40
6 Chili Davis .15 .40
7 Wade Boggs .25 .60
8 Jeff Bagwell .25 .60
59 Roberto Alomar .25 .60
60 Dennis Eckersley .15 .40
61 Ryan Klesko .15 .40
62 Manny Ramirez .25 .60
63 John Wetteland .15 .40
64 Cal Ripken 1.25 3.00
65 Edgar Renteria .15 .40
66 Tino Martinez .25 .60
67 Larry Walker .15 .40
68 Gregg Jefferies .15 .40
69 Lance Johnson .15 .40
70 Carlos Delgado .15 .40
71 Craig Biggio .25 .60
72 Jose Canseco .25 .60
73 Barry Bonds 1.00 2.50
74 Juan Gonzalez .15 .40
75 Eric Karros .15 .40
76 Reggie Sanders .15 .40
77 Robin Ventura .15 .40
78 Hideo Nomo .40 1.00
79 David Justice .15 .40
80 Vinny Castilla .15 .40
81 Travis Fryman .15 .40
82 Derek Jeter 1.00 2.50
83 Sammy Sosa .40 1.00
84 Ivan Rodriguez .25 .60
85 Rafael Palmeiro .25 .60
86 Roger Clemens .75 2.00
87 Jason Giambi .15 .40
88 Andres Galarraga .15 .40
89 Jermaine Dye .15 .40
90 Joe Carter .15 .40
91 Brady Anderson .15 .40
92 Derek Bell .15 .40
93 Randy Johnson .40 1.00
94 Fred McGriff .25 .60
95 John Smoltz .25 .60
96 Harold Baines .15 .40
97 Raul Mondesi .15 .40
98 Tim Salmon .25 .60
99 Carlos Baerga .15 .40
100 Dante Bichette .15 .40
101 Vladimir Guerrero .40 1.00
102 Richard Hidalgo .15 .40
103 Paul Konerko .25 .60
104 Alex Gonzalez RC .40 1.00
105 Jason Dickson .15 .40
106 Jose Rosado .15 .40
107 Todd Walker .15 .40
108 Seth Greisinger RC .15 .40
109 Todd Helton .40 1.00
110 Ben Davis .15 .40
111 Bartolo Colon .15 .40
112 Eliesel Marrero .15 .40
113 Jeff D'Amico .15 .40
114 Miguel Tejada RC 1.50 4.00
115 Darin Erstad .15 .40
116 Kris Benson RC .40 1.00
117 Adrian Beltre RC 5.00 12.00
118 Neifi Perez .15 .40
119 Pokey Reese .15 .40
120 Carl Pavano .15 .40
121 Juan Melo .15 .40
122 Kevin McGlinchy RC .15 .40
123 Pat Cline .15 .40
124 Felix Heredia RC .15 .40
125 Aaron Boone .15 .40
126 Glendon Rusch .15 .40
127 Mike Cameron .15 .40
128 Justin Thompson .15 .40
129 Chad Hermansen RC .15 .40
130 Sidney Ponson RC .40 1.00
131 Willie Martinez RC .15 .40
132 Paul Wilder RC .15 .40
133 Geoff Jenkins .15 .40
134 Roy Halladay RC 6.00 15.00
135 Carlos Guillen .15 .40
136 Tony Batista .15 .40
137 Todd Greene .15 .40
138 Luis Castillo .15 .40
139 Jimmy Anderson RC .15 .40
140 Edgard Velazquez .15 .40
141 Chris Snopek .15 .40
142 Ruben Rivera .15 .40
143 Javier Valentin .15 .40
144 Brian Rose .15 .40
145 Fernando Tatis RC .15 .40
146 Dean Crow RC .15 .40
147 Karim Garcia .15 .40
148 Dante Powell .15 .40
149 Hideki Irabu RC .25 .60
150 Matt Morris .15 .40
151 Wes Helms .15 .40
152 Russ Johnson .15 .40
153 Jarrod Washburn .15 .40
154 Kerry Wood RC 1.50 4.00
155 Joe Fontenot RC .15 .40
156 Eugene Kingsale .15 .40
157 Terrence Long .15 .40
158 Calvin Maduro .15 .40
159 Jeff Suppan .15 .40
160 DaRond Stovall .15 .40
161 Mark Redman .15 .40
162 Ken Cloude RC .15 .40
163 Bobby Estalella .15 .40
164 Abraham Nunez RC .15 .40
165 Derrick Gibson .15 .40
166 Mike Drumright RC .15 .40
167 Katsuhiro Maeda .15 .40
168 Jeff Liefer .15 .40
169 Ben Grieve .15 .40
170 Bob Abreu .25 .60
171 Shannon Stewart .15 .40
172 Braden Looper RC .30 .75
173 Brant Brown .15 .40
174 Marlon Anderson .15 .40
175 Brad Fullmer .15 .40
176 Carlos Beltran .75 2.00
177 Nomar Garciaparra .60 1.50
178 Derrek Lee .25 .60
179 Valerio De Los Santos RC .15 .40
180 Dmitri Young .15 .40
181 Jamey Wright .15 .40
182 Hiram Bocachica RC .15 .40
183 Wilton Guerrero .15 .40
184 Chris Carpenter .15 .40
185 Scott Spiezio .15 .40
186 Andruw Jones .25 .60
187 Travis Lee RC .25 .60
188 Jose Cruz Jr. RC .25 .60
189 Jose Guillen .15 .40
190 Jeff Abbott .15 .40
191 Ricky Ledee RC .25 .60
192 Mike Sweeney .15 .40
193 Donnie Sadler .15 .40
194 Scott Rolen .25 .60
195 Kevin Orie .15 .40
196 Jason Conti RC .15 .40
197 Mark Kotsay RC .60 1.50
198 Eric Milton RC .25 .60
199 Russell Branyan .15 .40
200 Alex Sanchez RC .25 .60

1997 Bowman's Best Atomic Refractors

*STARS: 5X TO 12X BASIC CARDS
*ROOKIES: 3X TO 8X BASIC CARDS
STATED ODDS 1:24
117 Adrian Beltre 100.00 250.00

1997 Bowman's Best Refractors

*STARS: 2.5X TO 6X BASIC CARDS
*ROOKIES: 1.5X TO 4X BASIC CARDS
STATED ODDS 1:12
117 Adrian Beltre 40.00 100.00

1997 Bowman's Best Autographs

Randomly inserted in packs at a rate of 1:170, this 10-card set features five silver rookie cards and five gold veteran cards with authentic autographs and a "Certified Autograph Issue" stamp.

COMPLETE SET (10) 125.00 250.00
STATED ODDS 1:170
*REFRACTOR: .75X TO 2X BASIC AUTO
REFRACTOR STATED ODDS 1:2036
*ATOMIC: 1.5X TO 4X BASIC AUTO
ATOMIC STATED ODDS 1:6107
SKIP-NUMBERED 10-CARD SET
29 Tony Gwynn 15.00 40.00
33 Paul Molitor 10.00 25.00
82 Derek Jeter 125.00 300.00
91 Brady Anderson 6.00 15.00
98 Tim Salmon 6.00 15.00
107 Todd Walker 6.00 15.00
183 Wilton Guerrero 2.00 5.00
185 Scott Spiezio 2.00 5.00
188 Jose Cruz Jr. 6.00 15.00
194 Scott Rolen 6.00 15.00

1997 Bowman's Best Best Cuts

Randomly inserted in packs at a rate of one in 24, this 20-card set features color player photos printed on intricate, Laser Cut Chromium card stock.

COMPLETE SET (20) 75.00 150.00
STATED ODDS 1:24
*REFRACTOR: .6X TO 1.5X BASIC CUTS
REFRACTOR STATED ODDS 1:48
*ATOMIC: 1X TO 2.5X BASIC CUTS
ATOMIC STATED ODDS 1:96
BC1 Derek Jeter 6.00 15.00
BC2 Chipper Jones 2.50 6.00
BC3 Frank Thomas 2.50 6.00
BC4 Cal Ripken 8.00 20.00
BC5 Mark McGwire 8.00 20.00
BC6 Ken Griffey Jr. 5.00 12.00
BC7 Jeff Bagwell 1.50 4.00
BC8 Mike Piazza 4.00 10.00
BC9 Ken Caminiti 1.00 2.50
BC10 Albert Belle 1.00 2.50
BC11 Jose Cruz Jr. 1.00 2.50
BC12 Wilton Guerrero 1.00 2.50
BC13 Darin Erstad 1.00 2.50
BC14 Andruw Jones 1.50 4.00
BC15 Scott Rolen 1.50 4.00
BC16 Jose Guillen 1.00 2.50
BC17 Bob Abreu 1.50 4.00
BC18 Vladimir Guerrero 2.50 6.00
BC19 Todd Walker 1.00 2.50
BC20 Nomar Garciaparra 4.00 10.00

1997 Bowman's Best Mirror Image

Randomly inserted in packs at a rate of one in 48, this 10-card set features color photos of four of the best players in the same position printed on double-sided chromium card stock. Two veterans and two rookies appear on each card. The veteran players are displayed in the larger photos with the rookies appearing in smaller corner photos.

COMPLETE SET (10) 30.00 80.00
STATED ODDS 1:48
*REFRACTORS: .6X TO 1.5X BASIC MI
REFRACTOR STATED ODDS 1:96
*ATOMIC REF: 1.25X TO 3X BASIC MI
ATOMIC STATED ODDS 1:192
*INVERTED: 2X VALUE OF NON-INVERTED
INVERTED: RANDOM INSERTS IN PACKS
INVERTED HAVE LARGER ROOKIE PHOTOS
MI1 Nomar 5.00 12.00
Jeter
Boca
Larkin
MI2 T.Lee 2.00 5.00
Thomas
D.Lee
Bag
MI3 K.Wood 2.00 5.00
Maddux
Benson
MI4 M.Piazza 3.00 8.00
I.Rod
E.Marrero
MI5 J.Cruz 6.00 15.00
Grif
Jones
Bonds
MI6 J.Gonz 1.25 3.00
Guillen
Hidalgo
Shef
MI7 Konor 5.00 12.00
McGwire
Helt
Palm
MI8 W.Guer 1.25 3.00
Biggio
Sadl
Knob
MI9 A.Beltre 1.50 4.00
C.Jones
Branyan
MI10 V.Guer 2.00 5.00
Abreu
Lofl
Belle

1997 Bowman's Best Jumbo

This 16-card set features selected cards from the 1997 regular Bowman's Best set in a 4" by 6" jumbo version available to Stadium Club members only by mail. Only 675 of each of the 16 cards were produced for this jumbo version. The cards are checklisted according to their number in the regular size set.

*REFRACTORS: 4X BASIC CARDS
*ATOMIC REFRACTORS: 8X BASIC CARDS
1 Ken Griffey Jr. 4.00 10.00
5 Mike Piazza 3.00 8.00
9 Chipper Jones 3.00 8.00
11 Kenny Lofton .75 2.00
29 Tony Gwynn 3.00 8.00
33 Paul Molitor 1.50 4.00
38 Frank Thomas 1.25 3.00
45 Mark McGwire 3.00 8.00
64 Cal Ripken Jr. 6.00 15.00
73 Barry Bonds 3.00 8.00
74 Juan Gonzalez .75 2.00
82 Derek Jeter 6.00 15.00
101 Vladimir Guerrero 1.50 4.00
177 Nomar Garciaparra 2.50 6.00
186 Andruw Jones 2.00 5.00
188 Jose Cruz Jr. .75 2.00

1998 Bowman's Best

The 1998 Bowman's Best set (produced by Topps) consists of 200 standard size cards and was released in August, 1998. The six-card packs retailed for a suggested price of $5 each. The card fronts feature 100 action photos with a gold background showcasing today's veteran players and 100 photos (combining posed shots with action shots) with a silver background showcasing rookies. The Bowman's Best logo sits in the upper right corner and the featured player's name sits in the lower left corner. Rookie Cards include Ryan Anderson, Troy Glaus, Orlando Hernandez, Carlos Lee, Ruben Mateo and Magglio Ordonez.

COMPLETE SET (200) 15.00 40.00
1 Mark McGwire 1.00 2.50
2 Jeromy Burnitz .15 .40
3 Barry Bonds 1.00 2.50
4 Dante Bichette .15 .40
5 Chipper Jones .40 1.00
6 Frank Thomas .40 1.00
7 Kevin Brown .25 .60
8 Juan Gonzalez .15 .40
9 Jay Buhner .15 .40
10 Chuck Knoblauch .15 .40
11 Cal Ripken 1.25 3.00
12 Matt Williams .15 .40
13 Jim Edmonds .15 .40
14 Manny Ramirez .25 .60
15 Tony Clark .15 .40
16 Mo Vaughn .15 .40
17 Bernie Williams .25 .60
18 Scott Rolen .25 .60
19 Gary Sheffield .15 .40
20 Albert Belle .15 .40
21 Mike Piazza .60 1.50
22 John Olerud .15 .40
23 Tony Gwynn .50 1.25
24 Jay Bell .15 .40
25 Jose Cruz Jr. .15 .40
26 Justin Thompson .15 .40
27 Ken Griffey Jr. .75 2.00
28 Sandy Alomar Jr. .15 .40
29 Mark Grudzielanek .15 .40
30 Mark Grace .25 .60
31 Ron Gant .15 .40
32 Javy Lopez .15 .40
33 Jeff Bagwell .25 .60
34 Fred McGriff .25 .60
35 Rafael Palmeiro .25 .60
36 Vinny Castilla .15 .40
37 Andy Benes .15 .40
38 Pedro Martinez .25 .60
39 Andy Pettitte .25 .60
40 Marty Cordova .15 .40
41 Rusty Greer .15 .40
42 Kevin Orie .15 .40
43 Chan Ho Park .15 .40
44 Ryan Klesko .15 .40
45 Alex Rodriguez .60 1.50
46 Travis Fryman .15 .40
47 Jeff King .15 .40
48 Roger Clemens .75 2.00
49 Darin Erstad .15 .40
50 Brady Anderson .15 .40
51 Jason Kendall .15 .40
52 John Valentin .15 .40
53 Ellis Burks .15 .40
54 Brian Hunter .15 .40
55 Paul O'Neill .25 .60
56 Ken Caminiti .15 .40
57 David Justice .15 .40
58 Eric Karros .15 .40
59 Pat Hentgen .15 .40
60 Greg Maddux .60 1.50
61 Craig Biggio .25 .60
62 Edgar Martinez .25 .60
63 Mike Mussina .25 .60
64 Larry Walker .15 .40
65 Tino Martinez .25 .60
66 Jim Thome .25 .60
67 Tom Glavine .25 .60
68 Raul Mondesi .15 .40
69 Marquis Grissom .15 .40
70 Randy Johnson .40 1.00
71 Steve Finley .15 .40
72 Jose Guillen .15 .40
73 Nomar Garciaparra .60 1.50
74 Wade Boggs .25 .60
75 Bobby Higginson .15 .40
76 Robin Ventura .15 .40
77 Derek Jeter 1.00 2.50
78 Andruw Jones .25 .60
79 Ray Lankford .15 .40
80 Vladimir Guerrero .40 1.00
81 Kenny Lofton .15 .40
82 Ivan Rodriguez .25 .60
83 Neifi Perez .15 .40
84 John Smoltz .25 .60
85 Tim Salmon .25 .60
86 Carlos Delgado .15 .40
87 Sammy Sosa .40 1.00
88 Jaret Wright .15 .40
89 Roberto Alomar .25 .60
90 Paul Molitor .15 .40
91 Dean Palmer .15 .40
92 Barry Larkin .25 .60
93 Jason Giambi .15 .40
94 Curt Schilling .15 .40
95 Eric Young .15 .40
96 Denny Neagle .15 .40
97 Moises Alou .15 .40
98 Livan Hernandez .15 .40
99 Todd Hundley .15 .40
100 Andres Galarraga .15 .40
101 Travis Lee .15 .40
102 Lance Berkman .15 .40
103 Orlando Cabrera .15 .40
104 Mike Lowell RC 1.25 3.00
105 Ben Grieve .15 .40
106 Jae Weong Seo RC .25 .60
107 Richie Sexson .15 .40
108 Eli Marrero .15 .40
109 Aramis Ramirez .15 .40
110 Paul Konerko .15 .40
111 Carl Pavano .15 .40
112 Brad Fullmer .15 .40
113 Matt Clement .15 .40
114 Donzell McDonald .15 .40
115 Todd Helton .25 .60
116 Mike Caruso .15 .40
117 Donnie Sadler .15 .40
118 Bruce Chen .15 .40
119 Jarrod Washburn .15 .40
120 Adrian Beltre .15 .40
121 Ryan Jackson RC .15 .40
122 Kevin Millar RC .60 1.50
123 Corey Koskie RC .40 1.00
124 Dermal Brown .15 .40
125 Kerry Wood .15 .40
126 Juan Melo .15 .40
127 Ramon Hernandez .15 .40
128 Roy Halladay .75 2.00
129 Ron Wright .15 .40
130 Darnell McDonald RC .25 .60
131 Odalis Perez RC .60 1.50
132 Alex Cora RC 1.00 2.50
133 Justin Towle .15 .40
134 Juan Encarnacion .15 .40
135 Brian Rose .15 .40
136 Russell Branyan .15 .40
137 Cesar King RC .15 .40
138 Ruben Rivera .15 .40
139 Ricky Ledee .15 .40
140 Vernon Wells .15 .40
141 Luis Rivas RC .40 1.00
142 Brent Butler .15 .40
143 Karim Garcia .15 .40
144 George Lombard .15 .40
145 Masato Yoshii RC .25 .60
146 Braden Looper .15 .40
147 Alex Sanchez .15 .40
148 Kris Benson .15 .40
149 Mark Kotsay .15 .40
150 Richard Hidalgo .15 .40
151 Scott Elarton .15 .40
152 Ryan Minor RC .15 .40
153 Troy Glaus RC 1.50 4.00
154 Carlos Lee RC 1.25 3.00
155 Michael Coleman .15 .40
156 Jason Grilli RC .15 .40
157 Julio Ramirez RC .15 .40
158 Randy Wolf RC .25 .60
159 Ryan Brannan .15 .40
160 Edgard Clemente .15 .40
161 Miguel Tejada .40 1.00
162 Chad Hermansen .15 .40
163 Ryan Anderson RC .15 .40
164 Ben Petrick .15 .40
165 Alex Gonzalez .15 .40
166 Ben Davis .15 .40
167 John Patterson .15 .40
168 Cliff Politte .15 .40
169 Randall Simon .15 .40
170 Javier Vazquez .15 .40
171 Kevin Witt .15 .40
172 Geoff Jenkins .15 .40
173 David Ortiz 1.50 4.00
174 Derrick Gibson .15 .40
175 Abraham Nunez .15 .40
176 A.J. Hinch .15 .40
177 Ruben Mateo RC .15 .40
178 Magglio Ordonez RC 2.00 5.00
179 Todd Dunwoody .15 .40
180 Daryle Ward .15 .40
181 Mike Kinkade RC .15 .40
182 Willie Martinez .15 .40
183 Orlando Hernandez RC .75 2.00
184 Eric Milton .15 .40
185 Eric Chavez .15 .40
186 Damian Jackson .15 .40
187 Jim Parque RC .25 .60
188 Dan Reichert RC .25 .60
189 Mike Drumright .15 .40
190 Todd Walker .15 .40
191 Shane Monahan .15 .40
192 Derrek Lee .25 .60
193 Jeremy Giambi RC .25 .60
194 Dan McKinley RC .40 1.00
195 Tony Armas Jr. RC .25 .60
196 Matt Anderson RC .15 .40
197 Jim Chamblee RC .15 .40
198 Francisco Cordero RC .40 1.00
199 Calvin Pickering .15 .40
200 Reggie Taylor .15 .40

1998 Bowman's Best Atomic Refractors

*STARS: 10X TO 25X BASIC CARDS
*YNG.STARS: 10X TO 25X BASIC CARDS
*PROSPECTS: 10X TO 25X BASIC CARDS
*ROOKIES: 6X TO 15X BASIC CARDS
STATED ODDS 1:82
STATED PRINT RUN 100 SERIAL #'d SETS
27 Ken Griffey Jr. 125.00 300.00
43 Chan Ho Park 100.00 200.00
45 Alex Rodriguez 75.00 150.00

1998 Bowman's Best Refractors

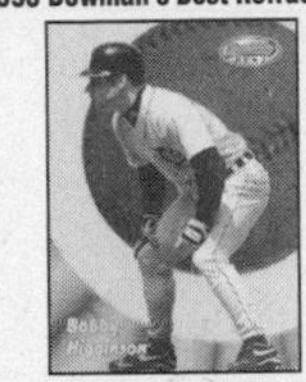

COMPLETE SET (200) 1500.00 3000.00
*STARS: 5X TO 12X BASIC CARDS
*ROOKIES: 2.5X TO 6X BASIC CARDS
STATED ODDS 1:20
STATED PRINT RUN 400 SERIAL #'d SETS
122 Kevin Millar 4.00 10.00

1998 Bowman's Best Autographs

Randomly inserted in packs at a rate of one in 180, this 10-card set is an insert to the 1998 Bowman's Best brand. The fronts feature five gold veteran and five silver prospect cards sporting a Topps "Certified Autograph Issue" logo for authentication. The cards are designed in an identical manner to the basic issue 1998 Bowman's Best set except, of course, for the autograph and the certification logo.

COMPLETE SET (10) 200.00 400.00
STATED ODDS 1:180
*REFRACTORS: .75X TO 2X BASIC AU'S
REFRACTOR STATED ODDS 1:2158
*ATOMICS: 2X TO 4X BASIC AU'S
ATOMIC STATED ODDS 1:6437
SKIP-NUMBERED 10-CARD SET
5 Chipper Jones 25.00 60.00
10 Chuck Knoblauch 6.00 15.00
15 Tony Clark 4.00 10.00
20 Albert Belle 6.00 15.00
25 Jose Cruz Jr. 4.00 10.00
105 Ben Grieve 4.00 10.00
110 Paul Konerko 10.00 25.00
115 Todd Helton 6.00 15.00
120 Adrian Beltre 60.00 150.00
125 Kerry Wood 6.00 15.00

1998 Bowman's Best Mirror Image Fusion

Randomly inserted in packs at a rate of one in 12, this 20-card set is an insert to the 1998 Bowman's Best brand. The fronts feature a Major League veteran player with his positional protégé on the flip side. The player's name runs along the bottom of the card.

COMPLETE SET (20) 15.00 40.00
STATED ODDS 1:12
*REFRACTORS: 1.25X TO 3X BASIC MIRROR
REFRACTOR STATED ODDS 1:809
REF.PRINT RUN 100 SERIAL #'d SETS
ATOMIC STATED ODDS 1:3237
ATOMIC PRINT RUN 25 SERIAL #'d SETS
NO ATOMIC PRICING DUE TO SCARCITY
MI1 F.Thomas 1.50 4.00
D.Ortiz
MI2 C.Knoblauch .50 1.25
E.Wilson
MI3 N.Garciaparra 1.25 3.00
M.Tejada
MI4 A.Rodriguez 1.50 4.00
M.Caruso
MI5 C.Ripken 4.00 10.00
R.Minor
MI6 K.Griffey Jr. 2.50 6.00
B.Grieve
MI7 J.Gonzalez .50 1.25
J.Encarnacion
MI8 J.Cruz Jr. .50 1.25
R.Mateo
MI9 R.Johnson 1.25 3.00
R.Anderson
MI10 I.Rodriguez .75 2.00
A.Hinch
MI11 J.Bagwell .75 2.00
P.Konerko
MI12 M.McGwire 2.00 5.00
T.Lee
MI13 C.Biggio .75 2.00
C.Hermansen
MI14 M.Grudzielanek .40 1.00
A.Gonzalez
MI15 C.Jones 1.25 3.00
A.Beltre
MI16 L.Walker .75 2.00
M.Kotsay
MI17 T.Gwynn 1.25 3.00
G.Lombard
MI18 B.Bonds 2.00 5.00
R.Hidalgo
MI19 G.Maddux 1.50 4.00
K.Wood
MI20 M.Piazza 1.25 3.00
B.Petrick

1998 Bowman's Best Performers

Randomly inserted in packs at a rate of one in six, this 10-card set is an insert to the 1998 Bowman's Best brand. The card fronts feature full color game-action photos of ten players with the best Minor League stats of 1997. The featured player's name is found below the photo with both Bowman's Best logo and the team logo above the photo.

COMPLETE SET (10) 6.00 15.00
STATED ODDS 1:6
*REFRACTORS: 5X TO 12X BASIC PERF.
REFRACTOR STATED ODDS 1:809
REF.PRINT RUN 200 SERIAL #'d SETS
*ATOMIC: 12.5X TO 30X BASIC PERF.
ATOMIC STATED ODDS 1:3237
ATOMIC PRINT RUN 50 SERIAL #'d SETS
BP1 Ben Grieve .60 1.50
BP2 Travis Lee .60 1.50
BP3 Ryan Minor .60 1.50
BP4 Todd Helton 1.00 2.50
BP5 Brad Fullmer .60 1.50
BP6 Paul Konerko .60 1.50
BP7 Adrian Beltre .60 1.50
BP8 Richie Sexson .60 1.50
BP9 Aramis Ramirez .60 1.50
BP10 Russell Branyan .60 1.50

1999 Bowman's Best Pre-Production

These three cards were distributed as a complete set in a sealed poly-bag and sent to dealers and hobby media several weeks prior to the national release of 1999 Bowman's Best. The cards were created to preview the upcoming product and are almost identical in design to their basic issue counterparts. The key difference is the card numbering. These pre-production cards are numbered PP1-PP3, whereas the basic issue cards of Anderson, Lopez and Gold are all numbered within the context of the 180-card standard set.

COMPLETE SET (3) .75 2.00
PP1 Javy Lopez .40 1.00
PP2 Marlon Anderson .40 1.00
PP3 J.M. Gold .40 1.00

1999 Bowman's Best

The 1999 Bowman's Best set (produced by Topps) consists of 200 standard size cards. The six-card packs, released in August, 1999, retailed for a suggested price of $5 each. The cards are printed on 27-pt. Serillusion stock and feature 85 veteran stars in a striking gold series, 15 Best Performers bonus subset captured in a bronze series, 50 rookies highlighted in a brilliant blue series and 50 prospects shown in a captivating silver series. The fifty rookies and prospects (cards 151-200) were seeded at a rate of one per pack. Notable Rookie Cards included Pat Burrell, Sean Burroughs, Nick Johnson, Austin Kearns, Corey Patterson and Alfonso Soriano.

COMPLETE SET (200) 15.00 40.00
COMP.SET w/o SP's (150) 10.00 25.00
COMMON CARD (1-150) .15 .40
COMMON ROOKIE (151-200) .20 .50
ONE ROOKIE CARD PER PACK
1 Chipper Jones .40 1.00
2 Brian Jordan .15 .40
3 David Justice .15 .40
4 Jason Kendall .15 .40
5 Mo Vaughn .15 .40
6 Jim Edmonds .25 .60
7 Wade Boggs .25 .60
8 Jeromy Burnitz .15 .40
9 Todd Hundley .15 .40
10 Rondell White .15 .40
11 Cliff Floyd .15 .40
12 Sean Casey .15 .40

13 Bernie Williams .25 .60
14 Dante Bichette .15 .40
15 Greg Vaughn .15 .40
16 Andres Galarraga .25 .60
17 Ray Durham .15 .40
18 Jim Thome .25 .60
19 Gary Sheffield .15 .40
20 Frank Thomas .40 1.00
21 Orlando Hernandez .15 .40
22 Ivan Rodriguez .25 .60
23 Jose Cruz Jr. .15 .40
24 Jason Giambi .15 .40
25 Craig Biggio .25 .60
26 Kerry Wood .15 .40
27 Manny Ramirez .40 1.00
28 Curt Schilling .15 .40
29 Mike Mussina .25 .60
30 Tim Salmon .15 .40
31 Mike Piazza .40 1.00
32 Roberto Alomar .25 .60
33 Larry Walker .25 .60
34 Barry Larkin .25 .60
35 Nomar Garciaparra .25 .60
36 Paul O'Neill .25 .60
37 Todd Walker .15 .40
38 Eric Karros .15 .40
39 Brad Fullmer .15 .40
40 John Olerud .15 .40
41 Todd Helton .25 .60
42 Raul Mondesi .15 .40
43 Jose Canseco .25 .60
44 Matt Williams .15 .40
45 Ray Lankford .15 .40
46 Carlos Delgado .15 .40
47 Darin Erstad .15 .40
48 Vladimir Guerrero .25 .60
49 Robin Ventura .15 .40
50 Alex Rodriguez .50 1.25
51 Vinny Castilla .15 .40
52 Tony Clark .15 .40
53 Pedro Martinez .25 .60
54 Rafael Palmeiro .25 .60
55 Scott Rolen .25 .60
56 Tino Martinez .15 .40
57 Tony Gwynn .40 1.00
58 Barry Bonds .60 1.50
59 Kenny Lofton .15 .40
60 Javy Lopez .15 .40
61 Mark Grace .25 .60
62 Travis Lee .15 .40
63 Kevin Brown .15 .40
64 Al Leiter .15 .40
65 Albert Belle .15 .40
66 Sammy Sosa .40 1.00
67 Greg Maddux .50 1.25
68 Mark Kotsay .15 .40
69 Dmitri Young .15 .40
70 Mark McGwire .60 1.50
71 Juan Gonzalez .15 .40
72 Andruw Jones .15 .40
73 Derek Jeter 1.00 2.50
74 Randy Johnson .40 1.00
75 Cal Ripken 1.25 3.00
76 Shawn Green .15 .40
77 Moises Alou .15 .40
78 Tom Glavine .25 .60
79 Sandy Alomar Jr. .15 .40
80 Ken Griffey Jr. .75 2.00
81 Ryan Klesko .15 .40
82 Jeff Bagwell .25 .60
83 Ben Grieve .15 .40
84 John Smoltz .25 .60
85 Roger Clemens .50 1.25
86 Ken Griffey Jr. BP .75 2.00
87 Roger Clemens BP .50 1.25
88 Derek Jeter BP 1.00 2.50
89 Nomar Garciaparra BP .25 .60
90 Mark McGwire BP .60 1.50
91 Sammy Sosa BP .40 1.00
92 Alex Rodriguez BP .50 1.25
93 Greg Maddux BP .50 1.25
94 Vladimir Guerrero BP .25 .60
95 Chipper Jones BP .40 1.00
96 Kerry Wood BP .15 .40
97 Ben Grieve BP .15 .40
98 Tony Gwynn BP .40 1.00
99 Juan Gonzalez BP .15 .40
100 Mike Piazza BP .40 1.00
101 Eric Chavez .15 .40
102 Billy Koch .15 .40
103 Dernell Stenson .15 .40
104 Marlon Anderson .15 .40
105 Ron Belliard .15 .40
106 Bruce Chen .15 .40
107 Carlos Beltran .25 .60
108 Chad Hermansen .15 .40
109 Ryan Anderson .15 .40
110 Michael Barrett .15 .40
111 Matt Clement .15 .40
112 Ben Davis .15 .40
113 Calvin Pickering .15 .40
114 Brad Penny .15 .40
115 Paul Konerko .15 .40
116 Alex Gonzalez .15 .40
117 George Lombard .15 .40
118 John Patterson .15 .40
119 Rob Bell .15 .40
120 Ruben Mateo .15 .40
121 Troy Glaus .15 .40
122 Ryan Bradley .15 .40
123 Carlos Lee .15 .40
124 Gabe Kapler .15 .40
125 Ramon Hernandez .15 .40
126 Carlos Febles .15 .40
127 Mitch Meluskey .15 .40
128 Michael Cuddyer .15 .40
129 Pablo Ozuna .15 .40
130 Jayson Werth .25 .60
131 Ricky Ledee .15 .40
132 Jeremy Giambi .15 .40
133 Danny Klassen .15 .40
134 Mark DeRosa .15 .40
135 Randy Wolf .15 .40
136 Roy Halladay .25 .60
137 Derrick Gibson .15 .40
138 Ben Petrick .15 .40
139 Warren Morris .15 .40
140 Lance Berkman .25 .60
141 Russell Branyan .15 .40
142 Adrian Beltre .40 1.00
143 Juan Encarnacion .15 .40
144 Fernando Seguignol .15 .40
145 Corey Koskie .15 .40
146 Preston Wilson .15 .40
147 Homer Bush .15 .40
148 Daryle Ward .15 .40
149 Joe McEwing RC .20 .50
150 Peter Bergeron RC .20 .50
151 Pat Burrell RC .75 2.00
152 Choo Freeman RC .20 .50
153 Matt Belisle RC .20 .50
154 Carlos Pena RC .60 1.50
155 A.J. Burnett RC .30 .75
156 Doug Mientkiewicz RC .30 .75
157 Sean Burroughs RC .20 .50
158 Mike Zywica RC .20 .50
159 Corey Patterson RC .50 1.25
160 Austin Kearns RC .75 2.00
161 Chip Ambres RC .20 .50
162 Kelly Dransfeldt RC .20 .50
163 Mike Nannini RC .20 .50
164 Mark Mulder RC .60 1.50
165 Jason Tyner RC .20 .50
166 Bobby Seay RC .20 .50
167 Alex Escobar RC .20 .50
168 Nick Johnson RC .50 1.25
169 Alfonso Soriano RC 2.00 5.00
170 Clayton Andrews RC .20 .50
171 C.C. Sabathia RC 1.50 4.00
172 Matt Holliday RC 1.00 2.50
173 Brad Lidge RC .60 1.50
174 Kit Pellow RC .20 .50
175 J.M. Gold RC .20 .50
176 Roosevelt Brown RC .20 .50
177 Eric Valent RC .20 .50
178 Adam Everett RC .30 .75
179 Jorge Toca RC .20 .50
180 Matt Roney RC .20 .50
181 Andy Brown RC .20 .50
182 Phil Norton RC .20 .50
183 Mickey Lopez RC .20 .50
184 Chris George RC .20 .50
185 Arturo McDowell RC .20 .50
186 Jose Fernandez RC .20 .50
187 Seth Etherton RC .20 .50
188 Josh McKinley RC .20 .50
189 Nate Cornejo RC .20 .50
190 Giuseppe Chiaramonte RC .20 .50
191 Mamon Tucker RC .20 .50
192 Ryan Mills RC .20 .50
193 Chad Moeller RC .20 .50
194 Tony Torcato RC .20 .50
195 Jeff Winchester RC .20 .50
196 Rick Elder RC .20 .50
197 Matt Burch RC .20 .50
198 Jeff Urban RC .20 .50
199 Chris Jones RC .20 .50
200 Masao Kida RC .20 .50

1999 Bowman's Best Atomic Refractors

*ATOMIC: 10X TO 25X BASIC CARDS
*ROOKIES: 8X TO 20X BASIC CARDS
STATED ODDS 1:62
STATED PRINT RUN 100 SERIAL #'d SETS
73 Derek Jeter 75.00 150.00

1999 Bowman's Best Refractors

*STARS: 5X TO 12X BASIC CARDS
*ROOKIES: 4X TO 10X BASIC CARDS
STATED ODDS 1:15
STATED PRINT RUN 400 SERIAL #'d SETS
80 Ken Griffey Jr. 25.00 60.00

1999 Bowman's Best Franchise Best Mach I

Randomly inserted in packs at the rate of one in 41, this 10-card set features color photos of some of the Major's top stars printed on die-cut Serillusion stock and sequentially numbered to 3,000.
COMPLETE SET (10) 10.00 25.00
STATED ODDS 1:41
STATED PRINT RUN 3000 SERIAL #'d SETS
*MACH II: .75X TO 2X MACH I
MACH II STATED ODDS 1:124
MACH II PRINT RUN 1000 SERIAL #'d SETS
*MACH III: 1.25X TO 3X MACH I
MACH III STATED ODDS 1:248
MACH III PRINT RUN 500 SERIAL #'d SETS
FB1 Mark McGwire 2.00 5.00
FB2 Ken Griffey Jr. 2.50 6.00
FB3 Sammy Sosa 1.25 3.00
FB4 Nomar Garciaparra .75 2.00
FB5 Alex Rodriguez 1.50 4.00
FB6 Derek Jeter 3.00 8.00
FB7 Mike Piazza 1.25 3.00
FB8 Frank Thomas 1.25 3.00
FB9 Chipper Jones 1.25 3.00
FB10 Juan Gonzalez .50 1.25

1999 Bowman's Best Franchise Favorites

Randomly inserted in packs at the rate of one in 40, this six-card set features color photos of retired legends and current stars in three versions. Version A pictures the current star; Version B, a retired great; and Version C pairs the current star with the retired legend.
COMPLETE SET (6) 12.50 30.00
STATED ODDS 1:40
FR1A Derek Jeter 4.00 10.00
FR1B Don Mattingly 3.00 8.00
FR1C D.Jeter 4.00 10.00
D.Mattingly
FR2A Scott Rolen 1.00 2.50
FR2B Mike Schmidt 2.50 6.00
FR2C S.Rolen 2.50 6.00
M.Schmidt

1999 Bowman's Best Franchise Favorites Autographs

This six-card set is an autographed parallel version of the regular insert set with the "Topps Certified Autograph Issue" stamp. The insertion rate for these cards are: Versions A and B, 1:1550 packs; and Version C, 1:6174. Version C cards feature autographs from both players.
FR1A/FR2A STATED ODDS 1:1550
FR1B/FR2B STATED ODDS 1:1550
FR1C/FR2C STATED ODDS 1:6174
FR1A Derek Jeter 100.00 200.00
FR1B Don Mattingly 30.00 60.00
FR1C D.Jeter/D.Mattingly 200.00 400.00
FR2A Scott Rolen 6.00 51.00
FR2B Mike Schmidt 15.00 40.00
FR2C S.Rolen/M.Schmidt 30.00 60.00

1999 Bowman's Best Future Foundations Mach I

Randomly inserted into packs at the rate of one in 41, this 10-card set features color photos of some of the top young stars printed on die-cut Serillusion stock and sequentially numbered to 3,000.
COMPLETE SET (10) 6.00 15.00
STATED ODDS 1:41
STATED PRINT RUN 3000 SERIAL #'d SETS
*MACH II: .75X TO 2X MACH I
MACH II STATED ODDS 1:124
MACH II PRINT RUN 1000 SERIAL #'d SETS
*MACH III: 1.25X TO 3X MACH I
MACH III STATED ODDS 1:248
MACH III PRINT RUN 500 SERIAL #'d SETS
FF1 Ruben Mateo .40 1.00
FF2 Troy Glaus .40 1.00
FF3 Eric Chavez .40 1.00
FF4 Pat Burrell 1.50 4.00
FF5 Adrian Beltre 1.00 2.50
FF6 Ryan Anderson .40 1.00
FF7 Alfonso Soriano 4.00 10.00
FF8 Brad Penny .40 1.00
FF9 Derrick Gibson .40 1.00
FF10 Bruce Chen .40 1.00

1999 Bowman's Best Mirror Image

Randomly inserted into packs at the rate of one in 24, this 10-card double-sided set features color photos of a veteran ballplayer on one side and a hot prospect on the other.
COMPLETE SET (10) 10.00 25.00
*REFRACTORS: .75X TO 2X BASIC MIR.IMAGE
REFRACTOR STATED ODDS 1:96
*ATOMIC: 1.25X TO 3X BASIC MIR.IMAGE
ATOMIC STATED ODDS 1:192
M1 A.Rodriguez 1.25 3.00
A.Gonzalez
M2 K.Griffey Jr. 2.00 5.00
R.Mateo
M3 D.Jeter 4.00 10.00
A.Soriano
M4 S.Sosa 1.00 2.50
C.Patterson
M5 G.Maddux 1.25 3.00
B.Chen
M6 C.Jones 1.00 2.50
E.Chavez
M7 V.Guerrero .60 1.50
C.Beltran
M8 F.Thomas 1.00 2.50
N.Johnson
M9 N.Garciaparra .60 1.50
P.Ozuna
M10 M.McGwire 1.50 4.00
P.Burrell

1999 Bowman's Best Rookie Locker Room Autographs

Randomly inserted into packs at the rate of one in 248, this five-card set features autographed color photos of top prospects with the "Topps Certified Autograph Issue" logo stamp.
STATED ODDS 1:248
RA1 Pat Burrell 8.00 20.00
RA2 Michael Barrett 4.00 10.00
RA3 Troy Glaus 6.00 15.00
RA4 Gabe Kapler 4.00 10.00
RA5 Eric Chavez 4.00 10.00

1999 Bowman's Best Rookie Locker Room Game Used Bats

Randomly inserted into packs at the rate of one in 517, this six-card set features color photos of top players with pieces of game-used bats embedded into the cards.
STATED ODDS 1:517
RB1 Pat Burrell 6.00 15.00
RB2 Michael Barrett 3.00 8.00
RB3 Troy Glaus 4.00 10.00
RB4 Gabe Kapler 3.00 8.00
RB5 Eric Chavez 3.00 8.00
RB6 Richie Sexson 3.00 8.00

1999 Bowman's Best Rookie Locker Room Game Worn Jerseys

Randomly inserted into packs at the rate of one in 538, this four-card set features color photos of some of the hottest young stars with pieces of their game-used jerseys embedded in the cards.
STATED ODDS 1:538
RJ1 Richie Sexson 4.00 10.00
RJ2 Michael Barrett 4.00 10.00
RJ3 Troy Glaus 6.00 15.00
RJ4 Eric Chavez 4.00 10.00

1999 Bowman's Best Rookie of the Year

Randomly inserted into packs at the rate of one in 95, this two-card set features color photos of the 1998 American and National League Rookies of the Year printed on Serillusion card stock. An autographed version of Ben Grieve's card with the "Topps Certified Autograph Issue" stamp was inserted at the rate of 1:1239 packs.
STATED ODDS 1:95
GRIEVE AU STATED ODDS 1:1239
ROY1 Ben Grieve .75 2.00
ROY2 Kerry Wood .75 2.00
ROY1A Ben Grieve AU 6.00 15.00

2000 Bowman's Best Pre-Production

This three card set of sample cards was distributed within a sealed, clear, cello poly-wrap to dealers and hobby media several weeks prior to the national release of 2000 Bowman's Best.
COMPLETE SET (3) 1.50 4.00
PP1 Larry Walker .60 1.50
PP2 Adam Dunn .60 1.50
PP3 Brett Myers 1.25 3.00

2000 Bowman's Best Previews

Randomly inserted into Bowman hobby/retail packs at one in 18, this 10-card insert set features preview cards from the 2000 Bowman's Best product. Card backs carry a "BB" prefix.
COMPLETE SET (10) 8.00 20.00
STATED ODDS 1:18 HOB/RET, 1:8 HTC
BB1 Derek Jeter 2.50 6.00
BB2 Ken Griffey Jr. 2.00 5.00
BB3 Nomar Garciaparra .60 1.50
BB4 Mike Piazza 1.00 2.50
BB5 Alex Rodriguez 1.25 3.00
BB6 Sammy Sosa 1.00 2.50
BB7 Mark McGwire 1.50 4.00
BB8 Pat Burrell .40 1.00
BB9 Josh Hamilton 1.25 3.00
BB10 Adam Piatt .40 1.00

2000 Bowman's Best

The 2000 Bowman's Best set (produced by Topps) was released in early August, 2000 and features a 200-card base set broken into tiers as follows: Base Veterans/Prospects (1-150) and Rookies (151-200) which were serial numbered to 2999. Each pack contained four cards, and carried a suggested retail of $5.00. Rookie Cards include Rick Asadoorian, Willie Bloomquist, Bobby Bradley, Ben Broussard, Chin-Feng Chen and Barry Zito. The added element of serial-numbered Rookie Cards was extremely popular with collectors and a much-need jolt of life for the Bowman's Best brand (which had been badly overshadowed for two years by the Bowman Chrome Brand).
COMP.SET w/o RC's (150) 10.00 25.00
COMMON CARD (1-150) .15 .40
COMMON ROOKIE (151-200) .50 1.25
RC 151-200 STATED ODDS 1:7
RC 151-200 PRINT RUN 2999 SERIAL #'d SETS
1 Nomar Garciaparra .25 .60
2 Chipper Jones .40 1.00
3 Tony Clark .15 .40
4 Bernie Williams .25 .60
5 Barry Bonds .60 1.50
6 Jermaine Dye .15 .40
7 John Olerud .15 .40
8 Mike Hampton .15 .40
9 Cal Ripken 1.25 3.00
10 Jeff Bagwell .25 .60
11 Troy Glaus .15 .40
12 J.D. Drew .15 .40
13 Jeromy Burnitz .15 .40
14 Carlos Delgado .15 .40
15 Shawn Green .15 .40
16 Kevin Millwood .15 .40
17 Rondell White .15 .40
18 Scott Rolen .25 .60
19 Jeff Cirillo .15 .40
20 Barry Larkin .25 .60
21 Brian Giles .15 .40
22 Roger Clemens .50 1.25
23 Manny Ramirez .40 1.00
24 Alex Gonzalez .15 .40
25 Mark Grace .25 .60
26 Fernando Tatis .15 .40
27 Randy Johnson .40 1.00
28 Roger Cedeno .15 .40
29 Brian Jordan .15 .40
30 Kevin Brown .15 .40
31 Greg Vaughn .15 .40
32 Roberto Alomar .25 .60
33 Larry Walker .25 .60
34 Rafael Palmeiro .25 .60
35 Curt Schilling .25 .60
36 Orlando Hernandez .15 .40
37 Todd Walker .15 .40
38 Juan Gonzalez .15 .40
39 Sean Casey .15 .40
40 Tony Gwynn .40 1.00
41 Albert Belle .15 .40
42 Gary Sheffield .15 .40
43 Michael Barrett .15 .40
44 Preston Wilson .15 .40
45 Jim Thome .25 .60
46 Shannon Stewart .15 .40
47 Mo Vaughn .15 .40
48 Ben Grieve .15 .40
49 Adrian Beltre .40 1.00
50 Sammy Sosa .40 1.00
51 Bob Abreu .15 .40
52 Edgardo Alfonzo .15 .40
53 Carlos Febles .15 .40
54 Frank Thomas .40 1.00
55 Alex Rodriguez .50 1.25
56 Cliff Floyd .15 .40
57 Jose Canseco .25 .60
58 Erubiel Durazo .15 .40
59 Tim Hudson .25 .60
60 Craig Biggio .25 .60
61 Eric Karros .15 .40
62 Mike Mussina .25 .60
63 Robin Ventura .15 .40
64 Carlos Beltran .25 .60
65 Pedro Martinez .25 .60
66 Gabe Kapler .15 .40
67 Jason Kendall .15 .40
68 Derek Jeter 1.00 2.50
69 Magglio Ordonez .25 .60
70 Mike Piazza .40 1.00
71 Mike Lieberthal .15 .40
72 Andres Galarraga .25 .60
73 Raul Mondesi .15 .40
74 Eric Chavez .15 .40
75 Greg Maddux .50 1.25
76 Matt Williams .15 .40
77 Kris Benson .15 .40
78 Ivan Rodriguez .25 .60
79 Pokey Reese .15 .40
80 Vladimir Guerrero .25 .60
81 Mark McGwire .60 1.50
82 Vinny Castilla .15 .40
83 Todd Helton .25 .60
84 Andruw Jones .15 .40
85 Ken Griffey Jr. .75 2.00
86 Mark McGwire BP .60 1.50
87 Derek Jeter BP 1.00 2.50
88 Chipper Jones BP .40 1.00
89 Nomar Garciaparra BP .25 .60
90 Sammy Sosa BP .40 1.00
91 Cal Ripken BP 1.25 3.00
92 Juan Gonzalez BP .15 .40
93 Alex Rodriguez BP .50 1.25
94 Barry Bonds BP .60 1.50
95 Sean Casey BP .15 .40
96 Vladimir Guerrero BP .25 .60
97 Mike Piazza BP .40 1.00
98 Shawn Green BP .15 .40
99 Jeff Bagwell BP .25 .60
100 Ken Griffey Jr. BP .75 2.00
101 Rick Ankiel .25 .60
102 John Patterson .15 .40
103 David Walling .15 .40
104 Michael Restovich .15 .40
105 A.J. Burnett .15 .40
106 Pablo Ozuna .15 .40
107 Chad Hermansen .15 .40
108 Choo Freeman .15 .40
109 Mark Quinn .15 .40
110 Corey Patterson .15 .40
111 Ramon Ortiz .15 .40
112 Vernon Wells .15 .40
113 Milton Bradley .15 .40
114 Gookie Dawkins .15 .40
115 Sean Burroughs .15 .40
116 Wily Mo Pena .15 .40
117 Dee Brown .15 .40
118 C.C. Sabathia .25 .60
119 Adam Kennedy .15 .40
120 Octavio Dotel .15 .40
121 Kip Wells .15 .40
122 Ben Petrick .15 .40
123 Mark Mulder .15 .40
124 Jason Standridge .15 .40
125 Adam Piatt .15 .40
126 Steve Lomasney .15 .40
127 Jayson Werth .25 .60
128 Alex Escobar .15 .40
129 Ryan Anderson .15 .40
130 Adam Dunn .25 .60
131 Ted Lilly .15 .40
132 Brad Penny .15 .40
133 Daryle Ward .15 .40
134 Eric Munson .15 .40
135 Nick Johnson .15 .40
136 Jason Jennings .15 .40
137 Tim Raines Jr. .15 .40
138 Ruben Mateo .15 .40
139 Jack Cust .15 .40
140 Rafael Furcal .25 .60
141 Eric Gagne .15 .40
142 Tony Armas Jr. .15 .40
143 Mike Paradis .15 .40
144 Peter Bergeron .15 .40
145 Alfonso Soriano .40 1.00
146 Josh Hamilton .50 1.25
147 Michael Cuddyer .15 .40
148 Jay Gehrke .15 .40
149 Josh Girdley .15 .40
150 Pat Burrell .15 .40
151 Brett Myers RC 1.50 4.00
152 Scott Seabol RC .50 1.25
153 Keith Reed RC .50 1.25
154 Francisco Rodriguez RC 3.00 8.00
155 Barry Zito RC 4.00 10.00
156 Pat Manning RC .50 1.25
157 Ben Christensen RC .50 1.25
158 Corey Myers RC .50 1.25
159 Wascar Serrano RC .50 1.25
160 Wes Anderson RC .50 1.25
161 Andy Tracy RC .50 1.25
162 Cesar Saba RC .50 1.25
163 Mike Lamb RC .50 1.25
164 Bobby Bradley RC .50 1.25
165 Vince Faison RC .50 1.25
166 Ty Howington RC .50 1.25
167 Ken Harvey RC .50 1.25
168 Josh Kalinowski RC .50 1.25
169 Ruben Salazar RC .50 1.25
170 Aaron Rowand RC 2.50 6.00
171 Ramon Santiago RC .50 1.25
172 Scott Sobkowiak RC .50 1.25
173 Lyle Overbay RC .75 2.00
174 Rico Washington RC .50 1.25
175 Rick Asadoorian RC .50 1.25
176 Matt Ginter RC .50 1.25
177 Jason Stumm RC .50 1.25
178 B.J. Garbe RC .50 1.25
179 Mike MacDougal RC .75 2.00
180 Ryan Christianson RC .50 1.25
181 Kurt Ainsworth RC .50 1.25
182 Brad Baisley RC .50 1.25
183 Ben Broussard RC .75 2.00
184 Aaron McNeal RC .50 1.25
185 John Sneed RC .50 1.25
186 Junior Brignac RC .50 1.25
187 Chance Caple RC .50 1.25
188 Scott Downs RC .50 1.25
189 Matt Cepicky RC .50 1.25
190 Chin-Feng Chen RC 1.50 4.00
191 Johan Santana RC 8.00 20.00
192 Brad Baker RC .50 1.25
193 Jason Repko RC .50 1.25
194 Craig Dingman RC .50 1.25
195 Chris Wakeland RC .50 1.25
196 Rogelio Arias RC .50 1.25
197 Luis Matos RC .50 1.25
198 Rob Ramsay .50 1.25
199 Willie Bloomquist RC 5.00 12.00
200 Tony Pena Jr. RC .50 1.25

2000 Bowman's Best Autographed Baseball Redemptions

Randomly inserted into packs at one in 688, this five-card insert features exchange cards for actual autographed baseballs from some of the Major League's hottest prospects. Please note the deadline to return these cards to Topps was June 30th, 2001.
STATED ODDS 1:688
EXCHANGE DEADLINE 06/30/01
PRICES REFER TO SIGNED BASEBALLS
1 Josh Hamilton 10.00 25.00
2 Rick Ankiel 15.00 40.00
3 Alfonso Soriano 12.00 30.00
4 Nick Johnson 15.00 40.00
5 Corey Patterson 15.00 40.00

2000 Bowman's Best Bets

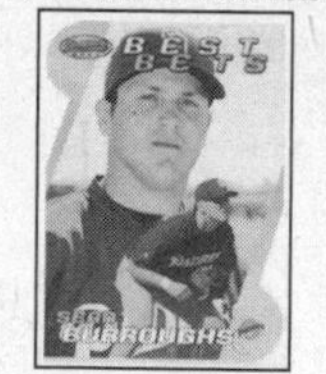

Randomly inserted into packs at one in 15, this 10-card insert features prospects that are sure bets to excel at the Major League level. Card backs carry a "BBB" prefix.
COMPLETE SET (10) 3.00 8.00
STATED ODDS 1:15
BBB1 Pat Burrell .40 1.00
BBB2 Alfonso Soriano 1.00 2.50
BBB3 Corey Patterson .40 1.00
BBB4 Eric Munson .40 1.00
BBB5 Sean Burroughs .40 1.00
BBB6 Rafael Furcal .60 1.50
BBB7 Rick Ankiel .60 1.50
BBB8 Nick Johnson .40 1.00
BBB9 Ruben Mateo .40 1.00
BBB10 Josh Hamilton 1.25 3.00

2000 Bowman's Best Franchise 2000

Randomly inserted into packs at one in 18, this 25-card set features players that teams build around. Card backs carry an "F" prefix.
COMPLETE SET (25) 20.00 50.00
STATED ODDS 1:18
F1 Cal Ripken 3.00 8.00
F2 Nomar Garciaparra .60 1.50
F3 Frank Thomas 1.00 2.50
F4 Manny Ramirez 1.00 2.50
F5 Juan Gonzalez .40 1.00
F6 Carlos Beltran .60 1.50
F7 Derek Jeter 2.50 6.00

8 Alex Rodriguez 1.25 3.00
9 Ben Grieve .40 1.00
10 Jose Canseco .60 1.50
11 Ivan Rodriguez .60 1.50
12 Mo Vaughn .40 1.00
13 Randy Johnson 1.00 2.50
14 Chipper Jones 1.00 2.50
15 Sammy Sosa 1.00 2.50
16 Ken Griffey Jr. 2.00 5.00
17 Larry Walker .60 1.50
18 Preston Wilson .40 1.00
19 Jeff Bagwell .60 1.50
20 Shawn Green .40 1.00
21 Vladimir Guerrero .60 1.50
22 Mike Piazza 1.00 2.50
23 Scott Rolen .60 1.50
24 Tony Gwynn 1.00 2.50
25 Barry Bonds 1.50 4.00

2000 Bowman's Best Franchise Favorites

Randomly inserted into packs at one in 17, this six-card insert features players (past and present) that are franchise favorites. Card backs carry a "FR" prefix.

COMPLETE SET (6) 6.00 15.00
STATED ODDS 1:17
FR1A Sean Casey .40 1.00
FR1B Johnny Bench 1.00 2.50
FR1C S.Casey 1.00 2.50
J.Bench
FR2A Cal Ripken 3.00 8.00
FR2B Brooks Robinson .60 1.50
FR2C C.Ripken 3.00 8.00
B.Robinson

2000 Bowman's Best Franchise Favorites Autographs

Randomly inserted into packs, this six-card insert is a complete parallel of the Franchise Favorites insert. Each of these cards were autographed by the players, and the set was broken into tiers as folllows: Group A (Sean Casey and Cal Ripken) were inserted at one in 1291, Group B (Johnny Bench and Brooks Robinson) were inserted at one in 1291, and Group C (Casey/Bench, and Ripken/Robinson) were inserted into packs at one in 1,513. The overall odds of getting an autograph cards were one in 574. Card backs carry a "FR" prefix.

GROUP A STATED ODDS 1:1291
GROUP B STATED ODDS 1:1291
GROUP C STATED ODDS 1:5153
OVERALL STATED ODDS 1:574
FR1A Sean Casey A 10.00 25.00
FR1B Johnny Bench B 30.00 60.00
FR1C S.Casey/J.Bench C 30.00 60.00
FR2A Cal Ripken A 40.00 80.00
FR2B Brooks Robinson B 15.00 40.00
FR2C C.Ripken/B.Robinson C 150.00 250.00

2000 Bowman's Best Locker Room Collection Autographs

Randomly inserted into packs, this 19-card insert features autographed cards of top Major League prospects. Card backs carry an "LRCA" prefix. Please note that these cards were broken into two groups. Group A cards were inserted at one in 1033 packs, and Group B cards were inserted at one in 61.

GROUP A STATED ODDS 1:1033
GROUP B STATED ODDS 1:61
OVERALL STATED ODDS 1:57
LRCA1 Carlos Beltran B 8.00 20.00
LRCA2 Rick Ankiel A 6.00 15.00
LRCA3 Vernon Wells A 6.00 15.00
LRCA4 Ruben Mateo A 4.00 10.00
LRCA5 Ben Petrick A 4.00 10.00
LRCA6 Adam Piatt A 4.00 10.00
LRCA7 Eric Munson A 4.00 10.00
LRCA8 Alfonso Soriano A 4.00 10.00
LRCA9 Kerry Wood B 6.00 15.00
LRCA10 Jack Cust A 4.00 10.00
LRCA11 Rafael Furcal A 4.00 10.00
LRCA12 Josh Hamilton 12.50 30.00
LRCA13 Brad Penny A 6.00 15.00
LRCA14 Dee Brown A 4.00 10.00
LRCA15 Milton Bradley A 6.00 15.00
LRCA16 Ryan Anderson A 4.00 10.00
LRCA17 John Patterson A 6.00 15.00
LRCA18 Nick Johnson A 6.00 15.00
LRCA19 Peter Bergeron A 4.00 10.00

2000 Bowman's Best Locker Room Collection Bats

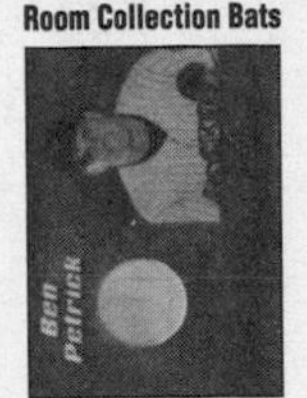

Randomly inserted into packs at one in 376, this 11-card insert features game-used bat cards of some of the hottest prospects in baseball. Card backs carry a "LRCL" prefix.

STATED ODDS 1:376
LRCLAP Adam Piatt 3.00 8.00
LRCLBP Ben Petrick 3.00 8.00
LRCLBP Brad Penny 4.00 10.00
LRCLCB Carlos Beltran 4.00 10.00
LRCLDB Dee Brown 3.00 8.00
LRCLEM Eric Munson 3.00 8.00
LRCLJD J.D. Drew 4.00 10.00
LRCLPB Pat Burrell 4.00 10.00
LRCLRA Rick Ankiel 6.00 15.00
LRCLRF Rafael Furcal 4.00 10.00
LRCLVW Vernon Wells 4.00 10.00

2000 Bowman's Best Locker Room Collection Jerseys

Randomly inserted into packs at one in 206, this five-card insert features swatches from actual game-used jerseys. Card backs carry a "LRCJ" prefix.

STATED ODDS 1:206
LRCJ1 Carlos Beltran 4.00 10.00
LRCJ2 Rick Ankiel 6.00 15.00
LRCJ3 Mark Quinn 3.00 8.00
LRCJ4 Ben Petrick 3.00 8.00
LRCJ5 Adam Piatt 3.00 8.00

2000 Bowman's Best Selections

Randomly inserted into packs at one in 30, this 15-card insert features players that turned out to be outstanding draft selections. Card backs carry a "BBS" prefix.

COMPLETE SET (15) 20.00 50.00
STATED ODDS 1:30
BBS1 Alex Rodriguez 2.00 5.00
BBS2 Ken Griffey Jr. 3.00 8.00
BBS3 Pat Burrell .60 1.50
BBS4 Mark McGwire 2.50 6.00
BBS5 Derek Jeter 4.00 10.00
BBS6 Nomar Garciaparra 1.00 2.50
BBS7 Mike Piazza 1.50 4.00
BBS8 Josh Hamilton 2.00 5.00
BBS9 Cal Ripken 5.00 12.00
BBS10 Jeff Bagwell 1.00 2.50
BBS11 Chipper Jones 1.50 4.00
BBS12 Jose Canseco 1.00 2.50
BBS13 Carlos Beltran 1.00 2.50
BBS14 Kerry Wood .60 1.50
BBS15 Ben Grieve .60 1.50

2000 Bowman's Best Year by Year

Randomly inserted into packs at one in 23, this 10-card insert features duos that made their Major League debuts in the same year. Card backs carry a "YY" prefix.

COMPLETE SET (10) 8.00 20.00
STATED ODDS 1:23
YY1 S.Sosa 2.00 5.00
K.Griffey Jr.
YY2 N.Garciaparra .60 1.50
V.Guerrero
YY3 A.Rodriguez 1.25 3.00
J.Cirillo
YY4 M.Piazza 1.00 2.50
P.Martinez
YY5 D.Jeter 2.50 6.00
E.Alfonzo
YY6 A.Soriano 1.00 2.50
R.Ankiel
YY7 M.McGwire 1.50 4.00
B.Bonds
YY8 J.Gonzalez .60 1.50
L.Walker
YY9 I.Rodriguez .60 1.50
J.Bagwell
YY10 S.Green 1.00 2.50
M.Ramirez

2001 Bowman's Best Promos

This three-card set was distributed in a sealed plastic cello wrap to dealers and hobby media a few months prior to the release of 2001 Bowman's Best to allow a sneak preview of the upcoming brand. The promos can be readily identified from base issue cards by their PP prefixed numbering on back.

COMPLETE SET (3) 2.00 5.00
PP1 Todd Helton .80 2.00
PP2 Tim Hudson .80 2.00
PP3 Vernon Wells .40 1.00

2001 Bowman's Best

This 200-card set features color action player photos printed in an all new design and leading technology. The set was distributed in five-card packs with a suggested retail price of $5 and includes 35 Rookie and 15 Exclusive Rookie cards sequentially numbered to 2,999.

COMP.SET w/o SP's (150) 20.00 50.00
COMMON CARD (1-150) .15 .40
COMMON CARD (151-200) 2.00 5.00
151-185 STATED ODDS 1:7
186-200 EXCLUSIVE RC ODDS 1:15
151-200 PRINT RUN 2999 SERIAL #'d SETS
1 Vladimir Guerrero .40 1.00
2 Miguel Tejada .15 .40
3 Geoff Jenkins .15 .40
4 Jeff Bagwell .25 .60
5 Todd Helton .25 .60
6 Ken Griffey Jr. .75 2.00
7 Nomar Garciaparra .60 1.50
8 Chipper Jones .40 1.00
9 Darin Erstad .15 .40
10 Frank Thomas .40 1.00
11 Jim Thome .25 .60
12 Preston Wilson .15 .40
13 Kevin Brown .15 .40
14 Derek Jeter 1.00 2.50
15 Scott Rolen .25 .60
16 Ryan Klesko .15 .40
17 Jeff Kent .15 .40
18 Raul Mondesi .15 .40
19 Greg Vaughn .15 .40
20 Bernie Williams .25 .60
21 Mike Piazza .60 1.50
22 Richard Hidalgo .15 .40
23 Dean Palmer .15 .40
24 Roberto Alomar .25 .60
25 Sammy Sosa .40 1.00
26 Randy Johnson .40 1.00
27 Manny Ramirez Sox .25 .60
28 Roger Clemens .75 2.00
29 Terrence Long .15 .40
30 Jason Kendall .15 .40
31 Richie Sexson .15 .40
32 David Wells .15 .40
33 Andruw Jones .25 .60
34 Pokey Reese .15 .40
35 Juan Gonzalez .15 .40
36 Carlos Beltran .15 .40
37 Shawn Green .15 .40
38 Mariano Rivera .40 1.00
39 John Olerud .15 .40
40 Jim Edmonds .15 .40
41 Andres Galarraga .15 .40
42 Carlos Delgado .15 .40
43 Kris Benson .15 .40
44 Andy Pettitte .25 .60
45 Jeff Cirillo .15 .40
46 Magglio Ordonez .15 .40
47 Tom Glavine .25 .60
48 Garret Anderson .15 .40
49 Cal Ripken 1.25 3.00
50 Pedro Martinez .25 .60
51 Barry Bonds 1.00 2.50
52 Alex Rodriguez .50 1.25
53 Ben Grieve .15 .40
54 Edgar Martinez .25 .60
55 Jason Giambi .15 .40
56 Jeromy Burnitz .15 .40
57 Mike Mussina .25 .60
58 Moises Alou .15 .40
59 Sean Casey .15 .40
60 Greg Maddux .60 1.50
61 Tim Hudson .15 .40
62 Mark McGwire 1.00 2.50
63 Rafael Palmeiro .25 .60
64 Tony Batista .15 .40
65 Kazuhiro Sasaki .15 .40
66 Jorge Posada .25 .60
67 Johnny Damon .25 .60
68 Brian Giles .15 .40
69 Jose Vidro .15 .40
70 Jermaine Dye .15 .40
71 Craig Biggio .25 .60
72 Larry Walker .15 .40
73 Eric Chavez .15 .40
74 David Segui .15 .40
75 Tim Salmon .25 .60
76 Javy Lopez .15 .40
77 Paul Konerko .15 .40
78 Barry Larkin .25 .60
79 Mike Hampton .15 .40
80 Bobby Higginson .15 .40
81 Mark Mulder .15 .40
82 Pat Burrell .15 .40
83 Kerry Wood .15 .40
84 J.T. Snow .15 .40
85 Ivan Rodriguez .25 .60
86 Edgardo Alfonzo .15 .40
87 Orlando Hernandez .15 .40
88 Gary Sheffield .15 .40
89 Mike Sweeney .15 .40
90 Carlos Lee .15 .40
91 Rafael Furcal .15 .40
92 Troy Glaus .15 .40
93 Bartolo Colon .15 .40
94 Cliff Floyd .15 .40
95 Barry Zito .25 .60
96 J.D. Drew .15 .40
97 Eric Karros .15 .40
98 Jose Valentin .15 .40
99 Ellis Burks .15 .40
100 David Justice .15 .40
101 Larry Barnes .15 .40
102 Rod Barajas .15 .40
103 Tony Pena Jr. .15 .40
104 Jerry Hairston Jr. .15 .40
105 Keith Ginter .15 .40
106 Corey Patterson .15 .40
107 Aaron Rowand .15 .40
108 Miguel Olivo .15 .40
109 Gookie Dawkins .15 .40
110 C.C. Sabathia .15 .40
111 Ben Petrick .15 .40
112 Eric Munson .15 .40
113 Ramon Castro .15 .40
114 Alex Escobar .15 .40
115 Josh Hamilton/2 .30 .75
116 Jason Marquis .15 .40
117 Ben Davis .15 .40
118 Alex Cintron .15 .40
119 Julio Zuleta .15 .40
120 Ben Broussard .15 .40
121 Adam Everett .15 .40
122 Ramon Carvajal RC .15 .40
123 Felipe Lopez .15 .40
124 Alfonso Soriano .25 .60
125 Jayson Werth .15 .40
126 Donzell McDonald .15 .40
127 Jason Hart .15 .40
128 Joe Crede .40 1.00
129 Sean Burroughs .15 .40
130 Jack Cust .15 .40
131 Corey Smith .15 .40
132 Adrian Gonzalez 1.00 2.50
133 J.R. House .15 .40
134 Steve Lomasney .15 .40
135 Tim Raines Jr. .15 .40
136 Tony Alvarez .15 .40
137 Doug Mientkiewicz .15 .40
138 Rocco Baldelli .15 .40
139 Jason Romano .15 .40
140 Vernon Wells .15 .40
141 Mike Bynum .15 .40
142 Xavier Nady .15 .40
143 Brad Wilkerson .15 .40
144 Ben Diggins .15 .40
145 Aubrey Huff .15 .40
146 Eric Byrnes .15 .40
147 Alex Gordon .15 .40
148 Roy Oswalt .40 1.00
149 Brian Esposito .15 .40
150 Scott Seabol .15 .40
151 Erick Almonte RC 2.00 5.00
152 Gary Johnson RC 2.00 5.00
153 Pedro Liriano RC 2.00 5.00
154 Matt White RC 2.00 5.00
155 Luis Montanez RC 2.50 6.00
156 Brad Cresse 2.00 5.00
157 Wilson Betemit RC 3.00 8.00
158 Octavio Martinez RC 2.00 5.00
159 Adam Pettyjohn RC 2.00 5.00
160 Corey Spencer RC 2.00 5.00
161 Mark Burnett RC 2.00 5.00
162 Ichiro Suzuki RC 30.00 80.00
163 Alexis Gomez RC 2.00 5.00
164 Greg Nash RC 2.00 5.00
165 Roberto Miniel RC 2.00 5.00
166 Justin Morneau RC 4.00 10.00
167 Ben Washburn RC 2.00 5.00
168 Bob Keppel RC 2.00 5.00
169 Deivi Mendez RC 2.00 5.00
170 Tsuyoshi Shinjo RC 3.00 8.00
171 Jared Abruzzo RC 2.00 5.00
172 Derrick Van Dusen RC 2.00 5.00
173 Hee Seop Choi RC 3.00 8.00
174 Albert Pujols RC 60.00 150.00
175 Travis Hafner RC 6.00 15.00
176 Ron Davenport RC 2.00 5.00
177 Luis Torres RC 2.00 5.00
178 Jake Peavy RC 5.00 12.00
179 Elvis Corporan RC 2.00 5.00
180 Dave Krynzel 2.00 5.00
181 Tony Blanco RC 2.00 5.00
182 Elpidio Guzman RC 2.00 5.00
183 Matt Butler RC 2.00 5.00
184 Joe Thurston RC 2.00 5.00
185 Andy Beal RC 2.00 5.00
186 Kevin Nulton RC 2.00 5.00
187 Sneideer Santos RC 2.00 5.00
188 Joe Dillon RC 2.00 5.00
189 Jeremy Blevins RC 2.00 5.00
190 Chris Amador RC 2.00 5.00
191 Mark Hendrickson RC 2.00 5.00
192 Willy Aybar RC 2.00 5.00
193 Antoine Cameron RC 2.00 5.00
194 J.J. Johnson RC 2.00 5.00
195 Ryan Ketchner RC 2.00 5.00
196 Bjorn Ivy RC 2.00 5.00
197 Josh Kroeger RC 2.00 5.00
198 Ty Wigginton RC 3.00 8.00
199 Stubby Clapp RC 2.00 5.00
200 Jerrod Riggan RC 2.00 5.00

2001 Bowman's Best Autographs

Randomly inserted in packs at the rate of one in 95, this seven-card set features autographed photos of top players.

STATED ODDS 1:95
BBAAG Adrian Gonzalez 10.00 25.00
BBABC Brad Cresse 4.00 10.00
BBAJH Josh Hamilton 10.00 25.00
BBAJR Jon Rauch 4.00 10.00
BBAJRH J.R. House 4.00 10.00
BBASB Sean Burroughs 4.00 10.00
BBATL Terrence Long 4.00 10.00

2001 Bowman's Best Exclusive Autographs

Randomly inserted in packs at the rate of one in 50, this nine-card set features autographed player photos. Stubby Clapp was an exchange card.

STATED ODDS 1:50
BBEABI Bjorn Ivy 3.00 8.00
BBEAJB Jeremy Blevins 3.00 8.00
BBEAJJ J.J. Johnson 3.00 8.00
BBEAJR Jerrod Riggan 3.00 8.00
BBEAMH Mark Hendrickson 3.00 8.00
BBEASC Stubby Clapp 3.00 8.00
BBEASS Sneideer Santos 3.00 8.00
BBEATW Ty Wigginton 4.00 10.00
BBEAWA Willy Aybar 3.00 8.00

2001 Bowman's Best Franchise Favorites

Randomly inserted in packs at the rate of one in 16, this nine-card set features color photos of past and present players that are franchise favorites.

COMPLETE SET (9) 20.00 50.00
STATED ODDS 1:16
FFAR Alex Rodriguez 2.50 6.00
FFDE Darin Erstad 1.50 4.00
FFDM Don Mattingly 5.00 12.00
FFDW Dave Winfield 1.50 4.00
FFEJ D.Erstad 1.50 4.00
R.Jackson
FFMW D.Mattingly 5.00 12.00
D.Winfield
FFNR Nolan Ryan 5.00 12.00
FFRJ Reggie Jackson 1.50 4.00
FFRR N.Ryan 4.00 10.00
A.Rodriguez

2001 Bowman's Best Franchise Favorites Autographs

Randomly inserted in packs, this nine-card set is an autographed parallel version of the regular insert set.

SINGLE STATED ODDS 1:556
DOUBLE STATED ODDS 1:4436
FFAAR Alex Rodriguez 30.00 60.00
FFADE Darin Erstad 6.00 15.00
FFADM Don Mattingly 30.00 60.00
FFADW Dave Winfield 15.00 40.00
FFAEJ D.Erstad/R.Jackson 40.00 80.00
FFAMW Mattingly/Winfield 125.00 200.00
FFANR Nolan Ryan 50.00 100.00
FFARJ Reggie Jackson 15.00 40.00
FFARR N.Ryan/A.Rodriguez 175.00 350.00

2001 Bowman's Best Franchise Favorites Relics

Randomly inserted in packs at the rate of one in 58, this 12-card set features color player photos of franchise favorites along with memorabilia pieces.

STATED JSY ODDS 1:139
STATED JSY/JSY ODDS 1:1114
STATED UNIFORM ODDS 1:307
STATED UNIFORM/UNIFORM ODDS 1:2456
FFRAR Alex Rodriguez Jsy 12.50 30.00
FFRBB Biggio U/Bagwell U 15.00 40.00
FFRCB Craig Biggio Uni 6.00 15.00
FFRDE Darin Erstad Jsy 4.00 10.00
FFRDM Don Mattingly Jsy 15.00 40.00
FFRDW Dave Winfield Jsy 4.00 10.00
FFREJ D.Erstad J/R.Jackson J 15.00 40.00
FFRJB Jeff Bagwell Uni 6.00 15.00
FFRMW Mattingly J/Winfield J 15.00 40.00
FFRNR Nolan Ryan Jsy 10.00 25.00
FFRRJ Reggie Jackson Jsy 6.00 15.00
FFRRR N.Ryan J/A.Rod J 20.00 50.00

2001 Bowman's Best Franchise Futures

Randomly inserted into packs at the rate of one in 24, this 12-card set displays color photos of top young players.

COMPLETE SET (12) 12.50 30.00
STATED ODDS 1:24
FF1 Josh Hamilton 1.50 4.00
FF2 Wes Helms .75 2.00
FF3 Alfonso Soriano .75 2.00
FF4 Nick Johnson .75 2.00
FF5 Jose Ortiz .75 2.00
FF6 Ben Sheets .75 2.00
FF7 Sean Burroughs .75 2.00
FF8 Ben Petrick .75 2.00
FF9 Corey Patterson .75 2.00
FF10 J.R. House .75 2.00
FF11 Alex Escobar .75 2.00
FF12 Travis Hafner 2.50 6.00

2001 Bowman's Best Impact Players

Randomly inserted in packs at the rate of one in seven, this 20-card set features color action photos of top players who have made their mark on the game.

COMPLETE SET (20) 12.50 30.00
STATED ODDS 1:7
IP1 Mark McGwire 2.00 5.00
IP2 Sammy Sosa .75 2.00
IP3 Manny Ramirez .50 1.25
IP4 Troy Glaus .40 1.00
IP5 Ken Griffey Jr. 1.50 4.00
IP6 Gary Sheffield .40 1.00
IP7 Vladimir Guerrero .75 2.00
IP8 Carlos Delgado .40 1.00
IP9 Jason Giambi .40 1.00
IP10 Frank Thomas .75 2.00
IP11 Vernon Wells .40 1.00
IP12 Carlos Pena .40 1.00
IP13 Joe Crede .75 2.00
IP14 Keith Ginter .40 1.00
IP15 Aubrey Huff .40 1.00
IP16 Brad Cresse .40 1.00
IP17 Austin Kearns .40 1.00
IP18 Nick Johnson .40 1.00
IP19 Josh Hamilton .75 2.00
IP20 Corey Patterson .40 1.00

2001 Bowman's Best Locker Room Collection Jerseys

Randomly inserted in packs at the rate of one in 133, this five-card set features color player photos with swatches of jerseys embedded in the cards and carry the "LRCL" prefix.

STATED ODDS 1:133
LRCJEC Eric Chavez 4.00 10.00
LRCJJP Jay Payton 3.00 8.00
LRCJMM Mark Mulder 4.00 10.00
LRCJPR Pokey Reese 3.00 8.00
LRCJPW Preston Wilson 4.00 10.00

2001 Bowman's Best Locker Room Collection Lumber

Randomly inserted in packs at the rate of one in 267, this five-card set features color player photos with pieces of actual bats embedded in the cards and carry the "LRCL" prefix.

STATED ODDS 1:267
LRCLAG Adrian Gonzalez 3.00 8.00
LRCLCP Corey Patterson 3.00 8.00
LRCLEM Eric Munson 3.00 8.00
LRCLPB Pat Burrell 4.00 10.00
LRCLSB Sean Burroughs 3.00 8.00

2001 Bowman's Best Rookie Fever

Randomly inserted in packs at the rate of one in 10, this 10-card set features color photos of top players during their rookie year. Card backs display the "RF" prefix.

COMPLETE SET (10) 6.00 15.00
STATED ODDS 1:10
RF1 Chipper Jones .60 1.50
RF2 Preston Wilson .40 1.00
RF3 Todd Helton .40 1.00
RF4 Jay Payton .40 1.00
RF5 Ivan Rodriguez .40 1.00
RF6 Manny Ramirez .40 1.00
RF7 Derek Jeter 1.50 4.00
RF8 Orlando Hernandez .40 1.00
RF9 Mark Quinn .40 1.00
RF10 Terrence Long .40 1.00

2002 Bowman's Best

This 181 card set was released in August, 2002. The set was issued in five card packs which were issued 10 packs to a box and 10 boxes to a case with an SRP of $15. The first 90 cards of the set featured veteran players while cards 91 through 181 featured prospects or rookies along with either an autograph or a game-used bat piece of the featured player. The higher numbered cards were issued in different seeding ratios and we have notated the group the player belongs to next to their name in our checklist. Card number 181 features Kaz Ishii and was issued as an exchange card which could be redeemed until December 31, 2002.

COMP.SET w/o SP's (90) 40.00 100.00
COMMON CARD (1-90) .30 .75
COMMON AUTO A (91-180) 3.00 8.00
AUTO GROUP A ODDS 1:3
COMMON AUTO B (91-180) 4.00 10.00
AUTO GROUP B ODDS 1:19
COMMON BAT (91-180) 2.00 5.00
91-180 BAT STATED ODDS 1:5
181 ISHII BAT EXCHANGE ODDS 1:131
ISHII EXCHANGE DEADLINE 12/31/02
1 Josh Dockott .30 .75
2 Derek Jeter 2.00 5.00
3 Alex Rodriguez 1.00 2.50
4 Miguel Tejada .30 .75
5 Nomar Garciaparra 1.25 3.00
6 Aramis Ramirez .30 .75
7 Jeremy Giambi .30 .75
8 Bernie Williams .50 1.25
9 Juan Pierre .30 .75
10 Chipper Jones .75 2.00
11 Jimmy Rollins .30 .75
12 Alfonso Soriano .30 .75
13 Mark Prior .50 1.25
14 Paul Konerko .30 .75
15 Tim Hudson .30 .75
16 Doug Mientkiewicz .30 .75
17 Todd Helton .50 1.25
18 Moises Alou .30 .75
19 Juan Gonzalez .30 .75
20 Jorge Posada .50 1.25
21 Jeff Kent .30 .75
22 Roger Clemens 1.50 4.00
23 Phil Nevin .30 .75
24 Brian Giles .30 .75
25 Carlos Delgado .30 .75
26 Jason Giambi .30 .75
27 Vladimir Guerrero .75 2.00
28 Cliff Floyd .30 .75
29 Shea Hillenbrand .30 .75
30 Ken Griffey Jr. 1.50 4.00
31 Mike Piazza 1.25 3.00
32 Carlos Pena .30 .75
33 Larry Walker .30 .75
34 Magglio Ordonez .30 .75
35 Mike Mussina .50 1.25
36 Andruw Jones .50 1.25
37 Nick Johnson .30 .75
38 Curt Schilling .30 .75
39 Eric Chavez .30 .75
40 Bartolo Colon .30 .75
41 Eric Hinske .30 .75
42 Sean Burroughs .30 .75
43 Randy Johnson .75 2.00
44 Adam Dunn .30 .75
45 Pedro Martinez .50 1.25
46 Garret Anderson .30 .75
47 Jim Thome .50 1.25
48 Gary Sheffield .30 .75
49 Tsuyoshi Shinjo .30 .75
50 Albert Pujols 1.50 4.00
51 Ichiro Suzuki 1.50 4.00
52 C.C. Sabathia .30 .75
53 Bobby Abreu .30 .75
54 Ivan Rodriguez .50 1.25
55 J.D. Drew .30 .75
56 Jacque Jones .30 .75
57 Jason Kendall .30 .75
58 Javier Vazquez .30 .75
59 Jeff Bagwell .50 1.25
60 Greg Maddux 1.25 3.00
61 Jim Edmonds .30 .75
62 Hank Blalock .50 1.25
63 Jose Vidro .30 .75
64 Kevin Brown .30 .75
65 Mark Teixeira .75 2.00
66 Sammy Sosa .75 2.00
67 Lance Berkman .30 .75
68 Mark Mulder .30 .75
69 Marty Cordova .30 .75
70 Frank Thomas .75 2.00
71 Mike Cameron .30 .75
72 Mike Sweeney .30 .75

73 Barry Bonds 2.00 5.00
74 Troy Glaus .30 .75
75 Barry Zito .30 .75
76 Pat Burrell .30 .75
77 Paul LoDuca .30 .75
78 Rafael Palmeiro .50 1.25
79 Austin Kearns .30 .75
80 Darin Erstad .30 .75
81 Richie Sexson .30 .75
82 Roberto Alomar .50 1.25
83 Roy Oswalt .30 .75
84 Ryan Klesko .30 .75
85 Luis Gonzalez .30 .75
86 Scott Rolen .50 1.25
87 Shannon Stewart .30 .75
88 Shawn Green .30 .75
89 Toby Hall .30 .75
90 Bret Boone .30 .75
91 Casey Kotchman Bat RC 3.00 8.00
92 Jose Valverde AU A RC 3.00 8.00
93 Cole Barthel Bat RC 2.00 5.00
94 Brad Nelson AU A RC 3.00 8.00
95 Mauricio Lara AU A RC 3.00 8.00
96 Ryan Gripp Bat RC 2.00 5.00
97 Brian West AU A RC 3.00 8.00
98 Chris Piersoll AU B RC 4.00 10.00
99 Ryan Church AU B RC 6.00 15.00
100 Javier Colina AU A 3.00 8.00
101 Juan M. Gonzalez AU A RC 3.00 8.00
102 Benito Baez AU A 3.00 8.00
103 Mike Hill Bat RC 2.00 5.00
104 Jason Grove AU B RC 4.00 10.00
105 Koyie Hill AU B 4.00 10.00
106 Mark Outlaw AU A RC 3.00 8.00
107 Jason Bay Bat RC 6.00 15.00
108 Jorge Padilla AU A RC 3.00 8.00
109 Pete Zamora AU A RC 3.00 8.00
110 Joe Mauer AU B RC 15.00 40.00
111 Franklyn German AU A RC 3.00 8.00
112 Chris Flinn AU A RC 3.00 8.00
113 David Wright Bat RC 6.00 15.00
114 Anastacio Martinez AU A RC 3.00 8.00
115 Nic Jackson Bat RC 2.00 5.00
116 Rene Reyes AU A RC 3.00 8.00
117 Colin Young AU A RC 3.00 8.00
118 Joe Orloski AU A RC 3.00 8.00
119 Mike Wilson AU A RC 3.00 8.00
120 Rich Thompson AU A RC 3.00 8.00
121 Jake Mauer AU B RC 4.00 10.00
122 Mario Ramos AU A RC 3.00 8.00
123 Doug Sessions AU B RC 4.00 10.00
124 Doug Devore Bat RC 2.00 5.00
125 Travis Foley AU A RC 3.00 8.00
126 Chris Baker AU A RC 3.00 8.00
127 Michael Floyd AU A RC 3.00 8.00
128 Josh Barfield Bat RC 4.00 10.00
129 Jose Bautista Bat RC 5.00 12.00
130 Gavin Floyd AU A RC 3.00 8.00
131 Jason Botts Bat RC 2.00 5.00
132 Clint Nageotte AU A RC 4.00 10.00
133 Jesus Cota AU B RC 4.00 10.00
134 Ron Calloway Bat RC 2.00 5.00
135 Kevin Cash Bat RC 2.00 5.00
136 Jonny Gomes AU B RC 8.00 20.00
137 Dennis Ulacia AU A RC 3.00 8.00
138 Ryan Snare AU A RC 3.00 8.00
139 Kevin Deaton AU A RC 3.00 8.00
140 Bobby Jenks AU B RC 3.00 8.00
141 Casey Kotchman AU A RC 6.00 15.00
142 Adam Walker AU A RC 3.00 8.00
143 Mike Gonzalez AU A RC 3.00 8.00
144 Ruben Gotay Bat RC 3.00 8.00
145 Jason Grove Bat RC 2.00 5.00
146 Freddy Sanchez AU B RC 5.00 12.00
147 Jason Arnold AU B RC 4.00 10.00
148 Scott Hairston AU A RC 4.00 10.00
149 Jason St. Clair AU B RC 4.00 10.00
150 Chris Tritle Bat RC 2.00 5.00
151 Edwin Yan Bat RC 2.00 5.00
152 Freddy Sanchez Bat RC 5.00 12.00
153 Greg Sain Bat RC 2.00 5.00
154 Yurendell De Caster Bat RC 2.00 5.00
155 Noochie Varner Bat RC 2.00 5.00
156 Nelson Castro AU B RC 4.00 10.00
157 Randall Shelley Bat RC 2.00 5.00
158 Reed Johnson Bat RC 3.00 8.00
159 Ryan Raburn AU A RC 3.00 8.00
160 Jose Morban Bat RC 2.00 5.00
161 Justin Schuda AU A RC 3.00 8.00
162 Henry Pichardo AU A RC 3.00 8.00
163 Josh Bard AU A RC 3.00 8.00
164 Josh Bonifay AU A RC 3.00 8.00
165 Brandon League AU B RC 4.00 10.00
166 Jorge-Julio DePaula AU A RC 3.00 8.00
167 Todd Linden AU B RC 6.00 15.00
168 Francisco Liriano AU A RC 6.00 15.00
169 Chris Snelling AU A RC 5.00 12.00
170 Blake McGinley AU A RC 3.00 8.00
171 Cody McKay AU A RC 3.00 8.00
172 Jason Stanford AU A RC 3.00 8.00
173 Lenny Dinardo AU A RC 3.00 8.00
174 Greg Montalbano AU A RC 3.00 8.00
175 Earl Snyder AU A RC 3.00 8.00
176 Justin Huber AU A RC 3.00 8.00
177 Chris Narveson AU A RC 3.00 8.00
178 Jon Switzer AU A RC 3.00 8.00
179 Ronald Acuna AU A RC 3.00 8.00
180 Chris Duffy Bat RC 3.00 8.00
181 Kazuhisa Ishii Bat RC 3.00 8.00

2002 Bowman's Best Blue

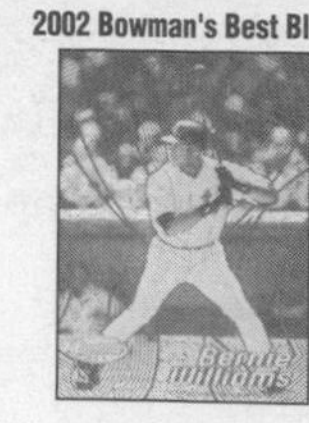

*BLUE 1-90: 1X TO 2.5X BASIC
1-90 STATED ODDS 1:6
1-90 PRINT RUN 300 SERIAL #'d SETS
*BLUE AUTO: .4X TO 1X BASIC AU A
*BLUE AUTO: .3X TO .8X BASIC AU B
AUTO STATED ODDS 1:6
*BLUE BAT: .4X TO 1X BASIC BAT
BAT STATED ODDS 1:14
ISHII BAT EXCHANGE ODDS 1:335
ISHII BAT EXCHANGE DEADLINE 12/31/02
BLUE BATS FEATURE TEAM LOGOS!
140 Bobby Jenks AU 6.00 15.00
181 Kazuhisa Ishii Bat 3.00 8.00

2002 Bowman's Best Gold

*GOLD 1-90: 3X TO 8X BASIC
1-90 STATED ODDS 1:31
1-90 PRINT RUN 50 SERIAL #'d SETS
*GOLD AUTO: 1X TO 2.5X BASIC AU A
*GOLD AUTO: .75X TO 2X BASIC AU B
GOLD AUTO STATED ODDS 1:51
*GOLD BAT: 1X TO 2.5X BASIC BAT
GOLD BAT STATED ODDS 1:115
ISHII BAT EXCHANGE ODDS 1:3444
ISHII BAT EXCHANGE DEADLINE 12/31/02
GOLD BATS FEATURE FACSIMILE AUTOS!
181 Kazuhisa Ishii Bat 8.00 20.00

2002 Bowman's Best Red

*RED 1-90: 1.25X TO 3X BASIC
1-90 STATED ODDS 1:8
1-90 PRINT RUN 200 SERIAL #'d SETS
*RED AUTO: .6X TO 1.5X BASIC AU A
*RED AUTO: .5X TO 1.2X BASIC AU B
AUTO STATED ODDS 1:17
*RED BATS: .6X TO 1.5X BASIC BATS
BAT STATED ODDS 1:39
ISHII BAT EXCHANGE ODDS 1:1117
ISHII BAT EXCHANGE DEADLINE 12/31/02
RED BATS FEATURE STATISTICS!
181 Kazuhisa Ishii Bat 5.00 12.00

2002 Bowman's Best Uncirculated

COMMON EXCH
AU STATED ODDS 1:129
BAT STATED ODDS 1:322
OVERALL STATED ODDS 1:92

2003 Bowman's Best

This 130 card set was released in September, 2003. This set was issued in five card packs which contained an autograph card. Each of these packs had an SRP of $15 and these packs were issued 10 to a box and 10 boxes to a case. This set was designed to be checklisted alphabetically as no numbering was used for this set. The first year cards which are autographed have the lettering FY AU RC after their name in the checklist. A few first year players had some cards issued with an bat piece included. Those bat cards were issued one per box-loader pack. In addition, high draft pick Bryan Bullington signed some of the actual boxes and those boxes were issued at a stated rate of one in 106.

COMP.SET w/o SP's (50) 15.00 40.00
COMMON CARD .40 1.00
COMMON RC .40 1.00
COMMON AUTO 3.00 8.00
AUTO ODDS ONE PER PACK
COMMON BAT 1.50 4.00
BAT ODDS ONE PER BOX-LOADER PACK
BULLINGTON BOX AU ODDS 1:106 BOXES
AB Andrew Brown FY AU RC 4.00 10.00
AK Austin Kearns .40 1.00
AM Aneudis Mateo FY AU RC 3.00 8.00
AP Albert Pujols 1.25 3.00
AR Alex Rodriguez 1.25 3.00
AS Alfonso Soriano .60 1.50
AW Aron Weston FY AU RC 3.00 8.00
BB Bryan Bullington FY AU RC 3.00 8.00
BC Bernie Castro FY RC .40 1.00
BFL Branden Florence FY AU RC 3.00 8.00
BFR Ben Francisco FY AU RC 3.00 8.00
BH Brendan Harris FY AU RC 4.00 10.00
BJH Bo Hart FY RC .40 1.00
BK Beau Kemp FY AU RC 3.00 8.00
BLB Barry Bonds 1.50 4.00
BM Brian McCann FY AU RC 4.00 10.00
BSG Brian Giles .40 1.00
BWB Bobby Basham FY AU RC 3.00 8.00
BZ Barry Zito .60 1.50
CAD Carlos Duran FY AU RC 3.00 8.00
CDC Chris De La Cruz FY AU RC 3.00 8.00
CJ Chipper Jones 1.00 2.50
CJW C.J. Wilson FY AU 3.00 8.00
CM Charlie Manning FY AU RC 3.00 8.00
CMS Curt Schilling .60 1.50
CS Cory Stewart FY AU RC 3.00 8.00
CSS Corey Shafer FY AU RC 3.00 8.00
CW Chien-Ming Wang FY RC 1.50 4.00
CWA Chien-Ming Wang FY AU 20.00 50.00
DAM Dustin Moseley FY AU RC 3.00 8.00
DC David Cash FY AU RC 3.00 8.00
DH Dan Haren FY AU RC 3.00 8.00
DJ Derek Jeter 2.50 6.00
DM David Martinez FY AU RC 3.00 8.00
DMM Dust. McGowan FY AU RC 4.00 10.00
DR Darrell Rasner FY AU RC 3.00 8.00
DW Doug Waechter FY AU RC 4.00 10.00
DY Dustin Yount FY RC .40 1.00
ERA Elizardo Ramirez FY AU RC 4.00 10.00
ERI Eric Riggs FY AU RC 4.00 10.00
ET Eider Torres FY AU RC 3.00 8.00
FP Felix Pie FY AU RC 3.00 8.00
FS Felix Sanchez FY AU RC 3.00 8.00
FT Ferdin Tejeda FY AU RC 3.00 8.00
GA Greg Aquino FY AU RC 3.00 8.00
GB Gregor Blanco FY AU RC 3.00 8.00
GJA Garret Anderson .40 1.00
GM Greg Maddux 1.25 3.00
GS Gary Schneidmiller FY AU RC 3.00 8.00
HR Hanley Ramirez FY AU RC 12.00 30.00
HRB Hanley Ramirez FY Bat 10.00 25.00
HT Haj Turay FY RC .40 1.00
IS Ichiro Suzuki 1.25 3.00
JB Jeremy Bonderman FY RC 1.50 4.00
JC Jose Contreras FY RC 1.00 2.50
JDD J.D. Durbin FY AU RC 3.00 8.00
JFK Jeff Kent .40 1.00
JG Joey Gomes FY AU RC 3.00 8.00
JGB Joey Gomes FY Bat 1.50 4.00
JGG Jason Giambi .40 1.00
JK Jason Kubel FY AU RC 4.00 10.00
JKB Jason Kubel FY Bat 2.50 6.00
JLB Jaime Bubela FY AU RC 3.00 8.00
JM Jose Morales FY AU RC 3.00 8.00
JMS Jon-Mark Sprowl FY RC .40 1.00
JRG Jeremy Griffiths FY AU RC 3.00 8.00
JT Jim Thome .60 1.50
JV Joe Valentine FY AU RC 3.00 8.00
JW Josh Willingham FY AU RC 6.00 15.00
KBS Kelly Shoppach FY Bat 2.00 5.00
KG Ken Griffey Jr. 2.00 5.00
KJ Kade Johnson FY AU RC 3.00 8.00
KS Kelly Shoppach FY AU RC 4.00 10.00
KY Kevin Youkilis FY AU RC 6.00 15.00
KYE Kevin Youkilis FY Bat 5.00 12.00
LB Lance Berkman .60 1.50
LF Lew Ford FY AU RC 4.00 10.00
LFJ Lew Ford FY Bat 2.00 5.00
LW Larry Walker .60 1.50
MB Matt Brubaek FY RC .40 1.00
MD Matt Diaz FY RC .60 1.50
MDA Matt Diaz FY AU 3.00 8.00
MDH Matt Hensley FY AU RC 3.00 8.00
MDM Mark Malaska FY AU RC 3.00 8.00
MH Michel Hernandez FY AU RC 3.00 8.00
MHI Michael Hinckley FY AU RC 4.00 10.00
MJP Mike Piazza 1.00 2.50
MK Matt Kata FY AU RC 3.00 8.00
MMH Matt Hagen FY AU RC 3.00 8.00
MO Mike O'Keefe FY RC .40 1.00
MOR Magglio Ordonez .60 1.50
MP Mark Prior .60 1.50
MR Manny Ramirez 1.00 2.50
MS Mike Sweeney .40 1.00
MT Miguel Tejada .60 1.50
NG Nomar Garciaparra .60 1.50
NL Nook Logan FY AU RC 4.00 10.00
OC Ozzie Chavez FY AU RC 3.00 8.00
PB Pat Burrell .40 1.00
PL Pete LaForest FY AU RC 3.00 8.00
PM Pedro Martinez .60 1.50
PR Prentice Redman FY AU RC 3.00 8.00
RC Ryan Cameron FY AU RC 3.00 8.00
RD Rajai Davis FY AU RC 3.00 8.00
RH Ryan Howard FY AU RC 10.00 25.00
RHJ Ryan Howard FY Bat 4.00 10.00
RJ Randy Johnson 1.00 2.50
RLD Rajai Davis FY Bat 1.50 4.00
RM Ramon Nivar-Martinez FY RC .40 1.00
RS Ryan Shealy FY AU RC 3.00 8.00
RSB Ryan Shealy FY Bat 5.00 12.00
RWH Robbie Hammock FY AU RC 3.00 8.00
SS Sammy Sosa 1.00 2.50
ST Scott Tyler FY AU RC 4.00 10.00
SV Shane Victorino FY RC 1.25 3.00
TA Tyler Adamczyk FY AU RC 3.00 8.00
TH Todd Helton .60 1.50
TI Travis Ishikawa FY AU RC 10.00 25.00
TJ Tyler Johnson FY AU RC 3.00 8.00
TJB T.J. Bohn FY RC .40 1.00
TKH Torii Hunter .40 1.00
TO Tim Olson FY AU RC 3.00 8.00
TS T.Story-Harden FY AU RC 3.00 8.00
TSB T.Story-Harden FY Bat 1.50 4.00
TT Terry Tiffee FY RC .40 1.00
VG Vladimir Guerrero .60 1.50
WE Willie Eyre FY AU RC 3.00 8.00
WL Wil Ledezma FY AU RC 3.00 8.00
WRC Roger Clemens 1.25 3.00
NNO B.Bullington Opened Box AU 10.00 25.00

2003 Bowman's Best Blue

*BLUE: 1.5X TO 4X BASIC
*BLUE FY: 3X TO 8X BASIC FY
BLUE STATED ODDS 1:28
BLUE PRINT RUN 100 SERIAL #'d SETS
*BLUE AUTO: 1X TO 2.5X BASIC AUTO
BLUE AUTO ODDS 1:32
BLUE AUTO PRINT RUN 50 SETS
BLUE AUTO'S NOT SERIAL-NUMBERED
BLUE AU PRINT RUNS PROVIDED BY TOPPS
*BLUE BAT: 1X TO 2.5X BASIC FY BAT
BLUE BAT ODDS 1:22 BOXLOADER PACKS
BLUE BAT PRINT RUN 50 SETS
BLUE BATS NOT SERIAL-NUMBERED
BLUE BAT PRINTS PROVIDED BY TOPPS

2003 Bowman's Best Red

*RED: 3X TO 8X BASIC RED
*RED FY: 3X TO 8X BASIC FY
RED STATED ODDS 1:55
RED STATED PRINT RUN 50 SERIAL #'d SETS
RED AUTO ODDS 1:63
RED AUTO PRINT RUN 25 SETS
RED AU PRINT RUNS PROVIDED BY TOPPS
RED AUTOS NOT SERIAL-NUMBERED
NO RED AUTO PRICING DUE TO SCARCITY
RED BAT ODDS 1:44 BOXLOADER PACKS
RED BAT PRINT RUN 25 SETS
RED BAT PRINT RUNS PROVIDED BY TOPPS
RED BATS NOT SERIAL-NUMBERED
NO RED BAT PRICING DUE TO SCARCITY

2003 Bowman's Best Double Play Autographs

STATED ODDS 1:55
EB Elizardo Ramirez 6.00 15.00
Bryan Bullington
GK Joey Gomes 6.00 15.00
Jason Kubel
HV Dan Haren 6.00 15.00
Joe Valentine
LL Nook Logan 6.00 15.00
Wil Ledezma
RS Prentice Redman 6.00 15.00
Gary Schneidmiller
SB Corey Shafer 6.00 15.00
Gregor Blanco
SR Felix Sanchez 6.00 15.00
Darrell Rasner
YS Kevin Youkilis 6.00 15.00
Kelly Shoppach

2003 Bowman's Best Triple Play Autographs

STATED ODDS 1:219
BCS Brown/Cash/Stewart 10.00 25.00
DRS Rajai/Hanley/Shealy 8.00 20.00

2004 Bowman's Best

This 108-card set was released in September, 2004. The set was issued in five-card packs with an $15 SRP which came 10 packs to a box and 10 boxes to a case. In an interesting twist, the cards are numbered using the initials of the players instead of using a numbering system. Fifty cards in this set feature veteran players and the rest of the set features either rookie cards some of whom signed cardd for this product.

COMP.SET w/o SP'S (50) 10.00 25.00
COMMON CARD .30 .75
COMMON RC .40 1.00
COMMON AUTO 3.00 8.00
ONE AUTO PER HOBBY PACK
COMMON RELIC 2.00 5.00
RELIC MINORS 2.00 5.00
RELIC SEMIS 3.00 8.00
RELIC UNLISTED 3.00 8.00
ONE RELIC PER BOX-LOADER PACK
ONE BOX-LOADER PACK PER HOBBY BOX
COMMON AU BOX 6.00 15.00
STAUFFER BOX RANDOM IN HOBBY CASES
OVERALL AU PLATE ODDS 1:391 HOBBY
AU PLATE PRINT RUN 1 SET PER COLOR
BLACK-CYAN-MAGENTA-YELLOW ISSUED
NO AU PLATE PRICING DUE TO SCARCITY
AER Alex Rodriguez 1.00 2.50
AG Adam Greenberg FY AU RC 4.00 10.00
AL Anthony Lerew FY RC .40 1.00
AO Akinori Otsuka FY RC .40 1.00
AP Albert Pujols 1.00 2.50
AS Alfonso Soriano .50 1.25
BB Bobby Brownlie FY AU RC 4.00 10.00
BEM Brandon Medders FY AU RC 3.00 8.00
BG Brian Giles .30 .75
BMS Brad Snyder FY AU RC 4.00 10.00
BP Brayan Pena FY AU RC 3.00 8.00
BS Brad Sullivan FY AU RC 4.00 10.00
CB Carlos Beltran .50 1.25
CD Carlos Delgado .30 .75
CJ Conor Jackson FY AU RC 4.00 10.00
CLH Chin-Lung Hu FY RC .40 1.00
CMA Craig Ansman FY AU RC 3.00 8.00
CMS Curt Schilling .50 1.25
CZ Charlie Zink FY AU RC 3.00 8.00
DA David Aardsma FY AU RC 4.00 10.00
DC Dave Crouthers FY AU RC 3.00 8.00
DDN Dustin Nippert FY AU RC 4.00 10.00
DG Danny Gonzalez FY RC .40 1.00
DK Donald Kelly FY AU RC 3.00 8.00
DL Donald Levinski FY AU RC 3.00 8.00
DM David Murphy FY AU RC 6.00 15.00
DN Dioner Navarro FY AU RC 4.00 10.00
DS Don Sutton FY RC .40 1.00
EA Erick Aybar FY AU RC 4.00 10.00
EC Eric Chavez .30 .75
EH Estee Harris FY AU RC 4.00 10.00
ES Ervin Santana FY AU RC 5.00 12.00
FH Felix Hernandez FY AU RC 20.00 50.00
GA Garret Anderson .30 .75
HB Hank Blalock .30 .75
HM Hector Made FY RC .40 1.00
IR Ivan Rodriguez .50 1.25
IS Ichiro Suzuki 1.00 2.50
JA Joaquin Arias FY AU RC 6.00 10.00
JAV Jose Vidro .30 .75
JC Juan Cedeno FY AU RC 3.00 8.00
JDS Jason Schmidt .30 .75
JE Jesse English FY AU RC 3.00 8.00
JGG Jason Giambi .30 .75
JH Jason Hirsh FY AU RC 10.00 25.00
JJC Jon Connolly FY RC .40 1.00
JK Jon Knott FY AU RC 3.00 8.00
JL Josh Labandeira FY AU RC 3.00 8.00
JLO Javy Lopez .30 .75
JP Jorge Posada .50 1.25
JRG Joey Gathright FY RC .40 1.00
JS Jeff Salazar FY AU RC 4.00 10.00
JSZ Jason Szuminski FY AU RC 3.00 8.00
JT Jim Thome .50 1.25
KC Kory Casto FY AU RC 3.00 8.00
KK Kevin Kouzmanoff FY AU RC 3.00 8.00
KM Kazuo Matsui FY Uni RC 2.00 5.00
KRK Kody Kirkland FY Bat RC 2.00 5.00
KS Kyle Sleeth FY RC .40 1.00
KT Kazuhito Tadano FY Jsy RC 3.00 8.00
LK Logan Kensing FY AU RC 3.00 8.00
LM Lastings Milledge FY AU RC 3.00 8.00
LO Lyle Overbay .30 .75
LTH Luke Hughes FY AU RC 4.00 10.00
LWJ Chipper Jones .75 2.00
MAR Manny Ramirez .75 2.00
MDC Matt Creighton FY AU RC 3.00 8.00
MG Mike Gosling FY RC .40 1.00
MJP Mike Piazza .75 2.00
MO Magglio Ordonez .50 1.25
MT Miguel Tejada .50 1.25
MTC Miguel Cabrera .75 2.00
MV Merkin Valdez FY AU RC 3.00 8.00
MWP Mark Prior .50 1.25
MY Michael Young .30 .75
NAG Nomar Garciaparra .50 1.25
NG Nick Gorneault FY RC .40 1.00
NU Nic Ungs FY AU RC 3.00 8.00
OQ Omar Quintanilla FY AU RC 4.00 10.00
PM Paul Maholm FY AU RC 4.00 10.00
PMM Paul McAnulty FY RC .40 1.00
RB Ryan Budde FY AU RC 3.00 8.00
RC Roger Clemens 1.00 2.50
RG Rudy Guillen FY AU RC 4.00 10.00
RJ Randy Johnson .75 2.00
RN Ricky Nolasco FY AU RC 4.00 10.00
RR Ramon Ramirez FY AU RC 3.00 8.00
RS Richie Sexson .30 .75
RT Rob Tejeda FY AU RC 6.00 15.00
SH Shawn Hill FY AU RC 3.00 8.00
SR Scott Rolen .50 1.25
SS Sammy Sosa .75 2.00
ST Shingo Takatsu FY Jsy RC 3.00 8.00
TB Travis Blackley FY Jsy RC 2.00 5.00
TD Tyler Davidson FY AU RC 4.00 10.00
TJ Terry Jones FY RC .40 1.00
TJS Tim Stauffer FY AU RC 4.00 10.00
TLH Todd Helton .50 1.25
TOH Travis Hanson FY AU RC 4.00 10.00
TRM Tom Mastny FY AU RC 3.00 8.00
TS Todd Self FY RC .40 1.00
VC Vito Chiaravalloti FY AU RC 3.00 8.00
VG Vladimir Guerrero .50 1.25
WM Warner Madrigal FY RC .60 1.50
WS Wardell Starling FY AU RC 3.00 8.00
YM Yadier Molina FY AU RC 100.00 250.00
ZD Zach Duke FY AU RC 5.00 12.00
NNO Tim Stauffer AU Box/100 10.00 25.00

2004 Bowman's Best Green

*GREEN: 1.5X TO 4X BASIC
*GREEN RC'S: 3X TO 8X BASIC RC'S
GREEN ODDS 1:18
GREEN PRINT RUN 100 SERIAL #'d SETS
*GREEN AU'S: 1X TO 2.5X BASIC AU'S
GREEN AU ODDS 1:32 HOBBY
GREEN AU PRINT RUN 50 SETS
GREEN AUTOS NOT SERIAL-NUMBERED
AUTO PRINT RUNS PROVIDED BY TOPPS
RELIC MINORS
RELIC SEMIS
RELIC UNLISTED
*GREEN RELICS: .75X TO 2X BASIC RELICS
GREEN RELIC ODDS 1:31 HOBBY BOXES
GREEN RELIC PRINT RUN 50 SETS
GREEN RELICS NOT SERIAL-NUMBERED
RELIC PRINT RUNS PROVIDED BY TOPPS

2004 Bowman's Best Red

*RED: 5X TO 12X BASIC
RED ODDS 1:90 HOBBY
RED PRINT RUN 20 SERIAL #'d SETS
NO RED RC PRICING DUE TO SCARCITY
RED AUTO ODDS 1:156 HOBBY
RED AU PRINT RUN 10 SETS
RED AU'S ARE NOT SERIAL-NUMBERED
PRINT RUN INFO PROVIDED BY TOPPS
NO RED AU PRICING DUE TO SCARCITY
RED RELIC ODDS 1:154 HOBBY BOXES
RED RELIC PRINT RUN 10 SETS
RED RELICS ARE NOT SERIAL-NUMBERED
PRINT RUN INFO PROVIDED BY TOPPS
NO RED RELIC PRICING DUE TO SCARCITY

2004 Bowman's Best Double Play Autographs

STATED ODDS 1:33 HOBBY
STATED PRINT RUN 236 SETS
CARDS ARE NOT SERIAL NUMBERED
PRINT RUN INFO PROVIDED BY TOPPS
CC M.Creighton/D.Crouthers 8.00 20.00
EN J.English/R.Nolasco 10.00 25.00
HJ T.Hanson/C.Jackson 10.00 25.00
MH L.Milledge/E.Harris 10.00 25.00
MN B.Medders/D.Nippert 6.00 15.00
QS O.Quintanilla/B.Snyder 6.00 15.00
SC T.Stauffer/V.Chiaravalloti 6.00 15.00
SK J.Salazar/J.Knott 6.00 15.00
SV E.Santana/M.Valdez 6.00 15.00
UK N.Ungs/K.Kouzmanoff 12.50 30.00

2004 Bowman's Best Triple Play Autographs

STATED ODDS 1:109 HOBBY
STATED PRINT RUN 236 SETS
CARDS ARE NOT SERIAL NUMBERED
PRINT RUN INFO PROVIDED BY TOPPS
ALS Aardsma/Levinski/Sullivan 6.00 15.00
CBA Cedeno/Brownlie/Arias 6.00 15.00
SSV Stauffer/Santana/Valdez 6.00 15.00

2005 Bowman's Best

This 143-card set was released in September, 2005. The set was issued in five-card packs with an $10 SRP which came 10 packs to a box and 10 boxes to case. The first 30 cards in the set feature active veterans while cards 31 through 143 feature Rookie Cards. Cards 101 through 143 are all autographed, and while most of them are Rookie Cards, a few of the cards are not Rookie Cards as the players had cards in the 31-100 grouping. Cards number 101 through 143 were issued at a stated rate of one in five hobby packs and those cards were issued to a stated print run of 974 serial numbered sets.

COMP.SET w/o SP's (100) 25.00 50.00
COMMON CARD (1-30) .20 .50
COMMON CARD (31-100) .40 1.00
COMMON AU (101-143) 3.00 8.00
101-143 ODDS 1:5 HOBBY
101-143 PRINT RUN 974 SERIAL #'d SETS
OVERALL 1-100 PLATE ODDS 1:345 H
OVERALL 101-143 AU PLATE ODDS 1:805 H
PLATE PRINT RUN 1 SET PER COLOR
BLACK-CYAN-MAGENTA-YELLOW ISSUED
NO PLATE PRICING DUE TO SCARCITY
1 Jose Vidro .20 .50
2 Adam Dunn .30 .75
3 Manny Ramirez .50 1.25
4 Miguel Tejada .30 .75
5 Ken Griffey Jr. 1.00 2.50
6 Pedro Martinez .30 .75
7 Alex Rodriguez .60 1.50
8 Ichiro Suzuki .60 1.50
9 Alfonso Soriano .30 .75
10 Brian Giles .20 .50
11 Roger Clemens .60 1.50
12 Todd Helton .30 .75
13 Ivan Rodriguez .30 .75
14 David Ortiz .50 1.25
15 Sammy Sosa .50 1.25
16 Chipper Jones .50 1.25
17 Mark Buehrle .30 .75
18 Miguel Cabrera .50 1.25
19 Johan Santana .30 .75
20 Randy Johnson .50 1.25
21 Jim Thome .30 .75
22 Vladimir Guerrero .30 .75
23 Dontrelle Willis .20 .50
24 Nomar Garciaparra .30 .75
25 Barry Bonds .75 2.00
26 Curt Schilling .30 .75
27 Carlos Beltran .30 .75
28 Albert Pujols .60 1.50
29 Mark Prior .30 .75
30 Derek Jeter 1.25 3.00
31 Ryan Garko FY RC .40 1.00
32 Eulogio De La Cruz FY RC .40 1.00
33 Luke Scott FY RC 1.00 2.50
34 Shane Costa FY RC .40 1.00
35 Casey McGehee FY RC .60 1.50
36 Jered Weaver FY RC 2.00 5.00
37 Kevin Melillo FY RC .40 1.00
38 D.J. Houlton FY RC .40 1.00
39 Brandon Moorhead FY RC .40 1.00
40 Jerry Owens FY RC .40 1.00
41 Elliot Johnson FY RC .40 1.00
42 Kevin West FY RC .40 1.00
43 Hernan Iribarren FY RC .40 1.00
44 Miguel Montero FY RC 1.25 3.00
45 Craig Tatum FY RC .40 1.00
46 Ryan Sweeney FY RC .60 1.50
47 Micah Furtado FY RC .40 1.00
48 Cody Haerther FY RC .40 1.00
49 Erick Abreu FY RC .40 1.00
50 Chuck Tiffany FY RC 1.00 2.50
51 Tadahito Iguchi FY RC .60 1.50
52 Frank Diaz FY RC .40 1.00
53 Errol Simonitsch FY RC .40 1.00
54 Wade Robinson FY RC .40 1.00
55 Adam Boeve FY RC .40 1.00
56 Steven Bondurant FY RC .40 1.00
57 Jason Motte FY RC .60 1.50
58 Juan Senreiso FY RC .40 1.00
59 Vinny Rottino FY RC .40 1.00
60 Jai Miller FY RC .40 1.00
61 Thomas Pauly FY RC .40 1.00
62 Tony Giarratano FY RC .40 1.00
63 Alexander Smit FY RC .40 1.00
64 Keiichi Yabu FY RC .40 1.00
65 Brian Bannister FY RC .60 1.50
66 Kennard Bibbs FY RC .40 1.00
67 Anthony Reyes FY RC .60 1.50
68 Thomas Oldham FY RC .40 1.00
69 Ben Harrison FY .40 1.00
70 Daryl Thompson FY RC .40 1.00
71 Kevin Collins FY RC .40 1.00
72 Wes Swackhamer FY RC .40 1.00
73 Landon Powell FY RC .40 1.00
74 Matt Brown FY RC .40 1.00
75 Russ Martin FY RC 1.25 3.00
76 Nick Touchstone FY RC .40 1.00
77 Steven White FY RC .40 1.00
78 Ian Bladergroen FY RC .40 1.00
79 Sean Marshall FY RC 1.00 2.50
80 Nick Masset FY RC .40 1.00
81 Ryan Goleski FY RC .40 1.00
82 Matt Campbell FY RC .40 1.00
83 Manny Parra FY RC 1.00 2.50
84 Melky Cabrera FY RC 1.25 3.00
85 Ryan Feierabend FY RC .40 1.00
86 Nate McLouth FY RC .60 1.50
87 Glen Perkins FY RC .40 1.00
88 Kila Kaaihue FY RC 1.00 2.50
89 Dana Eveland FY RC .40 1.00
90 Tyler Pelland FY RC .40 1.00
91 Matt Van Der Bosch FY RC .40 1.00
92 Andy Santana FY RC .40 1.00

3 Eric Nielsen FY RC .40 1.00
4 Brendan Ryan FY RC .40 1.00
5 Ian Kinsler FY RC 2.00 5.00
6 Matthew Kemp FY RC 2.00 5.00
7 Stephen Drew FY RC 1.25 3.00
8 Peeter Ramos FY RC .40 1.00
9 Chris Seddon FY RC .40 1.00
00 Chuck James FY RC 1.00 2.50
01 Travis Chick FY AU RC 3.00 8.00
02 Justin Verlander FY AU RC 50.00 120.00
03 Billy Butler FY AU RC 8.00 20.00
04 Chris B.Young FY AU RC 3.00 8.00
05 Jake Postlewait FY AU RC 3.00 8.00
06 C.J. Smith FY AU RC 3.00 8.00
07 Mike Rodriguez FY AU RC 3.00 8.00
108 Philip Humber FY AU RC 10.00 25.00
109 Jeff Niemann FY AU RC 3.00 8.00
110 Brian Miller FY AU RC 3.00 8.00
111 Chris Vines FY AU RC 3.00 8.00
112 Andy LaRoche FY AU RC 3.00 8.00
113 Mike Bourn FY AU RC 3.00 8.00
114 Wlad Balentein FY AU RC 3.00 8.00
115 Ismael Ramirez FY AU RC 3.00 8.00
116 Hayden Penn FY AU RC 3.00 8.00
117 Pedro Lopez FY AU RC 3.00 8.00
118 Shawn Bowman FY AU RC 3.00 8.00
119 Chad Orvella FY AU RC 3.00 8.00
120 Sean Tracey FY AU RC 3.00 8.00
121 Bobby Livingston FY AU RC 3.00 8.00
122 Michael Rogers FY AU RC 3.00 8.00
123 Willy Mota FY AU RC 3.00 8.00
124 Bran McCarthy FY AU RC 5.00 12.00
125 Mike Morse FY AU RC 8.00 20.00
126 Matt Lindstrom FY AU RC 3.00 8.00
127 Brian Stavisky FY AU RC 3.00 8.00
128 Richie Gardner FY AU RC 3.00 8.00
129 Scott Mitchinson FY AU RC 3.00 8.00
130 Billy McCarthy FY AU RC 3.00 8.00
131 Brandon Sing FY AU RC 3.00 8.00
132 Matt Albers FY AU RC 3.00 8.00
133 George Kottaras FY AU RC 3.00 8.00
134 Luis Hernandez FY AU RC 3.00 8.00
135 Hum Sanchez FY AU RC 3.00 8.00
136 Buck Coats FY AU RC 3.00 8.00
137 Jon Barratt FY AU RC 3.00 8.00
138 Raul Tablado FY AU RC 3.00 8.00
139 Jake Mullinax FY AU RC 3.00 8.00
140 Edgar Varela FY AU RC 3.00 8.00
141 Ryan Garko FY AU 3.00 8.00
142 Nate McLouth FY AU 6.00 15.00
143 Shane Costa FY AU 3.00 8.00

2005 Bowman's Best Black

STATED ODDS 1:1386 HOBBY
STATED PRINT RUN 1 SERIAL #'d SET
NO PRICING DUE TO SCARCITY

2005 Bowman's Best Blue

*BLUE 1-30: 1.25X TO 3X BASIC
*BLUE 31-100: .6X TO 1.5X BASIC
1-100 ODDS 1:4 HOBBY
1-100 PRINT RUN 499 #'d SETS
*BLUE AU 101-143: .5X TO 1.2X BASIC
AU 101-143 PRINT RUN 299 #'d SETS
AU 101-143 ODDS 1:14 HOBBY

2005 Bowman's Best Gold

*GOLD 1-30: 6X TO 15X BASIC
1-100 ODDS 1:69 HOBBY
1-100 PRINT RUN 25 #'d SETS
31-100 NO PRICING DUE TO SCARCITY
AU 101-143 ODDS 1:159 HOBBY
AU 101-143 PRINT RUN 25 #'d SETS
AU 101-143 NO PRICING DUE TO SCARCITY

2005 Bowman's Best Green

*GREEN 1-30: 1X TO 2.5X BASIC
*GREEN 31-100: .5X TO 1.2X BASIC
1-100 ODDS 1:2 HOBBY
1-100 PRINT RUN 899 #'d SETS
*GREEN AU 101-143: .5X TO 1.2X BASIC
AU 101-143 ODDS 1:10 HOBBY
AU 101-143 PRINT RUN 399 #'d SETS

2005 Bowman's Best Red

*RED 1-30: 1.5X TO 4X BASIC
*RED 31-100: 1X TO 2.5X BASIC
1-100 ODDS 1:9 HOBBY
1-100 PRINT RUN 199 #'d SETS
*RED AU 101-143: .6X TO 1.5X BASIC
AU 101-143 ODDS 1:20 HOBBY
AU 101-143 PRINT RUN 199 #'d SETS

2005 Bowman's Best Silver

*SILVER 1-30: 2.5X TO 6X BASIC
*SILVER 31-100: 1.25X TO 3X BASIC
1-100 ODDS 1:18 HOBBY
1-100 PRINT RUN 99 #'d SETS
*SILVER AU 101-143: .75X TO 2X BASIC
AU 101-143 ODDS 1:41 HOBBY
AU 101-143 PRINT RUN 99 #'d SETS

2005 Bowman's Best A-Rod Throwback Autograph

STATED ODDS 1:1402 HOBBY
STATED PRINT RUN 100 SERIAL #'d CARDS
AR Alex Rodriguez 1994 50.00 120.00

2005 Bowman's Best Mirror Image Spokesmen Dual Autograph

STATED ODDS 1:16,300 HOBBY
STATED PRINT RUN 10 SERIAL #'d CARDS
NO PRICING DUE TO SCARCITY

2005 Bowman's Best Mirror Image Throwback Dual Autograph

STATED ODDS 1:2835 HOBBY
STATED PRINT RUN 50 SERIAL #'d CARDS
RR A.Rodriguez/C.Ripken 175.00 350.00

2005 Bowman's Best Shortstops Triple Autograph

STATED ODDS 1:5927 HOBBY
STATED PRINT RUN 25 SERIAL #'d CARDS
NO PRICING DUE TO SCARCITY

2007 Bowman's Best

This 117-card set was released in January, 2008. The set consists of 33 base veteran cards, the last 11 of those cards also come in an autographed form. In addition, cards numbered 34-51 feature signed veterans. Cards numbered 52-81 are 2007 rookies which were inserted at a stated rate of one in two packs and those cards were issued to a stated print run of 799 serial numbered sets. The last 10 numbers in those rookies also come in a signed version which were inserted at a stated rate of one in 11. The set concludes with 18 signed 2007 rookie cards and those cards were also inserted at a stated rate of one in two. This set was issued in five-card packs with an $20 SRP which came five packs to a mini-box, three mini-boxes per full box and eight full boxes per case.

COMP.SET w/o AU (33) 6.00 15.00
COMMON CARD (1-33) .20 .50
COMMON AU VET VAR (23-33) 3.00 8.00
AU VET VAR GROUP A 1:15 PACKS
AU VET VAR GROUP B 1:122 PACKS
AU VET VAR GROUP C 1:381 PACKS
AU VET VAR GROUP D 1:113 PACKS
COMMON AU VET (34-51) 3.00 8.00
AU VET ODDS 1:2 PACKS
COMMON RC (52-81) .40 1.00
RC ODDS 1:2 PACKS
RC PRINT RUN 799 SER.#'D SETS
GU-RC ODDS 1:35 PACKS
COMMON AU VAR RC (71-81) 3.00 8.00
AU VAR RC ODDS 1:11 PACKS
COMMON AU RC (82-99) 3.00 8.00
AU RC ODDS 1:2 PACKS
PRINTING PLATE ODDS 1:88 PACKS
PRINTING PLATE AU ODDS 1:173 PACKS
PRINTING PLATE GU ODDS 1:8945 PACKS
PLATE PRINT RUN 1 SET PER COLOR
BLACK-CYAN-MAGENTA-YELLOW ISSUED
NO PLATE PRICING DUE TO SCARCITY
1 Jose Reyes .30 .75
2 Derek Jeter 1.25 3.00
3 Vladimir Guerrero .30 .75
4 Ichiro Suzuki .60 1.50
5 Jason Bay .30 .75
6 Joe Mauer .40 1.00
7 Alfonso Soriano .30 .75
8 David Ortiz .50 1.25
9 Andruw Jones .20 .50
10 Roger Clemens .60 1.50
11 Grady Sizemore .30 .75
12 Magglio Ordonez .30 .75
13 Carl Crawford .30 .75
14 Chase Utley .30 .75
15 Mark Teixeira .30 .75
16 Ryan Zimmerman .30 .75
17 Ken Griffey Jr. 1.00 2.50
18 Derrek Lee .20 .50
19 Barry Bonds .75 2.00
20 Chipper Jones .50 1.25
21 Vernon Wells .20 .50
22 Manny Ramirez .50 1.25
23a Alex Rodriguez .60 1.50
23b Alex Rodriguez AU A 25.00 80.00
24a Ryan Howard .40 1.00
24b Ryan Howard AU B 4.00 10.00
25a Tom Glavine .30 .75
25b Tom Glavine AU D 5.00 12.00
26a Gary Sheffield .20 .50
26b Gary Sheffield AU A 8.00 20.00
27a Miguel Cabrera .50 1.25
27b Miguel Cabrera AU A 12.00 30.00
28a Robinson Cano .30 .75
28b Robinson Cano AU A 10.00 25.00
29a David Wright .40 1.00
29b David Wright AU A 6.00 15.00
30a Jim Thome .30 .75
30b Jim Thome AU A 20.00 50.00
31a Albert Pujols .60 1.50
31b Albert Pujols AU C 50.00 120.00
32 Jorge Posada .30 .75
33a Brian McCann .20 .50
33b Brian McCann AU A 6.00 15.00
34 Josh Barfield AU 3.00 8.00
35 Melky Cabrera AU 4.00 10.00
36 Bill Hall AU 3.00 8.00
37 Cole Hamels AU 10.00 25.00
38 Adam LaRoche AU 3.00 8.00
39 Matt Holliday AU 4.00 10.00
40 Jeremy Hermida AU 3.00 8.00
41 Jonathan Papelbon AU 4.00 10.00
42 Hanley Ramirez AU 3.00 8.00
43 Justin Verlander AU 25.00 60.00
44 Andre Ethier AU 3.00 8.00
46 Erik Bedard AU 3.00 8.00
47 Freddy Sanchez AU 3.00 8.00
48 Adrian Gonzalez AU 4.00 10.00
49 Russell Martin AU 5.00 12.00
50 B.J. Upton AU 3.00 8.00
51 Prince Fielder AU 5.00 12.00
52 Tony Abreu RC 1.00 2.50
53 Ben Francisco (RC) .40 1.00
54 Billy Butler (RC) .60 1.50
55 Phillip Hughes (RC) 1.00 2.50
56 Josh Fields (RC) .40 1.00
57 Carlos Gomez RC .75 2.00
58 Akinori Iwamura RC 1.00 2.50
59 Matt Brown (RC) .40 1.00
60 Jesus Flores RC .40 1.00
61 Mike Fontenot (RC) .40 1.00
62 Ryan Feierabend (RC) .40 1.00
63 Miguel Montero (RC) .40 1.00
64a Daisuke Matsuzaka RC 1.50 4.00
64b Daisuke Matsuzaka Jsy 5.00 12.00
65 Kei Igawa RC 1.00 2.50
66 Shawn Riggans (RC) .40 1.00
67 Masumi Kuwata RC .40 1.00
68 Kevin Slowey (RC) 1.00 2.50
69 Josh Hamilton (RC) 1.25 3.00
70 Curtis Thigpen (RC) .40 1.00
71a Justin Upton RC 1.25 3.00
71b Justin Upton AU 5.00 12.00
72a Delmon Young (RC) .60 1.50
72b Delmon Young AU 3.00 8.00
73a Brandon Wood (RC) .40 1.00
73b Brandon Wood AU 6.00 15.00
74a Felix Pie (RC) .50 1.25
74b Felix Pie AU 4.00 10.00
75a Alex Gordon RC 1.25 3.00
75b Alex Gordon AU 6.00 15.00
76a Mark Reynolds RC 1.25 3.00
76b Mark Reynolds AU 3.00 8.00
77a Tyler Clippard (RC) .60 1.50
77b Tyler Clippard AU 4.00 10.00
78a Adam Lind (RC) .40 1.00
78b Adam Lind AU 3.00 8.00
79a Hunter Pence (RC) 1.25 3.00
79b Hunter Pence AU 5.00 12.00
80 Micah Owings (RC) .40 1.00
81a Jarrod Saltalamacchia (RC) .60 1.50
81b Jarrod Saltalamacchia AU 6.00 15.00
82 Kevin Kouzmanoff AU (RC) 3.00 8.00
83 Glen Perkins AU (RC) 3.00 8.00
84 Michael Bourn AU (RC) 3.00 8.00
85 Andrew Miller AU RC 4.00 10.00
86 Fred Lewis AU (RC) 3.00 8.00
88 Joba Chamberlain AU RC 5.00 12.00
89 Hideki Okajima AU RC 3.00 8.00
90 TroyTulowitzki AU (RC) 6.00 15.00
91 Ryan Sweeney AU (RC) 3.00 8.00
92 Matt Lindstrom AU (RC) 3.00 8.00
93 T.Lincecum AU RC UER 10.00 25.00
94 Homer Bailey AU (RC) 4.00 10.00
95 Matt DeSalvo AU (RC) 3.00 8.00
96 Alejandro De Aza AU RC 3.00 8.00
97 Ryan Braun AU (RC) 5.00 12.00
99 Andy LaRoche AU (RC) 3.00 8.00

2007 Bowman's Best Blue

*VET BLUE: 3X TO 8X BASIC VET
VET ODDS 1:11 PACKS
*AU VET BLUE: .5X TO 1.2X BASIC AU VET
AU VET ODDS 1:14 PACKS
*RC BLUE: 1X TO 2.5X BASIC RC
RC ODDS 1:12 PACKS
*AU RC BLUE: .5X TO 1.2X BASIC AU RC
AU RC ODDS 1:15 PACKS
*GU-RC BLUE: .75X TO 2X BASIC GU-RC
GU-RC ODDS 1:361 PACKS
STATED PRINT RUN 99 SER.#'d SETS

2007 Bowman's Best Gold

*VET GOLD: 4X TO 10X BASIC VET
VET ODDS 1:22 PACKS
*AU VET GOLD: .6X TO 1.5X BASIC AU VET
AU VET ODDS 1:28 PACKS
*RC GOLD: 1.5X TO 4X BASIC RC
RC ODDS 1:24 PACKS
*AU RC GOLD: .6X TO 1.5X BASIC AU RC
AU RC ODDS 1:29 PACKS
*GU-RC GOLD: 1X TO 2.5X BASIC GU-RC
GU-RC ODDS 1:715 PACKS
STATED PRINT RUN 50 SER.#'d SETS

2007 Bowman's Best Green

*VET GREEN: 1.5X TO 4X BASIC VET
VET ODDS 1:5 PACKS
*RC GREEN: .75X TO 2X BASIC RC
RC ODDS 1:5 PACKS
STATED PRINT RUN 249 SER.#'d SETS

2007 Bowman's Best Red

VET ODDS 1:1073 PACKS
AU VET ODDS 1:1325 PACKS
RC ODDS 1:1221 PACKS
AU RC ODDS 1:1376 PACKS
GU-RC ODDS 1:27,456 PACKS
STATED PRINT RUN 1 SER.#'d SET
NO PRICING DUE TO SCARCITY

2007 Bowman's Best Alex Rodriguez 500

COMPLETE SET (1) 1.50 4.00
COMMON CARD 1.50 4.00
STATED ODDS 1:
COMMON BLUE 8.00 20.00
BLUE ODDS 1:1107 PACKS
BLUE PRINT RUN 33 SER.#'d SETS
GOLD ODDS 1:2532 PACKS
GOLD PRINT RUN 15 SER.#'d SETS
NO GOLD PRICING DUE TO SCARCITY
COMMON GREEN 5.00 12.00
GREEN ODDS 1:361 PACKS
GREEN PRINT RUN 99 SER.#'d SETS
AR Alex Rodriguez 1.25 3.00

2007 Bowman's Best Barry Bonds 756

COMPLETE SET (1) 1.25 3.00
STATED ODDS 1:20 PACKS
PRINTING PLATE ODDS 1:8945 PACKS
PLATE PRINT RUN 1 SET PER COLOR
BLACK-CYAN-MAGENTA-YELLOW ISSUED
NO PLATE PRICING DUE TO SCARCITY
BB Barry Bonds 1.00 2.50

2007 Bowman's Best Prospects

COMMON PROSPECT (1-40) .25 .60
PROSPECT STATED ODDS 1:2 PACKS
PROSPECT PRINT RUN 499 SER.#'d SETS
COMMON PROS.AU VAR (37-40) 3.00 8.00
PROS AU VAR ODDS 1:26 PACKS
COMMON PROS.AUTO (41-60) 3.00 8.00
PROS.AUTO ODDS 1:26 PACKS
PRINTING PLATE ODDS 1:88 PACKS
PRINTING PLATE AU ODDS 1:173 PACKS
PLATE PRINT RUN 1 SET PER COLOR
BLACK-CYAN-MAGENTA-YELLOW ISSUED
NO PLATE PRICING DUE TO SCARCITY
BBP1 Greg Smith .40 1.00
BBP2 J.R. Towles .75 2.00
BBP3 Jeff Locke .60 1.50
BBP4 Henry Sosa .40 1.00
BBP5 Ivan De Jesus Jr. .40 1.00
BBP6 Brad Lincoln .25 .60
BBP7 Josh Papelbon .25 .60
BBP8 Mark Hamilton .25 .60
BBP9 Sam Fuld .75 2.00
BBP10 Thomas Fairchild .25 .60
BBP11 Chris Carter .75 2.00
BBP12 Chuck Lofgren .60 1.50
BBP13 Joe Gaetti .25 .60
BBP14 Zach McAllister .40 1.00
BBP15 Cole Gillespie .40 1.00
BBP16 Jeremy Papelbon .25 .60
BBP17 Mike Carp .75 2.00
BBP18 Cody Strait .25 .60
BBP19 Gorkys Hernandez .60 1.50
BBP20 Andrew Fie .25 .60
BBP21 Erik Lis .40 1.00
BBP22 Chance Douglass .25 .60
BBP23 Vasili Spanos .25 .60
BBP24 Desmond Jennings 1.00 2.50
BBP25 Vic Buttler .25 .60
BBP26 Cedric Hunter .60 1.50
BBP27 Emerson Frostad .25 .60
BBP28 Mike Devaney .25 .60
BBP29 Eric Young Jr. .40 1.00
BBP30 Evan Englebrook .25 .60
BBP31 Aaron Cunningham .40 1.00
BBP32 Dellin Betances .75 2.00
BBP33 Michael Saunders .75 2.00
BBP34 Deolis Guerra .50 1.25
BBP35 Brian Bocock .25 .60
BBP36 Rich Thompson .25 .60
BBP37a Greg Reynolds .60 1.50
BBP37b Greg Reynolds AU 5.00 12.00
BBP38a Jeff Samardzija 1.00 2.50
BBP38b Jeff Samardzija AU 5.00 12.00
BBP39a Evan Longoria 3.00 8.00
BBP39b Evan Longoria AU 10.00 25.00
BBP40a Luke Hochevar .75 2.00
BBP40b Luke Hochevar AU 6.00 15.00
BBP41 James Avery AU 3.00 8.00
BBP42 Joe Mather AU 3.00 8.00
BBP43 Hank Conger AU 4.00 10.00
BBP44 Adam Miller AU 3.00 8.00
BBP45 Clayton Kershaw AU 60.00 150.00
BBP46 Adam Ottavino AU 3.00 8.00
BBP47 Jason Place AU 5.00 12.00
BBP48 Billy Rowell AU 3.00 8.00
BBP49 Brett Sinkbell AU 3.00 8.00
BBP50 Colton Willems AU 3.00 8.00
BBP51 Cameron Maybin AU 3.00 8.00
BBP52 Jeremy Jeffress AU 3.00 8.00
BBP53 Fernando Martinez AU 3.00 8.00
BBP54 Chris Marrero AU 3.00 8.00
BBP55 Kyle McCulloch AU 3.00 8.00
BBP56 Chris Parmelee AU 3.00 8.00
BBP57 Emmanuel Burris AU 3.00 8.00
BBP58 Chris Coghlan AU 3.00 8.00
BBP59 Chris Perez AU 4.00 10.00
BBP60 David Huff AU 3.00 8.00

2007 Bowman's Best Prospects Blue

*PROS BLUE: .6X TO 1.5X BASIC PROS
PROS ODDS 1:9 PACKS
*PROS AU BLUE: .6X TO 1.5X BASIC PROS AU
PROS AU ODDS 1:16 PACKS
STATED PRINT RUN 99 SER.#'d SETS

2007 Bowman's Best Prospects Gold

*PROS GOLD: .75X TO 2X BASIC PROS
PROS ODDS 1:18 PACKS
*PROS AU GOLD: .75X TO 2X BASIC PROS AU
PROS AU ODDS 1:31 PACKS
STATED PRINT RUN 50 SER.#'d SETS

2007 Bowman's Best Prospects Green

PROS GREEN: .5X TO 1.2X BASIC PROS
STATED ODDS 1:4 PACKS
STATED PRINT RUN 249 SER.#'d SETS

2007 Bowman's Best Prospects Red

PROS. ODDS 1:908 PACKS
PROS. AU ODDS 1:1453 PACKS
STATED PRINT RUN 1 SER.#'d SET
NO PRICING DUE TO SCARCITY

2015 Bowman's Best

COMPLETE SET (100) 30.00 80.00
STATED PLATE ODDS 1:133 MINI BOX
PLATE PRINT RUN 1 SET PER COLOR
BLACK-CYAN-MAGENTA-YELLOW ISSUED
NO PLATE PRICING DUE TO SCARCITY
1 Mike Trout 2.00 5.00
2 James Shields .25 .60
3 Francisco Lindor RC 3.00 8.00
4 Chi Chi Gonzalez RC .75 2.00
5 Felix Hernandez .30 .75
6 Addison Russell RC 1.50 4.00
7 Joey Votto .40 1.00
8 Michael Brantley .30 .75
9 Robinson Cano .30 .75
10 Yasiel Puig .40 1.00
11 Edwin Encarnacion .40 1.00
12 Joey Gallo RC 1.00 2.50
13 Troy Tulowitzki .40 1.00
14 Nelson Cruz .40 1.00
15 Maikel Franco RC .60 1.50
16 Jake Arrieta .30 .75
17 Chris Archer .25 .60
18 Jacob deGrom .40 1.00
19 Adam Jones .30 .75
20 Daniel Norris RC .50 1.25
21 Jose Abreu .40 1.00
22 Masahiro Tanaka .30 .75
23 Yoenis Cespedes .30 .75
24 Anthony Rizzo .60 1.50
25 Bryce Harper .60 1.50
26 Starling Marte .30 .75
27 Byron Buxton RC .75 2.00
28 Joc Pederson RC 1.00 2.50
29 Adrian Gonzalez .30 .75
30 Buster Posey .50 1.25
31 Dee Gordon .25 .60
32 Noah Syndergaard RC 1.00 2.50
33 Michael Pineda .25 .60
34 Giancarlo Stanton .40 1.00
35 Freddie Freeman .50 1.25
36 George Springer .30 .75
37 Jose Bautista .30 .75
38 Brian Dozier .30 .75
39 Paul Goldschmidt .40 1.00
40 Eddie Rosario .50 1.25
41 Matt Wisler RC .50 1.25
42 Johnny Cueto .30 .75
43 Dustin Pedroia .40 1.00
44 Alex Meyer RC .50 1.25
45 Chris Sale .40 1.00
46 Yasmany Tomas RC .60 1.50
47 Mookie Betts .60 1.50
48 Zack Greinke .30 .75
49 Jung Ho Kang RC .50 1.25
50 Kris Bryant RC 3.00 8.00
51 Kyle Seager .25 .60
52 Sonny Gray .30 .75
53 Eric Hosmer .30 .75
54 Devon Travis RC .50 1.25
55 Rusney Castillo RC .60 1.50
56 Jose Altuve .30 .75
57 Matt Harvey .30 .75
58 Carlos Correa RC 2.50 6.00
59 Anthony Rendon .40 1.00
60 Michael Wacha .30 .75
61 Miguel Cabrera .40 1.00
62 Ryan Braun .30 .75
63 Garrett Richards .30 .75
64 Justin Upton .30 .75
65 Brett Gardner .30 .75
66 Todd Frazier .30 .75
67 Archie Bradley RC .50 1.25
68 Dallas Keuchel .30 .75
69 Jacoby Ellsbury .30 .75
70 Adam Wainwright .30 .75
71 Eduardo Rodriguez RC .50 1.25
72 Carlos Beltran .30 .75
73 Cole Hamels .30 .75
74 Charlie Blackmon .40 1.00
75 Josh Donaldson .30 .75
76 Jose Reyes .30 .75
77 Corey Kluber .30 .75
78 Prince Fielder .30 .75
79 Carlos Rodon RC .75 2.00
80 A.J. Cole RC .50 1.25
81 Jason Kipnis .30 .75
82 Albert Pujols .50 1.25
83 Max Scherzer .40 1.00
84 Blake Swihart RC .60 1.50
85 Aroldis Chapman .40 1.00
86 Adrian Beltre .40 1.00
87 Trevor Rosenthal .30 .75
88 Madison Bumgarner .30 .75
89 Carlos Gomez .25 .60
90 Andrew McCutchen .40 1.00
91 Hanley Ramirez .30 .75
92 Steven Matz RC .75 2.00
93 Jorge Soler RC .75 2.00
94 David Price .30 .75
95 Billy Hamilton .30 .75
96 Nolan Arenado .50 1.25
97 Gerrit Cole .40 1.00
98 Craig Kimbrel .30 .75
99 Manny Machado .40 1.00
100 Clayton Kershaw .75 2.00

2015 Bowman's Best Atomic Refractors

*ATOMIC REF: 3X TO 8X BASIC
*ATOMIC REF RC: 1.5X TO 4X BASIC
STATED ODDS 1:2 MINI BOXES

2015 Bowman's Best Blue Refractors

*BLUE REF: 2.5X TO 6X BASIC
*BLUE REF RC: 1.2X TO 3X BASIC
STATED ODDS 1:4 MINI BOXES
STATED PRINT RUN 150 SER.#'D SETS
50 Kris Bryant 10.00 25.00
58 Carlos Correa 20.00 50.00

2015 Bowman's Best Gold Refractors

*GOLD REF: 4X TO 10X BASIC
*GOLD REF RC: 2X TO 5X BASIC
STATED ODDS 1:11 MINI BOX
STATED PRINT RUN 50 SER.#'d SETS
30 Buster Posey 12.00 30.00
49 Jung Ho Kang 10.00 25.00
50 Kris Bryant 15.00 40.00
58 Carlos Correa 40.00 100.00
100 Clayton Kershaw 15.00 40.00

2015 Bowman's Best Green Refractors

*GREEN REF: 2.5X TO 6X BASIC
*GREEN REF RC: 1.2X TO 3X BASIC
STATED ODDS 1:6 MINI BOXES
STATED PRINT RUN 99 SER.#'d SETS
50 Kris Bryant 10.00 25.00
58 Carlos Correa 20.00 50.00

2015 Bowman's Best Orange Refractors

*ORANGE REF: 5X TO 12X BASIC
*ORANGE REF RC: 2.5X TO 6X BASIC
STATED ODDS 1:22 MINI BOX
STATED PRINT RUN 25 SER.#'d SETS
30 Buster Posey 15.00 40.00
49 Jung Ho Kang 12.00 30.00
50 Kris Bryant 50.00 120.00
58 Carlos Correa 50.00 120.00
100 Clayton Kershaw 20.00 50.00

2015 Bowman's Best Refractors

*REFRACTOR: 1.2X TO 3X BASIC
*REFRACTOR RC: .6X TO 1.5X BASIC
RANDOM INSERTS IN MINI BOXES
50 Kris Bryant 5.00 12.00

2015 Bowman's Best '95 Bowman's Best Autographs Refractors

STATED ODDS 1:66 MINI BOX
PRINT RUNS B/WN 30-50 COPIES PER
EXCHANGE DEADLINE 12/31/2017
*ORANGE/25: .5X TO 1.2X BASIC
95BBAG Adrian Gonzalez/50 15.00 40.00
95BBAJ Adam Jones/50 8.00 20.00
95BBAR Anthony Rizzo/50 25.00 60.00
95BBCH Cole Hamels/50 40.00 100.00
95BBDO David Ortiz/30 30.00 80.00
95BBEE Edwin Encarnacion/50 10.00 25.00
95BBFF Freddie Freeman/50 20.00 50.00
95BBGS George Springer/50 15.00 40.00
95BBJA Jose Abreu/50 20.00 50.00
95BBJD Jacob deGrom/50 25.00 60.00
95BBJV Joey Votto/50 25.00 60.00
95BBPS Pablo Sandoval/50 8.00 20.00
95BBRB Ryan Braun/50 12.00 30.00
95BBSM Shelby Miller/50 15.00 40.00

2015 Bowman's Best Best of '15 Autographs

OVERALL AUTO ODDS TWO PER MINI BOX
STATED PLATE ODDS 1:233 MINI BOX
PLATE PRINT RUN 1 SET PER COLOR
BLACK-CYAN-MAGENTA-YELLOW ISSUED
NO PLATE PRICING DUE TO SCARCITY
EXCHANGE DEADLINE 12/31/2017
B15AB Alex Blandino 3.00 8.00
B15AG Adrian Gonzalez 6.00 15.00
B15AJ Alex Jackson 4.00 10.00
B15ANB Andrew Benintendi 10.00 25.00
B15ANO Aaron Nola 8.00 20.00
B15AR Alex Reyes 4.00 10.00
B15ARI Anthony Rizzo 20.00 50.00
B15ASR Ashe Russell 3.00 8.00
B15BB Byron Buxton 8.00 20.00
B15BD Braxton Davidson 3.00 8.00
B15BEB Beau Burrows 4.00 10.00
B15BR Brendan Rodgers 6.00 15.00
B15BSN Blake Snell 10.00 25.00
B15BZ Bradley Zimmer 5.00 12.00
B15CD Chase De Jong 4.00 10.00
B15CF Carson Fulmer 3.00 8.00
B15CH Chris Heston 3.00 8.00
B15CR Carlos Rodon 5.00 12.00
B15CRA Cornelius Randolph 3.00 8.00
B15CT Cole Tucker 3.00 8.00
B15DF Derek Fisher 4.00 10.00
B15DM Dixon Machado 4.00 10.00
B15DS Dansby Swanson 10.00 25.00
B15DST D.J. Stewart 3.00 8.00
B15DTA Dillon Tate 4.00 10.00
B15ER Eduardo Rodriguez 3.00 8.00
B15FL Francisco Lindor 40.00 100.00
B15FM Frankie Montas 4.00 10.00
B15GH Grant Holmes 4.00 10.00

B15GW Garrett Whitley 5.00 12.00
B15HR Hanley Ramirez 4.00 10.00
B15IH Ian Happ 8.00 20.00
B15JAL Jose Altuve 15.00 40.00
B15JHK Jung Ho Kang EXCH 15.00 40.00
B15JK James Kaprielian 5.00 12.00
B15JM Jorge Mateo 5.00 12.00
B15JNA Josh Naylor 4.00 10.00
B15JP Joc Pederson 4.00 10.00
B15JW Jacob Wilson 3.00 8.00
B15KA Kolby Allard 3.00 8.00
B15KB Kris Bryant 50.00 120.00
B15KM Kevonte Mitchell 3.00 8.00
B15KME Kodi Medeiros 3.00 8.00
B15KN Kevin Newman 5.00 12.00
B15KT Kyle Tucker 10.00 25.00
B15LG Lucas Giolito 6.00 15.00
B15LW Luke Weaver 5.00 12.00
B15MC Michael Chavis 10.00 25.00
B15MCH Matt Chapman 10.00 25.00
B15MMA Manuel Margot 3.00 8.00
B15MN Mike Nikorak 3.00 8.00
B15MO Matt Olson 4.00 10.00
B15MP Max Pentecost 3.00 8.00
B15MR Mariano Rivera 6.00 15.00
B15MS Miguel Sano 6.00 15.00
B15MSC Max Scherzer 40.00 100.00
B15MWI Matt Wisler 3.00 8.00
B15NG Nick Gordon 4.00 10.00
B15NP Nick Plummer 4.00 10.00
B15NS Noah Syndergaard 20.00 50.00
B15OA Orlando Arcia 4.00 10.00
B15PB Phil Bickford 3.00 8.00
B15PV Pat Venditte 3.00 8.00
B15RD Rafael Devers 20.00 50.00
B15RM Richie Martin 3.00 8.00
B15SG Stephen Gonsalves 3.00 8.00
B15SMA Steven Matz 5.00 12.00
B15SN Sean Newcomb 4.00 10.00
B15TC Trent Clark 3.00 8.00
B15TJ Tyler Jay 3.00 8.00
B15TS Tyler Stephenson 4.00 10.00
B15TT Trea Turner 10.00 25.00
B15TTO Touki Toussaint 4.00 10.00
B15TWA Taylor Ward 5.00 12.00
B15WB Walker Buehler 25.00 60.00
B15WD Wilmer Difo 3.00 8.00
B15YL Yoan Lopez 3.00 8.00

2015 Bowman's Best Best of '15 Autographs Atomic Refractors

*ATOMIC REF: .75X TO 2X BASIC
STATED ODDS 1:20 MINI BOX
STATED PRINT RUN 50 SER.#'d SETS
EXCHANGE DEADLINE 12/31/2017
B15AG Adrian Gonzalez 12.00 30.00
B15CC Carlos Correa 150.00 300.00
B15JG Joey Gallo 12.00 30.00
B15KS Kyle Schwarber 60.00 150.00
B15MT Mike Trout 200.00 400.00
B15SGR Sonny Gray EXCH 8.00 20.00

2015 Bowman's Best Best of '15 Autographs Green Refractors

*GREEN REF: .6X TO 1.5X BASIC
STATED ODDS 1:11 MINI BOX
STATED PRINT RUN 99 SER.#'d SETS
EXCHANGE DEADLINE 12/31/2017
B15CC Carlos Correa 125.00 250.00
B15JG Joey Gallo 10.00 25.00
B15KS Kyle Schwarber 50.00 120.00
B15MT Mike Trout 175.00 350.00
B15SGR Sonny Gray EXCH 6.00 15.00

2015 Bowman's Best Best of '15 Autographs Orange Refractors

*ORANGE REF: 1X TO 2.5X BASIC
STATED ODDS 1:38 MINI BOX
STATED PRINT RUN 25 SER.#'d SETS
EXCHANGE DEADLINE 12/31/2017
B15AG Adrian Gonzalez 15.00 40.00
B15CC Carlos Correa 175.00 350.00
B15JG Joey Gallo 15.00 40.00
B15KS Kyle Schwarber 75.00 200.00
B15MT Mike Trout 250.00 500.00
B15SGR Sonny Gray EXCH 10.00 25.00

2015 Bowman's Best Best of '15 Autographs Refractors

*REFRACTORS: .5X TO 1.2X BASIC
RANDOM INSERTS IN PACKS
EXCHANGE DEADLINE 12/31/2017
B15SGR Sonny Gray EXCH 5.00 12.00

2015 Bowman's Best First Impressions Refractors

STATED ODDS 1:2 MINI BOX
*ATOMIC/50: 1.5X TO 4X BASIC
*ORANGE/25: 2.5X TO 6X BASIC
FIAB Andrew Benintendi 2.50 6.00
FIBR Brendan Rodgers 2.00 5.00
FICF Carson Fulmer .50 1.25
FICR Cornelius Randolph .50 1.25
FIDS Dansby Swanson 3.00 8.00
FIDT Dillon Tate .60 1.50
FIGW Garrett Whitley .75 2.00
FIIH Ian Happ 2.00 5.00
FIJK James Kaprielian .75 2.00
FIJN Josh Naylor .60 1.50
FIKA Kolby Allard .50 1.25
FIKT Kyle Tucker 3.00 8.00
FIPB Phil Bickford .50 1.25
FITJ Tyler Jay .50 1.25
FITS Tyler Stephenson .60 1.50

2015 Bowman's Best First Impressions Autographs

STATED ODDS 1:53 MINI BOX
STATED PRINT RUN 99 SER.#'d SETS
EXCHANGE DEADLINE 12/31/2017
*ORANGE/25: .6X TO 1.5X BASIC
FIAB Andrew Benintendi 50.00 120.00
FIBR Brendan Rodgers 20.00 50.00
FICF Carson Fulmer 6.00 15.00
FICR Cornelius Randolph 6.00 15.00
FIDS Dansby Swanson 50.00 120.00
FIDT Dillon Tate 8.00 20.00
FIGW Garrett Whitley 10.00 25.00
FIIH Ian Happ 20.00 50.00
FIJK James Kaprielian 10.00 25.00
FIJN Josh Naylor 8.00 20.00
FIKA Kolby Allard 6.00 15.00
FIKT Kyle Tucker 40.00 100.00
FIPB Phil Bickford 6.00 15.00
FITJ Tyler Jay 6.00 15.00
FITS Tyler Stephenson 8.00 20.00

2015 Bowman's Best Hi Def Heritage Refractors

RANDOM INSERTS IN PACKS
*ATOMIC: 1X TO 2.5X BASIC
*ORANGE/25: 1.5X TO 4X BASIC
HDHAB Archie Bradley .50 1.25
HDHAG Adrian Gonzalez .60 1.50
HDHAJ Alex Jackson .60 1.50
HDHAJO Adam Jones .60 1.50
HDHAP Albert Pujols 1.00 2.50
HDHAR Addison Russell 1.50 4.00
HDHARI Anthony Rizzo 1.25 3.00
HDHBB Byron Buxton .75 2.00
HDHBH Bryce Harper 1.25 3.00
HDHBP Buster Posey 1.00 2.50
HDHBS Blake Swihart .60 1.50
HDHCC Carlos Correa 2.50 6.00
HDHCK Corey Kluber .60 1.50
HDHCKE Clayton Kershaw 1.50 4.00
HDHCR Carlos Rodon .75 2.00
HDHCS Corey Seager 2.00 5.00
HDHCSA Chris Sale .75 2.00
HDHDO David Ortiz .75 2.00
HDHFL Francisco Lindor 3.00 8.00
HDHGS Giancarlo Stanton .75 2.00
HDHHH Hunter Harvey .50 1.25
HDHHO Henry Owens .50 1.25
HDHJA Jose Abreu .75 2.00
HDHJB Jose Bautista .60 1.50
HDHJC J.P. Crawford .50 1.25
HDHJD Jacob deGrom .75 2.00
HDHJG Joey Gallo 1.00 2.50
HDHJL Jon Lester .60 1.50
HDHJP Joc Pederson 1.00 2.50
HDHJS Jorge Soler .75 2.00
HDHJU Julio Urias 1.50 4.00
HDHJV Joey Votto .75 2.00
HDHKB Kris Bryant 3.00 8.00
HDHKP Kevin Plawecki .50 1.25
HDHKS Kyle Schwarber 2.00 5.00
HDHLG Lucas Giolito 1.00 2.50
HDHLS Luis Severino .60 1.50
HDHMC Miguel Cabrera .75 2.00
HDHMS Miguel Sano .60 1.50
HDHMSC Max Scherzer .75 2.00
HDHMT Mike Trout 4.00 10.00
HDHNC Nelson Cruz .75 2.00
HDHNG Nick Gordon .60 1.50
HDHNS Noah Syndergaard 1.00 2.50
HDHPG Paul Goldschmidt .75 2.00
HDHRC Robinson Cano .60 1.50
HDHRD Rafael Devers 3.00 8.00
HDHTG Tyler Glasnow .60 1.50
HDHTT Touki Toussaint .60 1.50
HDHYT Yasmany Tomas .60 1.50

2015 Bowman's Best Hi Def Heritage Autographs

STATED ODDS 1:55 MINI BOX
STATED PRINT RUN 50 SER.#'d SETS
EXCHANGE DEADLINE 12/31/2017
HDHAB Archie Bradley 15.00 40.00
HDHAG Adrian Gonzalez 8.00 20.00
HDHAJO Adam Jones 25.00 60.00
HDHAP Albert Pujols 200.00 300.00
HDHARI Anthony Rizzo 20.00 50.00
HDHBB Byron Buxton 25.00 60.00
HDHBS Blake Swihart 6.00 15.00
HDHCC Carlos Correa 150.00 250.00
HDHCK Corey Kluber 8.00 20.00
HDHCR Carlos Rodon 12.00 30.00
HDHHO Henry Owens EXCH 8.00 20.00
HDHJG Joey Gallo 12.00 30.00
HDHJL Jon Lester 15.00 40.00
HDHJP Joc Pederson 25.00 60.00
HDHJS Jorge Soler 15.00 40.00
HDHKB Kris Bryant 150.00 250.00
HDHLG Lucas Giolito 12.00 30.00
HDHLS Luis Severino 25.00 60.00
HDHMS Miguel Sano 20.00 50.00
HDHMSC Max Scherzer EXCH 20.00 50.00
HDHNS Noah Syndergaard 25.00 60.00

2015 Bowman's Best Hi Def Heritage Autographs Orange Refractors

*ORANGE REF: .5X TO 1.2X BASIC
STATED ODDS 1:116 MINI BOX
STATED PRINT RUN 25 SER.#'d SETS
EXCHANGE DEADLINE 12/31/2017

2015 Bowman's Best Mirror Image

COMP.SET w/o UER (20) 10.00 25.00
RANDOM INSERTS IN MINI BOX
BELTRAN UER ODDS 1:399 MINI BOX
MI1 G.Stanton/A.Judge 6.00 15.00
MI2 C.Seager/T.Tulowitzki 1.00 2.50
MI3 K.Schwarber/B.Posey 1.00 2.50
MI4 S.Strasburg/L.Giolito .50 1.25
MI5 J.Bell/E.Hosmer .50 1.25
MI6 J.Urias/C.Kershaw .75 2.00
MI7 K.Bryant/N.Arenado 1.50 4.00
MI8 B.Buxton/C.Blackmon .40 1.00
MI9 C.Correa/A.Rodriguez 1.25 3.00
MI10 J.Gallo/J.Donaldson .50 1.25
MI11 J.Pederson/R.Braun .50 1.25
MI12 M.Sano/T.Frazier .30 .75
MI13 C.Rodon/D.Price .40 1.00
MI14 A.Nola/J.Shields .40 1.00
MI15 D.Swanson/B.Crawford 1.50 4.00
MI16 B.Rodgers/X.Bogaerts 1.00 2.50
MI17 D.Tate/F.Hernandez .30 .75
MI18 P.Tucker/K.Tucker 1.50 4.00
MI19 M.Trout/A.Benintendi 2.00 5.00
MI20 B.McCann/T.Stephenson .30 .75
MILG Beltran/Gonzalez UER 2.00 5.00

2015 Bowman's Best Top Prospects

COMPLETE SET (50) 15.00 40.00
STATED PLATE ODDS 1:133 MINI BOX
PLATE PRINT RUN 1 SET PER COLOR
BLACK-CYAN-MAGENTA-YELLOW ISSUED
NO PLATE PRICING DUE TO SCARCITY
TP1 Corey Seager 1.00 2.50
TP2 Miguel Sano .30 .75
TP3 Robert Stephenson .25 .60
TP4 Raul Mondesi
TP5 Luis Severino .30 .75
TP6 Henry Owens .25 .60
TP7 Alex Reyes .30 .75
TP8 Hunter Harvey .25 .60
TP9 Dillon Tate .30 .75
TP10 Carson Fulmer .25 .60
TP11 Tyler Stephenson .30 .75
TP12 Kolby Allard .25 .60
TP13 Kevin Newman .40 1.00
TP14 Beau Burrows .30 .75
TP15 Frankie Montas .30 .75
TP16 Kyle Schwarber 1.00 2.50
TP17 Braden Shipley .25 .60
TP18 Mark Appel .25 .60
TP19 Austin Meadows .40 1.00
TP20 Jesse Winker .25 .60
TP21 Aaron Judge 4.00 10.00
TP22 Nick Gordon .30 .75
TP23 Ian Happ 1.00 2.50
TP24 Josh Naylor .30 .75
TP25 Lucas Giolito .50 1.25
TP26 James Kaprielian .40 1.00
TP27 Ashe Russell .25 .60
TP28 Michael Conforto .30 .75
TP29 Rafael Devers 1.50 4.00
TP30 Tyler Glasnow .30 .75
TP31 Jon Gray .25 .60
TP32 Jameson Taillon .30 .75
TP33 Aaron Nola .40 1.00
TP34 Tyler Kolek .25 .60
TP35 Dansby Swanson 1.50 4.00
TP36 Tyler Jay .25 .60
TP37 Andrew Benintendi 1.25 3.00
TP38 Garrett Whitley .40 1.00
TP39 Phil Bickford .25 .60
TP40 Richie Martin .25 .60
TP41 Bradley Zimmer .40 1.00
TP42 J.P. Crawford .25 .60
TP43 Aaron Blair .25 .60
TP44 Brandon Nimmo .40 1.00
TP45 Brendan Rodgers 1.00 2.50
TP46 Kyle Tucker 1.50 4.00
TP47 Cornelius Randolph .25 .60
TP48 Trent Clark .25 .60
TP49 Josh Bell .50 1.25
TP50 Julio Urias .75 2.00

2015 Bowman's Best Top Prospects Atomic Refractors

*ATOMIC REF: 1.5X TO 4X BASIC
RANDOM INSERST IN MINI BOXES
TP37 Andrew Benintendi 12.00 30.00

2015 Bowman's Best Top Prospects Blue Refractors

*BLUE REF: 1.5X TO 4X BASIC
RANDOM INSERTS IN MINI BOXES
STATED PRINT RUN 150 SER.#'d SETS
TP37 Andrew Benintendi 15.00 40.00

2015 Bowman's Best Top Prospects Gold Refractors

*GOLD REF: 5X TO 12X BASIC
RANDOM INSERTS IN MINI BOXES
STATED PRINT RUN 50 SER.#'d SETS

2015 Bowman's Best Top Prospects Green Refractors

*GREEN REF: 1.5X TO 4X BASIC
RANDOM INSERTS IN MINI BOXES
STATED PRINT RUN 99 SER.#'d SETS
TP37 Andrew Benintendi 20.00 50.00

2015 Bowman's Best Top Prospects Orange Refractors

*ORANGE REF: 6X TO 15X BASIC
RANDOM INSERTS IN MINI BOXES
STATED PRINT RUN 25 SER.#'d SETS

2015 Bowman's Best Top Prospects Refractors

*REFRACTORS: .5X TO 1.2X BASIC
RANDOM INSERST IN MINI BOXES

2016 Bowman's Best

COMPLETE SET (65) 10.00 25.00
1 Mike Trout 2.00 5.00
2 Albert Almora RC .50 1.25
3 Gary Sanchez RC 1.25 3.00
4 Michael Conforto RC .50 1.25
5 Evan Longoria .30 .75
6 Luis Severino RC .50 1.25
7 Dellin Betances .30 .75
8 Carlos Correa .40 1.00
9 Aaron Nola RC .75 2.00
10 Jose Altuve .30 .75
11 Paul Goldschmidt .40 1.00
12 Trevor Story RC 1.50 4.00
13 Dae-Ho Lee RC .60 1.50
14 Blake Snell RC .50 1.25
15 Miguel Sano RC .60 1.50
16 Wil Myers .25 .60
17 Josh Donaldson .30 .75
18 Freddie Freeman .50 1.25
19 Xander Bogaerts .40 1.00
20 Lucas Giolito RC .60 1.50
21 Nomar Mazara RC .60 1.50
22 Andrew McCutchen .40 1.00
23 Ryan Braun .30 .75
24 Julio Urias RC 1.25 3.00
25 Corey Seager RC 3.00 8.00
26 Manny Machado .40 1.00
27 Madison Bumgarner .30 .75
28 Ben Zobrist .30 .75
29 Aledmys Diaz RC .60 1.50
30 Clayton Kershaw .75 2.00
31 Max Scherzer .40 1.00
32 Mookie Betts .60 1.50
33 Nolan Arenado .50 1.25
34 Bryce Harper .60 1.50
35 Chris Sale .40 1.00
36 Jose Berrios RC .50 1.25
37 Jameson Taillon RC .50 1.25
38 Noah Syndergaard .30 .75
39 Kenta Maeda RC .75 2.00
40 Francisco Lindor .40 1.00
41 Jake Arrieta .30 .75
42 Tim Anderson RC 1.50 4.00
43 Rob Refsnyder RC .50 1.25
44 Anthony Rizzo .60 1.50
45 Jon Gray RC .40 1.00
46 Michael Fulmer RC .60 1.50
47 Yoenis Cespedes .40 1.00
48 Yu Darvish .40 1.00
49 Giancarlo Stanton .40 1.00
50 David Ortiz .40 1.00
51 Willson Contreras RC 2.50 6.00
52 Stephen Strasburg .40 1.00
53 Starling Marte .30 .75
54 Buster Posey .50 1.25
55 Tyler Naquin RC .50 1.25
56 Miguel Cabrera .40 1.00
57 Ichiro Suzuki .50 1.25
58 Trea Turner RC 1.25 3.00
59 Stephen Piscotty RC .60 1.50
60 Jose Bautista .30 .75
61 Daniel Murphy .30 .75
62 Felix Hernandez .30 .75
63 Robinson Cano .30 .75
64 Kyle Schwarber RC 1.25 3.00
65 Kris Bryant .50 1.25

2016 Bowman's Best Atomic Refractors

*ATOMIC REF: 3X TO 8X BASIC
*ATOMIC REF RC: 2X TO 5X BASIC RC
STATED ODDS 1:12 HOBBY

2016 Bowman's Best Blue Refractors

*BLUE REF: 2.5X TO 6X BASIC
*BLUE REF RC: 1.5X TO 4X BASIC RC
STATED ODDS 1:16 HOBBY
STATED PRINT RUN 250 SER.#'d SETS

2016 Bowman's Best Gold Refractors

*GOLD REF: 5X TO 12X BASIC
*GOLD REF RC: 3X TO 8X BASIC RC
STATED ODDS 1:79 HOBBY
STATED PRINT RUN 50 SER.#'d SETS

2016 Bowman's Best Green Refractors

*GRN REF: 3X TO 8X BASIC
*GRN REF RC: 2X TO 5X BASIC RC
STATED ODDS 1:49 HOBBY
STATED PRINT RUN 99 SER.#'d SETS

2016 Bowman's Best Orange Refractors

*ORANGE REF: 6X TO 15X BASIC
*ORANGE REF RC: 4X TO 10X BASIC RC
STATED ODDS 1:113 HOBBY
STATED PRINT RUN 25 SER.#'d SETS

2016 Bowman's Best Refractors

*REF: 1X TO 2.5X BASIC
*REF RC: .6X TO 1.5X BASIC RC

2016 Bowman's Best '96 Bowman's Best

STATED ODDS 1:6 HOBBY
96BBI Ichiro Suzuki 1.25 3.00
96BBAA Anthony Alford .60 1.50
96BBAB Andrew Benintendi 2.00 5.00
96BBAE Anderson Espinoza .60 1.50
96BBAG Andres Galarraga .75 2.00
96BBAP Andy Pettitte .75 2.00
96BBAR Alex Reyes .75 2.00
96BBBH Bryce Harper 1.50 4.00
96BBBS Blake Snell .75 2.00
96BBCC Carlos Correa 1.00 2.50
96BBDS Dansby Swanson 2.00 5.00
96BBDW David Wright .75 2.00
96BBHA Hank Aaron 2.00 5.00
96BBJB Jose Berrios .75 2.00
96BBJC Jose Canseco .75 2.00
96BBJD Johnny Damon .75 2.00
96BBJM Jorge Mateo .75 2.00
96BBJS John Smoltz 1.00 2.50
96BBKB Kris Bryant 1.25 3.00
96BBKM Kenta Maeda 1.25 3.00
96BBKS Kyle Schwarber 2.00 5.00
96BBLG Lucas Giolito 1.00 2.50
96BBMM Mark McGwire 1.50 4.00
96BBMT Mike Trout 5.00 12.00
96BBNA Nolan Arenado 1.25 3.00
96BBOA Orlando Arcia .75 2.00
96BBOV Omar Vizquel .75 2.00
96BBRD Rafael Devers 2.00 5.00
96BBSN Sean Newcomb .75 2.00
96BBYM Yoan Moncada 1.50 4.00

2016 Bowman's Best '96 Bowman's Best Atomic Refractors

*ATOMIC REF: 1X TO 2.5X BASIC
STATED ODDS 1:96 HOBBY
96BBKB Kris Bryant 20.00 50.00
96BBKS Kyle Schwarber 10.00 25.00
96BBMT Mike Trout 20.00 50.00

2016 Bowman's Best '96 Bowman's Best Orange Refractors

*ORANGE REF: 2X TO 5X BASIC
STATED ODDS 1:375 HOBBY
STATED PRINT RUN 35 SER.#'d SETS
96BBKB Kris Bryant 40.00 100.00
96BBKS Kyle Schwarber 20.00 50.00
96BBMT Mike Trout 40.00 100.00

2016 Bowman's Best '96 Bowman's Best Autographs

STATED ODDS 1:385 HOBBY
PRINT RUNS B/WN 30-99 COPIES PER
EXCHANGE DEADLINE 11/30/2018
96BBAAA Anthony Alford/99 4.00 10.00
96BBAAE Anderson Espinoza/99 4.00 10.00
96BBAAG Andres Galarraga/50 6.00 15.00
96BBAAR Alex Reyes/75 20.00 50.00
96BBADS Dansby Swanson/50 50.00 120.00
96BBAJC Jose Canseco/75 15.00 40.00
96BBAJD Johnny Damon/30 30.00 80.00
96BBAJM Jorge Mateo/99 5.00 12.00
96BBAKS Kyle Schwarber/50 15.00 40.00
96BBALG Lucas Giolito/75 6.00 15.00
96BBAOA Orlando Arcia/99 5.00 12.00
96BBAOV Omar Vizquel/75 5.00 12.00
96BBARD Rafael Devers/75 20.00 50.00
96BBASN Sean Newcomb/99 5.00 12.00

2016 Bowman's Best '96 Bowman's Best Autographs Atomic Refractors

*ATOMIC REF: .6X TO 1.5X BASIC
STATED ODDS 1:768 HOBBY
STATED PRINT RUN 25 SER.#'d SETS
EXCHANGE DEADLINE 11/30/2018
96BBAAP Andy Pettitte 20.00 50.00
96BBABH Bryce Harper 200.00 400.00
96BBACC Carlos Correa 75.00 200.00
96BBADW David Wright 25.00 60.00
96BBAHA Hank Aaron 250.00 400.00
96BBAI Ichiro Suzuki 300.00 600.00
96BBAJD Johnny Damon 30.00 80.00
96BBAJS John Smoltz 25.00 60.00
96BBAKB Kris Bryant 400.00 600.00
96BBAMM Mark McGwire 100.00 250.00
96BBAMT Mike Trout 175.00 350.00

2016 Bowman's Best Baseball America Prospect Forecast

STATED ODDS 1:262 HOBBY
STATED PRINT RUN 150 SER.#'d SETS
*ORANGE/35: .5X TO 1.2X BASIC
BAPFAE Anderson Espinoza 1.50 4.00
BAPFBR Brendan Rodgers 2.50 6.00
BAPFDS Dansby Swanson 5.00 12.00
BAPFGT Gleyber Torres 8.00 20.00
BAPFJM Jorge Mateo 2.00 5.00
BAPFLF Lucius Fox 2.50 6.00
BAPFRD Rafael Devers 4.00 10.00
BAPFSN Sean Newcomb 2.00 5.00
BAPFVR Victor Robles 6.00 15.00
BAPFYM Yoan Moncada 4.00 10.00

2016 Bowman's Best Baseball America Prospect Forecast Autographs

STATED ODDS 1:1,284 HOBBY
STATED PRINT RUN 50 SER.#'d SETS
EXCHANGE DEADLINE 11/30/2018
BAPFAE Anderson Espinoza
BAPFDS Dansby Swanson 20.00 50.00
BAPFGT Gleyber Torres 60.00 150.00
BAPFJM Jorge Mateo 6.00 15.00
BAPFSN Sean Newcomb 4.00 10.00
BAPFYM Yoan Moncada 30.00 80.00

2016 Bowman's Best Best of '16 Autographs

STATED ODDS 1:XX HOBBY
STATED PLATE ODDS 1:1,696 HOBBY
PLATE PRINT RUN 1 SET PER COLOR
BLACK-CYAN-MAGENTA-YELLOW ISSUED
NO PLATE PRICING DUE TO SCARCITY
EXCHANGE DEADLINE 11/30/2018
B16AA Anthony Alford 3.00 8.00
B16AB Anthony Banda 3.00 8.00
B16ABR Alex Bregman 20.00 50.00
B16ABE Andrew Benintendi 40.00 100.00
B16ABL Aaron Blair 3.00 8.00
B16AD Aledmys Diaz 5.00 12.00
B16AE Anderson Espinoza 3.00 8.00
B16AJ Aaron Judge 75.00 200.00
B16AK Alex Kirilloff 15.00 40.00
B16AP A.J. Puk 5.00 12.00
B16AR Alex Reyes 4.00 10.00
B16AR A.J. Reed 3.00 8.00
B16ARO Amed Rosario 5.00 12.00
B16BG Braxton Garrett 3.00 8.00
B16BH Bryce Harper 40.00 100.00
B16BP Buster Posey 30.00 80.00
B16BR Brendan Rodgers 5.00 12.00
B16BS Blake Snell 3.00 8.00
B16CC Carlos Correa 25.00 60.00
B16COR Corey Ray 6.00 15.00
B16CQ Cal Quantrill 3.00 8.00
B16CR Carlos Rodon 5.00 12.00
B16CS Corey Seager 20.00 50.00
B16DD David Dahl 4.00 10.00
B16DJ Drew Jackson 3.00 8.00
B16DS Dansby Swanson 10.00 25.00
B16ED Elias Diaz 3.00 8.00
B16FB Franklin Barreto 3.00 8.00
B16FL Francisco Lindor 20.00 50.00
B16FW Forrest Whitley 6.00 15.00
B16GD Garrett Davila 3.00 8.00
B16GL Gavin Lux 25.00 60.00
B16HOW Henry Owens 4.00 10.00
B16IA Ian Anderson 20.00 50.00
B16JD Justin Dunn 3.00 8.00
B16JH Josh Hader 4.00 10.00
B16JL Joshua Lowe 3.00 8.00
B16JM Jorge Mateo 4.00 10.00
B16JT Jameson Taillon 4.00 10.00
B16JU Julio Urias
B16KA Kolby Allard 3.00 8.00
B16KB Kris Bryant 75.00 200.00
B16KL Kyle Lewis 25.00 60.00
B16KM Kenta Maeda
B16KN Kevin Newman 5.00 12.00
B16KS Kyle Schwarber 12.00 30.00
B16LG Lucas Giolito 6.00 15.00
B16LS Luis Severino 10.00 25.00
B16MAS Mallex Smith
B16MC Michael Conforto
B16MCL Mike Clevinger 6.00 15.00
B16MM Mickey Moniak 4.00 10.00
B16MMA Matt Manning 10.00 25.00
B16MS Miguel Sano 5.00 12.00
B16MT Mike Trout
B16MTH Matt Thaiss 3.00 8.00
B16NA Nolan Arenado 15.00 40.00
B16NM Nomar Mazara
B16OA Ozzie Albies 15.00 40.00
B16OAR Orlando Arcia 4.00 10.00
B16RD Rafael Devers 25.00 60.00
B16RP Riley Pint 3.00 8.00
B16RS Robert Stephenson 3.00 8.00
B16SM Steven Matz 4.00 10.00
B16SN Sean Newcomb 4.00 10.00
B16ST Sam Travis 5.00 12.00
B16TA Tim Anderson 25.00 60.00
B16TO Tyler O'Neill 4.00 10.00
B16TS Trevor Story 15.00 40.00
B16TT Touki Toussaint EXCH 4.00 10.00
B16VG Vladimir Guerrero Jr. 75.00 200.00
B16WB Will Benson 5.00 12.00
B16WC Will Craig 3.00 8.00
B16WCO Willson Contreras 12.00 30.00
B16YG Yulieski Gurriel 8.00 20.00
B16YM Yoan Moncada 15.00 40.00
B16ZC Zack Collins 4.00 10.00

2016 Bowman's Best Best of '16 Autographs Atomic Refractors

*ATOMIC REF: 1X TO 2.5X BASIC
STATED ODDS 1:271 HOBBY
STATED PRINT RUN 25 SER.#'d SETS
EXCHANGE DEADLINE 11/30/2018
B16BP Buster Posey 60.00 150.00
B16JU Julio Urias 60.00 150.00
B16KM Kenta Maeda 15.00 40.00
B16MAS Mallex Smith 15.00 40.00
B16MC Michael Conforto 20.00 50.00
B16MT Mike Trout 150.00 400.00
B16NM Nomar Mazara 30.00 80.00
B16VG Vladimir Guerrero Jr. 400.00 800.00

2016 Bowman's Best Best of '16 Autographs Green Refractors

*GREEN REF: .6X TO 1.5X BASIC
STATED ODDS 1:69 HOBBY
STATED PRINT RUN 99 SER.#'d SETS
EXCHANGE DEADLINE 11/30/2018
B16JU Julio Urias 40.00 100.00
B16KM Kenta Maeda 10.00 25.00
B16MAS Mallex Smith 10.00 25.00
B16MC Michael Conforto 12.00 30.00
B16NM Nomar Mazara 20.00 50.00
B16VG Vladimir Guerrero Jr. 200.00 500.00

2016 Bowman's Best Best of '16 Autographs Orange Refractors

*ORANGE REF: .75X TO 2X BASIC
STATED ODDS 1:135 HOBBY
STATED PRINT RUN 50 SER.#'d SETS
EXCHANGE DEADLINE 11/30/2018
B16BP Buster Posey 50.00 120.00
B16JU Julio Urias 50.00 120.00
B16KM Kenta Maeda 12.00 30.00
B16MAS Mallex Smith 12.00 30.00
B16MC Michael Conforto 15.00 40.00
B16MT Mike Trout 125.00 300.00
B16NM Nomar Mazara 25.00 60.00
B16VG Vladimir Guerrero Jr. 300.00 600.00

2016 Bowman's Best Best of '16 Autographs Refractors

*REFRACTORS: .5X TO 1.2X BASIC
STATED ODDS 1:14 HOBBY
EXCHANGE DEADLINE 11/30/2018

2016 Bowman's Best Bowman Choice Autographs

STATED ODDS 1:768 HOBBY
STATED PRINT RUN 50 SER.#'d SETS
EXCHANGE DEADLINE 11/30/2018
BCAAB Alex Bregman 30.00 80.00
BCAAE Anderson Espinoza 8.00 20.00
BCACC Carlos Correa 30.00 80.00
BCACK Clayton Kershaw 50.00 120.00
BCACS Corey Seager 40.00 100.00
BCACSA Chris Sale
BCADO David Ortiz 40.00 100.00
BCAKB Kris Bryant 150.00 300.00
BCALG Lucas Giolito 8.00 20.00
BCANM Nomar Mazara 30.00 80.00
BCAOA Ozzie Albies 12.00 30.00
BCASM Steven Matz 10.00 25.00
BCATO Tyler O'Neill 6.00 15.00
BCAYM Yoan Moncada

2016 Bowman's Best Dual Autographs

STATED ODDS 1:3,072 HOBBY
STATED PRINT RUN 25 SER.#'d SETS
EXCHANGE DEADLINE 11/30/2018
BDAAB O.Arcia/R.Braun
BDABC A.Bregman/C.Correa 125.00 250.00
BDABH K.Bryant/M.Trout 1000.00 1500.00
BDAGH L.Giolito/B.Harper 30.00 80.00
BDAMS K.Maeda/C.Seager EXCH 125.00 250.00
BDAPM D.Pedroia/Y.Moncada 125.00 250.00
BDARF C.Rodon/C.Fulmer 20.00 50.00
BDASF D.Swanson/F.Freeman

2016 Bowman's Best First Impressions Autographs

STATED ODDS 1:385 HOBBY
STATED PRINT RUN 50 SER.#'d SETS
EXCHANGE DEADLINE 11/30/2018
*ATOMIC/25: .6X TO 1.5X BASIC
FIAAK Alex Kirilloff 40.00 100.00
FIAAP A.J. Puk 6.00 15.00
FIABG Braxton Garrett 12.00 30.00
FIACQ Cal Quantrill 4.00 10.00
FIACR Corey Ray 6.00 15.00
FIAFW Forrest Whitley 30.00 80.00
FIAGL Gavin Lux 40.00 100.00
FIAIA Ian Anderson 8.00 20.00
FIAJD Justin Dunn 4.00 10.00
FIAJL Joshua Lowe
FIAKL Kyle Lewis 40.00 100.00
FIAMM Mickey Moniak 25.00 60.00
FIAMMA Matt Manning 6.00 15.00
FIAMT Matt Thaiss 15.00 40.00
FIARP Riley Pint 4.00 10.00
FIAWB Will Benson 6.00 15.00
FIAZC Zack Collins 10.00 25.00

2016 Bowman's Best Mirror Image

COMPLETE SET (20) 8.00 20.00
STATED ODDS 1:4 HOBBY
*ATOMIC: .75X TO 2X BASIC
*ORANGE/25: 2.5X TO 6X BASIC
MI1 M.Moniak/J.Ellsbury 1.25 3.00
MI2 I.Anderson/J.deGrom .60 1.50
MI3 R.Pint/J.Verlander .40 1.00
MI4 C.Ray/J.Heyward .40 1.00
MI5 A.Puk/A.Miller .40 1.00
MI6 G.Stanton/J.Bour .40 1.00
MI7 M.Manning/N.Syndergaard .40 1.00
MI8 B.Posey/Z.Collins .50 1.25
MI9 A.Jones/K.Lewis 5.00 12.00
MI10 C.Yelich/A.Kirilloff 2.50 6.00
MI11 C.Seager/T.Tulowitzki 2.00 5.00
MI12 B.McCann/W.Contreras 1.50 4.00
MI13 L.Giolito/M.Scherzer .40 1.00
MI14 C.Kershaw/J.Urias .75 2.00
MI15 J.Lester/S.Matz .30 .75
MI16 J.Altuve/Y.Moncada .60 1.50
MI17 F.Lindor/O.Arcia .40 1.00
MI18 X.Bogaerts/D.Swanson .75 2.00
MI19 A.Reyes/J.Arrieta .30 .75
MI20 Carpenter/Devers .75 2.00

2016 Bowman's Best Stat Lines

COMPLETE SET (35) 10.00 25.00
STATED ODDS 1:3 HOBBY
*ATOMIC: 1X TO 2.5X BASIC
*ORANGE/25: 2.5X TO 6X BASIC
SLAB Anthony Banda .25 .60
SLABR Alex Bregman 1.50 4.00
SLAE Anderson Espinoza .25 .60
SLAJ Aaron Judge 2.00 5.00
SLAR Alex Reyes .30 .75
SLBH Bryce Harper .60 1.50
SLBP Buster Posey .50 1.25
SLBR Brendan Rodgers .40 1.00
SLBS Blake Snell .30 .75
SLCC Carlos Correa .40 1.00
SLCK Clayton Kershaw .75 2.00
SLCS Corey Seager 2.00 5.00
SLDO David Ortiz .40 1.00
SLDS Dansby Swanson .75 2.00
SLFL Francisco Lindor .40 1.00
SLGS Gary Sanchez .75 2.00

SLJA Jake Arrieta .30 .75
SLJAL Jose Altuve .30 .75
SLJH Josh Hader .30 .75
SLJT Jameson Taillon .30 .75
SLJU Julio Urias .75 2.00
SLKB Kris Bryant .50 1.25
SLKM Kenta Maeda .50 1.25
SLLG Lucas Giolito .40 1.00
SLMB Madison Bumgarner .30 .75
SLMC Michael Conforto .30 .75
SLMF Michael Fulmer .40 1.00
SLNA Nolan Arenado .50 1.25
SLNM Nomar Mazara .40 1.00
SLOA Orlando Arcia .30 .75
SLSN Sean Newcomb .30 .75
SLTA Tim Anderson 1.00 2.50
SLTO Tyler O'Neill .30 .75
SLTS Trevor Story 1.00 2.50
SLYM Yoan Moncada .60 1.50

2016 Bowman's Best Stat Lines Autographs

STATED ODDS 1:308 HOBBY
STATED PRINT RUN 50 SER.#'d SETS
EXCHANGE DEADLINE 11/30/2018
SLABR Alex Bregman 15.00 40.00
SLAJ Aaron Judge 40.00 100.00
SLBH Bryce Harper 75.00 200.00
SLBP Buster Posey 30.00 80.00
SLBS Blake Snell 6.00 15.00
SLCC Carlos Correa 30.00 80.00
SLCK Clayton Kershaw 30.00 80.00
SLDO David Ortiz 40.00 100.00
SLDS Dansby Swanson
SLFL Francisco Lindor 20.00 50.00
SLJH Josh Hader
SLJT Jameson Taillon 6.00 15.00
SLKM Kenta Maeda 15.00 40.00
SLMF Michael Fulmer 15.00 40.00
SLNA Nolan Arenado 20.00 50.00
SLNM Nomar Mazara 15.00 40.00
SLOA Orlando Arcia 6.00 15.00
SLSN Sean Newcomb 6.00 15.00
SLTA Tim Anderson 20.00 50.00
SLTO Tyler O'Neill 12.00 30.00
SLTS Trevor Story 15.00 40.00
SLYM Yoan Moncada 60.00 150.00

2016 Bowman's Best Top Prospects

COMPLETE SET (35) 6.00 15.00
*REF: .5X TO 1.2X BASIC
*BLUE/250: 1X TO 2.5X BASIC
*ATOMIC: 1X TO 2.5X BASIC
*GREEN/99: 1.2X TO 3X BASIC
*GOLD/50: 2X TO 5X BASIC
*ORANGE/35: 2.5X TO 6X BASIC
TP1 Yoan Moncada .60 1.50
TP2 Brendan Rodgers .40 1.00
TP3 Jorge Mateo .30 .75
TP4 Anderson Espinoza .25 .60
TP5 Orlando Arcia .30 .75
TP6 Cal Quantrill .25 .60
TP7 Joshua Lowe .25 .60
TP8 Bradley Zimmer .40 1.00
TP9 A.J. Puk .40 1.00
TP10 Will Craig .25 .60
TP11 Rafael Devers .75 2.00
TP12 J.P. Crawford .25 .60
TP13 Gleyber Torres 4.00 10.00
TP14 Riley Pint .25 .60
TP15 Will Benson .40 1.00
TP16 Dansby Swanson .75 2.00
TP17 Manny Margot .25 .60
TP18 Zack Collins .30 .75
TP19 Ian Anderson .60 1.50
TP20 Clint Frazier 1.00 2.50
TP21 Corey Ray .40 1.00
TP22 Kyle Lewis 5.00 12.00
TP23 Tyler Glasnow .30 .75
TP24 Francis Martes .30 .75
TP25 Alex Bregman 1.50 4.00
TP26 Braxton Garrett .30 .75
TP27 Alex Kirilloff 2.50 6.00
TP28 Aaron Judge 6.00 15.00
TP29 Andrew Benintendi .75 2.00
TP30 Alex Reyes .30 .75
TP31 Matt Manning .40 1.00
TP32 David Dahl .30 .75
TP33 Jose De Leon .25 .60
TP34 Austin Meadows .40 1.00
TP35 Mickey Moniak 1.25 3.00

2017 Bowman's Best

COMPLETE SET (65) 10.00 25.00
1 Aaron Judge RC 5.00 12.00
2 Max Scherzer .40 1.00
3 Tyler Glasnow RC .50 1.25
4 Daniel Murphy .30 .75
5 Freddie Freeman .50 1.25
6 Alex Reyes RC .50 1.25
7 Clayton Kershaw .75 2.00
8 Manny Machado .40 1.00
9 Jose Altuve .30 .75
10 Corey Seager .40 1.00
11 David Dahl RC .50 1.25
12 Jose De Leon RC .40 1.00
13 Franklin Barreto RC .40 1.00
14 Andrew Benintendi RC 1.25 3.00
15 Paul Goldschmidt .40 1.00
16 Jose Berrios .30 .75
17 Robinson Cano .30 .75
18 Miguel Sano .30 .75
19 Chris Sale .40 1.00
20 Giancarlo Stanton .40 1.00
21 Yoan Moncada RC 1.25 3.00
22 Brett Phillips RC .50 1.25
23 Miguel Cabrera .40 1.00
24 Jose Ramirez .30 .75
25 Mike Trout 2.00 5.00
26 Buster Posey .50 1.25
27 Craig Kimbrel .30 .75
28 Nolan Arenado .50 1.25
29 Yu Darvish .40 1.00
30 Jorge Alfaro RC .50 1.25
31 Bryce Harper .60 1.50
32 Luke Weaver RC .50 1.25
33 Noah Syndergaard .30 .75
34 Christian Arroyo RC .60 1.50
35 Anthony Rizzo .60 1.50
36 Joey Votto .40 1.00
37 Hunter Renfroe RC .50 1.25
38 Ian Happ RC .75 2.00
39 Charlie Blackmon .40 1.00
40 Kenley Jansen .30 .75
41 Yulieski Gurriel RC .60 1.50
42 Lewis Brinson RC .60 1.50
43 Sean Newcomb RC .50 1.25
44 Francisco Lindor .40 1.00
45 Aroldis Chapman .40 1.00
46 Mookie Betts .60 1.50
47 Trey Mancini RC .75 2.00
48 Carlos Correa .40 1.00
49 Josh Donaldson .30 .75
50 Kris Bryant .50 1.25
51 Andrew McCutchen .40 1.00
52 Ichiro .50 1.25
53 Khris Davis .40 1.00
54 Alex Bregman RC 1.50 4.00
55 Raimel Tapia RC .50 1.25
56 George Springer .30 .75
57 Corey Kluber .30 .75
58 Ryon Healy RC .50 1.25
59 Josh Bell RC 1.00 2.50
60 Jake Lamb .30 .75
61 Dansby Swanson RC 1.00 2.50
62 Yoenis Cespedes .40 1.00
63 Wil Myers .25 .60
64 Bradley Zimmer RC .50 1.25
65 Cody Bellinger RC 6.00 15.00

2017 Bowman's Best Atomic Refractors

*ATOMIC REF: 2X TO 5X BASIC
*ATOMIC REF RC: 1.2X TO 3X BASIC RC

2017 Bowman's Best Blue Refractors

*BLUE REF: 2.5X TO 6X BASIC
*BLUE REF RC: 1.5X TO 4X BASIC RC
STATED PRINT RUN 150 SER.#'d SETS

2017 Bowman's Best Gold Refractors

*GOLD REF: 5X TO 12X BASIC
*GOLD REF RC: 3X TO 8X BASIC RC
STATED PRINT RUN 50 SER.#'d SETS

2017 Bowman's Best Green Refractors

*GRN REF: 3X TO 8X BASIC
*GRN REF RC: 2X TO 5X BASIC RC
STATED PRINT RUN 99 SER.#'d SETS

2017 Bowman's Best Orange Refractors

*ORANGE REF: 6X TO 15X BASIC
*ORANGE REF RC: 4X TO 10X BASIC RC
STATED PRINT RUN 25 SER.#'d SETS

2017 Bowman's Best Purple Refractors

*PURPLE REF: 2.5X TO 6X BASIC
*PURPLE REF RC: 1.5X TO 4X BASIC RC
STATED PRINT RUN 250 SER.#'d SETS

2017 Bowman's Best Refractors

*REF: 1X TO 2.5X BASIC
*REF RC: .6X TO 1.5X BASIC RC

2017 Bowman's Best '97 Best Cuts

COMPLETE SET (30) 12.00 30.00
97BCAB Alex Bregman 2.00 5.00
97BCABE Andrew Benintendi 1.50 4.00
97BCAG Andres Galarraga .60 1.50
97BCAJ Aaron Judge 6.00 15.00
97BCBH Bryce Harper 1.25 3.00
97BCCB Cody Bellinger 8.00 20.00
97BCCC Carlos Correa .75 2.00
97BCCS Corey Seager .75 2.00
97BCDC Dylan Cozens .50 1.25
97BCDJ Derek Jeter 2.00 5.00
97BCDS Dominic Smith .50 1.25
97BCEJ Eloy Jimenez 2.00 5.00
97BCGT Gleyber Torres 8.00 20.00
97BCHA Hank Aaron 1.50 4.00
97BCJB Jeff Bagwell .60 1.50
97BCJT Jim Thome .60 1.50
97BCKB Kris Bryant 1.00 2.50
97BCKGJ Ken Griffey Jr. 1.50 4.00
97BCLA Lazarito Armenteros 1.25 3.00
97BCLB Lewis Brinson .75 2.00
97BCMM Mark McGwire 1.25 3.00
97BCMP Mike Piazza .75 2.00
97BCMT Mike Trout 4.00 10.00
97BCNG Nomar Garciaparra .60 1.50
97BCNS Nick Senzel 1.50 4.00
97BCPG Paul Goldschmidt .75 2.00
97BCRH Rhys Hoskins 2.00 5.00
97BCTO Tyler O'Neill .75 2.00
97BCWC Willie Calhoun .75 2.00
97BCYM Yoan Moncada 1.50 4.00

2017 Bowman's Best '97 Best Cuts Atomic Refractors

*ATOMIC REF: 1.2X TO 3X BASIC
97BCKGJ Ken Griffey Jr. 10.00 25.00

2017 Bowman's Best '97 Best Cuts Gold Refractors

*GOLD REF: 2X TO 5X BASIC
STATED PRINT RUN 50 SER.#'d SETS
97BCKB Kris Bryant 15.00 40.00
97BCKGJ Ken Griffey Jr. 30.00 80.00
97BCMP Mike Piazza 15.00 40.00
97BCMT Mike Trout 20.00 50.00

2017 Bowman's Best '97 Best Cuts Autographs

PRINT RUNS B/WN 9-150 COPIES PER
NO PRICING ON QTY 9
EXCHANGE DEADLINE 9/30/2019
97BCAAB Alex Bregman/150 20.00 50.00
97BCAABE Andrew Benintendi EXCH 25.00 60.00
97BCACB Cody Bellinger/150 75.00 200.00
97BCACC Carlos Correa/40 40.00 100.00
97BCADO David Ortiz/30 40.00 100.00
97BCAGT Gleyber Torres/150 60.00 150.00
97BCAHA Hank Aaron/20 200.00 400.00
97BCAJB Jeff Bagwell/50 20.00 50.00
97BCAJT Jim Thome/50 40.00 100.00
97BCAKB Kris Bryant/30 75.00 200.00
97BCALA Lazarito Armenteros/150 12.00 30.00
97BCAMM Mark McGwire/30 40.00 100.00
97BCAMT Mike Trout/20 300.00 500.00
97BCANG Nomar Garciaparra/50 15.00 40.00
97BCANS Nick Senzel/150 25.00 60.00
97BCAPG Paul Goldschmidt/50 25.00 60.00
97BCAYM Yoan Moncada/40 30.00 80.00

2017 Bowman's Best '97 Best Cuts Autographs Atomic Refractors

*ATOMIC REF: .6X TO 1.5X p/r 150
*ATOMIC REF: .5X TO 1.2X p/r 40-50
*ATOMIC REF: .4X TO 1X p/r 20-30
STATED PRINT RUN 50 SER.#'d SETS
EXCHANGE DEADLINE 11/30/2019
97BCAGT Gleyber Torres 125.00 300.00

2017 Bowman's Best '97 Best Cuts Autographs Gold Refractors

*GOLD REF: .5X TO 1.2X p/r 150
*GOLD REF: .4X TO 1X p/r 40-50
STATED PRINT RUN 50 SER.#'d SETS
EXCHANGE DEADLINE 11/30/2019

2017 Bowman's Best Baseball America's Dean's List

COMPLETE SET (40) 12.00 30.00
*ATOMIC REF: 1.5X TO 4X BASIC
*GOLD REF/50: 2.5X TO 6X BASIC
BADLAR Amed Rosario .50 1.25
BADLAS Tony Santillan .30 .75
BADLAV Alex Verdugo .50 1.25
BADLBD Bobby Dalbec .75 2.00
BADLBH Bryce Harper .75 2.00
BADLBHO Brent Honeywell .40 1.00
BADLBR Blake Rutherford .50 1.25
BADLCF Clint Frazier .60 1.50
BADLCS Corey Seager .50 1.25
BADLCST Christin Stewart .40 1.00
BADLDC Dylan Cozens .30 .75
BADLDS Dominic Smith .30 .75
BADLEJ Eloy Jimenez 1.25 3.00
BADLFM Francisco Mejia .50 1.25
BADLGT Gleyber Torres 5.00 12.00
BADLJD Jon Duplantier .50 1.25
BADLJG Jason Groome .60 1.50
BADLJM Jorge Mateo .30 .75
BADLJN Josh Naylor .40 1.00
BADLJS Justus Sheffield .50 1.25
BADLJSA Jesus Sanchez 1.50 4.00
BADLKB Kris Bryant .60 1.50
BADLKM Kevin Maitan .75 2.00
BADLLA Lazarito Armenteros .75 2.00
BADLLE Lucas Erceg .40 1.00
BADLMK Mitch Keller .40 1.00
BADLMM Mickey Moniak .75 2.00
BADLMT Mike Trout 2.50 6.00
BADLNS Nick Senzel 1.00 2.50
BADLPW Patrick Weigel .30 .75
BADLRA Ronald Acuna 6.00 15.00
BADLRD Rafael Devers .60 1.50
BADLRH Rhys Hoskins 1.25 3.00
BADLRM Ryan Mountcastle .50 1.25
BADLSK Scott Kingery .50 1.25
BADLSS Sixto Sanchez .75 2.00
BADLTM Triston McKenzie .30 .75
BADLTO Tyler O'Neill .40 1.00
BADLTT Taylor Trammell .50 1.25
BADLWC Willie Calhoun .50 1.25

2017 Bowman's Best Baseball America's Dean's List Autographs

STATED PRINT RUN 75 SER.#'d SETS
EXCHANGE DEADLINE 11/30/2019
BADLAS Tony Santillan 4.00 10.00
BADLAV Alex Verdugo 10.00 25.00
BADLBD Bobby Dalbec 10.00 25.00
BADLCF Clint Frazier 8.00 20.00
BADLDC Dylan Cozens 4.00 10.00
BADLDS Dominic Smith 4.00 10.00
BADLEJ Eloy Jimenez 20.00 50.00
BADLFM Francisco Mejia 10.00 25.00
BADLGT Gleyber Torres 30.00 80.00
BADLJG Jason Groome 8.00 20.00
BADLJM Jorge Mateo 8.00 20.00
BADLJN Josh Naylor 8.00 20.00
BADLJS Justus Sheffield 8.00 20.00
BADLKM Kevin Maitan 12.00 30.00
BADLLA Lazarito Armenteros 15.00 40.00
BADLLE Lucas Erceg 5.00 12.00
BADLMK Mitch Keller 5.00 12.00
BADLMM Mickey Moniak 15.00 40.00
BADLNS Nick Senzel 20.00 50.00
BADLPW Patrick Weigel 4.00 10.00
BADLRA Ronald Acuna 150.00 400.00
BADLRD Rafael Devers 10.00 25.00
BADLSK Scott Kingery 20.00 50.00
BADLTM Triston McKenzie 4.00 10.00
BADLTT Taylor Trammell 10.00 25.00
BADLWC Willie Calhoun 10.00 15.00

2017 Bowman's Best Best of '17 Autographs

PLATE PRINT RUN 1 SET PER COLOR
BLACK-CYAN-MAGENTA-YELLOW ISSUED
NO PLATE PRICING DUE TO SCARCITY
EXCHANGE DEADLINE 11/30/2019
B17AB Alex Bregman
B17ABE Andrew Benintendi 20.00 50.00
B17AE Anderson Espinoza 3.00 8.00
B17AF Alex Faedo 4.00 10.00
B17AH Adam Haseley 6.00 15.00
B17AJ Aaron Judge 100.00 250.00
B17AR Anthony Rizzo 20.00 50.00
B17ARO Amed Rosario 8.00 20.00
B17AUB Austin Beck 5.00 12.00
B17AV Alex Verdugo 6.00 15.00
B17BH Bryce Harper 75.00 200.00
B17BM Brendan McKay 10.00 25.00
B17BMC Brendan McKay 10.00 25.00
B17BP Brett Phillips 4.00 10.00
B17BR Blake Rutherford 5.00 12.00
B17CA Christian Arroyo 5.00 12.00
B17CAD Chance Adams 5.00 12.00
B17CB Cody Bellinger
B17CC Carlos Correa 20.00 50.00
B17CF Clint Frazier 8.00 20.00
B17CR Cole Ragans 3.00 8.00
B17CSA Chris Sale 8.00 20.00
B17CSC Clarke Schmidt 8.00 20.00
B17CSE Christopher Seise 4.00 10.00
B17DC Dylan Cozens 3.00 8.00
B17DD Dane Dunning 3.00 8.00
B17DE Drew Ellis 4.00 10.00
B17DF Dustin Fowler 4.00 10.00
B17DF Derek Fisher 5.00 12.00
B17DH D.L. Hall 4.00 10.00
B17DM Daniel Murphy 4.00 10.00
B17DPE David Peterson 4.00 10.00
B17DS Dansby Swanson 15.00 40.00
B17EW Evan White 8.00 20.00
B17FM Francisco Mejia 5.00 12.00
B17GT Gleyber Torres 40.00 100.00
B17HR Heliot Ramos 5.00 12.00
B17JA Jo Adell 50.00 120.00
B17JB Jorge Bonifacio 3.00 8.00
B17JBU Jake Burger 5.00 12.00
B17JC J.P. Crawford 6.00 12.00
B17JD Jeter Downs 4.00 10.00
B17JDU Jon Duplantier 4.00 10.00
B17JG Jason Groome 5.00 12.00
B17JMO Jordan Montgomery 5.00 12.00
B17JS Justus Sheffield 5.00 12.00
B17KB Kris Bryant 60.00 150.00
B17KH Keston Hiura 8.00 20.00
B17KM Kevin Maitan 8.00 20.00
B17KME Kevin Merrell 4.00 10.00
B17KW Kyle Wright 6.00 15.00
B17LA Lazarito Armenteros 5.00 12.00
B17LB Lewis Brinson 5.00 12.00
B17LE Lucas Erceg 4.00 10.00
B17LGJ Lourdes Gurriel Jr. 4.00 10.00
B17LW Logan Warmoth 4.00 10.00
B17MG MacKenzie Gore 15.00 40.00
B17MK Mitch Keller 5.00 12.00
B17MKO Michael Kopech 5.00 12.00
B17MMA Manny Machado
B17MS Matt Sauer 4.00 10.00
B17MT Mike Trout 250.00 600.00
B17MW Mitchell White 3.00 8.00
B17NPE Nate Pearson 20.00 50.00
B17NS Noah Syndergaard 10.00 25.00
B17NSE Nick Senzel 10.00 25.00
B17PC P.J. Conlon 3.00 8.00
B17PS Pavin Smith 4.00 10.00
B17QH Quentin Holmes 3.00 8.00
B17RA Ronald Acuna 100.00 250.00
B17RL Royce Lewis 15.00 40.00
B17RM Ryan Mountcastle 5.00 12.00
B17RR Roniel Raudes 3.00 8.00
B17SB Shane Baz 3.00 8.00
B17TC Trevor Clifton 3.00 8.00
B17TH Tanner Houck 12.00 30.00
B17TL Tristen Lutz 4.00 10.00
B17TM Triston McKenzie 12.00 30.00
B17TR Trevor Rogers 8.00 20.00
B17TTR Taylor Trammell 6.00 15.00
B17YG Yulieski Gurriel 6.00 15.00
B17YM Yoan Moncada

2017 Bowman's Best Best of '17 Autographs Atomic Refractors

*ATOMIC REF: 1X TO 2.5X BASIC
STATED PRINT RUN 25 SER.#'d SETS
EXCHANGE DEADLINE 11/30/2019
B17AB Alex Bregman 50.00 120.00
B17ABE Andrew Benintendi 60.00 150.00
B17AF Alex Faedo 15.00 40.00
B17AJ Aaron Judge 200.00 500.00
B17AR Anthony Rizzo 40.00 100.00
B17ARO Amed Rosario 25.00 60.00
B17BH Bryce Harper 125.00 300.00
B17BM Brendan McKay 50.00 120.00
B17BMC Brendan McKay 50.00 120.00
B17BR Blake Rutherford 20.00 50.00
B17CB Cody Bellinger 125.00 300.00
B17CC Carlos Correa 50.00 120.00
B17CSA Chris Sale 20.00 50.00
B17GT Gleyber Torres 100.00 250.00
B17JBU Jake Burger 25.00 60.00
B17JD Jeter Downs 30.00 80.00
B17KB Kris Bryant 125.00 300.00
B17LA Lazarito Armenteros 25.00 60.00
B17MK Mitch Keller 25.00 60.00
B17MMA Manny Machado 40.00 100.00
B17MT Mike Trout 250.00 600.00
B17RL Royce Lewis 50.00 120.00
B17TL Tristen Lutz 30.00 80.00
B17TM Triston McKenzie 30.00 80.00
B17TTR Taylor Trammell 30.00 80.00
B17YG Yulieski Gurriel 12.00 30.00
B17YM Yoan Moncada 40.00 100.00

2017 Bowman's Best Best of '17 Autographs Gold Refractors

*GOLD REF: .75X TO 2X BASIC
STATED PRINT RUN 50 SER.#'d SETS
EXCHANGE DEADLINE 11/30/2019
B17AB Alex Bregman 40.00 100.00
B17ABE Andrew Benintendi 40.00 100.00
B17AF Alex Faedo 12.00 30.00
B17AJ Aaron Judge 150.00 400.00
B17AR Anthony Rizzo 30.00 80.00
B17ARO Amed Rosario 15.00 40.00
B17BH Bryce Harper 100.00 250.00
B17BM Brendan McKay 40.00 100.00
B17BMC Brendan McKay 40.00 100.00
B17BR Blake Rutherford 15.00 40.00
B17CB Cody Bellinger 100.00 250.00
B17CC Carlos Correa 40.00 100.00
B17CSA Chris Sale 15.00 40.00
B17GT Gleyber Torres 75.00 200.00
B17JBU Jake Burger 20.00 50.00
B17JD Jeter Downs 25.00 60.00
B17KB Kris Bryant 100.00 250.00
B17LA Lazarito Armenteros 20.00 50.00
B17MK Mitch Keller 20.00 50.00
B17MMA Manny Machado 30.00 80.00
B17MT Mike Trout 200.00 500.00
B17RL Royce Lewis 40.00 100.00
B17TL Tristen Lutz 25.00 60.00
B17TM Triston McKenzie 25.00 60.00
B17TTR Taylor Trammell 25.00 60.00
B17YG Yulieski Gurriel 10.00 25.00
B17YM Yoan Moncada 30.00 80.00

2017 Bowman's Best Best of '17 Autographs Green Refractors

*GREEN REF: .6X TO 1.5X BASIC
STATED PRINT RUN 99 SER.#'d SETS
EXCHANGE DEADLINE 11/30/2019
B17AB Alex Bregman 30.00 80.00
B17ABE Andrew Benintendi 30.00 80.00
B17AJ Aaron Judge 125.00 300.00
B17AR Anthony Rizzo 25.00 60.00
B17BM Brendan McKay 30.00 80.00
B17BMC Brendan McKay 30.00 80.00
B17BR Blake Rutherford 12.00 30.00
B17CB Cody Bellinger 75.00 200.00
B17CC Carlos Correa 30.00 80.00
B17GT Gleyber Torres 60.00 150.00
B17JBU Jake Burger 12.00 30.00
B17JD Jeter Downs 20.00 50.00
B17KB Kris Bryant 75.00 200.00
B17LA Lazarito Armenteros 12.00 30.00
B17MMA Manny Machado 25.00 60.00
B17YG Yulieski Gurriel 8.00 20.00
B17YM Yoan Moncada 25.00 60.00

2017 Bowman's Best Best of '17 Autographs Refractors

*REFRACTORS: .5X TO 1.2X BASIC
EXCHANGE DEADLINE 11/30/2019

2017 Bowman's Best Dual Autographs

STATED PRINT RUN 25 SER.#'d SETS
EXCHANGE DEADLINE 11/30/2019
BDACB Correa/Bregman 75.00 200.00
BDAGG Gurriel/Gurriel 75.00 200.00
BDAJF Judge/Frazier 300.00 500.00
BDASG Sale/Groome 30.00 80.00
BDASM Swanton/Maitan 25.00 60.00
BDATB Trout/Bryant 600.00 800.00

2017 Bowman's Best Mirror Image

COMPLETE SET (20) 12.00 30.00
MI1 Stanton/Judge 4.00 10.00
MI2 Bellinger/Votto 5.00 12.00
MI3 Benintendi/Yelich 1.00 2.50
MI4 Odor/Moncada 1.00 2.50
MI5 Faria/Fulmer .30 .75
MI6 Pollock/Robles .75 2.00
MI7 Devers/Moustakas .60 1.50
MI8 Scherzer/Kopech .60 1.50
MI9 Sano/Maitan .75 2.00
MI10 Rosario/Lindor .50 1.25
MI11 McKay/Rizzo 1.25 3.00
MI12 McKay/Kershaw 1.25 3.00
MI13 Gore/Sale 2.00 5.00
MI14 Wright/Kluber 1.00 2.50
MI15 Beck/Trout 2.50 6.00
MI16 Hosmer/Smith 1.00 2.50
MI17 Brantley/Haseley .60 1.50
MI18 Hiura/Pedroia 1.50 4.00
MI19 Adell/Betts 2.50 6.00
MI20 Correa/Lewis 2.50 6.00

2017 Bowman's Best Mirror Image Atomic Refractors

*ATOMIC REF: .75X TO 2X BASIC
MI1 Stanton/Judge 12.00 30.00

2017 Bowman's Best Mirror Image Gold Refractors

*GOLD REF: 1.2X TO 3X BASIC
STATED PRINT RUN 50 SER.#'d SETS
MI1 Stanton/Judge 30.00 80.00

2017 Bowman's Best Monochrome Autographs

PRINT RUNS B/WN 30-150 COPIES PER
EXCHANGE DEADLINE 11/30/2019
MAAB Austin Beck/125 10.00 25.00
MAABE Andrew Benintendi EXCH 20.00 50.00
MAABR Alex Bregman/100 15.00 40.00
MAAH Adam Haseley/125 8.00 20.00
MAAJ Aaron Judge/125 60.00 150.00
MAAV Alex Verdugo/125 6.00 15.00
MABM Brendan McKay/125 20.00 50.00
MABMC Brendan McKay/125 20.00 50.00
MABR Blake Rutherford/125 12.00 30.00
MACB Cody Bellinger/100 40.00 100.00
MACF Clint Frazier/125 20.00 50.00
MACS Clarke Schmidt/125 6.00 15.00
MADF Dustin Fowler/125 6.00 15.00
MADH D.L. Hall/150 8.00 20.00
MAEW Evan White/125 6.00 15.00
MAGT Gleyber Torres/125 40.00 100.00
MAJA Jo Adell/125 40.00 100.00
MAJB Jake Burger/125 8.00 20.00
MAJG Jason Groome/125 10.00 25.00
MAKB Kris Bryant/50 75.00 200.00
MAKH Keston Hiura/125 20.00 50.00
MAKM Kevin Maitan/125 12.00 30.00
MAKW Kyle Wright/125 10.00 25.00
MALB Lewis Brinson/125 10.00 25.00
MALG Lourdes Gurriel Jr./125 6.00 15.00
MAMG MacKenzie Gore/125 15.00 40.00
MAMK Michael Kopech/125 8.00 20.00
MAMM Mickey Moniak/100 12.00 30.00
MAMT Mike Trout/30 150.00 400.00
MANS Nick Senzel/100 12.00 30.00
MAPS Pavin Smith/125 5.00 12.00
MARL Royce Lewis/100 25.00 60.00
MASB Shane Baz/125 10.00 25.00
MATR Trevor Rogers/125 6.00 15.00

2017 Bowman's Best Monochrome Autographs Atomic Refractors

*ATOMIC REF: .6X TO 1.5X BASE
STATED PRINT RUN 25 SER.#'d SETS
EXCHANGE DEADLINE 11/30/2019
MAAB Austin Beck 30.00 80.00
MAAH Adam Haseley 25.00 60.00
MAAJ Aaron Judge 125.00 300.00
MAKM Kevin Maitan 30.00 80.00
MAMT Mike Trout 150.00 400.00

2017 Bowman's Best Monochrome Autographs Gold Refractors

*GOLD REF: .5X TO 1.2X BASE
STATED PRINT RUN 50 SER.#'d SETS
EXCHANGE DEADLINE 11/30/2019
MAAB Austin Beck 20.00 50.00
MAAH Adam Haseley 20.00 50.00
MAAJ Aaron Judge 100.00 250.00
MAKM Kevin Maitan 20.00 50.00

2017 Bowman's Best Raking Rookies

COMPLETE SET (10) 12.00 30.00
*ATOMIC REF: .75X TO 2X BASIC
*GOLD REF/50: 1.5X TO 4X BASIC
RRAB Alex Bregman 2.00 5.00
RRABE Andrew Benintendi 1.50 4.00
RRAJ Aaron Judge 6.00 15.00
RRBZ Bradley Zimmer .60 1.50
RRCB Cody Bellinger 8.00 20.00
RRFB Franklin Barreto .50 1.25
RRHR Hunter Renfroe .60 1.50
RRIH Ian Happ 1.00 2.50
RRRH Ryon Healy .60 1.50
RRYG Yulieski Gurriel .75 2.00

2017 Bowman's Best Raking Rookies Autographs

STATED PRINT RUN 99 SER.#'d SETS
EXCHANGE DEADLINE 11/30/2019
RRABE Andrew Benintendi EXCH 50.00 120.00
RRAJ Aaron Judge 100.00 250.00
RRBZ Bradley Zimmer 10.00 25.00
RRCB Cody Bellinger EXCH 40.00 100.00
RRHR Hunter Renfroe 8.00 20.00
RRIH Ian Happ 10.00 25.00
RRRH Ryon Healy 5.00 12.00
RRYG Yulieski Gurriel 6.00 15.00

2017 Bowman's Best Top Prospects

COMPLETE SET (35) 10.00 25.00
*REF: .5X TO 1.2X BASIC
*ATOMIC: 1X TO 2.5X BASIC
*PURPLE/250: 1X TO 2.5X BASIC
*BLUE/150: 1X TO 2.5X BASIC
*GREEN/99: 1.2X TO 3X BASIC
TP1 Amed Rosario .40 1.00
TP2 Austin Meadows .40 1.00
TP3 Mickey Moniak .60 1.50
TP4 Jo Adell 2.00 5.00
TP5 Alex Faedo .40 1.00
TP6 Austin Beck 1.00 2.50
TP7 Clint Frazier .50 1.25
TP8 Victor Robles .60 1.50
TP9 Michael Kopech .50 1.25
TP10 Ronald Acuna 5.00 12.00
TP11 Kyle Wright .75 2.00
TP12 Rafael Devers .50 1.25
TP13 Kevin Maitan .60 1.50
TP14 Jay Groome .50 1.25
TP15 Adam Haseley .50 1.25
TP16 Gleyber Torres 4.00 10.00
TP17 Shane Baz .40 1.00
TP18 Brendan Rodgers .30 .75
TP19 MacKenzie Gore 1.50 4.00
TP20 Brendan McKay 1.00 2.50
TP21 Brendan McKay 1.00 2.50
TP22 Eloy Jimenez 1.00 2.50
TP23 Kyle Tucker .50 1.25
TP24 Clarke Schmidt .40 1.00
TP25 Keston Hiura 1.25 3.00
TP26 Brent Honeywell .30 .75
TP27 Nick Senzel .75 2.00
TP28 Pavin Smith .75 2.00
TP29 Blake Rutherford .40 1.00
TP30 Jake Burger .50 1.25
TP31 Triston McKenzie .25 .60
TP32 Willy Adames .30 .75
TP33 Vladimir Guerrero Jr. 3.00 8.00
TP34 Evan White .40 1.00
TP35 Royce Lewis 2.00 5.00

2017 Bowman's Best Top Prospects Gold Refractors

*GOLD REF: 2X TO 5X BASIC
STATED PRINT RUN 50 SER.#'d SETS

2017 Bowman's Best Top Prospects Orange Refractors

*ORANGE REF: 2.5X TO 6X BASIC
STATED PRINT RUN 25 SER.#'d SETS

2018 Bowman's Best

1 Shohei Ohtani RC 2.50 6.00
2 Walker Buehler RC 2.00 5.00
3 George Springer .30 .75
4 Rafael Devers RC 1.25 3.00
5 Bryce Harper .60 1.50
6 Andrew McCutchen .40 1.00
7 Chris Sale .40 1.00
8 Cody Bellinger .75 2.00
9 Austin Meadows RC .60 1.50
10 Manny Machado .40 1.00
11 Carlos Correa .40 1.00
12 Fernando Romero RC .40 1.00
13 Carlos Carrasco .25 .60
14 Craig Kimbrel .30 .75
15 Justin Verlander .40 1.00
16 Khris Davis .40 1.00
17 Mookie Betts .60 1.50
18 Francisco Lindor .40 1.00
19 Jose Ramirez .30 .75
20 Brian Dozier .30 .75
21 Harrison Bader RC .60 1.50
22 Andrew Benintendi .40 1.00
23 Dustin Fowler RC .40 1.00
24 Joey Votto .40 1.00
25 Aaron Judge 1.00 2.50
26 Nick Williams RC .50 1.25
27 Jose Altuve .30 .75
28 Josh Donaldson .30 .75
29 Juan Soto RC 10.00 25.00
30 Amed Rosario RC .50 1.25
31 Luis Severino .30 .75
32 Didi Gregorius .30 .75
33 Alex Verdugo RC .60 1.50
34 Jose Abreu .40 1.00
35 Trea Turner .30 .75
36 Rhys Hoskins RC 1.50 4.00
37 Victor Robles RC 1.00 2.50
38 J.P. Crawford RC .40 1.00
39 Justin Upton .30 .75
40 Mike Soroka RC 1.25 3.00
41 Jack Flaherty RC .60 1.50
42 Jacob deGrom .40 1.00
43 Eddie Rosario .40 1.00
44 Jean Segura .25 .60
45 Aroldis Chapman .40 1.00
46 Clint Frazier RC .75 2.00
47 Charlie Blackmon .40 1.00
48 J.D. Martinez .40 1.00
49 Miguel Andujar RC 1.50 4.00
50 Gleyber Torres RC 5.00 12.00
51 Ronald Acuna Jr. RC 8.00 20.00
52 Anthony Rizzo .60 1.50
53 Freddie Freeman .50 1.25
54 Ozzie Albies RC 1.25 3.00
55 Willy Adames RC .50 1.25
56 Francisco Mejia RC .50 1.25
57 Nolan Arenado .50 1.25
58 Giancarlo Stanton .40 1.00
59 Clayton Kershaw .75 2.00
60 Scott Kingery RC .60 1.50
61 Corey Kluber .30 .75
62 Brian Anderson RC .50 1.25
63 Max Scherzer .40 1.00
64 Paul Goldschmidt .40 1.00
65 Mike Trout 2.00 5.00
66 Javier Baez .50 1.25
67 Christian Yelich .50 1.25
68 Whit Merrifield .40 1.00
69 Blake Snell .30 .75
70 Noah Syndergaard .30 .75

2018 Bowman's Best Atomic Refractors
*ATOMIC REF: 1X TO 2.5X BASIC
*ATOMIC REF RC: .6X TO 1.5X BASIC RC
STATED ODDS 1:12 HOBBY

2018 Bowman's Best Blue Refractors
*BLUE REF: 2.5X TO 6X BASIC
*BLUE REF RC: 1.5X TO 4X BASIC RC
STATED ODDS 1:33 HOBBY
STATED PRINT RUN 150 SER.#'d SETS

2018 Bowman's Best Gold Refractors
*GOLD REF: 5X TO 12X BASIC
*GOLD REF RC: 3X TO 8X BASIC RC
STATED ODDS 1:99 HOBBY
STATED PRINT RUN 50 SER.#'d SETS

2018 Bowman's Best Green Refractors
*GRN REF: 2.5X TO 6X BASIC
*GRN REF RC: 1.5X TO 4X BASIC RC
STATED ODDS 1:50 HOBBY
STATED PRINT RUN 99 SER.#'d SETS

2018 Bowman's Best Orange Refractors
*ORANGE REF: 6X TO 15X BASIC
*ORANGE REF RC: 4X TO 10X BASIC RC
STATED ODDS 1:197 HOBBY
STATED PRINT RUN 25 SER.#'d SETS

2018 Bowman's Best Purple Refractors
*PURPLE REF: 1.2X TO 3X BASIC
*PURPLE REF RC: .75X TO 2X BASIC RC
STATED ODDS 1:20 HOBBY
STATED PRINT RUN 250 SER.#'d SETS

2018 Bowman's Best Refractors
*REF: .75X TO 2X BASIC
*REF RC: .5X TO 1.2X BASIC RC
RANDOM INSERTS IN PACKS

2018 Bowman's Best '98 Best Performers Refractors
STATED ODDS 1:3 HOBBY
*ATOMIC: X TO X BASIC
*GOLD REF/50: X TO X BASIC
98BPAB Alec Bohm 1.25 3.00
98BPAM Austin Meadows .40 1.00
98BPAR Anthony Rizzo .60 1.50
98BPARO Alex Rodriguez .50 1.25
98BPBM Brendan McKay .40 1.00
98BPBS Brady Singer .50 1.25
98BPBT Brice Turang .75 2.00
98BPCM Casey Mize 2.00 5.00
98BPCSC Connor Scott .30 .75
98BPDG Didi Gregorius .30 .75
98BPEF Estevan Florial .40 1.00
98BPFL Francisco Lindor .40 1.00
98BPGM Greg Maddux .50 1.25
98BPGR Grayson Rodriguez .50 1.25
98BPGT Gleyber Torres 2.50 6.00
98BPHG Hunter Greene .75 2.00
98BPJA Jordyn Adams 1.50 4.00
98BPJAD Jo Adell .75 2.00
98BPJC Jose Canseco .30 .75
98BPJG Jordan Groshans .75 2.00
98BPJI Jonathan India .40 1.00
98BPJK Jarred Kelenic 2.50 6.00
98BPJS Juan Soto 5.00 12.00
98BPKB Kris Bryant .50 1.25
98BPML Matthew Liberatore .30 .75
98BPMM Mark McGwire .60 1.50
98BPMT Mike Trout 2.00 5.00
98BPNM Nick Madrigal 1.50 4.00
98BPNN Noah Naylor .40 1.00
98BPOA Ozzie Albies .75 2.00
98BPPM Pedro Martinez .30 .75
98BPRAJ Ronald Acuna Jr. 5.00 12.00
98BPRC Roger Clemens .50 1.25
98BPRH Rhys Hoskins 1.00 2.50
98BPRJ Randy Johnson .40 1.00
98BPRL Royce Lewis 1.00 2.50
98BPRW Ryan Weathers .30 .75
98BPSO Shohei Ohtani 1.50 4.00
98BPTS Travis Swaggerty .75 2.00
98BPWA Willy Adames .30 .75

2018 Bowman's Best '98 Best Performers Autographs
STATED ODDS 1:121 HOBBY
PRINT RUNS B/WN 10-150 COPIES PER
NO PRICING ON QTY 10
EXCHANGE DEADLINE 11/30/2020
*GOLD/50: .5X TO 1.2X BASIC
*ATOMIC/25: .6X TO 1.5X BASIC
98BPAAB Alec Bohm/100 10.00 25.00
98BPAAM Austin Meadows/100 8.00 20.00
98BPAAT Alek Thomas/150 8.00 20.00
98BPABM Brendan McKay/100 6.00 15.00
98BPABS Brady Singer/150 8.00 20.00
98BPACM Casey Mize/75 15.00 40.00
98BPACP Cristian Pache/150 12.00 30.00
98BPACSC Connor Scott/150 4.00 10.00
98BPACW Cole Winn/150 6.00 15.00
98BPACWE Colton Welker/150 4.00 10.00
98BPAEF Estevan Florial/150 15.00 40.00
98BPAGR Grayson Rodriguez/150 8.00 20.00
98BPAHG Hunter Greene/100 20.00 50.00
98BPAJA Jordyn Adams/150 25.00 60.00
98BPAJG Jordan Groshans/150 12.00 30.00
98BPAJI Jonathan India/100 20.00 50.00
98BPAJK Jarred Kelenic/100 20.00 50.00
98BPAJS Juan Soto/100 200.00 500.00
98BPAKB Kris Bryant/50 50.00 120.00
98BPAKR Keibert Ruiz/100 10.00 25.00
98BPALG Logan Gilbert/150 6.00 15.00
98BPALR Luis Robert/150 60.00 150.00
98BPAML Matthew Liberatore/150 5.00 12.00
98BPAMT Mike Trout/30 300.00 500.00
98BPANG Nolan Gorman/150 25.00 60.00
98BPANM Nick Madrigal/100 25.00 60.00
98BPANN Noah Naylor/150 8.00 20.00
98BPAOA Ozzie Albies/100 15.00 40.00
98BPARA Ronald Acuna Jr./50 100.00 250.00
98BPARL Royce Lewis/75 15.00 40.00
98BPARW Ryan Weathers/150 5.00 12.00
98BPASK Scott Kingery/100 6.00 15.00
98BPATC Triston Casas/150 10.00 25.00
98BPATS Travis Swaggerty/150 10.00 25.00

2018 Bowman's Best Best of '18 Autographs
PRINTING PLATE ODDS 1:1442 HOBBY
PLATE PRINT RUN 1 SET PER COLOR
BLACK-CYAN-MAGENTA-YELLOW ISSUED
NO PLATE PRICING DUE TO SCARCITY
EXCHANGE DEADLINE 11/30/2020
B18AA Adbert Alzolay 3.00 8.00
B18AAL Aramis Ademan 4.00 10.00
B18ABO Alec Bohm 25.00 60.00
B18AG Andres Gimenez 3.00 8.00
B18AJ Aaron Judge 60.00 150.00
B18AM Austin Meadows 12.00 30.00
B18AR Anthony Rizzo 20.00 50.00
B18ARO Amed Rosario 3.00 8.00
B18AS Anthony Seigler 4.00 10.00
B18AT Alek Thomas 6.00 15.00
B18AV Alex Verdugo 6.00 15.00
B18BG Brusdar Graterol 3.00 8.00
B18BM Brendan McKay 5.00 12.00
B18BMA Brandon Marsh 3.00 8.00
B18BS Brady Singer 6.00 15.00
B18BSN Blake Snell 3.00 8.00
B18BT Brice Turang 5.00 12.00
B18CK Carter Kieboom 8.00 20.00
B18CM Casey Mize 20.00 50.00
B18CP Cristian Pache 10.00 25.00
B18CSC Connor Scott 3.00 8.00
B18CV Christian Villanueva 2.50 6.00
B18CW Colton Welker 2.50 6.00
B18CWI Cole Winn 4.00 10.00
B18DL Daniel Lynch 3.00 8.00
B18EF Estevan Florial 12.00 30.00
B18EH Ethan Hankins 5.00 12.00
B18EW Evan White 6.00 15.00
B18FP Franklin Perez 2.50 6.00
B18FR Fernando Romero 2.50 6.00
B18FT Fernando Tatis Jr. 100.00 250.00
B18GR Grayson Rodriguez 5.00 12.00
B18HG Hunter Greene 12.00 30.00
B18HR Heliot Ramos 5.00 12.00
B18JA Jose Altuve 12.00 30.00
B18JAD Jo Adell 20.00 50.00
B18JAD Jordyn Adams 4.00 10.00
B18JALEI Jose Albertos 2.50 6.00
B18JD Jeter Downs 4.00 10.00
B18JG Jordan Groshans 8.00 20.00
B18JH Jordan Hicks 6.00 15.00
B18JI Jonathan India 8.00 20.00
B18JK Jeren Kendall 3.00 8.00
B18JKE Jarred Kelenic 25.00 60.00
B18JL Jesus Luzardo 4.00 10.00
B18JS Jose Siri 2.50 6.00
B18JSO Juan Soto 75.00 200.00
B18JST Josh Stowers 3.00 8.00
B18JW Justin Williams 2.50 6.00
B18KB Kris Bryant 50.00 120.00
B18KD Khris Davis 4.00 10.00
B18KH Keston Hiura 6.00 15.00
B18KK Kevin Kramer 2.50 6.00
B18KR Keibert Ruiz 15.00 40.00
B18KRO Josh Breaux 3.00 8.00
B18LE Luis Escobar 2.50 6.00
B18LG Logan Gilbert 4.00 10.00
B18LR Luis Robert 75.00 200.00
B18LU Luis Urias 15.00
B18MD Mason Denaburg 3.00 8.00
B18MG MacKenzie Gore 6.00 15.00
B18ML Matthew Liberatore 6.00 15.00
B18MO Matt Olson 2.50 6.00
B18MT Mike Trout 150.00 400.00
B18NG Nolan Gorman 15.00 40.00
B18NH Nico Hoerner 8.00 20.00
B18NM Nick Madrigal 12.00 30.00
B18NN Noah Naylor 4.00 10.00
B18NSC Nick Schnell 3.00 8.00
B18OA Ozzie Albies 12.00 30.00
B18PD Paul DeJong 4.00 10.00
B18PS Pavin Smith 2.50 6.00
B18RA Ronald Acuna Jr. 75.00 200.00
B18RAD Riley Adams 3.00 8.00
B18RL Royce Lewis 12.00 30.00
B18RR Ryan Rolison 3.00 8.00
B18RW Ryan Weathers 3.00 8.00
B18SA Sandy Alcantara 2.50 6.00
B18SK Scott Kingery 4.00 10.00
B18SM Shane McClanahan 4.00 10.00
B18SO Shohei Ohtani 150.00 400.00
B18TC Triston Casas 12.00 30.00
B18TL Trevor Larnach 8.00 20.00
B18TST Trevor Stephan 2.50 6.00
B18VR Victor Robles 12.00 30.00
B18YA Yordan Alvarez 75.00 200.00

2018 Bowman's Best Best of '18 Autographs Atomic Refractors
*ATOMIC REF: 1X TO 2.5X BASIC
STATED ODDS 1:227 HOBBY
STATED PRINT RUN 25 SER.#'d SETS
EXCHANGE DEADLINE 11/30/2019
B18ABO Alec Bohm 60.00 150.00
B18CF Clint Frazier 20.00 50.00
B18MT Mike Trout 250.00 500.00
B18NG Nolan Gorman 125.00 300.00
B18SO Shohei Ohtani 400.00 800.00

2018 Bowman's Best Best of '18 Autographs Gold Refractors
*GOLD REF: .75X TO 2X BASIC
STATED ODDS 1:115 HOBBY
STATED PRINT RUN 50 SER.#'d SETS
EXCHANGE DEADLINE 11/30/2020
B18CF Clint Frazier 15.00 40.00
B18MT Mike Trout 200.00 500.00
B18NG Nolan Gorman 60.00 150.00
B18SO Shohei Ohtani 300.00 600.00

2018 Bowman's Best Best of '18 Autographs Green Refractors
*GREEN REF: .6X TO 1.5X BASIC
STATED ODDS 1:61 HOBBY
STATED PRINT RUN 99 SER.#'d SETS
EXCHANGE DEADLINE 11/30/2020
B18CF Clint Frazier 12.00 30.00
B18NG Nolan Gorman 50.00 120.00
B18SO Shohei Ohtani 200.00 500.00

2018 Bowman's Best Best of '18 Autographs Refractors
*REFRACTORS: .5X TO 1.2X BASIC
STATED ODDS 1:20 HOBBY
EXCHANGE DEADLINE 11/30/2020
B18CF Clint Frazier 10.00 25.00

2018 Bowman's Best Dual Autographs
STATED ODDS 1:2398 HOBBY
STATED PRINT RUN 25 SER.#'d SETS
EXCHANGE DEADLINE 11/30/2020
DAAA Albertos/Alzolay 40.00 100.00
DAAAL Acuna/Albies 200.00 400.00
DAAM Marsh/Adell 60.00 150.00
DABR Rizzo/Bryant EXCH 125.00 300.00
DAGM McKay/Greene 60.00 150.00
DAVR Ruiz/Verdugo EXCH 30.00 80.00

2018 Bowman's Best Early Indications Refractors
STATED ODDS 1:4 HOBBY
*ATOMIC: .75X TO 2X BASIC
*GOLD REF/50: 1.5X TO 4X BASIC
EI1 Fernando Tatis Jr. 2.00 5.00
EI2 Keston Hiura .60 1.50
EI3 Luis Robert 5.00 12.00
EI4 Brandon Marsh .30 .75
EI5 Cristian Pache 1.25 3.00
EI6 Jose Siri .25 .60
EI7 Brendan McKay .40 1.00
EI8 Hunter Greene .75 2.00
EI9 Franklin Perez .25 .60
EI10 Brent Rooker .30 .75
EI11 Jeter Downs .40 1.00
EI12 Kevin Kramer .25 .60
EI13 Estevan Florial .40 1.00
EI14 MacKenzie Gore .50 1.25
EI15 Jeren Kendall .30 .75
EI16 Pavin Smith .25 .60
EI17 Corbin Burnes .40 1.00
EI18 Jesus Luzardo .40 1.00
EI19 Carter Kieboom .40 1.00
EI20 Keibert Ruiz .75 2.00
EI21 Jo Adell .75 2.00
EI22 Jose Albertos .25 .60
EI23 Justin Williams .25 .60
EI24 Heliot Ramos .40 1.00
EI25 Yordan Alvarez 2.00 5.00
EI26 Colton Welker .25 .60
EI27 Luis Urias .50 1.25
EI28 Adbert Alzolay .30 .75
EI29 Michel Baez .25 .60
EI30 Royce Lewis 1.00 2.50

2018 Bowman's Best Early Indications Autographs
STATED ODDS 1:193 HOBBY
STATED PRINT RUN 100 SER.#'d SETS
EXCHANGE DEADLINE 11/30/2020
*GOLD/50: .5X TO 1.2X BASIC
*ATOMIC/25: .6X TO 1.5X BASIC
EIAAA Adbert Alzolay 5.00 12.00
EIABM Brendan McKay 6.00 15.00
EIACK Carter Kieboom 12.00 30.00
EIACP Cristian Pache 12.00 30.00
EIACW Colton Welker 4.00 10.00
EIAEF Estevan Florial 12.00 30.00
EIAFP Franklin Perez 4.00 10.00
EIAHG Hunter Greene 20.00 50.00
EIAHR Heliot Ramos 6.00 15.00
EIAJA Jo Adell 25.00 60.00
EIAJAL Jose Albertos 4.00 10.00
EIAJK Jeren Kendall 5.00 12.00
EIAJL Jesus Luzardo 10.00 25.00
EIAJS Jose Siri 4.00 10.00
EIAJW Justin Williams 4.00 10.00
EIAKH Keston Hiura 10.00 25.00
EIAKR Keibert Ruiz 10.00 25.00
EIALR Luis Robert 25.00 60.00
EIALU Luis Urias 10.00 25.00
EIAMB Michel Baez 4.00 10.00
EIAMG MacKenzie Gore 8.00 20.00
EIAPS Pavin Smith 4.00 10.00
EIARL Royce Lewis 15.00 40.00
EIAYA Yordan Alvarez 25.00 60.00

2018 Bowman's Best Neophyte Sensations Refractors
STATED ODDS 1:18 HOBBY
*ATOMIC: .75X TO 2X BASIC
*GOLD REF/50: 2X TO 5X BASIC
NSAR Amed Rosario .50 1.25
NSGT Gleyber Torres 4.00 10.00
NSJS Juan Soto 8.00 20.00
NSMA Miguel Andujar 1.50 4.00
NSOA Ozzie Albies 1.25 3.00
NSRAJ Ronald Acuna Jr. 8.00 20.00
NSRD Rafael Devers 1.25 3.00
NSRH Rhys Hoskins 1.50 4.00
NSSO Shohei Ohtani 2.50 6.00
NSWB Walker Buehler 2.00 5.00

2018 Bowman's Best Neophyte Sensations Autographs
STATED ODDS 1:512 HOBBY
PRINT RUNS B/WN 50-99 COPIES PER
EXCHANGE DEADLINE 11/30/2020
NSAR Amed Rosario/99 4.00 10.00
NSJS Juan Soto/99 125.00 300.00
NSMA Miguel Andujar/99 12.00 30.00
NSOA Ozzie Albies/99 12.00 30.00
NSRAJ Ronald Acuna Jr./99 75.00 200.00
NSRH Rhys Hoskins/99 20.00 50.00
NSSO Shohei Ohtani/50 200.00 400.00
NSWB Walker Buehler/99 25.00 60.00

2018 Bowman's Best Power Producers Refractors
STATED ODDS 1:6 HOBBY
*ATOMIC: .75X TO 2X BASIC
*GOLD REF/50: 2X TO 5X BASIC
PPAB Alec Bohm 2.00 5.00
PPAJ Aaron Judge 1.50 4.00
PPAR Anthony Rizzo 1.00 2.50
PPBH Bryce Harper 1.00 2.50
PPBM Brendan McKay .60 1.50
PPEJ Eloy Jimenez 1.50 4.00
PPGT Gleyber Torres 4.00 10.00
PPJA Jo Adell 1.25 3.00
PPJAL Jose Altuve .50 1.25
PPJK Jarred Kelenic 4.00 10.00
PPJS Juan Soto 8.00 20.00
PPKL Kyle Lewis .75 2.00
PPMT Mike Trout 3.00 8.00
PPNG Nolan Gorman 2.50 6.00
PPRAJ Ronald Acuna Jr. 8.00 20.00
PPRH Rhys Hoskins 1.50 4.00
PPSO Shohei Ohtani 2.50 6.00
PPTC Triston Casas 3.00 8.00
PPTL Trevor Larnach 2.50 6.00
PPVGJ Vladimir Guerrero Jr. 4.00 10.00

2018 Bowman's Best Power Producers Autographs
STATED ODDS 1:487 HOBBY
PRINT RUNS B/WN 15-99 COPIES PER
NO PRICING ON QTY 15
EXCHANGE DEADLINE 11/30/2020
PPAB Alec Bohm/99 12.00 30.00
PPAR Anthony Rizzo/35 40.00 100.00
PPBM Brendan McKay/50 10.00 25.00
PPJA Jo Adell/99 25.00 60.00
PPJAL Jose Altuve/40 20.00 50.00
PPJK Jarred Kelenic/99 15.00 40.00
PPJS Juan Soto/99 125.00 300.00
PPNG Nolan Gorman/99 25.00 60.00
PPRAJ Ronald Acuna Jr./40 100.00 250.00
PPRH Rhys Hoskins/75 20.00 50.00
PPTC Triston Casas/99 12.00 30.00
PPTL Trevor Larnach/99 12.00 30.00

2018 Bowman's Best Top Prospects
*REF: .5X TO 1.2X BASIC
*ATOMIC: 1X TO 2.5X BASIC
*PURPLE/250: 1X TO 2.5X BASIC
*BLUE/150: 1X TO 2.5X BASIC
*GREEN/99: 1.2X TO 3X BASIC
TP1 Vladimir Guerrero Jr. 2.50 6.00
TP2 Mitch Keller .30 .75
TP3 Kyle Tucker .50 1.25
TP4 Michael Kopech .50 1.25
TP5 Austin Riley .75 2.00
TP6 Jo Adell .75 2.00
TP7 Eloy Jimenez 1.00 2.50
TP8 Alec Bohm 1.25 3.00
TP9 Logan Gilbert .40 1.00
TP10 Justus Sheffield .30 .75
TP11 Sixto Sanchez .60 1.50
TP12 Connor Scott .30 .75
TP13 Brendan Rodgers .30 .75
TP14 Jonathan India .40 1.00
TP15 Jarred Kelenic 2.50 6.00
TP16 Nick Madrigal 1.50 4.00
TP17 Matthew Liberatore .30 .75
TP18 Royce Lewis 1.00 2.50
TP19 Taylor Trammell .40 1.00
TP20 Travis Swaggerty .75 2.00
TP21 Grayson Rodriguez .50 1.25
TP22 Alek Thomas .30 .75
TP23 Ryan Weathers .30 .75
TP24 Fernando Tatis Jr. 2.00 5.00
TP25 Brendan McKay .40 1.00
TP26 Jordyn Adams 1.50 4.00
TP27 Jordan Groshans .75 2.00
TP29 Triston Casas 2.00 5.00
TP30 Casey Mize 2.00 5.00

2018 Bowman's Best Top Prospects Gold Refractors
*GOLD REF: 2X TO 5X BASIC
STATED ODDS 1:99 HOBBY
STATED PRINT RUN 50 SER.#'d SETS
TP1 Vladimir Guerrero Jr. 40.00 100.00
TP8 Alec Bohm 25.00 60.00

2018 Bowman's Best Top Prospects Orange Refractors
*ORANGE REF: 2.5X TO 6X BASIC
STATED ODDS 1:197
STATED PRINT RUN 25 SER.#'d SETS
TP1 Vladimir Guerrero Jr. 50.00 120.00
TP8 Alec Bohm 30.00 80.00

2019 Bowman's Best
1 Mike Trout 2.00 5.00
2 Chris Paddack RC .75 2.00
3 Michael Kopech RC .75 2.00
4 Austin Riley RC 2.00 5.00
5 Nolan Arenado .50 1.25
6 Khris Davis .40 1.00
7 Gary Sanchez .40 1.00
8 Mookie Betts .60 1.50
9 Jacob deGrom .40 1.00
10 Yusei Kikuchi RC .60 1.50
11 Hyun-Jin Ryu .30 .75
12 Nick Senzel RC 1.25 3.00
13 Freddie Freeman .50 1.25
14 Clayton Kershaw .75 2.00
15 Charlie Blackmon .40 1.00
16 Gerrit Cole .40 1.00
17 Josh Bell .30 .75
18 Eloy Jimenez RC 1.50 4.00
19 Paul Goldschmidt .40 1.00
20 Chris Sale .40 1.00
21 Carter Kieboom RC .60 1.50
22 Michael Chavis RC .60 1.50
23 Yasiel Puig .40 1.00
24 Brendan Rodgers RC .60 1.50
25 Aaron Judge 1.00 2.50
26 Vladimir Guerrero Jr. RC 4.00 10.00
27 Kyle Wright RC .60 1.50
28 Jon Duplantier RC .40 1.00
29 Jose Abreu .40 1.00
30 Kris Bryant .50 1.25
31 Joey Gallo .30 .75
32 Pete Alonso RC 5.00 12.00
33 Shohei Ohtani .50 1.25
34 Justus Sheffield RC .60 1.50
35 Francisco Lindor .40 1.00
36 Jeff McNeil RC 1.00 2.50
37 Brandon Lowe RC .60 1.50
38 Alex Bregman .40 1.00
39 Xander Bogaerts .40 1.00
40 Max Scherzer .40 1.00
41 Will Smith RC 1.00 2.50
42 Rhys Hoskins .50 1.25
43 Kyle Tucker RC .75 2.00
44 Mitch Keller RC .50 1.25
45 Manny Machado .40 1.00
46 Anthony Rizzo .60 1.50
47 Walker Buehler .50 1.25
48 Trea Turner .30 .75
49 Whit Merrifield .40 1.00
50 Cody Bellinger .75 2.00
51 Justin Verlander .40 1.00
52 Javier Baez .50 1.25
53 Keston Hiura RC 1.25 3.00
54 Ozzie Albies .40 1.00
55 John Means RC .60 1.50
56 Bryce Harper .60 1.50
57 Paul DeJong .40 1.00
58 Fernando Tatis Jr. RC 5.00 12.00
59 Juan Soto 1.25 3.00
60 DJ LeMahieu .40 1.00
61 Ronald Acuna Jr. 2.00 5.00
62 Eugenio Suarez .30 .75
63 Griffin Canning RC .60 1.50
64 Gleyber Torres .75 2.00
65 Yoan Moncada .40 1.00
66 Ramon Laureano RC .75 2.00
67 J.D. Martinez .40 1.00
68 Rowdy Tellez RC .60 1.50
69 Jose Altuve .40 1.00
70 Christian Yelich .50 1.25

2019 Bowman's Best Atomic Refractors
*ATOMIC REF: 1X TO 2.5X BASIC
*ATOMIC REF RC: .6X TO 1.5X BASIC RC
STATED ODDS 1:12 HOBBY
26 Vladimir Guerrero Jr. 8.00 20.00
32 Pete Alonso 10.00 25.00
58 Fernando Tatis Jr. 15.00 40.00

2019 Bowman's Best Blue Refractors
*BLUE REF: 2X TO 5X BASIC
*BLUE REF RC: 1.2X TO 3X BASIC RC
STATED ODDS 1:34 HOBBY
STATED PRINT RUN 150 SER.#'d SETS
26 Vladimir Guerrero Jr. 15.00 40.00
32 Pete Alonso 15.00 40.00
58 Fernando Tatis Jr. 25.00 60.00

2019 Bowman's Best Gold Refractors
*GOLD REF: 4X TO 10X BASIC
*GOLD REF RC: 2.5X TO 6X BASIC RC
STATED ODDS 1:101 HOBBY
STATED PRINT RUN 50 SER.#'d SETS
26 Vladimir Guerrero Jr. 25.00 60.00
32 Pete Alonso 30.00 80.00
58 Fernando Tatis Jr. 50.00 120.00

2019 Bowman's Best Green Refractors
*GRN REF: 2.5X TO 6X BASIC
*GRN REF RC: 1.5X TO 4X BASIC RC
STATED ODDS 1:51 HOBBY
STATED PRINT RUN 99 SER.#'d SETS
26 Vladimir Guerrero Jr. 20.00 50.00
32 Pete Alonso 20.00 50.00
58 Fernando Tatis Jr. 30.00 80.00

2019 Bowman's Best Orange Refractors
*ORNG REF: 6X TO 15X BASIC
*ORNG REF RC: 4X TO 10X BASIC RC
STATED ODDS 1:202 HOBBY
STATED PRINT RUN 25 SER.#'d SETS
18 Eloy Jimenez 25.00 60.00
26 Vladimir Guerrero Jr. 50.00 120.00
32 Pete Alonso 40.00 100.00
53 Keston Hiura 20.00 50.00
58 Fernando Tatis Jr. 60.00 150.00

2019 Bowman's Best Purple Refractors
*PRPL REF: 1.2X TO 3X BASIC
*PRPL REF RC: .8X TO 2X BASIC RC
STATED ODDS 1:21 HOBBY
STATED PRINT RUN 250 SER.#'d SETS
26 Vladimir Guerrero Jr. 10.00 25.00
32 Pete Alonso 12.00 30.00
58 Fernando Tatis Jr. 20.00 50.00

2019 Bowman's Best '99 Franchise Favorites Refractors
STATED ODDS 1:3 HOBBY
*ATOMIC REF: 1.2X TO 3X BASIC
*GOLD REF/50: 3X TO 8X BASIC
99FFAM Alek Manoah .50 1.25
99FFAR Adley Rutschman 1.50 4.00
99FFAV Andrew Vaughn .75 2.00
99FFBB Brett Baty .50 1.25
99FFBR Brendan Rodgers .40 1.00
99FFCB Cavan Biggio 1.25 3.00
99FFCC Corbin Carroll .40 1.00
99FFCJ Chipper Jones .40 1.00
99FFCM Casey Mize .60 1.50
99FFEJ Eloy Jimenez 1.00 2.50
99FFHB Hunter Bishop .75 2.00
99FFJB Joey Bart .75 2.00
99FFJI Jonathan India .30 .75
99FFJJ Josh Jung .75 2.00
99FFJS Juan Soto 1.25 3.00
99FFKC Keoni Cavaco .60 1.50
99FFKH Keston Hiura .75 2.00
99FFMC Michael Chavis .40 1.00
99FFMM Mark McGwire .60 1.50
99FFMT Mike Trout 4.00 10.00
99FFNG Nolan Gorman .75 2.00
99FFNL Nick Lodolo .50 1.25
99FFNS Nick Senzel .75 2.00
99FFPM Pedro Martinez .30 .75
99FFRG Riley Greene 1.00 2.50
99FFSL Shea Langeliers .50 1.25
99FFSO Shohei Ohtani .50 1.25
99FFWF Wander Franco 4.00 10.00
99FFARI Austin Riley 1.25 3.00
99FFAVO Anthony Volpe .75 2.00
99FFBWJ Bobby Witt Jr. 1.00 2.50
99FFCJA CJ Abrams 1.25 3.00
99FFFTJ Fernando Tatis Jr. 8.00 20.00
99FFJBJ J.J. Bleday 1.25 3.00
99FFJPM Julio Pablo Martinez .25 .60
99FFKGJ Ken Griffey Jr. .75 2.00
99FFRAJ Ronald Acuna Jr. 2.00 5.00
99FFVGJ Vladimir Guerrero Jr. 1.50 4.00
99FFVMJ Victor Mesa Jr. .60 1.50
99FFVVM Victor Victor Mesa .50 1.25

2019 Bowman's Best '99 Franchise Favorites Atomic Refractors
*ATOMIC REF: 1.2X TO 3X BASIC
STATED ODDS 1:48 HOBBY
99FFAR Adley Rutschman 8.00 20.00
99FFMT Mike Trout 15.00 40.00
99FFBWJ Bobby Witt Jr. 12.00 30.00
99FFFTJ Fernando Tatis Jr. 40.00 100.00
99FFKGJ Ken Griffey Jr. 12.00 30.00
99FFRAJ Ronald Acuna Jr. 8.00 20.00

2019 Bowman's Best '99 Franchise Favorites Gold Refractors
*GOLD REF/50: 3X TO 8X BASIC
STATED ODDS 1:253 HOBBY
STATED PRINT RUN 50 SER.#'d SETS
99FFAR Adley Rutschman 15.00 40.00
99FFMT Mike Trout 40.00 100.00
99FFBWJ Bobby Witt Jr. 30.00 80.00
99FFFTJ Fernando Tatis Jr. 100.00 250.00
99FFKGJ Ken Griffey Jr. 15.00 40.00
99FFRAJ Ronald Acuna Jr. 20.00 50.00

2019 Bowman's Best '99 Franchise Favorites Autographs
STATED ODDS 1:155 HOBBY
PRINT RUNS B/WN 30-150 COPIES PER
EXCHANGE DEADLINE 11/30/2021
99FFAAM Alek Manoah/150 8.00 20.00
99FFAAR Adley Rutschman/60 75.00 200.00
99FFAAV Andrew Vaughn/50 40.00 100.00
99FFABB Brett Baty/150 15.00 40.00
99FFABR Brendan Rodgers/50 8.00 20.00
99FFABS Braden Shewmake/150 10.00 25.00
99FFACB Cavan Biggio/150 15.00 40.00
99FFACC Corbin Carroll/150 12.00 30.00
99FFACJ Chipper Jones/40 75.00 200.00
99FFACM Casey Mize/60 20.00 50.00
99FFAEJ Eloy Jimenez/60 25.00 60.00
99FFAHB Hunter Bishop 15.00 40.00
99FFAJB Joey Bart/50 40.00 100.00
99FFAJJ Josh Jung/120 12.00 30.00
99FFAKC Keoni Cavaco/150 12.00 30.00
99FFAKH Keston Hiura/75 40.00 100.00
99FFAMC Michael Chavis/75 12.00 30.00
99FFANG Nolan Gorman/150 12.00 30.00
99FFANL Nick Lodolo/120 15.00 40.00
99FFANS Nick Senzel/60 15.00 40.00
99FFAPM Pedro Martinez/30 30.00 80.00
99FFAQP Quinn Priester/150 5.00 12.00
99FFARG Riley Greene/50 30.00 80.00
99FFASL Shea Langeliers/100 15.00 40.00
99FFASO Shohei Ohtani/30 75.00 200.00
99FFATS Travis Swaggerty/150 5.00 12.00
99FFAWF Wander Franco/120 60.00 150.00
99FFAZT Zack Thompson/150 5.00 12.00
99FFAARI Austin Riley/60 25.00 60.00
99FFACJA CJ Abrams/100 25.00 60.00
99FFAFTJ Fernando Tatis Jr./60 125.00 300.00
99FFAJJB J.J. Bleday/50 25.00 60.00
99FFAKGJ Ken Griffey Jr. EXCH
99FFAKHO Kody Hoese/150 10.00 25.00
99FFARAJ Ronald Acuna Jr./50 75.00 200.00
99FFAVGJ Vladimir Guerrero Jr./60 50.00 120.00
99FFAVMJ Victor Mesa Jr./150 8.00 20.00
99FFAVVM Victor Victor Mesa/150 6.00 15.00

2019 Bowman's Best '99 Franchise Favorites Autographs Atomic Refractors
*ATOMIC REF: .8X TO 2X p/r 150
*ATOMIC REF: .6X TO 1.5X p/r 100-120
*ATOMIC REF: .5X TO 1.2X p/r 50-75
*ATOMIC REF: .4X TO 1X p/r 30-40
STATED ODDS 1:565 HOBBY
STATED PRINT RUN 25 SER.#'d SETS
EXCHANGE DEADLINE 11/30/2021
99FFACC Corbin Carroll 40.00 100.00
99FFAEJ Eloy Jimenez 75.00 200.00
99FFAHB Hunter Bishop 40.00 100.00
99FFAJJ Josh Jung 30.00 80.00
99FFANS Nick Senzel 25.00 60.00
99FFAWF Wander Franco 200.00 400.00
99FFAFTJ Fernando Tatis Jr. 250.00 600.00

2019 Bowman's Best '99 Franchise Favorites Autographs Gold Refractors
*GOLD REF: .6X TO 1.5X p/r 150
*GOLD REF: .5X TO 1.2X p/r 100-120
*GOLD REF: .4X TO 1X p/r 50-75
STATED ODDS 1:449 HOBBY
STATED PRINT RUN 50 SER.#'d SETS
EXCHANGE DEADLINE 11/30/2021
99FFAJJ Josh Jung 25.00 60.00
99FFAWF Wander Franco 125.00 300.00

2019 Bowman's Best Best of '19 Autographs
STATED ODDS 1:1 HOBBY
EXCHANGE DEADLINE 11/30/2021
B19AB Alec Bohm 25.00 60.00
B19AK Andrew Knizner 4.00 10.00
B19AM Alek Manoah 5.00 12.00
B19AR Adley Rutschman 60.00 150.00
B19ARI Austin Riley 12.00 30.00
B19AV Andrew Vaughn 20.00 50.00
B19BA Blaze Alexander 2.50 6.00
B19BB Brett Baty 10.00 25.00
B19BD Brock Deatherage 2.50 6.00
B19BH Bryce Harper 75.00 200.00
B19BM Brennan Malone 2.50 6.00
B19BR Brendan Rodgers 5.00 12.00
B19BS Bryson Stott 8.00 20.00
B19BSH Braden Shewmake 5.00 12.00
B19CB Cavan Biggio 15.00 40.00
B19CC Corbin Carroll 6.00 15.00
B19CJA CJ Abrams 15.00 40.00
B19CK Carter Kieboom 10.00 25.00
B19CM Casey Mize 12.00 30.00
B19CMI Cal Mitchell 4.00 10.00
B19DC Diego Cartaya 8.00 20.00
B19DE Daniel Espino 3.00 8.00
B19DG Deivi Garcia 15.00 40.00
B19DK Dean Kremer 6.00 15.00
B19DM Dustin May 15.00 40.00
B19EJ Eloy Jimenez 25.00 60.00
B19FTJ Fernando Tatis Jr. 100.00 250.00
B19GC Genesis Cabrera 4.00 10.00
B19GJ Greg Jones 3.00 8.00
B19GK George Kirby 4.00 10.00
B19GL Grant Lavigne 3.00 8.00
B19HB Hunter Bishop 10.00 25.00
B19HG Hunter Greene 10.00 25.00
B19JA Jose Altuve 15.00 40.00
B19JAD Jordyn Adams 3.00 8.00
B19JB Joey Bart 20.00 50.00
B19JBA Jake Bauers 4.00 10.00
B19JD Jon Duplantier 2.50 6.00
B19JI Jonathan India 3.00 8.00
B19JJ Josh James 4.00 10.00
B19JJB J.J. Bleday 10.00 25.00
B19JJU Josh Jung 12.00 30.00
B19JK Jarred Kelenic 20.00 50.00
B19JR Julio Rodriguez 30.00 80.00
B19JS Justus Sheffield 4.00 10.00
B19KB Kris Bryant 30.00 80.00
B19KC Keoni Cavaco 6.00 15.00
B19KH Kody Hoese 8.00 20.00
B19KHI Keston Hiura 15.00 40.00
B19KS Kyle Schwarber 4.00 10.00
B19LG Luis Gil 4.00 10.00
B19MB Michael Busch 4.00 10.00
B19MCH Michael Chavis 12.00 30.00
B19MKE Mitch Keller 5.00 12.00
B19MT Mike Trout 200.00 500.00

B19MTO Michael Toglia 4.00 10.00
B19MW Matt Wallner 5.00 12.00
B19NG Nolan Gorman 12.00 30.00
B19NH Nico Hoerner 12.00 30.00
B19NL Nate Lowe 3.00 8.00
B19NLO Nick Lodolo 10.00 25.00
B19OM Owen Miller 3.00 8.00
B19PA Pete Alonso 50.00 120.00
B19QP Quinn Priester 4.00 10.00
B19RB Rylan Bannon 3.00 8.00
B19RG Riley Greene 25.00 60.00
B19RH Rhys Hoskins 8.00 20.00
B19RHE Ronaldo Hernandez 2.50 6.00
B19RHI Rece Hinds 5.00 12.00
B19ROH Ryan O'Hearn 2.50 6.00
B19RT Rowdy Tellez 4.00 10.00
B19SB Seth Beer 6.00 15.00
B19SL Shea Langeliers 5.00 12.00
B19SN Shervyen Newton 4.00 10.00
B19SO Shohei Ohtani 100.00 250.00
B19TJS TJ Sikkema 4.00 10.00
B19TON Tyler O'Neill 3.00 8.00
B19TS Travis Swaggerty 4.00 10.00
B19VGJ Vladimir Guerrero Jr. 50.00 120.00
B19VMJ Victor Mesa Jr. 10.00 25.00
B19VVM Victor Victor Mesa 5.00 12.00
B19WA Willians Astudillo 2.50 6.00
B19WF Wander Franco 75.00 200.00
B19WS Will Smith 12.00 30.00
B19WW Will Wilson 4.00 10.00
B19YK Yusei Kikuchi 4.00 10.00
B19ZT Zack Thompson 4.00 10.00

2019 Bowman's Best Best of '19 Autographs Atomic Refractors

*ATOMIC REF: 1X TO 2.5X BASIC
STATED ODDS 1:233 HOBBY
STATED PRINT RUN 25 SER.#'d SETS
EXCHANGE DEADLINE 11/30/2021
B19AV Andrew Vaughn 75.00 200.00
B19BH Bryce Harper 200.00 500.00
B19CB Cavan Biggio 60.00 150.00
B19JJB J.J. Bleday 50.00 120.00
B19JJU Josh Jung 60.00 150.00
B19JR Julio Rodriguez 150.00 400.00
B19MT Mike Trout 400.00 800.00
B19PA Pete Alonso 200.00 500.00
B19RG Riley Greene 75.00 200.00

2019 Bowman's Best Best of '19 Autographs Blue Refractors

*BLUE REF: .5X TO 1.2X BASIC
STATED ODDS 1:43 HOBBY
STATED PRINT RUN 150 SER.#'d SETS
EXCHANGE DEADLINE 11/30/2021
B19AV Andrew Vaughn 40.00 100.00
B19CB Cavan Biggio 30.00 80.00
B19JJB J.J. Bleday 20.00 50.00
B19RG Riley Greene 40.00 100.00

2019 Bowman's Best Best of '19 Autographs Gold Refractors

*GOLD REF: .75X TO 2X BASIC
STATED ODDS 1:117 HOBBY
STATED PRINT RUN 50 SER.#'d SETS
EXCHANGE DEADLINE 11/30/2021
B19AV Andrew Vaughn 60.00 150.00
B19BH Bryce Harper 150.00 400.00
B19CB Cavan Biggio 50.00 120.00
B19JJB J.J. Bleday 30.00 80.00
B19JJU Josh Jung 50.00 120.00
B19MT Mike Trout 250.00 600.00
B19PA Pete Alonso 125.00 300.00
B19RG Riley Greene 60.00 150.00

2019 Bowman's Best Best of '19 Autographs Green Refractors

*GRN REF: .6X TO 1.5X BASIC
STATED ODDS 1:64 HOBBY
STATED PRINT RUN 99 SER.#'d SETS
EXCHANGE DEADLINE 11/30/2021
B19AV Andrew Vaughn 50.00 120.00
B19CB Cavan Biggio 40.00 100.00
B19JJB J.J. Bleday 25.00 60.00
B19RG Riley Greene 50.00 120.00

2019 Bowman's Best Best of '19 Autographs Refractors

*REF: .5X TO 1.2X BASIC
STATED ODDS 1:21 HOBBY
EXCHANGE DEADLINE 11/30/2021
B19AV Andrew Vaughn 40.00 100.00
B19CB Cavan Biggio 30.00 80.00
B19JJB J.J. Bleday 20.00 50.00
B19RG Riley Greene 40.00 100.00

2019 Bowman's Best Dual Autographs

STATED ODDS 1:3278 HOBBY
STATED PRINT RUN 25 SER.#'d SETS
EXCHANGE DEADLINE 11/30/2021
DAGJ V.Guerrero Jr./E.Jimenez 125.00 300.00
DAHH R.Hoskins/B.Harper 150.00 400.00
DAMM V.Mesa Jr./V.Mesa 75.00 200.00
DATO M.Trout/S.Ohtani 500.00 1000.00

2019 Bowman's Best Future Foundations Refractors

STATED ODDS 1:4 HOBBY
*ATOMIC REF: 1.2X TO 3X BASIC
*GOLD REF/50: 3X TO 8X BASIC
FFAB Alec Bohm 1.00 2.50
FFAK Andrew Knizner .40 1.00
FFBA Blaze Alexander .25 .60
FFBB Bo Bichette .75 2.00
FFBD Brock Deatherage .25 .60
FFCK Carter Kieboom .40 1.00
FFCM Casey Mize .60 1.50
FFDK Dean Kremer .30 .75
FFEJ Eloy Jimenez 1.00 2.50
FFEM Elehuris Montero .40 1.00
FFGL Grant Lavigne .30 .75
FFHG Hunter Greene .40 1.00
FFJA Jordyn Adams .30 .75
FFJB Joey Bart .75 2.00
FFJI Jonathan India .30 .75
FFJR Julio Rodriguez 2.00 5.00
FFNG Nolan Gorman .75 2.00
FFNH Nico Hoerner .75 2.00
FFNL Nate Lowe .30 .75
FFRB Rylan Bannon .30 .75
FFRH Ronaldo Hernandez .25 .60
FFSB Seth Beer .60 1.50
FFSN Shervyen Newton .40 1.00
FFTS Travis Swaggerty .40 1.00
FFWF Wander Franco 2.00 5.00
FFFTJ Fernando Tatis Jr. 2.50 6.00
FFJPM Julio Pablo Martinez .25 .60
FFVGJ Vladimir Guerrero Jr. 1.50 4.00
FFVMJ Victor Mesa Jr. .60 1.50
FFVVM Victor Victor Mesa .50 1.25

2019 Bowman's Best Future Foundations Atomic Refractors

*ATOMIC REF: 1.2X TO 3X BASIC
STATED ODDS 1:48 HOBBY
FFWF Wander Franco 6.00 15.00
FFFTJ Fernando Tatis Jr. 12.00 30.00

2019 Bowman's Best Future Foundations Gold Refractors

*GOLD REF/50: 3X TO 8X BASIC
STATED ODDS 1:336 HOBBY
STATED PRINT RUN 50 SER.#'d SETS
FFAB Alec Bohm 10.00 25.00
FFWF Wander Franco 15.00 40.00

2019 Bowman's Best Future Foundations Autographs

STATED ODDS 1:174 HOBBY
PRINT RUNS B/WN 50-150 COPIES PER
EXCHANGE DEADLINE 11/30/2021
FFAAB Alec Bohm/80 25.00 60.00
FFAAK Andrew Knizner/150 6.00 15.00
FFABA Blaze Alexander/150 8.00 20.00
FFABD Brock Deatherage/150 4.00 10.00
FFACK Carter Kieboom/100 12.00 30.00
FFACM Casey Mize/50 12.00 30.00
FFADK Dean Kremer/150 5.00 12.00
FFAEJ Eloy Jimenez/50 30.00 80.00
FFAHG Hunter Greene/50 15.00 40.00
FFAJA Jordyn Adams/150 5.00 12.00
FFAJB Joey Bart/80 30.00 80.00
FFAJI Jonathan India
FFAJR Julio Rodriguez/150 30.00 80.00
FFANG Nolan Gorman/100 15.00 40.00
FFANH Nico Hoerner/150 12.00 30.00
FFANL Nate Lowe/150 5.00 12.00
FFARH Ronaldo Hernandez/150 4.00 10.00
FFASB Seth Beer/150 10.00 25.00
FFASN Shervyen Newton/150 6.00 15.00
FFATS Travis Swaggerty/100 6.00 15.00
FFAWF Wander Franco/100 60.00 150.00
FFAFTJ Fernando Tatis Jr./150 100.00 250.00
FFAJPM Julio Pablo Martinez/100 4.00 10.00
FFAVGJ Vladimir Guerrero Jr./50 60.00 150.00
FFAVMJ Victor Mesa Jr./150 10.00 25.00
FFAVVM Victor Victor Mesa/100 8.00 20.00

2019 Bowman's Best Future Foundations Autographs Atomic Refractors

STATED ODDS 1:789 HOBBY
STATED PRINT RUN 25 SER.#'d SETS
EXCHANGE DEADLINE 11/30/2021
FFACK Carter Kieboom 25.00 60.00
FFAJI Jonathan India 15.00 40.00
FFAJR Julio Rodriguez 75.00 200.00
FFAWF Wander Franco 125.00 300.00
FFAVGJ Vladimir Guerrero Jr. 100.00 250.00

2019 Bowman's Best Future Foundations Autographs Gold Refractors

STATED ODDS 1:395 HOBBY
STATED PRINT RUN 50 SER.#'d SETS
EXCHANGE DEADLINE 11/30/2021
FFAJI Jonathan India 12.00 30.00
FFAWF Wander Franco 100.00 250.00

2019 Bowman's Best Neophyte Sensations Refractors

STATED ODDS 1:18 HOBBY
*ATOMIC REF: 1.2X TO 3X BASIC
*GOLD REF/50: 3X TO 8X BASIC
NS1 Vladimir Guerrero Jr. 1.50 4.00
NS2 Will Smith .60 1.50
NS3 Austin Riley .75 2.00
NS4 Brandon Lowe .40 1.00
NS5 Pete Alonso 2.00 5.00
NS6 Keston Hiura .75 2.00
NS7 Chris Paddack .50 1.25
NS8 Nick Senzel .75 2.00
NS9 Eloy Jimenez 1.00 2.50
NS10 Fernando Tatis Jr. 2.50 6.00

2019 Bowman's Best Neophyte Sensations Autographs

STATED ODDS 1:499 HOBBY
STATED PRINT RUN 99 SER.#'d SETS
EXCHANGE DEADLINE 11/30/2021
NS1 Vladimir Guerrero Jr. 50.00 120.00
NS2 Will Smith 10.00 25.00
NS3 Austin Riley 20.00 50.00
NS4 Brandon Lowe 10.00 25.00
NS5 Pete Alonso 50.00 120.00
NS6 Keston Hiura 15.00 40.00
NS7 Chris Paddack 15.00 40.00
NS8 Nick Senzel 12.00 30.00
NS9 Eloy Jimenez 20.00 50.00
NS10 Fernando Tatis Jr. 60.00 150.00

2019 Bowman's Best Power Producers Refractors

STATED ODDS 1:6 HOBBY
*ATOMIC REF: 1.2X TO 3X BASIC
*GOLD REF/50: 3X TO 8X BASIC
PPAR Adley Rutschman 1.50 4.00
PPAV Andrew Vaughn .75 2.00
PPBH Bryce Harper .60 1.50
PPCY Christian Yelich .50 1.25
PPEJ Eloy Jimenez 1.00 2.50
PPJB Josh Bell .30 .75
PPJJ Josh Jung .75 2.00
PPMM Manny Machado .40 1.00
PPMT Mike Trout 2.00 5.00
PPNA Nolan Arenado .50 1.25
PPPA Pete Alonso 2.00 5.00
PPRG Riley Greene 1.00 2.50
PPSO Shohei Ohtani .50 1.25
PPANR Anthony Rizzo .60 1.50
PPARI Austin Riley 1.25 3.00
PPFTJ Fernando Tatis Jr. 2.50 6.00
PPJDM J.D. Martinez .40 1.00
PPJJB J.J. Bleday 1.25 3.00
PPRAJ Ronald Acuna Jr. 2.00 5.00
PPVGJ Vladimir Guerrero Jr. 1.50 4.00

2019 Bowman's Best Power Producers Autographs

STATED ODDS 1:399 HOBBY
PRINT RUNS B/WN 25-99 COPIES PER
EXCHANGE DEADLINE 11/30/2021
PPAR Adley Rutschman/99 50.00 120.00
PPAV Andrew Vaughn/99 20.00 50.00
PPCY Christian Yelich/99 30.00 80.00
PPJJ Josh Jung/99 12.00 30.00
PPMM Manny Machado/99 20.00 50.00
PPMT Mike Trout/25 250.00 500.00
PPNA Nolan Arenado/50 20.00 50.00
PPPA Pete Alonso/99 60.00 150.00
PPRG Riley Greene/99 15.00 40.00
PPSO Shohei Ohtani/25 75.00 200.00
PPANR Anthony Rizzo/50 12.00 30.00
PPARI Austin Riley/99 20.00 50.00
PPFTJ Fernando Tatis Jr./99 100.00 250.00
PPRAJ Ronald Acuna Jr./99 50.00 120.00

2019 Bowman's Best Top Prospects

*REF: .6X TO 1.5X BASIC
TP1 Wander Franco 4.00 10.00
TP2 CJ Abrams 1.25 3.00
TP3 Alek Manoah .50 1.25
TP4 Luis Robert 2.50 6.00
TP5 Cristian Pache .60 1.50
TP6 Bryson Stott .75 2.00
TP7 Riley Greene 1.00 2.50
TP8 Josh Jung .75 2.00
TP9 Taylor Trammell .30 .75
TP10 Bo Bichette .75 2.00
TP11 Corbin Carroll .40 1.00
TP12 Shea Langeliers .50 1.25
TP13 Casey Mize .60 1.50
TP14 Jarred Kelenic 1.00 2.50
TP15 Nolan Gorman .75 2.00
TP16 Keoni Cavaco .60 1.50
TP17 Nick Lodolo .50 1.25
TP18 J.J. Bleday 1.25 3.00
TP19 Sixto Sanchez .30 .75
TP20 Forrest Whitley .40 1.00
TP21 Joey Bart .75 2.00
TP22 Royce Lewis .50 1.25
TP23 Will Wilson .40 1.00
TP24 MacKenzie Gore .50 1.25
TP25 Andrew Vaughn .75 2.00
TP26 Deivi Garcia 1.25 3.00
TP27 Jo Adell .75 2.00
TP28 Hunter Bishop .75 2.00
TP29 Brett Baty .50 1.25
TP30 Adley Rutschman 1.50 4.00

2019 Bowman's Best Top Prospects Atomic Refractors

*ATOMIC REF: 1X TO 2.5X BASIC
STATED ODDS 1:12 HOBBY
TP30 Adley Rutschman 8.00 20.00

2019 Bowman's Best Top Prospects Blue Refractors

*BLUE REF/150: 1.2X TO 3X BASIC
STATED ODDS 1:34 HOBBY
STATED PRINT RUN 150 SER.#'d SETS
TP30 Adley Rutschman 10.00 25.00

2019 Bowman's Best Top Prospects Gold Refractors

*GOLD REF/50: 2X TO 5X BASIC
STATED ODDS 1:101 HOBBY
STATED PRINT RUN 50 SER.#'d SETS
TP30 Adley Rutschman 15.00 40.00

2019 Bowman's Best Top Prospects Green Refractors

*GRN REF/99: 1.5X TO 4X BASIC
STATED ODDS 1:51 HOBBY
STATED PRINT RUN 99 SER.#'d SETS
TP30 Adley Rutschman 12.00 30.00

2019 Bowman's Best Top Prospects Orange Refractors

*ORNG REF/25: 2.5X TO 6X BASIC
STATED ODDS 1:202 HOBBY
STATED PRINT RUN 25 SER.#'d SETS
TP30 Adley Rutschman 20.00 50.00

2019 Bowman's Best Top Prospects Purple Refractors

*PRPL REF/250: 1X TO 2.5X BASIC
STATED ODDS 1:21 HOBBY
STATED PRINT RUN 250 SER.#'d SETS
TP30 Adley Rutschman 8.00 20.00

2020 Bowman's Best

1 Shun Yamaguchi RC .50 1.25
2 Mike Trout 2.00 5.00
3 Fernando Tatis Jr. 1.50 4.00
4 Buster Posey .50 1.25
5 Bo Bichette RC 4.00 10.00
6 Justin Verlander .40 1.00
7 Xander Bogaerts .40 1.00
8 Anthony Rizzo .60 1.50
9 Christian Yelich .50 1.25
10 Luis Robert RC 6.00 15.00
11 Justin Dunn RC .50 1.25
12 Yoshi Tsutsugo RC .50 1.25
13 Bobby Bradley RC .50 1.25
14 Kris Bryant .50 1.25
15 Manny Machado .40 1.00
16 Jordan Yamamoto RC .50 1.25
17 Corey Kluber .30 .75
18 Nolan Arenado .50 1.25
19 Dustin May RC 1.50 4.00
20 Mookie Betts .75 2.00
21 Sean Murphy RC .60 1.50
22 Shohei Ohtani .50 1.25
23 Pete Alonso 1.00 2.50
24 Jorge Alfaro .25 .60
25 Gerrit Cole .60 1.50
26 Vladimir Guerrero Jr. .75 2.00
27 Rhys Hoskins .50 1.25
28 Blake Snell .30 .75
29 Jacob deGrom .40 1.00
30 A.J. Puk RC .75 2.00
31 Kyle Lewis RC 5.00 12.00
32 Aristides Aquino RC .75 2.00
33 Josh Bell .30 .75
34 Yadier Molina .40 1.00
35 Zac Gallen RC 1.00 2.50
36 Nick Solak RC .60 1.50
37 Juan Soto 1.25 3.00
38 J.D. Martinez .40 1.00
39 Max Scherzer .40 1.00
40 Brendan McKay RC .60 1.50
41 Gavin Lux RC 2.50 6.00
42 Starling Marte .30 .75
43 Tim Anderson .40 1.00
44 Francisco Lindor .40 1.00
45 Yordan Alvarez RC 2.00 5.00
46 Nico Hoerner RC 1.50 4.00
47 Trent Grisham RC 1.50 4.00
48 Jesus Luzardo RC .75 2.00
49 Brusdar Graterol RC .60 1.50
50 Adbert Alzolay RC .50 1.25
51 Bryce Harper .60 1.50
52 Dylan Cease RC .75 2.00
53 Ronald Acuna Jr. 1.50 4.00
54 Freddie Freeman .50 1.25
55 Joey Votto .40 1.00
56 Anthony Rendon .40 1.00
57 Dan Vogelbach .25 .60
58 Trey Mancini .40 1.00
59 Albert Pujols .50 1.25
60 Paul Goldschmidt .40 1.00
61 Aaron Judge 1.00 2.50
62 Eddie Rosario .30 .75
63 Cody Bellinger .75 2.00
64 Austin Meadows .30 .75
65 Jose Altuve .30 .75
66 Mauricio Dubon RC .50 1.25
67 Miguel Cabrera .40 1.00
68 Jorge Soler .40 1.00
69 Matt Chapman .40 1.00
70 Shogo Akiyama RC .60 1.50

2020 Bowman's Best Atomic Refractors

*ATOMIC: 1X TO 2.5X BASIC
*ATOMIC RC: .6X TO 1.5X BASIC
STATED ODDS 1:XX HOBBY
2 Mike Trout 10.00 25.00
5 Bo Bichette 15.00 40.00
10 Luis Robert 20.00 50.00
31 Kyle Lewis 12.00 30.00

2020 Bowman's Best Blue Refractors

*BLUE: 2X TO 5X BASIC
*BLUE RC: 1.2X TO 3X BASIC
STATED ODDS 1:XX HOBBY
STATED PRINT RUN 150 SER.#'d SETS
2 Mike Trout 20.00 50.00
5 Bo Bichette 30.00 80.00
10 Luis Robert 50.00 120.00
31 Kyle Lewis 25.00 60.00

2020 Bowman's Best Gold Refractors

*GOLD: 4X TO 1X BASIC
*GOLD RC: 2.5X TO 6X BASIC
STATED ODDS 1:XX HOBBY
STATED PRINT RUN 50 SER.#'d SETS
2 Mike Trout 40.00 100.00
5 Bo Bichette 60.00 150.00
10 Luis Robert 100.00 250.00
31 Kyle Lewis 50.00 120.00
45 Yordan Alvarez 15.00 40.00

2020 Bowman's Best Green Refractors

*GREEN: 2.5X TO 6X BASIC
*GREEN RC: 1.5X TO 4X BASIC
STATED ODDS 1:XX HOBBY
STATED PRINT RUN 99 SER.#'d SETS
2 Mike Trout 25.00 60.00
5 Bo Bichette 40.00 100.00
10 Luis Robert 60.00 150.00
31 Kyle Lewis 30.00 80.00
45 Yordan Alvarez 10.00 25.00

2020 Bowman's Best Orange Refractors

*ORANGE: 6X TO 15X BASIC
*ORANGE RC: 4X TO 10X BASIC
STATED ODDS 1:XX HOBBY
STATED PRINT RUN 25 SER.#'d SETS
2 Mike Trout 60.00 150.00
5 Bo Bichette 100.00 250.00
10 Luis Robert 150.00 400.00
31 Kyle Lewis 75.00 200.00
45 Yordan Alvarez 25.00 60.00

2020 Bowman's Best Purple Refractors

*PURPLE: 1.2X TO 3X BASIC
*PURPLE RC: .8X TO 2X BASIC
STATED ODDS 1:XX HOBBY
STATED PRINT RUN 250 SER.#'d SETS
2 Mike Trout 12.00 30.00
5 Bo Bichette 20.00 50.00
10 Luis Robert 30.00 80.00
31 Kyle Lewis 15.00 40.00

2020 Bowman's Best Refractors

*REF: .8X TO 2X BASIC
*REF. RC: .5X TO 1.2X BASIC
STATED ODDS 1:XX HOBBY
5 Bo Bichette 6.00 15.00
10 Luis Robert 10.00 25.00

2020 Bowman's Best Best of '20 Autographs

STATED ODDS 1:XX HOBBY
EXCHANGE DEADLINE 11/30/22
B20AA Adbert Alzolay 3.00 8.00
B20AB Andrew Benintendi 8.00 20.00
B20AC Antonio Cabello 5.00 12.00
B20AH Austin Hendrick 30.00 80.00
B20AJ Aaron Judge 75.00 200.00
B20AK Anthony Kay 2.50 6.00
B20AV Andrew Vaughn 15.00 40.00
B20AW Austin Wells 10.00 25.00
B20BG Brusdar Graterol 6.00 15.00
B20BJ Bryce Jarvis 2.50 6.00
B20BM Brendan McKay 6.00 15.00
B20BR Bryan Reynolds 3.00 8.00
B20BW Bobby Witt Jr. 40.00 100.00
B20CC Cade Cavalli 5.00 12.00
B20CK Carter Kieboom 3.00 8.00
B20CS Casey Schmitt 5.00 12.00
B20CY Christian Yelich 25.00 60.00
B20DC Dylan Cease 5.00 12.00
B20DD Dillon Dingler 8.00 20.00
B20DF Daxton Fulton 4.00 10.00
B20DM Dustin May 10.00 25.00
B20EH Emerson Hancock 10.00 25.00
B20EP Everson Pereira 6.00 15.00
B20FT Fernando Tatis Jr.
B20GC Garrett Crochet 20.00 50.00
B20GM Garrett Mitchell 12.00 30.00
B20HK Heston Kjerstad 25.00 60.00
B20IH Ivan Herrera 10.00 25.00
B20JD Jasson Dominguez 100.00 250.00
B20JF Justin Foscue 6.00 15.00
B20JL Jesus Luzardo 5.00 12.00
B20JM Jeff McNeil 12.00 30.00
B20JR Jake Rogers 4.00 10.00
B20JS Juan Soto 60.00 150.00
B20JT J.T. Realmuto 8.00 20.00
B20JW Jordan Walker 25.00 50.00
B20JY Jordan Yamamoto 3.00 8.00
B20LA Logan Allen 2.50 6.00
B20LC Luis Castillo 3.00 8.00
B20LR Luis Robert 100.00 250.00
B20LW Logan Webb 3.00 8.00
B20MC Michael Chavis 5.00 12.00
B20MD Mauricio Dubon 3.00 8.00
B20MK Mitch Keller 4.00 10.00
B20MM Max Muncy 5.00 12.00
B20MT Mike Trout
B20NB Nick Bitsko 5.00 12.00
B20NG Nick Gonzales 15.00 40.00
B20NH Nico Hoerner 12.00 30.00
B20NS Nick Solak 6.00 15.00
B20NY Nick Yorke 12.00 30.00
B20OC Owen Caissie 15.00 40.00
B20PA Pete Alonso 30.00 80.00
B20PB Patrick Bailey 6.00 15.00
B20PC Pete Crow-Armstrong 15.00 40.00
B20RA Ronald Acuna Jr. 60.00 150.00
B20RD Rafael Devers
B20RH Robert Hassell 15.00 40.00
B20RL Ramon Laureano 5.00 12.00
B20RP Robert Puason 15.00 40.00
B20SA Shogo Akiyama 8.00 20.00
B20SM Sean Murphy 5.00 12.00
B20ST Spencer Torkelson 75.00 200.00
B20SY Shun Yamaguchi EXCH 5.00 12.00
B20TA Tim Anderson 10.00 25.00
B20TG Trent Grisham 15.00 40.00
B20TS Tarik Skubal 8.00 20.00
B20WM Whit Merrifield 6.00 15.00
B20WS Will Smith 6.00 15.00
B20YA Yordan Alvarez 25.00 60.00
B20ZD Zach DeLoach 8.00 20.00
B20ZV Zac Veen 30.00 80.00
B20AAQ Aristides Aquino 10.00 25.00
B20ADR Adley Rutschman 25.00 60.00
B20AMU Andres Munoz 4.00 10.00
B20BBB Bobby Bradley 3.00 8.00
B20BHE Ben Hernandez 4.00 10.00
B20BTY Brett Baty 8.00 20.00
B20CML Carmen Mlodzinski 4.00 10.00
B20EHO Ed Howard 30.00 80.00
B20JDA Jaylin Davis 4.00 10.00
B20JDU Jarren Duran 10.00 25.00
B20JLA Justin Lange 2.50 6.00
B20JSH Jared Shuster 6.00 15.00
B20JST Josh Staumont 2.50 6.00
B20MME Max Meyer 8.00 20.00
B20NGO Nolan Gorman 10.00 25.00
B20NLO Nick Loftin 5.00 12.00
B20RDE Reid Detmers 8.00 20.00
B20TSO Tyler Soderstrom 10.00 25.00

2020 Bowman's Best Best of '20 Autographs Atomic Refractors

*ATOMIC: 1X TO 2.5X BASIC
STATED ODDS 1:XX HOBBY
STATED PRINT RUN 25 SER.#'d SETS
EXCHANGE DEADLINE 11/30/22
B20AW Austin Wells 30.00 80.00
B20BR Bryan Reynolds 15.00 40.00
B20BW Bobby Witt Jr. 200.00 500.00
B20CK Carter Kieboom 20.00 50.00
B20EH Emerson Hancock 30.00 80.00
B20EP Everson Pereira 25.00 60.00
B20FT Fernando Tatis Jr. 150.00 400.00
B20HK Heston Kjerstad 100.00 250.00
B20IH Ivan Herrera 50.00 120.00
B20JD Jasson Dominguez 300.00 800.00
B20JL Jesus Luzardo 25.00 60.00
B20JT J.T. Realmuto 60.00 150.00
B20MC Michael Chavis 15.00 40.00
B20MT Mike Trout 600.00 1200.00
B20NG Nick Gonzales 75.00 200.00
B20NY Nick Yorke 40.00 100.00
B20PC Pete Crow-Armstrong 75.00 200.00
B20RA Ronald Acuna Jr. 150.00 400.00
B20RH Robert Hassell 60.00 150.00
B20RP Robert Puason 60.00 150.00
B20SM Sean Murphy 25.00 60.00
B20ST Spencer Torkelson 300.00 800.00
B20TG Trent Grisham 50.00 120.00
B20WS Will Smith 20.00 50.00
B20ADR Adley Rutschman 75.00 200.00
B20EHO Ed Howard 125.00 300.00
B20MME Max Meyer 40.00 100.00
B20NGO Nolan Gorman 40.00 100.00
B20TSO Tyler Soderstrom 75.00 200.00

2020 Bowman's Best Best of '20 Autographs Blue Refractors

*BLUE: .5X TO 1.2X BASIC
STATED ODDS 1:XX HOBBY
STATED PRINT RUN 150 SER.#'d SETS
EXCHANGE DEADLINE 11/30/22
B20BR Bryan Reynolds 8.00 20.00
B20BW Bobby Witt Jr. 60.00 150.00
B20EP Everson Pereira 10.00 25.00
B20HK Heston Kjerstad 40.00 100.00
B20IH Ivan Herrera 20.00 50.00
B20NG Nick Gonzales 40.00 100.00
B20NY Nick Yorke 20.00 50.00
B20PC Pete Crow-Armstrong 30.00 80.00
B20ST Spencer Torkelson 150.00 400.00
B20EHO Ed Howard 50.00 120.00
B20NGO Nolan Gorman 20.00 50.00
B20TSO Tyler Soderstrom 20.00 50.00

2020 Bowman's Best Best of '20 Autographs Gold Refractors

*GOLD: .8X TO 2X BASIC
STATED ODDS 1:XX HOBBY
STATED PRINT RUN 50 SER.#'d SETS
EXCHANGE DEADLINE 11/30/22
B20AW Austin Wells 25.00 60.00
B20BR Bryan Reynolds 12.00 30.00
B20BW Bobby Witt Jr. 125.00 300.00
B20CK Carter Kieboom 15.00 40.00
B20EH Emerson Hancock 25.00 60.00
B20EP Everson Pereira 20.00 50.00
B20FT Fernando Tatis Jr. 125.00 300.00
B20HK Heston Kjerstad 60.00 150.00
B20IH Ivan Herrera 40.00 100.00
B20JD Jasson Dominguez 250.00 600.00
B20JL Jesus Luzardo 15.00 40.00
B20LR Luis Robert 250.00 600.00
B20NG Nick Gonzales 60.00 150.00
B20NY Nick Yorke 30.00 80.00
B20PC Pete Crow-Armstrong 60.00 150.00
B20RH Robert Hassell 50.00 120.00
B20RP Robert Puason 50.00 120.00
B20SM Sean Murphy 15.00 40.00
B20ST Spencer Torkelson 250.00 600.00
B20TG Trent Grisham 40.00 100.00
B20WS Will Smith 15.00 40.00
B20ADR Adley Rutschman 60.00 150.00
B20EHO Ed Howard 100.00 250.00
B20NGO Nolan Gorman 30.00 80.00
B20TSO Tyler Soderstrom 30.00 80.00

2020 Bowman's Best Best of '20 Autographs Green Refractors

*GREEN: .6X TO 1.5X BASIC
STATED ODDS 1:XX HOBBY
STATED PRINT RUN 99 SER.#'d SETS
EXCHANGE DEADLINE 11/30/22
B20BR Bryan Reynolds 10.00 25.00
B20BW Bobby Witt Jr. 75.00 200.00
B20EH Emerson Hancock 20.00 50.00
B20EP Everson Pereira 12.00 30.00
B20HK Heston Kjerstad 50.00 120.00
B20IH Ivan Herrera 30.00 80.00
B20JL Jesus Luzardo 12.00 30.00
B20NG Nick Gonzales 50.00 120.00
B20NY Nick Yorke 25.00 60.00
B20PC Pete Crow-Armstrong 40.00 100.00
B20ST Spencer Torkelson 200.00 500.00
B20WS Will Smith 12.00 30.00
B20EHO Ed Howard 60.00 150.00
B20NGO Nolan Gorman 25.00 60.00
B20TSO Tyler Soderstrom 25.00 60.00

2020 Bowman's Best Decade's Best

STATED ODDS 1:XX HOBBY
DB1 Yoshi Tsutsugo .30 .75
DB2 Gavin Lux 1.50 4.00
DB3 Dustin May 1.00 2.50
DB4 Shogo Akiyama .40 1.00
DB5 Yordan Alvarez 1.25 3.00
DB6 Luis Robert 8.00 20.00
DB7 Jesus Luzardo .50 1.25
DB8 Nico Hoerner 1.00 2.50
DB9 Brendan McKay .40 1.00
DB10 Aristides Aquino .50 1.25

2020 Bowman's Best Decade's Best Atomic Refractors

*ATOMIC: 1.2X TO 3X BASIC
STATED ODDS 1:XX HOBBY
DB6 Luis Robert 50.00 120.00

2020 Bowman's Best Decade's Best Gold Refractors

*GOLD: 3X TO 8X BASIC
STATED ODDS 1:XX HOBBY
STATED PRINT RUN 50 SER.#'d SETS
DB6 Luis Robert 125.00 300.00

2020 Bowman's Best Decade's Best Autographs

STATED ODDS 1:XX HOBBY
STATED PRINT RUN 99 SER.#'d SETS
EXCHANGE DEADLINE 11/30/22
DB1 Yoshi Tsutsugo 10.00 25.00
DB2 Gavin Lux EXCH 40.00 100.00
DB3 Dustin May 40.00 100.00
DB4 Shogo Akiyama 12.00 30.00
DB5 Yordan Alvarez 40.00 100.00
DB6 Luis Robert 300.00 600.00
DB7 Jesus Luzardo 12.00 30.00
DB8 Nico Hoerner 20.00 50.00
DB9 Brendan McKay 12.00 30.00
DB10 Aristides Aquino 12.00 30.00

2020 Bowman's Best Franchise '20 Die Cuts

STATED ODDS 1:XX HOBBY
FFDCAA Aristides Aquino .50 1.25
FFDCAB Alec Bohm 1.50 4.00
FFDCAR Adley Rutschman 1.50 4.00
FFDCBB Bo Bichette 5.00 12.00
FFDCBR Brendan Rodgers .40 1.00
FFDCBW Bobby Witt Jr. 4.00 10.00
FFDCCK Carter Kieboom .30 .75
FFDCCM Casey Mize .75 2.00
FFDCCP Cristian Pache .75 2.00
FFDCFT Fernando Tatis Jr. 1.50 4.00
FFDCGL Gavin Lux 1.50 4.00
FFDCJA Jo Adell 1.00 2.50
FFDCJB Joey Bart .75 2.00
FFDCJD Jeter Downs .40 1.00
FFDCJK Jarred Kelenic 1.50 4.00
FFDCKH Ke'Bryan Hayes .25 .60
FFDCLR Luis Robert 8.00 20.00
FFDCNG Nolan Gorman .50 1.25
FFDCNH Nico Hoerner 1.00 2.50
FFDCNJ Nolan Jones .40 1.00
FFDCNS Nick Solak .40 1.00
FFDCPA Pete Alonso 1.00 2.50
FFDCRP Robert Puason .75 2.00
FFDCYA Yordan Alvarez 1.25 3.00
FFDCZG Zac Gallen .60 1.50
FFDCJBL JJ Bleday .75 2.00
FFDCJDO Jasson Dominguez 10.00 25.00
FFDCKHI Keston Hiura .50 1.25
FFDCRLA Ramon Laureano .40 1.00
FFDCRLE Royce Lewis .60 1.50

2020 Bowman's Best Franchise '20 Die Cuts Gold Refractors

*GOLD: 3X TO 8X BASIC
STATED ODDS 1:XX HOBBY
STATED PRINT RUN 50 SER.#'d SETS
FFDCFT Fernando Tatis Jr. 50.00 120.00

2020 Bowman's Best Franchise '20 Die Cuts Inverse Color Refractors

*INVRSE CLR: 1.2X TO 3X BASIC
STATED ODDS 1:XX HOBBY
FFDCFT Fernando Tatis Jr. 20.00 50.00

2020 Bowman's Best Franchise '20 Die Cuts Autographs
STATED ODDS 1:XX HOBBY
PRINT RUNS B/WN 100-150 COPIES PER
EXCHANGE DEADLINE 11/30/22
F20AA Aristides Aquino 10.00 25.00
F20AB Alec Bohm EXCH 40.00 100.00
F20AR Adley Rutschman 100.00 250.00
F20BR Brendan Rodgers 6.00 15.00
F20CK Carter Kieboom 10.00 25.00
F20DC Nolan Gorman 20.00 50.00
F20GL Gavin Lux 30.00 80.00
F20JA Jo Adell 20.00 50.00
F20JJ JJ Bleday 20.00 50.00
F20KH Keston Hiura 12.00 30.00
F20LR Luis Robert 150.00 400.00
F20NH Nico Hoerner 15.00 40.00
F20NS Nick Solak 6.00 15.00
F20PA Pete Alonso 40.00 100.00
F20RP Robert Puason 30.00 80.00
F20YA Yordan Alvarez

2020 Bowman's Best Franchise '20 Die Cuts Autographs Atomic Refractors
*ATOMIC: .6X TO 1.5X BASIC
RANDOM INSERTS IN PACKS
STATED PRINT RUN 25 SER.#'d SETS
F20AB Alec Bohm EXCH 100.00 250.00
F20DC Nolan Gorman 40.00 100.00
F20GL Gavin Lux 60.00 150.00
F20JA Jo Adell 40.00 100.00
F20KH Keston Hiura 25.00 60.00
F20NH Nico Hoerner 40.00 100.00

2020 Bowman's Best Franchise '20 Die Cuts Autographs Gold Refractors
*GOLD: .5X TO 1.2X BASIC
RANDOM INSERTS IN PACKS
STATED PRINT RUN 50 SER.#'d SETS
F20AB Alec Bohm EXCH 75.00 200.00
F20DC Nolan Gorman 30.00 80.00
F20JA Jo Adell 30.00 80.00
F20KH Keston Hiura 20.00 50.00

2020 Bowman's Best Franchise Favorites
STATED ODDS 1:XX HOBBY
FFAAA Aristides Aquino .50 1.25
FFAAH Austin Hendrick 2.50 6.00
FFAAL Asa Lacy 1.50 4.00
FFAAV Andrew Vaughn 1.00 2.50
FFABJ Bryce Jarvis .25 .60
FFABM Brendan McKay .40 1.00
FFABW Bobby Witt Jr. 4.00 10.00
FFACJ Chipper Jones .40 1.00
FFACR Cal Ripken Jr. 1.25 3.00
FFAEH Emerson Hancock 1.00 2.50
FFAFT Fernando Tatis Jr. 1.50 4.00
FFAGL Gavin Lux 1.50 4.00
FFAGM Garrett Mitchell 2.00 5.00
FFAHK Heston Kjerstad 1.25 3.00
FFAJF Justin Foscue 1.00 2.50
FFAJJ Josh Jung .60 1.50
FFAJL Jesus Luzardo .50 1.25
FFAJS Juan Soto 1.25 3.00
FFAKG Ken Griffey Jr. .75 2.00
FFALR Luis Robert 8.00 20.00
FFAMM Max Meyer 1.00 2.50
FFAMT Mike Trout 2.00 5.00
FFANG Nick Gonzales 1.25 3.00
FFANH Nico Hoerner 1.00 2.50
FFANY Nick Yorke 1.25 3.00
FFAPB Patrick Bailey .75 2.00
FFAPM Pedro Martinez .30 .75
FFARA Ronald Acuna Jr. 1.50 4.00
FFARD Reid Detmers .60 1.50
FFARG Riley Greene 1.00 2.50
FFARH Robert Hassell 2.00 5.00
FFASA Shogo Akiyama .40 1.00
FFASO Shohei Ohtani .50 1.25
FFAST Spencer Torkelson 2.50 6.00
FFAWF Wander Franco 2.50 6.00
FFAYA Yordan Alvarez 1.25 3.00
FFAZV Zac Veen 1.25 3.00
FFAEHO Ed Howard 2.00 5.00
FFANGO Nolan Gorman .50 1.25

2020 Bowman's Best Franchise Favorites Atomic Refractors
*ATOMIC: 1.2X TO 3X BASIC
STATED ODDS 1:XX HOBBY
FFAFT Fernando Tatis Jr. 20.00 50.00
FFAKG Ken Griffey Jr. 15.00 40.00
FFAMT Mike Trout 12.00 30.00
FFAWF Wander Franco 10.00 25.00

2020 Bowman's Best Franchise Favorites Gold Refractors
*GOLD: 3X TO 8X BASIC
STATED ODDS 1:XX HOBBY
STATED PRINT RUN 50 SER.#'d SETS
FFAFT Fernando Tatis Jr. 50.00 120.00
FFAKG Ken Griffey Jr. 40.00 100.00
FFAMT Mike Trout 30.00 80.00
FFARA Ronald Acuna Jr. 15.00 40.00
FFAWF Wander Franco 25.00 60.00

2020 Bowman's Best Franchise Favorites Autographs
STATED ODDS 1:XX HOBBY
PRINT RUNS B/WN 40-250 COPIES PER
EXCHANGE DEADLINE 11/30/22
FFABJ Bryce Jarvis/250 5.00 12.00
FFACJ Chipper Jones
FFACR Cal Ripken Jr./40 60.00 150.00
FFAEH Emerson Hancock/250 12.00 30.00
FFAGL Gavin Lux
FFAHK Heston Kjerstad/250 40.00 100.00
FFAJF Justin Foscue/250 12.00 30.00
FFAJJ Josh Jung/250 15.00 40.00
FFAJL Jesus Luzardo/250 6.00 15.00
FFAJS Juan Soto/50 100.00 250.00
FFALR Luis Robert
FFAMM Max Meyer/108 12.00 30.00
FFANG Nick Gonzales/250 30.00 80.00
FFANH Nico Hoerner/160
FFANY Nick Yorke/250 15.00 40.00
FFAPB Patrick Bailey/250 10.00 25.00
FFARA Ronald Acuna Jr.
FFARD Reid Detmers/250 8.00 20.00
FFARG Riley Greene/200 30.00 80.00
FFARH Robert Hassell/250 25.00 60.00
FFASA Shogo Akiyama/250 10.00 25.00
FFAST Spencer Torkelson/60
FFAVB Vidal Brujan/250 15.00 40.00
FFAJJB JJ Bleday
FFANGO Nolan Gorman

2020 Bowman's Best Franchise Favorites Autographs Atomic Refractors
*ATOMIC: .8X TO 2X p/r 108-250
*ATOMIC: .5X TO 1.2X p/r 40-60
RANDOM INSERTS IN PACKS
STATED PRINT RUN 25 SER.#'d SETS
FFANY Nick Yorke 30.00 80.00
FFARA Ronald Acuna Jr. 150.00 400.00

2020 Bowman's Best Franchise Favorites Autographs Gold Refractors
*GOLD: .6X TO 1.5X p/r 108-250
*GOLD: .4X TO 1X p/r 40-60
RANDOM INSERTS IN PACKS
STATED PRINT RUN 50 SER.#'d SETS
FFANY Nick Yorke 25.00 60.00

2020 Bowman's Best Power Producers
STATED ODDS 1:XX HOBBY
PPAA Aristides Aquino .50 1.25
PPAJ Aaron Judge 1.00 2.50
PPBH Bryce Harper .60 1.50
PPCB Cody Bellinger .75 2.00
PPCY Christian Yelich .50 1.25
PPES Eugenio Suarez .30 .75
PPJD Jasson Dominguez 10.00 25.00
PPJS Juan Soto 1.25 3.00
PPLR Luis Robert 8.00 20.00
PPMT Mike Trout 2.00 5.00
PPNA Nolan Arenado .50 1.25
PPNG Nick Gonzales 1.25 3.00
PPPA Pete Alonso 1.00 2.50
PPRA Ronald Acuna Jr. 1.50 4.00
PPRH Robert Hassell 2.00 5.00
PPSO Shohei Ohtani .50 1.25
PPST Spencer Torkelson 2.50 6.00
PPVG Vladimir Guerrero Jr. .75 2.00
PPYA Yordan Alvarez 1.25 3.00
PPZV Zac Veen 1.25 3.00

2020 Bowman's Best Power Producers Atomic Refractors
*ATOMIC: 1.2X TO 3X BASIC
STATED ODDS 1:XX HOBBY
PPBH Bryce Harper 6.00 15.00
PPMT Mike Trout 12.00 30.00

2020 Bowman's Best Power Producers Gold Refractors
*GOLD: 3X TO 8X BASIC
STATED ODDS 1:XX HOBBY
STATED PRINT RUN 50 SER.#'d SETS
PPBH Bryce Harper 15.00 40.00
PPMT Mike Trout 30.00 80.00
PPRA Ronald Acuna Jr. 15.00 40.00

2020 Bowman's Best Power Producers Autographs
STATED ODDS 1:XX HOBBY
STATED PRINT RUN 99 SER.#'d SETS
EXCHANGE DEADLINE 11/30/22
PPCB Cody Bellinger 60.00 150.00
PPJD Jasson Dominguez 125.00 300.00
PPJS Juan Soto 75.00 200.00
PPLR Luis Robert 100.00 250.00
PPMT Mike Trout 400.00 800.00
PPNA Nolan Arenado 30.00 80.00
PPNG Nick Gonzales 50.00 120.00
PPPA Pete Alonso 30.00 80.00
PPRA Ronald Acuna Jr. 60.00 150.00
PPRH Robert Hassell 30.00 80.00
PPSO Shohei Ohtani 60.00 150.00
PPST Spencer Torkelson
PPVG Vladimir Guerrero Jr. 30.00 80.00
PPYA Yordan Alvarez 25.00 60.00
PPZV Zac Veen 25.00 60.00

2020 Bowman's Best Top Prospects
STATED ODDS 1:XX HOBBY
TP1 Wander Franco 2.50 6.00
TP2 Emerson Hancock 1.00 2.50
TP3 Garrett Crochet .60 1.50
TP4 Casey Mize .75 2.00
TP5 Jarred Kelenic 1.50 4.00
TP6 Justin Foscue 1.00 2.50
TP7 Heston Kjerstad 1.25 3.00
TP8 Robert Hassell 2.00 5.00
TP9 Dylan Carlson 1.00 2.50
TP10 Royce Lewis .60 1.50
TP11 Nick Yorke 1.25 3.00
TP12 Zac Veen 1.25 3.00
TP13 Adley Rutschman 1.50 4.00
TP14 Joey Bart .75 2.00
TP15 Julio Rodriguez 1.50 4.00
TP16 Patrick Bailey .75 2.00
TP17 Nick Gonzales 1.25 3.00
TP18 Asa Lacy 1.50 4.00
TP19 Andrew Vaughn 1.00 2.50
TP20 Bobby Witt Jr. 1.25 3.00
TP21 Cristian Pache .75 2.00
TP22 Nate Pearson .50 1.25
TP23 Ed Howard 2.00 5.00
TP24 MacKenzie Gore .50 1.25
TP25 Max Meyer 1.00 2.50
TP26 Forrest Whitley .25 .60
TP27 Jo Adell 1.00 2.50
TP28 Reid Detmers .60 1.50
TP29 Austin Hendrick 2.50 6.00
TP30 Spencer Torkelson 4.00 10.00

2020 Bowman's Best Top Prospects Atomic Refractors
*ATOMIC: 1X TO 2.5X BASIC
STATED ODDS 1:XX HOBBY
TP30 Spencer Torkelson 15.00 40.00

2020 Bowman's Best Top Prospects Blue Refractors
*BLUE: 1.2X TO 3X BASIC
STATED ODDS 1:XX HOBBY
STATED PRINT RUN 150 SER.#'d SETS
TP13 Adley Rutschman 8.00 20.00
TP20 Bobby Witt Jr. 6.00 15.00
TP30 Spencer Torkelson 20.00 50.00

2020 Bowman's Best Top Prospects Gold Refractors
*GOLD: 2X TO 5X BASIC
STATED ODDS 1:XX HOBBY
STATED PRINT RUN 50 SER.#'d SETS
TP13 Adley Rutschman 12.00 30.00
TP16 Patrick Bailey 5.00 12.00
TP19 Andrew Vaughn 6.00 15.00
TP20 Bobby Witt Jr. 15.00 40.00
TP30 Spencer Torkelson 40.00 100.00

2020 Bowman's Best Top Prospects Green Refractors
*GREEN: 1.5X TO 4X BASIC
STATED ODDS 1:XX HOBBY
STATED PRINT RUN 99 SER.#'d SETS
TP13 Adley Rutschman 10.00 25.00
TP19 Andrew Vaughn 5.00 12.00
TP20 Bobby Witt Jr. 8.00 20.00
TP30 Spencer Torkelson 25.00 60.00

2020 Bowman's Best Top Prospects Orange Refractors
*ORANGE: 2.5X TO 6X BASIC
STATED ODDS 1:XX HOBBY
STATED PRINT RUN 25 SER.#'d SETS
TP13 Adley Rutschman 15.00 40.00
TP16 Patrick Bailey 6.00 15.00
TP19 Andrew Vaughn 8.00 20.00
TP20 Bobby Witt Jr. 20.00 50.00
TP30 Spencer Torkelson 50.00 120.00

2020 Bowman's Best Top Prospects Purple Refractors
*PURPLE: 1X TO 2.5X BASIC
STATED ODDS 1:XX HOBBY
STATED PRINT RUN 250 SER.#'d SETS
TP13 Adley Rutschman 6.00 15.00
TP20 Bobby Witt Jr. 5.00 12.00
TP30 Spencer Torkelson 15.00 40.00

2020 Bowman's Best Top Prospects Refractors
*REF.: .6X TO 1.5X BASIC
STATED ODDS 1:XX HOBBY
TP30 Spencer Torkelson 10.00 25.00

2019 Certified
RANDOM INSERTS IN PACKS
*GREEN: 1X TO 2.5X
*BLUE/99: 1.2X TO 3X
*RED/25: 2.5X TO 6X
*MIRROR GOLD/25: 2.5X TO 6X
1 Mike Trout 1.25 3.00
2 Bryce Harper .40 1.00
3 Aaron Judge .60 1.50
4 Kris Bryant .30 .75
5 Shohei Ohtani .30 .75
6 Yadier Molina .25 .60
7 Anthony Rizzo .40 1.00
8 Mookie Betts .40 1.00
9 Ichiro .30 .75
10 Giancarlo Stanton .25 .60
11 Jose Altuve .20 .50
12 Christian Yelich .30 .75
13 Francisco Lindor .25 .60
14 Albert Pujols .30 .75
15 Joey Votto .25 .60
16 Cody Bellinger .50 1.25
17 Ronald Acuna Jr. 1.25 3.00
18 Khris Davis .25 .60
19 Brendan Rodgers .25 .60
20 Chris Paddack RC .30 .75
21 Eloy Jimenez RC .60 1.50
22 Fernando Tatis Jr. 2.00 5.00
23 Kyle Tucker RC .30 .75
24 Michael Kopech RC .30 .75
25 Pete Alonso RC 3.00 8.00
26 Yusei Kikuchi RC .25 .60
27 Christin Stewart RC .20 .50
28 Jeff McNeil RC .40 1.00
29 Mitch Keller RC .20 .50
30 Brandon Lowe RC .25 .60
31 Cole Tucker RC .25 .60
32 Michael Chavis RC .25 .60
33 Bryan Reynolds RC .50 1.25
34 Darwinzon Hernandez RC .15 .40
35 Vladimir Guerrero Jr. RC 3.00 8.00

2020 Certified
RANDOM INSERTS IN PACKS
1 Pete Alonso .60 1.50
2 Shun Yamaguchi RC .30 .75
3 Luis Robert RC 4.00 10.00
4 Giancarlo Stanton .25 .60
5 Kwang-Hyun Kim RC .75 2.00
6 Yadier Molina .25 .60
7 Yordan Alvarez RC 1.25 3.00
8 Bryce Harper .40 1.00
9 Brendan McKay RC .40 1.00
10 Bo Bichette RC 3.00 8.00
11 Aristides Aquino RC .50 1.25
12 Sean Murphy RC .40 1.00
13 Ronald Acuna Jr. 1.50 4.00
14 Mike Trout 2.00 5.00
15 Kris Bryant .30 .75
16 Juan Soto .75 2.00
17 Yoshitomo Tsutsugo RC .30 .75
18 Robinson Cano .20 .50
19 Shogo Akiyama RC .40 1.00
20 Vladimir Guerrero Jr. .50 1.25
21 Cody Bellinger .50 1.25
22 Nolan Arenado .30 .75
23 Aaron Judge .60 1.50
24 Christian Yelich .30 .75
25 Gavin Lux RC 1.50 4.00
26 Austin Riley .40 1.00
27 Bobby Bradley RC .30 .75
28 Dillon Tate .15 .40
29 Brian Anderson .15 .40
30 Danny Mendick RC .30 .75

2014 Classics
COMPLETE SET (200) 15.00 40.00
1 Adam Jones .20 .50
2 Adam Wainwright .20 .50
3 Adrian Beltre .25 .60
4 Adrian Gonzalez .20 .50
5 Al Kaline .25 .60
6 Herb Pennock .20 .50
7 Albert Pujols .30 .75
8 Andrew McCutchen .25 .60
9 Arky Vaughan .15 .40
10 Bill Dickey .15 .40
11 Bill Terry .15 .40
12 Billy Herman .15 .40
13 Bob Feller .20 .50
14 Bob Gibson .20 .50
15 Brandon Belt .20 .50
16 Brooks Robinson .20 .50
17 Bryce Harper .40 1.00
18 Burleigh Grimes .20 .50
19 Buster Posey .30 .75
20 Cal Ripken .75 2.00
21 Carl Yastrzemski .40 1.00
22 Carlos Gomez .15 .40
23 Carlton Fisk .20 .50
24 Lefty Gomez .15 .40
25 Chipper Jones .25 .60
26 Chris Davis .15 .40
27 Chris Sale .25 .60
28 Chuck Klein .15 .40
29 Clayton Kershaw .50 1.25
30 Dave Bancroft .15 .40
31 David Ortiz .25 .60
32 David Wright .20 .50
33 Derek Jeter .60 1.50
34 Dizzy Dean .20 .50
35 Duke Snider .20 .50
36 Dustin Pedroia .25 .60
37 Earl Averill .15 .40
38 Eddie Collins .20 .50
39 Eddie Murray .20 .50
40 Edwin Encarnacion .25 .60
41 Elston Howard .15 .40
42 Eric Hosmer .20 .50
43 Ernie Banks .25 .60
44 Evan Longoria .20 .50
45 Felix Hernandez .20 .50
46 Frank Chance .20 .50
47 Frank Robinson .20 .50
48 Frank Thomas .25 .60
49 Lefty O'Doul .15 .40
50 Freddie Freeman .30 .75
51 Gabby Hartnett .15 .40
52 George Brett .50 1.25
53 George Kelly .15 .40
54 George Sisler .20 .50
55 Giancarlo Stanton .25 .60
56 Goose Goslin .20 .50
57 Greg Maddux .30 .75
58 Hack Wilson .20 .50
59 Hank Greenberg .25 .60
60 Hanley Ramirez .20 .50
61 Harmon Killebrew .25 .60
62 Harry Heilmann .20 .50
63 Honus Wagner .25 .60
64 Ichiro Suzuki .40 1.00
65 Jackie Robinson .25 .60
66 Jim Bottomley .15 .40
67 Jim Palmer .20 .50
68 Jim Thorpe .40 1.00
69 Jimmie Foxx .25 .60
70 Joe DiMaggio .50 1.25
71 Joe Jackson .30 .75
72 Joe Mauer .20 .50
73 Joe Medwick .15 .40
74 Joe Morgan .20 .50
75 Joey Votto .25 .60
76 Johnny Bench .25 .60
77 Jose Bautista .20 .50
78 Jose Fernandez .25 .60
79 Josh Donaldson .20 .50
80 Josh Gibson .25 .60
81 Juan Marichal .20 .50
82 Justin Upton .20 .50
83 Justin Verlander .25 .60
84 Ken Griffey Jr. .50 1.25
85 Lefty Grove .20 .50
86 Leo Durocher .15 .40
87 Lloyd Waner .20 .50
88 Carl Furillo .15 .40
89 Luke Appling .20 .50
90 Manny Machado .25 .60
91 Mariano Rivera .30 .75
92 Mark McGwire .50 1.25
93 Max Scherzer .25 .60
94 Mel Ott .25 .60
95 Miguel Cabrera .25 .60
96 Mike Piazza .25 .60
97 Mike Trout 1.25 3.00
98 Miller Huggins .15 .40
99 Nap Lajoie .25 .60
100 Nellie Fox .20 .50
101 Nolan Ryan .75 2.00
102 Orlando Cepeda .20 .50
103 Paul Goldschmidt .25 .60
104 Paul Molitor .25 .60
105 Paul Waner .20 .50
106 Pee Wee Reese .20 .50
107 Pete Rose .50 1.25
108 Phil Rizzuto .20 .50
109 Reggie Jackson .20 .50
110 Rick Ferrell .15 .40
111 Rickey Henderson .25 .60
112 Robinson Cano .20 .50
113 Robin Yount .25 .60
114 Rod Carew .20 .50
115 Roger Bresnahan .20 .50
116 Roger Clemens .30 .75
117 Roger Maris .25 .60
118 Barry Bonds .40 1.00
119 Roy Campanella .25 .60
120 Ryan Braun .20 .50
121 Ryne Sandberg .50 1.25
122 Sam Crawford .20 .50
123 Satchel Paige .25 .60
124 Stan Musial .40 1.00
125 Stephen Strasburg .25 .60
126 Steve Carlton .20 .50
127 Ted Kluszewski .20 .50
128 Sonny Gray .20 .50
129 Thurman Munson .25 .60
130 Todd Helton .20 .50
131 Tom Glavine .20 .50
132 Tom Seaver .20 .50
133 Tommy Henrich .15 .40
134 Tony Gwynn .25 .60
135 Tony Lazzeri .20 .50
136 Tony Perez .20 .50
137 Tris Speaker .20 .50
138 Troy Tulowitzki .25 .60
139 Ty Cobb .40 1.00
140 Wade Boggs .20 .50
141 Warren Spahn .20 .50
142 Whitey Ford .20 .50
143 Wil Myers .15 .40
144 Willie Keeler .15 .40
145 Willie McCovey .20 .50
146 Willie Stargell .20 .50
147 Yasiel Puig .25 .60
148 Yoenis Cespedes .25 .60
149 Yogi Berra .25 .60
150 Yu Darvish .25 .60
151 Arismendy Alcantara RC .25 .60
152 Alex Guerrero RC .30 .75
153 Andrew Heaney RC .25 .60
154 Anthony DeSclafani RC .25 .60
155 Billy Hamilton RC .30 .75
156 C.J. Cron RC .25 .60
157 Chris Owings RC .25 .60
158 Christian Bethancourt RC .25 .60
159 Danny Santana RC .30 .75
160 David Hale RC .25 .60
161 Kevin Kiermaier RC .40 1.00
162 Eddie Butler RC .25 .60
163 Aaron Sanchez RC .25 .60
164 Erisbel Arruebarrena RC .25 .60
165 Eugenio Suarez RC 1.00 2.50
166 Garin Cecchini RC .25 .60
167 George Springer RC 1.00 2.50
168 Gregory Polanco RC .40 1.00
169 Mookie Betts RC 8.00 20.00
170 J.R. Murphy RC .25 .60
171 Jace Peterson RC .25 .60
172 Jake Marisnick RC .25 .60
173 James Paxton RC .40 1.00
174 Jimmy Nelson RC .25 .60
175 Jon Singleton RC .30 .75
176 Jonathan Schoop RC .25 .60
177 Jose Abreu RC 2.00 5.00
178 Jose Ramirez RC 2.00 5.00
179 Kolten Wong RC .30 .75
180 Luis Sardinas RC .25 .60
181 Andrew Susac RC .30 .75
182 Marcus Stroman RC .40 1.00
183 Masahiro Tanaka RC .75 2.00
184 Matt Davidson RC .30 .75
185 Robbie Ray RC .25 .60
186 Nick Castellanos RC .75 2.00
187 Oscar Taveras RC .30 .75
188 Rafael Montero RC .25 .60
189 Randal Grichuk RC .40 1.00
190 Rougned Odor RC .50 1.25
191 Christian Vazquez RC .25 .60
192 Taijuan Walker RC .25 .60
193 Odrisamer Despaigne RC .25 .60
194 Tommy La Stella RC .25 .60
195 Travis d'Arnaud RC .30 .75
196 Chris Taylor RC 1.25 3.00
197 Domingo Santana RC .40 1.00
198 Xander Bogaerts RC .75 2.00
199 Kyle Parker RC .30 .75
200 Yordano Ventura RC .30 .75

2014 Classics Timeless Tributes Gold
*GOLD VET: 8X TO 20X BASIC
*GOLD RC: 5X TO 12X BASIC RC
RANDOM INSERTS IN PACKS
STATED PRINT RUN 25 SER.#'d SETS

2014 Classics Timeless Tributes Silver
*SILVER VET: 4X TO 10X BASIC
*SILVER RC: 2.5X TO 6X BASIC RC
RANDOM INSERTS IN PACKS
STATED PRINT RUN 149 SER.#'d SETS
177 Jose Abreu 6.00 15.00

2014 Classics Champion Materials
RANDOM INSERTS IN PACKS
STATED PRINT RUN 99 SER.#'d SETS
1 Bill Dickey 6.00 15.00
3 Carl Furillo 6.00 15.00
7 Lefty Gomez 10.00 25.00
15 Herb Pennock 8.00 20.00
18 Lefty O'Doul 20.00 50.00

2014 Classics Champion Materials Bats
RANDOM INSERTS IN PACKS
PRINT RUNS B/WN 10-99 SER.#'d SETS
NO PRICING ON QTY 10
2 Bob Meusel/25 6.00 15.00
3 Carl Furillo/99 6.00 15.00
4 Dave Bancroft/99 6.00 15.00
5 Eddie Collins/25 40.00 80.00
6 Frank Chance/25 25.00 60.00
8 George Kelly/99 6.00 15.00
9 Goose Goslin/99 20.00 50.00
10 Heinie Groh/99 6.00 15.00
11 Honus Wagner/25 40.00 100.00
12 Jake Daubert/99 6.00 15.00
13 Jim Bottomley/99 6.00 15.00
14 Joe Jackson/25 150.00 250.00
16 Miller Huggins/25 6.00 15.00
17 Roger Bresnahan/99 75.00 150.00
19 Tony Lazzeri/99 8.00 20.00
20 Tris Speaker/99 8.00 20.00

2014 Classics Classic Combos Bats
RANDOM INSERTS IN PACKS
PRINT RUNS B/WN 5-99 SER.#'d SETS
NO PRICING ON QTY 10 OR LESS
6 H.Groh/J.Daubert/25 10.00 25.00
12 G.Goslin/J.Cronin/25 30.00 80.00
13 E.Averill/W.Kamm/25 15.00 40.00
14 F.Frisch/J.Bottomley/25 40.00 80.00
21 Joe DiMaggio 25.00 60.00
Bill Dickey/25
22 J.Mize/M.Ott/99 12.00 30.00
23 F.Robinson/T.Kluszewski/99 6.00 15.00
27 A.Pujols/M.Trout/99 15.00 40.00
29 D.Jeter/I.Suzuki/99 10.00 25.00

2014 Classics Classic Combos Jerseys
RANDOM INSERTS IN PACKS
PRINT RUNS B/WN 5-99 SER.#'d SETS
NO PRICING ON QTY 5
23 F.Robinson/T.Kluszewski/99 15.00 40.00
25 B.Campaneris/R.Jackson/99 15.00 40.00
26 G.Springer/J.Singleton/99 5.00 12.00
27 A.Pujols/M.Trout/99 15.00 40.00
28 Stanton/Fernandez/99 5.00 12.00
29 D.Jeter/I.Suzuki/99 20.00 50.00
30 M.Tanaka/Y.Darvish/99 20.00 50.00

2014 Classics Classic Cuts
RANDOM INSERTS IN PACKS
PRINT RUNS B/WN 1-99 SER.#'d SETS
NO PRICING ON QTY 10 OR LESS
EXCHANGE DEADLINE 5/19/2016
7 Bobby Thomson/99 10.00 25.00
25 Johnny Pesky/99 15.00 40.00
34 Stan Musial/99 20.00 50.00
36 Lou Boudreau/25 15.00 40.00
39 Warren Spahn/25 40.00 100.00

2014 Classics Classic Lineups
RANDOM INSERTS IN PACKS
PRINT RUNS B/WN 25-99 COPIES PER
1 Ghrngr/Hlmnn/Cbb/99 30.00 80.00
2 Sthwrth/Bttmly/Hrnsby/25 100.00 200.00
3 Msl/Hlmnn/Drchr/99 12.00 30.00
4 Hrtntt/Wlsn/Hrnsby/99 20.00 50.00
5 Frsch/Mdwck/Drchr/25 75.00 150.00
6 Hrmn/Kln/Hrtntt/99 50.00 100.00
7 Ghrngr/Gsln/Grnbrg/99 50.00 100.00
8 Smmns/Ghrngr/Gsln/99 25.00 60.00
9 Hrmn/Grbrg/Knr/99 30.00 80.00
10 Frllo/Sndr/Rbnsn/25 75.00 150.00
11 Mzrski/Hk/Clmnt/99 20.00 50.00
12 Hwrd/Mrs/Brra/99 12.00 30.00
13 Mzrski/Clmnt/Strgll/99 30.00 80.00
14 Kllbrw/Crw/Olva/99 50.00 100.00
15 Pwll/Rbnsn/Rbnsn/99 12.00 30.00
16 Bncrft/Frsch/Klly/99 20.00 50.00
17 Musl/Ghrig/Lzzri/27 60.00 150.00
18 Smmns/Cllns/Fxx/99 30.00 80.00
19 DMggo/Fxx/Wllms/99 25.00 60.00
20 Hdgs/Gllam/Cmpnlla/99 15.00 40.00

2014 Classics Classic Quads Bats
RANDOM INSERTS IN PACKS
PRINT RUNS B/WN 5-99 COPIES PER
NO PRICING ON QTY 10 OR LESS
2 Frsch/Klly/Wlsn/Grh/25 75.00 150.00
8 DMggo/Fxx/Crnn/Wllms/25 60.00 120.00
12 Frllo/Stnky/Rbnsn/Rsr/25 40.00 100.00
16 Pwll/Rbnsn/Rbnsn/Aprco/99 12.00 30.00
19 Gnzlz/Krshw/Rmrz/Pg/75 15.00 40.00

2014 Classics Classic Quads Jerseys
RANDOM INSERTS IN PACKS
PRINT RUNS B/WN 5-99 COPIES PER
NO PRICING ON QTY 5
12 Frllo/Stnky/Rbnsn/Rsr/47 50.00 100.00
15 Pttte/Wllms/Jtr/Psda/98 30.00 60.00
17 Mrgn/Bnch/Rse/Prz/25 50.00 120.00
18 Whtly/Mrphy/Tnka/Slrte/99 12.00 30.00
19 Gnzlz/Krshw/Rmrz/Puig/99 12.00 30.00

2014 Classics Classic Triples Bats
RANDOM INSERTS IN PACKS
PRINT RUNS B/WN 15-99 COPIES PER
NO PRICING ON QTY 15
10 Herman/Greenberg/Kiner/25 60.00 120.00
14 Mazeroski/Clemente/Stargell/99 50.00 100.00
16 Powell/Robinson/Robinson/99 15.00 40.00
21 Jones/Davis/Machado/99 12.00 30.00
22 Ortiz/Pedroia/Bogaerts/99 12.00 30.00
25 Terry/Klein/Frisch/25 15.00 40.00

2014 Classics Classic Triples Jerseys
RANDOM INSERTS IN PACKS
PRINT RUNS B/WN 5-99 COPIES PER
NO PRICING ON QTY 10 OR LESS
9 Sthwrth/Slghtr/Msl/25 150.00 250.00
11 Frllo/Sndr/Rbnsn/25 75.00 150.00
13 Hwrd/Mrs/Brra/25 12.00 30.00
14 Maz/Clmnte/Strgll/25 50.00 100.00
15 Kllbrw/Crw/Olva/25 20.00 50.00
16 Pwll/Rbnsn/Rbnsn/99 10.00 25.00
17 Strwbrry/Crtr/Hrnndz/99 20.00 50.00
18 Abru/Pg/Cspds/99 12.00 30.00
19 McCtchn/Plnco/Mrte/99 25.00 60.00
20 Sprngr/Plnco/Tvrs/99 12.00 30.00
21 Jns/Dvs/Mchdo/99 12.00 30.00
22 Ortz/Pdra/Bgrts/99 20.00 50.00
23 Smmns/Dcky/Ghrngr/25 40.00 80.00

2014 Classics Home Run Heroes
COMPLETE SET (25) 12.00 30.00
RANDOM INSERTS IN PACKS
1 Adrian Beltre .50 1.25
2 Miguel Cabrera .50 1.25
3 Albert Pujols .60 1.50
4 Bill Terry .30 .75
5 Jose Abreu 2.50 6.00
6 Chris Davis .30 .75
7 Chuck Klein .30 .75
8 David Ortiz .50 1.25
9 Eddie Murray .40 1.00
10 Frank Howard .30 .75
11 Frank Thomas .50 1.25
12 Giancarlo Stanton .50 1.25
13 Hack Wilson .40 1.00
14 Hank Greenberg .50 1.25
15 Mike Trout 2.50 6.00
16 Joe DiMaggio 1.00 2.50
17 Johnny Mize .40 1.00
18 Justin Upton .40 1.00
19 Ken Griffey Jr. 1.00 2.50
20 Mel Ott .50 1.25
21 Roger Maris .50 1.25
22 Barry Bonds .75 2.00
23 Sam Crawford .40 1.00
24 Mark McGwire 1.00 2.50
25 Tony Lazzeri .40 1.00

2014 Classics Home Run Heroes Bats
RANDOM INSERTS IN PACKS
PRINT RUNS B/WN 10-99 COPIES PER
NO PRICING ON QTY 10 OR LESS
2 Al Simmons/99 10.00 25.00
3 Albert Pujols/99 5.00 12.00
4 Bill Terry/25 20.00 50.00
5 Bob Meusel/25 10.00 25.00
7 Chuck Klein/25 15.00 40.00
9 Eddie Murray/99 4.00 10.00
10 Frank Howard/99 3.00 8.00
11 Frank Thomas/99 5.00 12.00
12 Giancarlo Stanton/99 5.00 12.00
13 Hack Wilson/25 40.00 80.00
14 Hank Greenberg/25 50.00 100.00
16 Joe DiMaggio/25 20.00 50.00
17 Johnny Mize/25 10.00 25.00
18 Justin Upton/99 4.00 10.00
23 Sam Crawford/25 12.00 30.00
24 Ted Williams/25 20.00 50.00

2014 Classics Home Run Heroes Jerseys
RANDOM INSERTS IN PACKS
PRINT RUNS B/WN 4-99 COPIES PER
NO PRICING ON QTY 10 OR LESS

1 Adrian Beltre/99 5.00 12.00
3 Albert Pujols/99 5.00 12.00
6 Chris Davis/99 3.00 8.00
9 Eddie Murray/99 6.00 15.00
10 Frank Howard/99 6.00 15.00
11 Frank Thomas/99 5.00 12.00
12 Giancarlo Stanton/99 5.00 12.00
16 Joe DiMaggio/25 30.00 60.00
17 Johnny Mize/25 8.00 20.00
18 Justin Upton/99 4.00 10.00
24 Ted Williams/99 20.00 50.00

2014 Classics Home Run Heroes Jerseys HR

RANDOM INSERTS IN PACKS
PRINT RUNS B/WN 4-99 COPIES PER
NO PRICING ON QTY 10 OR LESS
1 Adrian Beltre/99 5.00 12.00
3 Albert Pujols/99 6.00 15.00
8 David Ortiz/99 5.00 12.00
9 Eddie Murray/99 6.00 15.00
10 Frank Howard/25 15.00 40.00
11 Frank Thomas/99 8.00 20.00
12 Giancarlo Stanton/99 5.00 12.00
17 Johnny Mize/25 15.00 40.00
24 Ted Williams/99 20.00 50.00

2014 Classics Home Run Heroes Materials Combos

RANDOM INSERTS IN PACKS
PRINT RUNS B/WN 4-99 COPIES PER
NO PRICING ON QTY 10 OR LESS
1 Adrian Beltre/99 5.00 12.00
2 Al Simmons/25 40.00 80.00
3 Albert Pujols/99 6.00 15.00
6 Chris Davis/99 3.00 8.00
8 David Ortiz/99 5.00 12.00
9 Eddie Murray/99 4.00 10.00
11 Frank Thomas/99 5.00 12.00
12 Giancarlo Stanton/99 5.00 12.00
18 Justin Upton/99 4.00 10.00
24 Ted Williams/25 30.00 60.00

2014 Classics Legendary Lumberjacks

COMPLETE SET (25) 12.00 30.00
RANDOM INSERTS IN PACKS
1 Albert Pujols .60 1.50
2 Ernie Banks .50 1.25
3 Cal Ripken 1.50 4.00
4 Tony Gwynn .50 1.25
5 Derek Jeter 1.25 3.00
6 Dustin Pedroia .50 1.25
7 Earl Averill .30 .75
8 Lefty O'Doul .30 .75
9 Eddie Murray .40 1.00
10 Frank Robinson .40 1.00
11 George Brett 1.00 2.50
12 George Sisler .40 1.00
13 Jose Abreu 2.50 6.00
14 Harry Heilmann .40 1.00
15 Honus Wagner .50 1.25
16 Ichiro Suzuki .75 2.00
17 Giancarlo Stanton .50 1.25
18 Lloyd Waner .40 1.00
19 Miguel Cabrera .50 1.25
20 Nap Lajoie .50 1.25
21 Paul Waner .40 1.00
22 Mike Trout 2.50 6.00
23 Tris Speaker .40 1.00
24 Ty Cobb .75 2.00
25 Willie Keeler .30 .75

2014 Classics Legendary Lumberjacks Bats

RANDOM INSERTS IN PACKS
PRINT RUNS B/WN 10-99 COPIES PER
NO PRICING ON QTY 10
1 Albert Pujols/99 6.00 15.00
2 Bill Dickey/25 8.00 20.00
3 Cal Ripken/99 6.00 15.00
5 Derek Jeter/99 12.00 30.00
6 Dustin Pedroia/99 5.00 12.00
7 Earl Averill/99 3.00 8.00
9 Eddie Murray/99 4.00 10.00
10 Frank Robinson/99 4.00 10.00
11 George Brett/99 6.00 15.00
12 George Sisler/99 8.00 20.00
15 Honus Wagner/25 50.00 100.00
16 Ichiro Suzuki/99 6.00 15.00
17 Joe Jackson/25 50.00 120.00
18 Lloyd Waner/99 4.00 10.00
19 Miguel Cabrera/99 6.00 15.00
20 Nap Lajoie/25 30.00 80.00
21 Paul Waner/25 20.00 50.00
22 Roberto Clemente/25 20.00 50.00

2014 Classics Legendary Lumberjacks Bats Combos

RANDOM INSERTS IN PACKS
PRINT RUNS B/WN 10-99 COPIES PER
NO PRICING ON QTY 10
3 Cal Ripken/99 10.00 25.00
5 Derek Jeter/99 20.00 50.00
6 Dustin Pedroia/99 5.00 12.00
7 Earl Averill/25 15.00 40.00
9 Eddie Murray/99 4.00 10.00
10 Frank Robinson/99 4.00 10.00
16 Ichiro Suzuki/99 8.00 20.00
18 Lloyd Waner/25 10.00 25.00
19 Miguel Cabrera/99 5.00 12.00

2014 Classics Legendary Lumberjacks Bats Signatures

RANDOM INSERTS IN PACKS
PRINT RUNS B/WN 5-25 COPIES PER
NO PRICING ON QTY 10 OR LESS
EXCHANGE DEADLINE 5/19/2016

2014 Classics Legendary Lumberjacks Jerseys

RANDOM INSERTS IN PACKS
PRINT RUNS B/WN 10-99 COPIES PER
NO PRICING ON QTY 10
1 Albert Pujols/99 6.00 15.00
3 Cal Ripken/99 10.00 25.00
4 Charlie Gehringer/25 15.00 40.00
5 Derek Jeter/99 15.00 40.00
6 Dustin Pedroia/99 5.00 12.00
9 Eddie Murray/99 5.00 12.00
10 Frank Robinson/99 4.00 10.00
11 George Brett/25 6.00 15.00
16 Ichiro Suzuki/99 8.00 20.00
19 Miguel Cabrera/99 5.00 12.00
22 Roberto Clemente/25 30.00 60.00

2014 Classics Legendary Players Bats

RANDOM INSERTS IN PACKS
PRINT RUNS B/WN 10-99 COPIES PER
NO PRICING ON QTY 10
8 George Kelly 20.00 50.00
9 Gil Hodges 12.00 30.00
11 Joe DiMaggio 25.00 60.00
15 Miller Huggins 15.00 40.00
16 Paul Waner 5.00 12.00
17 Pee Wee Reese 4.00 10.00
19 Roberto Clemente 12.00 30.00
20 Roger Maris 12.00 30.00
23 Thurman Munson 8.00 20.00
24 Tommy Henrich 3.00 8.00

2014 Classics Legendary Players Materials

RANDOM INSERTS IN PACKS
PRINT RUNS B/WN 25-99 COPIES PER
2 Bob Feller/25 50.00 100.00
3 Lefty O'Doul/99 20.00 50.00
5 Elston Howard/99 25.00 60.00
6 Enos Slaughter/99 6.00 15.00
7 Gabby Hartnett/99 50.00 100.00
9 Gil Hodges/99 10.00 25.00
13 Leo Durocher/99 6.00 15.00
14 Luke Appling/99 4.00 10.00
18 Rick Ferrell/99 10.00 25.00
19 Roberto Clemente/25 20.00 50.00
20 Roger Maris/25 20.00 50.00
21 Herb Pennock/99 12.00 30.00
22 Lefty Gomez/99 50.00 100.00
23 Thurman Munson/99 20.00 50.00
24 Tommy Henrich/99 3.00 8.00
25 Walter Alston/99 6.00 15.00

2014 Classics Membership Materials HOF

RANDOM INSERTS IN PACKS
PRINT RUNS B/WN 1-25 COPIES PER
NO PRICING ON QTY 10 OR LESS
5 George Sisler/25 60.00 120.00
8 Paul Waner/25 15.00 40.00
9 Jim Bottomley/25 30.00 80.00
10 Herb Pennock/25 50.00 100.00
12 Chuck Klein/25 10.00 25.00
15 Gabby Hartnett/25 75.00 150.00
16 Charlie Gehringer/25 20.00 50.00
18 Joe DiMaggio/25 75.00 150.00
19 Ted Williams/25 60.00 150.00
22 Roberto Clemente/25 100.00 200.00
24 Warren Spahn/25 75.00 150.00
25 Early Wynn/25 30.00 60.00

2014 Classics Membership Materials MVP

RANDOM INSERTS IN PACKS
PRINT RUNS B/WN 1-25 COPIES PER
NO PRICING ON QTY 10 OR LESS
3 Jake Daubert/25 40.00 80.00
23 Thurman Munson/25 40.00 80.00

2014 Classics October Heroes

COMPLETE SET (25) 12.00 30.00
RANDOM INSERTS IN PACKS
1 Don Larsen .30 .75
2 Albert Pujols .60 1.50
3 Bill Mazeroski .40 1.00
4 Bob Gibson .40 1.00
5 Herb Pennock .40 1.00
6 Carlos Ruiz .30 .75
7 Carlton Fisk .40 1.00
8 Catfish Hunter .40 1.00
9 David Ortiz .50 1.25
10 Derek Jeter 1.25 3.00
11 Eddie Collins .40 1.00
12 Frank Chance .40 1.00
13 Heinie Groh .30 .75
14 Joe Jackson .60 1.50
15 Johnny Bench .50 1.25
16 Luis Gonzalez .30 .75
17 Pablo Sandoval .40 1.00
18 Lefty Gomez .30 .75
19 Ted Kluszewski .40 1.00
20 Thurman Munson .50 1.25
21 Frank Robinson .40 1.00
22 Mariano Rivera .60 1.50
23 Mike Schmidt .75 2.00
24 Pete Rose 1.00 2.50
25 Reggie Jackson .40 1.00

2014 Classics October Heroes Bats

RANDOM INSERTS IN PACKS
PRINT RUNS B/WN 10-99 COPIES PER
NO PRICING ON QTY 10
2 Albert Pujols/99 5.00 12.00
3 Bill Mazeroski/25 12.00 30.00
5 Bob Meusel/25 6.00 15.00
7 Carlton Fisk/99 4.00 10.00
9 David Ortiz/99 5.00 12.00
10 Derek Jeter/99 8.00 20.00
13 Heinie Groh/99 6.00 15.00
14 Joe Jackson/25 125.00 250.00
17 Pablo Sandoval/99 4.00 10.00
18 Roberto Clemente/25 30.00 80.00
19 Ted Kluszewski/99 4.00 10.00
20 Thurman Munson/99 10.00 25.00

2014 Classics October Heroes Bats Signatures

RANDOM INSERTS IN PACKS
PRINT RUNS B/WN 5-25 COPIES PER
NO PRICING ON QTY 10 OR LESS
EXCHANGE DEADLINE 5/19/2016
4 Bill Mazeroski/25 20.00 50.00
10 David Freese/25 5.00 12.00
15 Joe Carter/25 15.00 40.00

2014 Classics October Heroes Jerseys

RANDOM INSERTS IN PACKS
PRINT RUNS B/WN 4-99 COPIES PER
NO PRICING ON QTY 4
1 Herb Pennock/99 6.00 15.00
4 Bob Gibson/99 10.00 25.00
7 Carlton Fisk/99 4.00 10.00
9 David Ortiz/99 5.00 12.00
10 Derek Jeter/99 12.00 30.00
18 Roberto Clemente/25 40.00 100.00
20 Thurman Munson/99 15.00 40.00

2014 Classics October Heroes Jerseys Signatures

RANDOM INSERTS IN PACKS
PRINT RUNS B/WN 5-25 COPIES PER
NO PRICING ON QTY 10 OR LESS
EXCHANGE DEADLINE 5/19/2016
1 Alan Trammell/25 12.00 30.00
3 Andy Pettitte/25 20.00 50.00
7 Carlos Ruiz/25 5.00 12.00

2014 Classics October Heroes Materials Combos

RANDOM INSERTS IN PACKS
PRINT RUNS B/WN 5-99 COPIES PER
NO PRICING ON QTY 10 OR LESS
1 Herb Pennock/25 50.00 100.00
2 Albert Pujols/99 5.00 12.00
3 Bill Mazeroski/25 20.00 50.00
4 Bob Gibson/99 15.00 40.00
6 Carlos Ruiz/99 3.00 8.00
7 Carlton Fisk/99 4.00 10.00
9 David Ortiz/99 5.00 12.00
10 Derek Jeter/99 12.00 30.00
12 Frank Chance/25 30.00 60.00
13 Heinie Groh/99 10.00 25.00
14 Joe Jackson/25 150.00 250.00
17 Pablo Sandoval/99 10.00 25.00
18 Roberto Clemente/25 50.00 100.00
19 Ted Kluszewski/99 15.00 40.00
20 Thurman Munson/25 50.00 100.00

2014 Classics October Heroes Materials Combos Signatures

RANDOM INSERTS IN PACKS
PRINT RUNS B/WN 5-25 COPIES PER
NO PRICING ON QTY 10 OR LESS
EXCHANGE DEADLINE 5/19/2016
3 Andy Pettitte/25 6.00 15.00
4 Bill Mazeroski/20 12.00 30.00
7 Carlos Ruiz/25 5.00 12.00
10 David Freese/25 5.00 12.00

2014 Classics Players Collection

RANDOM INSERTS IN PACKS
PRINT RUNS B/WN 5-99 COPIES PER
NO PRICING ON QTY 5
2 Derek Jeter/99 15.00 40.00
10 Jose Abreu/25 30.00 80.00
14 Nolan Ryan/25 20.00 50.00
15 Pete Rose/25 15.00 40.00
18 Tony Gwynn/99 6.00 15.00

2014 Classics Significant Signatures Bats Gold

RANDOM INSERTS IN PACKS
PRINT RUNS B/WN 1-25 COPIES PER
NO PRICING ON QTY 10 OR LESS
EXCHANGE DEADLINE 5/19/2016
36 Carlos Sanchez/25 5.00 12.00
73 Jose Abreu/25 40.00 100.00
77 Rougned Odor/25 10.00 25.00

2014 Classics Significant Signatures Bats Silver

RANDOM INSERTS IN PACKS
PRINT RUNS B/WN 5-99 COPIES PER
NO PRICING ON QTY 10 OR LESS
EXCHANGE DEADLINE 5/19/2016
8 Buster Posey 25.00 60.00
36 Carlos Sanchez 4.00 10.00
73 Jose Abreu 15.00 40.00
75 C.J. Cron 4.00 10.00
77 Rougned Odor 8.00 20.00
80 George Springer 10.00 25.00
90 Michael Choice 4.00 10.00

2014 Classics Significant Signatures Silver

*GOLD/25: .5X TO 1.2X SILVER
RANDOM INSERTS IN PACKS
PRINT RUNS B/WN 10-299 COPIES PER
NO PRICING ON QTY 10
EXCHANGE DEADLINE 5/19/2016
1 Aaron Sanchez/299 3.00 8.00
3 Alan Trammell/99 6.00 15.00
5 Austin Hedges/299 3.00 8.00
8 Boog Powell/299 3.00 8.00
10 Carlos Correa/299 20.00 50.00
14 Dave Parker/149 5.00 12.00
19 Doug Harvey/99 5.00 12.00
21 Dylan Bundy/99 4.00 10.00
22 Edgar Martinez/99 12.00 30.00
25 Francisco Lindor/299 20.00 50.00
35 Joe Charboneau/299 6.00 15.00
37 Joey Gallo/299 6.00 15.00
41 Jose Canseco/299 4.00 10.00
45 Kris Bryant/299 50.00 120.00
46 Lance Lynn/299 3.00 8.00
50 Maikel Franco/299 4.00 10.00
51 Matt Adams/299 3.00 8.00
52 Maury Wills/299 3.00 8.00
53 Michael Wacha/299 4.00 10.00
54 Miguel Sano/299 4.00 10.00
56 Mookie Betts/299 60.00 150.00
62 Robert Stephenson/299 3.00 8.00
64 Ron Guidry/25 10.00 25.00
67 Shelby Miller/149 4.00 10.00
70 Steve Garvey/199 3.00 8.00
74 Tony La Russa/25 5.00 12.00
75 Whitey Herzog/25 4.00 10.00
76 Willie Horton/89 3.00 8.00
79 Danny Santana/299 20.00 50.00
80 Robbie Ray/299 3.00 8.00
81 Anthony DeSclafani/299 3.00 8.00
82 Christian Bethancourt/299 3.00 8.00
83 Eddie Butler/299 3.00 8.00
84 Nick Ahmed/299 3.00 8.00
85 Erisbel Arruebarrena/299 6.00 15.00
86 Eugenio Suarez/299 8.00 20.00
87 Garin Cecchini/299 3.00 8.00
88 Alex Guerrero/299 4.00 10.00
89 Jace Peterson/299 3.00 8.00
90 Jacob deGrom/299 30.00 80.00
91 Jake Marisnick/299 3.00 8.00
92 James Paxton/299 5.00 12.00
93 Jon Singleton/299 4.00 10.00
94 Luis Sardinas/299 3.00 8.00
95 Marcus Stroman/299 5.00 12.00
96 Rafael Montero/299 3.00 8.00
97 Randal Grichuk/299 10.00 25.00
98 Arismendy Alcantara/299 3.00 8.00
99 Tanner Roark/299 3.00 8.00
100 Tommy La Stella/299 3.00 8.00

2014 Classics Significant Signatures Jerseys Silver

RANDOM INSERTS IN PACKS
PRINT RUNS B/WN 3-299 COPIES PER
NO PRICING ON QTY 10 OR LESS
EXCHANGE DEADLINE 5/19/2016
3 Andrew McCutchen/149 25.00 60.00
5 Anthony Rizzo/299 20.00 50.00
9 Byron Buxton/299 8.00 20.00
12 Carlos Gomez/199 3.00 8.00
20 Enny Romero/299 3.00 8.00
26 Joe Panik/299 4.00 10.00
29 Freddie Freeman/25 10.00 25.00
30 Gaylord Perry/25 5.00 12.00
35 Harold Baines/299 4.00 10.00
36 Carlos Sanchez/299 3.00 8.00
37 Jameson Taillon/299 4.00 10.00
38 Javier Baez/299 12.00 30.00
42 Jonathan Gray/299 4.00 10.00
45 Josh Donaldson/299 10.00 25.00
47 Kyle Zimmer/299 3.00 8.00
53 Mark Trumbo/25 4.00 10.00
63 Starling Marte/199 6.00 15.00
66 Tony Perez/25 20.00 50.00
71 Tyler Collins/299 3.00 8.00
73 Jose Abreu/299 12.00 30.00
74 Billy Hamilton/299 4.00 10.00
75 C.J. Cron/299 3.00 8.00
76 Chris Owings/299 3.00 8.00
77 Rougned Odor/299 4.00 10.00
78 David Hale/299 3.00 8.00
79 David Holmberg/299 3.00 8.00
80 George Springer/299 12.00 30.00
81 Gregory Polanco/299 5.00 12.00
82 J.R. Murphy/299 3.00 8.00
83 Jimmy Nelson/299 3.00 8.00
84 Jonathan Schoop/299 3.00 8.00
85 Andrew Heaney/299 3.00 8.00
86 Jose Ramirez/299 25.00 60.00
87 Kolten Wong/299 4.00 10.00
88 Marcus Semien/299 3.00 8.00
89 Matt Davidson/299 4.00 10.00
90 Michael Choice/299 3.00 8.00
91 Nick Castellanos/299 10.00 25.00
93 Roenis Elias/299 3.00 8.00
94 Taijuan Walker/299 3.00 8.00
95 Travis d'Arnaud/299 6.00 15.00
96 Wei-Chung Wang/299 15.00 40.00
97 Wilmer Flores/299 4.00 10.00
98 Xander Bogaerts/299 20.00 50.00
99 Yangervis Solarte/299 3.00 8.00
100 Yordano Ventura/299 8.00 20.00

2014 Classics Significant Signatures Jerseys Gold Prime

*GOLD: .5X TO 1.2X SILVER
RANDOM INSERTS IN PACKS
PRINT RUNS B/WN 5-25 COPIES PER
NO PRICING ON QTY 10 OR LESS
EXCHANGE DEADLINE 5/19/2016

2014 Classics Stars of Summer

COMPLETE SET (25) 12.00 30.00
RANDOM INSERTS IN PACKS
1 Adam Jones .40 1.00
2 Adrian Beltre .50 1.25
3 Albert Pujols .60 1.50
4 Andrew McCutchen .50 1.25
5 Anthony Rizzo .75 2.00
6 Aroldis Chapman .50 1.25
7 Bryce Harper .75 2.00
8 Buster Posey .60 1.50
9 Chris Davis .30 .75
10 David Ortiz .50 1.25
11 David Wright .40 1.00
12 Derek Jeter 1.25 3.00
13 Dustin Pedroia .50 1.25
14 Edwin Encarnacion .50 1.25
15 Evan Longoria .40 1.00
16 Felix Hernandez .40 1.00
17 Joey Votto .50 1.25
18 Jose Bautista .40 1.00
19 Justin Upton .40 1.00
20 Masahiro Tanaka 1.00 2.50
21 Miguel Cabrera .50 1.25
22 Paul Goldschmidt .50 1.25
23 Starlin Castro .30 .75
24 Yasiel Puig .50 1.25
25 Yu Darvish .50 1.25

2014 Classics Stars of Summer Bats

RANDOM INSERTS IN PACKS
STATED PRINT RUN 99 SER.#'d SETS
1 Adam Jones 2.50 6.00
2 Adrian Beltre 3.00 8.00
5 Anthony Rizzo 5.00 12.00
7 Bryce Harper 8.00 20.00
8 Buster Posey 4.00 10.00
9 Chris Davis 2.00 5.00
10 David Ortiz 3.00 8.00
11 David Wright 2.50 6.00
12 Derek Jeter 8.00 20.00
13 Dustin Pedroia 3.00 8.00
14 Edwin Encarnacion 3.00 8.00
15 Evan Longoria 2.50 6.00
17 Joey Votto 3.00 8.00
21 Miguel Cabrera 3.00 8.00
23 Starlin Castro 2.00 5.00
24 Yasiel Puig 3.00 8.00

2014 Classics Stars of Summer Bats Signatures

RANDOM INSERTS IN PACKS
PRINT RUNS B/WN 5-25 COPIES PER
NO PRICING ON QTY 10 OR LESS
EXCHANGE DEADLINE 5/19/2016
3 Anthony Rizzo/25 20.00 50.00
4 Buster Posey/25 40.00 80.00
18 Jose Abreu/25 40.00 100.00

2014 Classics Stars of Summer Jerseys

RANDOM INSERTS IN PACKS
STATED PRINT RUN 99 SER.#'d SETS
3 Albert Pujols 5.00 12.00
4 Andrew McCutchen 6.00 15.00
5 Anthony Rizzo 8.00 20.00
7 Bryce Harper 8.00 20.00
8 Buster Posey 6.00 15.00
10 David Ortiz 5.00 12.00
11 David Wright 4.00 10.00
12 Derek Jeter 12.00 30.00
15 Evan Longoria 4.00 10.00
16 Felix Hernandez 4.00 10.00
17 Joey Votto 5.00 12.00
19 Justin Upton 4.00 10.00
20 Masahiro Tanaka 12.00 30.00
21 Miguel Cabrera 5.00 12.00
22 Paul Goldschmidt 5.00 12.00
23 Starlin Castro 3.00 8.00
24 Yasiel Puig 5.00 12.00
25 Yu Darvish 5.00 12.00

2014 Classics Stars of Summer Jerseys Signatures

RANDOM INSERTS IN PACKS
PRINT RUNS B/WN 10-99 COPIES PER
NO PRICING ON QTY 10 OR LESS
EXCHANGE DEADLINE 5/19/2016
3 Anthony Rizzo/25 20.00 50.00
4 Buster Posey/25 40.00 80.00
12 Evan Gattis/99 5.00 12.00
15 George Springer/99 20.00 50.00
17 Gregory Polanco/99 8.00 20.00
18 Jose Abreu/99 40.00 100.00

2014 Classics Stars of Summer Materials Combos

RANDOM INSERTS IN PACKS
STATED PRINT RUN 99 SER.#'d SETS
2 Adrian Beltre 5.00 12.00
3 Albert Pujols 5.00 12.00
5 Anthony Rizzo 8.00 20.00
7 Bryce Harper 8.00 20.00
8 Buster Posey 6.00 15.00
11 David Wright 4.00 10.00
12 Derek Jeter 20.00 50.00
13 Dustin Pedroia 5.00 12.00
14 Edwin Encarnacion 5.00 12.00
15 Evan Longoria 4.00 10.00
16 Felix Hernandez 4.00 10.00
17 Joey Votto 5.00 12.00
19 Justin Upton 4.00 10.00
20 Masahiro Tanaka 20.00 50.00
21 Miguel Cabrera 6.00 15.00
22 Paul Goldschmidt 5.00 12.00
23 Starlin Castro 3.00 8.00
24 Yasiel Puig 6.00 15.00
25 Yu Darvish 8.00 20.00

2014 Classics Stars of Summer Materials Combos Signatures

RANDOM INSERTS IN PACKS
PRINT RUNS B/WN 5-25 COPIES PER
NO PRICING ON QTY 10 OR LESS
EXCHANGE DEADLINE 5/19/2016
3 Anthony Rizzo/25 20.00 50.00
4 Buster Posey/25 40.00 80.00
5 Carlos Gomez/25 8.00 20.00
15 George Springer/25 20.00 50.00
18 Jose Abreu/25 40.00 100.00

2014 Classics Timeless Treasures Bats

RANDOM INSERTS IN PACKS
PRINT RUNS B/WN 25-99 COPIES PER
1 Albert Pujols/99 5.00 12.00
2 Bill Dickey/25 20.00 50.00
4 Bob Meusel/25 2.50 6.00
5 Cal Ripken/99 10.00 25.00
13 Joe Jackson/25 100.00 200.00
15 Mark McGwire/99 5.00 16.00
16 Mike Schmidt/99 5.00 12.00
18 Nolan Ryan/25 8.00 20.00
20 Roger Bresnahan/99 12.00 30.00
22 Ryne Sandberg/99 5.00 12.00
23 Tony Gwynn/99 4.00 10.00
24 Tony Lazzeri/99 3.00 8.00

2014 Classics Timeless Treasures Jerseys

RANDOM INSERTS IN PACKS
PRINT RUNS B/WN 5-99 COPIES PER
NO PRICING ON QTY 5
*PRIME/25: .5X TO 1.2X BASIC
1 Albert Pujols/99 5.00 12.00
3 Bob Gibson/99 8.00 20.00
5 Cal Ripken/99 15.00 40.00
6 Herb Pennock/99 8.00 20.00
8 Elston Howard/99 10.00 25.00
10 Gabby Hartnett/99 40.00 80.00
11 Jackie Robinson/42 20.00 50.00
14 Leo Durocher/99 8.00 20.00
15 Mark McGwire/99 15.00 40.00
16 Mike Schmidt/99 8.00 20.00
18 Nolan Ryan/99 10.00 25.00
19 Rick Ferrell/99 10.00 25.00
21 Rogers Hornsby/25 25.00 60.00
22 Ryne Sandberg/99 10.00 25.00
23 Tony Gwynn/99 5.00 12.00
25 Warren Spahn/25 60.00 120.00

2018 Classics

INSERTED IN '18 CHRONICLES PACKS
*TRIB/199: 1X TO 2.5X BASE
*TRIB RC/199: .6X TO 1.5X BASE RC
*GOLD/99: 1.2X TO 3X BASE
*GOLD RC/99: .75X TO 2X BASE RC
*RED/25: 2X TO 5X BASE
*RED RC/25: 1.2X TO 3X BASE RC
1 Cole Hamels .20 .50
2 Victor Robles RC .60 1.50
3 Andrew McCutchen .25 .60
4 Ryan McMahon RC .30 .75
5 Nick Williams RC .30 .75
6 Alex Verdugo RC .40 1.00
7 Shohei Ohtani RC 1.50 4.00
8 Madison Bumgarner .20 .50
9 Dominic Smith RC .25 .60
10 Kris Bryant .30 .75
11 Aaron Judge .60 1.50
12 Rafael Devers RC .75 2.00
13 Shohei Ohtani RC 1.50 4.00
14 Josh Donaldson .20 .50
15 Francisco Lindor .25 .60
16 Clint Frazier RC .50 1.25
17 Jose Altuve .20 .50
18 Amed Rosario RC .30 .75
19 Charlie Blackmon .25 .60
20 Yoenis Cespedes .25 .60
21 Bryce Harper .40 1.00
22 Gleyber Torres RC 2.50 6.00
23 Ronald Acuna Jr. RC 5.00 12.00
24 Miguel Andujar RC 1.00 2.50
25 J.P. Crawford RC .25 .60
26 Rhys Hoskins RC 1.00 2.50
27 Anthony Rizzo .40 1.00
28 Austin Hays RC .40 1.00
29 Mookie Betts .40 1.00
30 Ozzie Albies RC .75 2.00

2018 Classics Classic Singles

INSERTED IN '18 CHRONICLES PACKS
*HOLO GLD/49: .6X TO 1.5X
*HOLO GLD/25: .75X TO 2X
*RED/25: .75X TO 2X BASIC
1 Mickey Mantle
2 Al Kaline 6.00 15.00
3 Mike Piazza 2.50 6.00
4 Mike Trout 12.00 30.00
5 Yoenis Cespedes 2.50 6.00
6 David Ortiz 2.50 6.00
7 Madison Bumgarner 2.00 5.00
8 Max Scherzer 2.50 6.00
9 Frank Thomas
10 Cal Ripken 8.00 20.00
11 Eddie Mathews
12 Harmon Killebrew
13 Aaron Judge 4.00 10.00
14 Jose Altuve 2.00 5.00
15 Gary Sheffield 1.50 4.00
16 Greg Maddux 3.00 8.00
17 Ryne Sandberg 5.00 12.00
18 Reggie Jackson 4.00 10.00
19 Bob Feller 2.00 5.00
20 Tony Gwynn

2018 Classics Classic Singles Blue

*BLUE/99: .5X TO 1.2X BASIC
*BLUE/49: .6X TO 1.5X BASIC
*BLUE/25: .75X TO 2X BASIC
INSERTED IN '18 CHRONICLES PACKS
PRINT RUNS B/WN 10-99 COPIES PER
NO PRICING ON QTY 15 OR LESS
11 Eddie Mathews/25 6.00 15.00

2018 Classics Classic Singles Gold

*GOLD/99-149: .5X TO 1.2X BASIC
*GOLD/49: .6X TO 1.5X BASIC
*GOLD/25: .75X TO 2X BASIC
INSERTED IN '18 CHRONICLES PACKS
PRINT RUNS B/WN 15-149 COPIES PER
NO PRICING ON QTY 15
1 Mickey Mantle/25 20.00 50.00
20 Tony Gwynn/49 4.00 10.00

2019 Classics

RANDOM INSERTS IN PACKS
*RED/99: 1.5X TO 4X
*BLUE/50: 2X TO 5X
*PINK/25: 3X TO 8X
1 Mike Trout 1.25 3.00
2 Fernando Tatis Jr. RC 2.00 5.00
3 Carlos Correa .25 .60
4 Ryan O'Hearn RC .15 .40
5 Pete Alonso RC 2.00 5.00
6 Kyle Tucker RC .30 .75
7 Chris Paddack RC .30 .75
8 Bryce Harper .40 1.00
9 Shohei Ohtani .30 .75
10 Javier Baez .30 .75
11 Aaron Judge .60 1.50
12 Yusei Kikuchi RC .25 .60
13 Eloy Jimenez RC .60 1.50
14 Michael Kopech RC .30 .75
15 Kris Bryant .30 .75
16 Austin Riley RC .75 2.00
17 Keston Hiura RC .50 1.25
18 Corbin Martin RC .25 .60
19 Nick Senzel RC .50 1.25
20 Carter Kieboom RC .25 .60

2020 Classics

RANDOM INSERTS IN PACKS
1 Yordan Alvarez RC 1.25 3.00
2 Bo Bichette RC 3.00 8.00
3 Aristides Aquino RC .50 1.25
4 Gavin Lux RC 1.50 4.00
5 Luis Robert RC 4.00 10.00
6 Brendan McKay RC .40 1.00
7 Shogo Akiyama RC .40 1.00
8 Yoshitomo Tsutsugo RC .30 .75
9 Joe Palumbo RC .25 .60
10 Yonathan Daza RC .30 .75
11 Jaylin Davis RC .40 1.00
12 Abraham Toro RC .30 .75
13 Donnie Walton RC .60 1.50
14 Jonathan Hernandez RC .25 .60
15 Rico Garcia RC .40 1.00
16 Cody Bellinger .50 1.25
17 J.D. Martinez .25 .60
18 Adalberto Mondesi .25 .60
19 Aaron Nola .25 .60
20 Mike Clevinger .20 .50
21 Ken Griffey Jr. .50 1.25
22 Jacob deGrom .25 .60
23 Christian Yelich .30 .75
24 Juan Soto .75 2.00
25 Ronald Acuna Jr. 1.50 4.00

2020 Classics Autographs

RANDOM INSERTS IN PACKS
EXCHANGE DEADLINE 3/18/2022
*RED/50: .6X TO 1.5X BASIC
*RED/25: .8X TO 2X BASIC
*BLUE/25: .8X TO 2X BASIC
1 Victor Caratini 2.50 6.00
2 Rosell Herrera 2.50 6.00
5 Dakota Hudson 3.00 8.00
7 Brad Keller 2.50 6.00
8 Evan White 2.50 6.00
9 Jharel Cotton 2.50 6.00
10 Nick Ciuffo 2.50 6.00
11 Mallex Smith 2.50 6.00
12 Michael Perez 2.50 6.00
13 Randy Dobnak 5.00 12.00
15 Jacob Nix 3.00 8.00
16 A.J. Minter 3.00 8.00
17 David Fletcher 4.00 10.00
18 Kevin Newman 3.00 8.00
20 Nomar Mazara 2.50 6.00
21 Jordan Hicks 3.00 8.00
22 Terrance Gore 2.50 6.00
23 Christin Stewart 2.50 6.00
24 Greg Allen 3.00 8.00
25 Raimel Tapia 2.50 6.00

2020 Classics Autographs Gold

*GOLD/99: .5X TO 1.2X BASIC
*GOLD/50: .6X TO 1.5X BASIC
*GOLD/25: .8X TO 2X BASIC
RANDOM INSERTS IN PACKS
PRINT RUNS B/WN 5-99 COPIES PER
NO PRICING QTY 15 OR LESS
EXCHANGE DEADLINE 3/18/2022
3 Mike Schmidt/25 25.00 60.00
6 Alex Bregman/25 10.00 25.00

1914 Cracker Jack

The cards in this 144-card set measure approximately 2 1/4" by 3". This "Series of colored pictures of Famous Ball Players and Managers" was issued in packages of Cracker Jack in 1914. The cards have tinted photos set against red backgrounds and many are commonly found with caramel stains. The set contains American, National, and Federal League players. The company claims to have printed 15 million cards as noted on the backs. Most of the cards were issued in both 1914 and 1915, but each year can easily be distinguished from the other by the notation of the number of cards in the series as printed on the back (144 for 1914 and 176 for 1915) and by the orientation of the text on the back of the cards. For 1914, the cardback text is right side up when the card is turned over but will be upside down for the 1915 release. Team names are included below for some players to show more specific differences between the 1914 and 1915 issues on those cards.

COMPLETE SET (144) 60000.00 120000.00
1 Otto Knabe 300.00 600.00
2 Frank Baker 750.00 1500.00
3 Joe Tinker 1000.00 2000.00
4 Larry Doyle 200.00 400.00
5 Ward Miller 200.00 400.00
6 Eddie Plank 750.00 1500.00
7 Eddie Collins 750.00 1500.00
8 Rube Oldring 200.00 400.00
9 Artie Hoffman 200.00 400.00
10 John McInnis 200.00 400.00
11 George Stovall 200.00 400.00
12 Connie Mack MG 750.00 1500.00
13 Art Wilson 200.00 400.00
14 Sam Crawford 750.00 1500.00
15 Reb Russell 200.00 400.00
16 Howie Camnitz 200.00 400.00
17 Roger Bresnahan 750.00 1500.00
17B Roger Bresnahan NNO 2000.00 4000.00
18 Johnny Evers 750.00 1500.00
19 Chief Bender 750.00 1500.00
20 Cy Falkenberg 200.00 400.00
21 Heinie Zimmerman 200.00 400.00
22 Joe Wood 1250.00 2500.00
23 Charles Comiskey 750.00 1500.00
24 George Mullen 200.00 400.00
25 Michael Simon 200.00 400.00
26 James Scott 200.00 400.00
27 Bill Carrigan 200.00 400.00
28 Jack Barry 200.00 400.00
29 Vean Gregg 200.00 400.00
30 Ty Cobb 5000.00 10000.00
31 Heinie Wagner 200.00 400.00
32 Mordecai Brown 750.00 1500.00
33 Amos Strunk 200.00 400.00
34 Ira Thomas 300.00 600.00
35 Harry Hooper 750.00 1500.00
36 Ed Walsh 750.00 1500.00
37 Grover C. Alexander 2000.00 4000.00
38 Red Dooin 200.00 400.00
39 Chick Gandil 750.00 1500.00
40 Jimmy Austin 200.00 400.00
41 Tommy Leach 200.00 400.00
42 Al Bridwell 200.00 400.00
43 Rube Marquard 750.00 1500.00
44 Jeff (Charles) Tesreau 200.00 400.00
45 Fred Luderus 200.00 400.00
46 Bob Groom 200.00 400.00
47 Josh Devore 200.00 400.00
48 Harry Lord 300.00 600.00
49 John Miller 200.00 400.00
50 John Hummell 200.00 400.00
51 Nap Rucker 200.00 400.00
52 Zach Wheat 750.00 1500.00
53 Otto Miller 200.00 400.00
54 Marty O'Toole 200.00 400.00
55 Dick Hoblitzel 200.00 400.00
56 Clyde Milan 200.00 400.00
57 Walter Johnson 2000.00 4000.00
58 Wally Schang 200.00 400.00
59 Harry Gessler 200.00 400.00
60 Rollie Zeider 300.00 600.00
61 Ray Schalk 1000.00 2000.00
62 Jay Cashion 300.00 600.00
63 Babe Adams 200.00 400.00
64 Jimmy Archer 200.00 400.00
65 Tris Speaker 750.00 1500.00
66 Napoleon Lajoie 1250.00 2500.00
67 Otis Crandall 200.00 400.00
68 Honus Wagner 4000.00 8000.00
69 John McGraw 750.00 1500.00
70 Fred Clarke 600.00 1200.00
71 Chief Meyers 200.00 400.00
72 John Boehling 200.00 400.00
73 Max Carey 750.00 1500.00
74 Frank Owens 200.00 400.00
75 Miller Huggins 600.00 1200.00
76 Claude Hendrix 200.00 400.00
77 Hughie Jennings MG 750.00 1500.00
78 Fred Merkle 200.00 400.00
79 Ping Bodie 200.00 400.00
80 Ed Ruelbach 200.00 400.00
81 Jim Delahanty 200.00 400.00
82 Gavvy Cravath 200.00 400.00
83 Russ Ford 200.00 400.00
84 Elmer E. Knetzer 200.00 400.00
85 Buck Herzog 200.00 400.00
86 Burt Shotton 200.00 400.00
87 Forrest Cady 200.00 400.00
88 Christy Mathewson 20000.00 50000.00
89 Lawrence Cheney 200.00 400.00
90 Frank Smith 200.00 400.00
91 Roger Peckinpaugh 200.00 400.00
92 Al Demaree 200.00 400.00
93 Del Pratt 200.00 400.00
94 Eddie Cicotte 750.00 1500.00
95 Ray Keating 200.00 400.00
96 Beals Becker 200.00 400.00
97 John (Rube) Benton 200.00 400.00
98 Frank LaPorte 200.00 400.00
99 Frank Chance 2000.00 4000.00
100 Thomas Seaton 200.00 400.00
101 Frank Schulte 200.00 400.00
102 Ray Fisher 200.00 400.00
103 Joe Jackson 10000.00 20000.00
104 Vic Saier 200.00 400.00
105 James Lavender 200.00 400.00
106 Joe Birmingham 200.00 400.00
107 Tom Downey 200.00 400.00
108 Sherry Magee 200.00 400.00
109 Fred Blanding 200.00 400.00
110 Bob Bescher 200.00 400.00
111 Jim Callahan 200.00 400.00
112 Ed Sweeney 200.00 400.00
113 George Suggs 200.00 400.00
114 George Moriarity 200.00 400.00
115 Addison Brennan 200.00 400.00
116 Rollie Zeider 200.00 400.00
117 Ted Easterly 200.00 400.00
118 Ed Konetchy 200.00 400.00
119 George Perring 200.00 400.00
120 Mike Doolan 200.00 400.00
121 Hub Perdue 200.00 400.00
122 Owen Bush 200.00 400.00
123 Slim Sallee 200.00 400.00
124 Earl Moore 200.00 400.00
125 Bert Niehoff 200.00 400.00
126 Walter Blair 200.00 400.00
127 Butch Schmidt 200.00 400.00
128 Steve Evans 200.00 400.00
129 Ray Caldwell 200.00 400.00
130 Ivy Wingo 200.00 400.00
131 George Baumgardner 200.00 400.00
132 Les Nunamaker 200.00 400.00
133 Branch Rickey MG 1000.00 2000.00
134 Armando Marsans 200.00 400.00
135 Bill Killefer 200.00 400.00
136 Rabbit Maranville 750.00 1500.00
137 William Rariden 200.00 400.00
138 Hank Gowdy 200.00 400.00
139 Rebel Oakes 200.00 400.00
140 Danny Murphy 200.00 400.00
141 Cy Barger 200.00 400.00
142 Eugene Packard 200.00 400.00
143 Jake Daubert 200.00 400.00
144 James C. Walsh 400.00 800.00

1915 Cracker Jack

The cards in this 176-card set measure approximately 2 1/4" by 3". The cards were available in boxes of Cracker Jack or from the company for "100 Cracker Jack coupons, or one coupon and 25 cents." An album was available for "50 coupons or one coupon and 10 cents." Most of the cards were issued in both 1914 and 1915, but each year can easily be distinguished from the other by the notation of the number of cards in the series as printed on the back (144 for 1914 and 176 for 1915) and by the orientation of the text on the back of the cards. For 1914, the cardback text is right side up when the card is turned over but will be upside down for the 1915 release. The 1915 Cracker Jack cards are noticeably easier to find than the 1914 Cracker Jack cards due to the mail-in offer, although neither set is plentiful. The set essentially duplicates E145-1 (1914 Cracker Jack) except for some additional cards and new poses. Players in the Federal League are indicated by FED in the checklist below.

COMPLETE SET (176) 25000.00 60000.00
COMMON CARD (1-144) 100.00 200.00
COMMON CARD(145-176) 125.00 250.00
1 Otto Knabe 300.00 600.00
2 Frank Baker 500.00 1000.00
3 Joe Tinker 400.00 800.00
4 Larry Doyle 125.00 250.00
5 Ward Miller 100.00 200.00
6 Eddie Plank 750.00 1500.00
7 Eddie Collins 400.00 800.00
8 Rube Oldring 100.00 200.00
9 Artie Hoffman 100.00 200.00
10 John McInnis 100.00 200.00
11 George Stovall 100.00 200.00
12 Connie Mack MG 400.00 800.00
13 Art Wilson 100.00 200.00
14 Sam Crawford 400.00 800.00
15 Reb Russell 100.00 200.00
16 Howie Camnitz 100.00 200.00
17 Roger Bresnahan 300.00 600.00
18 Johnny Evers 400.00 800.00
19 Chief Bender 400.00 800.00
20 Cy Falkenberg 100.00 200.00
21 Heinie Zimmerman 100.00 200.00
22 Joe Wood 500.00 1000.00
23 Charles Comiskey 500.00 1000.00
24 George Mullen 100.00 200.00
25 Michael Simon 100.00 200.00
26 James Scott 100.00 200.00
27 Bill Carrigan 100.00 200.00
28 Jack Barry 125.00 250.00
29 Vean Gregg 100.00 200.00
30 Ty Cobb 3000.00 6000.00
31 Heinie Wagner 100.00 200.00
32 Mordecai Brown 500.00 1000.00
33 Amos Strunk 100.00 200.00
34 Ira Thomas 100.00 200.00
35 Harry Hooper 300.00 600.00
36 Ed Walsh 400.00 800.00
37 Grover C. Alexander 1000.00 2000.00
38 Red Dooin 100.00 200.00
39 Chick Gandil 400.00 800.00
40 Jimmy Austin 125.00 250.00
41 Tommy Leach 100.00 200.00
42 Al Bridwell 100.00 200.00
43 Rube Marquard 300.00 600.00
44 Jeff (Charles) Tesreau 100.00 200.00
45 Fred Luderus 100.00 200.00
46 Bob Groom 100.00 200.00
47 Josh Devore 100.00 200.00
48 Steve O'Neill 100.00 200.00
49 John Miller 100.00 200.00
50 John Hummell 100.00 200.00
51 Nap Rucker 100.00 200.00
52 Zach Wheat 300.00 600.00
53 Otto Miller 100.00 200.00
54 Marty O'Toole 100.00 200.00
55 Dick Hoblitzel 100.00 200.00
56 Clyde Milan 100.00 200.00
57 Walter Johnson 1500.00 3000.00
58 Wally Schang 100.00 200.00
59 Harry Gessler 100.00 200.00
60 Oscar Dugey 100.00 200.00
61 Ray Schalk 400.00 800.00
62 Willie Mitchell 100.00 200.00
63 Babe Adams 100.00 200.00
64 Jimmy Archer 100.00 200.00
65 Tris Speaker 750.00 1500.00
66 Napoleon Lajoie 600.00 1200.00
67 Otis Crandall 100.00 200.00
68 Honus Wagner 3000.00 6000.00
69 John McGraw MG 400.00 800.00
70 Fred Clarke 300.00 600.00
71 Chief Meyers 125.00 250.00
72 John Boehling 100.00 200.00
73 Max Carey 400.00 800.00
74 Frank Owens 100.00 200.00
75 Miller Huggins 300.00 600.00
76 Claude Hendrix 100.00 200.00
77 Hughie Jennings MG 300.00 600.00
78 Fred Merkle 100.00 200.00
79 Ping Bodie 100.00 200.00
80 Ed Ruelbach 100.00 200.00
81 Jim Delahanty 100.00 200.00
82 Gavvy Cravath 100.00 200.00
83 Russ Ford 100.00 200.00
84 Elmer E. Knetzer 100.00 200.00
85 Buck Herzog 100.00 200.00
86 Burt Shotton 100.00 200.00
87 Forrest Cady 100.00 200.00
88 Christy Mathewson 1750.00 3500.00
89 Lawrence Cheney 100.00 200.00
90 Frank Smith 100.00 200.00
91 Roger Peckinpaugh 100.00 200.00
92 Al Demaree 100.00 200.00
93 Del Pratt 125.00 250.00
94 Eddie Cicotte 450.00 900.00
95 Ray Keating 100.00 200.00
96 Beals Becker 125.00 250.00
97 John (Rube) Benton 100.00 200.00
98 Frank LaPorte 100.00 200.00
99 Hal Chase 250.00 500.00
100 Thomas Seaton 100.00 200.00
101 Frank Schulte 100.00 200.00
102 Ray Fisher 100.00 200.00
103 Joe Jackson 7500.00 15000.00
104 Vic Saier 100.00 200.00
105 James Lavender 100.00 200.00
106 Joe Birmingham 100.00 200.00
107 Thomas Downey 100.00 200.00
108 Sherry Magee 100.00 200.00
109 Fred Blanding 100.00 200.00
110 Bob Bescher 100.00 200.00
111 Herbie Moran 100.00 200.00
112 Ed Sweeney 100.00 200.00
113 George Suggs 100.00 200.00
114 George Moriarity 100.00 200.00
115 Addison Brennan 100.00 200.00
116 Rollie Zeider 100.00 200.00
117 Ted Easterly 100.00 200.00
118 Ed Konetchy 100.00 200.00
119 George Perring 100.00 200.00
120 Mike Doolan 100.00 200.00
121 Hub Perdue 100.00 200.00
122 Owen Bush 100.00 200.00
123 Slim Sallee 100.00 200.00
124 Earl Moore 100.00 200.00
125 Bert Niehoff 100.00 200.00
126 Walter Blair 100.00 200.00
127 Butch Schmidt 100.00 200.00
128 Steve Evans 100.00 200.00
129 Ray Caldwell 100.00 200.00
130 Ivy Wingo 100.00 200.00
131 Geo. Baumgardner 100.00 200.00
132 Les Nunamaker 100.00 200.00
133 Branch Rickey MG 600.00 1200.00
134 Armando Marsans 125.00 250.00
135 William Killefer 100.00 200.00
136 Rabbit Maranville 300.00 600.00
137 William Rariden 100.00 200.00
138 Hank Gowdy 100.00 200.00
139 Rebel Oakes 100.00 200.00
140 Danny Murphy 100.00 200.00
141 Cy Barger 100.00 200.00
142 Eugene Packard 100.00 200.00
143 Jake Daubert 100.00 200.00
144 James C. Walsh 100.00 200.00
145 Ted Cather 125.00 250.00
146 George Tyler 125.00 250.00
147 Lee Magee 125.00 250.00
148 Owen Wilson 125.00 250.00
149 Hal Janvrin 125.00 250.00
150 Doc Johnston 125.00 250.00
151 George Whitted 125.00 250.00
152 George McQuillen 125.00 250.00
153 Bill James 125.00 250.00
154 Dick Rudolph 125.00 250.00
155 Joe Connolly 125.00 250.00
156 Jean Dubuc 125.00 250.00
157 George Kaiserling 125.00 250.00
158 Fritz Maisel 125.00 250.00
159 Heinie Groh 125.00 250.00
160 Benny Kauff 125.00 250.00
161 Edd Roush 500.00 1000.00
162 George Stallings MG 125.00 250.00
163 Bert Whaling 125.00 250.00
164 Bob Shawkey 125.00 250.00
165 Eddie Murphy 125.00 250.00
166 Joe Bush 125.00 250.00
167 Clark Griffith 300.00 600.00
168 Vin Campbell 125.00 250.00
169 Raymond Collins 125.00 250.00
170 Hans Lobert 125.00 250.00
171 Earl Hamilton 125.00 250.00
172 Erskine Mayer 125.00 250.00
173 Tilly Walker 125.00 250.00
174 Robert Veach 125.00 250.00
175 Joseph Benz 125.00 250.00
176 Hippo Vaughn 300.00 600.00

1982 Cracker Jack

The cards in this 16-card set measure 2 1/2" by 3 1/2"; cards came in two sheets of eight cards, plus an advertising card with a title in the center, which measured approximately 7 1/2" by 10 1/2". Cracker Jack reentered the baseball card market for the first time since 1915 to promote the first "Old Timers Baseball Classic" held July 19, 1982. The color player photos have a Cracker Jack border and have either green (NL) or red (AL) frame lines and name panels. The Cracker Jack logo appears on both sides of each card, with AL players numbered 1-8 and NL players numbered 9-16. Of the 16 ballplayers pictured, five did not appear at the game. At first, the two sheets were available only through the mail but are now commonly found in hobby circles. The set was prepared for Cracker Jack by Topps. The prices below reflect individual card prices; the price for complete panels would be about the same as the sum of the card prices for those players on the panel due to the easy availability of uncut sheets.

COMPLETE SET (16) 4.00 10.00
1 Larry Doby .30 .75
2 Bob Feller .40 1.00
3 Whitey Ford .40 1.00
4 Al Kaline .40 1.00
5 Harmon Killebrew .20 .50
6 Mickey Mantle 2.00 5.00
7 Tony Oliva .08 .25
8 Brooks Robinson .40 1.00
9 Hank Aaron 1.25 3.00
10 Ernie Banks .60 1.50
11 Ralph Kiner .20 .50
12 Ed Mathews .20 .50
13 Willie Mays 1.25 3.00
14 Robin Roberts .30 .75
15 Duke Snider .60 1.50
16 Warren Spahn .30 .75

2015 Diamond Kings

COMP.SET w/o SP's (200) 15.00 40.00
SPs RANDOMLY INSERTED
1 Adam Jones .25 .60
2 Adam Wainwright .25 .60
3 Adrian Beltre .30 .75
4 Adrian Gonzalez .25 .60
5 Al Simmons .25 .60
6 Albert Pujols .40 1.00
7 Alex Gordon .25 .60
8 Alexei Ramirez .25 .60
9 Andrew McCutchen .30 .75
10 Anthony Rendon .30 .75
11 Anthony Rizzo .50 1.25
12 Aroldis Chapman .30 .75
13 Babe Ruth .75 2.00
14 Bill Dickey .20 .50
15 Billy Butler .20 .50
16 Bob Feller .25 .60
17 Bobby Murcer .20 .50
18 Bobby Thomson .25 .60
19 Brock Holt .20 .50
20 Bryce Harper .50 1.25
21 Buster Posey .40 1.00
22 Cal Ripken 1.00 2.50
23 Carl Furillo .20 .50
24 Carlos Gomez .20 .50
25 Charlie Blackmon .30 .75
26 Charlie Gehringer .25 .60
27 Chase Utley .25 .60
28 Chris Davis .20 .50
29 Chris Sale .30 .75
30 Clayton Kershaw .60 1.50
31 Collin McHugh .20 .50
32 Corey Kluber .25 .60
33 Dallas Keuchel .25 .60
34 Danny Santana .20 .50
35 Dave Bancroft .20 .50
36 David Ortiz .30 .75
37 David Wright .25 .60
38 Devin Mesoraco .20 .50
39 Don Drysdale .25 .60
40 Duke Snider .25 .60
41 Dustin Pedroia .30 .75
42 Eddie Mathews .30 .75
43 Edwin Encarnacion .30 .75
44 Elston Howard .20 .50
45 Eric Hosmer .25 .60
46 Evan Gattis .20 .50
47 Evan Longoria .25 .60
48 Felix Hernandez .25 .60
49 Frank Chance .25 .60
50 Frankie Frisch .25 .60
51 Freddie Freeman .40 1.00
52 Gabby Hartnett .20 .50
53 Garrett Richards .25 .60
54 Gary Carter .25 .60
55 George Brett .60 1.50
56 George Kelly .20 .50
57 George Springer .25 .60
58 Giancarlo Stanton .30 .75
59 Gil Hodges .25 .60
60 Gil McDougald .20 .50
61 Gregory Polanco .25 .60
62 Harmon Killebrew .30 .75
63 Herb Pennock .25 .60
64 Honus Wagner .30 .75
65 Ichiro Suzuki .40 1.00
66 Jacoby Ellsbury .25 .60
67 Jake Arrieta .25 .60
68 Jason Heyward .25 .60
69 Jim Gilliam .20 .50
70 Jimmie Foxx .30 .75
71 Joe Cronin .20 .50
72 Joe DiMaggio .60 1.50
73 Joe Jackson .40 1.00
74 Joe Mauer .25 .60
75 Johnny Cueto .25 .60
76 Jonathan Lucroy .25 .60
77 Jose Abreu .30 .75
78 Jose Altuve .25 .60
79 Jose Bautista .25 .60
80 Jose Fernandez .30 .75
81 Josh Donaldson .25 .60
82 Jon Lester .25 .60
83 Justin Upton .25 .60
84 Ken Boyer .20 .50
85 Kirby Puckett .30 .75
86 Kyle Seager .20 .50
87 Lefty Gomez .20 .50
88 Lefty O'Doul .20 .50
89 Lefty Williams .20 .50
90 Leo Durocher .20 .50
91 Lloyd Waner .25 .60
92 Lou Gehrig .60 1.50
93 Luke Appling .25 .60
94 Madison Bumgarner .25 .60
95 Manny Machado .30 .75
96 Mark McGwire .50 1.25
97 Masahiro Tanaka .25 .60
98 Matt Adams .20 .50
99 Matt Shoemaker .25 .60
100 Max Scherzer .30 .75
101 Mel Ott .30 .75
102 Michael Brantley .25 .60
103 Mike Trout 1.50 4.00
104 Miller Huggins .20 .50
105 Miguel Cabrera .30 .75
106 Mookie Betts .50 1.25
107 Nap Lajoie .30 .75
108 Nellie Fox .25 .60
109 Nelson Cruz .30 .75
110 Nolan Ryan 1.00 2.50
111 Paul Goldschmidt .30 .75
112 Paul Waner .25 .60
113 Pee Wee Reese .25 .60
114 Rickey Henderson .30 .75
115 Roberto Clemente .75 2.00
116 Robinson Cano .25 .60
117 Roger Maris .30 .75
118 Rogers Hornsby .25 .60
119 Ron Santo .25 .60
120 Ryan Braun .25 .60
121 Salvador Perez .25 .60
122 Sam Crawford .25 .60
123 Shelby Miller .25 .60
124 Sonny Gray .25 .60
125 Stan Musial .50 1.25
126 Starling Marte .25 .60
127 Stephen Strasburg .30 .75
128 Ted Kluszewski .25 .60
129 Ted Williams .60 1.50
130 Thurman Munson .30 .75
131 Todd Frazier .25 .60
132 Tommy Henrich .20 .50
133 Tony Gwynn .30 .75
134 Tony Lazzeri .20 .50
135 Tris Speaker .25 .60
136 Troy Tulowitzki .30 .75
137 Ty Cobb .50 1.25
138 Victor Martinez .25 .60
139 Walter Alston .25 .60
140 Warren Spahn .25 .60
141 Wei-Yin Chen .20 .50
142 Whitey Ford .25 .60
143 Willie Kamm .20 .50
144 Willie Keeler .20 .50
145 Willie Stargell .25 .60
146 Xander Bogaerts .30 .75
147 Yadier Molina .30 .75
148 Yasiel Puig .30 .75
149 Yoenis Cespedes .25 .60
150 Yu Darvish .30 .75
151A Andy Wilkins RC .25 .60
151B Andy Wilkins SP .40 1.00
Black jsy
152A Anthony Ranaudo RC .25 .60
152B Anthony Ranaudo SP .40 1.00
No ball
153 Brandon Finnegan RC .25 .60
154 Buck Farmer RC .25 .60
155A Christian Walker RC .50 1.25
155B Walker SP Bat back .75 2.00
156A Cory Spangenberg RC .25 .60
156B Cory Spangenberg SP .40 1.00
Batting
157A Dalton Pompey RC .30 .75
157B Dalton Pompey SP .50 1.25
White jsy
158A Daniel Norris RC .25 .60
158B Daniel Norris SP .40 1.00
Leg up
159A Dilson Herrera RC .30 .75
159B Dilson Herrera SP .50 1.25
Batting
160 Edwin Escobar RC .25 .60
161 Gary Brown RC .25 .60
162A Jake Lamb RC .40 1.00
162B Jake Lamb SP .60 1.50
Bat Back
163 James McCann RC .40 1.00
164A Javier Baez RC 2.00 5.00
164B Javier Baez SP 3.00 8.00
Looking up
165A Joc Pederson RC .50 1.25
165B Joc Pederson SP .75 2.00
Bunting
166A Jorge Soler RC .40 1.00
166B Jorge Soler SP .60 1.50
Facing left
167A Kendall Graveman RC .25 .60
167B Kendall Graveman SP .40 1.00
Leg up
168A Kennys Vargas RC .25 .60
168B Kennys Vargas SP .40 1.00
Black jsy
169 Lane Adams RC .25 .60
170A Maikel Franco RC .30 .75
170B Franco SP Swing .50 1.25
171 Matt Barnes RC .25 .60
172 Matt Clark RC .25 .60
173 Matt Szczur RC .30 .75
174A Michael Taylor RC .25 .60
174B Michael Taylor SP .40 1.00
White jsy
175A Mike Foltynewicz RC .25 .60
175B Mike Foltynewicz SP .40 1.00
Ball above head
176 R.J. Alvarez RC .25 .60
177A Rusney Castillo RC .30 .75
177B Rusney Castillo SP .50 1.25
Purple sleeves
178 Ryan Rua RC .25 .60
179A Rymer Liriano RC .25 .60
179B Rymer Liriano SP .40 1.00
Facing right
180A Steven Moya RC .30 .75
180B Steven Moya SP .50 1.25
Facing left
181 Terrance Gore RC .25 .60
182 Trevor May RC .25 .60
183A Yorman Rodriguez RC .25 .60
183B Yorman Rodriguez SP .40 1.00
Black jsy
184 Andrew Chafin RC .25 .60
185 Bryce Brentz RC .25 .60
186 Carson Smith RC .25 .60
187 Daniel Corcino RC .25 .60
188 Melvin Mercedes RC .25 .60
189 Alexander Claudio RC .25 .60
190 Bryan Mitchell RC .25 .60
191 Carlos Rivero RC .25 .60
192 Chris Bassitt RC .25 .60
193 Eric Jokisch RC .25 .60
194 Jose Pirela RC .25 .60
195 Kyle Lobstein RC .25 .60
196 Kyle Ryan RC .25 .60
197 Lisalverto Bonilla RC .25 .60
198 Nick Tropeano RC .25 .60
199 Phil Klein RC .25 .60
200 Tomas Telis RC .25 .60

2015 Diamond Kings Framed Blue

*FRMD BLUE: 2X TO 5X BASIC
*FRMD BLUE RC: 1.5X TO 4X BASIC RC
RANDOM INSERTS IN PACKS
STATED PRINT RUN 99 SER.#'d SETS

2015 Diamond Kings Framed Red

*FRMD RED: 1.2X TO 3X BASIC
*FRMD RED RC: 1X TO 2.5X BASIC RC
RANDOM INSERTS IN PACKS

2015 Diamond Kings Gold

*GOLD: 5X TO 12X BASIC
*GOLD: RC: 4X TO 10X BASIC RC
RANDOM INSERTS IN PACKS
STATED PRINT RUN 25 SER.#'d SETS

2015 Diamond Kings Rookie Sapphire

*SAPPHIRE 1.5X TO 4X BASIC SP
RANDOM INSERTS IN PACKS
STATED PRINT RUN 25 SER.#'d SETS

2015 Diamond Kings Silver

*SILVER: 2X TO 5X BASIC
*SILVER: RC: 1.5X TO 4X BASIC RC
RANDOM INSERTS IN PACKS
STATED PRINT RUN 99 SER.#'d SETS

2015 Diamond Kings Aficionado

COMPLETE SET (20) 12.00 30.00
RANDOM INSERTS IN PACKS
*SAPPHIRE/25: 1.5X TO 4X BASIC
1 Mike Trout 3.00 8.00
2 Yasiel Puig .60 1.50
3 Clayton Kershaw 1.25 3.00
4 Bryce Harper 1.00 2.50
5 Yu Darvish .60 1.50
6 Madison Bumgarner .50 1.25
7 Buster Posey .75 2.00
8 Jose Abreu .60 1.50
9 Masahiro Tanaka .50 1.25
10 Ichiro Suzuki .75 2.00
11 Giancarlo Stanton .60 1.50
12 Corey Kluber .50 1.25
13 Yasmany Tomas .50 1.25
14 Rusney Castillo .50 1.25
15 David Ortiz .60 1.50
16 Miguel Cabrera .60 1.50
17 Andrew McCutchen .60 1.50
18 Yadier Molina .60 1.50
19 David Wright .50 1.25
20 Freddie Freeman .75 2.00

2015 Diamond Kings Also Known As

COMPLETE SET (20) 12.00 30.00
RANDOM INSERTS IN PACKS
*SAPPHIRE/25: 1.5X TO 4X BASIC
1 Nolan Ryan 2.00 5.00
2 Frank Thomas .60 1.50
3 Mariano Rivera .75 2.00
4 Babe Ruth 1.50 4.00
5 Lou Gehrig 1.25 3.00
6 Yasiel Puig .60 1.50
7 Ty Cobb 1.00 2.50
8 Honus Wagner .60 1.50
9 Tris Speaker .50 1.25
10 Rogers Hornsby .50 1.25
11 Frank Chance .50 1.25
12 Sam Crawford .50 1.25
13 Reggie Jackson .50 1.25
14 Joe Jackson .75 2.00
15 Stan Musial 1.00 2.50
16 Albert Pujols .75 2.00
17 Mike Trout 3.00 8.00
18 David Ortiz .60 1.50
19 Tony Gwynn .60 1.50
20 Johnny Bench .60 1.50

2015 Diamond Kings Diamond Cuts Signatures

RANDOM INSERTS IN PACKS
PRINT RUNS B/WN 1-99 COPIES PER
NO PRICING ON QTY 15 OR LESS
1 Stan Musial/99 20.00 50.00
2 Bobby Thomson/99 25.00 60.00
3 Johnny Pesky/99 10.00 25.00
7 Lou Boudreau/49 12.00 30.00
11 Rick Ferrell/25 25.00 60.00
14 Harmon Killebrew/49 15.00 40.00
15 Ralph Kiner/99 12.00 30.00

2015 Diamond Kings DK Materials Silver

RANDOM INSERTS IN PACKS
PRINT RUNS B/WN 10-99 COPIES PER
NO PRICING ON QTY 10
*BLUE p/r 25: .6X TO 1.5X BASE p/r 49-99
*BLUE p/r 25: .4X TO 1X BASE p/r 25
*RED p/r 49-99: .4X TO 1X BASE p/r 49-99
*RED p/r 49-99: .25X TO .6X BASE p/r 25
*RED p/r 25: .6X TO 1.5X BASE p/r 49-99
*RED p/r 25: .4X TO 1X BASE p/r 25
1 Adam Jones/99 3.00 8.00
3 Adrian Beltre/99 4.00 10.00
4 Adrian Gonzalez/99 3.00 8.00
6 Albert Pujols/49 5.00 12.00
7 Alex Gordon/99 3.00 8.00
8 Alexei Ramirez/99 3.00 8.00
9 Andrew McCutchen/99 10.00 25.00
10 Anthony Rendon/25 6.00 15.00
11 Anthony Rizzo/99 6.00 15.00
12 Aroldis Chapman/99 4.00 10.00

15 Billy Butler/99 2.50 6.00
19 Brock Holt/25 4.00 10.00
21 Buster Posey/49 10.00 25.00
24 Carlos Gomez/99 2.50 6.00
27 Chase Utley/99 3.00 8.00
28 Chris Davis/49 2.50 6.00
29 Chris Sale/49 4.00 10.00
30 Clayton Kershaw/49 8.00 20.00
33 Dallas Keuchel/99 3.00 8.00
34 Danny Santana/99 2.50 6.00
36 David Ortiz/99 4.00 10.00
37 David Wright/49 3.00 8.00
38 Devin Mesoraco/99 2.50 6.00
41 Dustin Pedroia/99 4.00 10.00
43 Edwin Encarnacion/99 4.00 10.00
45 Eric Hosmer/99 4.00 10.00
46 Evan Gattis/99 2.50 6.00
47 Evan Longoria/49 3.00 8.00
48 Felix Hernandez/25 5.00 12.00
51 Freddie Freeman/49 5.00 12.00
53 Garrett Richards/49 3.00 8.00
57 George Springer/99 3.00 8.00
58 Giancarlo Stanton/49 4.00 10.00
61 Gregory Polanco/25 5.00 12.00
62 Harmon Killebrew/25 6.00 15.00
63 Herb Pennock/25 15.00 40.00
66 Jacoby Ellsbury/25 5.00 12.00
74 Joe Mauer/49 3.00 8.00
75 Johnny Cueto/99 3.00 8.00
77 Jose Abreu/25 6.00 15.00
78 Jose Altuve/99 3.00 8.00
79 Jose Bautista/99 3.00 8.00
80 Jose Fernandez/25 6.00 15.00
81 Josh Donaldson/99 3.00 8.00
83 Justin Upton/99 3.00 8.00
86 Kyle Seager/25 4.00 10.00
94 Madison Bumgarner/49 3.00 8.00
95 Manny Machado/25 6.00 15.00
97 Masahiro Tanaka/25 5.00 12.00
98 Matt Adams/99 2.50 6.00
100 Max Scherzer/99 4.00 10.00
102 Michael Brantley/99 3.00 8.00
103 Mike Trout/49 20.00 50.00
105 Miguel Cabrera/99 4.00 10.00
106 Mookie Betts/99 6.00 15.00
109 Nelson Cruz/99 4.00 10.00
111 Paul Goldschmidt/49 4.00 10.00
116 Robinson Cano/99 3.00 8.00
120 Ryan Braun/99 3.00 8.00
121 Salvador Perez/99 3.00 8.00
123 Shelby Miller/99 3.00 8.00
124 Sonny Gray/99 3.00 8.00
126 Starling Marte/49 3.00 8.00
127 Stephen Strasburg/25 6.00 15.00
136 Troy Tulowitzki/49 4.00 10.00
138 Victor Martinez/99 3.00 8.00
141 Wei-Yin Chen/25 4.00 10.00
146 Xander Bogaerts/25 6.00 15.00
147 Yadier Molina/25 12.00 30.00
148 Yasiel Puig/25 6.00 15.00
150 Yu Darvish/99 4.00 10.00
201 Aaron Sanchez/99 3.00 8.00
202 Addison Russell/25 10.00 25.00
203 Archie Bradley/99 2.50 6.00
204 Barry Bonds/99 10.00 25.00
205 Billy Hamilton/99 3.00 8.00
206 Byron Buxton/99 4.00 10.00
207 Corey Seager/99 5.00 12.00
208 Devon Marrero/99 2.50 6.00
209 Francisco Lindor/99 4.00 10.00
210 Hunter Harvey/99 2.50 6.00
211 Jacob deGrom/99 4.00 10.00
212 Jake Marisnick/99 2.50 6.00
213 Jameson Taillon/99 3.00 8.00
214 Jesse Winker/99 2.50 6.00
215 Jonathan Gray/99 2.50 6.00
216 Kevin Plawecki/99 2.50 6.00
217 Kolten Wong/99 3.00 8.00
218 Kyle Zimmer/99 2.50 6.00
219 Luis Severino/99 4.00 10.00
220 Nick Castellanos/99 4.00 10.00
221 Peter O'Brien/99 4.00 10.00
223 Robert Stephenson/99 2.50 6.00
224 Travis d'Arnaud/99 3.00 8.00

2015 Diamond Kings DK Minis

RANDOM INSERTS IN PACKS
1 Adam Jones 1.25 3.00
2 Adam Wainwright 1.25 3.00
3 Adrian Beltre 1.50 4.00
4 Adrian Gonzalez 1.25 3.00
5 Al Simmons 1.25 3.00
6 Albert Pujols 2.00 5.00
7 Alex Gordon 1.25 3.00
8 Alexei Ramirez 1.25 3.00
9 Andrew McCutchen 1.50 4.00
10 Anthony Rendon 1.50 4.00
11 Anthony Rizzo 2.50 6.00
12 Aroldis Chapman 1.50 4.00
13 Babe Ruth 4.00 10.00
14 Bill Dickey 1.00 2.50
15 Billy Butler 1.00 2.50
16 Bob Feller 1.25 3.00
17 Bobby Murcer 1.00 2.50
18 Bobby Thomson 1.25 3.00
19 Brock Holt 1.00 2.50
20 Bryce Harper 2.50 6.00
21 Buster Posey 2.00 5.00
22 Cal Ripken 6.00 15.00
23 Carl Furillo 1.00 2.50
24 Carlos Gomez 1.00 2.50
26 Charlie Gehringer 1.00 2.50
27 Chase Utley 1.25 3.00
28 Chris Davis 1.00 2.50
29 Chris Sale 1.50 4.00
30 Clayton Kershaw 3.00 8.00
32 Corey Kluber 1.25 3.00
33 Dallas Keuchel 1.25 3.00
34 Danny Santana 1.00 2.50
35 Dave Bancroft 1.00 2.50
36 David Ortiz 1.50 4.00
37 David Wright 1.25 3.00
38 Devin Mesoraco 1.00 2.50
39 Don Drysdale 1.25 3.00
40 Duke Snider 1.25 3.00
41 Dustin Pedroia 1.50 4.00
42 Eddie Mathews 1.25 3.00
43 Edwin Encarnacion 1.50 4.00
44 Elston Howard 1.00 2.50
45 Eric Hosmer 1.25 3.00
46 Evan Gattis 1.00 2.50
47 Evan Longoria 1.25 3.00
48 Felix Hernandez 1.25 3.00
49 Frank Chance 1.25 3.00
50 Frankie Frisch 1.25 3.00
51 Freddie Freeman 2.00 5.00
52 Gabby Hartnett 1.00 2.50
53 Garrett Richards 1.25 3.00
54 Gary Carter 1.25 3.00
55 George Brett 3.00 8.00
56 George Kelly 1.00 2.50
57 George Springer 1.25 3.00
58 Giancarlo Stanton 1.50 4.00
59 Gil Hodges 1.25 3.00
60 Gil McDougald 1.00 2.50
61 Gregory Polanco 1.25 3.00
62 Harmon Killebrew 1.50 4.00
63 Herb Pennock 1.25 3.00
64 Honus Wagner 1.50 4.00
65 Ichiro Suzuki 2.00 5.00
66 Jacoby Ellsbury 1.25 3.00
68 Jason Heyward 1.25 3.00
69 Jim Gilliam 1.00 2.50
70 Jimmie Foxx 1.50 4.00
71 Joe Cronin 1.00 2.50
72 Joe DiMaggio 3.00 8.00
73 Joe Jackson 2.00 5.00
74 Joe Mauer 1.25 3.00
75 Johnny Cueto 1.25 3.00
76 Johnathan Lucroy 1.25 3.00
77 Jose Abreu 1.50 4.00
78 Jose Altuve 1.25 3.00
79 Jose Bautista 1.25 3.00
80 Jose Fernandez 1.50 4.00
81 Josh Donaldson 1.25 3.00
82 Jon Lester 1.25 3.00
83 Justin Upton 1.25 3.00
84 Ken Boyer 1.00 2.50
85 Kirby Puckett 1.50 4.00
86 Kyle Seager 1.00 2.50
87 Lefty Gomez 1.00 2.50
88 Lefty O'Doul 1.00 2.50
89 Lefty Williams 1.00 2.50
90 Leo Durocher 1.00 2.50
91 Lloyd Waner 1.25 3.00
92 Lou Gehrig 3.00 8.00
93 Luke Appling 1.25 3.00
94 Madison Bumgarner 1.25 3.00
95 Manny Machado 1.50 4.00
96 Mark McGwire 2.50 6.00
97 Masahiro Tanaka 1.25 3.00
98 Matt Adams 1.00 2.50
99 Matt Shoemaker 1.25 3.00
100 Max Scherzer 1.50 4.00
101 Mel Ott 1.50 4.00
102 Michael Brantley 1.25 3.00
103 Mike Trout 8.00 20.00
104 Miller Huggins 1.25 3.00
105 Miguel Cabrera 1.50 4.00
106 Mookie Betts 2.50 6.00
107 Nap Lajoie 1.50 4.00
108 Nellie Fox 1.25 3.00
109 Nelson Cruz 1.50 4.00
110 Nolan Ryan 5.00 12.00
111 Paul Goldschmidt 1.50 4.00
112 Paul Waner 1.25 3.00
113 Pee Wee Reese 1.25 3.00
114 Rickey Henderson 1.50 4.00
115 Roberto Clemente 4.00 10.00
116 Robinson Cano 1.25 3.00
117 Roger Maris 1.50 4.00
118 Rogers Hornsby 1.25 3.00
119 Ron Santo 1.25 3.00
120 Ryan Braun 1.25 3.00
121 Salvador Perez 1.25 3.00
122 Sam Crawford 1.25 3.00
123 Shelby Miller 1.25 3.00
124 Sonny Gray 1.25 3.00
125 Stan Musial 2.50 6.00
126 Starling Marte 1.25 3.00
127 Stephen Strasburg 1.50 4.00
128 Ted Kluszewski 1.25 3.00
129 Ted Williams 3.00 8.00
130 Thurman Munson 1.50 4.00
132 Tommy Henrich 1.00 2.50
133 Tony Gwynn 1.25 3.00
134 Tony Lazzeri 1.25 3.00
135 Tris Speaker 1.25 3.00
136 Troy Tulowitzki 1.50 4.00
137 Ty Cobb 2.50 6.00
138 Victor Martinez 1.25 3.00
139 Walter Alston 1.25 3.00
140 Warren Spahn 1.25 3.00
141 Wei-Yin Chen 1.00 2.50
142 Whitey Ford 1.25 3.00
143 Willie Kamm 1.00 2.50
144 Willie Keeler 1.00 2.50
145 Willie Stargell 1.25 3.00
146 Xander Bogaerts 1.50 4.00
147 Yadier Molina 1.50 4.00
148 Yasiel Puig 1.50 4.00
149 Yoenis Cespedes 1.25 3.00
150 Yu Darvish 1.50 4.00
151 Andy Wilkins 1.00 2.50
152 Anthony Ranaudo 1.00 2.50
153 Brandon Finnegan 1.00 2.50
159 Dilson Herrera 1.25 3.00
160 Edwin Escobar 1.00 2.50
161 Gary Brown 1.00 2.50
162 Jake Lamb 1.50 4.00
164 Javier Baez 8.00 20.00
165 Joc Pederson 2.00 5.00
166 Jorge Soler 1.50 4.00
168 Kennys Vargas 1.00 2.50
170 Maikel Franco 1.25 3.00
171 Matt Barnes 1.00 2.50
173 Matt Szczur 1.25 3.00
174 Michael Taylor 1.00 2.50
175 Mike Foltynewicz 1.00 2.50
176 R.J. Alvarez 1.00 2.50
177 Rusney Castillo 1.25 3.00
178 Ryan Rua 1.00 2.50
179 Rymer Liriano 1.00 2.50
180 Steven Moya 1.25 3.00
182 Trevor May 1.00 2.50
183 Yorman Rodriguez 1.00 2.50
201 Aaron Sanchez 1.25 3.00
202 Addison Russell 3.00 8.00
203 Archie Bradley 1.00 2.50
204 Barry Bonds 2.50 6.00
205 Billy Hamilton 1.25 3.00
206 Byron Buxton 1.50 4.00
207 Corey Seager 4.00 10.00
208 Deven Marrero 1.00 2.50
209 Francisco Lindor 6.00 15.00
210 Hunter Harvey 1.00 2.50
211 Jacob deGrom 1.50 4.00
212 Jake Marisnick 1.00 2.50
213 Jameson Taillon 1.25 3.00
214 Jesse Winker 1.00 2.50
215 Jonathan Gray 1.00 2.50
216 Kevin Plawecki 1.00 2.50
217 Kolten Wong 1.25 3.00
218 Kyle Zimmer 1.00 2.50
219 Luis Severino 1.25 3.00
220 Nick Castellanos 1.50 4.00
221 Peter O'Brien 1.50 4.00
222 Robert Refsnyder 1.25 3.00
223 Robert Stephenson 1.00 2.50
224 Travis d'Arnaud 1.25 3.00
231 Yasmany Tomas 1.25 3.00
232 Todd Frazier 1.25 3.00
233 Randy Johnson 1.50 4.00
234 Craig Biggio 1.25 3.00
235 Frank Thomas 1.50 4.00
236 Frankie Crosetti 1.00 2.50
237 Greg Maddux 2.00 5.00
238 Raisel Iglesias 1.25 3.00
239A Kris Bryant 6.00 15.00
Facing Left
239B Kris Bryant 6.00 15.00
Facing Right
240 Mariano Rivera 2.00 5.00
241 Matt Kemp 1.25 3.00
242 Pedro Martinez 1.25 3.00

2015 Diamond Kings DK Minis Framed Materials

RANDOM INSERTS IN PACKS
PRINT RUNS B/WN 5-99 COPIES PER
NO PRICING ON QTY 15 OR LESS
5 Al Simmons/25 10.00 25.00
6 Albert Pujols/25 8.00 20.00
9 Andrew McCutchen/49 10.00 25.00
14 Bill Dickey/49 6.00 15.00
16 Bob Feller/25 8.00 20.00
20 Bryce Harper/49 10.00 25.00
22 Cal Ripken/49 12.00 30.00
23 Carl Furillo/49 6.00 15.00
26 Charlie Gehringer/25 12.00 30.00
29 Chris Sale/49 4.00 10.00
30 Clayton Kershaw/49 6.00 15.00
39 Don Drysdale/49 8.00 20.00
40 Duke Snider/49 3.00 8.00
42 Eddie Mathews/49 6.00 15.00
44 Elston Howard/49 5.00 12.00
48 Felix Hernandez/49 3.00 8.00
50 Frankie Frisch/25 15.00 40.00
51 Freddie Freeman/49 5.00 12.00
52 Gabby Hartnett/49 20.00 50.00
55 George Brett/49 15.00 40.00
56 George Kelly/49 15.00 40.00
57 George Springer/49 3.00 8.00
58 Giancarlo Stanton/49 4.00 10.00
64 Honus Wagner/99 8.00 20.00
65 Ichiro Suzuki/49 5.00 12.00
73 Joe Jackson/25 100.00 200.00
77 Jose Abreu/25 6.00 15.00
88 Lefty O'Doul/49 50.00 100.00
90 Leo Durocher/25 15.00 40.00
91 Lloyd Waner/49 6.00 15.00
92 Lou Gehrig/25 40.00 100.00
94 Madison Bumgarner/49 3.00 8.00
96 Mark McGwire/49 6.00 15.00
97 Masahiro Tanaka/49 10.00 25.00
101 Mel Ott/25 20.00 50.00
102 Michael Brantley/49 3.00 8.00
103 Mike Trout/49 15.00 40.00
104 Miller Huggins/25 12.00 30.00
105 Miguel Cabrera/49 6.00 15.00
106 Mookie Betts/49 6.00 15.00
107 Nap Lajoie/25 40.00 80.00
108 Nellie Fox/25 10.00 25.00
110 Nolan Ryan/49 25.00 60.00
111 Paul Goldschmidt/49 4.00 10.00
112 Paul Waner/25 12.00 30.00
113 Pee Wee Reese/49 6.00 15.00
114 Rickey Henderson/49 5.00 12.00
115 Roberto Clemente/25 40.00 100.00
116 Robinson Cano/49 3.00 8.00
117 Roger Maris/49 10.00 25.00
118 Rogers Hornsby/25 30.00 60.00
119 Ron Santo/49 3.00 8.00
122 Sam Crawford/25 15.00 40.00
124 Sonny Gray/49 3.00 8.00
125 Stan Musial/49 12.00 30.00
129 Ted Williams/49 20.00 50.00
130 Thurman Munson/49 12.00 30.00
132 Tommy Henrich/49 6.00 15.00
133 Tony Gwynn/49 4.00 10.00
134 Tony Lazzeri/25 10.00 25.00
135 Tris Speaker/25 10.00 25.00
136 Troy Tulowitzki/49 4.00 10.00
137 Ty Cobb/25 40.00 100.00
139 Walter Alston/49 6.00 15.00
144 Willie Keeler/49 10.00 25.00
148 Yasiel Puig/49 4.00 10.00
150 Yu Darvish/49 4.00 10.00
161 Gary Brown/49 2.50 6.00
164 Javier Baez/49 20.00 50.00
165 Joc Pederson/49 5.00 12.00
166 Jorge Soler/49 4.00 10.00
168 Kennys Vargas/49 2.50 6.00
170 Maikel Franco/49 3.00 8.00
174 Michael Taylor/49 2.50 6.00
177 Rusney Castillo/49 3.00 8.00
180 Steven Moya/49 3.00 8.00
204 Barry Bonds/49 10.00 25.00
206 Byron Buxton/49 4.00 10.00
207 Corey Seager/49 10.00 25.00
209 Francisco Lindor/49 15.00 40.00
211 Jacob deGrom/49 4.00 10.00
219 Luis Severino/49 3.00 8.00
235 Frank Thomas/49 15.00 40.00
236 Frankie Crosetti/49 8.00 20.00
240 Mariano Rivera/49 5.00 12.00
243 Pedro Martinez/49 3.00 8.00
245 Randy Johnson/49 8.00 20.00

2015 Diamond Kings DK Minis Materials

RANDOM INSERTS IN PACKS
PRINT RUNS B/WN 10-99 COPIES PER
NO PRICING ON QTY 10
*PRIME/25: .5X TO 1.2X BASE p/r 49-99
*PRIME/25: .4X TO 1X BASE p/r 25
1 Adam Jones/99 3.00 8.00
2 Adrian Beltre/99 4.00 10.00
3 Adrian Gonzalez/99 3.00 8.00
7 Alex Gordon/99 3.00 8.00
8 Alexei Ramirez/99 3.00 8.00
10 Anthony Rendon/99 4.00 10.00
11 Anthony Rizzo/99 6.00 15.00
12 Aroldis Chapman/99 4.00 10.00
15 Billy Butler/99 2.50 6.00
17 Bobby Murcer/99 8.00 20.00
18 Bobby Thomson/99 6.00 15.00
19 Brock Holt/49 2.50 6.00
21 Buster Posey/99 5.00 12.00
24 Carlos Gomez/99 2.50 6.00
27 Chase Utley/99 3.00 8.00
28 Chris Davis/99 2.50 6.00
33 Dallas Keuchel/99 3.00 8.00
34 Danny Santana/49 2.50 6.00
36 David Ortiz/99 4.00 10.00
37 David Wright/99 3.00 8.00
38 Devin Mesoraco/99 2.50 6.00
41 Dustin Pedroia/99 4.00 10.00
43 Edwin Encarnacion/99 4.00 10.00
45 Eric Hosmer/99 3.00 8.00
46 Evan Gattis/99 2.50 6.00
47 Evan Longoria/99 3.00 8.00
53 Garrett Richards/99 3.00 8.00
54 Gary Carter/99 6.00 15.00
60 Gil McDougald/99 6.00 15.00
61 Gregory Polanco/99 3.00 8.00
62 Harmon Killebrew/99 4.00 10.00
66 Jacoby Ellsbury/99 3.00 8.00
68 Jason Heyward/99 3.00 8.00
69 Jim Gilliam/99 2.50 6.00
74 Joe Mauer/99 3.00 8.00
75 Johnny Cueto/99 3.00 8.00
78 Jose Altuve/99 3.00 8.00
79 Jose Bautista/99 3.00 8.00
81 Josh Donaldson/99 3.00 8.00
83 Justin Upton/99 3.00 8.00
84 Ken Boyer/99 2.50 6.00
85 Kirby Puckett/99 15.00 40.00
89 Lefty Williams/99 12.00 30.00
93 Luke Appling/25 8.00 20.00
95 Manny Machado/99 6.00 15.00
98 Matt Adams/99 2.50 6.00
100 Max Scherzer/99 4.00 10.00
109 Nelson Cruz/99 4.00 10.00
120 Ryan Braun/99 3.00 8.00
121 Salvador Perez/99 3.00 8.00
123 Shelby Miller/99 3.00 8.00
126 Starling Marte/99 3.00 8.00
127 Stephen Strasburg/99 4.00 10.00
128 Ted Kluszewski/99 3.00 8.00
138 Victor Martinez/99 3.00 8.00
142 Whitey Ford/99 3.00 8.00
143 Willie Kamm/99 5.00 12.00
145 Willie Stargell/99 8.00 20.00
146 Xander Bogaerts/99 4.00 10.00
147 Yadier Molina/99 6.00 15.00
151 Andy Wilkins/99 2.50 6.00
152 Anthony Ranaudo/99 2.50 6.00
153 Brandon Finnegan/99 2.50 6.00
159 Dilson Herrera/99 3.00 8.00
160 Edwin Escobar/99 2.50 6.00
162 Jake Lamb/99 4.00 10.00
171 Matt Barnes/99 2.50 6.00
173 Matt Szczur/99 3.00 8.00
175 Mike Foltynewicz/99 2.50 6.00
176 R.J. Alvarez/99 2.50 6.00
178 Ryan Rua/25 4.00 10.00
179 Rymer Liriano/99 2.50 6.00
182 Trevor May/99 2.50 6.00
183 Yorman Rodriguez/99 2.50 6.00
201 Aaron Sanchez/99 3.00 8.00
202 Addison Russell/99 4.00 10.00
203 Archie Bradley/99 2.50 6.00
205 Billy Hamilton/99 3.00 8.00
208 Deven Marrero/99 2.50 6.00
210 Hunter Harvey/99 2.50 6.00
212 Jake Marisnick/99 2.50 6.00
213 Jameson Taillon/99 3.00 8.00
214 Jesse Winker/99 2.50 6.00
215 Jonathan Gray/99 2.50 6.00
216 Kevin Plawecki/99 2.50 6.00
217 Kolten Wong/99 3.00 8.00
218 Kyle Zimmer/99 2.50 6.00
220 Nick Castellanos/99 4.00 10.00
221 Peter O'Brien/99 4.00 10.00
223 Robert Stephenson/99 2.50 6.00
224 Travis d'Arnaud/99 3.00 8.00
234 Craig Biggio/49 3.00 8.00
237 Greg Maddux/99 5.00 12.00
247 Wei-Yin Chen/99 2.50 6.00

2015 Diamond Kings DK Originals

COMPLETE SET (20) 10.00 25.00
RANDOM INSERTS IN PACKS
*SAPPHIRE/25: 1.5X TO 4X BASIC
1 Mike Trout 3.00 8.00
2 Yasiel Puig .60 1.50
3 Clayton Kershaw 1.25 3.00
4 Bryce Harper 1.00 2.50
5 Yu Darvish .60 1.50
6 Madison Bumgarner .50 1.25
7 Buster Posey .75 2.00
8 Jose Abreu .60 1.50
9 Masahiro Tanaka .50 1.25
10 Ichiro Suzuki .75 2.00
11 Giancarlo Stanton .60 1.50
12 Corey Kluber .50 1.25
13 Yasmany Tomas .50 1.25
14 Rusney Castillo .50 1.25
15 Dustin Pedroia .60 1.50
16 Miguel Cabrera .60 1.50
17 Andrew McCutchen .60 1.50
18 Yadier Molina .60 1.50
19 Robinson Cano .50 1.25
20 Jacob deGrom .60 1.50

2015 Diamond Kings DK Signature Materials Framed Blue

*FRMD BLUE: .6X TO 1.5X BASIC
RANDOM INSERTS IN PACKS
PRINT RUNS B/WN 5-25 COPIES PER
NO PRICING ON QTY 15 OR LESS
1 Adam Jones/25 12.00 30.00
4 Adrian Gonzalez/25 12.00 3.00
10 Anthony Rendon/25 12.00 30.00
11 Anthony Rizzo/25 20.00 50.00
29 Chris Sale/25 12.00 30.00
36 David Ortiz/25 30.00 80.00
203 Archie Bradley/25 6.00 15.00
206 Byron Buxton/25 25.00 60.00

2015 Diamond Kings DK Signature Materials Framed Red

*FRMD RED: .5X TO 1.2X BASIC
RANDOM INSERTS IN PACKS
PRINT RUNS B/WN 5-99 COPIES PER
NO PRICING ON QTY 15 OR LESS
1 Adam Jones/75 10.00 25.00
4 Adrian Gonzalez/49 10.00 25.00
10 Anthony Rendon/75 10.00 25.00
11 Anthony Rizzo/49 15.00 40.00
36 David Ortiz/49 25.00 60.00
203 Archie Bradley/49 5.00 12.00
225 Carlos Rodon/75 8.00 20.00
226 D.J. Peterson/49 5.00 12.00

2015 Diamond Kings DK Signature Materials Silver

RANDOM INSERTS IN PACKS
PRINT RUNS B/WN 10-299 COPIES PER
NO PRICING ON QTY 10 OR LESS
15 Billy Butler/99 4.00 10.00
19 Brock Holt/299 4.00 10.00
33 Dallas Keuchel/299 5.00 12.00
34 Danny Santana/299 4.00 10.00
201 Aaron Sanchez/299 4.00 10.00
202 Addison Russell/199 12.00 30.00
207 Corey Seager/299 20.00 50.00
208 Deven Marrero/99 6.00 15.00
209 Francisco Lindor/99 25.00 60.00
210 Hunter Harvey/99 4.00 10.00
211 Jacob deGrom/99 12.00 30.00
212 Jake Marisnick/99 4.00 10.00
213 Jameson Taillon/99 5.00 12.00
214 Jesse Winker/99 6.00 15.00
215 Jonathan Gray/99 4.00 10.00
216 Kevin Plawecki/99 4.00 10.00
217 Kolten Wong/99 5.00 12.00
218 Kyle Zimmer/99 4.00 10.00
219 Luis Severino/99 5.00 12.00
220 Nick Castellanos/99 6.00 15.00
221 Peter O'Brien/99 6.00 15.00
223 Robert Stephenson/99 4.00 10.00
228 Kendall Graveman/299 4.00 10.00
230 Kris Bryant/99 40.00 100.00

2015 Diamond Kings HOF Heroes Materials Framed Blue

RANDOM INSERTS IN PACKS
PRINT RUNS B/WN 1-25 COPIES PER
NO PRICING ON QTY 10 OR LESS
4 Bob Feller/25 15.00 40.00
5 Charlie Gehringer/25 12.00 30.00

2015 Diamond Kings HOF Heroes Signature Materials Framed Blue

*FRMD BLUE: .5X TO 1.2X BASIC
RANDOM INSERTS IN PACKS
PRINT RUNS B/WN 8-25 COPIES PER
NO PRICING ON QTY 10 OR LESS
14 Carlton Fisk/25 12.00 30.00

2015 Diamond Kings HOF Heroes Signature Materials Framed Red

RANDOM INSERTS IN PACKS
PRINT RUNS B/WN 15-49 COPIES PER
NO PRICING ON QTY 15
10 Al Kaline/49 25.00 50.00
11 Andre Dawson/49 10.00 25.00
12 Billy Williams/49 10.00 25.00
13 Brooks Robinson/49 20.00 50.00
17 Bert Blyleven/49 15.00 40.00
18 Barry Larkin/49 25.00 60.00
19 Bob Gibson/25 20.00 50.00

2015 Diamond Kings HOF Sluggers

COMPLETE SET (20) 10.00 25.00
RANDOM INSERTS IN PACKS
*SAPPHIRE/25: 1.5X TO 4X BASIC
1 Babe Ruth 1.50 4.00
2 Frank Robinson .50 1.25
3 Harmon Killebrew .60 1.50
4 Reggie Jackson .50 1.25
5 Frank Thomas .60 1.50
6 Eddie Mathews .60 1.50
7 Mel Ott .60 1.50
8 Eddie Murray .50 1.25
9 Lou Gehrig 1.25 3.00
10 Stan Musial 1.00 2.50
11 Willie Stargell .50 1.25
12 Carl Yastrzemski 1.00 2.50
13 Andre Dawson .50 1.25
14 Cal Ripken 2.00 5.00
15 Billy Williams .50 1.25
16 Duke Snider .50 1.25
17 Al Kaline .60 1.50
18 Johnny Bench .60 1.50
19 Ty Cobb 1.00 2.50
20 Jimmie Foxx .60 1.50

2015 Diamond Kings Masters of the Game Materials

RANDOM INSERTS IN PACKS
PRINT RUNS B/WN 10-99 COPIES PER
NO PRICING ON QTY 10
1 Nap Lajoie/25 30.00 60.00
5 Chuck Klein/99 10.00 25.00
6 Lou Gehrig/25 30.00 80.00
7 Frank Robinson/99 4.00 10.00
8 Carl Yastrzemski/49 15.00 40.00
9 Miguel Cabrera/99 5.00 12.00
11 Bob Feller/99 6.00 15.00
12 Steve Carlton/99 4.00 10.00
13 Dwight Gooden/99 3.00 8.00
14 Roger Clemens/99 6.00 15.00
15 Pedro Martinez/99 4.00 10.00
16 Randy Johnson/99 5.00 12.00
17 Clayton Kershaw/99 10.00 25.00
18 Mike Trout/99 15.00 40.00
19 Tony Gwynn/99 5.00 12.00
20 Ken Griffey Jr./99 6.00 15.00

2015 Diamond Kings Rookie Signature Materials Silver

RANDOM INSERTS IN PACKS
PRINT RUNS B/WN 99-299 COPIES PER
*FRMD RED/99: .5X TO 1.2X BASIC
*FRMD RED/25: .6X TO 1.5X BASIC
*BLUE/25: .6X TO 1.5X BASIC
151 Andy Wilkins/299 4.00 10.00
152 Anthony Ranaudo/299 4.00 10.00
153 Brandon Finnegan/299 4.00 10.00
157 Dalton Pompey/299 5.00 12.00
159 Dilson Herrera/299 5.00 12.00
160 Edwin Escobar/299 4.00 10.00
161 Gary Brown/299 4.00 10.00
162 Jake Lamb/299 6.00 15.00
164 Javier Baez/299 12.00 30.00
165 Joc Pederson/299 6.00 15.00
166 Jorge Soler/299 6.00 15.00
168 Kennys Vargas/299 4.00 10.00
170 Maikel Franco/299 6.00 15.00
171 Matt Barnes/299 4.00 10.00
173 Matt Szczur/299 5.00 12.00
174 Michael Taylor/299 4.00 10.00
175 Mike Foltynewicz/299 4.00 10.00
176 R.J. Alvarez/299 4.00 10.00
177 Rusney Castillo/299 5.00 12.00
178 Ryan Rua/99 4.00 10.00
179 Rymer Liriano/299 4.00 10.00
180 Steven Moya/299 5.00 12.00
182 Trevor May/299 4.00 10.00
183 Yorman Rodriguez/99 4.00 10.00

2015 Diamond Kings Sketches and Swatches

RANDOM INSERTS IN PACKS
PRINT RUNS B/WN 5-99 COPIES PER
NO PRICING ON QTY 5
*PRIME/25: .5X TO 1.2X BASIC
2 Chris Sale/25 12.00 30.00
3 Dustin Pedroia/25 20.00 50.00
4 Freddie Freeman/49 12.00 30.00
5 Jose Abreu/25 10.00 25.00
7 Paul Goldschmidt/25 12.00 30.00
8 Sonny Gray/25 12.00 30.00
9 Troy Tulowitzki/25 20.00 50.00
10 Jacob deGrom/25 15.00 40.00
11 Brock Holt/99 8.00 20.00
13 Anthony Rendon/49 12.00 30.00
14 Starling Marte/25 20.00 50.00
15 Matt Adams/25 6.00 15.00
17 Eric Hosmer/25 20.00 50.00
18 Edwin Encarnacion/25 10.00 25.00
19 Dallas Keuchel/99 12.00 30.00
20 Adrian Gonzalez/49 8.00 20.00

2015 Diamond Kings Sovereign Signatures Materials

RANDOM INSERTS IN PACKS
PRINT RUNS B/WN 5-99 COPIES PER
NO PRICING ON QTY 15 OR LESS
*PRIME/25: .6X TO 1.5X BASIC
10 Anthony Rizzo/49 12.00 30.00
11 Danny Santana/99 6.00 15.00
19 Adam Jones/49 12.00 30.00

2015 Diamond Kings Studio Portraits Materials Silver

RANDOM INSERTS IN PACKS
PRINT RUNS B/WN 25-99 COPIES PER
1 Yu Darvish/99 4.00 10.00
2 Yasiel Puig/99 10.00 25.00
3 Mike Trout/99 15.00 40.00
4 Bryce Harper/99 8.00 20.00
5 Clayton Kershaw/49 8.00 20.00
6 Madison Bumgarner/99 6.00 15.00
7 Masahiro Tanaka/25 10.00 25.00
8 Ichiro Suzuki/99 8.00 20.00
9 Albert Pujols/99 8.00 20.00
10 David Ortiz/99 4.00 10.00
11 Yadier Molina/99 4.00 10.00
12 Andrew McCutchen/99 10.00 25.00
13 Hyun-Jin Ryu/99 3.00 8.00
14 Jose Bautista/99 3.00 8.00
15 Edwin Encarnacion/99 4.00 10.00
16 Giancarlo Stanton/99 4.00 10.00
17 Felix Hernandez/99 3.00 8.00
18 Miguel Cabrera/99 8.00 20.00
19 Jose Abreu/25 6.00 15.00
20 Robinson Cano/99 3.00 8.00
21 Buster Posey/99 10.00 25.00
22 Paul Goldschmidt/99 4.00 10.00
23 Stephen Strasburg/99 4.00 10.00
24 Evan Longoria/99 3.00 8.00
25 Troy Tulowitzki/99 4.00 10.00

2015 Diamond Kings Studio Portraits Signature Materials Silver

RANDOM INSERTS IN PACKS
PRINT RUNS B/WN 25-99 COPIES PER
*FRMD RED: .4X TO 1X BASIC
1 Andy Wilkins/99 4.00 10.00
2 Anthony Ranaudo/99 4.00 10.00
3 Dalton Pompey/99 5.00 12.00
4 Dilson Herrera/99 5.00 12.00
5 Gary Brown/99 4.00 10.00
6 Jake Lamb/99 6.00 15.00
7 Javier Baez/99 15.00 40.00
8 Joc Pederson/99 15.00 40.00
9 Jorge Soler/99 15.00 40.00
10 Kennys Vargas/99 4.00 10.00
11 Maikel Franco/99 5.00 12.00
12 Matt Barnes/99 4.00 10.00
13 Matt Szczur/99 5.00 12.00
14 Michael Taylor/99 4.00 10.00
15 Mike Foltynewicz/99 4.00 10.00
16 R.J. Alvarez/99 4.00 10.00
17 Rusney Castillo/99 5.00 12.00
19 Rymer Liriano/99 4.00 10.00
20 Steven Moya/99 5.00 12.00
21 Trevor May/99 4.00 10.00
22 Yorman Rodriguez/99 4.00 10.00
23 Edwin Escobar/99 4.00 10.00
25 Kris Bryant/49 75.00 150.00

2015 Diamond Kings Timeline Materials

RANDOM INSERTS IN PACKS
PRINT RUNS B/WN 10-99 COPIES PER
NO PRICING ON QTY 10
*PRIME/25: .75X TO 2X BASIC
2 Abreu/deGrom/25 6.00 15.00
3 Kershaw/Trout/49 20.00 50.00
4 Posey/Bumgarner/99 10.00 25.00
7 Kershaw/Verlander/25 12.00 30.00
9 Castillo/Abreu/25 6.00 15.00
10 Soler/Baez/99 6.00 15.00
11 Pederson/Puig/99 12.00 30.00
12 D.Ortiz/K.Vargas/99 6.00 15.00
13 Harper/Taylor/99 6.00 15.00
15 Suzuki/Tanaka/25 15.00 40.00
16 Johnson/Martinez/99 10.00 25.00
18 Seager/Pederson/49 15.00 40.00
19 Buxton/Vargas/99 6.00 15.00
20 Russell/Bryant/49 20.00 50.00

2016 Diamond Kings

COMP.SET w/o SP (185)	20.00	50.00
1 Babe Ruth	.75	2.00
2 Bill Dickey	.20	.50
3 Billy Martin	.25	.60
4 Frank Chance	.25	.60
5 George Kelly	.20	.50
6 Gil Hodges	.25	.60
7A Honus Wagner	.30	.75
7B Honus Wagner SP w/Glove	.75	2.00
8 Jimmie Foxx	.30	.75
9A Joe DiMaggio	.60	1.50
9B DMggo SP Empty stnd	1.50	4.00
10 Joe Jackson	.40	1.00
11 Lefty Gomez	.20	.50
12 Leo Durocher	.20	.50
13A Lou Gehrig	.60	1.50
13B Gehrig SP Green	1.50	4.00
14 Luke Appling	.25	.60
15 Mel Ott	.30	.75
16 Pee Wee Reese	.25	.60
17A Roberto Clemente	.75	2.00
17B Clmnte SP SP Green	2.00	5.00
18 Roger Maris	.30	.75
19 Rogers Hornsby	.25	.60
20 Stan Musial	.50	1.25
21A Ted Williams	.60	1.50
21B Wllms SP Blk slvs	1.50	4.00
22 Tony Lazzeri	.25	.60
23A Ty Cobb	.50	1.25
23B Cobb SP Bat on shldr	1.25	3.00
24 Walter O'Malley	.20	.50
25 Don Hoak	.20	.50
26 Earl Averill	.20	.50
27 Elston Howard	.20	.50
28 Frankie Crosetti	.20	.50
29 Frankie Frisch	.25	.60
30 Gabby Hartnett	.20	.50
31 Gil McDougald	.20	.50
32 Goose Goslin	.25	.60
33 Bob Meusel	.20	.50
34 Bob Turley	.20	.50
35 Chuck Klein	.20	.50
36 Dom DiMaggio	.20	.50
37 Harry Brecheen	.20	.50
38 Heinie Groh	.20	.50
39 Jake Daubert	.20	.50
40 Jim Bottomley	.20	.50
41 John McGraw	.25	.60
42 Johnny Sain	.20	.50
43 Moose Skowron	.20	.50
44 Roger Bresnahan	.25	.60
45 Tom Yawkey	.20	.50
46A Kirby Puckett	.30	.75
46B Kirby Puckett SP No bat	.75	2.00
47 Jim Gilliam	.20	.50
48 Miller Huggins	.20	.50
49 Nap Lajoie	.30	.75
50 Lefty O'Doul	.20	.50
51 Adam Jones	.25	.60
52 Adam Wainwright	.25	.60
53 Adrian Beltre	.30	.75
54 Adrian Gonzalez	.25	.60
55 Albert Pujols	.40	1.00
56 Andrew McCutchen	.30	.75
57 Anthony Rendon	.30	.75
58 Anthony Rizzo	.50	1.25
59A Bryce Harper	.50	1.25
59B Harper SP Thrwng	1.25	3.00
60 Buster Posey	.40	1.00
61 Chris Davis	.20	.50
62 Clayton Kershaw	.60	1.50
63 Dallas Keuchel	.25	.60
64 David Ortiz	.30	.75
65 David Wright	.25	.60
66 Dustin Pedroia	.30	.75
67 Edwin Encarnacion	.30	.75
68 Eric Hosmer	.25	.60
69 Evan Gattis	.20	.50
70 Evan Longoria	.25	.60
71 Felix Hernandez	.25	.60
72 Freddie Freeman	.40	1.00
73 Garrett Richards	.25	.60
74 George Springer	.25	.60
75 Giancarlo Stanton	.30	.75
76 Ichiro Suzuki	.40	1.00
77 Jake Arrieta	.25	.60
78 Jason Heyward	.25	.60
79 Joe Mauer	.25	.60
80 Jonathan Lucroy	.25	.60
81 Jose Abreu	.30	.75
82 Jose Altuve	.25	.60
83 Jose Bautista	.25	.60
84 Josh Donaldson	.25	.60
85 Justin Upton	.25	.60
86 Madison Bumgarner	.25	.60
87 Manny Machado	.30	.75
88 Max Scherzer	.30	.75
89 Michael Brantley	.25	.60
90 Miguel Cabrera	.30	.75
91A Mike Trout	1.50	4.00
91B Trout SP Swngng	4.00	10.00
92 Mookie Betts	.50	1.25
93 Nelson Cruz	.30	.75
94 Paul Goldschmidt	.30	.75
95 Robinson Cano	.25	.60
96 Salvador Perez	.25	.60
97 Sonny Gray	.25	.60
98 Starling Marte	.25	.60
99 Stephen Strasburg	.30	.75
100 Todd Frazier	.25	.60
101 Troy Tulowitzki	.30	.75
102 Wei-Yin Chen	.20	.50
103 Xander Bogaerts	.30	.75
104 Yadier Molina	.30	.75
105 Yoenis Cespedes	.30	.75
106 Yu Darvish	.30	.75
107 Matt Kemp	.25	.60
108 David Price	.25	.60
109A Kris Bryant	.40	1.00
109B Bryant SP Blue slvs	1.00	2.50
110 Yasmany Tomas	.20	.50
111 Rusney Castillo	.20	.50
112 Jorge Soler	.30	.75
113 Joc Pederson	.25	.60
114 Maikel Franco	.25	.60
115 Noah Syndergaard	.25	.60
116 Prince Fielder	.25	.60
117 Zack Greinke	.25	.60
118 Chris Archer	.20	.50
119 Corey Kluber	.25	.60
120 Matt Carpenter	.30	.75
121 Michael Taylor	.20	.50
122 Carlos Correa	.30	.75
123 Vladimir Guerrero	.25	.60
124 A.J. Pollock	.20	.50
125 Nolan Arenado	.40	1.00
126 Ken Griffey Jr.	.60	1.50
127 George Brett	.60	1.50
128 Cal Ripken	1.00	2.50
129 Nolan Ryan	1.00	2.50
130 Rickey Henderson	.30	.75
131 Mariano Rivera	.40	1.00
132 Dave Winfield	.25	.60
133 Jung-Ho Kang	.20	.50
134 Roger Clemens	.40	1.00
135 Bob Gibson	.25	.60
136 Addison Russell	.30	.75
137 James McCann	.25	.60
138 Dalton Pompey	.25	.60
139 Joey Gallo	.25	.60
140 Carlos Rodon	.30	.75
141A Kyle Schwarber RC	.75	2.00
141B Schwrbr SP Bttng	1.50	4.00
142A Corey Seager RC	2.00	5.00
142B Seager SP Bttng	4.00	10.00
143A Miguel Sano RC	.40	1.00
143B Sano SP Drk jsy	.75	2.00
144A Michael Conforto RC	.30	.75
144B Conforto SP Gry jsy	.60	1.50
145A Stephen Piscotty RC	.40	1.00
145B Piscotty SP Swngng	.75	2.00
146 Trea Turner RC	.75	2.00
147 Aaron Nola RC	.50	1.25
148 Ketel Marte RC	.50	1.25
149 Raul Mondesi RC	.30	.75
150 Henry Owens RC	.30	.75
151 Greg Bird RC	.30	.75
152 Richie Shaffer RC	.25	.60
153 Brandon Drury RC	.40	1.00
154 Kaleb Cowart RC	.25	.60
155 Travis Jankowski RC	.25	.60
156 Colin Rea RC	.25	.60
157 Dariel Alvarez RC	.25	.60
158 Zach Davies RC	.30	.75
159 Rob Refsnyder RC	.30	.75
160 Peter O'Brien RC	.25	.60
161 Brian Johnson RC	.25	.60
162 Kyle Waldrop RC	.30	.75
163 Luis Severino RC	.30	.75
164 Jose Peraza RC	.30	.75
165 Jonathan Gray RC	.25	.60
166 Hector Olivera RC	.30	.75
167 Max Kepler RC	.40	1.00
168 Carl Edwards Jr. RC	.30	.75
169 Tom Murphy RC	.25	.60
170 Mac Williamson RC	.25	.60
171 Gary Sanchez RC	.75	2.00
172 Miguel Almonte RC	.25	.60
173 Michael Reed RC	.25	.60
174 Jorge Lopez RC	.25	.60
175 Zach Lee RC	.25	.60
176 Elias Diaz RC	.25	.60
177 Luke Jackson RC	.25	.60
178 John Lamb RC	.25	.60
179 Pedro Severino RC	.25	.60
180 Alex Dickerson RC	.25	.60
181 Brian Ellington RC	.25	.60
182 Socrates Brito RC	.25	.60
183 Kelby Tomlinson RC	.25	.60
184 Trayce Thompson RC	.40	1.00
185 Frankie Montas RC	.30	.75

2016 Diamond Kings Artist's Proofs

*AP 1-140: 2.5X TO 6X BASIC
*AP SP: 1X TO 2.5X BASIC
*AP 141-185: 2X TO 5X BASIC
RANDOM INSERTS IN PACKS
STATED PRINT RUN 99 SER.#'d SETS

2016 Diamond Kings Artist's Proofs Silver

*AP SILVER 1-140: 4X TO 10X BASIC
*AP SILVER SP: 1.5X TO 4X BASIC
*AP SILVER 141-185: 3X TO 8X BASIC
RANDOM INSERTS IN PACKS
STATED PRINT RUN 25 SER.#'d SETS

2016 Diamond Kings Framed

*FRMD 1-140: 1.2X TO 3X BASIC
*FRMD SP: .5X TO 1.2X BASIC
*FRMD 141-185: 1X TO 2.5X BASIC
RANDOM INSERTS IN PACKS

2016 Diamond Kings Framed Blue

*FRMD BLUE 1-140: 2.5X TO 6X BASIC
*FRMD BLUE SP: 1X TO 2.5X BASIC
*FRMD BLUE 141-185: 2X TO 5X BASIC
RANDOM INSERTS IN PACKS
STATED PRINT RUN 99 SER.#'d SETS

2016 Diamond Kings Framed Red

*FRMD RED 1-140: 2.5X TO 6X BASIC
*FRMD RED SP: 1X TO 2.5X BASIC
*FRMD RED 141-185: 2X TO 5X BASIC
RANDOM INSERTS IN PACKS
STATED PRINT RUN 99 SER.#'d SETS

2016 Diamond Kings Aficionado

COMPLETE SET (20)	10.00	25.00
RANDOM INSERTS IN PACKS		
*SAPPHIRE/25: 2.5X TO 6X BASIC		
A1 Albert Pujols	.60	1.50
A2 Josh Donaldson	.40	1.00
A3 Jake Arrieta	.40	1.00
A4 Dallas Keuchel	.40	1.00
A5 Joey Votto	.50	1.25
A6 Chris Davis	.30	.75
A7 Paul Goldschmidt	.50	1.25
A8 Kris Bryant	.60	1.50
A9 Carlos Correa	.50	1.25
A10 Nolan Arenado	.60	1.50
A11 Jose Bautista	.40	1.00
A12 Gerrit Cole	.50	1.25
A13 Adam Wainwright	.40	1.00
A14 Felix Hernandez	.40	1.00
A15 Jacob deGrom	.50	1.25
A16 Adrian Beltre	.50	1.25
A17 Todd Frazier	.40	1.00
A18 Dee Gordon	.30	.75
A19 Nelson Cruz	.50	1.25
A20 A.J. Pollock	.30	.75

2016 Diamond Kings Diamond Cuts Signatures

RANDOM INSERTS IN PACKS
PRINT RUNS B/WN 1-99 COPIES PER
NO PRICING ON QTY 20 OR LESS
EXCHANGE DEADLINE 10/6/2017

DCJP Johnny Pesky/99	8.00	20.00
DCSM Stan Musial/99	20.00	50.00

2016 Diamond Kings Diamond Deco Materials

RANDOM INSERTS IN PACKS
PRINT RUNS B/WN 15-99 COPIES PER
NO PRICING ON QTY 20 OR LESS
*PRIME/25: .75X TO 2X BASIC

DDBB Byron Buxton/99	5.00	12.00
DDCS Corey Seager/49	12.00	30.00
DDGM Greg Maddux/25	10.00	25.00
DDIS Ichiro Suzuki/25		
DDJD Josh Donaldson/25	10.00	25.00
DDKB Kris Bryant/25		
DDKG Ken Griffey Jr./49	25.00	60.00
DDKS Kyle Schwarber/99	8.00	20.00
DDMC Michael Conforto/99	10.00	20.00
DDMS Miguel Sano/99	6.00	15.00
DDMS Mike Schmidt/25	10.00	25.00
DDMT Mike Trout/25	25.00	60.00
DDRH Rickey Henderson/25	15.00	40.00
DDSP Stephen Piscotty/49		
DDVG Vladimir Guerrero/25		
DDYM Yoan Moncada/25	15.00	40.00
DDYM Yadier Molina/25	6.00	15.00

2016 Diamond Kings DK Jumbo Materials Silver

RANDOM INSERTS IN PACKS
PRINT RUNS B/WN 5-99 COPIES PER
NO PRICING ON QTY 15 OR LESS

DKJMBH Bryce Harper/25	6.00	15.00
DKJMCC Carlos Correa/25	20.00	50.00
DKJMDK Dallas Keuchel/25	4.00	10.00
DKJMJD Josh Donaldson/25	6.00	15.00
DKJMKB Kris Bryant/99	5.00	12.00
DKJMKG Ken Griffey Jr./25		

2016 Diamond Kings DK Jumbo Materials Framed

RANDOM INSERTS IN PACKS
PRINT RUNS B/WN 5-99 COPIES PER
NO PRICING ON QTY 15 OR LESS

DKJMBH Bryce Harper/25	6.00	15.00
DKJMDK Dallas Keuchel/49	3.00	8.00
DKJMDO David Ortiz/25	10.00	25.00
DKJMJD Josh Donaldson/25	6.00	15.00
DKJMKB Kris Bryant/99	5.00	12.00
DKJMKG Ken Griffey Jr./49		

2016 Diamond Kings DK Jumbo Materials Framed Blue

RANDOM INSERTS IN PACKS
PRINT RUNS B/WN 3-25 COPIES PER
NO PRICING ON QTY 10 OR LESS

DKJMDK Dallas Keuchel/25	4.00	10.00
DKJMKB Kris Bryant/25	6.00	15.00
DKJMKG Ken Griffey Jr./25		

2016 Diamond Kings DK Materials Silver

RANDOM INSERTS IN PACKS
PRINT RUNS B/WN 5-99 COPIES PER
NO PRICING ON QTY 15 OR LESS

9 Adam Wainwright/99	2.50	6.00
10 Adrian Beltre/25	4.00	10.00
11 Adrian Gonzalez/25	3.00	8.00
12 Albert Pujols/25	10.00	25.00
13 Andrew McCutchen/49	8.00	20.00
14 Bryce Harper/25	12.00	30.00
15 Buster Posey/25	8.00	20.00
18 Dallas Keuchel/99	2.50	6.00
19 David Ortiz/25	4.00	10.00
20 David Wright/25	3.00	8.00
21 Dustin Pedroia/25	4.00	10.00
22 Edwin Encarnacion/25	4.00	10.00
24 Felix Hernandez/25	3.00	8.00
25 Freddie Freeman/25	5.00	12.00
26 George Springer/99	2.50	6.00
27 Giancarlo Stanton/25	4.00	10.00
32 Jose Altuve/49	2.50	6.00
33 Jose Bautista/25	3.00	8.00
36 Madison Bumgarner/25	3.00	8.00
39 Miguel Cabrera/25	4.00	10.00
42 Nelson Cruz/25	4.00	10.00
45 Salvador Perez/25	3.00	8.00
46 Sonny Gray/25	3.00	8.00
47 Starling Marte/25	3.00	8.00
49 Xander Bogaerts/99	6.00	15.00
51 Yu Darvish/25	4.00	10.00
52 Matt Kemp/25	3.00	8.00
53 David Price/25	3.00	8.00
54 Kris Bryant/99	4.00	10.00
55 Yasmany Tomas/49	2.00	5.00
57 Jorge Soler/25	4.00	10.00
58 Joc Pederson/25	3.00	8.00
59 Maikel Franco/49	4.00	10.00
60 Noah Syndergaard/25	3.00	8.00
61 Prince Fielder/25	3.00	8.00
62 Chris Archer/25	2.50	6.00
63 Matt Carpenter/25	4.00	10.00
64 Michael Taylor/49	2.00	5.00
65 Carlos Correa/99	6.00	15.00
66 Vladimir Guerrero/25	3.00	8.00
67 A.J. Pollock/99	2.00	5.00
68 Ken Griffey Jr./49	8.00	20.00
70 Jung-Ho Kang/99	5.00	12.00
71 Addison Russell/99	3.00	8.00
72 James McCann/25	12.00	30.00
73 Dalton Pompey/49	2.50	6.00
75 Carlos Rodon/49	3.00	8.00
76 Lucas Giolito/99	3.00	8.00
77 Yoan Moncada/49	8.00	20.00
78 Tyler Glasnow/25	3.00	8.00
79 Dansby Swanson/99	5.00	12.00
80 Blake Snell/99	2.50	6.00
82 Nomar Mazara/99	5.00	12.00
83 Aaron Judge/99	10.00	25.00
84 Wei-Chieh Huang/25	2.50	6.00
85 Alex Bregman/99	6.00	15.00
86 Josh Bell/25	5.00	12.00
87 Willy Adames/25	4.00	10.00
88 Brett Phillips/99	2.00	5.00
89 Jameson Taillon/49	2.50	6.00
90 Rafael Devers/99	4.00	10.00

2016 Diamond Kings DK Materials Bronze

RANDOM INSERTS IN PACKS
PRINT RUNS B/WN 3-49 COPIES PER
NO PRICING ON QTY 15 OR LESS

DKMAB Alex Bregman/49	6.00	15.00
DKMAJ Aaron Judge/49	10.00	25.00
DKMAM Andrew McCutchen/25	10.00	25.00
DKMAP A.J. Pollock/49	2.00	5.00
DKMAR Addison Russell/49	3.00	8.00
DKMAW Adam Wainwright/49	2.50	6.00
DKMBP Brett Phillips/49	2.00	5.00
DKMBS Blake Snell/49	2.50	6.00
DKMCC Carlos Correa/49	6.00	15.00
DKMCR Carlos Rodon/25	4.00	10.00
DKMDP Dalton Pompey/25	3.00	8.00
DKMDS Dansby Swanson/49	5.00	12.00
DKMJK Jung-Ho Kang/49	5.00	12.00
DKMJT Jameson Taillon/25	3.00	8.00
DKMKB Kris Bryant/49	4.00	10.00
DKMLG Lucas Giolito/49	3.00	8.00
DKMMF Maikel Franco/25	5.00	12.00
DKMNM Nomar Mazara/49	5.00	12.00
DKMRD Rafael Devers/49	4.00	10.00
DKMXB Xander Bogaerts/49	6.00	15.00
DKMYM Yoan Moncada/25	10.00	25.00
DKMYT Yasmany Tomas/25	2.50	6.00

2016 Diamond Kings DK Materials Framed

RANDOM INSERTS IN PACKS
PRINT RUNS B/WN 5-99 COPIES PER
NO PRICING ON QTY 15 OR LESS

DKMAB Adrian Beltre/49	3.00	8.00
DKMAB Alex Bregman/99	6.00	15.00
DKMAG Adrian Gonzalez/25	3.00	8.00
DKMAJ Aaron Judge/99	10.00	25.00
DKMAM Andrew McCutchen/99	8.00	20.00
DKMAP A.J. Pollock/99	2.00	5.00
DKMAP Albert Pujols/25	10.00	25.00
DKMAR Addison Russell/99	3.00	8.00
DKMAW Adam Wainwright/99	2.50	6.00
DKMBH Bryce Harper/25	12.00	30.00
DKMBP Buster Posey/25	8.00	20.00
DKMBP Brett Phillips/99	2.00	5.00
DKMBS Blake Snell/99	2.50	6.00
DKMCA Chris Archer/49	2.00	5.00
DKMCC Carlos Correa/99	6.00	15.00
DKMCK Clayton Kershaw/25	8.00	20.00
DKMCR Carlos Rodon/99	3.00	8.00
DKMDK Dallas Keuchel/99	2.50	6.00
DKMDO David Ortiz/49	3.00	8.00
DKMDP Dustin Pedroia/49	3.00	8.00
DKMDP Dalton Pompey/99	2.50	6.00
DKMDP David Price/49	2.50	6.00
DKMDS Dansby Swanson/99	5.00	12.00
DKMDW David Wright/99	2.50	6.00
DKMEE Edwin Encarnacion/49	3.00	8.00
DKMEH Eric Hosmer/25	3.00	8.00
DKMFF Freddie Freeman/49	4.00	10.00
DKMFH Felix Hernandez/25	3.00	8.00
DKMGS George Springer/99	2.50	6.00
DKMGS Giancarlo Stanton/49	3.00	8.00
DKMIS Ichiro Suzuki/25	12.00	30.00
DKMJA Jake Arrieta/25	3.00	8.00
DKMJA Jose Abreu/25	4.00	10.00
DKMJA Jose Altuve/99	2.50	6.00
DKMJB Jose Bautista/49	2.50	6.00
DKMJB Josh Bell/99	4.00	10.00
DKMJD Josh Donaldson/25	3.00	8.00
DKMJG Joey Gallo/25	3.00	8.00
DKMJK Jung-Ho Kang/99	5.00	121.00
DKMJM James McCann/25	12.00	30.00
DKMJM Joe Mauer/25	3.00	8.00
DKMJP Joc Pederson/49	2.50	6.00
DKMJS Jorge Soler/49	3.00	8.00
DKMJT Jameson Taillon/99	2.50	6.00
DKMKB Kris Bryant/99	4.00	10.00
DKMKG Ken Griffey Jr./99	8.00	20.00
DKMLG Lucas Giolito/99	3.00	8.00
DKMMB Madison Bumgarner/25	3.00	8.00
DKMMB Michael Brantley/25	3.00	8.00
DKMMC Miguel Cabrera/49	3.00	8.00
DKMMC Matt Carpenter/49	3.00	8.00
DKMMF Maikel Franco/99	4.00	10.00
DKMMK Matt Kemp/49	2.50	6.00
DKMMM Manny Machado/49	6.00	15.00
DKMMT Mike Trout/25	20.00	50.00
DKMMT Michael Taylor/99	2.00	5.00
DKMNC Nelson Cruz/49	3.00	8.00
DKMNM Nomar Mazara/99	5.00	12.00
DKMNS Noah Syndergaard/49	2.50	6.00
DKMPF Prince Fielder/49	2.50	6.00
DKMPG Paul Goldschmidt/49	3.00	8.00
DKMRC Robinson Cano/25	3.00	8.00
DKMRC Rusney Castillo/25	2.50	6.00
DKMRD Rafael Devers/99	4.00	10.00
DKMSG Sonny Gray/25	3.00	8.00
DKMSM Starling Marte/49	2.50	6.00
DKMSM Stan Musial/25	10.00	25.00
DKMSP Salvador Perez/49	2.50	6.00
DKMTG Tyler Glasnow/25	3.00	8.00
DKMVG Vladimir Guerrero/49	2.50	6.00
DKMWA Willy Adames/49	3.00	8.00
DKMWH Wei-Chieh Huang/25	2.50	6.00
DKMXB Xander Bogaerts/99	6.00	15.00
DKMYD Yu Darvish/49	3.00	8.00
DKMYM Yadier Molina/25	4.00	10.00
DKMYM Yoan Moncada/99	8.00	20.00
DKMYT Yasmany Tomas/49	2.00	5.00

2016 Diamond Kings DK Materials Framed Blue

RANDOM INSERTS IN PACKS
PRINT RUNS B/WN 5-25 COPIES PER
NO PRICING ON QTY 15 OR LESS

DKMAB Adrian Beltre/25	4.00	10.00
DKMAB Alex Bregman/25	8.00	20.00
DKMAJ Aaron Judge/25	12.00	30.00
DKMAM Andrew McCutchen/25	10.00	25.00
DKMAP A.J. Pollock/25	2.50	6.00
DKMAR Addison Russell/25	4.00	10.00
DKMAW Adam Wainwright/25	3.00	8.00
DKMBP Brett Phillips/25	2.50	6.00
DKMBS Blake Snell/25	3.00	8.00
DKMCC Carlos Correa/25	8.00	20.00
DKMDK Dallas Keuchel/25	3.00	8.00
DKMDO David Ortiz/25	4.00	10.00
DKMDP Dalton Pompey/25	3.00	8.00
DKMDS Dansby Swanson/25	6.00	15.00
DKMEE Edwin Encarnacion/25	4.00	10.00
DKMFF Freddie Freeman/25	5.00	12.00
DKMJA Jose Altuve/25	3.00	8.00
DKMJB Jose Bautista/25	3.00	8.00
DKMJB Josh Bell/25	5.00	12.00
DKMJK Jung-Ho Kang/25	6.00	15.00
DKMJP Joc Pederson/25	3.00	8.00
DKMKB Kris Bryant/25	5.00	12.00
DKMKG Ken Griffey Jr./25	10.00	25.00
DKMLG Lucas Giolito/25	4.00	10.00
DKMMF Maikel Franco/25	5.00	12.00
DKMMT Michael Taylor/25	2.50	6.00
DKMNM Nomar Mazara/25	6.00	15.00
DKMPF Prince Fielder/25	3.00	8.00
DKMRD Rafael Devers/25	5.00	12.00
DKMSP Salvador Perez/25	3.00	8.00
DKMXB Xander Bogaerts/25	8.00	20.00
DKMYM Yoan Moncada/25	10.00	25.00
DKMYT Yasmany Tomas/25	2.50	6.00

2016 Diamond Kings DK Materials Signatures Silver

RANDOM INSERTS IN PACKS
PRINT RUNS B/WN 5-299 COPIES PER
NO PRICING ON QTY 20 OR LESS
EXCHANGE DEADLINE 10/6/2017
*BRONZE/99: .4X TO 1X p/r 49-99
*BRONZE/99: .5X TO 1.2X p/r 199-299
*BRONZE/25: .5X TO 1.2X p/r 49-99
*BRONZE/25: .6X TO 1.5X p/r 199-299

DKSAJ Aaron Judge/199	60.00	150.00
DKSAP A.J. Pollock/49	4.00	10.00
DKSAR Addison Russell/49	15.00	40.00
DKSBP Brett Phillips/199	5.00	12.00
DKSBS Blake Snell/199	4.00	10.00
DKSCR Carlos Rodon/25	8.00	20.00
DKSDP Dalton Pompey/49	5.00	12.00
DKSEG Evan Gattis/49	4.00	10.00
DKSGS George Springer/49	8.00	20.00
DKSJA Jake Arrieta/49 EXCH	25.00	60.00
DKSJA Jose Abreu/99	12.00	30.00
DKSJB Josh Bell/99	8.00	20.00
DKSJG Joey Gallo/25	12.00	30.00
DKSJH Jason Heyward/49	5.00	12.00
DKSJK Jung-Ho Kang/49	15.00	40.00
DKSJM James McCann/299	6.00	15.00
DKSJP Joc Pederson/199	10.00	25.00
DKSJS Jorge Soler/199	6.00	15.00
DKSKB Kris Bryant/25	60.00	150.00
DKSLG Lucas Giolito/199	6.00	15.00
DKSMB Michael Brantley/99	5.00	12.00
DKSMB Mookie Betts/299	40.00	100.00
DKSMC Matt Carpenter/99	8.00	20.00
DKSMF Maikel Franco/299	4.00	10.00
DKSMT Michael Taylor/199	3.00	8.00
DKSNS Noah Syndergaard/25	10.00	25.00
DKSSG Sonny Gray/99	5.00	12.00
DKSTF Todd Frazier/49	8.00	20.00
DKSTG Tyler Glasnow/25	15.00	40.00
DKSWH Wei-Chieh Huang/199	3.00	8.00
DKSXB Xander Bogaerts/49	15.00	40.00

2016 Diamond Kings DK Materials Signatures Framed

*FRAMED/49-99: .4X TO 1X p/r 49-99
*FRAMED/49-99: .5X TO 1.2X p/r 199-299
*FRAMED/25: .4X TO 1X p/r 25
*FRAMED/25: .5X TO 1.2X p/r 49-99
*FRAMED/25: .6X TO 1.5X p/r 199-299
RANDOM INSERTS IN PACKS
PRINT RUNS B/WN 5-99 COPIES PER
NO PRICING ON QTY 20 OR LESS
EXCHANGE DEADLINE 10/6/2017

DKSDK Dallas Keuchel/49	8.00	20.00
DKSGR Garrett Richards/99	5.00	12.00
DKSMS Max Scherzer/25		
DKSRC Rusney Castillo/49	4.00	10.00

2016 Diamond Kings DK Materials Signatures Framed Blue

*FRM BLUE/49: .4X TO 1X p/r 49-99
*FRM BLUE/49: .5X TO 1.2X p/r 199-299
*FRM BLUE/25: .4X TO 1X p/r 25
*FRM BLUE/25: .5X TO 1.2X p/r 49-99
*FRM BLUE/25: .6X TO 1.5X p/r 199-299
RANDOM INSERTS IN PACKS
PRINT RUNS B/WN 5-49 COPIES PER
NO PRICING ON QTY 15 OR LESS
EXCHANGE DEADLINE 10/6/2017

DKSGR Garrett Richards/25	6.00	15.00
DKSRC Rusney Castillo/25	5.00	12.00

2016 Diamond Kings DK Minis

RANDOM INSERTS IN PACKS
*BLACK/25: .75X TO 2X BASIC

1 Babe Ruth	3.00	8.00
2 Bill Dickey	.75	2.00
3 Billy Martin	1.00	2.50
4 Frank Chance	1.00	2.50
5 George Kelly	.75	2.00
6 Gil Hodges	1.00	2.50
7 Honus Wagner	1.25	3.00
8 Jimmie Foxx	1.25	3.00
9 Joe DiMaggio	2.50	6.00
10 Joe Jackson	1.50	4.00
11 Lefty Gomez	.75	2.00
12 Leo Durocher	.75	2.00
13 Lou Gehrig	2.50	6.00
14 Luke Appling	1.00	2.50
15 Mel Ott	1.25	3.00
16 Pee Wee Reese	1.00	2.50
17 Roberto Clemente	3.00	8.00
18 Roger Maris	1.25	3.00
19 Rogers Hornsby	1.00	2.50
20 Stan Musial	2.00	5.00
21 Ted Williams	2.50	6.00
22 Tony Lazzeri	1.00	2.50
23 Ty Cobb	2.00	5.00
24 Walter O'Malley	.75	2.00
25 Don Hoak	.75	2.00
26 Earl Averill	.75	2.00
27 Elston Howard	.75	2.00
28 Frankie Crosetti	.75	2.00
29 Frankie Frisch	1.00	2.50
30 Gabby Hartnett	.75	2.00
31 Gil McDougald	.75	2.00
32 Goose Goslin	1.00	2.50
33 Bob Meusel	.75	2.00
34 Bob Turley	.75	2.00
35 Chuck Klein	.75	2.00
36 Dom DiMaggio	.75	2.00
37 Harry Brecheen	.75	2.00
38 Heinie Groh	.75	2.00
39 Jake Daubert	.75	2.00
40 Jim Bottomley	.75	2.00
41 John McGraw	1.00	2.50
42 Johnny Sain	.75	2.00
43 Moose Skowron	.75	2.00
44 Roger Bresnahan	1.00	2.50
45 Tom Yawkey	.75	2.00
46 Kirby Puckett	1.25	3.00
47 Jim Gilliam	.75	2.00
48 Miller Huggins	.75	2.00
49 Nap Lajoie	1.25	3.00
50 Lefty O'Doul	.75	2.00
51 Adam Jones	1.00	2.50
52 Adam Wainwright	1.00	2.50
53 Adrian Beltre	1.25	3.00
54 Adrian Gonzalez	1.00	2.50
55 Albert Pujols	1.50	4.00
56 Andrew McCutchen	1.25	3.00
57 Anthony Rendon	1.25	3.00
58 Anthony Rizzo	2.00	5.00
59 Bryce Harper	2.00	5.00
60 Buster Posey	1.50	4.00
61 Chris Davis	.75	2.00
62 Clayton Kershaw	2.50	6.00
63 Dallas Keuchel	1.00	2.50
64 David Ortiz	1.25	3.00
65 David Wright	1.00	2.50
66 Dustin Pedroia	1.25	3.00
67 Edwin Encarnacion	1.25	3.00
68 Eric Hosmer	1.00	2.50
69 Evan Gattis	.75	2.00
70 Evan Longoria	1.00	2.50
71 Felix Hernandez	1.00	2.50
72 Freddie Freeman	1.50	4.00
73 Garrett Richards	1.00	2.50
74 George Springer	1.00	2.50
75 Giancarlo Stanton	1.25	3.00
76 Ichiro Suzuki	1.50	4.00
77 Jake Arrieta	1.00	2.50
78 Jason Heyward	1.00	2.50
79 Joe Mauer	1.00	2.50
80 Jonathan Lucroy	1.00	2.50
81 Jose Abreu	1.25	3.00
82 Jose Altuve	1.00	2.50
83 Jose Bautista	1.00	2.50
84 Josh Donaldson	1.00	2.50
85 Justin Upton	1.00	2.50
86 Madison Bumgarner	1.00	2.50
87 Manny Machado	1.25	3.00
88 Max Scherzer	1.25	3.00
89 Michael Brantley	1.00	2.50
90 Miguel Cabrera	1.25	3.00
91 Mike Trout	6.00	15.00
92 Mookie Betts	2.00	5.00
93 Nelson Cruz	1.25	3.00
94 Paul Goldschmidt	1.25	3.00
95 Robinson Cano	1.00	2.50
96 Salvador Perez	1.00	2.50
97 Sonny Gray	1.00	2.50
98 Starling Marte	1.00	2.50
99 Stephen Strasburg	1.25	3.00
100 Todd Frazier	1.00	2.50
101 Troy Tulowitzki	1.25	3.00
102 Wei-Yin Chen	.75	2.00
103 Xander Bogaerts	1.25	3.00
104 Yadier Molina	1.25	3.00
105 Yoenis Cespedes	1.25	3.00
106 Yu Darvish	1.25	3.00
107 Matt Kemp	1.00	2.50
108 David Price	1.00	2.50
109 Kris Bryant	1.50	4.00
110 Yasmany Tomas	.75	2.00
111 Rusney Castillo	.75	2.00
112 Jorge Soler	1.25	3.00
113 Joc Pederson	1.00	2.50
114 Maikel Franco	1.00	2.50
115 Noah Syndergaard	1.00	2.50
116 Prince Fielder	1.00	2.50
117 Zack Greinke	1.00	2.50
118 Chris Archer	.75	2.00
119 Corey Kluber	1.00	2.50
120 Matt Carpenter	1.25	3.00
121 Michael Taylor	.75	2.00
122 Carlos Correa	1.25	3.00
123 Vladimir Guerrero	1.00	2.50
124 A.J. Pollock	.75	2.00
125 Nolan Arenado	1.50	4.00
126 Ken Griffey Jr.	2.50	6.00
127 George Brett	2.50	6.00
128 Cal Ripken	4.00	10.00
129 Nolan Ryan	4.00	10.00
130 Rickey Henderson	1.25	3.00
131 Mariano Rivera	1.50	4.00
132 Dave Winfield	1.00	2.50
133 Jung-Ho Kang	.75	2.00
134 Roger Clemens	1.50	4.00
135 Bob Gibson	1.00	2.50
136 Addison Russell	1.25	3.00
137 James McCann	1.00	2.50
138 Dalton Pompey	1.00	2.50
139 Joey Gallo	1.00	2.50
140 Carlos Rodon	1.25	3.00
141 Kyle Schwarber	2.50	6.00
142 Corey Seager	6.00	15.00
143 Miguel Sano	1.25	3.00
144 Michael Conforto	1.00	2.50
145 Stephen Piscotty	1.25	3.00
146 Trea Turner	2.50	6.00
147 Aaron Nola	1.50	4.00
148 Ketel Marte	1.50	4.00
149 Raul Mondesi	1.00	2.50
150 Henry Owens	1.00	2.50
151 Greg Bird	1.00	2.50
152 Richie Shaffer	.75	2.00
153 Brandon Drury	1.25	3.00
154 Kaleb Cowart	.75	2.00
155 Travis Jankowski	.75	2.00
156 Colin Rea	.75	2.00
157 Dariel Alvarez	.75	2.00
158 Zach Davies	1.00	2.50
159 Rob Refsnyder	1.00	2.50
160 Peter O'Brien	.75	2.00
161 Brian Johnson	.75	2.00
162 Kyle Waldrop	1.00	2.50
163 Luis Severino	1.00	2.50
164 Jose Peraza	1.00	2.50
165 Jonathan Gray	.75	2.00
166 Hector Olivera	1.00	2.50
167 Max Kepler	1.25	3.00
168 Carl Edwards Jr.	1.00	2.50
169 Tom Murphy	.75	2.00
170 Mac Williamson	.75	2.00
171 Gary Sanchez	2.50	6.00
172 Miguel Almonte	.75	2.00
173 Michael Reed	.75	2.00
174 Jorge Lopez	.75	2.00
175 Zach Lee	.75	2.00

176 Elias Diaz .75 2.00
177 Luke Jackson .75 2.00
178 John Lamb .75 2.00
179 Pedro Severino .75 2.00
180 Alex Dickerson .75 2.00
181 Brian Ellington .75 2.00
182 Socrates Brito .75 2.00
183 Kelby Tomlinson .75 2.00
184 Trayce Thompson 1.25 3.00
185 Frankie Montas 1.00 2.50
186 Lucas Giolito 1.25 3.00
187 Yoan Moncada 2.00 5.00
188 Tyler Glasnow 1.00 2.50
189 Dansby Swanson 2.50 6.00
190 Blake Snell 1.00 2.50
191 Nomar Mazara 1.25 3.00
192 Aaron Judge 6.00 15.00
193 Wei-Chieh Huang .75 2.00
194 Alex Bregman 5.00 12.00
195 Josh Bell 1.50 4.00
196 Willy Adames 1.25 3.00
197 Brett Phillips .75 2.00
198 Jameson Taillon 1.00 2.50
199 Rafael Devers 2.50 6.00
200 Ken Griffey Jr. 2.50 6.00
201 Frank Robinson 1.00 2.50
202 Andy Pettitte 1.00 2.50
203 Omar Vizquel 1.00 2.50
204 Rickey Henderson 1.25 3.00
205 Johnny Bench 1.25 3.00
206 Greg Maddux 1.50 4.00
207 Randy Johnson 1.25 3.00
208 Roger Clemens 1.50 4.00

2016 Diamond Kings DK Minis Materials

RANDOM INSERTS IN PACKS
PRINT RUNS B/WN 5-99 COPIES PER
NO PRICING ON QTY 15 OR LESS
*PRIME/25: .75X TO 2X BASIC
51 Adam Jones/25 3.00 8.00
54 Adrian Gonzalez/25 3.00 8.00
57 Anthony Rendon/49 3.00 8.00
58 Anthony Rizzo/99 5.00 12.00
65 David Wright/49 2.50 6.00
67 Edwin Encarnacion/99 3.00 8.00
68 Eric Hosmer/49 2.50 6.00
69 Evan Gattis/25 2.50 6.00
72 Freddie Freeman/25 5.00 12.00
73 Garrett Richards/25 3.00 8.00
78 Jason Heyward/25 3.00 8.00
85 Justin Upton/25 3.00 8.00
88 Max Scherzer/25 4.00 10.00
89 Michael Brantley/25 3.00 8.00
92 Mookie Betts/25 6.00 15.00
93 Nelson Cruz/25 4.00 10.00
96 Salvador Perez/25 3.00 8.00
97 Sonny Gray/49 2.50 6.00
98 Starling Marte/25 3.00 8.00
100 Todd Frazier/25 3.00 8.00
102 Wei-Yin Chen/25 2.50 6.00
103 Xander Bogaerts/25 10.00 25.00
106 Yu Darvish/25 4.00 10.00
107 Matt Kemp/49 2.50 6.00
110 Yasmany Tomas/99 2.00 5.00
114 Maikel Franco/99 2.50 6.00
116 Prince Fielder/99 2.50 6.00
118 Chris Archer/25 2.50 6.00
120 Matt Carpenter/25 4.00 10.00
121 Michael Taylor/99 2.00 5.00
124 A.J. Pollock/99 2.00 5.00
136 Addison Russell/99 3.00 8.00
137 James McCann/99 10.00 25.00
138 Dalton Pompey/25 3.00 8.00
139 Joey Gallo/99 2.50 6.00
140 Carlos Rodon/99 3.00 8.00
143 Miguel Sano/99 3.00 8.00
144 Michael Conforto/99 4.00 10.00
145 Stephen Piscotty/49 3.00 8.00
146 Trea Turner/99 6.00 15.00
147 Aaron Nola/99 4.00 10.00
148 Ketel Marte/99 4.00 10.00
149 Raul Mondesi/99 2.50 6.00
151 Greg Bird/25 3.00 8.00
152 Richie Shaffer/99 2.00 5.00
153 Brandon Drury/99 3.00 8.00
154 Kaleb Cowart/99 2.00 5.00
157 Dariel Alvarez/25 2.50 6.00
158 Zach Davies/99 2.50 6.00
159 Rob Refsnyder/99 2.50 6.00
160 Peter O'Brien/99 2.00 5.00
161 Brian Johnson/99 2.00 5.00
162 Kyle Waldrop/49 2.50 6.00
163 Luis Severino/99 2.50 6.00
164 Jose Peraza/99 2.50 6.00
165 Jonathan Gray/99 2.00 5.00
170 Mac Williamson/99 2.00 5.00
171 Gary Sanchez/99 6.00 15.00
173 Michael Reed/25 2.50 6.00
186 Lucas Giolito/99 3.00 8.00
188 Tyler Glasnow/99 2.50 6.00
189 Dansby Swanson/99 6.00 15.00

2016 Diamond Kings DK Minis Materials Framed

RANDOM INSERTS IN PACKS
PRINT RUNS B/WN 5-99 COPIES PER
NO PRICING ON QTY 20 OR LESS
6 Gil Hodges/99 5.00 12.00
12 Leo Durocher/99 6.00 15.00
14 Luke Appling/99 6.00 15.00
15 Mel Ott/99 10.00 25.00
16 Pee Wee Reese/99 6.00 15.00
18 Roger Maris/99 12.00 30.00
19 Rogers Hornsby/25 20.00 50.00
20 Stan Musial/49 10.00 25.00
22 Tony Lazzeri/49 10.00 25.00
25 Don Hoak/99 6.00 15.00
26 Earl Averill/49
27 Elston Howard/99 6.00 15.00
28 Frankie Crosetti/99 6.00 15.00
29 Frankie Frisch/25
31 Gil McDougald/99 6.00 15.00
32 Goose Goslin/99 15.00 40.00
33 Bob Meusel/49 20.00 50.00
34 Bob Turley/99 4.00 10.00
35 Chuck Klein/25 15.00 40.00
37 Harry Brecheen/49 12.00 30.00
38 Heinie Groh/99 8.00 20.00
39 Jake Daubert/49 10.00 25.00
40 Jim Bottomley/25 10.00 25.00
41 John McGraw/25
42 Johnny Sain/99 5.00 12.00
43 Moose Skowron/99 5.00 12.00
44 Roger Bresnahan/49 12.00 30.00
45 Tom Yawkey/99 6.00 15.00
46 Kirby Puckett/99 20.00 50.00
47 Jim Gilliam/99 2.00 5.00
48 Miller Huggins/99 10.00 25.00
50 Lefty O'Doul/99 12.00 30.00
52 Adam Wainwright/99 2.50 6.00
55 Albert Pujols/99 4.00 10.00
56 Andrew McCutchen/99 12.00 30.00
59 Bryce Harper/49 10.00 25.00
60 Buster Posey/99 5.00 12.00
62 Clayton Kershaw/99 6.00 15.00
63 Dallas Keuchel/99 2.50 6.00
64 David Ortiz/99 6.00 15.00
71 Felix Hernandez/99 2.50 6.00
75 Giancarlo Stanton/99 3.00 8.00
76 Ichiro Suzuki/25 20.00 50.00
77 Jake Arrieta/99 3.00 8.00
81 Jose Abreu/99 3.00 8.00
82 Jose Altuve/99 6.00 15.00
83 Jose Bautista/99 2.50 6.00
84 Josh Donaldson/99 2.50 6.00
86 Madison Bumgarner/99 5.00 12.00
87 Manny Machado/99 8.00 20.00
90 Miguel Cabrera/99 10.00 25.00
91 Mike Trout/25 20.00 50.00
94 Paul Goldschmidt/99 3.00 8.00
101 Troy Tulowitzki/99 3.00 8.00
104 Yadier Molina/25 4.00 10.00
108 David Price/99 3.00 8.00
109 Kris Bryant/99 8.00 20.00
113 Joc Pederson/99 3.00 8.00
115 Noah Syndergaard/99 4.00 10.00
122 Carlos Correa/99 12.00 30.00
123 Vladimir Guerrero/99 2.50 6.00
126 Ken Griffey Jr./99 10.00 25.00
127 George Brett/99 12.00 30.00
128 Cal Ripken/99 8.00 20.00
129 Nolan Ryan/99 10.00 25.00
130 Rickey Henderson/99 6.00 15.00
131 Mariano Rivera/49 10.00 25.00
132 Dave Winfield/99 6.00 15.00
133 Jung-Ho Kang/99 8.00 20.00
134 Roger Clemens/99 6.00 15.00
135 Bob Gibson/25 10.00 25.00
141 Kyle Schwarber/99 10.00 25.00
142 Corey Seager/99 6.00 15.00

2016 Diamond Kings DK Minis Signatures

RANDOM INSERTS IN PACKS
PRINT RUNS B/WN 5-99 COPIES PER
NO PRICING ON QTY 15 OR LESS
EXCHANGE DEADLINE 10/6/2017
DMSCK Clayton Kershaw/49 40.00 100.00
DMSDG Dwight Gooden/25 10.00 25.00
DMSJC Jose Canseco/99 12.00 30.00
DMSLC Lorenzo Cain/25 10.00 25.00

2016 Diamond Kings DK Minis Signatures Framed

*FRMD/25-49: .5X TO 1.2X BASIC
RANDOM INSERTS IN PACKS
PRINT RUNS B/WN 5-49 COPIES PER
NO PRICING ON QTY 15 OR LESS
EXCHANGE DEADLINE 10/6/2017
DMSBP Buster Posey/25 60.00 120.00
DMSKB Kris Bryant/49 75.00 150.00

2016 Diamond Kings DK Originals

COMPLETE SET (20) 10.00 25.00
RANDOM INSERTS IN PACKS
*SAPPHIRE/25: 2.5X TO 6X BASIC
DKO1 Mike Trout 2.50 6.00
DKO2 Buster Posey .60 1.50
DKO3 Bryce Harper .75 2.00
DKO4 Clayton Kershaw 1.00 2.50
DKO5 Jake Arrieta .40 1.00
DKO6 Giancarlo Stanton .50 1.25
DKO7 Josh Donaldson .40 1.00
DKO8 Albert Pujols .60 1.50
DKO9 Kris Bryant .60 1.50
DKO10 Carlos Correa .50 1.25
DKO11 Ken Griffey Jr. 1.00 2.50
DKO12 George Brett 1.00 2.50
DKO13 Cal Ripken 1.50 4.00
DKO14 Rickey Henderson .50 1.25
DKO15 Nolan Ryan 1.50 4.00
DKO16 Kirby Puckett .50 1.25
DKO17 Pete Rose 1.00 2.50
DKO18 Frank Thomas .50 1.25
DKO19 Bo Jackson .50 1.25
DKO20 Mariano Rivera .60 1.50

2016 Diamond Kings Elements of Royalty Material Signatures Framed

RANDOM INSERTS IN PACKS
STATED PRINT RUN 49 SER.#'d SETS
EXCHANGE DEADLINE 10/6/2017
ERDE Dennis Eckersley 8.00 20.00
ERFT Frank Thomas 25.00 60.00
ERJP Jim Palmer

2016 Diamond Kings Elements of Royalty Material Signatures Framed Blue

RANDOM INSERTS IN PACKS
PRINT RUNS B/WN 3-25 COPIES PER
NO PRICING ON QTY 10 OR LESS
EXCHANGE DEADLINE 10/6/2017
ERPR Pete Rose/25 30.00 80.00

2016 Diamond Kings Elements of Royalty Materials Silver

RANDOM INSERTS IN PACKS
PRINT RUNS B/WN 5-99 COPIES PER
NO PRICING ON QTY 10 OR LESS
*FRAMED/99: .4X TO 1X BASIC
*FRAMED/25: .5X TO 1.2X BASIC
*FRM BLUE/25: .5X TO 1.2X BASIC
ERBM Billy Martin/99 6.00 15.00
EREH Elston Howard/99 5.00 12.00
ERGH Gil Hodges/99 6.00 15.00
ERLA Luke Appling/99 6.00 15.00
ERLD Leo Durocher/99 5.00 12.00
ERMO Mel Ott/99 6.00 15.00
ERPR Pee Wee Reese/99 6.00 15.00
ERRM Roger Maris/99 15.00 40.00
ERTL Tony Lazzeri/99 8.00 20.00

2016 Diamond Kings Expressionists

COMPLETE SET (20) 8.00 20.00
RANDOM INSERTS IN PACKS
*SAPPHIRE/25: 2.5X TO 6X BASIC
E1 Robinson Cano .40 1.00
E2 Ken Griffey Jr. 1.00 2.50
E3 Randy Johnson .50 1.25
E4 Andy Pettitte .40 1.00
E5 Troy Tulowitzki .50 1.25
E6 Jose Bautista .40 1.00
E7 Alex Gordon .40 1.00
E8 Felix Hernandez .40 1.00
E9 Andrew McCutchen .50 1.25
E10 Yadier Molina .50 1.25
E11 David Ortiz .50 1.25
E12 Salvador Perez .40 1.00
E13 Ozzie Smith .60 1.50
E14 Justin Upton .40 1.00
E15 Kris Bryant .60 1.50
E16 Rickey Henderson .50 1.25
E17 Addison Russell .50 1.25
E18 Miguel Sano .50 1.25
E19 Gregory Polanco .40 1.00
E20 David Wright .40 1.00

2016 Diamond Kings Heritage Collection

COMPLETE SET (20) 8.00 20.00
RANDOM INSERTS IN PACKS
*SAPPHIRE/25: 2.5X TO 6X BASIC
HC1 Robin Yount .50 1.25
HC2 Brooks Robinson .40 1.00
HC3 Frank Robinson .40 1.00
HC4 Reggie Jackson .40 1.00
HC5 Steve Carlton .40 1.00
HC6 Johnny Bench .50 1.25
HC7 Jose Canseco .40 1.00
HC8 Will Clark .40 1.00
HC9 Paul Molitor .50 1.25
HC10 Greg Maddux .60 1.50
HC11 Gaylord Perry .40 1.00
HC12 Orlando Cepeda .40 1.00
HC13 Jim Palmer .40 1.00
HC14 Tim Raines .40 1.00
HC15 Andre Dawson .40 1.00
HC16 Eddie Murray .40 1.00
HC17 Mike Schmidt .75 2.00
HC18 Ryne Sandberg 1.00 2.50
HC19 Lou Brock .40 1.00
HC20 Dennis Eckersley .40 1.00

2016 Diamond Kings Limited Lithos Material Signatures Silver

RANDOM INSERTS IN PACKS
PRINT RUNS B/WN 5-99 COPIES PER
NO PRICING ON QTY 15 OR LESS
EXCHANGE DEADLINE 10/6/2017
*FRM BLUE/25: .4X TO 1X BASIC p/r 25
1 Jose Canseco/99 10.00 25.00
3 Juan Gonzalez/25 12.00 30.00
6 Rollie Fingers/25 20.00 50.00
8 Tim Raines/99 10.00 25.00

2016 Diamond Kings Limited Lithos Material Signatures Framed

*FRAMED/99: .4X TO 1X BASIC p/r 99
*FRAMED/49: .3X TO .8X BASIC p/r 25
*FRAMED/25: .5X TO 1.2X BASIC p/r 99
RANDOM INSERTS IN PACKS
PRINT RUNS B/WN 1-25 COPIES PER
NO PRICING ON QTY 15 OR LESS
EXCHANGE DEADLINE 10/6/2017
5 Paul Molitor/25

2016 Diamond Kings Limited Lithos Materials Silver

RANDOM INSERTS IN PACKS
PRINT RUNS B/WN 15-99 COPIES PER
NO PRICING ON QTY 15
*FRAMED/99: .4X TO 1X BASIC
*FRM BLUE/25: .5X TO 1.2X BASIC
1 Kyle Schwarber/99 6.00 15.00
2 Corey Seager/99 15.00 40.00
3 Miguel Sano/99 3.00 8.00
4 Michael Conforto/99 2.50 6.00
5 Stephen Piscotty/25 5.00 12.00
6 Trea Turner/99 4.00 10.00
7 Aaron Nola/99 4.00 10.00
8 Raul Mondesi/99 2.50 6.00
10 Luis Severino/99 2.50 6.00

2016 Diamond Kings Masters of The Game Materials

RANDOM INSERTS IN PACKS
PRINT RUNS B/WN 5-99 COPIES PER
NO PRICING ON QTY 15 OR LESS
MGBH Bryce Harper/25 8.00 20.00
MGCF Carlton Fisk/99 4.00 10.00
MGCR Cal Ripken/99 15.00 40.00
MGFT Frank Thomas/99 5.00 12.00
MGGB George Brett/99 6.00 15.00
MGJB Johnny Bench/99 6.00 15.00
MGJD Josh Donaldson/99 4.00 10.00
MGJS John Smoltz/99 6.00 15.00
MGKP Kirby Puckett/99 6.00 15.00
MGLG Lou Gehrig/25 40.00 100.00
MGMR Mariano Rivera/99 5.00 12.00
MGNR Nolan Ryan/99 8.00 20.00
MGRJ Reggie Jackson/99 4.00 10.00
MGRM Roger Maris/99 10.00 25.00
MGRS Ryne Sandberg/99 6.00 15.00
MGWF Whitey Ford/99 10.00 25.00

2016 Diamond Kings Memorable Feats

COMPLETE SET (20) 8.00 20.00
RANDOM INSERTS IN PACKS
*SAPPHIRE/25: 2.5X TO 6X BASIC
MF1 Babe Ruth 1.25 3.00
MF2 Roberto Clemente 1.25 3.00
MF3 Lou Gehrig 1.00 2.50
MF4 Ty Cobb .75 2.00
MF5 Honus Wagner .50 1.25
MF6 Jimmie Foxx .50 1.25
MF7 Joe Jackson .60 1.50
MF8 Roger Maris .50 1.25
MF9 Stan Musial .75 2.00
MF10 Ted Williams 1.00 2.50
MF11 Rogers Hornsby .40 1.00
MF12 Mel Ott .50 1.25
MF13 Bill Dickey .30 .75
MF14 Walter O'Malley .30 .75
MF15 Gil Hodges .40 1.00
MF16 Tony Lazzeri .40 1.00
MF17 Nap Lajoie .50 1.25
MF18 Frankie Frisch .40 1.00
MF19 Elston Howard .30 .75
MF20 Hack Wilson .40 1.00

2016 Diamond Kings Rookie Material Signatures Silver

RANDOM INSERTS IN PACKS
PRINT RUNS B/WN 49-99
EXCHANGE DEADLINE 10/6/2017
*BRNZE/49-99: .5X TO 1.2X p/r 299
*BRNZE/49-99: .4X TO 1X p/r 49-99
*FRMD/99: .5X TO 1.2X p/r 299
*FRMD/99: .4X TO 1X p/r 49-99
RSAN Aaron Nola/299 8.00 20.00
RSBD Brandon Drury/299 6.00 15.00
RSBJ Brian Johnson/299 4.00 10.00
RSCS Corey Seager/299 25.00 60.00
RSDA Dariel Alvarez/299 4.00 10.00
RSJP Jose Peraza/299 5.00 12.00
RSKC Kaleb Cowart/299 4.00 10.00
RSKM Ketel Marte/299 8.00 20.00
RSKS Kyle Schwarber/299 20.00 50.00
RSKS Michael Reed/99 10.00 25.00
RSKW Kyle Waldrop/299 5.00 12.00
RSMS Miguel Sano/299 6.00 15.00
RSMW Mac Williamson/299 4.00 10.00
RSPO Peter O'Brien/299 4.00 10.00
RSRR Rob Refsnyder/299 5.00 12.00
RSRS Richie Shaffer/299 4.00 10.00
RSSP Stephen Piscotty/299 4.00 10.00
RSTM Tom Murphy/49 5.00 12.00
RSTT Trea Turner/299 12.00 30.00

2016 Diamond Kings Rookie Material Signatures Framed Blue

*FRMD BLUE: .5X TO 1.2X p/r 299
*FRMD BLUE: .4X TO 1X p/r 49-99
RANDOM INSERTS IN PACKS
STATED PRINT RUN 49 SER.#'d SETS
EXCHANGE DEADLINE 10/6/2017
RSLS Luis Severino

2016 Diamond Kings Sketches And Swatches

RANDOM INSERTS IN PACKS
PRINT RUNS B/WN 10-99 COPIES PER
NO PRICING ON QTY 15 OR LESS
EXCHANGE DEADLINE 10/6/2017
*PRIME/25: .4X TO 1X BASIC p/r 25
*PRIME/25: .5X TO 1.2X BASIC p/r 99
SASCS Chris Sale/49 12.00 30.00
SASDS Dansby Swanson/25
SASJF Jose Fernandez/49 6.00 15.00
SASJK Jung-Ho Kang/49 20.00 50.00
SASJP Joe Panik/99 5.00 12.00
SASJP Joc Pederson/99 8.00 20.00
SASLC Lorenzo Cain/49 20.00 50.00
SASMS Miguel Sano/25 12.00 30.00
SASRC Rusney Castillo/99 4.00 10.00
SASSP Stephen Piscotty/99 6.00 15.00
SASTT Trea Turner/99 12.00 30.00

2016 Diamond Kings Sovereign Material Signatures

RANDOM INSERTS IN PACKS
PRINT RUNS B/WN 5-99 COPIES PER
NO PRICING ON QTY 20 OR LESS
EXCHANGE DEADLINE 10/6/2017
SSAP Andy Pettitte/25 10.00 25.00
SSDG Dwight Gooden/25 12.00 30.00
SSFL Fred Lynn/99 4.00 10.00
SSMG Mark Grace/49 10.00 25.00
SSPM Paul Molitor/99 10.00 25.00
SSRP Rafael Palmeiro/99 6.00 15.00

2016 Diamond Kings Studio Portraits Material Signatures Silver

RANDOM INSERTS IN PACKS
PRINT RUNS B/WN 15-99 COPIES PER
NO PRICING ON QTY 15
EXCHANGE DEADLINE 10/6/2017
*FRAMED/99: .4X TO 1X BASIC
SPSAN Aaron Nola/99 10.00 25.00
SPSDA Dariel Alvarez/99 4.00 10.00
SPSKC Kaleb Cowart/99 4.00 10.00
SPSKM Ketel Marte/99 8.00 20.00
SPSKS Kyle Schwarber/99 15.00 40.00
SPSMS Miguel Sano/99 10.00 25.00
SPSPO Peter O'Brien/99 4.00 10.00
SPSRR Rob Refsnyder/99 5.00 12.00
SPSRS Richie Shaffer/99 4.00 10.00
SPSSP Stephen Piscotty/99 10.00 25.00
SPSTT Trea Turner/99 8.00 20.00

2016 Diamond Kings Studio Portraits Material Signatures Framed Blue

*FRM BLUE: .5X TO 1.2X BASIC
RANDOM INSERTS IN PACKS
PRINT RUNS B/WN 10-25 COPIES PER
NO PRICING ON QTY 10
EXCHANGE DEADLINE 10/6/2017
SPSLS Luis Severino/25 12.00 30.00

2016 Diamond Kings Studio Portraits Materials Silver

RANDOM INSERTS IN PACKS
PRINT RUNS B/WN 49-99 COPIES PER
*FRAMED/99: .4X TO 1X BASIC
*FRM BLUE/25: .5X TO 1.2X BASIC
SPAG Alex Gordon 4.00 10.00
SPAJ Adam Jones 4.00 10.00
SPAR Anthony Rizzo 8.00 20.00
SPAR Alex Rodriguez 5.00 12.00
SPCG Carlos Gonzalez 4.00 10.00
SPDG Dee Gordon 3.00 8.00
SPGC Gerrit Cole 5.00 12.00
SPJD Jacob deGrom 5.00 12.00
SPJM J.D. Martinez 5.00 12.00
SPJV Joey Votto 5.00 12.00
SPLC Lorenzo Cain 3.00 8.00
SPMH Matt Harvey 4.00 10.00
SPMS Max Scherzer 5.00 12.00

2017 Diamond Kings

COMPLETE SET (200) 60.00 150.00
1 Babe Ruth .75 2.00
2A Bill Dickey .20 .50
2B Bill Dickey VAR .60 1.50
Catchers equipment
3 Billy Herman .20 .50
4 Billy Martin .25 .60
5 Harry Brecheen .20 .50
6 Carl Erskine .20 .50
7 Carl Furillo .20 .50
8A Don Larsen .20 .50
8B Don Larsen VAR .60 1.50
Standing
9 Grover Alexander .25 .60
10A Ernie Banks .30 .75
10B Ernie Banks VAR 1.00 2.50
Face showing
11 George Kelly .20 .50
12 Harry Hooper .20 .50
13 Herb Pennock .25 .60
14 Honus Wagner .30 .75
15A Jackie Robinson .30 .75
15B Jackie Robinson VAR 1.00 2.50
42 on front
16 Jim Thorpe .50 1.25
17 Joe Cronin .20 .50
18A Joe DiMaggio .60 1.50
18B DiMaggio VAR Face lft 2.00 5.00
19 Joe Jackson .40 1.00
20 Kiki Cuyler .25 .60
21 Lefty Gomez .20 .50
22 Leo Durocher .20 .50
23 Lloyd Waner .25 .60
24 Lou Gehrig .60 1.50
25 Luke Appling .25 .60
26 Max Carey .20 .50
27A Kirby Puckett .30 .75
27B Kirby Puckett VAR 1.00 2.50
Throwback jersey
28 Nellie Fox .25 .60
29 Paul Waner .25 .60
30A Pee Wee Reese .25 .60
30B Pee Wee Reese VAR .75 2.00
Batting
31A Roberto Clemente .75 2.00
31B Clmnte VAR Solid jrsy 2.50 6.00
32 Roger Maris .30 .75
33A Stan Musial .50 1.25
33B Musial VAR Red belt 1.50 4.00
34 Ted Lyons .20 .50
35 Ted Williams .60 1.50
36 Tommy Henrich .20 .50
37 Ty Cobb .50 1.25
38 Tony Lazzeri .25 .60
39A Hack Wilson .25 .60
39B Hack Wilson VAR .75 2.00
Standing with bat
40 Earl Averill .20 .50
41 Nap Lajoie .30 .75
42 Goose Goslin .25 .60
43 Jim Bottomley .20 .50
44 Harry Walker .20 .50
45 Gabby Hartnett .20 .50
46 Heinie Groh .20 .50
47 Johnny Pesky .20 .50
48 John McGraw .25 .60
49 Moose Skowron .20 .50
50 Chuck Klein .20 .50
51 Paul Goldschmidt .30 .75
52 Freddie Freeman .40 1.00
53 Mark Trumbo .20 .50
54A Mookie Betts .50 1.25
54B Betts VAR Face lft 1.50 4.00
55A Kris Bryant .40 1.00
55B Bryant VAR No glss 1.25 3.00
56A Anthony Rizzo .50 1.25
56B Rizzo VAR Solid jrsy 1.50 4.00
57 Jake Arrieta .25 .60
58 Kyle Schwarber .30 .75
59 Jose Abreu .30 .75
60 Joey Votto .30 .75
61 Francisco Lindor .30 .75
62A Corey Kluber .25 .60
62B Corey Kluber VAR .75 2.00
Facing forward
63 Trevor Story .30 .75
64 Nolan Arenado .40 1.00
65 Justin Verlander .30 .75
66A Jose Altuve .25 .60
66B Altuve Ornge jrsy .75 2.00
67A Mike Trout 1.50 4.00
67B Trout VAR Red jrsy 5.00 12.00
68 Albert Pujols .40 1.00
69A Corey Seager .30 .75
69B Seager VAR Pre-swing 1.00 2.50
70 Clayton Kershaw .60 1.50
71 Christian Yelich .40 1.00
72 Ryan Braun .25 .60
73 Brian Dozier .30 .75
74 Yoenis Cespedes .30 .75
75 Didi Gregorius .25 .60
76 Khris Davis .30 .75
77 Maikel Franco .25 .60
78 Andrew McCutchen .30 .75
79 Wil Myers .20 .50
80A Madison Bumgarner .25 .60
80B Bmgrnr VAR Grey jrsy .75 2.00
81 Robinson Cano .25 .60
82 Stephen Piscotty .25 .60
83 Carlos Martinez .25 .60
84 Evan Longoria .25 .60
85 Adrian Beltre .30 .75
86 Cole Hamels .25 .60
87A Josh Donaldson .25 .60
87B Josh Donaldson VAR .75 2.00
Leg up
88 Edwin Encarnacion .30 .75
89 Bryce Harper .50 1.25
90A Daniel Murphy .25 .60
90B Daniel Murphy VAR .75 2.00
Red jersey
91 Don Mattingly .60 1.50
92 Al Oliver .20 .50
93 Andy Pettitte .25 .60
94 Chipper Jones .30 .75
95 Curt Schilling .25 .60
96 Fergie Jenkins .25 .60
97 Craig Biggio .25 .60
98 Brooks Robinson .25 .60
99 Larry Doby .25 .60
100 Billy Williams .25 .60
101 A.J. Pollock SP .60 1.50
102 Addison Russell SP 1.00 2.50
103 Anthony Rendon SP 1.00 2.50
104 Carlos Gonzalez SP .75 2.00
105 Charlie Blackmon SP 1.00 2.50
106 Chris Davis SP .60 1.50
107 Chris Sale SP 1.00 2.50
108 Eric Hosmer SP .75 2.00
109 Gerrit Cole SP 1.00 2.50
110 Gregory Polanco SP .75 2.00
111 Hanley Ramirez SP
112 J.D. Martinez SP 1.00 2.50
113 Jacob deGrom SP 1.00 2.50
114 Jason Kipnis SP .75 2.00
115 Jon Lester SP .75 2.00
116 Jonathan Villar SP .60 1.50
117 Kyle Hendricks SP 1.00 2.50
118 Kyle Seager SP .60 1.50
119 Matt Carpenter SP 1.00 2.50
120 Miguel Cabrera SP 1.00 2.50
121 Miguel Sano SP .75 2.00
122 Rougned Odor SP .75 2.00
123 Stephen Strasburg SP 1.00 2.50
124 Trea Turner SP .75 2.00
125 Nelson Cruz SP 1.00 2.50
126A Yoan Moncada RC 1.25 3.00
126B Mncda VAR Legs sprd 2.00 5.00
127A Alex Reyes RC .50 1.25
127B Reyes VAR Tan glv .75 2.00
128 Tyler Glasnow RC .50 1.25
129A Dansby Swanson RC 1.00 2.50
129B Swnsn VAR Back: Hype 1.50 4.00
130 Alex Bregman RC 1.50 4.00
131A Andrew Benintendi RC 1.25 3.00
131B Bnntndi VAR Blue jrsy 2.00 5.00
132 Orlando Arcia RC .60 1.50
133 David Dahl RC .50 1.25
134 Jose De Leon RC .40 1.00
135 Joe Musgrove RC .40 1.00
136 Josh Bell RC 1.00 2.50
137 Manuel Margot RC .40 1.00
138 Aaron Judge RC 5.00 12.00
139 David Paulino RC .50 1.25
140 Reynaldo Lopez RC .40 1.00
141 Jeff Hoffman RC .40 1.00
142 Braden Shipley RC .40 1.00
143 Hunter Renfroe RC .50 1.25
144 Jorge Alfaro RC .50 1.25
145A Carson Fulmer RC .40 1.00
145B Carson Fulmer VAR .60 1.50
Throwback
146 Luke Weaver RC .50 1.25
147 Raimel Tapia RC .50 1.25
148 Adalberto Mejia RC .40 1.00
149 Gavin Cecchini RC .40 1.00
150 Renato Nunez RC .75 2.00
151 Jacoby Jones RC .50 1.25
152 Yohander Mendez RC .40 1.00
153 Chad Pinder RC .40 1.00
154 Carson Kelly RC .50 1.25
155 Trey Mancini RC .75 2.00
156 Jose Rondon RC .40 1.00
157 Teoscar Hernandez RC 1.25 3.00
158 Ryon Healy RC .50 1.25
159 Erik Gonzalez RC .40 1.00
160 Roman Quinn RC .40 1.00
161 Matt Olson RC .60 1.50
162 Rio Ruiz RC .40 1.00
163 German Marquez RC .60 1.50
164 Jharel Cotton RC .40 1.00
165 Jake Thompson RC .40 1.00
166 Mitch Haniger RC .60 1.50
167 Robert Gsellman RC .40 1.00
168 Jordan Patterson RC .40 1.00
169 Hunter Dozier RC .40 1.00
170 Carlos Asuaje RC .40 1.00
171 Adam Plutko RC .40 1.00
172 Koda Glover RC .40 1.00
173 Austin Brice RC .40 1.00
174 Gabriel Ynoa RC .40 1.00
175 Jake Esch RC .40 1.00

2017 Diamond Kings Artist's Proof Blue

*FRM.BLUE: 3X TO 8X BASIC
*FRM.BLUE RC: 1.5X TO 4X BASIC RC
*FRM.BLUE SP: 1X TO 2.5X BASIC SP
*FRM.BLUE VAR: 1X TO 2.5X BASIC VAR
STATED PRINT RUN 25 SER.#'d SETS
27A Kirby Puckett 20.00 50.00
27B Puckett VAR Thrwbck jrsy 20.00 50.00
31A Roberto Clemente 12.00 30.00
31B Clmnte VAR Solid jrsy 12.00 30.00

2017 Diamond Kings Artist's Proof Gold

*AP GOLD: 2X TO 5X BASIC
*AP GOLD RC: 1X TO 2.5X BASIC RC
*AP GOLD SP: .6X TO 1.5X BASIC SP
*AP GOLD VAR: .6X TO 1.5X BASIC VAR
STATED PRINT RUN 99 SER.#'d SETS
27A Kirby Puckett 8.00 20.00
27B Puckett VAR Thrwbck jrsy 8.00 20.00
31A Roberto Clemente 8.00 20.00
31B Clmnte VAR Solid jrsy 8.00 20.00

2017 Diamond Kings Framed Brown

*FRM.BRWN: 2.5X TO 6X BASIC
*FRM.BRWN RC: 1.2X TO 3X BASIC RC
*FRM.BRWN SP: .75X TO 2X BASIC SP
*FRM.BRWN VAR: .75X TO 2X BASIC VAR
STATED PRINT RUN 49 SER.#'d SETS
27A Kirby Puckett 15.00 40.00
27B Puckett VAR Thrwbck jrsy 15.00 40.00
31A Roberto Clemente 10.00 25.00
31B Clmnte VAR Solid jrsy 10.00 25.00

2017 Diamond Kings Framed Green

*FRM.GRN: 1.5X TO 4X BASIC
*FRM.GRN RC: .75X TO 2X BASIC RC
*FRM.GRN SP: .5X TO 1.2X BASIC SP
*FRM.GRN VAR: .5X TO 1.2X BASIC VAR

2017 Diamond Kings Framed Grey

*FRM.GREY: 1.2X TO 3X BASIC
*FRM.GREY RC: .6X TO 1.5X BASIC RC
*FRM.GREY SP: .4X TO 1X BASIC SP
*FRM.GREY VAR: .4X TO 1X BASIC VAR

2017 Diamond Kings Framed Red

*FRM.RED: 2X TO 5X BASIC
*FRM.RED RC: 1X TO 2.5X BASIC RC
*FRM.RED SP: .6X TO 1.5X BASIC SP
*FRM.RED VAR: .6X TO 1.5X BASIC VAR
STATED PRINT RUN 99 SER.#'d SETS
27A Kirby Puckett 8.00 20.00
27B Puckett VAR Thrwbck jrsy 8.00 20.00
31A Roberto Clemente 8.00 20.00
31B Clmnte VAR Solid jrsy 8.00 20.00

2017 Diamond Kings Aurora

COMPLETE SET (20) 10.00 25.00
*HOLO BLUE/25: 1.5X TO 4X BASIC
A1 Brian Dozier .60 1.50
A2 Charlie Blackmon .60 1.50
A3 Clayton Kershaw 1.25 3.00

A4 Corey Seager .60 1.50
A5 Edwin Encarnacion .60 1.50
A6 Joey Votto .60 1.50
A7 Jon Lester .50 1.25
A8 Jonathan Villar .40 1.00
A9 Jose Altuve .50 1.25
A10 Josh Donaldson .50 1.25
A11 Justin Verlander .60 1.50
A12 Kris Bryant .75 2.00
A13 Madison Bumgarner .50 1.25
A14 Max Scherzer .60 1.50
A15 Miguel Cabrera .60 1.50
A16 Mike Trout 3.00 8.00
A17 Mookie Betts 1.00 2.50
A18 Nolan Arenado .75 2.00
A19 Paul Goldschmidt .60 1.50
A20 Robinson Cano .50 1.25

2017 Diamond Kings Bat Kings

RANDOM INSERTS IN PACKS
PRINT RUNS B/WN 10-99 COPIES PER
NO PRICING ON QTY 15 OR LESS
*GOLD/49: .5X TO 1.2X BASIC
*GOLD/25: .6X TO 1.5X BASIC
*BLUE/25: .6X TO 1.5X BASIC
BKAP Albert Pujols/49 6.00 15.00
BKCB Craig Biggio/49 4.00 10.00
BKCC Carlos Correa/99 4.00 10.00
BKCS Corey Seager/99 10.00 25.00
BKCY Christian Yelich/99 5.00 12.00
BKDM Don Mattingly/25 12.00 30.00
BKI Ichiro/25 12.00 30.00
BKIR Ivan Rodriguez/99 3.00 8.00
BKJB Johnny Bench/49 4.00 10.00
BKJB Jose Bautista/25 5.00 12.00
BKJC Joe Carter/49 3.00 8.00
BKKG Ken Griffey Jr./25 15.00 40.00
BKMC Miguel Cabrera/25 6.00 15.00
BKMN Mike Napoli/49 3.00 8.00
BKMT Mike Trout/99 15.00 40.00
BKRS Ryne Sandberg/49 10.00 25.00
BKSM Stan Musial/25 10.00 25.00
BKTC Rod Carew/49 4.00 10.00
BKTH Todd Helton/49 4.00 10.00
BKTS Trevor Story/99 4.00 10.00
BKTT Trea Turner/99 3.00 8.00
BKWB Wade Boggs/25
BKYT Yasmany Tomas/99 2.50 6.00

2017 Diamond Kings Bat Kings Signatures

RANDOM INSERTS IN PACKS
PRINT RUNS B/WN 7-99 COPIES PER
NO PRICING ON QTY 15 OR LESS
*GOLD/49: .5X TO 1.2X BASIC
*GOLD/25: .6X TO 1.5X BASIC
*BLUE/25: .6X TO 1.5X BASIC
BKSDF David Freese/20 8.00 20.00
BKSDS Darryl Strawberry/20 15.00 40.00
BKSEB Ernie Banks/25 25.00 60.00
BKSFF Freddie Freeman/20
BKSHR Hanley Ramirez/25 6.00 15.00
BKSMF Maikel Franco/49 5.00 12.00
BKSMN Mike Napoli/99 8.00 20.00
BKSPA Pedro Alvarez/25 6.00 15.00
BKSPM Paul Molitor/20 12.00 30.00
BKSTT Trea Turner/49 10.00 25.00
BKSYS Yangervis Solarte/99 3.00 8.00

2017 Diamond Kings Diamond Cuts Signatures

RANDOM INSERTS IN PACKS
PRINT RUNS B/WN 5-99 COPIES PER
NO PRICING ON QTY 15 OR LESS
*BLUE/25: .6X TO 1.5X BASIC
DCGC Gary Carter/99 12.00 30.00
DCGC Gary Carter/99 12.00 30.00
DCHK Harmon Killebrew/25 20.00 50.00
DCHK Harmon Killebrew/25 20.00 50.00
DCRK Ralph Kiner/25 20.00 50.00
DCRK Ralph Kiner/25 20.00 50.00
DCSM Stan Musial/25 20.00 50.00
DCSM Stan Musial/25 20.00 50.00

2017 Diamond Kings Diamond Cuts Signatures Holo Gold

*GOLD/49: .5X TO 1.2X BASIC
PRINT RUNS B/WN 4-49 COPIES PER
NO PRICING ON QTY 15 OR LESS
DCJP Johnny Pesky/20 20.00 50.00

2017 Diamond Kings Diamond Deco Materials

RANDOM INSERTS IN PACKS
PRINT RUNS B/WN 7-99 COPIES PER
NO PRICING ON QTY 7
*GOLD/49: .5X TO 1.2X BASIC
*GOLD/25: .6X TO 1.5X BASIC
*BLUE/25: .6X TO 1.5X BASIC
2 Willson Contreras/99 4.00 10.00
3 Francisco Lindor/99 6.00 15.00
5 Trea Turner/99 3.00 8.00
6 Corey Seager/99 6.00 15.00
7 Kyle Schwarber/99 4.00 10.00
8 Tony Gwynn/49 20.00 50.00
9 Kirby Puckett/25 40.00 100.00
10 Ken Griffey Jr./49 12.00 30.00

2017 Diamond Kings DK Materials

*SILVER/99: .4X TO 1X BASIC
*SILVER/49: .5X TO 1.2X BASIC
*SILVER/25: .6X TO 1.5X BASIC
*GOLD/49: .5X TO 1.2X BASIC
*GOLD/25: .6X TO 1.5X BASIC
*BLUE/25: .6X TO 1.5X BASIC
DKMAA Anthony Alford 2.50 6.00
DKMAB Adrian Beltre 4.00 10.00
DKMAG Adrian Gonzalez 3.00 8.00
DKMAJ Adam Jones 3.00 8.00
DKMAM Andrew McCutchen 6.00 15.00
DKMAM Austin Meadows 4.00 10.00
DKMAR Addison Russell 4.00 10.00
DKMAW Adam Wainwright 3.00 8.00
DKMBA Brian Anderson 3.00 8.00
DKMBH Bryce Harper 6.00 15.00
DKMBH Brent Honeywell 3.00 8.00
DKMBJ Bo Jackson 6.00 15.00
DKMBM Billy Martin 5.00 12.00
DKMBP Buster Posey 5.00 12.00
DKMBR Babe Ruth 250.00 400.00
DKMBZ Bradley Zimmer 3.00 8.00
DKMCA Chris Archer 2.50 6.00
DKMCB Cody Bellinger 8.00 20.00
DKMCB Charlie Blackmon 4.00 10.00
DKMCC Carlos Correa 4.00 10.00
DKMCH Cole Hamels 3.00 8.00
DKMCJ Chipper Jones 5.00 12.00
DKMCK Clayton Kershaw 5.00 12.00
DKMCS Curt Schilling 3.00 8.00
DKMCS Corey Seager 6.00 15.00
DKMCS Chris Sale 4.00 10.00
DKMCY Christian Yelich 5.00 12.00
DKMDM Daniel Murphy 3.00 8.00
DKMDM Don Mattingly 6.00 15.00
DKMDP David Price 3.00 8.00
DKMDW Dave Winfield 3.00 8.00
DKMEA Elvis Andrus 3.00 8.00
DKMEB Ernie Banks 8.00 20.00
DKMEJ Eloy Jimenez 5.00 12.00
DKMFB Franklin Barreto 2.50 6.00
DKMFF Freddie Freeman 5.00 12.00
DKMFH Felix Hernandez 3.00 8.00
DKMFL Francisco Lindor 5.00 12.00
DKMFM Francis Martes 2.50 6.00
DKMFT Frank Thomas 5.00 12.00
DKMGH Gabby Hartnett 20.00 50.00
DKMGS Giancarlo Stanton 4.00 10.00
DKMHB Harold Baines 3.00 8.00
DKMHG Heinie Groh 6.00 15.00
DKMIH Ian Happ 5.00 12.00
DKMJA Jose Altuve 3.00 8.00
DKMJA Jake Arrieta 3.00 8.00
DKMJB Javier Baez 5.00 12.00
DKMJB Jackie Bradley Jr. 4.00 10.00
DKMJC Joe Carter 2.50 6.00
DKMJC Joe Cronin 8.00 20.00
DKMJC Johnny Cueto 3.00 8.00
DKMJD Josh Donaldson 3.00 8.00
DKMJK Jason Kipnis 3.00 8.00
DKMJM J.D. Martinez 4.00 10.00
DKMJP Jorge Posada 3.00 8.00
DKMJP Jose Peraza 3.00 8.00
DKMJR Jose Ramirez 3.00 8.00
DKMJV Joey Votto 4.00 10.00
DKMJV Justin Verlander 4.00 10.00
DKMKB Kris Bryant 5.00 12.00
DKMKB Kris Bryant 5.00 12.00
DKMKC Kiki Cuyler 8.00 20.00
DKMKG Ken Griffey Jr. 5.00 12.00
DKMKL Corey Kluber 3.00 8.00
DKMKM Kenta Maeda 3.00 8.00
DKMKS Kyle Schwarber 4.00 10.00
DKMLG Lou Gehrig 50.00 120.00
DKMMB Mookie Betts 6.00 15.00
DKMMB Madison Bumgarner 3.00 8.00
DKMMC Matt Carpenter 4.00 10.00
DKMMC Miguel Cabrera 4.00 10.00
DKMMC Max Carey
DKMMF Michael Fulmer 2.50 6.00
DKMMM Manny Machado 4.00 10.00
DKMMS Max Scherzer 4.00 10.00
DKMMT Mike Trout 15.00 40.00
DKMMT Masahiro Tanaka 3.00 8.00
DKMMT Mike Trout 15.00 40.00
DKMNA Nolan Arenado 5.00 12.00
DKMNG Nick Gordon 2.50 6.00
DKMNG Nomar Garciaparra 3.00 8.00
DKMNS Noah Syndergaard 3.00 8.00
DKMRC Robinson Cano 3.00 8.00
DKMRM Roger Maris
DKMRO Rougned Odor 3.00 8.00
DKMRP Rick Porcello 3.00 8.00
DKMTL Tony Lazzeri 25.00 60.00
DKMTO Tyler O'Neill 3.00 8.00
DKMTS Trevor Story 4.00 10.00
DKMTT Trea Turner 3.00 8.00
DKMTT Tim Tebow 5.00 12.00
DKMXB Xander Bogaerts 4.00 10.00
DKMYD Yu Darvish 4.00 10.00
DKMYM Yadier Molina 6.00 15.00
DKMJTR J.T. Realmuto 4.00 10.00

2017 Diamond Kings DK Originals

COMPLETE SET (25) 6.00 15.00
*HOLO BLUE/25: 1.5X TO 4X BASIC
DO1 Anthony Rizzo 1.00 2.50
DO2 Corey Kluber .50 1.25
DO3 Corey Seager .60 1.50
DO4 Daniel Murphy .50 1.25
DO5 Freddie Freeman .75 2.00
DO6 Jose Altuve .50 1.25
DO7 Josh Donaldson .50 1.25
DO8 Kris Bryant .75 2.00
DO9 Manny Machado .60 1.50
DO10 Max Scherzer .60 1.50
DO11 Mike Trout 3.00 8.00
DO12 Mookie Betts 1.00 2.50
DO13 Rick Porcello .50 1.25
DO14 Bill Mazeroski .50 1.25
DO15 Dave Winfield .50 1.25
DO16 Jim Palmer .50 1.25
DO17 Mike Schmidt 1.00 2.50
DO18 Ozzie Smith .75 2.00
DO19 Paul Molitor .60 1.50
DO20 Pedro Martinez .50 1.25
DO21 Reggie Jackson .50 1.25
DO22 Robin Yount .60 1.50
DO23 Ryne Sandberg 1.25 3.00
DO24 Tony Gwynn .60 1.50
DO25 Wade Boggs .50 1.25

2017 Diamond Kings DK Rookie Signature Materials

*SILVER/99: .4X TO 1X BASIC
*SILVER/49: .5X TO 1.2X BASIC
*GOLD/49: .5X TO 1.2X BASIC
*GOLD/25: .6X TO 1.5X BASIC
RANDOM INSERTS IN PACKS
PRINT RUNS B/WN 99-299 COPIES PER
RSAB Andrew Benintendi/299 30.00 80.00
RSAJ Aaron Judge/299 75.00 200.00
RSAM Adalberto Mejia/299 3.00 8.00
RSAR Alex Reyes/299 8.00 20.00
RSAX Alex Bregman/299 15.00 40.00
RSBS Braden Shipley/299 3.00 8.00
RSCF Carson Fulmer/299 3.00 8.00
RSCK Carson Kelly/299 4.00 10.00
RSCP Chad Pinder/299 3.00 8.00
RSDD David Dahl/299 4.00 10.00
RSDD David Dahl/99 4.00 10.00
RSDP David Paulino/299 4.00 10.00
RSDS Dansby Swanson/299 5.00 12.00
RSEG Erik Gonzalez/299 3.00 8.00
RSGC Gavin Cecchini/299 3.00 8.00
RSHR Hunter Renfroe/299 4.00 10.00
RSJA Jorge Alfaro/299 6.00 15.00
RSJB Josh Bell/299 10.00 25.00
RSJC Jharel Cotton/299 8.00 20.00
RSJDL Jose De Leon/299 3.00 8.00
RSJH Jeff Hoffman/299 3.00 8.00
RSJJ Jacoby Jones/299 4.00 10.00
RSJM Joe Musgrove/299 3.00 8.00
RSJT Jake Thompson/299 3.00 8.00
RSLW Luke Weaver/299 4.00 10.00
RSMM Manuel Margot/299 5.00 12.00
RSMO Matt Olson/299 6.00 15.00
RSRH Ryon Healy/299 4.00 10.00
RSRL Reynaldo Lopez/299 3.00 8.00
RSRQ Roman Quinn/299 3.00 8.00
RSRT Raimel Tapia/299 5.00 12.00
RSTG Tyler Glasnow/299 8.00 20.00
RSTH Teoscar Hernandez/299 10.00 25.00
RSTM Trey Mancini/299 15.00 40.00
RSYM1 Yoan Moncada/242 15.00 40.00
RSYM2 Yoan Moncada/299 15.00 40.00
RSYO Yohander Mendez/299 3.00 8.00

2017 Diamond Kings DK Rookie Signature Materials Holo Blue

*BLUE/25: .6X TO 1.5X BASIC
PRINT RUNS B/WN 5-25 COPIES PER
NO PRICING ON QTY 10 OR LESS
RSAB Andrew Benintendi/25 100.00 250.00

2017 Diamond Kings DK Signature Materials

RANDOM INSERTS IN PACKS
PRINT RUNS B/WN 10-299 COPIES PER
NO PRICING ON QTY 10
*BLUE/25: .6X TO 1.5X BASIC
DKSAB Adrian Beltre/49 25.00 60.00
DKSAD Aledmys Diaz/299 4.00 10.00
DKSAM Austin Meadows/299 6.00 15.00
DKSAS Aaron Sanchez/99 10.00 25.00
DKSBB Bill Buckner/99 4.00 10.00
DKSBK Charlie Blackmon/49 6.00 15.00
DKSBN Brandon Nimmo/299 4.00 10.00
DKSCB Cody Bellinger/99 40.00 100.00
DKSCH Cole Hamels/25 10.00 25.00
DKSCK Corey Kluber/49 6.00 15.00
DKSCO Corey Seager/49 30.00 80.00
DKSCR Cameron Rupp/199 3.00 8.00
DKSCS Cory Spangenberg/199 3.00 8.00
DKSDW David Wright/25 12.00 30.00
DKSEH Eric Hosmer/49 12.00 30.00
DKSEJ Eloy Jimenez/299 15.00 40.00
DKSEL Evan Longoria/25 15.00 40.00
DKSGS George Springer/49 10.00 25.00
DKSJA Jake Arrieta/25 20.00 50.00
DKSJC John Cusack/49 20.00 50.00
DKSJH Jason Heyward/20 10.00 25.00
DKSJM Joe Mauer/25 8.00 20.00
DKSJP Joe Panik/199 4.00 10.00
DKSJR Jose Ramirez/49 5.00 12.00
DKSJS Jorge Soler/149 5.00 12.00
DKSJU Julio Urias/49 10.00 25.00
DKSKG Kendall Graveman/199 3.00 8.00
DKSKS Kyle Schwarber/49 20.00 50.00
DKSKY Kyle Seager/199 5.00 12.00
DKSLS Luis Severino/99 8.00 20.00
DKSMB Michael Brantley/49 6.00 15.00
DKSMF Mike Foltynewicz/299 3.00 8.00
DKSMM Manny Machado/99 15.00 40.00
DKSMS Max Scherzer/49 20.00 50.00
DKSMS Matt Szczur/299 4.00 10.00
DKSNC Nelson Cruz/25 8.00 20.00
DKSNS Noah Syndergaard/49 12.00 30.00
DKSOA Ozhaino Albies/299 12.00 30.00
DKSRB Robert Stephenson/199 3.00 8.00
DKSRS Richie Shaffer/199 3.00 8.00
DKSSZ Gary Sanchez/99 40.00 100.00
DKSTR Tanner Roark/99 3.00 8.00
DKSTT Trea Turner/149 12.00 30.00
DKSWR Wilin Rosario/199 3.00 8.00
DKSXB Xander Bogaerts/49 20.00 50.00
DKSYM Yadier Molina/49 30.00 80.00
DKSYT Yasmany Tomas/49 4.00 10.00

2017 Diamond Kings DK Signature Materials Holo Gold

*GOLD/49: .5X TO 1.2X BASIC
*GOLD/20-25: .6X TO 1.5X BASIC
PRINT RUNS B/WN 5-49 COPIES PER
NO PRICING ON QTY 15 OR LESS
DKSTS Trevor Story/49 12.00 30.00

2017 Diamond Kings DK Signature Materials Holo Silver

*SILVER/99: .4X TO 1X BASIC
*SILVER/49: .5X TO 1.2X BASIC
*SILVER/20-25: .6X TO 1.5X BASIC
PRINT RUNS B/WN 7-99 COPIES PER
NO PRICING ON QTY 15 OR LESS
DKSGT Gleyber Torres/25 60.00 150.00
DKSSG Sonny Gray/20 6.00 15.00
DKSTS Trevor Story/99 10.00 25.00

2017 Diamond Kings Heritage Collection

COMPLETE SET (28) 10.00 25.00
*HOLO BLUE/25: 1.5X TO 4X BASIC
HC1 Al Kaline .60 1.50
HC2 Bill Mazeroski .50 1.25
HC3 Bob Feller .50 1.25
HC4 Bruce Sutter .50 1.25
HC5 Cal Ripken 2.00 5.00
HC6 Carlton Fisk .50 1.25
HC7 Catfish Hunter .50 1.25
HC8 Frank Thomas .60 1.50
HC9 George Brett 1.25 3.00
HC10 Jim Bunning .50 1.25
HC11 Jim Rice .50 1.25
HC12 Joe Morgan .50 1.25
HC13 John Smoltz .60 1.50
HC14 Juan Marichal .50 1.25
HC15 Ken Griffey Jr. 1.25 3.00
HC16 Kirby Puckett .60 1.50
HC17 Mike Piazza .60 1.50
HC18 Nolan Ryan 2.00 5.00
HC19 Ozzie Smith .75 2.00
HC20 Phil Niekro .50 1.25
HC21 Eddie Murray .50 1.25
HC22 Rickey Henderson .60 1.50
HC23 Rod Carew .50 1.25
HC24 Rollie Fingers .50 1.25
HC25 Tony Gwynn .60 1.50
HC26 Tony Perez .50 1.25
HC27 Wade Boggs .50 1.25
HCWM Willie McCovey .50 1.25

2017 Diamond Kings Heritage Collection Material Signatures

RANDOM INSERTS IN PACKS
PRINT RUNS B/WN 7-49 COPIES PER
NO PRICING ON QTY 15 OR LESS
*GOLD/25: .5X TO 1.2X BASIC
HCMSBB Bill Buckner/25 12.00 30.00
HCMSCD Carlos Delgado/25 6.00 15.00
HCMSGP Gaylord Perry/49 8.00 20.00
HCMSWB Wade Boggs/25 20.00 50.00

2017 Diamond Kings Jersey Kings

RANDOM INSERTS IN PACKS
PRINT RUNS B/WN 10-99 COPIES PER
NO PRICING ON QTY 15 OR LESS
*GOLD/49: .5X TO 1.2X BASIC
*GOLD/25: .6X TO 1.5X BASIC
*BLUE/25: .6X TO 1.5X BASIC
JKAD Aledmys Diaz/49 5.00 12.00
JKAG Adrian Gonzalez/49 4.00 10.00
JKBD Brandon Drury/99 2.50 6.00
JKCB Charlie Blackmon/99 4.00 10.00
JKCH Cole Hamels/99 3.00 8.00
JKDM Daniel Murphy/99 3.00 8.00
JKGS Giancarlo Stanton/49 5.00 12.00
JKGS Gary Sanchez/99 8.00 20.00
JKHP Herb Pennock/49 6.00 15.00
JKID Ian Desmond/99 2.50 6.00
JKKP Kirby Puckett/25 40.00 100.00
JKKS Kyle Schwarber/99 4.00 10.00
JKMC Matt Carpenter/49 5.00 12.00
JKMF Michael Fulmer/99 2.50 6.00
JKMM Manny Machado/49 5.00 12.00
JKNM Nomar Mazara/99 2.50 6.00
JKSP Stephen Piscotty/99 3.00 8.00
JKTA Tim Anderson/99 4.00 10.00
JKTR Tim Raines/49 4.00 10.00
JKTT Trea Turner/99 3.00 8.00
JKHSK Hyun Soo Kim/49 4.00 10.00
JKPWR Pee Wee Reese/49 6.00 15.00
JKSHO Seung-Hwan Oh/49 5.00 12.00

2017 Diamond Kings Jersey Kings Signatures

RANDOM INSERTS IN PACKS
PRINT RUNS B/WN 7-99 COPIES PER
NO PRICING ON QTY 15 OR LESS
*GOLD/49: .5X TO 1.2X BASIC
*GOLD/25: .6X TO 1.5X BASIC
*BLUE/25: .6X TO 1.5X BASIC
JKSAG Alex Gordon/20 12.00 30.00
JKSBD Brian Dozier/25 15.00 40.00
JKSBF Brandon Finnegan/99 8.00 20.00
JKSBG Brett Gardner/49 6.00 15.00
JKSDP David Price/25 10.00 25.00
JKSDT Devon Travis/99 3.00 8.00
JKSGR Garrett Richards/25 6.00 15.00
JKSGS Gary Sanchez/25 40.00 100.00
JKSHI Hisashi Iwakuma/25 6.00 15.00
JKSJK Jason Kipnis/25 10.00 25.00
JKSJL Jake Lamb/99 4.00 10.00
JKSJP Joe Panik/99 4.00 10.00
JKSJR J.T. Realmuto/99 20.00 50.00
JKSJS Jonathan Schoop/25 15.00 40.00
JKSMB Matt Barnes/99 3.00 8.00
JKSMC Matt Carpenter/25 10.00 25.00
JKSMF Maikel Franco/99 4.00 10.00
JKSMS Marcus Semien/79
JKSNC Nick Castellanos/25
JKSRG Randal Grichuk/99 8.00 20.00
JKSSM Steven Matz/99 4.00 10.00
JKSSS Steven Souza/49 5.00 12.00
JKSTK Tom Koehler/49 4.00 10.00
JKSTT Trea Turner/49 15.00 40.00
JKSWB Wade Boggs/25 20.00 50.00

2017 Diamond Kings Limited Lithos Signature Materials

RANDOM INSERTS IN PACKS
PRINT RUNS B/WN 7-99 COPIES PER
NO PRICING ON QTY 15 OR LESS
*BLUE/25: .6X TO 1.5X BASIC
LLAN Aaron Nola/99 4.00 10.00
LLBB Bill Buckner/25 8.00 20.00
LLDS Darryl Strawberry/25 15.00 40.00
LLEM Edgar Martinez/25 20.00 50.00
LLGS George Springer/25 12.00 30.00
LLMC Matt Carpenter/25 10.00 25.00
LLMG Mark Grace/25 20.00 50.00
LLMS Matt Szczur/99 4.00 10.00
LLMT Michael Taylor/99 3.00 8.00
LLRS Ross Stripling/49 4.00 10.00
LLSM Steven Matz/99 4.00 10.00
LLWC Willson Contreras/99 15.00 40.00

2017 Diamond Kings Limited Lithos Signature Materials Holo Gold

*GOLD/49: .5X TO 1.2X BASIC
PRINT RUNS B/WN 5-49 COPIES PER
NO PRICING ON QTY 15 OR LESS
LLTS Trevor Story/49 12.00 30.00

2017 Diamond Kings Memorable Moment

COMPLETE SET (18) 10.00 25.00
*HOLO BLUE/25: 1.5X TO 4X BASIC
MM1 Babe Ruth 1.50 4.00
MM2 Nolan Ryan 2.00 5.00
MM3 Grover Alexander .50 1.25
MM4 Ernie Banks .60 1.50
MM5 Honus Wagner .60 1.50
MM6 Jackie Robinson .60 1.50
MM7 Jim Bottomley .40 1.00
MM8 Joe DiMaggio 1.25 3.00
MM9 Kirby Puckett .60 1.50
MM10 Lefty Gomez .40 1.00
MM11 Lou Gehrig 1.25 3.00
MM12 Luke Appling .50 1.25
MM13 Reggie Jackson .50 1.25
MM14 Nellie Fox .50 1.25
MM15 Paul Waner .50 1.25
MM16 Roberto Clemente 1.50 4.00
MM17 Ted Williams 1.25 3.00
MM18 Ty Cobb 1.00 2.50

2017 Diamond Kings Sketches and Swatches

RANDOM INSERTS IN PACKS
PRINT RUNS B/WN 7-99 COPIES PER
NO PRICING ON QTY 15 OR LESS
*GOLD/49: .5X TO 1.2X BASIC
*GOLD/20-25: .6X TO 1.5X BASIC
*BLUE/25: .6X TO 1.5X BASIC
SSAG Andres Galarraga/25 10.00 25.00
SSAG Adrian Gonzalez/20 5.00 12.00
SSAJ Andruw Jones/49 8.00 20.00
SSBC Bert Campaneris/99 5.00 12.00
SSBW Bernie Williams/25 20.00 50.00
SSCB Charlie Blackmon/25 8.00 20.00
SSCD Chris Davis/20
SSCH Cole Hamels/20 10.00 25.00
SSDS Don Sutton/25 6.00 15.00
SSDW David Wright/20 12.00 30.00
SSEE Edwin Encarnacion/25 12.00 30.00
SSEL Evan Longoria/20 15.00 40.00
SSJA Jose Abreu/20 6.00 15.00
SSJB Jeff Bagwell/20
SSJR Jose Ramirez/25 6.00 15.00
SSJS Jonathan Schoop/25 15.00 40.00
SSJT Josh Tomlin/99 3.00 8.00
SSKW Kerry Wood/25
SSLC Lorenzo Cain/25 10.00 25.00
SSNS Noah Syndergaard/20 15.00 40.00
SSRP Rafael Palmeiro/20
SSTL Tommy Lasorda/20 25.00 60.00

2017 Diamond Kings Studio Portraits Materials

RANDOM INSERTS IN PACKS
PRINT RUNS B/WN 7-99 COPIES PER
NO PRICING ON QTY 15 OR LESS
*GOLD/49: .5X TO 1.2X BASIC
*GOLD/25: .6X TO 1.5X BASIC
*BLUE/25: .6X TO 1.5X BASIC
SPMBF Bob Feller/49 6.00 15.00
SPMCK Corey Kluber/49 3.00 8.00
SPMCR Cal Ripken/99 10.00 25.00
SPMDG Dwight Gooden/99 4.00 10.00
SPMFL Francisco Lindor/99 6.00 15.00
SPMGB George Brett/25 15.00 40.00
SPMGC Gary Carter/99 5.00 15.00
SPMJB Javier Baez/99 5.00 12.00
SPMJR Jim Rice/49 5.00 12.00
SPMKB Kris Bryant/99 5.00 12.00
SPMMT Mike Trout/25 25.00 60.00
SPMNR Nolan Ryan/25 20.00 50.00
SPMPM Paul Molitor/99 6.00 15.00
SPMRA Roberto Alomar/49 4.00 10.00
SPMRJ Reggie Jackson/49 8.00 20.00

2017 Diamond Kings Ted Williams Collection

COMPLETE SET (3) 4.00 10.00
*HOLO BLUE/25: 1.2X TO 3X BASIC
1 Ted Williams 1.50 4.00
2 Ted Williams 1.50 4.00
3 Ted Williams 1.50 4.00

2017 Diamond Kings Ted Williams Collection Materials

RANDOM INSERTS IN PACKS
PRINT RUNS B/WN 25-99 COPIES PER
*GOLD/49: .5X TO 1.2X BASIC
*GOLD/25: .6X TO 1.5X BASIC
*BLUE/25: .6X TO 1.5X BASIC
TWCM1 Ted Williams/25 40.00 100.00
TWCM2 Ted Williams/99 25.00 60.00
TWCM3 Ted Williams/49 30.00 80.00

2018 Diamond Kings

COMPLETE SET (150)
1 Babe Ruth .75 2.00
2 Honus Wagner .30 .75
3 Stan Musial .50 1.25
4 Lou Gehrig .60 1.50
5 Bobby Thomson .25 .60
6 George Kelly .30 .75
7 Mickey Mantle 1.00 2.50
8 Harry Hooper .20 .50
9 Ted Williams .60 1.50
10 Joe Cronin .20 .50
11 Joe DiMaggio .60 1.50
12 Kiki Cuyler .25 .60
13 Lloyd Waner .25 .60
14 Luke Appling .25 .60
15 Max Carey .20 .50
16 Carl Furillo .20 .50
17 Nellie Fox .25 .60
18 Paul Waner .25 .60
19 Roberto Clemente .75 2.00
20 Roger Maris .30 .75
21 Ted Lyons .20 .50
22 Tommy Henrich .20 .50
23 Pee Wee Reese .25 .60
24 Don Larsen .20 .50
25 Ernie Banks .30 .75
26 Herb Pennock .20 .50
27 Lefty Gomez .20 .50
28 Jackie Robinson .30 .75
29 Jim Thorpe .50 1.25
30 Joe Jackson .40 1.00
31 Leo Durocher .20 .50
32 Gabby Hartnett .20 .50
33 Tony Lazzeri .25 .60
34 Ty Cobb .50 1.25
35 Billy Herman .20 .50
36 Carl Erskine .20 .50
37 Chuck Klein .20 .50
38 Earl Averill .20 .50
39 Dom DiMaggio .20 .50
40 John McGraw .25 .60
41 Goose Goslin .25 .60
42 Grover Alexander .25 .60
43 Hack Wilson .25 .60
44 Harry Brecheen .20 .50
45 Harry Walker .20 .50
46 Heinie Groh .20 .50
47 Jim Bottomley .20 .50
48 Johnny Pesky .20 .50
49 Frank Thomas .30 .75
50 Kirby Puckett .30 .75
51 Moose Skowron .20 .50
52 Luis Severino .25 .60
53 Alex Bregman .30 .75
54 Trey Mancini .25 .60
55 Paul DeJong .30 .75
56 Max Scherzer .30 .75
57 Chris Sale .30 .75
58 George Springer .25 .60
59 Carlos Correa .30 .75
60 Sam Crawford .25 .60
61 Paul Goldschmidt .30 .75
62 Mookie Betts .50 1.25
63 Kris Bryant .40 1.00
64 Anthony Rizzo .40 1.00
65 Francisco Lindor .30 .75
66 Corey Kluber .25 .60
67 Nolan Arenado .40 1.00
68 Justin Verlander .30 .75
69 Jose Altuve .25 .60
70 Mike Trout 1.50 4.00
71 Corey Seager .30 .75
72 Clayton Kershaw .60 1.50
73 Shohei Ohtani RC 2.50 6.00
74 Andrew McCutchen .30 .75
75 Robinson Cano .25 .60
76 Shohei Ohtani RC 2.50 6.00
77 Josh Donaldson .25 .60
78 Bryce Harper .50 1.25
79 Buster Posey .40 1.00
80 Aaron Judge .75 2.00
81 Andrew Benintendi .30 .75
82 Cody Bellinger .60 1.50
83 Anthony Banda RC .40 1.00
84 Luiz Gohara RC .40 1.00
85 Max Fried RC 1.50 4.00
86 Lucas Sims RC .40 1.00
87 Anthony Santander RC .40 1.00
88 Victor Caratini RC .40 1.00
89 Nicky Delmonico RC .40 1.00
90 Tyler Mahle RC .50 1.25
91 Greg Allen RC .40 1.00
92 Ryan McMahon RC .50 1.25
93 Dillon Peters RC .40 1.00
94 Brandon Woodruff RC .50 1.25
95 Dominic Smith RC .40 1.00
96 Chris Flexen RC .40 1.00
97 Tyler Wade RC .50 1.25
98 J.P. Crawford RC .40 1.00
99 Nick Williams RC .50 1.25
100 Victor Robles RC 1.00 2.50
101 Ozzie Albies SP RC 2.50 6.00
102 Austin Hays SP RC 1.25 3.00
103 Chance Sisco SP RC 1.00 2.50
104 Rafael Devers SP RC 2.50 6.00
105 Francisco Mejia SP RC 1.00 2.50
106 J.D. Davis SP RC 1.00 2.50
107 Cameron Gallagher SP RC .75 2.00
108 Walker Buehler SP RC 4.00 10.00
109 Alex Verdugo SP RC 1.25 3.00
110 Kyle Farmer SP RC .75 2.00
111 Brian Anderson SP RC 1.00 2.50
112 Mitch Garver SP RC .75 2.00
113 Zack Granite SP RC .75 2.00
114 Felix Jorge SP RC .75 2.00
115 Tomas Nido SP RC .75 2.00
116 Amed Rosario SP RC 1.00 2.50
117 Clint Frazier SP RC 1.50 4.00
118 Miguel Andujar SP RC 3.00 8.00
119 Dustin Fowler SP RC .75 2.00
120 Paul Blackburn SP RC .75 2.00
121 Rhys Hoskins SP RC 3.00 8.00
122 Thyago Vieira SP RC .75 2.00
123 Reyes Moronta SP RC .75 2.00
124 Jack Flaherty SP RC 1.25 3.00
125 Harrison Bader SP RC 1.25 3.00
126 Willie Calhoun SP RC 1.00 2.50
127 Richard Urena SP RC .75 2.00
128 Erick Fedde SP RC .75 2.00
129 Andrew Stevenson SP RC .75 2.00
130 Odubel Herrera SP .50 1.25
131 Evan Longoria SP .50 1.25
132 David Ortiz SP .60 1.50
133 Manny Machado SP .60 1.50
134 Jose Ramirez SP .50 1.25
135 George Brett SP 1.25 3.00
136 Nolan Ryan SP 2.00 5.00
137 J.D. Martinez SP .60 1.50
138 Ichiro SP .75 2.00
139 Shohei Ohtani SP 2.50 6.00
140 Dustin Pedroia SP .60 1.50
141 Giancarlo Stanton SP .60 1.50
142 Brooks Robinson SP .50 1.25
143 Freddie Freeman SP .75 2.00
144 Noah Syndergaard SP .50 1.25
145 Shohei Ohtani SP 2.50 6.00
146 Madison Bumgarner SP .50 1.25
147 Josh Bell SP .50 1.25
148 Joey Votto SP .60 1.50
149 Manuel Margot SP .40 1.00
150 Charlie Blackmon SP .60 1.50

2018 Diamond Kings Artist Proof Blue

*AP BLUE: 4X TO 10X BASIC
*AP BLUE RC: 2X TO 5X BASIC
*AP BLUE SP: 2X TO 5X BASIC
*AP BLUE SP RC: 1X TO 2.5X BASIC
RANDOM INSERTS IN PACKS
STATED PRINT RUN 25 SER. #'D SETS

2018 Diamond Kings Artist Proof Gold

*AP GOLD: 2X TO 5X BASIC
*AP GOLD RC: 1X TO 2.5X BASIC
*AP GOLD SP: 1X TO 2.5X BASIC
*AP GOLD SP RC: .5X TO 1.2X BASIC
RANDOM INSERTS IN PACKS
STATED PRINT RUN 99 SER. #'D SETS

2018 Diamond Kings Artist Proof Red

*AP RED: 1.5X TO 4X BASIC
*AP RED RC: .75X TO 2X BASIC
*AP RED SP: .75X TO 2X BASIC
*AP RED SP RC: .4X TO 1X BASIC
RANDOM INSERTS IN PACKS

2018 Diamond Kings Blue Frame

*BLUE FRAME: 1.5X TO 4X BASIC
*BLUE FRAME RC: .75X TO 2X BASIC
*BLUE FRAME SP: .75X TO 2X BASIC
*BLUE FRAME SP RC: .4X TO 1X BASIC
RANDOM INSERTS IN PACKS

2018 Diamond Kings Brown Frame

*BRWN FRAME: 2.5X TO 6X BASIC
*BRWN FRAME RC: 1.2X TO 3X BASIC
*BRWN FRAME SP: 1.2X TO 3X BASIC
*BRWN FRAME SP RC: .6X TO 1.5X BASIC
RANDOM INSERTS IN PACKS
STATED PRINT RUN 49 SER. #'D SETS

2018 Diamond Kings Gray Frame

*GRAY FRAME: 2X TO 5X BASIC
*GRAY FRAME RC: 1X TO 2.5X BASIC
*GRAY FRAME SP: 1X TO 2.5X BASIC
*GRAY FRAME SP RC: .5X TO 1.2X BASIC
STATED PRINT RUN 99 SER. #'D SETS

2018 Diamond Kings Red Frame

*RED FRAME: 1.5X TO 4X BASIC
*RED FRAME RC: .75X TO 2X BASIC
*RED FRAME SP: .75X TO 2X BASIC
*RED FRAME SP RC: .4X TO 1X BASIC
RANDOM INSERTS IN PACKS

2018 Diamond Kings Black and White Variations

P RED: .75X TO 2X BASIC
LUE FRAME: .75X TO 2X BASIC
ED FRAME: .75X TO 2X BASIC
P GOLD/99: 1X TO 2X BASIC
RAY FRAME/99: 1X TO 2.5X BASIC
RN FRAME/49: 1.2X TO 3X BASIC
P BLUE/25: 1.5X TO 4X BASIC
NDOM INSERTS IN PACKS
Shohei Ohtani 2.50 6.00
Shohei Ohtani 2.50 6.00
0 Victor Robles 1.00 2.50
4 Rafael Devers 1.25 3.00
5 Francisco Mejia .50 1.25
8 Walker Buehler 1.50 4.00
6 Amed Rosario .50 1.25
7 Clint Frazier .75 2.00
8 Miguel Andujar 1.50 4.00
1 Rhys Hoskins 1.50 4.00

2018 Diamond Kings Name Variations

P RED: .75X TO 2X BASIC
LUE FRAME: .75X TO 2X BASIC
ED FRAME: .75X TO 2X BASIC
P GOLD/99: 1X TO 2.5X BASIC
RAY FRAME/99: 1X TO 2.5X BASIC
RN FRAME/49: 1.2X TO 3X BASIC
P BLUE/25: 1.5X TO 4X BASIC
NDOM INSERTS IN PACKS
abe Ruth 1.50 4.00
Honus Wagner .60 1.50
Mickey Mantle 2.00 5.00
ed Williams 1.25 3.00
Ernie Banks .60 1.50
Frank Thomas .60 1.50
Shohei Ohtani 2.50 6.00
Shohei Ohtani 2.50 6.00
Aaron Judge 1.50 4.00
6 Nolan Ryan 2.00 5.00

2018 Diamond Kings Photo Variations

NDOM INSERTS IN PACKS
P RED: .75X TO 2X BASIC
LUE FRAME: .75X TO 2X BASIC
ED FRAME: .75X TO 2X BASIC
P GOLD/99: 1X TO 2.5X BASIC
RAY FRAME/99: 1X TO 2.5X BASIC
RN FRAME/49: 1.2X TO 3X BASIC
P BLUE/25: 1.5X TO 4X BASIC
Honus Wagner .60 1.50
Stan Musial 1.00 2.50
Lou Gehrig 1.25 3.00
Mickey Mantle 2.00 5.00
Harry Hooper .40 1.00
Ted Williams 1.25 3.00
Joe Cronin .40 1.00
Joe DiMaggio 1.25 3.00
Lloyd Waner .50 1.25
Paul Waner .50 1.25
Roberto Clemente 1.50 4.00
Roger Maris .60 1.50
Pee Wee Reese .50 1.25
Ernie Banks .60 1.50
Lefty Gomez .40 1.00
Jackie Robinson .60 1.50
Joe Jackson .75 2.00
Ty Cobb 1.00 2.50
Shohei Ohtani 2.50 6.00
Shohei Ohtani 2.50 6.00

2018 Diamond Kings Sepia Variations

P RED: .75X TO 2X BASIC
LUE FRAME: .75X TO 2X BASIC
ED FRAME: .75X TO 2X BASIC
P GOLD/99: 1X TO 2.5X BASIC
RAY FRAME/99: 1X TO 2.5X BASIC
RN FRAME/49: 1.2X TO 3X BASIC
P BLUE/25: 1.5X TO 4X BASIC
NDOM INSERTS IN PACKS
Francisco Lindor .60 1.50
Jose Altuve .50 1.25
Mike Trout 3.00 8.00
Shohei Ohtani 2.50 6.00
Shohei Ohtani 2.50 6.00
Bryce Harper 1.00 2.50
Buster Posey .75 2.00
Aaron Judge 1.50 4.00
Andrew Benintendi .60 1.50
Cody Bellinger 1.25 3.00

2018 Diamond Kings '82 DK Materials Signatures

NDOM INSERTS IN PACKS
INT RUNS B/WN 10-99 COPIES PER
PRICING ON QTY 15 OR LESS
OLO BLUE/25: .6X TO 1.5X BASE p/r 99
OLO GOLD/49: .5X TO 1.2X BASE p/r 99
OLO GOLD/25: .5X TO 1.2X BASE p/r 49
Nolan Ryan/49 50.00 120.00
Reggie Jackson/49 30.00 80.00
Dennis Eckersley/25 12.00 30.00
Josh Donaldson/25 8.00 20.00
Shohei Ohtani/99 300.00 600.00
Joey Votto/49 15.00 40.00
Josh Tomlin/99 10.00 25.00
Tommy Lasorda/99 20.00 50.00
Mark Grace/20 15.00 40.00
Max Scherzer/49 25.00 60.00
Ryne Sandberg/99 20.00 50.00
Terry Francona/25 15.00 40.00
Wade Boggs/99 12.00 30.00
19 Roberto Alomar/99 10.00 25.00
20 Frank Thomas/25 30.00 80.00

2018 Diamond Kings '82 DK Signatures

RANDOM INSERTS IN PACKS
STATED PRINT RUN 50 SER.#'d SETS
DKSS01 Shohei Ohtani 800.00 1200.00
DKSS02 Shohei Ohtani 800.00 1200.00

2018 Diamond Kings Aurora

COMPLETE SET (10)
RANDOM INSERTS IN PACKS
1 George Springer .40 1.00
2 Yadier Molina .50 1.25
3 Mookie Betts .75 2.00
4 Francisco Lindor .50 1.25
5 Andrew McCutchen .50 1.25
6 Carlos Correa .50 1.25
7 Buster Posey .60 1.50
8 Albert Pujols .60 1.50
9 Ichiro .60 1.50
10 Shohei Ohtani 2.00 5.00

2018 Diamond Kings Aurora Holo Blue

*HOLO BLUE: 2X TO 5X BASIC
RANDOM INSERTS IN PACKS
STATED PRINT RUN 25 SER.#'d SET
10 Shohei Ohtani 50.00 120.00

2018 Diamond Kings Bat Kings

RANDOM INSERTS IN PACKS
*HOLO BLUE/25: .75X TO 2X BASIC
*HOLO GOLD/49: .6X TO 1.5X BASIC
*HOLO GOLD/25: .75X TO 2X BASIC
*HOLO SILVER/99: .5X TO 1.2X BASIC
*HOLO SILVER/49: .6X TO 1.5X BASIC
*HOLO SILVER/25: .75X TO 2X BASIC
1 George Brett 6.00 15.00
2 Cal Ripken 15.00 40.00
3 Ted Williams 40.00 100.00
4 Manny Ramirez 3.00 8.00
5 Gary Sheffield 2.00 5.00
6 Barry Larkin 2.50 6.00
7 Alex Rodriguez 4.00 10.00
8 Babe Ruth 75.00 200.00
9 Pee Wee Reese 5.00 12.00
10 Mickey Mantle 25.00 60.00
12 Stan Musial 15.00 40.00
13 Harry Hooper
14 Joe Cronin
15 Ernie Banks 3.00 8.00
16 Heinie Groh 6.00 15.00
17 Sam Crawford 10.00 25.00
18 Kiki Cuyler 12.00 30.00
19 George Kelly 8.00 20.00
20 Frank Thomas 5.00 12.00
21 Rod Carew 2.50 6.00
22 George Springer 2.50 6.00
23 Giancarlo Stanton 3.00 8.00
24 Logan Morrison 2.00 5.00
25 Joey Votto 3.00 8.00

2018 Diamond Kings Diamond Cuts Signatures

RANDOM INSERTS IN PACKS
PRINT RUNS B/WN 2-25 COPIES PER
NO PRICING ON QTY 5 OR LESS
2 Gary Carter/25 20.00 50.00
3 Al Barlick/25 15.00 40.00
5 Bobby Thomson/25 12.00 30.00
17 Buck Leonard/25 10.00 25.00

2018 Diamond Kings Diamond Deco Materials

RANDOM INSERTS IN PACKS
*HOLO BLUE/25: .75X TO 2X BASIC
2 Tony Gwynn 10.00 25.00
3 Don Mattingly 15.00 40.00
4 Aaron Judge 12.00 30.00
5 Cody Bellinger 5.00 12.00
6 Alex Bregman 5.00 12.00
7 Andrew Benintendi 3.00 8.00
10 Alex Rodriguez 6.00 15.00

2018 Diamond Kings Diamond Deco Materials Holo Gold

*HOLO GOLD/49: .6X TO 1.5X BASIC
*HOLO GOLD/25: .75X TO 2X BASIC
RANDOM INSERTS IN PACKS
PRINT RUNS B/WN 5-49 COPIES PER
NO PRICING ON QTY 5
8 Ken Griffey Jr./25 40.00 100.00
9 Mike Trout/25 25.00 60.00

2018 Diamond Kings Diamond Deco Materials Holo Silver

*HOLO SILVER/99: .5X TO 1.2X BASIC
*HOLO SILVER/49: .6X TO 1.5X BASIC
RANDOM INSERTS IN PACKS
PRINT RUNS B/WN 49-99 COPIES PER
8 Ken Griffey Jr./49 30.00 80.00
9 Mike Trout/49 20.00 50.00

2018 Diamond Kings Diamond Material Cuts Signatures

RANDOM INSERTS IN PACKS
PRINT RUNS B/WN X-X COPIES PER
NO PRICING ON QTY X OR LESS
3 Gary Carter/49 12.00 30.00
4 Lloyd Waner/25 30.00 80.00
5 Stan Musial/25 25.00 60.00

2018 Diamond Kings DK Jumbo Materials Signatures

RANDOM INSERTS IN PACKS
PRINT RUNS B/WN 15-75 COPIES PER
NO PRICING ON QTY 15 OR LESS
1 Dwight Gooden/49 8.00 20.00
2 Eric Hosmer/49 5.00 12.00
3 Kyle Schwarber/49 12.00 30.00
5 Mariano Rivera/25 60.00 150.00
11 Wade Boggs/49 15.00 40.00
12 Paul Goldschmidt/75 10.00 25.00
13 Noah Syndergaard/49 5.00 12.00
14 Mike Napoli/25 5.00 12.00
15 Mike Piazza/75 20.00 50.00
17 Addison Russell/49 5.00 12.00
18 Brandon Belt/25 6.00 15.00
19 Edgar Martinez/49 10.00 25.00
20 George Springer/49 5.00 12.00

2018 Diamond Kings DK Jumbo Materials Signatures Holo Gold

*HOLO GOLD/49: .5X TO 1.2X BASE p/r 75
*HOLO GOLD/25: .5X TO 1.2X BASE p/r 49
RANDOM INSERTS IN PACKS
PRINT RUNS B/WN 5-49 COPIES PER
NO PRICING ON QTY 15 OR LESS
7 Ronald Acuna/25 100.00 250.00

2018 Diamond Kings DK Jumbo Rookie Materials Signatures

RANDOM INSERTS IN PACKS
PRINT RUNS B/WN 49-99 COPIES PER
*HOLO GOLD/25: .6X TO 1.5X BASE p/r 99
1 Max Fried/99 12.00 30.00
2 Ozzie Albies/99 10.00 25.00
3 Austin Hays/99 5.00 12.00
4 Shohei Ohtani/49 350.00 700.00
5 Rafael Devers/99 12.00 30.00
6 Francisco Mejia/99 4.00 10.00
7 Walker Buehler/99 15.00 40.00
8 Alex Verdugo/99 5.00 12.00
9 Kyle Farmer/99 6.00 15.00
10 Zack Granite/99 3.00 8.00
11 Anthony Banda/99 3.00 8.00
12 Amed Rosario/99 4.00 10.00
13 Clint Frazier/99 6.00 15.00
14 Miguel Andujar/99 20.00 50.00
15 J.P. Crawford/99 3.00 8.00
16 Nick Williams/99 4.00 10.00
17 Rhys Hoskins/99 25.00 60.00
18 Harrison Bader/99 5.00 12.00
19 Willie Calhoun/99 4.00 10.00
20 Victor Robles/99 8.00 20.00

2018 Diamond Kings DK Materials

RANDOM INSERTS IN PACKS
1 Anthony Banda 2.00 5.00
2 Luiz Gohara 2.00 5.00
3 Max Fried 8.00 20.00
4 Ozzie Albies 5.00 12.00
5 Lucas Sims 2.00 5.00
6 Austin Hays 3.00 8.00
7 Chance Sisco 2.50 6.00
8 Anthony Santander 2.00 5.00
9 Rafael Devers 5.00 12.00
10 Victor Caratini 2.50 6.00
11 Nicky Delmonico 2.00 5.00
12 Tyler Mahle 2.00 5.00
13 Francisco Mejia 2.50 6.00
14 Greg Allen 2.00 5.00
15 Ryan McMahon 2.50 6.00
16 J.D. Davis 2.50 6.00
17 Cameron Gallagher 2.00 5.00
18 Walker Buehler 5.00 12.00
19 Alex Verdugo 3.00 8.00
20 Kyle Farmer 2.00 5.00
21 Brian Anderson 2.50 6.00
22 Dillon Peters 2.00 5.00
23 Brandon Woodruff 2.50 6.00
24 Mitch Garver 2.00 5.00
25 Zack Granite 2.00 5.00
26 Felix Jorge 2.00 5.00
27 Tomas Nido 2.00 5.00
28 Greg Bird 2.50 6.00
29 Chris Flexen 2.00 5.00
30 Amed Rosario 2.50 6.00
31 Clint Frazier 4.00 10.00
32 Miguel Andujar 5.00 12.00
33 Tyler Wade 2.50 6.00
34 Dustin Fowler 2.00 5.00
35 Paul Blackburn 2.00 5.00
36 J.P. Crawford 2.00 5.00
37 Nick Williams 2.50 6.00
38 Rhys Hoskins 5.00 12.00
39 Thyago Vieira 2.00 5.00
40 Reyes Moronta 2.00 5.00
41 Jack Flaherty 3.00 8.00
42 Harrison Bader 3.00 8.00
43 Willie Calhoun 2.50 6.00
44 Richard Urena 2.00 5.00
45 Victor Robles 4.00 10.00
46 Erick Fedde 2.00 5.00
47 Andrew Stevenson 2.00 5.00
48 Mark McGwire 5.00 12.00
49 Ernie Banks 3.00 8.00
50 Herb Pennock 6.00 15.00
52 Leo Durocher 6.00 15.00
53 Lou Gehrig 60.00 150.00
54 Pee Wee Reese 5.00 12.00
55 Tony Lazzeri 12.00 30.00
56 Babe Ruth 75.00 200.00
57 Billy Martin 5.00 12.00
58 Carl Furillo
59 George Kelly 8.00 20.00
60 Harry Hooper
61 Joe Cronin
62 Joe DiMaggio 15.00 40.00
63 Kiki Cuyler 12.00 30.00
64 Lloyd Waner
65 Luke Appling 4.00 10.00
66 Max Carey
67 Mickey Mantle 25.00 60.00
70 Roger Maris
71 Stan Musial 15.00 40.00
73 Ted Williams 40.00 100.00
74 Tommy Henrich 5.00 12.00
75 Mike Trout 15.00 40.00
76 Ken Griffey Jr. 8.00 20.00
77 Gary Sheffield 2.00 5.00
78 Aaron Judge 10.00 25.00
80 Reggie Jackson 5.00 12.00
81 Andrew Benintendi 4.00 10.00
82 Jose Altuve 2.50 6.00
83 Cody Bellinger 4.00 10.00
84 Adrian Beltre 3.00 8.00
85 Addie Joss
86 Justin Turner 2.50 6.00
87 Shohei Ohtani 10.00 25.00
88 Marcell Ozuna 3.00 8.00
89 Mookie Betts 5.00 12.00
90 Joey Votto 3.00 8.00
91 Clayton Kershaw 6.00 15.00
92 Corey Kluber 2.50 6.00
93 Max Scherzer 3.00 8.00
94 Jose Abreu 3.00 8.00
95 Lorenzo Cain 2.00 5.00
96 Andrew McCutchen 3.00 8.00
97 Dallas Keuchel 2.50 6.00
99 Albert Pujols 4.00 10.00

2018 Diamond Kings DK Materials Holo Blue

*HOLO BLUE/25: .75X TO 2X BASIC
RANDOM INSERTS IN PACKS
PRINT RUNS B/WN 3-25 COPIES PER
NO PRICING ON QTY 10 OR LESS
79 Giancarlo Stanton/25 6.00 15.00

2018 Diamond Kings DK Materials Holo Gold

*HOLO GOLD/49: .6X TO 1.5X BASIC
*HOLO GOLD/20-25: .75X TO 2X BASIC
RANDOM INSERTS IN PACKS
PRINT RUNS B/WN 5-49 COPIES PER
NO PRICING ON QTY 15 OR LESS
79 Giancarlo Stanton/49 5.00 12.00
100 Mike Piazza/25 6.00 15.00

2018 Diamond Kings DK Materials Holo Silver

*HOLO SILVER/99: .5X TO 1.2X BASIC
*HOLO SILVER/49: .6X TO 1.5X BASIC
*HOLO SILVER/25: .75X TO 2X BASIC
RANDOM INSERTS IN PACKS
PRINT RUNS B/WN 7-99 COPIES PER
NO PRICING ON QTY 15 OR LESS
79 Giancarlo Stanton/99 4.00 10.00
100 Mike Piazza/99 4.00 10.00

2018 Diamond Kings DK Materials Signatures

RANDOM INSERTS IN PACKS
PRINT RUNS B/WN 10-299 COPIES PER
NO PRICING ON QTY 15 OR LESS
*HOLO BLUE/25: .6X TO 1.5X BASE p/r 75-299
*HOLO GOLD/49: .5X TO 1.2X BASE p/r 75-299
*HOLO GOLD/25: .6X TO 1.5X BASE p/r 75-299
*HOLO SLVR/99: .4X TO 1X BASE p/r 75-299
*HOLO SLVR/49: .5X TO 1.2X BASE p/r 75-299
*HOLO SLVR/25: .5X TO 1.2X BASE p/r 49
1 Rafael Palmeiro/49 12.00 30.00
2 Rickey Henderson/99 20.00 50.00
3 David Dahl/99 3.00 8.00
4 Roger Clemens/75 15.00 40.00
5 Ryne Sandberg/99 20.00 50.00
6 Stephen Piscotty/49
7 Todd Helton/99 8.00 20.00
8 Trea Turner/25 6.00 15.00
9 Trey Mancini/49 5.00 12.00
10 Wil Myers/30 5.00 12.00
11 Byron Buxton/35 6.00 15.00
12 Carlos Gonzalez/25 10.00 25.00
13 Cole Hamels/99 4.00 10.00
14 Craig Kimbrel/49 10.00 25.00
15 Eric Hosmer/49 12.00 30.00
17 Fergie Jenkins/99 4.00 10.00
18 Maikel Franco/299 4.00 10.00
19 Alex Bregman/150 12.00 30.00
20 Derek Fisher/299 3.00 8.00
21 Franklin Barreto/299 3.00 8.00
22 Jordan Montgomery/166 5.00 12.00
23 Ian Happ/196 4.00 10.00
24 Matt Olson/299 3.00 8.00
25 Ryon Healy/49 8.00 20.00
26 Bradley Zimmer/49 4.00 10.00
28 Jake Thompson/299 3.00 8.00
29 Antonio Senzatela/150 3.00 8.00
30 Joe Musgrove/299 3.00 8.00
31 Juan Gonzalez/299 5.00 12.00
32 Gary Sheffield/99 6.00 15.00
33 Yoenis Cespedes/75 8.00 20.00
34 Gerrit Cole/99 12.00 30.00
35 Jason Kipnis/49 5.00 12.00
36 Luke Weaver/299 4.00 10.00
37 Reynaldo Lopez/226 4.00 10.00
38 Carson Kelly/299 3.00 8.00
39 Jeff Hoffman/299 3.00 8.00

2018 Diamond Kings DK Originals Materials

RANDOM INSERTS IN PACKS
1 Carlos Gonzalez 2.50 6.00
2 Joey Gallo 2.50 6.00
3 Cody Bellinger 4.00 10.00
4 Aaron Judge 10.00 25.00
5 Andrew Benintendi 4.00 10.00
6 Josh Bell 2.50 6.00
7 Alex Bregman 3.00 8.00
8 Charlie Blackmon 3.00 8.00
9 Joey Votto 3.00 8.00
11 J.D. Martinez 3.00 8.00
12 Rhys Hoskins 5.00 12.00
13 Nolan Arenado 4.00 10.00
14 Manny Machado 3.00 8.00
15 Gary Sanchez 4.00 10.00
16 Paul Goldschmidt 3.00 8.00
17 Anthony Rizzo 5.00 12.00
18 Jose Abreu 3.00 8.00
19 Ozzie Albies 5.00 12.00
20 Victor Robles 4.00 10.00
21 Rafael Devers 5.00 12.00
22 Clint Frazier 4.00 10.00
23 Amed Rosario 2.50 6.00
24 Greg Bird 2.50 6.00
25 J.P. Crawford 2.00 5.00
26 Miguel Andujar 5.00 12.00
27 Chance Sisco 2.50 6.00
28 Kyle Farmer 2.00 5.00
29 Jonathan Schoop 2.00 5.00
30 Ryan Zimmerman 2.50 6.00
31 Corey Kluber 2.50 6.00
32 Stephen Strasburg 3.00 8.00
33 Luis Severino 2.50 6.00
34 Clayton Kershaw 6.00 15.00
35 Chris Sale 3.00 8.00
36 Max Scherzer 3.00 8.00
37 Craig Kimbrel 2.50 6.00
38 Kirby Puckett 12.00 30.00
39 Dom DiMaggio
40 Mickey Mantle 25.00 60.00

2018 Diamond Kings DK Originals Materials Holo Blue

*HOLO BLUE/25: .75X TO 2X BASIC
RANDOM INSERTS IN PACKS
PRINT RUNS B/WN 3-25 COPIES PER
NO PRICING ON QTY 10 OR LESS
10 Giancarlo Stanton/25 6.00 15.00

2018 Diamond Kings DK Originals Materials Holo Gold

*HOLO GOLD/49: .6X TO 1.5X BASIC
*HOLO GOLD/25: .75X TO 2X BASIC
RANDOM INSERTS IN PACKS
PRINT RUNS B/WN 5-49 COPIES PER
NO PRICING ON QTY 15 OR LESS
10 Giancarlo Stanton/49 5.00 12.00
14 Manny Machado/25 6.00 15.00

2018 Diamond Kings DK Originals Materials Holo Silver

*HOLO SILVER/99: .5X TO 1.2X BASIC
*HOLO SILVER/49: .6X TO 1.5X BASIC
*HOLO SILVER/25: .75X TO 2X BASIC
RANDOM INSERTS IN PACKS
PRINT RUNS B/WN 25-99 COPIES PER
10 Giancarlo Stanton/99 4.00 10.00
14 Manny Machado/49 5.00 12.00

2018 Diamond Kings DK Rookie Materials Signatures

RANDOM INSERTS IN PACKS
PRINT RUNS B/WN 99-299 COPIES PER
*HOLO GOLD/25: .6X TO 1.5X BASE
*HOLO SILVER/49: .5X TO 1.2X BASE
1 Anthony Banda/299 3.00 0.00
2 Luiz Gohara/199 6.00 15.00
3 Max Fried/299 12.00 30.00
4 Ozzie Albies/299 20.00 50.00
5 Lucas Sims/299 3.00 8.00
6 Austin Hays/299 5.00 12.00
7 Chance Sisco/299 4.00 10.00
8 Anthony Santander/299 3.00 8.00
9 Rafael Devers/299 10.00 25.00
10 Victor Caratini/299 4.00 10.00
11 Nicky Delmonico/299 3.00 8.00
12 Tyler Mahle/299 4.00 10.00
13 Francisco Mejia/299 4.00 10.00
14 Greg Allen/299 3.00 8.00
15 Ryan McMahon/299 4.00 10.00
16 J.D. Davis/299 4.00 10.00
17 Cameron Gallagher/199 3.00 8.00
18 Walker Buehler/299 12.00 30.00
19 Alex Verdugo/299 6.00 15.00
20 Kyle Farmer/299 6.00 15.00
21 Brian Anderson/299 4.00 10.00
22 Dillon Peters/299 3.00 8.00
23 Brandon Woodruff/299 4.00 10.00
24 Mitch Garver/299 3.00 8.00
25 Zack Granite/299 3.00 8.00
26 Felix Jorge/299 3.00 8.00
27 Tomas Nido/299 3.00 8.00
28 Ozzie Albies/299 20.00 50.00
29 Chris Flexen/299 3.00 8.00
30 Amed Rosario/299 4.00 10.00
31 Clint Frazier/299 6.00 15.00
32 Miguel Andujar/299 12.00 30.00
33 Tyler Wade/299 4.00 10.00
34 Dustin Fowler/299 3.00 8.00
35 Paul Blackburn/299 3.00 8.00
36 J.P. Crawford/199 3.00 8.00
37 Nick Williams/299 4.00 10.00
38 Rhys Hoskins/299 10.00 50.00
39 Thyago Vieira/299 3.00 8.00
40 Reyes Moronta/299 3.00 8.00
41 Jack Flaherty/299 5.00 12.00
42 Harrison Bader/299 5.00 12.00
43 Willie Calhoun/299 4.00 10.00
44 Richard Urena/299 3.00 8.00
45 Victor Robles/299 8.00 20.00
46 Erick Fedde/299 3.00 8.00
47 Andrew Stevenson/299 3.00 8.00
48 Shohei Ohtani/99 300.00 600.00

2018 Diamond Kings DK Rookie Signatures

RANDOM INSERTS IN PACKS
*HOLO SILVER/49: .5X TO 1.2X BASIC
*HOLO GOLD/25: .6X TO 1.5X BASIC
1 Anthony Banda 3.00 8.00
2 Luiz Gohara 3.00 8.00
3 Max Fried 12.00 30.00
4 Ozzie Albies 6.00 15.00
5 Lucas Sims 3.00 8.00
6 Austin Hays 4.00 10.00
7 Chance Sisco 4.00 10.00
8 Anthony Santander 3.00 8.00
9 Rafael Devers 5.00 12.00
10 Victor Caratini 4.00 10.00
11 Nicky Delmonico 3.00 8.00
12 Tyler Mahle 4.00 10.00
13 Francisco Mejia 4.00 10.00
14 Greg Allen 3.00 8.00
15 Ryan McMahon 4.00 10.00
16 J.D. Davis 4.00 10.00
17 Cameron Gallagher 3.00 8.00
18 Walker Buehler 8.00 20.00
19 Alex Verdugo 5.00 12.00
20 Kyle Farmer 3.00 8.00
21 Brian Anderson 4.00 10.00
22 Dillon Peters 3.00 8.00
23 Brandon Woodruff 4.00 10.00
24 Mitch Garver 3.00 8.00
25 Zack Granite 3.00 8.00
26 Felix Jorge 3.00 8.00
27 Tomas Nido 3.00 8.00
28 Dominic Smith 3.00 8.00
29 Chris Flexen 3.00 8.00
30 Amed Rosario 4.00 10.00
31 Clint Frazier 5.00 12.00
32 Miguel Andujar 20.00 50.00
33 Tyler Wade 4.00 10.00
34 Dustin Fowler 3.00 8.00
35 Paul Blackburn 3.00 8.00
36 J.P. Crawford 3.00 8.00
37 Nick Williams 4.00 10.00
38 Rhys Hoskins 15.00 40.00
39 Thyago Vieira 3.00 8.00
40 Reyes Moronta 3.00 8.00
41 Jack Flaherty 10.00 25.00
42 Harrison Bader 5.00 12.00
43 Willie Calhoun 4.00 10.00
44 Richard Urena 3.00 8.00
45 Victor Robles 6.00 15.00
46 Erick Fedde 3.00 8.00
47 Shohei Ohtani 125.00 300.00

2018 Diamond Kings DK Rookie Signatures Purple

*PURPLE/20: .6X TO 1.5X BASIC
RANDOM INSERTS IN PACKS
PRINT RUNS B/WN 10-20 COPIES PER
NO PRICING ON QTY 10

2018 Diamond Kings DK Signatures

RANDOM INSERTS IN PACKS
*HOLO BLUE/25: .75X TO 2X BASIC
*HOLO GOLD/49: .5X TO 1.2X BASIC
*HOLO GOLD/25: .6X TO 1.5X BASIC
*HOLO SILVER/49-99: .5X TO 1.2X BASIC
*HOLO SILVER/25: .6X TO 1.5X BASIC
*PURPLE/20: .6X TO 1.5X BASIC
1 Wade Boggs 10.00 25.00
2 Bob Gibson 12.00 30.00
3 David Dahl 3.00 8.00
4 Jose Abreu 4.00 10.00
5 Aaron Judge 60.00 150.00
6 Jose Altuve 12.00 30.00
7 Adam Frazier 3.00 8.00
8 Andre Dawson 6.00 15.00
9 Bill Mazeroski 12.00 30.00
10 Aaron Hicks 5.00 12.00
11 Bert Blyleven 4.00 10.00
12 Al Kaline 15.00 40.00
13 Jacoby Jones 4.00 10.00
14 Josh Bell 4.00 10.00
15 Raimel Tapia 3.00 8.00
16 Mike Foltynewicz 3.00 8.00
17 Carson Fulmer 3.00 8.00
18 Yasmany Tomas 3.00 8.00
19 Luke Weaver 4.00 10.00
20 Gavin Cecchini 3.00 8.00
21 Joe Musgrove 3.00 8.00
22 Tyler Glasnow 3.00 8.00
23 Matt Olson 3.00 8.00
24 Odubel Herrera 8.00 20.00
25 Ivan Rodriguez 10.00 25.00
26 Tom Glavine 6.00 15.00
27 Dansby Swanson 8.00 20.00
28 Sean Newcomb 4.00 10.00
29 Matt Carpenter 5.00 12.00
30 Chris Taylor 5.00 12.00
31 Brooks Robinson 12.00 30.00
32 Manuel Margot 3.00 8.00
33 Luis Robert 20.00 50.00
34 Justin Turner 15.00 40.00
35 Ozzie Smith 15.00 40.00
36 David Ortiz 20.00 50.00
37 Braden Shipley 3.00 8.00
38 Willie McGee 8.00 20.00
39 Adam Duvall 5.00 12.00
40 Chipper Jones 30.00 80.00
41 Chris Sale
42 Corey Seager 8.00 20.00
43 Darrell Evans 3.00 8.00
44 Darryl Strawberry 5.00 12.00
45 George Springer 10.00 25.00
46 Ian Kinsler 4.00 10.00
47 Jacob deGrom
48 Johnny Damon 5.00 12.00
49 Josh Donaldson
50 Kyle Seager 3.00 8.00
51 Manny Machado 15.00 40.00
52 Michael Kopech 6.00 15.00
53 Carlos Correa 15.00 40.00

2018 Diamond Kings DK Triple Materials Signatures

RANDOM INSERTS IN PACKS
PRINT RUNS B/WN 10-150 COPIES PER
NO PRICING ON QTY 10
*HOLO GOLD/25: .6X TO 1.5X BASE p/r 97
*HOLO SILVER/99: .4X TO 1X BASE p/r 150
*HOLO SILVER/49: .5X TO 1.2X BASE p/r 97-99
*HOLO SILVER/25: .5X TO 1.2X BASE p/r 49
1 Yoan Moncada/150 10.00 25.00
2 Craig Kimbrel/49 10.00 25.00
3 Don Mattingly/99 20.00 50.00
4 Greg Maddux/49 25.00 60.00
5 Nomar Mazara/97 3.00 8.00
6 Josh Donaldson/25 8.00 20.00
7 Barry Larkin/99 20.00 50.00
8 Joe Torre/49 12.00 30.00
9 Kyle Schwarber/99 8.00 20.00
10 Lou Brock/49 20.00 50.00
12 Shohei Ohtani/49 250.00 500.00
13 Nomar Garciaparra/49 20.00 50.00

2018 Diamond Kings Gallery of Stars

COMPLETE SET (18)
RANDOM INSERTS IN PACKS
1 Daniel Murphy .40 1.00
2 Justin Turner .40 1.00
3 Jose Ramirez .40 1.00
4 Nolan Arenado .60 1.50
5 Alex Bregman .50 1.25
6 Miguel Cabrera .50 1.25
7 Paul Goldschmidt .50 1.25
8 Brian Dozier .40 1.00
9 Joey Gallo .40 1.00
10 J.D. Martinez .50 1.25
11 Shohei Ohtani 2.00 5.00
12 Chris Sale .50 1.25
13 Jacob deGrom .50 1.25
14 Willie Stargell .40 1.00
15 Tony Gwynn .50 1.25
16 Reggie Jackson .40 1.00
17 Ozzie Smith .60 1.50
18 Orlando Cepeda .40 1.00

2018 Diamond Kings Gallery of Stars Holo Blue

*HOLO BLUE: 2X TO 5X BASIC
RANDOM INSERTS IN PACKS
STATED PRINT RUN 25 SER.#'d SET
11 Shohei Ohtani 50.00 120.00
16 Reggie Jackson 10.00 25.00
17 Ozzie Smith 10.00 25.00

2018 Diamond Kings Jersey Kings

RANDOM INSERTS IN PACKS
*HOLO BLUE/25: .75X TO 2X BASIC
*HOLO GOLD/49: .6X TO 1.5X BASIC
*HOLO GOLD/20-25: .75X TO 2X BASIC
*HOLO SILVER/99: .5X TO 1.2X BASIC
*HOLO SILVER/49: .6X TO 1.5X BASIC
*HOLO SILVER/25: .75X TO 2X BASIC
1 George Springer 2.50 6.00
2 Kris Bryant 6.00 15.00
3 Bryce Harper 5.00 12.00
4 Carlos Correa 3.00 8.00
5 Harmon Killebrew 5.00 12.00
6 George Brett 6.00 15.00
7 Johnny Bench 6.00 15.00
8 Ryne Sandberg 5.00 12.00
9 Juan Gonzalez 2.00 5.00
10 Greg Maddux 4.00 10.00
11 Yoenis Cespedes 3.00 8.00
12 Jeff Bagwell 2.50 6.00
13 Matt Carpenter 3.00 8.00
14 Marcell Ozuna 3.00 8.00
15 Babe Ruth 75.00 200.00
16 Lou Gehrig 60.00 150.00
17 Ted Williams 40.00 100.00
18 Jackie Robinson 25.00 60.00
19 Leo Durocher 6.00 15.00
20 Gabby Hartnett 8.00 20.00
21 Tony Gwynn 3.00 8.00
22 Aaron Judge 10.00 25.00
23 Cody Bellinger 4.00 10.00
24 Jose Altuve 2.50 6.00
25 Justin Turner 2.50 6.00

2018 Diamond Kings Mickey Mantle Collection

COMPLETE SET (8)
*HOLO BLUE/25: 1.5X TO 4X BASIC
1 Mickey Mantle 1.50 4.00
2 Mickey Mantle 1.50 4.00
3 Mickey Mantle 1.50 4.00
4 Mickey Mantle 1.50 4.00
5 Mickey Mantle 1.50 4.00
6 Mickey Mantle 1.50 4.00
7 Mickey Mantle 1.50 4.00
8 Mickey Mantle 1.50 4.00

2018 Diamond Kings Past and Present

COMPLETE SET (15)
RANDOM INSERTS IN PACKS
*HOLO BLUE/25: 1X TO 2.5X BASIC
1 Judge/Ruth 1.00 2.50

2 Bobby Doerr .40 1.00
Dustin Pedroia
3 Gonzalez/Bellinger .75 2.00
4 Brooks Robinson .40 1.00
Manny Machado
5 Verlander/Ryan 1.25 3.00
6 Frank Thomas .40 1.00
Jose Abreu
7 J.Ramriez/R.Alomar .30 .75
8 Mantle/Trout 2.00 5.00
9 Biggio/Altuve .30 .75
10 Ruth/Ohtani 1.50 4.00
11 Rizo/Banks .60 1.50
12 Lindor/Brock .40 1.00
13 Juan Marichal .30 .75
Madison Bumgarner
14 Benintendi/Lynn .40 1.00
15 Sanchez/Posada .40 1.00

2018 Diamond Kings Portraits

COMPLETE SET (15)
RANDOM INSERTS IN PACKS
1 Ken Griffey Jr. 1.00 2.50
2 David Ortiz .50 1.25
3 Cal Ripken 1.50 4.00
4 Chipper Jones .50 1.25
5 George Brett 1.00 2.50
6 Nolan Ryan 1.50 4.00
7 Mickey Mantle 1.50 4.00
8 Tony Gwynn .50 1.25
9 Ty Cobb .75 2.00
10 Ted Williams 1.00 2.50
11 Honus Wagner .50 1.25
12 Jackie Robinson .50 1.25
13 Greg Maddux .60 1.50
14 Joe Morgan .40 1.00
15 Shohei Ohtani 2.00 5.00

2018 Diamond Kings Portraits Holo Blue

*HOLO BLUE: 2X TO 5X BASIC
RANDOM INSERTS IN PACKS
STATED PRINT RUN 25 SER.#'d SET
15 Shohei Ohtani 50.00 120.00

2018 Diamond Kings Recollection Buyback Autographs

RANDOM INSERTS IN PACKS
PRINT RUNS B/WN 1-30 COPIES PER
NO PRICING ON QTY 10 OR LESS
102 Jeff Bagwell/23 20.00 50.00
119 Matt Carpenter/30 10.00 25.00

2018 Diamond Kings Royalty

RANDOM INSERTS IN PACKS
*HOLO BLUE/25: 4X TO 10X BASIC
1 Babe Ruth 1.25 3.00

2018 Diamond Kings The 500

RANDOM INSERTS IN PACKS
*HOLO BLUE/25: 2X TO 5X BASIC
1 Albert Pujols .60 1.50
2 Alex Rodriguez .60 1.50
3 Babe Ruth 1.25 3.00
4 Mark McGwire .75 2.00
5 David Ortiz .50 1.25
6 Eddie Mathews .50 1.25
7 Eddie Murray .40 1.00
8 Ernie Banks .50 1.25
9 Frank Thomas .50 1.25
10 Gary Sheffield .30 .75
11 Harmon Killebrew .50 1.25
12 Ken Griffey Jr. 1.00 2.50
13 Manny Ramirez .50 1.25
14 Mickey Mantle 1.50 4.00
15 Rafael Palmeiro .40 1.00
16 Reggie Jackson .40 1.00
17 Ted Williams 1.00 2.50
18 Willie McCovey .40 1.00

2018 Diamond Kings Trophy Club

COMPLETE SET (15)
RANDOM INSERTS IN PACKS
*HOLO BLUE/25: 1.5X TO 4X BASIC
1 George Springer .40 1.00
2 Aaron Judge 1.25 3.00
3 Cody Bellinger 1.00 2.50
4 Corey Seager .50 1.25
5 Justin Verlander .50 1.25
6 Corey Kluber .40 1.00
7 Max Scherzer .50 1.25
8 Clayton Kershaw 1.00 2.50
9 Mickey Mantle 1.50 4.00
10 Kris Bryant .60 1.50
11 Mike Trout 2.50 6.00
12 Bryce Harper .75 2.00
13 Dallas Keuchel .40 1.00
14 Josh Donaldson .40 1.00
15 Carlos Correa .50 1.25

2019 Diamond Kings

1 Stan Musial .50 1.25
2 Hank Greenberg .30 .75
3 Babe Ruth .75 2.00
4 Roger Maris .30 .75
5 Roberto Clemente .75 2.00
6 Mel Ott .30 .75
7 Walter Alston .25 .60
8 Mickey Cochrane .25 .60
9 Eddie Stanky .20 .50
10 Joe Wood .20 .50
11 Al Simmons .25 .60
12 Tris Speaker .25 .60
13 Grover Alexander .25 .60
14 Rogers Hornsby .25 .60
15 Mickey Mantle 1.00 2.50
16 Lou Gehrig .60 1.50
17 Yogi Berra .30 .75
18 Carl Erskine .20 .50
19 Joe DiMaggio .60 1.50
20 Jimmie Foxx .30 .75
21 Satchel Paige .30 .75
22 Ted Williams .60 1.50
23 Carl Hubbell .25 .60
24 Christy Mathewson .30 .75
25 Joe Jackson .40 1.00
26 Ty Cobb .50 1.25
27 Honus Wagner .30 .75
28 Joe Sewell .25 .60
29 Jackie Robinson .30 .75
30 Charlie Keller .20 .50
31 Enyel De Los Santos RC .40 1.00
32 Brad Keller RC .40 1.00
33 Nolan Ryan 1.00 2.50
34 Miguel Cabrera .30 .75
35 Brandon Lowe RC .60 1.50
36 Chipper Jones .30 .75
37 Tony Gwynn .30 .75
38 Jose Altuve .25 .60
39 J.D. Martinez .30 .75
40 Ronald Acuna Jr. 1.50 4.00
41 Kiki Cuyler .25 .60
42 Max Scherzer .30 .75
43 Corbin Burnes RC .60 1.50
44 Roger Clemens .40 1.00
45 Kevin Kramer RC .50 1.25
46 Khris Davis .30 .75
47 Paul Goldschmidt .30 .75
48 Johnny Bench .30 .75
49 Jacob deGrom .30 .75
50 Michael Kopech RC .75 2.00
51 Walker Buehler .40 1.00
52 Garrett Hampson RC .40 1.00
53 Kyle Freeland .25 .60
54 Jeff McNeil RC 1.00 2.50
55 Luis Severino .25 .60
56 Brooks Robinson .25 .60
57 Ramon Laureano RC .75 2.00
58 Jake Bauers RC .60 1.50
59 Andrew Benintendi .30 .75
60 Alex Bregman .30 .75
61 Kolby Allard RC .60 1.50
62 Kevin Newman RC .60 1.50
63 Josh James RC .60 1.50
64 Ryan O'Hearn RC .40 1.00
65 Juan Soto 1.00 2.50
66 Justus Sheffield .30 .75
67 Aaron Judge .75 2.00
68 Chris Shaw RC .60 1.50
69 Dakota Hudson RC .50 1.25
70 Giancarlo Stanton .30 .75
71 Joey Votto .30 .75
72 Sean Reid-Foley RC .40 1.00
73 Matt Carpenter .30 .75
74 Al Kaline .30 .75
75 Salvador Perez .25 .60
76 Kyle Wright RC .60 1.50
77 Cedric Mullins RC .60 1.50
78 Jonathan Loaisiga RC .50 1.25
79 Jacob Nix RC .50 1.25
80 Ichiro .40 1.00
81 Ozzie Albies .30 .75
82 Luis Urias RC .60 1.50
83 Sam Crawford .25 .60
84 Chris Sale .30 .75
85 Rickey Henderson .30 .75
86 Corey Kluber .25 .60
87 Aaron Nola .25 .60
88 Justin Verlander .30 .75
89 Rhys Hoskins .40 1.00
90 David Fletcher RC 1.25 3.00
91 Vladimir Guerrero .25 .60
92 Pee Wee Reese .25 .60
93 Freddie Freeman .40 1.00
94 Jonathan Davis RC .50 1.25
95 Mookie Betts .50 1.25
96 Bryse Wilson RC .50 1.25
97 Cionel Perez RC .40 1.00
98 Chance Adams RC .40 1.00
99 Christin Stewart RC .50 1.25
100 Miguel Andujar .30 .75
101 Framber Valdez SP RC .60 1.50
102 Noah Syndergaard SP .50 1.25
103 Touki Toussaint SP RC .75 2.00
104 Patrick Wisdom SP RC .60 1.50
105 Ryne Sandberg SP 1.25 3.00
106 Ryan Borucki SP RC .60 1.50
107 Nolan Arenado SP .75 2.00
108 Luis Ortiz SP RC .60 1.50
109 Steven Duggar SP RC .75 2.00
110 Kirby Puckett SP .60 1.50
111 Stephen Gonsalves SP RC .60 1.50
112 Yusei Kikuchi SP RC 1.00 2.50
113 Ken Griffey Jr. SP 1.25 3.00
114 Jake Cave SP RC .75 2.00
115 Albert Pujols SP .75 2.00
116 Jesus Aguilar SP .40 1.00
117 Taylor Ward SP RC .60 1.50
118 Kyle Tucker SP RC 1.25 3.00
119 Dennis Santana SP RC .60 1.50
120 Danny Jansen SP RC .60 1.50
121 Cal Ripken SP 2.00 5.00
122 Reese McGuire SP RC 1.00 2.50
123 Bob Gibson SP .50 1.25
124 Shohei Ohtani SP .75 2.00
125 Mariano Rivera SP .75 2.00
126 Matt Chapman SP .60 1.50
127 Yadier Molina SP .60 1.50
128 Adrian Beltre SP .60 1.50
129 Paul Waner SP .50 1.25
130 Jose Ramirez SP .50 1.25
131 Caleb Ferguson SP RC .75 2.00
132 Larry Doby SP .50 1.25
133 Mike Trout SP 3.00 8.00
134 Daniel Ponce de Leon SP RC 1.00 2.50
135 Anthony Rizzo SP 1.00 2.50
136 J.T. Realmuto SP .60 1.50
137 George Brett SP 1.25 3.00
138 Christian Yelich SP .75 2.00
139 Kris Bryant SP .75 2.00
140 Myles Straw SP RC 1.00 2.50
141 Rowdy Tellez SP RC 1.00 2.50
142 Clayton Kershaw SP 1.25 3.00
143 Bryce Harper SP 1.00 2.50
144 Gleyber Torres SP 1.25 3.00
145 Francisco Lindor SP .60 1.50
146 Blake Snell SP .50 1.25
147 Trevor Story SP .60 1.50
148 Frank Thomas SP .60 1.50
149 Manny Machado SP .60 1.50
150 Javier Baez SP .75 2.00

2019 Diamond Kings Artist Proof

*AP: 1.2X TO 3X BASIC
*AP RC: .6X TO 1.5X BASIC
*AP SP: .6X TO 1.5X BASIC
*AP SP RC: .4X TO 1X BASIC
RANDOM INSERTS IN PACKS

2019 Diamond Kings Artist Proof Blue

*AP BLUE: 1.5X TO 4X BASIC
*AP BLUE RC: .75X TO 2X BASIC
*AP BLUE SP: .75X TO 2X BASIC
*AP BLUE SP RC: .5X TO 1.2X BASIC
RANDOM INSERTS IN PACKS

2019 Diamond Kings Blue Frame

*BLUE FRAME: 1.5X TO 4X BASIC
*BLUE FRAME RC: .75X TO 2X BASIC
*BLUE FRAME SP: .75X TO 2X BASIC
*BLUE FRAME SP RC: .5X TO 1.2X BASIC
RANDOM INSERTS IN PACKS

2019 Diamond Kings Plum Frame

*PLUM FRAME: 1.2X TO 3X BASIC
*PLUM FRAME RC: .6X TO 1.5X BASIC
*PLUM FRAME SP: .6X TO 1.5X BASIC
*PLUM FRAME SP RC: .4X TO 1X BASIC
RANDOM INSERTS IN PACKS

2019 Diamond Kings Red Frame

*RED FRAME: 1.5X TO 4X BASIC
*RED FRAME RC: .75X TO 2X BASIC
*RED FRAME SP: .75X TO 2X BASIC
*RED FRAME SP RC: .5X TO 1.2X BASIC
RANDOM INSERTS IN PACKS

2019 Diamond Kings Variations

RANDOM INSERTS IN PACKS
*AP: .6X TO 1.5X BASIC
*PLUM FRAME: .6X TO 1.5X BASIC
*AP BLUE: .75X TO 2X BASIC
*BLUE FRAME: .75X TO 2X BASIC
*RED FRAME: .75X TO 2X BASIC
21 Satchel Paige .60 1.50
22 Wade Boggs .50 1.25
26 Ty Cobb 1.00 2.50
33 Nolan Ryan 2.00 5.00
43 Gleyber Torres 1.25 3.00
44 Javier Baez .75 2.00
60 Alex Bregman .60 1.50
64 Ryan O'Hearn .40 1.00
65 Juan Soto 2.00 5.00
80 Ichiro .75 2.00
81 Ozzie Albies .60 1.50
85 Rickey Henderson .60 1.50
91 Vladimir Guerrero .50 1.25
95 Mookie Betts 1.00 2.50
105 Ryne Sandberg 1.25 3.00
112 Yusei Kikuchi .60 1.50
124 Shohei Ohtani .75 2.00
130 Jose Ramirez .50 1.25
139 Kris Bryant .75 2.00
144 Gleyber Torres 1.25 3.00

2019 Diamond Kings '02 DK Retro

RANDOM INSERTS IN PACKS
*AP: .75X TO 2X BASIC
*PLUM FRAME: .75X TO 2X BASIC
*AP BLUE: 1X TO 2.5X BASIC
*BLUE FRAME: 1X TO 2.5X BASIC
*RED FRAME: 1X TO 2.5X BASIC
1 Randy Johnson .50 1.25
2 Pedro Martinez .40 1.00
3 Jason Giambi .30 .75
4 Miguel Tejada .30 .75
5 Ichiro .60 1.50
6 Albert Pujols .60 1.50
7 Paul Goldschmidt .50 1.25
8 Giancarlo Stanton .50 1.25
9 Joey Votto .50 1.25
10 Mookie Betts .75 2.00

2019 Diamond Kings '03 DK Retro

RANDOM INSERTS IN PACKS
*AP: .75X TO 2X BASIC
*PLUM FRAME: .75X TO 2X BASIC
*AP BLUE: 1X TO 2.5X BASIC
*BLUE FRAME: 1X TO 2.5X BASIC
*RED FRAME: 1X TO 2.5X BASIC
1 Alex Rodriguez .60 1.50
2 Hideki Matsui .50 1.25
3 Dontrelle Willis .30 .75
4 Jose Reyes .40 1.00
5 Miguel Cabrera .50 1.25
6 Max Scherzer .50 1.25
7 Freddie Freeman .60 1.50
8 Vladimir Guerrero Jr. 2.00 5.00
9 Jose Ramirez .40 1.00
10 Mike Trout 2.50 6.00

2019 Diamond Kings '04 DK Retro

RANDOM INSERTS IN PACKS
*AP: .75X TO 2X BASIC
*PLUM FRAME: .75X TO 2X BASIC
*AP BLUE: 1X TO 2.5X BASIC
*BLUE FRAME: 1X TO 2.5X BASIC
*RED FRAME: 1X TO 2.5X BASIC
1 David Wright .40 1.00
2 Vladimir Guerrero .40 1.00
3 Roger Clemens .60 1.50
4 Zack Greinke .40 1.00
5 Adrian Beltre .50 1.25
6 Justin Verlander .50 1.25
7 Anthony Rizzo .75 2.00
8 Clayton Kershaw 1.00 2.50
9 Bryce Harper .75 2.00
10 Francisco Lindor .50 1.25

2019 Diamond Kings '19 Diamond Kings

RANDOM INSERTS IN PACKS
*HOLO BLUE/25: 1.5X TO 4X BASIC
1 Babe Ruth 1.25 3.00
2 Joe Jackson .60 1.50
3 Jake Daubert .30 .75
4 Eddie Collins .40 1.00
5 Frank Baker .50 1.25
6 Honus Wagner .50 1.25
7 Ty Cobb .75 2.00
8 Tris Speaker .40 1.00
9 Walter Johnson .50 1.25
10 Eddie Cicotte .30 .75
11 Bob Shawkey .30 .75
12 Sam Rice .40 1.00
13 George Sisler .40 1.00
14 Lefty Williams .30 .75
15 Harry Heilmann .40 1.00

2019 Diamond Kings Diamond Cuts

RANDOM INSERTS IN PACKS
EXCHANGE DEADLINE 10/10/2020
8 Harmon Killebrew 25.00 60.00
10 Gary Carter 25.00 60.00
12 Elmer Flick

2019 Diamond Kings Diamond Cuts Materials

RANDOM INSERTS IN PACKS
EXCHANGE DEADLINE 10/10/2020
*HOLO BLUE/25: .6X TO 1.5X BASIC
1 Gary Carter 20.00 50.00
4 Harmon Killebrew 20.00 50.00

2019 Diamond Kings Diamond Deco

RANDOM INSERTS IN PACKS
2 Tony Gwynn 10.00 25.00
3 Mookie Betts 5.00 12.00
4 Ken Griffey Jr. 10.00 25.00
5 Ronald Acuna Jr. 8.00 20.00
6 Shohei Ohtani 4.00 10.00
7 Juan Soto 4.00 10.00
8 Rhys Hoskins 6.00 15.00
10 Max Muncy 2.50 6.00
11 Justin Verlander 3.00 8.00
12 Jesus Aguilar 2.00 5.00
13 Buster Posey 4.00 10.00
14 Michael Brantley 2.50 6.00
15 Noah Syndergaard 2.50 6.00
16 Jose Ramirez 2.50 6.00
17 Rickey Henderson 15.00 40.00
18 Reggie Jackson 6.00 15.00

2019 Diamond Kings Diamond Deco Holo Blue

*HOLO BLUE/25: .75X TO 2X BASIC
RANDOM INSERTS IN PACKS
PRINT RUNS B/WN 10-25 COPIES PER
NO PRICING ON QTY 15 OR LESS
9 Willie McCovey/25 12.00 30.00

2019 Diamond Kings DK 205

RANDOM INSERTS IN PACKS
*HOLO GOLD: .6X TO 1.5X BASIC
1 Cal Ripken 1.50 4.00
2 Aaron Judge 1.25 3.00
3 Ken Griffey Jr. 1.00 2.50
4 Mike Trout 2.50 6.00
5 Kirby Puckett .50 1.25
6 Shohei Ohtani .60 1.50
7 Justin Verlander .50 1.25
8 Javier Baez .60 1.50
9 Nolan Arenado .60 1.50
10 Ronald Acuna Jr. 2.50 6.00
11 Nolan Ryan 1.50 4.00
12 Christian Yelich .60 1.50
13 Max Scherzer .50 1.25
14 Gleyber Torres 1.00 2.50
15 Mike Piazza .50 1.25
16 Frank Thomas .50 1.25
17 Jacob deGrom .50 1.25
18 Blake Snell .40 1.00
19 Juan Soto 1.50 4.00
20 Mookie Betts .75 2.00
21 Jose Altuve .40 1.00
22 Clayton Kershaw 1.00 2.50
23 Anthony Rizzo .75 2.00
24 Bryce Harper .75 2.00
25 Mickey Mantle 1.50 4.00

2019 Diamond Kings DK 205 Holo Blue

*HOLO BLUE: 1.5X TO 4X BASIC
RANDOM INSERTS IN PACKS
STATED PRINT RUN 25 SER.#'d SETS
1 Cal Ripken 12.00 30.00
3 Ken Griffey Jr. 20.00 50.00
4 Mike Trout 10.00 25.00
11 Nolan Ryan 10.00 25.00
16 Frank Thomas 10.00 25.00

2019 Diamond Kings DK 205 Signatures

RANDOM INSERTS IN PACKS
EXCHANGE DEADLINE 10/10/2020
*HOLO BLUE/25: .6X TO 1.5X BASIC
*HOLO GOLD/49: .5X TO 1.2X BASIC
*HOLO GOLD/25: .6X TO 1.5X BASIC
*HOLO SLVR/49-99: .5X TO 1.2X BASIC
*HOLO SLVR/25: .6X TO 1.5X BASIC
2 Aaron Judge 50.00 120.00
3 Cal Ripken 25.00 60.00
4 Shohei Ohtani 50.00 120.00
5 Gleyber Torres 15.00 40.00
6 Juan Soto 10.00 25.00
7 Jacob deGrom 15.00 40.00
8 Ronald Acuna Jr. 40.00 100.00
9 Nolan Arenado 20.00 50.00
10 Ken Griffey Jr. 75.00 200.00
11 Clayton Kershaw 15.00 40.00
12 Frank Thomas 15.00 40.00
13 Nolan Ryan 40.00 100.00
14 Kyle Tucker 6.00 15.00
15 Michael Kopech 5.00 12.00
16 Bobby Richardson 12.00 30.00
17 Paul Goldschmidt 25.00 60.00
18 Francisco Lindor 10.00 25.00
19 Alex Bregman 15.00 40.00
20 Freddie Freeman 10.00 25.00

2019 Diamond Kings DK Flashbacks

RANDOM INSERTS IN PACKS
1 Albert Pujols .60 1.50
2 Miguel Cabrera .50 1.25
3 Tony Gwynn .50 1.25
4 Cal Ripken 1.50 4.00
5 Greg Maddux .60 1.50
6 Mark McGwire .75 2.00
7 Roger Clemens .60 1.50
8 Vladimir Guerrero .40 1.00
9 Kirby Puckett .50 1.25
10 Adrian Beltre .50 1.25
11 Frank Thomas .50 1.25
12 Nolan Ryan 1.50 4.00
13 Larry Walker .40 1.00
14 Alex Rodriguez .60 1.50
15 Jason Giambi .30 .75
16 Mike Piazza .50 1.25
17 Chipper Jones .50 1.25
18 Randy Johnson .50 1.25
19 Pedro Martinez .40 1.00
20 Wade Boggs .40 1.00

2019 Diamond Kings DK Flashbacks Holo Blue

*HOLO BLUE: 1.5X TO 4X BASIC
RANDOM INSERTS IN PACKS
STATED PRINT RUN 25 SER.#'d SETS
3 Tony Gwynn 8.00 20.00
4 Cal Ripken 12.00 30.00
11 Frank Thomas 10.00 25.00
12 Nolan Ryan 10.00 25.00
17 Chipper Jones 8.00 20.00

2019 Diamond Kings DK Jumbo Material Signatures

RANDOM INSERTS IN PACKS
EXCHANGE DEADLINE 10/10/2020
1 Robin Yount 20.00 50.00
2 Vladimir Guerrero Jr. 60.00 150.00
3 Addison Russell 4.00 10.00
4 Rickey Henderson 25.00 60.00
5 David Ortiz 20.00 50.00
6 Carlos Correa 12.00 30.00
7 Aaron Judge 50.00 120.00
8 Max Muncy 8.00 20.00
9 Rhys Hoskins 15.00 40.00
10 Nick Williams 3.00 8.00
12 Victor Robles 10.00 25.00
13 Gleyber Torres 15.00 40.00
14 Fernando Tatis Jr. 40.00 100.00
15 Trevor Story 8.00 20.00
16 Eloy Jimenez 20.00 50.00
17 Andrew Benintendi 10.00 25.00
18 Justin Turner 8.00 20.00
19 Edgar Martinez 12.00 30.00
20 Albert Pujols 40.00 100.00

2019 Diamond Kings DK Jumbo Material Signatures Holo Blue

*HOLO BLUE: .6X TO 1.5X BASIC
RANDOM INSERTS IN PACKS
PRINT RUNS B/WN 3-25 COPIES PER
NO PRICING ON QTY 15 OR LESS
EXCHANGE DEADLINE 10/10/2020
11 Yoan Moncada/25 25.00 60.00

2019 Diamond Kings DK Material Signatures

RANDOM INSERTS IN PACKS
EXCHANGE DEADLINE 10/10/2020
1 Brad Keller 3.00 8.00
2 Brandon Lowe 8.00 20.00
3 Bryse Wilson 4.00 10.00
4 Caleb Ferguson 4.00 10.00
5 Cedric Mullins 5.00 12.00
6 Chance Adams 3.00 8.00
7 Chris Shaw 5.00 12.00
8 Christin Stewart 4.00 10.00
9 Cionel Perez 3.00 8.00
10 Corbin Burnes 5.00 12.00
11 Dakota Hudson 4.00 10.00
12 Daniel Ponce de Leon 5.00 12.00
13 Danny Jansen 3.00 8.00
14 David Fletcher 10.00 25.00
15 Dennis Santana 3.00 8.00
16 Eloy Jimenez 12.00 30.00
18 Fernando Tatis Jr. 60.00 150.00
19 Framber Valdez 3.00 8.00
20 Garrett Hampson 3.00 8.00
21 Jacob Nix 4.00 10.00
22 Jake Bauers 5.00 12.00
23 Jake Cave 4.00 10.00
24 Jeff McNeil 15.00 40.00
25 Jonathan Davis 4.00 10.00
26 Jonathan Loaisiga 6.00 15.00
27 Josh James 5.00 12.00
28 Justus Sheffield 6.00 15.00
29 Kevin Kramer 4.00 10.00
30 Kevin Newman 5.00 12.00
31 Kolby Allard 5.00 12.00
32 Kyle Tucker 8.00 20.00
33 Kyle Wright 5.00 12.00
34 Luis Ortiz 3.00 8.00
35 Luis Urias 5.00 12.00
36 Michael Kopech 8.00 20.00
37 Myles Straw 5.00 12.00
39 Patrick Wisdom 3.00 8.00
40 Ramon Laureano 12.00 30.00
41 Reese McGuire 5.00 12.00
42 Rowdy Tellez 5.00 12.00
43 Ryan Borucki 3.00 8.00
44 Ryan O'Hearn 3.00 8.00
45 Sean Reid-Foley 3.00 8.00
46 Stephen Gonsalves 3.00 8.00
47 Steven Duggar 4.00 10.00
48 Taylor Ward 3.00 8.00
49 Touki Toussaint 4.00 10.00
50 Vladimir Guerrero Jr. 30.00 80.00
51 Eddie Murray 12.00 30.00
52 Byron Buxton 4.00 10.00
53 Masahiro Tanaka 40.00 100.00
54 Clayton Kershaw 40.00 100.00
55 Gary Sanchez 15.00 40.00
56 Clint Frazier 10.00 25.00
57 Willie McCovey 20.00 50.00
58 Joey Votto 20.00 50.00
59 Xander Bogaerts 10.00 25.00
60 Larry Walker 12.00 30.00

2019 Diamond Kings DK Material Signatures Holo Blue

*HOLO BLUE: .6X TO 1.5X BASIC
RANDOM INSERTS IN PACKS
PRINT RUNS B/WN 5-25 COPIES PER
NO PRICING ON QTY 15 OR LESS
EXCHANGE DEADLINE 10/10/2020
17 Enyel De Los Santos/25 5.00 12.00

2019 Diamond Kings DK Materials

RANDOM INSERTS IN PACKS
1 Brad Keller 2.00 5.00
2 Brandon Lowe 3.00 8.00
3 Bryse Wilson 2.50 6.00
4 Caleb Ferguson 2.50 6.00
5 Cedric Mullins 3.00 8.00
6 Chance Adams 2.00 5.00
7 Chris Shaw 3.00 8.00
8 Christin Stewart 2.50 6.00
9 Cionel Perez 2.00 5.00
10 Corbin Burnes 3.00 8.00
11 Dakota Hudson 2.50 6.00
12 Daniel Ponce de Leon 3.00 8.00
13 Danny Jansen 2.00 5.00
14 David Fletcher 6.00 15.00
15 Dennis Santana 2.00 5.00
16 Eloy Jimenez 8.00 20.00
17 Enyel De Los Santos 2.00 5.00
18 Fernando Tatis Jr. 4.00 10.00
19 Framber Valdez 2.00 5.00
20 Garrett Hampson 2.00 5.00
21 Jacob Nix 2.50 6.00
22 Jake Bauers 3.00 8.00
23 Jake Cave 2.50 6.00
24 Jeff McNeil 5.00 12.00
25 Jonathan Davis 2.50 6.00
26 Jonathan Loaisiga 2.50 6.00
27 Josh James 3.00 8.00
28 Justus Sheffield 3.00 8.00
29 Kevin Kramer 2.50 6.00
30 Kevin Newman 3.00 8.00
31 Kolby Allard 3.00 8.00
32 Kyle Tucker 4.00 10.00
33 Kyle Wright 3.00 8.00
34 Luis Ortiz 2.00 5.00
35 Luis Urias 3.00 8.00
36 Michael Kopech 4.00 10.00
37 Myles Straw 3.00 8.00
38 Nick Senzel 5.00 12.00
39 Patrick Wisdom 2.00 5.00
40 Ramon Laureano 4.00 10.00
41 Reese McGuire 3.00 8.00
42 Rowdy Tellez 3.00 8.00
43 Ryan Borucki 3.00 8.00
44 Ryan O'Hearn 2.00 5.00
45 Sean Reid-Foley 2.00 5.00
46 Stephen Gonsalves 2.00 5.00
47 Steven Duggar 2.50 6.0
48 Taylor Ward 2.00 5.0
49 Touki Toussaint 2.50 6.0
50 Vladimir Guerrero Jr. 6.00 15.0
51 Charlie Keller 3.00 8.0
52 Eddie Stanky 3.00 8.0
75 Patrick Corbin 2.50 6.0
76 Robinson Cano 2.50 6.0
77 Cal Ripken 6.00 15.0
78 Jonathan Schoop 2.00 5.0
80 Craig Kimbrel 2.50 6.0
81 Dallas Keuchel 2.50 6.0
82 Daniel Murphy 2.50 6.0
83 Ronald Acuna Jr. 5.00 12.0
84 Juan Soto 4.00 10.0
85 George Brett 8.00 20.0
87 Harvey Kuenn 2.00 5.0
89 Ichiro 4.00 10.0
91 Adrian Beltre 3.00 8.0
92 Frank Thomas 3.00 8.0
93 Paul Molitor 5.00 12.0
94 Willie McCovey 5.00 12.0
95 Al Kaline 4.00 10.0
98 Alex Rodriguez 4.00 10.0
99 Joe Morgan 2.50 6.0

2019 Diamond Kings DK Materials Holo Blue

*HOLO BLUE/25: .75X TO 2X BASIC
RANDOM INSERTS IN PACKS
PRINT RUNS B/WN 3-25 COPIES PER
NO PRICING ON QTY 15 OR LESS
2 Brandon Lowe/25 6.00 15.0
97 Rickey Henderson/25 12.00 30.0

2019 Diamond Kings DK Materials Holo Gold

*HOLO GOLD/49: .6X TO 1.5X BASIC
*HOLO GOLD/20-25: .75X TO 2X BASIC
RANDOM INSERTS IN PACKS
PRINT RUNS B/WN 4-49 COPIES PER
NO PRICING ON QTY 15 OR LESS
2 Brandon Lowe/49 5.00 12.0
61 Stan Musial/25 10.00 25.0
62 Ted Williams/25 40.00 100.0
64 Yogi Berra/20 6.00 15.0
65 Ernie Banks/25 6.00 15.0
86 Catfish Hunter/25 5.00 12.0
90 Nolan Ryan/25 25.00 60.0
96 Lee Smith/49 4.00 10.0
97 Rickey Henderson/49 10.00 25.0

2019 Diamond Kings DK Materials Holo Silver

*HOLO SLVR/60-99: .5X TO 1.2X BASIC
*HOLO SLVR/49: .6X TO 1.5X BASIC
*HOLO SLVR/20-25: .75X TO 2X BASIC
RANDOM INSERTS IN PACKS
PRINT RUNS B/WN 10-99 COPIES PER
NO PRICING ON QTY 15 OR LESS
2 Brandon Lowe/99 4.00 10.0
57 Mickey Mantle/25 40.00 100.0
66 Jackie Robinson/25 30.00 80.0
86 Catfish Hunter/49 4.00 10.0
90 Nolan Ryan/49 20.00 50.0
96 Lee Smith/99 3.00 8.0
97 Rickey Henderson/99 8.00 20.0

2019 Diamond Kings DK Signatures

RANDOM INSERTS IN PACKS
EXCHANGE DEADLINE 10/10/2020
*HOLO GOLD/35-49: .5X TO 1.2X BASIC
*HOLO GOLD/25: .6X TO 1.5X BASIC
*HOLO SLVR/49-99: .5X TO 1.2X BASIC
*HOLO SLVR/20-25: .6X TO 1.5X BASIC
1 Brad Keller 2.50 6.0
2 Brandon Lowe 6.00 15.0
3 Bryse Wilson 3.00 8.0
4 Caleb Ferguson 3.00 8.0
5 Cedric Mullins 4.00 10.0
6 Chance Adams 2.50 6.0
7 Chris Shaw 4.00 10.0
8 Christin Stewart 3.00 8.0
9 Cionel Perez 2.50 6.0
10 Corbin Burnes 4.00 10.0
11 Dakota Hudson 3.00 8.0
12 Daniel Ponce de Leon 4.00 10.0
13 Danny Jansen 2.50 6.0
14 David Fletcher 8.00 20.0
15 Dennis Santana 2.50 6.0
16 Eloy Jimenez 15.00 40.0
18 Fernando Tatis Jr. 50.00 120.0
19 Framber Valdez 2.50 6.0
20 Garrett Hampson 2.50 6.0
21 Jacob Nix 3.00 8.0
22 Jake Bauers 4.00 10.0
23 Jake Cave 3.00 8.0
24 Jeff McNeil 10.00 25.0
25 Jonathan Davis 3.00 8.0
26 Jonathan Loaisiga 3.00 8.0
27 Josh James 4.00 10.0
28 Justus Sheffield 4.00 10.0
29 Kevin Kramer 3.00 8.0
30 Kevin Newman 4.00 10.0
31 Kolby Allard 4.00 10.0
32 Kyle Tucker 5.00 12.0
33 Kyle Wright 4.00 10.0
34 Luis Ortiz 2.50 6.0
35 Luis Urias 4.00 10.0
36 Michael Kopech 5.00 12.0
37 Myles Straw 4.00 10.0
39 Patrick Wisdom 2.50 6.0
40 Ramon Laureano 6.00 15.0
41 Reese McGuire 4.00 10.0
42 Rowdy Tellez 4.00 10.0

Ryan Borucki 2.50 6.00
Ryan O'Hearn 2.50 6.00
Sean Reid-Foley 2.50 6.00
Stephen Gonsalves 2.50 6.00
Steven Duggar 3.00 8.00
Taylor Ward 2.50 6.00
Touki Toussaint 3.00 8.00
Vladimir Guerrero Jr. 30.00 80.00
Vin Scully 100.00 250.00
Ronald Acuna Jr. 40.00 100.00
Gleyber Torres 15.00 40.00
Rafael Devers 10.00 25.00
Rhys Hoskins 8.00 20.00
Ozzie Albies 6.00 15.00
Juan Soto 15.00 40.00
Miguel Andujar 6.00 15.00
Walker Buehler 12.00 30.00
Shohei Ohtani 50.00 120.00
Cody Bellinger 40.00 100.00
Victor Robles 5.00 12.00
Willy Adames 2.50 6.00
David Bote 6.00 15.00
Harrison Bader 3.00 8.00
Ryan McMahon 2.50 6.00
Yusei Kikuchi 12.00 30.00
Anthony Rizzo 15.00 40.00
Trea Turner 6.00 15.00
Yoan Moncada 4.00 10.00

2019 Diamond Kings DK Signatures Holo Blue

OLO BLUE/25: .6X TO 1.5X BASIC
NDOM INSERTS IN PACKS
NT RUNS BW/N 10-25 COPIES PER
PRICING ON QTY 10
CHANGE DEADLINE 10/10/2020
Enyel De Los Santos/25 4.00 10.00

019 Diamond Kings Downtown

NDOM INSERTS IN PACKS
hohei Ohtani 30.00 80.00
avier Baez 20.00 50.00
hristian Yelich 20.00 50.00
ookie Betts 25.00 60.00
ike Trout 80.00 200.00
att Carpenter 15.00 40.00
lex Bregman 30.00 80.00
aron Judge 40.00 100.00
olan Arenado 20.00 50.00
Francisco Lindor 15.00 40.00

019 Diamond Kings Gallery of Stars

NDOM INSERTS IN PACKS
ose Altuve .50 1.25
onald Acuna Jr. 3.00 8.00
Valker Buehler .75 2.00
ndrew Benintendi .60 1.50
lex Bregman .60 1.50
uan Soto 2.00 5.00
aron Judge 1.50 4.00
hiro .75 2.00
aron Nola .50 1.25
Nolan Arenado .75 2.00
Ken Griffey Jr. 1.25 3.00
Shohei Ohtani .75 2.00
Mike Trout 3.00 8.00
Clayton Kershaw 1.25 3.00
Christian Yelich .75 2.00

019 Diamond Kings Gallery of Stars Holo Blue

LO BLUE: 1.5X TO 4X BASIC
DOM INSERTS IN PACKS
TED PRINT RUN 25 SER.#'d SETS
Ken Griffey Jr 20.00 50.00
Mike Trout 10.00 25.00

2019 Diamond Kings Heirs to the Throne

NDOM INSERTS IN PACKS
hris Sale .50 1.25
edro Martinez
sh Donaldson 2.00 5.00
adimir Guerrero Jr.
aron Judge 1.25 3.00
be Ruth
hiro .60 1.50
hohei Ohtani
oy Jimenez 1.25 3.00
ank Thomas
ickey Mantle 2.50 6.00
ike Trout
orrest Whitley 1.50 4.00
olan Ryan
yce Harper 1.50 4.00
an Soto
is Severino .60 1.50
ger Clemens
Blake Snell .40 1.00
avid Price
avier Baez 1.00 2.50
ne Sandberg
Adrian Beltre .50 1.25
att Chapman
Craig Biggio .40 1.00
se Altuve
Brooks Robinson .60 1.50
lan Arenado
Vladimir Guerrero 2.00 5.00
adimir Guerrero Jr.

2019 Diamond Kings Heirs to the Throne Holo Blue

LO BLUE: 1.5X TO 4X BASIC
DOM INSERTS IN PACKS

STATED PRINT RUN 25 SER.#'d SETS
5 Jimenez/Thomas 10.00 25.00

2019 Diamond Kings HOF Heroes

RANDOM INSERTS IN PACKS
*HOLO GOLD: .6X TO 1.5X BASIC
*HOLO BLUE/25: 1.5X TO 4X BASIC
1 Honus Wagner .50 1.25
2 Joe DiMaggio 1.00 2.50
3 Roberto Clemente 1.25 3.00
4 Stan Musial .75 2.00
5 Ted Williams 1.00 2.50
6 Yogi Berra .50 1.25
7 Mariano Rivera .60 1.50
8 Jackie Robinson .50 1.25
9 Mel Ott .50 1.25
10 Ty Cobb .75 2.00

2019 Diamond Kings Jersey Kings

RANDOM INSERTS IN PACKS
*HOLO BLUE/20-25: .75X TO 2X BASIC
1 Shohei Ohtani 5.00 12.00
2 Ichiro 4.00 10.00
4 Jacob deGrom 3.00 8.00
5 Christian Yelich 4.00 10.00
6 Juan Gonzalez 2.00 5.00
7 Tony Gwynn 3.00 8.00
8 Aaron Judge 6.00 15.00
9 Gleyber Torres 4.00 10.00
10 Max Muncy 2.50 6.00
11 Charlie Blackmon 3.00 8.00
12 Alex Rodriguez 4.00 10.00
13 Rhys Hoskins 4.00 10.00
14 Starling Marte 2.50 6.00
15 Frank Thomas 3.00 8.00
16 Whit Merrifield 3.00 8.00
17 Patrick Corbin 2.50 6.00
18 Michael Brantley 2.50 6.00
19 Pee Wee Reese 6.00 15.00

2019 Diamond Kings Joe Jackson Collection

RANDOM INSERTS IN PACKS
*HOLO GOLD: .6X TO 1.5X BASIC
*HOLO BLUE/25: 1.5X TO 4X BASIC
1 Joe Jackson .60 1.50
2 Joe Jackson .60 1.50
3 Joe Jackson .60 1.50
4 Joe Jackson .60 1.50
5 Joe Jackson .60 1.50

2019 Diamond Kings Masters of the Game

RANDOM INSERTS IN PACKS
*HOLO GOLD: .6X TO 1.5X BASIC
1 Mookie Betts .75 2.00
2 Max Scherzer .50 1.25
3 Mike Trout 2.50 6.00
4 Clayton Kershaw 1.00 2.50
5 Matt Chapman .50 1.25
6 Justin Verlander .50 1.25
7 Francisco Lindor .50 1.25
8 Christian Yelich .60 1.50
9 Jose Ramirez .40 1.00
10 Javier Baez .60 1.50
11 Alex Bregman .50 1.25
12 Nolan Arenado .60 1.50
13 Aaron Nola .40 1.00
14 Freddie Freeman .60 1.50
15 Jacob deGrom .50 1.25

2019 Diamond Kings Masters of the Game Holo Blue

*HOLO BLUE: 1.5X TO 4X BASIC
RANDOM INSERTS IN PACKS
STATED PRINT RUN 25 SER.#'d SETS
3 Mike Trout 10.00 25.00

2019 Diamond Kings Portraits

RANDOM INSERTS IN PACKS
1 Rickey Henderson .50 1.25
2 Gleyber Torres 1.00 2.50
3 Albert Pujols .60 1.50
4 Mariano Rivera .60 1.50
5 Yadier Molina .50 1.25
6 Jose Ramirez .40 1.00
7 George Brett 1.00 2.50
8 Kris Bryant .60 1.50
9 Bryce Harper .75 2.00
10 Francisco Lindor .50 1.25
11 Trevor Story .50 1.25
12 Javier Baez .60 1.50
13 Robinson Cano .40 1.00
14 Mookie Betts .75 2.00
15 Noah Syndergaard .40 1.00

2019 Diamond Kings Portraits Holo Blue

*HOLO BLUE: 1.5X TO 4X BASIC
RANDOM INSERTS IN PACKS
STATED PRINT RUN 25 SER.#'d SETS
1 Rickey Henderson 10.00 25.00
7 George Brett 8.00 20.00

2019 Diamond Kings Recollection Buyback Autographs

RANDOM INSERTS IN PACKS
PRINT RUNS B/WN 1-23 COPIES PER
NO PRICING ON QTY 15 OR LESS
EXCHANGE DEADLINE 10/10/2020
4 Joey Votto/23 12.00 30.00

2019 Diamond Kings Retro '83 DK Material Signatures

RANDOM INSERTS IN PACKS
EXCHANGE DEADLINE 10/10/2020
1 Randy Johnson
2 Dave Concepcion 10.00 25.00
3 Vladimir Guerrero 15.00 40.00
4 John Smoltz 15.00 40.00
6 Frank Robinson 15.00 40.00
7 Mike Mussina 20.00 50.00
9 Kirk Gibson
10 Steve Garvey
11 Larry Walker 12.00 30.00
12 Dale Murphy 15.00 40.00
13 Wade Boggs 15.00 40.00
14 David Ortiz 20.00 50.00
15 Ivan Rodriguez 15.00 40.00
16 Dave Winfield 12.00 30.00
17 Luis Aparicio 10.00 25.00
19 Edgar Martinez 12.00 30.00
20 George Brett 50.00 120.00

2019 Diamond Kings Retro '83 DK Material Signatures Holo Blue

*HOLO BLUE: .6X TO 1.5X BASIC
RANDOM INSERTS IN PACKS
PRINT RUNS B/WN 10-25 COPIES PER
NO PRICING ON QTY 15 OR LESS
EXCHANGE DEADLINE 10/10/2020
8 Lee Smith/25 10.00 25.00

2019 Diamond Kings Squires

RANDOM INSERTS IN PACKS
*HOLO GOLD: .6X TO 1.5X BASIC
*HOLO BLUE/25: 1.5X TO 4X BASIC
1 Shohei Ohtani .60 1.50
2 Miguel Andujar .50 1.25
3 Gleyber Torres 1.00 2.50
4 Ronald Acuna Jr. 2.50 6.00
5 Juan Soto 1.50 4.00
6 Walker Buehler .60 1.50
7 Jack Flaherty .40 1.00
8 Vladimir Guerrero Jr. 2.00 5.00
9 Eloy Jimenez 1.25 3.00
10 Victor Robles .60 1.50
11 Kyle Tucker .60 1.50
12 Forrest Whitley .50 1.25
13 Jo Adell 1.00 2.50
14 Royce Lewis .60 1.50
15 Fernando Tatis Jr. 3.00 8.00
16 Nick Senzel 1.00 2.50
17 Brendan Rodgers .50 1.25
18 Ozzie Albies .50 1.25
19 Alex Verdugo .40 1.00
20 Sean Newcomb .30 .75

2019 Diamond Kings Team Heroes

RANDOM INSERTS IN PACKS
*HOLO GOLD: .6X TO 1.5X BASIC
*HOLO BLUE/25: 1.5X TO 4X BASIC
1 Mookie Betts .75 2.00
2 Alex Bregman .50 1.25
3 Aaron Judge 1.25 3.00
4 Matt Chapman .50 1.25
5 Christian Yelich .60 1.50
6 Javier Baez .60 1.50
7 Clayton Kershaw 1.00 2.50
8 Jose Ramirez .40 1.00
9 Nolan Arenado .60 1.50
10 Ronald Acuna Jr. 2.50 6.00
11 Blake Snell .40 1.00
12 Felix Hernandez .40 1.00
13 Yadier Molina .50 1.25
14 Starling Marte .40 1.00
15 Juan Soto 1.50 4.00
16 David Peralta .30 .75
17 Shohei Ohtani .60 1.50
18 Aaron Nola .40 1.00
19 Joe Mauer .40 1.00
20 Jacob deGrom .50 1.25
21 Justin Smoak .30 .75
22 Madison Bumgarner .40 1.00
23 Adrian Beltre .50 1.25
24 Joey Votto .50 1.25
25 Eric Hosmer .40 1.00
26 Miguel Cabrera .50 1.25
27 J.T. Realmuto .50 1.25
28 Jose Abreu .50 1.25
29 Whit Merrifield .50 1.25
30 Adam Jones .40 1.00

2019 Diamond Kings The 300

RANDOM INSERTS IN PACKS
1 Grover Alexander .40 1.00
2 Christy Mathewson .50 1.25
3 Warren Spahn .40 1.00
4 Greg Maddux .60 1.50
5 Roger Clemens .60 1.50
6 Early Wynn .40 1.00
7 Randy Johnson .50 1.25
8 Nolan Ryan 1.50 4.00
9 Tom Seaver .40 1.00
10 Tom Glavine .40 1.00

2019 Diamond Kings The 300 Holo Blue

*HOLO BLUE: 1.5X TO 4X BASIC
RANDOM INSERTS IN PACKS
STATED PRINT RUN 25 SER.#'d SETS
8 Nolan Ryan 10.00 25.00

2019 Diamond Kings Babe Ruth Collection

RANDOM INSERTS IN PACKS
*HOLO GOLD: .6X TO 1.5X BASIC
*HOLO BLUE/25: 1.5X TO 4X BASIC
BR1 Babe Ruth 1.25 3.00
BR2 Babe Ruth 1.25 3.00
BR3 Babe Ruth 1.25 3.00
BR4 Babe Ruth 1.25 3.00
BR5 Babe Ruth 1.25 3.00

2019 Diamond Kings Babe Ruth DK Materials Holo Blue

RANDOM INSERTS IN PACKS
STATED PRINT RUN 25 SER.#'d SETS
1 Babe Ruth

2019 Diamond Kings Bat Kings

RANDOM INSERTS IN PACKS
1 Mike Trout 12.00 30.00
3 Christian Yelich 4.00 10.00
4 Reggie Jackson 2.50 6.00
5 Juan Soto 4.00 10.00
6 Kris Bryant 4.00 10.00
7 Nick Senzel 5.00 12.00
8 Kirk Gibson 2.00 5.00
9 Matt Chapman 3.00 8.00
10 Alex Bregman 3.00 8.00
11 Dave Winfield 2.50 6.00
12 Eddie Murray 5.00 12.00
13 Ken Griffey Sr. 2.00 5.00
14 Luis Aparicio 2.50 6.00
15 Willie Stargell 2.50 6.00
17 Jimmie Foxx
20 Joe Jackson

2019 Diamond Kings Bat Kings Holo Blue

*HOLO BLUE/25: .75X TO 2X BASIC
RANDOM INSERTS IN PACKS
PRINT RUNS B/WN 15-25 COPIES PER
NO PRICING ON QTY 15 OR LESS
16 Roberto Clemente/25 60.00 150.00
17 Jimmie Foxx/25 15.00 40.00
18 Roger Maris/25
19 Tris Speaker/25 12.00 30.00
20 Joe Jackson/25 40.00 100.00

2020 Diamond Kings

RANDOM INSERTS IN PACKS
1 Joe Sewell .25 .60
2 Honus Wagner .30 .75
3 Mel Ott .30 .75
4 Walter Alston .25 .60
5 Don Larsen .20 .50
6 Roger Maris .30 .75
7 Mule Suttles .30 .75
8 Joe McCarthy .20 .50
9 Mickey Cochrane .25 .60
10 Joe Jackson .40 1.00
11 Stan Musial .50 1.25
12 Yogi Berra .30 .75
13 Ty Cobb .50 1.25
14 Satchel Paige .30 .75
15 Babe Ruth .75 2.00
16 Tris Speaker .25 .60
17 Christy Mathewson .30 .75
18 Lou Gehrig .60 1.50
19 Carl Hubbell .25 .60
20 Joe DiMaggio .60 1.50
21 Hank Greenberg .30 .75
22 Roberto Clemente .75 2.00
23 Harvey Kuenn .20 .50
24 Carl Erskine .20 .50
25 Charlie Keller .20 .50
26 Jimmie Foxx .30 .75
27 Jackie Robinson .30 .75
28 Joe Cronin .20 .50
29 Joe Wood .20 .50
30 Eddie Stanky .20 .50
31 Grover Alexander .25 .60
32 Rogers Hornsby .25 .60
33 Mickey Mantle 1.00 2.50
34 Ted Williams .60 1.50
35 Bill Terry .20 .50
36 Dom DiMaggio .20 .50
37 Elston Howard .20 .50
38 Frank Baker .30 .75
39 Goose Goslin .25 .60
40 Hack Wilson .25 .60
41 Johnny Pesky .20 .50
42 Bert Blyleven .25 .60
43 Billy Williams .25 .60
44 Cal Ripken 1.00 2.50
45 Eddie Mathews .30 .75
46 Frank Thomas .30 .75
47 Harmon Killebrew .30 .75
48 Adbert Alzolay RC .50 1.25
49 Zack Collins RC .50 1.25
50 Josh Rojas RC .40 1.00
51 Zac Gallen RC 1.00 2.50
52 Yu Chang RC .60 1.50
53 Cody Bellinger .60 1.50
54 Aristides Aquino RC .75 2.00
55 Logan Allen RC .40 1.00
56 Larry Walker .25 .60
57 Clayton Kershaw .60 1.50
58 Yordan Alvarez RC 2.00 5.00
59 Joey Votto .30 .75
60 Patrick Sandoval RC .60 1.50
61 Sam Hilliard RC .60 1.50
62 Tony Gonsolin RC 1.50 4.00
63 Yonathan Daza RC .50 1.25
64 Dylan Cease RC .75 2.00
65 Willi Castro RC .60 1.50
66 Bryce Harper .50 1.25
67 Jordan Yamamoto RC .50 1.25
68 Domingo Leyba RC .50 1.25
69 Ketel Marte .25 .60
70 Danny Mendick RC .50 1.25
71 Keston Hiura .40 1.00
72 Kris Bryant .40 1.00
73 Dustin May RC 1.50 4.00
74 Pete Alonso .75 2.00
75 Jake Rogers RC .40 1.00
76 Gavin Lux RC 2.50 6.00
77 Paul Goldschmidt .30 .75
78 Curt Schilling .25 .60
79 Bryan Abreu RC .40 1.00
80 Javier Baez .40 1.00
81 Isan Diaz RC .60 1.50
82 Pete Rose .60 1.50
83 Christian Yelich .40 1.00
84 Matt Thaiss RC .50 1.25
85 Travis Demeritte RC .50 1.25
86 Josh Bell .25 .60
87 Madison Bumgarner .25 .60
88 Aaron Civale RC .60 1.50
89 Anthony Rizzo .50 1.25
90 Nico Hoerner RC 1.50 4.00
91 Edwin Rios RC 1.00 2.50
92 Randy Johnson .30 .75
93 Tyrone Taylor RC .40 1.00
94 Bobby Bradley RC .50 1.25
95 Luis Robert RC 4.00 10.00
96 Buster Posey .40 1.00
97 Aaron Nola .30 .75
98 Brian Anderson .20 .50
99 Abraham Toro .25 .60
100 Jack Flaherty .25 .60
101 Tres Barrera SP .75 2.00
102 Sean Murphy SP RC 1.00 2.50
103 Albert Pujols SP .75 2.00
104 Mookie Betts SP 1.25 3.00
105 Adrian Morejon SP RC .60 1.50
106 Kyle Seager SP .40 1.00
107 Jose Altuve SP .50 1.25
108 Jonathan Hernandez SP RC .60 1.50
109 Reggie Jackson SP .50 1.25
110 Ronald Bolanos SP .60 1.50
111 Michael King SP RC 1.00 2.50
112 Tony Gwynn SP .60 1.50
113 Donnie Walton SP RC 1.50 4.00
114 Mike Trout SP 3.00 8.00
115 Ozzie Smith SP .75 2.00
116 Aaron Judge SP 1.50 4.00
117 Ronald Acuna Jr. SP 2.50 6.00
118 Johnny Bench SP .60 1.50
119 Mike Piazza SP .60 1.50
120 Randy Arozarena SP RC 5.00 12.00
121 Billy Williams SP .50 1.25
122 Joe Palumbo SP RC .60 1.50
123 Miguel Cabrera SP .60 1.50
124 Joey Gallo SP .60 1.50
125 Justin Dunn SP RC .75 2.00
126 Manny Machado SP .60 1.50
127 Trent Grisham SP RC 2.50 6.00
128 A.J. Puk SP RC 1.25 3.00
129 Whit Merrifield SP .60 1.50
130 Brusdar Graterol SP RC 1.00 2.50
131 Jake Fraley SP RC .75 2.00
132 Jose Berrios SP .50 1.25
133 T.J. Zeuch SP RC .60 1.50
134 Francisco Lindor SP .60 1.50
135 Vladimir Guerrero Jr. SP 1.25 3.00
136 Nolan Ryan SP 2.00 5.00
137 Fernando Tatis Jr. SP 2.50 6.00
138 Trevor Story SP .60 1.50
139 Nick Solak SP RC 1.00 2.50
140 Anthony Kay SP RC .60 1.50
141 Juan Soto SP 2.00 5.00
142 Joe Morgan SP .50 1.25
143 Ken Griffey Jr. SP 1.25 3.00
144 Bo Bichette SP RC 5.00 12.00
145 Mauricio Dubon SP RC .75 2.00
146 Sheldon Neuse SP RC .75 2.00
147 Justin Verlander SP .60 1.50
148 Kirby Puckett SP .60 1.50
149 Nolan Arenado SP .75 2.00
150 Jaylin Davis SP RC 1.00 2.50
151 Lewis Thorpe SP RC .60 1.50
152 Jesus Luzardo SP RC 1.25 3.00
153 Rico Garcia SP .60 1.50
154 Michel Baez SP RC .60 1.50
155 Deivy Grullon SP .40 1.00
156 Logan Webb SP RC .75 2.00
157 Kyle Lewis SP RC 5.00 12.00
158 Eloy Jimenez SP 1.25 3.00
159 Trey Mancini SP .60 1.50
160 Blake Snell SP .50 1.25
161 Sam Crawford SP .50 1.25
162 Brendan McKay SP RC 1.00 2.50
163 Nap Lajoie SP .60 1.50
164 Jose Ramirez SP .50 1.25
165 Shohei Ohtani SP .75 2.00
166 Ryne Sandberg SP 1.25 3.00
167 Sam Rice SP .50 1.25
168 Ichiro SP .75 2.00
169 Andres Munoz SP RC .75 2.00
170 Brock Burke SP RC .60 1.50

2020 Diamond Kings Artist Proof Gold

*AP GOLD 1-100: 2.5X TO 6X BASIC
*AP GOLD 1-100 RC: 1.2X TO 3X BASIC RC
*AP GOLD 101-170 SP: 1.2X TO 3X BASIC SP
*AP GOLD 101-170 SP RC: .8X TO 2X BASIC
RANDOM INSERTS IN PACKS
STATED PRINT RUN 49 SER. #'d SETS
22 Roberto Clemente 10.00 25.00
44 Cal Ripken 12.00 30.00
47 Harmon Killebrew 12.00 30.00
76 Gavin Lux 20.00 50.00
114 Mike Trout SP 20.00 50.00
143 Ken Griffey Jr. SP 12.00 30.00

2020 Diamond Kings Aficionado

RANDOM INSERTS IN PACKS
*BLUE: 1.5X TO 4X BASIC
1 Kirby Puckett .50 1.25
2 Mike Piazza .50 1.25
3 Cal Ripken 1.50 4.00
4 Nolan Arenado .60 1.50
5 Miguel Cabrera .50 1.25
6 Bryce Harper .75 2.00
7 Mike Trout 2.50 6.00
8 Ichiro .60 1.50
9 Jose Altuve .40 1.00
10 Anthony Rizzo .75 2.00
11 Mookie Betts 1.00 2.50
12 Rhys Hoskins .60 1.50
13 Justin Verlander .50 1.25
14 Pete Alonso 1.25 3.00
15 Gleyber Torres 1.00 2.50

2020 Diamond Kings All-Time Diamond Kings

RANDOM INSERTS IN PACKS
1 Tony Gwynn .50 1.25
2 Larry Walker .40 1.00
3 Mel Ott .50 1.25
4 Randy Johnson .50 1.25
5 Jackie Robinson .50 1.25
6 Craig Biggio .40 1.00
7 Rickey Henderson .50 1.25
8 Nolan Ryan 1.50 4.00
9 Mike Trout 2.50 6.00
10 Ken Griffey Jr. 1.00 2.50
11 Stan Musial .75 2.00
12 Robin Yount .50 1.25
13 Ryne Sandberg 1.00 2.50
14 Pete Rose 1.00 2.50
15 Roberto Clemente 1.25 3.00
16 Harmon Killebrew .50 1.25
17 Bob Feller .40 1.00
18 Frank Thomas .50 1.25
19 George Brett 1.00 2.50
20 Ty Cobb .75 2.00
21 Chipper Jones .50 1.25
22 Vladimir Guerrero .40 1.00
23 Mike Piazza .50 1.25
24 Richie Ashburn .40 1.00
25 Miguel Cabrera .50 1.25
26 Babe Ruth 1.25 3.00
27 Evan Longoria .40 1.00
28 Ted Williams 1.00 2.50
29 Roberto Alomar .40 1.00
30 Cal Ripken 1.50 4.00

2020 Diamond Kings All-Time Diamond Kings Artist Proof Blue

*AP BLUE: 1X TO 2.5X BASIC
RANDOM INSERTS IN PACKS
10 Ken Griffey Jr. 5.00 12.00

2020 Diamond Kings All-Time Diamond Kings Artist Proof Gold

*AP GOLD: 1.5X TO 4X BASIC
RANDOM INSERTS IN PACKS
STATED PRINT RUN 49 COPIES PER
7 Rickey Henderson 10.00 25.00
9 Mike Trout 15.00 40.00
10 Ken Griffey Jr. 25.00 60.00
11 Stan Musial 8.00 20.00
12 Robin Yount 6.00 15.00
15 Roberto Clemente 10.00 25.00
24 Richie Ashburn 10.00 25.00

2020 Diamond Kings All-Time Diamond Kings Blue Frame

*BLUE: 1X TO 2.5X BASIC
RANDOM INSERTS IN PACKS
10 Ken Griffey Jr. 5.00 12.00

2020 Diamond Kings All-Time Diamond Kings Gray Frame

*GRAY: 1X TO 2.5X BASIC
RANDOM INSERTS IN PACKS
10 Ken Griffey Jr. 5.00 12.00

2020 Diamond Kings All-Time Diamond Kings Litho Proof

*LITHO: 2.5X TO 6X BASIC
RANDOM INSERTS IN PACKS
STATED PRINT RUN 25 COPIES PER
7 Rickey Henderson 15.00 40.00
9 Mike Trout 25.00 60.00
10 Ken Griffey Jr. 40.00 100.00
11 Stan Musial 12.00 30.00
12 Robin Yount 10.00 25.00
15 Roberto Clemente 15.00 40.00
23 Mike Piazza 10.00 25.00
24 Richie Ashburn 15.00 40.00
30 Cal Ripken 20.00 50.00

2020 Diamond Kings All-Time Diamond Kings Plum Frame

*PLUM: 1X TO 2.5X BASIC
RANDOM INSERTS IN PACKS
10 Ken Griffey Jr. 5.00 12.00

2020 Diamond Kings All-Time Diamond Kings Red Frame

*RED: 1X TO 2.5X BASIC
RANDOM INSERTS IN PACKS
10 Ken Griffey Jr. 5.00 12.00

2020 Diamond Kings Artist's Palette

RANDOM INSERTS IN PACKS
*BLUE: 1.5X TO 4X BASIC
1 Ken Griffey Jr. 1.00 2.50
2 Ronald Acuna Jr. 2.00 5.00
3 Vladimir Guerrero Jr. 1.00 2.50
4 Francisco Lindor .50 1.25
5 Javier Baez .60 1.50
6 Mike Trout 2.50 6.00
7 Yadier Molina .50 1.25
8 Yordan Alvarez 1.50 4.00
9 Fernando Tatis Jr. 2.00 5.00
10 Aaron Judge 1.25 3.00

2020 Diamond Kings Bat Kings

RANDOM INSERTS IN PACKS
1 Joe DiMaggio
2 Joe Jackson 10.00 25.00
3 Roger Maris
4 Hank Greenberg 12.00 30.00
5 Honus Wagner
6 Joe Sewell 2.50 6.00
7 Mike Trout 12.00 30.00
8 Ronald Acuna Jr. 8.00 20.00
9 Alex Bregman 3.00 8.00
10 Eugenio Suarez 2.50 6.00
11 Ozzie Albies 3.00 8.00
12 Eddie Murray 6.00 15.00
13 Manny Machado 3.00 8.00
14 Anthony Rizzo 5.00 12.00
15 Whit Merrifield 3.00 8.00
16 Rickey Henderson 3.00 8.00
17 Gary Carter 6.00 15.00
18 Dave Concepcion 2.00 5.00
19 Orlando Cepeda 2.50 6.00
20 Kirby Puckett 12.00 30.00
21 Fernando Tatis Jr. 4.00 10.00
22 Vladimir Guerrero Jr. 4.00 10.00
23 Paul Molitor 6.00 15.00
24 Matt Chapman 3.00 8.00
25 J.D. Martinez 3.00 8.00
26 Trevor Story 3.00 8.00
27 Eloy Jimenez 4.00 10.00
28 Mookie Betts 6.00 15.00
29 Rhys Hoskins 4.00 10.00
30 Trea Turner 2.50 6.00
31 Yordan Alvarez 6.00 15.00
32 Jose Ramirez 2.50 6.00
33 Carl Yastrzemski 6.00 15.00
34 Doc Cramer 3.00 8.00
35 Pete Rose 10.00 25.00
36 Reggie Jackson 5.00 12.00
37 Richie Ashburn 4.00 10.00
38 Robin Yount
39 Tris Speaker
40 Wade Boggs 4.00 10.00

2020 Diamond Kings Bat Kings Holo Blue

*BLUE/25: .8X TO 2X BASIC
RANDOM INSERTS IN PACKS
PRINT RUN BTW 10-25 COPIES PER
NO PRICING QTY 15 OR LESS
7 Mike Trout/25 40.00 100.00
11 Ozzie Albies/25 10.00 25.00
14 Anthony Rizzo/25 15.00 40.00
23 Paul Molitor/25 15.00 40.00
35 Pete Rose/25 20.00 50.00
36 Reggie Jackson/25 12.00 30.00
37 Richie Ashburn/25 40.00 100.00

2020 Diamond Kings Bat Kings Purple

RANDOM INSERTS IN PACKS
STATED PRINT RUN 20 COPIES PER
1 Joe DiMaggio 20.00 50.00
2 Joe Jackson 30.00 80.00
3 Roger Maris 15.00 40.00
5 Honus Wagner 30.00 80.00
7 Mike Trout 40.00 100.00
11 Ozzie Albies 10.00 25.00
14 Anthony Rizzo 15.00 40.00
23 Paul Molitor 15.00 40.00
35 Pete Rose 20.00 50.00
36 Reggie Jackson 12.00 30.00
37 Richie Ashburn 40.00 100.00

2020 Diamond Kings DK 206

RANDOM INSERTS IN PACKS
1 Ken Griffey Jr. 1.00 2.50
2 Aaron Judge 1.25 3.00
3 Anthony Rizzo .75 2.00
4 Bryce Harper .75 2.00
5 Cal Ripken 1.50 4.00
6 Mookie Betts 1.00 2.50
7 Nolan Ryan 1.50 4.00
8 Ronald Acuna Jr. 2.00 5.00
9 Shohei Ohtani .60 1.50
10 Frank Thomas .50 1.25
11 Javier Baez .60 1.50
12 Jose Altuve .40 1.00
13 Justin Verlander .50 1.25
14 Kirby Puckett .50 1.25
15 Yordan Alvarez 1.50 4.00
16 Mickey Mantle 1.50 4.00
17 Mike Trout 2.50 6.00
18 Pete Alonso 1.25 3.00
19 Vladimir Guerrero Jr. 1.00 2.50
20 George Brett 1.00 2.50

2020 Diamond Kings DK 206 Holo Blue

*BLUE: 1.5X TO 4X BASIC
RANDOM INSERTS IN PACKS
STATED PRINT RUN 99 COPIES PER
1 Ken Griffey Jr. 15.00 40.00
17 Mike Trout 15.00 40.00
19 Vladimir Guerrero Jr. 10.00 25.00
20 George Brett 10.00 25.00

2020 Diamond Kings DK 206 Signatures

RANDOM INSERTS IN PACKS
EXCHANGE DEADLINE 12/10/2021
7 Yordan Alvarez 25.00 60.00

2020 Diamond Kings DK 206 Signatures Holo Blue

RANDOM INSERTS IN PACKS

PRINT RUN BTW 5-25 COPIES PER
NO PRICING QTY 15 OR LESS
EXCHANGE DEADLINE 12/10/2021
3 Ronald Acuna Jr./25 75.00 200.00
5 Frank Thomas/25 60.00 150.00
6 Jose Altuve/25 20.00 50.00
8 Pete Alonso/25 60.00 150.00

2020 Diamond Kings DK 206 Signatures Holo Gold
*GOLD/35-50: .6X TO 1.5X BASIC
*GOLD/25: .8X TO 2X BASIC
RANDOM INSERTS IN PACKS
PRINT RUN BTW 10-50 COPIES PER
NO PRICING QTY 15 OR LESS
EXCHANGE DEADLINE 12/10/2021
2 Nolan Ryan/25 75.00 200.00
3 Ronald Acuna Jr./50
5 Frank Thomas/50 50.00 120.00
6 Jose Altuve/35 15.00 40.00
8 Pete Alonso/50 40.00 100.00

2020 Diamond Kings DK 206 Signatures Holo Silver
*SLVR/99: .5X TO 1.2X BASIC
RANDOM INSERTS IN PACKS
PRINT RUN BTW 15-99 COPIES PER
NO PRICING QTY 15 OR LESS
EXCHANGE DEADLINE 12/10/2021
5 Frank Thomas/99 40.00 100.00
8 Pete Alonso/99 30.00 80.00

2020 Diamond Kings DK 206 Signatures Purple
*PRPL/20: .8X TO 2X BASIC
RANDOM INSERTS IN PACKS
PRINT RUN BTW 10-20 COPIES PER
NO PRICING QTY 15 OR LESS
EXCHANGE DEADLINE 12/10/2021
2 Nolan Ryan/20 75.00 200.00
3 Ronald Acuna Jr./20 75.00 200.00
4 Shohei Ohtani/20
5 Frank Thomas/20 60.00 150.00
6 Jose Altuve/20 20.00 50.00
8 Pete Alonso/20 60.00 150.00

2020 Diamond Kings DK Material Signatures
RANDOM INSERTS IN PACKS
EXCHANGE DEADLINE 12/10/2021
1 Josh Rojas 6.00 15.00
2 Matt Thaiss 4.00 10.00
3 Logan Allen 3.00 8.00
4 Kyle Lewis 20.00 50.00
5 Jesus Luzardo 8.00 20.00
6 Brendan McKay 5.00 12.00
7 Tony Gonsolin 5.00 12.00
8 Andres Munoz 4.00 10.00
9 Yonathan Daza 4.00 10.00
10 Yu Chang 5.00 12.00
11 Logan Webb 4.00 10.00
12 Michel Baez 3.00 8.00
13 Tyrone Taylor 3.00 8.00
14 Dylan Cease 6.00 15.00
15 Patrick Sandoval 5.00 12.00
16 Jaylin Davis 4.00 10.00
17 Sean Murphy 5.00 12.00
18 Jake Fraley 4.00 10.00
19 Jordan Yamamoto 4.00 10.00
20 Ronald Bolanos 5.00 12.00
21 Mauricio Dubon 4.00 10.00
22 Dustin May 12.00 30.00
23 Isan Diaz 5.00 12.00
24 Randy Arozarena 25.00 60.00
25 Michael King 5.00 12.00
26 Zac Gallen 8.00 20.00
27 Jake Rogers 3.00 8.00
28 Donnie Walton 4.00 10.00
29 Danny Mendick 4.00 10.00
30 Deivy Grullon 3.00 8.00
31 Brusdar Graterol 5.00 12.00
32 Bryan Abreu 3.00 8.00
33 Bo Bichette 25.00 60.00
34 Aristides Aquino 10.00 25.00
35 T.J. Zeuch 3.00 8.00
36 Lewis Thorpe 3.00 8.00
37 Justin Dunn 4.00 10.00
38 Joe Palumbo 3.00 8.00
39 Abraham Toro 4.00 10.00
40 Adrian Morejon 3.00 8.00
41 Rico Garcia 5.00 12.00
42 Willi Castro 5.00 12.00
43 Jonathan Hernandez 3.00 8.00
44 Adbert Alzolay 4.00 10.00
45 Yordan Alvarez 15.00 40.00
46 Anthony Kay 3.00 8.00
47 Domingo Leyba 4.00 10.00
48 Gavin Lux 15.00 40.00
49 Tres Barrera 6.00 15.00
50 Bobby Bradley 6.00 15.00
51 Trent Grisham 6.00 15.00
52 Sheldon Neuse 4.00 10.00
53 Nick Solak 6.00 15.00
54 Nico Hoerner 8.00 20.00
55 Zack Collins 4.00 10.00
56 Aaron Civale 6.00 15.00
57 Travis Demeritte 3.00 8.00
58 Sam Hilliard 5.00 12.00
59 Edwin Rios 8.00 20.00
60 A.J. Puk 6.00 15.00
61 Brock Burke 3.00 8.00

2020 Diamond Kings DK Material Signatures Gold
*GOLD: .5X TO 1.2X BASIC
RANDOM INSERTS IN PACKS
PRINT RUN BTW 15-49 COPIES PER
NO PRICING QTY 15 OR LESS
EXCHANGE DEADLINE 12/10/2021
45 Yordan Alvarez/49 60.00 150.00

2020 Diamond Kings DK Material Signatures Purple
RANDOM INSERTS IN PACKS
PRINT RUN BTW 15-20 COPIES PER
NO PRICING QTY 15 OR LESS
EXCHANGE DEADLINE 12/10/2021
6 Brendan McKay/20 12.00 30.00
45 Yordan Alvarez/20 75.00 200.00

2020 Diamond Kings DK Materials
RANDOM INSERTS IN PACKS
*SILVER/99: .5X TO 1.2X BASIC
*GOLD/50: .6X TO 1.5X BASIC
1 Josh Rojas 2.00 5.00
2 Matt Thaiss 2.50 6.00
3 Logan Allen 2.00 5.00
4 Kyle Lewis 15.00 40.00
5 Jesus Luzardo 5.00 12.00
6 Brendan McKay 3.00 8.00
7 Tony Gonsolin 8.00 20.00
8 Andres Munoz 2.50 6.00
9 Yonathan Daza 2.50 6.00
10 Yu Chang 3.00 8.00
11 Logan Webb 2.50 6.00
12 Michel Baez 2.00 5.00
13 Tyrone Taylor 2.00 5.00
14 Dylan Cease 4.00 10.00
15 Patrick Sandoval 3.00 8.00
16 Jaylin Davis 3.00 8.00
17 Sean Murphy 3.00 8.00
18 Jake Fraley 2.50 6.00
19 Jordan Yamamoto 2.50 6.00
20 Ronald Bolanos 3.00 8.00
21 Mauricio Dubon 2.50 6.00
22 Dustin May 5.00 12.00
23 Isan Diaz 3.00 8.00
24 Randy Arozarena 6.00 15.00
25 Michael King 3.00 8.00
26 Zac Gallen 5.00 12.00
27 Jake Rogers 2.00 5.00
28 Donnie Walton 5.00 12.00
29 Danny Mendick 2.50 6.00
30 Deivy Grullon 2.00 5.00
31 Brusdar Graterol 3.00 8.00
32 Bryan Abreu 2.00 5.00
33 Bo Bichette 6.00 15.00
34 Aristides Aquino 4.00 10.00
35 T.J. Zeuch 2.00 5.00
36 Lewis Thorpe 2.00 5.00
37 Justin Dunn 2.50 6.00
38 Joe Palumbo 2.00 5.00
39 Abraham Toro 2.50 6.00
40 Adrian Morejon 2.50 6.00
41 Rico Garcia 3.00 8.00
42 Willi Castro 3.00 8.00
43 Jonathan Hernandez 2.00 5.00
44 Adbert Alzolay 2.50 6.00
45 Yordan Alvarez 6.00 15.00
46 Anthony Kay 2.00 5.00
47 Domingo Leyba 2.50 6.00
48 Gavin Lux 10.00 25.00
49 Tres Barrera 4.00 10.00
50 Bobby Bradley 2.50 6.00
51 Trent Grisham 8.00 20.00
52 Sheldon Neuse 2.50 6.00
53 Nick Solak 3.00 8.00
54 Nico Hoerner 5.00 12.00
55 Zack Collins 2.50 6.00
56 Aaron Civale 3.00 8.00
57 Travis Demeritte 2.50 6.00
58 Sam Hilliard 3.00 8.00
59 Edwin Rios 5.00 12.00
60 A.J. Puk 4.00 10.00
61 Brock Burke 2.00 5.00
62 Mule Suttles 5.00 12.00
63 Babe Ruth 100.00 250.00
64 Jackie Robinson 20.00 50.00
65 Jimmie Foxx 12.00 30.00
66 Ty Cobb 20.00 50.00
67 Lou Gehrig 40.00 100.00
68 Mel Ott
69 Charlie Keller
70 Mickey Mantle 25.00 60.00
71 Roberto Clemente 60.00 150.00
72 Roger Maris
73 Ted Williams
74 Yogi Berra
75 Tris Speaker
76 Walter Alston 4.00 10.00
77 Eddie Stanky 2.00 5.00
78 Harvey Kuenn
79 Joe Cronin
80 Joe McCarthy 2.00 5.00
81 Ken Griffey Jr. 10.00 25.00
82 Mike Trout 12.00 30.00
83 Juan Soto 10.00 25.00
84 Ronald Acuna Jr. 8.00 20.00
85 Aaron Judge 5.00 12.00
86 Vladimir Guerrero Jr. 4.00 10.00
87 Pete Alonso 8.00 20.00
88 Walker Buehler 4.00 10.00
89 Eloy Jimenez 4.00 10.00
91 Nolan Arenado 4.00 10.00
92 Rafael Devers 4.00 10.00
93 Kris Bryant 10.00 25.00
94 Shohei Ohtani 4.00 10.00
95 Alex Bregman 3.00 8.00
96 Justin Verlander 3.00 8.00
97 Stephen Strasburg 3.00 8.00
98 Mookie Betts 6.00 15.00
99 Max Scherzer 3.00 8.00
100 Javier Baez 8.00 20.00

2020 Diamond Kings DK Materials Holo Blue
*BLUE/25: .8X TO 2X BASIC
RANDOM INSERTS IN PACKS
PRINT RUN BTW 3-25 COPIES PER
NO PRICING QTY 15 OR LESS
82 Mike Trout/25 40.00 100.00
85 Aaron Judge/25 15.00 40.00
87 Pete Alonso/25 15.00 40.00

2020 Diamond Kings DK Originals
RANDOM INSERTS IN PACKS
*BLUE: 1.5X TO 4X BASIC
1 Alex Bregman .50 1.25
2 Clayton Kershaw 1.00 2.50
3 Anthony Rizzo .75 2.00
4 Mel Ott .50 1.25
5 Joe DiMaggio 1.00 2.50
6 Ted Williams 1.00 2.50
7 Anthony Rendon .50 1.25
8 Keston Hiura .60 1.50
9 Justin Verlander .50 1.25
10 Ty Cobb .75 2.00

2020 Diamond Kings DK Originals Signatures
RANDOM INSERTS IN PACKS
EXCHANGE DEADLINE 12/10/2021
5 Curt Schilling
8 Alec Bohm 15.00 40.00
12 Luis Robert 60.00 150.00
13 Jose Abreu 4.00 10.00
15 Barry Larkin 12.00 30.00
17 Keith Hernandez 5.00 12.00
19 Anthony Rizzo
21 Trevor Hoffman EXCH 8.00 20.00
23 Corey Seager 4.00 10.00
24 Josh Donaldson 3.00 8.00
27 Blake Snell 3.00 8.00
28 Luis Severino 6.00 15.00
29 Andre Dawson
30 Walker Buehler EXCH 8.00 20.00

2020 Diamond Kings DK Originals Signatures Holo Blue
*BLUE/25: .8X TO 2X BASIC
RANDOM INSERTS IN PACKS
PRINT RUN BTW 10-25 COPIES PER
NO PRICING QTY 15 OR LESS
EXCHANGE DEADLINE 12/10/2021
1 Vladimir Guerrero Jr./25 40.00 100.00
2 Alan Trammell/25 25.00 60.00
3 Kenny Lofton/25 20.00 50.00
7 Xander Bogaerts/25 20.00 50.00
9 Forrest Whitley/25 8.00 20.00
10 Ben Zobrist/25 10.00 25.00
16 Dale Murphy/25 20.00 50.00
18 Aaron Judge/25 EXCH 40.00 100.00
20 J.D. Martinez/25 15.00 40.00
22 Kyle Hendricks/25 20.00 50.00
26 David Wright/25 20.00 50.00

2020 Diamond Kings DK Originals Signatures Holo Gold
*GOLD/30-50: .6X TO 1.5X BASIC
*GOLD/25: .8X TO 2X BASIC
RANDOM INSERTS IN PACKS
PRINT RUN BTW 15-50 COPIES PER
NO PRICING QTY 15 OR LESS
EXCHANGE DEADLINE 12/10/2021
1 Vladimir Guerrero Jr./50 30.00 80.00
2 Alan Trammell/50 20.00 50.00
3 Kenny Lofton/50
4 Clayton Kershaw/25 40.00 100.00
7 Xander Bogaerts/50 12.00 30.00
9 Forrest Whitley/50 4.00 10.00
11 John Smoltz/25 15.00 40.00
14 Jose Ramirez/25
16 Dale Murphy/50 15.00 40.00
20 J.D. Martinez/50 12.00 30.00
22 Kyle Hendricks/50 15.00 40.00
26 David Wright/50 15.00 40.00

2020 Diamond Kings DK Originals Signatures Holo Silver
*SLVR/75-99: .5X TO 1.2X BASIC
*SLVR/49-50: .6X TO 1.5X BASIC
*SLVR/25: .8X TO 2X BASIC
RANDOM INSERTS IN PACKS
PRINT RUN BTW 25-99 COPIES PER
EXCHANGE DEADLINE 12/10/2021
1 Vladimir Guerrero Jr./99 25.00 60.00
4 Clayton Kershaw/49 25.00 60.00
9 Forrest Whitley/99 3.00 8.00
11 John Smoltz/50 12.00 30.00
14 Jose Ramirez/75
16 Dale Murphy/99 12.00 30.00
19 Anthony Rizzo/25 15.00 40.00
20 J.D. Martinez/99 10.00 25.00
22 Kyle Hendricks/99 12.00 30.00
26 David Wright/99 12.00 30.00

2020 Diamond Kings DK Originals Signatures Purple
*PRPL: .8X TO 2X BASIC
RANDOM INSERTS IN PACKS
STATED PRINT RUN 25 COPIES PER
EXCHANGE DEADLINE 12/10/2021
1 Vladimir Guerrero Jr. 40.00 100.00
2 Alan Trammell 25.00 60.00
3 Kenny Lofton 20.00 50.00
4 Clayton Kershaw 40.00 100.00
5 Curt Schilling 20.00 50.00
6 Steve Garvey 30.00 80.00
7 Xander Bogaerts 20.00 50.00
9 Forrest Whitley 8.00 20.00
10 Ben Zobrist 10.00 25.00
11 John Smoltz 15.00 40.00
14 Jose Ramirez
16 Dale Murphy 20.00 50.00
18 Aaron Judge EXCH 40.00 100.00
19 Anthony Rizzo 15.00 40.00
20 J.D. Martinez 15.00 40.00
22 Kyle Hendricks 20.00 50.00
25 Josh Hader 5.00 12.00
26 David Wright 20.00 50.00

2020 Diamond Kings DK Quad Material Signatures
RANDOM INSERTS IN PACKS
EXCHANGE DEADLINE 12/10/2021
3 Yordan Alvarez 15.00 40.00
4 Bo Bichette 40.00 100.00
5 Cody Bellinger 50.00 120.00
6 Rickey Henderson 40.00 100.00
7 Chipper Jones 30.00 80.00
9 Frank Robinson 15.00 40.00
11 Eloy Jimenez
13 Mike Soroka 8.00 20.00
14 Gleyber Torres 30.00 80.00
15 Omar Vizquel 15.00 40.00
17 Jose Berrios 8.00 20.00
18 Brendan McKay 5.00 12.00
19 Chris Sale 10.00 25.00

2020 Diamond Kings DK Quad Material Signatures Gold
*GOLD/49: .5X TO 1.2X BASIC
*GOLD/25: .6X TO 1.5X BASIC
RANDOM INSERTS IN PACKS
PRINT RUN BTW 25-50 COPIES PER
EXCHANGE DEADLINE 12/10/2021
1 Aaron Judge/49
2 Ken Griffey Jr./25
3 Yordan Alvarez/49 60.00 150.00
8 Shohei Ohtani/49 50.00 120.00
10 Ronald Acuna Jr./49 50.00 120.00
11 Eloy Jimenez/49
12 Xander Bogaerts/49 20.00 50.00

2020 Diamond Kings DK Quad Material Signatures Holo Blue
*BLUE/23-25: .6X TO 1.5X BASIC
RANDOM INSERTS IN PACKS
PRINT RUN BTW 15-25 COPIES PER
NO PRICING QTY 15 OR LESS
EXCHANGE DEADLINE 12/10/2021
1 Aaron Judge/25 50.00 120.00
3 Yordan Alvarez/25 75.00 200.00
7 Chipper Jones/25 60.00 150.00
8 Shohei Ohtani/25 75.00 200.00
10 Ronald Acuna Jr./25 100.00 250.00
11 Eloy Jimenez/25 40.00 100.00
12 Xander Bogaerts/25 40.00 100.00
13 Mike Soroka/25 30.00 80.00
16 Scooter Gennett/25 15.00 40.00
18 Brendan McKay/25 12.00 30.00
19 Chris Sale/25 20.00 50.00

2020 Diamond Kings DK Quad Material Signatures Purple
*PRPL/20: .6X TO 1.5X BASIC
RANDOM INSERTS IN PACKS
PRINT RUN BTW 10-20 COPIES PER
NO PRICING QTY 15 OR LESS
EXCHANGE DEADLINE 12/10/2021
1 Aaron Judge/20 50.00 120.00
3 Yordan Alvarez/20 75.00 200.00
7 Chipper Jones/20 60.00 150.00
8 Shohei Ohtani/20 75.00 200.00
10 Ronald Acuna Jr./20 100.00 250.00
11 Eloy Jimenez/20 40.00 100.00
12 Xander Bogaerts/20 40.00 100.00
13 Mike Soroka/20 30.00 80.00
16 Scooter Gennett/20 15.00 40.00
18 Brendan McKay/20 12.00 30.00
19 Chris Sale/20 20.00 50.00

2020 Diamond Kings DK Quad Materials
RANDOM INSERTS IN PACKS
1 Jeff McNeil 2.50 6.00
2 Yordan Alvarez 6.00 15.00
3 Pete Alonso 6.00 15.00
4 Tony Gwynn 6.00 15.00
5 Aristides Aquino 5.00 12.00
6 Bo Bichette 10.00 25.00
7 Brendan McKay 3.00 8.00
8 Gavin Lux 10.00 25.00
9 Dustin May 8.00 20.00
10 Fernando Tatis Jr. 4.00 10.00
11 Eloy Jimenez 4.00 10.00
12 Mookie Betts 12.00 30.00
13 Shohei Ohtani 4.00 10.00
14 Hyun-Jin Ryu 2.50 6.00
15 Jacob deGrom 3.00 8.00
16 Gerrit Cole 5.00 12.00
17 Buster Posey 8.00 20.00
18 Miguel Cabrera 6.00 15.00
19 Adrian Beltre 3.00 8.00
20 Max Scherzer 3.00 8.00
21 Clayton Kershaw 6.00 15.00
22 Yadier Molina 5.00 12.00
23 David Ortiz 5.00 12.00
24 Justin Verlander 3.00 8.00
25 Robinson Cano 2.50 6.00

2020 Diamond Kings DK Quad Materials Holo Blue
*BLUE: .8X TO 2X BASIC
RANDOM INSERTS IN PACKS
STATED PRINT RUN 25 COPIES PER
3 Pete Alonso 15.00 40.00

2020 Diamond Kings DK Signatures
RANDOM INSERTS IN PACKS
EXCHANGE DEADLINE 12/10/2021
1 Josh Rojas 2.50 6.00
2 Matt Thaiss 3.00 8.00
3 Logan Allen 2.50 6.00
4 Kyle Lewis 10.00 25.00
5 Jesus Luzardo
6 Brendan McKay 10.00 25.00
7 Tony Gonsolin 10.00 25.00
8 Andres Munoz 3.00 8.00
9 Yonathan Daza 3.00 8.00
10 Yu Chang 4.00 10.00
11 Logan Webb 5.00 12.00
12 Michel Baez 2.50 6.00
13 Tyrone Taylor 2.50 6.00
14 Dylan Cease 5.00 12.00
15 Patrick Sandoval 4.00 10.00
16 Jaylin Davis 4.00 10.00
17 Sean Murphy 4.00 10.00
18 Jake Fraley 3.00 8.00
19 Jordan Yamamoto 3.00 8.00
20 Ronald Bolanos 4.00 10.00
21 Mauricio Dubon
22 Dustin May 10.00 25.00
23 Isan Diaz 4.00 10.00
24 Randy Arozarena 20.00 50.00
25 Michael King 4.00 10.00
26 Zac Gallen 4.00 10.00
27 Jake Rogers 2.50 6.00
28 Donnie Walton 6.00 15.00
29 Danny Mendick 3.00 8.00
30 Deivy Grullon 2.50 6.00
31 Brusdar Graterol 4.00 10.00
32 Bryan Abreu 2.50 6.00
33 Bo Bichette 20.00 50.00
34 Aristides Aquino 5.00 12.00
35 T.J. Zeuch 2.50 6.00
36 Lewis Thorpe 2.50 6.00
37 Justin Dunn 3.00 8.00
38 Joe Palumbo 2.50 6.00
39 Abraham Toro 3.00 8.00
40 Adrian Morejon 2.50 6.00
41 Rico Garcia 4.00 10.00
42 Willi Castro 5.00 12.00
43 Jonathan Hernandez 2.50 6.00
44 Adbert Alzolay 3.00 8.00
45 Yordan Alvarez 40.00 100.00
46 Anthony Kay 2.50 6.00
47 Domingo Leyba 3.00 8.00
48 Gavin Lux 25.00 60.00
49 Tres Barrera 5.00 12.00
50 Bobby Bradley 5.00 12.00
51 Trent Grisham 10.00 25.00
52 Sheldon Neuse 3.00 8.00
53 Nick Solak 2.50 6.00
54 Nico Hoerner 10.00 25.00
55 Zack Collins 3.00 8.00
56 Aaron Civale 4.00 10.00
57 Travis Demeritte 3.00 8.00
58 Sam Hilliard 4.00 10.00
59 Edwin Rios 6.00 15.00
60 A.J. Puk 5.00 12.00
61 Brock Burke 2.50 6.00
62 Yoshitomo Tsutsugo EXCH 20.00 50.00

2020 Diamond Kings DK Signatures Holo Gold
*GOLD/25: .8X TO 2X BASIC
RANDOM INSERTS IN PACKS
PRINT RUN BTW 10-25 COPIES PER
NO PRICING QTY 15 OR LESS
EXCHANGE DEADLINE 12/10/2021
48 Gavin Lux/25 60.00 150.00

2020 Diamond Kings DK Signatures Holo Silver
*SLVR/49: .6X TO 1.5X BASIC
RANDOM INSERTS IN PACKS
PRINT RUN BTW 15-49 COPIES PER
NO PRICING QTY 15 OR LESS
EXCHANGE DEADLINE 12/10/2021

2020 Diamond Kings DK Signatures Purple
*PRPL/20: .8X TO 2X BASIC
RANDOM INSERTS IN PACKS
PRINT RUN BTW 5-20 COPIES PER
NO PRICING QTY 15 OR LESS
EXCHANGE DEADLINE 12/10/2021
48 Gavin Lux/20 60.00 150.00

2020 Diamond Kings Downtown
RANDOM INSERTS IN PACKS
1 Mike Trout 100.00 250.00
2 Aaron Judge 25.00 60.00
3 Cody Bellinger 20.00 50.00
4 Yordan Alvarez 30.00 80.00
5 Fernando Tatis Jr. 75.00 200.00
6 Anthony Rendon 10.00 25.00
7 Yadier Molina 25.00 60.00
8 Rafael Devers 25.00 60.00
9 Anthony Rizzo 25.00 60.00
10 Bo Bichette 50.00 120.00
11 Wander Franco 30.00 80.00
12 Luis Robert 50.00 120.00
13 Jo Adell 40.00 100.00
14 Aristides Aquino 20.00 50.00
15 Gleyber Torres 40.00 100.00
16 Ronald Acuna Jr. 40.00 100.00
17 Pete Alonso 40.00 100.00
18 Juan Soto 40.00 100.00
19 Bryce Harper 30.00 80.00
20 Vladimir Guerrero Jr. 20.00 50.00

2020 Diamond Kings Gallery of Stars
RANDOM INSERTS IN PACKS
*BLUE: 1.5X TO 4X BASIC
1 Aaron Judge 1.25 3.00
2 Mookie Betts 1.00 2.50
3 Vladimir Guerrero Jr. 1.00 2.50
4 Francisco Lindor .50 1.25
5 Jose Altuve .40 1.00
6 Mike Trout 2.50 6.00
7 Shohei Ohtani .60 1.50
8 Ronald Acuna Jr. 2.00 5.00
9 Juan Soto 1.50 4.00
10 Pete Alonso 1.25 3.00
11 Bryce Harper .75 2.00
12 Javier Baez .60 1.50
13 Cody Bellinger 1.00 2.50
14 Christian Yelich .60 1.50
15 Fernando Tatis Jr. 2.00 5.00

2020 Diamond Kings In The Zone
RANDOM INSERTS IN PACKS
*BLUE: 1.5X TO 4X BASIC
1 Tony Gwynn .50 1.25
2 Reggie Jackson 1.00 2.50
3 Tim Anderson .50 1.25
4 Roger Maris .50 1.25
5 Matt Chapman .50 1.25
6 Alex Rodriguez .60 1.50
7 Pedro Martinez .40 1.00
8 Manny Machado .50 1.25
9 Shohei Ohtani .60 1.50
10 Juan Soto 1.50 4.00
11 Christian Yelich .60 1.50
12 Anthony Rendon .50 1.25
13 Jose Ramirez .40 1.00
14 Gerrit Cole .75 2.00
15 George Brett 1.20 3.00

2020 Diamond Kings Jersey Kings
RANDOM INSERTS IN PACKS
1 Stan Musial 8.00 20.00
2 Satchel Paige 25.00 60.00
3 Jorge Polanco 2.50 6.00
4 Yordan Alvarez 5.00 12.00
5 Pete Alonso 5.00 12.00
6 Ken Griffey Jr. 10.00 25.00
7 Mike Trout 12.00 30.00
8 Mickey Mantle 25.00 60.00
9 Nolan Arenado 4.00 10.00
10 Aaron Judge 5.00 12.00
11 Jose Altuve 2.50 6.00
12 Juan Soto 10.00 25.00
13 Miguel Cabrera 6.00 15.00
14 Jose Abreu 3.00 8.00
15 Andrew Benintendi 3.00 8.00
16 Frank Thomas 5.00 12.00
17 Elroy Face 2.00 5.00
18 Tim Anderson 3.00 8.00
19 J.D. Martinez 3.00 8.00
20 Anthony Rizzo 5.00 12.00
21 Giancarlo Stanton 3.00 8.00
22 Freddie Freeman 4.00 10.00
23 Kris Bryant 4.00 10.00
24 Craig Biggio 2.50 6.00
25 Aaron Nola 3.00 8.00
26 Max Muncy 2.50 6.00
27 Larry Walker 2.50 6.00
28 Lou Gehrig 40.00 100.00
29 Jackie Robinson 20.00 50.00
30 Babe Ruth 100.00 250.00
31 Ted Williams
32 Gil McDougald
33 Elston Howard
34 Kirby Puckett 12.00 30.00
35 Joe McCarthy 2.00 5.00

2020 Diamond Kings Jersey Kings Holo Blue
*BLUE: .8X TO 2X BASIC
RANDOM INSERTS IN PACKS
STATED PRINT RUN 25 COPIES PER
6 Ken Griffey Jr. 40.00 100.00
7 Mike Trout 50.00 120.00
10 Aaron Judge 15.00 40.00
16 Frank Thomas 25.00 60.00
20 Anthony Rizzo 15.00 40.00
29 Jackie Robinson 50.00 120.00
30 Babe Ruth 125.00 300.00
31 Ted Williams 50.00 120.00

2020 Diamond Kings Jersey Kings Purple
*PURPLE/19-20: .8X TO 2X BASIC
RANDOM INSERTS IN PACKS
PRINT RUN BTW 8-20 COPIES PER
NO PRICING QTY 15 OR LESS
6 Ken Griffey Jr./20 40.00 100.00
7 Mike Trout/20 50.00 120.00
10 Aaron Judge/20 15.00 40.00
16 Frank Thomas/20 25.00 60.00
20 Anthony Rizzo/20 15.00 40.00
29 Jackie Robinson/20 50.00 120.00
30 Babe Ruth/20 125.00 300.00
31 Ted Williams/20 50.00 120.00

2020 Diamond Kings Litho Proof
*LITHO 1-100: 4X TO 10X BASIC
*LITHO 1-100 RC: 2X TO 5X BASIC RC
*LITHO 101-170 SP: 2X TO 5X BASIC SP
*LITHO 101-170 SP RC: 1.2X TO 3X BASIC
RANDOM INSERTS IN PACKS
STATED PRINT RUN 25 SER. #'d SETS
22 Roberto Clemente 15.00 40.0
44 Cal Ripken 20.00 50.
47 Harmon Killebrew 20.00 50.
76 Gavin Lux 30.00 80.
114 Mike Trout SP 30.00 80.
143 Ken Griffey Jr. SP 20.00 50.

2020 Diamond Kings Pixel Ar
RANDOM INSERTS IN PACKS 3.00 8.
1 Mookie Betts 12.00 30.
2 Juan Soto 20.00 50.
3 Jose Altuve 6.00 15.
4 Javier Baez 10.00 25.
5 Shohei Ohtani 15.00 40.
6 Clayton Kershaw 10.00 25.
7 Yoshitomo Tsutsugo 4.00 10.
8 Miguel Cabrera 20.00 50.
9 Manny Machado 10.00 25.
10 Yadier Molina 8.00 20.
11 Ketel Marte 4.00 10.
12 Francisco Lindor 5.00 12.
13 Ozzie Albies 5.00 12.
14 Isan Diaz 5.00 12.
15 Joey Votto 12.00 30.
16 Josh Bell 4.00 10.
17 Kirby Puckett 40.00 100.
18 Josh Donaldson 10.00 25
19 Trey Mancini 5.00 12.
20 Trevor Story 5.00 12.

2020 Diamond Kings The 300
RANDOM INSERTS IN PACKS
*BLUE: 1.5X TO 4X BASIC
1 George Brett 1.00 2
2 Honus Wagner .50 1
3 Roberto Clemente 3.00 8
4 Al Kaline .50 1
5 Ty Cobb .75 2
6 Tris Speaker .40 1
7 Stan Musial .75 2
8 Pete Rose 1.00 2
9 Paul Molitor .50 1
10 Nap Lajoie .50 1
11 Eddie Murray .40 1
12 Albert Pujols .60 1
13 Cal Ripken 1.50 4
14 Tony Gwynn .50 1
15 Ichiro .60 1

1981 Donruss

In 1981 Donruss launched itself into the baseball card market with a 600-card set. Wax packs contained 15 cards as well as a piece of gum. Th would be the only year that Donruss was allowed have any confectionary product in their packs. Th standard-size cards are printed on thin stock and more than one pose exists for several popular players. Numerous errors of the first print run we later corrected by the company. These are marke and P2 in our checklist below. According to published reports at the time, approximately 500 were made available in uncut sheet form. The key Rookie Cards in this set are Danny Ainge, Tim Raines, and Jeff Reardon.

COMPLETE SET (605) 20.00 5
COMMON CARD (1-605) .02
COMMON RC .05
1 Ozzie Smith 1.25 3
2 Rollie Fingers .08
3 Rick Wise .02
4 Gene Richards .02
5 Alan Trammell .20
6 Tom Brookens .02
7A Duffy Dyer P1 .08
7B Duffy Dyer P2 .02
8 Mark Fidrych .08
9 Dave Rozema .02
10 Ricky Peters RC .02
11 Mike Schmidt 1.00 2
12 Willie Stargell .20
13 Tim Foli .02
14 Manny Sanguillen .08
15 Grant Jackson .02
16 Eddie Solomon .02
17 Omar Moreno .02
18 Joe Morgan .20
19 Rafael Landestoy .02
20 Bruce Bochy .02
21 Joe Sambito .02
22 Manny Trillo .02
23A Dave Smith P1 .20
23B Dave Smith P2 RC .20
24 Terry Puhl .02
25 Bump Wills .02
26A John Ellis P1 ERR .20
26B John Ellis P2 COR .08
27 Jim Kern .02
28 Richie Zisk .02
29 John Mayberry .02
30 Bob Davis .02
31 Jackson Todd .02
32 Alvis Woods .02

33 Steve Carlton .20 .50
34 Lee Mazzilli .08 .25
35 John Stearns .02 .10
36 Roy Lee Jackson RC .02 .10
37 Mike Scott .08 .25
38 Lamar Johnson .02 .10
39 Kevin Bell .02 .10
40 Ed Farmer .02 .10
41 Ross Baumgarten .02 .10
42 Leo Sutherland RC .02 .10
43 Dan Meyer .02 .10
44 Ron Reed .02 .10
45 Mario Mendoza .02 .10
46 Rick Honeycutt .02 .10
47 Glenn Abbott .02 .10
48 Leon Roberts .02 .10
49 Rod Carew .20 .50
50 Bert Campaneris .08 .25
51A Tom Donahue P1 ERR .08 .25
51B Tom Donohue P2 RC .02 .10
52 Dave Frost .02 .10
53 Ed Halicki .02 .10
54 Dan Ford .02 .10
55 Garry Maddox .02 .10
56A Steve Garvey P1 25HR .08 .25
56B Steve Garvey P2 21HR .08 .25
57 Bill Russell .08 .25
58 Don Sutton .08 .25
59 Reggie Smith .08 .25
60 Rick Monday .08 .25
61 Ray Knight .08 .25
62 Johnny Bench .40 1.00
63 Mario Soto .08 .25
64 Doug Bair .02 .10
65 George Foster .08 .25
66 Jeff Burroughs .08 .25
67 Keith Hernandez .08 .25
68 Tom Herr .02 .10
69 Bob Forsch .02 .10
70 John Fulgham .02 .10
71A Bobby Bonds P1 ERR .40 1.00
71B Bobby Bonds P2 COR .20 .50
72A Rennie Stennett P1 .08 .25
72B Rennie Stennett P2 .02 .10
73 Joe Strain .02 .10
74 Ed Whitson .02 .10
75 Tom Griffin .02 .10
76 Billy North .02 .10
77 Gene Garber .02 .10
78 Mike Hargrove .02 .10
79 Dave Rosello .02 .10
80 Ron Hassey .02 .10
81 Sid Monge .02 .10
82A Joe Charboneau P1 .40 1.00
82B Joe Charboneau P2 RC .40 1.00
83 Cecil Cooper .08 .25
84 Sal Bando .08 .25
85 Moose Haas .02 .10
86 Mike Caldwell .02 .10
87A Larry Hisle P1 .08 .25
87B Larry Hisle P2 .02 .10
88 Luis Gomez .02 .10
89 Larry Parrish .02 .10
90 Gary Carter .20 .50
91 Bill Gullickson RC .20 .50
92 Fred Norman .02 .10
93 Tommy Hutton .02 .10
94 Carl Yastrzemski .60 1.50
95 Glenn Hoffman RC .02 .10
96 Dennis Eckersley .20 .50
97A Tom Burgmeier P1 .08 .25
97B Tom Burgmeier P2 .02 .10
98 Win Remmerswaal RC .02 .10
99 Bob Horner .08 .25
100 George Brett 1.00 2.50
101 Dave Chalk .02 .10
102 Dennis Leonard .02 .10
103 Renie Martin .02 .10
104 Amos Otis .08 .25
105 Graig Nettles .08 .25
106 Eric Soderholm .02 .10
107 Tommy John .08 .25
108 Tom Underwood .02 .10
109 Lou Piniella .08 .25
110 Mickey Klutts .02 .10
111 Bobby Murcer .08 .25
112 Eddie Murray .60 1.50
113 Rick Dempsey .02 .10
114 Scott McGregor .02 .10
115 Ken Singleton .08 .25
116 Gary Roenicke .02 .10
117 Dave Revering .02 .10
118 Mike Norris .02 .10
119 Rickey Henderson 2.50 6.00
120 Mike Heath .02 .10
121 Dave Cash .02 .10
122 Randy Jones .08 .25
123 Eric Rasmussen .02 .10
124 Jerry Mumphrey .02 .10
125 Richie Hebner .02 .10
126 Mark Wagner .02 .10
127 Jack Morris .20 .50
128 Dan Petry .02 .10
129 Bruce Robbins .02 .10
130 Champ Summers .02 .10
131 Pete Rose 1.25 3.00
131B Pete Rose P2 .75 2.00
132 Willie Stargell .20 .50
133 Ed Ott .02 .10
134 Jim Bibby .02 .10
135 Bert Blyleven .08 .25
136 Dave Parker .08 .25
137 Bill Robinson .02 .10
138 Enos Cabell .02 .10
139 Dave Bergman .02 .10
140 J.R. Richard .08 .25
141 Ken Forsch .02 .10
142 Larry Bowa UER .08 .25
143 Frank LaCorte UER .02 .10
144 Denny Walling .02 .10
145 Buddy Bell .08 .25
146 Fergie Jenkins .08 .25
147 Dannny Darwin .08 .25
148 John Grubb .02 .10
149 Alfredo Griffin .02 .10
150 Jerry Garvin .02 .10
151 Paul Mirabella RC .02 .10
152 Rick Bosetti .02 .10
153 Dick Ruthven .02 .10
154 Frank Taveras .02 .10
155 Craig Swan .02 .10
156 Jeff Reardon RC .40 1.00
157 Steve Henderson .02 .10
158 Jim Morrison .02 .10
159 Glenn Borgmann .02 .10
160 LaMarr Hoyt RC .20 .50
161 Rich Wortham .02 .10
162 Thad Bosley .02 .10
163 Julio Cruz .02 .10
164A Del Unser P1 .08 .25
164B Del Unser P2 .02 .10
165 Jim Anderson .02 .10
166 Jim Beattie .02 .10
167 Shane Rawley .02 .10
168 Joe Simpson .02 .10
169 Rod Carew .20 .50
170 Fred Patek .02 .10
171 Frank Tanana .08 .25
172 Alfredo Martinez RC .02 .10
173 Chris Knapp .02 .10
174 Joe Rudi .08 .25
175 Greg Luzinski .08 .25
176 Steve Garvey .20 .50
177 Joe Ferguson .02 .10
178 Bob Welch .08 .25
179 Dusty Baker .08 .25
180 Rudy Law .02 .10
181 Dave Concepcion .08 .25
182 Johnny Bench .40 1.00
183 Mike LaCoss .02 .10
184 Ken Griffey .08 .25
185 Dave Collins .02 .10
186 Brian Asselstine .02 .10
187 Garry Templeton .08 .25
188 Mike Phillips .02 .10
189 Pete Vuckovich .02 .10
190 John Urrea .02 .10
191 Tony Scott .02 .10
192 Darrell Evans .08 .25
193 Milt May .02 .10
194 Bob Knepper .02 .10
195 Randy Moffitt .02 .10
196 Larry Herndon .02 .10
197 Rick Camp .02 .10
198 Andre Thornton .08 .25
199 Tom Veryzer .02 .10
200 Gary Alexander .02 .10
201 Rick Waits .02 .10
202 Rick Manning .02 .10
203 Paul Molitor .40 1.00
204 Jim Gantner .02 .10
205 Paul Mitchell .02 .10
206 Reggie Cleveland .02 .10
207 Sixto Lezcano .02 .10
208 Bruce Benedict .02 .10
209 Rodney Scott .02 .10
210 John Tamargo .02 .10
211 Bill Lee .08 .25
212 Andre Dawson .20 .50
213 Rowland Office .02 .10
214 Carl Yastrzemski .60 1.50
215 Jerry Remy .02 .10
216 Mike Torrez .02 .10
217 Skip Lockwood .02 .10
218 Fred Lynn .08 .25
219 Chris Chambliss .08 .25
220 Willie Aikens .02 .10
221 John Wathan .02 .10
222 Dan Quisenberry .08 .25
223 Willie Wilson .08 .25
224 Clint Hurdle .02 .10
225 Bob Watson .02 .10
226 Jim Spencer .02 .10
227 Ron Guidry .08 .25
228 Reggie Jackson .40 1.00
229 Oscar Gamble .02 .10
230 Jeff Cox RC .02 .10
231 Luis Tiant .08 .25
232 Rich Dauer .02 .10
233 Dan Graham .02 .10
234 Mike Flanagan .02 .10
235 John Lowenstein .02 .10
236 Benny Ayala .02 .10
237 Wayne Gross .02 .10
238 Rick Langford .02 .10
239 Tony Armas .08 .25
240A Bob Lacy P1 ERR .02 .10
240B Bob Lacey P2 COR .02 .10
241 Gene Tenace .08 .25
242 Bob Shirley .02 .10
243 Gary Lucas RC .02 .10
244 Jerry Turner .02 .10
245 John Wockenfuss .02 .10
246 Stan Papi .02 .10
247 Milt Wilcox .02 .10
248 Dan Schatzeder .02 .10
249 Steve Kemp .02 .10
250 Jim Lentine RC .02 .10
251 Pete Rose 1.25 3.00
252 Bill Madlock .08 .25
253 Dale Berra .02 .10
254 Kent Tekulve .02 .10
255 Enrique Romo .02 .10
256 Mike Easler .02 .10
257 Chuck Tanner MG .02 .10
258 Art Howe .02 .10
259 Alan Ashby .02 .10
260 Nolan Ryan 2.00 5.00
261A Vern Ruhle P1 ERR .20 .50
261B Vern Ruhle P2 COR .08 .25
262 Bob Boone .08 .25
263 Cesar Cedeno .08 .25
264 Jeff Leonard .08 .25
265 Pat Putnam .02 .10
266 Jon Matlack .02 .10
267 Dave Rajsich .02 .10
268 Billy Sample .02 .10
269 Damaso Garcia RC .02 .10
270 Tom Buskey .02 .10
271 Joey McLaughlin .02 .10
272 Barry Bonnell .02 .10
273 Tug McGraw .08 .25
274 Mike Jorgensen .02 .10
275 Pat Zachry .02 .10
276 Neil Allen .02 .10
277 Joel Youngblood .02 .10
278 Greg Pryor .02 .10
279 Britt Burns RC .02 .10
280 Rich Dotson RC .02 .10
281 Chet Lemon .08 .25
282 Rusty Kuntz RC .02 .10
283 Ted Cox .02 .10
284 Sparky Lyle .08 .25
285 Larry Cox .02 .10
286 Floyd Bannister .02 .10
287 Byron McLaughlin .02 .10
288 Rodney Craig .02 .10
289 Bobby Grich .08 .25
290 Dickie Thon .08 .25
291 Mark Clear .02 .10
292 Dave Lemanczyk .02 .10
293 Jason Thompson .02 .10
294 Rick Miller .02 .10
295 Lonnie Smith .08 .25
296 Ron Cey .08 .25
297 Steve Yeager .08 .25
298 Bobby Castillo .02 .10
299 Manny Mota .08 .25
300 Jay Johnstone .08 .25
301 Dan Driessen .02 .10
302 Joe Nolan .02 .10
303 Paul Householder RC .02 .10
304 Harry Spilman .02 .10
305 Cesar Geronimo .02 .10
306A Gary Mathews P1 ERR .20 .50
306B Gary Mathews P2 COR .08 .25
307 Ken Reitz .02 .10
308 Ted Simmons .08 .25
309 John Littlefield RC .02 .10
310 George Frazier .02 .10
311 Dane Iorg .02 .10
312 Mike Ivie .02 .10
313 Dennis Littlejohn .02 .10
314 Gary Lavelle .02 .10
315 Jack Clark .08 .25
316 Jim Wohlford .02 .10
317 Rick Matula .02 .10
318 Toby Harrah .08 .25
319A Dwane Kuiper P1 ERR .08 .25
319B Duane Kuiper P2 COR .02 .10
320 Len Barker .08 .25
321 Victor Cruz .02 .10
322 Dell Alston .02 .10
323 Robin Yount .60 1.50
324 Charlie Moore .02 .10
325 Lary Sorensen .02 .10
326A Gorman Thomas P1 .20 .50
326B Gorman Thomas P2 .08 .25
327 Bob Rodgers MG .02 .10
328 Phil Niekro .08 .25
329 Chris Speier .02 .10
330A Steve Rodgers P1 .08 .25
330B Steve Rogers P2 COR .08 .25
331 Woodie Fryman .02 .10
332 Warren Cromartie .02 .10
333 Jerry White .02 .10
334 Tony Perez .08 .25
335 Carlton Fisk .40 1.00
336 Dick Drago .02 .10
337 Steve Renko .02 .10
338 Jim Rice .08 .25
339 Jerry Royster .02 .10
340 Frank White .08 .25
341 Jamie Quirk .02 .10
342A Paul Spittorff P1 ERR .08 .25
342B Paul Splittorff P2 COR .02 .10
343 Marty Pattin .02 .10
344 Pete LaCock .02 .10
345 Willie Randolph .08 .25
346 Rick Cerone .02 .10
347 Rich Gossage .08 .25
348 Reggie Jackson .40 1.00
349 Ruppert Jones .02 .10
350 Dave McKay .02 .10
351 Yogi Berra CO .40 1.00
352 Doug DeCinces .02 .10
353 Jim Palmer .20 .50
354 Tippy Martinez .02 .10
355 Al Bumbry .02 .10
356 Earl Weaver MG .08 .25
357A Bob Picciolo P1 ERR .08 .25
357B Rob Picciolo P2 COR .02 .10
358 Matt Keough .02 .10
359 Dwayne Murphy .02 .10
360 Brian Kingman .02 .10
361 Bill Fahey .02 .10
362 Steve Mura .02 .10
363 Dennis Kinney RC .02 .10
364 Dave Winfield .20 .50
365 Lou Whitaker .20 .50
366 Lance Parrish .08 .25
367 Tim Corcoran .02 .10
368 Pat Underwood .02 .10
369 Al Cowens .02 .10
370 Sparky Anderson MG .08 .25
371 Pete Rose 1.25 3.00
372 Phil Garner .08 .25
373 Steve Nicosia .02 .10
374 John Candelaria .08 .25
375 Don Robinson .02 .10
376 Lee Lacy .02 .10
377 John Milner .02 .10
378 Craig Reynolds .02 .10
379A Luis Pujols P1 ERR .08 .25
379B Luis Pujols P2 COR .02 .10
380 Joe Niekro .02 .10
381 Joaquin Andujar .02 .10
382 Keith Moreland RC .02 .10
383 Jose Cruz .08 .25
384 Bill Virdon MG .02 .10
385 Jim Sundberg .08 .25
386 Doc Medich .02 .10
387 Al Oliver .08 .25
388 Jim Norris .02 .10
389 Bob Bailor .02 .10
390 Ernie Whitt .02 .10
391 Otto Velez .02 .10
392 Roy Howell .02 .10
393 Bob Walk RC .20 .50
394 Doug Flynn .02 .10
395 Pete Falcone .02 .10
396 Tom Hausman .02 .10
397 Elliott Maddox .02 .10
398 Mike Squires .02 .10
399 Marvis Foley RC .02 .10
400 Steve Trout .02 .10
401 Wayne Nordhagen .02 .10
402 Tony LaRussa MG .08 .25
403 Bruce Bochte .02 .10
404 Bake McBride .08 .25
405 Jerry Narron .02 .10
406 Rob Dressler .02 .10
407 Dave Heaverlo .02 .10
408 Tom Paciorek .02 .10
409 Carney Lansford .08 .25
410 Brian Downing .08 .25
411 Don Aase .02 .10
412 Jim Barr .02 .10
413 Don Baylor .08 .25
414 Jim Fregosi MG .02 .10
415 Dallas Green MG .02 .10
416 Dave Lopes .08 .25
417 Jerry Reuss .08 .25
418 Rick Sutcliffe .08 .25
419 Derrel Thomas .02 .10
420 Tom Lasorda MG .20 .50
421 Charlie Leibrandt RC .20 .50
422 Tom Seaver .40 1.00
423 Ron Oester .02 .10
424 Junior Kennedy .02 .10
425 Tom Seaver .40 1.00
426 Bobby Cox MG .08 .25
427 Leon Durham RC .08 .25
428 Terry Kennedy .02 .10
429 Silvio Martinez .02 .10
430 George Hendrick .08 .25
431 Red Schoendienst MG .20 .50
432 Johnnie LeMaster .02 .10
433 Vida Blue .08 .25
434 John Montefusco .02 .10
435 Terry Whitfield .02 .10
436 Dave Bristol MG .02 .10
437 Dale Murphy .20 .50
438 Jerry Dybzinski RC .02 .10
439 Jorge Orta .02 .10
440 Wayne Garland .02 .10
441 Miguel Dilone .02 .10
442 Dave Garcia MG .02 .10
443 Don Money .02 .10
444A Buck Martinez P1 ERR .08 .25
444B Buck Martinez P2 COR .02 .10
445 Jerry Augustine .02 .10
446 Ben Oglivie .08 .25
447 Jim Slaton .02 .10
448 Doyle Alexander .02 .10
449 Tony Bernazard .02 .10
450 Scott Sanderson .02 .10
451 David Palmer .02 .10
452 Stan Bahnsen .02 .10
453 Dick Williams MG .02 .10
454 Rick Burleson .02 .10
455 Gary Allenson .02 .10
456 Bob Stanley .02 .10
457A John Tudor ERR .40 1.00
457B John Tudor RC .40 1.00
458 Dwight Evans .20 .50
459 Glenn Hubbard .02 .10
460 U.L. Washington .02 .10
461 Larry Gura .02 .10
462 Rich Gale .02 .10
463 Hal McRae .08 .25
464 Jim Frey MG RC .02 .10
465 Bucky Dent .08 .25
466 Dennis Werth RC .02 .10
467 Ron Davis .02 .10
468 Reggie Jackson .40 1.00
469 Bobby Brown .02 .10
470 Mike Davis RC .20 .50
471 Gaylord Perry .08 .25
472 Mark Belanger .02 .10
473 Jim Palmer .20 .50
474 Sammy Stewart .02 .10
475 Tim Stoddard .02 .10
476 Steve Stone .02 .10
477 Jeff Newman .02 .10
478 Steve McCatty .02 .10
479 Billy Martin MG .20 .50
480 Mitchell Page .02 .10
481 Steve Carlton CY .08 .25
482 Bill Buckner .08 .25
483A Ivan DeJesus P1 ERR .08 .25
483B Ivan DeJesus P2 COR .02 .10
484 Cliff Johnson .02 .10
485 Lenny Randle .02 .10
486 Larry Milbourne .02 .10
487 Roy Smalley .02 .10
488 John Castino .02 .10
489 Ron Jackson .02 .10
490A Dave Roberts P1 .08 .25
490B Dave Roberts P2 .02 .10
491 George Brett MVP .60 1.50
492 Mike Cubbage .02 .10
493 Rob Wilfong .02 .10
494 Danny Goodwin .02 .10
495 Jose Morales .02 .10
496 Mickey Rivers .02 .10
497 Mike Edwards .02 .10
498 Mike Sadek .02 .10
499 Lenn Sakata .02 .10
500 Gene Michael MG .02 .10
501 Dave Roberts .02 .10
502 Steve Dillard .02 .10
503 Jim Essian .02 .10
504 Rance Mulliniks .02 .10
505 Darrell Porter .02 .10
506 Joe Torre MG .08 .25
507 Terry Crowley .02 .10
508 Bill Travers .02 .10
509 Nelson Norman .02 .10
510 Bob McClure .02 .10
511 Steve Howe RC .20 .50
512 Dave Rader .02 .10
513 Mick Kelleher .02 .10
514 Kiko Garcia .02 .10
515 Larry Biittner .02 .10
516A Willie Norwood P1 .08 .25
516B Willie Norwood P2 .02 .10
517 Bo Diaz .02 .10
518 Juan Beniquez .02 .10
519 Scot Thompson .02 .10
520 Jim Tracy RC .40 1.00
521 Carlos Lezcano RC .02 .10
522 Joe Amalfitano MG .02 .10
523 Preston Hanna .02 .10
524A Ray Burris P1 .08 .25
524B Ray Burris P2 .02 .10
525 Broderick Perkins .02 .10
526 Mickey Hatcher .02 .10
527 John Goryl MG .02 .10
528 Dick Davis .02 .10
529 Butch Wynegar .02 .10
530 Sal Butera RC .02 .10
531 Jerry Koosman .08 .25
532A Geoff Zahn P1 .08 .25
532B Geoff Zahn P2 .02 .10
533 Dennis Martinez .08 .25
534 Gary Thomasson .02 .10
535 Steve Macko .02 .10
536 Jim Kaat .08 .25
537 G.Brett/R.Carew .60 1.50
538 Tim Raines RC 1.00 2.50
539 Keith Smith .02 .10
540 Ken Macha .02 .10
541 Burt Hooton .02 .10
542 Butch Hobson .02 .10
543 Bill Stein .02 .10
544 Dave Stapleton RC .02 .10
545 Bob Pate RC .02 .10
546 Doug Corbett RC .02 .10
547 Darrell Jackson .02 .10
548 Pete Redfern .02 .10
549 Roger Erickson .02 .10
550 Al Hrabosky .08 .25
551 Dick Tidrow .02 .10
552 Dave Ford .02 .10
553 Dave Kingman .08 .25
554A Mike Vail P1 .08 .25
554B Mike Vail P2 .02 .10
555A Jerry Martin P1 .02 .10
555B Jerry Martin P2 .02 .10
556A Jesus Figueroa P1 .08 .25
556B Jesus Figueroa P2 RC .02 .10
557 Don Stanhouse .02 .10
558 Barry Foote .02 .10
559 Tim Blackwell .02 .10
560 Bruce Sutter .20 .50
561 Rick Reuschel .08 .25
562 Lynn McGlothen .02 .10
563A Bob Owchinko P1 .08 .25
563B Bob Owchinko P2 .02 .10
564 John Verhoeven .02 .10
565 Ken Landreaux .02 .10
566A Glen Adams P1 ERR .08 .25
566B Glenn Adams P2 COR .02 .10
567 Hosken Powell .02 .10
568 Dick Noles .02 .10
569 Danny Ainge RC 1.25 3.00
570 Bobby Mattick MG RC .02 .10
571 Joe Lefebvre RC .02 .10
572 Bobby Clark .02 .10
573 Dennis Lamp .02 .10
574 Randy Lerch .02 .10
575 Mookie Wilson RC 1.25 3.00
576 Ron LeFlore .08 .25
577 Jim Dwyer .02 .10
578 Bill Castro .02 .10
579 Greg Minton .02 .10
580 Mark Littell .02 .10
581 Andy Hassler .02 .10
582 Dave Stieb .08 .25
583 Ken Oberkfell .02 .10
584 Larry Bradford .02 .10
585 Fred Stanley .02 .10
586 Bill Caudill .02 .10
587 Doug Capilla .02 .10
588 George Riley RC .02 .10
589 Willie Hernandez .02 .10
590 Mike Schmidt MVP 1.00 2.50
591 Steve Stone CY .02 .10
592 Rick Sofield .02 .10
593 Bombo Rivera .02 .10
594 Gary Ward .02 .10
595A Dave Edwards P1 .08 .25
595B Dave Edwards P2 .02 .10
596 Mike Proly .02 .10
597 Tommy Boggs .02 .10
598 Greg Gross .02 .10
599 Elias Sosa .02 .10
600 Pat Kelly .02 .10
601A Checklist 1-120 P1 .08 .25
601B Checklist 1-120 P2 .20 .50
602 Checklist 121-240 NNO .08 .25
603A Checklist 241-360 P1 .08 .25
603B Checklist 241-360 P2 .08 .25
604A Checklist 361-480 P1 .08 .25
604B Checklist 361-480 P2 .08 .25
605A Checklist 481-600 P1 .08 .25
605B Checklist 481-600 P2 .08 .25

1982 Donruss

The 1982 Donruss set contains 653 numbered standard-size cards and seven unnumbered checklists. The first 26 cards of this set are entitled Diamond Kings (DK) and feature the artwork of Dick Perez of Perez-Steele Galleries. The set was marketed with puzzle pieces in 15-card packs rather than with bubble gum. Those 15-card packs with an 30 cent SRP were issued 36 packs to a box and 20 boxes to a case. There are 63 pieces to the puzzle, which, when put together, make a collage of Babe Ruth entitled "Hall of Fame Diamond King." The card stock in this year's Donruss cards is considerably thicker than the 1981 cards. The seven unnumbered checklist cards are arbitrarily assigned numbers 654 through 660 and are listed at the end of the list below. Notable Rookie Cards in this set include Brett Butler, Cal Ripken Jr., Lee Smith and Dave Stewart.

COMPLETE SET (660) 20.00 50.00
COMP.FACT.SET (660) 20.00 50.00
COMP.RUTH PUZZLE 5.00 10.00
1 Pete Rose DK 1.00 2.50
2 Gary Carter DK .07 .20
3 Steve Garvey DK .07 .20
4 Vida Blue DK .07 .20
5 Alan Trammell DK COR .07 .20
5A Alan Trammel DK ERR Name misspelled .07 .20
6 Len Barker DK .02 .10
7 Dwight Evans DK .15 .40
8 Rod Carew DK .15 .40
9 George Hendrick DK .07 .20
10 Phil Niekro DK .07 .20
11 Richie Zisk DK .02 .10
12 Dave Parker DK .07 .20
13 Nolan Ryan DK 1.50 4.00
14 Ivan DeJesus DK .02 .10
15 George Brett DK .75 2.00
16 Tom Seaver DK .15 .40
17 Dave Kingman DK .07 .20
18 Dave Winfield DK .07 .20
19 Mike Norris DK .02 .10
20 Carlton Fisk DK .15 .40
21 Ozzie Smith DK .60 1.50
22 Roy Smalley DK .02 .10
23 Buddy Bell DK .07 .20
24 Ken Singleton DK .07 .20
25 John Mayberry DK .02 .10
26 Gorman Thomas DK .07 .20
27 Earl Weaver MG .07 .20
28 Rollie Fingers .07 .20
29 Sparky Anderson MG .07 .20
30 Dennis Eckersley .15 .40
31 Dave Winfield .07 .20
32 Burt Hooton .02 .10
33 Rick Waits .02 .10
34 George Brett .75 2.00
35 Steve McCatty .02 .10
36 Steve Rogers .07 .20
37 Bill Stein .02 .10
38 Steve Renko .02 .10
39 Mike Squires .02 .10
40 George Hendrick .07 .20
41 Bob Knepper .02 .10
42 Steve Carlton .15 .40
43 Larry Biittner .02 .10
44 Chris Welsh .02 .10
45 Steve Nicosia .02 .10
46 Jack Clark .07 .20
47 Chris Chambliss .07 .20
48 Ivan DeJesus .02 .10
49 Lee Mazzilli .07 .20
50 Julio Cruz .02 .10
51 Pete Redfern .02 .10
52 Dave Stieb .07 .20
53 Doug Corbett .02 .10
54 Jorge Bell RC George Bell .40 1.00
55 Joe Simpson .02 .10
56 Rusty Staub .07 .20
57 Hector Cruz .02 .10
58 Claudell Washington .02 .10
59 Enrique Romo .02 .10
60 Gary Lavelle .02 .10
61 Tim Flannery .02 .10
62 Joe Nolan .02 .10
63 Larry Bowa .07 .20
64 Sixto Lezcano .02 .10
65 Joe Sambito .02 .10
66 Bruce Kison .02 .10
67 Wayne Nordhagen .02 .10
68 Woodie Fryman .02 .10
69 Billy Sample .02 .10
70 Amos Otis .07 .20
71 Matt Keough .02 .10
72 Toby Harrah .07 .20
73 Dave Righetti RC .60 1.50
74 Carl Yastrzemski .50 1.25
75 Bob Welch .07 .20
76 Alan Trammell COR .07 .20
76A Alan Trammel ERR Name misspelled .07 .20
77 Rick Dempsey .02 .10
78 Paul Molitor .07 .20
79 Dennis Martinez .07 .20
80 Jim Slaton .02 .10
81 Champ Summers .02 .10
82 Carney Lansford .07 .20
83 Barry Foote .02 .10
84 Steve Garvey .07 .20
85 Rick Manning .02 .10
86 John Wathan .02 .10
87 Brian Kingman .02 .10
88 Andre Dawson UER Middle name Fernando should be Nolan .07 .20
89 Jim Kern .02 .10
90 Bobby Grich .07 .20
91 Bob Forsch .02 .10
92 Art Howe .02 .10
93 Marty Bystrom .02 .10
94 Ozzie Smith .60 1.50
95 Dave Parker .07 .20
96 Doyle Alexander .02 .10
97 Al Hrabosky .02 .10
98 Frank Taveras .02 .10
99 Tim Blackwell .02 .10
100 Floyd Bannister .02 .10
101 Alfredo Griffin .02 .10
102 Dave Engle .02 .10
103 Mario Soto .07 .20
104 Ross Baumgarten .02 .10
105 Ken Singleton .07 .20
106 Ted Simmons .07 .20
107 Jack Morris .07 .20
108 Bob Watson .02 .10
109 Dwight Evans .15 .40
110 Tom Lasorda MG .15 .40
111 Bert Blyleven .07 .20
112 Dan Quisenberry .02 .10
113 Rickey Henderson 1.00 2.50
114 Gary Carter .07 .20
115 Brian Downing .07 .20
116 Al Oliver .07 .20
117 LaMarr Hoyt .02 .10
118 Cesar Cedeno .07 .20
119 Keith Moreland .02 .10
120 Bob Shirley .02 .10
121 Terry Kennedy .02 .10
122 Frank Pastore .02 .10
123 Gene Garber .02 .10
124 Tony Pena .07 .20
125 Allen Ripley .02 .10
126 Randy Martz .02 .10
127 Richie Zisk .02 .10
128 Mike Scott .07 .20
129 Lloyd Moseby .02 .10
130 Rob Wilfong .02 .10
131 Tim Stoddard .02 .10
132 Gorman Thomas .07 .20
133 Dan Petry .02 .10
134 Bob Stanley .02 .10
135 Lou Piniella .07 .20
136 Pedro Guerrero .07 .20
137 Len Barker .02 .10
138 Rich Gale .02 .10
139 Wayne Gross .02 .10
140 Tim Wallach RC .40 1.00
141 Gene Mauch MG .02 .10
142 Doc Medich .02 .10

143 Tony Bernazard .02 .10
144 Bill Virdon MG .02 .10
145 John Littlefield .02 .10
146 Dave Bergman .02 .10
147 Dick Davis .02 .10
148 Tom Seaver .30 .75
149 Matt Sinatro .02 .10
150 Chuck Tanner MG .02 .10
151 Leon Durham .02 .10
152 Gene Tenace .07 .20
153 Al Bumbry .02 .10
154 Mark Brouhard .02 .10
155 Rick Peters .02 .10
156 Jerry Remy .02 .10
157 Rick Reuschel .07 .20
158 Steve Howe .02 .10
159 Alan Bannister .02 .10
160 U.L. Washington .02 .10
161 Rick Langford .02 .10
162 Bill Gullickson .02 .10
163 Mark Wagner .02 .10
164 Geoff Zahn .02 .10
165 Ron LeFlore .07 .20
166 Dane Iorg .02 .10
167 Joe Niekro .02 .10
168 Pete Rose 1.00 2.50
169 Dave Collins .02 .10
170 Rick Wise .02 .10
171 Jim Bibby .02 .10
172 Larry Herndon .02 .10
173 Bob Horner .07 .20
174 Steve Dillard .02 .10
175 Mookie Wilson .07 .20
176 Dan Meyer .02 .10
177 Fernando Arroyo .02 .10
178 Jackson Todd .02 .10
179 Darrell Jackson .02 .10
180 Alvis Woods .02 .10
181 Jim Anderson .02 .10
182 Dave Kingman .07 .20
183 Steve Henderson .02 .10
184 Brian Asselstine .02 .10
185 Rod Scurry .02 .10
186 Fred Breining .02 .10
187 Danny Boone .02 .10
188 Junior Kennedy .02 .10
189 Sparky Lyle .07 .20
190 Whitey Herzog MG .07 .20
191 Dave Smith .02 .10
192 Ed Ott .02 .10
193 Greg Luzinski .07 .20
194 Bill Lee .07 .20
195 Don Zimmer MG .07 .20
196 Hal McRae .07 .20
197 Mike Norris .02 .10
198 Duane Kuiper .02 .10
199 Rick Cerone .02 .10
200 Jim Rice .07 .20
201 Steve Yeager .07 .20
202 Tom Brookens .07 .20
203 Jose Morales .02 .10
204 Roy Howell .02 .10
205 Tippy Martinez .02 .10
206 Moose Haas .02 .10
207 Al Cowens .02 .10
208 Dave Stapleton .02 .10
209 Bucky Dent .07 .20
210 Ron Cey .07 .20
211 Jorge Orta .02 .10
212 Jamie Quirk .02 .10
213 Jeff Jones .02 .10
214 Tim Raines .15 .40
215 Jon Matlack .02 .10
216 Rod Carew .15 .40
217 Jim Kaat .07 .20
218 Joe Pittman .02 .10
219 Larry Christenson .02 .10
220 Juan Bonilla RC .05 .15
221 Mike Easler .02 .10
222 Vida Blue .07 .20
223 Rick Camp .02 .10
224 Mike Jorgensen .02 .10
225 Jody Davis RC .02 .10
226 Mike Parrott .02 .10
227 Jim Clancy .02 .10
228 Hosken Powell .02 .10
229 Tom Hume .02 .10
230 Britt Burns .02 .10
231 Jim Palmer .07 .20
232 Bob Rodgers MG .02 .10
233 Milt Wilcox .02 .10
234 Dave Revering .02 .10
235 Mike Torrez .02 .10
236 Robert Castillo .02 .10
237 Von Hayes RC .20 .50
238 Renie Martin .02 .10
239 Dwayne Murphy .02 .10
240 Rodney Scott .02 .10
241 Fred Patek .02 .10
242 Mickey Rivers .02 .10
243 Steve Trout .02 .10
244 Jose Cruz .07 .20
245 Manny Trillo .02 .10
246 Lary Sorensen .02 .10
247 Dave Edwards .02 .10
248 Dan Driessen .02 .10
249 Tommy Boggs .02 .10
250 Dale Berra .02 .10
251 Ed Whitson .02 .10
252 Lee Smith RC .75 2.00
253 Tom Paciorek .02 .10
254 Pat Zachry .02 .10
255 Luis Leal .02 .10
256 John Castino .02 .10
257 Rich Dauer .02 .10
258 Cecil Cooper .07 .20
259 Dave Rozema .02 .10
260 John Tudor .07 .20
261 Jerry Mumphrey .02 .10
262 Jay Johnstone .02 .10
263 Bo Diaz .02 .10
264 Dennis Leonard .02 .10
265 Jim Spencer .02 .10
266 John Milner .02 .10
267 Don Aase .02 .10
268 Jim Sundberg .07 .20
269 Lamar Johnson .02 .10
270 Frank LaCorte .02 .10
271 Barry Evans .02 .10
272 Enos Cabell .02 .10
273 Del Unser .02 .10
274 George Foster .07 .20
275 Brett Butler RC .40 1.00
276 Lee Lacy .02 .10
277 Ken Reitz .02 .10
278 Keith Hernandez .07 .20
279 Doug DeCinces .02 .10
280 Charlie Moore .02 .10
281 Lance Parrish .07 .20
282 Ralph Houk MG .02 .10
283 Rich Gossage .07 .20
284 Jerry Reuss .02 .10
285 Mike Stanton .02 .10
286 Frank White .07 .20
287 Bob Owchinko .02 .10
288 Scott Sanderson .02 .10
289 Bump Wills .02 .10
290 Dave Frost .02 .10
291 Chet Lemon .07 .20
292 Tito Landrum .02 .10
293 Vern Ruhle .02 .10
294 Mike Schmidt .75 2.00
295 Sam Mejias .02 .10
296 Gary Lucas .02 .10
297 John Candelaria .02 .10
298 Jerry Martin .02 .10
299 Dale Murphy .15 .40
300 Mike Lum .02 .10
301 Tom Hausman .02 .10
302 Glenn Abbott .02 .10
303 Roger Erickson .02 .10
304 Otto Velez .02 .10
305 Danny Goodwin .02 .10
306 John Mayberry .02 .10
307 Lenny Randle .02 .10
308 Bob Bailor .02 .10
309 Jerry Morales .02 .10
310 Rufino Linares .02 .10
311 Kent Tekulve .02 .10
312 Joe Morgan .07 .20
313 John Urrea .02 .10
314 Paul Householder .02 .10
315 Garry Maddox .02 .10
316 Mike Ramsey .02 .10
317 Alan Ashby .02 .10
318 Bob Clark .02 .10
319 Tony LaRussa MG .07 .20
320 Charlie Lea .02 .10
321 Danny Darwin .02 .10
322 Cesar Geronimo .02 .10
323 Tom Underwood .02 .10
324 Andre Thornton .02 .10
325 Rudy May .02 .10
326 Frank Tanana .07 .20
327 Dave Lopes .07 .20
328 Richie Hebner .02 .10
329 Mike Flanagan .02 .10
330 Mike Caldwell .02 .10
331 Scott McGregor .02 .10
332 Jerry Augustine .02 .10
333 Stan Papi .02 .10
334 Rick Miller .02 .10
335 Graig Nettles .07 .20
336 Dusty Baker .07 .20
337 Dave Garcia MG .02 .10
338 Larry Gura .02 .10
339 Cliff Johnson .02 .10
340 Warren Cromartie .02 .10
341 Steve Comer .02 .10
342 Rick Burleson .02 .10
343 John Martin RC .05 .15
344 Craig Reynolds .02 .10
345 Mike Proly .02 .10
346 Ruppert Jones .02 .10
347 Omar Moreno .02 .10
348 Greg Minton .02 .10
349 Rick Mahler .02 .10
350 Alex Trevino .02 .10
351 Mike Krukow .02 .10
352A Shane Rawley ERR .15 .40
Photo actually
Jim Anderson
352B Shane Rawley COR .02 .10
353 Garth Iorg .02 .10
354 Pete Mackanin .02 .10
355 Paul Moskau .02 .10
356 Richard Dotson .02 .10
357 Steve Stone .02 .10
358 Larry Hisle .02 .10
359 Aurelio Lopez .02 .10
360 Oscar Gamble .02 .10
361 Tom Burgmeier .02 .10
362 Terry Forster .07 .20
363 Joe Charboneau .07 .20
364 Ken Brett .02 .10
365 Tony Armas .07 .20
366 Chris Speier .02 .10
367 Fred Lynn .07 .20
368 Buddy Bell .07 .20
369 Jim Essian .02 .10
370 Terry Puhl .02 .10
371 Greg Gross .02 .10
372 Bruce Sutter .15 .40
373 Joe Lefebvre .02 .10
374 Ray Knight .07 .20
375 Bruce Benedict .02 .10
376 Tim Foli .02 .10
377 Al Holland .02 .10
378 Ken Kravec .02 .10
379 Jeff Burroughs .02 .10
380 Pete Falcone .02 .10
381 Ernie Whitt .02 .10
382 Brad Havens .02 .10
383 Terry Crowley .02 .10
384 Don Money .07 .20
385 Dan Schatzeder .02 .10
386 Gary Allenson .02 .10
387 Yogi Berra CO .30 .75
388 Ken Landreaux .02 .10
389 Mike Hargrove .02 .10
390 Darryl Motley .02 .10
391 Dave McKay .02 .10
392 Stan Bahnsen .02 .10
393 Ken Forsch .02 .10
394 Mario Mendoza .02 .10
395 Jim Morrison .02 .10
396 Mike Ivie .02 .10
397 Broderick Perkins .02 .10
398 Darrell Evans .07 .20
399 Ron Reed .02 .10
400 Johnny Bench .30 .75
401 Steve Bedrosian RC .20 .50
402 Bill Robinson .02 .10
403 Bill Buckner .07 .20
404 Ken Oberkfell .02 .10
405 Cal Ripken RC 10.00 25.00
406 Jim Gantner .02 .10
407 Kirk Gibson .30 .75
408 Tony Perez .15 .40
409 Tommy John UER .07 .20
Text says 52-56 as
Yankee, should be
52-26
410 Dave Stewart RC .60 1.50
411 Dan Spillner .02 .10
412 Willie Aikens .02 .10
413 Mike Heath .02 .10
414 Ray Burris .02 .10
415 Leon Roberts .02 .10
416 Mike Witt .20 .50
417 Bob Molinaro .02 .10
418 Steve Braun .02 .10
419 Nolan Ryan UER 1.50 4.00
420 Tug McGraw .07 .20
421 Dave Concepcion .07 .20
422A Juan Eichelberger .15 .40
ERR Photo actually
Gary Lucas
422B Juan Eichelberger .02 .10
COR
423 Rick Rhoden .02 .10
424 Frank Robinson MG .15 .40
425 Eddie Miller .02 .10
426 Bill Caudill .02 .10
427 Doug Flynn .02 .10
428 Larry Andersen UER .02 .10
Misspelled Anderson
on card front
429 Al Williams .02 .10
430 Jerry Garvin .02 .10
431 Glenn Adams .02 .10
432 Barry Bonnell .02 .10
433 Jerry Narron .02 .10
434 John Stearns .02 .10
435 Mike Tyson .02 .10
436 Glenn Hubbard .02 .10
437 Eddie Solomon .02 .10
438 Jeff Leonard .02 .10
439 Randy Bass .20 .50
440 Mike LaCoss .02 .10
441 Gary Matthews .07 .20
442 Mark Littell .02 .10
443 Don Sutton .07 .20
444 John Harris .02 .10
445 Vada Pinson CO .07 .20
446 Elias Sosa .02 .10
447 Charlie Hough .07 .20
448 Willie Wilson .07 .20
449 Fred Stanley .02 .10
450 Tom Veryzer .02 .10
451 Ron Davis .02 .10
452 Mark Clear .02 .10
453 Bill Russell .07 .20
454 Lou Whitaker .07 .20
455 Dan Graham .02 .10
456 Reggie Cleveland .02 .10
457 Sammy Stewart .02 .10
458 Pete Vuckovich .02 .10
459 John Wockenfuss .02 .10
460 Glenn Hoffman .02 .10
461 Willie Randolph .07 .20
462 Fernando Valenzuela .30 .75
463 Ron Hassey .02 .10
464 Paul Splittorff .02 .10
465 Rob Picciolo .02 .10
466 Larry Parrish .07 .20
467 Johnny Grubb .02 .10
468 Dan Ford .02 .10
469 Silvio Martinez .02 .10
470 Kiko Garcia .02 .10
471 Bob Boone .07 .20
472 Luis Salazar .02 .10
473 Randy Niemann UER .02 .10
Card says Pirate, but in an Astro uniform
474 Tom Griffin .02 .10
475 Phil Niekro .07 .20
476 Hubie Brooks .02 .10
477 Dick Tidrow .02 .10
478 Jim Beattie .02 .10
479 Damaso Garcia .02 .10
480 Mickey Hatcher .02 .10
481 Joe Price .02 .10
482 Ed Farmer .02 .10
483 Eddie Murray .30 .75
484 Ben Oglivie .07 .20
485 Kevin Saucier .02 .10
486 Bobby Murcer .07 .20
487 Bill Campbell .02 .10
488 Reggie Smith .07 .20
489 Wayne Garland .02 .10
490 Jim Wright .02 .10
491 Billy Martin MG .15 .40
492 Jim Fanning MG .02 .10
493 Don Baylor .07 .20
494 Rick Honeycutt .02 .10
495 Carlton Fisk .15 .40
496 Denny Walling .02 .10
497 Bake McBride .07 .20
498 Darrell Porter .02 .10
499 Gene Richards .02 .10
500 Ron Oester .02 .10
501 Ken Dayley .02 .10
502 Jason Thompson .02 .10
503 Milt May .02 .10
504 Doug Bird .02 .10
505 Bruce Bochte .02 .10
506 Neil Allen .02 .10
507 Joey McLaughlin .02 .10
508 Butch Wynegar .02 .10
509 Gary Roenicke .02 .10
510 Robin Yount .50 1.25
511 Dave Tobik .02 .10
512 Rich Gedman .20 .50
513 Gene Nelson .02 .10
514 Rick Monday .07 .20
515 Miguel Dilone .02 .10
516 Clint Hurdle .02 .10
517 Jeff Newman .02 .10
518 Grant Jackson .02 .10
519 Andy Hassler .02 .10
520 Pat Putnam .02 .10
521 Greg Pryor .02 .10
522 Tony Scott .02 .10
523 Steve Mura .02 .10
524 Johnnie LeMaster .02 .10
525 Dick Ruthven .02 .10
526 John McNamara MG .02 .10
527 Larry McWilliams .02 .10
528 Johnny Ray RC .20 .50
529 Pat Tabler .02 .10
530 Tom Herr .02 .10
531A San Diego Chicken .40 1.00
ERR Without TM
531B San Diego Chicken .40 1.00
COR With TM
532 Sal Butera .02 .10
533 Mike Griffin .02 .10
534 Kelvin Moore .02 .10
535 Reggie Jackson .15 .40
536 Ed Romero .02 .10
537 Derrel Thomas .02 .10
538 Mike O'Berry .02 .10
539 Jack O'Connor .02 .10
540 Bob Ojeda RC .20 .50
541 Roy Lee Jackson .02 .10
542 Lynn Jones .02 .10
543 Gaylord Perry .07 .20
544A Phil Garner ERR .07 .20
Reverse negative
544B Phil Garner COR .07 .20
545 Garry Templeton .07 .20
546 Rafael Ramirez .02 .10
547 Jeff Reardon .07 .20
548 Ron Guidry .07 .20
549 Tim Laudner .02 .10
550 John Henry Johnson .02 .10
551 Chris Bando .02 .10
552 Bobby Brown .02 .10
553 Larry Bradford .02 .10
554 Scott Fletcher RC .20 .50
555 Jerry Royster .02 .10
556 Shooty Babitt UER .02 .10
Spelled Babbitt
on front
557 Kent Hrbek RC .40 1.00
558 Ron Guidry .07 .20
Tommy John
559 Mark Bomback .02 .10
560 Julio Valdez .02 .10
561 Buck Martinez .02 .10
562 Mike A. Marshall RC .20 .50
563 Rennie Stennett .02 .10
564 Steve Crawford .02 .10
565 Bob Babcock .02 .10
566 Johnny Podres CO .07 .20
567 Paul Serna .02 .10
568 Harold Baines .07 .20
569 Dave LaRoche .02 .10
570 Lee May .07 .20
571 Gary Ward .02 .10
572 John Denny .02 .10
573 Roy Smalley .02 .10
574 Bob Brenly RC .40 1.00
575 Reggie Jackson .07 .20
Dave Winfield
576 Luis Pujols .02 .10
577 Butch Hobson .02 .10
578 Harvey Kuenn MG .02 .10
579 Cal Ripken Sr. CO .07 .20
580 Juan Berenguer .02 .10
581 Benny Ayala .02 .10
582 Vance Law .02 .10
583 Rick Leach .02 .10
584 George Frazier .02 .10
585 P.Rose/M.Schmidt .60 1.50
586 Joe Rudi .07 .20
587 Juan Beniquez .02 .10
588 Luis DeLeon .02 .10
589 Craig Swan .02 .10
590 Dave Chalk .02 .10
591 Billy Gardner MG .02 .10
592 Sal Bando .07 .20
593 Bert Campaneris .07 .20
594 Steve Kemp .02 .10
595A Randy Lerch ERR .15 .40
Braves
595B Randy Lerch COR .02 .10
Brewers
596 Bryan Clark RC .05 .15
597 Dave Ford .02 .10
598 Mike Scioscia .07 .20
599 John Lowenstein .02 .10
600 Rene Lachemann MG .02 .10
601 Mick Kelleher .02 .10
602 Ron Jackson .02 .10
603 Jerry Koosman .07 .20
604 Dave Goltz .02 .10
605 Ellis Valentine .02 .10
606 Lonnie Smith .02 .10
607 Joaquin Andujar .07 .20
608 Garry Hancock .02 .10
609 Jerry Turner .02 .10
610 Bob Bonner .02 .10
611 Jim Dwyer .02 .10
612 Terry Bulling .02 .10
613 Joel Youngblood .02 .10
614 Larry Milbourne .02 .10
615 Gene Roof UER .02 .10
Name on front
is Phil Roof
616 Keith Drumwright .02 .10
617 Dave Rosello .02 .10
618 Rickey Keeton .02 .10
619 Dennis Lamp .02 .10
620 Sid Monge .02 .10
621 Jerry White .02 .10
622 Luis Aguayo .02 .10
623 Jamie Easterly .02 .10
624 Steve Sax RC .40 1.00
625 Dave Roberts .02 .10
626 Rick Bosetti .02 .10
627 Terry Francona RC 1.25 3.00
628 Tom Seaver .30 .75
Johnny Bench
629 Paul Mirabella .02 .10
630 Rance Mulliniks .02 .10
631 Kevin Hickey RC .05 .15
632 Reid Nichols .02 .10
633 Dave Geisel .02 .10
634 Ken Griffey .07 .20
635 Bob Lemon MG .15 .40
636 Orlando Sanchez .02 .10
637 Bill Almon .02 .10
638 Danny Ainge .07 .20
639 Willie Stargell .15 .40
640 Bob Sykes .02 .10
641 Ed Lynch .02 .10
642 John Ellis .02 .10
643 Fergie Jenkins .07 .20
644 Lenn Sakata .02 .10
645 Julio Gonzalez .02 .10
646 Jesse Orosco .02 .10
647 Jerry Dybzinski .02 .10
648 Tommy Davis CO .07 .20
649 Ron Gardenhire RC .20 .50
650 Felipe Alou CO .07 .20
651 Harvey Haddix CO .07 .20
652 Willie Upshaw .20 .50
653 Bill Madlock .07 .20
654A DK Checklist 1-26 .15 .40
ERR Unnumbered
With Trammel
654B DK Checklist 1-26 .07 .20
COR Unnumbered
With Trammell
655 Checklist 27-130 .07 .20
Unnumbered
656 Checklist 131-234 .07 .20
Unnumbered
657 Checklist 235-338 .07 .20
Unnumbered
658 Checklist 339-442 .07 .20
Unnumbered
659 Checklist 443-544 .07 .20
Unnumbered
660 Checklist 545-653 .07 .20
Unnumbered

1982 Donruss Babe Ruth Puzzle

1 Ruth Puzzle 1-3 .20 .50
4 Ruth Puzzle 4-6 .20 .50
7 Ruth Puzzle 7-10 .20 .50
10 Ruth Puzzle 10-12 .20 .50
13 Ruth Puzzle 13-15 .20 .50
16 Ruth Puzzle 16-18 .20 .50
19 Ruth Puzzle 19-21 .20 .50
22 Ruth Puzzle 22-24 .20 .50
25 Ruth Puzzle 25-27 .20 .50
28 Ruth Puzzle 28-30 .20 .50
31 Ruth Puzzle 29-31 .20 .50
34 Ruth Puzzle 34-36 .20 .50
37 Ruth Puzzle 37-39 .20 .50
40 Ruth Puzzle 40-42 .20 .50
43 Ruth Puzzle 43-45 .20 .50
46 Ruth Puzzle 46-48 .20 .50
49 Ruth Puzzle 49-51 .20 .50
52 Ruth Puzzle 52-54 .20 .50
55 Ruth Puzzle 55-57 .20 .50
58 Ruth Puzzle 58-60 .20 .50
61 Ruth Puzzle 61-63 .20 .50

1983 Donruss

The 1983 Donruss baseball set leads off with a 26-card Diamond Kings (DK) series. Of the remaining 634 standard-size cards, two are combination cards, one portrays the San Diego Chicken, one shows the completed Ty Cobb puzzle, and seven are unnumbered checklist cards. The seven unnumbered checklist cards are arbitrarily assigned numbers 654 through 660 and are listed at the end of the list below. All cards measure the standard size. Card fronts feature full color photos around a framed white broder. Several printing variations are available but, the complete set price below includes only the more common of each variation pair. Cards were issued in 15-card packs which included a three-piece Ty Cobb puzzle panel (21 different panels were needed to complete the puzzle). Notable Rookie Cards include Wade Boggs, Tony Gwynn and Ryne Sandberg.

COMPLETE SET (660) 25.00 60.00
COMP.FACT.SET (660) 30.00 80.00
COMP.COBB PUZZLE 2.00 5.00
1 Fernando Valenzuela DK .07 .20
2 Rollie Fingers DK .07 .20
3 Reggie Jackson DK .15 .40
4 Jim Palmer DK .07 .20
5 Jack Morris DK .07 .20
6 George Foster DK .07 .20
7 Jim Sundberg DK .07 .20
8 Willie Stargell DK .15 .40
9 Dave Stieb DK .07 .20
10 Joe Niekro DK .02 .10
11 Rickey Henderson DK .60 1.50
12 Dale Murphy DK .15 .40
13 Toby Harrah DK .07 .20
14 Bill Buckner DK .07 .20
15 Willie Wilson DK .07 .20
16 Steve Carlton DK .15 .40
17 Ron Guidry DK .07 .20
18 Steve Rogers DK .07 .20
19 Kent Hrbek DK .07 .20
20 Keith Hernandez DK .07 .20
21 Floyd Bannister DK .02 .10
22 Johnny Bench DK .30 .75
23 Britt Burns DK .02 .10
24 Joe Morgan DK .07 .20
25 Carl Yastrzemski DK .30 .75
26 Terry Kennedy DK .02 .10
27 Gary Roenicke .02 .10
28 Dwight Bernard .02 .10
29 Pat Underwood .02 .10
30 Gary Allenson .02 .10
31 Ron Guidry .07 .20
32 Burt Hooton .02 .10
33 Chris Bando .02 .10
34 Vida Blue .07 .20
35 Rickey Henderson .60 1.50
36 Ray Burris .02 .10
37 John Butcher .02 .10
38 Don Aase .02 .10
39 Jerry Koosman .07 .20
40 Bruce Sutter .15 .40
41 Jose Cruz .07 .20
42 Pete Rose 1.00 2.50
43 Cesar Cedeno .07 .20
44 Floyd Chiffer .02 .10
45 Larry McWilliams .02 .10
46 Alan Fowlkes .02 .10
47 Dale Murphy .15 .40
48 Doug Bird .02 .10
49 Hubie Brooks .02 .10
50 Floyd Bannister .02 .10
51 Jack O'Connor .02 .10
52 Steve Senteney .02 .10
53 Gary Gaetti RC .40 1.00
54 Damaso Garcia .02 .10
55 Gene Nelson .02 .10
56 Mookie Wilson .07 .20
57 Allen Ripley .02 .10
58 Bob Horner .07 .20
59 Tony Pena .02 .10
60 Gary Lavelle .02 .10
61 Tim Lollar .02 .10
62 Frank Pastore .02 .10
63 Garry Maddox .02 .10
64 Bob Forsch .02 .10
65 Harry Spilman .02 .10
66 Geoff Zahn .02
67 Salome Barojas .02
68 David Palmer .02
69 Charlie Hough .07
70 Dan Quisenberry .02
71 Tony Armas .07
72 Rick Sutcliffe .07
73 Steve Balboni .02
74 Jerry Remy .02
75 Mike Scioscia .07
76 John Wockenfuss .02
77 Jim Palmer .07
78 Rollie Fingers .07
79 Joe Nolan .02
80 Pete Vuckovich .02
81 Rick Leach .02
82 Rick Miller .02
83 Graig Nettles .07
84 Ron Cey .07
85 Miguel Dilone .02
86 John Wathan .02
87 Kelvin Moore .02
88A Byrn Smith ERR .07
Sic, Bryn
88B Bryn Smith FDC COR .15
89 Dave Hostetler RC .02
90 Rod Carew .15
91 Lonnie Smith .02
92 Bob Knepper .02
93 Marty Bystrom .02
94 Chris Welsh .02
95 Jason Thompson .02
96 Tom O'Malley .02
97 Phil Niekro .07
98 Neil Allen .02
99 Bill Buckner .07
100 Ed VandeBerg .02
101 Jim Clancy .02
102 Robert Castillo .02
103 Bruce Berenyi .02
104 Carlton Fisk .15
105 Mike Flanagan .02
106 Cecil Cooper .07
107 Jack Morris .07
108 Mike Morgan .02
109 Luis Aponte .02
110 Pedro Guerrero .07
111 Len Barker .02
112 Willie Wilson .07
113 Dave Beard .02
114 Mike Gates .02
115 Reggie Jackson .15
116 George Wright RC .20
117 Vance Law .02
118 Nolan Ryan 1.50 4.0
119 Mike Krukow .02
120 Ozzie Smith .50 1.2
121 Broderick Perkins .02
122 Tom Seaver .30
123 Chris Chambliss .07
124 Chuck Tanner MG .02
125 Johnnie LeMaster .02
126 Mel Hall RC .20
127 Bruce Bochte .02
128 Charlie Puleo .02
129 Luis Leal .02
130 John Pacella .02
131 Glenn Gulliver .02
132 Don Money .02
133 Dave Rozema .02
134 Bruce Hurst .02
135 Rudy May .02
136 Tom Lasorda MG .15
137 Dan Spillner UER .02
Photo actually
Ed Whitson
138 Jerry Martin .02
139 Mike Norris .02
140 Al Oliver .07
141 Daryl Sconiers .02
142 Lamar Johnson .02
143 Harold Baines .07
144 Alan Ashby .02
145 Garry Templeton .07
146 Al Holland .02
147 Bo Diaz .02
148 Dave Concepcion .07
149 Rick Camp .02
150 Jim Morrison .02
151 Randy Martz .02
152 Keith Hernandez .07
153 John Lowenstein .02
154 Mike Caldwell .02
155 Milt Wilcox .02
156 Rich Gedman .02
157 Rich Gossage .07
158 Jerry Reuss .02
159 Ron Hassey .02
160 Larry Gura .02
161 Dwayne Murphy .02
162 Woodie Fryman .02
163 Steve Comer .02
164 Ken Forsch .02
165 Dennis Lamp .02
166 David Green RC .20
167 Terry Puhl .02
168 Mike Schmidt .75 2.
169 Eddie Milner .02
170 John Curtis .02
171 Don Robinson .02
172 Rich Gale .02
173 Steve Bedrosian .02
174 Willie Hernandez .02

175 Ron Gardenhire .02 .10
176 Jim Beattie .02 .10
177 Tim Laudner .02 .10
178 Buck Martinez .02 .10
179 Kent Hrbek .07 .20
180 Alfredo Griffin .02 .10
181 Larry Andersen .02 .10
182 Pete Falcone .02 .10
183 Jody Davis .02 .10
184 Glenn Hubbard .02 .10
185 Dale Berra .02 .10
186 Greg Minton .02 .10
187 Gary Lucas .02 .10
188 Dave Van Gorder .02 .10
189 Bob Dernier .02 .10
190 Willie McGee RC .60 1.50
191 Dickie Thon .02 .10
192 Bob Boone .07 .20
193 Britt Burns .02 .10
194 Jeff Reardon .07 .20
195 Jon Matlack .02 .10
196 Don Slaught RC .20 .50
197 Fred Stanley .02 .10
198 Rick Manning .02 .10
199 Dave Righetti .07 .20
200 Dave Stapleton .02 .10
201 Steve Yeager .07 .20
202 Enos Cabell .02 .10
203 Sammy Stewart .02 .10
204 Moose Haas .02 .10
205 Lenn Sakata .02 .10
206 Charlie Moore .02 .10
207 Alan Trammell .07 .20
208 Jim Rice .07 .20
209 Roy Smalley .02 .10
210 Bill Russell .07 .20
211 Andre Thornton .02 .10
212 Willie Aikens .02 .10
213 Dave McKay .02 .10
214 Tim Blackwell .02 .10
215 Buddy Bell .07 .20
216 Doug DeCinces .02 .10
217 Tom Herr .02 .10
218 Frank LaCorte .02 .10
219 Steve Carlton .15 .40
220 Terry Kennedy .02 .10
221 Mike Easler .02 .10
222 Jack Clark .07 .20
223 Gene Garber .02 .10
224 Scott Holman .02 .10
225 Mike Proly .02 .10
226 Terry Bulling .02 .10
227 Jerry Garvin .02 .10
228 Ron Davis .02 .10
229 Tom Hume .02 .10
230 Marc Hill .02 .10
231 Dennis Martinez .07 .20
232 Jim Gantner .02 .10
233 Larry Pashnick .02 .10
234 Dave Collins .02 .10
235 Tom Burgmeier .02 .10
236 Ken Landreaux .02 .10
237 John Denny .02 .10
238 Hal McRae .07 .20
239 Matt Keough .02 .10
240 Doug Flynn .02 .10
241 Fred Lynn .07 .20
242 Billy Sample .02 .10
243 Tom Paciorek .02 .10
244 Joe Sambito .02 .10
245 Sid Monge .02 .10
246 Ken Oberkfell .02 .10
247 Joe Pittman UER .02 .10
Photo actually
Juan Eichelberger
248 Mario Soto .07 .20
249 Claudell Washington .02 .10
250 Rick Rhoden .02 .10
251 Darrell Evans .07 .20
252 Steve Henderson .02 .10
253 Manny Castillo .02 .10
254 Craig Swan .02 .10
255 Joey McLaughlin .02 .10
256 Pete Redfern .02 .10
257 Ken Singleton .07 .20
258 Robin Yount .50 1.25
259 Elias Sosa .02 .10
260 Bob Ojeda .02 .10
261 Bobby Murcer .07 .20
262 Candy Maldonado RC .20 .50
263 Rick Waits .02 .10
264 Greg Pryor .02 .10
265 Bob Owchinko .02 .10
266 Chris Speier .02 .10
267 Bruce Kison .02 .10
268 Mark Wagner .02 .10
269 Steve Kemp .02 .10
270 Phil Garner .07 .20
271 Gene Richards .02 .10
272 Renie Martin .02 .10
273 Dave Roberts .02 .10
274 Dan Driessen .02 .10
275 Rufino Linares .02 .10
276 Lee Lacy .02 .10
277 Ryne Sandberg RC 6.00 15.00
278 Darrell Porter .02 .10
279 Cal Ripken 4.00 10.00
280 Jamie Easterly .02 .10
281 Bill Fahey .02 .10
282 Glenn Hoffman .02 .10
283 Willie Randolph .07 .20
284 Fernando Valenzuela .07 .20
285 Alan Bannister .02 .10
286 Paul Splittorff .02 .10
287 Joe Rudi .07 .20
288 Bill Gullickson .02 .10
289 Danny Darwin .02 .10
290 Andy Hassler .02 .10
291 Ernesto Escarrega .02 .10
292 Steve Mura .02 .10
293 Tony Scott .02 .10
294 Manny Trillo .02 .10
295 Greg Harris .02 .10
296 Luis DeLeon .02 .10
297 Kent Tekulve .02 .10
298 Atlee Hammaker .02 .10
299 Bruce Benedict .02 .10
300 Fergie Jenkins .07 .20
301 Dave Kingman .07 .20
302 Bill Caudill .02 .10
303 John Castino .02 .10
304 Ernie Whitt .02 .10
305 Randy Johnson RC .02 .10
306 Garth Iorg .02 .10
307 Gaylord Perry .07 .20
308 Ed Lynch .02 .10
309 Keith Moreland .02 .10
310 Rafael Ramirez .02 .10
311 Bill Madlock .07 .20
312 Milt May .02 .10
313 John Montefusco .02 .10
314 Wayne Krenchicki .02 .10
315 George Vukovich .02 .10
316 Joaquin Andujar .07 .20
317 Craig Reynolds .02 .10
318 Rick Burleson .02 .10
319 Richard Dotson .02 .10
320 Steve Rogers .07 .20
321 Dave Schmidt .02 .10
322 Bud Black RC .20 .50
323 Jeff Burroughs .02 .10
324 Von Hayes .02 .10
325 Butch Wynegar .02 .10
326 Carl Yastrzemski .50 1.25
327 Ron Roenicke .02 .10
328 Howard Johnson RC .40 1.00
329 Rick Dempsey UER .02 .10
Posing as a left-
handed batter
330A Jim Slaton .02 .10
Bio printed
black on white
330B Jim Slaton .07 .20
Bio printed
black on yellow
331 Benny Ayala .02 .10
332 Ted Simmons .07 .20
333 Lou Whitaker .07 .20
334 Chuck Rainey .02 .10
335 Lou Piniella .07 .20
336 Steve Sax .07 .20
337 Toby Harrah .07 .20
338 George Brett .75 2.00
339 Dave Lopes .07 .20
340 Gary Carter .07 .20
341 John Grubb .02 .10
342 Tim Foli .02 .10
343 Jim Kaat .07 .20
344 Mike LaCoss .02 .10
345 Larry Christenson .02 .10
346 Juan Bonilla .02 .10
347 Omar Moreno .02 .10
348 Chili Davis .07 .20
349 Tommy Boggs .02 .10
350 Rusty Staub .07 .20
351 Bump Wills .02 .10
352 Rick Sweet .02 .10
353 Jim Gott RC .20 .50
354 Terry Felton .02 .10
355 Jim Kern .02 .10
356 Bill Almon UER .02 .10
Expos
Mets in 1980,
not Padres
Mets
357 Tippy Martinez .02 .10
358 Roy Howell .02 .10
359 Dan Petry .02 .10
360 Jerry Mumphrey .02 .10
361 Mark Clear .02 .10
362 Mike Marshall .02 .10
363 Lary Sorensen .02 .10
364 Amos Otis .07 .20
365 Rick Langford .02 .10
366 Brad Mills .02 .10
367 Brian Downing .07 .20
368 Mike Richardt .02 .10
369 Aurelio Rodriguez .02 .10
370 Dave Smith .02 .10
371 Tug McGraw .07 .20
372 Doug Bair .02 .10
373 Ruppert Jones .02 .10
374 Alex Trevino .02 .10
375 Ken Dayley .02 .10
376 Rod Scurry .02 .10
377 Bob Brenly .02 .10
378 Scot Thompson .02 .10
379 Julio Cruz .02 .10
380 John Stearns .02 .10
381 Dale Murray .02 .10
382 Frank Viola RC .60 1.50
383 Al Bumbry .02 .10
384 Ben Oglivie .07 .20
385 Dave Tobik .02 .10
386 Bob Stanley .02 .10
387 Andre Robertson .02 .10
388 Jorge Orta .02 .10
389 Ed Whitson .02 .10
390 Don Hood .02 .10
391 Tom Underwood .02 .10
392 Tim Wallach .07 .20
393 Steve Renko .02 .10
394 Mickey Rivers .02 .10
395 Greg Luzinski .07 .20
396 Art Howe .02 .10
397 Alan Wiggins .02 .10
398 Jim Barr .02 .10
399 Ivan DeJesus .02 .10
400 Tom Lawless .02 .10
401 Bob Walk .02 .10
402 Jimmy Smith .02 .10
403 Lee Smith .15 .40
404 George Hendrick .07 .20
405 Eddie Murray .30 .75
406 Marshall Edwards .02 .10
407 Lance Parrish .07 .20
408 Carney Lansford .07 .20
409 Dave Winfield .07 .20
410 Bob Welch .07 .20
411 Larry Milbourne .02 .10
412 Dennis Leonard .02 .10
413 Dan Meyer .02 .10
414 Charlie Lea .02 .10
415 Rick Honeycutt .02 .10
416 Mike Witt .02 .10
417 Steve Trout .02 .10
418 Glenn Brummer .02 .10
419 Denny Walling .02 .10
420 Gary Matthews .02 .10
421 Charlie Leibrandt UER .02 .10
Liebrandt on
front of card
422 Juan Eichelberger UER .02 .10
Photo actually
Joe Pittman
423 Cecilio Guante UER .02 .10
Listed as Matt
on card
424 Bill Laskey .02 .10
425 Jerry Royster .02 .10
426 Dickie Noles .02 .10
427 George Foster .07 .20
428 Mike Moore RC .20 .50
429 Gary Ward .02 .10
430 Barry Bonnell .02 .10
431 Ron Washington RC .10 .25
432 Rance Mulliniks .02 .10
433 Mike Stanton .02 .10
434 Jesse Orosco .02 .10
435 Larry Bowa .07 .20
436 Biff Pocoroba .02 .10
437 Johnny Ray .02 .10
438 Joe Morgan .07 .20
439 Eric Show RC .20 .50
440 Larry Biittner .02 .10
441 Greg Gross .02 .10
442 Gene Tenace .07 .20
443 Danny Heep .02 .10
444 Bobby Clark .02 .10
445 Kevin Hickey .02 .10
446 Scott Sanderson .07 .20
447 Frank Tanana .07 .20
448 Cesar Geronimo .02 .10
449 Jimmy Sexton .02 .10
450 Mike Hargrove .02 .10
451 Doyle Alexander .02 .10
452 Dwight Evans .15 .40
453 Terry Forster .07 .20
454 Tom Brookens .02 .10
455 Rich Dauer .02 .10
456 Rob Picciolo .02 .10
457 Terry Crowley .02 .10
458 Ned Yost .02 .10
459 Kirk Gibson .07 .20
460 Reid Nichols .02 .10
461 Oscar Gamble .02 .10
462 Dusty Baker .07 .20
463 Jack Perconte .02 .10
464 Frank White .07 .20
465 Mickey Klutts .02 .10
466 Warren Cromartie .02 .10
467 Larry Parrish .02 .10
468 Bobby Grich .07 .20
469 Dane Iorg .02 .10
470 Joe Niekro .02 .10
471 Ed Farmer .02 .10
472 Tim Flannery .02 .10
473 Dave Parker .07 .20
474 Jeff Leonard .02 .10
475 Al Hrabosky .02 .10
476 Ron Hodges .02 .10
477 Leon Durham .02 .10
478 Jim Essian .02 .10
479 Roy Lee Jackson .02 .10
480 Brad Havens .02 .10
481 Joe Price .02 .10
482 Tony Bernazard .02 .10
483 Scott McGregor .02 .10
484 Paul Molitor .07 .20
485 Mike Ivie .02 .10
486 Ken Griffey .07 .20
487 Dennis Eckersley .15 .40
488 Steve Garvey .07 .20
489 Mike Fischlin .02 .10
490 U.L. Washington .02 .10
491 Steve McCatty .02 .10
492 Roy Johnson .02 .10
493 Don Baylor .07 .20
494 Bobby Johnson .02 .10
495 Mike Squires .02 .10
496 Bert Roberge .02 .10
497 Dick Ruthven .02 .10
498 Tito Landrum .02 .10
499 Sixto Lezcano .02 .10
500 Johnny Bench .30 .75
501 Larry Whisenton .02 .10
502 Manny Sarmiento .02 .10
503 Fred Breining .02 .10
504 Bill Campbell .02 .10
505 Todd Cruz .02 .10
506 Bob Bailor .02 .10
507 Dave Stieb .07 .20
508 Al Williams .02 .10
509 Dan Ford .02 .10
510 Gorman Thomas .07 .20
511 Chet Lemon .07 .20
512 Mike Torrez .02 .10
513 Shane Rawley .02 .10
514 Mark Belanger .02 .10
515 Rodney Craig .02 .10
516 Onix Concepcion .02 .10
517 Mike Heath .02 .10
518 Andre Dawson UER .07 .20
Middle name Fernando,
should be Nolan
519 Luis Sanchez .02 .10
520 Terry Bogener .02 .10
521 Rudy Law .02 .10
522 Ray Knight .07 .20
523 Joe Lefebvre .02 .10
524 Jim Wohlford .02 .10
525 Julio Franco RC 2.50 6.00
526 Ron Oester .02 .10
527 Rick Mahler .02 .10
528 Steve Nicosia .02 .10
529 Junior Kennedy .02 .10
530A Whitey Herzog MG .07 .20
Bio printed
black on white
530B Whitey Herzog MG .07 .20
Bio printed
black on yellow
531A Don Sutton .07 .20
Blue border
on photo
531B Don Sutton .07 .20
Green border
on photo
532 Mark Brouhard .02 .10
533A Sparky Anderson MG .07 .20
Bio printed
black on white
533B Sparky Anderson MG .07 .20
Bio printed
black on yellow
534 Roger LaFrancois .02 .10
535 George Frazier .02 .10
536 Tom Niedenfuer .02 .10
537 Ed Glynn .02 .10
538 Lee May .02 .10
539 Bob Kearney .02 .10
540 Tim Raines .07 .20
541 Paul Mirabella .02 .10
542 Luis Tiant .07 .20
543 Ron LeFlore .07 .20
544 Dave LaPoint .02 .10
545 Randy Moffitt .02 .10
546 Luis Aguayo .02 .10
547 Brad Lesley .02 .10
548 Luis Salazar .02 .10
549 John Candelaria .02 .10
550 Dave Bergman .02 .10
551 Bob Watson .02 .10
552 Pat Tabler .02 .10
553 Brent Gaff .02 .10
554 Al Cowens .02 .10
555 Tom Brunansky .07 .20
556 Lloyd Moseby .02 .10
557A Pascual Perez ERR .75 2.00
557B Pascual Perez COR .07 .20
Braves in glove
558 Willie Upshaw .02 .10
559 Richie Zisk .02 .10
560 Pat Zachry .02 .10
561 Jay Johnstone .02 .10
562 Carlos Diaz RC .05 .15
563 John Tudor .07 .20
564 Frank Robinson MG .15 .40
565 Dave Edwards .02 .10
566 Paul Householder .02 .10
567 Ron Reed .02 .10
568 Mike Ramsey .02 .10
569 Kiko Garcia .02 .10
570 Tommy John .07 .20
571 Tony LaRussa MG .07 .20
572 Joel Youngblood .02 .10
573 Wayne Tolleson .02 .10
574 Keith Creel .02 .10
575 Billy Martin MG .15 .40
576 Jerry Dybzinski .02 .10
577 Rick Cerone .02 .10
578 Tony Perez .15 .40
579 Greg Brock .02 .10
580 Glenn Wilson .20 .50
581 Tim Stoddard .02 .10
582 Bob McClure .02 .10
583 Jim Dwyer .02 .10
584 Ed Romero .02 .10
585 Larry Herndon .02 .10
586 Wade Boggs RC 5.00 12.00
587 Jay Howell .02 .10
588 Dave Stewart .07 .20
589 Bert Blyleven .07 .20
590 Dick Howser MG .02 .10
591 Wayne Gross .02 .10
592 Terry Francona .07 .20
593 Don Werner .02 .10
594 Bill Stein .02 .10
595 Jesse Barfield .07 .20
596 Bob Molinaro .02 .10
597 Mike Vail .02 .10
598 Tony Gwynn RC 8.00 20.00
599 Gary Rajsich .02 .10
600 Jerry Ujdur .02 .10
601 Cliff Johnson .02 .10
602 Jerry White .02 .10
603 Bryan Clark .02 .10
604 Joe Ferguson .02 .10
605 Guy Sularz .02 .10
606A Ozzie Virgil .07 .20
Green border
on photo
606B Ozzie Virgil .07 .20
Orange border
on photo
607 Terry Harper .02 .10
608 Harvey Kuenn MG .02 .10
609 Jim Sundberg .07 .20
610 Willie Stargell .15 .40
611 Reggie Smith .07 .20
612 Rob Wilfong .02 .10
613 Joe Niekro .07 .20
Phil Niekro
614 Lee Elia MG .02 .10
615 Mickey Hatcher .02 .10
616 Jerry Hairston .02 .10
617 John Martin .02 .10
618 Wally Backman .02 .10
619 Storm Davis RC .20 .50
620 Alan Knicely .02 .10
621 John Stuper .02 .10
622 Matt Sinatro .02 .10
623 Geno Petralli .20 .50
624 Duane Walker RC .02 .10
625 Dick Williams MG .02 .10
626 Pat Corrales MG .02 .10
627 Vern Ruhle .02 .10
628 Joe Torre MG .07 .20
629 Anthony Johnson .02 .10
630 Steve Howe .02 .10
631 Gary Woods .02 .10
632 LaMarr Hoyt .02 .10
633 Steve Swisher .02 .10
634 Terry Leach .02 .10
635 Jeff Newman .02 .10
636 Brett Butler .07 .20
637 Gary Gray .02 .10
638 Lee Mazzilli .07 .20
639A Ron Jackson ERR 8.00 20.00
639B Ron Jackson COR .02 .10
Angels in glove,
red border
on photo
639C Ron Jackson COR .15 .40
Angels in glove,
green border
on photo
640 Juan Beniquez .02 .10
641 Dave Rucker .02 .10
642 Luis Pujols .02 .10
643 Rick Monday .07 .20
644 Hosken Powell .02 .10
645 The Chicken .15 .40
646 Dave Engle .02 .10
647 Dick Davis .02 .10
648 Frank Robinson .15 .40
Vida Blue
Joe Morgan
649 Al Chambers .02 .10
650 Jesus Vega .02 .10
651 Jeff Jones .02 .10
652 Marvis Foley .02 .10
653 Ty Cobb Puzzle Card .30 .75
654A Dick Perez .15 .40
Diamond
King Checklist 1-26
Unnumbered ERR
Word 'checklist'
omitted from back
654B Dick Perez .15 .40
Diamond
King Checklist 1-26
Unnumbered COR
Word 'checklist'
is on back
655 Checklist 27-130 .02 .10
Unnumbered
656 Checklist 131-234 .02 .10
Unnumbered
657 Checklist 235-338 .02 .10
Unnumbered
658 Checklist 339-442 .02 .10
Unnumbered
659 Checklist 443-544 .02 .10
Unnumbered
660 Checklist 545-653 .02 .10
Unnumbered

1983 Donruss Mickey Mantle Puzzle

1 Mantle Puzzle 1-3 .10 .25
4 Mantle Puzzle 4-6 .10 .25
7 Mantle Puzzle 7-9 .10 .25
10 Mantle Puzzle 10-12 .10 .25
13 Mantle Puzzle 13-15 .10 .25
16 Mantle Puzzle 16-18 .10 .25
19 Mantle Puzzle 19-21 .10 .25
22 Mantle Puzzle 22-24 .10 .25
25 Mantle Puzzle 25-27 .10 .25
28 Mantle Puzzle 28-30 .10 .25
31 Mantle Puzzle 31-33 .10 .25
34 Mantle Puzzle 34-36 .10 .25
37 Mantle Puzzle 37-39 .10 .25
40 Mantle Puzzle 40-42 .10 .25
43 Mantle Puzzle 43-45 .10 .25
46 Mantle Puzzle 46-48 .10 .25
49 Mantle Puzzle 49-51 .10 .25
52 Mantle Puzzle 52-54 .10 .25
55 Mantle Puzzle 55-57 .10 .25
58 Mantle Puzzle 58-60 .10 .25
61 Mantle Puzzle 61-63 .10 .25

1983 Donruss Ty Cobb Puzzle

1 Cobb Puzzle 1-3 .10 .25
4 Cobb Puzzle 4-6 .10 .25
7 Cobb Puzzle 7-10 .10 .25
10 Cobb Puzzle 10-12 .10 .25
13 Cobb Puzzle 13-15 .10 .25
16 Cobb Puzzle 16-18 .10 .25
19 Cobb Puzzle 19-21 .10 .25
22 Cobb Puzzle 22-24 .10 .25
25 Cobb Puzzle 25-27 .10 .25
28 Cobb Puzzle 28-30 .10 .25
31 Cobb Puzzle 29-31 .10 .25
34 Cobb Puzzle 34-36 .10 .25
37 Cobb Puzzle 37-39 .10 .25
40 Cobb Puzzle 40-42 .10 .25
43 Cobb Puzzle 43-45 .10 .25
46 Cobb Puzzle 46-48 .10 .25
49 Cobb Puzzle 49-51 .10 .25
52 Cobb Puzzle 52-54 .10 .25
55 Cobb Puzzle 55-57 .10 .25
58 Cobb Puzzle 58-60 .10 .25
61 Cobb Puzzle 61-63 .10 .25

1983 Donruss Action All-Stars

The cards in this 60-card set measure approximately 3 1/2" by 5". The 1983 Action All-Stars series depicts 60 major leagers in a distinctive new style. A 63-piece Mickey Mantle puzzle (three pieces on one card per pack) was marketed as an insert premium; the complete puzzle card set is one of the more difficult of the Donruss insert puzzles.

COMPLETE SET (60) 3.00 8.00
COMP.MANTLE PUZZLE 6.00 15.00
1 Eddie Murray .25 .60
2 Dwight Evans .02 .10
3A Reggie Jackson ERR/(Red screen on back 1.25 3.00
covers so
3B Reggie Jackson COR .20 .50
4 Greg Luzinski .02 .10
5 Larry Herndon .01 .05
6 Al Oliver .02 .10
7 Bill Buckner .02 .10
8 Jason Thompson .01 .05
9 Andre Dawson .15 .40
10 Greg Minton .01 .05
11 Terry Kennedy .01 .05
12 Phil Niekro .15 .40
13 Willie Wilson .01 .05
14 Johnny Bench .20 .50
15 Ron Guidry .02 .10
16 Hal McRae .01 .05
17 Damaso Garcia .01 .05
18 Gary Ward .01 .05
19 Cecil Cooper .02 .10
20 Keith Hernandez .02 .10
21 Ron Cey .02 .10
22 Rickey Henderson .20 .50
23 Nolan Ryan 1.25 3.00
24 Steve Carlton .15 .40
25 John Stearns .01 .05
26 Jim Sundberg .01 .05
27 Joaquin Andujar .01 .05
28 Gaylord Perry .10 .30
29 Jack Clark .02 .10
30 Bill Madlock .02 .10
31 Pete Rose .30 .75
32 Mookie Wilson .02 .10
33 Rollie Fingers .10 .30
34 Lonnie Smith .01 .05
35 Tony Pena .01 .05
36 Dave Winfield .15 .40
37 Tim Lollar .01 .05
38 Rod Carew .15 .40
39 Toby Harrah .01 .05
40 Buddy Bell .02 .10
41 Bruce Sutter .07 .20
42 George Brett .50 1.25
43 Carlton Fisk .20 .50
44 Carl Yastrzemski .20 .50
45 Dale Murphy .07 .20
46 Bob Horner .01 .05
47 Dave Concepcion .02 .10
48 Dave Stieb .01 .05
49 Kent Hrbek .02 .10
50 Lance Parrish .02 .10
51 Joe Niekro .01 .05
52 Cal Ripken 1.25 3.00
53 Fernando Valenzuela .02 .10
54 Richie Zisk .01 .05
55 Leon Durham .01 .05
56 Robin Yount .20 .50
57 Mike Schmidt .30 .75
58 Gary Carter .20 .50
59 Fred Lynn .02 .10
60 Checklist Card .01 .05

1983 Donruss HOF Heroes

The cards in this 44-card set measure 2 1/2" by 3 1/2". Although it was issued with the same Mantle puzzle as the Action All Stars set, the Donruss Hall of Fame Heroes set is completely different in content and design. Of the 44 cards in the set, 42 are Dick Perez artwork portraying Hall of Fame members, while one card depicts the completed Mantle puzzle and the last card is a checklist. The red, white, and blue backs contain the card number and a short player biography. The cards were packaged eight cards plus one puzzle card (three pieces) for 30 cents in the summer of 1983.

COMPLETE SET (44) 4.00 10.00
1 Ty Cobb .40 1.00
2 Walter Johnson .15 .40
3 Christy Mathewson .15 .40
4 Josh Gibson .15 .40
5 Honus Wagner .30 .75
6 Jackie Robinson .50 1.25
7 Mickey Mantle 1.00 2.50
8 Luke Appling .01 .05
9 Ted Williams .40 1.00
10 Johnny Mize .05 .15
11 Satchel Paige .15 .40
12 Lou Boudreau .01 .05
13 Jimmie Foxx .05 .15
14 Duke Snider .15 .40
15 Monte Irvin .05 .15
16 Hank Greenberg .08 .25
17 Roberto Clemente .50 1.25
18 Al Kaline .15 .40
19 Frank Robinson .15 .40
20 Joe Cronin .05 .15
21 Burleigh Grimes .01 .05
22 The Waner Brothers .01 .05
Paul Waner
Lloyd Waner
23 Grover Alexander .05 .15
24 Yogi Berra .15 .40
25 Cool Papa Bell .05 .15
26 Bill Dickey .05 .15
27 Cy Young .08 .25
28 Charlie Gehringer .01 .05
29 Dizzy Dean .15 .40
30 Bob Lemon .05 .15
31 Red Ruffing .01 .05
32 Stan Musial .30 .75
33 Carl Hubbell .08 .25
34 Hank Aaron .30 .75
35 John McGraw .01 .05
36 Bob Feller .15 .40
37 Casey Stengel .15 .40
38 Ralph Kiner .05 .15
39 Roy Campanella .15 .40
40 Mel Ott .05 .15
41 Robin Roberts .05 .15
42 Early Wynn .01 .05
43 Mantle Puzzle Card 1.00 2.50
44 Checklist Card .01 .05

1984 Donruss

The 1984 Donruss set contains a total of 660 standard-size cards; however, only 658 are numbered. The first 26 cards in the set are again Diamond Kings (DK). A new feature, Rated Rookies (RR), was introduced with this set with Bill Madden's 20 selections comprising numbers 27 through 46. Two "Living Legend" cards designated A (featuring Gaylord Perry and Rollie Fingers) and B (featuring Johnny Bench and Carl Yastrzemski) were issued as bonus cards in wax packs, but were not issued in the factory sets sold to hobby dealers. The seven unnumbered checklist cards are arbitrarily assigned numbers 652 through 658 and are listed at the end of the list below. The attractive card front designs changed considerably from the previous two years. This set has since grown in stature to be recognized as one of the finest produced in the 1980's. The backs contain statistics and are printed in green and black ink. The cards, issued amongst other ways in

15 card packs which had a 30 cent SRP, were distributed with a three-piece puzzle panel of Duke Snider. There are no extra variation cards included in the complete set price below. The variation cards apparently resulted from a different printing for the factory sets as the Darling and Stenhouse no number variations as well as the Perez-Steele errors were corrected in the factory sets which were released later in the year. The factory sets were shipped 15 to a case. The Diamond King cards found in packs spelled Perez-Steele as Perez-Steel. Rookie Cards in this set include Joe Carter, Don Mattingly, Darryl Strawberry, and Andy Van Slyke. The Joe Carter card is almost never found well centered.

COMPLETE SET (660) 60.00 120.00
COMP.FACT.SET (658) 100.00 175.00
COMP.SNIDER PUZZLE 2.00 5.00
1 Robin Yount DK COR 1.00 2.50
1A Robin Yount DK ERR 2.00 5.00
2 Dave Concepcion DK COR .30 .75
2A Dave Concepcion DK ERR Perez Steel .30 .75
3 Dwayne Murphy DK COR .08 .25
3A Dwayne Murphy DK ERR Perez Steel .08 .25
4 John Castino DK COR .08 .25
4A John Castino DK ERR Perez Steel .08 .25
5 Leon Durham DK COR .30 .75
5A Leon Durham DK ERR Perez Steel .08 .25
6 Rusty Staub DK COR .30 .75
6A Rusty Staub DK ERR Perez Steel .30 .75
7 Jack Clark DK COR .30 .75
7A Jack Clark DK ERR Perez Steel .30 .75
8 Dave Dravecky DK COR .08 .25
8A Dave Dravecky DK ERR Perez Steel .08 .25
9 Al Oliver DK COR .30 .75
9A Al Oliver DK ERR Perez Steel .30 .75
10 Dave Righetti DK COR .30 .75
10A Dave Righetti DK ERR Perez Steel .30 .75
11 Hal McRae DK COR .30 .75
11A Hal McRae DK ERR Perez Steel .30 .75
12 Ray Knight DK COR .30 .75
12A Ray Knight DK ERR Perez Steel .30 .75
13 Bruce Sutter DK COR .60 1.50
13A Bruce Sutter DK ERR Perez Steel .60 1.50
14 Bob Horner DK COR .30 .75
14A Bob Horner DK ERR Perez Steel .30 .75
15 Lance Parrish DK COR .30 .75
15A Lance Parrish DK ERR Perez Steel .30 .75
16 Matt Young DK COR .30 .75
16A Matt Young DK ERR Perez Steel .30 .75
17 Fred Lynn DK COR .30 .75
17A Fred Lynn DK ERR Perez Steel A's logo on back .30 .75
18 Ron Kittle DK COR .08 .25
18A Ron Kittle DK ERR Perez Steel .08 .25
19 Jim Clancy DK COR .08 .25
19A Jim Clancy DK ERR Perez Steel .08 .25
20 Bill Madlock DK COR .30 .75
20A Bill Madlock DK ERR Perez Steel .30 .75
21 Larry Parrish DK COR .08 .25
21A Larry Parrish DK ERR Perez Steel .08 .25
22 Eddie Murray DK COR 1.25 3.00
22A Eddie Murray DK ERR 1.25 3.00
23 Mike Schmidt DK COR 2.00 5.00
23A Mike Schmidt DK ERR 2.00 5.00
24 Pedro Guerrero DK COR .30 .75
24A Pedro Guerrero DK ERR Perez Steel .30 .75
25 Andre Thornton DK COR .08 .25
25A Andre Thornton DK ERR Perez Steel .08 .25
26 Wade Boggs DK COR 1.25 3.00
26A Wade Boggs DK ERR 1.25 3.00
27 Joel Skinner RC .08 .25
28 Tommy Dunbar RC .08 .25
29A Mike Stenhouse RC ERR No number on back .08 .25
29B M.Stenhouse RR COR 1.25 3.00
30A Ron Darling RC ERR No number on back .75 2.00
30B Ron Darling RR COR Numbered on back 1.25 3.00
31 Dion James RC .08 .25
32 Tony Fernandez RC .75 2.00
33 Angel Salazar RC .08 .25
34 Kevin McReynolds RC .75 2.00
35 Dick Schofield RC .40 1.00
36 Brad Komminsk RC .08 .25
37 Tim Teufel RR RC .40 1.00
38 Doug Frobel RC .08 .25
39 Greg Gagne RC .40 1.00
40 Mike Fuentes RC .08 .25
41 Joe Carter RR RC 5.00 12.00
42 Mike C. Brown RC Angels OF .08 .25
43 Mike Jeffcoat RC .08 .25
44 Sid Fernandez RC ! .75 2.00
45 Brian Dayett RC .08 .25
46 Chris Smith RC .08 .25
47 Eddie Murray 1.25 3.00
48 Robin Yount 2.00 5.00
49 Lance Parrish .60 1.50
50 Jim Rice .30 .75
51 Dave Winfield .30 .75
52 Fernando Valenzuela .30 .75
53 George Brett 3.00 8.00
54 Rickey Henderson 2.00 5.00
55 Gary Carter .30 .75
56 Buddy Bell .30 .75
57 Reggie Jackson .60 1.50
58 Harold Baines .30 .75
59 Ozzie Smith 2.00 5.00
60 Nolan Ryan UER 4.00 10.00
61 Pete Rose 4.00 10.00
62 Ron Oester .08 .25
63 Steve Garvey .30 .75
64 Jason Thompson .08 .25
65 Jack Clark .30 .75
66 Dale Murphy .60 1.50
67 Leon Durham .08 .25
68 Darryl Strawberry RC 5.00 12.00
69 Richie Zisk .08 .25
70 Kent Hrbek .30 .75
71 Dave Stieb .30 .75
72 Ken Schrom .08 .25
73 George Bell .30 .75
74 John Moses .08 .25
75 Ed Lynch .08 .25
76 Chuck Rainey .08 .25
77 Biff Pocoroba .08 .25
78 Cecilio Guante .08 .25
79 Jim Barr .08 .25
80 Kurt Bevacqua .08 .25
81 Tom Foley .08 .25
82 Joe Lefebvre .08 .25
83 Andy Van Slyke RC 1.50 4.00
84 Bob Lillis MG .08 .25
85 Ricky Adams .08 .25
86 Jerry Hairston .08 .25
87 Bob James .08 .25
88 Joe Altobelli MG .08 .25
89 Ed Romero .08 .25
90 John Grubb .08 .25
91 John Henry Johnson .08 .25
92 Juan Espino .08 .25
93 Candy Maldonado .08 .25
94 Andre Thornton .08 .25
95 Onix Concepcion .08 .25
96 Donnie Hill UER Listed as P, should be 2B .08 .25
97 Andre Dawson UER Wrong middle name, should be Nolan .30 .75
98 Frank Tanana .30 .75
99 Curtis Wilkerson .08 .25
100 Larry Gura .08 .25
101 Dwayne Murphy .08 .25
102 Tom Brennan .08 .25
103 Dave Righetti .30 .75
104 Steve Sax .30 .75
105 Dan Petry .30 .75
106 Cal Ripken 5.00 12.00
107 Paul Molitor UER '83 stats should say .270 BA, 608 AB, and 164 hits .30 .75
108 Fred Lynn .30 .75
109 Neil Allen .08 .25
110 Joe Niekro .08 .25
111 Steve Carlton .60 1.50
112 Terry Kennedy .08 .25
113 Bill Madlock .30 .75
114 Chili Davis .30 .75
115 Jim Gantner .08 .25
116 Tom Seaver 1.25 3.00
117 Bill Buckner .30 .75
118 Bill Caudill .08 .25
119 Jim Clancy .08 .25
120 John Castino .08 .25
121 Dave Concepcion .30 .75
122 Greg Luzinski .30 .75
123 Mike Boddicker .08 .25
124 Pete Ladd .08 .25
125 Juan Berenguer .08 .25
126 John Montefusco .08 .25
127 Ed Jurak .08 .25
128 Tom Niedenfuer .08 .25
129 Bert Blyleven .30 .75
130 Bud Black .08 .25
131 Gorman Heimueller .08 .25
132 Dan Schatzeder .08 .25
133 Ron Jackson .08 .25
134 Tom Henke RC .75 2.00
135 Kevin Hickey .08 .25
136 Mike Scott .30 .75
137 Bo Diaz .08 .25
138 Glenn Brummer .08 .25
139 Sid Monge .08 .25
140 Rich Gale .08 .25
141 Brett Butler .30 .75
142 Brian Harper RC .40 1.00
143 John Rabb .08 .25
144 Gary Woods .08 .25
145 Pat Putnam .08 .25
146 Jim Acker .08 .25
147 Mickey Hatcher .08 .25
148 Todd Cruz .08 .25
149 Tom Tellmann .08 .25
150 John Wockenfuss .08 .25
151 Wade Boggs UER 3.00 8.00
152 Don Baylor .30 .75
153 Bob Welch .30 .75
154 Alan Bannister .08 .25
155 Willie Aikens .08 .25
156 Jeff Burroughs .08 .25
157 Bryan Little .08 .25
158 Bob Boone .30 .75
159 Dave Hostetler .08 .25
160 Jerry Dybzinski .08 .25
161 Mike Madden .08 .25
162 Luis DeLeon .08 .25
163 Willie Hernandez .08 .25
164 Frank Pastore .08 .25
165 Rick Camp .08 .25
166 Lee Mazzilli .30 .75
167 Scot Thompson .08 .25
168 Bob Forsch .08 .25
169 Mike Flanagan .08 .25
170 Rick Manning .08 .25
171 Chet Lemon .30 .75
172 Jerry Remy .08 .25
173 Ron Guidry .30 .75
174 Pedro Guerrero .30 .75
175 Willie Wilson .30 .75
176 Carney Lansford .30 .75
177 Al Oliver .30 .75
178 Jim Sundberg .30 .75
179 Bobby Grich .30 .75
180 Rich Dotson .08 .25
181 Joaquin Andujar .30 .75
182 Jose Cruz .30 .75
183 Mike Schmidt 3.00 8.00
184 Gary Redus RC .40 1.00
185 Garry Templeton .30 .75
186 Tony Pena .08 .25
187 Greg Minton .08 .25
188 Phil Niekro .30 .75
189 Ferguson Jenkins .30 .75
190 Mookie Wilson .30 .75
191 Jim Beattie .08 .25
192 Gary Ward .08 .25
193 Jesse Barfield .30 .75
194 Pete Filson .08 .25
195 Roy Lee Jackson .08 .25
196 Rick Sweet .08 .25
197 Jesse Orosco .08 .25
198 Steve Lake .08 .25
199 Ken Dayley .08 .25
200 Manny Sarmiento .08 .25
201 Mark Davis .08 .25
202 Tim Flannery .08 .25
203 Bill Scherrer .08 .25
204 Al Holland .08 .25
205 Dave Von Ohlen .08 .25
206 Mike LaCoss .08 .25
207 Juan Beniquez .08 .25
208 Juan Agosto .08 .25
209 Bobby Ramos .08 .25
210 Al Bumbry .08 .25
211 Mark Brouhard .08 .25
212 Howard Bailey .08 .25
213 Bruce Hurst .08 .25
214 Bob Shirley .08 .25
215 Pat Zachry .08 .25
216 Julio Franco 1.25 3.00
217 Mike Armstrong .08 .25
218 Dave Beard .08 .25
219 Steve Rogers .30 .75
220 John Butcher .08 .25
221 Mike Smithson .08 .25
222 Frank White .30 .75
223 Mike Heath .08 .25
224 Chris Bando .08 .25
225 Roy Smalley .08 .25
226 Dusty Baker .30 .75
227 Lou Whitaker .30 .75
228 John Lowenstein .08 .25
229 Ben Oglivie .08 .25
230 Doug DeCinces .08 .25
231 Lonnie Smith .08 .25
232 Ray Knight .30 .75
233 Gary Matthews .30 .75
234 Juan Bonilla .08 .25
235 Rod Scurry .08 .25
236 Atlee Hammaker .08 .25
237 Mike Caldwell .08 .25
238 Keith Hernandez .30 .75
239 Larry Bowa .30 .75
240 Tony Bernazard .08 .25
241 Damaso Garcia .08 .25
242 Tom Brunansky .30 .75
243 Dan Driessen .08 .25
244 Ron Kittle .08 .25
245 Tim Stoddard .08 .25
246 Bob L. Gibson RC/(Brewers Pitcher) .08 .25
247 Marty Castillo .08 .25
248 Don Mattingly RC 25.00 60.00
249 Jeff Newman .08 .25
250 Alejandro Pena RC .75 2.00
251 Toby Harrah .30 .75
252 Cesar Geronimo .08 .25
253 Tom Underwood .08 .25
254 Doug Flynn .08 .25
255 Andy Hassler .08 .25
256 Odell Jones .08 .25
257 Rudy Law .08 .25
258 Harry Spilman .08 .25
259 Marty Bystrom .08 .25
260 Dave Rucker .08 .25
261 Ruppert Jones .08 .25
262 Jeff R. Jones/(Reds OF) .08 .25
263 Gerald Perry .40 1.00
264 Gene Tenace .30 .75
265 Brad Wellman .08 .25
266 Dickie Noles .08 .25
267 Jamie Allen .08 .25
268 Jim Gott .08 .25
269 Ron Davis .08 .25
270 Benny Ayala .08 .25
271 Ned Yost .08 .25
272 Dave Rozema .08 .25
273 Dave Stapleton .08 .25
274 Lou Piniella .30 .75
275 Jose Morales .08 .25
276 Broderick Perkins .08 .25
277 Butch Davis RC .08 .25
278 Tony Phillips RC .75 2.00
279 Jeff Reardon .30 .75
280 Ken Forsch .08 .25
281 Pete O'Brien RC .40 1.00
282 Tom Paciorek .08 .25
283 Frank LaCorte .08 .25
284 Tim Lollar .08 .25
285 Greg Gross .08 .25
286 Alex Trevino .08 .25
287 Gene Garber .08 .25
288 Dave Parker .30 .75
289 Lee Smith .30 .75
290 Dave LaPoint .08 .25
291 John Shelby .08 .25
292 Charlie Moore .08 .25
293 Alan Trammell .30 .75
294 Tony Armas .30 .75
295 Shane Rawley .08 .25
296 Greg Brock .08 .25
297 Hal McRae .30 .75
298 Mike Davis .08 .25
299 Tim Raines .30 .75
300 Bucky Dent .30 .75
301 Tommy John .30 .75
302 Carlton Fisk .60 1.50
303 Darrell Porter .08 .25
304 Dickie Thon .08 .25
305 Garry Maddox .08 .25
306 Cesar Cedeno .30 .75
307 Gary Lucas .08 .25
308 Johnny Ray .08 .25
309 Andy McGaffigan .08 .25
310 Claudell Washington .08 .25
311 Ryne Sandberg 5.00 12.00
312 George Foster .30 .75
313 Spike Owen RC .40 1.00
314 Gary Gaetti .60 1.50
315 Willie Upshaw .08 .25
316 Al Williams .08 .25
317 Jorge Orta .08 .25
318 Orlando Mercado .08 .25
319 Junior Ortiz .08 .25
320 Mike Proly .08 .25
321 Randy Johnson UER '72-'82 stats are from Twins' Randy Johnson, '83 stats are from Braves' Randy Johnson .08 .25
322 Jim Morrison .08 .25
323 Max Venable .08 .25
324 Tony Gwynn 5.00 12.00
325 Duane Walker .08 .25
326 Ozzie Virgil .08 .25
327 Jeff Lahti .08 .25
328 Bill Dawley .08 .25
329 Rob Wilfong .08 .25
330 Marc Hill .08 .25
331 Ray Burris .08 .25
332 Allan Ramirez .08 .25
333 Chuck Porter .08 .25
334 Wayne Krenchicki .08 .25
335 Gary Allenson .08 .25
336 Bobby Meacham .08 .25
337 Joe Beckwith .08 .25
338 Rick Sutcliffe .30 .75
339 Mark Huismann .08 .25
340 Tim Conroy .08 .25
341 Scott Sanderson .08 .25
342 Larry Biittner .08 .25
343 Dave Stewart .30 .75
344 Darryl Motley .08 .25
345 Chris Codiroli .08 .25
346 Rich Behenna .08 .25
347 Andre Robertson .08 .25
348 Mike Marshall .08 .25
349 Larry Herndon .30 .75
350 Rich Dauer .08 .25
351 Cecil Cooper .30 .75
352 Rod Carew .60 1.50
353 Willie McGee .30 .75
354 Phil Garner .30 .75
355 Joe Morgan .30 .75
356 Luis Salazar .08 .25
357 John Candelaria .08 .25
358 Bill Laskey .08 .25
359 Bob McClure .08 .25
360 Dave Kingman .30 .75
361 Ron Cey .30 .75
362 Matt Young RC .40 1.00
363 Lloyd Moseby .08 .25
364 Frank Viola .60 1.50
365 Eddie Milner .08 .25
366 Floyd Bannister .08 .25
367 Dan Ford .08 .25
368 Moose Haas .08 .25
369 Doug Bair .08 .25
370 Ray Fontenot .08 .25
371 Luis Aponte .08 .25
372 Jack Fimple .08 .25
373 Neal Heaton .08 .25
374 Greg Pryor .08 .25
375 Wayne Gross .08 .25
376 Charlie Lea .08 .25
377 Steve Lubratich .08 .25
378 Jon Matlack .08 .25
379 Julio Cruz .08 .25
380 John Mizerock .08 .25
381 Kevin Gross RC .40 1.00
382 Mike Ramsey .08 .25
383 Doug Gwosdz .08 .25
384 Kelly Paris .08 .25
385 Pete Falcone .08 .25
386 Milt May .08 .25
387 Fred Breining .08 .25
388 Craig Lefferts RC .08 .25
389 Steve Henderson .08 .25
390 Randy Moffitt .08 .25
391 Ron Washington .08 .25
392 Gary Roenicke .08 .25
393 Tom Candiotti RC .75 2.00
394 Larry Pashnick .08 .25
395 Dwight Evans .60 1.50
396 Rich Gossage .30 .75
397 Derrel Thomas .08 .25
398 Juan Eichelberger .08 .25
399 Leon Roberts .08 .25
400 Dave Lopes .30 .75
401 Bill Gullickson .08 .25
402 Geoff Zahn .08 .25
403 Billy Sample .08 .25
404 Mike Squires .08 .25
405 Craig Reynolds .08 .25
406 Eric Show .08 .25
407 John Denny .08 .25
408 Dann Bilardello .08 .25
409 Bruce Benedict .08 .25
410 Kent Tekulve .08 .25
411 Mel Hall .30 .75
412 John Stuper .08 .25
413 Rick Dempsey .08 .25
414 Don Sutton .30 .75
415 Jack Morris .30 .75
416 John Tudor .30 .75
417 Willie Randolph .30 .75
418 Jerry Reuss .08 .25
419 Don Slaught .30 .75
420 Steve McCatty .08 .25
421 Tim Wallach .30 .75
422 Larry Parrish .08 .25
423 Brian Downing .30 .75
424 Britt Burns .08 .25
425 David Green .08 .25
426 Jerry Mumphrey .08 .25
427 Ivan DeJesus .08 .25
428 Mario Soto .30 .75
429 Gene Richards .08 .25
430 Dale Berra .08 .25
431 Darrell Evans .30 .75
432 Glenn Hubbard .08 .25
433 Jody Davis .08 .25
434 Danny Heep .08 .25
435 Ed Nunez RC .08 .25
436 Bobby Castillo .08 .25
437 Ernie Whitt .08 .25
438 Scott Ullger .08 .25
439 Doyle Alexander .08 .25
440 Domingo Ramos .08 .25
441 Craig Swan .08 .25
442 Warren Brusstar .08 .25
443 Len Barker .08 .25
444 Mike Easler .08 .25
445 Renie Martin .08 .25
446 Dennis Rasmussen RC .40 1.00
447 Ted Power .08 .25
448 Charles Hudson .08 .25
449 Danny Cox RC .08 .25
450 Kevin Bass .08 .25
451 Daryl Sconiers .08 .25
452 Scott Fletcher .08 .25
453 Bryn Smith .08 .25
454 Jim Dwyer .08 .25
455 Rob Picciolo .08 .25
456 Enos Cabell .08 .25
457 Dennis Boyd .30 .75
458 Butch Wynegar .08 .25
459 Burt Hooton .08 .25
460 Ron Hassey .08 .25
461 Danny Jackson RC .40 1.00
462 Bob Kearney .08 .25
463 Terry Francona .30 .75
464 Wayne Tolleson .08 .25
465 Mickey Rivers .08 .25
466 John Wathan .08 .25
467 Bill Almon .08 .25
468 George Vukovich .08 .25
469 Steve Kemp .08 .25
470 Ken Landreaux .08 .25
471 Milt Wilcox .08 .25
472 Tippy Martinez .08 .25
473 Ted Simmons .30 .75
474 Tim Foli .08 .25
475 George Hendrick .30 .75
476 Terry Puhl .08 .25
477 Von Hayes .08 .25
478 Bobby Brown .08 .25
479 Lee Lacy .08 .25
480 Joel Youngblood .08 .25
481 Jim Slaton .08 .25
482 Mike Fitzgerald .08 .25
483 Keith Moreland .08 .25
484 Ron Roenicke .08 .25
485 Luis Leal .08 .25
486 Bryan Oelkers .08 .25
487 Bruce Berenyi .08 .25
488 LaMarr Hoyt .08 .25
489 Joe Nolan .08 .25
490 Marshall Edwards .08 .25
491 Mike Laga .30 .75
492 Rick Cerone .08 .25
493 Rick Miller UER Listed as Mike on card front .08 .25
494 Rick Honeycutt .08 .25
495 Mike Hargrove .08 .25
496 Joe Simpson .08 .25
497 Keith Atherton .08 .25
498 Chris Welsh .08 .25
499 Bruce Kison .08 .25
500 Bobby Johnson .08 .25
501 Jerry Koosman .30 .75
502 Frank DiPino .08 .25
503 Tony Perez .60 1.50
504 Ken Oberkfell .08 .25
505 Mark Thurmond .08 .25
506 Joe Price .08 .25
507 Pascual Perez .08 .25
508 Marvell Wynne .40 1.00
509 Mike Krukow .08 .25
510 Dick Ruthven .08 .25
511 Al Cowens .08 .25
512 Cliff Johnson .08 .25
513 Randy Bush .08 .25
514 Sammy Stewart .08 .25
515 Bill Schroeder .08 .25
516 Aurelio Lopez .30 .75
517 Mike C. Brown .08 .25
518 Graig Nettles .30 .75
519 Dave Sax .08 .25
520 Jerry Willard .08 .25
521 Paul Splittorff .08 .25
522 Tom Burgmeier .08 .25
523 Chris Speier .08 .25
524 Bobby Clark .08 .25
525 George Wright .08 .25
526 Dennis Lamp .08 .25
527 Tony Scott .08 .25
528 Ed Whitson .08 .25
529 Ron Reed .08 .25
530 Charlie Puleo .08 .25
531 Jerry Royster .08 .25
532 Don Robinson .08 .25
533 Steve Trout .08 .25
534 Bruce Sutter .60 1.50
535 Bob Horner ! .30 .75
536 Pat Tabler .08 .25
537 Chris Chambliss .30 .75
538 Bob Ojeda .08 .25
539 Alan Ashby .08 .25
540 Jay Johnstone .08 .25
541 Bob Dernier .08 .25
542 Brook Jacoby .40 1.00
543 U.L. Washington .08 .25
544 Danny Darwin .08 .25
545 Kiko Garcia .08 .25
546 Vance Law UER Listed as P on card front .08 .25
547 Tug McGraw .30 .75
548 Dave Smith .08 .25
549 Len Matuszek .08 .25
550 Tom Hume .08 .25
551 Dave Dravecky .08 .25
552 Rick Rhoden .08 .25
553 Duane Kuiper .08 .25
554 Rusty Staub .30 .75
555 Bill Campbell .08 .25
556 Mike Torrez .08 .25
557 Dave Henderson .30 .75
558 Len Whitehouse .08 .25
559 Barry Bonnell .08 .25
560 Rick Lysander .08 .25
561 Garth Iorg .08 .25
562 Bryan Clark .08 .25
563 Brian Giles .08 .25
564 Vern Ruhle .08 .25
565 Steve Bedrosian .08 .25
566 Larry McWilliams .08 .25
567 Jeff Leonard UER Listed as P on card front .08 .25
568 Alan Wiggins .08 .25
569 Jeff Russell RC .40 1.00
570 Salome Barojas .08 .25
571 Dane Iorg .08 .25
572 Bob Knepper .08 .25
573 Gary Lavelle .08 .25
574 Gorman Thomas .30 .75
575 Manny Trillo .08 .25
576 Jim Palmer .30 .75
577 Dale Murray .08 .25
578 Tom Brookens .30 .75
579 Rich Gedman .08 .25
580 Bill Doran RC .40 1.00
581 Steve Yeager .30 .75
582 Dan Spillner .08 .25
583 Dan Quisenberry .08 .25
584 Rance Mulliniks .08 .25
585 Storm Davis .08 .25
586 Dave Schmidt .08 .25
587 Bill Russell .30 .75
588 Pat Sheridan .08 .25
589 Rafael Ramirez UER (A's on front) .08 .25
590 Bud Anderson .08 .25
591 George Frazier .08 .25
592 Lee Tunnell .08 .25
593 Kirk Gibson 1.25 3.00
594 Scott McGregor .08 .25
595 Bob Bailor .08 .25
596 Tom Herr .08 .25
597 Luis Sanchez .08 .25
598 Dave Engle .08 .25
599 Craig McMurtry .08 .25
600 Carlos Diaz .08 .25
601 Tom O'Malley .08 .25
602 Nick Esasky .08 .25
603 Ron Hodges .08 .25
604 Ed VandeBerg .08 .25
605 Alfredo Griffin .08 .25
606 Glenn Hoffman .08 .25
607 Hubie Brooks .08 .25
608 Richard Barnes UER Photo actually Neal Heaton .08 .25
609 Greg Walker .40 1.00
610 Ken Singleton .30 .75
611 Mark Clear .08 .25
612 Buck Martinez .08 .25
613 Ken Griffey .30 .75
614 Reid Nichols .08 .25
615 Doug Sisk .08 .25
616 Bob Brenly .08 .25
617 Joey McLaughlin .08 .25
618 Glenn Wilson .30 .75
619 Bob Stoddard .08 .25
620 Lenn Sakata UER Listed as Len on card front .08 .25
621 Mike Young RC .08 .25
622 John Stefero .08 .25
623 Carmelo Martinez .08 .25
624 Dave Bergman .08 .25
625 Runnin' Reds UER Sic, Redbirds David Green Willie McGee Lonnie Smith Ozzie Smith 1.25 3.0
626 Rudy May .08 .2
627 Matt Keough .08 .2
628 Jose DeLeon RC .40 1.0
629 Jim Essian .08 .2
630 Darnell Coles RC .40 1.0
631 Mike Warren .08 .2
632 Del Crandall MG .08 .2
633 Dennis Martinez .30 .7
634 Mike Moore .08 .2
635 Lary Sorensen .08 .2
636 Ricky Nelson .08 .2
637 Omar Moreno .08 .2
638 Charlie Hough .30 .7
639 Dennis Eckersley ! .60 1.5
640 Walt Terrell .08 .2
641 Denny Walling .08 .2
642 Dave Anderson RC .08 .2
643 Jose Oquendo RC .40 1.0
644 Bob Stanley .08 .2
645 Dave Geisel .08 .2
646 Scott Garrelts .08 .2
647 Gary Pettis .08 .2
648 Duke Snider Puzzle Card .60 1.5
649 Johnnie LeMaster .08 .2
650 Dave Collins .08 .2
651 The Chicken .60 1.5
652 DK Checklist 1-26 Unnumbered .30 .7
653 Checklist 27-130 Unnumbered .08 .2
654 Checklist 131-234 Unnumbered .08 .2
655 Checklist 235-338 Unnumbered .08 .2
656 Checklist 339-442 Unnumbered .08 .2
657 Checklist 443-546 Unnumbered .08 .2
658 Checklist 547-651 Unnumbered .08 .2
A Living Legends A 1.00 2.
B Living Legends B 2.00 5.

1984 Donruss Duke Snider Puzzle

1 Snider Puzzle 1-3 .10
4 Snider Puzzle 4-6 .10
7 Snider Puzzle 7-10 .10
10 Snider Puzzle 10-12 .10
13 Snider Puzzle 13-15 .10
16 Snider Puzzle 16-18 .10
19 Snider Puzzle 19-21 .10
22 Snider Puzzle 22-24 .10
25 Snider Puzzle 25-27 .10
28 Snider Puzzle 28-30 .10
31 Snider Puzzle 29-31 .10
34 Snider Puzzle 34-36 .10
37 Snider Puzzle 37-39 .10

40 Snider Puzzle 40-42 .10 .25
43 Snider Puzzle 43-45 .10 .25
46 Snider Puzzle 46-48 .10 .25
49 Snider Puzzle 49-51 .10 .25
52 Snider Puzzle 52-54 .10 .25
55 Snider Puzzle 55-57 .10 .25
58 Snider Puzzle 58-60 .10 .25
61 Snider Puzzle 61-63 .10 .25

1984 Donruss Ted Williams Puzzle

1 Williams Puzzle 1-3 .10 .25
4 Williams Puzzle 4-6 .10 .25
7 Williams Puzzle 7-10 .10 .25
10 Williams Puzzle 10-12 .10 .25
13 Williams Puzzle 13-15 .10 .25
16 Williams Puzzle 16-18 .10 .25
19 Williams Puzzle 19-21 .10 .25
22 Williams Puzzle 22-24 .10 .25
25 Williams Puzzle 25-27 .10 .25
28 Williams Puzzle 28-30 .10 .25
31 Williams Puzzle 29-31 .10 .25
34 Williams Puzzle 34-36 .10 .25
37 Williams Puzzle 37-39 .10 .25
40 Williams Puzzle 40-42 .10 .25
43 Williams Puzzle 43-45 .10 .25
46 Williams Puzzle 46-48 .10 .25
49 Williams Puzzle 49-51 .10 .25
52 Williams Puzzle 52-54 .10 .25
55 Williams Puzzle 55-57 .10 .25
58 Williams Puzzle 58-60 .10 .25
61 Williams Puzzle 61-63 .10 .25

1984 Donruss Action All-Stars

The cards in this 60-card set measure approximately 3 1/2" by 5". For the second year in a row, Donruss issued a postcard-size card set. Unlike last year, when the fronts of the cards contained both an action and a portrait shot of the player, the fronts of this year's cards contain only an action photo. On the backs, the top section contains the card number and a full-color portrait of the player pictured on the front. The bottom half features the player's career statistics. The set was distributed with a 63-piece Ted Williams puzzle. This puzzle is the toughest of all the Donruss puzzles.

COMPLETE SET (60) 3.00 8.00
COMP.WILLIAMS PUZZLE 12.50 25.00
Gary Lavelle .01 .05
Willie McGee .10 .30
Tony Pena .01 .05
Lou Whitaker .07 .20
Robin Yount .15 .40
Doug DeCinces .01 .05
John Castino .01 .05
Terry Kennedy .01 .05
Rickey Henderson .30 1.00
Bob Horner .01 .05
Harold Baines .02 .10
Buddy Bell .02 .10
Fernando Valenzuela .02 .10
Nolan Ryan 1.00 2.50
Andre Thornton .01 .05
Gary Redus .01 .05
Pedro Guerrero .02 .10
Andre Dawson .10 .30
Dave Stieb .01 .05
Cal Ripken 1.00 2.50
Ken Griffey .02 .10
Wade Boggs .30 1.00
Keith Hernandez .02 .10
Steve Carlton .20 .50
Hal McRae .01 .05
John Lowenstein .01 .05
Fred Lynn .02 .10
Bill Buckner .02 .10
Chris Chambliss .01 .05
Richie Zisk .01 .05
Jack Clark .02 .10
George Hendrick .01 .05
Bill Madlock .01 .05
Lance Parrish .07 .20
Paul Molitor .20 .50
Reggie Jackson .20 .50
Kent Hrbek .02 .10
Steve Garvey .02 .10
Carney Lansford .02 .10
Dale Murphy .10 .30
Greg Luzinski .02 .10
Larry Parrish .01 .05
Ryne Sandberg .50 1.25
Dickie Thon .01 .05
Bert Blyleven .02 .10
Ron Oester .01 .05
Dusty Baker .02 .10
Steve Rogers .01 .05
Jim Clancy .01 .05
Eddie Murray .25 .60
Ron Guidry .02 .10
Jim Rice .02 .10
Tom Seaver .20 .50
Pete Rose .30 .75
George Brett .50 1.25
56 Dan Quisenberry .01 .05
57 Mike Schmidt .25 .60
58 Ted Simmons .02 .10
59 Dave Righetti .01 .05
60 Checklist Card .01 .05

1984 Donruss Champions

The cards in this 60-card set measure approximately 3 1/2" by 5". The 1984 Donruss Champions set is a hybrid photo/artwork issue. Grand Champions, listed GC in the checklist below, feature the artwork of Dick Perez of Perez-Steele Galleries. Current players in the set feature photographs. The theme of this postcard-size set features a Grand Champion and those current players that are directly behind him in a baseball statistical category, for example, Season Home Runs (1-7), Career Home Runs (8-13), Season Batting Average (14-19), Career Batting Average (20-25), Career Hits (26-30), Career Victories (31-36), Career Strikeouts (37-42), Most Valuable Players (43-49), World Series stars (50-54), and All-Star heroes (55-59). The cards were issued in cello packs with pieces of the Duke Snider puzzle.

COMPLETE SET (60) 5.00 12.00
1 Babe Ruth GC .75 2.00
2 George Foster .02 .10
3 Dave Kingman .02 .10
4 Jim Rice .02 .10
5 Gorman Thomas .01 .05
6 Ben Oglivie .01 .05
7 Jeff Burroughs .01 .05
8 Hank Aaron GC .30 .75
9 Reggie Jackson .20 .50
10 Carl Yastrzemski .20 .50
11 Mike Schmidt .25 .60
12 Graig Nettles .02 .10
13 Greg Luzinski .02 .10
14 Ted Williams GC .60 1.50
15 George Brett .50 1.25
16 Wade Boggs .20 .50
17 Hal McRae .01 .05
18 Bill Buckner .02 .10
19 Eddie Murray .25 .60
20 Rogers Hornsby GC .20 .50
21 Rod Carew .15 .40
22 Bill Madlock .02 .10
23 Lonnie Smith .01 .05
24 Cecil Cooper .02 .10
25 Ken Griffey .02 .10
26 Ty Cobb GC .40 1.00
27 Pete Rose .30 .75
28 Rusty Staub .02 .10
29 Tony Perez .02 .10
30 Al Oliver .02 .10
31 Cy Young GC .20 .50
32 Gaylord Perry .15 .40
33 Ferguson Jenkins .15 .40
34 Phil Niekro .15 .40
35 Jim Palmer .15 .40
36 Tommy John .02 .10
37 Walter Johnson GC .20 .50
38 Steve Carlton .15 .40
39 Nolan Ryan 1.00 2.50
40 Tom Seaver .15 .40
41 Don Sutton .15 .40
42 Bert Blyleven .02 .10
43 Frank Robinson GC .15 .40
44 Joe Morgan .15 .40
45 Rollie Fingers .10 .30
46 Keith Hernandez .02 .10
47 Robin Yount .10 .30
48 Cal Ripken 1.00 2.50
49 Dale Murphy .10 .30
50 Mickey Mantle GC 1.25 3.00
51 Johnny Bench .20 .50
52 Carlton Fisk .20 .50
53 Tug McGraw .02 .10
54 Paul Molitor .20 .50
55 Carl Hubbell GC .10 .30
56 Steve Garvey .02 .10
57 Dave Parker .02 .10
58 Gary Carter .20 .50
59 Fred Lynn .02 .10
60 Checklist Card .01 .05

1985 Donruss

The 1985 Donruss set consists of 660 standard-size cards. The wax packs, packed 36 packs to a box and 20 boxes to a case, contained 15 cards and a Lou Gehrig puzzle panel. The fronts feature full color photos framed by jet black borders (making the cards condition sensitive). The first 26 cards of the set feature Diamond Kings (DK), for the fourth year in a row; the artwork on the Diamond Kings was again produced by the Perez-Steele Galleries. Cards 27-46 feature Rated Rookies (RR). The unnumbered checklist cards are arbitrarily numbered below as numbers 654 through 660. Rookie Cards in this set include Roger Clemens, Eric Davis, Shawon Dunston, Dwight Gooden, Orel Hershiser, Jimmy Key, Terry Pendleton, Kirby Puckett and Bret Saberhagen.

COMPLETE SET (660) 20.00 50.00
COMP.FACT.SET (660) 30.00 60.00
COMP.GEHRIG PUZZLE 1.50 4.00
1 Ryne Sandberg DK .50 1.25
2 Doug DeCinces DK .05 .15
3 Richard Dotson DK .05 .15
4 Bert Blyleven DK .15 .40
5 Lou Whitaker DK .15 .40
6 Dan Quisenberry DK .05 .15
7 Don Mattingly DK 1.00 2.50
8 Carney Lansford DK .15 .40
9 Frank Tanana DK .15 .40
10 Willie Upshaw DK .05 .15
11 C.Washington DK .05 .15
12 Mike Marshall DK .05 .15
13 Joaquin Andujar DK .15 .40
14 Cal Ripken DK 1.00 2.50
15 Jim Rice DK .15 .40
16 Don Sutton DK .15 .40
17 Frank Viola DK .15 .40
18 Alvin Davis DK .15 .40
19 Mario Soto DK .15 .40
20 Jose Cruz DK .15 .40
21 Charlie Lea DK .05 .15
22 Jesse Orosco DK .05 .15
23 Juan Samuel DK .05 .15
24 Tony Pena DK .05 .15
25 Tony Gwynn DK .50 1.25
26 Bob Brenly DK .05 .15
27 Danny Tartabull RC .40 1.00
28 Mike Bielecki RC .08 .25
29 Steve Lyons RC .20 .50
30 Jeff Reed RC .08 .25
31 Tony Brewer RC .08 .25
32 John Morris RC .08 .25
33 Daryl Boston RC .08 .25
34 Al Pulido RC .08 .25
35 Steve Kiefer RC .08 .25
36 Larry Sheets RC .08 .25
37 Scott Bradley RC .08 .25
38 Calvin Schiraldi RC .20 .50
39 Shawon Dunston RC .40 1.00
40 Charlie Mitchell RC .08 .25
41 Billy Hatcher RC .20 .50
42 Russ Stephans RC .08 .25
43 Alejandro Sanchez RC .08 .25
44 Steve Jeltz RC .08 .25
45 Jim Traber RC .08 .25
46 Doug Loman RC .08 .25
47 Eddie Murray .50 1.25
48 Robin Yount .75 2.00
49 Lance Parrish .15 .40
50 Jim Rice .15 .40
51 Dave Winfield .15 .40
52 Fernando Valenzuela .15 .40
53 George Brett 1.25 3.00
54 Dave Kingman .15 .40
55 Gary Carter .15 .40
56 Buddy Bell .15 .40
57 Reggie Jackson .30 .75
58 Harold Baines .15 .40
59 Ozzie Smith .75 2.00
60 Nolan Ryan UER 2.50 6.00
61 Mike Schmidt 1.25 3.00
62 Dave Parker .15 .40
63 Tony Gwynn 1.00 2.50
64 Tony Pena .05 .15
65 Jack Clark .15 .40
66 Dale Murphy .30 .75
67 Ryne Sandberg 1.00 2.50
68 Keith Hernandez .15 .40
69 Alvin Davis RC* .20 .50
70 Kent Hrbek .15 .40
71 Willie Upshaw .05 .15
72 Dave Engle .05 .15
73 Alfredo Griffin .05 .15
74A Jack Perconte .05 .15
Career Highlights
takes four lines
74B Jack Perconte .05 .15
Career Highlights
takes three lines
75 Jesse Orosco .05 .15
76 Jody Davis .05 .15
77 Bob Horner .15 .40
78 Larry McWilliams .05 .15
79 Joel Youngblood .05 .15
80 Alan Wiggins .05 .15
81 Ron Oester .05 .15
82 Ozzie Virgil .05 .15
83 Ricky Horton .05 .15
84 Bill Doran .05 .15
85 Rod Carew .30 .75
86 LaMarr Hoyt .05 .15
87 Tim Wallach .05 .15
88 Mike Flanagan .05 .15
89 Jim Sundberg .15 .40
90 Chet Lemon .15 .40
91 Bob Stanley .05 .15
92 Willie Randolph .15 .40
93 Bill Russell .15 .40
94 Julio Franco .15 .40
95 Dan Quisenberry .05 .15
96 Bill Caudill .05 .15
97 Bill Gullickson .05 .15
98 Danny Darwin .05 .15
99 Curtis Wilkerson .05 .15
100 Bud Black .05 .15
101 Tony Phillips .05 .15
102 Tony Bernazard .05 .15
103 Jay Howell .05 .15
104 Burt Hooton .05 .15
105 Milt Wilcox .05 .15
106 Rich Dauer .05 .15
107 Don Sutton .15 .40
108 Mike Witt .05 .15
109 Bruce Sutter .15 .40
110 Enos Cabell .05 .15
111 John Denny .05 .15
112 Dave Dravecky .05 .15
113 Marvell Wynne .05 .15
114 Johnnie LeMaster .05 .15
115 Chuck Porter .05 .15
116 John Gibbons RC .05 .15
117 Keith Moreland .05 .15
118 Darnell Coles .05 .15
119 Dennis Lamp .05 .15
120 Ron Davis .05 .15
121 Nick Esasky .05 .15
122 Vance Law .05 .15
123 Gary Roenicke .05 .15
124 Bill Schroeder .05 .15
125 Dave Rozema .05 .15
126 Bobby Meacham .05 .15
127 Marty Barrett .05 .15
128 R.J. Reynolds .05 .15
129 Ernie Camacho UER .05 .15
Photo actually
Rich Thompson
130 Jorge Orta .05 .15
131 Lary Sorensen .05 .15
132 Terry Francona .15 .40
133 Fred Lynn .15 .40
134 Bob Jones .05 .15
135 Jerry Hairston .05 .15
136 Kevin Bass .05 .15
137 Garry Maddox .05 .15
138 Dave LaPoint .05 .15
139 Kevin McReynolds .15 .40
140 Wayne Krenchicki .05 .15
141 Rafael Ramirez .05 .15
142 Rod Scurry .05 .15
143 Greg Minton .05 .15
144 Tim Stoddard .05 .15
145 Steve Henderson .05 .15
146 George Bell .15 .40
147 Dave Meier .05 .15
148 Sammy Stewart .05 .15
149 Mark Brouhard .05 .15
150 Larry Herndon .05 .15
151 Oil Can Boyd .05 .15
152 Brian Dayett .05 .15
153 Tom Niedenfuer .05 .15
154 Brook Jacoby .05 .15
155 Onix Concepcion .05 .15
156 Tim Conroy .05 .15
157 Joe Hesketh .05 .15
158 Brian Downing .15 .40
159 Tommy Dunbar .05 .15
160 Marc Hill .05 .15
161 Phil Garner .15 .40
162 Jerry Davis .05 .15
163 Bill Campbell .05 .15
164 John Franco RC .40 1.00
165 Len Barker .05 .15
166 Benny Distefano .05 .15
167 George Frazier .05 .15
168 Tito Landrum .05 .15
169 Cal Ripken 2.00 5.00
170 Cecil Cooper .15 .40
171 Alan Trammell .15 .40
172 Wade Boggs .50 1.25
173 Don Baylor .15 .40
174 Pedro Guerrero .15 .40
175 Frank White .15 .40
176 Rickey Henderson .60 1.50
177 Charlie Lea .05 .15
178 Pete O'Brien .05 .15
179 Doug DeCinces .05 .15
180 Ron Kittle .05 .15
181 George Hendrick .15 .40
182 Joe Niekro .05 .15
183 Juan Samuel .05 .15
184 Mario Soto .15 .40
185 Rich Gossage .15 .40
186 Johnny Ray .05 .15
187 Bob Brenly .05 .15
188 Craig McMurtry .05 .15
189 Leon Durham .05 .15
190 Dwight Gooden RC 1.25 3.00
191 Barry Bonnell .05 .15
192 Tim Teufel .05 .15
193 Dave Stieb .15 .40
194 Mickey Hatcher .05 .15
195 Jesse Barfield .15 .40
196 Al Cowens .05 .15
197 Hubie Brooks .05 .15
198 Steve Trout .05 .15
199 Glenn Hubbard .05 .15
200 Bill Madlock .15 .40
201 Jeff D. Robinson .05 .15
202 Eric Show .05 .15
203 Dave Concepcion .15 .40
204 Ivan DeJesus .05 .15
205 Neil Allen .05 .15
206 Jerry Mumphrey .05 .15
207 Mike C. Brown .05 .15
208 Carlton Fisk .30 .75
209 Bryn Smith .05 .15
210 Tippy Martinez .05 .15
211 Dion James .05 .15
212 Willie Hernandez .05 .15
213 Mike Easler .05 .15
214 Ron Guidry .15 .40
215 Rick Honeycutt .05 .15
216 Brett Butler .15 .40
217 Larry Gura .05 .15
218 Ray Burris .05 .15
219 Steve Rogers .15 .40
220 Frank Tanana UER .15 .40
Bats Left listed
twice on card back
221 Ned Yost .05 .15
222 B.Saberhagen RC UER .60 1.50
223 Mike Davis .05 .15
224 Bert Blyleven .15 .40
225 Steve Kemp .05 .15
226 Jerry Reuss .05 .15
227 Darrell Evans UER .15 .40
80 homers in 1980
228 Wayne Gross .05 .15
229 Jim Gantner .05 .15
230 Bob Boone .15 .40
231 Lonnie Smith .05 .15
232 Frank DiPino .05 .15
233 Jerry Koosman .15 .40
234 Graig Nettles .15 .40
235 John Tudor .15 .40
236 John Rabb .05 .15
237 Rick Manning .05 .15
238 Mike Fitzgerald .05 .15
239 Gary Matthews .15 .40
240 Jim Presley .20 .50
241 Dave Collins .05 .15
242 Gary Gaetti .15 .40
243 Dann Bilardello .05 .15
244 Rudy Law .05 .15
245 John Lowenstein .05 .15
246 Tom Tellmann .05 .15
247 Howard Johnson .15 .40
248 Ray Fontenot .05 .15
249 Tony Armas .15 .40
250 Candy Maldonado .05 .15
251 Mike Jeffcoat .05 .15
252 Dane Iorg .05 .15
253 Bruce Bochte .05 .15
254 Pete Rose Expos 1.50 4.00
255 Don Aase .05 .15
256 George Wright .05 .15
257 Britt Burns .05 .15
258 Mike Scott .15 .40
259 Len Matuszek .05 .15
260 Dave Rucker .05 .15
261 Craig Lefferts .05 .15
262 Jay Tibbs .05 .15
263 Bruce Benedict .05 .15
264 Don Robinson .05 .15
265 Gary Lavelle .05 .15
266 Scott Sanderson .05 .15
267 Matt Young .05 .15
268 Ernie Whitt .05 .15
269 Houston Jimenez .05 .15
270 Ken Dixon .05 .15
271 Pete Ladd .05 .15
272 Juan Berenguer .05 .15
273 Roger Clemens RC 8.00 20.00
274 Rick Cerone .05 .15
275 Dave Anderson .05 .15
276 George Vukovich .05 .15
277 Greg Pryor .05 .15
278 Mike Warren .05 .15
279 Bob James .05 .15
280 Bobby Grich .15 .40
281 Mike Mason RC .08 .25
282 Ron Reed .05 .15
283 Alan Ashby .05 .15
284 Mark Thurmond .05 .15
285 Joe Lefebvre .05 .15
286 Ted Power .05 .15
287 Chris Chambliss .15 .40
288 Lee Tunnell .05 .15
289 Rich Bordi .05 .15
290 Glenn Brummer .05 .15
291 Mike Boddicker .05 .15
292 Rollie Fingers .15 .40
293 Lou Whitaker .15 .40
294 Dwight Evans .30 .75
295 Don Mattingly 2.00 5.00
296 Mike Marshall .05 .15
297 Willie Wilson .15 .40
298 Mike Heath .05 .15
299 Tim Raines .15 .40
300 Larry Parrish .05 .15
301 Geoff Zahn .05 .15
302 Rich Dotson .05 .15
303 David Green .05 .15
304 Jose Cruz .15 .40
305 Steve Carlton .15 .40
306 Gary Redus .05 .15
307 Steve Garvey .15 .40
308 Jose DeLeon .05 .15
309 Randy Lerch .05 .15
310 Claudell Washington .05 .15
311 Lee Smith .15 .40
312 Darryl Strawberry .50 1.25
313 Jim Beattie .05 .15
314 John Butcher .05 .15
315 Damaso Garcia .05 .15
316 Mike Smithson .05 .15
317 Luis Leal .05 .15
318 Ken Phelps .05 .15
319 Wally Backman .05 .15
320 Ron Cey .15 .40
321 Brad Komminsk .05 .15
322 Jason Thompson .05 .15
323 Frank Williams .05 .15
324 Tim Lollar .05 .15
325 Eric Davis RC 1.25 3.00
326 Von Hayes .05 .15
327 Andy Van Slyke .30 .75
328 Craig Reynolds .05 .15
329 Dick Schofield .05 .15
330 Scott Fletcher .05 .15
331 Jeff Reardon .15 .40
332 Rick Dempsey .05 .15
333 Ben Oglivie .15 .40
334 Dan Petry .05 .15
335 Jackie Gutierrez .05 .15
336 Dave Righetti .15 .40
337 Alejandro Pena .05 .15
338 Mel Hall .05 .15
339 Pat Sheridan .05 .15
340 Keith Atherton .05 .15
341 David Palmer .05 .15
342 Gary Ward .05 .15
343 Dave Stewart .15 .40
344 Mark Gubicza RC .20 .50
345 Carney Lansford .15 .40
346 Jerry Willard .05 .15
347 Ken Griffey .15 .40
348 Franklin Stubbs .05 .15
349 Aurelio Lopez .05 .15
350 Al Bumbry .05 .15
351 Charlie Moore .05 .15
352 Luis Sanchez .05 .15
353 Darrell Porter .05 .15
354 Bill Dawley .05 .15
355 Charles Hudson .05 .15
356 Garry Templeton .15 .40
357 Cecilio Guante .05 .15
358 Jeff Leonard .05 .15
359 Paul Molitor .15 .40
360 Ron Gardenhire .05 .15
361 Larry Bowa .15 .40
362 Bob Kearney .05 .15
363 Garth Iorg .05 .15
364 Tom Brunansky .05 .15
365 Brad Gulden .05 .15
366 Greg Walker .05 .15
367 Mike Young .05 .15
368 Rick Waits .05 .15
369 Doug Bair .05 .15
370 Bob Shirley .05 .15
371 Bob Ojeda .05 .15
372 Bob Welch .15 .40
373 Neal Heaton .05 .15
374 Danny Jackson UER .05 .15
Photo actually
Frank Wills
375 Donnie Hill .05 .15
376 Mike Stenhouse .05 .15
377 Bruce Kison .05 .15
378 Wayne Tolleson .05 .15
379 Floyd Bannister .05 .15
380 Vern Ruhle .05 .15
381 Tim Corcoran .05 .15
382 Kurt Kepshire .05 .15
383 Bobby Brown .05 .15
384 Dave Van Gorder .05 .15
385 Rick Mahler .05 .15
386 Lee Mazzilli .15 .40
387 Bill Laskey .05 .15
388 Thad Bosley .05 .15
389 Al Chambers .05 .15
390 Tony Fernandez .15 .40
391 Ron Washington .05 .15
392 Bill Swaggerty .05 .15
393 Bob L. Gibson .05 .15
394 Marty Castillo .05 .15
395 Steve Crawford .05 .15
396 Clay Christiansen .05 .15
397 Bob Bailor .05 .15
398 Mike Hargrove .05 .15
399 Charlie Leibrandt .05 .15
400 Tom Burgmeier .05 .15
401 Razor Shines .05 .15
402 Rob Wilfong .05 .15
403 Tom Henke .15 .40
404 Al Jones .05 .15
405 Mike LaCoss .05 .15
406 Luis DeLeon .05 .15
407 Greg Gross .05 .15
408 Tom Hume .05 .15
409 Rick Camp .05 .15
410 Milt May .05 .15
411 Henry Cotto RC .08 .25
412 David Von Ohlen .05 .15
413 Scott McGregor .05 .15
414 Ted Simmons .15 .40
415 Jack Morris .15 .40
416 Bill Buckner .15 .40
417 Butch Wynegar .05 .15
418 Steve Sax .05 .15
419 Steve Balboni .05 .15
420 Dwayne Murphy .05 .15
421 Andre Dawson .15 .40
422 Charlie Hough .15 .40
423 Tommy John .15 .40
424A Tom Seaver ERR .30 .75
Photo actually
Floyd Bannister
424B Tom Seaver COR 4.00 10.00
425 Tom Herr .05 .15
426 Terry Puhl .05 .15
427 Al Holland .05 .15
428 Eddie Milner .05 .15
429 Terry Kennedy .05 .15
430 John Candelaria .05 .15
431 Manny Trillo .05 .15
432 Ken Oberkfell .05 .15
433 Rick Sutcliffe .15 .40
434 Ron Darling .15 .40
435 Spike Owen .05 .15
436 Frank Viola .15 .40
437 Lloyd Moseby .05 .15
438 Kirby Puckett RC 6.00 15.00
439 Jim Clancy .05 .15
440 Mike Moore .05 .15
441 Doug Sisk .05 .15
442 Dennis Eckersley .30 .75
443 Gerald Perry .05 .15
444 Dale Berra .05 .15
445 Dusty Baker .15 .40
446 Ed Whitson .05 .15
447 Cesar Cedeno .15 .40
448 Rick Schu .05 .15
449 Joaquin Andujar .15 .40
450 Mark Bailey .05 .15
451 Ron Romanick .05 .15
452 Julio Cruz .05 .15
453 Miguel Dilone .05 .15
454 Storm Davis .05 .15
455 Jaime Cocanower .05 .15
456 Barbaro Garbey .05 .15
457 Rich Gedman .05 .15
458 Phil Niekro .15 .40
459 Mike Scioscia .15 .40
460 Pat Tabler .05 .15
461 Darryl Motley .05 .15
462 Chris Codiroli .05 .15
463 Doug Flynn .05 .15
464 Billy Sample .05 .15
465 Mickey Rivers .05 .15
466 John Wathan .05 .15
467 Bill Krueger .05 .15
468 Andre Thornton .05 .15
469 Rex Hudler .05 .15
470 Sid Bream RC .20 .50
471 Kirk Gibson .15 .40
472 John Shelby .05 .15
473 Moose Haas .05 .15
474 Doug Corbett .05 .15
475 Willie McGee .15 .40
476 Bob Knepper .05 .15
477 Kevin Gross .05 .15
478 Carmelo Martinez .05 .15
479 Kent Tekulve .05 .15
480 Chili Davis .15 .40
481 Bobby Clark .05 .15
482 Mookie Wilson .15 .40
483 Dave Owen .05 .15
484 Ed Nunez .05 .15
485 Rance Mulliniks .05 .15
486 Ken Schrom .05 .15
487 Jeff Russell .05 .15
488 Tom Paciorek .05 .15
489 Dan Ford .05 .15
490 Mike Caldwell .05 .15
491 Scottie Earl .05 .15
492 Jose Rijo RC .40 1.00
493 Bruce Hurst .05 .15
494 Ken Landreaux .05 .15
495 Mike Fischlin .05 .15
496 Don Slaught .05 .15
497 Steve McCatty .05 .15
498 Gary Lucas .05 .15
499 Gary Pettis .05 .15
500 Marvis Foley .05 .15
501 Mike Squires .05 .15
502 Jim Pankovits .05 .15
503 Luis Aguayo .05 .15
504 Ralph Citarella .05 .15
505 Bruce Bochy .05 .15
506 Bob Owchinko .05 .15
507 Pascual Perez .05 .15
508 Lee Lacy .05 .15
509 Atlee Hammaker .05 .15
510 Bob Dernier .05 .15
511 Ed VandeBerg .05 .15
512 Cliff Johnson .05 .15
513 Len Whitehouse .05 .15
514 Dennis Martinez .15 .40
515 Ed Romero .05 .15
516 Rusty Kuntz .05 .15
517 Rick Miller .05 .15
518 Dennis Rasmussen .05 .15
519 Steve Yeager .15 .40
520 Chris Bando .05 .15
521 U.L. Washington .05 .15
522 Curt Young .05 .15
523 Angel Salazar .05 .15
524 Curt Kaufman .05 .15
525 Odell Jones .05 .15
526 Juan Agosto .05 .15
527 Denny Walling .05 .15
528 Andy Hawkins .05 .15
529 Sixto Lezcano .05 .15
530 Skeeter Barnes RC .08 .25
531 Randy Johnson .05 .15
532 Jim Morrison .05 .15
533 Warren Brusstar .05 .15
534A Terry Pendleton RC .40 1.00
ERR Wrong first name as Jeff
534B Terry Pendleton COR .40 1.00
535 Vic Rodriguez .05 .15

536 Bob McClure .05 .15
537 Dave Bergman .05 .15
538 Mark Clear .05 .15
539 Mike Pagliarulo .05 .15
540 Terry Whitfield .05 .15
541 Joe Beckwith .05 .15
542 Jeff Burroughs .05 .15
543 Dan Schatzeder .05 .15
544 Donnie Scott .05 .15
545 Jim Slaton .05 .15
546 Greg Luzinski .15 .40
547 Mark Salas .05 .15
548 Dave Smith .05 .15
549 John Wockenfuss .05 .15
550 Frank Pastore .05 .15
551 Tim Flannery .05 .15
552 Rick Rhoden .05 .15
553 Mark Davis .05 .15
554 Jeff Dedmon .05 .15
555 Gary Woods .05 .15
556 Danny Heep .05 .15
557 Mark Langston RC .40 1.00
558 Darrell Brown .05 .15
559 Jimmy Key RC .40 1.00
560 Rick Lysander .05 .15
561 Doyle Alexander .05 .15
562 Mike Stanton .05 .15
563 Sid Fernandez .15 .40
564 Richie Hebner .05 .15
565 Alex Trevino .05 .15
566 Brian Harper .05 .15
567 Dan Gladden RC .20 .50
568 Luis Salazar .05 .15
569 Tom Foley .05 .15
570 Larry Andersen .05 .15
571 Danny Cox .05 .15
572 Joe Sambito .05 .15
573 Juan Beniquez .05 .15
574 Joel Skinner .05 .15
575 Randy St.Claire .05 .15
576 Floyd Rayford .05 .15
577 Roy Howell .05 .15
578 John Grubb .05 .15
579 Ed Jurak .05 .15
580 John Montefusco .05 .15
581 Orel Hershiser RC 1.25 3.00
582 Tom Waddell .05 .15
583 Mark Huismann .05 .15
584 Joe Morgan .15 .40
585 Jim Wohlford .05 .15
586 Dave Schmidt .05 .15
587 Jeff Kunkel .05 .15
588 Hal McRae .15 .40
589 Bill Almon .05 .15
590 Carmelo Castillo .05 .15
591 Omar Moreno .05 .15
592 Ken Howell .05 .15
593 Tom Brookens .05 .15
594 Joe Nolan .05 .15
595 Willie Lozado .05 .15
596 Tom Nieto .05 .15
597 Walt Terrell .05 .15
598 Al Oliver .15 .40
599 Shane Rawley .05 .15
600 Denny Gonzalez .05 .15
601 Mark Grant .05 .15
602 Mike Armstrong .05 .15
603 George Foster .15 .40
604 Dave Lopes .15 .40
605 Salome Barojas .05 .15
606 Roy Lee Jackson .05 .15
607 Pete Filson .05 .15
608 Duane Walker .05 .15
609 Glenn Wilson .05 .15
610 Rafael Santana .05 .15
611 Roy Smith .05 .15
612 Ruppert Jones .05 .15
613 Joe Cowley .05 .15
614 Al Nipper UER Photo actually Mike Brown .05 .15
615 Gene Nelson .05 .15
616 Joe Carter .50 1.25
617 Ray Knight .15 .40
618 Chuck Rainey .05 .15
619 Dan Driessen .05 .15
620 Daryl Sconiers .05 .15
621 Bill Stein .05 .15
622 Roy Smalley .05 .15
623 Ed Lynch .05 .15
624 Jeff Stone RC .05 .15
625 Bruce Berenyi .05 .15
626 Kelvin Chapman .05 .15
627 Joe Price .05 .15
628 Steve Bedrosian .05 .15
629 Vic Mata .05 .15
630 Mike Krukow .05 .15
631 Phil Bradley .20 .50
632 Jim Gott .05 .15
633 Randy Bush .05 .15
634 Tom Browning RC .20 .50
635 Lou Gehrig Puzzle Card .50 1.25
636 Reid Nichols .05 .15
637 Dan Pasqua RC .20 .50
638 German Rivera .05 .15
639 Don Schulze .05 .15
640A Mike Jones Career Highlights, takes five lines .05 .15
640B Mike Jones Career Highlights, takes four lines .05 .15
641 Pete Rose 1.50 4.00
642 Wade Rowdon .05 .15
643 Jerry Narron .05 .15
644 Darrell Miller .05 .15
645 Tim Hulett RC .08 .25
646 Andy McGaffigan .05 .15
647 Kurt Bevacqua .05 .15
648 John Russell .05 .15
649 Ron Robinson .05 .15
650 Donnie Moore .05 .15
651A Two for the Title YL .75 2.00
651B Two for the Title WL 2.00 5.00
652 Tim Laudner .05 .15
653 Steve Farr RC .20 .50
654 DK Checklist 1-26 Unnumbered .05 .15
655 Checklist 27-130 Unnumbered .05 .15
656 Checklist 131-234 Unnumbered .05 .15
657 Checklist 235-338 Unnumbered .05 .15
658 Checklist 339-442 Unnumbered .05 .15
659 Checklist 443-546 Unnumbered .05 .15
660 Checklist 547-653 Unnumbered .05 .15

1985 Donruss Lou Gehrig Puzzle

1 Gehrig Puzzle 1-3 .10 .25
4 Gehrig Puzzle 4-6 .10 .25
7 Gehrig Puzzle 7-9 .10 .25
10 Gehrig Puzzle 10-12 .10 .25
13 Gehrig Puzzle 13-15 .10 .25
16 Gehrig Puzzle 16-18 .10 .25
19 Gehrig Puzzle 19-21 .10 .25
22 Gehrig Puzzle 22-24 .10 .25
25 Gehrig Puzzle 25-27 .10 .25
28 Gehrig Puzzle 28-30 .10 .25
31 Gehrig Puzzle 31-33 .10 .25
34 Gehrig Puzzle 34-36 .10 .25
37 Gehrig Puzzle 37-39 .10 .25
40 Gehrig Puzzle 40-42 .10 .25
43 Gehrig Puzzle 43-45 .10 .25
46 Gehrig Puzzle 46-48 .10 .25
49 Gehrig Puzzle 49-51 .10 .25
52 Gehrig Puzzle 52-54 .10 .25
55 Gehrig Puzzle 55-57 .10 .25
58 Gehrig Puzzle 58-60 .10 .25
61 Gehrig Puzzle 61-63 .10 .25

1985 Donruss Wax Box Cards

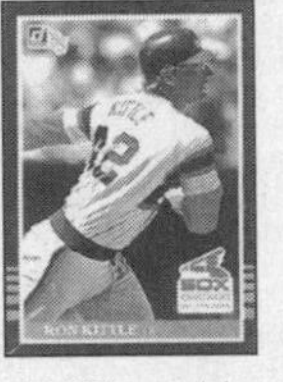

The boxes of the 1985 Donruss regular issue baseball cards, in which the wax packs were contained, featured four standard-size cards, with backs. The complete set price of the regular issue set does not include these cards; they are considered a separate set. The cards are styled the same as the regular Donruss cards. The cards are numbered but with the prefix PC before the number. The value of the panel uncut is slightly greater, perhaps by 25 percent greater, than the value of the individual cards cut up carefully.

COMPLETE SET (4) 1.50 4.00
PC1 Dwight Gooden .40 1.00
PC2 Ryne Sandberg 1.25 3.00
PC3 Ron Kittle .08 .25
PUZ Lou Gehrig Puzzle Card .30 .75

1985 Donruss Action All-Stars

The cards in this 60-card set measure approximately 3 1/2" by 5". For the third year in a row, Donruss issued a set of Action All-Stars. This set features action photos on the obverse which also contains a portrait inset of the player. The backs, unlike the year before, do not contain a full color picture of the player but list, if space is available, full statistical data, biographical data, career highlights, and acquisition and contract status. The cards were issued with a Lou Gehrig puzzle card.

COMPLETE SET (60) 3.00 8.00
1 Tim Raines .02 .10
2 Jim Gantner .01 .05
3 Mario Soto .01 .05
4 Spike Owen .01 .05
5 Lloyd Moseby .01 .05
6 Damaso Garcia .01 .05
7 Cal Ripken 1.00 2.50
8 Dan Quisenberry .01 .05
9 Eddie Murray .25 .60
10 Tony Pena .02 .10
11 Buddy Bell .02 .10
12 Dave Winfield .15 .40
13 Ron Kittle .01 .05
14 Rich Gossage .02 .10
15 Dwight Evans .02 .10
16 Alvin Davis .01 .05
17 Mike Schmidt .25 .60
18 Pascual Perez .01 .05
19 Tony Gwynn .75 2.00
20 Nolan Ryan 1.00 2.50
21 Robin Yount .15 .40
22 Mike Marshall .01 .05
23 Brett Butler .02 .10
24 Ryne Sandberg .30 .75
25 Dale Murphy .10 .30
26 George Brett .50 1.25
27 Jim Rice .02 .10
28 Ozzie Smith .40 1.00
29 Larry Parrish .01 .05
30 Jack Clark .02 .10
31 Manny Trillo .01 .05
32 Dave Kingman .07 .20
33 Geoff Zahn .01 .05
34 Pedro Guerrero .02 .10
35 Dave Parker .02 .10
36 Rollie Fingers .15 .40
37 Fernando Valenzuela .07 .20
38 Wade Boggs .20 .50
39 Reggie Jackson .20 .50
40 Kent Hrbek .02 .10
41 Keith Hernandez .02 .10
42 Lou Whitaker .02 .10
43 Tom Herr .01 .05
44 Alan Trammell .07 .20
45 Butch Wynegar .01 .05
46 Leon Durham .01 .05
47 Dwight Gooden .20 .50
48 Don Mattingly .60 1.50
49 Phil Niekro .15 .40
50 Johnny Ray .01 .05
51 Doug DeCinces .01 .05
52 Willie Upshaw .01 .05
53 Lance Parrish .02 .10
54 Jody Davis .01 .05
55 Steve Carlton .15 .40
56 Juan Samuel .01 .05
57 Gary Carter .20 .50
58 Harold Baines .10 .30
59 Eric Show .01 .05
60 Checklist Card .01 .05

1985 Donruss Highlights

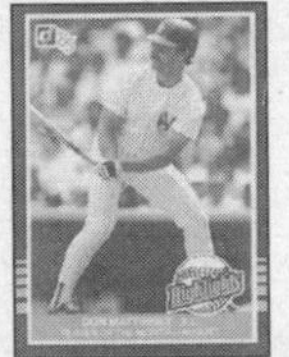

This 56-card standard-size set features the players and pitchers of the month for each league as well as a number of highlight cards commemorating the 1985 season. The Donruss Company dedicated the last two cards to their own selections for Rookies of the Year (ROY). This set proved to be more popular than the Donruss Company had predicted, as their first and only print run was exhausted before card dealers' initial orders were filled.

COMPLETE SET (56) 6.00 15.00
1 Tom Seaver .30 .75
2 Rollie Fingers .20 .50
3 Mike Davis .02 .10
4 Charlie Leibrandt .02 .10
5 Dale Murphy .20 .50
6 Fernando Valenzuela .07 .20
7 Larry Bowa .07 .20
8 Dave Concepcion .07 .20
9 Tony Perez .20 .50
10 Pete Rose .60 1.50
11 George Brett .60 1.50
12 Dave Stieb .02 .10
13 Dave Parker .07 .20
14 Andy Hawkins .02 .10
15 Andy Hawkins .02 .10
16 Von Hayes .02 .10
17 Rickey Henderson .30 .75
18 Jay Howell .02 .10
19 Pedro Guerrero .07 .20
20 John Tudor .02 .10
21 Keith Hernandez and Gary Carter: Marathon Game I .20 .50
22 Nolan Ryan 2.00 5.00
23 LaMarr Hoyt .02 .10
24 Oddibe McDowell .02 .10
25 George Brett .60 1.50
26 Bret Saberhagen .20 .50
27 Keith Hernandez .07 .20
28 Fernando Valenzuela .07 .20
29 Willie McGee and Vince Coleman: Record Setting B .07 .20
30 Tom Seaver .20 .50
31 Rod Carew .20 .50
32 Dwight Gooden .30 .75
33 Dwight Gooden .30 .75
34 Eddie Murray .20 .50
35 Don Baylor .07 .20
36 Don Mattingly .60 1.50
37 Dave Righetti .07 .20
38 Willie McGee .07 .20
39 Shane Rawley .02 .10
40 Pete Rose .60 1.50
41 Andre Dawson .20 .50
42 Rickey Henderson .30 .75
43 Tom Browning .07 .20
44 Don Mattingly .60 1.50
45 Don Mattingly .60 1.50
46 Charlie Leibrandt .02 .10
47 Gary Carter .20 .50
48 Dwight Gooden .30 .75
49 Wade Boggs .30 .75
50 Phil Niekro .20 .50
51 Darrell Evans .07 .20
52 Willie McGee .10 .30
53 Dave Winfield .20 .50
54 Vince Coleman .07 .20
55 Ozzie Guillen .20 .50
NNO Checklist Card .02 .10

1985 Donruss HOF Sluggers

This eight-card set of Hall of Fame players features the artwork of resident Donruss artist Dick Perez. These oversized (3 1/2" by 6 1/2", blank backed cards actually form part of a box of gum distributed by the Donruss Company through supermarket type outlets. These cards are reminiscent of the Bazooka issues. The players in the set were ostensibly chosen based on their career slugging percentage. The cards themselves are numbered by (slugging percentage) rank. The boxes are also numbered on one of the white side tabs of the complete box; this completely different numbering system is not used.

COMPLETE SET (8) 4.00 10.00
1 Babe Ruth 1.25 3.00
2 Ted Williams .75 2.00
3 Lou Gehrig .75 2.00
4 Johnny Mize .20 .50
5 Stan Musial .30 .75
6 Mickey Mantle 1.25 3.00
7 Hank Aaron .60 1.50
8 Frank Robinson .20 .50

1985 Donruss Super DK's

The cards in this 28-card set measure approximately 4 15/16 by 6 3/4". The 1985 Donruss Diamond Kings Supers set contains enlarged cards of the first 26 cards of the Donruss regular set of this year. In addition, the Diamond Kings checklist card, a card of artist Dick Perez and a Lou Gehrig puzzle card are included in the set. The set was the brain-child of the Perez-Steele Galleries and could be obtained via a write-in offer on the wrappers of the Donruss regular cards of this year. The Gehrig puzzle card is actually a 12-piece jigsaw puzzle. The back of the checklist card is blank; however, the Dick Perez card back gives a short history of Dick Perez and the Perez-Steele Galleries. The offer for obtaining this set was detailed on the wax pack wrappers; three wrappers plus $9.00 was required for this mail-in offer.

COMPLETE SET (28) 5.00 12.00
1 Ryne Sandberg .75 2.00
2 Doug DeCinces .08 .25
3 Richard Dotson .08 .25
4 Bert Blyleven .20 .50
5 Lou Whitaker .30 .75
6 Dan Quisenberry .08 .25
7 Don Mattingly 1.25 3.00
8 Carney Lansford .20 .50
9 Frank Tanana .08 .25
10 Willie Upshaw .08 .25
11 Claudell Washington .08 .25
12 Mike Marshall .08 .25
13 Joaquin Andujar .08 .25
14 Cal Ripken 2.00 5.00
15 Jim Rice .20 .50
16 Don Sutton .40 1.00
17 Frank Viola .20 .50
18 Alvin Davis .08 .25
19 Mario Soto .08 .25
20 Jose Cruz .08 .25
21 Charlie Lea .08 .25
22 Jesse Orosco .20 .50
23 Juan Samuel .08 .25
24 Tony Pena .20 .50
25 Tony Gwynn 1.25 3.00
26 Bob Brenly .08 .25
NNO Checklist Card .08 .25
NNO Dick Perez/(History of DK's) .08 .25

1986 Donruss

The 1986 Donruss set consists of 660 standard-size cards. Wax packs, packed 36 packs to a box and 20 boxes to a case, contained 15 cards plus a Hank Aaron puzzle panel. The card fronts feature blue borders, the standard team logo, player's name, position, and Donruss logo. The first 26 cards of the set are Diamond Kings (DK), for the fifth year in a row; the artwork on the Diamond Kings was again produced by the Perez-Steele Galleries. Cards 27-46 again feature Rated Rookies (RR). The unnumbered checklist cards are arbitrarily numbered below as numbers 654 through 660. Rookie Cards in this set include Jose Canseco, Darren Daulton, Len Dykstra, Cecil Fielder, Andres Galarraga, Fred McGriff and Paul O'Neill.

COMPLETE SET (660) 15.00 40.00
COMP.FACT.SET (660) 15.00 40.00
COMP.AARON PUZZLE .75 2.00
1 Kirk Gibson DK .08 .25
2 Goose Gossage DK .08 .25
3 Willie McGee DK .08 .25
4 George Bell DK .08 .25
5 Tony Armas DK .08 .25
6 Chili Davis DK .08 .25
7 Cecil Cooper DK .08 .25
8 Mike Boddicker DK .05 .15
9 Dave Lopes DK .08 .25
10 Bill Doran DK .05 .15
11 Bret Saberhagen DK .08 .25
12 Brett Butler DK .08 .25
13 Harold Baines DK .08 .25
14 Mike Davis DK .05 .15
15 Tony Perez DK .20 .50
16 Willie Randolph DK .08 .25
17 Bob Boone DK .08 .25
18 Orel Hershiser DK .20 .50
19 Johnny Ray DK .05 .15
20 Gary Ward DK .05 .15
21 Rick Mahler DK .05 .15
22 Phil Bradley DK .05 .15
23 Jerry Koosman DK .08 .25
24 Tom Brunansky DK .05 .15
25 Andre Dawson DK .05 .15
26 Dwight Gooden DK .30 .75
27 Kal Daniels RC .20 .50
28 Fred McGriff RC 3.00 8.00
29 Cory Snyder .05 .15
30 Jose Guzman RC .05 .15
31 Ty Gainey RC .05 .15
32 Johnny Abrego RC .05 .15
33A Andres Galarraga RC .60 1.50
33B Andre's Galarraga RC .60 1.50
34 Dave Shipanoff RC .05 .15
35 Mark McLemore RC .40 1.00
36 Marty Clary RC .05 .15
37 Paul O'Neill RC 1.50 4.00
38 Danny Tartabull .08 .25
39 Jose Canseco RC 10.00 25.00
40 Juan Nieves RC .05 .15
41 Lance McCullers RC .05 .15
42 Rick Surhoff RC .05 .15
43 Todd Worrell RC .20 .50
44 Bob Kipper RC .05 .15
45 John Habyan RC .05 .15
46 Mike Woodard RC .05 .15
47 Mike Boddicker .05 .15
48 Robin Yount .50 1.25
49 Lou Whitaker .08 .25
50 Oil Can Boyd .05 .15
51 Rickey Henderson .30 .75
52 Mike Marshall .05 .15
53 George Brett .75 2.00
54 Dave Kingman .08 .25
55 Hubie Brooks .05 .15
56 Oddibe McDowell .05 .15
57 Doug DeCinces .05 .15
58 Britt Burns .05 .15
59 Ozzie Smith .50 1.25
60 Jose Cruz .08 .25
61 Mike Schmidt .75 2.00
62 Pete Rose 1.00 2.50
63 Steve Garvey .08 .25
64 Tony Pena .05 .15
65 Chili Davis .08 .25
66 Dale Murphy .20 .50
67 Ryne Sandberg .60 1.50
68 Gary Carter .08 .25
69 Alvin Davis .05 .15
70 Kent Hrbek .08 .25
71 George Bell .08 .25
72 Kirby Puckett .75 2.00
73 Lloyd Moseby .05 .15
74 Bob Kearney .05 .15
75 Dwight Gooden .30 .75
76 Gary Matthews .08 .25
77 Rick Mahler .05 .15
78 Benny Distefano .05 .15
79 Jeff Leonard .05 .15
80 Kevin McReynolds .08 .25
81 Ron Oester .05 .15
82 John Russell .05 .15
83 Tommy Herr .05 .15
84 Jerry Mumphrey .05 .15
85 Ron Romanick .05 .15
86 Daryl Boston .05 .15
87 Andre Dawson .08 .25
88 Eddie Murray .30 .75
89 Dion James .05 .15
90 Chet Lemon .08 .25
91 Bob Stanley .05 .15
92 Willie Randolph .08 .25
93 Mike Scioscia .08 .25
94 Tom Waddell .05 .15
95 Danny Jackson .05 .15
96 Mike Davis .05 .15
97 Mike Fitzgerald .05 .15
98 Gary Ward .05 .15
99 Pete O'Brien .05 .15
100 Bret Saberhagen .08 .25
101 Alfredo Griffin .05 .15
102 Brett Butler .08 .25
103 Ron Guidry .08 .25
104 Jerry Reuss .05 .15
105 Jack Morris .08 .25
106 Rick Dempsey .05 .15
107 Ray Burris .05 .15
108 Brian Downing .08 .25
109 Willie McGee .08 .25
110 Bill Doran .05 .15
111 Kent Tekulve .05 .15
112 Tony Gwynn .50 1.25
113 Marvell Wynne .05 .15
114 David Green .05 .15
115 Jim Gantner .05 .15
116 George Foster .08 .25
117 Steve Trout .05 .15
118 Mark Langston .08 .25
119 Tony Fernandez .05 .15
120 John Butcher .05 .15
121 Ron Robinson .05 .15
122 Dan Spillner .05 .15
123 Mike Young .05 .15
124 Paul Molitor .08 .25
125 Kirk Gibson .08 .25
126 Ken Griffey .08 .25
127 Tony Armas .08 .25
128 Mariano Duncan RC .20 .50
129 Pat Tabler .05 .15
130 Frank White .08 .25
131 Carney Lansford .08 .25
132 Vance Law .05 .15
133 Dick Schofield .05 .15
134 Wayne Tolleson .05 .15
135 Greg Walker .05 .15
136 Denny Walling .05 .15
137 Ozzie Virgil .05 .15
138 Ricky Horton .05 .15
139 LaMarr Hoyt .05 .15
140 Wayne Krenchicki .05 .15
141 Glenn Hubbard .05 .15
142 Cecilio Guante .05 .15
143 Mike Krukow .05 .15
144 Lee Smith .08 .25
145 Edwin Nunez .05 .15
146 Dave Stieb .08 .25
147 Mike Smithson .05 .15
148 Ken Dixon .05 .15
149 Danny Darwin .05 .15
150 Chris Pittaro .05 .15
151 Bill Buckner .08 .25
152 Mike Pagliarulo .05 .15
153 Bill Russell .08 .25
154 Brook Jacoby .05 .15
155 Pat Sheridan .05 .15
156 Mike Gallego RC .05 .15
157 Jim Wohlford .05 .15
158 Gary Pettis .05 .15
159 Toby Harrah .08 .25
160 Richard Dotson .05 .15
161 Bob Knepper .05 .15
162 Dave Dravecky .05 .15
163 Greg Gross .05 .15
164 Eric Davis .30 .75
165 Gerald Perry .05 .15
166 Rick Rhoden .05 .15
167 Keith Moreland .05 .15
168 Jack Clark .08 .25
169 Storm Davis .05 .15
170 Cecil Cooper .08 .25
171 Alan Trammell .08 .25
172 Roger Clemens 2.00 5.00
173 Don Mattingly 1.00 2.50
174 Pedro Guerrero .08 .25
175 Willie Wilson .08 .25
176 Dwayne Murphy .05 .15
177 Tim Raines .08 .25
178 Larry Parrish .05 .15
179 Mike Witt .05 .15
180 Harold Baines .08 .25
181 Vince Coleman UER RC .40 1.00
182 Jeff Heathcock .05 .15
183 Steve Carlton .08 .25
184 Mario Soto .08 .25
185 Goose Gossage .08 .25
186 Johnny Ray .05 .15
187 Dan Gladden .05 .15
188 Bob Horner .08 .25
189 Rick Sutcliffe .08 .25
190 Keith Hernandez .08 .25
191 Phil Bradley .05 .15
192 Tom Brunansky .05 .15
193 Jesse Barfield .08 .25
194 Frank Viola .08 .25
195 Willie Upshaw .05 .15
196 Jim Beattie .05 .15
197 Darryl Strawberry .20 .50
198 Ron Cey .08 .25
199 Steve Bedrosian .05 .15
200 Steve Kemp .05 .15
201 Manny Trillo .05 .15
202 Garry Templeton .08 .25
203 Dave Parker .08 .25
204 John Denny .05 .15
205 Terry Pendleton .08 .25
206 Terry Puhl .05 .15
207 Bobby Grich .08 .25
208 Ozzie Guillen RC .75 2.00
209 Jeff Reardon .08 .25
210 Cal Ripken 1.25 3.00
211 Bill Schroeder .05
212 Dan Petry .05
213 Jim Rice .08
214 Dave Righetti .08
215 Fernando Valenzuela .08
216 Julio Franco .08
217 Darryl Motley .05
218 Dave Collins .05
219 Tim Wallach .05
220 George Wright .05
221 Tommy Dunbar .05
222 Steve Balboni .05
223 Jay Howell .05
224 Joe Carter .08
225 Ed Whitson .05
226 Orel Hershiser .30
227 Willie Hernandez .05
228 Lee Lacy .05
229 Rollie Fingers .08
230 Bob Boone .08
231 Joaquin Andujar .08
232 Craig Reynolds .05
233 Shane Rawley .05
234 Eric Show .05
235 Jose DeLeon .05
236 Jose Uribe .05
237 Moose Haas .05
238 Wally Backman .05
239 Dennis Eckersley .20
240 Mike Moore .05
241 Damaso Garcia .05
242 Tim Teufel .05
243 Dave Concepcion .08
244 Floyd Bannister .05
245 Fred Lynn .08
246 Charlie Moore .05
247 Walt Terrell .05
248 Dave Winfield .08
249 Dwight Evans .20
250 Dennis Powell .05
251 Andre Thornton .05
252 Onix Concepcion .05
253 Mike Heath .05
254A David Palmer ERR/(Position 2B) .05
254B David Palmer COR/(Position P) .20
255 Donnie Moore .05
256 Curtis Wilkerson .05
257 Julio Cruz .05
258 Nolan Ryan 1.50
259 Jeff Stone .05
260 John Tudor .08
261 Mark Thurmond .05
262 Jay Tibbs .05
263 Rafael Ramirez .05
264 Larry McWilliams .05
265 Mark Davis .05
266 Bob Dernier .05
267 Matt Young .05
268 Jim Clancy .05
269 Mickey Hatcher .05
270 Sammy Stewart .05
271 Bob L. Gibson .05
272 Nelson Simmons .05
273 Rich Gedman .05
274 Butch Wynegar .05
275 Ken Howell .05
276 Mel Hall .05
277 Jim Sundberg .08
278 Chris Codiroli .05
279 Herm Winningham .05
280 Rod Carew .20
281 Don Slaught .05
282 Scott Fletcher .05
283 Bill Dawley .05
284 Andy Hawkins .05
285 Glenn Wilson .05
286 Nick Esasky .05
287 Claudell Washington .05
288 Lee Mazzilli .08
289 Jody Davis .05
290 Darrell Porter .05
291 Scott McGregor .05
292 Ted Simmons .08
293 Aurelio Lopez .05
294 Marty Barrett .05
295 Dale Berra .05
296 Greg Brock .05
297 Charlie Leibrandt .05
298 Bill Krueger .05
299 Bryn Smith .05
300 Burt Hooton .05
301 Stu Cliburn .05
302 Luis Salazar .05
303 Ken Dayley .05
304 Frank DiPino .05
305 Von Hayes .05
306 Gary Redus .05

307 Craig Lefferts .05 .15
308 Sammy Khalifa .05 .15
309 Scott Garrelts .05 .15
310 Rick Cerone .05 .15
311 Shawon Dunston .08 .25
312 Howard Johnson .08 .25
313 Jim Presley .05 .15
314 Gary Gaetti .08 .25
315 Luis Leal .05 .15
316 Mark Salas .05 .15
317 Bill Caudill .05 .15
318 Dave Henderson .05 .15
319 Rafael Santana .05 .15
320 Leon Durham .05 .15
321 Bruce Sutter .08 .25
322 Jason Thompson .05 .15
323 Bob Brenly .05 .15
324 Carmelo Martinez .05 .15
325 Eddie Milner .05 .15
326 Juan Samuel .05 .15
327 Tom Nieto .05 .15
328 Dave Smith .05 .15
329 Urbano Lugo .05 .15
330 Joel Skinner .05 .15
331 Bill Gullickson .05 .15
332 Floyd Rayford .05 .15
333 Ben Oglivie .08 .25
334 Lance Parrish .08 .25
335 Jackie Gutierrez .05 .15
336 Dennis Rasmussen .05 .15
337 Terry Whitfield .05 .15
338 Neal Heaton .05 .15
339 Jorge Orta .05 .15
340 Donnie Hill .05 .15
341 Joe Hesketh .05 .15
342 Charlie Hough .08 .25
343 Dave Rozema .05 .15
344 Greg Pryor .05 .15
345 Mickey Tettleton RC .20 .50
346 George Vukovich .05 .15
347 Don Baylor .08 .25
348 Carlos Diaz .05 .15
349 Barbaro Garbey .05 .15
350 Larry Sheets .05 .15
351 Teddy Higuera RC* .20 .50
352 Juan Beniquez .05 .15
353 Bob Forsch .05 .15
354 Mark Bailey .05 .15
355 Larry Andersen .05 .15
356 Terry Kennedy .05 .15
357 Don Robinson .05 .15
358 Jim Gott .05 .15
359 Earnie Riles .05 .15
360 John Christensen .05 .15
361 Ray Fontenot .05 .15
362 Spike Owen .05 .15
363 Jim Acker .05 .15
364 Ron Davis .05 .15
365 Tom Hume .05 .15
366 Carlton Fisk .20 .50
367 Nate Snell .05 .15
368 Rick Manning .05 .15
369 Darrell Evans .08 .25
370 Ron Hassey .05 .15
371 Wade Boggs .20 .50
372 Rick Honeycutt .05 .15
373 Chris Bando .05 .15
374 Bud Black .05 .15
375 Steve Henderson .05 .15
376 Charlie Lea .05 .15
377 Reggie Jackson .20 .50
378 Dave Schmidt .05 .15
379 Bob James .05 .15
380 Glenn Davis .05 .15
381 Tim Corcoran .05 .15
382 Danny Cox .05 .15
383 Tim Flannery .05 .15
384 Tom Browning .05 .15
385 Rick Camp .05 .15
386 Jim Morrison .05 .15
387 Dave LaPoint .05 .15
388 Dave Lopes .08 .25
389 Al Cowens .05 .15
390 Doyle Alexander .05 .15
391 Tim Laudner .05 .15
392 Don Aase .05 .15
393 Jaime Cocanower .05 .15
394 Randy O'Neal .05 .15
395 Mike Easler .05 .15
396 Scott Bradley .05 .15
397 Tom Niedenfuer .05 .15
398 Jerry Willard .05 .15
399 Lonnie Smith .05 .15
400 Bruce Bochte .05 .15
401 Terry Francona .08 .25
402 Jim Slaton .05 .15
403 Bill Stein .05 .15
404 Tim Hulett .05 .15
405 Alan Ashby .05 .15
406 Tim Stoddard .05 .15
407 Garry Maddox .05 .15
408 Ted Power .05 .15
409 Len Barker .05 .15
410 Denny Gonzalez .05 .15
411 George Frazier .05 .15
412 Andy Van Slyke .20 .50
413 Jim Dwyer .05 .15
414 Paul Householder .05 .15
415 Alejandro Sanchez .05 .15
416 Steve Crawford .05 .15
417 Dan Pasqua .05 .15
418 Enos Cabell .05 .15
419 Mike Jones .05 .15
420 Steve Kiefer .05 .15
421 Tim Burke .05 .15
422 Mike Mason .05 .15
423 Ruppert Jones .05 .15
424 Jerry Hairston .05 .15
425 Tito Landrum .05 .15
426 Jeff Calhoun .05 .15
427 Don Carman .05 .15
428 Tony Perez .20 .50
429 Jerry Davis .05 .15
430 Bob Walk .05 .15
431 Brad Wellman .05 .15
432 Terry Forster .08 .25
433 Billy Hatcher .05 .15
434 Clint Hurdle .05 .15
435 Ivan Calderon RC* .20 .50
436 Pete Filson .05 .15
437 Tom Henke .08 .25
438 Dave Engle .05 .15
439 Tom Filer .05 .15
440 Gorman Thomas .08 .25
441 Rick Aguilera RC .20 .50
442 Scott Sanderson .05 .15
443 Jeff Dedmon .05 .15
444 Joe Orsulak RC* .20 .50
445 Atlee Hammaker .05 .15
446 Jerry Royster .05 .15
447 Buddy Bell .08 .25
448 Dave Rucker .05 .15
449 Ivan DeJesus .05 .15
450 Jim Pankovits .05 .15
451 Jerry Narron .05 .15
452 Bryan Little .05 .15
453 Gary Lucas .05 .15
454 Dennis Martinez .08 .25
455 Ed Romero .05 .15
456 Bob Melvin .05 .15
457 Glenn Hoffman .05 .15
458 Bob Shirley .05 .15
459 Bob Welch .08 .25
460 Carmen Castillo .05 .15
461 Dave Leeper OF .05 .15
462 Tim Birtsas .05 .15
463 Randy St.Claire .05 .15
464 Chris Welsh .05 .15
465 Greg Harris .05 .15
466 Lynn Jones .05 .15
467 Dusty Baker .08 .25
468 Roy Smith .05 .15
469 Andre Robertson .05 .15
470 Ken Landreaux .05 .15
471 Dave Bergman .05 .15
472 Gary Roenicke .05 .15
473 Pete Vuckovich .05 .15
474 Kirk McCaskill RC .20 .50
475 Jeff Lahti .05 .15
476 Mike Scott .08 .25
477 Darren Daulton RC .40 1.00
478 Graig Nettles .08 .25
479 Bill Almon .05 .15
480 Greg Minton .05 .15
481 Randy Ready .05 .15
482 Len Dykstra RC .60 1.50
483 Thad Bosley .05 .15
484 Harold Reynolds RC .60 1.50
485 Al Oliver .08 .25
486 Roy Smalley .05 .15
487 John Franco .08 .25
488 Juan Agosto .05 .15
489 Al Pardo .05 .15
490 Bill Wegman RC .05 .15
491 Frank Tanana .08 .25
492 Brian Fisher RC .05 .15
493 Mark Clear .05 .15
494 Len Matuszek .05 .15
495 Ramon Romero .05 .15
496 John Wathan .05 .15
497 Rob Picciolo .05 .15
498 U.L. Washington .05 .15
499 John Candelaria .05 .15
500 Duane Walker .05 .15
501 Gene Nelson .05 .15
502 John Mizerock .05 .15
503 Luis Aguayo .05 .15
504 Kurt Kepshire .05 .15
505 Ed Wojna .05 .15
506 Joe Price .05 .15
507 Milt Thompson RC .20 .50
508 Junior Ortiz .05 .15
509 Vida Blue .08 .25
510 Steve Engel .05 .15
511 Karl Best .05 .15
512 Cecil Fielder RC .75 2.00
513 Frank Eufemia .05 .15
514 Tippy Martinez .05 .15
515 Billy Joe Robidoux .05 .15
516 Bill Scherrer .05 .15
517 Bruce Hurst .05 .15
518 Rich Bordi .05 .15
519 Steve Yeager .08 .25
520 Tony Bernazard .05 .15
521 Hal McRae .08 .25
522 Jose Rijo .08 .25
523 Mitch Webster .05 .15
524 Jack Howell .05 .15
525 Alan Bannister .05 .15
526 Ron Kittle .05 .15
527 Phil Garner .08 .25
528 Kurt Bevacqua .05 .15
529 Kevin Gross .05 .15
530 Bo Diaz .05 .15
531 Ken Oberkfell .05 .15
532 Rick Reuschel .08 .25
533 Ron Meridith .05 .15
534 Steve Braun .05 .15
535 Wayne Gross .05 .15
536 Ray Searage .05 .15
537 Tom Brookens .05 .15
538 Al Nipper .05 .15
539 Billy Sample .05 .15
540 Steve Sax .05 .15
541 Dan Quisenberry .05 .15
542 Tony Phillips .05 .15
543 Floyd Youmans .05 .15
544 Steve Buechele RC .20 .50
545 Craig Gerber .05 .15
546 Joe DeSa .05 .15
547 Brian Harper .05 .15
548 Kevin Bass .05 .15
549 Tom Foley .05 .15
550 Dave Van Gorder .05 .15
551 Bruce Bochy .05 .15
552 R.J. Reynolds .05 .15
553 Chris Brown RC .05 .15
554 Bruce Benedict .05 .15
555 Warren Brusstar .05 .15
556 Danny Heep .05 .15
557 Darnell Coles .05 .15
558 Greg Gagne .05 .15
559 Ernie Whitt .05 .15
560 Ron Washington .05 .15
561 Jimmy Key .08 .25
562 Bill Swift .05 .15
563 Ron Darling .08 .25
564 Dick Ruthven .05 .15
565 Zane Smith .05 .15
566 Sid Bream .05 .15
567A Joel Youngblood ERR/(Position P) .05 .15
567B Joel Youngblood COR
(Position IF) .20 .50
568 Mario Ramirez .05 .15
569 Tom Runnells .05 .15
570 Rick Schu .05 .15
571 Bill Campbell .05 .15
572 Dickie Thon .05 .15
573 Al Holland .05 .15
574 Reid Nichols .05 .15
575 Bert Roberge .05 .15
576 Mike Flanagan .05 .15
577 Tim Leary .05 .15
578 Mike Laga .05 .15
579 Steve Lyons .05 .15
580 Phil Niekro .08 .25
581 Gilberto Reyes .05 .15
582 Jamie Easterly .05 .15
583 Mark Gubicza .05 .15
584 Stan Javier RC .20 .50
585 Bill Laskey .05 .15
586 Jeff Russell .05 .15
587 Dickie Noles .05 .15
588 Steve Farr .05 .15
589 Steve Ontiveros RC .05 .15
590 Mike Hargrove .05 .15
591 Marty Bystrom .05 .15
592 Franklin Stubbs .05 .15
593 Larry Herndon .05 .15
594 Bill Swaggerty .05 .15
595 Carlos Ponce .05 .15
596 Pat Perry .05 .15
597 Ray Knight .08 .25
598 Steve Lombardozzi .05 .15
599 Brad Havens .05 .15
600 Pat Clements .05 .15
601 Joe Niekro .05 .15
602 Hank Aaron Puzzle .30 .75
603 Dwayne Henry .05 .15
604 Mookie Wilson .08 .25
605 Buddy Biancalana .05 .15
606 Rance Mulliniks .05 .15
607 Alan Wiggins .05 .15
608 Joe Cowley .05 .15
609 Tom Seaver .20 .50
609B Tom Seaver YL .75 2.00
610 Neil Allen .05 .15
611 Don Sutton .08 .25
612 Fred Toliver .05 .15
613 Jay Baller .05 .15
614 Marc Sullivan .05 .15
615 John Grubb .05 .15
616 Bruce Kison .05 .15
617 Bill Madlock .08 .25
618 Chris Chambliss .08 .25
619 Dave Stewart .08 .25
620 Tim Lollar .05 .15
621 Gary Lavelle .05 .15
622 Charles Hudson .05 .15
623 Joel Davis .05 .15
624 Joe Johnson .05 .15
625 Sid Fernandez .05 .15
626 Dennis Lamp .05 .15
627 Terry Harper .05 .15
628 Jack Lazorko .05 .15
629 Roger McDowell RC* .20 .50
630 Mark Funderburk .05 .15
631 Ed Lynch .05 .15
632 Rudy Law .05 .15
633 Roger Mason RC .05 .15
634 Mike Felder RC .05 .15
635 Ken Schrom .05 .15
636 Bob Ojeda .05 .15
637 Ed VandeBerg .05 .15
638 Bobby Meacham .05 .15
639 Cliff Johnson .05 .15
640 Garth Iorg .05 .15
641 Dan Driessen .05 .15
642 Mike Brown OF .05 .15
643 John Shelby .05 .15
644 Pete Rose RB .30 .75
645 The Knuckle Brothers .08 .25
646 Jesse Orosco .05 .15
647 Billy Beane RC .40 1.00
648 Cesar Cedeno .08 .25
649 Bert Blyleven .08 .25
650 Max Venable .05 .15
651 Fleet Feet .05 .15
Vince Coleman
Willie McGee
652 Calvin Schiraldi .05 .15
653 Pete Rose KING .30 .75
654 Diamond Kings CL 1-26
(Unnumbered) .05 .15
655A CL 1: 27-130/(Unnumbered)
(45 Beane ERR) .05 .15
655B CL 1: 27-130/(Unnumbered)
(45 Habyan COR) .05 .15
656 CL 2: 131-234/(Unnumbered) .05 .15
657 CL 3: 235-338/(Unnumbered) .05 .15
658 CL 4: 339-442/(Unnumbered) .05 .15
659 CL 5: 443-546/(Unnumbered) .05 .15
660 CL 6: 547-653/(Unnumbered) .05 .15

1986 Donruss Hank Aaron Puzzle

1 Aaron Puzzle 1-3 .10 .25
4 Aaron Puzzle 4-6 .10 .25
7 Aaron Puzzle 7-10 .10 .25
10 Aaron Puzzle 10-12 .10 .25
13 Aaron Puzzle 13-15 .10 .25
16 Aaron Puzzle 16-18 .10 .25
19 Aaron Puzzle 19-21 .10 .25
22 Aaron Puzzle 22-24 .10 .25
25 Aaron Puzzle 25-27 .10 .25
28 Aaron Puzzle 28-30 .10 .25
31 Aaron Puzzle 29-31 .10 .25
34 Aaron Puzzle 34-36 .10 .25
37 Aaron Puzzle 37-39 .10 .25
40 Aaron Puzzle 40-42 .10 .25
43 Aaron Puzzle 43-45 .10 .25
46 Aaron Puzzle 46-48 .10 .25
49 Aaron Puzzle 49-51 .10 .25
52 Aaron Puzzle 52-54 .10 .25
55 Aaron Puzzle 55-57 .10 .25
58 Aaron Puzzle 58-60 .10 .25
61 Aaron Puzzle 61-63 .10 .25

1986 Donruss Wax Box Cards

The cards in this four-card set measure the standard 2 1/2" by 3 1/2". Cards have essentially the same design as the 1986 Donruss regular issue set. The cards were printed on the bottoms of the regular issue wax pack boxes. The four cards (PC4 to PC6 plus a Hank Aaron puzzle card) are considered a separate set in their own right and are not typically included in a complete set of the regular issue 1986 Donruss cards. The value of the panel uncut is slightly greater, perhaps by 25 percent greater, than the value of the individual cards cut up carefully.

COMPLETE SET (4) .40 1.00
PC4 Kirk Gibson .15 .40
PC5 Willie Hernandez .02 .10
PC6 Doug DeCinces .02 .10
PUZ Hank Aaron .30 .75
Puzzle Card

1986 Donruss Rookies

The 1986 Donruss "The Rookies" set features 56 full-color standard-size cards plus a 15-piece puzzle of Hank Aaron. The set was distributed through hobby dealers, packed in 60-set cases, in a small green, cellophane wrapped factory box. Although the set was wrapped in cellophane, the top card was number one Joyner, resulting in a percentage of the Joyner cards arriving in less than perfect condition. Donruss fixed the problem after it was called to their attention and even went so far as to include a customer service phone number in their second printing. Card fronts are similar in design to the 1986 Donruss regular issue except for the presence of "The Rookies" logo in the lower left corner and a bluish green border instead of a blue border. The key extended Rookie Cards in this set are Barry Bonds, Bobby Bonilla, Will Clark, Bo Jackson, Wally Joyner and John Kruk.

COMP.FACT.SET (56) 10.00 25.00
1 Wally Joyner XRC .40 1.00
2 Tracy Jones .05 .15
3 Allan Anderson XRC .05 .15
4 Ed Correa .05 .15
5 Reggie Williams .05 .15
6 Charlie Kerfeld .05 .15
7 Andres Galarraga .60 1.50
8 Bob Tewksbury XRC .20 .50
9 Al Newman XRC .08 .25
10 Andres Thomas .05 .15
11 Barry Bonds XRC 5.00 12.00
12 Juan Nieves .05 .15
13 Mark Eichhorn .05 .15
14 Dan Plesac XRC .20 .50
15 Cory Snyder .05 .15
16 Kelly Gruber .05 .15
17 Kevin Mitchell XRC .40 1.00
18 Steve Lombardozzi .05 .15
19 Mitch Williams XRC .20 .50
20 John Cerutti .05 .15
21 Todd Worrell .20 .50
22 Jose Canseco 1.50 4.00
23 Pete Incaviglia XRC .20 .50
24 Jose Guzman .05 .15
25 Scott Bailes .05 .15
26 Greg Mathews .05 .15
27 Eric King .05 .15
28 Paul Assenmacher .20 .50
29 Jeff Sellers .05 .15
30 Bobby Bonilla XRC .40 1.00
31 Doug Drabek XRC .40 1.00
32 Will Clark XRC .75 2.00
33 Bip Roberts XRC .20 .50
34 Jim Deshaies XRC .05 .15
35 Mike LaValliere XRC .20 .50
36 Scott Bankhead .05 .15
37 Dale Sveum .05 .15
38 Bo Jackson XRC 2.00 5.00
39 Robby Thompson XRC .20 .50
40 Eric Plunk .05 .15
41 Bill Bathe .05 .15
42 John Kruk XRC .60 1.50
43 Andy Allanson XRC .05 .15
44 Mark Portugal XRC .20 .50
45 Danny Tartabull .08 .25
46 Bob Kipper .05 .15
47 Gene Walter .05 .15
48 Rey Quinones UER
(Misspelled Quinonez) .05 .15
49 Bobby Witt XRC .20 .50
50 Bill Mooneyham .05 .15
51 John Cangelosi .05 .15
52 Ruben Sierra XRC .60 1.50
53 Rob Woodward .05 .15
54 Ed Hearn XRC .05 .15
55 Joel McKeon .05 .15
56 Checklist 1-56 .05 .15

1986 Donruss All-Stars

The cards in this 60-card set measure approximately 3 1/2" by 5". Players featured were involved in the 1985 All-Star game played in Minnesota. Cards are very similar in design to the 1986 Donruss regular issue set. The backs give each player's All-Star game statistics and have an orange-yellow border.

COMPLETE SET (60) 2.50 6.00
1 Tony Gwynn .50 1.25
2 Tommy Herr .01 .05
3 Steve Garvey .07 .20
4 Dale Murphy .07 .20
5 Darryl Strawberry .02 .10
6 Graig Nettles .02 .10
7 Terry Kennedy .01 .05
8 Ozzie Smith .30 .75
9 LaMarr Hoyt .01 .05
10 Rickey Henderson .25 .60
11 Lou Whitaker .02 .10
12 George Brett .40 1.00
13 Eddie Murray .20 .50
14 Cal Ripken .75 2.00
15 Dave Winfield .20 .50
16 Jim Rice .02 .10
17 Carlton Fisk .20 .50
18 Jack Morris .02 .10
19 Jose Cruz .01 .05
20 Tim Raines .02 .10
21 Nolan Ryan .75 2.00
22 Tony Pena .02 .10
23 Jack Clark .02 .10
24 Dave Parker .02 .10
25 Tim Wallach .01 .05
26 Ozzie Virgil .01 .05
27 Fernando Valenzuela .02 .10
28 Dwight Gooden .07 .20
29 Glenn Wilson .01 .05
30 Garry Templeton .01 .05
31 Goose Gossage .02 .10
32 Ryne Sandberg .30 .75
33 Jeff Reardon .02 .10
34 Pete Rose .20 .50
35 Scott Garrelts .01 .05
36 Willie McGee .02 .10
37 Ron Darling .01 .05
38 Dick Williams MG .01 .05
39 Paul Molitor .20 .50
40 Damaso Garcia .01 .05
41 Phil Bradley .01 .05
42 Dan Petry .01 .05
43 Willie Hernandez .01 .05
44 Tom Brunansky .01 .05
45 Alan Trammell .07 .20
46 Donnie Moore .01 .05
47 Wade Boggs .20 .50
48 Ernie Whitt .01 .05
49 Harold Baines .02 .10
50 Don Mattingly .30 .75
51 Gary Ward .01 .05
52 Bert Blyleven .02 .10
53 Jimmy Key .02 .10
54 Cecil Cooper .02 .10
55 Dave Stieb .01 .05
56 Rich Gedman .01 .05
57 Jay Howell .01 .05
58 Sparky Anderson MG .01 .05
59 Minneapolis Metrodome .01 .05
NNO Checklist Card .01 .05

1986 Donruss All-Star Box

The cards in this four-card set measure the standard size in spite of the fact that they form the bottom of the wax pack box for the larger Donruss All-Star cards. These box cards have essentially the same design as the 1986 Donruss regular issue set. The cards were printed on the bottoms of the Donruss All-Star (3 1/2" by 5") wax pack boxes. The four cards (PC7 to PC9 plus a Hank Aaron puzzle card) are considered a separate set in their own right and are not typically included in a complete set of the regular issue 1986 Donruss All-Star (or regular) cards. The value of the panel uncut is slightly greater, perhaps by 25 percent greater, than the value of the individual cards cut up carefully.

COMPLETE SET (4) .75 2.00
PC7 Wade Boggs .40 1.00
PC8 Lee Smith .20 .50
PC9 Cecil Cooper .08 .25
PUZ Hank Aaron .30 .75
Puzzle Card

1986 Donruss Highlights

Donruss' second edition of Highlights was released late in 1986. These glossy-coated cards are standard size. Cards commemorate events during the 1986 season, as well as players and pitchers of the month from each league. The set was distributed in its own red, white, blue, and gold box along with a small Hank Aaron puzzle. Card fronts are similar to the regular 1986 Donruss issue except that the Highlights logo is positioned in the lower left-hand corner and the borders are in gold instead of blue. The backs are printed in black and gold on white card stock. A first year card of Jose Canseco highlights this set.

COMP.FACT.SET (56) 2.00 5.00
DISTRIBUTED IN FACTORY SET ONLY
1 Will Clark .40 1.00
2 Jose Rijo .02 .10
3 George Brett .25 .60
4 Mike Schmidt .15 .40
5 Roger Clemens .75 2.00
6 Roger Clemens .75 2.00
7 Kirby Puckett .20 .50
8 Dwight Gooden .15 .40
9 Johnny Ray .02 .10
10 M.Mantle .75 2.00
R.Jackson
11 Wade Boggs .08 .25
12 Don Aase .02 .10
13 Wade Boggs .08 .25
14 Jeff Reardon .02 .10
15 Hubie Brooks .02 .10
16 Don Sutton .15 .40
17 Roger Clemens .75 2.00
18 Roger Clemens .75 2.00
19 Kent Hrbek .05 .15
20 Rick Rhoden .02 .10
21 Kevin Bass .02 .10
22 Bob Horner .02 .10
23 Wally Joyner .08 .25
24 Darryl Strawberry .08 .25
25 Fernando Valenzuela .05 .15
26 Roger Clemens .75 2.00
27 Jack Morris .05 .15
28 Scott Fletcher .02 .10
29 Todd Worrell .05 .15
30 Eric Davis .15 .40
31 Bert Blyleven .05 .15
32 Bobby Doerr .08 .25
33 Ernie Lombardi .05 .15
34 Willie McCovey .05 .15
35 Steve Carlton .05 .15
36 Mike Schmidt .15 .40
37 Juan Samuel .02 .10
38 Mike Witt .02 .10
39 Doug DeCinces .02 .10
40 Bill Gullickson .02 .10
41 Dale Murphy .08 .25
42 Joe Carter .15 .40
43 Bo Jackson .40 1.00
44 Joe Cowley .02 .10
45 Jim Deshaies .02 .10
46 Mike Scott .02 .10
47 Bruce Hurst .02 .10
48 Don Mattingly .25 .60
49 Mike Krukow .02 .10
50 Steve Sax .02 .10
51 John Cangelosi .02 .10
52 Dave Righetti .02 .10
53 Don Mattingly .25 .60
54 Todd Worrell .05 .15
55 Jose Canseco 1.25 3.00
56 Checklist Card .02 .10

1986 Donruss Pop-Ups

This set is the companion of the 1986 Donruss All-Star (60) set; as such it features the first 18 cards of that set (the All-Star starting line-ups) in a pop-up, die-cut type of card. These cards (measuring (2 1/2" X 5") can be "popped up" to feature a standing card showing the player in action in front of the Metrodome ballpark background. Although this set is unnumbered it is numbered in the same order as its companion set, presumably according to the respective batting orders of the starting line-ups. The first nine numbers below are National Leaguers and the last nine are American Leaguers. See also the Donruss All-Star checklist card which contains a checklist for the Pop-Ups as well

COMPLETE SET (18) 2.00 5.00
1 Tony Gwynn .60 1.50
2 Tommy Herr .01 .05
3 Steve Garvey .07 .20
4 Dale Murphy .10 .30
5 Darryl Strawberry .02 .10
6 Graig Nettles .02 .10
7 Terry Kennedy .01 .05
8 Ozzie Smith .40 1.00
9 LaMarr Hoyt .01 .05
10 Rickey Henderson .20 .50
11 Lou Whitaker .02 .10
12 George Brett .50 1.25
13 Eddie Murray .25 .60
14 Cal Ripken 1.00 2.50
15 Dave Winfield .20 .50
16 Jim Rice .02 .10
17 Carlton Fisk .20 .50
18 Jack Morris .02 .10

1986 Donruss Super DK's

This 29-card set of large Diamond Kings features the full-color artwork of Dick Perez. The set could be obtained from Perez-Steele Galleries by sending three Donruss wrappers and $9.00. The cards measure 4 7/8" by 6 13/16" and are identical in design to the Diamond King cards in the Donruss regular issue.

COMPLETE SET (27) 5.00 12.00
1 Kirk Gibson .20 .50
2 Goose Gossage .20 .50
3 Willie McGee .20 .50
4 George Bell .08 .25
5 Tony Armas .08 .25
6 Chili Davis .20 .50
7 Cecil Cooper .08 .25
8 Mike Boddicker .08 .25
9 Dave Lopes .08 .25
10 Bill Doran .08 .25
11 Bret Saberhagen .20 .50
12 Brett Butler .20 .50
13 Harold Baines .30 .75
14 Mike Davis .08 .25
15 Tony Perez .40 1.00
16 Willie Randolph .20 .50
17 Bob Boone .20 .50
18 Orel Hershiser .30 .75
19 Johnny Ray .08 .25
20 Gary Ward .08 .25
21 Rick Mahler .08 .25
22 Phil Bradley .08 .25
23 Jerry Koosman .20 .50
24 Tom Brunansky .08 .25
25 Andre Dawson .30 .75
26 Dwight Gooden .40 1.00
27 Pete Rose 1.00 2.50
King of Kings
NNO Checklist Card .08 .25
NNO Aaron Large Puzzle .40 1.00

1987 Donruss

This set consists of 660 standard-size cards. Cards were primarily distributed in 15-card wax packs, rack packs and a factory set. All packs included a Roberto Clemente puzzle panel and the factory sets contained a complete puzzle. The regular-issue cards feature a black and gold border on the front. The backs of the cards in the factory sets are oriented differently than cards taken from wax packs, giving the appearance that one version or the other is upside down when sorting from the card backs. There are no premiums or discounts for either version. The popular Diamond King subset returns for the sixth consecutive year. Some of the Diamond King (1-26) selections are repeats from prior years; Perez-Steele Galleries had indicated in 1987 that a five-year rotation would be maintained in order to avoid depleting the pool of available worthy "kings" on some of the teams. The rich selection of Rookie Cards in this set include Barry Bonds, Bobby Bonilla, Kevin Brown, Will Clark, David Cone, Chuck Finley, Bo Jackson, Wally Joyner, Barry Larkin, Greg Maddux and Rafael Palmeiro.

COMPLETE SET (660) 15.00 40.00
COMP.FACT.SET (660) 20.00 50.00
COMP.CLEMENTE PUZZLE .60 1.50
1 Wally Joyner DK .15 .40
2 Roger Clemens DK .75 2.00
3 Dale Murphy DK .08 .25
4 Darryl Strawberry DK .05 .15
5 Ozzie Smith DK .25 .60
6 Jose Canseco DK .40 1.00
7 Charlie Hough DK .05 .15
8 Brook Jacoby DK .02 .10
9 Fred Lynn DK .05 .15
10 Rick Rhoden DK .02 .10
11 Chris Brown DK .02 .10
12 Von Hayes DK .02 .10
13 Jack Morris DK .05 .15
14A Kevin McReynolds DK ERR .15 .40
14B Kevin McReynolds DK COR .02 .10
15 George Brett DK .40 1.00
16 Ted Higuera DK .02 .10
17 Hubie Brooks DK .02 .10
18 Mike Scott DK .05 .15
19 Kirby Puckett DK .30 .75
20 Dave Winfield DK .05 .15
21 Lloyd Moseby DK .02 .10
22A Eric Davis DK ERR .15 .40
22B Eric Davis DK COR .08 .25
23 Jim Presley DK .02 .10
24 Keith Moreland DK .02 .10
25A Greg Walker DK ERR .15 .40
No color in DK banner on card back
25B Greg Walker DK COR .02 .10
DK banner on back colored yellow
26 Steve Sax DK .02 .10
27 DK Checklist 1-26 .02 .10
28 B.J. Surhoff RC .25 .60
29 Randy Myers RC .25 .60
30 Ken Gerhart RC .05 .15
31 Benito Santiago .05 .15
32 Greg Swindell RC .15 .40
33 Mike Birkbeck RC .05 .15
34 Terry Steinbach RC .25 .60
35 Bo Jackson RC 2.50 6.00
36 Greg Maddux RC 4.00 10.00
37 Jim Lindeman RC .05 .15
38 Devon White RC .25 .60
39 Eric Bell RC .05 .15
40 Willie Fraser RC .05 .15
41 Jerry Browne RC .05 .15
42 Chris James RC * .05 .15
43 Rafael Palmeiro RC 2.00 5.00
44 Pat Dodson RC .05 .15
45 Duane Ward RC * .15 .40
46 Mark McGwire 3.00 8.00
47 Bruce Fields UER RC .05 .15
48 Eddie Murray .15 .40
49 Ted Higuera .02 .10
50 Kirk Gibson .05 .15
51 Oil Can Boyd .02 .10
52 Don Mattingly .50 1.25
53 Pedro Guerrero .05 .15
54 George Brett .40 1.00
55 Jose Rijo .05 .15
56 Tim Raines .05 .15
57 Ed Correa .02 .10
58 Mike Witt .02 .10
59 Greg Walker .02 .10
60 Ozzie Smith .25 .60
61 Glenn Davis .02 .10
62 Glenn Wilson .02 .10
63 Tom Browning .02 .10
64 Tony Gwynn .25 .60
65 R.J. Reynolds .02 .10
66 Will Clark RC .60 1.50
67 Ozzie Virgil .02 .10
68 Rick Sutcliffe .05 .15
69 Gary Carter .05 .15
70 Mike Moore .02 .10
71 Bert Blyleven .05 .15
72 Tony Fernandez .02 .10
73 Kent Hrbek .05 .15
74 Lloyd Moseby .02 .10
75 Alvin Davis .02 .10
76 Keith Hernandez .05 .15
77 Ryne Sandberg .30 .75
78 Dale Murphy .08 .25
79 Sid Bream .02 .10
80 Chris Brown .02 .10
81 Steve Garvey .05 .15
82 Mario Soto .05 .15
83 Shane Rawley .02 .10
84 Willie McGee .05 .15
85 Jose Cruz .05 .15
86 Brian Downing .05 .15
87 Ozzie Guillen .08 .25
88 Hubie Brooks .02 .10
89 Cal Ripken .60 1.50
90 Juan Nieves .02 .10
91 Lance Parrish .05 .15
92 Jim Rice .05 .15
93 Ron Guidry .05 .15
94 Fernando Valenzuela .05 .15
95 Andy Allanson RC .02 .10
96 Willie Wilson .05 .15
97 Jose Canseco .40 1.00
98 Jeff Reardon .05 .15
99 Bobby Witt RC .15 .40
100 Checklist 28-133 .02 .10
101 Jose Guzman .02 .10
102 Steve Balboni .02 .10
103 Tony Phillips .02 .10
104 Brook Jacoby .02 .10
105 Dave Winfield .05 .15
106 Orel Hershiser .08 .25
107 Lou Whitaker .05 .15
108 Fred Lynn .05 .15
109 Bill Wegman .02 .10
110 Donnie Moore .02 .10
111 Jack Clark .05 .15
112 Bob Knepper .02 .10
113 Von Hayes .02 .10
114 Bip Roberts RC .15 .40
115 Tony Pena .02 .10
116 Scott Garrelts .02 .10
117 Paul Molitor .05 .15
118 Darryl Strawberry .05 .15
119 Shawon Dunston .02 .10
120 Jim Presley .02 .10
121 Jesse Barfield .05 .15
122 Gary Gaetti .05 .15
123 Kurt Stillwell .02 .10
124 Joel Davis .02 .10
125 Mike Boddicker .02 .10
126 Robin Yount .25 .60
127 Alan Trammell .05 .15
128 Dave Righetti .05 .15
129 Dwight Evans .08 .25
130 Mike Scioscia .05 .15
131 Julio Franco .05 .15
132 Bret Saberhagen .05 .15
133 Mike Davis .02 .10
134 Joe Hesketh .02 .10
135 Wally Joyner RC .25 .60
136 Don Slaught .02 .10
137 Daryl Boston .02 .10
138 Nolan Ryan .75 2.00
139 Mike Schmidt .40 1.00
140 Tommy Herr .02 .10
141 Garry Templeton .05 .15
142 Kal Daniels .02 .10
143 Billy Sample .02 .10
144 Johnny Ray .02 .10
145 Robby Thompson RC * .15 .40
146 Bob Dernier .02 .10
147 Danny Tartabull .02 .10
148 Ernie Whitt .02 .10
149 Kirby Puckett .30 .75
150 Mike Young .02 .10
151 Ernest Riles .02 .10
152 Frank Tanana .02 .10
153 Rich Gedman .02 .10
154 Willie Randolph .05 .15
155 Bill Madlock .05 .15
156 Joe Carter .05 .15
157 Danny Jackson .02 .10
158 Carney Lansford .05 .15
159 Bryn Smith .02 .10
160 Gary Pettis .02 .10
161 Oddibe McDowell .02 .10
162 John Cangelosi .02 .10
163 Mike Scott .05 .15
164 Eric Show .02 .10
165 Juan Samuel .02 .10
166 Nick Esasky .02 .10
167 Zane Smith .02 .10
168 Mike C. Brown OF .02 .10
169 Keith Moreland .02 .10
170 John Tudor .05 .15
171 Ken Dixon .02 .10
172 Jim Gantner .02 .10
173 Jack Morris .05 .15
174 Bruce Hurst .02 .10
175 Dennis Rasmussen .02 .10
176 Mike Marshall .02 .10
177 Dan Quisenberry .02 .10
178 Eric Plunk .02 .10
179 Tim Wallach .02 .10
180 Steve Buechele .02 .10
181 Don Sutton .05 .15
182 Dave Schmidt .02 .10
183 Terry Pendleton .05 .15
184 Jim Deshaies RC * .05 .15
185 Steve Bedrosian .02 .10
186 Pete Rose .50 1.25
187 Dave Dravecky .02 .10
188 Rick Reuschel .05 .15
189 Dan Gladden .02 .10
190 Rick Mahler .02 .10
191 Thad Bosley .02 .10
192 Ron Darling .05 .15
193 Matt Young .02 .10
194 Tom Brunansky .02 .10
195 Dave Stieb .05 .15
196 Frank Viola .05 .15
197 Tom Henke .02 .10
198 Karl Best .02 .10
199 Dwight Gooden .08 .25
200 Checklist 134-239 .02 .10
201 Steve Trout .02 .10
202 Rafael Ramirez .02 .10
203 Bob Walk .02 .10
204 Roger Mason .02 .10
205 Terry Kennedy .02 .10
206 Ron Oester .02 .10
207 John Russell .02 .10
208 Greg Mathews .02 .10
209 Charlie Kerfeld .02 .10
210 Reggie Jackson .08 .25
211 Floyd Bannister .02 .10
212 Vance Law .02 .10
213 Rich Bordi .02 .10
214 Dan Plesac .02 .10
215 Dave Collins .02 .10
216 Bob Stanley .02 .10
217 Joe Niekro .02 .10
218 Tom Niedenfuer .02 .10
219 Brett Butler .05 .15
220 Charlie Leibrandt .02 .10
221 Steve Ontiveros .02 .10
222 Tim Burke .02 .10
223 Curtis Wilkerson .02 .10
224 Pete Incaviglia RC * .15 .40
225 Lonnie Smith .02 .10
226 Chris Codiroli .02 .10
227 Scott Bailes .02 .10
228 Rickey Henderson .15 .40
229 Ken Howell .02 .10
230 Darnell Coles .02 .10
231 Don Aase .02 .10
232 Tim Leary .02 .10
233 Bob Boone .05 .15
234 Ricky Horton .02 .10
235 Mark Bailey .02 .10
236 Kevin Gross .02 .10
237 Lance McCullers .02 .10
238 Cecilio Guante .02 .10
239 Bob Melvin .02 .10
240 Billy Joe Robidoux .02 .10
241 Roger McDowell .02 .10
242 Leon Durham .02 .10
243 Ed Nunez .02 .10
244 Jimmy Key .05 .15
245 Mike Smithson .02 .10
246 Bo Diaz .02 .10
247 Carlton Fisk .08 .25
248 Larry Sheets .02 .10
249 Juan Castillo RC .02 .10
250 Eric King .02 .10
251 Doug Drabek RC .25 .60
252 Wade Boggs .08 .25
253 Mariano Duncan .02 .10
254 Pat Tabler .02 .10
255 Frank White .05 .15
256 Alfredo Griffin .02 .10
257 Floyd Youmans .02 .10
258 Rob Wilfong .02 .10
259 Pete O'Brien .02 .10
260 Tim Hulett .02 .10
261 Dickie Thon .02 .10
262 Darren Daulton .05 .15
263 Vince Coleman .02 .10
264 Andy Hawkins .02 .10
265 Eric Davis .08 .25
266 Andres Thomas .02 .10
267 Mike Diaz .02 .10
268 Chili Davis .05 .15
269 Jody Davis .05 .15
270 Phil Bradley .02 .10
271 George Bell .05 .15
272 Keith Atherton .02 .10
273 Storm Davis .02 .10
274 Rob Deer .02 .10
275 Walt Terrell .02 .10
276 Roger Clemens .75 2.00
277 Mike Easler .02 .10
278 Steve Sax .02 .10
279 Andre Thornton .02 .10
280 Jim Sundberg .05 .15
281 Bill Bathe .02 .10
282 Jay Tibbs .02 .10
283 Dick Schofield .05 .15
284 Mike Mason .02 .10
285 Jerry Hairston .02 .10
286 Bill Doran .05 .15
287 Tim Flannery .02 .10
288 Gary Redus .02 .10
289 John Franco .02 .10
290 Paul Assenmacher .15 .40
291 Joe Orsulak .02 .10
292 Lee Smith .05 .15
293 Mike Laga .02 .10
294 Rick Dempsey .05 .15
295 Mike Felder .02 .10
296 Tom Brookens .02 .10
297 Al Nipper .02 .10
298 Mike Pagliarulo .02 .10
299 Franklin Stubbs .02 .10
300 Checklist 240-345 .02 .10
301 Steve Farr .02 .10
302 Bill Mooneyham .02 .10
303 Andres Galarraga .05 .15
304 Scott Fletcher .02 .10
305 Jack Howell .02 .10
306 Russ Morman .02 .10
307 Todd Worrell .02 .10
308 Dave Smith .02 .10
309 Jeff Stone .02 .10
310 Ron Robinson .02 .10
311 Bruce Bochy .02 .10
312 Jim Winn .02 .10
313 Mark Davis .02 .10
314 Jeff Dedmon .02 .10
315 Jamie Moyer RC .40 1.00
316 Wally Backman .02 .10
317 Ken Phelps .02 .10
318 Steve Lombardozzi .02 .10
319 Rance Mulliniks .02 .10
320 Tim Laudner .02 .10
321 Mark Eichhorn .02 .10
322 Lee Guetterman .02 .10
323 Sid Fernandez .02 .10
324 Jerry Mumphrey .02 .10
325 David Palmer .02 .10
326 Bill Almon .02 .10
327 Candy Maldonado .02 .10
328 John Kruk RC .40 1.00
329 John Denny .02 .10
330 Milt Thompson .02 .10
331 Mike LaValliere RC * .15 .40
332 Alan Ashby .02 .10
333 Doug Corbett .02 .10
334 Ron Karkovice RC .15 .40
335 Mitch Webster .02 .10
336 Lee Lacy .02 .10
337 Glenn Braggs RC .05 .15
338 Dwight Lowry .02 .10
339 Don Baylor .05 .15
340 Brian Fisher .02 .10
341 Reggie Williams .02 .10
342 Tom Candiotti .02 .10
343 Rudy Law .02 .10
344 Curt Young .02 .10
345 Mike Fitzgerald .02 .10
346 Ruben Sierra RC .40 1.00
347 Mitch Williams RC * .15 .40
348 Jorge Orta .02 .10
349 Mickey Tettleton .02 .10
350 Ernie Camacho .02 .10
351 Ron Kittle .02 .10
352 Ken Landreaux .02 .10
353 Chet Lemon .05 .15
354 John Shelby .02 .10
355 Mark Clear .02 .10
356 Doug DeCinces .02 .10
357 Ken Dayley .02 .10
358 Phil Garner .05 .15
359 Steve Jeltz .02 .10
360 Ed Whitson .02 .10
361 Barry Bonds RC 4.00 10.00
362 Vida Blue .05 .15
363 Cecil Cooper .05 .15
364 Bob Ojeda .02 .10
365 Dennis Eckersley .08 .25
366 Mike Morgan .02 .10
367 Willie Upshaw .02 .10
368 Allan Anderson RC .02 .10
369 Bill Gullickson .02 .10
370 Bobby Thigpen RC .15 .40
371 Juan Beniquez .02 .10
372 Charlie Moore .02 .10
373 Dan Petry .02 .10
374 Rod Scurry .02 .10
375 Tom Seaver .05 .15
376 Ed VandeBerg .02 .10
377 Tony Bernazard .02 .10
378 Greg Pryor .02 .10
379 Dwayne Murphy .02 .10
380 Andy McGaffigan .02 .10
381 Kirk McCaskill .02 .10
382 Greg Harris .02 .10
383 Rich Dotson .02 .10
384 Craig Reynolds .02 .10
385 Greg Gross .02 .10
386 Tito Landrum .02 .10
387 Craig Lefferts .02 .10
388 Dave Parker .05 .15
389 Bob Horner .05 .15
390 Pat Clements .02 .10
391 Jeff Leonard .02 .10
392 Chris Speier .02 .10
393 John Moses .02 .10
394 Garth Iorg .02 .10
395 Greg Gagne .02 .10
396 Nate Snell .02 .10
397 Bryan Clutterbuck .02 .10
398 Darrell Evans .05 .15
399 Steve Crawford .02 .10
400 Checklist 346-451 .02 .10
401 Phil Lombardi .02 .10
402 Rick Honeycutt .02 .10
403 Ken Schrom .02 .10
404 Bud Black .02 .10
405 Donnie Hill .02 .10
406 Wayne Krenchicki .02 .10
407 Chuck Finley RC .25 .60
408 Toby Harrah .05 .15
409 Steve Lyons .02 .10
410 Kevin Bass .02 .10
411 Marvell Wynne .02 .10
412 Ron Roenicke .02 .10
413 Tracy Jones .02 .10
414 Gene Garber .02 .10
415 Mike Bielecki .02 .10
416 Frank DiPino .02 .10
417 Andy Van Slyke .08 .25
418 Jim Dwyer .02 .10
419 Ben Oglivie .05 .15
420 Dave Bergman .02 .10
421 Joe Sambito .02 .10
422 Bob Tewksbury RC * .15 .40
423 Len Matuszek .02 .10
424 Mike Kingery RC .05 .15
425 Dave Kingman .05 .15
426 Al Newman RC .02 .10
427 Gary Ward .02 .10
428 Ruppert Jones .02 .10
429 Harold Baines .05 .15
430 Pat Perry .02 .10
431 Terry Puhl .02 .10
432 Don Carman .02 .10
433 Eddie Milner .02 .10
434 LaMarr Hoyt .02 .10
435 Rick Rhoden .02 .10
436 Jose Uribe .02 .10
437 Ken Oberkfell .02 .10
438 Ron Davis .02 .10
439 Jesse Orosco .02 .10
440 Scott Bradley .02 .10
441 Randy Bush .02 .10
442 John Cerutti .02 .10
443 Roy Smalley .02 .10
444 Kelly Gruber .02 .10
445 Bob Kearney .02 .10
446 Ed Hearn RC .02 .10
447 Scott Sanderson .02 .10
448 Bruce Benedict .02 .10
449 Junior Ortiz .02 .10
450 Mike Aldrete .02 .10
451 Kevin McReynolds .02 .10
452 Rob Murphy .02 .10
453 Kent Tekulve .02 .10
454 Curt Ford .02 .10
455 Dave Lopes .05 .15
456 Bob Grich .05 .15
457 Jose DeLeon .02 .10
458 Andre Dawson .05 .15
459 Mike Flanagan .02 .10
460 Joey Meyer .05 .15
461 Chuck Cary .02 .10
462 Bill Buckner .05 .15
463 Bob Shirley .02 .10
464 Jeff Hamilton .02 .10
465 Phil Niekro .05 .15
466 Mark Gubicza .02 .10
467 Jerry Willard .02 .10
468 Bob Sebra .02 .10
469 Larry Parrish .02 .10
470 Charlie Hough .05 .15
471 Hal McRae .05 .15
472 Dave Leiper .02 .10
473 Mel Hall .02 .10
474 Dan Pasqua .02 .10
475 Bob Welch .05 .15
476 Johnny Grubb .02 .10
477 Jim Traber .02 .10
478 Chris Bosio RC .15 .40
479 Mark McLemore .02 .10
480 John Morris .02 .10
481 Billy Hatcher .02 .10
482 Dan Schatzeder .02 .10
483 Rich Gossage .05 .15
484 Jim Morrison .02 .10
485 Bob Brenly .02 .10
486 Bill Schroeder .02 .10
487 Mookie Wilson .05 .15
488 Dave Martinez RC .15 .40
489 Harold Reynolds .05 .15
490 Jeff Hearron .02 .10
491 Mickey Hatcher .02 .10
492 Barry Larkin RC 1.50 4.00
493 Bob James .02 .10
494 John Habyan .02 .10
495 Jim Adduci .02 .10
496 Mike Heath .02 .10
497 Tim Stoddard .02 .10
498 Tony Armas .05 .15
499 Dennis Powell .02 .10
500 Checklist 452-557 .02 .10
501 Chris Bando .02 .10
502 David Cone RC .40 1.00
503 Jay Howell .02 .10
504 Tom Foley .02 .10
505 Ray Chadwick .02 .10
506 Mike Loynd RC .02 .10
507 Neil Allen .02 .10
508 Danny Darwin .02 .10
509 Rick Schu .02 .10
510 Jose Oquendo .02 .10
511 Gene Walter .02 .10
512 Terry McGriff .02 .10
513 Ken Griffey .05 .15
514 Benny Distefano .02 .10
515 Terry Mulholland RC .15 .40
516 Ed Lynch .02 .10
517 Bill Swift .02 .10
518 Manny Lee .02 .10
519 Andre David .02 .10
520 Scott McGregor .02 .10
521 Rick Manning .02 .10
522 Willie Hernandez .02 .10
523 Marty Barrett .02 .10
524 Wayne Tolleson .02 .10
525 Jose Gonzalez RC .05 .15
526 Cory Snyder .02 .10
527 Buddy Biancalana .02 .10
528 Moose Haas .02 .10
529 Wilfredo Tejada .02 .10
530 Stu Cliburn .02 .10
531 Dale Mohorcic .02 .10
532 Ron Hassey .02 .10
533 Ty Gainey .02 .10
534 Jerry Royster .02 .10
535 Mike Maddux RC .02 .10
536 Ted Power .02 .10
537 Ted Simmons .05 .15
538 Rafael Belliard RC .15 .40
539 Chico Walker .02 .10
540 Bob Forsch .02 .10
541 John Stefero .02 .10
542 Dale Sveum .02 .10
543 Mark Thurmond .02 .10
544 Jeff Sellers .02 .10
545 Joel Skinner .02 .10
546 Alex Trevino .02 .10
547 Randy Kutcher .02 .10
548 Joaquin Andujar .05 .15
549 Casey Candaele .02 .10
550 Jeff Russell .02 .10
551 John Candelaria .02 .10
552 Joe Cowley .02 .10
553 Danny Cox .02 .10
554 Denny Walling .02 .10
555 Bruce Ruffin RC .05 .15
556 Buddy Bell .05 .15
557 Jimmy Jones RC .05 .15
558 Bobby Bonilla RC .25 .60
559 Jeff D. Robinson .02 .10
560 Ed Olwine .02 .10
561 Glenallen Hill RC .15 .40
562 Lee Mazzilli .05 .15
563 Mike G. Brown P .02 .10
564 George Frazier .02 .10
565 Mike Sharperson RC .05 .15
566 Mark Portugal RC * .15 .40
567 Rick Leach .02 .10
568 Mark Langston .02 .10
569 Rafael Santana .02 .10
570 Manny Trillo .02 .10
571 Cliff Speck .02 .10
572 Bob Kipper .02 .10
573 Kelly Downs RC .05 .15
574 Randy Asadoor .02 .10
575 Dave Magadan RC .15 .40
576 Marvin Freeman RC .05 .15
577 Jeff Lahti .02 .10
578 Jeff Calhoun .02 .10
579 Gus Polidor .02 .10
580 Gene Nelson .02 .10
581 Tim Teufel .02 .10
582 Odell Jones .02 .10
583 Mark Ryal .02 .10
584 Randy O'Neal .02 .10
585 Mike Greenwell RC .15 .40
586 Ray Knight .05 .15
587 Ralph Bryant .02 .10
588 Carmen Castillo .02 .10
589 Ed Wojna .02 .10
590 Stan Javier .02 .10
591 Jeff Musselman .02 .10
592 Mike Stanley RC .15 .40
593 Darrell Porter .02 .10
594 Drew Hall .02 .10
595 Rob Nelson .02 .10
596 Bryan Oelkers .02 .10
597 Scott Nielsen .02 .10
598 Brian Holton .02 .10
599 Kevin Mitchell RC * .25 .60
600 Checklist 558-660 .02 .10
601 Jackie Gutierrez .02 .10
602 Barry Jones .02 .10
603 Jerry Narron .02 .10
604 Steve Lake .02 .10
605 Jim Pankovits .02 .10
606 Ed Romero .02 .10
607 Dave LaPoint .02 .10
608 Don Robinson .02 .10
609 Mike Krukow .02 .10
610 Dave Valle RC ** .05 .15
611 Len Dykstra .05 .15
612 Roberto Clemente PUZ .20 .50
613 Mike Trujillo .02 .10
614 Damaso Garcia .02 .10
615 Neal Heaton .02 .10
616 Juan Berenguer .02 .10
617 Steve Carlton .05 .15
618 Gary Lucas .02 .10
619 Geno Petralli .02 .10
620 Rick Aguilera .02 .10
621 Fred McGriff .30 .75
622 Dave Henderson .02 .10
623 Dave Clark RC .05 .15
624 Angel Salazar .02 .10
625 Randy Hunt .02 .10
626 John Gibbons .02 .10
627 Kevin Brown RC .60 1.50
628 Bill Dawley .02 .10
629 Aurelio Lopez .02 .10
630 Charles Hudson .02 .10
631 Ray Soff .02 .10
632 Ray Hayward .02 .10
633 Spike Owen .02 .10
634 Glenn Hubbard .02 .10
635 Kevin Elster RC .15 .40
636 Mike LaCoss .02 .10
637 Dwayne Henry .02 .10
638 Rey Quinones .02 .10
639 Jim Clancy .02 .10
640 Larry Andersen .02 .10
641 Calvin Schiraldi .02 .10
642 Stan Jefferson .02 .10
643 Marc Sullivan .02 .10
644 Mark Grant .02 .10
645 Cliff Johnson .02 .10
646 Howard Johnson .05 .15
647 Dave Sax .02 .10
648 Dave Stewart .05 .15
649 Danny Heep .02 .10
650 Joe Johnson .02 .10
651 Bob Brower .02 .10
652 Rob Woodward .02 .10
653 John Mizerock .02 .10
654 Tim Pyznarski .02 .10
655 Luis Aquino .02 .10
656 Mickey Brantley .02 .10
657 Doyle Alexander .02 .10
658 Sammy Stewart .02 .10
659 Jim Acker .02 .10
660 Pete Ladd .02 .10

1987 Donruss Roberto Clemente Puzzle

1 Clemente Puzzle 1-3 .10 .25
4 Clemente Puzzle 4-6 .10 .25
7 Clemente Puzzle 7-10 .10 .25
10 Clemente Puzzle 10-12 .10 .25
13 Clemente Puzzle 13-15 .10 .2
16 Clemente Puzzle 16-18 .10 .2
19 Clemente Puzzle 19-21 .10 .25
22 Clemente Puzzle 22-24 .10 .2
25 Clemente Puzzle 25-27 .10 .2
28 Clemente Puzzle 28-30 .10 .25
31 Clemente Puzzle 31-33 .10 .2
34 Clemente Puzzle 34-36 .10 .2
37 Clemente Puzzle 37-39 .10 .2
40 Clemente Puzzle 40-42 .10 .2
43 Clemente Puzzle 43-45 .10 .2
46 Clemente Puzzle 46-48 .10 .2
49 Clemente Puzzle 49-51 .10 .2
52 Clemente Puzzle 52-54 .10 .2
55 Clemente Puzzle 55-57 .10 .2
58 Clemente Puzzle 58-60 .10 .2
61 Clemente Puzzle 61-63 .10 .2

1987 Donruss Wax Box Cards

The cards in this four-card set measure the standa 2 1/2" by 3 1/2". Cards have essentially the same design as the 1987 Donruss regular issue set. The cards were printed on the bottoms of the regular issue wax pack boxes. The four cards (PC10 to PC plus a Roberto Clemente puzzle card) are considere a separate set in their own right and are not typical included in a complete set of the regular issue 198 Donruss cards. The value of the panel uncut is slightly greater, perhaps by 25 percent greater, tha the value of the individual cards cut up carefully.

COMPLETE SET (4) .75 2.
PC10 Dale Murphy .20
PC11 Jeff Reardon .08
PC12 Jose Canseco .50 1.
PUZ Roberto Clemente/(Puzzle Card) .30

1987 Donruss Rookies

The 1987 Donruss "The Rookies" set features 56 f color standard-size cards plus a 15-piece puzzle o Roberto Clemente. The set was distributed in facto set form packaged in a small green and black box through hobby dealers. Card fronts are similar in design to the 1987 Donruss regular issue except f the presence of "The Rookies" logo in the lower le corner and a green border instead of a black borde The key extended Rookie Cards in this set are Ellis Burks and Matt Williams. The second Donruss-issued cards of Greg Maddux and Rafael Palmeiro are also in this set. Because it's the first card in th set (of which came in a tightly-sealed cello wrap, Mark McGwire card is quite condition sensitive.

COMP.FACT.SET (56) 10.00 25
1 Mark McGwire 4.00 10
2 Eric Bell .05
3 Mark Williamson .02
4 Mike Greenwell .15
5 Ellis Burks XRC .25
6 DeWayne Buice .02
7 Mark McLemore .08
8 Devon White .25

Willie Fraser .05 .15
0 Les Lancaster .02 .10
1 Ken Williams .02 .10
2 Matt Nokes XRC .15 .40
3 Jeff M. Robinson .02 .10
4 Bo Jackson 2.00 5.00
5 Kevin Seitzer XRC .15 .40
6 Bill Ripken XRC .15 .40
7 B.J. Surhoff .25 .60
8 Chuck Crim .02 .10
9 Mike Birkbeck .05 .15
Chris Bosio .15 .40
1 Les Straker .02 .10
2 Mark Davidson .02 .10
3 Gene Larkin XRC .15 .40
4 Ken Gerhart .02 .10
5 Luis Polonia XRC .15 .40
Terry Steinbach .25 .60
Mickey Brantley .02 .10
Mike Stanley .15 .40
Jerry Browne .05 .15
Todd Benzinger XRC .15 .40
Fred McGriff .60 1.50
Mike Henneman XRC .15 .40
Casey Candaele .02 .10
Dave Magadan .15 .40
David Cone .40 1.00
Mike Jackson XRC .15 .40
John Mitchell XRC .05 .15
Mike Dunne .05 .15
John Smiley XRC .15 .40
Joe Magrane XRC .05 .15
Jim Lindeman .05 .15
Shane Mack .02 .10
Stan Jefferson .02 .10
Benito Santiago .08 .25
Matt Williams XRC 1.00 2.50
Dave Meads .02 .10
Rafael Palmeiro 2.00 5.00
Bill Long .02 .10
Bob Brower .02 .10
James Steels .02 .10
Paul Noce .02 .10
Greg Maddux 3.00 8.00
Jeff Musselman .02 .10
Brian Holton .02 .10
Chuck Jackson .02 .10
Checklist 1-56 .02 .10
Roberto Clemente 1.25 3.00
Puzzle

1987 Donruss All-Stars

is 60-card set features cards measuring proximately 3 1/2" by 5". Card fronts are in full lor with a black border. The card backs are printed black and blue on white card stock. Cards are mbered on the back. Card backs feature statistical ormation about the player's performance in past -Star games. The set was distributed in packs ich also contained a Pop-Up.

MPLETE SET (60) 2.50 6.00
Wally Joyner .10 .30
ave Winfield .20 .50
ou Whitaker .02 .10
irby Puckett .30 .75
al Ripken .75 2.00
ickey Henderson .20 .50
ade Boggs .20 .50
oger Clemens .30 .75
ance Parrish .02 .10
Dick Howser MG .01 .05
Keith Hernandez .02 .10
Darryl Strawberry .02 .10
Ryne Sandberg .20 .50
Dale Murphy .10 .30
Ozzie Smith .30 .75
Tony Gwynn .40 1.00
Mike Schmidt .20 .50
Dwight Gooden .02 .10
Gary Carter .20 .50
Whitey Herzog MG .02 .10
Jose Canseco .20 .50
John Franco .02 .10
Jesse Barfield .01 .05
Rick Rhoden .01 .05
Harold Baines .07 .20
Sid Fernandez .01 .05
George Brett .40 1.00
Steve Sax .01 .05
Jim Presley .01 .05
Dave Smith .01 .05
Eddie Murray .20 .50
Mike Scott .01 .05
Don Mattingly .40 1.00
Dave Parker .02 .10
Tony Fernandez .01 .05
Tim Raines .07 .20
Brook Jacoby .01 .05
Chili Davis .02 .10
Rich Gedman .01 .05
Kevin Bass .01 .05
Frank White .02 .10

42 Glenn Davis .01 .05
43 Willie Hernandez .01 .05
44 Chris Brown .01 .05
45 Jim Rice .02 .10
46 Tony Pena .02 .10
47 Don Aase .01 .05
48 Hubie Brooks .01 .05
49 Charlie Hough .01 .05
50 Jody Davis .01 .05
51 Mike Witt .01 .05
52 Jeff Reardon .02 .10
53 Ken Schrom .01 .05
54 Fernando Valenzuela .02 .10
55 Dave Righetti .01 .05
56 Shane Rawley .01 .05
57 Ted Higuera .01 .05
58 Mike Krukow .01 .05
59 Lloyd Moseby .01 .05
60 Checklist Card .01 .05

1987 Donruss All-Star Box

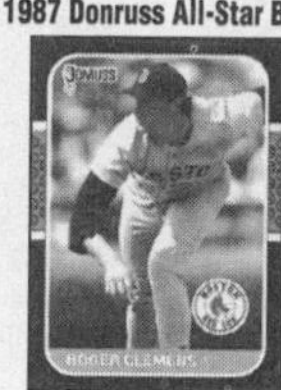

The cards in this four-card set measure the standard 2 1/2" by 3 1/2" in spite of the fact that they form the bottom of the wax pack box for the larger Donruss All-Star cards. These box cards have essentially the same design as the 1987 Donruss regular issue set. The cards were printed on the bottoms of the Donruss All-Star (3 1/2" by 5") wax pack boxes. The four cards (PC13 to PC15 plus a Roberto Clemente puzzle card) are considered a separate set in their own right and are not typically included in a complete set of the 1987 Donruss All-Star (or regular) cards. The value of the panel uncut is slightly greater, perhaps by 25 percent greater, than the value of the individual cards cut up carefully.

COMPLETE SET (4) 1.00 2.50
PC13 Mike Scott .08 .25
PC14 Roger Clemens .50 1.25
PC15 Mike Krukow .08 .25
PUZ Roberto Clemente .40 1.00
Puzzle Card

1987 Donruss Highlights

Donruss' third (and last) edition of Highlights was released late in 1987. The cards are standard size and are glossy in appearance. Cards commemorate events during the 1987 season, as well as players and pitchers of the month from each league. The set was distributed in its own red, black, blue, and gold box along with a small Roberto Clemente puzzle. Card fronts are similar to the regular 1987 Donruss issue except that the Highlights logo is positioned in the lower right-hand corner and the borders are in blue instead of black. The backs are printed in black and gold on white card stock.

COMP.FACT.SET (56) 4.00 10.00
ISSUED ONLY IN FACTORY SET FORM
1 Juan Nieves .02 .10
2 Mike Schmidt .15 .40
3 Eric Davis .08 .25
4 Sid Fernandez .02 .10
5 Brian Downing .02 .10
6 Bret Saberhagen .05 .15
7 Tim Raines .05 .15
8 Eric Davis .08 .25
9 Steve Bedrosian .02 .10
10 Larry Parrish .02 .10
11 Jim Clancy .02 .10
12 Tony Gwynn .15 .40
13 Orel Hershiser .08 .25
14 Wade Boggs .08 .25
15 Steve Ontiveros .02 .10
16 Tim Raines .05 .15
17 Don Mattingly .30 .75
18 Ray Dandridge .05 .15
19 Jim Hunter .08 .25
20 Billy Williams .05 .15
21 Bo Diaz .02 .10
22 Floyd Youmans .02 .10
23 Don Mattingly .30 .75
24 Frank Viola .02 .10
25 Bobby Witt .05 .15
26 Kevin Seitzer .15 .40
27 Mark McGwire .75 2.00
28 Andre Dawson .05 .15
29 Paul Molitor .05 .15
30 Kirby Puckett .30 .75
31 Andre Dawson .05 .15
32 Doug Drabek .15 .40
33 Dwight Evans .08 .25
34 Mark Langston .02 .10
35 Wally Joyner .08 .25
36 Vince Coleman .02 .10
37 Eddie Murray .15 .40
38 Cal Ripken .30 .75
39 F.McGriff .05 .15
R.Ducey
E.Whitt
40 M.McGwire 2.00 5.00
J.Canseco
41 Bob Boone .05 .15
42 Darryl Strawberry .05 .15
43 Howard Johnson .02 .10
44 Wade Boggs .08 .25
45 Benito Santiago .05 .15
46 Mark McGwire .75 2.00
47 Kevin Seitzer .15 .40
48 Don Mattingly .30 .75
49 Darryl Strawberry .05 .15
50 Pascual Perez .02 .10
51 Alan Trammell .05 .15
52 Doyle Alexander .02 .10
53 Nolan Ryan .40 1.00
54 Mark McGwire .75 2.00
55 Benito Santiago .05 .15
56 Checklist 1-56 .02 .10

1987 Donruss Opening Day

This innovative set of 272 standard-size cards features a card for each of the players in the starting line-ups of all the teams on Opening Day 1987. The set was packaged in a specially designed box. Cards are very similar in design to the 1987 regular Donruss issue except that these "OD" cards have a maroon border instead of a black border. Teams in the same city share a checklist card. A 15-piece puzzle of Roberto Clemente is also included with every complete set. The error on Barry Bonds (picturing Johnny Ray by mistake) was corrected very early in the press run; supposedly less than one percent of the sets have the error. Players in this set in their Rookie Card year include Will Clark, Bo Jackson, Wally Joyner and Barry Larkin.

COMP.FACT.SET (272) 12.50 30.00
163A LISTED IN NEAR MINT CONDITION
1 Doug DeCinces .02 .10
2 Mike Witt .02 .10
3 George Hendrick .05 .15
4 Dick Schofield .02 .10
5 Devon White .25 .60
6 Butch Wynegar .02 .10
7 Wally Joyner .08 .25
8 Mark McLemore .05 .15
9 Brian Downing .05 .15
10 Gary Pettis .02 .10
11 Bill Doran .02 .10
12 Phil Garner .05 .15
13 Jose Cruz .05 .15
14 Kevin Bass .02 .10
15 Mike Scott .05 .15
16 Glenn Davis .05 .15
17 Alan Ashby .02 .10
18 Billy Hatcher .02 .10
19 Craig Reynolds .02 .10
20 Carney Lansford .05 .15
21 Mike Davis .02 .10
22 Reggie Jackson .08 .25
23 Mickey Tettleton .02 .10
24 Jose Canseco .60 1.50
25 Rob Nelson .02 .10
26 Tony Phillips .02 .10
27 Dwayne Murphy .02 .10
28 Alfredo Griffin .02 .10
29 Curt Young .02 .10
30 Willie Upshaw .02 .10
31 Mike Sharperson .02 .10
32 Rance Mulliniks .02 .10
33 Ernie Whitt .02 .10
34 Jesse Barfield .05 .15
35 Tony Fernandez .02 .10
36 Lloyd Moseby .02 .10
37 Jimmy Key .05 .15
38 Fred McGriff .30 .75
39 George Bell .05 .15
40 Dale Murphy .08 .25
41 Rick Mahler .02 .10
42 Ken Griffey .05 .15
43 Andres Thomas .02 .10
44 Dion James .02 .10
45 Ozzie Virgil .02 .10
46 Ken Oberkfell .02 .10
47 Gary Roenicke .02 .10
48 Glenn Hubbard .02 .10
49 Bill Schroeder .02 .10
50 Greg Brock .02 .10
51 Billy Jo Robidoux .02 .10
52 Glenn Braggs .05 .15
53 Jim Gantner .02 .10
54 Paul Molitor .05 .15
55 Dale Sveum .02 .10
56 Ted Higuera .02 .10
57 Rob Deer .02 .10
58 Robin Yount .25 .60
59 Jim Lindeman .05 .15
60 Vince Coleman .02 .10
61 Tommy Herr .02 .10
62 Terry Pendleton .05 .15
63 John Tudor .05 .15
64 Tony Pena .02 .10
65 Ozzie Smith .25 .60
66 Tito Landrum .02 .10
67 Jack Clark .05 .15
68 Bob Dernier .02 .10
69 Rick Sutcliffe .05 .15
70 Andre Dawson .05 .15
71 Keith Moreland .02 .10
72 Jody Davis .02 .10
73 Brian Dayett .02 .10
74 Leon Durham .02 .10
75 Ryne Sandberg .30 .75
76 Shawon Dunston .02 .10
77 Mike Marshall .02 .10
78 Bill Madlock .05 .15
79 Orel Hershiser .08 .25
80 Mike Ramsey .02 .10
81 Ken Landreaux .02 .10
82 Mike Scioscia .05 .15
83 Franklin Stubbs .02 .10
84 Mariano Duncan .02 .10
85 Steve Sax .02 .10
86 Mitch Webster .02 .10
87 Reid Nichols .02 .10
88 Tim Wallach .02 .10
89 Floyd Youmans .02 .10
90 Andres Galarraga .05 .15
91 Hubie Brooks .02 .10
92 Jeff Reed .02 .10
93 Alonzo Powell .02 .10
94 Vance Law .02 .10
95 Bob Brenly .02 .10
96 Will Clark .75 2.00
97 Chili Davis .05 .15
98 Mike Krukow .02 .10
99 Jose Uribe .02 .10
100 Chris Brown .02 .10
101 Robby Thompson .15 .40
102 Candy Maldonado .02 .10
103 Jeff Leonard .02 .10
104 Tom Candiotti .02 .10
105 Chris Bando .02 .10
106 Cory Snyder .02 .10
107 Pat Tabler .02 .10
108 Andre Thornton .02 .10
109 Joe Carter .05 .15
110 Tony Bernazard .02 .10
111 Julio Franco .05 .15
112 Brook Jacoby .02 .10
113 Brett Butler .05 .15
114 Donell Nixon .02 .10
115 Alvin Davis .02 .10
116 Mark Langston .02 .10
117 Harold Reynolds .05 .15
118 Ken Phelps .02 .10
119 Mike Kingery .05 .15
120 Dave Valle .02 .10
121 Rey Quinones .02 .10
122 Phil Bradley .02 .10
123 Jim Presley .02 .10
124 Keith Hernandez * .05 .15
125 Kevin McReynolds .02 .10
126 Rafael Santana .02 .10
127 Bob Ojeda .02 .10
128 Darryl Strawberry .05 .15
129 Mookie Wilson .05 .15
130 Gary Carter .05 .15
131 Tim Teufel .02 .10
132 Howard Johnson .05 .15
133 Cal Ripken .60 1.50
134 Rick Burleson .02 .10
135 Fred Lynn .05 .15
136 Eddie Murray .15 .40
137 Ray Knight .05 .15
138 Alan Wiggins .02 .10
139 John Shelby .02 .10
140 Mike Boddicker .02 .10
141 Ken Gerhart .02 .10
142 Terry Kennedy .02 .10
143 Steve Garvey .05 .15
144 Marvell Wynne .02 .10
145 Kevin Mitchell .08 .25
146 Tony Gwynn .25 .60
147 Joey Cora .15 .40
148 Benito Santiago .05 .15
149 Eric Show .02 .10
150 Garry Templeton .05 .15
151 Carmelo Martinez .02 .10
152 Von Hayes .02 .10
153 Lance Parrish .05 .15
154 Milt Thompson .02 .10
155 Mike Easler .05 .15
156 Juan Samuel .02 .10
157 Steve Jeltz .02 .10
158 Glenn Wilson .02 .10
159 Shane Rawley .02 .10
160 Mike Schmidt .40 1.00
161 Andy Van Slyke .08 .25
162 Johnny Ray .02 .10
163A B.Bonds ERR J.Ray 300.00 500.00
163B Barry Bonds COR 5.00 12.00
164 Junior Ortiz .02 .10
165 Rafael Belliard .15 .40
166 Bob Patterson .02 .10
167 Bobby Bonilla .25 .60
168 Sid Bream .02 .10
169 Jim Morrison .02 .10
170 Jerry Browne .05 .15
171 Scott Fletcher .02 .10
172 Ruben Sierra .40 1.00
173 Larry Parrish .02 .10
174 Pete O'Brien .02 .10
175 Pete Incaviglia .15 .40
176 Don Slaught .02 .10
177 Oddibe McDowell .02 .10
178 Charlie Hough .05 .15
179 Steve Buechele .02 .10
180 Bob Stanley .02 .10
181 Wade Boggs .08 .25
182 Jim Rice .05 .15
183 Bill Buckner .05 .15
184 Dwight Evans .08 .25
185 Spike Owen .02 .10
186 Don Baylor .05 .15
187 Marc Sullivan .02 .10
188 Marty Barrett .02 .10
189 Dave Henderson .02 .10
190 Bo Diaz .02 .10
191 Barry Larkin .75 2.00
192 Kal Daniels .02 .10
193 Terry Francona .05 .15
194 Tom Browning .02 .10
195 Ron Oester .02 .10
196 Buddy Bell .05 .15
197 Eric Davis .08 .25
198 Dave Parker .05 .15
199 Steve Balboni .02 .10
200 Danny Tartabull .02 .10
201 Ed Hearn .02 .10
202 Buddy Biancalana .02 .10
203 Danny Jackson .02 .10
204 Frank White .05 .15
205 Bo Jackson 2.00 5.00
206 George Brett .40 1.00
207 Kevin Seitzer .05 .15
208 Willie Wilson .05 .15
209 Orlando Mercado .02 .10
210 Darrell Evans .05 .15
211 Larry Herndon .02 .10
212 Jack Morris .05 .15
213 Chet Lemon .05 .15
214 Mike Heath .02 .10
215 Darnell Coles .02 .10
216 Alan Trammell .05 .15
217 Terry Harper .02 .10
218 Lou Whitaker .05 .15
219 Gary Gaetti .05 .15
220 Tom Nieto .02 .10
221 Kirby Puckett .30 .75
222 Tom Brunansky .02 .10
223 Greg Gagne .02 .10
224 Dan Gladden .02 .10
225 Mark Davidson .02 .10
226 Bert Blyleven .05 .15
227 Steve Lombardozzi .02 .10
228 Kent Hrbek .05 .15
229 Gary Redus .02 .10
230 Ivan Calderon .02 .10
231 Tim Hulett .02 .10
232 Carlton Fisk .08 .25
233 Greg Walker .02 .10
234 Ron Karkovice .15 .40
235 Ozzie Guillen .08 .25
236 Harold Baines .05 .15
237 Donnie Hill .02 .10
238 Rich Dotson .02 .10
239 Mike Pagliarulo .05 .15
240 Joel Skinner .02 .10
241 Don Mattingly .50 1.25
242 Gary Ward .02 .10
243 Dave Winfield .05 .15
244 Dan Pasqua .02 .10
245 Wayne Tolleson .02 .10
246 Willie Randolph .05 .15
247 Dennis Rasmussen .02 .10
248 Rickey Henderson .15 .40
249 Angels Logo .01 .05
250 Astros Logo .01 .05
251 A's Logo .01 .05
252 Blue Jays Logo .01 .05
253 Braves Logo .01 .05
254 Brewers Logo .01 .05
255 Cardinals Logo .01 .05
256 Dodgers Logo .01 .05
257 Expos Logo .01 .05
258 Giants Logo .01 .05
259 Indians Logo .01 .05
260 Mariners Logo .01 .05
261 Orioles Logo .01 .05
262 Padres Logo .01 .05
263 Phillies Logo .01 .05
264 Pirates Logo .01 .05
265 Rangers Logo .01 .05
266 Red Sox Logo .01 .05
267 Reds Logo .01 .05
268 Royals Logo .01 .05
269 Tigers Logo .01 .05
270 Twins Logo .01 .05
271 Chicago Logos .01 .05
272 New York Logos .01 .05

1987 Donruss Pop-Ups

This 20-card set features "fold-out" cards measuring approximately 2 1/2" X 5". Card fronts are in full color. Cards are unnumbered but are listed in the same order as the Donruss All-Stars on the All-Star checklist card. Card backs present essentially no information about the player. The set was distributed in packs which also contained All-Star cards (3 1/2" by 5").

COMPLETE SET (20) 2.00 5.00
1 Wally Joyner .10 .30
2 Dave Winfield .15 .40
3 Lou Whitaker .02 .10
4 Kirby Puckett .30 .75
5 Cal Ripken .75 2.00
6 Rickey Henderson .20 .50
7 Wade Boggs .20 .50
8 Roger Clemens .50 1.25
9 Lance Parrish .02 .10
10 Dick Howser MG .01 .05
11 Keith Hernandez .02 .10
12 Darryl Strawberry .02 .10
13 Ryne Sandberg .20 .50
14 Dale Murphy .10 .30
15 Ozzie Smith .30 .75
16 Tony Gwynn .40 1.00
17 Mike Schmidt .20 .50
18 Dwight Gooden .07 .20
19 Gary Carter .15 .40
20 Whitey Herzog MG .02 .10

1987 Donruss Super DK's

This 28-card set was available through a mail-in offer detailed on the wax packs. The set was sent in return for $8.00 and three wrappers plus $1.50 postage and handling. The set features the popular Diamond King subseries in large (approximately 4 7/8" X 6 13/16") form. Dick Perez of Perez-Steele Galleries did the original artwork from which these cards were taken. The cards are essentially a large version of the Donruss regular issue Diamond Kings.

COMPLETE SET (26) 5.00 12.00
1 Wally Joyner .60 1.50
2 Roger Clemens 1.00 2.50
3 Dale Murphy .60 1.50
4 Darryl Strawberry .30 .75
5 Ozzie Smith .75 2.00
6 Jose Canseco 1.00 2.50
7 Charlie Hough .20 .50
8 Brook Jacoby .20 .50
9 Fred Lynn .30 .75
10 Rick Rhoden .20 .50
11 Chris Brown .20 .50
12 Von Hayes .20 .50
13 Jack Morris .30 .75
14 Kevin McReynolds .20 .50
15 George Brett 1.25 3.00
16 Ted Higuera .20 .50
17 Hubie Brooks .20 .50
18 Mike Scott .20 .50
19 Kirby Puckett 1.00 2.50
20 Dave Winfield .75 2.00
21 Lloyd Moseby .20 .50
22 Eric Davis .40 1.00
23 Jim Presley .20 .50
24 Keith Moreland .20 .50
25 Greg Walker .20 .50
26 Steve Sax .20 .50
NNO Roberto Clemente .60 1.50
Large Puzzle
NNO DK Checklist 1-26 .20 .50

1988 Donruss

This set consists of 660 standard-size cards. For the seventh straight year, wax packs consisted of 15 cards plus a puzzle panel (featuring Stan Musial this time around). Cards were also distributed in rack packs and retail and hobby factory sets. Card fronts feature a distinctive black and blue border on the front. The card front border design pattern of the factory set card fronts is oriented differently from that of the regular wax pack cards. No premium or discount exists for either version. Subsets include Diamond Kings (1-27) and Rated Rookies (28-47). Cards marked as SP (short printed) from 648-660 are more difficult to find than the other 13 SP's in the lower 600s. These 26 cards listed as SP were apparently pulled from the printing sheet to make room for the 26 Bonus MVP cards. Six of the checklist cards were done two different ways to reflect the inclusion or exclusion of the Bonus MVP cards in the wax packs. In the checklist below, the A variations (for the checklist cards) are from the wax packs and the B variations are from the factory-collated sets. The key Rookie Cards in this set are Roberto Alomar, Jay Bell, Jay Buhner, Ellis Burks, Ken Caminiti, Tom Glavine, Mark Grace and Matt Williams. There was also a Kirby Puckett card issued as the package back of Donruss blister packs; it uses a different photo from both of Kirby's regular and Bonus MVP cards and is unnumbered on the back.

COMPLETE SET (660) 4.00 10.00
COMP.FACT.SET (660) 6.00 15.00
COMMON CARD (1-660) .01 .05
COMMON SP (648-660) .02 .10
1 Mark McGwire DK .30 .75
2 Tim Raines DK .02 .10
3 Benito Santiago DK .02 .10
4 Alan Trammell DK .02 .10
5 Danny Tartabull DK .01 .05
6 Ron Darling DK .02 .10
7 Paul Molitor DK .02 .10
8 Devon White DK .02 .10
9 Andre Dawson DK .01 .05
10 Julio Franco DK .02 .10
11 Scott Fletcher DK .01 .05
12 Tony Fernandez DK .01 .05
13 Shane Rawley DK .01 .05
14 Kal Daniels DK .01 .05
15 Jack Clark DK .02 .10
16 Dwight Evans DK .05 .15
17 Tommy John DK .02 .10
18 Andy Van Slyke DK .05 .15
19 Gary Gaetti DK .02 .10
20 Mark Langston DK .01 .05
21 Will Clark DK .07 .20
22 Glenn Hubbard DK .01 .05
23 Billy Hatcher DK .01 .05
24 Bob Welch DK .02 .10
25 Ivan Calderon DK .01 .05
26 Cal Ripken DK .15 .40
27 DK Checklist 1-26 .01 .05
28 Mackey Sasser RC .08 .25
29 Jeff Treadway RC .08 .25
30 Mike Campbell RR RC .01 .05
31 Lance Johnson RC .08 .25
32 Nelson Liriano RR RC .01 .05
33 Shawn Abner RR .01 .05
34 Roberto Alomar RC .75 2.00
35 Shawn Hillegas RR RC .01 .05
36 Joey Meyer RR .01 .05
37 Kevin Elster RR .01 .05
38 Jose Lind RC .08 .25
39 Kirt Manwaring RC .08 .25
40 Mark Grace RC .75 2.00
41 Jody Reed RC .08 .25
42 John Farrell RR RC .02 .10
43 Al Leiter RC .30 .75
44 Gary Thurman RR RC .01 .05
45 Vicente Palacios RR RC .01 .05
46 Eddie Williams RC .02 .10
47 Jack McDowell RC .15 .40
48 Ken Dixon .01 .05
49 Mike Birkbeck .01 .05
50 Eric King .01 .05
51 Roger Clemens .40 1.00
52 Pat Clements .01 .05
53 Fernando Valenzuela .02 .10
54 Mark Gubicza .01 .05
55 Jay Howell .01 .05
56 Floyd Youmans .01 .05
57 Ed Correa .01 .05
58 DeWayne Buice .01 .05
59 Jose DeLeon .01 .05
60 Danny Cox .01 .05
61 Nolan Ryan .40 1.00
62 Steve Bedrosian .01 .05
63 Tom Browning .01 .05
64 Mark Davis .01 .05
65 R.J. Reynolds .01 .05
66 Kevin Mitchell .02 .10
67 Ken Oberkfell .01 .05
68 Rick Sutcliffe .02 .10
69 Dwight Gooden .02 .10
70 Scott Bankhead .01 .05
71 Bert Blyleven .02 .10
72 Jimmy Key .02 .10
73 Les Straker .01 .05
74 Jim Clancy .01 .05
75 Mike Moore .01 .05
76 Ron Darling .02 .10
77 Ed Lynch .01 .05
78 Dale Murphy .05 .15
79 Doug Drabek .01 .05
80 Scott Garrelts .01 .05
81 Ed Whitson .01 .05
82 Rob Murphy .01 .05
83 Shane Rawley .01 .05
84 Greg Mathews .01 .05
85 Jim Deshaies .01 .05
86 Mike Witt .01 .05
87 Donnie Hill .01 .05
88 Jeff Reed .01 .05
89 Mike Boddicker .01 .05
90 Ted Higuera .01 .05
91 Walt Terrell .01 .05
92 Bob Stanley .01 .05
93 Dave Righetti .02 .10
94 Orel Hershiser .02 .10
95 Chris Bando .01 .05
96 Bret Saberhagen .02 .10
97 Curt Young .01 .05
98 Tim Burke .01 .05
99 Charlie Hough .02 .10
100A Checklist 28-137 .01 .05
100B Checklist 28-133 .01 .05
101 Bobby Witt .01 .05
102 George Brett .20 .50
103 Mickey Tettleton .01 .05
104 Scott Bailes .01 .05
105 Mike Pagliarulo .01 .05
106 Mike Scioscia .02 .10
107 Tom Brookens .01 .05
108 Ray Knight .02 .10
109 Dan Plesac .01 .05
110 Wally Joyner .02 .10

Card	Low	High
111 Bob Forsch	.01	.05
112 Mike Scott	.02	.10
113 Kevin Gross	.01	.05
114 Benito Santiago	.02	.10
115 Bob Kipper	.01	.05
116 Mike Krukow	.01	.05
117 Chris Bosio	.01	.05
118 Sid Fernandez	.01	.05
119 Jody Davis	.01	.05
120 Mike Morgan	.01	.05
121 Mark Eichhorn	.01	.05
122 Jeff Reardon	.02	.10
123 John Franco	.02	.10
124 Richard Dotson	.01	.05
125 Eric Bell	.01	.05
126 Juan Nieves	.01	.05
127 Jack Morris	.02	.10
128 Rick Rhoden	.01	.05
129 Rich Gedman	.01	.05
130 Ken Howell	.01	.05
131 Brook Jacoby	.01	.05
132 Danny Jackson	.01	.05
133 Gene Nelson	.01	.05
134 Neal Heaton	.01	.05
135 Willie Fraser	.01	.05
136 Jose Guzman	.01	.05
137 Ozzie Guillen	.02	.10
138 Bob Knepper	.01	.05
139 Mike Jackson RC*	.08	.25
140 Joe Magrane RC*	.08	.25
141 Jimmy Jones	.01	.05
142 Ted Power	.01	.05
143 Ozzie Virgil	.01	.05
144 Felix Fermin	.01	.05
145 Kelly Downs	.01	.05
146 Shawon Dunston	.01	.05
147 Scott Bradley	.01	.05
148 Dave Stieb	.02	.10
149 Frank Viola	.02	.10
150 Terry Kennedy	.01	.05
151 Bill Wegman	.01	.05
152 Matt Nokes RC*	.08	.25
153 Wade Boggs	.05	.15
154 Wayne Tolleson	.01	.05
155 Mariano Duncan	.01	.05
156 Julio Franco	.02	.10
157 Charlie Leibrandt	.01	.05
158 Terry Steinbach	.02	.10
159 Mike Fitzgerald	.01	.05
160 Jack Lazorko	.01	.05
161 Mitch Williams	.01	.05
162 Greg Walker	.01	.05
163 Alan Ashby	.01	.05
164 Tony Gwynn	.10	.30
165 Bruce Ruffin	.01	.05
166 Ron Robinson	.01	.05
167 Zane Smith	.01	.05
168 Junior Ortiz	.01	.05
169 Jamie Moyer	.02	.10
170 Tony Pena	.01	.05
171 Cal Ripken	.30	.75
172 B.J. Surhoff	.02	.10
173 Lou Whitaker	.02	.10
174 Ellis Burks RC	.15	.40
175 Ron Guidry	.02	.10
176 Steve Sax	.01	.05
177 Danny Tartabull	.01	.05
178 Carney Lansford	.02	.10
179 Casey Candaele	.01	.05
180 Scott Fletcher	.01	.05
181 Mark McLemore	.01	.05
182 Ivan Calderon	.01	.05
183 Jack Clark	.02	.10
184 Glenn Davis	.01	.05
185 Luis Aguayo	.01	.05
186 Bo Diaz	.01	.05
187 Stan Jefferson	.01	.05
188 Sid Bream	.01	.05
189 Bob Brenly	.01	.05
190 Dion James	.01	.05
191 Leon Durham	.01	.05
192 Jesse Orosco	.01	.05
193 Alvin Davis	.01	.05
194 Gary Gaetti	.02	.10
195 Fred McGriff	.07	.20
196 Steve Lombardozzi	.01	.05
197 Rance Mulliniks	.01	.05
198 Rey Quinones	.01	.05
199 Gary Carter	.02	.10
200A Checklist 138-247	.01	.05
200B Checklist 134-239	.01	.05
201 Keith Moreland	.01	.05
202 Ken Griffey	.02	.10
203 Tommy Gregg	.01	.05
204 Will Clark	.07	.20
205 John Kruk	.02	.10
206 Buddy Bell	.02	.10
207 Von Hayes	.01	.05
208 Tommy Herr	.01	.05
209 Craig Reynolds	.01	.05
210 Gary Pettis	.01	.05
211 Harold Baines	.02	.10
212 Vance Law	.01	.05
213 Ken Gerhart	.01	.05
214 Jim Gantner	.01	.05
215 Chet Lemon	.02	.10
216 Dwight Evans	.02	.10
217 Don Mattingly	.25	.60
218 Franklin Stubbs	.01	.05
219 Pat Tabler	.01	.05
220 Bo Jackson	.07	.20
221 Tony Phillips	.01	.05
222 Tim Wallach	.01	.05
223 Ruben Sierra	.02	.10
224 Steve Buechele	.01	.05
225 Frank White	.02	.10
226 Alfredo Griffin	.01	.05
227 Greg Swindell	.01	.05
228 Willie Randolph	.02	.10
229 Mike Marshall	.01	.05
230 Alan Trammell	.02	.10
231 Eddie Murray	.07	.20
232 Dale Sveum	.01	.05
233 Dick Schofield	.01	.05
234 Jose Oquendo	.01	.05
235 Bill Doran	.01	.05
236 Milt Thompson	.01	.05
237 Marvell Wynne	.01	.05
238 Bobby Bonilla	.02	.10
239 Chris Speier	.01	.05
240 Glenn Braggs	.01	.05
241 Wally Backman	.01	.05
242 Ryne Sandberg	.15	.40
243 Phil Bradley	.01	.05
244 Kelly Gruber	.01	.05
245 Tom Brunansky	.01	.05
246 Ron Oester	.01	.05
247 Bobby Thigpen	.01	.05
248 Fred Lynn	.02	.10
249 Paul Molitor	.02	.10
250 Darrell Evans	.02	.10
251 Gary Ward	.01	.05
252 Bruce Hurst	.01	.05
253 Bob Welch	.02	.10
254 Joe Carter	.02	.10
255 Willie Wilson	.02	.10
256 Mark McGwire	.60	1.50
257 Mitch Webster	.01	.05
258 Brian Downing	.02	.10
259 Mike Stanley	.01	.05
260 Carlton Fisk	.05	.15
261 Billy Hatcher	.01	.05
262 Glenn Wilson	.01	.05
263 Ozzie Smith	.10	.30
264 Randy Ready	.01	.05
265 Kurt Stillwell	.01	.05
266 David Palmer	.01	.05
267 Mike Diaz	.01	.05
268 Robby Thompson	.02	.10
269 Andre Dawson	.02	.10
270 Lee Guetterman	.01	.05
271 Willie Upshaw	.01	.05
272 Randy Bush	.01	.05
273 Larry Sheets	.01	.05
274 Rob Deer	.01	.05
275 Kirk Gibson	.07	.20
276 Marty Barrett	.01	.05
277 Rickey Henderson	.07	.20
278 Pedro Guerrero	.02	.10
279 Brett Butler	.02	.10
280 Kevin Seitzer	.01	.05
281 Mike Davis	.01	.05
282 Andres Galarraga	.02	.10
283 Devon White	.02	.10
284 Pete O'Brien	.01	.05
285 Jerry Hairston	.01	.05
286 Kevin Bass	.01	.05
287 Carmelo Martinez	.01	.05
288 Juan Samuel	.01	.05
289 Kal Daniels	.01	.05
290 Albert Hall	.01	.05
291 Andy Van Slyke	.05	.15
292 Lee Smith	.02	.10
293 Vince Coleman	.01	.05
294 Tom Niedenfuer	.01	.05
295 Robin Yount	.10	.30
296 Jeff M. Robinson	.01	.05
297 Todd Benzinger RC*	.08	.25
298 Dave Winfield	.02	.10
299 Mickey Hatcher	.01	.05
300A Checklist 248-357	.01	.05
300B Checklist 240-345	.01	.05
301 Bud Black	.01	.05
302 Jose Canseco	.20	.50
303 Tom Foley	.01	.05
304 Pete Incaviglia	.01	.05
305 Bob Boone	.02	.10
306 Bill Long	.01	.05
307 Willie McGee	.02	.10
308 Ken Caminiti RC	.75	2.00
309 Darren Daulton	.02	.10
310 Tracy Jones	.01	.05
311 Greg Booker	.01	.05
312 Mike LaValliere	.01	.05
313 Chili Davis	.02	.10
314 Glenn Hubbard	.01	.05
315 Paul Noce	.01	.05
316 Keith Hernandez	.02	.10
317 Mark Langston	.01	.05
318 Keith Atherton	.01	.05
319 Tony Fernandez	.01	.05
320 Kent Hrbek	.02	.10
321 John Cerutti	.01	.05
322 Mike Kingery	.01	.05
323 Dave Magadan	.01	.05
324 Rafael Palmeiro	.15	.40
325 Jeff Dedmon	.01	.05
326 Barry Bonds	.75	2.00
327 Jeffrey Leonard	.01	.05
328 Tim Flannery	.01	.05
329 Dave Concepcion	.02	.10
330 Mike Schmidt	.20	.50
331 Bill Dawley	.01	.05
332 Larry Andersen	.01	.05
333 Jack Howell	.01	.05
334 Ken Williams	.01	.05
335 Bryn Smith	.01	.05
336 Bill Ripken RC*	.08	.25
337 Greg Brock	.01	.05
338 Mike Heath	.01	.05
339 Mike Greenwell	.01	.05
340 Claudell Washington	.01	.05
341 Jose Gonzalez	.01	.05
342 Mel Hall	.01	.05
343 Jim Eisenreich	.01	.05
344 Tony Bernazard	.01	.05
345 Tim Raines	.02	.10
346 Bob Brower	.01	.05
347 Larry Parrish	.01	.05
348 Thad Bosley	.01	.05
349 Dennis Eckersley	.05	.15
350 Cory Snyder	.01	.05
351 Rick Cerone	.01	.05
352 John Shelby	.01	.05
353 Larry Herndon	.01	.05
354 John Habyan	.01	.05
355 Chuck Crim	.01	.05
356 Gus Polidor	.01	.05
357 Ken Dayley	.01	.05
358 Danny Darwin	.01	.05
359 Lance Parrish	.02	.10
360 James Steels	.01	.05
361 Al Pedrique	.01	.05
362 Mike Aldrete	.01	.05
363 Juan Castillo	.01	.05
364 Len Dykstra	.02	.10
365 Luis Quinones	.01	.05
366 Jim Presley	.01	.05
367 Lloyd Moseby	.01	.05
368 Kirby Puckett	.07	.20
369 Eric Davis	.02	.10
370 Gary Redus	.01	.05
371 Dave Schmidt	.01	.05
372 Mark Clear	.01	.05
373 Dave Bergman	.01	.05
374 Charles Hudson	.01	.05
375 Calvin Schiraldi	.01	.05
376 Alex Trevino	.01	.05
377 Tom Candiotti	.01	.05
378 Steve Farr	.01	.05
379 Mike Gallego	.01	.05
380 Andy McGaffigan	.01	.05
381 Kirk McCaskill	.01	.05
382 Oddibe McDowell	.01	.05
383 Floyd Bannister	.01	.05
384 Denny Walling	.01	.05
385 Don Carman	.01	.05
386 Todd Worrell	.01	.05
387 Eric Show	.01	.05
388 Dave Parker	.02	.10
389 Rick Mahler	.01	.05
390 Mike Dunne	.01	.05
391 Candy Maldonado	.01	.05
392 Bob Dernier	.01	.05
393 Dave Valle	.01	.05
394 Ernie Whitt	.01	.05
395 Juan Berenguer	.01	.05
396 Mike Young	.01	.05
397 Mike Felder	.01	.05
398 Willie Hernandez	.01	.05
399 Jim Rice	.02	.10
400A Checklist 358-467	.01	.05
400B Checklist 346-451	.01	.05
401 Tommy John	.02	.10
402 Brian Holton	.01	.05
403 Carmen Castillo	.01	.05
404 Jamie Quirk	.01	.05
405 Dwayne Murphy	.01	.05
406 Jeff Parrett	.01	.05
407 Don Sutton	.02	.10
408 Jerry Browne	.01	.05
409 Jim Winn	.01	.05
410 Dave Smith	.01	.05
411 Shane Mack	.01	.05
412 Greg Gross	.01	.05
413 Nick Esasky	.01	.05
414 Damaso Garcia	.01	.05
415 Brian Fisher	.01	.05
416 Brian Dayett	.01	.05
417 Curt Ford	.01	.05
418 Mark Williamson	.01	.05
419 Bill Schroeder	.01	.05
420 Mike Henneman RC*	.08	.25
421 John Marzano	.01	.05
422 Ron Kittle	.01	.05
423 Matt Young	.01	.05
424 Steve Balboni	.01	.05
425 Luis Polonia RC*	.08	.25
426 Randy St.Claire	.01	.05
427 Greg Harris	.01	.05
428 Johnny Ray	.01	.05
429 Ray Searage	.01	.05
430 Ricky Horton	.01	.05
431 Gerald Young	.01	.05
432 Rick Schu	.01	.05
433 Paul O'Neill	.05	.15
434 Rich Gossage	.02	.10
435 John Cangelosi	.01	.05
436 Mike LaCoss	.01	.05
437 Gerald Perry	.01	.05
438 Dave Martinez	.01	.05
439 Darryl Strawberry	.02	.10
440 John Moses	.01	.05
441 Greg Gagne	.01	.05
442 Jesse Barfield	.02	.10
443 George Frazier	.01	.05
444 Garth Iorg	.01	.05
445 Ed Nunez	.01	.05
446 Rick Aguilera	.01	.05
447 Jerry Mumphrey	.01	.05
448 Rafael Ramirez	.01	.05
449 John Smiley RC*	.08	.25
450 Atlee Hammaker	.01	.05
451 Lance McCullers	.01	.05
452 Guy Hoffman	.01	.05
453 Chris James	.01	.05
454 Terry Pendleton	.02	.10
455 Dave Meads	.01	.05
456 Bill Buckner	.02	.10
457 John Pawlowski	.01	.05
458 Bob Sebra	.01	.05
459 Jim Dwyer	.01	.05
460 Jay Aldrich	.01	.05
461 Frank Tanana	.02	.10
462 Oil Can Boyd	.01	.05
463 Dan Pasqua	.01	.05
464 Tim Crews RC	.08	.25
465 Andy Allanson	.01	.05
466 Bill Pecota RC*	.02	.10
467 Steve Ontiveros	.01	.05
468 Hubie Brooks	.01	.05
469 Paul Kilgus	.01	.05
470 Dale Mohorcic	.01	.05
471 Dan Quisenberry	.01	.05
472 Dave Stewart	.02	.10
473 Dave Clark	.01	.05
474 Joel Skinner	.01	.05
475 Dave Anderson	.01	.05
476 Dan Petry	.01	.05
477 Carl Nichols	.01	.05
478 Ernest Riles	.01	.05
479 George Hendrick	.02	.10
480 John Morris	.01	.05
481 Manny Hernandez	.01	.05
482 Jeff Stone	.01	.05
483 Chris Brown	.01	.05
484 Mike Bielecki	.01	.05
485 Dave Dravecky	.01	.05
486 Rick Manning	.01	.05
487 Bill Almon	.01	.05
488 Jim Sundberg	.02	.10
489 Ken Phelps	.01	.05
490 Tom Henke	.01	.05
491 Dan Gladden	.01	.05
492 Barry Larkin	.05	.15
493 Fred Manrique	.01	.05
494 Mike Griffin	.01	.05
495 Mark Knudson	.01	.05
496 Bill Madlock	.02	.10
497 Tim Stoddard	.01	.05
498 Sam Horn RC	.02	.10
499 Tracy Woodson RC	.02	.10
500A Checklist 468-577	.01	.05
500B Checklist 452-557	.01	.05
501 Ken Schrom	.01	.05
502 Angel Salazar	.01	.05
503 Eric Plunk	.01	.05
504 Joe Hesketh	.01	.05
505 Greg Minton	.01	.05
506 Geno Petralli	.01	.05
507 Bob James	.01	.05
508 Robbie Wine	.01	.05
509 Jeff Calhoun	.01	.05
510 Steve Lake	.01	.05
511 Mark Grant	.01	.05
512 Frank Williams	.01	.05
513 Jeff Blauser RC	.08	.25
514 Bob Walk	.01	.05
515 Craig Lefferts	.01	.05
516 Manny Trillo	.01	.05
517 Jerry Reed	.01	.05
518 Rick Leach	.01	.05
519 Mark Davidson	.01	.05
520 Jeff Ballard RC	.01	.05
521 Dave Stapleton RC	.01	.05
522 Pat Sheridan	.01	.05
523 Al Nipper	.01	.05
524 Steve Trout	.01	.05
525 Jeff Hamilton	.01	.05
526 Tommy Hinzo	.01	.05
527 Lonnie Smith	.01	.05
528 Greg Cadaret	.01	.05
529 Bob McClure UER/(Rob- on front)	.01	.05
530 Chuck Finley	.02	.10
531 Jeff Russell	.01	.05
532 Steve Lyons	.01	.05
533 Terry Puhl	.01	.05
534 Eric Nolte	.01	.05
535 Kent Tekulve	.01	.05
536 Pat Pacillo	.01	.05
537 Charlie Puleo	.01	.05
538 Tom Prince	.01	.05
539 Greg Maddux	.40	1.00
540 Jim Lindeman	.01	.05
541 Pete Stanicek RC	.01	.05
542 Steve Kiefer	.01	.05
543A Jim Morrison ERR (No decimal before lifetime ave	.05	.15
543B Jim Morrison COR	.01	.05
544 Spike Owen	.01	.05
545 Jay Buhner RC	.20	.50
546 Mike Devereaux RC	.08	.25
547 Jerry Don Gleaton	.01	.05
548 Jose Rijo	.02	.10
549 Dennis Martinez	.02	.10
550 Mike Loynd	.01	.05
551 Darrell Miller	.01	.05
552 Dave LaPoint	.01	.05
553 John Tudor	.02	.10
554 Rocky Childress	.01	.05
555 Wally Ritchie	.01	.05
556 Terry McGriff	.01	.05
557 Dave Leiper	.01	.05
558 Jeff D. Robinson	.01	.05
559 Jose Uribe UER	.01	.05
560 Ted Simmons	.02	.10
561 Les Lancaster	.01	.05
562 Keith Miller RC	.08	.25
563 Harold Reynolds	.02	.10
564 Gene Larkin RC*	.08	.25
565 Cecil Fielder	.02	.10
566 Roy Smalley	.01	.05
567 Duane Ward	.01	.05
568 Bill Wilkinson	.01	.05
569 Howard Johnson	.02	.10
570 Frank DiPino	.01	.05
571 Pete Smith RC	.02	.10
572 Darnell Coles	.01	.05
573 Don Robinson	.01	.05
574 Rob Nelson UER/(Career 0 RBI& but 1 RBI in '87)	.01	.05
575 Dennis Rasmussen	.01	.05
576 Steve Jeltz UER (Photo actually Juan Samuel; Sam	.01	.05
577 Tom Pagnozzi RC	.02	.10
578 Ty Gainey	.01	.05
579 Gary Lucas	.01	.05
580 Ron Hassey	.01	.05
581 Herm Winningham	.01	.05
582 Rene Gonzales RC	.02	.10
583 Brad Komminsk	.01	.05
584 Doyle Alexander	.01	.05
585 Jeff Sellers	.01	.05
586 Bill Gullickson	.01	.05
587 Tim Belcher	.01	.05
588 Doug Jones RC	.08	.25
589 Melido Perez RC	.08	.25
590 Rick Honeycutt	.01	.05
591 Pascual Perez	.01	.05
592 Curt Wilkerson	.01	.05
593 Steve Howe	.01	.05
594 John Davis RC	.01	.05
595 Storm Davis	.01	.05
596 Sammy Stewart	.01	.05
597 Neil Allen	.01	.05
598 Alejandro Pena	.01	.05
599 Mark Thurmond	.01	.05
600A Checklist 578-660 BC1-BC26	.01	.05
600B Checklist 558-660	.01	.05
601 Jose Mesa RC	.08	.25
602 Don August	.01	.05
603 Terry Leach SP	.02	.10
604 Tom Newell	.01	.05
605 Randall Byers SP	.02	.10
606 Jim Gott	.01	.05
607 Harry Spilman	.01	.05
608 John Candelaria	.01	.05
609 Mike Brumley	.01	.05
610 Mickey Brantley	.01	.05
611 Jose Nunez SP	.02	.10
612 Tom Nieto	.01	.05
613 Rick Reuschel	.02	.10
614 Lee Mazzilli SP	.02	.10
615 Scott Lusader	.01	.05
616 Bobby Meacham	.01	.05
617 Kevin McReynolds SP	.02	.10
618 Gene Garber	.01	.05
619 Barry Lyons SP	.02	.10
620 Randy Myers	.02	.10
621 Donnie Moore	.01	.05
622 Domingo Ramos	.01	.05
623 Ed Romero	.01	.05
624 Greg Myers RC	.08	.25
625 The Ripken Family	.15	.40
626 Pat Perry	.01	.05
627 Andres Thomas SP	.02	.10
628 Matt Williams RC	.30	.75
629 Dave Hengel	.01	.05
630 Jeff Musselman SP	.02	.10
631 Tim Laudner	.01	.05
632 Bob Ojeda SP	.02	.10
633 Rafael Santana	.01	.05
634 Wes Gardner	.01	.05
635 Roberto Kelly SP RC	.08	.25
636 Mike Flanagan SP	.02	.10
637 Jay Bell RC	.15	.40
638 Bob Melvin	.01	.05
639 Damon Berryhill RC	.08	.25
640 David Wells RC	.40	1.00
641 Stan Musial Puzzle	.07	.20
642 Doug Sisk	.01	.05
643 Keith Hughes RC	.01	.05
644 Tom Glavine RC	1.25	3.00
645 Al Newman	.01	.05
646 Scott Sanderson	.01	.05
647 Scott Terry	.01	.05
648 Tim Teufel SP	.02	.10
649 Garry Templeton SP	.02	.10
650 Manny Lee SP	.02	.10
651 Roger McDowell SP	.02	.10
652 Mookie Wilson SP	.02	.10
653 David Cone	.02	.10
654 Ron Gant RC	.15	.40
655 Joe Price SP	.02	.10
656 George Bell SP	.02	.10
657 Gregg Jefferies RC	.08	.25
658 Todd Stottlemyre RC	.08	.25
659 Geronimo Berroa RC	.08	.25
660 Jerry Royster SP	.02	.10
XX Kirby Puckett Blister Pack	.50	1.25

1988 Donruss Bonus MVP's

Numbered with the prefix "BC" for bonus card, this 26-card set featuring the most valuable player from each major league team was randomly inserted in the wax and rack packs. The cards are distinguished by the MVP logo in the upper left corner of the obverse, and cards BC14-BC26 are considered to be very slightly more difficult to find than cards BC1-BC13.

Card	Low	High
COMPLETE SET (26)	1.25	3.00
RANDOM INSERTS IN PACKS		
BC1 Cal Ripken	.30	.75
BC2 Eric Davis	.02	.10
BC3 Paul Molitor	.02	.10
BC4 Mike Schmidt	.20	.50
BC5 Ivan Calderon	.01	.05
BC6 Tony Gwynn	.10	.30
BC7 Wade Boggs	.05	.15
BC8 Andy Van Slyke	.05	.15
BC9 Joe Carter	.02	.10
BC10 Andre Dawson	.02	.10
BC11 Alan Trammell	.02	.10
BC12 Mike Scott	.02	.10
BC13 Wally Joyner	.02	.10
BC14 Dale Murphy SP	.05	.15
BC15 Kirby Puckett SP	.07	.20
BC16 Pedro Guerrero SP	.02	.10
BC17 Kevin Seitzer SP	.01	.05
BC18 Tim Raines SP	.02	.10
BC19 George Bell SP	.02	.10
BC20 Darryl Strawberry SP	.02	.10
BC21 Don Mattingly SP	.25	.60
BC22 Ozzie Smith SP	.10	.30
BC23 Mark McGwire SP	.60	1.50
BC24 Will Clark SP	.07	.20
BC25 Alvin Davis SP	.01	.05
BC26 Ruben Sierra SP	.02	.10

1988 Donruss Rookies

The 1988 Donruss "The Rookies" set features 56 standard-size full-color cards plus a 15-piece puzzle of Stan Musial. This set was distributed exclusively in factory set form in a small, cellophane-wrapped, green and black through hobby dealers. Card fronts are similar in design to the 1988 Donruss regular issue except for the presence of "The Rookies" logo in the lower right corner and a green and black border instead of a blue and black border on the fronts. Extended Rookie Cards in this set include Brady Anderson, Edgar Martinez, and Walt Weiss. Notable early cards were issued of Roberto Alomar, Mark Grace and Jay Buhner.

Card	Low	High
COMP.FACT.SET (56)	4.00	10.00
1 Mark Grace	.75	2.00
2 Mike Campbell	.05	.15
3 Todd Frohwirth	.05	.15
4 Dave Stapleton	.05	.15
5 Shawn Abner	.05	.15
6 Jose Cecena	.05	.15
7 Dave Gallagher	.05	.15
8 Mark Parent XRC	.05	.15
9 Cecil Espy XRC	.05	.15
10 Pete Smith	.05	.15
11 Jay Buhner	.40	1.00
12 Pat Borders XRC	.20	.50
13 Doug Jennings XRC	.05	.15
14 Brady Anderson XRC	.30	.75
15 Pete Stanicek	.05	.15
16 Roberto Kelly	.20	.50
17 Jeff Treadway	.05	.15
18 Walt Weiss XRC*	.30	.75
19 Paul Gibson	.05	.15
20 Tim Crews	.05	.15
21 Melido Perez	.05	.15
22 Steve Peters	.05	.15
23 Craig Worthington	.05	.15
24 John Trautwein	.05	.15
25 DeWayne Vaughn	.05	.15
26 David Wells	.60	1.50
27 Al Leiter	.40	1.00
28 Tim Belcher	.05	.15
29 Johnny Paredes	.05	.15
30 Chris Sabo XRC	.15	.40
31 Damon Berryhill	.05	.15
32 Randy Milligan XRC*	.08	.25
33 Gary Thurman	.05	.15
34 Kevin Elster	.05	.15
35 Roberto Alomar	1.50	4.00
36 Edgar Martinez XRC	2.50	6.00
37 Todd Stottlemyre	.05	.15
38 Joey Meyer	.05	.15
39 Carl Nichols	.05	.15
40 Jack McDowell	.30	.75
41 Jose Bautista XRC	.08	.25
42 Sil Campusano	.05	.15
43 John Dopson	.05	.15
44 Jody Reed	.20	.50
45 Darrin Jackson XRC*	.08	.25
46 Mike Capel	.05	.15
47 Ron Gant	.30	.75
48 John Davis	.05	.15
49 Kevin Coffman	.05	.15
50 Cris Carpenter XRC	.08	.25
51 Mackey Sasser	.05	.15
52 Luis Alicea XRC	.20	.50
53 Bryan Harvey XRC	.10	.30
54 Steve Ellsworth	.05	.15
55 Mike Macfarlane XRC	.20	.50
56 Checklist 1-56	.05	.15

1988 Donruss Stan Musial Puzzle

Card	Low	High
1 Musial Puzzle 1-3	.10	.2
4 Musial Puzzle 4-6	.10	.2
7 Musial Puzzle 7-10	.10	.2
10 Musial Puzzle 10-12	.10	.2
13 Musial Puzzle 13-15	.10	.2
16 Musial Puzzle 16-18	.10	.2
19 Musial Puzzle 19-21	.10	.2
22 Musial Puzzle 22-24	.10	.2
25 Musial Puzzle 25-27	.10	.2
28 Musial Puzzle 28-30	.10	.2
31 Musial Puzzle 31-33	.10	.2
34 Musial Puzzle 34-36	.10	.2
37 Musial Puzzle 37-39	.10	.2
40 Musial Puzzle 40-42	.10	.2
43 Musial Puzzle 43-45	.10	.2
46 Musial Puzzle 46-48	.10	.2
49 Musial Puzzle 49-51	.10	.2
52 Musial Puzzle 52-54	.10	.2
55 Musial Puzzle 55-57	.10	.2
58 Musial Puzzle 58-60	.10	.2
61 Musial Puzzle 61-63	.10	.2

1988 Donruss All-Stars

This 64-card set features cards measures the standard size. Card fronts are in full color with a solid blue and black border. The card backs are printed in black and blue on white card stock. Card are numbered on the back inside a blue star in the upper right hand corner. Card backs feature statistical information about the player's performar in past All-Star games. The set was distributed in packs which also contained a Pop-Up. The AL Checklist card number 32 has two uncorrected err on it, Wade Boggs is erroneously listed as the AL Leftfielder and Dan Plesac is erroneously listed as being on the Tigers.

Card	Low	High
COMPLETE SET (64)	3.00	8.
1 Don Mattingly	.40	1.
2 Dave Winfield	.20	
3 Willie Randolph	.02	
4 Rickey Henderson	.20	
5 Cal Ripken	1.00	2.
6 George Bell	.01	
7 Wade Boggs	.20	
8 Bret Saberhagen	.02	
9 Terry Kennedy	.01	
10 John McNamara MG	.01	
11 Jay Howell	.01	
12 Harold Baines	.07	
13 Harold Reynolds	.02	
14 Bruce Hurst	.01	
15 Kirby Puckett	.40	1.
16 Matt Nokes	.01	
17 Pat Tabler	.01	
18 Dan Plesac	.01	
19 Mark McGwire	.75	2
20 Mike Witt	.01	
21 Larry Parrish	.01	
22 Alan Trammell	.07	
23 Dwight Evans	.02	
24 Jack Morris	.02	
25 Tony Fernandez	.01	
26 Mark Langston	.01	
27 Kevin Seitzer	.02	
28 Tom Henke	.01	
29 Dave Righetti	.01	
30 Oakland Stadium	.01	
31 Wade Boggs/(Top AL Vote Getter)	.20	
32 AL Checklist UER	.01	
33 Jack Clark	.02	
34 Darryl Strawberry	.02	
35 Ryne Sandberg	.30	
36 Andre Dawson	.10	
37 Ozzie Smith	.40	
38 Eric Davis	.02	
39 Mike Schmidt	.30	
40 Mike Scott	.01	
41 Gary Carter	.20	
42 Davey Johnson MG	.01	
43 Rick Sutcliffe	.01	
44 Willie McGee	.02	
45 Hubie Brooks	.01	
46 Dale Murphy	.10	

az .01 .05
Guerrero .01 .05
Hernandez .02 .10
Virgil UER/(Phillies logo .01 .05
back&
Gwynn .50 1.25
Reuschel UER/(Pirates logo .01 .05
back)
Franco .02 .10
Leonard .01 .05
Samuel .01 .05
Hershiser .02 .10
aines .02 .10
ernandez .01 .05
Vallach .01 .05
mith .02 .10
Bedrosian .01 .05
aines .02 .10
Smith/(Top NL Vote Getter) .40 1.00
hecklist .01 .05

8 Donruss Baseball's Best

ovative set of 336 standard-size cards was by Donruss very late in the 1988 season to n large national retail chains as a complete d set. The set was packaged in a specially d box. Cards are very similar in design to the gular Donruss issue except that these cards nge and black borders instead of blue and rders. The set is also sometimes referred to alloween set because of the orange box and f the cards. Six (2 1/2" by 3 1/2") 15-piece of Stan Musial are also included with every e set.

ACT.SET (336) 10.00 25.00
Mattingly .40 1.00
ant .20 .50
oone .07 .20
Grace .75 2.00
Allanson .02 .10
niels .02 .10
Bannister .02 .10
shby .02 .10
Barrett .02 .10
Belcher .07 .20
d Baines .07 .20
e Brooks .02 .10
e Alexander .02 .10
Carter .20 .50
n Braggs .02 .10
e Bedrosian .02 .10
Bonds .50 1.00
Blyleven .07 .20
Brunansky .02 .10
Candelaria .02 .10
n Abner .02 .10
Canseco .20 .50
Butler .07 .20
t Bradley .02 .10
Calderon .02 .10
Gossage .07 .20
Downing .02 .10
Rice .07 .20
James .02 .10
Kennedy .02 .10
ge Bell .02 .10
t Fletcher .02 .10
y Bonilla .07 .20
Burke .02 .10
ell Evans .07 .20
e Davis .02 .10
von Dunston .02 .10
n Bass .02 .10
ge Brett .50 1.25
d Cone .15 .40
Darling .02 .10
erto Alomar .75 2.00
nis Eckersley .20 .50
e Coleman .02 .10
Bream .02 .10
Gaetti .07 .20
Bradley .02 .10
Clancy .02 .10
Clark .07 .20
e Krukow .02 .10
y Cotto .02 .10
Dotson .02 .10
Gantner .02 .10
Franco .07 .20
Incaviglia .02 .10
Carter .15 .40
er Clemens .30 1.00
ld Perry .02 .10
Howell .02 .10
ce Law .02 .10
Bell .20 .50
Davis .07 .20
e Garber .07 .20
n Davis .02 .10
e Boggs .20 .50
Gibson .07 .20

67 Carlton Fisk .20 .50
68 Casey Candaele .02 .10
69 Mike Heath .02 .10
70 Kevin Elster .02 .10
71 Greg Brock .02 .10
72 Don Carman .02 .10
73 Doug Drabek .07 .20
74 Greg Gagne .02 .10
75 Danny Cox .02 .10
76 Rickey Henderson .20 .50
77 Chris Brown .02 .10
78 Terry Steinbach .07 .20
79 Will Clark .20 .50
80 Mickey Brantley .02 .10
81 Ozzie Guillen .07 .20
82 Greg Maddux .50 1.25
83 Kirk McCaskill .02 .10
84 Dwight Evans .07 .20
85 Ozzie Virgil .02 .10
86 Mike Morgan .02 .10
87 Tony Fernandez .07 .20
88 Jose Guzman .02 .10
89 Mike Dunne .02 .10
90 Andres Galarraga .15 .40
91 Mike Henneman .07 .20
92 Alfredo Griffin .02 .10
93 Rafael Palmeiro .30 .75
94 Jim Deshaies .02 .10
95 Mark Gubicza .02 .10
96 Dwight Gooden .07 .20
97 Howard Johnson .02 .10
98 Mark Davis .02 .10
99 Dave Stewart .07 .20
100 Joe Magrane .02 .10
101 Brian Fisher .02 .10
102 Kent Hrbek .07 .20
103 Kevin Gross .02 .10
104 Tom Henke .02 .10
105 Mike Pagliarulo .02 .10
106 Kelly Downs .02 .10
107 Alvin Davis .02 .10
108 Willie Randolph .07 .20
109 Rob Deer .02 .10
110 Bo Diaz .02 .10
111 Paul Kilgus .02 .10
112 Tom Candiotti .02 .10
113 Dale Murphy .15 .40
114 Rick Mahler .02 .10
115 Wally Joyner .10 .30
116 Ryne Sandberg .20 .50
117 John Farrell .02 .10
118 Nick Esasky .02 .10
119 Bo Jackson .15 .40
120 Bill Doran .02 .10
121 Ellis Burks .30 .75
122 Pedro Guerrero .02 .10
123 Dave LaPoint .02 .10
124 Neal Heaton .02 .10
125 Willie Hernandez .02 .10
126 Roger McDowell .02 .10
127 Ted Higuera .02 .10
128 Von Hayes .02 .10
129 Mike LaValliere .02 .10
130 Dan Gladden .02 .10
131 Willie McGee .07 .20
132 Al Leiter .20 .50
133 Mark Grant .02 .10
134 Bob Welch .02 .10
135 Dave Dravecky .07 .20
136 Mark Langston .02 .10
137 Dan Pasqua .02 .10
138 Rick Sutcliffe .07 .20
139 Dan Petry .02 .10
140 Rich Gedman .02 .10
141 Ken Griffey .07 .20
142 Eddie Murray .20 .50
143 Jimmy Key .07 .20
144 Dale Mohorcic .02 .10
145 Jose Lind .02 .10
146 Dennis Martinez .07 .20
147 Chet Lemon .02 .10
148 Orel Hershiser .07 .20
149 Dave Martinez .02 .10
150 Billy Hatcher .02 .10
151 Charlie Leibrandt .02 .10
152 Keith Hernandez .07 .20
153 Kevin McReynolds .02 .10
154 Tony Gwynn .30 1.00
155 Stan Javier .02 .10
156 Tony Pena .02 .10
157 Andy Van Slyke .07 .20
158 Gene Larkin .02 .10
159 Chris James .02 .10
160 Fred McGriff .30 .75
161 Rick Rhoden .02 .10
162 Scott Garrelts .02 .10
163 Mike Campbell .02 .10
164 Dave Righetti .02 .10
165 Paul Molitor .20 .50
166 Danny Jackson .02 .10
167 Pete O'Brien .02 .10
168 Julio Franco .07 .20
169 Mark McGwire .75 2.00
170 Zane Smith .02 .10
171 Johnny Ray .02 .10
172 Les Lancaster .02 .10
173 Mel Hall .02 .10
174 Tracy Jones .02 .10
175 Kevin Seitzer .07 .20
176 Bob Knepper .02 .10
177 Mike Greenwell .07 .20
178 Mike Marshall .02 .10
179 Melido Perez .02 .10
180 Tim Raines .07 .20
181 Jack Morris .07 .20
182 Darryl Strawberry .07 .20
183 Robin Yount .20 .50
184 Lance Parrish .02 .10
185 Darnell Coles .02 .10
186 Kirby Puckett .20 .50
187 Terry Pendleton .07 .20
188 Don Slaught .02 .10
189 Jimmy Jones .02 .10
190 Dave Parker .07 .20
191 Mike Aldrete .02 .10
192 Mike Moore .02 .10
193 Greg Walker .02 .10
194 Calvin Schiraldi .02 .10
195 Dick Schofield .02 .10
196 Jody Reed .07 .20
197 Pete Smith .02 .10
198 Cal Ripken .75 2.00
199 Lloyd Moseby .02 .10
200 Ruben Sierra .07 .20
201 R.J. Reynolds .02 .10
202 Bryn Smith .02 .10
203 Gary Pettis .02 .10
204 Steve Sax .02 .10
205 Frank DiPino .02 .10
206 Mike Scott UER .02 .10
1977 Jackson losses
say 1.10, should be 1
207 Kurt Stillwell .02 .10
208 Mookie Wilson .07 .20
209 Lee Mazzilli .07 .20
210 Lance McCullers .02 .10
211 Rick Honeycutt .02 .10
212 John Tudor .02 .10
213 Jim Gott .02 .10
214 Frank Viola .02 .10
215 Juan Samuel .02 .10
216 Jesse Barfield .02 .10
217 Claudell Washington .02 .10
218 Rick Reuschel .07 .20
219 Jim Presley .02 .10
220 Tommy John .07 .20
221 Dan Plesac .02 .10
222 Barry Larkin .15 .40
223 Mike Stanley .02 .10
224 Cory Snyder .02 .10
225 Andre Dawson .15 .40
226 Ken Oberkfell .02 .10
227 Devon White .07 .20
228 Jamie Moyer .20 .50
229 Brook Jacoby .02 .10
230 Rob Murphy .02 .10
231 Bret Saberhagen .07 .20
232 Nolan Ryan .75 2.00
233 Bruce Hurst .02 .10
234 Jesse Orosco .07 .20
235 Bobby Thigpen .02 .10
236 Pascual Perez .02 .10
237 Matt Nokes .07 .20
238 Bob Ojeda .02 .10
239 Joey Meyer .02 .10
240 Shane Rawley .02 .10
241 Jeff Robinson .02 .10
242 Jeff Reardon .07 .20
243 Ozzie Smith .20 .50
244 Dave Winfield .20 .50
245 John Kruk .08 .25
246 Carney Lansford .07 .20
247 Candy Maldonado .02 .10
248 Ken Phelps .02 .10
249 Ken Williams .02 .10
250 Al Nipper .02 .10
251 Mark McLemore .02 .10
252 Lee Smith .07 .20
253 Albert Hall .02 .10
254 Billy Ripken .02 .10
255 Kelly Gruber .02 .10
256 Charlie Hough .07 .20
257 John Smiley .07 .20
258 Tim Wallach .02 .10
259 Frank Tanana .07 .20
260 Mike Scioscia .07 .20
261 Damon Berryhill .02 .10
262 Dave Smith .07 .20
263 Willie Wilson .02 .10
264 Len Dykstra .07 .20
265 Randy Myers .10 .30
266 Keith Moreland .02 .10
267 Eric Plunk .02 .10
268 Todd Worrell .07 .20
269 Bob Walk .02 .10
270 Keith Atherton .02 .10
271 Mike Schmidt .20 .50
272 Mike Flanagan .02 .10
273 Rafael Santana .02 .10
274 Robby Thompson .02 .10
275 Rey Quinones .02 .10
276 Cecilio Guante .02 .10
277 B.J. Surhoff .10 .30
278 Chris Sabo .07 .20
279 Mitch Williams .02 .10
280 Greg Swindell .02 .10
281 Alan Trammell .10 .30
282 Storm Davis .02 .10
283 Chuck Finley .10 .30
284 Dave Stieb .07 .20
285 Scott Bailes .02 .10
286 Larry Sheets .02 .10
287 Danny Tartabull .02 .10
288 Checklist Card .02 .10
289 Todd Benzinger .02 .10
290 John Shelby .02 .10
291 Steve Lyons .07 .20
292 Mitch Webster .02 .10
293 Walt Terrell .02 .10
294 Pete Stanicek .02 .10
295 Chris Bosio .02 .10
296 Milt Thompson .02 .10
297 Fred Lynn .02 .10
298 Juan Berenguer .02 .10
299 Ken Dayley .02 .10
300 Joel Skinner .02 .10
301 Benito Santiago .07 .20
302 Ron Hassey .02 .10
303 Jose Uribe .02 .10
304 Harold Reynolds .07 .20
305 Dale Sveum .02 .10
306 Glenn Wilson .02 .10
307 Mike Witt .02 .10
308 Ron Robinson .02 .10
309 Denny Walling .02 .10
310 Joe Orsulak .02 .10
311 David Wells .60 1.50
312 Steve Buechele .02 .10
313 Jose Oquendo .02 .10
314 Floyd Youmans .02 .10
315 Lou Whitaker .07 .20
316 Fernando Valenzuela .07 .20
317 Mike Boddicker .02 .10
318 Gerald Young .02 .10
319 Frank White .07 .20
320 Bill Wegman .02 .10
321 Tom Niedenfuer .02 .10
322 Ed Whitson .02 .10
323 Curt Young .02 .10
324 Greg Mathews .02 .10
325 Doug Jones .15 .40
326 Tommy Herr .02 .10
327 Kent Tekulve .02 .10
328 Rance Mulliniks .02 .10
329 Checklist Card .02 .10
330 Craig Lefferts .02 .10
331 Franklin Stubbs .02 .10
332 Rick Cerone .02 .10
333 Dave Schmidt .02 .10
334 Larry Parrish .02 .10
335 Tom Browning .02 .10
336 Checklist Card .02 .10

1988 Donruss Pop-Ups

This 20-card set features "fold-out" cards measures the standard size. Card fronts are in full color. Cards are unnumbered but are listed in the same order as the Donruss All-Stars on the All-Star checklist card. Card backs present essentially no information about the player. The set was distributed in packs which also contained All-Star cards. In order to remain in mint condition, the cards should not be popped up.

COMPLETE SET (20) 2.00 5.00
1 Don Mattingly .50 1.25
2 Dave Winfield .15 .40
3 Willie Randolph .02 .10
4 Rickey Henderson .25 .60
5 Cal Ripken .75 2.00
6 George Bell .01 .05
7 Wade Boggs .20 .50
8 Bret Saberhagen .02 .10
9 Terry Kennedy .01 .05
10 John McNamara MG .01 .05
11 Jack Clark .02 .10
12 Darryl Strawberry .02 .10
13 Ryne Sandberg .20 .50
14 Andre Dawson .10 .30
15 Ozzie Smith .30 .75
16 Eric Davis .02 .10
17 Mike Schmidt .20 .50
18 Mike Scott .01 .05
19 Gary Carter .15 .40
20 Davey Johnson MG .01 .05

1988 Donruss Super DK's

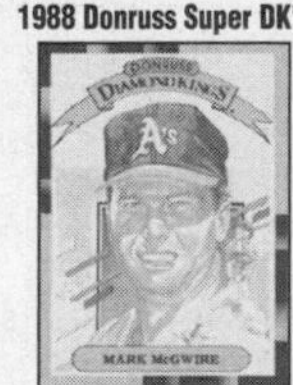

This 26-player card set was available through a mail-in offer detailed on the wax packs. The set was sent in return for 8.00 and three wrappers plus 1.50 postage and handling. The set features the popular Diamond King subseries in large (approximately 4 7/8" by 6 13/16") form. Dick Perez of Perez-Steele Galleries did another outstanding job on the artwork. The cards are essentially a large version of the Donruss regular issue Diamond Kings.

COMPLETE SET (26) 6.00 15.00
1 Mark McGwire 1.25 3.00
2 Tim Raines .30 .75
3 Benito Santiago .30 .75
4 Alan Trammell .40 1.00
5 Danny Tartabull .20 .50
6 Ron Darling .20 .50
7 Paul Molitor .75 2.00
8 Devon White .30 .75
9 Andre Dawson .60 1.50
10 Julio Franco .30 .75
11 Scott Fletcher .20 .50
12 Tony Fernandez .20 .50
13 Shane Rawley .20 .50
14 Kal Daniels .20 .50
15 Jack Clark .30 .75
16 Dwight Evans .30 .75
17 Tommy John .30 .75
18 Andy Van Slyke .20 .50
19 Gary Gaetti .30 .75
20 Mark Langston .20 .50
21 Will Clark .75 2.00
22 Glenn Hubbard .20 .50
23 Billy Hatcher .20 .50
24 Bob Welch .20 .50
25 Ivan Calderon .20 .50
26 Cal Ripken 2.00 5.00

1989 Donruss

This set consists of 660 standard-size cards. The cards were primarily issued in 15-card wax packs, rack packs and hobby and retail factory sets. Each wax pack also contained a puzzle panel (featuring Warren Spahn this year). The wax packs were issued 36 packs to a box and 20 boxes to a case. The cards feature a distinctive black side border with an alternating coating. Subsets include Diamond Kings (1-27) and Rated Rookies (28-47). There are two variations that occur throughout most of the set. On the card backs "Denotes Led League" can be found with one asterisk to the left or with an asterisk on each side. On the card fronts the horizontal lines on the left and right borders can be glossy or non-glossy. Since both of these variation types are relatively minor and seem equally common, there is no premium value for either type. Rather than short-printing 26 cards in order to make room for printing the Bonus MVP's this year, Donruss apparently chose to double print 106 cards. These double prints are listed below by DP. Rookie Cards in this set include Sandy Alomar Jr., Brady Anderson, Dante Bichette, Craig Biggio, Ken Griffey Jr., Randy Johnson, Curt Schilling, Gary Sheffield and John Smoltz. Similar to the 1988 Donruss set, a special card was issued on blister packs, and features the card number as "Bonus Card".

COMPLETE SET (660) 10.00 25.00
COMP.FACT.SET (672) 10.00 25.00
1 Mike Greenwell DK .01 .05
2 Bobby Bonilla DK DP .02 .10
3 Pete Incaviglia DK .01 .05
4 Chris Sabo DK DP .02 .10
5 Robin Yount DK .15 .40
6 Tony Gwynn DK DP .05 .15
7 Carlton Fisk DK UER .05 .15
O.F. on back
8 Cory Snyder DK .01 .05
9 David Cone DK UER .02 .10
'hurdlers'
10 Kevin Seitzer DK .01 .05
11 Rick Reuschel DK .02 .10
12 Johnny Ray DK .01 .05
13 Dave Schmidt DK .01 .05
14 Andres Galarraga DK .02 .10
15 Kirk Gibson DK .02 .10
16 Fred McGriff DK .05 .15
17 Mark Grace DK .08 .25
18 Jeff M. Robinson DK .01 .05
19 Vince Coleman DK DP .01 .05
20 Dave Henderson DK .01 .05
21 Harold Reynolds DK .02 .10
22 Gerald Perry DK .01 .05
23 Frank Viola DK .02 .10
24 Steve Bedrosian DK .01 .05
25 Glenn Davis DK .01 .05
26 Don Mattingly DK UER .10 .30
27 DK Checklist 1-26 DP .01 .05
28 Sandy Alomar Jr. RC .15 .40
29 Steve Searcy RR .01 .05
30 Cameron Drew RR .01 .05
31 Gary Sheffield RR RC .60 1.50
32 Erik Hanson RR RC .08 .25
33 Ken Griffey Jr. RR RC 5.00 12.00
34 Greg W. Harris RR RC .02 .10
35 Gregg Jefferies RR .01 .05
36 Luis Medina RR .01 .05
37 Carlos Quintana RR RC .02 .10
38 Felix Jose RR RC .02 .10
39 Cris Carpenter RR RC* .02 .10
40 Ron Jones RR .02 .10
41 Dave West RR RC .02 .10
42 R.Johnson RC RR UER .75 2.00
43 Mike Harkey RR RC .02 .10
44 Pete Harnisch RC .08 .25
45 Tom Gordon RR DP RC .20 .50
46 Gregg Olson RC RR DP .08 .25
47 Alex Sanchez RC .01 .05
48 Ruben Sierra .02 .10
49 Rafael Palmeiro .08 .25
50 Ron Gant .02 .10
51 Cal Ripken .30 .75
52 Wally Joyner .02 .10
53 Gary Carter .02 .10
54 Andy Van Slyke .05 .15
55 Robin Yount .15 .40
56 Pete Incaviglia .01 .05
57 Greg Brock .01 .05
58 Melido Perez .01 .05
59 Craig Lefferts .01 .05
60 Gary Pettis .01 .05
61 Danny Tartabull .01 .05
62 Guillermo Hernandez .01 .05
63 Ozzie Smith .15 .40
64 Gary Gaetti .02 .10
65 Mark Davis .01 .05
66 Lee Smith .02 .10
67 Dennis Eckersley .05 .15
68 Wade Boggs .05 .15
69 Mike Scott .02 .10
70 Fred McGriff .05 .15
71 Tom Browning .01 .05
72 Claudell Washington .01 .05
73 Mel Hall .01 .05
74 Don Mattingly .25 .60
75 Steve Bedrosian .01 .05
76 Juan Samuel .01 .05
77 Mike Scioscia .02 .10
78 Dave Righetti .02 .10
79 Alfredo Griffin .01 .05
80 Eric Davis UER .02 .10
165 games in 1988,
should be 135
81 Juan Berenguer .01 .05
82 Todd Worrell .01 .05
83 Joe Carter .02 .10
84 Steve Sax .01 .05
85 Frank White .02 .10
86 John Kruk .02 .10
87 Rance Mulliniks .01 .05
88 Alan Ashby .01 .05
89 Charlie Leibrandt .01 .05
90 Frank Tanana .02 .10
91 Jose Canseco .08 .25
92 Barry Bonds .60 1.50
93 Harold Reynolds .02 .10
94 Mark McLemore .01 .05
95 Mark McGwire .40 1.00
96 Eddie Murray .08 .25
97 Tim Raines .02 .10
98 Robby Thompson .01 .05
99 Kevin McReynolds .01 .05
100 Checklist 28-137 .01 .05
101 Carlton Fisk .05 .15
102 Dave Martinez .01 .05
103 Glenn Braggs .01 .05
104 Dale Murphy .05 .15
105 Ryne Sandberg .15 .40
106 Dennis Martinez .02 .10
107 Pete O'Brien .01 .05
108 Dick Schofield .01 .05
109 Henry Cotto .01 .05
110 Mike Marshall .01 .05
111 Keith Moreland .01 .05
112 Tom Brunansky .01 .05
113 Kelly Gruber UER .01 .05
Wrong birthdate
114 Brook Jacoby .01 .05
115 Keith Brown .01 .05
116 Matt Nokes .01 .05
117 Keith Hernandez .02 .10
118 Bob Forsch .01 .05
119 Bert Blyleven UER .02 .10
120 Willie Wilson .02 .10
121 Tommy Gregg .01 .05
122 Jim Rice .02 .10
123 Bob Knepper .01 .05
124 Danny Jackson .01 .05
125 Eric Plunk .01 .05
126 Brian Fisher .01 .05
127 Mike Pagliarulo .01 .05
128 Tony Gwynn .10 .30
129 Lance McCullers .01 .05
130 Andres Galarraga .02 .10
131 Jose Uribe .01 .05
132 Kirk Gibson UER .02 .10
Wrong birthdate
133 David Palmer .01 .05
134 R.J. Reynolds .01 .05
135 Greg Walker .01 .05
136 Kirk McCaskill UER .01 .05
Wrong birthdate
137 Shawon Dunston .01 .05
138 Andy Allanson .01 .05
139 Rob Murphy .01 .05
140 Mike Aldrete .01 .05
141 Terry Kennedy .01 .05
142 Scott Fletcher .01 .05
143 Steve Balboni .01 .05
144 Bret Saberhagen .02 .10
145 Ozzie Virgil .01 .05
146 Dale Sveum .01 .05
147 Darryl Strawberry .02 .10
148 Harold Baines .02 .10
149 George Bell .02 .10
150 Dave Parker .02 .10
151 Bobby Bonilla .02 .10
152 Mookie Wilson .02 .10
153 Ted Power .01 .05
154 Nolan Ryan .40 1.00
155 Jeff Reardon .02 .10
156 Tim Wallach .01 .05
157 Jamie Moyer .02 .10
158 Rich Gossage .02 .10
159 Dave Winfield .02 .10
160 Von Hayes .01 .05
161 Willie McGee .02 .10
162 Rich Gedman .01 .05
163 Tony Pena .01 .05
164 Mike Morgan .01 .05
165 Charlie Hough .02 .10
166 Mike Stanley .01 .05
167 Andre Dawson .02 .10
168 Joe Boever .01 .05
169 Pete Stanicek .01 .05
170 Bob Boone .02 .10
171 Ron Darling .02 .10
172 Bob Walk .01 .05
173 Rob Deer .01 .05
174 Steve Buechele .01 .05
175 Ted Higuera .01 .05
176 Ozzie Guillen .02 .10
177 Candy Maldonado .01 .05
178 Doyle Alexander .01 .05
179 Mark Gubicza .01 .05
180 Alan Trammell .02 .10
181 Vince Coleman .01 .05
182 Kirby Puckett .08 .25
183 Chris Brown .01 .05
184 Marty Barrett .01 .05
185 Stan Javier .01 .05
186 Mike Greenwell .01 .05
187 Billy Hatcher .01 .05
188 Jimmy Key .02 .10
189 Nick Esasky .01 .05
190 Don Slaught .01 .05
191 Cory Snyder .01 .05
192 John Candelaria .01 .05
193 Mike Schmidt .20 .50
194 Kevin Gross .01 .05
195 John Tudor .02 .10
196 Neil Allen .01 .05
197 Orel Hershiser .02 .10
198 Kal Daniels .01 .05
199 Kent Hrbek .02 .10
200 Checklist 138-247 .01 .05
201 Joe Magrane .01 .05
202 Scott Bailes .01 .05
203 Tim Belcher .01 .05
204 George Brett .25 .60
205 Benito Santiago .02 .10
206 Tony Fernandez .01 .05
207 Gerald Young .01 .05
208 Bo Jackson .08 .25
209 Chet Lemon .02 .10
210 Storm Davis .01 .05
211 Doug Drabek .01 .05
212 Mickey Brantley UER .01 .05
Photo actually
Nelson Simmons
213 Devon White .02 .10
214 Dave Stewart .02 .10
215 Dave Schmidt .01 .05
216 Bryn Smith .01 .05
217 Brett Butler .02 .10
218 Bob Ojeda .01 .05
219 Steve Rosenberg .01 .05
220 Hubie Brooks .01 .05
221 B.J. Surhoff .02 .10
222 Rick Mahler .01 .05
223 Rick Sutcliffe .02 .10
224 Neal Heaton .01 .05
225 Mitch Williams .01 .05
226 Chuck Finley .02 .10
227 Mark Langston .01 .05
228 Jesse Orosco .01 .05
229 Ed Whitson .01 .05
230 Terry Pendleton .02 .10
231 Lloyd Moseby .01 .05
232 Greg Swindell .01 .05
233 John Franco .02 .10
234 Jack Morris .02 .10
235 Howard Johnson .02 .10
236 Glenn Davis .01 .05
237 Frank Viola .02 .10
238 Kevin Seitzer .01 .05
239 Gerald Perry .01 .05
240 Dwight Evans .05 .15
241 Jim Deshaies .01 .05
242 Bo Diaz .01 .05
243 Carney Lansford .02 .10
244 Mike LaValliere .01 .05
245 Rickey Henderson .08 .25
246 Roberto Alomar .08 .25
247 Jimmy Jones .01 .05
248 Pascual Perez .01 .05
249 Will Clark .05 .15
250 Fernando Valenzuela .02 .10
251 Shane Rawley .01 .05
252 Sid Bream .01 .05
253 Steve Lyons .01 .05
254 Brian Downing .02 .10
255 Mark Grace .08 .25
256 Tom Candiotti .01 .05
257 Barry Larkin .05 .15
258 Mike Krukow .01 .05
259 Billy Ripken .01 .05
260 Cecilio Guante .01 .05
261 Scott Bradley .01 .05
262 Floyd Bannister .01 .05
263 Pete Smith .01 .05
264 Jim Gantner UER .01 .05

Wrong birthdate
265 Roger McDowell .01 .05
266 Bobby Thigpen .01 .05
267 Jim Clancy .01 .05
268 Terry Steinbach .02 .10
269 Mike Dunne .01 .05
270 Dwight Gooden .02 .10
271 Mike Heath .01 .05
272 Dave Smith .01 .05
273 Keith Atherton .01 .05
274 Tim Burke .01 .05
275 Damon Berryhill .01 .05
276 Vance Law .01 .05
277 Rich Dotson .01 .05
278 Lance Parrish .02 .10
279 Denny Walling .01 .05
280 Roger Clemens .40 1.00
281 Greg Mathews .01 .05
282 Tom Niedenfuer .01 .05
283 Paul Kilgus .01 .05
284 Jose Guzman .01 .05
285 Calvin Schiraldi .01 .05
286 Charlie Puleo UER .01 .05
Career ERA 4.24,
should be 4.23
287 Joe Orsulak .01 .05
288 Jack Howell .01 .05
289 Kevin Elster .01 .05
290 Jose Lind .01 .05
291 Paul Molitor .02 .10
292 Cecil Espy .01 .05
293 Bill Wegman .01 .05
294 Dan Pasqua .01 .05
295 Scott Garrelts UER .01 .05
Wrong birthdate
296 Walt Terrell .01 .05
297 Ed Hearn .01 .05
298 Lou Whitaker .02 .10
299 Ken Dayley .01 .05
300 Checklist 248-357 .01 .05
301 Tommy Herr .01 .05
302 Mike Brumley .01 .05
303 Ellis Burks .02 .10
304 Curt Young UER .01 .05
Wrong birthdate
305 Jody Reed .01 .05
306 Bill Doran .01 .05
307 David Wells .02 .10
308 Ron Robinson .01 .05
309 Rafael Santana .01 .05
310 Julio Franco .02 .10
311 Jack Clark .02 .10
312 Chris James .01 .05
313 Milt Thompson .01 .05
314 John Shelby .01 .05
315 Al Leiter .08 .25
316 Mike Davis .01 .05
317 Chris Sabo RC .15 .40
318 Greg Gagne .01 .05
319 Jose Oquendo .01 .05
320 John Farrell .01 .05
321 Franklin Stubbs .01 .05
322 Kurt Stillwell .01 .05
323 Shawn Abner .01 .05
324 Mike Flanagan .01 .05
325 Kevin Bass .01 .05
326 Pat Tabler .01 .05
327 Mike Henneman .01 .05
328 Rick Honeycutt .01 .05
329 John Smiley .01 .05
330 Rey Quinones .01 .05
331 Johnny Ray .01 .05
332 Bob Welch .02 .10
333 Larry Sheets .01 .05
334 Jeff Parrett .01 .05
335 Rick Reuschel UER .02 .10
For Don Robinson&
should be Jeff
336 Randy Myers .02 .10
337 Ken Williams .01 .05
338 Andy McGaffigan .01 .05
339 Joey Meyer .01 .05
340 Dion James .01 .05
341 Les Lancaster .01 .05
342 Tom Foley .01 .05
343 Geno Petralli .01 .05
344 Dan Petry .01 .05
345 Alvin Davis .01 .05
346 Mickey Hatcher .01 .05
347 Marvell Wynne .01 .05
348 Danny Cox .01 .05
349 Dave Stieb .02 .10
350 Jay Bell .02 .10
351 Jeff Treadway .01 .05
352 Luis Salazar .01 .05
353 Len Dykstra .02 .10
354 Juan Agosto .01 .05
355 Gene Larkin .01 .05
356 Steve Farr .01 .05
357 Paul Assenmacher .01 .05
358 Todd Benzinger .01 .05
359 Larry Andersen .01 .05
360 Paul O'Neill .05 .15
361 Ron Hassey .01 .05
362 Jim Gott .01 .05
363 Ken Phelps .01 .05
364 Tim Flannery .01 .05
365 Randy Ready .01 .05
366 Nelson Santovenia .01 .05
367 Kelly Downs .01 .05
368 Danny Heep .01 .05
369 Phil Bradley .01 .05
370 Jeff D. Robinson .01 .05
371 Ivan Calderon .01 .05
372 Mike Witt .01 .05
373 Greg Maddux .20 .50
374 Carmen Castillo .01 .05
375 Jose Rijo .02 .10
376 Joe Price .01 .05
377 Rene Gonzales .01 .05
378 Oddibe McDowell .01 .05
379 Jim Presley .01 .05
380 Brad Wellman .01 .05
381 Tom Glavine .08 .25
382 Dan Plesac .01 .05
383 Wally Backman .01 .05
384 Dave Gallagher .01 .05
385 Tom Henke .01 .05
386 Luis Polonia .01 .05
387 Junior Ortiz .01 .05
388 David Cone .02 .10
389 Dave Bergman .01 .05
390 Danny Darwin .01 .05
391 Dan Gladden .01 .05
392 John Dopson .01 .05
393 Frank DiPino .01 .05
394 Al Nipper .01 .05
395 Willie Randolph .02 .10
396 Don Carman .01 .05
397 Scott Terry .01 .05
398 Rick Cerone .01 .05
399 Tom Pagnozzi .01 .05
400 Checklist 358-467 .01 .05
401 Mickey Tettleton .01 .05
402 Curtis Wilkerson .01 .05
403 Jeff Russell .01 .05
404 Pat Perry .01 .05
405 Jose Alvarez RC .02 .10
406 Rick Schu .01 .05
407 Sherman Corbett RC .01 .05
408 Dave Magadan .01 .05
409 Bob Kipper .01 .05
410 Don August .01 .05
411 Bob Brower .01 .05
412 Chris Bosio .01 .05
413 Jerry Reuss .01 .05
414 Atlee Hammaker .01 .05
415 Jim Walewander .01 .05
416 Mike Macfarlane RC * .08 .25
417 Pat Sheridan .01 .05
418 Pedro Guerrero .02 .10
419 Allan Anderson .01 .05
420 Mark Parent RC .01 .05
421 Bob Stanley .01 .05
422 Mike Gallego .01 .05
423 Bruce Hurst .01 .05
424 Dave Meads .01 .05
425 Jesse Barfield .02 .10
426 Rob Dibble RC .15 .40
427 Joel Skinner .01 .05
428 Ron Kittle .01 .05
429 Rick Rhoden .01 .05
430 Bob Dernier .01 .05
431 Steve Jeltz .01 .05
432 Rick Dempsey .01 .05
433 Roberto Kelly .01 .05
434 Dave Anderson .01 .05
435 Herm Winningham .01 .05
436 Al Newman .01 .05
437 Jose DeLeon .01 .05
438 Doug Jones .01 .05
439 Brian Holton .01 .05
440 Jeff Montgomery .01 .05
441 Dickie Thon .01 .05
442 Cecil Fielder .02 .10
443 John Fishel RC .01 .05
444 Jerry Don Gleaton .01 .05
445 Paul Gibson .01 .05
446 Walt Weiss .01 .05
447 Glenn Wilson .01 .05
448 Mike Moore .01 .05
449 Chili Davis .02 .10
450 Dave Henderson .01 .05
451 Jose Bautista RC .01 .05
452 Rex Hudler .01 .05
453 Bob Brenly .01 .05
454 Mackey Sasser .01 .05
455 Daryl Boston .01 .05
456 Mike R. Fitzgerald .01 .05
457 Jeffrey Leonard .01 .05
458 Bruce Sutter .02 .10
459 Mitch Webster .01 .05
460 Joe Hesketh .01 .05
461 Bobby Witt .01 .05
462 Stu Cliburn .01 .05
463 Scott Bankhead .01 .05
464 Ramon Martinez RC .08 .25
465 Dave Leiper .01 .05
466 Luis Alicea RC * .08 .25
467 John Cerutti .01 .05
468 Ron Washington .01 .05
469 Jeff Reed .01 .05
470 Jeff M. Robinson .01 .05
471 Sid Fernandez .01 .05
472 Terry Puhl .01 .05
473 Charlie Lea .01 .05
474 Israel Sanchez .01 .05
475 Bruce Benedict .01 .05
476 Oil Can Boyd .01 .05
477 Craig Reynolds .01 .05
478 Frank Williams .01 .05
479 Greg Cadaret .01 .05
480 Randy Kramer .01 .05
481 Dave Eiland .01 .05
482 Eric Show .01 .05
483 Garry Templeton .02 .10
484 Wallace Johnson .01 .05
485 Kevin Mitchell .02 .10
486 Tim Crews .01 .05
487 Mike Maddux .01 .05
488 Dave LaPoint .01 .05
489 Fred Manrique .01 .05
490 Greg Minton .01 .05
491 Doug Dascenzo UER .01 .05
Photo actually
Damon Berryhill
492 Willie Upshaw .01 .05
493 Jack Armstrong RC * .08 .25
494 Kirt Manwaring .01 .05
495 Jeff Ballard .01 .05
496 Jeff Kunkel .01 .05
497 Mike Campbell .01 .05
498 Gary Thurman .01 .05
499 Zane Smith .01 .05
500 Checklist 468-577 DP .01 .05
501 Mike Birkbeck .01 .05
502 Terry Leach .01 .05
503 Shawn Hillegas .01 .05
504 Manny Lee .01 .05
505 Doug Jennings RC .01 .05
506 Ken Oberkfell .01 .05
507 Tim Teufel .01 .05
508 Tom Brookens .01 .05
509 Rafael Ramirez .01 .05
510 Fred Toliver .01 .05
511 Brian Holman RC * .02 .10
512 Mike Bielecki .01 .05
513 Jeff Pico .01 .05
514 Charles Hudson .01 .05
515 Bruce Ruffin .01 .05
516 L.McWilliams UER .01 .05
New Richland, should
be North Richland
517 Jeff Sellers .01 .05
518 John Costello RC .01 .05
519 Brady Anderson RC .15 .40
520 Craig McMurtry .01 .05
521 Ray Hayward DP .01 .05
522 Drew Hall DP .01 .05
523 Mark Lemke DP RC .15 .40
524 Oswald Peraza DP RC .01 .05
525 Bryan Harvey DP RC * .08 .25
526 Rick Aguilera DP .01 .05
527 Tom Prince DP .01 .05
528 Mark Clear DP .01 .05
529 Jerry Browne DP .01 .05
530 Juan Castillo DP .01 .05
531 Jack McDowell DP .02 .10
532 Chris Speier DP .01 .05
533 Darrell Evans DP .02 .10
534 Luis Aquino DP .01 .05
535 Eric King DP .01 .05
536 Ken Hill DP RC .08 .25
537 Randy Bush DP .01 .05
538 Shane Mack DP .01 .05
539 Tom Bolton DP .01 .05
540 Gene Nelson DP .01 .05
541 Wes Gardner DP .01 .05
542 Ken Caminiti DP .05 .15
543 Duane Ward DP .01 .05
544 Norm Charlton DP RC .08 .25
545 Hal Morris DP RC .08 .25
546 Rich Yett DP .01 .05
547 Hensley Meulens DP RC .02 .10
548 Greg A. Harris DP .01 .05
549 Darren Daulton DP .02 .10
Posing as right-
handed hitter
550 Jeff Hamilton DP .01 .05
551 Luis Aguayo DP .01 .05
552 Tim Leary DP .01 .05
553 Ron Oester DP .01 .05
554 Steve Lombardozzi DP .01 .05
555 Tim Jones DP .01 .05
556 Bud Black DP .01 .05
557 Alejandro Pena DP .01 .05
558 Jose DeJesus DP .01 .05
559 Dennis Rasmussen DP .01 .05
560 Pat Borders DP RC* .08 .25
561 Craig Biggio DP RC 1.25 3.00
562 Luis DeLosSantos DP .01 .05
563 Fred Lynn DP .02 .10
564 Todd Burns DP .01 .05
565 Felix Fermin DP .01 .05
566 Darnell Coles DP .01 .05
567 Willie Fraser DP .01 .05
568 Glenn Hubbard DP .01 .05
569 Craig Worthington DP .01 .05
570 Johnny Paredes DP .01 .05
571 Don Robinson DP .01 .05
572 Barry Lyons DP .01 .05
573 Bill Long DP .01 .05
574 Tracy Jones DP .01 .05
575 Juan Nieves DP .01 .05
576 Andres Thomas DP .01 .05
577 Rolando Roomes DP .01 .05
578 Luis Rivera UER DP .01 .05
Wrong birthdate
579 Chad Kreuter DP RC .08 .25
580 Tony Armas DP .02 .10
581 Jay Buhner .02 .10
582 Ricky Horton DP .01 .05
583 Andy Hawkins DP .01 .05
584 Sil Campusano .01 .05
585 Dave Clark .01 .05
586 Van Snider DP .01 .05
587 Todd Frohwirth DP .01 .05
588 Warren Spahn Puzzle DP .05 .15
589 William Brennan .01 .05
590 German Gonzalez .01 .05
591 Ernie Whitt DP .01 .05
592 Jeff Blauser .01 .05
593 Spike Owen DP .01 .05
594 Matt Williams .08 .25
595 Lloyd McClendon DP .01 .05
596 Steve Ontiveros .01 .05
597 Scott Medvin .01 .05
598 Hipolito Pena DP .01 .05
599 Jerald Clark DP RC .02 .10
600A CL 578-660 DP .01 .05
635 Kurt Schilling
600B CL 578-660 DP .01 .05
635 Curt Schilling;
MVP's not listed
on checklist card
600C CL 578-660 DP .01 .05
635 Curt Schilling;
MVP's listed
following 660
601 Carmelo Martinez DP .01 .05
602 Mike LaCoss .01 .05
603 Mike Devereaux .01 .05
604 Alex Madrid DP .01 .05
605 Gary Redus DP .01 .05
606 Lance Johnson .01 .05
607 Terry Clark DP .01 .05
608 Manny Trillo DP .01 .05
609 Scott Jordan RC .08 .25
610 Jay Howell DP .01 .05
611 Francisco Melendez .01 .05
612 Mike Boddicker .01 .05
613 Kevin Brown DP .08 .25
614 Dave Valle .01 .05
615 Tim Laudner DP .01 .05
616 Andy Nezelek UER .01 .05
Wrong birthdate
617 Chuck Crim .01 .05
618 Jack Savage DP .01 .05
619 Adam Peterson .01 .05
620 Todd Stottlemyre .01 .05
621 Lance Blankenship RC .02 .10
622 Miguel Garcia DP .01 .05
623 Keith A. Miller DP .01 .05
624 Ricky Jordan DP RC* .08 .25
625 Ernest Riles DP .01 .05
626 John Moses DP .01 .05
627 Nelson Liriano DP .01 .05
628 Mike Smithson DP .01 .05
629 Scott Sanderson .01 .05
630 Dale Mohorcic .01 .05
631 Marvin Freeman DP .01 .05
632 Mike Young DP .01 .05
633 Dennis Lamp .01 .05
634 Dante Bichette DP RC .15 .40
635 Curt Schilling DP RC 1.50 4.00
636 Scott May DP .01 .05
637 Mike Schooler .01 .05
638 Rick Leach .01 .05
639 Tom Lampkin UER .01 .05
Throws Left, should
be Throws Right
640 Brian Meyer .01 .05
641 Brian Harper .01 .05
642 John Smoltz RC .60 1.50
643 Jose Canseco .08 .25
40-40 Club
644 Bill Schroeder .01 .05
645 Edgar Martinez .08 .25
646 Dennis Cook RC .08 .25
647 Barry Jones .01 .05
648 Orel Hershiser .02 .10
59 and Counting
649 Rod Nichols .01 .05
650 Jody Davis .01 .05
651 Bob Milacki .01 .05
652 Mike Jackson .01 .05
653 Derek Lilliquist RC .02 .10
654 Paul Mirabella .01 .05
655 Mike Diaz .01 .05
656 Jeff Musselman .01 .05
657 Jerry Reed .01 .05
658 Kevin Blankenship .01 .05
659 Wayne Tolleson .01 .05
660 Eric Hetzel .01 .05
BC Jose Canseco .75 2.00
Blister Pack

1989 Donruss Bonus MVP's

Rather than short-printing 26 cards in order to make room for printing the Bonus MVP's this year, Donruss apparently chose to double print 106 cards. Numbered with the prefix "BC" for bonus card, the 26-card set featuring the most valuable player from each of the 26 teams was randomly inserted in the wax and rack packs. These cards are distinguished by the bold MVP logo in the upper background of the obverse, and the four doubleprinted cards are denoted by "DP" in the checklist below.

COMPLETE SET (26) .60 1.50
RANDOM INSERTS IN PACKS
BC1 Kirby Puckett .08 .25
BC2 Mike Scott .02 .10
BC3 Joe Carter .02 .10
BC4 Orel Hershiser .02 .10
BC5 Jose Canseco .08 .25
BC6 Darryl Strawberry .02 .10
BC7 George Brett .25 .60
BC8 Andre Dawson .02 .10
BC9 Paul Molitor UER .02 .10
Brewers logo missing
the word Milwaukee
BC10 Andy Van Slyke .05 .15
BC11 Dave Winfield .02 .10
BC12 Kevin Gross .01 .05
BC13 Mike Greenwell .01 .05
BC14 Ozzie Smith .15 .40
BC15 Cal Ripken .30 .75
BC16 Andres Galarraga .02 .10
BC17 Alan Trammell .02 .10
BC18 Kal Daniels .01 .05
BC19 Fred McGriff .05 .15
BC20 Tony Gwynn .10 .30
BC21 Wally Joyner DP .02 .10
BC22 Will Clark DP .05 .15
BC23 Ozzie Guillen .02 .10
BC24 Gerald Perry DP .01 .05
BC25 Alvin Davis DP .01 .05
BC26 Ruben Sierra .02 .10

1989 Donruss Grand Slammers

The 1989 Donruss Grand Slammers set contains 12 standard-size cards. Each card in the set can be found with five different colored border combinations, but no color combination of borders appears to be scarcer than any other. The set includes cards for each player who hit one or more grand slams in 1988. The backs detail the players' grand slams. The cards were distributed one per cello pack as well as an insert (complete) set in each factory set.

COMPLETE SET (12) .75 2.00
ONE PER CELLO PACK
ONE SET PER FACTORY SET
1 Jose Canseco .08 .25
2 Mike Marshall .01 .05
3 Walt Weiss .01 .05
4 Kevin McReynolds .01 .05
5 Mike Greenwell .01 .05
6 Dave Winfield .02 .10
7 Mark McGwire .40 1.00
8 Keith Hernandez .02 .10
9 Franklin Stubbs .01 .05
10 Danny Tartabull .01 .05
11 Jesse Barfield .02 .10
12 Ellis Burks .02 .10

1989 Donruss Rookies

The 1989 Donruss Rookies set contains 56 standard-size cards. The cards were distributed exclusively in factory set form in small, emerald green, cellophane-wrapped boxes through hobby dealers. The cards are almost identical in design to regular 1989 Donruss except for the green borders. Rookie Cards in this set include Jim Abbott, Steve Finley, Kenny Rogers and Deion Sanders. Ken Griffey Jr. and Randy Johnson are also featured on a card within the set.

COMP.FACT.SET (56) 6.00 15.00
1 Gary Sheffield .75 2.00
2 Gregg Jefferies .02 .10
3 Ken Griffey Jr.! 5.00 12.00
4 Tom Gordon .08 .25
5 Billy Spiers RC .08 .25
6 Deion Sanders RC .60 1.50
7 Donn Pall .01 .05
8 Steve Carter RC .01 .05
9 Francisco Oliveras .01 .05
10 Steve Wilson RC .02 .10
11 Bob Geren RC .01 .05
12 Tony Castillo RC .02 .10
13 Kenny Rogers RC 1.00 2.50
14 Carlos Martinez RC .02 .10
15 Edgar Martinez .08 .25
16 Jim Abbott RC .40 1.00
17 Torey Lovullo RC .02 .10
18 Mark Carreon .01 .05
19 Geronimo Berroa .01 .05
20 Luis Medina .01 .05
21 Sandy Alomar Jr. .05 .15
22 Bob Milacki .01 .05
23 Joe Girardi RC .15 .40
24 German Gonzalez .01 .05
25 Craig Worthington .01 .05
26 Jerome Walton RC .08 .25
27 Gary Wayne .01 .05
28 Tim Jones .01 .05
29 Dante Bichette .05 .15
30 Alexis Infante RC .01 .05
31 Ken Hill .08 .25
32 Dwight Smith RC .08 .25
33 Luis de los Santos .01 .05
34 Eric Yelding .01 .05
35 Gregg Olson .08 .25
36 Phil Stephenson .01 .05
37 Ken Patterson .01 .05
38 Rick Wrona .01 .05
39 Mike Brumley .01 .05
40 Cris Carpenter .01 .05
41 Jeff Brantley RC .08 .25
42 Ron Jones .01 .05
43 R.Johnson UER .75 2.00
44 Kevin Brown .08 .25
45 Ramon Martinez .02 .10
46 Greg W.Harris .01 .05
47 Steve Finley RC .30 .75
48 Randy Kramer .01 .05
49 Erik Hanson .02 .10
50 Matt Merullo .01 .05
51 Mike Devereaux .01 .05
52 Clay Parker .01 .05
53 Omar Vizquel RC .40 1.00
54 Derek Lilliquist .01 .05
55 Junior Felix RC .02 .10
56 Checklist 1-56 .01 .05

1989 Donruss Warren Spahn Puzzle

1 Spahn Puzzle 1-3 .10 .25
4 Spahn Puzzle 4-6 .10 .25
7 Spahn Puzzle 7-10 .10 .25
10 Spahn Puzzle 10-12 .10 .25
13 Spahn Puzzle 13-15 .10 .25
16 Spahn Puzzle 16-18 .10 .25
19 Spahn Puzzle 19-21 .10 .25
22 Spahn Puzzle 22-24 .10 .25
25 Spahn Puzzle 25-27 .10 .25
28 Spahn Puzzle 28-30 .10 .25
31 Spahn Puzzle 31-33 .10 .25
34 Spahn Puzzle 34-36 .10 .25
37 Spahn Puzzle 37-39 .10 .25
40 Spahn Puzzle 40-42 .10 .25
43 Spahn Puzzle 43-45 .10 .25
46 Spahn Puzzle 46-48 .10 .25
49 Spahn Puzzle 49-51 .10 .25
52 Spahn Puzzle 52-54 .10 .25
55 Spahn Puzzle 55-57 .10 .25
58 Spahn Puzzle 58-60 .10 .25
61 Spahn Puzzle 61-63 .10 .25

1989 Donruss All-Stars

These All-Stars are standard size and very similar in design to the regular issue of 1989 Donruss. The set is distinguished by the presence of the respective League logos in the lower right corner of each obverse. The cards are numbered on the backs. The players chosen for the set are essentially the participants at the previous year's All-Star Game. Individual wax packs of All Stars (suggested retail price of 35 cents) contained one Pop-Up, five All-Star cards, and a Warren Spahn puzzle card.

COMPLETE SET (64) 3.00 8.00
1 Mark McGwire .50 1.25
2 Jose Canseco .20 .50
3 Paul Molitor .20 .50
4 Rickey Henderson .25 .60
5 Cal Ripken .75 2.00
6 Dave Winfield .08 .25
7 Wade Boggs .08 .25
8 Frank Viola .01 .05
9 Terry Steinbach .02 .10
10 Tom Kelly MG .01 .05
11 George Brett .40 1.00
12 Doyle Alexander .01 .05
13 Gary Gaetti .02 .10
14 Roger Clemens .40 1.00
15 Mike Greenwell .01 .05
16 Dennis Eckersley .20 .50
17 Carney Lansford .02 .10
18 Mark Gubicza .01 .05
19 Tim Laudner .01 .05
20 Doug Jones .01 .05
21 Don Mattingly .40 1.00
22 Dan Plesac .01 .05
23 Kirby Puckett .20 .50
24 Jeff Reardon .02 .10
25 Johnny Ray .01 .05
26 Jeff Russell .01 .05
27 Harold Reynolds .02 .10
28 Dave Stieb .01 .05
29 Kurt Stillwell .01 .05
30 Jose Canseco/(Top AL Vote Getter) .02 .10
31 Terry Steinbach/(All-Star Game MVP) .01 .05
32 AL Checklist 1-32 .01 .05
33 Will Clark .15 .40
34 Darryl Strawberry .02 .10
35 Ryne Sandberg .40 1.00
36 Andre Dawson .07 .20
37 Ozzie Smith .40
38 Vince Coleman .01
39 Bobby Bonilla .01
40 Dwight Gooden .02
41 Gary Carter .15
42 Whitey Herzog MG .01
43 Shawon Dunston .01
44 David Cone .05
45 Andres Galarraga .07
46 Mark Davis .01
47 Barry Larkin .07
48 Kevin Gross .01
49 Vance Law .01
50 Orel Hershiser .02
51 Willie McGee .02
52 Danny Jackson .01
53 Rafael Palmeiro .15
54 Bob Knepper .01
55 Lance Parrish .01
56 Greg Maddux .60
57 Gerald Perry .01
58 Bob Walk .01
59 Chris Sabo .01
60 Todd Worrell .01
61 Andy Van Slyke .02
62 Ozzie Smith/(Top AL Vote Getter) .20
63 Riverfront Stadium .01
64 NL Checklist 33-64 .01

1989 Donruss Baseball's

The 1989 Donruss Baseball's Best set conta
standard-size glossy cards. The fronts are g
yellow, and the backs feature career highligh
information. The backs are green, and featur
vertically oriented career stats. The cards we
distributed as a set in a blister pack through
retail and department store chains. The Sam
card in this set is the only major league lice
issued of him in 1989. In addition, early car
Griffey Jr. and Randy Johnson are featured i
set.

COMP.FACT.SET (336) 20.00
1 Don Mattingly .60
2 Tom Glavine .25
3 Bert Blyleven .08
4 Andre Dawson .08
5 Pete O'Brien .05
6 Eric Davis .08
7 George Brett .60
8 Glenn Davis .05
9 Ellis Burks .08
10 Kirk Gibson .08
11 Carlton Fisk .15
12 Andres Galarraga .08
13 Alan Trammell .08
14 Dwight Gooden .08
15 Paul Molitor .08
16 Roger McDowell .05
17 Doug Drabek .05
18 Kent Hrbek .08
19 Vince Coleman .05
20 Steve Sax .05
21 Roberto Alomar .25
22 Carney Lansford .08
23 Will Clark .15
24 Alvin Davis .05
25 Bobby Thigpen .05
26 Ryne Sandberg .40
27 Devon White .08
28 Mike Greenwell .05
29 Dale Murphy .15
30 Jeff Ballard .05
31 Kelly Gruber .05
32 Julio Franco .08
33 Bobby Bonilla .08
34 Tim Wallach .05
35 Lou Whitaker .08
36 Jay Howell .05
37 Greg Maddux .50
38 Bill Doran .05
39 Danny Tartabull .05
40 Darryl Strawberry .08
41 Ron Darling .08
42 Tony Gwynn .30
43 Mark McGwire 1.00
44 Ozzie Smith .40
45 Andy Van Slyke .15
46 Juan Berenguer .05
47 Von Hayes .05
48 Tony Fernandez .05
49 Eric Plunk .05
50 Ernest Riles .05
51 Harold Reynolds .08
52 Andy Hawkins .05
53 Robin Yount .40
54 Danny Jackson .05
55 Nolan Ryan 1.00
56 Joe Carter .08
57 Jose Canseco .25
58 Jody Davis .05
59 Lance Parrish .08
60 Mitch Williams .05

Jacoby .05 .15
rowning. .05 .15
illwell .05 .15
Ramirez .05 .15
Clemens 1.00 2.50
Scioscia .08 .25
Gallagher .05 .15
Langston .05 .15
Lemon .08 .25
McReynolds .05 .15
eer .05 .15
y Herr .05 .15
Bonds 1.25 3.00
Viola .08 .25
Guerrero .08 .25
Righetti UER/(ML total of 7 .05 .15
correct)
Hurst .05 .15
Henderson .25 .60
Thompson .05 .15
Johnson 2.00 5.00
Baines .08 .25
Schiraldi .05 .15
cCaskill .05 .15
mith .08 .25
Smoltz 1.50 4.00
y Tettleton .05 .15
Key .08 .25
Palmeiro .25 .60
eam .05 .15
s Martinez .08 .25
Tanana .08 .25
Murray .25 .60
on Dunston .05 .15
Scott .08 .25
aberhagen .08 .25
Cone .08 .25
Fister .05 .15
Clark .08 .25
Stewart .08 .25
Oquendo .05 .15
Lind .05 .15
Gaetti .08 .25
y Jordan .20 .50
McGriff .15 .40
Slaught .05 .15
Uribe .05 .15
ey Leonard .05 .15
Guetterman .05 .15
s Bosio .05 .15
y Larkin .15 .40
en Sierra .08 .25
Swindell .05 .15
y Sheffield 1.50 4.00
nie Smith .05 .15
i Davis .08 .25
non Berryhill .05 .15
Candiotti .05 .15
Daniels .05 .15
k Gubicza .05 .15
Deshaies .05 .15
ght Evans .15 .40
e Morgan .05 .15
Pasqua .05 .15
Smith .05 .15
yle Alexander .05 .15
ward Johnson .08 .25
ck Crim .05 .15
ren Daulton .08 .25
Robinson .05 .15
by Puckett .25 .60
Magrane .05 .15
se Barfield .08 .25
k Davis UER/(Photo actually .05 .15
Leiper)
nis Eckersley .15 .40
e Krukow .05 .15
Buhner .08 .25
ie Guillen .08 .25
k Sutcliffe .08 .25
lly Joyner .08 .25
de Boggs .15 .40
Treadway .05 .15
Ripken .75 2.00
e Stieb .08 .25
e Incaviglia .05 .15
Walk .05 .15
son Santovenia .05 .15
e Heath .05 .15
lie Randolph .08 .25
l Kilgus .05 .15
y Hatcher .05 .15
ve Farr .05 .15
egg Jefferies .05 .15
ndy Myers .08 .25
rry Templeton .08 .25
lt Weiss .05 .15
rry Pendleton .08 .25
nn Smiley .05 .15
eg Gagne .05 .15
n Dykstra .08 .25
lson Liriano .05 .15
aro Espinoza .08 .25
ck Reuschel .08 .25
ar Vizquel UER .75 2.00
ay Parker .05 .15
n Plesac .05 .15
n Franco .08 .25
ott Fletcher .05 .15
ory Snyder .05 .15
Jackson .25 .60
mmy Gregg .05 .15
n Abbott .75 2.00
172 Jerome Walton .20 .50
173 Doug Jones .05 .15
174 Todd Benzinger .05 .15
175 Frank White .08 .25
176 Craig Biggio 1.25 3.00
177 John Dopson .05 .15
178 Alfredo Griffin .05 .15
179 Melido Perez .05 .15
180 Tim Burke .08 .25
181 Matt Nokes .05 .15
182 Gary Carter .08 .25
183 Ted Higuera .05 .15
184 Ken Howell .05 .15
185 Rey Quinones .05 .15
186 Wally Backman .05 .15
187 Tom Brunansky .05 .15
188 Steve Balboni .05 .15
189 Marvell Wynne .05 .15
190 Dave Henderson .05 .15
191 Don Robinson .05 .15
192 Ken Griffey Jr. 4.00 10.00
193 Ivan Calderon .05 .15
194 Mike Bielecki .05 .15
195 Johnny Ray .05 .15
196 Rob Murphy .05 .15
197 Andres Thomas .05 .15
198 Phil Bradley .05 .15
199 Junior Felix .08 .25
200 Jeff Russell .05 .15
201 Mike LaValliere .05 .15
202 Kevin Gross .05 .15
203 Keith Moreland .05 .15
204 Mike Marshall .05 .15
205 Dwight Smith .20 .50
206 Jim Clancy .05 .15
207 Kevin Seitzer .05 .15
208 Keith Hernandez .08 .25
209 Bob Ojeda .05 .15
210 Ed Whitson .05 .15
211 Tony Phillips .05 .15
212 Milt Thompson .05 .15
213 Randy Kramer .05 .15
214 Randy Bush .05 .15
215 Randy Ready .05 .15
216 Duane Ward .05 .15
217 Jimmy Jones .05 .15
218 Scott Garrelts .05 .15
219 Scott Bankhead .05 .15
220 Lance McCullers .05 .15
221 B.J. Surhoff .08 .25
222 Chris Sabo .30 .75
223 Steve Buechele .05 .15
224 Joel Skinner .05 .15
225 Orel Hershiser .08 .25
226 Derek Lilliquist .08 .25
227 Claudell Washington .05 .15
228 Lloyd McClendon .05 .15
229 Felix Fermin .05 .15
230 Paul O'Neill .15 .40
231 Charlie Leibrandt .05 .15
232 Dave Smith .05 .15
233 Bob Stanley .05 .15
234 Tim Belcher .05 .15
235 Eric King .05 .15
236 Spike Owen .05 .15
237 Mike Henneman .05 .15
238 Juan Samuel .05 .15
239 Greg Brock .05 .15
240 John Kruk .08 .25
241 Glenn Wilson .05 .15
242 Jeff Reardon .08 .25
243 Todd Worrell .05 .15
244 Dave LaPoint .05 .15
245 Walt Terrell .05 .15
246 Mike Moore .05 .15
247 Kelly Downs .05 .15
248 Dave Valle .05 .15
249 Ron Kittle .05 .15
250 Steve Wilson .08 .25
251 Dick Schofield .05 .15
252 Marty Barrett .05 .15
253 Dion James .05 .15
254 Bob Milacki .05 .15
255 Ernie Whitt .05 .15
256 Kevin Brown .25 .60
257 R.J. Reynolds .05 .15
258 Tim Raines .08 .25
259 Frank Williams .05 .15
260 Jose Gonzalez .05 .15
261 Mitch Webster .05 .15
262 Ken Caminiti .15 .40
263 Bob Boone .08 .25
264 Dave Magadan .05 .15
265 Rick Aguilera .05 .15
266 Chris James .05 .15
267 Bob Welch .08 .25
268 Ken Dayley .05 .15
269 Junior Ortiz .05 .15
270 Allan Anderson .05 .15
271 Steve Jeltz .05 .15
272 George Bell .08 .25
273 Roberto Kelly .05 .15
274 Brett Butler .08 .25
275 Mike Schooler .08 .25
276 Ken Phelps .05 .15
277 Glenn Braggs .05 .15
278 Jose Rijo .08 .25
279 Bobby Witt .05 .15
280 Jerry Browne .05 .15
281 Kevin Mitchell .08 .25
282 Craig Worthington .05 .15
283 Greg Minton .05 .15
284 Nick Esasky .05 .15
285 John Farrell .05 .15
286 Rick Mahler .05 .15
287 Tom Gordon .40 1.00
288 Gerald Young .05 .15
289 Jody Reed .05 .15
290 Jeff Hamilton .05 .15
291 Gerald Perry .05 .15
292 Hubie Brooks .05 .15
293 Bo Diaz .05 .15
294 Terry Puhl .05 .15
295 Jim Gantner .05 .15
296 Jeff Parrett .05 .15
297 Mike Boddicker .05 .15
298 Dan Gladden .05 .15
299 Tony Pena .05 .15
300 Checklist Card .05 .15
301 Tom Henke .05 .15
302 Pascual Perez .05 .15
303 Steve Bedrosian .05 .15
304 Ken Hill .20 .50
305 Jerry Reuss .05 .15
306 Jim Eisenreich .05 .15
307 Jack Howell .05 .15
308 Rick Cerone .05 .15
309 Tim Leary .05 .15
310 Joe Orsulak .05 .15
311 Jim Dwyer .05 .15
312 Geno Petralli .05 .15
313 Rick Honeycutt .05 .15
314 Tom Foley .05 .15
315 Kenny Rogers 1.25 3.00
316 Mike Flanagan .05 .15
317 Bryan Harvey .05 .15
318 Billy Ripken .05 .15
319 Jeff Montgomery .05 .15
320 Erik Hanson .20 .50
321 Brian Downing .08 .25
322 Gregg Olson .20 .50
323 Terry Steinbach .08 .25
324 Sammy Sosa 4.00 10.00
325 Gene Harris .05 .15
326 Mike Devereaux .05 .15
327 Dennis Cook .20 .50
328 David Wells .08 .25
329 Checklist Card .05 .15
330 Kirt Manwaring .05 .15
331 Jim Presley .05 .15
332 Checklist Card .05 .15
333 Chuck Finley .08 .25
334 Rob Dibble .30 .75
335 Cecil Espy .05 .15
336 Dave Parker .08 .25

1989 Donruss Pop-Ups

These Pop-Ups are borderless and standard size. The cards are unnumbered; however the All Star checklist card lists the same numbers as the All Star cards. Those numbers are used below for reference. The players chosen for the set are essentially the starting lineups for the previous year's All-Star Game. Individual wax packs of All Stars (suggested retail price of 35 cents) contained one Pop-Up, five All-Star cards and a puzzle card.

COMPLETE SET (20) 2.00 5.00
1 Mark McGwire .75 2.00
2 Jose Canseco .20 .50
3 Paul Molitor .20 .50
4 Rickey Henderson .30 1.00
5 Cal Ripken 1.25 3.00
6 Dave Winfield .20 .50
7 Wade Boggs .20 .50
8 Frank Viola .02 .10
9 Terry Steinbach .02 .10
10 Tom Kelly MG .02 .10
33 Will Clark .20 .50
34 Darryl Strawberry .07 .20
35 Ryne Sandberg .40 1.00
36 Andre Dawson .15 .40
37 Ozzie Smith .40 1.00
38 Vince Coleman .02 .10
39 Bobby Bonilla .07 .20
40 Dwight Gooden .07 .20
41 Gary Carter .20 .50
42 Whitey Herzog MG .02 .10

1989 Donruss Super DK's

This 26-player card set was available through a mail-in offer detailed on the wax packs. The set was sent in return for $8.00 and three wrappers plus $2.00 postage and handling. The set features the popular Diamond King subseries in the large (approximately 4 7/8" X 6 13/16") form. Dick Perez of Perez-Steele Galleries did another outstanding job on the artwork. The cards are essentially a large version of the Donruss regular issue Diamond Kings.

COMPLETE SET (26) 6.00 15.00
1 Mike Greenwell .02 .10
2 Bobby Bonilla .07 .20
3 Pete Incaviglia .02 .10
4 Chris Sabo .02 .10
5 Robin Yount .40 1.00
6 Tony Gwynn 1.50 4.00
7 Carlton Fisk 1.25 3.00
8 Cory Snyder .02 .10
9 David Cone .10 .30
10 Kevin Seitzer .02 .10
11 Rick Reuschel .02 .10
12 Johnny Ray .02 .10
13 Dave Schmidt .02 .10
14 Andres Galarraga .15 .40
15 Kirk Gibson .07 .20
16 Fred McGriff .40 1.00
17 Mark Grace 1.50 4.00
18 Jeff M. Robinson .02 .10
19 Vince Coleman .02 .10
20 Dave Henderson .02 .10
21 Harold Reynolds .07 .20
22 Gerald Perry .02 .10
23 Frank Viola .02 .10
24 Steve Bedrosian .02 .10
25 Glenn Davis .02 .10
26 Don Mattingly 2.00 5.00

1989 Donruss Traded

The 1989 Donruss Traded set contains 56 standard-size cards. The fronts have yellowish-orange borders; the backs are yellow and feature recent statistics. The set was distributed as a boxed set. The set was never very popular with collectors since it included (as the name implies) only traded players rather than rookies. The cards are numbered with a "T" prefix.

COMP.FACT.SET (56) 1.25 3.00
1 Jeffrey Leonard .02 .10
2 Jack Clark .07 .20
3 Kevin Gross .02 .10
4 Tommy Herr .02 .10
5 Bob Boone .07 .20
6 Rafael Palmeiro .20 .50
7 John Dopson .02 .10
8 Willie Randolph .07 .20
9 Chris Brown .02 .10
10 Wally Backman .02 .10
11 Steve Ontiveros .02 .10
12 Eddie Murray .20 .50
13 Lance McCullers .02 .10
14 Spike Owen .02 .10
15 Rob Murphy .02 .10
16 Pete O'Brien .02 .10
17 Ken Williams .02 .10
18 Nick Esasky .02 .10
19 Nolan Ryan .60 1.50
20 Brian Holton .02 .10
21 Mike Moore .02 .10
22 Joel Skinner .02 .10
23 Steve Sax .02 .10
24 Rick Mahler .02 .10
25 Mike Aldrete .02 .10
26 Jesse Orosco .02 .10
27 Dave LaPoint .02 .10
28 Walt Terrell .02 .10
29 Eddie Williams .02 .10
30 Mike Devereaux .02 .10
31 Julio Franco .07 .20
32 Jim Clancy .02 .10
33 Felix Fermin .02 .10
34 Curt Wilkerson .02 .10
35 Bert Blyleven .07 .20
36 Mel Hall .02 .10
37 Eric King .02 .10
38 Mitch Williams .02 .10
39 Jamie Moyer .07 .20
40 Rick Rhoden .02 .10
41 Phil Bradley .02 .10
42 Paul Kilgus .02 .10
43 Milt Thompson .02 .10
44 Jerry Browne .02 .10
45 Bruce Hurst .02 .10
46 Claudell Washington .02 .10
47 Todd Benzinger .02 .10
48 Steve Balboni .02 .10
49 Oddibe McDowell .02 .10
50 Charles Hudson .02 .10
51 Ron Kittle .02 .10
52 Andy Hawkins .02 .10
53 Tom Brookens .02 .10
54 Tom Niedenfuer .02 .10
55 Jeff Parrett .02 .10
56 Checklist Card .02 .10

1989 Donruss Blue Chips

COMPLETE SET (12)
1 Jose Canseco
2 Mike Marshall
3 Walt Weiss
4 Kevin McReynolds
5 Mike Greenwell
6 Dave Winfield
7 Mark McGwire
8 Keith Hernandez
9 Franklin Stubbs
10 Danny Tartabull
11 Jesse Barfield
12 Ellis Burks

1990 Donruss Previews

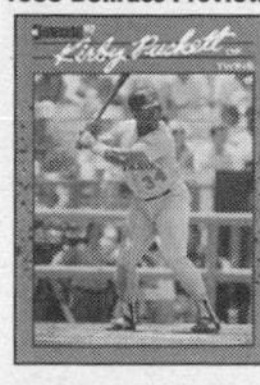

COMPLETE SET (12) 200.00 400.00
1 Todd Zeile/(Not shown as Rated 6.00 15.00
Rookie on front)
2 Ben McDonald 4.00 10.00
3 Bo Jackson 15.00 40.00
4 Will Clark 20.00 50.00
5 Dave Stewart 6.00 15.00
6 Kevin Mitchell 4.00 10.00
7 Nolan Ryan 60.00 120.00
8 Howard Johnson 4.00 10.00
9 Tony Gwynn 30.00 80.00
10 Jerome Walton/(Shown ready to bunt) 4.00
10.00
11 Wade Boggs 20.00 50.00
12 Kirby Puckett 15.00 40.00

1990 Donruss

The 1990 Donruss set contains 716 standard-size cards. Cards were issued in wax packs and hobby and retail factory sets. The card fronts feature bright red borders. Subsets include Diamond Kings (1-27) and Rated Rookies (28-47). The set was the largest ever produced by Donruss, unfortunately it also had a large number of errors which were corrected after the cards were released. Most of these feature minor printing flaws and insignificant variations that collectors have found unworthy of price differentials. There are several double-printed cards indicated in our checklist with the set indicated with a "DP" coding. Rookie Cards of note include Juan Gonzalez, David Justice, John Olerud, Dean Palmer, Sammy Sosa, Larry Walker and Bernie Williams.

COMPLETE SET (716) 6.00 15.00
COMP.FACT.SET (728) 6.00 15.00
COMP.YAZ PUZZLE .40 1.00
1 Bo Jackson DK .05 .15
2 Steve Sax DK .01 .05
3A Ruben Sierra DK ERR .02 .10
No small line on top
border on card back
3B Ruben Sierra DK COR .02 .10
4 Ken Griffey Jr. DK .20 .50
5 Mickey Tettleton DK .01 .05
6 Dave Stewart DK .01 .05
7 Jim Deshaies DK DP .01 .05
8 John Smoltz DK .08 .25
9 Mike Bielecki DK .01 .05
10A Brian Downing DK ERR .05 .15
10B Brian Downing DK COR .01 .05
11 Kevin Mitchell DK .01 .05
12 Kelly Gruber DK .01 .05
13 Joe Magrane DK .01 .05
14 John Franco DK .02 .10
15 Ozzie Guillen DK .02 .10
16 Lou Whitaker DK .01 .05
17 John Smiley DK .01 .05
18 Howard Johnson DK .01 .05
19 Willie Randolph DK .01 .05
20 Chris Bosio DK .01 .05
21 Tommy Herr DK DP .01 .05
22 Dan Gladden DK .01 .05
23 Ellis Burks DK .02 .10
24 Pete O'Brien DK .01 .05
25 Bryn Smith DK .01 .05
26 Ed Whitson DK DP .01 .05
27 DK Checklist 1-27 DP .01 .05
Comments on Perez-
Steele on back
28 Robin Ventura .08 .25
29 Todd Zeile RR .02 .10
30 Sandy Alomar Jr. .02 .10
31 Kent Mercker RC .08 .25
32 Ben McDonald RC UER .08 .25
Middle name Benard
not Benjamin
33A Juan Gonzalez RevNg RC .75 2.00
33B Juan Gonzalez COR RC .40 1.00
34 Eric Anthony RC .02 .10
35 Mike Fetters RC .08 .25
36 Marquis Grissom RC .15 .40
37 Greg Vaughn .01 .05
38 Brian DuBois RC .02 .10
39 Steve Avery RR UER .01 .05
Born in MI, not NJ
40 Mark Gardner RC .02 .10
41 Andy Benes .02 .10
42 Delino DeShields RC .08 .25
43 Scott Coolbaugh RC .02 .10
44 Pat Combs DP .01 .05
45 Alex Sanchez DP .01 .05
46 Kelly Mann DP RC .02 .10
47 Julio Machado RC .02 .10
48 Pete Incaviglia .01 .05
49 Shawon Dunston .01 .05
50 Jeff Treadway .01 .05
51 Jeff Ballard .01 .05
52 Claudell Washington .01 .05
53 Juan Samuel .01 .05
54 John Smiley .01 .05
55 Rob Deer .01 .05
56 Geno Petralli .01 .05
57 Chris Bosio .01 .05
58 Carlton Fisk .05 .15
59 Kirt Manwaring .01 .05
60 Chet Lemon .01 .05
61 Bo Jackson .08 .25
62 Doyle Alexander .01 .05
63 Pedro Guerrero .01 .05
64 Allan Anderson .01 .05
65 Greg W. Harris .01 .05
66 Mike Greenwell .01 .05
67 Walt Weiss .01 .05
68 Wade Boggs .05 .15
69 Jim Clancy .01 .05
70 Junior Felix .01 .05
71 Barry Larkin .05 .15
72 Dave LaPoint .01 .05
73 Joel Skinner .01 .05
74 Jesse Barfield .01 .05
75 Tommy Herr .01 .05
76 Ricky Jordan .01 .05
77 Eddie Murray .08 .25
78 Steve Sax .01 .05
79 Tim Belcher .01 .05
80 Danny Jackson .01 .05
81 Kent Hrbek .02 .10
82 Milt Thompson .01 .05
83 Brook Jacoby .01 .05
84 Mike Marshall .01 .05
85 Kevin Seitzer .01 .05
86 Tony Gwynn .10 .30
87 Dave Stieb .02 .10
88 Dave Smith .01 .05
89 Bret Saberhagen .02 .10
90 Alan Trammell .02 .10
91 Tony Phillips .01 .05
92 Doug Drabek .01 .05
93 Jeffrey Leonard .01 .05
94 Wally Joyner .02 .10
95 Carney Lansford .02 .10
96 Cal Ripken .30 .75
97 Andres Galarraga .02 .10
98 Kevin Mitchell .01 .05
99 Howard Johnson .01 .05
100A Checklist 28-129 .01 .05
100B Checklist 28-125 .01 .05
101 Melido Perez .01 .05
102 Spike Owen .01 .05
103 Paul Molitor .02 .10
104 Geronimo Berroa .01 .05
105 Ryne Sandberg .15 .40
106 Bryn Smith .01 .05
107 Steve Buechele .01 .05
108 Jim Abbott .05 .15
109 Alvin Davis .01 .05
110 Lee Smith .02 .10
111 Roberto Alomar .05 .15
112 Rick Reuschel .01 .05
113A Kelly Gruber ERR .01 .05
Born 2/22
113B Kelly Gruber COR .01 .05
Born 2/26; corrected
in factory sets
114 Joe Carter .02 .10
115 Jose Rijo .01 .05
116 Greg Minton .01 .05
117 Bob Ojeda .01 .05
118 Glenn Davis .01 .05
119 Jeff Reardon .02 .10
120 Kurt Stillwell .01 .05
121 John Smoltz .08 .25
122 Dwight Evans .05 .15
123 Eric Yelding RC .01 .05
124 John Franco .02 .10
125 Jose Canseco .05 .15
126 Barry Bonds .40 1.00
127 Lee Guetterman .01 .05
128 Jack Clark .02 .10
129 Dave Valle .01 .05
130 Hubie Brooks .01 .05
131 Ernest Riles .01 .05
132 Mike Morgan .01 .05
133 Steve Jeltz .01 .05
134 Jeff D. Robinson .01 .05
135 Ozzie Guillen .02 .10
136 Chili Davis .02 .10
137 Mitch Webster .01 .05
138 Jerry Browne .01 .05
139 Bo Diaz .01 .05
140 Robby Thompson .01 .05
141 Craig Worthington .01 .05
142 Julio Franco .02 .10
143 Brian Holman .01 .05
144 George Brett .25 .60
145 Tom Glavine .05 .15
146 Robin Yount .15 .40
147 Gary Carter .02 .10
148 Ron Kittle .01 .05
149 Tony Fernandez .01 .05
150 Dave Stewart .02 .10
151 Gary Gaetti .02 .10
152 Kevin Elster .01 .05
153 Gerald Perry .01 .05
154 Jesse Orosco .01 .05
155 Wally Backman .01 .05
156 Dennis Martinez .02 .10
157 Rick Sutcliffe .02 .10
158 Greg Maddux .15 .40
159 Andy Hawkins .01 .05
160 John Kruk .02 .10
161 Jose Oquendo .01 .05
162 John Dopson .01 .05
163 Joe Magrane .01 .05
164 Bill Ripken .01 .05
165 Fred Manrique .01 .05
166 Nolan Ryan UER .40 1.00
167 Damon Berryhill .01 .05
168 Dale Murphy .05 .15
169 Mickey Tettleton .01 .05
170A Kirk McCaskill ERR .01 .05
Born 4/19
170B Kirk McCaskill COR .01 .05
Born 4/9; corrected
in factory sets
171 Dwight Gooden .02 .10
172 Jose Lind .01 .05
173 B.J. Surhoff .02 .10
174 Ruben Sierra .02 .10
175 Dan Plesac .01 .05
176 Dan Pasqua .01 .05
177 Kelly Downs .01 .05
178 Matt Nokes .01 .05
179 Luis Aquino .01 .05
180 Frank Tanana .01 .05
181 Tony Pena .01 .05
182 Dan Gladden .01 .05
183 Bruce Hurst .01 .05
184 Roger Clemens .40 1.00
185 Mark McGwire .40 1.00
186 Rob Murphy .01 .05
187 Jim Deshaies .01 .05
188 Fred McGriff .08 .25
189 Rob Dibble .02 .10
190 Don Mattingly .25 .60
191 Felix Fermin .01 .05
192 Roberto Kelly .01 .05
193 Dennis Cook .01 .05
194 Darren Daulton .02 .10
195 Alfredo Griffin .01 .05
196 Eric Plunk .01 .05
197 Orel Hershiser .02 .10
198 Paul O'Neill .05 .15
199 Randy Bush .01 .05
200A Checklist 130-231 .01 .05
200B Checklist 126-223 .01 .05
201 Ozzie Smith .15 .40
202 Pete O'Brien .01 .05
203 Jay Howell .01 .05
204 Mark Gubicza .01 .05
205 Ed Whitson .01 .05
206 George Bell .01 .05
207 Mike Scott .01 .05
208 Charlie Leibrandt .01 .05
209 Mike Heath .01 .05
210 Dennis Eckersley .02 .10
211 Mike LaValliere .01 .05
212 Darnell Coles .01 .05
213 Lance Parrish .01 .05
214 Mike Moore .01 .05
215 Steve Finley .02 .10
216 Tim Raines .02 .10
217A Scott Garrelts ERR .01 .05
Born 10/20
217B Scott Garrelts COR .01 .05
Born 10/30; corrected
in factory sets
218 Kevin McReynolds .01 .05
219 Dave Gallagher .01 .05
220 Tim Wallach .01 .05
221 Chuck Crim .01 .05
222 Lonnie Smith .01 .05
223 Andre Dawson .02 .10
224 Nelson Santovenia .01 .05
225 Rafael Palmeiro .05 .15
226 Devon White .02 .10
227 Harold Reynolds .02 .10
228 Ellis Burks .05 .15
229 Mark Parent .01 .05
230 Will Clark .05 .15
231 Jimmy Key .02 .10
232 John Farrell .01 .05
233 Eric Davis .02 .10
234 Johnny Ray .01 .05
235 Darryl Strawberry .02 .10
236 Bill Doran .01 .05
237 Greg Gagne .01 .05
238 Jim Eisenreich .01 .05
239 Tommy Gregg .01 .05
240 Marty Barrett .01 .05
241 Rafael Ramirez .01 .05
242 Chris Sabo .01 .05
243 Dave Henderson .01 .05
244 Andy Van Slyke .05 .15
245 Alvaro Espinoza .01 .05
246 Garry Templeton .01 .05
247 Gene Harris .01 .05
248 Kevin Gross .01 .05
249 Brett Butler .02 .10

250 Willie Randolph .02 .10
251 Roger McDowell .01 .05
252 Rafael Belliard .01 .05
253 Steve Rosenberg .01 .05
254 Jack Howell .01 .05
255 Marvell Wynne .01 .05
256 Tom Candiotti .01 .05
257 Todd Benzinger .01 .05
258 Don Robinson .01 .05
259 Phil Bradley .01 .05
260 Cecil Espy .01 .05
261 Scott Bankhead .01 .05
262 Frank White .02 .10
263 Andres Thomas .01 .05
264 Glenn Braggs .01 .05
265 David Cone .02 .10
266 Bobby Thigpen .01 .05
267 Nelson Liriano .01 .05
268 Terry Steinbach .01 .05
269 Kirby Puckett UER .08 .25
Back doesn't consider
Joe Torre's .363 in '71
270 Gregg Jefferies .02 .10
271 Jeff Blauser .01 .05
272 Cory Snyder .01 .05
273 Roy Smith .01 .05
274 Tom Foley .01 .05
275 Mitch Williams .01 .05
276 Paul Kilgus .01 .05
277 Don Slaught .01 .05
278 Von Hayes .01 .05
279 Vince Coleman .01 .05
280 Mike Boddicker .01 .05
281 Ken Dayley .01 .05
282 Mike Devereaux .01 .05
283 Kenny Rogers .02 .10
284 Jeff Russell .01 .05
285 Jerome Walton .01 .05
286 Derek Lilliquist .01 .05
287 Joe Orsulak .01 .05
288 Dick Schofield .01 .05
289 Ron Darling .01 .05
290 Bobby Bonilla .02 .10
291 Jim Gantner .01 .05
292 Bobby Witt .01 .05
293 Greg Brock .01 .05
294 Ivan Calderon .01 .05
295 Steve Bedrosian .01 .05
296 Mike Henneman .01 .05
297 Tom Gordon .02 .10
298 Lou Whitaker .02 .10
299 Terry Pendleton .02 .10
300A Checklist 232-333 .01 .05
300B Checklist 224-321 .01 .05
301 Juan Berenguer .01 .05
302 Mark Davis .01 .05
303 Nick Esasky .01 .05
304 Rickey Henderson .08 .25
305 Rick Cerone .01 .05
306 Craig Biggio .08 .25
307 Duane Ward .01 .05
308 Tom Browning .01 .05
309 Walt Terrell .01 .05
310 Greg Swindell .01 .05
311 Dave Righetti .01 .05
312 Mike Maddux .01 .05
313 Len Dykstra .02 .10
314 Jose Gonzalez .01 .05
315 Steve Balboni .01 .05
316 Mike Scioscia .01 .05
317 Ron Oester .01 .05
318 Gary Wayne .01 .05
319 Todd Worrell .01 .05
320 Doug Jones .01 .05
321 Jeff Hamilton .01 .05
322 Danny Tartabull .01 .05
323 Chris James .01 .05
324 Mike Flanagan .01 .05
325 Gerald Young .01 .05
326 Bob Boone .02 .10
327 Frank Williams .01 .05
328 Dave Parker .02 .10
329 Sid Bream .01 .05
330 Mike Schooler .01 .05
331 Bert Blyleven .02 .10
332 Bob Welch .01 .05
333 Bob Milacki .01 .05
334 Tim Burke .01 .05
335 Jose Uribe .01 .05
336 Randy Myers .02 .10
337 Eric King .01 .05
338 Mark Langston .01 .05
339 Teddy Higuera .01 .05
340 Oddibe McDowell .01 .05
341 Lloyd McClendon .01 .05
342 Pascual Perez .01 .05
343 Kevin Brown UER .02 .10
Signed is misspelled
as signeed on back
344 Chuck Finley .02 .10
345 Erik Hanson .01 .05
346 Rich Gedman .01 .05
347 Bip Roberts .01 .05
348 Matt Williams .02 .10
349 Tom Henke .01 .05
350 Brad Komminsk .01 .05
351 Jeff Reed .01 .05
352 Brian Downing .01 .05
353 Frank Viola .01 .05
354 Terry Puhl .01 .05
355 Brian Harper .01 .05
356 Steve Farr .01 .05
357 Joe Boever .01 .05
358 Danny Heep .01 .05
359 Larry Andersen .01 .05
360 Rolando Roomes .01 .05
361 Mike Gallego .01 .05
362 Bob Kipper .01 .05
363 Clay Parker .01 .05
364 Mike Pagliarulo .01 .05
365 Ken Griffey Jr. UER .40 1.00
366 Rex Hudler .01 .05
367 Pat Sheridan .01 .05
368 Kirk Gibson .02 .10
369 Jeff Parrett .01 .05
370 Bob Walk .01 .05
371 Ken Patterson .01 .05
372 Bryan Harvey .01 .05
373 Mike Bielecki .01 .05
374 Tom Magrann RC .01 .05
375 Rick Mahler .01 .05
376 Craig Lefferts .01 .05
377 Gregg Olson .02 .10
378 Jamie Moyer .02 .10
379 Randy Johnson .20 .50
380 Jeff Montgomery .02 .10
381 Marty Clary .01 .05
382 Bill Spiers .01 .05
383 Dave Magadan .01 .05
384 Greg Hibbard RC .02 .10
385 Ernie Whitt .01 .05
386 Rick Honeycutt .01 .05
387 Dave West .01 .05
388 Keith Hernandez .02 .10
389 Jose Alvarez .01 .05
390 Albert Belle .08 .25
391 Rick Aguilera .02 .10
392 Mike Fitzgerald .01 .05
393 Dwight Smith .01 .05
394 Steve Wilson .01 .05
395 Bob Geren .01 .05
396 Randy Ready .01 .05
397 Ken Hill .02 .10
398 Jody Reed .01 .05
399 Tom Brunansky .01 .05
400A Checklist 334-435 .01 .05
400B Checklist 322-419 .01 .05
401 Rene Gonzales .01 .05
402 Harold Baines .02 .10
403 Cecilio Guante .01 .05
404 Joe Girardi .05 .15
405A Sergio Valdez ERR RC .01 .05
405B Sergio Valdez COR RC .01 .05
406 Mark Williamson .01 .05
407 Glenn Hoffman .01 .05
408 Jeff Innis RC .01 .05
409 Randy Kramer .01 .05
410 Charlie O'Brien .01 .05
411 Charlie Hough .02 .10
412 Gus Polidor .01 .05
413 Ron Karkovice .01 .05
414 Trevor Wilson .01 .05
415 Kevin Ritz RC .01 .05
416 Gary Thurman .01 .05
417 Jeff M. Robinson .01 .05
418 Scott Terry .01 .05
419 Tim Laudner .01 .05
420 Dennis Rasmussen .01 .05
421 Luis Rivera .01 .05
422 Jim Corsi .01 .05
423 Dennis Lamp .01 .05
424 Ken Caminiti .02 .10
425 David Wells .02 .10
426 Norm Charlton .01 .05
427 Deion Sanders .08 .25
428 Dion James .01 .05
429 Chuck Cary .01 .05
430 Ken Howell .01 .05
431 Steve Lake .01 .05
432 Kal Daniels .01 .05
433 Lance McCullers .01 .05
434 Lenny Harris .01 .05
435 Scott Scudder .01 .05
436 Gene Larkin .01 .05
437 Dan Quisenberry .01 .05
438 Steve Olin RC .08 .25
439 Mickey Hatcher .01 .05
440 Willie Wilson .01 .05
441 Mark Grant .01 .05
442 Mookie Wilson .02 .10
443 Alex Trevino .01 .05
444 Pat Tabler .01 .05
445 Dave Bergman .01 .05
446 Todd Burns .01 .05
447 R.J. Reynolds .01 .05
448 Jay Buhner .02 .10
449 Lee Stevens .02 .10
450 Ron Hassey .01 .05
451 Bob Melvin .01 .05
452 Dave Martinez .01 .05
453 Greg Litton .01 .05
454 Mark Carreon .01 .05
455 Scott Fletcher .01 .05
456 Otis Nixon .01 .05
457 Tony Fossas RC .01 .05
458 John Russell .01 .05
459 Paul Assenmacher .01 .05
460 Zane Smith .01 .05
461 Jack Daugherty RC .01 .05
462 Rich Monteleone .01 .05
463 Greg Briley .01 .05
464 Mike Smithson .01 .05
465 Benito Santiago .02 .10
466 Jeff Brantley .01 .05
467 Jose Nunez .01 .05
468 Scott Bailes .01 .05
469 Ken Griffey Sr. .02 .10
470 Bob McClure .01 .05
471 Mackey Sasser .01 .05
472 Glenn Wilson .01 .05
473 Kevin Tapani RC .08 .25
474 Bill Buckner .01 .05
475 Ron Gant .02 .10
476 Kevin Romine .01 .05
477 Juan Agosto .01 .05
478 Herm Winningham .01 .05
479 Storm Davis .01 .05
480 Jeff King .01 .05
481 Kevin Mmahat RC .01 .05
482 Carmelo Martinez .01 .05
483 Omar Vizquel .08 .25
484 Jim Dwyer .01 .05
485 Bob Knepper .01 .05
486 Dave Anderson .01 .05
487 Ron Jones .01 .05
488 Jay Bell .02 .10
489 Sammy Sosa RC 1.00 2.50
490 Kent Anderson .01 .05
491 Domingo Ramos .01 .05
492 Dave Clark .01 .05
493 Tim Birtsas .01 .05
494 Ken Oberkfell .01 .05
495 Larry Sheets .01 .05
496 Jeff Kunkel .01 .05
497 Jim Presley .01 .05
498 Mike Macfarlane .01 .05
499 Pete Smith .01 .05
500A Checklist 436-537 DP .01 .05
500B Checklist 420-517 .01 .05
501 Gary Sheffield .08 .25
502 Terry Bross RC .01 .05
503 Jerry Kutzler RC .01 .05
504 Lloyd Moseby .01 .05
505 Curt Young .01 .05
506 Al Newman .01 .05
507 Keith Miller .01 .05
508 Mike Stanton RC .08 .25
509 Rich Yett .01 .05
510 Tim Drummond RC .01 .05
511 Joe Hesketh .01 .05
512 Rick Wrona .01 .05
513 Luis Salazar .01 .05
514 Hal Morris .01 .05
515 Terry Mulholland .01 .05
516 John Morris .01 .05
517 Carlos Quintana .01 .05
518 Frank DiPino .01 .05
519 Randy Milligan .01 .05
520 Chad Kreuter .01 .05
521 Mike Jeffcoat .01 .05
522 Mike Harkey .01 .05
523A Andy Nezelek ERR .01 .05
Wrong birth year
523B Andy Nezelek COR .05 .15
Finally corrected
in factory sets
524 Dave Schmidt .01 .05
525 Tony Armas .01 .05
526 Barry Lyons .01 .05
527 Rick Reed RC .08 .25
528 Jerry Reuss .01 .05
529 Dean Palmer RC .08 .25
530 Jeff Peterek RC .01 .05
531 Carlos Martinez .01 .05
532 Atlee Hammaker .01 .05
533 Mike Brumley .01 .05
534 Terry Leach .01 .05
535 Doug Strange RC .01 .05
536 Jose DeLeon .01 .05
537 Shane Rawley .01 .05
538 Joey Cora .02 .10
539 Eric Hetzel .01 .05
540 Gene Nelson .01 .05
541 Wes Gardner .01 .05
542 Mark Portugal .01 .05
543 Al Leiter .08 .25
544 Jack Armstrong .01 .05
545 Greg Cadaret .01 .05
546 Rod Nichols .01 .05
547 Luis Polonia .01 .05
548 Charlie Hayes .01 .05
549 Dickie Thon .01 .05
550 Tim Crews .01 .05
551 Dave Winfield .02 .10
552 Mike Davis .01 .05
553 Ron Robinson .01 .05
554 Carmen Castillo .01 .05
555 John Costello .01 .05
556 Bud Black .01 .05
557 Rick Dempsey .01 .05
558 Jim Acker .01 .05
559 Eric Show .01 .05
560 Pat Borders .01 .05
561 Danny Darwin .01 .05
562 Rick Luecken RC .01 .05
563 Edwin Nunez .01 .05
564 Felix Jose .01 .05
565 John Cangelosi .01 .05
566 Bill Swift .01 .05
567 Bill Schroeder .01 .05
568 Stan Javier .01 .05
569 Jim Traber .01 .05
570 Wallace Johnson .01 .05
571 Donell Nixon .01 .05
572 Sid Fernandez .01 .05
573 Lance Johnson .01 .05
574 Andy McGaffigan .01 .05
575 Mark Knudson .01 .05
576 Tommy Greene RC .02 .10
577 Mark Grace .05 .15
578 Larry Walker RC .40 1.00
579 Mike Stanley .01 .05
580 Mike Witt DP .01 .05
581 Scott Bradley .01 .05
582 Greg A. Harris .01 .05
583A Kevin Hickey ERR .08 .25
583B Kevin Hickey COR .01 .05
584 Lee Mazzilli .01 .05
585 Jeff Pico .01 .05
586 Joe Oliver .01 .05
587 Willie Fraser DP .01 .05
588 Carl Yastrzemski .08 .25
Puzzle Card DP
589 Kevin Bass DP .01 .05
590 John Moses DP .01 .05
591 Tom Pagnozzi DP .01 .05
592 Tony Castillo DP .01 .05
593 Jerald Clark DP .01 .05
594 Dan Schatzeder .01 .05
595 Luis Quinones DP .01 .05
596 Pete Harnisch DP .01 .05
597 Gary Redus .01 .05
598 Mel Hall .01 .05
599 Rick Schu .01 .05
600A Checklist 538-639 .01 .05
600B Checklist 518-617 .01 .05
601 Mike Kingery DP .01 .05
602 Terry Kennedy DP .01 .05
603 Mike Sharperson DP .01 .05
604 Don Carman DP .01 .05
605 Jim Gott .01 .05
606 Donn Pall DP .01 .05
607 Rance Mulliniks .01 .05
608 Curt Wilkerson DP .01 .05
609 Mike Felder DP .01 .05
610 Guillermo Hernandez DP .01 .05
611 Candy Maldonado DP .01 .05
612 Mark Thurmond DP .01 .05
613 Rick Leach DP RC .01 .05
614 Jerry Reed DP .01 .05
615 Franklin Stubbs .01 .05
616 Billy Hatcher DP .01 .05
617 Don August DP .01 .05
618 Tim Teufel .01 .05
619 Shawn Hillegas DP .01 .05
620 Manny Lee .01 .05
621 Gary Ward DP .01 .05
622 Mark Guthrie DP RC .01 .05
623 Jeff Musselman DP .01 .05
624 Mark Lemke DP .01 .05
625 Fernando Valenzuela .02 .10
626 Paul Sorrento DP RC .08 .25
627 Glenallen Hill DP .01 .05
628 Les Lancaster DP .01 .05
629 Vance Law DP .01 .05
630 Randy Velarde DP .01 .05
631 Todd Frohwirth DP .01 .05
632 Willie McGee .02 .10
633 Dennis Boyd DP .01 .05
634 Cris Carpenter DP .01 .05
635 Brian Holton .01 .05
636 Tracy Jones DP .01 .05
637A Terry Steinbach AS .01 .05
Recent Major
League Performance
637B Terry Steinbach AS .01 .05
All-Star Game
Performance
638 Brady Anderson .02 .10
639A Jack Morris ERR .02 .10
Card front shows
black line crossing
J in Jack
639B Jack Morris COR .02 .10
640 Jaime Navarro .01 .05
641 Darrin Jackson .01 .05
642 Mike Dyer RC .01 .05
643 Mike Schmidt .20 .50
644 Henry Cotto .01 .05
645 John Cerutti .01 .05
646 Francisco Cabrera .01 .05
647 Scott Sanderson .01 .05
648 Brian Meyer .01 .05
649 Ray Searage .01 .05
650A Bo Jackson AS .08 .25
Recent Major
League Performance
650B Bo Jackson AS .08 .25
All-Star Game
Performance
651 Steve Lyons .01 .05
652 Mike LaCoss .01 .05
653 Ted Power .01 .05
654A Howard Johnson AS .01 .05
Recent Major
League Performance
654B Howard Johnson AS .01 .05
All-Star Game
Performance
655 Mauro Gozzo RC .01 .05
656 Mike Blowers RC .02 .10
657 Paul Gibson .01 .05
658 Neal Heaton .01 .05
659 N.Ryan 5000K COR .20 .50
659A Nolan Ryan 5000K .60 1.50
660A Harold Baines AS .30 .75
660B Harold Baines AS .40 1.00
660C Harold Baines AS .08 .25
Black line behind
star on front;
Recent Major
League Performance
660D Harold Baines AS .01 .05
Black line behind
star on front;
All-Star Game
Performance
661 Gary Pettis .01 .05
662 Clint Zavaras RC .01 .05
663A Rick Reuschel AS .01 .05
Recent Major
League Performance
663B Rick Reuschel AS .01 .05
All-Star Game
Performance
664 Alejandro Pena .01 .05
665 Nolan Ryan KING COR .20 .50
665A N.Ryan KING .60 1.50
665C N.Ryan KING ERR .30 .75
666 Ricky Horton .01 .05
667 Curt Schilling .40 1.00
668 Bill Landrum .01 .05
669 Todd Stottlemyre .02 .10
670 Tim Leary .01 .05
671 John Wetteland .08 .25
672 Calvin Schiraldi .01 .05
673A Ruben Sierra AS .01 .05
Recent Major
League Performance
673B Ruben Sierra AS .01 .05
All-Star Game
Performance
674A Pedro Guerrero AS .01 .05
Recent Major
League Performance
674B Pedro Guerrero AS .01 .05
All-Star Game
Performance
675 Ken Phelps .01 .05
676A Cal Ripken AS .15 .40
676B Cal Ripken AS .30 .75
677 Denny Walling .01 .05
678 Goose Gossage .02 .10
679 Gary Mielke RC .01 .05
680 Bill Bathe .01 .05
681 Tom Lawless .01 .05
682 Xavier Hernandez RC .01 .05
683A Kirby Puckett AS .05 .15
Recent Major
League Performance
683B Kirby Puckett AS .05 .15
All-Star Game
Performance
684 Mariano Duncan .01 .05
685 Ramon Martinez .01 .05
686 Tim Jones .01 .05
687 Tom Filer .01 .05
688 Steve Lombardozzi .01 .05
689 Bernie Williams RC .60 1.50
690 Chip Hale RC .01 .05
691 Beau Allred RC .01 .05
692A Ryne Sandberg AS .08 .25
Recent Major
League Performance
692B Ryne Sandberg AS .08 .25
All-Star Game
Performance
693 Jeff Huson RC .02 .10
694 Curt Ford .01 .05
695A Eric Davis AS .01 .05
Recent Major
League Performance
695B Eric Davis AS .01 .05
All-Star Game
Performance
696 Scott Lusader .01 .05
697A Mark McGwire AS .20 .50
697B Mark McGwire AS .20 .50
698 Steve Cummings RC .01 .05
699 George Canale RC .01 .05
700A Checklist 640-715 .08 .25
and BC1-BC26
700B Checklist 640-716 .02 .10
and BC1-BC26
700C Checklist 618-716 .01 .05
701A Julio Franco AS .01 .05
Recent Major
League Performance
701B Julio Franco AS .01 .05
All-Star Game
Performance
702 Dave Wayne Johnson RC .01 .05
703A Dave Stewart AS ERR .01 .05
703B Dave Stewart AS COR .01 .05
704 Dave Justice RC .20 .50
705 Tony Gwynn AS .05 .15
All-Star Game
Performance
705A Tony Gwynn AS .05 .15
Recent Major
League Performance
706 Greg Myers .01 .05
707A Will Clark AS .05 .15
Recent Major
League Performance
707B Will Clark AS .05 .15
All-Star Game
Performance
708A Benito Santiago AS .01 .05
Recent Major
League Performance
708B Benito Santiago AS .01 .05
All-Star Game
Performance
709 Larry McWilliams .01 .05
710A Ozzie Smith AS .08 .25
Recent Major
League Performance
710B Ozzie Smith AS Perf .08 .25
711 John Olerud RC .20 .50
712A Wade Boggs AS .02 .10
Recent Major
League Performance
712B Wade Boggs AS .02 .10
All-Star Game
Performance
713 Gary Eave RC .01 .05
714 Bob Tewksbury .01 .05
715A Kevin Mitchell AS .01 .05
Recent Major
League Performance
715B Kevin Mitchell AS .01 .05
All-Star Game
Performance
716 Bart Giamatti MEM .08 .25

1990 Donruss Bonus MVP's

Numbered with the prefix "BC" for bonus card, a 26-card set featuring the most valuable player from each of the 26 teams was randomly inserted in all 1990 Donruss unopened pack formats. The factory sets were distributed without the Bonus Cards; thus there were again new checklist cards printed to reflect the exclusion of the Bonus Cards.

COMPLETE SET (26) .60 1.50
RANDOM INSERTS IN PACKS
BC1 Bo Jackson .08 .25
BC2 Howard Johnson .01 .05
BC3 Dave Stewart .02 .10
BC4 Tony Gwynn .10 .30
BC5 Orel Hershiser .02 .10
BC6 Pedro Guerrero .01 .05
BC7 Tim Raines .02 .10
BC8 Kirby Puckett .08 .25
BC9 Alvin Davis .01 .05
BC10 Ryne Sandberg .15 .40
BC11 Kevin Mitchell .01 .05
BC12A J.Smoltz ERR Glavine .05 .15
BC12B John Smoltz COR .08 .25
BC13 George Bell .01 .05
BC14 Julio Franco .02 .10
BC15 Paul Molitor .02 .10
BC16 Bobby Bonilla .02 .10
BC17 Mike Greenwell .01 .05
BC18 Cal Ripken .30 .75
BC19 Carlton Fisk .05 .15
BC20 Chili Davis .02 .10
BC21 Glenn Davis .01 .05
BC22 Steve Sax .01 .05
BC23 Eric Davis DP .02 .10
BC24 Greg Swindell DP .01 .05
BC25 Von Hayes DP .01 .05
BC26 Alan Trammell .02 .10

1990 Donruss Carl Yastrzemski Puzzle

1 Yastrzemski Puzzle 1-3 .10 .25
4 Yastrzemski Puzzle 4-6 .10 .25
7 Yastrzemski Puzzle 7-10 .10 .25
10 Yastrzemski Puzzle 10-12 .10 .25
13 Yastrzemski Puzzle 13-15 .10 .25
16 Yastrzemski Puzzle 16-18 .10 .25
19 Yastrzemski Puzzle 19-21 .10 .25
22 Yastrzemski Puzzle 22-24 .10 .25
25 Yastrzemski Puzzle 25-27 .10 .25
28 Yastrzemski Puzzle 28-30 .10 .25
31 Yastrzemski Puzzle 31-33 .10 .25
34 Yastrzemski Puzzle 34-36 .10 .25
37 Yastrzemski Puzzle 37-39 .10 .25
40 Yastrzemski Puzzle 40-42 .10 .25
43 Yastrzemski Puzzle 43-45 .10 .25
46 Yastrzemski Puzzle 46-48 .10 .25
49 Yastrzemski Puzzle 49-51 .10 .25
52 Yastrzemski Puzzle 52-54 .10 .25
55 Yastrzemski Puzzle 55-57 .10 .25
58 Yastrzemski Puzzle 58-60 .10 .25
61 Yastrzemski Puzzle 61-63 .10 .25
NNO Complete Puzzle 1.00 2.50

1990 Donruss Grand Slammers

This 12-card standard size set was in the 1990 Donruss set as a special card deliniating each 55-card section of the 1990 Factory Set. This set honors those players who connected for grand slam homers during the 1989 season. The cards are in the 1990 Donruss design and the back describes the grand slam homer hit by each player.

COMPLETE SET (12) .60 1.50
ONE SET PER FACTORY SET
1 Matt Williams .02
2 Jeffrey Leonard .01
3 Chris James .01
4 Mark McGwire .40
5 Dwight Evans .05
6 Will Clark .05
7 Mike Scioscia .01
8 Todd Benzinger .01
9 Fred McGriff .08
10 Kevin Bass .01
11 Jack Clark .02
12 Bo Jackson .08

1990 Donruss Rookie

The 1990 Donruss Rookies set marked the
consecutive year that Donruss issued a box
season's end honoring the best rookies of t
season. This set, which used the 1990 Don
design but featured a green border, was iss
exclusively through the Donruss dealer netw
hobby dealers. This 56-card, standard size
in its own box and the words "The Rookies"
featured prominently on the front of the car
are no notable Rookie Cards in this set.

COMP.FACT.SET (56) .75
1 Sandy Alomar Jr. .02
2 John Olerud .20
3 Pat Combs .01
4 Brian DuBois .01
5 Felix Jose .01
6 Delino DeShields .08
7 Mike Stanton .01
8 Mike Munoz RC .01
9 Craig Grebeck RC .02
10 Joe Kraemer RC .01
11 Jeff Huson .01
12 Bill Sampen RC .01
13 Brian Bohanon RC .02
14 David Justice .20
15 Robin Ventura .08
16 Greg Vaughn .01
17 Wayne Edwards RC .01
18 Shawn Boskie RC .02
19 Carlos Baerga RC .08
20 Mark Gardner .01
21 Kevin Appier .02
22 Mike Harkey .01
23 Tim Layana RC .01
24 Glenallen Hill .01
25 Jerry Kutzler .01
26 Mike Blowers .02
27 Scott Ruskin RC .01
28 Dana Kiecker RC .01
29 Willie Blair RC .02
30 Ben McDonald .01
31 Todd Zeile .02
32 Scott Coolbaugh RC .01
33 Xavier Hernandez .01
34 Mike Hartley RC .01
35 Kevin Tapani .08
36 Kevin Wickander .01
37 Carlos Hernandez RC .08
38 Brian Traxler RC .02
39 Marty Brown .01
40 Scott Radinsky RC .02
41 Julio Machado .01
42 Steve Avery .01
43 Mark Lemke .01
44 Alan Mills RC .02
45 Marquis Grissom .08
46 Greg Olson (C) RC .02
47 Dave Hollins RC .08
48 Jerald Clark .01
49 Eric Anthony .01
50 Tim Drummond .01
51 John Burkett .01
52 Brent Knackert RC .02
53 Jeff Shaw .01
54 John Orton RC .02
55 Terry Shumpert RC .01
56 Checklist 1-56 .01

1990 Donruss Aqueous T

These cards are remarkably similar to the 19
Donruss issue except that the words "Aqueou
are printed in black ink on the back. It is poss
but not confirmed that all cards may exist in t
Any additions to this checklist is greatly appr

1 Bo Jackson DK 20.00
3 Ruben Sierra DK 12.50
6 Dave Stewart DK 10.00

ielecki DK	10.00	25.00
Vhitaker DK	12.50	30.00
rd Johnson DK	10.00	25.00
ladden DK	10.00	25.00
Alomar Jr RR	10.00	25.00
lcDonald RR	10.00	25.00
Gonzalez RR	50.00	120.00
nthony RR	10.00	25.00
Fetters RR	10.00	25.00
ncaviglia	10.00	25.00
allard	10.00	25.00
ell Washington	10.00	25.00
Deer	10.00	25.00
Petralli	10.00	25.00
Bosio	10.00	25.00
Lemon	10.00	25.00
Harris	10.00	25.00
Larkin	20.00	50.00
LaPoint	10.00	25.00
Murray	30.00	80.00
Sax	10.00	25.00
Belcher	10.00	25.00
Hrbek	12.50	30.00
Jacoby	10.00	25.00
Seitzer	10.00	25.00
Gwynn	40.00	100.00
Saberhagen	12.50	30.00
Phillips	10.00	25.00
Leonard	10.00	25.00
Joyner	10.00	25.00
ey Lansford	12.50	30.00
ipken Jr.	75.00	600.00
Mitchell	10.00	25.00
cklist	10.00	25.00
ke Owen	10.00	25.00
Molitor	25.00	60.00
e Sandberg	40.00	100.00
ve Buechele	10.00	25.00
Abbott	15.00	40.00
n Davis	10.00	25.00
Reuschel	12.50	30.00
Carter	12.50	30.00
by Ojeda	10.00	25.00
nn Davis	10.00	25.00
t Stillwell	10.00	25.00
e Canseco	25.00	60.00
ry Bonds	50.00	120.00
ve Valle	10.00	25.00
ke Morgan	10.00	25.00
Robinson	10.00	25.00
Diaz	10.00	25.00
by Thompson	10.00	25.00
ig Worthington	10.00	25.00
in Yount	25.00	60.00
ry Carter	25.00	60.00
n Kittle	10.00	25.00
ny Fernandez	12.50	30.00
sse Orosco	12.50	30.00
lly Backman	10.00	25.00
eg Maddux	50.00	120.00
n Dopson	10.00	25.00
Ripken	10.00	25.00
ed Manrique	10.00	25.00
lan Ryan	75.00	200.00
mon Berryhill	10.00	25.00
le Murphy	20.00	50.00
ckey Tettleton	10.00	25.00
k McCaskill	10.00	25.00
ight Gooden	12.50	30.00
se Lind	10.00	25.00
J. Surhoff	12.50	30.00
ben Sierra	12.50	30.00
n Plesac	10.00	25.00
n Pasqua	10.00	25.00
lly Downs	10.00	25.00
att Nokes	10.00	25.00
is Aquino	10.00	25.00
ank Tanana	12.50	30.00
ny Pena	10.00	25.00
n Gladden	10.00	25.00
uce Hurst	10.00	25.00
ger Clemens	40.00	100.00
ark McGwire	50.00	120.00
b Murphy	10.00	25.00
n Deshaies	10.00	25.00
ed McGriff	20.00	50.00
b Dibble	10.00	25.00
n Mattingly	40.00	100.00
lix Fermin	10.00	25.00
berto Kelly	10.00	25.00
ennis Cook	10.00	25.00
rren Daulton	10.00	25.00
fredo Griffin	10.00	25.00
ic Plunk	10.00	25.00
el Hershiser	12.50	30.00
aul O'Neill	15.00	40.00
andy Bush	10.00	25.00
zzie Smith	30.00	80.00
ete O'Brien	10.00	25.00
ay Howell	10.00	25.00
ark Gubicza	10.00	25.00
d Whitson	10.00	25.00
eorge Bell	10.00	25.00
like Scott	10.00	25.00
harlie Liebrandt	10.00	25.00
Mike Heath	10.00	25.00
ennis Eckersley	15.00	40.00
Mike LaVallilere	10.00	25.00
arnell Coles	10.00	25.00
ance Parrish	10.00	25.00
Mike Moore	10.00	25.00
teve Finley	12.50	30.00
im Raines	12.50	30.00
217 Scott Garrelts	10.00	25.00
218 Kevin McReynolds	10.00	25.00
219 Dave Gallagher	10.00	25.00
220 Tim Wallach	10.00	25.00
221 Chuck Crim	10.00	25.00
222 Lonnie Smith	12.50	30.00
223 Andre Dawson	30.00	80.00
224 Nelson Santovenia	10.00	25.00
225 Rafael Palmeiro	20.00	50.00
226 Devon White	10.00	25.00
227 Harold Reynolds	12.50	30.00
228 Ellis Burks	12.50	30.00
229 Mark Parent	10.00	25.00
230 Will Clark	25.00	60.00
231 Jimmy Key	10.00	25.00
232 John Farrell	10.00	25.00
233 Eric Davis	12.50	30.00
234 Johnny Ray	10.00	25.00
235 Darryl Strawberry	12.50	30.00
236 Bill Doran	10.00	25.00
237 Greg Gagne	10.00	25.00
238 Jim Eisenreich	10.00	25.00
239 Tommy Gregg	10.00	25.00
240 Marty Barrett	10.00	25.00
241 Rafael Ramirez	10.00	25.00
242 Chris Sabo	10.00	25.00
243 Dave Henderson	10.00	25.00
245 Alvaro Espinoza	10.00	25.00
246 Garry Templeton	10.00	25.00
247 Gene Harris	10.00	25.00
248 Kevin Gross	10.00	25.00
249 Brett Butler	12.50	30.00
250 Willie Randolph	12.50	30.00
251 Roger McDowell	10.00	25.00
252 Rafael Belliard	10.00	25.00
253 Steve Rosenberg	10.00	25.00
254 Jack Howell	10.00	25.00
255 Marvell Wynne	10.00	25.00
256 Tom Candiotti	10.00	25.00
257 Todd Benzinger	10.00	25.00
258 Don Robinson	10.00	25.00
259 Phil Bradley	10.00	25.00
260 Cecil Espy	10.00	25.00
261 Scott Bankhead	10.00	25.00
262 Rafael Belliard	10.00	25.00
262 Frank White	12.50	30.00
263 Andres Thomas	10.00	25.00
264 Glenn Braggs	10.00	25.00
265 David Cone	15.00	40.00
266 Bobby Thigpen	10.00	25.00
267 Nelson Liriano	10.00	25.00
268 Terry Steinbach	10.00	25.00
269 Kirby Puckett	40.00	100.00
270 Gregg Jefferies	10.00	25.00
271 Jeff Blauser	10.00	25.00
272 Cory Snyder	10.00	25.00
273 Roy Smith	10.00	25.00
274 Tom Foley	10.00	25.00
275 Mitch Williams	10.00	25.00
276 Paul Kilgus	10.00	25.00
277 Don Slaught	10.00	25.00
278 Von Hayes	10.00	25.00
279 Vince Coleman	10.00	25.00
280 Mike Boddicker	10.00	25.00
281 Ken Dayley	10.00	25.00
282 Mike Devereaux	10.00	25.00
BC1 Bo Jackson MVP	20.00	50.00
BC3 Dave Stewart MVP	12.50	30.00
BC6 Pedro Guerrero MVP	12.50	30.00
BC7 Tim Raines MVP	12.50	30.00
BC8 Kirby Puckett MVP	40.00	100.00
BC9 Alvin Davis MVP	10.00	25.00

1990 Donruss Best AL

The 1990 Donruss Best of the American League set consists of 144 standard-size cards. This was Donruss' latest version of what had been titled the previous two years as Baseball's Best. In 1990, the sets were split into National and American League and marketed separately. The front design was similar to the regular issue Donruss set except for the front borders being blue while the backs have complete major and minor league statistics as compared to the regular Donruss cards which only cover the past five major-league seasons. An early Sammy Sosa card is featured within this set.

COMP.FACT.SET (144)	15.00	40.00
1 Ken Griffey Jr.	.60	1.50
2 Bob Milacki	.05	.15
3 Mike Boddicker	.05	.15
4 Bert Blyleven	.07	.20
5 Carlton Fisk	.10	.30
6 Greg Swindell	.05	.15
7 Alan Trammell	.07	.20
8 Mark Davis	.05	.15
9 Chris Bosio	.05	.15
10 Gary Gaetti	.07	.20
11 Matt Nokes	.05	.15
12 Dennis Eckersley	.07	.20
13 Kevin Brown	.07	.20
14 Tom Henke	.05	.15
15 Mickey Tettleton	.05	.15
16 Jody Reed	.05	.15
17 Mark Langston	.05	.15
18 Melido Perez UER	.05	.15
Listed as an Expo		
rather than White Sox		
19 John Farrell	.05	.15
20 Tony Phillips	.05	.15
21 Bret Saberhagen	.07	.20
22 Robin Yount	.30	.75
23 Kirby Puckett	.20	.50
24 Steve Sax	.05	.15
25 Dave Stewart	.07	.20
26 Alvin Davis	.05	.15
27 Geno Petralli	.05	.15
28 Mookie Wilson	.07	.20
29 Jeff Ballard	.05	.15
30 Ellis Burks	.07	.20
31 Wally Joyner	.07	.20
32 Bobby Thigpen	.05	.15
33 Keith Hernandez	.07	.20
34 Jack Morris	.07	.20
35 George Brett	.50	1.25
36 Dan Plesac	.05	.15
37 Brian Harper	.05	.15
38 Don Mattingly	.50	1.25
39 Dave Henderson	.05	.15
40 Scott Bankhead UER	.05	.15
Asheboro misspelled		
as Ashboro on card		
41 Rafael Palmeiro	.10	.30
42 Jimmy Key	.07	.20
43 Gregg Olson	.05	.15
44 Tony Pena	.05	.15
45 Jack Howell	.05	.15
46 Eric King	.05	.15
47 Cory Snyder	.05	.15
48 Frank Tanana	.07	.20
49 Nolan Ryan	.60	1.50
50 Bob Boone	.07	.20
51 Dave Parker	.07	.20
52 Allan Anderson	.05	.15
53 Tim Leary	.05	.15
54 Mark McGwire	.60	1.50
55 Dave Valle	.05	.15
56 Fred McGriff	.10	.30
57 Cal Ripken	.60	1.50
58 Roger Clemens	.60	1.50
59 Lance Parrish	.07	.20
60 Robin Ventura	.20	.50
61 Doug Jones	.05	.15
62 Lloyd Moseby	.05	.15
63 Bo Jackson	.20	.50
64 Paul Molitor	.07	.20
65 Kent Hrbek	.07	.20
66 Mel Hall	.05	.15
67 Bob Welch	.07	.20
68 Erik Hanson	.05	.15
69 Harold Baines	.07	.20
70 Junior Felix	.05	.15
71 Craig Worthington	.05	.15
72 Jeff Reardon	.07	.20
73 Johnny Ray	.05	.15
74 Ozzie Guillen	.07	.20
75 Brook Jacoby	.05	.15
76 Chet Lemon	.05	.15
77 Mark Gubicza	.05	.15
78 B.J. Surhoff	.07	.20
79 Rick Aguilera	.07	.20
80 Pascual Perez	.05	.15
81 Jose Canseco	.10	.30
82 Mike Schooler	.05	.15
83 Jeff Huson	.05	.15
84 Kelly Gruber	.05	.15
85 Randy Milligan	.05	.15
86 Wade Boggs	.10	.30
87 Dave Winfield	.07	.20
88 Scott Fletcher	.05	.15
89 Tom Candiotti	.05	.15
90 Mike Heath	.05	.15
91 Kevin Seitzer	.05	.15
92 Ted Higuera	.05	.15
93 Kevin Tapani	.20	.50
94 Roberto Kelly	.05	.15
95 Walt Weiss	.05	.15
96 Checklist Card	.05	.15
97 Sandy Alomar Jr.	.07	.20
98 Pete O'Brien	.05	.15
99 Jeff Russell	.05	.15
100 John Olerud	.60	1.50
101 Pete Harnisch	.05	.15
102 Dwight Evans	.10	.30
103 Chuck Finley	.07	.20
104 Sammy Sosa	2.50	6.00
105 Mike Henneman	.05	.15
106 Kurt Stillwell	.05	.15
107 Greg Vaughn	.05	.15
108 Dan Gladden	.05	.15
109 Jesse Barfield	.05	.15
110 Willie Randolph	.07	.20
111 Randy Johnson	.30	.75
112 Julio Franco	.07	.20
113 Tony Fernandez	.05	.15
114 Ben McDonald	.05	.15
115 Mike Greenwell	.05	.15
116 Luis Polonia	.05	.15
117 Carney Lansford	.07	.20
118 Bud Black	.05	.15
119 Lou Whitaker	.07	.20
120 Jim Eisenreich	.05	.15
121 Gary Sheffield	.20	.50
122 Shane Mack	.05	.15
123 Alvaro Espinoza	.05	.15
124 Rickey Henderson	.20	.50
125 Jeffrey Leonard	.05	.15
126 Gary Pettis	.05	.15
127 Dave Stieb	.07	.20
128 Danny Tartabull	.05	.15
129 Joe Orsulak	.05	.15
130 Tom Brunansky	.05	.15
131 Dick Schofield	.05	.15
132 Candy Maldonado	.05	.15
133 Cecil Fielder	.07	.20
134 Terry Shumpert	.05	.15
135 Greg Gagne	.05	.15
136 Dave Righetti	.07	.20
137 Terry Steinbach	.05	.15
138 Harold Reynolds	.07	.20
139 George Bell	.05	.15
140 Carlos Quintana	.05	.15
141 Ivan Calderon	.05	.15
142 Greg Brock	.05	.15
143 Ruben Sierra	.07	.20
144 Checklist Card	.05	.15

1990 Donruss Best NL

The 1990 Donruss Best of the National League set consists of 144 standard-size cards. This was Donruss' latest version of what had been titled the previous two years as Baseball's Best. In 1990, the sets were split into National and American League and marketed separately. The front design was similar to the regular issue Donruss set except for the front borders being blue while the backs have complete major and minor league statistics as compared to the regular Donruss cards which only cover the past five major-league seasons. An early Larry Walker card is featured within this set.

COMP.FACT.SET (144)	3.00	8.00
1 Eric Davis	.07	.20
2 Tom Glavine	.10	.30
3 Mike Bielecki	.05	.15
4 Jim Deshaies	.05	.15
5 Mike Scioscia	.05	.15
6 Spike Owen	.05	.15
7 Dwight Gooden	.07	.20
8 Ricky Jordan	.05	.15
9 Doug Drabek	.05	.15
10 Bryn Smith	.05	.15
11 Tony Gwynn	.25	.60
12 John Burkett	.05	.15
13 Nick Esasky	.05	.15
14 Greg Maddux	.30	.75
15 Joe Oliver	.05	.15
16 Mike Scott	.05	.15
17 Tim Belcher	.05	.15
18 Kevin Gross	.05	.15
19 Howard Johnson	.05	.15
20 Darren Daulton	.07	.20
21 John Smiley	.05	.15
22 Ken Dayley	.05	.15
23 Craig Lefferts	.05	.15
24 Will Clark	.10	.30
25 Greg Olson	.05	.15
26 Ryne Sandberg	.25	.60
27 Tom Browning	.05	.15
28 Eric Anthony	.05	.15
29 Juan Samuel	.05	.15
30 Dennis Martinez	.07	.20
31 Kevin Elster	.05	.15
32 Tom Herr	.05	.15
33 Sid Bream	.05	.15
34 Terry Pendleton	.07	.20
35 Roberto Alomar	.10	.30
36 Kevin Bass	.05	.15
37 Jim Presley	.05	.15
38 Les Lancaster	.05	.15
39 Paul O'Neill	.10	.30
40 Dave Smith	.05	.15
41 Kirk Gibson	.07	.20
42 Tim Burke	.05	.15
43 David Cone	.07	.20
44 Ken Howell	.05	.15
45 Barry Bonds	.60	1.50
46 Joe Magrane	.05	.15
47 Andy Benes	.07	.20
48 Gary Carter	.07	.20
49 Pat Combs	.05	.15
50 John Smoltz	.20	.50
51 Mark Grace	.10	.30
52 Barry Larkin	.10	.30
53 Danny Darwin	.05	.15
54 Orel Hershiser	.07	.20
55 Tim Wallach	.05	.15
56 Dave Magadan	.05	.15
57 Roger McDowell	.05	.15
58 Bill Landrum	.05	.15
59 Jose DeLeon	.05	.15
60 Bip Roberts	.05	.15
61 Matt Williams	.07	.20
62 Dale Murphy	.10	.30
63 Dwight Smith	.05	.15
64 Chris Sabo	.05	.15
65 Glenn Davis	.05	.15
66 Jay Howell	.05	.15
67 Andres Galarraga	.07	.20
68 Frank Viola	.07	.20
69 John Kruk	.07	.20
70 Bobby Bonilla	.07	.20
71 Todd Zeile	.07	.20
72 Joe Carter	.07	.20
73 Robby Thompson	.05	.15
74 Jeff Blauser	.05	.15
75 Mitch Williams	.05	.15
76 Rob Dibble	.07	.20
77 Rafael Ramirez	.05	.15
78 Eddie Murray	.20	.50
79 Dave Martinez	.05	.15
80 Darryl Strawberry	.07	.20
81 Dickie Thon	.05	.15
82 Jose Lind	.05	.15
83 Ozzie Smith	.30	.75
84 Bruce Hurst	.05	.15
85 Kevin Mitchell	.05	.15
86 Lonnie Smith	.05	.15
87 Joe Girardi	.05	.15
88 Randy Myers	.07	.20
89 Craig Biggio	.20	.50
90 Fernando Valenzuela	.07	.20
91 Larry Walker	.75	2.00
92 John Franco	.07	.20
93 Dennis Cook	.05	.15
94 Bob Walk	.05	.15
95 Pedro Guerrero	.07	.20
96 Checklist Card	.05	.15
97 Andre Dawson	.07	.20
98 Ed Whitson	.05	.15
99 Steve Bedrosian	.05	.15
100 Oddibe McDowell	.05	.15
101 Todd Benzinger	.05	.15
102 Bill Doran	.05	.15
103 Alfredo Griffin	.05	.15
104 Tim Raines	.07	.20
105 Sid Fernandez	.05	.15
106 Charlie Hayes	.05	.15
107 Mike LaValliere	.05	.15
108 Jose Oquendo	.05	.15
109 Jack Clark	.07	.20
110 Scott Garrelts	.05	.15
111 Ron Gant	.07	.20
112 Shawon Dunston	.05	.15
113 Mariano Duncan	.05	.15
114 Eric Yelding	.05	.15
115 Hubie Brooks	.05	.15
116 Delino DeShields	.07	.20
117 Gregg Jefferies	.05	.15
118 Len Dykstra	.07	.20
119 Andy Van Slyke	.10	.30
120 Lee Smith	.07	.20
121 Benito Santiago	.07	.20
122 Jose Uribe	.05	.15
123 Jeff Treadway	.05	.15
124 Jerome Walton	.05	.15
125 Billy Hatcher	.05	.15
126 Ken Caminiti	.07	.20
127 Kal Daniels	.05	.15
128 Marquis Grissom	.20	.50
129 Kevin McReynolds	.05	.15
130 Wally Backman	.05	.15
131 Willie McGee	.07	.20
132 Terry Kennedy	.05	.15
133 Garry Templeton	.05	.15
134 Lloyd McClendon	.05	.15
135 Daryl Boston	.05	.15
136 Jay Bell	.07	.20
137 Mike Pagliarulo	.05	.15
138 Vince Coleman	.05	.15
139 Brett Butler	.07	.20
140 Von Hayes	.05	.15
141 Ramon Martinez	.05	.15
142 Jack Armstrong	.05	.15
143 Franklin Stubbs	.05	.15
144 Checklist Card	.05	.15

1990 Donruss Learning Series

The 1990 Donruss Learning Series consists of 55 standard-size cards that served as part of an educational packet for elementary and middle school students. The cards were issued in two formats. Grades Three and Four received the cards, a historical timeline that relates events in baseball to major historical events, additional Donruss cards from wax packs, and a teacher's guide that focused on several academic subjects. Grades 5 through 8 received the cards, a teacher's guide designed for older students, and a 14-minute video shot at Chicago's Wrigley Field. The fronts feature color head shots of the players and bright red borders. The horizontally oriented backs are amber and present biography, statistics, and career highlights.

COMPLETE SET (55)	15.00	40.00
1 George Brett DK	1.00	2.50
2 Kevin Mitchell	.02	.10
3 Andy Van Slyke	.07	.20
4 Benito Santiago	.07	.20
5 Gary Carter	.40	1.00
6 Jose Canseco	.50	1.25
7 Rickey Henderson	.50	1.25
8 Ken Griffey Jr.	2.00	5.00
9 Ozzie Smith	1.00	2.50
10 Dwight Gooden	.07	.20
11 Ryne Sandberg DK	1.00	2.50
12 Don Mattingly	1.00	2.50
13 Ozzie Guillen	.07	.20
14 Dave Righetti	.02	.10
15 Rick Dempsey	.02	.10
16 Tom Herr	.02	.10
17 Julio Franco	.07	.20
18 Von Hayes	.02	.10
19 Cal Ripken	3.00	8.00
20 Alan Trammell	.30	.75
21 Wade Boggs	.40	1.00
22 Glenn Davis	.02	.10
23 Will Clark	.60	1.50
24 Nolan Ryan	3.00	8.00
25 George Bell	.02	.10
26 Cecil Fielder	.20	.50
27 Gregg Olson	.02	.10
28 Tim Wallach	.02	.10
29 Ron Darling	.02	.10
30 Kelly Gruber	.02	.10
31 Shawn Boskie	.02	.10
32 Mike Greenwell	.02	.10
33 Dave Parker	.07	.20
34 Joe Magrane	.02	.10
35 Dave Stewart	.07	.20
36 Kent Hrbek	.07	.20
37 Robin Yount	.40	1.00
38 Bo Jackson	.20	.50
39 Fernando Valenzuela	.07	.20
40 Sandy Alomar Jr.	.07	.20
41 Lance Parrish	.02	.10
42 Candy Maldonado	.02	.10
43 Mike LaValliere	.02	.10
44 Jim Abbott	.07	.20
45 Edgar Martinez	.10	.30
46 Kirby Puckett	.40	1.00
47 Delino DeShields	.20	.50
48 Tony Gwynn	1.00	2.50
49 Carlton Fisk	.40	1.00
50 Mike Scott	.02	.10
51 Barry Larkin	.30	.75
52 Andre Dawson	.20	.50
53 Tom Glavine	.30	.75
54 Tom Browning	.02	.10
55 Checklist Card	.02	.10

1990 Donruss Super DK's

This 26 player card set was available through a mail-in offer detailed on the wax packs. The set was sent in return for 10.00 and three wrappers plus 2.00 postage and handling. The set features the popular Diamond King subseries in large (approximately 4 7/8" by 6 13/16") form. Dick Perez of Perez-Steele Galleries did another outstanding job on the artwork. The cards are essentially a large version of the Donruss regular issue Diamond Kings. There is also a jumbo sized Ryan King of Kings card. Although not listed with the regular set; it is heavily sought after by Ryan collectors.

COMPLETE SET (26)	12.50	30.00
1 Bo Jackson	.40	1.00
2 Steve Sax	.08	.25
3 Ruben Sierra	.20	.50
4 Ken Griffey Jr.	5.00	12.00
5 Mickey Tettleton	.20	.50
6 Dave Stewart	.20	.50
7 Jim Deshaies	.08	.25
8 John Smoltz	.30	.75
9 Mike Bielecki	.08	.25
10 Brian Downing	.08	.25
11 Kevin Mitchell	.08	.25
12 Kelly Gruber	.08	.25
13 Joe Magrane	.08	.25
14 John Franco	.20	.50
15 Ozzie Guillen	.08	.25
16 Lou Whitaker	.20	.50
17 John Smiley	.08	.25
18 Howard Johnson	.08	.25
19 Willie Randolph	.20	.50
20 Chris Bosio	.08	.25
21 Tommy Herr	.08	.25
22 Dan Gladden	.08	.25
23 Ellis Burks	.30	.75
24 Pete O'Brien	.08	.25
25 Bryn Smith	.08	.25
26 Ed Whitson	.08	.25
NNO Nolan Ryan	6.00	15.00
King of Kings		

1991 Donruss Previews

COMPLETE SET (12)	125.00	250.00
1 Dave Justice	5.00	12.00
2 Doug Drabek	2.00	5.00
3 Scott Chiamparino	2.00	5.00
4 Ken Griffey Jr.	20.00	50.00
5 Bob Welch	2.00	5.00
6 Tino Martinez	5.00	12.00
7 Nolan Ryan	15.00	40.00
8 Dwight Gooden	3.00	8.00
9 Ryne Sandberg	20.00	50.00
10 Barry Bonds	15.00	40.00
11 Jose Canseco	8.00	20.00
12 Eddie Murray	8.00	20.00

1991 Donruss

The 1991 Donruss set was issued in two series of 386 and 384 for a total of 770 standard-size cards. This set marked the first time Donruss issued cards in multiple series. The second series was issued approximately three months after the first series was issued. Cards were issued in wax packs and factory sets. As a separate promotion, wax packs were also given away with six and 12-packs of Coke and Diet Coke. First series cards feature blue borders and second series green borders with some stripes and the players name in white against a red background. Subsets include Diamond Kings (1-27), Rated Rookies (28-47/413-432), AL All-Stars (48-56), MVP's (387-412) and NL All-Stars (433-441). There were also special cards to honor the award winners and the heroes of the World Series. On cards 60, 70, 127, 182, 239, 294, 355, 368, and 377, the border stripes are red and yellow. There are no notable Rookie Cards in this set.

COMPLETE SET (770)	3.00	8.00
COMP.FACT.w/LEAF PREV	4.00	10.00
COMP.FACT.w/STUDIO PREV	4.00	10.00
SUBSET CARDS HALF VALUE OF BASE CARDS		
COMP.STARGELL PUZZLE	.40	1.00
1 Dave Stieb DK	.01	.05
2 Craig Biggio DK	.02	.10
3 Cecil Fielder DK	.01	.05
4 Barry Bonds DK	.20	.50
5 Barry Larkin DK	.02	.10
6 Dave Parker DK	.01	.05
7 Len Dykstra DK	.01	.05
8 Bobby Thigpen DK	.01	.05
9 Roger Clemens DK	.15	.40
10 Ron Gant DK UER	.02	.10
11 Delino DeShields DK	.01	.05
12 Roberto Alomar DK UER	.02	.10
13 Sandy Alomar Jr. DK	.01	.05
14 Ryne Sandberg DK UER	.08	.25
15 Ramon Martinez DK	.01	.05
16 Edgar Martinez DK	.05	.15
17 Dave Magadan DK	.01	.05
18 Matt Williams DK	.01	.05
19 Rafael Palmeiro DK UER	.02	.10
20 Bob Welch DK	.01	.05
21 Dave Righetti DK	.01	.05
22 Brian Harper DK	.01	.05
23 Gregg Olson DK	.01	.05
24 Kurt Stillwell DK	.01	.05
25 Pedro Guerrero DK UER	.01	.05
26 Chuck Finley DK UER	.02	.10
27 DK Checklist 1-27	.01	.05
28 Tino Martinez RR	.08	.25
29 Mark Lewis RR	.01	.05
30 Bernard Gilkey RR	.01	.05
31 Hensley Meulens RR	.01	.05
32 Derek Bell RR	.02	.10
33 Jose Offerman RR	.01	.05
34 Terry Bross RR	.01	.05
35 Leo Gomez RR	.01	.05
36 Derrick May RR	.01	.05
37 Kevin Morton RR RC	.01	.05
38 Moises Alou RR	.02	.10
39 Julio Valera RR	.01	.05
40 Milt Cuyler RR	.01	.05
41 Phil Plantier RR RC	.08	.25
42 Scott Chiamparino RR	.01	.05
43 Ray Lankford RR	.02	.10
44 Mickey Morandini RR	.01	.05
45 Dave Hansen RR	.01	.05
46 Kevin Belcher RR RC	.01	.05
47 Darrin Fletcher RR	.01	.05
48 Steve Sax AS	.01	.05
49 Ken Griffey Jr. AS	.10	.30
50A Jose Canseco AS ERR	.02	.10
50B Jose Canseco AS COR	.05	.15

51 Sandy Alomar Jr. AS .01 .05
52 Cal Ripken AS .15 .40
53 Rickey Henderson AS .05 .15
54 Bob Welch AS .01 .05
55 Wade Boggs AS .02 .10
56 Mark McGwire AS .15 .40
57A Jack McDowell ERR .08 .25
57B Jack McDowell COR .20 .50
58 Jose Lind .01 .05
59 Alex Fernandez .01 .05
60 Pat Combs .01 .05
61 Mike Walker .01 .05
62 Juan Samuel .01 .05
63 Mike Blowers UER .01 .05
64 Mark Guthrie .01 .05
65 Mark Salas .01 .05
66 Tim Jones .01 .05
67 Tim Leary .01 .05
68 Andres Galarraga .02 .10
69 Bob Milacki .01 .05
70 Tim Belcher .01 .05
71 Todd Zeile .01 .05
72 Jerome Walton .01 .05
73 Kevin Seitzer .01 .05
74 Jerald Clark .01 .05
75 John Smoltz UER .05 .15
76 Mike Henneman .01 .05
77 Ken Griffey Jr. .25 .60
78 Jim Abbott .05 .15
79 Gregg Jefferies .01 .05
80 Kevin Reimer .01 .05
81 Roger Clemens .30 .75
82 Mike Fitzgerald .01 .05
83 Bruce Hurst UER .01 .05
84 Eric Davis .02 .10
85 Paul Molitor .02 .10
86 Will Clark .05 .15
87 Mike Bielecki .01 .05
88 Bret Saberhagen .02 .10
89 Nolan Ryan .40 1.00
90 Bobby Thigpen .01 .05
91 Dickie Thon .01 .05
92 Duane Ward .01 .05
93 Luis Polonia .01 .05
94 Terry Kennedy .01 .05
95 Kent Hrbek .02 .10
96 Danny Jackson .01 .05
97 Sid Fernandez .01 .05
98 Jimmy Key .02 .10
99 Franklin Stubbs .01 .05
100 Checklist 28-103 .01 .05
101 R.J. Reynolds .01 .05
102 Dave Stewart .02 .10
103 Dan Pasqua .01 .05
104 Dan Plesac .01 .05
105 Mark McGwire .30 .75
106 John Farrell .01 .05
107 Don Mattingly .25 .60
108 Carlton Fisk .05 .15
109 Ken Oberkfell .01 .05
110 Darrel Akerfelds .01 .05
111 Gregg Olson .01 .05
112 Mike Scioscia .01 .05
113 Bryn Smith .01 .05
114 Bob Geren .01 .05
115 Tom Candiotti .01 .05
116 Kevin Tapani .01 .05
117 Jeff Treadway .01 .05
118 Alan Trammell .02 .10
119 Pete O'Brien UER .01 .05
120 Joel Skinner .01 .05
121 Mike LaValliere .01 .05
122 Dwight Evans .05 .15
123 Jody Reed .01 .05
124 Lee Guetterman .01 .05
125 Tim Burke .01 .05
126 Dave Johnson .01 .05
127 Fernando Valenzuela UER .02 .10
128 Jose DeLeon .01 .05
129 Andre Dawson .02 .10
130 Gerald Perry .01 .05
131 Greg W. Harris .01 .05
132 Tom Glavine .05 .15
133 Lance McCullers .01 .05
134 Randy Johnson .10 .30
135 Lance Parrish UER .02 .10
136 Mackey Sasser .01 .05
137 Geno Petralli .01 .05
138 Dennis Lamp .01 .05
139 Dennis Martinez .02 .10
140 Mike Pagliarulo .01 .05
141 Hal Morris .01 .05
142 Dave Parker .02 .10
143 Brett Butler .02 .10
144 Paul Assenmacher .01 .05
145 Mark Gubicza .01 .05
146 Charlie Hough .02 .10
147 Sammy Sosa .08 .25
148 Randy Ready .01 .05
149 Kelly Gruber .01 .05
150 Devon White .02 .10
151 Gary Carter .02 .10
152 Gene Larkin .01 .05
153 Chris Sabo .01 .05
154 David Cone .02 .10
155 Todd Stottlemyre .01 .05
156 Glenn Wilson .01 .05
157 Bob Walk .01 .05
158 Mike Gallego .01 .05
159 Greg Hibbard .01 .05
160 Chris Bosio .01 .05
161 Mike Moore .01 .05
162 Jerry Browne UER .01 .05
163 Steve Sax UER .01 .05
164 Melido Perez .01 .05
165 Danny Darwin .01 .05
166 Roger McDowell .01 .05
167 Bill Ripken .01 .05
168 Mike Sharperson .01 .05
169 Lee Smith .02 .10
170 Matt Nokes .01 .05
171 Jesse Orosco .01 .05
172 Rick Aguilera .02 .10
173 Jim Presley .01 .05
174 Lou Whitaker .02 .10
175 Harold Reynolds .02 .10
176 Brook Jacoby .01 .05
177 Wally Backman .01 .05
178 Wade Boggs .05 .15
179 Chuck Cary UER .01 .05
180 Tom Foley .01 .05
181 Pete Harnisch .01 .05
182 Mike Morgan .01 .05
183 Bob Tewksbury .01 .05
184 Joe Girardi .01 .05
185 Storm Davis .01 .05
186 Ed Whitson .01 .05
187 Steve Avery UER .01 .05
188 Lloyd Moseby .01 .05
189 Scott Bankhead .01 .05
190 Mark Langston .01 .05
191 Kevin McReynolds .01 .05
192 Julio Franco .02 .10
193 John Dopson .01 .05
194 Dennis Boyd .01 .05
195 Bip Roberts .01 .05
196 Billy Hatcher .01 .05
197 Edgar Diaz .01 .05
198 Greg Litton .01 .05
199 Mark Grace .05 .15
200 Checklist 104-179 .01 .05
201 George Brett .25 .60
202 Jeff Russell .01 .05
203 Ivan Calderon .01 .05
204 Ken Howell .01 .05
205 Tom Henke .01 .05
206 Bryan Harvey .01 .05
207 Steve Bedrosian .01 .05
208 Al Newman .01 .05
209 Randy Myers .01 .05
210 Daryl Boston .01 .05
211 Manny Lee .01 .05
212 Dave Smith .01 .05
213 Don Slaught .01 .05
214 Walt Weiss .01 .05
215 Donn Pall .01 .05
216 Jaime Navarro .01 .05
217 Willie Randolph .02 .10
218 Rudy Seanez .01 .05
219 Jim Leyritz .01 .05
220 Ron Karkovice .01 .05
221 Ken Caminiti .02 .10
222 Von Hayes .01 .05
223 Cal Ripken .30 .75
224 Lenny Harris .01 .05
225 Milt Thompson .01 .05
226 Alvaro Espinoza .01 .05
227 Chris James .01 .05
228 Dan Gladden .01 .05
229 Jeff Blauser .01 .05
230 Mike Heath .01 .05
231 Omar Vizquel .05 .15
232 Doug Jones .01 .05
233 Jeff King .01 .05
234 Luis Rivera .01 .05
235 Ellis Burks .02 .10
236 Greg Cadaret .01 .05
237 Dave Martinez .01 .05
238 Mark Williamson .01 .05
239 Stan Javier .01 .05
240 Ozzie Smith .15 .40
241 Shawn Boskie .01 .05
242 Tom Gordon .01 .05
243 Tony Gwynn .10 .30
244 Tommy Gregg .01 .05
245 Jeff M. Robinson .01 .05
246 Keith Comstock .01 .05
247 Jack Howell .01 .05
248 Keith Miller .01 .05
249 Bobby Witt .01 .05
250 Rob Murphy UER .01 .05
251 Spike Owen .01 .05
252 Garry Templeton .01 .05
253 Glenn Braggs .01 .05
254 Ron Robinson .01 .05
255 Kevin Mitchell .01 .05
256 Les Lancaster .01 .05
257 Mel Stottlemyre Jr. .01 .05
258 Kenny Rogers UER .02 .10
259 Lance Johnson .01 .05
260 John Kruk .02 .10
261 Fred McGriff .05 .15
262 Dick Schofield .01 .05
263 Trevor Wilson .01 .05
264 David West .01 .05
265 Scott Scudder .01 .05
266 Dwight Gooden .02 .10
267 Willie Blair .01 .05
268 Mark Portugal .01 .05
269 Doug Drabek .01 .05
270 Dennis Eckersley .02 .10
271 Eric King .01 .05
272 Robin Yount .15 .40
273 Carney Lansford .02 .10
274 Carlos Baerga .01 .05
275 Dave Righetti .02 .10
276 Scott Fletcher .01 .05
277 Eric Yelding .01 .05
278 Charlie Hayes .01 .05
279 Jeff Ballard .01 .05
280 Orel Hershiser .02 .10
281 Jose Oquendo .01 .05
282 Mike Witt .01 .05
283 Mitch Webster .01 .05
284 Greg Gagne .01 .05
285 Greg Olson .01 .05
286 Tony Phillips UER .01 .05
287 Scott Bradley .01 .05
288 Cory Snyder .01 .05
289 Jay Bell UER .02 .10
290 Kevin Romine .01 .05
291 Jeff D. Robinson .01 .05
292 Steve Frey UER .01 .05
293 Craig Worthington .01 .05
294 Tim Crews .01 .05
295 Joe Magrane .01 .05
296 Hector Villanueva .01 .05
297 Terry Shumpert .01 .05
298 Joe Carter .02 .10
299 Kent Mercker UER .01 .05
300 Checklist 180-255 .01 .05
301 Chet Lemon .01 .05
302 Mike Schooler .01 .05
303 Dante Bichette .02 .10
304 Kevin Elster .01 .05
305 Jeff Huson .01 .05
306 Greg A. Harris .01 .05
307 Marquis Grissom UER .02 .10
308 Calvin Schiraldi .01 .05
309 Mariano Duncan .01 .05
310 Bill Spiers .01 .05
311 Scott Garrelts .01 .05
312 Mitch Williams .01 .05
313 Mike Macfarlane .01 .05
314 Kevin Brown .02 .10
315 Robin Ventura .02 .10
316 Darren Daulton .02 .10
317 Pat Borders .01 .05
318 Mark Eichhorn .01 .05
319 Jeff Brantley .01 .05
320 Shane Mack .01 .05
321 Rob Dibble .02 .10
322 John Franco .02 .10
323 Junior Felix .01 .05
324 Casey Candaele .01 .05
325 Bobby Bonilla .02 .10
326 Dave Henderson .01 .05
327 Wayne Edwards .01 .05
328 Mark Knudson .01 .05
329 Terry Steinbach .01 .05
330 Colby Ward UER RC .01 .05
331 Oscar Azocar .01 .05
332 Scott Radinsky .01 .05
333 Eric Anthony .01 .05
334 Steve Lake .01 .05
335 Bob Melvin .01 .05
336 Kal Daniels .01 .05
337 Tom Pagnozzi .01 .05
338 Alan Mills .01 .05
339 Steve Olin .01 .05
340 Juan Berenguer .01 .05
341 Francisco Cabrera .01 .05
342 Dave Bergman .01 .05
343 Henry Cotto .01 .05
344 Sergio Valdez .01 .05
345 Bob Patterson .01 .05
346 John Marzano .01 .05
347 Dana Kiecker .01 .05
348 Dion James .01 .05
349 Hubie Brooks .01 .05
350 Bill Landrum .01 .05
351 Bill Sampen .01 .05
352 Greg Briley .01 .05
353 Paul Gibson .01 .05
354 Dave Eiland .01 .05
355 Steve Finley .02 .10
356 Bob Boone .02 .10
357 Steve Buechele .01 .05
358 Chris Hoiles FDC .01 .05
359 Larry Walker .08 .25
360 Frank DiPino .01 .05
361 Mark Grant .01 .05
362 Dave Magadan .01 .05
363 Robby Thompson .01 .05
364 Lonnie Smith .01 .05
365 Steve Farr .01 .05
366 Dave Valle .01 .05
367 Tim Naehring .01 .05
368 Jim Acker .01 .05
369 Jeff Reardon UER .02 .10
370 Tim Teufel .01 .05
371 Juan Gonzalez .08 .25
372 Luis Salazar .01 .05
373 Rick Honeycutt .01 .05
374 Greg Maddux .15 .40
375 Jose Uribe UER .01 .05
376 Donnie Hill .01 .05
377 Don Carman .01 .05
378 Craig Grebeck .01 .05
379 Willie Fraser .01 .05
380 Glenallen Hill .01 .05
381 Joe Oliver .01 .05
382 Randy Bush .01 .05
383 Alex Cole .01 .05
384 Norm Charlton .01 .05
385 Gene Nelson .01 .05
386 Checklist 256-331 .01 .05
387 Rickey Henderson MVP .05 .15
388 Lance Parrish MVP .01 .05
389 Fred McGriff MVP .02 .10
390 Dave Parker MVP .01 .05
391 Candy Maldonado MVP .01 .05
392 Ken Griffey Jr. MVP .10 .30
393 Gregg Olson MVP .01 .05
394 Rafael Palmeiro MVP .02 .10
395 Roger Clemens MVP .15 .40
396 George Brett MVP .08 .25
397 Cecil Fielder MVP .01 .05
398 Brian Harper MVP UER .01 .05
399 Bobby Thigpen MVP .01 .05
400 Roberto Kelly MVP UER .01 .05
401 Danny Darwin MVP .01 .05
402 Dave Justice MVP .01 .05
403 Lee Smith MVP .01 .05
404 Ryne Sandberg MVP .08 .25
405 Eddie Murray MVP .05 .15
406 Tim Wallach MVP .01 .05
407 Kevin Mitchell MVP .01 .05
408 D. Strawberry MVP .01 .05
409 Joe Carter MVP .01 .05
410 Len Dykstra MVP .01 .05
411 Doug Drabek MVP .01 .05
412 Chris Sabo MVP .01 .05
413 Paul Marak RR RC .01 .05
414 Tim McIntosh RR .01 .05
415 Brian Barnes RR RC .02 .10
416 Eric Gunderson RR .01 .05
417 Mike Gardiner RR RC .01 .05
418 Steve Carter RR .01 .05
419 Gerald Alexander RR RC .01 .05
420 Rich Garces RR RC .02 .10
421 Chuck Knoblauch RR .02 .10
422 Scott Aldred RR .01 .05
423 Wes Chamberlain RR RC .08 .25
424 Lance Dickson RR RC .02 .10
425 Greg Colbrunn RR RC .08 .25
426 Rich DeLucia RR UER RC .01 .05
427 Jeff Conine RR RC .15 .40
428 Steve Decker RR RC .01 .05
429 Turner Ward RR RC .08 .25
430 Mo Vaughn RR .02 .10
431 Steve Chitren RR RC .01 .05
432 Mike Benjamin RR .01 .05
433 Ryne Sandberg AS .08 .25
434 Len Dykstra AS .01 .05
435 Andre Dawson AS .01 .05
436A Mike Scioscia AS White .01 .05
436B Mike Scioscia AS Yellow .01 .05
437 Ozzie Smith AS .08 .25
438 Kevin Mitchell AS .01 .05
439 Jack Armstrong AS .01 .05
440 Chris Sabo AS .01 .05
441 Will Clark AS .02 .10
442 Mel Hall .01 .05
443 Mark Gardner .01 .05
444 Mike Devereaux .01 .05
445 Kirk Gibson .02 .10
446 Terry Pendleton .02 .10
447 Mike Harkey .01 .05
448 Jim Eisenreich .01 .05
449 Benito Santiago .02 .10
450 Oddibe McDowell .01 .05
451 Cecil Fielder .02 .10
452 Ken Griffey Sr. .02 .10
453 Bert Blyleven .02 .10
454 Howard Johnson .01 .05
455 Monty Fariss UER .01 .05
456 Tony Pena .01 .05
457 Tim Raines .02 .10
458 Dennis Rasmussen .01 .05
459 Luis Quinones .01 .05
460 B.J. Surhoff .02 .10
461 Ernest Riles .01 .05
462 Rick Sutcliffe .02 .10
463 Danny Tartabull .01 .05
464 Pete Incaviglia .01 .05
465 Carlos Martinez .01 .05
466 Ricky Jordan .01 .05
467 John Cerutti .01 .05
468 Dave Winfield .02 .10
469 Francisco Oliveras .01 .05
470 Roy Smith .01 .05
471 Barry Larkin .05 .15
472 Ron Darling .01 .05
473 David Wells .02 .10
474 Glenn Davis .01 .05
475 Neal Heaton .01 .05
476 Ron Hassey .01 .05
477 Frank Thomas .08 .25
478 Greg Vaughn .01 .05
479 Todd Burns .01 .05
480 Candy Maldonado .01 .05
481 Dave LaPoint .01 .05
482 Alvin Davis .01 .05
483 Mike Scott .01 .05
484 Dale Murphy .05 .15
485 Ben McDonald .01 .05
486 Jay Howell .01 .05
487 Vince Coleman .01 .05
488 Alfredo Griffin .01 .05
489 Sandy Alomar Jr. .01 .05
490 Kirby Puckett .08 .25
491 Andres Thomas .01 .05
492 Jack Morris .02 .10
493 Matt Young .01 .05
494 Greg Myers .01 .05
495 Barry Bonds .40 1.00
496 Scott Cooper UER .01 .05
497 Dan Schatzeder .01 .05
498 Jesse Barfield .01 .05
499 Jerry Goff .01 .05
500 Checklist 332-408 .01 .05
501 Anthony Telford RC .01 .05
502 Eddie Murray .08 .25
503 Omar Olivares RC .08 .25
504 Ryne Sandberg .15 .40
505 Jeff Montgomery .01 .05
506 Mark Parent .01 .05
507 Ron Gant .02 .10
508 Frank Tanana .01 .05
509 Jay Buhner .02 .10
510 Max Venable .01 .05
511 Wally Whitehurst .01 .05
512 Gary Pettis .01 .05
513 Tom Brunansky .01 .05
514 Tim Wallach .01 .05
515 Craig Lefferts .01 .05
516 Tim Layana .01 .05
517 Darryl Hamilton .01 .05
518 Rick Reuschel .01 .05
519 Steve Wilson .01 .05
520 Kurt Stillwell .01 .05
521 Rafael Palmeiro .05 .15
522 Ken Patterson .01 .05
523 Len Dykstra .02 .10
524 Tony Fernandez .01 .05
525 Kent Anderson .01 .05
526 Mark Leonard RC .01 .05
527 Allan Anderson .01 .05
528 Tom Browning .01 .05
529 Frank Viola .02 .10
530 John Olerud .02 .10
531 Juan Agosto .01 .05
532 Zane Smith .01 .05
533 Scott Sanderson .01 .05
534 Barry Jones .01 .05
535 Mike Felder .01 .05
536 Jose Canseco .05 .15
537 Felix Fermin .01 .05
538 Roberto Kelly .01 .05
539 Brian Holman .01 .05
540 Mark Davidson .01 .05
541 Terry Mulholland .01 .05
542 Randy Milligan .01 .05
543 Jose Gonzalez .01 .05
544 Craig Wilson RC .01 .05
545 Mike Hartley .01 .05
546 Greg Swindell .01 .05
547 Gary Gaetti .02 .10
548 Dave Justice .02 .10
549 Steve Searcy .01 .05
550 Erik Hanson .01 .05
551 Dave Stieb .01 .05
552 Andy Van Slyke .05 .15
553 Mike Greenwell .01 .05
554 Kevin Maas .01 .05
555 Delino DeShields .02 .10
556 Curt Schilling .08 .25
557 Ramon Martinez .01 .05
558 Pedro Guerrero .02 .10
559 Dwight Smith .01 .05
560 Mark Davis .01 .05
561 Shawn Abner .01 .05
562 Charlie Leibrandt .01 .05
563 John Shelby .01 .05
564 Bill Swift .01 .05
565 Mike Fetters .01 .05
566 Alejandro Pena .01 .05
567 Ruben Sierra .02 .10
568 Carlos Quintana .01 .05
569 Kevin Gross .01 .05
570 Derek Lilliquist .01 .05
571 Jack Armstrong .01 .05
572 Greg Brock .01 .05
573 Mike Kingery .01 .05
574 Greg Smith .01 .05
575 Brian McRae RC .08 .25
576 Jack Daugherty .01 .05
577 Ozzie Guillen .02 .10
578 Joe Boever .01 .05
579 Luis Sojo .01 .05
580 Chili Davis .02 .10
581 Don Robinson .01 .05
582 Brian Harper .01 .05
583 Paul O'Neill .05 .15
584 Bob Ojeda .01 .05
585 Mookie Wilson .02 .10
586 Rafael Ramirez .01 .05
587 Gary Redus .01 .05
588 Jamie Quirk .01 .05
589 Shawn Hillegas .01 .05
590 Tom Edens RC .01 .05
591 Joe Klink .01 .05
592 Charles Nagy .01 .05
593 Eric Plunk .01 .05
594 Tracy Jones .01 .05
595 Craig Biggio .05 .15
596 Jose DeJesus .01 .05
597 Mickey Tettleton .01 .05
598 Chris Gwynn .01 .05
599 Rex Hudler .01 .05
600 Checklist 409-506 .01 .05
601 Jim Gott .01 .05
602 Jeff Manto .01 .05
603 Nelson Liriano .01 .05
604 Mark Lemke .01 .05
605 Clay Parker .01 .05
606 Edgar Martinez .05 .15
607 Mark Whiten .01 .05
608 Ted Power .01 .05
609 Tom Bolton .01 .05
610 Tom Herr .01 .05
611 Andy Hawkins UER .01 .05
612 Scott Ruskin .01 .05
613 Ron Kittle .01 .05
614 John Wetteland .02 .10
615 Mike Perez RC .02 .10
616 Dave Clark .01 .05
617 Brent Mayne .01 .05
618 Jack Clark .02 .10
619 Marvin Freeman .01 .05
620 Edwin Nunez .01 .05
621 Russ Swan .01 .05
622 Johnny Ray .01 .05
623 Charlie O'Brien .01 .05
624 Joe Bitker RC .01 .05
625 Mike Marshall .01 .05
626 Otis Nixon .01 .05
627 Andy Benes .01 .05
628 Ron Oester .01 .05
629 Ted Higuera .01 .05
630 Kevin Bass .01 .05
631 Damon Berryhill .01 .05
632 Bo Jackson .08 .25
633 Brad Arnsberg .01 .05
634 Jerry Willard .01 .05
635 Tommy Greene .01 .05
636 Bob MacDonald RC .01 .05
637 Kirk McCaskill .01 .05
638 John Burkett .01 .05
639 Paul Abbott RC .01 .05
640 Todd Benzinger .01 .05
641 Todd Hundley .01 .05
642 George Bell .01 .05
643 Javier Ortiz .01 .05
644 Sid Bream .01 .05
645 Bob Welch .01 .05
646 Phil Bradley .01 .05
647 Bill Krueger .01 .05
648 Rickey Henderson .08 .25
649 Kevin Wickander .01 .05
650 Steve Balboni .01 .05
651 Gene Harris .01 .05
652 Jim Deshaies .01 .05
653 Jason Grimsley .01 .05
654 Joe Orsulak .01 .05
655 Jim Poole .01 .05
656 Felix Jose .01 .05
657 Denis Cook .01 .05
658 Tom Brookens .01 .05
659 Junior Ortiz .01 .05
660 Jeff Parrett .01 .05
661 Jerry Don Gleaton .01 .05
662 Brent Knackert .01 .05
663 Rance Mulliniks .01 .05
664 John Smiley .01 .05
665 Larry Andersen .01 .05
666 Willie McGee .02 .10
667 Chris Nabholz .01 .05
668 Brady Anderson .02 .10
669 Darren Holmes UER RC .08 .25
670 Ken Hill .01 .05
671 Gary Varsho .01 .05
672 Bill Pecota .01 .05
673 Fred Lynn .01 .05
674 Kevin D. Brown .01 .05
675 Dan Petry .01 .05
676 Mike Jackson .01 .05
677 Wally Joyner .02 .10
678 Danny Jackson .01 .05
679 Bill Haselman RC .01 .05
680 Mike Boddicker .01 .05
681 Mel Rojas .01 .05
682 Roberto Alomar .05 .15
683 Dave Justice ROY .01 .05
684 Chuck Crim .01 .05
685 Matt Williams .02 .10
686 Shawon Dunston .01 .05
687 Jeff Schulz RC .01 .05
688 John Barfield .01 .05
689 Gerald Young .01 .05
690 Luis Gonzalez RC .20 .50
691 Frank Wills .01 .05
692 Chuck Finley .02 .10
693 Sandy Alomar Jr. ROY .01 .05
694 Tim Drummond .01 .05
695 Herm Winningham .01 .05
696 Darryl Strawberry .02 .10
697 Al Leiter .02 .10
698 Karl Rhodes .01 .05
699 Stan Belinda .01 .05
700 Checklist 507-604 .01 .05
701 Lance Blankenship .01 .05
702 Willie Stargell PUZ .05 .15
703 Jim Gantner .01 .05
704 Reggie Harris .01 .05
705 Rob Ducey .01 .05
706 Tim Hulett .01 .05
707 Atlee Hammaker .01 .05
708 Xavier Hernandez .01 .05
709 Chuck McElroy .01 .05
710 John Mitchell .01 .05
711 Carlos Hernandez .01 .05
712 Geronimo Pena .01 .05
713 Jim Neidlinger RC .01 .05
714 John Orton .01 .05
715 Terry Leach .01 .05
716 Mike Stanton .01 .05
717 Walt Terrell .01 .05
718 Luis Aquino .01 .05
719 Bud Black UER .01 .05
720 Bob Kipper .01 .05
721 Jeff Gray RC .01 .05
722 Jose Rijo .01 .05
723 Curt Young .01 .05
724 Jose Vizcaino .01 .05
725 Randy Tomlin RC .02 .10
726 Junior Noboa .01 .05
727 Bob Welch CY .01
728 Gary Ward .01
729 Rob Deer UER .01
730 David Segui .01
731 Mark Carreon .01
732 Vicente Palacios .01
733 Sam Horn .01
734 Howard Farmer .01
735 Ken Dayley UER .01
736 Kelly Mann .01
737 Joe Grahe RC .02
738 Kelly Downs .01
739 Jimmy Kremers .01
740 Kevin Appier .02
741 Jeff Reed .01
742 Jose Rijo WS .01
743 Dave Rohde .01
744 L.Dykstra/D.Murphy UER .05
745 Paul Sorrento .01
746 Thomas Howard .01
747 Matt Stark RC .01
748 Harold Baines .02
749 Doug Dascenzo .01
750 Doug Drabek CY .01
751 Gary Sheffield .02
752 Terry Lee RC .01
753 Jim Vatcher RC .01
754 Lee Stevens .01
755 Randy Veres .01
756 Bill Doran .01
757 Gary Wayne .01
758 Pedro Munoz RC .02
759 Chris Hammond FDC .01
760 Checklist 605-702 .01
761 Rickey Henderson MVP .05
762 Barry Bonds MVP .20
763 Billy Hatcher WS UER .01
764 Julio Machado .01
765 Jose Mesa .01
766 Willie Randolph WS .01
767 Scott Erickson .01
768 Travis Fryman .02
769 Rich Rodriguez RC .01
770 Checklist 703-770 .01
BC1-BC22
793 Bozo T. Clown

1991 Donruss Bonus Car

These bonus cards are standard size and were randomly inserted in Donruss packs and high outstanding player achievements, the first ten first series and the remaining 12 in the secon picking up in time beginning with Valenzuela' hitter and continuing until the end of the seas

COMPLETE SET (22) .60
RANDOM INSERTS IN PACKS
BC1 M.Langston/M.Witt .01
BC2 Randy Johnson .10
BC3 Nolan Ryan NH .40
BC4 Dave Stewart .02
BC5 Cecil Fielder .02
BC6 Carlton Fisk .05
BC7 Ryne Sandberg .15
BC8 Gary Carter .02
BC9 Mark McGwire UER .30
BC10 Bo Jackson .08
BC11 Fernando Valenzuela .02
BC12A Andy Hawkins ERR .01
BC12B Andy Hawkins COR .01
BC13 Melido Perez .01
BC14 Terry Mulholland UER .01
BC15 Nolan Ryan 300W .40
BC16 Delino DeShields .10
BC17 Cal Ripken .30
BC18 Eddie Murray .08
BC19 George Brett .25
BC20 Bobby Thigpen .01
BC21 Dave Stieb .01
BC22 Willie McGee .02

1991 Donruss Elite

These special cards were randomly inserted in 1991 Donruss first and second series wax pac These cards marked the beginning of an eight- run of Elite inserts. Production was limited to maximum of 10,000 serial-numbered cards fo card in the Elite series, and lesser production f Sandberg Signature (5,000) and Ryan Legend (7,500) cards. This was the first time that main insert cards were ever serial numbered allowin verifiable proof of print runs. The regular Elite are photos enclosed in a bronze marble border

surround an evenly squared photo of the
s. The Sandberg Signature card has a green border and is signed in a blue sharpie. The Ryan Legend card is a Dick Perez drawing with borders. The cards are all numbered on the out of 10,000, etc.
OM INSERTS IN PACKS
D PRINT RUN 10,000 SERIAL #'d SETS
y Bonds 12.00 30.00
ge Brett 20.00 50.00
Canseco 12.00 30.00
e Dawson 10.00 25.00
Drabek 12.00 30.00
Fielder 12.00 30.00
ey Henderson 20.00 50.00
Williams 10.00 25.00
lan Ryan LGD/7500 40.00 100.00
e Sandberg AU/5000 100.00 250.00

91 Donruss Grand Slammers

4-card standard-size set commemorates s who hit grand slams in 1990. They were uted in complete set form within factory sets in on to being seeded at a rate of one per cello

PLETE SET (14) .75 2.00
SET PER FACTORY SET
Carter .02 .10
by Bonilla .02 .10
Daniels .01 .05
e Canseco .05 .15
y Bonds .40 1.00
Buhner .02 .10
l Fielder .02 .10
t Williams .02 .10
res Galarraga .02 .10
is Polonia .01 .05
ark McGwire .30 .75
n Karkovice .01 .05
arryl Strawberry UER .02 .10
ke Greenwell .01 .05

991 Donruss Willie Stargell Puzzle

rgell Puzzle 1-3 .10 .25
rgell Puzzle 4-6 .10 .25
rgell Puzzle 7-10 .10 .25
argell Puzzle 10-12 .10 .25
argell Puzzle 13-15 .10 .25
argell Puzzle 16-18 .10 .25
argell Puzzle 19-21 .10 .25
argell Puzzle 22-24 .10 .25
argell Puzzle 25-27 .10 .25
argell Puzzle 28-30 .10 .25
argell Puzzle 29-31 .10 .25
argell Puzzle 34-36 .10 .25
argell Puzzle 37-39 .10 .25
argell Puzzle 40-42 .10 .25
argell Puzzle 43-45 .10 .25
argell Puzzle 46-48 .10 .25
argell Puzzle 49-51 .10 .25
argell Puzzle 52-54 .10 .25
argell Puzzle 55-57 .10 .25
argell Puzzle 58-60 .10 .25
argell Puzzle 61-63 .10 .25

1991 Donruss Rookies

56-card 1991 Donruss Rookies set was issued usively in factory set form through hobby ers. The cards measure the standard size and a puzzle featuring Hall of Famer Willie Stargell included with the set. The fronts feature color on player photos, with white and red borders. kie Cards include Jeff Bagwell and Ivan riguez.

MP.FACT.SET (56) 2.00 5.00
t Kelly RC .02 .10
ch DeLucia .02 .10
es Chamberlain .02 .10
cott Leius .02 .10
arryl Kile .08 .25
ilt Cuyler .02 .10
odd Van Poppel RC .02 .10
ay Lankford .08 .25
rian R.Hunter RC .08 .25
Tony Perezchica .02 .10
Ced Landrum RC .02 .10
Dave Burba RC .08 .25
Ramon Garcia RC .02 .10
Ed Sprague .02 .10
Warren Newson RC .02 .10
Paul Faries RC .02 .10
Luis Gonzalez .20 .50
18 Charles Nagy .02 .10
19 Chris Hammond .02 .10
20 Frank Castillo RC .08 .25
21 Pedro Munoz .02 .10
22 Orlando Merced RC .02 .10
23 Jose Melendez RC .02 .10
24 Kirk Dressendorfer RC .02 .10
25 Heathcliff Slocumb RC .08 .25
26 Doug Simons RC .02 .10
27 Mike Timlin RC .08 .25
28 Jeff Fassero RC .08 .25
29 Mark Leiter RC .02 .10
30 Jeff Bagwell RC .60 1.50
31 Brian McRae .08 .25
32 Mark Whiten .02 .10
33 Ivan Rodriguez RC .75 2.00
34 Wade Taylor RC .02 .10
35 Darren Lewis FDC .02 .10
36 Mo Vaughn .08 .25
37 Mike Remlinger .02 .10
38 Rick Wilkins RC .02 .10
39 Chuck Knoblauch .08 .25
40 Kevin Morton .02 .10
41 Carlos Rodriguez RC .02 .10
42 Mark Lewis .02 .10
43 Brent Mayne .02 .10
44 Chris Haney RC .02 .10
45 Denis Boucher RC .02 .10
46 Mike Gardiner .02 .10
47 Jeff Johnson RC .02 .10
48 Dean Palmer .08 .25
49 Chuck McElroy .02 .10
50 Chris Jones RC .02 .10
51 Scott Kamieniecki RC .02 .10
52 Al Osuna RC .02 .10
53 Rusty Meacham RC .02 .10
54 Chito Martinez RC .02 .10
55 Reggie Jefferson .02 .10
56 Checklist 1-56 .02 .10

1991 Donruss Super DK's

For the seventh consecutive year Donruss issued a card set featuring the players used in the current year's Diamond King subset in a larger size, approximately 5" X 7". The set again featured the art work of famed sports artist Dick Perez and was available through a postpaid mail-in offer detailed on the 1991 Donruss wax packs involving $14.00 and three wax wrappers.

COMPLETE SET (26) 15.00 40.00
1 Dave Stieb .30 .75
2 Craig Biggio 1.00 2.50
3 Cecil Fielder .30 .75
4 Barry Bonds 4.00 10.00
5 Barry Larkin .60 1.50
6 Dave Parker .30 .75
7 Len Dykstra .30 .75
8 Bobby Thigpen .20 .50
9 Roger Clemens 3.00 8.00
10 Ron Gant .30 .75
11 Delino DeShields .30 .75
12 Roberto Alomar .60 1.50
13 Sandy Alomar Jr. .30 .75
14 Ryne Sandberg 2.50 6.00
15 Ramon Martinez .30 .75
16 Edgar Martinez .40 1.00
17 Dave Magadan .20 .50
18 Matt Williams .40 1.00
19 Rafael Palmeiro .60 1.50
20 Bob Welch .20 .50
21 Dave Righetti .20 .50
22 Brian Harper .20 .50
23 Gregg Olson .20 .50
24 Kurt Stillwell .20 .50
25 Pedro Guerrero .20 .50
26 Chuck Finley .30 .75

1992 Donruss Previews

COMPLETE SET (12) 100.00 200.00
1 Wade Boggs 6.00 15.00
2 Barry Bonds 10.00 25.00
3 Will Clark 5.00 12.00
4 Andre Dawson 5.00 12.00
5 Dennis Eckersley 6.00 15.00
6 Robin Ventura 3.00 8.00
7 Ken Griffey Jr. 15.00 40.00
8 Kelly Gruber 2.00 5.00
9 Ryan Klesko 4.00 10.00
10 Cal Ripken 20.00 50.00
11 Nolan Ryan 20.00 50.00
12 Todd Van Poppel 2.00 5.00

1992 Donruss

The 1992 Donruss set contains 784 standard-size cards issued in two separate series of 396. Cards were issued in first and second series foil wrapped packs in addition to hobby and retail factory sets. One of 21 different puzzle panels featuring Hall of Famer Rod Carew was inserted into each pack. The basic card design features glossy color player photos with white borders. Two-toned blue stripes overlay the top and bottom of the picture. Subsets include Rated Rookies (1-20, 397-421), All-Stars (21-30/422-431) and Highlights (33, 94, 154, 215, 276, 434, 495, 555, 616, 677). The only notable Rookie Card in the set features Scott Brosius.

COMPLETE SET (784) 4.00 10.00
COMP.HOBBY SET (788) 4.00 10.00
COMP.RETAIL SET (788) 4.00 10.00
COMPLETE SERIES 1 (396) 2.00 5.00
COMPLETE SERIES 2 (388) 2.00 5.00
COMP.CAREW PUZZLE .40 1.00
1 Mark Wohlers RR .01 .05
2 Wil Cordero .01 .05
3 Kyle Abbott RR .01 .05
4 Dave Nilsson .01 .05
5 Kenny Lofton .05 .15
6 Luis Mercedes RR .01 .05
7 Roger Salkeld RR .01 .05
8 Eddie Zosky RR .01 .05
9 Todd Van Poppel .01 .05
10 Frank Seminara RR RC .02 .10
11 Andy Ashby .01 .05
12 Reggie Jefferson RR .01 .05
13 Ryan Klesko .02 .10
14 Carlos Garcia .01 .05
15 John Ramos RR .01 .05
16 Eric Karros .02 .10
17 Patrick Lennon RR .01 .05
18 Eddie Taubensee RR RC .08 .25
19 Roberto Hernandez RR .01 .05
20 D.J. Dozier RR .01 .05
21 Dave Henderson AS .01 .05
22 Cal Ripken AS .15 .40
23 Wade Boggs AS .02 .10
24 Ken Griffey Jr. AS .10 .30
25 Jack Morris AS .01 .05
26 Danny Tartabull AS .01 .05
27 Cecil Fielder AS .01 .05
28 Roberto Alomar AS .02 .10
29 Sandy Alomar Jr. AS .01 .05
30 Rickey Henderson AS .05 .15
31 Ken Hill .01 .05
32 John Habyan .01 .05
33 Otis Nixon HL .01 .05
34 Tim Wallach .01 .05
35 Cal Ripken .30 .75
36 Gary Carter .02 .10
37 Juan Agosto .01 .05
38 Doug Dascenzo .01 .05
39 Kirk Gibson .02 .10
40 Benito Santiago .02 .10
41 Otis Nixon .01 .05
42 Andy Allanson .01 .05
43 Brian Holman .01 .05
44 Dick Schofield .01 .05
45 Dave Magadan .01 .05
46 Rafael Palmeiro .05 .15
47 Jody Reed .01 .05
48 Ivan Calderon .01 .05
49 Greg W. Harris .01 .05
50 Chris Sabo .01 .05
51 Paul Molitor .02 .10
52 Robby Thompson .01 .05
53 Dave Smith .01 .05
54 Mark Davis .01 .05
55 Kevin Brown .02 .10
56 Donn Pall .01 .05
57 Len Dykstra .02 .10
58 Roberto Alomar .05 .15
59 Jeff D. Robinson .01 .05
60 Willie McGee .02 .10
61 Jay Buhner .02 .10
62 Mike Pagliarulo .01 .05
63 Paul O'Neill .05 .15
64 Hubie Brooks .01 .05
65 Kelly Gruber .01 .05
66 Ken Caminiti .02 .10
67 Gary Redus .01 .05
68 Harold Baines .02 .10
69 Charlie Hough .02 .10
70 B.J. Surhoff .02 .10
71 Walt Weiss .01 .05
72 Shawn Hillegas .01 .05
73 Roberto Kelly .01 .05
74 Jeff Ballard .01 .05
75 Craig Biggio .05 .15
76 Pat Combs .01 .05
77 Jeff M. Robinson .01 .05
78 Tim Belcher .01 .05
79 Cris Carpenter .01 .05
80 Checklist 1-79 .01 .05
81 Steve Avery .01 .05
82 Chris James .01 .05
83 Brian Harper .01 .05
84 Charlie Leibrandt .01 .05
85 Mickey Tettleton .01 .05
86 Pete O'Brien .01 .05
87 Danny Darwin .01 .05
88 Bob Walk .01 .05
89 Jeff Reardon .02 .10
90 Bobby Rose .01 .05
91 Danny Jackson .01 .05
92 John Morris .01 .05
93 Bud Black .01 .05
94 Tommy Greene HL .01 .05
95 Rick Aguilera .02 .10
96 Gary Gaetti .02 .10
97 David Cone .02 .10
98 John Olerud .02 .10
99 Joel Skinner .01 .05
100 Jay Bell .02 .10
101 Bob Milacki .01 .05
102 Norm Charlton .01 .05
103 Chuck Crim .01 .05
104 Terry Steinbach .01 .05
105 Juan Samuel .01 .05
106 Steve Howe .01 .05
107 Rafael Belliard .01 .05
108 Joey Cora .01 .05
109 Tommy Greene .01 .05
110 Gregg Olson .01 .05
111 Frank Tanana .01 .05
112 Lee Smith .02 .10
113 Greg A. Harris .01 .05
114 Dwayne Henry .01 .05
115 Chili Davis .02 .10
116 Kent Mercker .01 .05
117 Brian Barnes .01 .05
118 Rich DeLucia .01 .05
119 Andre Dawson .02 .10
120 Carlos Baerga .01 .05
121 Mike LaValliere .01 .05
122 Jeff Gray .01 .05
123 Bruce Hurst .01 .05
124 Alvin Davis .01 .05
125 John Candelaria .01 .05
126 Matt Nokes .01 .05
127 George Bell .01 .05
128 Bret Saberhagen .02 .10
129 Jeff Russell .01 .05
130 Jim Abbott .05 .15
131 Bill Gullickson .01 .05
132 Todd Zeile .01 .05
133 Dave Winfield .02 .10
134 Wally Whitehurst .01 .05
135 Matt Williams .02 .10
136 Tom Browning .01 .05
137 Marquis Grissom .02 .10
138 Erik Hanson .01 .05
139 Rob Dibble .02 .10
140 Don August .01 .05
141 Tom Henke .01 .05
142 Dan Pasqua .01 .05
143 George Brett .25 .60
144 Jerald Clark .01 .05
145 Robin Ventura .02 .10
146 Dale Murphy .05 .15
147 Dennis Eckersley .02 .10
148 Eric Yelding .01 .05
149 Mario Diaz .01 .05
150 Casey Candaele .01 .05
151 Steve Olin .01 .05
152 Luis Salazar .01 .05
153 Kevin Maas .01 .05
154 Nolan Ryan HL .20 .50
155 Barry Jones .01 .05
156 Chris Hoiles .01 .05
157 Bob Ojeda .01 .05
158 Pedro Guerrero .02 .10
159 Paul Assenmacher .01 .05
160 Checklist 80-157 .01 .05
161 Mike Macfarlane .01 .05
162 Craig Lefferts .01 .05
163 Brian Hunter .01 .05
164 Alan Trammell .02 .10
165 Ken Griffey Jr. .20 .50
166 Lance Parrish .02 .10
167 Brian Downing .01 .05
168 John Barfield .01 .05
169 Jack Clark .02 .10
170 Chris Nabholz .01 .05
171 Tim Teufel .01 .05
172 Chris Hammond .01 .05
173 Robin Yount .15 .40
174 Dave Righetti .02 .10
175 Joe Girardi .01 .05
176 Mike Boddicker .01 .05
177 Dean Palmer .02 .10
178 Greg Hibbard .01 .05
179 Randy Ready .01 .05
180 Devon White .02 .10
181 Mark Eichhorn .01 .05
182 Mike Felder .01 .05
183 Joe Klink .01 .05
184 Steve Bedrosian .01 .05
185 Barry Larkin .05 .15
186 John Franco .02 .10
187 Ed Sprague .01 .05
188 Mark Portugal .01 .05
189 Jose Lind .01 .05
190 Bob Welch .01 .05
191 Alex Fernandez .01 .05
192 Gary Sheffield .02 .10
193 Rickey Henderson .08 .25
194 Rod Nichols .01 .05
195 Scott Kamieniecki .01 .05
196 Mike Flanagan .01 .05
197 Steve Finley .02 .10
198 Darren Daulton .02 .10
199 Leo Gomez .01 .05
200 Mike Morgan .01 .05
201 Bob Tewksbury .01 .05
202 Sid Bream .01 .05
203 Sandy Alomar Jr. .01 .05
204 Greg Gagne .01 .05
205 Juan Berenguer .01 .05
206 Cecil Fielder .02 .10
207 Randy Johnson .08 .25
208 Tony Pena .01 .05
209 Doug Drabek .01 .05
210 Wade Boggs .05 .15
211 Bryan Harvey .01 .05
212 Jose Vizcaino .01 .05
213 Alonzo Powell .01 .05
214 Will Clark .05 .15
215 Rickey Henderson HL .05 .15
216 Jack Morris .02 .10
217 Junior Felix .01 .05
218 Vince Coleman .01 .05
219 Jimmy Key .02 .10
220 Alex Cole .01 .05
221 Bill Landrum .01 .05
222 Randy Milligan .01 .05
223 Jose Rijo .01 .05
224 Greg Vaughn .01 .05
225 Dave Stewart .02 .10
226 Lenny Harris .01 .05
227 Scott Sanderson .01 .05
228 Jeff Blauser .01 .05
229 Ozzie Guillen .02 .10
230 John Kruk .02 .10
231 Bob Melvin .01 .05
232 Milt Cuyler .01 .05
233 Felix Jose .01 .05
234 Ellis Burks .02 .10
235 Pete Harnisch .01 .05
236 Kevin Tapani .01 .05
237 Terry Pendleton .02 .10
238 Mark Gardner .01 .05
239 Harold Reynolds .02 .10
240 Checklist 158-237 .01 .05
241 Mike Harkey .01 .05
242 Felix Fermin .01 .05
243 Barry Bonds .40 1.00
244 Roger Clemens .20 .50
245 Dennis Rasmussen .01 .05
246 Jose DeLeon .01 .05
247 Orel Hershiser .02 .10
248 Mel Hall .01 .05
249 Rick Wilkins .01 .05
250 Tom Gordon .01 .05
251 Kevin Reimer .01 .05
252 Luis Polonia .01 .05
253 Mike Henneman .01 .05
254 Tom Pagnozzi .01 .05
255 Chuck Finley .02 .10
256 Mackey Sasser .01 .05
257 John Burkett .01 .05
258 Hal Morris .01 .05
259 Larry Walker .05 .15
260 Bill Swift .01 .05
261 Joe Oliver .01 .05
262 Julio Machado .01 .05
263 Todd Stottlemyre .01 .05
264 Matt Merullo .01 .05
265 Brent Mayne .01 .05
266 Thomas Howard .01 .05
267 Lance Johnson .01 .05
268 Terry Mulholland .01 .05
269 Rick Honeycutt .01 .05
270 Luis Gonzalez .02 .10
271 Jose Guzman .01 .05
272 Jimmy Jones .01 .05
273 Mark Lewis .01 .05
274 Rene Gonzales .01 .05
275 Jeff Johnson .01 .05
276 Dennis Martinez HL .01 .05
277 Delino DeShields .01 .05
278 Sam Horn .01 .05
279 Kevin Gross .01 .05
280 Jose Oquendo .01 .05
281 Mark Grace .05 .15
282 Mark Gubicza .01 .05
283 Fred McGriff .05 .15
284 Ron Gant .02 .10
285 Lou Whitaker .02 .10
286 Edgar Martinez .05 .15
287 Ron Tingley .01 .05
288 Kevin McReynolds .01 .05
289 Ivan Rodriguez .08 .25
290 Mike Gardiner .01 .05
291 Chris Haney .01 .05
292 Darrin Jackson .01 .05
293 Bill Doran .01 .05
294 Ted Higuera .01 .05
295 Jeff Brantley .01 .05
296 Les Lancaster .01 .05
297 Jim Eisenreich .01 .05
298 Ruben Sierra .02 .10
299 Scott Radinsky .01 .05
300 Jose DeJesus .01 .05
301 Mike Timlin .01 .05
302 Luis Sojo .01 .05
303 Kelly Downs .01 .05
304 Scott Bankhead .01 .05
305 Pedro Munoz .01 .05
306 Scott Scudder .01 .05
307 Kevin Elster .01 .05
308 Duane Ward .01 .05
309 Darryl Kile .02 .10
310 Orlando Merced .01 .05
311 Dave Henderson .01 .05
312 Tim Raines .02 .10
313 Mark Lee .01 .05
314 Mike Gallego .01 .05
315 Charles Nagy .01 .05
316 Jesse Barfield .01 .05
317 Todd Frohwirth .01 .05
318 Al Osuna .01 .05
319 Darrin Fletcher .01 .05
320 Checklist 238-316 .01 .05
321 David Segui .01 .05
322 Stan Javier .01 .05
323 Bryn Smith .01 .05
324 Jeff Treadway .01 .05
325 Mark Whiten .01 .05
326 Kent Hrbek .02 .10
327 David Justice .02 .10
328 Tony Phillips .01 .05
329 Rob Murphy .01 .05
330 Kevin Morton .01 .05
331 John Smiley .01 .05
332 Luis Rivera .01 .05
333 Wally Joyner .02 .10
334 Heathcliff Slocumb .01 .05
335 Rick Cerone .01 .05
336 Mike Remlinger .01 .05
337 Mike Moore .01 .05
338 Lloyd McClendon .01 .05
339 Al Newman .01 .05
340 Kirk McCaskill .01 .05
341 Howard Johnson .01 .05
342 Greg Myers .01 .05
343 Kal Daniels .01 .05
344 Bernie Williams .05 .15
345 Shane Mack .01 .05
346 Gary Thurman .01 .05
347 Dante Bichette .02 .10
348 Mark McGwire .25 .60
349 Travis Fryman .02 .10
350 Ray Lankford .02 .10
351 Mike Jeffcoat .01 .05
352 Jack McDowell .01 .05
353 Mitch Williams .01 .05
354 Mike Devereaux .01 .05
355 Andres Galarraga .02 .10
356 Henry Cotto .01 .05
357 Scott Bailes .01 .05
358 Jeff Bagwell .08 .25
359 Scott Leius .01 .05
360 Zane Smith .01 .05
361 Bill Pecota .01 .05
362 Tony Fernandez .01 .05
363 Glenn Braggs .01 .05
364 Bill Spiers .01 .05
365 Vicente Palacios .01 .05
366 Tim Burke .01 .05
367 Randy Tomlin .01 .05
368 Kenny Rogers .02 .10
369 Brett Butler .02 .10
370 Pat Kelly .01 .05
371 Bip Roberts .01 .05
372 Gregg Jefferies .01 .05
373 Kevin Bass .01 .05
374 Ron Karkovice .01 .05
375 Paul Gibson .01 .05
376 Bernard Gilkey .01 .05
377 Dave Gallagher .01 .05
378 Bill Wegman .01 .05
379 Pat Borders .01 .05
380 Ed Whitson .01 .05
381 Gilberto Reyes .01 .05
382 Russ Swan .01 .05
383 Andy Van Slyke .05 .15
384 Wes Chamberlain .01 .05
385 Steve Chitren .01 .05
386 Greg Olson .01 .05
387 Brian McRae .01 .05
388 Rich Rodriguez .01 .05
389 Steve Decker .01 .05
390 Chuck Knoblauch .02 .10
391 Bobby Witt .01 .05
392 Eddie Murray .08 .25
393 Juan Gonzalez .05 .15
394 Scott Ruskin .01 .05
395 Jay Howell .01 .05
396 Checklist 317-396 .01 .05
397 Royce Clayton RR .01 .05
398 John Jaha RR RC .08 .25
399 Dan Wilson RR .01 .05
400 Archie Corbin .01 .05
401 Barry Manuel RR .01 .05
402 Kim Batiste RR .01 .05
403 Pat Mahomes RR RC .08 .25
404 Dave Fleming .01 .05
405 Jeff Juden RR .01 .05
406 Jim Thome .08 .25
407 Sam Militello RR .01 .05
408 Jeff Nelson RR RC .15 .40
409 Anthony Young .01 .05
410 Tino Martinez RR .05 .15
411 Jeff Mutis RR .01 .05
412 Rey Sanchez RR RC .08 .25
413 Chris Gardner RR .01 .05
414 John Vander Wal RR .01 .05
415 Reggie Sanders .02 .10
416 Brian Williams RR RC .02 .10
417 Mo Sanford RR .01 .05
418 David Weathers RR RC .15 .40
419 Hector Fajardo RR RC .02 .10
420 Steve Foster RR .01 .05
421 Lance Dickson RR .01 .05
422 Andre Dawson AS .01 .05
423 Ozzie Smith AS .08 .25
424 Chris Sabo AS .01 .05
425 Tony Gwynn AS .05 .15
426 Tom Glavine AS .02 .10
427 Bobby Bonilla AS .01 .05
428 Will Clark AS .02 .10
429 Ryne Sandberg AS .08 .25
430 Benito Santiago AS .01 .05
431 Ivan Calderon AS .01 .05
432 Ozzie Smith .15 .40
433 Tim Leary .01 .05
434 Bret Saberhagen HL .01 .05
435 Mel Rojas .01 .05
436 Ben McDonald .01 .05
437 Tim Crews .01 .05
438 Rex Hudler .01 .05
439 Chico Walker .01 .05
440 Kurt Stillwell .01 .05
441 Tony Gwynn .10 .30
442 John Smoltz .05 .15
443 Lloyd Moseby .01 .05
444 Mike Schooler .01 .05
445 Joe Grahe .01 .05
446 Dwight Gooden .02 .10
447 Oil Can Boyd .01 .05
448 John Marzano .01 .05
449 Bret Barberie .01 .05
450 Mike Maddux .01 .05
451 Jeff Reed .01 .05
452 Dale Sveum .01 .05
453 Jose Uribe .01 .05
454 Bob Scanlan .01 .05
455 Kevin Appier .02 .10
456 Jeff Huson .01 .05
457 Ken Patterson .01 .05
458 Ricky Jordan .01 .05
459 Tom Candiotti .01 .05
460 Lee Stevens .01 .05
461 Rod Beck RC .08 .25
462 Dave Valle .01 .05
463 Scott Erickson .01 .05
464 Chris Jones .01 .05
465 Mark Carreon .01 .05
466 Rob Ducey .01 .05
467 Jim Corsi .01 .05
468 Jeff King .01 .05
469 Curt Young .01 .05
470 Bo Jackson .08 .25
471 Chris Bosio .01 .05
472 Jamie Quirk .01 .05
473 Jesse Orosco .01 .05
474 Alvaro Espinoza .01 .05
475 Joe Orsulak .01 .05
476 Checklist 397-477 .01 .05
477 Gerald Young .01 .05
478 Wally Backman .01 .05
479 Juan Bell .01 .05
480 Mike Scioscia .01 .05
481 Omar Olivares .01 .05
482 Francisco Cabrera .01 .05
483 Greg Swindell UER (Shown on Indians& but listed .01 .05
484 Terry Leach .01 .05
485 Tommy Gregg .01 .05
486 Scott Aldred .01 .05
487 Greg Briley .01 .05
488 Phil Plantier .01 .05
489 Curtis Wilkerson .01 .05
490 Tom Brunansky .01 .05
491 Mike Fetters .01 .05
492 Frank Castillo .01 .05
493 Joe Boever .01 .05
494 Kirt Manwaring .01 .05
495 Wilson Alvarez HL .01 .05
496 Gene Larkin .01 .05
497 Gary DiSarcina .01 .05
498 Frank Viola .02 .10
499 Manuel Lee .01 .05
500 Albert Belle .02 .10
501 Stan Belinda .01 .05
502 Dwight Evans .05 .15
503 Eric Davis .02 .10
504 Darren Holmes .01 .05
505 Mike Bordick .01 .05
506 Dave Hansen .01 .05
507 Lee Guetterman .01 .05
508 Keith Mitchell .01 .05
509 Melido Perez .01 .05
510 Dickie Thon .01 .05
511 Mark Williamson .01 .05
512 Mark Salas .01 .05
513 Milt Thompson .01 .05
514 Mo Vaughn .02 .10
515 Jim Deshaies .01 .05
516 Rich Garces .01 .05
517 Lonnie Smith .01 .05
518 Spike Owen .01 .05
519 Tracy Jones .01 .05
520 Greg Maddux .15 .40
521 Carlos Martinez .01 .05
522 Neal Heaton .01 .05
523 Mike Greenwell .01 .05
524 Andy Benes .01 .05
525 Jeff Schaefer UER .01 .05
526 Mike Sharperson .01 .05
527 Wade Taylor .01 .05
528 Jerome Walton .01 .05
529 Storm Davis .01 .05
530 Jose Hernandez RC .08 .25
531 Mark Langston .01 .05

532 Rob Deer .01 .05
533 Geronimo Pena .01 .05
534 Juan Guzman .01 .05
535 Pete Schourek .01 .05
536 Todd Benzinger .01 .05
537 Billy Hatcher .01 .05
538 Tom Foley .01 .05
539 Dave Cochrane .01 .05
540 Mariano Duncan .01 .05
541 Edwin Nunez .01 .05
542 Rance Mulliniks .01 .05
543 Carlton Fisk .05 .15
544 Luis Aquino .01 .05
545 Ricky Bones .01 .05
546 Craig Grebeck .01 .05
547 Charlie Hayes .01 .05
548 Jose Canseco .05 .15
549 Andujar Cedeno .01 .05
550 Geno Petralli .01 .05
551 Javier Ortiz .01 .05
552 Rudy Seanez .01 .05
553 Rich Gedman .01 .05
554 Eric Plunk .01 .05
555 N.Ryan .15 .40
G.Gossage HL
556 Checklist 478-555 .01 .05
557 Greg Colbrunn .01 .05
558 Chito Martinez .01 .05
559 Darryl Strawberry .02 .10
560 Luis Alicea .01 .05
561 Dwight Smith .01 .05
562 Terry Shumpert .01 .05
563 Jim Vatcher .01 .05
564 Deion Sanders .05 .15
565 Walt Terrell .01 .05
566 Dave Burba .01 .05
567 Dave Howard .01 .05
568 Todd Hundley .01 .05
569 Jack Daugherty .01 .05
570 Scott Cooper .01 .05
571 Bill Sampen .01 .05
572 Jose Melendez .01 .05
573 Freddie Benavides .01 .05
574 Jim Gantner .01 .05
575 Trevor Wilson .01 .05
576 Ryne Sandberg .15 .40
577 Kevin Seitzer .01 .05
578 Gerald Alexander .01 .05
579 Mike Huff .01 .05
580 Von Hayes .01 .05
581 Derek Bell .02 .10
582 Mike Stanley .01 .05
583 Kevin Mitchell .01 .05
584 Mike Jackson .01 .05
585 Dan Gladden .01 .05
586 Ted Power UER
(Wrong year given for .01 .05
signing with
587 Jeff Innis .01 .05
588 Bob MacDonald .01 .05
589 Jose Tolentino .01 .05
590 Bob Patterson .01 .05
591 Scott Brosius RC .15 .40
592 Frank Thomas .08 .25
593 Darryl Hamilton .01 .05
594 Kirk Dressendorfer .01 .05
595 Jeff Shaw .01 .05
596 Don Mattingly .25 .60
597 Glenn Davis .01 .05
598 Andy Mota .01 .05
599 Jason Grimsley .01 .05
600 Jim Poole .01 .05
601 Jim Gott .01 .05
602 Stan Royer .01 .05
603 Marvin Freeman .01 .05
604 Denis Boucher .01 .05
605 Denny Neagle .02 .10
606 Mark Lemke .01 .05
607 Jerry Don Gleaton .01 .05
608 Brent Knackert .01 .05
609 Carlos Quintana .01 .05
610 Bobby Bonilla .02 .10
611 Joe Hesketh .01 .05
612 Daryl Boston .01 .05
613 Shawon Dunston .01 .05
614 Danny Cox .01 .05
615 Darren Lewis .01 .05
616 Mercker/Pena/Wohlers UER .01 .05
617 Kirby Puckett .08 .25
618 Franklin Stubbs .01 .05
619 Chris Donnels .01 .05
620 David Wells UER .02 .10
621 Mike Aldrete .01 .05
622 Bob Kipper .01 .05
623 Anthony Telford .01 .05
624 Randy Myers .01 .05
625 Willie Randolph .02 .10
626 Joe Slusarski .01 .05
627 John Wetteland .02 .10
628 Greg Cadaret .01 .05
629 Tom Glavine .05 .15
630 Wilson Alvarez .02 .10
631 Wally Ritchie .01 .05
632 Mike Mussina .08 .25
633 Mark Leiter .01 .05
634 Gerald Perry .01 .05
635 Matt Young .01 .05
636 Checklist 556-635 .01 .05
637 Scott Hemond .01 .05
638 David West .01 .05
639 Jim Clancy .01 .05
640 Doug Platt UER
(Not born in 1955 as .01 .05
on card; inc
641 Omar Vizquel .05 .15
642 Rick Sutcliffe .02 .10
643 Glenallen Hill .01 .05
644 Gary Varsho .01 .05
645 Tony Fossas .01 .05
646 Jack Howell .01 .05
647 Jim Campanis .01 .05
648 Chris Gwynn .01 .05
649 Jim Leyritz .01 .05
650 Chuck McElroy .01 .05
651 Sean Berry .01 .05
652 Donald Harris .01 .05
653 Don Slaught .01 .05
654 Rusty Meacham .01 .05
655 Scott Terry .01 .05
656 Ramon Martinez .01 .05
657 Keith Miller .01 .05
658 Ramon Garcia .01 .05
659 Milt Hill .01 .05
660 Steve Frey .01 .05
661 Bob McClure .01 .05
662 Ced Landrum .01 .05
663 Doug Henry RC .02 .10
664 Candy Maldonado .01 .05
665 Carl Willis .01 .05
666 Jeff Montgomery .01 .05
667 Craig Shipley .01 .05
668 Warren Newson .01 .05
669 Mickey Morandini .01 .05
670 Brook Jacoby .01 .05
671 Ryan Bowen .01 .05
672 Bill Krueger .01 .05
673 Rob Mallicoat .01 .05
674 Doug Jones .01 .05
675 Scott Livingstone .01 .05
676 Danny Tartabull .01 .05
677 Joe Carter HL .01 .05
678 Cecil Espy .01 .05
679 Randy Velarde .01 .05
680 Bruce Ruffin .01 .05
681 Ted Wood .01 .05
682 Dan Plesac .01 .05
683 Eric Bullock .01 .05
684 Junior Ortiz .01 .05
685 Dave Hollins .01 .05
686 Dennis Martinez .02 .10
687 Larry Andersen .01 .05
688 Doug Simons .01 .05
689 Tim Spehr .01 .05
690 Calvin Jones .01 .05
691 Mark Guthrie .01 .05
692 Alfredo Griffin .01 .05
693 Joe Carter .02 .10
694 Terry Mathews .01 .05
695 Pascual Perez .01 .05
696 Gene Nelson .01 .05
697 Gerald Williams .01 .05
698 Chris Cron .01 .05
699 Steve Buechele .01 .05
700 Paul McClellan .01 .05
701 Jim Lindeman .01 .05
702 Francisco Oliveras .01 .05
703 Rob Maurer RC .01 .05
704 Pat Hentgen .01 .05
705 Jaime Navarro .01 .05
706 Mike Magnante RC .02 .10
707 Nolan Ryan .40 1.00
708 Bobby Thigpen .01 .05
709 John Cerutti .01 .05
710 Steve Wilson .01 .05
711 Hensley Meulens .01 .05
712 Rheal Cormier .01 .05
713 Scott Bradley .01 .05
714 Mitch Webster .01 .05
715 Roger Mason .01 .05
716 Checklist 636-716 .01 .05
717 Jeff Fassero .01 .05
718 Cal Eldred .01 .05
719 Sid Fernandez .01 .05
720 Bob Zupcic RC .02 .10
721 Jose Offerman .01 .05
722 Cliff Brantley .01 .05
723 Ron Darling .01 .05
724 Dave Stieb .01 .05
725 Hector Villanueva .01 .05
726 Mike Hartley .01 .05
727 Arthur Rhodes .01 .05
728 Randy Bush .01 .05
729 Steve Sax .01 .05
730 Dave Otto .01 .05
731 John Wehner .01 .05
732 Dave Martinez .01 .05
733 Ruben Amaro .01 .05
734 Billy Ripken .01 .05
735 Steve Farr .01 .05
736 Shawn Abner .01 .05
737 Gil Heredia RC .08 .25
738 Ron Jones .01 .05
739 Tony Castillo .01 .05
740 Sammy Sosa .08 .25
741 Julio Franco .02 .10
742 Tim Naehring .01 .05
743 Steve Wapnick .01 .05
744 Craig Wilson .01 .05
745 Darrin Chapin .01 .05
746 Chris George .01 .05
747 Mike Simms .01 .05
748 Rosario Rodriguez .01 .05
749 Skeeter Barnes .01 .05
750 Roger McDowell .01 .05
751 Dann Howitt .01 .05
752 Paul Sorrento .01 .05
753 Braulio Castillo .01 .05
754 Yorkis Perez .01 .05
755 Willie Fraser .01 .05
756 Jeremy Hernandez RC .02 .10
757 Curt Schilling .05 .15
758 Steve Lyons .01 .05
759 Dave Anderson .01 .05
760 Willie Banks .01 .05
761 Mark Leonard .01 .05
762 Jack Armstrong/(Listed on Indians&.01 .05
but shown on
763 Scott Servais .01 .05
764 Ray Stephens .01 .05
765 Junior Noboa .01 .05
766 Jim Olander .01 .05
767 Joe Magrane .01 .05
768 Lance Blankenship .01 .05
769 Mike Humphreys .01 .05
770 Jarvis Brown .01 .05
771 Damon Berryhill .01 .05
772 Alejandro Pena .01 .05
773 Jose Mesa .01 .05
774 Gary Cooper .01 .05
775 Carney Lansford .02 .10
776 Mike Bielecki/(Shown on Cubs& .01 .05
but listed on Brav
777 Charlie O'Brien .01 .05
778 Carlos Hernandez .01 .05
779 Howard Farmer .01 .05
780 Mike Stanton .01 .05
781 Reggie Harris .01 .05
782 Xavier Hernandez .01 .05
783 Bryan Hickerson RC .02 .10
784 Checklist 717-784 .01 .05
and BC1-BC8

1992 Donruss Bonus Cards

The 1992 Donruss Bonus Cards set contains eight standard-size. The cards are numbered on the back and checklisted below accordingly. The cards were randomly inserted in foil packs of 1992 Donruss baseball cards.

COMPLETE SET (8) .75 2.00
RANDOM INSERTS IN FOIL PACKS
BC1 Cal Ripken MVP .30 .75
BC2 Terry Pendleton MVP .02 .10
BC3 Roger Clemens CY .20 .50
BC4 Tom Glavine CY .05 .15
BC5 Chuck Knoblauch ROY .02 .10
BC6 Jeff Bagwell ROY .08 .25
BC7 Colorado Rockies .01 .05
BC8 Florida Marlins .01 .05

1992 Donruss Diamond Kings

These standard-size cards were randomly inserted in 1992 Donruss I foil packs (cards 1-13 and the checklist only) and in 1992 Donruss II foil packs (cards 14-26). The decision at the time to transform the popular Diamond King subset into an limieted distribution insert set created notable groups of supporters and dissenters. The attractive fronts feature player portraits by noted sports artist Dick Perez. The words "Donruss Diamond Kings" are superimposed at the card top in a gold-trimmed blue and black banner, with the player's name in a similarly designed black stripe at the card bottom. A very limited amount of 5" by 7" cards were produced. These issues were never formally released but these cards were intended to be premiums in retail products.

COMPLETE SET (27) 8.00 20.00
COMPLETE SERIES 1 (14) 8.00 20.00
COMPLETE SERIES 2 (13) 2.00 4.00
RANDOM INSERTS IN PACKS
DK1 Paul Molitor .30 .75
DK2 Will Clark .50 1.25
DK3 Joe Carter .30 .75
DK4 Julio Franco .30 .75
DK5 Cal Ripken 2.50 6.00
DK6 David Justice .30 .75
DK7 George Bell .15 .40
DK8 Frank Thomas .75 2.00
DK9 Wade Boggs .50 1.25
DK10 Scott Sanderson .15 .40
DK11 Jeff Bagwell .75 2.00
DK12 John Kruk .30 .75
DK13 Felix Jose .15 .40
DK14 Harold Baines .30 .75
DK15 Dwight Gooden .30 .75
DK16 Brian McRae .15 .40
DK17 Jay Bell .30 .75
DK18 Brett Butler .30 .75
DK19 Hal Morris .15 .40
DK20 Mark Langston .15 .40
DK21 Scott Erickson .15 .40
DK22 Randy Johnson .75 2.00
DK23 Greg Swindell .15 .40
DK24 Dennis Martinez .30 .75
DK25 Tony Phillips .15 .40
DK26 Fred McGriff .50 1.25
DK27 Checklist 1-26 DP/(Dick Perez).15 .40

1992 Donruss Elite

These cards were random inserts in 1992 Donruss first and second series foil packs. Like the previous year, the cards were individually numbered of 10,000. Card fronts feature dramatic prismatic borders encasing a full color action or posed shot of the player. The numbering of the set is essentially a continuation of the series started the year before. Only 5,000 Ripken Signature Series cards were printed and only 7,500 Henderson Legends cards were printed. The complete set price does not include cards L2 and S2.

RANDOM INSERTS IN PACKS
STATED PRINT RUN 10,000 SERIAL #'d SETS
9 Wade Boggs 10.00 25.00
10 Joe Carter 10.00 25.00
11 Will Clark 12.50 30.00
12 Dwight Gooden 12.50 30.00
13 Ken Griffey Jr. 40.00 100.00
14 Tony Gwynn 15.00 40.00
15 Howard Johnson 10.00 25.00
16 Terry Pendleton 8.00 20.00
17 Kirby Puckett 12.00 30.00
18 Frank Thomas 25.00 60.00
L2 R.Henderson LGD/7500 30.00 60.00
S2 Cal Ripken AU/5000 175.00 350.00

1992 Donruss Rod Carew Puzzle

1 Carew Puzzle 1-3 .10 .25
4 Carew Puzzle 4-6 .10 .25
7 Carew Puzzle 7-10 .10 .25
10 Carew Puzzle 10-12 .10 .25
13 Carew Puzzle 13-15 .10 .25
16 Carew Puzzle 16-18 .10 .25
19 Carew Puzzle 19-21 .10 .25
22 Carew Puzzle 22-24 .10 .25
25 Carew Puzzle 25-27 .10 .25
28 Carew Puzzle 28-30 .10 .25
31 Carew Puzzle 29-31 .10 .25
34 Carew Puzzle 34-36 .10 .25
37 Carew Puzzle 37-39 .10 .25
40 Carew Puzzle 40-42 .10 .25
43 Carew Puzzle 43-45 .10 .25
46 Carew Puzzle 46-48 .10 .25
49 Carew Puzzle 49-51 .10 .25
52 Carew Puzzle 52-54 .10 .25
55 Carew Puzzle 55-57 .10 .25
58 Carew Puzzle 58-60 .10 .25
61 Carew Puzzle 61-63 .10 .25

1992 Donruss Update

Four cards from this 22-card standard-size set were included in each retail factory set. Card design is identical to regular issue 1992 Donruss cards except for the U-prefixed numbering on back. Card numbers U1-U6 are Rated Rookie cards, while card numbers U7-U9 are Highlights cards. A tough early Kenny Lofton card, his first as a member of the Cleveland Indians, highlights this set.

COMPLETE SET (22) 20.00 50.00
FOUR PER RETAIL FACTORY SET
U1 Pat Listach .60 1.50
U2 Andy Stankiewicz .40 1.00
U3 Brian Jordan 1.00 2.50
U4 Dan Walters RR .40 1.00
U5 Chad Curtis .60 1.50
U6 Kenny Lofton .60 1.50
U7 Mark McGwire HL 4.00 10.00
U8 Eddie Murray HL 1.50 4.00
U9 Jeff Reardon HL .60 1.50
U10 Frank Viola .60 1.50
U11 Gary Sheffield .60 1.50
U12 George Bell .40 1.00
U13 Rick Sutcliffe .60 1.50
U14 Wally Joyner .60 1.50
U15 Kevin Seitzer .40 1.00
U16 Bill Krueger .40 1.00
U17 Danny Tartabull .40 1.00
U18 Dave Winfield .60 1.50
U19 Gary Carter .60 1.50
U20 Bobby Bonilla .60 1.50
U21 Cory Snyder .40 1.00
U22 Bill Swift .40 1.00

1992 Donruss Rookies

After six years of issuing "The Rookies" as a 56-card boxed set, Donruss expanded it to a 132-card standard-size set and distributed the cards in hobby and retail foil packs. The card design is the same as the 1992 Donruss regular issue except that the two-tone blue color bars have been replaced by green, as in the previous six Donruss Rookies sets. The cards are arranged in alphabetical order and numbered on the back. Rookie Cards in this set include Jeff Kent, Manny Ramirez and Eric Young. In addition an early card of Pedro Martinez is featured.

COMPLETE SET (132) 4.00 10.00
1 Kyle Abbott .01 .05
2 Troy Afenir .01 .05
3 Rich Amaral RC .02 .10
4 Ruben Amaro .01 .05
5 Billy Ashley RC .02 .10
6 Pedro Astacio RC .08 .25
7 Jim Austin .01 .05
8 Robert Ayrault .01 .05
9 Kevin Baez .01 .05
10 Esteban Beltre .01 .05
11 Brian Bohanon .01 .05
12 Kent Bottenfield RC .08 .25
13 Jeff Branson .01 .05
14 Brad Brink .01 .05
15 John Briscoe .01 .05
16 Doug Brocail RC .02 .10
17 Rico Brogna .01 .05
18 J.T. Bruett .01 .05
19 Jacob Brumfield .01 .05
20 Jim Bullinger .01 .05
21 Kevin Campbell .01 .05
22 Pedro Castellano RC .02 .10
23 Mike Christopher .01 .05
24 Archi Cianfrocco RC .02 .10
25 Mark Clark RC .02 .10
26 Craig Colbert .01 .05
27 Victor Cole RC .02 .10
28 Steve Cooke RC .02 .10
29 Tim Costo .01 .05
30 Chad Curtis RC .08 .25
31 Doug Davis .01 .05
32 Gary DiSarcina .01 .05
33 John Doherty RC .02 .10
34 Mike Draper .01 .05
35 Monty Fariss .01 .05
36 Bien Figueroa .01 .05
37 John Flaherty RC .02 .10
38 Tim Fortugno .01 .05
39 Eric Fox RC .02 .10
40 Jeff Frye RC .02 .10
41 Ramon Garcia .01 .05
42 Brent Gates RC .02 .10
43 Tom Goodwin .01 .05
44 Buddy Groom RC .02 .10
45 Jeff Grotewold .01 .05
46 Juan Guerrero .01 .05
47 Johnny Guzman RC .02 .10
48 Shawn Hare RC .02 .10
49 Ryan Hawblitzel RC .02 .10
50 Bert Heffernan .01 .05
51 Butch Henry .01 .05
52 Cesar Hernandez RC .02 .10
53 Vince Horsman .01 .05
54 Steve Hosey .01 .05
55 Pat Howell .01 .05
56 Peter Hoy .01 .05
57 Jonathan Hurst RC .02 .10
58 Mark Hutton RC .02 .10
59 Shawn Jeter RC .02 .10
60 Joel Johnston .01 .05
61 Jeff Kent RC 1.00 2.50
62 Kurt Knudsen RC .02 .10
63 Kevin Koslofski .01 .05
64 Danny Leon .01 .05
65 Jesse Levis .01 .05
66 Tom Marsh RC .02 .10
67 Ed Martel .01 .05
68 Al Martin RC .08 .25
69 Pedro Martinez .75 2.00
70 Derrick May .01 .05
71 Matt Maysey .01 .05
72 Russ McGinnis .01 .05
73 Tim McIntosh .01 .05
74 Jim McNamara .01 .05
75 Jeff McNeely .01 .05
76 Rusty Meacham .01 .05
77 Tony Menendez .01 .05
78 Henry Mercedes .01 .05
79 Paul Miller .01 .05
80 Joe Millette .01 .05
81 Blas Minor .01 .05
82 Dennis Moeller .01 .05
83 Raul Mondesi .02 .10
84 Rob Natal .01 .05
85 Troy Neel RC .02 .10
86 David Nied RC .02 .10
87 Jerry Nielson .01 .05
88 Donovan Osborne .01 .05
89 John Patterson RC .02 .10
90 Roger Pavlik RC .02 .10
91 Dan Peltier .01 .05
92 Jim Pena .01 .05
93 William Pennyfeather .01 .05
94 Mike Perez .01 .05
95 Hipolito Pichardo RC .02 .10
96 Greg Pirkl RC .02 .10
97 Harvey Pulliam .01 .05
98 Manny Ramirez RC 1.50 4.00
99 Pat Rapp RC .02 .10
100 Jeff Reboulet .01 .05
101 Darren Reed .01 .05
102 Shane Reynolds RC .08 .25
103 Bill Risley .01 .05
104 Ben Rivera .01 .05
105 Henry Rodriguez .01 .05
106 Rico Rossy .01 .05
107 Johnny Ruffin .01 .05
108 Steve Scarsone .01 .05
109 Tim Scott .01 .05
110 Steve Shifflett .01 .05
111 Dave Silvestri .01 .05
112 Matt Stairs RC .08 .25
113 William Suero .01 .05
114 Jeff Tackett .01 .05
115 Eddie Taubensee .02 .10
116 Rick Trlicek RC .02 .10
117 Scooter Tucker .01 .05
118 Shane Turner .01 .05
119 Julio Valera .01 .05
120 Paul Wagner RC .02 .10
121 Tim Wakefield RC 1.25 3.00
122 Mike Walker .01 .05
123 Bruce Walton .01 .05
124 Lenny Webster .01 .05
125 Bob Wickman .08 .25
126 Mike Williams RC .08 .25
127 Kerry Woodson .01 .05
128 Eric Young RC .08 .25
129 Kevin Young RC .08 .25
130 Pete Young .01 .05
131 Checklist 1-66 .01 .05
132 Checklist 67-132 .01 .05

1992 Donruss Rookies Phenoms

This 20-card standard size set features a selection young prospects. The first twelve cards were randomly inserted into 1992 Donruss The Rookies 12-card foil packs. The last eight were inserted one per 1992 Donruss Rookies 30-card jumbo pack. Each glossy card front features a black border surrounding a full color photo and gold foil type. One of only three MLB-licensed cards of Mike Piazza issued in 1992 is featured within this set.

COMP.FOIL SET (12) 12.50 30.00
COMP.JUMBO SET (8) 5.00 10.00
COMMON FOIL (BC1-BC12) .40 1.00
FOIL: RANDOM INSERTS IN PACKS
COMMON JUMBO (BC13-BC20) .40 1.00
JUMBOS: ONE PER JUMBO PACK
BC1 Moises Alou .60 1.50
BC2 Bret Boone .60 1.50
BC3 Jeff Conine .60 1.50
BC4 Dave Fleming .40 1.00
BC5 Tyler Green .40 1.00
BC6 Eric Karros .60 1.50
BC7 Pat Listach .60 1.50
BC8 Kenny Lofton .60 1.50
BC9 Mike Piazza 6.00 15.00
BC10 Tim Salmon .60 1.50
BC11 Andy Stankiewicz .40 1.00
BC12 Dan Walters .40 1.00
BC13 Ramon Caraballo .40 1.00
BC14 Brian Jordan .60 1.50
BC15 Ryan Klesko .60 1.50
BC16 Sam Militello .40 1.00
BC17 Frank Seminara .40 1.00
BC18 Salomon Torres .40 1.00
BC19 John Valentin .60 1.50
BC20 Wil Cordero .40 1.00

1992 Donruss Coke Ryan

This 26-card standard-size set was produced by Donruss to commemorate each year of Ryan's professional baseball career. Both sides of the card bear the Coca-Cola logo, and four-card cello packs with one Ryan card and three regular issue 1992 Donruss cards were inserted in 12-can packs of Coca-Cola classic, caffeine-free Coca-Cola classic, diet Coke, caffeine-free diet Coke, Sprite, and diet Sprite. An offer on the back panel of specially marked Coca-Cola multi-packs (and the labels of two- bottles) made available boxed factory sets thro mail-in offer for 8.95 and UPC symbols from pack wraps of Coca-Cola products. The prom ran from April to June and covered nearly 90 of the country. The cards are numbered on the in chronolgical order; each year Nolan is pictu with his then-current team, New York Mets (N Califomoia Angels (CA), Houston Astros (HA) Rangers (TR).

COMPLETE SET (26) 4.00
COMMON PLAYER (1-26) .20

1992 Donruss Cracker Jac

This 36-card set is the first of two series produ Donruss for Cracker Jack, and the micro cards protected by a paper sleeve and inserted into specially marked boxes of Cracker Jack. A side listed all 36 players in series I. The micro card measure approximately 1 1/4" by 1 3/4". The f design is the same as the Donruss regular issu cards, only different color player photos are displayed. The backs, however, have a complet different design than the regular issue Donruss cards; they are horizontally oriented and preser biography, major league pitching (or batting) r and brief career summary inside navy blue bor The cards are numbered on the back. On the pa sleeve was a mail-in offer for a mini card albun six top loading plastic pages for 4.95 per albur

COMPLETE SET (36) 4.00
1 Dennis Eckersley .20
2 Jeff Bagwell .40
3 Jim Abbott .02
4 Steve Avery .01
5 Kelly Gruber .01
6 Ozzie Smith .40
7 Lance Dickson .01
8 Robin Yount .20
9 Brett Butler .02
10 Sandy Alomar Jr. .02
11 Travis Fryman .02
12 Ken Griffey Jr. .75
13 Cal Ripken 1.00
14 Will Clark .08
15 Nolan Ryan 1.00
16 Tony Gwynn .40
17 Roger Clemens .50
18 Wes Chamberlain .01
19 Barry Larkin .07
20 Brian McRae .01
21 Marquis Grissom .02
22 Cecil Fielder .02
23 Dwight Gooden .02
24 Chuck Knoblauch .07
25 Jose Canseco .20
26 Terry Pendleton .01
27 Ivan Rodriguez .40
28 Ryne Sandberg .20
29 Kent Hrbek .02
30 Ramon Martinez .02
31 Todd Zeile .02
32 Hal Morris .01
33 Robin Ventura .07
34 Doug Drabek .01
35 Frank Thomas .20
36 Don Mattingly .50

1992 Donruss Cracker Jack

This 36-card set is the second of two series produced by Donruss for Cracker Jack. The min cards were protected by a paper sleeve and inse into specially marked boxes of Cracker Jacks. A panel listed all 36 players in series II. The micro cards measure 1 1/4" by 1 3/4". The front desig the same as the Donruss regular issue cards, or different color player photos are displayed. The backs, however, have a completely different desi than the regular issue Donruss cards; they are horizontally oriented and present biography, ma league pitching (or batting) record, and brief car summary inside red borders. The cards are numbered on the back. On the paper sleeve was mail-in offer for a mini card album with six top loading plastic pages for 4.95 per album.

COMPLETE SET (36) 2.50
1 Craig Biggio .05
2 Tom Glavine .02
3 David Justice .08
4 Lee Smith .02
5 Mark Grace .08
6 Andre Dawson .08

yl Strawberry .02 .10
Davis .02 .10
Calderon .01 .05
yce Clayton .01 .05
att Williams .05 .15
ed McGriff .05 .15
n Dykstra .02 .10
rry Bonds .40 1.00
ggie Sanders .02 .10
ris Sabo .01 .05
ward Johnson .01 .05
bby Bonilla .01 .05
ckey Henderson .30 .75
ark Langston .01 .05
e Carter .02 .10
ul Molitor .20 .50
enallen Hill .01 .05
dgar Martinez .05 .15
egg Olson .01 .05
ben Sierra .02 .10
lio Franco .02 .10
il Plantier .01 .05
ade Boggs .15 .40
orge Brett .40 1.00
an Trammell .05 .15
rby Puckett .20 .50
ott Erickson .01 .05
ck McDowell .05 .15
att Nokes .01 .05
enny Tartabull .01 .05

1992 Donruss McDonald's

33-card standard-size set was produced by rus for distribution by McDonald's Restaurants ughout Canada. For 39 cents with the purchase y sandwich or breakfast entree, the collector ived a four-card pack featuring three cards from MVP series and one card from the Blue Jays Gold es. A player from each MLB team is represented e numbered 26-card MVP subset. Checklist s were also randomly inserted throughout the foil ks. In addition, 1,000 packs included a randomly rted prize card. By filling it out, answering the stion and sending it to the address on the card, winner received one of 1,000 numbered cards ographed by Roberto Alomar. The cards have the e design as the regular issue cards, with color on photos bordered in white and accented by blue es above and below the picture. One difference is MVP logo with the McDonald's "Golden Arches" emark on the front. The backs present a head , biography, recent major league performance istics, career highlights and the card number ("X 6"). Again, the McDonald's "Golden Arches" emark appears on the back alongside the other os. One card from the six-card gold subset (of onto Blue Jays) was included in each 1992 nruss McDonald's MVP four-card foil pack. The d card fronts feature full-bleed color player photos ented by goil foil stamping. The gold cards are ed below with a "G" prefix below for reference& ough a "G" prefix does not appear anywhere on cards. The player's name appears in a dark blue that overlays the bottom gold foil border stripe. In orizontal format, the backs carry biography, ntract status information, recent major league formance statistics and career highlights. As with MVP series, the McDonald's "Golden Arches" demark adorns both sides of the card.

MPLETE SET (33) 6.00 15.00
MMON PLAYER (1-26) .04 .10
MMON PLAYER (G1-G6) .20 .50
al Ripken 1.00 2.50
rank Thomas .20 .50
George Brett .50 1.25
oberto Kelly .02 .10
olan Ryan 1.00 2.50
yne Sandberg .30 .75
Darryl Strawberry .07 .20
Len Dykstra .07 .20
Fred McGriff .10 .30
Roger Clemens .50 1.25
Sandy Alomar Jr. .07 .20
Robin Yount .20 .50
Jose Canseco .30 .75
Jimmy Key .07 .20
Barry Larkin .15 .40
Dennis Martinez .07 .20
Andy Van Slyke .07 .20
3 Will Clark .15 .40
Mark Langston .02 .10
0 Cecil Fielder .07 .20
Kirby Puckett .20 .50
2 Ken Griffey Jr. 1.00 2.50
David Justice .15 .40
Jeff Bagwell .40 1.00
5 Howard Johnson .02 .10
5 Ozzie Smith .30 .75
1 Roberto Alomar .75 2.00
2 Joe Carter .30 .75
3 Kelly Gruber .20 .50
4 Jack Morris .30 .75

G5 Tom Henke .20 .50
G6 Devon White .20 .50
GAU Roberto Alomar AU 15.00 40.00
NNO Checklist Card SP .02 .10

1992 Donruss Super DK's

These cards are larger (5" by 7") versions of the 1992 Donruss Diamond King insert set. Although not formally available in 1992, a decent number have entered the secondary market in recent years making them more accessible in the hobby.

COMPLETE SET (27) 250.00 500.00
COMPLETE SERIES 1 (14) 150.00 400.00
COMPLETE SERIES 2 (13) 40.00 100.00
RANDOM INSERTS IN PACKS
DK1 Paul Molitor 12.50 30.00
DK2 Will Clark 10.00 25.00
DK3 Joe Carter 4.00 10.00
DK4 Julio Franco 4.00 10.00
DK5 Cal Ripken 60.00 150.00
DK6 David Justice 5.00 12.00
DK7 George Bell 3.00 8.00
DK8 Frank Thomas 20.00 50.00
DK9 Wade Boggs 15.00 40.00
DK10 Scott Sanderson 3.00 8.00
DK11 Jeff Bagwell 25.00 60.00
DK12 John Kruk 4.00 10.00
DK13 Felix Jose 3.00 8.00
DK14 Harold Baines 5.00 12.00
DK15 Dwight Gooden 4.00 10.00
DK16 Brian McRae 3.00 8.00
DK17 Jay Bell 3.00 8.00
DK18 Brett Butler 4.00 10.00
DK19 Hal Morris 3.00 8.00
DK20 Mark Langston 3.00 8.00
DK21 Scott Erickson 3.00 8.00
DK22 Randy Johnson 15.00 40.00
DK23 Greg Swindell 3.00 8.00
DK24 Dennis Martinez 4.00 10.00
DK25 Tony Phillips 3.00 8.00
DK26 Fred McGriff 5.00 12.00
DK27 Checklist 1-26 DP/(Dick Perez) 3.00 8.00

1993 Donruss Previews

COMPLETE SET (22) 30.00 80.00
1 Tom Glavine 1.25 3.00
2 Ryne Sandberg 3.00 8.00
3 Barry Larkin 1.25 3.00
4 Jeff Bagwell 2.50 6.00
5 Eric Karros .60 1.50
6 Larry Walker 1.25 3.00
7 Eddie Murray 2.00 5.00
8 Darren Daulton .60 1.50
9 Andy Van Slyke .60 1.50
10 Gary Sheffield 1.50 4.00
11 Will Clark 1.25 3.00
12 Cal Ripken 6.00 15.00
13 Roger Clemens 4.00 10.00
14 Frank Thomas 2.00 5.00
15 Cecil Fielder .60 1.50
16 George Brett 3.00 8.00
17 Robin Yount 1.50 4.00
18 Don Mattingly 3.00 8.00
19 Dennis Eckersley 1.50 4.00
20 Ken Griffey Jr. 8.00 20.00
21 Jose Canseco 1.25 3.00
22 Roberto Alomar 1.25 3.00

1993 Donruss

The 792-card 1993 Donruss set was issued in two series, each with 396 standard-size cards. Cards were distributed in foil packs. The basic card fronts feature glossy color action photos with white borders. At the bottom of the picture, the team logo appears in a team color-coded diamond with the player's name in a color-coded bar extending to the right. A Rated Rookies (RR) subset, sprinkled throughout the set, spotlights 20 young prospects. There are no key Rookie Cards in this set.

COMPLETE SET (792) 12.50 30.00
COMPLETE SERIES 1 (396) 6.00 15.00
COMPLETE SERIES 2 (396) 6.00 15.00
1 Craig Lefferts .02 .10
2 Kent Mercker .02 .10
3 Phil Plantier .02 .10
4 Alex Arias .02 .10
5 Julio Valera .02 .10
6 Dan Wilson .07 .20
7 Frank Thomas .20 .50
8 Eric Anthony .02 .10
9 Derek Lilliquist .02 .10
10 Rafael Bournigal .02 .10
11 Manny Alexander .02 .10
12 Bret Barberie .02 .10
13 Mickey Tettleton .02 .10
14 Anthony Young .02 .10
15 Tim Spehr .02 .10
16 Bob Ayrault .02 .10
17 Bill Wegman .02 .10
18 Jay Bell .07 .20
19 Rick Aguilera .02 .10
20 Todd Zeile .02 .10
21 Steve Farr .02 .10
22 Andy Benes .02 .10
23 Lance Blankenship .02 .10
24 Ted Wood .02 .10
25 Omar Vizquel .10 .30
26 Steve Avery .02 .10
27 Brian Bohanon .02 .10
28 Rick Wilkins .02 .10
29 Devon White .07 .20
30 Bobby Ayala RC .02 .10
31 Leo Gomez .02 .10
32 Mike Simms .02 .10
33 Ellis Burks .07 .20
34 Steve Wilson .02 .10
35 Jim Abbott .10 .30
36 Tim Wallach .02 .10
37 Wilson Alvarez .02 .10
38 Daryl Boston .02 .10
39 Sandy Alomar Jr. .02 .10
40 Mitch Williams .02 .10
41 Rico Brogna .02 .10
42 Gary Varsho .02 .10
43 Kevin Appier .07 .20
44 Eric Wedge RC .02 .10
45 Dante Bichette .07 .20
46 Jose Oquendo .02 .10
47 Mike Trombley .02 .10
48 Dan Walters .02 .10
49 Gerald Williams .02 .10
50 Bud Black .02 .10
51 Bobby Witt .02 .10
52 Mark Davis .02 .10
53 Shawn Barton RC .02 .10
54 Paul Assenmacher .02 .10
55 Kevin Reimer .02 .10
56 Billy Ashley .02 .10
57 Eddie Zosky .02 .10
58 Chris Sabo .02 .10
59 Billy Ripken .02 .10
60 Scooter Tucker .02 .10
61 Tim Wakefield .20 .50
62 Mitch Webster .02 .10
63 Jack Clark .07 .20
64 Mark Gardner .02 .10
65 Lee Stevens .02 .10
66 Todd Hundley .02 .10
67 Bobby Thigpen .02 .10
68 Dave Hollins .02 .10
69 Jack Armstrong .02 .10
70 Alex Cole .02 .10
71 Mark Carreon .02 .10
72 Todd Worrell .02 .10
73 Steve Shifflett .02 .10
74 Jerald Clark .02 .10
75 Paul Molitor .07 .20
76 Larry Carter RC .02 .10
77 Rich Rowland .02 .10
78 Damon Berryhill .02 .10
79 Willie Banks .02 .10
80 Hector Villanueva .02 .10
81 Mike Gallego .02 .10
82 Tim Belcher .02 .10
83 Mike Bordick .02 .10
84 Craig Biggio .10 .30
85 Lance Parrish .07 .20
86 Brett Butler .07 .20
87 Mike Timlin .02 .10
88 Brian Barnes .02 .10
89 Brady Anderson .07 .20
90 D.J. Dozier .02 .10
91 Frank Viola .07 .20
92 Darren Daulton .07 .20
93 Chad Curtis .02 .10
94 Zane Smith .02 .10
95 George Bell .02 .10
96 Rex Hudler .02 .10
97 Mark Whiten .02 .10
98 Tim Teufel .02 .10
99 Kevin Ritz .02 .10
100 Jeff Brantley .02 .10
101 Jeff Conine .07 .20
102 Vinny Castilla .20 .50
103 Greg Vaughn .02 .10
104 Steve Buechele .02 .10
105 Darren Reed .02 .10
106 Bip Roberts .02 .10
107 John Habyan .02 .10
108 Scott Servais .02 .10
109 Walt Weiss .02 .10
110 J.T. Snow RC .10 .30
111 Jay Buhner .07 .20
112 Darryl Strawberry .07 .20
113 Roger Pavlik .02 .10
114 Chris Nabholz .02 .10
115 Pat Borders .02 .10
116 Pat Howell .02 .10
117 Gregg Olson .02 .10
118 Curt Schilling .07 .20
119 Roger Clemens .40 1.00
120 Victor Cole .02 .10
121 Gary DiSarcina .02 .10
122 Checklist 1-80 .02 .10
Gary Carter and
Kirt Manwaring
123 Steve Sax .02 .10
124 Chuck Carr .02 .10
125 Mark Lewis .02 .10
126 Tony Gwynn .25 .60
127 Travis Fryman .07 .20
128 Dave Burba .02 .10
129 Wally Joyner .07 .20
130 John Smoltz .10 .30
131 Cal Eldred .02 .10
132 Checklist 81-159 .07 .20
(Roberto Alomar and
Devon White
133 Arthur Rhodes .02 .10
134 Jeff Blauser .02 .10
135 Scott Cooper .02 .10
136 Doug Strange .02 .10
137 Luis Sojo .02 .10
138 Jeff Branson .02 .10
139 Alex Fernandez .02 .10
140 Ken Caminiti .07 .20
141 Charles Nagy .02 .10
142 Tom Candiotti .02 .10
143 Willie Greene .02 .10
144 John Vander Wal .02 .10
145 Kurt Knudsen .02 .10
146 John Franco .07 .20
147 Eddie Pierce RC .02 .10
148 Kim Batiste .02 .10
149 Darren Holmes .02 .10
150 Steve Cooke .02 .10
151 Terry Jorgensen .02 .10
152 Mark Clark .02 .10
153 Randy Velarde .02 .10
154 Greg W. Harris .02 .10
155 Kevin Campbell .02 .10
156 John Burkett .02 .10
157 Kevin Mitchell .02 .10
158 Deion Sanders .10 .30
159 Jose Canseco .10 .30
160 Jeff Hartsock .02 .10
161 Tom Quinlan RC .02 .10
162 Tim Pugh RC .02 .10
163 Glenn Davis .02 .10
164 Shane Reynolds .02 .10
165 Jody Reed .02 .10
166 Mike Sharperson .02 .10
167 Scott Lewis .02 .10
168 Dennis Martinez .07 .20
169 Scott Radinsky .02 .10
170 Dave Gallagher .02 .10
171 Jim Thome .10 .30
172 Terry Mulholland .02 .10
173 Milt Cuyler .02 .10
174 Bob Patterson .02 .10
175 Jeff Montgomery .02 .10
176 Tim Salmon .10 .30
177 Franklin Stubbs .02 .10
178 Donovan Osborne .02 .10
179 Jeff Reboulet .02 .10
180 Jeremy Hernandez .02 .10
181 Charlie Hayes .02 .10
182 Matt Williams .07 .20
183 Mike Raczka .02 .10
184 Francisco Cabrera .02 .10
185 Rich DeLucia .02 .10
186 Sammy Sosa .20 .50
187 Ivan Rodriguez .10 .30
188 Bret Boone .07 .20
189 Juan Guzman .02 .10
190 Tom Browning .02 .10
191 Randy Milligan .02 .10
192 Steve Finley .07 .20
193 John Patterson RR .02 .10
194 Kip Gross .02 .10
195 Tony Fossas .02 .10
196 Ivan Calderon .02 .10
197 Junior Felix .02 .10
198 Pete Schourek .02 .10
199 Craig Grebeck .02 .10
200 Juan Bell .02 .10
201 Glenallen Hill .02 .10
202 Danny Jackson .02 .10
203 John Kiely .02 .10
204 Bob Tewksbury .02 .10
205 Kevin Koslofski .02 .10
206 Craig Shipley .02 .10
207 John Jaha .02 .10
208 Royce Clayton .02 .10
209 Mike Piazza 1.25 3.00
210 Ron Gant .07 .20
211 Scott Erickson .02 .10
212 Doug Dascenzo .02 .10
213 Andy Stankiewicz .02 .10
214 Geronimo Berroa .02 .10
215 Dennis Eckersley .07 .20
216 Al Osuna .02 .10
217 Tino Martinez .10 .30
218 Henry Rodriguez .02 .10
219 Ed Sprague .02 .10
220 Ken Hill .02 .10
221 Chito Martinez .02 .10
222 Bret Saberhagen .07 .20
223 Mike Greenwell .02 .10
224 Mickey Morandini .02 .10
225 Chuck Finley .07 .20
226 Denny Neagle .07 .20
227 Kirk McCaskill .02 .10
228 Rheal Cormier .02 .10
229 Paul Sorrento .02 .10
230 Darrin Jackson .02 .10
231 Rob Deer .02 .10
232 Bill Swift .02 .10
233 Kevin McReynolds .02 .10
234 Terry Pendleton .07 .20
235 Dave Nilsson .02 .10
236 Chuck McElroy .02 .10
237 Derek Parks .02 .10
238 Norm Charlton .02 .10
239 Matt Nokes .02 .10
240 Juan Guerrero .02 .10
241 Jeff Parrett .02 .10
242 Ryan Thompson .02 .10
243 Dave Fleming .02 .10
244 Dave Hansen .02 .10
245 Monty Fariss .02 .10
246 Archi Cianfrocco .02 .10
247 Pat Hentgen .02 .10
248 Bill Pecota .02 .10
249 Ben McDonald .02 .10
250 Cliff Brantley .02 .10
251 John Valentin .02 .10
252 Jeff King .02 .10
253 Reggie Williams .02 .10
254 Checklist 160-238 .02 .10
Sammy Sosa
Damon Berryhill
255 Ozzie Guillen .07 .20
256 Mike Perez .02 .10
257 Thomas Howard .02 .10
258 Kurt Stillwell .02 .10
259 Mike Henneman .02 .10
260 Steve Decker .02 .10
261 Brent Mayne .02 .10
262 Otis Nixon .02 .10
263 Mark Kiefer .02 .10
264 Checklist 239-317 .10 .30
Don Mattingly
Mike Bordick CL
265 Richie Lewis RC .02 .10
266 Pat Gomez RC .02 .10
267 Scott Taylor .02 .10
268 Shawn Dunston .02 .10
269 Greg Myers .02 .10
270 Tim Costo .02 .10
271 Greg Hibbard .02 .10
272 Pete Harnisch .02 .10
273 Dave Mlicki .02 .10
274 Orel Hershiser .07 .20
275 Sean Berry RR .02 .10
276 Doug Simons .02 .10
277 John Doherty .02 .10
278 Eddie Murray .20 .50
279 Chris Haney .02 .10
280 Stan Javier .02 .10
281 Jaime Navarro .02 .10
282 Orlando Merced .02 .10
283 Kent Hrbek .07 .20
284 Bernard Gilkey .02 .10
285 Russ Springer .02 .10
286 Mike Maddux .02 .10
287 Eric Fox .02 .10
288 Mark Leonard .02 .10
289 Tim Leary .02 .10
290 Brian Hunter .02 .10
291 Donald Harris .02 .10
292 Bob Scanlan .02 .10
293 Turner Ward .02 .10
294 Hal Morris .02 .10
295 Jimmy Poole .02 .10
296 Doug Jones .02 .10
297 Tony Pena .02 .10
298 Ramon Martinez .02 .10
299 Tim Fortugno .02 .10
300 Marquis Grissom .07 .20
301 Lance Johnson .02 .10
302 Jeff Kent .20 .50
303 Reggie Jefferson .02 .10
304 Wes Chamberlain .02 .10
305 Shawn Hare .02 .10
306 Mike LaValliere .02 .10
307 Gregg Jefferies .02 .10
308 Troy Neel .02 .10
309 Pat Listach .02 .10
310 Geronimo Pena .02 .10
311 Pedro Munoz .02 .10
312 Guillermo Velasquez .02 .10
313 Roberto Kelly .02 .10
314 Mike Jackson .02 .10
315 Rickey Henderson .20 .50
316 Mark Lemke .02 .10
317 Erik Hanson .02 .10
318 Derrick May .02 .10
319 Geno Petralli .02 .10
320 Melvin Nieves .02 .10
321 Doug Linton .02 .10
322 Rob Dibble .07 .20
323 Chris Hoiles .02 .10
324 Jimmy Jones .02 .10
325 Dave Staton .02 .10
326 Pedro Martinez .40 1.00
327 Paul Quantrill .02 .10
328 Greg Colbrunn .02 .10
329 Hilly Hathaway RC .02 .10
330 Jeff Innis .02 .10
331 Ron Karkovice .02 .10
332 Keith Shepherd RC .02 .10
333 Alan Embree .02 .10
334 Paul Wagner .02 .10
335 Dave Haas .02 .10
336 Ozzie Canseco .02 .10
337 Bill Sampen .02 .10
338 Rich Rodriguez .02 .10
339 Dean Palmer .07 .20
340 Greg Litton .02 .10
341 Jim Tatum RC .02 .10
342 Todd Haney RC .02 .10
343 Larry Casian .02 .10
344 Ryne Sandberg .30 .75
345 Sterling Hitchcock RC .07 .20
346 Chris Hammond .02 .10
347 Vince Horsman .02 .10
348 Butch Henry .02 .10
349 Dann Howitt .02 .10
350 Roger McDowell .02 .10
351 Jack Morris .07 .20
352 Bill Krueger .02 .10
353 Cris Colon .02 .10
354 Joe Vitko .02 .10
355 Willie McGee .07 .20
356 Jay Baller .02 .10
357 Pat Mahomes .02 .10
358 Roger Mason .02 .10
359 Jerry Nielsen .02 .10
360 Tom Pagnozzi .02 .10
361 Kevin Baez .02 .10
362 Tim Scott .02 .10
363 Domingo Martinez RC .02 .10
364 Kirt Manwaring .02 .10
365 Rafael Palmeiro .10 .30
366 Ray Lankford .07 .20
367 Tim McIntosh .02 .10
368 Jessie Hollins .02 .10
369 Scott Leius .02 .10
370 Bill Doran .02 .10
371 Sam Militello .02 .10
372 Ryan Bowen .02 .10
373 Dave Henderson .02 .10
374 Dan Smith .02 .10
375 Steve Reed RC .02 .10
376 Jose Offerman .02 .10
377 Kevin Brown .07 .20
378 Darrin Fletcher .02 .10
379 Duane Ward .02 .10
380 Wayne Kirby .02 .10
381 Steve Scarsone .02 .10
382 Mariano Duncan .02 .10
383 Ken Ryan RC .02 .10
384 Lloyd McClendon .02 .10
385 Brian Holman .02 .10
386 Braulio Castillo .02 .10
387 Danny Leon .02 .10
388 Omar Olivares .02 .10
389 Kevin Wickander .02 .10
390 Fred McGriff .10 .30
391 Phil Clark .02 .10
392 Darren Lewis .02 .10
393 Phil Hiatt .02 .10
394 Mike Morgan .02 .10
395 Shane Mack .02 .10
396 Checklist 318-396 .07 .20
(Dennis Eckersley
and Art Kusn
397 David Segui .02 .10
398 Rafael Belliard .02 .10
399 Tim Naehring .02 .10
400 Frank Castillo .02 .10
401 Joe Grahe .02 .10
402 Reggie Sanders .07 .20
403 Roberto Hernandez .02 .10
404 Luis Gonzalez .07 .20
405 Carlos Baerga .02 .10
406 Carlos Hernandez .02 .10
407 Pedro Astacio .02 .10
408 Mel Rojas .02 .10
409 Scott Livingstone .02 .10
410 Chico Walker .02 .10
411 Brian McRae .02 .10
412 Ben Rivera .02 .10
413 Ricky Bones .02 .10
414 Andy Van Slyke .10 .30
415 Chuck Knoblauch .07 .20
416 Luis Alicea .02 .10
417 Bob Wickman .02 .10
418 Doug Brocail .02 .10
419 Scott Brosius .07 .20
420 Rod Beck .02 .10
421 Edgar Martinez .10 .30
422 Ryan Klesko .07 .20
423 Nolan Ryan .75 2.00
424 Rey Sanchez .02 .10
425 Roberto Alomar .10 .30
426 Barry Larkin .10 .30
427 Mike Mussina .10 .30
428 Jeff Bagwell .10 .30
429 Mo Vaughn .07 .20
430 Eric Karros .07 .20
431 John Orton .02 .10
432 Wil Cordero .02 .10
433 Jack McDowell .02 .10
434 Howard Johnson .02 .10
435 Albert Belle .07 .20
436 John Kruk .07 .20
437 Skeeter Barnes .02 .10
438 Don Slaught .02 .10
439 Rusty Meacham .02 .10
440 Tim Laker RC .02 .10
441 Robin Yount .30 .75
442 Brian Jordan .07 .20
443 Kevin Tapani .02 .10
444 Gary Sheffield .07 .20
445 Rich Monteleone .02 .10
446 Will Clark .10 .30
447 Jerry Browne .02 .10
448 Jeff Treadway .02 .10
449 Mike Schooler .02 .10
450 Mike Harkey .02 .10
451 Julio Franco .07 .20
452 Kevin Young .07 .20
453 Kelly Gruber .02 .10
454 Jose Rijo .02 .10
455 Mike Devereaux .02 .10
456 Andujar Cedeno .02 .10
457 Damion Easley RR .02 .10
458 Kevin Gross .02 .10
459 Matt Young .02 .10
460 Matt Stairs .02 .10
461 Luis Polonia .02 .10
462 Dwight Gooden .07 .20
463 Warren Newson .02 .10
464 Jose DeLeon .02 .10
465 Jose Mesa .02 .10
466 Danny Cox .02 .10
467 Dan Gladden .02 .10
468 Gerald Perry .02 .10
469 Mike Boddicker .02 .10
470 Jeff Gardner .02 .10
471 Doug Henry .02 .10
472 Mike Benjamin .02 .10
473 Dan Peltier .02 .10
474 Mike Stanton .02 .10
475 John Smiley .02 .10
476 Dwight Smith .02 .10
477 Jim Leyritz .02 .10
478 Dwayne Henry .02 .10
479 Mark McGwire .50 1.25
480 Pete Incaviglia .02 .10
481 Dave Cochrane .02 .10
482 Eric Davis .07 .20
483 John Olerud .07 .20
484 Kent Bottenfield .02 .10
485 Mark McLemore .02 .10
486 Dave Magadan .02 .10
487 John Marzano .02 .10
488 Ruben Amaro .02 .10
489 Rob Ducey .02 .10
490 Stan Belinda .02 .10
491 Dan Pasqua .02 .10
492 Joe Magrane .02 .10
493 Brook Jacoby .02 .10
494 Gene Harris .02 .10
495 Mark Leiter .02 .10
496 Bryan Hickerson .02 .10
497 Tom Gordon .02 .10
498 Pete Smith .02 .10
499 Chris Bosio .02 .10
500 Shawn Boskie .02 .10
501 Dave West .02 .10
502 Milt Hill .02 .10
503 Pat Kelly .02 .10
504 Joe Boever .02 .10
505 Terry Steinbach .02 .10
506 Butch Huskey .02 .10
507 David Valle .02 .10
508 Mike Scioscia .02 .10
509 Kenny Rogers .07 .20
510 Moises Alou .07 .20
511 David Wells .07 .20
512 Mackey Sasser .02 .10
513 Todd Frohwirth .02 .10
514 Ricky Jordan .02 .10
515 Mike Gardiner .02 .10
516 Gary Redus .02 .10
517 Gary Gaetti .07 .20
518 Cal Ripken Jr. .02 .10
Kenny Lofton CL
519 Carlton Fisk .10 .30
520 Ozzie Smith .30 .75
521 Rod Nichols .02 .10
522 Benito Santiago .07 .20
523 Bill Gullickson .02 .10
524 Robby Thompson .02 .10
525 Mike Macfarlane .02 .10
526 Sid Bream .02 .10
527 Darryl Hamilton .02 .10
528 Checklist .02 .10
529 Jeff Tackett .02 .10
530 Greg Olson .02 .10
531 Bob Zupcic .02 .10
532 Mark Grace .10 .30
533 Steve Frey .02 .10
534 Dave Martinez .02 .10
535 Robin Ventura .07 .20
536 Casey Candaele .02 .10
537 Kenny Lofton .07 .20
538 Jay Howell .02 .10
539 Fernando Ramsey RC .02 .10
540 Larry Walker .07 .20
541 Cecil Fielder .07 .20
542 Lee Guetterman .02 .10
543 Keith Miller .02 .10
544 Len Dykstra .07 .20
545 B.J. Surhoff .07 .20
546 Bob Walk .02 .10
547 Brian Harper .02 .10
548 Lee Smith .07 .20
549 Danny Tartabull .02 .10
550 Frank Seminara .02 .10
551 Henry Mercedes .02 .10
552 Dave Righetti .07 .20
553 Ken Griffey Jr. .40 1.00

Card	Low	High
554 Tom Glavine	.10	.30
555 Juan Gonzalez	.07	.20
556 Jim Bullinger	.02	.10
557 Derek Bell	.02	.10
558 Cesar Hernandez	.02	.10
559 Cal Ripken	.60	1.50
560 Eddie Taubensee	.02	.10
561 John Flaherty	.02	.10
562 Todd Benzinger	.02	.10
563 Hubie Brooks	.02	.10
564 Delino DeShields	.02	.10
565 Tim Raines	.07	.20
566 Sid Fernandez	.02	.10
567 Steve Olin	.02	.10
568 Tommy Greene	.02	.10
569 Buddy Groom	.02	.10
570 Randy Tomlin	.02	.10
571 Hipolito Pichardo	.02	.10
572 Rene Arocha RC	.07	.20
573 Mike Fetters	.02	.10
574 Felix Jose	.02	.10
575 Gene Larkin	.02	.10
576 Bruce Hurst	.02	.10
577 Bernie Williams	.10	.30
578 Trevor Wilson	.02	.10
579 Bob Welch	.02	.10
580 David Justice	.07	.20
581 Randy Johnson	.20	.50
582 Jose Vizcaino	.02	.10
583 Jeff Huson	.02	.10
584 Rob Maurer	.02	.10
585 Todd Stottlemyre	.02	.10
586 Joe Oliver	.02	.10
587 Bob Milacki	.02	.10
588 Rob Murphy	.02	.10
589 Greg Pirkl	.02	.10
590 Lenny Harris	.02	.10
591 Luis Rivera	.02	.10
592 John Wetteland	.07	.20
593 Mark Langston	.02	.10
594 Bobby Bonilla	.07	.20
595 Esteban Beltre	.02	.10
596 Mike Hartley	.02	.10
597 Felix Fermin	.02	.10
598 Carlos Garcia	.02	.10
599 Frank Tanana	.02	.10
600 Pedro Guerrero	.07	.20
601 Terry Shumpert	.02	.10
602 Wally Whitehurst	.02	.10
603 Kevin Seitzer	.02	.10
604 Chris James	.02	.10
605 Greg Gohr	.02	.10
606 Mark Wohlers	.02	.10
607 Kirby Puckett	.20	.50
608 Greg Maddux	.30	.75
609 Don Mattingly	.50	1.25
610 Greg Cadaret	.02	.10
611 Dave Stewart	.07	.20
612 Mark Portugal	.02	.10
613 Pete O'Brien	.02	.10
614 Bob Ojeda	.02	.10
615 Joe Carter	.07	.20
616 Pete Young	.02	.10
617 Sam Horn	.02	.10
618 Vince Coleman	.02	.10
619 Wade Boggs	.10	.30
620 Todd Pratt RC	.07	.20
621 Ron Tingley	.02	.10
622 Doug Drabek	.02	.10
623 Scott Hemond	.02	.10
624 Tim Jones	.02	.10
625 Dennis Cook	.02	.10
626 Jose Melendez	.02	.10
627 Mike Munoz	.02	.10
628 Jim Pena	.02	.10
629 Gary Thurman	.02	.10
630 Charlie Leibrandt	.02	.10
631 Scott Fletcher	.02	.10
632 Andre Dawson	.07	.20
633 Greg Gagne	.02	.10
634 Greg Swindell	.02	.10
635 Kevin Maas	.02	.10
636 Xavier Hernandez	.02	.10
637 Ruben Sierra	.07	.20
638 Dmitri Young	.07	.20
639 Harold Reynolds	.07	.20
640 Tom Goodwin	.02	.10
641 Todd Burns	.02	.10
642 Jeff Fassero	.02	.10
643 Dave Winfield	.07	.20
644 Willie Randolph	.07	.20
645 Luis Mercedes	.02	.10
646 Dale Murphy	.10	.30
647 Danny Darwin	.02	.10
648 Dennis Moeller	.02	.10
649 Chuck Crim	.02	.10
650 Carlos Baerga CL	.02	.10
651 Shawn Abner	.02	.10
652 Tracy Woodson	.02	.10
653 Scott Scudder	.02	.10
654 Tom Lampkin	.02	.10
655 Alan Trammell	.07	.20
656 Cory Snyder	.02	.10
657 Chris Gwynn	.02	.10
658 Lonnie Smith	.02	.10
659 Jim Austin	.02	.10
660 Rob Picciolo	.02	.10
Tony Gwynn		
Gary Sheffield CL		
661 Tim Hulett	.02	.10
662 Marvin Freeman	.02	.10
663 Greg A. Harris	.02	.10
664 Heathcliff Slocumb	.02	.10
665 Mike Butcher	.02	.10
666 Steve Foster	.02	.10
667 Donn Pall	.02	.10
668 Darryl Kile	.07	.20
669 Jesse Levis	.02	.10
670 Jim Gott	.02	.10
671 Mark Hutton	.02	.10
672 Brian Drahman	.02	.10
673 Chad Kreuter	.02	.10
674 Tony Fernandez	.02	.10
675 Jose Lind	.02	.10
676 Kyle Abbott	.02	.10
677 Dan Plesac	.02	.10
678 Barry Bonds	.60	1.50
679 Chili Davis	.07	.20
680 Stan Royer	.02	.10
681 Scott Kamieniecki	.02	.10
682 Carlos Martinez	.02	.10
683 Mike Moore	.02	.10
684 Candy Maldonado	.02	.10
685 Jeff Nelson	.02	.10
686 Lou Whitaker	.07	.20
687 Jose Guzman	.02	.10
688 Manuel Lee	.02	.10
689 Bob MacDonald	.02	.10
690 Scott Bankhead	.02	.10
691 Alan Mills	.02	.10
692 Brian Williams	.02	.10
693 Tom Brunansky	.02	.10
694 Lenny Webster	.02	.10
695 Greg Briley	.02	.10
696 Paul O'Neill	.10	.30
697 Joey Cora	.02	.10
698 Charlie O'Brien	.02	.10
699 Junior Ortiz	.02	.10
700 Ron Darling	.02	.10
701 Tony Phillips	.02	.10
702 William Pennyfeather	.02	.10
703 Mark Gubicza	.02	.10
704 Steve Hosey	.02	.10
705 Henry Cotto	.02	.10
706 David Hulse RC	.02	.10
707 Mike Pagliarulo	.02	.10
708 Dave Stieb	.02	.10
709 Melido Perez	.02	.10
710 Jimmy Key	.07	.20
711 Jeff Russell	.02	.10
712 David Cone	.07	.20
713 Russ Swan	.02	.10
714 Mark Guthrie	.02	.10
715 Mark Grace	.02	.10
Bip Roberts CL		
716 Al Martin	.02	.10
717 Randy Knorr	.02	.10
718 Mike Stanley	.02	.10
719 Rick Sutcliffe	.07	.20
720 Terry Leach	.02	.10
721 Chipper Jones	.20	.50
722 Jim Eisenreich	.02	.10
723 Tom Henke	.02	.10
724 Jeff Frye	.02	.10
725 Harold Baines	.07	.20
726 Scott Sanderson	.02	.10
727 Tom Foley	.02	.10
728 Bryan Harvey	.02	.10
729 Tom Edens	.02	.10
730 Eric Young	.02	.10
731 Dave Weathers	.02	.10
732 Spike Owen	.02	.10
733 Scott Aldred	.02	.10
734 Cris Carpenter	.02	.10
735 Dion James	.02	.10
736 Joe Girardi	.02	.10
737 Nigel Wilson	.02	.10
738 Scott Chiamparino	.02	.10
739 Jeff Reardon	.07	.20
740 Willie Blair	.02	.10
741 Jim Corsi	.02	.10
742 Ken Patterson	.02	.10
743 Andy Ashby	.02	.10
744 Rob Natal	.02	.10
745 Kevin Bass	.02	.10
746 Freddie Benavides	.02	.10
747 Chris Donnels	.02	.10
748 Kerry Woodson	.02	.10
749 Calvin Jones	.02	.10
750 Gary Scott	.02	.10
751 Joe Orsulak	.02	.10
752 Armando Reynoso	.02	.10
753 Monty Fariss	.02	.10
754 Billy Hatcher	.02	.10
755 Denis Boucher	.02	.10
756 Walt Weiss	.02	.10
757 Mike Fitzgerald	.02	.10
758 Rudy Seanez	.02	.10
759 Bret Barberie	.02	.10
760 Mo Sanford	.02	.10
761 Pedro Castellano	.02	.10
762 Chuck Carr	.02	.10
763 Steve Howe	.02	.10
764 Andres Galarraga	.07	.20
765 Jeff Conine	.07	.20
766 Ted Power	.02	.10
767 Butch Henry	.02	.10
768 Steve Decker	.02	.10
769 Storm Davis	.02	.10
770 Vinny Castilla	.20	.50
771 Junior Felix	.02	.10
772 Walt Terrell	.02	.10
773 Brad Ausmus	.20	.50
774 Jamie McAndrew	.02	.10
775 Milt Thompson	.02	.10
776 Charlie Hayes	.02	.10
777 Jack Armstrong	.02	.10
778 Dennis Rasmussen	.02	.10
779 Darren Holmes	.02	.10
780 Alex Arias	.02	.10
781 Randy Bush	.02	.10
782 Javy Lopez	.10	.30
783 Dante Bichette	.07	.20
784 John Johnstone RC	.02	.10
785 Rene Gonzales	.02	.10
786 Alex Cole	.02	.10
787 Jeromy Burnitz	.07	.20
788 Michael Huff	.02	.10
789 Anthony Telford	.02	.10
790 Jerald Clark	.02	.10
791 Joel Johnston	.02	.10
792 David Nied	.02	.10

1993 Donruss Diamond Kings

These standard-size cards, commemorating Donruss' annual selection of the games top players, were randomly inserted in 1993 Donruss packs. The first 15 cards were available in the first series of the 1993 Donruss and cards 16-31 were inserted with the second series. The cards are gold-foil stamped and feature player portraits by noted sports artist Dick Perez. Card numbers 27-28 honor the first draft picks of the new Florida Marlins and Colorado Rockies franchises. Collectors 16 years of age and younger could enter Donruss' Diamond King contest by writing an essay of 75 words or less explaining who their favorite Diamond King player was and why. Winners were awarded one of 30 framed watercolors at the National Convention, held in Chicago, July 22-25, 1993.

Card	Low	High
COMPLETE SET (31)	12.50	30.00
COMPLETE SERIES 1 (15)	8.00	20.00
COMPLETE SERIES 2 (16)	4.00	10.00
RANDOM INSERTS IN FOIL PACKS		
DK1 Ken Griffey Jr.	2.50	6.00
DK2 Ryne Sandberg	2.00	5.00
DK3 Roger Clemens	2.50	6.00
DK4 Kirby Puckett	1.25	3.00
DK5 Bill Swift	.25	.60
DK6 Larry Walker	.50	1.25
DK7 Juan Gonzalez	.50	1.25
DK8 Wally Joyner	.50	1.25
DK9 Andy Van Slyke	.75	2.00
DK10 Robin Ventura	.50	1.25
DK11 Bip Roberts	.25	.60
DK12 Roberto Kelly	.25	.60
DK13 Carlos Baerga	.25	.60
DK14 Orel Hershiser	.50	1.25
DK15 Cecil Fielder	.50	1.25
DK16 Robin Yount	2.00	5.00
DK17 Darren Daulton	.50	1.25
DK18 Mark McGwire	3.00	8.00
DK19 Tom Glavine	.75	2.00
DK20 Roberto Alomar	.75	2.00
DK21 Gary Sheffield	.50	1.25
DK22 Bob Tewksbury	.25	.60
DK23 Brady Anderson	.50	1.25
DK24 Craig Biggio	.75	2.00
DK25 Eddie Murray	1.25	3.00
DK26 Luis Polonia	.25	.60
DK27 Nigel Wilson	.25	.60
DK28 David Nied	.25	.60
DK29 Pat Listach ROY	.25	.60
DK30 Eric Karros	.50	1.25
DK31 Checklist 1-31	.40	1.00

1993 Donruss Elite

The numbering on the 1993 Elite cards follows consecutively after that of the 1992 Elite series cards, and each of the 10,000 Elite cards is serially numbered. Cards 19-27 were random inserts in 1993 Donruss series I foil packs while cards 28-36 were inserted in series II packs. The backs of the Elite cards also carry the serial number ("X" of 10,000) as well as the card number. The Signature Series Will Clark card was randomly inserted in 1993 Donruss foil packs; he personally autographed 5,000 cards. Featuring a Dick Perez portrait, the ten thousand Legends Series cards honor Robin Yount for his 3,000th hit achievement.

Card	Low	High
RANDOM INSERTS IN PACKS		
STATED PRINT RUN 10,000 SERIAL #'d SETS		
19 Fred McGriff	8.00	20.00
20 Ryne Sandberg	8.00	20.00
21 Eddie Murray	8.00	20.00
22 Paul Molitor	5.00	12.00
23 Barry Larkin	8.00	20.00
24 Don Mattingly	10.00	25.00
25 Dennis Eckersley	5.00	12.00
26 Roberto Alomar	8.00	20.00
27 Edgar Martinez	8.00	20.00
28 Gary Sheffield	5.00	12.00
29 Darren Daulton	5.00	12.00
30 Larry Walker	5.00	12.00
31 Barry Bonds	12.00	30.00
32 Andy Van Slyke	12.00	30.00
33 Mark McGwire	10.00	25.00
34 Cecil Fielder	8.00	20.00
35 Dave Winfield	5.00	12.00
36 Juan Gonzalez	5.00	12.00
L3 Robin Yount Legend	10.00	25.00
S3 Will Clark AU/5000	50.00	100.00

1993 Donruss Long Ball Leaders

Randomly inserted in 26-card magazine distributor packs (1-9 in series I and 10-18 in series II), these standard-size cards feature some of MLB's outstanding sluggers.

Card	Low	High
COMPLETE SET (18)	25.00	60.00
COMPLETE SERIES 1 (9)	12.50	30.00
COMPLETE SERIES 2 (9)	12.50	30.00
RANDOM INSERTS IN 26-CARD JUMBOS		
LL1 Rob Deer	.40	1.00
LL2 Fred McGriff	1.25	3.00
LL3 Albert Belle	.75	2.00
LL4 Mark McGwire	5.00	12.00
LL5 David Justice	.75	2.00
LL6 Jose Canseco	1.25	3.00
LL7 Kent Hrbek	.75	2.00
LL8 Roberto Alomar	1.25	3.00
LL9 Ken Griffey Jr.	4.00	10.00
LL10 Frank Thomas	2.00	5.00
LL11 Darryl Strawberry	.75	2.00
LL12 Felix Jose	.40	1.00
LL13 Cecil Fielder	.75	2.00
LL14 Juan Gonzalez	.75	2.00
LL15 Ryne Sandberg	3.00	8.00
LL16 Gary Sheffield	.75	2.00
LL17 Jeff Bagwell	1.25	3.00
LL18 Larry Walker	.75	2.00

1993 Donruss MVPs

These twenty-six standard size MVP cards were issued 13 cards in each series, and they were inserted one per 23-card jumbo packs.

Card	Low	High
COMPLETE SET (26)	10.00	25.00
COMPLETE SERIES 1 (13)	4.00	10.00
COMPLETE SERIES 2 (13)	8.00	20.00
ONE PER 23-CARD JUMBO PACK		
1 Luis Polonia	.15	.40
2 Frank Thomas	.75	2.00
3 George Brett	2.00	5.00
4 Paul Molitor	.30	.75
5 Don Mattingly	2.00	5.00
6 Roberto Alomar	.50	1.25
7 Terry Pendleton	.30	.75
8 Eric Karros	.30	.75
9 Larry Walker	.30	.75
10 Eddie Murray	.75	2.00
11 Darren Daulton	.30	.75
12 Ray Lankford	.30	.75
13 Will Clark	.50	1.25
14 Cal Ripken	2.50	6.00
15 Roger Clemens	1.50	4.00
16 Carlos Baerga	.15	.40
17 Cecil Fielder	.30	.75
18 Kirby Puckett	.75	2.00
19 Mark McGwire	2.00	5.00
20 Ken Griffey Jr.	1.50	4.00
21 Juan Gonzalez	.30	.75
22 Ryne Sandberg	1.25	3.00
23 Bip Roberts	.15	.40
24 Jeff Bagwell	.50	1.25
25 Barry Bonds	2.50	6.00
26 Gary Sheffield	.30	.75

1993 Donruss Spirit of the Game

These 20 standard-size cards were randomly inserted in 1993 Donruss packs and packed approximately two per box. Cards 1-10 were first-series inserts, and cards 11-20 were second-series inserts. The fronts feature borderless glossy color action player photos.

Card	Low	High
COMPLETE SET (20)	8.00	20.00
COMPLETE SERIES 1 (10)	3.00	8.00
COMPLETE SERIES 2 (10)	5.00	12.00
RANDOM INSERTS IN FOIL/JUMBO PACKS		
SG1 M.Bordick	.20	.50
D.Winfield		
SG2 David Justice	.40	1.00
SG3 Roberto Alomar	.60	1.50
SG4 Dennis Eckersley	.40	1.00
SG5 J.Gonzalez	.60	1.50
J.Canseco		
SG6 G.Bell	1.00	2.50
F.Thomas		
SG7 W.Boggs	.60	1.50
L.Polonia		
SG8 Will Clark	.60	1.50
SG9 Bip Roberts	.20	.50
SG10 Fielder	.20	.50
Deer		
Tettleton		
SG11 Kenny Lofton	.40	1.00
SG12 G.Sheffield	1.00	2.50
F.McGriff		
SG13 G.Gagne	.20	.50
B.Larkin		
SG14 Ryne Sandberg	1.50	4.00
SG15 C.Baerga	.20	.50
G.Gaetti		
SG16 Danny Tartabull	.20	.50
SG17 Brady Anderson	.40	1.00
SG18 Frank Thomas	1.00	2.50
SG19 Kevin Gross	.20	.50
SG20 Robin Yount	1.50	4.00

1993 Donruss Elite Dominators

In a series of programs broadcast Dec. 8-13, 1993, on the Shop at Home cable network, viewers were offered the opportunity to purchase a factory-sealed box of either 1993 Donruss I or II, which included one Elite Dominator card produced especially for the promotion."The set retailed for 99.00 plus 6.00 for postage and handling. 5,000 serial-numbered sets were produced and half of the cards for Nolan Ryan, Juan Gonzalez, Paul Molitor, and Don Mattingly were signed by the player. The entire print run of 100,000 cards were reportedly purchased by the Shop at Home network and were to be offered periodically over the network. The production number, out of a total of 5,000 produced, is shown at the bottom.

Card	Low	High
COMP.UNSIGNED SET (20)	125.00	250.00
1 Ryne Sandberg	10.00	25.00
2 Fred McGriff	2.00	5.00
3 Greg Maddux	8.00	20.00
4 Ron Gant	1.50	4.00
5 Dave Justice	6.00	15.00
6 Don Mattingly	8.00	20.00
7 Tim Salmon	4.00	10.00
8 Mike Piazza	8.00	20.00
9 John Olerud	1.50	4.00
10 Nolan Ryan	20.00	50.00
11 Juan Gonzalez	2.50	6.00
12 Ken Griffey Jr.	30.00	80.00
13 Frank Thomas	15.00	40.00
14 Tom Glavine	2.00	5.00
15 George Brett	10.00	25.00
16 Barry Bonds	8.00	20.00
17 Albert Belle	3.00	8.00
18 Paul Molitor	3.00	8.00
19 Cal Ripken	6.00	15.00
20 Roberto Alomar	6.00	15.00
AU6 Don Mattingly AU	50.00	120.00
AU10 Nolan Ryan AU	40.00	100.00
AU11 Juan Gonzalez AU	20.00	50.00
AU18 Paul Molitor AU	15.00	40.00

1993 Donruss Elite Supers

Sequentially numbered one through 5,000, these 20 oversized cards measure approximately 3 1/2" by 5" and have wide prismatic foil borders with an inner gray borders. The Elite Update set features all the players found in the regular Elite set, plus Nolan Ryan and Frank Thomas, whose cards replace numbers 19 and 20 from the earlier release, and an updated card of Barry Bonds in his Giants uniform. The backs carry the production number and the card number.

Card	Low	High
COMPLETE SET (20)	75.00	150.00
1 Fred McGriff	1.50	4.00
2 Ryne Sandberg	6.00	15.00
3 Eddie Murray	8.00	20.00
4 Paul Molitor	4.00	10.00
5 Barry Larkin	4.00	10.00
6 Don Mattingly	6.00	15.00
7 Dennis Eckersley	3.00	8.00
8 Roberto Alomar	2.00	5.00
9 Edgar Martinez	1.50	4.00
10 Gary Sheffield	3.00	8.00
11 Darren Daulton	1.00	2.50
12 Larry Walker	4.00	10.00
13 Barry Bonds	8.00	20.00
14 Andy Van Slyke	6.00	15.00
15 Mark McGwire	8.00	20.00
16 Cecil Fielder	1.00	2.50
17 Dave Winfield	5.00	12.00
18 Juan Gonzalez	2.00	5.00
19 Frank Thomas	8.00	20.00
20 Nolan Ryan	15.00	40.00

1993 Donruss Masters of the Game

These cards were issued in individual retail re-packs, and also were included in special 18-pack boxes of 1993 Donruss second series. The cards were originally available only at retail outlets such as WalMart along with a foil pack of 1993 Donruss. These 16 postcards measure approximately 3 1/2" by 5" and feature the work of artist Dick Perez on their fronts.

Card	Low	High
COMPLETE SET (16)	8.00	20.00
1 Frank Thomas	1.25	3.00
2 Nolan Ryan	4.00	10.00
3 Gary Sheffield	1.25	3.00
4 Fred McGriff	.75	2.00
5 Ryne Sandberg	1.50	4.00
6 Cal Ripken	4.00	10.00
7 Jose Canseco	1.00	2.50
8 Ken Griffey Jr.	3.00	8.00
9 Will Clark	1.00	2.50
10 Roberto Alomar	1.00	2.50
11 Juan Gonzalez	1.00	2.50
12 David Justice	1.00	2.50
13 Kirby Puckett	1.25	3.00
14 Barry Bonds	2.00	5.00
15 Robin Yount	1.25	3.00
16 Deion Sanders	.75	2.00

1994 Donruss Promos

Card	Low	High
COMPLETE SET (12)	25.00	60.00
COMMON PLAYER (1-10)	.40	1.00
COMMON SP	6.00	15.00
1 Barry Bonds	2.50	6.00
1SE Barry Bonds SP	8.00	20.00
2 Darren Daulton	.40	1.00
3 John Olerud	.40	1.00
4 Frank Thomas	1.50	4.00
4SE Frank Thomas SP	6.00	15.00
5 Mike Piazza	2.50	6.00
6 Tim Salmon	.40	1.00
7 Ken Griffey Jr.	5.00	12.00
8 Fred McGriff	.60	1.50
9 Don Mattingly	2.00	5.00
10 Gary Sheffield	1.00	2.50

1994 Donruss

The 1994 Donruss set was issued in two separate series of 330 standard-size cards for a total of 660. Cards were issued in foil wrapped packs. The fronts feature borderless color player action photos on front. There are no notable Rookie Cards in this set.

Card	Low	High
COMPLETE SET (660)	12.50	30.00
COMPLETE SERIES 1 (330)	6.00	15.00
COMPLETE SERIES 2 (330)	6.00	15.00
1 Nolan Ryan Salute	1.50	4.00
2 Mike Piazza	.60	1.50
3 Moises Alou	.10	.30
4 Ken Griffey Jr.	.60	1.50
5 Gary Sheffield	.10	.30
6 Roberto Alomar	.20	.50
7 John Kruk	.10	.30
8 Gregg Olson	.05	.15
9 Gregg Jefferies	.05	.15
10 Tony Gwynn	.40	1.00
11 Chad Curtis	.05	.15
12 Craig Biggio	.20	.50
13 John Burkett	.05	.15
14 Carlos Baerga	.05	.15
15 Robin Yount	.50	1.25
16 Dennis Eckersley	.10	.30
17 Dwight Gooden	.10	.30
18 Ryne Sandberg	.50	1.25
19 Rickey Henderson	.30	.75
20 Jack McDowell	.05	.15
21 Jay Bell	.10	.30
22 Kevin Brown	.10	.30
23 Robin Ventura	.10	.30
24 Paul Molitor	.10	.30
25 David Justice	.10	.30
26 Rafael Palmeiro	.20	.50
27 Cecil Fielder	.10	.30
28 Chuck Knoblauch	.10	.30
29 Dave Hollins	.05	.15
30 Jimmy Key	.10	.30
31 Mark Langston	.05	.15
32 Darryl Kile	.10	.30
33 Ruben Sierra	.10	.30
34 Ron Gant	.10	.30
35 Ozzie Smith	.50	1.25
36 Wade Boggs	.20	.50
37 Marquis Grissom	.10	.30
38 Will Clark	.20	.50
39 Kenny Lofton	.10	.30
40 Cal Ripken	1.00	2.50
41 Steve Avery	.05	.15
42 Mo Vaughn	.10	.30
43 Brian McRae	.05	.15
44 Mickey Tettleton	.05	.15
45 Barry Larkin	.20	.50
46 Charlie Hayes	.05	.15
47 Kevin Appier	.10	.30
48 Robby Thompson	.05	.15
49 Juan Gonzalez	.10	.30
50 Paul O'Neill	.20	.50
51 Marcos Armas	.05	.15
52 Mike Butcher	.05	.15
53 Ken Caminiti	.10	.30
54 Pat Borders	.05	.15
55 Pedro Munoz	.05	
56 Tim Belcher	.05	
57 Paul Assenmacher	.05	
58 Damon Berryhill	.05	
59 Ricky Bones	.05	
60 Rene Arocha	.05	
61 Shawn Boskie	.05	
62 Pedro Astacio	.05	
63 Frank Bolick	.05	
64 Bud Black	.05	
65 Sandy Alomar Jr.	.05	
66 Rich Amaral	.05	
67 Luis Aquino	.05	
68 Kevin Baez	.05	
69 Mike Devereaux	.05	
70 Andy Ashby	.05	
71 Larry Andersen	.05	
72 Steve Cooke	.05	
73 Mario Diaz	.05	
74 Rob Deer	.05	
75 Bobby Ayala	.05	
76 Freddie Benavides	.05	
77 Stan Belinda	.05	
78 John Doherty	.05	
79 Willie Banks	.05	
80 Spike Owen	.05	
81 Mike Bordick	.05	
82 Chili Davis	.10	
83 Luis Gonzalez	.10	
84 Ed Sprague	.05	
85 Jeff Reboulet	.05	
86 Jason Bere	.05	
87 Mark Hutton	.05	
88 Jeff Blauser	.05	
89 Cal Eldred	.05	
90 Bernard Gilkey	.05	
91 Frank Castillo	.05	
92 Jim Gott	.05	
93 Greg Colbrunn	.05	
94 Jeff Brantley	.05	
95 Jeremy Hernandez	.05	
96 Norm Charlton	.05	
97 Alex Arias	.05	
98 John Franco	.10	
99 Chris Hoiles	.05	
100 Brad Ausmus	.20	
101 Wes Chamberlain	.05	
102 Mark Dewey	.05	
103 Benji Gil	.05	
104 John Dopson	.05	
105 John Smiley	.05	
106 David Nied	.05	
107 George Brett Salute	.75	
108 Kirk Gibson	.10	
109 Larry Casian	.05	
110 Ryne Sandberg CL	.30	
111 Brent Gates	.05	
112 Damion Easley	.05	
113 Pete Harnisch	.05	
114 Danny Cox	.05	
115 Kevin Tapani	.05	
116 Roberto Hernandez	.05	
117 Domingo Jean	.05	
118 Sid Bream	.05	
119 Doug Henry	.05	
120 Omar Olivares	.05	
121 Mike Harkey	.05	
122 Carlos Hernandez	.05	
123 Jeff Fassero	.05	
124 Dave Burba	.05	
125 Wayne Kirby	.05	
126 John Cummings	.05	
127 Bret Barberie	.05	
128 Todd Hundley	.05	
129 Tim Hulett	.05	
130 Phil Clark	.05	
131 Danny Jackson	.05	
132 Tom Foley	.05	
133 Donald Harris	.05	
134 Scott Fletcher	.05	
135 Johnny Ruffin	.05	
136 Jerald Clark	.05	
137 Billy Brewer	.05	
138 Dan Gladden	.05	
139 Eddie Guardado	.10	
140 Cal Ripken CL	.30	
141 Scott Hemond	.05	
142 Steve Frey	.05	
143 Xavier Hernandez	.05	
144 Mark Eichhorn	.05	
145 Ellis Burks	.10	
146 Jim Leyritz	.05	
147 Mark Lemke	.05	
148 Pat Listach	.05	
149 Donovan Osborne	.05	
150 Glenallen Hill	.05	
151 Orel Hershiser	.10	
152 Darrin Fletcher	.05	
153 Royce Clayton	.05	
154 Derek Lilliquist	.05	
155 Mike Felder	.05	
156 Jeff Conine	.10	
157 Ryan Thompson	.05	
158 Ben McDonald	.05	
159 Ricky Gutierrez	.05	
160 Terry Mulholland	.05	
161 Carlos Garcia	.05	
162 Tom Henke	.05	
163 Mike Greenwell	.05	
164 Thomas Howard	.05	
165 Joe Girardi	.05	
166 Hubie Brooks	.05	
167 Greg Gohr	.05	

168 Chip Hale .05 .15
169 Rick Honeycutt .05 .15
170 Hilly Hathaway .05 .15
171 Todd Jones .05 .15
172 Tony Fernandez .05 .15
173 Bo Jackson .30 .75
174 Bobby Munoz .05 .15
175 Greg McMichael .05 .15
176 Graeme Lloyd .05 .15
177 Tom Pagnozzi .05 .15
178 Derrick May .05 .15
179 Pedro Martinez .30 .75
180 Ken Hill .05 .15
181 Bryan Hickerson .05 .15
182 Jose Mesa .05 .15
183 Dave Fleming .05 .15
184 Henry Cotto .05 .15
185 Jeff Kent .20 .50
186 Mark McLemore .05 .15
187 Trevor Hoffman .20 .50
188 Todd Pratt .05 .15
189 Blas Minor .05 .15
190 Charlie Leibrandt .05 .15
191 Tony Pena .05 .15
192 Larry Luebbers RC .05 .15
193 Greg W. Harris .05 .15
194 David Cone .10 .30
195 Bill Gullickson .05 .15
196 Brian Harper .05 .15
197 Steve Karsay .05 .15
198 Greg Myers .05 .15
199 Mark Portugal .05 .15
200 Pat Hentgen .05 .15
201 Mike LaValliere .05 .15
202 Mike Stanley .05 .15
203 Kent Mercker .05 .15
204 Dave Nilsson .05 .15
205 Erik Pappas .05 .15
206 Mike Morgan .05 .15
207 Roger McDowell .05 .15
208 Mike Lansing .05 .15
209 Kirt Manwaring .05 .15
210 Randy Milligan .05 .15
211 Erik Hanson .05 .15
212 Orestes Destrade .05 .15
213 Mike Maddux .05 .15
214 Alan Mills .05 .15
215 Tim Mauser .05 .15
216 Ben Rivera .05 .15
217 Don Slaught .05 .15
218 Bob Patterson .05 .15
219 Carlos Quintana .05 .15
220 Tim Raines CL .05 .15
221 Hal Morris .05 .15
222 Darren Holmes .05 .15
223 Chris Gwynn .05 .15
224 Chad Kreuter .05 .15
225 Mike Hartley .05 .15
226 Scott Lydy .05 .15
227 Eduardo Perez .05 .15
228 Greg Swindell .05 .15
229 Al Leiter .10 .30
230 Scott Radinsky .05 .15
231 Bob Wickman .05 .15
232 Otis Nixon .05 .15
233 Kevin Reimer .05 .15
234 Geronimo Pena .05 .15
235 Kevin Roberson .05 .15
236 Jody Reed .05 .15
237 Kirk Rueter .05 .15
238 Willie McGee .10 .30
239 Charles Nagy .05 .15
240 Tim Leary .05 .15
241 Carl Everett .10 .30
242 Charlie O'Brien .05 .15
243 Mike Pagliarulo .05 .15
244 Kerry Taylor .05 .15
245 Kevin Stocker .05 .15
246 Joel Johnston .05 .15
247 Geno Petralli .05 .15
248 Jeff Russell .05 .15
249 Joe Oliver .05 .15
250 Roberto Mejia .05 .15
251 Chris Haney .05 .15
252 Bill Krueger .05 .15
253 Shane Mack .05 .15
254 Terry Steinbach .05 .15
255 Luis Polonia .05 .15
256 Eddie Taubensee .05 .15
257 Dave Stewart .10 .30
258 Tim Raines .10 .30
259 Bernie Williams .20 .50
260 John Smoltz .20 .50
261 Kevin Seitzer .05 .15
262 Bob Tewksbury .05 .15
263 Bob Scanlan .05 .15
264 Henry Rodriguez .05 .15
265 Tim Scott .05 .15
266 Scott Sanderson .05 .15
267 Eric Plunk .05 .15
268 Edgar Martinez .20 .50
269 Charlie Hough .10 .30
270 Joe Orsulak .05 .15
271 Harold Reynolds .10 .30
272 Tim Teufel .05 .15
273 Bobby Thigpen .05 .15
274 Randy Tomlin .05 .15
275 Gary Redus .05 .15
276 Ken Ryan .05 .15
277 Tim Pugh .05 .15
278 Jayhawk Owens .05 .15
279 Phil Hiatt .05 .15
280 Alan Trammell .10 .30
281 David McCarty .05 .15
282 Bob Welch .05 .15
283 J.T.Snow .10 .30
284 Brian Williams .05 .15
285 Devon White .10 .30
286 Steve Sax .05 .15
287 Tony Tarasco .05 .15
288 Bill Spiers .05 .15
289 Allen Watson .05 .15
290 Rickey Henderson CL .20 .50
291 Jose Vizcaino .05 .15
292 Darryl Strawberry .10 .30
293 John Wetteland .10 .30
294 Bill Swift .05 .15
295 Jeff Treadway .05 .15
296 Tino Martinez .20 .50
297 Richie Lewis .05 .15
298 Bret Saberhagen .10 .30
299 Arthur Rhodes .05 .15
300 Guillermo Velasquez .05 .15
301 Milt Thompson .05 .15
302 Doug Strange .05 .15
303 Aaron Sele .05 .15
304 Bip Roberts .05 .15
305 Bruce Ruffin .05 .15
306 Jose Lind .05 .15
307 David Wells .10 .30
308 Bobby Witt .05 .15
309 Mark Wohlers .05 .15
310 B.J. Surhoff .10 .30
311 Mark Whiten .05 .15
312 Turk Wendell .05 .15
313 Raul Mondesi .10 .30
314 Brian Turang RC .05 .15
315 Chris Hammond .05 .15
316 Tim Bogar .05 .15
317 Brad Pennington .05 .15
318 Tim Worrell .05 .15
319 Mitch Williams .05 .15
320 Rondell White .10 .30
321 Frank Viola .10 .30
322 Manny Ramirez .30 .75
323 Gary Wayne .05 .15
324 Mike Macfarlane .05 .15
325 Russ Springer .05 .15
326 Tim Wallach .05 .15
327 Salomon Torres .05 .15
328 Omar Vizquel .20 .50
329 Andy Tomberlin RC .05 .15
330 Chris Sabo .05 .15
331 Mike Mussina .20 .50
332 Andy Benes .05 .15
333 Darren Daulton .10 .30
334 Orlando Merced .05 .15
335 Mark McGwire .75 2.00
336 Dave Winfield .10 .30
337 Sammy Sosa .30 .75
338 Eric Karros .10 .30
339 Greg Vaughn .05 .15
340 Don Mattingly .75 2.00
341 Frank Thomas .30 .75
342 Fred McGriff .20 .50
343 Kirby Puckett .30 .75
344 Roberto Kelly .05 .15
345 Wally Joyner .10 .30
346 Andres Galarraga .10 .30
347 Bobby Bonilla .10 .30
348 Benito Santiago .10 .30
349 Barry Bonds .75 2.00
350 Delino DeShields .05 .15
351 Albert Belle .10 .30
352 Randy Johnson .30 .75
353 Tim Salmon .20 .50
354 John Olerud .10 .30
355 Dean Palmer .10 .30
356 Roger Clemens .60 1.50
357 Jim Abbott .20 .50
358 Mark Grace .20 .50
359 Ozzie Guillen .10 .30
360 Lou Whitaker .10 .30
361 Jose Rijo .05 .15
362 Jeff Montgomery .05 .15
363 Chuck Finley .10 .30
364 Tom Glavine .20 .50
365 Jeff Bagwell .20 .50
366 Joe Carter .10 .30
367 Ray Lankford .10 .30
368 Ramon Martinez .05 .15
369 Jay Buhner .10 .30
370 Matt Williams .10 .30
371 Larry Walker .10 .30
372 Jose Canseco .20 .50
373 Lenny Dykstra .10 .30
374 Bryan Harvey .05 .15
375 Andy Van Slyke .20 .50
376 Ivan Rodriguez .20 .50
377 Kevin Mitchell .05 .15
378 Travis Fryman .10 .30
379 Duane Ward .05 .15
380 Greg Maddux .50 1.25
381 Scott Servais .05 .15
382 Greg Olson .05 .15
383 Rey Sanchez .05 .15
384 Tom Kramer .05 .15
385 David Valle .05 .15
386 Eddie Murray .30 .75
387 Kevin Higgins .05 .15
388 Dan Wilson .05 .15
389 Todd Frohwith .05 .15
390 Gerald Williams .05 .15
391 Hipolito Pichardo .05 .15
392 Pat Meares .05 .15
393 Luis Lopez .05 .15
394 Ricky Jordan .05 .15
395 Bob Walk .05 .15
396 Sid Fernandez .05 .15
397 Todd Worrell .05 .15
398 Darryl Hamilton .05 .15
399 Randy Myers .05 .15
400 Rod Brewer .05 .15
401 Lance Blankenship .05 .15
402 Steve Finley .10 .30
403 Phil Leftwich RC .05 .15
404 Juan Guzman .05 .15
405 Anthony Young .05 .15
406 Jeff Gardner .05 .15
407 Ryan Bowen .05 .15
408 Fernando Valenzuela .10 .30
409 David West .05 .15
410 Kenny Rogers .10 .30
411 Bob Zupcic .05 .15
412 Eric Young .05 .15
413 Bret Boone .10 .30
414 Danny Tartabull .05 .15
415 Bob MacDonald .05 .15
416 Ron Karkovice .05 .15
417 Scott Cooper .05 .15
418 Dante Bichette .10 .30
419 Tripp Cromer .05 .15
420 Billy Ashley .05 .15
421 Roger Smithberg .05 .15
422 Dennis Martinez .10 .30
423 Mike Blowers .05 .15
424 Darren Lewis .05 .15
425 Junior Ortiz .05 .15
426 Butch Huskey .05 .15
427 Jimmy Poole .05 .15
428 Walt Weiss .05 .15
429 Scott Bankhead .05 .15
430 Deion Sanders .20 .50
431 Scott Bullett .05 .15
432 Jeff Huson .05 .15
433 Tyler Green .05 .15
434 Billy Hatcher .05 .15
435 Bob Hamelin .05 .15
436 Reggie Sanders .10 .30
437 Scott Erickson .05 .15
438 Steve Reed .05 .15
439 Randy Velarde .05 .15
440 Tony Gwynn CL .20 .50
441 Terry Leach .05 .15
442 Danny Bautista .05 .15
443 Kent Hrbek .10 .30
444 Rick Wilkins .05 .15
445 Tony Phillips .05 .15
446 Dion James .05 .15
447 Joey Cora .05 .15
448 Andre Dawson .10 .30
449 Pedro Castellano .05 .15
450 Tom Gordon .05 .15
451 Rob Dibble .10 .30
452 Ron Darling .05 .15
453 Chipper Jones .30 .75
454 Joe Grahe .05 .15
455 Domingo Cedeno .05 .15
456 Tom Edens .05 .15
457 Mitch Webster .05 .15
458 Jose Bautista .05 .15
459 Troy O'Leary .05 .15
460 Todd Zeile .05 .15
461 Sean Berry .05 .15
462 Brad Holman RC .05 .15
463 Dave Martinez .05 .15
464 Mark Lewis .05 .15
465 Paul Carey .05 .15
466 Jack Armstrong .05 .15
467 David Telgheder .05 .15
468 Gene Harris .05 .15
469 Danny Darwin .05 .15
470 Kim Batiste .05 .15
471 Tim Wakefield .20 .50
472 Craig Lefferts .05 .15
473 Jacob Brumfield .05 .15
474 Lance Painter .05 .15
475 Milt Cuyler .05 .15
476 Melido Perez .05 .15
477 Derek Parks .05 .15
478 Gary DiSarcina .05 .15
479 Steve Bedrosian .05 .15
480 Eric Anthony .05 .15
481 Julio Franco .10 .30
482 Tommy Greene .05 .15
483 Pat Kelly .05 .15
484 Nate Minchey .05 .15
485 William Pennyfeather .05 .15
486 Harold Baines .10 .30
487 Howard Johnson .05 .15
488 Angel Miranda .05 .15
489 Scott Sanders .05 .15
490 Shawon Dunston .05 .15
491 Mel Rojas .05 .15
492 Jeff Nelson .05 .15
493 Archi Cianfrocco .05 .15
494 Al Martin .05 .15
495 Mike Gallego .05 .15
496 Mike Henneman .05 .15
497 Armando Reynoso .05 .15
498 Mickey Morandini .05 .15
499 Rick Renteria .05 .15
500 Rick Sutcliffe .10 .30
501 Bobby Jones .05 .15
502 Gary Gaetti .10 .30
503 Rick Aguilera .05 .15
504 Todd Stottlemyre .05 .15
505 Mike Mohler .05 .15
506 Mike Stanton .05 .15
507 Jose Guzman .05 .15
508 Kevin Rogers .05 .15
509 Chuck Carr .05 .15
510 Chris Jones .05 .15
511 Brent Mayne .05 .15
512 Greg Harris .05 .15
513 Dave Henderson .05 .15
514 Eric Hillman .05 .15
515 Dan Peltier .05 .15
516 Craig Shipley .05 .15
517 John Valentin .05 .15
518 Wilson Alvarez .05 .15
519 Andujar Cedeno .05 .15
520 Troy Neel .05 .15
521 Tom Candiotti .05 .15
522 Matt Mieske .05 .15
523 Jim Thome .20 .50
524 Lou Frazier .05 .15
525 Mike Jackson .05 .15
526 Pedro A.Martinez RC .05 .15
527 Roger Pavlik .05 .15
528 Kent Bottenfield .05 .15
529 Felix Jose .05 .15
530 Mark Guthrie .05 .15
531 Steve Farr .05 .15
532 Craig Paquette .05 .15
533 Doug Jones .05 .15
534 Luis Allcea .05 .15
535 Cory Snyder .05 .15
536 Paul Sorrento .05 .15
537 Nigel Wilson .05 .15
538 Jeff King .05 .15
539 Willie Greene .05 .15
540 Kirk McCaskill .05 .15
541 Al Osuna .05 .15
542 Greg Hibbard .05 .15
543 Brett Butler .10 .30
544 Jose Valentin .05 .15
545 Wil Cordero .05 .15
546 Chris Bosio .05 .15
547 Jamie Moyer .10 .30
548 Jim Eisenreich .05 .15
549 Vinny Castilla .10 .30
550 Dave Winfield CL .05 .15
551 John Roper .05 .15
552 Lance Johnson .05 .15
553 Scott Kamieniecki .05 .15
554 Mike Moore .05 .15
555 Steve Buechele .05 .15
556 Terry Pendleton .10 .30
557 Todd Van Poppel .05 .15
558 Rob Butler .05 .15
559 Zane Smith .05 .15
560 David Hulse .05 .15
561 Tim Costo .05 .15
562 John Habyan .05 .15
563 Terry Jorgensen .05 .15
564 Matt Nokes .05 .15
565 Kevin McReynolds .05 .15
566 Phil Plantier .05 .15
567 Chris Turner .05 .15
568 Carlos Delgado .20 .50
569 John Jaha .05 .15
570 Dwight Smith .05 .15
571 John Vander Wal .05 .15
572 Trevor Wilson .05 .15
573 Felix Fermin .05 .15
574 Marc Newfield .05 .15
575 Jeromy Burnitz .10 .30
576 Leo Gomez .05 .15
577 Curt Schilling .10 .30
578 Kevin Young .05 .15
579 Jerry Spradlin RC .05 .15
580 Curt Leskanic .05 .15
581 Carl Willis .05 .15
582 Alex Fernandez .05 .15
583 Mark Holzemer .05 .15
584 Domingo Martinez .05 .15
585 Pete Smith .05 .15
586 Brian Jordan .10 .30
587 Kevin Gross .05 .15
588 J.R. Phillips .05 .15
589 Chris Nabholz .05 .15
590 Bill Wertz .05 .15
591 Derek Bell .05 .15
592 Brady Anderson .10 .30
593 Matt Turner .05 .15
594 Pete Incaviglia .05 .15
595 Greg Gagne .05 .15
596 John Flaherty .05 .15
597 Scott Livingstone .05 .15
598 Rod Bolton .05 .15
599 Mike Perez .05 .15
600 Roger Clemens CL .30 .75
601 Tony Castillo .05 .15
602 Henry Mercedes .05 .15
603 Mike Fetters .05 .15
604 Rod Beck .05 .15
605 Damon Buford .05 .15
606 Matt Whiteside .05 .15
607 Shawn Green .30 .75
608 Midre Cummings .05 .15
609 Jeff McNeely .05 .15
610 Danny Sheaffer .05 .15
611 Paul Wagner .05 .15
612 Torey Lovullo .05 .15
613 Javier Lopez .10 .30
614 Mariano Duncan .05 .15
615 Doug Brocail .05 .15
616 Dave Hansen .05 .15
617 Ryan Klesko .10 .30
618 Eric Davis .10 .30
619 Scott Ruffcorn .05 .15
620 Mike Trombley .05 .15
621 Jaime Navarro .05 .15
622 Rheal Cormier .05 .15
623 Jose Offerman .05 .15
624 David Segui .05 .15
625 Robb Nen .10 .30
626 Dave Gallagher .05 .15
627 Julian Tavarez RC .10 .30
628 Chris Gomez .05 .15
629 Jeffrey Hammonds .05 .15
630 Scott Brosius .10 .30
631 Willie Blair .05 .15
632 Doug Drabek .05 .15
633 Bill Wegman .05 .15
634 Jeff McKnight .05 .15
635 Rich Rodriguez .05 .15
636 Steve Trachsel .05 .15
637 Buddy Groom .05 .15
638 Sterling Hitchcock .05 .15
639 Chuck McElroy .05 .15
640 Rene Gonzales .05 .15
641 Dan Plesac .05 .15
642 Jeff Branson .05 .15
643 Darrell Whitmore .05 .15
644 Paul Quantrill .05 .15
645 Rich Rowland .05 .15
646 Curtis Pride RC .10 .30
647 Erik Plantenberg RC .05 .15
648 Albie Lopez .05 .15
649 Rich Batchelor RC .05 .15
650 Lee Smith .10 .30
651 Cliff Floyd .10 .30
652 Pete Schourek .05 .15
653 Reggie Jefferson .05 .15
654 Bill Haselman .05 .15
655 Steve Hosey .05 .15
656 Mark Clark .05 .15
657 Mark Davis .05 .15
658 Dave Magadan .05 .15
659 Candy Maldonado .05 .15
660 Mark Langston CL .05 .15

1994 Donruss Special Edition

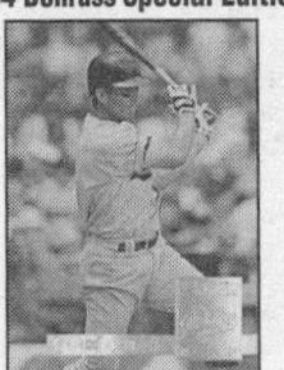

COMPLETE SET (100) 8.00 20.00
*STARS: .75X TO 2X BASIC CARDS
ONE PER PACK/TWO PER JUMBO
NUMBERS 51-100 CORRESPOND TO 331-380

1994 Donruss Anniversary '84

Randomly inserted in hobby foil packs at a rate of one in 12, this ten-card standard-size set reproduces selected cards from the 1984 Donruss baseball set. The cards feature white bordered color player photos on their fronts. The cards are numbered on the back at the bottom right as "X of 10," and also carry the numbers from the original 1984 set at the upper left.

COMPLETE SET (10) 12.50 30.00
RANDOM INSERTS IN SER.1 HOBBY PACKS
1 Joe Carter .75 2.00
2 Robin Yount 3.00 8.00
3 George Brett 5.00 12.00
4 Rickey Henderson 2.00 5.00
5 Nolan Ryan 10.00 25.00
6 Cal Ripken 6.00 15.00
7 Wade Boggs 1.25 3.00
8 Don Mattingly 5.00 12.00
9 Ryne Sandberg 3.00 8.00
10 Tony Gwynn 2.50 6.00

1994 Donruss Award Winner Jumbos

This 10-card set was issued one per jumbo foil and Canadian foil boxes and spotlights players that won various awards in 1993. Cards 1-5 were included in first series boxes and 6-10 with the second series. The cards measure approximately 3 1/2" by 5". Ten-thousand of each card were produced. Card fronts are full-bleed with a color player photo and the Award Winner logo at the top. The backs are individually numbered out of 10,000.

COMPLETE SET (10) 30.00 80.00
COMPLETE SERIES 1 (5) 25.00 60.00
COMPLETE SERIES 2 (5) 8.00 20.00
ONE PER JUMBO BOX OR CDN FOIL BOX
STATED PRINT RUN 10,000 SERIAL #'d SETS
1 Barry Bonds 8.00 20.00
2 Greg Maddux 5.00 12.00
3 Mike Piazza 6.00 15.00
4 Barry Bonds 8.00 20.00
5 Kirby Puckett 3.00 8.00
6 Frank Thomas 3.00 8.00
7 Jack McDowell CY .60 1.50
8 Tim Salmon 2.00 5.00
9 Juan Gonzalez 1.25 3.00
10 Paul Molitor WS MVP 2.50 6.00

1994 Donruss Diamond Kings

This 30-card standard-size set was split in two series. Cards 1-14 and 29 were randomly inserted in first series packs, while cards 15-28 and 30 were inserted in second series packs. With each series, the insertion rate was one in nine. The fronts feature full-bleed player portraits by noted sports artist Dick Perez. The cards are numbered on the back with the prefix DK.

COMPLETE SET (30) 20.00 50.00
COMPLETE SERIES 1 (15) 10.00 25.00
COMPLETE SERIES 2 (15) 10.00 25.00
STATED ODDS 1:9
*JUMBO DK's: .75X TO 2X BASIC DK'S
ONE JUMBO DK PER RETAIL BOX
DK1 Barry Bonds 2.50 6.00
DK2 Mo Vaughn .40 1.00
DK3 Steve Avery .20 .50
DK4 Tim Salmon .60 1.50
DK5 Rick Wilkins .20 .50
DK6 Brian Harper .20 .50
DK7 Andres Galarraga .40 1.00
DK8 Albert Belle .40 1.00
DK9 John Kruk .40 1.00
DK10 Ivan Rodriguez .60 1.50
DK11 Tony Gwynn 1.25 3.00
DK12 Brian McRae .20 .50
DK13 Bobby Bonilla .40 1.00
DK14 Ken Griffey Jr. 2.00 5.00
DK15 Mike Piazza 2.00 5.00
DK16 Don Mattingly 2.50 6.00
DK17 Barry Larkin .60 1.50
DK18 Ruben Sierra .40 1.00
DK19 Orlando Merced .20 .50
DK20 Greg Vaughn .20 .50
DK21 Gregg Jefferies .20 .50
DK22 Cecil Fielder .40 1.00
DK23 Moises Alou .40 1.00
DK24 John Olerud .40 1.00
DK25 Gary Sheffield .40 1.00
DK26 Mike Mussina .60 1.50
DK27 Jeff Bagwell .60 1.50
DK28 Frank Thomas 1.00 2.50
DK29 Dave Winfield .40 1.00
DK30 Checklist .20 .50

1994 Donruss Dominators

This 20-card, standard-size set was randomly inserted in all packs at a rate of one in 12. The 10 series 1 cards feature the top home run hitters of the '90s, while the 10 series 2 cards depict the decade's batting average leaders.

COMPLETE SET (20) 15.00 40.00
COMPLETE SERIES 1 (10) 8.00 20.00
COMPLETE SERIES 2 (10) 8.00 20.00
RANDOM INSERTS IN PACKS
*JUMBOS: .75X TO 2X BASIC DOM.
ONE JUMBO DOMINATOR PER HOBBY BOX
A1 Cecil Fielder .40 1.00
A2 Barry Bonds 2.50 6.00
A3 Fred McGriff .60 1.50
A4 Matt Williams .40 1.00
A5 Joe Carter .40 1.00
A6 Juan Gonzalez .40 1.00
A7 Jose Canseco .60 1.50
A8 Ron Gant .40 1.00
A9 Ken Griffey Jr. 2.00 5.00
A10 Mark McGwire 2.50 6.00
B1 Tony Gwynn 1.25 3.00
B2 Frank Thomas 1.00 2.50
B3 Paul Molitor .40 1.00
B4 Edgar Martinez .60 1.50
B5 Kirby Puckett 1.00 2.50
B6 Ken Griffey Jr. 2.00 5.00
B7 Barry Bonds 2.50 6.00
B8 Willie McGee .40 1.00
B9 Len Dykstra .40 1.00
B10 John Kruk .40 1.00

1994 Donruss Elite

This 12-card set was issued in two series of six. Using a continued numbering system from previous years, cards 37-42 were randomly inserted in first series foil packs with cards 43-48 a second series offering. The cards measure the standard size. Only 10,000 of each card were produced. .

COMPLETE SET (12) 30.00 80.00
COMPLETE SERIES 1 (6) 15.00 40.00
COMPLETE SERIES 2 (6) 15.00 40.00
RANDOM INSERTS IN HOBBY/RETAIL PACKS
STATED PRINT RUN 10,000 SERIAL #'d SETS
37 Frank Thomas 6.00 15.00
38 Tony Gwynn 4.00 10.00
39 Tim Salmon 1.50 4.00
40 Albert Belle 1.50 4.00
41 John Kruk 2.00 5.00
42 Juan Gonzalez 2.50 6.00
43 John Olerud 1.50 4.00
44 Barry Bonds 8.00 20.00
45 Ken Griffey Jr. 15.00 40.00
46 Mike Piazza 4.00 10.00
47 Jack McDowell 2.00 5.00
48 Andres Galarraga 2.50 6.00

1994 Donruss Long Ball Leaders

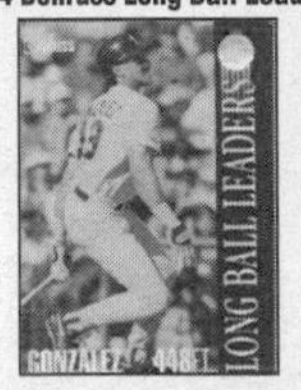

Inserted in second series hobby foil packs at a rate of one in 12, this 10-card standard-size set features some of top home run hitters and the distance of their longest home run of 1993.

COMPLETE SET (10) 12.50 30.00
RANDOM INSERTS IN SER.2 HOBBY PACKS
1 Cecil Fielder .60 1.50
2 Dean Palmer .60 1.50
3 Andres Galarraga .60 1.50
4 Bo Jackson 1.50 4.00
5 Ken Griffey Jr. 3.00 8.00
6 David Justice .60 1.50
7 Mike Piazza 3.00 8.00
8 Frank Thomas 1.50 4.00
9 Barry Bonds 4.00 10.00
10 Juan Gonzalez .60 1.50

1994 Donruss MVPs

Inserted at a rate of one per first and second series jumbo pack, this 28-card standard-size set was split into two series of 14; one player for each team. The first 14 are of National League players with the latter group being American Leaguers. Full-bleed card fronts feature an action photo of the player with "MVP" in large red (American League) or blue (National) letters at the bottom. The player's name and, for Amercian League player cards only, team name are beneath the "MVP".

COMPLETE SET (28) 25.00 60.00
COMPLETE SERIES 1 (14) 6.00 15.00
COMPLETE SERIES 2 (14) 20.00 50.00
ONE PER JUMBO PACK
1 David Justice .60 1.50
2 Mark Grace 1.00 2.50
3 Jose Rijo .30 .75
4 Andres Galarraga .60 1.50
5 Bryan Harvey .30 .75
6 Jeff Bagwell 1.00 2.50
7 Mike Piazza 3.00 8.00
8 Moises Alou .60 1.50
9 Bobby Bonilla .60 1.50
10 Len Dykstra .60 1.50
11 Jeff King .30 .75
12 Gregg Jefferies .30 .75
13 Tony Gwynn 2.00 5.00
14 Barry Bonds 4.00 10.00
15 Cal Ripken 5.00 12.00
16 Mo Vaughn .60 1.50
17 Tim Salmon 1.00 2.50
18 Frank Thomas 1.50 4.00
19 Albert Belle .60 1.50

20 Cecil Fielder .60 1.50
21 Wally Joyner .60 1.50
22 Greg Vaughn .30 .75
23 Kirby Puckett 1.50 4.00
24 Don Mattingly 4.00 10.00
25 Ruben Sierra .60 1.50
26 Ken Griffey Jr. 3.00 8.00
27 Juan Gonzalez .60 1.50
28 John Olerud .60 1.50

1994 Donruss Spirit of the Game

This ten card set features a selction of the games top stars. Cards 1-5 were randomly inserted in first-series magazine jumbo packs and cards 6-10 in second series magazine jumbo packs.

COMPLETE SET (10) 15.00 40.00
COMPLETE SERIES 1 (5) 10.00 25.00
COMPLETE SERIES 2 (5) 8.00 20.00
RANDOM INSERTS IN MAG.JUMBO PACKS
*JUMBOS: .75X TO 2X BASIC SOG
ONE JUMBO SPIRIT PER MAG.JUMBO BOX
JUMBO PRINT RUN 10,000 SERIAL #'d SETS
1 John Olerud .75 2.00
2 Barry Bonds 5.00 12.00
3 Ken Griffey Jr. 4.00 10.00
4 Mike Piazza 4.00 10.00
5 Juan Gonzalez .75 2.00
6 Frank Thomas 2.00 5.00
7 Tim Salmon 1.25 3.00
8 David Justice .75 2.00
9 Don Mattingly 5.00 12.00
10 Len Dykstra .75 2.00

1995 Donruss

The 1995 Donruss set consists of 550 standard-size cards. The first series had 330 cards while 220 cards comprised the second series. The fronts feature borderless color action player photos. A second, smaller color player photo in a homeplate shape with team color-coded borders appears in the lower left corner. There are no key Rookie Cards in this set. To preview the product prior to its public release, Donruss printed up additional quantities of cards 5, 8, 20, 42, 55, 275, 331 and 340 and mailed them to dealers and hobby media.

COMPLETE SET (550) 12.50 30.00
COMPLETE SERIES 1 (330) 8.00 20.00
COMPLETE SERIES 2 (220) 4.00 10.00
1 David Justice .10 .30
2 Rene Arocha .05 .15
3 Sandy Alomar Jr. .05 .15
4 Luis Lopez .05 .15
5 Mike Piazza .50 1.25
6 Bobby Jones .05 .15
7 Damion Easley .05 .15
8 Barry Bonds .75 2.00
9 Mike Mussina .20 .50
10 Kevin Seitzer .05 .15
11 John Smiley .05 .15
12 Wm.VanLandingham .05 .15
13 Ron Darling .05 .15
14 Walt Weiss .05 .15
15 Mike Lansing .05 .15
16 Allen Watson .05 .15
17 Aaron Sele .05 .15
18 Randy Johnson .30 .75
19 Dean Palmer .10 .30
20 Jeff Bagwell .20 .50
21 Curt Schilling .10 .30
22 Darrell Whitmore .05 .15
23 Steve Trachsel .05 .15
24 Dan Wilson .05 .15
25 Steve Finley .10 .30
26 Bret Boone .10 .30
27 Charles Johnson .10 .30
28 Mike Stanton .05 .15
29 Ismael Valdes .05 .15
30 Salomon Torres .05 .15
31 Eric Anthony .05 .15
32 Spike Owen .05 .15
33 Joey Cora .05 .15
34 Robert Eenhoorn .05 .15
35 Rick White .05 .15
36 Omar Vizquel .20 .50
37 Carlos Delgado .10 .30
38 Eddie Williams .05 .15
39 Shawon Dunston .05 .15
40 Darrin Fletcher .05 .15
41 Leo Gomez .05 .15
42 Juan Gonzalez .10 .30
43 Luis Alicea .05 .15
44 Ken Ryan .05 .15
45 Lou Whitaker .10 .30
46 Mike Blowers .05 .15
47 Willie Blair .05 .15
48 Todd Van Poppel .05 .15
49 Roberto Alomar .20 .50
50 Ozzie Smith .50 1.25
51 Sterling Hitchcock .05 .15
52 Mo Vaughn .10 .30
53 Rick Aguilera .05 .15
54 Kent Mercker .05 .15
55 Don Mattingly .75 2.00
56 Bob Scanlan .05 .15
57 Wilson Alvarez .05 .15
58 Jose Mesa .05 .15
59 Scott Kamieniecki .05 .15
60 Todd Jones .05 .15
61 John Kruk .10 .30
62 Mike Stanley .05 .15
63 Tino Martinez .20 .50
64 Eddie Zambrano .05 .15
65 Todd Hundley .05 .15
66 Jamie Moyer .10 .30
67 Rich Amaral .05 .15
68 Jose Valentin .05 .15
69 Alex Gonzalez .05 .15
70 Kurt Abbott .05 .15
71 Delino DeShields .05 .15
72 Brian Anderson .05 .15
73 John Vander Wal .05 .15
74 Turner Ward .05 .15
75 Tim Raines .10 .30
76 Mark Acre .05 .15
77 Jose Offerman .05 .15
78 Jimmy Key .10 .30
79 Mark Whiten .05 .15
80 Mark Gubicza .05 .15
81 Darren Hall .05 .15
82 Travis Fryman .10 .30
83 Cal Ripken 1.00 2.50
84 Geronimo Berroa .05 .15
85 Bret Barberie .05 .15
86 Andy Ashby .05 .15
87 Steve Avery .05 .15
88 Rich Becker .05 .15
89 John Valentin .05 .15
90 Glenallen Hill .05 .15
91 Carlos Garcia .05 .15
92 Dennis Martinez .10 .30
93 Pat Kelly .05 .15
94 Orlando Miller .05 .15
95 Felix Jose .05 .15
96 Mike Kingery .05 .15
97 Jeff Kent .10 .30
98 Pete Incaviglia .05 .15
99 Chad Curtis .05 .15
100 Thomas Howard .05 .15
101 Hector Carrasco .05 .15
102 Tom Pagnozzi .05 .15
103 Danny Tartabull .05 .15
104 Donnie Elliott .05 .15
105 Danny Jackson .05 .15
106 Steve Dunn .05 .15
107 Roger Salkeld .05 .15
108 Jeff King .05 .15
109 Cecil Fielder .10 .30
110 Paul Molitor CL .05 .15
111 Denny Neagle .10 .30
112 Troy Neel .05 .15
113 Rod Beck .05 .15
114 Alex Rodriguez .75 2.00
115 Joey Eischen .05 .15
116 Tom Candiotti .05 .15
117 Ray McDavid .05 .15
118 Vince Coleman .05 .15
119 Pete Harnisch .05 .15
120 David Nied .05 .15
121 Pat Rapp .05 .15
122 Sammy Sosa .30 .75
123 Steve Reed .05 .15
124 Jose Oliva .05 .15
125 Ricky Bottalico .05 .15
126 Jose DeLeon .05 .15
127 Pat Hentgen .05 .15
128 Will Clark .20 .50
129 Mark Dewey .05 .15
130 Greg Vaughn .05 .15
131 Darren Dreifort .05 .15
132 Ed Sprague .05 .15
133 Lee Smith .10 .30
134 Charles Nagy .05 .15
135 Phil Plantier .05 .15
136 Jason Jacome .05 .15
137 Jose Lima .05 .15
138 J.R. Phillips .05 .15
139 J.T. Snow .10 .30
140 Michael Huff .05 .15
141 Billy Brewer .05 .15
142 Jeromy Burnitz .10 .30
143 Ricky Bones .05 .15
144 Carlos Rodriguez .05 .15
145 Luis Gonzalez .10 .30
146 Mark Lemke .05 .15
147 Al Martin .05 .15
148 Mike Bordick .05 .15
149 Robb Nen .10 .30
150 Wil Cordero .05 .15
151 Edgar Martinez .20 .50
152 Gerald Williams .05 .15
153 Esteban Beltre .05 .15
154 Mike Moore .05 .15
155 Mark Langston .05 .15
156 Mark Clark .05 .15
157 Bobby Ayala .05 .15
158 Rick Wilkins .05 .15
159 Bobby Munoz .05 .15
160 Brett Butler CL .05 .15
161 Scott Erickson .05 .15
162 Paul Molitor .10 .30
163 Jon Lieber .05 .15
164 Jason Grimsley .05 .15
165 Norberto Martin .05 .15
166 Javier Lopez .10 .30
167 Brian McRae .05 .15
168 Gary Sheffield .10 .30
169 Marcus Moore .05 .15
170 John Hudek .05 .15
171 Kelly Stinnett .05 .15
172 Chris Gomez .05 .15
173 Rey Sanchez .05 .15
174 Juan Guzman .05 .15
175 Chan Ho Park .10 .30
176 Terry Shumpert .05 .15
177 Steve Ontiveros .05 .15
178 Brad Ausmus .10 .30
179 Tim Davis .05 .15
180 Billy Ashley .05 .15
181 Vinny Castilla .10 .30
182 Bill Spiers .05 .15
183 Randy Knorr .05 .15
184 Brian L.Hunter .05 .15
185 Pat Meares .05 .15
186 Steve Buechele .05 .15
187 Kirt Manwaring .05 .15
188 Tim Naehring .05 .15
189 Matt Mieske .05 .15
190 Josias Manzanillo .05 .15
191 Greg McMichael .05 .15
192 Chuck Carr .05 .15
193 Midre Cummings .05 .15
194 Darryl Strawberry .10 .30
195 Greg Gagne .05 .15
196 Steve Cooke .05 .15
197 Woody Williams .05 .15
198 Ron Karkovice .05 .15
199 Phil Leftwich .05 .15
200 Jim Thome .20 .50
201 Brady Anderson .10 .30
202 Pedro A.Martinez .05 .15
203 Steve Karsay .05 .15
204 Reggie Sanders .10 .30
205 Bill Risley .05 .15
206 Jay Bell .10 .30
207 Kevin Brown .10 .30
208 Tim Scott .05 .15
209 Lenny Dykstra .10 .30
210 Willie Greene .05 .15
211 Jim Eisenreich .05 .15
212 Cliff Floyd .10 .30
213 Otis Nixon .05 .15
214 Eduardo Perez .05 .15
215 Manuel Lee .05 .15
216 Armando Benitez .05 .15
217 Dave McCarty .05 .15
218 Scott Livingstone .05 .15
219 Chad Kreuter .05 .15
220 Don Mattingly CL .40 1.00
221 Brian Jordan .10 .30
222 Matt Whiteside .05 .15
223 Jim Edmonds .20 .50
224 Tony Gwynn .40 1.00
225 Jose Lind .05 .15
226 Marvin Freeman .05 .15
227 Ken Hill .05 .15
228 David Hulse .05 .15
229 Joe Hesketh .05 .15
230 Roberto Petagine .05 .15
231 Jeffrey Hammonds .05 .15
232 John Jaha .05 .15
233 John Burkett .05 .15
234 Hal Morris .05 .15
235 Tony Castillo .05 .15
236 Ryan Bowen .05 .15
237 Wayne Kirby .05 .15
238 Brent Mayne .05 .15
239 Jim Bullinger .05 .15
240 Mike Lieberthal .10 .30
241 Barry Larkin .20 .50
242 David Segui .05 .15
243 Jose Bautista .05 .15
244 Hector Fajardo .05 .15
245 Orel Hershiser .10 .30
246 James Mouton .10 .30
247 Scott Leius .05 .15
248 Tom Glavine .20 .50
249 Danny Bautista .05 .15
250 Jose Mercedes .05 .15
251 Marquis Grissom .10 .30
252 Charlie Hayes .10 .30
253 Ryan Klesko .10 .30
254 Vicente Palacios .05 .15
255 Matias Carrillo .05 .15
256 Gary DiSarcina .05 .15
257 Kirk Gibson .10 .30
258 Garey Ingram .10 .30
259 Alex Fernandez .05 .15
260 John Mabry .05 .15
261 Chris Howard .05 .15
262 Miguel Jimenez .05 .15
263 Heathcliff Slocumb .05 .15
264 Albert Belle .10 .30
265 Dave Clark .05 .15
266 Joe Orsulak .05 .15
267 Joey Hamilton .05 .15
268 Mark Portugal .05 .15
269 Kevin Tapani .05 .15
270 Sid Fernandez .05 .15
271 Steve Dreyer .05 .15
272 Denny Hocking .05 .15
273 Troy O'Leary .05 .15
274 Milt Cuyler .05 .15
275 Frank Thomas .30 .75
276 Jorge Fabregas .05 .15
277 Mike Gallego .05 .15
278 Mickey Morandini .05 .15
279 Roberto Hernandez .05 .15
280 Henry Rodriguez .05 .15
281 Garret Anderson .10 .30
282 Bob Wickman .05 .15
283 Gar Finnvold .05 .15
284 Paul O'Neill .20 .50
285 Royce Clayton .05 .15
286 Chuck Knoblauch .10 .30
287 Johnny Ruffin .05 .15
288 Dave Nilsson .05 .15
289 David Cone .10 .30
290 Chuck McElroy .05 .15
291 Kevin Stocker .05 .15
292 Jose Rijo .05 .15
293 Sean Berry .05 .15
294 Ozzie Guillen .10 .30
295 Chris Hoiles .05 .15
296 Kevin Foster .05 .15
297 Jeff Frye .05 .15
298 Lance Johnson .05 .15
299 Mike Kelly .05 .15
300 Ellis Burks .10 .30
301 Roberto Kelly .05 .15
302 Dante Bichette .10 .30
303 Alvaro Espinoza .05 .15
304 Alex Cole .05 .15
305 Rickey Henderson .30 .75
306 Dave Weathers .05 .15
307 Shane Reynolds .05 .15
308 Bobby Bonilla .10 .30
309 Junior Felix .05 .15
310 Jeff Fassero .05 .15
311 Darren Lewis .05 .15
312 John Doherty .05 .15
313 Scott Servais .05 .15
314 Rick Helling .05 .15
315 Pedro Martinez .20 .50
316 Wes Chamberlain .05 .15
317 Bryan Eversgerd .05 .15
318 Trevor Hoffman .10 .30
319 John Patterson .05 .15
320 Matt Walbeck .05 .15
321 Jeff Montgomery .05 .15
322 Mel Rojas .05 .15
323 Eddie Taubensee .05 .15
324 Ray Lankford .10 .30
325 Jose Vizcaino .05 .15
326 Carlos Baerga .05 .15
327 Jack Voigt .05 .15
328 Julio Franco .10 .30
329 Brent Gates .05 .15
330 Kirby Puckett CL .20 .50
331 Greg Maddux .50 1.25
332 Jason Bere .05 .15
333 Bill Wegman .05 .15
334 Tuffy Rhodes .05 .15
335 Kevin Young .05 .15
336 Andy Benes .05 .15
337 Pedro Astacio .05 .15
338 Reggie Jefferson .05 .15
339 Tim Belcher .05 .15
340 Ken Griffey Jr. .60 1.50
341 Mariano Duncan .05 .15
342 Andres Galarraga .10 .30
343 Rondell White .10 .30
344 Cory Bailey .05 .15
345 Bryan Harvey .05 .15
346 John Franco .10 .30
347 Greg Swindell .05 .15
348 David West .05 .15
349 Fred McGriff .20 .50
350 Jose Canseco .20 .50
351 Orlando Merced .05 .15
352 Rheal Cormier .05 .15
353 Carlos Pulido .05 .15
354 Terry Steinbach .05 .15
355 Wade Boggs .20 .50
356 B.J. Surhoff .10 .30
357 Rafael Palmeiro .20 .50
358 Anthony Young .05 .15
359 Tom Brunansky .05 .15
360 Todd Stottlemyre .05 .15
361 Chris Turner .05 .15
362 Joe Boever .05 .15
363 Jeff Blauser .05 .15
364 Derek Bell .05 .15
365 Matt Williams .10 .30
366 Jeremy Hernandez .05 .15
367 Joe Girardi .05 .15
368 Mike Devereaux .05 .15
369 Jim Abbott .20 .50
370 Manny Ramirez .20 .50
371 Kenny Lofton .10 .30
372 Mark Smith .05 .15
373 Dave Fleming .05 .15
374 Dave Stewart .10 .30
375 Roger Pavlik .05 .15
376 Hipolito Pichardo .05 .15
377 Bill Taylor .05 .15
378 Robin Ventura .10 .30
379 Bernard Gilkey .05 .15
380 Kirby Puckett .30 .75
381 Steve Howe .05 .15
382 Devon White .10 .30
383 Roberto Mejia .05 .15
384 Darrin Jackson .05 .15
385 Mike Morgan .05 .15
386 Rusty Meacham .05 .15
387 Bill Swift .05 .15
388 Lou Frazier .05 .15
389 Andy Van Slyke .20 .50
390 Brett Butler .10 .30
391 Bobby Witt .05 .15
392 Jeff Conine .10 .30
393 Tim Hyers .05 .15
394 Terry Pendleton .10 .30
395 Ricky Jordan .05 .15
396 Eric Plunk .05 .15
397 Melido Perez .05 .15
398 Darryl Kile .10 .30
399 Mark McLemore .05 .15
400 Greg W.Harris .05 .15
401 Jim Leyritz .05 .15
402 Doug Strange .05 .15
403 Tim Salmon .20 .50
404 Terry Mulholland .05 .15
405 Robby Thompson .05 .15
406 Ruben Sierra .10 .30
407 Tony Phillips .05 .15
408 Moises Alou .10 .30
409 Felix Fermin .05 .15
410 Pat Listach .05 .15
411 Kevin Bass .05 .15
412 Ben McDonald .05 .15
413 Scott Cooper .05 .15
414 Jody Reed .05 .15
415 Deion Sanders .20 .50
416 Ricky Gutierrez .05 .15
417 Gregg Jefferies .05 .15
418 Jack McDowell .05 .15
419 Al Leiter .10 .30
420 Tony Longmire .05 .15
421 Paul Wagner .05 .15
422 Geronimo Pena .05 .15
423 Ivan Rodriguez .20 .50
424 Kevin Gross .05 .15
425 Kirk McCaskill .05 .15
426 Greg Myers .05 .15
427 Roger Clemens .60 1.50
428 Chris Hammond .05 .15
429 Randy Myers .05 .15
430 Roger Mason .05 .15
431 Bret Saberhagen .10 .30
432 Jeff Reboulet .05 .15
433 John Olerud .10 .30
434 Bill Gullickson .05 .15
435 Eddie Murray .30 .75
436 Pedro Munoz .05 .15
437 Charlie O'Brien .05 .15
438 Jeff Nelson .05 .15
439 Mike Macfarlane .05 .15
440 Don Mattingly CL .40 1.00
441 Derrick May .05 .15
442 John Roper .05 .15
443 Darryl Hamilton .05 .15
444 Dan Miceli .05 .15
445 Tony Eusebio .05 .15
446 Jerry Browne .05 .15
447 Wally Joyner .10 .30
448 Brian Harper .05 .15
449 Scott Fletcher .05 .15
450 Bip Roberts .05 .15
451 Pete Smith .05 .15
452 Chili Davis .10 .30
453 Dave Hollins .05 .15
454 Tony Pena .05 .15
455 Butch Henry .05 .15
456 Craig Biggio .20 .50
457 Zane Smith .05 .15
458 Ryan Thompson .05 .15
459 Mike Jackson .05 .15
460 Mark McGwire .75 2.00
461 John Smoltz .20 .50
462 Steve Scarsone .05 .15
463 Greg Colbrunn .05 .15
464 Shawn Green .10 .30
465 David Wells .10 .30
466 Jose Hernandez .05 .15
467 Chip Hale .05 .15
468 Tony Tarasco .05 .15
469 Kevin Mitchell .05 .15
470 Billy Hatcher .05 .15
471 Jay Buhner .10 .30
472 Ken Caminiti .10 .30
473 Tom Henke .05 .15
474 Todd Worrell .05 .15
475 Mark Eichhorn .05 .15
476 Bruce Ruffin .05 .15
477 Chuck Finley .10 .30
478 Marc Newfield .05 .15
479 Paul Shuey .05 .15
480 Bob Tewksbury .05 .15
481 Ramon J.Martinez .05 .15
482 Melvin Nieves .05 .15
483 Todd Zeile .05 .15
484 Benito Santiago .10 .30
485 Stan Javier .05 .15
486 Kirk Rueter .05 .15
487 Andre Dawson .10 .30
488 Eric Karros .10 .30
489 Dave Magadan .05 .15
490 Joe Carter CL .05 .15
491 Randy Velarde .05 .15
492 Larry Walker .10 .30
493 Cris Carpenter .05 .15
494 Tom Gordon .05 .15
495 Dave Burba .05 .15
496 Darren Bragg .05 .15
497 Darren Daulton .10 .30
498 Don Slaught .05 .15
499 Pat Borders .05 .15
500 Lenny Harris .05 .15
501 Joe Ausanio .05 .15
502 Alan Trammell .10 .30
503 Mike Fetters .05 .15
504 Scott Ruffcorn .05 .15
505 Rich Rowland .05 .15
506 Juan Samuel .05 .15
507 Bo Jackson .30 .75
508 Jeff Branson .05 .15
509 Bernie Williams .20 .50
510 Paul Sorrento .05 .15
511 Dennis Eckersley .10 .30
512 Pat Mahomes .05 .15
513 Rusty Greer .10 .30
514 Luis Polonia .05 .15
515 Willie Banks .05 .15
516 John Wetteland .10 .30
517 Mike LaValliere .05 .15
518 Tommy Greene .05 .15
519 Mark Grace .20 .50
520 Bob Hamelin .05 .15
521 Scott Sanderson .05 .15
522 Joe Carter .10 .30
523 Jeff Brantley .05 .15
524 Andrew Lorraine .05 .15
525 Rico Brogna .05 .15
526 Shane Mack .05 .15
527 Mark Wohlers .05 .15
528 Scott Sanders .05 .15
529 Chris Bosio .05 .15
530 Andujar Cedeno .05 .15
531 Kenny Rogers .10 .30
532 Doug Drabek .05 .15
533 Curt Leskanic .05 .15
534 Craig Shipley .05 .15
535 Craig Grebeck .05 .15
536 Cal Eldred .05 .15
537 Mickey Tettleton .05 .15
538 Harold Baines .10 .30
539 Tim Wallach .05 .15
540 Damon Buford .05 .15
541 Lenny Webster .05 .15
542 Kevin Appier .10 .30
543 Raul Mondesi .10 .30
544 Eric Young .05 .15
545 Russ Davis .05 .15
546 Mike Benjamin .05 .15
547 Mike Greenwell .05 .15
548 Scott Brosius .10 .30
549 Brian Dorsett .05 .15
550 Chili Davis CL .05 .15

1995 Donruss Press Proofs

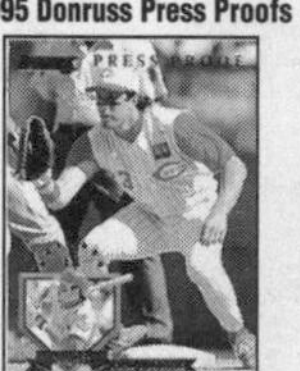

COMPLETE SET (550) 400.00 600.00
*STARS: 6X TO 15X BASIC CARDS
SER.1 ODDS 1:20 H/R, 1:18 JUM, 1:24 MAG
SER.2 ODDS 1:24 H/R, 1:18 JUM, 1:24 MAG
STATED PRINT RUN 2000 SETS

1995 Donruss Promos

1 Frank Thomas 1.00 2.50
2 Barry Bonds 1.50 4.00
3 Hideo Nomo 1.00 2.50
4 Ken Griffey Jr. 2.00 5.00
5 Cal Ripken Jr. 3.00 8.00
6 Manny Ramirez .60 1.50
7 Mike Piazza 1.00 2.50
8 Greg Maddux 1.50 4.00

1995 Donruss All-Stars

This 18-card standard-size set was randomly inserted into retail packs. The first series has the nine 1994 American League starters while the second series honored the National League starters. The cards are numbered in the upper right with either an "AL-X" or an "NL-X."

COMPLETE SET (18) 75.00 150.00
COMPLETE SERIES AL (9) 40.00 100.00
COMPLETE SERIES NL (9) 25.00 60.00
STATED ODDS 1:8 JUMBO
AL1 Jimmy Key 1.25 3.00
AL2 Ivan Rodriguez 2.00 5.00
AL3 Frank Thomas 3.00 8.00
AL4 Roberto Alomar 2.00 5.00
AL5 Wade Boggs 2.00 5.00
AL6 Cal Ripken 10.00 25.00
AL7 Joe Carter 1.25 3.00
AL8 Ken Griffey Jr. 6.00 15.00
AL9 Kirby Puckett 3.00 8.00
NL1 Greg Maddux 5.00 12.00
NL2 Mike Piazza 5.00 12.00
NL3 Gregg Jefferies .60 1.50
NL4 Mariano Duncan .60 1.50
NL5 Matt Williams 1.25 3.00
NL6 Ozzie Smith 5.00 12.00
NL7 Barry Bonds 8.00 20.00
NL8 Tony Gwynn 4.00 10.00
NL9 David Justice 1.25 3.00

1995 Donruss Bomb Squad

Randomly inserted one in every 24 retail packs a one in every 16 magazine packs, this set features top six home run hitters in the National and Ame League. These cards were only included in first series packs. Each of the six cards shows a diffe slugger on the either side of the card.

COMPLETE SET (6) 5.00 1
SER.1 STATED ODDS 1:24 RET, 1:16 MAG
1 K.Griffey 1.50
M.Williams
2 F.Thomas .75
J.Bagwell
3 B.Bonds 2.00
A.Belle
4 J.Canseco .50
F.McGriff
5 C.Fielder .30
A.Galarraga
6 J.Carter .30
K.Mitchell

1995 Donruss Diamond King

The 1995 Donruss Diamond King set consists of standard-size cards that were randomly inserted packs. The fronts feature water color player portra by noted sports artist Dick Perez. The player's na and "Diamond Kings" are in gold foil. The backs a dark blue border with a player photo and text. T cards are numbered on back with a DK prefix.

COMPLETE SET (29) 20.00 50
COMPLETE SERIES 1 (14) 8.00 20
COMPLETE SERIES 2 (15) 15.00 30
STATED ODDS 1:10 H/R, 1:9 JUM, 1:10 MAG
DK1 Frank Thomas 1.25 3
DK2 Jeff Bagwell .75 2
DK3 Chili Davis .50 1
DK4 Dante Bichette .50 1
DK5 Ruben Sierra .50 1
DK6 Jeff Conine .50 1
DK7 Paul O'Neill .75 2
DK8 Bobby Bonilla .50 1
DK9 Joe Carter .50 1
DK10 Moises Alou .50 1
DK11 Kenny Lofton .50 1
DK12 Matt Williams .50 1
DK13 Kevin Seitzer .25
DK14 Sammy Sosa 1.25 3
DK15 Scott Cooper .25
DK16 Raul Mondesi .50 1
DK17 Will Clark .75 2.
DK18 Lenny Dykstra .50 1.
DK19 Kirby Puckett 1.25 3
DK20 Hal Morris .25
DK21 Travis Fryman .50 1.
DK22 Greg Maddux 2.00 5.
DK23 Rafael Palmeiro .75 2.
DK24 Tony Gwynn 1.50 4.
DK25 David Cone .50 1.
DK26 Al Martin .25
DK27 Ken Griffey Jr. 2.50 6.
DK28 Gregg Jefferies .25
DK29 Checklist .25

1995 Donruss Dominators

This nine-card standard-size set was randomly inserted in second series hobby packs. Each of the cards features three of the leading players at each position. The horizontal fronts have photos of all three players and identify only their last name. The words "remove protective film" cover a significant portion of the fronts as well. The cards are numbe in the upper right corner as "X" of 9.

COMPLETE SET (9) 10.00 25.
SER.2 STATED ODDS 1:24 HOBBY
1 Maddux 1.25 3.
Cone
Mussina
2 Piazza 1.25 3.
Rodriguez
Daulton
3 Thomas .75 2.
Bagwell
McGriff
4 Alomar .50 1.
Baerga
Biggio
5 Ventura .30 .7
Fryman
Williams
6 Ripken 2.50 6.0
Larkin
Cordero
7 Bonds 2.00 5.0
Alou
Belle
8 Griffey 1.50 4.0
Lofton
Grissom
9 Gwynn 1.00 2.5
Puckett
O'Neill

1995 Donruss Elite

omly inserted one in every 210 Series 1 and 2 s, this set consists of 12 standard-size cards that umbered (49-60) based on where the previous s set left off. The fronts contain an action photo unded by a marble border. Silver holographic orders the card on all four sides. Limited to 0, the backs are individually numbered, contain ll photo and write-up.

PLETE SET (12) 40.00 100.00
PLETE SERIES 1 (6) 20.00 50.00
PLETE SERIES 2 (6) 20.00 50.00
ODDS 1:210 H/R, 1:120 J, 1:210 M
2 ODDS 1:180 H/R, 1:120 J, 1:180 M
ED PRINT RUN 10,000 SERIAL #'d SETS
ff Bagwell 3.00 8.00
ul O'Neill 3.00 8.00
eg Maddux 6.00 15.00
ke Piazza 5.00 12.00
att Williams 2.00 5.00
en Griffey Jr. 6.00 15.00
ank Thomas 5.00 12.00
rry Bonds 8.00 20.00
rby Puckett 5.00 12.00
ed McGriff 3.00 8.00
se Canseco 3.00 8.00
bert Belle 2.00 5.00

95 Donruss Long Ball Leaders

ted one in every 24 series one hobby packs, this eatures eight top home run hitters.

PLETE SET (8) 8.00 20.00
1 STATED ODDS 1:24 HOBBY
ank Thomas 1.00 2.50
d McGriff .60 1.50
n Griffey Jr. 2.00 5.00
tt Williams .40 1.00
ke Piazza 1.50 4.00
e Canseco .60 1.50
rry Bonds 2.50 6.00
f Bagwell .60 1.50

995 Donruss Mound Marvels

eight-card standard-size set was randomly ted into second series magazine jumbo and packs at a rate of one every 16 packs. This set ures eight of the leading major league starters.

MPLETE SET (8) 8.00 20.00
2 STATED ODDS 1:16 RET/MAG
eg Maddux 2.50 6.00
vid Cone .60 1.50
ke Mussina 1.00 2.50
et Saberhagen .60 1.50
mmy Key .60 1.50
ug Drabek .30 .75
ndy Johnson 1.50 4.00
son Bere .30 .75

995 Donruss Top of the Order

360-card standard-size set was distributed as a or League Baseball Card Game. The cards were kaged in 80-card starter decks with other cards lable in booster packs. The fronts carry player on photos with the player's name, team, position, other player information needed to play the e. The green backs carry the card logo. The first cards feature players in the American League the National League represented by the second cards. The cards are unnumbered and cklisted below in alphabetical order within each n. There are three levels of scarcity for these ds; common, uncommon and rare. All cards have n given either a designation of C (for common), U uncommon) or R (for rare).

MPLETE SET (360) 250.00 500.00
MMON CARD (1-360) .04 .10
COMMON CARD (1-360) .20 .50
RE CARD (1-360) .40 1.00
rady Anderson C .07 .20
arold Baines U .30 .75
ret Barberie U .20 .50
rmando Benitez C .07 .20
obby Bonilla U .20 .50
cott Erickson C .02 .10
eo Gomez C .02 .10
urtis Goodwin R .40 1.00
effrey Hammonds C .07 .20
Chris Hoiles C .02 .10
Doug Jones C .02 .10
Ben McDonald U .20 .50
Mike Mussina U 1.00 2.50
Rafael Palmeiro R 1.00 2.50
Cal Ripken Jr. R 15.00 40.00
Rick Aguilera C .07 .20
Luis Alicea C .02 .10
Jose Canseco U 1.00 2.50
Roger Clemens C .50 1.25
Mike Greenwell U .20 .50
Erik Hanson C .02 .10
Mike Macfarlane C .02 .10
Tim Naehring R .40 1.00
Troy O'Leary U .20 .50
Ken Ryan C .02 .10
Aaron Sele C .30 .75
Lee Tinsley U .20 .50
John Valentin R .40 1.00
Mo Vaughn R .40 1.00
Jim Abbott C .07 .20
Mike Butcher C .02 .10
Chili Davis R .60 1.50
Gary DiSarcina R .40 1.00
Damion Easley C .02 .10
Jim Edmonds R 1.00 2.50
Chuck Finley U .30 .75
Mark Langston C .02 .10

38 Greg Myers C .02 .10
39 Spike Owen C .02 .10
40 Troy Percival R .60 1.50
41 Tony Phillips U .20 .50
42 Tim Salmon R .75 2.00
43 Lee Smith R .60 1.50
44 J.T. Snow U .30 .75
45 Jason Bere C .02 .10
46 Mike Devereaux U .20 .50
47 Ray Durham C .30 .75
48 Alex Fernandez C .02 .10
49 Ozzie Guillen R .60 1.50
50 Roberto Hernandez C .07 .20
51 Lance Johnson U .20 .50
52 Ron Karkovice C .02 .10
53 Tim Raines U .30 .75
54 Frank Thomas R 3.00 8.00
55 Robin Ventura U .60 1.50
56 Sandy Alomar R .60 1.50
57 Carlos Baerga R .40 1.00
58 Albert Belle R .60 1.50
59 Kenny Lofton R .75 2.00
60 Dennis Martinez C .07 .20
61 Jose Mesa U .20 .50
62 Eddie Murray R 1.00 2.50
63 Charles Nagy C .02 .10
64 Tony Pena C .07 .20
65 Eric Plunk R .40 1.00
66 Manny Ramirez R 3.00 8.00
67 Paul Sorrento C .02 .10
68 Jim Thome R 1.00 2.50
69 Omar Vizquel C .07 .20
70 Danny Bautista C .02 .10
71 Joe Boever C .02 .10
72 Chad Curtis C .02 .10
73 Cecil Fielder U .30 .75
74 John Flaherty U .20 .50
75 Travis Fryman U .30 .75
76 Kirk Gibson C .07 .20
77 Chris Gomez C .02 .10
78 Mike Henneman R .40 1.00
79 Bob Higginson C .30 .75
80 Alan Trammell U .40 1.00
81 Lou Whitaker R .60 1.50
82 Kevin Appier R .60 1.50
83 Billy Brewer C .02 .10
84 Vince Coleman R .40 1.00
85 Gary Gaetti C .07 .20
86 Greg Gagne C .02 .10
87 Tom Goodwin R .40 1.00
88 Tom Gordon C .07 .20
89 Mark Gubicza C .02 .10
90 Bob Hamelin C .02 .10
91 Phil Hiatt C .02 .10
92 Wally Joyner R .40 1.00
93 Brent Mayne C .02 .10
94 Jeff Montgomery C .02 .10
95 Ricky Bones C .02 .10
96 Mike Fetters C .02 .10
97 Darryl Hamilton C .02 .10
98 Pat Listach C .02 .10
99 Matt Mieske C .02 .10
100 Dave Nilsson C .02 .10
101 Joe Oliver U .20 .50
102 Kevin Seitzer U .20 .50
103 B.J. Surhoff U .30 .75
104 Jose Valentin C .02 .10
105 Greg Vaughn C .07 .20
106 Bill Wegman C .02 .10
107 Alex Cole U .20 .50
108 Marty Cordova C .07 .20
109 Chuck Knoblauch R .60 1.50
110 Scott Leius C .02 .10
111 Pat Meares C .02 .10
112 Pedro Munoz C .02 .10
113 Kirby Puckett R 8.00 20.00
114 Scott Stahoviak C .02 .10
115 Mike Trombley C .02 .10
116 Matt Walbeck C .02 .10
117 Wade Boggs R 2.50 6.00
118 David Cone U .40 1.00
119 Tony Fernandez C .07 .20
120 Don Mattingly R 8.00 20.00
121 Jack McDowell C .02 .10
122 Paul O'Neill U .30 .75
123 Melido Perez C .02 .10
124 Luis Polonia C .02 .10
125 Ruben Sierra C .07 .20
126 Mike Stanley C .02 .10
127 Randy Velarde C .02 .10
128 John Wetteland R .60 1.50
129 Bob Wickman C .07 .20
130 Bernie Williams C .15 .40
131 Gerald Williams C .02 .10
132 Geronimo Berroa C .02 .10
133 Mike Bordick U .20 .50
134 Scott Brosius C .07 .20
135 Dennis Eckersley C .20 .50
136 Brent Gates C .02 .10
137 Rickey Henderson U 1.50 4.00
138 Stan Javier C .02 .10
139 Mark McGwire R 12.50 30.00
140 Steve Ontiveros U .20 .50
141 Terry Steinbach C .02 .10
142 Todd Stottlemyre R .40 1.00
143 Danny Tartabull C .07 .20
144 Bobby Ayala R .40 1.00
145 Andy Benes U .20 .50
146 Mike Blowers C .02 .10
147 Jay Buhner U .30 .75
148 Joey Cora U .20 .50
149 Alex Diaz C .02 .10
150 Ken Griffey Jr. R 10.00 25.00

151 Randy Johnson R 2.00 5.00
152 Edgar Martinez R .75 2.00
153 Tino Martinez U .40 1.00
154 Bill Risley R .40 1.00
155 Alex Rodriguez C 1.25 3.00
156 Dan Wilson C .02 .10
157 Will Clark R 1.00 2.50
158 Jeff Frye U .20 .50
159 Benji Gil C .02 .10
160 Juan Gonzalez C .30 .75
161 Rusty Greer C .07 .20
162 Mark McLemore R .40 1.00
163 Otis Nixon U .20 .50
164 Dean Palmer R .60 1.50
165 Ivan Rodriguez R 4.00 10.00
166 Kenny Rogers C .07 .20
167 Jeff Russell C .02 .10
168 Mickey Tettleton C .02 .10
169 Bob Tewksbury C .02 .10
170 Bobby Witt C .02 .10
171 Roberto Alomar R 1.00 2.50
172 Joe Carter R .60 1.50
173 Alex Gonzalez C .02 .10
174 Candy Maldonado C .02 .10
175 Paul Molitor C .20 .50
176 John Olerud C .07 .20
177 Lance Parrish C .07 .20
178 Ed Sprague C .02 .10
179 Devon White C .02 .10
180 Woody Williams C .02 .10
181 Steve Avery C .02 .10
182 Jeff Blauser C .02 .10
183 Tom Glavine U .60 1.50
184 Marquis Grissom R .40 1.00
185 Chipper Jones C .60 1.50
186 David Justice R 1.00 2.50
187 Ryan Klesko U .30 .75
188 Mark Lemke C .02 .10
189 Javy Lopez C .15 .40
190 Greg Maddux R 10.00 25.00
191 Fred McGriff R .75 2.00
192 Greg McMichael U .20 .50
193 John Smoltz R .60 1.50
194 Mark Wohlers R .40 1.00
195 Jim Bullinger U .20 .50
196 Shawon Dunston R .40 1.00
197 Kevin Foster C .02 .10
198 Luis Gonzalez C .20 .50
199 Mark Grace R 1.00 2.50
200 Brian McRae R .40 1.00
201 Randy Myers R .60 1.50
202 Jaime Navarro U .20 .50
203 Rey Sanchez U .20 .50
204 Scott Servais C .02 .10
205 Sammy Sosa R 8.00 20.00
206 Steve Trachsel U .30 .75
207 Todd Zeile C .07 .20
208 Bret Boone R .75 2.00
209 Jeff Branson U .20 .50
210 Jeff Brantley R .60 1.50
211 Hector Carrasco C .02 .10
212 Ron Gant R .60 1.50
213 Lenny Harris C .02 .10
214 Barry Larkin R 1.00 2.50
215 Darren Lewis C .02 .10
216 Hal Morris C .02 .10
217 Mark Portugal C .02 .10
218 Jose Rijo U .20 .50
219 Reggie Sanders R .60 1.50
220 Pete Schourek U .20 .50
221 John Smiley C .02 .10
222 Eddie Taubensee C .02 .10
223 David Wells C .10 .30
224 Jason Bates C .02 .10
225 Dante Bichette R .60 1.50
226 Vinny Castilla U .30 .75
227 Andres Galarraga R 1.00 2.50
228 Joe Girardi U .20 .50
229 Mike Kingery C .02 .10
230 Steve Reed R .40 1.00
231 Bruce Ruffin U .20 .50
232 Bret Saberhagen U .20 .50
233 Bill Swift C .02 .10
234 Larry Walker R 1.00 2.50
235 Walt Weiss C .02 .10
236 Eric Young C .02 .10
237 Kurt Abbott C .02 .10
238 John Burkett C .07 .20
239 Chuck Carr C .02 .10
240 Greg Colbrunn C .02 .10
241 Jeff Conine R .40 1.00
242 Andre Dawson C .15 .40
243 Chris Hammond R .40 1.00
244 Charles Johnson C .07 .20
245 Robb Nen C .07 .20
246 Terry Pendleton U .30 .75
247 Gary Sheffield R 1.50 4.00
248 Quilvio Veras C .02 .10
249 Jeff Bagwell U 1.50 4.00
250 Derek Bell R .40 1.00
251 Craig Biggio U .60 1.50
252 Doug Drabek C .02 .10
253 Tony Eusebio U .20 .50
254 John Hudek C .02 .10
255 Brian L. Hunter U .20 .50
256 Todd Jones R .60 1.50
257 Dave Magadan U .20 .50
258 Orlando Miller C .02 .10
259 James Mouton C .02 .10
260 Shane Reynolds C .02 .10
261 Greg Swindell C .02 .10
262 Billy Ashley C .02 .10
263 Tom Candiotti U .20 .50

264 Delino DeShields C .07 .20
265 Eric Karros R .60 1.50
266 Roberto Kelly C .02 .10
267 Ramon Martinez C .07 .20
268 Raul Mondesi R .60 1.50
269 Hideo Nomo R 15.00 40.00
270 Jose Offerman U .20 .50
271 Mike Piazza R 10.00 25.00
272 Ismael Valdes U .20 .50
273 Ismael Valdes U .20 .50
274 Tim Wallach C .02 .10
275 Todd Worrell R .40 1.00
276 Moises Alou R .60 1.50
277 Sean Berry U .20 .50
278 Wil Cordero U .20 .50
279 Jeff Fassero C .02 .10
280 Darrin Fletcher C .02 .10
281 Mike Lansing C .02 .10
282 Pedro Martinez R 3.00 8.00
283 Carlos Perez U .20 .50
284 Mel Rojas U .20 .50
285 Tim Scott R .40 1.00
286 David Segui U .30 .75
287 Tony Tarasco U .20 .50
288 Rondell White C .07 .20
289 Rico Brogna C .02 .10
290 Brett Butler C .07 .20
291 John Franco C .07 .20
292 Pete Harnisch C .02 .10
293 Todd Hundley C .07 .20
294 Bobby Jones C .02 .10
295 Jeff Kent C .15 .40
296 Joe Orsulak U .20 .50
297 Ryan Thompson U .20 .50
298 Jose Vizcaino C .02 .10
299 Ricky Bottalico U .20 .50
300 Darren Daulton C .07 .20
301 Mariano Duncan U .20 .50
302 Lenny Dykstra U .30 .75
303 Jim Eisenreich U .30 .75
304 Tyler Green U .20 .50
305 Charlie Hayes U .20 .50
306 Dave Hollins C .02 .10
307 Gregg Jefferies C .02 .10
308 Mickey Morandini U .20 .50
309 Curt Schilling R 2.00 5.00
310 Heathcliff Slocumb U .20 .50
311 Kevin Stocker C .02 .10
312 Jay Bell C .02 .10
313 Jacob Brumfield C .02 .10
314 Dave Clark U .20 .50
315 Carlos Garcia C .02 .10
316 Mark Johnson C .02 .10
317 Jeff King C .02 .10
318 Nelson Liriano U .20 .50
319 Al Martin U .20 .50
320 Orlando Merced U .20 .50
321 Dan Miceli U .20 .50
322 Denny Neagle C .07 .20
323 Mark Parent C .02 .10
324 Dan Plesac R .40 1.00
325 Scott Cooper C .02 .10
326 Bernard Gilkey R .40 1.00
327 Tom Henke R .40 1.00
328 Ken Hill C .02 .10
329 Danny Jackson C .02 .10
330 Brian Jordan R .60 1.50
331 Ray Lankford U .20 .50
332 John Mabry U .20 .50
333 Jose Oquendo C .02 .10
334 Tom Pagnozzi C .02 .10
335 Ozzie Smith U 2.00 5.00
336 Andy Ashby U .20 .50
337 Brad Ausmus U .02 .10
338 Ken Caminiti U .40 1.00
339 Andujar Cedeno C .02 .10
340 Steve Finley R .60 1.50
341 Tony Gwynn R 8.00 20.00
342 Joey Hamilton C .02 .10
343 Trevor Hoffman C .07 .20
344 Jody Reed C .02 .10
345 Bip Roberts R .40 1.00
346 Eddie Williams C .02 .10
347 Rod Beck U .30 .75
348 Mike Benjamin U .20 .50
349 Barry Bonds R 8.00 20.00
350 Royce Clayton C .02 .10
351 Glenallen Hill C .02 .10
352 Kirt Manwaring C .02 .10
353 Terry Mulholland C .02 .10
354 John Patterson C .02 .10
355 J.R. Phillips C .02 .10
356 Deion Sanders R .60 1.50
357 Steve Scarsone U .20 .50
358 Robby Thompson C .02 .10
359 William VanLandingham C .02 .10
360 Matt Williams R .75 2.00

1996 Donruss Samples

COMPLETE SET (8) 6.00 15.00
1 Frank Thomas .50 1.25
2 Barry Bonds 1.00 2.50
3 Hideo Nomo .40 1.00
4 Ken Griffey Jr. 1.50 4.00
5 Cal Ripken 2.00 5.00
6 Manny Ramirez .50 1.25
7 Mike Piazza 1.25 3.00
8 Greg Maddux 1.00 2.50

1996 Donruss

The 1996 Donruss set was issued in two series of 330 and 220 cards respectively, for a total of 550. The 12-card packs had a suggested retail price of $1.79. The full-bleed fronts feature full-color action photos with the player's name is in white ink in the upper right. The horizontal backs feature season and career stats, text, vital stats and another photo. Rookie Cards in this set include Mike Cameron.

COMPLETE SET (550) 15.00 40.00
COMPLETE SERIES 1 (330) 10.00 25.00
COMPLETE SERIES 2 (220) 6.00 15.00
SUBSET CARDS HALF VALUE OF BASE CARDS
1 Frank Thomas .30 .75
2 Jason Bates .10 .30
3 Steve Sparks .10 .30
4 Scott Servais .10 .30
5 Angelo Encarnacion RC .10 .30
6 Scott Sanders .10 .30
7 Billy Ashley .10 .30
8 Alex Rodriguez .60 1.50
9 Sean Bergman .10 .30
10 Brad Radke .10 .30
11 Andy Van Slyke .20 .50
12 Joe Girardi .10 .30
13 Mark Grudzielanek .10 .30
14 Rick Aguilera .10 .30
15 Randy Veres .10 .30
16 Tim Bogar .10 .30
17 Dave Veres .10 .30
18 Kevin Stocker .10 .30
19 Marquis Grissom .10 .30
20 Will Clark .20 .50
21 Jay Bell .10 .30
22 Allen Battle .10 .30
23 Frank Rodriguez .10 .30
24 Terry Steinbach .10 .30
25 Gerald Williams .10 .30
26 Sid Roberson .10 .30
27 Greg Zaun .10 .30
28 Ozzie Timmons .10 .30
29 Vaughn Eshelman .10 .30
30 Ed Sprague .10 .30
31 Gary DiSarcina .10 .30
32 Joe Boever .10 .30
33 Steve Avery .10 .30
34 Brad Ausmus .10 .30
35 Kirt Manwaring .10 .30
36 Gary Sheffield .10 .30
37 Jason Bere .10 .30
38 Jeff Manto .10 .30
39 David Cone .10 .30
40 Manny Ramirez .20 .50
41 Sandy Alomar Jr. .10 .30
42 Curtis Goodwin .10 .30
43 Tino Martinez .20 .50
44 Woody Williams .10 .30
45 Dean Palmer .10 .30
46 Hipolito Pichardo .10 .30
47 Jason Giambi .10 .30
48 Lance Johnson .10 .30
49 Bernard Gilkey .10 .30
50 Kirby Puckett .30 .75
51 Tony Fernandez .10 .30
52 Alex Gonzalez .10 .30
53 Bret Saberhagen .10 .30
54 Lyle Mouton .10 .30
55 Brian McRae .10 .30
56 Mark Gubicza .10 .30
57 Sergio Valdez .10 .30
58 Darrin Fletcher .10 .30
59 Steve Parris .10 .30
60 Johnny Damon .20 .50
61 Rickey Henderson .30 .75
62 Darrell Whitmore .10 .30
63 Roberto Petagine .10 .30
64 Trenidad Hubbard .10 .30
65 Heathcliff Slocumb .10 .30
66 Steve Finley .10 .30
67 Mariano Rivera .60 1.50
68 Brian L.Hunter .10 .30
69 Jamie Moyer .10 .30
70 Ellis Burks .10 .30
71 Pat Kelly .10 .30
72 Mickey Tettleton .10 .30
73 Garret Anderson .10 .30
74 Andy Pettitte .20 .50
75 Glenallen Hill .10 .30
76 Brent Gates .10 .30
77 Lou Whitaker .10 .30
78 David Segui .10 .30
79 Dan Wilson .10 .30
80 Pat Listach .10 .30
81 Jeff Bagwell .20 .50
82 Ben McDonald .10 .30

83 John Valentin .10 .30
84 John Jaha .10 .30
85 Pete Schourek .10 .30
86 Bryce Florie .10 .30
87 Brian Jordan .10 .30
88 Ron Karkovice .10 .30
89 Al Leiter .10 .30
90 Tony Longmire .10 .30
91 Nelson Liriano .10 .30
92 David Bell .10 .30
93 Kevin Gross .10 .30
94 Tom Candiotti .10 .30
95 Dave Martinez .10 .30
96 Greg Myers .10 .30
97 Rheal Cormier .10 .30
98 Chris Hammond .10 .30
99 Randy Myers .10 .30
100 Bill Pulsipher .10 .30
101 Jason Isringhausen .10 .30
102 Dave Stevens .10 .30
103 Roberto Alomar .20 .50
104 Bob Higginson .10 .30
105 Eddie Murray .30 .75
106 Matt Walbeck .10 .30
107 Mark Wohlers .10 .30
108 Jeff Nelson .10 .30
109 Tom Goodwin .10 .30
110 Cal Ripken CL .50 1.25
111 Rey Sanchez .10 .30
112 Hector Carrasco .10 .30
113 B.J. Surhoff .10 .30
114 Dan Miceli .10 .30
115 Dean Hartgraves .10 .30
116 John Burkett .10 .30
117 Gary Gaetti .10 .30
118 Ricky Bones .10 .30
119 Mike Macfarlane .10 .30
120 Bip Roberts .10 .30
121 Dave Mlicki .10 .30
122 Chili Davis .10 .30
123 Mark Whiten .10 .30
124 Herbert Perry .10 .30
125 Butch Henry .10 .30
126 Derek Bell .10 .30
127 Al Martin .10 .30
128 John Franco .10 .30
129 W. VanLandingham .10 .30
130 Mike Bordick .10 .30
131 Mike Mordecai .10 .30
132 Robby Thompson .10 .30
133 Greg Colbrunn .10 .30
134 Domingo Cedeno .10 .30
135 Chad Curtis .10 .30
136 Jose Hernandez .10 .30
137 Scott Klingenbeck .10 .30
138 Ryan Klesko .10 .30
139 John Smiley .10 .30
140 Charlie Hayes .10 .30
141 Jay Buhner .10 .30
142 Doug Drabek .10 .30
143 Roger Pavlik .10 .30
144 Todd Worrell .10 .30
145 Cal Ripken 1.00 2.50
146 Steve Reed .10 .30
147 Chuck Finley .10 .30
148 Mike Blowers .10 .30
149 Orel Hershiser .10 .30
150 Allen Watson .10 .30
151 Ramon Martinez .10 .30
152 Melvin Nieves .10 .30
153 Tripp Cromer .10 .30
154 Yorkis Perez .10 .30
155 Stan Javier .10 .30
156 Mel Rojas .10 .30
157 Aaron Sele .10 .30
158 Eric Karros .10 .30
159 Robb Nen .10 .30
160 Raul Mondesi .10 .30
161 John Wetteland .10 .30
162 Tim Scott .10 .30
163 Kenny Rogers .10 .30
164 Melvin Bunch .10 .30
165 Rod Beck .10 .30
166 Andy Benes .10 .30
167 Lenny Dykstra .10 .30
168 Orlando Merced .10 .30
169 Tomas Perez .10 .30
170 Xavier Hernandez .10 .30
171 Ruben Sierra .10 .30
172 Alan Trammell .10 .30
173 Mike Fetters .10 .30
174 Wilson Alvarez .10 .30
175 Erik Hanson .10 .30
176 Travis Fryman .10 .30
177 Jim Abbott .20 .50
178 Bret Boone .10 .30
179 Sterling Hitchcock .10 .30
180 Pat Mahomes .10 .30
181 Mark Acre .10 .30
182 Charles Nagy .10 .30
183 Rusty Greer .10 .30
184 Mike Stanley .10 .30
185 Jim Bullinger .10 .30
186 Shane Andrews .10 .30
187 Brian Keyser .10 .30
188 Tyler Green .10 .30
189 Mark Grace .20 .50
190 Bob Hamelin .10 .30
191 Luis Ortiz .10 .30
192 Joe Carter .10 .30
193 Eddie Taubensee .10 .30
194 Brian Anderson .10 .30
195 Edgardo Alfonzo .10 .30

196 Pedro Munoz .10 .30
197 David Justice .10 .30
198 Trevor Hoffman .10 .30
199 Bobby Ayala .10 .30
200 Tony Eusebio .10 .30
201 Jeff Russell .10 .30
202 Mike Hampton .10 .30
203 Walt Weiss .10 .30
204 Joey Hamilton .10 .30
205 Roberto Hernandez .10 .30
206 Greg Vaughn .10 .30
207 Felipe Lira .10 .30
208 Harold Baines .10 .30
209 Tim Wallach .10 .30
210 Manny Alexander .10 .30
211 Tim Laker .10 .30
212 Chris Haney .10 .30
213 Brian Maxcy .10 .30
214 Eric Young .10 .30
215 Darryl Strawberry .10 .30
216 Barry Bonds .75 2.00
217 Tim Naehring .10 .30
218 Scott Brosius .10 .30
219 Reggie Sanders .10 .30
220 Eddie Murray CL .20 .50
221 Luis Alicea .10 .30
222 Albert Belle .10 .30
223 Benji Gil .10 .30
224 Dante Bichette .10 .30
225 Bobby Bonilla .10 .30
226 Todd Stottlemyre .10 .30
227 Jim Edmonds .10 .30
228 Todd Jones .10 .30
229 Shawn Green .10 .30
230 Javier Lopez .10 .30
231 Ariel Prieto .10 .30
232 Tony Phillips .10 .30
233 James Mouton .10 .30
234 Jose Oquendo .10 .30
235 Royce Clayton .10 .30
236 Chuck Carr .10 .30
237 Doug Jones .10 .30
238 Mark McLemore .10 .30
239 Bill Swift .10 .30
240 Scott Leius .10 .30
241 Russ Davis .10 .30
242 Ray Durham .10 .30
243 Matt Mieske .10 .30
244 Brent Mayne .10 .30
245 Thomas Howard .10 .30
246 Troy O'Leary .10 .30
247 Jacob Brumfield .10 .30
248 Mickey Morandini .10 .30
249 Todd Hundley .10 .30
250 Chris Bosio .10 .30
251 Omar Vizquel .20 .50
252 Mike Lansing .10 .30
253 John Mabry .10 .30
254 Mike Perez .10 .30
255 Delino DeShields .10 .30
256 Wil Cordero .10 .30
257 Mike James .10 .30
258 Todd Van Poppel .10 .30
259 Joey Cora .10 .30
260 Andre Dawson .10 .30
261 Jerry DiPoto .10 .30
262 Rick Krivda .10 .30
263 Glenn Dishman .10 .30
264 Mike Mimbs .10 .30
265 John Ericks .10 .30
266 Jose Canseco .20 .50
267 Jeff Branson .10 .30
268 Curt Leskanic .10 .30
269 Jon Nunnally .10 .30
270 Scott Stahoviak .10 .30
271 Jeff Montgomery .10 .30
272 Hal Morris .10 .30
273 Esteban Loaiza .10 .30
274 Rico Brogna .10 .30
275 Dave Winfield .10 .30
276 J.R. Phillips .10 .30
277 Todd Zeile .10 .30
278 Tom Pagnozzi .10 .30
279 Mark Lemke .10 .30
280 Dave Magadan .10 .30
281 Greg McMichael .10 .30
282 Mike Morgan .10 .30
283 Moises Alou .10 .30
284 Dennis Martinez .10 .30
285 Jeff Kent .10 .30
286 Mark Johnson .10 .30
287 Darren Lewis .10 .30
288 Brad Clontz .10 .30
289 Chad Fonville .10 .30
290 Paul Sorrento .10 .30
291 Lee Smith .10 .30
292 Tom Glavine .20 .50
293 Antonio Osuna .10 .30
294 Kevin Foster .10 .30
295 Sandy Martinez .10 .30
296 Mark Leiter .10 .30
297 Julian Tavarez .10 .30
298 Mike Kelly .10 .30
299 Joe Oliver .10 .30
300 John Flaherty .10 .30
301 Don Mattingly .75 2.00
302 Pat Meares .10 .30
303 John Doherty .10 .30
304 Joe Vitiello .10 .30
305 Vinny Castilla .10 .30
306 Jeff Brantley .10 .30
307 Mike Greenwell .10 .30
308 Midre Cummings .10 .30

309 Curt Schilling .10 .30
310 Ken Caminiti .10 .30
311 Scott Erickson .10 .30
312 Carl Everett .10 .30
313 Charles Johnson .10 .30
314 Alex Diaz .10 .30
315 Jose Mesa .10 .30
316 Mark Carreon .10 .30
317 Carlos Perez .10 .30
318 Ismael Valdes .10 .30
319 Frank Castillo .10 .30
320 Tom Henke .10 .30
321 Spike Owen .10 .30
322 Joe Orsulak .10 .30
323 Paul Menhart .10 .30
324 Pedro Borbon .10 .30
325 Paul Molitor CL .10 .30
326 Jeff Cirillo .10 .30
327 Edwin Hurtado .10 .30
328 Orlando Miller .10 .30
329 Steve Ontiveros .10 .30
330 Kirby Puckett CL .20 .50
331 Scott Bullett .10 .30
332 Andres Galarraga .10 .30
333 Cal Eldred .10 .30
334 Sammy Sosa .30 .75
335 Don Slaught .10 .30
336 Jody Reed .10 .30
337 Roger Cedeno .10 .30
338 Ken Griffey Jr. .60 1.50
339 Todd Hollandsworth .10 .30
340 Mike Trombley .10 .30
341 Gregg Jefferies .10 .30
342 Larry Walker .10 .30
343 Pedro Martinez .20 .50
344 Dwayne Hosey .10 .30
345 Terry Pendleton .10 .30
346 Pete Harnisch .10 .30
347 Tony Castillo .10 .30
348 Paul Quantrill .10 .30
349 Fred McGriff .20 .50
350 Ivan Rodriguez .20 .50
351 Butch Huskey .10 .30
352 Ozzie Smith .50 1.25
353 Marty Cordova .10 .30
354 John Wasdin .10 .30
355 Wade Boggs .20 .50
356 Dave Nilsson .10 .30
357 Rafael Palmeiro .20 .50
358 Luis Gonzalez .10 .30
359 Reggie Jefferson .10 .30
360 Carlos Delgado .10 .30
361 Orlando Palmeiro .10 .30
362 Chris Gomez .10 .30
363 John Smoltz .20 .50
364 Marc Newfield .10 .30
365 Matt Williams .10 .30
366 Jesus Tavarez .10 .30
367 Bruce Ruffin .10 .30
368 Sean Berry .10 .30
369 Randy Velarde .10 .30
370 Tony Pena .10 .30
371 Jim Thome .20 .50
372 Jeffrey Hammonds .10 .30
373 Bob Wolcott .10 .30
374 Juan Guzman .10 .30
375 Juan Gonzalez .10 .30
376 Michael Tucker .10 .30
377 Doug Johns .10 .30
378 Mike Cameron RC .25 .60
379 Ray Lankford .10 .30
380 Jose Parra .10 .30
381 Jimmy Key .10 .30
382 John Olerud .10 .30
383 Kevin Ritz .10 .30
384 Tim Raines .10 .30
385 Rich Amaral .10 .30
386 Keith Lockhart .10 .30
387 Steve Scarsone .10 .30
388 Cliff Floyd .10 .30
389 Rich Aude .10 .30
390 Hideo Nomo .30 .75
391 Geronimo Berroa .10 .30
392 Pat Rapp .10 .30
393 Dustin Hermanson .10 .30
394 Greg Maddux .50 1.25
395 Darren Daulton .10 .30
396 Kenny Lofton .10 .30
397 Ruben Rivera .10 .30
398 Billy Wagner .10 .30
399 Kevin Brown .10 .30
400 Mike Kingery .10 .30
401 Bernie Williams .20 .50
402 Otis Nixon .10 .30
403 Damion Easley .10 .30
404 Paul O'Neill .20 .50
405 Deion Sanders .20 .50
406 Dennis Eckersley .10 .30
407 Tony Clark .10 .30
408 Rondell White .10 .30
409 Luis Sojo .10 .30
410 David Hulse .10 .30
411 Shane Reynolds .10 .30
412 Chris Hoiles .10 .30
413 Lee Tinsley .10 .30
414 Scott Karl .10 .30
415 Ron Gant .10 .30
416 Brian Johnson .10 .30
417 Jose Oliva .10 .30
418 Jack McDowell .10 .30
419 Paul Molitor .10 .30
420 Ricky Bottalico .10 .30
421 Paul Wagner .10 .30
422 Terry Bradshaw .10 .30
423 Bob Tewksbury .10 .30
424 Mike Piazza .50 1.25
425 Luis Andujar .10 .30
426 Mark Langston .10 .30
427 Stan Belinda .10 .30
428 Kurt Abbott .10 .30
429 Shawon Dunston .10 .30
430 Bobby Jones .10 .30
431 Jose Vizcaino .10 .30
432 Matt Lawton RC .15 .40
433 Pat Hentgen .10 .30
434 Cecil Fielder .10 .30
435 Carlos Baerga .10 .30
436 Rich Becker .10 .30
437 Chipper Jones .30 .75
438 Bill Risley .10 .30
439 Kevin Appier .10 .30
440 Wade Boggs CL .10 .30
441 Jaime Navarro .10 .30
442 Barry Larkin .20 .50
443 Jose Valentin .10 .30
444 Bryan Rekar .10 .30
445 Rick Wilkins .10 .30
446 Quilvio Veras .10 .30
447 Greg Gagne .10 .30
448 Mark Kiefer .10 .30
449 Bobby Witt .10 .30
450 Andy Ashby .10 .30
451 Alex Ochoa .10 .30
452 Jorge Fabregas .10 .30
453 Gene Schall .10 .30
454 Ken Hill .10 .30
455 Tony Tarasco .10 .30
456 Donnie Wall .10 .30
457 Carlos Garcia .10 .30
458 Ryan Thompson .10 .30
459 Marvin Benard RC .15 .40
460 Jose Herrera .10 .30
461 Jeff Blauser .10 .30
462 Chris Hook .10 .30
463 Jeff Conine .10 .30
464 Devon White .10 .30
465 Danny Bautista .10 .30
466 Steve Trachsel .10 .30
467 C.J. Nitkowski .10 .30
468 Mike Devereaux .10 .30
469 David Wells .10 .30
470 Jim Eisenreich .10 .30
471 Edgar Martinez .20 .50
472 Craig Biggio .20 .50
473 Jeff Frye .10 .30
474 Karim Garcia .10 .30
475 Jimmy Haynes .10 .30
476 Darren Holmes .10 .30
477 Tim Salmon .20 .50
478 Randy Johnson .30 .75
479 Eric Plunk .10 .30
480 Scott Cooper .10 .30
481 Chan Ho Park .10 .30
482 Ray McDavid .10 .30
483 Mark Petkovsek .10 .30
484 Greg Swindell .10 .30
485 George Williams .10 .30
486 Yamil Benitez .10 .30
487 Tim Wakefield .10 .30
488 Kevin Tapani .10 .30
489 Derrick May .10 .30
490 Ken Griffey Jr. CL .40 1.00
491 Derek Jeter .75 2.00
492 Jeff Fassero .10 .30
493 Benito Santiago .10 .30
494 Tom Gordon .10 .30
495 Jamie Brewington RC .10 .30
496 Vince Coleman .10 .30
497 Kevin Jordan .10 .30
498 Jeff King .10 .30
499 Mike Simms .10 .30
500 Jose Rijo .10 .30
501 Denny Neagle .10 .30
502 Jose Lima .10 .30
503 Kevin Seitzer .10 .30
504 Alex Fernandez .10 .30
505 Mo Vaughn .10 .30
506 Phil Nevin .10 .30
507 J.T. Snow .10 .30
508 Andujar Cedeno .10 .30
509 Ozzie Guillen .10 .30
510 Mark Clark .10 .30
511 Mark McGwire .75 2.00
512 Jeff Reboulet .10 .30
513 Armando Benitez .10 .30
514 LaTroy Hawkins .10 .30
515 Brett Butler .10 .30
516 Tavo Alvarez .10 .30
517 Chris Snopek .10 .30
518 Mike Mussina .20 .50
519 Darryl Kile .10 .30
520 Wally Joyner .10 .30
521 Willie McGee .10 .30
522 Kent Mercker .10 .30
523 Mike Jackson .10 .30
524 Troy Percival .10 .30
525 Tony Gwynn .40 1.00
526 Ron Coomer .10 .30
527 Darryl Hamilton .10 .30
528 Phil Plantier .10 .30
529 Norm Charlton .10 .30
530 Craig Paquette .10 .30
531 Dave Burba .10 .30
532 Mike Henneman .10 .30
533 Terrell Wade .10 .30
534 Eddie Williams .10 .30
535 Robin Ventura .10 .30
536 Chuck Knoblauch .10 .30
537 Les Norman .10 .30
538 Brady Anderson .10 .30
539 Roger Clemens .60 1.50
540 Mark Portugal .10 .30
541 Mike Matheny .10 .30
542 Jeff Parrett .10 .30
543 Roberto Kelly .10 .30
544 Damon Buford .10 .30
545 Chad Ogea .10 .30
546 Jose Offerman .10 .30
547 Brian Barber .10 .30
548 Danny Tartabull .10 .30
549 Duane Singleton .10 .30
550 Tony Gwynn CL .20 .50

1996 Donruss Press Proofs

*STARS: 6X TO 15X BASIC CARDS
*ROOKIES: 4X TO 10X BASIC CARDS
SER.1 STATED ODDS 1:12
SER.2 STATED ODDS 1:10
STATED PRINT RUN 2000 SETS
50 Kirby Puckett 12.50 30.00

1996 Donruss Diamond Kings

These 31 standard-size cards were randomly inserted into packs and issued in two series of 14 and 17 cards. They were inserted in first series packs at a ratio of approximately one every 60 packs. Second series cards were inserted one every 30 packs. The cards are sequentially numbered in the back lower right as "X" of 10,000. The fronts feature player portraits by noted sports artist Dick Perez. These cards are gold-foil stamped and the portraits are surrounded by gold-foil borders. The backs feature text about the player as well as a player photo. The cards are numbered on the back with a "DK" prefix.

COMPLETE SET (31) 20.00 50.00
COMPLETE SERIES 1 (14) 10.00 25.00
COMPLETE SERIES 2 (17) 10.00 25.00
SER.1 STATED ODDS 1:60
SER.2 STATED ODDS 1:30
STATED PRINT RUN 10,000 SERIAL #'d SETS
1 Frank Thomas 1.25 3.00
2 Mo Vaughn .50 1.25
3 Manny Ramirez .75 2.00
4 Mark McGwire 2.50 6.00
5 Juan Gonzalez .50 1.25
6 Roberto Alomar .75 2.00
7 Tim Salmon .50 1.25
8 Barry Bonds 2.00 5.00
9 Tony Gwynn 1.25 3.00
10 Reggie Sanders .50 1.25
11 Larry Walker .75 2.00
12 Pedro Martinez .75 2.00
13 Jeff King .50 1.25
14 Mark Grace .75 2.00
15 Greg Maddux 2.00 5.00
16 Don Mattingly 2.50 6.00
17 Gregg Jefferies .50 1.25
18 Chad Curtis .50 1.25
19 Jason Isringhausen .50 1.25
20 B.J. Surhoff .50 1.25
21 Jeff Conine .50 1.25
22 Kirby Puckett 1.25 3.00
23 Derek Bell .50 1.25
24 Wally Joyner .50 1.25
25 Brian Jordan .50 1.25
26 Edgar Martinez .75 2.00
27 Hideo Nomo 1.25 3.00
28 Mike Mussina .75 2.00
29 Eddie Murray 1.25 3.00
30 Cal Ripken 5.00 12.00
31 Checklist .50 1.25

1996 Donruss Elite

Randomly inserted approximately one in Donruss packs, this 12-card standard-size set is continuously numbered (61-72) from the previous year. First series cards were inserted one every 40 packs. Second series cards were inserted one every 75 packs. The fronts contain an action photo surrounded by a silver border. Limited to 10,000 and sequentially numbered, the backs contain a small photo and write up.

COMPLETE SET (12) 40.00 100.00
COMPLETE SERIES 1 (6) 20.00 50.00
COMPLETE SERIES 2 (6) 25.00 60.00
SER.1 STATED ODDS 1:140
SER.2 STATED ODDS 1:75
STATED PRINT RUN 10,000 SERIAL #'d SETS
61 Cal Ripken 12.50 30.00
62 Hideo Nomo 4.00 10.00
63 Reggie Sanders 1.50 4.00
64 Mo Vaughn 1.50 4.00
65 Tim Salmon 2.50 6.00
66 Chipper Jones 4.00 10.00
67 Manny Ramirez 2.50 6.00
68 Greg Maddux 6.00 15.00
69 Frank Thomas 4.00 10.00
70 Ken Griffey Jr. 15.00 40.00
71 Dante Bichette 1.50 4.00
72 Tony Gwynn 5.00 12.00

1996 Donruss Freeze Frame

Randomly inserted in second series packs at a rate of one in 60, this eight-card standard-size set features the top hitters and pitchers in baseball. Just 5,000 of each card were produced and sequentially numbered.

COMPLETE SET (8) 40.00 100.00
SER.2 STATED ODDS 1:60
STATED PRINT RUN 5000 SERIAL #'d SETS
1 Frank Thomas 4.00 10.00
2 Ken Griffey Jr. 8.00 20.00
3 Cal Ripken 12.50 30.00
4 Hideo Nomo 4.00 10.00
5 Greg Maddux 6.00 15.00
6 Albert Belle 1.50 4.00
7 Chipper Jones 4.00 10.00
8 Mike Piazza 6.00 15.00

1996 Donruss Hit List

This 16-card standard-size set was randomly inserted in 97 Donruss and salutes the most consistent hitters in the game. The first series cards were inserted one every 105 packs while the second series cards were inserted one every 60 packs. The cards are sequentially numbered out of 10,000.

COMPLETE SET (16) 20.00 50.00
COMPLETE SERIES 1 (8) 10.00 25.00
COMPLETE SERIES 2 (8) 10.00 25.00
SER.1 STATED ODDS 1:105
SER.2 STATED ODDS 1:60
STATED PRINT RUN 10,000 SERIAL #'d SETS
1 Tony Gwynn 1.50 4.00
2 Ken Griffey Jr. 3.00 8.00
3 Will Clark 1.00 2.50
4 Mike Piazza 1.50 4.00
5 Carlos Baerga .60 1.50
6 Mo Vaughn .60 1.50
7 Mark Grace 1.00 2.50
8 Kirby Puckett 1.50 4.00
9 Frank Thomas 1.50 4.00
10 Barry Bonds 2.50 6.00
11 Jeff Bagwell 1.00 2.50
12 Edgar Martinez 1.00 2.50
13 Tim Salmon .60 1.50
14 Wade Boggs 1.00 2.50
15 Don Mattingly 3.00 8.00
16 Eddie Murray 1.00 2.50

1996 Donruss Long Ball Leaders

This eight-card standard-size set was randomly inserted into series one retail packs. They were inserted at a rate of approximately one in every 96 packs. The cards are sequentially numbered out of 5,000. This set highlights eight top sluggers and their farthest home run distance of 1995. The fronts feature a player photo set against a silver-foil background.

COMPLETE SET (8) 15.00 40.00
SER.1 STATED ODDS 1:96 RETAIL
STATED PRINT RUN 5000 SERIAL #'d SETS
1 Barry Bonds 3.00 8.00
2 Ryan Klesko .75 2.00
3 Mark McGwire 3.00 8.00
4 Raul Mondesi .75 2.00
5 Cecil Fielder .75 2.00
6 Ken Griffey Jr. 4.00 10.00
7 Larry Walker 1.25 3.00
8 Frank Thomas 2.00 5.00

1996 Donruss Power Alley

This ten-card standard-size set was randomly inserted into series one hobby packs. They were inserted at a rate of approximately one in every 92 packs. These cards are all sequentially numbered out of 5,000.

COMPLETE SET (10) 15.00 40.00
SER.1 STATED ODDS 1:92 HOBBY
STATED PRINT RUN 4500 SERIAL #'d SETS
*DC'S: 3X TO 8X BASIC POWER ALLEY
DC SER.1 ODDS 1:920 HOBBY
DC PRINT RUN 500 SERIAL #'d SETS
1 Frank Thomas 2.00 5.00
2 Barry Bonds 3.00 8.00
3 Reggie Sanders .75 2.00
4 Albert Belle .75 2.00
5 Tim Salmon .75 2.00
6 Dante Bichette .75 2.00
7 Mo Vaughn .75 2.00
8 Jim Edmonds .75 2.00
9 Manny Ramirez 1.25 3.00
10 Ken Griffey Jr. 4.00 10.00

1996 Donruss Pure Power

Randomly inserted in retail and magazine packs only at a rate of one in eight, this eight-card set features color action player photos of eight of the most powerful players in Major League baseball.

COMPLETE SET (8) 30.00 80.00
RANDOM INSERTS IN SER.2 RETAIL PACKS
STATED PRINT RUN 5000 SETS
1 Raul Mondesi 2.00 5.00
2 Barry Bonds 12.50 30.00
3 Albert Belle 2.00 5.00
4 Frank Thomas 5.00 12.00
5 Mike Piazza 8.00 20.00
6 Dante Bichette 2.00 5.00
7 Manny Ramirez 3.00 8.00
8 Mo Vaughn 2.00 5.00

1996 Donruss Round Trippers

Randomly inserted in second series hobby packs at a rate of one in 55, this 10-card standard-size set honors ten of Baseball's top homerun hitters. Just 5,000 of each card were produced and consecutively numbered.

COMPLETE SET (10) 12.50 30.00
SER.2 STATED ODDS 1:55 HOBBY
STATED PRINT RUN 5000 SERIAL #'d SETS
1 Albert Belle 1.50 4.00
2 Barry Bonds 10.00 25.00
3 Jeff Bagwell 2.50 6.00
4 Tim Salmon 2.50 6.00
5 Mo Vaughn 1.50 4.00
6 Ken Griffey Jr. 8.00 20.00
7 Mike Piazza 6.00 15.00
8 Cal Ripken 12.50 30.00
9 Frank Thomas 4.00 10.00
10 Dante Bichette 1.50 4.00

1996 Donruss Showdown

This eight-card standard-size set was randomly inserted in series one packs at a rate of one every 105 packs. These cards feature one top hitter and one top pitcher from each league. The cards are sequentially numbered out of 10,000.

COMPLETE SET (8) 20.00 50.00
SER.1 STATED ODDS 1:105
STATED PRINT RUN 10,000 SERIAL #'d SETS
1 F.Thomas 3.00 8.00
H.Nomo
2 B.Bonds 4.00 10.00
R.Johnson
3 K.Griffey Jr. 6.00 15.00
G.Maddux
4 T.Gwynn 4.00 10.00
R.Clemens
5 M.Piazza 4.00 10.00
M.Mussina
6 C.Ripken 10.00 25.00
P.Martinez
7 T.Wakefield 1.25 3.00
M.Williams
8 M.Ramirez 2.00 5.00
C.Perez

1997 Donruss

The 1997 Donruss set was issued in two separate series of 270 and 180 cards respectively. Both first series and Update cards were distributed in 10-card packs carrying a suggested retail price of $1.99 each. Card fronts feature color action player photos while the backs carry another color player photo with player information and career statistics. The following subsets are included within the set: Checklists (267-270/448-450), Rookies (353-397), Hit List (398-422), King of the Hill (423-437) and Interleague Showdown (438-447). Rookie Cards in this set include Jose Cruz Jr., Brian Giles and Hideki Irabu.

COMPLETE SET (450) 20.00 50.00
COMPLETE SERIES 1 (270) 10.00 25.00
COMPLETE UPDATE (180) 10.00 25.00
SUBSET CARDS HALF VALUE OF BASE CARDS
1 Juan Gonzalez .10 .30
2 Jim Edmonds .10 .30
3 Tony Gwynn .40 1.00
4 Andres Galarraga .10 .30
5 Joe Carter .10 .30
6 Raul Mondesi .10 .30
7 Greg Maddux .50 1.25
8 Travis Fryman .10 .30
9 Brian Jordan .10 .30
10 Henry Rodriguez .10 .30
11 Manny Ramirez .20 .50
12 Mark McGwire .75 2.00
13 Marc Newfield .10 .30
14 Craig Biggio .20 .50
15 Sammy Sosa .30 .75
16 Brady Anderson .10 .30
17 Wade Boggs .20 .50
18 Charles Johnson .10 .30
19 Matt Williams .10 .30
20 Denny Neagle .10 .30
21 Ken Griffey Jr. .60 1.50
22 Robin Ventura .10 .30
23 Barry Larkin .20 .50
24 Todd Zeile .10 .30
25 Chuck Knoblauch .10 .30
26 Todd Hundley .10 .30
27 Roger Clemens .60 1.50
28 Michael Tucker .10 .30
29 Rondell White .10 .30
30 Osvaldo Fernandez .10 .30
31 Ivan Rodriguez .20 .50
32 Alex Fernandez .10 .30
33 Jason Isringhausen .10 .30
34 Chipper Jones .30 .75
35 Paul O'Neill .20 .50
36 Hideo Nomo .30 .75
37 Roberto Alomar .20 .50
38 Derek Bell .10 .30
39 Paul Molitor .10 .30
40 Andy Benes .10 .30
41 Steve Trachsel .10 .30
42 J.T. Snow .10 .30
43 Jason Kendall .10 .30
44 Alex Rodriguez .50 1.25
45 Joey Hamilton .10 .30
46 Carlos Delgado .10 .30
47 Jason Giambi .10 .30
48 Larry Walker .10 .30
49 Derek Jeter .75 2.00
50 Kenny Lofton .10 .30
51 Devon White .10 .30
52 Matt Mieske .10 .30
53 Melvin Nieves .10 .30
54 Jose Canseco .20 .50
55 Tino Martinez .20 .50
56 Rafael Palmeiro .20 .50
57 Edgardo Alfonzo .10 .30
58 Jay Buhner .10 .30
59 Shane Reynolds .10 .30
60 Steve Finley .10 .30
61 Bobby Higginson .10 .30
62 Dean Palmer .10 .30
63 Terry Pendleton .10 .30
64 Marquis Grissom .10 .30
65 Mike Stanley .10 .30
66 Moises Alou .10 .30
67 Ray Lankford .10 .30
68 Marty Cordova .10 .30
69 John Olerud .10 .30
70 David Cone .10 .30
71 Benito Santiago .10 .30
72 Ryne Sandberg .50 1.25
73 Rickey Henderson .30 .75
74 Roger Cedeno .10 .30
75 Wilson Alvarez .10 .30
76 Tim Salmon .20 .50
77 Orlando Merced .10 .30
78 Vinny Castilla .10 .30
79 Ismael Valdes .10 .30
80 Dante Bichette .10 .30
81 Kevin Brown .10 .30
82 Andy Pettitte .20 .50
83 Scott Stahoviak .10 .30
84 Mickey Tettleton .10 .30
85 Jack McDowell .10 .30
86 Tom Glavine .20 .50
87 Gregg Jefferies .10 .30
88 Chili Davis .10 .30
89 Randy Johnson .30 .75
90 John Mabry .10 .30
91 Billy Wagner .10 .30
92 Jeff Cirillo .10 .30
93 Trevor Hoffman .10 .30
94 Juan Guzman .10 .30
95 Geronimo Berroa .10 .30
96 Bernard Gilkey .10 .30
97 Danny Tartabull .10 .30
98 Johnny Damon .20 .50
99 Charlie Hayes .10 .30
100 Reggie Sanders .10 .30
101 Robby Thompson .10 .30
102 Bobby Bonilla .10 .30
103 Reggie Jefferson .10 .30
104 John Smoltz .20 .50
105 Jim Thome .20 .50
106 Ruben Rivera .10 .30
107 Darren Oliver .10 .30
108 Mo Vaughn .10 .30
109 Roger Pavlik .10 .30
110 Terry Steinbach .10 .30
111 Jermaine Dye .10 .30
112 Mark Grudzielanek .10 .30
113 Rick Aguilera .10 .30
114 Jamey Wright .10 .30
115 Eddie Murray .30 .75
116 Brian L. Hunter .10 .30
117 Hal Morris .10 .30
118 Tom Pagnozzi .10 .30
119 Mike Mussina .20 .50
120 Mark Grace .20 .50
121 Cal Ripken 1.00 2.50
122 Tom Goodwin .10 .30
123 Paul Sorrento .10 .30
124 Jay Bell .10 .30
125 Todd Hollandsworth .10 .30
126 Edgar Martinez .20 .50
127 George Arias .10 .30
128 Greg Vaughn .10 .30
129 Roberto Hernandez .10 .30
130 Delino DeShields .10 .30
131 Bill Pulsipher .10 .30
132 Joey Cora .10 .30
133 Mariano Rivera .30 .75
134 Mike Piazza .50 1.25
135 Carlos Baerga .10 .30
136 Jose Mesa .10
137 Will Clark .20
138 Frank Thomas .30
139 John Wetteland .10
140 Shawn Estes .10
141 Garret Anderson .10
142 Andre Dawson .10
143 Eddie Taubensee .10
144 Ryan Klesko .10
145 Rocky Coppinger .10
146 Jeff Bagwell .20
147 Donovan Osborne .10
148 Greg Myers .10
149 Brant Brown .10
150 Kevin Elster .10
151 Bob Wells .10
152 Wally Joyner .10
153 Rico Brogna .10
154 Dwight Gooden .10
155 Jermaine Allensworth .10
156 Ray Durham .10
157 Cecil Fielder .10
158 John Burkett .10
159 Gary Sheffield .10
160 Albert Belle .10
161 Tomas Perez .10
162 David Doster .10
163 John Valentin .10
164 Danny Graves .10
165 Jose Paniagua .10
166 Brian Giles RC .60
167 Barry Bonds .75
168 Sterling Hitchcock .10
169 Bernie Williams .20
170 Fred McGriff .20
171 George Williams .10
172 Amaury Telemaco .10
173 Ken Caminiti .10
174 Ron Gant .10
175 Dave Justice .10
176 James Baldwin .10
177 Pat Hentgen .10
178 Ben McDonald .10
179 Tim Naehring .10
180 Jim Eisenreich .10
181 Ken Hill .10
182 Paul Wilson .10
183 Marvin Benard .10
184 Alan Benes .10
185 Ellis Burks .10
186 Scott Servais .10
187 David Segui .10
188 Scott Brosius .10
189 Jose Offerman .10
190 Eric Davis .10
191 Brett Butler .10
192 Curtis Pride .10
193 Yamil Benitez .10
194 Chan Ho Park .10
195 Bret Boone .10
196 Omar Vizquel .20
197 Orlando Miller .10
198 Ramon Martinez .10
199 Harold Baines .10
200 Eric Young .10
201 Fernando Vina .10
202 Alex Gonzalez .10
203 Fernando Valenzuela .10
204 Steve Avery .10
205 Ernie Young .10
206 Kevin Appier .10
207 Randy Myers .10
208 Jeff Suppan .10
209 James Mouton .10
210 Russ Davis .10
211 Al Martin .10
212 Troy Percival .10
213 Al Leiter .10
214 Dennis Eckersley .10
215 Mark Johnson .10
216 Eric Karros .10
217 Royce Clayton .10
218 Tony Phillips .10
219 Tim Wakefield .10
220 Alan Trammell .10
221 Eduardo Perez .10
222 Butch Huskey .10
223 Tim Belcher .10
224 Jamie Moyer .10
225 F.P. Santangelo .10
226 Rusty Greer .10
227 Jeff Brantley .10
228 Mark Langston .10
229 Ray Montgomery .10
230 Rich Becker .10
231 Ozzie Smith .50
232 Rey Ordonez .10
233 Ricky Otero .10
234 Mike Cameron .10
235 Mike Sweeney .10
236 Mark Lewis .10
237 Luis Gonzalez .10
238 Marcus Jensen .10
239 Ed Sprague .10
240 Jose Valentin .10
241 Jeff Frye .10
242 Charles Nagy .10
243 Carlos Garcia .10
244 Mike Hampton .10
245 B.J. Surhoff .10
246 Wilton Guerrero .10
247 Frank Rodriguez .10
248 Gary Gaetti .10

ance Johnson .10 .30
arren Bragg .10 .30
arryl Hamilton .10 .30
ohn Jaha .10 .30
raig Paquette .10 .30
aime Navarro .10 .30
hawon Dunston .10 .30
ark Loretta .10 .30
m Belk .10 .30
eff Darwin .10 .30
uben Sierra .10 .30
huck Finley .10 .30
arryl Strawberry .10 .30
hannon Stewart .10 .30
edro Martinez .20 .50
eifi Perez .10 .30
eff Conine .10 .30
rel Hershiser .10 .30
ddie Murray CL .20 .50
aul Molitor CL .10 .30
arry Bonds CL .40 1.00
ark McGwire CL .40 1.00
att Williams .10 .30
odd Zeile .10 .30
oger Clemens .60 1.50
ichael Tucker .10 .30
.T. Snow .10 .30
enny Lofton .10 .30
ose Canseco .20 .50
arquis Grissom .10 .30
oises Alou .10 .30
enito Santiago .10 .30
illie McGee .10 .30
hili Davis .10 .30
on Coomer .10 .30
rlando Merced .10 .30
elino DeShields .10 .30
ohn Wetteland .10 .30
arren Daulton .10 .30
ee Stevens .10 .30
lbert Belle .10 .30
terling Hitchcock .10 .30
avid Justice .10 .30
ric Davis .10 .30
rian Hunter .10 .30
arryl Hamilton .10 .30
teve Avery .10 .30
oe Vitiello .10 .30
aime Navarro .10 .30
ddie Murray .30 .75
andy Myers .10 .30
rancisco Cordova .10 .30
avier Lopez .10 .30
eronimo Berroa .10 .30
effrey Hammonds .10 .30
eion Sanders .20 .50
eff Fassero .10 .30
urt Schilling .10 .30
obb Nen .10 .30
ark McLemore .10 .30
immy Key .10 .30
uilvio Veras .10 .30
ip Roberts .10 .30
steban Loaiza .10 .30
ndy Ashby .10 .30
andy Alomar Jr. .10 .30
hawn Green .10 .30
uis Castillo .10 .30
Benji Gil .10 .30
Otis Nixon .10 .30
Aaron Sele .10 .30
Brad Ausmus .10 .30
Troy O'Leary .10 .30
Terrell Wade .10 .30
Jeff King .10 .30
Kevin Seitzer .10 .30
Mark Wohlers .10 .30
Edgar Renteria .10 .30
Dan Wilson .10 .30
Brian McRae .10 .30
Rod Beck .10 .30
Julio Franco .10 .30
Dave Nilsson .10 .30
Glenallen Hill .10 .30
Kevin Elster .10 .30
Joe Girardi .10 .30
David Wells .10 .30
Jeff Blauser .10 .30
Darryl Kile .10 .30
Jeff Kent .10 .30
Jim Leyritz .10 .30
Todd Stottlemyre .10 .30
Tony Clark .10 .30
2 Chris Hoiles .10 .30
3 Mike Lieberthal .10 .30
4 Matt Lawton .10 .30
5 Alex Ochoa .10 .30
6 Chris Snopek .10 .30
7 Rudy Pemberton .10 .30
8 Eric Owens .10 .30
9 Joe Randa .10 .30
0 John Olerud .10 .30
1 Steve Karsay .10 .30
2 Mark Whiten .10 .30
3 Bob Abreu .20 .50
4 Bartolo Colon .10 .30
5 Vladimir Guerrero .30 .75
6 Darin Erstad .10 .30
7 Scott Rolen .20 .50
8 Andruw Jones .20 .50
9 Scott Spiezio .10 .30
0 Karim Garcia .10 .30
1 Hideki Irabu RC .15 .40
362 Nomar Garciaparra .50 1.25
363 Dmitri Young .10 .30
364 Bubba Trammell RC .15 .40
365 Kevin Orie .10 .30
366 Jose Rosado .10 .30
367 Jose Guillen .10 .30
368 Brooks Kieschnick .10 .30
369 Pokey Reese .10 .30
370 Glendon Rusch .10 .30
371 Jason Dickson .10 .30
372 Todd Walker .10 .30
373 Justin Thompson .10 .30
374 Todd Greene .10 .30
375 Jeff Suppan .10 .30
376 Trey Beamon .10 .30
377 Damon Mashore .10 .30
378 Wendell Magee .10 .30
379 Shigetoshi Hasegawa RC .20 .50
380 Bill Mueller RC .50 1.25
381 Chris Widger .10 .30
382 Tony Graffanino .10 .30
383 Derrek Lee .20 .50
384 Brian Moehler RC .15 .40
385 Quinton McCracken .10 .30
386 Matt Morris .10 .30
387 Marvin Benard .10 .30
388 Deivi Cruz RC .15 .40
389 Javier Valentin .10 .30
390 Todd Dunwoody .10 .30
391 Derrick Gibson .10 .30
392 Raul Casanova .10 .30
393 George Arias .10 .30
394 Tony Womack RC .15 .40
395 Antone Williamson .10 .30
396 Jose Cruz Jr. RC .15 .40
397 Desi Relaford .10 .30
398 Frank Thomas HIT .20 .50
399 Ken Griffey Jr. HIT .40 1.00
400 Cal Ripken HIT .50 1.25
401 Chipper Jones HIT .20 .50
402 Mike Piazza HIT .30 .75
403 Gary Sheffield HIT .10 .30
404 Alex Rodriguez HIT .30 .75
405 Wade Boggs HIT .10 .30
406 Juan Gonzalez HIT .10 .30
407 Tony Gwynn HIT .20 .50
408 Edgar Martinez HIT .10 .30
409 Jeff Bagwell HIT .10 .30
410 Larry Walker HIT .10 .30
411 Kenny Lofton HIT .10 .30
412 Manny Ramirez HIT .10 .30
413 Mark McGwire HIT .40 1.00
414 Roberto Alomar HIT .10 .30
415 Derek Jeter HIT .40 1.00
416 Brady Anderson HIT .10 .30
417 Paul Molitor HIT .10 .30
418 Dante Bichette HIT .10 .30
419 Jim Edmonds HIT .10 .30
420 Mo Vaughn HIT .10 .30
421 Barry Bonds HIT .40 1.00
422 Rusty Greer HIT .10 .30
423 Greg Maddux KING .30 .75
424 Andy Pettitte KING .10 .30
425 John Smoltz KING .10 .30
426 Randy Johnson KING .20 .50
427 Hideo Nomo KING .10 .30
428 Roger Clemens KING .30 .75
429 Tom Glavine KING .10 .30
430 Pat Hentgen KING .10 .30
431 Kevin Brown KING .10 .30
432 Mike Mussina KING .10 .30
433 Alex Fernandez KING .10 .30
434 Kevin Appier KING .10 .30
435 David Cone KING .10 .30
436 Jeff Fassero KING .10 .30
437 John Wetteland KING .10 .30
438 B.Bonds .40 1.00
I.Rodriguez IS
439 K.Griffey Jr. .40 1.00
A.Galarraga IS
440 F.McGriff .10 .30
R.Palmeiro IS
441 B.Larkin .20 .50
J.Thome IS
442 S.Sosa .20 .50
A.Belle IS
443 B.Williams .10 .30
T.Hundley IS
444 C.Knoblauch .10 .30
B.Jordan IS
445 M.Vaughn .10 .30
J.Conine IS
446 K.Caminiti .10 .30
J.Giambi IS
447 R.Mondesi .10 .30
T.Salmon IS
448 Cal Ripken CL .50 1.25
449 Greg Maddux CL .30 .75
450 Ken Griffey Jr. CL .40 1.00

1997 Donruss Gold Press Proofs

*STARS: 10X TO 25X BASIC CARDS
*ROOKIES: 3X TO 8X BASIC CARDS
SER.1 STATED ODDS 1:32
SER.2 STATED ODDS 1:64
STATED PRINT RUN 500 SETS

1997 Donruss Silver Press Proofs

*STARS: 4X TO 10X BASIC CARDS
*ROOKIES: 1.25X TO 3X BASIC CARDS
SER.1 STATED ODDS 1:8
SER.2 STATED ODDS 1:16
STATED PRINT RUN 2000 SETS

1997 Donruss Armed and Dangerous

Randomly inserted in hobby packs at a rate of one in 58 packs, this 15-card set features the League's hottest arms in the game. The fronts carry color action player photos with foil printing. The backs display player information and a color player head portrait at the end of a ribbon representing a medal. Only 5,000 of this set were produced and are sequentially numbered.

COMPLETE SET (15) 15.00 40.00
SER.1 STATED ODDS 1:58 HOBBY
STATED PRINT RUN 5000 SERIAL #'d SETS
1 Ken Griffey Jr. 3.00 8.00
2 Raul Mondesi .60 1.50
3 Chipper Jones 1.50 4.00
4 Ivan Rodriguez 1.00 2.50
5 Randy Johnson 1.50 4.00
6 Alex Rodriguez 2.00 5.00
7 Larry Walker 1.00 2.50
8 Cal Ripken 5.00 12.00
9 Kenny Lofton .60 1.50
10 Barry Bonds 2.50 6.00
11 Derek Jeter 4.00 10.00
12 Charles Johnson .60 1.50
13 Greg Maddux 2.50 6.00
14 Roberto Alomar 1.00 2.50
15 Barry Larkin 1.00 2.50

1997 Donruss Diamond Kings

Randomly inserted in all first series packs at a rate of one in 45, this 10-card set commemorates the 15th anniversary of the annual art cards in Donruss baseball sets. Only 10,000 sets were produced each of which is sequentially numbered. Ten cards were printed with the number 1,982 representing the year the insert began and could be redeemed for an original piece of artwork by Diamond Kings artist Dan Gardiner. This was the first year Gardiner painted the Diamond King series.

COMPLETE SET (10) 12.50 30.00
SER.1 STATED ODDS 1:45
STATED PRINT RUN 9500 SERIAL #'d SETS
*CANVAS: 2X TO 5X BASIC DK'S
CANVAS: RANDOM INS.IN SER.1 PACKS
CANVAS PRINT RUN 500 SERIAL #'d SETS
EACH CARD #1982 WINS ORIGINAL ART
1 Ken Griffey Jr. 4.00 10.00
2 Cal Ripken 6.00 15.00
3 Mo Vaughn .75 2.00
4 Chuck Knoblauch .75 2.00
5 Jeff Bagwell 1.25 3.00
6 Henry Rodriguez .75 2.00
7 Mike Piazza 2.00 5.00
8 Ivan Rodriguez 1.25 3.00
9 Frank Thomas 2.00 5.00
10 Chipper Jones 2.00 5.00

1997 Donruss Dominators

Randomly inserted in Update packs, cards from this 20-card set feature top stars with either incredible speed, awesome power, or unbelievable pitching ability. Card fronts feature red borders and silver foil stamping.

COMPLETE SET (20) 30.00 80.00
RANDOM INSERTS IN UPDATE PACKS
1 Frank Thomas 1.50 4.00
2 Ken Griffey Jr. 3.00 8.00
3 Greg Maddux 2.50 6.00
4 Cal Ripken 5.00 12.00
5 Alex Rodriguez 2.50 6.00
6 Albert Belle .60 1.50
7 Mark McGwire 4.00 10.00
8 Juan Gonzalez .60 1.50
9 Chipper Jones 1.50 4.00
10 Hideo Nomo 1.50 4.00
11 Roger Clemens 3.00 8.00
12 John Smoltz 1.00 2.50
13 Mike Piazza 2.50 6.00
14 Sammy Sosa 1.50 4.00
15 Matt Williams .60 1.50
16 Kenny Lofton .60 1.50
17 Barry Larkin 1.00 2.50
18 Rafael Palmeiro 1.00 2.50
19 Ken Caminiti .60 1.50
20 Gary Sheffield .60 1.50

1997 Donruss Elite Insert Promos

COMPLETE SET (12) 40.00 100.00
1 Frank Thomas 3.00 8.00
2 Paul Molitor 2.50 6.00
3 Sammy Sosa 4.00 10.00
4 Barry Bonds 4.00 10.00
5 Chipper Jones 4.00 10.00
6 Alex Rodriguez 6.00 15.00
7 Ken Griffey Jr. 5.00 12.00
8 Jeff Bagwell 2.50 6.00
9 Cal Ripken 8.00 20.00
10 Mo Vaughn .75 2.00
11 Mike Piazza 6.00 15.00
12 Juan Gonzalez 2.00 5.00

1997 Donruss Elite Inserts

Randomly inserted in all first series packs, this 12-card set honors perennial all-star players of the League. The fronts feature Micro-etched color action player photos, while the backs carry player information. Only 2,500 of this set were produced and are sequentially numbered.

COMPLETE SET (12) 125.00 250.00
SER.1 STATED ODDS 1:144
STATED PRINT RUN 2500 SERIAL #'d SETS
1 Frank Thomas 4.00 10.00
2 Paul Molitor 4.00 10.00
3 Sammy Sosa 2.50 6.00
4 Barry Bonds 6.00 15.00
5 Chipper Jones 4.00 10.00
6 Alex Rodriguez 5.00 12.00
7 Ken Griffey Jr. 8.00 20.00
8 Jeff Bagwell 2.50 6.00
9 Cal Ripken 12.00 30.00
10 Mo Vaughn 1.50 4.00
11 Mike Piazza 4.00 10.00
12 Juan Gonzalez 1.50 4.00

1997 Donruss Franchise Features

Randomly inserted in Update hobby packs only at an approximate rate of 1:48, cards from this 15-card set feature color player photos on a unique "movie-poster" style, double-front card design. Each card highlights a superstar veteran on one side displaying a "Now Playing" banner, while the other side features a rookie prospect with a "Coming Attraction" banner. Each card is printed on an all foil card stock and serial numbered to 3,000.

COMPLETE SET (15) 20.00 50.00
RANDOM INSERTS IN UPDATE PACKS
STATED PRINT RUN 3000 SERIAL #'d SETS
1 K.Griffey Jr. 3.00 8.00
A.Jones
2 F.Thomas 1.50 4.00
D.Erstad
3 A.Rodriguez 2.00 5.00
N.Garciaparra
4 C.Knoblauch .60 1.50
W.Guerrero
5 J.Gonzalez .60 1.50
B.Trammell
6 C.Jones 1.50 4.00
T.Walker
7 B.Bonds 2.50 6.00
V.Guerrero
8 M.McGwire 2.50 6.00
D.Young
9 M.Piazza 1.50 4.00
M.Sweeney
10 M.Vaughn .60 1.50
T.Clark
11 G.Sheffield .60 1.50
J.Guillen
12 K.Lofton .60 1.50
S.Stewart
13 C.Ripken 5.00 12.00
S.Rolen
14 D.Jeter 4.00 10.00
P.Reese
15 T.Gwynn 1.50 4.00
B.Abreu

1997 Donruss Longball Leaders

Randomly inserted in first series retail packs only, this 15-card set honors the league's most fearsome long-ball hitters. The fronts feature color action player photos and foil stamping. The backs carry player information. 5,000 serial-numbered sets were issued.

COMPLETE SET (15) 30.00 80.00
RANDOM INSERTS IN SER.1 RETAIL PACKS
STATED PRINT RUN 5000 SERIAL #'d SETS
1 Frank Thomas 2.50 6.00
2 Albert Belle 1.00 2.50
3 Mo Vaughn 1.00 2.50
4 Brady Anderson 1.00 2.50
5 Greg Vaughn 1.00 2.50
6 Ken Griffey Jr. 5.00 12.00
7 Jay Buhner 1.00 2.50
8 Juan Gonzalez 1.00 2.50
9 Mike Piazza 4.00 10.00
10 Jeff Bagwell 1.50 4.00
11 Sammy Sosa 2.50 6.00
12 Mark McGwire 6.00 15.00
13 Cecil Fielder 1.00 2.50
14 Ryan Klesko 1.00 2.50
15 Jose Canseco 1.50 4.00

1997 Donruss Power Alley

This 24-card set features color images of some of the league's top hitters printed on a micro-etched, all-foil card stock with holographic foil stamping. Using a "fractured" printing structure, 12 players utilize a green finish and are numbered to 4,000. Eight players are printed on all blue finish and number to 2,000, with the last four players utilizing a gold finish and are numbered to 1,000.

RANDOM INSERTS IN UPDATE PACKS
GREEN PRINT RUN 3750 SERIAL #'d SETS
BLUE PRINT RUN 1750 SERIAL #'d SETS
GOLD PRINT RUN 750 SERIAL #'d SETS
*GREEN DC's: 2X TO 5X BASIC GREEN
*BLUE DC's: 1.25X TO 3X BASIC BLUE
*GOLD DC's: .75X TO 2X BASIC GOLD
DIE CUTS: RANDOM INS.IN UPDATE PACKS
DIE CUTS PRINT RUN 250 SERIAL #'d SETS
1 Frank Thomas G 6.00 15.00
2 Ken Griffey Jr. G 25.00 60.00
3 Cal Ripken G 12.00 30.00
4 Jeff Bagwell B 2.50 6.00
5 Mike Piazza B 6.00 15.00
6 Andruw Jones GR 1.50 4.00
7 Alex Rodriguez G 10.00 25.00
8 Albert Belle GR 1.00 2.50
9 Mo Vaughn GR 1.00 2.50
10 Chipper Jones B 4.00 10.00
11 Juan Gonzalez B 1.50 4.00
12 Ken Caminiti GR 1.00 2.50
13 Manny Ramirez GR 1.50 4.00
14 Mark McGwire GR 6.00 15.00
15 Kenny Lofton B 1.50 4.00
16 Barry Bonds GR 6.00 15.00
17 Gary Sheffield GR 1.00 2.50
18 Tony Gwynn GR 3.00 8.00
19 Vladimir Guerrero B 4.00 10.00
20 Ivan Rodriguez B 2.50 6.00
21 Paul Molitor B 1.50 4.00
22 Sammy Sosa GR 2.50 6.00
23 Matt Williams GR 1.00 2.50
24 Derek Jeter GR 6.00 15.00

1997 Donruss Rated Rookies

Randomly inserted in all first series packs, this 30-card set honors the top rookie prospects as chosen by Donruss to be the most likely to succeed. The fronts feature color action player photos and silver foil printing. The backs carry a player portrait and player information.

COMPLETE SET (30) 15.00 40.00
RANDOM INSERTS IN SER.1 PACKS
WRAPPER ODDS 1:6
1 Jason Thompson .75 2.00
2 LaTroy Hawkins .75 2.00
3 Scott Rolen 1.25 3.00
4 Trey Beamon .75 2.00
5 Kimera Bartee .75 2.00
6 Nerio Rodriguez .75 2.00
7 Jeff D'Amico .75 2.00
8 Quinton McCracken .75 2.00
9 John Wasdin .75 2.00
10 Robin Jennings .75 2.00
11 Steve Gibralter .75 2.00
12 Tyler Houston .75 2.00
13 Tony Clark .75 2.00
14 Ugueth Urbina .75 2.00
15 Karim Garcia .75 2.00
16 Raul Casanova .75 2.00
17 Brooks Kieschnick .75 2.00
18 Luis Castillo .75 2.00
19 Edgar Renteria .75 2.00
20 Andruw Jones 1.25 3.00
21 Chad Mottola .75 2.00
22 Mac Suzuki .75 2.00
23 Justin Thompson .75 2.00
24 Darin Erstad .75 2.00
25 Todd Walker .75 2.00
26 Todd Greene .75 2.00
27 Vladimir Guerrero 2.00 5.00
28 Darren Dreifort .75 2.00
29 John Burke .75 2.00
30 Damon Mashore .75 2.00

1997 Donruss Ripken The Only Way I Know

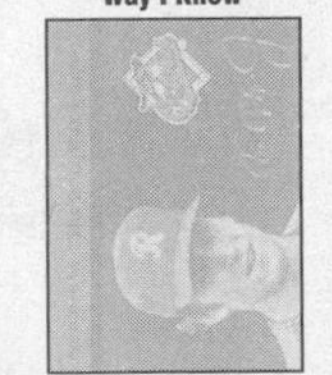

This special autobiographical tribute to Cal Ripken Jr. delivers a one-of-a-kind inside look at the modern day "Iron Man." Cards from this ten card set are printed on all foil card stock with foil stamping, utilizing exclusive photography and excerpts from his book. The first nine cards in the set were randomly seeded into packs of Donruss Update at an approximate rate of 1:24. Card number 10 was available exclusively in his book, "The Only Way I Know." Ripken autographed 2,131 of these number 10 cards and they were randomly inserted into the books. Because of it's separate distribution, card number 10 is not commonly included in complete sets, thus the mainstream set is considered complete with cards 1-9. Only 5,000 of each 1-9 card were produced, each of which are sequentially numbered on back.

COMPLETE SET (9) 40.00 100.00
COMMON CARD (1-9) 6.00 12.00
RANDOM INSERTS IN UPDATE PACKS
STATED PRINT RUN 5000 SERIAL #'d SETS
COMMON CARD (10) 10.00 20.00
CARD #10 DIST.ONLY W/RIPKEN'S BOOK
10A Cal Ripken BOOK AU/2131 100.00 200.00

1997 Donruss Rocket Launchers

Randomly inserted in first series magazine packs only, this 15-card set honors baseball's top power hitters. The fronts feature color player photos, while the backs carry player information. Only 5,000 sets were produced and all are sequentially numbered.

COMPLETE SET (15) 12.50 30.00
1 Frank Thomas 1.50 4.00
2 Albert Belle .60 1.50
3 Chipper Jones 1.50 4.00
4 Mike Piazza 1.50 4.00
5 Mo Vaughn .60 1.50
6 Juan Gonzalez .60 1.50
7 Fred McGriff 1.00 2.50
8 Jeff Bagwell 1.00 2.50
9 Matt Williams .60 1.50
10 Gary Sheffield .60 1.50
11 Barry Bonds 2.50 6.00
12 Manny Ramirez 1.00 2.50
13 Henry Rodriguez .60 1.50
14 Jason Giambi .60 1.50
15 Cal Ripken 5.00 12.00

1997 Donruss Rookie Diamond Kings

Randomly inserted in Update packs at an approximate rate of 1:24, cards from this 10-card set feature color portraits of some of the season's hottest rookie prospects in gold borders. Only 9,500 of each card were printed and are sequentially numbered. Please note that the numbering of each card runs to 10,000, but the first 500 of each card were Canvas parallels.

COMPLETE SET (10) 15.00 40.00
STATED PRINT RUN 9500 SERIAL #'d SETS
*CANVAS: 1.25X TO 3X BASIC DK'S
CANVAS PRINT RUN 500 SERIAL #'d SETS
RANDOM INSERTS IN UPDATE PACKS
1 Andruw Jones 2.50 6.00
2 Vladimir Guerrero 4.00 10.00
3 Scott Rolen 2.50 6.00
4 Todd Walker 1.50 4.00
5 Bartolo Colon 1.50 4.00
6 Jose Guillen 1.50 4.00
7 Nomar Garciaparra 6.00 15.00
8 Darin Erstad 1.50 4.00
9 Dmitri Young 1.50 4.00
10 Wilton Guerrero 1.50 4.00

1997 Donruss Update Ripken Info Card

This one-card set was inserted as the top card in prepackaged 1997 Donruss Update 14-card blister packs priced at $2.99 a package. The front features a borderless color action photo of Cal Ripken Jr. The back displays information about Donruss Update base and insert sets.

1 Cal Ripken Jr. 1.25 3.00

1998 Donruss

The 1998 Donruss set was issued in two series (series one numbers 1-170, series two numbers 171-420) and was distributed in 10-card packs with a suggested retail price of $1.99. The fronts feature color player photos with player information on the backs. The set contains the topical subsets: Fan Club (156-165), Hit List (346-375), The Untouchables (376-385), Spirit of the Game (386-415) and Checklists (416-420). Each Fan Club card carried instructions on how the fan could vote for their favorite players to be included in the 1998 Donruss Update set. Rookie Cards include Kevin Millwood and Magglio Ordonez. Sadly, after an eighteen year run, this was the last Donruss set to be issued due to card manufacturer Pinnacle's bankruptcy in 1998. In 2001, however, Donruss/Playoff procured a license to produce baseball cards and the Donruss brand was reinstituted after a two year break.

COMPLETE SET (420) 20.00 50.00
COMPLETE SERIES 1 (170) 8.00 20.00
COMPLETE UPDATE (250) 12.50 30.00
1 Paul Molitor .08 .25
2 Juan Gonzalez .08 .25
3 Darryl Kile .08 .25
4 Randy Johnson .25 .60
5 Tom Glavine .15 .40
6 Pat Hentgen .08 .25
7 David Justice .08 .25
8 Kevin Brown .15 .40
9 Mike Mussina .15 .40
10 Ken Caminiti .08 .25
11 Todd Hundley .08 .25
12 Frank Thomas .25 .60
13 Ray Lankford .08 .25
14 Justin Thompson .08 .25
15 Jason Dickson .08 .25
16 Kenny Lofton .08 .25
17 Ivan Rodriguez .15 .40
18 Pedro Martinez .15 .40
19 Brady Anderson .08 .25
20 Barry Larkin .15 .40
21 Chipper Jones .25 .60
22 Tony Gwynn .30 .75
23 Roger Clemens .50 1.25
24 Sandy Alomar Jr. .08 .25
25 Tino Martinez .15 .40
26 Jeff Bagwell .15 .40
27 Shawn Estes .08 .25
28 Ken Griffey Jr. .50 1.25
29 Javier Lopez .08 .25
30 Denny Neagle .08 .25
31 Mike Piazza .40 1.00
32 Andres Galarraga .08 .25
33 Larry Walker .08 .25
34 Alex Rodriguez .40 1.00
35 Greg Maddux .40 1.00
36 Albert Belle .08 .25
37 Barry Bonds .60 1.50
38 Mo Vaughn .08 .25
39 Kevin Appier .08 .25
40 Wade Boggs .15 .40
41 Garret Anderson .08 .25
42 Jeffrey Hammonds .08 .25
43 Marquis Grissom .08 .25
44 Jim Edmonds .08 .25
45 Brian Jordan .08 .25
46 Raul Mondesi .08 .25
47 John Valentin .08 .25
48 Brad Radke .08 .25
49 Ismael Valdes .08 .25
50 Matt Stairs .08 .25
51 Matt Williams .08 .25
52 Reggie Jefferson .08 .25
53 Alan Benes .08 .25
54 Charles Johnson .08 .25
55 Chuck Knoblauch .08 .25
56 Edgar Martinez .15 .40
57 Nomar Garciaparra .40 1.00
58 Craig Biggio .15 .40
59 Bernie Williams .15 .40
60 David Cone .08 .25
61 Cal Ripken .75 2.00
62 Mark McGwire .60 1.50
63 Roberto Alomar .15 .40
64 Fred McGriff .15 .40
65 Eric Karros .08 .25
66 Robin Ventura .08 .25
67 Darin Erstad .08 .25
68 Michael Tucker .08 .25
69 Jim Thome .15 .40
70 Mark Grace .15 .40
71 Lou Collier .08 .25
72 Karim Garcia .08 .25
73 Alex Fernandez .08 .25
74 J.T. Snow .08 .25
75 Reggie Sanders .08 .25
76 John Smoltz .15 .40
77 Tim Salmon .15 .40
78 Paul O'Neill .15 .40
79 Vinny Castilla .08 .25
80 Rafael Palmeiro .15 .40
81 Jaret Wright .08 .25
82 Jay Buhner .08 .25
83 Brett Butler .08 .25
84 Todd Greene .08 .25
85 Scott Rolen .15 .40
86 Sammy Sosa .25 .60
87 Jason Giambi .08 .25
88 Carlos Delgado .08 .25
89 Deion Sanders .15 .40
90 Wilton Guerrero .08 .25
91 Andy Pettitte .15 .40
92 Brian Giles .08 .25
93 Dmitri Young .08 .25
94 Ron Coomer .08 .25
95 Mike Cameron .08 .25
96 Edgardo Alfonzo .08 .25
97 Jimmy Key .08 .25
98 Ryan Klesko .08 .25
99 Andy Benes .08 .25
100 Derek Jeter .60 1.50
101 Jeff Fassero .08 .25
102 Neifi Perez .08 .25
103 Hideo Nomo .25 .60
104 Andruw Jones .15 .40
105 Todd Helton .15 .40
106 Livan Hernandez .08 .25

107 Brett Tomko .08 .25
108 Shannon Stewart .08 .25
109 Bartolo Colon .08 .25
110 Matt Morris .08 .25
111 Miguel Tejada .25 .60
112 Pokey Reese .08 .25
113 Fernando Tatis .08 .25
114 Todd Dunwoody .08 .25
115 Jose Cruz Jr. .08 .25
116 Chan Ho Park .08 .25
117 Kevin Young .08 .25
118 Rickey Henderson .25 .60
119 Hideki Irabu .08 .25
120 Francisco Cordova .08 .25
121 Al Martin .08 .25
122 Tony Clark .08 .25
123 Curt Schilling .08 .25
124 Rusty Greer .08 .25
125 Jose Canseco .15 .40
126 Edgar Renteria .08 .25
127 Todd Walker .08 .25
128 Wally Joyner .08 .25
129 Bill Mueller .08 .25
130 Jose Guillen .08 .25
131 Manny Ramirez .15 .40
132 Bobby Higginson .08 .25
133 Kevin Orie .08 .25
134 Will Clark .15 .40
135 Dave Nilsson .08 .25
136 Jason Kendall .08 .25
137 Ivan Cruz .08 .25
138 Gary Sheffield .08 .25
139 Bubba Trammell .08 .25
140 Vladimir Guerrero .25 .60
141 Dennis Reyes .08 .25
142 Bobby Bonilla .08 .25
143 Ruben Rivera .08 .25
144 Ben Grieve .08 .25
145 Moises Alou .08 .25
146 Tony Womack .08 .25
147 Eric Young .08 .25
148 Paul Konerko .08 .25
149 Dante Bichette .08 .25
150 Joe Carter .08 .25
151 Rondell White .08 .25
152 Chris Holt .08 .25
153 Shawn Green .08 .25
154 Mark Grudzielanek .08 .25
155 Jermaine Dye .08 .25
156 Ken Griffey Jr. FC .30 .75
157 Frank Thomas FC .15 .40
158 Chipper Jones FC .15 .40
159 Mike Piazza FC .25 .60
160 Cal Ripken FC .40 1.00
161 Greg Maddux FC .25 .60
162 Juan Gonzalez FC .08 .25
163 Alex Rodriguez FC .25 .60
164 Mark McGwire FC .30 .75
165 Derek Jeter FC .30 .75
166 Larry Walker CL .08 .25
167 Tony Gwynn CL .15 .40
168 Tino Martinez CL .08 .25
169 Scott Rolen CL .08 .25
170 Nomar Garciaparra CL .25 .60
171 Mike Sweeney .08 .25
172 Dustin Hermanson .08 .25
173 Darren Dreifort .08 .25
174 Ron Gant .08 .25
175 Todd Hollandsworth .08 .25
176 John Jaha .08 .25
177 Kerry Wood .10 .30
178 Chris Stynes .08 .25
179 Kevin Elster .08 .25
180 Derek Bell .08 .25
181 Darryl Strawberry .08 .25
182 Damion Easley .08 .25
183 Jeff Cirillo .08 .25
184 John Thomson .08 .25
185 Dan Wilson .08 .25
186 Jay Bell .08 .25
187 Bernard Gilkey .08 .25
188 Marc Valdes .08 .25
189 Ramon Martinez .08 .25
190 Charles Nagy .08 .25
191 Derek Lowe .08 .25
192 Andy Benes .08 .25
193 Delino DeShields .08 .25
194 Ryan Jackson RC .08 .25
195 Kenny Lofton .08 .25
196 Chuck Knoblauch .08 .25
197 Andres Galarraga .08 .25
198 Jose Canseco .15 .40
199 John Olerud .08 .25
200 Lance Johnson .08 .25
201 Darryl Kile .08 .25
202 Luis Castillo .08 .25
203 Joe Carter .08 .25
204 Dennis Eckersley .08 .25
205 Steve Finley .08 .25
206 Esteban Loaiza .08 .25
207 Ryan Christenson RC .08 .25
208 Deivi Cruz .08 .25
209 Mariano Rivera .25 .60
210 Mike Judd RC .10 .30
211 Billy Wagner .08 .25
212 Scott Spiezio .08 .25
213 Russ Davis .08 .25
214 Jeff Suppan .08 .25
215 Doug Glanville .08 .25
216 Dmitri Young .08 .25
217 Rey Ordonez .08 .25
218 Cecil Fielder .08 .25
219 Masato Yoshii RC .10 .30
220 Raul Casanova .08 .25
221 Rolando Arrojo RC .10 .30
222 Ellis Burks .08 .25
223 Butch Huskey .08 .25
224 Brian Hunter .08 .25
225 Marquis Grissom .08 .25
226 Kevin Brown .15 .40
227 Joe Randa .08 .25
228 Henry Rodriguez .08 .25
229 Omar Vizquel .15 .40
230 Fred McGriff .15 .40
231 Matt Williams .08 .25
232 Moises Alou .08 .25
233 Travis Fryman .08 .25
234 Wade Boggs .15 .40
235 Pedro Martinez .15 .40
236 Rickey Henderson .25 .60
237 Bubba Trammell .08 .25
238 Mike Caruso .08 .25
239 Wilson Alvarez .08 .25
240 Geronimo Berroa .08 .25
241 Eric Milton .08 .25
242 Scott Erickson .08 .25
243 Todd Erdos RC .08 .25
244 Bobby Hughes .08 .25
245 Dave Hollins .08 .25
246 Dean Palmer .08 .25
247 Carlos Baerga .08 .25
248 Jose Silva .08 .25
249 Jose Cabrera RC .08 .25
250 Tom Evans .08 .25
251 Marty Cordova .08 .25
252 Hanley Frias RC .08 .25
253 Javier Valentin .08 .25
254 Mario Valdez .08 .25
255 Joey Cora .08 .25
256 Mike Lansing .08 .25
257 Jeff Kent .08 .25
258 Dave Dellucci RC .20 .50
259 Curtis King RC .08 .25
260 David Segui .08 .25
261 Royce Clayton .08 .25
262 Jeff Blauser .08 .25
263 Manny Aybar RC .08 .25
264 Mike Cather RC .08 .25
265 Todd Zeile .08 .25
266 Richard Hidalgo .08 .25
267 Dante Powell .08 .25
268 Mike DeJean RC .08 .25
269 Ken Cloude .08 .25
270 Danny Klassen .08 .25
271 Sean Casey .08 .25
272 A.J. Hinch .08 .25
273 Rich Butler RC .08 .25
274 Ben Ford RC .08 .25
275 Billy McMillon .08 .25
276 Wilson Delgado .08 .25
277 Orlando Cabrera .08 .25
278 Geoff Jenkins .08 .25
279 Enrique Wilson .08 .25
280 Derrek Lee .15 .40
281 Marc Pisciotta RC .08 .25
282 Abraham Nunez .08 .25
283 Aaron Boone .08 .25
284 Brad Fullmer .08 .25
285 Rob Stanifer RC .08 .25
286 Preston Wilson .08 .25
287 Greg Norton .08 .25
288 Bobby Smith .08 .25
289 Josh Booty .08 .25
290 Russell Branyan .08 .25
291 Jeremi Gonzalez .08 .25
292 Michael Coleman .08 .25
293 Cliff Politte .08 .25
294 Eric Ludwick .08 .25
295 Rafael Medina .08 .25
296 Jason Varitek .25 .60
297 Ron Wright .08 .25
298 Mark Kotsay .08 .25
299 David Ortiz .30 .75
300 Frank Catalanotto RC .20 .50
301 Robinson Checo .08 .25
302 Kevin Millwood RC .30 .75
303 Jacob Cruz .08 .25
304 Javier Vazquez .08 .25
305 Magglio Ordonez RC 1.00 2.50
306 Kevin Witt .08 .25
307 Derrick Gibson .08 .25
308 Shane Monahan .08 .25
309 Brian Rose .08 .25
310 Bobby Estalella .08 .25
311 Felix Heredia .08 .25
312 Desi Relaford .08 .25
313 Esteban Yan RC .10 .30
314 Ricky Ledee .08 .25
315 Steve Woodard .08 .25
316 Pat Watkins .08 .25
317 Damian Moss .08 .25
318 Bob Abreu .08 .25
319 Jeff Abbott .08 .25
320 Miguel Cairo .08 .25
321 Rigo Beltran RC .08 .25
322 Tony Saunders .08 .25
323 Randall Simon .08 .25
324 Hiram Bocachica .08 .25
325 Richie Sexson .08 .25
326 Karim Garcia .08 .25
327 Mike Lowell RC .50 1.25
328 Pat Cline .08 .25
329 Matt Clement .08 .25
330 Scott Elarton .08 .25
331 Manuel Barrios RC .08 .25
332 Bruce Chen .08 .25
333 Juan Encarnacion .08 .25
334 Travis Lee .08 .25
335 Wes Helms .08 .25
336 Chad Fox RC .08 .25
337 Donnie Sadler .08 .25
338 Carlos Mendoza RC .08 .25
339 Damian Jackson .08 .25
340 Julio Ramirez RC .08 .25
341 John Halama RC .10 .30
342 Edwin Diaz .08 .25
343 Felix Martinez .08 .25
344 Eli Marrero .08 .25
345 Carl Pavano .08 .25
346 Vladimir Guerrero HL .15 .40
347 Barry Bonds HL .30 .75
348 Darin Erstad HL .08 .25
349 Albert Belle HL .08 .25
350 Kenny Lofton HL .08 .25
351 Mo Vaughn HL .08 .25
352 Jose Cruz Jr. HL .08 .25
353 Tony Clark HL .08 .25
354 Roberto Alomar HL .08 .25
355 Manny Ramirez HL .08 .25
356 Paul Molitor HL .08 .25
357 Jim Thome HL .08 .25
358 Tino Martinez HL .08 .25
359 Tim Salmon HL .08 .25
360 David Justice HL .08 .25
361 Raul Mondesi HL .08 .25
362 Mark Grace HL .08 .25
363 Craig Biggio HL .08 .25
364 Larry Walker HL .08 .25
365 Mark McGwire HL .30 .75
366 Juan Gonzalez HL .08 .25
367 Derek Jeter HL .30 .75
368 Chipper Jones HL .15 .40
369 Frank Thomas HL .15 .40
370 Alex Rodriguez HL .25 .60
371 Mike Piazza HL .25 .60
372 Tony Gwynn HL .15 .40
373 Jeff Bagwell HL .08 .25
374 Nomar Garciaparra HL .25 .60
375 Ken Griffey Jr. HL .30 .75
376 Livan Hernandez UN .08 .25
377 Chan Ho Park UN .08 .25
378 Mike Mussina UN .08 .25
379 Andy Pettitte UN .08 .25
380 Greg Maddux UN .25 .60
381 Hideo Nomo UN .15 .40
382 Roger Clemens UN .25 .60
383 Randy Johnson UN .15 .40
384 Pedro Martinez UN .15 .40
385 Jaret Wright UN .08 .25
386 Ken Griffey Jr. SG .30 .75
387 Todd Helton SG .08 .25
388 Paul Konerko SG .08 .25
389 Cal Ripken SG .40 1.00
390 Larry Walker SG .08 .25
391 Ken Caminiti SG .08 .25
392 Jose Guillen SG .08 .25
393 Jim Edmonds SG .08 .25
394 Barry Larkin SG .08 .25
395 Bernie Williams SG .08 .25
396 Tony Clark SG .08 .25
397 Jose Cruz Jr. SG .08 .25
398 Ivan Rodriguez SG .08 .25
399 Darin Erstad SG .08 .25
400 Scott Rolen SG .08 .25
401 Mark McGwire SG .30 .75
402 Andruw Jones SG .08 .25
403 Juan Gonzalez SG .08 .25
404 Derek Jeter SG .30 .75
405 Chipper Jones SG .15 .40
406 Greg Maddux SG .25 .60
407 Frank Thomas SG .15 .40
408 Alex Rodriguez SG .25 .60
409 Mike Piazza SG .25 .60
410 Tony Gwynn SG .15 .40
411 Jeff Bagwell SG .08 .25
412 Nomar Garciaparra SG .25 .60
413 Hideo Nomo SG .15 .40
414 Barry Bonds SG .30 .75
415 Ben Grieve SG .08 .25
416 Barry Bonds CL .30 .75
417 Mark McGwire CL .30 .75
418 Roger Clemens CL .25 .60
419 Livan Hernandez CL .08 .25
420 Ken Griffey Jr. CL .30 .75

1998 Donruss Gold Press Proofs

*STARS: 10X TO 25X BASIC CARDS
*ROOKIES: 5X TO 12X BASIC CARDS
RANDOM INSERTS IN PACKS
STATED PRINT RUN 500 SETS

1998 Donruss Silver Press Proofs

*STARS: 5X TO 12X BASIC CARDS
*ROOKIES: 3X TO 6X BASIC CARDS
RANDOM INSERTS IN PACKS
STATED PRINT RUN 1500 SETS

1998 Donruss Crusade Green

This 100-card set features a selection of the league's top stars. Cards were randomly inserted into three products as follows: 40 players into 1998 Donruss, 30 into 1998 Leaf, and 30 into 1998 Donruss Update. The fronts feature color player photos printed with Limited "refractive" technology. The backs carry player information. Only 250 of each of these Green cards were produced and sequentially numbered. Cards are designated below with a D, L or U suffix to denote their original distribution within Donruss, Leaf or Donruss Update packs. All of the "Call to Arms" (sic CTA) subset cards were mistakenly printed without numbers. Corrected copies were never made.

RANDOM INSERTS IN SEVERAL BRANDS
STATED PRINT RUN 250 SERIAL #'d SETS
D SUFFIX ON DONRUSS DISTRIBUTION
L SUFFIX ON LEAF DISTRIBUTION
U SUFFIX ON DON.UPDATE DISTRIBUTION
ALL CTA CARDS ARE UNNUMBERED ERRORS
1 Tim Salmon 10.00 25.00
2 Garret Anderson 6.00 15.00
3 Jim Edmonds CTA 6.00 15.00
4 Darin Erstad CTA 6.00 15.00
5 Jason Dickson 6.00 15.00
6 Todd Greene 6.00 15.00
7 Roberto Alomar CTA 10.00 25.00
8 Cal Ripken 50.00 100.00
9 Rafael Palmeiro CTA 10.00 25.00
10 Brady Anderson 6.00 15.00
11 Mike Mussina 10.00 25.00
12 Mo Vaughn CTA 6.00 15.00
13 Nomar Garciaparra 15.00 40.00
14 Frank Thomas CTA 12.50 30.00
15 Albert Belle CTA 6.00 15.00
16 Mike Cameron 6.00 15.00
17 Robin Ventura 6.00 15.00
18 Manny Ramirez 10.00 25.00
19 Jim Thome CTA 10.00 25.00
20 Sandy Alomar Jr. 6.00 15.00
21 David Justice 6.00 15.00
22 Matt Williams 6.00 15.00
23 Tony Clark 6.00 15.00
24 Bubba Trammell 6.00 15.00
25 Justin Thompson 6.00 15.00
26 Bobby Higginson 6.00 15.00
27 Kevin Appier 6.00 15.00
28 Paul Molitor 6.00 15.00
29 Chuck Knoblauch CTA 6.00 15.00
30 Todd Walker 6.00 15.00
31 Bernie Williams 10.00 25.00
32 Derek Jeter CTA 40.00 80.00
33 Tino Martinez 10.00 25.00
34 Andy Pettitte 10.00 25.00
35 Wade Boggs CTA 10.00 25.00
36 Hideki Irabu 6.00 15.00
37 Jose Canseco 10.00 25.00
38 Jason Giambi 6.00 15.00
39 Ken Griffey Jr. 100.00 200.00
40 Alex Rodriguez CTA 20.00 50.00
41 Randy Johnson 12.50 30.00
42 Edgar Martinez 10.00 25.00
43 Jay Buhner CTA 6.00 15.00
44 Juan Gonzalez CTA 6.00 15.00
45 Will Clark 15.00 40.00
46 Ivan Rodriguez 10.00 25.00
47 Rusty Greer 6.00 15.00
48 Roger Clemens 20.00 50.00
49 Carlos Delgado 6.00 15.00
50 Shawn Green 6.00 15.00
51 Jose Cruz Jr. 6.00 15.00
52 Kenny Lofton 6.00 15.00
53 Chipper Jones 30.00 60.00
54 Andruw Jones CTA 10.00 25.00
55 Greg Maddux 20.00 50.00
56 John Smoltz CTA 10.00 25.00
57 Tom Glavine 10.00 25.00
58 Javier Lopez 6.00 15.00
59 Fred McGriff 10.00 25.00
60 Mark Grace 10.00 25.00
61 Sammy Sosa CTA 12.50 30.00
62 Kevin Orie 6.00 15.00
63 Barry Larkin CTA 10.00 25.00
64 Pokey Reese 6.00 15.00
65 Deion Sanders 10.00 25.00
66 Andres Galarraga 6.00 15.00
67 Larry Walker 6.00 15.00
68 Dante Bichette CTA 6.00 15.00
69 Neifi Perez 6.00 15.00
70 Eric Young 6.00 15.00
71 Todd Helton 10.00 25.00
72 Gary Sheffield CTA 6.00 15.00
73 Moises Alou 6.00 15.00
74 Bobby Bonilla 6.00 15.00
75 Kevin Brown 10.00 25.00
76 Ben Grieve 6.00 15.00
77 Jeff Bagwell CTA 10.00 25.00
78 Craig Biggio 10.00 25.00
79 Mike Piazza 20.00 50.00
80 Raul Mondesi 6.00 15.00
81 Hideo Nomo CTA 12.50 30.00
82 Wilton Guerrero 6.00 15.00
83 Rondell White CTA 6.00 15.00
84 Vladimir Guerrero CTA 12.50 30.00
85 Pedro Martinez 10.00 25.00
86 Edgardo Alfonzo 6.00 15.00
87 Todd Hundley CTA 6.00 15.00
88 Scott Rolen 10.00 25.00
89 Francisco Cordova 6.00 15.00
90 Jose Guillen 6.00 15.00
91 Jason Kendall 6.00 15.00
92 Ray Lankford 6.00 15.00
93 Mark McGwire CTA 40.00 80.00
94 Matt Morris 6.00 15.00
95 Alan Benes 6.00 15.00
96 Brian Jordan CTA 6.00 15.00
97 Tony Gwynn 15.00 40.00
98 Ken Caminiti CTA 6.00 15.00
99 Barry Bonds CTA 40.00 80.00
100 Shawn Estes 6.00 15.00

1998 Donruss Crusade Purple

*PURPLE: 1X TO 2.5X GREEN
RANDOM INSERTS IN PACKS
STATED PRINT RUN 100 SERIAL #'d SETS

1998 Donruss Crusade Red

RANDOM INSERTS IN PACKS
STATED PRINT RUN 25 SERIAL #'d SETS
NO PRICING DUE TO SCARCITY

1998 Donruss Diamond Kings

Randomly inserted in packs, this 20-card set features color player portraits of some of the greatest names in baseball. Only 9,500 sets were produced and are sequentially numbered. The first 500 of each card were printed on actual canvas card stock. In addition, a Frank Thomas sample card was created as a promo for the 1998 Donruss 1 product. The card was sent to all wholesale accounts along with the order forms for the product. The large "SAMPLE" stamp across the back of the card makes it easy to differentiate from Thomas' standard 1998 Diamond King insert card.

COMPLETE SET (20) 25.00 60.00
RANDOM INSERTS IN PACKS
STATED PRINT RUN 9500 SERIAL #'d SETS
*CANVAS: 1.25X TO 3X BASIC DIAM.KINGS
CANVAS: RANDOM INSERTS IN PACKS
CANVAS PRINT RUN 500 SERIAL #'d SETS
1 Cal Ripken 5.00 12.00
2 Greg Maddux 2.00 5.00
3 Ivan Rodriguez 1.00 2.50
4 Tony Gwynn 1.50 4.00
5 Paul Molitor 1.50 4.00
6 Kenny Lofton .60 1.50
7 Andy Pettitte 1.00 2.50
8 Darin Erstad .60 1.50
9 Randy Johnson 1.50 4.00
10 Derek Jeter 4.00 10.00
11 Hideo Nomo 1.50 4.00
12 David Justice .60 1.50
13 Bernie Williams 1.00 2.50
14 Roger Clemens 2.00 5.00
15 Barry Larkin 1.00 2.50
16 Andruw Jones .60 1.50
17 Mike Piazza 1.50 4.00
18 Frank Thomas 1.50 4.00
19 Alex Rodriguez 2.00 5.00
20 Ken Griffey Jr. 3.00 8.00
S20 Frank Thomas Sample 1.50 4.00

1998 Donruss Dominators

Randomly inserted in update packs, this 30-card set is an insert to the Donruss base set. The holographic foil-stamped fronts feature color action photos surrounded by an orange background. The featured player's team name sits in the upper right corner and the Donruss logo sits in the upper left corner.

COMPLETE SET (30) 60.00 120.00
RANDOM INSERTS IN UPDATE PACKS
1 Roger Clemens 3.00 8.00
2 Tony Clark .60 1.50
3 Darin Erstad .60 1.50
4 Jeff Bagwell 1.00 2.50
5 Ken Griffey Jr 3.00 8.00
6 Andruw Jones 1.00 2.50
7 Juan Gonzalez .60 1.50
8 Ivan Rodriguez 1.00 2.50
9 Randy Johnson 1.50 4.00
10 Tino Martinez 1.00 2.50
11 Mark McGwire 4.00 10.00
12 Chuck Knoblauch .60 1.50
13 Jim Thome 1.00 2.50
14 Alex Rodriguez 2.50 6.00
15 Hideo Nomo 1.50 4.00
16 Jose Cruz Jr. .60 1.50
17 Chipper Jones 1.50 4.00
18 Tony Gwynn 2.00 5.00
19 Barry Bonds 4.00 10.00
20 Mo Vaughn .60 1.50
21 Cal Ripken 5.00 12.00
22 Greg Maddux 2.50 6.00
23 Manny Ramirez 1.00 2.50
24 Andres Galarraga .60 1.50
25 Vladimir Guerrero 1.50 4.00
26 Albert Belle .60 1.50
27 Nomar Garciaparra 2.50 6.00
28 Kenny Lofton .60 1.50
29 Mike Piazza 2.50 6.00
30 Frank Thomas 1.50 4.00

1998 Donruss Elite Inserts

Continuing the popular tradition begun in 1991, Donruss again inserted Elite cards in their packs. These cards which have the work "Elite" written in big cursive letters on the bottom and a small player photo, were serially numbered to 2500 and has the "cream of the crop" of the baseball players. This set was designed to be the last time Donruss would issue Elite cards ending the succsessful eight year run. It's interesting to note that unlike previous Elite inserts, the 1998 cards were not numbered in continuation of the Elite run.

COMPLETE SET (20) 50.00 100.00
RANDOM INSERTS IN UPDATE PACKS
STATED PRINT RUN 2500 SERIAL #'d SETS
1 Jeff Bagwell 1.50 4.00
2 Andruw Jones 1.00 2.50
3 Ken Griffey Jr. 5.00 12.00
4 Derek Jeter 6.00 15.00
5 Juan Gonzalez 1.00 2.50
6 Mark McGwire 4.00 10.00
7 Ivan Rodriguez 1.50 4.00
8 Paul Molitor 2.50 6.00
9 Hideo Nomo 2.50 6.00
10 Mo Vaughn 1.00 2.50
11 Chipper Jones 2.50 6.00
12 Nomar Garciaparra 1.50 4.00
13 Mike Piazza 2.50 6.00
14 Frank Thomas 2.50 6.00
15 Greg Maddux 3.00 8.00
16 Cal Ripken 8.00 20.00
17 Alex Rodriguez 3.00 8.00
18 Jose Cruz Jr. 1.00 2.50
19 Barry Bonds 4.00 10.00
20 Tony Gwynn 2.50 6.00

1998 Donruss FANtasy Team

Randomly inserted in update packs, this 20-card set features the leading votegetters from the on-line Fan Club. The top vote-getters make up the 1st team FANtasy Team and are sequentially numbered to 1750. The reamining players make up the 2nd team FANtasy Team and are sequentially numbered to 3750. The fronts carry color action photos surrounded by a red, white, and blue star-studded background. Cards number 1-10 feature members from the first team while cards numbered from 11-20 feature members of the second team.

COMPLETE SET (20) 75.00 150.00
1ST TEAM 1-10 PRINT 1750 SERIAL #'d SETS
2ND TEAM 11-20 PRINT 3750 SERIAL #'d SETS
*1ST TEAM DC's: .75X TO 2X BASIC FANTASY
*2ND TEAM DC's: 1X TO 2.5X BASIC FANTASY
DIE CUTS PRINT RUN 250 SERIAL #'d SETS
RANDOM INSERTS IN UPDATE PACKS
1 Frank Thomas 2.00 5.00
2 Ken Griffey Jr. 4.00 10.00
3 Cal Ripken 6.00 15.00
4 Jose Cruz Jr. .75 2.00
5 Travis Lee .75 2.00
6 Greg Maddux 2.50 6.00
7 Alex Rodriguez 2.50 6.00
8 Mark McGwire 3.00 8.00
9 Chipper Jones 2.00 5.00
10 Andruw Jones .75 2.00
11 Mike Piazza 1.50 4.00
12 Tony Gwynn 1.50 4.00
13 Larry Walker 1.00 2.50
14 Nomar Garciaparra 1.00 2.50
15 Jaret Wright .60 1.50
16 Livan Hernandez .60 1.50
17 Roger Clemens 2.00 5.00
18 Derek Jeter 4.00 10.00
19 Scott Rolen 1.00 2.50
20 Jeff Bagwell 1.00 2.50

1998 Donruss Longball Leaders

Randomly inserted in first series packs, this 24-card set features color photos of the top sluggers in baseball printed on micro-etched cards. Only 5000 of each card were produced and are sequentially numbered.

COMPLETE SET (24) 12.00 30.00
RANDOM INSERTS IN PACKS
STATED PRINT RUN 5000 SERIAL #'d SETS
1 Ken Griffey Jr. 2.00 5.00
2 Mark McGwire 1.50 4.00
3 Tino Martinez .40 1.00
4 Barry Bonds 1.50 4.00
5 Frank Thomas 1.00 2.50
6 Albert Belle .40 1.00
7 Mike Piazza 1.00 2.50
8 Chipper Jones 1.00 2.50
9 Vladimir Guerrero .60 1.50
10 Matt Williams .40 1.00
11 Sammy Sosa 1.00 2.50
12 Tim Salmon .40 1.00
13 Raul Mondesi .40
14 Jeff Bagwell .60
15 Mo Vaughn .40
16 Manny Ramirez 1.00
17 Jim Thome .60
18 Jim Edmonds .60
19 Tony Clark .40
20 Nomar Garciaparra .60
21 Juan Gonzalez .40
22 Scott Rolen .60
23 Larry Walker .60
24 Andres Galarraga .60

1998 Donruss MLB 99

This 20 card set was inserted into both Donruss Update and Studio packs. These cards feature 2[illegible] the leading Baseball players and were widely available because of the insertion into both of the aforementioned brands.

COMPLETE SET (20) 4.00 1[illegible]
UPDATE STATED ODDS 1:2
1 Cal Ripken .75
2 Nomar Garciaparra .40
3 Barry Bonds .60
4 Mike Mussina .15
5 Pedro Martinez .15
6 Derek Jeter .60
7 Andruw Jones .15
8 Kenny Lofton .08
9 Gary Sheffield .08
10 Raul Mondesi .08
11 Jeff Bagwell .15
12 Tim Salmon .15
13 Tom Glavine .15
14 Ben Grieve .08
15 Matt Williams .08
16 Juan Gonzalez .08
17 Mark McGwire .60 1[illegible]
18 Bernie Williams .15
19 Andres Galarraga .08
20 Jose Cruz Jr. .08

1998 Donruss Production Line On-Base

Randomly inserted in first series pre-priced packs only, this 20-card set features color player images printed on holographic board with green highlight[illegible] Each card is sequentially numbered according to t[illegible] player's on-base percentage. Print runs for each c[illegible] is matched with the player's 1997 on-base percentage and is listed individually below after ea[illegible] player's name in our checklist.

RANDOM INSERTS IN PRE-PRICED PACKS
PRINT RUN BASED ON PLAYER STATS
1 Frank Thomas/456 8.00 20.[illegible]
2 Edgar Martinez/456 5.00 12.[illegible]
3 Roberto Alomar/390 5.00 12.[illegible]
4 Chuck Knoblauch/390 3.00 8.[illegible]
5 Mike Piazza/431 12.50 30.[illegible]
6 Barry Larkin/440 5.00 12.[illegible]
7 Kenny Lofton/409 3.00 8.[illegible]
8 Jeff Bagwell/425 5.00 12.[illegible]
9 Barry Bonds/446 20.00 50.[illegible]
10 Rusty Greer/405 3.00 8.[illegible]
11 Gary Sheffield/424 3.00 8.[illegible]
12 Mark McGwire/393 20.00 50.[illegible]
13 Chipper Jones/371 8.00 20.[illegible]
14 Tony Gwynn/409 10.00 25.[illegible]
15 Craig Biggio/415 5.00 12.[illegible]
16 Mo Vaughn/420 3.00 8.[illegible]
17 Bernie Williams/408 5.00 12.[illegible]
18 Ken Griffey Jr./382 20.00 50.[illegible]
19 Brady Anderson/393 3.00 8.[illegible]
20 Derek Jeter/370 20.00 50.[illegible]

1998 Donruss Production Line Power Index

Randomly inserted in first series hobby packs only this 20-card set features color player images printe[illegible] on holographic board with blue highlights. Each ca[illegible] is sequentially numbered according to the player's power index. Print runs for each card is matched w[illegible] the player's 1997 power index percentage and is listed individually below after each player's name i[illegible] our checklist.

RANDOM INSERTS IN HOBBY PACKS
PRINT RUN BASED ON PLAYER STATS
1 Frank Thomas/1067 4.00 10.0[illegible]
2 Mark McGwire/1039 10.00 25.0[illegible]
3 Barry Bonds/1031 10.00 25.0[illegible]
4 Jeff Bagwell/1017 2.50 6.0[illegible]
5 Ken Griffey Jr./1028 12.00 30.0[illegible]
6 Alex Rodriguez/846 6.00 15.0[illegible]

per Jones/850 4.00 10.00
Piazza/1070 6.00 15.00
'aughn/980 1.50 4.00
dy Anderson/863 1.50 4.00
nny Ramirez/953 2.50 6.00
ert Belle/823 1.50 4.00
Thome/1001 2.50 6.00
nie Williams/952 2.50 6.00
tt Rolen/846 2.50 6.00
dimir Guerrero/833 4.00 10.00
ry Walker/1172 1.50 4.00
rid Justice/1013 1.50 4.00
o Martinez/948 2.50 6.00
y Gwynn/957 5.00 12.00

98 Donruss Production Line Slugging

mly inserted in first series retail packs only, -card set features color player images printed ographic board with red highlights. Each card uentially numbered according to the player's ng percentage and is detailed specifically in ecklist.
OM INSERTS IN RETAIL PACKS
RUN BASED ON PLAYER STATS
k McGwire/646 15.00 40.00
Griffey Jr./646 15.00 40.00
res Galarraga/585 2.50 6.00
y Bonds/585 15.00 40.00
n Gonzalez/589 2.50 6.00
e Piazza/638 10.00 25.00
Bagwell/592 4.00 10.00
nny Ramirez/538 4.00 10.00
Thome/579 4.00 10.00
Vaughn/560 2.50 6.00
rry Walker/720 2.50 6.00
no Martinez/577 4.00 10.00
ank Thomas/611 6.00 15.00
m Salmon/517 4.00 10.00
ul Mondesi/541 2.50 6.00
ex Rodriguez/496 10.00 25.00
omar Garciaparra/534 10.00 25.00
se Cruz Jr./499 2.50 6.00
ny Clark/500 2.50 6.00
l Ripken/402 20.00 50.00

998 Donruss Rated Rookies

omly inserted in packs, this 30-card set features r action photos of some of the top rookie pects as chosen by Donruss to be the most likely cceed. The backs carry player Information.
PLETE SET (30) 15.00 40.00
DALISTS: 2.5X TO 6X BASIC RR
DALIST PRINT RUN 250 SETS
DOM INSERTS IN PACKS
ark Kotsay .75 2.00
eifi Perez .75 2.00
ul Konerko .75 2.00
se Cruz Jr. .75 2.00
deki Irabu .75 2.00
ike Cameron .75 2.00
ff Suppan .75 2.00
evin Orie .75 2.00
okey Reese .75 2.00
Todd Dunwoody .75 2.00
Miguel Tejada 2.00 5.00
Jose Guillen .75 2.00
Bartolo Colon .75 2.00
Derrek Lee 1.25 3.00
Antone Williamson .75 2.00
Wilton Guerrero .75 2.00
Jaret Wright .75 2.00
Todd Helton 1.25 3.00
Shannon Stewart .75 2.00
Nomar Garciaparra 3.00 8.00
Brett Tomko .75 2.00
Fernando Tatis .75 2.00
Raul Ibanez .75 2.00
Dennis Reyes .75 2.00
Bobby Estalella .75 2.00
Lou Collier .75 2.00
Bubba Trammell .75 2.00
Ben Grieve .75 2.00
Ivan Cruz .75 2.00
Karim Garcia .75 2.00

1998 Donruss Rookie Diamond Kings

ese cards were randomly inserted in Donruss date packs. This 12-card set is an insert to the nruss base set. The set is sequentially numbered 10,000. The fronts feature head and shoulder lor prints surrounded by a four-sided border of the p young prospects in today's MLB.
OMPLETE SET (12) 12.50 30.00
ATED PRINT RUN 9500 SERIAL #'d SETS
CANVAS: 1.25X TO 3X BASIC ROOK.DK'S
NVAS PRINT RUN 500 SERIAL #'d SETS
NDOM INSERTS IN UPDATE PACKS
Travis Lee 1.50 4.00
Fernando Tatis 1.50 4.00
Livan Hernandez 1.50 4.00
Todd Helton 2.50 6.00
Derrek Lee 2.50 6.00
6 Jaret Wright 1.50 4.00
7 Ben Grieve 1.50 4.00
8 Paul Konerko 1.50 4.00
9 Jose Cruz Jr. 1.50 4.00
10 Mark Kotsay 1.50 4.00
11 Todd Greene 1.50 4.00
12 Brad Fullmer 1.50 4.00

1998 Donruss Signature Series Previews

Twenty-nine of these 34 cards were randomly inserted into Donruss Update packs. These 29 cards were previewing the then-upcoming 1998 Donruss Signature Series set. Each player signed a slightly different amount of cards so we have put the amount of cards signed next to the players name in our checklist. The five additional cards (Alou, Casey, Jenkins, Jeter and Wilson) were never intended for public release. It's believed that four players (all except Jeter) signed 100 or more cards but failed to return their cards to the manufacturer (Pinnacle Brands) in time for the Donruss Update packout. Apparently, the cards were stored in Pinnacle's card vault, but an unknown amount of each card made their way into the secondary market during Pinnacle's bankruptcy proceeding when Playoff Inc. bought the holdings. It's believed that a handful of the Jeter cards were erroneously sent to Jeter in his 1998 Donruss Signature card agreement (red, green and blue cards for a separate brand). Jeter simply signed all of the cards and sent them back to the manufacturer.
RANDOM INSERTS IN UPDATE PACKS
ALOU/CASEY/JENKINS/JETER/WILSON
WERE NOT PUBLICLY RELEASED
NO PRICING ON QTY OF 25 OR LESS
1 Sandy Alomar Jr./96 * 15.00 40.00
2 Moises Alou 10.00 25.00
3 Andy Benes/135 * 15.00 40.00
4 Russell Branyan/188 * 15.00 40.00
5 Sean Casey 8.00 20.00
6 Tony Clark/188 * 10.00 25.00
7 Juan Encarnacion/193 * 20.00 50.00
8 Brad Fullmer/396 * 8.00 20.00
9 Juan Gonzalez/108 * 20.00 50.00
10 Ben Grieve/100 * 15.00 40.00
11 Todd Helton/101 * 20.00 50.00
12 Richard Hidalgo/380 * 6.00 15.00
13 A.J. Hinch/400 * 6.00 15.00
14 Damian Jackson/15 *
15 Geoff Jenkins 60.00 120.00
16 Derek Jeter SP
17 Chipper Jones/112 * 30.00 80.00
18 Chuck Knoblauch/98 * 12.00 30.00
19 Travis Lee/101 * 10.00 25.00
20 Mike Lowell/450 * 6.00 15.00
21 Greg Maddux/92 * 250.00 400.00
22 Kevin Millwood/395 * 12.50 30.00
23 Magglio Ordonez/420 * 6.00 15.00
24 David Ortiz/393 * 25.00 60.00
25 Rafael Palmeiro/107 * 8.00 20.00
26 Cal Ripken/22 *
27 Alex Rodriguez/23 *
28 Curt Schilling/100 * 50.00 100.00
29 Randall Simon/380 * 6.00 15.00
30 Fernando Tatis/400 * 6.00 15.00
31 Miguel Tejada/375 * 6.00 15.00
32 Robin Ventura/95 * 20.00 50.00
33 Dan Wilson * 15.00 40.00
34 Kerry Wood/373 * 15.00 40.00

1998 Donruss Days

As a special mid-season promotion, Donruss/Leaf distributed these special Donruss Days cards to selected hobby shops in fourteen different areas of the nation. To obtain these cards, collectors had to redeem a special exchange card of which was handed out at local ballparks upon entrance into the stadium. Each hobby shop was supplied with a complete selection of all fourteen players, but received larger supplies of their local stars. Collectors were free to choose any player they wished until supplies ran out. The cards are somewhat similar in design to standard 1998 Donruss but have been upgraded with 20 point cardboard stock and foil fronts. According to Donruss representatives, no more than 10,000 of any of these cards were produced.
COMPLETE SET (14) 6.00 15.00
1 Frank Thomas .30 .75
2 Tony Clark .08 .25
3 Ivan Rodriguez .30 .75
4 David Justice .08 .25
5 Nomar Garciaparra .75 2.00
6 Mark McGwire 1.00 2.50
7 Travis Lee .08 .25
8 Cal Ripken 1.25 3.00
9 Jeff Bagwell .30 .75
10 Barry Bonds .60 1.50
11 Ken Griffey Jr. 1.00 2.50
12 Derek Jeter 1.25 3.00
13 Raul Mondesi .08 .25
14 Greg Maddux .75 2.00

2001 Donruss

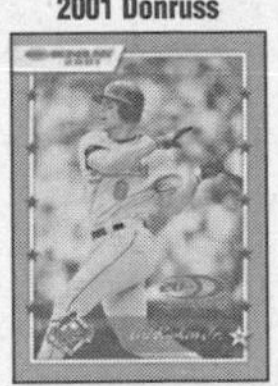

The 2001 Donruss product was released in early May, 2001. The 220-card base set was broken into tiers as follows: Base Veterans (1-150), short-printed Rated Rookies (151-200) serial numbered to 2001, and Fan Club cards (201-220) inserted approximatley one per box. Exchange cards with a redemption deadline of May 1st, 2003 was seeded into packs for card 156 Albert Pujols and 159 Ben Sheets. Each pack contained five cards, and a one card retro pack. Packs carried a suggested retail price of $1.99. Please note that 1999 Retro packs were inserted in Hobby packs, while 2000 Retro packs were inserted into Retail packs. One in every 720 packs contained an exchange card good for a complete set of 2001 Donruss Baseball's Best. One in every 72 packs contained and exchange card good for a complete set of 2001 Donruss the Rookies. The redemption deadline for both exchange cards was January 20th, 2002. The original exchange deadline was November 1st, 2001 but the manufacturer lengthened the redemption period.
COMP.SET w/o SP's (150) 10.00 25.00
COMMON CARD (1-150) .10 .30
COMMON CARD (151-200) 3.00 8.00
151-200 RANDOM INSERTS IN PACKS
151-200 PRINT RUN 2001 SERIAL #'d SETS
COMMON CARD (201-220) 1.00 2.50
FAN CLUB 201-220 APPX. ONE PER BOX
EXCHANGE DEADLINE 05/01/03
BASEBALL'S BEST COUPON 1:720
COUPON EXCHANGE DEADLINE 01/20/02
1 Alex Rodriguez .40 1.00
2 Barry Bonds .75 2.00
3 Cal Ripken 1.00 2.50
4 Chipper Jones .30 .75
5 Derek Jeter .75 2.00
6 Troy Glaus .10 .30
7 Frank Thomas .30 .75
8 Greg Maddux .50 1.25
9 Ivan Rodriguez .20 .50
10 Jeff Bagwell .20 .50
11 Jose Canseco .20 .50
12 Todd Helton .20 .50
13 Ken Griffey Jr. .60 1.50
14 Manny Ramirez Sox .20 .50
15 Mark McGwire .75 2.00
16 Mike Piazza .50 1.25
17 Nomar Garciaparra .50 1.25
18 Pedro Martinez .20 .50
19 Randy Johnson .30 .75
20 Rick Ankiel .10 .30
21 Rickey Henderson .30 .75
22 Roger Clemens .60 1.50
23 Sammy Sosa .30 .75
24 Tony Gwynn .40 1.00
25 Vladimir Guerrero .30 .75
26 Eric Davis .10 .30
27 Roberto Alomar .10 .30
28 Mark Mulder .10 .30
29 Pat Burrell .10 .30
30 Harold Baines .10 .30
31 Carlos Delgado .10 .30
32 J.D. Drew .10 .30
33 Jim Edmonds .10 .30
34 Darin Erstad .10 .30
35 Jason Giambi .10 .30
36 Tom Glavine .20 .50
37 Juan Gonzalez .10 .30
38 Mark Grace .20 .50
39 Shawn Green .10 .30
40 Tim Hudson .10 .30
41 Andruw Jones .20 .50
42 David Justice .10 .30
43 Jeff Kent .10 .30
44 Barry Larkin .20 .50
45 Pokey Reese .10 .30
46 Mike Mussina .20 .50
47 Hideo Nomo .30 .75
48 Rafael Palmeiro .20 .50
49 Adam Piatt .10 .30
50 Scott Rolen .20 .50
51 Gary Sheffield .10 .30
52 Bernie Williams .20 .50
53 Bob Abreu .10 .30
54 Edgardo Alfonzo .10 .30
55 Jermaine Clark RC .20 .50
56 Albert Belle .10 .30
57 Craig Biggio .20 .50
58 Andres Galarraga .10 .30
59 Edgar Martinez .20 .50
60 Fred McGriff .20 .50
61 Magglio Ordonez .10 .30
62 Jim Thome .20 .50
63 Matt Williams .10 .30
64 Kerry Wood .10 .30
65 Moises Alou .10 .30
66 Brady Anderson .10 .30
67 Garret Anderson .10 .30
68 Tony Armas Jr. .10 .30
69 Tony Batista .10 .30
70 Jose Cruz Jr. .10 .30
71 Carlos Beltran .10 .30
72 Adrian Beltre .10 .30
73 Kris Benson .10 .30
74 Lance Berkman .10 .30
75 Kevin Brown .10 .30
76 Jay Buhner .10 .30
77 Jeromy Burnitz .10 .30
78 Ken Caminiti .10 .30
79 Sean Casey .10 .30
80 Luis Castillo .10 .30
81 Eric Chavez .10 .30
82 Jeff Cirillo .10 .30
83 Bartolo Colon .10 .30
84 David Cone .10 .30
85 Freddy Garcia .10 .30
86 Johnny Damon .20 .50
87 Ray Durham .10 .30
88 Jermaine Dye .10 .30
89 Juan Encarnacion .10 .30
90 Terrence Long .10 .30
91 Carl Everett .10 .30
92 Steve Finley .10 .30
93 Cliff Floyd .10 .30
94 Brad Fullmer .10 .30
95 Brian Giles .10 .30
96 Luis Gonzalez .10 .30
97 Rusty Greer .10 .30
98 Jeffrey Hammonds .10 .30
99 Mike Hampton .10 .30
100 Orlando Hernandez .10 .30
101 Richard Hidalgo .10 .30
102 Geoff Jenkins .10 .30
103 Jacque Jones .10 .30
104 Brian Jordan .10 .30
105 Gabe Kapler .10 .30
106 Eric Karros .10 .30
107 Jason Kendall .10 .30
108 Adam Kennedy .10 .30
109 Byung-Hyun Kim .10 .30
110 Ryan Klesko .10 .30
111 Chuck Knoblauch .10 .30
112 Paul Konerko .10 .30
113 Carlos Lee .10 .30
114 Kenny Lofton .10 .30
115 Javy Lopez .10 .30
116 Tino Martinez .20 .50
117 Ruben Mateo .10 .30
118 Kevin Millwood .10 .30
119 Ben Molina .10 .30
120 Raul Mondesi .10 .30
121 Trot Nixon .10 .30
122 John Olerud .10 .30
123 Paul O'Neill .20 .50
124 Chan Ho Park .10 .30
125 Andy Pettitte .20 .50
126 Jorge Posada .20 .50
127 Mark Quinn .10 .30
128 Aramis Ramirez .10 .30
129 Mariano Rivera .30 .75
130 Tim Salmon .20 .50
131 Curt Schilling .10 .30
132 Richie Sexson .10 .30
133 John Smoltz .20 .50
134 J.T. Snow .10 .30
135 Jay Payton .10 .30
136 Shannon Stewart .10 .30
137 B.J. Surhoff .10 .30
138 Mike Sweeney .10 .30
139 Fernando Tatis .10 .30
140 Miguel Tejada .10 .30
141 Jason Varitek .30 .75
142 Greg Vaughn .10 .30
143 Mo Vaughn .10 .30
144 Robin Ventura .10 .30
145 Jose Vidro .10 .30
146 Omar Vizquel .20 .50
147 Larry Walker .10 .30
148 David Wells .10 .30
149 Rondell White .10 .30
150 Preston Wilson .10 .30
151 Brent Abernathy RR 3.00 8.00
152 Cory Aldridge RR RC 3.00 8.00
153 Gene Altman RR RC 3.00 8.00
154 Josh Beckett RR 4.00 10.00
155 Wilson Betemit RR RC 4.00 10.00
156 Albert Pujols RR/500 RC 75.00 200.00
157 Joe Crede RR 4.00 10.00
158 Jack Cust RR 3.00 8.00
159 Ben Sheets RR/500 15.00 40.00
160 Alex Escobar RR 3.00 8.00
161 Adrian Hernandez RR RC 3.00 8.00
162 Pedro Feliz RR 3.00 8.00
163 Nate Frese RR RC 3.00 8.00
164 Carlos Garcia RR RC 3.00 8.00
165 Marcus Giles RR 3.00 8.00
166 Alexis Gomez RR RC 3.00 8.00
167 Jason Hart RR 3.00 8.00
168 Eric Hinske RR RC 4.00 10.00
169 Cesar Izturis RR 3.00 8.00
170 Nick Johnson RR 3.00 8.00
171 Mike Young RR 4.00 10.00
172 Brian Lawrence RR RC 3.00 8.00
173 Steve Lomasney RR 3.00 8.00
174 Nick Maness RR 3.00 8.00
175 Jose Mieses RR RC 3.00 8.00
176 Greg Miller RR RC 3.00 8.00
177 Eric Munson RR 3.00 8.00
178 Xavier Nady RR 3.00 8.00
179 Blaine Neal RR RC 3.00 8.00
180 Abraham Nunez RR 3.00 8.00
181 Jose Ortiz RR 3.00 8.00
182 Jeremy Owens RR RC 3.00 8.00
183 Pablo Ozuna RR 3.00 8.00
184 Corey Patterson RR 3.00 8.00
185 Carlos Pena RR 3.00 8.00
186 Wily Mo Pena RR 3.00 8.00
187 Timo Perez RR 3.00 8.00
188 Adam Pettyjohn RR RC 3.00 8.00
189 Luis Rivas RR 3.00 8.00
190 Jackson Melian RR RC 3.00 8.00
191 Wilken Ruan RR RC 3.00 8.00
192 Duaner Sanchez RR RC 3.00 8.00
193 Alfonso Soriano RR 4.00 10.00
194 Rafael Soriano RR RC 3.00 8.00
195 Ichiro Suzuki RR RC 12.00 30.00
196 Billy Sylvester RR RC 3.00 8.00
197 Juan Uribe RR RC 4.00 10.00
198 Eric Valent RR 3.00 8.00
199 Carlos Valderrama RR RC 3.00 8.00
200 Matt White RR RC 3.00 8.00
201 Alex Rodriguez FC 2.00 5.00
202 Barry Bonds FC 4.00 10.00
203 Cal Ripken FC 5.00 12.00
204 Chipper Jones FC 1.50 4.00
205 Derek Jeter FC 4.00 10.00
206 Troy Glaus FC 1.00 2.50
207 Frank Thomas FC 1.50 4.00
208 Greg Maddux FC 2.50 6.00
209 Ivan Rodriguez FC 1.00 2.50
210 Jeff Bagwell FC 1.00 2.50
211 Todd Helton FC 1.00 2.50
212 Ken Griffey Jr. FC 3.00 8.00
213 Manny Ramirez Sox FC 1.00 2.50
214 Mark McGwire FC 4.00 10.00
215 Mike Piazza FC 2.50 6.00
216 Pedro Martinez FC 1.00 2.50
217 Sammy Sosa FC 1.50 4.00
218 Tony Gwynn FC 2.00 5.00
219 Vladimir Guerrero FC 1.50 4.00
220 Nomar Garciaparra FC 2.50 6.00
NNO BB Best Coupon .75 2.00
NNO The Rookies Coupon .20 .50

2001 Donruss Stat Line Career

*1-150 P/R b/wn 251-400: 2.5X TO 6X
*1-150 P/R b/wn 201-250: 2.5X TO 6X
*1-150 P/R b/wn 151-200: 3X TO 8X
*1-150 P/R b/wn 121 150: 3X TO 8X
*1-150 P/R b/wn 81-120: 4X TO 10X
*1-150 P/R b/wn 66-80: 5X TO 12X
*1-150 P/R b/wn 51-65: 5X TO 12X
*1-150 P/R b/wn 36-50: 6X TO 15X
*1 150 P/R b/wn 26-35: 8X TO 20X
*201-220 P/R b/wn 251-400 .5X TO 1.2X
*201-220 P/R b/wn 201-250 .5X TO 1.2X
*201-220 P/R b/wn 151-200 .6X TO 1.5X
*201-220 P/R b/wn 121-150 .6X TO 1.5X
*201-220 P/R b/wn 81-120 .75X TO 2X
*201-220 P/R b/wn 36-50 1.25X TO 3X
SEE BECKETT.COM FOR PRINT RUNS
NO PRICING ON QTY OF 25 OR LESS
EXCHANGE DEADLINE 05/01/03
152 Cory Aldridge RR/33 4.00 10.00
153 Gene Altman RR/351 .75 2.00
154 Josh Beckett RR/212 1.00 2.50
156 Albert Pujols RR/154 125.00 200.00
157 Joe Crede RR/357 1.25 3.00
158 Jack Cust RR/66 2.00 5.00
159 Ben Sheets RR/159 6.00 15.00
160 Alex Escobar RR/45 3.00 8.00
161 Adrian Hernandez RR/86 2.00 5.00
162 Pedro Feliz RR/286 .75 2.00
163 Nate Frese RR/119 2.00 5.00
164 Carlos Garcia RR/106 2.00 5.00
165 Marcus Giles RR/320 .75 2.00
166 Alexis Gomez RR/34 4.00 10.00
167 Jason Hart RR/303 .75 2.00
168 Eric Hinske RR/332 1.00 2.50
169 Cesar Izturis RR/60 2.50 6.00
170 Nick Johnson RR/308 .75 2.00
171 Mike Young RR/37 5.00 12.00
172 Brian Lawrence RR/281 .75 2.00
173 Steve Lomasney RR/229 1.00 2.50
175 Jose Mieses RR/265 .75 2.00
176 Greg Miller RR/328 .75 2.00
179 Blaine Neal RR/296 .75 2.00
180 Abraham Nunez RR/38 3.00 8.00
182 Jeremy Owens RR/273 .75 2.00
183 Pablo Ozuna RR/333 .75 2.00
185 Carlos Pena RR/52 2.50 6.00
186 Wily Mo Pena RR/114 2.00 5.00
187 Timo Perez RR/49 3.00 8.00
189 Luis Rivas RR/310 .75 2.00
190 Jackson Melian RR/26 4.00 10.00
191 Wilken Ruan RR/215 1.00 2.50
193 Alfonso Soriano RR/50 3.00 8.00
195 Ichiro Suzuki RR/106 60.00 120.00
197 Juan Uribe RR/157 1.25 3.00
198 Eric Valent RR/342 .75 2.00
200 Matt White RR/31 4.00 10.00

2001 Donruss Stat Line Season

*1-150 P/R b/wn 151-200: 3X TO 8X
*1-150 P/R b/wn 121-150: 3X TO 8X
*1-150 P/R b/wn 81-120: 4X TO 10X
*1-150 P/R b/wn 66-80: 5X TO 12X
*1-150 P/R b/wn 51-65: 5X TO 12X
*1-150 P/R b/wn 36-50: 6X TO 15X
*1-150 P/R b/wn 26-35: 8X TO 20X
*201-220 P/R b/wn 151-200 .6X TO 1.5X
*201-220 P/R b/wn 121-150 .6X TO 1.5X
*201-220 P/R b/wn 81-120 .75X TO 2X
*201-220 P/R b/wn 66-80 1X TO 2.5X
*201-220 P/R b/wn 36-50 1.25X TO 3X
*201-220 P/R b/wn 26-35 1.5X TO 4X
SEE BECKETT.COM FOR PRINT RUNS
NO PRICING ON QTY OF 25 OR LESS
151-200 NO PRICING ON QTY OF 25 OR LESS
EXCHANGE DEADLINE 05/01/03
151 Brent Abernathy RR/130 1.50 4.00
152 Cory Aldridge RR/100 2.00 5.00
154 Josh Beckett RR/61 2.50 6.00
155 Wilson Betemit RR/89 6.00 15.00
156B Albert Pujols RR AU 300.00 600.00
158 Jack Cust RR/131 1.50 4.00
159B Ben Sheets RR AU 30.00 60.00
160 Alex Escobar RR/126 1.50 4.00
163 Nate Frese RR/126 1.50 4.00
165 Marcus Giles RR/133 1.50 4.00
166 Alexis Gomez RR/117 2.00 5.00
167 Jason Hart RR/31 4.00 10.00
169 Cesar Izturis RR/95 2.00 5.00
170 Nick Johnson RR/145 1.50 4.00
171 Mike Young RR/155 2.00 5.00
172 Brian Lawrence RR/165 1.25 3.00
174 Nick Maness RR/127 1.50 4.00
179 Blaine Neal RR/65 2.50 6.00
180 Abraham Nunez RR/51 2.50 6.00
185 Carlos Pena RR/117 2.00 5.00
188 Adam Pettyjohn RR/68 2.00 5.00
190 Jackson Melian RR/73 2.00 5.00
191 Wilken Ruan RR/165 1.25 3.00
192 Duaner Sanchez RR/121 1.50 4.00
194 Rafael Soriano RR/90 2.00 5.00
195 Ichiro Suzuki RR/153 50.00 100.00
199 Carlos Valderrama RR/137 1.50 4.00
200 Matt White RR/126 1.50 4.00

2001 Donruss 1999 Retro

Inserted into hobby packs at one per hobby pack, this 100-card insert features cards that Donruss would have released in 1999 had they been producing baseball cards at the time. The set is broken into tiers as follows: Base Veterans (1-80), and Short-printed Prospects (81-100) serial numbered to 1999. Please note that these cards have a 2001 copyright, thus, are listed under the 2001 products.
COMPLETE SET (100) 75.00 150.00
COMP.SET w/o SP's (80) 20.00 50.00
COMMON CARD (1-80) .25 .60
1-80 ONE PER 1999 RETRO HOBBY PACK
COMMON CARD (81-100) 2.00 5.00
81-100 RANDOM IN '99 RETRO HOBBY PACKS
81-100 PRINT RUN 1999 SERIAL #'d SETS
1 Ken Griffey Jr. 1.25 3.00
2 Nomar Garciaparra 1.00 2.50
3 Alex Rodriguez .75 2.00
4 Mark McGwire 1.50 4.00
5 Sammy Sosa .60 1.50
6 Chipper Jones .60 1.50
7 Mike Piazza 1.00 2.50
8 Barry Larkin .40 1.00
9 Andruw Jones .40 1.00
10 Albert Belle .25 .60
11 Jeff Bagwell .40 1.00
12 Tony Gwynn .75 2.00
13 Manny Ramirez .40 1.00
14 Mo Vaughn .25 .60
15 Barry Bonds 1.50 4.00
16 Frank Thomas .60 1.50
17 Vladimir Guerrero .60 1.50
18 Derek Jeter 1.50 4.00
19 Randy Johnson .60 1.50
20 Greg Maddux 1.00 2.50
21 Pedro Martinez .40 1.00
22 Cal Ripken 2.00 5.00
23 Ivan Rodriguez .40 1.00
24 Matt Williams .25 .60
25 Javy Lopez .25 .60
26 Tim Salmon .40 1.00
27 Raul Mondesi .25 .60
28 Todd Helton .40 1.00
29 Magglio Ordonez .25 .60
30 Sean Casey .25 .60
31 Jeromy Burnitz .25 .60
32 Jeff Kent .25 .60
33 Jim Edmonds .25 .60
34 Jim Thome .40 1.00
35 Dante Bichette .25 .60
36 Larry Walker .25 .60
37 Will Clark .40 1.00
38 Omar Vizquel .40 1.00
39 Mike Mussina .40 1.00
40 Eric Karros .25 .60
41 Kenny Lofton .25 .60
42 David Justice .25 .60
43 Craig Biggio .40 1.00
44 J.D. Drew .25 .60
45 Rickey Henderson .60 1.50
46 Bernie Williams .40 1.00
47 Brian Giles .25 .60
48 Paul O'Neill .40 1.00
49 Orlando Hernandez .25 .60
50 Jason Giambi .25 .60
51 Curt Schilling .25 .60
52 Scott Rolen .40 1.00
53 Mark Grace .40 1.00
54 Moises Alou .25 .60
55 Jason Kendall .25 .60
56 Ray Lankford .25 .60
57 Kerry Wood .25 .60
58 Gary Sheffield .25 .60
59 Ruben Mateo .25 .60
60 Darin Erstad .25 .60
61 Troy Glaus .25 .60
62 Jose Canseco .40 1.00
63 Wade Boggs .40 1.00
64 Tom Glavine .40 1.00
65 Gabe Kapler .25 .60
66 Juan Gonzalez .25 .60
67 Rafael Palmeiro .40 1.00
68 Richie Sexson .25 .60
69 Carl Everett .25 .60
70 David Wells .25 .60
71 Carlos Delgado .25 .60
72 Eric Davis .25 .60
73 Shawn Green .25 .60
74 Andres Galarraga .25 .60
75 Edgar Martinez .40 1.00
76 Roberto Alomar .40 1.00
77 John Olerud .25 .60
78 Luis Gonzalez .25 .60
79 Kevin Brown .25 .60
80 Roger Clemens 1.25 3.00
81 Josh Beckett SP 3.00 8.00
82 Alfonso Soriano SP 3.00 8.00
83 Alex Escobar SP 2.00 5.00
84 Pat Burrell SP 2.00 5.00
85 Eric Chavez SP 2.00 5.00
86 Erubiel Durazo SP 2.00 5.00
87 Abraham Nunez SP 2.00 5.00
88 Carlos Pena SP 2.00 5.00
89 Nick Johnson SP 2.00 5.00
90 Eric Munson SP 2.00 5.00
91 Corey Patterson SP 2.00 5.00
92 Wily Mo Pena SP 2.00 5.00
93 Rafael Furcal SP 2.00 5.00
94 Eric Valent SP 2.00 5.00
95 Mark Mulder SP 2.00 5.00
96 Chad Hutchinson SP 2.00 5.00
97 Freddy Garcia SP 2.00 5.00
98 Tim Hudson SP 2.00 5.00
99 Rick Ankiel SP 2.00 5.00
100 Kip Wells SP 2.00 5.00

2001 Donruss 1999 Retro Stat Line Career

*1-80 P/R b/wn 251-400: 1.25X TO 3X
*1-80 P/R b/wn 201-250: 1.25X TO 3X
*1-80 P/R b/wn 151-200: 1.5X TO 4X
*1-80 P/R b/wn 121-150: 1.5X TO 4X
*1-80 P/R b/wn 81-120: 2X TO 5X
*1-80 P/R b/wn 66-80: 2.5X TO 6X
*1-80 P/R b/wn 51-65: 2.5X TO 6X
*1-80 P/R b/wn 36-50: 3X TO 8X
*1-80 P/R b/wn 26-35: 4X TO 10X
SEE BECKETT.COM FOR PRINT RUNS
NO PRICING ON QTY OF 25 OR LESS
81-100 NO PRICING ON QTY OF 25 OR LESS
82 Alfonso Soriano/113 1.50 4.00
83 Alex Escobar/181 1.00 2.50
84 Pat Burrell/303 .75 2.00
85 Eric Chavez/314 .75 2.00
86 Erubiel Durazo/147 1.25 3.00
87 Abraham Nunez/106 1.50 4.00
88 Carlos Pena/46 2.50 6.00
89 Nick Johnson/259 .75 2.00
90 Eric Munson/392 .75 2.00

91 Corey Patterson/117 1.50 4.00
92 Wily Mo Pena/247 .75 2.00
93 Rafael Furcal/137 1.25 3.00
94 Eric Valent/53 2.00 5.00
95 Mark Mulder/340 .75 2.00
97 Freddy Garcia/397 .75 2.00
99 Rick Ankiel/222 .75 2.00
100 Kip Wells/371 .75 2.00

2001 Donruss 1999 Retro Stat Line Season

*1-80 P/R b/wn 251-400: 1.25X TO 3X
*1-80 P/R b/wn 201-250: 1.25X TO 3X
*1-80 P/R b/wn 151-200: 1.5X TO 4X
*1-80 P/R b/wn 121-150: 1.5X TO 4X
*1-80 P/R b/wn 81-120: 2X TO 5X
*1-80 P/R b/wn 66-80: 2.5X TO 6X
*1-80 P/R b/wn 51-65: 2.5X TO 6X
*1-80 P/R b/wn 36-50: 3X TO 8X
*1-80 P/R b/wn 26-35: 4X TO 10X
PLEASE SEE BECKETT.COM FOR PRINT RUNS
NO PRICING ON QTY OF 25 OR LESS
81-100 NO PRICING ON QTY OF 25 OR LESS
81 Josh Beckett/178 1.00 2.50
83 Alex Escobar/27 3.00 8.00
85 Eric Chavez/33 3.00 8.00
87 Abraham Nunez/95 1.50 4.00
88 Carlos Pena/319 .75 2.00
93 Rafael Furcal/88 1.50 4.00
95 Mark Mulder/113 1.50 4.00
96 Chad Hutchinson/51 2.00 5.00
98 Tim Hudson/152 1.00 2.50
100 Kip Wells/135 1.00 2.50

2001 Donruss 1999 Retro Diamond Kings

Randomly inserted into 1999 Retro packs, this 5-card insert set features the "Diamond King" cards that Donruss would have produced had they been producing baseball cards in 1999. Each card is individually serial numbered to 2500.

COMPLETE SET (5) 30.00 60.00
STATED PRINT RUN 2,500 SERIAL #'d SETS
*STUDIO: .75X TO 2X BASIC RETRO DK
STUDIO PRINT RUN 250 SERIAL #'d SETS
1 Scott Rolen 4.00 10.00
2 Sammy Sosa 4.00 10.00
3 Juan Gonzalez 4.00 10.00
4 Ken Griffey Jr. 6.00 15.00
5 Derek Jeter 8.00 20.00

2001 Donruss 2000 Retro

Inserted into retail packs at one per retail pack, this 100-card insert features cards that Donruss would have released in 2000 had they been producing baseball cards at the time. The set is broken into tiers as follows: Base Veterans (1-80), and Short-printed Prospects (81-100) serial numbered to 2000. Please note that these cards have a 2001 copyright, thus, are listed under the 2001 products. Exchange cards originally intended for number 82 C.C. Sabathia and number 95 Ben Sheets were both issued in packs with an expiration date of 05/01/03. It's believed, however, two separate cards were made available for redemption card 95: Ben Sheets and Ichiro Suzuki.

COMPLETE SET (100) 125.00 250.00
COMP.SET w/o SP's (80) 40.00 80.00
COMMON CARD (1-80) .25 .60
1-80 ONE PER 2000 RETRO RETAIL PACK
COMMON CARD (81-100) 2.00 5.00
81-100 RANDOM IN 2000 RETRO RETAIL
81-100 PRINT RUN 2000 SERIAL #'d SETS
1 Vladimir Guerrero .60 1.50
2 Alex Rodriguez .75 2.00
3 Ken Griffey Jr. 1.25 3.00
4 Nomar Garciaparra 1.00 2.50
5 Mike Piazza 1.00 2.50
6 Mark McGwire 1.50 4.00
7 Sammy Sosa .60 1.50
8 Chipper Jones .60 1.50
9 Jim Edmonds .25 .60
10 Tony Gwynn .75 2.00
11 Andruw Jones .40 1.00
12 Albert Belle .25 .60
13 Jeff Bagwell .40 1.00
14 Manny Ramirez .40 1.00
15 Mo Vaughn .25 .60
16 Barry Bonds 1.50 4.00
17 Frank Thomas .60 1.50
18 Ivan Rodriguez .40 1.00
19 Derek Jeter 3.00 8.00
20 Randy Johnson .60 1.50
21 Greg Maddux 1.00 2.50
22 Pedro Martinez .40 1.00
23 Cal Ripken 2.00 5.00
24 Mark Grace .40 1.00
25 Javy Lopez .25 .60
26 Ray Durham .25 .60
27 Todd Helton .40 1.00
28 Magglio Ordonez .25 .60
29 Sean Casey .25 .60
30 Darin Erstad .25 .60
31 Barry Larkin .40 1.00
32 Will Clark .40 1.00
33 Jim Thome .40 1.00
34 Dante Bichette .25 .60
35 Larry Walker .25 .60
36 Ken Caminiti .25 .60
37 Omar Vizquel .40 1.00
38 Miguel Tejada .25 .60
39 Eric Karros .25 .60
40 Gary Sheffield .25 .60
41 Jeff Cirillo .25 .60
42 Rondell White .25 .60
43 Rickey Henderson .60 1.50
44 Bernie Williams .40 1.00
45 Brian Giles .25 .60
46 Paul O'Neill .40 1.00
47 Orlando Hernandez .25 .60
48 Ben Grieve .25 .60
49 Jason Giambi .25 .60
50 Curt Schilling .25 .60
51 Scott Rolen .40 1.00
52 Bobby Abreu .25 .60
53 Jason Kendall .25 .60
54 Fernando Tatis .25 .60
55 Jeff Kent .25 .60
56 Mike Mussina .40 1.00
57 Troy Glaus .25 .60
58 Jose Canseco .40 1.00
59 Wade Boggs .40 1.00
60 Fred McGriff .25 .60
61 Juan Gonzalez .25 .60
62 Rafael Palmeiro .40 1.00
63 Rusty Greer .25 .60
64 Carl Everett .25 .60
65 David Wells .25 .60
66 Carlos Delgado .25 .60
67 Shawn Green .25 .60
68 David Justice .25 .60
69 Edgar Martinez .40 1.00
70 Andres Galarraga .25 .60
71 Roberto Alomar .40 1.00
72 Jermaine Dye .25 .60
73 John Olerud .25 .60
74 Luis Gonzalez .25 .60
75 Craig Biggio .40 1.00
76 Kevin Millwood .25 .60
77 Kevin Brown .25 .60
78 John Smoltz .40 1.00
79 Roger Clemens 1.25 3.00
80 Mike Hampton .25 .60
81 Tomas De La Rosa SP 2.00 5.00
82 C.C. Sabathia SP 6.00 15.00
83 Ryan Christenson SP 2.00 5.00
84 Pedro Feliz SP 2.00 5.00
85 Jose Ortiz SP 2.00 5.00
86 Xavier Nady SP 2.00 5.00
87 Julio Zuleta SP 2.00 5.00
88 Jason Hart SP 2.00 5.00
89 Keith Ginter SP 2.00 5.00
90 Brent Abernathy SP 2.00 5.00
91 Timo Perez SP 2.00 5.00
92 Juan Pierre SP 2.00 5.00
93 Tike Redman SP 2.00 5.00
94 Mike Lamb SP 2.00 5.00
95A Ben Sheets 6.00 15.00
95B Ichiro Suzuki 20.00 50.00
96 Kazuhiro Sasaki SP 2.00 5.00
97 Barry Zito SP 3.00 8.00
98 Adam Bernero SP 2.00 5.00
99 Chad Durbin SP 2.00 5.00
100 Matt Ginter SP 2.00 5.00

2001 Donruss 2000 Retro Stat Line Career

*1-80 P/R b/wn 201-400: 1.2X TO 3X
*1-80 P/R b/wn 121-200: 1.5X TO 4X
*1-80 P/R b/wn 81-120: 2X TO 5X
*1-80 P/R b/wn 51-80: 2.5X TO 6X
*1-80 P/R b/wn 36-50: 3X TO 8X
*1-80 P/R b/wn 26-35: 4X TO 10X
19 Derek Jeter/63 20.00 50.00
81 Tomas De La Rosa/76 2.00 5.00
84 Pedro Feliz/45 2.00 5.00
85 Jose Ortiz/90 1.50 4.00
86 Xavier Nady/175 1.00 2.50
87 Julio Zuleta/295 .75 2.00
89 Keith Ginter/188 1.00 2.50
90 Brent Abernathy/254 .75 2.00
92 Juan Pierre/104 1.50 4.00
93 Tike Redman/151 1.00 2.50
94 Mike Lamb/240 .75 2.00
95A Ben Sheets/300 1.25 3.00
95B Ichiro Suzuki/159 10.00 25.00
96 Kazuhiro Sasaki/229 .75 2.00
98 Adam Bernero/254 .75 2.00
100 Matt Ginter/300 .75 2.00

2001 Donruss 2000 Retro Stat Line Season

*1-80 P/R b/wn 201-400: 1.2X TO 3X
*1-80 P/R b/wn 121-200: 1.5X TO 4X
*1-80 P/R b/wn 81-120: 2X TO 5X
*1-80 P/R b/wn 51-80: 2.5X TO 6X
*1-80 P/R b/wn 36-50: 3X TO 8X
*1-80 P/R b/wn 26-35: 4X TO 10X
19 Derek Jeter/37 30.00 80.00
81 Tomas De La Rosa/122 1.00 2.50
82 C.C. Sabathia/76 10.00 25.00
83 Ryan Christenson/56 2.00 5.00
85 Jose Ortiz/107 1.50 4.00
88 Jason Hart/168 1.00 2.50
90 Brent Abernathy/168 1.00 2.50
92 Juan Pierre/187 1.00 2.50
93 Tike Redman/143 1.00 2.50
94 Mike Lamb/177 1.00 2.50
96 Kazuhiro Sasaki/34 3.00 8.00
97 Barry Zito/97 1.50 4.00
98 Adam Bernero/80 2.00 5.00
100 Matt Ginter/66 2.00 5.00

2001 Donruss 2000 Retro Diamond Kings

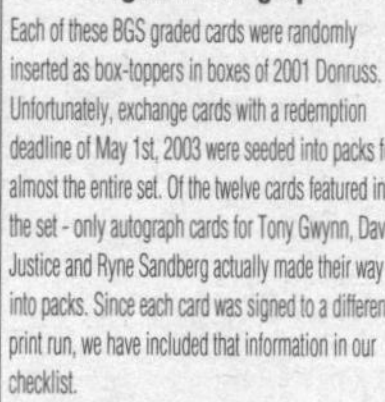

Randomly inserted into 2000 Retro packs, this 5-card insert set features the "Diamond King" cards that Donruss would have produced had they been producing baseball cards in 2000. Each card is individually serial numbered to 2500. Card backs carry a "DK" prefix.

COMPLETE SET (5) 30.00 60.00
STATED PRINT RUN 2,500 SERIAL #'d SETS
*STUDIO: .75X TO 2X BASIC RETRO DK
STUDIO PRINT RUN 250 SERIAL #'d SETS
DK1 Frank Thomas 4.00 10.00
DK2 Greg Maddux 5.00 12.00
DK3 Alex Rodriguez 4.00 10.00
DK4 Jeff Bagwell 4.00 10.00
DK5 Manny Ramirez 4.00 10.00

2001 Donruss 2000 Retro Diamond Kings Studio Series Autograph

An exchange card for an Alex Rodriguez autograph with a redemption deadline of May 1st, 2003 was randomly inserted in 2001 Donruss retro 2000 retail packs. The card is a signed version of A-Rod's basic Diamond King Studio Series insert and only 250 serial numbered copies were produced.

STATED PRINT RUN 50 SERIAL #'d SETS
DK3 Alex Rodriguez 100.00 200.00

2001 Donruss All-Time Diamond Kings

Randomly inserted into 2001 Donruss packs, this 10-card insert features some of the greatest players to have ever grace the front of a "Diamond Kings" card. Card backs carry a "ATDK" prefix. There were 2500 serial numbered sets produced. The Willie Mays and Hank Aaron cards both packed out as exchange cards with a redemption deadline of May 1st, 2003. The Mays card was originally intended to be card number ATDK-9 within this set, but was erroneously numbered ATDK-1 (the same number as the Frank Robinson card) when it was sent out by Donruss. Thus, this set has two card #1's and no card #9.

COMPLETE SET (10) 15.00 40.00
STATED PRINT RUN 2,500 SERIAL #'d SETS
*STUDIO: 1X TO 2.5X BASIC ALL-TIME DK
STUDIO PRINT RUN 200 SERIAL #'d SETS
STUDIO CARDS ARE SERIAL #'d 51-250
ATDK1 Willie Mays 3.00 8.00
ATDK1 Frank Robinson 1.00 2.50
ATDK2 Harmon Killebrew 1.50 4.00
ATDK3 Mike Schmidt 2.50 6.00
ATDK4 Reggie Jackson 1.25 3.00
ATDK5 Nolan Ryan 5.00 12.00
ATDK6 George Brett 3.00 8.00
ATDK7 Tom Seaver 1.00 2.50
ATDK8 Hank Aaron 3.00 8.00
ATDK10 Stan Musial 2.50 6.00

2001 Donruss All-Time Diamond Kings Studio Series Autograph

Randomly inserted into 2001 Donruss packs, this 10-card insert is a complete autographed parallel of the 2001 Donruss All-Time Diamond Kings. Card backs carry a "ATDK" prefix. Please note that the serial #ing for these cards is as follows: cards #'d 1/250 through 50/250 are from this Autograph set and cards #'d 51/250 to 250/250 are from the ATDK Studio Series (non-autographed set). Exchange cards with a redemption deadline of May 1st, 2003 were seeded into packs for Hank Aaron, Willie Mays and Nolan Ryan.

STATED PRINT RUN 50 SERIAL #'d SETS
AU CARDS ARE #'d 1/250 TO 50/250
MAYS & F.ROBINSON BOTH #'d ATDK-1
CARD ATDK-9 DOES NOT EXIST
ATDK1 Willie Mays 150.00 300.00
ATDK1 Frank Robinson 40.00 80.00
ATDK2 Harmon Killebrew 75.00 150.00
ATDK3 Mike Schmidt 100.00 175.00
ATDK4 Reggie Jackson 60.00 120.00
ATDK5 Nolan Ryan 150.00 250.00
ATDK6 George Brett 125.00 200.00
ATDK7 Tom Seaver 50.00 120.00
ATDK8 Hank Aaron 150.00 250.00
ATDK10 Stan Musial 75.00 150.00

2001 Donruss Anniversary Originals Autograph

Each of these BGS graded cards were randomly inserted as box-toppers in boxes of 2001 Donruss. Unfortunately, exchange cards with a redemption deadline of May 1st, 2003 were seeded into packs for almost the entire set. Of the twelve cards featured in the set - only autograph cards for Tony Gwynn, David Justice and Ryne Sandberg actually made their way into packs. Since each card was signed to a different print run, we have included that information in our checklist.

PRINT RUNS B/WN 2-250 COPIES PER
NO PRICING ON QTY OF 25 OR LESS
PRICES REFER TO BGS 7 AND BGS 8 CARDS
8743 Rafael Palmeiro/250 15.00 40.00
8834 Roberto Alomar/250 20.00 50.00
88644 Tom Glavine/250 30.00 60.00

2001 Donruss Bat Kings

Randomly inserted into packs, this 10-card insert features swatches of actual game-used bat. Card backs carry a "BK" prefix. Each card is individually serial numbered to 200. An exchange card with a redemption deadline of May 1st, 2003 was seeded into packs for Hank Aaron.

STATED PRINT RUN 250 SERIAL #'d SETS
BK1 Ivan Rodriguez 10.00 25.00
BK2 Tony Gwynn 15.00 40.00
BK3 Barry Bonds 10.00 25.00
BK4 Todd Helton 10.00 25.00
BK5 Troy Glaus 10.00 25.00
BK6 Mike Schmidt 10.00 25.00
BK7 Reggie Jackson 10.00 25.00
BK8 Harmon Killebrew 10.00 25.00
BK9 Frank Robinson 10.00 25.00
BK10 Hank Aaron 50.00 100.00

2001 Donruss Bat Kings Autograph

Randomly inserted into packs, this 10-card insert features swatches of actual game-used bat, as well as, an autograph from the depicted player. Card backs carry a "BK" prefix. Each card is individually serial numbered to 50. Exchange cards with a redemption deadline of May 1st, 2003 were seeded into packs for Barry Bonds, Troy Glaus, Todd Helton and Ivan Rodriguez. Unfortunately, Donruss was not able to get Barry Bonds to sign his Bat King cards - thus a non-autographed version of Bonds' card was sent out to collectors. Bonds did, however, agree to sign 100 of his vintage Donruss cards (1988 - 25 copies, 1989 -25 copies and 1990 - 50 copies). These 100 cards were stamped with a "Recollection Collection" logo and sent out to collectors - along with the unsigned Bonds Bat King card.

STATED PRINT RUN 50 SERIAL #'d SETS
BK1 Ivan Rodriguez 60.00 120.00
BK2 Tony Gwynn 75.00 150.00
BK3 Barry Bonds NO AUTO 30.00 60.00
BK4 Todd Helton 15.00 40.00
BK5 Troy Glaus 50.00 100.00
BK6 Mike Schmidt 100.00 175.00
BK7 Reggie Jackson 30.00 80.00
BK8 Harmon Killebrew 75.00 150.00
BK9 Frank Robinson 75.00 200.00
BK10 Hank Aaron 175.00 300.00

2001 Donruss Diamond Kings Hawaii Promos

COMPLETE SET (1) 100.00 200.00
HDK1 Alex Rodriguez SAMPLE 3.00 8.00
HDK1 Alex Rodriguez AU/100 100.00 200.00
HDK1 Alex Rodriguez 3.00 8.00

2001 Donruss Diamond Kings

Randomly inserted into 2001 Donruss packs, this 20-card insert features players that are leaders on and off the baseball field. Card backs carry a "DK" prefix. Each card is individually serial numbered to 2500.

COMPLETE SET (20) 30.00 60.00
STATED PRINT RUN 2,500 SERIAL #'d SETS
*STUDIO: .75X TO 2X BASIC DK
STUDIO NO AU PLAYER PRINT 250 #'d SETS
STUDIO AU PLAYER PRINT 200 #'d SETS
DK1 Alex Rodriguez 2.00 5.00
DK2 Cal Ripken 5.00 12.00
DK3 Mark McGwire 2.50 6.00
DK4 Ken Griffey Jr. 3.00 8.00
DK5 Derek Jeter 4.00 10.00
DK6 Nomar Garciaparra 1.00 2.50
DK7 Mike Piazza 1.50 4.00
DK8 Roger Clemens 2.50 6.00
DK9 Greg Maddux 2.50 6.00
DK10 Chipper Jones 1.50 4.00
DK11 Tony Gwynn 1.50 4.00
DK12 Barry Bonds 2.50 6.00
DK13 Sammy Sosa 1.00 2.50
DK14 Vladimir Guerrero 1.50 4.00
DK15 Frank Thomas 1.50 4.00
DK16 Troy Glaus .60 1.50
DK17 Todd Helton 1.00 2.50
DK18 Ivan Rodriguez 1.00 2.50
DK19 Pedro Martinez 1.00 2.50
DK20 Carlos Delgado .60 1.50

2001 Donruss Diamond Kings Studio Series Autograph

Randomly inserted into 2001 Donruss packs, this 11-card insert is a partial parallel of the 2001 Diamond Kings insert. Each of these autographed cards were serial numbered to 50. Exchange cards with a redemption deadline of May 1st, 2003 were seeded into packs for Barry Bonds, Roger Clemens, Troy Glaus, Vladimir Guerrero, Todd Helton, Chipper Jones, Alex Rodriguez and Ivan Rodriguez.

STATED PRINT RUN 50 SERIAL #'d SETS
SKIP-NUMBERED 11 CARD SET
DK1 Alex Rodriguez 25.00 60.00
DK2 Cal Ripken 150.00 300.00
DK8 Roger Clemens 100.00 175.00
DK9 Greg Maddux 100.00 200.00
DK10 Chipper Jones 60.00 150.00
DK11 Tony Gwynn 50.00 120.00
DK14 Vladimir Guerrero 30.00 60.00
DK16 Troy Glaus 12.00 30.00
DK17 Todd Helton 50.00 100.00
DK18 Ivan Rodriguez 40.00 80.00

2001 Donruss Diamond Kings Reprints

Randomly inserted into 2001 Donruss packs, this 20-card insert features reprints of past "Diamond King" cards. Card backs carry a "DKR" prefix. Print runs are listed in our checklist. An exchange card with a redemption deadline of May 1st, 2003 was seeded into packs for Will Clark.

COMPLETE SET (20) 100.00 200.00
STATED PRINT RUNS LISTED BELOW
DKR1 Rod Carew/1982 4.00 10.00
DKR2 Nolan Ryan/1982 10.00 25.00
DKR3 Tom Seaver/1982 4.00 10.00
DKR4 Carlton Fisk/1982 4.00 10.00
DKR5 Reggie Jackson/1983 4.00 10.00
DKR6 Steve Carlton/1983 4.00 10.00
DKR7 Johnny Bench/1983 4.00 10.00
DKR8 Joe Morgan/1983 4.00 10.00
DKR9 Mike Schmidt/1984 8.00 20.00
DKR10 Wade Boggs/1984 4.00 10.00
DKR11 Cal Ripken/1985 10.00 25.00
DKR12 Tony Gwynn/1985 5.00 12.00
DKR13 Andre Dawson/1986 4.00 10.00
DKR14 Ozzie Smith/1987 6.00 15.00
DKR15 George Brett/1987 8.00 20.00
DKR16 Dave Winfield/1987 4.00 10.00
DKR17 Paul Molitor/1988 4.00 10.00
DKR18 Will Clark/1988 6.00 15.00
DKR19 Robin Yount/1989 4.00 10.00
DKR20 Ken Griffey Jr./1989 8.00 20.00

2001 Donruss Diamond Kings Reprints Autographs

Randomly inserted into 2001 Donruss packs, this 20-card insert features autographed reprints of past "Diamond King" cards. Card backs carry a "DKR" prefix. Print runs are listed below. Exchange cards with a redemption deadline of May 1st, 2003 were seeded into packs for Wade Boggs, Rod Carew, Steve Carlton, Will Clark, Andre Dawson, Carlton Fisk, Cal Ripken, Nolan Ryan, Ozzie Smith, Dave Winfield and Robin Yount. Ken Griffey Jr. had a card issued serial #'d of 89 copies but he was the only player featured in the set to not sign any of his cards.

STATED PRINT RUNS LISTED BELOW
DKR1 Rod Carew/82 20.00 50.00
DKR2 Nolan Ryan/82 50.00 120.00
DKR3 Tom Seaver/82 40.00 100.00
DKR4 Carlton Fisk/82 20.00 50.00
DKR5 Reggie Jackson/83 40.00 80.00
DKR6 Steve Carlton/83 10.00 25.00
DKR7 Johnny Bench/83 40.00 80.00
DKR8 Joe Morgan/83 20.00 50.00
DKR9 Mike Schmidt/84 75.00 150.00
DKR10 Wade Boggs/84 20.00 50.00
DKR11 Cal Ripken/85 90.00 150.00
DKR12 Tony Gwynn/85 50.00 100.00
DKR13 Andre Dawson/86 10.00 25.00
DKR14 Ozzie Smith/87 30.00 60.00
DKR15 George Brett/87 60.00 120.00
DKR16 Dave Winfield/87 10.00 25.00
DKR17 Paul Molitor/88 10.00 25.00
DKR18 Will Clark/88 60.00 120.00
DKR19 Robin Yount/89 40.00 80.00
DKR20 Ken Griffey Jr./89 NO AU 20.00 50.00

2001 Donruss Elite Series

Randomly inserted into 2001 Donruss packs, this 20-card insert features many of the Major Leagues elite players. Card backs carry an "ES" prefix. Each card is individually serial numbered to 2500.

COMPLETE SET (20) 75.00 150.00
STATED PRINT RUN 2,500 SERIAL #'d SETS
*DOMINATORS: 6X TO 15X BASIC ELITE
DOMINATORS PRINT RUN 25 SERIAL #'d SETS
ES1 Vladimir Guerrero 2.00 5.00
ES2 Cal Ripken 6.00 15.00
ES3 Greg Maddux 3.00 8.00
ES4 Alex Rodriguez 2.50 6.00
ES5 Barry Bonds 5.00 12.00
ES6 Chipper Jones 2.00 5.00
ES7 Derek Jeter 5.00 12.00
ES8 Ivan Rodriguez 1.50 4.00
ES9 Ken Griffey Jr. 4.00 10.00
ES10 Mark McGwire 5.00 12.00
ES11 Mike Piazza 3.00 8.00
ES12 Nomar Garciaparra 3.00 8.00
ES13 Pedro Martinez 1.50 4.00
ES14 Randy Johnson 2.00 5.00
ES15 Roger Clemens 4.00 10.00
ES16 Sammy Sosa 2.00 5.00
ES17 Tony Gwynn 2.50 6.00
ES18 Darin Erstad 1.50
ES19 Andruw Jones 1.50
ES20 Bernie Williams 1.50

2001 Donruss Jersey King

Randomly inserted into packs, this 10-card ins
features swatches of actual game-used jerseys.
backs carry a "JK" prefix. Each card is individua
serial numbered to 250. Chipper Jones and Ozz
Smith were available only via mail redemption.
Exchange cards with a redemption deadline of M
1st, 2003 for "to be determined" players were se
originally into packs and many months passed
Chipper Jones and Ozzie Smith were revealed a
players that would be used to fulfill these cards

STATED PRINT RUN 250 SERIAL #'d SETS
JK1 Vladimir Guerrero 4.00 1
JK2 Cal Ripken 12.50 3
JK3 Greg Maddux 8.00 2
JK4 Chipper Jones 4.00 1
JK5 Roger Clemens 10.00 2
JK6 George Brett 8.00 2
JK7 Tom Seaver 4.00 1
JK8 Nolan Ryan 12.50 3
JK9 Stan Musial 5.00 1
JK10 Ozzie Smith 6.00 1

2001 Donruss Jersey Kings Autograph

Randomly inserted into packs, this 10-card inse
features swatches of actual game-used jerseys, a
well as, an autograph from the depicted player.
backs carry a "JK" prefix. Each card is individua
serial numbered to 50. The following players pla
did not return their cards in time for inclusion in
packs: Vladimir Guerrero, Cal Ripken, Chipper
Jones, Roger Clemens, Nolan Ryan and Ozzie S
Exchange cards with a redemption deadline of M
1st, 2003 were seeded into packs for these playe

STATED PRINT RUN 50 SERIAL #'d SETS
JK1 Vladimir Guerrero 75.00 15
JK2 Cal Ripken 175.00 30
JK3 Greg Maddux 60.00 15
JK4 Chipper Jones 75.00 15
JK5 Roger Clemens 125.00 20
JK6 George Brett 125.00 20
JK7 Tom Seaver 60.00 15
JK8 Nolan Ryan 150.00 25
JK9 Stan Musial 125.00 20
JK10 Ozzie Smith 75.00 15

2001 Donruss Longball Leade

Randomly inserted into packs, this 20-card insert
features some of the Major Leagues top power
hitters. Card backs carry a "LL" prefix. Each card
individually serial numbered to 1000.

COMPLETE SET (20) 75.00 150
STATED PRINT RUN 1000 SERIAL #'d SETS
SEASONAL PRINT RUN BASED ON '00 HR'S
LL1 Vladimir Guerrero 3.00 8
LL2 Alex Rodriguez 4.00 10
LL3 Barry Bonds 8.00 20.
LL4 Troy Glaus 1.50 4
LL5 Frank Thomas 3.00 8.
LL6 Jeff Bagwell 2.00 5.
LL7 Todd Helton 2.00 5.
LL8 Ken Griffey Jr. 6.00 15.
LL9 Manny Ramirez Sox 2.00 5.
LL10 Mike Piazza 5.00 12.
LL11 Sammy Sosa 3.00 8.
LL12 Carlos Delgado 1.50 4.
LL13 Jim Edmonds 1.50 4.
LL14 Jason Giambi 1.50 4.
LL15 David Justice 1.50 4.
LL16 Rafael Palmeiro 2.00 5.
LL17 Gary Sheffield 1.50 4.
LL18 Jim Thome 2.00 5.
LL19 Tony Batista 1.50 4.
LL20 Richard Hidalgo 1.50 4.0

2001 Donruss Production Line

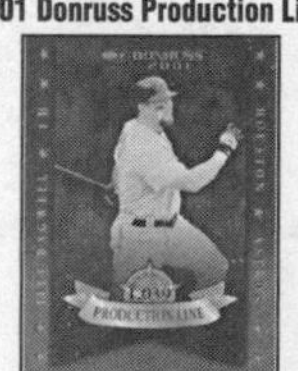

Randomly inserted into packs, this 60-card insert features some of the Major League's most feared hitters. Card backs carry a "PL" prefix. Each card is individually serial numbered to one of three offensi categories: OBP, SLG, and PI. Print runs are listed in our checklist.

COMPLETE SET (60) 200.00 400.0
COMMON SLG (21-40) 1.25 3.0
COMMON PI (41-60) 1.00 2.5
STATED PRINT RUNS LISTED BELOW
*DIE CUT OBP 1-20: .75X TO 2X BASIC PL
*DIE CUT SLG 21-40: 1X TO 2.5X BASIC PL

PI 41-60: 1.25X TO 3X BASIC PL
PRINT RUN 100 SERIAL #'d SETS
n Giambi OBP/476 1.50 4.00
os Delgado OBP/470 1.50 4.00
d Helton OBP/463 2.50 6.00
ny Ramirez Sox OBP/457 2.50 6.00
y Bonds OBP/440 10.00 25.00
Sheffield OBP/438 1.50 4.00
k Thomas OBP/436 4.00 10.00
ar Garciaparra OBP/434 6.00 15.00
n Giles OBP/432 1.50 4.00
gardo Alfonzo OBP/425 1.50 4.00
f Kent OBP/424 1.50 4.00
f Bagwell OBP/424 2.50 6.00
gar Martinez OBP/423 2.50 6.00
ex Rodriguez OBP/420 5.00 12.00
is Castillo OBP/418 1.50 4.00
ill Clark OBP/418 2.50 6.00
rge Posada OBP/417 2.50 6.00
rek Jeter OBP/416 10.00 25.00
b Abreu OBP/416 1.50 4.00
oises Alou OBP/416 1.50 4.00
dd Helton SLG/698 2.00 5.00
anny Ramirez Sox SLG/697 2.00 5.00
arry Bonds SLG/688 8.00 20.00
arlos Delgado SLG/664 1.25 3.00
adimir Guerrero SLG/664 3.00 8.00
son Giambi SLG/647 1.25 3.00
ary Sheffield SLG/643 1.25 3.00
chard Hidalgo SLG/636 1.25 3.00
ammy Sosa SLG/634 3.00 8.00
ank Thomas SLG/625 3.00 8.00
loises Alou SLG/623 1.25 3.00
eff Bagwell SLG/615 2.00 5.00
ike Piazza SLG/614 5.00 12.00
lex Rodriguez SLG/606 4.00 10.00
roy Glaus SLG/604 1.25 3.00
.Garciaparra SLG/599 5.00 12.00
eff Kent SLG/606 1.25 3.00
rian Giles SLG/594 1.25 3.00
eoff Jenkins SLG/588 1.25 3.00
arl Everett SLG/587 1.25 3.00
odd Helton PI/1161 1.50 4.00
Manny Ramirez Sox PI/1154 1.50 4.00
Carlos Delgado PI/1134 1.00 2.50
Barry Bonds PI/1128 6.00 15.00
ason Giambi PI/1123 1.00 2.50
Gary Sheffield PI/1081 1.00 2.50
Vladimir Guerrero PI/1074 2.50 6.00
Frank Thomas PI/1061 2.50 6.00
Sammy Sosa PI/1040 2.50 6.00
Moises Alou PI/1039 1.00 2.50
Jeff Bagwell PI/1039 1.50 4.00
Nomar Garciaparra PI/1033 4.00 10.00
Richard Hidalgo PI/1027 1.00 2.50
Alex Rodriguez PI/1026 3.00 8.00
Brian Giles PI/1026 1.00 2.50
Jeff Kent PI/1020 1.00 2.50
Mike Piazza PI/1012 4.00 10.00
Troy Glaus PI/1008 1.00 2.50
Edgar Martinez PI/1002 1.50 4.00
Jim Edmonds PI/994 1.50 4.00

001 Donruss Recollection Autographs

ifferent players signed cards for this program. Bonds and Alex Rodriguez each signed 100 ards.The Rodriguez cards were randomly ed in packs as exchange cards and the Bonds were issued as concessionary cards for tors that redeemed a Bat Kings Autograph s. According to representatives at Donruss, s refused to sign the memorabilia bat cards, but pprove signing these Recollection buybacks. xchange deadline for the Rodriguez cards was 1st, 2003. The Rodriguez exchange cards that into packs were numbered RC1-RC4, but the l autograph cards are not numbered as such. implicity's sake we have kept the original RC1- checklisting.

D RANDOM INSERTS IN PACKS
DS AVAIL VIA BAT KING AU EXCH
A.ROD'S ARE EXCH CARDS
RICING ON QTY OF 25 OR LESS
A.Rodriguez 01 Retro/30 60.00 120.00
A.Rodriguez 01 Don/40 60.00 120.00

001 Donruss Rookie Reprints

domly inserted into packs, this 40-card insert ures reprinted Donruss rookie cards from the -90s. Card backs carry a "RR" prefix. Please e that there was an error in production, and there two number 39's, no number 40. Print runs are ed in our checklist.

MPLETE SET (40) 150.00 300.00
ATED PRINT RUNS LISTED BELOW
RALLEL PRINT RUN BASED ON RC YEAR
Cal Ripken/1982 10.00 25.00
2 Wade Boggs/1983 2.00 5.00
3 Tony Gwynn/1983 5.00 12.00
4 Ryne Sandberg/1983 6.00 15.00
5 Don Mattingly/1984 10.00 25.00
6 Joe Carter/1984 2.00 5.00
RR7 Roger Clemens/1985 8.00 20.00
RR8 Kirby Puckett/1985 3.00 8.00
RR9 Orel Hershiser/1985 2.00 5.00
RR10 Andres Galarraga/1986 2.00 5.00
RR11 Jose Canseco/1986 2.00 5.00
RR12 Fred McGriff/1986 2.00 5.00
RR13 Paul O'Neill/1986 2.00 5.00
RR14 Mark McGwire/1987 8.00 20.00
RR15 Barry Bonds/1987 8.00 20.00
RR16 Kevin Brown/1987 2.00 5.00
RR17 David Cone/1987 2.00 5.00
RR18 Rafael Palmeiro/1987 2.00 5.00
RR19 Barry Larkin/1987 2.00 5.00
RR20 Bo Jackson/1987 3.00 8.00
RR21 Greg Maddux/1987 5.00 12.00
RR22 Roberto Alomar/1988 2.00 5.00
RR23 Mark Grace/1988 2.00 5.00
RR24 David Wells/1988 2.00 5.00
RR25 Tom Glavine/1988 2.00 5.00
RR26 Matt Williams/1988 2.00 5.00
RR27 Ken Griffey Jr./1989 6.00 15.00
RR28 Randy Johnson/1989 3.00 8.00
RR29 Gary Sheffield/1989 2.00 5.00
RR30 Craig Biggio/1989 2.00 5.00
RR31 Curt Schilling/1989 2.00 5.00
RR32 Larry Walker/1990 2.00 5.00
RR33 Bernie Williams/1990 2.00 5.00
RR34 Sammy Sosa/1990 3.00 8.00
RR35 Juan Gonzalez/1990 2.00 5.00
RR36 David Justice/1990 2.00 5.00
RR37 Ivan Rodriguez/1991 2.00 5.00
RR38 Jeff Bagwell/1991 2.00 5.00
RR39 Jeff Kent/1992 2.00 5.00
RR39 Manny Ramirez/1992 2.00 5.00

2001 Donruss Rookie Reprints Autograph

Randomly inserted into packs, this 26-card skip-numbered insert features autographed reprinted Donruss rookie cards from the 80's-90s. Card backs carry a "RR" prefix. Print runs are listed in our checklist. Nearly all of these cards packed out in the form of exchange cards - of which carried a May 1st, 2003 redemption deadline. Only autograph cards for Joe Carter, Tony Gwynn, David Justice, Greg Maddux and Ryne Sandberg actually made it into packs. Card RR24 was originally announced as a 1988 Donruss David Wells Reprint (with a print run of 88 copies) but due to contractual problems with the athlete the manufacturer substituted Diamondbacks outfielder Luis Gonzalez (reprinting 91 copies of his 1991 Donruss the Rookies RC).

STATED PRINT RUNS LISTED BELOW
SKIP-NUMBERED 18 CARD SET
RR1 Cal Ripken/82 200.00 400.00
RR2 Wade Boggs/83 30.00 60.00
RR3 Tony Gwynn/83 50.00 100.00
RR4 Ryne Sandberg/83 125.00 250.00
RR5 Don Mattingly/84 60.00 120.00
RR6 Joe Carter/84 15.00 40.00
RR7 Roger Clemens/85 175.00 300.00
RR8 Kirby Puckett/85 100.00 200.00
RR9 Orel Hershiser/85 30.00 60.00
RR10 Andres Galarraga/86 30.00 60.00
RR15 Barry Bonds/87 150.00 300.00
RR16 Kevin Brown/87 15.00 40.00
RR17 David Cone/87 15.00 40.00
RR18 Rafael Palmeiro/87 30.00 60.00
RR20 Bo Jackson/87 100.00 200.00
RR21 Greg Maddux/87 75.00 200.00
RR22 Roberto Alomar/88 30.00 60.00
RR24 Luis Gonzalez/91 15.00 40.00
RR25 Tom Glavine/88 50.00 120.00
RR28 Randy Johnson/89 150.00 300.00
RR29 Gary Sheffield/89 40.00 80.00
RR31 Curt Schilling/89 30.00 80.00
RR35 Juan Gonzalez/90 30.00 60.00
RR36 David Justice/90 15.00 40.00
RR37 Ivan Rodriguez/91 30.00 60.00
RR39 Manny Ramirez/92 75.00 150.00

2001 Donruss Rookies

This 110-card redemption set was issued via coupons in the 2001 Donruss product. The coupons were issued in packs at a rate of 1:72 and were good for a complete factory sealed set of 2001 Donruss the Rookies. Collector's were to send the coupon along with $24.99 to Playoff by January 20th, 2002. The set also came with one additional Diamond King card (106-110).

COMP.FACT.SET (106) 30.00 60.00
COMP.SET w/o SP's (105) 10.00 25.00
ONE SET PER COUPON VIA MAIL
COUPON ODDS 1:72 '01 DONRUSS PACKS
COUPON EXCHANGE DEADLINE 01/20/02
R1 Adam Dunn .30 .75
R2 Ryan Dresse RC .30 .75
R3 Bud Smith RC .15 .40
R4 Tsuyoshi Shinjo RC .30 .75
R5 Roy Oswalt .40 1.00
R6 Wilmy Caceres RC .20 .50
R7 Willie Harris RC .20 .50
R8 Andres Torres RC .15 .40
R9 Brandon Knight RC .15 .40
R10 Horacio Ramirez RC .30 .75
R11 Benito Baez RC .15 .40
R12 Jeremy Affeldt RC .20 .50
R13 Ryan Jensen RC .20 .50
R14 Casey Fossum RC .15 .40
R15 Ramon Vazquez RC .20 .50
R16 Dustan Mohr RC .20 .50
R17 Saul Rivera RC .20 .50
R18 Zach Day RC .20 .50
R19 Erik Hiljus RC .15 .40
R20 Cesar Crespo RC .15 .40
R21 Wilson Guzman RC .20 .50
R22 Travis Hafner RC 2.00 5.00
R23 Grant Balfour RC .15 .40
R24 Johnny Estrada RC .30 .75
R25 Morgan Ensberg RC .75 2.00
R26 Jack Wilson RC .30 .75
R27 Aubrey Huff .20 .50
R28 Endy Chavez RC .30 .75
R29 Delvin James RC .15 .40
R30 Michael Cuddyer .15 .40
R31 Jason Michaels RC .20 .50
R32 Martin Vargas RC .20 .50
R33 Donaldo Mendez RC .15 .40
R34 Jorge Julio RC .20 .50
R35 Tim Spooneybarger RC .20 .50
R36 Kurt Ainsworth .15 .40
R37 Josh Fogg RC .20 .50
R38 Brian Reith RC .15 .40
R39 Rick Bauer RC .15 .40
R40 Tim Redding .15 .40
R41 Erick Almonte RC .15 .40
R42 Juan A.Pena RC .15 .40
R43 Ken Harvey .15 .40
R44 David Brous RC .15 .40
R45 Kevin Olsen RC .20 .50
R46 Henry Mateo RC .15 .40
R47 Nick Neugebauer .15 .40
R48 Mike Penney RC .20 .50
R49 Jay Gibbons RC .30 .75
R50 Tim Christman RC .15 .40
R51 Brandon Duckworth RC .15 .40
R52 Brett Jodie RC .15 .40
R53 Christian Parker RC .15 .40
R54 Carlos Hernandez .15 .40
R55 Brandon Larson RC .15 .40
R56 Nick Punto RC .20 .50
R57 Elpidio Guzman RC .15 .40
R58 Joe Beimel RC .15 .40
R59 Junior Spivey RC .30 .75
R60 Will Ohman RC .20 .50
R61 Brandon Lyon RC .15 .40
R62 Stubby Clapp RC .15 .40
R63 Justin Duchscherer RC .20 .50
R64 Jimmy Rollins .20 .50
R65 Delvin Williams RC .15 .40
R66 Craig Monroe RC 1.00 2.50
R67 Jose Acevedo RC .15 .40
R68 Jason Jennings .15 .40
R69 Josh Phelps .15 .40
R70 Brian Roberts RC .75 2.00
R71 Claudio Vargas RC .15 .40
R72 Adam Johnson .15 .40
R73 Bart Miadich RC .15 .40
R74 Juan Rivera .15 .40
R75 Brad Voyles RC .15 .40
R76 Nate Cornejo .15 .40
R77 Juan Moreno RC .20 .50
R78 Brian Rogers RC .15 .40
R79 Ricardo Rodriguez RC .20 .50
R80 Geronimo Gil RC .15 .40
R81 Joe Kennedy RC .30 .75
R82 Kevin Joseph RC .20 .50
R83 Josue Perez RC .20 .50
R84 Victor Zambrano RC .30 .75
R85 Josh Towers RC .30 .75
R86 Mike Rivera RC .20 .50
R87 Mark Prior RC 2.00 5.00
R88 Juan Cruz RC .20 .50
R89 Dewon Brazelton RC .20 .50
R90 Angel Berroa RC .30 .75
R91 Mark Teixeira RC 4.00 10.00
R92 Cody Ransom RC .15 .40
R93 Angel Santos RC .15 .40
R94 Corky Miller RC .15 .40
R95 Brandon Berger RC .15 .40
R96 Corey Patterson UPD .15 .40
R97 Albert Pujols UPD 10.00 25.00
R98 Josh Beckett UPD .30 .75
R99 C.C. Sabathia UPD .20 .50
R100 Alfonso Soriano UPD .30 .75
R101 Ben Sheets UPD .30 .75
R102 Rafael Soriano UPD .20 .50
R103 Wilson Betemit UPD .75 2.00
R104 Ichiro Suzuki UPD 5.00 12.00
R105 Jose Ortiz UPD .15 .40

2001 Donruss Rookies Diamond Kings

Inserted one per Donruss Rookies set, these five cards feature some of the leading 2001 rookies in a special Diamond King format.

COMPLETE SET (5) 30.00 60.00
ONE DK PER ROOKIES FACTORY SET
RDK1 C.C. Sabathia DK 3.00 8.00
RDK2 Tsuyoshi Shinjo DK 4.00 10.00
RDK3 Albert Pujols DK 12.00 30.00
RDK4 Roy Oswalt DK 4.00 10.00
RDK5 Ichiro Suzuki DK 10.00 25.00

2002 Donruss Samples

*SAMPLES: 1.5X TO 4X BASIC CARDS
ONE PER SEALED BBCM 204
*GOLD SAMPLES: 1.5X TO 4X LISTED PRICE

2002 Donruss

This 220 card set was issued in four card packs which had an SRP of $1.99 per pack and were issued 24 to a box and 20 boxes to a case. Cards numbered 151-200 featured leading rookie prospect and were inserted at stated odds of one in four. Card numbered 201-220 were Fan Club subset cards and were inserted at stated odds of one in eight.

COMPLETE SET (220) 50.00 100.00
COMP.SET w/o SP'S (150) 10.00 25.00
COMMON CARD (1-150) .10 .30
COMMON CARD (151-200) 1.25 3.00
151-200 STATED ODDS 1:4
COMMON CARD (201-220) .60 1.50
201-220 STATED ODDS 1:8
1 Alex Rodriguez .40 1.00
2 Barry Bonds .75 2.00
3 Derek Jeter .75 2.00
4 Robert Fick .10 .30
5 Juan Pierre .10 .30
6 Torii Hunter .10 .30
7 Todd Helton .20 .50
8 Cal Ripken 1.00 2.50
9 Manny Ramirez .20 .50
10 Johnny Damon .20 .50
11 Mike Piazza .50 1.25
12 Nomar Garciaparra .50 1.25
13 Pedro Martinez .20 .50
14 Brian Giles .10 .30
15 Albert Pujols .60 1.50
16 Roger Clemens .60 1.50
17 Sammy Sosa .30 .75
18 Vladimir Guerrero .30 .75
19 Tony Gwynn .40 1.00
20 Pat Burrell .10 .30
21 Carlos Delgado .10 .30
22 Tino Martinez .20 .50
23 Jim Edmonds .10 .30
24 Jason Giambi .10 .30
25 Tom Glavine .20 .50
26 Mark Grace .20 .50
27 Tony Armas Jr. .10 .30
28 Andruw Jones .20 .50
29 Ben Sheets .10 .30
30 Jeff Kent .10 .30
31 Barry Larkin .20 .50
32 Joe Mays .10 .30
33 Mike Mussina .20 .50
34 Hideo Nomo .30 .75
35 Rafael Palmeiro .20 .50
36 Scott Brosius .10 .30
37 Scott Rolen .20 .50
38 Gary Sheffield .10 .30
39 Bernie Williams .20 .50
40 Bob Abreu .10 .30
41 Edgardo Alfonzo .10 .30
42 C.C. Sabathia .10 .30
43 Jeremy Giambi .10 .30
44 Craig Biggio .20 .50
45 Andres Galarraga .10 .30
46 Edgar Martinez .20 .50
47 Fred McGriff .20 .50
48 Magglio Ordonez .10 .30
49 Jim Thome .20 .50
50 Matt Williams .10 .30
51 Kerry Wood .10 .30
52 Moises Alou .10 .30
53 Brady Anderson .10 .30
54 Garret Anderson .10 .30
55 Juan Gonzalez .10 .30
56 Bret Boone .10 .30
57 Jose Cruz Jr. .10 .30
58 Carlos Beltran .10 .30
59 Adrian Beltre .10 .30
60 Joe Kennedy .10 .30
61 Lance Berkman .10 .30
62 Kevin Brown .10 .30
63 Tim Hudson .10 .30
64 Jeromy Burnitz .10 .30
65 Jarrod Washburn .10 .30
66 Sean Casey .10 .30
67 Eric Chavez .10 .30
68 Bartolo Colon .10 .30
69 Freddy Garcia .10 .30
70 Jermaine Dye .10 .30
71 Terrence Long .10 .30
72 Cliff Floyd .10 .30
73 Luis Gonzalez .10 .30
74 Ichiro Suzuki .60 1.50
75 Mike Hampton .10 .30
76 Richard Hidalgo .10 .30
77 Geoff Jenkins .10 .30
78 Gabe Kapler .10 .30
79 Ken Griffey Jr. .60 1.50
80 Jason Kendall .10 .30
81 Josh Towers .10 .30
82 Ryan Klesko .10 .30
83 Paul Konerko .10 .30
84 Carlos Lee .10 .30
85 Kenny Lofton .10 .30
86 Josh Beckett .10 .30
87 Raul Mondesi .10 .30
88 Trot Nixon .10 .30
89 John Olerud .10 .30
90 Paul O'Neill .20 .50
91 Chan Ho Park .10 .30
92 Andy Pettitte .20 .50
93 Jorge Posada .20 .50
94 Mark Quinn .10 .30
95 Aramis Ramirez .10 .30
96 Curt Schilling .10 .30
97 Richie Sexson .10 .30
98 John Smoltz .20 .50
99 Wilson Betemit .10 .30
100 Shannon Stewart .10 .30
101 Alfonso Soriano .10 .30
102 Mike Sweeney .10 .30
103 Miguel Tejada .10 .30
104 Greg Vaughn .10 .30
105 Robin Ventura .10 .30
106 Jose Vidro .10 .30
107 Larry Walker .10 .30
108 Preston Wilson .10 .30
109 Corey Patterson .10 .30
110 Mark Mulder .10 .30
111 Tony Clark .10 .30
112 Roy Oswalt .10 .30
113 Jimmy Rollins .10 .30
114 Kazuhiro Sasaki .10 .30
115 Barry Zito .10 .30
116 Javier Vazquez .10 .30
117 Mike Cameron .10 .30
118 Phil Nevin .10 .30
119 Bud Smith .10 .30
120 Cristian Guzman .10 .30
121 Al Leiter .10 .30
122 Brad Radke .10 .30
123 Bobby Higginson .10 .30
124 Robert Person .10 .30
125 Adam Dunn .10 .30
126 Ben Grieve .10 .30
127 Rafael Furcal .10 .30
128 Jay Gibbons .10 .30
129 Paul LoDuca .10 .30
130 Wade Miller .10 .30
131 Tsuyoshi Shinjo .10 .30
132 Eric Milton .10 .30
133 Rickey Henderson .30 .75
134 Roberto Alomar .20 .50
135 Darin Erstad .10 .30
136 J.D. Drew .10 .30
137 Shawn Green .10 .30
138 Randy Johnson .30 .75
139 Austin Kearns .10 .30
140 Jose Canseco .20 .50
141 Jeff Bagwell .20 .50
142 Greg Maddux .50 1.25
143 Mark Buehrle .10 .30
144 Ivan Rodriguez .20 .50
145 Frank Thomas .30 .75
146 Rich Aurilia .10 .30
147 Troy Glaus .10 .30
148 Ryan Dempster .10 .30
149 Chipper Jones .30 .75
150 Matt Morris .10 .30
151 Marlon Byrd RR 1.25 3.00
152 Ben Howard RR RC 1.25 3.00
153 Brandon Backe RR RC 1.25 3.00
154 Jorge De La Rosa RR RC 1.25 3.00
155 Corky Miller RR 1.25 3.00
156 Dennis Tankersley RR 1.25 3.00
157 Kyle Kane RR RC 1.25 3.00
158 Justin Duchscherer RR 1.25 3.00
159 Brian Mallette RR RC 1.25 3.00
160 Chris Baker RR RC 1.25 3.00
161 Jason Lane RR 1.25 3.00
162 Hee Seop Choi RR 1.25 3.00
163 Juan Cruz RR 1.25 3.00
164 Rodrigo Rosario RR RC 1.25 3.00
165 Matt Guerrier RR 1.25 3.00
166 Anderson Machado RR RC 1.25 3.00
167 Geronimo Gil RR 1.25 3.00
168 Dewon Brazelton RR 1.25 3.00
169 Mark Prior RR 1.50 4.00
170 Bill Hall RR 1.25 3.00
171 Jorge Padilla RR RC 1.25 3.00
172 Jose Cueto RR RC 1.25 3.00
173 Allan Simpson RR RC 1.25 3.00
174 Doug Devore RR RC 1.25 3.00
175 Josh Pearce RR 1.25 3.00
176 Angel Berroa RR 1.25 3.00
177 Steve Bechler RR RC 1.25 3.00
178 Antonio Perez RR 1.25 3.00
179 Mark Teixeira RR 1.50 4.00
180 Erick Almonte RR 1.25 3.00
181 Orlando Hudson RR 1.25 3.00
182 Michael Rivera RR 1.25 3.00
183 Raul Chavez RR RC 1.25 3.00
184 Juan Pena RR 1.25 3.00
185 Travis Hughes RR RC 1.25 3.00
186 Ryan Ludwick RR 1.25 3.00
187 Ed Rogers RR 1.25 3.00
188 Andy Pratt RR RC 1.25 3.00
189 Nick Neugebauer RR 1.25 3.00
190 Tom Shearn RR RC 1.25 3.00
191 Eric Cyr RR 1.25 3.00
192 Victor Martinez RR 1.50 4.00
193 Brandon Berger RR 1.25 3.00
194 Erik Bedard RR 1.25 3.00
195 Fernando Rodney RR 1.25 3.00
196 Joe Thurston RR 1.25 3.00
197 John Buck RR 1.25 3.00
198 Jeff Deardorff RR 1.25 3.00
199 Ryan Jamison RR 1.25 3.00
200 Alfredo Amezaga RR 1.25 3.00
201 Luis Gonzalez FC .60 1.50
202 Roger Clemens FC 2.00 5.00
203 Barry Zito FC .60 1.50
204 Bud Smith FC .60 1.50
205 Magglio Ordonez FC .60 1.50
206 Kerry Wood FC .60 1.50
207 Freddy Garcia FC .60 1.50
208 Adam Dunn FC .60 1.50
209 Curt Schilling FC .60 1.50
210 Lance Berkman FC .60 1.50
211 Rafael Palmeiro FC .60 1.50
212 Ichiro Suzuki FC 2.00 5.00
213 Bob Abreu FC .60 1.50
214 Mark Mulder FC .60 1.50
215 Roy Oswalt FC .60 1.50
216 Mike Sweeney FC .60 1.50
217 Paul LoDuca FC .60 1.50
218 Aramis Ramirez FC .60 1.50
219 Randy Johnson FC 1.00 2.50
220 Albert Pujols FC 2.00 5.00

2002 Donruss Autographs

Inserted randomly in packs, these 19 cards feature signatures of players in the Fan Club subset. Since the cards have different stated print runs, we have listed those print runs in our checklist. Cards with a print run of 25 or fewer are not priced due to market scarcity.

RANDOM INSERTS IN PACKS
SEE BECKETT.COM FOR PRINT RUNS
SKIP-NUMBERED 19-CARD SET
NO PRICING ON QTY OF 25 OR LESS
203 Barry Zito FC/200 15.00 40.00
204 Bud Smith FC/200 10.00 25.00
205 Magglio Ordonez FC/200 10.00 25.00
206 Kerry Wood FC/200 15.00 40.00
207 Freddy Garcia FC/200 10.00 25.00
208 Adam Dunn FC/200 15.00 40.00
210 Lance Berkman FC/175 15.00 40.00
213 Bob Abreu FC/200 10.00 25.00
214 Mark Mulder FC/200 10.00 25.00
215 Roy Oswalt FC/200 10.00 25.00
216 Mike Sweeney FC/200 10.00 25.00
217 Paul LoDuca FC/200 10.00 25.00
218 Aramis Ramirez FC/200 10.00 25.00
220 Albert Pujols FC/200 150.00 250.00

2002 Donruss Stat Line Career

*1-150 P/R b/wn 251-400: 2.5X TO 6X
*1-150 P/R b/wn 201-250: 2.5X TO 6X
*1-150 P/R b/wn 151-200: 3X TO 8X
*1-150 P/R b/wn 121-150: 3X TO 8X
*1-150 P/R b/wn 81-120: 4X TO 10X
*1-150 P/R b/wn 66-80: 5X TO 12X
*1-150 P/R b/wn 51-65: 5X TO 12X
*1-150 P/R b/wn 36-50: 6X TO 15X
*201-220 P/R b/wn 251-400 .5X TO 1.2X
*201-220 P/R b/wn 201-250 .6X TO 1.5X
*201-220 P/R b/wn 151-200 .75X TO 2X
*201-220 P/R b/wn 121-150 1X TO 2.5X
*201-220 P/R b/wn 51-65 1.5X TO 4X
SEE BECKETT.COM FOR PRINT RUNS
NO PRICING ON QTY OF 25 OR LESS
151 Marlon Byrd RR/232 1.00 2.50
152 Ben Howard RR/283 .75 2.00
153 Brandon Backe RR/94 2.00 5.00
154 Jorge De La Rosa RR/84 2.50 6.00
155 Corky Miller RR/184 1.25 3.00
156 Dennis Tankersley RR/253 .75 2.00
157 Kyle Kane RR/179 1.25 3.00
159 Brian Mallette RR/273 .75 2.00
160 Chris Baker RR/270 .75 2.00
161 Jason Lane RR/302 .75 2.00
162 Hee Seop Choi RR/286 .75 2.00
163 Juan Cruz RR/322 .75 2.00
164 Rodrigo Rosario RR/313 .75 2.00
165 Matt Guerrier RR/280 .75 2.00
166 Anderson Machado RR/252 .75 2.00
167 Geronimo Gil RR/293 .75 2.00
168 Dewon Brazelton RR/335 .75 2.00
169 Mark Prior RR/303 1.25 3.00
170 Bill Hall RR/373 .75 2.00
171 Jorge Padilla RR/273 .75 2.00
172 Jose Cueto RR/156 1.25 3.00
173 Allan Simpson RR/204 1.00 2.50
174 Doug Devore RR/287 .75 2.00
175 Josh Pearce RR/315 .75 2.00
176 Angel Berroa RR/268 .75 2.00
178 Antonio Perez RR/143 1.50 4.00
179 Mark Teixeira RR/165 2.00 5.00
181 Orlando Hudson RR/283 .75 2.00
182 Michael Rivera RR/333 .75 2.00
183 Raul Chavez RR/253 .75 2.00
184 Juan Pena RR/293 .75 2.00
185 Travis Hughes RR/174 1.25 3.00
186 Ryan Ludwick RR/264 .75 2.00
187 Ed Rogers RR/270 .75 2.00
188 Andy Pratt RR/203 1.00 2.50
190 Tom Shearn RR/251 .75 2.00
191 Eric Cyr RR/161 1.25 3.00
192 Victor Martinez RR/305 1.25 3.00
193 Brandon Berger RR/313 .75 2.00
194 Erik Bedard RR/279 .75 2.00
195 Fernando Rodney RR/309 .75 2.00
196 Joe Thurston RR/284 .75 2.00
197 John Buck RR/271 .75 2.00
198 Jeff Deardorff RR/201 1.00 2.50
199 Ryan Jamison RR/273 .75 2.00
200 Alfredo Amezaga RR/290 .75 2.00

2002 Donruss Stat Line Season

*1-150 P/R b/wn 151-200: 3X TO 8X
*1-150 P/R b/wn 121-150: 3X TO 8X
*1-150 P/R b/wn 81-120: 4X TO 10X
*1-150 P/R b/wn 66-80: 5X TO 12X
*1-150 P/R b/wn 51-65: 5X TO 12X
*1-150 P/R b/wn 36-50: 6X TO 15X
*1-150 P/R b/wn 26-35: 8X TO 20X
*201-220 P/R b/wn 81-120 1.25X TO 3X
*201-220 P/R b/wn 66-80 1.5X TO 4X
*201-220 P/R b/wn 51-65 1.5X TO 4X
*201-220 P/R b/wn 36-50 2X TO 5X
*201-220 P/R b/wn 26-35 2.5X TO 6X
SEE BECKETT.COM FOR PRINT RUNS
NO PRICING ON QTY OF 25 OR LESS
151 Marlon Byrd RR/89 2.00 5.00
152 Ben Howard RR/29 4.00 10.00
153 Brandon Backe RR/39 3.00 8.00
154 Jorge De La Rosa RR/32 4.00 10.00
156 Dennis Tankersley RR/30 4.00 10.00
157 Kyle Kane RR/75 2.50 6.00
159 Brian Mallette RR/94 2.00 5.00
160 Chris Baker RR/121 1.50 4.00
161 Jason Lane RR/38 3.00 8.00
162 Hee Seop Choi RR/45 3.00 8.00
163 Juan Cruz RR/39 3.00 8.00
164 Rodrigo Rosario RR/131 1.50 4.00
165 Matt Guerrier RR/118 2.00 5.00
166 Anderson Machado RR/36 3.00 8.00
170 Bill Hall RR/65 2.50 6.00
171 Jorge Padilla RR/66 2.50 6.00
172 Jose Cueto RR/62 2.50 6.00
173 Allan Simpson RR/77 2.50 6.00
174 Doug Devore RR/74 2.50 6.00
175 Josh Pearce RR/132 1.50 4.00
176 Angel Berroa RR/63 2.50 6.00
177 Steve Bechler RR/135 1.50 4.00
178 Antonio Perez RR/143 1.50 4.00
181 Orlando Hudson RR/79 2.50 6.00
184 Juan Pena RR/106 2.00 5.00
185 Travis Hughes RR/86 2.00 5.00
186 Ryan Ludwick RR/103 2.00 5.00
187 Ed Rogers RR/54 2.50 6.00
188 Andy Pratt RR/132 1.50 4.00
190 Tom Shearn RR/136 1.50 4.00
191 Eric Cyr RR/131 1.50 4.00
192 Victor Martinez RR/57 4.00 10.00
194 Erik Bedard RR/137 1.50 4.00
195 Fernando Rodney RR/52 2.50 6.00
196 Joe Thurston RR/46 3.00 8.00
197 John Buck RR/73 2.50 6.00
198 Jeff Deardorff RR/100 2.00 5.00
199 Ryan Jamison RR/95 2.00 5.00
200 Alfredo Amezaga RR/37 3.00 8.00

2002 Donruss All-Time Diamond Kings

Randomly inserted in packs, these 10 cards feature legendary baseball superstars reproduced on conventional stock with bronze foil. These cards have a stated print run of 2,500 copies.

STATED PRINT RUN 2500 SERIAL #'d SETS
*STUDIO: 1X TO 2.5X BASIC ALL-TIME DK
STUDIO PRINT RUN 250 SERIAL #'d SETS
1 Ted Williams 6.00 15.00
2 Cal Ripken 12.50 30.00
3 Lou Gehrig 6.00 15.00
4 Babe Ruth 10.00 25.00
5 Roberto Clemente 8.00 20.00
6 Don Mattingly 10.00 25.00
7 Kirby Puckett 4.00 10.00
8 Stan Musial 6.00 15.00
9 Yogi Berra 4.00 10.00
10 Ernie Banks 4.00 10.00

2002 Donruss Bat Kings

Randomly inserted in packs, these five cards feature a mix of active and retired superstars along with a sliver of each player's game-used bat. The active

players have a stated print run of 250 copies while the retired players have a stated print run of 125 copies.
1-3 PRINT RUN 250 SERIAL #'d SETS
4-5 PRINT RUN 125 SERIAL #'d SETS
*STUDIO 1-3: .75X TO 2X BASIC BAT KING
STUDIO 1-3 PRINT RUN 50 SERIAL #'d SETS
STUDIO 4-5 PRINT RUN 25 SERIAL #'d SETS
1 Jason Giambi 6.00 15.00
2 Alex Rodriguez 10.00 25.00
3 Mike Piazza 10.00 25.00
4 Roberto Clemente/125 25.00 60.00
5 Babe Ruth/125 50.00 100.00

2002 Donruss Diamond Kings Inserts

Randomly inserted in packs, these 20 cards feature leading players with silver foil stamping and stated sequential serial numbering to 2500.
STATED PRINT RUN 2500 SERIAL #'d SETS
*STUDIO: .75X TO 2X BASIC DK'S
STUDIO PRINT RUN 250 SERIAL #'d SETS
DK1 Nomar Garciaparra 5.00 12.00
DK2 Shawn Green 4.00 10.00
DK3 Randy Johnson 4.00 10.00
DK4 Derek Jeter 8.00 20.00
DK5 Carlos Delgado 4.00 10.00
DK6 Roger Clemens 6.00 15.00
DK7 Jeff Bagwell 4.00 10.00
DK8 Vladimir Guerrero 4.00 10.00
DK9 Luis Gonzalez 4.00 10.00
DK10 Mike Piazza 5.00 12.00
DK11 Ichiro Suzuki 6.00 15.00
DK12 Pedro Martinez 4.00 10.00
DK13 Todd Helton 4.00 10.00
DK14 Sammy Sosa 4.00 10.00
DK15 Ivan Rodriguez 4.00 10.00
DK16 Barry Bonds 8.00 20.00
DK17 Albert Pujols 6.00 15.00
DK18 Jim Thome 4.00 10.00
DK19 Alex Rodriguez 4.00 10.00
DK20 Jason Giambi 4.00 10.00

2002 Donruss Elite Series

Randomly inserted in packs, these 20 cards feature some of today's most storied performers. These cards are printed on metalized film board and are sequentially numbered to 2,500.
RANDOM INSERTS IN PACKS
STATED PRINT RUN 2500 SERIAL #'d SETS
1 Barry Bonds 5.00 12.00
2 Lance Berkman 1.50 4.00
3 Jason Giambi 1.50 4.00
4 Nomar Garciaparra 3.00 8.00
5 Curt Schilling 1.50 4.00
6 Vladimir Guerrero 2.00 5.00
7 Shawn Green 1.50 4.00
8 Troy Glaus 1.50 4.00
9 Jeff Bagwell 1.50 4.00
10 Manny Ramirez 1.50 4.00
11 Eric Chavez 1.50 4.00
12 Carlos Delgado 1.50 4.00
13 Mike Sweeney 1.50 4.00
14 Todd Helton 1.50 4.00
15 Luis Gonzalez 1.50 4.00
16 Enos Slaughter LGD 1.50 4.00
17 Frank Robinson LGD 1.50 4.00
17A Frank Robinson LGD AU/375 10.00 25.00
18 Bob Gibson LGD 1.50 4.00
19 Warren Spahn LGD 1.50 4.00
20 Whitey Ford LGD 1.50 4.00

2002 Donruss Elite Series Signatures

Randomly inserted in packs, these 18 cards feature players who signed cards for the 2002 Donruss Elite product. These cards have different print runs and we have notated that information in our checklist.
RANDOM INSERTS IN PACKS
STATED PRINT RUNS LISTED BELOW
SKIP-NUMBERED 18-CARD SET
NO PRICING ON QTY OF 25 OR LESS
16 Enos Slaughter LGD/250 15.00 40.00
17 Frank Robinson LGD/250 12.00 30.00
18 Bob Gibson LGD/250 15.00 40.00
19 Warren Spahn LGD/250 15.00 40.00
20 Whitey Ford LGD/250 15.00 40.00

2002 Donruss Jersey Kings

Randomly inserted in packs, these 15 cards feature game-worn jersey swatches of a mix all-time greats and active superstars. The active players have a stated print run of 250 serial numbered sets while the retired players have a stated print run of 125 sets.
1-12 PRINT RUN 250 SERIAL #'d SETS
13-15 PRINT RUN 125 SERIAL #'d SETS
*STUDIO 1-12: .75X TO 2X BASIC JSY KINGS
STUDIO 1-12 PRINT RUN 50 SERIAL #'d SETS
STUDIO 13-15 PRINT RUN 25 SERIAL #'d SETS
STUDIO 13-15 TOO SCARCE TO PRICE
1 Alex Rodriguez 5.00 12.00
2 Jason Giambi 1.50 4.00
3 Carlos Delgado 1.50 4.00
4 Barry Bonds 6.00 15.00
5 Randy Johnson 4.00 10.00
6 Jim Thome 2.50 6.00
7 Shawn Green 1.50 4.00
8 Pedro Martinez 2.50 6.00
9 Jeff Bagwell 2.50 6.00
10 Vladimir Guerrero 2.50 6.00
11 Ivan Rodriguez 2.50 6.00
12 Nomar Garciaparra 2.50 6.00
13 Don Mattingly/125 10.00 25.00
14 Ted Williams/125 10.00 25.00
15 Lou Gehrig/125 75.00 150.00

2002 Donruss Longball Leaders

Randomly inserted in packs, these 20 cards feature the majors most powerful hitters and they are featured on metalized film board and have a stated print run of 1,000 sequentially numbered sets.
STATED PRINT RUN 1000 SERIAL #'d SETS
SEASONAL PRINT RUN BASED ON '01 HR'S
1 Barry Bonds 8.00 20.00
2 Sammy Sosa 3.00 8.00
3 Luis Gonzalez 1.50 4.00
4 Alex Rodriguez 4.00 10.00
5 Shawn Green 1.50 4.00
6 Todd Helton 2.00 5.00
7 Jim Thome 2.00 5.00
8 Rafael Palmeiro 2.00 5.00
9 Richie Sexson 1.50 4.00
10 Troy Glaus 1.50 4.00
11 Manny Ramirez 2.00 5.00
12 Phil Nevin 1.50 4.00
13 Jeff Bagwell 2.00 5.00
14 Carlos Delgado 1.50 4.00
15 Jason Giambi 1.50 4.00
16 Chipper Jones 3.00 8.00
17 Larry Walker 1.50 4.00
18 Albert Pujols 6.00 15.00
19 Brian Giles 1.50 4.00
20 Bret Boone 1.50 4.00

2002 Donruss Production Line

Randomly inserted in packs, these 60 cards feature the msot productive sluggers in three categories: On-Base Percentage, Slugging Percentage and OPS. Cards numbered 1-20 feature On-Base Percentage, while cards numbered 21-40 feature Slugging Percentage and cards numbered 41-60 feature OPS. Since all the cards have different stated print runs, we have listed that information next to the card in our checklist.
COMMON OBP (1-20) 1.50 4.00
COMMON SLG (21-40) 1.25 3.00
COMMON OPS (41-60) 1.00 2.50
STATED PRINT RUNS LISTED BELOW
*DIE CUT OBP 1-20: .75X TO 2X BASIC PL
*DIE CUT SLG 21-40: 1X TO 2.5X BASIC PL
*DIE CUT OPS 41-60: 1.25X TO 3X BASIC PL
DIE CUT PRINT RUN 100 SERIAL #'d SETS
DC's ARE 1ST 100 #'d OF EACH PLAYER
1 Barry Bonds OBP/415* 10.00 25.00
2 Jason Giambi OBP/377* 1.50 4.00
3 Larry Walker OBP/349* 1.50 4.00
4 Sammy Sosa OBP/337* 4.00 10.00
5 Todd Helton OBP/332* 2.50 6.00
6 Lance Berkman OBP/330* 1.50 4.00
7 Luis Gonzalez OBP/329* 1.50 4.00
8 Chipper Jones OBP/327* 4.00 10.00
9 Edgar Martinez OBP/323* 2.50 6.00
10 Gary Sheffield OBP/317* 1.50 4.00
11 Jim Thome OBP/316* 2.50 6.00
12 Roberto Alomar OBP/315* 2.50 6.00
13 J.D. Drew OBP/314* 1.50 4.00
14 Jim Edmonds OBP/310* 1.50 4.00
15 Carlos Delgado OBP/308* 1.50 4.00
16 Manny Ramirez OBP/305* 2.50 6.00
17 Brian Giles OBP/304* 1.50 4.00
18 Albert Pujols OBP/303* 8.00 20.00
19 John Olerud OBP/301* 1.50 4.00
20 Alex Rodriguez OBP/299* 5.00 12.00
21 Barry Bonds SLG/763* 8.00 20.00
22 Sammy Sosa SLG/637* 4.00 10.00
23 Luis Gonzalez SLG/588* 1.25 3.00
24 Todd Helton SLG/685* 2.00 5.00
25 Larry Walker SLG/562* 1.25 3.00
26 Jason Giambi SLG/560* 1.25 3.00
27 Jim Thome SLG/524* 2.00 5.00
28 Alex Rodriguez SLG/522* 4.00 10.00
29 Lance Berkman SLG/520* 1.25 3.00
30 J.D. Drew SLG/513* 1.25 3.00
31 Albert Pujols SLG/510* 6.00 15.00
32 Manny Ramirez SLG/509* 2.00 5.00
33 Chipper Jones SLG/505* 3.00 8.00
34 Shawn Green SLG/498* 1.25 3.00
35 Brian Giles SLG/490* 1.25 3.00
36 Juan Gonzalez SLG/490* 1.25 3.00
37 Phil Nevin SLG/488* 1.25 3.00
38 Gary Sheffield SLG/483* 1.25 3.00
39 Bret Boone SLG/478* 1.25 3.00
40 Cliff Floyd SLG/478* 1.25 3.00
41 Barry Bonds OPS/1278* 6.00 15.00
42 Sammy Sosa OPS/1074* 4.00 10.00
43 Jason Giambi OPS/1037* 1.00 2.50
44 Todd Helton OPS/1017* 1.50 4.00
45 Luis Gonzalez OPS/1017* 1.00 2.50
46 Larry Walker OPS/1011* 1.00 2.50
47 Lance Berkman OPS/950* 1.00 2.50
48 Jim Thome OPS/940* 1.50 4.00
49 Chipper Jones OPS/932* 2.50 6.00
50 J.D. Drew OPS/927* 1.00 2.50
51 Alex Rodriguez OPS/921* 3.00 8.00
52 Manny Ramirez OPS/914* 1.50 4.00
53 Albert Pujols OPS/913* 5.00 12.00
54 Gary Sheffield OPS/900* 1.00 2.50
55 Brian Giles OPS/894* 1.00 2.50
56 Phil Nevin OPS/876* 1.00 2.50
57 Jim Edmonds OPS/874* 1.00 2.50
58 Shawn Green OPS/870* 1.00 2.50
59 Cliff Floyd OPS/868* 1.00 2.50
60 Edgar Martinez OPS/866* 1.50 4.00

2002 Donruss Recollection Autographs

Randomly inserted in packs, these 47 cards feature players who signed repurchased copies of their original cards for inclusion in the 2002 Donruss set. Since each player signed a different amount of cards, we have noted that information in our checklist. Please note that due to market scarcity, not all cards can be priced.
RANDOM INSERTS IN PACKS
STATED PRINT RUNS LISTED BELOW
NO PRICING ON QTY OF 40 OR LESS
8 Gary Carter 87/100 10.00 25.00
9 Gary Carter 89/100 10.00 25.00
24 Steve Garvey 87/75 8.00 20.00
46 Tom Seaver 87/60 30.00 80.00
47 Don Sutton 87/200 10.00 25.00

2002 Donruss Rookie Year Materials Bats

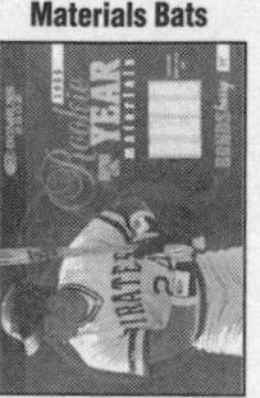

Randomly inserted into packs, these four cards feature a sliver of a game-used bat from the player's rookie season which includes silver holo-foil and are sequentially numbered a stated print run of 250 sequentially numbered sets.
STATED PRINT RUN 250 SERIAL #'d SETS
ERA PRINT RUNS BASED ON ROOKIE YR
1 Barry Bonds 20.00 50.00
2 Cal Ripken 15.00 40.00
3 Kirby Puckett 20.00 50.00
4 Johnny Bench 15.00 40.00

2002 Donruss Rookie Year Materials Bats ERA

These cards parallel the "Rookie Year Material Bats" insert set. These cards have gold holo-foil and have a stated print run sequentially numbered to the player's debut year. Since those years are all different, we have notated that information in our checklist.
RANDOM INSERTS IN PACKS
STATED PRINT RUNS LISTED BELOW
1 Barry Bonds/86 20.00 50.00
2 Cal Ripken/81 10.00 25.00
3 Kirby Puckett/84 25.00 50.00
4 Johnny Bench/68 40.00 80.00

2002 Donruss Rookie Year Materials Jersey

Randomly inserted into packs, these four cards feature a swatch of a game-used jersey from the player's rookie season which includes silver holo-foil and are sequentially numbered a stated print run of either 250 or 50 sequentially numbered sets. The active players have the print run of 250 while the retired players have the print run of 50 sets.
RANDOM INSERTS IN PACKS
1-4 PRINT RUN 250 SERIAL #'d SETS
5-6 PRINT RUN 50 SERIAL #'d SETS
1 Nomar Garciaparra 10.00 25.00
2 Randy Johnson 10.00 25.00
3 Ivan Rodriguez 10.00 25.00
4 Vladimir Guerrero 10.00 25.00
5 Stan Musial/50 40.00 80.00
6 Yogi Berra/50 40.00 80.00

2002 Donruss Rookie Year Materials Jersey Numbers

These cards parallel the "Rookie Year Material Jerseys" insert set. These cards have gold holo-foil and have a stated print run sequentially numbered to the player's jersey number his rookie season. We have notated that specific stated print information in our checklist.

2002 Donruss Rookies

This 110 card set was released in December, 2002. These cards were issued in five card packs which came 24 packs to a box and 16 boxes to a case with an SRP of $3.29 per pack. This set features the top rookies and prospects of the 2002 season.
COMPLETE SET (110) 10.00 25.00
1 Kazuhisa Ishii RC .20 .50
2 P.J. Bevis RC .15 .40
3 Jason Simontacchi RC .15 .40
4 John Lackey .08 .25
5 Travis Driskill RC .15 .40
6 Carl Sadler RC .15 .40
7 Tim Kalita RC .15 .40
8 Nelson Castro RC .15 .40
9 Francis Beltran RC .15 .40
10 So Taguchi RC .20 .50
11 Ryan Bukvich RC .15 .40
12 Brian Fitzgerald RC .15 .40
13 Kevin Frederick RC .15 .40
14 Chone Figgins RC .60 1.50
15 Marlon Byrd .08 .25
16 Ron Calloway RC .15 .40
17 Jason Lane .15 .40
18 Satoru Komiyama RC .15 .40
19 John Ennis RC .15 .40
20 Juan Brito RC .15 .40
21 Gustavo Chacin RC .30 .75
22 Josh Bard RC .15 .40
23 Brett Myers .15 .40
24 Mike Smith RC .15 .40
25 Eric Hinske .08 .25
26 Jake Peavy .20 .50
27 Todd Donovan RC .15 .40
28 Luis Ugueto RC .15 .40
29 Corey Thurman RC .15 .40
30 Takahito Nomura RC .15 .40
31 Andy Shibilo RC .15 .40
32 Mike Crudale RC .15 .40
33 Earl Snyder RC .15 .40
34 Brian Tallet RC .15 .40
35 Miguel Asencio RC .15 .40
36 Felix Escalona RC .15 .40
37 Drew Henson .08 .25
38 Steve Kent RC .15 .40
39 Rene Reyes RC .15 .40
40 Edwin Almonte RC .15 .40
41 Chris Snelling RC .25 .60
42 Franklyn German RC .15 .40
43 Jeriome Robertson RC .15 .40
44 Colin Young RC .15 .40
45 Jeremy Lambert RC .15 .40
46 Kirk Saarloos RC .15 .40
47 Matt Childers RC .15 .40
48 Justin Wayne .08 .25
49 Jose Valverde RC .15 .40
50 Wily Mo Pena .15 .40
51 Victor Alvarez RC .15 .40
52 Julius Matos RC .15 .40
53 Aaron Cook RC .15 .40
54 Jeff Austin RC .15 .40
55 Adrian Burnside RC .15 .40
56 Brandon Puffer RC .15 .40
57 Jeremy Hill RC .15 .40
58 Jaime Cerda RC .15 .40
59 Aaron Guiel RC .15 .40
60 Ron Chiavacci .08 .25
61 Kevin Cash RC .15 .40
62 Elio Serrano RC .15 .40
63 Julio Mateo RC .15 .40
64 Cam Esslinger RC .15 .40
65 Ken Huckaby RC .15 .40
66 Will Nieves RC .15 .40
67 Luis Martinez RC .15 .40
68 Scotty Layfield RC .15 .40
69 Jeremy Guthrie RC .30 .75
70 Hansel Izquierdo RC .15 .40
71 Shane Nance RC .15 .40
72 Jeff Baker RC .40 1.00
73 Cliff Bartosh RC .15 .40
74 Mitch Wylie RC .15 .40
75 Oliver Perez RC .30 .75
76 Matt Thornton RC .15 .40
77 John Foster RC .15 .40
78 Joe Borchard .08 .25
79 Eric Junge RC .15 .40
80 Jorge Sosa RC .20 .50
81 Runelvys Hernandez RC .15 .40
82 Kevin Mench .08 .25
83 Ben Kozlowski RC .15 .40
84 Trey Hodges RC .15 .40
85 Reed Johnson RC .30 .75
86 Eric Eckenstahler RC .15 .40
87 Franklin Nunez RC .15 .40
88 Victor Martinez .30 .75
89 Kevin Gryboski RC .15 .40
90 Jason Jennings .08 .25
91 Jim Rushford RC .15 .40
92 Jeremy Ward RC .15 .40
93 Adam Walker RC .15 .40
94 Freddy Sanchez RC .75 2.00
95 Wilson Valdez RC .15 .40
96 Lee Gardner RC .15 .40
97 Eric Good RC .15 .40
98 Hank Blalock .20 .50
99 Mark Corey RC .15 .40
100 Jason Davis RC .15 .40
101 Mike Gonzalez RC .15 .40
102 David Ross RC .25 .60
103 Tyler Yates RC .15 .40
104 Cliff Lee RC 1.50 4.00
105 Mike Moriarty RC .15 .40
106 Josh Hancock RC .20 .50
107 Jason Beverlin RC .15 .40
108 Clay Condrey RC .15 .40
109 Shawn Sedlacek RC .15 .40
110 Sean Burroughs .08 .25

2002 Donruss Rookies Autographs

Randomly inserted into packs, this is a partial parallel to the Donruss Rookies set. Each players signed between 15 and 100 cards for insertion in this product and cards with a stated print run of 25 or fewer are not priced due to market scarcity.
STATED PRINT RUNS LISTED BELOW
NO PRICING ON QTY OF 25 OR LESS
2 P.J. Bevis/50 10.00 25.00
9 Francis Beltran/100 4.00 10.00
13 Kevin Frederick/100 4.00 10.00
14 Chone Figgins/100 10.00 25.00
15 Marlon Byrd/100 4.00 10.00
17 Jason Lane/100 6.00 15.00
19 John Ennis/100 4.00 10.00
22 Josh Bard/100 4.00 10.00
25 Eric Hinske/100 4.00 10.00
28 Luis Ugueto/100 4.00 10.00
29 Corey Thurman/100 4.00 10.00
30 Takahito Nomura/100 10.00 25.00
33 Earl Snyder/100 4.00 10.00
34 Brian Tallet/100 4.00 10.00
37 Drew Henson/50 6.00 15.00
39 Rene Reyes/50 10.00 25.00
40 Edwin Almonte/50 10.00 25.00
41 Chris Snelling/50 12.50 30.00
42 Franklyn German/100 4.00 10.00
45 Jeremy Lambert/100 4.00 10.00
46 Kirk Saarloos/50 6.00 15.00
47 Matt Childers/100 4.00 10.00
50 Wily Mo Pena/100 6.00 15.00
51 Victor Alvarez/100 4.00 10.00
61 Kevin Cash/100 4.00 10.00
62 Elio Serrano/100 4.00 10.00
64 Cam Esslinger/100 4.00 10.00
69 Jeremy Guthrie/100 6.00 15.00
71 Shane Nance/100 4.00 10.00
72 Jeff Baker/100 10.00 25.00
76 Matt Thornton/100 4.00 10.00
78 Joe Borchard/100 4.00 10.00
82 Kevin Mench/100 6.00 15.00
83 Ben Kozlowski/100 4.00 10.00
84 Trey Hodges/100 4.00 10.00
85 Reed Johnson/100 6.00 15.00
88 Victor Martinez/100 15.00 40.00
90 Jason Jennings/100 4.00 10.00
95 Wilson Valdez/100 4.00 10.00
97 Eric Good/100 4.00 10.00
98 Hank Blalock/100 6.00 15.00
104 Cliff Lee/100 20.00 50.00
110 Sean Burroughs/50 6.00 15.00

2002 Donruss Rookies Crusade

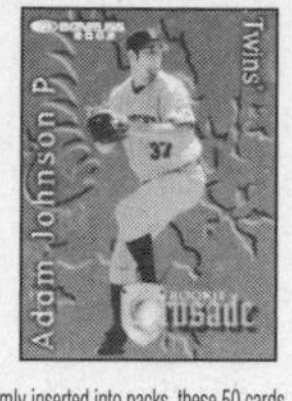

Randomly inserted into packs, these 50 cards, which were printed on metalized holo-foil board, were printed to a stated print run of 1500 serial numbered sets.
STATED PRINT RUN 1500 SERIAL #'d SETS
1 Corky Miller 1.50 4.00
2 Jack Cust 1.50 4.00
3 Erik Bedard 1.50 4.00
4 Andres Torres 1.50 4.00
5 Geronimo Gil 1.50 4.00
6 Rafael Soriano 1.50 4.00
7 Johnny Estrada 1.50 4.00
8 Steve Bechler 1.50 4.00
9 Adam Johnson 1.50 4.00
10 So Taguchi 1.50 4.00
11 Dee Brown 1.50 4.00
12 Kevin Frederick 1.50 4.00
13 Allan Simpson 1.50 4.00
14 Ricardo Rodriguez 1.50 4.00
15 Jason Hart 1.50 4.00
16 Matt Childers 1.50 4.00
17 Jason Jennings 1.50 4.00
18 Anderson Machado 1.50 4.00
19 Fernando Rodney 1.50 4.00
20 Brandon Larson 1.50 4.00
21 Satoru Komiyama 1.50 4.00
22 Francis Beltran 1.50 4.00
23 Joe Thurston 1.50 4.00
24 Josh Pearce 1.50 4.00
25 Carlos Hernandez 1.50 4.00
26 Ben Howard 1.50 4.00
27 Wilson Valdez 1.50 4.00
28 Victor Alvarez 1.50 4.00
29 Cesar Izturis 1.50 4.00
30 Endy Chavez 1.50 4.00
31 Michael Cuddyer 1.50 4.00
32 Bobby Hill 1.50 4.00
33 Willie Harris 1.50 4.00
34 Joe Crede 1.50 4.00
35 Jorge Padilla 1.50 4.00
36 Brandon Backe 1.50 4.00
37 Franklyn German 1.50 4.00
38 Xavier Nady 1.50 4.00
39 Raul Chavez 1.50 4.00
40 Shane Nance 1.50 4.00
41 Brandon Claussen 1.50 4.00
42 Tom Shearn 1.50 4.00
43 Freddy Sanchez 3.00 8.00
44 Chone Figgins 2.00 5.00
45 Cliff Lee 3.00 8.00
46 Brian Mallette 1.50 4.00
47 Mike Rivera 1.50 4.00
48 Elio Serrano 1.50 4.00
49 Rodrigo Rosario 1.50 4.00
50 Earl Snyder 1.50 4.00

2002 Donruss Rookies Crusade Autographs

These 49 cards basically parallel the Rookies Crusade set. These cards were issued to a stated print run of anywhere from 15 to 500 copies per. Cards with a print run of 25 or fewer are not priced due to market scarcity.
COMMON CARD p/r 300+ 4.00 10.00
COMMON ROOKIE p/r 300+ 4.00 10.00
COMMON CARD p/r 150-250 4.00 10.00
COMMON CARD p/r 100 4.00 10.00
STATED PRINT RUNS LISTED BELOW
NO PRICING ON QTY OF 25 OR LESS
1 Corky Miller/500 4.00 10.00
2 Jack Cust/500 4.00 10.00
3 Erik Bedard/100 4.00 10.00
4 Andres Torres/500 4.00 10.00
5 Geronimo Gil/500 4.00 10.00
6 Rafael Soriano/500 4.00 10.00
7 Johnny Estrada/400 4.00 10.00
8 Steve Bechler/500 4.00 10.00
9 Adam Johnson/500 4.00 10.00
11 Dee Brown/500 4.00 10.00
12 Kevin Frederick/150 4.00 10.00
13 Allan Simpson/150 4.00 10.00
14 Ricardo Rodriguez/500 4.00 10.00
15 Jason Hart/500 4.00 10.00
16 Matt Childers/150 4.00
17 Jason Jennings/500 4.00
18 Anderson Machado/500 4.00
19 Fernando Rodney/500 4.00
20 Brandon Larson/400 4.00
22 Francis Beltran/500 4.00
23 Joe Thurston/500 4.00
24 Josh Pearce/500 4.00
25 Carlos Hernandez/500 4.00
26 Ben Howard/500 4.00
27 Wilson Valdez/500 4.00
28 Victor Alvarez/500 4.00
29 Cesar Izturis/500 4.00
30 Endy Chavez/500 4.00
31 Michael Cuddyer/375 4.00
32 Bobby Hill/250 4.00
33 Willie Harris/300 4.00
34 Joe Crede/100 4.00
35 Jorge Padilla/475 4.00
36 Brandon Backe/350 6.00
37 Franklyn German/500 4.00
38 Xavier Nady/500 4.00
39 Raul Chavez/500 4.00
40 Shane Nance/500 4.00
41 Brandon Claussen/150 4.00
42 Tom Shearn/500 4.00
44 Chone Figgins/500 6.00
45 Cliff Lee/500 15.00
46 Brian Mallette/150 4.00
47 Mike Rivera/400 4.00
48 Elio Serrano/500 4.00
49 Rodrigo Rosario/100 4.00
50 Earl Snyder/100 4.00

2002 Donruss Rookies Phen

Randomly inserted into packs, these 25 cards, are set on shimmering double rainbow holo-fo board were sequentially numbered to 1000 ser numbered sets.
RANDOM INSERTS IN PACKS
STATED PRINT RUN 1000 SERIAL #'d SETS
1 Kazuhisa Ishii 2.00
2 Eric Hinske 2.00
3 Jason Lane 2.00
4 Victor Martinez 3.00
5 Mark Prior 2.00
6 Antonio Perez 2.00
7 John Buck 2.00
8 Joe Borchard 2.00
9 Alexis Gomez 2.00
10 Sean Burroughs 2.00
11 Carlos Pena 2.00
12 Bill Hall 2.00
13 Alfredo Amezaga 2.00
14 Ed Rogers 2.00
15 Mark Teixeira 3.00
16 Chris Snelling 2.50
17 Nick Johnson 2.00
18 Angel Berroa 2.00
19 Orlando Hudson 2.00
20 Drew Henson 2.00
21 Austin Kearns 2.00
22 Dewon Brazelton 2.00
23 Dennis Tankersley 2.00
24 Josh Beckett 2.00
25 Marlon Byrd 2.00

2002 Donruss Rookies Pheno Autographs

These cards parallel the Phenoms insert set. Eac these cards were issued to a stated print run of between 25 and 500 signed copies. As the Ishii w produced to a stated print run of 25 sets, no pric is provided for that card.
COMMON CARD p/r 300+ 4.00 1
COMMON CARD p/r 150-250 4.00 1
STATED PRINT RUNS LISTED BELOW
NO PRICING ON QTY OF 25 OR LESS
2 Eric Hinske/500 4.00 1
3 Jason Lane/500 6.00 15
4 Victor Martinez/225 10.00 25
5 Mark Prior/100 10.00 25
6 Antonio Perez/500 4.00 10
7 John Buck/100 4.00 10
8 Joe Borchard/100 4.00 10
9 Alexis Gomez/400 4.00 10
10 Sean Burroughs/150 4.00 10
11 Carlos Pena/150 4.00 10
12 Bill Hall/200 6.00 15
13 Alfredo Amezaga/500 4.00 10
14 Ed Rogers/500 4.00 10
15 Mark Teixeira/100 10.00 25
16 Chris Snelling/100 8.00 20
17 Nick Johnson/250 6.00 15
18 Angel Berroa/500 4.00 10
19 Orlando Hudson/400 4.00 10
20 Drew Henson/500 4.00 10
21 Austin Kearns/75 4.00 10
22 Dewon Brazelton/350 4.00 10
23 Dennis Tankersley/100 4.00 10
24 Josh Beckett/125 10.00 25
25 Marlon Byrd/500 4.00 10

2002 Donruss Rookies ecollection Autographs

y inserted into packs, these 55 cards feature m the 2001 and 2002 Donruss Rookie set re "bought-back" by Donruss/Playoff for n in this product. These cards were then y the player. Due to market scarcity, no s provided for these cards.

2003 Donruss Samples

LES: 1.5X TO 4X BASIC CARDS
R BBCM MAGAZINE

2003 Donruss

0 card set was released in December, 2002. was issued in 13 card packs with an SRP of which were packed 24 packs to a box and 20 o a case. Subsets in this set include cards red Diamond Kings (1-20) and Rated Rookies). For the first time since Donruss/Playoff ed to card production, this was a baseball set t short printed basc cards.

LETE SET (400)	25.00	50.00
MON CARD (71-400)	.10	.30
MON CARD (1-20)	.10	.30
MON CARD (21-70)	.20	.50
imir Guerrero DK	.20	.50
k Jeter DK	.75	2.00
n Dunn DK	.20	.50
g Maddux DK	.40	1.00
ce Berkman DK	.20	.50
ro Suzuki DK	.40	1.00
e Piazza DK	.30	.75
Rodriguez DK	.40	1.00
Glavine DK	.20	.50
ndy Johnson DK	.30	.75
mar Garciaparra DK	.20	.50
son Giambi DK	.12	.30
mmy Sosa DK	.30	.75
rry Zito DK	.20	.50
hipper Jones DK	.30	.75
agglio Ordonez DK	.20	.50
rry Walker DK	.20	.50
fonso Soriano DK	.20	.50
urt Schilling DK	.20	.50
rry Bonds DK	.50	1.25
e Borchard RR	.20	.50
hris Snelling RR	.20	.50
rian Tallet RR	.20	.50
liff Lee RR	1.25	3.00
reddy Sanchez RR	.20	.50
hone Figgans RR	.20	.50
evin Cash RR	.20	.50
osh Bard RR	.20	.50
eriome Robertson RR	.20	.50
eremy Hill RR	.20	.50
hane Nance RR	.20	.50
ake Peavy RR	.20	.50
Trey Hodges RR	.20	.50
Eric Eckenstahler RR	.20	.50
im Rushford RR	.20	.50
Oliver Perez RR	.20	.50
Kirk Saarloos RR	.20	.50
Hank Blalock RR	.20	.50
Francisco Rodriguez RR	.30	.75
Runelvys Hernandez RR	.20	.50
Aaron Cook RR	.20	.50
Josh Hancock RR	.20	.50
P.J. Bevis RR	.20	.50
Jon Adkins RR	.20	.50
Tim Kalita RR	.20	.50
Nelson Castro RR	.20	.50
Colin Young RR	.20	.50
Adrian Burnside RR	.20	.50
Luis Martinez RR	.20	.50
Pete Zamora RR	.20	.50
Todd Donovan RR	.20	.50
Jeremy Ward RR	.20	.50
Wilson Valdez RR	.20	.50
Eric Good RR	.20	.50
55 Jeff Baker RR	.20	.50
56 Mitch Wylie RR	.20	.50
57 Ron Calloway RR	.20	.50
58 Jose Valverde RR	.20	.50
59 Jason Davis RR	.20	.50
60 Scotty Layfield RR	.20	.50
61 Matt Thornton RR	.20	.50
62 Adam Walker RR	.20	.50
63 Gustavo Chacin RR	.20	.50
64 Ron Chiavacci RR	.20	.50
65 Wiki Nieves RR	.20	.50
66 Cliff Bartosh RR	.20	.50
67 Mike Gonzalez RR	.20	.50
68 Justin Wayne RR	.20	.50
69 Eric Junge RR	.20	.50
70 Ben Kozlowski RR	.20	.50
71 Darin Erstad	.12	.30
72 Garret Anderson	.12	.30
73 Troy Glaus	.12	.30
74 David Eckstein	.12	.30
75 Adam Kennedy	.12	.30
76 Kevin Appier	.12	.30
77 Jarrod Washburn	.12	.30
78 Scott Spiezio	.12	.30
79 Tim Salmon	.12	.30
80 Ramon Ortiz	.12	.30
81 Bengie Molina	.12	.30
82 Brad Fullmer	.12	.30
83 Troy Percival	.12	.30
84 David Segui	.12	.30
85 Jay Gibbons	.12	.30
86 Tony Batista	.12	.30
87 Scott Erickson	.12	.30
88 Jeff Conine	.12	.30
89 Melvin Mora	.12	.30
90 Buddy Groom	.12	.30
91 Rodrigo Lopez	.12	.30
92 Marty Cordova	.12	.30
93 Geronimo Gil	.12	.30
94 Kenny Lofton	.12	.30
95 Shea Hillenbrand	.12	.30
96 Manny Ramirez	.30	.75
97 Pedro Martinez	.20	.50
98 Nomar Garciaparra	.20	.50
99 Rickey Henderson	.30	.75
100 Johnny Damon	.20	.50
101 Trot Nixon	.12	.30
102 Derek Lowe	.12	.30
103 Hee Seop Choi	.12	.30
104 Mark Teixeira	.20	.50
105 Tim Wakefield	.20	.50
106 Jason Varitek	.30	.75
107 Frank Thomas	.30	.75
108 Joe Crede	.12	.30
109 Magglio Ordonez	.20	.50
110 Ray Durham	.12	.30
111 Mark Buehrle	.20	.50
112 Paul Konerko	.20	.50
113 Jose Valentin	.12	.30
114 Carlos Lee	.12	.30
115 Royce Clayton	.12	.30
116 C.C. Sabathia	.20	.50
117 Ellis Burks	.12	.30
118 Omar Vizquel	.20	.50
119 Jim Thome	.20	.50
120 Matt Lawton	.12	.30
121 Travis Fryman	.12	.30
122 Earl Snyder	.12	.30
123 Ricky Gutierrez	.12	.30
124 Einar Diaz	.12	.30
125 Danys Baez	.12	.30
126 Robert Fick	.12	.30
127 Bobby Higginson	.12	.30
128 Steve Sparks	.12	.30
129 Mike Rivera	.12	.30
130 Wendell Magee	.12	.30
131 Randall Simon	.12	.30
132 Carlos Pena	.20	.50
133 Mark Redman	.12	.30
134 Juan Acevedo	.12	.30
135 Mike Sweeney	.12	.30
136 Aaron Guiel	.12	.30
137 Carlos Beltran	.20	.50
138 Joe Randa	.12	.30
139 Paul Byrd	.12	.30
140 Shawn Sedlacek	.12	.30
141 Raul Ibanez	.20	.50
142 Michael Tucker	.12	.30
143 Torii Hunter	.12	.30
144 Jacque Jones	.12	.30
145 David Ortiz	.30	.75
146 Corey Koskie	.12	.30
147 Brad Radke	.12	.30
148 Doug Mientkiewicz	.12	.30
149 A.J. Pierzynski	.12	.30
150 Dustan Mohr	.12	.30
151 Michael Cuddyer	.12	.30
152 Eddie Guardado	.12	.30
153 Cristian Guzman	.12	.30
154 Derek Jeter	.75	2.00
155 Bernie Williams	.20	.50
156 Roger Clemens	.40	1.00
157 Mike Mussina	.20	.50
158 Jorge Posada	.20	.50
159 Alfonso Soriano	.20	.50
160 Jason Giambi	.12	.30
161 Robin Ventura	.12	.30
162 Andy Pettitte	.20	.50
163 David Wells	.12	.30
164 Nick Johnson	.12	.30
165 Jeff Weaver	.12	.30
166 Raul Mondesi	.12	.30
167 Rondell White	.12	.30
168 Tim Hudson	.20	.50
169 Barry Zito	.20	.50
170 Mark Mulder	.12	.30
171 Miguel Tejada	.20	.50
172 Eric Chavez	.12	.30
173 Billy Koch	.12	.30
174 Jermaine Dye	.12	.30
175 Scott Hatteberg	.12	.30
176 Terrence Long	.12	.30
177 David Justice	.12	.30
178 Ramon Hernandez	.12	.30
179 Ted Lilly	.12	.30
180 Ichiro Suzuki	.40	1.00
181 Edgar Martinez	.20	.50
182 Mike Cameron	.12	.30
183 John Olerud	.12	.30
184 Bret Boone	.12	.30
185 Dan Wilson	.12	.30
186 Freddy Garcia	.12	.30
187 Jamie Moyer	.12	.30
188 Carlos Guillen	.12	.30
189 Ruben Sierra	.12	.30
190 Kazuhiro Sasaki	.12	.30
191 Mark McLemore	.12	.30
192 John Halama	.12	.30
193 Joel Pineiro	.12	.30
194 Jeff Cirillo	.12	.30
195 Rafael Soriano	.12	.30
196 Ben Grieve	.12	.30
197 Aubrey Huff	.12	.30
198 Steve Cox	.12	.30
199 Toby Hall	.12	.30
200 Randy Winn	.12	.30
201 Brent Abernathy	.12	.30
202 Chris Gomez	.12	.30
203 John Flaherty	.12	.30
204 Paul Wilson	.12	.30
205 Chan Ho Park	.20	.50
206 Alex Rodriguez	.40	1.00
207 Juan Gonzalez	.12	.30
208 Rafael Palmeiro	.20	.50
209 Ivan Rodriguez	.20	.50
210 Rusty Greer	.12	.30
211 Kenny Rogers	.12	.30
212 Ismael Valdes	.12	.30
213 Frank Catalanotto	.12	.30
214 Hank Blalock	.12	.30
215 Michael Young	.12	.30
216 Kevin Mench	.12	.30
217 Herbert Perry	.12	.30
218 Gabe Kapler	.12	.30
219 Carlos Delgado	.12	.30
220 Shannon Stewart	.12	.30
221 Eric Hinske	.12	.30
222 Roy Halladay	.20	.50
223 Felipe Lopez	.12	.30
224 Vernon Wells	.12	.30
225 Josh Phelps	.12	.30
226 Jose Cruz	.12	.30
227 Curt Schilling	.20	.50
228 Randy Johnson	.30	.75
229 Luis Gonzalez	.12	.30
230 Mark Grace	.20	.50
231 Junior Spivey	.12	.30
232 Tony Womack	.12	.30
233 Matt Williams	.12	.30
234 Steve Finley	.12	.30
235 Byung-Hyun Kim	.12	.30
236 Craig Counsell	.12	.30
237 Greg Maddux	.40	1.00
238 Tom Glavine	.20	.50
239 John Smoltz	.30	.75
240 Chipper Jones	.30	.75
241 Gary Sheffield	.12	.30
242 Andruw Jones	.12	.30
243 Vinny Castilla	.12	.30
244 Damian Moss	.12	.30
245 Rafael Furcal	.12	.30
246 Javy Lopez	.12	.30
247 Kevin Millwood	.12	.30
248 Kerry Wood	.12	.30
249 Fred McGriff	.20	.50
250 Sammy Sosa	.30	.75
251 Alex Gonzalez	.12	.30
252 Corey Patterson	.12	.30
253 Moises Alou	.12	.30
254 Juan Cruz	.12	.30
255 Jon Lieber	.12	.30
256 Matt Clement	.12	.30
257 Mark Prior	.20	.50
258 Ken Griffey Jr.	.60	1.50
259 Barry Larkin	.20	.50
260 Adam Dunn	.20	.50
261 Sean Casey	.12	.30
262 Jose Rijo	.12	.30
263 Elmer Dessens	.12	.30
264 Austin Kearns	.12	.30
265 Corky Miller	.12	.30
266 Todd Walker	.12	.30
267 Chris Reitsma	.12	.30
268 Ryan Dempster	.12	.30
269 Aaron Boone	.12	.30
270 Danny Graves	.12	.30
271 Brandon Larson	.12	.30
272 Larry Walker	.20	.50
273 Todd Helton	.20	.50
274 Juan Uribe	.12	.30
275 Juan Pierre	.12	.30
276 Mike Hampton	.12	.30
277 Todd Zeile	.12	.30
278 Todd Hollandsworth	.12	.30
279 Jason Jennings	.12	.30
280 Josh Beckett	.12	.30
281 Mike Lowell	.12	.30
282 Derrek Lee	.12	.30
283 A.J. Burnett	.12	.30
284 Luis Castillo	.12	.30
285 Tim Raines	.12	.30
286 Preston Wilson	.12	.30
287 Juan Encarnacion	.12	.30
288 Charles Johnson	.12	.30
289 Jeff Bagwell	.20	.50
290 Craig Biggio	.20	.50
291 Lance Berkman	.20	.50
292 Daryle Ward	.12	.30
293 Roy Oswalt	.20	.50
294 Richard Hidalgo	.12	.30
295 Octavio Dotel	.12	.30
296 Wade Miller	.12	.30
297 Julio Lugo	.12	.30
298 Billy Wagner	.12	.30
299 Shawn Green	.12	.30
300 Adrian Beltre	.30	.75
301 Paul Lo Duca	.12	.30
302 Eric Karros	.12	.30
303 Kevin Brown	.12	.30
304 Hideo Nomo	.30	.75
305 Odalis Perez	.12	.30
306 Eric Gagne	.12	.30
307 Brian Jordan	.12	.30
308 Cesar Izturis	.12	.30
309 Mark Grudzielanek	.12	.30
310 Kazuhisa Ishii	.12	.30
311 Geoff Jenkins	.12	.30
312 Richie Sexson	.12	.30
313 Jose Hernandez	.12	.30
314 Ben Sheets	.12	.30
315 Ruben Quevedo	.12	.30
316 Jeffrey Hammonds	.12	.30
317 Alex Sanchez	.12	.30
318 Eric Young	.12	.30
319 Takahito Nomura	.12	.30
320 Vladimir Guerrero	.20	.50
321 Jose Vidro	.12	.30
322 Orlando Cabrera	.12	.30
323 Michael Barrett	.12	.30
324 Javier Vazquez	.12	.30
325 Tony Armas Jr.	.12	.30
326 Andres Galarraga	.20	.50
327 Tomo Ohka	.12	.30
328 Bartolo Colon	.12	.30
329 Fernando Tatis	.12	.30
330 Brad Wilkerson	.12	.30
331 Masato Yoshii	.12	.30
332 Mike Piazza	.30	.75
333 Jeromy Burnitz	.12	.30
334 Roberto Alomar	.20	.50
335 Mo Vaughn	.12	.30
336 Al Leiter	.12	.30
337 Pedro Astacio	.12	.30
338 Edgardo Alfonzo	.12	.30
339 Armando Benitez	.12	.30
340 Timo Perez	.12	.30
341 Jay Payton	.12	.30
342 Roger Cedeno	.12	.30
343 Rey Ordonez	.12	.30
344 Steve Trachsel	.12	.30
345 Satoru Komiyama	.12	.30
346 Scott Rolen	.20	.50
347 Pat Burrell	.12	.30
348 Bobby Abreu	.12	.30
349 Mike Lieberthal	.12	.30
350 Brandon Duckworth	.12	.30
351 Jimmy Rollins	.20	.50
352 Marlon Anderson	.12	.30
353 Travis Lee	.12	.30
354 Vicente Padilla	.12	.30
355 Randy Wolf	.12	.30
356 Jason Kendall	.12	.30
357 Brian Giles	.12	.30
358 Aramis Ramirez	.12	.30
359 Pokey Reese	.12	.30
360 Kip Wells	.12	.30
361 Josh Fogg	.12	.30
362 Mike Williams	.12	.30
363 Jack Wilson	.12	.30
364 Craig Wilson	.12	.30
365 Kevin Young	.12	.30
366 Ryan Klesko	.12	.30
367 Phil Nevin	.12	.30
368 Brian Lawrence	.12	.30
369 Mark Kotsay	.12	.30
370 Brett Tomko	.12	.30
371 Trevor Hoffman	.20	.50
372 Deivi Cruz	.12	.30
373 Bubba Trammell	.12	.30
374 Sean Burroughs	.12	.30
375 Barry Bonds	.50	1.25
376 Jeff Kent	.12	.30
377 Rich Aurilia	.12	.30
378 Tsuyoshi Shinjo	.12	.30
379 Benito Santiago	.12	.30
380 Kirk Rueter	.12	.30
381 Livan Hernandez	.12	.30
382 Russ Ortiz	.12	.30
383 David Bell	.12	.30
384 Jason Schmidt	.12	.30
385 Reggie Sanders	.12	.30
386 J.T. Snow	.12	.30
387 Robb Nen	.12	.30
388 Ryan Jensen	.12	.30
389 Jim Edmonds	.20	.50
390 J.D. Drew	.12	.30
391 Albert Pujols	.40	1.00
392 Fernando Vina	.12	.30
393 Tino Martinez	.12	.30
394 Edgar Renteria	.12	.30
395 Matt Morris	.12	.30
396 Woody Williams	.12	.30
397 Jason Isringhausen	.12	.30
398 Placido Polanco	.12	.30
399 Eli Marrero	.12	.30
400 Jason Simontacchi	.12	.30

2003 Donruss Chicago Collection

DISTRIBUTED AT CHICAGO SPORTSFEST
STATED PRINT RUN 5 SERIAL #'d SETS
NO PRICING DUE TO SCARCITY

2003 Donruss Stat Line Career

*STAT LINE 1-20: 2.5X TO 6X BASIC
*21-70 P/R b/wn 251-400: 1.25X TO 3X
*21-70 P/R b/wn 201-250: 1.25X TO 3X
*21-70 P/R b/wn 151-200 1.5X TO 4X
*21-70 P/R b/wn 121-150: 2X TO 5X
*21-70 P/R b/wn 81-120: 2.5X TO 6X
*21-70 P/R b/wn 51-65: 3X TO 8X
*21-70 P/R b/wn 36-50: 4X TO 10X
*21-70 P/R b/wn 26-35: 5X TO 12X
*71-400 P/R b/wn 251-400: 2.5X TO 6X
*71-400 P/R b/wn 201-250: 2.5X TO 6X
*71-400 P/R b/wn 151-200 3X TO 8X
*71-400 P/R b/wn 121-150: 3X TO 8X
*71-400 P/R b/wn 81-120: 4X TO 10X
*71-400 P/R b/wn 66-80: 5X TO 12X
*71-400 P/R b/wn 51-65: 5X TO 12X
*71-400 P/R b/wn 36-50: 6X TO 15X
*71-400 P/R b/wn 26-35: 8X TO 20X
SEE BECKETT.COM FOR FOR PRINT RUNS
NO PRICING ON QTY OF 25 OR LESS

2003 Donruss Stat Line Season

*1-20 P/R b/wn 121-150 3X TO 8X
*1-20 P/R b/wn 81-120 4X TO 10X
*1-20 P/R b/wn 66-80 5X TO 12X
*1-20 P/R b/wn 51-65 5X TO 12X
*1-20 P/R b/wn 36-50 6X TO 15X
*1-20 P/R b/wn 26-35 8X TO 20X
*21-70 P/R b/wn 81-120 2.5X TO 6X
*21-70 P/R b/wn 66-80 3X TO 8X
*21-70 P/R b/wn 51-65 3X TO 8X
*21-70 P/R b/wn 36-50 4X TO 10X
*21-70 P/R b/wn 26-35 5X TO 12X
*71-400 P/R b/wn 81-120 4X TO 10X
*71-400 P/R b/wn 66-80 5X TO 12X
*71-400 P/R b/wn 51-65 5X TO 12X
*71-400 P/R b/wn 36-50 6X TO 15X
*71-400 P/R b/wn 26-35 8X TO 20X
SEE BECKETT.COM FOR PRINT RUNS
NO PRICING ON QTY OF 25 OR LESS

2003 Donruss All-Stars

Issued at a stated rate of one in 12 retail packs, these 10 cards feature players who are projected to be mainstays on the All-Star team.

STATED ODDS 1:12 RETAIL

1 Ichiro Suzuki	1.25	3.00
2 Alex Rodriguez	1.25	3.00
3 Nomar Garciaparra	.60	1.50
4 Derek Jeter	2.50	6.00
5 Manny Ramirez	1.00	2.50
6 Barry Bonds	1.50	4.00
7 Adam Dunn	.60	1.50
8 Mike Piazza	1.00	2.50
9 Sammy Sosa	1.00	2.50
10 Todd Helton	.60	1.50

2003 Donruss Anniversary 1983

Issued at a stated rate of one in 12, this 20 card set features players who were among the most important players of that era. These cards use the 1983 Donruss design and photos.

COMPLETE SET (20)	20.00	50.00
STATED ODDS 1:12		
1 Dale Murphy	1.00	2.50
2 Jim Palmer	.60	1.50
3 Nolan Ryan	3.00	8.00
4 Ozzie Smith	1.25	3.00
5 Tom Seaver	.60	1.50
6 Mike Schmidt	1.50	4.00
7 Steve Carlton	.60	1.50
8 Robin Yount	1.00	2.50
9 Ryne Sandberg	2.00	5.00
10 Cal Ripken	3.00	8.00
11 Fernando Valenzuela	.40	1.00
12 Andre Dawson	.60	1.50
13 George Brett	2.00	5.00
14 Eddie Murray	.60	1.50
15 Dave Winfield	.60	1.50
16 Johnny Bench	1.00	2.50
17 Wade Boggs	.60	1.50
18 Tony Gwynn	1.00	2.50
19 San Diego Chicken	.40	1.00
20 Ty Cobb	1.50	4.00

2003 Donruss Bat Kings

Randomly inserted into packs, these 20 cards feature a game bat chip long with a reproduction of a previously used Diamond King card. Cards numbered 1 through 10 have a stated print run of 250 serial numbered sets while cards numbered 11 through 20 have a stated print run of 100 serial numbered sets.

1-10 PRINT RUN 250 SERIAL #'d SETS
11-20 PRINT RUN 100 SERIAL #'d SETS
*STUDIO 1-10: .75X TO 2X BASIC BAT KING
STUDIO 1-10 PRINT RUN 50 SERIAL #'d SETS
STUDIO 11-20 PRINT RUN 25 SERIAL #'d SETS
STUDIO 11-20 NO PRICING DUE TO SCARCITY

1 Scott Rolen 99 DK/250	8.00	20.00
2 Frank Thomas 00 DK/250	8.00	20.00
3 Chipper Jones 01 DK/250	8.00	20.00
4 Ivan Rodriguez 01 DK/250	8.00	20.00
5 Stan Musial 01 ATDK/100	20.00	50.00
6 Nomar Garciaparra 02 DK/250	10.00	25.00
7 Vladimir Guerrero 03 DK/250	8.00	20.00
8 Adam Dunn 03 DK/250	6.00	15.00
9 Lance Berkman 03 DK/250	6.00	15.00
10 Magglio Ordonez 03 DK/250	6.00	15.00
12 Manny Ramirez 95 DK/100	10.00	25.00
13 Mike Piazza 94 DK/100	15.00	40.00
14 Alex Rodriguez 97 DK/100	15.00	40.00
15 Todd Helton 97 RDK/100	10.00	25.00
16 Andre Dawson 85 DK/100	8.00	20.00
17 Cal Ripken 87 DK/100	25.00	60.00
18 Tony Gwynn 88 DK/100	12.50	30.00
19 Don Mattingly 02 ATDK/100	15.00	40.00
20 Ryne Sandberg 90 DK/100	12.00	30.00

2003 Donruss Diamond Kings Inserts

Randomly inserted into packs, these cards parallel the first 20 cards of the regular Donruss set except they are serial numbered to a stated print run of 2500 serial numbered sets. These cards can be easily seperated from the cards inserted into the regular packs as they were printed with a foil stamp.

STATED PRINT RUN 2500 SERIAL #'d SETS
*STUDIO: .75X TO 2X BASIC DK
STUDIO PRINT RUN 250 SERIAL #'d SETS

DK1 Vladimir Guerrero	1.00	2.50
DK2 Derek Jeter	4.00	10.00
DK3 Adam Dunn	1.00	2.50
DK4 Greg Maddux	2.00	5.00
DK5 Lance Berkman	1.00	2.50
DK6 Ichiro Suzuki	2.00	5.00
DK7 Mike Piazza	1.50	4.00
DK8 Alex Rodriguez	2.00	5.00
DK9 Tom Glavine	1.00	2.50
DK10 Randy Johnson	1.50	4.00
DK11 Nomar Garciaparra	1.00	2.50
DK12 Jason Giambi	.60	1.50
DK13 Sammy Sosa	1.50	4.00
DK14 Barry Zito	1.00	2.50
DK15 Chipper Jones	1.50	4.00
DK16 Magglio Ordonez	1.00	2.50
DK17 Larry Walker	1.00	2.50
DK18 Alfonso Soriano	1.00	2.50
DK19 Curt Schilling	1.00	2.50
DK20 Barry Bonds	2.50	6.00

2003 Donruss Elite Series

Randomly inserted into packs, this 15 card set, which is issued on metalized film board, features the elite 15 players in baseball. These cards were issued to a stated print run of 2500 serial numbered sets.

STATED PRINT RUN 2500 SERIAL #'d SETS
DOMINATORS PR.RUN 25 SERIAL #'d SETS
DOMINATORS NO PRICE DUE TO SCARCITY

1 Alex Rodriguez	1.25	3.00
2 Barry Bonds	1.50	4.00
3 Ichiro Suzuki	1.25	3.00
4 Vladimir Guerrero	.60	1.50
5 Randy Johnson	1.00	2.50
6 Pedro Martinez	.60	1.50
7 Adam Dunn	.60	1.50
8 Sammy Sosa	1.00	2.50
9 Jim Edmonds	.60	1.50
10 Greg Maddux	1.25	3.00
11 Kazuhisa Ishii	.40	1.00
12 Jason Giambi	.40	1.00
13 Nomar Garciaparra	.60	1.50
14 Tom Glavine	.60	1.50
15 Todd Helton	.60	1.50

2003 Donruss Gamers

Randomly inserted in DLP (Donruss/Leaf/Playoff) rookie packs, these 50 cards have game-worn memorabilia swatches of the featured players.

STATED PRINT RUN 500 SERIAL #'d SETS
*JSY NUM: .6X TO 1.5X BASIC
JSY NUM PRINT RUN 100 SERIAL #'d SETS
*POSITION: .6X TO 1.5X BASIC
POSITION PRINT RUN 100 SERIAL #'d SETS
PRIME PRINT RUN 25 SERIAL #'d SETS
NO PRIME PRICING DUE TO SCARCITY
REWARDS PRINT RUN 10 SERIAL #'d SETS
NO REWARDS PRICING DUE TO SCARCITY

1 Nomar Garciaparra	6.00	15.00
2 Alex Rodriguez	4.00	10.00
3 Mike Piazza	4.00	10.00
4 Greg Maddux	4.00	10.00
5 Roger Clemens	6.00	15.00
6 Sammy Sosa	3.00	8.00
7 Randy Johnson	3.00	8.00
8 Albert Pujols	6.00	15.00
9 Alfonso Soriano	2.00	5.00
10 Chipper Jones	3.00	8.00
11 Mark Prior	3.00	8.00
12 Hideo Nomo	3.00	8.00
13 Adam Dunn	2.00	5.00
14 Juan Gonzalez	2.00	5.00
15 Vladimir Guerrero	3.00	8.00
16 Pedro Martinez	3.00	8.00
17 Jim Thome	3.00	8.00
18 Brandon Webb/200	4.00	10.00
19 Mike Mussina	3.00	8.00
20 Mark Teixeira	3.00	8.00
21 Barry Larkin	3.00	8.00
22 Ivan Rodriguez	3.00	8.00
23 Hank Blalock	2.00	5.00
24 Rafael Palmeiro	3.00	8.00
25 Curt Schilling	2.00	5.00
26 Troy Glaus	2.00	5.00
27 Bernie Williams	3.00	8.00
28 Scott Rolen	3.00	8.00
29 Torii Hunter	2.00	5.00
30 Nick Johnson	2.00	5.00
31 Kazuhisa Ishii	2.00	5.00
32 Shawn Green	2.00	5.00
33 Jeff Bagwell	3.00	8.00
34 Lance Berkman	2.00	5.00
35 Roy Oswalt	2.00	5.00
36 Kerry Wood	2.00	5.00
37 Todd Helton	3.00	8.00
38 Manny Ramirez	3.00	8.00
39 Andruw Jones	3.00	8.00
40 Frank Thomas	3.00	8.00
41 Gary Sheffield	2.00	5.00
42 Magglio Ordonez	2.00	5.00
43 Mike Sweeney	2.00	5.00
44 Carlos Beltran	2.00	5.00
45 Richie Sexson	2.00	5.00
46 Jeff Kent	2.00	5.00
47 Carlos Delgado	2.00	5.00
48 Vernon Wells	2.00	5.00
49 Dontrelle Willis	3.00	8.00
50 Jae Weong Seo	2.00	5.00

2003 Donruss Gamers Autographs

PRINT RUNS B/WN 5-50 COPIES PER
NO PRICING ON QTY OF 25 OR LESS

20 Mark Teixeira/50	10.00	25.00
23 Hank Blalock/50	12.50	30.00
29 Torii Hunter/50	12.50	30.00
35 Roy Oswalt/50	12.50	30.00
43 Mike Sweeney/50	12.50	30.00
48 Vernon Wells/30	15.00	40.00
49 Dontrelle Willis/50	6.00	15.00
50 Jae Weong Seo/50	12.50	30.00

2003 Donruss Jersey Kings

Randomly inserted into packs, this set features cards which parallel previously issued Diamond King cards along with a game-worn jersey swatch. Cards were printed to a stated print run of either 100 or 250 serial numbered cards and we have put that information next to the player's name in our checklist.

1-10 PRINT RUN 250 SERIAL #'d SETS
11-20 PRINT RUN 100 SERIAL #'d SETS
*STUDIO 1-10: .75X TO 2X BASIC JSY KINGS
STUDIO 1-10 PRINT RUN 50 SERIAL #'d SETS
STUDIO 11-20 PRINT RUN 25 SERIAL #'d SETS
STUDIO 11-20 NO PRICE DUE TO SCARCITY

1 Juan Gonzalez 99 DK/250 6.00 15.00
2 Greg Maddux 00 DK/250 8.00 20.00
3 Nomar Garciaparra 01 DK/250 10.00 25.00
4 Troy Glaus 01 DK/250 6.00 15.00
5 Reggie Jackson 01 ATDK/100 10.00 25.00
6 Alex Rodriguez 01 DK/250 10.00 25.00
7 Alfonso Soriano 03 DK/250 6.00 15.00
8 Curt Schilling 03 DK/250 6.00 15.00
9 Vladimir Guerrero 03 DK/250 6.00 15.00
10 Adam Dunn 03 DK/250 6.00 15.00
11 Mark Grace 88 DK/100 10.00 25.00
12 Roger Clemens 90 DK/100 15.00 40.00
13 Jeff Bagwell 91 DK/100 10.00 25.00
14 Tom Glavine 92 DK/100 10.00 25.00
15 Mike Piazza 94 DK/100 12.50 30.00
16 Rod Carew 82 DK/100 10.00 25.00
17 Rickey Henderson 82 DK/100 10.00 25.00
18 Mike Schmidt 83 DK/100 15.00 40.00
19 Cal Ripken 85 DK/100 40.00 80.00
20 Dale Murphy 86 DK/100 10.00 25.00

2003 Donruss Longball Leaders

Randomly inserted into packs, these 10 cards, honoring some of the leading home run hitters, were printed on metalized film board and were issued to a stated print run of 1000 serial numbered sets.

STATED PRINT RUN 1000 SERIAL #'d SETS
*SEASON SUM: 1.5X TO 4X BASIC LL
SEASON PRINT RUN BASED ON 02 HR'S

1 Alex Rodriguez 2.00 5.00
2 Alfonso Soriano 1.00 2.50
3 Rafael Palmeiro 1.00 2.50
4 Jim Thome 1.00 2.50
5 Jason Giambi .60 1.50
6 Sammy Sosa 1.50 4.00
7 Barry Bonds 2.50 6.00
8 Lance Berkman 1.00 2.50
9 Shawn Green .60 1.50
10 Vladimir Guerrero 1.00 2.50

2003 Donruss Production Line

Randomly inserted into packs, these 30 cards feature players who excel in either on base percentage, slugging percentage, batting average or total bases. Each card is printed on metalized film board and was issued to that player's statistical information.

STATED PRINT RUNS LISTED BELOW
*DIE CUT OPS: 1.25X TO 3X BASIC PL
*DIE CUT OBP/SLG: 1X TO 2.5X BASIC PL
*DIE CUT AVG/TB: .75X TO 2X BASIC PL
DIE CUT PRINT RUN 100 SERIAL #'d SETS

1 Alex Rodriguez OPS/1015 2.00 5.00
2 Jim Thome OPS/1122 1.00 2.50
3 Lance Berkman OPS/982 1.00 2.50
4 Barry Bonds OPS/1381 2.50 6.00
5 Sammy Sosa OPS/993 1.50 4.00
6 Vladimir Guerrero OPS/1010 1.00 2.50
7 Barry Bonds OBP/582 3.00 8.00
8 Jason Giambi OBP/435 .75 2.00
9 Vladimir Guerrero OBP/417 1.25 3.00
10 Adam Dunn OBP/400 1.25 3.00
11 Chipper Jones OBP/435 2.00 5.00
12 Todd Helton OBP/429 1.25 3.00
13 Rafael Palmeiro SLG/571 1.25 3.00
14 Sammy Sosa SLG/594 2.00 5.00
15 Alex Rodriguez SLG/623 2.50 6.00
16 Larry Walker SLG/602 1.25 3.00
17 Lance Berkman SLG/578 1.25 3.00
18 Alfonso Soriano SLG/547 1.25 3.00
19 Ichiro Suzuki AVG/321 2.50 6.00
20 Mike Sweeney AVG/340 .75 2.00
21 Manny Ramirez AVG/349 2.00 5.00
22 Larry Walker AVG/338 1.25 3.00
23 Barry Bonds AVG/370 3.00 8.00
24 Jim Edmonds AVG/311 1.25 3.00
25 Alfonso Soriano TB/381 1.25 3.00
26 Jason Giambi TB/335 .75 2.00
27 Miguel Tejada TB/336 1.25 3.00
28 Brian Giles TB/309 .75 2.00
29 Vladimir Guerrero TB/364 1.25 3.00
30 Pat Burrell TB/319 .75 2.00

2003 Donruss Recollection Autographs

Randomly inserted into packs, these cards feature cards Donruss/Playoff "buy-backs" and were then autographed by the player. Each of these cards were issued to a stated print run of between one and 54 copies and for most of these cards no pricing is provided due to market scarcity.

RANDOM INSERTS IN PACKS
SEE BECKETT.COM FOR CHECKLIST
NO PRICING DUE TO SCARCITY

2003 Donruss Timber and Threads

Randomly inserted into packs, these 50 cards feature either a game-used jersey swatch or a game-use bat chip of the featured player. Since these cards have different stated print runs we have put that information next to the player's name in our checklist.

STATED PRINT RUNS LISTED BELOW

1 Al Kaline Bat/125 10.00 25.00
2 Alex Rodriguez Bat/350 8.00 20.00
3 Carlos Delgado Bat/250 4.00 10.00
4 Cliff Floyd Bat/250 4.00 10.00
5 Eddie Mathews Bat/125 10.00 25.00
6 Edgar Martinez Bat/125 10.00 25.00
7 Ernie Banks Bat/50 15.00 40.00
8 Ivan Rodriguez Bat/125 10.00 25.00
9 J.D. Drew Bat/125 6.00 15.00
10 Jorge Posada Bat/300 6.00 15.00
11 Lou Brock Bat/125 10.00 25.00
12 Mike Piazza Bat/125 10.00 25.00
13 Mike Schmidt Bat/125 15.00 40.00
14 Reggie Jackson Bat/125 10.00 25.00
15 Rickey Henderson Bat/125 10.00 25.00
16 Robin Yount Bat/125 10.00 25.00
17 Rod Carew Bat/125 10.00 25.00
18 Scott Rolen Bat/125 10.00 25.00
19 Shawn Green Bat/200 4.00 10.00
20 Willie Stargell Bat/125 10.00 25.00
21 Alex Rodriguez Jsy/175 12.50 30.00
22 Andruw Jones Jsy/275 6.00 15.00
23 Brooks Robinson Jsy/150 10.00 25.00
24 Chipper Jones Jsy/150 10.00 25.00
25 Greg Maddux Jsy/175 8.00 20.00
26 Hideo Nomo Jsy/300 15.00 40.00
27 Ivan Rodriguez Jsy/225 6.00 15.00
28 Jack Morris Jsy/150 6.00 15.00
29 J.D. Drew Jsy/150 6.00 15.00
30 Jeff Bagwell Jsy/500 6.00 15.00
31 Jim Thome Jsy/200 6.00 15.00
32 John Smoltz Jsy/175 6.00 15.00
33 John Olerud Jsy/450 4.00 10.00
34 Kerry Wood Jsy/200 4.00 10.00
36 Larry Walker Jsy/500 4.00 10.00
37 Magglio Ordonez Jsy/150 6.00 15.00
38 Manny Ramirez Jsy/500 6.00 15.00
39 Mike Piazza Jsy/300 6.00 15.00
40 Mike Sweeney Jsy/200 4.00 10.00
41 Nomar Garciaparra Jsy/200 10.00 25.00
42 Paul Konerko Jsy/500 4.00 10.00
43 Pedro Martinez Jsy/175 6.00 15.00
44 Randy Johnson Jsy/175 6.00 15.00
45 Roger Clemens Jsy/350 10.00 25.00
46 Shawn Green Jsy/250 4.00 10.00
47 Todd Helton Jsy/175 6.00 15.00
48 Tom Glavine Jsy/225 6.00 15.00
49 Tony Gwynn Jsy/150 10.00 25.00
50 Vladimir Guerrero Jsy/450 6.00 15.00

2003 Donruss Rookies

This 65-card set was released in December, 2003. This set was issued as part of the DLP (Donruss/Leaf/Playoff) Rookie Update product in which many of the products issued earlier in the year had Rookie Cards added. Each pack, contained eight cards and were sold at an $5 SRP with 24 packs in a box and 12 boxes in a case. In this Rookies set, cards 1-60 feature Rookie Cards while cards numbered 61-65 feature some of the most important players who changed teams during the 2003 season. As mentioned cards from the following DLP products were inserted into these packs: Donruss, Donruss Champions, Donruss Classics, Donruss Diamond Kings, Donruss Elite, Donruss Signature, Donruss Team Heroes, Leaf, Leaf Certified Materials, Leaf Limited, Playoff Absolute Memorablia, Playoff Prestige and Studio.

COMPLETE SET (65) 8.00 20.00
COMMON CARD (1-65) .10 .25
COMMON RC .10 .25

1 Jeremy Bonderman RC .40 1.00
2 Adam Loewen RC .10 .25
3 Dan Haren RC .50 1.25
4 Jose Contreras RC .25 .60
5 Hideki Matsui RC .50 1.25
6 Arnie Munoz RC .10 .25
7 Miguel Cabrera 1.25 3.00
8 Andrew Brown RC .10 .25
9 Josh Hall RC .10 .25
10 Josh Stewart RC .10 .25
11 Clint Barmes RC .25 .60
12 Luis Ayala RC .10 .25
13 Brandon Webb RC .30 .75
14 Greg Aquino RC .10 .25
15 Chien-Ming Wang RC .40 1.00
16 Rickie Weeks RC .30 .75
17 Edgar Gonzalez RC .10 .25
18 Dontrelle Willis .10 .25
19 Bo Hart RC .10 .25
20 Rosman Garcia RC .10 .25
21 Jeremy Griffiths RC .10 .25
22 Craig Brazell RC .10 .25
23 Daniel Cabrera RC .15 .40
24 Fernando Cabrera RC .10 .25
25 Termel Sledge RC .10 .25
26 Ramon Nivar RC .10 .25
27 Rob Hammock RC .10 .25
28 Francisco Rosario RC .10 .25
29 Cory Stewart RC .10 .25
30 Felix Sanchez RC .10 .25
31 Jorge Cordova RC .10 .25
32 Rocco Baldelli .10 .25
33 Beau Kemp RC .10 .25
34 Mike Nakamura RC .10 .25
35 Rett Johnson RC .10 .25
36 Guillermo Quiroz RC .10 .25
37 Hong-Chih Kuo RC .50 1.25
38 Ian Ferguson RC .10 .25
39 Franklin Perez RC .10 .25
40 Tim Olson RC .10 .25
41 Jerome Williams .10 .25
42 Rich Fischer RC .10 .25
43 Phil Seibel RC .10 .25
44 Aaron Looper RC .10 .25
45 Jae Weong Seo .10 .25
46 Chad Gaudin RC .10 .25
47 Matt Kata RC .10 .25
48 Ryan Wagner RC .10 .25
49 Michel Hernandez RC .10 .25
50 Diegomar Markwell RC .10 .25
51 Doug Waechter RC .10 .25
52 Mike Nicolas RC .10 .25
53 Prentice Redman RC .10 .25
54 Shane Bazzell RC .10 .25
55 Delmon Young RC .60 1.50
56 Brian Stokes RC .10 .25
57 Matt Bruback RC .10 .25
58 Nook Logan RC .10 .25
59 Oscar Villarreal RC .10 .25
60 Pete LaForest RC .10 .25
61 Shea Hillenbrand .10 .25
62 Aramis Ramirez .10 .25
63 Aaron Boone .10 .25
64 Roberto Alomar .15 .40
65 Rickey Henderson .25 .60

2003 Donruss Rookies Autographs

PRINT RUNS B/WN 10-1000 COPIES PER
NO PRICING ON QTY OF 25 OR LESS

1 Jeremy Bonderman/50 20.00 50.00
2 Adam Loewen/500 6.00 15.00
3 Dan Haren/100 10.00 25.00
4 Jose Contreras/100 12.50 30.00
6 Arnie Munoz/584 4.00 10.00
7 Miguel Cabrera/50 60.00 120.00
8 Andrew Brown/584 6.00 15.00
9 Josh Hall/1000 4.00 10.00
10 Josh Stewart/300 4.00 10.00
11 Clint Barmes/129 6.00 15.00
12 Luis Ayala/1000 4.00 10.00
13 Brandon Webb/100 12.50 30.00
14 Greg Aquino/1000 4.00 10.00
15 Chien-Ming Wang/100 60.00 120.00
17 Edgar Gonzalez/400 4.00 10.00
19 Bo Hart/150 4.00 10.00
20 Rosman Garcia/250 4.00 10.00
21 Jeremy Griffiths/812 4.00 10.00
22 Craig Brazell/205 4.00 10.00
23 Daniel Cabrera/383 10.00 25.00
24 Fernando Cabrera/1000 4.00 10.00
25 Termel Sledge/250 4.00 10.00
26 Ramon Nivar/100 4.00 10.00
27 Rob Hammock/201 4.00 10.00
29 Cory Stewart/1000 4.00 10.00
30 Felix Sanchez/1000 4.00 10.00
31 Jorge Cordova/1000 4.00 10.00
33 Beau Kemp/1000 4.00 10.00
34 Mike Nakamura/1000 4.00 10.00
35 Rett Johnson/1000 4.00 10.00
36 Guillermo Quiroz/90 4.00 10.00
37 Hong-Chih Kuo/50 100.00 200.00
38 Ian Ferguson/1000 4.00 10.00
39 Franklin Perez/1000 4.00 10.00
40 Tim Olson/150 4.00 10.00
41 Jerome Williams/50 6.00 15.00
42 Rich Fischer/734 4.00 10.00
43 Phil Seibel/1000 4.00 10.00
44 Aaron Looper/513 4.00 10.00
45 Jae Weong Seo/50 10.00 25.00
47 Matt Kata/203 4.00 10.00
48 Ryan Wagner/100 4.00 10.00
50 Diegomar Markwell/1000 4.00 10.00
51 Doug Waechter/583 6.00 15.00
52 Mike Nicolas/1000 4.00 10.00
53 Prentice Redman/425 4.00 10.00
54 Shane Bazzell/1000 4.00 10.00
55 Delmon Young/75 100.00 200.00
56 Brian Stokes/1000 4.00 10.00
57 Matt Bruback/513 4.00 10.00
58 Nook Logan/150 6.00 15.00
59 Oscar Villarreal/150 6.00 15.00
60 Pete LaForest/250 4.00 10.00

2003 Donruss Rookies Stat Line Career

*SLC P/R b/wn 201+: 3X TO 8X
*SLC P/R b/wn 121-200: 4X TO 10X
*SLC P/R b/wn 81-120: 5X TO 12X
*SLC P/R b/wn 66-80: 6X TO 15X
*SLC P/R b/wn 51-65: 6X TO 15X
*SLC RC's P/R b/wn 201+: 4X TO 10X
*SLC RC's P/R b/wn 121-200: 4X TO 10X
*SLC RC's P/R b/wn 81-120: 4X TO 10X
*SLC RC's P/R b/wn 66-80: 5X TO 12X
*SLC RC's P/R b/wn 51-65: 5X TO 12X
*SLC RC's P/R b/wn 36-50: 6X TO 15X
*SLC RC's P/R b/wn 26-35: 8X TO 20X
PRINT RUNS B/WN 1-245 COPIES PER
NO PRICING ON QTY OF 25 OR LESS

2003 Donruss Rookies Stat Line Season

*SLS P/R b/wn 201+: 3X TO 8X
*SLS P/R b/wn 121-200: 4X TO 10X
*SLS P/R b/wn 66-80: 6X TO 15X
*SLS P/R b/wn 36-50: 8X TO 20X
*SLS P/R b/wn 26-35: 10X TO 25X
*SLS RC's P/R b/wn 81-120: 4X TO 10X
*SLS RC's P/R b/wn 66-80: 5X TO 12X
*SLS RC's P/R b/wn 51-65: 5X TO 12X
*SLS RC's P/R b/wn 36-50: 6X TO 15X
*SLS RC's P/R b/wn 26-35: 8X TO 20X
PRINT RUNS B/WN 1-130 COPIES PER
NO PRICING ON QTY OF 25 OR LESS

2003 Donruss Rookies Recollection Autographs

RANDOM INSERTS IN DLP R/T PACKS
PRINT RUNS B/WN 1-75 COPIES PER
NO PRICING ON QTY OF 5 OR LESS

7 Jack McDowell 88/75 10.00 25.00

2004 Donruss

This 400-card standard-size set was released in November, 2003. This set was issued in 10 card packs with an $1.99 SRP and those cards came 24 packs to a box and 16 boxes to a case. Please note the following subsets were issued as part of this product: Diamond King (1-25); Rated Rookies (26-70) and Team Checklists (371-400).

COMPLETE SET (400) 40.00 100.00
COMP.SET w/o SP's (300) 10.00 25.00
COMMON CARD (71-370) .12 .30
COMMON CARD (1-25/371-400) .25 .60
COMMON CARD (26-70) .60 1.50
1-70/370-400 RANDOM INSERTS IN PACKS

1 Derek Jeter DK 1.50 4.00
2 Greg Maddux DK .75 2.00
3 Albert Pujols DK .75 2.00
4 Ichiro Suzuki DK .75 2.00
5 Alex Rodriguez DK .75 2.00
6 Roger Clemens DK .75 2.00
7 Andruw Jones DK .25 .60
8 Barry Bonds DK 1.00 2.50
9 Jeff Bagwell DK .40 1.00
10 Randy Johnson DK .60 1.50
11 Scott Rolen DK .40 1.00
12 Lance Berkman DK .40 1.00
13 Barry Zito DK .40 1.00
14 Manny Ramirez DK .60 1.50
15 Carlos Delgado DK .25 .60
16 Alfonso Soriano DK .40 1.00
17 Todd Helton DK .40 1.00
18 Mike Mussina DK .40 1.00
19 Austin Kearns DK .25 .60
20 Nomar Garciaparra DK .40 1.00
21 Chipper Jones DK .60 1.50
22 Mark Prior DK .40 1.00
23 Jim Thome DK .40 1.00
24 Vladimir Guerrero DK .40 1.00
25 Pedro Martinez DK .40 1.00
26 Sergio Mitre RR .60 1.50
27 Adam Loewen RR .60 1.50
28 Alfredo Gonzalez RR .60 1.50
29 Miguel Ojeda RR .60 1.50
30 Rosman Garcia RR .60 1.50
31 Arnie Munoz RR .60 1.50
32 Andrew Brown RR .60 1.50
33 Josh Hall RR .60 1.50
34 Josh Stewart RR .60 1.50
35 Clint Barmes RR 1.00 2.50
36 Brandon Webb RR .60 1.50
37 Chien-Ming Wang RR 2.50 6.00
38 Edgar Gonzalez RR .60 1.50
39 Alejandro Machado RR .60 1.50
40 Jeremy Griffiths RR .60 1.50
41 Craig Brazell RR .60 1.50
42 Daniel Cabrera RR .60 1.50
43 Fernando Cabrera RR .60 1.50
44 Termel Sledge RR .60 1.50
45 Rob Hammock RR .60 1.50
46 Francisco Rosario RR .60 1.50
47 Francisco Cruceta RR .60 1.50
48 Rett Johnson RR .60 1.50
49 Guillermo Quiroz RR .60 1.50
50 Hong-Chih Kuo RR .60 1.50
51 Ian Ferguson RR .60 1.50
52 Tim Olson RR .60 1.50
53 Todd Wellemeyer RR .60 1.50
54 Rich Fischer RR .60 1.50
55 Phil Seibel RR .60 1.50
56 Joe Valentine RR .60 1.50
57 Matt Kata RR .60 1.50
58 Michael Hessman RR .60 1.50
59 Michel Hernandez RR .60 1.50
60 Doug Waechter RR .60 1.50
61 Prentice Redman RR .60 1.50
62 Nook Logan RR .60 1.50
63 Oscar Villarreal RR .60 1.50
64 Pete LaForest RR .60 1.50
65 Matt Bruback RR .60 1.50
66 Dan Haren RR .60 1.50
67 Greg Aquino RR .60 1.50
68 Lew Ford RR .60 1.50
69 Jeff Duncan RR .60 1.50
70 Ryan Wagner RR .60 1.50
71 Bengie Molina .12 .30
72 Brad Fullmer .12 .30
73 Darin Erstad .12 .30
74 David Eckstein .12 .30
75 Garret Anderson .12 .30
76 Jarrod Washburn .12 .30
77 Kevin Appier .12 .30
78 Scott Spiezio .12 .30
79 Tim Salmon .12 .30
80 Troy Glaus .12 .30
81 Troy Percival .12 .30
82 Jason Johnson .12 .30
83 Jay Gibbons .12 .30
84 Melvin Mora .12 .30
85 Sidney Ponson .12 .30
86 Tony Batista .12 .30
87 Bill Mueller .12 .30
88 Byung-Hyun Kim .12 .30
89 David Ortiz .30 .75
90 Derek Lowe .12 .30
91 Johnny Damon .20 .50
92 Casey Fossum .12 .30
93 Manny Ramirez .30 .75
94 Nomar Garciaparra .20 .50
95 Pedro Martinez .20 .50
96 Todd Walker .12 .30
97 Trot Nixon .12 .30
98 Bartolo Colon .12 .30
99 Carlos Lee .12 .30
100 D'Angelo Jimenez .12 .30
101 Esteban Loaiza .12 .30
102 Frank Thomas .30 .75
103 Joe Crede .12 .30
104 Jose Valentin .12 .30
105 Magglio Ordonez .20 .50
106 Mark Buehrle .20 .50
107 Paul Konerko .20 .50
108 Brandon Phillips .12 .30
109 C.C Sabathia .20 .50
110 Ellis Burks .12 .30
111 Jeremy Guthrie .12 .30
112 Josh Bard .12 .30
113 Matt Lawton .12 .30
114 Milton Bradley .12 .30
115 Omar Vizquel .20 .50
116 Travis Hafner .12 .30
117 Bobby Higginson .12 .30
118 Carlos Pena .20 .50
119 Dmitri Young .12 .30
120 Eric Munson .12 .30
121 Jeremy Bonderman .12 .30
122 Nate Cornejo .12 .30
123 Omar Infante .12 .30
124 Ramon Santiago .12 .30
125 Angel Berroa .12 .30
126 Carlos Beltran .20 .50
127 Desi Relaford .12 .30
128 Jeremy Affeldt .12 .30
129 Joe Randa .12 .30
130 Ken Harvey .12 .30
131 Mike MacDougal .12 .30
132 Michael Tucker .12 .30
133 Mike Sweeney .12 .30
134 Raul Ibanez .20 .50
135 Runelvys Hernandez .12 .30
136 A.J. Pierzynski .12 .30
137 Brad Radke .12 .30
138 Corey Koskie .12 .30
139 Cristian Guzman .12 .30
140 Doug Mientkiewicz .12 .30
141 Dustan Mohr .12 .30
142 Jacque Jones .12 .30
143 Kenny Rogers .12 .30
144 Bobby Kielty .12 .30
145 Kyle Lohse .12 .30
146 Luis Rivas .12 .30
147 Torii Hunter .12 .30
148 Alfonso Soriano .20 .50
149 Andy Pettitte .20 .50
150 Bernie Williams .20 .50
151 David Wells .12 .30
152 Derek Jeter .75 2.00
153 Hideki Matsui .50 1.25
154 Jason Giambi .12 .30
155 Jorge Posada .20 .50
156 Jose Contreras .12 .30
157 Mike Mussina .20 .50
158 Nick Johnson .12 .30
159 Robin Ventura .12 .30
160 Roger Clemens .40 1.00
161 Barry Zito .20 .50
162 Chris Singleton .12 .30
163 Eric Byrnes .12 .30
164 Eric Chavez .12 .30
165 Erubiel Durazo .12 .30
166 Keith Foulke .12 .30
167 Mark Ellis .12 .30
168 Miguel Tejada .20 .50
169 Mark Mulder .12 .30
170 Ramon Hernandez .12 .30
171 Ted Lilly .12 .30
172 Terrence Long .12 .30
173 Tim Hudson .20 .50
174 Bret Boone .12 .30
175 Carlos Guillen .12 .30
176 Dan Wilson .12 .30
177 Edgar Martinez .20 .50
178 Freddy Garcia .12 .30
179 Gil Meche .12 .30
180 Ichiro Suzuki .40 1.00
181 Jamie Moyer .12 .30
182 Joel Pineiro .12 .30
183 John Olerud .12 .30
184 Mike Cameron .12 .30
185 Randy Winn .12 .30
186 Ryan Franklin .12 .30
187 Kazuhiro Sasaki .12 .30
188 Aubrey Huff .12 .30
189 Carl Crawford .20 .50
190 Joe Kennedy .12 .30
191 Marlon Anderson .12 .30
192 Rey Ordonez .12 .30
193 Rocco Baldelli .12 .30
194 Toby Hall .12 .30
195 Travis Lee .12 .30
196 Alex Rodriguez .40 1.00
197 Carl Everett .12 .30
198 Chan Ho Park .20 .50
199 Einar Diaz .12 .30
200 Hank Blalock .12 .30
201 Ismael Valdes .12 .30
202 Juan Gonzalez .12 .30
203 Mark Teixeira .20 .50
204 Mike Young .12 .30
205 Rafael Palmeiro .20 .50
206 Carlos Delgado .12 .30
207 Kelvim Escobar .12 .30
208 Eric Hinske .12 .30
209 Frank Catalanotto .12 .30
210 Josh Phelps .12 .30
211 Orlando Hudson .12 .30
212 Roy Halladay .20 .50
213 Shannon Stewart .12 .30
214 Vernon Wells .12 .30
215 Carlos Baerga .12 .30
216 Curt Schilling .20 .50
217 Junior Spivey .12 .30
218 Luis Gonzalez .12 .30
219 Lyle Overbay .12 .30
220 Mark Grace .20 .50
221 Matt Williams .12 .30
222 Randy Johnson .30 .75
223 Shea Hillenbrand .12
224 Steve Finley .12
225 Andruw Jones .12
226 Chipper Jones .30
227 Gary Sheffield .12
228 Greg Maddux .40
229 Javy Lopez .12
230 John Smoltz .30
231 Marcus Giles .12
232 Mike Hampton .12
233 Rafael Furcal .12
234 Robert Fick .12
235 Russ Ortiz .12
236 Alex Gonzalez .12
237 Carlos Zambrano .20
238 Corey Patterson .12
239 Hee Seop Choi .12
240 Kerry Wood .12
241 Mark Bellhorn .12
242 Mark Prior .20
243 Moises Alou .12
244 Sammy Sosa .30
245 Aaron Boone .12
246 Adam Dunn .20
247 Austin Kearns .12
248 Barry Larkin .20
249 Felipe Lopez .12
250 Jose Guillen .12
251 Ken Griffey Jr. .60
252 Jason LaRue .12
253 Scott Williamson .12
254 Sean Casey .12
255 Shawn Chacon .12
256 Chris Stynes .12
257 Jason Jennings .12
258 Jay Payton .12
259 Jose Hernandez .12
260 Larry Walker .20
261 Preston Wilson .12
262 Ronnie Belliard .12
263 Todd Helton .20
264 A.J. Burnett .12
265 Alex Gonzalez .12
266 Brad Penny .12
267 Derrek Lee .12
268 Ivan Rodriguez .20
269 Josh Beckett .12
270 Juan Encarnacion .12
271 Juan Pierre .12
272 Luis Castillo .12
273 Mike Lowell .12
274 Todd Hollandsworth .12
275 Billy Wagner .12
276 Brad Ausmus .12
277 Craig Biggio .20
278 Jeff Bagwell .20
279 Jeff Kent .12
280 Lance Berkman .20
281 Richard Hidalgo .12
282 Roy Oswalt .20
283 Wade Miller .12
284 Adrian Beltre .30
285 Brian Jordan .12
286 Cesar Izturis .12
287 Dave Roberts .20
288 Eric Gagne .12
289 Fred McGriff .12
290 Hideo Nomo .30
291 Kazuhisa Ishii .12
292 Kevin Brown .12
293 Paul Lo Duca .12
294 Shawn Green .12
295 Ben Sheets .12
296 Geoff Jenkins .12
297 Rey Sanchez .12
298 Richie Sexson .12
299 Wes Helms .12
300 Brad Wilkerson .12
301 Claudio Vargas .12
302 Endy Chavez .12
303 Fernando Tatis .12
304 Javier Vazquez .12
305 Jose Vidro .12
306 Michael Barrett .12
307 Orlando Cabrera .12
308 Tony Armas Jr. .12
309 Vladimir Guerrero .20
310 Zach Day .12
311 Al Leiter .12
312 Cliff Floyd .12
313 Jae Weong Seo .12
314 Jeromy Burnitz .12
315 Mike Piazza .30
316 Mo Vaughn .12
317 Roberto Alomar .20
318 Roger Cedeno .12
319 Tom Glavine .20
320 Jose Reyes .20
321 Bobby Abreu .12
322 Brett Myers .12
323 David Bell .12
324 Jim Thome .20
325 Jimmy Rollins .20
326 Kevin Millwood .12
327 Marlon Byrd .12
328 Mike Lieberthal .12
329 Pat Burrell .12
330 Randy Wolf .12
331 Aramis Ramirez .12
332 Brian Giles .12
333 Jason Kendall .12
334 Kenny Lofton .12
335 Kip Wells .12

Benson .12 .30
dall Simon .12 .30
ie Sanders .12 .30
rt Pujols .40 1.00
ar Renteria .12 .30
ando Vina .12 .30
Drew .12 .30
Edmonds .20 .50
t Morris .12 .30
e Matheny .12 .30
tt Rolen .20 .50
) Martinez .20 .50
ody Williams .12 .30
n Lawrence .12 .30
k Kotsay .12 .30
rk Loretta .12 .30
non Vazquez .12 .30
ndell White .12 .30
an Klesko .12 .30
an Burroughs .12 .30
vor Hoffman .20 .50
vier Nady .12 .30
dres Galarraga .20 .50
ry Bonds .50 1.25
nito Santiago .12 .30
ivi Cruz .12 .30
gardo Alfonzo .12 .30
. Snow .12 .30
son Schmidt .12 .30
k Rueter .12 .30
rt Ainsworth .12 .30
arquis Grissom .12 .30
y Durham .12 .30
ch Aurilia .12 .30
n Worrell .12 .30
oy Glaus TC .25 .60
elvin Mora TC .25 .60
omar Garciaparra TC .40 1.00
agglio Ordonez TC .40 1.00
mar Vizquel TC .40 1.00
mitri Young TC .25 .60
ike Sweeney TC .25 .60
rii Hunter TC .25 .60
erek Jeter TC 1.50 4.00
arry Zito TC .40 1.00
hiro Suzuki TC .75 2.00
occo Baldelli TC .25 .60
lex Rodriguez TC .75 2.00
arlos Delgado TC .25 .60
andy Johnson TC .60 1.50
reg Maddux TC .75 2.00
ammy Sosa TC .60 1.50
Ken Griffey Jr. TC 1.25 3.00
odd Helton TC .40 1.00
van Rodriguez TC .40 1.00
eff Bagwell TC .40 1.00
Hideo Nomo TC .60 1.50
Richie Sexson TC .25 .60
Vladimir Guerrero TC .40 1.00
Mike Piazza TC .60 1.50
Jim Thome TC .40 1.00
Jason Kendall TC .25 .60
Albert Pujols TC .75 2.00
Ryan Klesko TC .25 .60
Barry Bonds TC 1.00 2.50

2004 Donruss Autographs

DOM INSERTS IN PACKS
CARD PRINTS B/WN 5-141 COPIES PER
PRICING ON QTY OF 12 OR LESS
an Ferguson 4.00 10.00
Mark Buehrle/141 12.50 30.00
Josh Bard 4.00 10.00
Omar Infante 4.00 10.00
Terrence Long 4.00 10.00
Aubrey Huff/143 6.00 15.00
Toby Hall 4.00 10.00
Junior Spivey/132 4.00 10.00
Robert Fick 4.00 10.00
Brian Lawrence 4.00 10.00

2004 Donruss Press Proofs Black

ATED PRINT RUN 10 SERIAL #'d SETS
PRICING DUE TO SCARCITY

004 Donruss Press Proofs Blue

BLUE 71-370: 4X TO 10X BASIC
BLUE 1-25/371-400: 1.5X TO 4X BASIC
BLUE 26-70: .75X TO 2X BASIC
NDOM INSERTS IN RETAIL PACKS
ATED PRINT RUN 100 SERIAL #'d SETS

004 Donruss Press Proofs Gold

TATED PRINT RUN 25 SERIAL #'d SETS
O PRICING DUE TO SCARCITY

2004 Donruss Press Proofs Red

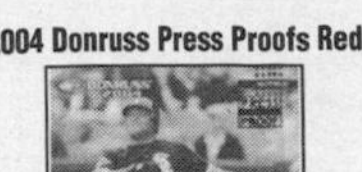

*PP RED 71-370: 2.5X TO 6X BASIC
*PP RED 1-25/371-400: 1X TO 2.5X BASIC
*PP RED 26-70: .5X TO 1.2X BASIC
STATED ODDS 1:12 RETAIL

2004 Donruss Stat Line Career

*71-370 p/r 200-443 2.5X TO 6X
*71-370 p/r 121-200: 3X TO 8X
*71-370 p/r 81-120: 4X TO 10X
*71-370 p/r 66-80: 5X TO 12X
*71-370 p/r 51-65: 5X TO 12X
*71-370 p/r 36-50: 6X TO 15X
*71-370 p/r 26-35: 8X TO 20X
*1-25/371-400 p/r 200-500: 1X TO 2.5X
*1-25/371-400 p/r 121-200: 1.25X TO 3X
*1-25/371-400 p/r 81-120: 1.5X TO 4X
*1-25/371-400 p/r 66-80: 2X TO 5X
*1-25/371-400 p/r 51-65: 2X TO 5X
*1-25/371-400 p/r 36-50: 2.5X TO 6X
*1-25/371-400 p/r 26-35: 3X TO 8X
*26-70 p/r 200-491: .5X TO 1.2X
*26-70 p/r 121-200: .6X TO 1.5X
*26-70 p/r 81-120: .75X TO 2X
*26-70 p/r 66-80: 1X TO 2.5X
*26-70 p/r 51-65: 1X TO 2.5X
*26-70 p/r 36-50: 1.25X TO 3X
*26-70 p/r 26-35: 1.5X TO 4X
RANDOM INSERTS IN PACKS
PRINT RUNS B/WN 6-500 COPIES PER
NO PRICING ON QTY OF 25 OR LESS

2004 Donruss Stat Line Season

*71-370 p/r 121-193: 3X TO 8X
*71-370 p/r 81-120: 4X TO 10X
*71-370 p/r 66-80: 5X TO 12X
*71-370 p/r 51-65: 5X TO 12X
*71-370 p/r 36-50: 6X TO 15X
*71-370 p/r 26-35: 8X TO 20X
*1-25/371-400 p/r 201-225:1X TO 2.5X
*1-25/371-400 p/r 121-200: 1.25X TO 3X
*1-25/371-400 p/r 81-120: 1.5X TO 4X
*1-25/371-400 p/r 66-80: 2X TO 5X
*1-25/371-400 p/r 51-65: 2X TO 5X
*1-25/371-400 p/r 36-50: 2.5X TO 6X
*1-25/371-400 p/r 26-35: 3X TO 8X
*26-70 p/r 201-261: .5X TO 1.2X
*26-70 p/r 121-200: .6X TO 1.5X
*26-70 p/r 81-120: .75X TO 2X
*26-70 p/r 66-80: 1X TO 2.5X
*26-70 p/r 51-65: 1X TO 2.5X
*26-70 p/r 36-50: 1.25X TO 3X
*26-70 p/r 26-35: 1.5X TO 4X
RANDOM INSERTS IN PACKS
PRINT RUNS B/WN 1-261 COPIES PER
NO PRICING ON QTY OF 25 OR LESS

2004 Donruss All-Stars American League

STATED PRINT RUN 1000 SERIAL #'d SETS
*BLACK: .6X TO 1.5X BASIC
BLACK PRINT RUN 250 SERIAL #'d SETS
RANDOM INSERTS IN PACKS
1 Alex Rodriguez 2.00 5.00
2 Roger Clemens 2.00 5.00
3 Ichiro Suzuki 2.00 5.00
4 Barry Zito 1.00 2.50
5 Garret Anderson .60 1.50
6 Derek Jeter 4.00 10.00
7 Manny Ramirez 1.50 4.00
8 Pedro Martinez 1.00 2.50
9 Alfonso Soriano 1.00 2.50
10 Carlos Delgado .60 1.50

2004 Donruss All-Stars National League

STATED PRINT RUN 1000 SERIAL #'d SETS
*BLACK: .6X TO 1.5X BASIC
BLACK PRINT RUN 250 SERIAL #'d SETS
RANDOM INSERTS IN PACKS
1 Barry Bonds 2.50 6.00
2 Andruw Jones .60 1.50
3 Scott Rolen 1.00 2.50
4 Austin Kearns .60 1.50
5 Mark Prior 1.00 2.50
6 Vladimir Guerrero 1.00 2.50
7 Jeff Bagwell 1.00 2.50
8 Mike Piazza 1.50 4.00
9 Albert Pujols 2.00 5.00
10 Randy Johnson 1.50 4.00

2004 Donruss Bat Kings

1-4 PRINT RUN 250 SERIAL #'d SETS
5-8 PRINT RUN 100 SERIAL #'d SETS
*STUDIO 1-4: .75X TO 2X BASIC
STUDIO 1-4 PRINT RUN 50 SERIAL #'d SETS
STUDIO 5-8 PRINT RUN 25 SERIAL #'d SETS
STUDIO 5-8 NO PRICING DUE TO SCARCITY
1 Alex Rodriguez 03 8.00 20.00
2 Albert Pujols 03 10.00 25.00
3 Chipper Jones 03 6.00 15.00
4 Lance Berkman 03 4.00 10.00
5 Cal Ripken 88 20.00 50.00
6 George Brett 87 15.00 40.00
7 Don Mattingly 89 15.00 40.00
8 Roberto Clemente 02 50.00 100.00

2004 Donruss Craftsmen

STATED PRINT RUN 2000 SERIAL #'d SETS
*BLACK: 1X TO 2.5X BASIC
BLACK PRINT RUN 275 SERIAL #'d SETS
*MASTER: 1.25X TO 3X BASIC
MASTER PRINT RUN 150 SERIAL #'d SETS
RANDOM INSERTS IN PACKS
1 Alex Rodriguez 1.25 3.00
2 Mark Prior .60 1.50
3 Ichiro Suzuki 1.25 3.00
4 Barry Bonds 1.50 4.00
5 Ken Griffey Jr. 2.00 5.00
6 Alfonso Soriano .60 1.50
7 Mike Piazza 1.00 2.50
8 Chipper Jones 1.00 2.50
9 Derek Jeter 2.50 6.00
10 Randy Johnson 1.00 2.50
11 Sammy Sosa 1.00 2.50
12 Roger Clemens 1.25 3.00
13 Nomar Garciaparra .60 1.50
14 Greg Maddux 1.25 3.00
15 Albert Pujols 1.25 3.00

2004 Donruss Diamond Kings Inserts

STATED PRINT RUN 2500 SERIAL #'d SETS
*BLACK: .75X TO 2X BASIC
BLACK PRINT RUN 100 SERIAL #'d SETS
*STUDIO: .6X TO 1.5X BASIC
STUDIO PRINT RUN 250 SERIAL #'d SETS
DK1 Derek Jeter 5.00 12.00
DK2 Greg Maddux 2.50 6.00
DK3 Albert Pujols 2.50 6.00
DK4 Ichiro Suzuki 2.50 6.00
DK5 Alex Rodriguez 2.50 6.00
DK6 Roger Clemens 2.50 6.00
DK7 Andruw Jones .75 2.00
DK8 Barry Bonds 3.00 8.00
DK9 Jeff Bagwell 1.25 3.00
DK10 Randy Johnson 2.00 5.00
DK11 Scott Rolen 1.25 3.00
DK12 Lance Berkman 1.25 3.00
DK13 Barry Zito 1.25 3.00
DK14 Manny Ramirez 2.00 5.00
DK15 Carlos Delgado .75 2.00
DK16 Alfonso Soriano 1.25 3.00
DK17 Todd Helton 1.25 3.00
DK18 Mike Mussina 1.25 3.00
DK19 Austin Kearns .75 2.00
DK20 Nomar Garciaparra 1.25 3.00
DK21 Chipper Jones 2.00 5.00
DK22 Mark Prior 1.25 3.00
DK23 Jim Thome 1.25 3.00
DK24 Vladimir Guerrero 1.25 3.00
DK25 Pedro Martinez 1.25 3.00

2004 Donruss Elite Series

RANDOM INSERTS IN PACKS
STATED PRINT RUN 1500 SERIAL #'d SETS
*BLACK: 1X TO 2.5X BASIC
BLACK PRINT RUN 150 SERIAL #'d SETS
DOMINATORS PRINT 25 SERIAL #'d SETS
DOMINATORS NO PRICE DUE TO SCARCITY
1 Albert Pujols 2.00 5.00
2 Barry Zito 1.00 2.50
3 Gary Sheffield .60 1.50
4 Mike Mussina 1.00 2.50
5 Lance Berkman 1.00 2.50
6 Alfonso Soriano 1.00 2.50
7 Randy Johnson 1.50 4.00
8 Nomar Garciaparra 1.00 2.50
9 Austin Kearns .60 1.50
10 Manny Ramirez 1.50 4.00
11 Mark Prior 1.00 2.50
12 Alex Rodriguez 2.00 5.00
13 Derek Jeter 4.00 10.00
14 Barry Bonds 2.50 6.00
15 Roger Clemens 2.00 5.00

2004 Donruss Inside View

RANDOM INSERTS IN PACKS
STATED PRINT RUN 1250 SERIAL #'d SETS
1 Derek Jeter 3.00 8.00
2 Greg Maddux 1.50 4.00
3 Albert Pujols 1.50 4.00
4 Ichiro Suzuki 1.50 4.00
5 Alex Rodriguez 1.50 4.00
6 Roger Clemens 1.50 4.00
7 Andruw Jones .50 1.25
8 Barry Bonds 2.00 5.00
9 Jeff Bagwell .75 2.00
10 Randy Johnson 1.25 3.00
11 Scott Rolen .75 2.00
12 Lance Berkman .75 2.00
13 Barry Zito .75 2.00
14 Manny Ramirez 1.25 3.00
15 Carlos Delgado .50 1.25
16 Alfonso Soriano .75 2.00
17 Todd Helton .75 2.00
18 Mike Mussina .75 2.00
19 Austin Kearns .50 1.25
20 Nomar Garciaparra .75 2.00
21 Chipper Jones 1.25 3.00
22 Mark Prior .75 2.00
23 Jim Thome .75 2.00
24 Vladimir Guerrero .75 2.00
25 Pedro Martinez .75 2.00

2004 Donruss Jersey Kings

1-6 PRINT RUN 250 SERIAL #'d SETS
7-12 PRINT RUN 100 SERIAL #'d SETS
*STUDIO 1-6: .75X TO 2X BASIC JSY KINGS
STUDIO 1-6 PRINT RUN 50 SERIAL #'d SETS
STUDIO 7-12 PRINT RUN 25 SERIAL #'d SETS
STUDIO 7-12 NO PRICING DUE TO SCARCITY
1 Alfonso Soriano 03 2.00 5.00
2 Sammy Sosa 03 3.00 8.00
3 Roger Clemens 03 4.00 10.00
4 Nomar Garciaparra 03 2.00 5.00
5 Mark Prior 03 2.00 5.00
6 Vladimir Guerrero 03 2.00 5.00
7 Don Mattingly 89 6.00 15.00
8 Roberto Clemente 02 40.00 100.00
9 George Brett 87 6.00 15.00
10 Nolan Ryan 01 10.00 25.00
11 Cal Ripken 01 15.00 40.00
12 Mike Schmidt 01 5.00 12.00

2004 Donruss Longball Leaders

STATED PRINT RUN 1500 SERIAL #'d SETS
*BLACK: .75X TO 2X BASIC LL
BLACK PRINT RUN 250 SERIAL #'d SETS
*DIE CUT: 1.25X TO 3X BASIC LL
DIE CUT PRINT RUN 50 SERIAL #'d SETS
1 Barry Bonds 2.00 5.00
2 Alfonso Soriano .75 2.00
3 Adam Dunn .75 2.00
4 Alex Rodriguez 1.50 4.00
5 Jim Thome .75 2.00
6 Garret Anderson .50 1.25
7 Juan Gonzalez .50 1.25
8 Jeff Bagwell .75 2.00
9 Gary Sheffield .50 1.25
10 Sammy Sosa 1.25 3.00

2004 Donruss Mound Marvels

STATED PRINT RUN 750 SERIAL #'d SETS
*BLACK: .75X TO 2X BASIC MM
BLACK PRINT RUN 175 SERIAL #'d SETS
RANDOM INSERTS IN PACKS
1 Mark Prior 1.25 3.00
2 Curt Schilling 1.25 3.00
3 Mike Mussina 1.25 3.00
4 Kevin Brown .75 2.00
5 Pedro Martinez 1.25 3.00
6 Mark Mulder .75 2.00
7 Kerry Wood .75 2.00
8 Greg Maddux 2.50 6.00
9 Kevin Millwood .75 2.00
10 Barry Zito 1.25 3.00
11 Roger Clemens 2.50 6.00
12 Randy Johnson 2.00 5.00
13 Hideo Nomo 2.00 5.00
14 Tim Hudson 1.25 3.00
15 Tom Glavine 1.25 3.00

2004 Donruss Power Alley Red

STATED PRINT RUN 2500 SERIAL #'d SETS
BLACK DC PRINT RUN 1 SERIAL #'d SET
BLACK DC NO PRICING DUE TO SCARCITY
*BLUE: .6X TO 1.5X BASIC RED
BLUE PRINT RUN 1000 SERIAL #'d SETS
*BLUE DC: 1.25X TO 3X BASIC RED
BLUE DC PRINT RUN 100 SERIAL #'d SETS
GREEN PRINT RUN 25 SERIAL #'d SETS
GREEN NO PRICING DUE TO SCARCITY
GREEN DC 5 SERIAL #'d SETS
GREEN DC NO PRICING DUE TO SCARCITY
*PURPLE: 1X TO 2.5X BASIC RED
PURPLE PRINT RUN 250 SERIAL #'d SETS
PURPLE DC PRINT RUN 25 SERIAL #'d SETS
PURPLE DC NO PRICING DUE TO SCARCITY
*RED DC: 1X TO 2.5X BASIC RED
RED DC PRINT RUN 250 SERIAL #'d SETS
*YELLOW: 1.25X TO 3X BASIC RED
YELLOW PRINT RUN 100 SERIAL #'d SETS
YELLOW DC PRINT RUN 10 SERIAL #'d SETS
YELLOW DC NO PRICING DUE TO SCARCITY
1 Albert Pujols 1.25 3.00
2 Mike Piazza 1.00 2.50
3 Carlos Delgado .40 1.00
4 Barry Bonds 1.50 4.00
5 Jim Edmonds .60 1.50
6 Nomar Garciaparra .60 1.50
7 Alfonso Soriano .60 1.50
8 Alex Rodriguez 1.25 3.00
9 Lance Berkman .60 1.50
10 Scott Rolen .60 1.50
11 Manny Ramirez 1.00 2.50
12 Rafael Palmeiro .60 1.50
13 Sammy Sosa 1.00 2.50
14 Adam Dunn .60 1.50
15 Andruw Jones .40 1.00
16 Jim Thome .60 1.50
17 Jason Giambi .40 1.00
18 Jeff Bagwell .60 1.50
19 Juan Gonzalez .40 1.00
20 Austin Kearns .40 1.00

2004 Donruss Production Line Average

PRINT RUNS B/WN 300-359 COPIES PER
*BLACK: .75X TO 2X BASIC AVG
BLACK PRINT RUN 35 SERIAL #'d SETS
*DIE CUT: .5X TO 1.2X BASIC AVG
DIE CUT PRINT RUN 100 SERIAL #'d SETS
1 Gary Sheffield/330 1.00 2.50
2 Ichiro Suzuki/312 3.00 8.00
3 Todd Helton/358 1.50 4.00
4 Manny Ramirez/325 2.50 6.00
5 Garret Anderson/315 1.00 2.50
6 Barry Bonds/341 4.00 10.00
7 Albert Pujols/359 3.00 8.00
8 Derek Jeter/324 6.00 15.00
9 Nomar Garciaparra/301 1.50 4.00
10 Hank Blalock/300 1.00 2.50

2004 Donruss Production Line OBP

PRINT RUNS B/WN 396-529 COPIES PER
*BLACK: 1X TO 2.5X BASIC OBP
BLACK PRINT RUN 40 SERIAL #'d SETS
*DIE CUT: .6X TO 1.5X BASIC OBP
DIE CUT PRINT RUN 100 SERIAL #'d SETS
1 Todd Helton/458 1.25 3.00
2 Albert Pujols/439 2.50 6.00
3 Larry Walker/422 1.25 3.00
4 Barry Bonds/529 3.00 8.00
5 Chipper Jones/402 2.00 5.00
6 Manny Ramirez/427 2.00 5.00
7 Gary Sheffield/419 .75 2.00
8 Lance Berkman/412 1.25 3.00
9 Alex Rodriguez/396 2.50 6.00
10 Jason Giambi/412 .75 2.00

2004 Donruss Production Line OPS

PRINT RUNS B/WN 910-1278 COPIES PER
*BLACK: .75X TO 2X BASIC OPS
BLACK PRINT RUN 125 SERIAL #'d SETS
*DIE CUT: .75X TO 2X BASIC OPS
DIE CUT PRINT RUN 100 SERIAL #'d SETS
1 Albert Pujols/1106 2.00 5.00
2 Barry Bonds/1278 2.50 6.00
3 Gary Sheffield/1023 .60 1.50
4 Todd Helton/1088 1.00 2.50
5 Scott Rolen/910 1.00 2.50
6 Manny Ramirez/1014 1.50 4.00
7 Alex Rodriguez/995 2.00 5.00
8 Jim Thome/958 1.00 2.50
9 Jason Giambi/939 .60 1.50
10 Frank Thomas/952 1.50 4.00

2004 Donruss Production Line Slugging

PRINT RUNS B/WN 541-749 COPIES PER
*BLACK: .75X TO 2X BASIC SLG
BLACK PRINT RUN 75 SERIAL #'d SETS
*DIE CUT: .6X TO 1.5X BASIC SLG
DIE CUT PRINT RUN 100 SERIAL #'d SETS
1 Alex Rodriguez/600 2.50 6.00
2 Frank Thomas/562 2.00 5.00
3 Garret Anderson/541 .75 2.00
4 Albert Pujols/667 2.50 6.00
5 Sammy Sosa/553 2.00 5.00
6 Gary Sheffield/604 .75 2.00
7 Manny Ramirez/587 2.00 5.00
8 Jim Edmonds/617 1.25 3.00
9 Barry Bonds/749 3.00 8.00
10 Todd Helton/630 1.25 3.00

2004 Donruss Recollection Autographs

PRINT RUNS B/WN 1-100 COPIES PER
NO PRICING ON QTY OF 50 OR LESS
27 John Candelaria 88 Black/83 6.00 15.00
39 Jack Clark 87/67 8.00 20.00
40 Jack Clark 88/75 6.00 15.00
69 Sid Fernandez 86/52 8.00 20.00
72 Sid Fernandez 88/58 8.00 20.00
83 George Foster 83/50 8.00 20.00
84 George Foster 84/70 8.00 20.00
85 George Foster 85/50 8.00 20.00
86 George Foster 86/83 6.00 15.00
91 Cliff Lee 03/100 8.00 20.00
92 Terrence Long 01/90 4.00 10.00
93 Melvin Mora 03/50 8.00 20.00
100 Jesse Orosco 86 Blue/65 5.00 12.00
102 Jesse Orosco 87 Blue/90 4.00 10.00
115 Jose Vidro 01/89 4.00 10.00

2004 Donruss Timber and Threads

STATED ODDS 1:40
*STUDIO: .75X TO 2X BASIC TT
STUDIO RANDOM INSERTS IN PACKS
STUDIO PRINT RUN 50 SERIAL #'d SETS
1 Adam Dunn Jsy 3.00 8.00
2 Alex Rodriguez Blue Jsy 6.00 15.00
3 Alex Rodriguez White Jsy 6.00 15.00
4 Andruw Jones Jsy 4.00 10.00
5 Austin Kearns Jsy 3.00 8.00
6 Carlos Beltran Jsy 3.00 8.00
7 Carlos Lee Jsy 3.00 8.00
8 Frank Thomas Jsy 4.00 10.00
9 Greg Maddux Jsy 4.00 10.00
10 Hideo Nomo Jsy 4.00 10.00
11 Jeff Bagwell Jsy 4.00 10.00
12 Lance Berkman Jsy 3.00 8.00
13 Magglio Ordonez Jsy 3.00 8.00
14 Mike Sweeney Jsy 3.00 8.00
15 Randy Johnson Jsy 4.00 10.00
16 Rocco Baldelli Jsy 3.00 8.00
17 Roger Clemens Jsy 6.00 15.00
18 Sammy Sosa Jsy 4.00 10.00
19 Shawn Green Jsy 3.00 8.00
20 Tom Glavine Jsy 4.00 10.00
21 Adam Dunn Bat 3.00 8.00
22 Andruw Jones Bat 4.00 10.00
23 Bobby Abreu Bat 3.00 8.00
24 Hank Blalock Bat 3.00 8.00
25 Ivan Rodriguez Bat 4.00 10.00
26 Jim Edmonds Bat 3.00 8.00
27 Josh Phelps Bat 3.00 8.00
28 Juan Gonzalez Bat 3.00 8.00
29 Lance Berkman Bat 3.00 8.00
30 Larry Walker Bat 3.00 8.00
31 Magglio Ordonez Bat 3.00 8.00
32 Manny Ramirez Bat 4.00 10.00
33 Mike Piazza Bat 4.00 10.00
34 Nomar Garciaparra Bat 6.00 15.00
35 Paul Lo Duca Bat 3.00 8.00
36 Roberto Alomar Bat 4.00 10.00
37 Rocco Baldelli Bat 3.00 8.00
38 Sammy Sosa Bat 4.00 10.00
39 Vernon Wells Bat 3.00 8.00
40 Vladimir Guerrero Bat 4.00 10.00

2004 Donruss Timber and Threads Autographs

RANDOM INSERTS IN PACKS
PRINT RUNS B/WN 5-50 COPIES PER
NO PRICING ON QTY OF 34 OR LESS
23 Bobby Abreu Bat/50 10.00 25.00
24 Hank Blalock Bat/50 10.00 25.00
27 Josh Phelps Bat/50 10.00 25.00
35 Paul Lo Duca Bat/50 10.00 25.00
40 Vladimir Guerrero Bat/50 30.00 60.00

2004 Donruss-Playoff Hawaii Fans of the Game Gandolfini

These cards, which were issued to select attendees of the 2004 Hawaii Trade Conference feature Sopranos star James Gandolfini. The cards were issued to promote the 2004 Donruss/Playoff initiative of having celebrity signatures within their 2004 products.

FG1 James Gandolfini/300

2005 Donruss

This 400-card set was released in November, 2004. The set was issued in 10-card packs with an $2 SRP which came 24 packs to a box and 16 boxes to a case. Subsets included: Diamond Kings (1-25), Rated Rookies (26-70), Team Checklists (371-400). All of these subets were issued at a stated rate of one in six.

COMPLETE SET (400) 40.00 100.00
COMP.SET w/o SP's (300) 10.00 25.00
COMMON CARD (71-370) .10 .30
COMMON (1-25/371-400) .40 1.00
COMMON CARD (26-70) .75 2.00
1-25 STATED ODDS 1:6
26-70 STATED ODDS 1:6
371-400 STATED ODDS 1:6
1 Garret Anderson DK .40 1.00
2 Vladimir Guerrero DK .60 1.50
3 Manny Ramirez DK 1.00 2.50
4 Kerry Wood DK .40 1.00
5 Sammy Sosa DK 1.00 2.50
6 Magglio Ordonez DK .60 1.50
7 Adam Dunn DK .60 1.50
8 Todd Helton DK .60 1.50
9 Josh Beckett DK .40 1.00
10 Miguel Cabrera DK 1.00 2.50
11 Lance Berkman DK .60 1.50
12 Carlos Beltran DK .60 1.50
13 Shawn Green DK .40 1.00
14 Roger Clemens DK 1.25 3.00
15 Mike Piazza DK 1.00 2.50
16 Alex Rodriguez DK 1.25 3.00
17 Derek Jeter DK 2.50 6.00
18 Mark Mulder DK .40 1.00
19 Jim Thome DK .60 1.50
20 Albert Pujols DK 1.25 3.00
21 Scott Rolen DK .60 1.50
22 Aubrey Huff DK .40 1.00
23 Alfonso Soriano DK .60 1.50
24 Hank Blalock DK .40 1.00
25 Vernon Wells DK .40 1.00
26 Kazuo Matsui RR .75 2.00
27 B.J. Upton RR 1.25 3.00
28 Charles Thomas RR .75 2.00
29 Akinori Otsuka RR .75 2.00
30 David Aardsma RR .75 2.00
31 Travis Blackley RR .75 2.00
32 Brad Halsey RR .75 2.00
33 David Wright RR 1.50 4.00
34 Kazuhito Tadano RR .75 2.00
35 Casey Kotchman RR .75 2.00
36 Khalil Greene RR .75 2.00
37 Adrian Gonzalez RR 1.50 4.00
38 Zack Greinke RR 2.00 5.00
39 Chad Cordero RR .75 2.00
40 Scott Kazmir RR 2.00 5.00
41 Jeremy Guthrie RR 1.25 3.00
42 Noah Lowry RR .75 2.00
43 Chase Utley RR 1.25 3.00
44 Billy Traber RR .75 2.00
45 Aarom Baldiris RR .75 2.00
46 Abe Alvarez RR .75 2.00
47 Angel Chavez RR .75 2.00
48 Joe Mauer RR 1.50 4.00
49 Joey Gathright RR .75 2.00
50 John Gall RR .75 2.00
51 Ronald Belisario RR .75 2.00
52 Ryan Wing RR .75 2.00
53 Scott Proctor RR .75 2.00
54 Yadier Molina RR 2.00 5.00
55 Carlos Hines RR .75 2.00
56 Frankie Francisco RR .75 2.00
57 Graham Koonce RR .75 2.00
58 Jake Woods RR .75 2.00
59 Jason Bartlett RR .75 2.00
60 Mike Rouse RR .75 2.00
61 Phil Stockman RR .75 2.00
62 Renyel Pinto RR .75 2.00
63 Roberto Novoa RR .75 2.00
64 Ryan Meaux RR .75 2.00
65 Dave Crouthers RR .75 2.00
66 Justin Knoedler RR .75 2.00
67 Justin Leone RR .75 2.00
68 Nick Regilio RR .75 2.00
69 Mike Gosling RR .75 2.00
70 Onil Joseph RR .75 2.00
71 Bartolo Colon .12 .30
72 Brad Fullmer .12 .30
73 Chone Figgins .12 .30
74 Darin Erstad .12 .30
75 Francisco Rodriguez .20 .50
76 Garret Anderson .12 .30
77 Jarrod Washburn .12 .30
78 John Lackey .20 .50
79 Jose Guillen .12 .30
80 Robb Quinlan .12 .30
81 Tim Salmon .12 .30
82 Troy Glaus .12 .30
83 Troy Percival .12 .30
84 Vladimir Guerrero .20 .50
85 Brandon Webb .20 .50
86 Casey Fossum .12 .30
87 Luis Gonzalez .12 .30
88 Randy Johnson .30 .75
89 Richie Sexson .12 .30
90 Robby Hammock .12 .30
91 Roberto Alomar .20 .50
92 Adam LaRoche .12 .30
93 Andruw Jones .12 .30
94 Bubba Nelson .12 .30
95 Chipper Jones .30 .75
96 J.D. Drew .12 .30
97 John Smoltz .30 .75
98 Johnny Estrada .12 .30
99 Marcus Giles .12 .30
100 Mike Hampton .12 .30
101 Nick Green .12 .30
102 Rafael Furcal .12 .30
103 Russ Ortiz .12 .30
104 Adam Loewen .12 .30
105 Brian Roberts .12 .30
106 Javy Lopez .12 .30
107 Jay Gibbons .12 .30
108 L.Bigbie UER Roberts .12 .30
109 Luis Matos .12 .30
110 Melvin Mora .12 .30
111 Miguel Tejada .20 .50
112 Rafael Palmeiro .20 .50
113 Rodrigo Lopez .12 .30
114 Sidney Ponson .12 .30
115 Bill Mueller .12 .30
116 Byung-Hyun Kim .12 .30
117 Curt Schilling .20 .50
118 David Ortiz .30 .75
119 Derek Lowe .12 .30
120 Doug Mientkiewicz .12 .30
121 Jason Varitek .30 .75

122 Johnny Damon .20 .50
123 Keith Foulke .12 .30
124 Kevin Youkilis .12 .30
125 Manny Ramirez .30 .75
126 Orlando Cabrera .12 .30
127 Pedro Martinez .20 .50
128 Trot Nixon .12 .30
129 Aramis Ramirez .12 .30
130 Carlos Zambrano .20 .50
131 Corey Patterson .12 .30
132 Derrek Lee .12 .30
133 Greg Maddux .40 1.00
134 Kerry Wood .12 .30
135 Mark Prior .20 .50
136 Matt Clement .12 .30
137 Moises Alou .12 .30
138 Nomar Garciaparra .20 .50
139 Sammy Sosa .30 .75
140 Todd Walker .12 .30
141 Angel Guzman .12 .30
142 Billy Koch .12 .30
143 Carlos Lee .12 .30
144 Frank Thomas .30 .75
145 Magglio Ordonez .20 .50
146 Mark Buehrle .20 .50
147 Paul Konerko .20 .50
148 Wilson Valdez .12 .30
149 Adam Dunn .20 .50
150 Austin Kearns .12 .30
151 Barry Larkin .20 .50
152 Benito Santiago .12 .30
153 Jason LaRue .12 .30
154 Ken Griffey Jr. .60 1.50
155 Ryan Wagner .12 .30
156 Sean Casey .12 .30
157 Brandon Phillips .12 .30
158 Brian Tallet .12 .30
159 C.C. Sabathia .20 .50
160 Cliff Lee .20 .50
161 Jeremy Guthrie .20 .50
162 Jody Gerut .12 .30
163 Matt Lawton .12 .30
164 Omar Vizquel .20 .50
165 Travis Hafner .12 .30
166 Victor Martinez .20 .50
167 Charles Johnson .12 .30
168 Garrett Atkins .12 .30
169 Jason Jennings .12 .30
170 Jay Payton .12 .30
171 Jeromy Burnitz .12 .30
172 Joe Kennedy .12 .30
173 Larry Walker .20 .50
174 Preston Wilson .12 .30
175 Todd Helton .20 .50
176 Vinny Castilla .12 .30
177 Bobby Higginson .12 .30
178 Brandon Inge .12 .30
179 Carlos Guillen .12 .30
180 Carlos Pena .20 .50
181 Craig Monroe .12 .30
182 Dmitri Young .12 .30
183 Eric Munson .12 .30
184 Fernando Vina .12 .30
185 Ivan Rodriguez .20 .50
186 Jeremy Bonderman .12 .30
187 Rondell White .12 .30
188 A.J. Burnett .12 .30
189 Dontrelle Willis .12 .30
190 Guillermo Mota .12 .30
191 Hee Seop Choi .12 .30
192 Jeff Conine .12 .30
193 Josh Beckett .12 .30
194 Juan Encarnacion .12 .30
195 Juan Pierre .12 .30
196 Luis Castillo .12 .30
197 Miguel Cabrera .30 .75
198 Mike Lowell .12 .30
199 Paul Lo Duca .12 .30
200 Andy Pettitte .20 .50
201 Brad Ausmus .12 .30
202 Carlos Beltran .20 .50
203 Chris Burke .12 .30
204 Craig Biggio .20 .50
205 Jeff Bagwell .20 .50
206 Jeff Kent .12 .30
207 Lance Berkman .20 .50
208 Morgan Ensberg .12 .30
209 Octavio Dotel .12 .30
210 Roger Clemens .40 1.00
211 Roy Oswalt .20 .50
212 Tim Redding .12 .30
213 Angel Berroa .12 .30
214 Juan Gonzalez .12 .30
215 Ken Harvey .12 .30
216 Mike Sweeney .12 .30
217 Adrian Beltre .30 .75
218 Brad Penny .12 .30
219 Eric Gagne .12 .30
220 Hideo Nomo .30 .75
221 Hong-Chih Kuo .12 .30
222 Jeff Weaver .12 .30
223 Kazuhisa Ishii .12 .30
224 Milton Bradley .12 .30
225 Shawn Green .12 .30
226 Steve Finley .12 .30
227 Danny Kolb .12 .30
228 Geoff Jenkins .12 .30
229 Junior Spivey .12 .30
230 Lyle Overbay .12 .30
231 Rickie Weeks .12 .30
232 Scott Podsednik .12 .30
233 Brad Radke .12 .30
234 Corey Koskie .12 .30
235 Cristian Guzman .12 .30
236 Dustan Mohr .12 .30
237 Eddie Guardado .12 .30
238 J.D. Durbin .12 .30
239 Jacque Jones .12 .30
240 Joe Nathan .12 .30
241 Johan Santana .20 .50
242 Lew Ford .12 .30
243 Michael Cuddyer .12 .30
244 Shannon Stewart .12 .30
245 Torii Hunter .12 .30
246 Brad Wilkerson .12 .30
247 Carl Everett .12 .30
248 Jeff Fassero .12 .30
249 Jose Vidro .12 .30
250 Livan Hernandez .12 .30
251 Michael Barrett .12 .30
252 Tony Batista .12 .30
253 Zach Day .12 .30
254 Al Leiter .12 .30
255 Cliff Floyd .12 .30
256 Jae Weong Seo .12 .30
257 John Olerud .12 .30
258 Jose Reyes .20 .50
259 Mike Cameron .12 .30
260 Mike Piazza .30 .75
261 Richard Hidalgo .12 .30
262 Tom Glavine .20 .50
263 Vance Wilson .12 .30
264 Alex Rodriguez .40 1.00
265 Armando Benitez .12 .30
266 Bernie Williams .20 .50
267 Bubba Crosby .12 .30
268 Chien-Ming Wang .50 1.25
269 Derek Jeter .75 2.00
270 Esteban Loaiza .12 .30
271 Gary Sheffield .12 .30
272 Hideki Matsui .50 1.25
273 Jason Giambi .12 .30
274 Javier Vazquez .12 .30
275 Jorge Posada .20 .50
276 Jose Contreras .12 .30
277 Kenny Lofton .12 .30
278 Kevin Brown .12 .30
279 Mariano Rivera .40 1.00
280 Mike Mussina .20 .50
281 Barry Zito .20 .50
282 Bobby Crosby .12 .30
283 Eric Byrnes .12 .30
284 Eric Chavez .12 .30
285 Erubiel Durazo .12 .30
286 Jermaine Dye .12 .30
287 Mark Kotsay .12 .30
288 Mark Mulder .12 .30
289 Rich Harden .12 .30
290 Tim Hudson .20 .50
291 Billy Wagner .12 .30
292 Bobby Abreu .12 .30
293 Brett Myers .12 .30
294 Eric Milton .12 .30
295 Jim Thome .20 .50
296 Jimmy Rollins .20 .50
297 Kevin Millwood .12 .30
298 Marlon Byrd .12 .30
299 Mike Lieberthal .12 .30
300 Pat Burrell .12 .30
301 Randy Wolf .12 .30
302 Craig Wilson .12 .30
303 Jack Wilson .12 .30
304 Jacob Cruz .12 .30
305 Jason Bay .12 .30
306 Jason Kendall .12 .30
307 Jose Castillo .12 .30
308 Kip Wells .12 .30
309 Brian Giles .12 .30
310 Brian Lawrence .12 .30
311 Chris Oxspring .12 .30
312 David Wells .12 .30
313 Freddy Guzman .12 .30
314 Jake Peavy .12 .30
315 Mark Loretta .12 .30
316 Ryan Klesko .12 .30
317 Sean Burroughs .12 .30
318 Trevor Hoffman .20 .50
319 Xavier Nady .12 .30
320 A.J. Pierzynski .12 .30
321 Edgardo Alfonzo .12 .30
322 J.T. Snow .12 .30
323 Jason Schmidt .12 .30
324 Jerome Williams .12 .30
325 Kirk Rueter .12 .30
326 Bret Boone .12 .30
327 Bucky Jacobsen .12 .30
328 Edgar Martinez .20 .50
329 Freddy Garcia .12 .30
330 Ichiro Suzuki .40 1.00
331 Jamie Moyer .12 .30
332 Joel Pineiro .12 .30
333 Scott Spiezio .12 .30
334 Shigetoshi Hasegawa .12 .30
335 Albert Pujols .40 1.00
336 Edgar Renteria .12 .30
337 Jason Isringhausen .12 .30
338 Jim Edmonds .20 .50
339 Matt Morris .12 .30
340 Mike Matheny .12 .30
341 Reggie Sanders .12 .30
342 Scott Rolen .20 .50
343 Woody Williams .12 .30
344 Jeff Suppan .12 .30
345 Aubrey Huff .12 .30
346 Carl Crawford .20 .50
347 Chad Gaudin .12 .30
348 Delmon Young .30 .75
349 Dewon Brazelton .12 .30
350 Jose Cruz Jr. .12 .30
351 Rocco Baldelli .12 .30
352 Tino Martinez .20 .50
353 Toby Hall .12 .30
354 Alfonso Soriano .20 .50
355 Brian Jordan .12 .30
356 Francisco Cordero .12 .30
357 Hank Blalock .12 .30
358 Kenny Rogers .12 .30
359 Kevin Mench .12 .30
360 Laynce Nix .12 .30
361 Mark Teixeira .20 .50
362 Michael Young .12 .30
363 Alex S. Gonzalez .12 .30
364 Alexis Rios .12 .30
365 Carlos Delgado .12 .30
366 Eric Hinske .12 .30
367 Frank Catalanotto .12 .30
368 Josh Phelps .12 .30
369 Roy Halladay .20 .50
370 Vernon Wells .12 .30
371 Vladimir Guerrero TC .60 1.50
372 Randy Johnson TC 1.00 2.50
373 Chipper Jones TC 1.00 2.50
374 Miguel Tejada TC .60 1.50
375 Pedro Martinez TC .60 1.50
376 Sammy Sosa TC 1.00 2.50
377 Frank Thomas TC 1.00 2.50
378 Ken Griffey Jr. TC 2.00 5.00
379 Victor Martinez TC .60 1.50
380 Todd Helton TC .60 1.50
381 Ivan Rodriguez TC .60 1.50
382 Miguel Cabrera TC 1.00 2.50
383 Roger Clemens TC 1.25 3.00
384 Ken Harvey TC .40 1.00
385 Eric Gagne TC .40 1.00
386 Lyle Overbay TC .40 1.00
387 Shannon Stewart TC .40 1.00
388 Brad Wilkerson TC .40 1.00
389 Mike Piazza TC 1.00 2.50
390 Alex Rodriguez TC 1.25 3.00
391 Mark Mulder TC .40 1.00
392 Jim Thome TC .60 1.50
393 Jack Wilson TC .40 1.00
394 Khalil Greene TC .40 1.00
395 Jason Schmidt TC .40 1.00
396 Ichiro Suzuki TC 1.25 3.00
397 Albert Pujols TC 1.25 3.00
398 Rocco Baldelli TC .40 1.00
399 Alfonso Soriano TC .60 1.50
400 Vernon Wells TC .40 1.00

2005 Donruss 25th Anniversary

*25th ANN 71-370: 10X TO 25X BASIC
*25th ANN 1-25/371-400: 4X TO 10X BASIC
*25th ANN 26-70: 2X TO 5X BASIC
RANDOM INSERTS IN PACKS
STATED PRINT RUN 25 SERIAL #'d SETS

2005 Donruss Press Proofs Black

STATED PRINT RUN 10 SERIAL #'d SETS
NO PRICING DUE TO SCARCITY

2005 Donruss Press Proofs Blue

*BLUE 71-370: 4X TO 10X BASIC
*BLUE 1-25/371-400: 1.5X TO 4X BASIC
*BLUE 26-70: .75X TO 2X BASIC
RANDOM INSERTS IN PACKS
STATED PRINT RUN 100 SERIAL #'d SETS

2005 Donruss Press Proofs Gold

*GOLD 71-370: 10X TO 25X BASIC
*GOLD 1-25/371-400: 4X TO 10X BASIC
*GOLD 26-70: 2X TO 5X BASIC
RANDOM INSERTS IN PACKS
STATED PRINT RUN 25 SERIAL #'d SETS

2005 Donruss Press Proofs Red

*RED 71-370: 2.5X TO 6X BASIC
*RED 1-25/371-400: 1X TO 2.5X BASIC
*RED 26-70: .5X TO 1.2X BASIC
RANDOM INSERTS IN PACKS
STATED PRINT RUN 200 SERIAL #'d SETS

2005 Donruss Stat Line Career

*71-370 p/r 200-394 2.5X TO 6X
*71-370 p/r 121-200: 3X TO 8X
*71-370 p/r 81-120: 4X TO 10X
*71-370 p/r 51-80: 5X TO 12X
*71-370 p/r 36-50: 6X TO 15X
*71-370 p/r 26-35: 8X TO 20X
*71-370 p/r 16-25: 10X TO 25X
*1-25/371-400 p/r 200-574:1X TO 2.5X
*1-25/371-400 p/r 121-200: 1.25X TO 3X
*1-25/371-400 p/r 81-120: 1.5X TO 4X
*1-25/371-400 p/r 51-80: 2X TO 5X
*1-25/371-400 p/r 36-50: 2.5X TO 6X
*1-25/371-400 p/r 26-35: 3X TO 8X
*26-70 p/r 200-263: .5X TO 1.2X
*26-70 p/r 121-200: .6X TO 1.5X
*26-70 p/r 81-120: .75X TO 2X
*26-70 p/r 51-80: 1X TO 2.5X
*26-70 p/r 36-50: 1.25X TO 3X
*26-70 p/r 26-35: 1.5X TO 4X
*26-70 p/r 16-25: 2X TO 5X
RANDOM INSERTS IN PACKS
PRINT RUNS B/WN 6-500 COPIES PER
NO PRICING ON QTY OF 15 OR LESS

2005 Donruss Stat Line Season

*71-370 p/r 121-158: 3X TO 8X
*71-370 p/r 81-120: 4X TO 10X
*71-370 p/r 51-80: 5X TO 12X
*71-370 p/r 36-50: 6X TO 15X
*71-370 p/r 26-35: 8X TO 20X
*71-370 p/r 16-25: 10X TO 25X
*1-25/371-400 p/r 81-120: 1.5X TO 4X
*1-25/371-400 p/r 51-80: 2X TO 5X
*1-25/371-400 p/r 36-50: 2.5X TO 6X
*1-25/371-400 p/r 26-35: 3X TO 8X
*1-25/371-400 p/r 16-25: 4X TO 10X
*26-70 p/r 121-200: .6X TO 1.5X
*26-70 p/r 81-120: .75X TO 2X
*26-70 p/r 51-80: 1X TO 2.5X
*26-70 p/r 36-50: 1.25X TO 3X
*26-70 p/r 26-35: 1.5X TO 4X
*26-70 p/r 16-25: 2X TO 5X
RANDOM INSERTS IN PACKS
PRINT RUNS B/WN 1-158 COPIES PER
NO PRICING ON QTY OF 15 OR LESS

2005 Donruss Autographs

RANDOM INSERTS IN PACKS
80 Robb Quinlan 4.00 10.00
101 Nick Green 4.00 10.00
141 Angel Guzman 4.00 10.00
148 Wilson Valdez 4.00 10.00
172 Joe Kennedy 4.00 10.00
178 Brandon Inge 6.00 15.00
181 Craig Monroe 4.00 10.00
263 Vance Wilson 4.00 10.00
304 Jacob Cruz 4.00 10.00
327 Bucky Jacobsen 4.00 10.00
344 Jeff Suppan 6.00 15.00

2005 Donruss '85 Reprints

RANDOM INSERTS IN PACKS
STATED PRINT RUN 1985 SERIAL #'d SETS
1 Eddie Murray 1.25 3.00
2 George Brett .75 2.00
3 Nolan Ryan 6.00 15.00
4 Mike Schmidt 4.00 10.00
5 Tony Gwynn 2.50 6.00
7 Cal Ripken 6.00 15.00
8 Dwight Gooden .75 2.00
9 Roger Clemens 2.50 6.00
10 Don Mattingly 4.00 10.00
11 Kirby Puckett 2.00 5.00
12 Orel Hershiser .75 2.00

2005 Donruss '85 Reprints Material

RANDOM INSERTS IN PACKS
STATED PRINT RUN 85 SERIAL #'d SETS
1 Eddie Murray Jsy 10.00 25.00
2 George Brett Jsy 15.00 40.00
3 Nolan Ryan Jkt 15.00 40.00
4 Mike Schmidt Jkt 15.00 40.00
5 Tony Gwynn Jsy 10.00 25.00
7 Cal Ripken Jsy 30.00 60.00
8 Dwight Gooden Jsy 6.00 15.00
9 Roger Clemens Jsy 15.00 40.00
10 Don Mattingly Jsy 15.00 40.00
11 Kirby Puckett Jsy 10.00 25.00
12 Orel Hershiser Jsy 6.00 15.00

2005 Donruss All-Stars AL

STATED PRINT RUN 1000 SERIAL #'d SETS
*GOLD: .75X TO 2X BASIC
GOLD PRINT RUN 100 SERIAL #'d SETS
RANDOM INSERTS IN PACKS
1 Alex Rodriguez 2.50 6.00
2 Alfonso Soriano 1.25 3.00
3 Curt Schilling 1.25 3.00
4 Derek Jeter 5.00 12.00
5 Hank Blalock .75 2.00
6 Hideki Matsui 3.00 8.00
7 Ichiro Suzuki 2.50 6.00
8 Ivan Rodriguez 1.25 3.00
9 Jason Giambi .75 2.00
10 Manny Ramirez 2.00 5.00
11 Mark Mulder .75 2.00
12 Michael Young .75 2.00
13 Tim Hudson 1.25 3.00
14 Victor Martinez 1.25 3.00
15 Vladimir Guerrero 1.25 3.00

2005 Donruss All-Stars NL

STATED PRINT RUN 1000 SERIAL #'d SETS
*GOLD: .75X TO 2X BASIC
GOLD PRINT RUN 100 SERIAL #'d SETS
RANDOM INSERTS IN PACKS
1 Albert Pujols 2.50 6.00
2 Ben Sheets .75 2.00
3 Edgar Renteria .75 2.00
4 Eric Gagne .75 2.00
5 Jack Wilson .75 2.00
6 Jason Schmidt .75 2.00
7 Jeff Kent .75 2.00
8 Jim Thome 1.25 3.00
9 Ken Griffey Jr. 4.00 10.00
10 Mike Piazza 2.00 5.00
11 Roger Clemens 2.50 6.00
12 Sammy Sosa 2.00 5.00
13 Scott Rolen 1.25 3.00
14 Sean Casey .75 2.00
15 Todd Helton 1.25 3.00

2005 Donruss Bat Kings

RANDOM INSERTS IN PACKS
PRINT RUNS B/WN 100-250 COPIES PER
1 Garret Anderson/250 3.00 8.00
2 Vladimir Guerrero/250 4.00 10.00
3 Cal Ripken/100 30.00 60.00
4 Manny Ramirez/250 4.00 10.00
5 Kerry Wood/250 3.00 8.00
6 Sammy Sosa/250 4.00 10.00
7 Magglio Ordonez/250 3.00 8.00
8 Adam Dunn/250 3.00 8.00
9 Todd Helton/250 4.00 10.00
10 Josh Beckett/250 3.00 8.00
11 Miguel Cabrera/250 4.00 10.00
12 Lance Berkman/250 3.00 8.00
13 Carlos Beltran/250 3.00 8.00
14 Shawn Green/250 3.00 8.00
15 Roger Clemens/100 8.00 20.00
16 Mike Piazza/250 4.00 10.00
17 Nolan Ryan/100 8.00 20.00
18 Mark Mulder/250 3.00 8.00
19 Jim Thome/250 4.00 10.00
20 Albert Pujols/250 8.00 20.00
21 Scott Rolen/250 4.00 10.00
22 Aubrey Huff/250 3.00 8.00
23 Alfonso Soriano/250 3.00 8.00

2005 Donruss Bat Kings Signatures

PRINT RUNS B/WN 5-10 COPIES PER
NO PRICING DUE TO SCARCITY

2005 Donruss Craftsmen

STATED PRINT RUN 2000 SERIAL #'d SETS
*BLACK: 1.25X TO 3X BASIC
BLACK PRINT RUN 100 SERIAL #'d SETS
*MASTER: 1X TO 2.5X BASIC
MASTER PRINT RUN 250 SERIAL #'d SETS
MASTER BLACK PRINT RUN 10 #'d SETS
NO MASTER BLACK PRICING AVAILABLE
RANDOM INSERTS IN PACKS
1 Albert Pujols 1.25 3.00
2 Alex Rodriguez 1.25 3.00
3 Alfonso Soriano .60 1.50
4 Andruw Jones .40 1.00
5 Carlos Beltran .60 1.50
6 Derek Jeter 2.50 6.00
7 Greg Maddux 1.25 3.00
8 Hank Blalock .40 1.00
9 Ichiro Suzuki 1.25 3.00
10 Jeff Bagwell .60 1.50
11 Jim Thome .60 1.50
12 Josh Beckett .40 1.00
13 Ken Griffey Jr. 2.00 5.00
14 Manny Ramirez 1.00 2.50
15 Mark Mulder .40 1.00
16 Mark Prior .60 1.50
17 Mark Teixeira .60 1.50
18 Miguel Tejada .60 1.50
19 Mike Mussina .60 1.50
20 Mike Piazza 1.00 2.50
21 Nomar Garciaparra .60 1.50
22 Pedro Martinez .60 1.50
23 Rafael Palmeiro .60 1.50
24 Randy Johnson 1.00 2.50
25 Roger Clemens 1.25 3.00
26 Sammy Sosa 1.00 2.50
27 Scott Rolen .60 1.50
28 Tim Hudson .60 1.50
29 Vernon Wells .40 1.00
30 Vladimir Guerrero .60 1.50

2005 Donruss Diamond Kings Inserts

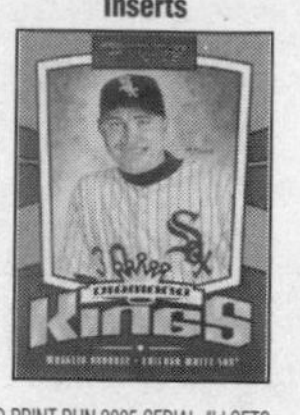

STATED PRINT RUN 2005 SERIAL #'d SETS
*STUDIO: 1X TO 2.5X BASIC
STUDIO PRINT RUN 250 SERIAL #'d SETS
*STUDIO BLACK: 1.25X TO 3X BASIC
STUDIO BLACK PRINT RUN 100 #'d SETS
RANDOM INSERTS IN PACKS
DK1 Garret Anderson .40 1.00
DK2 Vladimir Guerrero .60 1.50
DK3 Manny Ramirez 1.00 2.50
DK4 Kerry Wood .40 1.00
DK5 Sammy Sosa 1.00 2.50
DK6 Magglio Ordonez .60 1.50
DK7 Adam Dunn .60 1.50
DK8 Todd Helton .60 1.50
DK9 Josh Beckett .40 1.00
DK10 Miguel Cabrera 1.00 2.50
DK11 Lance Berkman .60 1.50
DK12 Carlos Beltran .60 1.50
DK13 Shawn Green .40 1.00
DK14 Roger Clemens 1.25 3.00
DK15 Mike Piazza 1.00 2.50
DK16 Alex Rodriguez 1.25 3.00
DK17 Derek Jeter 2.50 6.00
DK18 Mark Mulder .40 1.00
DK19 Jim Thome .60 1.50
DK20 Albert Pujols 1.25 3.00
DK21 Scott Rolen .60 1.50
DK22 Aubrey Huff .40 1.00
DK23 Alfonso Soriano .60 1.50
DK24 Hank Blalock .40 1.00
DK25 Vernon Wells .40 1.00

2005 Donruss Elite Series

STATED PRINT RUN 1500 SERIAL #'d SETS
*BLACK: .75X TO 2X BASIC
BLACK PRINT RUN 100 SERIAL #'d SETS
*DOMINATOR: .6X TO 1.5X BASIC
DOMINATOR PRINT RUN 250 #'d SETS
*DOM.BLACK: 1.5X TO 4X BASIC
DOM.BLACK PRINT RUN 25 #'d SETS
RANDOM INSERTS IN PACKS
1 Albert Pujols 2.00 5.00
2 Alex Rodriguez 2.00 5.00
3 Alfonso Soriano 1.00 2.50
4 Derek Jeter 4.00 10.00
5 Hank Blalock .60 1.50
6 Ichiro Suzuki 2.00 5.00
7 Ivan Rodriguez 1.00 2.50
8 Jim Thome 1.00 2.50
9 Ken Griffey Jr. 3.00 8.00
10 Manny Ramirez 1.50 4.00
11 Mark Mulder .60 1.50
12 Mark Prior 1.00 2.50
13 Michael Young .60 1.50
14 Miguel Cabrera 1.50 4.00
15 Miguel Tejada 1.00 2.50
16 Mike Piazza 1.50 4.00
17 Nomar Garciaparra 1.00 2.50
18 Rafael Palmeiro 1.00 2.50
19 Randy Johnson 1.50 4.00
20 Roger Clemens 2.00 5.00
21 Sammy Sosa 1.50 4.00
22 Scott Rolen 1.00 2.50
23 Tim Hudson 1.00 2.50
24 Todd Helton 1.00 2.50
25 Vladimir Guerrero 1.00 2.50

2005 Donruss Fans of the Game

COMPLETE SET (5) 4.00 10.00
RANDOM INSERTS IN PACKS
1 Jesse Ventura 1.25 3.00
2 John C. McGinley .75 2.00
3 Susie Essman .75 2.00
4 Dean Cain .75 2.00
5 Meat Loaf 1.25 3.00

2005 Donruss Fans of the G Autographs

RANDOM INSERTS IN PACKS
SP PRINT RUNS PROVIDED BY DONRUSS
SP'S ARE NOT SERIAL-NUMBERED
1 Jesse Ventura 25.00
2 John C. McGinley SP/300 12.00
3 Susie Essman 20.00
4 Dean Cain SP/250 40.00
5 Meat Loaf 25.00

2005 Donruss Inside Vie

NO PRICING DUE TO SCARCITY
NOT INTENDED FOR PUBLIC RELEASE

2005 Donruss Jersey King

RANDOM INSERTS IN PACKS
PRINT RUNS B/WN 100-250 COPIES PER
1 Garret Anderson/250 3.00
2 Vladimir Guerrero/250 4.00
3 Cal Ripken/100 30.00
4 Manny Ramirez/250 4.00
5 Kerry Wood/250 3.00
6 Sammy Sosa/250 4.00
7 Magglio Ordonez/250 3.00
8 Adam Dunn/250 3.00
9 Todd Helton/250 4.00
10 Josh Beckett/250 3.00
11 Miguel Cabrera/250 4.00
12 Lance Berkman/250 3.00
13 Carlos Beltran/250 3.00
14 Shawn Green/250 3.00
15 Roger Clemens/250 6.00
16 Mike Piazza/250 4.00
17 Nolan Ryan/100 20.00
18 Mark Mulder/250 3.00
19 Jim Thome/250 4.00
20 Albert Pujols/250 6.00
21 Scott Rolen/250 4.00
22 Aubrey Huff/250 3.00
23 Alfonso Soriano/250 3.00
24 Hank Blalock/250 3.00
25 Vernon Wells/250 3.00

2005 Donruss Jersey Kings Signatures

PRINT RUNS B/WN 5-10 COPIES PER
NO PRICING DUE TO SCARCITY

2005 Donruss Longball Lead

STATED PRINT RUN 1500 SERIAL #'d SETS
*BLACK: .75X TO 2X BASIC
BLACK PRINT RUN 250 SERIAL #'d SETS
*DIE CUT: 1.25X TO 3X BASIC
DIE CUT PRINT RUN 50 SERIAL #'d SETS
BLACK DC PRINT RUN 10 SERIAL #'d SETS
NO BLACK DC PRICING DUE TO SCARCITY
RANDOM INSERTS IN PACKS
1 Adam Dunn .75 2
2 Adrian Beltre 1.25 3
3 Albert Pujols 1.50 4
4 Alex Rodriguez 1.50 4
5 David Ortiz 1.25 3
6 Hank Blalock .50 1
7 J.D. Drew .50 1.
8 Jeromy Burnitz .50 1.
9 Jim Edmonds .75 2.
10 Jim Thome .75 2.
11 Manny Ramirez 1.25 3.
12 Mark Teixeira .75 2.
13 Moises Alou .50 1.
14 Paul Konerko .75 2.
15 Steve Finley .50 1.

2005 Donruss Mound Marvels

STATED PRINT RUN 1000 SERIAL #'d SETS
BLACK PRINT RUN 10 SERIAL #'d SETS
NO BLACK PRICING DUE TO SCARCITY
RANDOM INSERTS IN PACKS
1 Curt Schilling 1.00 2.5
2 Dontrelle Willis .60 1.
3 Eric Gagne .60 1.5
4 Greg Maddux 2.00 5.0
5 John Smoltz 1.50 4.0
6 Kenny Rogers .60 1.5
7 Kerry Wood .60 1.5
8 Mariano Rivera 2.00 5.0
9 Mark Mulder .60 1.5
10 Mark Prior 1.00 2.5
11 Mike Mussina 1.00 2.5
12 Pedro Martinez 1.00 2.5
13 Randy Johnson 1.50 4.0
14 Roger Clemens 2.00 5.0
15 Tim Hudson 1.00 2.5

2005 Donruss Power Alley Red

STATED PRINT RUN 2500 SERIAL #'d SETS
BLACK PRINT RUN 10 SERIAL #'d SETS
NO BLACK PRICING DUE TO SCARCITY
BLACK DC PRINT RUN 5 SERIAL #'d SETS
NO BLACK DC PRICING DUE TO SCARCITY
*BLUE: .6X TO 1.5X RED
BLUE PRINT RUN 1000 SERIAL #'d SETS
*BLUE DC: 1.25X TO 3X RED
BLUE DC PRINT RUN 100 SERIAL #'d SETS
*GREEN: 2.5X TO 6X RED

GREEN PRINT RUN 25 SERIAL #'d SETS
GREEN DC PRINT RUN 10 SERIAL #'d SETS
NO GREEN DC PRICING DUE TO SCARCITY
*PURPLE: 1X TO 2.5X RED
PURPLE PRINT RUN 250 SERIAL #'d SETS
*PURPLE DC: 1.5X TO 4X RED
PURPLE DC PRINT RUN 50 SERIAL #'d SETS
*RED DC: 1X TO 2.5X RED
RED DC PRINT RUN 250 SERIAL #'d SETS
*YELLOW: 1.25X TO 3X RED
YELLOW PRINT RUN 100 SERIAL #'d SETS
*YELLOW DC: 2.5X TO 6X RED
YELLOW DC PRINT RUN 25 #'d SETS
1 Adam Dunn .60 1.50
2 Adrian Beltre 1.00 2.50
3 Albert Pujols 1.25 3.00
4 Alex Rodriguez 1.25 3.00
5 Alfonso Soriano .60 1.50
6 Gary Sheffield .40 1.00
7 Hank Blalock .40 1.00
8 Hideki Matsui 1.50 4.00
9 J.D. Drew .40 1.00
10 Jeromy Burnitz .40 1.00
11 Jim Edmonds .60 1.50
12 Jim Thome .60 1.50
13 Ken Griffey Jr. 2.00 5.00
14 Manny Ramirez 1.00 2.50
15 Mark Teixeira .60 1.50
16 Miguel Cabrera 1.00 2.50
17 Miguel Tejada .60 1.50
18 Mike Lowell .40 1.00
19 Mike Piazza 1.00 2.50
20 Moises Alou .40 1.00
21 Paul Konerko .60 1.50
22 Sammy Sosa 1.00 2.50
23 Scott Rolen .60 1.50
24 Todd Helton .60 1.50
25 Vladimir Guerrero .60 1.50

2005 Donruss Production Line BA

PRINT RUNS B/WN 324-372 COPIES PER
*BLACK: 1X TO 2.5X BASIC PL
BLACK PRINT RUN 25 SERIAL #'d SETS
*DIE CUT: .5X TO 1.2X BASIC PL
DIE CUT PRINT RUN 100 SERIAL #'d SETS
BLACK DC PRINT RUN 10 SERIAL #'d SETS
NO BLACK DC PRICING DUE TO SCARCITY
RANDOM INSERTS IN PACKS
1 Ichiro Suzuki/372 3.00 8.00
2 Ivan Rodriguez/334 1.50 4.00
3 Juan Pierre/326 1.00 2.50
4 Adrian Beltre/334 2.50 6.00
5 Albert Pujols/331 3.00 8.00
6 Mark Loretta/335 1.00 2.50
7 Melvin Mora/340 1.00 2.50
8 Sean Casey/324 1.00 2.50
9 Todd Helton/347 1.50 4.00
10 Vladimir Guerrero/337 1.50 4.00

2005 Donruss Production Line OBP

RANDOM INSERTS IN PACKS
PRINT RUNS B/WN 397-469 COPIES PER
*BLACK: 1.25X TO 3X BASIC PL
BLACK PRINT RUN 25 SERIAL #'d SETS
*DIE CUT: .6X TO 1.5X BASIC PL
DIE CUT PRINT RUN 100 SERIAL #'d SETS
BLACK DC PRINT RUN 10 SERIAL #'d SETS
NO BLACK DC PRICING DUE TO SCARCITY
RANDOM INSERTS IN PACKS
1 Albert Pujols/415 2.50 6.00
2 Bobby Abreu/428 .75 2.00
3 Lance Berkman/450 1.25 3.00
4 J.D. Drew/436 .75 2.00
5 Jorge Posada/400 1.25 3.00
6 Ichiro Suzuki/414 2.50 6.00
7 Manny Ramirez/397 2.00 5.00
8 Melvin Mora/419 .75 2.00
9 Todd Helton/469 1.25 3.00
10 Travis Hafner/410 .75 2.00

2005 Donruss Production Line OPS

RANDOM INSERTS IN PACKS
PRINT RUNS B/WN 977-1088 COPIES PER
*BLACK: 1X TO 2.5X BASIC PL
BLACK PRINT RUN 50 SERIAL #'d SETS
*DIE CUT: .75X TO 2X BASIC PL
DIE CUT PRINT RUN 100 SERIAL #'d SETS
*BLACK DC: 1.5X TO 4X BASIC PL
BLACK DC PRINT RUN 25 SERIAL #'d SETS
RANDOM INSERTS IN PACKS
1 Albert Pujols/1072 2.00 5.00
2 David Ortiz/983 1.50 4.00
3 Adrian Beltre/1017 1.50 4.00
4 J.D. Drew/1006 .60 1.50
5 Jim Thome/977 1.00 2.50
6 Lance Berkman/1016 1.00 2.50
7 Manny Ramirez/1009 1.50 4.00
8 Scott Rolen/1007 1.00 2.50
9 Todd Helton/1088 1.00 2.50
10 Travis Hafner/993 .60 1.50

2005 Donruss Production Line Slugging

PRINT RUNS B/WN 569-657 COPIES PER
*BLACK: .75X TO 2X BASIC PL
BLACK PRINT RUN 50 SERIAL #'d SETS
*DIE CUT: .6X TO 1.5X BASIC PL
DIE CUT PRINT RUN 100 SERIAL #'d SETS
*BLACK DC: 1.2X TO 3X BASIC PL
BLACK DC PRINT RUN 25 SERIAL #'d SETS
RANDOM INSERTS IN PACKS
1 Adrian Beltre/629 2.00 5.00
2 Albert Pujols/657 2.50 6.00
3 Todd Helton/620 1.25 3.00
4 J.D. Drew/569 .75 2.00
5 Jim Edmonds/643 1.25 3.00
6 Jim Thome/581 1.25 3.00
7 Vladimir Guerrero/598 1.25 3.00
8 Manny Ramirez/613 2.00 5.00
9 Scott Rolen/598 1.25 3.00
10 Travis Hafner/583 .75 2.00

2005 Donruss Rookies

STATED ODDS 1:23
BLACK PRINT RUN 10 SERIAL #'d SETS
NO BLACK PRICING DUE TO SCARCITY
*BLUE: .5X TO 1.2X BASIC
BLUE PRINT RUN 100 SERIAL #'d SETS
*GOLD: 1.25X TO 3X BASIC
GOLD PRINT RUN 25 SERIAL #'d SETS
*RED: .4X TO 1X BASIC
RED PRINT RUN 200 SERIAL #'d SETS
1 Fernando Nieve .40 1.00
2 Frankie Francisco .40 1.00
3 Jorge Vasquez .40 1.00
4 Travis Blackley .40 1.00
5 Joey Gathright .40 1.00
6 Kazuhito Tadano .40 1.00
7 Edwin Moreno .40 1.00
8 Lance Cormier .40 1.00
9 Justin Knoedler .40 1.00
10 Orlando Rodriguez .40 1.00
11 Renyel Pinto .40 1.00
12 Justin Leone .40 1.00
13 Dennis Sarfate .40 1.00
14 Sam Narron .40 1.00
15 Yadier Molina 1.00 2.50
16 Carlos Vasquez .40 1.00
17 Ryan Wing .40 1.00
18 Brad Halsey .40 1.00
19 Ryan Meaux .40 1.00
20 Michael Wuertz .40 1.00
21 Shawn Camp .40 1.00
22 Ruddy Yan .40 1.00
23 Don Kelly .40 1.00
24 Jake Woods .40 1.00
25 Colby Miller .40 1.00
26 Abe Alvarez .40 1.00
27 Mike Rouse .40 1.00
28 Phil Stockman .40 1.00
29 Kevin Cave .40 1.00
30 Chris Shelton .40 1.00
31 Tim Bittner .40 1.00
32 Mariano Gomez .40 1.00
33 Angel Chavez .40 1.00
34 Carlos Hines .40 1.00
35 Aarom Baldiris .40 1.00
36 Kazuo Matsui .40 1.00
37 Nick Regilio .40 1.00
38 Ivan Ochoa .40 1.00
39 Graham Koonce .40 1.00
40 Merkin Valdez .40 1.00
41 Greg Dobbs .40 1.00
42 Chris Oxspring .40 1.00
43 Dave Crouthers .40 1.00
44 Freddy Guzman .40 1.00
45 Akinori Otsuka .40 1.00
46 Jesse Crain .40 1.00
47 Casey Daigle .40 1.00
48 Roberto Novoa .40 1.00
49 Eddy Rodriguez .40 1.00
50 Jason Bartlett .40 1.00

2005 Donruss Rookies Stat Line Career

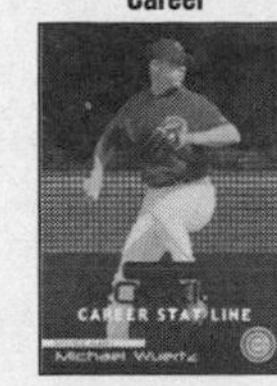

*SLC p/r 201-316: .4X TO 1X
*SLC p/r 121-200: .4X TO 1X
*SLC p/r 81-120: .5X TO 1.2X
*SLC p/r 51-80: .6X TO 1.5X
*SLC p/r 36-50: .75X TO 2X
*SLC p/r 26-35: 1X TO 2.5X
*SLC p/r 16-25: 1.25X TO 3X
RANDOM INSERTS IN DLP R/T PACKS
PRINT RUNS B/WN 1-316 COPIES PER
NO PRICING ON QTY OF 15 OR LESS

2005 Donruss Rookies Stat Line Season

*SLS p/r 121-200: .4X TO 1X
*SLS p/r 81-120: .5X TO 1.2X
*SLS p/r 51-80: .6X TO 1.5X
*SLS p/r 36-50: .75X TO 2X
*SLS p/r 26-35: 1X TO 2.5X
*SLS p/r 16-25: 1.25X TO 3X
RANDOM INSERTS IN DLP R/T PACKS
PRINT RUNS B/WN 1-188 COPIES PER
NO PRICING ON QTY OF 15 OR LESS

2005 Donruss Rookies Autographs

COMMON SP 4.00 10.00
RANDOM INSERTS IN PACKS
6/12/14/21/36/40-41/44-47 DO NOT EXIST
SP INFO PROVIDED BY DONRUSS
1 Fernando Nieve 3.00 8.00
2 Frankie Francisco 3.00 8.00
3 Jorge Vasquez 3.00 8.00
4 Travis Blackley 3.00 8.00
5 Joey Gathright 4.00 10.00
7 Edwin Moreno 3.00 8.00
8 Lance Cormier 3.00 8.00
9 Justin Knoedler 3.00 8.00
10 Orlando Rodriguez 3.00 8.00
11 Renyel Pinto 3.00 8.00
13 Dennis Sarfate 3.00 8.00
15 Yadier Molina 20.00 50.00
17 Ryan Wing SP 4.00 10.00
18 Brad Halsey 4.00 10.00
19 Ryan Meaux 3.00 8.00
20 Michael Wuertz 3.00 8.00
22 Ruddy Yan 3.00 8.00
23 Don Kelly 3.00 8.00
24 Jake Woods 3.00 8.00
25 Colby Miller 3.00 8.00
26 Abe Alvarez 4.00 10.00
27 Mike Rouse SP 4.00 10.00
28 Phil Stockman 3.00 8.00
29 Kevin Cave 3.00 8.00
30 Chris Shelton SP 10.00 25.00
31 Tim Bittner 3.00 8.00
32 Mariano Gomez 3.00 8.00
33 Angel Chavez 3.00 8.00
34 Carlos Hines 3.00 8.00
35 Aarom Baldiris 3.00 8.00
37 Nick Regilio 3.00 8.00
38 Ivan Ochoa 3.00 8.00
39 Graham Koonce 3.00 8.00
42 Chris Oxspring 3.00 8.00
43 Dave Crouthers 3.00 8.00
48 Roberto Novoa 3.00 8.00
49 Eddy Rodriguez 3.00 8.00
50 Jason Bartlett 3.00 8.00

2005 Donruss Timber and Threads Bat

RANDOM INSERTS IN PACKS
1 Albert Pujols 6.00 15.00
2 Alfonso Soriano 3.00 8.00
3 Andre Dawson 3.00 8.00
4 Austin Kearns 3.00 8.00
5 Brad Penny 3.00 8.00
6 Carlos Beltran 3.00 8.00
7 Carlos Lee 3.00 8.00
8 Chipper Jones 4.00 10.00
9 Dale Murphy 4.00 10.00
10 Don Mattingly 8.00 20.00
11 Frank Thomas 4.00 10.00
12 Garret Anderson 3.00 8.00
13 Gary Carter 3.00 8.00
14 Hank Blalock 3.00 8.00
15 Jacque Jones 3.00 8.00
17 Jay Gibbons 3.00 8.00
18 Jeff Bagwell 4.00 10.00
20 Jermaine Dye 3.00 8.00
21 Jim Thome 4.00 10.00
22 Jose Vidro 3.00 8.00
23 Lance Berkman 3.00 8.00
24 Laynce Nix 3.00 8.00
25 Magglio Ordonez 3.00 8.00
26 Marcus Giles 3.00 8.00
27 Mark Prior 4.00 10.00
28 Mark Teixeira 4.00 10.00
29 Melvin Mora 3.00 8.00
30 Michael Young 3.00 8.00
31 Miguel Cabrera 4.00 10.00
32 Mike Lowell 3.00 8.00
33 Roy Oswalt 3.00 8.00
34 Sammy Sosa 4.00 10.00
35 Scott Rolen 4.00 10.00
36 Sean Burroughs 3.00 8.00
37 Sean Casey 3.00 8.00
38 Shannon Stewart 3.00 8.00
39 Torii Hunter 3.00 8.00
40 Travis Hafner 3.00 8.00

2005 Donruss Timber and Threads Bat Signature

PRINT RUNS B/WN 5-10 COPIES PER
NO PRICING DUE TO SCARCITY

2005 Donruss Timber and Threads Combo

*COMBO: .6X TO 1.5X BAT
RANDOM INSERTS IN PACKS

2005 Donruss Timber and Threads Combo Signature

PRINT RUNS B/WN 5-10 COPIES PER
NO PRICING DUE TO SCARCITY

2005 Donruss Timber and Threads Jersey

*JSY: .4X TO 1X BAT
RANDOM INSERTS IN PACKS
19 Jeremy Bonderman 3.00 8.00

2005 Donruss Timber and Threads Jersey Signature

PRINT RUNS B/WN 5-10 COPIES PER
NO PRICING DUE TO SCARCITY

2014 Donruss

COMP.FACT.SET (356) 50.00 100.00
1 Bryce Harper DK 1.50 4.00
2 Mike Trout DK 5.00 12.00
3 Derek Jeter DK 2.50 6.00
4 Yasiel Puig DK 1.00 2.50
5 Chris Davis DK .60 1.50
6 Jose Bautista DK .75 2.00
7 Freddie Freeman DK 1.25 3.00
8 Eric Hosmer DK .75 2.00
9 Miguel Cabrera DK 1.00 2.50
10 Andrew McCutchen DK 1.00 2.50
11 Paul Goldschmidt DK 1.00 2.50
12 Adrian Beltre DK 1.00 2.50
13 David Ortiz DK 1.00 2.50
14 Buster Posey DK 1.25 3.00
15 David Wright DK .75 2.00
16 Jason Kipnis DK .75 2.00
17 Evan Longoria DK .75 2.00
18 Giancarlo Stanton DK 1.00 2.50
19 Chase Utley DK .75 2.00
20 Chris Sale DK 1.00 2.50
21 Joe Mauer DK .75 2.00
22 Anthony Rizzo DK 1.50 4.00
23 Jay Bruce DK .75 2.00
24 Jean Segura DK .75 2.00
25 Yadier Molina DK 1.00 2.50
26 Chris Carter DK .60 1.50
27 Josh Donaldson DK .75 2.00
28 Felix Hernandez DK .75 2.00
29 Troy Tulowitzki DK 1.00 2.50
30 Chase Headley DK .60 1.50
31 Michael Choice RC .50 1.25
32 Billy Hamilton RC .60 1.50
33 Nick Castellanos RC 1.50 4.00
34 Taijuan Walker RC .50 1.25
35 Kolten Wong RC .60 1.50
36 Travis d'Arnaud RC .60 1.50
37 Jonathan Schoop RC .50 1.25
38 Cameron Rupp RC .50 1.25
39 James Paxton RC .75 2.00
40 Tim Beckham RC .75 2.00
41 J.R. Murphy RC .50 1.25
42 Erik Johnson RC .50 1.25
43 Wilmer Flores RC .60 1.50
44 Xander Bogaerts RC 1.50 4.00
45 Tommy Medica RC .50 1.25
46 Jayson Werth .20 .50
47 Alex Gordon .20 .50
48 Allen Craig .20 .50
49 Buster Posey .30 .75
50 Prince Fielder .20 .50
51 Yadier Molina .25 .60
52 Justin Morneau .20 .50
53 Jacoby Ellsbury .20 .50
54 Ryan Zimmerman .20 .50
55 Michael Cuddyer .15 .40
56 Evan Longoria .20 .50
57 Justin Upton .20 .50
58 Chris Johnson .15 .40
59 Ichiro Suzuki .40 1.00
60 Joe Mauer .20 .50
61 Billy Butler .15 .40
62 Chase Utley UER .20 .50
Chase Headley name on back
63 Adam Dunn .20 .50
64 Brandon Phillips .15 .40
65 Joey Votto .25 .60
66 Jason Heyward .20 .50
67 Robinson Cano .20 .50
68 David Wright .20 .50
69 Clayton Kershaw .50 1.25
70 Troy Tulowitzki .25 .60
71 Kris Medlen .20 .50
72 Elvis Andrus .20 .50
73 Paul Konerko .20 .50
74 Josh Hamilton .20 .50
75 Felix Hernandez .20 .50
76 Nick Markakis .20 .50
77 Craig Kimbrel .20 .50
78 Max Scherzer .25 .60
79 Carlos Beltran .20 .50
80 Mike Napoli .15 .40
81 Travis Wood .15 .40
82 Adam Jones .20 .50
83 Jose Altuve .20 .50
84 Edwin Encarnacion .25 .60
85 Dustin Pedroia .25 .60
86 Shin-Soo Choo .20 .50
87 Hunter Pence .20 .50
88 Torii Hunter .15 .40
89 James Shields .15 .40
90 Yu Darvish .25 .60
91 Justin Verlander .25 .60
92 Adrian Gonzalez .20 .50
93 Matt Holliday .25 .60
94 Roy Halladay .20 .50
95 Albert Pujols .30 .75
96 Matt Carpenter .25 .60
97 Josh Donaldson .20 .50
98 Jason Kipnis .20 .50
99 Mark Trumbo .15 .40
100 Alfonso Soriano .20 .50
101 Carlos Gonzalez .20 .50
102 Adam Wainwright .20 .50
103 Jose Fernandez .25 .60
104 Jean Segura .20 .50
105 Evan Gattis .15 .40
106 Aroldis Chapman .25 .60
107 Nick Swisher .20 .50
108 Chris Sale .25 .60
109 Chris Carter .15 .40
110 Matt Harvey .20 .50
111 Cliff Lee .20 .50
112 Mike Trout 1.25 3.00
113 Everth Cabrera .15 .40
114 Matt Moore .20 .50
115 Andrew McCutchen .25 .60
116 Jordan Zimmermann .20 .50
117 Freddie Freeman .30 .75
118 Wei-Yin Chen .15 .40
119 Anthony Rizzo .40 1.00
120 Jon Lester .20 .50
121 Starlin Castro .15 .40
122 Gerardo Parra .15 .40
123 Ian Kennedy .15 .40
124 Stephen Strasburg .25 .60
125 Manny Machado .25 .60
126 Chase Headley .15 .40
127 Paul Goldschmidt .25 .60
128 Miguel Cabrera .25 .60
129 Adrian Beltre .25 .60
130 J.J. Hardy .15 .40
131 Eric Hosmer .20 .50
132 Giancarlo Stanton .25 .60
133 Hyun-Jin Ryu .20 .50
134 Shane Victorino .20 .50
135 R.A. Dickey .20 .50
136 Jhonny Peralta .15 .40
137 Alex Rodriguez .30 .75
138 Victor Martinez .20 .50
139 Shelby Miller .20 .50
140 Jose Reyes .20 .50
141 Jose Iglesias .20 .50
142 Yan Gomes .15 .40
143 Bryce Harper .40 1.00
144 Colby Rasmus .20 .50
145 Chris Archer .15 .40
146 Wil Myers .15 .40
147 Matt Kemp .20 .50
148 Pedro Alvarez .15 .40
149 Raul Ibanez .20 .50
150 Brandon Moss .15 .40
151 Marlon Byrd .15 .40
152 Zack Greinke .25 .60
153 Domonic Brown .20 .50
154 Derek Jeter .60 1.50
155 Yoenis Cespedes .25 .60
156 Kendrys Morales .15 .40
157 Hanley Ramirez .20 .50
158 Mitch Moreland .15 .40
159 Pablo Sandoval .20 .50
160 CC Sabathia .20 .50
161 Ian Kinsler .20 .50
162 Hisashi Iwakuma .20 .50
163 Michael Young .15 .40
164 Curtis Granderson .20 .50
165 Jered Weaver .20 .50
166 Zack Wheeler .20 .50
167 Glen Perkins .15 .40
168 Hiroki Kuroda .15 .40
169 Kyle Lohse .15 .40
170 Yasiel Puig .25 .60
171 C.J. Wilson .15 .40
172 Matt Wieters .25 .60
173 Trevor Bauer .25 .60
174 Aramis Ramirez .15 .40
175 Jay Bruce .20 .50
176 Carl Crawford .20 .50
177 B.J. Upton .20 .50
178 A.J. Pierzynski .15 .40
179 Chris Davis .15 .40
180 Jose Bautista .20 .50
181 David Ortiz .25 .60
182 Starling Marte .20 .50
183 Tim Lincecum .20 .50
184 Mariano Rivera .30 .75
185 Todd Helton .20 .50
186 Roberto Alomar .20 .50
187 Rickey Henderson .25 .60
188 Reggie Jackson .20 .50
189 Ozzie Smith .30 .75
190 Nolan Ryan .75 2.00
191 Mike Piazza .25 .60
192 Pete Rose .50 1.25
193 Nomar Garciaparra .20 .50
194 Chipper Jones .25 .60
195 Johnny Bench .25 .60
196 Ken Griffey Jr. .50 1.25
197 Frank Thomas .25 .60
198 Cal Ripken Jr. .75 2.00
199 George Brett .50 1.25
200 Don Mattingly .50 1.25
201A Tanaka English RC 10.00 25.00
201B Tanaka Japanese 60.00 120.00
202 Jose Abreu 8.00 20.00
203 Yordano Ventura 1.50 4.00
204 Stephen Strasburg DK 1.00 2.50
205 Albert Pujols DK 1.25 3.00
206 Masahiro Tanaka DK 2.00 5.00
207 Clayton Kershaw DK 2.00 5.00
208 Manny Machado DK 1.00 2.50
209 Edwin Encarnacion DK 1.00 2.50
210 Justin Upton DK .75 2.00
211 Yordano Ventura DK .75 2.00
212 Max Scherzer DK 1.00 2.50
213 Starling Marte DK .75 2.00
214 Mark Trumbo DK .60 1.50
215 Yu Darvish DK .75 2.00
216 Koji Uehara DK .60 1.50
217 Brandon Belt DK .75 2.00
218 Matt Harvey DK .75 2.00
219 Yan Gomes DK .60 1.50
220 Wil Myers DK .60 1.50
221 Jose Fernandez DK 1.00 2.50
222 Cliff Lee DK .75 2.00
223 Jose Abreu DK 5.00 12.00
224 Brian Dozier DK .75 2.00
225 Starlin Castro DK .60 1.50
226 Joey Votto DK 1.00 2.50
227 Carlos Gomez DK .60 1.50
228 Michael Wacha DK .75 2.00
229 Jose Altuve DK .75 2.00
230 Yoenis Cespedes DK 1.00 2.50
231 Robinson Cano DK .75 2.00
232 Carlos Gonzalez DK .75 2.00
233 Jedd Gyorko DK .60 1.50
234 Jose Abreu RC 4.00 10.00
235 Masahiro Tanaka RC 1.50 4.00
236 Alex Guerrero RC .60 1.50
237 Yordano Ventura RC .60 1.50
238 Rougned Odor RC 1.00 2.50
239 Nick Martinez RC .50 1.25
240 Oscar Taveras RC .60 1.50
241 Tucker Barnhart RC .50 1.25
242 Matt Davidson RC .60 1.50
243 Marcus Semien RC .50 1.25
244 Chris Owings RC .50 1.25
245 Yangervis Solarte RC .50 1.25
246 Wei-Chung Wang RC .50 1.25
247 Jimmy Nelson RC .50 1.25
248 Christian Bethancourt RC .50 1.25
249 George Springer RC 2.00 5.00
250 Jake Marisnick RC .50 1.25
251 Enny Romero RC .50 1.25
252 Chad Bettis RC .50 1.25
253 Erisbel Arruebarrena RC .50 1.25
254 Jon Singleton RC .60 1.50
255 David Holmberg RC .50 1.25
256 C.J. Cron RC .50 1.25
257 David Hale RC .50 1.25
258 Jose Ramirez RC 4.00 10.00
259 Patrick Corbin .20 .50
260 Paul Goldschmidt .25 .60
261 Wade Miley .15 .40
262 Alex Wood .15 .40
263 Andrelton Simmons .15 .40
264 Freddie Freeman .30 .75
265 Julio Teheran .20 .50
266 Chris Davis .15 .40
267 Chris Tillman .15 .40
268 Jonathan Schoop .15 .40
269 Nelson Cruz .25 .60
270 Clay Buchholz .15 .40
271 David Ortiz .25 .60
272 Grady Sizemore .20 .50
273 Koji Uehara .15 .40
274 Xander Bogaerts .50 1.25
275 Emilio Bonifacio .15 .40
276 Alejandro De Aza .15 .40
277 Alexei Ramirez .20 .50
278 Avisail Garcia .20 .50
279 Chris Sale .25 .60
280 Erik Johnson .15 .40
281 Billy Hamilton .25 .60
282 Joey Votto .25 .60
283 Johnny Cueto .20 .50
284 Mat Latos .20 .50
285 Tony Cingrani .20 .50
286 Carlos Santana .25 .60
287 Justin Masterson .15 .40
288 Michael Brantley .20 .50
289 Nolan Arenado .30 .75
290 Troy Tulowitzki .25 .60
291 Wilin Rosario .15 .40
292 Anibal Sanchez .15 .40
293 Austin Jackson .15 .40
294 Miguel Cabrera .25 .60
295 Nick Castellanos .50 1.25
296 Jason Castro .15 .40
297 Greg Holland .15 .40
298 Norichika Aoki .15 .40
299 Salvador Perez .20 .50
300 Kole Calhoun .15 .40
301 Mike Trout 1.25 3.00
302 Tyler Skaggs .15 .40
303 Dee Gordon .15 .40
304 Kenley Jansen .20 .50
305 Yasiel Puig .25 .60
306 Adeiny Hechavarria .15 .40
307 Christian Yelich .30 .75
308 Jose Fernandez .25 .60
309 Marcell Ozuna .25 .60
310 Carlos Gomez .15 .40
311 Ryan Braun .20 .50
312 Khris Davis .25 .60
313 Yovani Gallardo .15 .40
314 Brian Dozier .20 .50
315 Oswaldo Arcia .15 .40
316 Travis d'Arnaud .20 .50
317 Brian McCann .20 .50
318 Derek Jeter .60 1.50
319 Jed Lowrie .15 .40
320 Sonny Gray .20 .50
321 Carlos Ruiz .15 .40
322 Cole Hamels .20 .50
323 Ryan Howard .20 .50
324 Andrew McCutchen .25 .60
325 Francisco Liriano .15 .40
326 Gerrit Cole .25 .60
327 Andrew Cashner .15 .40
328 Jedd Gyorko .15 .40
329 Yonder Alonso .15 .40
330 Brandon Belt .20 .50
331 Buster Posey .30 .75
332 Madison Bumgarner .20 .50
333 Matt Cain .20 .50
334 James Paxton .25 .60
335 Robinson Cano .20 .50
336 Kolten Wong .20 .50
337 Lance Lynn .15 .40
338 Matt Adams .15 .40
339 Michael Wacha .20 .50
340 Trevor Rosenthal .20 .50
341 Yadier Molina .25 .60
342 Alex Cobb .15 .40
343 Ben Zobrist .20 .50
344 David Price .20 .50
345 Evan Longoria .20 .50
346 Yunel Escobar .15 .40
347 Alex Rios .20 .50
348 Jurickson Profar .20 .50
349 Leonys Martin .15 .40
350 Shin-Soo Choo .20 .50
351 Yu Darvish .25 .60
352 Brett Lawrie .20 .50
353 Jose Bautista .20 .50
354 Anthony Rendon .25 .60
355 Bryce Harper .40 1.00
356 Doug Fister .15 .40
357 Gio Gonzalez .20 .50
358 Ian Desmond .15 .40

2014 Donruss Press Proofs Silver

*SILVER DK: 1.2X TO 3X BASIC
*SILVER RC: 1.5X TO 4X BASIC
*SILVER VET: 5X TO 12X BASIC
STATED PRINT RUN 199 SER.#'d SETS
2 Mike Trout DK 12.00 30.00
112 Mike Trout 12.00 30.00
196 Ken Griffey Jr. 10.00 25.00
198 Cal Ripken Jr. 10.00 25.00
223 Jose Abreu DK 8.00 20.00
234 Jose Abreu 8.00 20.00
301 Mike Trout 10.00 25.00

2014 Donruss Press Proofs Gold

*GOLD DK: 1.5X TO 4X BASIC
*GOLD RC: 2X TO 5X BASIC
*GOLD VET: 6X TO 15X BASIC
STATED PRINT RUN 99 SER.#'d SETS
2 Mike Trout DK 15.00 40.00
112 Mike Trout 15.00 40.00
196 Ken Griffey Jr. 12.00 30.00
198 Cal Ripken Jr. 15.00 40.00
223 Jose Abreu DK 10.00 25.00
234 Jose Abreu 10.00 25.00
301 Mike Trout 12.00 30.00

2014 Donruss Stat Line Career

*CAR.DK p/r 251-400: 1X TO 2.5X BASIC
*CAR.DK p/r 100-248: 1.2X TO 3X BASIC
*CAR.DK p/r 51-99: 1.5X TO 4X BASIC
*CAR.DK p/r 26-50: 2X TO 5X BASIC
*CAR.RC p/r 251-400: 1.2X TO 3X BASIC
*CAR.RC p/r 51-99: 2X TO 5X BASIC
*CAR.RC p/r 26-50: 2.5X TO 6X BASIC
*CAR.VET p/r 251-400: 4X TO 10X BASIC
*CAR.VET p/r 100-248: 5X TO 12X BASIC
*CAR.VET p/r 51-99: 6X TO 15X BASIC
*CAR.VET p/r 26-50: 8X TO 20X BASIC
*CAR.VET p/r 20-25: 10X TO 25X BASIC
*CAR.VET p/r 17-19: 12X TO 30X BASIC
PRINT RUNS B/WN 4-400 COPIES PER
NO PRICING ON QTY 4
223 Jose Abreu DK/184 6.00 15.00
234 Jose Abreu/184 6.00 15.00

2014 Donruss Stat Line Season

*SEA.DK p/r 251-400: 1X TO 2.5X BASIC
*SEA.DK p/r 100-248: 1.2X TO 3X BASIC
*SEA.DK p/r 51-99: 1.5X TO 4X BASIC
*SEA.DK p/r 26-50: 2X TO 5X BASIC
*SEA.DK p/r 20-25: 2.5X TO 6X BASIC
*SEA.DK p/r 17-19: 3X TO 8X BASIC
*SEA.RC p/r 251-400: 1.2X TO 3X BASIC
*SEA.RC p/r 100-248: 1.5X TO 4X BASIC
*SEA.RC p/r 20-25: 3X TO 8X BASIC
*SEA.VET p/r 251-400: 4X TO 10X BASIC
*SEA.VET p/r 100-248: 5X TO 12X BASIC
*SEA.VET p/r 51-99: 6X TO 15X BASIC
*SEA.VET p/r 26-50: 8X TO 20X BASIC
*SEA.VET p/r 20-25: 10X TO 25X BASIC
*SEA.VET p/r 17-19: 12X TO 30X BASIC

PRINT RUNS B/WN 3-400 COPIES PER
NO PRICING ON QTY 13 OR LESS
223 Jose Abreu DK/37 20.00 50.00
234 Jose Abreu/33 20.00 50.00

2014 Donruss Bat Kings

RANDOM INSERTS IN PACKS
1 Hunter Pence 3.00 8.00
2 Ryan Howard 3.00 8.00
3 Shelby Miller 3.00 8.00
4 Robinson Cano 3.00 8.00
5 Mark Teixeira 3.00 8.00
6 Ichiro Suzuki 8.00 20.00
7 Jose Bautista 3.00 8.00
8 Justin Upton 3.00 8.00
9 David Wright 3.00 8.00
10 Ike Davis 2.50 6.00
11 Jay Bruce 3.00 8.00
12 Didi Gregorius 3.00 8.00
13 Logan Morrison 2.50 6.00
14 Devin Mesoraco 2.50 6.00
15 Hanley Ramirez 3.00 8.00
16 Dustin Ackley 2.50 6.00
17 Jose Reyes 3.00 8.00
18 Adam Jones 3.00 8.00
19 Derek Jeter 10.00 25.00
20 Alex Rodriguez 5.00 12.00
21 Yasiel Puig 6.00 15.00
22 Mike Trout 20.00 50.00
23 Albert Pujols 5.00 12.00
24 Adrian Gonzalez 3.00 8.00
25 Anthony Rizzo 6.00 15.00
26 B.J. Upton 3.00 8.00
27 Brandon Phillips 2.50 6.00
28 Christian Yelich 5.00 12.00
29 Edwin Encarnacion 4.00 10.00
30 Evan Gattis 2.50 6.00
31 Gerardo Parra 2.50 6.00
32 Miguel Cabrera 5.00 12.00
33 Jurickson Profar 3.00 8.00
34 Mike Napoli 2.50 6.00
35 Justin Morneau 3.00 8.00
36 David Freese 2.50 6.00
37 Starling Marte 3.00 8.00
38 Adam Dunn 3.00 8.00
39 Carl Crawford 3.00 8.00
40 Giancarlo Stanton 4.00 10.00
41 Dustin Pedroia 4.00 10.00
42 Evan Longoria 3.00 8.00
43 Jacoby Ellsbury 5.00 12.00
44 Joey Votto 4.00 10.00
45 Joe Mauer 3.00 8.00
46 Matt Kemp 3.00 8.00
47 Michael Bourn 2.50 6.00
48 Melky Cabrera 2.50 6.00
49 Nelson Cruz 4.00 10.00
50 Pedro Alvarez 2.50 6.00

2014 Donruss Bat Kings Studio Series

*STUDIO: .75X TO 2X BASIC
RANDOM INSERTS IN PACKS
STATED PRINT RUN 25 SER.#'d SETS

2014 Donruss Breakout Hitters

1 Chris Davis .60 1.50
2 Eric Hosmer .75 2.00
3 Josh Donaldson .75 2.00
4 Chris Johnson .60 1.50
5 Matt Carpenter 1.00 2.50
6 Paul Goldschmidt 1.00 2.50
7 Jean Segura .75 2.00
8 Yasiel Puig 1.00 2.50
9 Yadier Molina 1.00 2.50
10 Wil Myers .60 1.50
11 Jose Altuve .75 2.00
12 Jason Kipnis .75 2.00
13 Austin Jackson .60 1.50
14 Manny Machado 1.00 2.50
15 Allen Craig .75 2.00
16 Carlos Gomez .60 1.50
17 Ian Desmond .60 1.50
18 Anthony Rizzo 1.50 4.00
19 Starling Marte .75 2.00
20 Domonic Brown .75 2.00
21 Kyle Seager .60 1.50
22 Chris Carter .60 1.50
23 Pedro Alvarez .60 1.50
24 Denard Span .60 1.50
25 Giancarlo Stanton 1.00 2.50
26 Andrelton Simmons .60 1.50
27 Anthony Rendon 1.00 2.50
28 Edwin Encarnacion 1.00 2.50
29 Freddie Freeman 1.25 3.00
30 Mike Trout 5.00 12.00
31 Jedd Gyorko .60 1.50
32 Evan Gattis .60 1.50
33 Matt Adams .60 1.50
34 Jed Lowrie .60 1.50
35 Brandon Moss .60 1.50

2014 Donruss Breakout Pitchers

1 Max Scherzer 1.00 2.50
2 Homer Bailey .60 1.50
3 Jarrod Parker .60 1.50
4 Gerrit Cole 1.00 2.50
5 Hisashi Iwakuma .75 2.00
6 Craig Kimbrel .75 2.00
7 Yu Darvish 1.00 2.50
8 Matt Harvey .75 2.00
9 Patrick Corbin .75 2.00
10 Rick Porcello .75 2.00
11 Jose Fernandez 1.00 2.50
12 Madison Bumgarner .75 2.00
13 Jordan Zimmermann .75 2.00
14 Chris Sale 1.00 2.50
15 Derek Holland .60 1.50
16 Shelby Miller .75 2.00
17 David Price .75 2.00
18 Aroldis Chapman 1.00 2.50
19 Mike Leake .60 1.50
20 Andrew Cashner .60 1.50
21 Matt Moore .75 2.00
22 Mat Latos .75 2.00
23 A.J. Griffin .60 1.50
24 Adam Wainwright .75 2.00
25 Kris Medlen .75 2.00
26 Stephen Strasburg 1.00 2.50
27 Wade Miley .60 1.50
28 Travis Wood .60 1.50
29 Hyun-Jin Ryu .75 2.00
30 Dillon Gee .60 1.50
31 Anibal Sanchez .60 1.50
32 Martin Perez .75 2.00
33 Julio Teheran .75 2.00
34 Gio Gonzalez .75 2.00
35 Alex Cobb .60 1.50

2014 Donruss Diamond King Box Toppers

1 David Price 2.50 6.00
2 David Ortiz 3.00 8.00
3 Edwin Encarnacion 3.00 8.00
4 Max Scherzer 3.00 8.00
5 Matt Harvey 2.50 6.00
6 Nick Castellanos 5.00 12.00
7 Mike Zunino 2.00 5.00
8 Chris Sale 3.00 8.00
9 Cal Ripken Jr. 10.00 25.00
10 Craig Biggio 2.50 6.00
11 Evan Longoria 2.50 6.00
12 David Wright 2.50 6.00
13 Mike Trout 15.00 40.00
14 Jordan Zimmermann 2.50 6.00
15 Josh Donaldson 2.50 6.00
16 Ken Griffey Jr. 6.00 15.00
17 Jurickson Profar 2.50 6.00
18 Stephen Strasburg 3.00 8.00
19 Paul Goldschmidt 3.00 8.00
20 Kris Medlen 2.50 6.00
21 Manny Machado 3.00 8.00
22 Mark Trumbo 2.00 5.00
23 Chris Davis 2.00 5.00
24 Yoenis Cespedes 3.00 8.00
25 Gerrit Cole 3.00 8.00

2014 Donruss Diamond King Box Toppers Signatures

EXCHANGE DEADLINE 8/26/2015
3 Edwin Encarnacion EXCH 12.00 30.00
5 Matt Harvey EXCH 60.00 120.00
7 Mike Zunino 12.00 30.00
14 Jordan Zimmermann 8.00 20.00
17 Jurickson Profar EXCH 20.00 50.00
23 Chris Davis 40.00 80.00
24 Yoenis Cespedes 30.00 60.00
25 Gerrit Cole 30.00 60.00

2014 Donruss Elite Dominator

STATED PRINT RUN 999 SER.#'d SETS
1A Jered Weaver 1.50 4.00
1B Adrian Beltre 2.00 5.00
2A Chris Davis 1.25 3.00
2B Adrian Gonzalez 1.50 4.00
3A Stephen Strasburg 2.00 5.00
3B Brandon Belt 1.50 4.00
4A Jose Bautista 1.50 4.00
4B Clayton Kershaw 4.00 10.00
5A Miguel Cabrera 2.00 5.00
5B Cliff Lee 1.50 4.00
6A Matt Harvey 1.50 4.00
6B David Ortiz 2.00 5.00
7A Jarrod Parker 1.25 3.00
7B David Wright 1.50 4.00
8A Yasiel Puig 2.00 5.00
8B Derek Jeter 5.00 12.00
9A Robinson Cano 1.50 4.00
9B Eric Hosmer 1.50 4.00
10A Jose Fernandez 2.00 5.00
10B Felix Hernandez 1.50 4.00
11A Prince Fielder 1.50 4.00
11B Giancarlo Stanton 2.00 5.00
12A David Price 1.50 4.00
12B Hyun-Jin Ryu 1.50 4.00
13A Yoenis Cespedes 2.00 5.00
13B Ichiro Suzuki 3.00 8.00
14A Matt Kemp 1.50 4.00
14B Joe Mauer 1.50 4.00
15A James Shields 1.25 3.00
15B Joey Votto 2.00 5.00
16A Pablo Sandoval 1.50 4.00
16B Jose Abreu 10.00 25.00
17A Mark Trumbo 1.25 3.00
17B Josh Donaldson 1.50 4.00
18A Carlos Gonzalez 1.50 4.00
18B Madison Bumgarner 1.50 4.00
19A Edwin Encarnacion 2.00 5.00
19B Max Scherzer 2.00 5.00
20A Chad Billingsley 1.50 4.00
20B Masahiro Tanaka 4.00 10.00
21A Will Clark 1.50 4.00
21B Mike Trout 10.00 25.00
22A Craig Biggio 1.50 4.00
22B Nick Castellanos 4.00 10.00
23A Ken Griffey Jr. 4.00 10.00
23B Paul Goldschmidt 2.00 5.00
24A Mike Mussina 1.50 4.00
24B Ryan Braun 1.50 4.00
25A Tom Glavine 1.50 4.00
25B Sonny Gray 1.50 4.00
26A Tony Gwynn 2.00 5.00
26B Starling Marte 1.50 4.00
27A Pedro Martinez 1.50 4.00
27B Troy Tulowitzki 2.00 5.00
28A Curt Schilling 1.50 4.00
28B Wil Myers 1.25 3.00
29A Nolan Ryan 6.00 15.00
29B Yadier Molina 2.00 5.00
30A Jeff Bagwell 1.50 4.00
30B Yordano Ventura 1.50 4.00

2014 Donruss Game Gear

1 Derek Jeter 10.00 25.00
2 Buster Posey 6.00 15.00
3 Chris Davis 2.00 5.00
4 Bryce Harper 8.00 20.00
5 Drew Smyly 2.00 5.00
6 Hunter Pence 2.50 6.00
7 Paul Goldschmidt 3.00 8.00
8 Matt Wieters 3.00 8.00
9 Curtis Granderson 2.50 6.00
10 Jordan Lyles 2.00 5.00
11 Andy Dirks 2.00 5.00
12 Dillon Gee 2.00 5.00
13 Logan Morrison 2.00 5.00
14 Joey Votto 5.00 12.00
15 Brad Ziegler 2.00 5.00
16 Ian Kinsler 2.50 6.00
17 Dan Uggla 2.00 5.00
18 CC Sabathia 2.50 6.00
19 Chris Perez 2.00 5.00
20 Eric Hosmer 2.50 6.00
21 Jonathon Niese 2.00 5.00
22 Cliff Lee 2.50 6.00
23 Dustin Pedroia 3.00 8.00
24 Starlin Castro 2.00 5.00
25 Matt Moore 2.50 6.00
26 Josh Reddick 2.00 5.00
27 Devin Mesoraco 2.00 5.00
28 Austin Jackson 2.00 5.00
29 Madison Bumgarner 5.00 12.00
30 Jarrod Parker 2.00 5.00
31 Andrew McCutchen 3.00 8.00
32 Kendrys Morales 2.00 5.00
33 Paul Konerko 2.50 6.00
34 Johan Santana 2.50 6.00
35 Adrian Beltre 3.00 8.00
36 Leonys Martin 2.00 5.00
37 Felix Hernandez 2.50 6.00
38 Aroldis Chapman 2.50 6.00
39 Domonic Brown 2.50 6.00
40 Tim Hudson 2.50 6.00
41 Ike Davis 2.00 5.00
42 Brett Gardner 2.50 6.00
43 Matt Kemp 2.50 6.00
44 Edwin Encarnacion 3.00 8.00
45 Pedro Alvarez 2.00 5.00
46 Will Middlebrooks 2.00 5.00
47 Yoenis Cespedes 3.00 8.00
48 Anthony Rizzo 5.00 12.00
49 David Ortiz 5.00 12.00
50 Yasiel Puig 20.00 50.00

2014 Donruss Game Gear Prime

*PRIME: 1X TO 2.5X BASIC
PRINT RUNS B/WN 2-25 COPIES PER
NO PRICING ON QTY 10 OR LESS

2014 Donruss Hall Worthy

1 Mariano Rivera 1.50 4.00
2 Derek Jeter 3.00 8.00
3 Albert Pujols 1.50 4.00
4 Ichiro Suzuki 2.00 5.00
5 Carlos Beltran 1.00 2.50
6 Randy Johnson 1.25 3.00
7 Tim Hudson 1.00 2.50
8 Todd Helton 1.00 2.50
9 Roy Halladay 1.00 2.50
10 David Ortiz 1.25 3.00
11 Adrian Beltre 1.00 2.50
12 Miguel Cabrera 1.25 3.00
13 Johan Santana 1.00 2.50
14 Paul Konerko 1.00 2.50
15 CC Sabathia 1.00 2.50

2014 Donruss Jersey Kings

RANDOM INSERTS IN PACKS
1 Albert Pujols 5.00 12.00
2 Alex Rodriguez 5.00 12.00
3 David Ortiz 4.00 10.00
4 Brett Jackson 2.50 6.00
5 Joe Mauer 3.00 8.00
6 Miguel Cabrera 5.00 12.00
7 Mike Zunino 2.50 6.00
8 Neftali Feliz 2.50 6.00
9 Rick Porcello 3.00 8.00
10 Robinson Cano 3.00 8.00
11 Torii Hunter 2.50 6.00
12 Yovani Gallardo 2.50 6.00
13 Adrian Beltre 4.00 10.00
14 A.J. Burnett 2.50 6.00
15 Drew Smyly 2.50 6.00
16 Dustin Pedroia 4.00 10.00
17 Zoilo Almonte 3.00 8.00
18 Will Middlebrooks 2.50 6.00
19 Prince Fielder 3.00 8.00
20 Patrick Corbin 3.00 8.00
21 Matt Wieters 4.00 10.00
22 Matt Harvey 5.00 12.00
23 Justin Wilson 2.50 6.00
24 Derek Jeter 8.00 20.00
25 Alfonso Soriano 3.00 8.00
26 Derrick Robinson 2.50 6.00
27 Kyle Kendrick 2.50 6.00
28 Hanley Ramirez 3.00 8.00
29 Jose Fernandez 4.00 10.00
30 Ivan Nova 3.00 8.00
31 Jason Heyward 3.00 8.00
32 Nick Swisher 3.00 8.00
33 Russell Martin 2.50 6.00
34 Brandon Barnes 2.50 6.00
35 Pablo Sandoval 3.00 8.00
36 Zack Cozart 2.50 6.00
37 Nick Markakis 3.00 8.00
38 Alex Avila 3.00 8.00
39 Mike Napoli 2.50 6.00
40 Christian Yelich 5.00 12.00
41 Evan Longoria 3.00 8.00
42 Jeff Samardzija 2.50 6.00
43 Jose Reyes 3.00 8.00
44 John Mayberry 2.50 6.00
45 Robbie Ross 2.50 6.00
46 Aaron Hicks 3.00 8.00
47 Junior Lake 2.50 6.00
48 Jimmy Rollins 3.00 8.00
49 Kyle Seager 2.50 6.00
50 Michael Morse 2.50 6.00

2014 Donruss Jersey Kings Studio Series

*STUDIO: .75X TO 2X BASIC
RANDOM INSERTS IN PACKS
PRINT RUNS B/WN 3-25 COPIES PER
NO PRICING ON QTY 15 OR LESS

2014 Donruss National Convention Rated Rookies

201 Masahiro Tanaka 2.00 5.00
202 Jose Abreu 5.00 12.00
203 Yordano Ventura 3.00 8.00

2014 Donruss No No's

1 Nolan Ryan 4.00 10.00
2 Tim Lincecum 1.00 2.50
3 Homer Bailey .75 2.00
4 Dwight Gooden .75 2.00
5 Johan Santana 1.00 2.50
6 Jered Weaver 1.00 2.50
7 Roy Halladay 1.00 2.50
8 Justin Verlander 1.25 3.00
9 Mark Buehrle 1.00 2.50
10 Randy Johnson 1.25 3.00

2014 Donruss Power Plus

COMPLETE SET (12) 6.00 15.00
1 Mike Trout 3.00 8.00
2 Rickey Henderson .60 1.50
3 Josh Hamilton .50 1.25
4 Andrew McCutchen .60 1.50
5 Bryce Harper 1.00 2.50
6 Alex Rodriguez .75 2.00
7 Carlos Beltran .50 1.25
8 Alfonso Soriano .50 1.25
9 Joe Morgan .50 1.25
10 Ryne Sandberg 1.25 3.00
11 Yasiel Puig .60 1.50
12 Matt Kemp .50 1.25

2014 Donruss Power Plus Signatures

PRINT RUNS B/WN 5-25 COPIES PER
NO PRICING ON QTY 10 OR LESS
EXCHANGE DEADLINE 8/26/2015
3 Edwin Encarnacion/15 5.00 12.00
7 Alex Rios/25 10.00 25.00
10 Carlos Gomez/25 EXCH 15.00 40.00
11 Jason Kipnis/25 10.00 25.00
12 Starling Marte/25 EXCH 6.00 15.00
13 David Wright/15 60.00 120.00
14 Jose Canseco/25 150.00 250.00

2014 Donruss Recollection Buyback Autographs

PRINT RUNS B/WN 3-86 COPIES PER
NO PRICING ON QTY 10 OR LESS
EXCHANGE DEADLINE 8/26/2015
1 Tim Raines/45 12.00 30.00
179 Dusty Baker 81 Donruss/20 10.00 25.00
3 Alan Trammell/23 40.00 100.00
11 Ron Darling/18 EXCH 25.00 60.00
12 Don Mattingly/20 EXCH 100.00 200.00
13 Dusty Baker 84 Donruss/20 15.00 40.00
14 Darryl Strawberry 84 Donruss/26 30.00 80.00
293 Alan Trammell 84 Donruss/25 60.00 120.00
18 Eric Davis/40 EXCH 50.00 100.00
21 Vince Coleman 86 Donruss/66 10.00 25.00
24 Fred McGriff 86 Donruss/40 20.00 50.00
26 Wally Joyner 86 Donruss/48 30.00 60.00
30 Mark Grace 88 Donruss/66 15.00 40.00
32 Tom Glavine 88 Donruss/20 60.00 120.00
34 Craig Biggio 89 Donruss/50 15.00 40.00
667 Gregg Jefferies 88 Donruss/99 30.00 80.00

2014 Donruss Signatures

EXCHANGE DEADLINE 8/26/2015
1 Billy Hamilton 4.00 10.00
2 Dave Parker 5.00 12.00
3 Wil Myers 3.00 8.00
4 Jason Kipnis 3.00 8.00
5 Mike Zunino 3.00 8.00
6 Manny Machado 15.00 40.00
7 Bucky Dent 3.00 8.00
8 Kris Medlen 4.00 10.00
9 Chris Sale 5.00 12.00
10 Dusty Baker 3.00 8.00
11 Oscar Gamble 3.00 8.00
12 Willie Horton 3.00 8.00
13 Brandon Barnes 3.00 8.00
14 Martin Prado 3.00 8.00
15 Brandon Maurer 3.00 8.00
16 Alex Wilson 3.00 8.00
17 Andrew Brown 3.00 8.00
18 Starling Marte EXCH 4.00 10.00
19 Chris Rusin 3.00 8.00
20 Jordan Zimmermann 4.00 10.00
21 Evan Gattis EXCH 8.00 20.00
22 Mitch Moreland 3.00 8.00
23 Josh Donaldson 6.00 15.00
24 Bruce Rondon 3.00 8.00
25 Asdrubal Cabrera 4.00 10.00
26 Troy Glaus 8.00 20.00
27 James Shields 5.00 12.00
30 Didi Gregorius 4.00 10.00
31 Reymond Fuentes 3.00 8.00
32 Ivan Nova 4.00 10.00
33 Kevin Gausman 4.00 10.00
34 Jay Bruce 4.00 10.00
35 Michael Choice 3.00 8.00
36 Daniel Nava 6.00 15.00
38 Lance Lynn 6.00 15.00
39 Taijuan Walker 3.00 8.00
40 Xander Bogaerts 12.00 30.00
41 Kolten Wong 4.00 10.00
42 Jurickson Profar 8.00 20.00
43 Mike Napoli 6.00 15.00
44 Zack Wheeler 6.00 15.00
45 Vinnie Pestano 3.00 8.00
46 Michael Morse 3.00 8.00
47 Jay Buhner 4.00 10.00
48 Oscar Taveras 4.00 10.00
50 Miguel Sano 4.00 10.00

2014 Donruss Studio

1A Yasiel Puig 2.50 6.00
1B Adrian Beltre 2.50 6.00
2A Ichiro Suzuki 4.00 10.00
2B Albert Pujols 3.00 8.00
3A Andrew McCutchen 2.50 6.00
3B Chris Sale 2.50 6.00
4A Bryce Harper 4.00 10.00
4B Derek Jeter 6.00 15.00
5A Mike Trout 12.00 30.00
5B Dustin Pedroia 2.50 6.00
6A Chris Davis 1.50 4.00
6B Evan Longoria 2.50 6.00
7A Clayton Kershaw 5.00 12.00
7B Felix Hernandez 2.00 5.00
8A Buster Posey 3.00 8.00
8B Freddie Freeman 3.00 8.00
9A Yadier Molina 2.50 6.00
9B Giancarlo Stanton 2.50 6.00
10A David Ortiz 2.50 6.00
10B Joey Votto 2.50 6.00
11A Yu Darvish 2.50 6.00
11B Jose Abreu 6.00 15.00
12A Stephen Strasburg 2.50 6.00
12B Jose Bautista 2.00 5.00
13 Jose Fernandez 2.50 6.00
14 Masahiro Tanaka 5.00 12.00
15 Max Scherzer 2.50 6.00
16 Miguel Cabrera 2.50 6.00
17 Paul Goldschmidt 2.50 6.00
18 Robinson Cano 2.00 5.00
19 Troy Tulowitzki 2.50 6.00
20 Wil Myers 1.50 4.00

2014 Donruss Team MVPs

1 Buster Posey 2.50 6.00
2 Miguel Cabrera 2.50 6.00
3 Justin Verlander 2.00 5.00
4 Joey Votto 2.00 5.00
5 Josh Hamilton 1.50 4.00
6 Albert Pujols 2.50 6.00
7 Joe Mauer 1.50 4.00
8 Dustin Pedroia 2.00 5.00
9 Ryan Howard 1.50 4.00
10 Ichiro Suzuki 3.00 8.00
11 Chipper Jones 2.00 5.00
12 Ken Griffey Jr. 6.00 15.00
13 Frank Thomas 2.00 5.00
14 Dennis Eckersley 1.50 4.00
15 Cal Ripken Jr. 6.00 15.00
16 Rickey Henderson 2.00 5.00
17 Kirk Gibson 1.25 3.00
18 Roger Clemens 2.50 6.00
19 Don Mattingly 6.00 15.00
20 Dale Murphy 2.00 5.00
21 Robin Yount 2.00 5.00
22 Mike Schmidt 3.00 8.00
23 George Brett 4.00 10.00
24 Dave Parker 1.25 3.00
25 Rod Carew 1.50 4.00
26 Joe Morgan 1.50 4.00
27 Pete Rose 4.00 10.00
28 Reggie Jackson 1.50 4.00
29 Miguel Cabrera 2.50 6.00
30 Andrew McCutchen 2.00 5.00

2014 Donruss The Elite Series

STATED PRINT RUN 999 SER.#'d SETS
1A Brandon Phillips 1.50 4.00
1B Albert Pujols 3.00 8.00
2A Kris Medlen 2.00 5.00
2B Andrew McCutchen 2.50 6.00
3A David Ortiz 2.50 6.00
3B Bryce Harper 4.00 10.00
4A Mike Trout 12.00 30.00
4B Buster Posey 3.00 8.00
5A Evan Gattis 1.50 4.00
5B Carlos Beltran 2.00 5.00
6A Paul Konerko 2.00 5.00
6B Carlos Gomez 1.50 4.00
7A Yasiel Puig 2.50 6.00
7B Carlos Gonzalez 2.00 5.00
8A David Wright 2.00 5.00
8B Chris Archer 1.50 4.00
9A Paul Goldschmidt 2.50 6.00
9B Chris Davis 1.50 4.00
10A Jay Bruce 1.50 4.00
10B Chris Sale 2.50 6.00
11A Manny Machado 2.50 6.00
11B Derek Jeter 6.00 15.00
12A Adam Jones 2.00 5.00
12B Domonic Brown 2.00 5.00
13A Gerrit Cole 2.50 6.00
13B Edwin Encarnacion 2.50 6.00
14A Mariano Rivera 3.00 8.00
14B Evan Longoria 2.00 5.00
15A Stephen Strasburg 2.50 6.00
15B Freddie Freeman 3.00 8.00
16A Paul O'Neill 2.00 5.00
16B Hanley Ramirez 2.00 5.00
17A Cal Ripken Jr. 6.00 15.00
17B Jose Abreu 6.00 15.00
18A Johnny Damon 2.00 5.00
18B Jose Bautista 2.00 5.00
19A Chipper Jones 2.50 6.00
19B Jose Fernandez 2.50 6.00
20A Ozzie Smith 3.00 8.00
20B Jurickson Profar 2.00 5.00
21 Justin Verlander 2.50 6.00
22 Masahiro Tanaka 6.00 15.00
23 Miguel Cabrera 2.50 6.00
24 Nick Castellanos 5.00 12.00
25 Pablo Sandoval 2.00 5.00
26 Prince Fielder 2.00 5.00
27 Robinson Cano 2.00 5.00
28 Xander Bogaerts 5.00 12.00
29 Yordano Ventura 2.00 5.00
30 Yu Darvish 2.50 6.00

2014 Donruss The Rookies

42-100 ISSUED IN THE ROOKIES BOX SET
1 Michael Choice .40 1.00
2 Billy Hamilton .50 1.25
3 Nick Castellanos 1.25 3.00
4 Taijuan Walker .40 1.00
5 Kolten Wong .50 1.25
6 Travis d'Arnaud .50 1.25
7 Wilmer Flores .50 1.25
8 Xander Bogaerts 1.25 3.00
9 Tommy Medica .40 1.00
10 Tim Beckham .60 1.50
11 Cameron Rupp .40 1.00
12 Max Stassi .40 1.00
13 Tanner Roark .40 1.00
14 Enny Romero .40 1.00
15 Jonathan Schoop .40 1.00
16 Erik Johnson .40 1.00
17 Jose Abreu 3.00 8.00
18 Masahiro Tanaka 1.25 3.00
19 Alex Guerrero .50 1.25
20 Yordano Ventura .50 1.25
21 Abraham Almonte .40 1.00
22 Nick Martinez .40 1.00
23 Tyler Collins .40 1.00
24 Tucker Barnhart .40 1.00
25 Matt Davidson .50 1.25
26 Marcus Semien .40 1.00
27 Chris Owings .40 1.00
28 Yangervis Solarte .40 1.00
29 Wei-Chung Wang .40 1.00
30 Jimmy Nelson .40 1.00
31 Christian Bethancourt .40 1.00
32 George Springer 1.50 4.00
33 Jake Marisnick .40 1.00
34 Onelki Garcia .40 1.00
35 Chad Bettis .40 1.00
36 Ethan Martin .40 1.00
37 Brian Flynn .40 1.00
38 David Holmberg .40 1.00
39 Heath Hembree .75 2.00
40 David Hale .40 1.00
41 Jose Ramirez 3.00 8.00
42 Oscar Taveras .50 1.25
43 Gregory Polanco .60 1.50
44 Eddie Butler .40 1.00
45 Andrew Heaney .40 1.00
46 Rougned Odor .75 2.00
47 Marcus Stroman .60 1.50
48 Rafael Montero .40 1.00
49 Garin Cecchini .40 1.00
50 Mookie Betts 8.00 20.00
51 Jon Singleton .50 1.25
52 James Paxton .60 1.50
53 C.J. Cron .40 1.00
54 J.R. Murphy .40 1.00
55 Marco Gonzales .60 1.50
56 Kyle Parker .50 1.25
57 Anthony DeSclafani .40 1.00
58 Robbie Ray .40 1.00
59 Corey Knebel .40 1.00
60 Chris Withrow .40 1.00
61 Luis Sardinas .40 1.00
62 Eugenio Suarez 1.50 4.00
63 Jace Peterson .40 1.00
64 Carlos Contreras .40 1.00
65 Ryan Goins .50 1.25
66 Burch Smith .40 1.00
67 Aaron Altherr .40 1.00
68 Tommy La Stella .40 1.00
69 Danny Santana .50 1.25
70 Joe Panik .60 1.50
71 Matt Stites .40 1.00
72 Stolmy Pimentel .40 1.00
73 J.T. Realmuto 2.50 6.00
74 Jacob deGrom 2.50 6.00
75 Randal Grichuk .60 1.50
76 Kevin Kiermaier .60 1.50
77 Steven Souza .50 1.25
78 Jorge Polanco .40 1.00
79 Adrian Nieto .40 1.00
80 Erisbel Arruebarrena .40 1.00
81 Chase Whitley .40 1.00
82 Odrisamer Despaigne .40 1.00
83 Roenis Elias .40 1.00
84 Matt Shoemaker .60 1.50
85 Domingo Santana .60 1.50
86 Arismendy Alcantara .40 1.00
87 Nick Ahmed .40 1.00
89 Carlos Sanchez .40 1.00
90 C.C. Lee .40 1.00
91 Zach Walters .40 1.00
92 Enrique Hernandez .75 2.00
93 David Peralta .60 1.50
94 James Jones .40 1.00
95 Andrew Susac .50 1.25
96 Aaron Sanchez .40 1.00
97 Chris Taylor 2.00 5.00
98 Shane Greene 1.25 3.00
99 Jesse Hahn .50 1.25
100 Chase Anderson .40 1.00

2014 Donruss The Rookies Press Proofs Gold

*GOLD PROOF: 2.5X TO 6X BASIC
STATED PRINT RUN 99 SER.#'d SETS
RANDOM INSERTS IN PACKS
17 Jose Abreu 8.00 20.00

2014 Donruss The Rookies Press Proofs Silver

*SILVER PROOF: 2X TO 5X BASIC
STATED PRINT RUN 199 SER.#'d SETS
RANDOM INSERTS IN PACKS
17 Jose Abreu 6.00 15.00

2014 Donruss The Rookies Stat Line Career

*CAREER p/r 308-400: 1.5X TO 4X BASIC
*CAREER p/r 102-184: 2X TO 5X BASIC
*CAREER p/r 62-99: 2.5X TO 6X BASIC
*CAREER p/r 36-48: 3X TO 8X BASIC
*CAREER p/r 23: 4X TO 10X BASIC
RANDOM INSERTS IN PACKS
PRINT RUNS B/WN 23-400 COPIES PER
17 Jose Abreu/184 6.00 15.00

2014 Donruss The Rookies Stat Line Season

*SEASON p/r 116-180: 2X TO 5X BASIC
*SEASON p/r 67-77: 2.5X TO 6X BASIC
*SEASON p/r 31-44: 3X TO 8X BASIC
*SEASON p/r 21-24: 4X TO 10X BASIC
*SEASON p/r 15-19: 5X TO 12X BASIC
RANDOM INSERTS IN PACKS
PRINT RUNS B/WN 11-180 COPIES PER
NO PRICING ON QTY 12 OR LESS
17 Jose Abreu/37 10.00 25.00

2014 Donruss The Rookies Autographs

INSERTED IN THE ROOKIES UPDATE BOXES
1 Michael Choice 3.00 8.00
3 Nick Castellanos 10.00 25.00
4 Taijuan Walker 3.00 8.00
5 Kolten Wong 4.00 10.00
8 Xander Bogaerts 10.00 25.00
11 Cameron Rupp 3.00 8.00
17 Jose Abreu 25.00 60.00
19 Alex Guerrero 4.00 10.00
21 Abraham Almonte 3.00 8.00
22 Nick Martinez 3.00 8.00
23 Tyler Collins 3.00 8.00
24 Tucker Barnhart 3.00 8.00
26 Marcus Semien 3.00 8.00
27 Chris Owings 3.00 8.00
28 Yangervis Solarte 3.00 8.00
30 Jimmy Nelson 3.00 8.00
32 George Springer 8.00 20.00
33 Jake Marisnick 3.00 8.00
41 Jose Ramirez 20.00 50.00
42 Oscar Taveras 4.00 10.00
43 Gregory Polanco 5.00 12.00
44 Eddie Butler 3.00 8.00
45 Andrew Heaney 3.00 8.00
46 Rougned Odor 6.00 15.00
47 Marcus Stroman 5.00 12.00
48 Rafael Montero 3.00 8.00
49 Garin Cecchini 3.00 8.00
50 Mookie Betts 50.00 80.00
51 Jon Singleton 4.00 10.00
52 James Paxton 5.00 12.00
53 C.J. Cron 3.00 8.00
54 J.R. Murphy 3.00 8.00
56 Kyle Parker 4.00 10.00
57 Anthony DeSclafani 3.00 8.00
58 Robbie Ray 3.00 8.00
59 Corey Knebel 3.00 8.00
61 Luis Sardinas 3.00 8.00
62 Eugenio Suarez 10.00 25.00
63 Jace Peterson 3.00 8.00
64 Carlos Contreras 3.00 8.00
65 Ryan Goins 4.00 10.00
66 Burch Smith 3.00 8.00
67 Aaron Altherr 3.00 8.00
68 Tommy La Stella 3.00 8.00
69 Danny Santana 4.00 10.00
70 Joe Panik 5.00 12.00
72 Stolmy Pimentel 3.00 8.00
73 J.T. Realmuto 25.00 60.00
74 Jacob deGrom 15.00 40.00
75 Randal Grichuk 5.00 12.00
76 Kevin Kiermaier 8.00 20.00
77 Steven Souza 4.00 10.00
79 Adrian Nieto 3.00 8.00
80 Erisbel Arruebarrena 3.00 8.00
81 Chase Whitley 3.00 8.00
82 Odrisamer Despaigne 3.00 8.00
83 Roenis Elias 3.00 8.00

84 Matt Shoemaker 5.00 12.00
85 Domingo Santana 5.00 12.00
86 Arismendy Alcantara 3.00 8.00
87 Nick Ahmed 3.00 8.00
88 Christian Vazquez 6.00 15.00
89 Carlos Sanchez 3.00 8.00
90 C.C. Lee 3.00 8.00
92 Enrique Hernandez 8.00 20.00
94 James Jones 3.00 8.00
95 Andrew Susac 4.00 10.00
96 Aaron Sanchez 3.00 8.00
97 Chris Taylor 8.00 20.00
98 Shane Greene 5.00 12.00
99 Jesse Hahn 4.00 10.00
100 Chase Anderson 3.00 8.00

2015 Donruss

SPs RANDOMLY INSERTED
1 Paul Goldschmidt DK 1.00 2.50
2 Freddie Freeman DK 1.25 3.00
3 Adam Jones DK .75 2.00
4 Dustin Pedroia DK 1.00 2.50
5 Anthony Rizzo DK 1.50 4.00
6 Jose Abreu DK 1.00 2.50
7 Johnny Cueto DK .75 2.00
8 Corey Kluber DK .75 2.00
9 Nolan Arenado DK 1.25 3.00
10A Victor Martinez DK .75 2.00
10B Alex Gordon .20 .50
10C Gordon SP Back in KC 5.00 12.00
11 George Springer DK .75 2.00
12 Alex Gordon DK .75 2.00
13 Mike Trout DK 5.00 12.00
14 Clayton Kershaw DK 2.00 5.00
15 Giancarlo Stanton DK 1.00 2.50
16 Ryan Braun DK .75 2.00
17 Joe Mauer DK .75 2.00
18 David Wright DK .75 2.00
19 Jacoby Ellsbury DK .75 2.00
20 Sonny Gray DK .75 2.00
21 Ryan Howard DK .75 2.00
22 Gerrit Cole DK 1.00 2.50
23 Andrew Cashner DK .60 1.50
24 Madison Bumgarner DK .75 2.00
25 Felix Hernandez DK .75 2.00
26 Adam Wainwright DK .75 2.00
27 James Loney DK .60 1.50
28 Adrian Beltre DK 1.00 2.50
29 Jose Reyes DK .75 2.00
30 Jordan Zimmermann DK .75 2.00
31 Rusney Castillo RC .60 1.50
32 Joc Pederson RC 1.00 2.50
33 Dalton Pompey RC .60 1.50
34 Daniel Norris RC .50 1.25
35 Javier Baez RC 4.00 10.00
36 Kennys Vargas (RC) .50 1.25
37 Jorge Soler RC .75 2.00
38 Michael Taylor RC .50 1.25
39 Mike Foltynewicz RC .50 1.25
40 Brandon Finnegan RC .50 1.25
41 Maikel Franco RC .60 1.50
42 Yorman Rodriguez RC .50 1.25
43 Christian Walker RC 1.00 2.50
44 Jake Lamb RC .75 2.00
45 Rymer Liriano RC .50 1.25
46 Paul Goldschmidt .25 .60
47 Mark Trumbo .15 .40
48 Patrick Corbin .20 .50
49 Alex Wood .15 .40
50 Freddie Freeman .30 .75
51 Jason Heyward .20 .50
52 Justin Upton .20 .50
53 Julio Teheran .20 .50
54 Nelson Cruz .25 .60
55 Chris Davis .15 .40
56 Adam Jones .20 .50
57 Wei-Yin Chen .15 .40
58 Chris Tillman .15 .40
59 David Ortiz .25 .60
60 Dustin Pedroia .25 .60
61 Yoenis Cespedes .20 .50
62 Xander Bogaerts .25 .60
63 Anthony Rizzo .40 1.00
64 Junior Lake .15 .40
65 Starlin Castro .15 .40
66 Jake Arrieta .20 .50
67A Jose Abreu .25 .60
67B J.Abreu SP ROY 2.50 6.00
68 Chris Sale .25 .60
69 Alexei Ramirez .20 .50
70 Adam Eaton .15 .40
71 Joey Votto .25 .60
72 Todd Frazier .20 .50
73 Devin Mesoraco .15 .40
74 Billy Hamilton .20 .50
75 Johnny Cueto .20 .50
76 Aroldis Chapman .25 .60
77 Michael Brantley .20 .50
78 Corey Kluber .20 .50
79 Carlos Santana .20 .50
80 Yan Gomes .15 .40
81 Troy Tulowitzki .25 .60
82 Corey Dickerson .15 .40
83 Charlie Blackmon .25 .60
84 Nolan Arenado .30 .75
85 Justin Morneau .20 .50
86 Justin Verlander .25 .60
87A Miguel Cabrera .25 .60
87B Cabrera SP Marlins 2.50 6.00
88 Victor Martinez .20 .50
89 Max Scherzer .25 .60
90 David Price .25 .60
91 Dallas Keuchel .20 .50
92 Chris Carter .15 .40
93 George Springer .20 .50
94 Jose Altuve .20 .50
95 Eric Hosmer .20 .50
96 James Shields .15 .40
97 Alex Gordon .20 .50
98 Yordano Ventura .20 .50
99 Salvador Perez .20 .50
100A Mike Trout 1.25 3.00
100B Trout SP Rev Neg 15.00 40.00
100C Trout SP Fldng 15.00 40.00
100D Trout SP MVP 12.00 30.00
101 Albert Pujols .30 .75
102 Matt Shoemaker .20 .50
103 Jered Weaver .20 .50
104A Clayton Kershaw .50 1.25
104B Kershaw SP MVP 5.00 12.00
105 Adrian Gonzalez .20 .50
106A Yasiel Puig .25 .60
106B Puig SP White borders 6.00 15.00
107 Matt Kemp .20 .50
108 Zack Greinke .20 .50
109 Dee Gordon .15 .40
110 Giancarlo Stanton .25 .60
111 Marcell Ozuna .25 .60
112 Henderson Alvarez .15 .40
113 Jose Fernandez .25 .60
114 Ryan Braun .20 .50
115 Carlos Gomez .15 .40
116 Jonathan Lucroy .20 .50
117 Francisco Rodriguez .20 .50
118 Joe Mauer .20 .50
119 Brian Dozier .20 .50
120 Danny Santana .15 .40
121 Phil Hughes .15 .40
122 David Wright .20 .50
123 Zack Wheeler .20 .50
124 Matt Harvey .20 .50
125 Bartolo Colon .15 .40
126A Ichiro .30 .75
126B Ichiro SP Mariners 3.00 8.00
127 Brett Gardner .20 .50
128 Jacoby Ellsbury .20 .50
129A Masahiro Tanaka .20 .50
129B Tanaka SP No logo 2.00 5.00
130 David Robertson .20 .50
131 Josh Donaldson .20 .50
132 Sonny Gray .20 .50
133 Scott Kazmir .15 .40
134 Jon Lester .20 .50
135 Ryan Howard .20 .50
136 Jimmy Rollins .20 .50
137 Chase Utley .20 .50
138 Cole Hamels .20 .50
139 Gregory Polanco .20 .50
140A Andrew McCutchen .25 .60
140B McCutchen SP B/W 10.00 25.00
141 Neil Walker .20 .50
142 Starling Marte .20 .50
143 Edinson Volquez .15 .40
144 Gerrit Cole .25 .60
145 Seth Smith .15 .40
146 Everth Cabrera .15 .40
147 Ian Kennedy .15 .40
148A Buster Posey .30 .75
148B Posey SP Dynasty 3.00 8.00
149 Hunter Pence .20 .50
150 Madison Bumgarner .20 .50
151 Pablo Sandoval .20 .50
152 Brandon Belt .20 .50
153 Robinson Cano .20 .50
154 Kyle Seager .15 .40
155 Mike Zunino .15 .40
156 Felix Hernandez .20 .50
157 Hisashi Iwakuma .20 .50
158 Matt Adams .15 .40
159 Kolten Wong .20 .50
160 Yadier Molina .25 .60
161 Adam Wainwright .20 .50
162 Matt Carpenter .25 .60
163 Matt Holliday .25 .60
164 Evan Longoria .20 .50
165 Kevin Kiermaier .20 .50
166 Alex Cobb .15 .40
167 James Loney .15 .40
168 Adrian Beltre .25 .60
169 Yu Darvish .25 .60
170 Leonys Martin .15 .40
171 Rougned Odor .25 .60
172 Edwin Encarnacion .25 .60
173 Jose Bautista .20 .50
174 Melky Cabrera .15 .40
175 R.A. Dickey .20 .50
176A Bryce Harper .40 1.00
176B Harper SP Mohawk 10.00 25.00
177 Anthony Rendon .25 .60
178 Jordan Zimmermann .25 .60
179 Doug Fister .15 .40
180 Stephen Strasburg .25 .60
181 Rickey Henderson .25 .60
182 Mike Piazza .25 .60
183 Willie McCovey .20 .50
184 Mark McGwire .40 1.00
185A Frank Thomas .25 .60
185B Thomas SP NNOF 12.00 30.00
186 Frank Robinson .20 .50
187A Kirby Puckett .25 .60
187B Puckett SP Puck 10.00 25.00
188A Mariano Rivera .30 .75
188B Rivera SP B/W 10.00 25.00
189 George Brett .50 1.25
190 Wade Boggs .20 .50
191 Ryne Sandberg .50 1.25
192A Pete Rose .50 1.25
192B Rose SP '81 Design 20.00 50.00
193 Tony Gwynn .25 .60
194A Bo Jackson .25 .60
194B Jackson SP B/W 10.00 25.00
195 Ernie Banks .25 .60
196 Mike Trout 81 6.00 15.00
197 Miguel Cabrera 81 1.25 3.00
198 Andrew McCutchen 81 1.25 3.00
199 Albert Pujols 81 1.50 4.00
200 Yu Darvish 81 1.25 3.00
201 Bryce Harper 81 2.00 5.00
202 Jose Abreu 81 1.25 3.00
203 Masahiro Tanaka 81 1.00 2.50
204 Robinson Cano 81 1.00 2.50
205 Madison Bumgarner 81 1.00 2.50
206 Adam Wainwright 81 1.00 2.50
207 Yasiel Puig 81 1.25 3.00
208 Giancarlo Stanton 81 1.25 3.00
209 Evan Longoria 81 1.00 2.50
210 Yadier Molina 81 1.25 3.00
211 Joe Mauer 81 1.00 2.50
212 David Wright 81 1.00 2.50
213 Dustin Pedroia 81 1.25 3.00
214 Felix Hernandez 81 1.00 2.50
215 Clayton Kershaw 81 2.50 6.00
216 Chris Sale 81 1.25 3.00
217 Buster Posey 81 1.50 4.00
218 Alex Gordon 81 1.00 2.50
219 Freddie Freeman 81 1.50 4.00
220 David Ortiz 81 1.25 3.00
221 Ichiro 81 1.50 4.00
222 Nelson Cruz 81 1.25 3.00
223 Jose Bautista 81 1.00 2.50
224 Johnny Cueto 81 1.00 2.50
225 Ryan Howard 81 1.00 2.50
226 Eric Hosmer 81 1.00 2.50
227 Josh Donaldson 81 1.00 2.50
228 Troy Tulowitzki 81 1.25 3.00
229 Corey Kluber 81 1.00 2.50
230 Max Scherzer 81 1.25 3.00
231 Jose Altuve 81 1.00 2.50
232 Manny Machado 81 1.25 3.00
233 Yordano Ventura 81 1.00 2.50
234 Billy Hamilton 81 1.00 2.50
235 Adrian Beltre 81 1.25 3.00
236 Reggie Jackson 81 1.00 2.50
237 Johnny Bench 81 1.25 3.00
238 Cal Ripken 81 4.00 10.00
239 Bob Gibson 81 1.00 2.50
240 George Brett 81 2.50 6.00
241 Ozzie Smith 81 1.50 4.00
242 Don Mattingly 81 2.50 6.00
243 Greg Maddux 81 1.50 4.00
244 Ken Griffey Jr. 81 2.50 6.00
245 Nolan Ryan 81 4.00 10.00

2015 Donruss '81 Press Proofs Bronze

*PLAT.BRONZE: .6X TO 1.5X BASIC
RANDOM INSERTS IN PACKS
STATED PRINT RUN 299 SER.#'d SETS

2015 Donruss '81 Press Proofs Platinum Blue

*PLAT.BLUE: .75X TO 2X BASIC
RANDOM INSERTS IN PACKS
STATED PRINT RUN 199 SER.#'d SETS

2015 Donruss Press Proofs Gold

*GOLD DK: 1.2X TO 3X BASIC
*GOLD RC: 1.5X TO 4X BASIC
*GOLD VET: 5X TO 12X BASIC
RANDOM INSERTS IN PACKS
STATED PRINT RUN 99 SER.#'d SETS

2015 Donruss Press Proofs Silver

*SILVER DK: .75X TO 2X BASIC
*SILVER RC: 1X TO 2.5X BASIC
*SILVER VET: 3X TO 8X BASIC
RANDOM INSERTS IN PACKS
STATED PRINT RUN 199 SER.#'d SETS

2015 Donruss Stat Line Career

*CAR DK p/r 280-400: .6X TO 1.5X
*CAR DK p/r 154-230: .75X TO 2X
*CAR DK p/r 106-121: 1X TO 2.5X
*CAR DK p/r 63-71: 1.2X TO 3X
*CAR RR p/r 274-400: .75X TO 2X
*CAR RR p/r 150: 1X TO 2.5X
*CAR RR p/r 100: 1.2X TO 3X
*CAR RR p/r 19: 2.5X TO 6X
*CAR p/r 262-400: 2.5X TO 6X
*CAR p/r 136-248: 3X TO 8X
*CAR p/r 82-122: 4X TO 10X
*CAR p/r 50-73: 5X TO 12X
*CAR p/r 27: 6X TO 15X
*CAR p/r 17-23: 8X TO 20X
RANDOM INSERTS IN PACKS
PRINT RUNS B/WN 5-400 COPIES PER
NO PRICING ON QTY 15 OR LESS

2015 Donruss Stat Line Season

*SEA DK p/r 255-400: .6X TO 1.5X
*SEA DK p/r 138-248: .75X TO 2X
*SEA DK p/r 81-107: 1X TO 2.5X
*SEA DK p/r 29-36: 1.5X TO 4X
*SEA DK p/r 18-20: 2X TO 5X
*SEA RR p/r 255-400: .75X TO 2X
*SEA RR p/r 126-231: 1X TO 2.5X
*SEA RR p/r 84-106: 1.2X TO 3X
*SEA RR p/r 59: 1.5X TO 4X
*SEA RR p/r 30-46: 2X TO 5X
*SEA p/r 252-400: 2.5X TO 6X
*SEA p/r 130-246: 3X TO 8X
*SEA p/r 78-116: 4X TO 10X
*SEA p/r 53-70: 5X TO 12X
*SEA p/r 26-49: 6X TO 15X
*SEA p/r 16-25: 8X TO 20X
RANDOM INSERTS IN PACKS
PRINT RUNS B/WN 7-400 COPIES PER
NO PRICING ON QTY 15 OR LESS

2015 Donruss All Time Diamond Kings

RANDOM INSERTS IN PACKS
*SILVER/49: 3X TO 8X BASIC
1 Ken Griffey Jr. 2.50 6.00
2 Cal Ripken 4.00 10.00
3 Nolan Ryan 4.00 10.00
4 Frank Thomas 1.25 3.00
5 Greg Maddux 1.50 4.00
6 Pete Rose 2.50 6.00
7 George Brett 2.50 6.00
8 Robin Yount 1.25 3.00
9 Rickey Henderson 1.25 3.00
10 Kirby Puckett 1.25 3.00
11 Ozzie Smith 1.50 4.00
12 Tony Gwynn 1.25 3.00
13 Johnny Bench 1.25 3.00
14 Reggie Jackson 1.00 2.50
15 Ryne Sandberg 2.50 6.00
16 Willie McCovey 1.00 2.50
17 Brooks Robinson 1.00 2.50
18 Wade Boggs 1.00 2.50
19 Ernie Banks 1.25 3.00
20 Carl Yastrzemski 2.00 5.00
21 Mariano Rivera 1.50 4.00
22 Mike Piazza 1.25 3.00
23 Frank Robinson 1.00 2.50
24 Bob Gibson 1.00 2.50
25 Jim Palmer 1.00 2.50
26 Chipper Jones 1.25 3.00
27 Don Mattingly 2.50 6.00
28 Bo Jackson 1.25 3.00
29 Mark McGwire 2.00 5.00
30 Paul Molitor 1.25 3.00

2015 Donruss Bat Kings

RANDOM INSERTS IN PACKS
*STUDIO/25: .6X TO 1.5X BASIC
1 Albert Pujols 4.00 10.00
2 Brandon Belt 2.50 6.00
3 Evan Gattis 2.00 5.00
4 Carlos Beltran 2.50 6.00
5 Carlos Gonzalez 2.50 6.00
6 B.J. Upton 2.50 6.00
7 David Ortiz 3.00 8.00
8 Devin Mesoraco 2.00 5.00
9 Dustin Pedroia 3.00 8.00
10 Edwin Encarnacion 3.00 8.00
11 Evan Longoria 2.50 6.00
12 Gerardo Parra 2.00 5.00
13 Hanley Ramirez 2.50 6.00
14 Jacoby Ellsbury 2.50 6.00
15 Jose Bautista 2.50 6.00
16 Jose Reyes 2.50 6.00
17 Josh Donaldson 2.50 6.00
18 Justin Upton 2.50 6.00
19 Mark Teixeira 2.50 6.00
20 Matt Kemp 2.50 6.00
21 Mike Napoli 2.00 5.00
22 Nelson Cruz 3.00 8.00
23 Pedro Alvarez 2.00 5.00
24 Prince Fielder 2.50 6.00
25 Robinson Cano 2.50 6.00
26 Ryan Howard 2.50 6.00
27 Ryan Zimmerman 2.50 6.00
28 Troy Tulowitzki 3.00 8.00
29 Wil Myers 2.00 5.00
30 Adrian Gonzalez 2.50 6.00
31 Andrew McCutchen 3.00 8.00
32 Brandon Phillips 2.00 5.00
33 David Wright 2.50 6.00
34 George Springer 2.50 6.00
35 Hunter Pence 2.50 6.00
36 Joe Mauer 2.50 6.00
37 Joey Votto 3.00 8.00
38 Matt Adams 2.00 5.00
39 Melky Cabrera 2.00 5.00
40 Yasiel Puig 3.00 8.00
41 Giancarlo Stanton 3.00 8.00
42 Miguel Cabrera 3.00 8.00
43 Starlin Castro 2.00 5.00
44 Starling Marte 2.50 6.00
45 Mike Trout 6.00 15.00

2015 Donruss Elite Inserts

COMPLETE SET (36) 10.00 25.00
RANDOM INSERTS IN PACKS
*STAT.GLD/49: 1.5X TO 4X BASIC
*STAT.RED/25: 2.5X TO 6X BASIC
1 Patrick Corbin .50 1.25
2 Jason Heyward .50 1.25
3 Wei-Yin Chen .40 1.00
4 Yoenis Cespedes .50 1.25
5 Jose Abreu .60 1.50
6 Anthony Rizzo 1.00 2.50
7 Johnny Cueto .50 1.25
8 Corey Kluber .50 1.25
9 Nolan Arenado .75 2.00
10 Victor Martinez .50 1.25
11 Jose Altuve .50 1.25
12 Alex Gordon .50 1.25
13 Jered Weaver .50 1.25
14 Dee Gordon .40 1.00
15 Henderson Alvarez .40 1.00
16 Jonathan Lucroy .50 1.25
17 Brian Dozier .50 1.25
18 Zack Wheeler .50 1.25
19 Jacoby Ellsbury .50 1.25
20 Sonny Gray .50 1.25
21 Jimmy Rollins .50 1.25
22 Neil Walker .50 1.25
23 Matt Adams .40 1.00
24 Hisashi Iwakuma .50 1.25
25 Hunter Pence .50 1.25
26 Everth Cabrera .40 1.00
27 James Loney .40 1.00
28 Leonys Martin .40 1.00
29 R.A. Dickey .50 1.25
30 Anthony Rendon .60 1.50
31 Greg Holland .40 1.00
32 Francisco Lindor 2.50 6.00
33 Yasmany Tomas .50 1.25
34 Carlos Correa 2.00 5.00
35 Byron Buxton .60 1.50
36 Kris Bryant 2.50 6.00

2015 Donruss Elite Inserts Dominator

RANDOM INSERTS IN PACKS
STATED PRINT RUN 999 SER.#'d SETS
1 Freddie Freeman 2.00 5.00
2 Adam Jones 1.25 3.00
3 Yoenis Cespedes 1.25 3.00
4 Chris Sale 1.50 4.00
5 Andrew McCutchen 1.50 4.00
6 Buster Posey 2.00 5.00
7 Robinson Cano 1.25 3.00
8 Adam Wainwright 1.25 3.00
9 Bryce Harper 2.50 6.00
10 Jose Altuve 1.25 3.00
11 Salvador Perez 1.25 3.00
12 Albert Pujols 2.00 5.00
13 Ryan Howard 1.25 3.00
14 Yu Darvish 1.50 4.00
15 Javier Baez 8.00 20.00
16 Nolan Arenado 2.00 5.00
17 Zack Greinke 1.25 3.00
18 Mike Trout 8.00 20.00
19 Ichiro 2.00 5.00
20 Rusney Castillo 1.25 3.00
21 Kennys Vargas 1.00 2.50
22 Jorge Soler 1.50 4.00
23 Joc Pederson 2.00 5.00
24 Maikel Franco 1.25 3.00
25 Michael Taylor 1.00 2.50

2015 Donruss Hot off the Press

*HP DK: .6X TO 1.5X BASIC
*HP RC: .75X TO 2X BASIC
*SP VET: 2.5X TO 6X BASIC
*SP 81: .5X TO 1.2X BASIC
RANDOM INSERTS IN PACKS

2015 Donruss Jersey Kings

RANDOM INSERTS IN PACKS
*STUDIO/25: 1X TO 2.5X BASIC
1 Andrew McCutchen 4.00 10.00
2 Aaron Hicks 2.50 6.00
3 Adam Eaton 2.00 5.00
4 Anthony Rizzo 5.00 12.00
5 Billy Hamilton 2.50 6.00
6 Brad Ziegler 2.00 5.00
7 Brandon Belt 2.50 6.00
8 Brian Dozier 2.50 6.00
9 Bryce Harper 5.00 12.00
10 Carl Crawford 2.50 6.00
11 Carlos Gomez 2.00 5.00
12 Chase Headley 2.00 5.00
13 Chris Perez 2.00 5.00
14 Dallas Keuchel 2.50 6.00
15 Dan Uggla 2.00 5.00
16 David Ortiz 3.00 8.00
17 Dee Gordon 2.00 5.00
18 Dexter Fowler 2.50 6.00
19 Dillon Gee 2.00 5.00
20 Evan Longoria 2.50 6.00
21 Felix Hernandez 2.50 6.00
22 Ian Kinsler 2.50 6.00
23 Hunter Pence 2.50 6.00
24 Jackie Bradley Jr. 3.00 8.00
25 Jacoby Ellsbury 2.50 6.00
26 Albert Pujols 4.00 10.00
27 Jason Heyward 2.50 6.00
28 Jake Odorizzi 2.00 5.00
29 Jay Bruce 2.50 6.00
30 Jon Lester 2.50 6.00
31 Aramis Ramirez 2.00 5.00
32 Prince Fielder 2.50 6.00
33 Jason Kipnis 2.50 6.00
35 Josh Hamilton 2.50 6.00
36 Leonys Martin 2.00 5.00
37 Mark Trumbo 2.00 5.00
38 Matt Adams 2.00 5.00
39 Yovani Gallardo 2.00 5.00
40 Victor Martinez 2.50 6.00
41 Torii Hunter 2.50 6.00
42 Shane Victorino 2.50 6.00
43 Robinson Cano 2.50 6.00
44 Patrick Corbin 2.50 6.00
45 Nelson Cruz 3.00 8.00

2015 Donruss Long Ball Leaders

RANDOM INSERTS IN PACKS
*RED/99: 1.2X TO 3X BASIC
*GREEN/25: 2X TO 5X BASIC
1 Mike Trout 6.00 15.00
2 Giancarlo Stanton 1.25 3.00
3 David Ortiz 1.25 3.00
4 Justin Upton 1.00 2.50
5 Hanley Ramirez 1.00 2.50
6 Paul Goldschmidt 1.25 3.00
7 C.J. Cron .75 2.00
8 Anthony Rizzo 2.00 5.00
9 George Springer 1.00 2.50
10 Alex Gordon 1.00 2.50
11 Ian Desmond .75 2.00
12 Edwin Encarnacion 1.25 3.00
13 Hunter Pence 1.00 2.50
14 Buster Posey 1.50 4.00
15 Yasiel Puig 1.25 3.00

2015 Donruss Preferred Black

*BLACK: 1.5X TO 4X BASIC
RANDOM INSERTS IN PACKS
STATED PRINT RUN 99 SER.#'d SETS
2 George Brett 10.00 25.00
5 Kirby Puckett 10.00 25.00

2015 Donruss Preferred Bronze

COMPLETE SET (40) 10.00 25.00
RANDOM INSERTS IN PACKS
1 Ken Griffey Jr. 1.25 3.00
2 George Brett 1.25 3.00
3 Cal Ripken 2.00 5.00
4 Nolan Ryan 2.00 5.00
5 Kirby Puckett .60 1.50
6 Javier Baez 3.00 8.00
7 Kennys Vargas .40 1.00
8 Joc Pederson .75 2.00
9 Rusney Castillo .50 1.25
10 Dalton Pompey .50 1.25
11 Maikel Franco .50 1.25
12 Jorge Soler .60 1.50
13 Michael Taylor .40 1.00
14 Daniel Norris .40 1.00
15 Brandon Finnegan .40 1.00
16 Rymer Liriano .40 1.00
17 Mike Foltynewicz .40 1.00
18 Mike Trout 3.00 8.00
19 Ichiro .75 2.00
20 Clayton Kershaw 1.25 3.00
21 Jose Abreu .60 1.50
22 Yu Darvish .60 1.50
23 Bryce Harper 1.00 2.50
24 Chris Sale .60 1.50
25 Giancarlo Stanton .60 1.50
26 Masahiro Tanaka .50 1.25
27 George Springer .50 1.25
28 Eric Hosmer .50 1.25
29 Buster Posey .75 2.00
30 Felix Hernandez .50 1.25
31 Miguel Cabrera .60 1.50
32 Yasiel Puig .60 1.50
33 Adam Wainwright .50 1.25
34 Jose Altuve .50 1.25
35 David Ortiz .60 1.50
36 Francisco Lindor 2.50 6.00
37 Yasmany Tomas .50 1.25
38 Carlos Correa 2.00 5.00
39 Byron Buxton .60 1.50
40 Kris Bryant 2.50 6.00

2015 Donruss Preferred Cut to the Chase Bronze

*BRONZE: 2.5X TO 6X BASIC
RANDOM INSERTS IN PACKS
STATED PRINT RUN 49 SER.#'d SETS
2 George Brett 15.00 40.00
5 Kirby Puckett 15.00 40.00

2015 Donruss Preferred Cut to the Chase Gold

*GOLD: 3X TO 8X BASIC
RANDOM INSERTS IN PACKS
STATED PRINT RUN 25 SER.#'d SETS
2 George Brett 20.00 50.00
5 Kirby Puckett 20.00 50.00

2015 Donruss Preferred Gold

*GOLD: 1X TO 2.5X BASIC
RANDOM INSERTS IN PACKS
STATED PRINT RUN 299 SER.#'d SETS
2 George Brett 6.00 15.00
5 Kirby Puckett 6.00 15.00

2015 Donruss Preferred Red

*RED: 1.2X TO 3X BASIC
RANDOM INSERTS IN PACKS
STATED PRINT RUN 199 SER.#'d SETS
2 George Brett 8.00 20.00
5 Kirby Puckett 8.00 20.00

2015 Donruss Production Line Blue

RANDOM INSERTS IN PACKS
PRINT RUNS B/WN 427-581 COPIES PER
*RED: .75X TO 2X BASIC
*GREEN: 2.5X TO 6X BASIC
1 Jose Abreu/581 1.50 4.00
2 Giancarlo Stanton/555 1.50 4.00
3 Victor Martinez/565 1.25 3.00
4 Adrian Gonzalez/482 1.25 3.00
5 Adrian Beltre/492 1.50 4.00
6 Miguel Cabrera/524 1.50 4.00
7 Mike Trout/561 8.00 20.00
8 Adam LaRoche/455 1.00 2.50
9 Andrew McCutchen/542 1.50 4.00
10 Anthony Rizzo/527 2.50 6.00
11 Nelson Cruz/525 1.50 4.00
12 Jose Bautista/524 1.25 3.00
13 Chris Carter/491 1.00 2.50
14 David Ortiz/517 1.50 4.00
15 Albert Pujols/466 2.00 5.00
16 Justin Upton/491 1.25 3.00
17 Yoenis Cespedes/450 1.25 3.00
18 Carlos Santana/427 1.25 3.00
19 Freddie Freeman/461 2.00 5.00
20 Buster Posey/490 2.00 5.00

2015 Donruss Rated Rookies Die Cut Silver

RANDOM INSERTS IN PACKS
STATED PRINT RUN 750 SER.#'d SETS
*GOLD/25: 1X TO 2.5X BASIC
1 Rusney Castillo 1.50 4.00
2 Joc Pederson 2.50 6.00
3 Javier Baez 10.00 25.00
4 Jorge Soler 2.00 5.00
5 Maikel Franco 1.50 4.00
6 Kennys Vargas 1.25 3.00
7 Michael Taylor 1.25 3.00
8 Mike Foltynewicz 1.25 3.00
9 Daniel Norris 1.25 3.00
10 Dalton Pompey 1.50 4.00

2015 Donruss Signature Series

RANDOM INSERTS IN PACKS
1 Christian Walker 5.00 12.00
2 Rusney Castillo 3.00 8.00
3 Yasmany Tomas 3.00 8.00
4 Matt Barnes 2.50 6.00
5 Brandon Finnegan 2.50 6.00
6 Daniel Norris 2.50 6.00
7 Kendall Graveman 2.50 6.00
8 Yorman Rodriguez 2.50 6.00
9 Gary Brown 2.50 6.00
10 R.J. Alvarez 2.50 6.00
11 Dalton Pompey 3.00 8.00
14 Lane Adams 2.50 6.00
15 Joc Pederson 10.00 25.00
16 Steven Moya 3.00 8.00
17 Cory Spangenberg 2.50 6.00
18 Andy Wilkins 2.50 6.00
19 Terrance Gore 2.50 6.00
21 Dilson Herrera 3.00 8.00
23 Jorge Soler 4.00 10.00
24 Matt Szczur 3.00 8.00
25 Buck Farmer 2.50 6.00
26 Michael Taylor 2.50 6.00
28 Trevor May 2.50 6.00
29 Jake Lamb 4.00 10.00
30 Javier Baez 25.00 60.00
31 Mike Foltynewicz 2.50 6.00
32 Kennys Vargas 2.50 6.00
33 Anthony Ranaudo 2.50 6.00
34 Matt Carpenter 4.00 10.00
35 David Price 12.00 30.00
36 Alex Wood 2.50 6.00
37 Dante Bichette 2.50 6.00
38 Fernando Rodney 2.50 6.00
39 Ron Gant 2.50 6.00
40 Adam Eaton 2.50 6.00
41 Shane Victorino 3.00 8.00
42 Anthony Rendon 6.00 15.00
43 Max Scherzer 6.00 15.00
44 Daniel Murphy 3.00 8.00
45 Adam Jones 6.00 15.00
46 Adrian Beltre 6.00 15.00
48 Jered Weaver 3.00 8.00
49 Prince Fielder 6.00 15.00
50 R.A. Dickey 3.00 8.00
51 Victor Martinez 3.00 8.00
52 Brian McCann 3.00 8.00
53 David Freese 2.50 6.00
54 Gerrit Cole 4.00 10.00
55 Jason Kipnis 3.00 8.00
56 Wilin Rosario 2.50 6.00
57 Tanner Roark 2.50 6.00
58 Wil Myers 2.50 6.00
59 Matt den Dekker 2.50 6.00
60 Norichika Aoki 2.50 6.00
61 Junior Lake 2.50 6.00
62 Ehire Adrianza 2.50 6.00
64 Stephen Strasburg 10.00 25.00
65 Manny Machado 12.00 30.00
66 Evan Longoria 3.00 8.00
67 Alexi Ogando 2.50 6.00
69 Anthony Rizzo 12.00 30.00
70 Bob Horner 2.50 6.00
71 Bret Saberhagen 3.00 8.00
72 Curt Schilling 8.00 20.00
73 Jeff Conine 2.50 6.00
74 Jose Abreu 25.00 60.00
75 Mark Grace 10.00 25.00
76 Edgar Martinez 4.00 10.00
77 Paul Konerko 8.00 20.00
78 Kevin Millar 4.00 10.00
79 Willie McGee 10.00 25.00
80 Ryan Goins 4.00 10.00
81 Chuck Knoblauch 10.00 25.00
82 Archie Bradley 2.50 6.00
83 Danny Salazar 3.00 8.00
84 Darin Ruf 2.50 6.00
85 Harold Reynolds 3.00 8.00
86 John Franco 2.50 6.00
87 Fred McGriff 3.00 8.00
88 Steve Garvey 8.00 20.00
89 Kevin Mitchell 2.50 6.00
90 Steve Finley 2.50 6.00
91 Lance Parrish 2.50 6.00
93 Rob Dibble 4.00 10.00
94 Michael Young 2.50 6.00

2015 Donruss Signature Series Blue

*BLUE p/r 99: .5X TO 1.2X BASIC
*BLUE p/r 49: .6X TO 1.5X BASIC
*BLUE p/r 25: .75X TO 2X BASIC
RANDOM INSERTS IN PACKS
PRINT RUNS B/WN 15-99 COPIES PER
NO PRICING ON QTY 15 OR LESS

2015 Donruss Signature Series Green

*GREEN: .75X TO 2X BASIC
RANDOM INSERTS IN PACKS
PRINT RUNS B/WN 5-25 COPIES PER
NO PRICING ON QTY 15 OR LESS

12 Maikel Franco/25 6.00 15.00
32 Kennys Vargas/25 20.00 50.00

2015 Donruss Signature Series Red

*GREEN p/r 49: .6X TO 1.5X BASIC
*GREEN p/r 25-29: .75X TO 2X BASIC
RANDOM INSERTS IN PACKS
PRINT RUNS B/WN 10-49 COPIES PER
NO PRICING ON QTY 15 OR LESS

2015 Donruss Studio

RANDOM INSERTS IN PACKS
1 Yordano Ventura 1.25 3.00
2 Kennys Vargas 1.00 2.50
3 Javier Baez 8.00 20.00
4 Matt Shoemaker 1.25 3.00
5 Jorge Soler 1.50 4.00
6 Rusney Castillo 1.25 3.00
7 Jose Altuve 1.25 3.00
8 Joc Pederson 2.00 5.00
9 Michael Taylor 1.00 2.50
10 Pablo Sandoval 1.25 3.00

2015 Donruss The Elite Series

RANDOM INSERTS IN PACKS
STATED PRINT RUN 999 SER.#'d SET
1 Mark Trumbo 1.25 3.00
2 Javier Baez 3.00 8.00
3 Dustin Pedroia 2.00 5.00
4 Troy Tulowitzki 2.00 5.00
5 Max Scherzer 2.00 5.00
6 Rusney Castillo 1.50 4.00
7 Salvador Perez 1.50 4.00
8 Chase Utley 1.50 4.00
9 Madison Bumgarner 1.50 4.00
10 Adrian Beltre 2.00 5.00
11 Starling Marte 1.50 4.00
12 Clayton Kershaw 4.00 10.00
13 Giancarlo Stanton 2.00 5.00
14 Justin Upton 1.50 4.00
15 Josh Donaldson 1.50 4.00
16 Yadier Molina 2.00 5.00
17 Ichiro 2.50 6.00
18 Ryan Braun 1.50 4.00
19 Matt Harvey 1.50 4.00
20 Joey Votto 2.00 5.00
21 Kennys Vargas 1.25 3.00
22 Michael Taylor 1.25 3.00
23 Jorge Soler 2.00 5.00
24 Joc Pederson 2.50 6.00
25 Maikel Franco 1.50 4.00

2015 Donruss The Rookies

RANDOM INSERTS IN PACKS
*GOLD/99: 1X TO 2.5X
*SILVER/199: .75X TO 2X
*CAR p/r 276-400: .6X TO 1.5X
*CAR p/r 150: .75X TO 2X
*CAR p/r 100 : 1X TO 2.5X
*CAR p/r 19 : 2X TO 5X
*SEA p/r 255-400: .6X TO 1.5X
*SEA p/r 126-231: .75X TO 2X
*SEA p/r 84-106 : 1X TO 2.5X
*SEA p/r 59 : 1.2X TO 3X
*SEA p/r 30-46 : 1.5X TO 4X
1 Rusney Castillo .75 2.00
2 Joc Pederson 1.25 3.00
3 Javier Baez 5.00 12.00
4 Jorge Soler 1.00 2.50
5 Maikel Franco .75 2.00
6 Anthony Ranaudo .60 1.50
7 Michael Taylor .60 1.50
8 Mike Foltynewicz .60 1.50
9 Daniel Norris .60 1.50
10 Dalton Pompey .75 2.00
11 Brandon Finnegan .60 1.50
12 Yorman Rodriguez .60 1.50
13 Christian Walker 1.25 3.00
14 Jake Lamb 1.00 2.50
15 Rymer Liriano .60 1.50

2015 Donruss Tony Gwynn Tribute

COMPLETE SET (5) 5.00 12.00
RANDOM INSERTS IN PACKS
*RED/99: 2X TO 5X BASIC
*GREEN/25: 4X TO 10X BASIC
1 Tony Gwynn 1.25 3.00
2 Tony Gwynn 1.25 3.00
3 Tony Gwynn 1.25 3.00
4 Tony Gwynn 1.25 3.00
5 Tony Gwynn 1.25 3.00

2015 Donruss USA Collegiate National Team

RANDOM INSERTS IN PACKS
*RED/49: 1.2X TO 3X BASIC
*GOLD/25: 2X TO 5X BASIC
1 James Kaprielian 1.00 2.50
2 Jake Lemoine .60 1.50
3 Ryan Burr .60 1.50
4 Carson Fulmer .60 1.50
5 DJ Stewart .75 2.00
6 Chris Okey .60 1.50
7 Alex Bregman 2.50 6.00
8 Dansby Swanson 4.00 10.00
9 Blake Trahan .60 1.50
10 Thomas Eshelman .60 1.50
11 Kyle Funkhouser .75 2.00
12 A.J. Minter .75 2.00
13 Nicholas Banks .60 1.50
14 Zack Collins .75 2.00
15 Mark Mathias .75 2.00
16 Bryan Reynolds 2.00 5.00
17 Taylor Ward 1.00 2.50
18 Justin Garza .60 1.50
19 Tyler Jay .60 1.50
20 Tate Matheny .60 1.50
21 Trey Killian .60 1.50
22 Andrew Moore .75 2.00
23 Christin Stewart .75 2.00
24 Dillon Tate .75 2.00

2016 Donruss

COMP.SET w/o SPs (150) 10.00 25.00
SPs RANDOMLY INSERTED
COMP.SET ARE CARD 46-195
1 A.J. Pollock DK .60 1.50
2 Nick Markakis DK .75 2.00
3 Manny Machado DK 1.00 2.50
4 Xander Bogaerts DK 1.00 2.50
5 Jake Arrieta DK .75 2.00
6 Chris Sale DK 1.00 2.50
7 Todd Frazier DK .75 2.00
8 Michael Brantley DK .75 2.00
9 Carlos Gonzalez DK .75 2.00
10 Miguel Cabrera DK 1.00 2.50
11 Jose Altuve DK .75 2.00
12 Eric Hosmer DK .75 2.00
13 Albert Pujols DK 1.25 3.00
14 Zack Greinke DK .75 2.00
15 Jose Fernandez DK 1.00 2.50
16 Adam Lind DK .75 2.00
17 Brian Dozier DK .75 2.00
18 Jacob deGrom DK 1.00 2.50
19 Alex Rodriguez DK 1.25 3.00
20 Billy Burns DK .60 1.50
21 Odubel Herrera DK .75 2.00
22 Andrew McCutchen DK 1.00 2.50
23 Matt Kemp DK .75 2.00
24 Buster Posey DK 1.25 3.00
25 Nelson Cruz DK 1.00 2.50
26 Yadier Molina DK 1.00 2.50
27 Evan Longoria DK .75 2.00
28 Prince Fielder DK .75 2.00
29 Josh Donaldson DK .75 2.00
30 Bryce Harper DK 1.50 4.00
31 Kyle Schwarber RR RC 1.50 4.00
32 Corey Seager RR RC 4.00 10.00
33 Trea Turner RR RC 1.50 4.00
34 Rob Refsnyder RR RC .60 1.50
35 Miguel Sano RR RC .75 2.00
36 Stephen Piscotty RR RC .75 2.00
37 Aaron Nola RR RC 1.00 2.50
38 Michael Conforto RR RC .60 1.50
39 Ketel Marte RR RC .60 1.50
40 Luis Severino RR RC .60 1.50
41 Greg Bird RR RC .60 1.50
42 Hector Olivera RR RC .60 1.50
43 Jose Peraza RR RC .60 1.50
44 Henry Owens RR RC .60 1.50
45 Richie Shaffer RR RC .50 1.25
46 Edwin Encarnacion .25 .60
47A Josh Donaldson .20 .50
47B Donaldson SP MVP 1.50 4.00
47C Dnldsn SP Nickname 1.50 4.00
48 Robinson Cano .20 .50
49 David Price .20 .50
50 Sonny Gray .20 .50
51 Dallas Keuchel .20 .50
52 Jake Arrieta .20 .50
53 Clayton Kershaw .50 1.25
54 Zack Greinke .20 .50
55 Jose Bautista .20 .50
56 Paul Goldschmidt .25 .60
57A Bryce Harper .40 1.00
57B Harper SP MVP 3.00 8.00
58 Joey Votto .25 .60
59A Carlos Correa .25 .60
59B Correa SP ROY 2.00 5.00
60A Kris Bryant .30 .75
60B Bryant SP ROY 2.50 6.00
61 Andrew McCutchen .25 .60
62 Albert Pujols .30 .75
63 Prince Fielder .20 .50
64 Buster Posey .30 .75
65 Dee Gordon .15 .40
66 Nolan Arenado .30 .75
67 Miguel Cabrera .25 .60
68 Jose Altuve .20 .50
69 Xander Bogaerts .25 .60
70 Nelson Cruz .25 .60
71 Carlos Gonzalez .20 .50
72 Manny Machado .25 .60
73 Kevin Kiermaier .20 .50
74 Brandon Crawford .20 .50
75 Starling Marte .20 .50
76 A.J. Pollock .15 .40
77 Kole Calhoun .15 .40
78 Alcides Escobar .15 .40
79 Kevin Pillar .15 .40
80 Andrelton Simmons .15 .40
81 Lorenzo Cain .15 .40
82 Yadier Molina .25 .60
83A Mike Trout 1.25 3.00
83B Trout SP Hat off 10.00 25.00
83C Trout SP Nickname 10.00 25.00
84 David Ortiz .25 .60
85 Yoenis Cespedes .25 .60
86 Todd Frazier .20 .50
87 Anthony Rizzo .40 1.00
88 Jose Abreu .25 .60
89 Matt Carpenter .25 .60
90 Adrian Gonzalez .20 .50
91 Chris Davis .15 .40
92 Kendrys Morales .15 .40
93 J.D. Martinez .25 .60
94 Collin McHugh .15 .40
95 Madison Bumgarner .20 .50
96 Gerrit Cole .25 .60
97 Michael Wacha .20 .50
98 Colby Lewis .15 .40
99 Jacob deGrom .25 .60
100 Max Scherzer .25 .60
101 Ian Kinsler .20 .50
102 Ben Revere .15 .40
103 Charlie Blackmon .25 .60
104 Adam Eaton .15 .40
105 Jason Kipnis .20 .50
106 Joc Pederson .20 .50
107 Francisco Lindor .25 .60
108 Chris Sale .25 .60
109 Billy Hamilton .20 .50
110 Billy Burns .15 .40
111 Ryan Braun .20 .50
112 Jason Heyward .20 .50
113 Eddie Rosario .20 .50
114 Dexter Fowler .20 .50
115 Brian Dozier .20 .50
116 Curtis Granderson .20 .50
117 Shin-Soo Choo .20 .50
118 Mookie Betts .40 1.00
119 Kyle Seager .15 .40
120 Mark Melancon .15 .40
121 Trevor Rosenthal .20 .50
122 Jeurys Familia .20 .50
123 Corey Kluber .20 .50
124 Francisco Liriano .15 .40
125 Jon Lester .20 .50
126 Carlos Carrasco .15 .40
127 Carlos Martinez .20 .50
128 Cole Hamels .20 .50
129 Adrian Beltre .25 .60
130 James Shields .15 .40
131 Yordano Ventura .20 .50
132 Eric Hosmer .20 .50
133 Adam Wainwright .20 .50
134 Hisashi Iwakuma .20 .50
135 Chris Heston .15 .40
136 Alex Rodriguez .30 .75
137 Felix Hernandez .20 .50
138 CC Sabathia .20 .50
139 Aroldis Chapman .25 .60
140 Adam Jones .20 .50
141 Jonathan Lucroy .20 .50
142 Evan Longoria .20 .50
143 Troy Tulowitzki .25 .60
144 Matt Holliday .25 .60
145 Matt Duffy .15 .40
146 Pedro Alvarez .15 .40
147 Giancarlo Stanton .25 .60
148 Brian McCann .20 .50
149 Ichiro .30 .75
150 Evan Gattis .15 .40
151 Ted Giannoulas .25 .60
152 Chris Archer .15 .40
153 Johnny Cueto .20 .50
154 Stephen Strasburg .25 .60
155 Wei-Yin Chen .15 .40
156 Jose Fernandez .25 .60
157 Yasmany Tomas .15 .40
158 Addison Russell .25 .60
159 Maikel Franco .20 .50
160 Noah Syndergaard .20 .50
161 Jung-Ho Kang .20 .50
162 Rusney Castillo .15 .40
163 Carlos Rodon .25 .60
164 Odubel Herrera .20 .50
165 Yu Darvish .25 .60
166 Michael Taylor .15 .40
167 Jorge Soler .25 .60
168 Eduardo Rodriguez .15 .40
169 Delino DeShields Jr. .15 .40
170 David Wright .20 .50
171 Steven Matz .20 .50
172 Salvador Perez .20 .50
173 DJ LeMahieu .25 .60
174 Justin Upton .20 .50
175 Bo Jackson .25 .60
176 Mariano Rivera .30 .75
177 Ryne Sandberg .50 1.25
178A Kirby Puckett .25 .60
178B Puckett SP HOF 01 2.00 5.00
179A Ken Griffey Jr. .50 1.25
179B Griffey SP SEA 4.00 10.00
179C Grffy SP Nickname 4.00 10.00
180 Frank Thomas .25 .60
181A Cal Ripken .75 2.00
181B Rpkn SP Nickname 6.00 15.00
182A George Brett .50 1.25
182B Brett SP 80 MVP 4.00 10.00
183 Nolan Ryan .75 2.00
184 Rickey Henderson .25 .60
185 Carl Yastrzemski .40 1.00
186A Don Mattingly .50 1.25
186B Mttngly SP Nickname 4.00 10.00
187A Pete Rose .50 1.25
187B Rose SP Nickname 4.00 10.00
188 Pedro Martinez .20 .50
189 Craig Biggio .20 .50
190 John Smoltz .25 .60
191A Omar Vizquel .20 .50
191B Vzql SP Nickname 1.50 4.00
192 Andres Galarraga .20 .50
193 Checklist .15 .40
194 Checklist .15 .40
195 Checklist .15 .40

2016 Donruss Black Border

*BLK BRD DK: .75X TO 2X BASIC
*BLK BRD RR: 1X TO 2.5X BASIC
*BLK BRD VET: 3X TO 8X BASIC
RANDOM INSERTS IN PACKS
STATED PRINT RUN 199 SER.#'d SETS

2016 Donruss Pink Border

*PINK DK: .6X TO 1.5X BASIC
*PINK RR: .75X TO 2X BASIC
*PINK VET: 2.5X TO 6X BASIC
RANDOM INSERTS IN PACKS

2016 Donruss Press Proof Gold

*GLD PROOF DK: 1X TO 2.5X BASIC
*GLD PROOF RR: 1.2X TO 3X BASIC
*GLD PROOF VET: 4X TO 10X BASIC
RANDOM INSERTS IN PACKS
STATED PRINT RUN 99 SER.#'d SETS

2016 Donruss Stat Line Career

*CAR DK p/r 261-400: .6X TO 1.5X
*CAR DK p/r 166: .75X TO 2X
*CAR DK p/r 101-118: 1X TO 2.5X
*CAR RR p/r 351-400: .75X TO 2X
*CAR RR p/r 120: 1.2X TO 3X
*CAR RR p/r 63: 1.5X TO 4X
*CAR p/r 261-500: 2.5X TO 6X
*CAR p/r 126-243: 3X TO 8X
*CAR p/r 100-125: 4X TO 10X
*CAR p/r 42-58: 5X TO 12X
RANDOM INSERTS IN PACKS
PRINT RUNS B/WN 13-500 COPIES PER
NO PRICING ON QTY 13

2016 Donruss Stat Line Season

*SEA DK p/r 274-338: .6X TO 1.5X
*SEA DK p/r 166-236: .75X TO 2X
*SEA DK p/r 81-122: 1X TO 2.5X
*SEA DK p/r 38-45: 1.2X TO 3X
*SEA DK p/r 26-35: 1.5X TO 4X
*SEA DK p/r 20-23: 2X TO 5X
*SEA RR p/r 253-400: .75X TO 2X
*SEA RR p/r 50-68: 1.5X TO 4X
*SEA p/r 252-400: 2.5X TO 6X
*SEA p/r 130-248: 3X TO 8X
*SEA p/r 98-112: 4X TO 10X
*SEA p/r 36-70: 5X TO 12X
*SEA p/r 26-35: 6X TO 15X
*SEA p/r 20-25: 8X TO 20X
RANDOM INSERTS IN PACKS
PRINT RUNS B/WN 10-400 COPIES PER
NO PRICING ON QTY 19 OR LESS

2016 Donruss Test Proof Black

*PROOF BLK DK: 2X TO 5X BASIC
*PROOF BLK RR: 2.5X TO 6X BASIC
*PROOF BLK VET: 8X TO 20X BASIC
RANDOM INSERTS IN PACKS
STATED PRINT RUN 25 SER.#'d SETS

2016 Donruss Test Proof Cyan

*PROOF CYAN DK: 1.2X TO 3X BASIC
*PROOF CYAN RR: 1.5X TO 4X BASIC
*PROOF CYAN VET: 5X TO 12X BASIC
RANDOM INSERTS IN PACKS
STATED PRINT RUN 49 SER.#'d SETS

2016 Donruss '82

COMPLETE SET (50) 10.00 25.00
RANDOM INSERTS IN PACKS
*PINK: 1.5X TO 4X BASIC
*HOLMTRC/299: 1.2X TO 3X BASIC
*HOLOVIEW/199: 1.2X TO 3X BASIC
*BLK BRDR/99: 2.5X TO 6X BASIC
*CYAN/49: 2.5X TO 6X BASIC
*GLD PRF/49: 2.5X TO 6X BASIC
*BLCK PRF/25: 6X TO 15X BASIC
1 Mike Trout 2.50 6.00
2 Josh Donaldson .40 1.00
3 Lorenzo Cain .30 .75
4 David Price .40 1.00
5 Sonny Gray .40 1.00
6 Dallas Keuchel .40 1.00
7 Jake Arrieta .40 1.00
8 Clayton Kershaw 1.00 2.50
9 Zack Greinke .50 1.25
10 Yadier Molina .50 1.25
11 Paul Goldschmidt .50 1.25
12 Bryce Harper .75 2.00
13 Joey Votto .50 1.25
14 Carlos Correa .50 1.25
15 Kris Bryant .60 1.50
16 Andrew McCutchen .50 1.25
17 Matt Harvey .40 1.00
18 Prince Fielder .40 1.00
19 Buster Posey .60 1.50
20 Dee Gordon .30 .75
21 Nolan Arenado .60 1.50
22 Brandon Crawford .40 1.00
23 Madison Bumgarner .40 1.00
24 Miguel Cabrera .50 1.25
25 Jose Altuve .40 1.00
26 Xander Bogaerts .50 1.25
27 Nelson Cruz .50 1.25
28 Carlos Gonzalez .40 1.00
29 Eric Hosmer .40 1.00
30 Manny Machado .50 1.25
31 Kevin Kiermaier .40 1.00
32 Adrian Beltre .50 1.25
33 Starling Marte .40 1.00
34 A.J. Pollock .30 .75
35 Jason Heyward .40 1.00
36 Kole Calhoun .30 .75
37 Alcides Escobar .40 1.00
38 Kevin Pillar .30 .75
39 Jacob deGrom .50 1.25
40 Andrelton Simmons .30 .75
41 Cal Ripken 1.50 4.00
42 Kirby Puckett .50 1.25
43 George Brett 1.00 2.50
44 Ken Griffey Jr. 1.00 2.50
45 Nolan Ryan 1.50 4.00
46 Pete Rose 1.00 2.50
47 Rickey Henderson .50 1.25
48 Robin Yount .50 1.25
49 Frank Thomas .50 1.25
50 Steve Carlton .40 1.00

2016 Donruss Back to the Future Materials

RANDOM INSERTS IN PACKS
*GREEN/49-99: .5X TO 1.2X BASIC
*GREEN/25: .6X TO 1.5X BASIC
BFAB Adrian Beltre 3.00 8.00
BFAG Adrian Gonzalez 2.50 6.00
BFAR Alex Rodriguez 4.00 10.00
BFCB Carlos Beltran 2.50 6.00
BFCG Carlos Gomez 2.00 5.00
BFCG Curtis Granderson 2.50 6.00
BFCL Cliff Lee 2.50 6.00
BFCU Chase Utley 2.50 6.00
BFIK Ian Kinsler 2.50 6.00
BFJA Jake Arrieta 2.50 6.00
BFJC Johnny Cueto 2.50 6.00
BFJD Josh Donaldson 2.50 6.00
BFJL Jon Lester 2.50 6.00
BFJS Jeff Samardzija 2.00 5.00
BFJU Justin Upton 2.50 6.00
BFMC Miguel Cabrera 3.00 8.00
BFMK Matt Kemp 2.50 6.00
BFMS Max Scherzer 3.00 8.00
BFNC Nelson Cruz 3.00 8.00
BFNC Nelson Cruz 3.00 8.00
BFNS Nick Swisher 2.50 6.00
BFPF Prince Fielder 2.50 6.00
BFRC Robinson Cano 2.50 6.00
BFTT Troy Tulowitzki 2.50 6.00
BFYC Yoenis Cespedes 3.00 8.00

2016 Donruss Bat Kings

RANDOM INSERTS IN PACKS
*GREEN/49-99: .5X TO 1.2X BASIC
*GREEN/25: .6X TO 1.5X BASIC
*RED/49-199: .5X TO 1.2X BASIC
*RED/25: .6X TO 1.5X BASIC
*STUDIO/25: .6X TO 1.5X BASIC
BKI Ichiro 4.00 10.00
BKAG Adrian Gonzalez 2.50 6.00
BKAJ Adam Jones 2.50 6.00
BKAM Andrew McCutchen 3.00 8.00
BKAP Albert Pujols 4.00 10.00
BKAR Alex Rodriguez 4.00 10.00
BKAR Anthony Rizzo 5.00 12.00
BKBB Billy Burns 2.00 5.00
BKBH Bryce Harper 5.00 12.00
BKBM Brian McCann 2.50 6.00
BKCB Craig Biggio 2.50 6.00
BKCC Carlos Correa 5.00 12.00
BKCG Carlos Gomez 2.00 5.00
BKDO David Ortiz 3.00 8.00
BKDW Dave Winfield 2.50 6.00
BKER Eddie Rosario 2.50 6.00
BKGB George Brett 4.00 10.00
BKJA Jose Abreu 3.00 8.00
BKJB Jose Bautista 2.50 6.00
BKJB Javier Baez 4.00 10.00
BKJD Josh Donaldson 2.50 6.00
BKJH Josh Harrison 2.00 5.00
BKJP Joc Pederson 2.50 6.00
BKJS Jorge Soler 3.00 8.00
BKJV Joey Votto 3.00 8.00
BKKB Kris Bryant 6.00 15.00
BKKK Kevin Kiermaier 2.50 6.00
BKKW Kolten Wong 2.50 6.00
BKLM Logan Morrison 2.00 5.00
BKMB Mookie Betts 5.00 12.00
BKMB Michael Brantley 2.50 6.00
BKMC Matt Carpenter 3.00 8.00
BKMC Miguel Cabrera 3.00 8.00
BKMF Maikel Franco 2.50 6.00
BKMM Manny Machado 3.00 8.00
BKMN Mike Napoli 2.00 5.00
BKMT Mike Trout 8.00 20.00
BKNC Nelson Cruz 3.00 8.00
BKPF Prince Fielder 2.50 6.00
BKRC Robinson Cano 2.50 6.00
BKRH Rickey Henderson 6.00 15.00
BKVG Vladimir Guerrero 2.50 6.00
BKYT Yasmany Tomas 2.00 5.00
BKJHK Jung-Ho Kang 2.00 5.00

2016 Donruss Elite Dominators

RANDOM INSERTS IN PACKS
STATED PRINT RUN 999 SER.#'d SETS
ED1 Carlos Correa 1.00 2.50
ED2 Lorenzo Cain .60 1.50
ED3 Mike Trout 5.00 12.00
ED4 Kris Bryant 1.25 3.00
ED5 Giancarlo Stanton 1.00 2.50
ED6 Miguel Cabrera 1.00 2.50
ED7 Dee Gordon .60 1.50
ED8 Bryce Harper 1.50 4.00
ED9 Eric Hosmer .75 2.00
ED10 Nolan Arenado 1.25 3.00
ED11 Josh Donaldson .75 2.00
ED12 Corey Seager 5.00 12.00
ED13 Jake Arrieta .75 2.00
ED14 Dallas Keuchel .75 2.00
ED15 Madison Bumgarner .75 2.00
ED16 Buster Posey 1.25 3.00
ED 17 Alcides Escobar .75 2.00
ED18 Clayton Kershaw 2.00 5.00
ED19 Xander Bogaerts 1.00 2.50
ED20 Noah Syndergaard .75 2.00
ED21 Matt Duffy .60 1.50
ED22 Ichiro 1.25 3.00
ED23 Andrew McCutchen 1.00 2.50
ED24 Salvador Perez .75 2.00
ED25 Joey Votto 1.00 2.50

2016 Donruss Elite Series

RANDOM INSERTS IN PACKS
STATED PRINT RUN 999 SER.#'d SETS
ES1 Jacob deGrom 1.00 2.50
ES2 Mike Moustakas .75 2.00
ES3 Troy Tulowitzki 1.00 2.50
ES4 Jose Altuve .75 2.00
ES5 Manny Machado 1.00 2.50
ES6 Anthony Rizzo 1.50 4.00
ES7 Kevin Kiermaier .75 2.00
ES8 Brandon Crawford .75 2.00
ES9 A.J. Pollock .60 1.50
ES10 Paul Goldschmidt 1.00 2.50
ES11 Matt Harvey .75 2.00
ES12 Nelson Cruz 1.00 2.50
ES13 Kendrys Morales .60 1.50
ES14 Prince Fielder .75 2.00
ES15 Carlos Correa 1.00 2.50
ES16 Kyle Schwarber 2.00 5.00
ES17 Luis Severino .75 2.00
ES18 Corey Seager 5.00 12.00
ES19 Stephen Piscotty 1.00 2.50
ES20 Miguel Sano 1.00 2.50
ES21 Mike Trout 5.00 12.00
ES22 Bryce Harper 1.50 4.00
ES23 Carlos Gomez .60 1.50
ES24 Adam Jones .75 2.00
ES25 Robinson Cano .75 2.00

2016 Donruss Jersey Kings

RANDOM INSERTS IN PACKS
*GREEN/49-99: .5X TO 1.2X BASIC
*GREEN/25: .6X TO 1.5X BASIC
*RED/49-199: .5X TO 1.2X BASIC
*RED/25: .6X TO 1.5X BASIC
*STUDIO/25: .6X TO 1.5X BASIC
JKAB Archie Bradley 2.00 5.00
JKAC Aroldis Chapman 3.00 8.00
JKAJ Adam Jones 2.50 6.00
JKAM Andrew McCutchen 3.00 8.00
JKAP A.J. Pollock 2.00 5.00
JKAR Addison Russell 3.00 8.00
JKBB Byron Buxton 2.50 6.00
JKBD Brian Dozier 2.50 6.00
JKBH Bryce Harper 5.00 12.00
JKCA Chris Archer 2.00 5.00
JKCG Carlos Gonzalez 2.50 6.00
JKCK Clayton Kershaw 6.00 15.00
JKCR Cal Ripken 8.00 20.00
JKCS Chris Sale 3.00 8.00
JKDG Dee Gordon 2.00 5.00
JKDK Dallas Keuchel 2.50 6.00
JKEE Edwin Encarnacion 3.00 8.00
JKEH Eric Hosmer 2.50 6.00
JKFH Felix Hernandez 2.50 6.00
JKFL Francisco Lindor 3.00 8.00
JKGC Gerrit Cole 3.00 8.00
JKGS George Springer 2.50 6.00
JKJA Jose Altuve 2.50 6.00
JKJB Jeff Bagwell 2.50 6.00
JKJB Javier Baez 4.00 10.00
JKJD Josh Donaldson 2.50 6.00
JKJG Juan Gonzalez 2.00 5.00
JKJS Jorge Soler 3.00 8.00
JKKB Kris Bryant 6.00 15.00
JKKG Ken Griffey Jr. 6.00 15.00
JKLC Lorenzo Cain 2.00 5.00
JKMB Michael Brantley 2.50 6.00
JKMC Miguel Cabrera 3.00 8.00
JKMF Maikel Franco 2.50 6.00
JKMH Matt Harvey 2.50 6.00
JKMT Masahiro Tanaka 2.50 6.00
JKMT Michael Taylor 2.00 5.00
JKMT Mike Trout 15.00 40.00
JKNR Nolan Ryan 4.00 10.00
JKPS Pablo Sandoval 2.50 6.00
JKRH Rickey Henderson 3.00 8.00
JKSG Sonny Gray 2.50 6.00
JKSS Steven Souza 2.50 6.00
JKYT Yasmany Tomas 2.00 5.00

2016 Donruss Masters of the Game

COMPLETE SET (10) 3.00 8.00
RANDOM INSERTS IN PACKS
*BLUE/199: 1.5X TO 4X BASIC
*RED/99: 3X TO 8X BASIC
MG1 Rickey Henderson .50 1.25
MG2 Roger Clemens .60 1.50
MG3 Juan Gonzalez .30 .75
MG4 Frank Thomas .50 1.25
MG5 Steve Carlton .40 1.00
MG6 Mariano Rivera .60 1.50
MG7 Mark McGwire .75 2.00
MG8 Randy Johnson .50 1.25
MG9 Ken Griffey Jr. 1.00 2.50
MG10 Cal Ripken 1.50 4.00

2016 Donruss New Breed Autographs

RANDOM INSERTS IN PACKS
EXCHANGE DEADLINE 9/2/2017
*GREEN: .5X TO 1.2X BASIC
NBAC A.J. Cole 3.00 8.00
NBAR Anthony Ranaudo 3.00 8.00
NBBF Brandon Finnegan 3.00 8.00
NBBF Buck Farmer 3.00 8.00
NBCS Cory Spangenberg 3.00 8.00
NBDH Dilson Herrera 4.00 10.00
NBDN Daniel Norris 3.00 8.00
NBEE Edwin Escobar 3.00 8.00
NBGB Gary Brown 3.00 8.00
NBJL Jake Lamb 4.00 10.00
NBJM James McCann 4.00 10.00
NBKG Kendall Graveman 3.00 8.00
NBLA Lane Adams 3.00 8.00
NBMB Matt Barnes 3.00 8.00
NBMC Miguel Castro 3.00 8.00
NBMF Mike Foltynewicz 3.00 8.00
NBMS Matt Szczur 4.00 10.00
NBMT Michael Taylor 3.00 8.00
NBRA R.J. Alvarez 3.00 8.00
NBRL Rymer Liriano 3.00 8.00
NBRR Ryan Rua 3.00 8.00
NBSM Steven Moya 3.00 8.00
NBTG Terrance Gore 3.00 8.00
NBTM Trevor May 3.00 8.00
NBYR Yorman Rodriguez 3.00 8.00

2016 Donruss Power Alley

COMPLETE SET (10) 4.00 10.00
RANDOM INSERTS IN PACKS
*DISCO/299: 1X TO 2.5X BASIC
*BLUE/199: 1.2X TO 3X BASIC
*RED/99: 1.5X TO 4X BASIC
PA1 Bryce Harper .75 2.00
PA2 Mike Trout 2.50 6.00
PA3 Josh Donaldson .40 1.00
PA4 Carlos Correa .50 1.25
PA5 Miguel Sano .50 1.25
PA6 Giancarlo Stanton .50 1.25
PA7 Madison Bumgarner .40 1.00
PA8 Kyle Schwarber 1.00 2.50
PA9 Eric Hosmer .40 1.00
PA10 Jose Bautista .40 1.00

2016 Donruss Preferred Pairings Signatures Red

2 Schwarber/Seager/25 75.00 200.00
3 Gonzalez/IRod/25 20.00 50.00
5 Clemens/Vlad/25 25.00 60.00
6 Ripken/Brett/25 125.00 250.00

2016 Donruss Promising Pros Materials

RANDOM INSERTS IN PACKS
*GREEN/99: .5X TO 1.2X BASIC
*GREEN/25: .6X TO 1.5X BASIC
PPMAJ Aaron Judge 15.00 40.00
PPMAN Aaron Nola 4.00 10.00
PPMBS Rafael Devers 4.00 10.00
PPMBS Blake Snell 2.50 6.00
PPMCS Corey Seager 5.00 12.00
PPMGB Greg Bird 2.50 6.00
PPMJG Jonathan Gray 2.00 5.00
PPMKM Ketel Marte 4.00 10.00
PPMKS Kyle Schwarber 5.00 12.00
PPMLG Lucas Giolito 3.00 8.00
PPMLS Luis Severino 2.50 6.00
PPMMC Michael Conforto 4.00 10.00
PPMMO Matt Olson 4.00 10.00
PPMMS Miguel Sano 3.00 8.00
PPMNM Nomar Mazara 3.00 8.00
PPMOB Peter O'Brien 2.00 5.00
PPMRM Raul Mondesi 2.50 6.00
PPMRR Rob Refsnyder 2.50 6.00
PPMRS Richie Shaffer 2.00 5.00
PPMSP Stephen Piscotty 3.00 8.00
PPMTB Tyler Beede 2.50 6.00
PPMTM Tom Murphy 2.00 5.00
PPMTT Trea Turner 4.00 10.00
PPMWH Wei-Chieh Huang 2.00 5.00
PPMYM Yoan Moncada 5.00 12.00

2016 Donruss Promising Pros Materials Signatures

RANDOM INSERTS IN PACKS
PRINT RUNS B/WN 25-199 COPIES PER
EXCHANGE DEADLINE 9/2/2017
*GREEN/99: .5X TO 1.2X BASIC
PPMSAJ Aaron Judge/199 75.00 200.00
PPMSAN Aaron Nola/199 6.00 15.00
PPMSBS Blake Snell/199 4.00 10.00
PPMSCS Corey Seager/25 20.00 50.00
PPMSJG Jonathan Gray/99 3.00 8.00
PPMSKS Kyle Schwarber/25 30.00 80.00
PPMSLG Lucas Giolito/99 8.00 20.00
PPMSLS Luis Severino/25 10.00 25.00
PPMSMO Matt Olson/199 5.00 12.00
PPMSPO Peter O'Brien/199 3.00 8.00
PPMSRR Rob Refsnyder/199 6.00 15.00
PPMSRS Richie Shaffer/199 3.00 8.00
PPMSSP Stephen Piscotty/199 10.00 25.00
PPMSTB Tyler Beede/199 4.00 10.00
PPMSTM Tom Murphy/99 3.00 8.00
PPMSTT Trea Turner/199 10.00 25.00
PPMSWH Wei-Chieh Huang/199 3.00 8.00
PPMSYM Yoan Moncada/99 8.00 20.00

2016 Donruss Rated Rookies Die-Cut Blue

RANDOM INSERTS IN PACKS
STATED PRINT RUN 999 SER.#'d SETS
*RED/299: .5X TO 1.2X BASIC
*GREEN/99: .75X TO 2X BASIC
*BLACK/25: 1.5X TO 4X BASIC
RRDCAN Aaron Nola 2.00 5.00
RRDCCS Corey Seager 8.00 20.00
RRDCGB Greg Bird 1.25 3.00
RRDCHO Hector Olivera 1.25 3.00
RRDCKS Kyle Schwarber 3.00 8.00
RRDCLS Luis Severino 1.25 3.00
RRDCMC Michael Conforto 1.25 3.00
RRDCMS Miguel Sano 1.50 4.00
RRDCRR Rob Refsnyder 1.25 3.00
RRDCSP Stephen Piscotty 1.50 4.00

2016 Donruss San Diego Chicken Silhouette Materials
RANDOM INSERTS IN PACKS
STATED PRINT RUN 82 SER.#'d SETS
*GREEN/25: .5X TO 1.2X BASIC
1 Ted Giannoulas 30.00 80.00

2016 Donruss San Diego Chicken Silhouette Materials Autographs
RANDOM INSERTS IN PACKS
STATED PRINT RUN 82 SER.#'d SETS
*GREEN/25: .6X TO 1.5X BASIC
1 Ted Giannoulas 40.00 100.00

2016 Donruss Signature Series
RANDOM INSERTS IN PACKS
EXCHANGE DEADLINE 9/2/2017
SGSAG Andres Galarraga 8.00 20.00
SGSAN Aaron Nola 8.00 20.00
SGSBD Brandon Drury 4.00 10.00
SGSBE Brian Ellington 2.50 6.00
SGSBJ Brian Johnson 2.50 6.00
SGSBP Buster Posey 25.00 60.00
SGSCB Craig Biggio 10.00 25.00
SGSCE Carl Edwards Jr. 3.00 8.00
SGSCK Corey Kluber 3.00 8.00
SGSCL Clayton Kershaw 25.00 60.00
SGSCS Corey Seager 12.00 30.00
SGSCY Carl Yastrzemski 25.00 60.00
SGSDM Don Mattingly 20.00 50.00
SGSDO David Ortiz 20.00 50.00
SGSDP David Peralta 2.50 6.00
SGSDV Dave Winfield 6.00 15.00
SGSDW David Wright 3.00 8.00
SGSED Elias Diaz 2.50 6.00
SGSEL Evan Longoria 6.00 15.00
SGSFM Frankie Montas 3.00 8.00
SGSGS George Springer 5.00 12.00
SGSHO Henry Owens 4.00 10.00
SGSIG Juan Gonzalez 4.00 10.00
SGSJA Jake Arrieta 12.00 30.00
SGSJA Jose Abreu 12.00 30.00
SGSJC Jose Canseco 8.00 20.00
SGSJD Josh Donaldson 12.00 30.00
SGSJF Jeurys Familia 3.00 8.00
SGSJG Jonathan Gray 2.50 6.00
SGSJI Jimmy Wynn 2.50 6.00
SGSJL John Lamb 2.50 6.00
SGSJP Joc Pederson 3.00 8.00
SGSJP Jose Peraza
SGSJS Jorge Soler 4.00 10.00
SGSJW Jered Weaver 3.00 8.00
SGSKB Kris Bryant 30.00 80.00
SGSKG Ken Griffey Jr. 60.00 150.00
SGSKS Kyle Schwarber 15.00 40.00
SGSKT Kelby Tomlinson 2.50 6.00
SGSKW Kyle Waldrop 3.00 8.00
SGSLA Luis Aparicio 8.00 20.00
SGSLS Luis Severino 10.00 25.00
SGSMD Matt Duffy 2.50 6.00
SGSMF Maikel Franco 3.00 8.00
SGSMK Max Kepler 4.00 10.00
SGSMM Mark McGwire 40.00 100.00
SGSMO Mariano Rivera 40.00 100.00
SGSMR Michael Reed 2.50 6.00
SGSMW Mac Williamson 2.50 6.00
SGSNK Nathan Karns 2.50 6.00
SGSNS Nick Swisher 3.00 8.00
SGSOV Omar Vizquel EXCH 8.00 20.00
SGSPF Prince Fielder 3.00 8.00
SGSPM Pedro Martinez 20.00 50.00
SGSPO Peter O'Brien 2.50 6.00
SGSPR Pete Rose 10.00 25.00
SGSRC Roger Clemens 20.00 50.00
SGSRD R.A. Dickey 3.00 8.00
SGSRI Raul Ibanez 3.00 8.00
SGSRS Richie Shaffer 4.00 10.00
SGSRU Rusney Castillo 2.50 6.00
SGSSB Socrates Brito 2.50 6.00
SGSSM Steven Matz 3.00 8.00
SGSSP Stephen Piscotty 4.00 10.00
SGSSS Stephen Strasburg 12.00 30.00
SGSTD Tyler Duffey 2.50 6.00
SGSTJ Travis Jankowski 2.50 6.00
SGSTM Tom Murphy 2.50 6.00
SGSTR Trea Turner 6.00 15.00
SGSTT Trayce Thompson 4.00 10.00
SGSTZ Troy Tulowitzki 6.00 15.00
SGSVG Vladimir Guerrero 8.00 20.00
SGSWB Wade Boggs 15.00 40.00
SGSYM Yadier Molina 30.00 80.00
SGSYT Yasmany Tomas 4.00 10.00
SGSZG Zack Godley 2.50 6.00

2016 Donruss Signature Series Blue
*BLUE/99-199: .5X TO 1.2X BASIC
2016 Donruss Signature Series Blue
*BLUE/25: .75X TO 2X BASIC
RANDOM INSERTS IN PACKS
PRINT RUNS B/WN 20-199 COPIES PER
EXCHANGE DEADLINE 9/2/2017
SGSDA Dariel Alvarez/199 3.00 8.00
SGSOH Odubel Herrera/199 8.00 20.00
SGSRM Raul Mondesi/199 5.00 12.00

2016 Donruss Signature Series Green
*GREEN/25: .75X TO 2X BASIC
RANDOM INSERTS IN PACKS
PRINT RUNS B/WN 7-25 COPIES PER
NO PRICING ON QTY 15 OR LESS
EXCHANGE DEADLINE 9/2/2017
SGSDA Dariel Alvarez/25 5.00 12.00
SGSOH Odubel Herrera/25 12.00 30.00
SGSRM Raul Mondesi/25 8.00 20.00

2016 Donruss Signature Series Orange
*ORANGE/49: .6X TO 1.5X BASIC
*ORANGE/25: .75X TO 2X BASIC
RANDOM INSERTS IN PACKS
PRINT RUNS B/WN 10-49 COPIES PER
NO PRICING ON QTY 15 OR LESS
EXCHANGE DEADLINE 9/2/2017
SGSDA Dariel Alvarez/49 4.00 10.00
SGSOH Odubel Herrera/49 10.00 25.00
SGSRM Raul Mondesi/49 6.00 15.00
SGSRR Rob Refsnyder/49 6.00 15.00

2016 Donruss Signature Series Red
*RED/99: .5X TO 1.2X BASIC
*RED/49: .6X TO 1.5X BASIC
*RED/25: .75X TO 2X BASIC
RANDOM INSERTS IN PACKS
PRINT RUNS B/WN 15-99 COPIES PER
NO PRICING ON QTY 15
EXCHANGE DEADLINE 9/2/2017
SGSDA Dariel Alvarez/99 3.00 8.00
SGSOH Odubel Herrera/99 8.00 20.00
SGSRM Raul Mondesi/99 5.00 12.00
SGSRR Rob Refsnyder/99 5.00 12.00

2016 Donruss Signifcant Signatures Blue
RANDOM INSERTS IN PACKS
STATED PRINT RUN 99 SER.#'d SETS
EXCHANGE DEADLINE 9/2/2017
*RED/49: .5X TO 1.2X BASIC
*ORANGE/25: .6X TO 1.5X BASIC
SIGDN Don Newcombe 10.00 25.00
SIGAK Al Kaline 20.00 50.00
SIGJP Jim Palmer 8.00 20.00
SIGSC Steve Carlton 8.00 20.00
SIGGP Gaylord Perry 8.00 20.00

2016 Donruss Studio
RANDOM INSERTS IN PACKS
*RED/199: .75X TO 2X BASIC
*GLD PRF/99: 1X TO 2.5X BASIC
*CYAN/49: 1.2X TO 3X BASIC
*BLCK PRF/25: 1.5X TO 4X BASIC
S1 Kris Bryant .75 2.00
S2 Byron Buxton .50 1.25
S3 Michael Taylor .40 1.00
S4 Miguel Sano .60 1.50
S5 Corey Seager 3.00 8.00
S6 Kyle Schwarber 1.25 3.00
S7 Trea Turner 1.25 3.00
S8 Stephen Piscotty .60 1.50
S9 Luis Severino .50 1.25
S10 Michael Conforto .50 1.25

2016 Donruss Studio Signatures Blue
RANDOM INSERTS IN PACKS
PRINT RUNS B/WN 49-99 COPIES PER
EXCHANGE DEADLINE 9/2/2017
*RED/49: .5X TO 1.2X BASIC
*ORANGE/25: .6X TO 1.5X BASIC
SSCS Corey Seager/49 30.00 80.00
SSKB Kris Bryant/99 50.00 120.00
SSKS Kyle Schwarber/49 30.00 80.00
SSMT Michael Taylor/99

2016 Donruss The Prospects
COMPLETE SET (15) 10.00 25.00
RANDOM INSERTS IN PACKS
*CAREER: 1X TO 2.5X BASIC
*STAT/270-289: 1X TO 2.5X BASIC
*STAT/131-175: 1.2X TO 3X BASIC
*STAT/88: 1.5X TO 4X BASIC
*STAT/34-49: 2X TO 5X BASIC
*BLK BRDR/199: 1.2X TO 3X BASIC
*GLD PRF/99: 1.5X TO 4X BASIC
*CYAN PRF/49: 2X TO 5X BASIC
*BLCK PRF/25: 2.5X TO 6X BASIC
TP1 Lucas Giolito .50 1.25
TP2 Julio Urias 1.00 2.50
TP3 Yoan Moncada .75 2.00
TP4 Tyler Glasnow .40 1.00
TP5 Brendan Rodgers .50 1.25
TP6 Dansby Swanson 1.00 2.50
TP7 Orlando Arcia .40 1.00
TP8 Rafael Devers 1.00 2.50
TP9 Blake Snell .40 1.00
TP10 A.J. Reed .30 .75
TP11 Jose Berrios .40 1.00
TP12 Bradley Zimmer .50 1.25
TP13 Alex Reyes .40 1.00
TP14 Nomar Mazara .50 1.25
TP15 Josh Bell .60 1.50

2016 Donruss The Rookies
COMPLETE SET (15) 10.00 25.00
RANDOM INSERTS IN PACKS
*CAREER: 1X TO 2.5X BASIC
*STAT/253-337: 1X TO 2.5X BASIC
*STAT/56-68: 1.2X TO 3X BASIC
*BLK BRDR/199: 1.2X TO 3X BASIC
*GLD PRF/99: 1.5X TO 4X BASIC
*CYAN PRF/49: 2X TO 5X BASIC
*BLCK PRF/25: 2.5X TO 6X BASIC
TR1 Kyle Schwarber 1.00 2.50
TR2 Corey Seager 2.50 6.00
TR3 Trea Turner 1.00 2.50
TR4 Rob Refsnyder .40 1.00
TR5 Miguel Sano .50 1.25
TR6 Stephen Piscotty .50 1.25
TR7 Aaron Nola .60 1.50
TR8 Michael Conforto .40 1.00
TR9 Ketel Marte .60 1.50
TR10 Luis Severino .40 1.00
TR11 Greg Bird .40 1.00
TR12 Hector Olivera .40 1.00
TR13 Jose Peraza .40 1.00
TR14 Henry Owens .40 1.00
TR15 Richie Shaffer .30 .75

2016 Donruss USA Collegiate National Team
COMPLETE SET (24) 10.00 25.00
RANDOM INSERTS IN PACKS
*DISCO/299: .75X TO 2X BASIC
*BLUE/199: 1X TO 2.5X BASIC
*RED/99: 1.2X TO 3X BASIC
USA1 Buddy Reed .40 1.00
USA2 Robert Tyler .40 1.00
USA3 KJ Harrison .75 2.00
USA4 Bobby Dalbec 1.50 4.00
USA5 JJ Schwarz .50 1.25
USA6 Stephen Nogosek .40 1.00
USA7 Ryan Howard .40 1.00
USA8 Nick Banks .40 1.00
USA9 Bryson Brigman .40 1.00
USA10 Zack Burdi .50 1.25
USA11 Brendan McKay 1.00 2.50
USA12 A.J. Puk .60 1.50
USA13 Corey Ray .60 1.50
USA14 Matt Thaiss .40 1.00
USA15 Anfernee Grier .50 1.25
USA16 Garrett Hampson .75 2.00
USA17 Ryan Hendrix .40 1.00
USA18 Tanner Houck 1.00 2.50
USA19 Zach Jackson .50 1.25
USA20 Daulton Jefferies .50 1.25
USA21 Anthony Kay .40 1.00
USA22 Chris Okey .40 1.00
USA23 Mike Shawaryn .50 1.25
USA24 Logan Shore .50 1.25

2017 Donruss
COMP.SET w/o SPs (150) 10.00 25.00
196-245 INSERTED IN '17 CHRONICLES
SPs RANDOMLY INSERTED
COMP.SET ARE CARD 46-195
1 Paul Goldschmidt DK .60 1.50
2 Freddie Freeman DK .75 2.00
3 Mark Trumbo DK .40 1.00
4 Jackie Bradley Jr. DK .60 1.50
5 Anthony Rizzo DK 1.00 2.50
6 Jose Abreu DK .60 1.50
7 Joey Votto DK .60 1.50
8 Corey Kluber DK .50 1.25
9 Nolan Arenado DK .75 2.00
10 Justin Verlander DK .60 1.50
11 Carlos Correa DK .60 1.50
12 Salvador Perez DK .50 1.25
13 Mike Trout DK 3.00 8.00
14 Corey Seager DK .60 1.50
15 Christian Yelich DK .75 2.00
16 Jonathan Villar DK .40 1.00
17 Miguel Sano DK .50 1.25
18 Noah Syndergaard DK .50 1.25
19 Masahiro Tanaka DK .50 1.25
20 Khris Davis DK .60 1.50
21 Maikel Franco DK .50 1.25
22 Gregory Polanco DK .50 1.25
23 Wil Myers DK .40 1.00
24 Madison Bumgarner DK .50 1.25
25 Robinson Cano DK .50 1.25
26 Stephen Piscotty DK .50 1.25
27 Brad Miller DK .50 1.25
28 Rougned Odor DK .50 1.25
29 Edwin Encarnacion DK .60 1.50
30 Daniel Murphy DK .50 1.25
31 Yoan Moncada RR RC 1.25 3.00
32 David Dahl RR RC .50 1.25
33 Dansby Swanson RR RC 1.00 2.50
34 Andrew Benintendi RR RC 1.25 3.00
35 Alex Reyes RR RC .50 1.25
36 Tyler Glasnow RR RC .50 1.25
37 Josh Bell RR RC 1.00 2.50
38 Aaron Judge RR RC 10.00 25.00
39 Jose De Leon RR RC .40 1.00
40 Jeff Hoffman RR RC .40 1.00
41 Hunter Renfroe RR RC .40 1.00
42 Carson Fulmer RR RC .40 1.00
43 Alex Bregman RR RC 1.50 4.00
44 Orlando Arcia RR RC .40 1.00
45 Manny Margot RR RC .40 1.00
46 Paul Goldschmidt .25 .60
47 Jean Segura .20 .50
48 Zack Greinke .25 .60
49 Jake Lamb .20 .50
50 Yasmany Tomas .15 .40
51 Freddie Freeman .30 .75
52 Matt Kemp .20 .50
53 Nick Markakis .20 .50
54 Mark Trumbo .15 .40
55 Chris Davis .15 .40
56 Adam Jones .20 .50
57A Manny Machado .25 .60
57B Manny Machado SP 1.00 2.50
Hakuna Machado
58 Zach Britton .20 .50
59A Mookie Betts .40 1.00
59B Mookie Betts SP 1.50 4.00
back of jersey
60 Xander Bogaerts .25 .60
61 Dustin Pedroia .25 .60
62 Jackie Bradley Jr. .25 .60
63 Rick Porcello .20 .50
64 David Price .20 .50
65 Hanley Ramirez .20 .50
66 Jake Arrieta .20 .50
67 Javier Baez .30 .75
68A Kris Bryant .30 .75
68B Kris Bryant SP 1.25 3.00
black and white
68C Kris Bryant SP 1.25 3.00
MVP
68D Kris Bryant SP 1.25 3.00
Throwback Uniform
69 Kyle Hendricks .25 .60
70A Anthony Rizzo .40 1.00
70B Anthony Rizzo SP 1.50 4.00
Rizz
71 Ben Zobrist .20 .50
72 Addison Russell .25 .60
73 Jon Lester .20 .50
74 Kyle Schwarber .25 .60
75 Todd Frazier .20 .50
76 Melky Cabrera .15 .40
77 Chris Sale .25 .60
78 Jose Abreu .25 .60
79 Joey Votto .25 .60
80 Adam Duvall .25 .60
81 Dan Straily .15 .40
82 Jay Bruce .20 .50
83 Corey Kluber .20 .50
84 Francisco Lindor .25 .60
85 Jose Ramirez .20 .50
86 Mike Napoli .15 .40
87 Trevor Bauer .25 .60
88 Tyler Naquin .15 .40
89A Nolan Arenado .30 .75
89B Nolan Arenado SP 1.25 3.00
Grey Jersey
90 Trevor Story .25 .60
91 Charlie Blackmon .25 .60
92 D.J. LeMahieu .25 .60
93A Miguel Cabrera .25 .60
93B Miguel Cabrera SP 1.00 2.50
Miggy
94 Ian Kinsler .20 .50
95 Justin Verlander .25 .60
96A Michael Fulmer .15 .40
96B Michael Fulmer SP .60 1.50
ROY
97A Jose Altuve .20 .50
97B Altve SP Gigante .75 2.00
98 Carlos Correa .25 .60
99 George Springer .25 .60
100 Evan Gattis .15 .40
101 Eric Hosmer .20 .50
102 Salvador Perez .20 .50
103 Kendrys Morales .15 .40
104A Mike Trout 1.25 3.00
104B Mike Trout SP 5.00 12.00
Clapping
104C Mike Trout SP 5.00 12.00
MVP
105 Albert Pujols .30 .75
106A Corey Seager .25 .60
106B Corey Seager SP 1.00 2.50
ROY
107 Justin Turner .20 .50
108 Clayton Kershaw .50 1.25
109 Kenta Maeda .20 .50
110 Kenley Jansen .20 .50
111 Joc Pederson .20 .50
112 Adrian Gonzalez .20 .50
113 Christian Yelich .30 .75
114 Dee Gordon .15 .40
115 Marcell Ozuna .25 .60
116 Giancarlo Stanton .25 .60
117 Ryan Braun .20 .50
118 Jonathan Villar .15 .40
119 Chris Carter .15 .40
120 Brian Dozier .25 .60
121 Miguel Sano .20 .50
122 Noah Syndergaard .20 .50
123 Yoenis Cespedes .25 .60
124 Jacob deGrom .25 .60
125 Curtis Granderson .20 .50
126 Gary Sanchez .25 .60
127 Starlin Castro .15 .40
128 Masahiro Tanaka .20 .50
129 Khris Davis .25 .60
130 Marcus Semien .15 .40
131 Odubel Herrera .20 .50
132 Maikel Franco .20 .50
133 Freddy Galvis .15 .40
134 Starling Marte .25 .60
135 Andrew McCutchen .25 .60
136 Gregory Polanco .20 .50
137 Jung-Ho Kang .15 .40
138 Wil Myers .15 .40
139 Alex Dickerson .15 .40
140 Madison Bumgarner .20 .50
141 Buster Posey .30 .75
142 Johnny Cueto .20 .50
143 Brandon Belt .20 .50
144 Kyle Seager .15 .40
145 Robinson Cano .20 .50
146 Nelson Cruz .25 .60
147 Hisashi Iwakuma .20 .50
148 Felix Hernandez .20 .50
149 Matt Holliday .25 .60
150 Stephen Piscotty .25 .60
151 Randal Grichuk .15 .40
152 Yadier Molina .25 .60
153 Matt Carpenter .25 .60
154 Carlos Martinez .20 .50
155 Evan Longoria .20 .50
156 Brad Miller .20 .50
157 Jake Odorizzi .15 .40
158 Adrian Beltre .25 .60
159 Cole Hamels .20 .50
160 Ian Desmond .15 .40
161 Rougned Odor .20 .50
162 Elvis Andrus .20 .50
163 Nomar Mazara .15 .40
164 Edwin Encarnacion .25 .60
165A Josh Donaldson .20 .50
165B Josh Donaldson SP .75 2.00
Bringer of Rain
166 J.A. Happ .20 .50
167 Aaron Sanchez .20 .50
168 Devon Travis .15 .40
169 Troy Tulowitzki .25 .60
170 Jose Bautista .20 .50
171 Bryce Harper .40 1.00
172 Max Scherzer .25 .60
173A Daniel Murphy .20 .50
173B Daniel Murphy SP .75 2.00
Murphy
Black and White
174 Wilson Ramos .15 .40
175 Trea Turner .20 .50
176 Mark Melancon .15 .40
177A Cal Ripken .20 .50
177B Cal Ripken SP 3.00 8.00
Hall of Fame 2007
178A Dave Winfield .20 .50
178B Dave Winfield SP .75 2.00
12 Time All Star
179A Duke Snider .20 .50
179B Duke Snider SP .75 2.00
The Duke of Flatbush
180A Frank Thomas .25 .60
180B Frank Thomas SP 1.00 2.50
1993 MVP
Black and White
181 Jim Palmer .20 .50
182A Johnny Bench .25 .60
182B Johnny Bench SP 1.00 2.50
Little General
183 Ken Griffey Jr. .50 1.25
184 Kirby Puckett .25 .60
185A Nolan Ryan .75 2.00
185B Nolan Ryan .75 2.00
The Express
186A Pete Rose .50 1.25
186B Pete Rose SP 2.00 5.00
Charlie Hustle
187 Roberto Alomar .20 .50
188A Ryne Sandberg .50 1.25
188B Ryne Sandberg SP 2.00 5.00
Ryno
189 Tom Seaver .20 .50
190 Tony Gwynn .25 .60
191A Wade Boggs .20 .50
191B Wade Boggs SP .75 2.00
Chicken Man
192 Willie McCovey .20 .50
193A Willie Stargell .20 .50
193B Willie Stargell SP .75 2.00
Pops
194 Yu Darvish .25 .60
195 Carlos Gonzalez .20 .50
196 Cody Bellinger RR RC 6.00 15.00
197 Christian Arroyo RR RC .60 1.50
198 Ryon Healy RR RC .50 1.25
199 Mitch Haniger RR RC .60 1.50
200 Antonio Senzatela RR RC .40 1.00
201 Ian Happ RR RC .75 2.00
202 Trey Mancini RR RC .75 2.00
203 Jordan Montgomery RR RC .60 1.50
204 Bradley Zimmer RR RC .50 1.25
205 Jorge Bonifacio RR RC .40 1.00
206 Lewis Brinson RR RC .60 1.50
207 Jacoby Jones RR RC .50 1.25
208 Derek Fisher RR RC .50 1.25
209 Erik Gonzalez RR RC .40 1.00
210 Sam Travis RR RC .60 1.50
211 Franklin Barreto RR RC .40 1.00
212 Dinelson Lamet RR RC .40 1.00
213 Andrew Toles RR RC .40 1.00
214 Chad Pinder RR RC .40 1.00
215 Kyle Freeland RR RC .50 1.25
216 Yandy Diaz RR RC .75 2.00
217 Yulieski Gurriel RR RC .60 1.50
218 Magneuris Sierra RR RC .40 1.00
219 Marco Hernandez RR RC .40 1.00
220 Anthony Alford RR RC .40 1.00
221 Brock Stewart RR RC .40 1.00
222 Carson Kelly RR RC .50 1.25
223 Adam Frazier RR RC .40 1.00
224 Gavin Cecchini RR RC .40 1.00
225 Guillermo Heredia RR RC .40 1.00
226 German Marquez RR RC .60 1.50
227 Francis Martes RR RC .40 1.00
228 Matt Chapman RR RC .60 1.50
229 Hunter Dozier RR RC .40 1.00
230 Josh Hader RR RC .40 1.00
231 Luke Weaver RR RC .50 1.25
232 Jorge Alfaro RR RC .50 1.25
233 Matt Olson RR RC .60 1.50
234 Raimel Tapia RR RC .50 1.25
235 Teoscar Hernandez RR RC 1.25 3.00
236 Amir Garrett RR RC .40 1.00
237 Dan Vogelbach RR RC .60 1.50
238 Jharel Cotton RR RC .40 1.00
239 Roman Quinn RR RC .40 1.00
240 T.J. Rivera RR RC .60 1.50
241 Renato Nunez RR RC .75 2.00
242 Braden Shipley RR RC .40 1.00
243 Bruce Maxwell RR RC .40 1.00
244 Robert Gsellman RR RC .40 1.00
245 Paul DeJong RR RC 1.25 3.00

2017 Donruss Cyan Back
*CYAN BACK DK: .75X TO 2X BASIC
*CYAN BACK RR: .75X TO 2X BASIC
*CYAN BACK SP: .5X TO 1.2X BASIC
RANDOM INSERTS IN PACKS
196-245 INSERTED IN '17 CHRONICLES

2017 Donruss Gray Border
*GRAY DK: 1X TO 2.5X BASIC
*GRAY RR: 1X TO 2.5X BASIC
*GRAY VET: 2.5X TO 6X BASIC
*GRAY SP: .6X TO 1.5X BASIC
RANDOM INSERTS IN PACKS
196-245 INSERTED IN '17 CHRONICLES
STATED PRINT RUN 199 SER.#'d SETS
184 Kirby Puckett 8.00 20.00

2017 Donruss Magenta Back
*MAGENTA BACK: 2.5X TO 6X BASIC

2017 Donruss Pink Border
*PINK DK: 2X TO 5X BASIC
*PINK RR: 2X TO 5X BASIC
*PINK VET: 5X TO 12X BASIC
*PINK SP: 1.2X TO 3X BASIC
RANDOM INSERTS IN PACKS
196-245 INSERTED IN '17 CHRONICLES
STATED PRINT RUN 25 SER.#'d SETS
184 Kirby Puckett 25.00 60.00

2017 Donruss Press Proof Gold
*PROOF GLD DK: 1.5X TO 4X BASIC
*PROOF GLD RR: 1.5X TO 4X BASIC
*PROOF GLD VET: 4X TO 10X BASIC
*PROOF GLD SP: 1X TO 2.5X BASIC
RANDOM INSERTS IN PACKS
196-245 INSERTED IN '17 CHRONICLES
STATED PRINT RUN 99 SER.#'d SETS
184 Kirby Puckett 12.00 30.00

2017 Donruss Stat Line Career
*CAR p/r 126-515: 2X TO 5X BASIC
*CAR p/r 102-121: 2.5X TO 6X BASIC
RANDOM INSERTS IN PACKS
PRINT RUNS B/WN 102-515 COPIES PER
184 Kirby Puckett/318 6.00 15.00

2017 Donruss Stat Line Season
*SEA p/r 254-500: 2X TO 5X BASIC
*SEA p/r 127-234: 2.5X TO 6X BASIC
*SEA p/r 100-121: 3X TO 8X BASIC
*SEA p/r 51-98: 4X TO 10X BASIC
*SEA p/r 36-48: 5X TO 12X BASIC
*SEA p/r 26-34: 6X TO 15X BASIC
*SEA p/r 20-25: 8X TO 20X BASIC
RANDOM INSERTS IN PACKS
PRINT RUNS B/WN 14-500 COPIES PER
NO PRICING ON QTY 14
184 Kirby Puckett/234 8.00 20.00

2017 Donruss '83 Retro Materials
*GOLD/50-99: .5X TO 1.2X BASIC
*GOLD/25: .6X TO 1.5X BASIC
1 Ken Griffey Jr. 10.00 25.00
2 George Brett 5.00 12.00
3 Ryne Sandberg 6.00 15.00
4 Cal Ripken 8.00 20.00
5 Wade Boggs 4.00 10.00
6 Tony Gwynn 5.00 12.00
7 Gary Carter 2.50 6.00
8 Robin Yount 3.00 8.00
9 Lou Brock 4.00 10.00
10 Fergie Jenkins 2.50 6.00

2017 Donruss '83 Retro Signatures
*BLUE/49-99: .5X TO 1.2X BASIC
*RED/49: .5X TO 1.2X BASIC
*BLUE/20-25: .6X TO 1.5X BASIC
2017 Donruss New Breed Autographs Gold
*RED/25: .6X TO 1.5X BASIC
1 Omar Vizquel 6.00 15.00
2 Andres Galarraga 5.00 12.00
3 Wade Boggs 12.00 30.00
5 Ryne Sandberg 15.00 40.00
6 Todd Helton 6.00 15.00
7 George Springer 10.00 25.00
8 Cole Hamels
9 Manny Machado 20.00 50.00
10 Xander Bogaerts 12.00 30.00
11 Brian Dozier 4.00 10.00
12 Jose Ramirez 10.00 25.00
13 Anthony Rizzo 20.00 50.00
14 Evan Longoria 8.00 20.00
15 Jason Kipnis 8.00 20.00
17 Adam Eaton 4.00 10.00
18 Adrian Beltre 25.00 60.00
20 Edgar Renteria 5.00 12.00
22 Noah Syndergaard 10.00 25.00
23 Khris Davis 4.00 10.00

2017 Donruss '83 Retro Variations
*CAR p/r 282-500: 1.2X TO 3X
*CAR p/r 126-241: 1.5X TO 4X
*CAR p/r 102-117: 2X TO 5X
*SEA p/r 251-500: 1.2X TO 3X
*SEA p/r 140-210: 1.5X TO 4X
*SEA p/r 100-124: 2X TO 5X
*SEA p/r 73-98: 2.5X TO 6X
*SEA p/r 36-47: 3X TO 8X
*SEA p/r 28-34: 4X TO 10X
*SEA p/r 24-25: 5X TO 12X
*MGNTA BCK: 1X TO 2.5X BASIC
*GRAY/199: 1.5X TO 4X BASIC
*GOLD PP/99: 2.5X TO 6X BASIC
*AQS PP/49: 2.5X TO 6X BASIC
*PINK/25: 5X TO 12X BASIC
RV1 Paul Goldschmidt .40 1.00
RV2 Freddie Freeman .50 1.25
RV3 Mark Trumbo .25 .60
RV4 Mookie Betts .60 1.50
RV5 Kris Bryant .50 1.25
RV6 Kyle Hendricks .40 1.00
RV7 Todd Frazier .30 .75
RV8 Joey Votto .40 1.00
RV9 Corey Kluber .30 .75
RV10 Francisco Lindor .40 1.00
RV11 Nolan Arenado .50 1.25
RV12 Justin Verlander .40 1.00
RV13 Jose Altuve .30 .75
RV14 Eric Hosmer .30 .75
RV15 Mike Trout 2.00 5.00
RV16 Albert Pujols .50 1.25
RV17 Clayton Kershaw .75 2.00
RV18 Corey Seager .40 1.00
RV19 Christian Yelich .50 1.25
RV20 Ryan Braun .30 .75
RV21 Brian Dozier .40 1.00
RV22 Noah Syndergaard .30 .75
RV23 Masahiro Tanaka .30 .75
RV24 Khris Davis .40 1.00
RV25 Maikel Franco .30 .75
RV26 Andrew McCutchen .40 1.00
RV27 Wil Myers .25 .60
RV28 Madison Bumgarner .30 .75
RV29 Johnny Cueto .30 .75
RV30 Kyle Seager .25 .60
RV31 Robinson Cano .30 .75
RV32 Nelson Cruz .40 1.00
RV33 Stephen Piscotty .30 .75
RV34 Matt Carpenter .40 1.00
RV35 Evan Longoria .30 .75
RV36 Adrian Beltre .40 1.00
RV37 Rougned Odor .30 .75
RV38 Cole Hamels .30 .75
RV39 Josh Donaldson .30 .75
RV40 Daniel Murphy .30 .75
RV41 Mike Piazza .40 1.00
RV42 Pedro Martinez .30 .75
RV43 Robin Yount .40 1.00
RV44 Eddie Murray .30 .75
RV45 Ozzie Smith .50 1.25
RV46 Harmon Killebrew .40 1.00
RV47 Joe Morgan .30 .75
RV48 Goose Gossage .30 .75
RV49 Craig Biggio .30 .75
RV50 Brooks Robinson .30 .75

2017 Donruss All Stars
STATED PRINT RUN 999 SER.#'d SETS
*SILVER/349: .5X TO 1.2X BASIC
*BLUE/249: .6X TO 1.5X BASIC
*RED/149: .6X TO 1.5X BASIC
*GOLD/99: 1X TO 2.5X BASIC
*BLACK/25: 2X TO 5X BASIC
AS1 Addison Russell 1.00 2.50
AS2 Bryce Harper 1.50 4.00
AS3 Chris Sale 1.00 2.50
AS4 Eric Hosmer .75 2.00
AS5 Johnny Cueto .75 2.00
AS6 Jose Altuve .75 2.00
AS7 Kris Bryant 1.25 3.00
AS8 Manny Machado 1.00 2.50
AS9 Marcell Ozuna 1.00 2.50
AS10 Mike Trout 5.00 12.00
AS11 Mookie Betts 1.50 4.00
AS12 Yoenis Cespedes 1.00 2.50

2017 Donruss American Pride
RANDOM INSERTS IN PACKS
STATED PRINT RUN 999 SER.#'d SETS
*SILVER/349: .5X TO 1.2X BASIC
*BLUE/249: .6X TO 1.5X BASIC
*RED/149: .6X TO 1.5X BASIC
*GOLD/99: 1X TO 2.5X BASIC
*BLACK/25: 2X TO 5X BASIC
AP1 Darren McCaughan .75 2.00
AP2 Seth Beer 2.50 6.00
AP3 J.B. Bukauskas 1.00 2.50
AP4 Jake Burger 1.25 3.00
AP5 Tyler Johnson .75 2.00
AP6 Alex Faedo 1.00 2.50
AP7 TJ Friedl .60 1.50
AP8 Dalton Guthrie 1.00 2.50
AP9 Devin Hairston .75 2.00
AP10 KJ Harrison 1.00 2.50
AP11 Keston Hiura 3.00 8.00
AP12 Tanner Houck 3.00 8.00
AP13 Jeren Kendall 1.25 3.00
AP14 Alex Lange 1.00 2.50
AP15 Brendan McKay 2.50 6.00
AP16 Glenn Otto .60 1.50
AP17 David Peterson .75 2.00
AP18 Mike Rivera .60 1.50
AP19 Evan Skoug .75 2.00
AP20 Ricky Tyler Thomas .60 1.50
AP21 Taylor Walls .60 1.50
AP22 Tim Cate .75 2.00
AP23 Evan White 1.00 2.50
AP24 Kyle Wright 2.00 5.00

2017 Donruss Aqueous Test Proof
*AQUEOUS PROOF DK: 1.5X TO 4X BASIC
*AQUEOUS PROOF RR: 1.5X TO 4X BASIC
*AQUEOUS PROOF VET: 4X TO 10X BASIC
*AQUEOUS PROOF SP: 1X TO 2.5X BASIC
RANDOM INSERTS IN PACKS

196-245 INSERTED IN '17 CHRONICLES
STATED PRINT RUN 49 SER.#'d SETS
184 Kirby Puckett 15.00 40.00

2017 Donruss Back to the Future Materials

*GOLD/49-99: .5X TO 1.2X BASIC
*GOLD/25: .6X TO 1.5X BASIC
BFMAC Aroldis Chapman 3.00 8.00
BFMCB Carlos Beltran 2.50 6.00
BFMCS CC Sabathia 2.50 6.00
BFMDM Daniel Murphy 2.50 6.00
BFMDP David Price 2.50 6.00
BFMHP Hunter Pence 2.50 6.00
BFMJD Josh Donaldson 2.50 6.00
BFMJL Jon Lester 2.50 6.00
BFMMC Miguel Cabrera 3.00 8.00
BFMMK Matt Kemp 2.50 6.00
BFMMM Matt Moore 2.50 6.00
BFMMS Max Scherzer 3.00 8.00
BFMMT Mark Trumbo 2.00 5.00
BFMRC Robinson Cano 2.50 6.00
BFMRP Rick Porcello 2.50 6.00

2017 Donruss Diamond Collection Memorabilia

*GOLD/20-25: .6X TO 1.5X BASIC
DCAD Alex Dickerson 2.00 5.00
DCAJ Aaron Judge 12.00 30.00
DCAM Adalberto Mejia 2.00 5.00
DCAN Aaron Nola 2.50 6.00
DCAP Albert Pujols 4.00 10.00
DCAR A.J. Reed 2.00 5.00
DCAR Addison Russell 3.00 8.00
DCAX Alex Reyes 2.50 6.00
DCBB Bill Buckner 2.00 5.00
DCBD Brandon Drury 2.00 5.00
DCBE Brian Ellington 2.00 5.00
DCBH Bryce Harper 5.00 12.00
DCBJ Bo Jackson 3.00 8.00
DCBJ Brian Johnson 2.00 5.00
DCBL Barry Larkin 2.50 6.00
DCBN Brandon Nimmo 2.50 6.00
DCBP Byung-ho Park 2.00 5.00
DCCC Carlos Correa 3.00 8.00
DCCC C.J. Cron 2.00 5.00
DCCE Carl Edwards Jr. 2.00 5.00
DCCF Carson Fulmer 2.00 5.00
DCCK Carson Kelly 2.50 6.00
DCCK Corey Kluber 2.50 6.00
DCCK Clayton Kershaw 4.00 10.00
DCCR Colin Rea 2.00 5.00
DCCS Corey Seager 4.00 10.00
DCCY Christian Yelich 4.00 10.00
DCDD David Dahl 2.50 6.00
DCDP David Paulino 2.50 6.00
DCEL Evan Longoria 2.50 6.00
DCEM Eddie Murray 2.50 6.00
DCFF Freddie Freeman 4.00 10.00
DCFL Francisco Lindor 3.00 8.00
DCGB Greg Bird 2.50 6.00
DCGB George Brett 5.00 12.00
DCGC Gary Carter 2.50 6.00
DCGC Gavin Cecchini 2.00 5.00
DCGM Greg Maddux 4.00 10.00
DCGS Giancarlo Stanton 3.00 8.00
DCGS George Springer 2.50 6.00
DCGS Gary Sanchez 5.00 12.00
DCHR Hanley Ramirez 2.50 6.00
DCJB Jay Bruce 2.50 6.00
DCJB Javier Baez 4.00 10.00
DCJE Jacoby Ellsbury 2.50 6.00
DCJG Jonathan Gray 2.50 6.00
DCJJ Jacoby Jones 2.50 6.00
DCJL Jake Lamb 2.50 6.00
DCJM J.D. Martinez 3.00 8.00
DCJP Joe Panik 2.50 6.00
DCJP Joc Pederson 2.50 6.00
DCJT Jameson Taillon 2.50 6.00
DCJV Joey Votto 3.00 8.00
DCJV Justin Verlander 3.00 8.00
DCKB Kris Bryant 4.00 10.00
DCKG Kirk Gibson 2.00 5.00
DCKM Ketel Marte 2.50 6.00
DCKS Kyle Schwarber 5.00 12.00
DCLG Lucas Giolito 2.50 6.00
DCLS Luis Severino 2.50 6.00
DCMB Madison Bumgarner 2.50 6.00
DCMC Michael Conforto 2.50 6.00
DCMF Michael Fulmer 2.00 5.00
DCMK Max Kepler 2.50 6.00
DCMN Mike Napoli 2.00 5.00
DCMO Matt Olson 4.00 10.00
DCMP Mike Piazza 3.00 8.00
DCMS Mike Schmidt 5.00 12.00
DCMS Miguel Sano 2.50 6.00
DCMT Mike Trout 15.00 40.00
DCMW Mac Williamson 2.00 5.00
DCNA Nolan Arenado 4.00 10.00
DCOA Orlando Arcia 3.00 8.00
DCOH Orel Hershiser 2.00 5.00
DCPO Peter O'Brien 2.00 5.00
DCPR Pete Rose 5.00 12.00
DCRC Robinson Cano 2.50 6.00
DCRO Rougned Odor 2.50 6.00
DCRR Rob Refsnyder 2.00 5.00
DCRS Ryne Sandberg 6.00 15.00
DCRT Raimel Tapia 2.50 6.00
DCRY Robin Yount 3.00 8.00
DCSM Starling Marte 2.50 6.00
DCSP Stephen Piscotty 2.50 6.00
DCTA Tim Anderson 3.00 8.00
DCTD Tyler Duffey 2.00 5.00
DCTF Todd Frazier 2.50 6.00
DCTG Tony Gwynn 3.00 8.00
DCTH Todd Helton 2.50 6.00
DCTJ Travis Jankowski 2.00 5.00
DCTS Trevor Story 3.00 8.00
DCTT Trayce Thompson 2.50 6.00
DCTT Trea Turner 2.50 6.00
DCWC Willson Contreras 3.00 8.00
DCWC Will Clark 4.00 10.00
DCXB Xander Bogaerts 3.00 8.00
DCYM Yadier Molina 3.00 8.00
DCYM Yoan Moncada 3.00 8.00
DCZG Zack Godley 2.00 5.00

2017 Donruss Dominators

RANDOM INSERTS IN PACKS
STATED PRINT RUN 999 SER.#'d SETS
*SILVER/349: .5X TO 1.2X BASIC
*BLUE/249: .6X TO 1.5X BASIC
*RED/149: .6X TO 1.5X BASIC
*GOLD/99: 1X TO 2.5X BASIC
*BLACK/25: 2X TO 5X BASIC
D1 Kris Bryant 1.25 3.00
D2 Mike Trout 5.00 12.00
D3 Mookie Betts 1.50 4.00
D4 Jose Altuve .75 2.00
D5 D.J. LeMahieu 1.00 2.50
D6 Daniel Murphy .75 2.00
D7 Mark Trumbo .60 1.50
D8 Joey Votto 1.00 2.50
D9 Brian Dozier 1.00 2.50
D10 Max Scherzer 1.00 2.50
D11 Justin Verlander 1.00 2.50
D12 Rick Porcello .75 2.00
D13 Jon Lester .75 2.00
D14 Corey Kluber .75 2.00
D15 Miguel Cabrera 1.00 2.50
D16 Nolan Arenado 1.25 3.00
D17 Corey Seager 1.00 2.50
D18 Edwin Encarnacion 1.00 2.50
D19 Jean Segura .75 2.00
D20 Josh Donaldson .75 2.00
D21 Charlie Blackmon 1.00 2.50
D22 Robinson Cano .75 2.00
D23 Khris Davis 1.00 2.50
D24 Kyle Hendricks 1.00 2.50
D25 Jonathan Villar .60 1.50

2017 Donruss Elite Series

RANDOM INSERTS IN PACKS
STATED PRINT RUN 999 SER.#'d SETS
*SILVER/349: .5X TO 1.2X BASIC
*BLUE/249: .6X TO 1.5X BASIC
*RED/149: .6X TO 1.5X BASIC
*GOLD/99: 1X TO 2.5X BASIC
*BLACK/25: 2X TO 5X BASIC
ES1 Wil Myers .60 1.50
ES2 Freddie Freeman 1.25 3.00
ES3 Kris Bryant 1.25 3.00
ES4 Clayton Kershaw 2.00 5.00
ES5 Bryce Harper 1.50 4.00
ES6 Dustin Pedroia 1.00 2.50
ES7 Xander Bogaerts 1.00 2.50
ES8 Todd Frazier .75 2.00
ES9 Hanley Ramirez .75 2.00
ES10 Ian Kinsler .75 2.00
ES11 Manny Machado 1.00 2.50
ES12 Anthony Rizzo 1.50 4.00
ES13 Adrian Beltre 1.00 2.50
ES14 Kyle Seager .60 1.50
ES15 Tyler Naquin .60 1.50
ES16 Madison Bumgarner .75 2.00
ES17 Chris Sale 1.00 2.50
ES18 Gary Sanchez 1.00 2.50
ES19 Trevor Story 1.00 2.50
ES20 Trea Turner .75 2.00
ES21 Kenta Maeda .75 2.00
ES22 Buster Posey 1.25 3.00
ES23 Christian Yelich 1.25 3.00
ES24 Mike Trout 5.00 12.00
ES25 Jose Ramirez .75 2.00

2017 Donruss Masters of the Game

RANDOM INSERTS IN PACKS
STATED PRINT RUN 999 SER.#'d SETS
*SILVER/349: .5X TO 1.2X BASIC
*BLUE/249: .6X TO 1.5X BASIC
*RED/149: .6X TO 1.5X BASIC
*GOLD/99: 1X TO 2.5X BASIC
*BLACK/25: 2X TO 5X BASIC
MGCR Cal Ripken 3.00 8.00
MGFV Fernando Valenzuela .60 1.50
MGGB George Brett 2.00 5.00
MGLB Lou Brock .75 2.00
MGMM Mike Mussina .75 2.00
MGMP Mike Piazza 1.00 2.50
MGOS Ozzie Smith 1.25 3.00
MGPM Pedro Martinez .75 2.00
MGRC Rod Carew .75 2.00
MGRJ Reggie Jackson .75 2.00

2017 Donruss New Breed Autographs

*GOLD/99: .5X TO 1.2X BASIC
*GOLD/25: .6X TO 1.5X BASIC
NBAD Aledmys Diaz 10.00 25.00
NBAR A.J. Reed 2.50 6.00
NBBE Brett Eibner 2.50 6.00
NBBJ Brian Johnson 2.50 6.00
NBBN Brandon Nimmo 3.00 8.00
NBDA Dariel Alvarez 2.50 6.00
NBDR Daniel Robertson 2.50 6.00
NBFM Frankie Montas 5.00 12.00
NBGB Greg Bird 3.00 8.00
NBGM Greg Mahle 2.50 6.00
NBJB Jose Berrios 3.00 8.00
NBJE Jerad Eickhoff 2.50 6.00
NBJP Jose Peraza 3.00 8.00
NBJU Julio Urias 12.00 30.00
NBKM Ketel Marte 3.00 8.00
NBKW Kyle Waldrop
NBLJ Luke Jackson 2.50 6.00
NBMK Max Kepler 3.00 8.00
NBMS Mallex Smith 2.50 6.00
NBOA Ozhaino Albies 10.00 25.00
NBPS Pedro Severino 2.50 6.00
NBRS Ross Stripling 2.50 6.00
NBTT Trayce Thompson 3.00 8.00
NBZG Zack Godley 2.50 6.00

2017 Donruss Promising Pros Materials

*GOLD/49-99: .5X TO 1.2X BASIC
*GOLD/25: .6X TO 1.5X BASIC
PPMAD Aledmys Diaz 4.00 10.00
PPMAR A.J. Reed 2.00 5.00
PPMBE Brian Ellington 2.00 5.00
PPMBE Brett Eibner 2.00 5.00
PPMBN Brandon Nimmo 2.50 6.00
PPMDL Dae-ho Lee 3.00 8.00
PPMFM Frankie Montas 2.00 5.00
PPMGB Greg Bird 2.50 6.00
PPMGM Greg Mahle 2.00 5.00
PPMGK Hyun-soo Kim 2.50 6.00
PPMHO Henry Owens 2.00 5.00
PPMJB Jose Berrios 2.50 6.00
PPMJE Jerad Eickhoff 2.00 5.00
PPMJP Jose Peraza 2.50 6.00
PPMJR Joey Rickard 2.00 5.00
PPMJU Julio Urias 3.00 8.00
PPMKM Ketel Marte 2.50 6.00
PPMLJ Luke Jackson 2.00 5.00
PPMMS Mallex Smith 2.00 5.00
PPMPS Pedro Severino 2.00 5.00
PPMRS Ross Stripling 2.00 5.00
PPMSO Seung-Hwan Oh 4.00 10.00
PPMTT Trayce Thompson 2.50 6.00
PPMTW Tyler White 2.00 5.00
PPMWM Whit Merrifield 3.00 8.00

2017 Donruss Promising Pros Materials Signatures

PPMSAA Anthony Alford 3.00 8.00
PPMSAM Austin Meadows 5.00 12.00
PPMSBA Brian Anderson 4.00 10.00
PPMSBH Brent Honeywell 4.00 10.00
PPMSBZ Bradley Zimmer 5.00 12.00
PPMSCB Cody Bellinger 25.00 60.00
PPMSCF Clint Frazier 5.00 12.00
PPMSCS Christin Stewart
PPMSEJ Eloy Jimenez 12.00 30.00
PPMSFB Franklin Barreto 4.00 10.00
PPMSIH Ian Happ 12.00 30.00
PPMSJC Jeimer Candelario 6.00 15.00
PPMSJT Jake Thompson 3.00 8.00
PPMSLS Lucas Sims 5.00 12.00
PPMSMC Matt Chapman 5.00 12.00
PPMSNM Nomar Mazara 3.00 8.00
PPMSRD Rafael Devers 25.00 60.00
PPMSSN Sean Newcomb 4.00 10.00
PPMSTT Tim Tebow 40.00 100.00
PPMSTT Tyrone Taylor 3.00 8.00
PPMSWC Willson Contreras 8.00 20.00

2017 Donruss Promising Pros Materials Signatures Gold

*GOLD/40-99: .5X TO 1.2X BASIC
*GOLD/25: .6X TO 1.5X BASIC
PRINT RUNS B/WN 10-99 COPIES PER
NO PRICING ON QTY 10
PPMSJM Jorge Mateo/40 8.00 20.00

2017 Donruss San Diego Chicken Triple Material

1 Ted Giannoulas/83 20.00 50.00

2017 Donruss San Diego Chicken Triple Material Signatures

STATED PRINT RUN 83 SER.#'d SETS
1 Ted Giannoulas/83 50.00 120.00

2017 Donruss Signature Series

SOME ISSUED IN'17 CHRONICLES
*BLUE/49-199: .5X TO 1.2X BASIC
*BLUE/25-35: .6X TO 1.5X BASIC
*GOLD/49: .5X TO 1.2X BASIC
*GOLD/20-25: .6X TO 1.5X BASIC
*PURPLE/25: .6X TO 1.5X BASIC
*RED/49-99: .5X TO 1.2X BASIC
*RED/20-35: .6X TO 1.5X BASIC
CHRON.EXCH.DEADLINE 5/22/2019
1 Cody Bellinger
2 Ian Happ 6.00 15.00
3 Mitch Haniger 4.00 10.00
4 Sam Travis 2.50 6.00
6 Adam Frazier 2.50 6.00
7 Derek Fisher 3.00 8.00
8 Franklin Barreto 2.50 6.00
9 Jorge Bonifacio 2.50 6.00
10 Dinelson Lamet 2.50 6.00
12 Lewis Brinson 2.50 6.00
13 Magneuris Sierra 4.00 10.00
14 Juan Gonzalez 6.00 15.00
15 Andrew Toles 2.50 6.00
16 Bradley Zimmer 3.00 8.00
17 Antonio Senzatela 2.50 6.00
18 Brock Stewart 2.50 6.00
19 Yandy Diaz 5.00 12.00
20 Hunter Dozier 2.50 6.00
SSRR Rio Ruiz 2.50 6.00
22 Reggie Jackson 20.00 50.00
SS2RY Rhys Hoskins 5.00 12.00
24 Rickey Henderson 25.00 60.00
25 Wade Boggs 12.00 30.00
26 Adrian Beltre
27 Alex Rodriguez 30.00 80.00
28 Aaron Sanchez 3.00 8.00
29 Carlos Gonzalez 3.00 8.00
30 Jonathan Lucroy 3.00 8.00
31 Anthony Rizzo 25.00 60.00
32 David Ortiz 20.00 50.00
33 Hunter Pence 4.00 10.00
34 Ian Kinsler 3.00 8.00
35 Jonathan Villar 2.50 6.00
36 Rougned Odor 3.00 8.00
37 Frank Thomas
38 Jose Canseco 6.00 15.00
39 Alfonso Soriano 4.00 10.00
40 Ozzie Smith 12.00 30.00
41 Amed Rosario 4.00 10.00
42 Ozzie Albies 12.00 30.00
SS2GS George Springer 8.00 20.00
44 Jake Lamb 3.00 8.00
45 Charlie Blackmon 5.00 12.00
46 Logan Morrison 2.50 6.00
47 Ervin Santana 2.50 6.00
48 Lance McCullers 2.50 6.00
49 Craig Kimbrel 5.00 12.00
50 Kevin Pillar 2.50 6.00
SSAB Alex Bregman 15.00 40.00
SSAB Andrew Benintendi 30.00 80.00
SSAJ Aaron Judge 40.00 100.00
SSAM Adalberto Mejia 2.50 6.00
SSAR Alex Reyes 3.00 8.00
SSBR Brooks Robinson 10.00 25.00
SSBS Braden Shipley 2.50 6.00
SSCF Carson Fulmer 2.50 6.00
SSCK Carson Kelly 3.00 8.00
SSCP Chad Pinder 2.50 6.00
SSDD David Dahl 3.00 8.00
SSDM Don Mattingly 20.00 50.00
SSDP David Price 3.00 8.00
SSDP David Paulino 3.00 8.00
SSDS Dansby Swanson 6.00 15.00
SSEG Erik Gonzalez 2.50 6.00
SSGC Gavin Cecchini 2.50 6.00
SSHR Hunter Renfroe 3.00 8.00
SSJA Jorge Alfaro 3.00 8.00
SSJA Jose Abreu 5.00 12.00
SSJB Josh Bell 5.00 12.00
SSJC Jharel Cotton 2.50 6.00
SSJD Jose De Leon 2.50 6.00
SSJH Jeff Hoffman 2.50 6.00
SSJJ Jacoby Jones 3.00 8.00
SSJM Joe Musgrove 2.50 6.00
SSJR Jose Rondon 2.50 6.00
SSJT Josh Tomlin 5.00 12.00
SSJT Jake Thompson 2.50 6.00
SSLW Luke Weaver 3.00 8.00
SSMM Manny Margot 2.50 6.00
SSMO Matt Olson 6.00 15.00
SSMS Mike Schmidt 20.00 50.00
SSNC Nelson Cruz 4.00 10.00
SSNM Nomar Mazara 2.50 6.00
SSOA Orlando Arcia 4.00 10.00
SSRH Ryon Healy 3.00 8.00
SSRL Reynaldo Lopez
SSRQ Roman Quinn
SSRR Rio Ruiz 4.00 10.00
SSRT Raimel Tapia 3.00 8.00
SSSS Stephen Strasburg 12.00 30.00
SSTG Tom Glavine 8.00 20.00
SSTG Tyler Glasnow 3.00 8.00
SSTH Teoscar Hernandez
SSTM Trey Mancini 5.00 12.00
SSVG Vladimir Guerrero 8.00 20.00
SSYM Yohander Mendez 2.50 6.00
SSYM Yoan Moncada 15.00 40.00

2017 Donruss Significant Signatures

*BLUE/49: .5X TO 1.2X BASIC
*BLUE/20-25: .6X TO 1.5X BASIC
*RED/20-25: .6X TO 1.5X BASIC
SIGBG Bob Gibson 10.00 25.00
SIGBM Bill Mazeroski 10.00 25.00
SIGCY Carl Yastrzemski 30.00 80.00
SIGDW Dave Winfield 10.00 25.00
SIGEM Eddie Murray 15.00 40.00
SIGJM Juan Marichal 10.00 25.00
SIGJM Joe Morgan 10.00 25.00
SIGKG Ken Griffey Jr. 50.00 120.00
SIGOC Orlando Cepeda 6.00 15.00
SIGOS Ozzie Smith 10.00 25.00
SIGPR Pete Rose 15.00 40.00
SIGRC Rod Carew 12.00 30.00
SIGRC Roger Clemens 20.00 50.00
SIGRH Rickey Henderson 25.00 60.00
SIGRJ Reggie Jackson 20.00 50.00
SIGRS Ryne Sandberg 15.00 40.00
SIGSC Steve Carlton 10.00 25.00
SIGTL Tommy Lasorda 12.00 30.00
SIGWM Willie McCovey 15.00 40.00

2017 Donruss Studio Signatures

*BLUE/49: .5X TO 1.2X BASIC
*RED/25: .5X TO 1.2X BASIC
STSDW David Wright 5.00 12.00
STSFL Francisco Lindor
STSJA Jake Arrieta 15.00 40.00
STSMS Max Scherzer 10.00 25.00

2017 Donruss Studio Signatures Purple

PRINT RUNS B/WN 7-25 COPIES PER
NO PRICING ON QTY 15 OR LESS
STSDP Dustin Pedroia/25 15.00 40.00

2017 Donruss The Prospects

*CYAN BACK: .75X TO 2X BASIC
*GRAY/199: 1X TO 2.5X BASIC
*GOLD PP/99: 1.5X TO 4X BASIC
*AQS TEST/49: 1.5X TO 4X BASIC
*PINK/25: 3X TO 8X BASIC
TP1 Brendan Rodgers .40 1.00
TP2 Austin Meadows .50 1.25
TP3 Victor Robles .75 2.00
TP4 Ozhaino Albies 1.25 3.00
TP5 Anderson Espinoza .30 .75
TP6 Clint Frazier .60 1.50
TP7 Rafael Devers .60 1.50
TP8 Gleyber Torres 5.00 12.00
TP9 Jorge Mateo .30 .75
TP10 Ian Happ .60 1.50
TP11 Eloy Jimenez 1.25 3.00
TP12 Bradley Zimmer .40 1.00
TP13 Corey Ray .40 1.00
TP14 Cody Bellinger 5.00 12.00
TP15 Francis Martes .30 .75

2017 Donruss The Rookies

RANDOM INSERTS IN PACKS
*CYAN BACK: .75X TO 2X BASIC
*GRAY/199: 1X TO 2.5X BASIC
*GOLD PP/99: 1.5X TO 4X BASIC
*AQS TEST/49: 1.5X TO 4X BASIC
*PINK/25: 3X TO 8X BASIC
TR1 Yoan Moncada 1.00 2.50
TR2 David Dahl .40 1.00
TR3 Dansby Swanson .75 2.00
TR4 Andrew Benintendi 1.00 2.50
TR5 Alex Reyes .40 1.00
TR6 Tyler Glasnow .40 1.00
TR7 Josh Bell .75 2.00
TR8 Aaron Judge 4.00 10.00
TR9 Jose De Leon .30 .75
TR10 Jeff Hoffman .30 .75
TR11 Hunter Renfroe .40 1.00
TR12 Carson Fulmer .30 .75
TR13 Alex Bregman 1.25 3.00
TR14 Orlando Arcia .50 1.25
TR15 Manny Margot .30 .75

2017 Donruss Whammy

W1 Mike Trout 60.00 150.00
W2 Ken Griffey Jr. 25.00 60.00
W3 Kris Bryant 15.00 40.00
W4 Bryce Harper 20.00 50.00

2018 Donruss

1 Anthony Rizzo DK 1.00 2.50
2 Yoan Moncada DK .60 1.50
3 Evan Longoria DK .50 1.25
4 Joey Votto DK .60 1.50
5 Corey Kluber DK .50 1.25
6 Adrian Beltre DK .60 1.50
7 Jose Bautista DK .50 1.25
8 Nolan Arenado DK .75 2.00
9 Miguel Cabrera DK .60 1.50
10 Bryce Harper DK 1.00 2.50
11 Jose Altuve DK .50 1.25
12 Eric Hosmer DK .50 1.25
13 Mike Trout DK 3.00 8.00
14 Clayton Kershaw DK 1.25 3.00
15 Justin Bour DK .40 1.00
16 Ryan Braun DK .50 1.25
17 Brian Dozier DK .50 1.25
18 Noah Syndergaard DK .50 1.25
19 Aaron Judge DK 1.50 4.00
20 Matt Olson DK .40 1.00
21 Odubel Herrera DK .50 1.25
22 Paul Goldschmidt DK .60 1.50
23 Freddie Freeman DK .75 2.00
24 Andrew McCutchen DK .60 1.50
25 Adam Jones DK .50 1.25
26 Wil Myers DK .40 1.00
27 Mookie Betts DK 1.00 2.50
28 Madison Bumgarner DK .50 1.25
29 Robinson Cano DK .50 1.25
30 Adam Wainwright DK .50 1.25
31 Miguel Andujar RR RC 1.50 4.00
32 Nick Williams RR RC .50 1.25
33 Clint Frazier RR RC .75 2.00
34 Paul Blackburn RR RC .40 1.00
35 Rafael Devers RR RC 1.25 3.00
36 Ozzie Albies RR RC 1.25 3.00
37 Amed Rosario RR RC .50 1.25
38 Rhys Hoskins RR RC 1.50 4.00
39 Ryan McMahon RR RC .50 1.25
40 Willie Calhoun RR RC .50 1.25
41 Walker Buehler RR RC 2.00 5.00
42 Victor Robles RR RC 1.00 2.50
43 Luiz Gohara RR RC .40 1.00
44 J.P. Crawford RR RC .40 1.00
45 Alex Verdugo RR RC .60 1.50
46 Tyler Mahle RR RC .50 1.25
47 Dominic Smith RR RC .50 1.25
48 Brandon Woodruff RR RC .50 1.25
49 Chris Flexen RR RC .40 1.00
50 Dustin Fowler RR RC .40 1.00
51 Paul Goldschmidt .25 .60
52 David Peralta .15 .40
53 Zack Greinke .20 .50
54 Jake Lamb .20 .50
55 Robbie Ray .15 .40
56 Freddie Freeman .30 .75
57 Ender Inciarte .15 .40
58 Anthony Rendon .25 .60
59 Eddie Mathews .25 .60
60 Jonathan Schoop .15 .40
61 Trey Mancini .20 .50
62 Adam Jones .20 .50
63 J.A. Happ .20 .50
64 Cal Ripken .75 2.00
65 Jim Palmer .20 .50
66 Justin Smoak .15 .40
67 Xander Bogaerts .25 .60
68 Dustin Pedroia .25 .60
69 Jackie Bradley Jr. .25 .60
70 Jean Segura .15 .40
71 Drew Pomeranz .15 .40
72 Brian Dozier .20 .50
73 Wade Boggs .20 .50
74 Duke Snider .20 .50
75 Jake Arrieta .20 .50
76 Javier Baez .30 .75
77 Cole Hamels .20 .50
78 Kyle Hendricks .25 .60
79 Miguel Sano .20 .50
80 Willson Contreras .25 .60
81 Logan Morrison .15 .40
82 Jon Lester .20 .50
83 Kyle Schwarber .25 .60
84 Ryne Sandberg .50 1.25
85 Avisail Garcia .20 .50
86 Jose Abreu .25 .60
87 Frank Thomas .25 .60
88 Luis Castillo .20 .50
89 Tom Seaver .20 .50
90 Zack Cozart .15 .40
91 Barry Larkin .20 .50
92 Joe Morgan .20 .50
93 Jay Bruce .20 .50
94 Sonny Gray .20 .50
95 Odubel Herrera .20 .50
96 James Paxton .20 .50
97 Carlos Carrasco .15 .40
98 Andrew Miller .20 .50
99 Michael Brantley .20 .50
100 Roberto Alomar .20 .50
101 Edwin Encarnacion .25 .60
102 Nelson Cruz .25 .60
103 Trevor Story .25 .60
104 Charlie Blackmon .25 .60
105 DJ LeMahieu .25 .60
106 Kyle Freeland .20 .50
107 Jonathan Gray .15 .40
108 Reggie Jackson .20 .50
109 Michael Fulmer .15 .40
110 Al Kaline .25 .60
111 Justin Verlander .25 .60
112 Dave Winfield .20 .50
113 Madison Bumgarner .20 .50
114 Manuel Margot .15 .40
115 Juan Marichal .20 .50
116 Wil Myers .15 .40
117 Lorenzo Cain .15 .40
118 Eric Hosmer .20 .50
119 Marcus Stroman .20 .50
120 George Brett .50 1.25
121 Ryon Healy .15 .40
122 Andrelton Simmons .15 .40
123 Rod Carew .20 .50
124 Aaron Altherr .15 .40
125 Justin Turner .20 .50
126 Khris Davis .25 .60
127 Yu Darvish .25 .60
128 Kenley Jansen .20 .50
129 Alex Wood .15 .40
130 Didi Gregorius .25 .60
131 Justin Bour .15 .40
132 Christian Yelich .30 .75
133 Dee Gordon .15 .40
134 Marcell Ozuna .25 .60
135 Ervin Santana .15 .40
136 Ryan Braun .20 .50
137 Travis Shaw .15 .40
138 Eric Thames .15 .40
139 Orlando Arcia .15 .40
140 Chris Sale .25 .60
141 Anthony Rizzo .40 1.00
142 Kirby Puckett .25 .60
143 Giancarlo Stanton .25 .60
144 Noah Syndergaard .20 .50
145 Michael Conforto .20 .50
146 Jacob deGrom .25 .60
147 Joey Votto .25 .60
148 Aaron Judge .60 1.50
149 Cody Bellinger .50 1.25
150 Gary Sanchez .25 .60
151 Luis Severino .20 .50
152 Jordan Montgomery .25 .60
153 Corey Kluber .20 .50
154 Clayton Kershaw .50 1.25
155 Mike Trout 1.25 3.00
156 Miguel Cabrera .25 .60
157 Francisco Lindor .25 .60
158 Corey Seager .25 .60
159 Andrew McCutchen .25 .60
160 Josh Bell .20 .50
161 Gerrit Cole .25 .60
162 Alex Bregman .25 .60
163 Carlos Correa .25 .60
164 Dallas Keuchel .20 .50
165 Tony Gwynn .25 .60
166 Jose Altuve .20 .50
167 Buster Posey .30 .75
168 George Springer .20 .50
169 Andrew Benintendi .30 .75
170 Kyle Seager .15 .40
171 Robinson Cano .20 .50
172 Nolan Arenado .30 .75
173 Jose Ramirez .20 .50
174 Felix Hernandez .20 .50
175 Ken Griffey Jr. .50 1.25
176 Yadier Molina .25 .60
177 Matt Carpenter .25 .60
178 Carlos Martinez .20 .50
179 Evan Longoria .20 .50
180 Ian Happ .20 .50
181 Chris Archer .15 .40
182 Adrian Beltre .25 .60
183 Kris Bryant .30 .75
184 Joey Gallo .20 .50
185 Elvis Andrus .20 .50
186 Nomar Mazara .15 .40
187 Nolan Ryan .75 2.00
188 Josh Donaldson .20 .50
189 Manny Machado .25 .60
190 Salvador Perez .20 .50
191 Mookie Betts .40 1.00
192 Bryce Harper .40 1.00
193 Max Scherzer .25 .60
194 Daniel Murphy .25 .60
195 Chipper Jones .25 .60
196 Trea Turner .20 .50
197 Ryan Zimmerman .20 .50
198 Stephen Strasburg .25 .60
199 J.D. Martinez .25 .60
200 Mickey Mantle .75 2.00
201 A.Judge/C.Frazier .60 1.50
202 G.Maddux/T.Glavine .30 .75
203 Andre Dawson .20 .50
Gary Carter
204 A.Pujols/M.Trout 1.25 3.00
205 Eric Hosmer .20 .50
Lorenzo Cain
206 A.Pettitte/R.Clemens .30 .75
207 Gary Carter .20 .50
Dwight Gooden
208 M.Cabrera/N.Castellanos .25 .60
209 Harmon Killebrew .25 .60
Rod Carew
210 Nelson Cruz .25 .60
Yadier Molina
211 J.Altuve/C.Correa .25 .60
212 Manny Machado .25 .60
Byron Buxton
213 DJ LeMahieu .30 .75
Nolan Arenado
214 O.Smith/R.Sandberg .50 1.25
215 Barry Larkin .20 .50
Gary Sheffield
216 Dave Concepcion .20 .50
Tony Perez
217 Correa/Lindor/Molina .25 .60
218 G.Springer/C.Correa .25 .60
219 G.Brett/W.Boggs .50 1.25
220 C.Kershaw/C.Seager .50 1.25
221 Ted Giannoulas RETRO .15 .40
222 Paul Goldschmidt RETRO .25 .60
223 Freddie Freeman RETRO .30 .75
224 Trey Mancini RETRO .20 .50
225 Anthony Rizzo RETRO .40 1.00
226 Mookie Betts RETRO .40 1.00
227 Benintendi RETRO .25 .60
228 Kris Bryant RETRO .30 .75
229 Ian Happ RETRO .20 .50
230 Yoan Moncada RETRO .25 .60
231 Joey Votto RETRO .25 .60
232 Joe Morgan RETRO .20 .50
233 Corey Kluber RETRO .20 .50
234 Lindor RETRO .25 .60
235 Charlie Blackmon RETRO .25 .60
236 Nolan Arenado RETRO .30 .75
237 Miguel Cabrera RETRO .25 .60
238 Justin Verlander RETRO .25 .60
239 Jose Altuve RETRO .20 .50
240 George Springer RETRO .20 .50
241 George Brett RETRO .50 1.25
242 Mike Trout RETRO 1.25 3.00
243 Cody Bellinger RETRO .50 1.25
244 Kershaw RETRO .50 1.25
245 Corey Seager RETRO .25 .60
246 Marcell Ozuna RETRO .25 .60
247 Ryan Braun RETRO .20 .50
248 Eric Thames RETRO .20 .50
249 Brian Dozier RETRO .20 .50
250 Harmon Killebrew RETRO .25 .60
251 Noah Syndergaard RETRO .20 .50
252 Mike Piazza RETRO .25 .60
253 Aaron Judge RETRO .60 1.50
254 Mickey Mantle RETRO .75 2.00
255 Matt Olson RETRO .15 .40
256 Nolan Ryan RETRO .75 2.00
257 Andrew McCutchen RETRO .25 .60
258 Tony Gwynn RETRO .25 .60
259 Madison Bumgarner RETRO .20 .50
260 Kyle Seager RETRO .15 .40
261 Robinson Cano RETRO .20 .50
262 Adam Wainwright RETRO .20 .50
263 Matt Carpenter RETRO .25 .60
264 Ozzie Smith RETRO .30 .75
265 Evan Longoria RETRO .20 .50
266 Adrian Beltre RETRO .25 .60
267 Cole Hamels RETRO .20 .50
268 Josh Donaldson RETRO .20 .50
269 Max Scherzer RETRO .25 .60
270 Bryce Harper RETRO .40 1.00
271 Christian Villanueva RR RC .40 1.00
272 Shohei Ohtani RR 3.00 8.00
273 Austin Hays RR RC .60 1.50
274 Chance Sisco RR RC .50 1.25
275 Harrison Bader RR RC .60 1.50
276 Francisco Mejia RR RC .50 1.25
277 Erick Fedde RR RC .40 1.00
278 J.D. Davis RR RC .50 1.25
279 Scott Kingery RR RC .60 1.50
280 Juan Soto RR RC 4.00 10.00

281A Ohtani RR RC Eng 2.50 6.00
281B Ohtani RR Jpnse 4.00 10.00
282A G.Torres RR RC 4.00 10.00
282B Torres RR Twttr 6.00 15.00
283A R.Acuna RR RC 8.00 20.00
283B Acuna RR Full name 12.00 30.00

2018 Donruss Blank Backs

*BLANK DK: .75X TO 2X BASIC
*BLANK RR: .75X TO 2X BASIC
*BLANK VET: 2X TO 5X BASIC
*BLANK RET: 2X TO 5X BASIC
RANDOM INSERTS IN PACKS

2018 Donruss Career Stat Line

*CAR DK p/r 284-540: .75X TO 2X BASIC
*CAR RR p/r 317-500: .75X TO 2X BASIC
*CAR p/r 251-500: 2X TO 5X BASIC
*CAR DK p/r 231: 1X TO 2.5X BASIC
*CAR p/r 230-236: 2.5X TO 6X BASIC
*CAR DK p/r 100-201: 1.2X TO 3X BASIC
*CAR RR p/r 133-150: 1.2X TO 3X BASIC
*CAR p/r 114-203: 3X TO 8X BASIC
*CAR p/r 57-89: 4X TO 10X BASIC
RANDOM INSERTS IN PACKS
PRINT RUNS B/WN 17-540 COPIES PER
NO PRICING ON QTY 17

2018 Donruss Father's Day Ribbon

*FATHER DK: 1.2X TO 3X BASIC
*FATHER RR: 1.2X TO 3X BASIC
*FATHER VET: 3X TO 8X BASIC
*FATHER RET: 3X TO 8X BASIC
RANDOM INSERTS IN PACKS
STATED PRINT RUN 49 SER.#'d SETS

2018 Donruss Game Day Stat Line

*GAME DAY p/r 25: 8X TO 20X BASIC
RANDOM INSERTS IN PACKS
PRINT RUNS B/WN 1-25 COPIES PER
NO PRICING ON QTY 19 OR LESS

2018 Donruss Gold Press Proof

*GOLD PP DK: 1.2X TO 3X BASIC
*GOLD PP RR: 1.2X TO 3X BASIC
*GOLD PP VET: 3X TO 8X BASIC
*GOLD PP RET: 3X TO 8X BASIC
RANDOM INSERTS IN PACKS
STATED PRINT RUN 99 SER.#'d SETS

2018 Donruss Holo Blue

*HOLO BLUE: 1.2X TO 3X BASIC
RANDOM INSERTS IN PACKS

2018 Donruss Holo Green

*HOLO GREEN: 1.2X TO 3X BASIC
RANDOM INSERTS IN PACKS

2018 Donruss Mother's Day Ribbon

*MOTHER DK: 1.5X TO 4X BASIC
*MOTHER RR: 1.5X TO 4X BASIC
*MOTHER VET: 4X TO 10X BASIC
*MOTHER RET: 4X TO 10X BASIC
RANDOM INSERTS IN PACKS
STATED PRINT RUN 25 SER.#'d SETS

2018 Donruss Season Stat Line

*SEA DK p/r 265-307: .75X TO 2X BASIC
*SEA RR p/r 250-500: .75X TO 2X BASIC
*SEA p/r 250-500: 2X TO 5X BASIC
*SEA DK p/r 231 : 1X TO 2.5X BASIC
*SEA p/r 226-249: 2.5X TO 6X BASIC
*SEA DK p/r 100-204: 1.2X TO 3X BASIC
*SEA RR p/r 126: 1.2X TO 3X BASIC
*SEA p/r 100-225: 3X TO 8X BASIC
*SEA DK p/r 82-96: 1.5X TO 4X BASIC
*SEA p/r 52-97: 4X TO 10X BASIC
*SEA RR p/r 43-48: 2X TO 5X BASIC
*SEA p/r 36-47: 5X TO 12X BASIC
*SEA DK p/r 28-33: 2.5X TO 6X BASIC
*SEA p/r 26-34: 6X TO 15X BASIC
*SEA DK p/r 23-24: 3X TO 8X BASIC
*SEA RR p/r 23: 3X TO 8X BASIC
*SEA p/r 20-25: 8X TO 20X BASIC
RANDOM INSERTS IN PACKS
PRINT RUNS B/WN 4-500 COPIES PER
NO PRICING ON QTY 14

2018 Donruss Teal Border

*TEAL DK: .75X TO 2X BASIC
*TEAL RR: .75X TO 2X BASIC
*TEAL VET: 2X TO 5X BASIC
*TEAL RET: 2X TO 5X BASIC
RANDOM INSERTS IN PACKS
STATED PRINT RUN 199 SER.#'d SETS

2018 Donruss Variations

RANDOM INSERTS IN PACKS
*BLANK: .75X TO 2X BASIC
*CAR p/r 276-500: .75X TO 2X BASIC
*CAR p/r 231: .1X TO 2.5X BASIC
*CAR p/r 100-211: 1.2X TO 3X BASIC
*SEA p/r 250-312:.75X TO 2X BASIC
*SEA p/r 228-243:.1X TO 2.5X BASIC
*SEA p/r 101-220:1.2X TO 3X BASIC
*SEA p/r 54-95: 1.5X TO 4X BASIC
*SEA p/r 29-33: 2.5X TO 6X BASIC
*SEA p/r 20-24: 3X TO 8X BASIC
*TEAL/199: .75X TO 2X BASIC
*GOLD PP/99: 1.2X TO 3X BASIC
*FATHER/49 : 1.2X TO 3X BASIC
*MOTHER/25: 1.5X TO 4X BASIC
59 Eddie Mathews .60 1.50
64 Cal Ripken 2.00 5.00
65 Jim Palmer .50 1.25
69 Jackie Bradley Jr. .60 1.50
86 Jose Abreu .60 1.50
87 Frank Thomas .60 1.50
92 Joe Morgan .50 1.25
100 Roberto Alomar .50 1.25
104 Charlie Blackmon .60 1.50
108 Reggie Jackson .50 1.25
110 Al Kaline .60 1.50
120 George Brett 1.25 3.00
123 Rod Carew .50 1.25
134 Marcell Ozuna .60 1.50
141 Anthony Rizzo 1.00 2.50
142 Kirby Puckett .60 1.50
143 Giancarlo Stanton .60 1.50
144 Noah Syndergaard .50 1.25
148A Aaron Judge 1.50 4.00
NY 12th Judicial District
148B Aaron Judge 1.50 4.00
ROY
149A Cody Bellinger 1.25 3.00
Unanimous ROY
149B Cody Bellinger 1.25 3.00
Running
150 Gary Sanchez .60 1.50
153 Corey Kluber .50 1.25
154 Clayton Kershaw 1.25 3.00
155 Mike Trout 3.00 8.00
157 Francisco Lindor .60 1.50
158 Corey Seager .60 1.50
159 Andrew McCutchen .60 1.50
162 Alex Bregman .60 1.50
163 Carlos Correa .60 1.50
165 Tony Gwynn .60 1.50
166 Jose Altuve .50 1.25
167A Buster Posey .75 2.00
Gerald Dempsey Posey
167B Buster Posey .75 2.00
Red Sleeves
169A Andrew Benintendi .60 1.50
Sepia photo
169B Andrew Benintendi .60 1.50
Benny Baseball
172 Nolan Arenado .75 2.00
173 Jose Ramirez .50 1.25
175 Ken Griffey Jr. 1.25 3.00
176 Yadier Molina .60 1.50
183A Kris Bryant .75 2.00
Sepia photo
KB
183B Kris Bryant .75 2.00
no sunglasses
187 Nolan Ryan 2.00 5.00
189 Manny Machado .60 1.50
191A Mookie Betts 1.00 2.50
Markus Lynn Betts
191B Mookie Betts 1.00 2.50
Black Sleeves
192 Bryce Harper 1.00 2.50
195 Chipper Jones .60 1.50
200 Mickey Mantle 2.00 5.00
225 Anthony Rizzo RETRO 1.00 2.50
227 Andrew Benintendi RETRO .60 1.50
228 Kris Bryant RETRO .75 2.00
230 Yoan Moncada RETRO .60 1.50
234 Francisco Lindor RETRO .60 1.50
242 Mike Trout RETRO 3.00 8.00
243 Cody Bellinger RETRO 1.25 3.00
253 Aaron Judge RETRO 1.50 4.00
254 Mickey Mantle RETRO 2.00 5.00
256 Nolan Ryan RETRO 2.00 5.00

2018 Donruss '84 Retro Materials

RANDOM INSERTS IN PACKS
*GOLD/99: .5X TO 1.2X BASIC
R84CS Corey Seager 3.00 8.00
R84MM Manuel Margot 2.00 5.00
R84AB Alex Bregman 3.00 8.00
R84JA Jose Abreu 3.00 8.00
R84LS Luis Severino 2.50 6.00
R84JB Javier Baez 4.00 10.00
R84JG Jacob deGrom 3.00 8.00
R84JR Jose Ramirez 2.50 6.00
R84SM Sean Manaea 2.00 5.00
R84DP Dustin Pedroia 3.00 8.00
R84EH Eric Hosmer 2.50 6.00
R84AB Aaron Blair 2.00 5.00
R84KW Kolten Wong 2.50 6.00
R84MM Manny Machado 3.00 8.00
R84JG Jonathan Gray 2.00 5.00
R84AB Andrew Benintendi 4.00 10.00
R84VR Victor Robles 4.00 10.00
R84JG Juan Gonzalez 2.00 5.00
R84AJ Aaron Judge 8.00 20.00
R84KK Kevin Kiermaier 2.50 6.00
R84AR Alex Reyes 2.50 6.00
R84AB Archie Bradley 2.00 5.00
R84AR Addison Russell 2.50 6.00
R84MS Miguel Sano 2.50 6.00
R84KS Kyle Schwarber 3.00 8.00

2018 Donruss '84 Retro Signatures

RANDOM INSERTS IN PACKS
1 Bob Gibson 12.00 30.00
2 Ozzie Smith 15.00 40.00
3 Rickey Henderson 20.00 50.00
4 Darrell Evans 10.00 25.00
5 Keith Hernandez 15.00 40.00
6 Robin Yount 20.00 50.00
7 Jose Ramirez 3.00 8.00
8 Luis Severino 20.00 50.00
9 Alex Bregman 15.00 40.00
10 Carlos Correa 20.00 50.00
11 Kyle Seager 4.00 10.00
12 Marcell Ozuna 4.00 10.00
13 Paul Goldschmidt 12.00 30.00
14 David Wright 10.00 25.00
15 Yadier Molina 30.00 80.00
16 Carlton Fisk 10.00 25.00
17 Aaron Judge 75.00 200.00
18 Cody Bellinger 50.00 120.00
19 Greg Bird 3.00 8.00
20 John Franco 4.00 10.00
21 Salvador Perez 10.00 25.00
22 Joe Carter 10.00 25.00
23 Steve Carlton
24 Nomar Mazara

2018 Donruss '84 Retro Signatures Blue

*BLUE/35-99: .5X TO 1.2X BASIC
*BLUE/25: .6X TO 1.5X BASIC
RANDOM INSERTS IN PACKS
PRINT RUNS B/WN 25-99 COPIES PER
25 Al Kaline/25 25.00 50.00

2018 Donruss '84 Retro Signatures Red

*RED/20-25: .6X TO 1.5X BASIC
RANDOM INSERTS IN PACKS
PRINT RUNS B/WN 20-25 COPIES PER
25 Al Kaline/20 25.00 50.00

2018 Donruss All Stars

RANDOM INSERTS IN PACKS
STATED PRINT RUN 999 SER.#'d SETS
*CRYSTAL: .5X TO 1.2X BASIC
*SILVER/349: .5X TO 1.2X BASIC
*BLUE/249: .6X TO 1.5X BASIC
*RED/149: .6X TO 1.5X BASIC
*GOLD/99: 1X TO 2.5X BASIC
*GREEN/25: 1.5X TO 4X BASIC
1 Aaron Judge 1.50 4.00
2 Carlos Correa .60 1.50
3 Mookie Betts 1.00 2.50
4 Francisco Lindor .60 1.50
5 Corey Kluber .50 1.25
6 Chris Sale .60 1.50
7 Nolan Arenado .75 2.00
8 Charlie Blackmon .60 1.50
9 Corey Seager .60 1.50
10 Max Scherzer .60 1.50
11 Clayton Kershaw 1.25 3.00
12 Mike Trout 3.00 8.00

2018 Donruss American Pride

RANDOM INSERTS IN PACKS
STATED PRINT RUN 999 SER.#'d SETS
*CRYSTAL: .5X TO 1.2X BASIC
*SILVER/349: .5X TO 1.2X BASIC
*BLUE/249: .6X TO 1.5X BASIC
*RED/149: .6X TO 1.5X BASIC
*GOLD/99: 1X TO 2.5X BASIC
*GREEN/25: 1.5X TO 4X BASIC
AP1 Seth Beer 1.50 4.00
AP2 Steven Gingery .50 1.25
AP3 Nick Madrigal 2.50 6.00
AP4 Jake McCarthy .60 1.50
AP5 Nick Meyer .50 1.25
AP6 Casey Mize 3.00 8.00
AP7 Konnor Pilkington .50 1.25
AP8 Dallas Woolfolk .40 1.00
AP9 Tyler Frank .40 1.00
AP10 Cadyn Grenier .50 1.25
AP11 Gianluca Dalatri .40 1.00
AP12 Braden Shewmake 1.25 3.00
AP13 Bryce Tucker .40 1.00
AP14 Andrew Vaughn 1.25 3.00
AP15 Steele Walker .50 1.25
AP16 Jeremy Eierman .50 1.25
AP17 Patrick Raby .50 1.25
AP18 Grant Koch .40 1.00
AP19 Travis Swaggerty 1.25 3.00
AP20 Tim Cate .60 1.50
AP21 Nick Sprengel .40 1.00
AP22 Johnny Aiello .40 1.00
AP23 Ryley Gilliam .50 1.25
AP24 Jon Olsen .40 1.00
AP25 Tyler Holton .50 1.25
AP26 Sean Wymer .40 1.00

2018 Donruss Diamond Collection Memorabilia

*GOLD/99: .5X TO 1.2X BASIC
DCCP Chad Pinder 2.00 5.00
DCJE Jerad Eickhoff 2.00 5.00
DCOA Orlando Arcia 2.00 5.00
DCBP Brett Phillips 2.00 5.00
DCJL Jose De Leon 2.00 5.00
DCRT Raimel Tapia 2.00 5.00
DCJG Jonathan Gray 2.00 5.00
DCTG Tyler Glasnow 2.00 5.00
DCAS Antonio Senzatela 2.00 5.00
DCJB Josh Bell 2.50 6.00
DCDM Deven Marrero 2.00 5.00
DCJJ Jacoby Jones 2.50 6.00
DCCS Corey Seager 3.00 8.00
DCJC Jharel Cotton 2.00 5.00
DCJH Jeff Hoffman 2.00 5.00
DCJP Jose Peraza 2.50 6.00
DCBS Braden Shipley 2.00 5.00
DCJC Jeimer Candelario 2.50 6.00
DCDS Dansby Swanson 3.00 8.00
DCAG Amir Garrett 2.00 5.00
DCCF Carson Fulmer 2.00 5.00
DCTT Tim Tebow 5.00 12.00
DCJT Jake Thompson 2.00 5.00
DCDL Dinelson Lamet 2.00 5.00
DCTH Teoscar Hernandez 3.00 8.00
DCCR Colin Rea 2.00 5.00
DCHR Hunter Renfroe 2.00 5.00
DCGM German Marquez 2.00 5.00
DCPB Peter O'Brien 2.00 5.00
DCJM Joe Musgrove 2.00 5.00
DCDD David Dahl 2.00 5.00
DCLW Luke Weaver 2.50 6.00
DCMK Max Kepler 2.50 6.00
DCRD Rafael Devers 4.00 10.00
DCGB Greg Bird 2.50 6.00
DCKM Ketel Marte 2.50 6.00
DCRL Reynaldo Lopez 2.50 6.00
DCCJ Carl Edwards Jr. 2.00 5.00

2018 Donruss Dominators

RANDOM INSERTS IN PACKS
STATED PRINT RUN 999 SER.#'d SETS
*CRYSTAL: .5X TO 1.2X BASIC
*SILVER/349: .5X TO 1.2X BASIC
*BLUE/249: .6X TO 1.5X BASIC
*RED/149: .6X TO 1.5X BASIC
*GOLD/99: 1X TO 2.5X BASIC
*GREEN/25: 1.5X TO 4X BASIC
1 Mookie Betts 1.00 2.50
2 Jose Altuve .50 1.25
3 Joey Votto .60 1.50
4 Max Scherzer .60 1.50
5 Justin Verlander .60 1.50
6 Corey Kluber .50 1.25
7 Nolan Arenado .75 2.00
8 Corey Seager .60 1.50
9 Shohei Ohtani 2.50 6.00
10 Mickey Mantle 2.00 5.00

2018 Donruss Elite Series

RANDOM INSERTS IN PACKS
STATED PRINT RUN 999 SER.#'d SETS
*CRYSTAL: .5X TO 1.2X BASIC
*SILVER/349: .5X TO 1.2X BASIC
*BLUE/249: .6X TO 1.5X BASIC
*RED/149: .6X TO 1.5X BASIC
*GOLD/99: 1X TO 2.5X BASIC
*GREEN/25: 1.5X TO 4X BASIC
ES1 Kris Bryant .75 2.00
ES2 Clayton Kershaw 1.25 3.00
ES3 Bryce Harper 1.00 2.50
ES4 Manny Machado .60 1.50
ES5 Carlos Correa .60 1.50
ES6 Trea Turner .50 1.25
ES7 Buster Posey .75 2.00
ES8 Mike Trout 3.00 8.00
ES9 Jose Ramirez .50 1.25
ES10 Paul Goldschmidt .60 1.50

2018 Donruss Foundations

RANDOM INSERTS IN PACKS
STATED PRINT RUN 999 SER.#'d SETS
*CRYSTAL: .5X TO 1.2X BASIC
*SILVER/349: .5X TO 1.2X BASIC
*BLUE/249: .6X TO 1.5X BASIC
*RED/149: .6X TO 1.5X BASIC
*GOLD/99: 1X TO 2.5X BASIC
*GREEN/25: 1.5X TO 4X BASIC
F1 Cody Bellinger 1.25 3.00
F2 Aaron Judge 1.50 4.00
F3 Manny Machado .60 1.50
F4 Mike Trout 3.00 8.00
F5 Mookie Betts 1.00 2.50
F6 Bryce Harper 1.00 2.50
F7 Shohei Ohtani 2.50 6.00
F8 Jose Ramirez .50 1.25
F9 Jose Altuve .50 1.25

2018 Donruss Long Ball Leaders

RANDOM INSERTS IN PACKS
STATED PRINT RUN 999 SER.#'d SETS
*CRYSTAL: .5X TO 1.2X BASIC
*SILVER/349: .5X TO 1.2X BASIC
*BLUE/249: .6X TO 1.5X BASIC
*RED/149: .6X TO 1.5X BASIC
*GOLD/99: 1X TO 2.5X BASIC
*GREEN/25: 1.5X TO 4X BASIC
LBL1 Giancarlo Stanton .60 1.50
LBL2 Aaron Judge 1.50 4.00
LBL3 J.D. Martinez .60 1.50
LBL4 Khris Davis .60 1.50
LBL5 Joey Gallo .50 1.25
LBL6 Cody Bellinger 1.25 3.00
LBL7 Nelson Cruz .60 1.50
LBL8 Logan Morrison .40 1.00
LBL9 Nolan Arenado .75 2.00
LBL10 Justin Smoak .40 1.00

2018 Donruss Mound Marvels

RANDOM INSERTS IN PACKS
STATED PRINT RUN 999 SER.#'d SETS
*CRYSTAL: .5X TO 1.2X BASIC
*SILVER/349: .5X TO 1.2X BASIC
*BLUE/249: .6X TO 1.5X BASIC
*RED/149: .6X TO 1.5X BASIC
*GOLD/99: 1X TO 2.5X BASIC
*GREEN/25: 1.5X TO 4X BASIC
1 Clayton Kershaw 1.25 3.00
2 Max Scherzer .60 1.50
3 Shohei Ohtani 2.50 6.00
4 Corey Kluber .50 1.25
5 Chris Sale .60 1.50
6 Justin Verlander .60 1.50

2018 Donruss Out of this World

RANDOM INSERTS IN PACKS
STATED PRINT RUN 999 SER.#'d SETS
*CRYSTAL: .5X TO 1.2X BASIC
*SILVER/349: .5X TO 1.2X BASIC
*BLUE/249: .6X TO 1.5X BASIC
*RED/149: .6X TO 1.5X BASIC
*GOLD/99: 1X TO 2.5X BASIC
*GREEN/25: 1.5X TO 4X BASIC
OW1 Aaron Judge 1.50 4.00
OW2 Jose Altuve .50 1.25
OW3 Mike Trout 3.00 8.00
OW4 Joey Gallo .50 1.25
OW5 Shohei Ohtani 2.50 6.00
OW6 Giancarlo Stanton .60 1.50
OW7 Mickey Mantle 2.00 5.00
OW8 J.D. Martinez .60 1.50
OW9 Cody Bellinger 1.25 3.00
OW10 Nolan Arenado .75 2.00
OW11 Marcell Ozuna .60 1.50
OW12 Paul Goldschmidt .60 1.50

2018 Donruss Passing the Torch Signatures

RANDOM INSERTS IN PACKS
*BLUE/49: .5X TO 1.2X BASIC
*BLUE/25: .6X TO 1.5X BASIC
*RED/25: .6X TO 1.5X BASIC
1 deGrom/Glavine 20.00 50.00
2 Gonzalez/Bellinger
3 Jackson/Judge 50.00 120.00
4 Brock/Henderson 25.00 60.00
5 Garciaparra/Bogaerts 20.00 50.00
6 Baez/Sandberg 25.00 60.00
7 Griffey Sr/Griffey Jr
9 Sanchez/Posada 40.00 100.00
10 Gonzalez/Mazara 12.00 30.00

2018 Donruss Private Signings

RANDOM INSERTS IN PACKS
STATED PRINT RUN 50 SER.#'d SETS
PSS01 Shohei Ohtani 300.00 600.00
Issued in '18 Donruss
PSS02 Shohei Ohtani 300.00 600.00
Issued in '18 Diamond Kings
PSS03 Shohei Ohtani 300.00 600.00
Issued in '18 Donruss
PSS04 Shohei Ohtani 300.00 600.00
Issued in '18 Diamond Kings

2018 Donruss Promising Pros Materials

RANDOM INSERTS IN PACKS
*GOLD/99: .5X TO 1.2X BASIC
*BLACK/25: .6X TO 1.5X BASIC
PPMJR Jose Rondon 2.00 5.00
PPMMW Mac Williamson 2.00 5.00
PPMDP David Paulino 2.00 5.00
PPMJL Jorge Lopez 2.00 5.00
PPMTT Trayce Thompson 2.50 6.00
PPMTD Tyler Duffey 2.00 5.00
PPMGY Gabriel Ynoa 2.00 5.00
PPMKT Kelby Tomlinson 2.00 5.00
PPMSO Shohei Ohtani 10.00 25.00
PPMCW Christian Walker 2.50 6.00
PPMFM Frankie Montas 2.00 5.00
PPMAF Adam Frazier 2.00 5.00
PPMDA Dariel Alvarez 2.00 5.00
PPMAD Alex Dickerson 2.00 5.00
PPMJL John Lamb 2.00 5.00
PPMPS Pedro Severino 2.00 5.00
PPMED Elias Diaz 2.00 5.00
PPMFM Francis Martes 2.00 5.00
PPMKW Kyle Waldrop 2.00 5.00
PPMBE Brian Ellington 2.00 5.00
PPMBJ Brian Johnson 2.00 5.00
PPMDR Daniel Robertson 2.00 5.00
PPMLJ Luke Jackson 2.00 5.00
PPMEG Erik Gonzalez 2.00 5.00
PPMAM Adalberto Mejia 2.00 5.00

2018 Donruss Promising Pros Materials Signatures

RANDOM INSERTS IN PACKS
*GOLD/25: .75X TO 2X BASIC
PPMSAF Adam Frazier 3.00 8.00
PPMSBJ Brian Johnson 3.00 8.00
PPMSDR Daniel Robertson 3.00 8.00
PPMSJM Joe Musgrove 3.00 8.00
PPMSMM Manuel Margot 3.00 8.00
PPMSSO Shohei Ohtani 200.00 400.00
PPMSBS Braden Shipley 3.00 8.00
PPMSPS Pedro Severino 3.00 8.00
PPMSTT Trayce Thompson 4.00 10.00
PPMSTD Tyler Duffey 3.00 8.00

2018 Donruss Rated Prospects Signatures

RANDOM INSERTS IN PACKS
STATED PRINT RUN 50 SER.#'d SETS
1 Shohei Ohtani 300.00 600.00
2 Shohei Ohtani 300.00 600.00

2018 Donruss Recollection Buyback Autographs

RANDOM INSERTS IN PACKS
PRINT RUNS B/WN 1-50 COPIES PER
NO PRICING ON QTY 18 OR LESS
TBA3 Adam Duvall/25 6.00 15.00
TBA11 Matt Carpenter/50 5.00 12.00
TBA12 Matt Carpenter/50 5.00 12.00
TBA21 Odubel Herrera/25 5.00 12.00
TBA22 Wil Myers/23 4.00 10.00
TBA23 Wil Myers/25 4.00 10.00

2018 Donruss Signature Series

RANDOM INSERTS IN PACKS
*BLUE/99: .5X TO 1.2X BASIC
*RED/25: .6X TO 1.5X BASIC
1 Anthony Banda 2.50 6.00
SSMF Max Fried 10.00 25.00
SSOA Ozzie Albies 10.00 25.00
5 Lucas Sims 2.50 6.00
6 Austin Hays 4.00 10.00
SSCS Chance Sisco 3.00 8.00
8 Anthony Santander 4.00 10.00
SSRD Rafael Devers 12.00 30.00
10 Victor Caratini 3.00 8.00
11 Nicky Delmonico 2.50 6.00
12 Tyler Mahle 3.00 8.00
13 Francisco Mejia 6.00 15.00
14 Greg Allen 2.50 6.00
15 Ryan McMahon 3.00 8.00
16 J.D. Davis 3.00 8.00
17 Cameron Gallagher 2.50 6.00
SSWB Walker Buehler 15.00 40.00
SSAV Alex Verdugo 6.00 15.00
20 Kyle Farmer 4.00 10.00
21 Brian Anderson 3.00 8.00
22 Dillon Peters 2.50 6.00
23 Brandon Woodruff 3.00 8.00
24 Mitch Garver 2.50 6.00
25 Zack Granite 4.00 10.00
26 Felix Jorge 2.50 6.00
27 Tomas Nido 4.00 10.00
28 Dominic Smith 2.50 6.00
29 Chris Flexen 2.50 6.00
SSAR Amed Rosario 6.00 15.00
SSCL Clint Frazier 5.00 12.00
SSMA Miguel Andujar 8.00 20.00
33 Tyler Wade 3.00 8.00
34 Dustin Fowler 2.50 6.00
35 Paul Blackburn 2.50 6.00
36 J.P. Crawford 2.50 6.00
37 Nick Williams 3.00 8.00
38 Rhys Hoskins 15.00 40.00
39 Thyago Vieira 2.50 6.00
40 Reyes Moronta 2.50 6.00
41 Jack Flaherty 4.00 10.00
42 Harrison Bader 4.00 10.00
43 Willie Calhoun 3.00 8.00
44 Richard Urena 2.50 6.00
45 Victor Robles 5.00 12.00
46 Erick Fedde 2.50 6.00
47 Andrew Stevenson 2.50 6.00
48 Jimmie Sherfy 2.50 6.00
49 Shohei Ohtani 150.00 300.00
50 Jose Abreu 5.00 12.00

2018 Donruss Significant Signatures

RANDOM INSERTS IN PACKS
*BLUE/49-99: .5X TO 1.2X BASIC
*BLUE/25: .6X TO 1.5X BASIC
*RED/25: .6X TO 1.5X BASIC
1 Wade Boggs 8.00 20.00
2 Ivan Rodriguez 8.00 20.00
3 Willie McGee 8.00 20.00
4 Fergie Jenkins 6.00 15.00
5 Tony La Russa 3.00 8.00
6 Jerry Koosman 6.00 15.00
7 Frank Thomas 25.00 60.00
8 Alan Trammell 10.00 25.00
9 Paul Molitor 8.00 20.00
10 Jeff Bagwell 10.00 25.00
11 George Brett 100.00 250.00
12 Cal Ripken
13 Gary Sheffield 4.00 10.00
14 Pete Rose 12.00 30.00
15 Dwight Gooden 10.00 25.00

2018 Donruss Signing Day Signatures

RANDOM INSERTS IN PACKS
STATED PRINT RUN 50 SER.#'d SETS
1 Shohei Ohtani 300.00 600.00

2018 Donruss The Famous San Diego Chicken Dual Material

RANDOM INSERTS IN PACKS
STATED PRINT RUN 84 SER.#'d SETS
1 Ted Giannoulas 20.00 50.00

2018 Donruss The Famous San Diego Chicken Dual Material Signatures

RANDOM INSERTS IN PACKS
STATED PRINT RUN 84 SER.#'d SETS
1 Ted Giannoulas 50.00 120.00

2018 Donruss Whammy

RANDOM INSERTS IN PACKS
1 Mickey Mantle 20.00 50.00
2 Shohei Ohtani 50.00 120.00
3 Rhys Hoskins 12.00 30.00
4 Aaron Judge 25.00 60.00
5 Cody Bellinger 8.00 20.00

2019 Donruss

1 Mookie Betts DK 1.00 2.50
2 Aaron Judge DK 1.50 4.00
3 Blake Snell DK .50 1.25
4 Justin Smoak DK .40 1.00
5 Adam Jones DK .50 1.25
6 Jose Ramirez DK .50 1.25
7 Jose Berrios DK .50 1.25
8 Nicholas Castellanos DK .60 1.50
9 Yoan Moncada DK .60 1.50
10 Whit Merrifield DK .60 1.50
11 Alex Bregman DK .60 1.50
12 Matt Chapman DK .60 1.50
13 Mitch Haniger DK .50 1.25
14 Shohei Ohtani DK .75 2.00
15 Jurickson Profar DK .50 1.25
16 Ronald Acuna Jr. DK 3.00 8.00
17 Max Scherzer DK .60 1.50
18 Aaron Nola DK .50 1.25
19 Jacob deGrom DK .60 1.50
20 J.T. Realmuto DK .60 1.50
21 Christian Yelich DK .75 2.00
22 Javier Baez DK .75 2.00
23 Matt Carpenter DK .60 1.50
24 Starling Marte DK .50 1.25
25 Eugenio Suarez DK .50 1.25
26 Max Muncy DK .50 1.25
27 Trevor Story DK .60 1.50
28 Paul Goldschmidt DK .60 1.50
29 Brandon Crawford DK .50 1.25
30 Hunter Renfroe DK .40 1.00
31 Cedric Mullins RR RC .60 1.50
32 Christin Stewart RR RC .50 1.25
33 Corbin Burnes RR RC .60 1.50
34 Dakota Hudson RR RC .50 1.25
35 Danny Jansen RR RC .40 1.00
36 David Fletcher RR RC 1.25 3.00
37 Dennis Santana RR RC .40 1.00
38 Garrett Hampson RR RC .40 1.00
39 Jake Bauers RR RC .60 1.50
40 Jeff McNeil RR RC 1.00 2.50
41 Jonathan Loaisiga RR RC .50 1.25
42 Justus Sheffield RR RC .60 1.50
43 Kyle Tucker RR RC .75 2.00
44 Kyle Wright RR RC .60 1.50
45 Luis Urias RR RC .60 1.50
46 Michael Kopech RR RC .75 2.00
47 Ramon Laureano RR RC .75 2.00
48 Ryan O'Hearn RR RC .40 1.00
49 Steven Duggar RR RC .50 1.25
50 Touki Toussaint RR RC .50 1.25
51 Chris Sale .25 .60
52 Stephen Strasburg .25 .60
53 Cody Bellinger .50 1.25
54 David Peralta .15 .40
55 Jose Ramirez .20 .50
56 Brandon Nimmo .20 .50
57 Kris Bryant .30 .75
58 Nicholas Castellanos .25 .60
59 Ryan Yarbrough .15 .40
60 Whit Merrifield .25 .60
61 Juan Soto .75 2.00
62 J.D. Martinez .25 .60
63 Michael Brantley .20 .50
64 Jose Abreu .25 .60
65 George Springer .20 .50
66 Sean Manaea .15 .40
67 Brandon Belt .20 .50
68 Francisco Lindor .25 .60
69 Jaime Barria .15 .40
70 Jose Altuve .20 .50
71 Adam Jones .20 .50
72 Chris Archer .15 .40
73 Wade Davis .15 .40
74 Andrelton Simmons .15 .40
75 A.J. Pollock .15 .40
76 Andrew Benintendi .25 .60
77 Blake Treinen .15 .40
78 Carlos Correa .25 .60
79 Odubel Herrera .20 .50
80 Adrian Beltre .25 .60
81 Yadier Molina .25 .60
82 Austin Meadows .20 .50
83 Joey Wendle .15 .40
84 Felix Hernandez .20 .50
85 Edwin Diaz .20 .50
86 Corey Kluber .20 .50
87 Ronald Acuna Jr. 1.25 3.00
88 Clayton Kershaw .50 1.25
89 Albert Pujols .30 .75
90 Miles Mikolas .25 .60
91 Josh Donaldson .20 .50
92 David Wright .20 .50
93 Francisco Mejia .20 .50
94 Jeremy Jeffress .15 .40
95 Justin Turner .20 .50
96 Mallex Smith .15 .40
97 Justin Smoak .15 .40
98 Kyle Schwarber .25 .60
99 Matt Olson .15 .40
100 Miguel Cabrera .25 .60
101 Mookie Betts .40 1.00
102 Trevor Williams .15 .40
103 Eddie Rosario .20 .50
104 Rhys Hoskins .30 .75
105 J.T. Realmuto .25 .60
106 Adalberto Mondesi .20 .50
107 Shane Bieber .25 .60
108 Jon Lester .20 .50
109 Nick Williams .15 .40
110 Luis Severino .20 .50
111 Franmil Reyes .15 .40
112 Joey Gallo .20 .50
113 Yoan Moncada .25 .60
114 Jose Urena .15 .40
115 Hunter Renfroe .15 .40
116 Max Scherzer .25 .60
117 Sean Newcomb .15 .40
118 Mike Minor .15 .40
119 Starling Marte .20 .50
120 Manny Machado .25 .60
121 Aaron Judge .60 1.50
122 Robinson Cano .20 .50
123 Jacob deGrom .25 .60
124 Eugenio Suarez .20 .50
125 Nomar Mazara .15 .40
126 Kyle Freeland .20 .50
127 Miguel Sano .20 .50
128 Rafael Devers .30 .75
129 Miguel Andujar .25 .60
130 Nelson Cruz .25 .60
131 Charlie Blackmon .25 .60
132 Jose Berrios .20 .50
133 Walker Buehler .30 .75
134 Tyler O'Neill .20 .50
135 Mike Foltynewicz .25 .60
136 Noah Syndergaard .20 .50
137 Scooter Gennett .20 .50
138 David Bote .20 .50
139 Zack Greinke .20 .50
140 Kevin Pillar .15 .40

141 Trea Turner .20 .50
142 Carlos Rodon .20 .50
143 Willy Adames .15 .40
144 Jose Martinez .15 .40
145 Aaron Nola .20 .50
146 Mitch Haniger .20 .50
147 Freddy Peralta .25 .60
148 Joey Votto .25 .60
149 Ji-Man Choi .15 .40
150 Willie Calhoun .15 .40
151 Carlos Carrasco .15 .40
152 Paul Goldschmidt .25 .60
153 Trey Mancini .20 .50
154 Madison Bumgarner .20 .50
155 Amed Rosario .20 .50
156 Ozzie Albies .25 .60
157 Gleyber Torres .50 1.25
158 Wilson Ramos .15 .40
159 Brandon Crawford .20 .50
160 Andrew Heaney .15 .40
161 James Paxton .20 .50
162 Gerrit Cole .25 .60
163 Giancarlo Stanton .25 .60
164 Shohei Ohtani .30 .75
165 Javier Baez .30 .75
166 Jesus Aguilar .15 .40
167 Jackie Bradley Jr. .20 .50
168 Hunter Pence .20 .50
169 Khris Davis .25 .60
170 Mike Trout 1.25 3.00
171 Matt Carpenter .25 .60
172 Justin Verlander .25 .60
173 Brian Anderson .15 .40
174 Victor Robles .30 .75
175 Freddie Freeman .30 .75
176 Jack Flaherty .20 .50
177 Nick Markakis .20 .50
178 Dereck Rodriguez .15 .40
179 Salvador Perez .20 .50
180 Anthony Rendon .25 .60
181 Blake Snell .20 .50
182 Alex Bregman .25 .60
183 Bryce Harper .40 1.00
184 Lorenzo Cain .15 .40
185 Trevor Story .25 .60
186 Mike Moustakas .20 .50
187 Anthony Rizzo .40 1.00
188 Jameson Taillon .20 .50
189 Edwin Encarnacion .25 .60
190 Christian Yelich .30 .75
191 Michael Conforto .20 .50
192 Matt Chapman .25 .60
193 Teoscar Hernandez .25 .60
194 Eric Hosmer .20 .50
195 German Marquez .15 .40
196 Jeimer Candelario .15 .40
197 Xander Bogaerts .25 .60
198 Sandy Alcantara .15 .40
199 Harrison Bader .20 .50
200 Nolan Arenado .30 .75
201 Trevor Richards RETRO RC .40 1.00
202 Hoby Milner RETRO RC .40 1.00
203 Pablo Lopez RETRO RC .40 1.00
204 Trevor Oaks RETRO .15 .40
205 Grayson Greiner RETRO .15 .40
206 Johan Camargo RETRO .15 .40
207 Fernando Romero RETRO .15 .40
208 Heath Fillmyer RETRO RC .40 1.00
209 Tanner Rainey RETRO RC .40 1.00
210 Albert Almora Jr. RETRO RC .50 1.25
211 Max Muncy RETRO .20 .50
212 Arodys Vizcaino RETRO .15 .40
213 Daniel Palka RETRO .15 .40
214 Patrick Corbin RETRO .20 .50
215 Justin Williams RETRO RC .40 1.00
216 Taylor Ward RETRO RC .40 1.00
217 Kevin Newman RETRO RC .60 1.50
218 Stephen Gonsalves RETRO RC .40 1.00
219 Sean Reid-Foley RETRO RC .40 1.00
220 Kevin Kramer RETRO RC .50 1.25
221 Jonathan Davis RETRO RC .50 1.25
222 Daniel Ponce de Leon RETRO RC .60 1.50
223 Josh James RETRO RC .60 1.50
224 Jacob Nix RETRO RC .50 1.25
225 Patrick Wisdom RETRO RC .40 1.00
226 Brad Keller RETRO RC .40 1.00
227 Ryan Borucki RETRO RC .40 1.00
228 Luis Ortiz RETRO RC .40 1.00
229 Jake Cave RETRO RC .50 1.25
230 Kolby Allard RETRO RC .60 1.50
231 Framber Valdez RETRO RC .40 1.00
232 Brandon Lowe RETRO RC .60 1.50
233 Cionel Perez RETRO RC .40 1.00
234 Myles Straw RETRO RC .60 1.50
235 Reese McGuire RETRO RC .60 1.50
236 Enyel De Los Santos RETRO RC .40 1.00
237 Chris Shaw RETRO RC .60 1.50
238 Bryse Wilson RETRO RC .60 1.50
239 Rowdy Tellez RETRO RC .60 1.50
240 Chance Adams RETRO RC .40 1.00
241 Williams Astudillo RETRO RC .40 1.00
242 Kyle Gibson RETRO .20 .50
243 Matt Boyd RETRO .15 .40
244 Luke Voit RETRO .40 1.00
245 Caleb Ferguson RETRO RC .50 1.25
246 Eric Haase RETRO RC .40 1.00
247 Brett Kennedy RETRO RC .40 1.00
248 Ryan Meisinger RETRO RC .40 1.00
249 Nick Martini RETRO RC .40 1.00
250 Julio Urias RETRO .25 .60
251 Domingo Ayala FOIL 15.00 40.00
252 Yusei Kikuchi RR RC .60 1.50
253 Chris Paddack RR RC .75 2.00
254 Fernando Tatis Jr. RR RC 4.00 10.00
255 Pete Alonso RR RC 3.00 8.00
256 Vladimir Guerrero Jr. RR RC 2.50 6.00
257 Eloy Jimenez RR RC 1.50 4.00
258 Jon Duplantier RR RC .40 1.00
259 Carter Kieboom RR RC .60 1.50
260 Nick Senzel RR RC 1.25 3.00
261 Michael Chavis RR RC .60 1.50
262 Nathaniel Lowe RR RC .50 1.25

2019 Donruss 150th Anniversary

*150TH DK: 1X TO 2.5X BASIC
*150TH RR: 1X TO 2.5X BASIC
*150TH VET: 2.5X TO 6X BASIC
*150TH RET: 2.5X TO 6X BASIC
RANDOM INSERTS IN PACKS
STATED PRINT RUN 150 SER.#'d SETS

2019 Donruss 42 Tribute

*42 DK: 1.2X TO 3X BASIC
*42 RR: 1.2X TO 3X BASIC
*42 VET: 3X TO 8X BASIC
*42 RET: 3X TO 8X BASIC
RANDOM INSERTS IN PACKS
STATED PRINT RUN 42 SER.#'d SETS

2019 Donruss Career Stat Line

*CAR DK p/r 154-500: .75X TO 2X BASIC
*CAR RR p/r 154-500: .75X TO 2X BASIC
*CAR p/r 154-500: 2X TO 5X BASIC
*CAR DK p/r 100-146: 1X TO 2.5X BASIC
*CAR RR p/r 100-146: 1X TO 2.5X BASIC
*CAR p/r 100-146: 2.5X TO 6X BASIC
*CAR DK p/r 26-96: 1.2X TO 3X BASIC
*CAR RR p/r 26-96: 1.2X TO 3X BASIC
*CAR p/r 26-96: 3X TO 8X BASIC
*CAR DK p/r 20-25: 2X TO 5X BASIC
*CAR RR p/r 20-25: 2X TO 5X BASIC
*CAR p/r 20-25: 5X TO 12X BASIC
RANDOM INSERTS IN PACKS
PRINT RUNS B/WN 10-500 COPIES PER
NO PRICING ON QTY 19 OR LESS

2019 Donruss Father's Day Ribbon

*FD DK: 1.2X TO 3X BASIC
*FD RR: 1.2X TO 3X BASIC
*FD VET: 3X TO 8X BASIC
*FD RET: 3X TO 8X BASIC
RANDOM INSERTS IN PACKS
STATED PRINT RUN 49 SER.#'d SETS

2019 Donruss Holo Back

*HOLO BK DK: 1.2X TO 3X BASIC
*HOLO BK RR: 1.2X TO 3X BASIC
*HOLO BK VET: 3X TO 8X BASIC
*HOLO BK RET: 3X TO 8X BASIC
RANDOM INSERTS IN PACKS
STATED PRINT RUN 99 SER.#'d SETS

2019 Donruss Holo Orange

*HOLO ORNG RR: .5X TO 1.2X BASIC
*HOLO ORNG VET: 1.2X TO 3X BASIC
*HOLO ORNG RET: 1.2X TO 3X BASIC
RANDOM INSERTS IN PACKS

2019 Donruss Holo Pink

*HOLO PINK RR: .5X TO 1.2X BASIC
*HOLO PINK VET: 1.2X TO 3X BASIC
*HOLO PINK RET: 1.2X TO 3X BASIC
RANDOM INSERTS IN PACKS

2019 Donruss Holo Purple

*HOLO PRPL RR: .5X TO 1.2X BASIC
*HOLO PRPL VET: 1.2X TO 3X BASIC
*HOLO PRPL RET: 1.2X TO 3X BASIC
RANDOM INSERTS IN PACKS

2019 Donruss Holo Red

*HOLO RED RR: .5X TO 1.2X BASIC
*HOLO RED VET: 1.2X TO 3X BASIC
*HOLO RED RET: 1.2X TO 3X BASIC
RANDOM INSERTS IN PACKS

2019 Donruss Independence Day

*IND DAY RR: .5X TO 1.2X BASIC
*IND DAY DK: .5X TO 1.2X BASIC
*IND DAY VET: 1.2X TO 3X BASIC
*IND DAY RET: 1.2X TO 3X BASIC
RANDOM INSERTS IN PACKS

2019 Donruss Mother's Day Ribbon

*MD DK: 2X TO 5X BASIC
*MD RR: 2X TO 5X BASIC
*MD VET: 5X TO 12X BASIC
*MD RET: 5X TO 12X BASIC
RANDOM INSERTS IN PACKS
STATED PRINT RUN 25 SER.#'d SETS

2019 Donruss Season Stat Line

*SEA DK p/r 154-500: .75X TO 2X BASIC
*SEA RR p/r 154-500: .75X TO 2X BASIC
*SEA p/r 154-500: 2X TO 5X BASIC
*SEA DK p/r 100-149: 1X TO 2.5X BASIC
*SEA RR p/r 100-149: 1X TO 2.5X BASIC
*SEA p/r 100-149: 2.5X TO 6X BASIC
*SEA RR p/r 26-99: 1.2X TO 3X BASIC
*SEA RR p/r 26-99: 1.2X TO 3X BASIC
*SEA p/r 26-99: 3X TO 8X BASIC
*SEA DK p/r 20-25: 2X TO 5X BASIC
*SEA RR p/r 20-25: 2X TO 5X BASIC
*SEA p/r 20-25: 5X TO 12X BASIC
RANDOM INSERTS IN PACKS
PRINT RUNS B/WN 4-500 COPIES PER
NO PRICING ON QTY 19 OR LESS

2019 Donruss Variations

RANDOM INSERTS IN PACKS
*ID VAR: .5X TO 1.2X BASIC
*CAR p/r 156-500: .75X TO 2X BASIC
*CAR p/r 107-144: 1X TO 2.5X BASIC
*CAR p/r 27-93: 1.2X TO 3X BASIC
*CAR p/r 22-25: 2X TO 5X BASIC
*SEA p/r 151-500: .75X TO 2X BASIC
*SEA p/r 101-147: 1X TO 2.5X BASIC
*SEA p/r 27-96: 1.2X TO 3X BASIC
*SEA p/r 20-24: 2X TO 5X BASIC
*150 VAR/150: 1X TO 2.5X BASIC
*HOLO BCK VAR/99: 1.2X TO 3X BASIC
*FD VAR/49: 1.2X TO 3X BASIC
*42 VAR/42: 1.2X TO 3X BASIC
*MD VAR/25: 2X TO 5X BASIC
51 Chris Sale .60 1.50
55 Jose Ramirez .50 1.25
57 Kris Bryant .75 2.00
61 Juan Soto 2.00 5.00
62 J.D. Martinez .60 1.50
68 Francisco Lindor .60 1.50
70 Jose Altuve .50 1.25
76 Andrew Benintendi .60 1.50
80 Adrian Beltre .60 1.50
81 Yadier Molina .60 1.50
82 Austin Meadows .50 1.25
86 Corey Kluber .50 1.25
87 Ronald Acuna Jr. 3.00 8.00
90 Miles Mikolas .60 1.50
101 Mookie Betts 1.00 2.50
104 Rhys Hoskins .75 2.00
105 J.T. Realmuto .60 1.50
121 Aaron Judge 1.50 4.00
123 Jacob deGrom .60 1.50
126 Kyle Freeland .50 1.25
128 Rafael Devers .75 2.00
129 Miguel Andujar .60 1.50
133 Walker Buehler .75 2.00
145 Aaron Nola .50 1.25
152 Paul Goldschmidt .60 1.50
156 Ozzie Albies .60 1.50
157 Gleyber Torres 1.25 3.00
164 Shohei Ohtani .75 2.00
165 Javier Baez .75 2.00
166 Jesus Aguilar .40 1.00
170 Mike Trout 3.00 8.00
172 Justin Verlander .60 1.50
179 Salvador Perez .50 1.25
181 Blake Snell .50 1.25
182 Alex Bregman .60 1.50
183 Bryce Harper 1.00 2.50
185 Trevor Story .60 1.50
187 Anthony Rizzo 1.00 2.50
190 Christian Yelich .75 2.00
192 Matt Chapman .60 1.50
201 Trevor Richards RETRO .40 1.00
207 Fernando Romero RETRO .40 1.00
211 Max Muncy RETRO .50 1.25
213 Daniel Palka RETRO .40 1.00
215 Justin Williams RETRO .40 1.00
218 Stephen Gonsalves RETRO .40 1.00
223 Josh James RETRO .60 1.50
232 Brandon Lowe RETRO .60 1.50
239 Rowdy Tellez RETRO .60 1.50
244 Luke Voit RETRO 1.00 2.50

2019 Donruss '85 Retro Materials

RANDOM INSERTS IN PACKS
*GOLD/25-99: .5X TO 1.2X BASIC
1 Justin Verlander 2.50 6.00
2 Andrew McCutchen 2.50 6.00
3 Marcell Ozuna 2.50 6.00
4 Daniel Murphy 2.00 5.00
5 Christian Yelich 3.00 8.00
6 Gerrit Cole 2.50 6.00
7 Giancarlo Stanton 2.50 6.00
8 Lorenzo Cain 1.50 4.00
9 Mike Moustakas 2.00 5.00
10 Stephen Piscotty 1.50 4.00
11 Manny Machado 2.50 6.00
12 Nick Markakis 2.00 5.00
13 Starlin Castro 1.50 4.00
14 Eric Hosmer 2.00 5.00
15 Dee Gordon 1.50 4.00
16 Adrian Beltre 2.50 6.00
17 Adrian Gonzalez 2.00 5.00
18 Ian Desmond 1.50 4.00
19 Didi Gregorius 2.00 5.00
20 Tommy Pham 1.50 4.00
21 Albert Pujols 3.00 8.00
22 Chris Sale 2.50 6.00
23 J.A. Happ 2.00 5.00
24 Cole Hamels 2.00 5.00
25 Miguel Cabrera 2.50 6.00

2019 Donruss '85 Retro Rated Rookies Signatures

RANDOM INSERTS IN PACKS
EXCHANGE DEADLINE 09/06/2020
1 Yusei Kikuchi EXCH 15.00 100.00

2019 Donruss '85 Retro Signatures

RANDOM INSERTS IN PACKS
EXCHANGE DEADLINE 09/06/2020
*BLUE/49-99: .5X TO 1.2X BASIC
*BLUE/25: .75X TO 2X BASIC
*RED/25: .75X TO 2X BASIC
1 Aaron Judge EXCH 50.00 120.00
2 Anthony Rizzo 10.00 25.00
3 Ichiro 125.00 300.00
4 Clint Frazier 3.00 8.00
5 David Ortiz 30.00 80.00
6 Eddie Murray 12.00 30.00
7 Gary Sanchez 12.00 30.00
8 Rhys Hoskins 10.00 25.00
9 Trea Turner 8.00 20.00
10 Ivan Rodriguez 10.00 25.00
11 Cody Bellinger 12.00 30.00
12 Yoan Moncada 6.00 15.00
14 Phil Niekro 3.00 8.00
15 Ozzie Smith 20.00 50.00
16 Pedro Martinez 12.00 30.00
17 Roger Clemens 12.00 30.00
18 Dwight Gooden 6.00 15.00
19 Willie McGee 6.00 15.00
20 Don Mattingly 25.00 60.00

2019 Donruss Action All-Stars

RANDOM INSERTS IN PACKS
STATED PRINT RUN 999 SER.#'d SETS
*BRONZE/349: .5X TO 1.2X BASIC
*DIAMOND: .5X TO 1.2X BASIC
*PINK: .6X TO 1.5X BASIC
*BLUE/249: .6X TO 1.5X BASIC
*RAPTURE: .6X TO 1.5X BASIC
*RED/149: .6X TO 1.5X BASIC
*VECTOR: .6X TO 1.5X BASIC
*GOLD/99: 1X TO 2.5X BASIC
*GREEN/25: 1.5X TO 4X BASIC
1 Jose Altuve .50 1.25
2 Aaron Judge 1.50 4.00
3 Mike Trout 3.00 8.00
4 Shohei Ohtani .75 2.00
5 Mookie Betts 1.00 2.50
6 Clayton Kershaw 1.25 3.00
7 Kris Bryant .75 2.00
8 Bryce Harper 1.00 2.50
9 Khris Davis .60 1.50
10 Manny Machado .60 1.50
11 Charlie Blackmon .60 1.50
12 Ronald Acuna Jr. 3.00 8.00
13 Christian Yelich .75 2.00
14 J.D. Martinez .60 1.50
15 Francisco Lindor .60 1.50

2019 Donruss American Pride

RANDOM INSERTS IN PACKS
STATED PRINT RUN 999 SER.#'d SETS
*BRONZE/349: .5X TO 1.2X BASIC
*DIAMOND: .5X TO 1.2X BASIC
*PINK: .6X TO 1.5X BASIC
*BLUE/249: .6X TO 1.5X BASIC
*RAPTURE: .6X TO 1.5X BASIC
*RED/149: .6X TO 1.5X BASIC
*VECTOR: .6X TO 1.5X BASIC
*GOLD/99: 1X TO 2.5X BASIC
*GREEN/25: 1.5X TO 4X BASIC
1 Daniel Cabrera 1.50 4.00
2 Will Wilson .60 1.50
3 Braden Shewmake 1.25 3.00
4 John Doxakis .60 1.50
5 Bryson Stott 1.25 3.00
6 Andrew Vaughn 1.25 3.00
7 Mason Feole .40 1.00
8 Shea Langeliers .75 2.00
9 Spencer Torkelson 5.00 12.00
10 Josh Jung 1.25 3.00
11 Bryant Packard .60 1.50
12 Jake Agnos .60 1.50
13 Andre Pallante .50 1.25
14 Dominic Fletcher .40 1.00
15 Adley Rutschman 2.50 6.00
16 Graeme Stinson .40 1.00
17 Matt Cronin .40 1.00
18 Max Meyer 1.25 3.00
19 Kenyon Yovan .40 1.00
20 Tanner Burns .60 1.50
21 Drew Parrish .40 1.00
22 Kyle Brnovich .40 1.00
23 Zack Hess .40 1.00
24 Zach Watson .60 1.50
25 Zack Thompson .60 1.50
26 Parker Caracci .40 1.00

2019 Donruss Bleachers Inc. Autographs

RANDOM INSERTS IN PACKS
EXCHANGE DEADLINE 09/06/2020
*BLUE/49-99: .5X TO 1.2X BASIC
*RED/25: .75X TO 2X BASIC
1 Shohei Ohtani 75.00 200.00
2 Aaron Judge 40.00 100.00
3 Mike Soroka 4.00 10.00
4 Harrison Bader 3.00 8.00
5 Nick Williams 2.50 6.00
6 Dustin Fowler 2.50 6.00
7 Brian Anderson 2.50 6.00
8 J.D. Davis 2.50 6.00
9 Luiz Gohara 2.50 6.00
10 Anthony Banda 2.50 6.00
11 Willy Adames 2.50 6.00
12 Erick Fedde 2.50 6.00
13 Mitch Garver 2.50 6.00
14 Rhys Hoskins 12.00 30.00
15 Billy McKinney 2.50 6.00

2019 Donruss Dominators

RANDOM INSERTS IN PACKS
STATED PRINT RUN 999 SER.#'d SETS
*BRONZE/349: .5X TO 1.2X BASIC
*DIAMOND: .5X TO 1.2X BASIC
*PINK: .6X TO 1.5X BASIC
*BLUE/249: .6X TO 1.5X BASIC
*RAPTURE: .6X TO 1.5X BASIC
*RED/149: .6X TO 1.5X BASIC
*VECTOR: .6X TO 1.5X BASIC
*GOLD/99: 1X TO 2.5X BASIC
*GREEN/25: 1.5X TO 4X BASIC
1 Mike Trout 3.00 8.00
2 J.D. Martinez .60 1.50
3 Jacob deGrom .60 1.50
4 Manny Machado .60 1.50
5 Trevor Story .60 1.50
6 Alex Bregman .60 1.50
7 Miguel Andujar .60 1.50
8 Jose Ramirez .50 1.25
9 Freddie Freeman .75 2.00
10 Blake Snell .50 1.25

2019 Donruss Elite Series

RANDOM INSERTS IN PACKS
STATED PRINT RUN 999 SER.#'d SETS
*BRONZE/349: .5X TO 1.2X BASIC
*DIAMOND: .5X TO 1.2X BASIC
*PINK: .6X TO 1.5X BASIC
*BLUE/249: .6X TO 1.5X BASIC
*RAPTURE: .6X TO 1.5X BASIC
*RED/149: .6X TO 1.5X BASIC
*VECTOR: .6X TO 1.5X BASIC
*GOLD/99: 1.2X TO 3X BASIC
*GREEN/25: 2X TO 5X BASIC
1 Ronald Acuna Jr. 5.00 12.00
2 Shohei Ohtani 1.25 3.00
3 Christian Yelich 1.25 3.00
4 Gleyber Torres 2.00 5.00
5 Juan Soto 3.00 8.00
6 Javier Baez 1.25 3.00
7 Mookie Betts 1.50 4.00
8 Nolan Arenado 1.25 3.00
9 Francisco Lindor 1.00 2.50
10 Mike Trout 5.00 12.00

2019 Donruss Franchise Features

RANDOM INSERTS IN PACKS
STATED PRINT RUN 999 SER.#'d SETS
*BRONZE/349: .5X TO 1.2X BASIC
*DIAMOND: .5X TO 1.2X BASIC
*PINK: .6X TO 1.5X BASIC
*BLUE/249: .6X TO 1.5X BASIC
*RAPTURE: .6X TO 1.5X BASIC
*RED/149: .6X TO 1.5X BASIC
*VECTOR: .6X TO 1.5X BASIC
*GOLD/99: 1X TO 2.5X BASIC
*GREEN/25: 1.5X TO 4X BASIC
1 Arenado/Guerrero Jr. 2.50 6.00
2 Lindor/Tatis Jr. 4.00 10.00
3 Ozuna/Jimenez 1.50 4.00
4 Bryant/Senzel 1.25 3.00
5 Carlos Correa .75 2.00
Royce Lewis
6 Forrest Whitley .60 1.50
Justin Verlander
7 Corey Seager .60 1.50
Brendan Rodgers
8 Bo Bichette 1.25 3.00
Trevor Story
9 Turner/Franco 6.00 15.00
10 Judge/Kiriloff 1.50 4.00
11 Corey Kluber .50 1.25
Mitch Keller
12 Max Scherzer .60 1.50
Brent Honeywell
13 Rizzo/McKay 1.00 2.50
14 Puk/Kershaw 1.25 3.00
15 Adell/Trout 3.00 8.00
16 Posey/Bart 1.25 3.00
17 Goldschmidt/Alonso 3.00 8.00
18 Charlie Blackmon .60 1.50
Leody Taveras
19 deGrom/Duplantier .60 1.50
20 Altuve/Madrigal 1.25 3.00
21 George Springer .60 1.50
Estevan Florial

2019 Donruss Highlights

RANDOM INSERTS IN PACKS
STATED PRINT RUN 999 SER.#'d SETS
*BRONZE/349: .5X TO 1.2X BASIC
*DIAMOND: .5X TO 1.2X BASIC
*PINK: .6X TO 1.5X BASIC
*BLUE/249: .6X TO 1.5X BASIC
*RAPTURE: .6X TO 1.5X BASIC
*RED/149: .6X TO 1.5X BASIC
*VECTOR: .6X TO 1.5X BASIC
*GOLD/99: 1X TO 2.5X BASIC
*GREEN/25: 1.5X TO 4X BASIC
1 Shohei Ohtani .75 2.00
2 Albert Pujols .75 2.00
3 Sean Manaea .40 1.00
4 James Paxton .50 1.25
5 Max Scherzer .60 1.50
6 George Springer .50 1.25
7 Christian Yelich .75 2.00
8 Juan Soto 2.00 5.00
9 Mookie Betts 1.00 2.50
10 Jose Ramirez .50 1.25
11 Brock Holt .40 1.00
12 Walker Buehler .75 2.00

2019 Donruss Majestic Materials

RANDOM INSERTS IN PACKS
*GOLD/30-99: .5X TO 1.2X BASIC
1 Aaron Judge 8.00 20.00
2 Ronald Acuna Jr. 5.00 12.00
3 Juan Soto 4.00 10.00
4 Gleyber Torres 3.00 8.00
5 Ozzie Albies 2.50 6.00
6 Rhys Hoskins 3.00 8.00
7 Shohei Ohtani 5.00 12.00
8 Harrison Bader 2.00 5.00
9 Walker Buehler 3.00 8.00
10 Ryan McMahon 1.50 4.00
11 Jordan Hicks 2.00 5.00
12 Rafael Devers 3.00 8.00
13 Ronald Guzman 1.50 4.00
14 Austin Hays 2.50 6.00
15 Clint Frazier 2.00 5.00
16 Miguel Andujar 2.50 6.00
17 Jose Altuve 2.00 5.00
18 Victor Robles 3.00 8.00
19 Willy Adames 1.50 4.00
20 David Bote 2.00 5.00
21 Mike Trout 10.00 25.00
22 Khris Davis 2.50 6.00
23 Nolan Arenado 3.00 8.00
24 Christian Yelich 3.00 8.00
25 Alex Bregman 2.50 6.00
26 Trevor Story 2.50 6.00
27 Mookie Betts 4.00 10.00
28 Javier Baez 3.00 8.00
29 Jose Ramirez 2.00 5.00
30 Matt Olson 1.50 4.00
31 Jacob deGrom 2.50 6.00
32 Blake Snell 2.00 5.00
33 Whit Merrifield 2.50 6.00
34 Joey Votto 2.50 6.00
35 Freddie Freeman 3.00 8.00
36 Nicholas Castellanos 2.50 6.00
37 Matt Chapman 2.50 6.00
38 Bryce Harper 4.00 10.00

2019 Donruss Nicknames

RANDOM INSERTS IN PACKS
STATED PRINT RUN 999 SER.#'d SETS
*BRONZE/349: .5X TO 1.2X BASIC
*DIAMOND: .5X TO 1.2X BASIC
*PINK: .6X TO 1.5X BASIC
*BLUE/249: .6X TO 1.5X BASIC
*RAPTURE: .6X TO 1.5X BASIC
*RED/149: .6X TO 1.5X BASIC
*VECTOR: .6X TO 1.5X BASIC
*GOLD/99: 1X TO 2.5X BASIC
*GREEN/25: 1.5X TO 4X BASIC
1 Aaron Judge 2.50 6.00
2 Paul Goldschmidt 1.00 2.50
3 Mike Trout 5.00 12.00
4 Javier Baez 1.25 3.00
5 Juan Soto 3.00 8.00
6 Shohei Ohtani 1.25 3.00

2019 Donruss Rated Prospect Material Signatures

RANDOM INSERTS IN PACKS
EXCHANGE DEADLINE 09/06/2020
*GOLD/99: .5X TO 1.2X BASIC
1 Vladimir Guerrero Jr. 30.00 80.00
2 Fernando Tatis Jr. 75.00 200.00
3 Eloy Jimenez 15.00 40.00
4 Brendan McKay 4.00 10.00
5 Yordan Alvarez 20.00 50.00
6 Wander Franco 40.00 100.00
7 Julio Pablo Martinez 2.50 6.00
8 Peter Alonso 40.00 100.00
9 Taylor Trammell 8.00 20.00
10 Ke'Bryan Hayes 6.00 15.00

2019 Donruss Rated Prospect Materials

RANDOM INSERTS IN PACKS
*GOLD/99: .5X TO 1.2X BASIC
1 Eloy Jimenez 4.00 10.00
2 Vladimir Guerrero Jr. 8.00 20.00
3 Nick Senzel 3.00 8.00
4 Fernando Tatis Jr. 8.00 20.00
5 Taylor Trammell 2.00 5.00
6 Brendan McKay 2.50 6.00
7 Carter Kieboom 2.50 6.00
8 Jesus Sanchez 1.50 4.00
9 A.J. Puk 2.00 5.00
10 Yordan Alvarez 10.00 25.00
11 Ke'Bryan Hayes 1.50 4.00
12 Leody Taveras 1.50 4.00
13 Peter Alonso 8.00 20.00
14 Franklin Perez 1.50 4.00
15 Dustin May 3.00 8.00
16 Luis Robert 10.00 25.00
17 Wander Franco 8.00 20.00
18 Kaito Yuki 2.50 6.00
19 Julio Pablo Martinez 1.50 4.00
20 Francisco Morales 2.00 5.00
21 Noelvi Marte 6.00 15.00
22 Marco Luciano 6.00 15.00
23 Estanli Castillo 1.50 4.00
24 Keston Hiura 3.00 8.00
25 Austin Riley 5.00 12.00

2019 Donruss Rated Rookies Signatures

RANDOM INSERTS IN PACKS
EXCHANGE DEADLINE 09/06/2020
1 Yusei Kikuchi EXCH 30.00 80.00

2019 Donruss Sensational Signatures

RANDOM INSERTS IN PACKS
EXCHANGE DEADLINE 09/06/2020
*BLUE/49: .5X TO 1.2X BASIC
*RED/25: .6X TO 1.5X BASIC
1 Domingo Ayala 10.00 25.00

2019 Donruss Signature Series

RANDOM INSERTS IN PACKS
EXCHANGE DEADLINE 09/06/2020
*BLUE/99: .5X TO 1.2X BASIC
*RED/25: .75X TO 2X BASIC
1 Bryse Wilson 3.00 8.00
2 Kolby Allard 4.00 10.00
3 Kyle Wright 4.00 10.00
4 Touki Toussaint 3.00 8.00
5 Cedric Mullins 4.00 10.00
6 Luis Ortiz 2.50 6.00
7 Michael Kopech 5.00 12.00
8 Brandon Lowe 6.00 10.00
9 Garrett Hampson 2.50 6.00
10 Christin Stewart 3.00 8.00
11 Cionel Perez 2.50 6.00
12 Framber Valdez 2.50 6.00
13 Josh James 6.00 15.00
14 Myles Straw 4.00 10.00
15 Kyle Tucker 6.00 15.00
16 Brad Keller 2.50 6.00
17 Ryan O'Hearn 2.50 6.00
18 David Fletcher 8.00 20.00
19 Taylor Ward 2.50 6.00
20 Dennis Santana 2.50 6.00
21 Corbin Burnes 4.00 10.00
22 Jake Cave 3.00 8.00
23 Stephen Gonsalves 2.50 6.00
24 Caleb Ferguson 3.00 8.00
25 Jeff McNeil 6.00 15.00
26 Chance Adams 2.50 6.00
27 Jonathan Loaisiga
28 Justus Sheffield 4.00 10.00
29 Ramon Laureano 6.00 15.00
30 Enyel De Los Santos 2.50 6.00
31 Kevin Kramer 3.00 8.00
32 Kevin Newman 4.00 10.00
33 Jacob Nix 3.00 8.00
34 Luis Urias 4.00 10.00
35 Chris Shaw 4.00 10.00
36 Steven Duggar 3.00 8.00
37 Dakota Hudson 3.00 8.00
38 Daniel Ponce de Leon 4.00 10.00
39 Patrick Wisdom 2.50 6.00
40 Jake Bauers 4.00 10.00
41 Danny Jansen 2.50 6.00
42 Jonathan Davis 3.00 8.00
43 Reese McGuire 4.00 10.00
44 Rowdy Tellez 4.00 10.00
45 Ryan Borucki 2.50 6.00
46 Sean Reid-Foley 2.50 6.00
47 Eloy Jimenez 15.00 40.00
48 Vladimir Guerrero Jr. 30.00 80.00
49 Fernando Tatis Jr. 50.00 120.00
50 Nick Senzel EXCH 8.00 20.00

2019 Donruss The Famous San Diego Chicken 6 Piece

RANDOM INSERTS IN PACKS
STATED PRINT RUN 85 SER.#'d SETS
1 Ted Giannoulas 25.00 60.00
2 Ted Giannoulas 25.00 60.00
3 Ted Giannoulas 25.00 60.00
4 Ted Giannoulas 25.00 60.00
5 Ted Giannoulas 25.00 60.00
6 Ted Giannoulas 25.00 60.00

2019 Donruss The Famous San Diego Chicken 6 Piece Signatures

RANDOM INSERTS IN PACKS
STATED PRINT RUN 85 SER.#'d SETS
EXCHANGE DEADLINE 09/09/2020
1 Ted Giannoulas 50.00 120.00
2 Ted Giannoulas 50.00 120.00
3 Ted Giannoulas 50.00 120.00
4 Ted Giannoulas 50.00 120.00
5 Ted Giannoulas 50.00 120.00
6 Ted Giannoulas 50.00 120.00

2019 Donruss Whammy

RANDOM INSERTS IN PACKS
1 Mookie Betts 12.00 30.00
2 Ronald Acuna Jr. 20.00 50.00
3 Vladimir Guerrero Jr. 25.00 60.00
4 Juan Soto 15.00 40.00
5 Javier Baez 10.00 25.00

2020 Donruss

1 Fernando Tatis Jr. DK 2.50 6.00
2 Buster Posey DK .75 2.00
3 Cody Bellinger DK 1.25 3.00
4 Eugenio Suarez DK .50 1.25
5 Christian Yelich DK .75 2.00
6 Brian Anderson DK .40 1.00
7 Pete Alonso DK 1.50 4.00
8 Ronald Acuna Jr. DK 2.50 6.00
9 Mike Trout DK 3.00 8.00
10 Marcus Semien DK .40 1.00
11 Miguel Cabrera DK .60 1.50
12 Lucas Giolito DK .50 1.25
13 Nelson Cruz DK .60 1.50
14 Vladimir Guerrero Jr. DK 1.25 3.00
15 Austin Meadows DK .50 1.25
16 Rafael Devers DK .75 2.00
17 Trey Mancini DK .60 1.50
18 Shane Bieber DK .60 1.50
19 Jorge Soler DK .60 1.50
20 Alex Bregman DK .60 1.50
21 Lance Lynn DK .40 1.00
22 Marco Gonzales DK .40 1.00
23 Juan Soto DK 2.00 5.00
24 Bryce Harper DK 1.00 2.50
25 Paul Goldschmidt DK .60 1.50
26 Javier Baez DK .75 2.00
27 Josh Bell DK .50 1.25
28 Ketel Marte DK .50 1.25
29 Nolan Arenado DK .75 2.00
30 Aaron Judge DK 1.50 4.00
31 Bryan Abreu RR RC .40 1.00
32 Dustin May RR RC 1.50 4.00
33 Mauricio Dubon RR RC .50 1.25
34 Jesus Luzardo RR RC .75 2.00
35 Jordan Yamamoto RR RC .50 1.25
36 Brendan McKay RR RC .60 1.50
37 Bo Bichette RR RC 3.00 8.00
38 Nico Hoerner RR RC 1.50 4.00
39 Aristides Aquino RR RC .75 2.00
40 Brock Burke RR RC .40 1.00

41 Justin Dunn RR RC .50 1.25
42 Sean Murphy RR RC .60 1.50
43 Trent Grisham RR RC 1.50 4.00
44 Gavin Lux RR RC 2.50 6.00
45 Yordan Alvarez RR RC 2.00 5.00
46 Sam Hilliard RR RC .60 1.50
47 Patrick Sandoval RR RC .60 1.50
48 Isan Diaz RR RC .60 1.50
49 A.J. Puk RR RC .75 2.00
50 Logan Webb RR RC .50 1.25
51 Randy Arozarena RR RC 3.00 8.00
52 Anthony Kay RR RC .40 1.00
53 Dylan Cease RR RC .75 2.00
54 Zac Gallen RR RC 1.00 2.50
55 Adrian Morejon RR RC .40 1.00
56 Kyle Lewis RR RC 3.00 8.00
57 Nick Solak RR RC .60 1.50
58 Brusdar Graterol RR RC .60 1.50
59 Tony Gonsolin RR RC 1.50 4.00
60 Matt Thaiss RR RC .50 1.25
61 Eduardo Rodriguez .15 .40
62 Walker Buehler .30 .75
63 Michael Conforto .20 .50
64 Ozzie Albies .25 .60
65 Eric Hosmer .20 .50
66 Charlie Blackmon .25 .60
67 Stephen Strasburg .25 .60
68 Nick Senzel .25 .60
69 Yadier Molina .25 .60
70 Jean Segura .20 .50
71 Jacob deGrom .25 .60
72 Hunter Dozier .15 .40
73 Luis Severino .20 .50
74 Gary Sanchez .25 .60
75 Xander Bogaerts .25 .60
76 Lucas Giolito .20 .50
77 Mookie Betts .50 1.25
78 Ketel Marte .20 .50
79 Hyun-Jin Ryu .20 .50
80 Lorenzo Cain .15 .40
81 Corey Kluber .20 .50
82 Joey Votto .25 .60
83 Fernando Tatis Jr. 1.00 2.50
84 Cody Bellinger .50 1.25
85 Aroldis Chapman .25 .60
86 Robbie Ray .15 .40
87 Josh Donaldson .20 .50
88 Khris Davis .25 .60
89 Jeff McNeil .20 .50
90 Javier Baez .30 .75
91 Gleyber Torres .50 1.25
92 Marcus Semien .15 .40
93 Buster Posey .30 .75
94 Shohei Ohtani .30 .75
95 Mike Minor .15 .40
96 German Marquez .25 .60
97 Yu Darvish .25 .60
98 Charlie Morton .25 .60
99 Max Muncy .20 .50
100 Mitch Haniger .20 .50
101 Johnny Cueto .20 .50
102 Vladimir Guerrero Jr. .50 1.25
103 Matt Olson .15 .40
104 Shane Bieber .25 .60
105 Jorge Polanco .20 .50
106 Corey Seager .25 .60
107 Jose Abreu .25 .60
108 Trea Turner .20 .50
109 Justin Turner .20 .50
110 Christian Yelich .30 .75
111 Aaron Judge .60 1.50
112 Alex Bregman .25 .60
113 Nelson Cruz .25 .60
114 Chris Sale .25 .60
115 Gerrit Cole .40 1.00
116 Michael Brantley .20 .50
117 Madison Bumgarner .20 .50
118 Clayton Kershaw .50 1.25
119 DJ LeMahieu .25 .60
120 Masahiro Tanaka .25 .60
121 Eloy Jimenez .50 1.25
122 Cavan Biggio .30 .75
123 Max Scherzer .25 .60
124 Eugenio Suarez .20 .50
125 Jordan Hicks .20 .50
126 Aaron Nola .25 .60
127 Paul Goldschmidt .25 .60
128 Luke Weaver .15 .40
129 Mike Trout 1.25 3.00
130 Nomar Mazara .15 .40
131 Hunter Renfroe .15 .40
132 Anthony Rizzo .40 1.00
133 Josh Hader .15 .40
134 Marcell Ozuna .25 .60
135 Brandon Woodruff .15 .40
136 Luis Castillo .20 .50
137 Jonathan Villar .15 .40
138 David Fletcher .25 .60
139 Tim Anderson .25 .60
140 David Dahl .15 .40
141 Max Kepler .20 .50
142 Kyle Hendricks .25 .60
143 Max Fried .25 .60
144 Austin Meadows .20 .50
145 Yoan Moncada .25 .60
146 Josh Bell .20 .50
147 Nolan Arenado .30 .75
148 Francisco Lindor .25 .60
149 Matt Chapman .25 .60
150 Willie Calhoun .15 .40
151 Tyler Glasnow .15 .40
152 Mike Soroka .25 .60
153 Kevin Newman .20 .50
154 Anthony Rendon .25 .60
155 Trevor Bauer .25 .60
156 Elvis Andrus .20 .50
157 Justin Verlander .25 .60
158 Jose Ramirez .20 .50
159 Jose Altuve .20 .50
160 Bryan Reynolds .20 .50
161 Eddie Rosario .20 .50
162 Juan Soto .75 2.00
163 Chris Paddack .25 .60
164 Rafael Devers .30 .75
165 Brian Anderson .15 .40
166 Trevor Story .25 .60
167 Jose Berrios .20 .50
168 Brandon Lowe .25 .60
169 Freddie Freeman .30 .75
170 Ronald Acuna Jr. 1.00 2.50
171 Starling Marte .20 .50
172 Adalberto Mondesi .20 .50
173 Noah Syndergaard .20 .50
174 Tommy Pham .15 .40
175 Blake Snell .20 .50
176 George Springer .20 .50
177 Trey Mancini .20 .50
178 Kyle Schwarber .25 .60
179 Ramon Laureano .25 .60
180 Kris Bryant .30 .75
181 Rhys Hoskins .30 .75
182 Marco Gonzales .15 .40
183 J.D. Martinez .25 .60
184 Keston Hiura .30 .75
185 Manny Machado .25 .60
186 Carlos Santana .20 .50
187 David Peralta .15 .40
188 Albert Pujols .30 .75
189 Brandon Crawford .20 .50
190 Yandy Diaz .20 .50
191 Sandy Alcantara .15 .40
192 Jack Flaherty .20 .50
193 Bryce Harper .40 1.00
194 Yusei Kikuchi .20 .50
195 Giancarlo Stanton .25 .60
196 Joey Gallo .25 .60
197 Willson Contreras .25 .60
198 Mitch Garver .15 .40
199 Christian Vazquez .15 .40
200 Luis Arraez .30 .75
201 Sonny Gray .20 .50
202 Jorge Soler .25 .60
203 Matt Carpenter .25 .60
204 Pete Alonso .60 1.50
205 Whit Merrifield .25 .60
206 John Means .15 .40
207 Eduardo Escobar .15 .40
208 Kirby Yates .15 .40
209 Mike Yastrzemski .40 1.00
210 Tommy Edman .25 .60
211 Barry Larkin RETRO .20 .50
212 Jose Canseco RETRO .20 .50
213 Andres Galarraga RETRO .20 .50
214 Kevin Mitchell RETRO .15 .40
215 Wade Boggs RETRO .20 .50
216 Don Mattingly RETRO .50 1.25
217 Kirby Puckett RETRO .25 .60
218 Tony Gwynn RETRO .25 .60
219 Rickey Henderson RETRO .25 .60
220 Roger Clemens RETRO .30 .75
221 Bert Blyleven RETRO .20 .50
222 Dwight Gooden RETRO .15 .40
223 Nolan Ryan RETRO .75 2.00
224 Cal Ripken RETRO .75 2.00
225 Alan Trammell RETRO .20 .50
226 Jim Rice RETRO .20 .50
227 Keith Hernandez RETRO .15 .40
228 Eddie Murray RETRO .20 .50
229 George Brett RETRO .50 1.25
230 Gary Carter RETRO .20 .50
231 Darryl Strawberry RETRO .15 .40
232 Dave Winfield RETRO .20 .50
233 Robin Yount RETRO .25 .60
234 Dale Murphy RETRO .25 .60
235 Paul Molitor RETRO .25 .60
236 Willi Castro RETRO RC .60 1.50
237 Andres Munoz RETRO RC .50 1.25
238 Jonathan Hernandez RETRO RC .40 1.00
239 Josh Rojas RETRO RC .40 1.00
240 Sheldon Neuse RETRO RC .50 1.25
241 Yonathan Daza RETRO RC .50 1.25
242 Bobby Bradley RETRO RC .50 1.25
243 Logan Allen RETRO RC .40 1.00
244 Joe Palumbo RETRO RC .40 1.00
245 Jaylin Davis RETRO RC .60 1.50
246 Jake Fraley RETRO RC .50 1.25
247 Zack Collins RETRO RC .50 1.25
248 Danny Mendick RETRO RC .50 1.25
249 Edwin Rios RETRO RC 1.00 2.50
250 Travis Demeritte RETRO RC .50 1.25
251 Lewis Thorpe RETRO RC .40 1.00
252 Donnie Walton RETRO RC 1.00 2.50
253 Tyrone Taylor RETRO RC .40 1.00
254 Aaron Civale RETRO RC .60 1.50
255 Domingo Leyba RETRO RC .50 1.25
256 Michael King RETRO RC .60 1.50
257 Abraham Toro RETRO RC .50 1.25
258 Adbert Alzolay RETRO RC .50 1.25
259 Yu Chang RETRO RC .60 1.50
260 Jake Rogers RETRO RC .40 1.00
261 Ted Giannoulas .15 .40
262 Domingo Ayala 2.00 5.00
263 Yoshitomo Tsutsugo RR RC .50 1.25
264 Luis Robert RR RC 4.00 10.00

2020 Donruss Look At This

*LOOK AT THIS DK: 2X TO 5X BASIC
*LOOK AT THIS RR: 2X TO 5X BASIC
*LOOK AT THIS: 5X TO 12X BASIC
RANDOM INSERTS IN PACKS
STATED PRINT RUN 25 SER.#'d SETS
37 Bo Bichette RR 25.00 60.00
38 Nico Hoerner RR 25.00 60.00
44 Gavin Lux RR 20.00 50.00
264 Luis Robert RR 50.00 120.00

2020 Donruss Presidential Collection

*PRES DK: 1.2X TO 3X BASIC
*PRES RR: 1.2X TO 3X BASIC
*PRES: 3X TO 8X BASIC
RANDOM INSERTS IN PACKS
STATED PRINT RUN 50 SER.#'d SETS
38 Nico Hoerner RR 15.00 40.00
264 Luis Robert RR 30.00 80.00

2020 Donruss American Pride

RANDOM INSERTS IN PACKS
STATED PRINT RUN 999 SER.#'d SETS
*SILVER/349: .5X TO 1.2X BASIC
*DIAMOND: .5X TO 1.2X BASIC
*PINK: .6X TO 1.5X BASIC
*BLUE/249: .6X TO 1.5X BASIC
*RAPTURE: .6X TO 1.5X BASIC
*RED/149: .6X TO 1.5X BASIC
*VECTOR: .6X TO 1.5X BASIC
*GOLD/99: 1X TO 2.5X BASIC
*GREEN/25: 1.5X TO 4X BASIC
1 A.Rutschman/P.Bailey 2.50 6.00
2 B.McKay/R.Detmers 1.00 2.50
3 C.Cowser/D.Dahl .50 1.25
4 A.Lacy/C.Kershaw 2.50 6.00
5 A.Martin/C.Jones 1.25 3.00
6 M.Chapman/M.Meyer 1.50 4.00
7 G.Mitchell/M.Trout 3.00 8.00
8 A.Bregman/S.Torkelson 4.00 10.00
9 C.Wilcox/M.Scherzer .60 1.50
10 A.Williams/B.Witt Jr. 2.00 5.00
11 L.Allen/W.Buehler .75 2.00
12 A.Abbott/M.Stroman .50 1.25
13 G.Cole/T.Brown 1.00 2.50
14 B.Carraway/J.Verlander 1.00 2.50
15 A.Vaughn/J.Foscue 1.50 4.00
16 A.Bohm/N.Loftin 2.50 6.00
17 D.Nikhazy/N.Song .50 1.25
18 K.Griffey Jr./T.Allen 1.25 3.00
19 A.Burleson/J.Gallo .60 1.50
20 C.Cavalli/F.Whitley .75 2.00
21 J.Flaherty/J.Criswell .60 1.50
22 N.Frasso/S.Strasburg .60 1.50
23 H.Kjerstad/J.Adell 2.00 5.00
24 K.Bryant/L.Waddell .75 2.00
25 A.Puk/C.McMahon .75 2.00
26 C.Opitz/T.Grandal .60 1.50

2020 Donruss As Seen

RANDOM INSERTS IN PACKS
STATED PRINT RUN 999 SER.#'d SETS
*SILVER/349: .5X TO 1.2X BASIC
*DIAMOND: .5X TO 1.2X BASIC
*PINK: .6X TO 1.5X BASIC
*BLUE/249: .6X TO 1.5X BASIC
*RAPTURE: .6X TO 1.5X BASIC
*RED/149: .6X TO 1.5X BASIC
*VECTOR: .6X TO 1.5X BASIC
*GOLD/99: 1X TO 2.5X BASIC
*GREEN/25: 1.5X TO 4X BASIC
1 Fernando Tatis Jr. 2.50 6.00
2 Christian Yelich .75 2.00
3 Jose Altuve .50 1.25
4 Anthony Rizzo 1.00 2.50
5 Clayton Kershaw 1.25 3.00
6 Vladimir Guerrero Jr. 1.25 3.00

2020 Donruss Classics Autographs

RANDOM INSERTS IN PACKS
EXCHANGE DEADLINE 08/05/2021
*BLUE/99: .5X TO 1.2X BASIC
*BLUE/49-50: .6X TO 1.5X BASIC
*BLUE/25: .75X TO 2X BASIC
*GOLD/25: .75X TO 2X BASIC
1 Ken Griffey Jr. 50.00 120.00
2 Luis Arraez 6.00 15.00
3 Juan Soto 30.00 80.00
5 Kenny Lofton 8.00 20.00
6 Trevor Hoffman 8.00 20.00
7 Ryne Sandberg 10.00 25.00
8 Patrick Corbin 3.00 8.00
9 Adalberto Mondesi 4.00 10.00
10 Andres Galarraga 6.00 15.00
11 Gerrit Cole 15.00 40.00

2020 Donruss Classified Signatures

RANDOM INSERTS IN PACKS
EXCHANGE DEADLINE 08/05/2021
*BLUE/99: .5X TO 1.2X BASIC
*BLUE/49: .6X TO 1.5X BASIC
*GOLD/25: .75X TO 2X BASIC
1 Aaron Judge EXCH 40.00 100.00
2 Cody Bellinger 40.00 100.00
3 Josh Bell 6.00 15.00
4 Max Fried 4.00 10.00
5 Willy Adames 2.50 6.00
6 Hunter Dozier 2.50 6.00
7 Trea Turner 6.00 15.00
8 Fernando Tatis Jr. EXCH 50.00 120.00
9 Vladimir Guerrero Jr. 15.00 40.00
10 Eloy Jimenez 12.00 30.00

2020 Donruss Contenders

RANDOM INSERTS IN PACKS
STATED PRINT RUN 999 SER.#'d SETS
*BLUE/99: .6X TO 1.5X BASIC
*GOLD/25: 1X TO 2.5X BASIC
1 Rizz/Ross/Baez/Brynt 1.50 4.00
2 Bregmn/Correa/Sprngr/Altve 1.00 2.50
3 Benini/Sale/Martnz/Betts 2.00 5.00
4 Rendn/Parra/Soto/Schrzr/Stras 3.00 8.00

2020 Donruss Contenders Blue

*BLUE/99: .6X TO 1.5X BASIC
RANDOM INSERTS IN PACKS
STATED PRINT RUN 99 SER.#'d SETS
1 Rizz/Ross/Baez/Brynt 10.00 25.00
2 Bregmn/Correa/Sprngr/Altve 6.00 15.00
3 Benini/Sale/Martnz/Betts 4.00 10.00

2020 Donruss Contenders Gold

*GOLD/25: 1X TO 2.5X BASIC
RANDOM INSERTS IN PACKS
STATED PRINT RUN 25 SER.#'d SETS
1 Rizz/Ross/Baez/Brynt 15.00 40.00
2 Bregmn/Correa/Sprngr/Altve 10.00 25.00
3 Benini/Sale/Martnz/Betts 6.00 15.00

2020 Donruss Divisions

RANDOM INSERTS IN PACKS
1 Jdge/Snel/Bets/Mncni/Vlad Jr 5.00 12.00
2 Jimnz/Lndor/Solr/Keplr/Miggy 6.00 15.00
3 Vogel/Gallo/Altve/Davis/Trout 10.00 25.00
4 Andrsn/Harpr/Soto/Alnso/Acuna Jr. 8.00 20.00
5 Yelch/Baez/Votto/Gldschmdt/Mrte 8.00 20.00
6 Belli/Longo/Tatis Jr/Mrte/Arendo 6.00 15.00

2020 Donruss Dominators

RANDOM INSERTS IN PACKS
STATED PRINT RUN 999 SER.#'d SETS
*SILVER/349: .5X TO 1.2X BASIC
*DIAMOND: .5X TO 1.2X BASIC
*PINK: .6X TO 1.5X BASIC
*BLUE/249: .6X TO 1.5X BASIC
*RAPTURE: .6X TO 1.5X BASIC
*RED/149: .6X TO 1.5X BASIC
*VECTOR: .6X TO 1.5X BASIC
*GOLD/99: 1X TO 2.5X BASIC
*GREEN/25: 1.5X TO 4X BASIC
1 Max Scherzer .60 1.50
2 Pete Alonso 1.50 4.00
3 Gerrit Cole 1.00 2.50
4 Aaron Judge 1.50 4.00
5 Rafael Devers .75 2.00
6 Hyun-Jin Ryu .50 1.25
7 Jorge Soler .60 1.50
8 Austin Meadows .50 1.25
9 Ketel Marte .50 1.25
10 Jacob deGrom .60 1.50
11 Jorge Polanco .50 1.25
12 Josh Bell .50 1.25
13 Marcus Semien .40 1.00

2020 Donruss Domingo Ayala Material Signatures

RANDOM INSERTS IN PACKS
1 Domingo Ayala 15.00 40.00

2020 Donruss Elite Series

RANDOM INSERTS IN PACKS
STATED PRINT RUN 999 SER.#'d SETS
*SILVER/349: .5X TO 1.2X BASIC
*DIAMOND: .5X TO 1.2X BASIC
*PINK: .6X TO 1.5X BASIC
*BLUE/249: .6X TO 1.5X BASIC
*RAPTURE: .6X TO 1.5X BASIC
*RED/149: .6X TO 1.5X BASIC
*VECTOR: .6X TO 1.5X BASIC
1 Christian Yelich 1.25 3.00
2 Javier Baez 1.25 3.00
3 Nolan Arenado 1.25 3.00
4 Cody Bellinger 2.00 5.00
5 Mike Trout 5.00 12.00
6 Alex Bregman 1.00 2.50
7 Justin Verlander 1.00 2.50
8 Ronald Acuna Jr. 4.00 10.00
9 Juan Soto 3.00 8.00
10 Mookie Betts 2.00 5.00
11 Matt Chapman 1.00 2.50
12 Paul Goldschmidt 1.00 2.50
13 Yoan Moncada 1.00 2.50

2020 Donruss Elite Series Gold

*GOLD/99: 1X TO 2.5X BASIC
RANDOM INSERTS IN PACKS
STATED PRINT RUN 99 SER.#'d SETS
9 Juan Soto 10.00 25.00

2020 Donruss Elite Series Green

*GREEN/25: 1.5X TO 4X BASIC
RANDOM INSERTS IN PACKS
STATED PRINT RUN 25 SER.#'d SETS
5 Mike Trout 50.00 120.00
9 Juan Soto 15.00 40.00

2020 Donruss Highlights

RANDOM INSERTS IN PACKS
STATED PRINT RUN 999 SER.#'d SETS
*SILVER/349: .5X TO 1.2X BASIC
*DIAMOND: .5X TO 1.2X BASIC
*PINK: .6X TO 1.5X BASIC
*BLUE/249: .6X TO 1.5X BASIC
*RAPTURE: .6X TO 1.5X BASIC
*RED/149: .6X TO 1.5X BASIC
*VECTOR: .6X TO 1.5X BASIC
*GOLD/99: 1X TO 2.5X BASIC
*GREEN/25: 1.5X TO 4X BASIC
1 Justin Verlander .60 1.50
2 Joey Gallo .60 1.50
3 Albert Pujols .75 2.00
4 Pete Alonso 2.00 5.00
5 Trevor Story .60 1.50
6 Shohei Ohtani .75 2.00
7 Bryce Harper 1.00 2.50
8 Aristides Aquino 3.00 8.00
9 Ronald Acuna Jr. 4.00 10.00
10 Mike Trout 5.00 12.00
11 Eugenio Suarez .50 1.25
12 Bo Bichette 4.00 10.00

2020 Donruss Materials

RANDOM INSERTS IN PACKS
*RED/99: .5X TO 1.2X BASIC
*GOLD/25: .6X TO 1.5X BASIC
1 Aaron Judge 10.00 25.00
2 Rafael Devers 3.00 8.00
3 Ivan Rodriguez 4.00 10.00
4 Rhys Hoskins 3.00 8.00
5 Joe Torre 2.00 5.00
6 Randy Johnson 5.00 12.00
7 Kolten Wong 2.00 5.00
8 Masahiro Tanaka 2.50 6.00
9 Keston Hiura 3.00 8.00
10 Ronald Acuna Jr. 6.00 15.00
11 Red Schoendienst 3.00 8.00
12 Nolan Arenado 3.00 6.00
13 Matt Olson 1.50 4.00
14 Alex Verdugo 2.00 5.00
15 Adalberto Mondesi 2.50 6.00
16 Eloy Jimenez 5.00 12.00
17 Noah Syndergaard 2.00 5.00
18 Brendan Rodgers 2.50 6.00
19 Dansby Swanson 2.50 6.00
20 Corey Seager 3.00 8.00
21 Clayton Kershaw 5.00 12.00
22 Justin Verlander 2.50 6.00
23 Mookie Betts 6.00 15.00
24 Brandon Nimmo 2.00 5.00
25 David Bote 2.00 5.00
26 Ken Griffey Jr. 6.00 15.00
27 Kris Bryant 3.00 8.00
28 Austin Riley 4.00 10.00
29 Pete Alonso 5.00 12.00
30 Rickey Henderson 8.00 20.00
31 Jack Flaherty 2.00 5.00
32 Addison Russell 2.00 5.00
33 Brandon Lowe 2.50 6.00
34 Vladimir Guerrero Jr. 5.00 12.00
35 Joey Votto 2.50 6.00
36 Alex Bregman 4.00 10.00
37 Hunter Renfroe 1.50 4.00
38 Max Fried 2.50 6.00
39 Michael Chavis 2.00 5.00
40 Tony Gwynn 4.00 10.00
41 Joe Morgan 2.00 5.00
42 Brandon Woodruff 1.50 4.00
43 Walker Buehler 3.00 8.00
44 Kyle Schwarber 2.50 6.00
45 Joc Pederson 2.00 5.00
46 Hunter Dozier 1.50 4.00
47 Juan Soto 8.00 20.00

2020 Donruss Now Playing

RANDOM INSERTS IN PACKS
STATED PRINT RUN 999 SER.#'d SETS
*SILVER/349: .5X TO 1.2X BASIC
*DIAMOND: .5X TO 1.2X BASIC
*PINK: .6X TO 1.5X BASIC
*BLUE/249: .6X TO 1.5X BASIC
*RAPTURE: .6X TO 1.5X BASIC
*RED/149: .6X TO 1.5X BASIC
*VECTOR: .6X TO 1.5X BASIC
*GOLD/99: 1X TO 2.5X BASIC
*GREEN/25: 1.5X TO 4X BASIC
1 Vladimir Guerrero Jr. 1.25 3.00
2 Fernando Tatis Jr. 2.50 6.00
3 Pete Alonso 3.00 8.00
4 Yordan Alvarez 2.00 5.00
5 Bo Bichette 6.00 15.00
6 Eloy Jimenez 1.25 3.00
7 Jesus Luzardo .75 2.00
8 Aristides Aquino 4.00 10.00
9 Gavin Lux 2.50 6.00
10 Brendan McKay .60 1.50
11 Keston Hiura .75 2.00
12 Austin Riley 1.00 2.50

2020 Donruss Rated Prospects Blue

*BLUE/249: .6X TO 1.5X BASIC
RANDOM INSERTS IN PACKS
STATED PRINT RUN 249 SER.#'d SETS
2 Bobby Witt Jr. 8.00 20.00

2020 Donruss Rated Prospects Diamond

*DIAMOND: .5X TO 1.2X BASIC
RANDOM INSERTS IN PACKS
2 Bobby Witt Jr. 6.00 15.00

2020 Donruss Rated Prospects Gold

*GOLD/99: 1X TO 2.5X BASIC
RANDOM INSERTS IN PACKS
STATED PRINT RUN 99 SER.#'d SETS
2 Bobby Witt Jr. 15.00 40.00

2020 Donruss Rated Prospects Green

*GREEN/25: 1.5X TO 4X BASIC
RANDOM INSERTS IN PACKS
STATED PRINT RUN 25 SER.#'d SETS
2 Bobby Witt Jr. 25.00 60.00

2020 Donruss Rated Prospects Pink Fireworks

*PINK: .6X TO 1.5X BASIC
RANDOM INSERTS IN PACKS
2 Bobby Witt Jr. 8.00 20.00

2020 Donruss Rated Prospects Rapture

*RAPTURE: .6X TO 1.5X BASIC
RANDOM INSERTS IN PACKS
2 Bobby Witt Jr. 8.00 20.00

2020 Donruss Rated Prospects Red

*RED/149: .6X TO 1.5X BASIC
RANDOM INSERTS IN PACKS
STATED PRINT RUN 149 SER.#'d SETS
2 Bobby Witt Jr. 8.00 20.00

2020 Donruss Rated Prospects Silver

*SILVER: .5X TO 1.2X BASIC
RANDOM INSERTS IN PACKS
STATED PRINT RUN 349 SER.#'d SETS
2 Bobby Witt Jr. 6.00 15.00

2020 Donruss Rated Prospects Vector

*VECTOR: .6X TO 1.5X BASIC
RANDOM INSERTS IN PACKS
2 Bobby Witt Jr. 8.00 20.00

2020 Donruss Retro '86 Materials

RANDOM INSERTS IN PACKS
*GOLD/25: .6X TO 1.5X BASIC
1 Trey Mancini 2.50 6.00
2 Jung-Ho Kang 1.50 4.00
3 Josh Bell 2.00 5.00
4 Gary Sanchez 2.50 6.00
5 Freddie Freeman 3.00 8.00
6 Duke Snider 2.00 5.00
7 Vladimir Guerrero Jr. 5.00 12.00
8 Fernando Tatis Jr. 6.00 15.00
9 John Smoltz 2.50 6.00
10 Kyle Seager 1.50 4.00
11 Albert Pujols 4.00 10.00
12 Edgar Martinez 4.00 10.00
13 Luis Arraez 3.00 8.00
14 Jackie Bradley Jr. 2.50 6.00
15 Carlton Fisk 3.00 8.00
16 Aaron Judge 6.00 15.00
17 Cal Ripken 6.00 15.00
18 Mariano Rivera 5.00 12.00
19 Mike Piazza 2.50 6.00
20 Julio Teheran 2.00 5.00
21 Chipper Jones 2.50 6.00
22 Jacob deGrom 2.50 6.00
23 Alex Gordon 2.00 5.00
24 Javier Baez 3.00 8.00
25 Darryl Strawberry 1.50 4.00
26 Larry Walker 3.00 8.00
27 Mark McGwire 6.00 15.00
28 Luis Severino 2.00 5.00
29 Pete Rose 8.00 20.00
30 Barry Larkin 2.00 5.00
31 David Wright 2.00 5.00
32 Gerrit Cole 4.00 10.00
33 Jeff McNeil 2.00 5.00
34 David Ortiz 2.50 6.00
35 Shin-Soo Choo 2.00 5.00
36 Alex Rodriguez 3.00 8.00
37 Nomar Mazara 1.50 4.00
38 Frank Thomas 4.00 10.00
39 George Brett 5.00 12.00
40 Shohei Ohtani 3.00 8.00
41 Miguel Cabrera 2.50 6.00
42 Giancarlo Stanton 2.50 6.00
43 Don Mattingly 5.00 12.00
44 Ozzie Albies 4.00 10.00
45 Felix Hernandez 4.00 10.00
46 Greg Maddux 3.00 8.00
47 Gleyber Torres 6.00 15.00
48 Johnny Bench 2.50 6.00
49 Salvador Perez 2.00 5.00
50 Mike Soroka 2.50 6.00

2020 Donruss Retro '86 Signatures

RANDOM INSERTS IN PACKS
EXCHANGE DEADLINE 08/05/2021
*PINK/199: .4X TO 1X BASIC
*PINK/99-100: .5X TO 1.2X BASIC
*PINK/49-50: .6X TO 1.5X BASIC
*PINK/25: .75X TO 2X BASIC
*RED/99: .5X TO 1.2X BASIC
*RED/49: .6X TO 1.5X BASIC
*RED/25: .75X TO 2X BASIC
*GOLD/25: .75X TO 2X BASIC
1 Brusdar Graterol 4.00 10.00
2 Michael King 4.00 10.00
3 Deivy Grullon 2.50 6.00
4 Jonathan Hernandez 2.50 6.00
5 Isan Diaz 4.00 10.00
6 Lewis Thorpe 2.50 6.00
7 Aaron Civale 4.00 10.00
8 Willi Castro 4.00 10.00
9 Logan Webb 3.00 8.00
10 Sam Hilliard 4.00 10.00
11 Bobby Bradley 3.00 8.00
12 Jesus Luzardo 5.00 12.00
13 Zack Collins 3.00 8.00
14 Joe Palumbo 2.50 6.00
15 Anthony Kay 2.50 6.00
16 Travis Demeritte 3.00 8.00
17 Zac Gallen 6.00 15.00
18 Yu Chang 4.00 10.00
19 Sean Murphy 4.00 10.00
20 Yordan Alvarez 12.00 30.00
21 Justin Dunn 3.00 8.00
22 Dylan Cease 5.00 12.00
23 Mauricio Dubon 3.00 8.00
24 Jake Fraley 3.00 8.00
25 Logan Allen 2.50 6.00
26 Bo Bichette 25.00 60.00
27 Dustin May 10.00 25.00
28 Trent Grisham 10.00 25.00
29 Adrian Morejon 2.50 6.00
30 Aristides Aquino 5.00 12.00
31 Kyle Lewis 20.00 50.00
32 Patrick Sandoval 4.00 10.00
33 Sheldon Neuse 3.00 8.00
34 Brendan McKay 4.00 10.00
35 Gavin Lux 15.00 40.00
36 Randy Arozarena 20.00 50.00
37 Nick Solak 4.00 10.00
38 Brock Burke 2.50 6.00
39 Abraham Toro 3.00 8.00
40 Bryan Abreu 2.50 6.00
41 Nico Hoerner 10.00 25.00
42 Tony Gonsolin 10.00 25.00
43 Andres Munoz 3.00 8.00
44 Jake Rogers 2.50 6.00
45 A.J. Puk 5.00 12.00
46 Matt Thaiss 3.00 8.00
47 Adbert Alzolay 3.00 8.00
48 Domingo Leyba 3.00 8.00
49 Jordan Yamamoto 3.00 8.00
50 Edwin Rios 6.00 15.00
51 Ronald Bolanos 4.00 10.00
52 Tyrone Taylor 2.50 6.00
53 Jaylin Davis 4.00 10.00
54 Michel Baez 2.50 6.00
55 Danny Mendick 3.00 8.00
56 Donnie Walton 6.00 15.00
57 Tres Barrera 4.00 10.00
58 Josh Rojas 2.50 6.00
59 T.J. Zeuch 2.50 6.00
60 Rico Garcia 4.00 10.00
61 Yonathan Daza 3.00 8.00
62 Austin Dean 2.50 6.00
63 Luis Robert 50.00 120.00
64 Jalen Beeks 2.50 6.00
65 Jo Adell 20.00 50.00
66 Michael Shawaryn 2.50 6.00
67 Andrew Knizner 5.00 12.00
68 Ji-Man Choi 2.50 6.00
69 Taylor Hearn 2.50 6.00
70 Hanser Alberto 2.50 6.00
71 Genesis Cabrera 4.00 10.00
72 Anthony Santander 2.50 6.00
73 German Marquez 4.00 10.00
74 Bobby Dalbec 5.00 12.00
75 Royce Lewis 10.00 25.00
77 Taylor Clarke 2.50 6.00
78 Ryan Helsley 3.00 8.00
79 Shed Long Jr. 3.00 8.00
80 Darwinzon Hernandez 2.50 6.00
81 Oscar Mercado 5.00 12.00
82 Bryan Reynolds 10.00 25.00
83 Roger Clemens
84 Peter Lambert 3.00 8.00
85 Griffin Canning 4.00 10.00
87 Nicky Lopez 2.50 6.00
88 Yu Darvish 10.00 25.00
89 Alec Bohm 12.00 30.00
90 J.D. Davis 5.00 12.00
91 Forrest Whitley 2.50 6.00
92 Cole Tucker 4.00 10.00
93 Hunter Dozier 2.50 6.00
94 Eric Hosmer 3.00 8.00
95 Roberto Alomar 10.00 25.00
96 Omar Vizquel 3.00 8.00
97 Trey Mancini 4.00 10.00
98 Kyle Schwarber 10.00 25.00
99 Jack Flaherty 10.00 25.00
100 Sixto Sanchez 5.00 12.00

2020 Donruss Retro '86 Signatures Gold

*GOLD/25: .75X TO 2X BASIC
RANDOM INSERTS IN PACKS
PRINT RUNS B/WN 4-25 COPIES PER
NO PRICING ON QTY 15 OR LESS
EXCHANGE DEADLINE 08/05/2021
63 Luis Robert/25 125.00 300.00

2020 Donruss Retro '86 Signatures Pink Fireworks

*PINK/199: .4X TO 1X BASIC
*PINK/99-100: .5X TO 1.2X BASIC
*PINK/49-50: .6X TO 1.5X BASIC
*PINK/25: .75X TO 2X BASIC
RANDOM INSERTS IN PACKS
PRINT RUNS B/WN 25-199 COPIES PER
EXCHANGE DEADLINE 08/05/2021

2020 Donruss Retro '86 Signatures Red

*RED/99: .5X TO 1.2X BASIC
*RED/49: .6X TO 1.5X BASIC
*RED/25: .75X TO 2X BASIC
RANDOM INSERTS IN PACKS
PRINT RUNS B/WN 10-99 COPIES PER
NO PRICING ON QTY 15 OR LESS
EXCHANGE DEADLINE 08/05/2021
88 Yu Darvish/25 25.00 60.00

2020 Donruss Signature Series Blue

*BLUE/99: .5X TO 1.2X BASIC
*BLUE/49: .6X TO 1.5X BASIC
RANDOM INSERTS IN PACKS
PRINT RUNS B/WN 49-99 COPIES PER
EXCHANGE DEADLINE 08/05/2021

2020 Donruss Signature Series Gold

*GOLD/25: .75X TO 2X BASIC
RANDOM INSERTS IN PACKS
STATED PRINT RUN 25 SER.#'d SETS
EXCHANGE DEADLINE 08/05/2021

2020 Donruss Sky High Signatures

RANDOM INSERTS IN PACKS
EXCHANGE DEADLINE 08/05/2021
*BLUE/99: .5X TO 1.2X BASIC
*BLUE/50: .6X TO 1.5X BASIC
*BLUE/25: .75X TO 2X BASIC
*GOLD/25: .75X TO 2X BASIC

1 Shohei Ohtani 60.00 150.00
2 Ronald Acuna Jr. 40.00 100.00
3 J.P. Crawford 2.50 6.00
4 Paul DeJong 5.00 12.00
5 Cal Quantrill 2.50 6.00
6 David Dahl 2.50 6.00
7 Mitch Haniger 3.00 8.00
8 Charlie Blackmon 4.00 10.00
9 Michael Chavis 6.00 15.00
10 Bryan Reynolds 10.00 25.00

2020 Donruss The Rookies Green

*GREEN/25: 1.5X TO 4X BASIC
RANDOM INSERTS IN PACKS
STATED PRINT RUN 25 SER.#'d SETS

6 Bo Bichette 20.00 50.00
8 Gavin Lux 15.00 40.00

2020 Donruss Whammy

RANDOM INSERTS IN PACKS

1 Pete Alonso 20.00 50.00
2 Yordan Alvarez 25.00 60.00
3 Fernando Tatis Jr. 30.00 80.00
4 Alex Bregman 8.00 20.00
5 Albert Pujols 10.00 25.00

2004 Donruss Elite Extra Edition

This 286-card set was released in December, 2004. The set was issued in five card packs with an $6 SRP which came 12 packs to a box and 32 boxes to case. Cards numbered 1-150 featured active veterans while cards numbered 206 through 215 feature retired players and cards 216 through 355 are all Rookie Cards including many players drafted in 2004. This is the set in which Donruss had the right to picture any player drafted and later signed from the 2004 amateur draft. Each company, which the exception of Topps (who signs their players individually), was allowed to have one product with a full run of 2004 amateur draft in it. This was Donruss' product for that purpose.

COMP.SET w/o SP's (150) 10.00 25.00
COMMON CARD (1-150) .12 .30
COMMON CARD (206-215) .40 1.00
206-215 RANDOM INSERTS IN PACKS
206-215 PRINT RUN 1000 SERIAL #'d SETS
COMMON NO AU (234-254) .75 2.00
NO AU MINORS 234-254 .75 2.00
NO AU SEMIS 234-254 1.25 3.00
NO AU UNLISTED 234-254 2.00 5.00
NO AU 234-254 RANDOM IN PACKS
NO AU 234-254 PRINT RUN 1000 #'d SETS
COMMON AU p/r 803-1195 3.00 8.00
COMMON AU p/r 522-799 3.00 8.00
COMMON AU p/r 350-493 4.00 10.00
COMMON AU p/r 260 5.00 12.00
216-355 OVERALL AU-GU ODDS 1:4
216-355 PRINT RUNS B/WN 260-1617 PER
DO NOT EXIST: 151-205/232/236-238/240
DO NOT EXIST: 241/245/248-249/251/255
DO NOT EXIST: 274/339

1 Troy Glaus .12 .30
2 John Lackey .20 .50
3 Garret Anderson .12 .30
4 Francisco Rodriguez .20 .50
5 Casey Kotchman .12 .30
6 Jose Guillen .12 .30
7 Miguel Tejada .20 .50
8 Rafael Palmeiro .20 .50
9 Jay Gibbons .12 .30
10 Melvin Mora .12 .30
11 Javy Lopez .12 .30
12 Pedro Martinez .20 .50
13 Curt Schilling .20 .50
14 David Ortiz .30 .75
15 Manny Ramirez .30 .75
16 Nomar Garciaparra .20 .50
17 Magglio Ordonez .20 .50
18 Frank Thomas .30 .75
19 Esteban Loaiza .12 .30
20 Paul Konerko .20 .50
21 Mark Buehrle .20 .50
22 Jody Gerut .12 .30
23 Victor Martinez .20 .50
24 C.C. Sabathia .20 .50
25 Travis Hafner .12 .30
26 Cliff Lee .20 .50
27 Jeremy Bonderman .12 .30
28 Dallas McPherson .12 .30
29 Jermaine Dye .12 .30
30 Carlos Guillen .12 .30
31 Carlos Beltran .20 .50
32 Ken Harvey .12 .30
33 Mike Sweeney .12 .30
34 Angel Berroa .12 .30
35 Joe Nathan .12 .30
36 Johan Santana .20 .50
37 Jacque Jones .12 .30
38 Shannon Stewart .12 .30
39 Torii Hunter .12 .30
40 Derek Jeter .75 2.00
41 Jason Giambi .12 .30
42 Danny Graves .12 .30
43 Alfonso Soriano .20 .50
44 Gary Sheffield .12 .30
45 Mike Mussina .20 .50
46 Jorge Posada .20 .50
47 Hideki Matsui .50 1.25
48 Francisco Cordero .12 .30
49 Javier Vazquez .12 .30
50 Mariano Rivera .40 1.00
51 Eric Chavez .12 .30
52 Tim Hudson .20 .50
53 Mark Mulder .12 .30
54 Barry Zito .20 .50
55 Ichiro Suzuki .40 1.00
56 Edgar Martinez .20 .50
57 Bret Boone .12 .30
58 Lew Ford .12 .30
59 B.J. Upton .20 .50
60 Aubrey Huff .12 .30
61 Rocco Baldelli .12 .30
62 Carl Crawford .20 .50
63 Delmon Young .20 .50
64 Mark Teixeira .20 .50
65 Hank Blalock .12 .30
66 Michael Young .12 .30
67 Alex Rodriguez .40 1.00
68 Carlos Delgado .12 .30
69 Milton Bradley .12 .30
70 Roy Halladay .20 .50
71 Vernon Wells .12 .30
72 Randy Johnson .30 .75
73 Bobby Crosby .12 .30
74 Lyle Overbay .12 .30
75 Luis Gonzalez .12 .30
76 Steve Finley .12 .30
77 Chipper Jones .30 .75
78 Andruw Jones .12 .30
79 Marcus Giles .12 .30
80 Rafael Furcal .12 .30
81 J.D. Drew .12 .30
82 Sammy Sosa .30 .75
83 Kerry Wood .12 .30
84 Mark Prior .20 .50
85 Derrek Lee .12 .30
86 Moises Alou .12 .30
87 Carlos Zambrano .20 .50
88 Ken Griffey Jr. .60 1.50
89 Austin Kearns .12 .30
90 Adam Dunn .20 .50
91 Barry Larkin .20 .50
92 Todd Helton .20 .50
93 Larry Walker Cards .20 .50
94 Preston Wilson .12 .30
95 Sean Casey .12 .30
96 Luis Castillo .12 .30
97 Josh Beckett .12 .30
98 Mike Lowell .12 .30
99 Miguel Cabrera .30 .75
100 Brad Penny .12 .30
101 Dontrelle Willis .12 .30
102 Andy Pettitte .20 .50
103 Wade Miller .12 .30
104 Jeff Bagwell .20 .50
105 Craig Biggio .20 .50
106 Lance Berkman .20 .50
107 Jeff Kent .12 .30
108 Roy Oswalt .20 .50
109 Hideo Nomo .30 .75
110 Adrian Beltre .30 .75
111 Paul Lo Duca .12 .30
112 Shawn Green .12 .30
113 Roger Clemens .40 1.00
114 Eric Gagne .12 .30
115 Danny Kolb .12 .30
116 Rickie Weeks .12 .30
117 Scott Podsednik .12 .30
118 Livan Hernandez .12 .30
119 Orlando Cabrera .12 .30
120 Jose Vidro .12 .30
121 David Wright .25 .60
122 Tom Glavine .20 .50
123 Al Leiter .12 .30
124 Mike Piazza .30 .75
125 Jose Reyes .20 .50
126 Richard Hidalgo .12 .30
127 Eric Milton .12 .30
128 Jim Thome .20 .50
129 Mike Lieberthal .12 .30
130 Bobby Abreu .12 .30
131 Kip Wells .12 .30
132 Jack Wilson .12 .30
133 Jason Bay .20 .50
134 Brian Giles .12 .30
135 Sean Burroughs .12 .30
136 Khalil Greene .20 .50
137 Jake Peavy .12 .30
138 Jason Schmidt .12 .30
139 J.T. Snow .12 .30
140 Craig Wilson .12 .30
141 Chase Utley .20 .50
142 Jim Edmonds .20 .50
143 Albert Pujols .40 1.00
144 Edgar Renteria .12 .30
145 Scott Rolen .20 .50
146 Matt Morris .12 .30
147 Ivan Rodriguez .20 .50
148 Vladimir Guerrero .20 .50
149 Greg Maddux .40 1.00
150 Ben Sheets .12 .30
206 Will Clark RET .60 1.50
207 Nolan Ryan RET 3.00 8.00
208 Bob Feller RET .60 1.50
209 Red Schoendienst RET .60 1.50
210 Brooks Robinson RET .60 1.50
211 Al Kaline RET 1.00 2.50
212 Ozzie Smith RET 1.25 3.00
213 Maury Wills RET .40 1.00
214 Steve Carlton RET .60 1.50
215 Duke Snider RET .60 1.50
216 Scott Lewis AU/603 RC 8.00 20.00
217 Josh Johnson AU/597 RC 4.00 10.00
218 Jeff Fiorentino AU/597 RC 5.00 12.00
219 Grant Hansen AU/599 RC 3.00 8.00
220 Yov Gallardo AU/803 RC 4.00 10.00
221 Eddie Prasch AU/603 RC 4.00 10.00
222 Danny Hill AU/603 RC 3.00 8.00
223 Chuck Lofgren AU/803 RC 6.00 15.00
224 Blake Johnson AU/811 RC 4.00 10.00
225 Cory Dunlap AU/599 RC 6.00 15.00
226 Carlos Vasquez AU/869 RC 3.00 8.00
227 Jesse Crain AU/1000 RC 3.00 8.00
228 Yhency Brazoban AU/1000 3.00 8.00
229 Abe Alvarez AU/1000 RC 4.00 10.00
230 Scott Kazmir AU/350 RC 15.00 40.00
231 J.A. Happ AU/1195 RC 3.00 8.00
233 Mark Jecmen AU/1047 RC 3.00 8.00
234 Kameron Loe/1000 RC .75 2.00
235 Ervin Santana/1000 RC 2.00 5.00
239 Josh Karp/1000 RC .75 2.00
242 Alberto Callaspo/1000 RC 2.00 5.00
243 Jesse Hoyman AU/1191 RC 4.00 10.00
246 Just Hoyman AU/1124 RC 4.00 10.00
247 Juan Cedeno/1000 RC .75 2.00
250 Jake Dittler/1000 RC .75 2.00
252 Ben Zobrist AU/1178 RC 8.00 20.00
253 Jeff Salazar/1000 RC .75 2.00
254 Fausto Carmona/1000 RC 1.25 3.00
256 Jor Vasquez AU/1000 RC 3.00 8.00
257 Raf Gonzalez AU/603 RC 3.00 8.00
258 Andrew Dobies AU/601 RC 3.00 8.00
259 Colby Miller AU/997 RC 3.00 8.00
260 K.C. Herren AU/735 RC 3.00 8.00
261 Ryan Meaux AU/546 RC 3.00 8.00
262 Dust Pedroia AU/1114 RC 30.00 80.00
263 Fern Nieve AU/1000 RC 3.00 8.00
264 Mar Gomez AU/1000 RC 15.00 30.00
265 Eric Campbell AU/260 RC 70.00 120.00
266 Billy Killian AU/703 RC 4.00 10.00
267 Mike Rouse AU/999 RC 3.00 8.00
268 Kyle Bono AU/1203 RC 3.00 8.00
269 M.Einertson AU/1047 RC 6.00 15.00
270 Scott Proctor AU/1000 RC 3.00 8.00
271 Tim Bittner AU/1000 RC 3.00 8.00
272 Christian Garcia AU/799 RC 4.00 10.00
273 Yadier Molina AU/1000 RC 50.00 100.00
275 C.Thomas AU/907 RC 3.00 8.00
276 Trav Blackley AU/1000 RC 3.00 8.00
277 F.Francisco AU/1000 RC 3.00 8.00
278 Dion Navarro AU/1000 RC 3.00 8.00
279 Joey Gathright AU/1000 RC 3.00 8.00
280 Kaz Tadano AU/1000 RC 4.00 10.00
281 Matt Bush AU/1100 RC 3.00 8.00
282 David Haehnel AU/865 RC 4.00 10.00
283 Tommy Hottovy AU/825 RC 4.00 10.00
284 Chris Carter AU/973 RC 6.00 15.00
285 Mark Rogers AU/578 RC 8.00 20.00
286 Jeremy Sowers AU/537 RC 15.00 30.00
287 Homer Bailey AU/1571 RC 6.00 15.00
288 Mike Butia AU/825 RC 3.00 8.00
289 Chris Nelson AU/465 RC 5.00 12.00
290 T.Diamond AU/1055 RC 6.00 15.00
291 Neil Walker AU/1343 RC 4.00 10.00
292 Sean Gamble AU/1229 RC 3.00 8.00
293 Bill Bray AU/1073 RC 3.00 8.00
294 Reid Brignac AU/522 RC 8.00 20.00
295 R.Klosterman AU/865 RC 3.00 8.00
296 David Purcey AU/1485 RC 3.00 8.00
297 Scott Elbert AU/1617 RC 8.00 20.00
298 Josh Fields AU/961 RC 15.00 30.00
299 Chris Lambert AU/954 RC 4.00 10.00
300 Trevor Plouffe AU/1329 RC 3.00 8.00
301 Greg Golson AU/1334 RC 4.00 10.00
302 Josh Baker AU/525 RC 3.00 8.00
303 Philip Hughes AU/1485 RC 6.00 15.00
304 Matt Macri AU/979 RC 4.00 10.00
305 Kyle Waldrop AU/823 RC 6.00 15.00
306 Rich Robnett AU/1575 RC 4.00 10.00
307 T.Tankersley AU/1073 RC 4.00 10.00
308 Blake DeWitt AU/1562 RC 4.00 10.00
309 Daryl Jones AU/575 RC 12.50 30.00
310 Eric Hurley AU/1021 RC 10.00 25.00
311 J.P. Howell AU/1453 RC 4.00 10.00
312 Zach Jackson AU/1069 RC 3.00 8.00
313 Justin Orenduff AU/473 RC 12.50 30.00
314 Tyler Lumsden AU/473 RC 4.00 10.00
315 Matt Fox AU/473 RC 4.00 10.00
316 Danny Putnam AU/473 RC 4.00 10.00
317 Jon Poterson AU/464 RC 6.00 15.00
318 Gio Gonzalez AU/473 RC 5.00 12.00
319 Jay Rainville AU/823 RC 10.00 25.00
320 Huston Street AU/709 RC 6.00 15.00
321 Jeff Marquez AU/493 RC 4.00 10.00
322 Eric Beattie AU/930 RC 4.00 10.00
323 B.Szymanski AU/1327 RC 4.00 10.00
324 Seth Smith AU/1065 RC 3.00 8.00
325 Rob Johnson AU/790 RC 4.00 10.00
326 Wes Whisler AU/473 RC 4.00 10.00
327 Billy Buckner AU/673 RC 4.00 10.00
328 Jon Zeringue AU/473 RC 3.00 8.00
329 Curtis Thigpen AU/673 RC 12.50 30.00
330 Donny Lucy AU/573 RC 3.00 8.00
331 Mike Ferris AU/558 RC 4.00 10.00
332 Anthony Swarzak AU/370 RC 3.00 8.00
333 Jason Jaramillo AU/573 RC 4.00 10.00
334 Hunter Pence AU/672 RC 8.00 20.00
335 Mike Rozier AU/628 RC 4.00 10.00
336 Kurt Suzuki AU/473 RC 6.00 15.00
337 Jason Vargas AU/621 RC 6.00 15.00
338 Brian Bixler AU/665 RC 10.00 25.00
340 Dexter Fowler AU/623 RC 6.00 15.00
341 Mark Trumbo AU/1321 RC 5.00 12.00
342 Jeff Frazier AU/423 RC 4.00 10.00
343 Steve Register AU/673 RC 3.00 8.00
344 M.Schlact AU/477 RC 4.00 10.00
345 Garrett Mock AU/471 RC 4.00 10.00
346 Eric Haberer AU/473 RC 4.00 10.00
347 M.Tuiasosopo AU/473 RC 10.00 25.00
348 Jason Windsor AU/473 RC 4.00 10.00
349 Grant Johnson AU/815 RC 4.00 10.00
350 J.C. Holt AU/673 RC 4.00 10.00
351 Joe Bauserman AU/472 RC 4.00 10.00
352 Jamar Walton AU/481 RC 4.00 10.00
353 Eric Patterson AU/1571 RC 6.00 15.00
354 Tyler Johnson AU/775 RC 6.00 15.00
355 Nick Adenhart AU/653 RC 6.00 15.00

2004 Donruss Elite Extra Edition Aspirations

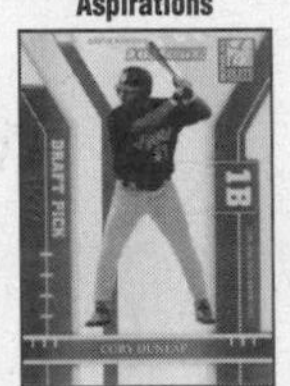

*1-150 p/r 81-99: 4X TO 10X
*1-150 p/r 51-80: 5X TO 12X
*1-150 p/r 36-50: 6X TO 15X
*1-150 p/r 26-35: 8X TO 20X
*1-150 p/r 16-25: 10X TO 25X
*206-215 p/r 81-99: 1.25X TO 3X
*206-215 p/r 51-80: 1.5X TO 4X
*216-355 p/r 51-80: .6X TO 1.5X NO AU
*216-355 p/r 36-50: .75X TO 2X NO AU
*216-355p/r81-99: .3X TO .8X AUp/r803-1617
*216-355p/r81-99: .25X TO .6X AUp/r522-799
*216-355p/r81-99: .2X TO .5X AU p/r 350-493
*216-355p/r51-80: .4X TO 1X AU p/r 803-1617
*216-355p/r51-80: .3X TO .8X AU p/r 522-799
*216-355p/r51-80: .25X TO .6X AUp/r350-493
*216-355 p/r 51-80: .15X TO .4X AU p/r 260
*216-355p/r36-50:.5X TO 1.2X AUp/r803-1617
*216-355 p/r 36-50: .4X TO 1X AU p/r 522-799
*216-355p/r36-50: .3X TO .8X AU p/r 350-493
*216-355 p/r 26-35: .4X TO 1X AU p/r 350-493
PRINT RUNS B/WN 4-99 COPIES PER
NO PRICING ON QTY OF 13 OR LESS

2004 Donruss Elite Extra Edition Aspirations Gold

*ASP.GOLD 1-150: 10X TO 25X
*ASP.GOLD 206-215: 3X TO 8X
RANDOM INSERTS IN PACKS
STATED PRINT RUN 25 SERIAL #'d SETS
216-355 NO PRICING DUE TO SCARCITY

2004 Donruss Elite Extra Edition Status

*1-150 p/r 51-80: 5X TO 12X
*1-150 p/r 36-50: 6X TO 15X
*1-150 p/r 26-35: 8X TO 20X
*1-150 p/r 16-25: 10X TO 25X
*206-215 p/r 26-35: 2.5X TO 6X
*206-215 p/r 16-25: 3X TO 8X
*216-355 p/r 36-50: .75X TO 2X NO AU
*216-355p/r81-96: .3X TO .8X AUp/r803-1617
*216-355p/r51-80: .4X TO 1X AU p/r 803-1617
*216-355p/r51-80: .3X TO .8X AU p/r 522-799
*216-355p/r51-80: .25X TO .6X AUp/r350-493
*216-355p/r36-50:.5X TO 1.2X AUp/r803-1617
*216-355 p/r 36-50: .4X TO 1X AU p/r 522-799
*216-355p/r36-50: .3X TO .8X AU p/r 350-493
*216-355p/r26-35:.6X TO 1.5X AUp/r803-1617
*216-355p/r26-35: .5X TO 1.2X AUp/r 522-799
*216-355 p/r 26-35: .4X TO 1X AU p/r 350-493
*216-355 p/r 26-35: .25X TO .6X AU p/r 260
PRINT RUNS B/WN 1-96 COPIES PER
1-215 NO PRICING ON QTY OF 15 OR LESS
216-355 NO PRICING ON QTY 25 OR LESS

2004 Donruss Elite Extra Edition Status Gold

STATED PRINT RUN 10 SERIAL #'d SETS
NO PRICING DUE TO SCARCITY

2004 Donruss Elite Extra Edition Turn of the Century

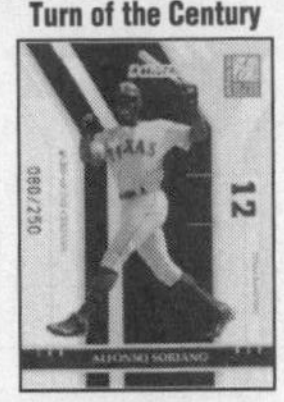

*1-150: 2.5X TO 6X BASIC
1-150 PRINT RUN 250 SERIAL #'d SETS
*206-215: 1.25X TO 3X BASIC
*216-355: .5X TO 1.2X NO AU p/r 1000
206-355 PRINT RUN 100 SERIAL #'d SETS
RANDOM INSERTS IN PACKS

2004 Donruss Elite Extra Edition Signature

*216-355 p/r 50: 1X TO 2.5X AU p/r 803-1617
OVERALL AU-GU ODDS 1:4
PRINT RUNS B/WN 1-50 #'d COPIES PER
NO PRICING ON QTY OF 10 OR LESS

132 Jack Wilson/25 12.50 30.00
133 Jason Bay/25 12.50 30.00
234 Kameron Loe ROO/50 10.00 25.00
235 Ervin Santana ROO/50 8.00 20.00
239 Josh Karp ROO/50 8.00 20.00
247 Juan Cedeno ROO/50 8.00 20.00
253 Jeff Salazar ROO/50 10.00 25.00
254 Fausto Carmona ROO/50 40.00 80.00

2004 Donruss Elite Extra Edition Signature Aspirations

*216-355 p/r 100: .6X TO 1.5X p/r 803-1617
*216-355 p/r 100: .6X TO 1.5X p/r 522-799
*216-355 p/r 100: .5X TO 1.2X p/r 350-493
*216-355 p/r 49-50: 1.25X TO 3X p/r 803-1617
*216-355 p/r 49-50: 1X TO 2.5X p/r 522-799
*216-355 p/r 49-50: .75X TO 2X p/r 350-493
OVERALL AU-GU ODDS 1:4
PRINT RUNS B/WN 1-100 COPIES PER
NO PRICING ON QTY OF 10 OR LESS

220 Yovani Gallardo ROO/50 40.00 80.00
273 Yadier Molina ROO/50 100.00 200.00
278 Dioner Navarro ROO/50 6.00 15.00
287 Homer Bailey DP/100 10.00 25.00
303 Philip Hughes DP/100 12.50 30.00
318 Gio Gonzalez DP/100 10.00 25.00
334 Hunter Pence DP/50 12.00 30.00
340 Dexter Fowler DP/50 20.00 50.00
341 Mark Trumbo DP/50 8.00 20.00
347 Matt Tuiasosopo DP/100 20.00 40.00
355 Nick Adenhart DP/100 12.50 30.00

2004 Donruss Elite Extra Edition Signature Aspirations Gold

OVERALL AU-GU ODDS 1:4
PRINT RUNS B/WN 1-25 COPIES PER
NO PRICING DUE TO SCARCITY

2004 Donruss Elite Extra Edition Signature Status

*216-355 p/r 50: 1.25X TO 3X p/r 803-1617
*216-355 p/r 50: 1X TO 2.5X p/r 522-799
*216-355 p/r 50: .75X TO 2X p/r 350-493
*216-355 p/r 50: .5X TO 1.2X p/r 260
OVERALL AU-GU ODDS 1:4
PRINT RUNS B/WN 1-50 COPIES PER
NO PRICING ON QTY OF 25 OR LESS

289 Chris Nelson DP/50 8.00 20.00
303 Philip Hughes DP/50 50.00 100.00
308 Blake DeWitt DP/50 15.00 40.00
318 Gio Gonzalez DP/50 12.50 30.00
334 Hunter Pence DP/50 12.00 30.00
340 Dexter Fowler DP/50 20.00 50.00
341 Mark Trumbo DP/50 8.00 20.00
347 Matt Tuiasosopo DP/50 30.00 60.00
355 Nick Adenhart DP/50 15.00 40.00

2004 Donruss Elite Extra Edition Signature Status Gold

OVERALL AU-GU ODDS 1:4
PRINT RUNS B/WN 1-10 COPIES PER
NO PRICING DUE TO SCARCITY

2004 Donruss Elite Extra Edition Signature Turn of the Century

*216-355p/r150-250: .6X TO 1.5X p/r803-1617
*216-355p/r150-250: .5X TO 1.2X p/r 522-799
*216-355p/r150-250: .4X TO 1X p/r 350-493
*216-355 p/r 100: .75X TO 2X p/r 803-1617
*216-355 p/r 100: .6X TO 1.5X p/r 522-799
*216-355 p/r 100: .5X TO 1.2X p/r 350-493
*216-355 p/r 50: .75X TO 2X p/r 350-493
OVERALL AU-GU ODDS 1:4
PRINT RUNS B/WN 1-250 COPIES PER
NO PRICING ON QTY OF 25 OR LESS

220 Yovani Gallardo ROO/100 12.50 30.00
252 Ben Zobrist DP/150 15.00 40.00
273 Yadier Molina ROO/100 40.00 80.00
274 Justin Leone ROO/100 6.00 15.00
281 Matt Bush DP/250 8.00 20.00
285 Mark Rogers DP/100 12.50 30.00
287 Homer Bailey DP/250 6.00 15.00
303 Philip Hughes DP/250 20.00 50.00
308 Blake DeWitt DP/250 10.00 25.00
310 Eric Hurley DP/250 12.50 30.00
318 Gio Gonzalez DP/250 6.00 15.00
334 Hunter Pence DP/200 10.00 25.00
340 Dexter Fowler DP/250 12.50 30.00
341 Mark Trumbo DP/250 6.00 15.00
347 Matt Tuiasosopo DP/250 6.00 15.00
355 Nick Adenhart DP/100 12.50 30.00

2004 Donruss Elite Extra Edition Back to Back Picks Signature

OVERALL AU-GU ODDS 1:4
1-10 PRINT RUNS B/WN 10-50 COPIES PER
11-20 PRINT RUNS B/WN 100-250 PER
NO PRICING ON QTY OF 10 OR LESS

1 D.Young/R.Weeks/25 8.00 20.00
3 A.Dunn/A.Kearns/25 30.00 60.00
5 M.Young/V.Wells/25 30.00 60.00
6 B.Roberts/L.Bigbie/50 6.00 15.00
7 R.Cey/S.Garvey/50 20.00 50.00
8 B.Madlock/D.Parker/50 40.00 80.00
9 D.Lee/Torii/Nixon/50 30.00 60.00
11 Nelson/Bush/Brignac/250 25.00 60.00
12 Szym/Golson/Frazier/250 15.00 40.00
13 Trumbo/Aden/T.Johns/100 20.00 50.00
14 Carter/Putnam/Jecmen/100 15.00 40.00
15 Killian/D.Jones/Bush/100 15.00 40.00
16 DeWitt/Orenduff/Elbert/250 12.50 30.00
17 R'ville/Waldrop/Plouffe/250 8.00 20.00
18 Marquez/Poter/Hughes/100 30.00 60.00
19 Gio/Lumsden/Whisler/100 12.50 30.00
20 Thigpen/Purcey/Z.Jack/100 12.50 30.00

2004 Donruss Elite Extra Edition Career Best All-Stars

RANDOM INSERTS IN PACKS
STATED PRINT RUN 500 SERIAL #'d SETS

1 Randy Johnson 1.50 4.00
2 David Ortiz 1.50 4.00
3 Edgar Renteria .60 1.50
4 Victor Martinez 1.00 2.50
5 Albert Pujols 2.00 5.00
6 Hideki Matsui 2.50 6.00
7 Mariano Rivera 2.00 5.00
8 Carlos Zambrano 1.00 2.50
9 Hank Blalock .60 1.50
10 Michael Young .60 1.50
11 Mike Piazza 1.50 4.00
12 Alfonso Soriano 1.00 2.50
13 Carl Crawford 1.00 2.50
14 Scott Rolen 1.00 2.50
15 Vladimir Guerrero 1.00 2.50
16 Lance Berkman 1.00 2.50
17 Todd Helton 1.00 2.50
18 Curt Schilling 1.00 2.50
19 Francisco Cordero .60 1.50
20 Mark Mulder .60 1.50
21 Sammy Sosa 1.50 4.00
22 Roger Clemens 2.00 5.00
23 Miguel Cabrera 1.50 4.00
24 Manny Ramirez 1.50 4.00
25 Jim Thome 1.00 2.50

2004 Donruss Elite Extra Edition Career Best All-Stars Jersey

STATED PRINT RUN 50 SERIAL #'d SETS
*PRIME p/r 25: .75X TO 2X BASIC
PRIME PRINT RUN B/WN 5-25 COPIES PER
NO PRIME PRICING ON QTY OF 5
OVERALL AU-GU ODDS 1:4

1 Randy Johnson 6.00 15.00
2 David Ortiz 6.00 15.00
3 Edgar Renteria 4.00 10.00
4 Victor Martinez 4.00 10.00
5 Albert Pujols 10.00 25.00
6 Hideki Matsui 12.50 30.00
7 Mariano Rivera 6.00 15.00
8 Carlos Zambrano 4.00 10.00
9 Hank Blalock 4.00 10.00
10 Michael Young 4.00 10.00
11 Mike Piazza 8.00 20.00
12 Alfonso Soriano 4.00 10.00
13 Carl Crawford 4.00 10.00
14 Scott Rolen 6.00 15.00
15 Vladimir Guerrero 6.00 15.00
16 Lance Berkman 4.00 10.00
17 Todd Helton 6.00 15.00
18 Curt Schilling 6.00 15.00
19 Francisco Cordero 4.00 10.00
20 Mark Mulder 4.00 10.00
21 Sammy Sosa 6.00 15.00
22 Roger Clemens 8.00 20.00
23 Miguel Cabrera 6.00 15.00
24 Manny Ramirez 6.00 15.00
25 Jim Thome 6.00 15.00

2004 Donruss Elite Extra Edition Career Best All-Stars Signature Jersey Gold

PRINT RUNS B/WN 1-25 COPIES PER
NO PRICING ON QTY OF 10 OR LESS
SIG BLACK PRINT RUN B/WN 1-5 PER
NO SIG BLACK PRICING DUE TO SCARCITY
SIG GOLD PRINT RUN B/WN 1-10 PER
NO SIG GOLD PRICING DUE TO SCARCITY
SIG JSY PRIME PRINT RUN B/WN 1-10 PER
NO SIG JSY PRIME PRICING AVAILABLE
OVERALL AU-GU ODDS 1:4

2 David Ortiz/25 40.00 80.00
3 Edgar Renteria/25 15.00 40.00
4 Victor Martinez/25 10.00 25.00
8 Carlos Zambrano/25 15.00 40.00
10 Michael Young/25 15.00 40.00
13 Carl Crawford/25 15.00 40.00
19 Francisco Cordero/25 10.00 25.00

2004 Donruss Elite Extra Edition Draft Class

RANDOM INSERTS IN PACKS
STATED PRINT RUN 500 SERIAL #'d SETS

1 J.Bench / N.Ryan 5.00 12.00
2 B.Blyleven / D.Evans 1.00 2.50
3 J.Rice / K.Hernandez 1.00 2.50
4 D.Eckersley / G.Carter 1.00 2.50
5 F.Lynn / R.Yount 1.50 4.00
6 A.Dawson / L.Smith 1.00 2.50
7 A.Trammell / J.Morris 1.00 2.50
8 H.Baines / P.Molitor 1.50 4.00
9 C.Ripken / K.Gibson 5.00 12.00
10 D.Mattingly / O.Hershiser 3.00 8.00
11 D.Strawberry / E.Davis .60 1.50
12 D.Gooden / J.Canseco 1.00 2.50
13 R.Palmeiro / R.Johnson 1.50 4.00
14 C.Schilling / G.Sheffield 1.00 2.50
15 M.Piazza / R.Ventura 1.50 4.00
16 F.Thomas / J.Bagwell 1.50 4.00
17 C.Jones / M.Mussina 1.50 4.00
18 G.Anderson / J.Posada 1.00 2.50
19 S.Rolen / T.Hunter 1.00 2.50
20 K.Wood / T.Helton 1.00 2.50
21 E.Chavez / R.Oswalt 1.00 2.50
22 J.Estrada / V.Wells .60 1.50
23 L.Berkman / T.Hudson 1.00 2.50
24 M.Buehrle / M.Mulder 1.00 2.50
25 C.Sabathia / S.Burroughs 1.00 2.50
26 A.Pujols / B.Zito 2.00 5.00
27 R.Harden / R.Baldelli .60 1.50
28 B.Crosby / M.Teixeira 1.00 2.50
29 C.Kotchman / M.Prior 1.00 2.50
30 D.Brazelton / J.Bonderman .60 1.50
31 J.Holt / J.Zeringue .60 1.50
32 K.Bono / M.Fox .60 1.50
33 D.Fowler / M.Rozier 2.00 5.00
34 H.Street / J.Howell 1.00 2.50

35 G.Johnson 1.00 2.50
M.Macri
36 E.Beattie .60 1.50
J.Frazier
37 J.Windsor 1.00 2.50
K.Suzuki
38 J.Fields 1.50 4.00
M.Tuiasosopo
39 J.Bauserman .60 1.50
K.Herren
40 C.Lambert .60 1.50
E.Haberer

2004 Donruss Elite Extra Edition Draft Class Signature

OVERALL AU-GU ODDS 1:4
1-30 PRINT RUNS B/WN 5-50 COPIES PER
31-40 PRINT RUNS B/WN 100-250 PER
NO PRICING ON QTY OF 10 OR LESS
2 B.Blyleven/D.Evans/50 10.00 25.00
3 J.Rice/K.Hernandez/50 15.00 40.00
4 D.Eckersley/G.Carter/25 30.00 60.00
5 A.Dawson/L.Smith/50 15.00 40.00
7 A.Trammell/J.Morris/50 15.00 40.00
H.Baines/P.Molitor/25 20.00 50.00
1 D.Strawberry/E.Davis/50 20.00 50.00
2 D.Gooden/J.Canseco/25 50.00 100.00
21 E.Chavez/R.Oswalt/25 20.00 50.00
22 J.Estrada/V.Wells/25 20.00 50.00
25 C.Sabathia/S.Burroughs/50 10.00 25.00
28 B.Crosby/M.Teixeira/25 30.00 60.00
29 C.Kotchman/M.Prior/25 20.00 50.00
30 D.Brazelton/J.Bonder/50 15.00 40.00
31 J.Holt/J.Zeringue/100 10.00 25.00
32 K.Bono/M.Fox/100 8.00 20.00
33 D.Fowler/M.Rozier/250 10.00 25.00
34 H.Street/J.Howell/100 10.00 25.00
35 G.Johnson/M.Macri/100 8.00 20.00
36 E.Beattie/J.Frazier/100 8.00 20.00
37 J.Windsor/K.Suzuki/100 10.00 25.00
38 J.Fields/M.Tuiasosopo/100 20.00 50.00
39 J.Bauserman/K.Herren/100 8.00 20.00
40 C.Lambert/E.Haberer/100 8.00 20.00

2004 Donruss Elite Extra Edition Passing the Torch

RANDOM INSERTS IN PACKS
STATED PRINT RUN 500 SERIAL #'d SETS
1 D.Eckersley 1.00 2.50
H.Street
2 M.Bush 1.50 4.00
T.Gwynn
3 H.Bailey 1.00 2.50
T.Seaver
4 B.Feller 1.00 2.50
J.Sowers
5 J.Fields 1.00 2.50
R.Ventura
6 N.Ryan 5.00 12.00
T.Diamond
7 E.Patterson 3.00 8.00
R.Sandberg
8 R.Robnett 1.50 4.00
R.Henderson
9 M.Ferris 2.50 6.00
S.Musial
10 B.Doerr 3.00 8.00
D.Pedroia

2004 Donruss Elite Extra Edition Passing the Torch Autograph Gold

PRINT RUNS B/WN 5-25 COPIES PER
BLACK PRINT RUNS B/WN 5-10 PER
OVERALL AU-GU ODDS 1:4
NO PRICING DUE TO SCARCITY

2004 Donruss Elite Extra Edition Round Numbers

RANDOM INSERTS IN PACKS
STATED PRINT RUN 500 SERIAL #'d SETS
1 Ozzie Smith 2.00 5.00
2 Derek Jeter 4.00 10.00
3 Alex Rodriguez 2.00 5.00
4 Paul Molitor 1.50 4.00
5 George Brett 3.00 8.00
6 Delmon Young 1.00 2.50
7 Dontrelle Willis .60 1.50
8 Gary Carter 1.00 2.50
9 Reggie Jackson 1.00 2.50
10 Andre Dawson 1.00 2.50
11 Neil Walker 3.00 8.00
12 Laynce Nix .60 1.50
13 Matt Bush 1.00 2.50
14 Lyle Overbay .60 1.50
15 Carlos Beltran 1.00 2.50
16 Todd Helton 1.00 2.50
17 Mark Grace 1.00 2.50
18 Fred Lynn .60 1.50
19 Robin Yount 1.50 4.00
20 Mike Schmidt 2.50 6.00
21 Roger Clemens 2.00 5.00
22 Will Clark 1.00 2.50
23 Don Mattingly 3.00 8.00
24 Blake DeWitt 1.00 2.50
25 Rafael Palmeiro 1.00 2.50
26 Wade Boggs 1.00 2.50
27 Mark Rogers 1.00 2.50
28 Billy Buckner .60 1.50
29 Jeff Baker .60 1.50
30 Nolan Ryan 5.00 12.00
31 Mike Piazza 1.50 4.00
32 Alexis Rios .60 1.50
33 Eddie Murray 1.00 2.50
34 Jose Canseco 1.00 2.50
35 Mike Mussina 1.00 2.50
36 Eric Beattie .60 1.50
37 Keith Hernandez .60 1.50
38 Michael Young .60 1.50
39 Dwight Evans .60 1.50
40 Scott Elbert .60 1.50
41 Adrian Gonzalez 1.25 3.00
42 Johnny Bench 1.50 4.00
43 Dennis Eckersley 1.00 2.50
44 Dale Murphy 1.50 4.00
45 Ryne Sandberg 3.00 8.00
46 David Wright 1.25 3.00
47 Hank Blalock .60 1.50
48 Orel Hershiser .60 1.50
49 Sean Casey .60 1.50
50 Albert Pujols 2.00 5.00

2004 Donruss Elite Extra Edition Round Numbers Signature

OVERALL AU-GU ODDS 1:4
PRINT RUNS B/WN 5-250 COPIES PER
NO PRICING ON QTY OF 10 OR LESS
1 Ozzie Smith/25 20.00 50.00
4 Paul Molitor/25 10.00 25.00
6 Delmon Young/50 12.50 30.00
7 Dontrelle Willis/25 15.00 40.00
8 Gary Carter/25 15.00 40.00
10 Andre Dawson/50 8.00 20.00
11 Neil Walker/250 6.00 15.00
12 Laynce Nix/50 5.00 12.00
13 Matt Bush/100 8.00 20.00
14 Lyle Overbay/50 5.00 12.00
15 Carlos Beltran/25 10.00 25.00
17 Mark Grace/25 15.00 40.00
18 Fred Lynn/50 5.00 12.00
20 Mike Schmidt/25 50.00 100.00
22 Will Clark/20 15.00 40.00
23 Don Mattingly/25 50.00 100.00
24 Blake DeWitt/250 6.00 15.00
27 Mark Rogers/100 12.50 30.00
28 Billy Buckner/100 6.00 15.00
32 Alexis Rios/50 8.00 20.00
34 Jose Canseco/25 20.00 50.00
36 Eric Beattie/100 6.00 15.00
37 Keith Hernandez/50 8.00 20.00
38 Michael Young/50 8.00 20.00
39 Dwight Evans/50 12.50 30.00
40 Scott Elbert/250 6.00 15.00
41 Adrian Gonzalez/50 10.00 25.00
43 Dennis Eckersley/50 12.50 30.00
44 Dale Murphy/50 12.50 30.00
46 David Wright/25 50.00 100.00
47 Hank Blalock/25 8.00 20.00
49 Sean Casey/25 8.00 20.00

2004 Donruss Elite Extra Edition Throwback Threads

OVERALL AU-GU ODDS 1:4
1 Roger Maris 30.00 60.00
2 Ted Williams 40.00 80.00
3 Cal Ripken 15.00 40.00
4 Duke Snider 10.00 25.00
5 George Brett 15.00 40.00

2004 Donruss Elite Extra Edition Throwback Threads Autograph

OVERALL AU-GU ODDS 1:4
PRINT RUNS B/WN 5-10 COPIES PER
NO PRICING DUE TO SCARCITY

2007 Donruss Elite Extra Edition

COMPLETE SET (142)
COMP.SET w/o AU's (92) 8.00 20.00
COMMON CARD (1-92) .20 .50
COMMON AU (92-142) 4.00 10.00
OVERALL AUTO/MEM ODDS 1:5
AU PRINT RUNS B/WN 374-999 COPIES PER
EXCHANGE DEADLINE 07/01/2009
1 Andrew Brackman .30 .75
2 Austin Gallagher .20 .50
3 Brett Cecil .20 .50
4 Darwin Barney .50 1.25
5 David Price 2.00 5.00
6 J. P. Arencibia .40 1.00
7 Josh Donaldson 1.25 3.00
8 Brandon Hicks .20 .50
9 Brian Rike .20 .50
10 Bryan Morris .20 .50
11 Cale Iorg .20 .50
12 Casey Weathers .20 .50
13 Corey Kluber .50 1.25
14 Daniel Moskos .20 .50
15 Danny Payne .20 .50
16 David Kopp .20 .50
17 Dellin Betances .75 2.00
18 Derrick Robinson .20 .50
19 Drew Stubbs .20 .50
20 Eric Eiland .20 .50
21 Francisco Pena .20 .50
22 Greg Reynolds .20 .50
23 Jeff Samardzija 1.25 3.00
24 Jess Todd .20 .50
25 John Tolisano .20 .50
26 Jordan Zimmerman UER .20 .50
27 Julian Sampson .20 .50
28 Luke Hochevar .50 1.25
29 Mat Latos .75 2.00
30 Matt Mangini .20 .50
31 Matt Spencer .30 .75
32 Matthew Sweeney .50 1.25
33 Max Scherzer .75 2.00
34 Mitch Canham .20 .50
35 Nick Schmidt .20 .50
36 Paul Kelly .20 .50
37 Ryan Pope .30 .75
38 Sam Runion .20 .50
39 Steven Souza .60 1.50
40 Travis Mattair .20 .50
41 Trystan Magnuson .20 .50
42 Will Middlebrooks .30 .75
43 Zack Cozart .60 1.50
44 James Adkins .20 .50
45 Cory Luebke .20 .50
46 Aaron Poreda .20 .50
47 Clayton Mortensen .20 .50
48 Bradley Suttle .30 .75
49 Tony Butler .30 .75
50 Zach Britton 1.25 3.00
51 Scott Cousins .20 .50
52 Wendell Fairley .50 1.25
53 Eric Sogard .20 .50
54 Jonathan Lucroy .30 .75
55 Lars Davis .20 .50
77 Jennie Finch .50 1.25
91 Charlie Culberson .60 1.50
92 Jacob Smolinski .20 .50
93 Blake Beaven AU/719 5.00 12.00
94 Brad Chalk AU/613 4.00 10.00
95 Brett Anderson AU/549 5.00 12.00
96 Chris Withrow AU/700 4.00 10.00
97 Clay Fuller AU/674 4.00 10.00
98 Damon Sublett AU/674 8.00 20.00
99 Devin Mesoraco AU/674 6.00 15.00
100 Drew Cumberland AU/744 4.00 10.00
101 Jack McGeary AU/674 6.00 15.00
102 Jake Arrieta AU/949 30.00 80.00
103 James Simmons AU/624 4.00 10.00
104 Jarrod Parker AU/499 10.00 25.00
105 Jason Dominguez AU/744 4.00 10.00
106 Jason Heyward AU/750 12.00 30.00
107 Joe Savery AU/750 5.00 12.00
108 Jon Gilmore AU/619 3.00 8.00
109 Jordan Walden AU/794 5.00 12.00
110 Josh Smoker AU/719 5.00 12.00
111 Josh Vitters AU/769 6.00 15.00
112 Julio Borbon AU/594 8.00 20.00
113 Justin Jackson AU/850 4.00 10.00
114 Kellen Kulbacki AU/549 5.00 12.00
115 Kevin Ahrens AU/794 8.00 20.00
116 Kyle Lotzkar AU/611 4.00 10.00
117 Madison Bumgarner AU/794 25.00 60.00
118 Matt Dominguez AU/769 4.00 10.00
119 Matt LaPorta AU/594 5.00 12.00
120 Matt Wieters AU/799 8.00 20.00
121 Michael Burgess AU/672 4.00 10.00
122 Michael Main AU/794 5.00 12.00
123 Mike Moustakas AU/999 8.00 20.00
124 Nathan Vineyard AU/700 5.00 12.00
125 Neil Ramirez AU/774 6.00 15.00
126 Nick Hagadone AU/544 4.00 10.00
127 Pete Kozma AU/719 5.00 12.00
128 Phillippe Aumont AU/674 5.00 12.00
129 Preston Mattingly AU/519 8.00 20.00
130 Joba Chamberlain AU/250 8.00 20.00
131 Ross Detwiler AU/650 5.00 12.00
132 Tim Alderson AU/719 8.00 20.00
133 Todd Frazier AU/774 15.00 40.00
134 Wes Roemer AU/694 5.00 12.00
135 Ben Revere AU/700 5.00 12.00
136 Chris Davis AU/374 12.00 30.00
138 Bryan Anderson AU/474 4.00 10.00
141 Austin Jackson AU/794 10.00 25.00
142 Beau Mills AU/624 8.00 20.00
149 Tommy Hunter AU/474 8.00 20.00

2007 Donruss Elite Extra Edition Aspirations

*ASP 1-92: 3X TO 8X BASIC
OVERALL INSERT ODDS 1:4
STATED PRINT RUN 100 SER.#'d SETS
5 David Price 30.00 60.00
23 Jeff Samardzija 8.00 20.00
33 Max Scherzer 8.00 20.00
92 Jacob Smolinski 1.50 4.00
93 Blake Beaven 1.50 4.00
94 Brad Chalk 1.50 4.00
95 Brett Anderson 2.50 6.00
96 Chris Withrow 1.50 4.00
97 Clay Fuller 1.50 4.00
98 Damon Sublett 2.50 6.00
99 Devin Mesoraco 2.00 5.00
100 Drew Cumberland 1.50 4.00
101 Jack McGeary 2.00 5.00
102 Jake Arrieta 6.00 15.00
103 James Simmons 1.50 4.00
104 Jarrod Parker 8.00 20.00
105 Jason Dominguez 1.50 4.00
106 Jason Heyward 50.00 100.00
107 Joe Savery 2.00 5.00
108 Jon Gilmore 2.00 5.00
109 Jordan Walden 2.50 6.00
110 Josh Smoker 2.50 6.00
111 Josh Vitters 5.00 12.00
112 Julio Borbon 2.00 5.00
113 Justin Jackson 1.50 4.00
114 Kellen Kulbacki 2.00 5.00
115 Kevin Ahrens 2.00 5.00
116 Kyle Lotzkar 1.50 4.00
117 Madison Bumgarner 12.00 30.00
118 Matt Dominguez 6.00 15.00
119 Matt LaPorta 8.00 20.00
120 Matt Wieters 6.00 15.00
121 Michael Burgess 6.00 15.00
122 Michael Main 2.00 5.00
123 Mike Moustakas 6.00 15.00
124 Nathan Vineyard 2.00 5.00
125 Neil Ramirez 1.50 4.00
126 Nick Hagadone 2.50 6.00
127 Pete Kozma 1.50 4.00
128 Phillippe Aumont 5.00 12.00
129 Preston Mattingly 4.00 10.00
131 Ross Detwiler 2.50 6.00
132 Tim Alderson 2.50 6.00
133 Todd Frazier 2.00 5.00
134 Wes Roemer 1.50 4.00
135 Ben Revere 2.50 6.00
141 Austin Jackson 4.00 10.00
142 Beau Mills 4.00 10.00
149 Tommy Hunter

2007 Donruss Elite Extra Edition Signature Aspirations

OVERALL AU/MEM ODDS 1:5
PRINT RUNS B/WN 5-100 COPIES PER
NO PRICING ON QTY 25 OR LESS
EXCHANGE DEADLINE 07/01/2007
1 Andrew Brackman/100 10.00 25.00
2 Austin Gallagher/100 12.50 30.00
3 Brett Cecil /100 6.00 15.00
4 Danny Worth/100 6.00 15.00
5 David Price/100 50.00 100.00
6 J. P. Arencibia/100 8.00 20.00
7 Josh Donaldson/100 20.00 50.00
8 Brandon Hicks/100 4.00 10.00
9 Brian Rike/100 4.00 10.00
10 Bryan Morris/100 4.00 10.00
11 Cale Iorg/100 12.50 30.00
12 Casey Weathers/100 6.00 15.00
13 Corey Kluber/100 40.00 100.00
14 Daniel Moskos/100 4.00 10.00
15 Danny Payne/50 6.00 15.00
16 David Kopp/36 6.00 15.00
17 Dellin Betances/50 8.00 20.00
18 Derrick Robinson/100 4.00 10.00
19 Drew Stubbs/100 15.00 40.00
20 Eric Eiland/100 6.00 15.00
21 Francisco Pena/100 8.00 20.00
22 Greg Reynolds/100 4.00 10.00
23 Jeff Samardzija/15
24 Jess Todd/50 12.50 30.00
25 John Tolisano/100 10.00 25.00
26 Jordan Zimmerman/75 12.50 30.00
27 Julian Sampson/50 4.00 10.00
28 Luke Hochevar/25
29 Mat Latos/34 50.00 100.00
30 Matt Mangini/80 10.00 25.00
31 Matt Spencer/30 6.00 15.00
32 Matthew Sweeney/100 EXCH 8.00 20.00
34 Mitch Canham/25
35 Nick Schmidt/25
36 Paul Kelly/100 4.00 10.00
37 Ryan Pope/100 12.50 30.00
38 Sam Runion/50 6.00 15.00
39 Steven Souza/100 10.00 25.00
40 Travis Mattair/50 6.00 15.00
41 Trystan Magnuson/50 4.00 10.00
42 Will Middlebrooks/25
43 Zack Cozart/25
44 James Adkins/100 10.00 25.00
45 Cory Luebke/100 4.00 10.00
46 Aaron Poreda/100 6.00 15.00
47 Clayton Mortensen/100 6.00 15.00
48 Bradley Suttle/100 12.50 30.00
49 Tony Butler/100 4.00 10.00
50 Zach Britton/100 15.00 40.00
51 Scott Cousins /50 6.00 15.00
52 Wendell Fairley/100 12.50 30.00
53 Eric Sogard/100 4.00 10.00
54 Jonathan Lucroy/100 20.00 50.00
55 Lars Davis/100 4.00 10.00
56 Tony Thomas/100 4.00 10.00
59 Nick Noonan/100 EXCH 4.00 10.00
60 Henry Sosa/100 EXCH 4.00 10.00
73 Corey Brown/5 EXCH
77 Jennie Finch/50 15.00 40.00
91 Charlie Culberson/100 15.00 40.00
92 Jacob Smolinski/100 8.00 20.00
93 Blake Beaven/100 6.00 15.00
94 Brad Chalk/100 4.00 10.00
95 Brett Anderson/100 5.00 12.00
96 Chris Withrow/100 6.00 15.00
97 Clay Fuller/100 4.00 10.00
98 Damon Sublett/50 6.00 15.00
99 Devin Mesoraco/100 10.00 25.00
100 Drew Cumberland/100 5.00 12.00
101 Jack McGeary/100 6.00 15.00
102 Jake Arrieta/100 50.00 120.00
103 James Simmons/50 EXCH 4.00 10.00
104 Jarrod Parker/50 20.00 50.00
105 Jason Dominguez/100 5.00 12.00
106 Jason Heyward/100 75.00 150.00
107 Joe Savery/100 5.00 12.00
108 Jon Gilmore/100 6.00 15.00
109 Jordan Walden/100 8.00 20.00
110 Josh Smoker/100 5.00 12.00
111 Josh Vitters/100 15.00 40.00
112 Julio Borbon/100 10.00 25.00
113 Justin Jackson/50 10.00 25.00
114 Kellen Kulbacki/100 8.00 20.00
115 Kevin Ahrens/50 15.00 40.00
116 Kyle Lotzkar/100 12.50 30.00
117 Madison Bumgarner/50 75.00 150.00
118 Matt Dominguez/50 10.00 25.00
119 Matt LaPorta/100 10.00 25.00
120 Matt Wieters/50 30.00 60.00
121 Michael Burgess/50 30.00 60.00
122 Michael Main/50 12.50 30.00
123 Mike Moustakas/100 12.00 30.00
124 Nathan Vineyard/100 5.00 12.00
125 Neil Ramirez/100 4.00 10.00
126 Nick Hagadone/50 12.50 30.00
127 Pete Kozma/100 6.00 15.00
128 Phillippe Aumont/100 12.50 30.00
129 Preston Mattingly/50 30.00 60.00
131 Ross Detwiler/100 4.00 10.00
132 Tim Alderson/100 15.00 40.00
133 Todd Frazier/100 25.00 60.00
134 Wes Roemer/100 6.00 15.00
135 Ben Revere/100 5.00 12.00
138 Bryan Anderson/50 EXCH 4.00 10.00
141 Austin Jackson/50 10.00 25.00
142 Beau Mills/50 EXCH 6.00 15.00
144 Chris Davis/50 25.00 60.00
149 Tommy Hunter/50

2007 Donruss Elite Extra Edition Signature Status

OVERALL AU/MEM ODDS 1:5
PRINT RUNS B/WN 1-50 COPIES PER
NO PRICING ON QTY 25 OR LESS
EXCHANGE DEADLINE 07/01/2007
1 Andrew Brackman/50 15.00 40.00
2 Austin Gallagher/50 20.00 50.00
3 Brett Cecil /50 20.00 50.00
4 Danny Worth/50 EXCH 8.00 20.00
5 David Price/50 60.00 120.00
6 J. P. Arencibia/50 30.00 60.00
7 Josh Donaldson/50 25.00 60.00
8 Brandon Hicks/50 6.00 15.00
9 Brian Rike/50 6.00 15.00
10 Bryan Morris/50 6.00 15.00
11 Cale Iorg/50 12.50 30.00
12 Casey Weathers/50 10.00 25.00
13 Corey Kluber/50 50.00 120.00
14 Daniel Moskos/50 6.00 15.00
15 Danny Payne/25
16 David Kopp/25
17 Dellin Betances/25
18 Derrick Robinson/50 6.00 15.00
19 Drew Stubbs/50 8.00 20.00
20 Eric Eiland/50 10.00 25.00
21 Francisco Pena/50 12.50 30.00
22 Greg Reynolds/50 6.00 15.00
23 Jeff Samardzija/10
24 Jess Todd/25
25 John Tolisano/50 15.00 40.00
26 Jordan Zimmerman/25
27 Julian Sampson/25
28 Luke Hochevar/10
29 Mat Latos/25
30 Matt Mangini/50 15.00 40.00
31 Matt Spencer/15
32 Matthew Sweeney/50 EXCH 12.50 30.00
33 Max Scherzer/12
34 Mitch Canham/10
35 Nick Schmidt/10
36 Paul Kelly/50 6.00 15.00
37 Ryan Pope/50 20.00 50.00
38 Sam Runion/25
39 Steven Souza/50 12.00 30.00
40 Travis Mattair/25
41 Trystan Magnuson/25
42 Will Middlebrooks/10
43 Zack Cozart/10
44 James Adkins/50 15.00 40.00
45 Cory Luebke/50 6.00 15.00
46 Aaron Poreda/50 10.00 25.00
47 Clayton Mortensen/50 10.00 25.00
48 Bradley Suttle/50 20.00 50.00
49 Tony Butler/50 6.00 15.00
50 Zach Britton/50 10.00 25.00
51 Scott Cousins /19
52 Wendell Fairley/50 20.00 50.00
53 Eric Sogard/50 6.00 15.00
54 Jonathan Lucroy/50 20.00 50.00
55 Lars Davis/50 6.00 15.00
56 Tony Thomas/50 EXCH 6.00 15.00
59 Nick Noonan/50 6.00 15.00
60 Henry Sosa/50 EXCH 6.00 15.00
73 Corey Brown/1 EXCH
77 Jennie Finch/25
91 Charlie Culberson/50 8.00 20.00
92 Jacob Smolinski/50 12.50 30.00
93 Blake Beaven/50 10.00 25.00
94 Brad Chalk/50 6.00 15.00
95 Brett Anderson/50 10.00 25.00
96 Chris Withrow/50 10.00 25.00
97 Clay Fuller/50 10.00 25.00
98 Damon Sublett/25
99 Devin Mesoraco/50 15.00 40.00
100 Drew Cumberland/50 8.00 20.00
101 Jack McGeary/50 10.00 25.00
102 Jake Arrieta/50 60.00 150.00
103 James Simmons/25 EXCH
104 Jarrod Parker/25
105 Jason Dominguez/50 8.00 20.00
106 Jason Heyward/50 60.00 120.00
107 Joe Savery/50 8.00 20.00
108 Jon Gilmore/50 10.00 25.00
109 Jordan Walden/25
110 Josh Smoker/50 50.00 100.00
111 Josh Vitters/50 12.50 30.00
112 Julio Borbon/50 12.50 30.00
113 Justin Jackson/25
114 Kellen Kulbacki/50 12.50 30.00
115 Kevin Ahrens/25
116 Kyle Lotzkar/50 10.00 25.00
117 Madison Bumgarner/25
118 Matt Dominguez/25
119 Matt LaPorta/50 15.00 40.00
120 Matt Wieters/25
121 Michael Burgess/25
122 Michael Main/25
123 Mike Moustakas/50 20.00 50.00
124 Nathan Vineyard/50 8.00 20.00
125 Neil Ramirez/50 12.50 30.00
126 Nick Hagadone/25
127 Pete Kozma/50 10.00 25.00
128 Phillippe Aumont/50 20.00 50.00
129 Preston Mattingly/25
131 Ross Detwiler/50 10.00 25.00
132 Tim Alderson/50 30.00 60.00
133 Todd Frazier/50 30.00 80.00
134 Wes Roemer/50 10.00 25.00
135 Ben Revere/50 8.00 20.00
138 Bryan Anderson/25 EXCH
141 Austin Jackson/25
142 Beau Mills/25 EXCH
144 Chris Davis/25
149 Tommy Hunter/25

2007 Donruss Elite Extra Edition Signature Turn of the Century

OVERALL AU/MEM ODDS 1:5
PRINT RUNS B/WN 10-500 COPIES PER
NO PRICING ON QTY 25 OR LESS
EXCHANGE DEADLINE 07/01/2007
1 Andrew Brackman/500 8.00 20.00
2 Austin Gallagher/500 10.00 25.00
3 Brett Cecil /500 8.00 20.00
4 Danny Worth/500 6.00 15.00
5 David Price/500 20.00 50.00
6 J. P. Arencibia/500 8.00 20.00
7 Josh Donaldson/500 20.00 50.00
8 Brandon Hicks/419 5.00 12.00
9 Brian Rike/500 5.00 12.00
10 Bryan Morris/500 4.00 10.00
11 Cale Iorg/397 6.00 15.00
12 Casey Weathers/500 5.00 12.00
13 Corey Kluber/419 20.00 50.00
14 Daniel Moskos/500 4.00 10.00
15 Danny Payne/394 4.00 10.00
16 David Kopp/449 4.00 10.00
17 Dellin Betances/494 6.00 15.00
18 Derrick Robinson/500 4.00 10.00
19 Drew Stubbs/494 4.00 10.00
20 Eric Eiland/419 6.00 15.00
21 Francisco Pena/396 6.00 15.00
22 Greg Reynolds/500 4.00 10.00
23 Jeff Samardzija/219 10.00 25.00
24 Jess Todd/394 12.50 30.00
25 John Tolisano/419 6.00 15.00
26 Jordan Zimmerman/469 6.00 15.00
27 Julian Sampson/494 4.00 10.00
28 Luke Hochevar/158 12.50 30.00
29 Mat Latos/499 6.00 15.00
30 Matt Mangini/500 5.00 12.00
31 Matt Spencer/500 4.00 10.00
32 Matthew Sweeney/500 6.00 15.00
33 Max Scherzer/250 60.00 150.00
34 Mitch Canham/209 5.00 12.00
35 Nick Schmidt/409 4.00 10.00
36 Paul Kelly/500 4.00 10.00
37 Ryan Pope/500 6.00 15.00
38 Sam Runion/494 5.00 12.00
39 Steven Souza/500 8.00 20.00
40 Travis Mattair/494 6.00 15.00
41 Trystan Magnuson/246 4.00 10.00
42 Will Middlebrooks/409 4.00 10.00
43 Zack Cozart/409 6.00 15.00
44 James Adkins/500 4.00 10.00
45 Cory Luebke/469 4.00 10.00
46 Aaron Poreda/500 5.00 12.00
47 Clayton Mortensen/500 4.00 10.00
48 Bradley Suttle/500 5.00 12.00
49 Tony Butler/419 4.00 10.00
50 Zach Britton/437 8.00 20.00
51 Scott Cousins /500 5.00 12.00
52 Wendell Fairley/500 10.00 25.00
53 Eric Sogard/500 5.00 12.00
54 Jonathan Lucroy/500 15.00 40.00
55 Lars Davis/500 4.00 10.00
56 Tony Thomas/300 4.00 10.00
59 Nick Noonan/300 EXCH 4.00 10.00
60 Henry Sosa/300 5.00 12.00
73 Corey Brown/10 EXCH
77 Jennie Finch/119 12.00 30.00
91 Charlie Culberson/500 10.00 25.00
92 Jacob Smolinski/500 6.00 15.00
93 Blake Beaven/500 6.00 15.00
94 Brad Chalk/100 5.00 12.00
95 Brett Anderson/145 5.00 12.00
96 Chris Withrow/168 5.00 12.00
97 Clay Fuller/145 5.00 12.00
98 Damon Sublett/220 10.00 25.00
99 Devin Mesoraco/145 5.00 12.00
100 Drew Cumberland/125 5.00 12.00
101 Jack McGeary/145 6.00 15.00
102 Jake Arrieta/145 50.00 120.00
103 James Simmons/100 EXCH 5.00 12.00
104 Jarrod Parker/55 20.00 50.00
105 Jason Dominguez/100 5.00 12.00
106 Jason Heyward/169 12.00 30.00
107 Joe Savery/119 6.00 15.00
108 Jon Gilmore/100 6.00 15.00
109 Jordan Walden/100 10.00 25.00
110 Josh Smoker/200 15.00 40.00
111 Josh Vitters/150 8.00 20.00
112 Julio Borbon/100 10.00 25.00
113 Justin Jackson/100 6.00 15.00
114 Kellen Kulbacki/145 5.00 12.00
115 Kevin Ahrens/100 10.00 25.00
116 Kyle Lotzkar/100 6.00 15.00
117 Madison Bumgarner/100 60.00 120.00
118 Matt Dominguez/100 10.00 25.00
119 Matt LaPorta/100 10.00 25.00
120 Matt Wieters/100 10.00 25.00
121 Michael Burgess/100 15.00 40.00
122 Michael Main/100 6.00 15.00
123 Mike Moustakas/345 10.00 25.00
124 Nathan Vineyard/119 6.00 15.00
125 Neil Ramirez/145 6.00 15.00
126 Nick Hagadone/100 6.00 15.00
127 Pete Kozma/100 5.00 12.00
128 Phillippe Aumont/120 5.00 12.00
129 Preston Mattingly/100 15.00 40.00
131 Ross Detwiler/119 10.00 25.00
132 Tim Alderson/100 15.00 40.00
133 Todd Frazier/145 8.00 20.00
134 Wes Roemer/100 5.00 12.00
135 Ben Revere/119 5.00 12.00
138 Bryan Anderson/100 EXCH 4.00 10.00
139 Marc Gasol EXCH 4.00 10.00
141 Austin Jackson/100 10.00 25.00
142 Beau Mills/100 EXCH 12.00 30.00
144 Chris Davis/100 20.00 50.00
149 Tommy Hunter 12.00 30.00

2007 Donruss Elite Extra Edition Status

*STATUS 1-92: 4X TO 10X BASIC
OVERALL INSERT ODDS 1:4
STATED PRINT RUN 50 SER.#'d SETS
92 Jacob Smolinski 2.00 5.00
93 Blake Beaven 2.00 5.00
94 Brad Chalk 2.00 5.00
95 Brett Anderson 3.00 8.00
96 Chris Withrow 2.00 5.00
97 Clay Fuller 2.00 5.00
98 Damon Sublett 3.00 8.00
99 Devin Mesoraco 2.50 6.00
100 Drew Cumberland 2.00 5.00
101 Jack McGeary 2.50 6.00
102 Jake Arrieta 8.00 20.00
103 James Simmons 2.00 5.00
104 Jarrod Parker 10.00 25.00
105 Jason Dominguez 2.00 5.00
106 Jason Heyward 60.00 120.00
107 Joe Savery 2.00 5.00
108 Jon Gilmore 2.00 5.00
109 Jordan Walden 3.00 8.00
110 Josh Smoker 3.00 8.00
111 Josh Vitters 6.00 15.00
112 Julio Borbon 2.50 6.00
113 Justin Jackson 2.00 5.00
114 Kellen Kulbacki 2.50 6.00
115 Kevin Ahrens 2.00 5.00
116 Kyle Lotzkar 2.00 5.00
117 Madison Bumgarner 15.00 40.00
118 Matt Dominguez 8.00 20.00
119 Matt LaPorta 10.00 25.00
120 Matt Wieters 6.00 15.00
121 Michael Burgess 8.00 20.00
122 Michael Main 2.50 6.00
123 Mike Moustakas 8.00 20.00
124 Nathan Vineyard 2.50 6.00
125 Neil Ramirez 2.00 5.00
126 Nick Hagadone 3.00 8.00
127 Pete Kozma 2.00 5.00
128 Phillippe Aumont 6.00 15.00
129 Preston Mattingly 5.00 12.00
131 Ross Detwiler 3.00 8.00
132 Tim Alderson 3.00 8.00
133 Todd Frazier 2.50 6.00
134 Wes Roemer 2.00 5.00
135 Ben Revere 3.00 8.00
141 Austin Jackson 12.50 30.00
142 Beau Mills 5.00 12.00

2007 Donruss Elite Extra Edition College Ties

STATED PRINT RUN 1500 SER.#'d SETS
*GOLD: .6X TO 1.5X BASIC
GOLD PRINT RUN 500 SER.#'d SETS
*RED: 1X TO 2.5X BASIC
RED PRINT RUN 100 SER.#'d SETS
OVERALL INSERT ODDS 1:4
1 D.Moskos/D.Kopp .75 2.00
2 N.Schmidt/J.Todd .75 2.00
3 J.Arencibia/J.Borbon .75 2.00
4 D.Price/C.Weathers 1.50 4.00
5 T.Green/M.LaPorta 1.25 3.00
6 J.Finch/A.Beard 1.50 4.00
7 J.Boehiem/D.Nichols .75 2.00
8 D.Payne/M.Wieters 1.50 4.00
9 D.Barney/M.Canham .75 2.00
10 L.Hochevar/J.Adkins .75 2.00
11 D.Cook/C.Luebke .75 2.00
12 D.Strawberry/B.Cecil .75 2.00

2007 Donruss Elite Extra Edition College Ties Autographs

OVERALL AUTO/MEM ODDS 1:5
PRINT RUNS B/WN 50-100 COPIES PER
EXCHANGE DEADLINE 07/01/2009
1 D.Moskos/D.Kopp 6.00 15.00
2 N.Schmidt/J.Todd 6.00 15.00
3 J.Arencibia/J.Borbon 10.00 25.00
4 D.Price/C.Weathers 8.00 20.00
5 T.Green/M.LaPorta 10.00 25.00
6 J.Finch/A.Beard 60.00 120.00
7 J.Boeheim/D.Nichols EXCH 6.00 15.00
8 D.Payne/M.Wieters 60.00 120.00
9 D.Barney/M.Canham EXCH 6.00 15.00
10 L.Hochevar/J.Adkins 6.00 15.00
11 D.Cook/C.Luebke 10.00 25.00
12 D.Strawberry/B.Cecil EXCH 6.00 15.00

2007 Donruss Elite Extra Edition College Ties Jerseys

OVERALL AUTO/MEM ODDS 1:5
PRINT RUNS B/WN 50-500 COPIES PER
1 D.Moskos/D.Kopp/75 4.00 10.00
6 J.Finch/A.Beard/50 6.00 15.00
9 D.Barney/M.Canham/500 3.00 8.00

2007 Donruss Elite Extra Edition College Ties Jerseys Prime

OVERALL AU/MEM ODDS 1:5
PRINT RUNS B/WN 5-50 COPIES PER
NO PRICING ON QTY 25 OR LESS
1 Daniel Moskos/David Kopp/5
6 Jennie Finch/Amanda Beard/25
9 Darwin Barney/Mitch Canham/50 4.00 10.00

2007 Donruss Elite Extra Edition Collegiate Patches

OVERALL AUTO/MEM ODDS 1:5
PRINT RUNS B/WN 25-250 COPIES PER
NO PRICING ON QTY 25 OR LESS
10 Jennie Finch/249 12.50 30.00
19 Josh Donaldson/250 20.00 50.00
25 Drew Stubbs/250 6.00 15.00
26 Andrew Brackman/250 6.00 15.00
27 Casey Weathers/250 10.00 25.00
28 Daniel Moskos/250 6.00 15.00
29 David Price/250 6.00 15.00
30 Greg Reynolds/250 6.00 15.00
31 J. P. Arencibia/249 6.00 15.00
32 Jeff Samardzija/150 12.50 30.00
33 Julio Borbon/250 6.00 15.00
34 Luke Hochevar/100 12.50 30.00
35 Matt LaPorta/250 6.00 15.00
36 Matt Mangini/250 6.00 15.00
37 Matt Wieters/250 12.50 30.00
38 Max Scherzer/182 30.00 80.00
39 Mitch Canham/250 6.00 15.00
40 Nick Schmidt/250 6.00 15.00
41 James Adkins/250 6.00 15.00
42 Tony Thomas/250 8.00 20.00
45 Tommy Hunter/250 8.00 20.00
52 Cale Iorg/250 6.00 15.00
54 Nick Hagadone/250 6.00 15.00
55 Trystan Magnuson/248 6.00 15.00
64 Matt Spencer/249 6.00 15.00
65 Corey Brown/250 EXCH 6.00 15.00
67 Connie Mack III/100 6.00 15.00

2007 Donruss Elite Extra Edition School Colors

OVERALL INSERT ODDS 1:4
STATED PRINT RUN 1500 SER.#'d SETS
1 David Price 2.00 5.00
2 Daniel Moskos .75 2.00
3 Greg Reynolds .75 2.00
4 Matt LaPorta 1.25 3.00
5 Matt Wieters 3.00 8.00
6 Luke Hochevar .75 2.00
7 Max Scherzer 2.00 5.00
26 Nick Schmidt .75 2.00
29 Beau Mills .75 2.00
30 James Simmons .75 2.00
31 Joe Savery .75 2.00
32 Ross Detwiler .75 2.00
33 J. P. Arencibia .75 2.00
34 Drew Stubbs .75 2.00

2007 Donruss Elite Extra Edition School Colors Autographs

OVERALL AUTO/MEM ODDS 1:5
PRINT RUNS B/WN 10-50 COPIES PER
NO PRICING ON QTY 25 OR LESS
EXCHANGE DEADLINE 07/01/2009
1 David Price/50 40.00 100.00
2 Daniel Moskos/50 6.00 15.00
3 Greg Reynolds/50 6.00 15.00
4 Matt LaPorta/50 6.00 15.00
5 Matt Wieters/50 12.50 30.00
6 Luke Hochevar/50 10.00 25.00
7 Max Scherzer/50 60.00 150.00
26 Nick Schmidt/50 6.00 15.00
29 Beau Mills/50 10.00 25.00
30 James Simmons/50 EXCH 6.00 15.00
31 Joe Savery/50 6.00 15.00
32 Ross Detwiler/50 10.00 25.00
33 J. P. Arencibia/50 30.00 60.00
34 Drew Stubbs/50 10.00 25.00
35 Josh Vitters/50 12.50 30.00

2007 Donruss Elite Extra Edition Throwback Threads

OVERALL AUTO/MEM ODDS 1:5
PRINT RUNS B/WN 44-500 COPIES PER
3 Drew Stubbs/500 3.00 8.00
4 Drew Cumberland/500 3.00 8.00
6 Mat Latos/500 6.00 15.00
7 Brett Cecil /500 3.00 8.00
9 Brett Anderson/500 3.00 8.00
10 Casey Weathers/75 4.00 10.00
11 Daniel Moskos/500 3.00 8.00
12 Darwin Barney/500 6.00 15.00
13 Kellen Kulbacki/500 3.00 8.00
14 Matt Dominguez/500 3.00 8.00
15 Matt Mangini/500 3.00 8.00
16 Mitch Canham/500 3.00 8.00
18 Will Middlebrooks/500 3.00 8.00
23 Nick Schmidt/500 3.00 8.00
24 Zack Cozart/500 3.00 8.00

2007 Donruss Elite Extra Edition Throwback Threads Prime

*PRIME: .75X TO 2X BASIC
OVERALL AUTO/MEM ODDS 1:5
PRINT RUNS B/WN 3-50 COPIES PER
NO PRICING ON QTY 25 OR LESS
10 Casey Weathers/3

2007 Donruss Elite Extra Edition Throwback Threads Autographs

OVERALL AUTO/MEM ODDS 1:5
PRINT RUNS B/WN 50-100 COPIES PER
EXCHANGE DEADLINE 07/01/2009
3 Drew Stubbs/100 8.00 20.00
4 Drew Cumberland/100 6.00 15.00
6 Mat Latos/100 20.00 50.00
9 Brett Anderson/100 6.00 15.00
10 Casey Weathers/100 10.00 25.00
11 Daniel Moskos/100 6.00 15.00
12 Josh Vitters/100 10.00 25.00
13 Kellen Kulbacki/100 6.00 15.00
14 Matt Dominguez/100 6.00 15.00
15 Matt Mangini/100 10.00 25.00
16 Mitch Canham/100 6.00 15.00
18 Will Middlebrooks/100 6.00 15.00
23 Nick Schmidt/100 6.00 15.00
24 Zack Cozart/100 6.00 15.00

2008 Donruss Elite Extra Edition

This set was released on November 26, 2008. The base set consists of 199 cards.
COMP.SET w/o AU's (100) 10.00 25.00
COMMON CARD (1-100) .20 .50
COMMON AU (101-200) 3.00 8.00
RANDOM INSERTS IN PACKS
PRINT RUNS B/WN 99-1495
EXCH DEADLINE 5/26/2010
1 Aaron Cunningham .20 .50
2 Aaron Pribanic .20 .50
3 Aaron Shafer .20 .50
4 Adam Mills .20 .50
5 Adam Moore .20 .50
6 Beamer Weems .20 .50
7 Beau Mills .20 .50
8 Blake Tekotte .30 .75
9 Bobby Lanigan .20 .50
10 Brad Hand .30 .75
11 Brandon Crawford .50 1.25
12 Brandon Waring .30 .75
13 Brent Morel .30 .75
14 Brett Jacobson .20 .50
15 Caleb Gindl .20 .50
16 Carlos Peguero .30 .75
17 Charlie Blackmon 1.50 4.00
18 Charlie Furbush .20 .50
19 Chris Davis .40 1.00
20 Chris Valaika .20 .50
21 Clark Murphy .30 .75
22 Clayton Cook .30 .75
23 Cody Adams .30 .75
24 Cody Satterwhite .30 .75
25 Cole St. Clair .20 .50
26 Corey Young .20 .50
27 Curtis Petersen .20 .50
28 Danny Rams .30 .75
29 Dennis Raben .30 .75
30 Derek Norris .30 .75
31 Tyson Brummett .20 .50
32 Dusty Coleman .20 .50
33 Edgar Olmos .20 .50
34 Engel Beltre .60 1.50
35 Eric Beaulac .20 .50
36 Geison Aguasviva .20 .50
37 Gerardo Parra .20 .50
38 Graham Hicks .30 .75
39 Greg Halman .30 .75
40 Hector Gomez .50 1.25
41 J.D. Alfaro .20 .50
42 Jack Egbert .30 .75
43 James Darnell .30 .75
44 Jay Austin .20 .50
45 Jeremy Beckham .30 .75
46 Jeremy Farrell .20 .50
47 Jeremy Hamilton .20 .50
48 Jericho Jones .20 .50
49 Jesse Darcy .20 .50
50 Jeudy Valdez .30 .75
51 Jharmidy De Jesus .20 .50
52 Joba Chamberlain .20 .50
53 Johnny Giavotella .60 1.50
54 Jon Mark Owings .30 .75
55 Jordan Meaker .30 .75
56 Jose Duran .30 .75
57 Josh Harrison .30 .75
58 Josh Lindblom .30 .75
59 Josh Reddick .60 1.50
60 Juan Carlos Sulbaran .20 .50
61 Justin Bristow .20 .50
62 Kenny Gilbert .20 .50
63 Kirk Nieuwenhuis .20 .50
64 Kyle Hudson .20 .50
65 Kyle Russell .20 .50
66 Kyle Weiland .50 1.25
67 L. J. Hoes .20 .50
68 Mark Cohoon .30 .75
69 Mark Sobolewski .50 1.25
70 Mat Gamel .50 1.25
71 Matt Harrison .30 .75
72 Max Ramirez .20 .50
73 Tony Delmonico .30 .75
74 Mike Stanton 3.00 8.00
75 Mitch Abeita .20 .50
76 Neftali Feliz .60 1.50
77 Neftali Soto .30 .75
78 Niko Vasquez .50 1.25
79 Omar Aguilar .30 .75
80 Petey Paramore .30 .75
81 Ray Kruml .20 .50
82 Rolando Gomez .30 .75
83 Ryan Chaffee .30 .75
84 Ryan Pressly .30 .75
85 Sam Freeman .50 1.25
86 Sawyer Carroll .30 .75
87 Scott Green .20 .50
88 Sean Ratliff .20 .50
89 Shane Peterson .30 .75
90 T.J. Steele .30 .75
91 Tim Federowicz .30 .75
92 Tyler Chatwood .30 .75
93 Tyler Cline .20 .50
94 Tyler Ladendorf .30 .75
95 Tyler Yockey .20 .50
96 Wilmer Flores .75 2.00
97 Wilson Ramos .60 1.50
98 Zach McAllister .30 .75
99 Zachary Stewart .20 .50
100 Zeke Spruill .50 1.25
101 Adrian Nieto AU/521 4.00 10.00
102 Alan Horne AU/349 6.00 15.00
103 Andrew Cashner AU/685 6.00 15.00
104 Anthony Hewitt AU/920 6.00 15.00
105 Brad Holt AU/432 5.00 12.00
106 Bryan Petersen AU/319 3.00 8.00
107 Bryan Price AU/572 4.00 10.00
108 Bud Norris AU/1095 3.00 8.00
109 Carlos Gutierrez AU/202 5.00 12.00
110 Chase D'Arnaud AU/1218 4.00 10.00
111 Chris Johnson AU/99 15.00 40.00
112 Christian Friedrich AU/402 8.00 20.00
113 Christian Marrero AU/662 4.00 10.00
114 Clayton Conner AU/819 3.00 8.00
115 Cole Rohrbough AU/719 4.00 10.00
116 Collin DeLome AU/819 3.00 8.00
117 Daniel Cortes AU/680 3.00 8.00
118 Daniel Schlereth AU/570 3.00 8.00
119 Denny Almonte AU/821 3.00 8.00
120 Allan Dykstra AU/1069 4.00 10.00
121 Dominic Brown AU/996 10.00 25.00
122 Evan Fredrickson AU/922 3.00 8.00
123 Gordon Beckham AU/710 5.00 12.00
124 Greg Veloz AU/819 3.00 8.00
125 Ike Davis AU/995 6.00 15.00
126 Isaac Galloway AU/1099 3.00 8.00
127 Jacob Jefferies AU/819 3.00 8.00
128 Michael Kohn AU/199 3.00 8.00
129 Jared Goedert AU/819 3.00 8.00
130 Jason Knapp AU/999 4.00 10.00
131 Jhoulys Chacin AU/821 4.00 10.00
132 Jordy Mercer AU/483 3.00 8.00
133 Jorge Bucardo AU/819 4.00 10.00
134 Jose Ceda AU/1470 3.00 8.00
135 Jose Martinez AU/868 3.00 8.00
136 Josh Roenicke AU/829 3.00 8.00
137 Juan Francisco AU/1495 5.00 12.00
138 Justin Parker AU/719 3.00 8.00
139 Kyle Ginley AU/819 3.00 8.00
140 Lance Lynn AU/570 3.00 8.00
141 Logan Forsythe AU/162 8.00 20.00
142 Logan Morrison AU/360 4.00 10.00
143 Logan Schafer AU/793 3.00 8.00
144 Lorenzo Cain AU/817 10.00 25.00
145 Lucas Duda AU/124 8.00 20.00
146 Matt Mitchell AU/719 3.00 8.00
147 Danny Espinosa AU/443 6.00 15.00
148 Michael Taylor AU/720 6.00 15.00
149 Michel Inoa AU/1199 6.00 15.00
150 Mike Montgomery AU/922 6.00 15.00
151 Cord Phelps AU/693 5.00 12.00
152 Pablo Sandoval AU/819 4.00 10.00
153 Quincy Latimore AU/819 3.00 8.00
154 R. J. Seidel AU/819 3.00 8.00
155 Rayner Contreras AU/1349 3.00 8.00
156 Rick Porcello AU/1299 4.00 10.00
157 Robert Hernandez AU/859 3.00 8.00
158 Ryan Kalish AU/1129 5.00 12.00
159 Ryan Perry AU/745 4.00 10.00
160 Shelby Ford AU/819 3.00 8.00
161 Shooter Hunt AU/397 8.00 20.00
162 Tyler Kolodny AU/819 4.00 10.00
163 Tyler Sample AU/619 4.00 10.00
164 Tyson Ross AU/999 3.00 8.00
166 Waldis Joaquin AU/819 3.00 8.00
167 Wellington Castillo AU/1319 3.00 8.00
168 Wilin Rosario AU/1099 6.00 15.00
169 Xavier Avery AU/199 10.00 25.00
170 Zach Collier AU/217 10.00 25.00
171 Zach Putnam AU/444 3.00 8.00
172 Anthony Gose AU/519 6.00 15.00
173 Roger Kieschnick AU/569 8.00 20.00
174 Andrew Liebel AU/219 5.00 12.00
175 Tim Murphy AU/244 4.00 10.00
176 Vance Worley AU/219 6.00 15.00
177 Buster Posey AU/934 25.00 60.00
178 Kenn Kasparek AU/694 3.00 8.00
179 J.P. Ramirez AU/719 5.00 12.00
180 Evan Bigley AU/819 3.00 8.00
181 Trey Haley AU/719 3.00 8.00
182 Robbie Grossman AU/719 3.00 8.00
183 Jordan Danks AU/254 12.50 30.00
184 Brett Hunter AU/269 4.00 10.00
185 Rafael Rodriguez AU/999 5.00 12.00
186 Yeicok Calderon AU/819 6.00 15.00
187 Gustavo Pierre AU/719 4.00 10.00
188 Will Smith AU/719 3.00 8.00
189 Daniel Thomas AU/719 3.00 8.00
190 Carson Blair AU/719 3.00 8.00
191 Chris Hicks AU/719 4.00 10.00
192 Rashun Dixon AU/199 5.00 12.00
193 Marcus Lemon AU/199 5.00 12.00
194 Kyle Nicholson AU/719 6.00 15.00
195 Mike Cisco AU/719 3.00 8.00
196 Jarek Cunningham AU/719 3.00 8.00
197 Cat Osterman AU/719 4.00 10.00
198 Derrick Rose AU/99 15.00 40.00
199 Michael Beasley AU/99 4.00 10.00
200 O.J. Mayo AU/99 4.00 10.00

2008 Donruss Elite Extra Edition Aspirations

*ASP 1-100: 2.5X TO 6X BASIC
RANDOM INSERTS IN PACKS
STATED PRINT RUN 150 SER.#'d SETS
101 Adrian Nieto 1.25 3.00
102 Alan Horne 1.25 3.00
103 Andrew Cashner 3.00 8.00
104 Anthony Hewitt 1.25 3.00
105 Brad Holt 1.25 3.00
106 Bryan Petersen 1.25 3.00
107 Bryan Price 1.25 3.00
108 Bud Norris 1.25 3.00
109 Carlos Gutierrez 3.00 8.00
110 Chase D'Arnaud 1.25 3.00
111 Chris Johnson 2.00 5.00
112 Christian Friedrich 3.00 8.00
113 Christian Marrero 2.00 5.00
114 Clayton Conner 1.25 3.00
115 Cole Rohrbough 1.25 3.00
116 Collin DeLome 2.00 5.00
117 Daniel Cortes 3.00 8.00
118 Daniel Schlereth 1.25 3.00
119 Denny Almonte 2.00 5.00
120 Allan Dykstra 1.25 3.00
121 Dominic Brown 5.00 12.00
122 Evan Fredrickson 1.25 3.00
123 Gordon Beckham 3.00 8.00
124 Greg Veloz 1.25 3.00
125 Ike Davis 2.50 6.00
126 Isaac Galloway 2.00 5.00
127 Jacob Jefferies 1.25 3.00
128 Michael Kohn 1.25 3.00
129 Jared Goedert 1.25 3.00
130 Jason Knapp 1.25 3.00
131 Jhoulys Chacin 6.00 15.00
132 Jordy Mercer 1.25 3.00
133 Jorge Bucardo 1.25 3.00
134 Jose Ceda 1.25 3.00
135 Jose Martinez 1.25 3.00
136 Josh Roenicke 1.25 3.00
137 Juan Francisco 6.00 15.00
138 Justin Parker 1.25 3.00
139 Kyle Ginley 1.25 3.00
140 Lance Lynn 3.00 8.00
141 Logan Forsythe 1.25 3.00
142 Logan Morrison 5.00 12.00
143 Logan Schafer 1.25 3.00
144 Lorenzo Cain 5.00 12.00
145 Lucas Duda 4.00 10.00
146 Matt Mitchell 1.25 3.00
147 Danny Espinosa 2.00 5.00
148 Michael Taylor 3.00 8.00
149 Michel Inoa 3.00 8.00
150 Mike Montgomery 2.00 5.00
151 Cord Phelps 1.25 3.00
152 Pablo Sandoval 5.00 12.00
153 Quincy Latimore 1.25 3.00
154 R. J. Seidel 1.25 3.00
155 Rayner Contreras 1.25 3.00
156 Rick Porcello 3.00 8.00
157 Robert Hernandez 1.25 3.00
158 Ryan Kalish 3.00 8.00
159 Ryan Perry 2.00 5.00
160 Shelby Ford 2.00 5.00
161 Shooter Hunt 1.25 3.00
162 Tyler Kolodny 3.00 8.00
163 Tyler Sample 1.25 3.00
164 Tyson Ross 2.00 5.00
166 Waldis Joaquin 1.25 3.00
167 Wellington Castillo 1.25 3.00
168 Wilin Rosario 2.00 5.00
169 Xavier Avery 3.00 8.00
170 Zach Collier 2.00 5.00
171 Zach Putnam 1.25 3.00
172 Anthony Gose 2.00 5.00
173 Roger Kieschnick 2.00 5.00
174 Andrew Liebel 1.25 3.00
175 Tim Murphy 1.25 3.00
176 Vance Worley 6.00 15.00
177 Buster Posey 4.00 10.00
178 Kenn Kasparek 3.00 8.00
179 J.P. Ramirez 1.25 3.00
180 Evan Bigley 1.25 3.00
181 Trey Haley 1.25 3.00
182 Robbie Grossman 2.00 5.00
183 Jordan Danks 3.00 8.00
184 Brett Hunter 1.25 3.00
185 Rafael Rodriguez 1.25 3.00
186 Yeicok Calderon 1.25 3.00
187 Gustavo Pierre 1.25 3.00
188 Will Smith
189 Daniel Thomas 1.25 3.00
190 Carson Blair 1.25 3.00
191 Chris Hicks 1.25 3.00
192 Rashun Dixon 1.25 3.00
193 Marcus Lemon 1.25 3.00
194 Kyle Nicholson 1.25 3.00
195 Mike Cisco 1.25 3.00
196 Jarek Cunningham 1.25 3.00
197 Cat Osterman 6.00 15.00
198 Derrick Rose 6.00 15.00
199 Michael Beasley 1.25 3.00
200 O.J. Mayo 3.00 8.00

2008 Donruss Elite Extra Edition Status

*STATUS 1-100: 4X TO 10X BASIC
*STATUS 101-200: .6X TO 1.5X ASP
RANDOM INSERTS IN PACKS
STATED PRINT RUN 50 SER.#'d SETS
101 Adrian Nieto 2.00 5.00
102 Alan Horne 2.00 5.00
103 Andrew Cashner 5.00 12.00
104 Anthony Hewitt 2.00 5.00
105 Brad Holt 2.00 5.00
106 Bryan Petersen 2.00 5.00
107 Bryan Price 2.00 5.00
108 Bud Norris 2.00 5.00
109 Carlos Gutierrez 5.00 12.00
110 Chase D'Arnaud 2.00 5.00
111 Chris Johnson 3.00 8.00
112 Christian Friedrich 5.00 12.00
113 Christian Marrero 3.00 8.00
114 Clayton Conner 2.00 5.00
115 Cole Rohrbough 2.00 5.00
116 Collin DeLome 3.00 8.00
117 Daniel Cortes 5.00 12.00
118 Daniel Schlereth 2.00 5.00
119 Denny Almonte 3.00 8.00
120 Allan Dykstra 2.00 5.00
121 Dominic Brown 8.00 20.00
122 Evan Fredrickson 2.00 5.00
123 Gordon Beckham 5.00 12.00
124 Greg Veloz 2.00 5.00
125 Ike Davis 4.00 10.00
126 Isaac Galloway 3.00 8.00
127 Jacob Jefferies 2.00 5.00
128 Michael Kohn 2.00 5.00
129 Jared Goedert 2.00 5.00
130 Jason Knapp 2.00 5.00
131 Jhoulys Chacin 10.00 25.00
132 Jordy Mercer 2.00 5.00
133 Jorge Bucardo 2.00 5.00
134 Jose Ceda 2.00 5.00
135 Jose Martinez 2.00 5.00
136 Josh Roenicke 2.00 5.00
137 Juan Francisco 4.00 10.00
138 Justin Parker 2.00 5.00
139 Kyle Ginley 2.00 5.00
140 Lance Lynn 5.00 12.00
141 Logan Forsythe 2.00 5.00
142 Logan Morrison 8.00 20.00
143 Logan Schafer 2.00 5.00
144 Lorenzo Cain 8.00 20.00
145 Lucas Duda 6.00 15.00
146 Matt Mitchell 2.00 5.00
147 Danny Espinosa 3.00 8.00
148 Michael Taylor 5.00 12.00
149 Michel Inoa 5.00 12.00
150 Mike Montgomery 3.00 8.00
151 Cord Phelps 2.00 5.00
152 Pablo Sandoval 8.00 20.00
153 Quincy Latimore 2.00 5.00
154 R. J. Seidel 2.00 5.00
155 Rayner Contreras 2.00 5.00
156 Rick Porcello 5.00 12.00
157 Robert Hernandez 2.00 5.00
158 Ryan Kalish 5.00 12.00
159 Ryan Perry 3.00 8.00
160 Shelby Ford 3.00 8.00
161 Shooter Hunt 2.00 5.00
162 Tyler Kolodny 5.00 12.00
163 Tyler Sample 2.00 5.00
164 Tyson Ross 3.00 8.00
166 Waldis Joaquin 2.00 5.00
167 Wellington Castillo 2.00 5.00
168 Wilin Rosario 3.00 8.00
169 Xavier Avery 5.00 12.00
170 Zach Collier 3.00 8.00
171 Zach Putnam 2.00 5.00
172 Anthony Gose 3.00 8.00
173 Roger Kieschnick 3.00 8.00
174 Andrew Liebel 2.00 5.00
175 Tim Murphy 2.00 5.00
176 Vance Worley 10.00 25.00
177 Buster Posey 25.00 60.00
178 Kenn Kasparek 5.00 12.00
179 J.P. Ramirez 2.00 5.00
180 Evan Bigley 2.00 5.00
181 Trey Haley 2.00 5.00
182 Robbie Grossman 3.00 8.00
183 Jordan Danks 5.00 12.00
184 Brett Hunter 2.00 5.00
185 Rafael Rodriguez 2.00 5.00
186 Yeicok Calderon 2.00 5.00
187 Gustavo Pierre 2.00 5.00
188 Will Smith
189 Daniel Thomas 2.00 5.00
190 Carson Blair 2.00 5.00
191 Chris Hicks 2.00 5.00
192 Rashun Dixon 2.00 5.00
193 Marcus Lemon 2.00 5.00
194 Kyle Nicholson 2.00 5.00
195 Mike Cisco 2.00 5.00
196 Jarek Cunningham 2.00 5.00
197 Cat Osterman 8.00 20.00
198 Derrick Rose 8.00 20.00
199 Michael Beasley 1.50 4.00
200 O.J. Mayo 6.00 15.00

2008 Donruss Elite Extra Edition Signature Aspirations

OVERALL AUTO/MEM ODDS 1:5
PRINT RUN B/WN 5-100 COPIES PER
NO PRICING ON QTY 25 OR LESS
EXCH DEADLINE 5/26/2010
1 Aaron Cunningham/50 6.00 15.00
2 Aaron Pribanic/100 5.00 12.00
3 Aaron Shafer/100 4.00 10.00
4 Adam Mills/100 4.00 10.00
5 Adam Moore/100 8.00 20.00
6 Beamer Weems/100 4.00 10.00
7 Beau Mills/50 6.00 15.00
9 Bobby Lanigan/100 4.00 10.00
10 Brad Hand/50 20.00 50.00
11 Brandon Crawford/50 15.00 40.00
12 Brandon Waring/100 5.00 12.00
13 Brent Morel/100 6.00 15.00
14 Brett Jacobson/100 5.00 12.00
15 Caleb Gindl/100 8.00 20.00
16 Carlos Peguero/100 12.50 30.00
17 Charlie Blackmon/50 20.00 50.00
18 Charlie Furbush/100 5.00 12.00
19 Chris Davis/100 20.00 50.00
20 Chris Valaika/100 4.00 10.00
21 Clark Murphy/50 4.00 10.00
22 Clayton Cook/100 4.00 10.00
23 Cody Adams/50 4.00 10.00
24 Cody Satterwhite/50 10.00 25.00
25 Cole St. Clair/100 5.00 12.00
26 Corey Young/100 4.00 10.00
27 Curtis Petersen/100 4.00 10.00
28 Danny Rams/100 5.00 12.00
29 Dennis Raben/50 8.00 20.00
30 Derek Norris/50 15.00 40.00
31 Tyson Brummett/100 4.00 10.00
32 Dusty Coleman/50 5.00 12.00
33 Edgar Olmos/100 4.00 10.00
35 Eric Beaulac/100 4.00 10.00
36 Geison Aguasviva/100 4.00 10.00
37 Gerardo Parra/100 6.00 15.00
38 Graham Hicks/100 4.00 10.00
39 Greg Halman/100 12.00 30.00
40 Hector Gomez/100 5.00 12.00
41 J.D. Alfaro/100 4.00 10.00
42 Jack Egbert/100 4.00 10.00
43 James Darnell/50 6.00 15.00
44 Jay Austin/50 5.00 12.00
45 Jeremy Beckham/100 EXCH 6.00 15.00
46 Jeremy Farrell/100 4.00 10.00
47 Jeremy Hamilton/100 4.00 10.00
48 Jericho Jones/100 8.00 20.00
49 Jesse Darcy/100 5.00 12.00
50 Jeudy Valdez/100 4.00 10.00
51 Jharmidy De Jesus/50 12.50 30.00
53 Johnny Giavotella/100 10.00 25.00
54 Jon Mark Owings/100 5.00 12.00
55 Jordan Meaker/100 4.00 10.00
56 Jose Duran/100 12.50 30.00
57 Josh Harrison/100 8.00 20.00
58 Josh Lindblom/50 4.00 10.00
59 Josh Reddick/100 6.00 15.00
60 Juan Carlos Sulbaran/100 5.00 12.00
61 Justin Bristow/100 4.00 10.00
62 Kenny Gilbert/100 4.00 10.00
63 Kirk Nieuwenhuis/100 5.00 12.00
64 Kyle Hudson/50 5.00 12.00
65 Kyle Russell/50 5.00 12.00
66 Kyle Weiland/50 5.00 12.00
67 L. J. Hoes/50 5.00 12.00
68 Mark Cohoon/100 5.00 12.00
69 Mark Sobolewski/100 15.00 40.00
70 Mat Gamel/50 12.50 30.00
71 Matt Harrison/100 10.00 25.00
72 Max Ramirez/100 8.00 20.00
73 Tony Delmonico/50 6.00 15.00
75 Mitch Abeita/100 4.00 10.00
76 Neftali Feliz/50 20.00 50.00
77 Neftali Soto/50 10.00 25.00
78 Niko Vasquez/50 6.00 15.00
79 Omar Aguilar/100 4.00 10.00
80 Petey Paramore/100 4.00 10.00
81 Ray Kruml/100 5.00 12.00
82 Rolando Gomez/50 4.00 10.00
83 Ryan Chaffee/100 5.00 12.00
84 Ryan Pressly/100 4.00 10.00
85 Sam Freeman/100 8.00 20.00
86 Sawyer Carroll/100 4.00 10.00
87 Scott Green/100 6.00 15.00
88 Sean Ratliff/100 8.00 20.00
89 Shane Peterson/50 8.00 20.00
90 T.J. Steele/50 8.00 20.00
91 Tim Federowicz/100 6.00 15.00
92 Tyler Chatwood/50 4.00 10.00
93 Tyler Cline/100 4.00 10.00
94 Tyler Ladendorf/50 5.00 12.00
95 Tyler Yockey/100 6.00 15.00
96 Wilmer Flores/50 12.00 30.00
97 Wilson Ramos/100 12.50 30.00
98 Zach McAllister/100 6.00 15.00
99 Zachary Stewart/100 4.00 10.00
100 Zeke Spruill/50 EXCH 12.50 30.00
102 Alan Horne/100 10.00 25.00
106 Bryan Petersen/50 4.00 10.00
108 Bud Norris/50 4.00 10.00
113 Christian Marrero/50 5.00 12.00
114 Clayton Conner/50 4.00 10.00
116 Collin DeLome/50 5.00 12.00
119 Denny Almonte/50 4.00 10.00
121 Dominic Brown/50 75.00 150.00
124 Greg Veloz/50 4.00 10.00
127 Jacob Jefferies/50 4.00 10.00
129 Jared Goedert/50 4.00 10.00
130 Jason Knapp/50 15.00 40.00
131 Jhoulys Chacin/50 10.00 25.00
132 Jordy Mercer/75 4.00 10.00
133 Jorge Bucardo/50 5.00 12.00
134 Jose Ceda/100 5.00 12.00
135 Jose Martinez/75 4.00 10.00
136 Josh Roenicke/50 4.00 10.00
137 Juan Francisco/100 EXCH 10.00 25.00
139 Kyle Ginley/50 4.00 10.00
143 Logan Schafer/50 8.00 20.00
144 Lorenzo Cain/50 20.00 50.00
148 Michael Taylor/50 5.00 12.00
152 Pablo Sandoval/50 50.00 120.00
153 Quincy Latimore/50 4.00 10.00
154 R. J. Seidel/50 4.00 10.00
155 Rayner Contreras/100 4.00 10.00
157 Robert Hernandez/50 4.00 10.00
158 Ryan Kalish/50 20.00 50.00
160 Shelby Ford/50 4.00 10.00
162 Tyler Kolodny/50 10.00 25.00
166 Waldis Joaquin/50 4.00 10.00
167 Wellington Castillo/50 4.00 10.00
173 Roger Kieschnick/50 5.00 12.00
180 Evan Bigley/50 6.00 15.00
186 Yeicok Calderon/50 12.50 30.00
200 O.J. Mayo/25 6.00 15.00

2008 Donruss Elite Extra Edition Signature Status

OVERALL AUTO/MEM ODDS 1:5
PRINT RUN B/WN 5-50 COPIES PER
NO PRICING ON QTY 25 OR LESS
EXCH DEADLINE 5/26/2010
2 Aaron Pribanic/50 6.00 15.00
3 Aaron Shafer/50 4.00 10.00
4 Adam Mills/50 4.00 10.00
5 Adam Moore/50 8.00 20.00
6 Beamer Weems/50 4.00 10.00
9 Bobby Lanigan/50 4.00 10.00
12 Brandon Waring/50 5.00 12.00
13 Brent Morel/50 8.00 20.00
14 Brett Jacobson/50 5.00 12.00
15 Caleb Gindl/50 8.00 20.00
16 Carlos Peguero/50 12.50 30.00
18 Charlie Furbush/50 5.00 12.00
19 Chris Davis/50 25.00 60.00
20 Chris Valaika/50 4.00 10.00
22 Clayton Cook/50 4.00 10.00
25 Cole St. Clair/50 5.00 12.00
26 Corey Young/50 4.00 10.00
27 Curtis Petersen/50 4.00 10.00
28 Danny Rams/50 5.00 12.00

31 Tyson Brummett/50 5.00 12.00
33 Edgar Olmos/50 4.00 10.00
35 Eric Beaulac/50 4.00 10.00
36 Geison Aguasviva/50 4.00 10.00
37 Gerardo Parra/50 5.00 12.00
38 Graham Hicks/50 4.00 10.00
39 Greg Halman/50 15.00 40.00
40 Hector Gomez/50 5.00 12.00
41 J.D. Alfaro/50 4.00 10.00
42 Jack Egbert/50 4.00 10.00
45 Jeremy Beckham/50 EXCH 6.00 15.00
46 Jeremy Farrell/50 4.00 10.00
47 Jeremy Hamilton/50 4.00 10.00
48 Jericho Jones/50 8.00 20.00
49 Jesse Darcy/50 5.00 12.00
50 Jeudy Valdez/50 4.00 10.00
53 Johnny Giavotella/50 12.50 30.00
54 Jon Mark Owings/50 5.00 12.00
55 Jordan Meaker/50 4.00 10.00
56 Jose Duran/50 12.50 30.00
57 Josh Harrison/50 10.00 25.00
59 Josh Reddick/50 20.00 50.00
60 Juan Carlos Sulbaran/50 5.00 12.00
61 Justin Bristow/50 4.00 10.00
62 Kenny Gilbert/50 4.00 10.00
63 Kirk Nieuwenhuis/50 12.50 30.00
68 Mark Cohoon/50 5.00 12.00
69 Mark Sobolewski/50 15.00 40.00
71 Matt Harrison/50 12.50 30.00
72 Max Ramirez/50 8.00 20.00
75 Mitch Abeita/50 4.00 10.00
79 Omar Aguilar/50 4.00 10.00
80 Petey Paramore/50 4.00 10.00
81 Ray Kruml/50 5.00 12.00
83 Ryan Chaffee/50 5.00 12.00
84 Ryan Pressly/50 4.00 10.00
85 Sam Freeman/50 5.00 12.00
86 Sawyer Carroll/50 4.00 10.00
87 Scott Green/50 6.00 15.00
88 Sean Ratliff/50 8.00 20.00
91 Tim Federowicz/50 6.00 15.00
93 Tyler Cline/50 4.00 10.00
95 Tyler Yockey/50 6.00 15.00
97 Wilson Ramos/50 15.00 40.00
98 Zach McAllister/50 6.00 15.00
99 Zachary Stewart/50 5.00 12.00
132 Jordy Mercer/40 5.00 12.00
134 Jose Ceda/50 5.00 12.00
135 Jose Martinez/50 4.00 10.00

2008 Donruss Elite Extra Edition Signature Turn of the Century

OVERALL AUTO/MEM ODDS 1:5
PRINT RUNS B/WN 8-999 COPIES PER
EXCH DEADLINE 5/26/2010
Aaron Cunningham/150 5.00 12.00
Aaron Pribanic/269 4.00 10.00
3 Aaron Shafer/117 4.00 10.00
4 Adam Mills/841 3.00 8.00
Adam Moore/844 4.00 10.00
Beamer Weems/844 3.00 8.00
Beau Mills/64 6.00 15.00
Blake Tekotte/194 4.00 10.00
Bobby Lanigan/594 3.00 8.00
0 Brad Hand/447 4.00 10.00
1 Brandon Crawford/718 6.00 15.00
2 Brandon Waring/369 4.00 10.00
3 Brent Morel/269 4.00 10.00
4 Brett Jacobson/488 4.00 10.00
5 Caleb Gindl/245 3.00 8.00
6 Carlos Peguero/344 4.00 10.00
7 Charlie Blackmon/122 25.00 60.00
8 Charlie Furbush/469 3.00 8.00
9 Chris Davis/399 10.00 25.00
0 Chris Valaika/309 3.00 8.00
1 Clark Murphy/644 3.00 8.00
2 Clayton Cook/844 3.00 8.00
3 Cody Adams/447 3.00 8.00
4 Cody Satterwhite/322 6.00 15.00
5 Cole St. Clair/342 4.00 10.00
6 Corey Young/594 3.00 8.00
7 Curtis Petersen/199 3.00 8.00
8 Danny Rams/594 3.00 8.00
9 Dennis Raben/172 6.00 15.00
0 Derek Norris/744 4.00 10.00
1 Tyson Brummett/919 3.00 8.00
2 Dusty Coleman/719 3.00 8.00
3 Edgar Olmos/594 3.00 8.00
5 Eric Beaulac/594 3.00 8.00
6 Geison Aguasviva/368 3.00 8.00
7 Gerardo Parra/421 5.00 12.00
8 Graham Hicks/594 3.00 8.00
9 Greg Halman/429 5.00 12.00
0 Hector Gomez/320 4.00 10.00
J.D. Alfaro/790 3.00 8.00
Jack Egbert/844 3.00 8.00
3 James Darnell/89 5.00 12.00
Jay Austin/207 4.00 10.00
Jeremy Beckham/199 5.00 12.00
Jeremy Farrell/844 3.00 8.00
Jeremy Hamilton/844 3.00 8.00
Jericho Jones/844 6.00 15.00
49 Jesse Darcy/594 3.00 8.00
50 Jeudy Valdez/374 3.00 8.00
51 Jharmidy De Jesus/269 10.00 25.00
52 Joba Chamberlain/39 10.00 25.00
53 Johnny Giavotella/844 6.00 15.00
54 Jon Mark Owings/844 4.00 10.00
55 Jordan Meaker/844 3.00 8.00
56 Jose Duran/262 10.00 25.00
57 Josh Harrison/844 5.00 12.00
58 Josh Lindblom/131 3.00 8.00
59 Josh Reddick/320 6.00 15.00
60 Juan Carlos Sulbaran/844 4.00 10.00
61 Justin Bristow/594 3.00 8.00
62 Kenny Gilbert/842 3.00 8.00
63 Kirk Nieuwenhuis/844 4.00 10.00
64 Kyle Hudson/419 4.00 10.00
65 Kyle Russell/594 4.00 10.00
66 Kyle Weiland/394 4.00 10.00
67 L. J. Hoes/494 5.00 12.00
68 Mark Cohoon/844 3.00 8.00
69 Mark Sobolewski/269 12.50 30.00
70 Mat Gamel/145 8.00 20.00
71 Matt Harrison/244 6.00 15.00
72 Max Ramirez/604 5.00 12.00
73 Tony Delmonico/744 5.00 12.00
74 Mike Stanton/100 100.00 250.00
75 Mitch Abeita/769 3.00 8.00
76 Neftali Feliz/999 8.00 20.00
77 Neftali Soto/645 5.00 12.00
78 Niko Vasquez/494 5.00 12.00
79 Omar Aguilar/594 4.00 10.00
80 Petey Paramore/519 3.00 8.00
81 Ray Kruml/844 4.00 10.00
82 Rolando Gomez/544 3.00 8.00
83 Ryan Chaffee/594 4.00 10.00
84 Ryan Pressly/844 5.00 12.00
85 Sam Freeman/819 3.00 8.00
86 Sawyer Carroll/544 3.00 8.00
87 Scott Green/294 3.00 8.00
88 Sean Ratliff/544 3.00 8.00
89 Shane Peterson/132 6.00 15.00
90 T.J. Steele/122 6.00 15.00
91 Tim Federowicz/844 4.00 10.00
92 Tyler Chatwood/257 5.00 12.00
93 Tyler Cline/594 3.00 8.00
94 Tyler Ladendorf/227 4.00 10.00
95 Tyler Yockey/844 3.00 8.00
96 Wilmer Flores/99 12.00 30.00
97 Wilson Ramos/745 3.00 8.00
98 Zach McAllister/844 3.00 8.00
99 Zachary Stewart/294 4.00 10.00
100 Zeke Spruill/99 EXCH 10.00 25.00
101 Adrian Nieto/50 10.00 25.00
102 Alan Horne/125 10.00 25.00
103 Andrew Cashner/50 8.00 20.00
104 Anthony Hewitt/50 8.00 20.00
105 Brad Holt/50 10.00 25.00
106 Bryan Petersen/100 4.00 10.00
107 Bryan Price/50 4.00 10.00
108 Bud Norris/100 4.00 10.00
109 Carlos Gutierrez/50 6.00 15.00
110 Chase D'Arnaud/50 5.00 12.00
111 Chris Johnson/50 12.50 30.00
112 Christian Friedrich/50 12.50 30.00
113 Christian Marrero/100 5.00 12.00
114 Clayton Conner/100 4.00 10.00
115 Cole Rohrbough/50 10.00 25.00
116 Collin DeLome/100 5.00 12.00
117 Daniel Cortes/50 8.00 20.00
118 Daniel Schlereth/50 4.00 10.00
119 Denny Almonte/100 4.00 10.00
120 Allan Dykstra/50 12.50 30.00
121 Dominic Brown/100 50.00 100.00
122 Evan Fredrickson/50 4.00 10.00
123 Gordon Beckham/50 12.50 30.00
124 Greg Veloz/100 4.00 10.00
125 Ike Davis/50 10.00 25.00
126 Isaac Galloway/50 10.00 25.00
127 Jacob Jefferies/100 4.00 10.00
128 Michael Kohn/40 4.00 10.00
129 Jared Goedert/100 4.00 10.00
130 Jason Knapp/125 10.00 25.00
131 Jhoulys Chacin/50 10.00 25.00
132 Jordy Mercer/50 5.00 12.00
133 Jorge Bucardo/100 5.00 12.00
134 Jose Ceda/250 4.00 10.00
135 Jose Martinez/100 4.00 10.00
136 Josh Roenicke/100 4.00 10.00
137 Juan Francisco/250 10.00 25.00
138 Justin Parker/50 5.00 12.00
139 Kyle Ginley/100 4.00 10.00
140 Lance Lynn/50 20.00 50.00
142 Logan Morrison/50 10.00 25.00
143 Logan Schafer/125 6.00 15.00
144 Lorenzo Cain/100 15.00 40.00
146 Matt Mitchell/50 4.00 10.00
147 Danny Espinosa/50 15.00 40.00
148 Michael Taylor/100 20.00 50.00
149 Michel Inoa/50 12.50 30.00
150 Mike Montgomery/50 20.00 50.00
151 Cord Phelps/50 6.00 15.00
152 Pablo Sandoval/100 20.00 50.00
153 Quincy Latimore/100 4.00 10.00
154 R. J. Seidel/100 4.00 10.00
155 Rayner Contreras/250 4.00 10.00
156 Rick Porcello/50 12.00 30.00
157 Robert Hernandez/100 4.00 10.00
158 Ryan Kalish/100 5.00 12.00
159 Ryan Perry/50 8.00 20.00
160 Shelby Ford/100 4.00 10.00
161 Shooter Hunt/50 15.00 40.00
162 Tyler Kolodny/100 10.00 25.00
163 Tyler Sample/50 5.00 12.00
164 Tyson Ross/50 4.00 10.00
166 Waldis Joaquin/100 4.00 10.00
167 Wellington Castillo/100 4.00 10.00
168 Wilin Rosario/50 10.00 25.00
169 Xavier Avery/50 3.00 8.00
170 Zach Collier/50 12.50 30.00
171 Zach Putnam/50 5.00 12.00
172 Anthony Gose/50 30.00 60.00
173 Roger Kieschnick/50 10.00 25.00
174 Andrew Liebel/50 6.00 15.00
175 Tim Murphy/50 5.00 12.00
176 Vance Worley/50 40.00 80.00
177 Buster Posey/50 125.00 250.00
178 Kenn Kasparek/50 4.00 10.00
179 J.P. Ramirez/50 4.00 10.00
180 Evan Bigley/100 6.00 15.00
181 Trey Haley/50 6.00 15.00
182 Robbie Grossman/50 6.00 15.00
183 Jordan Danks/40 EXCH 20.00 50.00
184 Brett Hunter/50 5.00 12.00
185 Rafael Rodriguez/50 20.00 50.00
186 Yeicok Calderon/100 12.50 30.00
187 Gustavo Pierre/50 6.00 15.00
188 Will Smith/50 4.00 10.00
189 Daniel Thomas/50 4.00 10.00
190 Carson Blair/50 8.00 20.00
191 Chris Hicks/50 8.00 20.00
193 Marcus Lemon/40 6.00 15.00
194 Kyle Nicholson/50 10.00 25.00
195 Mike Cisco/50 4.00 10.00
196 Jarek Cunningham/50 4.00 10.00
197 Cat Osterman/50 20.00 50.00
198 Derrick Rose/25 25.00 60.00
199 Michael Beasley/25 6.00 15.00
200 O.J. Mayo/25 6.00 15.00

2008 Donruss Elite Extra Edition College Ties Green

STATED PRINT RUN 1500 SER.#'d SETS
*GOLD: .75X TO 2X BASIC
OVERALL INSERT ODDS 1:2
GOLD PRINT RUN 100 SER.#'d SETS
*RED: 1.2X TO 3X BASIC
OVERALL INSERT ODDS 1:2
RED PRINT RUN 50 SER.#'d SETS
1 Cord Phelps/Sean Ratliff .75 2.00
2 Ryan Perry/T.J. Steele 1.25 3.00
3 Mitch Abeita/Aaron Pribanic .75 2.00
4 Ryan Perry/Daniel Schlereth 1.25 3.00
5 Daniel Schlereth/T.J. Steele 1.25 3.00
6 Matt Mangini/Jordy Mercer .75 2.00
7 Blake Tekotte/Mark Sobolewski 1.25 3.00
8 Nick Schmidt/Logan Forsythe .75 2.00
9 Wieters/Blackmon 4.00 10.00
10 M.Abeita/J.Chamberlain .50 1.25
11 Andrew Cashner/Andrew Walker 2.00 5.00
12 Sawyer Carroll/Scott Green .75 2.00
13 Taylor Teagarden/Kyle Russell .75 2.00
14 Carlos Gutierrez/Dennis Raben 2.00 5.00
15 Lance Lynn/Cody Satterwhite 1.25 3.00
16 Jordan Danks/Cat Osterman 1.25 3.00
17 Dusty Coleman/Aaron Shafer .75 2.00
18 J.Chamberlain/A.Pribanic .50 1.25
19 Bryan Price/Cole St. Clair .75 2.00
20 Cat Osterman/Kenn Kasparek 1.25 3.00
21 Jose Duran/Brandon Hicks .75 2.00
22 Roger Kieschnick/Zachary Stewart .75 2.00
23 Shane Peterson/Danny Espinosa 1.25 3.00
24 David Price/Brett Jacobson 1.00 2.50
25 Joe Savery/Bryan Price .50 1.25
26 Paramore/Davis 1.00 2.50
27 Brent Morel/Logan Schafer 1.25 3.00
28 Dennis Raben/Mark Sobolewski 1.25 3.00
29 Andrew Liebel/Shane Peterson 1.25 3.00
30 B.Posey/T.Thomas 2.00 5.00
31 Joe Savery/Cole St. Clair .50 1.25
32 Cat Osterman/Bradley Suttle .75 2.00
33 Dennis Raben/Blake Tekotte 1.25 3.00
34 Carlos Gutierrez/Mark Sobolewski 1.25 3.00
35 Carlos Gutierrez/Blake Tekotte 2.00 5.00

2008 Donruss Elite Extra Edition College Ties Autographs

OVERALL AUTO/MEM ODDS 1:5
PRINT RUNS B/N 20-44 COPIES PER
NO PRICING ON QTY 25 OR LESS
EXCH DEADLINE 5/26/2010
24 David Price/Brett Jacobson/44 10.00 25.00

2008 Donruss Elite Extra Edition College Ties Jerseys

OVERALL AU/MEM ODDS 1:5
PRINT RUNS B/WN 100-500 COPIES PER
6 Matt Mangini/Jordy Mercer/500 3.00 8.00
8 Nick Schmidt/Logan Forsythe/500 3.00 8.00
11 Andrew Cashner/Andrew Walker/500 3.00 8.00
15 Lance Lynn/Cody Satterwhite/500 3.00 8.00
16 J.Danks/C.Osterman/100 5.00 12.00
20 C.Osterman/K.Kasparek/100 6.00 15.00
21 Jose Duran/Brandon Hicks/100 4.00 10.00
30 B.Posey/T.Thomas/500 10.00 25.00

2008 Donruss Elite Extra Edition College Ties Jerseys Prime

OVERALL AU/MEM ODDS 1:5
STATED PRINT RUN 25 SER.#'d SETS
NO PRICING DUE TO SCARCITY

2008 Donruss Elite Extra Edition Collegiate Patches Autographs

OVERALL AUTO/MEM ODDS 1:5
PRINT RUNS B/WN 20-255 COPIES PER
NO PRICING ON QTY 25 OR LESS
EXCH DEADLINE 5/26/2010
1 Ryan Patterson/250 4.00 10.00
2 Mark Melancon/250 8.00 20.00
3 Buster Posey/250 20.00 50.00
4 O.J. Mayo/50 10.00 25.00
5 Gordon Beckham/250 10.00 25.00
6 Josh Roenicke/250 4.00 10.00
7 Michael Beasley/100 8.00 20.00
8 Jack Egbert/249 4.00 10.00
11 Tyson Brummett/250 4.00 10.00
12 Ike Davis/250 6.00 15.00
13 Andrew Cashner/250 5.00 12.00
14 Charlie Furbush/250 6.00 15.00
15 Ryan Perry/248 4.00 10.00
16 Sean Doolittle/250 4.00 10.00
17 Alan Horne/250 8.00 20.00
18 Daniel Schlereth/250 4.00 10.00
19 Carlos Gutierrez/249 8.00 20.00
20 Shooter Hunt/250 10.00 25.00
21 Cat Osterman/250 10.00 25.00
22 Lance Lynn/249 10.00 25.00
23 Byron Wiley/248 4.00 10.00
24 Brad Mills/249 4.00 10.00
25 Bryan Price/249 4.00 10.00
26 Logan Forsythe/249 4.00 10.00
27 Brian Duensing/50 6.00 15.00
28 Tyson Ross/255 5.00 12.00
29 Shane Peterson/250 6.00 15.00
30 Josh Lindblom/249 6.00 15.00
31 Aaron Shafer/250 4.00 10.00
32 Dennis Raben/250 4.00 10.00
33 Cody Satterwhite/250 4.00 10.00
34 James Darnell/250 6.00 15.00
35 Charlie Blackmon/240 15.00 40.00
36 Blake Wood/250 4.00 10.00
37 Jordan Danks/250 6.00 15.00
38 Jordy Mercer/247 5.00 12.00
39 Roger Kieschnick/250 5.00 12.00
40 Zachary Stewart/250 4.00 10.00
41 Daniel McCutchen/250 4.00 10.00
42 Brent Morel/250 4.00 10.00
43 Kyle Hudson/249 5.00 12.00
44 Tim Murphy/250 4.00 10.00
45 Petey Paramore/250 4.00 10.00
46 Kyle Russell/250 5.00 12.00
47 Logan Schafer/250 4.00 10.00
48 Andrew Liebel/248 6.00 15.00
49 Aaron Pribanic/250 4.00 10.00
50 Scott Green/250 6.00 15.00
51 Blake Tekotte/248 5.00 12.00
52 Vance Worley/250 8.00 20.00
53 Taylor Teagarden/250 5.00 12.00
54 Cord Phelps/250 4.00 10.00
55 Kyle Weiland/250 6.00 15.00
56 Allan Dykstra/250 5.00 12.00
57 Danny Espinosa/250 12.50 30.00
59 Zach Putnam/244 4.00 10.00
60 Mark Sobolewski/250 10.00 25.00
61 Regis Philbin/50 20.00 50.00
62 Randy Couture/50 30.00 60.00
63 Jose Duran/250 4.00 10.00
64 Lucas Duda/249 6.00 15.00

2008 Donruss Elite Extra Edition School Colors

OVERALL INSERT ODDS 1:2
STATED PRINT RUN 1500 SER.#'d SET
1 T.J. Steele 1.25 3.00
2 Brett Jacobson .50 1.25
3 Buster Posey 3.00 8.00
4 O.J. Mayo 1.25 3.00
5 Gordon Beckham 1.50 4.00
6 Sean Ratliff .75 2.00
7 Michael Beasley 1.25 3.00
8 Jose Duran .75 2.00
9 Derrick Rose 2.50 6.00
10 Joba Chamberlain .75 2.00
11 Sam Freeman 1.25 3.00
12 Ike Davis 1.50 4.00
13 Andrew Cashner 2.00 5.00
14 Chase D'Arnaud .75 2.00
15 Ryan Perry 1.25 3.00
16 Blake Tekotte 1.25 3.00
17 Cole St. Clair .75 2.00
18 Daniel Schlereth .75 2.00
19 Carlos Gutierrez 1.25 3.00
20 Shooter Hunt .75 2.00
21 Zach Putnam .75 2.00
22 Lance Lynn 1.25 3.00
23 Mitch Abeita .75 2.00
24 Jordan Danks 1.25 3.00
25 Bryan Price .75 2.00
26 Logan Forsythe .75 2.00
27 Brandon Crawford 2.00 5.00
28 Tyson Ross .75 2.00
29 Shane Peterson 1.25 3.00
30 Josh Lindblom .75 2.00
31 Aaron Shafer .75 2.00
32 Dennis Raben 1.25 3.00
33 Cody Satterwhite .75 2.00
34 James Darnell 1.25 3.00
35 Charlie Blackmon 6.00 15.00
36 Sawyer Carroll .75 2.00
37 Cat Osterman 2.00 5.00
38 Jordy Mercer .75 2.00
39 Roger Kieschnick .75 2.00
40 Zachary Stewart .75 2.00
41 Kyle Weiland 2.00 5.00
42 Brent Morel 1.25 3.00
43 Lucas Duda 1.50 4.00
44 Tim Murphy .75 2.00
45 Petey Paramore .75 2.00
46 Kyle Russell .75 2.00
47 Logan Schafer .75 2.00
48 Andrew Liebel .75 2.00
49 Aaron Pribanic .75 2.00
50 Scott Green .75 2.00

2008 Donruss Elite Extra Edition School Colors Autographs

OVERALL AUTO/MEM ODDS 1:5
PRINT RUNS B/WN 25-50 COPIES PER
NO PRICING ON QTY 25 OR LESS
EXCH DEADLINE 5/26/2010
3 Buster Posey/50 60.00 120.00
4 O.J. Mayo/25 6.00 15.00
5 Gordon Beckham/50 12.50 30.00
7 Michael Beasley/25 6.00 15.00
8 Jose Duran/50 4.00 10.00
9 Derrick Rose/25 25.00 60.00
12 Ike Davis/50 10.00 25.00
13 Andrew Cashner/50 10.00 25.00
14 Chase D'Arnaud/50 5.00 12.00
15 Ryan Perry/50 4.00 10.00
16 Blake Tekotte/50 4.00 10.00
18 Daniel Schlereth/50 4.00 10.00
22 Lance Lynn/50 6.00 15.00
25 Bryan Price/50 5.00 12.00
31 Aaron Shafer/50 4.00 10.00
32 Dennis Raben/50 10.00 25.00
33 Cody Satterwhite/50 8.00 20.00
35 Charlie Blackmon/50 20.00 50.00
42 Brent Morel/50 10.00 25.00
46 Kyle Russell/50 8.00 20.00
47 Logan Schafer/50 4.00 10.00

2008 Donruss Elite Extra Edition School Colors Materials

OVERALL AU/MEM ODDS 1:5
STATED PRINT RUN 100 SER.#'d SETS
3 Buster Posey 6.00 15.00
4 O.J. Mayo 4.00 10.00
5 Gordon Beckham 4.00 10.00
7 Michael Beasley 4.00 10.00
8 Jose Duran 4.00 10.00
9 Derrick Rose 6.00 15.00
13 Andrew Cashner 4.00 10.00
33 Cody Satterwhite 6.00 15.00
37 Cat Osterman 8.00 20.00

2008 Donruss Elite Extra Edition Throwback Threads

OVERALL AU/MEM ODDS 1:5
PRINT RUNS B/WN 15-500 COPIES PER
NO PRICING ON QTY 25 OR LESS
1 Rick Porcello/500 6.00 15.00
2 Gordon Beckham/500 4.00 10.00
3 Andrew Cashner/500 4.00 10.00
6 Cody Satterwhite/500 6.00 15.00
9 Jose Duran/500 3.00 8.00
10 Derrick Rose/500 4.00 10.00
11 Michael Beasley/500 3.00 8.00
12 O.J. Mayo/400 3.00 8.00
13 Buster Posey/250 12.50 30.00
20 Cat Osterman/100 6.00 15.00
24 Tim Alderson/500 3.00 8.00
25 Michael Burgess/500 3.00 8.00

2008 Donruss Elite Extra Edition Throwback Threads Prime

OVERALL AU/MEM ODDS 1:5
PRINT RUNS B/WN 1-50 COPIES PER
NO PRICING ON QTY 10 OR LESS
24 Tim Alderson/50 6.00 15.00
25 Michael Burgess/50 6.00 15.00

2008 Donruss Elite Extra Edition Throwback Threads Autographs

OVERALL AUTO/MEM ODDS 1:5
PRINT RUNS B/WN 4-100 COPIES PER
NO PRICING ON QTY 25 OR LESS
EXCH DEADLINE 5/26/2010
1 Rick Porcello/100 15.00 40.00
2 Gordon Beckham/100 10.00 25.00
3 Andrew Cashner/100 10.00 25.00
5 Xavier Avery/35 20.00 50.00
9 Jose Duran/100 10.00 25.00
10 Derrick Rose/25 40.00 100.00
11 Michael Beasley/25 12.00 30.00
12 O.J. Mayo/25 6.00 15.00
13 Buster Posey/100 50.00 100.00
20 Cat Osterman/50 10.00 25.00
24 Tim Alderson/40 10.00 25.00

2008 Donruss Elite Extra Edition Throwback Threads Autographs Prime

OVERALL AUTO/MEM ODDS 1:5
PRINT RUNS B/WN 1-25 COPIES PER
NO PRICING DUE TO SCARCITY
EXCH DEADLINE 5/26/2010

2009 Donruss Elite Extra Edition

COMP.SET w/o AU's (50) 6.00 15.00
COMMON CARD (1-50) .20 .50
COMMON AU (51-150) 3.00 8.00
AU SEMIS 4.00 10.00
AU UNLISTED 5.00 12.00
OVERALL AUTO ODDS 1:5 HOBBY
AU PRINT RUNS B/WN 99-999 COPIES PER
EXCHANGE DEADLINE 7/20/2011
1 Bobby Borchering .30 .75
2 Blake Smith .20 .50
3 Drew Storen .30 .75
4 J.R. Murphy .20 .50
5 Zack Wheeler .60 1.50
6 Nolan Arenado 2.50 6.00
7 Matt Bashore .20 .50
8 Josh Phegley .30 .75
9 Jacob Turner .75 2.00
10 Mike Leake .60 1.50
11 Kelly Dugan .20 .50
12 Bill Bullock .20 .50
13 Shelby Miller .60 1.50
14 Alex Wilson .20 .50
15 Ben Paulsen .20 .50
16 Max Stassi .30 .75
17 A.J. Pollock .50 1.25
18 Aaron Miller .20 .50
19 Brooks Pounders .30 .75
20 Shaver Hansen .20 .50
21 Tyler Skaggs .50 1.25
22 Jiovanni Mier .30 .75
23 Everett Williams .20 .50
24 Rich Poythress .20 .50
25 Chad Jenkins .20 .50
26 Rey Fuentes .20 .50
27 Ryan Jackson .20 .50
28 Eric Arnett .30 .75
29 Chris Owings .20 .50
30 Garrett Gould .20 .50
31 Tyler Matzek .30 .75
32 Donnie Joseph .20 .50
33 Brandon Belt .50 1.25
34 Jon Gaston .20 .50
35 Tracye Thompson .50 1.25
36 Marc Krauss .20 .50
37 Kyrell Hudson .30 .75
38 Ben Tootle .20 .50
39 Jake Marisnick .30 .75
40 Aaron Baker .20 .50
41 Kent Matthes .20 .50
42 Andrew Oliver .20 .50
43 Cameron Garfield .20 .50
44 Adam Warren .20 .50
45 Dustin Dickerson .30 .75
46 James Jones .20 .50
47 Brooks Raley .20 .50
48 Jenrry Mejia .30 .75
49 Brock Holt .30 .75
50 Wes Hatton .20 .50
51 Dustin Ackley AU/899 3.00 8.00
52 D.Tate AU/999 6.00 15.00
53 T.Sanchez AU/435 8.00 20.00
54 Matt Hobgood AU/681 5.00 12.00
55 Alex White AU/599 5.00 12.00
56 Jared Mitchell AU/370 6.00 15.00
57 Mike Trout AU/495 1000.00 2500.00
58 Brett Jackson AU/534 12.50 30.00
59 Mike Minor AU/570 3.00 8.00
60 S.Heathcott AU/754 3.00 8.00
61 T.Mendonca AU/569 4.00 10.00
62 Wil Myers AU/799 4.00 10.00
63 J.Kipnis AU/319 6.00 15.00
64 Robert Stock AU/569 3.00 8.00
65 Tim Wheeler AU/794 5.00 12.00
66 M.Givens AU/794 5.00 12.00
67 Grant Green AU/444 3.00 8.00
68 DLeMahieu AU/645 20.00 50.00
69 Rex Brothers AU/699 3.00 8.00
70 Thomas Joseph AU/99 20.00 50.00
71 Wade Gaynor AU/730 3.00 8.00
72 Ryan Wheeler AU/690 6.00 15.00
73 K.Heckathorn AU/599 4.00 10.00
74 C.James AU/99 15.00 40.00
75 Victor Black AU/694 4.00 10.00
76 T.Glaesmann AU/494 4.00 10.00
77 Tyler Kehrer AU/99 15.00 40.00
78 Steve Baron AU/700 3.00 8.00
79 M.Davidson AU/599 6.00 15.00
80 Jeff Kobernus AU/570 5.00 12.00
81 Kentrail Davis AU/655 4.00 10.00
82 Kyle Gibson AU/645 4.00 10.00
83 G.Richards AU/470 4.00 10.00
84 B.Boxberger AU/550 4.00 10.00
85 Evan Chambers AU/695 3.00 8.00
86 Telvin Nash AU/725 3.00 8.00
87 Austin Kirk AU/599 3.00 8.00
88 M.Cooper AU/99 10.00 25.00
89 Jason Christian AU/730 3.00 8.00
90 R.Grichuk AU/770 4.00 10.00
91 Nick Franklin AU/724 5.00 12.00
92 Eric Smith AU/99 12.50 30.00
93 J.Hazelbaker AU/640 3.00 8.00
94 Zach Dotson AU/699 3.00 8.00
95 Josh Fellhauer AU/494 4.00 10.00
96 Jeff Malm AU/650 4.00 10.00
97 Caleb Cotham AU/549 5.00 12.00
98 Trevor Holder AU/649 3.00 8.00
99 Joe Kelly AU/690 4.00 10.00
100 Robbie Shields AU/749 3.00 8.00
101 Kyle Bellamy AU/695 3.00 8.00
102 Braxton Lane AU/710 3.00 8.00
103 Justin Marks AU/99 3.00 8.00
104 Ryan Goins AU/599 3.00 8.00
105 Chase Anderson AU/619 3.00 8.00
106 Kyle Seager AU/744 4.00 10.00
107 C.Cain AU/99 20.00 50.00
108 D.Renfroe AU/695 6.00 15.00
109 Travis Banwart AU/645 3.00 8.00
110 Joe Testa AU/699 3.00 8.00
111 Brandon Jacobs AU/725 5.00 12.00
112 Brett Brach AU/699 3.00 8.00
113 Brad Brach AU/695 3.00 8.00
114 Keon Broxton AU/675 3.00 8.00
115 Nathan Karns AU/734 4.00 10.00
116 Kendal Volz AU/695 3.00 8.00
117 Charles Ruiz AU/594 3.00 8.00
118 Mike Spina AU/580 4.00 10.00
119 Jamie Johnson AU/619 3.00 8.00
120 B.Mitchell AU/699 4.00 10.00
121 Chad Bell AU/744 3.00 8.00
122 Dan Taylor AU/650 3.00 8.00
123 K.Davis AU/150 25.00 60.00
124 Ashur Tolliver AU/99 30.00 60.00
125 Cody Rogers AU/690 4.00 10.00
126 Trent Stevenson AU/744 3.00 8.00
127 Dean Weaver AU/599 3.00 8.00
128 Matt Helm AU/790 5.00 12.00
129 Andrew Doyle AU/640 3.00 8.00
130 Matt Graham AU/690 3.00 8.00
131 Kevan Hess AU/719 3.00 8.00
132 Luke Bailey AU/475 3.00 8.00
133 Steve Matz AU/790 10.00 25.00
134 Tanner Bushue AU/652 4.00 10.00
135 Neil Medchill AU/710 6.00 15.00
136 Edward Paredes AU/725 3.00 8.00
137 A.J. Jimenez AU/695 3.00 8.00
138 Grant Desme AU/744 5.00 12.00
139 Von Rosenberg AU/770 4.00 10.00
140 Daniel Fields AU/749 6.00 15.00
141 Graham Stoneburner AU/719 3.00 8.00
142 David Holmberg AU/710 3.00 8.00
143 C.Dominguez AU/719 4.00 10.00
144 Luke Murton AU/750 4.00 10.00
145 Danny Rosenbaum AU/695 6.00 15.00
146 T.Townsend AU/99 6.00 15.00
147 Louis Coleman AU/597 3.00 8.00
148 Patrick Schuster AU/695 3.00 8.00
149 Jeff Hunt AU/99 15.00 40.00
150 A.Chapman AU/695 12.00 30.00

2009 Donruss Elite Extra Edition Aspirations

*ASP 1-50: 2.5X TO 6X BASIC
RANDOM INSERTS IN PACKS
STATED PRINT RUN 150 SER.#'d SETS
51 Dustin Ackley 2.00 5.00
52 Donavan Tate 2.00 5.00
53 Tony Sanchez 3.00 8.00
54 Matt Hobgood 3.00 8.00
55 Alex White 3.00 8.00
56 Jared Mitchell 2.00 5.00
57 Mike Trout 75.00 150.00
58 Brett Jackson 4.00 10.00
59 Mike Minor 2.00 5.00
60 Slade Heathcott 4.00 10.00
61 Tom Mendonca 1.25 3.00
62 Wil Myers 3.00 8.00
63 Jason Kipnis 5.00 12.00
64 Robert Stock 2.00 5.00
65 Tim Wheeler 2.00 5.00
66 Mychal Givens 2.00 5.00
67 Grant Green 1.25 3.00
68 D.J. LeMahieu 8.00 20.00
69 Rex Brothers 2.00 5.00
70 Thomas Joseph 4.00 10.00
71 Wade Gaynor 1.25 3.00
72 Ryan Wheeler 2.00 5.00
73 Kyle Heckathorn 2.00 5.00
74 Chad James 2.00 5.00
75 Victor Black 2.00 5.00
76 Todd Glaesmann 1.25 3.00
77 Tyler Kehrer 2.00 5.00
78 Steve Baron 2.00 5.00
79 Matt Davidson 4.00 10.00
80 Jeff Kobernus 2.00 5.00
81 Kentrail Davis 2.00 5.00
82 Kyle Gibson 3.00 8.00
83 Garrett Richards 3.00 8.00
84 Brad Boxberger 2.00 5.00
85 Evan Chambers 1.25 3.00
86 Telvin Nash 4.00 10.00
87 Austin Kirk 1.25 3.00
88 Marquise Cooper 2.00 5.00
89 Jason Christian 1.25 3.00
90 Randal Grichuk 3.00 8.00
91 Nick Franklin 3.00 8.00
92 Eric Smith 2.00 5.00
93 Jeremy Hazelbaker 3.00 8.00
94 Zach Dotson 1.25 3.00
95 Josh Fellhauer 1.25 3.00
96 Jeff Malm 1.25 3.00
97 Caleb Cotham 2.00 5.00
98 Trevor Holder 1.25 3.00
99 Joe Kelly 1.25 3.00
100 Robbie Shields 1.25 3.00

101 Kyle Bellamy 1.25 3.00
102 Braxton Lane 1.25 3.00
103 Justin Marks 1.25 3.00
104 Ryan Goins 2.00 5.00
105 Chase Anderson 1.25 3.00
106 Kyle Seager 3.00 8.00
107 Colton Cain 2.00 5.00
108 David Renfroe 1.25 3.00
109 Travis Banwart 1.25 3.00
110 Joe Testa 1.25 3.00
111 Brandon Jacobs 2.00 5.00
112 Brett Brach 1.25 3.00
113 Brad Brach 1.25 3.00
114 Keon Broxton 1.25 3.00
115 Nathan Karns 1.25 3.00
116 Kendal Volz 2.00 5.00
117 Charles Ruiz 1.25 3.00
118 Mike Spina 1.25 3.00
119 Jamie Johnson 1.25 3.00
120 Bryan Mitchell 1.25 3.00
121 Chad Bell 3.00 8.00
122 Dan Taylor 1.25 3.00
123 Khris Davis 6.00 15.00
124 Ashur Tolliver 2.00 5.00
125 Cody Rogers 2.00 5.00
126 Trent Stevenson 1.25 3.00
127 Dean Weaver 1.25 3.00
128 Matt Helm 2.00 5.00
129 Andrew Doyle 1.25 3.00
130 Matt Graham 1.25 3.00
131 Kevan Hess 1.25 3.00
132 Luke Bailey 1.25 3.00
133 Steve Matz 4.00 10.00
134 Tanner Bushue 2.00 5.00
135 Neil Medchill 2.00 5.00
136 Edward Paredes 1.25 3.00
137 A.J. Jimenez 1.25 3.00
138 Grant Desme 1.25 3.00
139 Zack Von Rosenberg 1.25 3.00
140 Daniel Fields 1.25 3.00
141 Graham Stoneburner 1.25 3.00
142 David Holmberg 3.00 8.00
143 Chris Dominguez 1.25 3.00
144 Luke Murton 1.25 3.00
145 Danny Rosenbaum 2.00 5.00
146 Tyler Townsend 2.00 5.00
147 Louis Coleman 1.25 3.00
148 Patrick Schuster 1.25 3.00
149 Jeff Hunt 3.00 8.00
150 Aroldis Chapman 6.00 15.00

2009 Donruss Elite Extra Edition Status

*STATUS 1-50: 4X TO 10X BASIC
*STATUS 51-150: .6X TO 1.5X ASP
RANDOM INSERTS IN PACKS
STATED PRINT RUN 100 SER.#'d SETS
57 Mike Trout 150.00 250.00

2009 Donruss Elite Extra Edition Status Gold

*STAT.GOLD 1-50: 5X TO 12X BASIC
*STAT.GOLD 51-150: .75X TO 2X ASP
RANDOM INSERTS IN PACKS
STATED PRINT RUN 50 SER.#'d SETS
57 Mike Trout 200.00 400.00

2009 Donruss Elite Extra Edition Signature Aspirations

OVERALL AUTO ODDS 1:4 HOBBY
STATED PRINT RUN 100 SER.#'d SETS
EXCHANGE DEADLINE 7/20/2011
1 Bobby Borchering 4.00 10.00
2 Blake Smith 4.00 10.00
3 Drew Storen 6.00 15.00
4 J.R. Murphy 10.00 25.00
5 Zack Wheeler 25.00 60.00
6 Nolan Arenado 60.00 150.00
7 Matt Bashore 4.00 10.00
8 Josh Phegley 4.00 10.00
9 Jacob Turner 12.00 30.00
10 Mike Leake 8.00 20.00
11 Kelly Dugan 4.00 10.00
12 Bill Bullock 4.00 10.00
13 Shelby Miller 4.00 10.00
14 Alex Wilson 4.00 10.00
15 Ben Paulsen 4.00 10.00
16 Max Stassi 8.00 20.00
17 A.J. Pollock 6.00 15.00
18 Aaron Miller 6.00 15.00
19 Brooks Pounders 4.00 10.00
20 Shaver Hansen 3.00 8.00
21 Tyler Skaggs 8.00 20.00
22 Jiovanni Mier 6.00 15.00
23 Everett Williams 8.00 20.00
25 Chad Jenkins 6.00 15.00
27 Ryan Jackson 8.00 20.00
28 Eric Arnett 3.00 8.00
29 Chris Owings 12.00 30.00
30 Garrett Gould 8.00 20.00
32 Donnie Joseph 3.00 8.00
33 Brandon Belt 15.00 40.00
34 Jon Gaston 5.00 12.00
35 Tracye Thompson 15.00 40.00
36 Marc Krauss 3.00 8.00
38 Ben Tootle 3.00 8.00
39 Jake Marisnick 10.00 25.00
40 Aaron Baker 4.00 10.00
41 Kent Matthes 4.00 10.00
42 Andrew Oliver 5.00 12.00
43 Cameron Garfield 5.00 12.00
44 Adam Warren 8.00 20.00
45 Dustin Dickerson 4.00 10.00
47 Brooks Raley 4.00 10.00
48 Jenrry Mejia 6.00 15.00
49 Brock Holt 5.00 12.00
50 Wes Hatton 4.00 10.00
51 Dustin Ackley 5.00 12.00
52 Donavan Tate 3.00 8.00
53 Tony Sanchez 12.50 30.00
54 Matt Hobgood 8.00 20.00
55 Alex White 5.00 12.00
56 Jared Mitchell 3.00 8.00
57 Mike Trout 800.00 1500.00
58 Brett Jackson 6.00 15.00
59 Mike Minor 8.00 20.00
60 Slade Heathcott 8.00 20.00
61 Tom Mendonca 8.00 20.00
62 Wil Myers 6.00 15.00
63 Jason Kipnis 12.00 30.00
64 Robert Stock 10.00 25.00
65 Tim Wheeler 5.00 12.00
66 Mychal Givens 12.50 30.00
67 Grant Green 5.00 12.00
68 D.J. LeMahieu 30.00 80.00
69 Rex Brothers 5.00 12.00
71 Wade Gaynor 5.00 12.00
72 Ryan Wheeler 6.00 15.00
73 Kyle Heckathorn 5.00 12.00
75 Victor Black 4.00 10.00
76 Todd Glaesmann 5.00 12.00
78 Steve Baron 3.00 8.00
79 Matt Davidson 15.00 40.00
80 Jeff Kobernus 5.00 12.00
81 Kentrail Davis 10.00 25.00
82 Kyle Gibson 6.00 15.00
83 Garrett Richards 12.50 30.00
84 Brad Boxberger 10.00 25.00
85 Evan Chambers 3.00 8.00
86 Telvin Nash 8.00 20.00
87 Austin Kirk 4.00 10.00
89 Jason Christian 3.00 8.00
90 Randal Grichuk 25.00 60.00
91 Nick Franklin 8.00 20.00
93 Jeremy Hazelbaker 12.00 30.00
94 Zach Dotson 4.00 10.00
95 Josh Fellhauer 4.00 10.00
96 Jeff Malm 8.00 20.00
97 Caleb Cotham 10.00 25.00
98 Trevor Holder 6.00 15.00
99 Joe Kelly 12.50 30.00
100 Robbie Shields 3.00 8.00
101 Kyle Bellamy 4.00 10.00
102 Braxton Lane 5.00 12.00
104 Ryan Goins 5.00 12.00
105 Chase Anderson 6.00 15.00
106 Kyle Seager 12.00 30.00
108 David Renfroe 15.00 40.00
109 Travis Banwart 3.00 8.00
110 Joe Testa 6.00 15.00
111 Brandon Jacobs 8.00 20.00
112 Brett Brach 3.00 8.00
113 Brad Brach 3.00 8.00
114 Keon Broxton 5.00 12.00
115 Nathan Karns 4.00 10.00
116 Kendal Volz 5.00 12.00
117 Charles Ruiz 3.00 8.00
118 Mike Spina 8.00 20.00
119 Jamie Johnson 4.00 10.00
120 Bryan Mitchell 4.00 10.00
121 Chad Bell 3.00 8.00
122 Dan Taylor 3.00 8.00
125 Cody Rogers 6.00 15.00
126 Trent Stevenson 5.00 12.00
127 Dean Weaver 4.00 10.00
128 Matt Helm 10.00 25.00
129 Andrew Doyle 3.00 8.00
130 Matt Graham 4.00 10.00
131 Kevan Hess 4.00 10.00
132 Luke Bailey 5.00 12.00
133 Steve Matz 25.00 50.00
134 Tanner Bushue 6.00 15.00
135 Neil Medchill 10.00 25.00
136 Edward Paredes 4.00 10.00
137 A.J. Jimenez 6.00 15.00
138 Grant Desme 5.00 12.00
139 Zack Von Rosenberg 6.00 15.00
140 Daniel Fields 8.00 20.00
141 Graham Stoneburner 5.00 12.00
142 David Holmberg 8.00 20.00
143 Chris Dominguez 12.50 30.00
144 Luke Murton 8.00 20.00
145 Danny Rosenbaum 3.00 8.00
147 Louis Coleman 4.00 10.00
148 Patrick Schuster 4.00 10.00
150 Aroldis Chapman 15.00 40.00

2009 Donruss Elite Extra Edition Signature Status

OVERALL AUTO ODDS 1:4 HOBBY
STATED PRINT RUN 50 SER.#'d SETS
EXCHANGE DEADLINE 7/20/2011
1 Bobby Borchering 5.00 12.00
3 Drew Storen 6.00 15.00
4 J.R. Murphy 12.50 30.00
5 Zack Wheeler 30.00 80.00
6 Nolan Arenado 75.00 200.00
7 Matt Bashore 5.00 12.00
8 Josh Phegley 5.00 12.00
9 Jacob Turner 15.00 40.00
10 Mike Leake 15.00 40.00
11 Kelly Dugan 5.00 12.00
12 Bill Bullock 5.00 12.00
13 Shelby Miller 5.00 12.00
14 Alex Wilson 5.00 12.00
15 Ben Paulsen 5.00 12.00
16 Max Stassi 10.00 25.00
17 A.J. Pollock 8.00 20.00
18 Aaron Miller 15.00 40.00
19 Brooks Pounders 6.00 15.00
20 Shaver Hansen 3.00 8.00
21 Tyler Skaggs 10.00 25.00
22 Jiovanni Mier 12.50 30.00
23 Everett Williams 12.50 30.00
25 Chad Jenkins 10.00 25.00
27 Ryan Jackson 5.00 12.00
28 Eric Arnett 4.00 10.00
29 Chris Owings 12.00 30.00
30 Garrett Gould 6.00 15.00
32 Donnie Joseph 4.00 10.00
33 Brandon Belt 100.00 200.00
34 Jon Gaston 15.00 40.00
35 Tracye Thompson 20.00 50.00
36 Marc Krauss 4.00 10.00
38 Ben Tootle 3.00 8.00
39 Jake Marisnick 12.00 30.00
40 Aaron Baker 3.00 8.00
41 Kent Matthes 3.00 8.00
42 Andrew Oliver 8.00 20.00
43 Cameron Garfield 10.00 25.00
44 Adam Warren 8.00 20.00
45 Dustin Dickerson 4.00 10.00
47 Brooks Raley 5.00 12.00
48 Jenrry Mejia 6.00 15.00
49 Brock Holt 6.00 15.00
50 Wes Hatton 5.00 12.00
51 Dustin Ackley 6.00 15.00
52 Donavan Tate 4.00 10.00
53 Tony Sanchez 12.50 30.00
54 Matt Hobgood 15.00 40.00
55 Alex White 12.50 30.00
56 Jared Mitchell 3.00 8.00
57 Mike Trout 1000.00 2000.00
58 Brett Jackson 6.00 15.00
59 Mike Minor 12.50 30.00
60 Slade Heathcott 10.00 25.00
61 Tom Mendonca 5.00 12.00
62 Wil Myers 8.00 20.00
63 Jason Kipnis 15.00 40.00
64 Robert Stock 12.00 30.00
65 Tim Wheeler 6.00 15.00
66 Mychal Givens 15.00 40.00
67 Grant Green 6.00 15.00
68 D.J. LeMahieu 40.00 100.00
69 Rex Brothers 6.00 15.00
71 Wade Gaynor 6.00 15.00
72 Ryan Wheeler 10.00 25.00
73 Kyle Heckathorn 12.00 30.00
75 Victor Black 10.00 25.00
76 Todd Glaesmann 8.00 20.00
78 Steve Baron 5.00 12.00
79 Matt Davidson 25.00 60.00
80 Jeff Kobernus 4.00 10.00
81 Kentrail Davis 30.00 60.00
82 Kyle Gibson 20.00 50.00
83 Garrett Richards 20.00 50.00
84 Brad Boxberger 15.00 40.00
85 Evan Chambers 4.00 10.00
86 Telvin Nash 10.00 25.00
87 Austin Kirk 4.00 10.00
89 Jason Christian 4.00 10.00
90 Randal Grichuk 30.00 80.00
91 Nick Franklin 6.00 15.00
93 Jeremy Hazelbaker 15.00 40.00
94 Zach Dotson 6.00 15.00
95 Josh Fellhauer 8.00 20.00
96 Jeff Malm 15.00 40.00
97 Caleb Cotham 10.00 25.00
98 Trevor Holder 3.00 8.00
99 Joe Kelly 6.00 15.00
100 Robbie Shields 5.00 12.00
101 Kyle Bellamy 3.00 8.00
102 Braxton Lane 10.00 25.00
104 Ryan Goins 4.00 10.00
105 Chase Anderson 6.00 15.00
106 Kyle Seager 15.00 40.00
108 David Renfroe 30.00 60.00
109 Travis Banwart 3.00 8.00
110 Joe Testa 5.00 12.00
111 Brandon Jacobs 10.00 25.00
112 Brett Brach 10.00 25.00
113 Brad Brach 3.00 8.00
114 Keon Broxton 10.00 25.00
115 Nathan Karns 4.00 10.00
116 Kendal Volz 8.00 20.00
117 Charles Ruiz 3.00 8.00
118 Mike Spina 6.00 15.00
119 Jamie Johnson 4.00 10.00
120 Bryan Mitchell 6.00 15.00
121 Chad Bell 5.00 12.00
122 Dan Taylor 12.00 30.00
125 Cody Rogers 10.00 25.00
127 Dean Weaver 4.00 10.00
128 Matt Helm 6.00 15.00
129 Andrew Doyle 3.00 8.00
130 Matt Graham 4.00 10.00
131 Kevan Hess 6.00 15.00
132 Luke Bailey 6.00 15.00
133 Steve Matz 25.00 60.00
134 Tanner Bushue 12.00 30.00
135 Neil Medchill 15.00 40.00
136 Edward Paredes 4.00 10.00
137 A.J. Jimenez 4.00 10.00
138 Grant Desme 8.00 20.00
139 Zack Von Rosenberg 10.00 25.00
140 Daniel Fields 15.00 40.00
141 Graham Stoneburner 10.00 25.00
142 David Holmberg 10.00 25.00
143 Chris Dominguez 30.00 60.00
144 Luke Murton 10.00 25.00
145 Danny Rosenbaum 4.00 10.00
147 Louis Coleman 6.00 15.00
148 Patrick Schuster 8.00 20.00
150 Aroldis Chapman 25.00 60.00

2009 Donruss Elite Extra Edition Signature Turn of the Century

OVERALL AUTO ODDS 1:5 HOBBY
AU PRINT RUNS B/WN 10-844 COPIES PER
EXCHANGE DEADLINE 7/20/2011
1 B.Borchering AU/799 3.00 8.00
2 Blake Smith AU/794 3.00 8.00
3 Drew Storen AU/519 6.00 15.00
4 J.R. Murphy AU/840 6.00 15.00
5 Z.Wheeler AU/744 3.00 8.00
6 Nolan Arenado AU/844 40.00 100.00
7 Matt Bashore AU/655 3.00 8.00
8 Josh Phegley AU/613 3.00 8.00
9 Jacob Turner AU/799 6.00 15.00
10 Mike Leake AU/356 5.00 12.00
11 Kelly Dugan AU/799 3.00 8.00
12 Bill Bullock AU/370 3.00 8.00
13 Shelby Miller AU/690 3.00 8.00
14 Alex Wilson AU/710 3.00 8.00
15 Ben Paulsen AU/599 3.00 8.00
16 Max Stassi AU/810 5.00 12.00
17 A.J. Pollock AU/499 4.00 10.00
18 Aaron Miller AU/650 4.00 10.00
19 Brooks Pounders AU/844 3.00 8.00
20 Shaver Hansen AU/425 3.00 8.00
21 Tyler Skaggs AU/820 6.00 15.00
22 Jiovanni Mier AU/825 4.00 10.00
23 E.Williams AU/799 4.00 10.00
24 R.Poythress AU/150 10.00 25.00
25 Chad Jenkins AU/785 3.00 8.00
26 R.Fuentes AU/99 EXCH 15.00 40.00
27 Ryan Jackson AU/558 5.00 12.00
28 Eric Arnett AU/669 3.00 8.00
29 Chris Owings AU/799 6.00 15.00
30 Garrett Gould AU/799 3.00 8.00
31 T.Matzek AU/125 EXCH 15.00 40.00
32 Donnie Joseph AU/699 3.00 8.00
33 Brandon Belt AU/610 4.00 10.00
34 Jon Gaston AU/725 3.00 8.00
35 Tracye Thompson AU/699 6.00 15.00
36 Marc Krauss AU/619 3.00 8.00
37 K.Hudson AU/99 EXCH 20.00 50.00
38 Ben Tootle AU/825 3.00 8.00
39 Jake Marisnick AU/799 6.00 15.00
40 Aaron Baker AU/359 3.00 8.00
41 Kent Matthes AU/619 3.00 8.00
42 Andrew Oliver AU/710 3.00 8.00
43 Cameron Garfield AU/844 3.00 8.00
44 Adam Warren AU/675 4.00 10.00
45 Dustin Dickerson AU/650 3.00 8.00
46 James Jones AU/99 5.00 12.00
47 Brooks Raley AU/494 3.00 8.00
48 Jenrry Mejia AU/844 4.00 10.00
49 Brock Holt AU/619 4.00 10.00
50 Wes Hatton AU/790 3.00 8.00
51 Dustin Ackley AU/75 6.00 15.00
52 D.Tate AU/225 8.00 20.00
53 Tony Sanchez AU/50 20.00 50.00
54 M.Hobgood AU/75 8.00 20.00
55 Alex White AU/70 6.00 15.00
56 Jared Mitchell AU/60 10.00 25.00
57 Mike Trout AU/149 600.00 1000.00
58 Brett Jackson AU/49 6.00 15.00
60 S.Heathcott AU/40 30.00 60.00
61 Tom Mendonca AU/50 10.00 25.00
62 Wil Myers AU/50 8.00 20.00
64 Robert Stock AU/50 15.00 40.00
66 M.Givens AU/299 5.00 12.00
69 Rex Brothers AU/100 5.00 12.00
71 Wade Gaynor AU/110 3.00 8.00
72 R.Wheeler AU/150 6.00 15.00
73 K.Heckathorn AU/99 6.00 15.00
75 Victor Black AU/100 6.00 15.00
76 T.Glaesmann AU/50 4.00 10.00
78 Steve Baron AU/125 4.00 10.00
79 M.Davidson AU/125 12.50 30.00
80 Jeff Kobernus AU/99 5.00 12.00
81 Kentrail Davis AU/50 20.00 50.00
82 Kyle Gibson AU/99 10.00 25.00
83 G.Richards AU/99 12.00 30.00
84 B.Boxberger AU/110 5.00 12.00
85 Evan Chambers AU/149 3.00 8.00
86 Telvin Nash AU/100 8.00 20.00
87 Austin Kirk AU/199 4.00 10.00
89 Jason Christian AU/111 3.00 8.00
90 Randal Grichuk AU/50 30.00 80.00
91 N.Franklin AU/120 15.00 40.00
93 J.Hazelbaker AU/204 12.00 30.00
94 Zach Dotson AU/100 3.00 8.00
95 J.Fellhauer AU/125 4.00 10.00
96 Jeff Malm AU/149 10.00 25.00
97 Caleb Cotham AU/50 10.00 25.00
98 Trevor Holder AU/100 3.00 8.00
99 Joe Kelly AU/99 4.00 10.00
100 Robbie Shields AU/99 3.00 8.00
101 Kyle Bellamy AU/149 3.00 8.00
102 Braxton Lane AU/125 3.00 8.00
104 Ryan Goins AU/150 5.00 12.00
106 Kyle Seager AU/100 8.00 20.00
108 David Renfroe AU/149 8.00 20.00
109 Travis Banwart AU/199 3.00 8.00
110 Joe Testa AU/125 4.00 10.00
111 B.Jacobs AU/100 5.00 12.00
112 Brett Brach AU/75 3.00 8.00
113 Brad Brach AU/100 3.00 8.00
114 Keon Broxton AU/114 4.00 10.00
115 Nathan Karns AU/110 3.00 8.00
116 Kendal Volz AU/99 12.00 30.00
117 Charles Ruiz AU/125 3.00 8.00
118 Mike Spina AU/115 3.00 8.00
119 Jamie Johnson AU/100 4.00 10.00
120 Bryan Mitchell AU/125 4.00 10.00
121 Chad Bell AU/100 3.00 8.00
122 Dan Taylor AU/175 3.00 8.00
125 Cody Rogers AU/150 4.00 10.00
126 Trent Stevenson AU/100 3.00 8.00
127 Dean Weaver AU/199 3.00 8.00
128 Matt Helm AU/50 6.00 15.00
129 Andrew Doyle AU/155 3.00 8.00
130 Matt Graham AU/150 4.00 10.00
131 Kevan Hess AU/125 3.00 8.00
132 Luke Bailey AU/100 5.00 12.00
133 Steve Matz AU/50 20.00 50.00
134 T.Bushue AU/190 4.00 10.00
135 Neil Medchill AU/125 10.00 25.00
136 Edward Paredes AU/110 3.00 8.00
137 A.J. Jimenez AU/149 8.00 20.00
138 G.Desme AU/100 6.00 15.00
139 Von Rosenberg AU/50 8.00 20.00
140 Daniel Fields AU/90 15.00 40.00
141 G.Stoneburner AU/125 4.00 10.00
142 David Holmberg AU/110 8.00 20.00
143 C.Dominguez AU/125 8.00 20.00
144 Luke Murton AU/90 6.00 15.00
145 Danny Rosenbaum AU/149 6.00 15.00
147 L.Coleman AU/199 4.00 10.00
148 P.Schuster AU/149 4.00 10.00
150 A.Chapman AU/149 25.00 60.00

2009 Donruss Elite Extra Edition Back to Back Materials

RANDOM INSERTS IN PACKS
PRINT RUNS B/WN 35-250 COPIES PER
1 I.Davis/R.Jackson 5.00 12.00
2 J.Kipnis/R.Jackson 4.00 10.00
3 R.Grossman/Q.Latimore 3.00 8.00
4 B.Posey/W.Clark 15.00 40.00

2009 Donruss Elite Extra Edition Back to the Future Signatures

OVERALL AUTO ODDS 1:5 HOBBY
PRINT RUNS B/WN 1-99 COPIES PER
NO PRICING ON QTY 25 OR LESS
1 Allan Dykstra/99 3.00 8.00
2 Alan Horne/99 3.00 8.00
3 Jim Palmer/49 3.00 8.00
4 Andrew Cashner/99 4.00 10.00
5 Andrew Lambo/99 5.00 12.00
6 Anthony Hewitt/99 4.00 10.00
8 Brandon Crawford/99 8.00 20.00
9 Brett Hunter/99 3.00 8.00
10 Bryan Price/99 3.00 8.00
11 Buster Posey/99 15.00 40.00
12 Chase D'Arnaud/99 3.00 8.00
14 Christian Friedrich/99 6.00 15.00
16 Dwight Gooden/99 4.00 10.00
18 Evan Fredrickson/99 4.00 10.00
19 Mark Fidrych/49 8.00 20.00
20 George Brett/30 40.00 80.00
22 Ike Davis/99 15.00 40.00
23 Jason Knapp/99 3.00 8.00
26 Logan Schafer/99 3.00 8.00
27 Michael Ynoa/99 4.00 10.00
28 Mike Cisco/50 3.00 8.00
32 Pete Rose/99 15.00 40.00
33 Rafael Rodriguez/99 3.00 8.00
35 Robin Yount/49 15.00 40.00
37 Steve Garvey/50 15.00 40.00
39 Zach McAllister/99 4.00 10.00
40 Zeke Spruill/99 3.00 8.00

2009 Donruss Elite Extra Edition College Ties Green

COMPLETE SET (10) 8.00 20.00
RANDOM INSERTS IN PACKS
*GOLD: .6X TO 1.5X BASIC
GOLD RANDOMLY INSERTED
GOLD PRINT RUN 100 SER.#'d SETS
RED RANDOMLY INSERTED
RED PRINT RUN 25 SER.#'d SETS
NO RED PRICING AVAILABLE
1 D.Ackley/A.White 1.00 2.50
2 M.Leake/J.Kipnis 1.25 3.00
3 Mike Minor/Caleb Cotham .60 1.50
4 J.Kipnis/I.Davis 1.25 3.00
5 Brad Boxberger/Robert Stock .60 1.50
6 Garrett Richards/Jamie Johnson 1.00 2.50
7 Chase Anderson/Aaron Baker .40 1.00
8 Shaver Hansen/Dustin Dickerson .60 1.50
9 Kendal Volz/Aaron Miller .60 1.50
10 Brooks Raley/Jose Duran .60 1.50
11 Robert Stock/Grant Green .60 1.50
12 Chad Jenkins/Kyle Heckathorn .60 1.50
13 Eric Arnett/Josh Phegley .60 1.50
14 Matt Bashore/Josh Phegley .60 1.50
15 Jared Mitchell/D.J. LeMahieu 2.50 6.00
16 Victor Black/Ryan Goins .60 1.50
17 B.Jackson/J.Kobernus 1.25 3.00
18 B.Jackson/B.Smith 1.25 3.00
19 Trevor Holder/Rich Poythress .40 1.00
20 J.Danks/B.Belt 1.00 2.50

2009 Donruss Elite Extra Edition College Ties Autographs

OVERALL AUTO ODDS 1:5 HOBBY
PRINT RUNS B/WN 4-50 COPIES PER
NO PRICING ON QTY 25 OR LESS
EXCHANGE DEADLINE 7/20/2011
1 Ackley/White/50 20.00 50.00
2 Leake/Kipnis/50 EXCH 8.00 20.00
3 Minor/Cotham/50 5.00 12.00
4 Kipnis/Davis/50 10.00 25.00
5 Boxberger/Stock/50 8.00 20.00
7 Chase Anderson/Aaron Baker/50 5.00 12.00
8 Shaver Hansen/Dustin Dickerson/50 5.00 12.00
9 Kendal Volz/Aaron Miller/50 5.00 12.00
11 Stock/Green/50 8.00 20.00
12 Jenkins/Heckathorn/50 6.00 15.00
13 Arnett/Phegley/50 10.00 25.00
14 Bashore/Phegley/50 8.00 20.00
16 V.Black/RGoins/50 6.00 15.00
17 Jackson/Kobernus/50 6.00 15.00
18 B.Jackson/B.Smith/50 10.00 25.00
19 Holder/Poythress/50 8.00 20.00

2009 Donruss Elite Extra Edition College Ties Jerseys

RANDOM INSERTS IN PACKS
STATED PRINT RUN 250 SER.#'d SETS
7 Chase Anderson/Aaron Baker 3.00 8.00
10 Brooks Raley/Jose Duran 3.00 8.00

2009 Donruss Elite Extra Edition Collegiate Patches Autographs

OVERALL AUTO ODDS 1:5 HOBBY
PRINT RUNS B/WN 104-125 COPIES PER
EXCHANGE DEADLINE 7/20/2011
1 Dustin Ackley/118 5.00 12.00
2 Tony Sanchez/125 10.00 25.00
3 Mike Minor/125 8.00 20.00
4 Mike Leake/125 6.00 15.00
5 Drew Storen/125 8.00 20.00
6 Grant Green/125 8.00 20.00
7 Alex White/124 12.50 30.00
8 A.J. Pollock/123 12.00 30.00
9 Jared Mitchell/125 10.00 25.00
10 Eric Arnett/125 6.00 15.00
11 Brett Jackson/125 6.00 15.00
12 Aaron Miller/117 5.00 12.00
13 Josh Phegley/125 5.00 12.00
14 Kentrail Davis/125 8.00 20.00
15 Garrett Richards/104 12.00 30.00
16 Brad Boxberger/125 8.00 20.00
17 Matt Bashore/124 5.00 12.00
18 Jeff Kobernus/125 6.00 15.00
19 Rich Poythress/124 15.00 40.00
20 Blake Smith/125 4.00 10.00
21 Andrew Oliver/125 6.00 15.00
22 Tom Mendonca/125 5.00 12.00
23 Jason Kipnis/125 10.00 25.00
24 Marc Krauss/120 8.00 20.00
25 Robert Stock/125 8.00 20.00
26 Bill Bullock/125 5.00 12.00
27 Alex Wilson/125 4.00 10.00
28 D.J. LeMahieu/125 20.00 50.00
29 Trevor Holder/125 4.00 10.00
30 Donnie Joseph/125 4.00 10.00
31 Ben Paulsen/125 5.00 12.00
32 Kent Matthes/125 5.00 12.00
33 Adam Warren/125 8.00 20.00
34 Brandon Belt/125 15.00 40.00
35 Ryan Jackson/125 6.00 15.00
36 Caleb Cotham/125 10.00 25.00
37 Shaver Hansen/124 6.00 15.00
38 Josh Fellhauer/125 4.00 10.00
39 Jamie Johnson/125 4.00 10.00
40 Khris Davis/125 EXCH 30.00 80.00
41 Dustin Dickerson/125 4.00 10.00
42 Brock Holt/125 15.00 40.00
43 Charles Ruiz/125 4.00 10.00
44 Aaron Baker/125 3.00 8.00
45 Mike Spina/125 5.00 12.00
46 Jim Abbott/125 10.00 25.00
47 Fred Lynn/125 6.00 15.00
48 John Olerud/125 EXCH 10.00 25.00
49 Robin Ventura/125 5.00 12.00

2009 Donruss Elite Extra Edition Elite Series

RANDOM INSERTS IN PACKS
1 Dustin Ackley .75 2.00
2 Donavan Tate .75 2.00
3 Mike Leake 1.50 4.00
4 Tony Sanchez 1.25 3.00
5 Al Kaline 1.25 3.00
6 Mike Minor .75 2.00
7 A.J. Pollock 1.25 3.00
8 Nolan Ryan 4.00 10.00
9 Will Clark .75 2.00
10 Albert Pujols 1.50 4.00

2009 Donruss Elite Extra Edition Elite Series Autographs

OVERALL AUTO ODDS 1:5 HOBBY
PRINT RUNS B/WN 20-199 COPIES PER
NO PRICING ON QTY 20 OR LESS
1 Dustin Ackley/100 5.00 12.00
2 Donavan Tate/199 10.00 25.00
3 Mike Leake/100 6.00 15.00
4 Tony Sanchez/100 6.00 15.00
5 Al Kaline/100 20.00 50.00
6 Mike Minor/40 10.00 25.00
7 A.J. Pollock/100 8.00 20.00
8 Nolan Ryan/50 50.00 100.00
9 Will Clark/52 15.00 40.00

2009 Donruss Elite Extra Edition Passing the Torch Autographs

OVERALL AUTO ODDS 1:5 HOBBY
PRINT RUNS B/WN 5-100 COPIES PER
NO PRICING ON QTY 25 OR LESS
1 Posey/Sanchez/100 30.00 60.00

2009 Donruss Elite Extra Edition Private Signings

OVERALL AUTO ODDS 1:5 HOBBY
PRINT RUNS B/WN 5-250 COPIES PER
NO PRICING ON QTY 25 OR LESS
EXCHANGE DEADLINE 7/20/2011
3 Bobby Borchering/50 12.50 30.00
6 Donavan Tate/245 6.00 20.00
7 Drew Storen/100 6.00 15.00
8 Dustin Ackley/250 5.00 12.00
10 Grant Green/50 6.00 15.00
11 Jacob Turner/100 12.00 30.00
13 Kyle Gibson/50 10.00 25.00
15 Matt Hobgood/100 20.00 50.00
16 Mike Leake/50 10.00 25.00
18 Mike Minor/50 6.00 15.00
20 Slade Heathcott/50 20.00 50.00
23 Tony Sanchez/50 15.00 40.00
24 Tyler Matzek/100 6.00 15.00
25 Zack Wheeler/100 6.00 15.00

2009 Donruss Elite Extra Edition School Colors

COMPLETE SET (20) 8.00 20.00
RANDOM INSERTS IN PACKS
1 Dustin Ackley .60 1.50
2 Grant Green .40 1.00
3 Mike Leake 1.25 3.00
4 Drew Storen .60 1.50
5 Jared Mitchell .60 1.50
6 Ryan Jackson .40 1.00
7 Tom Mendonca .40 1.00
8 Josh Phegley .60 1.50
9 A.J. Pollock 1.00 2.50
10 Tony Sanchez 1.00 2.50
11 Marc Krauss .40 1.00
12 Garrett Richards 1.00 2.50
13 Shaver Hansen .40 1.00
14 Josh Fellhauer .40 1.00
15 Brandon Belt 1.00 2.50
16 Bill Bullock .40 1.00
17 Mike Minor .60 1.50
18 Kent Matthes .40 1.00
19 Ben Paulsen .40 1.00
20 Aaron Baker .40 1.00

2009 Donruss Elite Extra Edition School Colors Autographs

OVERALL AUTO ODDS 1:5 HOBBY
PRINT RUNS B/WN 20-100 COPIES PER
NO PRICING ON QTY 20 OR LESS
1 Dustin Ackley/100 5.00 12.00
2 Grant Green/100 5.00 12.00
3 Mike Leake/100 20.00 50.00
4 Drew Storen/100 6.00 15.00
5 Jared Mitchell/100 12.00 30.00
6 Ryan Jackson/100 4.00 10.00
7 Tom Mendonca/100 6.00 15.00
9 A.J. Pollock/100 8.00 20.00
10 Tony Sanchez/100 8.00 20.00
11 Marc Krauss/100 4.00 10.00
12 Garrett Richards/100 12.00 30.00
13 Shaver Hansen/100 3.00 8.00
14 Josh Fellhauer/100 3.00 8.00
15 Brandon Belt/100 6.00 15.00
16 Bill Bullock/100 3.00 8.00
18 Kent Matthes/100 6.00 15.00
19 Ben Paulsen/100 3.00 8.00
20 Aaron Baker/100 3.00 8.00

2009 Donruss Elite Extra Edition School Colors Materials

RANDOM INSERTS IN PACKS
STATED PRINT RUN 250 SER.#'d SETS
5 Jared Mitchell 3.00 8.00
13 Shaver Hansen 3.00 8.00
16 Bill Bullock 3.00 8.00
17 Mike Minor 3.00 8.00
20 Aaron Baker 3.00 8.00

2009 Donruss Elite Extra Edition Throwback Threads

RANDOM INSERTS IN PACKS
PRINT RUNS B/WN 50-250 COPIES PER
1 Mike Trout/250 50.00 100.0
2 Shelby Miller/250 6.00 15.0
3 Mike Minor/250 3.00 8.0
4 Jason Kipnis/250 4.00 10.0
5 Bill Bullock/250 3.00 8.0
6 Jared Mitchell/250 3.00 8.0
9 Kyle Russell/250 3.00 8.0
10 Jose Duran/250 3.00 8.0
11 Buster Posey/149 4.00 10.0
14 Pete Rose/250 10.00 25.0
16 Robbie Grossman/250 3.00 8.0
17 Shaver Hansen/250 3.00 8.0
18 Tim Wheeler/250 3.00 8.0
19 Josh Vitters/50 4.00 10.0
20 Todd Glaesmann/250 3.00 8.
21 Mike Cisco/250 3.00 8.
22 Aaron Baker/250 3.00 8.
23 Chase Anderson/250 3.00 8.
24 Brooks Raley/250 3.00 8.

2009 Donruss Elite Extra Edition Throwback Threads Autographs

OVERALL AUTO ODDS 1:5 HOBBY
PRINT RUNS B/WN 5-250 COPIES PER
NO PRICING ON QTY 25 OR LESS
EXCHANGE DEADLINE 7/20/2011
1 Mike Trout/100 500.00 800.
2 Shelby Miller/100 12.00 30.
3 Mike Minor/53 12.50 30.
4 Jason Kipnis/100 15.00 40.
5 Bill Bullock/199 4.00 10.
6 Jared Mitchell/149 10.00 25.
14 Pete Rose/149 20.00 50.
20 Todd Glaesmann/250 4.00 10.
21 Mike Cisco/250 4.00 10.
23 Chase Anderson/100 4.00 10
24 Brooks Raley/250 4.00 10

2009 Donruss Elite Extra Edition Throwback Threads Autographs Prime

*PRIME: .6X TO 1.5X BASIC

OVERALL AUTO ODDS 1:5 HOBBY
PRINT RUNS B/WN 1-50 COPIES PER
NO PRICING ON QTY 25 OR LESS

2010 Donruss Elite Extra Edition

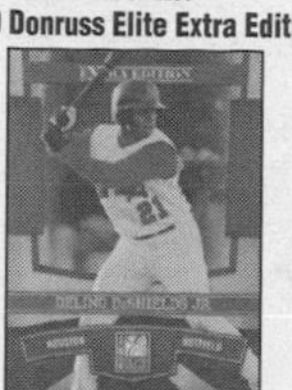

COMP.SET w/o AU's (100) 10.00 25.00
COMMON CARD (1-100) .20 .50
COMMON AUTO (101-200) 3.00 8.00
AU SEMIS 4.00 10.00
AU UNLISTED 5.00 12.00
OVERALL AUTO ODDS 6 PER BOX
AUTO PRINT RUNS B/WN 99-825 COPIES PER
EXCHANGE DEADLINE 4/6/2012
1 Bryce Brentz .50 1.25
2 Drew Vettleson .30 .75
3 Mike Olt .60 1.50
4 Tyrell Jenkins .60 1.50
5 Delino DeShields Jr. .30 .75
6 Asher Wojciechowski .50 1.25
7 Bobby Doran .20 .50
8 Hunter Morris .20 .50
9 J.R. Bradley .20 .50
10 Nick Castellanos 1.00 2.50
11 Chad Bettis .20 .50
12 Drew Robinson .20 .50
13 Aaron Sanchez .75 2.00
14 Brandon Workman .20 .50
15 Matt Moore 1.50 4.00
16 Cole Leonida .20 .50
17 Seth Rosin .30 .75
18 Josh Rutledge 1.25 3.00
19 Vincent Velasquez .75 2.00
20 Matt den Dekker .30 .75
21 Rett Varner .20 .50
22 Reggie Golden .20 .50
23 Derek Dietrich .50 1.25
24 Robbie Aviles .20 .50
25 DeAngelo Mack .30 .75
26 Alex Wimmers .30 .75
28 Mike Antonio .20 .50
29 Andy Wilkins .20 .50
30 Cody Buckel .50 1.25
31 Kevin Munson .20 .50
32 Chris Hawkins .20 .50
33 Drew Smyly .30 .75
34 Gary Sanchez 2.00 5.00
35 Dan Klein .20 .50
36 Yordy Cabrera .30 .75
37 Ralston Cash .20 .50
38 Jonathan Galvez .20 .50
39 Sam Dyson .20 .50
40 Rob Segedin .20 .50
41 Jimmy Nelson .20 .50
42 Daniel Tillman .20 .50
43 Raoul Torrez .20 .50
44 Sammy Solis .50 1.25
45 Austin Wates .20 .50
46 Matt Harvey 1.25 3.00
47 Connor Narron .30 .75
48 Bryan Morgado .30 .75
49 Chris Hernandez .20 .50
50 Hayden Simpson .30 .75
51 Brooks Hall .30 .75
52 Devin Lohman .20 .50
53 Pat Dean .20 .50
54 Gary Brown 1.00 2.50
55 Stetson Allie .30 .75
56 Griffin Murphy .30 .75
57 Jake Thompson .20 .50
58 Cody Wheeler .20 .50
59 Niko Goodrum .60 1.50
60 Rob Brantly .20 .50
61 Austin Ross .20 .50
62 Kevin Rath .20 .50
63 A.J. Cole .30 .75
64 Scott Lawson .30 .75
65 Logan Bawcom .20 .50
66 Connor Powers .20 .50
67 Mike Nesseth .30 .75
68 Jose Vinicio .30 .75
69 Ryan Casteel .20 .50
70 Rick Hague .20 .50
71 Kyle Blair .20 .50
72 Jordan Swagerty .50 1.25
73 Jake Anderson .20 .50
74 Brian Garman .20 .50
75 Mark Canha .50 1.25
76 Perci Garner .30 .75
77 Edinson Rincon .20 .50
78 Jonathan Jones .20 .50
79 Ross Wilson .20 .50
80 Mel Rojas Jr. .20 .50
81 Luke Jackson .30 .75
82 Cole Nelson .20 .50
83 David Filak .20 .50
84 Kyle Bellows .20 .50
85 Sam Tuivailala .30 .75
86 Cole Cook .20 .50
87 Jesse Hahn .20 .50
88 A.J. Griffin .20 .50
89 Max Walla .20 .50
90 Jurickson Profar .50 1.25
91 Zach Cates .20 .50
92 Ronald Torreyes .60 1.50
93 Marcus Littlewood .30 .75
94 Parker Bridwell .50 1.25
95 Tyler Austin .50 1.25
96 Rob Rasmussen .20 .50
97 Seth Blair .30 .75
98 Tyler Holt .20 .50
99 Micah Gibbs .30 .75
100 Pamela Anderson .50 1.25
101 Michael Choice AU/470 6.00 15.00
102 C.Colon AU/432 6.00 15.00
103 Chris Sale AU/655 30.00 80.00
104 Jake Skole AU/675 5.00 12.00
105 Mike Foltynewicz AU/653 6.00 15.00
106 Kolbrin Vitek AU/542 4.00 10.00
107 Kellin Deglan AU/640 3.00 8.00
108 Jesse Biddle AU/800 6.00 15.00
109 Justin O'Conner AU/794 4.00 10.00
110 Cito Culver AU/589 3.00 8.00
111 Mike Kvasnicka AU/530 3.00 8.00
112 Matt Lipka AU/722 5.00 12.00
113 N.Syndergaard AU/809 10.00 25.00
114 Ryan LaMarre AU/564 3.00 8.00
115 Josh Sale AU/536 6.00 15.00
116 Zack Cox AU/478 6.00 15.00
117 Bryan Holaday AU/500 3.00 8.00
118 Todd Cunningham AU/699 4.00 10.00
119 Jarrett Parker AU/580 4.00 10.00
120 Leon Landry AU/550 4.00 10.00
121 Cam Bedrosian AU/652 4.00 10.00
122 Ryan Bolden AU/799 3.00 8.00
123 Cameron Rupp AU/498 5.00 12.00
124 Jedd Gyorko AU/675 4.00 10.00
125 Matt Curry AU/209 3.00 8.00
126 Drew Pomeranz AU/527 8.00 20.00
127 Yasmani Grandal AU/395 4.00 10.00
128 Deck McGuire AU/441 10.00 25.00
129 Chevez Clarke AU/799 5.00 12.00
130 Jameson Taillon AU/699 6.00 15.00
131 Kaleb Cowart AU/750 4.00 10.00
132 Manny Machado AU/425 40.00 100.00
133 Tony Thompson AU/199 4.00 10.00
134 Dee Gordon AU/310 5.00 12.00
135 Chance Ruffin AU/550 3.00 8.00
136 J.Realmuto AU/99 50.00 120.00
137 Kevin Chapman AU/694 3.00 8.00
138 Kyle Roller AU/810 3.00 8.00
139 Stephen Pryor AU/819 5.00 12.00
140 Jonathan Singleton AU/699 4.00 10.00
141 Drew Cisco AU/399 4.00 10.00
142 Blake Forsythe AU/401 4.00 10.00
143 Kellen Sweeney AU/819 3.00 8.00
144 Brett Eibner AU/545 5.00 12.00
145 Martin Perez AU/494 10.00 25.00
146 Jean Segura AU/811 8.00 20.00
147 Christian Yelich AU/815 40.00 100.00
148 Robby Rowland AU/799 3.00 8.00
149 Trent Mummey AU/694 3.00 8.00
150 Zach Lee AU/650 6.00 15.00
151 Jason Mitchell AU/600 3.00 8.00
152 Nick Longmire AU/819 4.00 10.00
153 Robbie Erlin AU/699 3.00 8.00
154 Addison Reed AU/601 4.00 10.00
155 Austin Reed AU/499 4.00 10.00
156 Tyler Thornburg AU/819 5.00 12.00
157 Ty Linton AU/99 5.00 12.00
158 Chris Balcom-Miller AU/819 3.00 8.00
159 Wes Mugarian AU/799 3.00 8.00
161 Justin Grimm AU/99 8.00 20.00
162 Alex Lavisky AU/499 4.00 10.00
163 Taijuan Walker AU/819 6.00 15.00
164 Arodys Vizcaino AU/770 4.00 10.00
165 Brody Colvin AU/819 6.00 15.00
166 Christian Carmichael AU/815 3.00 8.00
167 Josh Spence AU/699 3.00 8.00
168 Joc Pederson AU/799 6.00 15.00
169 Justin Nicolino AU/399 8.00 20.00
170 Nick Tepesch AU/550 4.00 10.00
171 Joe Gardner AU/819 3.00 8.00
172 Taylor Morton AU/815 4.00 10.00
173 Jason Martinson AU/815 3.00 8.00
174 Matt Miller AU/585 3.00 8.00
175 Justin Bloxom AU/790 3.00 8.00
176 Matt Suschak AU/780 3.00 8.00
177 Zach Neal AU/750 3.00 8.00
178 Ben Gamel AU/801 5.00 12.00
179 Jimmy Reyes AU/810 3.00 8.00
180 Matt Price AU/699 3.00 8.00
181 Aaron Shipman AU/701 3.00 8.00
182 Hector Noesi AU/819 6.00 15.00
183 Peter Tago AU/649 3.00 8.00
184 Kyle Knudson AU/825 3.00 8.00
185 M.Kirkland AU/99 5.00 12.00
186 Mickey Wiswall AU/499 3.00 8.00
187 Steve Geltz AU/599 3.00 8.00
188 Shawn Tolleson AU/815 3.00 8.00
189 Greg Holle AU/810 3.00 8.00
190 Erik Goeddel AU/810 3.00 8.00
191 Paul Goldschmidt AU/820 25.00 60.00
192 L.Washington AU/199 6.00 15.00
193 Trey McNutt AU/249 8.00 20.00
194 Henry Rodriguez AU/620 5.00 12.00
195 Adrian Sanchez AU/620 4.00 10.00
196 Daniel Bibona AU/420 3.00 8.00
197 Chad Lewis AU/799 3.00 8.00
198 Brodie Greene AU/625 3.00 8.00
199 Carter Jurica AU/685 3.00 8.00
200 A.Ranaudo AU/150 12.50 30.00

2010 Donruss Elite Extra Edition Aspirations

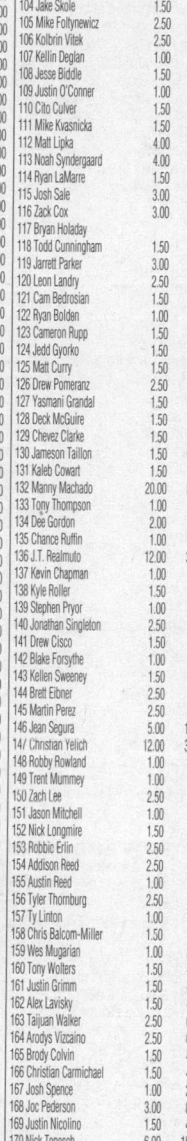

*ASP 1-100: 2X TO 5X BASIC
RANDOM INSERTS IN PACKS
STATED PRINT RUN 200 SER.#'d SETS
100 Pamela Anderson 8.00 20.00
101 Michael Choice 1.50 4.00
102 Christian Colon 1.50 4.00
103 Chris Sale 12.00 30.00
104 Jake Skole 1.50 4.00
105 Mike Foltynewicz 2.50 6.00
106 Kolbrin Vitek 2.50 6.00
107 Kellin Deglan 1.00 2.50
108 Jesse Biddle 1.50 4.00
109 Justin O'Conner 1.00 2.50
110 Cito Culver 1.50 4.00
111 Mike Kvasnicka 1.50 4.00
112 Matt Lipka 4.00 10.00
113 Noah Syndergaard 4.00 10.00
114 Ryan LaMarre 1.50 4.00
115 Josh Sale 3.00 8.00
116 Zack Cox 3.00 8.00
117 Bryan Holaday
118 Todd Cunningham 1.50 4.00
119 Jarrett Parker 3.00 8.00
120 Leon Landry 2.50 6.00
121 Cam Bedrosian 1.50 4.00
122 Ryan Bolden 1.00 2.50
123 Cameron Rupp 1.50 4.00
124 Jedd Gyorko 1.50 4.00
125 Matt Curry 1.50 4.00
126 Drew Pomeranz 2.50 6.00
127 Yasmani Grandal 1.50 4.00
128 Deck McGuire 1.50 4.00
129 Chevez Clarke 1.50 4.00
130 Jameson Taillon 1.50 4.00
131 Kaleb Cowart 1.50 4.00
132 Manny Machado 20.00 50.00
133 Tony Thompson 1.00 2.50
134 Dee Gordon 2.00 5.00
135 Chance Ruffin 1.00 2.50
136 J.T. Realmuto 12.00 30.00
137 Kevin Chapman 1.00 2.50
138 Kyle Roller 1.50 4.00
139 Stephen Pryor 1.00 2.50
140 Jonathan Singleton 2.50 6.00
141 Drew Cisco 1.50 4.00
142 Blake Forsythe 1.00 2.50
143 Kellen Sweeney 1.50 4.00
144 Brett Eibner 2.50 6.00
145 Martin Perez 2.50 6.00
146 Jean Segura 5.00 12.00
147 Christian Yelich 12.00 30.00
148 Robby Rowland 1.00 2.50
149 Trent Mummey 1.00 2.50
150 Zach Lee 2.50 6.00
151 Jason Mitchell 1.00 2.50
152 Nick Longmire 1.50 4.00
153 Robbie Erlin 2.50 6.00
154 Addison Reed 2.50 6.00
155 Austin Reed 1.00 2.50
156 Tyler Thornburg 2.50 6.00
157 Ty Linton 1.00 2.50
158 Chris Balcom-Miller 1.50 4.00
159 Wes Mugarian 1.00 2.50
160 Tony Wolters 1.50 4.00
161 Justin Grimm 1.50 4.00
162 Alex Lavisky 1.50 4.00
163 Taijuan Walker 2.50 6.00
164 Arodys Vizcaino 2.50 6.00
165 Brody Colvin 1.50 4.00
166 Christian Carmichael 1.50 4.00
167 Josh Spence 1.00 2.50
168 Joc Pederson 3.00 8.00
169 Justin Nicolino 1.50 4.00
170 Nick Tepesch 6.00 15.00
171 Joe Gardner 1.00 2.50
172 Taylor Morton 2.50 6.00
173 Jason Martinson 1.00 2.50
174 Matt Miller 1.00 2.50
175 Justin Bloxom 1.00 2.50
176 Matt Suschak 1.00 2.50
177 Zach Neal 1.00 2.50
178 Ben Gamel 1.50 4.00
179 Jimmy Reyes 1.00 2.50
180 Matt Price 1.00 2.50
181 Aaron Shipman 1.50 4.00
182 Hector Noesi 1.50 4.00
183 Peter Tago 1.50 4.00
184 Kyle Knudson 1.00 2.50
185 Matt Kirkland 1.00 2.50
186 Mickey Wiswall 1.00 2.50
187 Steve Geltz 1.00 2.50
188 Shawn Tolleson 1.00 2.50
189 Greg Holle 1.50 4.00
190 Erik Goeddel 1.50 4.00
191 Paul Goldschmidt 10.00 25.00
192 LeVon Washington 1.50 4.00
193 Trey McNutt 1.00 2.50
194 Henry Rodriguez 1.00 2.50
195 Adrian Sanchez 1.00 2.50
196 Daniel Bibona 1.50 4.00
197 Chad Lewis 1.50 4.00
198 Brodie Greene 1.00 2.50
199 Carter Jurica 1.00 2.50
200 Anthony Ranaudo 3.00 8.00

2010 Donruss Elite Extra Edition Status

*STATUS 1-100: 2.5X TO 6X BASIC
RANDOM INSERTS IN PACKS
STATED PRINT RUN 100 SER.#'d SETS
100 Pamela Anderson 10.00 25.00
101 Michael Choice 2.00 5.00
102 Christian Colon 2.00 5.00
103 Chris Sale 15.00 40.00
104 Jake Skole 2.00 5.00
105 Mike Foltynewicz 3.00 8.00
106 Kolbrin Vitek 3.00 8.00
107 Kellin Deglan 1.25 3.00
108 Jesse Biddle 2.00 5.00
109 Justin O'Conner 1.25 3.00
110 Cito Culver 2.00 5.00
111 Mike Kvasnicka 2.00 5.00
112 Matt Lipka 5.00 12.00
113 Noah Syndergaard 5.00 12.00
114 Ryan LaMarre 2.00 5.00
115 Josh Sale 4.00 10.00
116 Zack Cox 4.00 10.00
117 Bryan Holaday
118 Todd Cunningham 2.00 5.00
119 Jarrett Parker 4.00 10.00
120 Leon Landry 3.00 8.00
121 Cam Bedrosian 2.00 5.00
122 Ryan Bolden 1.25 3.00
123 Cameron Rupp 2.00 5.00
124 Jedd Gyorko 2.00 5.00
125 Matt Curry 2.00 5.00
126 Drew Pomeranz 3.00 8.00
127 Yasmani Grandal 2.00 5.00
128 Deck McGuire 2.00 5.00
129 Chevez Clarke 2.00 5.00
130 Jameson Taillon 2.00 5.00
131 Kaleb Cowart 2.00 5.00
132 Manny Machado 25.00 60.00
133 Tony Thompson 1.25 3.00
134 Dee Gordon 2.50 6.00
135 Chance Ruffin 1.25 3.00
136 J.T. Realmuto 15.00 40.00
137 Kevin Chapman 1.25 3.00
138 Kyle Roller 2.00 5.00
139 Stephen Pryor 1.25 3.00
140 Jonathan Singleton 3.00 8.00
141 Drew Cisco 2.00 5.00
142 Blake Forsythe 1.25 3.00
143 Kellen Sweeney 2.00 5.00
144 Brett Eibner 3.00 8.00
145 Martin Perez 3.00 8.00
146 Jean Segura 6.00 15.00
147 Christian Yelich 15.00 40.00
148 Robby Rowland 1.25 3.00
149 Trent Mummey 1.25 3.00
150 Zach Lee 3.00 8.00
151 Jason Mitchell 1.25 3.00
152 Nick Longmire 2.00 5.00
153 Robbie Erlin 3.00 8.00
154 Addison Reed 3.00 8.00
155 Austin Reed 1.25 3.00
156 Tyler Thornburg 3.00 8.00
157 Ty Linton 1.25 3.00
158 Chris Balcom-Miller 2.00 5.00
159 Wes Mugarian 1.25 3.00
160 Tony Wolters 2.00 5.00
161 Justin Grimm 2.00 5.00
162 Alex Lavisky 2.00 5.00
163 Taijuan Walker 3.00 8.00
164 Arodys Vizcaino 3.00 8.00
165 Brody Colvin 2.00 5.00
166 Christian Carmichael 2.00 5.00
167 Josh Spence 1.25 3.00
168 Joc Pederson 4.00 10.00
169 Justin Nicolino 2.00 5.00
170 Nick Tepesch 8.00 20.00
171 Joe Gardner 1.25 3.00
172 Taylor Morton 3.00 8.00
173 Jason Martinson 1.25 3.00
174 Matt Miller 1.25 3.00
175 Justin Bloxom 1.25 3.00
176 Matt Suschak 1.25 3.00
177 Zach Neal 1.25 3.00
178 Ben Gamel 2.00 5.00
179 Jimmy Reyes 1.25 3.00
180 Matt Price 1.25 3.00
181 Aaron Shipman 2.00 5.00
182 Hector Noesi 2.00 5.00
183 Peter Tago 2.00 5.00
184 Kyle Knudson 1.25 3.00
185 Matt Kirkland 1.25 3.00
186 Mickey Wiswall 1.25 3.00
187 Steve Geltz 1.25 3.00
188 Shawn Tolleson 1.25 3.00
189 Greg Holle 2.00 5.00
190 Erik Goeddel 2.00 5.00
191 Paul Goldschmidt 12.00 30.00
192 LeVon Washington 2.00 5.00
193 Trey McNutt 1.25 3.00
194 Henry Rodriguez 1.25 3.00
195 Adrian Sanchez 1.25 3.00
196 Daniel Bibona 2.00 5.00
197 Chad Lewis 2.00 5.00
198 Brodie Greene 1.25 3.00
199 Carter Jurica 1.25 3.00
200 Anthony Ranaudo 4.00 10.00

2010 Donruss Elite Extra Edition Signature Aspirations

OVERALL AUTO ODDS SIX PER BOX
STATED PRINT RUN 100 SER.#'d SETS
EXCHANGE DEADLINE 4/6/2012
1 Bryce Brentz 15.00 40.00
2 Drew Vettleson 10.00 25.00
3 Mike Olt 8.00 20.00
4 Tyrell Jenkins 6.00 15.00
5 Delino DeShields Jr. 8.00 20.00
6 Asher Wojciechowski 8.00 20.00
7 Bobby Doran 3.00 8.00
8 Hunter Morris 6.00 15.00
9 J.R. Bradley 4.00 10.00
10 Nick Castellanos 10.00 25.00
11 Chad Bettis 5.00 12.00
12 Drew Robinson 3.00 8.00
13 Aaron Sanchez 10.00 25.00
14 Brandon Workman 8.00 20.00
15 Matt Moore 6.00 15.00
16 Cole Leonida 5.00 12.00
17 Seth Rosin 3.00 8.00
18 Josh Rutledge 3.00 8.00
19 Vincent Velasquez 12.00 30.00
20 Matt den Dekker 8.00 20.00
21 Rett Varner 3.00 8.00
22 Reggie Golden 3.00 8.00
23 Derek Dietrich 40.00 100.00
24 Robbie Aviles 6.00 15.00
25 DeAngelo Mack 10.00 25.00
26 Alex Wimmers 6.00 15.00
28 Mike Antonio 5.00 12.00
29 Andy Wilkins 5.00 12.00
30 Cody Buckel 4.00 10.00
31 Kevin Munson 4.00 10.00
32 Chris Hawkins 10.00 25.00
33 Drew Smyly 12.50 30.00
34 Gary Sanchez 60.00 150.00
35 Dan Klein 3.00 8.00
36 Yordy Cabrera 8.00 20.00
37 Ralston Cash 4.00 10.00
38 Jonathan Galvez 3.00 8.00
39 Sam Dyson 4.00 10.00
40 Rob Segedin 5.00 12.00
41 Jimmy Nelson 8.00 20.00
42 Daniel Tillman 4.00 10.00
43 Raoul Torrez 3.00 8.00
44 Sammy Solis 4.00 10.00
45 Austin Wates 5.00 12.00
46 Matt Harvey 75.00 150.00
47 Connor Narron 4.00 10.00
48 Bryan Morgado 4.00 10.00
49 Chris Hernandez 4.00 10.00
50 Hayden Simpson 10.00 25.00
51 Brooks Hall 8.00 20.00
52 Devin Lohman 4.00 10.00
53 Pat Dean 10.00 25.00
54 Gary Brown 15.00 40.00
55 Stetson Allie 8.00 20.00
56 Griffin Murphy 8.00 20.00
57 Jake Thompson 4.00 10.00
58 Cody Wheeler 3.00 8.00
59 Niko Goodrum 10.00 25.00
60 Rob Brantly 5.00 12.00
61 Austin Ross 4.00 10.00
62 Kevin Rath 3.00 8.00
63 A.J. Cole 3.00 8.00
64 Scott Lawson 3.00 8.00
65 Logan Bawcom 3.00 8.00
66 Connor Powers 3.00 8.00
67 Mike Nesseth 3.00 8.00
68 Jose Vinicio 6.00 15.00
69 Ryan Casteel 4.00 10.00
70 Rick Hague 4.00 10.00
71 Kyle Blair 4.00 10.00
72 Swagerty UER Magic AU 15.00 40.00
73 Jake Anderson 5.00 12.00
74 Brian Garman 3.00 8.00
75 Mark Canha 5.00 12.00
76 Perci Garner 4.00 10.00
77 Edinson Rincon 4.00 10.00
78 Jonathan Jones 5.00 12.00
79 Ross Wilson 3.00 8.00
80 Mel Rojas Jr. 5.00 12.00
81 Luke Jackson 3.00 8.00
82 Cole Nelson 4.00 10.00
83 David Filak 4.00 10.00
84 Kyle Bellows 4.00 10.00
85 Sam Tuivailala 4.00 10.00
86 Cole Cook 4.00 10.00
87 Jesse Hahn 3.00 8.00
88 A.J. Griffin 10.00 25.00
89 Max Walla 8.00 20.00
90 Jurickson Profar 12.00 30.00
91 Zach Cates 4.00 10.00
92 Ronald Torreyes 12.00 30.00
93 Marcus Littlewood 6.00 15.00
94 Parker Bridwell 10.00 25.00
95 Tyler Austin 5.00 12.00
96 Rob Rasmussen 4.00 10.00
97 Seth Blair 5.00 12.00
98 Tyler Holt 6.00 15.00
99 Micah Gibbs 6.00 15.00
101 Michael Choice 6.00 15.00
102 Christian Colon 4.00 10.00
103 Chris Sale 40.00 100.00
104 Jake Skole 5.00 12.00
105 Mike Foltynewicz 12.00 30.00
106 Kolbrin Vitek 6.00 15.00
107 Kellin Deglan 3.00 8.00
108 Jesse Biddle 3.00 8.00
109 Justin O'Conner 5.00 12.00
110 Cito Culver 3.00 8.00
111 Mike Kvasnicka 5.00 12.00
112 Matt Lipka 3.00 8.00
113 Noah Syndergaard 15.00 40.00
114 Ryan LaMarre 6.00 15.00
115 Josh Sale 15.00 40.00
116 Zack Cox 6.00 15.00
117 Bryan Holaday 5.00 12.00
118 Todd Cunningham 6.00 15.00
119 Jarrett Parker 6.00 15.00
120 Leon Landry 6.00 15.00
121 Cam Bedrosian 6.00 15.00
122 Ryan Bolden 5.00 12.00
123 Cameron Rupp 6.00 15.00
124 Jedd Gyorko 20.00 50.00
125 Matt Curry 10.00 25.00
126 Drew Pomeranz 15.00 40.00
127 Yasmani Grandal 6.00 15.00
128 Deck McGuire 8.00 20.00
129 Chevez Clarke 5.00 12.00
130 Jameson Taillon 15.00 40.00
131 Kaleb Cowart 12.50 30.00
132 Manny Machado 75.00 200.00
133 Tony Thompson 4.00 10.00
134 Dee Gordon 12.00 30.00
135 Chance Ruffin 4.00 10.00
136 J.T. Realmuto 50.00 120.00
137 Kevin Chapman 4.00 10.00
138 Kyle Roller 6.00 15.00
139 Stephen Pryor 10.00 25.00
140 Jonathan Singleton 12.00 30.00
141 Drew Cisco 6.00 15.00
142 Blake Forsythe 4.00 10.00
143 Kellen Sweeney 10.00 25.00
144 Brett Eibner 8.00 20.00
145 Martin Perez 12.00 30.00
146 Jean Segura 12.00 30.00
147 Christian Yelich 40.00 100.00
148 Robby Rowland 4.00 10.00
149 Trent Mummey 4.00 10.00
150 Zach Lee 6.00 15.00
151 Jason Mitchell 3.00 8.00
152 Nick Longmire 6.00 15.00
153 Robbie Erlin 5.00 12.00
154 Addison Reed 6.00 15.00
155 Austin Reed 3.00 8.00
156 Tyler Thornburg 3.00 8.00
157 Ty Linton 5.00 12.00
158 Chris Balcom-Miller 5.00 12.00
159 Wes Mugarian 3.00 8.00
160 Tony Wolters 4.00 10.00
161 Justin Grimm 5.00 12.00
162 Alex Lavisky 6.00 15.00
163 Taijuan Walker 12.00 30.00
164 Arodys Vizcaino 6.00 15.00
165 Brody Colvin 6.00 15.00
166 Christian Carmichael 4.00 10.00
167 Josh Spence 5.00 12.00
168 Joc Pederson 8.00 20.00
169 Justin Nicolino 3.00 8.00
170 Nick Tepesch 8.00 20.00
171 Joe Gardner 4.00 10.00
172 Taylor Morton 8.00 20.00
173 Jason Martinson 3.00 8.00
174 Matt Miller 6.00 15.00
175 Justin Bloxom 4.00 10.00
176 Matt Suschak 3.00 8.00
177 Zach Neal 4.00 10.00
178 Ben Gamel 8.00 20.00
179 Jimmy Reyes 3.00 8.00
180 Matt Price 3.00 8.00
181 Aaron Shipman 5.00 12.00
182 Hector Noesi 10.00 25.00
183 Peter Tago 5.00 12.00
184 Kyle Knudson 4.00 10.00
185 Matt Kirkland 3.00 8.00
186 Mickey Wiswall 3.00 8.00
187 Steve Geltz 3.00 8.00
188 Shawn Tolleson 4.00 10.00
189 Greg Holle 5.00 12.00
190 Erik Goeddel 4.00 10.00
191 Paul Goldschmidt 40.00 100.00
192 LeVon Washington 6.00 15.00
193 Trey McNutt 4.00 10.00
194 Henry Rodriguez 5.00 12.00
195 Adrian Sanchez 4.00 10.00
196 Daniel Bibona 3.00 8.00
197 Chad Lewis 5.00 12.00
198 Brodie Greene 4.00 10.00
200 Anthony Ranaudo 10.00 25.00

2010 Donruss Elite Extra Edition Signature Status

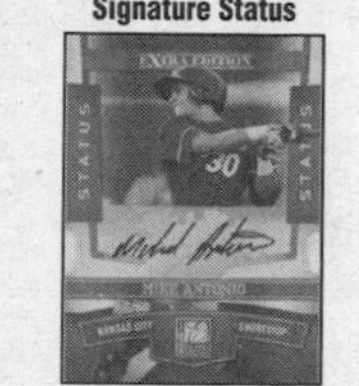

OVERALL AUTO ODDS SIX PER BOX
STATED PRINT RUN 50 SER.#'d SETS
EXCHANGE DEADLINE 4/6/2012
1 Bryce Brentz 15.00 40.00
2 Drew Vettleson 20.00 50.00
3 Mike Olt 10.00 25.00
4 Tyrell Jenkins 8.00 20.00
5 Delino DeShields Jr. 10.00 25.00
6 Asher Wojciechowski 5.00 12.00
7 Bobby Doran 4.00 10.00
8 Hunter Morris 8.00 20.00
9 J.R. Bradley 5.00 12.00
10 Nick Castellanos 12.00 30.00
11 Chad Bettis 10.00 25.00
12 Drew Robinson 4.00 10.00
13 Aaron Sanchez 12.00 30.00
14 Brandon Workman 5.00 12.00
15 Matt Moore 8.00 20.00
16 Cole Leonida 6.00 15.00
17 Seth Rosin 4.00 10.00
18 Josh Rutledge 8.00 20.00
19 Vincent Velasquez 15.00 40.00
20 Matt den Dekker 10.00 25.00
21 Rett Varner 4.00 10.00
22 Reggie Golden 4.00 10.00
23 Derek Dietrich 50.00 120.00
24 Robbie Aviles 8.00 20.00
25 DeAngelo Mack 6.00 15.00
26 Alex Wimmers 5.00 12.00
28 Mike Antonio 6.00 15.00
29 Andy Wilkins 6.00 15.00
30 Cody Buckel 15.00 40.00
31 Kevin Munson 5.00 12.00
32 Chris Hawkins 12.00 30.00
33 Drew Smyly 4.00 10.00
34 Gary Sanchez 100.00 250.00
35 Dan Klein 4.00 10.00
36 Yordy Cabrera 10.00 25.00
37 Ralston Cash 5.00 12.00
38 Jonathan Galvez 10.00 25.00
39 Sam Dyson 5.00 12.00
40 Rob Segedin 10.00 25.00
41 Jimmy Nelson 4.00 10.00
42 Daniel Tillman 8.00 20.00
43 Raoul Torrez 4.00 10.00
44 Sammy Solis 5.00 12.00
45 Austin Wates 10.00 25.00
46 Matt Harvey 100.00 200.00
47 Connor Narron 5.00 12.00
48 Bryan Morgado 5.00 12.00
49 Chris Hernandez 10.00 25.00
50 Hayden Simpson 12.00 30.00
51 Brooks Hall 6.00 15.00
52 Devin Lohman 8.00 20.00
53 Pat Dean 6.00 15.00
54 Gary Brown 20.00 50.00
55 Stetson Allie 5.00 12.00
56 Griffin Murphy 10.00 25.00
57 Jake Thompson 5.00 12.00
58 Cody Wheeler 4.00 10.00
59 Niko Goodrum 12.00 30.00
60 Rob Brantly 5.00 12.00
61 Austin Ross 5.00 12.00
62 Kevin Rath 4.00 10.00
63 A.J. Cole 10.00 25.00
64 Scott Lawson 6.00 15.00
65 Logan Bawcom 4.00 10.00
66 Connor Powers 4.00 10.00
67 Mike Nesseth 4.00 10.00
68 Jose Vinicio 6.00 15.00
69 Ryan Casteel 5.00 12.00
70 Rick Hague 5.00 12.00
71 Kyle Blair 5.00 12.00
72 Swagerty UER Magic AU 12.00 30.00
73 Jake Anderson 6.00 15.00
74 Brian Garman 4.00 10.00
75 Mark Canha 6.00 15.00
76 Perci Garner 5.00 12.00
77 Edinson Rincon 10.00 25.00
78 Jonathan Jones 6.00 15.00
79 Ross Wilson 4.00 10.00
80 Mel Rojas Jr. 6.00 15.00
81 Luke Jackson 10.00 25.00
82 Cole Nelson 5.00 12.00
83 David Filak 5.00 12.00
84 Kyle Bellows 5.00 12.00
85 Sam Tuivailala 5.00 12.00
86 Cole Cook 5.00 12.00
87 Jesse Hahn 4.00 10.00
88 A.J. Griffin 6.00 15.00
89 Max Walla 15.00 40.00
90 Jurickson Profar 15.00 40.00
91 Zach Cates 6.00 15.00
92 Ronald Torreyes 15.00 40.00
93 Marcus Littlewood 8.00 20.00
94 Parker Bridwell 12.00 30.00
95 Tyler Austin 6.00 15.00
96 Rob Rasmussen 5.00 12.00
97 Seth Blair 10.00 25.00

98 Tyler Holt 4.00 10.00
99 Micah Gibbs 8.00 20.00
101 Michael Choice 30.00 60.00
102 Christian Colon 12.00 30.00
103 Chris Sale 50.00 120.00
104 Jake Skole 10.00 25.00
105 Mike Foltynewicz 15.00 40.00
106 Kolbrin Vitek 5.00 12.00
107 Kellin Deglan 4.00 10.00
108 Jesse Biddle 20.00 50.00
109 Justin O'Conner 10.00 25.00
110 Cito Culver 4.00 10.00
111 Mike Kvasnicka 6.00 15.00
112 Matt Lipka 4.00 10.00
113 Noah Syndergaard 25.00 60.00
114 Ryan LaMarre 5.00 12.00
115 Josh Sale 20.00 50.00
116 Zack Cox 15.00 40.00
117 Bryan Holaday 6.00 15.00
118 Todd Cunningham 8.00 20.00
119 Jarrett Parker 8.00 20.00
120 Leon Landry 8.00 20.00
121 Cam Bedrosian EXCH 8.00 20.00
122 Ryan Bolden 6.00 15.00
123 Cameron Rupp 8.00 20.00
124 Jedd Gyorko 15.00 40.00
125 Matt Curry 5.00 12.00
126 Drew Pomeranz 10.00 25.00
127 Yasmani Grandal 8.00 20.00
128 Deck McGuire 5.00 12.00
129 Chevez Clarke 12.00 30.00
130 Jameson Taillon 20.00 50.00
131 Kaleb Cowart 15.00 40.00
132 Manny Machado 100.00 250.00
133 Tony Thompson 5.00 12.00
134 Dee Gordon 20.00 50.00
135 Chance Ruffin 5.00 12.00
136 J.T. Realmuto 60.00 150.00
137 Kevin Chapman 5.00 12.00
138 Kyle Roller 10.00 25.00
139 Stephen Pryor 8.00 20.00
140 Jonathan Singleton 20.00 50.00
141 Drew Cisco 8.00 20.00
142 Blake Forsythe 8.00 20.00
143 Kellen Sweeney 12.00 30.00
144 Brett Eibner 5.00 12.00
145 Martin Perez 15.00 40.00
146 Jean Segura 15.00 40.00
147 Christian Yelich 50.00 120.00
148 Robby Rowland 5.00 12.00
149 Trent Mummey 5.00 12.00
150 Zach Lee 8.00 20.00
151 Jason Mitchell 4.00 10.00
152 Nick Longmire 8.00 20.00
153 Robbie Erlin 5.00 12.00
154 Addison Reed 15.00 40.00
155 Austin Reed 4.00 10.00
156 Tyler Thornburg 4.00 10.00
157 Ty Linton 10.00 25.00
158 Chris Balcom-Miller 10.00 25.00
159 Wes Mugarian 4.00 10.00
160 Tony Wolters 5.00 12.00
161 Justin Grimm 5.00 12.00
162 Alex Lavisky 8.00 20.00
163 Taijuan Walker 20.00 50.00
164 Arodys Vizcaino 5.00 12.00
165 Brody Colvin 20.00 50.00
166 Christian Carmichael 5.00 12.00
167 Josh Spence 6.00 15.00
168 Joc Pederson 10.00 25.00
169 Justin Nicolino 4.00 10.00
170 Nick Tepesch 15.00 40.00
171 Joe Gardner 6.00 15.00
172 Taylor Morton 10.00 25.00
173 Jason Martinson 4.00 10.00
174 Matt Miller 4.00 10.00
175 Justin Bloxom 5.00 12.00
176 Matt Suschak 4.00 10.00
177 Zach Neal 5.00 12.00
178 Ben Gamel 10.00 25.00
179 Jimmy Reyes 4.00 10.00
180 Matt Price 4.00 10.00
181 Aaron Shipman 6.00 15.00
182 Hector Noesi 12.00 30.00
183 Peter Tago 6.00 15.00
184 Kyle Knudson 5.00 12.00
185 Matt Kirkland 6.00 15.00
186 Mickey Wiswall 4.00 10.00
187 Steve Geltz 4.00 10.00
188 Shawn Tolleson 5.00 12.00
189 Greg Holle 6.00 15.00
190 Erik Goeddel 4.00 10.00
191 Paul Goldschmidt 50.00 120.00
192 LeVon Washington 8.00 20.00
193 Trey McNutt 5.00 12.00
194 Henry Rodriguez 6.00 15.00
195 Adrian Sanchez 5.00 12.00
196 Daniel Bibona 4.00 10.00
197 Chad Lewis 6.00 15.00
198 Brodie Greene 5.00 12.00
200 Anthony Ranaudo 15.00 40.00

2010 Donruss Elite Extra Edition Back to the Future Signatures

OVERALL AUTO ODDS 6 PER BOX
PRINT RUNS B/WN 5-249 COPIES PER
EXCHANGE DEADLINE 4/6/2012
1 Pedro Baez/249 3.00 8.00
2 Colton Cain/249 3.00 8.00
3 Tyler Townsend/249 3.00 8.00
4 James Jones/249 8.00 20.00
5 Ashur Tolliver/249 4.00 10.00
6 Jeff Hunt/95 3.00 8.00
7 Aaron Baker/235 3.00 8.00
8 Tyler Matzek/150 8.00 20.00
9 Reymond Fuentes/249 3.00 8.00
10 Thomas Joseph/249 8.00 20.00
11 Chad James/244 3.00 8.00
12 Khris Davis/249 20.00 50.00
13 Eric Smith/249 3.00 8.00
14 Tyler Kehrer/249 3.00 8.00
17 Bob Gibson/50 12.50 30.00
19 Don Sutton/49 4.00 10.00
20 Frank Howard/30 12.50 30.00

2010 Donruss Elite Extra Edition College Ties

COMPLETE SET (10) 10.00 25.00
RANDOM INSERTS IN PACKS
1 Z.Cox/B.Eibner 1.25 3.00
2 Brandon Workman/Chance Ruffin .40 1.00
3 Matt Curry/Bryan Holaday .60 1.50
4 Micah Gibbs/Leon Landry 1.00 2.50
5 C.Colon/G.Brown 2.00 5.00
6 M.Choice/R.Varner .60 1.50
7 D.McGuire/D.Dietrich 1.00 2.50
8 Ryan LaMarre/Matt Miller .60 1.50
9 Dan Klein/Rob Rasmussen .40 1.00
10 Chad Bettis/Bobby Doran .40 1.00

2010 Donruss Elite Extra Edition College Ties Autographs

OVERALL AUTO ODDS 6 PER BOX
STATED PRINT RUN 50 SER.#'d SETS
EXCHANGE DEADLINE 4/6/2012
1 Z.Cox/B.Eibner 6.00 15.00
2 B.Workman/C.Ruffin 8.00 20.00
3 M.Curry/B.Holaday 8.00 20.00
5 Colon/Brown 8.00 20.00
6 M.Choice/R.Varner 6.00 15.00
7 D.McGuire/D.Dietrich 12.00 30.00
8 Ryan LaMarre/Matt Miller 6.00 15.00
9 Dan Klein/Rob Rasmussen 6.00 15.00
10 C.Bettis/B.Doran 12.50 30.00

2010 Donruss Elite Extra Edition Collegiate Patches Autographs

OVERALL AUTO ODDS 6 PER BOX
PRINT RUNS B/WN 49-150 COPIES PER
EXCHANGE DEADLINE 4/6/2012
ANW Andy Wilkins/125 5.00 12.00
AR A.Ranaudo/125 8.00 20.00
AUW Austin Wates/125 6.00 15.00
AW Alex Wimmers/125 10.00 25.00
BD Bobby Doran/125 5.00 12.00
BE Brett Eibner/125 10.00 25.00
BF Blake Forsythe/125 10.00 25.00
BG Brodie Greene/125 5.00 12.00
BH Bryan Holaday/125 8.00 20.00
BJS B.Surhoff/125 6.00 15.00
BMC Ben McDonald/125 10.00 25.00
BW B.Workman/125 5.00 12.00
CAR Cameron Rupp/124 5.00 12.00
CB Chad Bettis/125 4.00 10.00
CH Chris Hernandez/125 4.00 10.00
CJ Carter Jurica/125 4.00 10.00
CL Cole Leonida/140 4.00 10.00
CR Chance Ruffin/125 5.00 12.00
DD Derek Dietrich/125 10.00 25.00
DK Dan Klein/125 4.00 10.00
DL Devin Lohman/125 4.00 10.00
DM Deck McGuire/125 8.00 20.00
DP Drew Pomeranz/125 4.00 10.00
GB Gary Brown/49 50.00 100.00
HM Hunter Morris/150 8.00 20.00
JG Jedd Gyorko/125 10.00 25.00
JN Jimmy Nelson/125 4.00 8.00
JOS Swagerty/125 UER Magic AU 30.00 60.00
JP Jarrett Parker/125 10.00 25.00
JS Josh Spence/125 6.00 15.00
JT Jake Thompson/125 4.00 10.00
JUG Justin Grimm/125 6.00 15.00
KB Kyle Blair/125 4.00 10.00
KC Kevin Chapman/125 8.00 20.00
KG Kirk Gibson/125 12.50 30.00
LL Leon Landry/125 10.00 25.00
MC Matt Curry/125 4.00 10.00
MD Matt den Dekker/125 6.00 15.00
MG Micah Gibbs/125 5.00 12.00
MH Matt Harvey/125 40.00 80.00
MK Mike Kvasnicka/125 6.00 15.00
MN Mike Nesseth/125 4.00 10.00
MO Mike Olt/125 10.00 25.00
PD Pat Dean/125 5.00 12.00
PI P.Incaviglia/125 EXCH 5.00 12.00
RH Rick Hague/125 4.00 10.00
RL Ryan LaMarre/125 5.00 12.00
RR Rob Rasmussen/125 5.00 12.00
SB Seth Blair/125 4.00 10.00
SD Sam Dyson/125 4.00 10.00
SS Sammy Solis/125 5.00 12.00
TH Tyler Holt/125 5.00 12.00
TM Trent Mummey/125 6.00 15.00
YG Y.Grandal/125 15.00 40.00
ZC Zack Cox/125 12.50 30.00

2010 Donruss Elite Extra Edition Draft Hits Autographs

OVERALL AUTO ODDS 6 PER BOX
PRINT RUNS B/WN 5-299 COPIES PER
1 R.Monday/99 EXCH 4.00 10.00
2 Dale Murphy/99 8.00 20.00
7 Alan Trammell/40 10.00 25.00
8 B.Surhoff/299 4.00 10.00
9 Jack Morris/150 3.00 8.00
12 R.Ventura/99 8.00 20.00
14 P.Incaviglia/99 4.00 10.00
15 Ben McDonald/299 3.00 8.00
16 Ron Blomberg/299 3.00 8.00
17 Jeff Bagwell/35 EXCH 20.00 50.00
18 Jay Buhner/99 3.00 8.00
19 Tino Martinez/99 6.00 15.00

2010 Donruss Elite Extra Edition Elite Series

COMPLETE SET (20) 15.00 40.00
RANDOM INSERTS IN PACKS
1 Kaleb Cowart .60 1.50
2 Christian Colon .60 1.50
3 Brandon Workman .40 1.00
4 Michael Choice .60 1.50
5 Delino DeShields Jr. .60 1.50
6 Jarrett Parker 1.25 3.00
7 Kolbrin Vitek 1.00 2.50
8 Manny Machado 8.00 20.00
9 Dave Winfield .60 1.50
10 Yasmani Grandal .60 1.50
11 Chance Ruffin .40 1.00
12 Cito Culver .60 1.50
13 Zach Lee 1.00 2.50
14 Zack Cox 1.25 3.00
15 Drew Pomeranz 1.00 2.50
16 Josh Sale 1.25 3.00
17 Matt Harvey 2.50 6.00
18 Mike Olt 1.25 3.00
19 Jameson Taillon .60 1.50
20 Nick Castellanos 2.00 5.00

2010 Donruss Elite Extra Edition Elite Series Autographs

OVERALL AUTO ODDS 6 PER BOX
PRINT RUNS B/WN 19-100 COPIES PER
3 B.Workman/95 6.00 15.00
4 Michael Choice/100 10.00 25.00
5 D.DeShields Jr./75 10.00 25.00
6 Jarrett Parker/100 12.00 30.00
7 Kolbrin Vitek/100 8.00 20.00
10 Y.Grandal/100 8.00 20.00
13 Zach Lee/50 8.00 20.00
14 Zack Cox/49 40.00 80.00
15 Drew Pomeranz/49 12.50 30.00
18 Mike Olt/100 10.00 25.00
19 Jameson Taillon/49 12.00 30.00
20 Nick Castellanos/50 20.00 50.00

2010 Donruss Elite Extra Edition Franchise Futures Signatures

OVERALL AUTO ODDS 6 PER BOX
PRINT RUNS B/WN 49-150 COPIES PER
EXCHANGE DEADLINE 4/6/2012
1 Bryce Brentz/719 4.00 10.00
2 Drew Vettleson/690 3.00 8.00
3 Mike Olt/399 8.00 20.00
4 Tyrell Jenkins/599 4.00 10.00
5 D.DeShields Jr./499 3.00 8.00
6 A.Wojciechowski/675 5.00 12.00
7 Bobby Doran/644 4.00 10.00
8 Hunter Morris/619 6.00 15.00
9 J.R. Bradley/625 3.00 8.00
10 N.Castellanos/699 6.00 15.00
11 Chad Bettis/635 3.00 8.00
12 Drew Robinson/550 3.00 8.00
13 Aaron Sanchez/499 6.00 15.00
14 B.Workman/450 5.00 12.00
15 Matt Moore/819 5.00 12.00
16 Cole Leonida/669 3.00 8.00
17 Seth Rosin/710 3.00 8.00
18 Josh Rutledge/595 6.00 15.00
19 Vincent Velasquez/799 8.00 20.00
20 Matt den Dekker/694 3.00 8.00
21 Rett Varner/650 3.00 8.00
22 Reggie Golden/819 5.00 12.00
23 Derek Dietrich/490 20.00 50.00
24 Robbie Aviles/810 3.00 8.00
25 DeAngelo Mack/819 3.00 8.00
26 A.Wimmers/199 5.00 12.00
28 Mike Antonio/99 10.00 25.00
29 Andy Wilkins/494 3.00 8.00
30 Cody Buckel/816 6.00 15.00
31 Kevin Munson/819 3.00 8.00
32 Chris Hawkins/99 10.00 25.00
33 Drew Smyly/799 4.00 10.00
34 Gary Sanchez/669 40.00 100.00
35 Dan Klein/599 4.00 10.00
36 Yordy Cabrera/818 4.00 10.00
37 Ralston Cash/819 3.00 8.00
38 Jonathan Galvez/810 3.00 8.00
39 Sam Dyson/199 3.00 8.00
40 Rob Segedin/816 4.00 10.00
41 Jimmy Nelson/640 3.00 8.00
42 Daniel Tillman/816 3.00 8.00
43 Raoul Torrez/325 3.00 8.00
44 Sammy Solis/699 3.00 8.00
45 Austin Wates/99 12.50 30.00
46 Matt Harvey/149 50.00 100.00
47 Connor Narron/835 3.00 8.00
48 Bryan Morgado/601 4.00 10.00
49 Chris Hernandez/690 3.00 8.00
50 Hayden Simpson/599 5.00 12.00
51 Brooks Hall/819 4.00 10.00
52 Devin Lohman/694 3.00 8.00
53 Pat Dean/525 4.00 10.00
54 G.Brown/199 5.00 12.00
55 Stetson Allie/599 6.00 15.00
56 Griffin Murphy/775 3.00 8.00
57 Jake Thompson/699 3.00 8.00
58 Cody Wheeler/815 3.00 8.00
59 Niko Goodrum/819 8.00 20.00
60 Rob Brantly/819 4.00 10.00
61 Austin Ross/819 3.00 8.00
62 Kevin Rath/820 3.00 8.00
63 A.J. Cole/819 3.00 8.00
64 Scott Lawson/694 3.00 8.00
65 Logan Bawcom/790 3.00 8.00
66 Connor Powers/811 3.00 8.00
67 Mike Nesseth/590 3.00 8.00
68 Jose Vinicio/99 5.00 12.00
69 Ryan Casteel/817 3.00 8.00
70 Rick Hague/490 3.00 8.00
71 Kyle Blair/749 4.00 10.00
72 Swagerty/450 UER Magic AU 12.00 30.00
73 Jake Anderson/810 4.00 10.00
74 Brian Garman/810 3.00 8.00
75 Mark Canha/799 3.00 8.00
76 Perci Garner/799 3.00 8.00
77 Edinson Rincon/819 3.00 8.00
78 Jonathan Jones/694 3.00 8.00
79 Ross Wilson/815 3.00 8.00
80 Mel Rojas Jr./819 4.00 10.00
81 Luke Jackson/99 6.00 15.00
82 Cole Nelson/819 3.00 8.00
83 David Filak/817 3.00 8.00
84 Kyle Bellows/819 3.00 8.00
85 Sam Tuivailala/820 3.00 8.00
86 Cole Cook/840 3.00 8.00
87 Jesse Hahn/99 12.00 30.00
88 A.J. Griffin/99 12.00 30.00
89 Max Walla/819 3.00 8.00
90 Jurickson Profar/390 5.00 12.00
91 Zach Cates/816 3.00 8.00
92 Ronald Torreyes/599 10.00 25.00
93 M.Littlewood/825 4.00 10.00
94 Parker Bridwell/99 12.00 30.00
95 Tyler Austin/811 3.00 8.00
96 Rob Rasmussen/658 3.00 8.00
97 Seth Blair/99 4.00 10.00
98 Tyler Holt/694 4.00 10.00
99 Micah Gibbs/390 4.00 10.00
100 Pamela Anderson/35 125.00 250.00

2010 Donruss Elite Extra Edition Private Signings

OVERALL AUTO ODDS 6 PER BOX
PRINT RUNS B/WN 8-149 COPIES PER
1 Andy Wilkins/149 10.00 25.00
2 Bryan Holaday/50 10.00 25.00
3 Michael Choice/99 6.00 15.00
4 Cameron Rupp/50 8.00 20.00
5 Josh Sale/125 5.00 12.00
10 Kaleb Cowart/49 40.00 80.00
12 Jake Skole/125 5.00 12.00
13 Dee Gordon/100 5.00 12.00
14 Martin Perez/125 10.00 25.00
15 Hayden Simpson/125 6.00 15.00
16 Brandon Workman/99 5.00 12.00
18 Kolbrin Vitek/100 6.00 15.00
19 Rett Varner/99 3.00 8.00
20 Matt Lipka/100 8.00 20.00
21 Chris Sale/125 12.00 30.00
22 Cam Bedrosian/149 6.00 15.00
23 Cito Culver/149 12.50 30.00
24 Tyrell Jenkins/125 6.00 15.00
25 Mike Olt/125 4.00 10.00
26 Bryce Brentz/100 8.00 20.00
27 Wojciechowski/125 8.00 20.00
28 Zack Cox/99 10.00 25.00
29 Drew Vettleson/149 3.00 8.00
30 Gary Sanchez/149 50.00 120.00
31 Brett Eibner/99 8.00 20.00
32 J.R. Bradley/149 5.00 12.00
33 Micah Gibbs/99 8.00 20.00
34 Kellin Deglan/149 3.00 8.00
36 Matt Curry/100 6.00 15.00
37 Drew Pomeranz/100 3.00 8.00
38 Mike Foltynewicz/149 10.00 25.00
39 Aaron Sanchez/125 10.00 25.00
40 Zach Lee/110 6.00 15.00

2010 Donruss Elite Extra Edition School Colors

COMPLETE SET (20) 10.00 25.00
RANDOM INSERTS IN PACKS
1 Jordan Swagerty 1.00 2.50
2 Christian Colon .60 1.50
3 Michael Choice .60 1.50
4 Zack Cox 1.25 3.00
5 Yasmani Grandal .60 1.50
6 Kolbrin Vitek 1.00 2.50
7 Ryan LaMarre .60 1.50
8 Drew Pomeranz 1.00 2.50
9 Jarrett Parker 1.25 3.00
10 Blake Forsythe .40 1.00
11 Josh Rutledge 2.50 6.00
12 Sam Dyson .40 1.00
13 Hunter Morris .40 1.00
14 Deck McGuire .60 1.50
15 Mike Kvasnicka .60 1.50
16 Cameron Rupp .60 1.50
17 Todd Cunningham .60 1.50
18 Micah Gibbs .60 1.50
19 Alex Wimmers .60 1.50
20 Derek Dietrich 1.00 2.50

2010 Donruss Elite Extra Edition School Colors Autographs

OVERALL AUTO ODDS 6 PER BOX
PRINT RUNS B/WN 19-299 COPIES PER
1 Swagerty/149 UER Magic AU 10.00 25.00
2 Christian Colon/49 10.00 25.00
3 Michael Choice/99 10.00 25.00
5 Yasmani Grandal/99 6.00 15.00
6 Kolbrin Vitek/68 10.00 25.00
7 Ryan LaMarre/90 5.00 12.00
10 Blake Forsythe/49 6.00 15.00
11 Josh Rutledge/99 8.00 20.00
12 Sam Dyson/49 5.00 12.00
13 Hunter Morris/50 6.00 15.00
14 Deck McGuire/49 8.00 20.00
15 Mike Kvasnicka/165 4.00 10.00
16 Cameron Rupp/70 5.00 12.00
17 Todd Cunningham/82 3.00 8.00
18 Micah Gibbs/149 8.00 20.00
19 Alex Wimmers/49 5.00 12.00
20 Derek Dietrich/199 10.00 25.00

2011 Donruss Elite Extra Edition

COMPLETE SET (25) 5.00 12.00
COMMON CARD .20 .50
1 Josh Hamilton .30 .75
2 Adrian Gonzalez .40 1.00
3 Clayton Kershaw 1.00 2.50
4 Albert Pujols .60 1.50
5 Chris Perez .20 .50
6 Jeremy Hellickson RC .50 1.25
7 Curtis Granderson .40 1.00
8 Justin Upton .30 .75
9 Jordan Walden RC .20 .50
10 Brian McCann .30 .75
11 Starlin Castro .30 .75
12 Ichiro Suzuki .60 1.50
13 Trevor Cahill .20 .50
14 Justin Verlander .50 1.25
15 Danny Espinosa RC .20 .50
16 Andrew McCutchen .50 1.25
17 Dustin Pedroia .40 1.00
18 Adam Jones .30 .75
19 Ben Revere RC .30 .75
20 David Freese .20 .50
21 Michael Pineda RC .50 1.25
22 Heath Bell .20 .50
23 Andy Dirks RC .50 1.25
24 Troy Tulowitzki .50 1.25
25 Jay Bruce .30 .75

2011 Donruss Elite Extra Edition Aspirations

*ASPIRATIONS: 2X TO 5X BASIC
STATED PRINT RUN 200 SER.#'d SETS

2011 Donruss Elite Extra Edition Status

*STATUS: 2.5X TO 6X BASIC
STATED PRINT RUN 100 SER.#'d SETS

2011 Donruss Elite Extra Edition Back to the Future Signatures

OVERALL SIX AUTOS PER HOBBY BOX
PRINT RUNS B/WN 49-720 COPIES PER
EXCHANGE DEADLINE 06/28/2013
2 J.T. Realmuto 20.00 50.00
3 Jordan Swagerty 5.00 12.00
5 Austin Wates 5.00 12.00
6 Kyle Blair 6.00 15.00
7 A.J. Griffin 5.00 12.00
8 Jurickson Profar 5.00 12.00
10 Nick Castellanos 15.00 40.00
11 Chris Hawkins 6.00 15.00
12 Justin Nicolino 6.00 15.00
16 Jose Vinicio 3.00 8.00
19 Manny Machado 20.00 50.00
20 Stetson Allie 6.00 15.00
25 Jonathan Singleton 4.00 10.00

2011 Donruss Elite Extra Edition Best Compared To

RANDOM INSERTS IN PACKS
STATED PRINT RUN 499 SER.#'d SETS
1 Lincecum/Bauer 5.00 12.00
2 Bundy/Beckett 1.50 4.00
3 Cron/Trumbo 1.50 4.00
4 Starling/Hamilton .75 2.00
5 Spangenberg/Pedroia 1.00 2.50
6 Rendon/Zimmerman 4.00 10.00
7 Cole/Strasburg 5.00 12.00
8 Roy Oswalt/Sonny Gray 1.25 3.00
9 H.Ramirez/J.Baez 6.00 15.00
10 Colby Rasmus/Kes Carter .75 2.00
11 Granden Goetzman/Jayson Werth .75 2.00
12 T.Story/T.Tulowitzki 6.00 15.00

2011 Donruss Elite Extra Edition Building Blocks Dual

COMPLETE SET (15) 8.00 20.00
STATED ODDS 1:10 HOBBY
1 B.Starling/J.Bell 2.50 6.00
2 Brandon Drury 1.00 2.50
Kyle Kubitza
3 G.Cole/T.Bauer 4.00 10.00
4 Abel Baker .40 1.00
Pratt Maynard
5 Tyler Collins .40 1.00
Tyler Gibson
6 Logan Verrett .75 2.00
Phillip Evans
7 Nick Ramirez .60 1.50
Sean Halton
8 Jake Lowery .40 1.00
Jake Sisco
9 Jace Peterson .40 1.00
Lee Orr
10 Brandon Parrent .40 1.00
Nick Fleece
11 Jeff Ames .40 1.00
Steven Ames
12 Aaron Westlake .40 1.00
Dean Green
13 Chris Wallace .40 1.00
Michael Goodnight
14 Bryan Brickhouse 1.00 2.50
Cameron Gallagher
15 Cole Green .40 1.00
Kyle McMyne

2011 Donruss Elite Extra Edition Building Blocks Dual Signatures

PRINT RUNS B/WN 10-49 COPIES PER
NO PRICING ON QTY 20 OR LESS
EXCHANGE DEADLINE 06/28/2013
2 B.Drury/K.Kubitza 4.00 10.00
4 A.Baker/P.Maynard 8.00 20.00
5 T.Collins/T.Gibson 8.00 20.00
6 L.Verrett/P.Evans 6.00 15.00
7 N.Ramirez/S.Halton 10.00 25.00
8 J.Lowery/J.Sisco 12.50 30.00
9 J.Peterson/L.Orr 5.00 12.00
10 B.Parrent/N.Fleece 5.00 12.00
11 J.Ames/S.Ames 5.00 12.00
12 A.Westlake/D.Green 6.00 15.00
13 Chris Wallace 4.00 10.00
Michael Goodnight
14 B.Brickhouse/C.Gallagher 6.00 15.00
15 C.Green/K.McMyne 10.00 25.00

2011 Donruss Elite Extra Edition Building Blocks Quad

COMPLETE SET (10) 8.00 20.00
STATED ODDS 1:10 HOBBY
1 Aaron Westlake/Corey Williams/Grayson
Garvin/Sonny Gray 1.00 2.50
2 Lin/Hag/Baez/Mich 5.00 12.00
3 Brian Flynn/James McCann
Jason King/Jason Krizan 1.00 2.50
4 Erik Johnson/Keenyn Walker
Kyle McMillen/Scott Snodgress .40 1.00
5 Granden Goetzman/Johnny Eierman
Kes Carter/Mikie Mahtook 1.00 2.50
6 Andrew Susac/Blake Swihart
Jake Lowery/John Hicks .60 1.50
7 Hultz/Bundy/Cole/Bauer 4.00 10.00
8 Rend/Martin/Esposito/Dean 3.00 8.00
9 Nmm/Strlng/Smith/Bell 2.50 6.00
10 Austin Hedges/Jace Peterson
Joe Ross/Michael Kelly 1.00 2.50

2011 Donruss Elite Extra Edition Building Blocks Trio

COMPLETE SET (15) 8.00 20.00
STATED ODDS 1:10 HOBBY
1 Rendon/Goodwin/Purke 3.00 8.00
2 Bradley/Bundy/Fulmer 1.25 3.00
3 Dan Vogelbach/Dillon Maples
Matt Szczur 1.25 3.00
4 Hsr/Spingr/Hmbln 2.50 6.00
5 Cole Green/James Allen
Robert Stephenson .75 2.00
6 Snell/Ames/Guerrieri 1.50 4.00
7 Alex Hassan/Kendrick Perkins
Williams Jerez .40 1.00
8 Hultzen/Bradley/Anderson 2.00 5.00
9 Norris/Musgrove/Comer 1.25 3.00
10 Larry Greene/Mitch Walding
Roman Quinn 1.00 2.50

2011 Donruss Elite Extra Edition Elite Series

STATED ODDS 1:10 HOBBY
1 Jackie Bradley Jr. 1.50 4.00
2 Josh Bell 2.50 6.00
3 Angelo Songco .60 1.50
4 Brad Miller .40 1.00
5 Tyler Goeddel .40 1.00
6 Matt Purke 1.00 2.50
7 Blake Swihart .60 1.50
8 Roman Quinn 1.00 2.50
9 Jordan Cote 1.00 2.50
10 Anthony Rendon 3.00 8.00
11 Zeke DeVoss .60 1.50
12 Tyler Collins .40 1.00
13 Logan Verrett .75 2.00
14 Charlie Tilson 1.00 2.50
15 Brandon Nimmo 2.00 5.00
16 Taylor Jungmann .60 1.50
17 Joe Panik 1.00 2.50
18 Gerrit Cole 4.00 10.00
19 Abel Baker .40 1.00
20 Tyler Gibson .40 1.00

2011 Donruss Elite Extra Edition Elite Series Signatures

OVERALL SIX AUTOS PER HOBBY BOX
PRINT RUNS B/WN 25-228 COPIES PER
EXCHANGE DEADLINE 06/28/2013
1 Jackie Bradley Jr. 8.00 20.00
2 Josh Bell 15.00 40.00
3 Angelo Songco 6.00 15.00
5 Tyler Goeddel 4.00 10.00
6 Matt Purke 6.00 15.00
7 Blake Swihart 6.00 15.00
8 Roman Quinn 4.00 10.00
9 Jordan Cote 8.00 20.00
10 Anthony Rendon 15.00 40.00
11 Zeke DeVoss 6.00 15.00
12 Tyler Collins 6.00 15.00
13 Logan Verrett 8.00 20.00
14 Charlie Tilson 8.00 20.00
15 Brandon Nimmo 10.00 25.00
16 Taylor Jungmann 8.00 20.00
17 Joe Panik 12.00 30.00
18 Gerrit Cole 20.00 50.00
19 Abel Baker 8.00 20.00
20 Tyler Gibson 4.00 10.00

2011 Donruss Elite Extra Edition Franchise Futures Signatures

OVERALL SIX AUTOS PER HOBBY BOX
PRINT RUNS B/WN 137-1264 COPIES PER
EXCHANGE DEADLINE 06/28/2013
1 Tyler Goeddel 4.00 10.00
2 Dante Bichette Jr. 10.00 25.00
3 James Harris 5.00 12.00
4 Cory Mazzoni 5.00 12.00
5 Abel Baker 4.00 10.00
6 Alex Dickerson 5.00 12.00
7 Justin Bour 8.00 20.00
8 Tyler Anderson 4.00 10.00
9 Jeff Ames 4.00 10.00
10 Cristhian Adames 3.00 8.00
11 Jason Krizan 3.00 8.00
12 Michael Kelly 6.00 15.00
13 Kyle McMillen 3.00 8.00
14 Charlie Tilson 6.00 15.00
15 Brad Miller 4.00 10.00
16 Blake Snell 10.00 25.00
17 Daniel Norris 5.00 12.00
18 Williams Jerez 8.00 20.00
19 Erik Johnson 3.00 8.00
20 Gabriel Rosa 8.00 20.00
21 Adam Morgan 3.00 8.00
22 Aaron Westlake 4.00 10.00
23 Brandon Loy 3.00 8.00
24 Zach Good 3.00 8.00
25 Angelo Songco 5.00 12.00
26 Jordan Akins 4.00 10.00
27 Josh Osich 5.00 12.00
28 Austin Hedges 8.00 20.00
29 Jake Sisco 3.00 8.00
30 B.A. Vollmuth 3.00 8.00
31 Austin Wood 3.00 8.00
32 Dan Vogelbach 3.00 8.00
33 Carl Thomore 3.00 8.00
34 Blake Swihart 5.00 12.00
35 James Allen 4.00 10.00
36 Carlos Sanchez 3.00 8.00
37 Michael Goodnight 3.00 8.00
38 James McCann 6.00 15.00
39 Will Lamb 4.00 10.00
40 Taylor Featherston 4.00 10.00
41 Nick Ramirez 4.00 10.00
42 Johnny Eierman 4.00 10.00
43 Logan Verrett 12.00 30.00
44 Neftali Rosario 5.00 12.00
45 Kevin Comer 3.00 8.00
46 Kendrick Perkins 4.00 10.00
47 Tyler Grimes 5.00 12.00
48 Kyle Winkler 3.00 8.00
49 John Hicks 3.00 8.00
50 Taylor Guerrieri 5.00 12.00
51 Dillon Maples 4.00 10.00
52 Harold Martinez 4.00 10.00
53 Grayson Garvin 3.00 8.00
54 Zeke DeVoss 3.00 8.00
55 Mitch Walding 4.00 10.00
56 Clay Holmes 4.00 10.00
57 Hudson Boyd 4.00 10.00
58 Granden Goetzman 4.00 10.00
59 Bryan Brickhouse 3.00 8.00
60 Shane Opitz 4.00 10.00
61 Nick Fleece 3.00 8.00
62 Barret Loux 4.00 10.00
63 Jake Lowery 6.00 15.00
64 Madison Boer 5.00 12.00
65 Tony Zych 3.00 8.00
66 Sean Halton 3.00 8.00
67 Cavan Cohoes 4.00 10.00
68 Dean Green 6.00 15.00
69 Miles Hamblin 3.00 8.00
70 J.R. Graham 5.00 12.00
71 Tom Robson 3.00 8.00
72 Riccio Torrez 3.00 8.00

73 Adam Conley 3.00 8.00
74 Pratt Maynard 6.00 15.00
75 Jordan Cote 6.00 15.00
76 Kyle Gaedele 3.00 8.00
77 Christian Lopes 4.00 10.00
78 Travis Shaw 3.00 8.00
79 Parker Markel 3.00 8.00
80 Chad Comer 3.00 8.00
81 Adrian Houser 5.00 12.00
82 Corey Williams 3.00 8.00
83 Brian Flynn 3.00 8.00
84 Phillip Evans 3.00 8.00
85 Lee Orr 3.00 8.00
86 Brandon Parrent 3.00 8.00
87 Roman Quinn 5.00 12.00
88 Jake Floethe 3.00 8.00
89 Andrew Susac 6.00 15.00
90 Navery Moore 4.00 10.00
91 Chris Schwinden 4.00 10.00
92 Cole Green 4.00 10.00
93 Chris Wallace 3.00 8.00
94 Steven Ames 3.00 8.00
95 James Baldwin 4.00 10.00
96 Forrest Snow 3.00 8.00
97 Bobby Crocker 5.00 12.00
98 Dwight Smith Jr. 5.00 12.00
99 Greg Bird 15.00 40.00
100 Bryson Myles 4.00 10.00
151 Anthony Meo 4.00 10.00
152 Shawon Dunston Jr. 4.00 10.00
153 Rookie Davis 4.00 10.00
154 Rob Scahill 3.00 8.00
155 Chris Heston 6.00 15.00
156 Adam Jorgenson 3.00 8.00
157 Elliot Soto 3.00 8.00
158 Tyler Cloyd 5.00 12.00
159 Pierre LePage 3.00 8.00
160 Brett Jacobson 3.00 8.00
161 Casey Lawrence 3.00 8.00
162 Joe O'Gara 3.00 8.00
163 Mariekson Gregorius 30.00 80.00
164 Dan Osterbrock 3.00 8.00
165 Jared Hoying 3.00 8.00
166 Alan DeRatt 3.00 8.00
167 Charlie Leesman 5.00 12.00
168 Adam Davis 3.00 8.00
169 Danny Vasquez 6.00 15.00
170 Jon Griffin 4.00 10.00
171 Hernan Perez/810 4.00 10.00
172 Jeremy Cruz 3.00 8.00
173 Jose Osuna 4.00 10.00
174 Red Patterson 3.00 8.00
175 Jamaine Cotton 3.00 8.00
176 Pedro Villarreal 3.00 8.00
177 Justin Boudreaux 3.00 8.00
178 Chris Hanna 3.00 8.00
179 Mike Walker 4.00 10.00
180 David Herbek 3.00 8.00
181 Zack MacPhee 3.00 8.00
182 Ryan Tatusko 3.00 8.00
183 Dan Meadows 3.00 8.00
184 Albert Cartwright 4.00 10.00
185 Brandon Drury 5.00 12.00
186 Eddie Rosario 8.00 20.00
187 Jake Dunning 4.00 10.00
188 Miles Head 5.00 12.00
189 Duanel Jones 4.00 10.00
190 Rob Lyerly 4.00 10.00

2011 Donruss Elite Extra Edition Prospects

OVERALL SIX AUTOS PER HOBBY BOX
PRINT RUNS B/WN 334-865 COPIES PER
EXCHANGE DEADLINE 06/28/2013
1 Tyler Goeddel .20 .50
2 Dante Bichette Jr. .30 .75
3 James Harris .20 .50
4 Cory Mazzoni .20 .50
5 Abel Baker .20 .50
6 Alex Dickerson .30 .75
7 Justin Bour .50 1.25
8 Tyler Anderson .20 .50
9 Jeff Ames .20 .50
10 Cristhian Adames .20 .50
11 Jason Krizan .20 .50
12 Michael Kelly .20 .50
13 Kyle McMillen .20 .50
14 Charlie Tilson .50 1.25
15 Brad Miller .30 .75
16 Blake Snell .75 2.00
17 Daniel Norris .60 1.50
18 Williams Jerez .20 .50
19 Erik Johnson .20 .50
20 Gabriel Rosa .20 .50
21 Adam Morgan .30 .75
22 Aaron Westlake .20 .50
23 Brandon Loy .20 .50
24 Zach Good .20 .50
25 Angelo Songco .30 .75
26 Jordan Akins .20 .50
27 Josh Osich .30 .75
28 Austin Hedges .20 .50
29 Jake Sisco .20 .50
30 B.A. Vollmuth .20 .50
31 Austin Wood .20 .50
32 Dan Vogelbach .60 1.50
33 Carl Thomore .20 .50
34 Blake Swihart .30 .75
35 James Allen .20 .50
36 Carlos Sanchez .20 .50
37 Michael Goodnight .20 .50
38 James McCann .50 1.25
39 Will Lamb .20 .50
40 Taylor Featherston .20 .50
41 Nick Ramirez .30 .75
42 Johnny Eierman .20 .50
43 Logan Verrett .40 1.00
44 Neftali Rosario .20 .50
45 Kevin Comer .30 .75
46 Kendrick Perkins .20 .50
47 Tyler Grimes .20 .50
48 Kyle Winkler .20 .50
49 John Hicks .30 .75
50 Taylor Guerrieri .20 .50
51 Dillon Maples .20 .50
52 Harold Martinez .30 .75
53 Grayson Garvin .30 .75
54 Zeke DeVoss .30 .75
55 Mitch Walding .20 .50
56 Clay Holmes .20 .50
57 Hudson Boyd .20 .50
58 Granden Goetzman .20 .50
59 Bryan Brickhouse .50 1.25
60 Shane Opitz .30 .75
61 Nick Fleece .20 .50
62 Barret Loux .20 .50
63 Jake Lowery .20 .50
64 Madison Boer .20 .50
65 Tony Zych .20 .50
66 Sean Halton .20 .50
67 Cavan Cohoes .20 .50
68 Dean Green .20 .50
69 Miles Hamblin .20 .50
70 J.R. Graham .20 .50
71 Tom Robson .30 .75
72 Riccio Torrez .20 .50
73 Adam Conley .20 .50
74 Pratt Maynard .20 .50
75 Jordan Cote .50 1.25
76 Kyle Gaedele .20 .50
77 Christian Lopes .50 1.25
78 Travis Shaw .50 1.25
79 Parker Markel .20 .50
80 Chad Comer .20 .50
81 Adrian Houser .30 .75
82 Corey Williams .20 .50
83 Brian Flynn .20 .50
84 Phillip Evans .20 .50
85 Lee Orr .20 .50
86 Brandon Parrent .20 .50
87 Roman Quinn .50 1.25
88 Jake Floethe .20 .50
89 Andrew Susac .30 .75
90 Navery Moore .60 1.50
91 Chris Schwinden .20 .50
92 Cole Green .20 .50
93 Chris Wallace .30 .75
94 Steven Ames .20 .50
95 James Baldwin .20 .50
96 Forrest Snow .30 .75
97 Bobby Crocker .20 .50
98 Dwight Smith Jr. .20 .50
99 Greg Bird .40 1.00
100 Bryson Myles .30 .75
151 Anthony Meo .20 .50
152 Shawon Dunston Jr. .20 .50
153 Rookie Davis .50 1.25
154 Rob Scahill .20 .50
155 Chris Heston .30 .75
156 Adam Jorgenson .20 .50
157 Elliot Soto .20 .50
158 Tyler Cloyd .30 .75
159 Pierre LePage .20 .50
160 Brett Jacobson .20 .50
161 Casey Lawrence .30 .75
162 Joe O'Gara .30 .75
163 Mariekson Gregorius 5.00 12.00
164 Dan Osterbrock .20 .50
165 Jared Hoying .30 .75
166 Alan DeRatt .20 .50
167 Charlie Leesman .20 .50
168 Adam Davis .20 .50
169 Danny Vasquez .20 .50
170 Jon Griffin .20 .50
171 Hernan Perez .30 .75
172 Jeremy Cruz .20 .50
173 Jose Osuna .20 .50
174 Red Patterson .20 .50
175 Jamaine Cotton .20 .50
176 Pedro Villarreal .20 .50
177 Justin Boudreaux .20 .50
178 Chris Hanna .20 .50
179 Mike Walker .30 .75
180 David Herbek .20 .50
181 Zack MacPhee .30 .75
182 Ryan Tatusko .30 .75
183 Dan Meadows .20 .50
184 Albert Cartwright .20 .50
185 Brandon Drury .50 1.25
186 Eddie Rosario .60 1.50
187 Jake Dunning .20 .50
188 Miles Head .30 .75
189 Duanel Jones .20 .50
190 Rob Lyerly .20 .50
P1 Trevor Bauer AU/405 6.00 15.00
P2 Anthony Rendon AU/653 10.00 25.00
P3 Gerrit Cole AU/515 8.00 20.00
P4 Dylan Bundy AU/435 6.00 15.00
P5 C.J. Cron AU/465 6.00 15.00
P6 Tyler Collins AU/665 4.00 10.00
P7 C.Spangenberg AU/465 3.00 8.00
P8 Archie Bradley AU/464 4.00 10.00
P9 Jason Esposito AU/559 5.00 12.00
P10 Bubba Starling AU 6.00 15.00
P11 Joe Panik AU/572 3.00 8.00
P12 Kolten Wong AU/365 6.00 15.00
P13 Levi Michael AU/465 5.00 12.00
P14 Sonny Gray AU/364 6.00 15.00
P15 Javier Baez AU/565 25.00 60.00
P16 Danny Hultzen AU/642 6.00 15.00
P17 Alex Hassan AU/763 4.00 10.00
P18 Jace Peterson AU/665 3.00 8.00
P19 Jason King AU/862 3.00 8.00
P20 Kyle Kubitza AU/865 3.00 8.00
P21 Matt Szczur AU/783 5.00 12.00
P22 Sean Gilmartin AU/366 5.00 12.00
P23 Kevin Matthews AU/565 4.00 10.00
P24 Brandon Nimmo AU/565 3.00 8.00
P25 Jed Bradley AU/565 5.00 12.00
P26 C.Gallagher AU/760 4.00 10.00
P27 Mikie Mahtook AU/365 5.00 12.00
P28 Jacob Anderson AU/615 4.00 10.00
P29 Michael Fulmer AU/564 6.00 15.00
P30 Jackie Bradley Jr. AU/692 8.00 20.00
P31 T.Jungmann AU/465 3.00 8.00
P32 Matt Dean AU/855 4.00 10.00
P33 Joe Ross AU/365 6.00 15.00
P34 Jake Hager AU/665 4.00 10.00
P35 Josh Bell AU/692 15.00 40.00
P36 George Springer AU/537 10.00 25.00
P37 Chris Reed AU/500 3.00 8.00
P38 Brian Goodwin AU/750 3.00 8.00
P39 Francisco Lindor AU/557 30.00 80.00
P40 Tyler Gibson AU/665 4.00 10.00
P41 Robert Stephenson AU/334 6.00 15.00
P42 Brandon Martin AU/646 5.00 12.00
P43 Matt Purke AU/465 5.00 12.00
P44 Leonys Martin AU/746 4.00 10.00
P45 Keenyn Walker AU/665 3.00 8.00
P46 Kyle Parker AU/622 5.00 12.00
P47 Travis Harrison AU/664 3.00 8.00
P48 Matt Barnes AU/564 3.00 8.00
P49 Trevor Story AU/464 15.00 40.00
P50 Kyle Crick AU/614 5.00 12.00

2011 Donruss Elite Extra Edition Prospects Aspirations

*ASPIRATIONS: 2X TO 5X BASIC
COMMON CARD (P1-P50) 1.00 2.50
STATED PRINT RUN 200 SER.#'d SETS
74 Pratt Maynard 8.00 20.00
P1 Trevor Bauer 10.00 25.00
P2 Anthony Rendon 8.00 20.00
P3 Gerrit Cole 2.50 6.00
P4 Dylan Bundy 3.00 8.00
P5 C.J. Cron 5.00 12.00
P6 Tyler Collins 1.00 2.50
P7 Cory Spangenberg 1.50 4.00
P8 Archie Bradley 3.00 8.00
P9 Jason Esposito 2.50 6.00
P10 Bubba Starling 3.00 8.00
P11 Joe Panik 4.00 10.00
P12 Kolten Wong 1.50 4.00
P13 Levi Michael 1.50 4.00
P14 Sonny Gray 3.00 8.00
P15 Javier Baez 15.00 40.00
P16 Danny Hultzen 5.00 12.00
P17 Alex Hassan 1.00 2.50
P18 Jace Peterson 1.00 2.50
P19 Jason King 1.00 2.50
P20 Kyle Kubitza 1.00 2.50
P21 Matt Szczur 2.50 6.00
P22 Sean Gilmartin 1.00 2.50
P23 Kevin Matthews 1.00 2.50
P24 Brandon Nimmo 2.00 5.00
P25 Jed Bradley 1.50 4.00
P26 Cameron Gallagher 2.50 6.00
P27 Mikie Mahtook 2.50 6.00
P28 Jacob Anderson 3.00 8.00
P29 Michael Fulmer 2.50 6.00
P30 Jackie Bradley Jr. 4.00 10.00
P31 Taylor Jungmann 1.50 4.00
P32 Matt Dean 1.50 4.00
P33 Joe Ross 2.50 6.00
P34 Jake Hager 1.00 2.50
P35 Josh Bell 6.00 15.00
P36 George Springer 6.00 15.00
P37 Chris Reed 1.50 4.00
P38 Brian Goodwin 2.50 6.00
P39 Francisco Lindor 10.00 25.00
P40 Tyler Gibson 1.00 2.50
P41 Robert Stephenson 2.00 5.00
P42 Brandon Martin 1.50 4.00
P43 Matt Purke 2.50 6.00
P44 Leonys Martin 1.50 4.00
P45 Keenyn Walker 1.00 2.50
P46 Kyle Parker 1.50 4.00
P47 Travis Harrison 1.50 4.00
P48 Matt Barnes 1.50 4.00
P49 Trevor Story 12.00 30.00
P50 Kyle Crick 2.50 6.00

2011 Donruss Elite Extra Edition Prospects Status

*STATUS: 2.5X TO 6X BASIC
STATED PRINT RUN 100 SER.#'d SETS
74 Pratt Maynard 10.00 25.00
P1 Trevor Bauer 12.00 30.00
P2 Anthony Rendon 10.00 25.00
P3 Gerrit Cole 3.00 8.00
P4 Dylan Bundy 4.00 10.00
P5 C.J. Cron 6.00 15.00
P6 Tyler Collins 1.25 3.00
P7 Cory Spangenberg 2.00 5.00
P8 Archie Bradley 4.00 10.00
P9 Jason Esposito 3.00 8.00
P11 Joe Panik 5.00 12.00
P12 Kolten Wong 2.00 5.00
P13 Levi Michael 2.00 5.00
P14 Sonny Gray 4.00 10.00
P15 Javier Baez 15.00 40.00
P16 Danny Hultzen 6.00 15.00
P17 Alex Hassan 1.25 3.00
P18 Jace Peterson 1.25 3.00
P19 Jason King 1.25 3.00
P20 Kyle Kubitza 1.25 3.00
P21 Matt Szczur 3.00 8.00
P22 Sean Gilmartin 1.25 3.00
P23 Kevin Matthews 1.25 3.00
P24 Brandon Nimmo 3.00 6.00
P25 Jed Bradley 2.00 5.00
P26 Cameron Gallagher 3.00 8.00
P27 Mikie Mahtook 3.00 8.00
P28 Jacob Anderson 4.00 10.00
P29 Michael Fulmer 3.00 8.00
P30 Jackie Bradley Jr. 5.00 12.00
P31 Taylor Jungmann 2.00 5.00
P32 Matt Dean 2.00 5.00
P33 Joe Ross 3.00 8.00
P34 Jake Hager 1.25 3.00
P35 Josh Bell 8.00 20.00
P36 George Springer 8.00 20.00
P37 Chris Reed 2.00 5.00
P38 Brian Goodwin 3.00 8.00
P39 Francisco Lindor 12.00 30.00
P40 Tyler Gibson 1.25 3.00
P41 Robert Stephenson 2.50 6.00
P42 Brandon Martin 2.00 5.00
P43 Matt Purke 3.00 8.00
P44 Leonys Martin 2.00 5.00
P45 Keenyn Walker 1.25 3.00
P46 Kyle Parker 2.00 5.00
P47 Travis Harrison 2.00 5.00
P48 Matt Barnes 2.00 5.00
P49 Trevor Story 15.00 40.00
P50 Kyle Crick 3.00 8.00

2011 Donruss Elite Extra Edition Prospects Signature Aspirations

OVERALL SIX AUTOS PER HOBBY BOX
STATED PRINT RUN 100 SER.#'d SETS
EXCHANGE DEADLINE 06/28/2013
1 Tyler Goeddel 4.00 10.00
2 Dante Bichette Jr. 15.00 40.00
3 James Harris 5.00 12.00
4 Cory Mazzoni 10.00 25.00
5 Abel Baker 4.00 10.00
6 Alex Dickerson 8.00 20.00
7 Justin Bour 8.00 20.00
8 Tyler Anderson 10.00 25.00
9 Jeff Ames 4.00 10.00
10 Cristhian Adames 3.00 8.00
11 Jason Krizan 5.00 12.00
12 Michael Kelly 10.00 25.00
13 Kyle McMillen 3.00 8.00
14 Charlie Tilson 6.00 15.00
15 Brad Miller 6.00 15.00
16 Blake Snell 8.00 20.00
17 Daniel Norris 6.00 15.00
18 Williams Jerez 6.00 15.00
19 Erik Johnson 4.00 10.00
20 Gabriel Rosa 6.00 15.00
21 Adam Morgan 12.50 30.00
22 Aaron Westlake 6.00 15.00
23 Brandon Loy 4.00 10.00
24 Zach Good 5.00 12.00
25 Angelo Songco 8.00 20.00
26 Jordan Akins 5.00 12.00
27 Josh Osich 6.00 15.00
28 Austin Hedges 8.00 20.00
29 Jake Sisco 5.00 12.00
30 B.A. Vollmuth 8.00 20.00
31 Austin Wood 3.00 8.00
32 Dan Vogelbach 5.00 12.00
33 Carl Thomore 5.00 12.00
34 Blake Swihart 6.00 15.00
35 James Allen 3.00 8.00
36 Carlos Sanchez 3.00 8.00
37 Michael Goodnight 4.00 10.00
38 James McCann 8.00 20.00
39 Will Lamb 5.00 12.00
40 Taylor Featherston 3.00 8.00
41 Nick Ramirez 4.00 10.00
42 Johnny Eierman 8.00 20.00
43 Logan Verrett 6.00 15.00
44 Neftali Rosario 5.00 12.00
45 Kevin Comer 5.00 12.00
46 Kendrick Perkins 4.00 10.00
47 Tyler Grimes 3.00 8.00
48 Kyle Winkler 3.00 8.00
50 Taylor Guerrieri 5.00 12.00
51 Dillon Maples 6.00 15.00
52 Harold Martinez 3.00 8.00
53 Grayson Garvin 6.00 15.00
54 Zeke DeVoss 4.00 10.00
55 Mitch Walding 5.00 12.00
56 Clay Holmes 4.00 10.00
57 Hudson Boyd 5.00 12.00
58 Granden Goetzman 5.00 12.00
59 Bryan Brickhouse 4.00 10.00
60 Shane Opitz 4.00 10.00
61 Nick Fleece 4.00 10.00
62 Barret Loux 6.00 15.00
63 Jake Lowery 5.00 12.00
64 Madison Boer 4.00 10.00
65 Tony Zych 3.00 8.00
66 Sean Halton 5.00 12.00
67 Cavan Cohoes 6.00 15.00
68 Dean Green 4.00 10.00
69 Miles Hamblin 4.00 10.00
70 J.R. Graham 8.00 20.00
71 Tom Robson 5.00 12.00
72 Riccio Torrez 3.00 8.00
73 Adam Conley 3.00 8.00
74 Pratt Maynard 6.00 15.00
75 Jordan Cote 6.00 15.00
76 Kyle Gaedele 3.00 8.00
77 Christian Lopes 5.00 12.00
78 Travis Shaw 15.00 40.00
79 Parker Markel 3.00 8.00
80 Chad Comer 3.00 8.00
81 Adrian Houser 8.00 20.00
82 Corey Williams 5.00 12.00
84 Phillip Evans 4.00 10.00
85 Lee Orr 3.00 8.00
87 Roman Quinn 6.00 15.00
88 Jake Floethe 4.00 10.00
89 Andrew Susac 10.00 25.00
90 Navery Moore 5.00 12.00
91 Chris Schwinden 5.00 12.00
92 Cole Green 4.00 10.00
93 Chris Wallace 5.00 12.00
94 Steven Ames 5.00 12.00
95 James Baldwin 6.00 15.00
96 Forrest Snow 5.00 12.00
97 Bobby Crocker 6.00 15.00
98 Dwight Smith Jr. 8.00 20.00
99 Greg Bird 60.00 150.00
100 Bryson Myles 4.00 10.00
151 Anthony Meo 4.00 10.00
152 Shawon Dunston Jr. 6.00 15.00
153 Rookie Davis 30.00 60.00
154 Rob Scahill 3.00 8.00
155 Chris Heston 12.00 30.00
156 Adam Jorgenson 4.00 10.00
157 Elliot Soto 3.00 8.00
158 Tyler Cloyd 12.00 30.00
159 Pierre LePage 4.00 10.00
160 Brett Jacobson 3.00 8.00
161 Casey Lawrence 4.00 10.00
162 Joe O'Gara 5.00 12.00
163 Mariekson Gregorius 50.00 120.00
164 Dan Osterbrock 4.00 10.00
165 Jared Hoying 4.00 10.00
166 Alan DeRatt 3.00 8.00
167 Charlie Leesman 3.00 8.00
168 Adam Davis 3.00 8.00
169 Danny Vasquez 4.00 10.00
170 Jon Griffin 8.00 20.00
171 Hernan Perez 5.00 12.00
173 Jose Osuna 10.00 25.00
174 Red Patterson 4.00 10.00
175 Jamaine Cotton 4.00 10.00
176 Pedro Villarreal 5.00 12.00
177 Justin Boudreaux 4.00 10.00
180 David Herbek 3.00 8.00
181 Zack MacPhee 3.00 8.00
182 Ryan Tatusko 5.00 12.00
183 Dan Meadows 3.00 8.00
184 Albert Cartwright 4.00 10.00
185 Brandon Drury 8.00 20.00
186 Eddie Rosario 6.00 15.00
187 Jake Dunning 5.00 12.00
188 Miles Head 10.00 25.00
189 Duanel Jones 4.00 10.00
190 Rob Lyerly 4.00 10.00
P1 Trevor Bauer 5.00 12.00
P2 Anthony Rendon 10.00 25.00
P3 Gerrit Cole 12.00 30.00
P4 Dylan Bundy 30.00 60.00
P5 C.J. Cron 4.00 10.00
P6 Tyler Collins 4.00 10.00
P7 Cory Spangenberg 8.00 20.00
P8 Archie Bradley 5.00 12.00
P9 Jason Esposito 8.00 20.00
P10 Bubba Starling 12.50 30.00
P11 Joe Panik 6.00 15.00
P12 Kolten Wong 10.00 25.00
P13 Levi Michael 6.00 15.00
P14 Sonny Gray 5.00 12.00
P15 Javier Baez 40.00 100.00
P16 Danny Hultzen 30.00 60.00
P17 Alex Hassan 8.00 20.00
P18 Jace Peterson 3.00 8.00
P19 Jason King 3.00 8.00
P20 Kyle Kubitza 4.00 10.00
P21 Matt Szczur 6.00 15.00
P22 Sean Gilmartin 5.00 12.00
P23 Kevin Matthews 4.00 10.00
P24 Brandon Nimmo 4.00 10.00
P25 Jed Bradley 5.00 12.00
P26 Cameron Gallagher 5.00 12.00
P27 Mikie Mahtook 6.00 15.00
P28 Jacob Anderson 10.00 25.00
P29 Michael Fulmer 12.00 30.00
P30 Jackie Bradley Jr. 8.00 20.00
P31 Taylor Jungmann 6.00 15.00
P32 Matt Dean 8.00 20.00
P33 Joe Ross 8.00 20.00
P34 Jake Hager 3.00 8.00
P35 Josh Bell 15.00 40.00
P36 George Springer 25.00 60.00
P37 Chris Reed 10.00 25.00
P38 Brian Goodwin 4.00 10.00
P39 Francisco Lindor 40.00 100.00
P40 Tyler Gibson 6.00 15.00
P41 Robert Stephenson 10.00 25.00
P42 Brandon Martin 3.00 8.00
P43 Matt Purke 12.50 30.00
P44 Leonys Martin 4.00 10.00
P45 Keenyn Walker 4.00 10.00
P46 Kyle Parker 3.00 8.00
P47 Travis Harrison 6.00 15.00
P48 Matt Barnes 4.00 10.00
P49 Trevor Story 20.00 50.00
P50 Kyle Crick 4.00 10.00

2011 Donruss Elite Extra Edition Prospects Signature Status

OVERALL SIX AUTOS PER HOBBY BOX
STATED PRINT RUN 50 SER.#'d SETS
EXCHANGE DEADLINE 06/28/2013
1 Tyler Goeddel 6.00 15.00
2 Dante Bichette Jr. 60.00 120.00
3 James Harris 6.00 15.00
4 Cory Mazzoni 4.00 10.00
5 Abel Baker 5.00 12.00
6 Alex Dickerson 15.00 40.00
7 Justin Bour 10.00 25.00
8 Tyler Anderson 5.00 12.00
9 Jeff Ames 6.00 15.00
10 Cristhian Adames 6.00 15.00
11 Jason Krizan 5.00 12.00
12 Michael Kelly 5.00 12.00
13 Kyle McMillen 4.00 10.00
14 Charlie Tilson 10.00 25.00
15 Brad Miller 8.00 20.00
16 Blake Snell 10.00 25.00
17 Daniel Norris 15.00 40.00
18 Williams Jerez 5.00 12.00
19 Erik Johnson 6.00 15.00
20 Gabriel Rosa 10.00 25.00
21 Adam Morgan 6.00 15.00
22 Aaron Westlake 10.00 25.00
23 Brandon Loy 6.00 15.00
24 Zach Good 4.00 10.00
25 Angelo Songco 10.00 25.00
26 Jordan Akins 6.00 15.00
27 Josh Osich 6.00 15.00
28 Austin Hedges 8.00 20.00
29 Jake Sisco 5.00 12.00
30 B.A. Vollmuth 8.00 20.00
31 Austin Wood 4.00 10.00
32 Dan Vogelbach 6.00 15.00
33 Carl Thomore 8.00 20.00
34 Blake Swihart 10.00 25.00
35 James Allen 4.00 10.00
36 Carlos Sanchez 5.00 12.00
37 Michael Goodnight 5.00 12.00
38 James McCann 10.00 25.00
39 Will Lamb 6.00 15.00
40 Taylor Featherston 4.00 10.00
41 Nick Ramirez 6.00 15.00
42 Johnny Eierman 8.00 20.00
43 Logan Verrett 8.00 20.00
44 Neftali Rosario 5.00 12.00
45 Kevin Comer 8.00 20.00
46 Kendrick Perkins 4.00 10.00
47 Tyler Grimes 4.00 10.00
48 Kyle Winkler 4.00 10.00
50 Taylor Guerrieri 12.50 30.00
51 Dillon Maples 10.00 25.00
52 Harold Martinez 5.00 12.00
53 Grayson Garvin 10.00 25.00
54 Zeke DeVoss 6.00 15.00
55 Mitch Walding 8.00 20.00
56 Clay Holmes 8.00 20.00
57 Hudson Boyd 6.00 15.00
58 Granden Goetzman 8.00 20.00
59 Bryan Brickhouse 6.00 15.00
60 Shane Opitz 5.00 12.00
61 Nick Fleece 5.00 12.00
62 Barret Loux 6.00 15.00
63 Jake Lowery 5.00 12.00
64 Madison Boer 6.00 15.00
65 Tony Zych 4.00 10.00
66 Sean Halton 6.00 15.00
67 Cavan Cohoes 8.00 20.00
68 Dean Green 6.00 15.00
69 Miles Hamblin 5.00 12.00
70 J.R. Graham 10.00 25.00
71 Tom Robson 8.00 20.00
72 Riccio Torrez 4.00 10.00
73 Adam Conley 4.00 10.00
74 Pratt Maynard 6.00 15.00
75 Jordan Cote 12.50 30.00
76 Kyle Gaedele 6.00 15.00
77 Christian Lopes 10.00 25.00
78 Travis Shaw 20.00 50.00
79 Parker Markel 4.00 10.00
80 Chad Comer 5.00 12.00
81 Adrian Houser 8.00 20.00
82 Corey Williams 10.00 25.00
83 Brian Flynn 6.00 15.00
84 Phillip Evans 6.00 15.00
85 Lee Orr 4.00 10.00
87 Roman Quinn 6.00 15.00
88 Jake Floethe 8.00 20.00
89 Andrew Susac 10.00 25.00
90 Navery Moore 5.00 12.00
91 Chris Schwinden 6.00 15.00
92 Cole Green 8.00 20.00
93 Chris Wallace 5.00 12.00
94 Steven Ames 5.00 12.00
95 James Baldwin 5.00 12.00
96 Forrest Snow 8.00 20.00
97 Bobby Crocker 10.00 25.00
98 Dwight Smith Jr. 10.00 25.00
99 Greg Bird 75.00 200.00
100 Bryson Myles 8.00 20.00
151 Anthony Meo 5.00 12.00
152 Shawon Dunston Jr. 5.00 12.00
153 Rookie Davis 10.00 25.00
154 Rob Scahill 4.00 8.00
155 Chris Heston 12.00 30.00
156 Adam Jorgenson 4.00 10.00
157 Elliot Soto 5.00 12.00
158 Tyler Cloyd 20.00 50.00
159 Pierre LePage 8.00 20.00
160 Brett Jacobson 4.00 10.00
161 Casey Lawrence 8.00 20.00
162 Joe O'Gara 6.00 15.00
163 Mariekson Gregorius 60.00 15.00
164 Dan Osterbrock 4.00 10.00
165 Jared Hoying 8.00 20.00
166 Alan DeRatt 4.00 10.00
167 Charlie Leesman 4.00 10.00
168 Adam Davis 4.00 10.00
169 Danny Vasquez 8.00 20.00
170 Jon Griffin 8.00 20.00
171 Hernan Perez 6.00 15.00
172 Jeremy Cruz 4.00 10.00
173 Jose Osuna 12.00 30.00
174 Red Patterson 4.00 10.00
175 Jamaine Cotton 5.00 12.00
176 Pedro Villarreal 6.00 15.00
177 Justin Boudreaux 5.00 12.00
180 David Herbek 4.00 10.00
181 Zack MacPhee 4.00 10.00
182 Ryan Tatusko 5.00 12.00
183 Dan Meadows 5.00 12.00
184 Albert Cartwright 4.00 10.00
185 Brandon Drury 12.50 30.00
186 Eddie Rosario 10.00 25.00
187 Jake Dunning 5.00 12.00
188 Miles Head 10.00 25.00
189 Duanel Jones 5.00 12.00
190 Rob Lyerly 5.00 12.00
P1 Trevor Bauer 40.00 80.00
P2 Anthony Rendon 12.00 30.00
P3 Gerrit Cole 15.00 40.00
P4 Dylan Bundy 20.00 50.00
P5 C.J. Cron 5.00 12.00
P6 Tyler Collins 5.00 12.00
P7 Cory Spangenberg 8.00 20.00
P8 Archie Bradley 20.00 50.00
P9 Jason Esposito 4.00 10.00
P10 Bubba Starling 20.00 50.00
P11 Joe Panik 15.00 40.00
P12 Kolten Wong 12.00 30.00
P13 Levi Michael 8.00 20.00
P14 Sonny Gray 15.00 40.00
P15 Javier Baez 50.00 120.00
P16 Danny Hultzen 12.00 30.00
P17 Alex Hassan 6.00 15.00
P18 Jace Peterson 8.00 20.00
P19 Jason King 5.00 12.00
P20 Kyle Kubitza 8.00 20.00
P21 Matt Szczur 8.00 20.00
P22 Sean Gilmartin 8.00 20.00
P23 Kevin Matthews 8.00 20.00
P24 Brandon Nimmo 6.00 15.00
P25 Jed Bradley 6.00 15.00
P26 Cameron Gallagher 6.00 15.00
P27 Mikie Mahtook 20.00 50.00
P28 Jacob Anderson 20.00 50.00
P29 Michael Fulmer 15.00 40.00
P30 Jackie Bradley Jr. 10.00 25.00
P31 Taylor Jungmann 12.50 30.00
P32 Matt Dean 10.00 25.00
P33 Joe Ross 10.00 25.00
P34 Jake Hager 5.00 12.00
P35 Josh Bell 20.00 50.00
P36 George Springer 30.00 80.00
P37 Chris Reed 15.00 40.00
P38 Brian Goodwin 5.00 12.00
P39 Francisco Lindor 50.00 120.00
P40 Tyler Gibson 15.00 40.00
P41 Robert Stephenson 12.50 30.00
P42 Brandon Martin 5.00 12.00
P43 Matt Purke 15.00 40.00
P44 Leonys Martin 20.00 50.00
P45 Keenyn Walker 4.00 10.00
P46 Kyle Parker 4.00 10.00
P47 Travis Harrison 5.00 12.00
P48 Matt Barnes 30.00 60.00
P49 Trevor Story 25.00 60.00
P50 Kyle Crick 5.00 12.00

2011 Donruss Elite Extra Edition Two Sport Stars

RANDOM INSERTS IN PACKS
STATED PRINT RUN 499 SER.#'d SETS

1 Kyle Parker	.75	2.00
2 Jace Peterson	.50	1.25
3 Archie Bradley	1.50	4.00
4 Zach Lee	.75	2.00
5 Sonny Gray	1.25	3.00
6 Bubba Starling	.75	2.00
7 Matt Szczur	1.25	3.00
8 Shane Opitz	.75	2.00

2011 Donruss Elite Extra Edition Yearbook

STATED ODDS 1:10 HOBBY

1 Matt Purke	1.00	2.50
2 Christian Lopes	1.00	2.50
3 Andrew Susac	.60	1.50
4 Dante Bichette Jr.	.60	1.50
5 Brian Goodwin	1.00	2.50
6 Greg Bird	.75	2.00
7 Ty Linton	.40	1.00
8 Zach Cone	.60	1.50
9 Anthony Meo	.40	1.00
10 Sean Gilmartin	.40	1.00
11 Phillip Evans	.40	1.00
12 Justin O'Conner	.40	1.00
13 Tony Wolters	.40	1.00
14 Nick Castellanos	2.00	5.00
15 Dan Vogelbach	1.25	3.00
16 Williams Jerez	.40	1.00
17 Matt Skole	.60	1.50
18 Jackie Bradley Jr.	1.50	4.00
19 Tyler Goeddel	.40	1.00
20 Angelo Songco	.60	1.50

2011 Donruss Elite Extra Edition Yearbook Signatures

PRINT RUNS B/WN 25-899 COPIES PER
OVERALL SIX AUTOS PER HOBBY BOX
NO PRICING ON QTY 25 OR LESS
EXCHANGE DEADLINE 06/28/2013

2 Christian Lopes	4.00	10.00
3 Andrew Susac	5.00	12.00
4 Dante Bichette Jr.	5.00	12.00
5 Brian Goodwin	6.00	15.00
6 Greg Bird	20.00	50.00
7 Ty Linton	4.00	10.00
8 Zach Cone	4.00	10.00
9 Anthony Meo	3.00	8.00
10 Sean Gilmartin	6.00	15.00
14 Nick Castellanos	8.00	20.00
15 Dan Vogelbach	10.00	25.00
16 Williams Jerez	6.00	15.00
17 Matt Skole	5.00	12.00
18 Jackie Bradley Jr.	40.00	100.00
19 Tyler Goeddel	3.00	8.00
20 Angelo Songco	4.00	10.00

2012 Elite Extra Edition

COMP.SET w/o AU's (100)	12.50	30.00
COMMON CARD (1-100)	.20	.50
COMMON SP (1-100)	5.00	12.00
COMMON AU (101-200)	3.00	8.00
AU SEMIS	4.00	10.00
AU UNLISTED	5.00	12.00

AU PRINT RUNS B/WN 299-799 COPIES
EXCHANGE DEADLINE 07/16/2014

1A Addison Russell Batting	.50	1.25
1B Addison Russell Fielding SP	15.00	40.00
2A Albert Almora Facing left	.75	2.00
2B Albert Almora Facing right SP	15.00	40.00
3A Andrew Heaney Light jersey	.40	1.00
3B Andrew Heaney Dark jersey SP	5.00	12.00
4A Michael Wacha White jersey	.60	1.50
4B Michael Wacha Blue jersey SP	15.00	40.00
5 Marcus Stroman	.50	1.25
6 Pat Light	.20	.50
7 Keon Barnum	.30	.75
8 Mitch Gueller	.30	.75
9A Max White Facing left	.30	.75
9B Max White Facing right SP	5.00	12.00
10A Carson Kelly Hand up	.50	1.25
10B Carson Kelly Hands down SP	8.00	20.00
11 Nick Travieso	.40	1.00
12 Chris Stratton	.30	.75
13 Tyrone Taylor	.20	.50
14A Brian Johnson No ball	.30	.75
14B Brian Johnson Ball visible SP	5.00	12.00
15A Luke Bard Facing forward	.30	.75
16 Matt Smoral	.30	.75
17 Jesmuel Valentin	.40	1.00
18 Patrick Wisdom	.30	.75
19 Eddie Butler	.30	.75
20 Dane Phillips	.20	.50
21 Robert Refsnyder	.50	1.25
22 Nolan Fontana	.20	.50
23 Tyler Gonzales	.20	.50
24 Joe DeCarlo	.30	.75
25A Sam Selman Glove visible	.40	1.00
25B Sam Selman No glove SP	5.00	12.00
26 Dylan Cozens	.50	1.25
27 Duane Underwood	.20	.50
28 Chris Beck	.20	.50
29 Martin Agosta	.30	.75
30 Alex Wood	.20	.50
31 Adam Walker	.20	.50
32 Avery Romero	.30	.75
33 Ryan McNeil	.20	.50
34 Matt Koch	.20	.50
35 Austin Schotts	.30	.75
36 Edwin Diaz	.60	1.50
37 Kieran Lovegrove	.20	.50
38 Brett Mooneyham	.20	.50
39 Andrew Toles	.20	.50
40 Jake Barrett	.20	.50
41 Zach Quintana	.20	.50
42 Nathan Mikolas	.30	.75
43 Tyler Pike	.20	.50
44 Zach Green	.20	.50
45 Zack Jones	.20	.50
46 Patrick Kivlehan	.20	.50
47 Branden Kaupe	.30	.75
48 Alex Mejia	.20	.50
49 Ty Buttrey	.40	1.00
50 Charles Taylor	.20	.50
51 Drew VerHagen	.20	.50
52 Tyler Wagner	.20	.50
53 Chris Serritella	.20	.50
54 Corey Black	.30	.75
55A Royce Bolinger Facing left	.20	.50
55B Royce Bolinger Facing right SP	8.00	20.00
56 Adrian Sampson	.20	.50
57 Nick Basto	.20	.50
58 Dylan Baker	.30	.75
59 Spencer Kieboom	.20	.50
60 Ty Blach	.20	.50
61 Cory Jones	.20	.50
62 Ronnie Freeman	.30	.75
63 Lex Rutledge	.30	.75
64 Colin Rodgers	.20	.50
65 Kolby Copeland	.30	.75
66 Zach Lovvorn	.20	.50
67 Eric Stamets	.30	.75
68 Damion Carroll	.20	.50
69 Felipe Perez	.20	.50
70 Mason Melotakis	.20	.50
71 Rowan Wick	.30	.75
72 Jairo Beras	.30	.75
73 Dario Pizzano	.30	.75
74 Logan Taylor	.20	.50
75 Nick Kingham	.30	.75
76 Omar Luis Rodriguez	.20	.50
77 Rio Ruiz	.20	.50
78 Trey Lang	.20	.50
79 Alex Muren	.30	.75
80 D'Vone McClure	.30	.75
81 Matt Price	.20	.50
82 Alexis Rivera	.30	.75
83 Aaron West	.30	.75
84 Slade Smith	.20	.50
85 Matt Juengel	.20	.50
86 Kaleb Merck	.20	.50
87 Anthony Melchionda	.20	.50
88 J.O. Berrios	1.00	2.50
89 J.T. Chargois	.30	.75
90 Fernando Perez	.30	.75
91 Tom Murphy	.20	.50
92 Bryan De La Rosa	.30	.75
93 Angel Ortega	.20	.50
94 Seth Maness	.20	.50
95 Will Clinard	.20	.50
96 Scott Oberg	.30	.75
97 Jacob Wilson	.30	.75
98 Anthony Banda	.20	.50
99 Josh Conway	.20	.50
100 Andrew Lockett	.20	.50
101 Carlos Correa AU/470	60.00	150.00
102 Byron Buxton AU/599	12.00	30.00
103 Mike Zunino AU/677	4.00	10.00
104 Kevin Gausman AU/399	5.00	12.00
105 Kyle Zimmer AU/690	5.00	12.00
106 Max Fried AU/545	10.00	25.00
107 David Dahl AU/509	5.00	12.00
108 Gavin Cecchini AU/299	4.00	10.00
109 Courtney Hawkins AU/499	4.00	10.00
110 Tyler Naquin AU/612	6.00	15.00
111 Lucas Giolito AU/722	10.00	25.00
112 D.J. Davis AU/390	3.00	8.00
113 Corey Seager AU/330	40.00	100.00
114 Victor Roache AU/748	5.00	12.00
115 Deven Marrero AU/430	3.00	8.00
116 Lucas Sims AU/699	3.00	8.00
117 Stryker Trahan AU/597	4.00	10.00
118 Lewis Brinson AU/789	8.00	20.00
119 Kevin Plawecki AU/744	4.00	10.00
120 Richie Shaffer AU/722	3.00	8.00
121 Barrett Barnes AU/621	3.00	8.00
122 Shane Watson AU/799	3.00	8.00
123 Matt Olson AU/782	6.00	15.00
124 Lance McCullers AU/412	5.00	12.00
125 Mitch Haniger AU/750	5.00	12.00
126 Stephen Piscotty AU/680	5.00	12.00
127 Ty Hensley AU/790	3.00	8.00
128 Jesse Winker AU/494	4.00	10.00
129 Walker Weickel AU/597	3.00	8.00
130 James Ramsey AU/631	3.00	8.00
131 Joey Gallo AU/498	8.00	20.00
132 Mitch Nay AU/799	3.00	8.00
133 Alex Yarbrough AU/782	3.00	8.00
134 Preston Beck AU/782	3.00	8.00
135 Nick Goody AU/574	3.00	8.00
136 Daniel Robertson AU/589	3.00	8.00
137 Jake Thompson AU/740	3.00	8.00
138 Austin Nola AU/798	3.00	8.00
139 Tony Renda AU/598	3.00	8.00
140 Austin Aune AU/699	3.00	8.00
141 Tanner Rahier AU/612	3.00	8.00
142 Josh Elander AU/593	3.00	8.00
143 Tim Lopes AU/799	3.00	8.00
144 Ross Stripling AU/760	3.00	8.00
145 Bruce Maxwell AU/641	3.00	8.00
146 Mallex Smith AU/711	3.00	8.00
147 Collin Wiles AU/622	3.00	8.00
148 Pierce Johnson AU/799	3.00	8.00
149 Damien Magnifico AU/711	3.00	8.00
150 Travis Jankowski AU/641	3.00	8.00
151 Jeff Gelalich AU/497	3.00	8.00
152 Paul Blackburn AU/594	3.00	8.00
153 Steve Bean AU/397	3.00	8.00
154 Spencer Edwards AU/793	3.00	8.00
155 Branden Kline AU/588	3.00	8.00
156 Jeremy Baltz AU/799	3.00	8.00
157 Max White AU/510	3.00	8.00
158 Chase DeJong AU/799	3.00	8.00
159 Jamie Jarmon AU/580	3.00	8.00
160 Mitch Brown AU/610	3.00	8.00
161 Jamie Callahan AU/766	3.00	8.00
162 Joe Munoz AU/498	3.00	8.00
163 Peter O'Brien AU/360	3.00	8.00
164 Matt Koch AU/795	3.00	8.00
165 Patrick Cantwell AU/699	3.00	8.00
166 Blake Brown AU/651	3.00	8.00
167 Max Muncy AU/782	12.00	30.00
168 Justin Chigbogu AU/797	3.00	8.00
169 Alex Mejia AU/799	3.00	8.00
170 Jeff McVaney AU/710	3.00	8.00
171 Michael Earley AU/772	3.00	8.00
172 Steve Okert AU/780	3.00	8.00
173 Dan Langfield AU/799	3.00	8.00
174 Austin Maddox AU/352	3.00	8.00
175 Kenny Diekroeger AU/793	3.00	8.00
176 Brandon Brennan AU/749	3.00	8.00
177 Zach Isler AU/797	3.00	8.00
178 Stefen Romero AU/677	5.00	12.00
179 Mac Williamson AU/533	3.00	8.00
180 Seth Willoughby AU/749	3.00	8.00
181 Tyler Wagner AU/478	3.00	8.00
182 Jake Lamb AU/596	3.00	8.00
183 Preston Tucker AU/781	8.00	20.00
184 Josh Turley AU/799	3.00	8.00
185 Logan Vick AU/776	3.00	8.00
186 R.J. Alvarez AU/690	3.00	8.00
187 Clint Coulter AU/528	10.00	25.00
188 Joe Rogers AU/675	3.00	8.00
189 Evan Marzilli AU/791	3.00	8.00
190 Carlos Escobar AU/752	3.00	8.00
191 Wyatt Mathisen AU/739	8.00	20.00
192 Matt Reynolds AU/562	3.00	8.00
193 Nick Williams AU/490	4.00	10.00
194 Brady Rodgers AU/490	3.00	8.00
195 Tim Cooney AU/792	3.00	8.00
196 Brett Vertigan AU/554	4.00	10.00
197 Hoby Milner AU/799	3.00	8.00
198 Luke Maile AU/690	3.00	8.00
199 Darin Ruf AU/562	3.00	8.00
200 Adrian Marin AU/685	3.00	8.00

2012 Elite Extra Edition Aspirations

*ASPIRATIONS: 1.5X TO 4X BASIC
STATED PRINT RUN 200 SER.#'d SETS

101 Carlos Correa	8.00	20.00
102 Byron Buxton	3.00	8.00
103 Mike Zunino	2.00	5.00
104 Kevin Gausman	2.50	6.00
105 Kyle Zimmer	1.50	4.00
106 Max Fried	5.00	12.00
107 David Dahl	6.00	15.00
108 Gavin Cecchini	1.50	4.00
109 Courtney Hawkins	1.25	3.00
110 Tyler Naquin	1.50	4.00
111 Lucas Giolito	4.00	10.00
112 D.J. Davis	1.50	4.00
113 Corey Seager	5.00	12.00
114 Victor Roache	2.50	6.00
115 Deven Marrero	1.25	3.00
116 Lucas Sims	1.50	4.00
117 Stryker Trahan	1.25	3.00
118 Lewis Brinson	4.00	10.00
119 Kevin Plawecki	1.50	4.00
120 Richie Shaffer	1.50	4.00
121 Barrett Barnes	1.50	4.00
122 Shane Watson	1.50	4.00
123 Matt Olson	2.00	5.00
124 Lance McCullers	1.25	3.00
125 Mitch Haniger	3.00	8.00
126 Stephen Piscotty	2.50	6.00
127 Ty Hensley	1.50	4.00
128 Jesse Winker	1.50	4.00
129 Walker Weickel	.75	2.00
130 James Ramsey	1.25	3.00
131 Joey Gallo	4.00	10.00
132 Mitch Nay	.75	2.00
133 Alex Yarbrough	1.25	3.00
134 Preston Beck	.75	2.00
135 Nick Goody	1.25	3.00
136 Daniel Robertson	.75	2.00
137 Jake Thompson	.75	2.00
138 Austin Nola	.75	2.00
139 Tony Renda	.75	2.00
140 Austin Aune	1.50	4.00
141 Tanner Rahier	1.25	3.00
142 Josh Elander	.75	2.00
143 Tim Lopes	.75	2.00
144 Ross Stripling	.75	2.00
145 Bruce Maxwell	1.25	3.00
147 Collin Wiles	.75	2.00
148 Pierce Johnson	1.50	4.00
149 Damien Magnifico	.75	2.00
150 Travis Jankowski	1.50	4.00
151 Jeff Gelalich	.75	2.00
152 Paul Blackburn	1.25	3.00
153 Steve Bean	1.50	4.00
154 Spencer Edwards	1.25	3.00
155 Branden Kline	1.25	3.00
156 Jeremy Baltz	.75	2.00
157 Max White	1.25	3.00
158 Chase DeJong	1.50	4.00
159 Jamie Jarmon	1.25	3.00
160 Mitch Brown	1.25	3.00
161 Jamie Callahan	.75	2.00
162 Joe Munoz	.75	2.00
163 Peter O'Brien	2.00	5.00
164 Matt Koch	.75	2.00
165 Patrick Cantwell	.75	2.00
166 Blake Brown	.75	2.00
167 Max Muncy	6.00	15.00
168 Justin Chigbogu	1.25	3.00
169 Alex Mejia	.75	2.00
170 Jeff McVaney	.75	2.00
171 Michael Earley	1.25	3.00
172 Steve Okert	.75	2.00
173 Dan Langfield	.75	2.00
174 Austin Maddox	1.25	3.00
175 Kenny Diekroeger	.75	2.00
176 Brandon Brennan	1.25	3.00
177 Zach Isler	1.25	3.00
178 Stefen Romero	1.25	3.00
179 Mac Williamson	4.00	10.00
180 Seth Willoughby	.75	2.00
181 Tyler Wagner	.75	2.00
182 Jake Lamb	2.00	5.00
183 Preston Tucker	2.00	5.00
184 Josh Turley	1.25	3.00
185 Logan Vick	.75	2.00
186 R.J. Alvarez	1.25	3.00
187 Clint Coulter	1.25	3.00
188 Joe Rogers	.75	2.00
189 Evan Marzilli	.75	2.00
190 Carlos Escobar	.75	2.00
191 Wyatt Mathisen	1.25	3.00
192 Matt Reynolds	1.25	3.00
193 Nick Williams	1.25	3.00
194 Brady Rodgers	.75	2.00
195 Tim Cooney	.75	2.00
196 Brett Vertigan	.75	2.00
197 Hoby Milner	1.25	3.00
198 Luke Maile	.75	2.00
199 Darin Ruf	8.00	20.00
200 Adrian Marin	1.25	3.00

2012 Elite Extra Edition Back to the Future Signatures

PRINT RUNS B/WN 46-699 COPIES PER
EXCHANGE DEADLINE 07/16/2014

1 Dillon Maples/396	3.00	8.00
2 Hudson Boyd/73	3.00	8.00
3 Alex Dickerson/99	6.00	15.00
4 Christian Lopes/58	4.00	10.00
5 Barret Loux/599	3.00	8.00
6 Jordan Cote/51	8.00	20.00
7 Greg Bird/249	15.00	40.00
8 Elliot Soto/649	3.00	8.00
9 Austin Hedges/210	4.00	10.00
10 Rob Scahill/599	3.00	8.00
11 Travis Shaw/46	15.00	40.00
12 Daniel Norris/290	4.00	10.00
13 Justin Bour/499	3.00	8.00
14 Rob Lyerly/512	3.00	8.00
15 James McCann/61	8.00	20.00
16 Logan Verrett/48	6.00	15.00
17 Nick Ramirez/47	3.00	8.00
18 Eddie Rosario/699	4.00	10.00
19 Tommy Shirley/699	3.00	8.00
20 Didi Gregorius/621	12.00	30.00

2012 Elite Extra Edition Building Blocks Dual

1 Alex Wood/Lucas Sims	.75	2.00
2 M.Wacha/T.Naquin	1.25	3.00
3 L.Giolito/M.Fried	2.50	6.00
4 Spencer Edwards/Steve Bean	.75	2.00
5 D.J. Davis/Marcus Stroman	1.00	2.50
6 Alex Mejia/Robert Refsnyder	1.00	2.50
7 C.Correa/J.Berrios	4.00	10.00
8 B.Johnson/M.Zunino	1.00	2.50
9 Martin Agosta/Patrick Wisdom	.60	1.50
10 Courtney Hawkins/Wyatt Mathisen	.60	1.50
11 Aaron West/Jake Lamb	1.00	2.50
12 Brady Rodgers/Deven Marrero	.60	1.50
13 Patrick Cantwell/Travis Jankowski	.75	2.00
14 Evan Marzilli/Matt Price	.40	1.00
15 B.Buxton/C.Correa	4.00	10.00
16 Richie Shaffer/Spencer Kieboom	.75	2.00
17 James Ramsey/Preston Tucker	1.00	2.50
18 Damien Magnifico/Steve Okert	.40	1.00
19 M.Zunino/S.Trahan	1.00	2.50
20 D.Cozens/M.Nay	1.00	2.50

2012 Elite Extra Edition Building Blocks Dual Signatures

PRINT RUNS B/WN 5-49 COPIES PER
NO PRICING ON QTY 25 OR LESS
EXCHANGE DEADLINE 07/16/2014

4 Spencer Edwards/Steve Bean/49	5.00	12.00
6 Alex Mejia/Robert Refsnyder/49	10.00	25.00
9 Martin Agosta/Patrick Wisdom/49	5.00	12.00
11 A.West/J.Lamb/49	8.00	20.00
13 Patrick Cantwell/Travis Jankowski/49	5.00	12.00
14 E.Marzilli/M.Price/49	6.00	15.00
18 D.Magnifico/S.Okert/49	8.00	20.00

2012 Elite Extra Edition Building Blocks Trio

1 Turley/Vick/Muncy	3.00	8.00
2 Wacha/Stripling/Naquin	1.25	3.00
3 Yrbrgh/Muncy/Beck	3.00	8.00
4 Johnson/Zunino/Fontana	1.00	2.50
5 Drew VerHagen/Sam Selman Will Clinard	.75	2.00
6 Correa/Berrios/Valentin	4.00	10.00
7 Jake Thompson/Spencer Edwards Steve Bean	.75	2.00
8 Andrew Heaney/Damien Magnifico Steve Okert	.75	2.00
9 Austin Aune/Nathan Mikolas Peter O'Brien	1.00	2.50
10 Mnyhm/Psctty/Dkrgr	1.25	3.00

2012 Elite Extra Edition Diamond Kings

20 Jeff Gelalich	.40	1.00
DK1 Darin Ruf	4.00	10.00
DK2 Mike Zunino	1.00	2.50
DK3 Carlos Correa	4.00	10.00
DK4 Corey Seager	2.50	6.00
DK5 Kevin Gausman	1.25	3.00
DK6 Andrew Heaney	.75	2.00
DK7 David Dahl	2.00	5.00
DK8 Albert Almora	1.50	4.00
DK9 Stefen Romero	.60	1.50
DK10 Lance McCullers	.60	1.50
DK11 Joey Gallo	2.00	5.00
DK12 Byron Buxton	1.50	4.00
DK13 Kyle Zimmer	.75	2.00
DK14 Chris Stratton	.60	1.50
DK15 Gavin Cecchini	.75	2.00
DK16 Marcus Stroman	1.00	2.50
DK17 Omar Luis Rodriguez	.40	1.00
DK18 Tyler Naquin	.75	2.00
DK19 Courtney Hawkins	.60	1.50

2012 Elite Extra Edition Elite Series

1 Albert Almora	1.50	4.00
2 Andrew Heaney	.75	2.00
3 Joey Gallo	2.00	5.00
4 Lance McCullers	.60	1.50
5 David Dahl	2.00	5.00
6 Carlos Correa	4.00	10.00
7 Deven Marrero	.60	1.50
8 Byron Buxton	1.50	4.00
9 Corey Seager	2.50	6.00
10 Jake Thompson	.40	1.00
11 Travis Jankowski	.75	2.00
12 Kevin Gausman	1.25	3.00
13 Jesse Winker	.75	2.00
14 Lucas Giolito	2.00	5.00
15 Courtney Hawkins	.60	1.50
16 Victor Roache	1.25	3.00
17 Mike Zunino	1.00	2.50
18 Matt Reynolds	.60	1.50
19 Kyle Zimmer	.75	2.00
20 Nolan Fontana	.40	1.00

2012 Elite Extra Edition Elite Series Signatures

PRINT RUNS B/WN 25-199 COPIES PER
EXCHANGE DEADLINE 07/16/2014

1 Albert Almora/49	10.00	25.00
2 Andrew Heaney/125	5.00	12.00
3 Joey Gallo/199	12.00	30.00
4 Lance McCullers/99	8.00	20.00
5 David Dahl/125	6.00	15.00
6 Carlos Correa/49	60.00	150.00
7 Deven Marrero/99	6.00	15.00
8 Byron Buxton/49	60.00	120.00
9 Corey Seager/150	40.00	100.00
10 Jake Thompson/199	3.00	8.00
11 Travis Jankowski/50	4.00	10.00
12 Kevin Gausman/50	12.50	30.00
13 Jesse Winker/125	3.00	8.00
14 Lucas Giolito/149	12.00	30.00
15 Courtney Hawkins/50	10.00	25.00
16 Victor Roache/99	10.00	25.00
17 Mike Zunino/39	50.00	100.00
18 Matt Reynolds/199	4.00	10.00
19 Kyle Zimmer/25	20.00	50.00
20 Nolan Fontana/119	4.00	10.00

2012 Elite Extra Edition First Overall Pick Jersey

STATED PRINT RUN 999 SER.#'d SETS

1 Carlos Correa	6.00	15.00

2012 Elite Extra Edition Franchise Futures Signatures

PRINT RUNS B/WN 117-799 COPIES PER
EXCHANGE DEADLINE 07/16/2014

1 Addison Russell/250	6.00	15.00
2 Albert Almora/210	4.00	10.00
3 Andrew Heaney/175	3.00	8.00
4 Michael Wacha/210	4.00	10.00
5 Marcus Stroman/195	5.00	12.00
6 Pat Light/149	3.00	8.00
7 Keon Barnum/225	3.00	8.00
8 Mitch Gueller/220	4.00	10.00
9 Max White/229	3.00	8.00
10 Carson Kelly/205	4.00	10.00
11 Nick Travieso/125	6.00	15.00
12 Chris Stratton/120	10.00	25.00
13 Tyrone Taylor/192	8.00	20.00
14 Brian Johnson/212	3.00	8.00
15 Luke Bard/117	3.00	8.00
16 Matt Smoral/222	3.00	8.00
17 Jesmuel Valentin/180	8.00	20.00
18 Patrick Wisdom AU/161		
19 Eddie Butler/160	3.00	8.00
20 Dane Phillips/189	3.00	8.00
21 Robert Refsnyder/799	5.00	12.00
22 Nolan Fontana/210	3.00	8.00
23 Tyler Gonzales/151	6.00	15.00
24 Joe DeCarlo/190	3.00	8.00
25 Sam Selman/200	3.00	8.00
26 Dylan Cozens/199	12.00	30.00
27 Duane Underwood/152	8.00	20.00
28 Chris Beck/145	3.00	8.00
29 Martin Agosta/200	4.00	10.00
30 Alex Wood/200	8.00	20.00
31 Adam Walker/225	3.00	8.00
32 Avery Romero/275	3.00	8.00
33 Ryan McNeil/239	3.00	8.00
34 Matt Koch/300	3.00	8.00
35 Austin Schotts/499	5.00	12.00
36 Edwin Diaz AU/355	10.00	25.00
37 Kieran Lovegrove/249	3.00	8.00
38 Brett Mooneyham/350	3.00	8.00
39 Andrew Toles/317	3.00	8.00
40 Jake Barrett/319	3.00	8.00
41 Zach Quintana/381	3.00	8.00
42 Nathan Mikolas/355	5.00	12.00
43 Tyler Pike/799	3.00	8.00
44 Zach Green/419	6.00	15.00
45 Zack Jones/376	3.00	8.00
46 Patrick Kivlehan/352	3.00	8.00
47 Branden Kaupe/347	4.00	10.00
48 Alex Mejia/397	3.00	8.00
49 Ty Buttrey/499	3.00	8.00
50 Charles Taylor/492	3.00	8.00
51 Drew VerHagen/699	3.00	8.00
52 Tyler Wagner/481	3.00	8.00
53 Chris Serritella/312	3.00	8.00
54 Corey Black/283	3.00	8.00
55 Royce Bolinger/697	3.00	8.00
56 Adrian Sampson/180	3.00	8.00
57 Nick Basto/290	3.00	8.00
58 Dylan Baker AU/788	3.00	8.00
59 Spencer Kieboom/475	3.00	8.00
60 Ty Blach/560	3.00	8.00
61 Cory Jones/781	3.00	8.00
62 Ronnie Freeman/290	4.00	10.00
63 Lex Rutledge/471	3.00	8.00
64 Colin Rodgers/399	3.00	8.00
65 Kolby Copeland/433	3.00	8.00
66 Zach Lovvorn/592	3.00	8.00
67 Eric Stamets/590	3.00	8.00
68 Damion Carroll/649	3.00	8.00
69 Felipe Perez/799	3.00	8.00
70 Mason Melotakis/575	3.00	8.00
71 Rowan Wick/442	3.00	8.00
72 Jairo Beras/490	3.00	8.00
73 Dario Pizzano AU/490	4.00	10.00
74 Logan Taylor/712	3.00	8.00
75 Nick Kingham/599	3.00	8.00
76 Omar Luis Rodriguez/499	6.00	15.00
77 Rio Ruiz/590	3.00	8.00
78 Trey Lang/451	3.00	8.00
79 Alex Muren/788	3.00	8.00
80 D'Vone McClure AU/496	3.00	8.00
81 Matt Price/790	3.00	8.00
82 Alexis Rivera/797	3.00	8.00
83 Aaron West AU/788	3.00	8.00
84 Slade Smith AU/799	3.00	8.00
85 Matt Juengel AU/799	3.00	8.00
86 Kaleb Merck/799	3.00	8.00
87 Anthony Melchionda/791	3.00	8.00
88 J.O. Berrios/175	10.00	25.00
89 J.T. Chargois/175	4.00	10.00
90 Fernando Perez AU/692	3.00	8.00
91 Tom Murphy/371	3.00	8.00
92 Bryan De La Rosa/779	3.00	8.00
93 Angel Ortega/699	3.00	8.00
94 Seth Maness/722	3.00	8.00
95 Will Clinard/790	3.00	8.00
96 Scott Oberg/799	3.00	8.00
97 Jacob Wilson AU/749	3.00	8.00
98 Anthony Banda/500	3.00	8.00
99 Josh Conway/280	3.00	8.00
100 Andrew Lockett/299	3.00	8.00

2012 Elite Extra Edition Signature Aspirations

STATED PRINT RUN 100 SER.#'d SETS
EXCHANGE DEADLINE 07/16/2014

1 Addison Russell	20.00	50.00
2 Albert Almora	4.00	10.00
3 Andrew Heaney	4.00	10.00
4 Michael Wacha	4.00	10.00
5 Marcus Stroman	8.00	20.00
6 Pat Light	5.00	12.00
7 Keon Barnum	5.00	12.00
8 Mitch Gueller	6.00	15.00
9 Max White	3.00	8.00
10 Carson Kelly	6.00	15.00
11 Nick Travieso	4.00	10.00
12 Chris Stratton	6.00	15.00
13 Tyrone Taylor	5.00	12.00
14 Brian Johnson	4.00	10.00
15 Luke Bard	3.00	8.00
16 Matt Smoral	6.00	15.00
17 Jesmuel Valentin	8.00	20.00
18 Patrick Wisdom	4.00	10.00
19 Eddie Butler	3.00	8.00
20 Dane Phillips	3.00	8.00
21 Robert Refsnyder	25.00	60.00
22 Nolan Fontana	3.00	8.00
23 Tyler Gonzales	4.00	10.00
24 Joe DeCarlo	3.00	8.00
25 Sam Selman	4.00	10.00
26 Dylan Cozens	15.00	40.00
27 Duane Underwood	4.00	10.00
28 Chris Beck	4.00	10.00
29 Martin Agosta	6.00	15.00
30 Alex Wood	10.00	25.00
31 Adam Walker	5.00	12.00
32 Avery Romero	3.00	8.00
33 Ryan McNeil	5.00	12.00
34 Matt Koch	3.00	8.00
35 Austin Schotts	10.00	25.00
36 Edwin Diaz	12.00	30.00
37 Kieran Lovegrove	4.00	10.00
38 Brett Mooneyham	4.00	10.00
39 Andrew Toles	4.00	10.00
40 Jake Barrett	4.00	10.00
41 Zach Quintana	3.00	8.00
42 Nathan Mikolas	8.00	20.00
43 Tyler Pike	5.00	12.00
44 Zach Green	3.00	8.00
45 Zack Jones	3.00	8.00
46 Patrick Kivlehan	3.00	8.00
47 Branden Kaupe	5.00	12.00
49 Ty Buttrey	4.00	10.00
50 Charles Taylor	3.00	8.00
51 Drew VerHagen	3.00	8.00
52 Tyler Wagner	3.00	8.00
53 Chris Serritella	4.00	10.00
54 Corey Black	5.00	12.00
55 Royce Bolinger	3.00	8.00
56 Adrian Sampson	4.00	10.00
57 Nick Basto	3.00	8.00
58 Dylan Baker	6.00	15.00
60 Ty Blach	3.00	8.00
61 Cory Jones	3.00	8.00
62 Ronnie Freeman	3.00	8.00
63 Lex Rutledge	3.00	8.00
64 Colin Rodgers	5.00	12.00
65 Kolby Copeland	4.00	10.00
66 Zach Lovvorn	3.00	8.00
67 Eric Stamets	3.00	8.00
68 Damion Carroll	3.00	8.00
69 Felipe Perez	3.00	8.00
70 Mason Melotakis	3.00	8.00
71 Rowan Wick	3.00	8.00
72 Jairo Beras	6.00	15.00
73 Dario Pizzano	8.00	20.00
74 Logan Taylor	3.00	8.00
75 Nick Kingham	4.00	10.00
76 Omar Luis Rodriguez	10.00	25.00
77 Rio Ruiz	3.00	8.00
78 Trey Lang	3.00	8.00
79 Alex Muren	3.00	8.00
80 D'Vone McClure	10.00	25.00
81 Matt Price	3.00	8.00
82 Alexis Rivera	6.00	15.00
83 Aaron West	10.00	25.00
85 Matt Juengel	3.00	8.00
86 Kaleb Merck	3.00	8.00
87 Anthony Melchionda	3.00	8.00
88 J.O. Berrios	10.00	25.00
89 J.T. Chargois	3.00	8.00
90 Fernando Perez	5.00	12.00
91 Tom Murphy	3.00	8.00
92 Bryan De La Rosa	3.00	8.00
93 Angel Ortega	3.00	8.00
94 Seth Maness	4.00	10.00
95 Will Clinard	3.00	8.00
96 Scott Oberg	3.00	8.00
97 Jacob Wilson	4.00	10.00
98 Anthony Banda	3.00	8.00
100 Andrew Lockett	3.00	8.00
101 Carlos Correa	60.00	150.00
102 Byron Buxton	25.00	60.00
103 Mike Zunino	30.00	60.00
104 Kevin Gausman	4.00	10.00
105 Kyle Zimmer	8.00	20.00
106 Max Fried	12.00	30.00
107 David Dahl	15.00	40.00
108 Gavin Cecchini	5.00	12.00
109 Courtney Hawkins	6.00	15.00
110 Tyler Naquin	4.00	10.00
111 Lucas Giolito	15.00	40.00
112 D.J. Davis	8.00	20.00
113 Corey Seager	50.00	120.00
114 Victor Roache	6.00	15.00
115 Deven Marrero	5.00	12.00
116 Lucas Sims	8.00	20.00
117 Stryker Trahan	6.00	15.00
118 Lewis Brinson	10.00	25.00
119 Kevin Plawecki	5.00	12.00
120 Richie Shaffer	6.00	15.00
121 Barrett Barnes	5.00	12.00
122 Shane Watson	4.00	10.00
123 Matt Olson	10.00	25.00
124 Lance McCullers	8.00	20.00
125 Mitch Haniger	10.00	25.00
126 Stephen Piscotty	10.00	25.00
128 Jesse Winker	5.00	12.00
129 Walker Weickel	5.00	12.00
130 James Ramsey	5.00	12.00
131 Joey Gallo	12.00	30.00
132 Mitch Nay	3.00	8.00
133 Alex Yarbrough	5.00	12.00
134 Preston Beck	3.00	8.00
135 Nick Goody	4.00	10.00
136 Daniel Robertson	4.00	10.00
137 Jake Thompson	4.00	10.00
138 Austin Nola	3.00	8.00
140 Austin Aune	5.00	12.00

142 Josh Elander 3.00 8.00
144 Ross Stripling 10.00 25.00
145 Bruce Maxwell 3.00 8.00
146 Mallex Smith 3.00 8.00
147 Collin Wiles 4.00 10.00
148 Pierce Johnson 6.00 15.00
149 Damien Magnifico 3.00 8.00
151 Jeff Gelalich 3.00 8.00
152 Paul Blackburn 4.00 10.00
153 Steve Bean 4.00 10.00
154 Spencer Edwards 4.00 10.00
155 Branden Kline 5.00 12.00
156 Jeremy Baltz 3.00 8.00
157 Max White 3.00 8.00
158 Chase DeJong 4.00 10.00
159 Jamie Jarmon 4.00 10.00
160 Mitch Brown 4.00 10.00
161 Jamie Callahan 3.00 8.00
162 Joe Munoz 4.00 10.00
163 Peter O'Brien 6.00 15.00
164 Matt Koch 3.00 8.00
165 Patrick Cantwell 3.00 8.00
166 Blake Brown 4.00 10.00
167 Max Muncy 12.00 30.00
168 Justin Chigbogu 5.00 12.00
169 Alex Mejia 3.00 8.00
170 Jeff McVaney 3.00 8.00
171 Michael Earley 3.00 8.00
172 Steve Okert 5.00 12.00
173 Dan Langfield 4.00 10.00
174 Austin Maddox 4.00 10.00
175 Kenny Diekroeger 3.00 8.00
176 Brandon Brennan 3.00 8.00
177 Zach Isler 3.00 8.00
178 Stefen Romero 5.00 12.00
179 Mac Williamson 4.00 10.00
180 Seth Willoughby 3.00 8.00
181 Tyler Wagner 3.00 8.00
182 Jake Lamb 8.00 20.00
183 Preston Tucker 10.00 25.00
184 Josh Turley 5.00 12.00
185 Logan Vick 3.00 8.00
186 R.J. Alvarez 5.00 12.00
187 Clint Coulter 15.00 40.00
189 Evan Marzilli 3.00 8.00
190 Carlos Escobar 3.00 8.00
191 Wyatt Mathisen 5.00 12.00
192 Matt Reynolds 4.00 10.00
193 Nick Williams 6.00 15.00
194 Brady Rodgers 5.00 12.00
195 Tim Cooney 3.00 8.00
196 Brett Vertigan 3.00 8.00
197 Hoby Milner 6.00 15.00
198 Luke Maile 3.00 8.00
199 Darin Ruf 40.00 80.00
200 Adrian Marin 4.00 10.00

2012 Elite Extra Edition Signature Status Blue

STATED PRINT RUN 50 SER.#'d SETS
EXCHANGE DEADLINE 07/16/2014
1 Addison Russell 20.00 50.00
2 Albert Almora 5.00 12.00
3 Andrew Heaney 10.00 25.00
4 Michael Wacha 5.00 12.00
5 Marcus Stroman 10.00 25.00
7 Keon Barnum 10.00 25.00
8 Mitch Gueller 8.00 20.00
9 Max White 4.00 10.00
11 Nick Travieso 8.00 20.00
12 Chris Stratton 20.00 50.00
13 Tyrone Taylor 8.00 20.00
14 Brian Johnson 8.00 20.00
16 Matt Smoral 10.00 25.00
17 Jesmuel Valentin 12.50 30.00
18 Patrick Wisdom 4.00 10.00
19 Eddie Butler 6.00 15.00
20 Dane Phillips 3.00 8.00
21 Robert Refsnyder 30.00 80.00
22 Nolan Fontana 5.00 12.00
23 Tyler Gonzales 10.00 25.00
24 Joe DeCarlo 4.00 10.00
25 Sam Selman 10.00 25.00
26 Dylan Cozens 20.00 50.00
27 Duane Underwood 6.00 15.00
28 Chris Beck 3.00 8.00
30 Alex Wood 12.00 30.00
31 Adam Walker 15.00 40.00
32 Avery Romero 3.00 8.00
33 Ryan McNeil 5.00 12.00
34 Matt Koch 4.00 10.00
35 Austin Schotts 20.00 50.00
36 Edwin Diaz 15.00 40.00
37 Kieran Lovegrove 5.00 12.00
38 Brett Mooneyham 5.00 12.00
39 Andrew Toles 5.00 12.00
40 Jake Barrett 4.00 10.00
41 Zach Quintana 8.00 20.00
42 Nathan Mikolas 6.00 15.00
43 Tyler Pike 6.00 15.00
44 Zach Green 6.00 15.00
46 Patrick Kivlehan 4.00 10.00
47 Branden Kaupe 5.00 12.00
49 Ty Buttrey 4.00 10.00
50 Charles Taylor 3.00 8.00
51 Drew VerHagen 5.00 12.00
52 Tyler Wagner 4.00 10.00
53 Chris Serritella 6.00 15.00
54 Corey Black 8.00 20.00
55 Royce Bolinger 3.00 8.00
56 Adrian Sampson 5.00 12.00
57 Nick Basto 3.00 8.00
58 Dylan Baker 6.00 15.00
59 Spencer Kieboom 3.00 8.00
60 Ty Blach 3.00 8.00
61 Cory Jones 3.00 8.00
62 Ronnie Freeman 3.00 8.00
63 Lex Rutledge 4.00 10.00
65 Kolby Copeland 4.00 10.00
66 Zach Lovvorn 3.00 8.00
67 Eric Stamets 3.00 8.00
68 Damion Carroll 3.00 8.00
69 Felipe Perez 5.00 12.00
70 Mason Melotakis 3.00 8.00
71 Rowan Wick 5.00 12.00
72 Jairo Beras 12.50 30.00
73 Dario Pizzano 12.50 30.00
74 Logan Taylor 6.00 15.00
76 Omar Luis Rodriguez 10.00 25.00
77 Rio Ruiz 5.00 12.00
78 Trey Lang 5.00 12.00
80 D'Vone McClure 15.00 40.00
81 Matt Price 5.00 12.00
82 Alexis Rivera 10.00 25.00
84 Slade Smith 6.00 15.00
85 Matt Juengel 3.00 8.00
86 Kaleb Merck 3.00 8.00
87 Anthony Melchionda 4.00 10.00
88 J.O. Berrios 12.00 30.00
89 J.T. Chargois 5.00 12.00
90 Fernando Perez 6.00 15.00
91 Tom Murphy 6.00 15.00
92 Bryan De La Rosa 6.00 15.00
93 Angel Ortega 4.00 10.00
94 Seth Maness 8.00 20.00
95 Will Clinard 3.00 8.00
96 Scott Oberg 3.00 8.00
99 Josh Conway 6.00 15.00
100 Andrew Lockett 4.00 10.00
101 Carlos Correa 75.00 200.00
102 Byron Buxton 30.00 80.00
103 Mike Zunino 12.50 30.00
104 Kevin Gausman 6.00 15.00
105 Kyle Zimmer 12.50 30.00
106 Max Fried 15.00 40.00
107 David Dahl 20.00 50.00
108 Gavin Cecchini 6.00 15.00
109 Courtney Hawkins 10.00 25.00
110 Tyler Naquin 8.00 20.00
111 Lucas Giolito 20.00 50.00
112 D.J. Davis 8.00 20.00
113 Corey Seager 60.00 150.00
115 Deven Marrero 8.00 20.00
116 Lucas Sims 12.50 30.00
117 Stryker Trahan 12.50 30.00
118 Lewis Brinson 12.50 30.00
119 Kevin Plawecki 5.00 12.00
120 Richie Shaffer 12.50 30.00
121 Barrett Barnes 6.00 15.00
122 Shane Watson 5.00 12.00
123 Matt Olson 12.00 30.00
124 Lance McCullers 20.00 50.00
125 Mitch Haniger 12.00 30.00
126 Stephen Piscotty 12.00 30.00
128 Jesse Winker 8.00 20.00
129 Walker Weickel 5.00 12.00
130 James Ramsey 5.00 12.00
131 Joey Gallo 15.00 40.00
132 Mitch Nay 6.00 15.00
133 Alex Yarbrough 6.00 15.00
134 Preston Beck 3.00 8.00
135 Nick Goody 4.00 10.00
136 Daniel Robertson 8.00 20.00
137 Jake Thompson 5.00 12.00
138 Austin Nola 3.00 8.00
139 Tony Renda 4.00 10.00
140 Austin Aune 10.00 25.00
141 Tanner Rahier 4.00 10.00
142 Josh Elander 4.00
144 Ross Stripling 12.00 30.00
146 Mallex Smith 4.00 10.00
147 Collin Wiles 4.00 10.00
148 Pierce Johnson 5.00 12.00
149 Damien Magnifico 6.00 15.00
151 Jeff Gelalich 4.00 10.00
152 Paul Blackburn 4.00 10.00
153 Steve Bean 5.00 12.00
154 Spencer Edwards 5.00 12.00
155 Branden Kline 5.00 12.00
157 Max White 4.00 10.00
158 Chase DeJong 10.00 25.00
159 Jamie Jarmon 10.00 25.00
160 Mitch Brown 5.00 12.00
161 Jamie Callahan 3.00 8.00
162 Joe Munoz 4.00 10.00
163 Peter O'Brien 8.00 20.00
164 Matt Koch 4.00 10.00
165 Patrick Cantwell 3.00 8.00
166 Blake Brown 4.00 10.00
167 Max Muncy 15.00 40.00
168 Justin Chigbogu 5.00 12.00
169 Alex Mejia 4.00 10.00
170 Jeff McVaney 3.00 8.00
171 Michael Earley 4.00 10.00
173 Dan Langfield 4.00 10.00
174 Austin Maddox 5.00 12.00
175 Kenny Diekroeger 4.00 10.00
176 Brandon Brennan 4.00 10.00
177 Zach Isler 8.00 20.00
178 Stefen Romero 20.00 50.00
179 Mac Williamson 12.00 30.00
180 Seth Willoughby 3.00 8.00
181 Tyler Wagner 3.00 8.00
183 Preston Tucker 12.00 30.00
184 Josh Turley 5.00 12.00
185 Logan Vick 4.00 10.00
186 R.J. Alvarez 6.00 15.00
187 Clint Coulter 4.00 10.00
188 Joe Rogers 3.00 8.00
189 Evan Marzilli 3.00 8.00
190 Carlos Escobar 3.00 8.00
191 Wyatt Mathisen 6.00 15.00
192 Matt Reynolds 6.00 15.00
193 Nick Williams 10.00 25.00
194 Brady Rodgers 8.00 20.00
196 Brett Vertigan 5.00 12.00
197 Hoby Milner 8.00 20.00
198 Luke Maile 3.00 8.00
199 Darin Ruf 12.00 30.00
200 Adrian Marin 5.00 12.00

2012 Elite Extra Edition Status

*STATUS: 2.5X TO 6X BASIC
STATED PRINT RUN 100 SER.#'d SETS
101 Carlos Correa 12.00 30.00
102 Byron Buxton 5.00 12.00
103 Mike Zunino 3.00 8.00
104 Kevin Gausman 4.00 10.00
105 Kyle Zimmer 2.50 6.00
106 Max Fried 8.00 20.00
107 David Dahl 6.00 15.00
108 Gavin Cecchini 2.50 6.00
109 Courtney Hawkins 2.00 5.00
110 Tyler Naquin 2.50 6.00
111 Lucas Giolito 6.00 15.00
112 D.J. Davis 2.50 6.00
113 Corey Seager 8.00 20.00
114 Victor Roache 4.00 10.00
115 Deven Marrero 2.00 5.00
116 Lucas Sims 2.50 6.00
117 Stryker Trahan 2.00 5.00
118 Lewis Brinson 6.00 15.00
119 Kevin Plawecki 2.50 6.00
120 Richie Shaffer 2.50 6.00
121 Barrett Barnes 2.50 6.00
122 Shane Watson 2.50 6.00
123 Matt Olson 3.00 8.00
124 Lance McCullers 2.00 5.00
125 Mitch Haniger 5.00 12.00
126 Stephen Piscotty 4.00 10.00
127 Ty Hensley 2.50 6.00
128 Jesse Winker 2.50 6.00
129 Walker Weickel 1.25 3.00
130 James Ramsey 2.00 5.00
131 Joey Gallo 6.00 15.00
132 Mitch Nay 1.25 3.00
133 Alex Yarbrough 2.00 5.00
134 Preston Beck 1.25 3.00
135 Nick Goody 2.00 5.00
136 Daniel Robertson 1.25 3.00
137 Jake Thompson 1.25 3.00
138 Austin Nola 1.25 3.00
139 Tony Renda 1.25 3.00
140 Austin Aune 2.50 6.00
141 Tanner Rahier 2.00 5.00
142 Josh Elander 1.25 3.00
143 Tim Lopes 1.25 3.00
144 Ross Stripling 1.25 3.00
145 Bruce Maxwell 2.00 5.00
147 Collin Wiles 1.25 3.00
148 Pierce Johnson 2.50 6.00
149 Damien Magnifico 1.25 3.00
150 Travis Jankowski 2.50 6.00
151 Jeff Gelalich 1.25 3.00
152 Paul Blackburn 2.00 5.00
153 Steve Bean 2.50 6.00
154 Spencer Edwards 2.00 5.00
155 Branden Kline 2.00 5.00
156 Jeremy Baltz 1.25 3.00
157 Max White 2.00 5.00
158 Chase DeJong 2.50 6.00
159 Jamie Jarmon 2.00 5.00
160 Mitch Brown 2.00 5.00
161 Jamie Callahan 1.25 3.00
162 Joe Munoz 1.25 3.00
163 Peter O'Brien 3.00 8.00
164 Matt Koch 1.25 3.00
165 Patrick Cantwell 1.25 3.00
166 Blake Brown 1.25 3.00
167 Max Muncy 10.00 25.00
168 Justin Chigbogu 2.00 5.00
169 Alex Mejia 1.25 3.00
170 Jeff McVaney 1.25 3.00
171 Michael Earley 2.00 5.00
172 Steve Okert 1.25 3.00
173 Dan Langfield 1.25 3.00
174 Austin Maddox 2.00 5.00
175 Kenny Diekroeger 1.25 3.00
176 Brandon Brennan 2.00 5.00
177 Zach Isler 2.00 5.00
178 Stefen Romero 2.00 5.00
179 Mac Williamson 4.00 10.00
180 Seth Willoughby 1.25 3.00
181 Tyler Wagner 1.25 3.00
182 Jake Lamb 3.00 8.00
183 Preston Tucker 3.00 8.00
184 Josh Turley 2.00 5.00
185 Logan Vick 2.00 5.00
186 R.J. Alvarez 1.25 3.00
187 Clint Coulter 2.00 5.00
188 Joe Rogers 2.00 5.00
189 Evan Marzilli 1.25 3.00
190 Carlos Escobar 1.25 3.00
191 Wyatt Mathisen 2.00 5.00
192 Matt Reynolds 2.00 5.00
193 Nick Williams 2.00 5.00
194 Brady Rodgers 2.00 5.00
195 Tim Cooney 2.00 5.00
196 Brett Vertigan 1.25 3.00
197 Hoby Milner 2.00 5.00
198 Luke Maile 1.25 3.00
199 Darin Ruf 12.00 30.00
200 Adrian Marin 2.00 5.00

2012 Elite Extra Edition Team Panini

1 A.Russell/C.Correa 8.00 20.00
2 K.Plawecki/M.Zunino 2.00 5.00
3 A.Almora/B.Buxton 3.00 8.00
4 C.Seager/D.Marrero 5.00 12.00
5 C.Hawkins/D.Dahl 4.00 10.00
6 R.Shaffer/S.Piscotty 2.50 6.00
7 Kevin Gausman/Kyle Zimmer 2.50 6.00
8 J.Ramsey/J.Gallo 6.00 15.00
9 Jesse Winker/Nick Williams 1.50 4.00
10 D.J. Davis/Nolan Fontana 1.50 4.00
11 Andrew Heaney/Brian Johnson 1.50 4.00
12 Chris Stratton/Marcus Stroman 2.00 5.00
13 Barrett Barnes/Lewis Brinson 4.00 10.00
14 L.Giolito/T.Hensley 4.00 10.00
15 Gavin Cecchini/Daniel Robertson 1.50 4.00

2012 Elite Extra Edition USA Baseball 15U Game Jersey Signatures

STATED PRINT RUN 99 SER.#'d SETS
EXCHANGE DEADLINE 07/16/2014
1 John Aiello 5.00 12.00
2 Nick Anderson 4.00 10.00
3 Luken Baker 4.00 10.00
4 Solomon Bates 3.00 8.00
5 Chris Betts 5.00 12.00
6 Danny Casals 6.00 15.00
7 Chris Cullen 12.50 30.00
8 Kyle Dean 8.00 20.00
9 Bailey Falter 5.00 12.00
10 Isaak Gutierrez 3.00 8.00
11 Nico Hoerner 15.00 40.00
12 Parker Kelly 6.00 15.00
13 Nick Madrigal 12.00 30.00
15 Jio Orozco 3.00 8.00
16 Kyle Robeniol 5.00 12.00
17 Blake Rutherford 8.00 20.00
18 Cole Sands 6.00 15.00
19 Kyle Tucker 10.00 25.00
20 Coby Weaver 4.00 10.00

2012 Elite Extra Edition USA Baseball 15U Signatures

STATED PRINT RUN 125 SER.#'d SETS
EXCHANGE DEADLINE 07/16/2014
1 John Aiello 4.00 10.00
2 Nick Anderson 3.00 8.00
3 Luken Baker 4.00 10.00
4 Solomon Bates 3.00 8.00
5 Chris Betts 8.00 20.00
6 Danny Casals 3.00 8.00
7 Chris Cullen 5.00 12.00
8 Kyle Dean 3.00 8.00
9 Bailey Falter 3.00 8.00
10 Isaak Gutierrez 3.00 8.00
11 Nico Hoerner 10.00 25.00
12 Parker Kelly 4.00 10.00
13 Nick Madrigal 15.00 40.00
15 Jio Orozco 4.00 10.00
16 Kyle Robeniol 3.00 8.00
17 Blake Rutherford 10.00 25.00
18 Cole Sands 3.00 8.00
19 Kyle Tucker 12.00 30.00
20 Coby Weaver 4.00 10.00

2012 Elite Extra Edition USA Baseball 18U Game Jersey Signatures

STATED PRINT RUN 249 SER.#'d SETS
EXCHANGE DEADLINE 07/16/2014
1 Willie Abreu 5.00 12.00
2 Christian Arroyo 3.00 8.00
3 Cavan Biggio 8.00 20.00
4 Ryan Boldt 6.00 15.00
5 Bryson Brigman 3.00 8.00
6 Kevin Davis 3.00 8.00
7 Stephen Gonsalves 6.00 15.00
8 Connor Heady 4.00 10.00
9 John Kilichowski 3.00 8.00
10 Ian Clarkin 6.00 15.00
11 Jeremy Martinez 5.00 12.00
12 Reese McGuire 10.00 25.00
13 Dom Nunez 3.00 8.00
14 Chris Okey 3.00 8.00
15 Ryan Olson 4.00 10.00
16 Carson Sands 4.00 10.00
17 Dominic Taccolini 3.00 8.00
18 Keegan Thompson 3.00 8.00
19 Garrett Williams 4.00 10.00

2012 Elite Extra Edition USA Baseball 18U Signatures

STATED PRINT RUN 299 SER.#'d SETS
EXCHANGE DEADLINE 07/16/2014
1 Willie Abreu 3.00 8.00
2 Christian Arroyo 3.00 8.00
3 Cavan Biggio 10.00 25.00
4 Ryan Boldt 5.00 12.00
5 Bryson Brigman 6.00 15.00
6 Kevin Davis 3.00 8.00
7 Stephen Gonsalves 5.00 12.00
8 Connor Heady 3.00 8.00
9 John Kilichowski 3.00 8.00
10 Ian Clarkin 6.00 15.00
11 Jeremy Martinez 6.00 15.00
12 Reese McGuire 6.00 15.00
13 Dom Nunez 3.00 8.00
14 Chris Okey 3.00 8.00
15 Ryan Olson 3.00 8.00
16 Carson Sands 3.00 8.00
17 Dominic Taccolini 4.00 10.00
18 Keegan Thompson 4.00 10.00
19 Garrett Williams 4.00 10.00

2012 Elite Extra Edition Yearbook

1 Tyler Naquin .75 2.00
2 Nick Travieso .75 2.00
3 Addison Russell 1.00 2.50
4 Joey Gallo 2.00 5.00
5 Max Fried 2.50 6.00
6 Matt Olson 1.00 2.50
7 Jake Thompson .40 1.00
8 David Dahl 2.00 5.00
9 Preston Beck .40 1.00
10 Carlos Correa 4.00 10.00
11 Albert Almora 1.50 4.00
12 Gavin Cecchini .75 2.00
13 Deven Marrero .60 1.50
14 Lucas Giolito 2.00 5.00
15 Mike Zunino 1.00 2.50
16 Jesse Winker .75 2.00
17 Clint Coulter .60 1.50
18 Kyle Zimmer .75 2.00
19 Corey Seager 2.50 6.00
20 Byron Buxton 1.50 4.00

2013 Elite Extra Edition

AU PRINT RUNS B/WN 74-899 COPIES
EXCHANGE DEADLINE 07/09/2014
1A Colin Moran .25 .60
1B Colin Moran VAR
2A Trey Ball .30 .75
Green cap
2B Ball Grn Wht Cap SP
3A Hunter Renfroe .30 .75
Red jersey
3B Renfroe Pinstripes SP
4A Braden Shipley .20 .50
Red jersey
4B Chipley Wht jsy SP
5A Chris Anderson .25 .60
Ball visible
5B Anderson No ball SP
6A Marco Gonzales .30 .75
6B Marco Gonzales VAR
7A Ryan Walker .20 .50
7B Ryan Walker VAR
8A Phillip Ervin .20 .50
Red jersey
8B Ervin Dark jsy SP
9A Ryne Stanek .40 1.00
9B Ryne Stanek VAR
10A Sean Manaea .20 .50
Leg up
10B Manaea Hands together SP
11 Josh Hart .20 .50
12 Michael Lorenzen .25 .60
13 Andrew Thurman .25 .60
14 Trevor Williams .20 .50
15 Cody Reed .20 .50
16 Johnny Field .20 .50
17 Justin Williams .25 .60
18 Blake Taylor .20 .50
19 Chance Sisco .40 1.00
20 Tyler Danish .40 1.00
21 Victor Caratini .60 1.50
22 Marten Gasparini .20 .50
23 Jake Sweaney .20 .50
24 Alex Balog .20 .50
25 Tucker Neuhaus .20 .50
26 Dace Kime .20 .50
27 Ivan Wilson .20 .50
28 Carter Hope .25 .60
29 Barrett Astin .20 .50
30 Daniel Palka .20 .50
31 Keynan Middleton .20 .50
32 Carlos Salazar .20 .50
33 Mason Smith .20 .50
34 Cody Dickson .20 .50
35 Stephen Gonsalves .20 .50
36 K.J. Woods .20 .50
37 Jonah Heim .20 .50
38 Kean Wong .20 .50
39 Jared King .25 .60
40 Josh Uhen .20 .50
41 Cory Thompson .20 .50
42 Ryan Aper .20 .50
43 Cal Drummond .20 .50
44 Brian Navarreto .20 .50
45 Konner Wade .20 .50
46 Jake Bauers .30 .75
47 Tyler Horan .20 .50
48 Scott Brattvet .20 .50
49 David Napoli .20 .50
50 Mitch Garver .25 .60
51 D.J. Snelten .20 .50
52 Brad Goldberg .20 .50
53 Carlos Asuaje .20 .50
54 Erik Schoenrock .20 .50
55 Garrett Smith .20 .50
56 Domingo Tapia .20 .50
57 Bruce Kern .20 .50
58 Trae Arbet .20 .50
59 Amed Rosario .30 .75
60 Andy Burns .20 .50
61 Miguel Almonte .20 .50
62 Anthony DeSclafani .20 .50
63 Cameron Perkins .20 .50
64 Chris Taylor .30 .75
65 Dixon Machado .20 .50
66 Matt Duffy .30 .75
67 Joel Payamps .20 .50
68 Taylor Garrison .20 .50
69 Corey Black .25 .60
70 Junior Arias .20 .50
71 Gleyber Torres 3.00 8.00
72 Chad Rogers .20 .50
73 D.J. Baxendale .20 .50
74 Jason Coats .20 .50
75 Daniel Winkler .20 .50
76 Devon Travis .30 .75
77 Yoel Mecias .20 .50
78 Francisco Sosa .20 .50
79 Ronny Carvajal .20 .50
80 Eugenio Suarez .40 1.00
81 Akeel Morris .20 .50
82 Mike O'Neill .20 .50
83 Randy Rosario .20 .50
84 Orlando Castro .20 .50
85 Jesus Solorzano .20 .50
86 Rainy Lara .20 .50
87 Sam Moll .25 .60
88 Tyler Wade .30 .75
89 Roberto Osuna .20 .50
90 Rock Shoulders .20 .50
91 Jeremy Rathjen .20 .50
92 Luis Mateo .25 .60
93 Jose Abreu 1.50 4.00
94 Jordan Patterson .20 .50
95 Adrian De Horta .20 .50
96 David Garner .20 .50
97 Trey Michalczewski .20 .50
98 Drew Dosch .20 .50
99 Ryan Garvey .20 .50
100 Dereck Rodriguez .60 1.50
101 Mark Appel AU/320 4.00 10.00
102 Kris Bryant AU/324 40.00 100.00
103 Jonathan Gray AU/329 8.00 20.00
104 Kohl Stewart AU/275 6.00 15.00
105 Clint Frazier AU/324 8.00 20.00
106 Hunter Dozier AU/325 3.00 8.00
107 Austin Meadows AU/322 10.00 25.00
108 Dominic Smith AU/275 4.00 10.00
109 D.J. Peterson AU/299 6.00 15.00
110 Reese McGuire AU/324 8.00 20.00
111 J.P. Crawford AU/411 10.00 25.00
112 Tim Anderson AU/374 10.00 25.00
113 Jonathon Crawford AU/374 3.00 8.00
114 Nick Ciuffo AU/373 4.00 10.00
115 Hunter Harvey AU/499 3.00 8.00
116 Alex Gonzalez AU/420 10.00 25.00
117 Billy McKinney AU/322 4.00 10.00
118 Rob Kaminsky AU/364 3.00 8.00
119 Eric Jagielo AU/314 3.00 8.00
120 Travis Demeritte AU/599 4.00 10.00
121 Jason Hursh AU/227 4.00 10.00
122 Aaron Judge AU/599 60.00 150.00
123 Ian Clarkin AU/370 4.00 10.00
124 Aaron Blair AU/274 3.00 8.00
125 Corey Knebel AU/699 3.00 8.00
126 Rob Zastryzny AU/690 3.00 8.00
127 Ryan McMahon AU/899 3.00 8.00
128 Ryan Eades AU/674 3.00 8.00
129 Teddy Stankiewicz AU/674 3.00 8.00
130 Andrew Church AU/899 3.00 8.00
131 Austin Wilson AU/174 5.00 12.00
132 Dustin Peterson AU/599 3.00 8.00
133 Andrew Knapp AU/173 3.00 8.00
134 Devin Williams AU/655 6.00 15.00
135 Tom Windle AU/671 3.00 8.00
136 Oscar Mercado AU/799 4.00 10.00
137 Kevin Ziomek AU/669 3.00 8.00
138 Hunter Green AU/899 EXCH 3.00 8.00
139 Riley Unroe AU/590 3.00 8.00
140 Akeem Bostick AU/674 3.00 8.00
141 Dillon Overton AU/672 3.00 8.00
142 Ryder Jones AU/580 3.00 8.00
143 Gosuke Katoh AU/314 4.00 10.00
144 Kevin Franklin AU/799 3.00 8.00
145 Chad Pinder AU/671 3.00 8.00
146 Colby Suggs AU/674 3.00 8.00
147 Jacob Hannemann AU/669 3.00 8.00
148 Jonathan Denney AU/172 5.00 12.00
149 Patrick Murphy AU/670 3.00 8.00
150 Stuart Turner AU/674 3.00 8.00
151 Jacob May AU/899 3.00 8.00
152 Jacoby Jones AU/673 4.00 10.00
153 Brandon Dixon AU/672 4.00 10.00
154 Michael O'Neill AU/349 4.00 10.00
155 Drew Ward AU/371 4.00 10.00
156 Chris Kohler AU/672 3.00 8.00
157 Tyler Skulina AU/670 3.00 8.00
158 Cody Bellinger AU/673 100.00 250.00
159 Mason Katz AU/667 3.00 8.00
160 Brian Ragira AU/274 5.00 12.00
161 Tony Kemp AU/899 EXCH 3.00 8.00
162 Trey Masek AU/673 3.00 8.00
163 Aaron Slegers AU/662 3.00 8.00
164 Joe Jackson AU/664 EXCH 3.00 8.00
165 Dan Slania AU/670 5.00 12.00
166 Luke Farrell AU/673 3.00 8.00
167 Jacob Nottingham AU/899 3.00 8.00
168 Brandon Diaz AU/663 3.00 8.00
169 Kyle Farmer AU/670 3.00 8.00
170 Michael Ratterree AU/670 3.00 8.00
171 Kasey Coffman AU/668 3.00 8.00
172 Tyler Webb AU/673 3.00 8.00
173 Kendall Coleman AU/672 3.00 8.00
174 Chase Jensen AU/655 3.00 8.00
175 Mikey Reynolds AU/673 3.00 8.00
176 Ben Verlander AU/370 5.00 12.00
177 Austin Kubitza AU/600 3.00 8.00
178 Chris Garia AU/772 3.00 8.00
179 Alen Hanson AU/550 3.00 8.00
180 Micah Johnson AU/232 4.00 10.00
181 Anthony Garcia AU/272 4.00 10.00
182 Cameron Flynn AU/899 3.00 8.00
183 Gregory Polanco AU/667 8.00 20.00
184 Maikel Franco AU/299 5.00 12.00
185 Rosell Herrera AU/174 EXCH 12.00 30.00
186 Mike Yastrzemski AU/740 10.00 25.00
187 Cory Vaughn AU/74 5.00 12.00
188 Jayce Boyd AU/299 4.00 10.00
189 Matt Andriese AU/771 3.00 8.00
190 Luis Torrens AU/470 EXCH 3.00 8.00
191 Jorge Alfaro AU/74 8.00 20.00
192 Tim Atherton AU/765 3.00 8.00
193 Zach Borenstein AU/749 EXCH 3.00 8.00
194 Hunter Lockwood AU/773 3.00 8.00
195 Terry McClure AU/769 3.00 8.00
196 Cody Stubbs AU/322 3.00 8.00
197 Kyle Crockett AU/774 3.00 8.00
198 Kent Emanuel AU/670 3.00 8.00
199 Tanner Norton AU/760 3.00 8.00
200 Amaurys Minier AU/674 8.00 20.00

2013 Elite Extra Edition Aspirations

*ASPIRATIONS: 2.5X TO 6X BASIC
STATED PRINT RUN 200 SER.#'d SETS
101 Mark Appel 2.00 5.00
102 Kris Bryant 20.00 50.00
103 Jonathan Gray 1.50 4.00
104 Kohl Stewart 1.50 4.00
105 Clint Frazier 6.00 15.00
106 Hunter Dozier 1.25 3.00
107 Austin Meadows 2.50 6.00
108 Dominic Smith 2.00 5.00
109 D.J. Peterson 1.25 3.00
110 Reese McGuire 1.50 4.00
111 J.P. Crawford 2.00 5.00
112 Tim Anderson 5.00 12.00
113 Jonathon Crawford 1.25 3.00
114 Nick Ciuffo 1.25 3.00
115 Hunter Harvey 1.50 4.00
116 Alex Gonzalez 2.00 5.00
117 Billy McKinney 1.50 4.00
118 Rob Kaminsky 1.50 4.00
119 Eric Jagielo 1.50 4.00
120 Travis Demeritte 1.50 4.00
121 Jason Hursh 1.25 3.00
122 Aaron Judge 30.00 80.00
123 Ian Clarkin 1.25 3.00
124 Aaron Blair 1.25 3.00
125 Corey Knebel 2.00 5.00
126 Rob Zastryzny 2.00 5.00
127 Ryan McMahon 1.50 4.00
128 Ryan Eades 1.25 3.00
129 Teddy Stankiewicz 1.50 4.00
130 Andrew Church 1.25 3.00
131 Austin Wilson 1.50 4.00
132 Dustin Peterson 1.25 3.00
133 Andrew Knapp 1.25 3.00
134 Devin Williams 3.00 8.00
135 Tom Windle 1.25 3.00
136 Oscar Mercado 2.00 5.00
137 Kevin Ziomek 1.25 3.00
138 Hunter Green 1.25 3.00
139 Riley Unroe 1.25 3.00
140 Akeem Bostick .75 2.00
141 Dillon Overton 1.25 3.00
142 Ryder Jones 2.00 5.00
143 Gosuke Katoh 1.50 4.00
144 Kevin Franklin 1.25 3.00
145 Chad Pinder .75 2.00
146 Colby Suggs 1.50 4.00
147 Jacob Hannemann .75 2.00
148 Jonathan Denney 1.50 4.00
149 Patrick Murphy 1.25 3.00
150 Stuart Turner 1.25 3.00
151 Jacob May 1.25 3.00
152 Jacoby Jones 2.00 5.00
153 Brandon Dixon 1.50 4.00
154 Michael O'Neill 1.25 3.00
155 Drew Ward 1.50 4.00
156 Chris Kohler 1.50 4.00
157 Tyler Skulina .75 2.00
158 Cody Bellinger 20.00 50.00
159 Mason Katz 1.25 3.00
160 Brian Ragira 1.25 3.00
161 Tony Kemp .75 2.00
162 Trey Masek .75 2.00
163 Aaron Slegers 1.50 4.00
164 Joe Jackson .75 2.00
165 Dan Slania .75 2.00
166 Luke Farrell 1.25 3.00
167 Jacob Nottingham 1.25 3.00
168 Brandon Diaz 1.25 3.00
169 Kyle Farmer .75 2.00
170 Michael Ratterree .75 2.00
171 Kasey Coffman .75 2.00
172 Tyler Webb .75 2.00
173 Kendall Coleman 1.25 3.00
174 Chase Jensen .75 2.00
175 Mikey Reynolds .75 2.00
176 Ben Verlander 1.50 4.00
177 Austin Kubitza 1.25 3.00
178 Chris Garia .75 2.00
179 Alen Hanson 1.50 4.00
180 Micah Johnson 1.50 4.00
181 Anthony Garcia 2.00 5.00
182 Cameron Flynn 1.25 3.00
183 Gregory Polanco 2.50 6.00
184 Maikel Franco 2.00 5.00
185 Rosell Herrera 1.50 4.00
186 Mike Yastrzemski 4.00 10.00
187 Cory Vaughn 1.25 3.00
188 Jayce Boyd 1.25 3.00
189 Matt Andriese 1.50 4.00

190 Luis Torrens 1.25 3.00
191 Jorge Alfaro 2.50 6.00
192 Tim Atherton .75 2.00
193 Zach Borenstein 2.00 5.00
194 Hunter Lockwood .75 2.00
195 Terry McClure .75 2.00
196 Cody Stubbs 1.25 3.00
197 Kyle Crockett 1.25 3.00
198 Kent Emanuel .75 2.00
199 Tanner Norton .75 2.00
200 Amaurys Minier 1.25 3.00

2013 Elite Extra Edition Status

*STATUS: 3X TO 8X BASIC
STATED PRINT RUN 100 SER.#'d SETS
93 Jose Abreu 12.00 30.00
101 Mark Appel 2.50 6.00
102 Kris Bryant 15.00 40.00
103 Jonathan Gray 2.00 5.00
104 Kohl Stewart 2.00 5.00
105 Clint Frazier 8.00 20.00
106 Hunter Dozier 1.50 4.00
107 Austin Meadows 3.00 8.00
108 Dominic Smith 2.50 6.00
109 D.J. Peterson 1.50 4.00
110 Reese McGuire 2.00 5.00
111 J.P. Crawford 2.50 6.00
112 Tim Anderson 6.00 15.00
113 Jonathon Crawford 1.50 4.00
114 Nick Ciuffo 1.50 4.00
115 Hunter Harvey 2.00 5.00
116 Alex Gonzalez 2.50 6.00
117 Billy McKinney 2.00 5.00
118 Rob Kaminsky 2.00 5.00
119 Eric Jagielo 2.00 5.00
120 Travis Demeritte 2.00 5.00
121 Jason Hursh 1.50 4.00
122 Aaron Judge 40.00 100.00
123 Ian Clarkin 1.50 4.00
124 Aaron Blair 1.50 4.00
125 Corey Knebel 1.50 4.00
126 Rob Zastryzny 2.50 6.00
127 Ryan McMahon 2.00 5.00
128 Ryan Eades 1.50 4.00
129 Teddy Stankiewicz 2.00 5.00
130 Andrew Church 1.50 4.00
131 Austin Wilson 2.00 5.00
132 Dustin Peterson 1.50 4.00
133 Andrew Knapp 1.50 4.00
134 Devin Williams 4.00 10.00
135 Tom Windle 1.50 4.00
136 Oscar Mercado 2.50 6.00
137 Kevin Ziomek 1.50 4.00
138 Hunter Green 1.50 4.00
139 Riley Unroe 1.50 4.00
140 Akeem Bostick 1.00 2.50
141 Dillon Overton 1.50 4.00
142 Ryder Jones 2.50 6.00
143 Gosuke Katoh 2.00 5.00
144 Kevin Franklin 1.50 4.00
145 Chad Pinder 1.00 2.50
146 Colby Suggs 2.00 5.00
147 Jacob Hannemann 1.00 2.50
148 Jonathan Denney 2.00 5.00
149 Patrick Murphy 1.50 4.00
150 Stuart Turner 1.50 4.00
151 Jacob May 1.50 4.00
152 Jacoby Jones 2.50 6.00
153 Brandon Dixon 2.00 5.00
154 Michael O'Neill 1.50 4.00
155 Drew Ward 2.00 5.00
156 Chris Kohler 2.00 5.00
157 Tyler Skulina 1.00 2.50
158 Cody Bellinger 25.00 60.00
159 Mason Katz 1.50 4.00
160 Brian Ragira 1.50 4.00
161 Tony Kemp 1.00 2.50
162 Trey Masek 1.00 2.50
163 Aaron Slegers 2.00 5.00
164 Joe Jackson 1.00 2.50
165 Dan Slania 1.00 2.50
166 Luke Farrell 1.50 4.00
167 Jacob Nottingham 1.50 4.00
168 Brandon Diaz 1.50 4.00
169 Kyle Farmer 1.00 2.50
170 Michael Ratterree 1.00 2.50
171 Kasey Coffman 1.00 2.50
172 Tyler Webb 1.00 2.50
173 Kendall Coleman 1.50 4.00
174 Chase Jensen 1.00 2.50
175 Mikey Reynolds 1.00 2.50
176 Ben Verlander 2.00 5.00
177 Austin Kubitza 1.50 4.00
178 Chris Garia 1.00 2.50
179 Alen Hanson 2.00 5.00
180 Micah Johnson 2.00 5.00
181 Anthony Garcia 2.50 6.00
182 Cameron Flynn 1.50 4.00
183 Gregory Polanco 3.00 8.00
184 Maikel Franco 2.50 6.00
185 Rosell Herrera 2.00 5.00
186 Mike Yastrzemski 5.00 12.00
187 Cory Vaughn 1.50 4.00
188 Jayce Boyd 1.50 4.00
189 Matt Andriese 2.00 5.00
190 Luis Torrens 1.50 4.00
191 Jorge Alfaro 3.00 8.00
192 Tim Atherton 1.00 2.50
193 Zach Borenstein 2.50 6.00
194 Hunter Lockwood 1.00 2.50
195 Terry McClure 1.00 2.50
196 Cody Stubbs 1.50 4.00
197 Kyle Crockett 1.50 4.00
198 Kent Emanuel 1.00 2.50
199 Tanner Norton 1.00 2.50
200 Amaurys Minier 1.50 4.00

2013 Elite Extra Edition Status Emerald

*STATUS EMERALD: 6X TO 15X BASIC
STATED PRINT RUN 25 SER.#'d SETS
101 Mark Appel 5.00 12.00
102 Kris Bryant 30.00 80.00
103 Jonathan Gray 4.00 10.00
104 Kohl Stewart 4.00 10.00
105 Clint Frazier 15.00 40.00
106 Hunter Dozier 3.00 8.00
107 Austin Meadows 6.00 15.00
108 Dominic Smith 5.00 12.00
109 D.J. Peterson 3.00 8.00
110 Reese McGuire 4.00 10.00
111 J.P. Crawford 5.00 12.00
112 Tim Anderson 12.00 30.00
113 Jonathon Crawford 3.00 8.00
114 Nick Ciuffo 3.00 8.00
115 Hunter Harvey 4.00 10.00
116 Alex Gonzalez 5.00 12.00
117 Billy McKinney 4.00 10.00
118 Rob Kaminsky 4.00 10.00
119 Eric Jagielo 4.00 10.00
120 Travis Demeritte 4.00 10.00
121 Jason Hursh 3.00 8.00
122 Aaron Judge 75.00 200.00
123 Ian Clarkin 3.00 8.00
124 Aaron Blair 3.00 8.00
125 Corey Knebel 3.00 8.00
126 Rob Zastryzny 5.00 12.00
127 Ryan McMahon 4.00 10.00
128 Ryan Eades 3.00 8.00
129 Teddy Stankiewicz 4.00 10.00
130 Andrew Church 3.00 8.00
131 Austin Wilson 4.00 10.00
132 Dustin Peterson 3.00 8.00
133 Andrew Knapp 3.00 8.00
134 Devin Williams 8.00 20.00
135 Tom Windle 3.00 8.00
136 Oscar Mercado 5.00 12.00
137 Kevin Ziomek 3.00 8.00
138 Hunter Green 3.00 8.00
139 Riley Unroe 3.00 8.00
140 Akeem Bostick 2.00 5.00
141 Dillon Overton 3.00 8.00
142 Ryder Jones 5.00 12.00
143 Gosuke Katoh 4.00 10.00
144 Kevin Franklin 3.00 8.00
145 Chad Pinder 2.00 5.00
146 Colby Suggs 4.00 10.00
147 Jacob Hannemann 2.00 5.00
148 Jonathan Denney 4.00 10.00
149 Patrick Murphy 3.00 8.00
150 Stuart Turner 3.00 8.00
151 Jacob May 3.00 8.00
152 Jacoby Jones 5.00 12.00
153 Brandon Dixon 4.00 10.00
154 Michael O'Neill 3.00 8.00
155 Drew Ward 4.00 10.00
156 Chris Kohler 4.00 10.00
157 Tyler Skulina 2.00 5.00
158 Cody Bellinger 50.00 125.00
159 Mason Katz 3.00 8.00
160 Brian Ragira 3.00 8.00
161 Tony Kemp 2.00 5.00
162 Trey Masek 2.00 5.00
163 Aaron Slegers 4.00 10.00
164 Joe Jackson 2.00 5.00
165 Dan Slania 2.00 5.00
166 Luke Farrell 3.00 8.00
167 Jacob Nottingham 3.00 8.00
168 Brandon Diaz 3.00 8.00
169 Kyle Farmer 2.00 5.00
170 Michael Ratterree 2.00 5.00
171 Kasey Coffman 2.00 5.00
172 Tyler Webb 2.00 5.00
173 Kendall Coleman 3.00 8.00
174 Chase Jensen 2.00 5.00
175 Mikey Reynolds 2.00 5.00
176 Ben Verlander 4.00 10.00
177 Austin Kubitza 3.00 8.00
178 Chris Garia 2.00 5.00
179 Alen Hanson 4.00 10.00
180 Micah Johnson 4.00 10.00
181 Anthony Garcia 5.00 12.00
182 Cameron Flynn 3.00 8.00
183 Gregory Polanco 6.00 15.00
184 Maikel Franco 5.00 12.00
185 Rosell Herrera 4.00 10.00
186 Mike Yastrzemski 10.00 25.00
187 Cory Vaughn 3.00 8.00
188 Jayce Boyd 3.00 8.00
189 Matt Andriese 4.00 10.00
190 Luis Torrens 3.00 8.00
191 Jorge Alfaro 6.00 15.00
192 Tim Atherton 2.00 5.00
193 Zach Borenstein 5.00 12.00
194 Hunter Lockwood 2.00 5.00
195 Terry McClure 2.00 5.00
196 Cody Stubbs 3.00 8.00
197 Kyle Crockett 3.00 8.00
198 Kent Emanuel 2.00 5.00
199 Tanner Norton 2.00 5.00
200 Amaurys Minier 3.00 8.00

2013 Elite Extra Edition Back to the Future Signatures

PRINT RUNS B/WN 10-299 COPIES PER
NO PRICING ON QTY 10
EXCHANGE DEADLINE 07/09/2014
1 Nick Travieso/299 3.00 8.00
2 Courtney Hawkins/99 4.00 10.00
3 Keon Barnum/299 3.00 8.00
4 Josh Turley/299 3.00 8.00
5 Tom Murphy/299 3.00 8.00
6 Brian Johnson/150 3.00 8.00
7 Patrick Wisdom/199 3.00 8.00
8 Rio Ruiz/299 3.00 8.00
9 Dylan Cozens/99 4.00 10.00
10 Byron Buxton/25 50.00 100.00
11 J.O. Berrios/199 6.00 15.00
12 Jairo Beras/284 3.00 8.00
13 Stefen Romero/299 3.00 8.00
14 Wyatt Mathisen/99 3.00 8.00
15 Austin Nola/199 3.00 8.00
17 Drew VerHagen/99 5.00 12.00
18 Damion Carroll/99 3.00 8.00
19 Jeff McVaney/299 3.00 8.00
20 Charles Taylor/99 3.00 8.00

2013 Elite Extra Edition Bloodlines

COMPLETE SET (8) 4.00 10.00
1 C.Yaz/M.YaZ 1.25 3.00
2 D.Peterson/D.Peterson .50 1.25
3 M.O'Neill/P.O'Neill .60 1.50
4 D.Rodriguez/I.Rodriguez 1.50 4.00
5 R.Garvey/S.Garvey .50 1.25
6 B.Surhoff/C.Moran .60 1.50
7 B.Harvey/H.Harvey .60 1.50
8 J.May/L.May .50 1.25

2013 Elite Extra Edition Bloodlines Signatures

PRINT RUNS B/WN 5-25 COPIES PER
NO PRICING ON QTY 5
EXCHANGE DEADLINE 07/09/2014
2 D.Peterson/D.Peterson/25
3 M.O'Neill/P.O'Neill/25
4 D.Rodriguez/I.Rodriguez/25 50.00 120.00
5 R.Garvey/S.Garvey/25 40.00 100.00
6 B.Surhoff/C.Moran/25
7 Harvey/Harvey/25 EXCH 12.50 30.00
8 J.May/L.May/25 EXCH 5.00 12.00

2013 Elite Extra Edition Elite Series

1 Byron Buxton .60 1.50
2 Kris Bryant 6.00 15.00
3 Clint Frazier 1.25 3.00
4 Kohl Stewart .30 .75
5 Mark Appel .40 1.00
6 Colin Moran .30 .75
7 Trey Ball .40 1.00
8 Hunter Renfroe .40 1.00
9 Jonathan Gray .30 .75
10 D.J. Peterson .25 .60
11 Billy McKinney .30 .75
12 Hunter Dozier .25 .60
13 Miguel Sano .30 .75
14 Braden Shipley .25 .60
15 Phillip Ervin .25 .60
16 J.P. Crawford .40 1.00
17 Dominic Smith .40 1.00
18 Reese McGuire .30 .75
19 Hunter Harvey .30 .75
20 Maikel Franco .40 1.00

2013 Elite Extra Edition Elite Series Signatures

PRINT RUNS B/WN 25-199 COPIES PER
EXCHANGE DEADLINE 07/09/2014
1 Byron Buxton/199 10.00 25.00
2 Kris Bryant/25 100.00 250.00
3 Clint Frazier/50 30.00 60.00
4 Kohl Stewart/99 8.00 20.00
5 Mark Appel/50
6 Colin Moran/25 15.00 40.00
7 Trey Ball/99 12.50 30.00
8 Hunter Renfroe/49 4.00 10.00
9 Jonathan Gray/50 15.00 40.00
10 D.J. Peterson/50 10.00 25.00
11 Billy McKinney/50 12.50 30.00
12 Hunter Dozier/49 10.00 25.00
13 Miguel Sano/199 10.00 25.00
14 Braden Shipley/80 6.00 15.00
15 Phillip Ervin/80 10.00 25.00
16 J.P. Crawford/99 12.00 30.00
17 Dominic Smith/99 12.50 30.00
18 Reese McGuire/99 8.00 20.00
19 Hunter Harvey/149 6.00 15.00
20 Maikel Franco/99 8.00 20.00

2013 Elite Extra Edition Franchise Futures Signatures

PRINT RUNS B/WN 99-899 COPIES PER
EXCHANGE DEADLINE 07/09/2014
1 Colin Moran/250 3.00 8.00
2 Trey Ball/270 6.00 15.00
3 Hunter Renfroe/308 4.00 10.00
4 Braden Shipley/404 3.00 8.00
5 Chris Anderson/265 4.00 10.00
6 Marco Gonzales/298 4.00 10.00
7 Ryan Walker/699 3.00 8.00
8 Phillip Ervin/243 3.00 8.00
9 Ryne Stanek/530 4.00 10.00
10 Sean Manaea/565 3.00 8.00
11 Josh Hart/322 4.00 10.00
12 Michael Lorenzen/849 EXCH 3.00 8.00
13 Andrew Thurman/725 3.00 8.00
14 Trevor Williams/810 3.00 8.00
15 Cody Reed/672 3.00 8.00
16 Johnny Field/725 3.00 8.00
17 Justin Williams/672 3.00 8.00
18 Blake Taylor/672 3.00 8.00
19 Chance Sisco/672 4.00 10.00
20 Tyler Danish/670 EXCH 3.00 8.00
21 Victor Caratini/224 15.00 40.00
22 Marten Gasparini/652 3.00 8.00
23 Jake Sweaney/749 3.00 8.00
24 Alex Balog/661 3.00 8.00
25 Tucker Neuhaus/324 3.00 8.00
26 Dace Kime/669 3.00 8.00
27 Ivan Wilson/271 4.00 10.00
28 Carter Hope/672 3.00 8.00
29 Barrett Astin/899 3.00 8.00
30 Daniel Palka/549 3.00 8.00
31 Keynan Middleton/639 EXCH 3.00 8.00
32 Carlos Salazar/625 3.00 8.00
33 Mason Smith/668 3.00 8.00
34 Cody Dickson/672 3.00 8.00
35 Stephen Gonsalves/349 3.00 8.00
36 K.J. Woods/650 3.00 8.00
37 Jonah Heim/649 3.00 8.00
38 Kean Wong/625 3.00 8.00
39 Jared King/669 3.00 8.00
40 Josh Uhen/660 3.00 8.00
41 Cory Thompson/660 3.00 8.00
42 Ryan Aper/668 3.00 8.00
43 Cal Drummond/670 3.00 8.00
44 Brian Navarreto/710 3.00 8.00
45 Konner Wade/698 3.00 8.00
46 Jake Bauers/671 6.00 15.00
47 Tyler Horan/672 3.00 8.00
48 Scott Brattvet/671 3.00 8.00
49 David Napoli/671 3.00 8.00
50 Mitch Garver/655 3.00 8.00
51 D.J. Snelten/667 3.00 8.00
52 Brad Goldberg/672 3.00 8.00
53 Carlos Asuaje/672 3.00 8.00
54 Erik Schoenrock/662 3.00 8.00
55 Garrett Smith/801 3.00 8.00
56 Domingo Tapia/802 3.00 8.00
57 Bruce Kern/799 3.00 8.00
58 Trae Arbet/650 3.00 8.00
59 Amed Rosario/250 30.00 80.00
60 Andy Burns/399 3.00 8.00
61 Miguel Almonte/899 3.00 8.00
62 Anthony DeSclafani/603 3.00 8.00
63 Cameron Perkins/525 3.00 8.00
64 Chris Taylor/390 12.00 30.00
65 Dixon Machado/272 3.00 8.00
66 Matt Duffy/250 EXCH 12.00 30.00
67 Joel Payamps/749 3.00 8.00
68 Taylor Garrison/639 3.00 8.00
69 Corey Black/700 3.00 8.00
70 Junior Arias/671 3.00 8.00
71 Gleyber Torres/250 60.00 150.00
72 Chad Rogers/350 3.00 8.00
73 D.J. Baxendale/375 3.00 8.00
74 Jason Coats/499 3.00 8.00
75 Daniel Winkler/175 5.00 12.00
76 Devon Travis/115 10.00 25.00
77 Yoel Mecias/799 3.00 8.00
78 Francisco Sosa/250 EXCH 3.00 8.00
79 Ronny Carvajal/250 EXCH 3.00 8.00
80 Eugenio Suarez/299 12.00 30.00
81 Akeel Morris/720 3.00 8.00
82 Mike O'Neill/352 3.00 8.00
83 Randy Rosario/790 3.00 8.00
84 Orlando Castro/663 EXCH 3.00 8.00
85 Jesus Solorzano/199 EXCH 3.00 8.00
86 Rainy Lara/99 4.00 10.00
87 Sam Moll/699 3.00 8.00
88 Tyler Wade/699 4.00 10.00
89 Roberto Osuna/224 3.00 8.00
90 Rock Shoulders/267 5.00 12.00
91 Jeremy Rathjen/159 4.00 10.00
92 Luis Mateo/799 3.00 8.00
93 Jose Abreu/799 12.00 30.00
94 Jordan Patterson/670 3.00 8.00
95 Adrian De Horta/659 3.00 8.00
96 David Garner/670 3.00 8.00
97 Trey Michalczewski/312 3.00 8.00
98 Drew Dosch/665 3.00 8.00
99 Ryan Garvey/550 3.00 8.00
100 Dereck Rodriguez/200 25.00 60.00

2013 Elite Extra Edition Historic Picks

COMPLETE SET (10) 4.00 10.00
1 Craig Biggio .40 1.00
2 Shawn Green .30 .75
3 Ken Griffey Jr. 1.00 2.50
4 Roger Clemens .60 1.50
5 Chipper Jones .50 1.25
6 Joe Carter .30 .75
7 Johnny Damon .40 1.00
8 Jim Abbott .30 .75
9 Mike Piazza .50 1.25
10 Troy Glaus .30 .75

2013 Elite Extra Edition Historic Picks Signatures

PRINT RUNS B/WN 5-99 COPIES PER
NO PRICING ON QTY 10 OR LESS
EXCHANGE DEADLINE 07/09/2014
1 Craig Biggio/99 20.00 50.00
2 Shawn Green/99 3.00 8.00
6 Joe Carter/25 12.50 30.00
7 Johnny Damon/37 10.00 25.00
8 Jim Abbott/22 10.00 25.00

2013 Elite Extra Edition Panini High School All Stars

1 Clint Frazier 10.00 25.00
2 Josh Hart 2.00 5.00
3 Riley Unroe 2.00 5.00
4 Carlos Salazar 2.00 5.00
5 Trey Ball 3.00 8.00
6 Austin Meadows 4.00 10.00
7 Jake Bauers 3.00 8.00
8 Dustin Peterson 2.00 5.00
9 Jacob Nottingham 2.00 5.00
10 Kohl Stewart 2.50 6.00
11 Dominic Smith 3.00 8.00
12 Billy McKinney 2.50 6.00
13 Nick Ciuffo 2.00 5.00
14 Tyler Danish 4.00 10.00
15 Rob Kaminsky 2.50 6.00
16 Reese McGuire 2.50 6.00
17 J.P. Crawford 3.00 8.00
18 Hunter Harvey 2.50 6.00
19 Travis Demeritte 2.50 6.00
20 Ian Clarkin 2.00 5.00

2013 Elite Extra Edition Scouting 101

1 Austin Meadows .60 1.50
2 Nick Ciuffo .30 .75
3 Travis Demeritte .40 1.00
4 Eric Jagielo .40 1.00
5 Jake Bauers .50 1.25
6 Tim Anderson 1.25 3.00
7 Billy McKinney .40 1.00
8 Sean Manaea .30 .75
9 Ryne Stanek .60 1.50
10 Jonathon Crawford .30 .75
11 Riley Unroe .30 .75
12 Ian Clarkin .30 .75
13 Chris Anderson .40 1.00
14 Jonathan Denney .40 1.00
15 Jason Hursh .30 .75
16 Dominic Smith .50 1.25
17 Hunter Renfroe .50 1.25
18 Josh Hart .30 .75
19 Kris Bryant 1.50 4.00
20 Mark Appel .50 1.25

2013 Elite Extra Edition Signature Aspirations

STATED PRINT RUN 100 SER.#'d SETS
EXCHANGE DEADLINE 07/09/2014
1 Colin Moran 4.00 10.00
2 Trey Ball 10.00 25.00
3 Hunter Renfroe 12.00 30.00
4 Braden Shipley 3.00 8.00
5 Chris Anderson
6 Marco Gonzales 6.00 15.00
7 Ryan Walker 4.00 10.00
8 Phillip Ervin 8.00 20.00
9 Ryne Stanek 6.00 15.00
10 Sean Manaea 4.00 10.00
11 Josh Hart 4.00 10.00
12 Michael Lorenzen EXCH 4.00 10.00
13 Andrew Thurman 3.00 8.00
14 Trevor Williams 4.00 10.00
15 Cody Reed 12.50 30.00
16 Johnny Field 3.00 8.00
17 Justin Williams
18 Blake Taylor 3.00 8.00
19 Chance Sisco 4.00 10.00
20 Tyler Danish EXCH 4.00 10.00
21 Victor Caratini 15.00 40.00
22 Marten Gasparini 5.00 12.00
23 Jake Sweaney 3.00 8.00
24 Alex Balog 3.00 8.00
25 Tucker Neuhaus 3.00 8.00
26 Dace Kime 6.00 15.00
27 Ivan Wilson 4.00 10.00
28 Carter Hope 3.00 8.00
29 Barrett Astin 3.00 8.00
30 Daniel Palka 3.00 8.00
31 Keynan Middleton EXCH 5.00 12.00
32 Carlos Salazar 3.00 8.00
33 Mason Smith 3.00 8.00
34 Cody Dickson 3.00 8.00
35 Stephen Gonsalves 5.00 12.00
36 K.J. Woods 3.00 8.00
37 Jonah Heim 3.00 8.00
38 Kean Wong 3.00 8.00
39 Jared King 6.00 15.00
40 Josh Uhen 5.00 12.00
41 Cory Thompson 3.00 8.00
42 Ryan Aper 3.00 8.00
43 Cal Drummond
44 Brian Navarreto 3.00 8.00
45 Konner Wade
46 Jake Bauers 6.00 15.00
47 Tyler Horan 8.00 20.00
48 Scott Brattvet 3.00 8.00
49 David Napoli 3.00 8.00
50 Mitch Garver 3.00 8.00
51 D.J. Snelten 3.00 8.00
52 Brad Goldberg 5.00 12.00
53 Carlos Asuaje 3.00 8.00
54 Erik Schoenrock 3.00 8.00
55 Garrett Smith 3.00 8.00
56 Domingo Tapia 3.00 8.00
57 Bruce Kern
58 Trae Arbet 4.00 10.00
59 Amed Rosario 30.00 80.00
60 Andy Burns 3.00 8.00
61 Miguel Almonte 3.00 8.00
62 Anthony DeSclafani 3.00 8.00
63 Cameron Perkins 3.00 8.00
64 Chris Taylor 12.00 30.00
65 Dixon Machado 3.00 8.00
66 Matt Duffy EXCH 30.00 80.00
67 Joel Payamps 3.00 8.00
68 Taylor Garrison
69 Corey Black 3.00 8.00
70 Junior Arias 3.00 8.00
71 Gleyber Torres 60.00 150.00
72 Chad Rogers 3.00 8.00
73 D.J. Baxendale
74 Jason Coats 3.00 8.00
75 Daniel Winkler 5.00 12.00
76 Devon Travis 10.00 25.00
77 Yoel Mecias 4.00 10.00
78 Francisco Sosa EXCH 4.00 10.00
79 Ronny Carvajal EXCH 6.00 15.00
80 Eugenio Suarez 10.00 25.00
81 Akeel Morris 3.00 8.00
82 Mike O'Neill 4.00 10.00
83 Randy Rosario 3.00 8.00
84 Orlando Castro EXCH 3.00 8.00
85 Jesus Solorzano EXCH 4.00 10.00
86 Rainy Lara 15.00 40.00
87 Sam Moll 3.00 8.00
88 Tyler Wade 15.00 40.00
89 Roberto Osuna 5.00 12.00
90 Rock Shoulders
91 Jeremy Rathjen 4.00 10.00
92 Luis Mateo 3.00 8.00
93 Jose Abreu 15.00 40.00
94 Jordan Patterson 3.00 8.00
95 Adrian De Horta 3.00 8.00
96 David Garner 3.00 8.00
97 Trey Michalczewski 4.00 10.00
98 Drew Dosch
99 Ryan Garvey 5.00 12.00
100 Dereck Rodriguez 12.00 30.00
101 Mark Appel 6.00 15.00
102 Kris Bryant 50.00 120.00
103 Jonathan Gray 8.00 20.00
104 Kohl Stewart 6.00 15.00
105 Clint Frazier 15.00 40.00
106 Hunter Dozier 6.00 15.00
107 Austin Meadows 12.00 30.00
108 Dominic Smith 10.00 25.00
109 D.J. Peterson 10.00 25.00
110 Reese McGuire 8.00 20.00
111 J.P. Crawford 12.00 30.00
112 Tim Anderson 10.00 25.00
113 Jonathon Crawford 4.00 10.00
114 Nick Ciuffo 8.00 20.00
115 Hunter Harvey 3.00 8.00
116 Alex Gonzalez 10.00 25.00
117 Billy McKinney 8.00 20.00
118 Rob Kaminsky 4.00 10.00
119 Eric Jagielo 6.00 15.00
120 Travis Demeritte 4.00 10.00
121 Jason Hursh 6.00 15.00
122 Aaron Judge 75.00 200.00
123 Ian Clarkin 5.00 12.00
124 Aaron Blair 3.00 8.00
125 Corey Knebel 3.00 8.00
126 Rob Zastryzny 5.00 12.00
127 Ryan McMahon 10.00 25.00
128 Ryan Eades 3.00 8.00
129 Teddy Stankiewicz 6.00 15.00
130 Andrew Church 3.00 8.00
131 Austin Wilson 3.00 8.00
132 Dustin Peterson 5.00 12.00
133 Andrew Knapp 4.00 10.00
134 Devin Williams 8.00 20.00
135 Tom Windle 3.00 8.00
136 Oscar Mercado 4.00 10.00
137 Kevin Ziomek 3.00 8.00
138 Hunter Green EXCH 3.00 8.00
139 Riley Unroe 3.00 8.00
140 Akeem Bostick 5.00 12.00
141 Dillon Overton 3.00 8.00
142 Ryder Jones 6.00 15.00
143 Gosuke Katoh 5.00 12.00
144 Kevin Franklin 3.00 8.00
145 Chad Pinder 3.00 8.00
146 Colby Suggs 3.00 8.00
147 Jacob Hannemann 3.00 8.00
148 Jonathan Denney 5.00 12.00
149 Patrick Murphy 4.00 10.00
150 Stuart Turner 5.00 12.00
151 Jacob May 5.00 12.00
152 Jacoby Jones 5.00 12.00
153 Brandon Dixon 5.00 12.00
154 Michael O'Neill 4.00 10.00
155 Drew Ward 8.00 20.00
156 Chris Kohler 4.00 10.00
157 Tyler Skulina 3.00 8.00
158 Cody Bellinger 125.00 300.00
159 Mason Katz 3.00 8.00
160 Brian Ragira 5.00 12.00
161 Tony Kemp EXCH 4.00 10.00
162 Trey Masek 3.00 8.00
163 Aaron Slegers 20.00 50.00
164 Joe Jackson EXCH 4.00 10.00
165 Dan Slania 5.00 12.00
166 Luke Farrell 3.00 8.00
167 Jacob Nottingham 3.00 8.00
168 Brandon Diaz
169 Kyle Farmer 3.00 8.00
170 Michael Ratterree 4.00 10.00
171 Kasey Coffman 3.00 8.00
172 Tyler Webb 5.00 12.00
173 Kendall Coleman 3.00 8.00
174 Chase Jensen 3.00 8.00
175 Mikey Reynolds 4.00 10.00
176 Ben Verlander 6.00 15.00
177 Austin Kubitza 4.00 10.00
178 Chris Garia
179 Alen Hanson 3.00 8.00
180 Micah Johnson 4.00 10.00
181 Anthony Garcia 4.00 10.00
182 Cameron Flynn 3.00 8.00
183 Gregory Polanco 6.00 15.00
184 Maikel Franco 8.00 20.00
185 Rosell Herrera EXCH 12.00 30.00
186 Mike Yastrzemski 12.00 30.00
187 Cory Vaughn 5.00 12.00
188 Jayce Boyd 3.00 8.00
189 Matt Andriese 4.00 10.00
190 Luis Torrens EXCH 3.00 8.00
191 Jorge Alfaro 10.00 25.00
192 Tim Atherton 3.00 8.00
193 Zach Borenstein EXCH 10.00 25.00
194 Hunter Lockwood 3.00 8.00
195 Terry McClure 3.00 8.00
196 Cody Stubbs 3.00 8.00
197 Kyle Crockett 4.00 10.00
198 Kent Emanuel 3.00 8.00
199 Tanner Norton 3.00 8.00
200 Amaurys Minier 10.00 25.00

2013 Elite Extra Edition Signature Status Blue

STATED PRINT RUN 50 SER.#'d SETS
EXCHANGE DEADLINE 07/09/2014
1 Colin Moran 5.00 12.00
2 Trey Ball
3 Hunter Renfroe 15.00 40.00
4 Braden Shipley 4.00 10.00
5 Chris Anderson
6 Marco Gonzales 5.00 12.00
7 Ryan Walker
8 Phillip Ervin 12.50 30.00
9 Ryne Stanek 8.00 20.00
10 Sean Manaea 8.00 20.00
11 Josh Hart 5.00 12.00
12 Michael Lorenzen EXCH 5.00 12.00
13 Andrew Thurman 4.00 10.00
14 Trevor Williams 5.00 12.00
15 Cody Reed 15.00 40.00
16 Johnny Field
17 Justin Williams 4.00 10.00
18 Blake Taylor 4.00 10.00
19 Chance Sisco
20 Tyler Danish EXCH 5.00 12.00
21 Victor Caratini 20.00 50.00
22 Marten Gasparini 6.00 15.00
23 Jake Sweaney 4.00 10.00
24 Alex Balog
25 Tucker Neuhaus 4.00 10.00
26 Dace Kime 6.00 15.00
27 Ivan Wilson 5.00 12.00
28 Carter Hope 4.00 10.00
29 Barrett Astin 4.00 10.00
30 Daniel Palka 4.00 10.00
31 Keynan Middleton EXCH
32 Carlos Salazar 4.00 10.00
33 Mason Smith 4.00 10.00
34 Cody Dickson 4.00 10.00
35 Stephen Gonsalves 8.00 20.00
36 K.J. Woods 4.00 10.00
37 Jonah Heim
38 Kean Wong 4.00 10.00
39 Jared King 6.00 15.00
40 Josh Uhen 5.00 12.00
41 Cory Thompson 4.00 10.00
42 Ryan Aper
43 Cal Drummond 4.00 10.00
44 Brian Navarreto 4.00 10.00
45 Konner Wade
46 Jake Bauers 8.00 20.00
47 Tyler Horan 10.00 25.00
48 Scott Brattvet 4.00 10.00
49 David Napoli 4.00 10.00
50 Mitch Garver 4.00 10.00
51 D.J. Snelten 4.00 10.00
52 Brad Goldberg 4.00 10.00
53 Carlos Asuaje 4.00 10.00
54 Erik Schoenrock 4.00 10.00
55 Garrett Smith 4.00 10.00
56 Domingo Tapia
57 Bruce Kern 4.00 10.00
58 Trae Arbet 5.00 12.00
59 Amed Rosario 40.00 100.00
60 Andy Burns 4.00 10.00
61 Miguel Almonte 4.00 10.00
62 Anthony DeSclafani 4.00 10.00
63 Cameron Perkins 4.00 10.00
64 Chris Taylor 15.00 40.00
65 Dixon Machado 4.00 10.00
66 Matt Duffy EXCH 40.00 100.00
67 Joel Payamps
68 Taylor Garrison 4.00 10.00
69 Corey Black 4.00 10.00
70 Junior Arias 4.00 10.00
71 Gleyber Torres 150.00 300.00
72 Chad Rogers 4.00 10.00
73 D.J. Baxendale
74 Jason Coats
75 Daniel Winkler 6.00 15.00
76 Devon Travis 12.50 30.00
77 Yoel Mecias 5.00 12.00
78 Francisco Sosa EXCH 5.00 12.00
79 Ronny Carvajal EXCH 8.00 20.00
80 Eugenio Suarez 12.00 30.00
81 Akeel Morris 4.00 10.00
82 Mike O'Neill 5.00 12.00
83 Randy Rosario 4.00 10.00
84 Orlando Castro EXCH 4.00 10.00
85 Jesus Solorzano EXCH 5.00 12.00
86 Rainy Lara
87 Sam Moll 4.00 10.00
88 Tyler Wade 20.00 50.00
89 Roberto Osuna 6.00 15.00
90 Rock Shoulders 5.00 12.00
91 Jeremy Rathjen 4.00 10.00
92 Luis Mateo 4.00 10.00
93 Jose Abreu 20.00 50.00
94 Jordan Patterson 4.00 10.00

95 Adrian De Horta 6.00 15.00
96 David Garner 4.00 10.00
97 Trey Michalczewski
98 Drew Dosch
99 Ryan Garvey 4.00 10.00
100 Dereck Rodriguez 15.00 40.00
101 Mark Appel 8.00 20.00
102 Kris Bryant 75.00 200.00
103 Jonathan Gray 6.00 15.00
104 Kohl Stewart 8.00 20.00
105 Clint Frazier 50.00 120.00
106 Hunter Dozier 8.00 20.00
107 Austin Meadows 15.00 40.00
108 Dominic Smith 12.50 30.00
109 D.J. Peterson 12.50 30.00
110 Reese McGuire 10.00 25.00
111 J.P. Crawford 15.00 40.00
112 Tim Anderson 12.00 30.00
113 Jonathon Crawford 6.00 15.00
114 Nick Ciuffo 8.00 20.00
115 Hunter Harvey 5.00 12.00
116 Alex Gonzalez 12.00 30.00
117 Billy McKinney 10.00 25.00
118 Rob Kaminsky 6.00 15.00
119 Eric Jagielo 8.00 20.00
120 Travis Demeritte 5.00 12.00
121 Jason Hursh 6.00 15.00
122 Aaron Judge 150.00 400.00
123 Ian Clarkin
124 Aaron Blair 4.00 10.00
125 Corey Knebel 4.00 10.00
126 Rob Zastryzny 6.00 15.00
127 Ryan McMahon 15.00 40.00
128 Ryan Eades 4.00 10.00
129 Teddy Stankiewicz 5.00 12.00
130 Andrew Church 4.00 10.00
131 Austin Wilson 4.00 10.00
132 Dustin Peterson 6.00 15.00
133 Andrew Knapp 5.00 12.00
134 Devin Williams 10.00 25.00
135 Tom Windle 4.00 10.00
136 Oscar Mercado 5.00 12.00
137 Kevin Ziomek 4.00 10.00
138 Hunter Green EXCH 4.00 10.00
139 Riley Unroe 4.00 10.00
140 Akeem Bostick 6.00 15.00
141 Dillon Overton 4.00 10.00
142 Ryder Jones 4.00 10.00
143 Gosuke Katoh 5.00 12.00
144 Kevin Franklin 4.00 10.00
145 Chad Pinder 4.00 10.00
146 Colby Suggs 4.00 10.00
147 Jacob Hannemann 4.00 10.00
148 Jonathan Denney 6.00 15.00
149 Patrick Murphy 5.00 12.00
150 Stuart Turner 6.00 15.00
151 Jacob May
152 Jacoby Jones 6.00 15.00
153 Brandon Dixon 6.00 15.00
154 Michael O'Neill 5.00 12.00
155 Drew Ward 10.00 25.00
156 Chris Kohler 5.00 12.00
157 Tyler Skulina 4.00 10.00
158 Cody Bellinger 150.00 400.00
159 Mason Katz 4.00 10.00
160 Brian Ragira 4.00 10.00
161 Tony Kemp EXCH 5.00 12.00
162 Trey Masek 4.00 10.00
163 Aaron Slegers 25.00 60.00
164 Joe Jackson EXCH 5.00 12.00
165 Dan Slania
166 Luke Farrell 4.00 10.00
167 Jacob Nottingham
168 Brandon Diaz 5.00 12.00
169 Kyle Farmer 4.00 10.00
170 Michael Ratterree 5.00 12.00
171 Kasey Coffman 4.00 10.00
172 Tyler Webb
173 Kendall Coleman 4.00 10.00
174 Chase Jensen 4.00 10.00
175 Mikey Reynolds 5.00 12.00
176 Ben Verlander 8.00 20.00
177 Austin Kubitza 5.00 12.00
178 Chris Garia
179 Alen Hanson 4.00 10.00
180 Micah Johnson 5.00 12.00
181 Anthony Garcia 5.00 12.00
182 Cameron Flynn
183 Gregory Polanco 15.00 40.00
184 Maikel Franco 10.00 25.00
185 Rosell Herrera EXCH 20.00 50.00
186 Mike Yastrzemski 15.00 40.00
187 Cory Vaughn 6.00 15.00
188 Jayce Boyd 4.00 10.00
189 Matt Andriese 5.00 12.00
190 Luis Torrens EXCH
191 Jorge Alfaro 10.00 25.00
192 Tim Atherton
193 Zach Borenstein EXCH 8.00 20.00
194 Hunter Lockwood
195 Terry McClure 4.00 10.00
196 Cody Stubbs 4.00 10.00
197 Kyle Crockett 5.00 12.00
198 Kent Emanuel 4.00 10.00
199 Tanner Norton 4.00 10.00
200 Amaurys Minier

2013 Elite Extra Edition USA Baseball 15U Game Jerseys

1 Nick Allen 2.50 6.00
2 Jordan Butler 2.50 6.00
3 Daniel Cabrera 5.00 12.00
4 Sam Ferri 2.50 6.00
5 Isaak Gutierrez 2.50 6.00
6 Brandon Martorano 2.50 6.00
7 Mickey Moniak 4.00 10.00
8 Christian Moya 2.50 6.00
9 Manuel Perez 2.50 6.00
10 Todd Peterson 2.50 6.00
11 Logan Pouelsen 2.50 6.00
12 Nick Pratto 2.50 6.00
13 Ben Ramirez 2.50 6.00
14 DJ Roberts 2.50 6.00
15 Matthew Rudick 2.50 6.00
16 Blake Sabol 2.50 6.00
17 Chase Strumpf 2.50 6.00
18 Mason Thompson 2.50 6.00
19 Andrew Vaughn 4.00 10.00

2013 Elite Extra Edition USA Baseball 15U Game Jerseys Prime

*PRIME: .5X TO 1.2X BASIC
STATED PRINT RUN 49 SER.#'d SETS

2013 Elite Extra Edition USA Baseball 15U Signatures

PRINT RUNS B/WN 24-199 COPIES PER
EXCHANGE DEADLINE 07/09/2014
1 Nick Allen/199 3.00 8.00
2 Jordan Butler/199 3.00 8.00
3 Daniel Cabrera/188 6.00 15.00
4 Sam Ferri/161 3.00 8.00
5 Isaak Gutierrez/24 3.00 8.00
6 Brandon Martorano/199 3.00 8.00
7 Mickey Moniak/199 20.00 50.00
8 Christian Moya/197 3.00 8.00
9 Manuel Perez/199 3.00 8.00
10 Todd Peterson/189 3.00 8.00
11 Logan Pouelsen/199 3.00 8.00
12 Nick Pratto/199 3.00 8.00
13 Ben Ramirez/199 3.00 8.00
14 DJ Roberts/199 3.00 8.00
15 Matthew Rudick/199 3.00 8.00
16 Blake Sabol/199 3.00 8.00
17 Chase Strumpf/199 3.00 8.00
18 Mason Thompson/179 3.00 8.00
19 Andrew Vaughn/185 15.00 40.00

2013 Elite Extra Edition USA Baseball 18U Dual Game Jersey Signatures

PRINT RUNS B/WN 2-25 COPIES PER
NO PRICING ON QTY 3 OR LESS
EXCHANGE DEADLINE 07/09/2014
1 Brady Aiken/25 20.00 50.00
2 Bryson Brigman/25
3 Joe DeMers/25 4.00 10.00
4 Alex Destino/25 4.00 10.00
5 Jack Flaherty/25 6.00 15.00
6 Marvin Gorgas/25 4.00 10.00
7 Adam Haseley/25 5.00 12.00
8 Scott Hurst/25 4.00 10.00
9 Kel Johnson/25 10.00 25.00
10 Trace Loehr/25 4.00 10.00
11 Mac Marshall/25 5.00 12.00
13 Jacob Nix/25
14 Luis Ortiz/25 4.00 10.00
16 Michael Rivera/25 4.00 10.00
17 JJ Schwarz/25
18 Justus Sheffield/25 6.00 15.00
20 Cole Tucker/25

2013 Elite Extra Edition USA Baseball 18U Game Jerseys

1 Brady Aiken 6.00 15.00
2 Bryson Brigman 2.50 6.00
3 Joe DeMers 2.50 6.00
4 Alex Destino 2.50 6.00
5 Jack Flaherty 2.50 6.00
6 Marvin Gorgas 2.50 6.00
7 Adam Haseley 2.50 6.00
8 Scott Hurst 2.50 6.00
9 Kel Johnson 3.00 8.00
10 Trace Loehr 2.50 6.00
11 Mac Marshall 2.50 6.00
12 Keaton McKinney 2.50 6.00
13 Jacob Nix 2.50 6.00
14 Luis Ortiz 2.50 6.00
15 Jakson Reetz 6.00 15.00
16 Michael Rivera 2.50 6.00
17 JJ Schwarz 2.50 6.00
18 Justus Sheffield 2.50 6.00
19 Lane Thomas 2.50 6.00
20 Cole Tucker 2.50 6.00

2013 Elite Extra Edition USA Baseball 18U Game Jerseys Prime

*PRIME: .5X TO 1.2X BASIC
STATED PRINT RUN 49 SER.#'d SETS

2013 Elite Extra Edition USA Baseball 18U Signatures

PRINT RUNS B/WN 4-299 COPIES PER
NO PRICING ON QTY 5 OR LESS
EXCHANGE DEADLINE 07/09/2014
1 Brady Aiken/299 15.00 40.00
2 Bryson Brigman/299 3.00 8.00
3 Joe DeMers/299 3.00 8.00
4 Alex Destino/299 3.00 8.00
5 Jack Flaherty/299 4.00 10.00
6 Marvin Gorgas/299 3.00 8.00
7 Adam Haseley/299 3.00 8.00
8 Scott Hurst/299 3.00 8.00
9 Kel Johnson/299 4.00 10.00
10 Trace Loehr/299 3.00 8.00
11 Mac Marshall/299 3.00 8.00
13 Jacob Nix/299 3.00 8.00
14 Luis Ortiz/299 4.00 10.00
16 Michael Rivera/299 3.00 8.00
17 JJ Schwarz/299 3.00 8.00
18 Justus Sheffield/299 10.00 25.00
20 Cole Tucker/299 3.00 8.00

2014 Elite Extra Edition

COMP.SET w/o SP's (95) 12.00 30.00
SPs RANDOMLY INSERTED
NO SP PRICING DUE TO SCARCITY
1A Jose Pujols .20 .50
2A Jhoandro Alfaro .20 .50
3A Michael Kopech .50 1.25
4A Joey Pankake .20 .50
5A Forrest Wall .30 .75
6A Dermis Garcia .30 .75
7A James Norwood .20 .50
8A Luke Dykstra .40 1.00
9A Brandon Downes .25 .60
10A Chase Vallot .20 .50
11 Logan Moon .25 .60
12 Mark Payton .20 .50
13 Jonathan Holder .20 .50
14 Reed Reilly .20 .50
15 Deivi Grullon .20 .50
16 Ryan O'Hearn .40 1.00
17 Jordan Brink .25 .60
18 Derek Campbell .20 .50
19 Cole Lankford .20 .50
20 Javi Salas .20 .50
22 John Curtiss .20 .50
23 Gareth Morgan .20 .50
24 Casey Soltis .20 .50
25 Zach Thompson .20 .50
26 Jake Reed .20 .50
27 Dan Altavilla .20 .50
28 Lane Thomas .20 .50
29 Josh Prevost .20 .50
30 Jake Jewell .20 .50
31 Corey Ray .20 .50
32 Drew Van Orden .20 .50
33 Tejay Antone .20 .50
35 Jared Walker .20 .50
36 Lane Ratliff .20 .50
38 Trace Loehr .20 .50
39 Jake Peter .20 .50
40 Kevin McAvoy .20 .50
41 Austin Gomber .25 .60
42 Ross Kivett .20 .50
43 Grant Hockin .20 .50
44 Brett Graves .20 .50
45 Greg Mahle .20 .50
46 Chris Ellis .20 .50
47 Jeff Brigham .20 .50
48 Greg Allen .20 .50
49 A.J. Vanegas .20 .50
50 Marcus Wilson .20 .50
51 Kevin Padlo .20 .50
52 Danny Diekroeger .20 .50
53 Sam Coonrod .20 .50
54 Mac James .20 .50
55 Brian Anderson .20 .50
56 Jace Fry .20 .50
57 Mark Zagunis .20 .50
58 Cy Sneed .20 .50
59 Matt Railey .20 .50
60 Sam Hentges .20 .50
61 Eric Skoglund .20 .50
62 Brock Burke .20 .50
63 Grayson Greiner .20 .50
64 Jordan Luplow .20 .50
66 Jake Yacinich .20 .50
68 Richard Prigatano .20 .50
69 Brian Schales .20 .50
70 Dustin DeMuth .20 .50
71 Sam Clay .20 .50
72 Dillon Peters .20 .50
73 Skyler Ewing .25 .60
74 Gilbert Lara .20 .50
75 Michael Suchy .20 .50
76 Dalton Pompey .30 .75
77 Zech Lemond .20 .50
78 Troy Stokes .20 .50
79 Zac Curtis .20 .50
80 Austin Fisher .20 .50
81 Brandon Leibrandt .20 .50
82 Spencer Moran .20 .50
83 Jared Robinson .20 .50
84 Austin Coley .20 .50
85 Cody Reed .20 .50
86 Jose Trevino .20 .50
87 J.P. Feyereisen .20 .50
88 J.B. Kole .20 .50
89 Max Murphy .20 .50
90 Kevin Steen .20 .50
91 Keaton Steele .20 .50
92 Max George .20 .50
93 Andy Ferguson .20 .50
94 Dean Kiekhefer .20 .50
95 Carson Sands .20 .50
96 Justin Shafer .20 .50
97 Jorge Soler .40 1.00
98 Nelson Gomez .25 .60
99 Adrian Rondon .25 .60
100 Mike Strentz .20 .50

2014 Elite Extra Edition Inspirations

*INSPIRATIONS: 1.5X TO 4X BASIC
RANDOM INSERTS IN PACKS
STATED PRINT RUN 200 SER.#'d SETS

2014 Elite Extra Edition Status Blue

*BLUE: 2.5X TO 6X BASIC
RANDOM INSERTS IN PACKS
STATED PRINT RUN 150 SER.#'d SETS

2014 Elite Extra Edition Status Emerald

*EMERALD: 6X TO 15X BASIC
RANDOM INSERTS IN PACKS
STATED PRINT RUN 150 SER.#'d SETS

2014 Elite Extra Edition Status Purple

*PURPLE: 2X TO 5X BASIC
RANDOM INSERTS IN PACKS
STATED PRINT RUN 150 SER.#'d SETS

2014 Elite Extra Edition Signature Inspirations

*INSPRIATIONS: .5X TO 1.2X FUTURES
RANDOM INSERTS IN PACKS
STATED PRINT RUN 100 SER.#'d SETS
EXCHANGE DEADLINE 7/7/2016

2014 Elite Extra Edition Signature Status Blue

*BLUE: .6X TO 1.5X FUTURES
RANDOM INSERTS IN PACKS
STATED PRINT RUN 50 SER.#'d SETS
EXCHANGE DEADLINE 7/7/2016

2014 Elite Extra Edition Signature Status Emerald

*EMERALD: .75X TO 2X FUTURES
RANDOM INSERTS IN PACKS
STATED PRINT RUN 25 SER.#'d SETS
EXCHANGE DEADLINE 7/7/2016

2014 Elite Extra Edition Signature Status Purple

*PURPLE: .6X TO 1.5X FUTURES
RANDOM INSERTS IN PACKS
STATED PRINT RUN 75 SER.#'d SETS
EXCHANGE DEADLINE 7/7/2016

2014 Elite Extra Edition Back to the Future Signatures

RANDOM INSERTS IN PACKS
PRINT RUNS B/WN 10-99 COPIES PER
NO PRICING ON QTY 15 OR LESS
EXCHANGE DEADLINE 7/7/2016
4 Kyle Zimmer/49 3.00 8.00
8 Miguel Sano/25 12.00 30.00
16 Noah Syndergaard/99 10.00 25.00
19 Jorge Alfaro/49 4.00 10.00
20 Sean Manaea/49 8.00 20.00

2014 Elite Extra Edition Elite Expectations

RANDOM INSERTS IN PACKS
1 Adrian Rondon .60 1.50
2 Michael Chavis 2.50 6.00
3 Dalton Pompey .75 2.00
4 Tyler Kolek .50 1.25
5 Carlos Rodon 1.00 2.50
6 Alex Jackson .60 1.50
7 Kyle Schwarber 2.00 5.00
8 Kyle Freeland 1.00 2.50
9 Cole Tucker .50 1.25
10 Trea Turner 1.50 4.00
11 Erick Fedde .50 1.25
12 Bradley Zimmer .75 2.00
13 Michael Conforto 1.00 2.50
14 Jack Flaherty 2.00 5.00
15 Sean Newcomb .75 2.00
16 Aaron Nola 3.00 8.00
17 Max Pentecost .50 1.25
18 Jeff Hoffman .75 2.00
19 Kodi Medeiros .50 1.25
20 Rusney Castillo .60 1.50

2014 Elite Extra Edition Elite Expectations Signatures

RANDOM INSERTS IN PACKS
STATED PRINT RUN 25 SER.#'d SETS
EXCHANGE DEADLINE 7/7/2016
1 Adrian Rondon EXCH 12.00 30.00
2 Michael Chavis 40.00 100.00
4 Tyler Kolek 6.00 15.00
5 Carlos Rodon 25.00 60.00
8 Kyle Freeland 12.00 30.00
9 Cole Tucker 6.00 15.00
14 Jack Flaherty 12.00 30.00
17 Max Pentecost 6.00 15.00
18 Jeff Hoffman 10.00 25.00
19 Kodi Medeiros 6.00 15.00

2014 Elite Extra Edition Elite Series

COMPLETE SET (20)
RANDOM INSERTS IN PACKS
1 Alex Blandino .50 1.25
2 Derek Hill .50 1.25
3 Max Pentecost .50 1.25
4 Nick Howard .50 1.25
5 Luke Weaver 1.50 4.00
6 Derek Fisher .75 2.00
7 Aaron Nola 3.00 8.00
8 Trea Turner 1.50 4.00
9 Kodi Medeiros .50 1.25
10 Casey Gillaspie .75 2.00
11 Raisel Iglesias .60 1.50
12 Luis Ortiz .50 1.25
13 Grant Holmes .50 1.25
14 Michael Gettys .60 1.50
15 Joey Pankake .50 1.25
16 Austin Cousino .50 1.25
17 Jorge Soler 1.00 2.50
18 Luis Severino .75 2.00
19 J.D. Davis .75 2.00
20 Dylan Davis .60 1.50

2014 Elite Extra Edition Elite Series Signatures

RANDOM INSERTS IN PACKS
PRINT RUNS B/WN 4-149 COPIES PER
NO PRICING ON QTY 4 OR LESS
EXCHANGE DEADLINE 7/7/2016
1 Alex Blandino/49 3.00 8.00
2 Derek Hill/49 6.00 15.00
4 Nick Howard/49 8.00 20.00
8 Trea Turner/49 20.00 50.00
9 Kodi Medeiros/149 3.00 8.00
10 Casey Gillaspie/49 5.00 12.00
13 Grant Holmes/49 12.00 30.00
14 Michael Gettys/99 4.00 10.00
15 Joey Pankake/99 3.00 8.00
16 Austin Cousino/99 8.00 20.00
19 J.D. Davis/99 5.00 12.00
20 Dylan Davis/104 12.00 30.00

2014 Elite Extra Edition Franchise Futures Signatures

RANDOM INSERTS IN PACKS
PRINT RUNS B/WN 20-799 COPIES PER
EXCHANGE DEADLINE 7/7/2016
*EMERALD/25: .75X TO 2X BASIC
1 Jose Pujols/699 3.00 8.00
2 Jhoandro Alfaro/499 3.00 8.00
3 Michael Kopech/399 12.00 30.00
4 Joey Pankake/799 3.00 8.00
5 Forrest Wall/399 5.00 12.00
6 Dermis Garcia/634 5.00 12.00
7 James Norwood/799 3.00 8.00
9 Brandon Downes/799 4.00 10.00
10 Chase Vallot/399 3.00 8.00
11 Logan Moon/799 4.00 10.00
12 Mark Payton/799 3.00 8.00
13 Jonathan Holder/799 3.00 8.00
14 Reed Reilly/799 3.00 8.00
15 Deivi Grullon/799 3.00 8.00
16 Ryan O'Hearn/799 6.00 15.00
17 Jordan Brink/799 4.00 10.00
18 Derek Campbell/799 3.00 8.00
19 Cole Lankford/799 3.00 8.00
20 Javi Salas/799 3.00 8.00
23 Gareth Morgan/299 3.00 8.00
24 Casey Soltis/799 3.00 8.00
25 Zach Thompson/799 3.00 8.00
26 Jake Reed/799 3.00 8.00
27 Dan Altavilla/799 3.00 8.00
28 Lane Thomas/799 3.00 8.00
29 Josh Prevost/699 3.00 8.00
30 Jake Jewell/699 3.00 8.00
31 Corey Ray/699 3.00 8.00
32 Drew Van Orden/699 3.00 8.00
33 Tejay Antone/699 3.00 8.00
35 Jared Walker/799 3.00 8.00
36 Lane Ratliff/799 3.00 8.00
38 Trace Loehr/799 3.00 8.00
39 Jake Peter/799 3.00 8.00
40 Kevin McAvoy/799 3.00 8.00
41 Austin Gomber/799 4.00 10.00
42 Ross Kivett/799 3.00 8.00
43 Grant Hockin/499 3.00 8.00
44 Brett Graves/220 3.00 8.00
45 Greg Mahle/799 3.00 8.00
46 Chris Ellis/599 3.00 8.00
47 Jeff Brigham/799 3.00 8.00
48 Greg Allen/799 3.00 8.00
49 A.J. Vanegas/799 3.00 8.00
50 Marcus Wilson/499 5.00 12.00
51 Kevin Padlo/699 3.00 8.00
52 Danny Diekroeger/799 3.00 8.00
53 Sam Coonrod/699 3.00 8.00
54 Mac James/799 3.00 8.00
55 Brian Anderson/649 3.00 8.00
57 Mark Zagunis/799 6.00 15.00
58 Cy Sneed/799 3.00 8.00
59 Matt Railey/649 3.00 8.00
60 Sam Hentges/799 3.00 8.00
61 Eric Skoglund/649 3.00 8.00
62 Brock Burke/799 3.00 8.00
63 Grayson Greiner/599 3.00 8.00
64 Jordan Luplow/699 3.00 8.00
68 Richard Prigatano/799 3.00 8.00
69 Brian Schales/69 3.00 8.00
70 Dustin DeMuth/799 3.00 8.00
71 Sam Clay/799 3.00 8.00
72 Dillon Peters/699 3.00 8.00
73 Skyler Ewing/799 4.00 10.00
75 Michael Suchy/599 3.00 8.00
76 Dalton Pompey/524 5.00 12.00
77 Zech Lemond/699 3.00 8.00
79 Zac Curtis/799 3.00 8.00
80 Austin Fisher/799 3.00 8.00
81 Brandon Leibrandt/799 3.00 8.00
82 Spencer Moran/799 3.00 8.00
83 Jared Robinson/799 3.00 8.00
84 Austin Coley/799 3.00 8.00
86 Jose Trevino/699 3.00 8.00
87 J.P. Feyereisen/424 3.00 8.00
88 J.B. Kole/799 3.00 8.00
89 Max Murphy/799 3.00 8.00
90 Kevin Steen/799 3.00 8.00
91 Keaton Steele/799 3.00 8.00
92 Max George/799 3.00 8.00
93 Andy Ferguson/799 3.00 8.00
94 Dean Kiekhefer/799 3.00 8.00
95 Carson Sands/120 3.00 8.00
96 Justin Shafer/799 3.00 8.00
97 Jorge Soler/149 6.00 15.00
99 Adrian Rondon/499 10.00 25.00
100 Mike Strentz/799 3.00 8.00

2014 Elite Extra Edition Historic Picks

COMPLETE SET (10) 10.00 25.00
RANDOM INSERTS IN PACKS
1 Ken Griffey Jr. 3.00 8.00
2 Chipper Jones 1.50 4.00
3 Mike Piazza 1.50 4.00
4 Luis Gonzalez 1.00 2.50
5 Dusty Baker 1.00 2.50
6 Johnny Bench 1.50 4.00
7 Nolan Ryan 5.00 12.00
8 Mark Grace 1.25 3.00
9 Jorge Posada 1.25 3.00
10 Andy Pettitte 1.25 3.00

2014 Elite Extra Edition Passing the Torch Signatures

RANDOM INSERTS IN PACKS
STATED PRINT RUN 25 SER.#'d SETS
EXCHANGE DEADLINE 7/7/2016
6 G.Lara/M.Sano EXCH 20.00 50.00
8 N.Howard/R.Stephenson 15.00 40.00
9 J.Hoffman/M.Pentecost 25.00 60.00

2014 Elite Extra Edition Prospects Inspirations

RANDOM INSERTS IN PACKS
STATED PRINT RUN 200 SER.#'d SETS
*PURPLE/150: .5X TO 1.2X BASIC
*BLUE/100: .6X TO 1.5X BASIC
*EMERALD/25: 1.2X TO 3X BASIC
1 Braxton Davidson .75 2.00
2 Tyler Kolek .75 2.00
3 Carlos Rodon 1.50 4.00
4 Kyle Schwarber 3.00 8.00
5 Derek Fisher 1.25 3.00
6 Alex Jackson 1.00 2.50
7 Aaron Nola 5.00 12.00
8 Kyle Freeland 1.50 4.00
9 Jeff Hoffman 1.25 3.00
10 Michael Conforto 1.50 4.00
11 Max Pentecost .75 2.00
12 Kodi Medeiros .75 2.00
13 Trea Turner 2.50 6.00
14 Tyler Beede 1.25 3.00
15 Sean Newcomb 1.25 3.00
16 J.D. Davis 1.50 4.00
17 Brandon Finnegan .75 2.00
18 Erick Fedde .75 2.00
19 A.J. Reed 1.50 4.00
20 Casey Gillaspie 1.25 3.00
21 Bradley Zimmer 1.25 3.00
22 Grant Holmes .75 2.00
23 Derek Hill .75 2.00
24 Cole Tucker .75 2.00
25 Matt Chapman 4.00 10.00
26 Michael Chavis 4.00 10.00
27 Luke Weaver 2.50 6.00
28 Foster Griffin .75 2.00
29 Alex Blandino .75 2.00
30 Luis Ortiz .75 2.00
31 Michael Cederoth 1.00 2.50
32 Aramis Garcia .75 2.00
33 Joe Gatto .75 2.00
35 Jacob Lindgren 1.00 2.50
36 Scott Blewett .75 2.00
37 Austin Cousino .75 2.00
38 Taylor Sparks .75 2.00
39 Ti'Quan Forbes .75 2.00
40 Cameron Varga .75 2.00
41 Eudor Garcia .75 2.00
42 Alex Verdugo 1.50 4.00
43 Spencer Turnbull .75 2.00
44 Mitch Keller 1.25 3.00
45 John Richy .75 2.00
46 Aaron Brown .75 2.00
47 Sam Travis 1.50 4.00
48 Justin Twine .75 2.00
49 Chris Oliver .75 2.00
51 Raisel Iglesias 1.00 2.50
52 Nick Howard .75 2.00
53 Sam Howard .75 2.00
54 Dylan Davis 1.00 2.50
55 Wyatt Strahan .75 2.00
56 Daniel Mengden .75 2.00
57 Auston Bousfield .75 2.00
58 Logan Webb 1.25 3.00
59 Josh Ockimey 1.25 3.00
60 Adam Ravenelle 1.00 2.50
61 Shane Zeile .75 2.00
62 Jake Cosart 1.00 2.50
63 Michael Mader .75 2.00
64 Justin Steele .75 2.00
65 Jakson Reetz .75 2.00
66 Luis Severino 1.25 3.00
67 Rusney Castillo 1.00 2.50
68 Bobby Bradley 1.00 2.50
69 Jordan Montgomery 1.50 4.00
70 Dariel Alvarez .75 2.00
71 Taylor Gushue .75 2.00
72 Jordan Schwartz .75 2.00
73 Gilbert Lara .75 2.00
74 Justus Sheffield 1.50 4.00
75 Connor Joe .75 2.00
76 Spencer Adams 1.00 2.50
77 Nick Burdi .75 2.00
78 Matt Imhof .75 2.00
79 Mitch Watrous 1.00 2.50
80 Dylan Cease 2.00 5.00
81 Jake Stinnett .75 2.00
82 Jacob Gatewood .75 2.00
83 Monte Harrison 1.25 3.00
84 Nick Wells .75 2.00
85 Milton Ramos .75 2.00
86 Wes Rogers .75 2.00
87 Mason McCullough .75 2.00
88 Chris Diaz 1.00 2.50
89 Dalier Hinojosa .75 2.00
90 Josh Morgan .75 2.00
91 Michael Gettys 1.00 2.50
92 Ryan Castellani .75 2.00
93 Victor Arano .75 2.00
94 Trey Supak .75 2.00
95 Andrew Morales .75 2.00
96 Jack Flaherty 3.00 8.00
97 Daniel Gossett .75 2.00
98 Ronnie Williams .75 2.00
99 Isan Diaz 2.00 5.00
100 Sean Reid-Foley .75 2.00

2014 Elite Extra Edition Prospects Signatures

RANDOM INSERTS IN PACKS
PRINT RUNS B/WN 34-799 COPIES PER
EXCHANGE DEADLINE 7/7/2016
1 Braxton Davidson/499 3.00 8.00
2 Tyler Kolek/299 3.00 8.00
3 Carlos Rodon/299 6.00 15.00
4 Kyle Schwarber/299 25.00 60.00
5 Derek Fisher/499 5.00 12.00
6 Alex Jackson/299 4.00 10.00
7 Aaron Nola/399 6.00 15.00
8 Kyle Freeland/399 6.00 15.00
9 Jeff Hoffman/399 4.00 10.00
10 Michael Conforto/299 EXCH 12.00 30.00
11 Max Pentecost/399 3.00 8.00
12 Kodi Medeiros/399 3.00 8.00
13 Trea Turner/449 12.00 30.00
14 Tyler Beede/399 5.00 12.00
15 Sean Newcomb/399 5.00 12.00
16 J.D. Davis/799 5.00 12.00
17 Brandon Finnegan/399 3.00 8.00
18 Erick Fedde/399 3.00 8.00
19 A.J. Reed/599 6.00 15.00
20 Casey Gillaspie/399 5.00 12.00
21 Bradley Zimmer/399 3.00 8.00
22 Grant Holmes/199 8.00 20.00
23 Derek Hill/449 3.00 8.00
24 Cole Tucker/399 3.00 8.00
25 Matt Chapman/399 10.00 25.00
26 Michael Chavis/474 20.00 50.00
27 Luke Weaver/399 10.00 25.00
28 Foster Griffin/399 3.00 8.00
29 Alex Blandino/204 3.00 8.00
30 Luis Ortiz/399 3.00 8.00
31 Michael Cederoth/699 3.00 8.00
32 Aramis Garcia/499 3.00 8.00
33 Joe Gatto/599 3.00 8.00
35 Jacob Lindgren/499 3.00 8.00
36 Scott Blewett/349 3.00 8.00
37 Austin Cousino/599 3.00 8.00
38 Taylor Sparks/499 3.00 8.00
39 Ti'Quan Forbes/499 3.00 8.00
40 Cameron Varga/399 3.00 8.00
41 Eudor Garcia/799 3.00 8.00
42 Alex Verdugo/499 6.00 15.00
43 Spencer Turnbull/499 3.00 8.00
44 Mitch Keller/499 3.00 8.00
45 John Richy/799 3.00 8.00
46 Aaron Brown/599 3.00 8.00
47 Sam Travis/524 6.00 15.00
48 Justin Twine/399 3.00 8.00
49 Chris Oliver/799 3.00 8.00
51 Raisel Iglesias/399 8.00 20.00
52 Nick Howard/399 3.00 8.00
53 Sam Howard/799 3.00 8.00
54 Dylan Davis/799 4.00 10.00
55 Wyatt Strahan/599 3.00 8.00
56 Daniel Mengden/799 3.00 8.00
57 Auston Bousfield/699 3.00 8.00
58 Logan Webb/599 5.00 12.00
59 Josh Ockimey/799 5.00 12.00
60 Adam Ravenelle/599 4.00 10.00
61 Shane Zeile/599 3.00 8.00
62 Jake Cosart/799 3.00 8.00
63 Michael Mader/799 3.00 8.00
64 Justin Steele/799 3.00 8.00
65 Jakson Reetz/599 3.00 8.00
66 Luis Severino/399 10.00 25.00
67 Rusney Castillo/699 4.00 10.00
68 Bobby Bradley/799 4.00 10.00
69 Jordan Montgomery/699 3.00 8.00
70 Dariel Alvarez/499 3.00 8.00
71 Taylor Gushue/699 3.00 8.00
72 Jordan Schwartz/799 3.00 8.00
73 Gilbert Lara/34 EXCH 20.00 50.00
74 Justus Sheffield/449 6.00 15.00
75 Connor Joe/399 3.00 8.00
76 Spencer Adams/549 4.00 10.00
77 Nick Burdi/499 3.00 8.00
78 Matt Imhof/499 3.00 8.00
79 Mitch Watrous/799 4.00 10.00
80 Dylan Cease/799 8.00 20.00
81 Jake Stinnett/499 3.00 8.00
82 Jacob Gatewood/399 3.00 8.00
83 Monte Harrison/499 5.00 12.00
84 Nick Wells/599 3.00 8.00
85 Milton Ramos/599 3.00 8.00
86 Wes Rogers/699 3.00 8.00
87 Mason McCullough/699 3.00 8.00
88 Chris Diaz/699 4.00 10.00
89 Dalier Hinojosa/699 3.00 8.00
90 Josh Morgan/599 3.00 8.00
91 Michael Gettys/499 4.00 10.00
92 Ryan Castellani/499 3.00 8.00
93 Victor Arano/799 8.00 20.00
94 Trey Supak/499 3.00 8.00
95 Andrew Morales/499 3.00 8.00
96 Jack Flaherty/399 6.00 15.00
97 Daniel Gossett/499 3.00 8.00
98 Ronnie Williams/499 3.00 8.00
99 Isan Diaz/570 8.00 20.00
100 Sean Reid-Foley/499 3.00 8.00

2014 Elite Extra Edition Prospects Signatures Red Ink
*RED INK: .75X TO 2X BASIC
RANDOM INSERTS IN PACKS
STATED PRINT RUN 25 SER.#'d SETS
EXCHANGE DEADLINE 7/7/2016
73 Gilbert Lara EXCH 20.00 50.00

2014 Elite Extra Edition Prospects Signatures Inspirations
*INSPIRATIONS: .5X TO 1.2X BASIC
RANDOM INSERTS IN PACKS
STATED PRINT RUN 100 SER.#'d SETS
EXCHANGE DEADLINE 7/7/2016
73 Gilbert Lara EXCH 10.00 25.00

2014 Elite Extra Edition Prospects Signatures Status Blue
*BLUE: .6X TO 1.5X BASIC
RANDOM INSERTS IN PACKS
STATED PRINT RUN 50 SER.#'d SETS
EXCHANGE DEADLINE 7/7/2016
73 Gilbert Lara EXCH 15.00 40.00

2014 Elite Extra Edition Prospects Signatures Status Emerald
*EMERALD: .75X TO 2X BASIC
RANDOM INSERTS IN PACKS
STATED PRINT RUN 25 SER.#'d SETS
EXCHANGE DEADLINE 7/7/2016
73 Gilbert Lara EXCH 20.00 50.00

2014 Elite Extra Edition Prospects Signatures Status Purple
*PURPLE: .6X TO 1.5X BASIC
RANDOM INSERTS IN PACKS
STATED PRINT RUN 75 SER.#'d SETS
EXCHANGE DEADLINE 7/7/2016
73 Gilbert Lara EXCH 15.00 40.00

2014 Elite Extra Edition Throwback Threads
RANDOM INSERTS IN PACKS
STATED PRINT RUN 79 SER.#'d SETS
1 Jose Abreu 12.00 30.00

2014 Elite Extra Edition USA Baseball 15U Game Jerseys
RANDOM INSERTS IN PACKS
*PRIME/25: .5X TO 1.2X BASIC
1 Blake Paugh 2.50 6.00
2 Alejandro Toral 3.00 8.00
3 Hugh Fisher 2.50 6.00
4 Steven Williams 2.00 5.00
5 John Dearth 2.00 5.00
6 Doug Nikhazy 2.00 5.00
7 Raymond Gil 2.00 5.00
8 Noah Campbell 2.00 5.00
9 Mark Vientos 3.00 8.00
10 Justin Bullock 2.50 6.00
11 Christopher Austin Martin 4.00 10.00
12 Thomas Burbank 2.50 6.00
13 Ryan Vilade 4.00 10.00
14 Kristofer Armstrong 2.00 5.00
15 Royce Lewis 5.00 12.00
16 Devin Ortiz 2.00 5.00
17 Hunter Greene 6.00 15.00
18 Jacob Blas 2.00 5.00
19 Cordell Dunn Jr. 2.00 5.00
20 Brice Turang 6.00 15.00

2014 Elite Extra Edition USA Baseball 15U Signatures
RANDOM INSERTS IN PACKS
STATED PRINT RUN 199 SER.#'d SETS
EXCHANGE DEADLINE 7/7/2016
1 Blake Paugh 4.00 10.00
2 Alejandro Toral 5.00 12.00
3 Hugh Fisher 4.00 10.00
4 Steven Williams 3.00 8.00
5 John Dearth 3.00 8.00
6 Doug Nikhazy 3.00 8.00
7 Raymond Gil 3.00 8.00
8 Noah Campbell 3.00 8.00
9 Mark Vientos 5.00 12.00
10 Justin Bullock 4.00 10.00
11 Christopher Austin Martin 15.00 40.00
12 Thomas Burbank 4.00 10.00
13 Ryan Vilade 6.00 15.00
14 Kristofer Armstrong 3.00 8.00
15 Royce Lewis 15.00 40.00
16 Devin Ortiz 3.00 8.00
17 Hunter Greene 40.00 100.00
18 Jacob Blas 3.00 8.00
19 Cordell Dunn Jr. 3.00 8.00
20 Brice Turang 10.00 25.00

2014 Elite Extra Edition USA Baseball 18U Dual Game Jersey Signatures
RANDOM INSERTS IN PACKS
STATED PRINT RUN 25 SER.#'d SETS
EXCHANGE DEADLINE 7/7/2016
6 Peter Lambert 4.00 10.00
7 Lucas Herbert 4.00 10.00
19 Max Wotell 5.00 12.00

2014 Elite Extra Edition USA Baseball 18U Game Jerseys
RANDOM INSERTS IN PACKS
*PRIME/20-25: .5X TO 1.2X BASIC
1 L.T. Tolbert 2.00 5.00
2 Austin Smith 2.00 5.00
3 Blake Rutherford 4.00 10.00
4 Nick Madrigal 4.00 10.00
5 Xavier LeGrant 2.00 5.00
6 Peter Lambert 2.00 5.00
7 Lucas Herbert 2.00 5.00
8 Ke'Bryan Hayes 3.00 8.00
9 Mitchell Hansen 2.00 5.00
10 Gray Fenter 2.00 5.00
11 Joe DeMers 2.00 5.00
12 Trenton Clark 2.50 6.00
13 Daz Cameron 4.00 10.00
14 Kale Breaux 3.00 8.00
15 Austin Bergner 2.50 6.00
16 Luken Baker 3.00 8.00
17 Kolby Allard 4.00 10.00
18 Kyle Molnar 2.00 5.00
19 Max Wotell 2.50 6.00
20 Elih Marrero 2.00 5.00

2014 Elite Extra Edition USA Baseball 18U Signatures
RANDOM INSERTS IN PACKS
STATED PRINT RUN 199 SER.#'d SETS
EXCHANGE DEADLINE 7/7/2016
1 L.T. Tolbert 3.00 8.00
2 Austin Smith 3.00 8.00
3 Blake Rutherford 6.00 15.00
5 Xavier LeGrant 3.00 8.00
6 Peter Lambert 3.00 8.00
7 Lucas Herbert 3.00 8.00
8 Ke'Bryan Hayes 5.00 12.00
9 Mitchell Hansen 3.00 8.00
10 Gray Fenter 3.00 8.00
11 Joe DeMers 3.00 8.00
12 Trenton Clark 4.00 10.00
13 Daz Cameron 15.00 40.00
14 Kale Breaux 5.00 12.00
15 Austin Bergner 4.00 10.00
16 Luken Baker 5.00 12.00
17 Kolby Allard 6.00 15.00
18 Kyle Molnar 3.00 8.00
19 Max Wotell 4.00 10.00
20 Elih Marrero 3.00 8.00

2014 Elite Extra Edition Signature Status Dual
RANDOM INSERTS IN PACKS
PRINT RUNS B/WN 10-49 COPIES PER
NO PRICING ON QTY 15 OR LESS
EXCHANGE DEADLINE 7/7/2016
5 A.Reed/D.Fisher 20.00 50.00
7 G.Greiner/J.Montgomery 15.00 40.00
8 S.Travis/D.DeMuth 10.00 25.00

2015 Elite Extra Edition
COMPLETE SET (196) 60.00 150.00
1 Yoan Moncada 1.00 2.50
2 Dansby Swanson 1.25 3.00
3 Alex Bregman .75 2.00
4 Brendan Rodgers .75 2.00
5 Dillon Tate .25 .60
6 Kyle Tucker 1.25 3.00
7 Tyler Jay .20 .50
8 Andrew Benintendi 1.00 2.50
9 Carson Fulmer .20 .50
10 Ian Happ .75 2.00
11 Cornelius Randolph .25 .60
12 Tyler Stephenson .25 .60
13 Josh Naylor .25 .60
14 Garrett Whitley .30 .75
15 Kolby Allard .20 .50
16 Trenton Clark .20 .50
17 James Kaprielian .30 .75
18 Yadier Alvarez .30 .75
19 Phil Bickford .20 .50
20 Kevin Newman .30 .75
21 Richie Martin .20 .50
22 Ashe Russell .20 .50
23 Beau Burrows .25 .60
24 Nick Plummer .25 .60
25 Walker Buehler 1.25 3.00
26 DJ Stewart .25 .60
27 Taylor Ward .30 .75
28 Mike Nikorak .20 .50
29 Mike Soroka 1.25 3.00
30 Jon Harris .25 .60
31 Kyle Holder .25 .60
32 Chris Shaw .40 1.00
33 Ke'Bryan Hayes .30 .75
34 Nolan Watson .20 .50
35 Christin Stewart .20 .50
36 Lucius Fox .30 .75
37 Ryan Mountcastle .75 2.00
38 Daz Cameron .20 .50
39 Tyler Nevin .30 .75
40 Jake Woodford .20 .50
41 Nathan Kirby .20 .50
42 Austin Riley 2.50 6.00
43 Triston McKenzie .20 .50
44 Alex Young .20 .50
45 Peter Lambert .20 .50
46 Eric Jenkins .20 .50
47 Thomas Eshelman .20 .50
48 Donnie Dewees .30 .75
49 Scott Kingery .30 .75
50 Antonio Santillan .25 .60
51 Brett Lilek .20 .50
52 Austin Smith .20 .50
53 Chris Betts .25 .60
54 Desmond Lindsay .30 .75
55 Lucas Herbert .20 .50
56 Cody Ponce .20 .50
57 Harrison Bader .30 .75
58 Jeff Degano .25 .60
59 Andrew Stevenson .20 .50
60 Juan Hillman .20 .50
61 Nick Neidert .20 .50
62 Andrew Suarez .25 .60
63 Kevin Kramer .25 .60
64 Mikey White .25 .60
65 Josh Staumont .25 .60
66 Tyler Alexander .20 .50
67 Bryce Denton .30 .75
68 Mitchell Hansen .20 .50
69 Wei-Chieh Huang .25 .60
70 Blake Perkins .20 .50
71 Jahmai Jones .25 .60
72 Brent Honeywell .30 .75
73 Austin Byler .20 .50
74 Mariano Rivera III .30 .75
75 Tyler White .25 .60
76 A.J. Minter .25 .60
77 Taylor Clarke .20 .50
78 Javier Medina .20 .50
79 Michael Matuella .20 .50
80 Riley Ferrell .20 .50
81 Travis Blankenhorn 1.00 2.50
82 Austin Rei .25 .60
83 Bryan Hudson .20 .50
84 Lucas Williams .20 .50
85 Blake Trahan .20 .50
86 Joe McCarthy .20 .50
87 Jacob Nix .20 .50
88 Brandon Lowe .30 .75
89 Max Wotell .20 .50
90 Yoan Lopez .20 .50
91 Skye Bolt .25 .60
92 Justin Maese .20 .50
93 Drew Finley .20 .50
94 Mark Mathias .25 .60
95 Braden Bishop .20 .50
96 Jalen Miller .20 .50
97 Casey Hughston .20 .50
98 Dakota Chalmers .20 .50
99 Anderson Miller .30 .75
100 Josh Hader .20 .50
101 Ketel Marte .40 1.00
102 Philip Pfeifer .20 .50
103 Garrett Cleavinger .25 .60
104 Rhett Wiseman .20 .50
105 Grayson Long .20 .50
106 Jordan Hicks .40 1.00
107 Breckin Williams .20 .50
108 Domingo Acevedo .30 .75
109 Jake Lemoine .20 .50
110 Anthony Hermelyn .20 .50
111 Trey Cabbage .20 .50
112 Tate Matheny .20 .50
113 Zack Erwin .20 .50
114 Max Schrock .20 .50
115 Kyle Martin .20 .50
116 Miles Gordon .25 .60
117 Cody Poteet .20 .50
118 Austin Allen .25 .60
119 Brandon Koch .20 .50
120 David Thompson .25 .60
121 Josh Graham .25 .60
122 Demi Orimoloye .25 .60
123 Carl Wise .25 .60
124 Jeff Hendrix .20 .50
125 Tyler Krieger .20 .50
126 Alex Robinson .20 .50
127 Thomas Szapucki .20 .50
128 Elias Diaz .20 .50
129 Ryan Ripken .25 .60
130 Jeison Guzman .25 .60
131 Raffy Ozuna .25 .60
132 Brian Gonzalez .20 .50
133 Max Povse .20 .50
134 Brent Jones .20 .50
135 Chad Sobotka .20 .50
136 Julio Urias .60 1.50
137 Domingo Leyba .20 .50
138 Jarlin Garcia .25 .60
139 Orlando Arcia .25 .60
140 Justin Garza .20 .50
141 Richard Urena .30 .75
142 Reydel Medina .20 .50
143 Aristides Aquino 10.00 25.00
144 Yairo Munoz .25 .60
145 Ozhaino Albies 2.00 5.00
146 Edmundo Sosa .25 .60
147 Daniel Carbonell .25 .60
148 Magneuris Sierra .30 .75
149 Julian Leon .20 .50
150 Jesus Lopez .20 .50
151 Manuel Margot .20 .50
152 Francisco Mejia .50 1.25
153 Jairo Labourt .20 .50
154 Marcos Molina .20 .50
155 Teoscar Hernandez .60 1.50
156 Reynaldo Lopez .25 .60
157 Austin Voth .20 .50
158 Correlle Prime .20 .50
159 Andrew Faulkner .20 .50
160 Brett Phillips .20 .50
161 John Curtiss .20 .50
162 Tanner Rainey .20 .50
163 Jorge Mateo .60 1.50
164 Omar Carrizales .25 .60
165 Jace Fry .20 .50
166 Javier Guerra .40 1.00
167 Mauricio Dubon .30 .75
168 Jhailyn Ortiz .40 1.00
169 Vladimir Guerrero Jr. 3.00 8.00
170 Jose Lopez .20 .50
171 Wander Javier .30 .75
172 Jharel Cotton .30 .75
173 Nash Walters .20 .50
174 Steven Brault .20 .50
175 Fernando Tatis Jr. 8.00 20.00
176 Preston Morrison .20 .50
177 Christian Pache .50 1.25
178 Drew Jackson .25 .60
179 Rookie Davis .20 .50
180 Gleyber Torres 3.00 8.00
181 Gregory Guerrero .30 .75
182 Leodys Taveras .60 1.50
183 Anfernee Seymour .20 .50
184 Willson Contreras 1.25 3.00
185 Micker Adolfo .25 .60
186 Cristian Olivo .30 .75
187 Derian Cruz .25 .60
188 Carlos Vargas .20 .50
189 Jonathan Arauz .20 .50
190 Antonio Senzatela .25 .60
191 Ryan Burr .20 .50
192 Victor Robles .75 2.00
193 Domingo German .30 .75
194 Rafael Devers 1.25 3.00
195 Franklin Reyes .20 .50
196 Franklin Barreto .25 .60

2015 Elite Extra Edition Aspirations Die Cut
*ASPIRATIONS: 1.2X TO 3X BASIC
RANDOM INSERTS IN PACKS
STATED PRINT RUN 200 SER.#'d SETS
75 Tyler White .75 2.00

2015 Elite Extra Edition Status Blue Die Cut
*STATUS BLUE: 2X TO 5X BASIC
RANDOM INSERTS IN PACKS
STATED PRINT RUN 100 SER.#'d SETS
75 Tyler White 1.25 3.00

2015 Elite Extra Edition Status Emerald Die Cut
*STATUS EMERALD: 3X TO 8X BASIC
RANDOM INSERTS IN PACKS
STATED PRINT RUN 25 SER.#'d SETS
75 Tyler White 2.00 5.00

2015 Elite Extra Edition Status Purple Die Cut
*STATUS PURPLE: 1.5X TO 4X BASIC
RANDOM INSERTS IN PACKS
STATED PRINT RUN 150 SER.#'d SETS
75 Tyler White 1.00 2.50

2015 Elite Extra Edition Back to the Future Signatures
RANDOM INSERTS IN PACKS
STATED ODDS B/WN 10-149 COPIES PER
NO PRICING ON QTY 15 OR LESS
1 Kyle Schwarber/25 75.00 200.00
2 Corey Seager/30 30.00 80.00
5 Robert Stephenson/49 4.00 10.00
7 Hunter Harvey/25 4.00 10.00
8 Justus Sheffield/49 8.00 20.00
9 Bobby Bradley/149 8.00 20.00
10 Trevor Story/49 15.00 40.00
11 Austin Cousino/99 4.00 10.00
12 Grant Holmes/49 5.00 12.00
14 Kyle Zimmer/25 4.00 10.00
15 Aaron Judge/25 60.00 150.00
16 Logan Moon/75 12.00 30.00
17 Casey Gillaspie/25 6.00 15.00
22 Jhoandro Alfaro/25 4.00 10.00
24 Jorge Alfaro/49 3.00 8.00
30 Nick Williams/25 12.00 30.00

2015 Elite Extra Edition Collegiate Legacy
RANDOM INSERTS IN PACKS
1 Dansby Swanson 1.50 4.00
2 Alex Bregman 1.00 2.50
3 Tyler Jay .25 .60
4 Andrew Benintendi 1.25 3.00
5 Carson Fulmer .25 .60
6 Ian Happ 1.00 2.50
7 James Kaprielian .40 1.00
8 Kevin Newman .40 1.00
9 Richie Martin .25 .60
10 Walker Buehler 1.50 4.00
11 Taylor Ward .40 1.00
12 Aaron Nola .40 1.00
13 Tyler Naquin .30 .75
14 Kyle Schwarber 1.00 2.50
15 Jeff Degano .30 .75
16 Robert Refsnyder .30 .75
17 Hunter Renfroe .40 1.00
18 DJ Stewart .30 .75
19 Christin Stewart .30 .75
20 A.J. Reed .30 .75

2015 Elite Extra Edition Collegiate Legacy Signatures
RANDOM INSERTS IN PACKS
PRINT RUNS B/WN 10-99 COPIES PER
NO PRICING ON QTY 15 OR LESS
10 Walker Buehler/49 12.00 30.00
17 Hunter Renfroe/25 6.00 15.00

2015 Elite Extra Edition Elite Status Dual Signatures
RANDOM INSERTS IN PACKS
PRINT RUNS B/WN 10-25 COPIES PER
NO PRICING ON QTY 10
11 Woodford/Plummer/25 10.00 25.00
12 Alvarez/Lopez/25 12.00 30.00
17 Bradley/Zimmer/25 12.00 30.00

2015 Elite Extra Edition Future Threads Silhoutte Signatures
RANDOM INSERTS IN PACKS
PRINT RUNS B/WN 21-149 COPIES PER
*PRIME: X TO X BASIC
1 Yoan Moncada/25 60.00 150.00
2 Kyle Schwarber/49 60.00 150.00
3 Manuel Margot/49 4.00 10.00
5 Aaron Judge/49 75.00 200.00
8 Luis Encarnacion/149 10.00 25.00
9 Jorge Alfaro/49 8.00 20.00
10 Michael Conforto/25 30.00 80.00
11 Lucas Giolito/49 10.00 25.00
12 Tyler Beede/49 15.00 40.00
13 Trea Turner/25 15.00 40.00
14 Richard Urena/99 8.00 20.00
15 Jairo Labourt/149 4.00 10.00
17 Teoscar Hernandez/99 8.00 20.00
18 Reynaldo Lopez/49 5.00 12.00
19 Lucas Sims/49 4.00 10.00
22 Tyler Glasnow/25 20.00 50.00
23 Edmundo Sosa/149 5.00 12.00
25 Raul Mondesi/49
29 Rafael Devers/125 25.00 60.00
30 Matt Olson/49 12.00 30.00
31 Nomar Mazara/49 12.00 30.00
35 Aaron Nola/49 6.00 15.00
36 Corey Seager/75 15.00 40.00
37 Miguel Sano/49 5.00 12.00
38 Robert Refsnyder/49 8.00 20.00
39 Blake Snell/49 8.00 20.00

2015 Elite Extra Edition Future Threads Silhoutte Signatures Prime
*PRIME: X TO X BASIC
RANDOM INSERTS IN PACKS
PRINT RUNS B/WN 6-25 COPIES PER
NO PRICING ON QTY 10 OR LESS

2015 Elite Extra Edition Hype
RANDOM INSERTS IN PACKS
1 Vladimir Guerrero Jr. 4.00 10.00
2 Corey Seager 1.00 2.50
3 Orlando Arcia .30 .75
4 Kyle Schwarber 1.00 2.50
5 Yadier Alvarez .40 1.00
6 Lucius Fox .40 1.00
7 Jhailyn Ortiz .50 1.25
8 Lucas Giolito .50 1.25
9 Nomar Mazara .40 1.00
10 Rafael Devers 1.50 4.00
11 Ozhaino Albies 2.50 6.00
12 Cornelius Randolph .25 .60
13 Manuel Margot .25 .60
14 Julio Urias .75 2.00
15 Luis Severino .30 .75
16 Yoan Lopez .25 .60
17 Daz Cameron .40 1.00
18 Gilbert Lara .30 .75
19 Wander Javier .40 1.00
20 Franklin Barreto .30 .75

2015 Elite Extra Edition Hype Signatures
RANDOM INSERTS IN PACKS
PRINT RUN B/WN 10-149 COPIES PER
NO PRICING ON QTY 10 OR LESS
1 Vladimir Guerrero Jr./25 200.00 500.00
2 Corey Seager/30 25.00 60.00
5 Yadier Alvarez/49 20.00 50.00
6 Lucius Fox/25 40.00 100.00
9 Nomar Mazara/25 20.00 50.00
16 Yoan Lopez/149 4.00 10.00
17 Daz Cameron/40 10.00 25.00
19 Wander Javier/49 8.00 20.00

2015 Elite Extra Edition International Pride
RANDOM INSERTS IN PACKS
1 Yoan Moncada 1.25 3.00
2 Yoan Lopez .25 .60
3 Julio Urias .75 2.00
4 Domingo Leyba .25 .60
5 Jarlin Garcia .30 .75
6 Richard Urena .40 1.00
7 Mike Soroka 1.50 4.00
8 Yairo Munoz .30 .75
9 Yadier Alvarez .40 1.00
10 Edmundo Sosa .30 .75
11 Orlando Arcia .30 .75
12 Manuel Margot .25 .60
13 Teoscar Hernandez .75 2.00
14 Reynaldo Lopez .30 .75
15 Marcos Molina .25 .60
16 Ketel Marte .50 1.25
17 Magneuris Sierra .40 1.00
18 Daniel Carbonell .30 .75
19 Ozhaino Albies 2.50 6.00
20 Vladimir Guerrero Jr. 4.00 10.00
21 Jhailyn Ortiz .50 1.25
22 Lucius Fox .40 1.00
23 Jorge Alfaro .40 1.00
24 Wei-Chieh Huang .30 .75
25 Gilbert Lara .30 .75
26 Dariel Alvarez .25 .60
27 Franklin Barreto .30 .75
28 Carlos Vargas .25 .60
29 Gleyber Torres 4.00 10.00
30 Julian Leon .25 .60

2015 Elite Extra Edition International Pride Signatures
RANDOM INSERTS IN PACKS
STATED ODDS B/WN 10-149 COPIES PER
NO PRICING ON QTY 10
2 Yoan Lopez/99 4.00 10.00
4 Domingo Leyba/99 4.00 10.00
5 Jarlin Garcia/75 5.00 12.00
7 Mike Soroka/37 12.00 30.00
10 Edmundo Sosa/99 5.00 12.00
11 Orlando Arcia/49 5.00 12.00
13 Teoscar Hernandez/99 8.00 20.00
14 Reynaldo Lopez/25 5.00 12.00
16 Ketel Marte/149 8.00 20.00
17 Magneuris Sierra/149 6.00 15.00
18 Daniel Carbonell/99 5.00 12.00
19 Ozhaino Albies/99 40.00 100.00
22 Lucius Fox/49 6.00 15.00
23 Jorge Alfaro/99 6.00 15.00
24 Wei-Chieh Huang/99 8.00 20.00
25 Gilbert Lara/99 5.00 12.00
28 Carlos Vargas/49 4.00 10.00
29 Gleyber Torres/149 40.00 100.00
30 Julian Leon/25 4.00 10.00

2015 Elite Extra Edition Passing the Torch Signatures
RANDOM INSERTS IN PACKS
PRINT RUNS B/WN 10-20 COPIES PER
NO PRICING ON QTY 10

2015 Elite Extra Edition Prospect Autographs
RANDOM INSERTS IN PACKS
1 Yoan Moncada 20.00 60.00
2 Dansby Swanson 10.00 25.00
3 Alex Bregman 10.00 25.00
4 Brendan Rodgers 6.00 15.00
5 Dillon Tate 5.00 12.00
6 Kyle Tucker 10.00 25.00
7 Tyler Jay 8.00 20.00
8 Andrew Benintendi 40.00 100.00
9 Carson Fulmer 2.50 6.00
10 Ian Happ 12.00 30.00
11 Cornelius Randolph 12.00 30.00
12 Tyler Stephenson 3.00 8.00
14 Garrett Whitley 8.00 20.00
15 Kolby Allard 2.50 6.00
16 Trenton Clark 2.50 6.00
17 James Kaprielian 4.00 10.00
18 Yadier Alvarez 6.00 15.00
20 Kevin Newman 4.00 10.00
21 Richie Martin 2.50 6.00
23 Beau Burrows 3.00 8.00
24 Nick Plummer 3.00 8.00
25 Walker Buehler 20.00 50.00
26 DJ Stewart 3.00 8.00
27 Taylor Ward 4.00 10.00
28 Mike Nikorak 2.50 6.00
29 Mike Soroka 12.00 30.00
30 Jon Harris 3.00 8.00
31 Kyle Holder 3.00 8.00
33 Ke'Bryan Hayes 4.00 10.00
34 Nolan Watson 2.50 6.00
35 Christin Stewart 3.00 8.00
36 Lucius Fox 4.00 10.00
37 Ryan Mountcastle 5.00 12.00
38 Daz Cameron 12.00 30.00
39 Tyler Nevin 4.00 10.00
40 Jake Woodford 2.50 6.00
41 Nathan Kirby 3.00 8.00
42 Austin Riley 30.00 80.00
43 Triston McKenzie 5.00 12.00
44 Alex Young 2.50 6.00
45 Peter Lambert 2.50 6.00
46 Eric Jenkins 2.50 6.00
47 Thomas Eshelman 2.50 6.00
48 Donnie Dewees 4.00 10.00
49 Scott Kingery 10.00 25.00
51 Brett Lilek 2.50 6.00
52 Austin Smith 2.50 6.00
53 Chris Betts 3.00 8.00
54 Desmond Lindsay 4.00 10.00
55 Lucas Herbert 4.00 10.00
56 Cody Ponce 2.50 6.00
57 Harrison Bader 8.00 20.00
58 Jeff Degano 3.00 8.00
59 Andrew Stevenson 2.50 6.00
60 Juan Hillman 2.50 6.00
61 Nick Neidert 2.50 6.00
62 Andrew Suarez 3.00 8.00
63 Kevin Kramer 3.00 8.00
64 Mikey White 3.00 8.00
65 Josh Staumont 3.00 8.00
66 Tyler Alexander 2.50 6.00
67 Bryce Denton 4.00 10.00
68 Mitchell Hansen 2.50 6.00
69 Wei-Chieh Huang 3.00 8.00
70 Blake Perkins 2.50 6.00
71 Jahmai Jones 3.00 8.00
72 Brent Honeywell 4.00 10.00
73 Austin Byler 2.50 6.00
74 Mariano Rivera III 4.00 10.00
75 Tyler White 3.00 8.00
76 A.J. Minter 3.00 8.00
77 Taylor Clarke 2.50 6.00
78 Javier Medina 2.50 6.00
79 Michael Matuella 3.00 8.00
80 Riley Ferrell 2.50 6.00
81 Travis Blankenhorn 6.00 15.00
82 Austin Rei 3.00 8.00
83 Bryan Hudson 2.50 6.00
84 Lucas Williams 2.50 6.00
85 Blake Trahan 2.50 6.00
86 Joe McCarthy 2.50 6.00
87 Jacob Nix 2.50 6.00
88 Brandon Lowe 6.00 15.00
89 Max Wotell 2.50 6.00
90 Yoan Lopez 2.50 6.00
91 Skye Bolt 3.00 8.00
92 Justin Maese 2.50 6.00
93 Drew Finley 2.50 6.00
95 Braden Bishop 2.50 6.00
96 Jalen Miller 2.50 6.00
97 Casey Hughston 2.50 6.00
98 Dakota Chalmers 2.50 6.00
99 Anderson Miller 4.00 10.00
100 Josh Hader 2.50 6.00
101 Ketel Marte 5.00 12.00
102 Philip Pfeifer 2.50 6.00
103 Garrett Cleavinger 3.00 8.00
104 Rhett Wiseman 2.50 6.00
105 Grayson Long 2.50 6.00
106 Jordan Hicks 10.00 25.00
107 Breckin Williams 2.50 6.00
108 Domingo Acevedo 4.00 10.00
109 Jake Lemoine 2.50 6.00
110 Anthony Hermelyn 2.50 6.00
111 Trey Cabbage 2.50 6.00
112 Tate Matheny 2.50 6.00
113 Zack Erwin 2.50 6.00
114 Max Schrock 2.50 6.00
115 Kyle Martin 2.50 6.00
116 Miles Gordon 3.00 8.00
117 Cody Poteet 2.50 6.00
118 Austin Allen 3.00 8.00
119 Brandon Koch 2.50 6.00
120 David Thompson 3.00 8.00
121 Josh Graham 3.00 8.00
122 Demi Orimoloye 3.00 8.00
123 Carl Wise 3.00 8.00
124 Jeff Hendrix 3.00 8.00
125 Tyler Krieger 2.50 6.00
126 Alex Robinson 2.50 6.00
127 Thomas Szapucki 2.50 6.00
128 Elias Diaz 2.50 6.00
129 Ryan Ripken 3.00 8.00
130 Jeison Guzman 3.00 8.00
131 Raffy Ozuna 3.00 8.00
132 Brian Gonzalez 2.50 6.00
133 Max Povse 3.00 8.00
134 Brent Jones 2.50 6.00
135 Chad Sobotka 2.50 6.00
136 Julio Urias UER 8.00 20.00
137 Domingo Leyba 2.50 6.00
138 Jarlin Garcia 3.00 8.00
140 Justin Garza 2.50 6.00
142 Reydel Medina 2.50 6.00
143 Aristides Aquino 40.00 100.00
144 Yairo Munoz 3.00 8.00
145 Ozhaino Albies 25.00 60.00
146 Edmundo Sosa 3.00 8.00
147 Daniel Carbonell 3.00 8.00
148 Magneuris Sierra 3.00 8.00
149 Julian Leon 2.50 6.00
150 Jesus Lopez 2.50 6.00
151 Manuel Margot 2.50 6.00
152 Francisco Mejia 8.00 20.00
153 Jairo Labourt 2.50 6.00
154 Marcos Molina 2.50 6.00
155 Teoscar Hernandez 5.00 12.00
157 Austin Voth 2.50 6.00
158 Correlle Prime 2.50 6.00
159 Andrew Faulkner 2.50 6.00
160 Brett Phillips 2.50 6.00
161 John Curtiss 2.50 6.00
162 Tanner Rainey 2.50 6.00
163 Jorge Mateo 6.00 15.00
164 Omar Carrizales 3.00 8.00
165 Jace Fry 2.50 6.00
166 Javier Guerra 2.50 6.00
167 Mauricio Dubon 3.00 8.00
169 Vladimir Guerrero Jr. 60.00 150.00
170 Jose Lopez 2.50 6.00
171 Wander Javier 4.00 10.00
172 Jharel Cotton 4.00 10.00
174 Steven Brault 2.50 6.00
175 Tatis Jr. Sgnd in red 125.00 300.00
176 Preston Morrison 2.50 6.00
177 Christian Pache 8.00 20.00
178 Drew Jackson 3.00 8.00
179 Rookie Davis 2.50 6.00
180 Gleyber Torres 50.00 120.00
181 Gregory Guerrero 4.00 10.00
183 Anfernee Seymour 2.50 6.00
184 Willson Contreras 8.00 20.00
185 Micker Adolfo 3.00 8.00
187 Derian Cruz 6.00 15.00
188 Carlos Vargas 2.50 6.00
189 Jonathan Arauz 3.00 8.00
190 Antonio Senzatela 3.00 8.00
191 Ryan Burr 2.50 6.00
192 Victor Robles 8.00 20.00
193 Domingo German 12.00 30.00
194 Rafael Devers 15.00 40.00
195 Franklin Reyes 2.50 6.00
196 Franklin Barreto 3.00 8.00

2015 Elite Extra Edition Prospect Autographs Aspirations Die Cut
*ASPRTNS DC: .5X TO 1.2X BASIC
RANDOM INSERTS IN PACKS
PRINT RUNS B/WN 26-100 COPIES PER
1 Yoan Moncada/100 30.00 80.00
2 Dansby Swanson/100 12.00 30.00
3 Alex Bregman/100 12.00 30.00
4 Brendan Rodgers/100 8.00 20.00
5 Dillon Tate/100 6.00 15.00
6 Kyle Tucker/100 12.00 30.00
7 Tyler Jay/100 10.00 25.00
9 Carson Fulmer/100 3.00 8.00
10 Ian Happ/100 15.00 40.00
11 Cornelius Randolph/100 15.00 40.00
12 Tyler Stephenson/100 4.00 10.00
14 Garrett Whitley/100 10.00 25.00
15 Kolby Allard/100 3.00 8.00
16 Trenton Clark/100 3.00 8.00
17 James Kaprielian/100 5.00 12.00
18 Yadier Alvarez/100 8.00 20.00

20 Kevin Newman/100 5.00 12.00
21 Richie Martin/100 3.00 8.00
23 Beau Burrows/100 4.00 10.00
24 Nick Plummer/100 4.00 10.00
25 Walker Buehler/100 25.00 60.00
26 DJ Stewart/100 4.00 10.00
27 Taylor Ward/100 5.00 12.00
28 Mike Nikorak/100 3.00 8.00
29 Mike Soroka/100 15.00 40.00
30 Jon Harris/100 4.00 10.00
31 Kyle Holder/100 4.00 10.00
33 Ke'Bryan Hayes/98 5.00 12.00
34 Nolan Watson/100 3.00 8.00
35 Christin Stewart/100 4.00 10.00
36 Lucius Fox/100 5.00 12.00
37 Ryan Mountcastle/100 6.00 15.00
38 Daz Cameron/100 15.00 40.00
39 Tyler Nevin/100 5.00 12.00
40 Jake Woodford/100 3.00 8.00
41 Nathan Kirby/100 4.00 10.00
42 Austin Riley/100 40.00 100.00
43 Triston McKenzie/100 6.00 15.00
44 Alex Young/100 3.00 8.00
45 Peter Lambert/100 3.00 8.00
46 Eric Jenkins/100 3.00 8.00
47 Thomas Eshelman/100 3.00 8.00
48 Donnie Dewees/100 5.00 12.00
49 Scott Kingery/100 12.00 30.00
51 Brett Lilek/100 3.00 8.00
52 Austin Smith/100 3.00 8.00
53 Chris Betts/100 4.00 10.00
54 Desmond Lindsay/100 5.00 12.00
55 Lucas Herbert/100 5.00 12.00
56 Cody Ponce/100 3.00 8.00
57 Harrison Bader/100 10.00 25.00
58 Jeff Degano/100 4.00 10.00
59 Andrew Stevenson/100 3.00 8.00
60 Juan Hillman/100 3.00 8.00
61 Nick Neidert/100 3.00 8.00
62 Andrew Suarez/100 4.00 10.00
63 Kevin Kramer/100 4.00 10.00
64 Mikey White/100 4.00 10.00
65 Josh Staumont/100 4.00 10.00
66 Tyler Alexander/100 3.00 8.00
67 Bryce Denton/26 5.00 12.00
68 Mitchell Hansen/100 3.00 8.00
69 Wei-Chieh Huang/100 4.00 10.00
70 Blake Perkins/100 3.00 8.00
71 Jahmai Jones/100 4.00 10.00
72 Brent Honeywell/100 5.00 12.00
73 Austin Byler/100 3.00 8.00
74 Mariano Rivera III/100 5.00 12.00
75 Tyler White/100 4.00 10.00
76 A.J. Minter/100 4.00 10.00
77 Taylor Clarke/100 3.00 8.00
78 Javier Medina/96 3.00 8.00
79 Michael Matuella/100 4.00 10.00
80 Riley Ferrell/100 3.00 8.00
81 Travis Blankenhorn/100 8.00 20.00
82 Austin Rei/100 4.00 10.00
83 Bryan Hudson/100 3.00 8.00
84 Lucas Williams/100 3.00 8.00
85 Blake Trahan/100 3.00 8.00
86 Joe McCarthy/100 3.00 8.00
87 Jacob Nix/100 3.00 8.00
88 Brandon Lowe/100 8.00 20.00
89 Max Wotell/100 3.00 8.00
90 Yoan Lopez/100 3.00 8.00
91 Skye Bolt/100 4.00 10.00
92 Justin Maese/100 3.00 8.00
93 Drew Finley/100 3.00 8.00
95 Braden Bishop/100 3.00 8.00
96 Jalen Miller/100 3.00 8.00
97 Casey Hughston/100 3.00 8.00
98 Dakota Chalmers/100 3.00 8.00
99 Anderson Miller/100 5.00 12.00
100 Josh Hader/100 3.00 8.00
101 Ketel Marte/100 6.00 15.00
102 Philip Pfeifer/100 3.00 8.00
103 Garrett Cleavinger/100 4.00 10.00
104 Rhett Wiseman/100 3.00 8.00
105 Grayson Long/100 3.00 8.00
107 Breckin Williams/100 3.00 8.00
108 Domingo Acevedo/100 5.00 12.00
109 Jake Lemoine/100 3.00 8.00
110 Anthony Hermelyn/100 3.00 8.00
111 Trey Cabbage/100 3.00 8.00
112 Tate Matheny/100 3.00 8.00
113 Zack Erwin/100 3.00 8.00
114 Max Schrock/100 3.00 8.00
115 Kyle Martin/100 3.00 8.00
116 Miles Gordon/100 4.00 10.00
117 Cody Poteet/100 3.00 8.00
118 Austin Allen/100 4.00 10.00
119 Brandon Koch/100 3.00 8.00
120 David Thompson/100 4.00 10.00
121 Josh Graham/100 4.00 10.00
122 Demi Orimoloye/100 4.00 10.00
123 Carl Wise/100 4.00 10.00
124 Jeff Hendrix/100 4.00 10.00
125 Tyler Krieger/100 3.00 8.00
126 Alex Robinson/100 3.00 8.00
127 Thomas Szapucki/100 3.00 8.00
128 Elias Diaz/100 3.00 8.00
129 Ryan Ripken/100 4.00 10.00
130 Jeison Guzman/100 4.00 10.00
131 Raffy Ozuna/100 4.00 10.00
132 Brian Gonzalez/100 3.00 8.00
133 Max Povse/100 4.00 10.00
134 Brent Jones/100 3.00 8.00
135 Chad Sobotka/100 3.00 8.00
136 Julio Urias/100 10.00 25.00
UER Wrong position
137 Domingo Leyba/100 3.00 8.00
138 Jarlin Garcia/100 4.00 10.00
140 Justin Garza/100 3.00 8.00
141 Richard Urena/34 5.00 12.00
142 Reydel Medina/100 3.00 8.00
143 Aristides Aquino/100 50.00 120.00
144 Yairo Munoz/100 4.00 10.00
145 Ozhaino Albies/100 30.00 80.00
146 Edmundo Sosa/100 4.00 10.00
147 Daniel Carbonell/100 4.00 10.00
148 Magneuris Sierra/100 4.00 10.00
149 Julian Leon/100 3.00 8.00
150 Jesus Lopez/100 3.00 8.00
151 Manuel Margot/100 3.00 8.00
152 Francisco Mejia/100 10.00 25.00
153 Jairo Labourt/100 3.00 8.00
154 Marcos Molina/100 3.00 8.00
155 Teoscar Hernandez/100 8.00 20.00
157 Austin Voth/100 3.00 8.00
158 Correlle Prime/100 3.00 8.00
159 Andrew Faulkner/100 3.00 8.00
160 Brett Phillips/100 3.00 8.00
161 John Curtiss/100 3.00 8.00
162 Tanner Rainey/100 3.00 8.00
163 Jorge Mateo/100 8.00 20.00
164 Omar Carrizales/100 4.00 10.00
165 Jace Fry/100 3.00 8.00
166 Javier Guerra/100 3.00 8.00
167 Mauricio Dubon/100 4.00 10.00
169 Vladimir Guerrero Jr./100 75.00 200.00
170 Jose Lopez/100 3.00 8.00
171 Wander Javier/100 5.00 12.00
172 Jharel Cotton/100 5.00 12.00
174 Steven Brault/100 3.00 8.00
175 Fernando Tatis Jr./100 150.00 400.00
176 Preston Morrison/100 3.00 8.00
177 Christian Pache/100 10.00 25.00
178 Drew Jackson/100 4.00 10.00
179 Rookie Davis/100 3.00 8.00
180 Gleyber Torres/100 60.00 150.00
181 Gregory Guerrero/100 5.00 12.00
183 Antenee Seymour/100 3.00 8.00
184 Willson Contreras/100 10.00 25.00
185 Micker Adolfo/100 4.00 10.00
187 Derian Cruz/100 8.00 20.00
188 Carlos Vargas/100 3.00 8.00
189 Jonathan Arauz/100 4.00 10.00
190 Antonio Senzatela/100 4.00 10.00
191 Ryan Burr/100 3.00 8.00
192 Victor Robles/100 10.00 25.00
193 Domingo German/100 15.00 40.00
194 Rafael Devers/100 20.00 50.00
195 Franklin Reyes/100 3.00 8.00
196 Franklin Barreto/100 4.00 10.00

2015 Elite Extra Edition Prospect Autographs Red Ink

*RED INK: .75X TO 2X BASIC
RANDOM INSERTS IN PACKS
STATED PRINT RUN 25 SER.#'d SETS
141 Richard Urena/25 8.00 20.00

2015 Elite Extra Edition Prospect Autographs Status Blue Die Cut

*STAT BLUE DC: .6X TO 1.5X BASIC
RANDOM INSERTS IN PACKS
STATED PRINT RUN 50 SER.#'d SETS
141 Richard Urena/50 6.00 15.00

2015 Elite Extra Edition Prospect Autographs Status Emerald Die Cut

*STAT.EMRLD DC: .75X TO 2X BASIC
RANDOM INSERTS IN PACKS
PRINT RUNS B/WN 22-25 COPIES PER
141 Richard Urena/25 8.00 20.00

2015 Elite Extra Edition Prospect Autographs Status Purple Die Cut

*STAT PRPL DC: .5X TO 1.2X BASIC
RANDOM INSERTS IN PACKS
STATED PRINT RUN 75 SER.#'d SETS
141 Richard Urena 5.00 12.00

2015 Elite Extra Edition Prospect Status

RANDOM INSERTS IN PACKS
1 Aaron Judge 4.00 10.00
2 Corey Seager 1.00 2.50
3 Luis Severino .30 .75
4 Luke Weaver .40 1.00
5 Michael Kopech .60 1.50
6 Bobby Bradley .30 .75
7 Luis Ortiz .25 .60
8 Sean Reid-Foley .30 .75
9 Dillon Tate .30 .75
10 Willy Adames .40 1.00
11 Sean Newcomb .30 .75
12 Tyler Naquin .30 .75
13 Kyle Schwarber 1.00 2.50
14 Lucas Giolito .50 1.25
15 Eudor Garcia .25 .60
16 Dariel Alvarez .25 .60
17 Yoan Moncada 1.25 3.00
18 Tyler Glasnow .30 .75
19 Trea Turner .75 2.00
20 Orlando Arcia .30 .75
21 Nomar Mazara .40 1.00
22 Franklin Barreto .30 .75
23 Austin Meadows .40 1.00
24 Bradley Zimmer .40 1.00
25 Brett Phillips .25 .60
26 Raul Mondesi
27 Robert Stephenson .25 .60
28 Brent Honeywell .40 1.00
29 Julio Urias .75 2.00
30 Jorge Mateo .75 2.00

2015 Elite Extra Edition Prospect Status Signatures

RANDOM INSERTS IN PACKS
PRINT RUNS BW/N 10-149 COPIES PER
NO PRICING ON QTY 10
1 Aaron Judge/25 60.00 150.00
2 Corey Seager/30 25.00 60.00
4 Luke Weaver/25 6.00 15.00
6 Bobby Bradley/149 8.00 20.00
7 Luis Ortiz/25 4.00 10.00
8 Sean Reid-Foley/49 5.00 12.00
12 Tyler Naquin/49 5.00 12.00
13 Kyle Schwarber/25 30.00 80.00
16 Dariel Alvarez/49 4.00 10.00
18 Tyler Glasnow/25 25.00 60.00
19 Trea Turner/49 12.00 30.00
21 Nomar Mazara/49 15.00 40.00
26 Raul Mondesi/49 6.00 15.00
27 Robert Stephenson/49 4.00 10.00
28 Brent Honeywell/25 6.00 15.00
30 Jorge Mateo/49 8.00 20.00

2015 Elite Extra Edition USA Baseball 15U Jerseys

RANDOM INSERTS IN PACKS
*PRIME/25-49: .6X TO 1.5X BASIC
1 Brandon Walker 2.50 6.00
2 Luis Tuero 2.50 6.00
3 Lyon Richardson 4.00 10.00
4 Connor Ollio 2.50 6.00
5 Zachary Morgan 2.50 6.00
6 Chris McElvain 2.50 6.00
7 Justyn-Henry Malloy 2.50 6.00
8 Jeremiah Jackson 6.00 15.00
9 Jared Hart 2.50 6.00
10 Rohan Handa 2.50 6.00
11 Ryder Green 6.00 15.00
12 Jaden Fein 3.00 8.00
13 Jonathan Childress 2.50 6.00
14 Joseph Charles 2.50 6.00
15 Triston Casas 4.00 10.00
17 C.J. Brown 2.50 6.00
18 Gabe Briones 2.50 6.00
19 Colton Bowman 2.50 6.00
20 Branden Boissiere 2.50 6.00

2015 Elite Extra Edition USA Baseball 15U Signatures

RANDOM INSERTS IN PACKS
1 Brandon Walker 3.00 8.00
2 Luis Tuero 3.00 8.00
3 Lyon Richardson 5.00 12.00
4 Connor Ollio 3.00 8.00
5 Zachary Morgan 8.00 20.00
6 Chris McElvain 3.00 8.00
7 Justyn-Henry Malloy 6.00 15.00
8 Jeremiah Jackson 8.00 20.00
9 Jared Hart 3.00 8.00
10 Rohan Handa 3.00 8.00
11 Ryder Green 8.00 20.00
12 Jaden Fein 4.00 10.00
13 Jonathan Childress 3.00 8.00
14 Joseph Charles 3.00 8.00
15 Triston Casas 12.00 30.00
16 Kendrick Calilao 4.00 10.00
17 C.J. Brown 10.00 25.00
18 Gabe Briones 8.00 20.00
19 Colton Bowman 5.00 12.00
20 Branden Boissiere 3.00 8.00

2015 Elite Extra Edition USA Baseball 18U Dual Jerseys Signatures

RANDOM INSERTS IN PACKS
STATED PRINT RUN 50 SER.#'d SETS
1 Forrest Whitley 15.00 40.00
2 Cole Stobbe 5.00 12.00
3 Blake Rutherford 10.00 25.00
4 Ryan Rolison 10.00 25.00
5 Nicholas Quintana 10.00 25.00
6 Nicholas Pratto 5.00 12.00
7 Mickey Moniak 20.00 50.00
8 Morgan McCullough 5.00 12.00
9 Reggie Lawson 5.00 12.00
10 Cooper Johnson 5.00 12.00
11 Hunter Greene 15.00 40.00
12 Kevin Gowdy 8.00 20.00
13 Braxton Garrett 8.00 20.00
14 Hagen Danner 15.00 40.00
15 Jordan Butler 5.00 12.00
16 Austin Bergner 5.00 12.00
17 William Benson 10.00 25.00
19 Ian Anderson 6.00 15.00
20 Michael Amditis 5.00 12.00

2015 Elite Extra Edition USA Baseball 18U Jerseys

RANDOM INSERTS IN PACKS
*PRIME/25-49: .6X TO 1.5X BASIC
1 Forrest Whitley 5.00 12.00
2 Cole Stobbe 2.50 6.00
3 Blake Rutherford 5.00 12.00
4 Ryan Rolison 5.00 12.00
5 Nicholas Quintana 5.00 12.00
6 Nicholas Pratto 2.50 6.00
7 Mickey Moniak 6.00 15.00
8 Morgan McCullough 2.50 6.00
9 Reggie Lawson 2.50 6.00
10 Cooper Johnson 2.50 6.00
11 Hunter Greene 6.00 15.00
12 Kevin Gowdy 4.00 10.00
13 Braxton Garrett 4.00 10.00
14 Hagen Danner 5.00 12.00
15 Jordan Butler 2.50 6.00
16 Austin Bergner 2.50 6.00
17 William Benson 3.00 8.00
18 Daniel Bakst 2.50 6.00
19 Ian Anderson 12.00 30.00
20 Michael Amditis 2.50 6.00

2015 Elite Extra Edition USA Baseball 18U Signatures

RANDOM INSERTS IN PACKS
1 Forrest Whitley 15.00 40.00
2 Cole Stobbe 3.00 8.00
3 Blake Rutherford 10.00 25.00
4 Ryan Rolison 5.00 12.00
5 Nicholas Quintana 6.00 15.00
6 Nicholas Pratto 3.00 8.00
7 Mickey Moniak 20.00 50.00
8 Morgan McCullough 3.00 8.00
9 Reggie Lawson 3.00 8.00
10 Cooper Johnson 3.00 8.00
11 Hunter Greene 10.00 25.00
12 Kevin Gowdy 6.00 15.00
13 Braxton Garrett 5.00 12.00
14 Hagen Danner 15.00 40.00
15 Jordan Butler 3.00 8.00
16 Austin Bergner 3.00 8.00
17 William Benson 15.00 40.00
18 Daniel Bakst 6.00 15.00
19 Ian Anderson 6.00 15.00
20 Michael Amditis 3.00 8.00

2016 Elite Extra Edition

STATED PRINT RUN 999 SER.#'d SETS
1 Tyler O'Neill .50 1.25
2 Nick Senzel 5.00 12.00
3 Ian Anderson 1.00 2.50
4 Riley Pint .40 1.00
5 Corey Ray .60 1.50
6 A.J. Puk .60 1.50
7 Braxton Garrett .50 1.25
8 Cal Quantrill .40 1.00
9 Matt Manning .60 1.50
10 Nash Walters .40 1.00
11 Kyle Lewis 8.00 20.00
12 Jason Groome .75 2.00
13 Joshua Lowe .40 1.00
14 Will Benson .60 1.50
15 Alex Kirilloff 4.00 10.00
16 Matt Thaiss .40 1.00
17 Brandon Waddell .40 1.00
18 Bryson Brigman .40 1.00
19 Justin Dunn .40 1.00
20 Gavin Lux 4.00 10.00
21 T.J. Zeuch .50 1.25
22 Will Craig .40 1.00
23 Delvin Perez 1.25 3.00
24 Matt Strahm .60 1.50
25 Eric Lauer .50 1.25
26 Zack Burdi .50 1.25
27 Cody Sedlock .60 1.50
28 Carter Kieboom 2.50 6.00
29 Dane Dunning .50 1.25
30 Cole Ragans .50 1.25
31 Anthony Kay .40 1.00
32 Will Smith 3.00 8.00
33 Dylan Carlson 5.00 12.00
34 Dakota Hudson .60 1.50
35 Taylor Trammell 3.00 8.00
36 Jordan Sheffield .40 1.00
37 Daulton Jefferies .50 1.25
38 Robert Tyler .40 1.00
39 Anfernee Grier .50 1.25
40 Joey Wentz .60 1.50
41 Skylar Szynski .40 1.00
42 German Marquez .60 1.50
43 Chris Okey .40 1.00
44 Anderson Espinoza .40 1.00
45 Alex Reyes .50 1.25
46 Drew Harrington .40 1.00
48 Buddy Reed .40 1.00
49 Alec Hansen .50 1.25
50 Joe Rizzo .40 1.00
51 C.J. Chatham .50 1.25
52 Andrew Yerzy .40 1.00
53 Ryan Boldt .50 1.25
54 Andrew Yerzy .40 1.00
55 Nolan Jones .60 1.50
56 Ben Rortvedt .50 1.25
57 J.B. Woodman .60 1.50
58 Sheldon Neuse .50 1.25
59 Bryan Reynolds 1.25 3.00
60 Matt Thaiss .40 1.00
61 Ronnie Dawson .40 1.00
62 Nick Solak 1.25 3.00
63 Shawn Morimando
64 Peter Alonso 8.00 20.00
65 T.J. Zeuch .50 1.25
66 Bobby Dalbec 1.50 4.00
67 A.J. Puckett .50 1.25
68 Travis MacGregor .50 1.25
69 Cody Sedlock .60 1.50
70 Connor Jones .50 1.25
71 Willie Calhoun 1.25 3.00
72 Logan Ice .40 1.00
73 Jose Miranda .50 1.25
74 Braden Webb .40 1.00
75 Mario Feliciano .50 1.25
76 Jake Rogers 2.00 5.00
77 Luis Arraez 1.50 4.00
78 TJ Friedl .75 2.00
79 Raimel Tapia .50 1.25
80 Ryan Hendrix .40 1.00
81 Chris Paddack 1.00 2.50
82 Luis Urias .75 2.00
83 J.T. Riddle .40 1.00
84 Mitchell White .75 2.00
85 Jake Fraley .50 1.25
86 Cole Stobbe .40 1.00
87 Corbin Burnes .60 1.50
88 Andy Ibanez .60 1.50
89 Andrew Knapp .40 1.00
90 Payton Henry .40 1.00
91 Chris Rodriguez .40 1.00
92 Thomas Jones .40 1.00
93 Mason Thompson .40 1.00
94 Matthias Dietz .40 1.00
95 Nick Gordon .40 1.00
96 Shaun Anderson .50 1.25
97 Jon Duplantier .40 1.00
98 Austin Franklin .40 1.00
99 Tim Tebow 10.00 25.00
100 Bernardo Flores .40 1.00
101 Zack Trageton .50 1.25
102 Jesus Luzardo 2.50 6.00
103 Heath Quinn .75 2.00
104 Nolan Williams .40 1.00
105 Jace Vines .50 1.25
106 Nolan Martinez .50 1.25
107 Kole Enright .50 1.25
108 Matt Krook .40 1.00
109 Dustin May 2.50 6.00
110 Zach Jackson .40 1.00
111 Khalil Lee .60 1.50
112 Mitchell Kranson .60 1.50
113 Stephen Alemais .60 1.50
114 Zac Gallen .40 1.00
115 Hudson Potts .50 1.25
116 Josh Rogers .60 1.50
117 Andrew Velazquez .40 1.00
118 Clayton Blackburn .40 1.00
119 Francis Martes .50 1.25
120 David Martinelli .40 1.00
121 Adalberto Mejia .40 1.00
122 Tyler Eppler .40 1.00
123 Mike Gerber .40 1.00
124 Mark Mathias .40 1.00
125 Drew Smith .40 1.00
126 J.D. Busfield .40 1.00
127 Scott Heineman .40 1.00
128 Kyle Garlick .40 1.00
129 Eloy Jimenez 1.50 4.00
130 Nicholas Lopez .60 1.50
131 Stefan Crichton .50 1.25
132 Guillermo Heredia .50 1.25
133 Nick Longhi .40 1.00
134 Hoy Jun Park .50 1.25
135 Raudy Read .40 1.00
136 Kelvin Gutierrez .40 1.00
137 Hunter Wood .40 1.00
138 Trey Mancini 1.25 3.00
139 Austen Williams .40 1.00
141 Hunter Cole .40 1.00
142 Yandy Diaz .75 2.00
143 Lazaro Armenteros 1.00 2.50
144 Brandon Marsh 1.00 2.50
145 Jason Jester .40 1.00
146 Kade Scivicque .40 1.00
147 Forrest Whitley 3.00 8.00
148 Kevin Maitan 1.50 4.00
149 Blake Rutherford 1.50 4.00
150 Alex Speas .50 1.25
151 Nate Griep .40 1.00
152 Zack Collins .50 1.25
153 Kyle Muller .50 1.25
154 Jose Azocar .40 1.00
155 Yu-Cheng Chang 1.00 2.50
156 Albert Abreu .50 1.25
157 Jimmy Herget .40 1.00
158 Matt Gage .50 1.25
159 George Bryner Bell .40 1.00
160 Kyle Funkhouser .50 1.25
161 Connor Walsh .40 1.00
162 Jordan Balazovic .75 2.00
163 Eric Stout .40 1.00
164 Matt Cooper .40 1.00
165 Juan Soto 8.00 20.00
166 Miguelangel Sierra .75 2.00
167 Josh VanMeter .50 1.25
168 Max Kranick .60 1.50
169 Jake Newberry .40 1.00
170 Brody Koerner .40 1.00
171 Phil Maton .40 1.00
172 Braulio Ortiz .40 1.00
173 Reggie Lawson .40 1.00
174 Chih-Wei Hu .50 1.25
176 Willi Castro .40 1.00
177 Isaiah White .40 1.00
178 Nestor Cortes .40 1.00
179 Jeremy Martinez 1.00 2.50
180 Dietrich Enns .50 1.25
181 Rhys Hoskins 1.50 4.00
182 Junior Fernandez .60 1.50
183 Dawel Lugo .40 1.00
184 Steven Duggar .40 1.00

2016 Elite Extra Edition Aspirations Blue

*ASP BLUE: .75X TO 2X BASIC
STATED PRINT RUN 75 SER.#'d SETS

2016 Elite Extra Edition Aspirations Purple

*ASP PRPLE: .6X TO 1.5X BASIC
STATED PRINT RUN 200 SER.#'d SETS

2016 Elite Extra Edition Aspirations Tie Dye

*ASP TIE DYE: 1.2X TO 3X BASIC
STATED PRINT RUN 25 SER.#'d SETS

2016 Elite Extra Edition Status Black Die Cut

*STAT.BLK DC: .75X TO 2X BASIC
STATED PRINT RUN 99 SER.#'d SETS

2016 Elite Extra Edition Status Emerald Die Cut

*STAT.EMRLD.DC: 1X TO 2.5X BASIC
STATED PRINT RUN 49 SER.#'d SETS

2016 Elite Extra Edition Status Red Die Cut

*STAT.RED DC: .75X TO 2X BASIC
STATED PRINT RUN 99 SER.#'d SETS

2016 Elite Extra Edition Autographs

RANDOM INSERTS IN PACKS
PRINTING PLATES RANDOMLY INSERTED
PLATE PRINT RUN 1 SET PER COLOR
NO PLATE PRICING DUE TO SCARCITY
1 Tyler O'Neill 3.00 8.00
2 Nick Senzel 8.00 20.00
3 Ian Anderson 15.00 40.00
4 Riley Pint 2.50 6.00
6 A.J. Puk 4.00 10.00
7 Braxton Garrett 3.00 8.00
8 Cal Quantrill 2.50 6.00
9 Matt Manning 4.00 10.00
10 Nash Walters 2.50 6.00
12 Jason Groome 5.00 12.00
13 Joshua Lowe 2.50 6.00
14 Will Benson 4.00 10.00
15 Alex Kirilloff 8.00 20.00
16 Matt Thaiss 3.00 8.00
17 Brandon Waddell 2.50 6.00
18 Bryson Brigman 2.50 6.00
19 Justin Dunn 2.50 6.00
21 T.J. Zeuch 3.00 8.00
22 Will Craig 2.50 6.00
24 Matt Strahm 4.00 10.00
25 Eric Lauer 3.00 8.00
26 Zack Burdi 3.00 8.00
27 Cody Sedlock 4.00 10.00
28 Carter Kieboom 12.00 30.00
29 Dane Dunning 3.00 8.00
30 Cole Ragans 3.00 8.00
31 Anthony Kay 2.50 6.00
32 Will Smith 12.00 30.00
33 Dylan Carlson 20.00 50.00
34 Dakota Hudson 4.00 10.00
35 Taylor Trammell 10.00 25.00
36 Jordan Sheffield 2.50 6.00
37 Daulton Jefferies 3.00 8.00
38 Robert Tyler 2.50 6.00
39 Anfernee Grier 3.00 8.00
40 Joey Wentz 4.00 10.00
41 Skylar Szynski 2.50 6.00
42 German Marquez 4.00 10.00
43 Chris Okey 2.50 6.00
44 Anderson Espinoza 2.50 6.00
45 Alex Reyes 6.00 15.00
46 Drew Harrington 2.50 6.00
48 Buddy Reed 2.50 6.00
49 Alec Hansen 5.00 12.00
50 Joe Rizzo 2.50 6.00
51 C.J. Chatham 3.00 8.00
52 Andrew Yerzy 2.50 6.00
53 Ryan Boldt 3.00 8.00
54 Andrew Yerzy 2.50 6.00
55 Nolan Jones 4.00 10.00
56 Ben Rortvedt 3.00 8.00
57 J.B. Woodman 4.00 10.00
59 Bryan Reynolds 5.00 12.00
60 Matt Thaiss 3.00 8.00
61 Ronnie Dawson 2.50 6.00
62 Nick Solak 3.00 8.00
63 Shawn Morimando
64 Peter Alonso 25.00 60.00
65 T.J. Zeuch 3.00 8.00
66 Bobby Dalbec 8.00 20.00
67 A.J. Puckett 3.00 8.00
68 Travis MacGregor 3.00 8.00
69 Cody Sedlock 4.00 10.00
70 Connor Jones 3.00 8.00
72 Logan Ice 2.50 6.00
73 Jose Miranda 3.00 8.00
74 Braden Webb 2.50 6.00
75 Mario Feliciano 3.00 8.00
76 Jake Rogers 8.00 20.00
77 Luis Arraez 6.00 15.00
78 TJ Friedl 5.00 12.00
79 Raimel Tapia 3.00 8.00
80 Ryan Hendrix 2.50 6.00
82 Luis Urias 8.00 20.00
83 J.T. Riddle 2.50 6.00
84 Mitchell White 5.00 12.00
85 Jake Fraley 3.00 8.00
86 Cole Stobbe 2.50 6.00
87 Corbin Burnes 4.00 10.00
88 Andy Ibanez 5.00 12.00
89 Andrew Knapp 2.50 6.00
90 Payton Henry 2.50 6.00
91 Chris Rodriguez 2.50 6.00
92 Thomas Jones 2.50 6.00
93 Mason Thompson 2.50 6.00
95 Nick Gordon 2.50 6.00
96 Shaun Anderson 3.00 8.00
97 Jon Duplantier 2.50 6.00
98 Austin Franklin 2.50 6.00
99 Tim Tebow 40.00 100.00
100 Bernardo Flores 2.50 6.00
101 Zack Trageton 3.00 8.00
102 Jesus Luzardo 6.00 15.00
103 Heath Quinn 3.00 8.00
104 Nolan Williams 2.50 6.00
105 Jace Vines 3.00 8.00
106 Nolan Martinez 3.00 8.00
107 Kole Enright 3.00 8.00
108 Matt Krook 4.00 10.00
109 Dustin May 10.00 25.00
110 Zach Jackson 2.50 6.00
111 Khalil Lee 4.00 10.00
112 Mitchell Kranson 2.50 6.00
113 Stephen Alemais 4.00 10.00
114 Zac Gallen 2.50 6.00
115 Hudson Potts 3.00 8.00
116 Josh Rogers 4.00 10.00
117 Andrew Velazquez 2.50 6.00
118 Clayton Blackburn 2.50 6.00
119 Francis Martes 3.00 8.00
120 David Martinelli 2.50 6.00
122 Tyler Eppler 2.50 6.00
123 Mike Gerber 2.50 6.00
124 Mark Mathias 2.50 6.00
125 Drew Smith 2.50 6.00
126 J.D. Busfield 2.50 6.00
127 Scott Heineman 2.50 6.00
128 Kyle Garlick 2.50 6.00
129 Eloy Jimenez 15.00 40.00
131 Stefan Crichton 3.00 8.00
133 Nick Longhi 2.50 6.00
134 Hoy Jun Park 3.00 8.00
135 Raudy Read 2.50 6.00
136 Kelvin Gutierrez 2.50 6.00
137 Hunter Wood 2.50 6.00
138 Trey Mancini 5.00 12.00
139 Austen Williams 2.50 6.00
141 Hunter Cole 2.50 6.00
143 Lazaro Armenteros 6.00 15.00
144 Brandon Marsh 6.00 15.00
145 Jason Jester 2.50 6.00
146 Kade Scivicque 2.50 6.00
147 Forrest Whitley 15.00 40.00
148 Kevin Maitan 5.00 12.00
150 Alex Speas 3.00 8.00
151 Nate Griep 2.50 6.00
152 Zack Collins 3.00 8.00
153 Kyle Muller 3.00 8.00
154 Jose Azocar 2.50 6.00
157 Jimmy Herget 2.50 6.00
158 Matt Gage 3.00 8.00
159 George Bryner Bell 2.50 6.00
161 Connor Walsh 2.50 6.00
163 Eric Stout 2.50 6.00
164 Matt Cooper 2.50 6.00
166 Miguelangel Sierra 5.00 12.00
167 Josh VanMeter 3.00 8.00
168 Max Kranick 4.00 10.00
169 Jake Newberry 2.50 6.00
170 Brody Koerner 2.50 6.00
171 Phil Maton 2.50 6.00
172 Braulio Ortiz 2.50 6.00
173 Reggie Lawson 2.50 6.00
174 Chih-Wei Hu 3.00 8.00
177 Isaiah White 2.50 6.00
178 Nestor Cortes 2.50 6.00
179 Jeremy Martinez 3.00 8.00
180 Dietrich Enns 3.00 8.00
181 Rhys Hoskins 25.00 60.00
182 Junior Fernandez 4.00 10.00
183 Dawel Lugo 2.50 6.00
184 Steven Duggar 2.50 6.00

2016 Elite Extra Edition Autographs Aspirations Blue

*ASP BLUE/50: .6X TO 1.5X BASIC
*ASP BLUE/25: .75X TO 2X BASIC
RANDOM INSERTS IN PACKS
PRINT RUNS B/WN 10-50 COPIES PER
NO PRICING ON QTY 15 OR LESS

2016 Elite Extra Edition Autographs Aspirations Purple

*ASP PRPLE/100: .6X TO 1.5X BASIC
*ASP PRPLE/25: .75X TO 2X BASIC
RANDOM INSERTS IN PACKS
PRINT RUNS B/WN 15-100 COPIES PER
NO PRICING ON QTY 15

2016 Elite Extra Edition Autographs Charcoal

*CHARCOAL/25: .75X TO 2X BASIC
RANDOM INSERTS IN PACKS
PRINT RUNS BW/N 10-25 COPIES PER
NO PRICING ON QTY 10

2016 Elite Extra Edition Autographs Status Emerald Die Cut

*STAT.EMRLD.DC/25: .75X TO 2X BASIC
RANDOM INSERTS IN PACKS
PRINT RUNS B/WN 5-25 COPIES PER
NO PRICING ON QTY 10 OR LESS

2016 Elite Extra Edition Autographs Status Red Die Cut

*STAT.RED DC/75: .6X TO 1.5X BASIC
*STAT.RED DC/25: .75X TO 2X BASIC
RANDOM INSERTS IN PACKS
PRINT RUNS B/WN 10-75 COPIES PER
NO PRICING ON QTY 15 OR LESS

2016 Elite Extra Edition College Ticket Autographs

RANDOM INSERTS IN PACKS
*CRACKED ICE/24: .6X TO 1.5X BASIC
PRINTING PLATES RANDOMLY INSERTED
PLATE PRINT RUN 1 SET PER COLOR
BLACK-CYAN-MAGENTA-YELLOW ISSUED
NO PLATE PRICING DUE TO SCARCITY
1 Nick Senzel 20.00 50.00

3 A.J. Puk 10.00 25.00
4 Cal Quantrill 2.50 6.00
5 Daulton Jefferies 3.00 8.00
6 Robert Tyler 2.50 6.00
7 Zack Collins 3.00 8.00
9 Will Craig 2.50 6.00
10 T.J. Zeuch 3.00 8.00
11 Eric Lauer 6.00 15.00
12 Zack Burdi 3.00 8.00
13 Cody Sedlock 4.00 10.00
14 Dakota Hudson 4.00 10.00
15 Rhys Hoskins 25.00 60.00
16 Jordan Sheffield 2.50 6.00
18 Logan Shore 5.00 12.00
19 Buddy Reed 10.00 25.00
20 Alec Hansen 3.00 8.00
21 Ryan Boldt 3.00 8.00
23 Bryan Reynolds 5.00 12.00
24 Nick Solak 5.00 12.00
25 Connor Jones 3.00 8.00
26 Logan Ice 2.50 6.00
27 Kade Scivicque 2.50 6.00
28 Justin Dunn 2.50 6.00
29 Will Smith
30 Jason Jester 2.50 6.00
31 Dietrich Enns 3.00 8.00
32 C.J. Chatham 6.00 15.00
33 Connor Walsh 2.50 6.00
34 J.B. Woodman 4.00 10.00
35 Ronnie Dawson 2.50 6.00
36 Peter Alonso 75.00 200.00

2016 Elite Extra Edition Dual Materials

RANDOM INSERTS IN PACKS
STATED PRINT RUN 299 SER.#'d SETS
*SILVER/149: .4X TO 1X BASIC
*HOLO GLD/99: .5X TO 1.2X BASIC
*HOLO SLVR/49: .5X TO 1.2X BASIC
*PURPLE/25: .6X TO 1.5X BASIC
1 Jake Fraley 3.00 8.00
2 Cole Stobbe 2.50 6.00
3 Braden Shipley 2.50 6.00
4 Drew Harrington 2.50 6.00
5 Aaron Knapp 2.50 6.00
6 Braden Webb 2.50 6.00
7 Chris Rodriguez 2.50 6.00
8 Thomas Jones 2.50 6.00
9 Mason Thompson 2.50 6.00
10 Hoy Jun Park 3.00 8.00
11 Bryson Brigman 2.50 6.00
12 Shaun Anderson 3.00 8.00
13 Jon Duplantier 2.50 6.00
14 Austin Franklin 2.50 6.00
15 Hunter Cole 2.50 6.00
16 Nick Longhi 2.50 6.00
17 Jordan Balazovic 5.00 12.00
18 Jesus Luzardo 6.00 15.00
19 Heath Quinn 4.00 10.00
20 Nolan Williams 2.50 6.00

2016 Elite Extra Edition Future Threads Silhouette Autographs

RANDOM INSERTS IN PACKS
PRINT RUNS B/WN 115-299 COPIES PER
12 J.T. Riddle/299 3.00 8.00
25 Jake Fraley/149 4.00 10.00
26 Cole Stobbe/299 3.00 8.00
28 Drew Harrington/199 3.00 8.00
29 Aaron Knapp/299 3.00 8.00
31 Chris Rodriguez/199 3.00 8.00
35 Bryson Brigman/299 3.00 8.00
39 Hunter Cole/149 3.00 8.00
48 Matt Krook/115 3.00 8.00
49 Dustin May/199 12.00 30.00

2016 Elite Extra Edition Future Threads Silhouette Autographs Purple

*PURPLE/25: .6X TO 1.5X SILVER
RANDOM INSERTS IN PACKS
PRINT RUNS B/WN 10-25 COPIES PER
NO PRICING ON QTY 15 OR LESS
2 Yoan Moncada/25 15.00 40.00
5 Alex Reyes/25 15.00 40.00
14 Clint Frazier/25 15.00 40.00
16 Josh Bell/25 20.00 50.00
20 Carson Fulmer/25 6.00 15.00
21 David Dahl/25 8.00 20.00
22 Matt Olson/25 15.00 40.00
45 Sean Newcomb/25 8.00 20.00

2016 Elite Extra Edition Future Threads Silhouette Autographs Red

*RED/49: .5X TO 1.2X SILVER
*RED/25: .6X TO 1.5X SILVER
RANDOM INSERTS IN PACKS
PRINT RUNS B/WN 15-49 COPIES PER
NO PRICING ON QTY 15
3 Dansby Swanson/25 20.00 50.00
4 Tyler Glasnow/25
5 Alex Reyes/49 12.00 30.00
7 Andrew Benintendi/49 75.00 200.00
14 Clint Frazier/49 12.00 30.00
17 Alex Bregman/25 40.00 100.00
18 Aaron Judge/49 75.00 200.00
20 Carson Fulmer/49 5.00 12.00
21 David Dahl/49 6.00 15.00
22 Matt Olson/49 12.00 30.00
45 Sean Newcomb/49 6.00 15.00

2016 Elite Extra Edition Future Threads Silhouette Autographs Silver

RANDOM INSERTS IN PACKS
STATED PRINT RUN 99 SER.#'d SETS
1 Orlando Arcia 5.00 12.00
6 Rafael Devers 15.00 40.00
8 Manuel Margot 4.00 10.00
9 Clayton Blackburn 4.00 10.00
10 Francis Martes 5.00 12.00
11 Adalberto Mejia 4.00 10.00
12 J.T. Riddle 4.00 10.00
13 Mike Gerber 4.00 10.00
15 Raimel Tapia 5.00 12.00
23 Matt Chapman 6.00 15.00
24 Brett Phillips 4.00 10.00
25 Jake Fraley 5.00 12.00
26 Cole Stobbe 4.00 10.00
28 Drew Harrington 4.00 10.00
29 Aaron Knapp 4.00 10.00
31 Chris Rodriguez 4.00 10.00
32 Thomas Jones 4.00 10.00
33 Mason Thompson 4.00 10.00
34 Hoy Jun Park 5.00 12.00
35 Bryson Brigman 4.00 10.00
36 Shaun Anderson 5.00 12.00
37 Jon Duplantier 4.00 10.00
38 Austin Franklin 4.00 10.00
39 Hunter Cole 4.00 10.00
40 Nick Longhi 4.00 10.00
41 Jordan Balazovic 8.00 20.00
42 Jesus Luzardo 10.00 25.00
43 Heath Quinn 8.00 20.00
44 Nolan Williams 4.00 10.00
46 Nolan Martinez 5.00 12.00
47 Kole Enright 5.00 12.00
48 Matt Krook 4.00 10.00
49 Dustin May 15.00 40.00
50 Zach Jackson 4.00 10.00
51 Khalil Lee 6.00 15.00
52 Mitchell Kranson 4.00 10.00
53 Stephen Alemais 6.00 15.00
55 Josh Rogers 6.00 15.00
56 Andrew Velazquez 4.00 10.00

2016 Elite Extra Edition Future Threads Silhouettes Duals

RANDOM INSERTS IN PACKS
PRINT RUNS B/WN 125-299 COPIES PER
1 Devers/Moncada/125 5.00 12.00
4 Chapman/Olson/299 5.00 12.00
6 Fulmer/Glasnow/199 3.00 8.00
7 Dahl/Tapia/299 3.00 8.00
8 Martes/Newcomb/299 3.00 8.00
10 Rogers/Martinez/299 4.00 10.00
11 Margot/Thompson/299 2.50 6.00
12 Mejia/Blackburn/299 2.50 6.00
14 Manuel Margot/299 2.50 6.00
15 Brett Phillips/299 2.50 6.00
16 Reyes/Glasnow/299 3.00 8.00
18 Frazier/Gerber/299 10.00 25.00

2016 Elite Extra Edition Future Threads Silhouettes Duals Holo Gold

*HOLO GOLD: .5X TO 1.2X BASIC
5 Benintendi/Frazier 8.00 20.00
9 Phillips/Arcia 4.00 10.00

2016 Elite Extra Edition Future Threads Silhouettes Duals Holo Silver

*HOLO SILVER/49: .5X TO 1.2X BASIC
*HOLO SILVER/25: .6X TO 1.5X BASIC
RANDOM INSERTS IN PACKS
PRINT RUNS B/WN 25-49 COPIES PER
2 Bregman/Swanson/49 10.00 25.00
3 Judge/Mateo/49 10.00 25.00
5 Benintendi/Frazier/49 8.00 20.00
9 Phillips/Arcia/49 4.00 10.00
13 Dansby Swanson/25 10.00 25.00
17 Bell/Glasnow/49 6.00 15.00
19 Moncada/Benintendi/49 12.00 30.00
20 Arcia/Mateo/49 4.00 10.00

2016 Elite Extra Edition Future Threads Silhouettes Duals Purple

*PURPLE: .6X TO 1.5X BASIC
RANDOM INSERTS IN PACKS
PRINT RUNS B/WN 10-25 COPIES PER
NO PRICING ON QTY 15 OR LESS
2 Bregman/Swanson/25 12.00 30.00
3 Judge/Mateo/25 12.00 30.00
5 Benintendi/Frazier/25 10.00 25.00
9 Phillips/Arcia/25 5.00 12.00
17 Bell/Glasnow/25 8.00 20.00
20 Arcia/Mateo/25 5.00 12.00

2016 Elite Extra Edition Future Threads Silhouettes Duals Silver

*HOLO SILVER/149: .4X TO 1X BASIC
*HOLO SILVER/75: .5X TO 1.2X BASIC
RANDOM INSERTS IN PACKS
PRINT RUNS B/WN 75-149 COPIES PER
5 Benintendi/Frazier/149 6.00 15.00
9 Phillips/Arcia/149 3.00 8.00

2016 Elite Extra Edition Quad Materials

RANDOM INSERTS IN PACKS
STATED PRINT RUN 299 SER.#'d SETS
7 Manuel Margot 2.50 6.00
8 Clayton Blackburn 2.50 6.00
11 Mike Gerber 2.50 6.00
12 Clint Frazier 5.00 12.00
13 Raimel Tapia 3.00 8.00
15 Aaron Judge 15.00 40.00
19 Matt Olson 5.00 12.00

2016 Elite Extra Edition Quad Materials Holo Gold

*HOLO GLD/149: .5X TO 1.2X BASIC
RANDOM INSERTS IN PACKS
PRINT RUNS B/WN 49-99 COPIES PER
1 Orlando Arcia/99 4.00 10.00
2 Yoan Moncada/99 6.00 15.00
3 Tyler Glasnow/99 4.00 10.00
4 Alex Reyes/99 4.00 10.00
5 Rafael Devers/75 3.00 8.00
9 Francis Martes/99 4.00 10.00
10 Adalberto Mejia/99 3.00 8.00
14 Alex Bregman/99 8.00 20.00
16 Jorge Mateo/49 3.00 8.00
17 Carson Fulmer/99 3.00 8.00
18 David Dahl/99 4.00 10.00
20 Brett Phillips/99 3.00 8.00

2016 Elite Extra Edition Quad Materials Holo Silver

*HOLO SILVER/49: .5X TO 1.2X BASIC
*HOLO SILVER/25: .6X TO 1.5X BASIC
RANDOM INSERTS IN PACKS
PRINT RUNS B/WN 25-49 COPIES PER
1 Orlando Arcia/49 4.00 10.00
2 Yoan Moncada/49 6.00 15.00
3 Tyler Glasnow/49 4.00 10.00
4 Alex Reyes/49 4.00 10.00
5 Rafael Devers/49 4.00 10.00
6 Andrew Benintendi/49 6.00 15.00
9 Francis Martes/49 4.00 10.00
10 Adalberto Mejia/49 3.00 8.00
14 Alex Bregman/49 8.00 20.00
16 Jorge Mateo/25 4.00 10.00
17 Carson Fulmer/49 3.00 8.00
18 David Dahl/49 4.00 10.00
20 Brett Phillips/49 3.00 8.00

2016 Elite Extra Edition Quad Materials Purple

*PURPLE: .6X TO 1.5X BASIC
NO PRICING ON QTY 15
RANDOM INSERTS IN PACKS
PRINT RUNS B/WN 15-25 COPIES PER
1 Orlando Arcia/25 5.00 12.00
2 Yoan Moncada/25 8.00 20.00
3 Tyler Glasnow/25 5.00 12.00
4 Alex Reyes/25 5.00 12.00
5 Rafael Devers/25 5.00 12.00
9 Francis Martes/25 5.00 12.00
10 Adalberto Mejia/25 4.00 10.00
14 Alex Bregman/25 10.00 25.00
17 Carson Fulmer/25 4.00 10.00
18 David Dahl/25 5.00 12.00
20 Brett Phillips/25 4.00 10.00

2016 Elite Extra Edition Quad Materials Silver

*SILVER/149: .4X TO 1X BASIC
*SILVER/75-99: .5X TO 1.2X BASIC
RANDOM INSERTS IN PACKS
PRINT RUNS B/WN 75-149 COPIES PER
1 Orlando Arcia/149 3.00 8.00
2 Yoan Moncada/149 5.00 12.00
3 Tyler Glasnow/149 3.00 8.00
4 Alex Reyes/149 3.00 8.00
5 Rafael Devers/99 4.00 10.00
9 Francis Martes/149 3.00 8.00
10 Adalberto Mejia/149 2.50 6.00
16 Jorge Mateo/75 3.00 8.00
18 David Dahl/149 3.00 8.00
20 Brett Phillips/149 2.50 6.00

2016 Elite Extra Edition Triple Materials

RANDOM INSERTS IN PACKS
STATED PRINT RUN 299 SER.#'d SETS
1 Sean Newcomb/299 3.00 8.00
2 Nolan Martinez/299 3.00 8.00
3 Kole Enright/299 3.00 8.00
4 Matt Krook/299 2.50 6.00
5 Dustin May/299 6.00 15.00
6 Zach Jackson/299 2.50 6.00
7 Khalil Lee/299 4.00 10.00
8 Mitchell Kranson/299 2.50 6.00
9 Stephen Alemais/299 4.00 10.00
11 Josh Rogers/299 4.00 10.00
12 Andrew Velazquez/299 2.50 6.00
14 J.T. Riddle/299 2.50 6.00
16 Matt Chapman/299 4.00 10.00
17 Dansby Swanson/149 6.00 15.00

2016 Elite Extra Edition Triple Materials Holo Gold

*HOLO GOLD: .5X TO 1.2X BASIC
RANDOM INSERTS IN PACKS
PRINT RUNS B/WN 65-99 COPIES PER
18 Yoan Moncada/99 5.00 12.00
19 Andrew Benintendi/99 6.00 15.00
20 Alex Bregman/99 6.00 15.00

2016 Elite Extra Edition Triple Materials Holo Silver

*HOLO SILVER: .5X TO 1.2X BASIC
RANDOM INSERTS IN PACKS
STATED PRINT RUN 49 SER.#'d SETS
18 Yoan Moncada 5.00 12.00
19 Andrew Benintendi 6.00 15.00
20 Alex Bregman 6.00 15.00

2016 Elite Extra Edition Triple Materials Purple

*PURPLE: .6X TO 1.5X BASIC
RANDOM INSERTS IN PACKS
PRINT RUNS B/WN 15-25 COPIES PER
NO PRICING ON QTY 15 OR LESS
18 Yoan Moncada/25 6.00 15.00
20 Alex Bregman/25 8.00 20.00

2016 Elite Extra Edition Triple Materials Silver

*SILVER/125-149: .4X TO 1X BASIC
*SILVER/99: .5X TO 1.2X BASIC
RANDOM INSERTS IN PACKS
PRINT RUNS B/WN 99-149 COPIES PER
18 Yoan Moncada/99 4.00 10.00
19 Andrew Benintendi/125 5.00 12.00
20 Alex Bregman/149 5.00 12.00

2016 Elite Extra Edition USA 15U and Collegiate National Team Quad Materials

RANDOM INSERTS IN PACKS
STATED PRINT RUN 199 SER.#'d SETS
*SILVER/99: .6X TO 1.5X BASIC
*PURPLE/25: .75X TO 2X BASIC
1 Olasin/Hairston/Dixon/Friedl 3.00 8.00
2 Skoug/Briones/Rivera/Young 4.00 10.00
3 Volpe/Cairo/Burger/Guthrie 4.00 10.00
4 Brgmn/Olsn/White/Hra 6.00 15.00
5 Bukauskas/McCaughan/Long/Jones 4.00 10.00
6 Faedo/Campbell/Johnson/Scott 4.00 10.00
7 McKay/Naranjo/Gorby/Peterson 5.00 12.00
8 Berkwich/Cate/Thomas/Jacob 3.00 8.00
9 Lange/Faltine/Houck/Martinez 3.00 8.00
10 Wright/Sims/Wohlgemuth/Otto 3.00 8.00
11 Doughty/Faltine/Faedo/Houck 4.00 10.00
12 Olasin/Briones/Harrison/Walls 3.00 8.00
13 Brgmn/Beer/Dxn/Kndll 6.00 15.00
14 Cairo/Harrison/Young/Hairston 4.00 10.00
15 Peterson/Campbell/Otto/Gorby 3.00 8.00
16 Young/Rivera/Berkwich/Friedl 4.00 10.00
17 Long/Wright/Thomas/Naranjo 3.00 8.00
18 Brigman/Walls/Briones/Hiura 5.00 12.00
19 Guthrie/Gorby/Burger/Jacob 3.00 8.00

2016 Elite Extra Edition USA Baseball 18U Ticket Autographs

RANDOM INSERTS IN PACKS
*CRACKED ICE/24: .6X TO 1.5X BASIC
PRINTING PLATES RANDOMLY INSERTED
PLATE PRINT RUN 1 SET PER COLOR
BLACK-CYAN-MAGENTA-YELLOW ISSUED
NO PLATE PRICING DUE TO SCARCITY
1 Nick Allen 3.00 8.00
2 Hans Crouse 4.00 10.00
3 Hagen Danner 6.00 15.00
4 Hunter Greene 12.00 30.00
5 Quentin Holmes 3.00 8.00
6 Royce Lewis 6.00 15.00
7 Nick Pratto 3.00 8.00
8 Shane Baz 4.00 10.00
9 Logan Allen 2.50 6.00
10 Jordan Butler 2.50 6.00
11 Brice Turang 10.00 25.00
12 Mike Siani 2.50 6.00
14 Blayne Enlow 4.00 10.00
15 Patrick Bailey 5.00 12.00
16 Ryan Vilade 5.00 12.00
17 CJ Van Eyk 2.50 6.00
18 Mitchell Stone 2.50 6.00
19 M.J. Melendez 10.00 25.00
20 Triston Casas 10.00 25.00

2016 Elite Extra Edition USA Baseball Ticket Autographs

RANDOM INSERTS IN PACKS
*CRACKED ICE/24: .6X TO 1.5X BASIC
PRINTING PLATES RANDOMLY INSERTED
PLATE PRINT RUN 1 SET PER COLOR
BLACK-CYAN-MAGENTA-YELLOW ISSUED
NO PLATE PRICING DUE TO SCARCITY
1 Darren McCaughan 2.50 6.00
2 Seth Beer 8.00 20.00
3 J.B. Bukauskas 10.00 25.00
4 Jake Burger 6.00 15.00
5 Tyler Johnson 2.50 6.00
6 Alex Faedo 3.00 8.00
7 TJ Friedl 5.00 12.00
8 Dalton Guthrie 3.00 8.00
10 KJ Harrison 5.00 12.00
11 Keston Hiura 20.00 50.00
12 Tanner Houck 12.00 30.00
13 Jeren Kendall 10.00 25.00
14 Alex Lange 4.00 10.00
15 Brendan McKay 6.00 15.00
16 Glenn Otto 2.50 6.00
17 David Peterson 4.00 10.00
18 Mike Rivera
19 Evan Skoug 3.00 8.00
20 Ricky Tyler Thomas 2.50 6.00
21 Taylor Walls 3.00 8.00
22 Tim Cate 3.00 8.00
23 Evan White 4.00 10.00
24 Kyle Wright 8.00 20.00
25 Nelson Berkwich 3.00 8.00
26 Coleman Brigman 2.50 6.00
27 Gabe Briones 2.50 6.00
28 Christian Cairo 4.00 10.00
29 Justin Campbell 3.00 8.00
30 Jasiah Dixon 4.00 10.00
31 Cade Doughty 3.00 8.00
32 Sammy Faltine 2.50 6.00
33 Nick Gorby 4.00 10.00
34 Tony Jacob 4.00 10.00
35 Jared Jones 2.50 6.00
36 Ethan Long 4.00 10.00
37 Zach Martinez 5.00 12.00
38 Joe Naranjo 3.00 8.00
39 Colton Olasin 2.50 6.00
40 Wesley Scott 8.00 20.00
41 Landon Sims 3.00 8.00
42 Anthony Volpe 15.00 40.00
43 Nate Wohlgemuth 2.50 6.00
44 Carter Young 6.00 15.00

2016 Elite Extra Edition USA Collegiate Silhouette Autographs

RANDOM INSERTS IN PACKS
STATED PRINT RUN 99 SER.#'d SETS
*SILVER/49: .5X TO 1.2X BASIC
*PURPLE/25: .6X TO 1.5X BASIC
1 Darren McCaughan 4.00 10.00
2 Seth Beer 10.00 25.00
3 J.B. Bukauskas 10.00 25.00
4 Jake Burger 6.00 15.00
5 Tyler Johnson 4.00 10.00
6 Alex Faedo 6.00 15.00
7 TJ Friedl 4.00 10.00
8 Dalton Guthrie 5.00 12.00
9 Devin Hairston 4.00 10.00
10 KJ Harrison 8.00 20.00
11 Keston Hiura 10.00 25.00
12 Tanner Houck 10.00 25.00
13 Jeren Kendall 8.00 20.00
14 Alex Lange 8.00 20.00
15 Brendan McKay 10.00 25.00
16 Glenn Otto 4.00 10.00
17 David Peterson 6.00 15.00
18 Mike Rivera
19 Evan Skoug 6.00 15.00
20 Ricky Tyler Thomas 4.00 10.00
21 Taylor Walls 5.00 12.00
22 Tim Cate 5.00 12.00
23 Evan White 8.00 20.00
24 Kyle Wright 15.00 40.00

2017 Elite Extra Edition

STATED PRINT RUN 999 SER.#'d SETS
1 Royce Lewis 2.00 5.00
3 MacKenzie Gore 1.50 4.00
4 Brendan McKay 1.00 2.50
5 Kyle Wright .75 2.00
6 Austin Beck 1.00 2.50
7 Pavin Smith .75 2.00
8 Adam Haseley .50 1.25
9 Keston Hiura 1.25 3.00
10 Jo Adell 2.00 5.00
11 Jake Burger .50 1.25
12 Shane Baz .40 1.00
13 Trevor Rogers .40 1.00
14 Nick Pratto .40 1.00
15 J.B. Bukauskas .40 1.00
16 Clarke Schmidt .40 1.00
17 Evan White .40 1.00
18 Alex Faedo .40 1.00
19 Heliot Ramos 2.00 5.00
20 David Peterson .30 .75
21 DL Hall .30 .75
22 Logan Warmoth .40 1.00
23 Jeren Kendall .50 1.25
24 Tanner Houck 1.25 3.00
25 Seth Romero .25 .60
26 Bubba Thompson .40 1.00
27 Brendon Little .30 .75
28 Nate Pearson .60 1.50
29 Christopher Seise .40 1.00
30 Alex Lange .40 1.00
31 Ronald Acuna 5.00 12.00
32 Jeter Downs .50 1.25
33 Kevin Merrell .30 .75
34 Tristen Lutz .40 1.00
35 Brent Rooker .60 1.50
36 Brian Miller .30 .75
38 Stuart Fairchild .30 .75
39 Luis Campusano .30 .75
40 Michael Mercado .30 .75
41 Drew Waters 1.50 4.00
43 Greg Deichmann .50 1.25
44 Drew Ellis .40 1.00
45 Spencer Howard .25 .60
46 Tanner Scott .25 .60
47 Griffin Canning .40 1.00
48 Ryan Vilade .40 1.00
49 Gavin Sheets .40 1.00
50 Brett Netzer .50 1.25
51 Joseph Dunand .50 1.25
52 M.J. Melendez .40 1.00
53 Joe Perez .30 .75
54 Matt Sauer .30 .75
55 Sam Carlson .30 .75
56 Corbin Martin .25 .60
57 Tomas Nido .25 .60
58 Jacob Gonzalez .75 2.00
59 Mark Vientos .40 1.00
60 Ryan Lillie .25 .60
61 Hagen Danner .30 .75
62 Morgan Cooper .30 .75
63 Evan Steele .30 .75
64 Quentin Holmes .30 .75
65 Wil Crowe .40 1.00
66 Hans Crouse .60 1.50
67 Michel Baez .40 1.00
68 Daulton Varsho .30 .75
69 Blake Hunt .25 .60
70 Tommy Doyle .25 .60
71 Tyler Freeman .25 .60
72 Tyler Buffett .25 .60
73 Nathan Lukes .25 .60
74 Ernie Clement .30 .75
75 J.J. Matijevic .30 .75
76 Blayne Enlow .30 .75
77 Colton Hock .30 .75
78 Mason House .40 1.00
79 Aneury Tavarez .25 .60
80 Freddy Tarnok .30 .75
81 Tim Locastro .30 .75
82 Matt Tabor .25 .60
83 Connor Seabold .25 .60
84 KJ Harrison .40 1.00
85 Jacob Pearson .25 .60
86 Will Gaddis .25 .60
87 Nick Dini .25 .60
88 Dylan Busby .25 .60
89 Taylor Walls .25 .60
90 Charcer Burks .25 .60
91 Ronaldo Hernandez .40 1.00
92 Trevor Stephan .40 1.00
93 Brennon Lund .25 .60
94 Esteury Ruiz .40 1.00
95 Joey Morgan .30 .75
96 Seth Corry .25 .60
97 Quinn Brodey .25 .60
98 Mike Baumann .30 .75
100 Jaime Barria .30 .75
101 Trenton Kemp .40 1.00
102 JoJo Romero .60 1.50
103 Diego Castillo .40 1.00
104 Buddy Kennedy .40 1.00
105 Shed Long .25 .60
106 Daniel Tillo .40 1.00
107 Andres Gimenez .50 1.25
108 Brayan Hernandez .25 .60
109 Carlos Soto .25 .60
110 Ronald Bolanos .25 .60
111 Myles Straw .30 .75
112 Edwin Lora .30 .75
113 Joan Baez .25 .60
114 Adrian Morejon .40 1.00
115 Adonis Medina .40 1.00
116 Johan Oviedo .30 .75
117 Luis Almanzar .25 .60
118 Chance Adams .40 1.00
119 David Garcia .30 .75
120 Ronald Guzman .30 .75
121 Luis Alexander Basabe .40 1.00
122 Jesus Sanchez 1.25 3.00
123 Yasel Antuna 1.25 3.00
124 Estevan Florial 1.50 4.00
125 Luis Garcia .40 1.00
126 Jordan Holloway .25 .60
127 Abraham Gutierrez UER .40 1.00
Abrahan Gutierrez
128 Yefry Ramirez .25 .60
129 Dustin Fowler .30 .75
130 Joshua Palacios .25 .60
131 Carlos Rincon .25 .60
132 Nicky Lopez .40 1.00
133 Jelfry Marte .40 1.00
134 Luis V. Garcia .75 2.00
135 Ronny Mauricio 1.25 3.00
136 Julio Rodriguez 2.50 6.00
137 Larry Ernesto .25 .60
138 Adrian Hernandez .25 .60
139 Ynmanol Marinez .30 .75
140 George Valera .50 1.25
141 Ronny Rojas .25 .60
142 Carlos Aguiar .30 .75
143 Luis Robert 6.00 15.00
144 Kyri Washington .60 1.50
145 Jose Miguel Fernandez .25 .60
146 Bryan Mata .30 .75
147 Daniel Flores .25 .60
148 Oneil Cruz .40 1.00
149 Bryan Garcia .25 .60
150 Jake Junis .40 1.00
151 Freddy Peralta .40 1.00
152 Michael Rucker .50 1.25
153 Seby Zavala .40 1.00
154 Zack Granite .75 2.00
155 Nelson Beltran .25 .60
156 Junior Paniagua .40 1.00
157 Omar Florentino .25 .60
158 Ricardo Balogh Aybar .25 .60
159 Ayendi Ortiz .25 .60
160 Noelvi Marte 1.25 3.00
161 Wilmin Candelario .40 1.00
162 Juan Jerez .30 .75
163 Julio Heureaux .40 1.00
164 Ilvin Fernandez .25 .60
165 Moises Ramirez .25 .60
166 Frankely Hurtado .25 .60
167 Orlando Chivilli .25 .60
168 Marco Luciano 1.25 3.00
169 Jeferson Geraldo .25 .60
170 Alberto Fabian .25 .60
171 Henry Morales .25 .60
172 Jeffrey Diaz .25 .60
173 Estanli Castillo .40 1.00
174 Lucas Erceg .30 .75
175 Yeison Lemos .40 1.00
176 Jose Hernandez .25 .60
177 Robert Puason 1.25 3.00
178 Jhon Diaz .40 1.00
179 Bayron Lora .75 2.00
180 Emmanuel Rodriguez .25 .60
181 Franyel Baez .25 .60
182 Algenis Vasquez .25 .60
183 Junio Tilien .40 1.00
184 Malfrin Sosa .25 .60
185 Isaac Paredes .75 2.00
186 Seuly Matias .50 1.25
187 Cole Brannen .40 1.00
188 Connor Wong .40 1.00
189 Gerson Moreno .25 .60
190 Pedro Vasquez .25 .60
191 Antonio Valerio .40 1.00
192 Brendan Murphy .25 .60
193 Zach Kirtley .30 .75
194 Lincoln Henzman .25 .60
195 Dane Myers .40 1.00
196 Jonah Todd .40 1.00
197 Bryce Johnson .25 .60
198 Nick Allen .30 .75
199 Kevin Smith .25 .60
200 Jake Thompson .25 .60

2017 Elite Extra Edition Aspirations Blue

*ASP.BLUE: .75X TO 2X BASIC
RANDOM INSERTS IN PACKS
STATED PRINT RUN 75 SER.#'d SETS

2017 Elite Extra Edition Aspirations Orange

*ASP.ORANGE: .75X TO 2X BASIC
RANDOM INSERTS IN PACKS
STATED PRINT RUN 100 SER.#'d SETS

2017 Elite Extra Edition Aspirations Purple

*ASP PRPLE: .6X TO 1.5X BASIC
RANDOM INSERTS IN PACKS
STATED PRINT RUN 200 SER.#'d SETS

2017 Elite Extra Edition Aspirations Red

*ASP.RED: .6X TO 1.5X BASIC
RANDOM INSERTS IN PACKS
STATED PRINT RUN 150 SER.#'d SETS

2017 Elite Extra Edition Aspirations Tie Dye

*ASP.TIE DYE: 1.2X TO 3X BASIC
RANDOM INSERTS IN PACKS
STATED PRINT RUN 25 SER.#'d SETS

2017 Elite Extra Edition Status Die Cut Emerald

*STAT.EMRLD.DC: 1X TO 2.5X BASIC
RANDOM INSERTS IN PACKS
STATED PRINT RUN 49 SER.#'d SETS

2017 Elite Extra Edition Status Die Cut Red

*STAT.RED DC: .75X TO 2X BASIC
RANDOM INSERTS IN PACKS
STATED PRINT RUN 99 SER.#'d SETS

2017 Elite Extra Edition Autographs

RANDOM INSERTS IN PACKS
PRINTING PLATES RANDOMLY INSERTED
PLATE PRINT RUN 1 SET PER COLOR
BLACK-CYAN-MAGENTA-YELLOW ISSUED
NO PLATE PRICING DUE TO SCARCITY
EXCHANGE DEADLINE 6/6/2019
1 Royce Lewis 8.00 20.00
3 MacKenzie Gore 10.00 25.00
4 Brendan McKay 8.00 20.00
5 Kyle Wright 4.00 10.00
6 Austin Beck 5.00 12.00
7 Pavin Smith 8.00 20.00
8 Adam Haseley 5.00 12.00
9 Keston Hiura 8.00 20.00
10 Jo Adell 15.00 40.00
11 Jake Burger 5.00 12.00
12 Shane Baz 4.00 10.00
13 Trevor Rogers 4.00 10.00
14 Nick Pratto 8.00 20.00
15 J.B. Bukauskas 4.00 10.00
16 Clarke Schmidt 4.00 10.00
17 Evan White 4.00 10.00
18 Alex Faedo 4.00 10.00
19 Heliot Ramos 6.00 15.00
20 David Peterson 3.00 8.00
21 DL Hall 3.00 8.00
22 Logan Warmoth 8.00 20.00
23 Jeren Kendall 5.00 12.00
24 Tanner Houck 10.00 25.00
26 Bubba Thompson 4.00 10.00
27 Brendon Little 3.00 8.00
28 Nate Pearson 6.00 15.00
29 Christopher Seise 4.00 10.00
30 Alex Lange 4.00 10.00
31 Ronald Acuna 60.00 150.00
32 Jeter Downs 8.00 20.00
33 Kevin Merrell 3.00 8.00
34 Tristen Lutz 4.00 10.00
35 Brent Rooker 6.00 15.00
36 Brian Miller 3.00 8.00
38 Stuart Fairchild 3.00 8.00
39 Luis Campusano 3.00 8.00
40 Michael Mercado 3.00 8.00
41 Drew Waters 8.00 20.00
43 Greg Deichmann 5.00 12.00
44 Drew Ellis 4.00 10.00
45 Spencer Howard 2.50 6.00
46 Tanner Scott 2.50 6.00
47 Griffin Canning 4.00 10.00
48 Ryan Vilade 4.00 10.00
49 Gavin Sheets 4.00 10.00
50 Brett Netzer 3.00 8.00
51 Joseph Dunand 5.00 12.00
52 M.J. Melendez 4.00 10.00
53 Joe Perez 3.00 8.00
54 Matt Sauer 3.00 8.00
55 Sam Carlson 3.00 8.00
57 Tomas Nido 2.50 6.00
58 Jacob Gonzalez
59 Mark Vientos 4.00 10.00
60 Ryan Lillie 2.50 6.00
61 Hagen Danner 3.00 8.00
62 Morgan Cooper 3.00 8.00
63 Evan Steele 3.00 8.00
64 Quentin Holmes 3.00 8.00
65 Wil Crowe 4.00 10.00

Card	Low	High
Daulton Varsho	8.00	20.00
Blake Hunt	2.50	6.00
Tommy Doyle	2.50	6.00
Tyler Freeman	2.50	6.00
Tyler Buffett	2.50	6.00
Nathan Lukes	2.50	6.00
Ernie Clement	3.00	8.00
J.J. Matijevic	3.00	8.00
Blayne Enlow	3.00	8.00
Colton Hock	3.00	8.00
Mason House	4.00	10.00
Aneury Tavarez	2.50	6.00
Freddy Tarnok	3.00	8.00
Tim Locastro	3.00	8.00
Matt Tabor	2.50	6.00
Connor Seabold	2.50	6.00
KJ Harrison	4.00	10.00
Jacob Pearson	2.50	6.00
Will Gaddis	2.50	6.00
Nick Dini	2.50	6.00
Dylan Busby	2.50	6.00
Taylor Walls	2.50	6.00
Charcer Burks	2.50	6.00
Trevor Stephan	4.00	10.00
Brennon Lund	2.50	6.00
Joey Morgan	3.00	8.00
Seth Corry	2.50	6.00
Quinn Brodey	2.50	6.00
Mike Baumann	3.00	8.00
0 Jaime Barria	3.00	8.00
1 Trenton Kemp	4.00	10.00
2 JoJo Romero	4.00	10.00
3 Diego Castillo	4.00	10.00
4 Buddy Kennedy	4.00	10.00
5 Shed Long	2.50	6.00
6 Daniel Tillo	4.00	10.00
7 Andres Gimenez	4.00	10.00
0 Ronald Bolanos	2.50	6.00
1 Myles Straw	3.00	8.00
2 Edwin Lora	3.00	8.00
3 Joan Baez	2.50	6.00
4 Adrian Morejon	4.00	10.00
5 Adonis Medina	4.00	10.00
6 Johan Oviedo	3.00	8.00
7 Luis Almanzar	2.50	6.00
8 Chance Adams	6.00	15.00
9 David Garcia	3.00	8.00
20 Ronald Guzman	3.00	8.00
21 Luis Alexander Basabe	4.00	10.00
22 Jesus Sanchez	20.00	50.00
23 Yasel Antuna	12.00	30.00
24 Estevan Florial	15.00	40.00
25 Luis Garcia	4.00	10.00
26 Jordan Holloway	2.50	6.00
27 Abraham Gutierrez UER Abrahan Gutierrez	4.00	10.00
28 Yefry Ramirez	2.50	6.00
29 Dustin Fowler	3.00	8.00
31 Carlos Rincon	2.50	6.00
32 Nicky Lopez	3.00	8.00
33 Jelfry Marte	4.00	10.00
34 Luis V. Garcia	5.00	12.00
35 Ronny Mauricio	8.00	20.00
36 Julio Rodriguez	15.00	40.00
37 Larry Ernesto	2.50	6.00
38 Adrian Hernandez	2.50	6.00
39 Ynmanol Marinez	3.00	8.00
40 George Valera	5.00	12.00
41 Ronny Rojas	2.50	6.00
42 Carlos Aguiar	3.00	8.00
43 Luis Robert	100.00	250.00
44 Kyri Washington	6.00	15.00
45 Jose Miguel Fernandez	2.50	6.00
46 Bryan Mata	3.00	8.00
47 Daniel Flores	2.50	6.00
48 Oneil Cruz	4.00	10.00
49 Bryan Garcia	2.50	6.00
50 Jake Junis	4.00	10.00
51 Freddy Peralta	4.00	10.00
52 Michael Rucker	5.00	12.00
53 Seby Zavala	4.00	10.00
54 Zack Granite	8.00	20.00
55 Nelson Beltran	2.50	6.00
56 Junior Paniagua	4.00	10.00
57 Omar Florentino	2.50	6.00
58 Ricardo Balogh Aybar	2.50	6.00
59 Ayendi Ortiz	2.50	6.00
60 Noelvi Marte	5.00	12.00
61 Wilmin Candelario	4.00	10.00
62 Juan Jerez	3.00	8.00
63 Julio Heureaux	4.00	10.00
64 Ilvin Fernandez	2.50	6.00
65 Moises Ramirez	2.50	6.00
66 Frankely Hurtado	2.50	6.00
67 Orlando Chivilli	2.50	6.00
68 Marco Luciano	15.00	40.00
69 Jeferson Geraldo	2.50	6.00
70 Alberto Fabian	2.50	6.00
71 Henry Morales	2.50	6.00
72 Jeffrey Diaz	2.50	6.00
73 Estanli Castillo	4.00	10.00
75 Yeison Lemos	4.00	10.00
76 Jose Hernandez	2.50	6.00
77 Robert Puason	8.00	20.00
78 Jhon Diaz	4.00	10.00
79 Bayron Lora	15.00	40.00
80 Emmanuel Rodriguez	2.50	6.00
81 Franyel Baez	2.50	6.00
82 Algenis Vasquez	2.50	6.00
83 Junio Tilien	4.00	10.00
85 Isaac Paredes	8.00	20.00
86 Seuly Matias	4.00	10.00
87 Cole Brannen	4.00	10.00
188 Connor Wong	4.00	10.00
189 Gerson Moreno	2.50	6.00
190 Pedro Vasquez	2.50	6.00
191 Adrian Valerio	2.50	6.00
192 Brendan Murphy	2.50	6.00
193 Zach Kirtley	3.00	8.00
194 Lincoln Henzman	2.50	6.00
195 Dane Myers	4.00	10.00
196 Jonah Todd	4.00	10.00
197 Bryce Johnson	2.50	6.00
198 Nick Allen	3.00	8.00
199 Kevin Smith	2.50	6.00
200 Jake Thompson	2.50	6.00

2017 Elite Extra Edition Autographs Aspirations Blue

*ASP BLUE/50: .6X TO 1.5X BASIC
*ASP BLUE/25: .75X TO 2X BASIC
RANDOM INSERTS IN PACKS
PRINT RUNS B/WN 10-50 COPIES PER
NO PRICING ON QTY 10 OR LESS
EXCHANGE DEADLINE 6/6/2019

Card	Low	High
130 Joshua Palacios/50	8.00	20.00

2017 Elite Extra Edition Autographs Aspirations Purple

*ASP PRPLE/100: .5X TO 1.2X BASIC
*ASP PRPLE/50: .6X TO 1.5X BASIC
*ASP PRPLE/25: .75X TO 2X BASIC
RANDOM INSERTS IN PACKS
PRINT RUNS B/WN 25-100 COPIES PER
EXCHANGE DEADLINE 6/6/2019

Card	Low	High
130 Joshua Palacios/100	6.00	15.00

2017 Elite Extra Edition Autographs Emerald

*EMERALD: .75X TO 2X BASIC
RANDOM INSERTS IN PACKS
STATED PRINT RUN 25 SER.#'d SETS
EXCHANGE DEADLINE 6/6/2019

Card	Low	High
130 Joshua Palacios	10.00	25.00

2017 Elite Extra Edition Autographs Status Die Cut Emerald

*STAT.EMRLD.DC/25: .75X TO 2X BASIC
RANDOM INSERTS IN PACKS
PRINT RUNS B/WN 10-25 COPIES PER
NO PRICING ON QTY 10
EXCHANGE DEADLINE 6/6/2019

Card	Low	High
130 Joshua Palacios/25	10.00	25.00

2017 Elite Extra Edition Autographs Status Die Cut Red

*STAT.RED DC/75: .5X TO 1.2X BASIC
*STAT.RED DC/25-35: .75X TO 2X BASIC
RANDOM INSERTS IN PACKS
PRINT RUNS B/WN 25-75 COPIES PER
EXCHANGE DEADLINE 6/6/2019

Card	Low	High
130 Joshua Palacios/75	6.00	15.00

2017 Elite Extra Edition Dual Materials

RANDOM INSERTS IN PACKS
PRINT RUNS B/WN 299-399 COPIES PER

Card	Low	High
1 Tyler O'Neill/349	2.00	5.00
2 Kevin Maitan/349	3.00	8.00
3 Ronald Acuna/299	8.00	20.00
4 Gleyber Torres/299	4.00	10.00
5 Michael Kopech/299	3.00	8.00
6 Luis Robert/299	6.00	15.00
7 Willy Adames/399	2.00	5.00
8 Victor Robles/399	4.00	10.00
10 Dominic Smith/299	1.50	4.00
11 Lucius Fox/299	1.50	4.00
12 Dustin Peterson/399		
13 Austin Voth/399	1.50	4.00
14 Zack Collins/299	2.00	5.00
15 Luis Almanzar/399	1.50	4.00
16 Jomar Reyes/299	1.50	4.00
18 Nick Senzel/299	3.00	8.00
19 David Garcia/399	2.00	5.00
20 Dillon Peters/299	1.50	4.00

2017 Elite Extra Edition Dual Materials Holo Gold

*HOLO GOLD: .5X TO 1.2X BASIC
RANDOM INSERTS IN PACKS
STATED PRINT RUN 99 SER.#'d SETS

Card	Low	High
9 Nick Gordon	2.00	5.00

2017 Elite Extra Edition Dual Materials Holo Silver

*HOLO SILVER: .5X TO 1.2X BASIC
RANDOM INSERTS IN PACKS
STATED PRINT RUN 49 SER.#'d SETS

Card	Low	High
9 Nick Gordon	2.00	5.00

2017 Elite Extra Edition Dual Materials Purple

*PURPLE: .6X TO 1.5X BASIC
RANDOM INSERTS IN PACKS
PRINT RUNS B/WN 10-25 COPIES PER
NO PRICING ON QTY 10

Card	Low	High
9 Nick Gordon/25	2.50	6.00

2017 Elite Extra Edition Dual Materials Silver

*SILVER: .4X TO 1X BASIC
RANDOM INSERTS IN PACKS
STATED PRINT RUN 149 SER.#'d SETS

Card	Low	High
9 Nick Gordon	1.50	4.00

2017 Elite Extra Edition Future Threads Dual Silhouettes

RANDOM INSERTS IN PACKS
PRINT RUNS B/WN 299-399 COPIES PER

Card	Low	High
7 Peters/Garcia/295	1.50	4.00
9 Locastro/Alvarez/299	2.50	6.00
11 Sedlock/Scott/139	1.50	4.00
13 O'Neil/Robles/299	3.00	8.00
17 Bader/Oviedo/150	3.00	8.00
18 Garcia/Guzman/162	2.00	5.00
20 Adams/Torres/221	6.00	15.00

2017 Elite Extra Edition Future Threads Dual Silhouettes Holo Gold

*HOLO GOLD/65-99: .5X TO 1.2X BASIC
*HOLO GOLD/25: .6X TO 1.5X BASIC
RANDOM INSERTS IN PACKS
PRINT RUNS B/WN 25-49 COPIES PER

Card	Low	High
12 Maitan/Acuna/97	8.00	20.00
14 Fox/Adames/94	2.50	6.00
15 Honeywell/Kopech/99	4.00	10.00

2017 Elite Extra Edition Future Threads Dual Silhouettes Holo Silver

*HOLO SILVER/35-49: .5X TO 1.2X BASIC
*HOLO SILVER/25: .6X TO 1.5X BASIC
RANDOM INSERTS IN PACKS
PRINT RUNS B/WN 23-49 COPIES PER

Card	Low	High
10 Robert/Kopech/49	8.00	20.00
16 Smith/Gordon/23	2.50	6.00

2017 Elite Extra Edition Future Threads Dual Silhouettes Purple

*PURPLE/25: .6X TO 1.5X BASIC
RANDOM INSERTS IN PACKS
PRINT RUNS B/WN 5-25 COPIES PER
NO PRICING ON QTY 10 OR LESS

2017 Elite Extra Edition Future Threads Dual Silhouettes Silver

*SILVER: .4X TO 1X BASIC
RANDOM INSERTS IN PACKS
PRINT RUNS B/WN 99-149 COPIES PER

Card	Low	High
1 Hernandez/Aguiar/125	2.00	5.00
2 Marte/Garcia/149	3.00	8.00
3 Mauricio/Rojas/99	4.00	10.00
4 Fernandez/Marinez/149	2.00	5.00
5 Rodriguez/Ernesto/113	6.00	15.00
6 Tavarez/Mars/132	3.00	8.00
8 Rodgers/Torres/149	5.00	12.00
19 Gillaspie/Hoskins/136	4.00	10.00

2017 Elite Extra Edition Future Threads Silhouette Autographs

RANDOM INSERTS IN PACKS
PRINT RUNS B/WN 59-99 COPIES PER
EXCHANGE DEADLINE 6/6/2019

Card	Low	High
1 Tyler O'Neill/99	4.00	10.00
3 Victor Robles/99	10.00	25.00
5 Willy Adames/99	4.00	10.00
6 Brent Honeywell/99	4.00	10.00
7 Luis Robert/99	100.00	250.00
10 Dominic Smith/99	3.00	8.00
11 Danny Mars/99	8.00	20.00
12 Ronny Rojas/99	3.00	8.00
13 Jomar Reyes/99	3.00	8.00
14 Ronald Acuna/99	60.00	150.00
16 Carlos Aguiar/99	4.00	10.00
17 Abraham Gutierrez/99 UER Abrahan Gutierrez	5.00	12.00
18 Aneury Tavarez/99	3.00	8.00
19 Casey Gillaspie/99	3.00	8.00
20 Cody Sedlock/59	3.00	8.00
21 Dillon Peters/99	3.00	8.00
23 Tomas Nido/99	3.00	8.00
24 Luis V. Garcia/99	5.00	12.00
25 Luis Ortiz/99	3.00	8.00
27 A.J. Minter/99	4.00	10.00
28 Dustin Fowler/99	5.00	12.00
29 Austin Voth/99	3.00	8.00
30 Chance Adams/99	8.00	20.00
31 David Garcia/99	4.00	10.00
32 Dustin Peterson/99	3.00	8.00
33 Harrison Bader/99	5.00	12.00
34 Jarlin Garcia/99	3.00	8.00
35 Johan Oviedo/99	4.00	10.00
36 Jose Miguel Fernandez/99	3.00	8.00
37 Luis Almanzar/99	3.00	8.00
38 Rhys Hoskins/99	25.00	60.00
39 Ronald Guzman/99	4.00	10.00
40 Tanner Scott/99	3.00	8.00
41 Yasel Antuna/99	5.00	12.00
42 Jelfry Marte/99	5.00	12.00
43 Luis Garcia/99	5.00	12.00
44 Ronny Mauricio/99	6.00	15.00
45 Julio Rodriguez/99	25.00	60.00
46 Larry Ernesto/99	3.00	8.00
47 Adrian Hernandez/99	3.00	8.00
48 Ynmanol Marinez/99	4.00	10.00
51 Jaime Barria/99	4.00	10.00
52 Marco Luciano/99	12.00	30.00
53 Bayron Lora/99	10.00	25.00
54 Merandy Gonzalez/99	5.00	12.00
55 Nick Dini/99	3.00	8.00
56 Nathan Lukes/99	3.00	8.00
58 Tim Locastro/99	4.00	10.00

2017 Elite Extra Edition Future Threads Silhouette Autographs Red

*RED: .5X TO 1.2X BASIC
RANDOM INSERTS IN PACKS
PRINT RUNS B/WN 25-35 COPIES PER
EXCHANGE DEADLINE 6/6/2019

Card	Low	High
2 Gleyber Torres/35	60.00	150.00
4 Michael Kopech/35	8.00	20.00
9 Nick Gordon/35	4.00	10.00
15 Lucius Fox/35	4.00	10.00
22 Zack Collins/35	5.00	12.00
26 Yadier Alvarez/35	6.00	15.00
49 Brendan Rodgers/35	8.00	20.00
50 Ian Anderson/35	20.00	50.00

2017 Elite Extra Edition Future Threads Silhouette Autographs Silver

*SILVER: .5X TO 1.2X BASIC
RANDOM INSERTS IN PACKS
STATED PRINT RUN 49 SER.#'d SETS
EXCHANGE DEADLINE 6/6/2019

Card	Low	High
2 Gleyber Torres	60.00	150.00
4 Michael Kopech	8.00	20.00
8 Kevin Maitan	5.00	12.00
9 Nick Gordon	4.00	10.00
15 Lucius Fox	4.00	10.00
22 Zack Collins	5.00	12.00
26 Yadier Alvarez	6.00	15.00
49 Brendan Rodgers	8.00	20.00
50 Ian Anderson	20.00	50.00

2017 Elite Extra Edition Future Threads Silhouettes

RANDOM INSERTS IN PACKS
PRINT RUNS B/WN 99-399 COPIES PER

Card	Low	High
1 Tyler O'Neill/299	2.00	5.00
3 Victor Robles/399	4.00	10.00
4 Michael Kopech/149	3.00	8.00
5 Willy Adames/399	2.00	5.00
6 Brent Honeywell/399	2.00	5.00
8 Kevin Maitan/299	3.00	8.00
10 Dominic Smith/99	2.00	5.00
11 Danny Mars/149	3.00	8.00
12 Jomar Reyes/299	1.50	4.00
15 Zack Collins/299	2.00	5.00
17 Rhys Hoskins/125	5.00	12.00
18 Robert Puason/299	3.00	8.00
19 Yasel Antuna/318	3.00	8.00
20 Tom De Blok/399	1.50	4.00

2017 Elite Extra Edition Future Threads Silhouettes Holo Gold

*HOLO GOLD: .5X TO 1.2X p/r 125-399
*HOLO GOLD: .4X TO 1X p/r 99
RANDOM INSERTS IN PACKS
PRINT RUNS B/WN 49-99 COPIES PER

Card	Low	High
2 Gleyber Torres/99	5.00	12.00
7 Luis Robert/99	10.00	25.00
13 Ronald Acuna/99	8.00	20.00
14 Lucius Fox/49	2.00	5.00
16 Nick Senzel/49	4.00	10.00

2017 Elite Extra Edition Future Threads Silhouettes Holo Silver

*HOLO SILVER: .5X TO 1.2X p/r 125-399
*HOLO SILVER: .4X TO 1X p/r 99
RANDOM INSERTS IN PACKS
PRINT RUNS B/WN 25-49 COPIES PER

Card	Low	High
2 Gleyber Torres/49	5.00	12.00
7 Luis Robert/49	10.00	25.00
13 Ronald Acuna/49	8.00	20.00
14 Lucius Fox/25	2.50	6.00
16 Nick Senzel/25	5.00	12.00

2017 Elite Extra Edition Future Threads Silhouettes Purple

*PURPLE/25: .6X TO 1.5X p/r 125-399
RANDOM INSERTS IN PACKS
PRINT RUNS B/WN 10-25 COPIES PER
NO PRICING ON QTY 15 OR LESS

2017 Elite Extra Edition Future Threads Silhouettes Silver

*SILVER/149: .4X TO 1X BASIC
*SILVER/99: .5X TO 1.2X BASIC
RANDOM INSERTS IN PACKS
STATED PRINT RUN 140 SER.#'d SETS

Card	Low	High
2 Gleyber Torres/149	4.00	10.00
7 Luis Robert/149	10.00	25.00
13 Ronald Acuna/149	6.00	15.00
16 Nick Senzel/99	4.00	10.00

2017 Elite Extra Edition Jumbo Materials

RANDOM INSERTS IN PACKS
PRINT RUNS B/WN 99-299 COPIES PER

Card	Low	High
1 Tyler O'Neill/299	2.00	5.00
2 Gleyber Torres/175	4.00	10.00
3 Victor Robles/299	4.00	10.00
5 Willy Adames/299	2.00	5.00
6 Brent Honeywell/299	2.00	5.00
7 Luis Robert/149	10.00	25.00
8 Kevin Maitan/299	3.00	8.00
9 Nick Gordon/199	1.50	4.00
10 Dominic Smith/99	2.00	5.00
11 Danny Mars/199	3.00	8.00
13 J.P. Crawford/299	1.50	4.00
15 Richard Urena/299	2.50	6.00

2017 Elite Extra Edition Jumbo Materials Purple

*PURPLE/20-25: .6X TO 1.5X p/r 149-299
RANDOM INSERTS IN PACKS
PRINT RUNS B/WN 10-25 COPIES PER
NO PRICING ON QTY 15 OR LESS

Card	Low	High
4 Michael Kopech/20	5.00	12.00
12 Jomar Reyes/25	2.50	6.00
16 Ronald Acuna/25	12.00	30.00

2017 Elite Extra Edition Jumbo Materials Red

*RED/49: .5X TO 1.2X p/r 149-299
*RED/25: .6X TO 1.5X p/r 149-299
*RED/25: .5X TO 1.2X p/r 99
RANDOM INSERTS IN PACKS
PRINT RUNS B/WN 25-49 COPIES PER

Card	Low	High
4 Michael Kopech/49	4.00	10.00
12 Jomar Reyes/49	2.00	5.00
14 Nick Senzel/25	5.00	12.00
16 Ronald Acuna/49	10.00	25.00

2017 Elite Extra Edition Jumbo Materials Silver

*SILVER: .5X TO 1.2X p/r 149-299
*SILVER: .4X TO 1X p/r 99
RANDOM INSERTS IN PACKS
PRINT RUNS B/WN 49-99 COPIES PER

Card	Low	High
4 Michael Kopech/99	4.00	10.00
14 Nick Senzel/75	4.00	10.00
16 Ronald Acuna/99	10.00	25.00

2017 Elite Extra Edition Quad Materials

RANDOM INSERTS IN PACKS
PRINT RUNS B/WN 199-399 COPIES PER

Card	Low	High
1 Tyler O'Neill/299	2.00	5.00
2 Kevin Maitan/199	3.00	8.00
4 Gleyber Torres/299	4.00	10.00
5 Michael Kopech/299	3.00	8.00
6 Luis Robert/299	5.00	12.00
7 Willy Adames/399	2.00	5.00
8 Victor Robles/399	4.00	10.00
12 Casey Gillaspie/399	1.50	4.00
13 Cody Sedlock/299	1.50	4.00
14 Johan Oviedo/299	2.00	5.00
15 Harrison Bader/299	3.00	8.00
16 Ronald Guzman/299	2.00	5.00
17 Tanner Scott/399	1.50	4.00
19 Dustin Fowler/299	3.00	8.00
20 Jose Miguel Fernandez/399	1.50	4.00

2017 Elite Extra Edition Quad Materials Holo Gold

*HOLO GOLD: .5X TO 1.2X BASIC
RANDOM INSERTS IN PACKS
PRINT RUNS B/WN 49-99 COPIES PER

Card	Low	High
3 Ronald Acuna/49	8.00	20.00
10 Dominic Smith/49	2.00	5.00
11 Lucius Fox/49	2.00	5.00
18 Nick Senzel/99	4.00	10.00

2017 Elite Extra Edition Quad Materials Holo Silver

*HOLO SILVER/49: .5X TO 1.2X BASIC
*HOLO SILVER/25: .6X TO 1.5X BASIC
RANDOM INSERTS IN PACKS
PRINT RUNS B/WN 25-49 COPIES PER

Card	Low	High
3 Ronald Acuna/25	10.00	25.00
9 Nick Gordon/49	2.00	5.00
10 Dominic Smith/25	2.50	6.00
11 Lucius Fox/25	2.50	6.00
18 Nick Senzel/49	4.00	10.00

2017 Elite Extra Edition Quad Materials Purple

*PURPLE: .6X TO 1.5X BASIC
RANDOM INSERTS IN PACKS
PRINT RUNS B/WN 10-25 COPIES PER
NO PRICING ON QTY 10

Card	Low	High
9 Nick Gordon/25	2.50	6.00

2017 Elite Extra Edition Quad Materials Silver

*SILVER/149: .4X TO 1X BASIC
*SILVER/99: .5X TO 1.2X BASIC
RANDOM INSERTS IN PACKS
PRINT RUNS B/WN 99-149 COPIES PER

Card	Low	High
11 Lucius Fox/99	2.00	5.00
18 Nick Senzel/125	3.00	8.00

2017 Elite Extra Edition Triple Materials

RANDOM INSERTS IN PACKS
PRINT RUNS B/WN 99-399 COPIES PER

Card	Low	High
1 Tyler O'Neill/299	2.00	5.00
2 Kevin Maitan/299	3.00	8.00
4 Gleyber Torres/299	4.00	10.00
5 Michael Kopech/299	3.00	8.00
6 Luis Robert/299	5.00	12.00
7 Willy Adames/399	2.00	5.00
8 Victor Robles/399	4.00	10.00
10 Dominic Smith/99	2.00	5.00
11 Lucius Fox/299	1.50	4.00
12 A.J. Minter/399	2.00	5.00
13 Jarlin Garcia/349	1.50	4.00
14 Luis Ortiz/399	1.50	4.00
15 Rhys Hoskins/299	5.00	12.00
16 Yadier Alvarez/399	2.50	6.00
17 Yasel Antuna/325	3.00	8.00
18 Nick Senzel/299	3.00	8.00
19 Danny Mars/299	3.00	8.00
20 Chance Adams/299	3.00	8.00

2017 Elite Extra Edition Triple Materials Holo Gold

*HOLO GOLD: .5X TO 1.2X p/r 299-399
*HOLO GOLD: .4X TO 1X p/r 99
RANDOM INSERTS IN PACKS
PRINT RUNS B/WN 49-99 COPIES PER

Card	Low	High
3 Ronald Acuna/49	8.00	20.00
9 Nick Gordon/99	2.00	5.00

2017 Elite Extra Edition Triple Materials Holo Silver

*HOLO SILVER/49: .5X TO 1.2X p/r 299-399
*HOLO SILVER/25: .5X TO 1.2X p/r 99
RANDOM INSERTS IN PACKS
PRINT RUNS B/WN 25-49 COPIES PER

Card	Low	High
3 Ronald Acuna/25	10.00	25.00
9 Nick Gordon/49	2.00	5.00

2017 Elite Extra Edition Triple Materials Purple

*PURPLE/25: .6X TO 1.5X p/r 299-399
RANDOM INSERTS IN PACKS
PRINT RUNS B/WN 25-49 COPIES PER
NO PRICING ON QTY 10

Card	Low	High
9 Nick Gordon/25	2.50	6.00

2017 Elite Extra Edition Triple Materials Silver

*SILVER/125-149: .4X TO 1X p/r 299-399
RANDOM INSERTS IN PACKS
PRINT RUNS B/WN 99-149 COPIES PER

Card	Low	High
3 Ronald Acuna/99	8.00	20.00
9 Nick Gordon/125	1.50	4.00

2017 Elite Extra Edition USA Collegiate Silhouette Autographs

RANDOM INSERTS IN PACKS
STATED PRINT RUN 99 SER.#'d SETS
EXCHANGE DEADLINE 6/6/2019
*SILVER/49: .5X TO 1.2X BASIC
*PURPLE/25: .6X TO 1.5X BASIC

Card	Low	High
1 Seth Beer	10.00	25.00
2 Steven Gingery	6.00	15.00
3 Nick Madrigal	8.00	20.00
4 Jake McCarthy	5.00	12.00
5 Nick Meyer	5.00	12.00
6 Casey Mize	12.00	30.00
7 Konnor Pilkington	5.00	12.00
8 Dallas Woolfolk	4.00	10.00
9 Tyler Frank	5.00	12.00
10 Cadyn Grenier	5.00	12.00
11 Gianluca Dalatri	4.00	10.00
12 Braden Shewmake	12.00	30.00
13 Bryce Tucker	4.00	10.00
14 Andrew Vaughn	10.00	25.00
15 Steele Walker	5.00	12.00
16 Jeremy Eierman	6.00	15.00
17 Patrick Raby	6.00	15.00
18 Grant Koch	4.00	10.00
19 Travis Swaggerty	6.00	15.00
20 Tim Cate	5.00	12.00
21 Nick Sprengel	4.00	10.00
22 Johnny Aiello	5.00	12.00
23 Ryley Gilliam	4.00	10.00
24 Jon Olsen	8.00	20.00
25 Tylor Holton	4.00	10.00
26 Sean Wymer	4.00	10.00

2018 Elite Extra Edition

STATED PRINT RUN 999 SER.#'d SETS

Card	Low	High
1 Casey Mize	2.00	5.00
2 Joey Bart	2.50	6.00
3 Alec Bohm	1.25	3.00
4 Nick Madrigal	1.50	4.00
5 Jonathan India	.40	1.00
6 Jarred Kelenic	2.50	6.00
7 Ryan Weathers	.30	.75
8 Franklin Perez	.25	.60
9 Travis Swaggerty	.75	2.00
10 Grayson Rodriguez	.50	1.25
11 Jordan Groshans	.75	2.00
12 Connor Scott	.30	.75
13 Logan Gilbert	.40	1.00
14 Cole Winn	.40	1.00
15 Matthew Liberatore	.30	.75
16 Jordyn Adams	1.50	4.00
17 Brady Singer	.50	1.25
18 Nolan Gorman	1.50	4.00
19 Trevor Larnach	1.50	4.00
20 Brice Turang	.75	2.00
21 Ryan Rolison	.50	1.25
22 Anthony Seigler	.60	1.50
23 Nico Hoerner	1.25	3.00
24 Diego Cartaya	1.50	4.00
25 Triston Casas	2.00	5.00
26 Mason Denaburg	.30	.75
27 Seth Beer	1.00	2.50
28 Bo Naylor	.30	.75
29 Taylor Hearn	.25	.60
30 Shane McClanahan	.40	1.00
31 Nick Schnell	.30	.75
32 Jackson Kowar	.25	.60
33 Daniel Lynch	.30	.75
34 Ethan Hankins	.30	.75
35 Richard Palacios	.25	.60
36 Cadyn Grenier	.30	.75
37 Xavier Edwards	.40	1.00
38 Jake McCarthy	.40	1.00
39 Kris Bubic	.40	1.00
40 Lenny Torres Jr.	.30	.75
41 Grant Lavigne	1.25	3.00
42 Griffin Roberts	.25	.60
43 Parker Meadows	.50	1.25
44 Sean Hjelle	.30	.75
45 Steele Walker	.30	.75
46 Lyon Richardson	.40	1.00
47 Simeon Woods-Richardson	.30	.75
48 Greyson Jenista	.50	1.25
49 Jameson Hannah	.40	1.00
50 Braxton Ashcraft	.40	1.00
51 Griffin Conine	.50	1.25
52 Osiris Johnson	.30	.75
53 Josh Stowers	.60	1.50
54 Owen White	.40	1.00
55 Tyler Frank	.25	.60
56 Jeremiah Jackson	.40	1.00
57 Jonathan Bowlan	.25	.60
58 Ryan Jeffers	.50	1.25
59 Joe Gray	.40	1.00
60 Josh Breaux	.30	.75
61 Brennen Davis	2.00	5.00
62 Alek Thomas	1.00	2.50
63 Nick Decker	.50	1.25
64 Tim Cate	.40	1.00
65 Jayson Schroeder	.25	.60
66 Nick Sandlin	.25	.60
67 Wander Franco	5.00	12.00
68 Will Banfield	.25	.60
69 Jeremy Eierman	.30	.75
70 Tanner Dodson	.30	.75
71 Josiah Gray	.40	1.00
72 Micah Bello	.40	1.00
73 Grant Little	.25	.60
74 Luken Baker	.40	1.00
75 Mitchell Kilkenny	.25	.60
76 Cole Roederer	.75	2.00
77 Blaine Knight	.30	.75
78 Kody Clemens	.50	1.25
79 Jake Wong	.25	.60
80 Konnor Pilkington	.30	.75
81 Tristan Pompey	.40	1.00
82 Carlos Cortes	.30	.75
83 Owen Miller	.25	.60
84 Cal Raleigh	.25	.60
85 Connor Kaiser	.25	.60
86 Kevin Sanchez	.25	.60
87 Adbert Alzolay	.30	.75
88 Akil Baddoo	.30	.75
89 Jose Siri	.25	.60
90 Nick Margevicius	.25	.60
91 Jeisson Rosario	.40	1.00
92 Sandro Fabian	.25	.60
93 Aramis Ademan	.40	1.00
94 Miguel Aparicio	.25	.60
95 James Nelson	.25	.60
96 Bo Bichette	1.00	2.50
97 D.J. Wilson	.25	.60
98 Samir Duenez	.25	.60
99 Sixto Sanchez	.60	1.50
100 Samad Taylor	.25	.60
101 Lency Delgado	.50	1.25
102 Austin Listi	.25	.60
103 Yunior Severino	.30	.75
104 Jayce Easley	.25	.60
105 Ford Proctor	.30	.75
106 Kyle Isbel	.60	1.50
107 Mateo Gil	.25	.60
108 Terrin Vavra	.50	1.25
109 Jimmy Herron	.25	.60
110 Reid Schaller	.25	.60
111 Victor Victor Mesa	1.00	2.50
112 Orelvis Martinez	.50	1.25
113 Noelvi Marte	1.25	3.00
114 Marco Luciano	1.25	3.00
115 Jose de la Cruz	.40	1.00
116 Junior Sanquintin	.30	.75
117 Kevin Alcantara	.40	1.00
118 Francisco Morales	.30	.75
119 Omar Florentino	.30	.75
120 Sergio Campana	.25	.60
121 Landon Leach	.30	.75
122 Jose Suarez	.25	.60
123 Luis Escobar	.25	.60
124 Yordan Alvarez	5.00	12.00
125 Keibert Ruiz	.75	2.00
126 DJ Peters	.60	1.50
127 Francisco Alvarez	.50	1.25
128 Julio Pablo Martinez	.40	1.00
129 Jose Garcia	.25	.60
130 Alexander Canario	.25	.60
131 Freudis Nova	.50	1.25
132 Daniel Brito	.25	.60
133 Genesis Cabrera	.40	1.00
134 Erling Moreno	.50	1.25
135 Jose Mujica	.25	.60
136 Wadye Ynfante	.25	.60
137 Dean Kremer	.30	.75
138 Jonathan Ornelas	.60	1.50
139 Tony Gonsolin	.60	1.50
140 Ryder Green	.50	1.25
141 Jackson Goddard	.25	.60
142 Durbin Feltman	.40	1.00
143 Jeremy Pena	.50	1.25
144 John Rooney	.30	.75
145 Everson Pereira	.40	1.00
146 Jhoan Urena	.25	.60
147 Sandy Baez	.25	.60
148 Henry Henry	.25	.60
149 Taylor Widener	.25	.60
150 Trent Deveaux	.30	.75
151 Elehuris Montero	.50	1.25
152 Miguel Amaya	.40	1.00
153 Richard Gallardo	.50	1.25
154 Gabriel Rodriguez	.50	1.25
155 Luis Oviedo	.25	.60
156 Brewer Hicklen	.40	1.00
157 Peter Solomon	.25	.60
158 Chad Spanberger	.40	1.00
159 Andres Munoz	.40	1.00
160 Misael Urbina	.75	2.00
161 Luis Medina	.40	1.00
162 Osiel Rodriguez	.40	1.00
163 Roberto Ramos	.40	1.00
164 Tristan Beck	.30	.75
165 DaShawn Keirsey Jr.	.40	1.00
166 Eric Cole	.30	.75
167 Steven Jennings	.25	.60
168 Jose Cosma	.25	.60
169 Luis De La Cruz	.25	.60
170 Gregory Duran	.25	.60
171 Luis Encarnacion	.25	.60
172 Jose Pena	.25	.60
173 Lizandro Rodriguez	.30	.75
174 Leonel Sanchez	.25	.60
175 Luis Gil	.30	.75
176 Yonaldi Soto	.25	.60
177 Ariel Almonte	.25	.60
178 Jonathan Bautista	.25	.60
179 Saul Bautista	.25	.60
180 Luis Castillo	.25	.60
181 Armando Cruz	.25	.60
182 Danny De Andrande	.25	.60

183 Manny De La Rosa .25 .60
184 Yamal Encarnacion .25 .60
185 Willy Fana .25 .60
186 Yamal Flores .25 .60
187 Jayson Jimenez .25 .60
188 Fraidel Liriano .25 .60
189 Robelin Lopez .25 .60
190 Yendel Mateo .25 .60
191 Keiderson Pavon .25 .60
192 Victor Quezada .25 .60
193 Luis Ravelo .25 .60
194 Elias Reynoso .25 .60
195 Cristian Santana .60 1.50
196 Dervy Ventura .25 .60
197 Kaito Yuki .40 1.00
198 Jake Irvin .25 .60
199 Blaze Alexander .50 1.25
200 Zach Haake .25 .60

2018 Elite Extra Edition Aspirations Blue

*ASP.BLUE: .75X TO 2X BASIC
RANDOM INSERTS IN PACKS
STATED PRINT RUN 75 SER.#'d SETS

2018 Elite Extra Edition Aspirations Orange

*ASP ORANGE: .6X TO 1.5X BASIC
RANDOM INSERTS IN PACKS
STATED PRINT RUN 100 SER.#'d SETS

2018 Elite Extra Edition Aspirations Red

*ASP RED: .6X TO 1.5X BASIC
RANDOM INSERTS IN PACKS
STATED PRINT RUN 150 SER.#'d SETS

2018 Elite Extra Edition Aspirations Tie Dye

*ASP.TIE DYE: 1.2X TO 3X BASIC
RANDOM INSERTS IN PACKS
STATED PRINT RUN 25 SER.#'d SETS

2018 Elite Extra Edition Pink

*PINK: .6X TO 1.5X BASIC
RANDOM INSERTS IN PACKS

2018 Elite Extra Edition Status Die Cut Emerald

*STAT.EMRLD.DC: 1X TO 2.5X BASIC
RANDOM INSERTS IN PACKS
STATED PRINT RUN 49 SER.#'d SETS

2018 Elite Extra Edition Status Die Cut Red

*STAT.RED DC: .75X TO 2X BASIC
RANDOM INSERTS IN PACKS
STATED PRINT RUN 99 SER.#'d SETS

2018 Elite Extra Edition Autographs

RANDOM INSERTS IN PACKS
EXCHANGE DEADLINE 6/12/2020
*BLUE/50: .5X TO 1.2X BASIC
*BLUE/25: .6X TO 1.5X BASIC
*PURPLE/50-100: .5X TO 1.2X BASIC
*PURPLE/25: .6X TO 1.5X BASIC
*EMERALD/25: .6X TO 1.5X BASIC
*DC EMERALD/25: .6X TO 1.5X BASIC
*DC RED/50-75: .5X TO 1.2X BASIC
*DC RED/25: .6X TO 1.5X BASIC
1 Casey Mize 12.00 30.00
2 Joey Bart 40.00 100.00
3 Alec Bohm 12.00 30.00
4 Nick Madrigal 8.00 20.00
5 Jonathan India 15.00 40.00
6 Jarred Kelenic 10.00 25.00
8 Franklin Perez 2.50 6.00
9 Travis Swaggerty 5.00 12.00
10 Grayson Rodriguez 5.00 12.00
11 Jordan Groshans 12.00 30.00
13 Logan Gilbert 4.00 10.00
14 Cole Winn 4.00 10.00
15 Matthew Liberatore 3.00 8.00
16 Jordyn Adams 8.00 20.00
17 Brady Singer 5.00 12.00
18 Nolan Gorman 12.00 30.00
19 Trevor Larnach 6.00 15.00
20 Brice Turang 4.00 10.00
21 Ryan Rolison 3.00 8.00
22 Anthony Seigler 4.00 10.00
23 Nico Hoerner 10.00 25.00
24 Diego Cartaya 30.00 80.00
25 Triston Casas 6.00 15.00
26 Mason Denaburg 3.00 8.00
27 Seth Beer 6.00 15.00
28 Bo Naylor 3.00 8.00
29 Taylor Hearn 2.50 6.00
30 Shane McClanahan 4.00 10.00
31 Nick Schnell 3.00 8.00
32 Jackson Kowar 2.50 6.00
33 Daniel Lynch 3.00 8.00
34 Ethan Hankins 3.00 8.00
35 Richard Palacios 2.50 6.00
36 Cadyn Grenier 3.00 8.00
37 Xavier Edwards 4.00 10.00
38 Jake McCarthy 4.00 10.00
39 Kris Bubic 4.00 10.00
40 Lenny Torres Jr. 3.00 8.00
41 Grant Lavigne 5.00 12.00
42 Griffin Roberts 2.50 6.00
43 Parker Meadows 4.00 10.00
44 Sean Hjelle 3.00 8.00
45 Steele Walker 3.00 8.00
46 Lyon Richardson 4.00 10.00
47 Simeon Woods-Richardson 3.00 8.00
48 Greyson Jenista 3.00 8.00
49 Jameson Hannah 2.50 6.00
50 Braxton Ashcraft 4.00 10.00
51 Griffin Conine 3.00 8.00
52 Osiris Johnson 3.00 8.00
53 Josh Stowers 4.00 10.00
54 Owen White 4.00 10.00
55 Tyler Frank 2.50 6.00
56 Jeremiah Jackson 4.00 10.00
57 Jonathan Bowlan 2.50 6.00
58 Ryan Jeffers 3.00 8.00
59 Joe Gray 4.00 10.00
60 Josh Breaux 3.00 8.00
61 Brennen Davis 15.00 40.00
62 Alek Thomas 4.00 10.00
63 Nick Decker 3.00 8.00
64 Tim Cate 4.00 10.00
65 Jayson Schroeder 2.50 6.00
66 Nick Sandlin 2.50 6.00
67 Wander Franco 40.00 100.00
68 Will Banfield 2.50 6.00
69 Jeremy Eierman 3.00 8.00
70 Tanner Dodson 3.00 8.00
71 Josiah Gray 4.00 10.00
72 Micah Bello 4.00 10.00
74 Luken Baker 4.00 10.00
75 Mitchell Kilkenny 2.50 6.00
76 Cole Roederer 4.00 10.00
77 Blaine Knight 3.00 8.00
78 Kody Clemens 5.00 12.00
79 Jake Wong 2.50 6.00
80 Konnor Pilkington 3.00 8.00
81 Tristan Pompey 4.00 10.00
82 Carlos Cortes 3.00 8.00
83 Owen Miller 2.50 6.00
84 Cal Raleigh 2.50 6.00
85 Connor Kaiser 2.50 6.00
86 Kevin Sanchez 2.50 6.00
87 Adbert Alzolay 3.00 8.00
88 Akil Baddoo 3.00 8.00
90 Nick Margevicius 2.50 6.00
91 Jeisson Rosario 4.00 10.00
92 Sandro Fabian 4.00 10.00
93 Aramis Ademan 2.50 6.00
94 Miguel Aparicio 2.50 6.00
95 James Nelson 2.50 6.00
96 Bo Bichette 20.00 50.00
97 D.J. Wilson 2.50 6.00
98 Samir Duenez 2.50 6.00
99 Sixto Sanchez 8.00 20.00
100 Samad Taylor 2.50 6.00
101 Lency Delgado 2.50 6.00
102 Austin Listi 2.50 6.00
103 Yunior Severino 3.00 8.00
104 Jayce Easley 2.50 6.00
105 Ford Proctor 3.00 8.00
107 Mateo Gil 2.50 6.00
108 Terrin Vavra 3.00 8.00
109 Jimmy Herron 2.50 6.00
110 Reid Schaller 2.50 6.00
111 Victor Victor Mesa 30.00 80.00
112 Orelvis Martinez 6.00 15.00
113 Noelvi Marte 5.00 12.00
114 Marco Luciano 10.00 25.00
115 Jose de la Cruz 4.00 10.00
116 Junior Sanquintin 3.00 8.00
117 Kevin Alcantara 6.00 15.00
118 Francisco Morales 3.00 8.00
119 Omar Florentino 3.00 8.00
120 Sergio Campana 2.50 6.00
121 Landon Leach 3.00 8.00
122 Jose Suarez 2.50 6.00
123 Luis Escobar 2.50 6.00
124 Yordan Alvarez 25.00 60.00
125 Keibert Ruiz 6.00 15.00
126 DJ Peters 4.00 10.00
128 Julio Pablo Martinez 10.00 25.00
129 Jose Devers 2.50 6.00
130 Alexander Canario 2.50 6.00
131 Freudis Nova 8.00 20.00
132 Daniel Brito 2.50 6.00
133 Genesis Cabrera 4.00 10.00
134 Erling Moreno 10.00 25.00
135 Jose Mujica 2.50 6.00
136 Wadye Ynfante 2.50 6.00
137 Dean Kremer 3.00 8.00
138 Jonathan Ornelas 5.00 12.00
139 Tony Gonsolin 6.00 15.00
140 Ryder Green 2.50 6.00
141 Jackson Goddard 2.50 6.00
142 Durbin Feltman 4.00 10.00
143 Jeremy Pena 5.00 12.00
144 John Rooney 3.00 8.00
145 Everson Pereira 6.00 15.00
146 Jhoan Urena 2.50 6.00
147 Sandy Baez 2.50 6.00
148 Henry Henry 2.50 6.00
149 Taylor Widener 2.50 6.00
150 Trent Deveaux 3.00 8.00
151 Elehuris Montero 5.00 12.00
152 Miguel Amaya 12.00 30.00
153 Richard Gallardo 5.00 12.00
155 Luis Oviedo 2.50 6.00
156 Brewer Hicklen 4.00 10.00
157 Peter Solomon 2.50 6.00
158 Chad Spanberger 4.00 10.00
159 Andres Munoz 5.00 12.00
161 Luis Medina 4.00 10.00
162 Osiel Rodriguez 6.00 15.00
163 Roberto Ramos 4.00 10.00
164 Tristan Beck 3.00 8.00
165 DaShawn Keirsey Jr. 4.00 10.00
166 Eric Cole 5.00 12.00
167 Steven Jennings 2.50 6.00
168 Jose Cosma 2.50 6.00
169 Luis De La Cruz 2.50 6.00
170 Gregory Duran 2.50 6.00
171 Luis Encarnacion 2.50 6.00
172 Jose Pena 2.50 6.00
173 Lizandro Rodriguez 3.00 8.00
174 Leonel Sanchez 2.50 6.00
175 Luis Gil 3.00 8.00
176 Yonaldi Soto 2.50 6.00
177 Ariel Almonte 2.50 6.00
178 Jonathan Bautista 2.50 6.00
179 Saul Bautista 2.50 6.00
180 Luis Castillo 2.50 6.00
181 Armando Cruz 2.50 6.00
182 Danny De Andrande 2.50 6.00
183 Manny De La Rosa 2.50 6.00
184 Yamal Encarnacion 2.50 6.00
185 Willy Fana 2.50 6.00
186 Yamal Flores 2.50 6.00
187 Jayson Jimenez 2.50 6.00
188 Fraidel Liriano 2.50 6.00
189 Robelin Lopez 2.50 6.00
190 Yendel Mateo 2.50 6.00
191 Keiderson Pavon 2.50 6.00
192 Victor Quezada 2.50 6.00
193 Luis Ravelo 2.50 6.00
194 Elias Reynoso 2.50 6.00
195 Cristian Santana 5.00 12.00
196 Dervy Ventura 2.50 6.00
197 Kaito Yuki 4.00 10.00
198 Jake Irvin 2.50 6.00
199 Blaze Alexander 5.00 12.00
200 Zach Haake 2.50 6.00

2018 Elite Extra Edition Contenders College Tickets

RANDOM INSERTS IN PACKS
*HOLO: .5X TO 1.2X BASIC
1 Casey Mize 2.00 5.00
2 Blaine Knight .30 .75
3 Tristan Pompey .40 1.00
4 Cal Raleigh .25 .60
5 Ford Proctor .30 .75
6 Konnor Pilkington .30 .75
7 Kyle Isbel .60 1.50
8 Terrin Vavra .50 1.25
9 Jimmy Herron .25 .60
10 Jackson Goddard .25 .60
11 Durbin Feltman .40 1.00
12 Reid Schaller .25 .60
13 Jake Irvin .25 .60
14 Kody Clemens .50 1.25
15 Nick Madrigal 1.50 4.00
16 Logan Gilbert .40 1.00
17 Brady Singer .50 1.25
18 Trevor Larnach 1.50 4.00
19 Nico Hoerner 1.25 3.00
20 Seth Beer 1.00 2.50
21 Cadyn Grenier .30 .75
22 Jake McCarthy .30 .75
23 Luken Baker .40 1.00
24 Travis Swaggerty .75 2.00
25 Jeremy Eierman .30 .75
26 Ryan Rolison .50 1.25
27 Tim Cate .40 1.00
28 Steele Walker .30 .75
29 Tyler Frank .25 .60
30 Shane McClanahan .40 1.00
31 Casey Mize 2.00 5.00
32 Nick Madrigal 1.50 4.00
33 Seth Beer 1.00 2.50
34 Griffin Roberts .25 .60

2018 Elite Extra Edition Contenders College Tickets Signatures

RANDOM INSERTS IN PACKS
PRINT RUNS B/WN 5-99 COPIES PER
NO PRICING ON QTY 5
EXCHANGE DEADLINE 6/12/2020
*HOLO/25: .5X TO 1.2X p/r 40-99
1 Casey Mize/40 15.00 40.00
2 Blaine Knight/99 4.00 10.00
3 Tristan Pompey/99 5.00 12.00
4 Cal Raleigh/99 3.00 8.00
5 Ford Proctor/99 4.00 10.00
6 Konnor Pilkington/99 4.00 10.00
8 Terrin Vavra/99 4.00 10.00
9 Jimmy Herron/99 3.00 8.00
10 Jackson Goddard/99 3.00 8.00
11 Durbin Feltman/99 5.00 12.00
12 Reid Schaller/99 3.00 8.00
13 Jake Irvin/99 3.00 8.00
15 Nick Madrigal/25 12.00 30.00
20 Seth Beer/99 6.00 15.00
21 Cadyn Grenier/99 4.00 10.00
22 Jake McCarthy/99 5.00 12.00
23 Luken Baker/99 5.00 12.00
24 Travis Swaggerty/25 8.00 20.00
25 Jeremy Eierman/99 4.00 10.00
26 Ryan Rolison/99 4.00 10.00
27 Tim Cate/99 5.00 12.00
28 Steele Walker/99 4.00 10.00
29 Tyler Frank/99 3.00 8.00
31 Casey Mize/43 15.00 40.00
32 Nick Madrigal/25 12.00 30.00
33 Seth Beer/99 6.00 15.00
34 Griffin Roberts/99 3.00 8.00

2018 Elite Extra Edition Contenders USA Collegiate Tickets

RANDOM INSERTS IN PACKS
*HOLO: .5X TO 1.2X BASIC
1 Daniel Cabrera 1.00 2.50
2 Will Wilson .40 1.00
3 Braden Shewmake .75 2.00
4 John Doxakis .25 .60
5 Bryson Stott .75 2.00
6 Andrew Vaughn .75 2.00
7 Mason Feole .40 1.00
8 Shea Langeliers .50 1.25
9 Spencer Torkelson 1.50 4.00
10 Josh Jung .75 2.00
11 Bryant Packard .50 1.25
12 Jake Agnos .40 1.00
13 Andre Pallante .25 .60
14 Dominic Fletcher .30 .75
15 Adley Rutschman 1.50 4.00
16 Graeme Stinson .30 .75
17 Matt Cronin .25 .60
18 Max Meyer .75 2.00
19 Kenyon Yovan .30 .75
20 Tanner Burns .40 1.00
21 Drew Parrish .25 .60
22 Kyle Brnovich .25 .60
23 Zack Hess .30 .75
24 Zach Watson .25 .60
25 Zack Thompson .50 1.25
26 Parker Caracci .25 .60

2018 Elite Extra Edition Contenders USA Collegiate Tickets Signatures

RANDOM INSERTS IN PACKS
STATED PRINT RUN 99 SER.#'d SETS
EXCHANGE DEADLINE 6/12/2020
*RED/100: .4X TO 1X BASIC
*HOLO/25: .5X TO 1.2X BASIC
1 Daniel Cabrera 12.00 30.00
2 Will Wilson 5.00 12.00
3 Braden Shewmake 10.00 25.00
4 John Doxakis 3.00 8.00
5 Bryson Stott 10.00 25.00
6 Andrew Vaughn 12.00 30.00
7 Mason Feole 5.00 12.00
8 Shea Langeliers 12.00 30.00
9 Spencer Torkelson 50.00 120.00
10 Josh Jung 10.00 25.00
11 Bryant Packard 12.00 30.00
12 Jake Agnos 10.00 25.00
13 Andre Pallante 3.00 8.00
14 Dominic Fletcher 8.00 20.00
15 Adley Rutschman 100.00 250.00
16 Graeme Stinson 4.00 10.00
17 Matt Cronin 3.00 8.00
18 Max Meyer 10.00 25.00
19 Kenyon Yovan 4.00 10.00
20 Tanner Burns 5.00 12.00
21 Drew Parrish 3.00 8.00
22 Kyle Brnovich 3.00 8.00
23 Zack Hess 4.00 10.00
24 Zach Watson 3.00 8.00
25 Zack Thompson 6.00 15.00
26 Parker Caracci 3.00 8.00

2018 Elite Extra Edition Dual Materials

RANDOM INSERTS IN PACKS
PRINT RUNS B/WN 175-399 COPIES PER
1 Genesis Cabrera/199 2.50 6.00
2 Nick Senzel/199 4.00 10.00
3 Brendan Rodgers/399 2.00 5.00
4 Franklin Perez/199 1.50 4.00
5 Forrest Whitley/199 2.50 6.00
6 Kevin Maitan/399 2.00 5.00
7 Braxton Garrett/199 1.50 4.00
8 Corey Ray/199 2.00 5.00
10 Chris Shaw/199 1.50 4.00
11 Tyler Kolek/199 2.00 5.00
12 Bobby Bradley/199 2.00 5.00
13 Diego Infante/199 1.50 4.00
16 Luis Almanzar/199 1.50 4.00
17 Bo Bichette/399 3.00 8.00
18 Akil Baddoo/175 2.00 5.00
19 Cal Quantrill/399 1.50 4.00
20 Taylor Trammell/399 2.50 6.00

2018 Elite Extra Edition Dual Materials Gold

*GOLD: .4X TO 1X BASIC
RANDOM INSERTS IN PACKS
STATED PRINT RUN 99 SER.#'d SETS
14 Joshua Palacios 1.50 4.00
15 Kyle Lewis 3.00 8.00

2018 Elite Extra Edition Dual Materials Purple

*PURPLE: .6X TO 1.5X BASIC
RANDOM INSERTS IN PACKS
STATED PRINT RUN 25 SER.#'d SETS
14 Joshua Palacios 2.50 6.00
15 Kyle Lewis 5.00 12.00

2018 Elite Extra Edition Dual Materials Red

*RED: .4X TO 1X BASIC
RANDOM INSERTS IN PACKS
STATED PRINT RUN 49 SER.#'d SETS
14 Joshua Palacios 1.50 4.00
15 Kyle Lewis 3.00 8.00

2018 Elite Extra Edition Dual Materials Silver

*SILVER: .4X TO 1X BASIC
RANDOM INSERTS IN PACKS
STATED PRINT RUN 149 SER.#'d SETS
14 Joshua Palacios 1.50 4.00
15 Kyle Lewis 3.00 8.00

2018 Elite Extra Edition Dual Silhouettes

RANDOM INSERTS IN PACKS
STATED PRINT RUN 199 SER.#'d SETS
*GOLD/99: .4X TO 1X BASIC
*RED/49: .4X TO 1X BASIC
*SILVER/149: .4X TO 1X BASIC
*PURPLE/25: .6X TO 1.5X BASIC
1 Michael Chavis 2.50 6.00
2 Luis Robert 5.00 12.00
3 Eloy Jimenez 5.00 12.00
4 Yordan Alvarez 6.00 15.00
5 Brandon Marsh 2.00 5.00
6 DJ Peters 4.00 10.00
7 Nick Gordon 1.50 4.00
8 Justus Sheffield 2.00 5.00
9 Estevan Florial 6.00 15.00
10 Mitch Keller 2.00 5.00

2018 Elite Extra Edition Future Threads Silhouette Autographs

RANDOM INSERTS IN PACKS
PRINT RUNS B/WN 144-299 COPIES PER
EXCHANGE DEADLINE 6/12/2020
1 Fernando Tatis Jr./299 100.00 250.00
12 Jahmai Jones/268 3.00 8.00
14 Josh Staumont/299 3.00 8.00
15 Lucas Erceg/299 3.00 8.00
16 Estanli Castillo/299 3.00 8.00
18 Francisco Morales/299 4.00 10.00
22 Nathan Lukes/253 3.00 8.00
23 JoJo Romero/299 4.00 10.00
24 Yanio Perez/299 3.00 8.00
26 Kevin Sanchez/299 3.00 8.00
28 Akil Baddoo/199 4.00 10.00
29 Jose Siri/199 3.00 8.00
30 Nick Margevicius/286 3.00 8.00
31 Luis Escobar/299 3.00 8.00
32 Miguel Aparicio/144 3.00 8.00
34 James Nelson/144 3.00 8.00
35 DJ Peters/199 4.00 10.00
36 Samir Duenez/299 3.00 8.00
40 Daniel Brito/299 3.00 8.00
44 D.J. Wilson/299 3.00 8.00

2018 Elite Extra Edition Future Threads Silhouette Autographs Gold

*GOLD: .4X TO 1X BASIC
RANDOM INSERTS IN PACKS
STATED PRINT RUN 99 SER.#'d SETS
EXCHANGE DEADLINE 6/12/2020
4 Carter Kieboom 10.00 25.00
8 Estevan Florial 20.00 50.00
9 Kevin Newman 5.00 12.00
10 Leody Taveras 4.00 10.00
11 Jose de la Cruz 5.00 12.00
33 Yordan Alvarez 50.00 120.00

2018 Elite Extra Edition Future Threads Silhouette Autographs Purple

*PURPLE/25: .5X TO 1.2X BASIC
RANDOM INSERTS IN PACKS
PRINT RUNS B/WN 15-25 COPIES PER
NO PRICING ON QTY 15
EXCHANGE DEADLINE 6/12/2020
2 Ke'Bryan Hayes/25 10.00 25.00
5 Orelvis Martinez/25 15.00 40.00
6 Noelvi Marte/25 8.00 20.00
7 Marco Luciano/25 30.00 80.00
8 Estevan Florial/25 30.00 80.00
9 Kevin Newman/25 8.00 20.00
10 Leody Taveras/25 8.00 20.00
11 Jose de la Cruz/25 8.00 20.00
13 Austin Riley/25 50.00 120.00
17 Kevin Alcantara/25 20.00 50.00
19 Chris Shaw/25 5.00 12.00
20 Mitch Keller/25 10.00 25.00
21 Taylor Trammell/25 12.00 30.00
25 Peter Alonso/25 75.00 200.00
27 Omar Florentino/25 8.00 20.00
37 Julio Pablo Martinez/25 25.00 60.00
38 Jose Garcia/25 5.00 12.00
39 Freudis Nova/25 10.00 25.00
41 Sergio Campana/25 5.00 12.00
42 Wander Franco/25 125.00 300.00
43 Bo Bichette/25 20.00 50.00

2018 Elite Extra Edition Future Threads Silhouette Autographs Red

*RED/49: .4X TO 1X BASIC
*RED/25: .5X TO 1.2X BASIC
RANDOM INSERTS IN PACKS
PRINT RUNS B/WN 25-49 COPIES PER
EXCHANGE DEADLINE 6/12/2020
3 Shane Baz/25 6.00 15.00
6 Noelvi Marte/49 6.00 15.00
7 Marco Luciano/49 25.00 60.00
8 Estevan Florial/49 25.00 60.00
9 Kevin Newman/49 6.00 15.00
10 Leody Taveras/49 5.00 12.00
11 Jose de la Cruz/49 6.00 15.00
17 Kevin Alcantara/49 15.00 40.00
19 Chris Shaw/49 4.00 10.00
20 Mitch Keller/49 8.00 20.00
21 Taylor Trammell/49 10.00 25.00
25 Peter Alonso/49 25.00 60.00
27 Omar Florentino/49 6.00 15.00
38 Jose Garcia/49 4.00 10.00
39 Freudis Nova/49 8.00 20.00
41 Sergio Campana/49 4.00 10.00
42 Wander Franco/49 100.00 250.00

2018 Elite Extra Edition OptiChrome

RANDOM INSERTS IN PACKS
*HOLO: .5X TO 1.2X BASIC
1 Casey Mize 2.00 5.00
2 Joey Bart 2.50 6.00
3 Alec Bohm 1.25 3.00
4 Nick Madrigal 1.50 4.00
5 Jonathan India .40 1.00
6 Jarred Kelenic 2.50 6.00
7 Ryan Weathers .30 .75
8 Franklin Perez .25 .60
9 Travis Swaggerty .75 2.00
10 Grayson Rodriguez .50 1.25
12 Connor Scott .30 .75
15 Matthew Liberatore .30 .75
20 Brice Turang .75 2.00
22 Anthony Seigler .60 1.50
24 Diego Cartaya 1.50 4.00
25 Triston Casas 2.00 5.00
26 Mason Denaburg .30 .75
34 Ethan Hankins .30 .75
36 Cadyn Grenier .30 .75
38 Jake McCarthy .40 1.00
56 Jeremiah Jackson .40 1.00
62 Alek Thomas 1.00 2.50
68 Will Banfield .25 .60
78 Kody Clemens .50 1.25
86 Kevin Sanchez .25 .60
87 Adbert Alzolay .30 .75
88 Akil Baddoo .30 .75
89 Jose Siri .25 .60
90 Nick Margevicius .25 .60
91 Jeisson Rosario .40 1.00
92 Sandro Fabian .25 .60
94 Miguel Aparicio .25 .60
95 James Nelson .25 .60
96 Bo Bichette 1.00 2.50
99 Sixto Sanchez .60 1.50
100 Samad Taylor .25 .60
107 Mateo Gil .25 .60
111 Victor Victor Mesa 1.00 2.50
112 Casey Mize 2.00 5.00
113 Bo Bichette 1.00 2.50

2018 Elite Extra Edition OptiChrome Signatures

RANDOM INSERTS IN PACKS
PRINT RUNS B/WN 5-99 COPIES PER
NO PRICING ON QTY 10 OR LESS
EXCHANGE DEADLINE 6/12/2020
*HOLO/25: .5X TO 1.2X p/r 49-99
4 Nick Madrigal/99 10.00 25.00
5 Jonathan India/25 25.00 60.00
6 Jarred Kelenic/99 12.00 30.00
7 Ryan Weathers/99 4.00 10.00
15 Matthew Liberatore/99 4.00 10.00
20 Brice Turang/99 5.00 12.00
22 Anthony Seigler/99 5.00 12.00
25 Triston Casas/99 5.00 12.00
26 Mason Denaburg/99 4.00 10.00
34 Ethan Hankins/99 4.00 10.00
36 Cadyn Grenier/99 4.00 10.00
38 Jake McCarthy/52 5.00 12.00
56 Jeremiah Jackson/79 5.00 12.00
62 Alek Thomas/99 6.00 15.00
68 Will Banfield/99 3.00 8.00
78 Kody Clemens/99 6.00 15.00
86 Kevin Sanchez/49 3.00 8.00
91 Jeisson Rosario/49 5.00 12.00
92 Sandro Fabian/49 5.00 12.00
100 Samad Taylor/76 3.00 8.00
107 Mateo Gil/99 3.00 8.00

2018 Elite Extra Edition Prospect Materials

RANDOM INSERTS IN PACKS
STATED PRINT RUN 199 SER.#'d SETS
1 Austin Riley 3.00 8.00
2 Jose Siri 1.50 4.00
3 Taylor Trammell 2.50 6.00
4 Josh Staumont 1.50 4.00
5 Samir Duenez 1.50 4.00
6 Jahmai Jones 1.50 4.00
7 Brayan Hernandez 1.50 4.00
8 James Nelson 1.50 4.00
9 Lucas Erceg 1.50 4.00
11 Kevin Newman 2.50 6.00
13 Cal Quantrill 1.50 4.00
14 Bryan Reynolds 2.50 6.00
15 Heliot Ramos 2.50 6.00
16 Jesus Sanchez 1.50 4.00
18 Miguel Aparicio 1.50 4.00
19 Carter Kieboom 2.50 6.00
20 Fernando Tatis Jr. 12.00 30.00

2018 Elite Extra Edition Prospect Materials Gold

*GOLD: .4X TO 1X BASIC
RANDOM INSERTS IN PACKS
STATED PRINT RUN 99 SER.#'d SETS
10 JoJo Romero 2.00 5.00
12 Luis Escobar 1.50 4.00
17 Wei-Chieh Huang 2.50 6.00

2018 Elite Extra Edition Prospect Materials Purple

*PURPLE: .6X TO 1.5X BASIC
RANDOM INSERTS IN PACKS
STATED PRINT RUN 25 SER.#'d SETS
10 JoJo Romero 3.00 8.00
12 Luis Escobar 2.50 6.00
17 Wei-Chieh Huang 4.00 10.00

2018 Elite Extra Edition Prospect Materials Red

*RED: .4X TO 1X BASIC
RANDOM INSERTS IN PACKS
STATED PRINT RUN 49 SER.#'d SETS
10 JoJo Romero 2.00 5.00
17 Wei-Chieh Huang 2.50 6.00

2018 Elite Extra Edition Prospect Materials Silver

*SILVER: .4X TO 1X BASIC
RANDOM INSERTS IN PACKS
STATED PRINT RUN 149 SER.#'d SETS
10 JoJo Romero 2.00 5
12 Luis Escobar 1.50 4

2018 Elite Extra Edition Qua Materials

RANDOM INSERTS IN PACKS
PRINT RUNS B/WN 199-399 COPIES PER
1 Jon Duplantier/399 1.50 4
2 D.J. Wilson/399 1.50 4
3 Akil Baddoo/199 2.00 5
4 Luis Ortiz/249 1.50 4.
5 Brayan Hernandez/399 1.50 4
6 DJ Peters/399 4.00 10
8 Ke'Bryan Hayes/399 1.50 4.
9 Shane Baz/399 2.00 5.
11 Cal Quantrill/399 1.50 4.
13 Aneury Tavarez/399 1.50 4.
14 Max Pentecost/399 1.50 4
16 Thairo Estrada/299 4.00 10.
18 Yusniel Diaz/399 5.00 12
19 Erling Moreno/399 3.00 8.
20 Freudis Nova/399 5.00 12.

2018 Elite Extra Edition Quad Materials Gold

*GOLD: .4X TO 1X BASIC
RANDOM INSERTS IN PACKS
PRINT RUNS B/WN 75-99 COPIES PER
7 Jose Siri/99 1.50 4.
15 Nathan Lukes/99 1.50 4.
17 Yanio Perez/99 1.50 4.

2018 Elite Extra Edition Quad Materials Purple

*PURPLE: .6X TO 1.5X BASIC
RANDOM INSERTS IN PACKS
STATED PRINT RUN 25 SER.#'d SETS
7 Jose Siri 2.50 6.
10 Jomar Reyes 10.00 25.
12 Julio Pablo Martinez 8.00 20.
15 Nathan Lukes 2.50 6.
17 Yanio Perez 2.50 6.

2018 Elite Extra Edition Quad Materials Red

*RED: .4X TO 1X BASIC
RANDOM INSERTS IN PACKS
STATED PRINT RUN 49 SER.#'d SETS
15 Nathan Lukes 1.50 4.
17 Yanio Perez 1.50 4.

2018 Elite Extra Edition Quad Materials Silver

*SILVER: .4X TO 1X BASIC
RANDOM INSERTS IN PACKS
PRINT RUNS B/WN 99-149 COPIES PER
7 Jose Siri/125 1.50 4.
15 Nathan Lukes/149 1.50 4.
17 Yanio Perez/149 1.50 4.

2018 Elite Extra Edition Triple Materials

RANDOM INSERTS IN PACKS
STATED PRINT RUN 399 SER.#'d SETS
1 Wander Franco 6.00 15.
2 Justus Sheffield 2.00 5.
3 Franklin Perez 1.50 4.
5 James Nelson 1.50 4.
7 Austin Riley 3.00 8.
8 Chris Shaw 1.50 4.
9 Heliot Ramos 2.50 6.
10 Jahmai Jones 1.50 4.
11 Miguel Aparicio 1.50 4.
13 JoJo Romero 2.00 5.
14 Jesus Sanchez 1.50 4.
15 Carter Kieboom 2.50 6.
16 Sean Murphy 2.50 6.
17 Josh Staumont 1.50 4.
18 Lucas Erceg 1.50 4.
20 Luis Escobar 1.50 4.

2018 Elite Extra Edition Triple Materials Gold

*GOLD: .4X TO 1X BASIC
RANDOM INSERTS IN PACKS
STATED PRINT RUN 99 SER.#'d SETS
4 Yordan Alvarez 3.00 8.
6 Brandon Marsh 2.00 5.0
12 Kevin Newman 2.50 6.
19 Nick Margevicius 1.50 4.

2018 Elite Extra Edition Triple Materials Purple

*PURPLE: .6X TO 1.5X BASIC
RANDOM INSERTS IN PACKS
STATED PRINT RUN 25 SER.#'d SETS
4 Yordan Alvarez 5.00 12.
6 Brandon Marsh 3.00 8.
12 Kevin Newman 4.00 10.
19 Nick Margevicius 2.50 6.0

2018 Elite Extra Edition Triple Materials Red

*RED: .4X TO 1X BASIC
RANDOM INSERTS IN PACKS
STATED PRINT RUN 49 SER.#'d SETS
4 Yordan Alvarez 3.00 8.0
6 Brandon Marsh 2.00 5.0
12 Kevin Newman 2.50 6.0
19 Nick Margevicius 1.50 4.0

2018 Elite Extra Edition Triple Materials Silver

*SILVER: .4X TO 1X BASIC
RANDOM INSERTS IN PACKS

TED PRINT RUN 149 SER.#'d SETS
rdan Alvarez 3.00 8.00
andon Marsh 2.00 5.00
Kevin Newman 2.50 6.00
Nick Margevicius 1.50 4.00

2018 Elite Extra Edition USA Baseball 15U Signatures

DOM INSERTS IN PACKS
TED PRINT RUN 99 SER.#'d SETS
HANGE DEADLINE 6/12/2020
D/100: .4X TO 1X BASIC
UE/25: .5X TO 1.2X BASIC
an Spikes 3.00 8.00
vis Diaz 3.00 8.00
ree Reed 3.00 8.00
eego McIntosh 3.00 8.00
rson Bowen 8.00 20.00
stin Colon 4.00 10.00
ge Ziehl 3.00 8.00
le Lansville 3.00 8.00
Ryan Clifford 6.00 15.00
Samuel Dutton 3.00 8.00
Joseph Brown 3.00 8.00
Cody Schrier 3.00 8.00
Charlie Saum 3.00 8.00
Luke Leto 10.00 25.00
Andrew Painter 4.00 10.00
Brady House 4.00 10.00
Josh Hartle 4.00 10.00
Christian Little 3.00 8.00
Thomas DiLandri 4.00 10.00

2018 Elite Extra Edition USA Baseball 18U Signatures

NDOM INSERTS IN PACKS
ATED PRINT RUN 99 SER.#'d SETS
CHANGE DEADLINE 6/12/2020
ED/100: .4X TO 1X BASIC
LUE/25: .5X TO 1.2X BASIC
J Abrams 12.00 30.00
yler Callihan 4.00 10.00
orbin Carroll 8.00 20.00
Riley Cornelio 3.00 8.00
Pete Crow-Armstrong 6.00 15.00
Sammy Faltine 4.00 10.00
Riley Greene 12.00 30.00
Ryan Hawks 4.00 10.00
Jared Kelley 3.00 8.00
Jack Leiter 4.00 10.00
Brennan Malone 5.00 12.00
Jacob Meador 3.00 8.00
Max Rajcic 3.00 8.00
Avery Short 4.00 10.00
Anthony Volpe 6.00 15.00
Bobby Witt Jr. 30.00 80.00
Dylan Crews 8.00 20.00
Yohandy Morales 4.00 10.00
Drew Romo 8.00 20.00
Timmy Manning 5.00 12.00

2018 Elite Extra Edition USA Collegiate Silhouette Autographs

ANDOM INSERTS IN PACKS
TATED PRINT RUN 99 SER.#'d SETS
XCHANGE DEADLINE 6/12/2020
GOLD/49: .5X TO 1.2X BASIC
RED/25: .6X TO 1.5X BASIC
Daniel Cabrera 12.00 30.00
Will Wilson 5.00 12.00
Braden Shewmake 10.00 25.00
John Doxakis 3.00 8.00
Bryson Stott 10.00 25.00
Andrew Vaughn 15.00 40.00
Mason Feole 5.00 12.00
Shea Langeliers 12.00 30.00
Spencer Torkelson 50.00 120.00
0 Josh Jung 10.00 25.00
Bryant Packard 8.00 20.00
2 Jake Agnos 8.00 20.00
3 Andre Pallante 3.00 8.00
4 Dominic Fletcher 4.00 10.00
5 Adley Rutschman 60.00 150.00
6 Graeme Stinson 4.00 10.00
7 Matt Cronin 3.00 8.00
8 Max Meyer 10.00 25.00
9 Kenyon Yovan 4.00 10.00
0 Tanner Burns 5.00 12.00
1 Drew Parrish 3.00 8.00
2 Kyle Brnovich 3.00 8.00
3 Zack Hess 4.00 10.00
4 Zach Watson 3.00 8.00
5 Zack Thompson 6.00 15.00
6 Parker Caracci 3.00 8.00

2018 Elite Extra Edition USA Materials

ANDOM INSERTS IN PACKS
RINT RUNS B/WN 225-399 COPIES PER
0 Alex Faedo/399 2.50 6.00
1 A.J. Puk/225 2.00 5.00
2 Corey Ray/399 2.00 5.00

2018 Elite Extra Edition USA Materials Gold

GOLD: .4X TO 1X BASIC
ANDOM INSERTS IN PACKS
TATED PRINT RUN 99 SER.#'d SETS
Casey Mize/99 6.00 15.00
Jarred Kelenic/99 5.00 12.00
Ryan Weathers/99 2.00 5.00
Travis Swaggerty/99 4.00 10.00
Connor Scott/99 2.00 5.00
Matthew Liberatore/99 2.00 5.00
Nolan Gorman/99 6.00 15.00
Brice Turang/99 3.00 8.00
10 Ryan Rolison/99 3.00 8.00
11 Anthony Seigler/99 3.00 8.00
12 Nico Hoerner/99 4.00 10.00
13 Triston Casas/99 4.00 10.00
15 Seth Beer/99 8.00 20.00
17 Ethan Hankins/99 2.00 5.00
18 Cadyn Grenier/99 2.00 5.00
19 Jake McCarthy/99 2.50 6.00
20 Steele Walker/99 2.00 5.00
21 Tyler Frank/99 1.50 4.00
22 Jeremiah Jackson/99 3.00 8.00
23 Alek Thomas/99 3.00 8.00
24 Tim Cate/99 2.50 6.00
25 Will Banfield/99 1.50 4.00
26 Jeremy Eierman/99 2.00 5.00
27 Luken Baker/99 3.00 8.00
28 Brendan McKay/99 2.50 6.00
31 Shane Baz/99 2.00 5.00
33 Royce Lewis/99 6.00 15.00
35 Bryan Reynolds/99 2.50 6.00
36 Forrest Whitley/99 2.50 6.00
37 Braxton Garrett/99 1.50 4.00
38 Keston Hiura/99 3.00 8.00
39 Zack Collins/99 2.00 5.00
40 Evan White/99 2.50 6.00

2018 Elite Extra Edition USA Materials Purple

*PURPLE: .6X TO 1.5X BASIC
RANDOM INSERTS IN PACKS
STATED PRINT RUN 25 SER.#'d SETS
1 Casey Mize/25 10.00 25.00
2 Nick Madrigal/25 8.00 20.00
3 Jarred Kelenic/25 8.00 20.00
4 Ryan Weathers/25 3.00 8.00
5 Travis Swaggerty/25 6.00 15.00
6 Connor Scott/25 3.00 8.00
7 Matthew Liberatore/25 3.00 8.00
8 Nolan Gorman/25 10.00 25.00
10 Ryan Rolison/25 5.00 12.00
11 Anthony Seigler/25 5.00 12.00
12 Nico Hoerner/25 6.00 15.00
13 Triston Casas/25 6.00 15.00
15 Seth Beer/25 12.00 30.00
17 Ethan Hankins/25 3.00 8.00
19 Jake McCarthy/25 4.00 10.00
20 Steele Walker/25 3.00 8.00
21 Tyler Frank/25 2.50 6.00
22 Jeremiah Jackson/25 5.00 12.00
24 Tim Cate/25 4.00 10.00
25 Will Banfield/25 2.50 6.00
26 Jeremy Eierman/25 3.00 8.00
28 Brendan McKay/25 4.00 10.00
31 Shane Baz/25 3.00 8.00
33 Royce Lewis/25 10.00 25.00
34 Kyle Wright/25 5.00 12.00
38 Keston Hiura/25 5.00 12.00
40 Evan White/25 4.00 10.00

2018 Elite Extra Edition USA Materials Red

*RED: .4X TO 1X BASIC
RANDOM INSERTS IN PACKS
STATED PRINT RUN 49 SER.#'d SETS
1 Casey Mize/49 6.00 15.00
2 Nick Madrigal/49 5.00 12.00
3 Jarred Kelenic/49 5.00 12.00
4 Ryan Weathers/49 2.00 5.00
5 Travis Swaggerty/49 4.00 10.00
6 Connor Scott/49 2.00 5.00
7 Matthew Liberatore/49 2.00 5.00
8 Nolan Gorman/49 6.00 15.00
9 Brice Turang/49 3.00 8.00
10 Ryan Rolison/49 3.00 8.00
11 Anthony Seigler/49 3.00 8.00
12 Nico Hoerner/49 4.00 10.00
13 Triston Casas/49 4.00 10.00
15 Seth Beer/49 8.00 20.00
17 Ethan Hankins/49 2.00 5.00
18 Cadyn Grenier/49 2.00 5.00
19 Jake McCarthy/49 2.50 6.00
20 Steele Walker/49 2.00 5.00
21 Tyler Frank/49 1.50 4.00
22 Jeremiah Jackson/49 3.00 8.00
23 Alek Thomas/49 3.00 8.00
24 Tim Cate/49 2.50 6.00
25 Will Banfield/49 1.50 4.00
26 Jeremy Eierman/49 2.00 5.00
27 Luken Baker/49 3.00 8.00
28 Brendan McKay/49 2.50 6.00
31 Shane Baz/49 2.00 5.00
33 Royce Lewis/49 6.00 15.00
34 Kyle Wright/49 3.00 8.00
35 Bryan Reynolds/49 2.50 6.00
36 Forrest Whitley/49 2.50 6.00
37 Braxton Garrett/49 1.50 4.00
38 Keston Hiura/49 3.00 8.00
39 Zack Collins/49 2.00 5.00
40 Evan White/49 2.50 6.00

2018 Elite Extra Edition USA Materials Silver

*SILVER: .4X TO 1X BASIC
RANDOM INSERTS IN PACKS
PRINT RUNS B/WN 99-149 COPIES PER
1 Casey Mize/149 6.00 15.00
3 Jarred Kelenic/149 5.00 12.00
5 Travis Swaggerty/149 4.00 10.00
27 Luken Baker/149 3.00 8.00
28 Brendan McKay/149 2.50 6.00
36 Forrest Whitley/149 2.50 6.00
37 Braxton Garrett/149 1.50 4.00

2019 Elite Extra Edition

STATED PRINT RUN 999 SER.#'d SETS
1 Adley Rutschman 4.00 10.00
2 Bobby Witt Jr. 5.00 12.00
3 Andrew Vaughn .75 2.00
4 JJ Bleday 1.25 3.00
5 Riley Greene 1.00 2.50
6 CJ Abrams 1.25 3.00
7 Nick Lodolo .50 1.25
8 Josh Jung .75 2.00
9 Shea Langeliers .50 1.25
10 Hunter Bishop .75 2.00
11 Alek Manoah .50 1.25
12 Brett Baty .50 1.25
13 Keoni Cavaco .60 1.50
14 Bryson Stott .75 2.00
15 Will Wilson .40 1.00
16 Corbin Carroll .40 1.00
17 Jackson Rutledge .50 1.25
18 Quinn Priester .40 1.00
19 Zack Thompson .40 1.00
20 George Kirby .40 1.00
21 Braden Shewmake .75 2.00
22 Greg Jones .30 .75
23 Michael Toglia .40 1.00
24 Daniel Espino .30 .75
25 Kody Hoese .75 2.00
26 Blake Walston .40 1.00
27 Ryan Jensen .40 1.00
28 Ethan Small .30 .75
29 Logan Davidson .25 .60
30 Anthony Volpe .75 2.00
31 Michael Busch .75 2.00
32 Korey Lee .50 1.25
33 Brennan Malone .25 .60
34 Drey Jameson .25 .60
35 Kameron Misner .60 1.50
36 J.J. Goss .30 .75
37 Sammy Siani .30 .75
38 T.J. Sikkema .40 1.00
39 Matt Wallner .50 1.25
40 Seth Johnson .25 .60
41 Davis Wendzel .30 .75
42 Gunnar Henderson .50 1.25
43 Cameron Cannon .50 1.25
44 Brady McConnell .40 1.00
45 Matthew Thompson .30 .75
46 Nasim Nunez .25 .60
47 Nick Quintana .50 1.25
48 Joshua Mears .50 1.25
49 Rece Hinds .30 .75
50 Ryan Garcia .25 .60
51 Logan Wyatt .40 1.00
52 Kendall Williams .40 1.00
53 Josh Wolf .30 .75
54 Matt Canterino .30 .75
55 Will Holland .40 1.00
56 Glenallen Hill Jr. .40 1.00
57 Matt Gorski .40 1.00
58 Trejyn Fletcher .40 1.00
59 Brandon Williamson .40 1.00
60 Beau Philip .40 1.00
61 John Doxakis .40 1.00
62 Aaron Schunk .50 1.25
63 Yordys Valdes .50 1.25
64 Chase Strumpf .50 1.25
65 Antoine Kelly .50 1.25
66 Tyler Baum .30 .75
67 Josh Smith .50 1.25
68 Jacob Sanford .50 1.25
69 Matthew Lugo .40 1.00
70 Alec Marsh .30 .75
71 Kyle Stowers .40 1.00
72 Jared Triolo .40 1.00
73 Logan Driscoll .40 1.00
74 Tommy Henry .30 .75
75 Dominic Fletcher .25 .60
76 Isaiah Campbell .50 1.25
77 Karl Kauffmann .25 .60
78 Jimmy Lewis .25 .60
79 Zach Watson .40 1.00
80 Tyler Callihan .30 .75
81 Matthew Allan .50 1.25
82 Jack Kochanowicz .30 .75
83 Dasan Brown .60 1.50
84 Ryan Pepiot .25 .60
85 Tristin English .25 .60
86 Erik Miller .60 1.50
87 Matt Cronin .25 .60
88 Graeme Stinson .25 .60
89 Brandon Lewis .40 1.00
90 Kyle McCann .30 .75
91 Logan O'Hoppe .25 .60
92 D'Shawn Knowles .30 .75
93 Miguel Vargas 1.25 3.00
94 Shervyen Newton .40 1.00
95 Deivi Garcia 1.25 3.00
96 Brailyn Marquez .60 1.50
97 Bryan Rocchio 1.00 2.50
98 Shane Sasaki .25 .60
99 Randy Arozarena 8.00 20.00
100 Jarren Duran 1.50 4.00
114 Sherten Apostel .60 1.50
115 Noah Song .75 2.00
116 Andrew Dalquist .25 .60
117 Miguel Hiraldo .75 2.00
118 Jasseel De La Cruz .25 .60
119 Abraham Toro .40 1.00
120 Ismael Mena .40 1.00
121 Devin Mann 1.25 3.00
122 Austin Shenton .25 .60
123 Evan Fitterer .60 1.50
124 Antonio Cabello .50 1.25
125 Jhoan Duran .40 1.00
126 Kyren Paris .25 .60
127 Moises Gomez .40 1.00
128 Jose Devers .40 1.00
129 Carlos Rodriguez .25 .60
130 Jhon Torres .25 .60
131 Randy Florentino .25 .60
132 Ryne Nelson .30 .75
133 Livan Soto .30 .75
134 Gabriel Maciel .25 .60
135 Ronny Brito .25 .60
136 Yeison Coca .25 .60
137 Lenyn Sosa .25 .60
138 Oswaldo Cabrera .25 .60
139 Ivan Herrera .40 1.00
140 Michael Grove .25 .60
141 Aaron Hernandez .25 .60
142 CJ Alexander .75 2.00
143 Mason Englert .25 .60
144 Brenden Spillane .25 .60
145 Hogan Harris .25 .60
146 Tucker Davidson .25 .60
147 Michael Massey .30 .75
148 Jasson Dominguez 20.00 50.00
149 Spencer Steer .25 .60
150 Tyler Dyson .25 .60
151 Cody Bolton .40 1.00
152 Osleivis Basabe .25 .60
153 Eddy Diaz .25 .60
154 Michael Harris .25 .60
155 Ryan Zeferjahn .30 .75
156 Liover Peguero .40 1.00
157 Aaron Ashby .25 .60
158 Alvaro Seijas .30 .75
159 Canaan Smith .40 1.00
160 Jose Soriano
161 Sandy Gaston .25 .60
162 Gabriel Moreno .40 1.00
163 Gilberto Jimenez 1.50 4.00
164 Joe Ryan .40 1.00
165 Joey Cantillo .50 1.25
166 Jose Salas .40 1.00
167 David Parkinson .25 .60
168 Luis Matos .40 1.00
169 Luisangel Acuna .75 2.00
170 Tarik Skubal 1.25 3.00
171 Thad Ward .25 .60
172 Jose Rodriguez .25 .60
173 Drew Rom .25 .60
174 Israel Pineda .40 1.00
175 Wilderd Patino .25 .60
176 Trevor McDonald .25 .60
177 Avery Short .25 .60
178 Trey Harris .30 .75
179 Luis Toribio .25 .60
180 Nathan Patterson .25 .60
181 Leo Crawford .25 .60
182 Alejandro Kirk .40 1.00
183 Justin Dean .30 .75
184 Cristian Batista .25 .60
185 Jefferson De La Cruz .25 .60
186 Cristofer Espinola .25 .60
187 Wilton Lara .25 .60
188 Fidel Montero .40 1.00
189 Aneudis Mordan .25 .60
190 Joel Peguero .25 .60
191 John Peguero .25 .60
192 Bryan Pena .25 .60
193 Salvador Ramirez .25 .60
194 Rhaybel Roso .25 .60
195 Jay Vargas .25 .60
196 Wesley Zapata .25 .60
197 Josefrailin Alcantara .60 1.50
198 Rodolfo Caraballo .25 .60
199 Elizual Chalas .25 .60
200 Elian Cortorreal .25 .60
201 Randy De Jesus .25 .60
202 Aneudi Escanio .25 .60
203 Xavier Guillen .30 .75
204 Yanki Jean .25 .60
205 Maximo Maria .25 .60
206 Juan Martinez .25 .60
207 Yasser Mercedes .25 .60
208 Jeral Perez .30 .75
209 Jhonny Severino .25 .60
210 Ivan Sosa .30 .75
211 Miguel Tamares .25 .60
212 Braylin Tavera .25 .60
213 Sebastian Castro .25 .60

2019 Elite Extra Edition Aspirations Blue

*ASP.BLUE: .75X TO 2X BASIC
RANDOM INSERTS IN PACKS
STATED PRINT RUN 75 SER.#'d SETS

2019 Elite Extra Edition Aspirations Orange

*ASP ORANGE: .6X TO 1.5X BASIC
RANDOM INSERTS IN PACKS
STATED PRINT RUN 100 SER.#'d SETS

2019 Elite Extra Edition Aspirations Purple

*ASP PURPLE: .5X TO 1.2X BASIC
RANDOM INSERTS IN PACKS
STATED PRINT RUN 250 SER.#'d SETS

2019 Elite Extra Edition Aspirations Red

*ASP RED: .6X TO 1.5X BASIC
RANDOM INSERTS IN PACKS
STATED PRINT RUN 150 SER.#'d SETS

2019 Elite Extra Edition Aspirations Tie Dye

*ASP.TIE DYE: 1.2X TO 3X BASIC
RANDOM INSERTS IN PACKS
STATED PRINT RUN 25 SER.#'d SETS

2019 Elite Extra Edition Pink

*PINK: .6X TO 1.5X BASIC
RANDOM INSERTS IN PACKS

2019 Elite Extra Edition Status Die Cut Blue

*STAT.BLUE DC: .75X TO 2X BASIC
RANDOM INSERTS IN PACKS
STATED PRINT RUN 75 SER.#'d SETS

2019 Elite Extra Edition Status Die Cut Emerald

*STAT.EMRLD.DC: 1X TO 2.5X BASIC
RANDOM INSERTS IN PACKS
STATED PRINT RUN 49 SER.#'d SETS

2019 Elite Extra Edition Status Die Cut Purple

*STAT.PURPLE DC: .6X TO 1.5X BASIC
RANDOM INSERTS IN PACKS
STATED PRINT RUN 125 SER.#'d SETS

2019 Elite Extra Edition Status Die Cut Red

*STAT.RED DC: .75X TO 2X BASIC
RANDOM INSERTS IN PACKS
STATED PRINT RUN 99 SER.#'d SETS

2019 Elite Extra Edition Status Die Cut Tie Dye

*STAT.TIE DYE DC: 1.2X TO 3X BASIC
RANDOM INSERTS IN PACKS
STATED PRINT RUN 25 SER.#'d SETS

2019 Elite Extra Edition Autographs

1 Adley Rutschman 30.00 80.00
2 Bobby Witt Jr. 20.00 50.00
3 Andrew Vaughn 10.00 25.00
4 JJ Bleday 12.00 30.00
5 Riley Greene 10.00 25.00
6 CJ Abrams 10.00 25.00
7 Nick Lodolo 5.00 12.00
8 Josh Jung 10.00 25.00
9 Shea Langeliers 5.00 12.00
10 Hunter Bishop 8.00 20.00
11 Alek Manoah 6.00 15.00
12 Brett Baty
13 Keoni Cavaco 6.00 15.00
14 Bryson Stott 8.00 20.00
15 Will Wilson 6.00 15.00
16 Corbin Carroll 6.00 15.00
17 Jackson Rutledge 5.00 12.00
18 Quinn Priester 4.00 10.00
19 Zack Thompson 5.00 12.00
20 George Kirby 4.00 10.00
21 Braden Shewmake 5.00 12.00
22 Greg Jones 3.00 8.00
23 Michael Toglia 4.00 10.00
24 Daniel Espino 3.00 8.00
25 Kody Hoese 5.00 12.00
26 Blake Walston 4.00 10.00
27 Ryan Jensen 4.00 10.00
28 Ethan Small 3.00 8.00
29 Logan Davidson 2.50 6.00
30 Anthony Volpe 6.00 15.00
32 Korey Lee 5.00 12.00
34 Drey Jameson 2.50 6.00
35 Kameron Misner 5.00 12.00
36 J.J. Goss 3.00 8.00
37 Sammy Siani 3.00 8.00
38 T.J. Sikkema 4.00 10.00
39 Matt Wallner 5.00 12.00
40 Seth Johnson 2.50 6.00
41 Davis Wendzel 3.00 8.00
42 Gunnar Henderson 5.00 12.00
43 Cameron Cannon 5.00 12.00
44 Brady McConnell 4.00 10.00
45 Matthew Thompson 3.00 8.00
46 Nasim Nunez 2.50 6.00
47 Nick Quintana 5.00 12.00
48 Joshua Mears 5.00 12.00
49 Rece Hinds 3.00 8.00
50 Ryan Garcia 2.50 6.00
51 Logan Wyatt 4.00 10.00
52 Kendall Williams 4.00 10.00
53 Josh Wolf 3.00 8.00
54 Matt Canterino 3.00 8.00
55 Will Holland 4.00 10.00
56 Glenallen Hill Jr. 4.00 10.00
57 Matt Gorski 4.00 10.00
58 Trejyn Fletcher 4.00 10.00
59 Brandon Williamson 4.00 10.00
60 Beau Philip 4.00 10.00
62 Aaron Schunk 5.00 12.00
63 Yordys Valdes 5.00 12.00
64 Chase Strumpf 5.00 12.00
65 Antoine Kelly 5.00 12.00
66 Tyler Baum 3.00 8.00
67 Josh Smith 5.00 12.00
68 Jacob Sanford 5.00 12.00
69 Matthew Lugo 4.00 10.00
70 Alec Marsh 3.00 8.00
71 Kyle Stowers 4.00 10.00
72 Jared Triolo 4.00 10.00
73 Logan Driscoll 4.00 10.00
74 Tommy Henry 3.00 8.00
75 Dominic Fletcher 2.50 6.00
76 Isaiah Campbell 5.00 12.00
77 Karl Kauffmann 2.50 6.00
78 Jimmy Lewis 2.50 6.00
79 Zach Watson 4.00 10.00
80 Tyler Callihan 3.00 8.00
81 Matthew Allan 5.00 12.00
82 Jack Kochanowicz 3.00 8.00
83 Dasan Brown 6.00 15.00
84 Ryan Pepiot 2.50 6.00
85 Tristin English 2.50 6.00
87 Matt Cronin 2.50 6.00
88 Graeme Stinson 2.50 6.00
89 Brandon Lewis 4.00 10.00
90 Kyle McCann 3.00 8.00
91 Logan O'Hoppe 2.50 6.00
93 Miguel Vargas 10.00 25.00
94 Shervyen Newton 4.00 10.00
95 Deivi Garcia 12.00 30.00
96 Brailyn Marquez 6.00 15.00
97 Bryan Rocchio 10.00 25.00
98 Shane Sasaki 2.50 6.00
99 Randy Arozarena 50.00 120.00
100 Jarren Duran 8.00 20.00
114 Sherten Apostel 6.00 15.00
115 Noah Song 8.00 20.00
116 Andrew Dalquist 2.50 6.00
117 Miguel Hiraldo 8.00 20.00
118 Jasseel De La Cruz 2.50 6.00
119 Abraham Toro 4.00 10.00
121 Devin Mann 4.00 10.00
124 Antonio Cabello 5.00 12.00
125 Jhoan Duran 4.00 10.00
126 Kyren Paris 2.50 6.00
127 Moises Gomez 4.00 10.00
129 Carlos Rodriguez 2.50 6.00
130 Jhon Torres 2.50 6.00
131 Randy Florentino 2.50 6.00
133 Livan Soto 3.00 8.00
134 Gabriel Maciel 2.50 6.00
136 Yeison Coca 2.50 6.00
137 Lenyn Sosa 2.50 6.00
138 Oswaldo Cabrera 2.50 6.00
139 Ivan Herrera 4.00 10.00
140 Michael Grove 2.50 6.00
141 Aaron Hernandez 2.50 6.00
142 CJ Alexander 8.00 20.00
143 Mason Englert 2.50 6.00
144 Brenden Spillane 2.50 6.00
145 Hogan Harris 2.50 6.00
146 Tucker Davidson 2.50 6.00
147 Michael Massey 3.00 8.00
148 Jasson Dominguez 100.00 250.00
149 Spencer Steer 2.50 6.00
150 Tyler Dyson 2.50 6.00
151 Cody Bolton 4.00 10.00
152 Osleivis Basabe 2.50 6.00
154 Michael Harris 2.50 6.00
155 Ryan Zeferjahn 3.00 8.00
156 Liover Peguero 4.00 10.00
157 Aaron Ashby 2.50 6.00
158 Alvaro Seijas 2.50 6.00
159 Canaan Smith 4.00 10.00
160 Jose Soriano 4.00 10.00
161 Sandy Gaston 4.00 10.00
162 Gabriel Moreno 4.00 10.00
163 Gilberto Jimenez 12.00 30.00
164 Joe Ryan 4.00 10.00
165 Joey Cantillo 5.00 12.00
166 Jose Salas 4.00 10.00
167 David Parkinson 2.50 6.00
168 Luis Matos 4.00 10.00
169 Luisangel Acuna 8.00 20.00
170 Tarik Skubal 12.00 30.00
171 Thad Ward 2.50 6.00
172 Jose Rodriguez 2.50 6.00
173 Drew Rom 2.50 6.00
174 Israel Pineda 4.00 10.00
175 Wilderd Patino 2.50 6.00
176 Trevor McDonald 2.50 6.00
177 Avery Short 2.50 6.00
178 Trey Harris 3.00 8.00
179 Luis Toribio 2.50 6.00
180 Nathan Patterson 2.50 6.00
181 Leo Crawford 2.50 6.00
182 Alejandro Kirk 6.00 15.00
183 Justin Dean 3.00 8.00
184 Cristian Batista 2.50 6.00
185 Jefferson De La Cruz 2.50 6.00
186 Cristofer Espinola 2.50 6.00
187 Wilton Lara 2.50 6.00
188 Fidel Montero 4.00 10.00
189 Aneudis Mordan 2.50 6.00
190 Joel Peguero 2.50 6.00
191 John Peguero 2.50 6.00
192 Bryan Pena 2.50 6.00
193 Salvador Ramirez 2.50 6.00
194 Rhaybel Roso 2.50 6.00
195 Jay Vargas 2.50 6.00
196 Wesley Zapata 2.50 6.00
198 Rodolfo Caraballo 2.50 6.00
199 Elizual Chalas 2.50 6.00
200 Elian Cortorreal 2.50 6.00
201 Randy De Jesus 2.50 6.00
202 Aneudi Escanio 2.50 6.00
203 Xavier Guillen 3.00 8.00
204 Yanki Jean 2.50 6.00
205 Maximo Maria 2.50 6.00
206 Juan Martinez 2.50 6.00
207 Yasser Mercedes 2.50 6.00
208 Jeral Perez 3.00 8.00
209 Jhonny Severino 2.50 6.00
210 Ivan Sosa 3.00 8.00
211 Miguel Tamares 2.50 6.00
212 Braylin Tavera 2.50 6.00
213 Sebastian Castro 2.50 6.00

2019 Elite Extra Edition Autographs Aspirations Blue

148 Jasson Dominguez/25 300.00 800.00

2019 Elite Extra Edition Autographs Emerald

148 Jasson Dominguez/25 300.00 800.00

2019 Elite Extra Edition Autographs Status Die Cut Emerald

148 Jasson Dominguez/25 300.00 800.00

2019 Elite Extra Edition Base OptiChrome

RANDOM INSERTS IN PACKS
*HOLO: .5X TO 1.2X BASIC
1 Adley Rutschman 1.50 4.00
2 Bobby Witt Jr. 1.00 2.50
3 Andrew Vaughn .75 2.00
4 JJ Bleday 1.25 3.00
5 Riley Greene 1.00 2.50
6 CJ Abrams 1.25 3.00
7 Nick Lodolo .50 1.25
8 Josh Jung .75 2.00
9 Shea Langeliers .50 1.25
10 Hunter Bishop .75 2.00
11 Alek Manoah .50 1.25
14 Bryson Stott .75 2.00
15 Will Wilson .40 1.00
16 Corbin Carroll .40 1.00
22 Greg Jones .30 .75
24 Daniel Espino .30 .75
25 Kody Hoese .75 2.00
29 Logan Davidson .25 .60
30 Anthony Volpe .75 2.00
33 Brennan Malone .25 .60
35 Kameron Misner .60 1.50
49 Rece Hinds .30 .75
51 Logan Wyatt .40 1.00
80 Tyler Callihan .30 .75
81 Matthew Allan .50 1.25
84 Ryan Pepiot .25 .60
85 Tristin English .25 .60
86 Erik Miller .60 1.50
87 Matt Cronin .25 .60
88 Graeme Stinson .25 .60
89 Brandon Lewis .40 1.00
90 Kyle McCann .30 .75
91 Logan O'Hoppe .25 .60
93 Miguel Vargas 1.25 3.00
94 Shervyen Newton .40 1.00
96 Brailyn Marquez .60 1.50
97 Bryan Rocchio 1.00 2.50
99 Randy Arozarena 2.50 6.00
100 Jarren Duran 1.50 4.00
148 Jasson Dominguez 25.00 60.00

2019 Elite Extra Edition Base OptiChrome Signatures

1 Adley Rutschman 25.00 60.00
2 Bobby Witt Jr. 15.00 40.00
3 Andrew Vaughn 8.00 20.00
4 JJ Bleday 12.00 30.00
5 Riley Greene 10.00 25.00
6 CJ Abrams 12.00 30.00
7 Nick Lodolo 5.00 12.00
8 Josh Jung 8.00 20.00
9 Shea Langeliers 5.00 12.00
10 Hunter Bishop 8.00 20.00
11 Alek Manoah 5.00 12.00
14 Bryson Stott 8.00 20.00
15 Will Wilson 4.00 10.00
16 Corbin Carroll 4.00 10.00
22 Greg Jones 3.00 8.00
24 Daniel Espino 3.00 8.00
25 Kody Hoese 8.00 20.00
29 Logan Davidson 2.50 6.00
30 Anthony Volpe 8.00 20.00
33 Brennan Malone 2.50 6.00
35 Kameron Misner 6.00 15.00
49 Rece Hinds 3.00 8.00
51 Logan Wyatt 4.00 10.00
80 Tyler Callihan 3.00 8.00
81 Matthew Allan 5.00 12.00
84 Ryan Pepiot 2.50 6.00
86 Erik Miller 6.00 15.00
87 Matt Cronin 2.50 6.00
88 Graeme Stinson 2.50 6.00
89 Brandon Lewis 4.00 10.00
90 Kyle McCann 3.00 8.00
91 Logan O'Hoppe 2.50 6.00
93 Miguel Vargas 12.00 30.00
94 Shervyen Newton 4.00 10.00
96 Brailyn Marquez 6.00 15.00
97 Bryan Rocchio 10.00 25.00
99 Randy Arozarena 25.00 60.00
100 Jarren Duran 20.00 50.00
148 Jasson Dominguez 100.00 250.00

2019 Elite Extra Edition College Tickets

RANDOM INSERTS IN PACKS
*HOLO: .5X TO 1.2X BASIC
1 Adley Rutschman 1.50 4.00
2 Andrew Vaughn .75 2.00
3 JJ Bleday 1.25 3.00
4 Nick Lodolo .50 1.25
5 Josh Jung .75 2.00
6 Shea Langeliers .50 1.25
7 Hunter Bishop .75 2.00
8 Alek Manoah .50 1.25
9 Bryson Stott .75 2.00
10 Will Wilson .40 1.00
11 Zack Thompson .40 1.00
12 Michael Massey .30 .75
13 Braden Shewmake .75 2.00
14 Noah Song .75 2.00
15 Michael Toglia .40 1.00
16 Kody Hoese .75 2.00
17 Ryan Jensen .40 1.00
18 Ethan Small .30 .75
19 Logan Davidson .25 .60

20 Michael Busch .75 2.00
21 Korey Lee .50 1.25
22 Drey Jameson .25 .60
23 Kameron Misner .60 1.50
24 T.J. Sikkema .40 1.00
25 Matt Wallner .50 1.25
26 Tyler Dyson .25 .60
27 Davis Wendzel .30 .75
28 Cameron Cannon .50 1.25
29 Brady McConnell .40 1.00
30 Nick Quintana .50 1.25
31 Ryan Garcia .25 .60
32 Logan Wyatt .40 1.00
33 Matt Canterino .30 .75

2019 Elite Extra Edition College Tickets Signatures

1 Adley Rutschman 25.00 60.00
2 Andrew Vaughn 8.00 20.00
3 JJ Bleday 12.00 30.00
4 Nick Lodolo 5.00 12.00
5 Josh Jung 8.00 20.00
6 Shea Langeliers 5.00 12.00
7 Hunter Bishop 8.00 20.00
8 Alek Manoah 5.00 12.00
9 Bryson Stott 8.00 20.00
10 Will Wilson 4.00 10.00
11 Zack Thompson 4.00 10.00
12 Michael Massey 3.00 8.00
13 Braden Shewmake 8.00 20.00
14 Noah Song 8.00 20.00
15 Michael Toglia 4.00 10.00
16 Kody Hoese 8.00 20.00
17 Ryan Jensen 4.00 10.00
18 Ethan Small 3.00 8.00
19 Logan Davidson 2.50 6.00
20 Michael Busch 8.00 20.00
21 Korey Lee 5.00 12.00
22 Drey Jameson 2.50 6.00
23 Kameron Misner 6.00 15.00
24 T.J. Sikkema 4.00 10.00
25 Matt Wallner 5.00 12.00
26 Tyler Dyson 2.50 6.00
27 Davis Wendzel 3.00 8.00
28 Cameron Cannon 5.00 12.00
29 Brady McConnell 4.00 10.00
30 Nick Quintana 5.00 12.00
31 Ryan Garcia 2.50 6.00
32 Logan Wyatt 4.00 10.00
33 Matt Canterino 3.00 8.00

2019 Elite Extra Edition Dominican Prospect League Jumbo Materials Red

1 Robert Puason
2 Bayron Lora
3 Emmanuel Rodriguez
4 Dauris Lorenzo
5 Alexander Ramirez
6 Jose Pastrano
7 Christian Cardozo
8 Jhon Diaz
9 Adael Amador
10 Rikelvin Castro

2019 Elite Extra Edition Dominican Prospect League Signatures

RANDOM INSERTS IN PACKS
101 Robert Puason 8.00 20.00
102 Bayron Lora 8.00 20.00
103 Emmanuel Rodriguez 4.00 10.00
104 Alexander Ramirez 5.00 12.00
105 Jhon Diaz 5.00 12.00
106 Adael Amador 3.00 8.00
107 Malfrin Sosa 3.00 8.00
108 Dauris Lorenzo 3.00 8.00
109 Jose Pastrano 3.00 8.00
110 Brailin Minier 4.00 10.00
111 Rikelvin Castro 3.00 8.00
112 Junior Tilien 3.00 8.00
113 Christian Cardozo 3.00 8.00

2019 Elite Extra Edition Dual Prospect Materials Black

3 Antonio Santillan/399 1.50 4.00
4 Royce Lewis/399 3.00 8.00
10 Gabriel Arias/299 2.50 6.00
11 Evan White/399 2.50 6.00
13 Khalil Lee/249 1.50 4.00
14 Victor Victor Mesa/399 3.00 8.00
15 Sixto Sanchez/399 2.00 5.00
17 Vidal Brujan/399 10.00 25.00
18 Brent Rooker/399 2.00 5.00
19 Lazaro Armenteros/399 2.00 5.00
20 Leody Taveras/399 1.50 4.00

2019 Elite Extra Edition First Round Materials Black

1 Adley Rutschman/399 10.00 25.00
3 Andrew Vaughn/399 5.00 12.00
5 Riley Greene/399 6.00 15.00
6 CJ Abrams/399 8.00 20.00
7 Josh Jung/262 5.00 12.00

2019 Elite Extra Edition Future Threads Signatures Black

1 Victor Mesa Jr./299 8.00 20.00
2 Brent Rooker/249 4.00 10.00
3 Bryson Brigman/299 3.00 8.00
4 Eli White/299 12.00 30.00
5 Jordan Yamamoto/299 5.00 12.00
6 Sean Murphy/199 4.00 10.00
7 Brailyn Marquez/240 8.00 20.00
8 Kyle Lewis/99 10.00 25.00
9 Victor Victor Mesa/299 6.00 15.00
10 Deivi Garcia/199 10.00 25.00
11 Andres Gimenez/99 4.00 10.00
12 Bobby Dalbec/199 8.00 20.00
13 Dane Dunning/199 3.00 8.00
14 Domingo Acevedo/199 3.00 8.00
15 Gabriel Arias/199 5.00 12.00
16 Gavin Lux/199 20.00 50.00
17 Hudson Potts/199 3.00 8.00
18 Jonathan Hernandez/299 3.00 8.00
19 Keibert Ruiz/199 8.00 20.00
20 Kevin Smith/299 3.00 8.00
21 Luis V. Garcia/199 4.00 10.00
23 Nick Neidert/299 3.00 8.00
24 Ryan Mountcastle/299 4.00 10.00
26 Taylor Widener/199 3.00 8.00
27 Trent Grisham/249 6.00 15.00
28 Vidal Brujan/199 20.00 50.00
29 Brandon Marsh/199 3.00 8.00
30 Jarren Duran/299
31 Ben Braymer/199 3.00 8.00
33 Ryan McKenna/199 3.00 8.00
34 George Valera/199 6.00 15.00
36 Monte Harrison/249 3.00 8.00
39 Michael King/195 4.00 10.00
40 Evan White/149 5.00 12.00
41 Jesus Sanchez/125 3.00 8.00
42 Jasson Dominguez/74 150.00 400.00
44 Luis Garcia/249 12.00 30.00

2019 Elite Extra Edition Future Threads Signatures Purple

42 Jasson Dominguez/25 300.00 600.00

2019 Elite Extra Edition Hidden Gems Autographs Black

1 Bobby Bradley 4.00 10.00
2 Trevor McDonald 2.50 6.00
3 Avery Short 2.50 6.00
4 Osleivis Basabe 2.50 6.00
5 Carlos Rodriguez 2.50 6.00
6 Randy Florentino 2.50 6.00
7 Livan Soto 3.00 8.00
8 Gabriel Maciel 2.50 6.00
10 Yeison Coca 2.50 6.00
11 Lenyn Sosa 2.50 6.00
12 Oswaldo Cabrera 2.50 6.00
13 Ivan Herrera 4.00 10.00
14 Cody Bolton 4.00 10.00
15 Sam Hentges 2.50 6.00
16 Yu Chang 3.00 8.00
17 Bo Bichette 15.00 40.00
18 Mauricio Dubon 6.00 15.00
19 Logan O'Hoppe 2.50 6.00
20 Brayan Rocchio 10.00 25.00
21 Miguel Vargas 10.00 25.00
22 Yordan Alvarez 40.00 100.00
23 Canaan Smith 4.00 10.00
24 Aristides Aquino 10.00 25.00
25 Logan Webb 4.00 10.00
26 Brock Burke 2.50 6.00
27 A.J. Puk 3.00 8.00
28 Thad Ward 2.50 6.00
29 Willi Castro 2.50 6.00
30 Brendan McKay 4.00 10.00

2019 Elite Extra Edition Prospect Materials Black

1 Evan White 2.50 6.00
2 Victor Victor Mesa 3.00 8.00
3 Brent Rooker 2.00 5.00
4 Eli White 6.00 15.00
5 Sixto Sanchez 2.00 5.00
6 Royce Lewis 3.00 8.00
7 Tucker Davidson 1.50 4.00
8 Michael King 2.00 5.00
10 Antonio Santillan 1.50 4.00
12 Dane Dunning 1.50 4.00
13 Gabriel Arias 2.50 6.00
15 Taylor Trammell 2.00 5.00
16 Jonathan Hernandez 1.50 4.00
17 Keibert Ruiz 4.00 10.00
18 Kevin Smith 1.50 4.00
19 Nick Neidert 1.50 4.00
20 Taylor Widener 1.50 4.00
21 Trent Grisham 5.00 12.00
22 Vidal Brujan 10.00 25.00
23 Wander Franco 12.00 30.00
24 Khalil Lee 1.50 4.00
27 Luis Garcia 6.00 15.00
28 Braxton Garrett 1.50 4.00
29 Monte Harrison 1.50 4.00
30 Triston McKenzie 1.50 4.00

2019 Elite Extra Edition Triple Prospect Materials Black

1 Leody Taveras/399 1.50 4.00
2 Vidal Brujan/399 10.00 25.00
4 Ryan McKenna/399 1.50 4.00
5 Bobby Dalbec/399 4.00 10.00
6 Gabriel Arias/199 2.50 6.00
9 Royce Lewis/399 3.00 8.00

2019 Elite Extra Edition Triple Silhouettes Black

1 Wander Franco/399 12.00 30.00
2 Victor Mesa Jr./399 4.00 10.00
4 Kyle Lewis/399 3.00 8.00
5 Jo Adell/399 5.00 12.00
8 Sixto Sanchez/399 2.00 5.00
9 Ryan Mountcastle/399 2.00 5.00
10 Matt Manning/149 2.50 6.00
11 Forrest Whitley/399 2.50 6.00
12 Leody Taveras/399 1.50 4.00
13 Yusniel Diaz/363 2.50 6.00
15 Andres Gimenez/399 2.00 5.00
17 Sean Murphy/199 2.00 5.00
18 JoJo Romero/299 1.50 4.00
19 Royce Lewis/399 3.00 8.00

2019 Elite Extra Edition USA Baseball 15U Signatures Red

1 Brandon Barriera 2.50 6.00
2 Karson Bowen 2.50 6.00
3 Joseph Brown 2.50 6.00
4 Drew Burress 2.50 6.00
5 Spencer Butt 2.50 6.00
6 Kai Caranto 2.50 6.00
7 Duke Ekstrom 2.50 6.00
8 Termarr Johnson 5.00 12.00
9 Dylan Lina 3.00 8.00
10 Matthew Matthijs 4.00 10.00
11 Ethan McElvain 2.50 6.00
12 Steven Milam 2.50 6.00
13 Aidan Miller 2.50 6.00
14 Brandon Olivera 2.50 6.00
15 Benjamin Reiland 5.00 12.00
16 Louis Rodriguez 2.50 6.00
17 Mikey Romero 2.50 6.00
18 Logan Saloman 2.50 6.00
19 Nolan Schubart 2.50 6.00
20 Colton Wombles 5.00 12.00

2019 Elite Extra Edition USA Baseball 18U Signatures Red

1 Mick Abel 4.00 10.00
2 Drew Bowser 2.50 6.00
3 Jack Bulger 2.50 6.00
4 Pete Crow-Armstrong 5.00 12.00
5 Lucas Gordon 2.50 6.00
6 Hunter Haas 3.00 8.00
7 Colby Halter 2.50 6.00
8 Kyle Harrison 6.00 15.00
9 Robert Hassell 6.00 15.00
10 Rawley Hector 2.50 6.00
11 Austin Hendrick 10.00 25.00
12 Ben Hernandez 2.50 6.00
13 Nolan McLean 2.50 6.00
14 Max Rajcic 2.50 6.00
15 Drew Romo 6.00 15.00
16 Alejandro Rosario 5.00 12.00
17 Jason Savacool 4.00 10.00
18 Tyler Soderstrom 5.00 12.00
19 Milan Tolentino 3.00 8.00

2019 Elite Extra Edition USA Collegiate Material Signatures Black

1 Andrew Abbott 3.00 8.00
2 Logan Allen 3.00 8.00
3 Tanner Allen 3.00 8.00
4 Patrick Bailey 6.00 15.00
5 Tyler Brown 5.00 12.00
6 Alec Burleson 5.00 12.00
7 Burl Carraway 6.00 15.00
8 Cade Cavalli 6.00 15.00
9 Colton Cowser 4.00 10.00
10 Jeff Criswell 5.00 12.00
11 Reid Detmers 6.00 15.00
12 Justin Foscue 8.00 20.00
13 Nick Frasso 3.00 8.00
14 Heston Kjerstad 20.00 50.00
15 Asa Lacy 25.00 60.00
16 Nick Loftin 3.00 8.00
17 Austin Martin 20.00 50.00
18 Chris McMahon 3.00 8.00
19 Max Meyer 10.00 25.00
20 Doug Nikhazy 3.00 8.00
21 Casey Opitz 5.00 12.00
22 Spencer Torkelson 50.00 120.00
23 Luke Waddell 3.00 8.00
24 Cole Wilcox 4.00 10.00
25 Alika Williams 5.00 12.00
26 Lucas Dunn 3.00 8.00

2019 Elite Extra Edition USA Collegiate Tickets

RANDOM INSERTS IN PACKS
*HOLO: .5X TO 1.2X BASIC
1 Andrew Abbott .25 .60
2 Logan Allen .25 .60
3 Tanner Allen .25 .60
4 Patrick Bailey .75 2.00
5 Tyler Brown .40 1.00
6 Alec Burleson .40 1.00
7 Burl Carraway .50 1.25
8 Cade Cavalli .50 1.25
9 Colton Cowser .30 .75
10 Jeff Criswell .40 1.00
11 Reid Detmers .75 2.00
12 Justin Foscue 1.00 2.50
13 Nick Frasso .25 .60
14 Heston Kjerstad 1.25 3.00
15 Asa Lacy 1.25 3.00
16 Nick Loftin .25 .60
17 Austin Martin .75 2.00
18 Chris McMahon .25 .60
19 Max Meyer .75 2.00
20 Doug Nikhazy .25 .60
21 Casey Opitz .40 1.00
22 Spencer Torkelson 3.00 8.00
23 Luke Waddell .25 .60
24 Cole Wilcox .30 .75
25 Alika Williams .40 1.00
26 Lucas Dunn .25 .60
27 Garrett Mitchell 1.50 4.00

2019 Elite Extra Edition USA Collegiate Tickets Signatures

1 Andrew Abbott
2 Logan Allen
3 Tanner Allen
4 Patrick Bailey
5 Tyler Brown
6 Alec Burleson
7 Burl Carraway
8 Cade Cavalli
9 Colton Cowser
10 Jeff Criswell
11 Reid Detmers
12 Justin Foscue
13 Nick Frasso
14 Heston Kjerstad
15 Asa Lacy
16 Nick Loftin
17 Austin Martin
18 Chris McMahon
19 Max Meyer
20 Doug Nikhazy
21 Casey Opitz
22 Spencer Torkelson
23 Luke Waddell
24 Cole Wilcox
25 Alika Williams
26 Lucas Dunn
27 Garrett Mitchell

2019 Elite Extra Edition USA Materials Black

1 Adley Rutschman/199 10.00 25.00
2 Bobby Witt Jr./452 6.00 15.00
3 Andrew Vaughn/499 5.00 12.00
4 Riley Greene/499 6.00 15.00
5 CJ Abrams/499 8.00 20.00
6 Josh Jung/399 5.00 12.00
8 Bryson Stott/289 5.00 12.00
9 Will Wilson/499 2.50 6.00
10 Corbin Carroll/199 2.50 6.00
11 Zack Thompson/199 2.50 6.00
12 Braden Shewmake/499 5.00 12.00
13 Anthony Volpe/499 5.00 12.00
14 Brennan Malone/299 1.50 4.00
15 Bryson Brigman/499 1.50 4.00
16 Tyler Callihan/180 2.00 5.00
17 Matthew Thompson/499 2.00 5.00
18 Logan Allen/499 1.50 4.00
22 John Doxakis/499 2.50 6.00
23 Seth Beer/499 4.00 10.00
24 Nick Quintana/275 3.00 8.00
26 Jarred Kelenic/499 6.00 15.00
27 Matt Cronin/399 1.50 4.00
28 Graeme Stinson/231 1.50 4.00
29 Evan White/499 2.50 6.00
30 Triston Casas/499 6.00 15.00

2016 Donruss Optic

COMP.SET w/o SPs (165) 30.00 80.00
1 Zack Greinke DK .50 1.25
2 Nick Markakis DK .50 1.25
3 Manny Machado DK .60 1.50
4 David Price DK .50 1.25
5 Jason Heyward DK .50 1.25
6 Chris Sale DK .60 1.50
7 Brandon Phillips DK .40 1.00
8 Michael Brantley DK .50 1.25
9 Carlos Gonzalez DK .50 1.25
10 Miguel Cabrera DK .60 1.50
11 Jose Altuve DK .50 1.25
12 Eric Hosmer DK .50 1.25
13 Albert Pujols DK .75 2.00
14 Joc Pederson DK .50 1.25
15 Jose Fernandez DK .60 1.50
16 Jonathan Lucroy DK .50 1.25
17 Brian Dozier DK .50 1.25
18 Jacob deGrom DK .60 1.50
19 Alex Rodriguez DK .75 2.00
20 Billy Burns DK .40 1.00
21 Odubel Herrera DK .50 1.25
22 Andrew McCutchen DK .60 1.50
23 Matt Kemp DK .50 1.25
24 Buster Posey DK .75 2.00
25 Nelson Cruz DK .60 1.50
26 Yadier Molina DK .60 1.50
27 Evan Longoria DK .50 1.25
28 Prince Fielder DK .50 1.25
29 Josh Donaldson DK .50 1.25
30 Bryce Harper DK 1.00 2.50
31 Kyle Schwarber RR RC 1.25 3.00
32 Corey Seager RR RC 3.00 8.00
33 Trea Turner RR RC 1.25 3.00
34 Rob Refsnyder RR RC .50 1.25
35 Miguel Sano RR RC .60 1.50
36 Stephen Piscotty RR RC .60 1.50
37 Aaron Nola RR RC .75 2.00
38 Michael Conforto RR RC .50 1.25
39 Ketel Marte RR RC .75 2.00
40 Luis Severino RR RC .50 1.25
41 Greg Bird RR RC .50 1.25
42 Hector Olivera RR RC .50 1.25
43 Jose Peraza RR RC .50 1.25
44 Henry Owens RR RC .50 1.25
45 Richie Shaffer RR RC .40 1.00
46 Byung-ho Park RR RC .50 1.25
47 Tyler Naquin RR RC .50 1.25
48 Jonathan Gray RR RC .40 1.00
49 Peter O'Brien RR RC .40 1.00
50 Aledmys Diaz RR RC .60 1.50
51 Tyler White RR RC .40 1.00
52 Nomar Mazara RR RC .60 1.50
53 Trevor Story RR RC 1.50 4.00
54 Max Kepler RR RC .60 1.50
55 Ross Stripling RR RC .40 1.00
56 Tom Murphy RR RC .40 1.00
57 Travis Jankowski RR RC .40 1.00
58 Socrates Brito RR RC .40 1.00
59 Kenta Maeda RR RC .75 2.00
60 Tyler Duffey RR RC .40 1.00
61 Jeremy Hazelbaker RR RC .50 1.25
62 Brandon Drury RR RC .60 1.50
63 Jerad Eickhoff RR RC .60 1.50
64 Jorge Lopez RR RC .40 1.00
65 Zach Davies RR RC .50 1.25
66 Chris Sale .40 1.00
67 Adrian Gonzalez .30 .75
68 Ian Kinsler .30 .75
69 Justin Upton .30 .75
70 Todd Frazier .30 .75
71 Corey Kluber .30 .75
72 Carlos Gonzalez .30 .75
73 Yadier Molina .40 1.00
74A Kris Bryant .50 1.25
74B K.Bryant SP ROY 2.00 5.00
75 Evan Gattis .25 .60
76 Dallas Keuchel .30 .75
77 Lorenzo Cain .25 .60
78 Starling Marte .30 .75
79 Yoenis Cespedes .40 1.00
80 Odubel Herrera .30 .75
81 Paul Goldschmidt .40 1.00
82 Ichiro Suzuki .50 1.25
83 Yasmany Tomas .25 .60
84 Alcides Escobar .30 .75
85 Evan Longoria .30 .75
86 Aroldis Chapman .40 1.00
87 James Shields .25 .60
88 Yasiel Puig .40 1.00
89 Mike Trout 4.00 10.00
90 Kole Calhoun .25 .60
91 Brian McCann .30 .75
92 Yu Darvish .40 1.00
93 Eddie Rosario .30 .75
94 Jason Heyward .30 .75
95 Jake Arrieta .30 .75
96 Freddie Freeman .50 1.25
97 Max Scherzer .40 1.00
98 Jorge Soler .40 1.00
99 Gerrit Cole .40 1.00
100 Alex Rodriguez .50 1.25
101 Addison Russell .40 1.00
102 Adam Wainwright .30 .75
103 Billy Hamilton .30 .75
104 Chris Davis .25 .60
105 Joey Votto .40 1.00
106 Nelson Cruz .40 1.00
107 Nolan Arenado .50 1.25
108 Johnny Cueto .30 .75
109 Matt Kemp .30 .75
110 Brandon Crawford .30 .75
111 Steven Matz .30 .75
112 Jose Fernandez .40 1.00
113 Jason Kipnis .30 .75
114A Jose Bautista .30 .75
114B Btsta SP Joey Bats 1.25 3.00
115 Matt Carpenter .40 1.00
116 David Wright .30 .75
117A Bryce Harper .60 1.50
117B B.Harper SP MVP 2.50 6.00
118 Jacob deGrom .40 1.00
119 Sonny Gray .30 .75
120 David Price .30 .75
121 Adam Jones .30 .75
122 Prince Fielder .30 .75
123 Giancarlo Stanton .40 1.00
124 Zack Greinke .40 1.00
125 Troy Tulowitzki .40 1.00
126 David Ortiz .40 1.00
127 Andrew McCutchen .40 1.00
128 Joc Pederson .30 .75
129 Billy Burns .25 .60
130 Adrian Beltre .40 1.00
131 Edwin Encarnacion .40 1.00
132 Miguel Cabrera .40 1.00
133 Francisco Lindor .40 1.00
134 Charlie Blackmon .40 1.00
135 Ryan Braun .30 .75
136 Robinson Cano .30 .75
137 Stephen Strasburg .40 1.00
138 Eric Hosmer .30 .75
139A Carlos Correa .50 1.25
139B C.Correa SP ROY 1.50 4.00
140 Maikel Franco .30 .75
141 Albert Pujols .50 1.25
142 Manny Machado .40 1.00
143 Jeff Samardzija .25 .60
144 Dee Gordon .25 .60
145 Xander Bogaerts .40 1.00
146 Chris Archer .25 .60
147 Salvador Perez .25 .60
148 Andrelton Simmons .25 .60
149 Anthony Rizzo .60 1.50
150 Madison Bumgarner .30 .75
151 Jonathan Lucroy .30 .75
152 Adam Eaton .25 .60
153 Matt Holliday .40 1.00
154 Jose Altuve .30 .75
155 Buster Posey .50 1.25
156 Cole Hamels .30 .75
157 Mookie Betts .60 1.50
158 Felix Hernandez .30 .75
159 Brian Dozier .30 .75
160 A.J. Pollock .25 .60
161A Josh Donaldson .30 .75
161B J.Donaldson SP MVP 1.25 3.00
162 Clayton Kershaw .75 2.00
163 Jose Abreu .40 1.00
164 Noah Syndergaard .30 .75
165 The Famous San Diego Chicken .25 .60
Ted Giannoulas
166 Mac Williamson RR AU RC 2.50 6.00
167 Trayce Thompson RR AU RC 4.00 10.00
168 Zack Godley RR AU RC 2.50 6.00
169 John Lamb RR AU RC 2.50 6.00
170 Brian Ellington RR AU RC 2.50 6.00
171 Colin Rea RR AU RC 2.50 6.00
172 Frankie Montas RR AU RC 3.00 8.00
173 Alex Dickerson RR AU RC 2.50 6.00
174 Kaleb Cowart RR AU RC 2.50 6.00
175 Pedro Severino RR AU RC 2.50 6.00

2016 Donruss Optic Aqua

*AQUA DK: .75X TO 2X BASIC DK
*AQUA RR: .75X TO 2X BASIC RR
*AQUA VET: 1.2X TO 3X BASIC VET
*AQUA AU: .5X TO 1.2X BASIC AU
RANDOM INSERTS IN PACKS
STATED PRINT RUN 299 SER.#'d SETS
AU PRINT RUNS B/WN 4-125 COPIES PER
NO PRICING ON QTY 4
EXCHANGE DEADLINE 1/20/2018
50 Aledmys Diaz RR 10.00 25.00
89 Mike Trout 15.00 40.00

2016 Donruss Optic Black

*BLACK DK: 2X TO 5X BASIC DK
*BLACK RR: 2X TO 5X BASIC RR
*BLACK VET: 3X TO 8X BASIC VET
*BLACK AU: .75X TO 2X BASIC AU
RANDOM INSERTS IN PACKS
STATED PRINT RUN 25 SER.#'d SETS
EXCHANGE DEADLINE 1/20/2018
50 Aledmys Diaz RR 60.00 150.00
89 Mike Trout 60.00 150.00

2016 Donruss Optic Blue

*BLUE DK: 1X TO 2.5X BASIC DK
*BLUE RR: 1X TO 2.5X BASIC RR
*BLUE VET: 1.5X TO 4X BASIC VET
*BLUE SP: .4X TO 1X BASIC SP
*BLUE AU: .6X TO 1.5X BASIC AU
RANDOM INSERTS IN PACKS
STATED PRINT RUN 149 SER.#'d SETS
AU PRINT RUN 75 SER.#'d SETS
EXCHANGE DEADLINE 1/20/2018
50 Aledmys Diaz RR 20.00 50.00
89 Mike Trout 20.00 50.00

2016 Donruss Optic Carolina Blue

*CAR.BLU DK: 1.5X TO 4X BASIC DK
*CAR.BLU RR: 1.5X TO 4X BASIC RR
*CAR.BLU VET: 2.5X TO 6X BASIC VET
*CAR.BLU AU: .75X TO 2X BASIC AU
RANDOM INSERTS IN PACKS
STATED PRINT RUN 50 SER.#'d SETS
AU PRINT RUN 35 SER.#'d SETS
EXCHANGE DEADLINE 1/20/2018
50 Aledmys Diaz RR 50.00 120.00
89 Mike Trout 50.00 120.00

2016 Donruss Optic Holo

*HOLO DK: .5X TO 1.2X BASIC DK
*HOLO RR: .5X TO 1.2X BASIC RR
*HOLO VET: .75X TO 2X BASIC VET
*HOLO AU: .5X TO 1.2X BASIC AU
RANDOM INSERTS IN PACKS
AU PRINT RUNS B/WN 5-150 COPIES PER
NO PRICING ON QTY 5
EXCHANGE DEADLINE 1/20/2018
89 Mike Trout 25.00 60.00

2016 Donruss Optic Orange

*ORANGE DK: 1X TO 2.5X BASIC DK
*ORANGE RR: 1X TO 2.5X BASIC RR
*ORANGE VET: 1.5X TO 4X BASIC VET
*ORANGE AU: .6X TO 1.5X BASIC AU
RANDOM INSERTS IN PACKS
STATED PRINT RUN 199 SER.#'d SETS
AU PRINT RUNS B/WN 5-75 COPIES PER
NO PRICING ON QTY 5
EXCHANGE DEADLINE 1/20/2018
50 Aledmys Diaz RR 20.00 50.00
89 Mike Trout 20.00 50.00

2016 Donruss Optic Pink

*PINK DK: .6X TO 1.5X BASIC DK
*PINK RR: .6X TO 1.5X BASIC RR
*PINK VET: 1X TO 2.5X BASIC VET
RANDOM INSERTS IN PACKS

2016 Donruss Optic Purple

*PURPLE DK: .6X TO 1.5X BASIC DK
*PURPLE RR: .6X TO 1.5X BASIC RR
*PURPLE VET: 1X TO 2.5X BASIC VET
INSERTED IN RETAIL PACKS

2016 Donruss Optic Red

*RED DK: 1.2X TO 3X BASIC DK
*RED RR: 1.2X TO 3X BASIC RR
*RED VET: 2X TO 5X BASIC VET
*RED SP: .5X TO 1.2X BASIC SP
*RED AU: .6X TO 1.5X BASIC AU
RANDOM INSERTS IN PACKS
STATED PRINT RUN 99 SER.#'d SETS
AU PRINT RUN 50 SER.#'d SETS
EXCHANGE DEADLINE 1/20/2018
50 Aledmys Diaz RR 30.00 80.00
89 Mike Trout 25.00 60.00

2016 Donruss Optic Autographs

RANDOM INSERTS IN PACKS
*BLUE/50: .5X TO 1.2X BASIC
*BLUE/25: .6X TO 1.5X BASIC
*RED/25: .6X TO 1.5X BASIC
EXCHANGE DEADLINE 1/20/2018
OAAR Anthony Rizzo 15.00 40.00
OABH Billy Hamilton 4.00 10.00
OABJ Brian Johnson 2.50 6.00
OACK Clayton Kershaw 25.00 60.00
OACM Carlos Martinez 3.00 8.00
OADO David Ortiz
OADP David Price 8.00 20.00
OADW David Wright 6.00 15.00
OAED Elias Diaz 2.50 6.00
OAEG Evan Gattis 2.50 6
OAEL Evan Longoria 8.00 20
OAGC Gerrit Cole 10.00 25
OAGP Gregory Polanco 3.00 8
OAJA Jose Abreu 8.00 20
OAJB Jose Bautista 10.00 25
OAJD Josh Donaldson 10.00 25
OAJL Jorge Lopez 2.50 6
OAKM Ketel Marte 4.00 10
OAMA Matt Adams 2.50 6
OAMB Mookie Betts 50.00 120
OARS Richie Shaffer 2.50 6
OASM Starling Marte 3.00 8
OATJ Travis Jankowski 2.50 6
OATS Trevor Story 8.00 20
OATT Trea Turner 10.00 25

2016 Donruss Optic Back to the Future

RANDOM INSERTS IN PACKS
*BLUE/149: 1X TO 2.5X BASIC
*RED/99: 1.2X TO 3X BASIC
BF1 Adrian Beltre .60 1
BF2 Miguel Cabrera .60 1
BF3 Jason Heyward .50 1
BF4 Yoenis Cespedes .60 1
BF5 Chris Davis .40 1
BF6 Josh Donaldson .50 1
BF7 Albert Pujols .75 2
BF8 Jake Arrieta .50 1
BF9 Zack Greinke .50 1
BF10 David Price .50 1
BF11 Prince Fielder .50 1
BF12 Josh Hamilton .50 1
BF13 Anthony Rizzo 1.00 2
BF14 Max Scherzer .60 1
BF15 David Ortiz .60 1

2016 Donruss Optic Back to the Future Signatures

RANDOM INSERTS IN PACKS
*BLUE/50: .5X TO 1.2X BASIC
*BLUE/25: .6X TO 1.5X BASIC
*RED/25: .6X TO 1.5X BASIC
EXCHANGE DEADLINE 1/20/2018
BTFAG Adrian Gonzalez 3.00 8
BTFBB Bill Buckner 3.00 8
BTFDM Don Mattingly 25.00 60
BTFDO David Ortiz 15.00 40
BTFDP David Price 6.00 15
BTFFT Frank Thomas 20.00 50
BTFJD Josh Donaldson 10.00 25
BTFJU Justin Upton 3.00 8
BTFKG Ken Griffey Jr. 50.00 120
BTFKM Kris Medlen 4.00 10
BTFLG Luke Gregerson 2.50 6
BTFMG Mark Grace 6.00 15
BTFMS Max Scherzer 10.00 25
BTFNS Nick Swisher 6.00 15
BTFOV Omar Vizquel 5.00 12
BTFPF Prince Fielder
BTFRA Roberto Alomar 10.00 25
BTFRH Rickey Henderson 20.00 50
BTFRS Ryne Sandberg 15.00 40
BTFTF Todd Frazier 3.00 8
BTFTG Ted Giannoulas 25.00 60
BTFTT Troy Tulowitzki 8.00 20
BTFTW Tim Wakefield 15.00 40
BTFYC Yoenis Cespedes

2016 Donruss Optic Illusion

RANDOM INSERTS IN PACKS
*BLUE/149: 1X TO 2.5X BASIC
*RED/99: 1.2X TO 3X BASIC
1 Mike Trout 3.00 8
2 Bryce Harper 1.00 2
3 David Ortiz .60 1.5
4 Jose Bautista .50 1.2
5 Jose Abreu .60 1.5
6 Miguel Cabrera .60 1.5
7 Carlos Correa .60 1.5
8 Robinson Cano .50 1.2
9 Kris Bryant .75 2.0
10 Giancarlo Stanton .60 1.5
11 Andrew McCutchen .60 1.5
12 Chris Davis .40 1.0
13 Jason Heyward .50 1.2
14 Justin Upton .50 1.2
15 Clayton Kershaw 1.25 3.0
16 Jacob deGrom .60 1.5
17 Matt Harvey .50 1.2
18 Johnny Cueto .50 1.2
19 Noah Syndergaard .50 1.2
20 David Price .50 1.2

2016 Donruss Optic Masters of the Game

RANDOM INSERTS IN PACKS
*BLUE/149: 1X TO 2.5X BASIC
*RED/99: 1.2X TO 3X BASIC
1 Rickey Henderson .60 1.5
2 Roger Clemens .75 2.0
3 Juan Gonzalez .40 1.0
4 Frank Thomas .60 1.5
5 Steve Carlton .50 1.2
6 Mariano Rivera .75 2.0
7 Mark McGwire 1.00 2.5
8 Randy Johnson .60 1.5
9 Ken Griffey Jr. 1.25 3.0
10 Cal Ripken 2.00 5.0
11 Ryne Sandberg 1.25 3.0
12 Mike Piazza .60 1.5
13 Edgar Martinez .50 1.2
14 Pete Rose 1.25 3.0
15 Johnny Bench .60 1.5

016 Donruss Optic Power Alley
NDOM INSERTS IN PACKS
LUE/149: 1X TO 2.5X BASIC
ED/99: 1.2X TO 3X BASIC
ryce Harper 1.00 2.50
Aike Trout 3.00 8.00
osh Donaldson .50 1.25
arlos Correa .60 1.50
Aiguel Sano .60 1.50
iancarlo Stanton .60 1.50
Madison Bumgarner .50 1.25
yle Schwarber 1.25 3.00
ric Hosmer .50 1.25
Jose Bautista .50 1.25
Kris Bryant .75 2.00
Albert Pujols .75 2.00
Paul Goldschmidt .60 1.50
David Ortiz .60 1.50
Yoenis Cespedes .60 1.50

2016 Donruss Optic Rated Rookies Signatures
NDOM INSERTS IN PACKS
QUA/50-125: .5X TO 1.2X BASIC
LACK/25: .6X TO 1.5X BASIC
LUE/75: .5X TO 1.2X BASIC
LUE/25-35: .6X TO 1.5X BASIC
AR.BLUE/35: .6X TO 1.5X BASIC
OLO/75-150: .5X TO 1.2X BASIC
RNGE/50-99: .5X TO 1.2X BASIC
RNGE/35: .6X TO 1.5X BASIC
ED/50: .5X TO 1.2X BASIC
ED/25: .6X TO 1.5X BASIC
CHANGE DEADLINE 1/20/2018
Aaron Nola 5.00 12.00
Brandon Drury 4.00 10.00
Brian Johnson 2.50 6.00
Byung-ho Park 3.00 8.00
Carl Edwards Jr. 3.00 8.00
Corey Seager 60.00 150.00
Dariel Alvarez 2.50 6.00
Elias Diaz 2.50 6.00
Greg Bird 3.00 8.00
0 Henry Owens
Jerad Eickhoff 4.00 10.00
2 Jonathan Gray
3 Jorge Lopez
4 Jose Peraza 3.00 8.00
5 Kelby Tomlinson 2.50 6.00
7 Ketel Marte 5.00 12.00
3 Kyle Schwarber 8.00 20.00
9 Kyle Waldrop 3.00 8.00
0 Luis Severino 3.00 8.00
1 Luke Jackson
2 Max Kepler 5.00 12.00
3 Michael Conforto 15.00 40.00
4 Michael Reed 2.50 6.00
5 Miguel Sano 8.00 20.00
6 Peter O'Brien
7 Raul Mondesi 5.00 12.00
8 Richie Shaffer 2.50 6.00
9 Rob Refsnyder 5.00 12.00
0 Socrates Brito 2.50 6.00
1 Stephen Piscotty 4.00 10.00
2 Tom Murphy 2.50 6.00
3 Travis Jankowski 2.50 6.00
4 Trea Turner 8.00 20.00
5 Tyler Duffey 2.50 6.00
6 Zach Davies 6.00 15.00
7 A.J. Reed 6.00 15.00

2016 Donruss Optic Significant Signatures
ANDOM INSERTS IN PACKS
*BLUE/50: .5X TO 1.2X BASIC
BLUE/25: .6X TO 1.5X BASIC
RED/25: .6X TO 1.5X BASIC
XCHANGE DEADLINE 1/20/2018
Don Newcombe
2 Al Kaline 20.00 50.00
3 Jim Palmer 5.00 10.00
4 Steve Carlton 8.00 20.00
5 Gaylord Perry 4.00 10.00
6 Andres Galarraga 5.00 12.00
7 Fergie Jenkins 6.00 15.00
8 Alan Trammell 20.00 50.00
9 Andre Dawson
10 Andy Pettitte 12.00 30.00
11 Bernie Williams 10.00 25.00
12 Bert Blyleven 5.00 12.00
13 Bob Gibson 10.00 25.00
14 Phil Niekro 12.00 30.00
15 Edgar Martinez 8.00 20.00
16 Paul Molitor 6.00 15.00
17 Fred Lynn 4.00 10.00
18 Rollie Fingers
19 Jim Rice 6.00 15.00
20 Frank Thomas 20.00 50.00
21 Rocky Colavito 25.00 60.00
22 Todd Helton 12.00 30.00
23 Will Clark 30.00 80.00
24 Carlton Fisk
25 Billy Williams

2016 Donruss Optic Studio Signatures
RANDOM INSERTS IN PACKS
*BLUE/50: .5X TO 1.2X BASIC
*BLUE/25: .6X TO 1.5X BASIC
*RED/25: .6X TO 1.5X BASIC
EXCHANGE DEADLINE 1/20/2018
1 Kris Bryant 50.00 120.00
2 Michael Taylor 2.50 6.00
3 Miguel Sano 4.00 10.00
4 Corey Seager 8.00 20.00
5 Kyle Schwarber 10.00 25.00
6 Carl Edwards Jr. 3.00 8.00
7 Lucas Giolito 4.00 10.00
8 Charlie Blackmon 4.00 10.00
9 Evan Gattis 2.50 6.00
10 Evan Longoria 5.00 12.00
11 George Springer 3.00 8.00
12 Joe Mauer
13 Maikel Franco 3.00 8.00
14 Addison Russell 10.00 25.00
15 Vladimir Guerrero Jr. 125.00 300.00
16 Zack Wheeler 3.00 8.00
17 A.J. Reed 2.50 6.00
18 Anthony Ranaudo 2.50 6.00
19 Carlos Martinez 3.00 8.00
20 Didi Gregorius 3.00 8.00
21 Eddie Rosario 3.00 8.00
22 Jose Berrios 3.00 8.00
23 Josh Harrison 2.50 6.00
24 Kaleb Cowart 2.50 6.00
25 Orlando Arcia 3.00 8.00

2016 Donruss Optic The Prospects
RANDOM INSERTS IN PACKS
*BLUE/149: 1X TO 2.5X BASIC
*RED/99: 1.2X TO 3X BASIC
1 Lucas Giolito .60 1.50
2 Julio Urias 1.25 3.00
3 Yoan Moncada 1.00 2.50
4 Tyler Glasnow .50 1.25
5 Brendan Rodgers .60 1.50
6 Dansby Swanson 1.25 3.00
7 Orlando Arcia .50 1.25
8 Rafael Devers 1.25 3.00
9 Vladimir Guerrero Jr. 6.00 15.00
10 A.J. Reed .40 1.00
11 Andrew Benintendi 1.25 3.00
12 Bradley Zimmer .60 1.50
13 Alex Reyes .50 1.25
14 Clint Frazier 1.50 4.00
15 Josh Bell .75 2.00

2016 Donruss Optic The Rookies
RANDOM INSERTS IN PACKS
*BLUE/149: 1X TO 2.5X BASIC
*RED/99: 1.2X TO 3X BASIC
1 Kyle Schwarber 1.25 3.00
2 Corey Seager 3.00 8.00
3 Trea Turner 1.25 3.00
4 Rob Refsnyder .50 1.25
5 Miguel Sano .60 1.50
6 Stephen Piscotty .60 1.50
7 Aaron Nola .75 2.00
8 Michael Conforto .50 1.25
9 Ketel Marte .75 2.00
10 Luis Severino .50 1.25
11 Greg Bird .50 1.25
12 Hector Olivera .50 1.25
13 Jose Peraza .50 1.25
14 Henry Owens .50 1.25
15 Richie Shaffer .40 1.00

2017 Donruss Optic
COMP.SET w/o SPs (165) 30.00 80.00
EXCHANGE DEADLINE 1/19/2019
SPs RANDOMLY INSERTED
1 Paul Goldschmidt DK .50 1.25
2 Freddie Freeman DK .60 1.50
3 Mark Trumbo DK .30 .75
4 Chris Sale DK .50 1.25
5 Anthony Rizzo DK .75 2.00
6 Lucas Giolito DK .40 1.00
7 Mickey Mantle DK 1.50 4.00
8 Corey Kluber DK .40 1.00
9 Nolan Arenado DK .60 1.50
10 Justin Verlander DK .50 1.25
11 Carlos Correa DK .50 1.25
12 Salvador Perez DK .40 1.00
13 Mike Trout DK 2.50 6.00
14 Corey Seager DK .50 1.25
15 Christian Yelich DK .60 1.50
16 Jonathan Villar DK .30 .75
17 Miguel Sano DK .40 1.00
18 Noah Syndergaard DK .40 1.00
19 Joey Votto DK .50 1.25
20 Khris Davis DK .50 1.25
21 Maikel Franco DK .40 1.00
22 Gregory Polanco DK .40 1.00
23 Wil Myers DK .30 .75
24 Madison Bumgarner DK .40 1.00
25 Robinson Cano DK .40 1.00
26 Dexter Fowler DK .40 1.00
27 Kevin Kiermaier DK .40 1.00
28 Rougned Odor DK .40 1.00
29 Troy Tulowitzki DK .50 1.25
30 Daniel Murphy DK .40 1.00
31 Yoan Moncada RR RC 1.00 2.50
32 David Dahl RR RC .40 1.00
33 Dansby Swanson RR RC .75 2.00
34 Andrew Benintendi RR RC 1.00 2.50
35 Alex Reyes RR RC .40 1.00
36 Tyler Glasnow RR RC .40 1.00
37 Josh Bell RR RC .75 2.00
38 Aaron Judge RR RC 4.00 10.00
39 Jose De Leon RR RC .30 .75
40 Ian Happ RR RC .60 1.50
41 Hunter Renfroe RR RC .40 1.00
42 Carson Fulmer RR RC .30 .75
43 Alex Bregman RR RC 1.25 3.00
44 Orlando Arcia RR RC .50 1.25
45 Manuel Margot RR RC .30 .75
46 Joe Musgrove RR RC .30 .75
47 David Paulino RR RC .40 1.00
48 Reynaldo Lopez RR RC .30 .75
49 Jake Thompson RR RC .30 .75
50 Braden Shipley RR RC .30 .75
51 Jorge Alfaro RR RC .40 1.00
52 Luke Weaver RR RC .40 1.00
53 Raimel Tapia RR RC .40 1.00
54 Adalberto Mejia RR RC .30 .75
55 Gavin Cecchini RR RC .30 .75
56 Renato Nunez RR RC .60 1.50
57 Jacoby Jones RR RC .40 1.00
58 Magneuris Sierra RR RC .50 1.25
59 Trey Mancini RR RC .60 1.50
60 Ryon Healy RR RC .40 1.00
61 Jordan Montgomery RR RC .50 1.25
62 Teoscar Hernandez RR RC 1.00 2.50
63 Christian Arroyo RR RC .50 1.25
64 Mitch Haniger RR RC .50 1.25
65 Cody Bellinger RR RC 5.00 12.00
66 Paul Goldschmidt .30 .75
67 Yasmany Tomas .20 .50
68 Zack Greinke .25 .60
69 Freddie Freeman .40 1.00
70 Matt Kemp .25 .60
71 Nick Markakis .25 .60
72 Adam Jones .25 .60
73 Manny Machado .30 .75
74 Chris Sale .30 .75
75 Dustin Pedroia .30 .75
76 Jackie Bradley Jr. .30 .75
77 Mookie Betts .50 1.25
78 Rick Porcello .25 .60
79 Xander Bogaerts .30 .75
80 Addison Russell .30 .75
81A Anthony Rizzo .50 1.25
81B Rizzo SP Rizz .50 1.25
82 Javier Baez .40 1.00
83A Kris Bryant .40 1.00
83B Bryant SP MVP .40 1.00
84 Kyle Hendricks .30 .75
85 Kyle Schwarber .30 .75
86 Jose Abreu .30 .75
87 Todd Frazier .25 .60
88 Joey Votto .30 .75
89 Corey Kluber .25 .60
90 Francisco Lindor .30 .75
91 Tyler Naquin .20 .50
92 Andrew Miller .25 .60
93 Charlie Blackmon .30 .75
94 Nolan Arenado .40 1.00
95 Trevor Story .30 .75
96 Carlos Gonzalez .25 .60
97 Justin Verlander .30 .75
98 Michael Fulmer .20 .50
99 Miguel Cabrera .30 .75
100 Carlos Correa .30 .75
101 George Springer .25 .60
102 Jose Altuve .25 .60
103 Eric Hosmer .25 .60
104 Kendrys Morales .20 .50
105 Salvador Perez .20 .50
106 Albert Pujols .40 1.00
107A Mike Trout 1.50 4.00
107B Trout SP MVP 5.00 12.00
108 Clayton Kershaw .60 1.50
109A Corey Seager .30 .75
109B Seager SP ROY .30 .75
110 Kenta Maeda .25 .60
111 Christian Yelich .40 1.00
112 Dee Gordon .20 .50
113 Giancarlo Stanton .30 .75
114 Chris Carter .20 .50
115 Ryan Braun .25 .60
116 Brian Dozier .30 .75
117 Miguel Sano .25 .60
118 Jacob deGrom .25 .60
119 Jay Bruce .25 .60
120 Noah Syndergaard .25 .60
121 Yoenis Cespedes .30 .75
122 Gary Sanchez .30 .75
123 Masahiro Tanaka .25 .60
124 Khris Davis .30 .75
125 Marcus Semien .20 .50
126 Freddy Galvis .20 .50
127 Maikel Franco .25 .60
128 Andrew McCutchen .30 .75
129 Gregory Polanco .25 .60
130 Starling Marte .25 .60
131 Alex Dickerson .20 .50
132 Wil Myers .25 .60
133 Brandon Belt .25 .60
134 Buster Posey .40 1.00
135 Madison Bumgarner .25 .60
136 Felix Hernandez .25 .60
137 Robinson Cano .25 .60
138 Matt Carpenter .25 .60
139 Stephen Piscotty .25 .60
140 Yadier Molina .30 .75
141 Dexter Fowler .25 .60
142 Brad Miller .25 .60
143 Evan Longoria .25 .60
144 Kevin Kiermaier .25 .60
145 Adrian Beltre .30 .75
146 Nomar Mazara .20 .50
147 Rougned Odor .25 .60
148 Yu Darvish .30 .75
149 Jose Bautista .25 .60
150 Josh Donaldson .25 .60
151 Troy Tulowitzki .30 .75
152 Bryce Harper .50 1.25
153 Daniel Murphy .25 .60
154 Trea Turner .25 .60
155 Edwin Encarnacion .30 .75
156 Cal Ripken 1.00 2.50
157 Duke Snider .25 .60
158 Frank Thomas .30 .75
159 Ken Griffey Jr. .60 1.50
160 Kirby Puckett .30 .75
161 Nolan Ryan 1.00 2.50
162 Pete Rose .60 1.50
163 Ryne Sandberg .60 1.50
164 Tony Gwynn .30 .75
165A Mickey Mantle 1.00 2.50
165B Mantle SP The Mick 3.00 8.00
166 Roman Quinn RR AU 2.50 6.00
167 Matt Olson RR AU 6.00 15.00
168 Rio Ruiz RR AU 2.50 6.00
169 Chad Pinder RR AU 2.50 6.00
170 Teoscar Hernandez RR AU 8.00 20.00
171 Erik Gonzalez RR AU 2.50 6.00
172 German Marquez RR AU 4.00 10.00
173 Jharel Cotton RR AU 2.50 6.00
174 Carson Kelly RR AU 3.00 8.00
175 Jose Rondon RR AU 2.50 6.00

2017 Donruss Optic Aqua
*AQUA DK: .75X TO 2X BASIC DK
*AQUA RR: .75X TO 2X BASIC RR
*AQUA VET: 1.2X TO 3X BASIC VET
*AQUA AU: .5X TO 1.2X BASIC AU
RANDOM INSERTS IN PACKS
STATED PRINT RUN 299 SER.#'d SETS
AU PRINT RUN 125 SER.#'d SETS
EXCHANGE DEADLINE 1/19/2019

2017 Donruss Optic Black
*BLACK DK: 2.5X TO 6X BASIC DK
*BLACK RR: 2.5X TO 6X BASIC RR
*BLACK VET: 4X TO 10X BASIC VET
*BLACK AU: 1X TO 2.5X BASIC AU
RANDOM INSERTS IN PACKS
STATED PRINT RUN 25 SER.#'d SETS
EXCHANGE DEADLINE 1/19/2019

2017 Donruss Optic Blue
*BLUE DK: 1.2X TO 3X BASIC DK
*BLUE RR: 1.2X TO 3X BASIC RR
*BLUE VET: 2X TO 5X BASIC VET
*BLUE SP: .6X TO 1.5X BASIC SP
*BLUE AU: .6X TO 1.5X BASIC AU
RANDOM INSERTS IN PACKS
STATED PRINT RUN 149 SER.#'d SETS
AU PRINT RUN 75 SER.#'d SETS
EXCHANGE DEADLINE 1/19/2019

2017 Donruss Optic Carolina Blue
*CAR.BLU DK: 2X TO 5X BASIC DK
*CAR.BLU RR: 2X TO 5X BASIC RR
*CAR.BLU VET: 3X TO 8X BASIC VET
*CAR.BLU AU: .75X TO 2X BASIC AU
RANDOM INSERTS IN PACKS
STATED PRINT RUN 50 SER.#'d SETS
AU PRINT RUN 35 SER.#'d SETS
EXCHANGE DEADLINE 1/19/2019

2017 Donruss Optic Holo
*HOLO DK: .5X TO 1.2X BASIC DK
*HOLO RR: .5X TO 1.2X BASIC RR
*HOLO VET: .75X TO 2.5X BASIC VET
*HOLO AU: .5X TO 1.2X BASIC AU
RANDOM INSERTS IN PACKS
AU PRINT RUN 150 SER.#'d SETS
EXCHANGE DEADLINE 1/19/2019

2017 Donruss Optic Orange
*ORANGE DK: 1.2X TO 3X BASIC DK
*ORANGE RR: 1.2X TO 3X BASIC RR
*ORANGE VET: 2X TO 5X BASIC VET
*ORANGE SP: .6X TO 1.5X BASIC SP
*ORANGE AU: .6X TO 1.5X BASIC AU
RANDOM INSERTS IN PACKS
STATED PRINT RUN 199 SER.#'d SETS
AU PRINT RUN 99 SER.#'d SETS
EXCHANGE DEADLINE 1/19/2019

2017 Donruss Optic Pink
*PINK DK: .75X TO 2X BASIC DK
*PINK RR: .75X TO 2X BASIC RR
*PINK VET: 1.2X TO 3X BASIC VET
RANDOM INSERTS IN PACKS

2017 Donruss Optic Purple
*PURPLE DK: .75X TO 2X BASIC DK
*PURPLE RR: .75X TO 2X BASIC RR
*PURPLE VET: 1.2X TO 3X BASIC VET
INSERTED IN RETAIL PACKS

2017 Donruss Optic Red
*RED DK: 1.5X TO 4X BASIC DK
*RED RR: 1.5X TO 4X BASIC RR
*RED VET: 2.5X TO 6X BASIC VET
*RED SP: .75X TO 2X BASIC SP
*RED AU: .6X TO 1.5X BASIC AU
RANDOM INSERTS IN PACKS
STATED PRINT RUN 99 SER.#'d SETS
AU PRINT RUN 50 SER.#'d SETS
EXCHANGE DEADLINE 1/19/2019
38 Aaron Judge RR/99 30.00 80.00

2017 Donruss Optic All Stars
RANDOM INSERTS IN PACKS
*BLUE/149: 1X TO 2.5X BASIC
*RED/99: 1.2X TO 3X BASIC
AS1 Addison Russell .60 1.50
AS2 Bryce Harper 1.00 2.50
AS3 Chris Sale .60 1.50
AS4 Eric Hosmer .50 1.25
AS5 Johnny Cueto .50 1.25
AS6 Jose Altuve .50 1.25
AS7 Kris Bryant .75 2.00
AS8 Manny Machado .60 1.50
AS9 Marcell Ozuna .60 1.50
AS10 Mike Trout 3.00 8.00
AS11 Mookie Betts 1.00 2.50
AS12 Yoenis Cespedes .60 1.50
AS13 Salvador Perez .50 1.25
AS14 Corey Kluber .50 1.25
AS15 Aledmys Diaz .50 1.25

2017 Donruss Optic Autographs
RANDOM INSERTS IN PACKS
EXCHANGE DEADLINE 1/19/2019
OAAT Alan Trammell 6.00 15.00
OACB Cody Bellinger 40.00 100.00
OAER Eddie Rosario 3.00 8.00
OAFF Freddie Freeman 20.00 50.00
OAIH Ian Happ 6.00 15.00
OAIN Ivan Nova 3.00 8.00
OAJL Jorge Lopez 2.50 6.00
OAJM James McCann 3.00 8.00
OAKH Keith Hernandez 8.00 20.00
OAKP Kevin Pillar 2.50 6.00
OALT Leodys Taveras 8.00 20.00
OAMC Matt Carpenter 5.00 12.00
OAMF Mike Foltynewicz 2.50 6.00
OANA Norichika Aoki 4.00 10.00
OAPO Paulo Orlando 2.50 6.00
OAWM Willie McGee 5.00 12.00

2017 Donruss Optic Autographs Blue
*BLUE/50: .6X TO 1.5X BASIC
*BLUE/25: .75X TO 2X BASIC
RANDOM INSERTS IN PACKS
PRINT RUNS BWN 10-50 COPIES PER
NO PRICING ON QTY 15 OR LESS
EXCHANGE DEADLINE 1/19/2019
OAAN Aaron Nola/50 12.00 30.00

2017 Donruss Optic Autographs Red
*RED/25: .75X TO 2X BASIC
RANDOM INSERTS IN PACKS
PRINT RUNS BWN 7-25 COPIES PER
NO PRICING ON QTY 15 OR LESS
EXCHANGE DEADLINE 1/19/2019
OAAN Aaron Nola/25 15.00 40.00

2017 Donruss Optic Back to the Future Signatures
RANDOM INSERTS IN PACKS
EXCHANGE DEADLINE 1/19/2019
*RED/25: .75X TO 2X BASIC
1 Josh Donaldson 10.00 25.00
2 Max Scherzer 15.00 40.00
4 Michael Kopech 5.00 12.00
6 Jose De Leon 2.50 6.00
8 Lucas Giolito 3.00 8.00
10 Jorge Alfaro 3.00 8.00
12 Cole Hamels
13 Nelson Cruz 4.00 10.00
15 Willie McGee 5.00 12.00
17 Trea Turner 6.00 15.00
20 Khris Davis 4.00 10.00
23 John Lamb 2.50 6.00
24 Peter O'Brien 2.50 6.00
25 Jean Segura

2017 Donruss Optic Back to the Future Signatures Blue
*BLUE/50: .6X TO 1.5X BASIC
*BLUE/25: .75X TO 2X BASIC
RANDOM INSERTS IN PACKS
PRINT RUNS BWN 10-50 COPIES PER
NO PRICING ON QTY 15 OR LESS
EXCHANGE DEADLINE 1/19/2019
18 Justin Turner/25 12.00 20.00

2017 Donruss Optic Dominators
RANDOM INSERTS IN PACKS
*BLUE/149: 1X TO 2.5X BASIC
*RED/99: 1.2X TO 3X BASIC
D1 Kris Bryant .75 2.00
D2 Mike Trout 3.00 8.00
D3 Corey Seager .60 1.50
D4 Mookie Betts 1.00 2.50
D5 Jose Altuve .50 1.25
D6 Joey Votto .60 1.50
D7 Brian Dozier .60 1.50
D8 Rick Porcello .50 1.25
D9 Corey Kluber .50 1.25
D10 Miguel Cabrera .60 1.50
D11 Robinson Cano .50 1.25
D12 Khris Davis .60 1.50
D13 Kyle Hendricks .60 1.50
D14 Max Scherzer .60 1.50
D15 Nolan Arenado .75 2.00

2017 Donruss Optic Masters of the Game
RANDOM INSERTS IN PACKS
*BLUE/149: 1X TO 2.5X BASIC
*RED/99: 1.2X TO 3X BASIC
MG1 Cal Ripken 2.00 5.00
MG2 Fernando Valenzuela .40 1.00
MG3 George Brett 1.25 3.00
MG4 Lou Brock .50 1.25
MG5 Mike Mussina .50 1.25
MG6 Mike Piazza .60 1.50
MG7 Mickey Mantle 2.00 5.00
MG8 Pedro Martinez .50 1.25
MG9 Reggie Jackson .50 1.25
MG10 Rod Carew .50 1.25
MG11 Don Mattingly 1.25 3.00
MG12 Ken Griffey Jr. 1.25 3.00
MG13 Todd Helton .50 1.25
MG14 Ryne Sandberg 1.25 3.00
MG15 Greg Maddux .75 2.00

2017 Donruss Optic Rated Rookies Signatures
RANDOM INSERTS IN PACKS
EXCHANGE DEADLINE 1/19/2019
*AQUA/75-125: .5X TO 1.2X BASIC
*BLACK/25: .75X TO 2X BASIC
2017 Donruss Optic Autographs Blue
2017 Donruss Optic Autographs Blue
*CAR.BLU/35: .6X TO 1.5X BASIC
*CAR.BLU/20-25: .75X TO 2X BASIC
*HOLO/99-150: .5X TO 1.2X BASIC
*ORANGE/75-99: .5X TO 1.2X BASIC
*RED/35-50: .6X TO 1.5X BASIC
*RED/25: .75X TO 2X BASIC
RRSAB Alex Bregman 12.00 30.00
RRSAJ Aaron Judge 75.00 200.00
RRSAM Adalberto Mejia 2.50 6.00
RRSAR Alex Reyes 3.00 8.00
RRSAX Andrew Benintendi 10.00 25.00
RRSBS Braden Shipley 2.50 6.00
RRSCF Carson Fulmer 2.50 6.00
RRSCL Clint Frazier 12.00 30.00
RRSDD David Dahl 3.00 8.00
RRSDP David Paulino 3.00 8.00
RRSDS Dansby Swanson 15.00 40.00
RRSGC Gavin Cecchini 2.50 6.00
RRSHR Hunter Renfroe 3.00 8.00
RRSJA Jorge Alfaro 3.00 8.00
RRSJB Josh Bell 6.00 15.00
RRSJDL Jose De Leon 2.50 6.00
RRSJH Jeff Hoffman 2.50 6.00
RRSJJ Jacoby Jones 3.00 8.00
RRSJM Joe Musgrove 2.50 6.00
RRSJT Jake Thompson 2.50 6.00
RRSLB Lewis Brinson 5.00 12.00
RRSLW Luke Weaver 3.00 8.00
RRSMM Manuel Margot 2.50 6.00
RRSOA Orlando Arcia EXCH 5.00 12.00
RRSRH Ryon Healy 4.00 10.00
RRSRL Reynaldo Lopez 2.50 6.00
RRSRN Renato Nunez 5.00 12.00
RRSRT Raimel Tapia 3.00 8.00
RRSTG Tyler Glasnow 10.00 25.00
RRSTM Trey Mancini 5.00 12.00
RRSYM Yoan Moncada 30.00 80.00
RRSYO Yohander Mendez 2.50 6.00

2017 Donruss Optic Significant Signatures
RANDOM INSERTS IN PACKS
EXCHANGE DEADLINE 1/19/2019
*BLUE/50: .6X TO 1.5X BASIC
*RED/25: .75X TO 2X BASIC
21 Al Oliver 4.00 10.00
23 Pat Gillick 4.00 10.00

2017 Donruss Optic Studio Signatures
RANDOM INSERTS IN PACKS
EXCHANGE DEADLINE 1/19/2019
*RED/25: .75X TO 2X BASIC
6 Giannoulas SD Chicken 5.00 12.00
8 Matt Szczur 3.00 8.00
10 Tyler Naquin 2.50 6.00
11 Dilson Herrera 3.00 8.00
14 Willson Contreras 8.00 20.00
17 Michael Reed 2.50 6.00
21 Cory Spangenberg 2.50 6.00
22 Trevor May 2.50 6.00
23 Greg Bird 3.00 8.00
24 Jameson Taillon 4.00 10.00
25 Tim Anderson 4.00 10.00

2017 Donruss Optic Studio Signatures Blue
*BLUE/50: .6X TO 1.5X BASIC
*BLUE/25: .75X TO 2X BASIC
RANDOM INSERTS IN PACKS
PRINT RUNS BWN 10-50 COPIES PER
NO PRICING ON QTY 10
EXCHANGE DEADLINE 1/19/2019
9 Andres Galarraga/25 6.00 15.00
16 Corey Seager/25 20.00 50.00

2017 Donruss Optic The Elite Series
RANDOM INSERTS IN PACKS
*BLUE/149: 1X TO 2.5X BASIC
*RED/99: 1.2X TO 3X BASIC
ES1 Kris Bryant .75 2.00
ES2 Clayton Kershaw 1.25 3.00
ES3 Bryce Harper 1.00 2.50
ES4 Manny Machado .60 1.50
ES5 Anthony Rizzo 1.00 2.50
ES6 Adrian Beltre .60 1.50
ES7 Mickey Mantle 2.00 5.00
ES8 Chris Sale .60 1.50
ES9 Gary Sanchez .60 1.50
ES10 Trevor Story .60 1.50
ES11 Trea Turner .50 1.25
ES12 Kenta Maeda .50 1.25
ES13 Buster Posey .75 2.00
ES14 Mike Trout 3.00 8.00
ES15 Francisco Lindor .60 1.50
ES16 Kyle Schwarber .60 1.50
ES17 Dustin Pedroia .60 1.50
ES18 Corey Kluber .50 1.25
ES19 Yoenis Cespedes .60 1.50
ES20 Madison Bumgarner .50 1.25

2017 Donruss Optic The Prospects
RANDOM INSERTS IN PACKS
*BLUE/149: .6X TO 1.5X BASIC
*RED/99: .75X TO 2X BASIC
TP1 Brendan Rodgers .40 1.00
TP2 Austin Meadows .50 1.25
TP3 Victor Robles .75 2.00
TP4 Ozhaino Albies 1.25 3.00
TP5 Anderson Espinoza .30 .75
TP6 Clint Frazier .60 1.50
TP7 Rafael Devers .60 1.50
TP8 Gleyber Torres 5.00 12.00
TP9 Jorge Mateo .30 .75
TP10 Vladimir Guerrero Jr. 4.00 10.00
TP11 Eloy Jimenez 1.25 3.00
TP12 Bradley Zimmer .40 1.00
TP13 Corey Ray .40 1.00
TP14 Amed Rosario .50 1.25
TP15 Francis Martes .30 .75

2017 Donruss Optic The Rookies
RANDOM INSERTS IN PACKS
*BLUE/149: 1X TO 2.5X BASIC
*RED/99: 1.2X TO 3X BASIC
TR1 Yoan Moncada 1.00 2.50
TR2 David Dahl .40 1.00
TR3 Dansby Swanson .75 2.00
TR4 Andrew Benintendi 1.00 2.50
TR5 Alex Reyes .40 1.00
TR6 Tyler Glasnow .40 1.00
TR7 Josh Bell .75 2.00
TR8 Aaron Judge 4.00 10.00
TR9 Jose De Leon .30 .75
TR10 Ian Happ .60 1.50
TR11 Hunter Renfroe .40 1.00
TR12 Carson Fulmer .30 .75
TR13 Alex Bregman 1.25 3.00
TR14 Orlando Arcia .50 1.25
TR15 Cody Bellinger 5.00 12.00

2018 Donruss Optic
COMPLETE SET (185) 20.00 50.00
1 Anthony Rizzo DK .75 2.00
2 Yoan Moncada DK .50 1.25
3 Chris Archer DK .30 .75
4 Joey Votto DK .50 1.25
5 Corey Kluber DK .40 1.00
6 Adrian Beltre DK .50 1.25
7 Jose Bautista DK .40 1.00
8 Nolan Arenado DK .60 1.50
9 Miguel Cabrera DK .50 1.25
10 Bryce Harper DK .75 2.00
11 Jose Altuve DK .40 1.00
12 Eric Hosmer DK .40 1.00
13 Mike Trout DK 2.50 6.00
14 Clayton Kershaw DK 1.00 2.50
15 Justin Bour DK .30 .75
16 Ryan Braun DK .40 1.00
17 Brian Dozier DK .40 1.00
18 Noah Syndergaard DK .40 1.00
19 Aaron Judge DK 1.25 3.00
20 Matt Olson DK .30 .75
21 Odubel Herrera DK .40 1.00
22 Paul Goldschmidt DK .50 1.25
23 Freddie Freeman DK .60 1.50
24 Andrew McCutchen DK .50 1.25
25 Adam Jones DK .40 1.00
26 Salvador Perez DK .40 1.00
27 Mookie Betts DK .75 2.00
28 Josh Bell DK .40 1.00
29 Robinson Cano DK .40 1.00
30 Adam Wainwright DK .40 1.00
31 Miguel Andujar RR RC 1.25 3.00
32 Nick Williams RR RC .40 1.00
33 Clint Frazier RR RC .60 1.50
34 Paul Blackburn RR RC .30 .75
35 Rafael Devers RR RC 1.00 2.50
36 Ozzie Albies RR RC 1.00 2.50
37 Amed Rosario RR RC .40 1.00
38 Rhys Hoskins RR RC 1.25 3.00
39 Ryan McMahon RR RC .40 1.00
40 Willie Calhoun RR RC .40 1.00
41 Walker Buehler RR RC 1.50 4.00
42 Victor Robles RR RC .75 2.00
43 Luiz Gohara RR RC .30 .75
44 J.P. Crawford RR RC .30 .75
45 Alex Verdugo RR RC .50 1.25
46 Scott Kingery RR RC .50 1.25
47 Dominic Smith RR RC .30 .75
48 Yoshihisa Hirano RR RC .50 1.25
49 Ronald Guzman RR RC .30 .75
50 Dustin Fowler RR RC .30 .75
51 Chance Sisco RR RC .30 .75
52 Tyler Wade RR RC .40 1.00
53 Thyago Vieira RR RC .30 .75
54 Harrison Bader RR RC .50 1.25
55 Jack Flaherty RR RC .50 1.25
56 Shohei Ohtani RR RC 4.00 10.00
57 Tyler O'Neill RR RC .50 1.25
58 Austin Hays RR RC .50 1.25
59 Nicky Delmonico RR RC .30 .75
60 Greg Allen RR RC .30 .75
61 Mitch Garver RR RC .30 .75
62 Zack Granite RR RC .30 .75
63 Ronald Acuna Jr. RR RC 6.00 15.00
64 Cameron Gallagher RR RC .30 .75
65 Gleyber Torres RR RC 3.00 8.00
66 Paul Goldschmidt .30 .75
67 Zack Greinke .25 .60
68 Freddie Freeman .40 1.00
69 Eddie Mathews .30 .75
70 Adam Jones .25 .60
71 Cal Ripken 1.00 2.50
72 Dustin Pedroia .30 .75
73 Jean Segura .20 .50
74 Brian Dozier .25 .60
75 Javier Baez .40 1.00
76 Kyle Hendricks .30 .75
77 Miguel Sano .25 .60
78 Kyle Schwarber .30 .75
79 Ryne Sandberg .60 1.50
80 Jose Abreu .30 .75
81 Frank Thomas .30 .75
82 Zack Cozart .20 .50

83 Barry Larkin .25 .60
84 Joe Morgan .25 .60
85 Odubel Herrera .25 .60
86 Andrew Miller .25 .60
87 Edwin Encarnacion .30 .75
88 Trevor Story .30 .75
89 Charlie Blackmon .30 .75
90 Jonathan Gray .20 .50
91 Reggie Jackson .25 .60
92 Michael Fulmer .20 .50
93 Justin Verlander .30 .75
94 Madison Bumgarner .25 .60
95 Manuel Margot .20 .50
96 Marcus Stroman .25 .60
97 George Brett .60 1.50
98 Justin Turner .25 .60
99 Yu Darvish .30 .75
100 Kenley Jansen .25 .60
101 Christian Yelich .40 1.00
102 Dee Gordon .20 .50
103 Marcell Ozuna .30 .75
104 Ryan Braun .25 .60
105 Orlando Arcia .20 .50
106 Chris Sale .30 .75
107 Anthony Rizzo .50 1.25
108 Kirby Puckett .30 .75
109 Giancarlo Stanton .30 .75
110 Noah Syndergaard .25 .60
111 Michael Conforto .25 .60
112 Jacob deGrom .30 .75
113 Joey Votto .30 .75
114 Aaron Judge .75 2.00
115 Cody Bellinger .60 1.50
116 Gary Sanchez .30 .75
117 Luis Severino .25 .60
118 Jordan Montgomery .30 .75
119 Corey Kluber .25 .60
120 Clayton Kershaw .60 1.50
121 Mike Trout 1.50 4.00
122 Miguel Cabrera .30 .75
123 Francisco Lindor .30 .75
124 Corey Seager .30 .75
125 Andrew McCutchen .30 .75
126 Josh Bell .25 .60
127 Gerrit Cole .30 .75
128 Alex Bregman .30 .75
129 Carlos Correa .30 .75
130 Dallas Keuchel .25 .60
131 Tony Gwynn .30 .75
132 Jose Altuve .25 .60
133 Buster Posey .40 1.00
134 George Springer .25 .60
135 Andrew Benintendi .30 .75
136 Kyle Seager .20 .50
137 Robinson Cano .25 .60
138 Nolan Arenado .40 1.00
139 Jose Ramirez .25 .60
140 Felix Hernandez .25 .60
141 Ken Griffey Jr. .60 1.50
142 Yadier Molina .30 .75
143 Matt Carpenter .30 .75
144 Carlos Martinez .25 .60
145 Evan Longoria .25 .60
146 Ian Happ .25 .60
147 Chris Archer .20 .50
148 Adrian Beltre .30 .75
149 Kris Bryant .40 1.00
150 Joey Gallo .25 .60
151 Nomar Mazara .20 .50
152 Nolan Ryan 1.00 2.50
153 Josh Donaldson .25 .60
154 Manny Machado .30 .75
155 Salvador Perez .25 .60
156 Mookie Betts .50 1.25
157 Bryce Harper .50 1.25
158 Max Scherzer .30 .75
159 Daniel Murphy .25 .60
160 Chipper Jones .30 .75
161 Trea Turner .25 .60
162 Ryan Zimmerman .25 .60
163 Stephen Strasburg .30 .75
164 J.D. Martinez .30 .75
165 Mickey Mantle 1.00 2.50
166 Joey Votto AS .30 .75
167 Gary Sanchez AS .30 .75
168 Lance McCullers AS .20 .50
169 Jose Ramirez AS .25 .60
170 Carlos Correa AS .30 .75
171 Aaron Judge AS .75 2.00
172 Cody Bellinger AS .60 1.50
173 Bryce Harper AS .50 1.25
174 Yadier Molina AS .30 .75
175 Nolan Arenado AS .40 1.00
177 Erick Fedde RR RC .20 .50
178 Caleb Smith RR RC .20 .50
179 Francisco Mejia RR RC .25 .60
180 Shohei Ohtani RR 1.25 3.00
181 Juan Soto RR RC 4.00 10.00
182 Kyle Farmer RR RC .20 .50
183 Willy Adames RR RC .25 .60
184 Anthony Santander RR RC .20 .50
185 Brian Anderson RR RC .25 .60
186 Richard Urena RR RC .20 .50

2018 Donruss Optic Aqua

*AQUA DK: .75X TO 2X BASIC DK
*AQUA RR: .75X TO 2X BASIC RR
*AQUA VET: 1.2X TO 3X BASIC VET
RANDOM INSERTS IN PACKS
STATED PRINT RUN 299 SER.#'d SETS

2018 Donruss Optic Black

*BLACK DK: 1.5X TO 4X BASIC DK
*BLACK RR: 1.5X TO 4X BASIC RR
*BLACK VET: 2.5X TO 6X BASIC VET
RANDOM INSERTS IN PACKS
STATED PRINT RUN 25 SER.#'d SETS
13 Mike Trout DK 10.00 25.00
71 Cal Ripken 15.00 40.00
97 George Brett 10.00 25.00
108 Kirby Puckett 25.00 60.00
121 Mike Trout 10.00 25.00
131 Tony Gwynn 8.00 20.00
141 Ken Griffey Jr. 15.00 40.00
152 Nolan Ryan 15.00 40.00

2018 Donruss Optic Blue

*BLUE DK: .75X TO 2X BASIC DK
*BLUE RR: .75X TO 2X BASIC RR
*BLUE VET: 1.2X TO 3X BASIC VET
RANDOM INSERTS IN PACKS
STATED PRINT RUN 149 SER.#'d SETS

2018 Donruss Optic Bronze

*BRONZE DK: .5X TO 1.2X BASIC DK
*BRONZE RR: .5X TO 1.2X BASIC RR
*BRONZE VET: .75X TO 2.5X BASIC VET
RANDOM INSERTS IN PACKS

2018 Donruss Optic Carolina Blue

*CAR.BLU DK: 1X TO 2.5X BASIC DK
*CAR.BLU RR: 1X TO 2.5X BASIC RR
*CAR.BLU VET: 1.5X TO 4X BASIC VET
RANDOM INSERTS IN PACKS
STATED PRINT RUN 50 SER.#'d SETS
71 Cal Ripken 10.00 25.00
97 George Brett 6.00 15.00
108 Kirby Puckett 10.00 25.00
131 Tony Gwynn 5.00 12.00
152 Nolan Ryan 10.00 25.00

2018 Donruss Optic Holo

*HOLO DK: .5X TO 1.2X BASIC DK
*HOLO RR: .5X TO 1.2X BASIC RR
*HOLO VET: .75X TO 2.5X BASIC VET
RANDOM INSERTS IN PACKS

2018 Donruss Optic Orange

*ORANGE DK: .75X TO 2X BASIC DK
*ORANGE RR: .75X TO 2X BASIC RR
*ORANGE VET: 1.2X TO 3X BASIC VET
RANDOM INSERTS IN PACKS
STATED PRINT RUN 199 SER.#'d SETS

2018 Donruss Optic Pink

*PINK DK: .5X TO 1.2X BASIC DK
*PINK RR: .5X TO 1.2X BASIC RR
*PINK VET: .75X TO 2X BASIC VET
RANDOM INSERTS IN PACKS

2018 Donruss Optic Purple

*PURPLE DK: .5X TO 1.2X BASIC DK
*PURPLE RR: .5X TO 1.2X BASIC RR
*PURPLE VET: .75X TO 2X BASIC VET
INSERTED IN RETAIL PACKS

2018 Donruss Optic Red

*RED DK: 1X TO 2.5X BASIC DK
*RED RR: 1X TO 2.5X BASIC RR
*RED VET: 1.5X TO 4X BASIC VET
RANDOM INSERTS IN PACKS
STATED PRINT RUN 99 SER.#'d SETS
108 Kirby Puckett 10.00 25.00

2018 Donruss Optic Red and Yellow

*RED YEL DK: .5X TO 1.2X BASIC DK
*RED YEL RR: .5X TO 1.2X BASIC RR
*RED YEL VET: .75X TO 2X BASIC VET
RANDOM INSERTS IN PACKS

2018 Donruss Optic Shock

*SHOCK DK: .5X TO 1.2X BASIC DK
*SHOCK RR: .5X TO 1.2X BASIC RR
*SHOCK VET: .75X TO 2.5X BASIC VET
RANDOM INSERTS IN PACKS

2018 Donruss Optic Variations

RANDOM INSERTS IN PACKS
31 Miguel Andujar RR 1.25 3.00
32 Nick Williams RR .40 1.00
33 Clint Frazier RR .60 1.50
35 Rafael Devers RR 1.00 2.50
36 Ozzie Albies RR 1.00 2.50
37 Amed Rosario RR .40 1.00
38 Rhys Hoskins RR 1.25 3.00
39 Ryan McMahon RR .40 1.00
40 Willie Calhoun RR .40 1.00
41 Walker Buehler RR 1.50 4.00
42 Victor Robles RR .75 2.00
51 Chance Sisco RR .40 1.00
56 Shohei Ohtani RR 4.00 10.00
65 Gleyber Torres RR 3.00 8.00
109 Giancarlo Stanton .30 .75
114 Aaron Judge .75 2.00
115 Cody Bellinger .60 1.50
121 Mike Trout 1.50 4.00
122 Miguel Cabrera .30 .75
123 Francisco Lindor .30 .75
125 Andrew McCutchen .30 .75
135 Andrew Benintendi .30 .75
148 Adrian Beltre .30 .75
165 Mickey Mantle 1.00 2.50
176 Shohei Ohtani RR 4.00 10.00

2018 Donruss Optic Variations Aqua

*AQUA RR: .75X TO 2X BASIC RR
*AQUA VET: 1.2X TO 3X BASIC VET
RANDOM INSERTS IN PACKS
STATED PRINT RUN 299 SER.#'d SETS

2018 Donruss Optic Variations Black

*BLACK RR: 1.5X TO 4X BASIC RR
*BLACK VET: 2.5X TO 6X BASIC VET
RANDOM INSERTS IN PACKS
STATED PRINT RUN 25 SER.#'d SETS
121 Mike Trout 10.00 25.00

2018 Donruss Optic Variations Blue

*BLUE RR: .75X TO 2X BASIC RR
*BLUE VET: 1.2X TO 3X BASIC VET
RANDOM INSERTS IN PACKS
STATED PRINT RUN 149 SER.#'d SETS

2018 Donruss Optic Variations Bronze

*BRONZE RR: .5X TO 1.2X BASIC RR
*BRONZE VET: .75X TO 2.5X BASIC VET
RANDOM INSERTS IN PACKS

2018 Donruss Optic Variations Carolina Blue

*CAR.BLU RR: 1X TO 2.5X BASIC RR
*CAR.BLU VET: 1.5X TO 4X BASIC VET
RANDOM INSERTS IN PACKS
STATED PRINT RUN 50 SER.#'d SETS

2018 Donruss Optic Variations Holo

*HOLO RR: .5X TO 1.2X BASIC RR
*HOLO VET: .75X TO 2.5X BASIC VET
RANDOM INSERTS IN PACKS

2018 Donruss Optic Variations Orange

*ORANGE RR: .75X TO 2X BASIC RR
*ORANGE VET: 1.2X TO 3X BASIC VET
RANDOM INSERTS IN PACKS
STATED PRINT RUN 199 SER.#'d SETS

2018 Donruss Optic Variations Pink

*PINK RR: .5X TO 1.2X BASIC RR
*PINK VET: .75X TO 2X BASIC VET
RANDOM INSERTS IN PACKS

2018 Donruss Optic Variations Purple

*PURPLE RR: .5X TO 1.2X BASIC RR
*PURPLE VET: .75X TO 2X BASIC VET

2018 Donruss Optic Variations Red

*RED RR: 1X TO 2.5X BASIC RR
*RED VET: 1.5X TO 4X BASIC VET
RANDOM INSERTS IN PACKS
STATED PRINT RUN 99 SER.#'d SETS

2018 Donruss Optic Variations Red and Yellow

*RED YEL RR: .5X TO 1.2X BASIC RR
*RED YEL VET: .75X TO 2X BASIC VET
RANDOM INSERTS IN PACKS

2018 Donruss Optic Variations Shock

*SHOCK RR: .5X TO 1.2X BASIC RR
*SHOCK VET: .75X TO 2.5X BASIC VET
RANDOM INSERTS IN PACKS

2018 Donruss Optic Autographs

RANDOM INSERTS IN PACKS
EXCHANGE DEADLINE 01/18/2020
*BLUE/50: .6X TO 1.5X BASIC
*BLUE/20-25: .75X TO 2X BASIC
*RED/25: .75X TO 2X BASIC
1 Darryl Strawberry 5.00 12.00
2 David Cone
3 David Price 3.00 8.00
4 David Wells 6.00 15.00
5 Eric Hosmer 3.00 8.00
6 Fernando Valenzuela
7 Francisco Lindor 12.00 30.00
8 Gary Sanchez 10.00 25.00
9 George Springer 5.00 12.00
10 Graig Nettles 2.50 6.00
11 Hunter Pence 3.00 8.00
12 Jameson Taillon
13 Jim Bunning 5.00 12.00
14 Joey Votto
15 Jonathan Lucroy 3.00 8.00
16 Jose Abreu
17 Kyle Seager 2.50 6.00
18 Lorenzo Cain 6.00 15.00
19 Luke Weaver 3.00 8.00
20 Maikel Franco 3.00 8.00
21 Matt Carpenter 6.00 15.00
22 Max Scherzer
23 Ozzie Smith 12.00 30.00
24 Ron Guidry 5.00 12.00
25 Roy Oswalt 3.00 8.00
26 Ryan Braun 5.00 12.00
27 Shelby Miller
28 Willie McGee 5.00 12.00
29 Andres Gimenez 3.00 8.00
30 Aneury Tavarez 2.50 6.00
31 Austin Voth 2.50 6.00
32 Jesus Sanchez 4.00 10.00
33 Bobby Bradley 3.00 8.00
34 Brett Phillips 2.50 6.00
35 Bruce Maxwell 2.50 6.00
36 Casey Gillaspie
37 Christopher Seise 2.50 6.00
38 Dan Vogelbach 2.50 6.00
39 Derek Law 2.50 6.00
40 Diego Castillo 2.50 6.00
41 Leody Taveras 3.00 8.00
42 Dustin Peterson
43 Josh Hader 2.50 6.00
44 Michael Chavis 10.00 25.00
45 Nick Gordon 2.50 6.00
46 Kyle Lewis 20.00 50.00
47 Johan Oviedo 2.50 6.00
48 Tyler O'Neill 8.00 20.00
49 Kyle Tucker 6.00 15.00
50 Randal Grichuk 2.50 6.00

2018 Donruss Optic Long Ball Leaders

RANDOM INSERTS IN PACKS
*BLUE/149: .6X TO 1.5X BASIC
*RED/99: .75X TO 2X BASIC
1 Giancarlo Stanton .50 1.25
2 Aaron Judge 1.25 3.00
3 J.D. Martinez .50 1.25
4 Khris Davis .50 1.25
5 Joey Gallo .40 1.00
6 Cody Bellinger 1.00 2.50
7 Nelson Cruz .50 1.25
8 Logan Morrison .30 .75
9 Nolan Arenado .60 1.50
10 Justin Smoak .30 .75

2018 Donruss Optic Looking Back

RANDOM INSERTS IN PACKS
*BLUE/149: 1X TO 2.5X BASIC
*RED/99: 1.2X TO 3X BASIC
1 Griffey Jr/Griffey Sr. 1.00 2.50
2 Robinson/Machado .50 1.25
3 Judge/Jackson 1.25 3.00
4 Ichiro/Rose 1.00 2.50
5 Baez/Sandberg 1.00 2.50
6 Kershaw/Ryan 1.50 4.00
7 Biggio/Altuve .40 1.00
8 Thomas/Abreu .50 1.25
9 C.Sale/R.Clemens .60 1.50
10 Lindor/Vizquel .50 1.25

2018 Donruss Optic Mound Marvels

RANDOM INSERTS IN PACKS
*BLUE/149: .75X TO 2X BASIC
*RED/99: 1X TO 2.5X BASIC
1 Clayton Kershaw 1.00 2.50
2 Max Scherzer .50 1.25
3 Shohei Ohtani 2.00 5.00
4 Corey Kluber .40 1.00
5 Chris Sale .50 1.25
6 Justin Verlander .50 1.25
7 Noah Syndergaard .40 1.00
8 Nolan Ryan 1.50 4.00

2018 Donruss Optic Out of This World

RANDOM INSERTS IN PACKS
*BLUE/149: 1X TO 2.5X BASIC
*RED/99: 1.2X TO 3X BASIC
1 Aaron Judge 1.25 3.00
2 Jose Altuve .40 1.00
3 Mike Trout 2.50 6.00
4 Joey Gallo .40 1.00
5 Shohei Ohtani 2.00 5.00
6 Giancarlo Stanton .50 1.25
7 Mickey Mantle 1.50 4.00
8 J.D. Martinez .50 1.25
9 Cody Bellinger 1.00 2.50
10 Nolan Arenado .60 1.50
11 Marcell Ozuna .50 1.25
12 Paul Goldschmidt .50 1.25
13 Ken Griffey Jr. 1.00 2.50
14 Joey Votto .50 1.25
15 Nelson Cruz .50 1.25

2018 Donruss Optic Premiere Rookies

RANDOM INSERTS IN PACKS
*BLUE/149: 1X TO 2.5X BASIC
1 Rafael Devers 1.00 2.50
2 Clint Frazier .60 1.50
3 Victor Robles .75 2.00
4 Shohei Ohtani 2.00 5.00
5 Ozzie Albies 1.00 2.50
6 Francisco Mejia .40 1.00
7 Amed Rosario .40 1.00
8 Rhys Hoskins 1.25 3.00
9 Ryan McMahon .40 1.00
10 Miguel Andujar 1.25 3.00

2018 Donruss Optic Premiere Rookies Red

*RED: 1.2X TO 3X BASIC
RANDOM INSERTS IN PACKS
STATED PRINT RUN 99 SER.#'d SETS
4 Shohei Ohtani 20.00 50.00

2018 Donruss Optic Rated Prospects

RANDOM INSERTS IN PACKS
*BLUE/149: 1X TO 2.5X BASIC
*RED/99: 1.2X TO 3X BASIC
1 Vladimir Guerrero Jr. 3.00 8.00
2 Fernando Tatis Jr. 2.50 6.00
3 Eloy Jimenez 1.25 3.00
4 Bo Bichette 1.25 3.00
5 Nick Senzel 1.00 2.50
6 Brendan Rodgers .40 1.00
7 Kyle Tucker .60 1.50
8 Leody Taveras .40 1.00

2018 Donruss Optic Rated Prospects Signatures

RANDOM INSERTS IN PACKS
EXCHANGE DEADLINE 01/18/2020
*AQUA/75-100: .5X TO 1.2X BASIC
*BLACK/25: .75X TO 2X BASIC
*BLUE/75: .5X TO 1.2X BASIC
*BLUE/50: .6X TO 1.5X BASIC
*BRONZE: .4X TO 1X BASIC
*CAR.BLUE/35: .6X TO 1.5X BASIC
*CAR.BLUE/20-25: .75X TO 2X BASIC
*HOLO: .4X TO 1X BASIC
*ORANGE/ 60-99: .5X TO 1.2X BASIC
*RED/35-50: .6X TO 1.5X BASIC
1 Gleyber Torres 30.00 80.00
2 Vladimir Guerrero Jr. 100.00 250.00
3 Eloy Jimenez 15.00 40.00
4 Ronald Acuna Jr. 75.00 200.00
6 Kyle Tucker 6.00 15.00
7 Nick Senzel EXCH 15.00 40.00
8 Michael Kopech 6.00 15.00
9 Brent Honeywell 4.00 10.00
10 Luis Robert 30.00 80.00
11 Justus Sheffield 8.00 20.00
12 Kevin Maitan 3.00 8.00
13 Yadier Alvarez 3.00 8.00
14 Franklin Perez 5.00 12.00
15 Willy Adames 3.00 8.00

2018 Donruss Optic Rated Rookies '84 Retro

RANDOM INSERTS IN PACKS
*BLUE/149: 1X TO 2.5X BASIC
*RED/99: 1.2X TO 3X BASIC
1 Shohei Ohtani 2.00 5.00
2 Clint Frazier .60 1.50
3 Rafael Devers 1.00 2.50
4 Walker Buehler 1.50 4.00
5 Ozzie Albies 1.00 2.50
6 Francisco Mejia .40 1.00
7 Ryan McMahon .40 1.00
8 Rhys Hoskins 1.25 3.00
9 Victor Robles .75 2.00
10 Amed Rosario .40 1.00
11 Willie Calhoun .40 1.00
12 Nick Williams .40 1.00
13 Dominic Smith .30 .75
14 J.P. Crawford .30 .75
15 Dustin Fowler .30 .75

2018 Donruss Optic Rated Rookies '84 Retro Signatures

RANDOM INSERTS IN PACKS
EXCHANGE DEADLINE 01/18/2020
*AQUA/60-125: .5X TO 1.2X BASIC
*AQUA/35: .6X TO 1.5X BASIC
*BLACK/25: .75X TO 2X BASIC
*BLUE/60-75: .5X TO 1.2X BASIC
*BLUE/35-50: .6X TO 1.5X BASIC
*BLUE/25: .75X TO 2X BASIC
*BRONZE: .4X TO 1X BASIC
*CAR.BLUE/35: .6X TO 1.5X BASIC
*CAR.BLUE/20-25: .75X TO 2X BASIC
*HOLO: .4X TO 1X BASIC
*ORANGE/ 60-99: .5X TO 1.2X BASIC
*ORANGE/30-49: .6X TO 1.5X BASIC
*RED/35-50: .6X TO 1.5X BASIC
*RED/25: .75X TO 2X BASIC
1 Ozzie Albies 12.00 30.00
2 Austin Hays 4.00 10.00
3 Chance Sisco 3.00 8.00
4 Rafael Devers 10.00 25.00
5 Victor Caratini 3.00 8.00
6 Nicky Delmonico 2.50 6.00
7 Francisco Mejia 3.00 8.00
8 Cameron Gallagher 2.50 6.00
9 Walker Buehler 12.00 30.00
10 Alex Verdugo 4.00 10.00
11 Kyle Farmer 2.50 6.00
12 Zack Granite 2.50 6.00
13 Tomas Nido 2.50 6.00
14 Ryan McMahon 3.00 8.00
15 Amed Rosario 3.00 8.00
16 Clint Frazier 5.00 12.00
17 Miguel Andujar 15.00 40.00
18 Tyler Wade 3.00 8.00
19 J.P. Crawford EXCH 2.50 6.00
20 Nick Williams 3.00 8.00
21 Rhys Hoskins 15.00 40.00
22 Shohei Ohtani 150.00 300.00
23 Willie Calhoun 3.00 8.00
24 Victor Robles 6.00 15.00
25 Erick Fedde 2.50 6.00

2018 Donruss Optic Rated Rookies Signatures

RANDOM INSERTS IN PACKS
EXCHANGE DEADLINE 01/18/2020
*AQUA/75-125: .5X TO 1.2X BASIC
*AQUA/35: .6X TO 1.5X BASIC
*BLACK/25: .75X TO 2X BASIC
*BLUE/60-75: .5X TO 1.2X BASIC
*BLUE/50: .6X TO 1.5X BASIC
*BLUE/20: .75X TO 2X BASIC
*BRONZE: .4X TO 1X BASIC
*CAR.BLUE/35: .6X TO 1.5X BASIC
*CAR.BLUE/25: .75X TO 2X BASIC
*HOLO: .4X TO 1X BASIC
*ORANGE/ 60-99: .5X TO 1.2X BASIC
*ORANGE/25: .75X TO 2X BASIC
*RED/35-50: .6X TO 1.5X BASIC
RRSAB Anthony Banda 2.50 6.00
RRSAH Austin Hays 4.00 10.00
RRSAR Amed Rosario 3.00 8.00
RRSAS Andrew Stevenson 2.50 6.00
RRSAV Alex Verdugo 4.00 10.00
RRSAY Anthony Santander 2.50 6.00
RRSBA Brian Anderson 3.00 8.00
RRSBW Brandon Woodruff 3.00 8.00
RRSCF Chris Flexen 2.50 6.00
RRSCG Cameron Gallagher 2.50 6.00
RRSCL Clint Frazier 5.00 12.00
RRSCS Chance Sisco 3.00 8.00
RRSDF Dustin Fowler 2.50 6.00
RRSDP Dillon Peters 2.50 6.00
RRSEF Erick Fedde 2.50 6.00
RRSFJ Felix Jorge 2.50 6.00
RRSFM Francisco Mejia 3.00 8.00
RRSGA Greg Allen 2.50 6.00
RRSHB Harrison Bader 4.00 10.00
RRSJC J.P. Crawford EXCH 2.50 6.00
RRSJD J.D. Davis 3.00 8.00
RRSJF Jack Flaherty 4.00 10.00
RRSJS Jimmie Sherfy 2.50 6.00
RRSKF Kyle Farmer 2.50 6.00
RRSLG Luiz Gohara 2.50 6.00
RRSLS Lucas Sims 2.50 6.00
RRSMA Miguel Andujar 10.00 25.00
RRSMF Max Fried 10.00 25.00
RRSMG Mitch Garver 2.50 6.00
RRSND Nicky Delmonico 2.50 6.00
RRSNW Nick Williams 3.00 8.00
RRSOA Ozzie Albies 8.00 20.00
RRSPB Paul Blackburn 2.50 6.00
RRSRA Ronald Acuna 75.00 200.00
RRSRD Rafael Devers 10.00 25.00
RRSRH Rhys Hoskins 10.00 25.00
RRSRM Reyes Moronta 2.50 6.00
RRSRU Richard Urena 2.50 6.00
RRSRY Ryan McMahon 3.00 8.00
RRSSO Shohei Ohtani 75.00 200.00
RRSTM Tyler Mahle 3.00 8.00
RRSTN Tomas Nido 2.50 6.00
RRSTV Thyago Vieira 2.50 6.00
RRSTW Tyler Wade 3.00 8.00
RRSVC Victor Caratini 3.00 8.00
RRSVG Vladimir Guerrero Jr 30.00 80.00
Issued in '19 Donruss Optic
RRSVR Victor Robles 10.00 25.00
RRSWB Walker Buehler 15.00 40.00
RRSWC Willie Calhoun 3.00 8.00
RRSZG Zack Granite 2.50 6.00

2018 Donruss Optic '84 Retro Signatures

RANDOM INSERTS IN PACKS
EXCHANGE DEADLINE 01/18/2020
*BRONZE: .4X TO 1X BASIC
*HOLO: .4X TO 1X BASIC
1 Ken Griffey Jr. 100.00 250.00
2 Jose Altuve EXCH 20.00 50.00
3 Anthony Rizzo
4 Cal Ripken
5 Cody Bellinger EXCH 15.00 40.00
6 Aaron Judge 60.00 150.00
7 Mark McGwire

2018 Donruss Optic Signature Series

RANDOM INSERTS IN PACKS
EXCHANGE DEADLINE 01/18/2020
*BLUE/50: .6X TO 1.5X BASIC
*BLUE/20-25: .75X TO 2X BASIC
*RED/25: .75X TO 2X BASIC
1 Albert Almora Jr. 3.00 8.00
2 Alex Gordon 5.00 12.00
3 Brian Dozier 3.00 8.00
4 Carlos Correa 10.00 25.00
5 Chris Davis
7 Corey Kluber 6.00 15.00
8 Josh Donaldson 3.00 8.00
9 Juan Marichal
10 Justin Turner 8.00 20.00
11 Kyle Schwarber 6.00 15.00
12 Starling Marte 3.00 8.00
13 Yoan Moncada
14 Ryan Mountcastle 4.00 10.00
15 Jacoby Jones 3.00 8.00
16 Adrian Valerio 2.50 6.00
17 Albert Abreu 2.50 6.00
18 Brendan McKay 4.00 10.00
19 Brendan Rodgers 8.00 20.00
20 Keith Hernandez 5.00 12.00
21 Jarrett Parker 2.50 6.00
22 Guillermo Heredia 2.50 6.00
23 Willy Adames 3.00 8.00
24 Mitch Keller 3.00 8.00
25 Kyle Wright 4.00 10.00

2018 Donruss Optic Significant Signatures

RANDOM INSERTS IN PACKS
EXCHANGE DEADLINE 01/18/2020
*BLUE/50: .6X TO 1.5X BASIC
*BLUE/20: .75X TO 2X BASIC
*RED/25: .75X TO 2X BASIC
1 Adrian Beltre 12.00 30.00
2 Alan Trammell 8.00 20.00
4 Andre Dawson 5.00 12.00
5 Andruw Jones 4.00 10.00
6 Barry Larkin
7 Bernie Williams 8.00 20.00
8 Bill Mazeroski 8.00 20.00
10 Bob Gibson 10.00 25.00
11 Brooks Robinson 6.00 15.00
12 Curt Schilling 8.00 20.00
13 Dave Winfield
14 Eddie Murray 20.00 50.00
15 Fergie Jenkins 3.00 8.00
16 Paul Molitor 6.00 15.00
17 Phil Niekro 4.00 10.00
18 Rickey Henderson 20.00 50.00
19 Rollie Fingers 6.00 15.00
20 Roy Halladay 20.00 50.00
21 Steve Garvey 15.00 40.00
22 Todd Helton 8.00 20.00
23 Wade Boggs 6.00 15.00
24 Whitey Ford 25.00 60.00
25 Whitey Herzog 8.00 20.00

2018 Donruss Optic Standouts

RANDOM INSERTS IN PACKS
*BLUE/149: .6X TO 1.5X BASIC
*RED/99: .75X TO 2X BASIC
1 Giancarlo Stanton .50 1.
2 Aaron Judge 1.25 3.

2018 Donruss Optic Year in Review

RANDOM INSERTS IN PACKS
*BLUE/149: .6X TO 1.5X BASIC
*RED/99: .75X TO 2X BASIC
1 Aaron Judge 1.25 3.
2 Giancarlo Stanton .50 1.2
3 Cody Bellinger 1.00 2.5
4 Jose Altuve .40 1.
5 Albert Pujols .60 1.5
6 Miguel Cabrera .50 1.2
7 Aaron Judge 1.25 3.
8 Adrian Beltre .50 1.2
9 Rhys Hoskins 1.25 3.
10 Cody Bellinger 1.00 2.
11 Chris Sale .50 1.2
12 Jose Ramirez .40 1.

2019 Donruss Optic

1 Mookie Betts DK .75 2.
2 Aaron Judge DK 1.25 3.
3 Blake Snell DK .40 1.
4 Justin Smoak DK .30 .
5 Trey Mancini DK .40 1.
6 Jose Ramirez DK .40 1.
7 Jose Berrios DK .40 1.
8 Nicholas Castellanos DK .50 1.2
9 Yoan Moncada DK .50 1.2
10 Whit Merrifield DK .50 1.2
11 Alex Bregman DK .50 1.2
12 Matt Chapman DK .50 1.2
13 Mitch Haniger DK .40 1.
14 Shohei Ohtani DK .60 1.5
15 Joey Gallo DK .40 1.
16 Ronald Acuna Jr. DK 2.50 6.
17 Max Scherzer DK .50 1.2
18 Aaron Nola DK .40 1.
19 Jacob deGrom DK .50 1.2
20 Jose Urena DK .30 .7
21 Christian Yelich DK .60 1.5
22 Javier Baez DK .60 1.5
23 Matt Carpenter DK .50 1.2
24 Starling Marte DK .40 1.
25 Eugenio Suarez DK .40 1.
26 Max Muncy DK .40 1.
27 Trevor Story DK .50 1.2
28 David Peralta DK .30 .7
29 Brandon Crawford DK .40 1.
30 Manny Machado DK .50 1.2
31 Cedric Mullins RR RC .50 1.2
32 Christin Stewart RR RC .40 1.
33 Corbin Burnes RR RC .50 1.2
34 Dakota Hudson RR RC .40 1.
35 Danny Jansen RR RC .30 .7
36 David Fletcher RR RC 1.00 2.5
37 Dennis Santana RR RC .30 .7
38 Garrett Hampson RR RC .30 .7
39 Jake Bauers RR RC .50 1.2
40 Jeff McNeil RR RC .75 2.
41 Jonathan Loaisiga RR RC .40 1.
42 Justus Sheffield RR RC .50 1.2
43 Kyle Tucker RR RC .60 1.5
44 Kyle Wright RR RC .50 1.2
45 Luis Urias RR RC .50 1.2
46 Michael Kopech RR RC .60 1.5
47 Ramon Laureano RR RC .60 1.5
48 Ryan O'Hearn RR RC .30 .7
49 Steven Duggar RR RC .40 1.
50 Touki Toussaint RR RC .40 1.
51 Chris Shaw RR RC .40 1.
52 Rowdy Tellez RR RC .50 1.2
53 Brandon Lowe RR RC .50 1.2
54 Taylor Hearn RR RC .30 .7
55 Reese McGuire RR RC .50 1.2
56 Taylor Ward RR RC .30 .7
57 Jake Cave RR RC .40 1.
58 Ty France RR RC 1.00 2.5
59 Myles Straw RR RC .50 1.2
60 Brad Keller RR RC .30 .7
61 Bryse Wilson RR RC .40 1.0
62 Caleb Ferguson RR RC .40 1.00
63 Chance Adams RR RC .30 .75
64 Vladimir Guerrero Jr. RR RC 2.00 5.00
65 Daniel Ponce de Leon RR RC .50 1.25
66 Enyel De Los Santos RR RC .30 .75
67 Framber Valdez RR RC .30 .75
68 Jacob Nix RR RC .40 1.00
69 Josh James RR RC .50 1.25
70 Kolby Allard RR RC .50 1.25
71 Luis Ortiz RR RC .30 .75
72 Ryan Borucki RR RC .30 .75
73 Sean Reid-Foley RR RC .30 .75
74 Stephen Gonsalves RR RC .30 .75
75 Kevin Kramer RR RC .40 1.00
76 Kevin Newman RR RC .50 1.25
77 Yusei Kikuchi RR RC .50 1.25
78 Michael Perez RR RC .30 .75
79 Williams Astudillo RR RC .30 .75
80 Trevor Richards RR RC .30 .75
81 Michael Chavis RR RC .50 1.25
82 Pete Alonso RR RC 2.50 6.00
83 Eloy Jimenez RR RC 1.25 3.00
84 Fernando Tatis Jr. RR RC 10.00 25.00
85 Jon Duplantier RR RC .30 .75
86 Darwinzon Hernandez RR RC .30 .75
87 Cole Tucker RR RC .50 1.25
88 Chris Paddack RR RC .60 1.50
89 Nick Senzel RR RC 1.00 2.50
90 Griffin Canning RR RC .50 1.25
91 Cal Quantrill RR RC .30 .75

92 Carter Kieboom RR RC .50 1.25
93 Keston Hiura RR RC 1.00 2.50
94 Corbin Martin RR RC .50 1.25
95 Austin Riley RR RC 1.50 4.00
96 Brendan Rodgers RR RC .50 1.25
97 Bryce Harper AS .50 1.25
98 Aaron Judge AS .75 2.00
99 Mookie Betts AS .50 1.25
100 Mike Trout AS 1.50 4.00
101 Mookie Betts .50 1.25
102 Chris Sale .30 .75
103 Eddie Rosario .25 .60
104 Rhys Hoskins .40 1.00
105 J.T. Realmuto .30 .75
106 Cody Bellinger .60 1.50
107 Jose Ramirez .25 .60
108 Jon Lester .25 .60
109 Kris Bryant .40 1.00
110 Luis Severino .25 .60
111 Whit Merrifield .30 .75
112 Joey Gallo .25 .60
113 Juan Soto 1.00 2.50
114 Jose Urena .20 .50
115 J.D. Martinez .30 .75
116 Max Scherzer .30 .75
117 Sean Newcomb .20 .50
118 Francisco Lindor .30 .75
119 Starling Marte .25 .60
120 Manny Machado .30 .75
121 Aaron Judge .75 2.00
122 Robinson Cano .25 .60
123 Jacob deGrom .30 .75
124 Eugenio Suarez .25 .60
125 Nomar Mazara .20 .50
126 Kyle Freeland .20 .50
127 Miguel Sano .25 .60
128 Rafael Devers .40 1.00
129 Miguel Andujar .25 .60
130 Nelson Cruz .30 .75
131 Charlie Blackmon .30 .75
132 Jose Berrios .25 .60
133 Walker Buehler .40 1.00
134 Tyler O'Neill .25 .60
135 Mike Foltynewicz .30 .75
136 Noah Syndergaard .25 .60
137 Scooter Gennett .25 .60
138 David Bote .25 .60
139 Zack Greinke .25 .60
140 Andrew Benintendi .30 .75
141 Trea Turner .25 .60
142 Carlos Rodon .25 .60
143 Carlos Correa .30 .75
144 Jose Martinez .20 .50
145 Aaron Nola .25 .60
146 Mitch Haniger .25 .60
147 Yadier Molina .30 .75
148 Joey Votto .30 .75
149 Felix Hernandez .25 .60
150 Willie Calhoun .20 .50
151 Carlos Carrasco .20 .50
152 Paul Goldschmidt .30 .75
153 Trey Mancini .25 .60
154 Madison Bumgarner .25 .60
155 Amed Rosario .25 .60
156 Ozzie Albies .30 .75
157 Gleyber Torres .60 1.50
158 Wilson Ramos .20 .50
159 Brandon Crawford .25 .60
160 Andrew Heaney .20 .50
161 James Paxton .25 .60
162 Gerrit Cole .30 .75
163 Giancarlo Stanton .30 .75
164 Shohei Ohtani .40 1.00
165 Javier Baez .40 1.00
166 Jesus Aguilar .20 .50
167 Jackie Bradley Jr. .30 .75
168 Corey Kluber .25 .60
169 Khris Davis .30 .75
170 Mike Trout 1.50 4.00
171 Matt Carpenter .30 .75
172 Justin Verlander .30 .75
173 Brian Anderson .20 .50
174 Victor Robles .40 1.00
175 Freddie Freeman .40 1.00
176 Jack Flaherty .25 .60
177 Ronald Acuna Jr. 1.50 4.00
178 Clayton Kershaw .60 1.50
179 Salvador Perez .25 .60
180 Anthony Rendon .30 .75
181 Blake Snell .25 .60
182 Alex Bregman .30 .75
183 Bryce Harper .50 1.25
184 Lorenzo Cain .20 .50
185 Trevor Story .30 .75
186 Mike Moustakas .25 .60
187 Anthony Rizzo .50 1.25
188 Jameson Taillon .25 .60
189 Edwin Encarnacion .30 .75
190 Christian Yelich .40 1.00
191 Michael Conforto .25 .60
192 Matt Chapman .30 .75
193 Albert Pujols .40 1.00
194 Eric Hosmer .25 .60
195 German Marquez .20 .50
196 Jeimer Candelario .20 .50
197 Xander Bogaerts .30 .75
198 Miguel Cabrera .30 .75
199 Harrison Bader .25 .60
200 Nolan Arenado .40 1.00

2019 Donruss Optic Black
*BLACK DK: 1.5X TO 4X BASIC DK
*BLACK RR: 1.5X TO 4X BASIC RR
*BLACK VET: 2.5X TO 6X BASIC VET
RANDOM INSERTS IN PACKS
STATED PRINT RUN 25 SER.#'d SETS
40 Jeff McNeil RR 10.00 25.00
64 Vladimir Guerrero Jr. RR 25.00 60.00
82 Pete Alonso RR 40.00 100.00
83 Eloy Jimenez RR 10.00 25.00
84 Fernando Tatis Jr. RR 125.00 300.00

2019 Donruss Optic Blue
*BLUE DK: 1X TO 2.5X BASIC DK
*BLUE RR: 1X TO 2.5X BASIC RR
*BLUE VET: 1.5X TO 4X BASIC VET
RANDOM INSERTS IN PACKS
STATED PRINT RUN 75 SER.#'d SETS
64 Vladimir Guerrero Jr. RR 12.00 30.00
82 Pete Alonso RR 15.00 40.00
83 Eloy Jimenez RR 6.00 15.00
84 Fernando Tatis Jr. RR 50.00 120.00

2019 Donruss Optic Blue Pandora
*BLUE PAN. DK: 1X TO 2.5X BASIC DK
*BLUE PAN. RR: 1X TO 2.5X BASIC RR
*BLUE PAN. VET: 1.5X TO 4X BASIC VET
RANDOM INSERTS IN PACKS
STATED PRINT RUN 99 SER.#'d SETS
64 Vladimir Guerrero Jr. RR 12.00 30.00
82 Pete Alonso RR 15.00 40.00
83 Eloy Jimenez RR 6.00 15.00
84 Fernando Tatis Jr. RR 50.00 120.00

2019 Donruss Optic Carolina Blue
*CAR.BLU DK: 1.2X TO 3X BASIC DK
*CAR.BLU RR: 1.2X TO 3X BASIC RR
*CAR.BLU VET: 2X TO 5X BASIC VET
RANDOM INSERTS IN PACKS
STATED PRINT RUN 50 SER.#'d SETS
40 Jeff McNeil RR 8.00 20.00
64 Vladimir Guerrero Jr. RR 20.00 50.00
82 Pete Alonso RR 20.00 50.00
83 Eloy Jimenez RR 8.00 20.00
84 Fernando Tatis Jr. RR 60.00 150.00

2019 Donruss Optic Carolina Blue and White
*CAR.BLU.WHT DK: .5X TO 1.2X BASIC DK
*CAR.BLU.WHT RR: .5X TO 1.2X BASIC RR
*CAR.BLU.WHT VET: .75X TO 2.5X BASIC VET
RANDOM INSERTS IN PACKS
64 Vladimir Guerrero Jr. RR 6.00 15.00
82 Pete Alonso RR 6.00 15.00
83 Eloy Jimenez RR 3.00 8.00
84 Fernando Tatis Jr. RR 20.00 50.00

2019 Donruss Optic Holo
*HOLO DK: .5X TO 1.2X BASIC DK
*HOLO RR: .5X TO 1.2X BASIC RR
*HOLO VET: .75X TO 2.5X BASIC VET
RANDOM INSERTS IN PACKS
64 Vladimir Guerrero Jr. RR 6.00 15.00
82 Pete Alonso RR 6.00 15.00
83 Eloy Jimenez RR 3.00 8.00
84 Fernando Tatis Jr. RR 20.00 50.00

2019 Donruss Optic Lime Green
*LIME GRN DK: .5X TO 1.2X BASIC DK
*LIME GRN RR: .5X TO 1.2X BASIC RR
*LIME GRN VET: .75X TO 2.5X BASIC VET
RANDOM INSERTS IN PACKS
64 Vladimir Guerrero Jr. RR 6.00 15.00
82 Pete Alonso RR 6.00 15.00
83 Eloy Jimenez RR 3.00 8.00
84 Fernando Tatis Jr. RR 20.00 50.00

2019 Donruss Optic Orange
*ORANGE DK: 1X TO 2.5X BASIC DK
*ORANGE RR: 1X TO 2.5X BASIC RR
*ORANGE VET: 1.5X TO 4X BASIC VET
RANDOM INSERTS IN PACKS
STATED PRINT RUN 99 SER.#'d SETS
64 Vladimir Guerrero Jr. RR 12.00 30.00
82 Pete Alonso RR 15.00 40.00
83 Eloy Jimenez RR 6.00 15.00
84 Fernando Tatis Jr. RR 50.00 120.00

2019 Donruss Optic Pandora
*PANDORA DK: 1X TO 2.5X BASIC DK
*PANDORA RR: 1X TO 2.5X BASIC RR
*PANDORA VET: 1.5X TO 4X BASIC VET
RANDOM INSERTS IN PACKS
STATED PRINT RUN 99 SER.#'d SETS
64 Vladimir Guerrero Jr. RR 12.00 30.00
82 Pete Alonso RR 15.00 40.00
83 Eloy Jimenez RR 6.00 15.00
84 Fernando Tatis Jr. RR 50.00 120.00

2019 Donruss Optic Pink
*PINK DK: .5X TO 1.2X BASIC DK
*PINK RR: .5X TO 1.2X BASIC RR
*PINK VET: .75X TO 2.5X BASIC VET
RANDOM INSERTS IN PACKS
64 Vladimir Guerrero Jr. RR 6.00 15.00
82 Pete Alonso RR 6.00 15.00
83 Eloy Jimenez RR 3.00 8.00
84 Fernando Tatis Jr. RR 20.00 50.00

2019 Donruss Optic Pink Velocity
*PINK VEL. DK: .75X TO 2X BASIC DK
*PINK VEL. RR: .75X TO 2X BASIC RR
*PINK VEL. VET: 1.2X TO 3X BASIC VET
RANDOM INSERTS IN PACKS
STATED PRINT RUN 199 SER.#'d SETS
64 Vladimir Guerrero Jr. RR 10.00 25.00
82 Pete Alonso RR 12.00 30.00
83 Eloy Jimenez RR 5.00 12.00
84 Fernando Tatis Jr. RR 40.00 100.00

2019 Donruss Optic Purple Pandora
*PRPL PAN. DK: 1X TO 2.5X BASIC DK
*PRPL PAN. RR: 1X TO 2.5X BASIC RR
*PRPL PAN. VET: 1.5X TO 4X BASIC VET
RANDOM INSERTS IN PACKS
STATED PRINT RUN 99 SER.#'d SETS
64 Vladimir Guerrero Jr. RR 12.00 30.00
82 Pete Alonso RR 15.00 40.00
83 Eloy Jimenez RR 6.00 15.00
84 Fernando Tatis Jr. RR 50.00 120.00

2019 Donruss Optic Purple Stars
*PRPL STRS DK: .75X TO 2X BASIC DK
*PRPL STRS RR: .75X TO 2X BASIC RR
*PRPL STRS VET: 1.2X TO 3X BASIC VET
RANDOM INSERTS IN PACKS
STATED PRINT RUN 125 SER.#'d SETS
64 Vladimir Guerrero Jr. RR 10.00 25.00
82 Pete Alonso RR 12.00 30.00
83 Eloy Jimenez RR 5.00 12.00
84 Fernando Tatis Jr. RR 40.00 100.00

2019 Donruss Optic Red
*RED DK: 1X TO 2.5X BASIC DK
*RED RR: 1X TO 2.5X BASIC RR
*RED VET: 1.5X TO 4X BASIC VET
RANDOM INSERTS IN PACKS
STATED PRINT RUN 60 SER.#'d SETS
64 Vladimir Guerrero Jr. RR 12.00 30.00
82 Pete Alonso RR 15.00 40.00
83 Eloy Jimenez RR 6.00 15.00
84 Fernando Tatis Jr. RR 50.00 120.00

2019 Donruss Optic Red Pandora
*RED PAN. DK: 1X TO 2.5X BASIC DK
*RED PAN. RR: 1X TO 2.5X BASIC RR
*RED PAN. VET: 1.5X TO 4X BASIC VET
RANDOM INSERTS IN PACKS
STATED PRINT RUN 99 SER.#'d SETS
64 Vladimir Guerrero Jr. RR 12.00 30.00
82 Pete Alonso RR 15.00 40.00
83 Eloy Jimenez RR 6.00 15.00
84 Fernando Tatis Jr. RR 50.00 120.00

2019 Donruss Optic Red Wave
*RED WAVE DK: .5X TO 1.2X BASIC DK
*RED WAVE RR: .5X TO 1.2X BASIC RR
*RED WAVE VET: .75X TO 2.5X BASIC VET
RANDOM INSERTS IN PACKS
64 Vladimir Guerrero Jr. RR 6.00 15.00
82 Pete Alonso RR 6.00 15.00
83 Eloy Jimenez RR 3.00 8.00
84 Fernando Tatis Jr. RR 20.00 50.00

2019 Donruss Optic Red White and Blue 150th Anniversary
*RWB 150th DK: .75X TO 2X BASIC DK
*RWB 150th RR: .75X TO 2X BASIC RR
*RWB 150th VET: 1.2X TO 3X BASIC VET
RANDOM INSERTS IN PACKS
STATED PRINT RUN 150 SER.#'d SETS
64 Vladimir Guerrero Jr. RR 10.00 25.00
82 Pete Alonso RR 12.00 30.00
83 Eloy Jimenez RR 5.00 12.00
84 Fernando Tatis Jr. RR 40.00 100.00

2019 Donruss Optic Teal Velocity
*TEAL VEL. DK: 1.2X TO 3X BASIC DK
*TEAL VEL. RR: 1.2X TO 3X BASIC RR
*TEAL VEL. VET: 2X TO 5X BASIC VET
RANDOM INSERTS IN PACKS
STATED PRINT RUN 35 SER.#'d SETS
40 Jeff McNeil RR 8.00 20.00
64 Vladimir Guerrero Jr. RR 20.00 50.00
82 Pete Alonso RR 20.00 50.00
83 Eloy Jimenez RR 8.00 20.00
84 Fernando Tatis Jr. RR 60.00 150.00

2019 Donruss Optic '85 Retro Signatures
RANDOM INSERTS IN PACKS
EXCHANGE DEADLINE 01/17/2021
*HOLO p/r 75-99: .5X TO 1.2X BASIC
*HOLO/49: .6X TO 1.5X BASIC
*HOLO p/r 20-25: .75X TO 2X BASIC
*BLUE p/r 35-50: .6X TO 1.5X BASIC
*BLUE/25: .75X TO 2X BASIC
*RED/25: .75X TO 2X BASIC
2 Chris Sabo 2.50 6.00
3 Ted Simmons 15.00 40.00
5 Keith Hernandez 2.50 6.00
6 Ken Griffey Sr. 2.50 6.00
7 Darryl Strawberry 2.50 6.00
8 Dave Stewart 2.50 6.00
10 Ozzie Guillen 2.50 6.00
11 Pete Rose 10.00 25.00
12 Jose Canseco 3.00 8.00
14 Omar Vizquel 3.00 8.00
16 Dave Concepcion 2.50 6.00
17 Joe Carter 2.50 6.00
18 Jim Rice 3.00 8.00
19 Darrell Evans 2.50 6.00
20 Lou Whitaker 2.50 6.00

2019 Donruss Optic Action All-Stars
RANDOM INSERTS IN PACKS
*HOLO: 1X TO 2.5X BASIC
1 Jose Altuve .30 .75
2 Aaron Judge 1.00 2.50
3 Mike Trout 2.00 5.00
4 Shohei Ohtani .60 1.50
5 Mookie Betts .60 1.50
6 Clayton Kershaw .75 2.00
7 Kris Bryant .50 1.25
8 Bryce Harper .60 1.50
9 Khris Davis .40 1.00
10 Manny Machado .40 1.00
11 Charlie Blackmon .40 1.00
12 Ronald Acuna Jr. 2.00 5.00
13 Christian Yelich .50 1.25
14 J.D. Martinez .40 1.00
15 Francisco Lindor .40 1.00

2019 Donruss Optic Autographs
RANDOM INSERTS IN PACKS
EXCHANGE DEADLINE 01/17/2021
*HOLO/99: .5X TO 1.2X BASIC
*HOLO/25: .75X TO 2X BASIC
*BLUE/50: .6X TO 1.5X BASIC
*RED/25: .75X TO 2X BASIC
1 Stephen Piscotty 2.50 6.00
2 Salvador Perez 3.00 8.00
3 Ronald Acuna Jr. 40.00 100.00
4 Nolan Arenado 15.00 40.00
5 Francisco Lindor 10.00 25.00
6 Franklin Barreto 2.50 6.00
8 Aaron Nola 3.00 8.00
9 Brandon Belt 3.00 8.00
10 Cody Bellinger 25.00 60.00
12 Franmil Reyes 2.50 6.00
13 Jason Kipnis 3.00 8.00
14 Mitch Haniger 3.00 8.00
15 Paul Goldschmidt 4.00 10.00
16 Trea Turner 3.00 8.00
17 Xander Bogaerts 4.00 10.00
18 Yoshihisa Hirano 2.50 6.00
19 Pete Alonso 20.00 50.00
20 Jose Abreu 4.00 10.00

2019 Donruss Optic Highlights
RANDOM INSERTS IN PACKS
*HOLO: 1X TO 2.5X BASIC
1 Shohei Ohtani .50 1.25
2 Albert Pujols .50 1.25
3 Sean Manaea .25 .60
4 James Paxton .30 .75
5 Max Scherzer .40 1.00
6 George Springer .30 .75
7 Christian Yelich .50 1.25
8 Juan Soto 1.25 3.00
9 Mookie Betts .60 1.50
10 Jose Ramirez .30 .75

2019 Donruss Optic Illusions
RANDOM INSERTS IN PACKS
*HOLO: 1X TO 2.5X BASIC
1 Mike Trout 2.00 5.00
2 Paul Goldschmidt .40 1.00
3 Trea Turner .30 .75
4 Christian Yelich .50 1.25
5 Trevor Story .40 1.00
6 Ronald Acuna Jr. 2.00 5.00
7 Javier Baez .50 1.25
8 Juan Soto 1.25 3.00
9 Carlos Correa .40 1.00
10 Aaron Judge 1.00 2.50
11 Kris Bryant .50 1.25
12 Corey Seager .40 1.00

2019 Donruss Optic MVP
RANDOM INSERTS IN PACKS
*HOLO: 1X TO 2.5X BASIC
1 Mookie Betts .60 1.50
2 Christian Yelich .50 1.25
3 Giancarlo Stanton .40 1.00
4 Jose Altuve .30 .75
5 Kris Bryant .50 1.25
6 Mike Trout 2.50 6.00
7 Bryce Harper .60 1.50
8 Miguel Cabrera .40 1.00
9 Ichiro .50 1.25
10 Albert Pujols .50 1.25
11 Clayton Kershaw .75 2.00
12 Josh Donaldson .30 .75
13 Buster Posey .50 1.25
14 Joey Votto .40 1.00
15 Dustin Pedroia .40 1.00

2019 Donruss Optic MVP Signatures
RANDOM INSERTS IN PACKS
EXCHANGE DEADLINE 01/17/2021
*HOLO: .4X TO 1X BASIC
*PINK VEL.: .4X TO 1X BASIC
*BLUE p/r 17-33: .75X TO 2X BASIC
*LGHT BLUE p/r 17-33: .75X TO 2X BASIC
*ORANGE p/r 17-33: .75X TO 2X BASIC
*PURPLE p/r 17-33: .75X TO 2X BASIC
*RED p/r 17-33: .75X TO 2X BASIC
*TEAL VEL. p/r 17-33: .75X TO 2X BASIC
*BLK CRK ICE p/r 17-25: .75X TO 2X BASIC
MVPAM Andrew McCutchen 25.00 60.00
MVPAP Albert Pujols 40.00 100.00
MVPAR Alex Rodriguez
MVPBL Barry Larkin 12.00 30.00
MVPBR Brooks Robinson 12.00 30.00
MVPDE Dennis Eckersley 6.00 15.00
MVPDM Dale Murphy 15.00 40.00
MVPFT Frank Thomas 30.00 80.00
MVPGB George Brett 40.00 100.00
MVPIR Ivan Rodriguez 12.00 30.00
MVPJC Jose Canseco 8.00 20.00
MVPJG Jason Giambi 4.00 10.00
MVPJM Joe Morgan 10.00 25.00
MVPJR Ken Griffey Jr. 75.00 200.00
MVPJV Joey Votto 12.00 30.00
MVPKH Keith Hernandez 2.50 6.00
MVPKM Kevin Mitchell 2.50 6.00
MVPPR Pete Rose 12.00 30.00
MVPRC Rod Carew 10.00 25.00
MVPRH Rickey Henderson 20.00 50.00
MVPRS Ryne Sandberg 8.00 20.00
MVPSG Steve Garvey 10.00 25.00
MVPWM Willie McGee 2.50 6.00

2019 Donruss Optic Mythical
RANDOM INSERTS IN PACKS
*HOLO: 1X TO 2.5X BASIC
1 Mike Trout 2.00 5.00
2 Aaron Judge 1.00 2.50
3 Mookie Betts .60 1.50
4 Kris Bryant .50 1.25
5 Bryce Harper .60 1.50
6 Jose Altuve .30 .75
7 Nolan Arenado .50 1.25
8 Shohei Ohtani .50 1.25

2019 Donruss Optic Peak Performers
RANDOM INSERTS IN PACKS
*HOLO: 1X TO 2.5X BASIC
1 Shohei Ohtani .50 1.25
2 Christian Yelich .50 1.25
3 Mookie Betts .60 1.50
4 Blake Snell .30 .75
5 Jacob deGrom .40 1.00
6 Ronald Acuna Jr. 2.00 5.00
7 Edwin Diaz .30 .75
8 Josh Hader .25 .60
9 J.D. Martinez .40 1.00
10 Khris Davis .40 1.00
11 Aaron Nola .30 .75
12 Mike Trout 2.00 5.00
13 Max Scherzer .40 1.00
14 Vladimir Guerrero Jr. 1.50 4.00
15 Fernando Tatis Jr. 2.50 6.00
16 Nolan Arenado .50 1.25

2019 Donruss Optic Rated Prospects
RANDOM INSERTS IN PACKS
*HOLO: 1X TO 2.5X BASIC
1 Royce Lewis .50 1.25
2 Jo Adell .75 2.00
3 Alec Bohm 1.00 2.50
4 Victor Victor Mesa .50 1.25
5 Casey Mize .60 1.50
6 Estevan Florial .40 1.00
7 Wander Franco 4.00 10.00
8 Cavan Biggio 1.25 3.00
9 Everson Pereira .40 1.00
10 Nico Hoerner .75 2.00

2019 Donruss Optic Rated Prospects Signatures
RANDOM INSERTS IN PACKS
EXCHANGE DEADLINE 01/17/2021
*HOLO: .4X TO 1X BASIC
*PINK VEL.: .4X TO 1X BASIC
*PURPLE/125: .5X TO 1.2X BASIC
*PURPLE/60: .6X TO 1.5X BASIC
*ORANGE/99: .6X TO 1.5X BASIC
*ORANGE/49: .75X TO 2X BASIC
*BLUE/75: .6X TO 1.5X BASIC
*BLUE/35: .75X TO 2X BASIC
*BLACK/50: .75X TO 2X BASIC
*RED/50: .75X TO 2X BASIC
*RED/25: 1X TO 2.5X BASIC
1 Fernando Tatis Jr. 60.00 150.00
2 Wander Franco 60.00 150.00
3 Victor Victor Mesa 5.00 12.00
4 Taylor Trammell 3.00 8.00
5 Alex Kirilloff 6.00 15.00
7 Keston Hiura 12.00 30.00
8 Jon Duplantier 2.50 6.00
9 Dylan Cease 6.00 15.00
10 Yordan Alvarez 20.00 50.00
11 Jo Adell 25.00 60.00
12 Triston McKenzie 6.00 15.00
13 Brendan Rodgers 4.00 10.00
14 Forrest Whitley 4.00 10.00
15 Austin Riley 6.00 15.00

2019 Donruss Optic Rated Prospects Signatures Black Cracked Ice
*BLK CRK ICE/25: 1X TO 2.5X BASIC
RANDOM INSERTS IN PACKS
PRINT RUNS B/WN 15-25 COPIES PER
NO PRICING DUE TO SCARCITY
EXCHANGE DEADLINE 01/17/2021
4 Taylor Trammell/25 30.00 80.00
10 Yordan Alvarez/25 75.00 200.00

2019 Donruss Optic Rated Prospects Signatures Light Blue
*LGHT BLUE/35: .75X TO 2X BASIC
*LGHT BLUE/20: 1X TO 2.5X BASIC
RANDOM INSERTS IN PACKS
PRINT RUNS B/WN 5-35 COPIES PER
NO PRICING DUE TO SCARCITY
EXCHANGE DEADLINE 01/17/2021
4 Taylor Trammell/35 12.00 30.00

2019 Donruss Optic Rated Prospects Signatures Teal Velocity
*TEAL VEL./35: .75X TO 2X BASIC
*TEAL VEL./20: 1X TO 2.5X BASIC
RANDOM INSERTS IN PACKS
PRINT RUNS B/WN 20-35 COPIES PER
EXCHANGE DEADLINE 01/17/2021
4 Taylor Trammell/35 12.00 30.00

2019 Donruss Optic Rated Rookies '85 Retro Signatures
RANDOM INSERTS IN PACKS
EXCHANGE DEADLINE 01/17/2021
*HOLO/99: .5X TO 1.2X BASIC
*BLUE/50: .6X TO 1.5X BASIC
*BLUE/25: .75X TO 2X BASIC
*RED/25: .75X TO 2X BASIC
1 Yusei Kikuchi 8.00 20.00
2 Michael Kopech 5.00 12.00
3 Kyle Tucker 5.00 12.00
4 Corbin Burnes 4.00 10.00
5 Justus Sheffield 4.00 10.00
6 Ryan O'Hearn 2.50 6.00
7 Christin Stewart 3.00 8.00
8 Touki Toussaint 3.00 8.00
9 Luis Urias 4.00 10.00
10 Ramon Laureano 6.00 15.00
11 Jeff McNeil 6.00 15.00
12 Josh James 4.00 10.00
13 Stephen Gonsalves 2.50 6.00
14 Danny Jansen 2.50 6.00
15 Brandon Lowe 6.00 15.00
17 Myles Straw 4.00 10.00
18 Brad Keller 2.50 6.00
19 Chris Shaw 4.00 10.00
20 Chance Adams 2.50 6.00

2019 Donruss Optic Rated Rookies Signatures
RANDOM INSERTS IN PACKS
EXCHANGE DEADLINE 01/17/2021
*HOLO: .4X TO 1X BASIC
*PINK VEL.: .4X TO 1X BASIC
*PURPLE/125: .5X TO 1.2X BASIC
*PURPLE/60: .6X TO 1.5X BASIC
1 Brad Keller 2.50 6.00
2 Bryse Wilson 3.00 8.00
3 Cedric Mullins 4.00 10.00
4 Chance Adams 2.50 6.00
5 Chris Shaw 4.00 10.00
6 Christin Stewart 3.00 8.00
7 Cionel Perez 2.50 6.00
8 Corbin Burnes 4.00 10.00
9 Dakota Hudson 3.00 8.00
10 Daniel Ponce de Leon 4.00 10.00
11 Danny Jansen 2.50 6.00
12 David Fletcher 8.00 20.00
13 Dennis Santana 2.50 6.00
14 Enyel De Los Santos 2.50 6.00
15 Framber Valdez 2.50 6.00
16 Brandon Lowe 6.00 15.00
17 Garrett Hampson 2.50 6.00
18 Jacob Nix 3.00 8.00
19 Jake Bauers 4.00 10.00
20 Jake Cave 3.00 8.00
21 Jeff McNeil 8.00 20.00
22 Jonathan Davis 3.00 8.00
23 Jonathan Loaisiga 3.00 8.00
24 Josh James 4.00 10.00
25 Justus Sheffield 4.00 10.00
26 Kevin Kramer 3.00 8.00
27 Kevin Newman 4.00 10.00
28 Kolby Allard 4.00 10.00
29 Kyle Tucker 8.00 20.00
30 Kyle Wright 4.00 10.00
31 Luis Ortiz 2.50 6.00
32 Luis Urias 4.00 10.00
33 Michael Kopech 6.00 15.00
34 Myles Straw 4.00 10.00
35 Patrick Wisdom 2.50 6.00
36 Ramon Laureano 5.00 12.00
37 Reese McGuire 4.00 10.00
38 Rowdy Tellez 4.00 10.00
39 Ryan Borucki 2.50 6.00
40 Ryan O'Hearn 2.50 6.00
41 Sean Reid-Foley 2.50 6.00
42 Stephen Gonsalves 2.50 6.00
43 Steven Duggar 3.00 8.00
44 Taylor Ward 2.50 6.00
45 Touki Toussaint 3.00 8.00
46 Caleb Ferguson 3.00 8.00
47 Vladimir Guerrero Jr. 40.00 100.00
48 Fernando Tatis Jr. 75.00 200.00
49 Eloy Jimenez 15.00 40.00
50 Nick Senzel 15.00 40.00

2019 Donruss Optic Rated Rookies Signatures Black
*BLACK: .75X TO 2X BASIC
RANDOM INSERTS IN PACKS
STATED PRINT RUN 50 SER.#'d SETS
EXCHANGE DEADLINE 01/17/2021

2019 Donruss Optic Rated Rookies Signatures Blue
*BLUE/75: .6X TO 1.5X BASIC
*BLUE/35: .75X TO 2X BASIC
RANDOM INSERTS IN PACKS
PRINT RUNS B/WN 35-75 COPIES PER
EXCHANGE DEADLINE 01/17/2021

2019 Donruss Optic Rated Rookies Signatures Light Blue
*LGHT BLUE/35: .75X TO 2X BASIC
*LGHT BLUE/20: 1X TO 2.5X BASIC
RANDOM INSERTS IN PACKS
PRINT RUNS B/WN 20-35 COPIES PER
EXCHANGE DEADLINE 01/17/2021

2019 Donruss Optic Rated Rookies Signatures Orange
*ORANGE/99: .6X TO 1.5X BASIC
*ORANGE/49: .75X TO 2X BASIC
RANDOM INSERTS IN PACKS
PRINT RUNS B/WN 49-99 COPIES PER
EXCHANGE DEADLINE 01/17/2021

2019 Donruss Optic Rated Rookies Signatures Red
*RED/50: .75X TO 2X BASIC
*RED/25: 1X TO 2.5X BASIC
RANDOM INSERTS IN PACKS
PRINT RUNS B/WN 25-50 COPIES PER
EXCHANGE DEADLINE 01/17/2021

2019 Donruss Optic Rated Rookies Signatures Teal Velocity
*TEAL VEL./35: .75X TO 2X BASIC
*TEAL VEL./20: 1X TO 2.5X BASIC
RANDOM INSERTS IN PACKS
PRINT RUNS B/WN 20-35 COPIES PER
EXCHANGE DEADLINE 01/17/2021

2019 Donruss Optic Signature Series
RANDOM INSERTS IN PACKS
EXCHANGE DEADLINE 01/17/2021
*HOLO/99: .5X TO 1.2X BASIC
*HOLO/49: .6X TO 1.5X BASIC
*HOLO/25: .75X TO 2X BASIC
*BLUE/50: .6X TO 1.5X BASIC
*BLUE/25: .75X TO 2X BASIC
*RED/25: .75X TO 2X BASIC
1 Adbert Alzolay 2.50 6.00
2 Corey Ray 2.50 6.00
3 Sean Murphy 3.00 8.00
4 Yusniel Diaz 4.00 10.00
7 Ian Desmond 2.50 6.00
8 Shane Bieber 12.00 30.00
9 Wil Myers 2.50 6.00
10 Odubel Herrera 3.00 8.00
11 Kyle Schwarber 4.00 10.00
12 Josh Donaldson 3.00 8.00
13 Eric Thames 2.50 6.00
14 Carson Kelly 2.50 6.00
15 Matt Olson 2.50 6.00
17 Trevor Story 8.00 20.00
18 Chris Paddack 5.00 12.00
19 Victor Robles 5.00 12.00

2019 Donruss Optic Significant Signatures
RANDOM INSERTS IN PACKS
EXCHANGE DEADLINE 01/17/2021
*HOLO/99: .5X TO 1.2X BASIC
*HOLO/25: .75X TO 2X BASIC
1 Craig Biggio 8.00 20.00
2 Luis Tiant 2.50 6.00
3 Bobby Richardson 2.50 6.00
5 David Ross 2.50 6.00
6 Gary Sheffield 2.50 6.00
7 Larry Walker 3.00 8.00
10 Charles Johnson 2.50 6.00
11 Dontrelle Willis 2.50 6.00
14 Roberto Alomar 3.00 8.00
15 Don Sutton 3.00 8.00
16 Juan Gonzalez 6.00 15.00
18 Tim Wakefield 3.00 8.00
19 Bob Horner 2.50 6.00

2019 Donruss Optic Significant Signatures Blue
*BLUE p/r 35-50: .6X TO 1.5X BASIC
RANDOM INSERTS IN PACKS
PRINT RUNS B/WN 10-50 COPIES PER
NO PRICING ON QTY 15 OR LESS
EXCHANGE DEADLINE 01/17/2021
3 Bobby Richardson/35 12.00 30.00

2019 Donruss Optic Significant Signatures Red
*RED/25: .75X TO 2X BASIC
RANDOM INSERTS IN PACKS
PRINT RUNS B/WN 7-25 COPIES PER
NO PRICING ON QTY 15 OR LESS
EXCHANGE DEADLINE 01/17/2021
3 Bobby Richardson/25 15.00 40.00

2019 Donruss Optic The Rookies
RANDOM INSERTS IN PACKS
*HOLO: 1X TO 2.5X BASIC
1 Yusei Kikuchi .40 1.00
2 Kyle Tucker .50 1.25
3 Michael Kopech .50 1.25
4 Christin Stewart .30 .75
5 Justus Sheffield .40 1.00
6 Corbin Burnes .40 1.00
7 Jonathan Loaisiga .30 .75
8 Josh James .40 1.00
9 Touki Toussaint .30 .75
10 Danny Jansen .25 .60
11 Vladimir Guerrero Jr. 1.50 4.00
12 Eloy Jimenez 1.00 2.50
13 Fernando Tatis Jr. 2.50 6.00
14 Pete Alonso 2.00 5.00

2019 Donruss Optic We The People
*WTP DK: 1X TO 2.5X BASIC DK
*WTP RR: 1X TO 2.5X BASIC RR
*WTP VET: 1.5X TO 4X BASIC VET
RANDOM INSERTS IN PACKS
STATED PRINT RUN 76 SER.#'d SETS
64 Vladimir Guerrero Jr. RR 12.00 30.00
82 Pete Alonso RR 15.00 40.00
83 Eloy Jimenez RR 6.00 15.00
84 Fernando Tatis Jr. RR 12.00 30.00

2020 Donruss Optic
1 Fernando Tatis Jr. DK 2.00 5.00
2 Buster Posey DK .60 1.50
3 Cody Bellinger DK 1.00 2.50
4 Eugenio Suarez DK .40 1.00
5 Christian Yelich DK .60 1.50
6 Brian Anderson DK .30 .75
7 Pete Alonso DK 1.25 3.00
8 Ronald Acuna Jr. DK 2.00 5.00
9 Mike Trout DK 2.50 6.00
10 Marcus Semien DK .30 .75
11 Miguel Cabrera DK .50 1.25

12 Lucas Giolito DK .40 1.00
13 Nelson Cruz DK .50 1.25
14 Vladimir Guerrero Jr. DK 1.00 2.50
15 Austin Meadows DK .40 1.00
16 Rafael Devers DK .60 1.50
17 Trey Mancini DK .50 1.25
18 Shane Bieber DK .50 1.25
19 Jorge Soler DK .50 1.25
20 Alex Bregman DK .50 1.25
21 Lance Lynn DK .30 .75
22 Marco Gonzales DK .30 .75
23 Juan Soto DK 1.50 4.00
24 Bryce Harper DK .75 2.00
25 Paul Goldschmidt DK .50 1.25
26 Javier Baez DK .60 1.50
27 Josh Bell DK .40 1.00
28 Ketel Marte DK .40 1.00
29 Nolan Arenado DK .60 1.50
30 Aaron Judge DK 1.25 3.00
31 Bryan Abreu RR RC .30 .75
32 Dustin May RR RC 1.25 3.00
33 Mauricio Dubon RR RC .40 1.00
34 Jesus Luzardo RR RC .60 1.50
35 Jordan Yamamoto RR RC .40 1.00
36 Brendan McKay RR RC .50 1.25
37 Bo Bichette RR RC 6.00 15.00
38 Nico Hoerner RR RC 1.25 3.00
39 Aristides Aquino RR RC 4.00 10.00
40 Brock Burke RR RC .30 .75
41 Justin Dunn RR RC .40 1.00
42 Sean Murphy RR RC .50 1.25
43 Trent Grisham RR RC 1.25 3.00
44 Gavin Lux RR RC 2.00 5.00
45 Yordan Alvarez RR RC 3.00 8.00
46 Sam Hilliard RR RC .50 1.25
47 Patrick Sandoval RR RC .50 1.25
48 Isan Diaz RR RC .50 1.25
49 A.J. Puk RR RC .60 1.50
50 Logan Webb RR RC .40 1.00
51 Randy Arozarena RR RC 2.50 6.00
52 Anthony Kay RR RC .30 .75
53 Dylan Cease RR RC .50 1.25
54 Zac Gallen RR RC .75 2.00
55 Adrian Morejon RR RC .30 .75
56 Kyle Lewis RR RC 3.00 8.00
57 Nick Solak RR RC .50 1.25
58 Brusdar Graterol RR RC .50 1.25
59 Tony Gonsolin RR RC 1.25 3.00
60 Matt Thaiss RR RC .40 1.00
61 Yoshitomo Tsutsugo RR RC .40 1.00
62 Luis Robert RR RC 3.00 8.00
63 Bobby Bradley RR RC .40 1.00
64 Edwin Rios RR RC .75 2.00
65 Travis Demeritte RR RC .40 1.00
66 Domingo Leyba RR RC .40 1.00
67 Josh Rojas RR RC .30 .75
68 Abraham Toro RR RC .40 1.00
69 Sheldon Neuse RR RC .40 1.00
70 Donnie Walton RR RC .75 2.00
71 Zack Collins RR RC .40 1.00
72 Jake Rogers RR RC .30 .75
73 Deivy Grullon RR RC .30 .75
74 Tres Barrera RR RC .60 1.50
75 Logan Allen RR RC .30 .75
76 Lewis Thorpe RR RC .30 .75
77 Yonathan Daza RR RC .40 1.00
78 Tyrone Taylor RR RC .30 .75
79 Jaylin Davis RR RC .50 1.25
80 Jake Fraley RR RC .40 1.00
81 Michael King RR RC .50 1.25
82 Andres Munoz RR RC .40 1.00
83 Michel Baez RR RC .30 .75
84 Ronald Bolanos RR RC .50 1.25
85 Joe Palumbo RR RC .30 .75
86 T.J. Zeuch RR RC .30 .75
87 Adbert Alzolay RR RC .40 1.00
88 Aaron Civale RR RC .50 1.25
89 Rico Garcia RR RC .50 1.25
90 Jonathan Hernandez RR RC .30 .75
91 Danny Mendick RR RC .40 1.00
92 Willi Castro RR RC .50 1.25
93 Yu Chang RR RC .50 1.25
94 Kwang-Hyun Kim RR RC 1.00 2.50
95 Shun Yamaguchi RR RC .40 1.00
96 Shogo Akiyama RR RC .50 1.25
97 Walker Buehler .40 1.00
98 Ozzie Albies .30 .75
99 Charlie Blackmon .30 .75
100 Stephen Strasburg .30 .75
101 Nick Senzel .30 .75
102 Yadier Molina .30 .75
103 Jacob deGrom .30 .75
104 Luis Severino .25 .60
105 Mookie Betts .60 1.50
106 Ketel Marte .25 .60
107 Hyun-Jin Ryu .25 .60
108 Lorenzo Cain .20 .50
109 Corey Kluber .25 .60
110 Joey Votto .30 .75
111 Fernando Tatis Jr. 1.25 3.00
112 Cody Bellinger .60 1.50
113 Josh Donaldson .25 .60
114 Jeff McNeil .25 .60
115 Javier Baez .40 1.00
116 Gleyber Torres .60 1.50
117 Marcus Semien .20 .50
118 Shohei Ohtani .40 1.00
119 Buster Posey .40 1.00
120 Charlie Morton .30 .75
121 Mitch Haniger .25 .60
122 Johnny Cueto .25 .60
123 Vladimir Guerrero Jr. .60 1.50
124 Matt Olson .20 .50
125 Shane Bieber .30 .75
126 Jorge Polanco .25 .60
127 Jose Abreu .30 .75
128 Trea Turner .25 .60
129 Christian Yelich .40 1.00
130 Aaron Judge .75 2.00
131 Alex Bregman .30 .75
132 Chris Sale .30 .75
133 Gerrit Cole .50 1.25
134 Madison Bumgarner .25 .60
135 Clayton Kershaw .60 1.50
136 Eloy Jimenez .60 1.50
137 Cavan Biggio .40 1.00
138 Max Scherzer .30 .75
139 Eugenio Suarez .25 .60
140 Aaron Nola .30 .75
141 Paul Goldschmidt .30 .75
142 Mike Trout 1.50 4.00
143 Anthony Rizzo .50 1.25
144 Jonathan Villar .20 .50
145 Kyle Hendricks .30 .75
146 Austin Meadows .25 .60
147 Yoan Moncada .30 .75
148 Josh Bell .25 .60
149 Nolan Arenado .40 1.00
150 Francisco Lindor .30 .75
151 Matt Chapman .30 .75
152 Willie Calhoun .20 .50
153 Mike Soroka .30 .75
154 Kevin Newman .25 .60
155 Anthony Rendon .30 .75
156 Elvis Andrus .25 .60
157 Justin Verlander .30 .75
158 Jose Ramirez .25 .60
159 Jose Altuve .25 .60
160 Bryan Reynolds .25 .60
161 Juan Soto 1.00 2.50
162 Chris Paddack .30 .75
163 Rafael Devers .40 1.00
164 Brian Anderson .20 .50
165 Trevor Story .30 .75
166 Jose Berrios .25 .60
167 Brandon Lowe .30 .75
168 Freddie Freeman .40 1.00
169 Ronald Acuna Jr. 1.25 3.00
170 Starling Marte .25 .60
171 Adalberto Mondesi .30 .75
172 Blake Snell .25 .60
173 Trey Mancini .30 .75
174 Ramon Laureano .30 .75
175 Kris Bryant .40 1.00
176 Rhys Hoskins .40 1.00
177 Marco Gonzales .20 .50
178 J.D. Martinez .30 .75
179 Keston Hiura .40 1.00
180 Manny Machado .30 .75
181 Sandy Alcantara .20 .50
182 Jack Flaherty .25 .60
183 Bryce Harper .50 1.25
184 Joey Gallo .30 .75
185 Jorge Soler .30 .75
186 Matt Carpenter .30 .75
187 Pete Alonso .75 2.00
188 Whit Merrifield .30 .75
189 John Means .20 .50
190 Luis Arraez .40 1.00
191 Tommy Edman .30 .75
192 Max Muncy .25 .60
193 Albert Pujols .40 1.00
194 George Springer .25 .60
195 Tim Anderson .30 .75
196 Masahiro Tanaka .30 .75
197 Mike Trout AS 1.50 4.00
198 Christian Yelich AS .40 1.00
199 Ronald Acuna Jr. AS 1.25 3.00
200 Javier Baez AS .40 1.00

2020 Donruss Optic Black

*BLACK DK: 1.5X TO 4X BASIC DK
*BLACK RR: 1.5X TO 4X BASIC RR
*BLACK VET: 2.5X TO 6X BASIC VET
RANDOM INSERTS IN PACKS
STATED PRINT RUN 25 SER.#'d SETS
32 Dustin May RR 10.00 25.00
33 Mauricio Dubon RR 6.00 15.00
37 Bo Bichette RR 40.00 100.00
38 Nico Hoerner RR 12.00 30.00
44 Gavin Lux RR 10.00 25.00
45 Yordan Alvarez RR 25.00 60.00
56 Kyle Lewis RR 25.00 60.00
62 Luis Robert RR 60.00 150.00
96 Shogo Akiyama RR 15.00 40.00

2020 Donruss Optic Black Stars

*BLK STARS .75X TO 2X BASIC DK
*BLK STARS RR: .75X TO 2X BASIC RR
*BLK STARS VET: 1.2X TO 3X BASIC VET
RANDOM INSERTS IN PACKS
STATED PRINT RUN 125 SER.#'d SETS
32 Dustin May RR 5.00 12.00
33 Mauricio Dubon RR 3.00 8.00
37 Bo Bichette RR 15.00 40.00
38 Nico Hoerner RR 5.00 12.00
44 Gavin Lux RR 6.00 15.00
45 Yordan Alvarez RR 12.00 30.00
56 Kyle Lewis RR 12.00 30.00
62 Luis Robert RR 20.00 50.00
96 Shogo Akiyama RR 6.00 15.00

2020 Donruss Optic Blue

*BLUE DK: 1X TO 2.5X BASIC DK
*BLUE RR: 1X TO 2.5X BASIC DK
*BLUE VET: 1.5X TO 4X BASIC VET
RANDOM INSERTS IN PACKS
STATED PRINT RUN 75 SER.#'d SETS
32 Dustin May RR 6.00 15.00
33 Mauricio Dubon RR 4.00 10.00
37 Bo Bichette RR 20.00 50.00
38 Nico Hoerner RR 8.00 20.00
44 Gavin Lux RR 8.00 20.00
45 Yordan Alvarez RR 15.00 40.00
56 Kyle Lewis RR 15.00 40.00
62 Luis Robert RR 25.00 60.00
96 Shogo Akiyama RR 10.00 25.00

2020 Donruss Optic Carolina Blue

*CAR.BLUE DK: 1.2X TO 3X BASIC DK
*CAR.BLUE RR: 1.2X TO 3X BASIC DK
*CAR.BLUE VET: 2X TO 5X BASIC VET
RANDOM INSERTS IN PACKS
STATED PRINT RUN 50 SER.#'d SETS
32 Dustin May RR 8.00 20.00
33 Mauricio Dubon RR 5.00 12.00
37 Bo Bichette RR 30.00 80.00
38 Nico Hoerner RR 10.00 25.00
44 Gavin Lux RR 10.00 25.00
45 Yordan Alvarez RR 20.00 50.00
56 Kyle Lewis RR 20.00 50.00
62 Luis Robert RR 50.00 120.00
96 Shogo Akiyama RR 12.00 30.00

2020 Donruss Optic Carolina Blue and White

*CBW DK: .5X TO 1.2X BASIC DK
*CBW RR: .5X TO 1.2X BASIC RR
*CBW VET: .8X TO 2X BASIC VET
RANDOM INSERTS IN PACKS
32 Dustin May RR 3.00 8.00
33 Mauricio Dubon RR 2.00 5.00
37 Bo Bichette RR 10.00 25.00
44 Gavin Lux RR 4.00 10.00
45 Yordan Alvarez RR 8.00 20.00
56 Kyle Lewis RR 8.00 20.00
62 Luis Robert RR 12.00 30.00
96 Shogo Akiyama RR 4.00 10.00

2020 Donruss Optic Freedom

*FREEDOM DK: 1.2X TO 3X BASIC DK
*FREEDOM RR: 1.2X TO 3X BASIC DK
*FREEDOM VET: 2X TO 5X BASIC VET
RANDOM INSERTS IN PACKS
STATED PRINT RUN 45 SER.#'d SETS
32 Dustin May RR 8.00 20.00
33 Mauricio Dubon RR 5.00 12.00
37 Bo Bichette RR 30.00 80.00
38 Nico Hoerner RR 10.00 25.00
44 Gavin Lux RR 10.00 25.00
45 Yordan Alvarez RR 20.00 50.00
56 Kyle Lewis RR 20.00 50.00
62 Luis Robert RR 50.00 120.00
96 Shogo Akiyama RR 12.00 30.00

2020 Donruss Optic Green Dragon

*GRN DRGN DK: 1X TO 2.5X BASIC DK
*GRN DRGN RR: 1X TO 2.5X BASIC DK
*GRN DRGN VET: 1.5X TO 4X BASIC VET
RANDOM INSERTS IN PACKS
STATED PRINT RUN 84 SER.#'d SETS
32 Dustin May RR 6.00 15.00
33 Mauricio Dubon RR 4.00 10.00
37 Bo Bichette RR 20.00 50.00
38 Nico Hoerner RR 8.00 20.00
44 Gavin Lux RR 8.00 20.00
45 Yordan Alvarez RR 15.00 40.00
56 Kyle Lewis RR 15.00 40.00
62 Luis Robert RR 25.00 60.00
96 Shogo Akiyama RR 10.00 25.00

2020 Donruss Optic Holo

*HOLO DK: .5X TO 1.2X BASIC DK
*HOLO RR: .5X TO 1.2X BASIC RR
*HOLO VET: .8X TO 2X BASIC VET
RANDOM INSERTS IN PACKS
32 Dustin May RR 3.00 8.00
33 Mauricio Dubon RR 2.00 5.00
37 Bo Bichette RR 10.00 25.00
44 Gavin Lux RR 4.00 10.00
45 Yordan Alvarez RR 8.00 20.00
56 Kyle Lewis RR 8.00 20.00
62 Luis Robert RR 12.00 30.00
96 Shogo Akiyama RR 4.00 10.00

2020 Donruss Optic Liberty

*LIBERTY DK: 1.2X TO 3X BASIC DK
*LIBERTY RR: 1.2X TO 3X BASIC DK
*LIBERTY VET: 2X TO 5X BASIC VET
RANDOM INSERTS IN PACKS
STATED PRINT RUN 45 SER.#'d SETS
32 Dustin May RR 8.00 20.00
33 Mauricio Dubon RR 5.00 12.00
37 Bo Bichette RR 30.00 80.00
38 Nico Hoerner RR 10.00 25.00
44 Gavin Lux RR 10.00 25.00
45 Yordan Alvarez RR 20.00 50.00
56 Kyle Lewis RR 20.00 50.00
62 Luis Robert RR 50.00 120.00
96 Shogo Akiyama RR 12.00 30.00

2020 Donruss Optic Lime Green

*LIME GRN DK: .5X TO 1.2X BASIC DK
*LIME GRN RR: .5X TO 1.2X BASIC RR
*LIME GRN VET: .8X TO 2X BASIC VET
RANDOM INSERTS IN PACKS
32 Dustin May RR 3.00 8.00
33 Mauricio Dubon RR 2.00 5.00
37 Bo Bichette RR 10.00 25.00
44 Gavin Lux RR 4.00 10.00
45 Yordan Alvarez RR 8.00 20.00
56 Kyle Lewis RR 8.00 20.00
62 Luis Robert RR 12.00 30.00
96 Shogo Akiyama RR 4.00 10.00

2020 Donruss Optic Orange

*ORANGE DK: 1X TO 2.5X BASIC DK
*ORANGE RR: 1X TO 2.5X BASIC DK
*ORANGE VET: 1.5X TO 4X BASIC VET
RANDOM INSERTS IN PACKS
STATED PRINT RUN 100 SER.#'d SETS
32 Dustin May RR 6.00 15.00
33 Mauricio Dubon RR 4.00 10.00
37 Bo Bichette RR 20.00 50.00
38 Nico Hoerner RR 8.00 20.00
44 Gavin Lux RR 8.00 20.00
45 Yordan Alvarez RR 15.00 40.00
56 Kyle Lewis RR 15.00 40.00
62 Luis Robert RR 25.00 60.00
96 Shogo Akiyama RR 10.00 25.00

2020 Donruss Optic Pink

*PINK DK: .5X TO 1.2X BASIC DK
*PINK RR: .5X TO 1.2X BASIC RR
*PINK VET: .8X TO 2X BASIC VET
RANDOM INSERTS IN PACKS
32 Dustin May RR 3.00 8.00
33 Mauricio Dubon RR 2.00 5.00
37 Bo Bichette RR 10.00 25.00
44 Gavin Lux RR 4.00 10.00
45 Yordan Alvarez RR 8.00 20.00
56 Kyle Lewis RR 8.00 20.00
62 Luis Robert RR 12.00 30.00
96 Shogo Akiyama RR 4.00 10.00

2020 Donruss Optic Pink Velocity

*PINK VEL. DK: .75X TO 2X BASIC DK
*PINK VEL. RR: .75X TO 2X BASIC RR
*PINK VEL. VET: 1.2X TO 3X BASIC VET
RANDOM INSERTS IN PACKS
STATED PRINT RUN 199 SER.#'d SETS
32 Dustin May RR 5.00 12.00
33 Mauricio Dubon RR 3.00 8.00
37 Bo Bichette RR 15.00 40.00
38 Nico Hoerner RR 5.00 12.00
44 Gavin Lux RR 6.00 15.00
45 Yordan Alvarez RR 12.00 30.00
56 Kyle Lewis RR 12.00 30.00
62 Luis Robert RR 20.00 50.00
96 Shogo Akiyama RR 6.00 15.00

2020 Donruss Optic Red

*RED DK: 1X TO 2.5X BASIC DK
*RED RR: 1X TO 2.5X BASIC DK
*RED VET: 1.5X TO 4X BASIC VET
RANDOM INSERTS IN PACKS
STATED PRINT RUN 60 SER.#'d SETS
32 Dustin May RR 6.00 15.00
33 Mauricio Dubon RR 4.00 10.00
37 Bo Bichette RR 20.00 50.00
38 Nico Hoerner RR 8.00 20.00
44 Gavin Lux RR 8.00 20.00
45 Yordan Alvarez RR 15.00 40.00
56 Kyle Lewis RR 15.00 40.00
62 Luis Robert RR 25.00 60.00
96 Shogo Akiyama RR 10.00 25.00

2020 Donruss Optic Red Dragon

*RED DRGN DK: 1X TO 2.5X BASIC DK
*RED DRGN RR: 1X TO 2.5X BASIC DK
*RED DRGN VET: 1.5X TO 4X BASIC VET
RANDOM INSERTS IN PACKS
STATED PRINT RUN 88 SER.#'d SETS
32 Dustin May RR 6.00 15.00
33 Mauricio Dubon RR 4.00 10.00
37 Bo Bichette RR 20.00 50.00
38 Nico Hoerner RR 8.00 20.00
44 Gavin Lux RR 8.00 20.00
45 Yordan Alvarez RR 15.00 40.00
56 Kyle Lewis RR 15.00 40.00
62 Luis Robert RR 25.00 60.00
96 Shogo Akiyama RR 10.00 25.00

2020 Donruss Optic Red Wave

*RED WAVE DK: .5X TO 1.2X BASIC DK
*RED WAVE RR: .5X TO 1.2X BASIC RR
*RED WAVE VET: .8X TO 2X BASIC VET
RANDOM INSERTS IN PACKS
32 Dustin May RR 3.00 8.00
33 Mauricio Dubon RR 2.00 5.00
37 Bo Bichette RR 10.00 25.00
44 Gavin Lux RR 4.00 10.00
45 Yordan Alvarez RR 8.00 20.00
56 Kyle Lewis RR 8.00 20.00
62 Luis Robert RR 12.00 30.00
96 Shogo Akiyama RR 4.00 10.00

2020 Donruss Optic Red White and Blue

*RWB DK: .75X TO 2X BASIC DK
*RWB RR: .75X TO 2X BASIC RR
*RWB VET: 1.2X TO 3X BASIC VET
RANDOM INSERTS IN PACKS
STATED PRINT RUN 150 SER.#'d SETS
32 Dustin May RR 5.00 12.00
33 Mauricio Dubon RR 3.00 8.00
37 Bo Bichette RR 15.00 40.00
38 Nico Hoerner RR 5.00 12.00
44 Gavin Lux RR 6.00 15.00
45 Yordan Alvarez RR 12.00 30.00
56 Kyle Lewis RR 12.00 30.00
62 Luis Robert RR 20.00 50.00
96 Shogo Akiyama RR 6.00 15.00

2020 Donruss Optic Spirit of 76

*76 DK: 1X TO 2.5X BASIC DK
*76 RR: 1X TO 2.5X BASIC DK
*76 VET: 1.5X TO 4X BASIC VET
RANDOM INSERTS IN PACKS
STATED PRINT RUN 76 SER.#'d SETS
32 Dustin May RR 6.00 15.00
33 Mauricio Dubon RR 4.00 10.00
37 Bo Bichette RR 20.00 50.00
38 Nico Hoerner RR 8.00 20.00
44 Gavin Lux RR 8.00 20.00
45 Yordan Alvarez RR 15.00 40.00
56 Kyle Lewis RR 15.00 40.00
62 Luis Robert RR 25.00 60.00
96 Shogo Akiyama RR 10.00 25.00

2020 Donruss Optic Stars and Stripes

RANDOM INSERTS IN PACKS
1 Aaron Judge 15.00 40.00
2 Mike Trout 60.00 150.00
3 Yordan Alvarez 20.00 50.00
4 Javier Baez 15.00 40.00
5 Ken Griffey Jr. 40.00 100.00
6 Shohei Ohtani 8.00 20.00
7 Clayton Kershaw 15.00 40.00
8 Juan Soto 15.00 40.00
9 Francisco Lindor 10.00 25.00
10 Bryce Harper 12.00 30.00

2020 Donruss Optic Teal Velocity

*TEAL VEL. DK: 1.2X TO 3X BASIC DK
*TEAL VEL. RR: 1.2X TO 3X BASIC DK
*TEAL VEL. VET: 2X TO 5X BASIC VET
RANDOM INSERTS IN PACKS
STATED PRINT RUN 35 SER.#'d SETS
32 Dustin May RR 8.00 20.00
33 Mauricio Dubon RR 5.00 12.00
37 Bo Bichette RR 30.00 80.00
38 Nico Hoerner RR 10.00 25.00
44 Gavin Lux RR 10.00 25.00
45 Yordan Alvarez RR 20.00 50.00
56 Kyle Lewis RR 20.00 50.00
62 Luis Robert RR 50.00 120.00
96 Shogo Akiyama RR 12.00 30.00

2020 Donruss Optic Autographs

RANDOM INSERTS IN PACKS
EXCHANGE DEADLINE 01/22/2022
1 Robel Garcia 2.50 6.00
2 Kris Bubic 4.00 10.00
3 Nolan Gorman 5.00 12.00
5 Matt Manning 3.00 8.00
6 Triston Casas 6.00 15.00
7 MacKenzie Gore 5.00 12.00
8 Drew Waters 8.00 20.00
9 Trevor Rogers 2.50 6.00
10 JJ Bleday 8.00 20.00
11 Shane Baz 2.50 6.00
12 Bobby Dalbec 6.00 15.00
13 Adonis Medina 4.00 10.00
14 Erick Fedde 2.50 6.00
15 Bryan Mata 2.50 6.00
16 Luis Rodriguez 15.00 40.00
17 Alex Faedo 3.00 8.00
18 Yoshitomo Tsutsugo 3.00 8.00
19 Luis Robert EXCH 75.00 200.00
21 Andy Pettitte 3.00 8.00
22 Austin Meadows 3.00 8.00
23 Kevin Newman 3.00 8.00
24 Sean Murphy 4.00 10.00
25 Richard Urena 2.50 6.00
26 J.D. Davis 2.50 6.00
27 Jonathan Loaisiga 3.00 8.00
28 Michael Chavis 5.00 12.00
29 Dillon Peters 2.50 6.00
30 Nick Martini 2.50 6.00
31 Ryan Mountcastle 4.00 10.00
32 Josh James 4.00 10.00
33 Richie Martin 2.50 6.00
34 Reynaldo Lopez 3.00 8.00
35 Cesar Hernandez 2.50 6.00
36 Josh Donaldson 3.00 8.00
37 Reese McGuire 3.00 8.00
39 Shed Long Jr. 3.00 8.00
40 Corey Ray 2.50 6.00

2020 Donruss Optic Autographs Holo

*HOLO: .5X TO 1.2X BASIC
RANDOM INSERTS IN PACKS
EXCHANGE DEADLINE 01/22/2022
28 Michael Chavis 8.00 20.00

2020 Donruss Optic Fireworks Signatures

RANDOM INSERTS IN PACKS
EXCHANGE DEADLINE 01/22/2022
1 Nolan Jones 4.00 10.00
2 Brice Turang 2.50 6.00
3 Luisangel Acuna 20.00 50.00
5 Johan Rojas 5.00 12.00
6 Corbin Carroll 4.00 10.00
8 Kristian Robinson 8.00 20.00
9 Luis Matos 4.00 10.00
10 Josh Jung 6.00 15.00
11 Riley Greene 12.00 30.00
13 Julio Rodriguez 15.00 40.00
14 Luis V. Garcia 4.00 10.00
16 Shogo Akiyama 8.00 20.00
17 Yoshitomo Tsutsugo 3.00 8.00
18 Alex Bregman EXCH 10.00 25.00
19 Tommy Edman 4.00 10.00
20 Evan White 2.50 6.00
21 Dylan Carlson 15.00 40.00
24 Shohei Ohtani EXCH 40.00 100.00
25 Yoan Moncada 15.00 40.00
26 Yordan Alvarez EXCH 25.00 60.00
27 Aristides Aquino 5.00 12.00
28 Adrian Beltre 10.00 25.00
29 Troy Glaus 6.00 15.00
30 Eugenio Suarez 3.00 8.00
33 Frank Thomas EXCH 20.00 50.00
34 Eloy Jimenez EXCH 20.00 50.00
36 Bobby Bradley 3.00 8.00
37 Kyle Lewis 25.00 60.00
38 Christin Stewart 2.50 6.00
39 Ty France 4.00 10.00
40 Nathaniel Lowe 2.50 6.00

2020 Donruss Optic Fireworks Signatures Holo

*HOLO: .5X TO 1.2X BASIC
RANDOM INSERTS IN PACKS
EXCHANGE DEADLINE 01/22/2022
21 Dylan Carlson 25.00 60.00
25 Yoan Moncada 25.00 60.00
26 Yordan Alvarez EXCH 40.00 100.00
37 Kyle Lewis 40.00 100.00

2020 Donruss Optic Highlights Signatures

RANDOM INSERTS IN PACKS
EXCHANGE DEADLINE 01/22/2022
1 Aaron Judge
2 Jose Abreu EXCH 4.00 10.00
3 Austin Riley 6.00 15.00
4 Juan Soto
5 Jose Altuve
6 Blake Snell 3.00 8.00
7 Ronald Acuna Jr. 40.00 100.00
8 Justin Turner 3.00 8.00
9 Pete Alonso 30.00 80.00
10 Vladimir Guerrero Jr. 20.00 50.00
11 Rafael Devers 10.00 25.00
12 Matt Chapman 4.00 10.00
13 Paul DeJong 4.00 10.00
14 Clayton Kershaw
15 Ozzie Albies
16 Josh Hader 2.50 6.00
17 Anthony Rizzo 15.00 40.00
18 Fernando Tatis Jr.
19 Rhys Hoskins 12.00 30.00

2020 Donruss Optic Highlights Signatures Black

*BLACK/20-35: .8X TO 2X BASIC
RANDOM INSERTS IN PACKS
PRINT RUNS B/WN 3-35 COPIES PER
NO PRICING QTY 15 OR LESS
EXCHANGE DEADLINE 01/22/2022
8 Justin Turner/20 15.00 40.00

2020 Donruss Optic Highlights Signatures Black Cracked Ice

*BLK CRKD ICE/20-25: .8X TO 2X BASIC
RANDOM INSERTS IN PACKS
PRINT RUNS B/WN 3-25 COPIES PER
NO PRICING QTY 15 OR LESS
EXCHANGE DEADLINE 01/22/2022
8 Justin Turner/25 15.00 40.00
15 Ozzie Albies/25 15.00 40.00

2020 Donruss Optic Highlights Signatures Blue

*BLUE/50: .6X TO 1.5X BASIC
*BLUE/20-35: .8X TO 2X BASIC
RANDOM INSERTS IN PACKS
PRINT RUNS B/WN 3-50 COPIES PER
NO PRICING QTY 15 OR LESS
EXCHANGE DEADLINE 01/22/2022
8 Justin Turner/20 15.00 40.00
15 Ozzie Albies/50 12.00 30.00

2020 Donruss Optic Highlights Signatures Carolina Blue

*CAR.BLUE/20-35: .8X TO 2X BASIC
RANDOM INSERTS IN PACKS
PRINT RUNS B/WN 3-35 COPIES PER
EXCHANGE DEADLINE 01/22/2022
8 Justin Turner/20 15.00 40.00

2020 Donruss Optic Highlights Signatures Holo

*HOLO: .5X TO 1.2X BASIC
RANDOM INSERTS IN PACKS
EXCHANGE DEADLINE 01/22/2022
8 Justin Turner 8.00 20.00
15 Ozzie Albies

2020 Donruss Optic Highlights Signatures Orange

*ORANGE/50: .6X TO 1.5X BASIC
*ORANGE/20: .8X TO 2X BASIC
RANDOM INSERTS IN PACKS
PRINT RUNS B/WN 3-50 COPIES PER
NO PRICING QTY 15 OR LESS
EXCHANGE DEADLINE 01/22/2022
8 Justin Turner/20 15.00 40.00
15 Ozzie Albies/50 12.00 30.00

2020 Donruss Optic Highlights Signatures Pink Velocity

*PINK VEL.: .5X TO 1.2X BASIC
RANDOM INSERTS IN PACKS
EXCHANGE DEADLINE 01/22/2022
8 Justin Turner 8.00 20.00
14 Clayton Kershaw 40.00 100.00
15 Ozzie Albies 10.00 25.00

2020 Donruss Optic Highlights Signatures Purple

*PURPLE/50: .6X TO 1.5X BASIC
*PURPLE/20: .8X TO 2X BASIC
RANDOM INSERTS IN PACKS
PRINT RUNS B/WN 3-50 COPIES PER
NO PRICING QTY 15 OR LESS
EXCHANGE DEADLINE 01/22/2022
8 Justin Turner/20 15.00 40.00
15 Ozzie Albies/50 12.00 30.00

2020 Donruss Optic Highlights Signatures Red

*RED/50: .6X TO 1.5X BASIC
*RED/20-35: .8X TO 2X BASIC
RANDOM INSERTS IN PACKS
PRINT RUNS B/WN 3-50 COPIES PER
NO PRICING QTY 15 OR LESS
EXCHANGE DEADLINE 01/22/2022
8 Justin Turner/20 15.00 40.00
15 Ozzie Albies/50 12.00 30.00

2020 Donruss Optic Highlights Signatures Teal Velocity

*TEAL VEL./20-35: .8X TO 2X BASIC
RANDOM INSERTS IN PACKS
PRINT RUNS B/WN 3-35 COPIES PER
NO PRICING QTY 15 OR LESS
EXCHANGE DEADLINE 01/22/2022
8 Justin Turner/35 15.00 40.00
15 Ozzie Albies/35 15.00 40.00

2020 Donruss Optic Illusions

RANDOM INSERTS IN PACKS
1 Jacob deGrom .40 1.00
2 Paul Goldschmidt .40 1.00
3 Buster Posey .50 1.25
4 Isan Diaz .40 1.00
5 Whit Merrifield .40 1.00
6 Yordan Alvarez 1.25 3.00
7 Mookie Betts .75 2.00
8 Eloy Jimenez .75 2.00
9 Corey Kluber .30 .75
10 Joey Votto .40 1.00
11 Josh Bell .30 .75
12 Austin Meadows .30 .75
13 Shohei Ohtani .50 1.25
14 Trevor Story .40 1.00
15 Keston Hiura .50 1.25

2020 Donruss Optic Illusions Holo

*HOLO: 1X TO 2.5X BASIC
RANDOM INSERTS IN PACKS
15 Keston Hiura 2.00 5.00

2020 Donruss Optic Mythical

RANDOM INSERTS IN PACKS
*HOLO: 1X TO 2.5X BASIC
1 Luis Robert 5.00 12.00
2 Manny Machado .40 1.00
3 Francisco Lindor .40 1.00
4 Mike Trout 2.00 5.00
5 Cody Bellinger .75 2.00
6 Fernando Tatis Jr. 1.50 4.00
7 Wander Franco 2.50 6.00
8 Vladimir Guerrero Jr. .75 2.00
9 Javier Baez .50 1.25
10 Ronald Acuna Jr. 1.50 4.00
11 Alex Bregman .40 1.00
12 Aristides Aquino .50 1.25
13 Juan Soto 1.25 3.00
14 Aaron Judge 1.00 2.50
15 Pete Alonso 1.00 2.50

2020 Donruss Optic Pandora

*PANDORA DK: 1X TO 2.5X BASIC DK
*PANDORA RR: 1X TO 2.5X BASIC DK
*PANDORA VET: 1.5X TO 4X BASIC VET
RANDOM INSERTS IN PACKS
STATED PRINT RUN 99 SER.#'d SETS
32 Dustin May RR 6.00 15.00
33 Mauricio Dubon RR 4.00 10.00
37 Bo Bichette RR 20.00 50.00
38 Nico Hoerner RR 8.00 20.00
44 Gavin Lux RR 8.00 20.00
45 Yordan Alvarez RR 15.00 40.00
56 Kyle Lewis RR 15.00 40.00
62 Luis Robert RR 25.00 60.00
96 Shogo Akiyama RR 10.00 25.00

2020 Donruss Optic Pandora Blue

*PAND.BLUE DK: 1X TO 2.5X BASIC DK
*PAND.BLUE RR: 1X TO 2.5X BASIC DK
*PAND.BLUE VET: 1.5X TO 4X BASIC VET
RANDOM INSERTS IN PACKS
STATED PRINT RUN 99 SER.#'d SETS
32 Dustin May RR 6.00 15.00
33 Mauricio Dubon RR 4.00 10.00
37 Bo Bichette RR 20.00 50.00
38 Nico Hoerner RR 8.00 20.00
44 Gavin Lux RR 8.00 20.00
45 Yordan Alvarez RR 15.00 40.00
56 Kyle Lewis RR 15.00 40.00
62 Luis Robert RR 25.00 60.00
96 Shogo Akiyama RR 10.00 25.00

2020 Donruss Optic Pandora Purple

*PAND.PURP. DK: 1X TO 2.5X BASIC DK
*PAND.PURP.RR: 1X TO 2.5X BASIC DK
*PAND.PURP.VET: 1.5X TO 4X BASIC VET
RANDOM INSERTS IN PACKS
STATED PRINT RUN 99 SER.#'d SETS
32 Dustin May RR 6.00 15.00
33 Mauricio Dubon RR 4.00 10.00
37 Bo Bichette RR 20.00 50.00
38 Nico Hoerner RR 8.00 20.00
44 Gavin Lux RR 8.00 20.00
45 Yordan Alvarez RR 15.00 40.00
56 Kyle Lewis RR 15.00 40.00
62 Luis Robert RR 25.00 60.00
96 Shogo Akiyama RR 10.00 25.00

2020 Donruss Optic Pandora Red

*PAND.RED DK: 1X TO 2.5X BASIC DK
*PAND.RED RR: 1X TO 2.5X BASIC DK
*PAND.RED VET: 1.5X TO 4X BASIC VET
RANDOM INSERTS IN PACKS
STATED PRINT RUN 79 SER.#'d SETS
32 Dustin May RR 6.00 15.00

3 Mauricio Dubon RR 4.00 10.00
7 Bo Bichette RR 20.00 50.00
8 Nico Hoerner RR 8.00 20.00
4 Gavin Lux RR 8.00 20.00
5 Yordan Alvarez RR 15.00 40.00
6 Kyle Lewis RR 15.00 40.00
2 Luis Robert RR 25.00 60.00
6 Shogo Akiyama RR 10.00 25.00

2020 Donruss Optic Rated Prospects

RANDOM INSERTS IN PACKS
Wander Franco 2.50 6.00
Bobby Witt Jr. 1.25 3.00
Jo Adell 2.50 6.00
Casey Mize .75 2.00
Royce Lewis .60 1.50
Nate Pearson .50 1.25
Cristian Pache 2.00 5.00
Alex Kirilloff .50 1.25
Forrest Whitley .25 .60
0 Dylan Carlson 1.00 2.50
1 Jasson Dominguez 10.00 25.00
2 Tristen Lutz .30 .75
3 Adley Rutschman 3.00 8.00
4 MacKenzie Gore .50 1.25
5 Jarred Kelenic 5.00 12.00
6 Joey Bart .75 2.00
7 CJ Abrams 1.00 2.50
8 Andrew Vaughn 1.00 2.50
9 Ryan Mountcastle .40 1.00
20 Nick Madrigal .75 2.00

2020 Donruss Optic Rated Prospects Holo

*HOLO: 1X TO 2.5X BASIC
RANDOM INSERTS IN PACKS
4 Casey Mize 3.00 8.00
14 MacKenzie Gore 4.00 10.00
16 Joey Bart 4.00 10.00
17 CJ Abrams 3.00 8.00
20 Nick Madrigal 3.00 8.00

2020 Donruss Optic Rated Prospects Signatures

RANDOM INSERTS IN PACKS
EXCHANGE DEADLINE 01/22/2022
1 Wander Franco 25.00 60.00
2 Luis Robert
3 Forrest Whitley 2.50 6.00
4 Royce Lewis
5 Bobby Witt Jr. 50.00 120.00
6 Jo Adell 20.00 50.00
7 Alec Bohm 15.00 40.00
8 Alex Kirilloff 5.00 12.00
9 Dylan Carlson 15.00 40.00
10 Joey Bart 20.00 50.00
11 Jonathan India 5.00 12.00
12 Victor Mesa Jr. 6.00 15.00
13 JJ Bleday 6.00 15.00
14 Deivi Garcia 10.00 25.00
15 Jasson Dominguez 100.00 250.00
16 Miguel Amaya 3.00 8.00
17 Oneil Cruz 3.00 8.00
18 Andres Gimenez 6.00 15.00
19 Nick Neidert 2.50 6.00
20 Ronaldo Hernandez 2.50 6.00

2020 Donruss Optic Rated Prospects Signatures Black

*BLACK/50: .6X TO 1.5X BASIC
*BLACK/20-35: .8X TO 2X BASIC
RANDOM INSERTS IN PACKS
PRINT RUNS B/WN 15-50 COPIES PER
NO PRICING QTY 15 OR LESS
EXCHANGE DEADLINE 01/22/2022
1 Wander Franco/50 EXCH 75.00 200.00
6 Jo Adell/50 40.00 100.00
9 Dylan Carlson/50 30.00 80.00
15 Jasson Dominguez/50 250.00 600.00

2020 Donruss Optic Rated Prospects Signatures Black Cracked Ice

*BLK CRKD ICE: .8X TO 2X BASIC
RANDOM INSERTS IN PACKS
STATED PRINT RUN 25 SER.#'d SETS
EXCHANGE DEADLINE 01/22/2022
1 Wander Franco EXCH 125.00 300.00
2 Luis Robert 150.00 400.00
6 Jo Adell 50.00 120.00
9 Dylan Carlson 40.00 100.00
15 Jasson Dominguez 500.00 1000.00

2020 Donruss Optic Rated Prospects Signatures Blue

*BLUE/50-75: .6X TO 1.5X BASIC
*BLUE/20: .8X TO 2X BASIC
RANDOM INSERTS IN PACKS
PRINT RUNS B/WN 20-75 COPIES PER
EXCHANGE DEADLINE 01/22/2022
1 Wander Franco/75 EXCH 60.00 150.00
2 Luis Robert/20 200.00 500.00
6 Jo Adell/50 40.00 100.00
9 Dylan Carlson/50 30.00 80.00
15 Jasson Dominguez/50 250.00 600.00

2020 Donruss Optic Rated Prospects Signatures Blue Mojo

*BLUE MOJO/49-99: .6X TO 1.5X BASIC
RANDOM INSERTS IN PACKS
PRINT RUNS B/WN 49-99 COPIES PER
EXCHANGE DEADLINE 01/22/2022
1 Wander Franco/99 EXCH 60.00 150.00
2 Luis Robert/99 125.00 300.00
6 Jo Adell/99 40.00 100.00
9 Dylan Carlson/99 30.00 80.00
15 Jasson Dominguez/49 250.00 600.00

2020 Donruss Optic Rated Prospects Signatures Carolina Blue

*CAR.BLUE/20-35: .8X TO 2X BASIC
RANDOM INSERTS IN PACKS
PRINT RUNS B/WN 15-35 COPIES PER
NO PRICING QTY 15 OR LESS
EXCHANGE DEADLINE 01/22/2022
1 Wander Franco/35 EXCH 100.00 250.00
6 Jo Adell/35 50.00 120.00
9 Dylan Carlson/35 40.00 100.00
15 Jasson Dominguez/35 300.00 800.00

2020 Donruss Optic Rated Prospects Signatures Green Mojo

*GRN MOJO/49-99: .6X TO 1.5X BASIC
RANDOM INSERTS IN PACKS
PRINT RUNS B/WN 49-99 COPIES PER
EXCHANGE DEADLINE 01/22/2022
1 Wander Franco/99 EXCH 60.00 150.00
2 Luis Robert/99 125.00 300.00
6 Jo Adell/99 40.00 100.00
9 Dylan Carlson/99 30.00 80.00
15 Jasson Dominguez/49 250.00 600.00

2020 Donruss Optic Rated Prospects Signatures Holo

*HOLO: .5X TO 1.2X BASIC
RANDOM INSERTS IN PACKS
EXCHANGE DEADLINE 01/22/2022
1 Wander Franco EXCH 50.00 120.00
2 Luis Robert 100.00 250.00
6 Jo Adell 30.00 80.00
9 Dylan Carlson 25.00 60.00
15 Jasson Dominguez 150.00 400.00

2020 Donruss Optic Rated Prospects Signatures Orange

*ORANGE/50-75: .6X TO 1.5X BASIC
*ORANGE/20: .8X TO 2X BASIC
RANDOM INSERTS IN PACKS
PRINT RUNS B/WN 20-75 COPIES PER
EXCHANGE DEADLINE 01/22/2022
1 Wander Franco/75 EXCH 60.00 150.00
2 Luis Robert/20 200.00 500.00
6 Jo Adell/75 40.00 100.00
9 Dylan Carlson/75 30.00 80.00
15 Jasson Dominguez/75 200.00 500.00

2020 Donruss Optic Rated Prospects Signatures Pink Velocity

*PINK VEL.: .5X TO 1.2X BASIC
RANDOM INSERTS IN PACKS
EXCHANGE DEADLINE 01/22/2022
1 Wander Franco EXCH 50.00 120.00
2 Luis Robert 100.00 250.00
6 Jo Adell 30.00 80.00
9 Dylan Carlson 25.00 60.00
15 Jasson Dominguez 200.00 500.00

2020 Donruss Optic Rated Prospects Signatures Purple

*PURPLE/50-99: .6X TO 1.5X BASIC
*PURPLE/20: .8X TO 2X BASIC
RANDOM INSERTS IN PACKS
PRINT RUNS B/WN 20-99 COPIES PER
EXCHANGE DEADLINE 01/22/2022
1 Wander Franco/99 EXCH 60.00 150.00
2 Luis Robert/20 200.00 500.00
6 Jo Adell/75 40.00 100.00
9 Dylan Carlson/75 30.00 80.00
15 Jasson Dominguez/75 200.00 500.00

2020 Donruss Optic Rated Prospects Signatures Red

*RED/50: .6X TO 1.5X BASIC
*RED/20-35: .8X TO 2X BASIC
RANDOM INSERTS IN PACKS
PRINT RUNS B/WN 15-50 COPIES PER
NO PRICING QTY 15 OR LESS
EXCHANGE DEADLINE 01/22/2022
1 Wander Franco/50 EXCH 75.00 200.00
6 Jo Adell/50 40.00 100.00
9 Dylan Carlson/50 30.00 80.00
15 Jasson Dominguez/50 250.00 600.00

2020 Donruss Optic Rated Prospects Signatures Red Mojo

*RED MOJO/49-99: .6X TO 1.5X BASIC
RANDOM INSERTS IN PACKS
PRINT RUNS B/WN 49-99 COPIES PER
EXCHANGE DEADLINE 01/22/2022
1 Wander Franco/99 EXCH 60.00 150.00
2 Luis Robert/99 125.00 300.00
6 Jo Adell/99 40.00 100.00
9 Dylan Carlson/99 30.00 80.00
15 Jasson Dominguez/49 250.00 600.00

2020 Donruss Optic Rated Prospects Signatures Teal Velocity

*TEAL VEL./30-35: .8X TO 2X BASIC
RANDOM INSERTS IN PACKS
PRINT RUNS B/WN 15-35 COPIES PER
NO PRICING QTY 15 OR LESS
EXCHANGE DEADLINE 01/22/2022
1 Wander Franco/35 EXCH 100.00 250.00
6 Jo Adell/35 50.00 120.00
9 Dylan Carlson/35 40.00 100.00
15 Jasson Dominguez/35 300.00 800.00

2020 Donruss Optic Rated Prospects Signatures White Mojo

*WHT MOJO/49-99: .6X TO 1.5X BASIC
RANDOM INSERTS IN PACKS
PRINT RUNS B/WN 49-99 COPIES PER
EXCHANGE DEADLINE 01/22/2022
1 Wander Franco/99 EXCH 60.00 150.00
2 Luis Robert/99 125.00 300.00
6 Jo Adell/99 40.00 100.00
9 Dylan Carlson/99 30.00 80.00
15 Jasson Dominguez/49 250.00 600.00

2020 Donruss Optic Rated Rookies Signatures

RANDOM INSERTS IN PACKS
EXCHANGE DEADLINE 01/22/2022
1 Aristides Aquino 6.00 15.00
2 Brock Burke 2.50 6.00
3 Jesus Luzardo 8.00 20.00
4 Aaron Civale 4.00 10.00
5 Jake Rogers 2.50 6.00
6 Brendan McKay 4.00 10.00
7 Nick Solak 5.00 12.00
8 Matt Thaiss 3.00 8.00
9 Zack Collins 4.00 10.00
10 Dylan Cease 5.00 12.00
11 Kyle Lewis 20.00 50.00
12 Justin Dunn 3.00 8.00
14 Sheldon Neuse 3.00 8.00
15 Adbert Alzolay 3.00 8.00
16 Isan Diaz 4.00 10.00
17 Bobby Bradley 3.00 8.00
18 Zac Gallen 6.00 15.00
19 Nico Hoerner 10.00 25.00
20 Dustin May 10.00 25.00
21 Bo Bichette 30.00 80.00
22 Logan Webb 3.00 8.00
23 Willi Castro 5.00 12.00
24 Jonathan Hernandez 2.50 6.00
25 Jake Fraley 3.00 8.00
26 A.J. Puk 5.00 12.00
27 Mauricio Dubon 3.00 8.00
28 Logan Allen 2.50 6.00
29 Gavin Lux 25.00 60.00
30 Jordan Yamamoto 6.00 15.00
31 Domingo Leyba 3.00 8.00
32 Anthony Kay 2.50 6.00
33 Yu Chang 4.00 10.00
34 Adrian Morejon 2.50 6.00
35 Tony Gonsolin 6.00 15.00
36 Bryan Abreu 2.50 6.00
37 Sam Hilliard 4.00 10.00
38 Brusdar Graterol 4.00 10.00
39 Edwin Rios 6.00 15.00
40 Lewis Thorpe 2.50 6.00
41 Rico Garcia 4.00 10.00
42 Jaylin Davis 4.00 10.00
43 Patrick Sandoval 4.00 10.00
44 Abraham Toro 3.00 8.00
45 Michael King 4.00 10.00
46 Deivy Grullon 2.50 6.00
47 Donnie Walton 6.00 15.00
48 Tyrone Taylor 2.50 6.00
49 Ronald Bolanos 4.00 10.00
50 T.J. Zeuch 2.50 6.00
51 Randy Arozarena 50.00 120.00
52 Andres Munoz 3.00 8.00
53 Sean Murphy 4.00 10.00
54 Travis Demeritte 3.00 8.00
55 Yordan Alvarez 30.00 80.00
56 Tres Barrera 5.00 12.00
57 Danny Mendick 3.00 8.00
58 Josh Rojas 2.50 6.00
59 Michel Baez 2.50 6.00
60 Joe Palumbo 2.50 6.00
61 Yonathan Daza 3.00 8.00

2020 Donruss Optic Rated Rookies Signatures Black

*BLACK/50: .6X TO 1.5X BASIC
*BLACK/35: .8X TO 2X BASIC
RANDOM INSERTS IN PACKS
PRINT RUNS B/WN 35-50 COPIES PER
EXCHANGE DEADLINE 01/22/2022
11 Kyle Lewis/50 40.00 100.00
13 Trent Grisham/50 20.00 50.00
20 Dustin May/35 25.00 60.00
33 Yu Chang/50 10.00 25.00
53 Sean Murphy/50 10.00 25.00

2020 Donruss Optic Rated Rookies Signatures Black Cracked Ice

*BLK CRKD ICE: .8X TO 2X BASIC
RANDOM INSERTS IN PACKS
STATED PRINT RUN 25 SER.#'d SETS
EXCHANGE DEADLINE 01/22/2022
11 Kyle Lewis 50.00 120.00
13 Trent Grisham 25.00 60.00
20 Dustin May 30.00 80.00
33 Yu Chang 12.00 30.00
53 Sean Murphy 12.00 30.00

2020 Donruss Optic Rated Rookies Signatures Blue

*BLUE/50-75: .6X TO 1.5X BASIC
RANDOM INSERTS IN PACKS
PRINT RUNS B/WN 50-75 COPIES PER
EXCHANGE DEADLINE 01/22/2022
13 Trent Grisham/75 20.00 50.00
20 Dustin May/50 20.00 50.00
33 Yu Chang/75 10.00 25.00
53 Sean Murphy/75 10.00 25.00

2020 Donruss Optic Rated Rookies Signatures Blue Mojo

*BLUE MOJO/49-99: .6X TO 1.5X BASIC
RANDOM INSERTS IN PACKS
PRINT RUNS B/WN 49-99 COPIES PER
EXCHANGE DEADLINE 01/22/2022
13 Trent Grisham/99 20.00 50.00
20 Dustin May/49 20.00 50.00
33 Yu Chang/99 10.00 25.00
53 Sean Murphy/99 10.00 25.00

2020 Donruss Optic Rated Rookies Signatures Carolina Blue

*CAR.BLUE/35: .8X TO 2X BASIC
RANDOM INSERTS IN PACKS
STATED PRINT RUN 35 SER.#'d SETS
EXCHANGE DEADLINE 01/22/2022
11 Kyle Lewis 50.00 120.00
20 Dustin May 25.00 60.00
33 Yu Chang 12.00 30.00
53 Sean Murphy 12.00 30.00

2020 Donruss Optic Rated Rookies Signatures Green Mojo

*GRN MOJO/49-99: .6X TO 1.5X BASIC
RANDOM INSERTS IN PACKS
PRINT RUNS B/WN 49-99 COPIES PER
EXCHANGE DEADLINE 01/22/2022
13 Trent Grisham/99 20.00 50.00
20 Dustin May/49 20.00 50.00
33 Yu Chang/99 10.00 25.00
53 Sean Murphy/99 10.00 25.00

2020 Donruss Optic Rated Rookies Signatures Holo

*HOLO: .5X TO 1.2X BASIC
RANDOM INSERTS IN PACKS
EXCHANGE DEADLINE 01/22/2022
13 Trent Grisham 15.00 40.00
20 Dustin May 15.00 40.00
33 Yu Chang 8.00 20.00
53 Sean Murphy 8.00 20.00

2020 Donruss Optic Rated Rookies Signatures Orange

*ORANGE/50-99: .6X TO 1.5X BASIC
RANDOM INSERTS IN PACKS
PRINT RUNS B/WN 50-99 COPIES PER
EXCHANGE DEADLINE 01/22/2022
20 Dustin May/50 20.00 50.00
33 Yu Chang/99 10.00 25.00
53 Sean Murphy/99 10.00 25.00

2020 Donruss Optic Rated Rookies Signatures Pink Velocity

*PINK VEL.: .5X TO 1.2X BASIC
RANDOM INSERTS IN PACKS
EXCHANGE DEADLINE 01/22/2022
20 Dustin May 15.00 40.00
33 Yu Chang 8.00 20.00
53 Sean Murphy 8.00 20.00

2020 Donruss Optic Rated Rookies Signatures Purple

*PURPLE/75-125: .6X TO 1.5X BASIC
RANDOM INSERTS IN PACKS
PRINT RUNS B/WN 75-125 COPIES PER
EXCHANGE DEADLINE 01/22/2022
13 Trent Grisham/125 20.00 50.00
20 Dustin May/75 20.00 50.00
33 Yu Chang/125 10.00 25.00
53 Sean Murphy/125 10.00 25.00

2020 Donruss Optic Rated Rookies Signatures Red

*RED/50: .6X TO 1.5X BASIC
*RED/35: .8X TO 2X BASIC
RANDOM INSERTS IN PACKS
PRINT RUNS B/WN 35-50 COPIES PER
EXCHANGE DEADLINE 01/22/2022
11 Kyle Lewis/50 40.00 100.00
20 Dustin May/35 25.00 60.00
33 Yu Chang/50 10.00 25.00
53 Sean Murphy/50 10.00 25.00

2020 Donruss Optic Rated Rookies Signatures Red Mojo

*RED MOJO/49-99: .6X TO 1.5X BASIC
RANDOM INSERTS IN PACKS
PRINT RUNS B/WN 49-99 COPIES PER
EXCHANGE DEADLINE 01/22/2022
13 Trent Grisham/99 20.00 50.00
20 Dustin May/49 20.00 50.00
33 Yu Chang/99 10.00 25.00
53 Sean Murphy/99 10.00 25.00

2020 Donruss Optic Rated Rookies Signatures Teal Velocity

*TEAL VEL./30-35: .8X TO 2X BASIC
RANDOM INSERTS IN PACKS
PRINT RUNS B/WN 30-35 COPIES PER
EXCHANGE DEADLINE 01/22/2022
11 Kyle Lewis/35 50.00 120.00
13 Trent Grisham/35 25.00 60.00
20 Dustin May/30 25.00 60.00
33 Yu Chang/35 12.00 30.00
53 Sean Murphy/35 12.00 30.00

2020 Donruss Optic Rated Rookies Signatures White Mojo

*WHT MOJO/49-99: .6X TO 1.5X BASIC
RANDOM INSERTS IN PACKS
PRINT RUNS B/WN 49-99 COPIES PER
EXCHANGE DEADLINE 01/22/2022
13 Trent Grisham/99 20.00 50.00
20 Dustin May/49 20.00 50.00
33 Yu Chang/99 10.00 25.00
53 Sean Murphy/99 10.00 25.00

2020 Donruss Optic Retro '86

RANDOM INSERTS IN PACKS
*HOLO: 1X TO 2.5X BASIC
1 Cal Ripken 1.25 3.00
2 Kirby Puckett .40 1.00
3 George Brett .75 2.00
4 Rickey Henderson .40 1.00
5 Jose Canseco .30 .75
6 Nolan Ryan 1.25 3.00
7 Alan Trammell .30 .75
8 Tony Gwynn .40 1.00
9 Darryl Strawberry .25 .60
10 Paul Molitor .40 1.00
11 Roger Clemens .50 1.25
12 Wade Boggs .30 .75
13 Barry Larkin .30 .75
14 Andres Galarraga .30 .75
15 Kevin Mitchell .25 .60
16 Don Mattingly .75 2.00
17 Bert Blyleven .30 .75
18 Jim Rice .30 .75
19 Keith Hernandez .25 .60
20 Eddie Murray .30 .75
21 Gary Carter .30 .75
22 Dave Winfield .30 .75
23 Dale Murphy .40 1.00
24 Robin Yount .40 1.00
25 Dwight Gooden .25 .60

2020 Donruss Optic Retro '86 Signatures

RANDOM INSERTS IN PACKS
EXCHANGE DEADLINE 01/22/2022
*PANDORA/25: .8X TO 2X BASIC
*PAN.BLUE/25: .8X TO 2X BASIC
*PAN.PURP./25: .8X TO 2X BASIC
*PAN.RED/25: .8X TO 2X BASIC
1 Noelvi Marte 10.00 25.00
2 Daulton Varsho 2.50 6.00
3 Freudis Nova 2.50 6.00
4 Miguel Vargas 6.00 15.00
5 Matthew Liberatore 3.00 8.00
6 Alek Thomas 3.00 8.00
7 Deivi Garcia 10.00 25.00
8 Luis Robert EXCH 100.00 250.00
9 Nick Madrigal 12.00 30.00
10 Hunter Greene 10.00 25.00
11 Evan White 8.00 20.00
12 Cristian Pache EXCH 12.00 30.00
13 Triston McKenzie 4.00 10.00
14 CJ Abrams 10.00 25.00
15 Shun Yamaguchi 3.00 8.00
16 CC Sabathia
17 Stephen Piscotty 6.00 15.00
18 Fernando Tatis Jr. 50.00 120.00
19 Randy Johnson EXCH
20 Cody Bellinger EXCH 40.00 100.00
21 Andrew McCutchen 25.00 60.00
22 Alex Rodriguez EXCH
24 Chipper Jones
25 Anthony Rizzo EXCH
26 Joey Votto 15.00 40.00
27 Jose Altuve 12.00 30.00
28 Vladimir Guerrero 15.00 40.00
29 Wade Boggs 12.00 30.00
30 Juan Marichal 8.00 20.00
31 Don Mattingly 30.00 80.00
32 Jose Abreu EXCH 5.00 12.00
33 Dustin Pedroia 10.00 25.00
34 Corey Seager EXCH
35 Nomar Mazara 2.50 6.00
36 Dakota Hudson 3.00 8.00
37 Aaron Sanchez 3.00 8.00
38 Mike Zunino 2.50 6.00
39 Raimel Tapia 2.50 6.00
41 Ryan O'Hearn 2.50 6.00
42 Jake Cave 3.00 8.00
43 Austin Dean 2.50 6.00
44 Taylor Clarke 2.50 6.00
45 Domingo German 3.00 8.00
46 Yu Chang 4.00 10.00

2020 Donruss Optic Retro '86 Signatures Holo

*HOLO: .5X TO 1.2X BASIC
RANDOM INSERTS IN PACKS
EXCHANGE DEADLINE 01/22/2022
24 Chipper Jones 40.00 100.00
34 Corey Seager EXCH 10.00 25.00

2020 Donruss Optic Signature Series

RANDOM INSERTS IN PACKS
EXCHANGE DEADLINE 01/22/2022
3 Jarren Duran 10.00 25.00
4 Tyler Freeman 3.00 8.00
5 Tarik Skubal 10.00 25.00
6 Vidal Brujan 5.00 12.00
7 Logan Gilbert 3.00 8.00
8 Ke'Bryan Hayes 2.50 6.00
9 Jesus Sanchez 2.50 6.00
10 Jarred Kelenic 15.00 40.00
11 Taylor Trammell 3.00 8.00
12 Ryan Mountcastle 4.00 10.00
13 Victor Victor Mesa 4.00 10.00
14 Heliot Ramos 4.00 10.00
15 Kwang-Hyun Kim 10.00 25.00
16 Alex Bregman EXCH 10.00 25.00
17 CC Sabathia 12.00 30.00
18 Adam Haseley 4.00 10.00
19 Tanner Rainey 2.50 6.00
20 Joe Ryan 2.50 6.00
21 Luis Ortiz 2.50 6.00
22 Jose Suarez 2.50 6.00
23 Mauricio Dubon 2.50 6.00
24 Edmundo Sosa 3.00 8.00
25 Monte Harrison 2.50 6.00
26 Brent Honeywell 3.00 8.00
27 Jonathan Davis 3.00 8.00
28 Eric Haase 2.50 6.00
29 Brian Anderson 2.50 6.00
30 Dylan Cease 5.00 12.00
31 Thomas Pannone 4.00 10.00
32 Duane Underwood 2.50 6.00
33 Cole Tucker 4.00 10.00
34 Clint Frazier 8.00 20.00
35 Brandon Lowe 6.00 15.00
36 Jose Berrios 3.00 8.00
37 Xander Bogaerts EXCH
38 Wil Myers 2.50 6.00
39 Jonathan Lucroy 3.00 8.00
40 Cole Hamels 3.00 8.00
41 Adam Plutko 2.50 6.00
42 Josh Naylor 2.50 6.00
43 Yandy Diaz 3.00 8.00
44 Michael Taylor 2.50 6.00
45 Corbin Burnes 3.00 8.00
46 Gleyber Torres EXCH
47 Mitch Moreland 2.50 6.00
48 Rickey Henderson 25.00 60.00
49 Aaron Judge 50.00 120.00
50 Vladimir Guerrero Jr. 20.00 50.00

2020 Donruss Optic Signature Series Holo

*HOLO: .5X TO 1.2X BASIC
RANDOM INSERTS IN PACKS
EXCHANGE DEADLINE 01/22/2022
46 Gleyber Torres EXCH 30.00 80.00

2020 Donruss Optic Signature Series Pandora

*PANDORA/20-35: .8X TO 2X BASIC
RANDOM INSERTS IN PACKS
PRINT RUNS B/WN 5-35 COPIES PER
NO PRICING QTY 15 OR LESS
EXCHANGE DEADLINE 01/22/2022
15 Kwang-Hyun Kim/25 25.00 60.00

2020 Donruss Optic Signature Series Pandora Blue

*PAN.BLUE/20-35: .8X TO 2X BASIC
RANDOM INSERTS IN PACKS
PRINT RUNS B/WN 5-35 COPIES PER
NO PRICING QTY 15 OR LESS
EXCHANGE DEADLINE 01/22/2022
15 Kwang-Hyun Kim/25 25.00 60.00

2020 Donruss Optic Signature Series Pandora Purple

*PAN.PURP./20-35: .8X TO 2X BASIC
RANDOM INSERTS IN PACKS
PRINT RUNS B/WN 5-35 COPIES PER
NO PRICING QTY 15 OR LESS
EXCHANGE DEADLINE 01/22/2022
15 Kwang-Hyun Kim/25 25.00 60.00

2020 Donruss Optic Signature Series Pandora Red

*PAN.RED/20-35: .8X TO 2X BASIC
RANDOM INSERTS IN PACKS
PRINT RUNS B/WN 5-35 COPIES PER
NO PRICING QTY 15 OR LESS
EXCHANGE DEADLINE 01/22/2022
15 Kwang-Hyun Kim/25 25.00 60.00

2020 Donruss Optic Stained Glass

RANDOM INSERTS IN PACKS
1 Nolan Arenado .50 1.25
2 Christian Yelich .50 1.25
3 Trey Mancini .40 1.00
4 Miguel Cabrera .40 1.00
5 Ketel Marte .30 .75
6 Gavin Lux 4.00 10.00
7 Rafael Devers .50 1.25
8 Evan White .25 .60
9 Bo Bichette 3.00 8.00
10 Matt Chapman .40 1.00
11 Gleyber Torres .75 2.00
12 Bryce Harper .60 1.50
13 Josh Donaldson .30 .75
14 Yoshitomo Tsutsugo .30 .75
15 Kris Bryant .50 1.25

2020 Donruss Optic Stained Glass Holo

*HOLO: 1X TO 2.5X BASIC
RANDOM INSERTS IN PACKS
1 Nolan Arenado 5.00 12.00

2020 Donruss Optic The Rookies

RANDOM INSERTS IN PACKS
1 Yordan Alvarez 3.00 8.00
2 Dylan Cease .50 1.25
3 Dustin May 1.00 2.50
4 Aristides Aquino .50 1.25
5 A.J. Puk .50 1.25
6 Bo Bichette 3.00 8.00
7 Brendan McKay .40 1.00
8 Gavin Lux 1.50 4.00
9 Luis Robert 5.00 12.00
10 Yoshitomo Tsutsugo .30 .75

2020 Donruss Optic The Rookies Holo

*HOLO: 1X TO 2.5X BASIC
RANDOM INSERTS IN PACKS
3 Dustin May 3.00 8.00
5 A.J. Puk 3.00 8.00
8 Gavin Lux 5.00 12.00

1993 Finest

This 199-card standard-size single series set is widely recognized as one of the most important issues of the 1990's. The Finest brand was Topps first attempt at the super-premium card market. Production was announced at 4,000 cases and cards were distributed exclusively through hobby dealers in the fall of 1993. This was the first time in the history of the hobby that a major manufacturer publicly released production figures. Cards were issued in seven-card foil fin-wrapped packs that carried a suggested retail price of $3.99. The product was a smashing success upon release with pack prices immediately soaring well above suggested retail prices. The popularity of the product has continued to grow throughout the years as it's place in hobby lore is now well soldified. The cards have silver-blue metallic finishes on their fronts and feature color player action photos. The set's title appears at the top, and the player's name is shown at the bottom. J.T. Snow is the only Rookie Card of note in this set.

COMPLETE SET (199) 40.00 100.00
1 David Justice 1.00 2.50
2 Lou Whitaker 1.00 2.50
3 Bryan Harvey .60 1.50
4 Carlos Garcia .60 1.50
5 Sid Fernandez .60 1.50
6 Brett Butler 1.00 2.50
7 Scott Cooper .60 1.50
8 B.J. Surhoff 1.00 2.50
9 Steve Finley 1.00 2.50
10 Curt Schilling 1.00 2.50
11 Jeff Bagwell 1.50 4.00
12 Alex Cole .60 1.50
13 John Olerud 1.00 2.50
14 John Smiley .60 1.50
15 Bip Roberts .60 1.50
16 Albert Belle 1.00 2.50
17 Duane Ward .60 1.50
18 Alan Trammell 1.00 2.50
19 Andy Benes .60 1.50
20 Reggie Sanders 1.00 2.50
21 Todd Zeile .60 1.50
22 Rick Aguilera .60 1.50
23 Dave Hollins .60 1.50
24 Jose Rijo .60 1.50
25 Matt Williams 1.00 2.50
26 Sandy Alomar Jr. .60 1.50
27 Alex Fernandez .60 1.50
28 Ozzie Smith 4.00 10.00
29 Ramon Martinez .60 1.50
30 Bernie Williams 1.50 4.00
31 Gary Sheffield 1.00 2.50
32 Eric Karros 1.00 2.50
33 Frank Viola 1.00 2.50
34 Kevin Young 1.00 2.50
35 Ken Hill .60 1.50
36 Tony Fernandez .60 1.50
37 Tim Wakefield 2.50 6.00
38 John Kruk 1.00 2.50
39 Chris Sabo .60 1.50
40 Marquis Grissom 1.00 2.50
41 Glenn Davis .60 1.50
42 Jeff Montgomery .60 1.50
43 Kenny Lofton 1.00 2.50
44 John Burkett .60 1.50
45 Darryl Hamilton .60 1.50
46 Jim Abbott 1.50 4.00
47 Ivan Rodriguez 1.50 4.00
48 Eric Young .60 1.50
49 Mitch Williams .60 1.50
50 Harold Reynolds 1.00 2.50
51 Brian Harper .60 1.50
52 Rafael Palmeiro 1.50 4.00
53 Bret Saberhagen 1.00 2.50
54 Jeff Conine 1.00 2.50
55 Ivan Calderon .60 1.50
56 Juan Guzman .60 1.50
57 Carlos Baerga .60 1.50
58 Charles Nagy .60 1.50
59 Wally Joyner 1.00 2.50
60 Charlie Hayes .60 1.50
61 Shane Mack .60 1.50
62 Pete Harnisch .60 1.50
63 George Brett 6.00 15.00
64 Lance Johnson .60 1.50
65 Ben McDonald .60 1.50
66 Bobby Bonilla 1.00 2.50
67 Terry Steinbach .60 1.50
68 Ron Gant 1.00 2.50
69 Doug Jones .60 1.50
70 Paul Molitor 1.00 2.50
71 Brady Anderson 1.00 2.50
72 Chuck Finley 1.00 2.50
73 Mark Grace 1.50 4.00
74 Mike Devereaux .60 1.50
75 Tony Phillips .60 1.50
76 Chuck Knoblauch 1.00 2.50
77 Tony Gwynn 3.00 8.00
78 Kevin Appier 1.00 2.50
79 Sammy Sosa 2.50 6.00
80 Mickey Tettleton .60 1.50
81 Felix Jose .60 1.50
82 Mark Langston .60 1.50
83 Gregg Jefferies .60 1.50
84 Andre Dawson AS 1.00 2.50
85 Greg Maddux AS 4.00 10.00
86 Rickey Henderson AS 2.50 6.00
87 Tom Glavine AS 1.50 4.00
88 Roberto Alomar AS 1.50 4.00
89 Darryl Strawberry AS 1.00 2.50
90 Wade Boggs AS 1.50 4.00
91 Bo Jackson AS 2.50 6.00
92 Mark McGwire AS 6.00 15.00
93 Robin Ventura AS 1.00 2.50
94 Joe Carter AS 1.00 2.50
95 Lee Smith AS 1.00 2.50
96 Cal Ripken AS 8.00 20.00
97 Larry Walker AS 1.00 2.50
98 Don Mattingly AS 6.00 15.00
99 Jose Canseco AS 1.50 4.00
100 Dennis Eckersley AS 1.00 2.50
101 Terry Pendleton AS 1.00 2.50

102 Frank Thomas AS 2.50 6.00
103 Barry Bonds AS 6.00 15.00
104 Roger Clemens AS 5.00 12.00
105 Ryne Sandberg AS 4.00 10.00
106 Fred McGriff AS 1.50 4.00
107 Nolan Ryan AS 10.00 25.00
108 Will Clark AS 1.50 4.00
109 Pat Listach AS .60 1.50
110 Ken Griffey Jr. AS 5.00 12.00
111 Cecil Fielder AS 1.00 2.50
112 Kirby Puckett AS 2.50 6.00
113 Dwight Gooden AS 1.00 2.50
114 Barry Larkin AS 1.50 4.00
115 David Cone AS 1.00 2.50
116 Juan Gonzalez AS 1.00 2.50
117 Kent Hrbek 1.00 2.50
118 Tim Wallach .60 1.50
119 Craig Biggio 1.50 4.00
120 Roberto Kelly .60 1.50
121 Gregg Olson .60 1.50
122 Eddie Murray UER 2.50 6.00
122 career strikeouts
should be 1224
123 Wil Cordero .60 1.50
124 Jay Buhner 1.00 2.50
125 Carlton Fisk 1.50 4.00
126 Eric Davis 1.00 2.50
127 Doug Drabek .60 1.50
128 Ozzie Guillen 1.00 2.50
129 John Wetteland 1.00 2.50
130 Andres Galarraga 1.00 2.50
131 Ken Caminiti 1.00 2.50
132 Tom Candiotti .60 1.50
133 Pat Borders .60 1.50
134 Kevin Brown 1.00 2.50
135 Travis Fryman 1.00 2.50
136 Kevin Mitchell .60 1.50
137 Greg Swindell .60 1.50
138 Benito Santiago 1.00 2.50
139 Reggie Jefferson .60 1.50
140 Chris Bosio .60 1.50
141 Deion Sanders 1.50 4.00
142 Scott Erickson .60 1.50
143 Howard Johnson .60 1.50
144 Orestes Destrade .60 1.50
145 Jose Guzman .60 1.50
146 Chad Curtis .60 1.50
147 Cal Eldred .60 1.50
148 Willie Greene .60 1.50
149 Tommy Greene .60 1.50
150 Erik Hanson .60 1.50
151 Bob Welch .60 1.50
152 John Jaha .60 1.50
153 Harold Baines 1.00 2.50
154 Randy Johnson 2.50 6.00
155 Al Martin .60 1.50
156 J.T.Snow RC 1.50 4.00
157 Mike Mussina 1.50 4.00
158 Ruben Sierra 1.00 2.50
159 Dean Palmer 1.00 2.50
160 Steve Avery .60 1.50
161 Julio Franco 1.00 2.50
162 Dave Winfield 1.00 2.50
163 Tim Salmon 1.50 4.00
164 Tom Henke .60 1.50
165 Mo Vaughn 1.00 2.50
166 John Smoltz 1.50 4.00
167 Danny Tartabull .60 1.50
168 Delino DeShields .60 1.50
169 Charlie Hough 1.00 2.50
170 Paul O'Neill 1.50 4.00
171 Darren Daulton 1.00 2.50
172 Jack McDowell .60 1.50
173 Junior Felix .60 1.50
174 Jimmy Key 1.00 2.50
175 George Bell .60 1.50
176 Mike Stanton .60 1.50
177 Len Dykstra 1.00 2.50
178 Norm Charlton .60 1.50
179 Eric Anthony .60 1.50
180 Rob Dibble 1.00 2.50
181 Otis Nixon .60 1.50
182 Randy Myers .60 1.50
183 Tim Raines 1.00 2.50
184 Orel Hershiser 1.00 2.50
185 Andy Van Slyke 1.50 4.00
186 Mike Lansing RC 1.00 2.50
187 Ray Lankford 1.00 2.50
188 Mike Morgan .60 1.50
189 Moises Alou 1.00 2.50
190 Edgar Martinez 1.50 4.00
191 John Franco 1.00 2.50
192 Robin Yount 4.00 10.00
193 Bob Tewksbury .60 1.50
194 Jay Bell 1.00 2.50
195 Luis Gonzalez 1.00 2.50
196 Dave Fleming .60 1.50
197 Mike Greenwell .60 1.50
198 David Nied .60 1.50
199 Mike Piazza 6.00 15.00

1993 Finest Refractors

STATED ODDS 1:18
SP CL: 3/10/12/25/34/38-41/47/70/79-81/84
SP CL: 116/123/134/155/159/173/182/193
ASTERISK CARDS: PERCEIVED SCARCITY
28 Ozzie Smith 40.00 80.00
41 Glenn Davis* 60.00 120.00
47 Ivan Rodriguez * 75.00 150.00
63 George Brett 125.00 200.00
77 Tony Gwynn 60.00 120.00
79 Sammy Sosa * 30.00 60.00
81 Felix Jose* 40.00 80.00
85 Greg Maddux AS 100.00 200.00
88 Roberto Alomar AS 40.00 80.00
91 Bo Jackson AS 50.00 100.00
92 Mark McGwire AS 75.00 150.00
96 Cal Ripken AS 200.00 400.00
98 Don Mattingly AS 125.00 250.00
99 Jose Canseco AS ! 40.00 80.00
102 Frank Thomas AS 150.00 300.00
103 Barry Bonds AS 125.00 250.00
104 Roger Clemens AS 125.00 200.00
105 Ryne Sandberg AS 75.00 150.00
107 Nolan Ryan AS ! 300.00 500.00
108 Will Clark AS ! 40.00 80.00
110 Ken Griffey Jr. AS ! 250.00 600.00
112 Kirby Puckett AS 60.00 120.00
114 Barry Larkin AS 40.00 80.00
116 Juan Gonzalez AS * 150.00 250.00
122 Eddie Murray 60.00 120.00
144 Orestes Destrade 75.00 150.00
154 Randy Johnson 75.00 150.00
157 Mike Mussina 40.00 80.00
192 Robin Yount 60.00 120.00
199 Mike Piazza 100.00 200.00

1993 Finest Jumbos

*STARS: 1X TO 2.5X BASIC CARDS
ONE CARD PER SEALED BOX

1994 Finest Pre-Production

This 40-card preview standard-size set is identical in design to the basic Finest set. Cards were randomly inserted at a rate of one in 36 in second series Topps packs and three cards were issued with each Topps factory set. The card numbers on back correspond to those of the regular issue. The only way to distinguish between the preview and basic cards is "Pre-Production" in small red letters on back.

COMPLETE SET (40) 30.00 60.00
TOPPS SER.2 ODDS 1:36H/R,1:15J,1:28 CEL
THREE PER REGULAR TOPPS FACTORY SET
NUMBERS CORRESPOND TO BASIC SET
22P Deion Sanders 5.00 12.00
23P Jose Offerman 2.00 5.00
26P Alex Fernandez 2.00 5.00
31P Steve Finley 3.00 8.00
35P Andres Galarraga 3.00 8.00
43P Reggie Sanders 3.00 8.00
47P Dave Hollins 2.00 5.00
52P David Cone 3.00 8.00
59P Dante Bichette 3.00 8.00
61P Orlando Merced 2.00 5.00
62P Brian McRae 2.00 5.00
66P Mike Mussina 5.00 12.00
76P Mike Stanley 2.00 5.00
78P Mark McGwire 20.00 50.00
79P Pat Listach 2.00 5.00
82P Dwight Gooden 3.00 8.00
84P Phil Plantier 2.00 5.00
90P Jeff Russell 2.00 5.00
92P Gregg Jefferies 2.00 5.00
93P Jose Guzman 2.00 5.00
100P John Smoltz 5.00 12.00
102P Jim Thome 5.00 12.00
121P Moises Alou 3.00 8.00
125P Devon White 3.00 8.00
126P Ivan Rodriguez 5.00 12.00
130P Dave Magadan 2.00 5.00
136P Ozzie Smith 12.50 30.00
141P Chris Hoiles 2.00 5.00
149P Jim Abbott 5.00 12.00
151P Bill Swift 2.00 5.00
154P Edgar Martinez 5.00 12.00
157P J.T. Snow 3.00 8.00
159P Alan Trammell 3.00 8.00
163P Roberto Kelly 2.00 5.00
166P Scott Erickson 2.00 5.00
168P Scott Cooper 2.00 5.00
169P Rod Beck 2.00 5.00
177P Dean Palmer 3.00 8.00
182P Todd Van Poppel 2.00 5.00
185P Paul Sorrento 2.00 5.00

1994 Finest

The 1994 Topps Finest baseball set consists of two series of 220 cards each, for a total of 440 standard-size cards. Each series includes 40 special design Finest cards: 20 top 1993 rookies (1-20), 20 top 1994 rookies (421-440) and 40 top veterans (201-240). It's believed that these subset cards are in slightly shorter supply than the basic issue cards, but the manufacturer has never confirmed this. These glossy and metallic cards have a color photo on front with green and gold borders. A color photo on back is accompanied by statistics and a "Finest Moment" note. Some series 2 packs contained either one or two series 1 cards. The only notable Rookie Card is Chan Ho Park.

COMPLETE SET (440) 30.00 80.00
COMPLETE SERIES 1 (220) 15.00 40.00
COMPLETE SERIES 2 (220) 15.00 40.00
SOME SER.2 PACKS HAVE 1 OR 2 SER.1 CARDS
1 Mike Piazza FIN 2.50 6.00
2 Kevin Stocker FIN .30 .75
3 Greg McMichael FIN .30 .75
4 Jeff Conine FIN .50 1.25
5 Rene Arocha FIN .30 .75
6 Aaron Sele FIN .30 .75
7 Brent Gates FIN .30 .75
8 Chuck Carr FIN .30 .75
9 Kirk Rueter FIN .30 .75
10 Mike Lansing FIN .30 .75
11 Al Martin FIN .30 .75
12 Jason Bere FIN .30 .75
13 Troy Neel FIN .30 .75
14 Armando Reynoso FIN .30 .75
15 Jeromy Burnitz FIN .50 1.25
16 Rich Amaral FIN .30 .75
17 David McCarty FIN .30 .75
18 Tim Salmon FIN .75 2.00
19 Steve Cooke FIN .30 .75
20 Wil Cordero FIN .30 .75
21 Kevin Tapani .30 .75
22 Deion Sanders .75 2.00
23 Jose Offerman .30 .75
24 Mark Langston .30 .75
25 Ken Hill .30 .75
26 Alex Fernandez .30 .75
27 Jeff Blauser .30 .75
28 Royce Clayton .30 .75
29 Brad Ausmus .75 2.00
30 Ryan Bowen .30 .75
31 Steve Finley .50 1.25
32 Charlie Hayes .30 .75
33 Jeff Kent .75 2.00
34 Mike Henneman .30 .75
35 Andres Galarraga .50 1.25
36 Wayne Kirby .30 .75
37 Joe Oliver .30 .75
38 Terry Steinbach .30 .75
39 Ryan Thompson .30 .75
40 Luis Alicea .30 .75
41 Randy Velarde .30 .75
42 Bob Tewksbury .30 .75
43 Reggie Sanders .50 1.25
44 Brian Williams .30 .75
45 Joe Orsulak .30 .75
46 Jose Lind .30 .75
47 Dave Hollins .30 .75
48 Graeme Lloyd .30 .75
49 Jim Gott .30 .75
50 Andre Dawson .50 1.25
51 Steve Buechele .30 .75
52 David Cone .50 1.25
53 Ricky Gutierrez .30 .75
54 Lance Johnson .30 .75
55 Tino Martinez .75 2.00
56 Phil Hiatt .30 .75
57 Carlos Garcia .30 .75
58 Danny Darwin .30 .75
59 Dante Bichette .50 1.25
60 Scott Kamieniecki .30 .75
61 Orlando Merced .30 .75
62 Brian McRae .30 .75
63 Pat Kelly .30 .75
64 Tom Henke .30 .75
65 Jeff King .30 .75
66 Mike Mussina .75 2.00
67 Tim Pugh .30 .75
68 Robby Thompson .30 .75
69 Paul O'Neill .75 2.00
70 Hal Morris .30 .75
71 Ron Karkovice .30 .75
72 Joe Girardi .30 .75
73 Eduardo Perez .30 .75
74 Raul Mondesi .50 1.25
75 Mike Gallego .30 .75
76 Mike Stanley .30 .75
77 Kevin Roberson .30 .75
78 Mark McGwire 3.00 8.00
79 Pat Listach .30 .75
80 Eric Davis .50 1.25
81 Mike Bordick .30 .75
82 Dwight Gooden .50 1.25
83 Mike Moore .30 .75
84 Phil Plantier .30 .75
85 Darren Lewis .30 .75
86 Rick Wilkins .30 .75
87 Darryl Strawberry .50 1.25
88 Rob Dibble .50 1.25
89 Greg Vaughn .30 .75
90 Jeff Russell .30 .75
91 Mark Lewis .30 .75
92 Gregg Jefferies .30 .75
93 Jose Guzman .30 .75
94 Kenny Rogers .50 1.25
95 Mark Lemke .30 .75
96 Mike Morgan .30 .75
97 Andujar Cedeno .30 .75
98 Orel Hershiser .50 1.25
99 Greg Swindell .30 .75
100 John Smoltz .75 2.00
101 Pedro A.Martinez RC .30 .75
102 Jim Thome .75 2.00
103 David Segui .30 .75
104 Charles Nagy .30 .75
105 Shane Mack .30 .75
106 John Jaha .30 .75
107 Tom Candiotti .30 .75
108 David Wells .50 1.25
109 Bobby Jones .30 .75
110 Bob Hamelin .30 .75
111 Bernard Gilkey .30 .75
112 Chili Davis .50 1.25
113 Todd Stottlemyre .30 .75
114 Derek Bell .30 .75
115 Mark McLemore .30 .75
116 Mark Whiten .30 .75
117 Mike Devereaux .30 .75
118 Terry Pendleton .50 1.25
119 Pat Meares .30 .75
120 Pete Harnisch .30 .75
121 Moises Alou .50 1.25
122 Jay Buhner .50 1.25
123 Wes Chamberlain .30 .75
124 Mike Perez .30 .75
125 Devon White .50 1.25
126 Ivan Rodriguez .75 2.00
127 Don Slaught .30 .75
128 John Valentin .30 .75
129 Jaime Navarro .30 .75
130 Dave Magadan .30 .75
131 Brady Anderson .50 1.25
132 Juan Guzman .30 .75
133 John Wetteland .50 1.25
134 Dave Stewart .50 1.25
135 Scott Servais .30 .75
136 Ozzie Smith 2.00 5.00
137 Darrin Fletcher .30 .75
138 Jose Mesa .30 .75
139 Wilson Alvarez .30 .75
140 Pete Incaviglia .30 .75
141 Chris Hoiles .30 .75
142 Darryl Hamilton .30 .75
143 Chuck Finley .50 1.25
144 Archi Cianfrocco .30 .75
145 Bill Wegman .30 .75
146 Joey Cora .30 .75
147 Darrell Whitmore .30 .75
148 David Hulse .30 .75
149 Jim Abbott .75 2.00
150 Curt Schilling .50 1.25
151 Bill Swift .30 .75
152 Tommy Greene .30 .75
153 Roberto Mejia .30 .75
154 Edgar Martinez .75 2.00
155 Roger Pavlik .30 .75
156 Randy Tomlin .30 .75
157 J.T. Snow .50 1.25
158 Bob Welch .30 .75
159 Alan Trammell .50 1.25
160 Ed Sprague .30 .75
161 Ben McDonald .30 .75
162 Derrick May .30 .75
163 Roberto Kelly .30 .75
164 Bryan Harvey .30 .75
165 Ron Gant .50 1.25
166 Scott Erickson .30 .75
167 Anthony Young .30 .75
168 Scott Cooper .30 .75
169 Rod Beck .30 .75
170 John Franco .50 1.25
171 Gary DiSarcina .30 .75
172 Dave Fleming .30 .75
173 Wade Boggs .75 2.00
174 Kevin Appier .50 1.25
175 Jose Bautista .30 .75
176 Wally Joyner .50 1.25
177 Dean Palmer .50 1.25
178 Tony Phillips .30 .75
179 John Smiley .30 .75
180 Charlie Hough .50 1.25
181 Scott Fletcher .30 .75
182 Todd Van Poppel .30 .75
183 Mike Blowers .30 .75
184 Willie McGee .50 1.25
185 Paul Sorrento .30 .75
186 Eric Young .30 .75
187 Bret Barberie .30 .75
188 Manuel Lee .30 .75
189 Jeff Branson .30 .75
190 Jim Deshaies .30 .75
191 Ken Caminiti .50 1.25
192 Tim Raines .50 1.25
193 Joe Grahe .30 .75
194 Hipolito Pichardo .30 .75
195 Denny Neagle .50 1.25
196 Dave Staton .30 .75
197 Mike Benjamin .30 .75
198 Milt Thompson .30 .75
199 Bruce Ruffin .30 .75
200 Chris Hammond UER .30 .75
Back of card has Mariners;
should be Marlins
201 Tony Gwynn FIN 1.50 4.00
202 Robin Ventura FIN .50 1.25
203 Frank Thomas FIN 1.25 3.00
204 Kirby Puckett FIN 1.25 3.00
205 Roberto Alomar FIN .75 2.00
206 Dennis Eckersley FIN .50 1.25
207 Joe Carter FIN .50 1.25
208 Albert Belle FIN .50 1.25
209 Greg Maddux FIN 2.00 5.00
210 Ryne Sandberg FIN 2.00 5.00
211 Juan Gonzalez FIN .50 1.25
212 Jeff Bagwell FIN .75 2.00
213 Randy Johnson FIN 1.25 3.00
214 Matt Williams FIN .50 1.25
215 Dave Winfield FIN .50 1.25
216 Larry Walker FIN .50 1.25
217 Roger Clemens FIN 2.50 6.00
218 Kenny Lofton FIN .50 1.25
219 Cecil Fielder FIN .50 1.25
220 Darren Daulton FIN .50 1.25
221 John Olerud FIN .50 1.25
222 Jose Canseco FIN .75 2.00
223 Rickey Henderson FIN 1.25 3.00
224 Fred McGriff FIN .75 2.00
225 Gary Sheffield FIN .50 1.25
226 Jack McDowell FIN .50 1.25
227 Rafael Palmeiro FIN .75 2.00
228 Travis Fryman FIN .50 1.25
229 Marquis Grissom FIN .50 1.25
230 Barry Bonds FIN 3.00 8.00
231 Carlos Baerga FIN .30 .75
232 Ken Griffey Jr. FIN 2.50 6.00
233 David Justice FIN .50 1.25
234 Bobby Bonilla FIN .50 1.25
235 Cal Ripken FIN 4.00 10.00
236 Sammy Sosa FIN 1.25 3.00
237 Len Dykstra FIN .50 1.25
238 Will Clark FIN .75 2.00
239 Paul Molitor FIN .50 1.25
240 Barry Larkin FIN .75 2.00
241 Bo Jackson 1.25 3.00
242 Mitch Williams .30 .75
243 Ron Darling .30 .75
244 Darryl Kile .50 1.25
245 Geronimo Berroa .30 .75
246 Gregg Olson .30 .75
247 Brian Harper .30 .75
248 Rheal Cormier .30 .75
249 Rey Sanchez .30 .75
250 Jeff Fassero .30 .75
251 Sandy Alomar Jr. .30 .75
252 Chris Bosio .30 .75
253 Andy Stankiewicz .30 .75
254 Harold Baines .50 1.25
255 Andy Ashby .30 .75
256 Tyler Green .30 .75
257 Kevin Brown .50 1.25
258 Mo Vaughn .50 1.25
259 Mike Harkey .30 .75
260 Dave Henderson .30 .75
261 Kent Hrbek .50 1.25
262 Darrin Jackson .30 .75
263 Bob Wickman .30 .75
264 Spike Owen .30 .75
265 Todd Jones .30 .75
266 Pat Borders .30 .75
267 Tom Glavine .75 2.00
268 Dave Nilsson .30 .75
269 Rich Batchelor .30 .75
270 Delino DeShields .30 .75
271 Felix Fermin .30 .75
272 Orestes Destrade .30 .75
273 Mickey Morandini .30 .75
274 Otis Nixon .30 .75
275 Ellis Burks .50 1.25
276 Greg Gagne .30 .75
277 John Doherty .30 .75
278 Julio Franco .50 1.25
279 Bernie Williams .75 2.00
280 Rick Aguilera .30 .75
281 Mickey Tettleton .30 .75
282 David Nied .30 .75
283 Johnny Ruffin .30 .75
284 Dan Wilson .30 .75
285 Omar Vizquel .75 2.00
286 Willie Banks .30 .75
287 Erik Pappas .30 .75
288 Cal Eldred .30 .75
289 Bobby Witt .30 .75
290 Luis Gonzalez .50 1.25
291 Greg Pirkl .30 .75
292 Alex Cole .30 .75
293 Ricky Bones .30 .75
294 Denis Boucher .30 .75
295 John Burkett .30 .75
296 Steve Trachsel .30 .75
297 Ricky Jordan .30 .75
298 Mark Dewey .30 .75
299 Jimmy Key .50 1.25
300 Mike Macfarlane .30 .75
301 Tim Belcher .30 .75
302 Carlos Reyes .30 .75
303 Greg A. Harris .30 .75
304 Brian Anderson RC .50 1.25
305 Terry Mulholland .30 .75
306 Felix Jose .30 .75
307 Darren Holmes .30 .75
308 Jose Rijo .30 .75
309 Paul Wagner .30 .75
310 Bob Scanlan .30 .75
311 Mike Jackson .30 .75
312 Jose Vizcaino .30 .75
313 Rob Butler .30 .75
314 Kevin Seitzer .30 .75
315 Geronimo Pena .30 .75
316 Hector Carrasco .30 .75
317 Eddie Murray 1.25 3.00
318 Roger Salkeld .30 .75
319 Todd Hundley .30 .75
320 Danny Jackson .30 .75
321 Kevin Young .30 .75
322 Mike Greenwell .30 .75
323 Kevin Mitchell .30 .75
324 Chuck Knoblauch .50 1.25
325 Danny Tartabull .30 .75
326 Vince Coleman .30 .75
327 Marvin Freeman .30 .75
328 Andy Benes .30 .75
329 Mike Kelly .30 .75
330 Karl Rhodes .30 .75
331 Allen Watson .30 .75
332 Damion Easley .30 .75
333 Reggie Jefferson .30 .75
334 Kevin McReynolds .30 .75
335 Arthur Rhodes .30 .75
336 Brian Hunter .30 .75
337 Tom Browning .30 .75
338 Pedro Munoz .30 .75
339 Billy Ripken .30 .75
340 Gene Harris .30 .75
341 Fernando Vina .30 .75
342 Sean Berry .30 .75
343 Pedro Astacio .30 .75
344 B.J. Surhoff .50 1.25
345 Doug Drabek .30 .75
346 Jody Reed .30 .75
347 Ray Lankford .50 1.25
348 Steve Farr .30 .75
349 Eric Anthony .30 .75
350 Pete Smith .30 .75
351 Lee Smith .50 1.25
352 Mariano Duncan .30 .75
353 Doug Strange .30 .75
354 Tim Bogar .30 .75
355 Dave Weathers .30 .75
356 Eric Karros .50 1.25
357 Randy Myers .30 .75
358 Chad Curtis .30 .75
359 Steve Avery .30 .75
360 Brian Jordan .50 1.25
361 Tim Wallach .30 .75
362 Pedro Martinez 1.25 3.00
363 Bip Roberts .30 .75
364 Lou Whitaker .50 1.25
365 Luis Polonia .30 .75
366 Benito Santiago .50 1.25
367 Brett Butler .50 1.25
368 Shawon Dunston .30 .75
369 Kelly Stinnett RC .50 1.25
370 Chris Turner .30 .75
371 Ruben Sierra .50 1.25
372 Greg A. Harris .30 .75
373 Xavier Hernandez .30 .75
374 Howard Johnson .30 .75
375 Duane Ward .30 .75
376 Roberto Hernandez .30 .75
377 Scott Leius .30 .75
378 Dave Valle .30 .75
379 Sid Fernandez .30 .75
380 Doug Jones .30 .75
381 Zane Smith .30 .75
382 Craig Biggio .75 2.00
383 Rick White RC .30 .75
384 Tom Pagnozzi .30 .75
385 Chris James .30 .75
386 Bret Boone .50 1.25
387 Jeff Montgomery .30 .75
388 Chad Kreuter .30 .75
389 Greg Hibbard .30 .75
390 Mark Grace .75 2.00
391 Phil Leftwich RC .30 .75
392 Don Mattingly 3.00 8.00
393 Ozzie Guillen .50 1.25
394 Gary Gaetti .50 1.25
395 Erik Hanson .30 .75
396 Scott Brosius .50 1.25
397 Tom Gordon .30 .75
398 Bill Gullickson .30 .75
399 Matt Mieske .30 .75
400 Pat Hentgen .30 .75
401 Walt Weiss .30 .75
402 Greg Blosser .30 .75
403 Stan Javier .30 .75
404 Doug Henry .30 .75
405 Ramon Martinez .30 .75
406 Frank Viola .50 1.25
407 Mike Hampton .50 1.25
408 Andy Van Slyke .75 2.00
409 Bobby Ayala .30 .75
410 Todd Zeile .30 .75
411 Jay Bell .50 1.25
412 Dennis Martinez .50 1.25
413 Mark Portugal .30 .75
414 Bobby Munoz .30 .75
415 Kirt Manwaring .30 .75
416 John Kruk .50 1.25
417 Trevor Hoffman .75 2.00
418 Chris Sabo .30 .75
419 Bret Saberhagen .50 1.25
420 Chris Nabholz .30 .75
421 James Mouton FIN .30 .75
422 Tony Tarasco FIN .30 .75
423 Carlos Delgado FIN .75 2.00
424 Rondell White FIN .50 1.25
425 Javier Lopez FIN .50 1.25
426 Chan Ho Park FIN RC .75 2.00
427 Cliff Floyd FIN .50 1.25
428 Dave Staton FIN .30 .75
429 J.R. Phillips FIN .30 .75
430 Manny Ramirez FIN 1.25 3.00
431 Kurt Abbott FIN RC .30 .75
432 Melvin Nieves FIN .30 .75
433 Alex Gonzalez FIN .30 .75
434 Rick Helling FIN .30 .75
435 Danny Bautista FIN .30 .75
436 Matt Walbeck FIN .30 .75
437 Ryan Klesko FIN .50 1.25
438 Steve Karsay FIN .30 .75
439 Salomon Torres FIN .30 .75
440 Scott Ruffcorn FIN .30 .75

1994 Finest Refractors

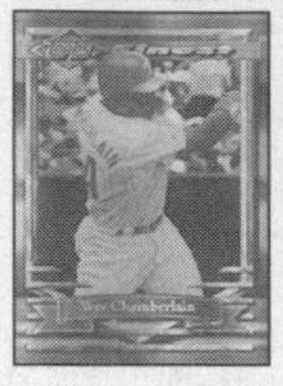

COMPLETE SET (440) 2000.00 3000.00
*STARS: 2.5X TO 6X BASIC CARDS
*ROOKIES: 1.5X TO 4X BASIC CARDS
STATED ODDS 1:9
240 Barry Larkin FIN 15.00 40.00

1994 Finest Jumbos

COMPLETE SET (80) 175.00 350.00
*JUMBOS: 1.25X TO 3X BASIC CARDS
ONE JUMBO PER BOX

1994 Finest Superstar Samplers

1 Mike Piazza 6.00 15.00
18 Tim Salmon 1.25 3.00
35 Andres Galarraga 2.50 6.00
74 Raul Mondesi 1.25 3.00
92 Gregg Jefferies .75 2.00
201 Tony Gwynn 6.00 15.00
203 Frank Thomas 4.00 10.00
204 Kirby Puckett 4.00 10.00
205 Roberto Alomar 2.50 6.00
207 Joe Carter 1.25 3.00
208 Albert Belle 1.25 3.00
209 Greg Maddux 8.00 20.00
210 Ryne Sandberg 5.00 12.00
211 Juan Gonzalez 2.50 6.00
212 Jeff Bagwell 4.00 10.00
213 Randy Johnson 5.00 12.00
214 Matt Williams 2.00 5.00
216 Larry Walker 3.00 8.00
217 Roger Clemens 6.00 15.00
219 Cecil Fielder 1.25 3.00
220 Darren Daulton 1.25 3.00
221 John Olerud 1.25 3.00
222 Jose Canseco 4.00 10.00
224 Fred McGriff 2.00 5.00
225 Gary Sheffield 4.00 10.00
226 Jack McDowell .75 2.00
227 Rafael Palmeiro 3.00 8.00
229 Marquis Grissom 1.25 3.00
230 Barry Bonds 6.00 15.00
231 Carlos Baerga .75 2.00
232 Ken Griffey Jr. 8.00 20.00
233 David Justice 2.50 6.00
234 Bobby Bonilla 1.25 3.00
235 Cal Ripken 12.00 30.00
237 Len Dykstra .75 2.00
238 Will Clark 2.50 6.00
239 Paul Molitor 3.00 8.00
240 Barry Larkin 2.50 6.00
258 Mo Vaughn 1.25 3.00
267 Tom Glavine 3.00 8.00
390 Mark Grace 2.00 5.00
392 Don Mattingly 3.00 8.00
408 Andy Van Slyke .75 2.00
427 Cliff Floyd 2.00 5.00
430 Manny Ramirez 4.00 10.00

1995 Finest

Consisting of 330 standard-size cards, this set (produced by Topps) was issued in series of 220 and 110. A protective film, designed to keep the card from scratching and to maintain original gloss, covers the front. With the Finest logo at the top, a silver baseball diamond design surrounded by green (field) form the background to an action photo. Horizontally designed backs have a photo to the right with statistical information to the left. A Finest Moment, or career highlight, is also included. Rookie Cards in this set include Bobby Higginson and Hideo Nomo.

Card	Low	High
COMPLETE SET (330)	25.00	60.00
COMPLETE SERIES 1 (220)	20.00	50.00
COMPLETE SERIES 2 (110)	6.00	15.00
1 Raul Mondesi	.40	1.00
2 Kurt Abbott	.20	.50
3 Chris Gomez	.20	.50
4 Manny Ramirez	.60	1.50
5 Rondell White	.40	1.00
6 William VanLandingham	.20	.50
7 Jon Lieber	.20	.50
8 Ryan Klesko	.40	1.00
9 John Hudek	.20	.50
10 Joey Hamilton	.20	.50
11 Bob Hamelin	.20	.50
12 Brian Anderson	.20	.50
13 Mike Lieberthal	.40	1.00
14 Rico Brogna	.20	.50
15 Rusty Greer	.40	1.00
16 Carlos Delgado	.40	1.00
17 Jim Edmonds	.60	1.50
18 Steve Trachsel	.20	.50
19 Matt Walbeck	.20	.50
20 Armando Benitez	.20	.50
21 Steve Karsay	.20	.50
22 Jose Oliva	.20	.50
23 Cliff Floyd	.40	1.00
24 Kevin Foster	.20	.50
25 Javier Lopez	.40	1.00
26 Jose Valentin	.20	.50
27 James Mouton	.20	.50
28 Hector Carrasco	.20	.50
29 Orlando Miller	.20	.50
30 Garret Anderson	.40	1.00
31 Marvin Freeman	.20	.50
32 Brett Butler	.40	1.00
33 Roberto Kelly	.20	.50
34 Rod Beck	.20	.50
35 Jose Rijo	.20	.50
36 Edgar Martinez	.60	1.50
37 Jim Thome	.60	1.50
38 Rick Wilkins	.20	.50
39 Wally Joyner	.40	1.00
40 Wil Cordero	.20	.50
41 Tommy Greene	.20	.50
42 Travis Fryman	.40	1.00
43 Don Slaught	.20	.50
44 Brady Anderson	.40	1.00
45 Matt Williams	.40	1.00
46 Rene Arocha	.20	.50
47 Rickey Henderson	1.00	2.50
48 Mike Mussina	.60	1.50
49 Greg McMichael	.20	.50
50 Jody Reed	.20	.50
51 Tino Martinez	.60	1.50
52 Dave Clark	.20	.50
53 John Valentin	.20	.50
54 Bret Boone	.40	1.00
55 Walt Weiss	.20	.50
56 Kenny Lofton	.40	1.00
57 Scott Leius	.20	.50
58 Eric Karros	.40	1.00
59 John Olerud	.40	1.00
60 Chris Hoiles	.20	.50
61 Sandy Alomar Jr.	.20	.50
62 Tim Wallach	.20	.50
63 Cal Eldred	.20	.50
64 Tom Glavine	.60	1.50
65 Mark Grace	.60	1.50
66 Rey Sanchez	.20	.50
67 Bobby Ayala	.20	.50
68 Dante Bichette	.40	1.00
69 Andres Galarraga	.40	1.00
70 Chuck Carr	.20	.50
71 Bobby Witt	.20	.50
72 Steve Avery	.20	.50
73 Bobby Jones	.20	.50
74 Delino DeShields	.20	.50
75 Kevin Tapani	.20	.50
76 Randy Johnson	1.00	2.50
77 David Nied	.20	.50
78 Pat Hentgen	.20	.50
79 Tim Salmon	.60	1.50
80 Todd Zeile	.20	.50
81 John Wetteland	.40	1.00
82 Albert Belle	.40	1.00
83 Ben McDonald	.20	.50
84 Bobby Munoz	.20	.50
85 Bip Roberts	.20	.50
86 Mo Vaughn	.40	1.00
87 Chuck Finley	.40	1.00
88 Chuck Knoblauch	.40	1.00
89 Frank Thomas	1.00	2.50
90 Danny Tartabull	.20	.50
91 Dean Palmer	.40	1.00
92 Len Dykstra	.40	1.00
93 J.R. Phillips	.20	.50
94 Tom Candiotti	.20	.50
95 Marquis Grissom	.40	1.00
96 Barry Larkin	.60	1.50
97 Bryan Harvey	.20	.50
98 David Justice	.40	1.00
99 David Cone	.40	1.00
100 Wade Boggs	.60	1.50
101 Jason Bere	.20	.50
102 Hal Morris	.20	.50
103 Fred McGriff	.60	1.50
104 Bobby Bonilla	.40	1.00
105 Jay Buhner	.40	1.00
106 Allen Watson	.20	.50
107 Mickey Tettleton	.20	.50
108 Kevin Appier	.40	1.00
109 Ivan Rodriguez	.60	1.50
110 Carlos Garcia	.20	.50
111 Andy Benes	.20	.50
112 Eddie Murray	1.00	2.50
113 Mike Piazza	1.50	4.00
114 Greg Vaughn	.20	.50
115 Paul Molitor	.40	1.00
116 Terry Steinbach	.20	.50
117 Jeff Bagwell	.60	1.50
118 Ken Griffey Jr.	4.00	10.00
119 Gary Sheffield	.40	1.00
120 Cal Ripken	3.00	8.00
121 Jeff Kent	.40	1.00
122 Jay Bell	.40	1.00
123 Will Clark	.60	1.50
124 Cecil Fielder	.40	1.00
125 Alex Fernandez	.20	.50
126 Don Mattingly	2.50	6.00
127 Reggie Sanders	.40	1.00
128 Moises Alou	.40	1.00
129 Craig Biggio	.60	1.50
130 Eddie Williams	.20	.50
131 John Franco	.40	1.00
132 John Kruk	.40	1.00
133 Jeff King	.20	.50
134 Royce Clayton	.20	.50
135 Doug Drabek	.20	.50
136 Ray Lankford	.40	1.00
137 Roberto Alomar	.60	1.50
138 Todd Hundley	.20	.50
139 Alex Cole	.20	.50
140 Shawon Dunston	.20	.50
141 John Roper	.20	.50
142 Mark Langston	.20	.50
143 Tom Pagnozzi	.20	.50
144 Wilson Alvarez	.20	.50
145 Scott Cooper	.20	.50
146 Kevin Mitchell	.20	.50
147 Mark Whiten	.20	.50
148 Jeff Conine	.40	1.00
149 Chili Davis	.40	1.00
150 Luis Gonzalez	.40	1.00
151 Juan Guzman	.20	.50
152 Mike Greenwell	.20	.50
153 Mike Henneman	.20	.50
154 Rick Aguilera	.20	.50
155 Dennis Eckersley	.40	1.00
156 Darrin Fletcher	.20	.50
157 Darren Lewis	.20	.50
158 Juan Gonzalez	.40	1.00
159 Dave Hollins	.20	.50
160 Jimmy Key	.40	1.00
161 Roberto Hernandez	.20	.50
162 Randy Myers	.20	.50
163 Joe Carter	.40	1.00
164 Darren Daulton	.40	1.00
165 Mike Macfarlane	.20	.50
166 Bret Saberhagen	.40	1.00
167 Kirby Puckett	1.00	2.50
168 Lance Johnson	.20	.50
169 Mark McGwire	2.50	6.00
170 Jose Canseco	.60	1.50
171 Mike Stanley	.20	.50
172 Lee Smith	.40	1.00
173 Robin Ventura	.40	1.00
174 Greg Gagne	.20	.50
175 Brian McRae	.20	.50
176 Mike Bordick	.20	.50
177 Rafael Palmeiro	.60	1.50
178 Kenny Rogers	.40	1.00
179 Chad Curtis	.20	.50
180 Devon White	.40	1.00
181 Paul O'Neill	.60	1.50
182 Ken Caminiti	.40	1.00
183 Dave Nilsson	.20	.50
184 Tim Naehring	.20	.50
185 Roger Clemens	2.00	5.00
186 Otis Nixon	.20	.50
187 Tim Raines	.40	1.00
188 Denny Martinez	.40	1.00
189 Pedro Martinez	.60	1.50
190 Jim Abbott	.60	1.50
191 Ryan Thompson	.20	.50
192 Barry Bonds	2.50	6.00
193 Joe Girardi	.20	.50
194 Steve Finley	.40	1.00
195 John Jaha	.20	.50
196 Tony Gwynn	1.25	3.00
197 Sammy Sosa	1.00	2.50
198 John Burkett	.20	.50
199 Carlos Baerga	.20	.50
200 Ramon Martinez	.20	.50
201 Aaron Sele	.20	.50
202 Eduardo Perez	.20	.50
203 Alan Trammell	.40	1.00
204 Orlando Merced	.20	.50
205 Deion Sanders	.60	1.50
206 Robb Nen	.40	1.00
207 Jack McDowell	.20	.50
208 Ruben Sierra	.40	1.00
209 Bernie Williams	.60	1.50
210 Kevin Seitzer	.20	.50
211 Charles Nagy	.40	1.00
212 Tony Phillips	.20	.50
213 Greg Maddux	1.50	4.00
214 Jeff Montgomery	.20	.50
215 Larry Walker	.40	1.00
216 Andy Van Slyke	.60	1.50
217 Ozzie Smith	1.50	4.00
218 Geronimo Pena	.20	.50
219 Gregg Jefferies	.20	.50
220 Lou Whitaker	.40	1.00
221 Chipper Jones	1.00	2.50
222 Benji Gil	.20	.50
223 Tony Phillips	.20	.50
224 Trevor Wilson	.20	.50
225 Tony Tarasco	.20	.50
226 Roberto Petagine	.20	.50
227 Mike Macfarlane	.20	.50
228 Hideo Nomo RC	4.00	10.00
229 Mark McLemore	.20	.50
230 Ron Gant	.40	1.00
231 Andujar Cedeno	.20	.50
232 Michael Mimbs RC	.20	.50
233 Jim Abbott	.60	1.50
234 Ricky Bones	.20	.50
235 Marty Cordova	.20	.50
236 Mark Johnson RC	.50	1.25
237 Marquis Grissom	.40	1.00
238 Tom Henke	.20	.50
239 Terry Pendleton	.40	1.00
240 John Wetteland	.40	1.00
241 Lee Smith	.40	1.00
242 Jaime Navarro	.20	.50
243 Luis Alicea	.20	.50
244 Scott Cooper	.20	.50
245 Gary Gaetti	.40	1.00
246 Edgardo Alfonzo UER	.20	.50
Incomplete career BA		
247 Brad Clontz	.20	.50
248 Dave Mlicki	.20	.50
249 Dave Winfield	.40	1.00
250 Mark Grudzielanek RC	.75	2.00
251 Alex Gonzalez	.20	.50
252 Kevin Brown	.40	1.00
253 Esteban Loaiza	.20	.50
254 Vaughn Eshelman	.20	.50
255 Bill Swift	.20	.50
256 Brian McRae	.20	.50
257 Bob Higginson RC	.75	2.00
258 Jack McDowell	.20	.50
259 Scott Stahoviak	.20	.50
260 Jon Nunnally	.20	.50
261 Charlie Hayes	.20	.50
262 Jacob Brumfield	.20	.50
263 Chad Curtis	.20	.50
264 Heathcliff Slocumb	.20	.50
265 Mark Whiten	.20	.50
266 Mickey Tettleton	.20	.50
267 Jose Mesa	.20	.50
268 Doug Jones	.20	.50
269 Trevor Hoffman	.40	1.00
270 Paul Sorrento	.20	.50
271 Shane Andrews	.20	.50
272 Brett Butler	.40	1.00
273 Curtis Goodwin	.20	.50
274 Larry Walker	.40	1.00
275 Phil Plantier	.20	.50
276 Ken Hill	.20	.50
277 Vinny Castilla UER	.40	1.00
Rockies spelled Rockie		
278 Billy Ashley	.20	.50
279 Derek Jeter	2.50	6.00
280 Bob Tewksbury	.20	.50
281 Jose Offerman	.20	.50
282 Glenallen Hill	.20	.50
283 Tony Fernandez	.20	.50
284 Mike Devereaux	.20	.50
285 John Burkett	.20	.50
286 Geronimo Berroa	.20	.50
287 Quilvio Veras	.20	.50
288 Jason Bates	.20	.50
289 Lee Tinsley	.20	.50
290 Derek Bell	.20	.50
291 Jeff Fassero	.20	.50
292 Ray Durham	.40	1.00
293 Chad Ogea	.20	.50
294 Bill Pulsipher	.20	.50
295 Phil Nevin	.40	1.00
296 Carlos Perez RC	.50	1.25
297 Roberto Kelly	.20	.50
298 Tim Wakefield	.40	1.00
299 Jeff Manto	.20	.50
300 Brian L.Hunter	.20	.50
301 C.J. Nitkowski	.20	.50
302 Dustin Hermanson	.20	.50
303 John Mabry	.20	.50
304 Orel Hershiser	.40	1.00
305 Ron Villone	.20	.50
306 Sean Bergman	.20	.50
307 Tom Goodwin	.20	.50
308 Al Reyes	.20	.50
309 Todd Stottlemyre	.20	.50
310 Rich Becker	.20	.50
311 Joey Cora	.20	.50
312 Ed Sprague	.20	.50
313 John Smoltz UER	.60	1.50
3rd line; from spelled as form		
314 Frank Castillo	.20	.50
315 Chris Hammond	.20	.50
316 Ismael Valdes	.20	.50
317 Pete Harnisch	.20	.50
318 Bernard Gilkey	.20	.50
319 John Kruk	.40	1.00
320 Marc Newfield	.20	.50
321 Brian Johnson	.20	.50
322 Mark Portugal	.20	.50
323 David Hulse	.20	.50
324 Luis Ortiz UER	.20	.50
Below spelled beloe		
325 Mike Benjamin	.20	.50
326 Brian Jordan	.40	1.00
327 Shawn Green	.40	1.00
328 Joe Oliver	.20	.50
329 Felipe Lira	.20	.50
330 Andre Dawson	.40	1.00

1995 Finest Refractors

Card	Low	High
*STARS: 4X TO 10X BASIC CARDS		
*ROOKIES: 3X TO 8X BASIC CARDS		
STATED ODDS 1:12		
118 Ken Griffey Jr.	75.00	200.00

1995 Finest Flame Throwers

Randomly inserted in first series packs at a rate of 1:48, this nine-card set showcases strikeout leaders who bring on the heat. With a protective coating, a player photo is superimposed over a fiery orange background.

Card	Low	High
COMPLETE SET (9)	15.00	40.00
SER.1 STATED ODDS 1:48		
FT1 Jason Bere	1.25	3.00
FT2 Roger Clemens	12.50	30.00
FT3 Juan Guzman	1.25	3.00
FT4 John Hudek	1.25	3.00
FT5 Randy Johnson	6.00	15.00
FT6 Pedro Martinez	4.00	10.00
FT7 Jose Rijo	1.25	3.00
FT8 Bret Saberhagen	2.50	6.00
FT9 John Wetteland	2.50	6.00

1995 Finest Power Kings

Randomly inserted in series one packs at a rate of one in 24, Power Kings is an 18-card set highlighting top sluggers. With a protective coating, the fronts feature chromium technology that allows the player photo to be further enhanced as if to jump out from a blue lightning bolt background.

Card	Low	High
COMPLETE SET (18)	75.00	150.00
SER.1 STATED ODDS 1:24		
PK1 Bob Hamelin	1.00	2.50
PK2 Raul Mondesi	2.00	5.00
PK3 Ryan Klesko	2.00	5.00
PK4 Carlos Delgado	2.00	5.00
PK5 Manny Ramirez	3.00	8.00
PK6 Mike Piazza	8.00	20.00
PK7 Jeff Bagwell	3.00	8.00
PK8 Mo Vaughn	2.00	5.00
PK9 Frank Thomas	5.00	12.00
PK10 Ken Griffey Jr.	10.00	25.00
PK11 Albert Belle	2.00	5.00
PK12 Sammy Sosa	5.00	12.00
PK13 Dante Bichette	2.00	5.00
PK14 Gary Sheffield	2.00	5.00
PK15 Matt Williams	2.00	5.00
PK16 Fred McGriff	3.00	8.00
PK17 Barry Bonds	12.50	30.00
PK18 Cecil Fielder	2.00	5.00

1995 Finest Bronze

Available exclusively direct from Topps, this six-card set features 1994 league leaders. The fronts feature chromium metallized graphics, mounted on bronze and factory sealed in clear resin. The cards are numbered on the back "X of 6."

Card	Low	High
COMPLETE SET (6)	30.00	80.00
1 Matt Williams	3.00	8.00
2 Tony Gwynn	10.00	25.00
3 Jeff Bagwell	6.00	15.00
4 Ken Griffey Jr.	15.00	40.00
5 Paul O'Neill	2.00	5.00
6 Frank Thomas	6.00	15.00

1996 Finest

The 1996 Finest set (produced by Topps) was issued in two series of 191 cards and 168 cards respectively, for a total of 359 cards. The six-card foil packs originally retailed for $5.00 each. A protective film, designed to keep the card from scratching and to maintain original gloss, covers the front. This product provides collectors with the opportunity to complete a number of sets within sets, each with a different degree of insertion. Each card is numbered twice to indicate the set count and the theme count. Series 1 set covers four distinct themes: Finest Phenoms, Finest Intimidators, Finest Gamers and Finest Sterling. Within the first three themes, some players will be common (bronze trim), some uncommon (silver) and some rare (gold). Finest Sterling consists of star players included within one of the other three themes, but featured with a new design and different photography. The breakdown for the player selection of common, uncommon and rare cards is completely random. There are 110 common, 55 uncommon (1:4 packs) and 25 rare cards (1:24 packs). Series 2 covers four distict themes also with common, uncommon and rare cards seeded at the same ratio. The four themes are: Finest Franchises which features 36 team leaders and bonafide superstars, Finest Additions which features 47 players who have switched teams in '96, Finest Prodigies which features 45 best up-and-coming players, and Finest Sterling with 39 top stars. In addition to the cards' special borders, each card will also have either "common," "uncommon", or "rare" written within the numbering box on the card backs to let collectors know which type of card they hold.

Card	Low	High
COMP.BRONZE SER.1 (110)	10.00	25.00
COMP.BRONZE SER.2 (110)	10.00	25.00
COMMON BRONZE	.20	.50
COMMON GOLD	2.00	5.00
COMMON G RC	2.00	5.00
GOLD STATED ODDS 1:24		
COMMON SILVER	1.00	2.50
SILVER STATED ODDS 1:4		
SETS SKIP-NUMBERED BY COLOR		
B5 Roberto Hernandez B	.20	.50
B8 Terry Pendleton B	.20	.50
B12 Ken Caminiti B	.20	.50
B15 Dan Miceli B	.20	.50
B16 Chipper Jones B	.50	1.25
B17 John Wetteland B	.20	.50
B19 Tim Naehring B	.20	.50
B21 Eddie Murray B	.50	1.25
B23 Kevin Appier B	.20	.50
B24 Ken Griffey Jr. B	1.00	2.50
B26 Brian McRae B	.20	.50
B27 Pedro Martinez B	.30	.75
B28 Brian Jordan B	.20	.50
B29 Mike Fetters B	.20	.50
B30 Carlos Delgado B	.20	.50
B31 Shane Reynolds B	.20	.50
B32 Terry Steinbach B	.20	.50
B34 Mark Leiter B	.20	.50
B36 David Segui B	.20	.50
B40 Fred McGriff B	.30	.75
B44 Glenallen Hill B	.20	.50
B45 Brady Anderson B	.20	.50
B47 Jim Thome B	.30	.75
B48 Frank Thomas B	.50	1.25
B49 Chuck Knoblauch B	.20	.50
B50 Len Dykstra B	.20	.50
B53 Tom Pagnozzi B	.20	.50
B55 Ricky Bones B	.20	.50
B56 David Justice B	.20	.50
B57 Steve Avery B	.20	.50
B58 Robby Thompson B	.20	.50
B61 Tony Gwynn B	.60	1.50
B63 Denny Neagle B	.20	.50
B67 Robin Ventura B	.20	.50
B70 Kevin Seitzer B	.20	.50
B71 Ramon Martinez B	.20	.50
B75 Brian L.Hunter B	.20	.50
B76 Alan Benes B	.20	.50
B80 Ozzie Guillen B	.20	.50
B82 Benji Gil B	.20	.50
B85 Todd Hundley B	.20	.50
B87 Pat Hentgen B	.20	.50
B89 Chuck Finley B	.20	.50
B92 Derek Jeter B	1.25	3.00
B93 Paul O'Neill B	.30	.75
B94 Darrin Fletcher B	.20	.50
B96 Delino DeShields B	.20	.50
B97 Tim Salmon B	.30	.75
B98 John Olerud B	.20	.50
B101 Tim Wakefield B	.20	.50
B103 Dave Stevens B	.20	.50
B104 Orlando Merced B	.20	.50
B106 Jay Bell B	.20	.50
B107 John Burkett B	.20	.50
B108 Chris Hoiles B	.20	.50
B110 Dave Nilsson B	.20	.50
B111 Rod Beck B	.20	.50
B113 Mike Piazza B	.75	2.00
B114 Mark Langston B	.20	.50
B116 Rico Brogna B	.20	.50
B118 Tom Goodwin B	.20	.50
B119 Bryan Rekar B	.20	.50
B120 David Cone B	.20	.50
B122 Andy Pettitte B	.30	.75
B123 Chili Davis B	.20	.50
B124 John Smoltz B	.30	.75
B125 Heathcliff Slocumb B	.20	.50
B126 Dante Bichette B	.20	.50
B128 Alex Gonzalez B	.20	.50
B129 Jeff Montgomery B	.20	.50
B131 Denny Martinez B	.20	.50
B132 Mel Rojas B	.20	.50
B133 Derek Bell B	.20	.50
B134 Trevor Hoffman B	.20	.50
B136 Darren Daulton B	.20	.50
B137 Pete Schourek B	.20	.50
B138 Phil Nevin B	.20	.50
B139 Andres Galarraga B	.20	.50
B140 Chad Fonville B	.20	.50
B144 J.T. Snow B	.20	.50
B146 Barry Bonds B	1.25	3.00
B147 Orel Hershiser B	.20	.50
B148 Quilvio Veras B	.20	.50
B149 Will Clark B	.30	.75
B150 Jose Rijo B	.20	.50
B152 Travis Fryman B	.20	.50
B154 Alex Fernandez B	.20	.50
B155 Wade Boggs B	.30	.75
B156 Troy Percival B	.20	.50
B157 Moises Alou B	.20	.50
B158 Javy Lopez B	.20	.50
B159 Jason Giambi B	.20	.50
B162 Mark McGwire B	1.25	3.00
B163 Eric Karros B	.20	.50
B166 Mickey Tettleton B	.20	.50
B167 Barry Larkin B	.30	.75
B169 Ruben Sierra B	.20	.50
B170 Bill Swift B	.20	.50
B172 Chad Curtis B	.20	.50
B173 Dean Palmer B	.20	.50
B175 Bobby Bonilla B	.20	.50
B176 Greg Colbrunn B	.20	.50
B177 Jose Mesa B	.20	.50
B178 Mike Greenwell B	.20	.50
B181 Doug Drabek B	.20	.50
B183 Wilson Alvarez B	.20	.50
B184 Marty Cordova B	.20	.50
B185 Hal Morris B	.20	.50
B187 Carlos Garcia B	.20	.50
B190 Marquis Grissom B	.20	.50
B193 Will Clark B	.30	.75
B194 Paul Molitor B	.20	.50
B195 Kenny Rogers B	.20	.50
B196 Reggie Sanders B	.20	.50
B199 Raul Mondesi B	.20	.50
B200 Lance Johnson B	.20	.50
B201 Alvin Morman B	.20	.50
B203 Jack McDowell B	.20	.50
B204 Randy Myers B	.20	.50
B205 Harold Baines B	.20	.50
B206 Marty Cordova B	.20	.50
B207 Rich Hunter B RC	.20	.50
B208 Al Leiter B	.20	.50
B209 Greg Gagne B	.20	.50
B210 Ben McDonald B	.20	.50
B212 Terry Adams B	.20	.50
B213 Paul Sorrento B	.20	.50
B214 Albert Belle B	.20	.50
B215 Mike Blowers B	.20	.50
B216 Jim Edmonds B	.20	.50
B217 Felipe Crespo B	.20	.50
B219 Shawon Dunston B	.20	.50
B220 Jimmy Haynes B	.20	.50
B221 Jose Canseco B	.30	.75
B222 Eric Davis B	.20	.50
B224 Tim Raines B	.20	.50
B225 Tony Phillips B	.20	.50
B226 Charlie Hayes B	.20	.50
B227 Eric Owens B	.20	.50
B228 Roberto Alomar B	.30	.75
B233 Kenny Lofton B	.20	.50
B236 Mark McGwire B	1.25	3.00
B237 Jay Buhner B	.20	.50
B238 Craig Biggio B	.30	.75
B240 Barry Bonds B	1.25	3.00
B244 Ron Gant B	.20	.50
B245 Paul Wilson B	.20	.50
B246 Todd Hollandsworth B	.20	.50
B247 Todd Zeile B	.20	.50
B248 David Justice B	.20	.50
B250 Moises Alou B	.20	.50
B251 Bob Wolcott B	.20	.50
B252 David Wells B	.20	.50
B253 Juan Gonzalez B	.20	.50
B254 Andres Galarraga B	.20	.50
B255 Dave Hollins B	.20	.50
B257 Sammy Sosa B	.50	1.25
B258 Ivan Rodriguez B	.30	.75
B259 Bip Roberts B	.20	.50
B260 Tino Martinez B	.30	.75
B262 Mike Stanley B	.20	.50
B264 Butch Huskey B	.20	.50
B265 Jeff Conine B	.20	.50
B267 Mark Grace B	.30	.75
B268 Jason Schmidt B	.30	.75
B269 Otis Nixon B	.20	.50
B271 Kirby Puckett B	.50	1.25
B273 Andy Benes B	.20	.50
B275 Mike Piazza B	.75	2.00
B276 Rey Ordonez B	.20	.50
B278 Gary Gaetti B	.20	.50
B280 Robin Ventura B	.20	.50
B281 Cal Ripken B	1.50	4.00
B282 Carlos Baerga B	.20	.50
B283 Roger Cedeno B	.20	.50
B285 Terrell Wade B	.20	.50
B286 Kevin Brown B	.20	.50
B287 Rafael Palmeiro B	.30	.75
B288 Mo Vaughn B	.20	.50
B292 Bob Tewksbury B	.20	.50
B297 T.J. Mathews B	.20	.50
B298 Manny Ramirez B	.30	.75
B299 Jeff Bagwell B	.30	.75
B301 Wade Boggs B	.30	.75
B303 Steve Gibralter B	.20	.50
B304 B.J. Surhoff B	.20	.50
B306 Royce Clayton B	.20	.50
B307 Sal Fasano B	.20	.50
B309 Gary Sheffield B	.20	.50
B310 Ken Hill B	.20	.50
B311 Joe Girardi B	.20	.50
B312 Matt Lawton B RC	.20	.50
B314 Julio Franco B	.20	.50
B315 Joe Carter B	.20	.50
B316 Brooks Kieschnick B	.20	.50
B318 Heathcliff Slocumb B	.20	.50
B319 Barry Larkin B	.30	.75
B320 Tony Gwynn B	.60	1.50
B322 Frank Thomas B	.50	1.25
B323 Edgar Martinez B	.30	.75
B325 Henry Rodriguez B	.20	.50
B326 Marvin Benard B RC	.20	.50
B329 Ugueth Urbina B	.20	.50
B331 Roger Salkeld B	.20	.50
B332 Edgar Renteria B	.20	.50
B333 Ryan Klesko B	.20	.50
B334 Ray Lankford B	.20	.50
B336 Justin Thompson B	.20	.50
B339 Mark Clark B	.20	.50
B340 Ruben Rivera B	.20	.50
B342 Matt Williams B	.20	.50
B343 Francisco Cordova B RC	.20	.50
B344 Cecil Fielder B	.20	.50
B348 Mark Grudzielanek B	.20	.50
B349 Ron Coomer B	.20	.50
B351 Rich Aurilia B RC	.20	.50
B352 Jose Herrera B	.20	.50
B356 Tony Clark B	.20	.50
B358 Dan Naulty B RC	.20	.50
B359 Checklist B	.20	.50
G4 Marty Cordova G	2.00	5.00
G6 Tony Gwynn G	6.00	15.00
G9 Albert Belle G	2.00	5.00
G18 Kirby Puckett G	5.00	12.00
G20 Karim Garcia G	2.00	5.00
G25 Cal Ripken G	15.00	40.00
G33 Hideo Nomo G	5.00	12.00
G39 Ryne Sandberg G	8.00	20.00
G42 Jeff Bagwell G	1.50	4.00
G51 Jason Isringhausen G	2.00	5.00
G64 Mo Vaughn G	2.00	5.00
G66 Dante Bichette G	2.00	5.00
G74 Mark McGwire G	12.50	30.00
G81 Kenny Lofton G	2.00	5.00
G83 Jim Edmonds G	2.00	5.00
G90 Mike Mussina G	3.00	8.00
G100 Jeff Conine G	2.00	5.00
G102 Johnny Damon G	3.00	8.00
G105 Barry Bonds G	12.50	30.00
G117 Jose Canseco G	3.00	8.00
G135 Ken Griffey Jr. G	10.00	25.00
G141 Chipper Jones G	5.00	12.00
G145 Greg Maddux G	8.00	20.00
G164 Jay Buhner G	2.00	5.00
G186 Frank Thomas G	5.00	12.00
G191 Checklist G	2.00	5.00
G192 Chipper Jones G	5.00	12.00
G197 Roberto Alomar G	3.00	8.00
G198 Dennis Eckersley G	2.00	5.00
G202 George Arias G	2.00	5.00
G232 Hideo Nomo G	5.00	12.00
G243 Chris Snopek G	2.00	5.00
G249 Tim Salmon G	3.00	8.00
G266 Matt Williams G	2.00	5.00
G270 Randy Johnson G	5.00	12.00
G279 Paul Molitor G	2.00	5.00
G290 Cecil Fielder G	2.00	5.00
G294 Livan Hernandez G RC	4.00	10.00
G300 Marty Janzen G RC	2.00	5.00
G308 Ron Gant G	2.00	5.00
G321 Ryan Klesko G	2.00	5.00
G324 Jermaine Dye G	2.00	5.00
G330 Jason Giambi G	2.00	5.00
G335 Edgar Martinez G	3.00	8.00
G338 Rey Ordonez G	2.00	5.00
G347 Sammy Sosa G	5.00	12.00
G354 Juan Gonzalez G	2.00	5.00
G355 Craig Biggio G	3.00	8.00
S1 G.Maddux S UER	4.00	10.00
S2 Bernie Williams S	1.50	4.00
S3 Ivan Rodriguez S	1.50	4.00
S7 Barry Larkin S	1.50	4.00
S10 Ray Lankford S	1.00	2.50
S11 Mike Piazza S	4.00	10.00
S13 Larry Walker S	1.00	2.50
S14 Matt Williams S	1.00	2.50
S22 Tim Salmon S	1.50	4.00
S35 Edgar Martinez S	1.50	4.00
S37 Gregg Jefferies S	1.00	2.50
S38 Bill Pulsipher S	1.00	2.50
S41 Shawn Green S	1.00	2.50
S43 Jim Abbott S	1.50	4.00
S46 Roger Clemens S	5.00	12.00
S52 Rondell White S	1.00	2.50
S54 Dennis Eckersley S	1.00	2.50
S59 Hideo Nomo S	2.50	6.00
S60 Gary Sheffield S	1.00	2.50
S62 Will Clark S	1.50	4.00
S65 Bret Boone S	1.00	2.50
S68 Rafael Palmeiro S	1.50	4.00
S69 Carlos Baerga S	1.00	2.50
S72 Tom Glavine S	1.50	4.00
S73 Garret Anderson S	1.00	2.50
S77 Randy Johnson S	2.50	6.00
S78 Jeff King S	1.00	2.50
S79 Kirby Puckett S	2.50	6.00
S84 Cecil Fielder S	1.00	2.50
S86 Reggie Sanders S	1.00	2.50
S88 Ryan Klesko S	1.00	2.50
S91 John Valentin S	1.00	2.50
S95 Manny Ramirez S	1.50	4.00
S99 Vinny Castilla S	1.00	2.50
S109 Carlos Perez S	1.00	2.50
S112 Craig Biggio S	1.50	4.00
S115 Juan Gonzalez S	1.00	2.50
S121 Ray Durham S	1.00	2.50
S127 C.J. Nitkowski S	1.00	2.50
S130 Raul Mondesi S	1.00	2.50
S142 Lee Smith S	1.00	2.50
S143 Joe Carter S	1.00	2.50
S151 Mo Vaughn S	1.00	2.50
S153 Frank Rodriguez S	1.00	2.50

S160 Steve Finley S 1.00 2.50
S161 Jeff Bagwell S 1.50 4.00
S165 Cal Ripken S 8.00 20.00
S168 Lyle Mouton S 1.00 2.50
S171 Sammy Sosa S 2.50 6.00
S174 John Franco S 1.00 2.50
S179 Greg Vaughn S 1.00 2.50
S180 Mark Wohlers S 1.00 2.50
S182 Paul O'Neill S 1.50 4.00
S188 Albert Belle S 1.00 2.50
S189 Mark Grace S 1.50 4.00
S211 Ernie Young S 1.00 2.50
S218 Fred McGriff S 1.50 4.00
S223 Kimera Bartee S 1.00 2.50
S229 Rickey Henderson S 2.50 6.00
S230 Sterling Hitchcock S 1.00 2.50
S231 Bernard Gilkey S 1.00 2.50
S234 Ryne Sandberg S 4.00 10.00
S235 Greg Maddux S 4.00 10.00
S239 Todd Stottlemyre S 1.00 2.50
S241 Jason Kendall S 1.00 2.50
S242 Paul O'Neill S 1.50 4.00
S256 Devon White S 1.00 2.50
S261 Chuck Knoblauch S 1.00 2.50
S263 Wally Joyner S 1.00 2.50
S272 Andy Fox S 1.00 2.50
S274 Sean Berry S 1.00 2.50
S277 Benito Santiago S 1.00 2.50
S284 Chad Mottola S 1.00 2.50
S289 Dante Bichette S 1.00 2.50
S291 Dwight Gooden S 1.00 2.50
S293 Kevin Mitchell S 1.00 2.50
S295 Russ Davis S 1.00 2.50
S296 Chan Ho Park S 1.00 2.50
S302 Larry Walker S 1.00 2.50
S305 Ken Griffey Jr. S 5.00 12.00
S313 Billy Wagner S 1.00 2.50
S317 Mike Grace S RC 1.00 2.50
S327 Kenny Lofton S 1.00 2.50
S328 Derek Bell S 1.00 2.50
S337 Gary Sheffield S 1.00 2.50
S341 Mark Grace S 1.50 4.00
S345 Andres Galarraga S 1.00 2.50
S346 Brady Anderson S 1.00 2.50
S350 Derek Jeter S 5.00 12.00
S353 Jay Buhner S 1.00 2.50
S357 Tino Martinez S 1.50 4.00

1996 Finest Refractors

*BRONZE: 4X TO 10X BASIC BRONZE
BRONZE STATED ODDS 1:12
*GOLD: .75X TO 2X BASIC GOLD
GOLD STATED ODDS 1:288
*SILVER: 1.25X TO 3X BASIC SILVER
SILVER STATED ODDS 1:48
B92 Derek Jeter B 40.00 80.00
S350 Derek Jeter S 40.00 80.00

1996 Finest Landmark

This four-card limited edition medallion set came with a Certificate of Authenticity and was produced by Topps. Only 2,000 sets were made. The fronts feature color action player photos on a gold ball and star metallic background. The backs carry player biographical and career information including batting records.

1 Greg Maddux 8.00 20.00
2 Albert Belle 2.00 5.00
3 Cal Ripken 15.00 40.00
4 Eddie Murray 3.00 8.00

1997 Finest Promos

COMPLETE SET (5) 3.00 8.00
1 Barry Bonds C .60 1.50
15 Derek Jeter C 1.25 3.00
30 Mark McGwire C 1.00 2.50
143 Hideo Nomo U .40 1.00
159 Jeff Bagwell R .60 1.50

1997 Finest

The 1997 Finest set (produced by Topps) was issued in two series of 175 cards each and was distributed in six-card packs with a suggested retail price of $5.00. The fronts feature a borderless action player photo while the backs carry player information with another player photo. Series one is divided into five distinct themes: Finest Hurlers (top pitchers), Finest Blue Chips (up-and-coming future stars), Finest Power (long-ball hitters), Finest Warriors (superstar players), and Finest Masters (hottest players). Series two is also divided into five distinct themes: Finest Power (power hitters and pitchers), Finest Masters (top players), Finest Blue Chips (top new players), Finest Competitors (hottest players), and Finest Acquisitions (latest trades and new signings). All five themes of each series have common cards (1-100 and 176-275) designated with bronze trim, uncommon (101-150 and 276-325) with silver trim and an insertion rate of one in four for both series, and rare (151-175 and 326-350) with gold trim and an insertion rate of one in 24 for both series. The cards are numbered on the backs within the whole set and within the theme set. Notable Rookie Cards include Brian Giles.

COMP.BRONZE SER.1 (100) 12.50 30.00
COMP.BRONZE SER.2 (100) 12.50 30.00
COM.BRON.(1-100/176-275) .20 .50
COMP.SILVER SER.1 (50)
COMP.SILVER SER.2 (50)
COM.SILV.(101-150/276-325) .75 2.00
SILVER STATED ODDS 1:4
COMP.GOLD SER.1 (25)
COMP.GOLD SER.2 (25)
COM.GOLD (151-175/326-350) 2.00 5.00
GOLD STATED ODDS 1:24
BICHETTE/JETER BOTH NUMBERED 155
BICHETTE UER SHOULD BE NUMBER 5
1 Barry Bonds B 1.25 3.00
2 Ryne Sandberg B .75 2.00
3 Brian Jordan B .20 .50
4 Rocky Coppinger B .20 .50
5 Dante Bichette B UER 155 .20 .50
6 Al Martin B .20 .50
7 Charles Nagy B .20 .50
8 Otis Nixon B .20 .50
9 Mark Johnson B .20 .50
10 Jeff Bagwell B .30 .75
11 Ken Hill B .20 .50
12 Willie Adams B .20 .50
13 Raul Mondesi B .20 .50
14 Reggie Sanders B .20 .50
15 Derek Jeter B 1.25 3.00
16 Jermaine Dye B .20 .50
17 Edgar Renteria B .20 .50
18 Travis Fryman B .20 .50
19 Roberto Hernandez B .20 .50
20 Sammy Sosa B .50 1.25
21 Garret Anderson B .20 .50
22 Rey Ordonez B .20 .50
23 Glenallen Hill B .20 .50
24 Dave Nilsson B .20 .50
25 Kevin Brown B .20 .50
26 Brian McRae B .20 .50
27 Joey Hamilton B .20 .50
28 Jamey Wright B .20 .50
29 Frank Thomas B .50 1.25
30 Mark McGwire B 1.25 3.00
31 Ramon Martinez B .20 .50
32 Jaime Bluma B .20 .50
33 Frank Rodriguez B .20 .50
34 Andy Benes B .20 .50
35 Jay Buhner B .20 .50
36 Justin Thompson B .20 .50
37 Darin Erstad B .20 .50
38 Gregg Jefferies B .20 .50
39 Jeff D'Amico B .20 .50
40 Pedro Martinez B .30 .75
41 Nomar Garciaparra B .75 2.00
42 Jose Valentin B .20 .50
43 Pat Hentgen B .20 .50
44 Will Clark B .30 .75
45 Bernie Williams B .30 .75
46 Luis Castillo B .20 .50
47 B.J. Surhoff B .20 .50
48 Greg Gagne B .20 .50
49 Pete Schourek B .20 .50
50 Mike Piazza B .75 2.00
51 Dwight Gooden B .20 .50
52 Javy Lopez B .20 .50
53 Chuck Finley B .20 .50
54 James Baldwin B .20 .50
55 Jack McDowell B .20 .50
56 Royce Clayton B .20 .50
57 Carlos Delgado B .20 .50
58 Neifi Perez B .20 .50
59 Eddie Taubensee B .20 .50
60 Rafael Palmeiro B .30 .75
61 Marty Cordova B .20 .50
62 Wade Boggs B .30 .75
63 Rickey Henderson B .50 1.25
64 Mike Hampton B .20 .50
65 Troy Percival B .20 .50
66 Barry Larkin B .30 .75
67 Jermaine Allensworth B .20 .50
68 Mark Clark B .20 .50
69 Mike Lansing B .20 .50
70 Mark Grudzielanek B .20 .50
71 Todd Stottlemyre B .20 .50
72 Juan Guzman B .20 .50
73 John Burkett B .20 .50
74 Wilson Alvarez B .20 .50
75 Ellis Burks B .20 .50
76 Bobby Higginson B .20 .50
77 Ricky Bottalico B .20 .50
78 Omar Vizquel B .30 .75
79 Paul Sorrento B .20 .50
80 Denny Neagle B .20 .50
81 Roger Pavlik B .20 .50
82 Mike Lieberthal B .20 .50
83 Devon White B .20 .50
84 John Olerud B .20 .50
85 Kevin Appier B .20 .50
86 Joe Girardi B .20 .50
87 Paul O'Neill B .30 .75
88 Mike Sweeney B .20 .50
89 John Smiley B .20 .50
90 Ivan Rodriguez B .30 .75
91 Randy Myers B .20 .50
92 Bip Roberts B .20 .50
93 Jose Mesa B .20 .50
94 Paul Wilson B .20 .50
95 Mike Mussina B .30 .75
96 Ben McDonald B .20 .50
97 John Mabry B .20 .50
98 Tom Goodwin B .20 .50
99 Edgar Martinez B .30 .75
100 Andruw Jones B .30 .75
101 Jose Canseco S 1.25 3.00
102 Billy Wagner S .75 2.00
103 Dante Bichette S .75 2.00
104 Curt Schilling S .75 2.00
105 Dean Palmer S .75 2.00
106 Larry Walker S .75 2.00
107 Bernie Williams S 1.25 3.00
108 Chipper Jones S 2.00 5.00
109 Gary Sheffield S .75 2.00
110 Randy Johnson S 2.00 5.00
111 Roberto Alomar S 1.25 3.00
112 Todd Walker S .75 2.00
113 Sandy Alomar Jr. S .75 2.00
114 John Jaha S .75 2.00
115 Ken Caminiti S .75 2.00
116 Ryan Klesko S .75 2.00
117 Mariano Rivera S 2.00 5.00
118 Jason Giambi S .75 2.00
119 Lance Johnson S .75 2.00
120 Robin Ventura S .75 2.00
121 Todd Hollandsworth S .75 2.00
122 Johnny Damon S 1.25 3.00
123 William VanLandingham S .75 2.00
124 Jason Kendall S .75 2.00
125 Vinny Castilla S .75 2.00
126 Harold Baines S .75 2.00
127 Joe Carter S .75 2.00
128 Craig Biggio S 1.25 3.00
129 Tony Clark S .75 2.00
130 Ron Gant S .75 2.00
131 David Segui S .75 2.00
132 Steve Trachsel S .75 2.00
133 Scott Rolen S 1.25 3.00
134 Mike Stanley S .75 2.00
135 Cal Ripken S 6.00 15.00
136 John Smoltz S 1.25 3.00
137 Bobby Jones S .75 2.00
138 Manny Ramirez S 1.25 3.00
139 Ken Griffey Jr. S 4.00 10.00
140 Chuck Knoblauch S .75 2.00
141 Mark Grace S 1.25 3.00
142 Chris Snopek S .75 2.00
143 Hideo Nomo S 2.00 5.00
144 Tim Salmon S 1.25 3.00
145 David Cone S .75 2.00
146 Eric Young S .75 2.00
147 Jeff Brantley S .75 2.00
148 Jim Thome S 1.25 3.00
149 Trevor Hoffman S .75 2.00
150 Juan Gonzalez S .75 2.00
151 Mike Piazza G 8.00 20.00
152 Ivan Rodriguez G 3.00 8.00
153 Mo Vaughn G 2.00 5.00
154 Brady Anderson G 2.00 5.00
155 Mark McGwire G 12.50 30.00
156 Rafael Palmeiro G 3.00 8.00
157 Barry Larkin G 3.00 8.00
158 Greg Maddux G 8.00 20.00
159 Jeff Bagwell G 3.00 8.00
160 Frank Thomas G 5.00 12.00
161 Ken Caminiti G 2.00 5.00
162 Andruw Jones G 3.00 8.00
163 Dennis Eckersley G 2.00 5.00
164 Jeff Conine G 2.00 5.00
165 Jim Edmonds G 2.00 5.00
166 Derek Jeter G 15.00 40.00
167 Vladimir Guerrero G 5.00 12.00
168 Sammy Sosa G 5.00 12.00
169 Tony Gwynn G 6.00 15.00
170 Andres Galarraga G 2.00 5.00
171 Todd Hundley G 2.00 5.00
172 Jay Buhner G UER 164 2.00 5.00
173 Paul Molitor G 2.00 5.00
174 Kenny Lofton G 2.00 5.00
175 Barry Bonds G 12.50 30.00
176 Gary Sheffield B .20 .50
177 Dmitri Young B .20 .50
178 Jay Bell B .20 .50
179 David Wells B .20 .50
180 Walt Weiss B .20 .50
181 Paul Molitor B .20 .50
182 Jose Guillen B .20 .50
183 Al Leiter B .20 .50
184 Mike Fetters B .20 .50
185 Mark Langston B .20 .50
186 Fred McGriff B .30 .75
187 Darrin Fletcher B .20 .50
188 Brant Brown B .20 .50
189 Geronimo Berroa B .20 .50
190 Jim Thome B .30 .75
191 Jose Vizcaino B .20 .50
192 Andy Ashby B .20 .50
193 Rusty Greer B .20 .50
194 Brian Hunter B .20 .50
195 Chris Hoiles B .20 .50
196 Orlando Merced B .20 .50
197 Brett Butler B .20 .50
198 Derek Bell B .20 .50
199 Bobby Bonilla B .20 .50
200 Alex Ochoa B .20 .50
201 Wally Joyner B .20 .50
202 Mo Vaughn B .20 .50
203 Doug Drabek B .20 .50
204 Tino Martinez B .30 .75
205 Roberto Alomar B .30 .75
206 Brian Giles B RC 1.25 3.00
207 Todd Worrell B .20 .50
208 Alan Benes B .20 .50
209 Jim Leyritz B .20 .50
210 Darryl Hamilton B .20 .50
211 Jimmy Key B .20 .50
212 Juan Gonzalez B .20 .50
213 Vinny Castilla B .20 .50
214 Chuck Knoblauch B .20 .50
215 Tony Phillips B .20 .50
216 Jeff Cirillo B .20 .50
217 Carlos Garcia B .20 .50
218 Brooks Kieschnick B .20 .50
219 Marquis Grissom B .20 .50
220 Dan Wilson B .20 .50
221 Greg Vaughn B .20 .50
222 John Wetteland B .20 .50
223 Andres Galarraga B .20 .50
224 Ozzie Guillen B .20 .50
225 Kevin Elster B .20 .50
226 Bernard Gilkey B .20 .50
227 Mike Macfarlane B .20 .50
228 Heathcliff Slocumb B .20 .50
229 Wendell Magee Jr. B .20 .50
230 Carlos Baerga B .20 .50
231 Kevin Seitzer B .20 .50
232 Henry Rodriguez B .20 .50
233 Roger Clemens B 1.00 2.50
234 Mark Wohlers B .20 .50
235 Eddie Murray B .50 1.25
236 Todd Zeile B .20 .50
237 J.T. Snow B .20 .50
238 Ken Griffey Jr. B 1.00 2.50
239 Sterling Hitchcock B .20 .50
240 Albert Belle B .20 .50
241 Terry Steinbach B .20 .50
242 Robb Nen B .20 .50
243 Mark McLemore B .20 .50
244 Jeff King B .20 .50
245 Tony Clark B .20 .50
246 Tim Salmon B .30 .75
247 Benito Santiago B .20 .50
248 Robin Ventura B .20 .50
249 Bubba Trammell B RC .20 .50
250 Chili Davis B .20 .50
251 John Valentin B .20 .50
252 Cal Ripken B 1.50 4.00
253 Matt Williams B .20 .50
254 Jeff Kent B .20 .50
255 Eric Karros B .20 .50
256 Ray Lankford B .20 .50
257 Ed Sprague B .20 .50
258 Shane Reynolds B .20 .50
259 Jaime Navarro B .20 .50
260 Eric Davis B .20 .50
261 Orel Hershiser B .20 .50
262 Mark Grace B .30 .75
263 Rod Beck B .20 .50
264 Ismael Valdes B .20 .50
265 Manny Ramirez B .30 .75
266 Ken Caminiti B .20 .50
267 Tim Naehring B .20 .50
268 Jose Rosado B .20 .50
269 Greg Colbrunn B .20 .50
270 Dean Palmer B .20 .50
271 David Justice B .20 .50
272 Scott Spiezio B .20 .50
273 Chipper Jones B .50 1.25
274 Mel Rojas B .20 .50
275 Bartolo Colon B .20 .50
276 Darin Erstad S .75 2.00
277 Sammy Sosa S 2.00 5.00
278 Rafael Palmeiro S 1.25 3.00
279 Frank Thomas S 2.00 5.00
280 Ruben Rivera S .75 2.00
281 Hal Morris S .75 2.00
282 Jay Buhner S .75 2.00
283 Kenny Lofton S .75 2.00
284 Jose Canseco S 1.25 3.00
285 Alex Fernandez S .75 2.00
286 Todd Helton S 2.00 5.00
287 Andy Pettitte S 1.25 3.00
288 John Franco S .75 2.00
289 Ivan Rodriguez S 1.25 3.00
290 Ellis Burks S .75 2.00
291 Julio Franco S .75 2.00
292 Mike Piazza S 3.00 8.00
293 Brian Jordan S .75 2.00
294 Greg Maddux S 3.00 8.00
295 Bob Abreu S 1.25 3.00
296 Rondell White S .75 2.00
297 Moises Alou S .75 2.00
298 Tony Gwynn S 2.50 6.00
299 Deion Sanders S 1.25 3.00
300 Jeff Montgomery S .75 2.00
301 Ray Durham S .75 2.00
302 John Wasdin S .75 2.00
303 Ryne Sandberg S 3.00 8.00
304 Delino DeShields S .75 2.00
305 Mark McGwire S 5.00 12.00
306 Andruw Jones S 1.25 3.00
307 Kevin Orie S .75 2.00
308 Matt Williams S .75 2.00
309 Karim Garcia S .75 2.00
310 Derek Jeter S 5.00 12.00
311 Mo Vaughn S .75 2.00
312 Brady Anderson S .75 2.00
313 Barry Bonds S 5.00 12.00
314 Steve Finley S .75 2.00
315 Vladimir Guerrero S 2.00 5.00
316 Matt Morris S .75 2.00
317 Tom Glavine S 1.25 3.00
318 Jeff Bagwell S 1.25 3.00
319 Albert Belle S .75 2.00
320 Hideki Irabu S RC .75 2.00
321 Andres Galarraga S .75 2.00
322 Cecil Fielder S .75 2.00
323 Barry Larkin S 1.25 3.00
324 Todd Hundley S .75 2.00
325 Fred McGriff S 1.25 3.00
326 Gary Sheffield G 2.00 5.00
327 Craig Biggio G 3.00 8.00
328 Raul Mondesi G 2.00 5.00
329 Edgar Martinez G 3.00 8.00
330 Chipper Jones G 5.00 12.00
331 Bernie Williams G 3.00 8.00
332 Juan Gonzalez G 2.00 5.00
333 Ron Gant G 2.00 5.00
334 Cal Ripken G 15.00 40.00
335 Larry Walker G 2.00 5.00
336 Matt Williams G 2.00 5.00
337 Jose Cruz Jr. G RC 2.00 5.00
338 Joe Carter G 2.00 5.00
339 Wilton Guerrero G 2.00 5.00
340 Cecil Fielder G 2.00 5.00
341 Todd Walker G 2.00 5.00
342 Ken Griffey Jr. G 10.00 25.00
343 Ryan Klesko G 2.00 5.00
344 Roger Clemens G 10.00 25.00
345 Hideo Nomo G 5.00 12.00
346 Dante Bichette G 2.00 5.00
347 Albert Belle G 2.00 5.00
348 Randy Johnson G 5.00 12.00
349 Manny Ramirez G 3.00 8.00
350 John Smoltz G 3.00 8.00

1997 Finest Embossed

*SILV.STARS: .60X TO 1.5X BASIC CARD
*SILVER ROOKIES: .5X TO 1.25X BASIC
SILVER STATED ODDS 1:16
ALL SILVER CARDS ARE NON DIE CUT
*GOLD STARS: .75X TO 2X BASIC CARD
*GOLD ROOKIES: .5X TO 1.2X BASIC CARD
GOLD STATED ODDS 1:96
ALL GOLD CARDS ARE DIE CUT

1997 Finest Embossed Refractors

*SILVER STARS: 2.5X TO 6X BASIC CARDS
*SILVER ROOKIES: 2X TO 5X BASIC CARDS
SILVER STATED ODDS 1:192
ALL SILVER CARDS ARE NON DIE CUT
*SER.1 GOLD STARS: 8X TO 20X BASIC
*SER.2 GOLD STARS: 8X TO 20X BASIC
*SER.2 GOLD RC'S: 5X TO 12X BASIC
GOLD STATED ODDS 1:1152
ALL GOLD CARDS ARE DIE CUT

1997 Finest Refractors

*BRONZE STARS: 4X TO 10X BASIC CARD
*BRONZE RC'S: 1.25X TO 3X BASIC CARD
BRONZE STATED ODDS 1:12
*SILVER STARS: 1.25X TO 3X BASIC CARD
*SILVER ROOKIES: 1X TO 2.5X BASIC CARD
SILVER STATED ODDS 1:48
*GOLD STARS: 1.25X TO 3X BASIC CARD
*GOLD ROOKIES: .75X TO 2X BASIC CARD
GOLD STATED ODDS 1:288

1998 Finest Pre-Production

COMPLETE SET (5) 4.00 10.00
PP1 Nomar Garciaparra 1.00 2.50
PP2 Mark McGwire 1.00 2.50
PP3 Ivan Rodriguez .60 1.50
PP4 Ken Griffey Jr 1.25 3.00
PP5 Roger Clemens 1.00 2.50

1998 Finest

This 275-card set (produced by Topps) was distributed in first and second series six-card packs with a suggested retail price of $5. Series one contains cards 1-150 and series two contains cards 151-275. Each card features action color player photos printed on 26 pt. card stock with each postion identified by a different card design. The backs carry player information and career statistics.

COMPLETE SET (275) 20.00 50.00
COMPLETE SERIES 1 (150) 10.00 25.00
COMPLETE SERIES 2 (125) 10.00 25.00
1 Larry Walker .15 .40
2 Andruw Jones .25 .60
3 Ramon Martinez .08 .25
4 Geronimo Berroa .08 .25
5 David Justice .15 .40
6 Rusty Greer .15 .40
7 Chad Ogea .08 .25
8 Tom Goodwin .08 .25
9 Tino Martinez .25 .60
10 Jose Guillen .15 .40
11 Jeffrey Hammonds .08 .25
12 Brian McRae .08 .25
13 Jeremi Gonzalez .08 .25
14 Craig Counsell .08 .25
15 Mike Piazza .60 1.50
16 Greg Maddux .60 1.50
17 Todd Greene .08 .25
18 Rondell White .15 .40
19 Kirk Rueter .08 .25
20 Tony Clark .08 .25
21 Brad Radke .15 .40
22 Jaret Wright .08 .25
23 Carlos Delgado .15 .40
24 Dustin Hermanson .08 .25
25 Gary Sheffield .15 .40
26 Jose Canseco .25 .60
27 Kevin Young .15 .40
28 David Wells .15 .40
29 Mariano Rivera .40 1.00
30 Reggie Sanders .15 .40
31 Mike Cameron .08 .25
32 Bobby Witt .08 .25
33 Kevin Orie .08 .25
34 Royce Clayton .08 .25
35 Edgar Martinez .25 .60
36 Neifi Perez .08 .25
37 Kevin Appier .15 .40
38 Darryl Hamilton .08 .25
39 Michael Tucker .08 .25
40 Roger Clemens .75 2.00
41 Carl Everett .15 .40
42 Mike Sweeney .15 .40
43 Pat Meares .08 .25
44 Brian Giles .15 .40
45 Matt Morris .15 .40
46 Jason Dickson .08 .25
47 Rich Loiselle RC .15 .40
48 Joe Girardi .08 .25
49 Steve Trachsel .08 .25
50 Ben Grieve .08 .25
51 Brian Johnson .08 .25
52 Hideki Irabu .08 .25
53 J.T. Snow .15 .40
54 Mike Hampton .15 .40
55 Dave Nilsson .08 .25
56 Alex Fernandez .08 .25
57 Brett Tomko .08 .25
58 Wally Joyner .15 .40
59 Kelvim Escobar .08 .25
60 Roberto Alomar .25 .60
61 Todd Jones .08 .25
62 Paul O'Neill .25 .60
63 Jamie Moyer .15 .40
64 Mark Wohlers .08 .25
65 Jose Cruz Jr. .08 .25
66 Troy Percival .15 .40
67 Rick Reed .08 .25
68 Will Clark .25 .60
69 Jamey Wright .08 .25
70 Mike Mussina .25 .60
71 David Cone .15 .40
72 Ryan Klesko .15 .40
73 Scott Hatteberg .08 .25
74 James Baldwin .08 .25
75 Tony Womack .08 .25
76 Carlos Perez .08 .25
77 Charles Nagy .08 .25
78 Jeromy Burnitz .15 .40
79 Shane Reynolds .08 .25
80 Cliff Floyd .15 .40
81 Jason Kendall .15 .40
82 Chad Curtis .08 .25
83 Matt Karchner .08 .25
84 Ricky Bottalico .08 .25
85 Sammy Sosa .40 1.00
86 Javy Lopez .15 .40
87 Jeff Kent .15 .40
88 Shawn Green .15 .40
89 Joey Cora .08 .25
90 Tony Gwynn .50 1.25
91 Bob Tewksbury .08 .25
92 Derek Jeter 1.00 2.50
93 Eric Davis .15 .40
94 Jeff Fassero .08 .25
95 Denny Neagle .08 .25
96 Ismael Valdes .08 .25
97 Tim Salmon .25 .60
98 Mark Grudzielanek .08 .25
99 Curt Schilling .15 .40
100 Ken Griffey Jr. .75 2.00
101 Edgardo Alfonzo .08 .25
102 Vinny Castilla .15 .40
103 Jose Rosado .08 .25
104 Scott Erickson .08 .25
105 Alan Benes .08 .25
106 Shannon Stewart .15 .40
107 Delino DeShields .08 .25
108 Mark Loretta .08 .25
109 Todd Hundley .08 .25
110 Chuck Knoblauch .15 .40
111 Todd Helton .25 .60
112 F.P. Santangelo .08 .25
113 Jeff Cirillo .08 .25
114 Omar Vizquel .25 .60
115 John Valentin .08 .25
116 Damion Easley .08 .25
117 Matt Lawton .08 .25
118 Jim Thome .25 .60
119 Sandy Alomar Jr. .08 .25
120 Albert Belle .15 .40
121 Chris Stynes .08 .25
122 Butch Huskey .08 .25
123 Shawn Estes .08 .25
124 Terry Adams .08 .25
125 Ivan Rodriguez .25 .60
126 Ron Gant .15 .40
127 John Mabry .08 .25
128 Jeff Shaw .08 .25
129 Jeff Montgomery .08 .25
130 Justin Thompson .08 .25
131 Livan Hernandez .15 .40
132 Ugueth Urbina .08 .25
133 Scott Servais .08 .25
134 Troy O'Leary .08 .25
135 Cal Ripken 1.25 3.00
136 Quilvio Veras .08 .25
137 Pedro Astacio .08 .25
138 Willie Greene .08 .25
139 Lance Johnson .08 .25
140 Nomar Garciaparra .60 1.50
141 Jose Offerman .08 .25
142 Scott Rolen .25 .60
143 Derek Bell .08 .25
144 Johnny Damon .25 .60
145 Mark McGwire 1.00 2.50
146 Chan Ho Park .15 .40
147 Edgar Renteria .15 .40
148 Eric Young .08 .25
149 Craig Biggio .25 .60
150 Checklist (1-150) .08 .25
151 Frank Thomas .40 1.00
152 John Wetteland .15 .40
153 Mike Lansing .08 .25
154 Pedro Martinez .25 .60
155 Rico Brogna .08 .25
156 Kevin Brown .25 .60
157 Alex Rodriguez .60 1.50
158 Wade Boggs .25 .60
159 Richard Hidalgo .08 .25
160 Mark Grace .25 .60
161 Jose Mesa .08 .25
162 John Olerud .15 .40
163 Tim Belcher .08 .25
164 Chuck Finley .15 .40
165 Brian Hunter .08 .25
166 Joe Carter .15 .40
167 Stan Javier .08 .25
168 Jay Bell .15 .40
169 Ray Lankford .15 .40
170 John Smoltz .25 .60
171 Ed Sprague .08 .25
172 Jason Giambi .15 .40
173 Todd Walker .08 .25
174 Paul Konerko .15 .40
175 Rey Ordonez .08 .25
176 Dante Bichette .15 .40
177 Bernie Williams .25 .60
178 Jon Nunnally .08 .25
179 Rafael Palmeiro .25 .60
180 Jay Buhner .15 .40
181 Devon White .15 .40
182 Jeff D'Amico .08 .25
183 Walt Weiss .15 .40
184 Scott Spiezio .08 .25
185 Moises Alou .15 .40
186 Carlos Baerga .08 .25
187 Todd Zeile .15 .40
188 Gregg Jefferies .08 .25
189 Mo Vaughn .15 .40
190 Terry Steinbach .08 .25
191 Ray Durham .15 .40
192 Robin Ventura .15 .40
193 Jeff Reed .08 .25
194 Ken Caminiti .15 .40
195 Eric Karros .15 .40
196 Wilson Alvarez .08 .25
197 Gary Gaetti .15 .40
198 Andres Galarraga .15 .40
199 Alex Gonzalez .08 .25
200 Garret Anderson .15 .40
201 Andy Benes .08 .25
202 Harold Baines .15 .40
203 Ron Coomer .08 .25
204 Dean Palmer .15 .40
205 Reggie Jefferson .08 .25
206 John Burkett .08 .25
207 Jermaine Allensworth .08 .25
208 Bernard Gilkey .08 .25
209 Jeff Bagwell .25 .60
210 Kenny Lofton .15 .40
211 Bobby Jones .08 .25
212 Bartolo Colon .15 .40
213 Jim Edmonds .15 .40
214 Pat Hentgen .08 .25
215 Matt Williams .15 .40
216 Bob Abreu .15 .40
217 Jorge Posada .25 .60
218 Marty Cordova .08 .25
219 Ken Hill .08 .25
220 Steve Finley .15 .40
221 Jeff King .08 .25
222 Quinton McCracken .08 .25
223 Matt Stairs .08 .25
224 Darin Erstad .15 .40
225 Fred McGriff .25 .60
226 Marquis Grissom .15 .40
227 Doug Glanville .08 .25
228 Tom Glavine .25 .60
229 John Franco .15 .40
230 Darren Bragg .08 .25
231 Barry Larkin .25 .60
232 Trevor Hoffman .15 .40
233 Brady Anderson .15 .40
234 Al Martin .08 .25
235 B.J. Surhoff .15 .40
236 Ellis Burks .15 .40
237 Randy Johnson .40 1.00
238 Mark Clark .08 .25
239 Tony Saunders .08 .25
240 Hideo Nomo .40 1.00
241 Brad Fullmer .08 .25
242 Chipper Jones .40 1.00

243 Jose Valentin .08 .25
244 Manny Ramirez .25 .60
245 Derrek Lee .25 .60
246 Jimmy Key .15 .40
247 Tim Naehring .08 .25
248 Bobby Higginson .15 .40
249 Charles Johnson .15 .40
250 Chili Davis .15 .40
251 Tom Gordon .08 .25
252 Mike Lieberthal .15 .40
253 Billy Wagner .15 .40
254 Juan Guzman .08 .25
255 Todd Stottlemyre .08 .25
256 Brian Jordan .15 .40
257 Barry Bonds 1.00 2.50
258 Dan Wilson .08 .25
259 Paul Molitor .15 .40
260 Juan Gonzalez .15 .40
261 Francisco Cordova .08 .25
262 Cecil Fielder .15 .40
263 Travis Lee .08 .25
264 Kevin Tapani .08 .25
265 Raul Mondesi .15 .40
266 Travis Fryman .15 .40
267 Armando Benitez .08 .25
268 Pokey Reese .08 .25
269 Rick Aguilera .08 .25
270 Andy Pettitte .25 .60
271 Jose Vizcaino .08 .25
272 Kerry Wood .20 .50
273 Vladimir Guerrero .40 1.00
274 John Smiley .08 .25
275 Checklist (151-275) .08 .25

1998 Finest No-Protectors

COMPLETE SET (275) 175.00 350.00
COMPLETE SERIES 1 (150) 100.00 200.00
COMPLETE SERIES 2 (125) 75.00 150.00
*STARS: 1.5X TO 4X BASIC CARDS
STATED ODDS 1:2, 1 PER HTA

1998 Finest Oversize

These sixteen 3" by 5" cards were inserted one every three hobby boxes. Though not actually on the cards, first series cards have been assigned an A prefix and second series a B prefix to clarify our listing. The cards are parallel to the regular Finest cards except numbering "of 8". They were issued as chiptoppers in the boxes.

COMPLETE SERIES 1 (8) 50.00 120.00
COMPLETE SERIES 2 (8) 30.00 80.00
STATED ODDS 1:3 HOBBY/HTA BOXES
*REFRACTORS: .75X TO 2X BASIC OVERSIZE
REF.ODDS 1:6 HOBBY/HTA BOXES
A1 Mark McGwire 6.00 15.00
A2 Cal Ripken 8.00 20.00
A3 Nomar Garciaparra 4.00 10.00
A4 Mike Piazza 4.00 10.00
A5 Greg Maddux 4.00 10.00
A6 Jose Cruz Jr. .60 1.50
A7 Roger Clemens 5.00 12.00
A8 Ken Griffey Jr. 5.00 12.00
B1 Frank Thomas 2.50 6.00
B2 Bernie Williams 1.50 4.00
B3 Randy Johnson 2.50 6.00
B4 Chipper Jones 2.50 6.00
B5 Manny Ramirez 1.50 4.00
B6 Barry Bonds 6.00 15.00
B7 Juan Gonzalez 1.00 2.50
B8 Jeff Bagwell 1.50 4.00

1998 Finest Refractors

COMPLETE SET (275) 550.00 1100.00
*STARS: 5X TO 12X BASIC CARDS
STATED ODDS 1:12, 1:5 HTA
NO-PROTECTOR REF.ODDS 1:24, 1:10 HTA

1998 Finest Centurions

Randomly inserted in Series one hobby packs at a rate of 1:153 and Home Team Advantage packs at a rate of 1:71, cards from this 20-card set feature action color photos of top players who will lead the game into the next century. Each card is sequentially numbered on back to 500. Unfortunately, an unknown quantity of unnumbered Centurions made their way into the secondary market in 1999. It's believed that these cards were quality control extras. To further compound this situation, some unscrupulous parties attempted to serial-number the cards. The fake cards have flat gold foil numbering. The real cards have bright foil numbering.

COMPLETE SET (20) 20.00 50.00
SER.1 ODDS 1:153 HOBBY, 1:71 HTA
STATED PRINT RUN 500 SERIAL #'d SETS
*REF: 2.5X TO 6X BASIC CENTURIONS
SER.1 REF.ODDS 1:1020 HOBBY, 1:471 HTA
REFRACTOR PR.RUN 75 SERIAL #'d SETS
BEWARE COUNTERFEITS
C1 Andruw Jones .75 2.00
C2 Vladimir Guerrero 1.25 3.00
C3 Nomar Garciaparra 1.25 3.00
C4 Scott Rolen 1.25 3.00
C5 Ken Griffey Jr. 25.00 60.00
C6 Jose Cruz Jr. .75 2.00
C7 Barry Bonds 3.00 8.00
C8 Mark McGwire 3.00 8.00
C9 Juan Gonzalez .75 2.00
C10 Jeff Bagwell 1.25 3.00
C11 Frank Thomas 2.00 5.00
C12 Paul Konerko .75 2.00
C13 Alex Rodriguez 2.50 6.00
C14 Mike Piazza 2.00 5.00
C15 Travis Lee .75 2.00
C16 Chipper Jones 2.00 5.00
C17 Larry Walker 1.25 3.00
C18 Mo Vaughn .75 2.00
C19 Livan Hernandez .75 2.00
C20 Jaret Wright .75 2.00

1998 Finest The Man

Randomly inserted in packs at a rate of one in 119, this 20-card set is an insert to the 1998 Finest base set. The entire set is sequentially numbered to 500.

COMPLETE SET (20) 200.00 400.00
SER.2 STATED ODDS 1:119
STATED PRINT RUN 500 SERIAL #'d SETS
*REF: 1X TO 2.5X BASIC THE MAN
REF.SER.2 ODDS 1:793
REFRACTOR PR.RUN 75 SERIAL #'d SETS
TM1 Ken Griffey Jr. 30.00 80.00
TM2 Barry Bonds 15.00 40.00
TM3 Frank Thomas 12.00 30.00
TM4 Chipper Jones 12.00 30.00
TM5 Cal Ripken 20.00 50.00
TM6 Nomar Garciaparra 10.00 25.00
TM7 Mark McGwire 15.00 40.00
TM8 Mike Piazza 12.50 30.00
TM9 Derek Jeter 15.00 40.00
TM10 Alex Rodriguez 10.00 25.00
TM11 Jose Cruz Jr. 1.50 4.00
TM12 Larry Walker 2.50 6.00
TM13 Jeff Bagwell 4.00 10.00
TM14 Tony Gwynn 8.00 20.00
TM15 Travis Lee 1.50 4.00
TM16 Juan Gonzalez 2.50 6.00
TM17 Scott Rolen 4.00 10.00
TM18 Randy Johnson 6.00 15.00
TM19 Roger Clemens 12.50 30.00
TM20 Greg Maddux 10.00 25.00

1998 Finest Mystery Finest 1

Randomly inserted in first series hobby packs at the rate of one in 36 and Home Team Advantage packs at the rate of one in 15, cards from this 50-card set feature color action photos of 20 top players on double-sided cards. Each player is matched with three different players on the opposite side or another photo of himself. Each side is covered with the Finest opaque protector.

SER.1 ODDS 1:36 HOBBY, 1:15 HTA
*REFRACTOR: 1X TO 2.5X BASIC MYSTERY
REF.SER.1 ODDS 1:144 HOBBY, 1:64 HTA
M1 F.Thomas 8.00 20.00
K.Griffey Jr.
M2 F.Thomas 4.00 10.00
M.Piazza
M3 F.Thomas 10.00 25.00
M.McGwire
M4 F.Thomas 4.00 10.00
F.Thomas
M5 K.Griffey Jr. 8.00 20.00
M.Piazza
M6 K.Griffey Jr. 12.50 30.00
M.McGwire
M7 K.Griffey Jr. 8.00 20.00
K.Griffey Jr.
M8 M.Piazza 10.00 25.00
M.McGwire
M9 M.Piazza 8.00 20.00
M.Piazza
M10 M.McGwire 12.50 30.00
M.McGwire
M11 N.Garciaparra 6.00 15.00
J.Cruz Jr.
M12 N.Garciaparra 8.00 20.00
D.Jeter
M13 N.Garciaparra 6.00 15.00
A.Jones
M14 N.Garciaparra 8.00 20.00
N.Garc
M15 J.Cruz Jr. 10.00 25.00
D.Jeter
M16 J.Cruz Jr. 2.50 6.00
A.Jones
M17 J.Cruz Jr. 1.50 4.00
J.Cruz Jr.
M18 D.Jeter 10.00 25.00
A.Jones
M19 D.Jeter 12.50 30.00
D.Jeter
M20 A.Jones 2.50 6.00
A.Jones
M21 C.Ripken 10.00 25.00
T.Gwynn
M22 C.Ripken 12.50 30.00
B.Bonds
M23 C.Ripken 12.50 30.00
G.Maddux
M24 C.Ripken 15.00 40.00
C.Ripken
M25 T.Gwynn 12.50 30.00
B.Bonds
M26 T.Gwynn 6.00 15.00
G.Maddux
M27 T.Gwynn 6.00 15.00
T.Gwynn
M28 B.Bonds 12.50 30.00
G.Maddux
M29 B.Bonds 12.50 30.00
B.Bonds
M30 G.Maddux 8.00 20.00
G.Maddux
M31 J.Gonzalez 1.50 4.00
L.Walker
M32 J.Gonzalez 1.50 4.00
A.Galarraga
M33 J.Gonzalez 4.00 10.00
C.Jones
M34 J.Gonzalez 1.50 4.00
J.Gonzalez
M35 L.Walker 1.50 4.00
A.Galarraga
M36 L.Walker 4.00 10.00
C.Jones
M37 L.Walker 1.50 4.00
L.Walker
M38 A.Galarraga 4.00 10.00
C.Jones
M39 A.Galarraga 1.50 4.00
A.Galarraga
M40 C.Jones 4.00 10.00
C.Jones
M41 G.Sheffield 4.00 10.00
S.Sosa
M42 G.Sheffield 2.50 6.00
J.Bagwell
M43 G.Sheffield 2.50 6.00
T.Martinez
M44 G.Sheffield 1.50 4.00
G.Sheffield
M45 S.Sosa 8.00 20.00
J.Bagwell
M46 S.Sosa 4.00 10.00
T.Martinez
M47 S.Sosa 4.00 10.00
S.Sosa
M48 J.Bagwell 2.50 6.00
T.Martinez
M49 J.Bagwell 2.50 6.00
J.Bagwell
M50 T.Martinez 2.50 6.00
T.Martinez

1998 Finest Mystery Finest 2

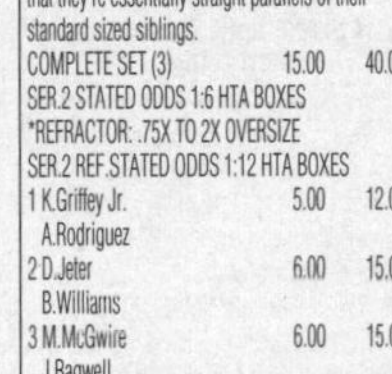

Randomly inserted in second series hobby packs at the rate of one in 36 and Home Team Advantage packs at the rate of one in 15, cards from this 50-card set feature color action photos of 20 top players on double-sided cards. Each player is matched with three different players on the opposite side or another photo of himself. Each side is covered with the Finest opaque protector.

COMPLETE SET (40) 150.00 300.00
SER.2 STATED ODDS 1:36
*REFRACTOR: 1X TO 2.5X BASIC MYSTERY
REF.SER.2 ODDS 1:144
M1 N.Garciaparra 4.00 10.00
F.Thomas
M2 N.Garciaparra 4.00 10.00
A.Belle
M3 N.Garciaparra 6.00 15.00
S.Rolen
M4 F.Thomas 4.00 10.00
A.Belle
M5 F.Thomas 4.00 10.00
S.Rolen
M6 A.Belle 2.50 6.00
S.Rolen
M7 K.Griffey Jr. 8.00 20.00
J.Cruz Jr.
M8 K.Griffey Jr. 8.00 20.00
A.Rodriguez
M9 K.Griffey Jr. 10.00 25.00
R.Clemens
M10 J.Cruz Jr. 6.00 15.00
A.Rodriguez
M11 J.Cruz Jr. 8.00 20.00
R.Clemens
M12 A.Rodriguez 6.00 15.00
R.Clemens
M13 M.Piazza 12.50 30.00
B.Bonds
M14 M.Piazza 10.00 25.00
D.Jeter
M15 M.Piazza 6.00 15.00
B.Williams
M16 B.Bonds 12.50 30.00
D.Jeter
M17 B.Bonds 6.00 15.00
B.Williams
M18 D.Jeter 10.00 25.00
B.Williams
M19 M.McGwire 10.00 25.00
J.Bagwell
M20 M.McGwire 10.00 25.00
M.Vaughn
M21 M.McGwire 10.00 25.00
J.Thome
M22 J.Bagwell 2.50 6.00
M.Vaughn
M23 J.Bagwell 2.50 6.00
J.Thome
M24 M.Vaughn 2.50 6.00
J.Thome
M25 J.Gonzalez 1.50 4.00
T.Lee
M26 J.Gonzalez 1.50 4.00
B.Grieve
M27 J.Gonzalez 2.50 6.00
F.McGriff
M28 T.Lee 1.50 4.00
B.Grieve
M29 T.Lee 2.50 6.00
F.McGriff
M30 B.Grieve 2.50 6.00
F.McGriff
M31 A.Belle 1.50 4.00
A.Belle
M32 S.Rolen 2.50 6.00
S.Rolen
M33 A.Rodriguez 8.00 20.00
A.Rodriguez
M34 R.Clemens 8.00 20.00
R.Clemens
M35 B.Williams 2.50 6.00
B.Williams
M36 M.Vaughn 1.50 4.00
M.Vaughn
M37 J.Thome 2.50 6.00
J.Thome
M38 T.Lee 1.50 4.00
T.Lee
M39 F.McGriff 2.50 6.00
F.McGriff
M40 B.Grieve 1.50 4.00
B.Grieve

1998 Finest Mystery Finest Oversize

One of these three different cards was randomly seeded as chiptoppers (lying on top of the packs, but within the sealed box) at a rate of 1:6 series two Home Team Collector boxes. Besides the obvious difference in size, these cards are also numbered differently than the standard-sized cards, but beyond that they're essentially straight parallels of their standard sized siblings.

COMPLETE SET (3) 15.00 40.00
SER.2 STATED ODDS 1:6 HTA BOXES
*REFRACTOR: .75X TO 2X OVERSIZE
SER.2 REF.STATED ODDS 1:12 HTA BOXES
1 K.Griffey Jr. 5.00 12.00
A.Rodriguez
2 D.Jeter 6.00 15.00
B.Williams
3 M.McGwire 6.00 15.00
J.Bagwell

1998 Finest Power Zone

Randomly inserted in series one hobby packs at the rate of one in 72 and in series one Home Team Advantage packs at the rate of one in 32, this 20-card set features color action photos of top players printed with new "Flop Inks" technology which actually changes the color of the card when it is held at different angles.

COMPLETE SET (20) 25.00 60.00
SER.1 STAT.ODDS 1:72 HOBBY, 1:32 HTA
P1 Ken Griffey Jr 5.00 12.00
P2 Jeff Bagwell 1.50 4.00
P3 Jose Cruz Jr. 1.00 2.50
P4 Barry Bonds 4.00 10.00
P5 Mark McGwire 4.00 10.00
P6 Jim Thome 1.50 4.00
P7 Mo Vaughn 1.00 2.50
P8 Gary Sheffield 1.00 2.50
P9 Andres Galarraga 1.50 4.00
P10 Nomar Garciaparra 1.50 4.00
P11 Rafael Palmeiro 1.50 4.00
P12 Sammy Sosa 2.50 6.00
P13 Jay Buhner 1.00 2.50
P14 Tony Clark 1.00 2.50
P15 Mike Piazza 2.50 6.00
P16 Larry Walker 1.50 4.00
P17 Albert Belle 1.00 2.50
P18 Tino Martinez 1.00 2.50
P19 Juan Gonzalez 1.00 2.50
P20 Frank Thomas 2.50 6.00

1998 Finest Stadium Stars

Randomly inserted in packs at a rate of one in 72, this 24-card set features a selection of the majors top hitters set against an attractive foil-glowing stadium background.

COMPLETE SET (24) 40.00 100.00
JUMBOS: RANDOM IN SER.2 JUMBO BOXES
SS1 Ken Griffey Jr. 5.00 12.00
SS2 Alex Rodriguez 3.00 8.00
SS3 Mo Vaughn 1.00 2.50
SS4 Nomar Garciaparra 1.50 4.00
SS5 Frank Thomas 2.50 6.00
SS6 Albert Belle 1.00 2.50
SS7 Derek Jeter 6.00 15.00
SS8 Chipper Jones 2.50 6.00
SS9 Cal Ripken 8.00 20.00
SS10 Jim Thome 1.50 4.00
SS11 Mike Piazza 2.50 6.00
SS12 Juan Gonzalez 1.00 2.50
SS13 Jeff Bagwell 1.50 4.00
SS14 Sammy Sosa 2.50 6.00
SS15 Jose Cruz Jr. 1.00 2.50
SS16 Gary Sheffield 1.00 2.50
SS17 Larry Walker 1.50 4.00
SS18 Tony Gwynn 2.50 6.00
SS19 Mark McGwire 4.00 10.00
SS20 Barry Bonds 4.00 10.00
SS21 Tino Martinez 1.00 2.50
SS22 Manny Ramirez 2.50 6.00
SS23 Ken Caminiti 1.00 2.50
SS24 Andres Galarraga 1.50 4.00

1999 Finest Pre-Production

This six-card set was issued to preview the 1999 Finest set. Six of the more popular players in baseball today were picked to represent the players in the set. The cards are numbered with a "PP" prefix.

COMPLETE SET (6) 3.00 8.00
PP1 Darin Erstad .75 2.00
PP2 Javy Lopez .75 2.00
PP3 Vinny Castilla .40 1.00
PP4 Jim Thome .60 1.50
PP5 Tino Martinez .40 1.00
PP6 Mark Grace .75 2.00

1999 Finest

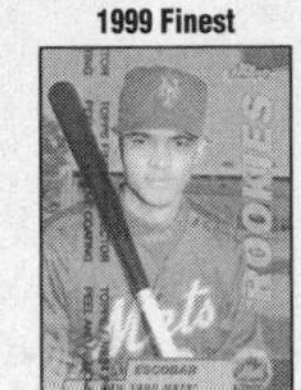

This 300-card set (produced by Topps) was distributed in first and second series six-card packs with a suggested retail price of $5. The fronts feature color action player photos printed on 27 pt. card stock using Chromium technology. The backs carry player information. The set includes the following subsets: Gems (101-120), Sensations (121-130) Rookies (131-150/277-299), Sterling (251-265) and Gamers (266-276). Card number 300 is a special Hank Aaron/Mark McGwire tribute. Cards numbered from 101 through 150 and 251 through 300 were short printed and seeded at a rate of one per hobby, one per retail and two per Home Team Advantage pack. Notable Rookie Cards include Pat Burrell, Sean Burroughs, Nick Johnson, Austin Kearns, Corey Patterson and Alfonso Soriano.

COMPLETE SET (300) 25.00 60.00
COMPLETE SERIES 1 (150) 15.00 40.00
COMPLETE SERIES 2 (150) 15.00 40.00
COMP.SER.1 w/o SP's (100) 6.00 15.00
COMP.SER.2 w/o SP's (100) 6.00 15.00
COMMON (1-100/151-250) .15 .40
COMMON (101-150/251-300) .20 .50
101-150/251-300 ODDS 1:1 H/R, 2:1 HTA
1 Darin Erstad .15 .40
2 Javy Lopez .15 .40
3 Vinny Castilla .15 .40
4 Jim Thome .25 .60
5 Tino Martinez .15 .40
6 Mark Grace .25 .60
7 Shawn Green .15 .40
8 Dustin Hermanson .15 .40
9 Kevin Young .15 .40
10 Tony Clark .15 .40
11 Scott Brosius .15 .40
12 Craig Biggio .25 .60
13 Brian McRae .15 .40
14 Chan Ho Park .25 .60
15 Manny Ramirez .40 1.00
16 Chipper Jones .40 1.00
17 Rico Brogna .15 .40
18 Quinton McCracken .15 .40
19 J.T. Snow .15 .40
20 Tony Gwynn .40 1.00
21 Juan Guzman .15 .40
22 John Valentin .15 .40
23 Rick Helling .15 .40
24 Sandy Alomar Jr. .15 .40
25 Frank Thomas .40 1.00
26 Jorge Posada .25 .60
27 Dmitri Young .15 .40
28 Rick Reed .15 .40
29 Kevin Tapani .15 .40
30 Troy Glaus .15 .40
31 Kenny Rogers .15 .40
32 Jeromy Burnitz .15 .40
33 Mark Grudzielanek .15 .40
34 Mike Mussina .25 .60
35 Scott Rolen .25 .60
36 Neifi Perez .15 .40
37 Brad Radke .15 .40
38 Darryl Strawberry .15 .40
39 Robb Nen .15 .40
40 Moises Alou .15 .40
41 Eric Young .15 .40
42 Livan Hernandez .15 .40
43 John Wetteland .15 .40
44 Matt Lawton .15 .40
45 Ben Grieve .15 .40
46 Fernando Tatis .15 .40
47 Travis Fryman .15 .40
48 David Segui .15 .40
49 Bob Abreu .15 .40
50 Nomar Garciaparra .25 .60
51 Paul O'Neill .25 .60
52 Jeff King .15 .40
53 Francisco Cordova .15 .40
54 John Olerud .15 .40
55 Vladimir Guerrero .25 .60
56 Fernando Vina .15 .40
57 Shane Reynolds .15 .40
58 Chuck Finley .15 .40
59 Rondell White .15 .40
60 Greg Vaughn .15 .40
61 Ryan Minor .15 .40
62 Tom Gordon .15 .40
63 Damion Easley .15 .40
64 Ray Durham .15 .40
65 Orlando Hernandez .15 .40
66 Bartolo Colon .15 .40
67 Jaret Wright .15 .40
68 Royce Clayton .15 .40
69 Tim Salmon .15 .40
70 Mark McGwire .60 1.50
71 Alex Gonzalez .15 .40
72 Tom Glavine .25 .60
73 David Justice .15 .40
74 Omar Vizquel .25 .60
75 Juan Gonzalez .15 .40
76 Bobby Higginson .15 .40
77 Todd Walker .15 .40
78 Dante Bichette .15 .40
79 Kevin Millwood .15 .40
80 Roger Clemens .50 1.25
81 Kerry Wood .15 .40
82 Cal Ripken 1.25 3.00
83 Jay Bell .15 .40
84 Barry Bonds .60 1.50
85 Alex Rodriguez .50 1.25
86 Doug Glanville .15 .40
87 Jason Kendall .15 .40
88 Sean Casey .15 .40
89 Aaron Sele .15 .40
90 Derek Jeter 1.00 2.50
91 Andy Ashby .15 .40
92 Rusty Greer .15 .40
93 Rod Beck .15 .40
94 Matt Williams .15 .40
95 Mike Piazza .40 1.00
96 Wally Joyner .15 .40
97 Barry Larkin .25 .60
98 Eric Milton .15 .40
99 Gary Sheffield .15 .40
100 Greg Maddux .50 1.25
101 Ken Griffey Jr. GEM 1.25 3.00
102 Frank Thomas GEM .60 1.50
103 Nomar Garciaparra GEM 1.00 2.50
104 Mark McGwire GEM 1.50 4.00
105 Alex Rodriguez GEM 1.00 2.50
106 Tony Gwynn GEM .75 2.00
107 Juan Gonzalez GEM .25 .60
108 Jeff Bagwell GEM .40 1.00
109 Sammy Sosa GEM .60 1.50
110 Vladimir Guerrero GEM .60 1.50
111 Roger Clemens GEM 1.25 3.00
112 Barry Bonds GEM 1.50 4.00
113 Darin Erstad GEM .25 .60
114 Mike Piazza GEM 1.00 2.50
115 Derek Jeter GEM 1.50 4.00
116 Chipper Jones GEM .60 1.50
117 Larry Walker GEM .25 .60
118 Scott Rolen GEM .40 1.00
119 Cal Ripken GEM 2.00 5.00
120 Greg Maddux GEM 1.00 2.50
121 Troy Glaus SENS .40 1.00
122 Ben Grieve SENS .20 .50
123 Ryan Minor SENS .20 .50
124 Kerry Wood SENS .25 .60
125 Travis Lee SENS .20 .50
126 Adrian Beltre SENS .25 .60
127 Brad Fullmer SENS .20 .50
128 Aramis Ramirez SENS .25 .60
129 Eric Chavez SENS .25 .60
130 Todd Helton SENS .40 1.00
131 Pat Burrell RC 1.25 3.00
132 Ryan Mills RC .20 .50
133 Austin Kearns RC 1.25 3.00
134 Josh McKinley RC .20 .50
135 Adam Everett RC .40 1.00
136 Marlon Anderson .20 .50
137 Bruce Chen .20 .50
138 Matt Clement .25 .60
139 Alex Gonzalez .20 .50
140 Roy Halladay .25 .60
141 Calvin Pickering .20 .50
142 Randy Wolf .20 .50
143 Ryan Anderson .20 .50
144 Ruben Mateo .20 .50
145 Alex Escobar RC .25 .60
146 Jeremy Giambi .20 .50
147 Lance Berkman .25 .60
148 Michael Barrett .20 .50
149 Preston Wilson .20 .50
150 Gabe Kapler .25 .60
151 Roger Clemens .75 2.00
152 Jay Buhner .15 .40
153 Brad Fullmer .15 .40
154 Ray Lankford .15 .40
155 Jim Edmonds .15 .40
156 Jason Giambi .15 .40
157 Bret Boone .15 .40
158 Jeff Cirillo .15 .40
159 Rickey Henderson .40 1.00
160 Edgar Martinez .25 .60
161 Ron Gant .15 .40
162 Mark Kotsay .15 .40
163 Trevor Hoffman .15 .40
164 Jason Schmidt .15 .40
165 Brett Tomko .15 .40
166 David Ortiz .40 1.00
167 Dean Palmer .15 .40
168 Hideki Irabu .15 .40
169 Mike Cameron .15 .40
170 Pedro Martinez .25 .60
171 Tom Goodwin .15 .40
172 Brian Hunter .15 .40
173 Al Leiter .15 .40
174 Charles Johnson .15 .40
175 Curt Schilling .15 .40
176 Robin Ventura .15 .40
177 Travis Lee .15 .40
178 Jeff Shaw .15 .40
179 Ugueth Urbina .15 .40
180 Roberto Alomar .25 .60
181 Cliff Floyd .15 .40
182 Adrian Beltre .15 .40
183 Tony Womack .15 .40
184 Brian Jordan .15 .40
185 Randy Johnson .40 1.00
186 Mickey Morandini .15 .40
187 Todd Hundley .15 .40
188 Jose Valentin .15 .40
189 Eric Davis .15 .40
190 Ken Caminiti .15 .40
191 David Wells .15 .40
192 Ryan Klesko .15 .40
193 Garret Anderson .15 .40
194 Eric Karros .15 .40
195 Ivan Rodriguez .25 .60
196 Aramis Ramirez .15 .40
197 Mike Lieberthal .15 .40
198 Will Clark .25 .60
199 Rey Ordonez .15 .40
200 Ken Griffey Jr. .75 2.00
201 Jose Guillen .15 .40
202 Scott Erickson .15 .40
203 Paul Konerko .15 .40
204 Johnny Damon .25 .60
205 Larry Walker .15 .40
206 Denny Neagle .15 .40
207 Jose Offerman .15 .40
208 Andy Pettitte .25 .60
209 Bobby Jones .15 .40
210 Kevin Brown .25 .60
211 John Smoltz .25 .60
212 Henry Rodriguez .15 .40
213 Tim Belcher .15 .40
214 Carlos Delgado .15 .40
215 Andruw Jones .25 .60
216 Andy Benes .15 .40
217 Fred McGriff .25 .60
218 Edgar Renteria .15 .40
219 Miguel Tejada .15 .40
220 Bernie Williams .25 .60
221 Justin Thompson .15 .40
222 Marty Cordova .15 .40
223 Delino DeShields .15 .40
224 Ellis Burks .15 .40
225 Kenny Lofton .15 .40
226 Steve Finley .15 .40
227 Eric Chavez .15 .40
228 Jose Cruz Jr. .15 .40
229 Marquis Grissom .15 .40
230 Jeff Bagwell .25 .60
231 Jose Canseco .25 .60
232 Edgardo Alfonzo .15 .40
233 Richie Sexson .15 .40
234 Jeff Kent .15 .40
235 Rafael Palmeiro .25 .60
236 David Cone .15 .40
237 Gregg Jefferies .15 .40
238 Mike Lansing .15 .40
239 Mariano Rivera .40 1.00
240 Albert Belle .15 .40
241 Chuck Knoblauch .15 .40
242 Derek Bell .15 .40
243 Pat Hentgen .15 .40
244 Andres Galarraga .15 .40
245 Mo Vaughn .15 .40
246 Wade Boggs .25 .60
247 Devon White .15 .40
248 Todd Helton .25 .60
249 Raul Mondesi .15 .40
250 Sammy Sosa .40 1.00
251 Nomar Garciaparra ST 1.00 2.50
252 Mark McGwire ST 1.50 4.00
253 Alex Rodriguez ST 1.00 2.50
254 Juan Gonzalez ST .25 .60
255 Vladimir Guerrero ST .60 1.50
256 Ken Griffey Jr. ST 1.25 3.00
257 Mike Piazza ST 1.00 2.50
258 Derek Jeter ST 1.50 4.00
259 Albert Belle ST .25 .60
260 Greg Vaughn ST .20 .50
261 Sammy Sosa ST .60 1.50
262 Greg Maddux ST 1.00 2.50
263 Frank Thomas ST .60 1.50
264 Mark Grace ST .40 1.00
265 Ivan Rodriguez ST .40 1.00
266 Roger Clemens GM 1.25 3.00
267 Mo Vaughn GM .25 .60
268 Jim Thome GM .40 1.00
269 Darin Erstad GM .25 .60
270 Chipper Jones GM .60 1.50
271 Larry Walker GM .25 .60
272 Cal Ripken GM 2.00 5.00
273 Scott Rolen GM .40 1.00
274 Randy Johnson GM .60 1.50

275 Tony Gwynn GM .75 2.00
276 Barry Bonds GM 1.50 4.00
277 Sean Burroughs RC .40 1.00
278 J.M. Gold RC .20 .50
279 Carlos Lee .25 .60
280 George Lombard .20 .50
281 Carlos Beltran .40 1.00
282 Fernando Seguignol .20 .50
283 Eric Chavez .25 .60
284 Carlos Pena RC .30 .75
285 Corey Patterson RC .60 1.50
286 Alfonso Soriano RC 3.00 8.00
287 Nick Johnson RC .60 1.50
288 Jorge Toca RC .25 .60
289 A.J. Burnett RC .60 1.50
290 Andy Brown RC .20 .50
291 Doug Mientkiewicz RC .40 1.00
292 Bobby Seay RC .20 .50
293 Chip Ambres RC .20 .50
294 C.C. Sabathia RC 1.50 4.00
295 Choo Freeman RC .25 .60
296 Eric Valent RC .25 .60
297 Matt Belisle RC .20 .50
298 Jason Tyner RC .20 .50
299 Masao Kida RC .25 .60
300 H.Aaron 1.25 3.00
M.McGwire

1999 Finest Gold Refractors

*STARS 1-100/151-250: 15X TO 40X BASIC
*STARS 101-150/251-300: 10X TO 25X BASIC
*ROOKIES: 6X TO 15X BASIC
SER.1 ODDS 1:82 HOB/RET, 1:38 HTA
SER.2 ODDS 1:57 HOB/RET, 1:26 HTA
STATED PRINT RUN 100 SERIAL #'d SETS

1999 Finest Refractors

*STARS 1-100/151-250: 3X TO 8X BASIC
*STARS 101-150/251-300: 2X TO 5X BASIC
*ROOKIES: 1.5X TO 4X BASIC
STATED ODDS 1:12 HOB/RET, 1:5 HTA

1999 Finest Aaron Award Contenders

Randomly inserted into Series two packs at different rates depending on the player, this nine-card set features color action photos of players vying for the Hank Aaron Award.

COMPLETE SET (9) 10.00 25.00
HA1 SER.2 ODDS 1:216, 1:108 HTA
HA2 SER.2 ODDS 1:108, 1:54 HTA
HA3 SER.2 ODDS 1:72, 1:36 HTA
HA4 SER.2 ODDS 1:54, 1:27 HTA
HA5 SER.2 ODDS 1:43, 1:21 HTA
HA6 SER.2 ODDS 1:36, 1:18 HTA
HA7 SER.2 ODDS 1:31, 1:15 HTA
HA8 SER.2 ODDS 1:27, 1:13 HTA
HA9 SER.2 ODDS 1:24, 1:12 HTA
*REF: 5X TO 1.2X BASIC AARON
REF HA1 SER.2 ODDS 1:1728, 1:864 HTA
REF HA2 SER.2 ODDS 1:864, 1:432 HTA
REF HA3 SER.2 ODDS 1:576, 1:288 HTA
REF HA4 SER.2 ODDS 1:432, 1:216 HTA
REF HA5 SER.2 ODDS 1:344, 1:172 HTA
REF HA6 SER.2 ODDS 1:288, 1:144 HTA
REF HA7 SER.2 ODDS 1:248, 1:124 HTA
REF HA8 SER.2 ODDS 1:216, 1:108 HTA
REF HA9 SER.2 ODDS 1:192, 1:96 HTA
HA1 Juan Gonzalez .60 1.50
HA2 Vladimir Guerrero 1.00 2.50
HA3 Nomar Garciaparra 1.00 2.50
HA4 Albert Belle .60 1.50
HA5 Frank Thomas 1.50 4.00
HA6 Sammy Sosa 1.50 4.00
HA7 Alex Rodriguez 2.00 5.00
HA8 Ken Griffey Jr. 3.00 8.00
HA9 Mark McGwire 2.50 6.00

1999 Finest Complements

Randomly inserted into Series two packs at the rate of one in 56, this seven-card set features color action photos of 14 stars who complement each other's skills and share a common bond paired together on cards printed with advanced "Split Screen" technology which combines Refractor and Non-Refractor technology on the same card. Each card has three variations as follows: 1) Non-Refractor/Refractor, 2) Refractor/Non-Refractor, and 3) Refractor/Refractor.

COMPLETE SET (7) 8.00 20.00
SER.2 STATED ODDS 1:56, 1:27 HTA
RIGHT/LEFT REF.VARIATIONS EQUAL VALUE
*DUAL REF: 1.2X TO 3X BASIC COMP.
DUAL REF.SER.2 ODDS 1:168, 1:81 HTA
C1 M.Piazza 1.00 2.50
I.Rodriguez
C2 Tony Gwynn 1.00 2.50
Wade Boggs
C3 Kerry Wood 1.25 3.00
Roger Clemens
C4 Juan Gonzalez 1.00 2.50
Sammy Sosa
C5 Derek Jeter 2.50 6.00
Nomar Garciaparra
C6 Mark McGwire 1.50 4.00
Frank Thomas
C7 Vladimir Guerrero .60 1.50
Andruw Jones

1999 Finest Double Feature

Randomly inserted into Series two packs at the rate of one in 56, this seven-card set features color photos of fourteen paired teammates printed on cards using Split Screen technology combining Refractor and Non-Refractor technology on the same card. There are three different versions of each card as follows: 1) Non-Refractor/Refractor, 2) Refractor/Non-Refractor, and 3) Refractor/Refractor.

COMPLETE SET (7) 15.00 40.00
SER.2 STATED ODDS 1:56, 1:27 HTA
RIGHT/LEFT REF.VARIATIONS EQUAL VALUE
*DUAL REF: 1.25X TO 3X BASIC DOUB.FEAT.
*DUAL REF BURRELL: 1.25X TO 3X HI COL.
DUAL REF.SER.2 ODDS 1:168, 1:81 HTA
DF1 K.Griffey Jr. 3.00 8.00
A.Rodriguez
DF2 C.Jones 1.50 4.00
A.Jones
DF3 D.Erstad .60 1.50
M.Vaughn
DF4 C.Biggio 1.00 2.50
J.Bagwell
DF5 B.Grieve .60 1.50
E.Chavez
DF6 A.Belle 5.00 12.00
C.Ripken
DF7 S.Rolen 1.25 3.00
P.Burrell

1999 Finest Franchise Records

Randomly inserted into Series two packs at the rate of one in 129, this ten-card set features color action photos of all-time and single-season franchise statistic holders. A refractive parallel version of this set was also produced and inserted in Series two packs at the rate of one in 378.

COMPLETE SET (10) 75.00 150.00
SER.2 STATED ODDS 1:129, 1:64 HTA
*REFRACTORS: .75X TO 2X BASIC FRAN.REC.
REF.SER.2 ODDS 1:378, 1:189 HTA
FR1 Frank Thomas 4.00 10.00
FR2 Ken Griffey Jr. 8.00 20.00
FR3 Mark McGwire 10.00 25.00
FR4 Juan Gonzalez 1.50 4.00
FR5 Nomar Garciaparra 6.00 15.00
FR6 Mike Piazza 6.00 15.00
FR7 Cal Ripken 12.50 30.00
FR8 Sammy Sosa 4.00 10.00
FR9 Barry Bonds 10.00 25.00
FR10 Tony Gwynn 5.00 12.00

1999 Finest Future's Finest

Randomly inserted into Series two packs at the rate of one in 171, this 10-card set features color photos of top young stars printed on card stock using Refractive Finest technology. The cards are sequentially numbered to 500.

COMPLETE SET (10) 40.00 100.00
SER.2 STATED ODDS 1:171, 1:79 HTA
STATED PRINT RUN 500 SERIAL #'d SETS
FF1 Pat Burrell 6.00 15.00
FF2 Troy Glaus 4.00 10.00
FF3 Eric Chavez 4.00 10.00
FF4 Ryan Anderson 4.00 10.00
FF5 Ruben Mateo 4.00 10.00
FF6 Gabe Kapler 4.00 10.00
FF7 Alex Gonzalez 4.00 10.00
FF8 Michael Barrett 4.00 10.00
FF9 Adrian Beltre 4.00 10.00
FF10 Fernando Seguignol 4.00 10.00

1999 Finest Leading Indicators

Randomly inserted in Series one packs at the rate of one in 24, this 10-card set features color action photos highlighting the 1998 home run totals of superstar players and printed on cards using a heat-sensitvie, thermal-ink technology. When a collector touched the baseball field background in left, center, or right field, the heat from his finger revealed the pictured player's '98 home run totals in that direction.

COMPLETE SET (10) 20.00 50.00
SER.1 ODDS 1:24 HOB/RET, 1:11 HTA
L1 Mark McGwire 4.00 10.00
L2 Sammy Sosa 1.50 4.00
L3 Ken Griffey Jr. 3.00 8.00
L4 Greg Vaughn .60 1.50
L5 Albert Belle .60 1.50
L6 Juan Gonzalez .60 1.50
L7 Andres Galarraga .60 1.50
L8 Alex Rodriguez 2.50 6.00
L9 Barry Bonds 4.00 10.00
L10 Jeff Bagwell 1.00 2.50

1999 Finest Milestones

Randomly inserted into packs at the rate of one in 29, this 40-card set features color photos of players who have the highest statistics in four categories: Hits, Home Runs, RBI's and Doubles. The cards are printed with Refractor technology and sequentially numbered based on the category as follows: Hits to 3,000, Home Runs to 500, RBIs to 1,400, and Doubles to 500.

HIT SER.2 ODDS 1:29, 1:13 HTA
HIT PRINT RUN 3000 SERIAL #'d SUBSETS
HR SER.2 ODDS 1:171, 1:79 HTA
HR PRINT RUN 500 SERIAL #'d SUBSETS
RBI SER.2 ODDS 1:61, 1:28 HTA
RBI PRINT RUN 1400 SERIAL #'d SUBSETS
2B SER.2 ODDS 1:171, 1:79 HTA
2B PRINT RUN 500 SERIAL #'d SUBSETS
M1 Tony Gwynn HIT 1.50 4.00
M2 Cal Ripken HIT 5.00 12.00
M3 Wade Boggs HIT 1.00 2.50
M4 Ken Griffey Jr. HIT 3.00 8.00
M5 Frank Thomas HIT 1.50 4.00
M6 Barry Bonds HIT 2.50 6.00
M7 Travis Lee HIT .60 1.50
M8 Alex Rodriguez HIT 2.00 5.00
M9 Derek Jeter HIT 4.00 10.00
M10 Vladimir Guerrero HIT 1.00 2.50
M11 Mark McGwire HR 10.00 25.00
M12 Ken Griffey Jr. HR 12.00 30.00
M13 Vladimir Guerrero HR 4.00 10.00
M14 Alex Rodriguez HR 8.00 20.00
M15 Barry Bonds HR 10.00 25.00
M16 Sammy Sosa HR 6.00 15.00
M17 Albert Belle HR 2.50 6.00
M18 Frank Thomas HR 6.00 15.00
M19 Jose Canseco HR 4.00 10.00
M20 Mike Piazza HR 6.00 15.00
M21 Jeff Bagwell RBI 2.00 5.00
M22 Barry Bonds RBI 5.00 12.00
M23 Ken Griffey Jr. RBI 6.00 15.00
M24 Albert Belle RBI 1.25 3.00
M25 Juan Gonzalez RBI 1.25 3.00
M26 Vinny Castilla RBI 1.25 3.00
M27 Mark McGwire RBI 5.00 12.00
M28 Alex Rodriguez RBI 4.00 10.00
M29 Nomar Garciaparra RBI 2.00 5.00
M30 Frank Thomas RBI 3.00 8.00
M31 Barry Bonds 2B 10.00 25.00
M32 Albert Belle 2B 2.50 6.00
M33 Ben Grieve 2B 2.50 6.00
M34 Craig Biggio 2B 4.00 10.00
M35 Vladimir Guerrero 2B 4.00 10.00
M36 Nomar Garciaparra 2B 4.00 10.00
M37 Alex Rodriguez 2B 8.00 20.00
M38 Derek Jeter 2B 15.00 40.00
M39 Ken Griffey Jr. 2B 12.00 30.00
M40 Brad Fullmer 2B 2.50 6.00

1999 Finest Peel and Reveal Sparkle

Randomly inserted in Series one packs at the rate of one in 30, this 20-card set features color action player images on a sparkle background. This set was considered Common and the protective coating had to be peeled from the card front and back to reveal the level.

COMPLETE SET (20) 60.00 120.00
SER.1 STATED ODDS 1:30 HOB/RET, 1:15 HTA
*HYPERPLAID: .6X TO 1.5X SPARKLE
HYPERPLAID SER.1 ODDS 1:60 H/R,1:30 HTA
*STADIUM STARS: 1.25X TO 3X SPARKLE
STAD.STAR SER.1 ODDS 1:120 H/R, 1:60 HTA
1 Kerry Wood .75 2.00
2 Mark McGwire 5.00 12.00
3 Sammy Sosa 2.00 5.00
4 Ken Griffey Jr. 4.00 10.00
5 Nomar Garciaparra 3.00 8.00
6 Greg Maddux 3.00 8.00
7 Derek Jeter 5.00 12.00
8 Andres Galarraga .75 2.00
9 Alex Rodriguez 3.00 8.00
10 Frank Thomas 2.00 5.00
11 Roger Clemens 4.00 10.00
12 Juan Gonzalez .75 2.00
13 Ben Grieve .75 2.00
14 Jeff Bagwell 1.25 3.00
15 Todd Helton 1.25 3.00
16 Chipper Jones 2.00 5.00
17 Barry Bonds 5.00 12.00
18 Travis Lee .75 2.00
19 Vladimir Guerrero 2.00 5.00
20 Pat Burrell 1.50 4.00

1999 Finest Prominent Figures

Randomly inserted in Series one packs with various insertion rates, this 50-card set features color action photos of ten superstars in each of five statistical categories and printed with Refractor technology. The categories are: Home Runs (with an insertion rate of 1:1,749) and sequentially numbered to 70, Slugging Percentage (1:145) numbered to 847, Batting Average (1:289) numbered to 424, Runs Batted In (1:644) numbered to 190, and Total Bases (1:268) numbered to 457.

HR SER.1 ODDS 1:1749 HOB/RET, 1:807 HTA
HR PRINT RUN 70 SERIAL #'d SUBSETS
SLUGGING SER.1 ODDS 1:145 H/R, 1:67 HTA
SLG PRINT RUN 847 SERIAL #'d SUBSETS
BAT SER.1 ODDS 1:289 HOB/RET, 1:133 HTA
BAT PRINT RUN 424 SERIAL #'d SUBSETS
RBI SER.1 ODDS 1:644 HOB/RET, 1:297 HTA
RBI PRINT RUN 190 SERIAL #'d SUBSETS
TOT.BASES SER.1 ODDS 1:268 H/R, 1:124 HTA
TB PRINT RUN 457 SERIAL #'d SUBSETS
PF1 Mark McGwire HR 50.00 120.00
PF2 Sammy Sosa HR 30.00 80.00
PF3 Ken Griffey Jr. HR 60.00 150.00
PF4 Mike Piazza HR 30.00 80.00
PF5 Juan Gonzalez HR 12.00 30.00
PF6 Greg Vaughn HR 12.00 30.00
PF7 Alex Rodriguez HR 40.00 100.00
PF8 Manny Ramirez HR 30.00 80.00
PF9 Jeff Bagwell HR 20.00 50.00
PF10 Andres Galarraga HR 20.00 50.00
PF11 Mark McGwire SLG 10.00 25.00
PF12 Sammy Sosa SLG 6.00 15.00
PF13 Juan Gonzalez SLG 2.50 6.00
PF14 Ken Griffey Jr. SLG 12.00 30.00
PF15 Barry Bonds SLG 10.00 25.00
PF16 Greg Vaughn SLG 2.50 6.00
PF17 Larry Walker SLG 4.00 10.00
PF18 Andres Galarraga SLG 4.00 10.00
PF19 Jeff Bagwell SLG 4.00 10.00
PF20 Albert Belle SLG 2.50 6.00
PF21 Tony Gwynn BAT 8.00 20.00
PF22 Mike Piazza BAT 8.00 20.00
PF23 Larry Walker BAT 5.00 12.00
PF24 Alex Rodriguez BAT 10.00 25.00
PF25 John Olerud BAT 3.00 8.00
PF26 Frank Thomas BAT 8.00 20.00
PF27 Bernie Williams BAT 5.00 12.00
PF28 Chipper Jones BAT 8.00 20.00
PF29 Jim Thome BAT 5.00 12.00
PF30 Barry Bonds BAT 12.00 30.00
PF31 Juan Gonzalez RBI 5.00 12.00
PF32 Sammy Sosa RBI 12.00 30.00
PF33 Mark McGwire RBI 20.00 50.00
PF34 Albert Belle RBI 5.00 12.00
PF35 Ken Griffey Jr. RBI 25.00 60.00
PF36 Jeff Bagwell RBI 8.00 20.00
PF37 Chipper Jones RBI 12.00 30.00
PF38 Vinny Castilla RBI 5.00 12.00
PF39 Alex Rodriguez RBI 15.00 40.00
PF40 Andres Galarraga RBI 8.00 20.00
PF41 Sammy Sosa TB 8.00 20.00
PF42 Mark McGwire TB 12.00 30.00
PF43 Albert Belle TB 3.00 8.00
PF44 Ken Griffey Jr. TB 15.00 40.00
PF45 Jeff Bagwell TB 5.00 12.00
PF46 Juan Gonzalez TB 3.00 8.00
PF47 Barry Bonds TB 12.00 30.00
PF48 Vladimir Guerrero TB 5.00 12.00
PF49 Larry Walker TB 5.00 12.00
PF50 Alex Rodriguez TB 10.00 25.00

1999 Finest Split Screen Single Refractors

Randomly inserted in Series one packs at the rate of one in 28, this 14-card set features action color photos of two players paired together on the same card and printed using a special refractor and non-refractor technology. Each card was printed with right/left refractor variations.

SER.1 STATED ODDS 1:28 HOB/RET, 1:14 HTA
RIGHT/LEFT REF.VARIATIONS EQUAL VALUE
*DUAL REF: .6X TO 1.5X BASIC SCREEN
DUAL REF.SER.1 ODDS 1:82 H/R, 1:42 HTA
SS1A McGwire REF/Sosa 1.50 4.00
SS1B McGwire/Sosa REF 1.50 4.00
SS2A Griffey REF/ARod 2.00 5.00
SS2B Griffey/ARod REF 2.00 5.00
SS3A Nomar REF/Jeter 2.50 6.00
SS3B Nomar/Jeter REF 2.50 6.00
SS4A Bonds REF/Belle 1.50 4.00
SS4B Bonds/Belle REF 1.50 4.00
SS5A Ripken REF/Gwynn 3.00 8.00
SS5B Ripken/Gwynn REF 3.00 8.00
SS6A Manny Ramirez REF 1.00 2.50
Juan Gonzalez
SS6B Manny Ramirez 1.00 2.50
Juan Gonzalez REF
SS7A Frank Thomas REF 1.00 2.50
Andres Galarraga
SS7B Frank Thomas 1.00 2.50
Andres Galarraga REF
SS8A Scott Rolen REF 1.00 2.50
Chipper Jones
SS8B Scott Rolen 1.00 2.50
Chipper Jones REF
SS9A Ivan Rodriguez REF 1.00 2.50
Mike Piazza
SS9B Ivan Rodriguez 1.00 2.50
Mike Piazza REF
SS10A Wood REF/Clemens 1.25 3.00
SS10B Wood/Clemens REF 1.25 3.00
SS11A Maddux REF/Glavine 1.25 3.00
SS11B Maddux/Glavine REF 1.25 3.00
SS12A Troy Glaus REF .40 1.00
Eric Chavez
SS12B Troy Glaus .40 1.00
Eric Chavez REF
SS13A Ben Grieve REF .60 1.50
Todd Helton
SS13B Ben Grieve .60 1.50
Todd Helton REF
SS14A Lee REF/Burrell 1.50 4.00
SS14B Lee/Burrell REF 1.50 4.00

1999 Finest Team Finest Blue

Randomly inserted in Series one and Series two packs at the rate of one in 82 first series and one in 57 second series. Also distributed in HTA packs at a rate of one in 38 first series and one in 26 second series. This 20-card set features color action player images printed using prismatic Chromium technology with blue highlights and is sequentially numbered to 1500. Cards 1-10 were distributed in first series packs and 11-20 in second series packs.

COMP.BLUE SET (20) 75.00 150.00
COMP.BLUE SER.2 (10) 30.00 80.00
BLUE SER.1 ODDS 1:82 HOB/RET, 1:38 HTA
BLUE SER.2 ODDS 1:57 HOB/RET, 1:26 HTA
BLUE PRINT RUN 1500 SERIAL #'d SETS
*BLUE REF: .75X TO 2X BASIC BLUE
BLUE REF.SER.1 ODDS 1:816 HOB, 1:377 HTA
BLUE REF.SER.2 ODDS 1:571 HOB, 1:263 HTA
BLUE REF.PRINT RUN 150 SERIAL #'d SETS
*RED: .5X TO 1.2X BASIC BLUE
RED SER.2 ODDS 1:18 HTA
RED SER.1 ODDS 1:25 HTA
RED PRINT RUN 500 SERIAL #'d SETS
*RED REF: 2.5X TO 6X BASIC BLUE
RED REF.SER.1 ODDS 1:254 HTA
RED REF.SER.2 ODDS 1:184 HTA
RED REF.PRINT RUN 50 SERIAL #'d SETS
*GOLD: .6X TO 1.5X BASIC BLUE
GOLD SER.1 ODDS 1:51 HTA
GOLD SER.2 ODDS 1:37 HTA
GOLD PRINT RUN 250 SERIAL #'d SETS
*GOLD REF: 4X TO 10X BASIC BLUE
GOLD REF.SER.1 ODDS 1:510 HTA
GOLD REF.SER.2 ODDS 1:369 HTA
GOLD REF.PRINT RUN 25 SERIAL #'d SETS
TF1 Greg Maddux 2.50 6.00
TF2 Mark McGwire 4.00 10.00
TF3 Sammy Sosa 1.50 4.00
TF4 Juan Gonzalez .75 2.00
TF5 Alex Rodriguez 2.50 6.00
TF6 Travis Lee .75 2.00
TF7 Roger Clemens 3.00 8.00
TF8 Darin Erstad .75 2.00
TF9 Todd Helton 1.00 2.50
TF10 Mike Piazza 2.50 6.00
TF11 Kerry Wood .75 2.00
TF12 Ken Griffey Jr. 3.00 8.00
TF13 Frank Thomas 1.50 4.00
TF14 Jeff Bagwell 1.00 2.50
TF15 Nomar Garciaparra 2.50 6.00
TF16 Derek Jeter 4.00 10.00
TF17 Chipper Jones 1.50 4.00
TF18 Barry Bonds 4.00 10.00
TF19 Tony Gwynn 2.00 5.00
TF20 Ben Grieve .75 2.00

2000 Finest Pre-Production

This five card standard-size set was issued to preview what the 2000 Finest set would look like. It was issued to the dealers and hobby media on Topps' mailing list several weeks before the release of 2000 Finest. The cards can be differentiated from the regular Finest cards by the "PP" numbering on the back.

COMPLETE SET (5) 2.50 6.00
PP1 Brian Jordan .40 1.00
PP2 Bernie Williams .60 1.50
PP3 Pat Burrell .40 1.00
PP4 Corey Myers .40 1.00
PP5 Derek Jeter GEM 2.50 6.00

2000 Finest

Produced by Topps, the 2000 Finest Series one product was released in April, 2000 as a 147-card set. The Finest Series two product was released in July, 2000 as a 140-card set. Each hobby and retail pack contained six cards and carried a suggested retail price of $4.99. Each HTA pack contained 13 cards and carried a suggested retail price of $10.00. The set includes 179-player cards, 20 first series Rookie Cards (cards 101-120) each serial numbered to 2000 and 20 second series Rookie Cards (cards 247-266) each serial numbered to 3000, 15 Features subset cards (cards 121-135), 10 Counterparts subset cards (numbers 267-276), and 20 Gems subset cards (numbers 136-145 and 277-286). The set also includes two versions of card number 146 Ken Griffey Jr. wearing his Reds uniform (a portrait and action shot). Rookie Cards were seeded at a rate of 1:23 hobby/retail packs and 1:6 HTA packs. Features and Counterparts subset cards were inserted one every eight hobby and retail packs and one every three HTA packs. Gems subset cards were inserted one every 24 hobby and retail packs and one every nine HTA packs. Finally, 20 "Graded Gems" exchange cards were randomly seeded into packs (10 per series). The lucky handful of collectors that found these cards could send them into Topps for a complete Gems subset, each of which was professionally graded "Gem Mint 10" by PSA.

COMP.SERIES 1 w/o SP's (100) 10.00 25.00
COMP.SERIES 2 w/o SP's (100) 10.00 25.00
COMMON (1-100/146-246) .15 .40
COMMON ROOKIE (101-120) .75 2.00
SER.1 ROOKIES ODDS 1:23 H/R, 1:6 HTA
SER.1 ROOKIES PRINT RUN 2000 #'d SETS
COMMON FEATURES (121-135) .40 1.00
FEATURES 121-135 ODDS 1:8 H/R, 1:3 HTA
COMM.GEM (136-145/277-286) .40 1.00
GEMS 136-145/277-268 1:24 H/R, 1:9 HTA
COMMON ROOKIE (247-266) .60 1.50
SER.2 ROOKIES ODDS 1:13 H/R, 1:5 HTA
SER.2 ROOKIES PRINT RUN 3000 #'d SETS
COMMON COUNTER (267-276) .40 1.00
COUNTER 267-276 ODDS 1:8 H/R 1:3 HTA
GRIFFEY 146 NOT INCL.IN 100-CARD SET
BOTH 146 GRIFFEY'S PRINTED EQUALLY
GRADED GEMS SER.1 ODDS 1:9344 HTA
GRADED GEMS SER.2 ODDS 1:8157 HTA
GRADED GEMS EXCH.DEADLINE 12/31/00
1 Nomar Garciaparra .25 .60
2 Chipper Jones .40 1.00
3 Erubiel Durazo .15 .40
4 Robin Ventura .15 .40
5 Garret Anderson .15 .40
6 Dean Palmer .15 .40
7 Mariano Rivera .50 1.25
8 Rusty Greer .15 .40
9 Jim Thome .25 .60
10 Jeff Bagwell .25 .60
11 Jason Giambi .15 .40
12 Jeromy Burnitz .15 .40
13 Mark Grace .25 .60
14 Russ Ortiz .15 .40
15 Kevin Brown .15 .40
16 Kevin Millwood .15 .40
17 Scott Williamson .15 .40
18 Orlando Hernandez .15 .40
19 Todd Walker .15 .40
20 Carlos Beltran .25 .60
21 Ruben Rivera .15 .40
22 Curt Schilling .25 .60
23 Brian Giles .15 .40
24 Eric Karros .15 .40
25 Preston Wilson .15 .40
26 Al Leiter .15 .40
27 Juan Encarnacion .15 .40
28 Tim Salmon .15 .40
29 B.J. Surhoff .15 .40
30 Bernie Williams .25 .60
31 Lee Stevens .15 .40
32 Pokey Reese .15 .40
33 Mike Sweeney .15 .40
34 Corey Koskie .15 .40
35 Roberto Alomar .25 .60
36 Tim Hudson .25 .60
37 Tom Glavine .25 .60
38 Jeff Kent .15 .40
39 Mike Lieberthal .15 .40
40 Barry Larkin .25 .60
41 Paul O'Neill .25 .60
42 Rico Brogna .15 .40
43 Brian Daubach .15 .40
44 Rich Aurilia .15 .40
45 Vladimir Guerrero .25 .60
46 Luis Castillo .15 .40
47 Bartolo Colon .15 .40
48 Kevin Appier .15 .40
49 Mo Vaughn .15 .40
50 Alex Rodriguez .50 1.25
51 Randy Johnson .40 1.00
52 Kris Benson .15 .40
53 Tony Clark .15 .40
54 Chad Allen .15 .40
55 Larry Walker .25 .60
56 Freddy Garcia .15 .40
57 Paul Konerko .15 .40
58 Edgardo Alfonzo .15 .40
59 Brady Anderson .15 .40
60 Derek Jeter 1.00 2.50
61 John Smoltz .40 1.00
62 Doug Glanville .15 .40
63 Shannon Stewart .15 .40
64 Greg Maddux .50 1.25
65 Mark McGwire .60 1.50
66 Gary Sheffield .15 .40
67 Kevin Young .15 .40
68 Tony Gwynn .40 1.00
69 Rey Ordonez .15 .40
70 Cal Ripken 1.25 3.00
71 Todd Helton .25 .60
72 Brian Jordan .15 .40
73 Jose Canseco .25 .60
74 Luis Gonzalez .15 .40
75 Barry Bonds .60 1.50
76 Jermaine Dye .15 .40
77 Jose Offerman .15 .40
78 Magglio Ordonez .25 .60
79 Fred McGriff .25 .60
80 Ivan Rodriguez .25 .60
81 Josh Hamilton .50 1.25
82 Vernon Wells .15 .40
83 Mark Mulder .15 .40
84 John Patterson .15 .40
85 Nick Johnson .15 .40
86 Pablo Ozuna .15 .40
87 A.J. Burnett .15 .40
88 Jack Cust .15 .40
89 Adam Piatt .15 .40
90 Rob Ryan .15 .40
91 Sean Burroughs .15 .40
92 D'Angelo Jimenez .15 .40
93 Chad Hermansen .15 .40
94 Robert Fick .15 .40
95 Ruben Mateo .15 .40
96 Alex Escobar .15 .40
97 Wily Pena .15 .40
98 Corey Patterson .15 .40
99 Eric Munson .15 .40
100 Pat Burrell .15 .40
101 Michael Tejera RC .75 2.00
102 Bobby Bradley RC .75 2.00
103 Larry Bigbie RC .75 2.00
104 B.J. Garbe RC .75 2.00
105 Josh Kalinowski RC .75 2.00
106 Brett Myers RC 2.50 6.00
107 Chris Mears RC .75 2.00
108 Aaron Rowand RC 4.00 10.00
109 Corey Myers RC .75 2.00
110 John Sneed RC .75 2.00
111 Ryan Christianson RC .75 2.00
112 Kyle Snyder .75 2.00
113 Mike Paradis .75 2.00
114 Chance Caple RC .75 2.00
115 Ben Christensen RC .75 2.00
116 Brad Baker RC .75 2.00
117 Rob Purvis RC .75 2.00
118 Rick Asadoorian RC .75 2.00
119 Ruben Salazar RC .75 2.00
120 Julio Zuleta RC .75 2.00
121 A.Rodriguez 2.00 5.00
K.Griffey Jr.
122 N.Garciaparra 2.50 6.00
D.Jeter
123 M.McGwire 1.50 4.00
S.Sosa
124 R.Johnson 1.00 2.50
P.Martinez
125 I.Rodriguez 1.00 2.50
M.Piazza
126 M.Ramirez 1.00 2.50
R.Alomar
127 C.Jones 1.00 2.50
A.Jones
128 C.Ripken 3.00 8.00
T.Gwynn
129 J.Bagwell .60 1.50
C.Biggio
130 B.Bonds 1.50 4.00
V.Guerrero
131 N.Johnson 1.00 2.50
A.Soriano
132 Josh Hamilton 1.25 3.00
133 C.Patterson .40 1.00
R.Mateo
134 L.Walker .60 1.50
T.Helton
135 R.Ordonez .40 1.00
E.Alfonzo
136 Derek Jeter GEM 2.50 6.00
137 Alex Rodriguez GEM 1.25 3.00
138 Chipper Jones GEM 1.00 2.50
139 Mike Piazza GEM 1.00 2.50
140 Mark McGwire GEM 1.50 4.00
141 Ivan Rodriguez GEM .60 1.50
142 Cal Ripken GEM 3.00 8.00
143 Vladimir Guerrero GEM .60 1.50
144 Randy Johnson GEM 1.00 2.50
145 Jeff Bagwell GEM .60 1.50
146 Ken Griffey Jr. ACTION .75 2.00
146A Ken Griffey Jr. PORT .75 2.00
147 Andruw Jones .15 .40
148 Kerry Wood .15 .40
149 Jim Edmonds .15 .40
150 Pedro Martinez .25 .60
151 Warren Morris .15 .40
152 Trevor Hoffman .25 .60
153 Ryan Klesko .15 .40
154 Andy Pettitte .25 .60
155 Frank Thomas .40 1.00
156 Damion Easley .15 .40
157 Cliff Floyd .15 .40
158 Ben Davis .15 .40
159 John Valentin .15 .40
160 Rafael Palmeiro .25 .60
161 Andy Ashby .15 .40
162 J.D. Drew .15 .40
163 Jay Bell .15 .40
164 Adam Kennedy .15 .40
165 Manny Ramirez .40 1.00
166 John Halama .15 .40
167 Octavio Dotel .15 .40
168 Darin Erstad .15 .40
169 Jose Lima .15 .40
170 Andres Galarraga .25 .60
171 Scott Rolen .25 .60
172 Delino DeShields .15 .40
173 J.T. Snow .15 .40
174 Tony Womack .15 .40
175 John Olerud .15 .40
176 Jason Kendall .15 .40
177 Carlos Lee .15 .40
178 Eric Milton .15 .40
179 Jeff Cirillo .15 .40
180 Gabe Kapler .15 .40
181 Greg Vaughn .15 .40
182 Denny Neagle .15 .40
183 Tino Martinez .15 .40
184 Doug Mientkiewicz .15 .40
185 Juan Gonzalez .15 .40
186 Ellis Burks .15 .40
187 Mike Hampton .15 .40

188 Royce Clayton .15 .40
189 Mike Mussina .25 .60
190 Carlos Delgado .15 .40
191 Ben Grieve .15 .40
192 Fernando Tatis .15 .40
193 Matt Williams .15 .40
194 Rondell White .15 .40
195 Shawn Green .15 .40
196 Hideki Irabu .15 .40
197 Troy Glaus .15 .40
198 Roger Cedeno .15 .40
199 Ray Lankford .15 .40
200 Sammy Sosa .40 1.00
201 Kenny Lofton .15 .40
202 Edgar Martinez .25 .60
203 Mark Kotsay .15 .40
204 David Wells .15 .40
205 Craig Biggio .25 .60
206 Ray Durham .15 .40
207 Troy O'Leary .15 .40
208 Rickey Henderson .40 1.00
209 Bob Abreu .15 .40
210 Neifi Perez .15 .40
211 Carlos Febles .15 .40
212 Chuck Knoblauch .15 .40
213 Moises Alou .15 .40
214 Omar Vizquel .25 .60
215 Vinny Castilla .15 .40
216 Javy Lopez .15 .40
217 Johnny Damon .25 .60
218 Roger Clemens .50 1.25
219 Miguel Tejada .25 .60
220 Carl Everett .15 .40
221 Matt Lawton .15 .40
222 Albert Belle .15 .40
223 Adrian Beltre .40 1.00
224 Dante Bichette .15 .40
225 Raul Mondesi .15 .40
226 Mike Piazza .40 1.00
227 Brad Penny .15 .40
228 Kip Wells .15 .40
229 Adam Everett .15 .40
230 Eddie Yarnall .15 .40
231 Matt LeCroy .15 .40
232 Jason Tyner .15 .40
233 Rick Ankiel .25 .60
234 Lance Berkman .25 .60
235 Rafael Furcal .25 .60
236 Dee Brown .15 .40
237 Gookie Dawkins .15 .40
238 Eric Valent .15 .40
239 Peter Bergeron .15 .40
240 Alfonso Soriano .40 1.00
241 Adam Dunn .25 .60
242 Jorge Toca .15 .40
243 Ryan Anderson .15 .40
244 Jason Dellaero .15 .40
245 Jason Grilli .15 .40
246 Milton Bradley .15 .40
247 Scott Downs RC .60 1.50
248 Keith Reed RC .60 1.50
249 Edgar Cruz RC .60 1.50
250 Wes Anderson RC .60 1.50
251 Lyle Overbay RC 1.00 2.50
252 Mike Lamb RC .60 1.50
253 Vince Faison RC .60 1.50
254 Chad Alexander .60 1.50
255 Chris Wakeland RC .60 1.50
256 Aaron McNeal RC .60 1.50
257 Tomo Ohka RC .60 1.50
258 Ty Howington RC .60 1.50
259 Javier Colina RC .60 1.50
260 Jason Jennings .60 1.50
261 Ramon Santiago RC .60 1.50
262 Johan Santana RC 6.00 15.00
263 Quincy Foster RC .60 1.50
264 Junior Brignac RC .60 1.50
265 Rico Washington RC .60 1.50
266 Scott Sobkowiak RC .60 1.50
267 P.Martinez .60 1.50
R.Ankiel
268 M.Ramirez 1.00 2.50
V.Guerrero
269 A.Burnett .40 1.00
M.Mulder
270 M.Piazza 1.00 2.50
E.Munson
271 Josh Hamilton 1.25 3.00
272 K.Griffey Jr. 2.00 5.00
S.Sosa
273 D.Jeter 2.50 6.00
A.Soriano
274 M.McGwire 1.50 4.00
P.Burrell
275 C.Jones 3.00 8.00
C.Ripken
276 N.Garciaparra 1.25 3.00
A.Rodriguez
277 Pedro Martinez GEM .60 1.50
278 Tony Gwynn GEM 1.00 2.50
279 Barry Bonds GEM 1.50 4.00
280 Juan Gonzalez GEM .40 1.00
281 Larry Walker GEM .60 1.50
282 Nomar Garciaparra GEM .60 1.50
283 Ken Griffey Jr. GEM 2.00 5.00
284 Manny Ramirez GEM 1.00 2.50
285 Shawn Green GEM .40 1.00
286 Sammy Sosa GEM 1.00 2.50

2000 Finest Gold Refractors

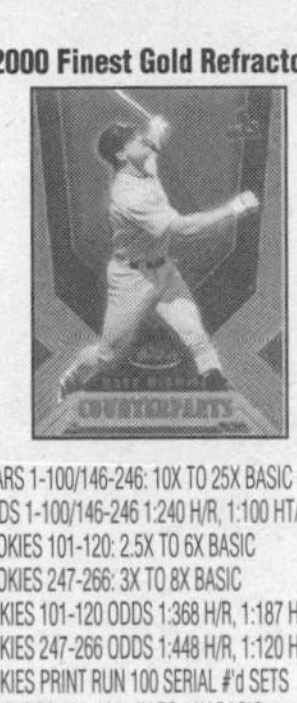

*STARS 1-100/146-246: 10X TO 25X BASIC
CARDS 1-100/146-246 1:240 H/R, 1:100 HTA
*ROOKIES 101-120: 2.5X TO 6X BASIC
*ROOKIES 247-266: 3X TO 8X BASIC
ROOKIES 101-120 ODDS 1:368 H/R, 1:187 HTA
ROOKIES 247-266 ODDS 1:448 H/R, 1:120 HTA
ROOKIES PRINT RUN 100 SERIAL #'d SETS
*FEATURES 121-135: 4X TO 10X BASIC
FEATURES ODDS 1:960 H/R, 1:400 HTA
*GEMS 136-145/277-286: 4X TO 10X BASIC
GEMS ODDS 1:2880 H/R, 1:1200 HTA
*COUNTER 267-276: 4X TO 10X BASIC
COUNTERPARTS ODDS 1:960 H/R 1:400 HTA
CARD 146 GRIFFEY REDS IS NOT AN SP
262 Johan Santana 60.00 120.00

2000 Finest Refractors

*STARS 1-100/146-246: 6X TO 15X BASIC
1-100/146-246 ODDS 1:24 H/R, 1:9 HTA
*ROOKIES 101-120: 2X TO 5X BASIC
SER.1 ROOKIES ODDS 1:93 H/R, 1:23 HTA
SER.1 ROOKIES PRINT RUN 500 #'d SETS
*FEATURES 121-135: 2.5X TO 6X BASIC
FEATURES ODDS 1:96 H/R, 1:40 HTA
*GEMS 136-145/277-286: 2.5X TO 6X BASIC
GEMS ODDS 1:288 H/R, 1:120 HTA
*ROOKIES 247-266: 2X TO 5X BASIC RC'S
SER.2 ROOKIES ODDS 1:49 H/R, 1:11 HTA
SER.2 ROOKIES PRINT RUN 1000 #'d SETS
*COUNTER 267-276: 2.5X TO 6X BASIC
COUNTERPARTS 1:96 H/R 1:40 HTA
CARD 146 GRIFFEY REDS IS NOT AN SP
262 Johan Santana 15.00 40.00

2000 Finest Gems Oversize

Randomly inserted as a "box-topper", this 20-card oversized set features some of the best players in major league baseball. Please note that cards 1-10 were inserted into series one boxes, and cards 11-20 were inserted into series two boxes.

COMPLETE SET (20) 25.00 60.00
COMPLETE SERIES 1 (10) 12.50 30.00
COMPLETE SERIES 2 (10) 12.50 30.00
ONE PER HOBBY/RETAIL BOX CHIP-TOPPER
*REF: .4X TO 1X BASIC GEMS OVERSIZE
REFRACTORS ONE PER HTA CHIP-TOPPER
1 Derek Jeter 4.00 10.00
2 Alex Rodriguez 2.00 5.00
3 Chipper Jones 1.50 4.00
4 Mike Piazza 1.50 4.00
5 Mark McGwire 2.50 6.00
6 Ivan Rodriguez 1.00 2.50
7 Cal Ripken 5.00 12.00
8 Vladimir Guerrero 1.00 2.50
9 Randy Johnson 1.50 4.00
10 Jeff Bagwell 1.00 2.50
11 Nomar Garciaparra 1.00 2.50
12 Ken Griffey Jr. 3.00 8.00
13 Manny Ramirez 1.50 4.00
14 Shawn Green .60 1.50
15 Sammy Sosa 1.50 4.00
16 Pedro Martinez 1.00 2.50
17 Tony Gwynn 1.50 4.00
18 Barry Bonds 2.50 6.00
19 Juan Gonzalez .60 1.50
20 Larry Walker 1.00 2.50

2000 Finest Ballpark Bounties

Randomly inserted into first and second series packs at one in 24 hobby/retail and 1:12 HTA, this insert set features 30 MLB players who are "wanted" for their pure talent. Card backs carry a "BB" prefix. Please note that cards 1-15 were inserted into series one packs, while cards 16-30 were inserted into series two packs.

COMPLETE SET (30) 40.00 100.00
COMPLETE SERIES 1 (15) 20.00 50.00
COMPLETE SERIES 2 (15) 20.00 50.00
STATED ODDS 1:24 HOB/RET, 1:12 HTA
BB1 Chipper Jones 2.00 5.00
BB2 Mike Piazza 2.00 5.00
BB3 Vladimir Guerrero 1.25 3.00
BB4 Sammy Sosa 2.00 5.00
BB5 Nomar Garciaparra 1.25 3.00
BB6 Manny Ramirez 2.00 5.00
BB7 Jeff Bagwell 1.25 3.00
BB8 Scott Rolen 1.25 3.00
BB9 Carlos Beltran 1.25 3.00
BB10 Pedro Martinez 1.25 3.00
BB11 Greg Maddux 2.50 6.00
BB12 Josh Hamilton 2.50 6.00
BB13 Adam Piatt .75 2.00
BB14 Pat Burrell .75 2.00
BB15 Alfonso Soriano 2.00 5.00
BB16 Alex Rodriguez 2.50 6.00
BB17 Derek Jeter 5.00 12.00
BB18 Cal Ripken 6.00 15.00
BB19 Larry Walker 1.25 3.00
BB20 Barry Bonds 3.00 8.00
BB21 Ken Griffey Jr. 4.00 10.00
BB22 Mark McGwire 3.00 8.00
BB23 Ivan Rodriguez 1.25 3.00
BB24 Andruw Jones .75 2.00
BB25 Todd Helton 1.25 3.00
BB26 Randy Johnson 2.00 5.00
BB27 Ruben Mateo .75 2.00
BB28 Corey Patterson .75 2.00
BB29 Sean Burroughs .75 2.00
BB30 Eric Munson .75 2.00

2000 Finest Dream Cast

Randomly inserted into series two packs at one in 36 hobby/retail packs and one in 13 HTA packs, this 10-card insert features players that have skills people dream about having. Card backs carry a "DC" prefix.

COMPLETE SET (10) 40.00 100.00
SER.2 STATED ODDS 1:36 HOB/RET, 1:13 HTA
DC1 Mark McGwire 4.00 10.00
DC2 Roberto Alomar 1.50 4.00
DC3 Chipper Jones 2.50 6.00
DC4 Derek Jeter 6.00 15.00
DC5 Barry Bonds 4.00 10.00
DC6 Ken Griffey Jr. 5.00 12.00
DC7 Sammy Sosa 2.50 6.00
DC8 Mike Piazza 2.50 6.00
DC9 Pedro Martinez 1.50 4.00
DC10 Randy Johnson 2.50 6.00

2000 Finest For the Record

Randomly inserted in first series packs at a rate of 1:71 hobby or retail and 1:33 HTA, this insert set features 30 serial-numbered cards. Each player has three versions that are sequentially numbered to the distance of the left, center, and right field walls of their home ballpark. Card backs carry a "FR" prefix.

SER.1 STATED ODDS 1:71 H/R, 1:33 HTA
PRINT RUNS B/WN 302-410 COPIES PER
FR1A Derek Jeter/318 12.00 30.00
FR1B Derek Jeter/408 12.00 30.00
FR1C Derek Jeter/314 12.00 30.00
FR2A Mark McGwire/330 3.00 8.00
FR2B Mark McGwire/402 3.00 8.00
FR2C Mark McGwire/330 3.00 8.00
FR3A Ken Griffey Jr./331 4.00 10.00
FR3B Ken Griffey Jr./405 4.00 10.00
FR3C Ken Griffey Jr./327 4.00 10.00
FR4A Alex Rodriguez/331 2.50 6.00
FR4B Alex Rodriguez/405 2.50 6.00
FR4C Alex Rodriguez/327 2.50 6.00
FR5A Nomar Garciaparra/310 1.25 3.00
FR5B Nomar Garciaparra/390 1.25 3.00
FR5C Nomar Garciaparra/302 1.25 3.00
FR6A Cal Ripken/333 6.00 15.00
FR6B Cal Ripken/410 6.00 15.00
FR6C Cal Ripken/318 6.00 15.00
FR7A Sammy Sosa/355 2.00 5.00
FR7B Sammy Sosa/400 2.00 5.00
FR7C Sammy Sosa/353 2.00 5.00
FR8A Manny Ramirez/325 2.00 5.00
FR8B Manny Ramirez/410 2.00 5.00
FR8C Manny Ramirez/325 2.00 5.00
FR9A Mike Piazza/338 2.00 5.00
FR9B Mike Piazza/410 2.00 5.00
FR9C Mike Piazza/338 2.00 5.00
FR10A Chipper Jones/335 2.00 5.00
FR10B Chipper Jones/401 2.00 5.00
FR10C Chipper Jones/330 2.00 5.00

2000 Finest Going the Distance

Randomly inserted in first series hobby and retail packs at one in 24 and HTA packs at a rate of one in 12, this 12-card insert set features some of the best hitters in major league baseball. Card backs carry a "GTD" prefix.

COMPLETE SET (12) 12.50 30.00
SER.1 ODDS 1:24 HOB/RET, 1:12 HTA
GTD1 Tony Gwynn 1.00 2.50
GTD2 Alex Rodriguez 1.25 3.00
GTD3 Derek Jeter 2.50 6.00
GTD4 Chipper Jones 1.00 2.50
GTD5 Nomar Garciaparra .60 1.50
GTD6 Sammy Sosa 1.00 2.50
GTD7 Ken Griffey Jr. 2.00 5.00
GTD8 Vladimir Guerrero .60 1.50
GTD9 Mark McGwire 1.50 4.00
GTD10 Mike Piazza 1.00 2.50
GTD11 Manny Ramirez 1.00 2.50
GTD12 Cal Ripken 3.00 8.00

2000 Finest Moments

Randomly inserted into series two hobby and retail packs at one in nine, and HTA packs at one in four, this four-card insert features great moments from the 1999 baseball season. Card backs carry a "FM" prefix.

COMPLETE SET (4) 2.50 6.00
SER.2 STATED ODDS 1:9 H/R 1:4 HTA
*REFRACTORS: .75X TO 2X BASIC MOMENTS
SER.2 REF.ODDS 1:20 H/R 1:9 HTA
FM1 Chipper Jones 1.00 2.50
FM2 Ivan Rodriguez .60 1.50
FM3 Tony Gwynn 1.00 2.50
FM4 Wade Boggs .60 1.50

2000 Finest Moments Refractors Autograph

Randomly inserted into series two hobby/retail packs at one in 425, and in HTA packs at one in 196, this four-card set is a complete parallel of the Finest Moments insert. This set is autographed by the player depicted on the card. Card backs carry a "FM" prefix.

SER.2 STATED ODDS 1:425 H/R 1:196 HTA
FM1 Chipper Jones 40.00 100.00
FM2 Ivan Rodriguez 15.00 40.00
FM3 Tony Gwynn 30.00 80.00
FM4 Wade Boggs 20.00 50.00

2001 Finest

This 140-card set was distributed in six-card hobby packs with a suggested retail price of $6. Printed on 27 pt. card stock, the set features color action photos of 100 veteran players, 30 draft picks and prospects printed with the "Rookie Card" logo and sequentially numbered to 999, and 10 standout veterans sequentially numbered to 1999.

COMP.SET w/o SP's (100) 10.00 25.00
COMMON CARD (1-110) .15 .40
SP ODDS 1:32 HOBBY, 1:15 HTA
SP PRINT RUN 1999 SERIAL #'d SETS
COMMON PROSPECT (111-140) 4.00 10.00
111-140 ODDS 1:21 HOBBY, 1:10 HTA
111-140 PRINT RUN 999 SERIAL #'d SETS
1 Mike Piazza SP 3.00 8.00
2 Andruw Jones .25 .60
3 Jason Giambi .15 .40
4 Fred McGriff .25 .60
5 Vladimir Guerrero SP 3.00 8.00
6 Adrian Gonzalez 1.00 2.50
7 Pedro Martinez .25 .60
8 Mike Lieberthal .15 .40
9 Warren Morris .15 .40
10 Juan Gonzalez .15 .40
11 Jose Canseco .25 .60
12 Jose Valentin .15 .40
13 Jeff Cirillo .15 .40
14 Pokey Reese .15 .40
15 Scott Rolen .25 .60
16 Greg Maddux .60 1.50
17 Carlos Delgado .15 .40
18 Rick Ankiel .15 .40
19 Steve Finley .15 .40
20 Shawn Green .15 .40
21 Orlando Cabrera .15 .40
22 Roberto Alomar .25 .60
23 John Olerud .15 .40
24 Albert Belle .15 .40
25 Edgardo Alfonzo .15 .40
26 Rafael Palmeiro .25 .60
27 Mike Sweeney .15 .40
28 Bernie Williams .25 .60
29 Larry Walker .15 .40
30 Barry Bonds SP 5.00 12.00
31 Orlando Hernandez .15 .40
32 Randy Johnson .40 1.00
33 Shannon Stewart .15 .40
34 Mark Grace .25 .60
35 Alex Rodriguez SP 4.00 10.00
36 Tino Martinez .25 .60
37 Carlos Febles .15 .40
38 Al Leiter .15 .40
39 Omar Vizquel .25 .60
40 Chuck Knoblauch .15 .40
41 Tim Salmon .25 .60
42 Brian Jordan .15 .40
43 Edgar Renteria .15 .40
44 Preston Wilson .15 .40
45 Mariano Rivera .40 1.00
46 Gabe Kapler .15 .40
47 Jason Kendall .15 .40
48 Rickey Henderson .40 1.00
49 Luis Gonzalez .15 .40
50 Tom Glavine .25 .60
51 Jeromy Burnitz .15 .40
52 Garret Anderson .15 .40
53 Craig Biggio .25 .60
54 Vinny Castilla .15 .40
55 Jeff Kent .15 .40
56 Gary Sheffield .15 .40
57 Jorge Posada .25 .60
58 Sean Casey .15 .40
59 Johnny Damon .25 .60
60 Dean Palmer .15 .40
61 Todd Helton .25 .60
62 Barry Larkin .25 .60
63 Robin Ventura .15 .40
64 Kenny Lofton .15 .40
65 Sammy Sosa SP 2.00 5.00
66 Rafael Furcal .15 .40
67 Jay Bell .15 .40
68 J.T. Snow .15 .40
69 Jose Vidro .15 .40
70 Ivan Rodriguez .25 .60
71 Jermaine Dye .15 .40
72 Chipper Jones SP 3.00 8.00
73 Fernando Vina .15 .40
74 Ben Grieve .15 .40
75 Mark McGwire SP 5.00 12.00
76 Matt Williams .15 .40
77 Mark Grudzielanek .15 .40
78 Mike Hampton .15 .40
79 Brian Giles .15 .40
80 Tony Gwynn .50 1.25
81 Carlos Beltran .15 .40
82 Ray Durham .15 .40
83 Brad Radke .15 .40
84 David Justice .15 .40
85 Frank Thomas .40 1.00
86 Todd Zeile .15 .40
87 Pat Burrell .15 .40
88 Jim Thome .25 .60
89 Greg Vaughn .15 .40
90 Ken Griffey Jr. SP 6.00 15.00
91 Mike Mussina .25 .60
92 Magglio Ordonez .15 .40
93 Bob Abreu .15 .40
94 Alex Gonzalez .15 .40
95 Kevin Brown .15 .40
96 Jay Buhner .15 .40
97 Roger Clemens .75 2.00
98 Nomar Garciaparra SP 2.00 5.00
99 Derrek Lee .25 .60
100 Derek Jeter SP 8.00 20.00
101 Adrian Beltre .15 .40
102 Geoff Jenkins .15 .40
103 Javy Lopez .15 .40
104 Raul Mondesi .15 .40
105 Troy Glaus .15 .40
106 Jeff Bagwell .25 .60
107 Eric Karros .15 .40
108 Mo Vaughn .15 .40
109 Cal Ripken 1.25 3.00
110 Manny Ramirez Sox .25 .60
111 Scott Heard PROS 4.00 10.00
112 Luis Montanez PROS RC 4.00 10.00
113 Ben Diggins PROS 4.00 10.00
114 Shaun Boyd PROS RC 4.00 10.00
115 Sean Burnett PROS 4.00 10.00
116 Carmen Cali PROS RC 4.00 10.00
117 Derek Thompson PROS 4.00 10.00
118 David Parrish PROS RC 4.00 10.00
119 Dominic Rich PROS RC 4.00 10.00
120 Chad Petty PROS RC 4.00 10.00
121 Steve Smyth PROS RC 4.00 10.00
122 John Lackey PROS 4.00 10.00
123 Matt Galante PROS RC 4.00 10.00
124 Danny Borrell PROS RC 4.00 10.00
125 Bob Keppel PROS RC 4.00 10.00
126 Justin Wayne PROS RC 4.00 10.00
127 J.R. House PROS 4.00 10.00
128 Brian Sellier PROS RC 4.00 10.00
129 Dan Moylan PROS RC 4.00 10.00
130 Scott Pratt PROS RC 4.00 10.00
131 Victor Hall PROS RC 4.00 10.00
132 Joel Pineiro PROS 4.00 10.00
133 Josh Axelson PROS RC 4.00 10.00
134 Jose Reyes PROS RC 10.00 25.00
135 Greg Runser PROS RC 4.00 10.00
136 Bryan Hebson PROS RC 4.00 10.00
137 Sammy Serrano PROS RC 4.00 10.00
138 Kevin Joseph PROS RC 4.00 10.00
139 Juan Richardson PROS RC 4.00 10.00
140 Mark Fischer PROS RC 4.00 10.00

2001 Finest Refractors

*1-110 REF: 4X TO 10X BASIC 1-110
1-110 ODDS 1:13 HOBBY, 1:6 HTA
1-110 PRINT RUN 499 SERIAL #'d SETS
*SP REF: .5X TO 1.2X BASIC SP
SP STATED ODDS 1:159 HOBBY, 1:73 HTA
SP STATED PRINT RUN 399 SERIAL #'d SETS
*111-140 REF: .75X TO 2X BASIC 111-140
111-140 ODDS 1:88 HOBBY, 1:40 HTA
111-140 PRINT RUN 241 SERIAL #'d SETS

2001 Finest All-Stars

Randomly inserted in packs at the rate of one in five, this 10-card set features color photos of the preeminent players at their respective positions. A refractive parallel version of this insert set was also produced and inserted in packs at the rate of one in 20.

COMPLETE SET (10) 30.00 60.00
STATED ODDS 1:10 HOBBY, 1:5 HTA
*REF: 1X TO 2.5X BASIC ALL-STARS
REFRACTOR ODDS 1:40 HOBBY, 1:20 HTA
FAS1 Mark McGwire 4.00 10.00
FAS2 Derek Jeter 4.00 10.00
FAS3 Alex Rodriguez 2.00 5.00
FAS4 Chipper Jones 1.50 4.00
FAS5 Nomar Garciaparra 2.50 6.00
FAS6 Sammy Sosa 1.50 4.00
FAS7 Mike Piazza 2.50 6.00
FAS8 Barry Bonds 4.00 10.00
FAS9 Vladimir Guerrero 1.50 4.00
FAS10 Ken Griffey Jr. 3.00 8.00

2001 Finest Autographs

Randomly inserted in packs at the rate of one in 22, this 29-card set features autographed color photos of players who made the moments. All of these cards are refractors and carry the Topps "Certified Autograph" stamp and the Topps "Genuine Issue" sticker.

STATED ODDS 1:22 HOBBY, 1:10 HTA
FAAG Adrian Gonzalez 4.00 10.00
FAAH Adam Hyzdu 4.00 10.00
FAAK Adam Kennedy 6.00 15.00
FAAP Albert Pujols 200.00 400.00
FABD Ben Diggins 4.00 10.00
FABM Ben Molina 6.00 15.00
FABS Ben Sheets 10.00 25.00
FABZ Barry Zito 6.00 15.00
FABKC Brian Cole 10.00 25.00
FACD Chad Durham 4.00 10.00
FACP Carlos Pena 6.00 15.00
FADK Dave Krynzel 4.00 10.00
FADCP Corey Patterson 4.00 10.00
FAJC Joe Crede 10.00 25.00
FAJH Jason Hart 4.00 10.00
FAJM Justin Morneau 6.00 15.00
FAJO Jose Ortiz 4.00 10.00
FAJP Jay Payton 4.00 10.00
FAJHH Josh Hamilton 6.00 15.00
FAJRH J.R. House 4.00 10.00
FAKG Keith Ginter 4.00 10.00
FAKM Kevin Mench 6.00 15.00
FAMB Milton Bradley 6.00 15.00
FAMQ Mark Quinn 4.00 10.00
FAMR Mark Redman 4.00 10.00
FARF Rafael Furcal 6.00 15.00
FASB Sean Burnett 4.00 10.00
FATF Troy Farnsworth 4.00 10.00
FATL Terrence Long 4.00 10.00

2001 Finest Moments

Randomly inserted in packs at the rate of one in 12, this 25-card set features color photos of players involved in great moments from the 2000 season plus both active and retired 3000 Hit Club members. A refractive parallel version of this set was also produced with an insertion rate of 1:40.

COMPLETE SET (25) 60.00 120.00
STATED ODDS 1:12 HOBBY, 1:6 HTA
*REF: .75X TO 2X BASIC MOMENTS
REFRACTOR ODDS 1:40 HOBBY, 1:20 HTA
FM1 Pat Burrell 1.00 2.50
FM2 Adam Kennedy 1.00 2.50
FM3 Mike Lamb 1.00 2.50
FM4 Rafael Furcal 1.00 2.50
FM5 Terrence Long 1.00 2.50
FM6 Jay Payton 1.00 2.50
FM7 Mark Quinn 1.00 2.50
FM8 Ben Molina 1.00 2.50
FM9 Kazuhiro Sasaki 1.00 2.50
FM10 Mark Redman 1.00 2.50
FM11 Barry Bonds 6.00 15.00
FM12 Alex Rodriguez 3.00 8.00
FM13 Roger Clemens 5.00 12.00
FM14 Jim Edmonds 1.00 2.50
FM15 Jason Giambi 1.00 2.50
FM16 Todd Helton 1.50 4.00
FM17 Troy Glaus 1.00 2.50
FM18 Carlos Delgado 1.00 2.50
FM19 Darin Erstad 1.00 2.50
FM20 Cal Ripken 8.00 20.00
FM21 Paul Molitor 1.00 2.50
FM22 Robin Yount 2.50 6.00
FM23 George Brett 5.00 12.00
FM24 Dave Winfield 1.00 2.50
FM25 Eddie Murray 2.50 6.00

2001 Finest Moments Refractors Autograph

Randomly inserted in packs at the rate of one in 250, this 10-card set features autographed player photos with the Topps "Certified Autograph" stamp and the Topps "Genuine Issue" sticker printed on these refractive cards. Exchange cards with a redemption deadline of April 30, 2003 were seeded into packs for Cal Ripken, Eddie Murray and Robin Yount.

STATED ODDS 1:250 HOBBY, 1:115 HTA
FMABB Barry Bonds 90.00 150.00
FMACR Cal Ripken 40.00 100.00
FMADW Dave Winfield 20.00 50.00
FMAEM Eddie Murray 15.00 40.00
FMAGB George Brett 30.00 80.00
FMAJG Jason Giambi 10.00 25.00
FMAPM Paul Molitor 15.00 40.00
FMARY Robin Yount 25.00 60.00
FMATG Troy Glaus 10.00 25.00
FMATH Todd Helton 10.00 25.00

2001 Finest Origins

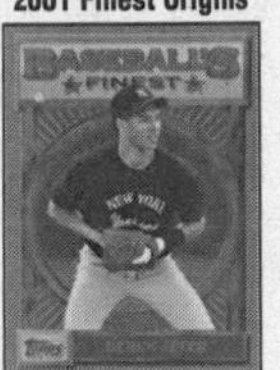

Randomly inserted in packs at the rate of one in seven, this 15-card set features some of today's best ballplayers who didn't make the 1993 Finest cut. These cards are printed in the 1993 classic Finest card design. A refractive parallel version of this set was also produced with an insertion rate of 1:40.

COMPLETE SET (15) 20.00 40.00
STATED ODDS 1:7 HOBBY, 1:4 HTA
*REF: 1X TO 2.5X BASIC ORIGINS
REFRACTOR ODDS 1:40 HOBBY, 1:20 HTA
FO1 Derek Jeter 5.00 12.00
FO2 Jason Kendall .75 2.00
FO3 Jose Vidro .75 2.00
FO4 Preston Wilson .75 2.00
FO5 Jim Edmonds .75 2.00
FO6 Vladimir Guerrero 2.00 5.00
FO7 Andruw Jones 1.25 3.00
FO8 Scott Rolen 1.25 3.00
FO9 Edgardo Alfonzo .75 2.00
FO10 Mike Sweeney .75 2.00
FO11 Alex Rodriguez 2.50 6.00
FO12 Jermaine Dye .75 2.00
FO13 Charles Johnson .75 2.00
FO14 Darren Dreifort .75 2.00
FO15 Neifi Perez .75 2.00

2002 Finest

This 110 card set was issued in five card pack with an SRP of $6 per pack which were packed six per mini box with three mini boxes per full box and twelve boxes per case. Cards number 101 through 110 are Rookie Cards which were all autographed by the featured player. One of these autograph cards were inserted into each six pack mini box.

COMP.SET w/o SP's (100) 10.00 25.00
COMMON CARD (1-100) .20 .50
COMMON CARD (101-110) 4.00 10.00
ONE AUTO OR RELIC PER 6-PACK MINI BOX
1 Mike Mussina .30 .75
2 Steve Sparks .20 .50
3 Randy Johnson .50 1.25
4 Orlando Cabrera .20 .50
5 Jeff Kent .20 .50
6 Carlos Delgado .20 .50
7 Ivan Rodriguez .30 .75
8 Jose Cruz .20 .50
9 Jason Giambi .20 .50
10 Brad Penny .20 .50
11 Moises Alou .20 .50
12 Mike Piazza .75 2.00
13 Ben Grieve .20 .50
14 Derek Jeter 1.25 3.00
15 Roy Oswalt .20 .50
16 Pat Burrell .20 .50
17 Preston Wilson .20 .50
18 Kevin Brown .20 .50
19 Barry Bonds 1.25 3.00
20 Phil Nevin .20 .50
21 Aramis Ramirez .20 .50
22 Carlos Beltran .20 .50
23 Chipper Jones .50 1.25
24 Curt Schilling .20 .50
25 Jorge Posada .30 .75
26 Alfonso Soriano .20 .50
27 Cliff Floyd .20 .50
28 Rafael Palmeiro .30 .75
29 Terrence Long .20 .50
30 Ken Griffey Jr. 1.00 2.50
31 Jason Kendall .20 .50
32 Jose Vidro .20 .50
33 Jermaine Dye .20 .50
34 Bobby Higginson .20 .50

2002 Finest

35 Albert Pujols 1.00 2.50
36 Miguel Tejada .20 .50
37 Jim Edmonds .20 .50
38 Barry Zito .20 .50
39 Jimmy Rollins .20 .50
40 Rafael Furcal .20 .50
41 Omar Vizquel .30 .75
42 Kazuhiro Sasaki .20 .50
43 Brian Giles .20 .50
44 Darin Erstad .20 .50
45 Mariano Rivera .50 1.25
46 Troy Percival .20 .50
47 Mike Sweeney .20 .50
48 Vladimir Guerrero .50 1.25
49 Troy Glaus .20 .50
50 So Taguchi RC 1.00 2.50
51 Edgardo Alfonzo .20 .50
52 Roger Clemens 1.00 2.50
53 Eric Chavez .20 .50
54 Alex Rodriguez .60 1.50
55 Cristian Guzman .20 .50
56 Jeff Bagwell .30 .75
57 Bernie Williams .30 .75
58 Kerry Wood .20 .50
59 Ryan Klesko .20 .50
60 Ichiro Suzuki 1.00 2.50
61 Larry Walker .20 .50
62 Nomar Garciaparra .75 2.00
63 Craig Biggio .30 .75
64 J.D. Drew .20 .50
65 Juan Pierre .20 .50
66 Roberto Alomar .30 .75
67 Luis Gonzalez .20 .50
68 Bud Smith .20 .50
69 Magglio Ordonez .20 .50
70 Scott Rolen .30 .75
71 Tsuyoshi Shinjo .20 .50
72 Paul Konerko .20 .50
73 Garret Anderson .20 .50
74 Tim Hudson .20 .50
75 Adam Dunn .20 .50
76 Gary Sheffield .20 .50
77 Johnny Damon Sox .30 .75
78 Todd Helton .30 .75
79 Geoff Jenkins .20 .50
80 Shawn Green .20 .50
81 C.C. Sabathia .20 .50
82 Kazuhisa Ishii RC 1.00 2.50
83 Rich Aurilia .20 .50
84 Mike Hampton .20 .50
85 Ben Sheets .20 .50
86 Andruw Jones .30 .75
87 Richie Sexson .20 .50
88 Jim Thome .30 .75
89 Sammy Sosa .50 1.25
90 Greg Maddux .75 2.00
91 Pedro Martinez .30 .75
92 Jeromy Burnitz .20 .50
93 Raul Mondesi .20 .50
94 Bret Boone .20 .50
95 Jerry Hairston .20 .50
96 Mike Rivera .20 .50
97 Juan Cruz .20 .50
98 Morgan Ensberg .20 .50
99 Nathan Haynes .20 .50
100 Xavier Nady .20 .50
101 Nic Jackson FY AU RC 4.00 10.00
102 Mauricio Lara FY AU RC 4.00 10.00
103 Freddy Sanchez FY AU RC 4.00 10.00
104 Clint Nageotte FY AU RC 4.00 10.00
105 Beltran Perez FY AU RC 4.00 10.00
106 Garrett Gentry FY AU RC 4.00 10.00
107 Chad Qualls FY AU RC 4.00 10.00
108 Jason Bay FY AU RC 4.00 10.00
109 Michael Hill FY AU RC 4.00 10.00
110 Brian Tallet FY AU RC 4.00 10.00

2002 Finest Refractors

*REFRACTORS 1-100: 2.5X TO 6X BASIC
*REF.RC'S 1-100: 1.5X TO 4X BASIC
STATED ODDS 1:2 MINI BOXES
STATED PRINT RUN 499 SERIAL #'d SETS
101 Nic Jackson FY 2.00 5.00
102 Mauricio Lara FY 2.00 5.00
103 Freddy Sanchez FY 3.00 8.00
104 Clint Nageotte FY 3.00 8.00
105 Beltran Perez FY 2.00 5.00
106 Garett Gentry FY 2.00 5.00
107 Chad Qualls FY 3.00 8.00
108 Jason Bay FY 3.00 8.00
109 Michael Hill FY 2.00 5.00
110 Brian Tallet FY 2.00 5.00

2002 Finest X-Fractors

*XF 1-100: 3X TO 8X BASIC
*XF RC'S 1-100: 2X TO 5X BASIC
*XF 101-110: .5X TO 1.2X REFRACTOR
STATED ODDS 1:3 MINI BOXES
STATED PRINT RUN 299 SERIAL #'d SETS

2002 Finest X-Fractors Protectors

*XF PROT. 1-100: 6X TO 15X BASIC
*XF PROT.RC'S 1-100: 4X TO 10X BASIC
*XF PROT 101-110: .75X TO 2X REFRACTOR
STATED ODDS 1:7 MINI BOXES
STATED PRINT RUN 99 SERIAL #'d SETS

2002 Finest Bat Relics

Inserted at a stated rate of one in 12 mini boxes these 15 cards feature a bat slice from the featured player.
STATED ODDS 1:12 MINI BOXES
FBRAJ Andruw Jones 6.00 15.00
FBRAP Albert Pujols 8.00 20.00
FBRAR Alex Rodriguez 6.00 15.00
FBRAS Alfonso Soriano 4.00 10.00
FBRBB Barry Bonds 10.00 25.00
FBRBO Bret Boone 4.00 10.00
FBRBW Bernie Williams 6.00 15.00
FBRCJ Chipper Jones 6.00 15.00
FBRIR Ivan Rodriguez 6.00 15.00
FBRLG Luis Gonzalez 4.00 10.00
FBRMP Mike Piazza 6.00 15.00
FBRNG Nomar Garciaparra 6.00 15.00
FBRTG Tony Gwynn 6.00 15.00
FBRTH Todd Helton 6.00 15.00
FBRTS Tsuyoshi Shinjo 4.00 10.00

2002 Finest Jersey Relics

Inserted at a stated rate of one in four mini boxes, these 24 cards feature the player photo along with a game-used jersey swatch.
STATED ODDS 1:4 MINI BOXES
FJRAJ Andruw Jones 6.00 15.00
FJRAR Alex Rodriguez 6.00 15.00
FJRBB Barry Bonds 10.00 25.00
FJRBO Bret Boone 4.00 10.00
FJRCD Carlos Delgado 4.00 10.00
FJRCJ Chipper Jones 6.00 15.00
FJRCS Curt Schilling 4.00 10.00
FJRFT Frank Thomas 6.00 15.00
FJRGM Greg Maddux 6.00 15.00
FJRHN Hideo Nomo 6.00 15.00
FJRIR Ivan Rodriguez 6.00 15.00
FJRJB Jeff Bagwell 6.00 15.00
FJRLG Luis Gonzalez 4.00 10.00
FJRLW Larry Walker 4.00 10.00
FJRMG Mark Grace 6.00 15.00
FJRMP Mike Piazza 6.00 15.00
FJRPM Pedro Martinez 6.00 15.00
FJRRA Roberto Alomar 6.00 15.00
FJRRH Rickey Henderson 6.00 15.00
FJRRP Rafael Palmeiro 6.00 15.00
FJRSG Shawn Green 4.00 10.00
FJRTG Tony Gwynn 6.00 15.00
FJRTH Todd Helton 6.00 15.00
FJRTS Tsuyoshi Shinjo 4.00 10.00

2002 Finest Moments Autographs

Inserted at a stated rate of one in three mini boxes, these cards feature leading retired players who signed cards honoring their greatest career moment.
STATED ODDS 1:3 MINI BOXES
FMABG Bob Gibson 30.00 80.00
FMABR Bobby Richardson 6.00 15.00
FMABRO Brooks Robinson 12.00 30.00
FMABT Bobby Thomson 10.00 25.00
FMADL Don Larsen 10.00 25.00
FMADM Don Mattingly 25.00 60.00
FMAFJ Fergie Jenkins 6.00 15.00
FMAGG Goose Gossage 8.00 20.00
FMAGP Gaylord Perry 8.00 20.00
FMAJB Jim Bunning 6.00 15.00
FMAJS Johnny Sain 8.00 20.00
FMALA Luis Aparicio 10.00 25.00
FMAMS Mike Schmidt 20.00 50.00
FMARS Red Schoendienst 12.00 30.00
FMAYB Yogi Berra 30.00 80.00

2003 Finest

This 110 card set was released in May, 2003. This product was issued in six pack mini-boxes with an SRP of $36. The first 100 cards are veterans while the final 10 cards featured autographed cards of leading rookies and prospects. Those cards (101-110) were issued at a stated rate of one in four mini boxes.
COMP.SET w/o SP's (100) 10.00 25.00
COMMON CARD (1-100) .20 .50
COMMON CARD (101-110) 6.00 15.00
COMMON RC (101-110) 4.00 10.00
101-110 STATED ODDS 1:4 MINI-BOXES
1993 FINEST BUYBACKS 1:333 MINI BOXES
1993 FINEST BUYBACKS ARE NOT STAMPED
1 Sammy Sosa .50 1.25
2 Paul Konerko .30 .75
3 Todd Helton .30 .75
4 Mike Lowell .20 .50
5 Lance Berkman .30 .75
6 Kazuhisa Ishii .20 .50
7 A.J. Pierzynski .20 .50
8 Jose Vidro .20 .50
9 Roberto Alomar .30 .75
10 Derek Jeter 1.25 3.00
11 Barry Zito .30 .75
12 Jimmy Rollins .30 .75
13 Brian Giles .20 .50
14 Ryan Klesko .20 .50
15 Rich Aurilia .20 .50
16 Jim Edmonds .30 .75
17 Aubrey Huff .20 .50
18 Ivan Rodriguez .30 .75
19 Eric Hinske .20 .50
20 Barry Bonds .75 2.00
21 Darin Erstad .20 .50
22 Curt Schilling .30 .75
23 Andruw Jones .20 .50
24 Jay Gibbons .20 .50
25 Nomar Garciaparra .30 .75
26 Kerry Wood .20 .50
27 Magglio Ordonez .20 .50
28 Austin Kearns .20 .50
29 Jason Jennings .20 .50
30 Jason Giambi .20 .50
31 Tim Hudson .30 .75
32 Edgar Martinez .30 .75
33 Carl Crawford .30 .75
34 Hee Seop Choi .20 .50
35 Vladimir Guerrero .30 .75
36 Jeff Kent .20 .50
37 John Smoltz .50 1.25
38 Frank Thomas .50 1.25
39 Cliff Floyd .20 .50
40 Mike Piazza .50 1.25
41 Mark Prior .30 .75
42 Tim Salmon .20 .50
43 Shawn Green .20 .50
44 Bernie Williams .30 .75
45 Jim Thome .30 .75
46 John Olerud .20 .50
47 Orlando Hudson .20 .50
48 Mark Teixeira .30 .75
49 Gary Sheffield .20 .50
50 Ichiro Suzuki .60 1.50
51 Tom Glavine .30 .75
52 Torii Hunter .20 .50
53 Craig Biggio .30 .75
54 Carlos Beltran .30 .75
55 Bartolo Colon .20 .50
56 Jorge Posada .30 .75
57 Pat Burrell .20 .50
58 Edgar Renteria .20 .50
59 Rafael Palmeiro .30 .75
60 Alfonso Soriano .20 .50
61 Brandon Phillips .20 .50
62 Luis Gonzalez .20 .50
63 Manny Ramirez .50 1.25
64 Garret Anderson .20 .50
65 Ken Griffey Jr. 1.00 2.50
66 A.J. Burnett .20 .50
67 Mike Sweeney .20 .50
68 Doug Mientkiewicz .20 .50
69 Eric Chavez .20 .50
70 Adam Dunn .20 .50
71 Shea Hillenbrand .20 .50
72 Troy Glaus .20 .50
73 Rodrigo Lopez .20 .50
74 Moises Alou .20 .50
75 Chipper Jones .50 1.25
76 Bobby Abreu .20 .50
77 Mark Mulder .20 .50
78 Kevin Brown .20 .50
79 Josh Beckett .20 .50
80 Larry Walker .30 .75
81 Randy Johnson .50 1.25
82 Greg Maddux .60 1.50
83 Johnny Damon .30 .75
84 Omar Vizquel .30 .75
85 Jeff Bagwell .30 .75
86 Carlos Pena .30 .75
87 Roy Oswalt .30 .75
88 Richie Sexson .20 .50
89 Roger Clemens .60 1.50
90 Miguel Tejada .30 .75
91 Vicente Padilla .20 .50
92 Phil Nevin .20 .50
93 Edgardo Alfonzo .20 .50
94 Bret Boone .20 .50
95 Albert Pujols .60 1.50
96 Carlos Delgado .20 .50
97 Jose Contreras RC .50 1.25
98 Scott Rolen .30 .75
99 Pedro Martinez .30 .75
100 Alex Rodriguez .60 1.50
101 Adam LaRoche AU 4.00 10.00
102 Andy Marte AU RC 4.00 10.00
103 Daryl Clark AU RC 4.00 10.00
104 J.D. Durbin AU RC 4.00 10.00
105 Craig Brazell AU RC 4.00 10.00
106 Brian Burgamy AU RC 4.00 10.00
107 Tyler Johnson AU RC 4.00 10.00
108 Joey Gomes AU RC 4.00 10.00
109 Bryan Bullington AU RC 4.00 10.00
110 Byron Gettis AU RC 4.00 10.00

2003 Finest Refractors

*REFRACTORS 1-100: 2X TO 5X BASIC
*REFRACTOR RC'S 1-100: 1.25X TO 3X BASIC
1-100 STATED ODDS ONE PER MINI-BOX
*REFRACTORS 101-110: .75X TO 2X BASIC
101-110 STATED ODDS 1:34 MINI-BOXES
101-110 STATED PRINT RUN 199 #'d SETS

2003 Finest X-Fractors

*X-FRACTORS 1-100: 6X TO 15X BASIC
*X-FRACTOR RC'S 1-100: 4X TO 10X BASIC
*X-FRACTORS 101-110: 1X TO 2.5X BASIC
STATED ODDS 1:7 MINI-BOXES
STATED PRINT RUN 99 SERIAL #'d SETS

2003 Finest Uncirculated Gold X-Fractors

*GOLD X-F 1-100: 5X TO 12X BASIC
*GOLD X-F RC'S 1-100: 3X TO 8X BASIC
*GOLD X-F 101-110: .75X TO 2X BASIC
ONE PER BASIC SEALED BOX
STATED PRINT RUN 199 SERIAL #'d SETS

2003 Finest Bat Relics

These cards were inserted at different rates depending on what group the bat relic belonged to. We have notated what group the player belonged to next to their name in our checklist.
GROUP A STATED ODDS 1:104 MINI-BOXES
GROUP B STATED ODDS 1:32 MINI-BOXES
GROUP C STATED ODDS 1:29 MINI-BOXES
GROUP D STATED ODDS 1:42 MINI-BOXES
GROUP E STATED ODDS 1:40 MINI-BOXES
GROUP F STATED ODDS 1:23 MINI-BOXES
GROUP G STATED ODDS 1:18 MINI-BOXES
GROUP H STATED ODDS 1:24 MINI-BOXES
GROUP I STATED ODDS 1:12 MINI-BOXES
GROUP J STATED ODDS 1:22 MINI-BOXES
GROUP K STATED ODDS 1:21 MINI-BOXES
AD Adam Dunn H 2.00 5.00
AK Austin Kearns F 1.25 3.00
AP Albert Pujols I 4.00 10.00
AR Alex Rodriguez E 4.00 10.00
AS Alfonso Soriano H 2.00 5.00
BB Barry Bonds F 5.00 12.00
CJ Chipper Jones G 3.00 8.00
CR Cal Ripken B 10.00 25.00
DM Dale Murphy I 3.00 8.00
GM Greg Maddux F 4.00 10.00
IR Ivan Rodriguez G 2.00 5.00
JB Jeff Bagwell D 2.00 5.00
JT Jim Thome D 2.00 5.00
KP Kirby Puckett K 3.00 8.00
LB Lance Berkman C 2.00 5.00
MP Mike Piazza E 3.00 8.00
MR Manny Ramirez I 3.00 8.00
MS Mike Schmidt C 5.00 12.00
MT Miguel Tejada I 2.00 5.00
NG Nomar Garciaparra A 2.00 5.00
PM Paul Molitor C 3.00 8.00
RC Rod Carew K 2.00 5.00
RCL Roger Clemens J 4.00 10.00
RH Rickey Henderson B 3.00 8.00
RP Rafael Palmeiro J 2.00 5.00
TH Todd Helton B 2.00 5.00
WB Wade Boggs G 2.00 5.00

2003 Finest Moments Refractors Autographs

Inserted at different odds depening on whether the card was issued as part of group A or group B, this 12 card set features authentic signatures of baseball legends. Johnny Sain did not return his card in time for inclusion in this product and the exchange cards could be redeemed until April 30th, 2005.
GROUP A STATED ODDS 1:113 MINI-BOXES
GROUP B STATED ODDS 1:5 MINI-BOXES
DL Don Larsen B 8.00 20.00
EB Ernie Banks A 40.00 100.00
GC Gary Carter B 6.00 15.00
GF George Foster B 6.00 15.00
GG Goose Gossage B 6.00 15.00
GP Gaylord Perry B 6.00 15.00
JP Jim Palmer B 6.00 15.00
JS Johnny Sain B 6.00 15.00
KH Keith Hernandez B 6.00 15.00
LB Lou Brock B 6.00 15.00
OC Orlando Cepeda B 6.00 15.00
PB Paul Blair B 6.00 15.00
WMA Willie Mays A 200.00 400.00

2003 Finest Uniform Relics

These 22 cards were inserted in different odds depending on what group the player belonged to. We have notated what group the player belonged to next to their name in our checklist.
GROUP A STATED ODDS 1:28 MINI-BOXES
GROUP B STATED ODDS 1:11 MINI-BOXES
GROUP C STATED ODDS 1:11 MINI-BOXES
GROUP D STATED ODDS 1:10 MINI-BOXES
GROUP E STATED ODDS 1:19 MINI-BOXES
GROUP F STATED ODDS 1:12 MINI-BOXES
GROUP G STATED ODDS 1:34 MINI-BOXES
GROUP H STATED ODDS 1:17 MINI-BOXES
AD Adam Dunn B 2.50 6.00
AJ Andruw Jones H 1.50 4.00
AP Albert Pujols D 5.00 12.00
AR Alex Rodriguez F 5.00 12.00
AS Alfonso Soriano A 2.50 6.00
BB Barry Bonds D 6.00 15.00
CJ Chipper Jones B 4.00 10.00
CS Curt Schilling B 2.50 6.00
EC Eric Chavez B 1.50 4.00
GM Greg Maddux C 5.00 12.00
LG Luis Gonzalez D 1.50 4.00
LW Larry Walker C 2.50 6.00
MM Mark Mulder C 1.50 4.00
MP Mike Piazza C 4.00 10.00
MR Manny Ramirez E 4.00 10.00
MSW Mike Sweeney F 1.50 4.00
RJ Randy Johnson H 4.00 10.00
RO Roy Oswalt G 2.50 6.00
RP Rafael Palmeiro E 2.50 6.00
SS Sammy Sosa D 4.00 10.00
TH Todd Helton F 2.50 6.00
WM Willie Mays A 12.00 30.00

2004 Finest

This 122 card set was released in May, 2004. The set was issued in 30-card packs with a $40 SRP. Those packs were issued three to a box and 12 boxes to a case. The first 100 cards in this set feature veterans while cards 101-110 feature veteran players with a game-used jersey swatch on the card and cards 111-122 feature autograph rookie cards. Please note that David Murphy and Lastings Milledge did not sign their cards in time for pack out and those cards could be redeemed until April 30, 2006. In addition, troubled Marlins prospect Jeff Allison also had an exchange card with a 4/30/06 redemption deadline seeded into packs, but Topps was unable to fulfill the redemption and sent 2004 Topps World Series Highlights Autographs Bobby Thomson cards in their place.
COMP.SET w/o SP's (100) 10.00 25.00
COMMON CARD (1-100) .20 .50
COMMON CARD (101-110) 3.00 8.00
101-110 STATED ODDS 1:7 MINI-BOXES
COMMON CARD (111-122) 4.00 10.00
111-122 STATED ODDS 1:3 MINI-BOXES
EXCHANGE DEADLINE 04/30/06
CARD 112 EXCH UNABLE TO BE FULFILLED
04 WS HL B.THOMSON AU SENT INSTEAD
1 Juan Pierre .20 .50
2 Derek Jeter 1.25 3.00
3 Garret Anderson .20 .50
4 Javy Lopez .20 .50
5 Corey Patterson .20 .50
6 Todd Helton .30 .75
7 Roy Oswalt .30 .75
8 Shawn Green .20 .50
9 Vladimir Guerrero .30 .75
10 Jorge Posada .30 .75
11 Jason Kendall .20 .50
12 Scott Rolen .30 .75
13 Randy Johnson .50 1.25
14 Bill Mueller .20 .50
15 Magglio Ordonez .30 .75
16 Larry Walker .30 .75
17 Lance Berkman .30 .75
18 Richie Sexson .20 .50
19 Orlando Cabrera .20 .50
20 Alfonso Soriano .30 .75
21 Kevin Millwood .20 .50
22 Edgar Martinez .30 .75
23 Aubrey Huff .20 .50
24 Carlos Delgado .20 .50
25 Vernon Wells .20 .50
26 Mark Teixeira .30 .75
27 Troy Glaus .20 .50
28 Jeff Kent .20 .50
29 Hideo Nomo .50 1.25
30 Torii Hunter .20 .50
31 Hank Blalock .20 .50
32 Brandon Webb .20 .50
33 Tony Batista .20 .50
34 Bret Boone .20 .50
35 Ryan Klesko .20 .50
36 Barry Zito .30 .75
37 Edgar Renteria .30 .75
38 Geoff Jenkins .20 .50
39 Jeff Bagwell .30 .75
40 Dontrelle Willis .20 .50
41 Adam Dunn .30 .75
42 Mark Buehrle .30 .75
43 Esteban Loaiza .20 .50
44 Angel Berroa .20 .50
45 Ivan Rodriguez .30 .75
46 Jose Vidro .20 .50
47 Mark Mulder .20 .50
48 Roger Clemens .60 1.50
49 Jim Edmonds .30 .75
50 Eric Gagne .20 .50
51 Marcus Giles .20 .50
52 Curt Schilling .30 .75
53 Ken Griffey Jr. 1.00 2.50
54 Jason Schmidt .20 .50
55 Miguel Tejada .30 .75
56 Dmitri Young .20 .50
57 Mike Lowell .20 .50
58 Mike Sweeney .20 .50
59 Scott Podsednik .20 .50
60 Miguel Cabrera .50 1.25
61 Johan Santana .30 .75
62 Bernie Williams .30 .75
63 Eric Chavez .20 .50
64 Bobby Abreu .20 .50
65 Brian Giles .20 .50
66 Michael Young .20 .50
67 Paul Lo Duca .20 .50
68 Austin Kearns .20 .50
69 Jody Gerut .20 .50
70 Kerry Wood .20 .50
71 Luis Matos .20 .50
72 Greg Maddux .60 1.50
73 Alex Rodriguez Yanks .60 1.50
74 Mike Lieberthal .20 .50
75 Jim Thome .30 .75
76 Javier Vazquez .20 .50
77 Bartolo Colon .20 .50
78 Manny Ramirez .50 1.25
79 Jacque Jones .20 .50
80 Johnny Damon .30 .75
81 Carlos Beltran .30 .75
82 C.C. Sabathia .30 .75
83 Preston Wilson .20 .50
84 Luis Castillo .20 .50
85 Kevin Brown .20 .50
86 Shannon Stewart .20 .50
87 Cliff Floyd .20 .50
88 Mike Mussina .30 .75
89 Rafael Furcal .20 .50
90 Roy Halladay .20 .50
91 Frank Thomas .50 1.25
92 Melvin Mora .20 .50
93 Andruw Jones .20 .50
94 Luis Gonzalez .20 .50
95 David Ortiz .50 1.25
96 Gary Sheffield .20 .50
97 Tim Hudson .30 .75
98 Phil Nevin .20 .50
99 Ichiro Suzuki .60 1.50
100 Albert Pujols .60 1.50
101 Nomar Garciaparra SR Jsy 6.00 15.00
102 Sammy Sosa SR Jsy 4.00 10.00
103 Josh Beckett SR Jsy 3.00 8.00
104 Jason Giambi SR Jsy 3.00 8.00
105 Rocco Baldelli SR Jsy 3.00 8.00
106 Jose Reyes SR Jsy 3.00 8.00
107 Chipper Jones SR Jsy 4.00 10.00
108 Pedro Martinez SR Jsy 4.00 10.00
109 Mike Piazza SR Jsy 6.00 15.00
110 Mark Prior SR Jsy 4.00 10.00
111 Craig Ansman AU RC 4.00 10.00
112 David Murphy AU RC 5.00 12.00
113 Jason Hirsh AU RC 6.00 15.00
114 Jason Hirsh AU RC 6.00 15.00
115 Matt Moses AU RC 4.00 10.00
116 Estee Harris AU RC 4.00 10.00
117 Logan Kensing AU RC 4.00 10.00
118 L.Milledge AU RC 3.00 8.00
119 Merkin Valdez AU RC 4.00 10.00
120 Travis Blackley AU RC 4.00 10.00
121 Vito Chiaravalloti AU RC 4.00 10.00
122 Dioner Navarro AU RC 4.00 10.00

2004 Finest Gold Refractors

*GOLD REF 1-100: 6X TO 15X BASIC
1-100 STATED ODDS 1:11
*GOLD REF 101-110: 1.25X TO 3X BASIC
101-110 STATED ODDS 1:102
*GOLD REF 111-122: 2X TO 4X BASIC
111-122 STATED ODDS 1:85
STATED PRINT RUN 50 SERIAL #'d SETS
CARD 112 EXCH UNABLE TO BE FULFILLED
EXCHANGE DEADLINE 04/30/06

2004 Finest Refractors

*REFRACTORS 1-100: 2X TO 5X BASIC
1-100 APPX.ODDS 3 IN EVERY 4 MINI-BOXES
*REFRACTORS 101-110: .5X TO 1.2X BASIC
101-110 STATED ODDS 1:26 MINI-BOXES
*REFRACTORS 111-122: .6X TO 1.5X BASIC
111-122 STATED ODDS 1:22 MINI-BOXES
EXCHANGE DEADLINE 04/30/06
CARD 112 EXCH UNABLE TO BE FULFILLED

2004 Finest Uncirculated Gold X-Fractors

*GOLD X-F 1-100: 4X TO 10X BASIC
*GOLD X-F 101-110: .75X TO 2X BASIC
*GOLD X-F 111-122: .75X TO 2.5X BASIC
ONE PER BASIC SEALED BOX
STATED PRINT RUN 139 SERIAL #'d SETS
EXCHANGE DEADLINE 04/30/06
CARD 112 EXCH UNABLE TO BE FULFILLED

2004 Finest Moments Autographs

GROUP A ODDS 1:86 MINI-BOXES
GROUP B ODDS 1:102 MINI-BOXES
GROUP C ODDS 1:5 MINI-BOXES
DS Duke Snider A 15.00 40.00
EK Ed Kranepool C 4.00 10.00
GS George Foster C 4.00 10.00
JA Jim Abbott A 20.00 50.00
JP Johnny Podres C 6.00 15.00
LD Lenny Dykstra C 4.00 10.00
OC Orlando Cepeda C 4.00 10.00
RY Robin Yount A 20.00 50.00
VB Vida Blue C 4.00 10.00
WM Willie Mays B 100.00 200.00

2004 Finest Relics

GROUP A ODDS 1:3 MINI-BOXES
GROUP B ODDS 1:4 MINI-BOXES
AB Angel Berroa Bat B 3.00 8.00
AD Adam Dunn Jsy A 3.00 8.00
AG Adrian Gonzalez Bat A 3.00 8.00
AJ Andruw Jones Bat A 4.00 10.00
AP Andy Pettitte Uni B 4.00 10.00
AP1 Albert Pujols Uni A 8.00 20.00
AP2 Albert Pujols Bat A 8.00 20.00
AR1 A.Rodriguez Rgr Jsy A 6.00 15.00
AR2 A.Rodriguez Yanks Jsy A 10.00 25.00
AS Alfonso Soriano Bat A 3.00 8.00
BM1 B.Myers Arm Down Jsy A 3.00 8.00
BM2 B.Myers Arm Up Jsy A 3.00 8.00
BW Bernie Williams Bat B 4.00 10.00
BZ Barry Zito Jsy A 3.00 8.00
CCS C.C. Sabathia Jsy A 3.00 8.00
CG Cristian Guzman Jsy A 3.00 8.00
CS Curt Schilling Jsy A 3.00 8.00
DE Darin Erstad Bat A 3.00 8.00
DL Derek Lowe Uni A 3.00 8.00
DW Dontrelle Willis Uni B 4.00 10.00
DY Delmon Young Bat B 4.00 10.00
EC Eric Chavez Uni B 3.00 8.00
FT Frank Thomas Jsy A 4.00 10.00
GM Greg Maddux Jsy A 6.00 15.00
GS Gary Sheffield Bat A 3.00 8.00
HB1 Hank Blalock Bat A 3.00 8.00
HB2 Hank Blalock Jsy B 3.00 8.00
IR1 I.Rodriguez Running Jsy A 4.00 10.00
IR2 I.Rodriguez w Glove Jsy A 4.00 10.00
IR3 Ivan Rodriguez Bat B 4.00 10.00
JB Jeff Bagwell Jsy A 4.00 10.00
JL Javy Lopez Jsy A 3.00 8.00
JP Juan Pierre Bat A 3.00 8.00
JPB1 Josh Beckett Jsy A 3.00 8.00
JR1 Jose Reyes White Jsy A 3.00 8.00
JR2 Jose Reyes Bat A 3.00 8.00
JR3 Jose Reyes Black Jsy B 3.00 8.00
JS John Smoltz Uni A 4.00 10.00
JT Jim Thome Jsy A 4.00 10.00
KI Kazuhisa Ishii Jsy A 3.00 8.00
KM Kevin Millwood Jsy A 3.00 8.00
KS Kazuhiro Sasaki Jsy A 3.00 8.00
KW1 Kerry Wood Jsy A 3.00 8.00
KW2 Kerry Wood Bat A 3.00 8.00
LB1 Lance Berkman Bat A 3.00 8.00
LB2 Lance Berkman Jsy A 3.00 8.00
LG Luis Gonzalez Jsy A 3.00 8.00
LW Larry Walker Jsy A 3.00 8.00
MB Marlon Byrd Jsy A 3.00 8.00
MC Miguel Cabrera Bat B 4.00 10.00
ML1 Mike Lowell Grey Jsy A 3.00 8.00
ML2 Mike Lowell Black Jsy B 3.00 8.00
MM Mark Mulder Uni B 3.00 8.00
MO1 Magglio Ordonez Jsy A 3.00 8.00
MO2 Magglio Ordonez Bat A 3.00 8.00
MP Mark Prior Bat A 4.00 10.00
MR Mariano Rivera Uni A 4.00 10.00
MT1 Miguel Tejada Bat A 3.00 8.00
MT2 Miguel Tejada Uni A 3.00 8.00
NG Nomar Garciaparra Bat A 6.00 15.00
PB Pat Burrell Jsy A 3.00 8.00
PW Preston Wilson Bat A 3.00 8.00
RB1 R.Baldelli Bat Down Jsy B 3.00 8.00
RB3 R.Baldelli Bat on Ball Jsy B 3.00 8.00
RH Rich Harden Uni B 3.00 8.00
RJ Randy Johnson Jsy A 4.00 10.00
RP1 Rafael Palmeiro Bat A 4.00 10.00
RP2 Rafael Palmeiro Uni A 4.00 10.00
RP3 Rafael Palmeiro Jsy B 4.00 10.00
SB Sean Burroughs Bat A 3.00 8.00
SG Shawn Green Jsy A 3.00 8.00
SR Scott Rolen Bat A 4.00 10.00
SS Sammy Sosa Bat A 4.00 10.00
TG Troy Glaus Bat A 3.00 8.00
TH Tim Hudson Uni B 3.00 8.00
TH1 Todd Helton Bat A 4.00 10.00
TH2 Todd Helton Jsy A 4.00 10.00
TKH1 Torii Hunter Bat A 3.00 8.00
TKH2 Torii Hunter Jsy B 3.00 8.00
VG Vladimir Guerrero Jsy B 4.00 10.00
VW Vernon Wells Jsy A 3.00 8.00

2005 Finest

This 166-card set was released in May, 2005. The set was issued in three "mini-boxes" which contained 30 total cards (or 10 cards per mini-box). These "full boxes" came eight to a case. Cards numbered 1 through 140 featured active veterans while cards numbered 141 through 156 feature signed Rookie

Cards which were issued to a varying print run amount and are noted in our checklist. Cards numbers 157 through 166 feature retired stars.
COMP.SET w/o SP's (150) 40.00 80.00
COMMON CARD (1-140) .20 .50
COMMON CARD (157-166) .30 .75
AU p/r 970 ODDS 1:3 MINI BOXES
AU p/r 970 PRINT RUN 970 #'d SETS
AU p/r 375 ODDS 1:41 MINI BOXES
AU p/r 375 PRINT RUN 375 #'d SETS
OVERALL PLATE ODDS 1:51 MINI BOX
OVERALL AU PLATE ODDS 1:478 MINI BOX
PLATE PRINT RUN 1 SET PER COLOR
BLACK-CYAN-MAGENTA-YELLOW ISSUED
NO PLATE PRICING DUE TO SCARCITY
1 Alexis Rios .20 .50
2 Hank Blalock .20 .50
3 Bobby Abreu .20 .50
4 Curt Schilling .30 .75
5 Albert Pujols .60 1.50
6 Aaron Rowand .20 .50
7 B.J. Upton .30 .75
8 Andruw Jones .20 .50
9 Jeff Francis .20 .50
10 Sammy Sosa .50 1.25
11 Aramis Ramirez .20 .50
12 Carl Pavano .20 .50
13 Bartolo Colon .20 .50
14 Greg Maddux .60 1.50
15 Scott Kazmir .50 1.25
16 Melvin Mora .20 .50
17 Brandon Backe .20 .50
18 Bobby Crosby .20 .50
19 Carlos Lee .20 .50
20 Carl Crawford .30 .75
21 Brian Giles .20 .50
22 Jeff Bagwell .30 .75
23 J.D. Drew .20 .50
24 C.C. Sabathia .30 .75
25 Alfonso Soriano .30 .75
26 Chipper Jones .50 1.25
27 Austin Kearns .20 .50
28 Carlos Delgado .20 .50
29 Jack Wilson .20 .50
30 Dmitri Young .20 .50
31 Carlos Guillen .20 .50
32 Jim Thome .30 .75
33 Eric Chavez .20 .50
34 Jason Schmidt .20 .50
35 Brad Radke .20 .50
36 Frank Thomas .50 1.25
37 Darin Erstad .20 .50
38 Javier Vazquez .20 .50
39 Garret Anderson .20 .50
40 David Ortiz .50 1.25
41 Javy Lopez .20 .50
42 Geoff Jenkins .20 .50
43 Jose Vidro .20 .50
44 Aubrey Huff .20 .50
45 Bernie Williams .30 .75
46 Dontrelle Willis .20 .50
47 Jim Edmonds .30 .75
48 Ivan Rodriguez .30 .75
49 Gary Sheffield .20 .50
50 Alex Rodriguez .60 1.50
51 John Buck .20 .50
52 Andy Pettitte .30 .75
53 Ichiro Suzuki .60 1.50
54 Johnny Estrada .20 .50
55 Jake Peavy .20 .50
56 Carlos Zambrano .30 .75
57 Jose Reyes .30 .75
58 Bret Boone .20 .50
59 Jason Bay .20 .50
60 David Wright .40 1.00
61 Jeromy Burnitz .20 .50
62 Corey Patterson .20 .50
63 Juan Pierre .20 .50
64 Zack Greinke .50 1.25
65 Mike Lowell .20 .50
66 Ken Griffey Jr. 1.00 2.50
67 Marcus Giles .20 .50
68 Edgar Renteria .20 .50
69 Ken Harvey .20 .50
70 Pedro Martinez .30 .75
71 Johnny Damon .30 .75
72 Lyle Overbay .20 .50
73 Mike Maroth .20 .50
74 Jorge Posada .30 .75
75 Carlos Beltran .30 .75
76 Mark Buehrle .30 .75
77 Khalil Greene .20 .50
78 Josh Beckett .20 .50
79 Mark Loretta .20 .50
80 Rafael Palmeiro .30 .75
81 Justin Morneau .30 .75
82 Rocco Baldelli .20 .50
83 Ben Sheets .20 .50
84 Kerry Wood .20 .50
85 Miguel Tejada .30 .75
86 Magglio Ordonez .30 .75
87 Livan Hernandez .20 .50
88 Kazuo Matsui .20 .50
89 Manny Ramirez .50 1.25
90 Hideki Matsui .75 2.00
91 Jeff Kent .20 .50
92 Matt Lawton .20 .50
93 Richie Sexson .20 .50
94 Mike Mussina .30 .75
95 Adam Dunn .30 .75
96 Johan Santana .30 .75
97 Nomar Garciaparra .30 .75
98 Michael Young .20 .50
99 Victor Martinez .30 .75
100 Barry Bonds .75 2.00
101 Oliver Perez .20 .50
102 Randy Johnson .50 1.25
103 Mark Mulder .20 .50
104 Pat Burrell .20 .50
105 Mike Sweeney .20 .50
106 Mark Teixeira .30 .75
107 Paul Lo Duca .20 .50
108 Jon Lieber .20 .50
109 Mike Piazza .50 1.25
110 Roger Clemens .60 1.50
111 Rafael Furcal .20 .50
112 Troy Glaus .20 .50
113 Miguel Cabrera .50 1.25
114 Randy Wolf .20 .50
115 Lance Berkman .30 .75
116 Mark Prior .30 .75
117 Rich Harden .20 .50
118 Preston Wilson .20 .50
119 Roy Oswalt .30 .75
120 Luis Gonzalez .20 .50
121 Ronnie Belliard .20 .50
122 Sean Casey .20 .50
123 Barry Zito .30 .75
124 Larry Walker .30 .75
125 Derek Jeter 1.25 3.00
126 Tim Hudson .30 .75
127 Tom Glavine .30 .75
128 Scott Rolen .30 .75
129 Torii Hunter .20 .50
130 Paul Konerko .30 .75
131 Shawn Green .20 .50
132 Travis Hafner .20 .50
133 Vernon Wells .20 .50
134 Sidney Ponson .20 .50
135 Vladimir Guerrero .30 .75
136 Mark Kotsay .20 .50
137 Todd Helton .30 .75
138 Adrian Beltre .50 1.25
139 Wily Mo Pena .20 .50
140 Joe Mauer .40 1.00
141 Brian Stavisky AU/970 RC 4.00 10.00
142 Nate McLouth AU/970 RC 4.00 10.00
143 Glen Perkins AU/375 RC 4.00 10.00
144 Chip Cannon AU/970 RC 4.00 10.00
145 Shane Costa AU/970 RC 4.00 10.00
146 W.Swackhamer AU/970 RC 4.00 10.00
147 Kevin Melillo AU/970 RC 4.00 10.00
148 Billy Butler AU/970 RC 4.00 10.00
149 Landon Powell AU/970 RC 4.00 10.00
150 Scott Mathieson AU/970 RC 4.00 10.00
151 Chris Roberson AU/970 4.00 10.00
152 Chad Orvella AU/375 RC 4.00 10.00
153 Eric Nielsen AU/970 RC 4.00 10.00
154 Matt Campbell AU/970 RC 4.00 10.00
155 Mike Rogers AU/970 RC 4.00 10.00
156 Melky Cabrera AU/970 RC 6.00 15.00
157 Nolan Ryan RET 2.50 6.00
158 Bo Jackson RET .75 2.00
159 Wade Boggs RET .50 1.25
160 Andre Dawson RET .50 1.25
161 Dave Winfield RET .50 1.25
162 Reggie Jackson RET .50 1.25
163 David Justice RET .30 .75
164 Dale Murphy RET .75 2.00
165 Paul O'Neill RET .50 1.25
166 Tom Seaver RET .50 1.25

2005 Finest Refractors

*REF 1-140: 1.5X TO 4X BASIC
*REF 157-166: 1X TO 2.5X BASIC
1-140/157-166 ODDS ONE PER MINI BOX
COMMON AUTO (141-156) 4.00 10.00
*REF AU 141-156: .4X TO 1X p/r 970
*REF AU 141-156: .3X TO .8X p/r 375
AU 141-156 ODDS 1:5 MINI BOX
STATED PRINT RUN 399 SERIAL #'d SETS

2005 Finest Refractors Black

*REF BLACK 1-140: 4X TO 10X BASIC
*REF BLACK 157-166: 2.5X TO 6X BASIC
1-140/157-166 ODDS 1:2 MINI BOX
COMMON AUTO (141-156) 10.00 25.00
*REF BLK AU 141-156: .6X TO 1.5X p/r 970
*REF BLK AU 141-156: .5X TO 1.2X p/r 375
AU 141-156 ODDS 1:19 MINI BOX
STATED PRINT RUN 99 SERIAL #'d SETS

2005 Finest Refractors Blue

*REF BLUE 1-140: 1.5X TO 4X BASIC
*REF BLUE 157-166: 1X TO 2.5X BASIC
1-140/157-166 ODDS ONE PER MINI BOX
COMMON AUTO (141-156) 4.00 10.00
*REF BLUE AU 141-156: .4X TO 1X p/r 970
*REF BLUE AU 141-156: .3X TO .8X p/r 375
AU 141-156 ODDS 1:7 MINI BOX
STATED PRINT RUN 299 SERIAL #'d SETS

2005 Finest Refractors Gold

*REF GOLD 1-140: 5X TO 12X BASIC
*REF GOLD 157-166: 3X TO 8X BASIC
1-140/157-166 ODDS 1:5 MINI BOX
COMMON AUTO (141-156) 15.00 40.00
*REF GOLD AU 141-156: 1X TO 2.5X p/r 970
*REF GOLD AU 141-156: .75X TO 2X p/r 375
AU 141-156 ODDS 1:39 MINI BOX
STATED PRINT RUN 49 SERIAL #'d SETS
125 Derek Jeter 15.00 40.00

2005 Finest Refractors Green

*REF GREEN 1-140: 2X TO 5X BASIC
*REF GREEN 157-166: 1.25X TO 3X BASIC
1-140/157-166 ODDS ONE PER MINI BOX
COMMON AUTO (141-156) 5.00 12.00
*REF GRN AU 141-156: .4X TO 1X p/r 970
*REF GRN AU 141-156: .3X TO 8X p/r 375
AU 141-156 ODDS 1:10 MINI BOX
STATED PRINT RUN 199 SERIAL #'d SETS

2005 Finest Refractors White Framed

1-140/157-166 ODDS 1:202 MINI BOX
AU 141-165 ODDS 1:1914 MINI BOX
STATED PRINT RUN 1 SERIAL #'d SET
NO PRICING DUE TO SCARCITY

2005 Finest X-Fractors

*XF 1-140: 2X TO 5X BASIC
*XF 157-166: 1.25X TO 3X BASIC
1-140/157-166 ODDS ONE PER MINI BOX
COMMON AUTO (141-156) 4.00 10.00
*XF AU 141-156: .4X TO 1X p/r 970
*XF AU 141-156: .3X TO 8X p/r 375
AU 141-156 ODDS 1:8 MINI BOX
STATED PRINT RUN 250 SERIAL #'d SETS

2005 Finest X-Fractors Black

*XF BLACK 1-140: 8X TO 20X BASIC
*XF BLACK 157-166: 5X TO 12X BASIC
1-140/157-166 ODDS 1:8 MINI BOX
AU 141-156 ODDS 1:76 MINI BOX
STATED PRINT RUN 25 SERIAL #'d SETS
AU 141-156 NO PRICING DUE TO SCARCITY
157 Nolan Ryan RET 30.00 80.00

2005 Finest X-Fractors Blue

*XF BLUE 1-140: 2.5X TO 6X BASIC
*XF BLUE 157-166: 1.5X TO 4X BASIC
1-140/157-166 ODDS 1:2 MINI BOX
COMMON AUTO (141-156) 6.00 15.00
*XF BLUE AU 141-156: .5X TO 1.2X p/r 970
*XF BLUE AU 141-156: .4X TO 1X p/r 375
AU 141-156 ODDS 1:13 MINI BOX
STATED PRINT RUN 150 SERIAL #'d SETS

2005 Finest X-Fractors Gold

1-140/157-166 ODDS 1:20 MINI BOX
AU 141-156 ODDS 1:190 MINI BOX
STATED PRINT RUN 10 SERIAL #'d SETS
NO PRICING DUE TO SCARCITY

2005 Finest X-Fractors Green

*XF GREEN 1-140: 5X TO 12X BASIC
*XF GREEN 157-166: 3X TO 8X BASIC
1-140/157-166 ODDS 1:2 MINI BOX
COMMON AUTO (141-156) 12.50 30.00
*XF GRN AU 141-156: .75X TO 2X p/r 970
*XF GRN AU 141-156: .6X TO 1.5X p/r 375
AU 141-156 ODDS 1:38 MINI BOX
STATED PRINT RUN 50 SERIAL #'d SETS

2005 Finest A-Rod Moments

COMMON CARD (1-49) 3.00 8.00
ONE PER MASTER BOX
STATED PRINT RUN 190 SERIAL #'d SETS

2005 Finest A-Rod Moments Autographs

COMMON CARD (1-49) 90.00 180.00
APPROXIMATE ODDS 1:15 MASTER BOXES
STATED PRINT RUN 13 SERIAL #'d SETS

2005 Finest Autograph Refractors

GROUP A ODDS 1:435 MINI BOX
GROUP B ODDS 1:13 MINI BOX
GROUP C ODDS 1:32 MINI BOX
GROUP D ODDS 1:15 MINI BOX
GROUP A PRINT RUN 70 CARDS
GROUP A CARD IS NOT SERIAL-NUMBERED
GROUP A PRINT RUN PROVIDED BY TOPPS
OVERALL PLATE ODDS 1:513 MINI BOX
PLATE PRINT RUN 1 SET PER COLOR
BLACK-CYAN-MAGENTA-YELLOW ISSUED
NO PLATE PRICING DUE TO SCARCITY
SUPERFRACTOR ODDS 1:2051 MINI BOX
SUPERFRACTOR PRINT RUN 1 #'d SET
NO SUPERFRACTOR PRICING AVAILABLE
*X-FRACTOR: 1.25X TO 3X BASIC D
*X-FRACTOR: .75X TO 2X BASIC C
*X-FRACTOR: .6X TO 1.5X BASIC B
*X-FRACTOR: .6X TO 1.5X BASIC A
X-FRACTOR ODDS 1:81 MINI BOX
X-FRACTOR PRINT RUN 25 SERIAL #'d SETS
EXCHANGE DEADLINE 04/30/07
AS Alfonso Soriano B 6.00 15.00
BB Barry Bonds A/70 * 125.00 250.00
DO David Ortiz B 10.00 25.00
DW David Wright C 20.00 50.00
EC Eric Chavez B 6.00 15.00
EG Eric Gagne B 6.00 15.00
GS Gary Sheffield C 6.00 15.00
JB Jason Bay B 10.00 25.00
JE Johnny Estrada B 6.00 15.00
JS Johan Santana B 8.00 20.00
JST Jacob Stevens D 4.00 10.00
KM Kevin Millar B 15.00 40.00
MB Milton Bradley B 6.00 15.00
MR Mariano Rivera B 100.00 250.00

2005 Finest Moments Autograph Gold Refractors

STATED ODDS 1:305 MINI BOX
PEDRO PRINT RUN 50 SERIAL #'d CARDS
SCHILLING PRINT RUN 50 CARDS
SCHILLING IS NOT SERIAL-NUMBERED
SCHILLING QTY PROVIDED BY TOPPS
CS Curt Schilling/50 * 100.00 175.00
PM Pedro Martinez/50 60.00 120.00

2006 Finest

This 155-card set was released in May, 2006. The set was issued in an "mini-box" form. There were three mini-boxes in a full box and each mini-box contained 30 cards. The SRP for an individual mini-box was $50 and there were eight full boxes in a case. Cards numbered 1-130 feature veterans while cards cards 131-155 feature 2006 rookies. Cards numbered 141 through 155 were all signed and all of those cards were issued to a stated print run of 963 signed copies.
COMP.SET w/o AU's (140) 30.00 60.00
COMMON CARD (1-131) .20 .50
COMMON ROOKIE (132-140) .30 .75
COMMON AUTO (141-155) 4.00 10.00
141-155 AU ODDS 1:4 MINI BOX
141-155 AU PRINT RUN 963 SETS
141-155 AU's NOT SERIAL NUMBERED
PRINT RUN INFO PROVIDED BY TOPPS
1-140 PLATES RANDOM INSERTS IN PACKS
AU 141-155 PLATE ODDS 1:792 MINI BOX
PLATE PRINT RUN 1 SET PER COLOR
BLACK-CYAN-MAGENTA-YELLOW ISSUED
NO PLATE PRICING DUE TO SCARCITY
1 Vladimir Guerrero .30 .75
2 Troy Glaus .20 .50
3 Andruw Jones .20 .50
4 Miguel Tejada .30 .75
5 Manny Ramirez .50 1.25
6 Curt Schilling .30 .75
7 Mark Prior .30 .75
8 Kerry Wood .20 .50
9 Tadahito Iguchi .20 .50
10 Freddy Garcia .20 .50
11 Ryan Howard .40 1.00
12 Mark Buehrle .30 .75
13 Wily Mo Pena .20 .50
14 C.C. Sabathia .30 .75
15 Garret Anderson .20 .50
16 Shawn Green .20 .50
17 Rafael Furcal .20 .50
18 Jeff Francoeur .50 1.25
19 Ken Griffey Jr. 1.00 2.50
20 Derrek Lee .20 .50
21 Paul Konerko .30 .75
22 Rickie Weeks .20 .50
23 Magglio Ordonez .30 .75
24 Juan Pierre .20 .50
25 Felix Hernandez .30 .75
26 Roger Clemens .60 1.50
27 Zack Greinke .30 .75
28 Johan Santana .30 .75
29 Jose Reyes .30 .75
30 Bobby Crosby .20 .50
31 Jason Schmidt .20 .50
32 Khalil Greene .20 .50
33 Richie Sexson .20 .50
34 Mark Mulder .20 .50
35 Mark Teixeira .30 .75
36 Nick Johnson .20 .50
37 Vernon Wells .20 .50
38 Scott Kazmir .30 .75
39 Jim Edmonds .30 .75
40 Adrian Beltre .50 1.25
41 Dan Johnson .20 .50
42 Carlos Lee .20 .50
43 Lance Berkman .30 .75
44 Josh Beckett .20 .50
45 Morgan Ensberg .20 .50
46 Garrett Atkins .20 .50
47 Chase Utley .30 .75
48 Joe Mauer .30 .75
49 Travis Hafner .20 .50
50 Alex Rodriguez .60 1.50
51 Austin Kearns .20 .50
52 Scott Podsednik .20 .50
53 Jose Contreras .20 .50
54 Greg Maddux .60 1.50
55 Hideki Matsui .50 1.25
56 Matt Clement .20 .50
57 Javy Lopez .20 .50
58 Tim Hudson .30 .75
59 Luis Gonzalez .20 .50
60 Bartolo Colon .20 .50
61 Marcus Giles .20 .50
62 Justin Morneau .30 .75
63 Nomar Garciaparra .30 .75
64 Robinson Cano .30 .75
65 Ervin Santana .20 .50
66 Brady Clark .20 .50
67 Edgar Renteria .20 .50
68 Jon Garland .20 .50
69 Felipe Lopez .20 .50
70 Ivan Rodriguez .30 .75
71 Dontrelle Willis .20 .50
72 Carlos Guillen .20 .50
73 J.D. Drew .20 .50
74 Rich Harden .20 .50
75 Albert Pujols .60 1.50
76 Livan Hernandez .20 .50
77 Roy Halladay .30 .75
78 Hank Blalock .20 .50
79 David Wright .40 1.00
80 Jimmy Rollins .30 .75
81 John Smoltz .50 1.25
82 Miguel Cabrera .50 1.25
83 David DeJesus .20 .50
83 Zach Duke .20 .50
84 Torii Hunter .20 .50
85 Adam Dunn .30 .75
86 Randy Johnson .50 1.25
87 Roy Oswalt .30 .75
88 Bobby Abreu .20 .50
89 Rocco Baldelli .20 .50
90 Ichiro Suzuki .60 1.50
91 Jorge Cantu .20 .50
92 Jack Wilson .20 .50
93 Jose Vidro .20 .50
94 Kevin Millwood .20 .50
95 David Ortiz .50 1.25
96 Victor Martinez .30 .75
97 Jeremy Bonderman .20 .50
98 Todd Helton .30 .75
99 Carlos Beltran .30 .75
100 Barry Bonds .75 2.00
101 Jeff Kent .20 .50
102 Mike Sweeney .20 .50
103 Ben Sheets .20 .50
104 Melvin Mora .20 .50
105 Gary Sheffield .20 .50
106 Craig Wilson .20 .50
107 Chris Carpenter .30 .75
108 Michael Young .20 .50
109 Gustavo Chacin .20 .50
110 Chipper Jones .50 1.25
111 Mark Loretta .20 .50
112 Andy Pettitte .30 .75
113 Carlos Delgado .20 .50
114 Pat Burrell .20 .50
115 Jason Bay .20 .50
116 Brian Roberts .20 .50
117 Joe Crede .20 .50
118 Jake Peavy .20 .50
119 Aubrey Huff .20 .50
120 Pedro Martinez .30 .75
121 Jorge Posada .30 .75
122 Barry Zito .30 .75
123 Scott Rolen .30 .75
124 Brett Myers .20 .50
125 Derek Jeter 1.25 3.00
126 Eric Chavez .20 .50
127 Carl Crawford .30 .75
128 Jim Thome .30 .75
129 Johnny Damon .30 .75
130 Alfonso Soriano .30 .75
131 Clint Barmes .20 .50
132 Dustin Nippert (RC) .30 .75
133 Hanley Ramirez (RC) .50 1.25
134 Matt Capps (RC) .30 .75
135 Miguel Perez (RC) .30 .75
136 Tom Gorzelanny (RC) .30 .75
137 Charlton Jimerson (RC) .30 .75
138 Bryan Bullington (RC) .30 .75
139 Kenji Johjima RC .75 2.00
140 Craig Hansen RC .75 2.00
141 Craig Breslow AU/963 RC * 4.00 10.00
142 A.Wainwright AU/963 (RC) * 6.00 15.00
143 Joey Devine AU/963 RC * 4.00 10.00
144 H.Kuo AU/963 (RC) * 20.00 50.00
145 Jason Botts AU/963 (RC) * 4.00 10.00
146 J.Johnson AU/963 (RC) * 6.00 15.00
147 J.Bergmann AU/963 RC * 4.00 10.00
148 Scott Olsen AU/963 (RC) * 4.00 10.00
149 D.Rasner AU/963 (RC) * 4.00 10.00
150 Dan Ortmeier AU/963 (RC) * 4.00 10.00
151 Chuck James AU/963 (RC) * 6.00 15.00
152 Ryan Garko AU/963 (RC) * 4.00 10.00
153 Nelson Cruz AU/963 (RC) * 12.00 30.00
154 A.Lerew AU/963 (RC) * 4.00 10.00
155 F.Liriano AU/963 (RC) * 4.00 10.00

2006 Finest Refractors

*REF 1-131: 1.5X TO 4X BASIC
*REF 132-140: 1.5X TO 4X BASIC
1-140 ODDS ONE PER MINI BOX
*REF AU 141-155: .4X TO 1X BASIC AU
AU 141-155 ODDS 1:8 MINI BOX
STATED PRINT RUN 399 SERIAL #'d SETS

2006 Finest Refractors Black

*REF BLACK 1-131: 4X TO 10X BASIC
*REF BLACK 132-140: 4X TO 10X BASIC
1-140 ODDS 1:4 MINI BOX
*REF BLK AU 141-155: .6X TO 1.5X BASIC AU
AU 141-155 ODDS 1:32 MINI BOX
STATED PRINT RUN 99 SERIAL #'d SETS

2006 Finest Refractors Blue

*REF BLUE 1-131: 1.5X TO 4X BASIC
*REF BLUE 132-140: 1.5X TO 4X BASIC
1-140 ODDS 1:2 MINI BOX
*REF BLUE AU 141-155: .4X TO 1X BASIC AU
AU 141-155 ODDS 1:11 MINI BOX
STATED PRINT RUN 299 SERIAL #'d SETS

2006 Finest Refractors Gold

*REF GOLD 1-131: 5X TO 12X BASIC
*REF GOLD 132-140: 5X TO 12X BASIC
1-140 ODDS 1:7 MINI BOX
*REF GOLD AU 141-155: 1X TO 2.5X BASIC AU
AU 141-155 ODDS 1:64 MINI BOX
STATED PRINT RUN 49 SERIAL #'d SETS

2006 Finest Refractors Green

*REF GREEN 1-131: 2X TO 5X BASIC
*REF GREEN 132-140: 2X TO 5X BASIC
1-140 ODDS 1:2 MINI BOX
*REF GRN AU 141-155: .4X TO 1X BASIC AU
AU 141-155 ODDS 1:16 MINI BOX
STATED PRINT RUN 199 SERIAL #'d SETS

2006 Finest Refractors White Framed

1-140 ODDS 1:340 MINI BOX
AU 141-155 ODDS 1:3342 MINI BOX
STATED PRINT RUN 1 SERIAL #'d SET
NO PRICING DUE TO SCARCITY

2006 Finest X-Fractors

*XF 1-131: 2X TO 5X BASIC
*XF 132-140: 2X TO 5X BASIC
1-140 ODDS 1:2 MINI BOX
*XF AU 141-155: .4X TO 1X BASIC AU
AU 141-155 ODDS 1:13 MINI BOX
STATED PRINT RUN 250 SERIAL #'d SETS

2006 Finest X-Fractors Black

*XF BLACK 1-131: 8X TO 20X BASIC
1-140 ODDS 1:14 MINI BOX
NO XF BLACK 132-140 PRICING
AU 141-155 ODDS 1:125 MINI BOX
STATED PRINT RUN 25 SERIAL #'d SETS
NO XF BLACK AU PRICING

2006 Finest X-Fractors Blue

*XF BLUE 1-131: 2.5X TO 6X BASIC
*XF BLUE 132-140: 2.5X TO 6X BASIC
1-140 ODDS 1:3 MINI BOX
*XF BLUE AU 141-155: .5X TO 1.2X BASIC AU
AU 141-155 ODDS 1:21 MINI BOX
STATED PRINT RUN 150 SERIAL #'d SETS

2006 Finest X-Fractors Green

*XF GREEN 1-131: 5X TO 12X BASIC
*XF GREEN 132-140: 5X TO 12X BASIC
1-140 ODDS 1:7 MINI BOX
*XF GREEN AU 141-155: .75X TO 2X BASIC AU
AU 141-155 ODDS 1:63 MINI BOX
STATED PRINT RUN 50 SERIAL #'d SETS

2006 Finest Autograph Refractors

GROUP A ODDS 1:22 MINI BOX
GROUP B ODDS 1:8 MINI BOX
GROUP C ODDS 1:214 MINI BOX
GROUP A PRINT RUN 720 CARDS
GROUP B PRINT RUN 470 CARDS
GROUP C PRINT RUN 220 CARDS
CARDS ARE NOT SERIAL NUMBERED
PRINT RUN INFO PROVIDED BY TOPPS
OVERALL PLATE ODDS 1:654 MINI BOX
PLATE PRINT RUN 1 SET PER COLOR
BLACK-CYAN-MAGENTA-YELLOW ISSUED
NO PLATE PRICING DUE TO SCARCITY
SUPERFRACTOR ODDS 1:2751 MINI BOX
SUPERFRACTOR PRINT RUN 1 #'d SET
NO SUPERFRACTOR PRICING AVAILABLE
*GROUP A-B XF: .75X TO 2X BASIC
*GROUP C XF: 1X TO 2X BASIC
X-FRACTOR ODDS 1:104 MINI BOX
X-FRACTOR PRINT RUN 25 SERIAL #'d SETS
X-F JOHJIMA PRICING NOT AVAILABLE
APPROX. 10 PERCENT OF D.LEE ARE EXCH
EXCHANGE DEADLINE 04/30/08
AJ Andruw Jones B/470 * 6.00 15.00
AR Alex Rodriguez C/220 * 40.00 100.00
CJ Chipper Jones B/470 * 60.00 150.00
CW Craig Wilson B/470 * 4.00 10.00
DL Derrek Lee A/720 * 4.00 10.00
DW David Wright B/470 * 6.00 15.00
DWI Dontrelle Willis B/470 * 6.00 15.00
EC Eric Chavez A/720 * 6.00 15.00
GS Gary Sheffield B/470 * 6.00 15.00
JB Jason Bay B/470 * 6.00 15.00
JG Jose Guillen B/470 * 4.00 10.00
KJ Kenji Johjima B/470 * 10.00 25.00
MC Miguel Cabrera B/470 * 15.00 40.00
MG Marcus Giles B/470 * 6.00 15.00
RC Robinson Cano B/470 * 10.00 25.00
RH Rich Harden B/470 * 6.00 15.00
RO Roy Oswalt B/470 * 6.00 15.00
VG Vladimir Guerrero A/720 * 10.00 25.00

2006 Finest Bonds Moments Refractors

COMMON CARD (M1-M25) 3.00 8.00
STATED ODDS 1:2 MASTER BOX
STATED PRINT RUN 425 SERIAL #'d SETS
*REF GOLD: .5X TO 1.25X BASIC
REF.GOLD STATED ODDS 1:4 MASTER BOX
REF.GOLD PRINT RUN 199 SERIAL #'d SETS

2006 Finest Mantle Moments

COMMON CARD (M1-M20) 2.50 0.00
STATED ODDS 1:3 MINI BOX
STATED PRINT RUN 850 SERIAL #'d SETS
PRINTING PLATES RANDOM IN PACKS
PLATE PRINT RUN 1 SET PER COLOR
BLACK-CYAN-MAGENTA-YELLOW ISSUCD
NO PLATE PRICING DUE TO SCARCITY
*REF: .5X TO 1.25X BASIC
REF ODDS 1:6 MINI BOX
REF PRINT RUN 399 SERIAL #'d SETS
*REF BLACK: 1.25X TO 3X BASIC
REF BLACK ODDS 1:24 MINI BOX
REF BLACK PRINT RUN 99 SERIAL #'d SETS
*REF BLUE: .6X TO 1.5X BASIC
REF BLUE ODDS 1:8 MINI BOX
REF BLUE PRINT RUN 299 SERIAL #'d SETS
*REF GOLD: 2.5X TO 6X BASIC
REF GOLD ODDS 1:49 MINI BOX
REF GOLD PRINT RUN 49 SERIAL #'d SETS
*REF GREEN: .75X TO 2X BASIC
REF GREEN ODDS 1:12 MINI BOX
REF GREEN PRINT RUN 199 SERIAL #'d SETS
REF WHITE FRAME ODDS 1:2482 MINI BOX
REF WHITE FRAME PRINT RUN 1 #'d SET
NO REF WF PRICING DUE TO SCARCITY
SUPERFRACTORS ODDS 1:2482 MINI BOX
SUPERFRACTORS PRINT RUN 1 #'d SET
NO SF PRICING DUE TO SCARCITY
*X-FRAC: .6X TO 1.5X BASIC
X-FRAC ODDS 1:10 MINI BOX
X-FRAC PRINT RUN 250 SERIAL #'d SETS
*X-FRAC BLACK: 3X TO 8X BASIC
X-FRAC BLACK ODDS 1:95 MINI BOX
X-FRAC BLACK PRINT RUN 25 #'d SETS
*X-FRAC BLUE: .75X TO 2X BASIC
X-FRAC BLUE ODDS 1:16 MINI BOX
X-FRAC BLUE PRINT RUN 150 #'d SETS
*X-FRAC GOLD: 8X TO 20X BASIC
X-FRAC GOLD ODDS 1:238 MINI BOX
X-FRAC GOLD PRINT RUN 10 SERIAL #'d SETS
*X-FRAC GREEN: 2.5X TO 6X BASIC
X-FRAC GREEN ODDS 1:48 MINI BOX
X-FRAC GREEN PRINT RUN 50 #'d SETS
X-FRAC WF ODDS 1:2482 MINI BOX
X-FRAC WF PRINT RUN 1 SERIAL #'d SET
NO X-F WF PRICING DUE TO SCARCITY

2007 Finest

This 166-card set was released in March, 2007. The set was issued in five-card packs, which were issued six packs per mini box (which had an $50 SRP) and those mini-boxes were issued three per master box and eight master boxes per case. Cards numbered 1-135 feature veterans while cards numbered 135-150 were 2007 rookies and cards numbered 151-166 feature 2007 signed rookies. The signed rookie cards were issued at a stated rate of one in three mini-boxes.

COMP.SET w/o AU's (150) 30.00 60.00
COMMON CARD (1-135) .15 .40
COMMON ROOKIE (136-150) .40 1.00
151-166 AU ODDS 1:3 MINI BOX
1-150 PLATE ODDS 1:96 MINI BOX
AU 151-166 PLATE ODDS 1:909 MINI BOX
PLATE PRINT RUN 1 SET PER COLOR
BLACK-CYAN-MAGENTA-YELLOW ISSUED
NO PLATE PRICING DUE TO SCARCITY
EXCHANGE DEADLINE 02/28/09
1 David Wright .30 .75
2 Jered Weaver .25 .60
3 Chipper Jones .40 1.00
4 Magglio Ordonez .25 .60
5 Ben Sheets .15 .40
6 Nick Johnson .15 .40
7 Melvin Mora .15 .40
8 Chien-Ming Wang .25 .60
9 Andre Ethier .25 .60
10 Carlos Beltran .25 .60
11 Ryan Zimmerman .25 .60
12 Troy Glaus .15 .40
13 Hanley Ramirez .25 .60
14 Mark Buehrle .25 .60
15 Dan Uggla .15 .40
16 Richie Sexson .15 .40
17 Scott Kazmir .25 .60
18 Garrett Atkins .15 .40
19 Matt Cain .25 .60
20 Jorge Posada .25 .60
21 Brett Myers .15 .40
22 Jeff Francoeur .40 1.00
23 Scott Rolen .25 .60
24 Derrek Lee .15 .40
25 Manny Ramirez .40 1.00
26 Johnny Damon .25 .60
27 Mark Teixeira .25 .60
28 Mark Prior .25 .60
29 Victor Martinez .25 .60
30 Greg Maddux .50 1.25
31 Prince Fielder .25 .60
32 Jeremy Bonderman .15 .40
33 Paul LoDuca .15 .40
34 Brandon Webb .25 .60
35 Robinson Cano .25 .60
36 Josh Beckett .15 .40
37 David DeJesus .15 .40
38 Kenny Rogers .15 .40
39 Jim Thome .25 .60
40 Brian McCann .15 .40
41 Lance Berkman .25 .60
42 Adam Dunn .25 .60
43 Rocco Baldelli .15 .40
44 Brian Roberts .15 .40
45 Vladimir Guerrero .25 .60
46 Dontrelle Willis .15 .40
47 Eric Chavez .15 .40
48 Carlos Zambrano .25 .60
49 Ivan Rodriguez .25 .60
50 Alex Rodriguez .50 1.25
51 Curt Schilling .25 .60
52 Carlos Delgado .15 .40
53 Matt Holliday .40 1.00
54 Mark Teahen .15 .40
55 Frank Thomas .40 1.00
56 Grady Sizemore .25 .60
57 Aramis Ramirez .15 .40
58 Rafael Furcal .15 .40
59 David Ortiz .40 1.00
60 Paul Konerko .25 .60
61 Barry Zito .25 .60
62 Travis Hafner .15 .40
63 Nick Swisher .25 .60
64 Johan Santana .25 .60
65 Miguel Tejada .25 .60
66 Carl Crawford .25 .60
67 Kenji Johjima .40 1.00
68 Derek Jeter 1.00 2.50
69 Francisco Liriano .15 .40
70 Ken Griffey Jr. .75 2.00
71 Pat Burrell .15 .40
72 Adrian Gonzalez .30 .75
73 Miguel Cabrera .40 1.00
74 Albert Pujols .50 1.25
75 Justin Verlander .40 1.00
76 Carlos Lee .15 .40
77 John Smoltz .40 1.00
78 Orlando Hudson .15 .40
79 Joe Mauer .30 .75
80 Freddy Sanchez .15 .40
81 Bobby Abreu .15 .40
82 Pedro Martinez .25 .60
83 Vernon Wells .15 .40
84 Justin Morneau .25 .60
85 Bill Hall .15 .40
86 Jason Schmidt .15 .40
87 Michael Young .15 .40
88 Tadahito Iguchi .15 .40
89 Kevin Millwood .15 .40
90 Randy Johnson .40 1.00
91 Roy Halladay .25 .60
92 Mike Lowell .15 .40
93 Jake Peavy .15 .40
94 Jason Varitek .40 1.00
95 Todd Helton .25 .60
96 Mark Loretta .15 .40
97 Gary Matthews Jr. .15 .40
98 Ryan Howard .30 .75
99 Jose Reyes .25 .60
100 Chris Carpenter .25 .60
101 Hideki Matsui .40 1.00
102 Brian Giles .15 .40
103 Torii Hunter .15 .40
104 Rich Harden .15 .40
105 Ichiro Suzuki .50 1.25
106 Chase Utley .25 .60
107 Nick Markakis .30 .75
108 Marcus Giles .15 .40
109 Gary Sheffield .15 .40
110 Jim Edmonds .25 .60
111 Brandon Phillips .15 .40
112 Roy Oswalt .25 .60
113 Jeff Kent .15 .40
114 Jason Bay .25 .60
115 Raul Ibanez .25 .60
116 Stephen Drew .15 .40
117 Hank Blalock .15 .40
118 Tom Glavine .25 .60
119 Andruw Jones .15 .40
120 Alfonso Soriano .25 .60
121 Mariano Rivera .50 1.25
122 Garret Anderson .15 .40
123 Erik Bedard UER .15 .40
124 Huston Street .15 .40
125 Austin Kearns .15 .40
126 Jermaine Dye .15 .40
127 C.C. Sabathia .25 .60
128 Joe Nathan .15 .40
129 Craig Monroe .15 .40
130 Aubrey Huff .15 .40
131 Billy Wagner .15 .40
132 Jorge Cantu .15 .40
133 Trevor Hoffman .25 .60
134 Ronnie Belliard .15 .40
135 B.J. Ryan .15 .40
136 Adam Lind (RC) .40 1.00
137 Hector Gimenez (RC) .40 1.00
138 Shawn Riggans UER (RC) .40 1.00
139 Joaquin Arias (RC) .40 1.00
140 Drew Anderson RC .40 1.00
141 Mike Rabelo RC .40 1.00
142 Chris Narveson (RC) .40 1.00
143 Ryan Feierabend (RC) .40 1.00
144 Vinny Rottino (RC) .40 1.00
145 Jon Knott (RC) .40 1.00
146 Oswaldo Navarro RC .40 1.00
147 Brian Stokes (RC) .40 1.00
148 Glen Perkins (RC) .40 1.00
149 Mitch Maier RC .40 1.00
150 Delmon Young (RC) .60 1.50
151 Andrew Miller AU RC 4.00 10.00
152 T.Tulowitzki AU (RC) 4.00 10.00
153 Philip Humber AU (RC) 4.00 10.00
154 K.Kouzmanoff AU (RC) 4.00 15.00
155 Michael Bourn AU (RC) 4.00 10.00
156 M.Montero AU (RC) 4.00 10.00
157 David Murphy AU (RC) 4.00 10.00
158 R.Sweeney AU (RC) 4.00 10.00
159 Jeff Baker AU (RC) 4.00 10.00
160 Jeff Salazar AU (RC) 4.00 10.00
161 J.Garcia AU RC 4.00 10.00
162 Josh Fields AU (RC) 4.00 10.00
163 Delwyn Young AU (RC) 4.00 10.00
164 Fred Lewis AU (RC) 4.00 10.00
165 Scott Moore AU (RC) 4.00 10.00
166 Chris Stewart AU RC 4.00 10.00

2007 Finest Refractors

*REF 1-135: .5X TO 1.2X BASIC
*REF 136-150: .5X TO 1.2X BASIC
1-150 ODDS TWO PER MINI BOX
*REF AU 151-166: .4X TO 1X BASIC AU
AU 151-166 ODDS 1:10 MINI BOX
AU 151-166 PRINT RUN 399 SER.#'d SETS
EXCHANGE DEADLINE 02/28/09

2007 Finest Refractors Black

*REF BLACK 1-135: 4X TO 10X BASIC
*REF BLACK 136-150: 2.5X TO 6X BASIC
1-150 ODDS 1:6 MINI BOX
*REF BLK AU 151-166: 1X TO 2.5X BASIC AU
AU 151-166 ODDS 1:37 MINI BOX
STATED PRINT RUN 99 SERIAL #'d SETS
EXCHANGE DEADLINE 02/28/09
159 Jeff Baker AU 5.00 12.00
160 Jeff Salazar AU 5.00 12.00
164 Fred Lewis AU 12.50 30.00

2007 Finest Refractors Blue

*REF BLUE 1-135: 1.5X TO 4X BASIC
*REF BLUE 136-150: 1X TO 2.5X BASIC
1-150 ODDS ONE PER MINI BOX
1-150 PRINT RUN 399 SER.#'d SETS
*REF BLUE AU 151-166: .5X TO 1.2X BASIC AU
AU 151-166 ODDS 1:13 MINI BOX
AU 151-166 PRINT RUN 299 SER.#'d SETS
EXCHANGE DEADLINE 02/28/09

2007 Finest Refractors Gold

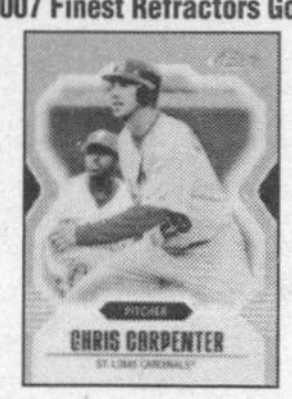

*REF GOLD 1-135: 5X TO 12X BASIC
*REF GOLD 136-150: 4X TO 10X BASIC
1-150 ODDS 1:8 MINI BOX
1-150 PRINT RUN 50 SER.#'d SETS
*REF GOLD AU 151-166: 1.25X TO 3X BASIC AU
AU 151-166 ODDS 1:74 MINI BOX
AU 151-166 PRINT RUN 49 SER.#'d SETS
EXCHANGE DEADLINE 02/28/09
155 Michael Bourn AU 15.00 40.00
158 Ryan Sweeney AU 15.00 40.00
162 Josh Fields AU 15.00 40.00
164 Fred Lewis AU 15.00 40.00
165 Scott Moore AU 15.00 40.00

2007 Finest Refractors Green

*REF GREEN 1-135: 2X TO 5X BASIC
*REF GREEN 136-150: 1.25X TO 3X BASIC
1-150 ODDS 1:2 MINI BOX
*REF GRN AU 151-166: .6X TO 1.5X BASIC AU
AU 151-166 ODDS 1:19 MINI BOX
STATED PRINT RUN 199 SERIAL #'d SETS
EXCHANGE DEADLINE 02/28/09

2007 Finest X-Fractors

*XF 1-135: 8X TO 20X BASIC
1-150 ODDS 1:16 MINI BOX
AU 151-166 ODDS 1:144 MINI BOX
STATED PRINT RUN 25 SER.#'d SETS
NO ROOKIE PRICING AVAILABLE
EXCHANGE DEADLINE 02/28/09

2007 Finest Rookie Finest Moments

STATED ODDS 2 PER MINI BOX
PRINTING PLATE ODDS 1:289 MINI BOX
PLATE PRINT RUN 1 SET PER COLOR
BLACK-CYAN-MAGENTA-YELLOW ISSUED
NO PLATE PRICING DUE TO SCARCITY
*REF: .6X TO 1.5X BASIC
REFRACTOR ODDS 1 PER MINI BOX
*REF BLACK: 2.5X TO 6X BASIC
REF BLACK ODDS 1:12 MINI BOX
REF BLACK PRINT RUN 99 SER.#'d SETS
*REF BLUE: 1X TO 2.5X BASIC
REF BLUE ODDS 1:4 MINI BOX
REF BLUE PRINT RUN 299 SER.#'d SETS
*REF GOLD: 5X TO 12X BASIC
REF GOLD ODDS 1:23 MINI BOX
REF GOLD PRINT RUN 50 SER.#'d SETS
*REF GREEN: 1.25X TO 3X BASIC
REF GREEN ODDS 1:6 MINI BOX
REF GREEN PRINT RUN 199 SER.#'d SETS
SUPERFRACTOR ODDS 1:1156 MINI BOX
SUPERFRACTOR PRINT RUN 1 SER.#'d SET
NO SUPERFRACTOR PRICING AVAILABLE
*X-FRACTOR: 8X TO 20X BASIC
X-FRACTOR ODDS 1:46 MINI BOX
X-FRACTOR PRINT RUN 25 SER.#'d SETS
X-F WHITE ODDS 1:1156 MINI BOX
X-F WHITE PRINT RUN 1 SER.#'d SET
NO X-F WHITE PRICING AVAILABLE
AD Adam Dunn .40 1.00
AE Andre Ethier .40 1.00
AJ Andruw Jones .25 .60
AP Albert Pujols .75 2.00
AR Alex Rodriguez .75 2.00
AS Anibal Sanchez .25 .60
AW Adam Wainwright .40 1.00
CB Carlos Beltran .40 1.00
CC Carl Crawford .40 1.00
CH Cole Hamels .50 1.25
CJ Chipper Jones .60 1.50
CQ Carlos Quentin .25 .60
DJ Derek Jeter 1.50 4.00
DL Derrek Lee .25 .60
DO David Ortiz .60 1.50
DU Dan Uggla .25 .60
DW David Wright .50 1.25
FL Francisco Liriano .25 .60
HM Hideki Matsui .60 1.50
HR Hanley Ramirez .40 1.00
IK Ian Kinsler .40 1.00
IS Ichiro Suzuki .75 2.00
JB Jason Bay .40 1.00
JH Jason Hirsh .25 .60
JM Joe Mauer .50 1.25
JP Jonathan Papelbon .60 1.50
JR Jose Reyes .40 1.00
JS Jeremy Sowers .25 .60
JV Justin Verlander .60 1.50
JW Jered Weaver .40 1.00
KG Ken Griffey Jr. 1.25 3.00
KJ Kenji Johjima .60 1.50
MC Miguel Cabrera .60 1.50
MK Matt Kemp .50 1.25
MN Mike Napoli .25 .60
MP Mike Piazza .60 1.50
MR Manny Ramirez .60 1.50
MT Miguel Tejada .40 1.00
NC Nelson Cruz .60 1.50
NG Nomar Garciaparra .40 1.00
NM Nick Markakis .50 1.25
PF Prince Fielder .40 1.00
RH Ryan Howard .50 1.25
RM Russ Martin .25 .60
SD Stephen Drew .25 .60
VG Vladimir Guerrero .40 1.00
DWW Dontrelle Willis .25 .60
JBA Josh Barfield .25 .60
JST Brian Stokes .25 .60
MCA Melky Cabrera .25 .60

2007 Finest Rookie Finest Moments Autographs

STATED ODDS 1:5 MINI BOX
PRINTING PLATE ODDS 1:482 MINI BOX
PLATE PRINT RUN 1 SET PER COLOR
BLACK-CYAN-MAGENTA-YELLOW ISSUED
NO PLATE PRICING DUE TO SCARCITY
REFRACTOR ODDS 1:77 MINI BOX
REFRACTOR PRINT RUN 25 #'d SETS
NO REFRACTOR PRICING AVAILABLE
SUPERFRACTOR ODDS 1:1975 MINI BOX
NO SUPERFRACTOR PRICING AVAILABLE
SUPERFRACTOR PRINT RUN 1 #'d SET
AR Alex Rodriguez 30.00 80.00
AS Anibal Sanchez 3.00 8.00
AW Adam Wainwright 12.00 30.00
BP Brandon Phillips 5.00 12.00
BW Brad Wilkerson 3.00 8.00
CH Cole Hamels 6.00 15.00
CJ Chuck James 4.00 10.00
CQ Carlos Quentin 6.00 15.00
DO David Ortiz 20.00 50.00
DU Dan Uggla 3.00 8.00
DW David Wright 12.00 30.00
DWW Dontrelle Willis 6.00 15.00
DY Delmon Young 10.00 25.00
ES Ervin Santana 3.00 8.00
FC Fausto Carmona 5.00 12.00
HR Hanley Ramirez 5.00 12.00
JM Justin Morneau 3.00 8.00
JN Joe Nathan 3.00 8.00
JP Jonathan Papelbon 5.00 12.00
LM Lastings Milledge 6.00 15.00
MC Melky Cabrera 3.00 8.00
MN Mike Napoli 6.00 15.00
MTC Matt Cain 10.00 25.00
RC Robinson Cano 6.00 15.00
RH Rich Hill 4.00 12.00
RH Ryan Howard 10.00 25.00
RM Russ Martin 6.00 15.00
RZ Ryan Zimmerman 5.00 12.00
TH Travis Hafner 6.00 15.00
YP Yusmeiro Petit 3.00 8.00

2007 Finest Rookie Finest Moments Autographs Dual

STATED ODDS 1:32 MINI BOX
STATED PRINT RUN 74 SER.#'d SETS
REFRACTOR ODDS 1:93 MINI BOX
REFRACTOR PRINT RUN 25 #'d SETS
NO REFRACTOR PRICING AVAILABLE
REF GOLD ODDS 1:2387 MINI BOX
REF GOLD PRINT RUN 1 #'d SET
NO REF GOLD PRICING AVAILABLE
EXCHANGE DEADLINE 02/28/09
BM J.Bay/J.Morneau 8.00 20.00
CC E.Chavez/M.Cabrera 30.00 60.00
CK N.Cruz/M.Kemp 10.00 25.00
CR M.Cain/A.Reyes 15.00 40.00
CY R.Cano/M.Young 15.00 40.00
HJ R.Hill/J.Johnson 15.00 40.00
HM C.Hamels/B.Myers 20.00 50.00
HR T.Hafner/M.Ramirez 20.00 50.00
JH C.James/C.Hamels 8.00 20.00
MC L.Milledge/M.Cabrera 15.00 40.00
MG R.Martin/R.Garko 8.00 20.00
MK L.Milledge/M.Kemp 12.50 30.00
MN K.Morales/M.Napoli 8.00 20.00
MNA R.Martin/M.Napoli 10.00 25.00
OP R.Oswalt/M.Prior 8.00 20.00
PO Y.Petit/S.Olsen 8.00 20.00
PP J.Papelbon/D.Pedroia 20.00 50.00
RP M.Rivera/J.Posada 100.00 200.00
RU H.Ramirez/D.Uggla 10.00 25.00
UG D.Uggla/M.Giles 8.00 20.00
US D.Uggla/A.Sanchez 10.00 25.00
VE J.Verlander/H.Ramirez 20.00 50.00
WW C.Wang/B.Webb 25.00 60.00
ZC J.Zumaya/F.Carmona 8.00 20.00

2007 Finest Rookie Photo Variation

STATED ODDS 1:5 MINI BOX
STATED PRINT RUN 439 SER.#'d SETS
*REF: .75X TO 2X BASIC
REFRACTOR ODDS 1:13 MINI BOX
REFRACTOR PRINT RUN 149 #'d SETS
REF GOLD ODDS 1:1975 MINI BOX
REF GOLD PRINT RUN 1 SER.#'d SET
NO REF GOLD PRICING AVAILABLE
*X-FRACTOR: 2X TO 5X BASIC
X-FRACTOR ODDS 1:39 MINI BOX
X-FRACTOR PRINT RUN 50 SER.#'d SETS
136 A.Lind Bat Up .75 2.00
136 A.Lind Bat Out .75 2.00
137 H.Gimenez Posed .75 2.00
137 H.Gimenez Batting .75 2.00
138 S.Riggans w/Bat .75 2.00
138 S.Riggans w/Glove .75 2.00
139 J.Arias w/Bat .75 2.00
139 J.Arias Throw .75 2.00
140 D.Anderson Run Away .75 2.00
140 D.Anderson w/Glove .75 2.00
141 M.Rabelo Bat Shoulder .75 2.00
141 M.Rabelo Bat Up .75 2.00
142 C.Narveson Portrait .75 2.00
142 C.Narveson w/Glove .75 2.00
143 R.Feierabend Catch .75 2.00
143 R.Feierabend Pitch .75 2.00
144 V.Rottino Swing .75 2.00
144 V.Rottino Field .75 2.00
145 J.Knott Run .75 2.00
145 J.Knott w/Bat .75 2.00
146 O.Navarro Posed .75 2.00
146 O.Navarro Swing .75 2.00
147 B.Stokes Windup .75 2.00
147 B.Stokes Throw .75 2.00
148 G.Perkins Windup .75 2.00
148 G.Perkins w/Jacket .75 2.00
149 M.Maier In OF .75 2.00
149 M.Maier On Deck .75 2.00
150 D.Young Running 1.25 3.00
150 D.Young Portirat 1.25 3.00

2007 Finest Rookie Redemption

This 10-card set was announced during the year as new 2007 rookies made an impact in the majors. These cards, which were inserted at a stated rate of one in three mini-boxes, could be redeemed until December 31, 2007.

STATED ODDS 1:3 MINI BOX
REDEEMABLE FOR 07 RC LOGO PLAYER
EXCHANGE DEADLINE 12/30/07
1 Hideki Okajima 4.00 10.00
2 Elijah Dukes 1.25 3.00
3 Akinori Iwamura 2.00 5.00
4 Tim Lincecum 4.00 10.00
5 Daisuke Matsuzaka 3.00 8.00
6 Ryan Braun 4.00 10.00
7 D.Matsuzaka/H.Okajima 4.00 10.00
8 Justin Upton 2.50 6.00
9 Philip Hughes 2.00 5.00
10 Joba Chamberlain AU 6.00 15.00

2007 Finest Ryan Howard Finest Moments

COMMON CARD 1.50 4.00
STATED ODDS 2 PER HOWARD BOX LOADER
STATED PRINT RUN 459 SER.#'d SETS
*REF: .6X TO 1.5X BASIC
REFRACTOR ODDS 1:3 BOXES
REFRACTOR PRINT RUN 149 SER.#'d SETS
REF GOLD ODDS 1:329 BOXES
REF GOLD PRINT RUN 1 SER.#'d SET
NO REF GOLD PRICING AVAILABLE
*X-FRACTOR: .75X TO 2X BASIC
X-FRACTOR ODDS 1:7 BOXES
X-FRACTOR PRINT RUN 50 SER.#'d SETS

2008 Finest

COMP.SET w/o AUs (150) 40.00 80.00
COMMON CARD (1-125) .15 .40
COMMON RC (126-150) .75 2.00
COMMON AU RC (151-166) 4.00 10.00
151-166 AU ODDS 1:3 MINI BOX
1-150 PLATE ODDS 1:82 MINI BOX
AU 151-166 PLATE ODDS 1:775 MINI BOX
PLATE PRINT RUN 1 SET PER COLOR
BLACK-CYAN-MAGENTA-YELLOW ISSUED
NO PLATE PRICING DUE TO SCARCITY
1 Daisuke Matsuzaka .25 .60
2 Justin Upton .25 .60
3 Andruw Jones .15 .40
4 John Lackey .25 .60
5 Brandon Phillips .15 .40
6 Ryan Zimmerman .25 .60
7 Tim Lincecum .25 .60
8 Johnny Damon .25 .60
9 Garrett Atkins .15 .40
10 Magglio Ordonez .25 .60
11 Tom Gorzelanny .15 .40
12 Eric Chavez .15 .40
13 Troy Tulowitzki .40 1.00
14 Mike Lowell .15 .40
15 Brandon Webb .25 .60
16 Chipper Jones .40 1.00
17 Alex Gordon .25 .60
18 Ken Griffey Jr. .75 2.00
19 Roy Oswalt .25 .60
20 Miguel Cabrera .40 1.00
21 Chase Utley .25 .60
22 Scott Kazmir .25 .60
23 Kenji Johjima .15 .40
24 Frank Thomas .40 1.00
25 Ryan Braun .25 .60
26 Carlos Pena .25 .60
27 Robinson Cano .25 .60
28 Ben Sheets .15 .40
29 Russell Martin .15 .40
30 Joe Mauer .30 .75
31 Gary Sheffield .15 .40
32 Carlos Zambrano .25 .60
33 Jermaine Dye .15 .40
34 Dan Uggla .15 .40
35 Erik Bedard .15 .40
36 Tim Hudson .25 .60
37 David Ortiz .40 1.00
38 Tom Glavine .25 .60
39 Adrian Gonzalez .25 .60
40 Jorge Posada .25 .60
41 Noah Lowry .15 .40
42 Vernon Wells .15 .40
43 Johan Santana .25 .60
44 Dmitri Young .15 .40
45 Manny Ramirez .40 1.00
46 Jim Edmonds .25 .60
47 Roy Halladay .25 .60
48 Delmon Young .25 .60
49 Nick Swisher .25 .60
50 David Wright .25 .60
51 Paul Konerko .25 .60
52 Curt Schilling .25 .60
53 Torii Hunter .15 .40
54 Gary Matthews .15 .40
55 Derrek Lee .15 .40
56 John Smoltz .40 1.00
57 Adam Dunn .25 .60
58 C.C Sabathia .25 .60
59 Chris Young .15 .40
60 Jake Peavy .15 .40
61 Joba Chamberlain .25 .60
62 Jason Bay .25 .60
63 Chris Carpenter .25 .60
64 Jimmy Rollins .25 .60
65 Grady Sizemore .25 .60
66 Joe Blanton .15 .40
67 Justin Morneau .25 .60
68 Lance Berkman .25 .60
69 Jeff Francis .15 .40
70 Nick Markakis .30 .75
71 Orlando Cabrera .25 .60
72 Barry Zito .25 .60
73 Eric Byrnes .15 .40
74 Brian McCann .25 .60
75 Albert Pujols .50 1.25
76 Josh Beckett .15 .40
77 Jim Thome .25 .60
78 Fausto Carmona .15 .40
79 Brad Hawpe .15 .40
80 Prince Fielder .25 .60
81 Justin Verlander .40 1.00
82 Billy Butler .15 .40
83 J.J. Hardy .15 .40
84 Hideki Matsui .40 1.00
85 Matt Holliday .40 1.00
86 Bobby Crosby .15 .40
87 Orlando Hudson .15 .40
88 Ichiro Suzuki .50 1.25
89 Troy Glaus .25 .60
90 Hanley Ramirez .25 .60
91 Carlos Beltran .25 .60
92 Mark Buehrle .25 .60
93 Andy Pettitte .25 .60
94 Mark Teixeira .25 .60
95 Curtis Granderson .25 .60
96 Cole Hamels .30 .75
97 Jarrod Saltalamacchia .15 .40
98 Carl Crawford .25 .60
99 Dontrelle Willis .15 .40
100 Alex Rodriguez .50 1.25
101 Brad Penny .15 .40
102 Michael Young .15 .40
103 Greg Maddux .50 1.25
104 Brian Roberts .15 .40
105 Hunter Pence .25 .60
106 Aaron Harang .15 .40
107 Ivan Rodriguez .25 .60
108 Dan Haren .15 .40
109 Freddy Sanchez .15 .40
110 Alfonso Soriano .25 .60
111 Hank Blalock .15 .40
112 Chien- Ming Wang .25 .60
113 Carlos Delgado .15 .40
114 Aramis Ramirez .15 .40
115 Jose Reyes .25 .60
116 Victor Martinez .25 .60
117 Carlos Lee .15 .40
118 Jeff Kent .15 .40
119 Miguel Tejada .25 .60
120 Vladimir Guerrero .25 .60
121 Travis Hafner .15 .40
122 Todd Helton .25 .60
123 Chris Young .15 .40
124 Derek Jeter 1.00 2.50
125 Ryan Howard .25 .60
126 Alberto Gonzalez RC 1.25 3.00
127 Felipe Paulino RC 1.25 3.00
128 Donny Lucy (RC) .75 2.00
129 Nick Blackburn RC 1.25 3.00
130 Luke Hochevar RC 1.25 3.00
131 Bronson Sardinha (RC) .75 2.00
132 Heath Phillips RC 1.25 3.00
133 Bryan Bullington (RC) .75 2.00
134 Jeff Clement (RC) 1.25 3.00
135 Josh Banks (RC) .75 2.00
136 Emilio Bonifacio RC 2.00 5.00
137 Ryan Hanigan RC 1.25 3.00
138 Erick Threets (RC) .75 2.00
139 Seth Smith (RC) .75 2.00
140 Billy Buckner (RC) .75 2.00
141 Bill Murphy (RC) .75 2.00
142 Radhames Liz RC 1.25 3.00
143 Joey Votto (RC) 3.00 8.00
144 Mel Stocker RC .75 2.00
145 Dan Meyer (RC) .75 2.00
146 Rob Johnson (RC) .75 2.00
147 Josh Newman RC 1.25 3.00
148 Dan Giese (RC) .75 2.00
149 Luis Mendoza (RC) .75 2.00
150 Wladimir Balentien (RC) .75 2.00
151 B.Jones AU RC 4.00 10.00
152 Rich Thompson AU RC 4.00 10.00
153 C.Hu AU (RC) 4.00 10.00
154 Chris Seddon AU (RC) 4.00 10.00
155 S.Pearce AU RC 10.00 25.00
156 Lance Broadway AU (RC) 4.00 10.00
157 Nyjer Morgan AU (RC) 4.00 10.00
158 Jonathan Meloan AU RC 4.00 10.00
159 Josh Anderson AU (RC) 4.00 10.00
160 C.Buchholz AU (RC) 4.00 10.00
161 Joe Koshansky AU (RC) 4.00 10.00
162 Clint Sammons AU (RC) 4.00 10.00
163 Daric Barton AU (RC) 5.00 12.00
164 Ross Detwiler AU RC 5.00 12.00
165 Sam Fuld AU RC 6.00 15.00
166 Justin Ruggiano AU RC 4.00 10.00

2008 Finest Refractors

*REF VET: 1X TO 2.5X BASIC
*REF RC: .5X TO 1.2X BASIC RC
1-150 REF.RANDOMLY INSERTED
*REF AU: .4X TO 1X BASIC AU
151-166 ODDS 1:7 MINI PACKS
151-166 PRINT RUN 499 SER.#'d SETS

2008 Finest Refractors Black

*BLACK VET: 4X TO 10X BASIC
*BLACK RC: 1X TO 2.5X BASIC RC
1-150 ODDS 1:4 MINI BOXES
1-150 PRINT RUN 99 SER.#'d SETS
*REF AU: .6X TO 1.5X BASIC AU
151-166 ODDS 1:32 MINI PACKS
151-166 PRINT RUN 99 SER.#'d SETS
164 Ross Detwiler AU 10.00 25.00

2008 Finest Refractors Blue

*BLUE VET: 1.5X TO 4X BASIC
*BLUE RC: .6X TO 1.5X BASIC RC
1-150 ODDS 1:2 MINI BOXES
1-150 PRINT RUN 299 SER.#'d SETS
*REF AU: .5X TO 1.2X BASIC AU
151-166 ODDS 1:8 MINI PACKS
151-166 PRINT RUN 399 SER.#'d SETS

2008 Finest Refractors Gold

*GOLD VET: 6X TO 15X BASIC
*GOLD RC: 2X TO 5X BASIC RC
1-150 ODDS 1:7 MINI BOXES

50 PRINT RUN 50 SER.#'d SETS
*F AU: 1X TO 2.5X BASIC AU
1-166 ODDS 1:64 MINI PACKS
1-166 PRINT RUN 50 SER.#'d SETS
Frank Thomas 20.00 50.00
Ichiro Suzuki 15.00 40.00
0 Alex Rodriguez 15.00 40.00
3 Greg Maddux 20.00 50.00
4 Derek Jeter 30.00 60.00
6 Alberto Gonzalez 10.00 25.00
9 Nick Blackburn 20.00 50.00
2 Heath Phillips 6.00 15.00
4 Jeff Clement 15.00 40.00
7 Josh Newman 6.00 15.00
8 Dan Giese 6.00 15.00
0 Wladimir Balentien 6.00 15.00
3 Daric Barton AU 15.00 40.00
4 Ross Detwiler AU 15.00 40.00

2008 Finest Refractors Green

GREEN VET: 2X TO 5X BASIC
GREEN RC: .75X TO 2X BASIC RC
-150 ODDS 1:2 MINI BOXES
-150 PRINT RUN 199 SER.#'d SETS
REF AU: .5X TO 1.2X BASIC AU
51-166 ODDS 1:16 MINI PACKS
51-166 PRINT RUN 199 SER.#'d SETS

2008 Finest Refractors Red

-150 ODDS 1:14 MINI BOXES
51-166 AU ODDS 1:128 MINI BOXES
STATED PRINT RUN 25 SER.#'d SETS
NO PRICING DUE TO SCARCITY

2008 Finest X-Fractors White Framed

-150 ODDS 1:327 MINI BOXES
51-166 AU ODDS 1:2036 MINI BOXES
STATED PRINT RUN 1 SER.#'d SET
NO PRICING DUE TO SCARCITY

2008 Finest Finest Moments

*REF: .6X TO 1.5X BASIC
REF.RANDOMLY INSERTED
STATED ODDS XX PER MINI BOX
*BLACK REF: 1.5X TO 4X BASIC
BLACK ODDS 1:10 MINI BOXES
BLACK PRINT RUN 99 SER.#'d SETS
*BLUE REF: .75X TO 2X BASIC
BLUE ODDS 1:4 MINI BOXES
BLUE PRINT RUN 399 SER.#'d SETS
*GOLD REF: 2.5X TO 6X BASIC
GOLD ODDS 1:20 MINI BOXES
GOLD PRINT RUN 50 SER.#'d SETS
*GREEN REF: 1X TO 2.5X BASIC
GREEN ODDS 1:5 MINI BOXES
GREEN PRINT RUN 199 SER.#'d SETS
PRINTING PLATE ODDS 1:245 MINI BOXES
PLATE PRINT RUN 1 SET PER COLOR
BLACK-CYAN-MAGENTA-YELLOW ISSUED
NO PLATE PRICING DUE TO SCARCITY
AG Adrian Gonzalez .60 1.50
AP Andy Pettitte .60 1.50
APU Albert Pujols 1.25 3.00
AR Alex Rodriguez 1.25 3.00
AS Andy Sonnanstine .40 1.00
BP Brandon Phillips .40 1.00
BPB Brian Bannister .40 1.00
BW Brandon Webb .60 1.50
CB Clay Buchholz .60 1.50
CF Chone Figgins .40 1.00
CG Curtis Granderson .60 1.50
CH Cole Hamels .75 2.00
CP Carlos Pena .60 1.50
CS C.C. Sabathia .60 1.50
DH Dan Haren .40 1.00
DJ Derek Jeter 2.50 6.00
DL Derrek Lee .40 1.00
DO David Ortiz 1.00 2.50
DW David Wright .60 1.50
EB Eric Byrnes .40 1.00
FC Fausto Carmona .40 1.00
FH Felix Hernandez .60 1.50
FT Frank Thomas 1.00 2.50
HP Hunter Pence .60 1.50
HR Hanley Ramirez .60 1.50
IS Ichiro Suzuki 1.25 3.00
ISS Ichiro Suzuki 1.25 3.00
JAS Johan Santana .60 1.50
JMC Miguel Cabrera 1.00 2.50
JR Jose Reyes .60 1.50
JS John Smoltz 1.00 2.50
JSA Jarrod Saltalamacchia .40 1.00
JT Jim Thome .60 1.50
JV Justin Verlander 1.00 2.50
MB Mark Buehrle .60 1.50
ME Mark Ellis .40 1.00
MH Matt Holliday 1.00 2.50
MR Mark Reynolds .40 1.00
PF Prince Fielder .60 1.50
PM Pedro Martinez .60 1.50
RA Rick Ankiel .40 1.00
RB Ryan Braun .60 1.50
RH Ryan Howard .60 1.50
ROH Roy Halladay .60 1.50
SS Sammy Sosa 1.00 2.50
TG Tom Glavine .60 1.50
TH Trevor Hoffman .60 1.50
TOH Todd Helton .60 1.50
TT Troy Tulowitzki 1.00 2.50
VG Vladimir Guerrero .60 1.50

2008 Finest Finest Moments Refractors Red

STATED ODDS 1:39 MINI BOXES
STATED PRINT RUN 25 SER.#'d SETS
NO PRICING DUE TO SCARCITY

2008 Finest Finest Moments X-Fractors White Framed

STATED ODDS 1:982 MINI BOXES
STATED PRINT RUN 1 SER.#'d SET
NO PRICING DUE TO SCARCITY

2008 Finest Finest Moments Autographs

GROUP A ODDS 1:5 MINI BOXES
GROUP B ODDS 1:282 MINI BOXES
AR Alex Rios A 6.00 15.00
AS Andy Sonnanstine A 3.00 8.00
BP Brandon Phillips A 6.00 15.00
BPB Brian Bannister A 6.00 15.00
CG Curtis Granderson A 5.00 12.00
CH Cole Hamels A 3.00 8.00
CMW Chien-Ming Wang A 12.50 30.00
DW David Wright A 10.00 25.00
FC Fausto Carmona A 6.00 15.00
HR Hanley Ramirez A 4.00 10.00
JA Jeremy Accardo A 3.00 8.00
JC Jack Cust A 3.00 8.00
JD Justin Duchscherer A 6.00 15.00
JH Josh Hamilton A 6.00 15.00
JMC Miguel Cabrera A 20.00 50.00
JR Jose Reyes A 5.00 12.00
JS Jarrod Saltalamacchia A 3.00 8.00
ME Mark Ellis A 3.00 8.00
MR Mark Reynolds A 8.00 20.00
NM Nick Markakis A 6.00 15.00
PH Phil Hughes A 4.00 10.00
RB Ryan Braun A 10.00 25.00
RH Ryan Howard B 8.00 20.00
RZ Ryan Zimmerman A 6.00 15.00
VG Vladimir Guerrero A 10.00 25.00

2008 Finest Finest Moments Autographs Refractors Red

STATED ODDS 1:79 MINI BOXES
STATED PRINT RUN 25 SER.#'d SETS
NO PRICING DUE TO SCARCITY

2008 Finest Finest Moments Autographs X-Fractors White Framed

STATED ODDS 1:3260 MINI BOXES
STATED PRINT RUN 1 SER.#'d SET
NO PRICING DUE TO SCARCITY

2008 Finest Rookie Redemption

STATED ODDS 1:3 MINI BOXES
EXCHANGE DEADLINE 4/30/2009
1 Johnny Cueto 2.50 6.00
2 Jay Bruce AU 12.00 30.00
3 Kosuke Fukudome 3.00 8.00
4 Jeff Samardzija 3.00 8.00
5 Chris Davis 2.00 5.00
6 Justin Masterson 2.50 6.00
7 Clayton Kershaw 8.00 20.00
8 Daniel Murphy 4.00 10.00
9 Denard Span 1.50 4.00
10 Jed Lowrie AU 4.00 10.00

2008 Finest Topps Team Favorites

COMPLETE SET (8) 5.00 12.00
RANDOM INSERTS IN PACKS
*REF: .5X TO 1.2X BASIC
REF.ODDS 1:4 MINI BOXES
AS Alfonso Soriano 1.00 2.50
BC Bobby Crosby .60 1.50
DW David Wright 1.00 2.50
EC Eric Chavez .60 1.50
FP Felix Pie .60 1.50
JR Jose Reyes 1.00 2.50
MC Melky Cabrera .60 1.50
RC Robinson Cano 1.00 2.50

2008 Finest Topps Team Favorites Autographs

STATED PRINT RUN 100 SER.#'d SETS
AS Alfonso Soriano 20.00 50.00
BC Bobby Crosby 6.00 15.00
DW David Wright 20.00 50.00
EC Eric Chavez 6.00 15.00
FP Felix Pie 6.00 15.00
JR Jose Reyes 8.00 20.00
MC Melky Cabrera 4.00 10.00
RC Robinson Cano 15.00 40.00

2008 Finest Topps Team Favorites Autographs Refractors Red

STATED ODDS 1:164 MINI BOXES
STATED PRINT RUN 25 SER.#'d SETS
NO PRICING DUE TO SCARCITY

2008 Finest Topps Team Favorites Autographs X-Fractors White Framed

STATED ODDS 1:4092 MINI BOXES
STATED PRINT RUN 1 SER.#'d SET
NO PRICING DUE TO SCARCITY

2008 Finest Topps Team Favorites Dual

COMPLETE SET (4) 3.00 8.00
RANDOM INSERTS IN PACKS
*REF: .5X TO 1.2X BASIC
REF.RANDOMLY INSERTED
CC Melky Cabrera 1.00 2.50
Robinson Cano
EB Eric Chavez .60 1.50
Bobby Crosby
RW Jose Reyes 1.00 2.50
David Wright
SP Alfonso Soriano 1.00 2.50
Felix Pie

2008 Finest Topps Team Favorites Dual Autographs

STATED ODDS 1:166 MINI BOXES
STATED PRINT RUN 74 SER.#'d SETS
CC M.Cabrera/R.Cano 10.00 25.00
EB E.Chavez/B.Crosby 6.00 15.00
RW J.Reyes/D.Wright 25.00 60.00
SP A.Soriano/F.Pie 6.00 15.00

2008 Finest Topps Team Favorites Dual Autographs X-Fractors White Framed

STATED ODDS 1:4092 MINI BOXES
STATED PRINT RUN 1 SER.#'d SET
NO PRICING DUE TO SCARCITY

2008 Finest Topps Team Favorites Dual Autographs Cuts

STATED ODDS 1:9821 MINI BOXES
STATED PRINT RUN 1 SER.#'d SET
NO PRICING DUE TO SCARCITY

2008 Finest Topps TV Autographs

STATED ODDS 1:11 MINI BOXES
RM Alan Narz 4.00 10.00
RGF Felicia 4.00 10.00
RGH Hollie 4.00 10.00
RGR Rachael 4.00 10.00
RGLS Lindsey 4.00 10.00
Stephanie

2008 Finest Topps TV Autographs Red Ink

RANDOM INSERTS IN PACKS
PRINT RUNS B/WN 5-10 COPIES PER
NO PRICING DUE TO SCARCITY

2008 Finest Topps TV Autographs Refractors

STATED ODDS 1:392 MINI BOXES
STATED PRINT RUN 1 SER.#'d SET
NO PRICING DUE TO SCARCITY

2009 Finest

COMP.SET w/o AU's (150) 40.00 80.00
COMMON CARD (1-125) .15 .40
COMMON RC (126-150) .75 2.00
COMMON AU RC (151-164) 5.00 12.00
AU RC ODDS 1:2 MINI BOX
LETTERS SER.#'d B/W 170-285 COPIES PER
TOTAL PRINT RUNS LISTED BELOW
EXCHANGE DEADLINE 4/30/2012
1-150 PLATE ODDS 1:45 MINI BOX
PLATE PRINT RUN 1 SET PER COLOR
BLACK-CYAN-MAGENTA-YELLOW ISSUED
NO PLATE PRICING DUE TO SCARCITY
1 Kosuke Fukudome .25 .60
2 Derek Jeter 1.00 2.50
3 Evan Longoria .25 .60
4 Alex Gordon .25 .60
5 David Wright .30 .75
6 Ryan Howard .30 .75
7 Jose Reyes .25 .60
8 Ryan Braun .25 .60
9 Hunter Pence .25 .60
10 Chipper Jones .40 1.00
11 Jimmy Rollins .25 .60
12 Alfonso Soriano .25 .60
13 Alex Rodriguez .50 1.25
14 Paul Konerko .25 .60
15 Dustin Pedroia .30 .75
16 Brian McCann .25 .60
17 Ken Griffey .75 2.00
18 Daisuke Matsuzaka .25 .60
19 Josh Beckett .15 .40
20 Jorge Posada .25 .60
21 Nick Markakis .30 .75
22 Xavier Nady .15 .40
23 Carlos Pena .25 .60
24 Grady Sizemore .25 .60
25 Mark Teixeira .25 .60
26 Chase Utley .25 .60
27 Vladimir Guerrero .25 .60
28 Prince Fielder .25 .60
29 Brian Roberts .15 .40
30 Magglio Ordonez .25 .60
31 Cliff Lee .25 .60
32 Josh Hamilton .25 .60
33 Justin Morneau .25 .60
34 David Ortiz .40 1.00
35 Cole Hamels .30 .75
36 Edinson Volquez .15 .40
37 Hanley Ramirez .25 .60
38 Carlos Zambrano .25 .60
39 Brett Myers .15 .40
40 Chien-Ming Wang .25 .60
41 John Lackey .25 .60
42 B.J. Upton .25 .60
43 Gary Sheffield .15 .40
44 Jake Peavy .15 .40
45 Carlos Lee .15 .40
46 Jacoby Ellsbury .30 .75
47 Francisco Liriano .15 .40
48 Torii Hunter .15 .40
49 Eric Chavez .15 .40
50 Jamie Moyer .15 .40
51 Ichiro Suzuki .50 1.25
52 CC Sabathia .25 .60
53 Matt Holliday .40 1.00
54 Ervin Santana .15 .40
55 Hideki Matsui .40 1.00
56 Mark Buehrle .25 .60
57 Johan Santana .25 .60
58 Francisco Rodriguez .25 .60
59 Jorge Cantu .15 .40
60 Joe Mauer .30 .75
61 Ian Kinsler .25 .60
62 Joba Chamberlain .15 .40
63 Stephen Drew .15 .40
64 J.D. Drew .15 .40
65 Justin Upton .25 .60
66 Troy Glaus .15 .40
67 Chone Figgins .15 .40
68 David DeJesus .15 .40
69 Joey Votto .40 1.00
70 Alex Rios .15 .40
71 Adam Jones .25 .60
72 Miguel Tejada .25 .60
73 Michael Young .15 .40
74 Vernon Wells .15 .40
75 Tim Lincecum .25 .60
76 Ryan Zimmerman .25 .60
77 Nate McLouth .15 .40
78 Carl Crawford .25 .60
79 Dan Haren .15 .40
80 Brandon Webb .25 .60
81 Tim Hudson .25 .60
82 Rafael Furcal .15 .40
83 Ryan Dempster .15 .40
84 Carlos Beltran .25 .60
85 Lance Berkman .25 .60
86 Jhonny Peralta .15 .40
87 Aramis Ramirez .15 .40
88 Aubrey Huff .15 .40
89 Johnny Damon .25 .60
90 Carlos Quentin .15 .40
91 Yunel Escobar .15 .40
92 Scott Kazmir .15 .40
93 Delmon Young .25 .60
94 Jermaine Dye .15 .40
95 Miguel Cabrera .40 1.00
96 Zack Greinke .25 .60
97 Chris Young .15 .40
98 Derrek Lee .15 .40
99 Orlando Hudson .15 .40
100 Jay Bruce .25 .60
101 Garrett Atkins .15 .40
102 Curtis Granderson .30 .75
103 Adrian Gonzalez .30 .75
104 Raul Ibanez .25 .60
105 Roy Halladay .25 .60
106 Jon Lester .25 .60
107 Adam Dunn .25 .60
108 A.J. Burnett .15 .40
109 Gavin Floyd .15 .40
110 Russ Martin .15 .40
111 Dan Uggla .15 .40
112 Andre Ethier .25 .60
113 Casey Kotchman .15 .40
114 Matt Garza .15 .40
115 Kevin Youkilis .15 .40
116 Felix Hernandez .25 .60
117 Rich Harden .15 .40
118 Roy Oswalt .25 .60
119 Jason Bay .25 .60
120 Geovany Soto .25 .60
121 Ryan Ludwick .25 .60
122 Joe Saunders .15 .40
123 Gil Meche .15 .40
124 Jim Thome .25 .60
125 Albert Pujols .50 1.25
126 Andrew Carpenter RC 1.25 3.00
127 Aaron Cunningham RC .75 2.00
128 Phil Coke RC 1.25 3.00
129 Alcides Escobar RC 1.25 3.00
130 Dexter Fowler (RC) 1.25 3.00
131 Michael Hinckley (RC) .75 2.00
132 Brad Nelson (RC) .75 2.00
133 Scott Lewis (RC) .75 2.00
134 Juan Miranda RC 1.25 3.00
135 Jason Motte (RC) 1.25 3.00
136 Travis Snider RC 1.25 3.00
137 Wade LeBlanc RC 1.25 3.00
138 Matt Tuiasosopo (RC) .75 2.00
139 Humberto Sanchez (RC) .75 2.00
140 Freddy Sandoval (RC) .75 2.00
141 Chris Lambert (RC) .75 2.00
142 John Jaso RC .75 2.00
143 James McDonald RC 2.00 5.00
144 Luis Valbuena RC 1.25 3.00
145 Rich Rundles (RC) .75 2.00
146 Josh Whitesell RC 1.25 3.00
147 Jeff Baisley RC .75 2.00
148 Ramon Ramirez (RC) .75 2.00
149 Jason Bourgeois (RC) .75 2.00
150 Jesus Delgado RC 1.25 3.00
151 M.Gamel AU/1425 * RC 3.00 8.00
152 Travis Snider AU 5.00 12.00
153 Angel Salome AU/1308 * (RC) 5.00 12.00
154 Will Venable AU/1190 * RC 5.00 12.00
155 M.Bowden AU/1308 * (RC) 5.00 12.00
156 Conor Gillaspie AU/963 * RC 5.00 12.00
157 Matt Antonelli AU/963 * RC 5.00 12.00
158 Greg Golson AU/1308 * (RC) 5.00 12.00
159 Kila Ka'aihue AU/1190 * (RC) 4.00 10.00
160 Bobby Parnell AU/1190 * RC 5.00 12.00
161 Gaby Sanchez AU/1190 * RC 6.00 15.00
162 Jonathon Niese AU/1425 * RC 6.00 15.00
163 Dexter Fowler AU EXCH 3.00 8.00
164 David Price AU/1425 * RC 10.00 25.00

2009 Finest Refractors

*REF VET: 1.2X TO 3X BASIC
*REF RC: .5X TO 1.2X BASIC RC
1-150 RANDOMLY INSERTED
*REF AU: .5X TO 1.2X BASIC AU
151-164 ODDS 1:4 MINI BOXES
EACH LETTER AU SER.#'d TO 75
TOTAL PRINT RUNS LISTED BELOW
EXCHANGE DEADLINE 4/30/2012

2009 Finest Refractors Blue

*BLUE REF VET: 1.5X TO 4X BASIC
*BLUE REF RC: .6X TO 1.5X BASIC RC
1-150 RANDOMLY INSERTED
1-150 PRINT RUN 399 SER.#'d SETS
*BLUE REF AU: .6X TO 1.5X BASIC AU
151-164 ODDS 1:12 MINI BOXES
EACH LETTER AU SER.#'d TO 25
TOTAL PRINT RUNS LISTED BELOW
EXCHANGE DEADLINE 4/30/2012

2009 Finest Refractors Gold

*GOLD REF VET: 6X TO 15X BASIC
*GOLD REF RC: 1.5X TO 4X BASIC RC
1-150 STATED ODDS 1:4 MINI BOXES
1-150 PRINT RUN 50 SER.#'d SETS
*GOLD REF AU: .75X TO 2X BASIC AU
151-164 ODDS 1:30 MINI BOXES
EACH LETTER AU SER.#'d TO 10
TOTAL PRINT RUNS LISTED BELOW
EXCHANGE DEADLINE 4/30/2012

2009 Finest Refractors Green

*GREEN REF VET: 4X TO 10X BASIC
*GREEN REF RC: 1X TO 2.5X BASIC RC
1-150 STATED ODDS 1:2 MINI BOXES
STATED PRINT RUN 99 SER.#'d SETS

2009 Finest Refractors Red

*RED REF VET: 12X TO 30X BASIC
*RED REF RC: 2.5X TO 6X BASIC RC
1-150 STATED ODDS 1:8 MINI BOXES
1-150 PRINT RUN 25 SER.#'d SETS
*RED REF AU: 1.5X TO 4X BASIC AU
151-164 ODDS 1:60 MINI BOXES
EACH LETTER AU SER.#'d TO 5
TOTAL PRINT RUNS LISTED BELOW
EXCHANGE DEADLINE 4/30/2012

2009 Finest X-Fractors

1-150 ODDS 1:180 MINI BOX
151-164 AU ODDS 1:298 MINI BOX
STATED PRINT RUN 1 SER.#'d SET
NO PRICING DUE TO SCARCITY
EXCHANGE DEADLINE 4/30/2012

2009 Finest Finest Moments Autographs

GROUP A ODDS 1:10 MINI BOX
GROUP B ODDS 1:61 MINI BOX
REF.ODDS 1:68 MINI BOXES
REF.PRINT RUN 25 SER.#'d SETS
NO REF.PRICING DUE TO SCARCITY
X-F ODDS 1:1797 MINI BOX
X-F PRINT RUN 1 SER.#'d SET
NO X-F PRICING DUE TO SCARCITY
AC Asdrubal Cabrera A 5.00 12.00
AI Akinori Iwamura A 5.00 12.00
AR Alex Rodriguez B 100.00 175.00
DO David Ortiz B 30.00 80.00
DW David Wright A 8.00 20.00
EV Evan Longoria A 6.00 15.00
HP Hunter Pence A 6.00 15.00
JB Jay Bruce A 5.00 12.00
JC Joba Chamberlain A 8.00 20.00
JL Jon Lester A 5.00 12.00
JR Jose Reyes A 5.00 12.00
JT Jim Thome B 12.50 30.00
JV Joey Votto B 30.00 60.00
RC Robinson Cano A 10.00 25.00
RH Ryan Howard B 8.00 20.00
JBA Jason Bay B 5.00 12.00

2009 Finest Rookie Redemption

STATED ODDS 1:3 MINI BOXES
*REF: .5X TO 1.2X BASIC
REF.ODDS 1:14 MINI BOXES
*GOLD REF: 1.2X TO 3X BASIC
GOLD REF.ODDS 1:54 MINI BOXES
EXCHANGE DEADLINE 4/30/2010
1 Matt LaPorta 2.00 5.00
2 Tommy Hanson 3.00 8.00
3 Andrew Bailey 3.00 8.00
4 Julio Borbon 1.25 3.00
5 Colby Rasmus 2.00 5.00
6 Kyle Blanks 2.00 5.00
7 Neftali Feliz 2.00 5.00
8 Nolan Reimold 1.25 3.00
9 Rick Porcello 4.00 10.00
10 Tommy Hanson AU 6.00 15.00

2010 Finest

COMP.SET w/o AU's (150) 30.00 60.00
COMMON CARD (1-125) .15 .40
COMMON RC (126-150) .75 2.00
COMMON AU RC (151-164) 4.00 10.00
AU RC ODDS 1:2 MINI BOX
LETTERS SER.#'d B/W 106-284 COPIES PER
TOTAL PRINT RUNS LISTED BELOW
1-150 PLATE ODDS 1:50 MINI BOX
1 Tim Lincecum .25 .60
2 Evan Longoria .25 .60
3 Alex Rodriguez .50 1.25
4 Ryan Braun .25 .60
5 Grady Sizemore .25 .60
6 David Wright .30 .75
7 Albert Pujols .50 1.25
8 Derrek Lee .15 .40
9 Ichiro Suzuki .50 1.25
10 Justin Morneau .25 .60
11 Johan Santana .25 .60
12 Matt Kemp .30 .75
13 Daisuke Matsuzaka .25 .60
14 Derek Jeter 1.00 2.50
15 Mark Buehrle .25 .60
16 Chipper Jones .40 1.00
17 Prince Fielder .25 .60
18 Ryan Howard .30 .75
19 Vladimir Guerrero .25 .60
20 Alexei Ramirez .25 .60
21 Joba Chamberlain .15 .40
22 Russell Martin .15 .40
23 CC Sabathia .25 .60
24 Adam Dunn .25 .60
25 Jose Reyes .25 .60
26 Michael Young .15 .40
27 Joe Mauer .30 .75
28 Mark Teixeira .25 .60
29 Jason Bartlett .15 .40
30 Johnny Damon .25 .60
31 Miguel Cabrera .40 1.00
32 Adam Wainwright .25 .60
33 Brandon Webb .25 .60
34 Carlos Pena .25 .60
35 Jorge Posada .25 .60
36 Pablo Sandoval .25 .60
37 Manny Ramirez .40 1.00
38 Robinson Cano .25 .60
39 Nick Markakis .30 .75
40 Justin Upton .25 .60
41 Adrian Gonzalez .30 .75
42 Ian Kinsler .25 .60
43 Ryan Zimmerman .25 .60
44 Mark Reynolds .15 .40
45 Raul Ibanez .25 .60
46 Jason Bay .25 .60
47 Kendry Morales .15 .40
48 Todd Helton .25 .60
49 Dan Uggla .15 .40
50 Adam Lind .25 .60
51 Victor Martinez .25 .60
52 Mariano Rivera .50 1.25
53 Chase Utley .25 .60
54 Kevin Youkilis .15 .40
55 Carlos Lee .15 .40
56 Josh Hamilton .25 .60
57 Brad Hawpe .15 .40
58 Brandon Inge .25 .60
59 Bobby Abreu .15 .40
60 Nelson Cruz .40 1.00
61 James Loney .15 .40
62 Jason Kubel .15 .40
63 Russell Branyan .15 .40
64 Curtis Granderson .30 .75
65 Ken Griffey Jr. .75 2.00
66 Troy Tulowitzki .40 1.00
67 Jermaine Dye .15 .40
68 Paul Konerko .25 .60
69 Josh Johnson .25 .60
70 David Ortiz .40 1.00
71 Hideki Matsui .40 1.00
72 Dustin Pedroia .30 .75
73 Jon Lester UER .25 .60
74 Joey Votto .40 1.00
75 Josh Beckett .15 .40
76 Billy Butler .15 .40
77 David DeJesus .15 .40
78 Nick Swisher .25 .60
79 Brian Roberts .15 .40
80 Felix Hernandez .25 .60
81 J.A. Happ .25 .60
82 Marco Scutaro .25 .60
83 Hanley Ramirez .25 .60
84 Lance Berkman .25 .60
85 Dan Haren .15 .40
86 Yunel Escobar .15 .40
87 Justin Verlander .40 1.00
88 Carlos Beltran .25 .60
89 Shane Victorino .25 .60
90 Carl Crawford .25 .60
91 Adam Jones .25 .60
92 Jason Marquis .15 .40
93 Everth Cabrera .15 .40
94 B.J. Upton .25 .60
95 Ted Lilly .15 .40
96 Ubaldo Jimenez .15 .40
97 Aaron Hill .15 .40
98 Kosuke Fukudome .25 .60
99 Jorge Cantu .15 .40
100 Jose Lopez .15 .40
101 Rick Porcello .25 .60
102 Matt Cain .25 .60
103 Chone Figgins .15 .40
104 Tommy Hanson .25 .60
105 Jacoby Ellsbury .30 .75
106 Clayton Kershaw .75 2.00
107 Miguel Tejada .25 .60
108 Yovani Gallardo .15 .40
109 Andrew McCutchen .40 1.00
110 Felipe Lopez .15 .40
111 Asdrubal Cabrera .25 .60
112 Roy Halladay .25 .60
113 Hunter Pence .25 .60
114 Gordon Beckham .15 .40
115 Cole Hamels .30 .75
116 Brian McCann .25 .60
117 Michael Cuddyer .15 .40
118 Cliff Lee .25 .60
119 Roy Oswalt .25 .60
120 A.J. Pierzynski .15 .40
121 Jayson Werth .25 .60
122 Mike Lowell .15 .40
123 John Lannan .15 .40
124 Luis Castillo .15 .40
125 Andy Pettitte .25 .60
126 Neil Walker (RC) 1.25 3.00
127 Brad Kilby RC .75 2.00
128 Chris Johnson RC 1.25 3.00
129 Tommy Manzella (RC) .75 2.00
130 Sergio Escalona (RC) .75 2.00
131 Chris Pettit RC .75 2.00
132 Kevin Richardson (RC) .75 2.00
133 Armando Gabino RC .75 2.00
134 Reid Gorecki (RC) 1.25 3.00
135 Justin Turner RC 4.00 10.00
136 Adam Moore RC .75 2.00
137 Kyle Phillips RC .75 2.00
138 John Hester RC .75 2.00
139 Dusty Hughes RC .75 2.00
140 Waldis Joaquin RC .75 2.00
141 Jeff Manship (RC) .75 2.00
142 Dan Runzler RC 1.25 3.00
143 Pedro Viola RC .75 2.00
144 Craig Gentry RC .75 2.00
145 Brent Dlugach (RC) .75 2.00
146 Esmil Rogers RC .75 2.00
147 Josh Butler RC .75 2.00
148 Dustin Richardson RC .75 2.00
149 Matt Carson (RC) .75 2.00
150 Henry Rodriguez RC .75 2.00
151 Brandon Allen AU/1420 * (RC) 4.00 10.00
152 Colvin AU/1302 * RC 4.00 10.00
153 Hudson AU/1302 * RC 4.00 10.00
154 Francisco AU/954 * RC 4.00 10.00
155 Stubbs AU/1302 * RC 4.00 10.00
156 Brantley AU/1072 * RC 6.00 15.00
157 Stoner AU/1302 * RC 4.00 10.00
158 Thole AU/1420 * RC 4.00 10.00
159 McCutchen AU/954 * RC 4.00 10.00
160 Eric Hacker AU/1302 * RC 4.00 10.00
161 Bumgarner AU/954 * RC 30.00 80.00
162 Posey AU/1420 * RC 50.00 120.00
163 Dan Runzler AU/1190 * 4.00 10.00
164 Desmond AU/1190 * (RC) 5.00 12.00
165 Richardson AU/2170 * 4.00 10.00

2010 Finest Rookie Logo Patch

STATED ODDS 1:26 MINI BOX
STATED PRINT RUN 50 SER.#'d SETS
PURPLE ODDS 1:1197 MINI BOX
PURPLE PRINT RUN 1 SER.#'d SET
126 Neil Walker 8.00 20.00
127 Brad Kilby 5.00 12.00
128 Chris Johnson 8.00 20.00
129 Tommy Manzella 5.00 12.00
130 Sergio Escalona 5.00 12.00
131 Chris Pettit 5.00 12.00

132 Kevin Richardson 5.00 12.00
133 Armando Gabino 5.00 12.00
134 Reid Gorecki 8.00 20.00
135 Justin Turner 25.00 60.00
136 Adam Moore 5.00 12.00
137 Kyle Phillips 5.00 12.00
138 John Hester 5.00 12.00
139 Dusty Hughes 5.00 12.00
140 Waldis Joaquin 5.00 12.00
141 Jeff Manship 5.00 12.00
142 Dan Runzler 8.00 20.00
143 Pedro Viola 5.00 12.00
144 Craig Gentry 5.00 12.00
145 Brent Dlugach 5.00 12.00
146 Esmil Rogers 5.00 12.00
147 Josh Butler 5.00 12.00
148 Dustin Richardson 5.00 12.00
149 Matt Carson 5.00 12.00
150 Henry Rodriguez 5.00 12.00

2010 Finest Refractors

*REF VET: 1.2X TO 3X BASIC
*REF RC: .5X TO 1.2X BASIC RC
1-150 RANDOMLY INSERTED
1-150 PRINT RUN 599 SER.#'d SETS
*REF AU: .5X TO 1.2X BASIC AU
151-165 ODDS 1:4 MINI BOX
EACH LETTER AU SER.#'d TO 75
TOTAL LETTER PRINT RUNS LISTED

2010 Finest Refractors Blue

*BLUE REF VET: 2.5X TO 6X BASIC
*BLUE REF RC: .6X TO 1.5X BASIC RC
1-150 STATED RANDOMLY INSERTED
1-150 PRINT RUN 299 SER.#'d SETS
*BLUE REF AU: .6X TO 1.5X BASIC AU
151-165 ODDS 1:13 MINI BOX
EACH LETTER AU SER.#'d TO 25
TOTAL LETTER PRINT RUNS LISTED

2010 Finest Refractors Gold

*GOLD REF VET: 10X TO 25X BASIC
*GOLD REF RC: 2X TO 5X BASIC RC
1-150 STATED ODDS 1:4 MINI BOX
1-150 PRINT RUN 50 SER.#'d SETS
*GOLD REF AU: 1X TO 2.5X BASIC AU
151-165 ODDS 1:32 MINI BOX
EACH LETTER AU SER.#'d TO 10
TOTAL LETTER PRINT RUNS LISTED

2010 Finest Refractors Green

*GREEN REF VET: 5X TO 12X BASIC
*GREEN REF RC: 1X TO 2.5X BASIC RC
STATED ODDS 1:3 MINI BOXES
STATED PRINT RUN 99 SER.#'d SETS

2010 Finest Refractors Red

*RED REF VET: 12X TO 30X BASIC
*RED REF RC: 2.5X TO 6X BASIC RC
1-150 STATED ODDS 1:8 MINI BOX
1-150 PRINT RUN 25 SER.#'d SETS
*RED REF AU: 1.5X TO 4X BASIC AU
151-165 ODDS 1:60 MINI BOX
EACH LETTER AU SER.#'d TO 5
TOTAL LETTER PRINT RUNS LISTED

2010 Finest Finest Moments Autographs

GROUP A ODDS 1:10 MINI BOX
GROUP B ODDS 1:58 MINI BOX
PURPLE ODDS 1:1662 MINI BOX
PURPLE PRINT RUN 1 SER.#'d SET
RED ODDS 1:67 MINI BOX
RED PRINT RUN 25 SER.#'d SETS
AE Andre Ethier A 6.00 15.00
AH Aaron Hill A 5.00 12.00
CF Chone Figgins A 4.00 10.00
CJ Chipper Jones B 40.00 80.00
CK Clayton Kershaw A 15.00 40.00
DP Dustin Pedroia A 12.50 30.00
DW David Wright B 15.00 40.00
JF Jeff Francoeur A 8.00 20.00
JM Justin Morneau B 12.50 30.00
JS Joe Saunders A 4.00 10.00
MS Max Scherzer A 20.00 50.00
PF Prince Fielder B 8.00 20.00
RC Robinson Cano A 10.00 25.00
RH Ryan Howard B 10.00 25.00
RP Rick Porcello B 4.00 10.00
UJ Ubaldo Jimenez A 8.00 20.00
YG Yovani Gallardo A 5.00 12.00
ZG Zack Greinke B 10.00 25.00

2010 Finest Rookie Redemption

COMPLETE SET (11) 175.00 350.00
STATED ODDS 1:3 MINI BOX
*BLUE REF: .6X TO 1.5X BASIC
BLUE REF.ODDS 1:15 MINI BOX
*GOLD REF: 2.5X TO 6X BASIC
GOLD REF.ODDS 1:60 MINI BOX
EXCHANGE DEADLINE 4/30/2011
1a Jason Heyward 2.50 6.00
1b Jason Heyward AU 40.00 80.00
2 Ike Davis 1.25 3.00
3 Starlin Castro 1.50 4.00
4 Mike Leake 2.00 5.00
5 Mike Stanton 8.00 20.00
6 Stephen Strasburg 4.00 10.00
7 Andrew Cashner AU 3.00 8.00
8 Dayan Viciedo 1.00 2.50
9 Domonic Brown 2.50 6.00
10 Ryan Kalish 1.00 2.50

2011 Finest

COMPLETE SET (100) 20.00 50.00
COMMON CARD (1-60) .15 .40
COMMON RC (61-100) .40 1.00
1-100 PLATE ODDS 1:103 MINI BOX
PLATE PRINT RUN 1 SET PER COLOR
BLACK-CYAN-MAGENTA-YELLOW ISSUED
NO PLATE PRICING DUE TO SCARCITY
1 Hanley Ramirez .25 .60
2 Jason Heyward .30 .75
3 Buster Posey .50 1.25
4 Mark Teixeira .25 .60
5 Evan Longoria .25 .60
6 Chase Utley .25 .60
7 Ryan Braun .25 .60
8 Felix Hernandez .25 .60
9 Hunter Pence .25 .60
10 Adrian Gonzalez .30 .75
11 Nick Markakis .30 .75
12 Miguel Cabrera .40 1.00
13 Paul Konerko .25 .60
14 Ryan Zimmerman .25 .60
15 Troy Tulowitzki .40 1.00
16 Chipper Jones .40 1.00
17 Torii Hunter .15 .40
18 B.J. Upton .25 .60
19 Michael Young .15 .40
20 Ryan Howard .30 .75
21 Andre Ethier .25 .60
22 Justin Verlander .40 1.00
23 Clay Buchholz .15 .40
24 Cole Hamels .30 .75
25 Albert Pujols .50 1.25
26 Adrian Beltre .40 1.00
27 Zack Greinke .25 .60
28 Derek Jeter 1.00 2.50
29 Jacoby Ellsbury .30 .75
30 Dan Uggla .15 .40
31 Adam Dunn .25 .60
32 Matt Kemp .30 .75
33 Starlin Castro .25 .60
34 Brian McCann .25 .60
35 David Wright .30 .75
36 Tim Lincecum .25 .60
37 David Price .30 .75
38 Jayson Werth .25 .60
39 Roy Oswalt .25 .60
40 Ichiro Suzuki .50 1.25
41 Jose Bautista .25 .60
42 Robinson Cano .25 .60
43 David Ortiz .40 1.00
44 Mike Stanton .40 1.00
45 Roy Halladay .25 .60
46 Justin Upton .25 .60
47 Joey Votto .40 1.00
48 Andrwe McCutchen .40 1.00
49 Matt Holliday .40 1.00
50 Alex Rodriguez .50 1.25
51 Jon Lester .25 .60
52 Jered Weaver .25 .60
53 Kevin Youkilis .15 .40
54 Ike Davis .15 .40
55 Joe Mauer .30 .75
56 Carl Crawford .25 .60
57 Cliff Lee .25 .60
58 Josh Hamilton .25 .60
59 Stephen Strasburg .40 1.00
60 Prince Fielder .25 .60
61 Sergio Santos .40 1.00
62 Randall Delgado RC .60 1.50
63 Eric Hosmer RC 2.50 6.00
64 Julio Teheran RC .60 1.50
65 Danny Duffy RC .60 1.50
66 J.P. Arencibia (RC) .40 1.00
67 Domonic Brown (RC) .75 2.00
68 Mike Minor (RC) .40 1.00
69 Brett Wallace (RC) .40 1.00
70 Jerry Sands RC 1.00 2.50
71 Mark Trumbo (RC) 1.00 2.50
72 Freddie Freeman RC 6.00 15.00
73 Tsuyoshi Nishioka RC 1.25 3.00
74 Jeremy Hellickson RC 1.00 2.50
75 Kyle Drabek RC .60 1.50
76 Dustin Ackley RC .60 1.50
77 Brandon Beachy RC 1.00 2.50
78 Brent Morel RC .40 1.00
79 Dillon Gee RC .60 1.50
80 Chris Sale RC 2.50 6.00
81 Alex Cobb RC .40 1.00
82 Dee Gordon RC .60 1.50
83 Brandon Belt RC 1.00 2.50
84 Zach Britton RC 1.00 2.50
85 Craig Kimbrel RC 1.00 2.50
86 Michael Pineda RC 1.00 2.50
87 Andrew Cashner (RC) .40 1.00
88 Jordan Walden RC .40 1.00
89 Alexi Ogando RC 1.00 2.50
90 Jake McGee (RC) .40 1.00
91 Hector Noesi RC .60 1.50
92 Darwin Barney RC 1.25 3.00
93 Ben Revere RC .60 1.50
94 Mike Trout RC 150.00 400.00
95 Danny Espinosa RC .40 1.00
96 Aaron Crow RC .60 1.50
97 Anthony Rizzo RC 4.00 10.00
98 Mike Moustakas RC 1.00 2.50
99 Eduardo Sanchez RC .60 1.50
100 Daniel Descalso RC .40 1.00

2011 Finest Refractors

*REF: 1.2X TO 3X BASIC
*REF RC: .5X TO 1.2X BASIC RC
STATED PRINT RUN 549 SER.#'d SETS
94 Mike Trout 300.00 800.00

2011 Finest Gold Refractors

*GOLD: 6X TO 15X BASIC
*GOLD RC: 2.5X TO 6X BASIC RC
STATED ODDS 1:9 MINI BOX
STATED PRINT RUN 50 SER.#'d SETS
25 Albert Pujols 20.00 50.00
28 Derek Jeter 20.00 50.00
94 Mike Trout 1500.00 4000.00

2011 Finest Green Refractors

*GREEN: 2.5X TO 6X BASIC
*GREEN RC: 1X TO 2.5X BASIC RC
STATED ODDS 1:3 MINI BOX
STATED PRINT RUN 199 SER.#'d SETS
94 Mike Trout 600.00 1500.00

2011 Finest Orange Refractors

*ORANGE: 3X TO 8X BASIC
*ORANGE RC: 1.2X TO 3X BASIC RC
STATED ODDS 1:5 MINI BOX
STATED PRINT RUN 99 SER.#'d SETS
94 Mike Trout 750.00 2000.00

2011 Finest X-Fractors

*XF: 2.5X TO 6X BASIC
*XF RC: 1X TO 2.5X BASIC RC
STATED ODDS 1:2 MINI BOX
STATED PRINT RUN 299 SER.#'d SETS
94 Mike Trout 600.00 1500.00

2011 Finest Foundations

STATED ODDS 1:6 MINI BOX
ORANGE ODDS 1:12 MINI BOX
PURPLE ODDS 1:96 MINI BOX
NO PURPLE PRICING DUE TO SCARCITY
FF1 Albert Pujols 1.25 3.00
FF2 Roy Halladay .60 1.50
FF3 Adrian Gonzalez .75 2.00
FF4 Ryan Howard .75 2.00
FF5 Alex Rodriguez 1.25 3.00
FF6 Evan Longoria .60 1.50
FF7 Buster Posey 1.25 3.00
FF8 Robinson Cano .60 1.50
FF9 Tim Lincecum .60 1.50
FF10 Jason Heyward .75 2.00
FF11 Troy Tulowitzki 1.00 2.50
FF12 Ichiro Suzuki 1.25 3.00
FF13 Stephen Strasburg 1.00 2.50
FF14 Hanley Ramirez .60 1.50
FF15 Derek Jeter 2.50 6.00

2011 Finest Foundations Orange Refractors

*ORANGE: .6X TO 1.5X BASIC
STATED ODDS 1:12 MINI BOX
FF12 Ichiro Suzuki 5.00 12.00
FF15 Derek Jeter 10.00 25.00

2011 Finest Freshmen

STATED ODDS 1:6 MINI BOX
*ORANGE: .6X TO 1.5X BASIC
ORANGE ODDS 1:12 MINI BOX
PURPLE ODDS 1:96 MINI BOX
NO PURPLE PRICING DUE TO SCARCITY
FFR1 Freddie Freeman 6.00 15.00
FFR2 Domonic Brown .75 2.00
FFR3 Jordan Walden .40 1.00
FFR4 Aroldis Chapman 1.25 3.00
FFR5 Zach Britton 1.00 2.50
FFR6 Mark Trumbo 1.00 2.50
FFR7 Brett Wallace .40 1.00
FFR8 Alexi Ogando 1.00 2.50
FFR9 Tsuyoshi Nishioka 1.25 3.00
FFR10 Jeremy Hellickson 1.00 2.50
FFR11 Brent Morel .40 1.00
FFR12 J.P. Arencibia .40 1.00
FFR13 Andrew Cashner .40 1.00
FFR14 Eric Hosmer 2.50 6.00
FFR15 Craig Kimbrel 1.00 2.50
FFR16 Kyle Drabek .60 1.50
FFR17 Michael Pineda 1.00 2.50

2011 Finest Moments

STATED ODDS 1:6 MINI BOX
*ORANGE: .6X TO 1.5X BASIC
ORANGE ODDS 1:12 MINI BOX
PURPLE ODDS 1:96 MINI BOX
NO PURPLE PRICING DUE TO SCARCITY
FM1 Joe Mauer .75 2.00
FM2 Carl Crawford .60 1.50
FM3 Robinson Cano .60 1.50
FM4 Andrew McCutchen 1.00 2.50
FM5 Cliff Lee .60 1.50
FM6 Nick Markakis .75 2.00
FM7 Roy Halladay .60 1.50
FM8 Ryan Howard .75 2.00
FM9 David Wright .75 2.00
FM10 Buster Posey 1.25 3.00
FM11 Jason Heyward .75 2.00
FM12 Josh Hamilton .60 1.50
FM13 Alex Rodriguez 1.25 3.00
FM14 Chase Utley .60 1.50
FM15 David Ortiz 1.00 2.50
FM16 CC Sabathia .60 1.50
FM17 Stephen Strasburg 1.00 2.50
FM18 Ike Davis .40 1.00

2011 Finest Moments Relic Autographs

GROUP A ODDS 1:25 MINI BOX
GROUP B ODDS 1:93 MINI BOX
GROUP C ODDS 1:342 MINI BOX
GROUP A PRINT RUN 274 SER.#'d SETS
GROUP B PRINT RUN 74 SER.#'d SETS
GROUP C PRINT RUN 24 SER.#'d SETS
NO PRICING ON QTY 25 OR LESS
EXCHANGE DEADLINE 10/31/2014
FMA1 Joe Mauer/274 10.00 25.00
FMA2 Carl Crawford/274 6.00 15.00
FMA3 Robinson Cano/274 15.00 40.00
FMA5 Cliff Lee/274 4.00 10.00
FMA6 Nick Markakis/274 6.00 15.00
FMA7 Roy Halladay/74 12.00 30.00
FMA8 Ryan Howard/74 12.50 30.00
FMA9 David Wright/74 15.00 40.00
FMA11 Jason Heyward/74 10.00 25.00
FMA12 Josh Hamilton/74 12.50 30.00
FMA13 Alex Rodriguez/74 50.00 100.00
FMA22 Adrian Gonzalez/74 10.00 25.00

2011 Finest Rookie Autographs Refractors

STATED ODDS 1:5 MINI BOX
STATED PRINT RUN 499 SER.#'d SETS
PRINTING PLATE ODDS 1:603 MINI BOX
PLATE PRINT RUN 1 SET PER COLOR
BLACK-CYAN-MAGENTA-YELLOW ISSUED
NO PLATE PRICING DUE TO SCARCITY
EXCHANGE DEADLINE 10/31/2014
62 Randall Delgado 4.00 10.00
66 Brandon Belt 4.00 10.00
69 Brett Wallace 5.00 12.00
70 Jerry Sands 4.00 10.00
71 Mark Trumbo 8.00 20.00
72 Freddie Freeman 30.00 80.00
76 Dustin Ackley 5.00 12.00
78 Brent Morel 4.00 10.00
79 Dillon Gee 4.00 10.00
82 Dee Gordon 4.00 10.00
83 Zach Britton 5.00 12.00
84 Mike Trout 1000.00 2000.00
86 Michael Pineda 4.00 10.00
88 Jordan Walden 4.00 10.00
93 Eric Sogard 4.00 10.00
96 Aaron Crow 5.00 12.00
97 Anthony Rizzo 30.00 80.00
98 Mike Moustakas EXCH 8.00 20.00
99 Eduardo Sanchez 4.00 10.00
100 Daniel Descalso 4.00 10.00
105 Eduardo Nunez 5.00 12.00

2011 Finest Rookie Autographs Gold Refractors

*GOLD: .75X TO 2X BASIC
STATED ODDS 1:33 MINI BOX
STATED PRINT RUN 75 SER.#'d SETS
EXCHANGE DEADLINE 10/31/2014

2011 Finest Rookie Autographs Green Refractors

*GREEN: .5X TO 1.2X BASIC
STATED ODDS 1:13 MINI BOX
STATED PRINT RUN 199 SER.#'d SETS
EXCHANGE DEADLINE 10/31/2014

2011 Finest Rookie Autographs Orange Refractors

*ORANGE: .6X TO 1.5X BASIC
STATED ODDS 1:25 MINI BOX
STATED PRINT RUN 99 SER.#'d SETS
EXCHANGE DEADLINE 10/31/2014

2011 Finest Rookie Autographs X-Fractors

*XF: .5X TO 1.2X BASIC
STATED ODDS 1:9 MINI BOX
STATED PRINT RUN 299 SER.#'d SETS
EXCHANGE DEADLINE 10/31/2014

2011 Finest Rookie Dual Relic Autographs Refractors

STATED ODDS 1:4 MINI BOX
STATED PRINT RUN 499 SER.#'d SETS
PRINTING PLATE ODDS 1:427 MINI BOX
PLATE PRINT RUN 1 SET PER COLOR
BLACK-CYAN-MAGENTA-YELLOW ISSUED
NO PLATE PRICING DUE TO SCARCITY
EXCHANGE DEADLINE 10/31/2014
62 Eduardo Nunez 4.00 10.00
63 Eric Hosmer 10.00 25.00
64 Julio Teheran 4.00 10.00
68 Mike Minor 6.00 15.00
72 Freddie Freeman 25.00 60.00
77 Brandon Beachy 8.00 20.00
79 Dillon Gee 4.00 10.00
82 Dee Gordon 10.00 25.00
84 Zach Britton 5.00 12.00
85 Craig Kimbrel 4.00 10.00
86 Michael Pineda 5.00 12.00
87 Andrew Cashner 4.00 10.00
88 Jordan Walden 4.00 10.00
89 Alexi Ogando 6.00 15.00
91 Hector Noesi 4.00 10.00
92 Darwin Barney 4.00 10.00
96 Aaron Crow 5.00 12.00
98A Mike Moustakas 10.00 25.00
98B Ivan DeJesus Jr. 4.00 10.00
100 Alex Cobb 4.00 10.00

2011 Finest Rookie Dual Relic Autographs Gold Refractors

*GOLD: .75X TO 2X BASIC
STATED ODDS 1:26 MINI BOX
STATED PRINT RUN 69 SER.#'d SETS
EXCHANGE DEADLINE 10/31/2014

2011 Finest Rookie Dual Relic Autographs Green Refractors

*GREEN: .4X TO 1X BASIC
STATED ODDS 1:12 MINI BOX
STATED PRINT RUN 149 SER.#'d SETS
EXCHANGE DEADLINE 10/31/2014

2011 Finest Rookie Dual Relic Autographs Orange Refractors

*ORANGE: .6X TO 1.5X BASIC
STATED ODDS 1:18 MINI BOX
STATED PRINT RUN 99 SER.#'d SETS
EXCHANGE DEADLINE 10/31/2014

2012 Finest

COMPLETE SET (100) 20.00 50.00
1-100 PLATE ODDS 1:90 MINI BOX
PLATE PRINT RUN 1 SET PER COLOR
BLACK-CYAN-MAGENTA-YELLOW ISSUED
NO PLATE PRICING DUE TO SCARCITY
1 Albert Pujols .50 1.25
2 Alex Rodriguez .50 1.25
3 Michael Pineda .25 .60
4 Jay Bruce .30 .75
5 Derek Jeter 1.00 2.50
6 Tom Milone RC .60 1.50
7 Justin Upton .30 .75
8 Cliff Lee .30 .75
9 Giancarlo Stanton .40 1.00
10 Justin Verlander .40 1.00
11 Ichiro Suzuki .50 1.25
12 Drew Pomeranz RC .60 1.50
13 Josh Hamilton .30 .75
14 David Freese .25 .60
15 Robinson Cano .30 .75
16 Wilin Rosario RC .60 1.50
17 Paul Goldschmidt .40 1.00
18 Drew Hutchison RC .75 2.00
19 Michael Young .25 .60
20 Ryan Braun .25 .60
21 David Price .30 .75
22 Jordan Pacheco RC .60 1.50
23 Ian Kennedy .25 .60
24 Jacoby Ellsbury .30 .75
25 Troy Tulowitzki .40 1.00
26 Evan Longoria .30 .75
27 Nelson Cruz .40 1.00
28 Jered Weaver .30 .75
29 Kirk Nieuwenhuis RC .60 1.50
30 Prince Fielder .30 .75
31 Mark Teixeira .30 .75
32 Ryan Zimmerman .30 .75
33 Steve Lombardozzi RC .60 1.50
34 Drew Smyly RC .60 1.50
35 Yu Darvish RC 1.50 4.00
36 Yovani Gallardo .30 .75
37 Felix Hernandez .30 .75
38 David Wright .30 .75
39 Dan Uggla .30 .75
40 Matt Kemp .30 .75
41 Zack Cozart .25 .60
42 Mariano Rivera .50 1.25
43 Jarrod Parker RC .75 2.00
44 Jon Lester .25 .60
45 Adrian Beltre .40 1.00
46 Lance Berkman .30 .75
47 Kevin Youkilis .40 1.00
48 CC Sabathia .30 .75
49 Dustin Pedroia .30 .75
50 Clayton Kershaw .75 2.00
51 Brad Peacock RC .60 1.50
52 Tyler Pastornicky RC .60 1.50
53 Buster Posey .50 1.25
54 Chase Utley .30 .75
55 Hanley Ramirez .30 .75
56 Devin Mesoraco RC .60 1.50
57 Paul Konerko .25 .60
58 Chipper Jones .40 1.00
59 Mark Trumbo .25 .60
60 Jose Bautista .30 .75
61 Carlos Gonzalez .30 .75
62 Ryan Howard .30 .75
63 Eric Hosmer .30 .75
64 Matt Dominguez RC .75 2.00
65 Brett Lawrie .30 .75
66 Hisashi Iwakuma RC 1.25 3.00
67 Matt Moore RC 1.00 2.50
68 Wily Peralta RC .60 1.50
69 Pablo Sandoval .30 .75
70 Miguel Cabrera .40 1.00
71 Dellin Betances RC 1.00 2.50
72 Jesus Montero RC .60 1.50
73 Bryce Harper RC 6.00 15.00
74 Tsuyoshi Wada RC .60 1.50
75 Cole Hamels .30 .75
76 Wade Miley .30 .75
77 Liam Hendriks RC .60 1.50
78 Mike Trout 12.00 30.00
79 Ian Kinsler .30 .75
80 Joey Votto .40 1.00
81 Austin Romine RC .60 1.50
82 Starlin Castro .30 .75
83 Joe Mauer .30 .75
84 Tim Lincecum .30 .75
85 Curtis Granderson .30 .75
86 Addison Reed RC .60 1.50
87 Eric Surkamp RC 1.00 2.50
88 Chris Parmelee RC .60 1.50
89 Adrian Gonzalez .30 .75
90 Jose Reyes .25 .60
91 Brett Pill RC 1.00 2.50
92 Trevor Bauer RC 2.00 5.00
93 Leonys Martin RC .60 1.50
94 Josh Beckett .25 .60
95 Brian Wilson .40 1.00
96 Joe Benson RC .60 1.50
97 Yoenis Cespedes RC 1.50 4.00
98 Mike Napoli .25 .60
99 Alex Liddi RC .25 .60
100 Roy Halladay .30 .75

2012 Finest Refractors

*REF: 1.2X TO 3X BASIC
*REF RC: .5X TO 1.2X BASIC RC

2012 Finest Gold Refractors

*GOLD REF: 8X TO 20X BASIC
*GOLD REF RC: 3X TO 8X BASIC RC
STATED ODDS 1:8 MINI BOX
STATED PRINT RUN 50 SER.#'d SETS
78 Mike Trout 400.00 1000.00

2012 Finest Green Refractors

*GREEN REF: 2X TO 5X BASIC
*GREEN REF RC: .75X TO 2X BASIC RC
STATED ODDS 1:2 MINI BOX
STATED PRINT RUN 199 SER.#'d SETS
78 Mike Trout 100.00 250.00

2012 Finest Orange Refractors

*ORANGE REF: 3X TO 8X BASIC
*ORANGE REF RC: 1.2X TO 3X BASIC RC
STATED ODDS 1:4 MINI BOX
STATED PRINT RUN 99 SER.#'d SETS
78 Mike Trout 150.00 400.00

2012 Finest X-Fractors

*X-FRAC: 2X TO 5X BASIC
*X-FRAC RC: .75X TO 2X BASIC RC

2012 Finest Autograph Rookie Mystery Exchange

STATED ODDS 1:72 MINI BOX
EXCHANGE DEADLINE 06/22/2013
SM Starling Marte 20.00 50.00
BJ Brett Jackson 4.00 10.00
MT Mike Trout 500.00 1200.00
JR Josh Rutledge 4.00 10.00
JS Jean Segura 10.00 25.00

2012 Finest Faces of the Franchise

AM Andrew McCutchen 1.50 4.00
AP Albert Pujols 2.00 5.00
BP Buster Posey 2.00 5.00
CJ Chipper Jones 1.50 4.00
DJ Derek Jeter 4.00 10.00
DP Dustin Pedroia 1.25 3.00
DW David Wright 1.25 3.00
EH Eric Hosmer 1.25 3.00
EHO Eric Hosmer 1.25 3.00
EL Evan Longoria 1.25 3.00
FH Felix Hernandez 1.25 3.00
HR Hanley Ramirez 1.25 3.00
JB Jose Bautista 1.25 3.00
JH Josh Hamilton 1.25 3.00
JM Joe Mauer 1.25 3.00
JU Justin Upton 1.25 3.00
JV Justin Verlander 1.50 4.00
JVO Joey Votto 1.50 4.00
MK Matt Kemp 1.25 3.00
RB Ryan Braun 1.00 2.50
RH Roy Halladay 1.25 3.00
RZ Ryan Zimmerman .75 2.00
SC Starlin Castro 1.25 3.00
TL Tim Lincecum 1.25 3.00
TT Troy Tulowitzki 1.50 4.00

2012 Finest Game Changers

AG Adrian Gonzalez 1.25 3.00
AP Albert Pujols 2.00 5.00
BP Buster Posey 2.00 5.00
CG Carlos Gonzalez 1.25 3.00
CJ Chipper Jones 1.50 4.00
GS Giancarlo Stanton 1.50 4.00
JB Jose Bautista 1.25 3.00
JH Jason Heyward 1.25 3.00
JMA Joe Mauer 1.25 3.00
JV Justin Verlander 1.50 4.00
MC Miguel Cabrera 1.00 2.50
MT Mike Trout 20.00 50.00
PF Prince Fielder 1.25 3.00
RB Ryan Braun 1.00 2.50
RH Roy Halladay 1.25 3.00

2012 Finest Moments

AG Adrian Gonzalez .75 2.00
BL Brett Lawrie .75 2.00
CH Cole Hamels .75 2.00
CK Clayton Kershaw 2.00 5.00
DA Dustin Ackley .60 1.50
DF David Freese .60 1.50
DU Dan Uggla .75 2.00
IK Ian Kennedy .60 1.50
JH Jeremy Hellickson .60 1.50
JJ Josh Johnson .75 2.00
JM Jason Motte .60 1.50
JV Justin Verlander 1.00 2.50
MC Miguel Cabrera 1.00 2.50
MM Matt Moore 1.00 2.50
MP Michael Pineda .60 1.50
NC Nelson Cruz 1.00 2.5
RC Robinson Cano .75 2.0
SS Stephen Strasburg 1.00 2.5
UJ Ubaldo Jimenez .60 1.5
YD Yu Darvish 1.50 4.0

2012 Finest Rookie Autographs Refractors

STATED ODDS 1:9 MINI BOX
PRINTING PLATE ODDS 1:427 MINI BOX
PLATE PRINT RUN 1 SET PER COLOR
BLACK-CYAN-MAGENTA-YELLOW ISSUED
NO PLATE PRICING DUE TO SCARCITY
EXCHANGE DEADLINE 07/31/2015
AR Addison Reed 4.00 10.0
ARO Austin Romine 4.00 10.0
BD Brian Dozier 20.00 50.0
BH Bryce Harper 125.00 300.0
BP Brad Peacock 4.00 10.0
DB Dellin Betances 5.00 12.0
DH Drew Hutchison 4.00 10.0
DM Devin Mesoraco 4.00 10.0
DS Drew Smyly 6.00 15.0
JM Jesus Montero 6.00 15.0
JP Jordan Pacheco 4.00 10.0
JPA Jarrod Parker 5.00 12.0
JT Jacob Turner 4.00 10.0
KS Kirk Nieuwenhuis 4.00 10.0
LH Liam Hendriks 4.00 10.00
MM Matt Moore 4.00 10.00
RL Ryan Lavarnway 5.00 12.00
TM Tom Milone 4.00 10.0
TW Tsuyoshi Wada 6.00 15.0
WP Wily Peralta 4.00 10.00
YD Yu Darvish 40.00 100.00

2012 Finest Rookie Autographs Gold Refractors

*GOLD REF: 1X TO 2.5X BASIC REF
STATED ODDS 1:35 MINI BOX
STATED PRINT RUN 50 SER.#'d SETS
EXCHANGED DEADLINE 07/31/2015
BH Bryce Harper 200.00 500.00
YD Yu Darvish 75.00 200.00

2012 Finest Rookie Autographs Green Refractors

*GREEN REF: .4X TO 1X BASIC REF
STATED ODDS 1:10 MINI BOX
STATED PRINT RUN 199 SER.#'d SETS
EXCHANGED DEADLINE 07/31/2015

2012 Finest Rookie Autographs Orange Refractors

*ORANGE REF: .5X TO 1.2X BASIC REF
STATED ODDS 1:18 MINI BOX
STATED PRINT RUN 99 SER.#'d SETS
EXCHANGED DEADLINE 07/31/2015
BH Bryce Harper 150.00 400.00
YD Yu Darvish 60.00 150.00

2012 Finest Rookie Autographs X-Fractors

*X-FRAC: .4X TO 1X BASIC REF
STATED ODDS 1:7 MINI BOX
STATED PRINT RUN 299 SER.#'d SETS
EXCHANGED DEADLINE 07/31/2015

2012 Finest Rookie Jumbo Relic Autographs Refractors

STATED ODDS 1:18 MINI BOX
1-100 PLATE ODDS 1:358 MINI BOX
PLATE PRINT RUN 1 SET PER COLOR
NO PLATE PRICING DUE TO SCARCITY
EXCHANGE DEADLINE 07/31/2015
ARO Austin Romine 4.00 10.00
BH Bryce Harper 100.00 200.00
BL Brett Lawrie 5.00 12.00
BP Brad Peacock 4.00 10.00
CP Chris Parmelee 5.00 12.00
DM Devin Mesoraco 5.00 12.00
DP Drew Pomeranz 4.00 10.00
JM Jesus Montero 6.00 15.00
JP Jordan Pacheco 4.00 10.00
JPA Jarrod Parker 8.00 20.00
JVN Jordany Valdespin 4.00 10.00
LH Liam Hendriks 4.00 10.00
LM Leonys Martin 4.00 10.00
MA Matt Adams 12.50 30.00
MD Matt Dominguez 4.00 10.00
MM Matt Moore 8.00 20.00
RL Ryan Lavarnway 5.00 12.00
TB Trevor Bauer 12.00 30.00
TM Tom Milone 5.00 12.00
TP Tyler Pastornicky 5.00 12.00
WMI Will Middlebrooks 6.00 15.00
YA Yonder Alonso 4.00 10.00
YC Yoenis Cespedes 20.00 50.00
YD Yu Darvish 75.00 150.00
ZC Zack Cozart 6.00 15.00

2012 Finest Rookie Jumbo Relic Autographs Gold Refractors

*GOLD REF: .6X TO 1.5X BASIC REF
STATED ODDS 1:30 MINI BOX
STATED PRINT RUN 50 SER.#'d SETS
EXCHANGE DEADLINE 07/31/2015
DP Drew Pomeranz 10.00 25.00
YD Yu Darvish 100.00 200.00

2012 Finest Rookie Jumbo Relic Autographs Green Refractors

*GREEN REF: .4X TO 1X BASIC REF
STATED ODDS 1:8 MINI BOX
STATED PRINT RUN 199 SER.#'d SETS
EXCHANGE DEADLINE 07/31/2015

2012 Finest Rookie Jumbo Relic Autographs Orange Refractors

*ORANGE REF: .5X TO 1.2X BASIC REF

ATED ODDS 1:15 MINI BOX
ATED PRINT RUN 99 SER.#'d SETS
CHANGE DEADLINE 07/31/2015
Bryce Harper 150.00 300.00
Yu Darvish 100.00 200.00

12 Finest Rookie Jumbo Relic Autographs X-Fractors
RAC: .4X TO 1X BASIC REF
ATED ODDS 1:6 MINI BOX
ATED PRINT RUN 299 SER.#'d SETS
CHANGE DEADLINE 07/31/2015

1993 Flair Promos
MPLETE SET (8) 150.00 300.00
Will Clark 15.00 40.00
Darren Daulton 6.00 15.00
Andres Galarraga 8.00 20.00
Bryan Harvey 4.00 10.00
David Justice 8.00 20.00
Jody Reed 4.00 10.00
Nolan Ryan 125.00 250.00
Sammy Sosa 30.00 80.00

2013 Finest
MPLETE SET (100) 15.00 40.00
100 PLATE ODDS 1:151 MINI BOX
ATE PRINT RUN 1 SET PER COLOR
ACK-CYAN-MAGENTA-YELLOW ISSUED
PLATE PRICING DUE TO SCARCITY
Mike Trout 2.00 5.00
Derek Jeter .60 1.50
Michael Wacha RC .40 1.00
Ryan Howard .20 .50
Adrian Beltre .25 .60
CC Sabathia .20 .50
Avisail Garcia RC .40 1.00
Prince Fielder .20 .50
David Price .20 .50
Clayton Kershaw .50 1.25
Roy Halladay .20 .50
2 Carlos Gonzalez .20 .50
3 Andrew McCutchen .40 1.00
4 Dustin Pedroia .20 .50
5 Allen Webster RC .40 1.00
6 Dylan Bundy RC .40 1.00
7 David Freese .15 .40
8 Johnny Cueto .20 .50
9 Yadier Molina .40 1.00
0 Stephen Strasburg .25 .60
1 Kevin Gausman RC .50 1.25
2 Pablo Sandoval .20 .50
3 Adrian Gonzalez .20 .50
4 Jake Odorizzi RC .40 1.00
25 Matt Kemp .20 .50
26 Paul Goldschmidt .40 1.00
27 Tony Cingrani RC .60 1.50
28 Cliff Lee .30 .75
29 Will Middlebrooks .25 .60
30 Buster Posey .30 .75
31 Aroldis Chapman .25 .60
32 Mike Zunino RC .50 1.25
33 Wil Myers RC .40 1.00
34 Jason Heyward .20 .50
35 Troy Tulowitzki .40 1.00
36 Billy Butler .15 .40
37 Nolan Arenado RC 1.50 4.00
38 Adeiny Hechavarria RC .40 1.00
39 Jackie Bradley Jr. RC .75 2.00
40 Felix Hernandez .30 .75
41 Bruce Rondon RC .30 .75
42 Mariano Rivera .50 1.25
43 Joey Votto .40 1.00
44 Kyuji Fujikawa RC .50 1.25
45 Didi Gregorius RC 1.25 3.00
46 Edwin Encarnacion .25 .60
47 Hyun-Jin Ryu RC .75 2.00
48 Cole Hamels .20 .50
49 Austin Jackson .15 .40
50 Justin Verlander .25 .60
51 Tyler Skaggs RC .50 1.25
52 Evan Longoria .30 .75
53 Chris Sale .40 1.00
54 Evan Gattis RC .60 1.50
55 David Wright .20 .50
56 Rob Brantly RC .30 .75
57 Kyle Gibson RC .50 1.25
58 Marcell Ozuna RC .75 2.00
59 Jose Fernandez RC .75 2.00
60 Yu Darvish .25 .60
61 Albert Pujols .50 1.25
62 Jurickson Profar RC .40 1.00
63 Jered Weaver .30 .75
64 Anthony Rendon RC 1.50 4.00
65 Robinson Cano .20 .50
66 Jose Bautista .20 .50
67 Joe Mauer .30 .75
68 Jose Reyes .20 .50
69 Shelby Miller RC .75 2.00
70 Miguel Cabrera .25 .60
71 Zack Wheeler RC .60 1.50
72 Anthony Rizzo .40 1.00
73 Yoenis Cespedes .25 .60
74 R.A. Dickey .30 .75
75 Justin Upton .20 .50
76 Matt Harvey .20 .50
77 Carlos Beltran .20 .50
78 Jacoby Ellsbury .20 .50
79 Mike Olt RC .40 1.00
80 Manny Machado RC 2.00 5.00
81 Giancarlo Stanton .40 1.00
82 Oswaldo Arcia RC .30 .75
83 Freddie Freeman .50 1.25
84 Tim Lincecum .20 .50
85 Adam Wainwright .30 .75
86 Adam Jones .20 .50
87 Josh Hamilton .30 .75
88 Matt Cain .20 .50
89 Carlos Martinez RC .50 1.25
90 Ryan Braun .20 .50
91 Yasiel Puig RC 1.25 3.00
92 Mark Trumbo .25 .60
93 Nick Franklin RC .40 1.00
94 Adam Eaton RC .50 1.25
95 Trevor Rosenthal RC .60 1.50
96 Jedd Gyorko RC .40 1.00
97 Jeurys Familia RC .50 1.25
98 Starlin Castro .15 .40
99 Gerrit Cole RC 2.00 5.00
100 Bryce Harper .40 1.00

2013 Finest Gold Refractors
*GOLD REF: 10X TO 25X BASIC
*GOLD REF RC: 5X TO 12X BASIC RC
STATED ODDS 1:13 MINI BOX
STATED PRINT RUN 50 SER.#'d SETS
80 Manny Machado 30.00 60.00
91 Yasiel Puig 60.00 120.00

2013 Finest Green Refractors
*GREEN REF: 2.5X TO 6X BASIC
*GREEN REF RC: 1.2X TO 3X BASIC RC
STATED ODDS 1:4 MINI BOX
STATED PRINT RUN 199 SER.#'d SETS
91 Yasiel Puig 15.00 40.00

2013 Finest Orange Refractors
*ORANGE REF: 5X TO 12X BASIC
*ORANGE REF RC: 2.5X TO 6X BASIC RC
STATED ODDS 1:7 MINI BOX
STATED PRINT RUN 99 SER.#'d SETS
1 Mike Trout 12.50 30.00
2 Derek Jeter 12.50 30.00
91 Yasiel Puig 20.00 50.00

2013 Finest Refractors
*REF: 1.5X TO 4X BASIC
*REF RC: .75X TO 2X BASIC

2013 Finest X-Fractors
*X-FRACTOR: 2X TO 5X BASIC
*X-FRACTOR RC: 1X TO 2.5X BASIC
91 Yasiel Puig 10.00 25.00

2013 Finest 93 Finest
STATED ODDS 1:4 MINI BOX
AC Aroldis Chapman 1.50 4.00
AG Adrian Gonzalez 1.25 3.00
AJ Austin Jackson 1.00 2.50
AP Andy Pettitte 1.25 3.00
AR Alex Rodriguez 2.00 5.00
ARI Anthony Rizzo 2.50 6.00
AS Andrelton Simmons 1.00 2.50
AW Adam Wainwright 1.25 3.00
BB Billy Butler 1.00 2.50
BL Brett Lawrie 1.25 3.00
BP Brandon Phillips 1.00 2.50
CB Carlos Beltran 1.25 3.00
CD Chris Davis 1.25 3.00
CG Curtis Granderson 1.25 3.00
CH Cole Hamels 1.25 3.00
CK Clayton Kershaw 3.00 8.00
CL Cliff Lee 1.25 3.00
CR Carlos Ruiz 1.00 2.50
CS Carlos Santana 1.25 3.00
CU Chase Utley 1.25 3.00
DB Dylan Bundy 2.50 6.00
DO David Ortiz 1.50 4.00
DP David Price 1.25 3.00
DPE Dustin Pedroia 1.25 3.00
EE Edwin Encarnacion 1.50 4.00
EH Eric Hosmer 1.25 3.00
FF Freddie Freeman 2.00 5.00
GG Gio Gonzalez 1.25 3.00
HJR Hyun-Jin Ryu 2.50 6.00
HR Hanley Ramirez 1.25 3.00
IK Ian Kinsler 1.25 3.00
JB Jackie Bradley Jr. 2.50 6.00
JC Johnny Cueto 1.25 3.00
JE Jacoby Ellsbury 1.25 3.00
JF Jose Fernandez 2.50 6.00
JH Jason Heyward 1.25 3.00
JP Jurickson Profar 1.25 3.00
JR Josh Reddick 1.00 2.50
JRO Jimmy Rollins 1.25 3.00
JS James Shields 1.00 2.50
JSM Jeff Samardzija 1.00 2.50
JU Justin Upton 1.25 3.00
JV Joey Votto 1.50 4.00
JZ Jordan Zimmermann 1.25 3.00
KM Kris Medlen 1.25 3.00
MB Madison Bumgarner 1.25 3.00
MH Matt Holliday 1.50 4.00
MHA Matt Harvey 1.25 3.00
MK Matt Kemp 1.25 3.00
MM Manny Machado 6.00 15.00
MMO Matt Moore 1.25 3.00
MN Mike Napoli 1.00 2.50
MR Mariano Rivera 8.00 20.00
MT Mike Trout 20.00 50.00
MTE Mark Teixeira 1.25 3.00
MTR Mark Trumbo 1.00 2.50
RH Ryan Howard 1.25 3.00
RHA Roy Halladay 1.25 3.00
RZ Ryan Zimmerman 1.25 3.00
SC Starlin Castro 1.00 2.50
SP Salvador Perez 1.25 3.00
TH Torii Hunter 1.00 2.50
TL Tim Lincecum 1.25 3.00
WM Will Middlebrooks 1.00 2.50
YC Yoenis Cespedes 1.50 4.00
YM Yadier Molina 1.50 4.00
YP Yasiel Puig 12.50 30.00
ZG Zack Greinke 1.25 3.00

2013 Finest 93 Finest All-Star
STATED ODDS 1:12 MINI BOX
AB Adrian Beltre 3.00 8.00
AJ Adam Jones 2.50 6.00
AM Andrew McCutchen 3.00 8.00
AP Albert Pujols 4.00 10.00
BH Bryce Harper 20.00 50.00
BP Buster Posey 4.00 10.00
CC CC Sabathia 2.50 6.00
CG Carlos Gonzalez 2.50 6.00
CK Craig Kimbrel 2.50 6.00
CS Chris Sale 3.00 8.00
DF David Freese 2.00 5.00
DJ Derek Jeter 20.00 50.00
DW David Wright 2.50 6.00
EL Evan Longoria 2.50 6.00
FH Felix Hernandez 2.50 6.00
GS Giancarlo Stanton 3.00 8.00
JB Jose Bautista 2.50 6.00
JH Josh Hamilton 2.50 6.00
JM Joe Mauer 2.50 6.00
JR Jose Reyes 2.50 6.00
JV Justin Verlander 3.00 8.00
JW Jered Weaver 2.50 6.00
MC Matt Cain 2.50 6.00
MCA Miguel Cabrera 3.00 8.00
PF Prince Fielder 2.50 6.00
PS Pablo Sandoval 2.50 6.00
RB Ryan Braun 2.50 6.00
RC Robinson Cano 2.50 6.00
RD R.A. Dickey 2.50 6.00
SS Stephen Strasburg 3.00 8.00
TT Troy Tulowitzki 3.00 8.00
YD Yu Darvish 3.00 8.00

2013 Finest Autograph Rookie Mystery Exchange
STATED ODDS 1:201 MINI BOX
STATED PRINT RUN 100 SER.#'d SETS
EXCHANGE DEADLINE 9/30/2016
RR1 Wil Myers 10.00 25.00
RR2 Shelby Miller 5.00 12.00
RR3 Evan Gattis 12.00 30.00

2013 Finest Masters Refractors
STATED ODDS 1:61 MINI BOX
STATED PRINT RUN 50 SER.#'d SETS
AP Albert Pujols 8.00 20.00
BH Bryce Harper 10.00 25.00
BP Buster Posey 20.00 50.00
CG Carlos Gonzalez 5.00 12.00
CK Clayton Kershaw 12.00 30.00
DJ Derek Jeter 75.00 150.00
DP David Price 5.00 12.00
EL Evan Longoria 5.00 12.00
FH Felix Hernandez 5.00 12.00
GS Giancarlo Stanton 6.00 15.00
JH Josh Hamilton 5.00 12.00
JV Justin Verlander 6.00 15.00
JW Jered Weaver 5.00 12.00
MC Miguel Cabrera 8.00 20.00
MR Mariano Rivera 20.00 50.00
MT Mike Trout 50.00 125.00
RB Ryan Braun 5.00 12.00
RC Robinson Cano 5.00 12.00
SS Stephen Strasburg 6.00 15.00
YD Yu Darvish 6.00 15.00

2013 Finest Prodigies Die Cut Refractors
STATED ODDS 1:24 MINI BOX
PBH Bryce Harper 12.50 30.00
PGS Giancarlo Stanton 2.00 5.00
PJP Jurickson Profar 1.50 4.00
PMH Matt Harvey 1.50 4.00
PMM Manny Machado 8.00 20.00
PMT Mike Trout 12.50 30.00
PSS Stephen Strasburg 2.00 5.00
PYC Yoenis Cespedes 2.00 5.00
PYD Yu Darvish 2.00 5.00
PYP Yasiel Puig 25.00 60.00

2013 Finest Rookie Autographs Gold Refractors
*GOLD REF: .6X TO 1.5X BASIC
STATED ODDS 1:21 MINI BOX
STATED PRINT RUN 50 SER.#'d SETS
EXCHANGE DEADLINE 9/30/2016
DR Darin Ruf 12.50 30.00
MZ Mike Zunino 20.00 50.00

2013 Finest Rookie Autographs Green Refractors
*GREEN REF: .4X TO 1X BASIC
STATED ODDS 1:21 HOBBY
STATED PRINT RUN 125 SER.#'d SETS
EXCHANGE DEADLINE 9/30/2016

2013 Finest Rookie Autographs Orange Refractors
*ORANGE REF: .5X TO 1.2X BASIC
STATED ODDS 1:27 HOBBY
STATED PRINT RUN 99 SER.#'d SETS
EXCHANGE DEADLINE 9/30/2016

2013 Finest Rookie Autographs Refractors
PRINTING PLATE ODDS 1:655 MINI BOX
PLATE PRINT RUN 1 SET PER COLOR
BLACK-CYAN-MAGENTA-YELLOW ISSUED
NO PLATE PRICING DUE TO SCARCITY
EXCHANGE DEADLINE 09/30/2016
AE Adam Eaton 5.00 12.00
AG Avisail Garcia 4.00 10.00
AH Adeiny Hechavarria 3.00 8.00
AM Alfredo Marte 3.00 8.00
BM Brandon Maurer 3.00 8.00
CM Carlos Martinez 6.00 15.00
DB Dylan Bundy 6.00 15.00
DG Didi Gregorius 15.00 40.00
DR Darin Ruf 4.00 10.00
EG Evan Gattis 5.00 12.00
JF Jeurys Familia 3.00 8.00
JFZ Jose Fernandez 20.00 50.00
JG Jedd Gyorko 3.00 8.00
JO Jake Odorizzi 3.00 8.00
JP Jurickson Profar 5.00 12.00
KG Kyle Gibson 3.00 8.00
LH L.J. Hoes 3.00 8.00
MM Manny Machado 25.00 60.00
MO Mike Olt 4.00 10.00
MZ Mike Zunino 4.00 10.00
SM Shelby Miller 4.00 10.00
TCI Tony Cingrani 3.00 8.00
TS Tyler Skaggs 3.00 8.00
WM Wil Myers 8.00 20.00

2013 Finest Rookie Autographs X-Fractors
*X-FRACTORS: .4X TO 1X BASIC
STATED ODDS 1:18 HOBBY
STATED PRINT RUN 149 SER.#'d SETS
EXCHANGE DEADLINE 9/30/2016

2013 Finest Rookie Jumbo Relic Autographs Gold Refractors
*GOLD REF: .6X TO 1.5X BASIC
STATED ODDS 1:29 MINI BOX
STATED PRINT RUN 50 SER.#'d SETS
EXCHANGE DEADLINE 9/30/2016
YP Yasiel Puig 50.00 120.00

2013 Finest Rookie Jumbo Relic Autographs Green Refractors
*GREEN REF: .4X TO 1X BASIC
STATED ODDS 1:14 HOBBY
STATED PRINT RUN 125 SER.#'d SETS
EXCHANGE DEADLINE 9/30/2016

2013 Finest Rookie Jumbo Relic Autographs Orange Refractors
*ORANGE REF: .5X TO 1.2X BASIC
STATED ODDS 1:15 HOBBY
STATED PRINT RUN 99 SER.#'d SETS
EXCHANGE DEADLINE 9/30/2016
YP Yasiel Puig 40.00 100.00

2013 Finest Rookie Jumbo Relic Autographs Refractors
PRINTING PLATE ODDS 1:359 MINI BOX
PLATE PRINT RUN 1 SET PER COLOR
BLACK-CYAN-MAGENTA-YELLOW ISSUED
NO PLATE PRICING DUE TO SCARCITY
EXCHANGE DEADLINE 09/30/2016
AE Adam Eaton 4.00 10.00
AG Avisail Garcia 5.00 12.00
AG2 Avisail Garcia 4.00 10.00
AHI Aaron Hicks 5.00 12.00
AR Anthony Rendon 20.00 50.00
AR2 Anthony Rendon 20.00 50.00
AW Allen Webster 4.00 10.00
BM Brandon Maurer 4.00 10.00
BR Bruce Rondon 4.00 10.00
CK Casey Kelly 4.00 10.00
CM Carlos Martinez 8.00 20.00
CY Christian Yelich 75.00 200.00
DB Dylan Bundy 10.00 25.00
DG Didi Gregorius 4.00 10.00
DG2 Didi Gregorius 4.00 10.00
DR Darin Ruf 4.00 10.00
EG Evan Gattis 5.00 12.00
GC Gerrit Cole 20.00 50.00
HJR Hyun-Jin Ryu 12.00 30.00
JB Jackie Bradley Jr. 20.00 50.00
JC Jarred Cosart 4.00 10.00
JFE Jose Fernandez 20.00 50.00
JG Jedd Gyorko 4.00 10.00
JO Jake Odorizzi 4.00 10.00
JP Jurickson Profar 6.00 15.00
KF Kyuji Fujikawa 4.00 10.00
MM Manny Machado 30.00 80.00
MO Mike Olt 4.00 10.00
MO2 Mike Olt 4.00 10.00
MZ Mike Zunino 6.00 15.00
NA Nolan Arenado 40.00 100.00
OA Oswaldo Arcia EXCH 4.00 10.00
PR Paco Rodriguez 4.00 10.00
RB Rob Brantly 4.00 10.00
SM Shelby Miller 5.00 12.00
TC Tony Cingrani EXCH 5.00 12.00
TCL Tyler Cloyd 4.00 10.00
TR Trevor Rosenthal 6.00 15.00
TS Tyler Skaggs 4.00 10.00
WM Wil Myers 10.00 25.00
YP Yasiel Puig EXCH 30.00 80.00
ZW Zack Wheeler 6.00 15.00

2013 Finest Rookie Jumbo Relic Autographs X-Fractors
*X-FRACTORS: .4X TO 1X BASIC
STATED ODDS 1:12 HOBBY
STATED PRINT RUN 149 SER.#'d SETS
EXCHANGE DEADLINE 9/30/2016

2014 Finest
COMPLETE SET (100) 15.00 40.00
1-100 PLATE ODDS 1:110 MINI BOX
PLATE PRINT RUN 1 SET PER COLOR
BLACK-CYAN-MAGENTA-YELLOW ISSUED
NO PLATE PRICING DUE TO SCARCITY
1 Miguel Cabrera .30 .75
2 Adam Wainwright .25 .60
3 Luis Sardinas RC .40 1.00
4 Alex Rios .25 .60
5 Alex Guerrero RC .50 1.25
6 Michael Choice RC .40 1.00
7 Tim Beckham RC .60 1.50
8 Jay Bruce .25 .60
9 Matt Kemp .25 .60
10 Jimmy Nelson RC .40 1.00
11 Max Scherzer .30 .75
12 Buster Posey .40 1.00
13 Adrian Beltre .30 .75
14 Carlos Gomez .20 .50
15 Kolten Wong RC .50 1.25
16 Andre Rienzo RC .40 1.00
17 Matt Davidson RC .50 1.25
18 Chris Davis .20 .50
19 Madison Bumgarner .25 .60
20 Paul Goldschmidt .30 .75
21 Billy Hamilton RC .50 1.25
22 Jose Abreu RC 3.00 8.00
23 Prince Fielder .25 .60
24 Andrew McCutchen .30 .75
25 Clayton Kershaw .60 1.50
26 Rafael Montero RC .40 1.00
27 David Wright .25 .60
28 Chris Owings RC .40 1.00
29 Dustin Pedroia .30 .75
30 Carlos Gonzalez .25 .60
31 Marcus Semien RC .40 1.00
32 John Ryan Murphy RC .40 1.00
33 Ian Kinsler .25 .60
34 Enny Romero RC .40 1.00
35 Wil Myers .20 .50
36 C.J. Cron RC .40 1.00
37 Ryan Braun .25 .60
38 Yu Darvish .30 .75
39 George Springer RC 1.50 4.00
40 Rougned Odor RC .75 2.00
41 Jason Heyward .25 .60
42 Michael Wacha .25 .60
43 Joey Votto .30 .75
44 Josmil Pinto RC .40 1.00
45 Freddie Freeman .40 1.00
46 Cliff Lee .25 .60
47 Jacoby Ellsbury .25 .60
48 Bryce Harper .50 1.25
49 Gerrit Cole .30 .75
50 Yasiel Puig .30 .75
51 Taijuan Walker RC .40 1.00
52 Christian Bethancourt RC .40 1.00
53 Jose Bautista .25 .60
54 Derek Jeter .75 2.00
55 David Ortiz .30 .75
56 Manny Machado .30 .75
57 Felix Hernandez .25 .60
58 Adam Jones .25 .60
59 Jonathan Schoop RC .40 1.00
60 Joe Mauer .25 .60
61 Jason Kipnis .25 .60
62 Josh Donaldson .25 .60
63 Yangervis Solarte RC .40 1.00
64 David Price .25 .60
65 Ian Desmond .20 .50
66 Yadier Molina .30 .75
67 Eric Hosmer .25 .60
68 Edwin Encarnacion .30 .75
69 Shin-Soo Choo .25 .60
70 Robinson Cano .25 .60
71 Aroldis Chapman .30 .75
72 Pedro Alvarez .20 .50
73 Craig Kimbrel .25 .60
74 Trevor Rosenthal .25 .60
75 Masahiro Tanaka RC 1.25 3.00
76 Erisbel Arruebarrena RC .40 1.00
77 Anthony Rizzo .50 1.25
78 Chris Sale .30 .75
79 Erik Johnson RC .40 1.00
80 Troy Tulowitzki .30 .75
81 Jose Ramirez RC 3.00 8.00
82 Yordano Ventura RC .50 1.25
83 Giancarlo Stanton .30 .75
84 Travis d'Arnaud RC .50 1.25
85 Justin Verlander .30 .75
86 Matt Holliday .30 .75
87 Carlos Santana .25 .60
88 Stephen Strasburg .30 .75
89 Xander Bogaerts RC 1.25 3.00
90 Marcus Stroman RC .60 1.50
91 Nick Castellanos .60 1.50
92 Evan Longoria .25 .60
93 Albert Pujols .40 1.00
94 Jake Marisnick RC .40 1.00
95 Jose Reyes .25 .60
96 Justin Upton .25 .60
97 Jose Fernandez .30 .75
98 Wilmer Flores RC .50 1.25
99 Hanley Ramirez .25 .60
100 Mike Trout 1.50 4.00

2014 Finest Black Refractors
*BLACK REF: 4X TO 10X BASIC
*BLACK REF RC: 2X TO 5X BASIC RC
STATED ODDS 1:5 MINI BOXES
STATED PRINT RUN 99 SER.#'d SETS
22 Jose Abreu 15.00 40.00
100 Mike Trout 15.00 40.00

2014 Finest Blue Refractors
*BLUE REF: 3X TO 8X BASIC
*BLUE REF RC: 1.5X TO 4X BASIC RC
STATED ODDS 1:4 MINI BOXES
STATED PRINT RUN 125 SER.#'d SETS

2014 Finest Gold Refractors
*GOLD REF: 5X TO 12X BASIC
*GOLD REF RC: 2.5X TO 6X BASIC RC
STATED ODDS 1:9 MINI BOXES
STATED PRINT RUN 50 SER.#'d SETS
22 Jose Abreu 20.00 50.00
54 Derek Jeter 15.00 40.00
100 Mike Trout 15.00 40.00

2014 Finest Green Refractors
*GREEN REF: 3X TO 8X BASIC
*GREEN REF RC: 1.5X TO 4X BASIC RC
STATED ODDS 1:3 MINI BOXES
STATED PRINT RUN 199 SER.#'d SETS
100 Mike Trout 12.00 30.00

2014 Finest Orange Refractors
*ORANGE REF: 2.5X TO 6X BASIC
*ORANGE REF RC: 1.2X TO 3X BASIC RC
RANDOM INSERTS IN HOT BOXES
54 Derek Jeter 10.00 25.00

2014 Finest Red Refractors
*RED REF: 8X TO 20X BASIC
*RED REF RC: 4X TO 10X BASIC RC
STATED ODDS 1:18 MINI BOXES
STATED PRINT RUN 25 SER.#'d SETS
100 Mike Trout 60.00 120.00

2014 Finest Refractors
*REF: 1X TO 2.5X BASIC
*REF RC: .5X TO 1.2X BASIC RC
RANDOM INSERTS IN MINI BOXES

2014 Finest X-Fractors
*X-FACTOR: 1.5X TO 4X BASIC
*X-FACTOR RC: .75X TO 2X BASIC RC
RANDOM INSERTS IN MINI BOXES

2014 Finest 94 Finest
RANDOM INSERTS IN PACKS
94FAJ Adam Jones .75 2.00
94FAM Andrew McCutchen 1.00 2.50
94FBH Bryce Harper 1.50 4.00
94FBHA Billy Hamilton .75 2.00
94FBP Buster Posey 1.25 3.00
94FCK Clayton Kershaw 2.00 5.00
94FDJ Derek Jeter 2.50 6.00
94FDP Dustin Pedroia 1.00 2.50
94FEL Evan Longoria .75 2.00
94FFH Felix Hernandez .75 2.00
94FGS George Springer 2.50 6.00
94FJA Jose Abreu 5.00 12.00
94FJF Jose Fernandez 1.00 2.50
94FJM Joe Mauer .75 2.00
94FJU Justin Upton .75 2.00
94FMC Miguel Cabrera 1.00 2.50
94FMM Manny Machado 1.00 2.50
94FMT Mike Trout 5.00 12.00
94FMTA Masahiro Tanaka 3.00 8.00
94FSS Stephen Strasburg 1.00 2.50
94FTT Troy Tulowitzki 1.00 2.50
94FTW Taijuan Walker .60 1.50
94FWM Wil Myers .60 1.50
94FXB Xander Bogaerts 2.00 5.00
94FYP Yasiel Puig 1.00 2.50

2014 Finest 94 Finest Refractors
*REFRACTORS: 10X TO 25X BASIC
STATED ODDS 1:71 MINI BOX
STATED PRINT RUN 25 SER.#'d SETS
94FDJ Derek Jeter 125.00 250.00
94FJA Jose Abreu 75.00 150.00
94FMT Mike Trout 125.00 250.00

2014 Finest Competitors Refractors
STATED ODDS 1:44 MINI BOX
FCAJ Adam Jones 4.00 10.00
FCAM Andrew McCutchen 5.00 12.00
FCBH Bryce Harper 10.00 25.00
FCBP Buster Posey 6.00 15.00
FCCK Clayton Kershaw 10.00 25.00
FCDO David Ortiz 5.00 12.00
FCDP Dustin Pedroia 5.00 12.00
FCDW David Wright 4.00 10.00
FCEL Evan Longoria 4.00 10.00
FCJE Jacoby Ellsbury 4.00 10.00
FCJF Jose Fernandez 5.00 12.00
FCJV Justin Verlander 5.00 12.00
FCMC Miguel Cabrera 5.00 12.00
FCMT Mike Trout 75.00 150.00
FCPG Paul Goldschmidt 5.00 12.00
FCRC Robinson Cano 4.00 10.00
FCTT Troy Tulowitzki 5.00 12.00
FCWM Wil Myers 3.00 8.00
FCYD Yu Darvish 5.00 12.00
FCYP Yasiel Puig 5.00 12.00

2014 Finest Competitors Gold Refractors
*GOLD REFRACTORS: 1X TO 2.5X BASIC
STATED ODDS 1:88 MINI BOX
STATED PRINT RUN 25 SER.#'d SETS
FCMT Mike Trout 150.00 300.00

2014 Finest Greats Autographs Black Refractors
STATED ODDS 1:222 MINI BOX
STATED PRINT RUN 99 SER.#'d SETS
FGAEB Ernie Banks 50.00 120.00
FGAMR Mariano Rivera 100.00 250.00
FGAMS Mike Schmidt 40.00 100.00
FGAOS Ozzie Smith 25.00 60.00
FGARY Robin Yount 30.00 80.00
FGASC Steve Carlton 15.00 40.00
FGASK Sandy Koufax 200.00 300.00

2014 Finest Greats Autographs Blue Refractors
STATED ODDS 1:176 MINI BOX
STATED PRINT RUN 125 SER.#'d SETS
FGABJ Bo Jackson 50.00 150.00
FGAEB Ernie Banks 50.00 120.00
FGAMS Mike Schmidt 40.00 100.00
FGAOS Ozzie Smith 25.00 60.00
FGASC Steve Carlton 15.00 40.00

2014 Finest Greats Autographs Gold Refractors
STATED ODDS 1:176 MINI BOX
STATED PRINT RUN 50 SER.#'d SETS
FGABJ Bo Jackson 60.00 150.00
FGAEB Ernie Banks 60.00 150.00
FGAKG Ken Griffey Jr. 200.00 300.00
FGALB Lou Brock 15.00 40.00
FGAMM Mark McGwire 100.00 250.00
FGAMR Mariano Rivera 125.00 300.00
FGAMS Mike Schmidt 50.00 120.00
FGAOS Ozzie Smith 40.00 100.00
FGARJ Randy Johnson 100.00 200.00
FGARY Robin Yount 40.00 100.00
FGASC Steve Carlton 20.00 50.00
FGASK Sandy Koufax 300.00 400.00

2014 Finest Greats Autographs Red Refractors
STATED ODDS 1:352 MINI BOX
STATED PRINT RUN 25 SER.#'d SETS
FGABJ Bo Jackson 75.00 200.00
FGAEB Ernie Banks 75.00 200.00
FGAKG Ken Griffey Jr. 250.00 400.00
FGALB Lou Brock 20.00 50.00
FGAMM Mark McGwire 150.00 300.00
FGAMR Mariano Rivera 150.00 400.00
FGAMS Mike Schmidt 60.00 150.00
FGAOS Ozzie Smith 50.00 120.00
FGARJ Randy Johnson 125.00 250.00
FGARY Robin Yount 60.00 150.00
FGASC Steve Carlton 25.00 60.00
FGASK Sandy Koufax 350.00 500.00

2014 Finest Greats Autographs X-Fractors
STATED ODDS 1:148 MINI BOX
STATED PRINT RUN 149 SER.#'d SETS
FGALB Lou Brock 12.00 30.00
FGAMR Mariano Rivera 100.00 250.00
FGARY Robin Yount 30.00 80.00

2014 Finest Rookie Autographs
OVERALL ONE AUTO PER MINI BOX
RAAG Alex Guerrero 4.00 10.00
RAAL Andrew Lambo 3.00 8.00
RACB Christian Bethancourt 3.00 8.00
RACO Chris Owings 3.00 8.00
RAEB Eddie Butler 3.00 8.00
RAEM Ethan Martin 3.00 8.00
RAER Enny Romero 3.00 8.00
RAGP Gregory Polanco 6.00 15.00
RAGS George Springer 20.00 50.00
RAJA Jose Abreu 20.00 50.00
RAJM J.R. Murphy 3.00 8.00
RAJMA Jake Marisnick 3.00 8.00
RAJPI Josmil Pinto 3.00 8.00
RAJR Jose Ramirez 40.00 100.00
RAJS Jonathan Schoop 3.00 8.00
RAKW Kolten Wong 4.00 10.00
RAMC Michael Choice 3.00 8.00
RAMD Matt Davidson 4.00 10.00
RANC Nick Castellanos 10.00 25.00
RAOG Onelki Garcia 3.00 8.00
RATM Tommy Medica 3.00 8.00
RATW Taijuan Walker 3.00 8.00
RAWF Wilmer Flores 4.00 10.00
RAYV Yordano Ventura 4.00 10.00

2014 Finest Rookie Autographs Refractors
*REF: .5X TO 1.2X BASIC
OVERALL ONE AUTO PER MINI BOX

2014 Finest Rookie Autographs Black Refractors
*BLACK REF: .6X TO 1.5X BASIC
STATED ODDS 1:18 MINI BOX
STATED PRINT RUN 99 SER.#'d SETS
RAAH Andrew Heaney 5.00 12.00
RAEA Erisbel Arruebarrena 20.00 50.00
RAOT Oscar Taveras 6.00 15.00
RAXB Xander Bogaerts 20.00 50.00

2014 Finest Rookie Autographs Blue Refractors
*BLUE REF: .6X TO 1.5X BASIC
STATED ODDS 1:14 MINI BOX
STATED PRINT RUN 125 SER.#'d SETS
RAAH Andrew Heaney 5.00 12.00
RAEA Erisbel Arruebarrena 20.00 50.00
RAOT Oscar Taveras 6.00 15.00
RAXB Xander Bogaerts 20.00 50.00

2014 Finest Rookie Autographs Gold Refractors
*GOLD REF: .75X TO 2X BASIC
STATED ODDS 1:34 MINI BOX
STATED PRINT RUN 50 SER.#'d SETS
RAAH Andrew Heaney 6.00 15.00
RAEA Erisbel Arruebarrena 25.00 60.00
RAOT Oscar Taveras 8.00 20.00
RAXB Xander Bogaerts 25.00 60.00

2014 Finest Rookie Autographs Red Refractors
*RED REF: 1X TO 2.5X BASIC
STATED ODDS 1:68 MINI BOX
STATED PRINT RUN 25 SER.#'d SETS
RAAH Andrew Heaney 8.00 20.00
RAEA Erisbel Arruebarrena 30.00 80.00
RAOT Oscar Taveras 10.00 25.00

2014 Finest Rookie Autographs X-Fractors
*X-FRACTORS: .6X TO 1.5X BASIC
STATED ODDS 1:12 MINI BOX

STATED PRINT RUN 149 SER.#'d SETS
RAAH Andrew Heaney 5.00 12.00
RAEA Erisbel Arruebarrena 15.00 40.00
RAOT Oscar Taveras 6.00 15.00
RAXB Xander Bogaerts 20.00 50.00

2014 Finest Rookie Autographs Mystery Exchange

RANDOM INSERTS IN PACKS
1 Sandy Koufax EXCH 150.00 300.00
2 Jacob deGrom EXCH 250.00 400.00
3 Kennys Vargas EXCH 15.00 40.00

2014 Finest Sterling Refractors

STATED ODDS 1:2 MINI BOX
TSAJ Adam Jones 1.00 2.50
TSAM Andrew McCutchen 1.25 3.00
TSBH Bryce Harper 2.00 5.00
TSBHA Billy Hamilton 1.00 2.50
TSBP Buster Posey 1.50 4.00
TSCD Chris Davis .75 2.00
TSCG Carlos Gonzalez 1.00 2.50
TSCK Clayton Kershaw 2.50 6.00
TSDJ Derek Jeter 3.00 8.00
TSDO David Ortiz 1.25 3.00
TSDW David Wright 1.00 2.50
TSFH Felix Hernandez 1.00 2.50
TSGS Giancarlo Stanton 1.25 3.00
TSJA Jose Abreu 6.00 15.00
TSJF Jose Fernandez 1.25 3.00
TSMC Miguel Cabrera 1.25 3.00
TSMM Manny Machado 1.25 3.00
TSMT Mike Trout 6.00 15.00
TSMTA Masahiro Tanaka 2.50 6.00
TSMW Michael Wacha 1.00 2.50
TSPG Paul Goldschmidt 1.25 3.00
TSRC Robinson Cano 1.00 2.50
TSTW Taijuan Walker .75 2.00
TSYD Yu Darvish 1.25 3.00
TSYP Yasiel Puig 1.25 3.00

2014 Finest Sterling Gold Refractors

*GOLD REF: 3X TO 8X BASIC
STATED ODDS 1:71 MINI BOX
STATED PRINT RUN 25 SER.#'d SETS
TSDJ Derek Jeter 150.00 250.00
TSJA Jose Abreu 75.00 150.00
TSMT Mike Trout 150.00 250.00

2014 Finest Vintage Refractors

STATED ODDS 1:2 MINI BOX
FVBG Bob Gibson .75 2.00
FVDS Duke Snider .75 2.00
FVGS Greg Maddux 1.25 3.00
FVHA Hank Aaron 2.00 5.00
FVJB Johnny Bench 1.00 2.50
FVMP Mike Piazza 1.00 2.50
FVMS Mike Schmidt 1.50 4.00
FVNR Nolan Ryan 3.00 8.00
FVOZ Ozzie Smith 1.25 3.00
FVRH Rickey Henderson 1.00 2.50
FVSK Sandy Koufax 2.00 5.00
FVTG Tony Gwynn 1.00 2.50
FVTS Tom Seaver .75 2.00
FVWM Willie Mays 2.00 5.00
FVYB Yogi Berra 1.00 2.50

2014 Finest Vintage Gold Refractors

*GOLD REF: 3X TO 8X BASIC
STATED ODDS 1:117 MINI BOX
STATED PRINT RUN 25 SER.#'d SETS

2014 Finest Warriors Die Cut Refractors

STATED ODDS 1:4 MINI BOX
FWBH Billy Hamilton 1.25 3.00
FWJA Jose Abreu 4.00 10.00
FWKW Kolten Wong 1.25 3.00
FWMC Michael Choice 1.00 2.50
FWMD Matt Davidson 1.25 3.00
FWMT Masahiro Tanaka 3.00 8.00
FWNC Nick Castellanos 3.00 8.00
FWTD Travis d'Arnaud 1.25 3.00
FWTW Taijuan Walker 1.00 2.50
FWXB Xander Bogaerts 3.00 8.00

2014 Finest Warriors Die Cut Gold Refractors

*GOLD: 2X TO 5X BASIC
STATED ODDS 1:176 MINI BOX
STATED PRINT RUN 25 SER.#'d SETS
FWJA Jose Abreu 40.00 100.00

2015 Finest

COMP.SET w/o SP's (100) 12.00 30.00
1-100 PLATE ODDS 1:114 MINI BOX
PLATE PRINT RUN 1 SET PER COLOR
BLACK-CYAN-MAGENTA-YELLOW ISSUED
NO PLATE PRICING DUE TO SCARCITY
1 Albert Pujols .40 1.00
2 Christian Yelich .40 1.00
3 Cory Spangenberg RC .30 .75
4 Mike Foltynewicz RC .30 .75
5 Miguel Cabrera .30 .75
6 Jonathan Lucroy .25 .60
7 Dustin Pedroia .30 .75
8 Samuel Tuivailala RC .30 .75
9 Hanley Ramirez .25 .60
10 Joe Mauer .25 .60
11 David Ortiz .30 .75
12 Michael Taylor RC .30 .75
13 Clayton Kershaw .60 1.50
14 Dalton Pompey RC .40 1.00
15 Eric Hosmer .25 .60
16 Jose Abreu .30 .75
17 Troy Tulowitzki .30 .75
18 Andrelton Simmons .20 .50
19 Giancarlo Stanton .30 .75
20 Jose Pirela RC .30 .75
21 Joc Pederson RC .60 1.50
22 Buster Posey .40 1.00
23 Josh Reddick .20 .50
24 Matt Barnes RC .30 .75
25 Stephen Strasburg .30 .75
26 David Peralta .20 .50
27 Jose Altuve .25 .60
28 Starling Marte .25 .60
29 Yu Darvish .30 .75
30 Jason Heyward .25 .60
31 Jose Fernandez .30 .75
32 Kyle Seager .20 .50
33 Michael Brantley .25 .60
34 Yoenis Cespedes .25 .60
35 Gregory Polanco .25 .60
36 Daniel Norris RC .30 .75
37 Jorge Soler RC .50 1.25
38 Nelson Cruz .30 .75
39 Buck Farmer RC .30 .75
40 Alex Gordon .25 .60
41 Yordano Ventura .25 .60
42 Bryce Harper .50 1.25
43 Chris Sale .30 .75
44 Javier Baez RC 2.50 6.00
45 Jacoby Ellsbury .25 .60
46 Cole Hamels .25 .60
47 Joey Votto .30 .75
48 Anthony Ranaudo RC .30 .75
49 Christian Walker RC .60 1.50
50 Rymer Liriano RC .30 .75
51 Freddie Freeman .40 1.00
52 Josh Harrison .20 .50
53 Justin Verlander .30 .75
54 Koji Uehara .20 .50
55 Evan Longoria .25 .60
56 Anthony Rendon .30 .75
57 Kolten Wong .25 .60
58 Brandon Phillips .20 .50
59 Elvis Andrus .25 .60
60 Rusney Castillo RC .40 1.00
61 Manny Machado .30 .75
62 Madison Bumgarner .25 .60
63 David Wright .25 .60
64 Anthony Rizzo .50 1.25
65 Josh Donaldson .25 .60
66 Phil Hughes .20 .50
67 Felix Hernandez .25 .60
68 Mike Trout 1.50 4.00
69 Salvador Perez .25 .60
70 Brandon Finnegan RC .30 .75
71 Brandon Crawford .25 .60
72 Edwin Escobar RC .30 .75
73 Max Scherzer .30 .75
74 Adam Jones .25 .60
75 Carlos Gonzalez .25 .60
76 Adrian Gonzalez .25 .60
77 Maikel Franco RC .40 1.00
78 Daniel Corcino RC .30 .75
79 Jake Lamb RC .50 1.25
80 Julio Teheran .25 .60
81 Matt Carpenter .30 .75
82 Trevor May RC .30 .75
83 Yasiel Puig .30 .75
84 Chase Utley .25 .60
85 Gary Brown RC .30 .75
86 Jose Bautista .25 .60
87 CC Sabathia .25 .60
88 George Springer .25 .60
89 Matt Kemp .25 .60
90 Yimi Garcia RC .30 .75
91 Dilson Herrera RC .40 1.00
92 Jacob deGrom .30 .75
93 Zack Wheeler .25 .60
94 Sonny Gray .25 .60
95 Charlie Blackmon .30 .75
96 Masahiro Tanaka .25 .60
97 Joe Panik .25 .60
98 Corey Kluber .25 .60
99 Kennys Vargas .20 .50
100 Matt Adams .20 .50
101 Josh Hamilton SP 3.00 8.00
102 Wil Myers SP 2.50 6.00
103 Adam Wainwright SP 3.00 8.00
104 Edwin Encarnacion SP 4.00 10.00
105 Adrian Beltre SP 4.00 10.00
106 Andrew McCutchen SP 4.00 10.00
107 Paul Goldschmidt SP 4.00 10.00
108 Ryan Braun SP 3.00 8.00
109 Mark Teixeira SP 3.00 8.00
110 Robinson Cano SP 3.00 8.00
111 Kris Bryant SP RC 75.00 200.00

2015 Finest Black Refractors

*BLACK REF: 2X TO 5X BASIC
*BLACK REF RC: 1.2X TO 3X BASIC
RANDOM INSERTS IN MINI BOXES

2015 Finest Blue Refractors

*BLUE REF: 2.5X TO 6X BASIC
*BLUE REF RC: 1.5X TO 4X BASIC
STATED ODDS 1:4 MINI BOX
STATED PRINT RUN 150 SER.#'d SETS

2015 Finest Gold Refractors

*GOLD REF: 6X TO 15X BASIC
*GOLD REF RC: 4X TO 10X BASIC
STATED ODDS 1:10 MINI BOX
STATED PRINT RUN 50 SER.#'d SETS
68 Mike Trout 25.00 60.00

2015 Finest Green Refractors

*GREEN REF: 3X TO 8X BASIC
*GREEN REF RC: 2X TO 5X BASIC
STATED ODDS 1:5 MINI BOX
STATED PRINT RUN 99 SER.#'d SETS

2015 Finest Orange Refractors

*ORANGE REF: 8X TO 20X BASIC
*ORANGE REF RC: 5X TO 12X BASIC
STATED ODDS 1:19 MINI BOX
STATED PRINT RUN 25 SER.#'d SETS
68 Mike Trout 30.00 80.00

2015 Finest Prism Refractors

*PRISM REF: 1.2X TO 3X BASIC
*PRISM REF RC: .75X TO 2X BASIC
RANDOM INSERTS IN MINI BOXES

2015 Finest Purple Refractors

*PRPLE REF: 2X TO 5X BASIC
*PRPLE REF RC: 1.2X TO 3X BASIC
STATED ODDS 1:2 MINI BOX
STATED PRINT RUN 250 SER.#'d SETS

2015 Finest Refractors

*REF: 1X TO 2.5X BASIC
*REF RC: .6X TO 1.5X BASIC
RANDOM INSERTS IN MINI BOXES
*REF SP: .6X TO 1.5X BASIC
REF SP ODDS 1:183 MINI BOXES
REF SP PRINT RUN 25 SER.#'d SETS
106 Andrew McCutchen 20.00 50.00
111 Kris Bryant 250.00 400.00

2015 Finest '95 Topps Finest

COMPLETE SET (20) 6.00 15.00
RANDOM INSERTS IN MINI BOXES
*REF/25: 12X TO 30X BASIC
94F01 Clayton Kershaw 1.25 3.00
94F02 Jose Abreu .60 1.50
94F03 Mike Trout 3.00 8.00
94F04 Albert Pujols .75 2.00
94F05 Robinson Cano .50 1.25
94F06 Masahiro Tanaka .50 1.25
94F07 Adam Jones .50 1.25
94F08 Freddie Freeman .75 2.00
94F09 Matt Kemp .50 1.25
94F10 David Ortiz .60 1.50
94F11 Brandon Phillips .40 1.00
94F12 Troy Tulowitzki .60 1.50
94F13 Giancarlo Stanton .60 1.50
94F14 Ryan Braun .50 1.25
94F15 David Wright .50 1.25
94F16 Chase Utley .50 1.25
94F17 Madison Bumgarner .50 1.25
94F18 Adrian Beltre .60 1.50
94F19 Max Scherzer .60 1.50
94F20 Jose Bautista .50 1.25

2015 Finest Affiliations Autographs

STATED ODDS 1:92 MINI BOX
STATED PRINT RUN 50 SER.#'d SETS
EXCHANGE DEADLINE 5/31/2018
FAABSR J.Baez/J.Soler 125.00 300.00
FAACP D.Pedroia/R.Cano 25.00 60.00
FAAGS J.Smoltz/T.Glavine 50.00 120.00
FAAJM M.McGwire/R.Jackson 50.00 120.00
FAAKS C.Sale/C.Kershaw 50.00 125.00
FAAMP M.Mussina/J.Posada 40.00 100.00
FAASD R.Sandberg/A.Dawson 50.00 125.00
FAATA J.Abreu/F.Thomas 75.00 150.00

2015 Finest Autographs

RANDOM INSERTS IN PACKS
*BLUE REF/150: .5X TO 1.2X BASIC
*GREEN REF/99: .6X TO 1.5X BASIC
*GOLD REF/50: .75X TO 2X BASIC
*ORNGE REF/25: 1X TO 2.5X BASIC
PRINTING PLATE ODDS 1:197 MINI BOX
PLATE PRINT RUN 1 SET PER COLOR
BLACK-CYAN-MAGENTA-YELLOW ISSUED
NO PLATE PRICING DUE TO SCARCITY
EXCHANGE DEADLINE 5/31/2018
FAAR Anthony Rizzo 20.00 50.00
FABB Bryce Brentz 3.00 8.00
FABC Brandon Crawford 5.00 12.00
FABF Buck Farmer 3.00 8.00
FACR Carlos Rodon 5.00 12.00
FACSG Cory Spangenberg 3.00 8.00
FACW Christian Walker 6.00 15.00
FACY Christian Yelich 20.00 50.00
FADC Daniel Corcino 3.00 8.00
FADH Dilson Herrera 4.00 10.00
FAEE Edwin Escobar 3.00 8.00
FAGB Gary Brown 3.00 8.00
FAGSR George Springer 10.00 25.00
FAJDN Josh Donaldson 10.00 25.00
FAJF Jose Fernandez 25.00 60.00
FAJL Jake Lamb 5.00 12.00
FAJMN James McCann 5.00 12.00
FAJT Julio Teheran 4.00 10.00
FAKB Kris Bryant 75.00 200.00
FAKG Kendall Graveman 3.00 8.00
FAKL Kyle Lobstein 3.00 8.00
FAKW Kolten Wong 4.00 10.00
FAMA Matt Adams 3.00 8.00
FAMTR Michael Taylor 3.00 8.00
FARCA Rusney Castillo 4.00 10.00
FARCO Robinson Cano 5.00 12.00
FARL Rymer Liriano 3.00 8.00
FASG Sonny Gray 4.00 10.00
FASM Steven Moya 4.00 10.00
FAST Samuel Tuivailala 3.00 8.00
FATM Trevor May 3.00 8.00
FAXS Xavier Scruggs 3.00 8.00
FAYG Yimi Garcia 3.00 8.00

2015 Finest Autographs Blue Refractors

*BLUE REF: .5X TO 1.2X BASIC
STATED ODDS 1:7 MINI BOX
STATED PRINT RUN 150 SER.#'d SETS
EXCHANGE DEADLINE 5/31/2018
FAAG Adrian Gonzalez 10.00 25.00
FACSE Chris Sale 12.00 30.00
FADP Dustin Pedroia 12.00 3.00
FAFF Freddie Freeman 20.00 50.00
FAHR Hanley Ramirez 5.00 12.00
FAJDM Jacob deGrom 25.00 60.00
FARB Ryan Braun 8.00 20.00
FARCO Robinson Cano 6.00 15.00
FAYT Yasmany Tomas 6.00 15.00

2015 Finest Autographs Gold Refractors

*GOLD REF: .75X TO 2X BASIC
STATED ODDS 1:19 MINI BOX
STATED PRINT RUN 50 SER.#'d SETS
EXCHANGE DEADLINE 5/31/2018
FAAG Adrian Gonzalez 15.00 40.00
FAAJ Adam Jones 12.00 30.00
FACSE Chris Sale 20.00 50.00
FADP Dustin Pedroia 20.00 50.00
FAFF Freddie Freeman 30.00 80.00
FAHR Hanley Ramirez 8.00 20.00
FAJA Jose Abreu 30.00 80.00
FAJDM Jacob deGrom 40.00 100.00
FAKU Koji Uehara 8.00 20.00
FARB Ryan Braun 12.00 30.00
FARCO Robinson Cano 10.00 25.00
FAYT Yasmany Tomas 10.00 25.00

2015 Finest Autographs Green Refractors

*GREEN REF: .6X TO 1.5X BASIC
STATED ODDS 1:10 MINI BOX
STATED PRINT RUN 99 SER.#'d SETS
EXCHANGE DEADLINE 5/31/2018
FAAG Adrian Gonzalez 12.00 30.00
FAAJ Adam Jones 10.00 25.00
FACSE Chris Sale 15.00 40.00
FADP Dustin Pedroia 15.00 40.00
FAFF Freddie Freeman 25.00 60.00
FAHR Hanley Ramirez 6.00 15.00
FAJA Jose Abreu 25.00 60.00
FAJDM Jacob deGrom 30.00 80.00
FAKU Koji Uehara 6.00 15.00
FARB Ryan Braun 10.00 25.00
FARCO Robinson Cano 8.00 20.00
FAYT Yasmany Tomas 8.00 20.00

2015 Finest Autographs Orange Refractors

*ORANGE REF: 1X TO 2.5X BASIC
STATED ODDS 1:32 MINI BOX
STATED PRINT RUN 25 SER.#'d SETS
EXCHANGE DEADLINE 5/31/2018
FAAG Adrian Gonzalez 20.00 50.00
FAAJ Adam Jones 15.00 40.00
FACK Clayton Kershaw 60.00 150.00
FACSE Chris Sale 25.00 60.00
FADP Dustin Pedroia 25.00 60.00
FAFF Freddie Freeman 40.00 100.00
FAHR Hanley Ramirez 10.00 25.00
FAJA Jose Abreu 40.00 100.00
FAJDM Jacob deGrom 50.00 120.00
FAJV Joey Votto 50.00 120.00
FAKB Kris Bryant 200.00 500.00
FAKU Koji Uehara 10.00 25.00
FAMTT Mike Trout 300.00 500.00
FARB Ryan Braun 15.00 40.00
FARCO Robinson Cano 60.00 150.00
FATT Troy Tulowitzki 20.00 50.00
FAYT Yasmany Tomas 12.00 30.00

2015 Finest Careers Die Cut

RANDOM INSERTS IN PACKS
*REF/25: 1.5X TO 4X BASIC
JETER1 Derek Jeter 8.00 20.00
JETER2 Derek Jeter 8.00 20.00
JETER3 Derek Jeter 8.00 20.00
JETER4 Derek Jeter 8.00 20.00
JETER5 Derek Jeter 8.00 20.00
JETER6 Derek Jeter 8.00 20.00
JETER7 Derek Jeter 8.00 20.00
JETER8 Derek Jeter 8.00 20.00
JETER9 Derek Jeter 8.00 20.00
JETER10 Derek Jeter 8.00 20.00

2015 Finest Firsts

RANDOM INSERTS IN MINI BOXES
*REF/25: 2.5X TO 6X BASIC
FF1 Joc Pederson 1.00 2.50
FF2 Maikel Franco .60 1.50
FF3 Anthony Ranaudo .50 1.25
FF4 Dalton Pompey .60 1.50
FF5 Brandon Finnegan .50 1.25
FF6 Javier Baez 4.00 10.00
FF7 Jorge Soler .75 2.00
FF8 Daniel Norris .50 1.25
FF9 Trevor May .50 1.25
FF10 Rusney Castillo .60 1.50

2015 Finest Firsts Autographs

STATED ODDS 1:25 MINI BOX
*BLUE REF/150: .5X TO 1.2X BASIC
*GREEN REF/99: .5X TO 1.2X BASIC
*GOLD REF/50: 1X TO 2.5X BASIC
*ORNGE REF/25: 1.2X TO 3X BASIC
PRINTING PLATE ODDS 1:1612 MINI BOX
PLATE PRINT RUN 1 SET PER COLOR
BLACK-CYAN-MAGENTA-YELLOW ISSUED
NO PLATE PRICING DUE TO SCARCITY
EXCHANGE DEADLINE 5/31/2018
FFABF Brandon Finnegan 5.00 12.00
FFADP Dalton Pompey 6.00 15.00
FFAJB Javier Baez 20.00 50.00
FFAJP Joc Pederson 10.00 25.00
FFAJS Jorge Soler 8.00 20.00
FFAMF Maikel Franco 8.00 20.00

2015 Finest Generations

COMPLETE SET (50) 30.00 80.00
RANDOM INSERTS IN MINI BOXES
*REF/25: 4X TO 10X BASIC
FG01 Stan Musial 1.25 3.00
FG02 Tom Glavine .60 1.50
FG03 Steve Carlton .60 1.50
FG04 Ozzie Smith 1.00 2.50
FG05 Ernie Banks .75 2.00
FG06 Frank Robinson .60 1.50
FG07 Barry Larkin .60 1.50
FG08 Chipper Jones .75 2.00
FG09 Mike Schmidt 1.25 3.00
FG10 Rickey Henderson .75 2.00
FG11 Mark McGwire 1.25 3.00
FG12 Nolan Ryan 2.50 6.00
FG13 Cal Ripken Jr. 2.50 6.00
FG14 Roger Clemens 1.00 2.50
FG15 Mike Piazza .75 2.00
FG16 Sandy Koufax 1.50 4.00
FG17 Johnny Bench .75 2.00
FG18 Ken Griffey Jr. 1.50 4.00
FG19 Tom Seaver .60 1.50
FG20 Robin Yount .75 2.00
FG21 Phil Niekro .60 1.50
FG22 Juan Marichal .60 1.50
FG23 Bo Jackson .75 2.00
FG24 Frank Thomas .75 2.00
FG25 Mariano Rivera 1.00 2.50
FG26 Lou Brock .60 1.50
FG27 Orlando Cepeda .60 1.50
FG28 Dennis Eckersley .60 1.50
FG29 Luis Aparicio .60 1.50
FG30 Andre Dawson .60 1.50
FG31 Rod Carew .60 1.50
FG32 Alex Rodriguez 1.00 2.50
FG33 Randy Johnson .75 2.00
FG34 Albert Pujols 1.00 2.50
FG35 Greg Maddux 1.00 2.50
FG36 Tony Gwynn .75 2.00
FG37 Chase Utley .60 1.50
FG38 Derek Jeter 2.00 5.00
FG39 Wade Boggs .60 1.50
FG40 Joe Morgan .60 1.50
FG41 Willie Mays 1.50 4.00
FG42 Clayton Kershaw 1.50 4.00
FG43 Mike Trout 4.00 10.00
FG44 Cole Hamels .60 1.50
FG45 David Price .60 1.50
FG46 Andrew McCutchen .75 2.00
FG47 Adrian Beltre .75 2.00
FG48 Giancarlo Stanton .75 2.00
FG49 Miguel Cabrera .75 2.00
FG50 Robinson Cano .60 1.50

2015 Finest Generations Autographs

STATED ODDS 1:122 MINI BOX
STATED PRINT RUN 25 SER.#'d SETS
EXCHANGE DEADLINE 5/31/2018
FGABL Barry Larkin 30.00 80.00
FGACR Cal Ripken Jr. 125.00 300.00
FGADE Dennis Eckersley 30.00 80.00
FGAFR Frank Robinson 30.00 80.00
FGAJB Johnny Bench 40.00 100.00
FGAKG Ken Griffey Jr. 200.00 400.00
FGALB Lou Brock 30.00 80.00
FGAMM Mark McGwire 125.00 250.00
FGAMP Mike Piazza 75.00 200.00
FGAMR Mariano Rivera 150.00 250.00
FGANR Nolan Ryan 125.00 300.00
FGAOS Ozzie Smith 30.00 80.00
FGARCS Roger Clemens 50.00 125.00
FGARH Rickey Henderson 60.00 150.00
FGASC Steve Carlton 30.00 80.00
FGASK Sandy Koufax 300.00 400.00
FGATG Tom Glavine 60.00 150.00

2015 Finest Greats Autographs

STATED ODDS 1:29 MINI BOX
PRINTING PLATE ODDS 1:764 MINI BOX
PLATE PRINT RUN 1 SET PER COLOR
BLACK-CYAN-MAGENTA-YELLOW ISSUED
NO PLATE PRICING DUE TO SCARCITY
EXCHANGE DEADLINE 5/31/2018
FGABL Barry Larkin 25.00 60.00
FGACF Carlton Fisk 12.00 30.00
FGACJ Chipper Jones 50.00 120.00
FGAFR Frank Robinson 15.00 40.00
FGAFT Frank Thomas 25.00 60.00
FGAJB Johnny Bench 20.00 50.00
FGALB Lou Brock 15.00 40.00
FGAOS Ozzie Smith 12.00 30.00
FGARH Rickey Henderson 50.00 120.00
FGATG Tom Glavine 15.00 40.00

2015 Finest Greats Autographs Gold Refractors

*GOLD REF: .5X TO 1.2X BASIC
STATED ODDS 1:61 MINI BOX
STATED PRINT RUN 50 SER.#'d SETS
EXCHANGE DEADLINE 5/31/2018
FGAGM Greg Maddux 40.00 100.00
FGAHA Hank Aaron 150.00 400.00
FGAKG Ken Griffey Jr. 125.00 300.00
FGANR Nolan Ryan 75.00 200.00

2015 Finest Greats Autographs Orange Refractors

*ORANGE REF: .6X TO 1.5X BASIC
STATED ODDS 1:122 MINI BOX
STATED PRINT RUN 25 SER.#'d SETS
EXCHANGE DEADLINE 5/31/2018
FGAGM Greg Maddux 50.00 120.00
FGAHA Hank Aaron 250.00 500.00
FGAKG Ken Griffey Jr. 200.00 400.00
FGANR Nolan Ryan 100.00 250.00
FGARC Roger Clemens 40.00 100.00
FGARJ Randy Johnson 60.00 150.00

2015 Finest Rookie Autographs Mystery Exchange

STATED ODDS 1:154 MINI BOX
EXCHANGE DEADLINE 5/31/2018
RR1 Byron Buxton 75.00 150.00
RR2 Joc Pederson 12.00 30.00
RR3 Francsico Lindor 75.00 200.00

2016 Finest

COMP.SET w/o SP's (100) 25.00 60.00
SP ODDS 1:5 MINI BOX
PRINTING PLATE ODDS 1:87 MINI BOX
BLACK-CYAN-MAGENTA-YELLOW ISSUED
PLATE PRINT RUN 1 SET PER COLOR
NO PLATE PRICING DUE TO SCARCITY
1 Mike Trout 1.50 4.00
2 Ryan Howard .25 .60
3 Edwin Encarnacion .30 .75
4 Dee Gordon .20 .50
5 Evan Longoria .25 .60
6 Jake Arrieta .25 .60
7 Jose Abreu .30 .75
8 Frankie Montas RC .40 1.00
9 Matt Harvey .25 .60
10 Ichiro Suzuki .40 1.00
11 A.J. Pollock .20 .50
12 Ian Kinsler .25 .60
13 Salvador Perez .25 .60
14 Buster Posey .40 1.00
15 Corey Kluber .25 .60
16 Jose Peraza RC .40 1.00
17 Greg Bird RC .40 1.00
18 Trea Turner RC 1.00 2.50
19 Joc Pederson .25 .60
20 J.D. Martinez .30 .75
21 Carl Edwards Jr. RC .40 1.00
22 Carlos Correa .30 .75
23 Cole Hamels .25 .60
24 Joey Votto .30 .75
25 Kenta Maeda RC .60 1.50
26 Dellin Betances .25 .60
27 Ketel Marte RC .60 1.50
28 Brian McCann .25 .60
29 Troy Tulowitzki .30 .75
30 Dallas Keuchel .25 .60
31 Byron Buxton .25 .60
32 David Ortiz .30 .75
33 Rob Refsnyder RC .40 1.00
34 Tyson Ross .20 .50
35 Mookie Betts .50 1.25
36 Charlie Blackmon .30 .75
37 Francisco Lindor .30 .75
38 Sonny Gray .25 .60
39 Jose Altuve .25 .60
40 Chris Sale .30 .75
41 Brian Dozier .25 .60
42 Luis Severino RC .40 1.00
43 Robinson Cano .25 .60
44 Josh Donaldson .25 .60
45 Adrian Beltre .30 .75
46 Jose Fernandez .30 .75
47 Andrew McCutchen .30 .75
48 Ryan Braun .25 .60
49 Noah Syndergaard .25 .60
50 Clayton Kershaw .60 1.50
51 Michael Brantley .25 .60
52 Felix Hernandez .25 .60
53 Yu Darvish .30 .75
54 Andrew Miller .25 .60
55 Eric Hosmer .25 .60
56 Peter O'Brien RC .30 .75
57 Wil Myers .20 .50
58 Corey Seager RC 2.50 6.00
59 George Springer .25 .60
60 Brandon Crawford .25 .60
61 Jacob deGrom .30 .75
62 Alcides Escobar .25 .60
63 Yoenis Cespedes .30 .75
64 Gary Sanchez RC 1.00 2.50
65 Miguel Cabrera .30 .75
66 Gerrit Cole .30 .75
67 Kyle Schwarber RC 1.00 2.50
68 Jorge Soler .30 .75
69 Miguel Sano RC .50 1.25
70 Brandon Phillips .20 .50
71 Maikel Franco .25 .60
72 Craig Kimbrel .25 .60
73 Dustin Pedroia .30 .75
74 Matt Holliday .30 .75
75 Henry Owens RC .40 1.00
76 Anthony Rizzo .50 1.25
77 David Wright .25 .60
78 Giancarlo Stanton .30 .75
79 Nolan Arenado .40 1.00
80 Kyle Seager .20 .50
81 Mark Melancon .20 .50
82 Raul Mondesi Jr. RC .40 1.00
83 Carlos Carrasco .20 .50
84 Matt Carpenter .30 .75
85 David Price .25 .60
86 Todd Frazier .25 .60
87 Rusney Castillo .20 .50
88 Madison Bumgarner .25 .60
89 Starling Marte .25 .60
90 Zack Greinke .25 .60
91 Hector Olivera RC .40 1.00
92 Kolten Wong .25 .60
93 Christian Yelich .40 1.
94 Max Kepler RC .50 1.
95 Jason Kipnis .25
96 Prince Fielder .25
97 Stephen Piscotty RC .50 1.
98 Jorge Lopez RC .30
99 Jon Lester .25
100 Bryce Harper .50 1.
101 Adam Jones SP 8.00 20.
102 Aroldis Chapman SP 10.00 25.
103 Aaron Nola SP RC 12.00 30.
104 Matt Harvey SP 8.00 20.
105 Wade Davis SP 6.00 15.
106 Paul Goldschmidt SP 10.00 25.
107 Max Scherzer SP 10.00 25.
108 Michael Conforto SP RC 8.00 20.
109 Freddie Freeman SP 12.00 30.
110 Kris Bryant SP 12.00 30.0

2016 Finest Blue Refractors

*BLUE REF: 2.5X TO 6X BASIC
*BLUE REF RC: 1.5X TO 4X BASIC
STATED ODDS 1:3 MINI BOX
STATED PRINT RUN 150 SER.#'d SETS

2016 Finest Gold Refractors

*GOLD REF: 6X TO 15X BASIC
*GOLD REF RC: 4X TO 10X BASIC
STATED ODDS 1:7 MINI BOX
STATED PRINT RUN 50 SER.#'d SETS

2016 Finest Green Refractors

*GREEN REF: 3X TO 8X BASIC
*GREEN REF RC: 2X TO 5X BASIC
STATED ODDS 1:4 MINI BOX
STATED PRINT RUN 99 SER.#'d SETS

2016 Finest Orange Refractors

*ORANGE REF: 8X TO 20X BASIC
*ORANGE REF RC: 5X TO 12X BASIC
*ORANGE REF SP: .75X TO 2X BASIC
STATED ODDS 1:14 MINI BOX
SP ODDS 1:139 MINI BOX
STATED PRINT RUN 25 SER.#'d SETS

2016 Finest Purple Refractors

*PRPLE REF: 2X TO 5X BASIC
*PRPLE REF RC: 1.2X TO 3X BASIC
STATED ODDS 1:2 MINI BOX
STATED PRINT RUN 250 SER.#'d SETS

2016 Finest Refractors

*REF: 1X TO 2.5X BASIC
*REF RC: .6X TO 1.5X BASIC
RANDOM INSERTS IN PACKS

2016 Finest '96 Finest Intimidators Autographs

STATED ODDS 1:136 MINI BOX
STATED PRINT RUN 25 SER.#'d SETS
PRINTING PLATE ODDS 1:847 MINI BOX
PLATE PRINT RUN 1 SET PER COLOR
NO PLATE PRICING DUE TO SCARCITY
EXCHANGE DEADLINE 4/30/2018
96FIABJ Bo Jackson 100.00 250.00
96FIAMM Mark McGwire
96FIANR Nolan Ryan
96FIARC Roger Clemens 30.00 80.00
96FIAYD Yu Darvish

2016 Finest '96 Finest Intimidators Refractors

RANDOM INSERTS IN PACKS
*ORANGE/25: 8X TO 20X BASIC
96FII Ichiro Suzuki .75 2.00
96FIAP Albert Pujols .75 2.00
96FIBJ Bo Jackson .60 1.50
96FICS Chris Sale .60 1.50
96FIDO David Ortiz .60 1.50
96FIEE Edwin Encarnacion .60 1.50
96FIEG Evan Gattis .40 1.00
96FIFT Frank Thomas .60 1.50
96FIGS Giancarlo Stanton .60 1.50
96FIJC Jose Canseco .50 1.25
96FIMH Matt Harvey .50 1.25
96FIMM Mark McGwire 1.00 2.50
96FIMP Mike Piazza .60 1.50
96FINR Nolan Ryan 2.00 5.00
96FIPF Prince Fielder .50 1.25
96FIRC Roger Clemens .75 2.00
96FIRJ Randy Johnson .60 1.50
96FIVG Vladimir Guerrero .50 1.25
96FIYC Yoenis Cespedes .60 1.50
96FIYD Yu Darvish .60 1.50

2016 Finest Autographs

OVERALL AUTO ODDS 1:1 MINI BOX
PRINTING PLATE ODDS 1:187 MINI BOX
PLATE PRINT RUN 1 SET PER COLOR
NO PLATE PRICING DUE TO SCARCITY
EXCHANGE DEADLINE 4/30/2018
FAAG Andres Galarraga 6.00 15.00
FAAJ Andruw Jones 5.00 12.00
FAAM Andrew Miller 4.00 10.00
FAAP A.J. Pollock 3.00 8.00
FABH Bryce Harper 50.00 120.00
FABPA Byung-Ho Park 40.00 100.00
FABPO Buster Posey 40.00 100.00
FABS Blake Swihart 4.00 10.00
FACB Craig Biggio 12.00 30.00
FACC Carlos Correa 60.00 150.00
FACD Carlos Delgado 3.00 8.00
FACDI Corey Dickerson 4.00 10.00
FACE Carl Edwards Jr. 4.00 10.00
FACKL Corey Kluber 5.00 12.00
FACM Carlos Martinez 4.00 10.00
FACR Cal Ripken Jr. 60.00 150.00
FADK Dallas Keuchel 10.00 25.00
FADN Daniel Norris 3.00 8.00

FF Freddie Freeman 12.00 30.00
FL Francisco Lindor 15.00 40.00
HO Hector Olivera 4.00 10.00
Ichiro Suzuki 200.00 400.00
JAL Jose Altuve 12.00 30.00
JD Jacob deGrom 12.00 30.00
JKR John Kruk 5.00 12.00
JR J.T. Realmuto 12.00 30.00
KB Kris Bryant 40.00 100.00
KC Kole Calhoun 3.00 8.00
KMA Kenta Maeda 40.00 100.00
KW Kolten Wong 4.00 10.00
MC Matt Cain 4.00 10.00
MT Mike Trout 200.00 300.00
OV Omar Vizquel 4.00 10.00
RB Ryan Braun 8.00 20.00
RF Rollie Fingers 5.00 12.00
RM Raul Mondesi Jr. 8.00 20.00
RR Rob Refsnyder 4.00 10.00
SM Starling Marte 4.00 10.00
SMA Steven Matz 3.00 8.00
SP Stephen Piscotty 5.00 12.00
TT Trea Turner 25.00 60.00
WD Wade Davis 3.00 8.00
YD Yu Darvish 30.00 80.00

2016 Finest Autographs Blue Refractors
BLUE REF: .5X TO 1.2X BASIC
TATED ODDS 1:8 MINI BOX
TATED PRINT RUN 150 SER.#'d SETS
XCHANGE DEADLINE 4/30/2018

2016 Finest Autographs Gold Refractors
GOLD REF: .75X TO 2X BASIC
STATED ODDS 1:18 MINI BOX
STATED PRINT RUN 50 SER.#'d SETS
EXCHANGE DEADLINE 4/30/2018
FAAJ Andruw Jones 10.00 25.00

2016 Finest Autographs Green Refractors
GREEN REF: .6X TO 1.5X BASIC
STATED ODDS 1:11 MINI BOX
STATED PRINT RUN 99 SER.#'d SETS
EXCHANGE DEADLINE 4/30/2018

2016 Finest Autographs Orange Refractors
*ORANGE REF: 1X TO 2.5X BASIC
STATED ODDS 1:30 MINI BOX
STATED PRINT RUN 25 SER.#'d SETS
EXCHANGE DEADLINE 4/30/2018
FAAJ Andruw Jones 12.00 30.00

2016 Finest Autographs Purple Refractors
*PURPLE REF: 1X TO 2.5X BASIC
STATED ODDS 1:32 MINI BOX
STATED PRINT RUN 30 SER.#'d SETS
EXCHANGE DEADLINE 4/30/2018
FAAJ Andruw Jones 12.00 30.00

2016 Finest Careers Die Cut Refractors
STATED ODDS 1:16 MINI BOX
*ORANGE/25: 1X TO 2.5X BASIC
*RED/5: 3X TO 8X BASIC
FCAKG1 Ken Griffey Jr. 12.00 30.00
FCAKG2 Ken Griffey Jr. 12.00 30.00
FCAKG3 Ken Griffey Jr. 12.00 30.00
FCAKG4 Ken Griffey Jr. 12.00 30.00
FCAKG5 Ken Griffey Jr. 12.00 30.00
FCAKG6 Ken Griffey Jr. 12.00 30.00
FCAKG7 Ken Griffey Jr. 12.00 30.00
FCAKG8 Ken Griffey Jr. 12.00 30.00
FCAKG9 Ken Griffey Jr. 12.00 30.00
FCAKG10 Ken Griffey Jr. 12.00 30.00

2016 Finest Firsts Autographs
STATED ODDS 1:23 MINI BOX
PRINTING PLATE ODDS 1:1180 MINI BOX
PLATE PRINT RUN 1 SET PER COLOR
NO PLATE PRICING DUE TO SCARCITY
EXCHANGE DEADLINE 4/30/2018
FFAAN Aaron Nola 8.00 20.00
FFACS Corey Seager
FFAHOW Henry Owens EXCH 6.00 15.00
FFAKS Kyle Schwarber
FFALS Luis Severino 6.00 15.00
FFAMC Michael Conforto
FFAMS Miguel Sano 6.00 15.00

2016 Finest Firsts Autographs Blue Refractors
*BLUE REF: .5X TO 1.2X BASIC
STATED ODDS 1:38 MINI BOX
STATED PRINT RUN 150 SER.#'d SETS
EXCHANGE DEADLINE 4/30/2018

2016 Finest Firsts Autographs Gold Refractors
*GOLD REF: .75X TO 2X BASIC
STATED ODDS 1:97 MINI BOX
STATED PRINT RUN 50 SER.#'d SETS
EXCHANGE DEADLINE 4/30/2018
FFACS Corey Seager 125.00 300.00
FFAKS Kyle Schwarber 25.00 60.00
FFAMC Michael Conforto 15.00 40.00

2016 Finest Firsts Autographs Green Refractors
*GREEN REF: .6X TO 1.5X BASIC
STATED ODDS 1:49 MINI BOX
STATED PRINT RUN 99 SER.#'d SETS
EXCHANGE DEADLINE 4/30/2018
FFAKS Kyle Schwarber 20.00 50.00
FFAMC Michael Conforto 12.00 30.00

2016 Finest Firsts Autographs Orange Refractors
*ORANGE REF: 1.2X TO 3X BASIC
STATED ODDS 1:192 MINI BOX
STATED PRINT RUN 25 SER.#'d SETS
EXCHANGE DEADLINE 4/30/2018
FFACS Corey Seager 300.00 500.00
FFAKS Kyle Schwarber 40.00 100.00

2016 Finest Firsts Refractors
STATED ODDS 1:2 MINI BOX
*ORANGE/25: 6X TO 15X BASIC
FFAN Aaron Nola 1.00 2.50
FFCS Corey Seager 4.00 10.00
FFHO Hector Olivera .60 1.50
FFHOW Henry Owens .60 1.50
FFKS Kyle Schwarber 1.50 4.00
FFLS Luis Severino .60 1.50
FFMC Michael Conforto .60 1.50
FFMS Miguel Sano .75 2.00
FFSP Stephen Piscotty .75 2.00
FFTT Trea Turner 1.50 4.00

2016 Finest Franchise Finest Autographs
STATED ODDS 1:66 MINI BOX
PRINT RUNS B/WN 40-150 COPIES PER
PRINTING PLATE ODDS 1:1032 MINI BOX
PLATE PRINT RUN 1 SET PER COLOR
NO PLATE PRICING DUE TO SCARCITY
EXCHANGE DEADLINE 4/30/2018
*ORNGE REF: .6X TO 1.5X BASIC
FFIABP Buster Posey/40 40.00 100.00
FFIACK Clayton Kershaw/50 30.00 80.00
FFIAEL Evan Longoria/50 12.00 30.00
FFIAFH Felix Hernandez 30.00 80.00
FFIAJA Jose Altuve/150 15.00 40.00
FFIAMT Mike Trout/40 150.00 400.00
FFIAWM Wil Myers/100 6.00 15.00

2016 Finest Franchise Finest Refractors
RANDOM INSERTS IN PACKS
*ORANGE/25: 6X TO 15X BASIC
FFAJ Adam Jones .60 1.50
FFAM Andrew McCutchen .75 2.00
FFAR Anthony Rizzo 1.25 3.00
FFBD Brian Dozier .60 1.50
FFBH Bryce Harper 1.25 3.00
FFBM Brian McCann .60 1.50
FFBP Buster Posey 1.00 2.50
FFCK Clayton Kershaw 1.50 4.00
FFCS Chris Sale .75 2.00
FFDO David Ortiz .75 2.00
FFEH Eric Hosmer .60 1.50
FFEL Evan Longoria .60 1.50
FFFF Freddie Freeman 1.00 2.50
FFFH Felix Hernandez .60 1.50
FFGS Giancarlo Stanton .75 2.00
FFJA Jose Altuve .60 1.50
FFJD Josh Donaldson .60 1.50
FFJV Joey Votto .75 2.00
FFMB Michael Brantley .60 1.50
FFMC Miguel Cabrera .75 2.00
FFMCA Matt Carpenter .75 2.00
FFMH Matt Harvey .60 1.50
FFMT Mike Trout 4.00 10.00
FFNA Nolan Arenado 1.00 2.50
FFPF Prince Fielder .60 1.50
FFPG Paul Goldschmidt .75 2.00
FFRB Ryan Braun .60 1.50
FFRH Ryan Howard .60 1.50
FFSG Sonny Gray .60 1.50
FFWM Wil Myers .50 1.25

2016 Finest Greats Autographs
STATED ODDS 1:18 MINI BOX
PRINT RUNS B/WN 40-300 COPIES PER
PRINTING PLATE ODDS 1:702 MINI BOX
PLATE PRINT RUN 1 SET PER COLOR
NO PLATE PRICING DUE TO SCARCITY
EXCHANGE DEADLINE 4/30/2018
FGAAK Al Kaline/200 20.00 50.00
FGACR Cal Ripken Jr./60 50.00 120.00
FGADM Don Mattingly/60 25.00 60.00
FGAEM Edgar Martinez/300 10.00 25.00
FGAHA Hank Aaron/40 150.00 300.00
FGAJG Juan Gonzalez/300 8.00 20.00
FGAJS John Smoltz/90 20.00 50.00
FGAMP Mike Piazza/50 60.00 150.00
FGANR Nolan Ryan/60 75.00 200.00
FGARC Rod Carew/150 10.00 25.00
FGASK Sandy Koufax/40 150.00 300.00
FGAVG Vladimir Guerrero/150 15.00 40.00

2016 Finest Greats Autographs Gold Refractors
*GOLD REF: 1X TO 2.5X BASIC
STATED ODDS 1:75 MINI BOX
STATED PRINT RUN 50 SER.#'d SETS
EXCHANGE DEADLINE 4/30/2018
FGACR Cal Ripken Jr. 60.00 150.00
FGADM Don Mattingly 30.00 80.00
FGANR Nolan Ryan 100.00 250.00
FGARC Rod Carew 25.00 60.00

2016 Finest Greats Autographs Orange Refractors
*ORANGE REF: 1.2X TO 3X BASIC
STATED ODDS 1:135 MINI BOX
STATED PRINT RUN 25 SER.#'d SETS
EXCHANGE DEADLINE 4/30/2018
FGACR Cal Ripken Jr. 75.00 200.00
FGADM Don Mattingly 40.00 100.00
FGAMP Mike Piazza 100.00 250.00
FGANR Nolan Ryan 125.00 300.00
FGARC Rod Carew 30.00 80.00

2016 Finest Mystery Redemption Autograph
COMMON CARD 60.00 150.00
SEMISTARS 75.00 200.00
UNLISTED STARS 100.00 250.00
STATED ODDS 1:337 MINI BOX
EXCHANGE DEADLINE 4/30/2018
FMR1 Trevor Story
FMR2 Normar Mazara
FMR3 Julio Urias 60.00 150.00

2016 Finest Originals Buyback Autographs
STATED ODDS 1:170 MINI BOX
STATED PRINT RUN 20 SER.#'d SETS
EXCHANGE DEADLINE 4/30/2018
BW Billy Wagner 20.00 50.00
CJ Ghipper Jones 60.00 150.00
CR Cal Ripken Jr.
JS John Smoltz
RJ Randy Johnson 30.00 120.00

2017 Finest
COMP.SET w/o SP's (100) 20.00 50.00
STATED SP ODDS 1:22 HOBBY
1 Mike Trout 1.50 4.00
2 Aaron Judge RC 6.00 15.00
3 Gregory Polanco .25 .60
4 Masahiro Tanaka .25 .60
5 Evan Longoria .25 .60
6 Todd Frazier .25 .60
7 Trea Turner .25 .60
8 Manny Machado .30 .75
9 Max Scherzer .30 .75
10 Edwin Encarnacion .30 .75
11 Jonathan Villar .20 .50
12 Hanley Ramirez .25 .60
13 Billy Hamilton .25 .60
14 Kenta Maeda .25 .60
15 Joey Votto .30 .75
16 Carlos Correa .30 .75
17 Carlos Santana .25 .60
18 Jose Bautista .25 .60
19 Seth Lugo RC .30 .75
20 Carlos Carrasco .20 .50
21 Christian Yelich .40 1.00
22 Tyler Austin RC .50 1.25
23 Jorge Alfaro RC .40 1.00
24 Yoan Moncada RC 1.00 2.50
25 Corey Seager .30 .75
26 Zack Greinke .25 .60
27 Ryan Braun .25 .60
28 Brian Dozier .30 .75
29 Giancarlo Stanton .30 .75
30 Carlos Martinez .25 .60
31 David Price .25 .60
32 Dansby Swanson RC .75 2.00
33 Willson Contreras .30 .75
34 Ryon Healy RC .40 1.00
35 Reynaldo Lopez RC .30 .75
36 Chris Archer .20 .50
37 D.J. LeMahieu .30 .75
38 Chris Sale .30 .75
39 Jean Segura .25 .60
40 Orlando Arcia RC .50 1.25
41 Braden Shipley RC .30 .75
42 Jon Lester .25 .60
43 Francisco Lindor .30 .75
44 Josh Donaldson .25 .60
45 Kenley Jansen .25 .60
46 Aroldis Chapman .30 .75
47 Adam Jones .25 .60
48 Jake Arrieta .25 .60
49 Stephen Strasburg .30 .75
50 Clayton Kershaw .60 1.50
51 Joe Musgrove RC .30 .75
52 Rick Porcello .25 .60
53 Ichiro .40 1.00
54 Kyle Schwarber .30 .75
55 Manny Margot RC .30 .75
56 Dustin Pedroia .30 .75
57 Jose De Leon RC .30 .75
58 Alex Reyes RC .40 1.00
59 Kyle Seager .20 .50
60 Justin Verlander .30 .75
61 Miguel Cabrera .30 .75
62 Adrian Beltre .30 .75
63 Nelson Cruz .30 .75
64 Michael Fulmer .20 .50
65 Ian Kinsler .25 .60
66 Andrew Benintendi RC 1.00 2.50
67 Nolan Arenado .40 1.00
68 Jason Kipnis .25 .60
69 Stephen Piscotty .25 .60
70 Andrew Miller .25 .60
71 Mookie Betts .50 1.25
72 Yu Darvish .30 .75
73 J.D. Martinez .30 .75
74 Gerrit Cole .30 .75
75 Raimel Tapia RC .40 1.00
76 Robinson Cano .25 .60
77 Carlos Gonzalez .25 .60
78 Rougned Odor .25 .60
79 Bryce Harper .50 1.25
80 Noah Syndergaard .25 .60
81 Johnny Cueto .25 .60
82 Charlie Blackmon .30 .75
83 Buster Posey .40 1.00
84 Matt Harvey .25 .60
85 Freddie Freeman .40 1.00
86 Paul Goldschmidt .30 .75
87 Hunter Renfroe RC .40 1.00
88 Robert Gsellman RC .30 .75
89 Alex Bregman RC 1.25 3.00
90 Yulieski Gurriel RC .50 1.25
91 Wil Myers .20 .50
92 Justin Upton .25 .60
93 Matt Carpenter .30 .75
94 Starling Marte .25 .60
95 Craig Kimbrel .25 .60
96 Xander Bogaerts .30 .75
97 George Springer .25 .60
98 Roberto Osuna .20 .50
99 Dee Gordon .20 .50
100 Kris Bryant .40 1.00
101 Jose Altuve SP 5.00 12.00
102 Dellin Betances SP 5.00 12.00
103 Jackie Bradley Jr. SP 6.00 15.00
104 Yoenis Cespedes SP 6.00 15.00
105 Gavin Cecchini SP RC 4.00 10.00
106 Jharel Cotton SP RC 4.00 10.00
107 Albert Pujols SP 8.00 20.00
108 Daniel Murphy SP 5.00 12.00
109 Tyler Glasnow SP RC 5.00 12.00
110 Chris Davis SP 4.00 10.00
111 A.J. Pollock SP 4.00 10.00
112 Gary Sanchez SP 6.00 15.00
113 Kyle Hendricks SP 6.00 15.00
114 Eric Hosmer SP 5.00 12.00
115 Andrew McCutchen SP 6.00 15.00
116 Luke Weaver SP RC 5.00 12.00
117 Zach Britton SP 5.00 12.00
118 Jacob deGrom SP 6.00 15.00
119 Edwin Diaz SP 5.00 12.00
120 Corey Kluber SP 5.00 12.00
121 Danny Duffy SP 4.00 10.00
122 Jose Abreu SP 6.00 15.00
123 David Dahl SP RC 5.00 12.00
124 Trevor Story SP 6.00 15.00
125 Anthony Rizzo SP 10.00 25.00

2017 Finest Blue Refractors
*BLUE REF: 3X TO 8X BASIC
*BLUE REF RC: 2X TO 5X BASIC RC
STATED ODDS 1:19 HOBBY
STATED PRINT RUN 150 SER.#'d SETS

2017 Finest Gold Refractors
*GOLD REF: 6X TO 15X BASIC
*GOLD REF RC: 4X TO 10X BASIC RC
STATED ODDS 1:55 HOBBY
STATED PRINT RUN 50 SER.#'d SETS

2017 Finest Green Refractors
*GREEN REF: 4X TO 10X BASIC
*GREEN REF RC: 2.5X TO 6X BASIC RC
STATED ODDS 1:28 HOBBY
STATED PRINT RUN 99 SER.#'d SETS

2017 Finest Orange Refractors
*ORANGE REF: 8X TO 20X BASIC
*ORANGE REF RC: 5X TO 12X BASIC RC
*ORANGE REF SP: .6X TO 1.5X BASIC SP
STATED ODDS 1:110 HOBBY
STATED SP ODDS 1:438 HOBBY
STATED PRINT RUN 25 SER.#'d SETS

2017 Finest Purple Refractors
*PURPLE REF: 2.5X TO 6X BASIC
*PURPLE REF RC: 1.5X TO 4X BASIC RC
STATED ODDS 1:11 HOBBY
STATED PRINT RUN 250 SER.#'d SETS

2017 Finest Refractors
*REF: 1.2X TO 3X BASIC
*REF RC: .75X TO 2X BASIC RC
STATED ODDS 1:3 HOBBY

2017 Finest '94-'95 Finest Recreates
STATED ODDS 1:6 HOBBY
*ORANGE/25: 6X TO 15X BASIC
BRAG Andres Galarraga .50 1.25
BRAR Anthony Rizzo 1.00 2.50
BRBH Bryce Harper 1.00 2.50
BRBP Buster Posey .75 2.00
BRCJ Chipper Jones .60 1.50
BRCS Corey Seager .60 1.50
BRFL Francisco Lindor .60 1.50
BRGM Greg Maddux .75 2.00
BRIR Ivan Rodriguez .50 1.25
BRI Ichiro .75 2.00
BRJA Jose Altuve .50 1.25
BRKB Kris Bryant .75 2.00
BRKGJ Ken Griffey Jr. 1.25 3.00
BRMF Michael Fulmer .40 1.00
BRNA Nolan Arenado .75 2.00
BRNS Noah Syndergaard .50 1.25
BROV Omar Vizquel .50 1.25
BRSP Stephen Piscotty .50 1.25
BRTS Trevor Story .60 1.50
BRWC Willson Contreras .60 1.50

2017 Finest '94-'95 Finest Recreates Autographs
STATED ODDS 1:508 HOBBY
EXCHANGE DEADLINE 5/31/2019
*ORANGE/25: .6X TO 1.5X BASIC
BRAAG Andres Galarraga 12.00 30.00
BRAAR Anthony Rizzo 30.00 80.00
BRABP Buster Posey
BRACJ Chipper Jones
BRACS Corey Seager 60.00 150.00
BRAFL Francisco Lindor 30.00 80.00
BRAGM Greg Maddux 75.00 200.00
BRAIR Ivan Rodriguez 25.00 60.00
BRAJA Jose Altuve 40.00 100.00
BRAKB Kris Bryant EXCH 200.00 400.00
BRANS Noah Syndergaard EXCH 30.00 80.00
BRAOV Omar Vizquel EXCH 20.00 50.00
BRASP Stephen Piscotty 20.00 50.00
BRATS Trevor Story 12.00 30.00
BRAWC Willson Contreras 20.00 50.00

2017 Finest Autographs Refractors
STATED ODDS 1:22 HOBBY
EXCHANGE DEADLINE 5/31/2019
FAAB Andrew Benintendi 30.00 80.00
FAABR Alex Bregman 20.00 50.00
FAAD Adam Duvall 12.00 30.00
FAAJ Aaron Judge 250.00 500.00
FAAR Anthony Rizzo 20.00 50.00
FAARE Alex Reyes 5.00 12.00
FAARU Addison Russell 10.00 25.00
FABB Barry Bonds 200.00 400.00
FABH Bryce Harper 150.00 300.00
FABP Buster Posey 30.00 80.00
FABS Blake Snell 4.00 10.00
FACC Carlos Correa 30.00 80.00
FACJ Chipper Jones
FACK Clayton Kershaw 50.00 120.00
FACR Cody Reed 3.00 8.00
FACS Corey Seager 60.00 150.00
FADD Danny Duffy 3.00 8.00
FADDA David Dahl 4.00 10.00
FADJ Derek Jeter
FADP David Price 10.00 25.00
FADS Dansby Swanson 15.00 40.00
FAER Eddie Rosario 4.00 10.00
FAFL Francisco Lindor 20.00 50.00
FAHO Henry Owens 3.00 8.00
FAHR Hunter Renfroe 4.00 10.00
FAIR Ivan Rodriguez 12.00 30.00
FAJA Jose Altuve 30.00 80.00
FAJAL Jorge Alfaro 4.00 10.00
FAJDL Jose De Leon 3.00 8.00
FAJH Jason Heyward 8.00 20.00
FAJMU Joe Musgrove 3.00 8.00
FAJT Justin Turner 20.00 50.00
FAKB Kris Bryant 100.00 200.00
FAKGJ Ken Griffey Jr. EXCH 100.00 250.00
FAKM Kendrys Morales 3.00 8.00
FALG Lucas Giolito 4.00 10.00
FALS Luis Severino 5.00 12.00
FALW Luke Weaver 4.00 10.00
FAMF Michael Fulmer 8.00 20.00
FAMK Max Kepler 4.00 10.00
FAMT Mike Trout 300.00 600.00
FAMTA Masahiro Tanaka 75.00 200.00
FANM Nomar Mazara 3.00 8.00
FANS Noah Syndergaard 10.00 25.00
FAOA Orlando Arcia 5.00 12.00
FAOV Omar Vizquel 4.00 10.00
FARH Ryon Healy 4.00 10.00
FARS Rob Segedin 3.00 8.00
FASP Stephen Piscotty 4.00 10.00
FASW Steven Wright 3.00 8.00
FATA Tyler Austin 5.00 12.00
FATN Tyler Naquin 3.00 8.00
FATS Trevor Story 5.00 12.00
FATT Trea Turner 8.00 20.00
FAWC Willson Contreras 12.00 30.00
FAYG Yulieski Gurriel 8.00 20.00
FAYM Yoan Moncada 60.00 150.00

2017 Finest Autographs Blue Refractors
*BLUE REF: .5X TO 1.2X BASIC
STATED ODDS 1:36 HOBBY
STATED PRINT RUN 150 SER.#'d SETS
EXCHANGE DEADLINE 5/31/2019

2017 Finest Autographs Blue Wave Refractors
*BLUE WAVE REF: 1X TO 2.5X BASIC
STATED ODDS 1:214 HOBBY
STATED PRINT RUN 25 SER.#'d SETS
EXCHANGE DEADLINE 5/31/2019
FABH Bryce Harper 200.00 400.00
FACJ Chipper Jones 150.00 300.00
FACK Clayton Korshaw 60.00 150.00
FACS Corey Seager 75.00 200.00
FADP David Price 12.00 30.00
FAIR Ivan Rodriguez 15.00 40.00
FAJA Jose Altuve 40.00 100.00
FAJH Jason Heyward 10.00 25.00
FAKB Kris Bryant 250.00 500.00
FAKGJ Ken Griffey Jr. EXCH 200.00 500.00
FAMT Mike Trout 400.00 800.00
FAMTA Masahiro Tanaka 100.00 250.00
FAYM Yoan Moncada 100.00 250.00

2017 Finest Autographs Gold Refractors
*GOLD REF: .75X TO 2X BASIC
STATED ODDS 1:107 HOBBY
STATED PRINT RUN 50 SER.#'d SETS
EXCHANGE DEADLINE 5/31/2019

2017 Finest Autographs Green Refractors
*GREEN REF: .6X TO 1.5X BASIC
STATED ODDS 1:54 HOBBY
STATED PRINT RUN 99 SER.#'d SETS
EXCHANGE DEADLINE 5/31/2019

2017 Finest Autographs Orange Refractors
*ORANGE REF: 1X TO 2.5X BASIC
STATED ODDS 1:214 HOBBY
STATED PRINT RUN 25 SER.#'d SETS
EXCHANGE DEADLINE 5/31/2019
FABH Bryce Harper 200.00 400.00
FACJ Chipper Jones 150.00 300.00
FACK Clayton Kershaw 60.00 150.00
FACS Corey Seager 75.00 200.00
FADP David Price 12.00 30.00
FAIR Ivan Rodriguez 15.00 40.00
FAJA Jose Altuve 40.00 100.00
FAJH Jason Heyward 10.00 25.00
FAKB Kris Bryant 250.00 500.00
FAKGJ Ken Griffey Jr. EXCH 200.00 500.00
FAMT Mike Trout 400.00 800.00
FAMTA Masahiro Tanaka 100.00 250.00
FAYM Yoan Moncada 100.00 250.00

2017 Finest Autographs Red Wave Refractors
*RED WAVE REF: 1X TO 2.5X BASIC
STATED ODDS 1:214 HOBBY
STATED PRINT RUN 25 SER.#'d SETS
EXCHANGE DEADLINE 5/31/2019
FABH Bryce Harper 200.00 400.00
FACJ Chipper Jones 150.00 300.00
FACK Clayton Kershaw 60.00 150.00
FACS Corey Seager 75.00 200.00
FADP David Price 12.00 30.00
FAIR Ivan Rodriguez 15.00 40.00
FAJA Jose Altuve 40.00 100.00
FAJH Jason Heyward 10.00 25.00
FAKB Kris Bryant 250.00 500.00
FAKGJ Ken Griffey Jr. EXCH 200.00 500.00
FAMT Mike Trout 400.00 800.00
FAMTA Masahiro Tanaka 100.00 250.00
FAYM Yoan Moncada 100.00 250.00

2017 Finest Breakthroughs
STATED ODDS 1:3 HOBBY
*ORANGE/25: 4X TO 10X BASIC
FBAD Aledmys Diaz .50 1.25
FBAN Aaron Nola .50 1.25
FBAR Anthony Rizzo 1.00 2.50
FBARU Addison Russell .60 1.50
FBBH Bryce Harper 1.00 2.50
FBCC Carlos Correa .60 1.50
FBCS Corey Seager .60 1.50
FBFL Francisco Lindor .60 1.50
FBJA Jose Altuve .50 1.25
FBJD Jacob deGrom .60 1.50
FBKB Kris Bryant .75 2.00
FRKM Kenta Maeda .50 1.25
FBMT Mike Trout 3.00 8.00
FBNA Nolan Arenado .75 2.00
FBNM Nomar Mazara .40 1.00
FBNS Noah Syndergaard .50 1.25
FBSM Steven Matz .50 1.25
FBSP Stephen Piscotty .50 1.25
FBTS Trevor Story .60 1.50
FBWC Willson Contreras .60 1.50

2017 Finest Breakthroughs Autographs
STATED ODDS 1:356 HOBBY
PRINT RUNS B/WN 10-50 COPIES PER
NO PRICING ON QTY 20 OR LESS
EXCHANGE DEADLINE 5/31/2019
*ORANGE/25: .5X TO 1.2X BASIC
FBAAD Aledmys Diaz/50 8.00 20.00
FBAAR Anthony Rizzo/30 25.00 60.00
FBACS Corey Seager/30 75.00 200.00
FBAFL Francisco Lindor EXCH 25.00 60.00
FBAJA Jose Altuve/50 30.00 80.00
FBAKB Kris Bryant
FBANM Nomar Mazara/50 20.00 50.00
FBANS Noah Syndergaard EXCH
FBASP Stephen Piscotty/50 12.00 30.00
FBATS Trevor Story/50 12.00 30.00
FBAWC Willson Contreras/50 10.00 25.00

2017 Finest Careers Die Cut
STATED ODDS 1:48 HOBBY
*ORANGE/25: 2X TO 5X BASIC
FCIDO1 David Ortiz 2.00 5.00
FCIDO2 David Ortiz 2.00 5.00
FCIDO3 David Ortiz 2.00 5.00
FCIDO4 David Ortiz 2.00 5.00
FCIDO5 David Ortiz 2.00 5.00
FCIDO6 David Ortiz 2.00 5.00
FCIDO7 David Ortiz 2.00 5.00
FCIDO8 David Ortiz 2.00 5.00
FCIDO9 David Ortiz 2.00 5.00
FCIDO10 David Ortiz 2.00 5.00

2017 Finest Careers Die Cut Autographs
COMMON CARD 100.00 250.00
STATED ODDS 1:2666 HOBBY
STATED PRINT RUN 10 SER.#'d SETS
EXCHANGE DEADLINE 5/31/2019

2017 Finest Finishes Autographs
STATED ODDS 1:122 HOBBY
EXCHANGE DEADLINE 5/31/2019
*ORANGE/25: .6X TO 1.5X BASIC
FINABB Barry Bonds 100.00 250.00
FINACF Carlton Fisk 20.00 50.00
FINACRJ Cal Ripken Jr. 50.00 120.00
FINADJ Derek Jeter 400.00 700.00
FINAEM Edgar Martinez 12.00 30.00
FINAFL Francisco Lindor 10.00 25.00
FINAFV Fernando Valenzuela 15.00 40.00
FINAHA Hank Aaron
FINAIR Ivan Rodriguez 10.00 25.00
FINAJA Jake Arrieta EXCH 20.00 50.00
FINAKB Kris Bryant 100.00 200.00
FINAKGJ Ken Griffey Jr. EXCH 200.00 300.00
FINALG Luis Gonzalez 4.00 10.00
FINAMM Mark McGwire 60.00 150.00
FINANR Nolan Ryan
FINAOS Ozzie Smith 15.00 40.00
FINAOV Omar Vizquel 5.00 12.00
FINAPM Pedro Martinez 40.00 100.00
FINARJ Reggie Jackson 40.00 100.00
FINASK Sandy Koufax 100.00 250.00

2017 Finest Firsts
STATED ODDS 1:12 HOBBY
*ORANGE/25: 2.5X TO 6X BASIC
FFIAB Andrew Benintendi 1.50 4.00
FFIABR Alex Bregman 2.00 5.00
FFIAJ Aaron Judge 10.00 25.00
FFIAR Alex Reyes .60 1.50
FFIDD David Dahl .60 1.50
FFIDS Dansby Swanson 1.25 3.00
FFIOA Orlando Arcia .75 2.00
FFITG Tyler Glasnow .60 1.50
FFIYG Yulieski Gurriel .75 2.00
FFIYM Yoan Moncada 1.50 4.00

2017 Finest Firsts Autographs
STATED ODDS 1:77 HOBBY
EXCHANGE DEADLINE 5/31/2019
FFAB Andrew Benintendi 25.00 60.00
FFABR Alex Bregman 15.00 40.00
FFAJ Aaron Judge
FFAR Alex Reyes 5.00 12.00
FFDD David Dahl 5.00 12.00
FFDS Dansby Swanson 20.00 50.00
FFHR Hunter Renfroe 5.00 12.00
FFJDL Jose De Leon 4.00 10.00
FFOA Orlando Arcia
FFTA Tyler Austin 6.00 15.00
FFYG Yulieski Gurriel 6.00 15.00
FFYM Yoan Moncada 40.00 100.00

2017 Finest Firsts Autographs Blue Refractors
*BLUE REF: .5X TO 1.2X BASIC
STATED ODDS 1:178 HOBBY
STATED PRINT RUN 150 SER.#'d SETS
EXCHANGE DEADLINE 5/31/2019
FFAJ Aaron Judge 175.00 350.00

2017 Finest Firsts Autographs Blue Wave Refractors
*BLUE WAVE: 1X TO 2.5X BASIC
STATED ODDS 1:1067 HOBBY
STATED PRINT RUN 25 SER.#'d SETS
EXCHANGE DEADLINE 5/31/2019
FFAJ Aaron Judge 350.00 700.00
FFOA Orlando Arcia 20.00 50.00

2017 Finest Firsts Autographs Gold Refractors
*GOLD REF: .75X TO 2X BASIC
STATED ODDS 1:534 HOBBY
STATED PRINT RUN 50 SER.#'d SETS
EXCHANGE DEADLINE 5/31/2019
FFAJ Aaron Judge 250.00 500.00
FFOA Orlando Arcia 12.00 30.00

2017 Finest Firsts Autographs Green Refractors
*GREEN REF: .6X TO 1.5X BASIC
STATED ODDS 1:270 HOBBY
STATED PRINT RUN 99 SER.#'d SETS
EXCHANGE DEADLINE 5/31/2019
FFAJ Aaron Judge 200.00 400.00

2017 Finest Firsts Autographs Orange Refractors
*ORANGE REF: 1X TO 2.5X BASIC
STATED ODDS 1:1067 HOBBY
STATED PRINT RUN 25 SER.#'d SETS
EXCHANGE DEADLINE 5/31/2019
FFAJ Aaron Judge 350.00 700.00
FFOA Orlando Arcia 20.00 50.00

2017 Finest Firsts Autographs Red Wave Refractors
*RED WAVE: 1X TO 2.5X BASIC
STATED ODDS 1:1067 HOBBY
STATED PRINT RUN 25 SER.#'d SETS
EXCHANGE DEADLINE 5/31/2019
FFAJ Aaron Judge 350.00 700.00
FFOA Orlando Arcia 20.00 50.00

2017 Finest Mystery Redemption Autographs
STATED ODDS 1:898 HOBBY
EXCHANGE DEADLINE 5/31/2019
FMR1 Cody Bellinger 125.00 300.00
FMR2 Ian Happ 75.00 200.00
FMR3 Bradley Zimmer 75.00 200.00

2018 Finest
COMP.SET w/o SP's (100) 20.00 50.00
STATED SP ODDS 1:28 HOBBY
1 Aaron Judge .75 2.00
2 Francisco Lindor .30 .75
3 Brandon Woodruff RC .40 1.00
4 Rougned Odor .25 .60
5 Jose Abreu .30 .75
6 Chris Archer .20 .50
7 Andrew Benintendi .30 .75
8 Evan Longoria .25 .60
9 Joey Gallo .25 .60
10 Dallas Keuchel .25 .60
11 Austin Hays RC .50 1.25
12 Nicky Delmonico RC .30 .75
13 Elvis Andrus .25 .60
14 Jack Flaherty RC .50 1.25
15 Domingo Santana .25 .60
16 Anthony Rendon .30 .75
17 Alex Wood .20 .50
18 Eric Thames .25 .60
19 Jacob deGrom .30 .75
20 Nomar Mazara .20 .50
21 Tommy Pham .20 .50
22 Didi Gregorius .25 .60
23 Tim Beckham .25 .60
24 Yadier Molina .30 .75
25 Kris Bryant .40 1.00
26 Carlos Carrasco .20 .50

27 Jose Ramirez .25 .60
28 Lucas Sims RC .30 .75
29 Giancarlo Stanton .30 .75
30 Charlie Blackmon .30 .75
31 Albert Pujols .40 1.00
32 Ervin Santana .20 .50
33 Billy Hamilton .25 .60
34 Marcus Stroman .25 .60
35 Robinson Cano .25 .60
36 Dominic Smith RC .30 .75
37 Anthony Rizzo .50 1.25
38 Mookie Betts .50 1.25
39 Wil Myers .20 .50
40 Clayton Kershaw .60 1.50
41 Travis Shaw .20 .50
42 Kevin Pillar .20 .50
43 Yuli Gurriel .25 .60
44 Paul DeJong .30 .75
45 George Springer .25 .60
46 Buster Posey .40 1.00
47 Craig Kimbrel .25 .60
48 Andrelton Simmons .20 .50
49 Justin Verlander .30 .75
50 Mike Trout 1.50 4.00
51 Adrian Beltre .30 .75
52 Raisel Iglesias .25 .60
53 Dustin Fowler RC .30 .75
54 Salvador Perez .25 .60
55 Stephen Strasburg .30 .75
56 Ryan McMahon RC .40 1.00
57 Edwin Encarnacion .30 .75
58 Noah Syndergaard .25 .60
59 Nolan Arenado .40 1.00
60 Maikel Franco .25 .60
61 Rafael Devers RC 1.00 2.50
62 Khris Davis .30 .75
63 J.P. Crawford RC .30 .75
64 Chris Sale .30 .75
65 Odubel Herrera .25 .60
66 Alex Bregman .30 .75
67 Justin Turner .25 .60
68 Michael Fulmer .20 .50
69 Brian Dozier .25 .60
70 Freddie Freeman .40 1.00
71 Avisail Garcia .25 .60
72 Adam Jones .25 .60
73 Jose Altuve .25 .60
74 Francisco Mejia RC .40 1.00
75 Rhys Hoskins RC 1.25 3.00
76 Max Scherzer .30 .75
77 Miguel Cabrera .30 .75
78 Corey Knebel .20 .50
79 Jackie Bradley Jr. .30 .75
80 Kenley Jansen .25 .60
81 Amed Rosario RC .40 1.00
82 Bryce Harper .50 1.25
83 Nick Williams RC .40 1.00
84 David Robertson .20 .50
85 Chance Sisco RC .40 1.00
86 Robbie Ray .20 .50
87 Nelson Cruz .30 .75
88 Ryan Braun .25 .60
89 Cody Bellinger .60 1.50
90 Miguel Andujar RC 1.25 3.00
91 Willson Contreras .30 .75
92 Andrew McCutchen .30 .75
93 Gary Sanchez .30 .75
94 Yoenis Cespedes .30 .75
95 Matt Olson .20 .50
96 Brett Gardner .25 .60
97 Paul Goldschmidt .30 .75
98 Manny Machado .30 .75
99 Alex Verdugo RC .50 1.25
100 Shohei Ohtani RC 6.00 15.00
101 Joey Votto SP 5.00 12.00
102 Yoan Moncada SP 5.00 12.00
103 Ozzie Albies SP RC 10.00 25.00
104 Corey Kluber SP 4.00 10.00
105 Jake Lamb SP 4.00 10.00
106 Aaron Altherr SP 3.00 8.00
107 Harrison Bader SP RC 5.00 12.00
108 Jose Berrios SP 4.00 10.00
109 Jonathan Schoop SP 3.00 8.00
110 Marcell Ozuna SP 5.00 12.00
111 J.D. Davis SP RC 4.00 10.00
112 Willie Calhoun SP RC 4.00 10.00
113 Hunter Renfroe SP 3.00 8.00
114 Michael Conforto SP 4.00 10.00
115 Brandon Crawford SP 4.00 10.00
116 Whit Merrifield SP 5.00 12.00
117 Josh Donaldson SP 4.00 10.00
118 Josh Bell SP 4.00 10.00
119 Clint Frazier SP RC 6.00 15.00
120 Nicholas Castellanos SP 5.00 12.00
121 Byron Buxton SP 4.00 10.00
122 Luis Severino SP 4.00 10.00
123 Corey Seager SP 5.00 12.00
124 Zack Greinke SP 4.00 10.00
125 Carlos Correa SP 5.00 12.00

2018 Finest Blue Refractors

*BLUE REF: 2X TO 5X BASIC
*BLUE REF RC: 1.2X TO 3X BASIC RC
STATED ODDS 1:28 HOBBY
STATED PRINT RUN 150 SER.#'d SETS
50 Mike Trout 10.00 25.00
100 Shohei Ohtani 40.00 100.00

2018 Finest Gold Refractors

*GOLD REF: 5X TO 12X BASIC
*GOLD REF RC: 3X TO 8X BASIC RC
*GOLD SP REF RC: .6X TO 1.5X BASIC RC
1-100 STATED ODDS 1:84 HOBBY
101-125 STATED ODDS 1:333 HOBBY
STATED PRINT RUN 50 SER.#'d SETS
50 Mike Trout 25.00 60.00
100 Shohei Ohtani 200.00 400.00

2018 Finest Green Refractors

*GREEN REF: 3X TO 8X BASIC
*GREEN REF RC: 2X TO 5X BASIC RC
STATED ODDS 1:43 HOBBY
STATED PRINT RUN 99 SER.#'d SETS
50 Mike Trout 15.00 40.00
100 Shohei Ohtani 60.00 150.00

2018 Finest Orange Refractors

*ORANGE REF: 6X TO 15X BASIC
*ORANGE REF RC: 4X TO 10X BASIC RC
STATED ODDS 1:167 HOBBY
STATED PRINT RUN 25 SER.#'d SETS
50 Mike Trout 30.00 80.00
100 Shohei Ohtani 250.00 500.00

2018 Finest Purple Refractors

*PURPLE REF: 1.5X TO 4X BASIC
*PURPLE REF RC: 1X TO 2.5X BASIC RC
STATED ODDS 1:11 HOBBY
STATED PRINT RUN 250 SER.#'d SETS
50 Mike Trout 8.00 20.00
100 Shohei Ohtani 25.00 60.00

2018 Finest Refractors

*REF: 1X TO 2.5X BASIC
*REF RC: .6X TO 1.5X BASIC RC
STATED ODDS 1:3 HOBBY

2018 Finest Autographs

STATED ODDS 1:14 HOBBY
EXCHANGE DEADLINE 5/31/2020
FAAB Adrian Beltre 20.00 50.00
FAABA Anthony Banda 2.50 6.00
FAAH Austin Hays 4.00 10.00
FAAP Andy Pettitte 12.00 30.00
FAAR Amed Rosario 3.00 8.00
FAAV Alex Verdugo 6.00 15.00
FABA Brian Anderson 5.00 12.00
FABD Brian Dozier 5.00 12.00
FABW Brandon Woodruff 3.00 8.00
FACA Christian Arroyo 2.50 6.00
FACS Chris Sale 10.00 25.00
FACT Chris Taylor 3.00 8.00
FADF Dustin Fowler 2.50 6.00
FADG Didi Gregorius 10.00 25.00
FADJ Derek Jeter 300.00 600.00
FADS Dominic Smith 2.50 6.00
FAFM Francisco Mejia 6.00 15.00
FAGA Greg Allen 2.50 6.00
FAGC Garrett Cooper 2.50 6.00
FAHB Harrison Bader 4.00 10.00
FAIH Ian Happ 5.00 12.00
FAJC J.P. Crawford 2.50 6.00
FAJF Jack Flaherty 10.00 25.00
FAJL Jake Lamb 3.00 8.00
FAJR Jose Ramirez 3.00 8.00
FAJT Jim Thome 50.00 120.00
FAKB Kris Bryant EXCH 60.00 150.00
FAKD Khris Davis 6.00 15.00
FALG Lucas Giolito 6.00 15.00
FALSI Lucas Sims 2.50 6.00
FAMA Miguel Andujar 10.00 25.00
FAMFR Max Fried 12.00 30.00
FAMM Manny Machado 15.00 40.00
FAMO Matt Olson 2.50 6.00
FAMR Mariano Rivera 100.00 250.00
FAMT Mike Trout
FAOA Ozzie Albies 12.00 30.00
FAPBL Paul Blackburn 2.50 6.00
FARD Rafael Devers 20.00 50.00
FARI Raisel Iglesias 3.00 8.00
FARM Ryan McMahon 3.00 8.00
FASA Sandy Alcantara 2.50 6.00
FASN Sean Newcomb 3.00 8.00
FASO Shohei Ohtani 200.00 400.00
FATM Tyler Mahle 3.00 8.00
FATP Tommy Pham 2.50 6.00
FATS Travis Shaw 3.00 8.00
FATW Tyler Wade 3.00 8.00
FATWL Tzu-Wei Lin 5.00 12.00
FAVR Victor Robles 12.00 30.00
FAWB Walker Buehler 25.00 60.00

2018 Finest Autographs Blue Refractors

*BLUE REF: .5X TO 1.2X BASIC
STATED ODDS 1:55 HOBBY
STATED PRINT RUN 150 SER.#'d SETS
EXCHANGE DEADLINE 5/31/2020
FABA Brian Anderson 10.00 25.00
FAWM Whit Merrifield 10.00 25.00

2018 Finest Autographs Gold Refractors

*GOLD REF: .75X TO 2X BASIC
STATED ODDS 1:164 HOBBY
STATED PRINT RUN 50 SER.#'d SETS
EXCHANGE DEADLINE 5/31/2020
FABA Brian Anderson 20.00 50.00
FACS Chris Sale 12.00 30.00
FACSI Chance Sisco 10.00 25.00
FAOA Ozzie Albies 25.00 60.00
FAPD Paul DeJong 12.00 30.00
FARD Rafael Devers 50.00 120.00
FASO Shohei Ohtani 400.00 800.00
FATS Travis Shaw 10.00 25.00
FATWL Tzu-Wei Lin 25.00 60.00
FAWM Whit Merrifield 15.00 40.00

2018 Finest Autographs Green Refractors

*GREEN REF: .6X TO 1.5X BASIC
STATED ODDS 1:83 HOBBY
STATED PRINT RUN 99 SER.#'d SETS
EXCHANGE DEADLINE 5/31/2020
FABA Brian Anderson 12.00 30.00
FACSI Chance Sisco 8.00 20.00
FAPD Paul DeJong 8.00 20.00
FAWM Whit Merrifield 12.00 30.00

2018 Finest Autographs Green Wave Refractors

*GREEN WAVE REF: .6X TO 1.5X BASIC
STATED ODDS 1:83 HOBBY
STATED PRINT RUN 99 SER.#'d SETS
EXCHANGE DEADLINE 5/31/2020
FABA Brian Anderson 12.00 30.00
FACSI Chance Sisco 8.00 20.00
FAPD Paul DeJong 8.00 20.00
FAWM Whit Merrifield 12.00 30.00

2018 Finest Autographs Orange Refractors

*ORANGE REF: 1X TO 2.5X BASIC
STATED ODDS 1:370 HOBBY
STATED PRINT RUN 25 SER.#'d SETS
EXCHANGE DEADLINE 5/31/2020
FAAB Adrian Beltre 30.00 80.00
FAAV Alex Verdugo 30.00 80.00
FABA Brian Anderson 25.00 60.00
FACS Chris Sale 15.00 40.00
FACSI Chance Sisco 20.00 50.00
FADF Dustin Fowler 20.00 50.00
FADS Dominic Smith 10.00 25.00
FAFM Francisco Mejia 30.00 80.00
FAJT Jim Thome 60.00 150.00
FAKB Kris Bryant EXCH 125.00 300.00
FAOA Ozzie Albies 30.00 80.00
FAPD Paul DeJong 15.00 40.00
FARD Rafael Devers 60.00 150.00
FASN Sean Newcomb 20.00 50.00
FASO Shohei Ohtani 600.00 1000.00
FATS Travis Shaw 12.00 30.00
FATWL Tzu-Wei Lin 30.00 80.00
FAWM Whit Merrifield 20.00 50.00

2018 Finest Autographs Orange Wave Refractors

*ORANGE WAVE REF: 1X TO 2.5X BASIC
STATED ODDS 1:370 HOBBY
STATED PRINT RUN 25 SER.#'d SETS
EXCHANGE DEADLINE 5/31/2020
FAAB Adrian Beltre 30.00 80.00
FAAV Alex Verdugo 30.00 80.00
FABA Brian Anderson 25.00 60.00
FACS Chris Sale 15.00 40.00
FACSI Chance Sisco 20.00 50.00
FADF Dustin Fowler 20.00 50.00
FADS Dominic Smith 10.00 25.00
FAFM Francisco Mejia 30.00 80.00
FAJT Jim Thome 60.00 150.00
FAKB Kris Bryant EXCH 125.00 300.00
FAOA Ozzie Albies 30.00 80.00
FAPD Paul DeJong 15.00 40.00
FARD Rafael Devers 60.00 150.00
FASN Sean Newcomb 20.00 50.00
FASO Shohei Ohtani 600.00 1000.00
FATS Travis Shaw 12.00 30.00
FATWL Tzu-Wei Lin 30.00 80.00
FAWM Whit Merrifield 20.00 50.00

2018 Finest Careers Die Cut

STATED ODDS 1:48 HOBBY
*GOLD/50: 1.5X TO 4X BASIC
*RED/5: 5X TO 12X BASIC
FCCR1 Cal Ripken Jr. 4.00 10.00
FCCR2 Cal Ripken Jr. 4.00 10.00
FCCR3 Cal Ripken Jr. 4.00 10.00
FCCR4 Cal Ripken Jr. 4.00 10.00
FCCR5 Cal Ripken Jr. 4.00 10.00
FCCR6 Cal Ripken Jr. 4.00 10.00
FCCR7 Cal Ripken Jr. 4.00 10.00
FCCR8 Cal Ripken Jr. 4.00 10.00
FCCR9 Cal Ripken Jr. 4.00 10.00
FCCR10 Cal Ripken Jr. 4.00 10.00

2018 Finest Careers Die Cut Autographs

STATED ODDS 1:4056 HOBBY
STATED PRINT RUN 10 SER.#'d SETS
EXCHANGE DEADLINE 5/31/2020
FCACR1 Cal Ripken Jr. 80.00 200.00
FCACR2 Cal Ripken Jr. 80.00 200.00
FCACR3 Cal Ripken Jr. 80.00 200.00
FCACR4 Cal Ripken Jr. 80.00 200.00
FCACR5 Cal Ripken Jr. 80.00 200.00
FCACR6 Cal Ripken Jr. 80.00 200.00
FCACR7 Cal Ripken Jr. 80.00 200.00
FCACR8 Cal Ripken Jr. 80.00 200.00
FCACR9 Cal Ripken Jr. 80.00 200.00
FCACR10 Cal Ripken Jr. 80.00 200.00

2018 Finest Cornerstones

STATED ODDS 1:3 HOBBY
*GOLD/50: 2.5X TO 6X BASIC
FCAB Andrew Benintendi .60 1.50
FCAJ Aaron Judge 1.50 4.00
FCBH Bryce Harper 1.00 2.50
FCBP Buster Posey .75 2.00
FCCA Chris Archer .40 1.00
FCCB Cody Bellinger 1.25 3.00
FCCC Carlos Correa .60 1.50
FCFF Freddie Freeman .75 2.00
FCFL Francisco Lindor .60 1.50
FCJA Jose Abreu .60 1.50
FCJB Josh Bell .50 1.25
FCJD Josh Donaldson .50 1.25
FCJUB Justin Bour .40 1.00
FCJV Joey Votto .60 1.50
FCKB Kris Bryant .75 2.00
FCMC Miguel Cabrera .60 1.50
FCMM Manny Machado .60 1.50
FCMO Matt Olson .40 1.00
FCMS Miguel Sano .50 1.25
FCMT Mike Trout 3.00 8.00
FCNA Nolan Arenado .75 2.00
FCNM Nomar Mazara .40 1.00
FCNS Noah Syndergaard .50 1.25
FCPG Paul Goldschmidt .60 1.50
FCRB Ryan Braun .50 1.25
FCRC Robinson Cano .50 1.25
FCRH Rhys Hoskins 1.50 4.00
FCSP Salvador Perez .50 1.25
FCWM Wil Myers .40 1.00
FCYM Yadier Molina .60 1.50

2018 Finest Cornerstones Autographs

STATED ODDS 1:314 HOBBY
EXCHANGE DEADLINE 5/31/2020
FCABH Bryce Harper 125.00 300.00
FCAEL Evan Longoria 10.00 25.00
FCAFF Freddie Freeman 25.00 60.00
FCAJV Joey Votto 30.00 80.00
FCAKB Kris Bryant EXCH 125.00 300.00
FCAMM Manny Machado 25.00 60.00
FCAMO Matt Olson 5.00 12.00
FCAMT Mike Trout 250.00 500.00
FCAPG Paul Goldschmidt
FCARB Ryan Braun 10.00 25.00
FCAYM Yadier Molina 50.00 120.00

2018 Finest Cornerstones Autographs Orange Refractors

*ORANGE REF: .6X TO 1.5X BASIC
STATED ODDS 1:815 HOBBY
STATED PRINT RUN 25 SER.#'d SETS
EXCHANGE DEADLINE 5/31/2020
FCAPG Paul Goldschmidt 40.00 100.00

2018 Finest Finest Hour Autographs

STATED ODDS 1:156 HOBBY
EXCHANGE DEADLINE 5/31/2020
FHAABE Adrian Beltre 20.00 50.00
FHAAJ Aaron Judge 75.00 200.00
FHAAP Andy Pettitte 10.00 25.00
FHAAR Amed Rosario 5.00 12.00
FHABH Bryce Harper 150.00 400.00
FHABJ Bo Jackson 40.00 100.00
FHABL Barry Larkin 15.00 40.00
FHACF Clint Frazier 12.00 30.00
FHACK Clayton Kershaw
FHACS Chris Sale 10.00 25.00
FHADJ Derek Jeter 300.00 600.00
FHADS Dominic Smith 4.00 10.00
FHAFL Francisco Lindor 20.00 50.00
FHAFT Frank Thomas 25.00 60.00
FHAGS Gary Sanchez EXCH 15.00 40.00
FHAI Ichiro 150.00 300.00
FHAKB Kris Bryant EXCH 60.00 150.00
FHAMR Mariano Rivera 75.00 200.00
FHAMT Mike Trout 300.00 600.00
FHAOS Ozzie Smith 20.00 50.00
FHAPM Pedro Martinez 30.00 80.00
FHARD Rafael Devers 12.00 30.00
FHARH Rhys Hoskins 20.00 50.00
FHARHE Rickey Henderson
FHAVR Victor Robles 10.00 25.00

2018 Finest Finest Hour Autographs Gold Refractors

*GOLD REF: .5X TO 1.2X BASIC
STATED ODDS 1:407 HOBBY
STATED PRINT RUN 50 SER.#'d SETS
EXCHANGE DEADLINE 5/31/2020

2018 Finest Finest Hour Autographs Orange Refractors

*ORANGE REF: .6X TO 1.5X BASIC
STATED ODDS 1:813 HOBBY
STATED PRINT RUN 25 SER.#'d SETS
EXCHANGE DEADLINE 5/31/2020
FHACK Clayton Kershaw 60.00 150.00
FHARHE Rickey Henderson 40.00 100.00

2018 Finest Firsts

STATED ODDS 1:12 HOBBY
*GOLD/50: 4X TO 10X BASIC
FFAR Amed Rosario .60 1.50
FFAV Alex Verdugo .75 2.00
FFCF Clint Frazier 1.00 2.50
FFDS Dominic Smith .50 1.25
FFNW Nick Williams .60 1.50
FFOA Ozzie Albies 1.50 4.00
FFRD Rafael Devers 1.50 4.00
FFRH Rhys Hoskins 2.00 5.00
FFSO Shohei Ohtani 3.00 8.00
FFVR Victor Robles 1.25 3.00

2018 Finest Firsts Autographs

STATED ODDS 1:204 HOBBY
EXCHANGE DEADLINE 5/31/2020
*BLUE/150: .5X TO 1.2X BASIC
*GREEN/99: .6X TO 1.5X BASIC
*GREEN WAVE/99: .6X TO 1.5X BASIC
*GOLD/50: .75X TO 2X BASIC
*ORANGE/25: 1X TO 2.5X BASIC
*ORNGE WAVE/25: 1X TO 2.5X BASIC
FFAAR Amed Rosario 5.00 12.00
FFAAV Alex Verdugo 6.00 15.00
FFADS Dominic Smith 4.00 10.00
FFAFM Francisco Mejia 8.00 20.00
FFAHB Harrison Bader 6.00 15.00
FFAJC J.P. Crawford 4.00 10.00
FFAJF Jack Flaherty 6.00 15.00
FFAMA Miguel Andujar 15.00 40.00
FFAOA Ozzie Albies 12.00 30.00
FFARD Rafael Devers 254.00 60.00
FFAVR Victor Robles 12.00 30.00

2018 Finest Mystery Redemption Autographs

STATED ODDS 1:1390 HOBBY
EXCHANGE DEADLINE 5/31/2020
1 Shohei Ohtani 200.00 500.00
2 Gleyber Torres 50.00 120.00
3 Ronald Acuna Jr. 200.00 500.00

2018 Finest Sitting Red

STATED ODDS 1:6 HOBBY
*GOLD/50: 2.5X TO 6X BASIC
SRAJ Aaron Judge 1.50 4.00
SRBH Bryce Harper 1.00 2.50
SRCB Cody Bellinger 1.25 3.00
SREE Edwin Encarnacion .60 1.50
SRGS Gary Sanchez .60 1.50
SRGST Giancarlo Stanton .60 1.50
SRJD Josh Donaldson .50 1.25
SRJG Joey Gallo .50 1.25
SRJV Joey Votto .60 1.50
SRKB Kris Bryant .75 2.00
SRKD Khris Davis .60 1.50
SRMM Manny Machado .60 1.50
SRMO Matt Olson .40 1.00
SRMS Miguel Sano .50 1.25
SRMT Mike Trout 3.00 8.00
SRNA Nolan Arenado .75 2.00
SRNC Nelson Cruz .60 1.50
SRPG Paul Goldschmidt .60 1.50
SRRH Rhys Hoskins 1.50 4.00
SRYC Yoenis Cespedes .60 1.50

2018 Finest Sitting Red Autographs

STATED ODDS 1:544 HOBBY
STATED PRINT RUN 50 SER.#'d SETS
EXCHANGE DEADLINE 5/31/2020
SRABH Bryce Harper
SRAEE Edwin Encarnacion 10.00 25.00
SRAJV Joey Votto
SRAKB Kris Bryant EXCH
SRAKD Khris Davis 10.00 25.00
SRAMM Manny Machado
SRAMO Matt Olson 10.00 25.00
SRAMT Mike Trout
SRAPG Paul Goldschmidt
SRAYC Yoenis Cespedes 12.00 30.00

2018 Finest Sitting Red Autographs Orange Refractors

*ORANGE REF: .5X TO 1.2X BASIC
STATED ODDS 1:1089 HOBBY
STATED PRINT RUN 25 SER.#'d SETS
EXCHANGE DEADLINE 5/31/2020
SRAJV Joey Votto 60.00 150.00
SRAKB Kris Bryant EXCH 125.00 300.00
SRAMM Manny Machado 40.00 100.00
SRAPG Paul Goldschmidt 30.00 80.00

2019 Finest

COMP.SET w/o SP's (100) 20.00 50.00
STATED SP ODDS 1:30 HOBBY
1 Mookie Betts .50 1.25
2 Salvador Perez .25 .60
3 Kyle Tucker RC .60 1.50
4 Wil Myers .20 .50
5 Matt Chapman .30 .75
6 Aaron Nola .25 .60
7 Walker Buehler .40 1.00
8 Steven Duggar RC .40 1.00
9 Ryan O'Hearn RC .30 .75
10 Trevor Story .30 .75
11 Buster Posey .40 1.00
12 Albert Pujols .40 1.00
13 Javier Baez .40 1.00
14 Miguel Cabrera .30 .75
15 Marcus Stroman .25 .60
16 Michael Kopech RC .60 1.50
17 Maikel Franco .25 .60
18 Eloy Jimenez RC 1.25 3.00
19 Paul DeJong .30 .75
20 J.D. Martinez .30 .75
21 Paul Goldschmidt .30 .75
22 Ramon Laureano RC .60 1.50
23 Clayton Kershaw .60 1.50
24 Christin Stewart RC .40 1.00
25 Mike Trout 1.50 4.00
26 Joey Votto .30 .75
27 Kolby Allard RC .50 1.25
28 David Peralta .20 .50
29 Brandon Crawford .25 .60
30 Rhys Hoskins .40 1.00
31 Carlos Correa .30 .75
32 Jose Abreu .30 .75
33 Ronald Acuna Jr. 1.50 4.00
34 Robinson Cano .25 .60
35 Miguel Andujar .30 .75
36 Blake Snell .25 .60
37 Chris Davis .20 .50
38 Francisco Lindor .30 .75
39 Corbin Burnes RC .50 1.25
40 Willy Adames .20 .50
41 Ryan Borucki RC .30 .75
42 Christian Yelich .40 1.00
43 Whit Merrifield .30 .75
44 Pete Alonso RC 2.50 6.00
45 Trey Mancini .25 .60
46 DJ Stewart RC .40 1.00
47 Yadier Molina .30 .75
48 Josh Bell .25 .60
49 Brian Anderson .20 .50
50 Jacob deGrom .30 .75
51 Aaron Judge .75 2.00
52 Rowdy Tellez RC .50 1.25
53 Gleyber Torres .60 1.50
54 Dee Gordon .20 .50
55 Jose Berrios .25 .60
56 Luis Urias RC .50 1.25
57 Mitch Haniger .25 .60
58 Scooter Gennett .25 .60
59 Ozzie Albies .30 .75
60 Lucas Giolito .25 .60
61 Starlin Castro .20 .50
62 Joey Gallo .25 .60
63 Charlie Blackmon .30 .75
64 Justus Sheffield RC .50 1.25
65 Anthony Rizzo .50 1.25
66 Tim Anderson .30 .75
67 Juan Soto 1.00 2.50
68 Xander Bogaerts .30 .75
69 Max Kepler .25 .60
70 Ronald Guzman .20 .50
71 Chris Shaw RC .50 1.25
72 Corey Kluber .25 .60
73 Cedric Mullins RC .50 1.25
74 Kris Bryant .40 1.00
75 Nolan Arenado .40 1.00
76 Danny Jansen RC .30 .75
77 Eric Hosmer .25 .60
78 Byron Buxton .25 .60
79 Gregory Polanco .25 .60
80 Zack Greinke .25 .60
81 Trea Turner .25 .60
82 Justin Smoak .20 .50
83 Chance Adams RC .30 .75
84 Cody Bellinger .60 1.50
85 Fernando Tatis Jr. RC 8.00 20.00
86 Jake Bauers RC .50 1.25
87 Kyle Wright RC .50 1.25
88 Touki Toussaint RC .40 1.00
89 Jose Ramirez .25 .60
90 Jose Altuve .25 .60
91 Billy Hamilton .25 .60
92 Alex Bregman .30 .75
93 Matt Olson .20 .50
94 Josh Hader .20 .50
95 Noah Syndergaard .25 .60
96 Nicholas Castellanos .30 .75
97 Max Scherzer .30 .75
98 Dansby Swanson .30 .75
99 Willians Astudillo RC .30 .75
100 Shohei Ohtani .40 1.00
101 Vladimir Guerrero Jr. RC 6.00 15.00
101 Yusei Kikuchi SP RC 3.00 8.00
102 Eddie Rosario SP 2.50 6.00
103 Marcell Ozuna SP 3.00 8.00
104 Kevin Newman SP RC 3.00 8.00
105 Brad Keller SP RC 2.00 5.00
106 Heath Fillmyer SP RC 2.00 5.00
107 Justin Verlander SP 3.00 8.00
108 Freddie Freeman SP 4.00 10.00
109 Stephen Strasburg SP 3.00 8.00
110 Chris Sale SP 3.00 8.00
111 Jonathan Loaisiga SP RC 2.50 6.00
112 Anthony Rendon SP 3.00 8.00
113 Kevin Kramer SP RC 2.50 6.00
114 Andrew Benintendi SP 3.00 8.00
115 Taylor Ward SP RC 2.00 5.00
116 Starling Marte SP 2.50 6.00
117 George Springer SP 2.50 6.00
118 Daniel Ponce de Leon SP RC 3.00 8.00
119 Luis Severino SP 2.50 6.00
120 Dakota Hudson SP RC 2.50 6.00
121 Josh James SP RC 3.00 8.00
122 Khris Davis SP 3.00 8.00
123 Eugenio Suarez SP 2.50 6.00
124 Carlos Carrasco SP 2.00 5.00
125 Giancarlo Stanton SP 3.00 8.00

2019 Finest Blue Refractors

*BLUE REF: 3X TO 8X BASIC
*BLUE REF RC: 2X TO 5X BASIC RC
STATED ODDS 1:30 HOBBY
STATED PRINT RUN 150 SER.#'d SETS
33 Ronald Acuna Jr. 10.00 25.00
44 Pete Alonso 15.00 40.00

2019 Finest Gold Refractors

*GOLD REF: 6X TO 15X BASIC
*GOLD REF RC: 4X TO 10X BASIC RC
*GOLD SP REF RC: .75X TO 2X BASIC RC
1-100 STATED ODDS 1:88 HOBBY
101-125 STATED ODDS 1:350 HOBBY
STATED PRINT RUN 50 SER.#'d SETS
25 Mike Trout 40.00 100.00
33 Ronald Acuna Jr. 20.00 50.00
44 Pete Alonso 30.00 80.00

2019 Finest Green Refractors

*GREEN REF: 4X TO 10X BASIC
*GREEN REF RC: 2.5X TO 6X BASIC RC
STATED ODDS 1:45 HOBBY
STATED PRINT RUN 99 SER.#'d SETS
33 Ronald Acuna Jr. 12.00 30.00
44 Pete Alonso 20.00 50.00

2019 Finest Orange Refractors

*ORANGE REF: 8X TO 20X BASIC
*ORANGE REF RC: 5X TO 12X BASIC RC
STATED ODDS 1:176 HOBBY
STATED PRINT RUN 25 SER.#'d SETS
25 Mike Trout 50.00 120.00
33 Ronald Acuna Jr. 25.00 60.00
44 Pete Alonso 40.00 100.00

2019 Finest Purple Refractors

*PURPLE REF: 2.5X TO 6X BASIC
*PURPLE REF RC: 1.5X TO 4X BASIC RC
STATED ODDS 1:18 HOBBY
STATED PRINT RUN 250 SER.#'d SETS
44 Pete Alonso 12.00 30.00

2019 Finest Refractors

*REF: 1.5X TO 4X BASIC
*REF RC: 1X TO 2.5X BASIC RC
STATED ODDS 1:3 HOBBY

2019 Finest Autographs

STATED ODDS 1:12 HOBBY
EXCHANGE DEADLINE 5/31/2021
FAAB Alex Bregman 12.00 30.00
FAAJ Aaron Judge 75.00 200.00
FAAR Anthony Rizzo 20.00 50.00
FABK Brad Keller 2.50 6.00
FABL Brandon Lowe 6.00 15.00
FABN Brandon Nimmo 3.00 8.00
FABW Bryse Wilson 3.00 8.00
FACA Chance Adams 2.50 6.00
FACB Corbin Burnes 6.00 15.00
FACJ Chipper Jones 50.00 120.00
FACM Cedric Mullins 4.00 10.00
FACS Chris Shaw 4.00 10.00
FACSA Carlos Santana 3.00 8.00
FACST Christin Stewart 4.00 10.00
FACY Christian Yelich 40.00 100.00
FADJ Derek Jeter 150.00 400.00
FADJA Danny Jansen 2.50 6.00
FADL Dawel Lugo 4.00 10.00
FAEJ Eloy Jimenez 30.00 80.00
FAER Eddie Rosario 6.00 15.00
FAFA Francisco Arcia 4.00 10.00
FAFL Francisco Lindor 12.00 30.00
FAFR Franmil Reyes 10.00 25.00
FAFTJ Fernando Tatis Jr. 100.00 250.00
FAGS George Springer 12.00 30.00
FAI Ichiro 125.00 300.00
FAJA Jose Altuve 15.00 40.00
FAJAG Jesus Aguilar 2.50 6.00
FAJB Jake Bauers 4.00 10.00
FAJD Jacob deGrom 20.00 50.00
FAJM Jose Martinez 2.50 6.00
FAJMC Jeff McNeil 15.00 40.00
FAJP Jorge Posada 20.00 50.00
FAJS Juan Soto 50.00 120.00
FAJSH Justus Sheffield 4.00 10.00
FAKA Kolby Allard 4.00 10.00
FAKB Kris Bryant 50.00 120.00
FAKT Kyle Tucker 10.00 25.00
FAKW Kyle Wright 4.00 10.00
FALU Luis Urias 8.00 20.00
FALV Luke Voit 15.00 40.00
FAMA Miguel Andujar 10.00 25.00
FAMC Matt Chapman EXCH 6.00 15.00
FAMH Mitch Haniger 3.00 8.00
FAMK Michael Kopech 8.00 20.00
FAMR Mariano Rivera 75.00 200.00
FAMT Mike Trout 200.00 500.00
FANR Nolan Ryan 50.00 120.00
FAOA Ozzie Albies 12.00 30.00
FAPA Pete Alonso 75.00 200.00
FAPD Paul DeJong 5.00 12.00
FARAJ Ronald Acuna Jr. 50.00 120.00
FARB Ryan Borucki 2.50 6.00
FAROH Ryan O'Hearn 2.50 6.00
FART Rowdy Tellez 4.00 10.00
FASD Steven Duggar 3.00 8.00
FASO Shohei Ohtani 125.00 300.00
FATA Tim Anderson 8.00 20.00
FATHU Torii Hunter 8.00 20.00
FATON Tyler O'Neill 6.00 15.00
FATT Touki Toussaint 3.00 8.00
FAVGJ Vladimir Guerrero Jr. 100.00 250.00
FAWA Willians Astudillo 6.00 15.00
FAYK Yusei Kikuchi EXCH 12.00 30.00
FAYM Yadier Molina 30.00 80.00

2019 Finest Autographs Blue Refractors

*BLUE REF: .5X TO 1.2X BASIC
STATED ODDS 1:87 HOBBY
STATED PRINT RUN 150 SER.#'d SETS
EXCHANGE DEADLINE 5/31/2021

2019 Finest Autographs Gold Refractors

*GOLD REF: .75X TO 2X BASIC
STATED ODDS 1:176 HOBBY
STATED PRINT RUN 50 SER.#'d SETS
EXCHANGE DEADLINE 5/31/2021
FAAB Alex Bregman 25.00 60.00
FAEJ Eloy Jimenez 60.00 150.00
FAFL Francisco Lindor 20.00 50.00
FAJA Jose Altuve 20.00 50.00
FAJP Jorge Posada 25.00 60.00
FAJS Juan Soto 100.00 250.00
FAMA Miguel Andujar 15.00 40.00
FAYM Yadier Molina 40.00 100.00

2019 Finest Autographs Green Refractors

*GREEN REF: .6X TO 1.5X BASIC
STATED ODDS 1:112 HOBBY
STATED PRINT RUN 99 SER.#'d SETS
EXCHANGE DEADLINE 5/31/2021
FAEJ Eloy Jimenez 40.00 100.00

2019 Finest Autographs Green Wave Refractors

*GREEN WAVE REF: .6X TO 1.5X BASIC
STATED ODDS 1:112 HOBBY
STATED PRINT RUN 99 SER.#'d SETS
EXCHANGE DEADLINE 5/31/2021
FAEJ Eloy Jimenez 40.00 100.00

2019 Finest Autographs Orange Refractors

*ORANGE REF: 1X TO 2.5X BASIC

TATED ODDS 1:313 HOBBY
TATED PRINT RUN 25 SER.#'d SETS
XCHANGE DEADLINE 5/31/2021
AAB Alex Bregman 30.00 80.00
AAJ Aaron Judge 125.00 300.00
AAR Anthony Rizzo 30.00 80.00
ACJ Chipper Jones 75.00 200.00
ACY Christian Yelich 60.00 150.00
AEJ Eloy Jimenez 75.00 200.00
AFL Francisco Lindor 25.00 60.00
AGS George Springer 20.00 50.00
AJA Jose Altuve 30.00 80.00
AJP Jorge Posada 30.00 80.00
AJS Juan Soto 125.00 300.00
FAKB Kris Bryant 100.00 250.00
FAMA Miguel Andujar 20.00 50.00
FANR Nolan Ryan 75.00 200.00
FAYM Yadier Molina 50.00 120.00

2019 Finest Autographs Orange Wave Refractors

*ORANGE WAVE REF: 1X TO 2.5X BASIC
STATED ODDS 1:313 HOBBY
STATED PRINT RUN 25 SER.#'d SETS
EXCHANGE DEADLINE 5/31/2021
FAAB Alex Bregman 30.00 80.00
FAAJ Aaron Judge 125.00 300.00
FAAR Anthony Rizzo 30.00 80.00
FACJ Chipper Jones 75.00 200.00
FACY Christian Yelich 60.00 150.00
FAEJ Eloy Jimenez 75.00 200.00
FAFL Francisco Lindor 25.00 60.00
FAGS George Springer 20.00 50.00
FAJA Jose Altuve 30.00 80.00
FAJP Jorge Posada 30.00 80.00
FAJS Juan Soto 125.00 300.00
FAKB Kris Bryant 100.00 250.00
FAMA Miguel Andujar 20.00 50.00
FANR Nolan Ryan 75.00 200.00
FAYM Yadier Molina 50.00 120.00

2019 Finest Blue Chips

STATED ODDS 1:3 HOBBY
*GOLD/50: 2.5X TO 6X BASIC
FBCAB Alex Bregman .60 1.50
FBCABE Andrew Benintendi .60 1.50
FBCAJ Aaron Judge 1.50 4.00
FBCAM Austin Meadows .50 1.25
FBCAR Amed Rosario .50 1.25
FBCBN Brandon Nimmo .50 1.25
FBCBS Blake Snell .50 1.25
FBCFL Francisco Lindor .60 1.50
FBCGS Gary Sanchez .60 1.50
FBCGT Gleyber Torres 1.25 3.00
FBCIH Ian Happ .50 1.25
FBCJA Jesus Aguilar .40 1.00
FBCJH Josh Hader .40 1.00
FBCJM Jose Martinez .40 1.00
FBCJS Juan Soto 2.00 5.00
FBCLGJ Lourdes Gurriel Jr. .50 1.25
FBCLV Luke Voit 1.00 2.50
FBCMA Miguel Andujar .60 1.50
FBCMC Matt Chapman .60 1.50
FBCMH Mitch Haniger .50 1.25
FBCMM Miles Mikolas .60 1.50
FBCMO Matt Olson .40 1.00
FBCOA Ozzie Albies .60 1.50
FBCPD Paul DeJong .60 1.50
FBCRAJ Ronald Acuna Jr. 3.00 8.00
FBCRI Raisel Iglesias .40 1.00
FBCSK Scott Kingery .50 1.25
FBCSO Shohei Ohtani .75 2.00
FBCTM Trey Mancini .50 1.25
FBCWA Willy Adames .40 1.00

2019 Finest Blue Chips Autographs

STATED ODDS 1:284 HOBBY
PRINT RUNS B/WN 10-99 COPIES PER
NO PRICING ON QTY 15 OR LESS
EXCHANGE DEADLINE 5/31/2021
*ORANGE/25: .6X TO 1.5X p/r 99
*ORANGE/25: .5X TO 1.2X p/r 40
*ORANGE/25: .4X TO 1X p/r 25
FBCABN Brandon Nimmo/99 4.00 10.00
FBCABS Blake Snell/99 10.00 25.00
FBCAFL Francisco Lindor/25 40.00 100.00
FBCAGS Gary Sanchez/30 15.00 40.00
FBCAJA Jesus Aguilar/99 3.00 8.00
FBCAJH Josh Hader/99 3.00 8.00
FBCAJM Jose Martinez/99 6.00 15.00
FBCAJS Juan Soto/40 50.00 120.00
FBCALV Luke Voit/99 50.00 120.00
FBCAMA Miguel Andujar/25
FBCAMC Matt Chapman EXCH 10.00 25.00
FBCAMH Mitch Haniger/99 8.00 20.00
FBCAOA Ozzie Albies/99 12.00 30.00
FBCAPD Paul DeJong/99 5.00 12.00
FBCARAJ Ronald Acuna Jr./40 100.00 250.00
FBCARI Raisel Iglesias/99 3.00 8.00
FBCASK Scott Kingery/99 12.00 30.00
FBCAWA Willy Adames/99 3.00 8.00

2019 Finest Career Die Cuts

STATED ODDS 1:48 HOBBY
*GOLD/50: 2X TO 5X BASIC
*RED/5: 30X TO 80X BASIC
FCMR1 Mariano Rivera 1.50 4.00
FCMR2 Mariano Rivera 1.50 4.00
FCMR3 Mariano Rivera 1.50 4.00
FCMR4 Mariano Rivera 1.50 4.00
FCMR5 Mariano Rivera 1.50 4.00
FCMR6 Mariano Rivera 1.50 4.00
FCMR7 Mariano Rivera 1.50 4.00
FCMR8 Mariano Rivera 1.50 4.00
FCMR9 Mariano Rivera 1.50 4.00
FCMR10 Mariano Rivera 1.50 4.00

2019 Finest Career Die Cuts Autographs

STATED ODDS 1:4275 HOBBY
STATED PRINT RUN 10 SER.#'d SETS
EXCHANGE DEADLINE 5/31/2021
FCAMR1 Mariano Rivera 100.00 250.00
FCAMR2 Mariano Rivera 100.00 250.00
FCAMR3 Mariano Rivera 100.00 250.00
FCAMR4 Mariano Rivera 100.00 250.00
FCAMR5 Mariano Rivera 100.00 250.00
FCAMR6 Mariano Rivera 100.00 250.00
FCAMR7 Mariano Rivera 100.00 250.00
FCAMR8 Mariano Rivera 100.00 250.00
FCAMR9 Mariano Rivera 100.00 250.00
FCAMR10 Mariano Rivera 100.00 250.00

2019 Finest Firsts

STATED ODDS 1:12 HOBBY
*GOLD/50: 2.5X TO 6X BASIC
FFCB Corbin Burnes .60 1.50
FFCS Chris Shaw .60 1.50
FFJB Jake Bauers .60 1.50
FFJS Justus Sheffield .60 1.50
FFKT Kyle Tucker .75 2.00
FFLU Luis Urias .60 1.50
FFMK Michael Kopech .75 2.00
FFRB Ryan Borucki .40 1.00
FFRT Rowdy Tellez .60 1.50
FFYK Yusei Kikuchi .60 1.50

2019 Finest Firsts Autographs

STATED ODDS 1:117 HOBBY
EXCHANGE DEADLINE 5/31/2021
*BLUE/150: .5X TO 1.2X BASIC
*GREEN/99: .6X TO 1.5X BASIC
*GREEN WAVE/99: .6X TO 1.5X BASIC
*GOLD/50: .75X TO 2X BASIC
*ORANGE/25: 1X TO 2.5X BASIC
*ORNGE WAVE/25: 1X TO 2.5X BASIC
FFACB Corbin Burnes 5.00 12.00
FFACS Chris Shaw 5.00 12.00
FFADF David Fletcher 10.00 25.00
FFAJB Jake Bauers 5.00 12.00
FFAJM Jeff McNeil 12.00 30.00
FFAJS Justus Sheffield 5.00 12.00
FFAKT Kyle Tucker 20.00 50.00
FFALU Luis Urias 8.00 20.00
FFAMK Michael Kopech 6.00 15.00
FFARB Ryan Borucki 3.00 8.00
FFART Rowdy Tellez 5.00 12.00

2019 Finest Mystery Redemption Autographs

FMA1 Austin Riley 15.00 40.00
FMA2 Nick Senzel 25.00 60.00
FMA3 Vladimir Guerrero Jr 75.00 200.00

2019 Finest Origins Autographs

STATED ODDS 1:128 HOBBY
EXCHANGE DEADLINE 5/31/2021
*GOLD REF/50: .5X TO 1.2X BASIC
*ORANGE REF/25: .6X TO 1.5X BASIC
FOAABE Adrian Beltre 25.00 60.00
FOAAJ Aaron Judge 75.00 200.00
FOAAR Anthony Rizzo 25.00 60.00
FOACJ Chipper Jones 50.00 120.00
FOAEJ Eloy Jimenez 30.00 80.00
FOAFL Francisco Lindor 12.00 30.00
FOAHA Hank Aaron 250.00 500.00
FOAJA Jose Altuve 15.00 40.00
FOAJD Jacob deGrom 12.00 30.00
FOAJP Jorge Posada 20.00 50.00
FOAJS Juan Soto 60.00 150.00
FOAKB Kris Bryant 50.00 120.00
FOAMA Miguel Andujar 10.00 25.00
FOAMT Mike Trout 400.00 800.00
FOANR Nolan Ryan 100.00 250.00
FOAOS Ozzie Smith 15.00 40.00
FOARAJ Ronald Acuna Jr. 60.00 150.00
FOASC Steve Carlton 12.00 30.00
FOASO Shohei Ohtani 100.00 250.00
FOATH Todd Helton 15.00 40.00
FOAYM Yadier Molina 40.00 100.00

2019 Finest Prized Performers

STATED ODDS 1:6 HOBBY
*GOLD/50: 2.5X TO 6X BASIC
PPAR Anthony Rizzo 1.00 2.50
PPBH Bryce Harper 1.00 2.50
PPCK Corey Kluber .50 1.25
PPCKE Clayton Kershaw 1.25 3.00
PPCS Carlos Santana .50 1.25
PPCY Christian Yelich .75 2.00
PPDG Didi Gregorius .50 1.25
PPED Edwin Diaz .50 1.25
PPGS George Springer .50 1.25
PPJA Jose Altuve .50 1.25
PPJD Jacob deGrom .60 1.50
PPJS Justin Smoak .40 1.00
PPJU Justin Upton .50 1.25
PPJV Joey Votto .60 1.50
PPKB Kris Bryant .75 2.00
PPMT Mike Trout 3.00 8.00
PPNS Noah Syndergaard .50 1.25
PPPG Paul Goldschmidt .60 1.50
PPSP Salvador Perez .50 1.25
PPYM Yadier Molina .60 1.50

2019 Finest Prized Performers Autographs

STATED ODDS 1:659 HOBBY
STATED PRINT RUN 50 SER.#'d SETS
EXCHANGE DEADLINE 5/31/2021
*ORANGE/25: .5X TO 1.2X BASIC
PPAAR Anthony Rizzo 25.00 60.00
PPACK Corey Kluber 8.00 20.00
PPACS Carlos Santana 8.00 20.00
PPACY Christian Yelich 40.00 100.00
PPADG Didi Gregorius 10.00 25.00
PPAGS George Springer 8.00 20.00
PPAJA Jose Altuve 8.00 20.00
PPAJD Jacob deGrom 20.00 50.00
PPAJU Justin Upton 12.00 30.00
PPAKB Kris Bryant 50.00 120.00
PPAMT Mike Trout
PPAPG Paul Goldschmidt 10.00 25.00
PPASP Salvador Perez 10.00 25.00
PPAYM Yadier Molina 25.00 60.00

2020 Finest

STATED SP ODDS 1:32 HOBBY
1 Mike Trout 3.00 8.00
2 Ryan Braun .25 .60
3 Bryce Harper .50 1.25
4 Keston Hiura .40 1.00
5 Xander Bogaerts .30 .75
6 Vladimir Guerrero Jr. .60 1.50
7 Bobby Bradley RC .40 1.00
8 Paul Goldschmidt .50 1.20
9 Jose Berrios .25 .60
10 Kris Bryant .40 1.00
11 Lucas Giolito .25 .60
12 Giancarlo Stanton .30 .75
13 Francisco Lindor .30 .75
14 Juan Soto 1.00 2.50
15 Jorge Polanco .25 .60
16 Dylan Cease RC .60 1.50
17 Noah Syndergaard .25 .60
18 Tim Anderson .30 .75
19 Brusdar Graterol RC .50 1.25
20 Trent Grisham RC 1.25 3.00
21 Aristides Aquino RC 2.00 5.00
22 Kyle Schwarber .30 .75
23 Charlie Blackmon .30 .75
24 Rafael Devers .40 1.00
25 Ronald Acuna Jr. 2.00 5.00
26 Trea Turner .25 .60
27 Bo Bichette RC 6.00 15.00
28 Yasmani Grandal .20 .50
29 Max Muncy .25 .60
30 A.J. Puk RC .60 1.50
31 Abraham Toro .25 .60
32 Franmil Reyes .20 .50
33 Matt Chapman .30 .75
34 Manny Machado .30 .75
35 Isan Diaz RC .50 1.25
36 Lorenzo Cain .20 .50
37 Gleyber Torres .60 1.50
38 Rhys Hoskins .40 1.00
39 Jorge Soler .30 .75
40 Shohei Ohtani .40 1.00
41 Kyle Lewis RC 2.50 6.00
42 Eric Hosmer .25 .60
43 Adbert Alzolay RC .40 1.00
44 Sean Murphy RC .50 1.25
45 Nico Hoerner RC 3.00 8.00
46 Will Smith .40 1.00
47 Freddie Freeman .40 1.00
48 Zack Collins RC .40 1.00
49 J.D. Martinez .30 .75
50 Yordan Alvarez RC 5.00 12.00
51 Anthony Rizzo .50 1.25
52 Yu Darvish .30 .75
53 Yuli Gurriel .25 .60
54 Marcus Semien .20 .50
55 Jesus Luzardo RC .60 1.50
56 George Springer .25 .60
57 Eloy Jimenez .60 1.50
58 Cody Bellinger .60 1.50
59 Gerrit Cole .50 1.25
60 Dansby Swanson .30 .75
61 Austin Meadows .25 .60
62 Pete Alonso .75 2.00
63 Trevor Story .30 .75
64 Javier Baez .40 1.00
65 Whit Merrifield .30 .75
66 Anthony Rendon .30 .75
67 Charlie Morton .30 .75
68 Alex Bregman .30 .75
69 Stephen Strasburg .30 .75
70 Aaron Civale RC .50 1.25
71 Justin Verlander .30 .75
72 Sheldon Neuse RC .40 1.00
73 Mauricio Dubon RC .40 1.00
74 Jacob deGrom .30 .75
75 Amed Rosario .25 .60
76 Dustin May RC 1.25 3.00
77 Gavin Lux RC 3.00 8.00
78 Max Scherzer .30 .75
79 Aaron Nola .30 .75
80 Josh Hader .20 .50
81 Justin Turner .25 .60
82 Jose Altuve .25 .60
83 Aaron Judge 1.50 4.00
84 Mookie Betts .60 1.50
85 J.T. Realmuto .30 .75
86 Nolan Arenado .40 1.00
87 Yoan Moncada .30 .75
88 Seth Brown RC .30 .75
89 Clayton Kershaw .60 1.50
90 Zack Greinke .25 .60
91 Masahiro Tanaka .30 .75
92 Michel Baez RC .30 .75
93 Nick Solak RC .50 1.25
94 Walker Buehler .40 1.00
95 Victor Robles .40 1.00
96 James Paxton .25 .60
97 Luis Robert RC 6.00 15.00
98 Mike Clevinger .25 .60
99 Adrian Morejon RC .30 .75
100 Christian Yelich .40 1.00
101 Ozzie Albies SP 8.00 20.00
102 Khris Davis SP 12.00 30.00
103 DJ LeMahieu SP 12.00 30.00
104 Shane Bieber SP 3.00 8.00
105 Tommy Pham SP 6.00 15.00
106 Matt Olson SP 2.00 5.00
107 Paul DeJong SP 3.00 8.00
108 Josh Bell SP 2.50 6.00
109 Eddie Rosario SP 2.50 6.00
110 Gary Sanchez SP 10.00 25.00
111 Jeff McNeil SP 2.50 6.00
112 Trey Mancini SP 3.00 8.00
113 Kirby Yates SP 8.00 20.00
114 Mike Soroka SP 3.00 8.00
115 Michael Conforto SP 2.50 6.00
116 Adalberto Mondesi SP 3.00 8.00
117 Michael Brantley SP 8.00 20.00
118 Hyun-Jin Ryu SP 2.50 6.00
119 Jose Abreu SP 8.00 20.00
120 Didi Gregorius SP 6.00 15.00
121 Patrick Corbin SP 5.00 12.00
122 Carlos Santana SP 5.00 12.00
123 Andrew Benintendi SP 6.00 15.00
124 Jack Flaherty SP 2.50 6.00
125 Ketel Marte SP 2.50 6.00

2020 Finest Autographs

STATED ODDS 1:13 HOBBY
EXCHANGE DEADLINE 5/31/2022
FAAA Aristides Aquino 15.00 40.00
FAAJ Aaron Judge 60.00 150.00
FAAP A.J. Puk EXCH 5.00 12.00
FAAR Austin Riley 12.00 30.00
FAAT Abraham Toro 3.00 8.00
FABH Bryce Harper 125.00 300.00
FABM Brendan McKay 8.00 20.00
FABR Bryan Reynolds 3.00 8.00
FACB Cavan Biggio 12.00 30.00
FACC Carlos Carrasco 2.50 6.00
FACJ Chipper Jones 50.00 120.00
FACK Carter Kieboom 8.00 20.00
FACY Christian Yelich 30.00 80.00
FADC Dylan Cease 5.00 12.00
FADL Domingo Leyba 3.00 8.00
FADM Dustin May 20.00 50.00
FAEJ Eloy Jimenez 12.00 30.00
FAGL Gavin Lux 40.00 100.00
FAID Isan Diaz 10.00 25.00
FAI Ichiro
FAJA Jose Altuve 12.00 30.00
FAJB Jake Bauers 3.00 8.00
FAJL Jesus Luzardo 12.00 30.00
FAJM John Means 2.50 6.00
FAJR Jake Rogers 2.50 6.00
FAJS Juan Soto 60.00 150.00
FAJY Jordan Yamamoto 3.00 8.00
FAKB Kris Bryant 30.00 80.00
FAKH Keston Hiura 10.00 25.00
FALA Logan Allen 4.00 10.00
FAMC Michael Chavis 6.00 15.00
FAMD Mauricio Dubon 3.00 8.00
FAMK Mitch Keller 4.00 10.00
FAMM Mike Mussina 20.00 50.00
FAMT Mike Trout 400.00 800.00
FAMY Mike Yastrzemski 12.00 30.00
FANH Nico Hoerner 12.00 30.00
FANS Nick Solak 6.00 15.00
FAPA Pete Alonso 40.00 100.00
FAPD Paul DeJong 5.00 12.00
FARA Rogelio Armenteros 3.00 8.00
FARD Rafael Devers 12.00 30.00
FARG Robel Garcia 2.50 6.00
FARH Rhys Hoskins 12.00 30.00
FASN Sheldon Neuse 3.00 8.00
FASO Shohei Ohtani 100.00 250.00
FATA Tim Anderson 8.00 20.00
FATD Travis Demeritte 4.00 10.00
FATG Trent Grisham 12.00 30.00
FAWS Will Smith 6.00 15.00
FAZC Zack Collins 5.00 12.00
FAAAL Adbert Alzolay 3.00 8.00
FAAMU Andres Munoz 3.00 8.00
FABBR Bobby Bradley 5.00 12.00
FABBU Brock Burke 2.50 6.00
FAFTJ Fernando Tatis Jr. 100.00 250.00
FAJSO Jorge Soler 4.00 10.00
FAKGJ Ken Griffey Jr. 200.00 500.00
FALGJ Lourdes Gurriel Jr. 6.00 15.00
FAMBE Matt Beaty 5.00 12.00
FAMTH Matt Thaiss 3.00 8.00
FASBR Seth Brown 2.50 6.00
FASSC Shin-Soo Choo 12.00 30.00

2020 Finest Autographs Blue Refractors

*BLUE REF: .5X TO 1.2X BASIC
STATED ODDS 1:83 HOBBY
STATED PRINT RUN 150 SER.#'d SETS
EXCHANGE DEADLINE 5/31/2022
FADC Dylan Cease 10.00 25.00
FAGL Gavin Lux 60.00 150.00

2020 Finest Autographs Gold Refractors

*GOLD REF: .75X TO 2X BASIC
STATED ODDS 1:158 HOBBY
STATED PRINT RUN 50 SER.#'d SETS
EXCHANGE DEADLINE 5/31/2022
FABB Bo Bichette 100.00 250.00
FABM Brendan McKay 20.00 50.00
FADC Dylan Cease 15.00 40.00
FAEJ Eloy Jimenez 25.00 60.00
FAGL Gavin Lux 100.00 250.00
FAMD Mauricio Dubon 20.00 50.00
FAMTH Matt Thaiss 10.00 25.00

2020 Finest Autographs Green Refractors

*GREEN REF: .6X TO 1.5X BASIC
STATED ODDS 1:103 HOBBY
STATED PRINT RUN 99 SER.#'d SETS
EXCHANGE DEADLINE 5/31/2022
FABB Bo Bichette 75.00 200.00
FADC Dylan Cease 12.00 30.00
FAGL Gavin Lux 75.00 200.00
FAMD Mauricio Dubon 15.00 40.00

2020 Finest Autographs Green Wave Refractors

*GREEN WAVE REF: .6X TO 1.5X BASIC
STATED ODDS 1:103 HOBBY
STATED PRINT RUN 99 SER.#'d SETS
EXCHANGE DEADLINE 5/31/2022
FABB Bo Bichette 75.00 200.00
FADC Dylan Cease 12.00 30.00
FAGL Gavin Lux 75.00 200.00
FAMD Mauricio Dubon 15.00 40.00

2020 Finest Autographs Orange Refractors

*ORANGE REF: 1X TO 2.5X BASIC
STATED ODDS 1:301 HOBBY
STATED PRINT RUN 25 SER.#'d SETS
EXCHANGE DEADLINE 5/31/2022
FABB Bo Bichette 200.00 500.00
FABM Brendan McKay 30.00 80.00
FACK Carter Kieboom 30.00 80.00
FADC Dylan Cease 20.00 50.00
FAEJ Eloy Jimenez 30.00 80.00
FAGL Gavin Lux 150.00 400.00
FAMD Mauricio Dubon 40.00 100.00
FARD Rafael Devers 40.00 100.00
FAAMU Andres Munoz 15.00 40.00
FAMBE Matt Beaty 15.00 40.00
FAMTH Matt Thaiss 12.00 30.00
FASSC Shin-Soo Choo 50.00 120.00

2020 Finest Autographs Orange Wave Refractors

*ORANGE WAVE REF: 1X TO 2.5X BASIC
STATED ODDS 1:301 HOBBY
STATED PRINT RUN 25 SER.#'d SETS
EXCHANGE DEADLINE 5/31/2022
FABB Bo Bichette 200.00 500.00
FABM Brendan McKay 30.00 80.00
FACK Carter Kieboom 30.00 80.00
FADC Dylan Cease 20.00 50.00
FAEJ Eloy Jimenez 30.00 80.00
FAGL Gavin Lux 150.00 400.00
FAMD Mauricio Dubon 40.00 100.00
FARD Rafael Devers 40.00 100.00
FAAMU Andres Munoz 15.00 40.00
FAMBE Matt Beaty 15.00 40.00
FAMTH Matt Thaiss 12.00 30.00
FASSC Shin-Soo Choo 50.00 120.00

2020 Finest Duals

STATED ODDS 1:6 HOBBY
FD1 S.Ohtani/M.Trout 5.00 12.00
FD2 M.Chavis/R.Devers .75 2.00
FD3 A.Riley/R.Acuna 2.50 6.00
FD4 S.Bieber/C.Carrasco .60 1.50
FD5 A.Rizzo/K.Bryant 1.00 2.50
FD6 I.Diaz/J.Yamamoto .60 1.50
FD7 J.Soto/C.Kieboom 2.00 5.00
FD8 C.Yelich/K.Hiura .75 2.00
FD9 B.Reynolds/M.Keller .60 1.50
FD10 S.Brown/A.Puk .75 2.00
FD11 W.Merrifield/J.Soler .60 1.50
FD12 B.Rodgers/N.Arenado .75 2.00
FD13 C.Paddack/F.Tatis Jr 2.50 6.00
FD14 T.Anderson/E.Jimenez 1.25 3.00
FD15 M.Muncy/W.Smith .75 2.00
FD16 B.Harper/R.Hoskins 1.00 2.50
FD17 Y.Alvarez/J.Altuve 2.00 5.00
FD18 V.Guerrero Jr/B.Bichette 3.00 8.00
FD19 N.Senzel/A.Aquino .75 2.00
FD20 A.Judge/G.Torres 1.50 4.00

2020 Finest Duals Gold Refractors

*GOLD REF: 3X TO 8X BASIC
STATED ODDS 1:468 HOBBY
STATED PRINT RUN 50 SER.#'d SETS
FD18 V.Guerrero Jr/B.Bichette 30.00 80.00

2020 Finest Duals Autographs

STATED ODDS 1:126 HOBBY
EXCHANGE DEADLINE 5/31/2022
FDAAJ T.Anderson/E.Jimenez 40.00 100.00
FDAAS N.Senzel/A.Aquino 50.00 120.00
FDADY J.Yamamoto/I.Diaz 20.00 50.00
FDARK B.Reynolds/M.Keller 20.00 50.00
FDASM M.Muncy/W.Smith 20.00 50.00
FDATP C.Paddack/F.Tatis Jr EXCH 125.00 300.00
FDASOM J.Soler/W.Merrifield 30.00 80.00

2020 Finest Duals Autographs Orange Refractors

*ORANGE REF/25: 1X TO 2.5X BASIC
STATED ODDS 1:964 HOBBY
STATED PRINT RUN 25 SER.#'d SETS
EXCHANGE DEADLINE 5/31/2022
FDAAA Y.Alvarez/J.Altuve 100.00 250.00
FDAAR A.Riley/R.Acuna 100.00 250.00
FDABR A.Rizzo/K.Bryant 100.00 250.00
FDAGB V.Guerrero Jr/B.Bichette EXCH
FDAHH R.Hoskins/B.Harper 200.00 500.00
FDAJT G.Torres/A.Judge 300.00 600.00
FDASK J.Soto/C.Kieboom 100.00 250.00
FDAYH K.Hiura/C.Yelich 125.00 300.00

2020 Finest Firsts

STATED ODDS 1:12 HOBBY
*GOLD REF: 3X TO 8X BASIC
FF1 Yordan Alvarez 2.00 5.00
FF2 A.J. Puk .75 2.00
FF3 Gavin Lux 4.00 10.00
FF4 Kyle Lewis 3.00 8.00
FF5 Nico Hoerner 1.50 4.00
FF6 Dylan Cease .75 2.00
FF7 Brendan McKay .60 1.50
FF8 Dustin May 1.50 4.00
FF9 Aristides Aquino .75 2.00
FF10 Bo Bichette 3.00 8.00

2020 Finest Firsts Autographs

STATED ODDS 1:117 HOBBY
EXCHANGE DEADLINE 5/31/2022
*BLUE/150: .5X TO 1.2X BASIC
FFAAA Aristides Aquino 20.00 50.00
FFAAT Abraham Toro 4.00 10.00
FFABB Bo Bichette
FFABM Brendan McKay 10.00 25.00
FFADC Dylan Cease 6.00 15.00
FFAGL Gavin Lux 60.00 150.00
FFAJY Jordan Yamamoto 3.00 8.00
FFANH Nico Hoerner 12.00 30.00
FFASB Seth Brown 3.00 8.00
FFAYA Yordan Alvarez 30.00 80.00
FFAAJP A.J. Puk EXCH 10.00 25.00

2020 Finest Firsts Autographs Gold Refractors

*GOLD REF: .75X TO 2X BASIC
STATED ODDS 1:762 HOBBY
STATED PRINT RUN 50 SER.#'d SETS
EXCHANGE DEADLINE 5/31/2022
FFABB Bo Bichette 100.00 250.00

2020 Finest Firsts Autographs Green Refractors

*GREEN REF: .6X TO 1.5X BASIC
STATED ODDS 1:385 HOBBY
STATED PRINT RUN 99 SER.#'d SETS
EXCHANGE DEADLINE 5/31/2022
FFABB Bo Bichette 75.00 200.00

2020 Finest Firsts Autographs Green Wave Refractors

*GREEN WAVE REF: .6X TO 1.5X BASIC
STATED ODDS 1:385 HOBBY
STATED PRINT RUN 99 SER.#'d SETS
EXCHANGE DEADLINE 5/31/2022
FFABB Bo Bichette 75.00 200.00

2020 Finest Firsts Autographs Orange Refractors

*ORANGE REF: 1X TO 2.5X BASIC
STATED ODDS 1:1520 HOBBY
STATED PRINT RUN 25 SER.#'d SETS
EXCHANGE DEADLINE 5/31/2022
FFABB Bo Bichette 125.00 300.00
FFAYA Yordan Alvarez 100.00 250.00

2020 Finest Firsts Autographs Orange Wave Refractors

*ORANGE WAVE REF: 1X TO 2.5X BASIC
STATED ODDS 1:1520 HOBBY
STATED PRINT RUN 25 SER.#'d SETS
EXCHANGE DEADLINE 5/31/2022
FFABB Bo Bichette 125.00 300.00
FFAYA Yordan Alvarez 100.00 250.00

2020 Finest Ichiro Careers

STATED ODDS 1:48 HOBBY
*GOLD REF: 2X TO 5X BASIC
FCI1 Ichiro 5.00 12.00
FCI2 Ichiro 5.00 12.00
FCI3 Ichiro 5.00 12.00
FCI4 Ichiro 5.00 12.00
FCI5 Ichiro 5.00 12.00
FCI6 Ichiro 5.00 12.00
FCI7 Ichiro 5.00 12.00
FCI8 Ichiro 5.00 12.00
FCI9 Ichiro 5.00 12.00
FCI10 Ichiro 5.00 12.00

2020 Finest Moments Autographs

STATED ODDS 1:126 HOBBY
EXCHANGE DEADLINE 5/31/2022
MOMAAA Aristides Aquino 10.00 25.00
MOMABB Bo Bichette EXCH 50.00 120.00
MOMABH Bryce Harper 125.00 300.00
MOMACJ Chipper Jones 50.00 120.00
MOMADO David Ortiz 40.00 100.00
MOMAFT Frank Thomas 30.00 80.00
MOMAHA Hank Aaron 125.00 300.00
MOMAJA Jose Altuve 15.00 40.00
MOMAKB Kris Bryant
MOMAMM Mark McGwire 50.00 120.00
MOMAMT Mike Trout 400.00 800.00
MOMANR Nolan Ryan 60.00 150.00
MOMAOS Ozzie Smith 25.00 60.00
MOMAPA Pete Alonso 40.00 100.00
MOMARH Rhys Hoskins 15.00 40.00
MOMARJ Reggie Jackson 30.00 80.00
MOMASK Sandy Koufax 125.00 300.00
MOMASO Shohei Ohtani 100.00 250.00
MOMAVG Vladimir Guerrero 20.00 50.00
MOMAYA Yordan Alvarez 30.00 80.00
MOMACRJ Cal Ripken Jr. 75.00 200.00
MOMAKGJ Ken Griffey Jr. 200.00 500.00
MOMARAJ Ronald Acuna Jr. 60.00 150.00
MOMAVGJ Vladimir Guerrero Jr. 30.00 80.00

2020 Finest Moments Autographs Gold Refractors

*GOLD REF: .6X TO 1.5X BASIC
STATED ODDS 1:831 HOBBY
STATED PRINT RUN 50 SER.#'d SETS
EXCHANGE DEADLINE 5/31/2022
MOMAKB Kris Bryant 40.00 100.00

2020 Finest Moments Autographs Orange Refractors

*ORANGE REF/25: 1X TO 2.5X BASIC
STATED ODDS 1:1016 HOBBY
STATED PRINT RUN 25 SER.#'d SETS
EXCHANGE DEADLINE 5/31/2022
MOMABB Bo Bichette EXCH 150.00 400.00
MOMAKB Kris Bryant 75.00 200.00
MOMAPA Pete Alonso 125.00 300.00

2020 Finest The Man

STATED ODDS 1:3 HOBBY
FTM1 Mike Trout 6.00 15.00
FTM2 Bryan Reynolds .50 1.25
FTM3 Carter Kieboom .50 1.25
FTM4 Dustin May 1.50 4.00
FTM5 Will Smith .75 2.00
FTM6 Jorge Soler .60 1.50
FTM7 Juan Soto 3.00 8.00
FTM8 Gleyber Torres 2.50 6.00
FTM9 Luis Robert 12.00 30.00
FTM10 Gavin Lux 4.00 10.00
FTM11 Ronald Acuna Jr. 6.00 15.00
FTM12 Yordan Alvarez 2.00 5.00
FTM13 Rhys Hoskins .75 2.00
FTM14 Matt Beaty .50 1.25
FTM15 Austin Riley 2.00 5.00
FTM16 Keston Hiura .75 2.00
FTM17 Bo Bichette 8.00 20.00
FTM18 Brendan McKay .60 1.50
FTM19 Aristides Aquino .75 2.00
FTM20 Fernando Tatis Jr. 5.00 12.00
FTM21 Vladimir Guerrero Jr. 2.50 6.00
FTM22 Francisco Lindor 1.50 4.00
FTM23 Shane Bieber .60 1.50
FTM24 Dylan Cease .75 2.00
FTM25 Cavan Biggio .75 2.00
FTM26 Tim Anderson .60 1.50
FTM27 A.J. Puk .75 2.00
FTM28 Pete Alonso 5.00 12.00
FTM29 Mike Yastrzemski 1.00 2.50
FTM30 Bryce Harper 3.00 8.00

2020 Finest The Man Gold Refractors

*GOLD REF: 3X TO 8X BASIC
STATED ODDS 1:312 HOBBY
STATED PRINT RUN 50 SER.#'d SETS
FTM1 Mike Trout 100.00 250.00
FTM7 Juan Soto 60.00 150.00
FTM8 Gleyber Torres 60.00 150.00
FTM10 Gavin Lux 40.00 100.00
FTM11 Ronald Acuna Jr. 100.00 250.00
FTM13 Rhys Hoskins 15.00 40.00
FTM17 Bo Bichette 60.00 150.00
FTM25 Cavan Biggio 15.00 40.00
FTM30 Bryce Harper 30.00 80.00

2020 Finest The Man Autographs

STATED ODDS 1:325 HOBBY
PRINT RUNS B/WN 10-99 COPIES PER
NO PRICING ON QTY 15 OR LESS
EXCHANGE DEADLINE 5/31/2022
FTMAAA Aristides Aquino 30.00 80.00
FTMAAR Austin Riley 30.00 80.00
FTMABB Bo Bichette EXCH 125.00 300.00
FTMABH Bryce Harper/10
FTMABM Brendan McKay 12.00 30.00
FTMACB Cavan Biggio 25.00 60.00
FTMACK Carter Kieboom 15.00 40.00
FTMADM Dustin May 15.00 40.00
FTMAGL Gavin Lux 60.00 150.00
FTMAGT Gleyber Torres/45 125.00 300.00
FTMAJB Jake Bauers 6.00 15.00
FTMAJS Juan Soto/40 100.00 250.00
FTMAMB Matt Beaty 5.00 12.00
FTMAMT Mike Trout/10
FTMAPA Pete Alonso 60.00 150.00
FTMARH Rhys Hoskins/30 25.00 60.00
FTMATA Tim Anderson 12.00 30.00
FTMAWS Will Smith 12.00 30.00
FTMAYA Yordan Alvarez 75.00 200.00
FTMAFTJ Fernando Tatis Jr. 125.00 300.00

2020 Finest The Man Autographs Orange Refractors

*ORANGE/25: .8X TO 2X p/r 60-99
*ORANGE/25: .5X TO 1.2X p/r 30-50
STATED ODDS 1:964 HOBBY
STATED PRINT RUN 25 SER.#'d SETS
EXCHANGE DEADLINE 5/31/2022
FTMABM Brendan McKay 40.00 100.00
FTMATA Tim Anderson 30.00 80.00

2020 Finest Flashbacks

1 Walker Buehler 1.25 3.00
2 John Means .60 1.50
3 Miguel Cabrera 1.00 2.50
4 Will Smith 1.25 3.00
5 Yu Chang RC 1.50 4.00
6 Charlie Blackmon 1.00 2.50
7 Andrelton Simmons .60 1.50
8 Hunter Harvey 1.00 2.50
9 Whit Merrifield 1.00 2.50
10 Alex Young RC 1.00 2.50
11 Cedric Mullins 1.00 2.50
12 Eloy Jimenez 2.00 5.00
13 Shohei Ohtani 1.25 3.00
14 Zack Collins RC 1.25 3.00
15 Tyler Alexander RC 1.50 4.00
16 Harold Ramirez .60 1.50
17 Bobby Bradley .75 2.00

18 Gavin Lux RC 10.00 25.00
19 Josh Reddick .60 1.50
20 Carlos Correa 1.00 2.50
21 J.D. Martinez 1.00 2.50
22 Eduardo Escobar .60 1.50
23 Jorge Soler 1.00 2.50
24 Austin Riley 1.50 4.00
25 Jake Rogers RC 1.00 2.50
26 Michael Chavis .75 2.00
27 Hunter Dozier .60 1.50
28 Nick Senzel 1.00 2.50
29 Isan Diaz RC 1.50 4.00
30 Bubba Starling RC 2.00 5.00
31 Matt Thaiss RC 1.25 3.00
32 Rafael Devers 1.25 3.00
33 A.J. Minter .75 2.00
34 Robbie Ray .60 1.50
35 Zack Greinke .75 2.00
36 Travis Demeritte RC 1.25 3.00
37 Yuli Gurriel .75 2.00
38 Keston Hiura 1.25 3.00
39 Mookie Betts 2.00 5.00
40 Yordan Alvarez RC 10.00 25.00
41 Logan Allen .60 1.50
42 Javier Baez 1.25 3.00
43 Ozzie Albies 1.00 2.50
44 Tim Anderson 1.00 2.50
45 Willi Castro 1.00 2.50
46 Aaron Civale 1.00 2.50
47 Albert Pujols 1.25 3.00
48 Trevor Bauer 1.00 2.50
49 Jon Lester .75 2.00
50 Corey Seager 1.00 2.50
51 Ender Inciarte .60 1.50
52 David Price .75 2.00
53 Lorenzo Cain .60 1.50
54 Zac Gallen RC 2.50 6.00
55 Trey Mancini 1.00 2.50
56 Jordan Yamamoto RC 1.25 3.00
57 Dylan Cease RC 2.00 5.00
58 Anthony Rendon 1.00 2.50
59 Luis Robert RC 40.00 100.00
60 Sandy Alcantara .60 1.50
61 Kyle Schwarber 1.00 2.50
62 Max Muncy .75 2.00
63 Sam Hilliard RC 1.50 4.00
64 Jose Altuve .75 2.00
65 Mike Soroka 1.00 2.50
66 Robel Garcia RC 1.00 2.50
67 Nico Hoerner RC 4.00 10.00
68 Brandon Woodruff .60 1.50
69 Dustin May RC 4.00 10.00
70 Oscar Mercado RC 1.25 3.00
71 Aristides Aquino RC 2.00 5.00
72 Adalberto Mondesi 1.00 2.50
73 Dwight Smith Jr. .60 1.50
74 Brian Anderson .60 1.50
75 Eugenio Suarez .75 2.00
76 David Dahl .60 1.50
77 Dom Nunez RC 1.25 3.00
78 Dansby Swanson 1.00 2.50
79 Raisel Iglesias .60 1.50
80 Adbert Alzolay RC 1.25 3.00
81 Domingo Leyba RC 1.25 3.00
82 Trevor Story 1.00 2.50
83 Andrew Benintendi 1.00 2.50
84 Aroldis Chapman 1.00 2.50
85 Christian Yelich 1.25 3.00
86 Freddie Freeman 1.25 3.00
87 Carlos Santana .75 2.00
88 Ketel Marte .75 2.00
89 Javier Baez 1.25 3.00
90 Paul DeJong 1.00 2.50
91 Xander Bogaerts 1.00 2.50
92 DJ LeMahieu 1.00 2.50
93 Clayton Kershaw 2.00 5.00
94 Masahiro Tanaka 1.00 2.50
95 Max Scherzer 1.00 2.50
96 Jose Abreu 1.00 2.50
97 Pete Alonso 2.50 6.00
98 Gary Sanchez 1.00 2.50
99 Ronald Acuna Jr. 6.00 15.00
100 Alex Bregman 1.00 2.50
101 Nolan Arenado 1.25 3.00
102 Jacob deGrom 1.00 2.50
103 Justin Verlander 1.00 2.50
104 Willson Contreras 1.00 2.50
105 George Springer .75 2.00
106 Michael Brantley .75 2.00
107 Gleyber Torres 2.00 5.00
108 Cody Bellinger 2.00 5.00
109 J.T. Realmuto 1.00 2.50
110 Jorge Polanco .75 2.00
111 Lucas Giolito .75 2.00
112 Shane Bieber 1.00 2.50
113 Kris Bryant 1.25 3.00
114 Joey Gallo 1.00 2.50
115 Francisco Lindor 1.00 2.50
116 Mike Trout 15.00 40.00
117 Paul Goldschmidt 1.00 2.50
118 Willians Astudillo .60 1.50
119 Tommy Pham .60 1.50
120 Colin Moran .60 1.50
121 Victor Robles 1.25 3.00
122 Jack Flaherty .75 2.00
123 Jeff McNeil .75 2.00
124 Gerrit Cole 1.50 4.00
125 Lourdes Gurriel Jr. .75 2.00
126 Brusdar Graterol RC 1.50 4.00
127 Rougned Odor .75 2.00
128 Shin-Soo Choo .75 2.00
129 Kean Wong RC 1.25 3.00
130 Tyler Glasnow .60 1.50
131 Bryan Reynolds .75 2.00
132 Austin Nola RC 1.50 4.00
133 Kyle Lewis RC 15.00 40.00
134 Marcus Semien .60 1.50
135 Carter Kieboom .75 2.00
136 Josh Bell .75 2.00
137 Brandon Crawford .75 2.00
138 Fernando Tatis Jr. 6.00 15.00
139 Tommy Edman 1.00 2.50
140 Justin Dunn RC 1.25 3.00
141 Stephen Strasburg 1.00 2.50
142 James Paxton .75 2.00
143 Mike Minor .60 1.50
144 Nelson Cruz 1.00 2.50
145 Trent Grisham RC 4.00 10.00
146 A.J. Puk RC 2.00 5.00
147 Blake Snell .75 2.00
148 Max Kepler .75 2.00
149 Yadier Molina 1.00 2.50
150 Adam Haseley 1.00 2.50
151 Jose Berrios .75 2.00
152 Patrick Corbin .75 2.00
153 Jonathan Hernandez RC 1.00 2.50
154 Nick Solak RC 1.50 4.00
155 Trea Turner .75 2.00
156 Buster Posey 1.25 3.00
157 Marcus Stroman .75 2.00
158 Wilson Ramos .60 1.50
159 Seth Brown .60 1.50
160 Andres Munoz RC 1.25 3.00
161 Adam Ottavino .60 1.50
162 Chris Archer .60 1.50
163 Gio Urshela 1.00 2.50
164 Steven Matz .75 2.00
165 Kevin Kiermaier .75 2.00
166 Jeff Samardzija .60 1.50
167 Juan Soto 3.00 8.00
168 Cavan Biggio 1.25 3.00
169 Mike Yastrzemski 1.50 4.00
170 Matt Chapman 1.00 2.50
171 Mitch Keller 1.00 2.50
172 Hyun-Jin Ryu .75 2.00
173 Willy Adames .60 1.50
174 Amed Rosario .75 2.00
175 Rhys Hoskins 1.25 3.00
176 Junior Fernandez RC 1.00 2.50
177 Khris Davis 1.00 2.50
178 Mitch Haniger .75 2.00
179 Ronald Guzman .60 1.50
180 Brendan McKay RC 1.50 4.00
181 Ryan Braun .75 2.00
182 Kevin Newman .75 2.00
183 Kirby Yates .60 1.50
184 Didi Gregorius .75 2.00
185 Josh Hader .60 1.50
186 Bryce Harper 1.50 4.00
187 Jesus Luzardo RC 2.00 5.00
188 Austin Meadows .75 2.00
189 Miles Mikolas .60 1.50
190 Bo Bichette RC 20.00 50.00
191 Manny Machado 1.00 2.50
192 J.D. Davis .60 1.50
193 J.T. Realmuto 1.00 2.50
194 Eddie Rosario .75 2.00
195 Brandon Belt .75 2.00
196 Aaron Judge 2.50 6.00
197 Giancarlo Stanton 1.00 2.50
198 Vladimir Guerrero Jr. 2.00 5.00
199 Evan Longoria .75 2.00

2020 Finest Flashbacks Black Refractors

*BLACK REF.: 5X TO 12X BASIC
*BLACK REF.RC: 3X TO 8X BASIC RC
STATED ODDS 1:36 HOBBY
STATED PRINT RUN 25 SER.#'d SETS
1 Walker Buehler 25.00 60.00
4 Will Smith 25.00 60.00
12 Eloy Jimenez 50.00 120.00
13 Shohei Ohtani 100.00 250.00
18 Gavin Lux 250.00 600.00
32 Rafael Devers 40.00 100.00
38 Keston Hiura 30.00 80.00
39 Mookie Betts 125.00 300.00
40 Yordan Alvarez 400.00 1000.00
42 Javier Baez 50.00 120.00
47 Albert Pujols 125.00 300.00
54 Zac Gallen 40.00 100.00
59 Luis Robert 1000.00 2500.00
67 Nico Hoerner 75.00 200.00
69 Dustin May 50.00 120.00
71 Aristides Aquino 40.00 100.00
83 Andrew Benintendi 20.00 50.00
85 Christian Yelich 60.00 150.00
86 Freddie Freeman 50.00 120.00
89 Javier Baez 60.00 150.00
93 Clayton Kershaw 60.00 150.00
97 Pete Alonso 60.00 150.00
99 Ronald Acuna Jr. 250.00 600.00
101 Nolan Arenado 50.00 120.00
107 Gleyber Torres 150.00 400.00
108 Cody Bellinger 100.00 250.00
113 Kris Bryant 60.00 150.00
116 Mike Trout 1000.00 2500.00
124 Gerrit Cole 50.00 120.00
133 Kyle Lewis 200.00 500.00
138 Fernando Tatis Jr. 150.00 400.00
145 Trent Grisham 50.00 120.00
146 A.J. Puk 30.00 80.00
156 Buster Posey 30.00 80.00
167 Juan Soto 250.00 600.00
168 Cavan Biggio 30.00 80.00
169 Mike Yastrzemski 40.00 100.00
175 Rhys Hoskins 25.00 60.00
180 Brendan McKay 30.00 80.00
186 Bryce Harper 125.00 300.00
187 Jesus Luzardo 50.00 120.00
190 Bo Bichette 400.00 1000.00
196 Aaron Judge 125.00 300.00
198 Vladimir Guerrero Jr. 75.00 200.00

2020 Finest Flashbacks Gold Refractors

*GOLD REF.: 4X TO 10X BASIC
*GOLD REF.RC: 2.5X TO 6X BASIC RC
STATED ODDS 1:18 HOBBY
STATED PRINT RUN 50 SER.#'d SETS
1 Walker Buehler 20.00 50.00
4 Will Smith 20.00 50.00
12 Eloy Jimenez 40.00 100.00
13 Shohei Ohtani 75.00 200.00
18 Gavin Lux 200.00 500.00
32 Rafael Devers 30.00 80.00
38 Keston Hiura 25.00 60.00
39 Mookie Betts 100.00 250.00
40 Yordan Alvarez 300.00 600.00
42 Javier Baez 40.00 100.00
47 Albert Pujols 100.00 250.00
54 Zac Gallen 30.00 80.00
59 Luis Robert 750.00 2000.00
67 Nico Hoerner 60.00 150.00
69 Dustin May 40.00 100.00
71 Aristides Aquino 30.00 80.00
83 Andrew Benintendi 15.00 40.00
85 Christian Yelich 50.00 120.00
86 Freddie Freeman 40.00 100.00
89 Javier Baez 40.00 100.00
93 Clayton Kershaw 50.00 120.00
97 Pete Alonso 50.00 120.00
99 Ronald Acuna Jr. 200.00 500.00
101 Nolan Arenado 40.00 100.00
107 Gleyber Torres 125.00 300.00
108 Cody Bellinger 75.00 200.00
113 Kris Bryant 50.00 120.00
116 Mike Trout 750.00 2000.00
124 Gerrit Cole 40.00 100.00
133 Kyle Lewis 150.00 400.00
138 Fernando Tatis Jr. 125.00 300.00
145 Trent Grisham 40.00 100.00
146 A.J. Puk 25.00 60.00
156 Buster Posey 25.00 60.00
167 Juan Soto 200.00 500.00
168 Cavan Biggio 25.00 60.00
169 Mike Yastrzemski 30.00 80.00
175 Rhys Hoskins 20.00 50.00
180 Brendan McKay 25.00 60.00
186 Bryce Harper 100.00 250.00
187 Jesus Luzardo 40.00 100.00
190 Bo Bichette 300.00 800.00
196 Aaron Judge 100.00 250.00
198 Vladimir Guerrero Jr. 60.00 150.00

2020 Finest Flashbacks Refractors

*REF.: 3X TO 8X BASIC
*REF.RC: 2X TO 5X BASIC RC
STATED ODDS 1:18 HOBBY
1 Walker Buehler 15.00 40.00
4 Will Smith 15.00 40.00
12 Eloy Jimenez 30.00 80.00
13 Shohei Ohtani 60.00 150.00
18 Gavin Lux 150.00 400.00
32 Rafael Devers 25.00 60.00
38 Keston Hiura 20.00 50.00
39 Mookie Betts 75.00 200.00
40 Yordan Alvarez 250.00 500.00
42 Javier Baez 30.00 80.00
47 Albert Pujols 75.00 200.00
54 Zac Gallen 25.00 60.00
59 Luis Robert 600.00 1500.00
67 Nico Hoerner 50.00 120.00
69 Dustin May 30.00 80.00
71 Aristides Aquino 25.00 60.00
83 Andrew Benintendi 12.00 30.00
85 Christian Yelich 40.00 100.00
86 Freddie Freeman 30.00 80.00
89 Javier Baez 30.00 80.00
93 Clayton Kershaw 40.00 100.00
97 Pete Alonso 40.00 100.00
99 Ronald Acuna Jr. 150.00 400.00
101 Nolan Arenado 30.00 80.00
107 Gleyber Torres 100.00 250.00
108 Cody Bellinger 60.00 150.00
113 Kris Bryant 40.00 100.00
116 Mike Trout 600.00 1500.00
124 Gerrit Cole 30.00 80.00
133 Kyle Lewis 125.00 300.00
138 Fernando Tatis Jr. 100.00 250.00
145 Trent Grisham 30.00 80.00
146 A.J. Puk 20.00 50.00
156 Buster Posey 20.00 50.00
167 Juan Soto 150.00 400.00
168 Cavan Biggio 20.00 50.00
169 Mike Yastrzemski 25.00 60.00
175 Rhys Hoskins 15.00 40.00
180 Brendan McKay 20.00 50.00
186 Bryce Harper 75.00 200.00
187 Jesus Luzardo 30.00 80.00
190 Bo Bichette 250.00 600.00
196 Aaron Judge 75.00 200.00
198 Vladimir Guerrero Jr. 50.00 120.00

1959 Fleer Ted Williams

The cards in this 80-card set measure 2 1/2" by 3 1/2". The 1959 Fleer set, with a catalog designation of R418-1, portrays the life of Ted Williams. The wording of the wrapper, "Baseball's Greatest Series," has led to speculation that Fleer contemplated similar sets honoring other baseball immortals, but chose to develop instead the format of the 1960 and 1961 issues. These packs contained either six or eight cards. The packs cost a nickel and were packed 24 to a box which were packed 24 to a case. Card number 68, which was withdrawn early in production, is considered scarce and has even been counterfeited; the fake has a rosy coloration and a cross-hatch pattern visible over the picture area. The card numbering is arranged essentially in chronological order.

COMPLETE SET (80) 900.00 1500.00
WRAPPER (6-CARD) 100.00 125.00
WRAPPER (8-CARD) 100.00 150.00
1 The Early Years 60.00 100.00
2 Ted's Idol Babe Ruth 60.00 100.00
3 Practice Makes Perfect 7.50 15.00
4 Learns Fine Points 7.50 15.00
5 Ted's Fame Spreads 7.50 15.00
6 Ted Turns Pro 12.50 25.00
7 From Mound to Plate 7.50 15.00
8 1937 First Full Season 7.50 15.00
9 Williams 10.00 20.00
E.Collins
10 Gunning as Pastime 7.50 15.00
11 T.Williams 20.00 40.00
J.Foxx
12 Burning Up Minors 10.00 20.00
13 1939 Shows Will Stay 7.50 15.00
14 Outstanding Rookie '39 7.50 15.00
15 Licks Sophomore Jinx 10.00 20.00
16 1941 Greatest Year 7.50 15.00
17 How Ted Hit .400 20.00 40.00
18 1941 All Star Hero 10.00 20.00
19 Ted Wins Triple Crown 7.50 15.00
20 On to Naval Training 7.50 15.00
21 Honors for Williams 7.50 15.00
22 1944 Ted Solos 7.50 15.00
23 Williams Wins Wings 7.50 15.00
24 1945 Sharpshooter# 7.50 15.00
25 1945 Ted Discharged 7.50 15.00
26 Off to Flying Start 7.50 15.00
27 7/9/46 One Man Show 7.50 15.00
28 The Williams Shift 7.50 15.00
29 Ted Hits for Cycle 10.00 20.00
30 Beating Williams Shift 7.50 15.00
31 Sox Lose Series 10.00 20.00
32 Most Valuable Player 7.50 15.00
33 Another Triple Crown 7.50 15.00
34 Runs Scored Record 7.50 15.00
35 Sox Miss Pennant 7.50 15.00
36 Banner Year for Ted 7.50 15.00
37 1949 Sox Miss Again 7.50 15.00
38 1949 Power Rampage 7.50 15.00
39 1950 Great Start 12.50 25.00
40 Ted Crashes into Wall 7.50 15.00
41 1950 Ted Recovers 7.50 15.00
42 Williams 7.50 15.00
Tom Yawkey
43 Double Play Lead 7.50 15.00
44 Back to Marines 7.50 15.00
45 Farewell to Baseball 7.50 15.00
46 Ready for Combat 7.50 15.00
47 Ted Crash Lands Jet 7.50 15.00
48 1953 Ted Returns 10.00 20.00
49 Smash Return 7.50 15.00
50 1954 Spring Injury 12.50 25.00
51 Ted is Patched Up 7.50 15.00
52 1954 Ted's Comeback 10.00 20.00
53 Comeback is Success 7.50 15.00
54 Ted Hooks Big One 7.50 15.00
55 Retirement No Go 10.00 20.00
56 2,000th Hit 8/11/55 7.50 15.00
57 400th Homer 10.00 20.00
58 Williams Hits .388 7.50 15.00
59 Hot September for Ted 7.50 15.00
60 More Records for Ted 7.50 15.00
61 1957 Outfielder Ted 10.00 20.00
62 1958 Sixth Batting Title 7.50 15.00
63 AS Record w 50.00 80.00
Auto
64 Daughter and Daddy 7.50 15.00
65 1958 August 30 10.00 20.00
66 1958 Powerhouse 7.50 15.00
67 Fam.Fishermen w 20.00 40.00
Ned
68 Signs for 1959 SP 400.00 700.00
69 A Future Ted Williams 7.50 15.00
70 T.Williams 20.00 40.00
J.Thorpe
71 Hitting Fundamental 1 7.50 15.00
72 Hitting Fundamental 2 7.50 15.00
73 Hitting Fundamental 3 7.50 15.00
74 Here's How 7.50 15.00
75 Williams' Value to Sox 30.00 50.00
76 On Base Record 7.50 15.00
77 Ted Relaxes 7.50 15.00
78 Honors for Williams 7.50 15.00
79 Where Ted Stands 12.50 25.00
80 Ted's Goals for 1959 20.00 40.00

1960 Fleer

The cards in this 79-card set measure 2 1/2" by 3 1/2". The cards from the 1960 Fleer series of Baseball Greats are sometimes mistaken for 1930s cards by collectors not familiar with this set. The cards each contain a tinted photo of a baseball immortal, and were issued in one series. There are no known scarcities, although a number 80 card (Pepper Martin reverse with Eddie Collins, Joe Tinker or Lefty Grove obverse) exists (this is not considered part of the set). The catalog designation for 1960 Fleer is R418-2. The cards were printed on a 96-card sheet with 17 double prints. These are noted in the checklist below by DP. On the sheet the second Eddie Collins card is typically found in the number 80 position. According to correspondence sent from Fleers at the time -- no card 80 was issued because of contract problems. Some cards have been discovered with wrong backs. The cards were issued in nickel packs which were packed 24 to a box.

COMPLETE SET (79) 250.00 600.00
WRAPPER (5-CENT) 50.00 100.00
1 Napoleon Lajoie DP 12.50 30.00
2 Christy Mathewson 8.00 20.00
3 Babe Ruth 60.00 150.00
4 Carl Hubbell 3.00 8.00
5 Grover C. Alexander 3.00 8.00
6 Walter Johnson DP 4.00 10.00
7 Chief Bender 1.50 4.00
8 Roger Bresnahan 1.50 4.00
9 Mordecai Brown 1.50 4.00
10 Tris Speaker 3.00 8.00
11 Arky Vaughan DP 1.50 4.00
12 Zach Wheat 1.50 4.00
13 George Sisler 1.50 4.00
14 Connie Mack 3.00 8.00
15 Clark Griffith 1.50 4.00
16 Lou Boudreau DP 3.00 8.00
17 Ernie Lombardi 1.50 4.00
18 Heinie Manush 1.50 4.00
19 Marty Marion 2.50 6.00
20 Eddie Collins DP 1.50 4.00
21 Rabbit Maranville DP 1.50 4.00
22 Joe Medwick 1.50 4.00
23 Ed Barrow 1.50 4.00
24 Mickey Cochrane 2.50 6.00
25 Jimmy Collins 1.50 4.00
26 Bob Feller DP 6.00 15.00
27 Luke Appling 2.50 6.00
28 Lou Gehrig 30.00 80.00
29 Gabby Hartnett 1.50 4.00
30 Chuck Klein 1.50 4.00
31 Tony Lazzeri DP 2.50 6.00
32 Al Simmons 1.50 4.00
33 Wilbert Robinson 1.50 4.00
34 Sam Rice 1.50 4.00
35 Herb Pennock 1.50 4.00
36 Mel Ott DP 3.00 8.00
37 Lefty O'Doul 1.50 4.00
38 Johnny Mize 3.00 8.00
39 Edmund (Bing) Miller 1.50 4.00
40 Joe Tinker 1.50 4.00
41 Frank Baker DP 1.50 4.00
42 Ty Cobb 25.00 60.00
43 Paul Derringer 1.50 4.00
44 Cap Anson 1.50 4.00
45 Jim Bottomley 1.50 4.00
46 Eddie Plank DP 1.50 4.00
47 Denton (Cy) Young 12.00 30.00
48 Hack Wilson 2.50 6.00
49 Ed Walsh UER 1.50 4.00
50 Frank Chance 1.50 4.00
51 Dazzy Vance DP 1.50 4.00
52 Bill Terry 2.50 6.00
53 Jimmie Foxx 4.00 10.00
54 Lefty Gomez 3.00 8.00
55 Branch Rickey 1.50 4.00
56 Ray Schalk DP 1.50 4.00
57 Johnny Evers 1.50 4.00
58 Charley Gehringer 2.50 6.00
59 Burleigh Grimes 1.50 4.00
60 Lefty Grove 3.00 8.00
61 Rube Waddell DP 1.50 4.00
62 Honus Wagner 12.00 30.00
63 Red Ruffing 1.50 4.00
64 Kenesaw M. Landis 1.50 4.00
65 Harry Heilmann 1.50 4.00
66 John McGraw DP 1.50 4.00
67 Hughie Jennings 1.50 4.00
68 Hal Newhouser 2.50 6.00
69 Waite Hoyt 1.50 4.00
70 Bobo Newsom 1.50 4.00
71 Earl Averill DP 1.50 4.00
72 Ted Williams 40.00 80.00
73 Warren Giles 2.50 6.00
74 Ford Frick 2.50 6.00
75 Kiki Cuyler 1.50 4.00
76 Paul Waner DP 2.50 6.00
77 Pie Traynor 1.50 4.00
78 Lloyd Waner 1.50 4.00
79 Ralph Kiner 4.00 10.00
80A P.Martin SP/Eddie Collins 1250.00 2500.00
80B P.Martin SP/Lefty Grove 1000.00 2000.00
80C P.Martin SP/Joe Tinker 1000.00 2000.00

1960 Fleer Stickers

This 20-sticker set measures the standard size. The fronts feature a cartoon depicting the title of the card. The pictures are framed with red and black stars and the words "All Star" printed in blue. First names are printed below and are used to place in the blank box of each sticker to represent the person the sticker depicts. The stickers are unnumbered and checklisted below in alphabetical order.

COMPLETE SET (20) 20.00 50.00
COMMON CARD (1-20) 1.25 3.00

1961 Fleer

The cards in this 154-card set measure 2 1/2" by 3 1/2". In 1961, Fleer continued its Baseball Greats format by issuing this series of cards. The set was released in two distinct series, 1-88 and 89-154 (of which the latter is more difficult to obtain). The players within each series are conveniently numbered in alphabetical order. The catalog number for this set is F418-3. In each first series pack Fleer inserted a Major League team decal and a pennant sticker honoring past World Series winners. The cards were issued in nickel packs which were issued 24 to a box.

COMPLETE SET (154) 1000.00 1000.00
COMMON CARD (1-88) 1.25 3.00
COMMON CARD (89-154) 3.00 8.00
WRAPPER (5-CENT) 50.00 100.00
1 Baker/Cobb/Wheat 20.00 50.00
2 Grover C. Alexander 2.50 6.00
3 Nick Altrock 1.25 3.00
4 Cap Anson 1.50 4.00
5 Earl Averill 1.50 4.00
6 Frank Baker 1.50 4.00
7 Dave Bancroft 1.50 4.00
8 Chief Bender 1.50 4.00
9 Jim Bottomley 1.50 4.00
10 Roger Bresnahan 1.50 4.00
11 Mordecai Brown 1.50 4.00
12 Max Carey 1.50 4.00
13 Jack Chesbro 1.50 4.00
14 Ty Cobb 20.00 50.00
15 Mickey Cochrane 1.50 4.00
16 Eddie Collins 2.50 6.00
17 Earle Combs 1.50 4.00
18 Charles Comiskey 1.50 4.00
19 Kiki Cuyler 1.50 4.00
20 Paul Derringer 1.25 3.00
21 Howard Ehmke 1.25 3.00
22 Billy Evans UMP 1.50 4.00
23 Johnny Evers 1.50 4.00
24 Urban Faber 1.50 4.00
25 Bob Feller 5.00 12.00
26 Wes Ferrell 1.25 3.00
27 Lew Fonseca 1.25 3.00
28 Jimmie Foxx 2.50 6.00
29 Ford Frick 1.25 3.00
30 Frankie Frisch 1.50 4.00
31 Lou Gehrig 25.00 60.00
32 Charley Gehringer 1.50 4.00
33 Warren Giles 1.25 3.00
34 Lefty Gomez 1.50 4.00
35 Goose Goslin 1.50 4.00
36 Clark Griffith 1.50 4.00
37 Burleigh Grimes 1.50 4.00
38 Lefty Grove 2.50 6.00
39 Chick Haley 1.50 4.00
40 Jesse Haines 1.50 4.00
41 Gabby Hartnett 1.50 4.00
42 Harry Heilmann 1.50 4.00
43 Rogers Hornsby 2.50 6.00
44 Waite Hoyt 1.50 4.00
45 Carl Hubbell 2.50 6.00
46 Miller Huggins 1.50 4.00
47 Hughie Jennings 1.50 4.00
48 Ban Johnson 1.50 4.00
49 Walter Johnson 5.00 12.00
50 Ralph Kiner 2.50 6.00
51 Chuck Klein 1.50 4.00
52 Johnny Kling 1.25 3.00
53 Kenesaw M. Landis 1.50 4.00
54 Tony Lazzeri 1.50 4.00
55 Ernie Lombardi 1.50 4.00
56 Dolf Luque 1.25 3.00
57 Heinie Manush 1.50 4.00
58 Marty Marion 1.25 3.00
59 Christy Mathewson 5.00 12.00
60 John McGraw 1.50 4.00
61 Joe Medwick 1.50 4.00
62 Edmund (Bing) Miller 1.25 3.00
63 Johnny Mize 1.50 4.00
64 John Mostil 1.25 3.00
65 Art Nehf 1.25 3.00
66 Hal Newhouser 1.50 4.00
67 Bobo Newsom 1.25 3.00
68 Mel Ott 2.50 6.00
69 Allie Reynolds 1.25 3.00
70 Sam Rice 1.50 4.00
71 Eppa Rixey 1.50 4.00
72 Edd Roush 1.50 4.00
73 Schoolboy Rowe 1.25 3.00
74 Red Ruffing 1.50 4.00
75 Babe Ruth 60.00 150.00
76 Joe Sewell 1.50 4.00
77 Al Simmons 1.50 4.00
78 George Sisler 1.50 4.00
79 Tris Speaker 2.50 6.00
80 Fred Toney 1.25 3.00
81 Dazzy Vance 1.50 4.00
82 Hippo Vaughn 1.25 3.00
83 Ed Walsh 1.50 4.00
84 Lloyd Waner 1.50 4.00
85 Paul Waner 1.50 4.00
86 Zack Wheat 1.50 4.00
87 Hack Wilson 1.50 4.00
88 Jimmy Wilson 1.25 3.00
89 G.Sisler/P.Traynor 30.00 60.00
90 Babe Adams 3.00 8.00
91 Dale Alexander 3.00 8.00
92 Jim Bagby 3.00 8.00
93 Ossie Bluege 3.00 8.00
94 Lou Boudreau 4.00 10.00
95 Tommy Bridges 3.00 8.00
96 Donie Bush 3.00 8.00
97 Dolph Camilli 3.00 8.00
98 Frank Chance 4.00 10.00
99 Jimmy Collins 4.00 10.00
100 Stan Coveleskie 4.00 10.00
101 Hugh Critz 3.00 8.00
102 Alvin Crowder 3.00 8.00
103 Joe Dugan 3.00 8.00
104 Bibb Falk 3.00 8.00
105 Rick Ferrell 4.00 10.00
106 Art Fletcher 3.00 8.00
107 Dennis Galehouse 3.00 8.00
108 Chick Galloway 3.00 8.00
109 Mule Haas 3.00 8.00
110 Stan Hack 3.00 8.00
111 Bump Hadley 3.00 8.00
112 Billy Hamilton 4.00 10.00
113 Joe Hauser 3.00 8.00
114 Babe Herman 3.00 8.00
115 Travis Jackson 4.00 10.00
116 Eddie Joost 3.00 8.00
117 Addie Joss 4.00 10.00
118 Joe Judge 3.00 8.00
119 Joe Kuhel 3.00 8.00
120 Napoleon Lajoie 5.00 12.00
121 Dutch Leonard 3.00 8.00
122 Ted Lyons 4.00 10.00
123 Connie Mack 5.00 12.00
124 Rabbit Maranville 4.00 10.00
125 Fred Marberry 3.00 8.00
126 Joe McGinnity 4.00 10.00
127 Oscar Melillo 3.00 8.00
128 Ray Mueller 3.00 8.00
129 Kid Nichols 4.00 10.00
130 Lefty O'Doul 4.00 10.00
131 Bob O'Farrell 3.00 8.00
132 Roger Peckinpaugh 3.00 8.00
133 Herb Pennock 4.00 10.00
134 George Pipgras 3.00 8.00
135 Eddie Plank 4.00 10.00
136 Ray Schalk 4.00 10.00
137 Hal Schumacher 3.00 8.00
138 Luke Sewell 3.00 8.00
139 Bob Shawkey 3.00 8.00
140 Riggs Stephenson 3.00 8.00
141 Billy Sullivan 3.00 8.00
142 Bill Terry 5.00 12.00
143 Joe Tinker 4.00 10.00
144 Pie Traynor 4.00 10.00
145 Hal Trosky 3.00 8.00
146 George Uhle 3.00 8.00
147 Johnny VanderMeer 4.00 10.00
148 Arky Vaughan 4.00 10.00
149 Rube Waddell 4.00 10.00
150 Honus Wagner 20.00 50.00
151 Dixie Walker 3.00 8.00
152 Ted Williams 40.00 100.00
153 Cy Young 15.00 40.00
154 Ross Youngs 15.00 40.00

1963 Fleer

The Fleer set of current baseball players was marketed in 1963 in a gum card-style waxed wrapper package which contained a cherry cookie instead of gum. The five cent packs were packaged 24 to a box. The cards were printed in sheets of 66 with the scarce card of Joe Adcock (number 46) replaced by the unnumbered checklist card for the final press run. The complete set price includes the checklist card. The catalog designation for this set is R418-4. The key Rookie Card in this set is Maury Wills. The set is basically arranged numerically in alphabetical order by teams which are also in alphabetical order.

COMPLETE SET (67) 600.00 1500.00
WRAPPER (5-CENT) 50.00 100.00
1 Steve Barber 10.00 25.00
2 Ron Hansen 6.00 15.00
3 Milt Pappas 8.00 20.00
4 Brooks Robinson 25.00 60.00
5 Willie Mays 60.00 150.00
6 Lou Clinton 6.00 15.00
7 Bill Monbouquette 6.00 15.00
8 Carl Yastrzemski 25.00 60.00
9 Ray Herbert 6.00 15.00
10 Jim Landis 6.00 15.00
11 Dick Donovan 6.00 15.00
12 Tito Francona 6.00 15.00
13 Jerry Kindall 6.00 15.00

14 Frank Lary 8.00 20.00
15 Dick Howser 8.00 20.00
16 Jerry Lumpe 6.00 15.00
17 Norm Siebern 6.00 15.00
18 Don Lee 6.00 15.00
19 Albie Pearson 8.00 20.00
20 Bob Rodgers 8.00 20.00
21 Leon Wagner 6.00 15.00
22 Jim Kaat 10.00 25.00
23 Vic Power 8.00 20.00
24 Rich Rollins 8.00 20.00
25 Bobby Richardson 10.00 25.00
26 Ralph Terry 8.00 20.00
27 Tom Cheney 6.00 15.00
28 Chuck Cottier 6.00 15.00
29 Jimmy Piersall 8.00 20.00
30 Dave Stenhouse 6.00 15.00
31 Glen Hobbie 6.00 15.00
32 Ron Santo 15.00 40.00
33 Gene Freese 6.00 15.00
34 Vada Pinson 10.00 25.00
35 Bob Purkey 6.00 15.00
36 Joe Amalfitano 6.00 15.00
37 Bob Aspromonte 6.00 15.00
38 Dick Farrell 6.00 15.00
39 Al Spangler 6.00 15.00
40 Tommy Davis 8.00 20.00
41 Don Drysdale 20.00 50.00
42 Sandy Koufax 50.00 120.00
43 Maury Wills RC 30.00 80.00
44 Frank Bolling 6.00 15.00
45 Warren Spahn 15.00 40.00
46 Joe Adcock SP 25.00 60.00
47 Roger Craig 8.00 20.00
48 Al Jackson 8.00 20.00
49 Rod Kanehl 8.00 20.00
50 Ruben Amaro 6.00 15.00
51 Johnny Callison 8.00 20.00
52 Clay Dalrymple 6.00 15.00
53 Don Demeter 6.00 15.00
54 Art Mahaffey 6.00 15.00
55 Smoky Burgess 8.00 20.00
56 Roberto Clemente 60.00 150.00
57 Roy Face 8.00 20.00
58 Vern Law 8.00 20.00
59 Bill Mazeroski 8.00 20.00
60 Ken Boyer 10.00 25.00
61 Bob Gibson 25.00 60.00
62 Gene Oliver 6.00 15.00
63 Bill White 8.00 20.00
64 Orlando Cepeda 12.50 30.00
65 Jim Davenport 6.00 15.00
66 Billy O'Dell 10.00 25.00
NNO Checklist SP 250.00 500.00

1981 Fleer

This issue of cards marks Fleer's first modern era entry into the current player baseball card market since 1963. Unopened packs contained 17 cards as well as a piece of gum. Unopened boxes contained 38 packs. As a matter of fact, the boxes actually told the retailer there was extra profit as they were charged as if there were 36 packs in the box. These cards were packed 20 boxes to a case. Cards are grouped in team order and teams are ordered based upon their standings from the 1980 season with the World Series champion Philadelphia Phillies starting off the set. Cards 638-660 feature specials and checklists. The cards of pitchers in this set erroneously show a heading (on the card backs) of "Batting Record" over their career pitching statistics. There were three distinct printings: the two following the primary run were designed to correct numerous errors. The variations caused by these multiple printings are noted in the checklist below (P1, P2, or P3). The Craig Nettles variation was corrected before the end of the first printing and thus is not included in the complete set consideration due to scarcity. The key Rookie Cards in this set are Danny Ainge, Harold Baines, Kirk Gibson, Jeff Reardon, and Fernando Valenzuela, whose first name was erroneously spelled Fernand on the card front.

COMPLETE SET (660) 15.00 40.00
1 Pete Rose 1.25 3.00
2 Larry Bowa .08 .25
3 Manny Trillo .02 .10
4 Bob Boone .08 .25
5A M.Schmidt Batting 1.00 2.50
5B M.Schmidt Portrait P1 1.00 2.50
6 Steve Carlton P1 .20 .50
6B Steve Carlton P2 .60 1.50
6C Steve Carlton P3 .75 2.00
7 Tug McGraw .08 .25
8 Larry Christenson .02 .10
9 Bake McBride .08 .25
10 Greg Luzinski .08 .25
11 Ron Reed .02 .10
12 Dickie Noles .02 .10
13 Keith Moreland RC .02 .10
14 Bob Walk RC .20 .50
15 Lonnie Smith .08 .25
16 Dick Ruthven .02 .10
17 Sparky Lyle .08 .25
18 Greg Gross .02 .10
19 Garry Maddox .02 .10
20 Nino Espinosa .02 .10
21 George Vukovich RC .02 .10
22 John Vukovich .02 .10
23 Ramon Aviles .02 .10
24A Kevin Saucier P1 .02 .10
24B Kevin Saucier P3 .20 .50
25 Randy Lerch .02 .10
26 Del Unser .02 .10
27 Tim McCarver .08 .25
28A George Brett 1.00 2.50
28B George Brett 1.00 2.50
(MVP Third Base
29A Willie Wilson .08 .25
29B Willie Wilson .08 .25
Outfield
30 Paul Splittorff .02 .10
31 Dan Quisenberry .02 .10
32A Amos Otis P1 Batting .08 .25
32B Amos Otis P2 Portrait .08 .25
33 Steve Busby .02 .10
34 U.L. Washington .02 .10
35 Dave Chalk .02 .10
36 Darrell Porter .02 .10
37 Marty Pattin .02 .10
38 Larry Gura .02 .10
39 Renie Martin .02 .10
40 Rich Gale .02 .10
41A Hal McRae P1 .20 .50
41B Hal McRae P2 .08 .25
42 Dennis Leonard .02 .10
43 Willie Aikens .02 .10
44 Frank White .08 .25
45 Clint Hurdle .02 .10
46 John Wathan .02 .10
47 Pete LaCock .02 .10
48 Rance Mulliniks .02 .10
49 Jeff Twitty RC .02 .10
50 Jamie Quirk .02 .10
51 Art Howe .02 .10
52 Ken Forsch .02 .10
53 Vern Ruhle .02 .10
54 Joe Niekro .02 .10
55 Frank LaCorte .02 .10
56 J.R. Richard .08 .25
57 Nolan Ryan 2.00 5.00
58 Enos Cabell .02 .10
59 Cesar Cedeno .08 .25
60 Jose Cruz .08 .25
61 Bill Virdon MG .02 .10
62 Terry Puhl .02 .10
63 Joaquin Andujar .08 .25
64 Alan Ashby .02 .10
65 Joe Sambito .02 .10
66 Denny Walling .02 .10
67 Jeff Leonard .08 .25
68 Luis Pujols .02 .10
69 Bruce Bochy .02 .10
70 Rafael Landestoy .02 .10
71 Dave Smith RC .20 .50
72 Danny Heep RC .02 .10
73 Julio Gonzalez .02 .10
74 Craig Reynolds .02 .10
75 Gary Woods .02 .10
76 Dave Bergman .02 .10
77 Randy Niemann .02 .10
78 Joe Morgan .20 .50
79A Reggie Jackson .40 1.00
79B Reggie Jackson .40 1.00
Mr.Baseball
80 Bucky Dent .08 .25
81 Tommy John .08 .25
82 Luis Tiant .08 .25
83 Rick Cerone .02 .10
84 Dick Howser MG .02 .10
85 Lou Piniella .08 .25
86 Ron Davis .02 .10
87A Craig Nettles P1 2.00 5.00
87B Graig Nettles COR .08 .25
88 Ron Guidry .08 .25
89 Rich Gossage .08 .25
90 Rudy May .02 .10
91 Gaylord Perry .08 .25
92 Eric Soderholm .02 .10
93 Bob Watson .02 .10
94 Bobby Murcer .08 .25
95 Bobby Brown .02 .10
96 Jim Spencer .02 .10
97 Tom Underwood .02 .10
98 Oscar Gamble .02 .10
99 Johnny Oates .08 .25
100 Fred Stanley .02 .10
101 Ruppert Jones .02 .10
102 Dennis Werth RC .02 .10
103 Joe Lefebvre RC .02 .10
104 Brian Doyle .02 .10
105 Aurelio Rodriguez .02 .10
106 Doug Bird .02 .10
107 Mike Griffin RC .05 .15
108 Tim Lollar RC .02 .10
109 Willie Randolph .08 .25
110 Steve Garvey .20 .50
111 Reggie Smith .08 .25
112 Don Sutton .08 .25
113 Burt Hooton .02 .10
114A Dave Lopes P1 .20 .50
114B Dave Lopes P2 .08 .25
115 Dusty Baker .08 .25
116 Tom Lasorda MG .20 .50
117 Bill Russell .08 .25
118 Jerry Reuss UER .08 .25
119 Terry Forster .08 .25
120A Bob Welch .08 .25
120B Bob Welch (Robert) .08 .25
121 Don Stanhouse .02 .10
122 Rick Monday .08 .25
123 Derrel Thomas .02 .10
124 Joe Ferguson .02 .10
125 Rick Sutcliffe .08 .25
126A Ron Cey P1 .08 .25
126B Ron Cey P2 .08 .25
127 Dave Goltz .02 .10
128 Jay Johnstone .02 .10
129 Steve Yeager .08 .25
130 Gary Weiss RC .02 .10
131 Mike Scioscia RC .60 1.50
132 Vic Davalillo .02 .10
133 Doug Rau .02 .10
134 Pepe Frias .02 .10
135 Mickey Hatcher .02 .10
136 Steve Howe RC .20 .50
137 Robert Castillo RC .02 .10
138 Gary Thomasson .02 .10
139 Rudy Law .02 .10
140 Fernando Valenzuela RC 2.50 6.00
141 Manny Mota .08 .25
142 Gary Carter .20 .50
143 Steve Rogers .08 .25
144 Warren Cromartie .02 .10
145 Andre Dawson .20 .50
146 Larry Parrish .02 .10
147 Rowland Office .02 .10
148 Ellis Valentine .02 .10
149 Dick Williams MG .02 .10
150 Bill Gullickson RC .20 .50
151 Elias Sosa .02 .10
152 John Tamargo .02 .10
153 Chris Speier .02 .10
154 Ron LeFlore .08 .25
155 Rodney Scott .02 .10
156 Stan Bahnsen .02 .10
157 Bill Lee .08 .25
158 Fred Norman .02 .10
159 Woodie Fryman .02 .10
160 David Palmer .02 .10
161 Jerry White .02 .10
162 Roberto Ramos RC .02 .10
163 John D'Acquisto .02 .10
164 Tommy Hutton .02 .10
165 Charlie Lea RC .02 .10
166 Scott Sanderson .02 .10
167 Ken Macha .02 .10
168 Tony Bernazard .02 .10
169 Jim Palmer .20 .50
170 Steve Stone .02 .10
171 Mike Flanagan .02 .10
172 Al Bumbry .02 .10
173 Doug DeCinces .02 .10
174 Scott McGregor .02 .10
175 Mark Belanger .02 .10
176 Tim Stoddard .02 .10
177A Rick Dempsey P1 .08 .25
177B Rick Dempsey P2 .02 .10
178 Earl Weaver MG .08 .25
179 Tippy Martinez .02 .10
180 Dennis Martinez .08 .25
181 Sammy Stewart .02 .10
182 Rich Dauer .02 .10
183 Lee May .02 .10
184 Eddie Murray .60 1.50
185 Benny Ayala .02 .10
186 John Lowenstein .02 .10
187 Gary Roenicke .02 .10
188 Ken Singleton .08 .25
189 Dan Graham .02 .10
190 Terry Crowley .02 .10
191 Kiko Garcia .02 .10
192 Dave Ford .02 .10
193 Mark Corey .02 .10
194 Lenn Sakata .02 .10
195 Doug DeCinces .02 .10
196 Johnny Bench .40 1.00
197 Dave Concepcion .08 .25
198 Ray Knight .08 .25
199 Ken Griffey .08 .25
200 Tom Seaver .40 1.00
201 Dave Collins .02 .10
202 George Foster .20 .50
203 Junior Kennedy .02 .10
204 Frank Pastore .02 .10
205 Dan Driessen .02 .10
206 Hector Cruz .02 .10
207 Paul Moskau .02 .10
208 Charlie Leibrandt RC .20 .50
209 Harry Spilman .02 .10
210 Joe Price RC .02 .10
211 Tom Hume .02 .10
212 Joe Nolan RC .02 .10
213 Doug Bair .02 .10
214 Mario Soto .08 .25
215A Bill Bonham P1 .20 .50
215B Bill Bonham P2 .02 .10
216A George Foster SLG .08 .25
216B George Foster P2 .20 .50
217 Paul Householder RC .02 .10
218 Ron Oester .02 .10
219 Sam Mejias .02 .10
220 Sheldon Burnside RC .02 .10
221 Carl Yastrzemski .60 1.50
222 Jim Rice .08 .25
223 Fred Lynn .08 .25
224 Carlton Fisk .20 .50
225 Rick Burleson .02 .10
226 Dennis Eckersley .20 .50
227 Butch Hobson .02 .10
228 Tom Burgmeier .02 .10
229 Garry Hancock .02 .10
230 Don Zimmer MG .02 .10
231 Steve Renko .02 .10
232 Dwight Evans .20 .50
233 Mike Torrez .02 .10
234 Bob Stanley .02 .10
235 Jim Dwyer .02 .10
236 Dave Stapleton RC .02 .10
237 Glenn Hoffman RC .02 .10
238 Jerry Remy .02 .10
239 Dick Drago .02 .10
240 Bill Campbell .02 .10
241 Tony Perez .20 .50
242 Phil Niekro .08 .25
243 Dale Murphy .20 .50
244 Bob Horner .08 .25
245 Jeff Burroughs .08 .25
246 Rick Camp .02 .10
247 Bobby Cox MG .08 .25
248 Bruce Benedict .02 .10
249 Gene Garber .02 .10
250 Jerry Royster .02 .10
251A Gary Matthews P1 .20 .50
251B Gary Matthews P2 .08 .25
252 Chris Chambliss .08 .25
253 Luis Gomez .02 .10
254 Bill Nahorodny .02 .10
255 Doyle Alexander .02 .10
256 Brian Asselstine .02 .10
257 Biff Pocoroba .02 .10
258 Mike Lum .02 .10
259 Charlie Spikes .02 .10
260 Glenn Hubbard .02 .10
261 Tommy Boggs .02 .10
262 Al Hrabosky .08 .25
263 Rick Matula .02 .10
264 Preston Hanna .02 .10
265 Larry Bradford .02 .10
266 Rafael Ramirez RC .02 .10
267 Larry McWilliams .02 .10
268 Rod Carew .20 .50
269 Bobby Grich .08 .25
270 Carney Lansford .08 .25
271 Don Baylor .08 .25
272 Joe Rudi .08 .25
273 Dan Ford .02 .10
274 Jim Fregosi MG .02 .10
275 Dave Frost .02 .10
276 Frank Tanana .08 .25
277 Dickie Thon .02 .10
278 Jason Thompson .02 .10
279 Rick Miller .02 .10
280 Bert Campaneris .08 .25
281 Tom Donohue .02 .10
282 Brian Downing .08 .25
283 Fred Patek .02 .10
284 Bruce Kison .02 .10
285 Dave LaRoche .02 .10
286 Don Aase .02 .10
287 Jim Barr .02 .10
288 Alfredo Martinez RC .02 .10
289 Larry Harlow .02 .10
290 Andy Hassler .02 .10
291 Dave Kingman .08 .25
292 Bill Buckner .08 .25
293 Rick Reuschel .08 .25
294 Bruce Sutter .20 .50
295 Jerry Martin .02 .10
296 Scot Thompson .02 .10
297 Ivan DeJesus .02 .10
298 Steve Dillard .02 .10
299 Dick Tidrow .02 .10
300 Randy Martz RC .02 .10
301 Lenny Randle .02 .10
302 Lynn McGlothen .02 .10
303 Cliff Johnson .02 .10
304 Tim Blackwell .02 .10
305 Dennis Lamp .02 .10
306 Bill Caudill .02 .10
307 Carlos Lezcano RC .02 .10
308 Jim Tracy RC .40 1.00
309 Doug Capilla UER .02 .10
310 Willie Hernandez .02 .10
311 Mike Vail .02 .10
312 Mike Krukow RC .02 .10
313 Barry Foote .02 .10
314 Larry Biittner .02 .10
315 Mike Tyson .02 .10
316 Lee Mazzilli .08 .25
317 John Stearns .02 .10
318 Alex Trevino .02 .10
319 Craig Swan .02 .10
320 Frank Taveras .02 .10
321 Steve Henderson .02 .10
322 Neil Allen .02 .10
323 Mark Bomback RC .02 .10
324 Mike Jorgensen .02 .10
325 Joe Torre MG .08 .25
326 Elliott Maddox .02 .10
327 Pete Falcone .02 .10
328 Ray Burris .02 .10
329 Claudell Washington .02 .10
330 Doug Flynn .02 .10
331 Joel Youngblood .02 .10
332 Bill Almon .02 .10
333 Tom Hausman .02 .10
334 Pat Zachry .02 .10
335 Jeff Reardon RC .40 1.00
336 Wally Backman RC .20 .50
337 Dan Norman .02 .10
338 Jerry Morales .02 .10
339 Ed Farmer .02 .10
340 Bob Molinaro .02 .10
341 Todd Cruz .02 .10
342A Britt Burns P1 .20 .50
342B Britt Burns P2 RC .08 .25
343 Kevin Bell .02 .10
344 Tony LaRussa MG .08 .25
345 Steve Trout .02 .10
346 Harold Baines RC .75 2.00
347 Richard Wortham .02 .10
348 Wayne Nordhagen .02 .10
349 Mike Squires .02 .10
350 Lamar Johnson .02 .10
351 Rickey Henderson SB 1.25 3.00
352 Francisco Barrios .02 .10
353 Thad Bosley .02 .10
354 Chet Lemon .08 .25
355 Bruce Kimm .02 .10
356 Richard Dotson RC .02 .10
357 Jim Morrison .02 .10
358 Mike Proly .08 .25
359 Greg Pryor .02 .10
360 Dave Parker .08 .25
361 Omar Moreno .02 .10
362A Kent Tekulve P1 .02 .10
362B Kent Tekulve P2 .08 .25
363 Willie Stargell .20 .50
364 Phil Garner .08 .25
365 Ed Ott .02 .10
366 Don Robinson .02 .10
367 Chuck Tanner MG .02 .10
368 Jim Rooker .02 .10
369 Dale Berra .02 .10
370 Jim Bibby .02 .10
371 Steve Nicosia .02 .10
372 Mike Easler .02 .10
373 Bill Robinson .02 .10
374 Lee Lacy .02 .10
375 John Candelaria .08 .25
376 Manny Sanguillen .08 .25
377 Rick Rhoden .02 .10
378 Grant Jackson .02 .10
379 Tim Foli .02 .10
380 Rod Scurry RC .02 .10
381 Bill Madlock .08 .25
382A Kurt Bevacqua P1 .08 .25
382B Kurt Bevacqua P2 .02 .10
383 Bert Blyleven .08 .25
384 Eddie Solomon .02 .10
385 Enrique Romo .02 .10
386 John Milner .02 .10
387 Mike Hargrove .02 .10
388 Jorge Orta .02 .10
389 Toby Harrah .08 .25
390 Tom Veryzer .02 .10
391 Miguel Dilone .02 .10
392 Dan Spillner .02 .10
393 Jack Brohamer .02 .10
394 Wayne Garland .02 .10
395 Sid Monge .02 .10
396 Rick Waits .02 .10
397 Joe Charboneau RC .40 1.00
398 Gary Alexander .02 .10
399 Jerry Dybzinski RC .02 .10
400 Mike Stanton RC .02 .10
401 Mike Paxton .02 .10
402 Gary Gray RC .02 .10
403 Rick Manning .02 .10
404 Bo Diaz .02 .10
405 Ron Hassey .02 .10
406 Ross Grimsley .02 .10
407 Victor Cruz .02 .10
408 Len Barker .08 .25
409 Bob Bailor .02 .10
410 Otto Velez .02 .10
411 Ernie Whitt .02 .10
412 Jim Clancy .02 .10
413 Barry Bonnell .02 .10
414 Dave Stieb .08 .25
415 Damaso Garcia RC .02 .10
416 John Mayberry .02 .10
417 Roy Howell .02 .10
418 Danny Ainge RC 1.25 3.00
419A Jesse Jefferson P1 .02 .10
419B Jesse Jefferson P3 .20 .50
420 Joey McLaughlin .02 .10
421 Lloyd Moseby RC .20 .50
422 Alvis Woods .02 .10
423 Garth Iorg .02 .10
424 Doug Ault .02 .10
425 Ken Schrom RC .02 .10
426 Mike Willis .02 .10
427 Steve Braun .02 .10
428 Bob Davis .02 .10
429 Jerry Garvin .02 .10
430 Alfredo Griffin .02 .10
431 Bob Mattick MG RC .02 .10
432 Vida Blue .08 .25
433 Jack Clark .08 .25
434 Willie McCovey .20 .50
435 Mike Ivie .02 .10
436A Darrel Evans P1 ERR .20 .50
436B Darrell Evans P2 COR .20 .50
437 Terry Whitfield .02 .10
438 Rennie Stennett .02 .10
439 John Montefusco .02 .10
440 Jim Wohlford .02 .10
441 Bill North .02 .10
442 Milt May .02 .10
443 Max Venable RC .02 .10
444 Ed Whitson .02 .10
445 Al Holland RC .02 .10
446 Randy Moffitt .02 .10
447 Bob Knepper .02 .10
448 Gary Lavelle .02 .10
449 Greg Minton .02 .10
450 Johnnie LeMaster .02 .10
451 Larry Herndon .02 .10
452 Rich Murray RC .02 .10
453 Joe Pettini RC .02 .10
454 Allen Ripley .02 .10
455 Dennis Littlejohn .02 .10
456 Tom Griffin .02 .10
457 Alan Hargesheimer RC .02 .10
458 Joe Strain .02 .10
459 Steve Kemp .02 .10
460 Sparky Anderson MG .08 .25
461 Alan Trammell .20 .50
462 Mark Fidrych .08 .25
463 Lou Whitaker .20 .50
464 Dave Rozema .02 .10
465 Milt Wilcox .02 .10
466 Champ Summers .02 .10
467 Lance Parrish .08 .25
468 Dan Petry .02 .10
469 Pat Underwood .02 .10
470 Rick Peters RC .02 .10
471 Al Cowens .02 .10
472 John Wockenfuss .02 .10
473 Tom Brookens .02 .10
474 Richie Hebner .02 .10
475 Jack Morris .20 .50
476 Jim Lentine RC .02 .10
477 Bruce Robbins .02 .10
478 Mark Wagner .02 .10
479 Tim Corcoran .02 .10
480A Stan Papi P1 .08 .25
480B Stan Papi P2 .02 .10
481 Kirk Gibson RC 2.00 5.00
482 Dan Schatzeder .02 .10
483 Amos Otis .08 .25
484 Dave Winfield .20 .50
485 Rollie Fingers .08 .25
486 Gene Richards .02 .10
487 Randy Jones .02 .10
488 Ozzie Smith 1.25 3.00
489 Gene Tenace .08 .25
490 Bill Fahey .02 .10
491 John Curtis .02 .10
492 Dave Cash .02 .10
493A Tim Flannery P1 .08 .25
493B Tim Flannery P2 .02 .10
494 Jerry Mumphrey .02 .10
495 Bob Shirley .02 .10
496 Steve Mura .02 .10
497 Eric Rasmussen .02 .10
498 Broderick Perkins .02 .10
499 Barry Evans RC .02 .10
500 Chuck Baker .02 .10
501 Luis Salazar RC .20 .50
502 Gary Lucas RC .02 .10
503 Mike Armstrong RC .02 .10
504 Jerry Turner .02 .10
505 Dennis Kinney RC .02 .10
506 Willie Montanez UER .02 .10
507 Gorman Thomas .08 .25
508 Ben Oglivie .08 .25
509 Larry Hisle .02 .10
510 Sal Bando .08 .25
511 Robin Yount .60 1.50
512 Mike Caldwell .02 .10
513 Sixto Lezcano .02 .10
514A Bill Travers P1 ERR .08 .25
514B Bill Travers P2 COR .02 .10
515 Paul Molitor .40 1.00
516 Moose Haas .02 .10
517 Bill Castro .02 .10
518 Jim Slaton .02 .10
519 Lary Sorensen .02 .10
520 Bob McClure .02 .10
521 Charlie Moore .02 .10
522 Jim Gantner .08 .25
523 Reggie Cleveland .02 .10
524 Don Money .02 .10
525 Bill Travers .02 .10
526 Buck Martinez .02 .10
527 Dick Davis .02 .10
528 Ted Simmons .08 .25
529 Garry Templeton .08 .25
530 Ken Reitz .02 .10
531 Tony Scott .02 .10
532 Ken Oberkfell .02 .10
533 Bob Sykes .02 .10
534 Keith Smith .02 .10
535 John Littlefield RC .02 .10
536 Jim Kaat .08 .25
537 Bob Forsch .02 .10
538 Mike Phillips .02 .10
539 Terry Landrum RC .02 .10
540 Leon Durham RC .20 .50
541 Terry Kennedy .02 .10
542 George Hendrick .08 .25
543 Dane Iorg .02 .10
544 Mark Littell .02 .10
545 Keith Hernandez .08 .25
546 Silvio Martinez .02 .10
547A Don Hood P1 ERR .08 .25
547B Don Hood P2 COR .02 .10
548 Bobby Bonds .08 .25
549 Mike Ramsey RC .05 .15
550 Tom Herr .02 .10
551 Roy Smalley .02 .10
552 Jerry Koosman .08 .25
553 Ken Landreaux .02 .10
554 John Castino .02 .10
555 Doug Corbett RC .02 .10
556 Bombo Rivera .02 .10
557 Ron Jackson .02 .10
558 Butch Wynegar .02 .10
559 Hosken Powell .02 .10
560 Pete Redfern .02 .10
561 Roger Erickson .02 .10
562 Glenn Adams .02 .10
563 Rick Sofield .02 .10
564 Geoff Zahn .02 .10
565 Pete Mackanin .02 .10
566 Mike Cubbage .02 .10
567 Darrell Jackson .02 .10
568 Dave Edwards .02 .10
569 Rob Wilfong .02 .10
570 Sal Butera RC .02 .10
571 Jose Morales .02 .10
572 Rick Langford .02 .10
573 Mike Norris .02 .10
574 Rickey Henderson 2.50 6.00
575 Tony Armas .08 .25
576 Dave Revering .02 .10
577 Jeff Newman .02 .10
578 Bob Lacey .02 .10
579 Brian Kingman .02 .10
580 Mitchell Page .02 .10
581 Billy Martin MG .20 .50
582 Rob Picciolo .02 .10
583 Mike Heath .02 .10
584 Mickey Klutts .02 .10
585 Orlando Gonzalez .02 .10
586 Mike Davis RC .20 .50
587 Wayne Gross .02 .10
588 Matt Keough .02 .10
589 Steve McCatty .02 .10
590 Dwayne Murphy .02 .10
591 Mario Guerrero .02 .10
592 Dave McKay RC .02 .10
593 Jim Essian .02 .10
594 Dave Heaverlo .02 .10
595 Maury Wills MG .08 .25
596 Juan Beniquez .02 .10
597 Rodney Craig .02 .10
598 Jim Anderson .02 .10
599 Floyd Bannister .02 .10
600 Bruce Bochte .02 .10
601 Julio Cruz .02 .10
602 Ted Cox .02 .10
603 Dan Meyer .02 .10
604 Larry Cox .02 .10
605 Bill Stein .02 .10
606 Steve Garvey .20 .50
607 Dave Roberts .02 .10
608 Leon Roberts .02 .10
609 Reggie Walton RC .02 .10
610 Dave Edler RC .02 .10
611 Larry Milbourne .02 .10
612 Kim Allen RC .02 .10
613 Mario Mendoza .02 .10
614 Tom Paciorek .02 .10
615 Glenn Abbott .02 .10
616 Joe Simpson .02 .10
617 Mickey Rivers .02 .10
618 Jim Kern .02 .10
619 Jim Sundberg .08 .25
620 Richie Zisk .02 .10
621 Jon Matlack .02 .10
622 Fergie Jenkins .08 .25
623 Pat Corrales MG .02 .10
624 Ed Figueroa .02 .10
625 Buddy Bell .08 .25
626 Al Oliver .08 .25
627 Doc Medich .02 .10
628 Bump Wills .02 .10
629 Rusty Staub .08 .25
630 Pat Putnam .02 .10
631 John Grubb .02 .10
632 Danny Darwin .02 .10
633 Ken Clay .02 .10
634 Jim Norris .02 .10
635 John Butcher RC .02 .10
636 Dave Roberts .02 .10
637 Billy Sample .02 .10
638 Carl Yastrzemski .60 1.50
639 Cecil Cooper .08 .25
640 M.Schmidt Portrait P2 1.00 2.50
641A CL: Phils/Royals P1 .08 .25
641B CL: Phils/Royals P2 .08 .25
642 CL: Astros .02 .10
Yankees
643 CL: Expos .02 .10
Dodgers
644A CL: Reds/Orioles P1 .08 .25
644B CL: Reds/Orioles P2 .08 .25
645A Rose/Bowa/Schmidt .60 1.50
645B Rose/Bowa/Schmidt 1.00 2.50
646 CL: Braves .02 .10
Red Sox
647 CL: Cubs .02 .10
Angels
648 CL: Mets .02 .10
White Sox
649 CL: Indians .02 .10
Pirates
650 Reggie Jackson Mr. BB .40 1.00
651 CL: Giants .02 .10
Blue Jays
652A CL: Tigers/Padres P1 .08 .25
652B CL: Tigers/Padres P2 .08 .25
653 Willie Wilson Most Hits .08 .25
654A CL:Brewers/Cards P1 .08 .25
654B CL:Brewers/Cards P2 .08 .25
655 George Brett .390 Avg. 1.00 2.50
656 CL: Twins/Oakland A's .08 .25
657 T.McGraw Saver P2 .08 .25
658 CL: Rangers .02 .10
Mariners
659A Checklist P1 .02 .10
659B Checklist P2 .02 .10
660A S.Carlton Gold Arm P1 .20 .50
660B S.Carlton Golden Arm .75 2.00

1981 Fleer Star Stickers

The stickers in this 128-sticker standard-size set were distributed in wax packs. The 1981 Fleer Baseball Star Stickers consist of numbered cards with peelable, full-color sticker fronts and three unnumbered checklists. The backs of the numbered player cards are the same as the 1981 Fleer regular issue cards except for the numbers, while the checklist cards (cards 126-128 below) have sticker fronts of Jackson (1-42), Brett (43-83), and Schmidt (84-125).

COMPLETE SET (128)	10.00	25.00
1 Steve Garvey	.20	.50
2 Ron LeFlore	.02	.10
3 Ron Cey	.05	.15
4 Dave Revering	.02	.10
5 Tony Armas	.02	.10
6 Mike Norris	.02	.10
7 Steve Kemp	.02	.10
8 Bruce Bochte	.02	.10
9 Mike Schmidt	1.00	2.50
10 Scott McGregor	.02	.10
11 Buddy Bell	.05	.15
12 Carney Lansford	.05	.15
13 Carl Yastrzemski	.40	1.00
14 Ben Oglivie	.02	.10
15 Willie Stargell	.20	.50
16 Cecil Cooper	.05	.15
17 Gene Richards	.02	.10
18 Jim Kern	.02	.10
19 Jerry Koosman	.05	.15
20 Larry Bowa	.05	.15
21 Kent Tekulve	.05	.15
22 Dan Driessen	.02	.10
23 Phil Niekro	.20	.50
24 Dan Quisenberry	.05	.15
25 Dave Winfield	.40	1.00
26 Dave Parker	.05	.15
27 Rick Langford	.02	.10
28 Amos Otis	.05	.15
29 Bill Buckner	.05	.15
30 Al Bumbry	.02	.10
31 Bake McBride	.02	.10
32 Mickey Rivers	.05	.15
33 Rick Burleson	.02	.10
34 Dennis Eckersley	.20	.50
35 Cesar Cedeno	.05	.15
36 Enos Cabell	.02	.10
37 Johnny Bench	.40	1.00
38 Robin Yount	.40	1.00
39 Mark Belanger	.05	.15
40 Rod Carew	.30	.75
41 George Foster	.05	.15
42 Lee Mazzilli	.02	.10
43 Triple Threat: Pete Rose Larry Bowa Mike Schmid	.75	2.00
44 J.R. Richard	.02	.10
45 Lou Piniella	.05	.15
46 Ken Landreaux	.02	.10
47 Rollie Fingers	.20	.50
48 Joaquin Andujar	.05	.15
49 Tom Seaver	.40	1.00
50 Bobby Grich	.05	.15
51 Jon Matlack	.02	.10
52 Jack Clark	.05	.15
53 Jim Rice	.05	.15
54 Rickey Henderson	1.50	4.00
55 Roy Smalley	.02	.10
56 Mike Flanagan	.02	.10
57 Steve Rogers	.02	.10
58 Carlton Fisk	.60	1.50
59 Don Sutton	.20	.50
60 Ken Griffey	.05	.15
61 Burt Hooton	.02	.10
62 Dusty Baker	.05	.15
63 Vida Blue	.05	.15
64 Al Oliver	.05	.15
65 Jim Bibby	.02	.10
66 Tony Perez	.10	.30
67 Davey Lopes	.05	.15
68 Bill Russell	.05	.15
69 Larry Parrish	.02	.10
70 Garry Maddox	.02	.10
71 Phil Garner	.05	.15
72 Graig Nettles	.07	.20
73 Gary Carter	.30	.75
74 Pete Rose	.60	1.50
75 Greg Luzinski	.05	.15
76 Ron Guidry	.05	.15
77 Gorman Thomas	.02	.10
78 Jose Cruz	.05	.15
79 Bob Boone	.05	.15
80 Bruce Sutter	.05	.15
81 Chris Chambliss	.05	.15
82 Paul Molitor	.75	2.00
83 Tug McGraw	.05	.15
84 Ferguson Jenkins	.10	.30
85 Steve Carlton	.30	.75
86 Miguel Dilone	.02	.10
87 Reggie Smith	.05	.15
88 Rick Cerone	.02	.10
89 Alan Trammell	.20	.50
90 Doug DeCinces	.02	.10
91 Sparky Lyle	.05	.15
92 Warren Cromartie	.02	.10
93 Rick Reuschel	.05	.15
94 Larry Hisle	.02	.10
95 Paul Splittorff	.02	.10
96 Manny Trillo	.02	.10
97 Frank White	.05	.15
98 Fred Lynn	.05	.15
99 Bob Horner	.02	.10
100 Omar Moreno	.02	.10
101 Dave Concepcion	.05	.15
102 Larry Gura	.02	.10
103 Ken Singleton	.05	.15
104 Steve Stone	.02	.10
105 Richie Zisk	.05	.15
106 Willie Wilson	.05	.15
107 Willie Randolph	.05	.15
108 Nolan Ryan	3.00	8.00
109 Joe Morgan	.30	.75
110 Bucky Dent	.05	.15
111 Dave Kingman	.07	.20
112 John Castino	.02	.10
113 Joe Rudi	.02	.10
114 Ed Farmer	.02	.10
115 Reggie Jackson	.40	1.00
116 George Brett	1.25	3.00
117 Eddie Murray	.75	2.00
118 Rich Gossage	.20	.50
119 Dale Murphy	.30	.75
120 Ted Simmons	.05	.15
121 Tommy John	.08	.25
122 Don Baylor	.07	.20
123 Andre Dawson	.30	.75
124 Jim Palmer	.30	.75
125 Garry Templeton	.02	.10
126 Reggie Jackson CL 1 Unnumbered	.20	.50
127 George Brett CL 2 Unnumbered	.60	1.50
128 Mike Schmidt CL3 Unnumbered	.40	1.00

1982 Fleer

The 1982 Fleer set contains 660-card standard-size cards, of which are grouped in team order based upon standings from the previous season. Cards numbered 628 through 646 are special cards highlighting some of the stars and leaders of the 1981 season. The last 14 cards in the set (647-660) are checklist cards. The backs feature player statistics and a full-color team logo in the upper right-hand corner of each card. The complete set price below does not include any of the more valuable variation cards listed. Fleer was not allowed to insert bubble gum or other confectionary products into these packs; therefore logo stickers were included in these 15-card packs. Those 15-card packs with an SRP of 30 cents were packed 36 packs to a box and 20 boxes to a case. Notable Rookie Cards in this set include Cal Ripken Jr., Lee Smith, and Dave Stewart.

COMPLETE SET (660)	20.00	50.00
1 Dusty Baker	.07	.20
2 Robert Castillo	.02	.10
3 Ron Cey	.07	.20
4 Terry Forster	.07	.20
5 Steve Garvey	.07	.20
6 Dave Goltz	.02	.10
7 Pedro Guerrero	.07	.20
8 Burt Hooton	.02	.10
9 Steve Howe	.02	.10
10 Jay Johnstone	.02	.10
11 Ken Landreaux	.02	.10
12 Dave Lopes	.07	.20
13 Mike A. Marshall RC	.20	.50
14 Bobby Mitchell	.02	.10
15 Rick Monday	.07	.20
16 Tom Niedenfuer RC	.20	.50
17 Ted Power RC	.05	.15
18 Jerry Reuss UER	.02	.10
19 Ron Roenicke	.02	.10
20 Bill Russell	.07	.20
21 Steve Sax RC	.40	1.00
22 Mike Scioscia	.07	.20
23 Reggie Smith	.07	.20
24 Dave Stewart RC	.60	1.50
25 Rick Sutcliffe	.07	.20
26 Derrel Thomas	.02	.10
27 Fernando Valenzuela	.30	.75
28 Bob Welch	.07	.20
29 Steve Yeager	.07	.20
30 Bobby Brown	.02	.10
31 Rick Cerone	.02	.10
32 Ron Davis	.02	.10
33 Bucky Dent	.07	.20
34 Barry Foote	.02	.10
35 George Frazier	.02	.10
36 Oscar Gamble	.02	.10
37 Rich Gossage	.07	.20
38 Ron Guidry	.07	.20
39 Reggie Jackson	.15	.40
40 Tommy John	.07	.20
41 Rudy May	.02	.10
42 Larry Milbourne	.02	.10
43 Jerry Mumphrey	.02	.10
44 Bobby Murcer	.07	.20
45 Gene Nelson	.02	.10
46 Graig Nettles	.07	.20
47 Johnny Oates	.07	.20
48 Lou Piniella	.07	.20
49 Willie Randolph	.07	.20
50 Rick Reuschel	.07	.20
51 Dave Revering	.02	.10
52 Dave Righetti RC	.60	1.50
53 Aurelio Rodriguez	.02	.10
54 Bob Watson	.02	.10
55 Dennis Werth	.02	.10
56 Dave Winfield	.07	.20
57 Johnny Bench	.30	.75
58 Bruce Berenyi	.02	.10
59 Larry Biittner	.02	.10
60 Scott Brown	.02	.10
61 Dave Collins	.02	.10
62 Geoff Combe	.02	.10
63 Dave Concepcion	.07	.20
64 Dan Driessen	.02	.10
65 Joe Edelen	.02	.10
66 George Foster	.07	.20
67 Ken Griffey	.07	.20
68 Paul Householder	.02	.10
69 Tom Hume	.02	.10
70 Junior Kennedy	.02	.10
71 Ray Knight	.07	.20
72 Mike LaCoss	.02	.10
73 Rafael Landestoy	.02	.10
74 Charlie Leibrandt	.02	.10
75 Sam Mejias	.02	.10
76 Paul Moskau	.02	.10
77 Joe Nolan	.02	.10
78 Mike O'Berry	.02	.10
79 Ron Oester	.02	.10
80 Frank Pastore	.02	.10
81 Joe Price	.02	.10
82 Tom Seaver	.30	.75
83 Mario Soto	.07	.20
84 Mike Vail	.02	.10
85 Tony Armas	.07	.20
86 Shooty Babitt	.02	.10
87 Dave Beard	.02	.10
88 Rick Bosetti	.02	.10
89 Keith Drumwright	.02	.10
90 Wayne Gross	.02	.10
91 Mike Heath	.02	.10
92 Rickey Henderson	1.00	2.50
93 Cliff Johnson	.02	.10
94 Jeff Jones	.02	.10
95 Matt Keough	.02	.10
96 Brian Kingman	.02	.10
97 Mickey Klutts	.02	.10
98 Rick Langford	.02	.10
99 Steve McCatty	.02	.10
100 Dave McKay	.02	.10
101 Dwayne Murphy	.02	.10
102 Jeff Newman	.02	.10
103 Mike Norris	.02	.10
104 Bob Owchinko	.02	.10
105 Mitchell Page	.02	.10
106 Rob Picciolo	.02	.10
107 Jim Spencer	.02	.10
108 Fred Stanley	.02	.10
109 Tom Underwood	.02	.10
110 Joaquin Andujar	.07	.20
111 Steve Braun	.02	.10
112 Bob Forsch	.02	.10
113 George Hendrick	.07	.20
114 Keith Hernandez	.07	.20
115 Tom Herr	.02	.10
116 Dane Iorg	.02	.10
117 Jim Kaat	.07	.20
118 Tito Landrum	.02	.10
119 Sixto Lezcano	.02	.10
120 Mark Littell	.02	.10
121 John Martin RC	.05	.15
122 Silvio Martinez	.02	.10
123 Ken Oberkfell	.02	.10
124 Darrell Porter	.02	.10
125 Mike Ramsey	.02	.10
126 Orlando Sanchez	.02	.10
127 Bob Shirley	.02	.10
128 Lary Sorensen	.02	.10
129 Bruce Sutter	.15	.40
130 Bob Sykes	.02	.10
131 Garry Templeton	.07	.20
132 Gene Tenace	.07	.20
133 Jerry Augustine	.02	.10
134 Sal Bando	.07	.20
135 Mark Brouhard	.02	.10
136 Mike Caldwell	.02	.10
137 Reggie Cleveland	.02	.10
138 Cecil Cooper	.07	.20
139 Jamie Easterly	.02	.10
140 Marshall Edwards	.02	.10
141 Rollie Fingers	.07	.20
142 Jim Gantner	.02	.10
143 Moose Haas	.02	.10
144 Larry Hisle	.02	.10
145 Roy Howell	.02	.10
146 Rickey Keeton	.02	.10
147 Randy Lerch	.02	.10
148 Paul Molitor	.07	.20
149 Don Money	.02	.10
150 Charlie Moore	.02	.10
151 Ben Oglivie	.07	.20
152 Ted Simmons	.07	.20
153 Jim Slaton	.02	.10
154 Gorman Thomas	.07	.20
155 Robin Yount	.50	1.25
156 Pete Vuckovich Should precede Yount in the team order	.02	.10
157 Benny Ayala	.02	.10
158 Mark Belanger	.02	.10
159 Al Bumbry	.02	.10
160 Terry Crowley	.02	.10
161 Rich Dauer	.02	.10
162 Doug DeCinces	.02	.10
163 Rick Dempsey	.02	.10
164 Jim Dwyer	.02	.10
165 Mike Flanagan	.02	.10
166 Dave Ford	.02	.10
167 Dan Graham	.02	.10
168 Wayne Krenchicki	.02	.10
169 John Lowenstein	.02	.10
170 Dennis Martinez	.07	.20
171 Tippy Martinez	.02	.10
172 Scott McGregor	.02	.10
173 Jose Morales	.02	.10
174 Eddie Murray	.30	.75
175 Jim Palmer	.07	.20
176 Cal Ripken RC	10.00	25.00
177 Gary Roenicke	.02	.10
178 Lenn Sakata	.02	.10
179 Ken Singleton	.07	.20
180 Sammy Stewart	.02	.10
181 Tim Stoddard	.02	.10
182 Steve Stone	.02	.10
183 Stan Bahnsen	.02	.10
184 Ray Burris	.02	.10
185 Gary Carter	.07	.20
186 Warren Cromartie	.02	.10
187 Andre Dawson	.07	.20
188 Terry Francona RC	1.25	3.00
189 Woodie Fryman	.02	.10
190 Bill Gullickson	.02	.10
191 Grant Jackson	.02	.10
192 Wallace Johnson	.02	.10
193 Charlie Lea	.02	.10
194 Bill Lee	.07	.20
195 Jerry Manuel	.02	.10
196 Brad Mills	.02	.10
197 John Milner	.02	.10
198 Rowland Office	.02	.10
199 David Palmer	.02	.10
200 Larry Parrish	.02	.10
201 Mike Phillips	.02	.10
202 Tim Raines	.15	.40
203 Bobby Ramos	.02	.10
204 Jeff Reardon	.07	.20
205 Steve Rogers	.07	.20
206 Scott Sanderson	.02	.10
207 Rodney Scott UER Photo actually Tim Raines	.15	.40
208 Elias Sosa	.02	.10
209 Chris Speier	.02	.10
210 Tim Wallach RC	.40	1.00
211 Jerry White	.02	.10
212 Alan Ashby	.02	.10
213 Cesar Cedeno	.07	.20
214 Jose Cruz	.07	.20
215 Kiko Garcia	.02	.10
216 Phil Garner	.07	.20
217 Danny Heep	.02	.10
218 Art Howe	.02	.10
219 Bob Knepper	.02	.10
220 Frank LaCorte	.02	.10
221 Joe Niekro	.02	.10
222 Joe Pittman	.02	.10
223 Terry Puhl	.02	.10
224 Luis Pujols	.02	.10
225 Craig Reynolds	.02	.10
226 J.R. Richard	.07	.20
227 Dave Roberts	.02	.10
228 Vern Ruhle	.02	.10
229 Nolan Ryan	1.50	4.00
230 Joe Sambito	.02	.10
231 Tony Scott	.02	.10
232 Dave Smith	.02	.10
233 Harry Spilman	.02	.10
234 Don Sutton	.07	.20
235 Dickie Thon	.02	.10
236 Denny Walling	.02	.10
237 Gary Woods	.02	.10
238 Luis Aguayo	.02	.10
239 Ramon Aviles	.02	.10
240 Bob Boone	.07	.20
241 Larry Bowa	.07	.20
242 Warren Brusstar	.02	.10
243 Steve Carlton	.15	.40
244 Larry Christenson	.02	.10
245 Dick Davis	.02	.10
246 Greg Gross	.02	.10
247 Sparky Lyle	.07	.20
248 Garry Maddox	.02	.10
249 Gary Matthews	.07	.20
250 Bake McBride	.07	.20
251 Tug McGraw	.07	.20
252 Keith Moreland	.02	.10
253 Dickie Noles	.02	.10
254 Mike Proly	.02	.10
255 Ron Reed	.02	.10
256 Pete Rose	1.00	2.50
257 Dick Ruthven	.02	.10
258 Mike Schmidt	.75	2.00
259 Lonnie Smith	.02	.10
260 Manny Trillo	.02	.10
261 Del Unser	.02	.10
262 George Vukovich	.02	.10
263 Tom Brookens	.02	.10
264 George Cappuzzello	.02	.10
265 Marty Castillo	.02	.10
266 Al Cowens	.02	.10
267 Kirk Gibson	.30	.75
268 Richie Hebner	.02	.10
269 Ron Jackson	.02	.10
270 Lynn Jones	.02	.10
271 Steve Kemp	.02	.10
272 Rick Leach	.02	.10
273 Aurelio Lopez	.02	.10
274 Jack Morris	.07	.20
275 Kevin Saucier	.02	.10
276 Lance Parrish	.07	.20
277 Rick Peters	.02	.10
278 Dan Petry	.02	.10
279 Dave Rozema	.02	.10
280 Stan Papi	.02	.10
281 Dan Schatzeder	.02	.10
282 Champ Summers	.02	.10
283 Alan Trammell	.07	.20
284 Lou Whitaker	.07	.20
285 Milt Wilcox	.02	.10
286 John Wockenfuss	.02	.10
287 Gary Allenson	.02	.10
288 Tom Burgmeier	.02	.10
289 Bill Campbell	.02	.10
290 Mark Clear	.02	.10
291 Steve Crawford	.02	.10
292 Dennis Eckersley	.15	.40
293 Dwight Evans	.15	.40
294 Rich Gedman	.20	.50
295 Garry Hancock	.02	.10
296 Glenn Hoffman	.02	.10
297 Bruce Hurst	.02	.10
298 Carney Lansford	.07	.20
299 Rick Miller	.02	.10
300 Reid Nichols	.02	.10
301 Bob Ojeda RC	.20	.50
302 Tony Perez	.15	.40
303 Chuck Rainey	.02	.10
304 Jerry Remy	.02	.10
305 Jim Rice	.07	.20
306 Joe Rudi	.07	.20
307 Bob Stanley	.02	.10
308 Dave Stapleton	.02	.10
309 Frank Tanana	.07	.20
310 Mike Torrez	.02	.10
311 John Tudor	.07	.20
312 Carl Yastrzemski	.50	1.25
313 Buddy Bell	.07	.20
314 Steve Comer	.02	.10
315 Danny Darwin	.02	.10
316 John Ellis	.02	.10
317 John Grubb	.02	.10
318 Rick Honeycutt	.02	.10
319 Charlie Hough	.07	.20
320 Ferguson Jenkins	.07	.20
321 John Henry Johnson	.02	.10
322 Jim Kern	.02	.10
323 Jon Matlack	.02	.10
324 Doc Medich	.02	.10
325 Mario Mendoza	.02	.10
326 Al Oliver	.07	.20
327 Pat Putnam	.02	.10
328 Mickey Rivers	.02	.10
329 Leon Roberts	.02	.10
330 Billy Sample	.02	.10
331 Bill Stein	.02	.10
332 Jim Sundberg	.07	.20
333 Mark Wagner	.02	.10
334 Bump Wills	.02	.10
335 Bill Almon	.02	.10
336 Harold Baines	.07	.20
337 Ross Baumgarten	.02	.10
338 Tony Bernazard	.02	.10
339 Britt Burns	.02	.10
340 Richard Dotson	.02	.10
341 Jim Essian	.02	.10
342 Ed Farmer	.02	.10
343 Carlton Fisk	.15	.40
344 Kevin Hickey RC	.05	.15
345 LaMarr Hoyt	.02	.10
346 Lamar Johnson	.02	.10
347 Jerry Koosman	.07	.20
348 Rusty Kuntz	.02	.10
349 Dennis Lamp	.02	.10
350 Ron LeFlore	.07	.20
351 Chet Lemon	.07	.20
352 Greg Luzinski	.07	.20
353 Bob Molinaro	.02	.10
354 Jim Morrison	.02	.10
355 Wayne Nordhagen	.02	.10
356 Greg Pryor	.02	.10
357 Mike Squires	.02	.10
358 Steve Trout	.02	.10
359 Alan Bannister	.02	.10
360 Len Barker	.02	.10
361 Bert Blyleven	.07	.20
362 Joe Charboneau	.07	.20
363 John Denny	.02	.10
364 Bo Diaz	.02	.10
365 Miguel Dilone	.02	.10
366 Jerry Dybzinski	.02	.10
367 Wayne Garland	.02	.10
368 Mike Hargrove	.02	.10
369 Toby Harrah	.07	.20
370 Ron Hassey	.02	.10
371 Von Hayes RC	.20	.50
372 Pat Kelly	.02	.10
373 Duane Kuiper	.02	.10
374 Rick Manning	.02	.10
375 Sid Monge	.02	.10
376 Jorge Orta	.02	.10
377 Dave Rosello	.02	.10
378 Dan Spillner	.02	.10
379 Mike Stanton	.02	.10
380 Andre Thornton	.02	.10
381 Tom Veryzer	.02	.10
382 Rick Waits	.02	.10
383 Doyle Alexander	.02	.10
384 Vida Blue	.07	.20
385 Fred Breining	.02	.10
386 Enos Cabell	.02	.10
387 Jack Clark	.07	.20
388 Darrell Evans	.07	.20
389 Tom Griffin	.02	.10
390 Larry Herndon	.02	.10
391 Al Holland	.02	.10
392 Gary Lavelle	.02	.10
393 Johnnie LeMaster	.02	.10
394 Jerry Martin	.02	.10
395 Milt May	.02	.10
396 Greg Minton	.02	.10
397 Joe Morgan	.07	.20
398 Joe Pettini	.02	.10
399 Allen Ripley	.02	.10
400 Billy Smith	.02	.10
401 Rennie Stennett	.02	.10
402 Ed Whitson	.02	.10
403 Jim Wohlford	.02	.10
404 Willie Aikens	.02	.10
405 George Brett	.75	2.00
406 Ken Brett	.02	.10
407 Dave Chalk	.02	.10
408 Rich Gale	.02	.10
409 Cesar Geronimo	.02	.10
410 Larry Gura	.02	.10
411 Clint Hurdle	.02	.10
412 Mike Jones	.02	.10
413 Dennis Leonard	.02	.10
414 Renie Martin	.02	.10
415 Lee May	.02	.10
416 Hal McRae	.07	.20
417 Darryl Motley	.02	.10
418 Rance Mulliniks	.02	.10
419 Amos Otis	.07	.20
420 Ken Phelps	.02	.10
421 Jamie Quirk	.02	.10
422 Dan Quisenberry	.02	.10
423 Paul Splittorff	.02	.10
424 U.L. Washington	.02	.10
425 John Wathan	.02	.10
426 Frank White	.07	.20
427 Willie Wilson	.07	.20
428 Brian Asselstine	.02	.10
429 Bruce Benedict	.02	.10
430 Tommy Boggs	.02	.10
431 Larry Bradford	.02	.10
432 Rick Camp	.02	.10
433 Chris Chambliss	.07	.20
434 Gene Garber	.02	.10
435 Preston Hanna	.02	.10
436 Bob Horner	.07	.20
437 Glenn Hubbard	.02	.10
438A All Hrabosky ERR	3.00	8.00
438B Al Hrabosky ERR Height 5'1	.15	.40
438C Al Hrabosky Height 5'10	.07	.20
439 Rufino Linares	.02	.10
440 Rick Mahler	.02	.10
441 Ed Miller	.02	.10
442 John Montefusco	.02	.10
443 Dale Murphy	.15	.40
444 Phil Niekro	.07	.20
445 Gaylord Perry	.07	.20
446 Biff Pocoroba	.02	.10
447 Rafael Ramirez	.02	.10
448 Jerry Royster	.02	.10
449 Claudell Washington	.02	.10
450 Don Aase	.02	.10
451 Don Baylor	.07	.20
452 Juan Beniquez	.02	.10
453 Rick Burleson	.02	.10
454 Bert Campaneris	.07	.20
455 Rod Carew	.15	.40
456 Bob Clark	.02	.10
457 Brian Downing	.07	.20
458 Dan Ford	.02	.10
459 Ken Forsch	.02	.10
460A Dave Frost 5 mm space before ERA	.02	.10
460B Dave Frost 1 mm space	.02	.10
461 Bobby Grich	.07	.20
462 Larry Harlow	.02	.10
463 John Harris	.02	.10
464 Andy Hassler	.02	.10
465 Butch Hobson	.02	.10
466 Jesse Jefferson	.02	.10
467 Bruce Kison	.02	.10
468 Fred Lynn	.07	.20
469 Angel Moreno	.02	.10
470 Ed Ott	.02	.10
471 Fred Patek	.02	.10
472 Steve Renko	.02	.10
473 Mike Witt	.20	.50
474 Geoff Zahn	.02	.10
475 Gary Alexander	.02	.10
476 Dale Berra	.02	.10
477 Kurt Bevacqua	.02	.10
478 Jim Bibby	.02	.10
479 John Candelaria	.02	.10
480 Victor Cruz	.02	.10
481 Mike Easler	.02	.10
482 Tim Foli	.02	.10
483 Lee Lacy	.02	.10
484 Vance Law	.02	.10
485 Bill Madlock	.07	.20
486 Willie Montanez	.02	.10
487 Omar Moreno	.02	.10
488 Steve Nicosia	.02	.10
489 Dave Parker	.07	.20
490 Tony Pena	.07	.20
491 Pascual Perez	.02	.10
492 Johnny Ray RC	.20	.50
493 Rick Rhoden	.02	.10
494 Bill Robinson	.02	.10
495 Don Robinson	.02	.10
496 Enrique Romo	.02	.10
497 Rod Scurry	.02	.10
498 Eddie Solomon	.02	.10
499 Willie Stargell	.15	.40
500 Kent Tekulve	.02	.10
501 Jason Thompson	.02	.10
502 Glenn Abbott	.02	.10
503 Jim Anderson	.02	.10
504 Floyd Bannister	.02	.10
505 Bruce Bochte	.02	.10
506 Jeff Burroughs	.02	.10
507 Bryan Clark RC	.05	.15
508 Ken Clay	.02	.10
509 Julio Cruz	.02	.10
510 Dick Drago	.02	.10
511 Gary Gray	.02	.10
512 Dan Meyer	.02	.10
513 Jerry Narron	.02	.10
514 Tom Paciorek	.02	.10
515 Casey Parsons	.02	.10
516 Lenny Randle	.02	.10
517 Shane Rawley	.02	.10
518 Joe Simpson	.02	.10
519 Richie Zisk	.02	.10
520 Neil Allen	.02	.10
521 Bob Bailor	.02	.10
522 Hubie Brooks	.02	.10
523 Mike Cubbage	.02	.10
524 Pete Falcone	.02	.10
525 Doug Flynn	.02	.10
526 Tom Hausman	.02	.10
527 Ron Hodges	.02	.10
528 Randy Jones	.02	.10
529 Mike Jorgensen	.02	.10
530 Dave Kingman	.07	.20
531 Ed Lynch	.02	.10
532 Mike G. Marshall	.02	.10
533 Lee Mazzilli	.07	.20
534 Dyar Miller	.02	.10
535 Mike Scott	.07	.20
536 Rusty Staub	.07	.20
537 John Stearns	.02	.10
538 Craig Swan	.02	.10
539 Frank Taveras	.02	.10
540 Alex Trevino	.02	.10
541 Ellis Valentine	.02	.10
542 Mookie Wilson	.07	.20
543 Joel Youngblood	.02	.10
544 Pat Zachry	.02	.10
545 Glenn Adams	.02	.10
546 Fernando Arroyo	.02	.10
547 John Verhoeven	.02	.10
548 Sal Butera	.02	.10
549 John Castino	.02	.10
550 Don Cooper	.02	.10
551 Doug Corbett	.02	.10
552 Dave Engle	.02	.10
553 Roger Erickson	.02	.10
554 Danny Goodwin	.02	.10
555A Darrell Jackson Black cap	.15	.40
555B Darrell Jackson Red cap with T	.07	.20
555C Darrell Jackson	1.25	3.00
556 Pete Mackanin	.02	.10
557 Jack O'Connor	.02	.10
558 Hosken Powell	.02	.10
559 Pete Redfern	.02	.10
560 Roy Smalley	.02	.10
561 Chuck Baker UER Shortshop on front	.02	.10
562 Gary Ward	.02	.10
563 Rob Wilfong	.02	.10
564 Al Williams	.02	.10
565 Butch Wynegar	.02	.10
566 Randy Bass	.20	.50
567 Juan Bonilla RC	.05	.15
568 Danny Boone	.02	.10
569 John Curtis	.02	.10
570 Juan Eichelberger	.02	.10
571 Barry Evans	.02	.10
572 Tim Flannery	.02	.10
573 Ruppert Jones	.02	.10
574 Terry Kennedy	.02	.10
575 Joe Lefebvre	.02	.10
576A John Littlefield ERR	30.00	60.00
576B John Littlefield COR Right handed	.07	.20
577 Gary Lucas	.02	.10
578 Steve Mura	.02	.10
579 Broderick Perkins	.02	.10
580 Gene Richards	.02	.10
581 Luis Salazar	.02	.10
582 Ozzie Smith	.60	1.50
583 John Urrea	.02	.10
584 Chris Welsh	.02	.10

585 Rick Wise .02 .10
586 Doug Bird .02 .10
587 Tim Blackwell .02 .10
588 Bobby Bonds .07 .20
589 Bill Buckner .07 .20
590 Bill Caudill .02 .10
591 Hector Cruz .02 .10
592 Jody Davis RC .02 .10
593 Ivan DeJesus .02 .10
594 Steve Dillard .02 .10
595 Leon Durham .02 .10
596 Rawly Eastwick .07 .20
597 Steve Henderson .02 .10
598 Mike Krukow .02 .10
599 Mike Lum .02 .10
600 Randy Martz .02 .10
601 Jerry Morales .02 .10
602 Ken Reitz .02 .10
603 Lee Smith RC ERR .75 2.00
603B Lee Smith RC COR 2.50 6.00
604 Dick Tidrow .02 .10
605 Jim Tracy .07 .20
606 Mike Tyson .02 .10
607 Ty Waller .02 .10
608 Danny Ainge .07 .20
609 Jorge Bell RC .40 1.00
George Bell
610 Mark Bomback .02 .10
611 Barry Bonnell .02 .10
612 Jim Clancy .02 .10
613 Damaso Garcia .02 .10
614 Jerry Garvin .02 .10
615 Alfredo Griffin .02 .10
616 Garth Iorg .02 .10
617 Luis Leal .02 .10
618 Ken Macha .02 .10
619 John Mayberry .02 .10
620 Joey McLaughlin .02 .10
621 Lloyd Moseby .02 .10
622 Dave Stieb .07 .20
623 Jackson Todd .02 .10
624 Willie Upshaw .20 .50
625 Otto Velez .02 .10
626 Ernie Whitt .02 .10
627 Alvis Woods .02 .10
628 All Star Game .07 .20
Cleveland, Ohio
629 Frank White .07 .20
Bucky Dent
630 Dan Driessen .07 .20
Dave Concepcion
George Foster
631 Bruce Sutter .07 .20
Top NL Relief Pitcher
632 Steve Carlton .07 .20
Carlton Fisk
633 Carl Yastrzemski .30 .75
3000th Game
634 Johnny Bench .30 .75
Tom Seaver
635 Fernando Valenzuela .02 .10
Gary Carter
636A Fernando Valenzuela: .15 .40
NL SO King 'he' NL
636B Fernando Valenzuela .15 .40
NL SO King 'the' NL
637 Mike Schmidt .30 .75
Home Run King
638 Gary Carter .02 .10
Dave Parker
639 Perfect Game UER .07 .20
Len Barker
Bo Diaz
Catcher actually
Ron Hassey
640 Pete Rose .30 .75
Pete Rose Jr.
641 Lonnie Smith .30 .75
Mike Schmidt
Steve Carlton
642 Fred Lynn .15 .40
Dwight Evans
643 Rickey Henderson .50 1.25
644 Rollie Fingers .07 .20
Most Saves AL
645 Tom Seaver .07 .20
Most 1981 Wins
646 Yankee Powerhouse .07 .20
Reggie Jackson
Dave Winfield
Comma on back
after outfielder
646B Yankee Powerhouse .07 .20
Reggie Jackson
Dave Winfield
No comma
647 CL: Yankees .02 .10
Dodgers
648 CL: A's .02 .10
Reds
649 CL: Cards .02 .10
Brewers
650 CL: Expos .02 .10
Orioles
651 CL: Astros .02 .10
Phillies
652 CL: Tigers .02 .10
Red Sox
653 CL: Rangers .02 .10
White Sox
654 CL: Giants .02 .10
Indians
655 CL: Royals .02 .10
Braves
656 CL: Angels .02 .10
Pirates
657 CL: Mariners .02 .10
Mets
658 CL: Padres .02 .10
Twins
659 CL: Blue Jays .02 .10
Cubs
660 Specials Checklist .02 .10

1982 Fleer Stamps

The stamps in this 242-piece set measure 1 13/16" by 2 1/2". The 1982 Fleer stamp set consists of different individual stamps issued in strips of 10 stamps each. The stamps were issued in packages with the Fleer team logo stickers. The backs are blank and an inexpensive album is available in which to place the stamps. A checklist is provided in the back of the album which lists 25 strips of 10 stamps. The checklist below lists the individual stamps plus the strip (with prefix G) to which the stamps are supposed to belong based on the album strip checklist. Complete strips have equal value to the sum of the individual stamps on the strip. Eight stamps have been doubly printed and are noted by two different strip numbers below. The numbering is essentially in team order.

COMPLETE SET (242) 8.00 20.00
COMMON SHEET .30 .75
1 Fern. Valenzuela G20 .20 .50
2 Rick Monday G16 .01 .05
3 Ron Cey G9 .02 .10
4 Dusty Baker G20 .02 .10
5 Burt Hooton G10 .01 .05
6 Pedro Guerrero G23 .02 .10
7 Jerry Reuss G12 .01 .05
8 Bill Russell G7 .01 .05
9 Steve Garvey G21 .05 .15
10 Davey Lopes G19 .02 .10
11 Tom Seaver G7 .40 1.00
12 George Foster G17 .02 .10
13 Frank Pastore G12 .01 .05
14 Dave Collins G5 .01 .05
15 Dave Concepcion G21 .02 .10
16 Ken Griffey G6 .02 .10
17 Johnny Bench G20 .40 1.00
18 Ray Knight G16 .01 .05
19 Mario Soto G9 .01 .05
20 Ron Oester G19 .01 .05
21 Ken Oberkfell G21 .01 .05
22 Bob Forsch G4 .01 .05
23 Keith Hernandez G19 .02 .10
24 Dane Iorg G9 .01 .05
25 George Hendrick G2 .01 .05
26 Gene Tenace G24 .01 .05
27 Garry Templeton G12 .01 .05
28 Bruce Sutter G18 .02 .10
29 Darrell Porter G14 .01 .05
30 Tom Herr G3 .01 .05
31 Tim Raines G11 .20 .50
32 Chris Speier G13 .01 .05
33 Warren Cromartie G22 .01 .05
34 Larry Parrish G15 .01 .05
35 Andre Dawson G10 .30 .75
36 Steve Rogers G1 .01 .05
G25
37 Jeff Reardon G23 .05 .15
38 Rodney Scott G12 .01 .05
39 Gary Carter G14 .25 .60
40 Scott Sanderson G6 .01 .05
41 Cesar Cedeno G7 .01 .05
42 Nolan Ryan G10 2.50 6.00
43 Don Sutton G24 .08 .25
44 Terry Puhl G15 .01 .05
45 Joe Niekro G13 .02 .10
46 Tony Scott G16 .01 .05
47 Joe Sambito G1 .01 .05
48 Art Howe G9 .01 .05
49 Bob Knepper G18 .01 .05
50 Jose Cruz G22 .02 .10
51 Pete Rose G16 .75 2.00
52 Dick Ruthven G12 .01 .05
53 Mike Schmidt G14 .75 2.00
54 Steve Carlton G17 .40 1.00
55 Tug McGraw G4 .02 .10
56 Larry Bowa G4 .02 .10
57 Garry Maddox G18 .01 .05
58 Gary Matthews G4 .01 .05
59 Manny Trillo G15 .01 .05
60 Lonnie Smith G20 .01 .05
61 Vida Blue G11 .02 .10
62 Milt May G12 .01 .05
63 Joe Morgan G16 .20 .50
64 Enos Cabell G8 .01 .05
65 Jack Clark G18 .02 .10
66 Claud.Washington G19 .01 .05
67 Gaylord Perry G16 .20 .50
68 Phil Niekro G22 .20 .50
69 Bob Horner G7 .01 .05
70 Chris Chambliss G11 .01 .05
71 Dave Parker G15 .05 .15
72 Tony Pena G11 .02 .10
73 Kent Tekulve G23 .01 .05
74 Mike Easler G18 .01 .05
75 Tim Foli G13 .01 .05
76 Willie Stargell G21 .20 .50
77 Bill Madlock G5 .02 .10
78 Jim Bibby G14 .01 .05
79 Omar Moreno G17 .01 .05
80 Lee Lacy G2 .01 .05
81 Hubie Brooks G24 .01 .05
82 Rusty Staub G4 .02 .10
83 Ellis Valentine G13 .01 .05
84 Neil Allen G1 .01 .05
85 Dave Kingman G9 .05 .15
86 Mookie Wilson G3 .05 .15
87 Doug Flynn G11 .01 .05
88 Pat Zachry G8 .01 .05
89 John Stearns G6 .01 .05
90 Lee Mazzilli G2 .02 .10
91 Ken Reitz G23 .01 .05
92 Mike Krukow G11 .01 .05
93 Jerry Morales G10 .01 .05
94 Leon Durham G22 .01 .05
95 Ivan DeJesus G2 .01 .05
96 Bill Buckner G17 .02 .10
97 Jim Tracy G12 .01 .05
98 Steve Henderson G14 .01 .05
99 Dick Tidrow G14 .01 .05
100 Mike Tyson G5 .01 .05
101 Ozzie Smith G12 1.00 2.50
102 Ruppert Jones G24 .01 .05
103 Brod Perkins G10 .01 .05
104 Gene Richards G15 .01 .05
105 Terry Kennedy G22 .01 .05
106 Jim Bibby and .05 .15
Willie Stargell G4
107 Pete Rose and .30 .75
Larry Bowa G21
108 Fern.Valenzuela and .08 .25
Warren Spahn G1
G25
109 Pete Rose and .30 .75
Dave Concepcion G8
110 Reggie Jackson and .60 1.50
Dave Winfield G3
111 Fernando Valenzuela .05 .15
and Tom Lasorda G4
112 Reggie Jackson G6 .75 2.00
113 Dave Winfield G3 .60 1.50
114 Lou Piniella G2 .02 .10
115 Tommy John G9 .02 .10
116 Rich Gossage G1 .02 .10
G25
117 Ron Davis G10 .01 .05
118 Rick Cerone G5 .01 .05
119 Graig Nettles G8 .02 .10
120 Ron Guidry G24 .02 .10
121 Willie Randolph G24 .02 .10
122 Dwayne Murphy G15 .01 .05
123 Rickey Henderson G16 1.00 2.50
124 Wayne Gross G6 .01 .05
125 Mike Norris G8 .01 .05
126 Rick Langford G20 .01 .05
127 Jim Spencer G17 .01 .05
128 Tony Armas G12 .01 .05
129 Matt Keough G7 .01 .05
130 Jeff Jones G19 .01 .05
131 Steve McCatty G3 .01 .05
132 Rollie Fingers G7 .10 .30
133 Jim Gantner G15 .01 .05
134 Gorman Thomas G6 .01 .05
135 Robin Yount G13 .40 1.00
136 Paul Molitor G22 .60 1.50
137 Ted Simmons G10 .02 .10
138 Ben Oglivie G23 .01 .05
139 Moose Haas G21 .01 .05
140 Cecil Cooper G24 .02 .10
141 Pete Vuckovich G10 .01 .05
142 Doug DeCinces G21 .01 .05
143 Jim Palmer G9 .20 .50
144 Steve Stone G16 .01 .05
145 Mike Flanagan G19 .01 .05
146 Rick Dempsey G9 .01 .05
147 Al Bumbry G14 .01 .05
148 Mark Belanger G8 .01 .05
149 Scott McGregor G23 .01 .05
150 Ken Singleton G10 .01 .05
151 Eddie Murray G5 1.00 2.50
152 Lance Parrish G20 .05 .15
153 Dave Rozema G15 .01 .05
154 Champ Summers G13 .01 .05
155 Alan Trammell G2 .20 .50
156 Lou Whitaker G1 .08 .25
G25
157 Milt Wilcox G5 .01 .05
158 Kevin Saucier G24 .01 .05
159 Jack Morris G14 .02 .10
160 Steve Kemp G7 .01 .05
161 Kirk Gibson G3 .08 .25
162 Carl Yastrzemski G3 .30 .75
163 Jim Rice G21 .05 .15
164 Carney Lansford G15 .02 .10
165 Dennis Eckersley G6 .20 .50
166 Mike Torrez G5 .01 .05
167 Dwight Evans G19 .02 .10
168 Glenn Hoffman G18 .01 .05
169 Bob Stanley G20 .01 .05
170 Tony Perez G16 .08 .25
171 Jerry Remy G13 .01 .05
172 Buddy Bell G5 .02 .10
173 Fergie Jenkins G17 .08 .25
174 Mickey Rivers G9 .01 .05
175 Bump Wills G2 .01 .05
176 Jon Matlack G20 .01 .05
177 Steve Comer G23 .01 .05
178 Al Oliver G1 .02 .10
G25
179 Bill Stein G3 .01 .05
180 Pat Putnam G14 .01 .05
181 Jim Sundberg G4 .01 .05
182 Ron LeFlore G4 .02 .10
183 Carlton Fisk G11 .40 1.00
184 Harold Baines G18 .08 .25
185 Bill Almon G2 .01 .05
186 Richard Dotson G9 .01 .05
187 Greg Luzinski G14 .02 .10
188 Mike Squires G13 .01 .05
189 Britt Burns G19 .01 .05
190 LaMarr Hoyt G6 .01 .05
191 Chet Lemon G22 .01 .05
192 Joe Charboneau G20 .01 .05
193 Toby Harrah G16 .01 .05
194 John Denny G22 .01 .05
195 Rick Manning G8 .01 .05
196 Miguel Dilone G15 .01 .05
197 Bo Diaz G13 .01 .05
198 Mike Hargrove G17 .02 .10
199 Bert Blyleven G11 .02 .10
200 Len Barker G7 .01 .05
201 Andre Thornton G18 .01 .05
202 George Brett G24 .75 2.00
203 U.L. Washington G25 .01 .05
204 Dan Quisenberry G17 .01 .05
205 Larry Gura G17 .01 .05
206 Willie Aikens G22 .01 .05
207 Willie Wilson G21 .01 .05
208 Dennis Leonard G8 .01 .05
209 Frank White G6 .02 .10
210 Hal McRae G23 .02 .10
211 Amos Otis G18 .01 .05
212 Don Aase G23 .01 .05
213 Butch Hobson G6 .01 .05
214 Fred Lynn G18 .02 .10
215 Brian Downing G10 .01 .05
216 Dan Ford G5 .01 .05
217 Rod Carew G5 .30 .75
218 Bobby Grich G19 .02 .10
219 Rick Burleson G11 .01 .05
220 Don Baylor G3 .02 .10
221 Ken Forsch G17 .01 .05
222 Bruce Bochte .01 .05
223 Richie Zisk .01 .05
224 Tom Paciorek .01 .05
225 Julio Cruz .01 .05
226 Jeff Burroughs .01 .05
227 Doug Corbett .01 .05
228 Roy Smalley .01 .05
229 Gary Ward .01 .05
230 John Castino .01 .05
231 Rob Wilfong .01 .05
232 Dave Stieb .02 .10
233 Otto Velez .01 .05
234 Damaso Garcia .01 .05
235 John Mayberry .01 .05
236 Alfredo Griffin .01 .05
237 Ted Williams .75 2.00
Carl Yastrzemski
238 Rick Cerone .02 .10
Graig Nettles
239 Buddy Bell .60 1.50
George Brett
240 Steve Carlton .08 .25
Jim Kaat
241 Steve Carlton .08 .25
Dave Parker
242 Ron Davis 1.50 4.00
Nolan Ryan
XX Stamp Album .75 2.00

1983 Fleer Promo Sheet

This sheet, which measures approximately 7 1/2" by 10 1/2" featured information on the 1983 Fleer wax, cello and rack packs. The cards shown on the sheet are the same as their regular card from the set. Six different players are featured on this set.

1 Rod Carew 1.25 3.00
Tom Paciorek
Jerry Dybzinski
Dan Drie

1983 Fleer

In 1983, for the third straight year, Fleer produced a baseball series of 660 standard-size cards. Of these, 1-628 are player cards, 629-646 are special cards, and 647-660 are checklist cards. The player cards are again ordered alphabetically within team and teams seeded in descending order based upon the previous season's standings. The front of each card has a colorful team logo at bottom left and the player's name and position at lower right. The reverses are done in shades of brown on white. Wax packs consisted of 15 cards plus logo stickers in a 38-pack box. Notable Rookie Cards include Wade Boggs, Tony Gwynn and Ryne Sandberg.

COMPLETE SET (660) 25.00 60.00
1 Joaquin Andujar .07 .20
2 Doug Bair .02 .10
3 Steve Braun .02 .10
4 Glenn Brummer .02 .10
5 Bob Forsch .02 .10
6 David Green RC .20 .50
7 George Hendrick .07 .20
8 Keith Hernandez .07 .20
9 Tom Herr .02 .10
10 Dane Iorg .02 .10
11 Jim Kaat .07 .20
12 Jeff Lahti .02 .10
13 Tito Landrum .02 .10
14 Dave LaPoint .02 .10
15 Willie McGee RC .60 1.50
16 Steve Mura .02 .10
17 Ken Oberkfell .02 .10
18 Darrell Porter .02 .10
19 Mike Ramsey .02 .10
20 Gene Roof .02 .10
21 Lonnie Smith .02 .10
22 Ozzie Smith .50 1.25
23 John Stuper .02 .10
24 Bruce Sutter .15 .40
25 Gene Tenace .07 .20
26 Jerry Augustine .02 .10
27 Dwight Bernard .02 .10
28 Mark Brouhard .02 .10
29 Mike Caldwell .02 .10
30 Cecil Cooper .07 .20
31 Jamie Easterly .02 .10
32 Marshall Edwards .02 .10
33 Rollie Fingers .07 .20
34 Jim Gantner .02 .10
35 Moose Haas .02 .10
36 Roy Howell .02 .10
37 Pete Ladd .02 .10
38 Bob McClure .02 .10
39 Doc Medich .02 .10
40 Paul Molitor .07 .20
41 Don Money .02 .10
42 Charlie Moore .02 .10
43 Ben Oglivie .07 .20
44 Ed Romero .02 .10
45 Ted Simmons .07 .20
46 Jim Slaton .02 .10
47 Don Sutton .07 .20
48 Gorman Thomas .07 .20
49 Pete Vuckovich .02 .10
50 Ned Yost .02 .10
51 Robin Yount .50 1.25
52 Benny Ayala .02 .10
53 Bob Bonner .02 .10
54 Al Bumbry .02 .10
55 Terry Crowley .02 .10
56 Storm Davis RC .20 .50
57 Rich Dauer .02 .10
58 Rick Dempsey UER .02 .10
Posing batting lefty
59 Jim Dwyer .02 .10
60 Mike Flanagan .02 .10
61 Dan Ford .02 .10
62 Glenn Gulliver .02 .10
63 John Lowenstein .02 .10
64 Dennis Martinez .07 .20
65 Tippy Martinez .02 .10
66 Scott McGregor .02 .10
67 Eddie Murray .30 .75
68 Joe Nolan .02 .10
69 Jim Palmer .07 .20
70 Cal Ripken 2.50 6.00
71 Gary Roenicke .02 .10
72 Lenn Sakata .02 .10
73 Ken Singleton .07 .20
74 Sammy Stewart .02 .10
75 Tim Stoddard .02 .10
76 Don Aase .02 .10
77 Don Baylor .07 .20
78 Juan Beniquez .02 .10
79 Bob Boone .07 .20
80 Rick Burleson .02 .10
81 Rod Carew .15 .40
82 Bobby Clark .02 .10
83 Doug Corbett .02 .10
84 John Curtis .02 .10
85 Doug DeCinces .02 .10
86 Brian Downing .07 .20
87 Joe Ferguson .02 .10
88 Tim Foli .02 .10
89 Ken Forsch .02 .10
90 Dave Goltz .02 .10
91 Bobby Grich .07 .20
92 Andy Hassler .02 .10
93 Reggie Jackson .15 .40
94 Ron Jackson .02 .10
95 Tommy John .07 .20
96 Bruce Kison .02 .10
97 Fred Lynn .07 .20
98 Ed Ott .02 .10
99 Steve Renko .02 .10
100 Luis Sanchez .02 .10
101 Rob Wilfong .02 .10
102 Mike Witt .02 .10
103 Geoff Zahn .02 .10
104 Willie Aikens .02 .10
105 Mike Armstrong .02 .10
106 Vida Blue .07 .20
107 Bud Black RC .20 .50
108 George Brett .75 2.00
109 Bill Castro .02 .10
110 Onix Concepcion .02 .10
111 Dave Frost .02 .10
112 Cesar Geronimo .02 .10
113 Larry Gura .02 .10
114 Steve Hammond .02 .10
115 Don Hood .02 .10
116 Dennis Leonard .02 .10
117 Jerry Martin .02 .10
118 Lee May .02 .10
119 Hal McRae .07 .20
120 Amos Otis .07 .20
121 Greg Pryor .02 .10
122 Dan Quisenberry .07 .20
123 Don Slaught RC .20 .50
124 Paul Splittorff .02 .10
125 U.L. Washington .02 .10
126 John Wathan .02 .10
127 Frank White .07 .20
128 Willie Wilson .07 .20
129 Steve Bedrosian UER .02 .10
Height 6'33
130 Bruce Benedict .02 .10
131 Tommy Boggs .02 .10
132 Brett Butler .07 .20
133 Rick Camp .02 .10
134 Chris Chambliss .07 .20
135 Ken Dayley .02 .10
136 Gene Garber .02 .10
137 Terry Harper .02 .10
138 Bob Horner .07 .20
139 Glenn Hubbard .02 .10
140 Rufino Linares .02 .10
141 Rick Mahler .02 .10
142 Dale Murphy .15 .40
143 Phil Niekro .07 .20
144 Pascual Perez .02 .10
145 Biff Pocoroba .02 .10
146 Rafael Ramirez .02 .10
147 Jerry Royster .02 .10
148 Ken Smith .02 .10
149 Bob Walk .02 .10
150 Claudell Washington .02 .10
151 Bob Watson .02 .10
152 Larry Whisenton .02 .10
153 Porfirio Altamirano .02 .10
154 Marty Bystrom .02 .10
155 Steve Carlton .15 .40
156 Larry Christenson .02 .10
157 Ivan DeJesus .02 .10
158 John Denny .02 .10
159 Bob Dernier .02 .10
160 Bo Diaz .02 .10
161 Ed Farmer .02 .10
162 Greg Gross .02 .10
163 Mike Krukow .02 .10
164 Garry Maddox .02 .10
165 Gary Matthews .07 .20
166 Tug McGraw .07 .20
167 Bob Molinaro .02 .10
168 Sid Monge .02 .10
169 Ron Reed .02 .10
170 Bill Robinson .02 .10
171 Pete Rose 1.00 2.50
172 Dick Ruthven .02 .10
173 Mike Schmidt .75 2.00
174 Manny Trillo .02 .10
175 Ozzie Virgil .02 .10
176 George Vukovich .02 .10
177 Gary Allenson .02 .10
178 Luis Aponte .02 .10
179 Wade Boggs RC 6.00 15.00
180 Tom Burgmeier .02 .10
181 Mark Clear .02 .10
182 Dennis Eckersley .15 .40
183 Dwight Evans .15 .40
184 Rich Gedman .02 .10
185 Glenn Hoffman .02 .10
186 Bruce Hurst .02 .10
187 Carney Lansford .07 .20
188 Rick Miller .02 .10
189 Reid Nichols .02 .10
190 Bob Ojeda .02 .10
191 Tony Perez .15 .40
192 Chuck Rainey .02 .10
193 Jerry Remy .02 .10
194 Jim Rice .07 .20
195 Bob Stanley .02 .10
196 Dave Stapleton .02 .10
197 Mike Torrez .02 .10
198 John Tudor .07 .20
199 Julio Valdez .02 .10
200 Carl Yastrzemski .50 1.25
201 Dusty Baker .07 .20
202 Joe Beckwith .02 .10
203 Greg Brock .02 .10
204 Ron Cey .07 .20
205 Terry Forster .07 .20
206 Steve Garvey .07 .20
207 Pedro Guerrero .07 .20
208 Burt Hooton .02 .10
209 Steve Howe .02 .10
210 Ken Landreaux .02 .10
211 Mike Marshall .02 .10
212 Candy Maldonado RC .20 .50
213 Rick Monday .07 .20
214 Tom Niedenfuer .02 .10
215 Jorge Orta .02 .10
216 Jerry Reuss UER .02 .10
217 Ron Roenicke .02 .10
218 Vicente Romo .02 .10
219 Bill Russell .07 .20
220 Steve Sax .07 .20
221 Mike Scioscia .07 .20
222 Dave Stewart .07 .20
223 Derrel Thomas .02 .10
224 Fernando Valenzuela .07 .20
225 Bob Welch .07 .20
226 Ricky Wright .02 .10
227 Steve Yeager .07 .20
228 Bill Almon .02 .10
229 Harold Baines .07 .20
230 Salome Barojas .02 .10
231 Tony Bernazard .02 .10
232 Britt Burns .02 .10
233 Richard Dotson .02 .10
234 Ernesto Escarrega .02 .10
235 Carlton Fisk .15 .40
236 Jerry Hairston .02 .10
237 Kevin Hickey .02 .10
238 LaMarr Hoyt .02 .10
239 Steve Kemp .02 .10
240 Jim Kern .02 .10
241 Ron Kittle RC .40 1.00
242 Jerry Koosman .07 .20
243 Dennis Lamp .02 .10
244 Rudy Law .02 .10
245 Vance Law .02 .10
246 Ron LeFlore .07 .20
247 Greg Luzinski .07 .20
248 Tom Paciorek .02 .10
249 Aurelio Rodriguez .02 .10
250 Mike Squires .02 .10
251 Steve Trout .02 .10
252 Jim Barr .02 .10
253 Dave Bergman .02 .10
254 Fred Breining .02 .10
255 Bob Brenly .02 .10
256 Jack Clark .07 .20
257 Chili Davis .07 .20
258 Darrell Evans .07 .20
259 Alan Fowlkes .02 .10
260 Rich Gale .02 .10
261 Atlee Hammaker .02 .10
262 Al Holland .02 .10
263 Duane Kuiper .02 .10
264 Bill Laskey .02 .10
265 Gary Lavelle .02 .10
266 Johnnie LeMaster .02 .10
267 Renie Martin .02 .10
268 Milt May .02 .10
269 Greg Minton .02 .10
270 Joe Morgan .07 .20
271 Tom O'Malley .02 .10
272 Reggie Smith .07 .20
273 Guy Sularz .02 .10
274 Champ Summers .02 .10
275 Max Venable .02 .10
276 Jim Wohlford .02 .10
277 Ray Burris .02 .10
278 Gary Carter .07 .20
279 Warren Cromartie .02 .10
280 Andre Dawson .07 .20
281 Terry Francona .07 .20
282 Doug Flynn .02 .10
283 Woodie Fryman .02 .10
284 Bill Gullickson .02 .10
285 Wallace Johnson .02 .10
286 Charlie Lea .02 .10
287 Randy Lerch .02 .10
288 Brad Mills .02 .10
289 Dan Norman .02 .10
290 Al Oliver .07 .20
291 David Palmer .02 .10
292 Tim Raines .07 .20
293 Jeff Reardon .07 .20
294 Steve Rogers .07 .20
295 Scott Sanderson .02 .10
296 Dan Schatzeder .02 .10
297 Bryn Smith .02 .10
298 Chris Speier .02 .10
299 Tim Wallach .07 .20
300 Jerry White .02 .10
301 Joel Youngblood .02 .10
302 Ross Baumgarten .02 .10
303 Dale Berra .02 .10
304 John Candelaria .02 .10
305 Dick Davis .02 .10
306 Mike Easler .02 .10
307 Richie Hebner .02 .10
308 Lee Lacy .02 .10
309 Bill Madlock .07 .20
310 Larry McWilliams .02 .10
311 John Milner .02 .10
312 Omar Moreno .02 .10
313 Jim Morrison .02 .10
314 Steve Nicosia .02 .10
315 Dave Parker .07 .20
316 Tony Pena .02 .10
317 Johnny Ray .02 .10
318 Rick Rhoden .02 .10
319 Don Robinson .02 .10
320 Enrique Romo .02 .10
321 Manny Sarmiento .02 .10
322 Rod Scurry .02 .10
323 Jimmy Smith .02 .10
324 Willie Stargell .15 .40
325 Jason Thompson .02 .10
326 Kent Tekulve .02 .10
327A Tom Brookens .02 .10
Short .375-inch brown box
shaded in on card back
327B Tom Brookens .02 .10
Longer 1.25-inch brown box
shaded in on card back
328 Enos Cabell .02 .10
329 Kirk Gibson .07 .20
330 Larry Herndon .02 .10
331 Mike Ivie .02 .10
332 Howard Johnson RC .40 1.00
333 Lynn Jones .02 .10
334 Rick Leach .02 .10
335 Chet Lemon .07 .20
336 Jack Morris .07 .20
337 Lance Parrish .07 .20
338 Larry Pashnick .02 .10
339 Dan Petry .02 .10
340 Dave Rozema .02 .10
341 Dave Rucker .02 .10
342 Elias Sosa .02 .10
343 Dave Tobik .02 .10
344 Alan Trammell .07 .20

345 Jerry Turner .02 .10
346 Jerry Ujdur .02 .10
347 Pat Underwood .02 .10
348 Lou Whitaker .07 .20
349 Milt Wilcox .02 .10
350 Glenn Wilson .20 .50
351 John Wockenfuss .02 .10
352 Kurt Bevacqua .02 .10
353 Juan Bonilla .02 .10
354 Floyd Chiffer .02 .10
355 Luis DeLeon .02 .10
356 Dave Dravecky RC .40 1.00
357 Dave Edwards .02 .10
358 Juan Eichelberger .02 .10
359 Tim Flannery .02 .10
360 Tony Gwynn RC 8.00 20.00
361 Ruppert Jones .02 .10
362 Terry Kennedy .02 .10
363 Joe Lefebvre .02 .10
364 Sixto Lezcano .02 .10
365 Tim Lollar .02 .10
366 Gary Lucas .02 .10
367 John Montefusco .02 .10
368 Broderick Perkins .02 .10
369 Joe Pittman .02 .10
370 Gene Richards .02 .10
371 Luis Salazar .02 .10
372 Eric Show RC .20 .50
373 Garry Templeton .07 .20
374 Chris Welsh .02 .10
375 Alan Wiggins .02 .10
376 Rick Cerone .02 .10
377 Dave Collins .02 .10
378 Roger Erickson .02 .10
379 George Frazier .02 .10
380 Oscar Gamble .02 .10
381 Rich Gossage .07 .20
382 Ken Griffey .07 .20
383 Ron Guidry .07 .20
384 Dave LaRoche .02 .10
385 Rudy May .02 .10
386 John Mayberry .02 .10
387 Lee Mazzilli .07 .20
388 Mike Morgan .02 .10
389 Jerry Mumphrey .02 .10
390 Bobby Murcer .07 .20
391 Graig Nettles .07 .20
392 Lou Piniella .07 .20
393 Willie Randolph .07 .20
394 Shane Rawley .02 .10
395 Dave Righetti .07 .20
396 Andre Robertson .02 .10
397 Roy Smalley .02 .10
398 Dave Winfield .07 .20
399 Butch Wynegar .02 .10
400 Chris Bando .02 .10
401 Alan Bannister .02 .10
402 Len Barker .02 .10
403 Tom Brennan .02 .10
404 Carmelo Castillo .02 .10
405 Miguel Dilone .02 .10
406 Jerry Dybzinski .02 .10
407 Mike Fischlin .02 .10
408 Ed Glynn UER .02 .10
Photo actually
Bud Anderson
409 Mike Hargrove .02 .10
410 Toby Harrah .07 .20
411 Ron Hassey .02 .10
412 Von Hayes .02 .10
413 Rick Manning .02 .10
414 Bake McBride .07 .20
415 Larry Milbourne .02 .10
416 Bill Nahorodny .02 .10
417 Jack Perconte .02 .10
418 Lary Sorensen .02 .10
419 Dan Spillner .02 .10
420 Rick Sutcliffe .07 .20
421 Andre Thornton .02 .10
422 Rick Waits .02 .10
423 Eddie Whitson .02 .10
424 Jesse Barfield .07 .20
425 Barry Bonnell .02 .10
426 Jim Clancy .02 .10
427 Damaso Garcia .02 .10
428 Jerry Garvin .02 .10
429 Alfredo Griffin .02 .10
430 Garth Iorg .02 .10
431 Roy Lee Jackson .02 .10
432 Luis Leal .02 .10
433 Buck Martinez .02 .10
434 Joey McLaughlin .02 .10
435 Lloyd Moseby .02 .10
436 Rance Mulliniks .02 .10
437 Dale Murray .02 .10
438 Wayne Nordhagen .02 .10
439 Geno Petralli .20 .50
440 Hosken Powell .02 .10
441 Dave Stieb .07 .20
442 Willie Upshaw .02 .10
443 Ernie Whitt .02 .10
444 Alvis Woods .02 .10
445 Alan Ashby .02 .10
446 Jose Cruz .07 .20
447 Kiko Garcia .02 .10
448 Phil Garner .07 .20
449 Danny Heep .02 .10
450 Art Howe .02 .10
451 Bob Knepper .02 .10
452 Alan Knicely .02 .10
453 Ray Knight .07 .20
454 Frank LaCorte .02 .10
455 Mike LaCoss .02 .10
456 Randy Moffitt .02 .10
457 Joe Niekro .02 .10
458 Terry Puhl .02 .10
459 Luis Pujols .02 .10
460 Craig Reynolds .02 .10
461 Bert Roberge .02 .10
462 Vern Ruhle .02 .10
463 Nolan Ryan 1.50 4.00
464 Joe Sambito .02 .10
465 Tony Scott .02 .10
466 Dave Smith .02 .10
467 Harry Spilman .02 .10
468 Dickie Thon .02 .10
469 Denny Walling .02 .10
470 Larry Andersen .02 .10
471 Floyd Bannister .02 .10
472 Jim Beattie .02 .10
473 Bruce Bochte .02 .10
474 Manny Castillo .02 .10
475 Bill Caudill .02 .10
476 Bryan Clark .02 .10
477 Al Cowens .02 .10
478 Julio Cruz .02 .10
479 Todd Cruz .02 .10
480 Gary Gray .02 .10
481 Dave Henderson .02 .10
482 Mike Moore RC .20 .50
483 Gaylord Perry .07 .20
484 Dave Revering .02 .10
485 Joe Simpson .02 .10
486 Mike Stanton .02 .10
487 Rick Sweet .02 .10
488 Ed VandeBerg .02 .10
489 Richie Zisk .02 .10
490 Doug Bird .02 .10
491 Larry Bowa .07 .20
492 Bill Buckner .07 .20
493 Bill Campbell .02 .10
494 Jody Davis .02 .10
495 Leon Durham .02 .10
496 Steve Henderson .02 .10
497 Willie Hernandez .02 .10
498 Ferguson Jenkins .07 .20
499 Jay Johnstone .02 .10
500 Junior Kennedy .02 .10
501 Randy Martz .02 .10
502 Jerry Morales .02 .10
503 Keith Moreland .02 .10
504 Dickie Noles .02 .10
505 Mike Proly .02 .10
506 Allen Ripley .02 .10
507 Ryne Sandberg RC UER 8.00 20.00
508 Lee Smith .15 .40
509 Pat Tabler .02 .10
510 Dick Tidrow .02 .10
511 Bump Wills .02 .10
512 Gary Woods .02 .10
513 Tony Armas .07 .20
514 Dave Beard .02 .10
515 Jeff Burroughs .02 .10
516 John D'Acquisto .02 .10
517 Wayne Gross .02 .10
518 Mike Heath .02 .10
519 Rickey Henderson UER .60 1.50
520 Cliff Johnson .02 .10
521 Matt Keough .02 .10
522 Brian Kingman .02 .10
523 Rick Langford .02 .10
524 Dave Lopes .07 .20
525 Steve McCatty .02 .10
526 Dave McKay .02 .10
527 Dan Meyer .02 .10
528 Dwayne Murphy .02 .10
529 Jeff Newman .02 .10
530 Mike Norris .02 .10
531 Bob Owchinko .02 .10
532 Joe Rudi .07 .20
533 Jimmy Sexton .02 .10
534 Fred Stanley .02 .10
535 Tom Underwood .02 .10
536 Neil Allen .02 .10
537 Wally Backman .02 .10
538 Bob Bailor .02 .10
539 Hubie Brooks .02 .10
540 Carlos Diaz RC .08 .25
541 Pete Falcone .02 .10
542 George Foster .07 .20
543 Ron Gardenhire .02 .10
544 Brian Giles .02 .10
545 Ron Hodges .02 .10
546 Randy Jones .02 .10
547 Mike Jorgensen .02 .10
548 Dave Kingman .07 .20
549 Ed Lynch .02 .10
550 Jesse Orosco .02 .10
551 Rick Ownbey .02 .10
552 Charlie Puleo .02 .10
553 Gary Rajsich .02 .10
554 Mike Scott .07 .20
555 Rusty Staub .07 .20
556 John Stearns .02 .10
557 Craig Swan .02 .10
558 Ellis Valentine .02 .10
559 Tom Veryzer .02 .10
560 Mookie Wilson .07 .20
561 Pat Zachry .02 .10
562 Buddy Bell .07 .20
563 John Butcher .02 .10
564 Steve Comer .02 .10
565 Danny Darwin .02 .10
566 Bucky Dent .07 .20
567 John Grubb .02 .10
568 Rick Honeycutt .02 .10
569 Dave Hostetler RC .02 .10
570 Charlie Hough .07 .20
571 Lamar Johnson .02 .10
572 Jon Matlack .02 .10
573 Paul Mirabella .02 .10
574 Larry Parrish .02 .10
575 Mike Richardt .02 .10
576 Mickey Rivers .02 .10
577 Billy Sample .02 .10
578 Dave Schmidt .02 .10
579 Bill Stein .02 .10
580 Jim Sundberg .07 .20
581 Frank Tanana .07 .20
582 Mark Wagner .02 .10
583 George Wright RC .20 .50
584 Johnny Bench .30 .75
585 Bruce Berenyi .02 .10
586 Larry Biittner .02 .10
587 Cesar Cedeno .07 .20
588 Dave Concepcion .07 .20
589 Dan Driessen .02 .10
590 Greg Harris .02 .10
591 Ben Hayes .02 .10
592 Paul Householder .02 .10
593 Tom Hume .02 .10
594 Wayne Krenchicki .02 .10
595 Rafael Landestoy .02 .10
596 Charlie Leibrandt .02 .10
597 Eddie Milner .02 .10
598 Ron Oester .02 .10
599 Frank Pastore .02 .10
600 Joe Price .02 .10
601 Tom Seaver .30 .75
602 Bob Shirley .02 .10
603 Mario Soto .07 .20
604 Alex Trevino .02 .10
605 Mike Vail .02 .10
606 Duane Walker RC .02 .10
607 Tom Brunansky .07 .20
608 Bobby Castillo .02 .10
609 John Castino .02 .10
610 Ron Davis .02 .10
611 Lenny Faedo .02 .10
612 Terry Felton .02 .10
613 Gary Gaetti RC .40 1.00
614 Mickey Hatcher .02 .10
615 Brad Havens .02 .10
616 Kent Hrbek .07 .20
617 Randy Johnson RC .02 .10
618 Tim Laudner .02 .10
619 Jeff Little .02 .10
620 Bobby Mitchell .02 .10
621 Jack O'Connor .02 .10
622 John Pacella .02 .10
623 Pete Redfern .02 .10
624 Jesus Vega .02 .10
625 Frank Viola RC .60 1.50
626 Ron Washington RC .10 .25
627 Gary Ward .02 .10
628 Al Williams .02 .10
629 Carl Yastrzemski .30 .75
Dennis Eckersley
Mark Clear
630 Gaylord Perry .02 .10
Terry Bulling
631 Dave Concepcion .07 .20
Manny Trillo
632 Robin Yount .30 .75
Buddy Bell
633 Dave Winfield .02 .10
Kent Hrbek
634 Willie Stargell .30 .75
Pete Rose
635 Toby Harrah .07 .20
Andre Thornton
636 Ozzie Smith .30 .75
Lonnie Smith
637 Bo Diaz .02 .10
Gary Carter
638 Carlton Fisk .07 .20
Gary Carter
639 Rickey Henderson IA .30 .75
640 Ben Oglivie .15 .40
Reggie Jackson
641 Joel Youngblood .02 .10
August 4, 1982
642 Ron Hassey .07 .20
Len Barker
643 Black and Blue .07 .20
Vida Blue
644 Black and Blue .02 .10
Bud Black
645 Reggie Jackson Power .07 .20
646 Rickey Henderson Speed .30 .75
647 CL: Cards .02 .10
Brewers
648 CL: Orioles .02 .10
Angels
649 CL: Royals .02 .10
Braves
650 CL: Phillies .02 .10
Red Sox
651 CL: Dodgers .02 .10
White Sox
652 CL: Giants .02 .10
Expos
653 CL: Pirates .02 .10
Tigers
654 CL: Padres .02 .10
Yankees
655 CL: Indians .02 .10
Blue Jays
656 CL: Astros .02 .10
Mariners
657 CL: Cubs .02 .10
A's
658 CL: Mets .02 .10
Rangers
659 CL: Reds .02 .10
Twins
660 CL: Specials .02 .10
Teams

1983 Fleer Stamps

This 250-stamp set features color photos of players and team logos on stamps measuring approximately 1 1/4" by 1 13/16" each. The stamps were issued on four different sheets of 72 stamps each. There are 224 player stamps and 26 team logo stamps. The team logo stamps have double and triple prints. Baseball trivia quiz questions were also included with the stamps. The stamps are unnumbered and checklisted below in alphabetical order. Stamps were issued in three different colored Vend-A-Strip dispensors. Each row in a dispensor consisted of 18 stamps and 11 quizes.

COMPLETE SET (250) 4.00 10.00
1 Willie Aikens .01 .05
2 Neil Allen .01 .05
3 Joaquin Andujar .01 .05
4 Alan Ashby .01 .05
5 Bob Bailor .01 .05
6 Harold Baines .05 .15
7 Dusty Baker .02 .10
8 Floyd Bannister .01 .05
9 Len Barker .01 .05
10 Don Baylor .02 .10
11 Dave Beard .01 .05
12 Jim Beattie .01 .05
13 Buddy Bell .02 .10
14 Johnny Bench .30 .75
15 Dale Berra .01 .05
16 Larry Biittner .01 .05
17 Vida Blue .02 .10
18 Bruce Bochte .01 .05
19 Wade Boggs 2.00 5.00
20 Bob Boone .02 .10
21 Larry Bowa .01 .05
22 George Brett .75 2.00
23 Hubie Brooks .01 .05
24 Tom Brunansky .01 .05
25 Bill Buckner .02 .10
26 Al Bumbry .01 .05
27 Jeff Burroughs .01 .05
28 Enos Cabell .01 .05
29 Rod Carew .20 .50
30 Steve Carlton .15 .40
31 Gary Carter .15 .40
32 Bobby Castillo .01 .05
33 Bill Caudill .01 .05
34 Cesar Cedeno .02 .10
35 Rick Cerone .01 .05
36 Ron Cey .02 .10
37 Chris Chambliss .02 .10
38 Larry Christenson .01 .05
39 Jim Clancy .01 .05
40 Jack Clark .02 .10
41 Mark Clear .01 .05
42 Dave Concepcion .02 .10
43 Cecil Cooper .02 .10
44 Warren Cromartie .01 .05
45 Jose Cruz .02 .10
46 Danny Darwin .01 .05
47 Rich Dauer .01 .05
48 Ron Davis .01 .05
49 Andre Dawson .20 .50
50 Doug DeCinces .01 .05
51 Ivan DeJesus .01 .05
52 Luis DeLeon .01 .05
53 Bo Diaz .01 .05
54 Brian Downing .02 .10
55 Dan Driessen .01 .05
56 Leon Durham .01 .05
57 Mike Easler .01 .05
58 Dennis Eckersley .20 .50
59 Dwight Evans .05 .15
60 Rollie Fingers .15 .40
61 Carlton Fisk .20 .50
62 Mike Flanagan .01 .05
63 Bob Forsch .01 .05
64 Ken Forsch .01 .05
65 George Foster .02 .10
66 Gene Garber .02 .10
67 Damaso Garcia .01 .05
68 Phil Garner .02 .10
69 Steve Garvey .05 .15
70 Goose Gossage .05 .15
71 Ken Griffey .02 .10
72 John Grubb .01 .05
73 Ron Guidry .02 .10
74 Atlee Hammaker .01 .05
75 Mike Hargrove .02 .10
76 Toby Harrah .01 .05
77 Rickey Henderson .75 2.00
78 Keith Hernandez .05 .15
79 Larry Herndon .01 .05
80 Tom Herr .01 .05
81 Al Holland .01 .05
82 Burt Hooton .01 .05
83 Bob Horner .01 .05
84 Art Howe .01 .05
85 Steve Howe .01 .05
86 LaMarr Hoyt .01 .05
87 Kent Hrbek .08 .25
88 Tom Hume .01 .05
89 Garth Iorg .01 .05
90 Reggie Jackson .30 .75
91 Ferguson Jenkins .10 .30
92 Tommy John .05 .15
93 Ruppert Jones .01 .05
94 Steve Kemp .01 .05
95 Bruce Kison .01 .05
96 Ray Knight .01 .05
97 Jerry Koosman .02 .10
98 Duane Kuiper .01 .05
99 Ken Landreaux .01 .05
100 Carney Lansford .01 .05
101 Bill Laskey .01 .05
102 Gary Lavelle .01 .05
103 Charlie Lea .01 .05
104 Ron LeFlore .01 .05
105 Dennis Leonard .01 .05
106 Sixto Lezcano .01 .05
107 Davey Lopes .02 .10
108 John Lowenstein .01 .05
109 Greg Luzinski .02 .10
110 Fred Lynn .05 .15
111 Garry Maddox .01 .05
112 Bill Madlock .02 .10
113 Rick Manning .01 .05
114 Dennis Martinez .02 .10
115 Tippy Martinez .01 .05
116 Randy Martz .01 .05
117 John Matlack .01 .05
118 Gary Matthews .02 .10
119 Milt May .01 .05
120 Lee Mazzilli .02 .10
121 Bob McClure .01 .05
122 Tug McGraw .02 .10
123 Scott McGregor .01 .05
124 Hal McRae .02 .10
125 Eddie Milner .01 .05
126 Greg Minton .01 .05
127 Paul Molitor .30 .75
128 Rick Monday .01 .05
129 John Montefusco .01 .05
130 Keith Moreland .01 .05
131 Joe Morgan .20 .50
132 Jerry Mumphrey .01 .05
133 Steve Mura .01 .05
134 Dale Murphy .15 .40
135 Dwayne Murphy .01 .05
136 Eddie Murray .20 .50
137 Graig Nettles .05 .15
138 Joe Niekro .02 .10
139 Phil Niekro .10 .30
140 Ken Oberkfell .01 .05
141 Ben Oglivie .01 .05
142 Al Oliver .05 .15
143 Amos Otis .02 .10
144 Tom Paciorek .01 .05
145 Jim Palmer .15 .40
146 Dave Parker .02 .10
147 Lance Parrish .05 .15
148 Larry Parrish .02 .10
149 Tony Pena .02 .10
150 Gaylord Perry .10 .30
151 Lou Piniella .02 .10
152 Darrell Porter .01 .05
153 Hosken Powell .01 .05
154 Dan Quisenberry .02 .10
155 Tim Raines .08 .25
156 Rafael Ramirez .01 .05
157 Willie Randolph .02 .10
158 Johnny Ray .01 .05
159 Jeff Reardon .02 .10
160 Ron Reed .01 .05
161 Jerry Reuss .02 .10
162 Rick Rhoden .01 .05
163 Jim Rice .02 .10
164 Mike Richardt .01 .05
165 Cal Ripken Jr. 1.50 4.00
166 Ron Roenicke .01 .05
167 Steve Rogers .01 .05
168 Pete Rose .40 1.00
169 Jerry Royster .01 .05
170 Nolan Ryan 1.50 4.00
171 Manny Sarmiento .01 .05
172 Steve Sax .01 .05
173 Mike Schmidt .40 1.00
174 Tom Seaver .20 .50
175 Eric Show .01 .05
176 Ted Simmons .05 .15
177 Ken Singleton .01 .05
178 Roy Smalley .01 .05
179 Lonnie Smith .01 .05
180 Ozzie Smith .75 2.00
181 Reggie Smith .02 .10
182 Mario Soto .01 .05
183 Chris Speier .01 .05
184 Dan Spillner .01 .05
185 Bob Stanley .01 .05
186 Willie Stargell .10 .30
187 Rusty Staub .05 .15
188 Dave Stieb .02 .10
189 Jim Sundberg .01 .05
190 Rick Sutcliffe .01 .05
191 Bruce Sutter .02 .10
192 Don Sutton .10 .30
193 Craig Swan .01 .05
194 Kent Tekulve .01 .05
195 Gorman Thomas .01 .05
196 Jason Thompson .01 .05
197 Dickie Thon .01 .05
198 Andre Thornton .01 .05
199 Dick Tidrow .01 .05
200 Manny Trillo .01 .05
201 John Tudor .01 .05
202 Tom Underwood .01 .05
203 Willie Upshaw .01 .05
204 Ellis Valentin .01 .05
205 Fernando Valenzuela .10 .30
206 Ed VandeBerg .01 .05
207 Pete Vuckovich .01 .05
208 Gary Ward .01 .05
209 Claudell Washington .01 .05
210 U.L. Washington .01 .05
211 Bob Watson .02 .10
212 Lou Whitaker .08 .25
213 Frank White .01 .05
214 Milt Wilcox .01 .05
215 Al Williams .01 .05
216 Bump Wills .01 .05
217 Mookie Wilson .02 .10
218 Willie Wilson .01 .05
219 Dave Winfield .30 .75
220 John Wockenfuss .01 .05
221 Carl Yastrzemski .20 .50
222 Robin Yount .20 .50
223 Pat Zachry .01 .05
224 Richie Zisk .01 .05
225 Atlanta Braves TP .01 .05
226 Baltimore Orioles DP .01 .05
227 Boston Red Sox DP .01 .05
228 California Angels TP .01 .05
229 Chicago Cubs DP .01 .05
230 Chicago White Sox TP .01 .05
231 Cincinnati Reds TP .01 .05
232 Cleveland Indians TP .01 .05
233 Detroit Tigers DP .01 .05
234 Houston Astros DP .01 .05
235 Los Angeles Dodgers TP .01 .05
236 Kansas City Royals TP .01 .05
237 Milwaukee Brewers DP .01 .05
238 Minnesota Twins TP .01 .05
239 Montreal Expos TP .01 .05
240 New York Mets DP .01 .05
241 New York Yankees DP .01 .05
242 Oakland A's DP .01 .05
243 Philadelphia Phillies TP .01 .05
244 Pittsburgh Pirates TP .01 .05
245 St. Louis Cardinals DP .01 .05
246 San Diego Padres DP .01 .05
247 San Francisco Giants TP .01 .05
248 Seattle Mariners DP .01 .05
249 Texas Rangers DP .01 .05
250 Toronto Blue Jays DP .01 .05

1983 Fleer Stickers

The stickers in this 270-sticker set measure approximately 1 13/16" by 2 1/2". The 1983 Fleer stickers set was issued in strips of ten stickers plus two team logos per strip. No album was issued for the stickers. The fronts contain player photos surrounded by a blue border with two red stars on the upper portion of a yellow frameline. While all of the players could be attained on 27 different strips, it was necessary to have 30 different strips to obtain all of the team logos. There are a few instances where the logo pictured on the front of the card relates to a different team checklisted on the back of the card. The backs of the logo stamps feature either a team checklist (CL) or poster offer (PO).

COMPLETE SET 5.00 12.00
1 Bruce Sutter .02 .10
2 Willie McGee .10 .30
3 Darrell Porter .01 .05
4 Lonnie Smith .01 .05
5 Dane Iorg .01 .05
6 Keith Hernandez .02 .10
7 Joaquin Andujar .01 .05
8 Ken Oberkfell .01 .05
9 John Stuper .01 .05
10 Ozzie Smith .60 1.50
11 Bob Forsch .01 .05
12 Jim Gantner .01 .05
13 Rollie Fingers .10 .30
14 Pete Vuckovich .01 .05
15 Ben Oglivie .01 .05
16 Don Sutton .10 .30
17 Bob McClure .01 .05
18 Robin Yount .15 .40
19 Paul Molitor .20 .50
20 Gorman Thomas .01 .05
21 Mike Caldwell .01 .05
22 Ted Simmons .02 .10
23 Cecil Cooper .02 .10
24 Steve Renko .01 .05
25 Tommy John .05 .15
26 Rod Carew .15 .40
27 Bruce Kison .01 .05
28 Ken Forsch .01 .05
29 Geoff Zahn .01 .05
30 Doug DeCinces .01 .05
31 Fred Lynn .02 .10
32 Reggie Jackson .30 .75
33 Don Baylor .02 .10
34 Bob Boone .02 .10
35 Brian Downing .01 .05
36 Rich Gossage .05 .15
37 Roy Smalley .01 .05
38 Graig Nettles .05 .15
39 Dave Winfield .20 .50
40 Lee Mazzilli .02 .10
41 Jerry Mumphrey .01 .05
42 Dave Collins .01 .05
43 Rick Cerone .01 .05
44 Willie Randolph .02 .10
45 Lou Piniella .02 .10
46 Ken Griffey .02 .10
47 Ron Guidry .02 .10
48 Jack Clark .01 .05
49 Reggie Smith .01 .05
50 Atlee Hammaker .01 .05
51 Fred Breining .01 .05
52 Gary Lavelle .01 .05
53 Chili Davis .08 .25
54 Greg Minton .01 .05
55 Joe Morgan .10 .30
56 Al Holland .01 .05
57 Bill Laskey .01 .05
58 Duane Kuiper .01 .05
59 Tom Burgmeier .01 .05
60 Carl Yastrzemski .20 .50
61 Mark Clear .01 .05
62 Mike Torrez .01 .05
63 Dennis Eckersley .10 .30
64 Wade Boggs 1.25 3.00
65 Bob Stanley .01 .05
66 Jim Rice .02 .10
67 Carney Lansford .01 .05
68 Jerry Remy .01 .05
69 Dwight Evans .05 .15
70 John Candelaria .01 .05
71 Bill Madlock .02 .10
72 Dave Parker .02 .10
73 Kent Tekulve .01 .05
74 Tony Pena .02 .10
75 Manny Sarmiento .01 .05
76 Johnny Ray .01 .05
77 Dale Berra .01 .05
78 Lee Lacy .01 .05
79 Jason Thompson .01 .05
80 Mike Easler .01 .05
81 Willie Stargell .10 .30
82 Rick Camp .01 .05
83 Bob Watson .02 .10
84 Bob Horner .01 .05
85 Rafael Ramirez .01 .05
86 Chris Chambliss .02 .10
87 Gene Garber .02 .10
88 Claudell Washington .01 .05
89 Steve Bedrosian .01 .05
90 Dale Murphy .20 .50
91 Phil Niekro .10 .30
92 Jerry Royster .01 .05
93 Bob Walk .01 .05
94 Frank White .01 .05
95 Dennis Leonard .01 .05
96 Vida Blue .02 .10
97 U.L. Washington .01 .05
98 George Brett 1.25 3.00
99 Amos Otis .01 .05
100 Dan Quisenberry .01 .05
101 Willie Aikens .01 .05
102 Hal McRae .01 .05
103 Larry Gura .01 .05
104 Willie Wilson .01 .05
105 Damaso Garcia .01 .05
106 Hosken Powell .01 .05
107 Joey McLaughlin .01 .05
108 Jim Clancy .01 .05
109 Barry Bonnell .01 .05
110 Garth Iorg .01 .05
111 Dave Stieb .02 .10
112 Fernando Valenzuela .05 .15
113 Steve Garvey .08 .25
114 Rick Monday .01 .05
115 Burt Hooten .01 .05
116 Bill Russell .01 .05
117 Pedro Guerrero .02 .10
118 Steve Sax .01 .05
119 Steve Howe .01 .05
120 Ken Landreaux .01 .05
121 Dusty Baker .02 .10
122 Ron Cey .02 .10
123 Jerry Reuss .02 .10
124 Bump Wills .01 .05
125 Keith Moreland .01 .05
126 Dick Tidrow .01 .05
127 Bill Campbell .01 .05
128 Larry Bowa .01 .05
129 Randy Martz .01 .05
130 Ferguson Jenkins .10 .30
131 Leon Durham .01 .05
132 Bill Buckner .02 .10
133 Ron Davis .01 .05
134 Jack O'Connor .01 .05
135 Kent Hrbek .02 .10
136 Gary Ward .01 .05
137 Al Williams .01 .05
138 Tom Brunansky .01 .05
139 Bobby Castillo .01 .05
140 Dusty Baker .05 .15
Dale Murphy
141 Nolan Ryan 1.00 2.50
Alan Ashby
142 Omar Moreno .01 .05
Lee Lacy
sic, Lacey
143 Al Oliver .20 .50
Pete Rose
144 Rickey Henderson .30 .75
145 Ray Knight .20 .50

ike Schmidt
ete Rose
Ben Oglivie .01 .05
al McRae
Ray Knight .01 .05
m Hume
Buddy Bell .08 .25
arlton Fisk
Steve Kemp .01 .05
Rudy Law .01 .05
Ron LeFlore .01 .05
Jerry Koosman .02 .10
Carlton Fisk .20 .50
Salome Barojas .01 .05
Harold Baines .02 .10
Britt Burns .01 .05
Tom Paciorek .01 .05
Greg Luzinski .01 .05
LaMarr Hoyt .01 .05
George Wright .01 .05
Danny Darwin .01 .05
Lamar Johnson .01 .05
3 Charlie Hough .02 .10
Buddy Bell .02 .10
5 Jon Matlack .01 .05
Billy Sample .01 .05
Johnny Grubb .01 .05
3 Larry Parrish .02 .10
Ivan DeJesus .01 .05
Mike Schmidt .40 1.00
Tug McGraw .01 .05
2 Ron Reed .01 .05
3 Garry Maddox .01 .05
4 Pete Rose .60 1.50
5 Manny Trillo .01 .05
6 Steve Carlton .30 .75
7 Bo Diaz .01 .05
8 Gary Matthews .01 .05
9 Bill Caudill .01 .05
0 Ed VandeBerg .01 .05
1 Gaylord Perry .10 .30
2 Floyd Bannister .01 .05
3 Richie Zisk .01 .05
4 Al Cowens .01 .05
5 Bruce Bochte .01 .05
6 Jeff Burroughs .01 .05
7 Dave Beard .01 .05
8 Dave Lopes .01 .05
9 Dwayne Murphy .01 .05
0 Rick Langford .01 .05
1 Tom Underwood .01 .05
2 Rickey Henderson .75 2.00
3 Mike Flanagan .01 .05
4 Scott McGregor .01 .05
5 Ken Singleton .01 .05
6 Rich Dauer .01 .05
7 John Lowenstein .01 .05
8 Cal Ripken 2.00 5.00
9 Dennis Martinez .02 .10
0 Jim Palmer .20 .50
1 Tippy Martinez .01 .05
2 Eddie Murray .40 1.00
3 Al Bumbry .01 .05
4 Dickie Thon .01 .05
5 Phil Garner .02 .10
6 Jose Cruz .02 .10
7 Nolan Ryan 2.00 5.00
08 Ray Knight .01 .05
09 Terry Puhl .01 .05
10 Joe Niekro .01 .05
11 Art Howe .01 .05
12 Alan Ashby .01 .05
13 Tom Hume .01 .05
14 Johnny Bench .20 .50
15 Larry Biittner .01 .05
16 Mario Soto .01 .05
17 Dan Driessen .01 .05
18 Tom Seaver .20 .50
19 Dave Concepcion .02 .10
20 Wayne Krenchicki .01 .05
21 Cesar Cedeno .01 .05
22 Ruppert Jones .01 .05
23 Terry Kennedy .01 .05
24 Luis DeLeon .01 .05
25 Eric Show .01 .05
26 Tim Flannery .01 .05
27 Garry Templeton .01 .05
28 Tim Lollar .01 .05
29 Sixto Lezcano .01 .05
230 Bob Bailor .01 .05
231 Craig Swan .01 .05
232 Dave Kingman .02 .10
233 Mookie Wilson .02 .10
234 John Stearns .01 .05
235 Ellis Valentine .01 .05
236 Neil Allen .01 .05
237 Pat Zachry .01 .05
238 Rusty Staub .02 .10
239 George Foster .01 .05
240 Rick Sutcliffe .01 .05
241 Andre Thornton .01 .05
242 Mike Hargrove .02 .10
243 Dan Spillner .01 .05
244 Lary Sorensen .01 .05
245 Len Barker .01 .05
246 Rick Manning .01 .05
247 Toby Harrah .01 .05
248 Milt Wilcox .01 .05
249 Lou Whitaker .02 .10
250 Tom Brookens .01 .05
251 Chet Lemon .01 .05
252 Jack Morris .02 .10
253 Alan Trammell .08 .25
254 Johnny Wockenfuss .01 .05
255 Lance Parrish .05 .15
256 Larry Herndon .01 .05
257 Chris Speier .01 .05
258 Woodie Fryman .01 .05
259 Scott Sanderson .01 .05
260 Steve Rogers .01 .05
261 Warren Cromartie .01 .05
262 Gary Carter .15 .40
263 Bill Gullickson .01 .05
264 Andre Dawson .10 .30
265 Tim Raines .05 .15
266 Charlie Lea .01 .05
267 Jeff Reardon .02 .10
268 Al Oliver .02 .10
269 George Hendrick .01 .05
270 John Montefusco .01 .05
NNO Oakland A's CL .01 .05
NNO Pittsburgh Pirates PO .01 .05
NNO St. Louis Cardinals CL .01 .05
NNO Los Angeles Dodgers CL .01 .05
NNO St. Louis Cardinals PO .01 .05
NNO Baltimore Orioles CL .01 .05
NNO Montreal Expos PO .01 .05
NNO Philadelphia Phillies CL .01 .05
NNO Chicago White Sox PO .01 .05
NNO New York Yankees PO .01 .05
NNO San Diego Padres PO .01 .05
NNO Atlanta Braves PO .01 .05
NNO Texas Rangers CL .01 .05
NNO Los Angeles Dodgers PO .01 .05
NNO Detroit Tigers CL .01 .05
NNO Milwaukee Brewers PO .01 .05
NNO Toronto Blue Jays PO .01 .05
NNO Kansas City Royals CL .01 .05
NNO Montreal Expos CL .01 .05
NNO Boston Red Sox CL .01 .05
NNO California Angels PO .01 .05
NNO California Angels CL .01 .05
NNO Minnesota Twins PO .01 .05
NNO Pittsburgh Pirates CL .01 .05
NNO San Diego Padres CL .01 .05
NNO Cleveland Indians PO .01 .05
NNO Baltimore Orioles PO .01 .05
NNO New York Mets PO .01 .05
NNO Cincinnati Reds CL .01 .05
NNO Houston Astros PO .01 .05
NNO San Francisco Giants PO .01 .05
NNO Atlanta Braves CL .01 .05
NNO Toronto Blue Jays CL .01 .05
NNO Minnesota Twins CL .01 .05
NNO Chicago Cubs CL .01 .05
NNO Boston Red Sox PO .01 .05
NNO Kansas City Royals PO .01 .05
NNO New York Yankees CL .01 .05
NNO Philadelphia Phillies PO .01 .05
NNO Cincinnati Reds PO .01 .05
NNO Detroit Tigers PO .01 .05
NNO New York Mets CL .01 .05
NNO Milwaukee Brewers CL .01 .05
NNO Cleveland Indians CL .01 .05
NNO Seattle Mariners CL .01 .05
NNO Seattle Mariners PO .01 .05

1984 Fleer

The 1984 Fleer card 660-card standard-size set featured fronts with full-color team logos along with the player's name and position and the Fleer identification. Wax packs again consisted of 15 cards plus logo stickers. The set features many imaginative photos, several multi-player cards, and many more action shots than the 1983 card set. The backs are quite similar to the 1983 backs except that blue rather than brown ink is used. The player cards are alphabetized within team and the teams are ordered by their 1983 season finish and won-lost record. Specials (626-646) and checklist cards (647-660) make up the end of the set. The key Rookie Cards in this set are Don Mattingly, Darryl Strawberry and Andy Van Slyke.

COMPLETE SET (660) 20.00 50.00
1 Mike Boddicker .05 .15
2 Al Bumbry .05 .15
3 Todd Cruz .05 .15
4 Rich Dauer .05 .15
5 Storm Davis .05 .15
6 Rick Dempsey .05 .15
7 Jim Dwyer .05 .15
8 Mike Flanagan .05 .15
9 Dan Ford .05 .15
10 John Lowenstein .05 .15
11 Dennis Martinez .15 .40
12 Tippy Martinez .05 .15
13 Scott McGregor .05 .15
14 Eddie Murray .60 1.50
15 Joe Nolan .05 .15
16 Jim Palmer .15 .40
17 Cal Ripken 4.00 10.00
18 Gary Roenicke .05 .15
19 Lenn Sakata .05 .15
20 John Shelby .05 .15
21 Ken Singleton .15 .40
22 Sammy Stewart .05 .15
23 Tim Stoddard .05 .15
24 Marty Bystrom .05 .15
25 Steve Carlton .30 .75
26 Ivan DeJesus .05 .15
27 John Denny .05 .15
28 Bob Dernier .05 .15
29 Bo Diaz .05 .15
30 Kiko Garcia .05 .15
31 Greg Gross .05 .15
32 Kevin Gross RC .20 .50
33 Von Hayes .05 .15
34 Willie Hernandez .05 .15
35 Al Holland .05 .15
36 Charles Hudson .05 .15
37 Joe Lefebvre .05 .15
38 Sixto Lezcano .05 .15
39 Garry Maddox .05 .15
40 Gary Matthews .05 .15
41 Len Matuszek .05 .15
42 Tug McGraw .15 .40
43 Joe Morgan .15 .40
44 Tony Perez .30 .75
45 Ron Reed .05 .15
46 Pete Rose 2.00 5.00
47 Juan Samuel RC .40 1.00
48 Mike Schmidt 1.50 4.00
49 Ozzie Virgil .05 .15
50 Juan Agosto .05 .15
51 Harold Baines .15 .40
52 Floyd Bannister .05 .15
53 Salome Barojas .05 .15
54 Britt Burns .05 .15
55 Julio Cruz .05 .15
56 Richard Dotson .05 .15
57 Jerry Dybzinski .05 .15
58 Carlton Fisk .30 .75
59 Scott Fletcher .05 .15
60 Jerry Hairston .05 .15
61 Kevin Hickey .05 .15
62 Marc Hill .05 .15
63 LaMarr Hoyt .05 .15
64 Ron Kittle .05 .15
65 Jerry Koosman .15 .40
66 Dennis Lamp .05 .15
67 Rudy Law .05 .15
68 Vance Law .05 .15
69 Greg Luzinski .15 .40
70 Tom Paciorek .05 .15
71 Mike Squires .05 .15
72 Dick Tidrow .05 .15
73 Greg Walker .20 .50
74 Glenn Abbott .05 .15
75 Howard Bailey .05 .15
76 Doug Bair .05 .15
77 Juan Berenguer .05 .15
78 Tom Brookens .15 .40
79 Enos Cabell .05 .15
80 Kirk Gibson .60 1.50
81 John Grubb .05 .15
82 Larry Herndon .15 .40
83 Wayne Krenchicki .05 .15
84 Rick Leach .05 .15
85 Chet Lemon .15 .40
86 Aurelio Lopez .15 .40
87 Jack Morris .15 .40
88 Lance Parrish .30 .75
89 Dan Petry .15 .40
90 Dave Rozema .05 .15
91 Alan Trammell .15 .40
92 Lou Whitaker .15 .40
93 Milt Wilcox .05 .15
94 Glenn Wilson .15 .40
95 John Wockenfuss .05 .15
96 Dusty Baker .15 .40
97 Joe Beckwith .05 .15
98 Greg Brock .05 .15
99 Jack Fimple .05 .15
100 Pedro Guerrero .15 .40
101 Rick Honeycutt .05 .15
102 Burt Hooton .05 .15
103 Steve Howe .05 .15
104 Ken Landreaux .05 .15
105 Mike Marshall .15 .40
106 Rick Monday .15 .40
107 Jose Morales .05 .15
108 Tom Niedenfuer .05 .15
109 Alejandro Pena RC* .40 1.00
110 Jerry Reuss UER .05 .15
111 Bill Russell .15 .40
112 Steve Sax .05 .15
113 Mike Scioscia .15 .40
114 Derrel Thomas .05 .15
115 Fernando Valenzuela .15 .40
116 Bob Welch .15 .40
117 Steve Yeager .15 .40
118 Pat Zachry .05 .15
119 Don Baylor .15 .40
120 Bert Campaneris .15 .40
121 Rick Cerone .05 .15
122 Ray Fontenot .05 .15
123 George Frazier .05 .15
124 Oscar Gamble .05 .15
125 Rich Gossage .15 .40
126 Ken Griffey .15 .40
127 Ron Guidry .15 .40
128 Jay Howell .05 .15
129 Steve Kemp .05 .15
130 Matt Keough .05 .15
131 Don Mattingly RC 8.00 20.00
132 John Montefusco .05 .15
133 Omar Moreno .05 .15
134 Dale Murray .05 .15
135 Graig Nettles .15 .40
136 Lou Piniella .15 .40
137 Willie Randolph .15 .40
138 Shane Rawley .05 .15
139 Dave Righetti .15 .40
140 Andre Robertson .05 .15
141 Bob Shirley .05 .15
142 Roy Smalley .05 .15
143 Dave Winfield .15 .40
144 Butch Wynegar .05 .15
145 Jim Acker .05 .15
146 Doyle Alexander .05 .15
147 Jesse Barfield .15 .40
148 Jorge Bell .15 .40
149 Barry Bonnell .05 .15
150 Jim Clancy .05 .15
151 Dave Collins .05 .15
152 Tony Fernandez RC .40 1.00
153 Damaso Garcia .05 .15
154 Dave Geisel .05 .15
155 Jim Gott .05 .15
156 Alfredo Griffin .05 .15
157 Garth Iorg .05 .15
158 Roy Lee Jackson .05 .15
159 Cliff Johnson .05 .15
160 Luis Leal .05 .15
161 Buck Martinez .05 .15
162 Joey McLaughlin .05 .15
163 Randy Moffitt .05 .15
164 Lloyd Moseby .05 .15
165 Rance Mulliniks .05 .15
166 Jorge Orta .05 .15
167 Dave Stieb .15 .40
168 Willie Upshaw .05 .15
169 Ernie Whitt .05 .15
170 Len Barker .05 .15
171 Steve Bedrosian .05 .15
172 Bruce Benedict .05 .15
173 Brett Butler .15 .40
174 Rick Camp .05 .15
175 Chris Chambliss .15 .40
176 Ken Dayley .05 .15
177 Pete Falcone .05 .15
178 Terry Forster .05 .15
179 Gene Garber .05 .15
180 Terry Harper .05 .15
181 Bob Horner .05 .15
182 Glenn Hubbard .05 .15
183 Randy Johnson .05 .15
184 Craig McMurtry .05 .15
185 Donnie Moore .05 .15
186 Dale Murphy .30 .75
187 Phil Niekro .15 .40
188 Pascual Perez .05 .15
189 Biff Pocoroba .05 .15
190 Rafael Ramirez .05 .15
191 Jerry Royster .05 .15
192 Claudell Washington .05 .15
193 Bob Watson .05 .15
194 Jerry Augustine .05 .15
195 Mark Brouhard .05 .15
196 Mike Caldwell .05 .15
197 Tom Candiotti RC .40 1.00
198 Cecil Cooper .15 .40
199 Rollie Fingers .15 .40
200 Jim Gantner .05 .15
201 Bob L. Gibson RC .08 .25
202 Moose Haas .05 .15
203 Roy Howell .05 .15
204 Pete Ladd .05 .15
205 Rick Manning .05 .15
206 Bob McClure .05 .15
207 Paul Molitor UER .15 .40
'83 stats should say
270 BA and 608 AB
208 Don Money .05 .15
209 Charlie Moore .05 .15
210 Ben Oglivie .15 .40
211 Chuck Porter .05 .15
212 Ed Romero .05 .15
213 Ted Simmons .15 .40
214 Jim Slaton .05 .15
215 Don Sutton .15 .40
216 Tom Tellmann .05 .15
217 Pete Vuckovich .05 .15
218 Ned Yost .05 .15
219 Robin Yount 1.00 2.50
220 Alan Ashby .05 .15
221 Kevin Bass .05 .15
222 Jose Cruz .15 .40
223 Bill Dawley .05 .15
224 Frank DiPino .05 .15
225 Bill Doran RC .20 .50
226 Phil Garner .15 .40
227 Art Howe .05 .15
228 Bob Knepper .05 .15
229 Ray Knight .15 .40
230 Frank LaCorte .05 .15
231 Mike LaCoss .05 .15
232 Mike Madden .05 .15
233 Jerry Mumphrey .05 .15
234 Joe Niekro .05 .15
235 Terry Puhl .05 .15
236 Luis Pujols .05 .15
237 Craig Reynolds .05 .15
238 Vern Ruhle .05 .15
239 Nolan Ryan 4.00 10.00
240 Mike Scott .15 .40
241 Tony Scott .05 .15
242 Dave Smith .05 .15
243 Dickie Thon .05 .15
244 Denny Walling .05 .15
245 Dale Berra .05 .15
246 Jim Bibby .05 .15
247 John Candelaria .05 .15
248 Jose DeLeon RC .20 .50
249 Mike Easler .05 .15
250 Cecilio Guante .05 .15
251 Richie Hebner .05 .15
252 Lee Lacy .05 .15
253 Bill Madlock .15 .40
254 Milt May .05 .15
255 Lee Mazzilli .15 .40
256 Larry McWilliams .05 .15
257 Jim Morrison .05 .15
258 Dave Parker .15 .40
259 Tony Pena .05 .15
260 Johnny Ray .05 .15
261 Rick Rhoden .05 .15
262 Don Robinson .05 .15
263 Manny Sarmiento .05 .15
264 Rod Scurry .05 .15
265 Kent Tekulve .05 .15
266 Gene Tenace .15 .40
267 Jason Thompson .05 .15
268 Lee Tunnell .05 .15
269 Marvell Wynne .20 .50
270 Ray Burris .05 .15
271 Gary Carter .15 .40
272 Warren Cromartie .05 .15
273 Andre Dawson .15 .40
274 Doug Flynn .05 .15
275 Terry Francona .15 .40
276 Bill Gullickson .05 .15
277 Bob James .05 .15
278 Charlie Lea .05 .15
279 Bryan Little .05 .15
280 Al Oliver .15 .40
281 Tim Raines .15 .40
282 Bobby Ramos .05 .15
283 Jeff Reardon .15 .40
284 Steve Rogers .15 .40
285 Scott Sanderson .05 .15
286 Dan Schatzeder .05 .15
287 Bryn Smith .05 .15
288 Chris Speier .05 .15
289 Manny Trillo .05 .15
290 Mike Vail .05 .15
291 Tim Wallach .05 .15
292 Chris Welsh .05 .15
293 Jim Wohlford .05 .15
294 Kurt Bevacqua .05 .15
295 Juan Bonilla .05 .15
296 Bobby Brown .05 .15
297 Luis DeLeon .05 .15
298 Dave Dravecky .05 .15
299 Tim Flannery .05 .15
300 Steve Garvey .15 .40
301 Tony Gwynn 2.50 6.00
302 Andy Hawkins .05 .15
303 Ruppert Jones .05 .15
304 Terry Kennedy .05 .15
305 Tim Lollar .05 .15
306 Gary Lucas .05 .15
307 Kevin McReynolds RC .40 1.00
308 Sid Monge .05 .15
309 Mario Ramirez .05 .15
310 Gene Richards .05 .15
311 Luis Salazar .05 .15
312 Eric Show .05 .15
313 Elias Sosa .05 .15
314 Garry Templeton .15 .40
315 Mark Thurmond .05 .15
316 Ed Whitson .05 .15
317 Alan Wiggins .05 .15
318 Neil Allen .05 .15
319 Joaquin Andujar .15 .40
320 Steve Braun .05 .15
321 Glenn Brummer .05 .15
322 Bob Forsch .05 .15
323 David Green .05 .15
324 George Hendrick .15 .40
325 Tom Herr .05 .15
326 Dane Iorg .05 .15
327 Jeff Lahti .05 .15
328 Dave LaPoint .05 .15
329 Willie McGee .15 .40
330 Ken Oberkfell .05 .15
331 Darrell Porter .05 .15
332 Jamie Quirk .05 .15
333 Mike Ramsey .05 .15
334 Floyd Rayford .05 .15
335 Lonnie Smith .05 .15
336 Ozzie Smith 1.00 2.50
337 John Stuper .05 .15
338 Bruce Sutter .30 .75
339 A.Van Slyke RC UER 1.00 2.50
340 Dave Von Ohlen .05 .15
341 Willie Aikens .05 .15
342 Mike Armstrong .05 .15
343 Bud Black .05 .15
344 George Brett 1.50 4.00
345 Onix Concepcion .05 .15
346 Keith Creel .05 .15
347 Larry Gura .05 .15
348 Don Hood .05 .15
349 Dennis Leonard .05 .15
350 Hal McRae .15 .40
351 Amos Otis .15 .40
352 Gaylord Perry .15 .40
353 Greg Pryor .05 .15
354 Dan Quisenberry .05 .15
355 Steve Renko .05 .15
356 Leon Roberts .05 .15
357 Pat Sheridan .05 .15
358 Joe Simpson .05 .15
359 Don Slaught .15 .40
360 Paul Splittorff .05 .15
361 U.L. Washington .05 .15
362 John Wathan .05 .15
363 Frank White .15 .40
364 Willie Wilson .15 .40
365 Jim Barr .05 .15
366 Dave Bergman .05 .15
367 Fred Breining .05 .15
368 Bob Brenly .05 .15
369 Jack Clark .15 .40
370 Chili Davis .15 .40
371 Mark Davis .05 .15
372 Darrell Evans .15 .40
373 Atlee Hammaker .05 .15
374 Mike Krukow .05 .15
375 Duane Kuiper .05 .15
376 Bill Laskey .05 .15
377 Gary Lavelle .05 .15
378 Johnnie LeMaster .05 .15
379 Jeff Leonard .05 .15
380 Randy Lerch .05 .15
381 Renie Martin .05 .15
382 Andy McGaffigan .05 .15
383 Greg Minton .05 .15
384 Tom O'Malley .05 .15
385 Max Venable .05 .15
386 Brad Wellman .05 .15
387 Joel Youngblood .05 .15
388 Gary Allenson .05 .15
389 Luis Aponte .05 .15
390 Tony Armas .15 .40
391 Doug Bird .05 .15
392 Wade Boggs 1.50 4.00
393 Dennis Boyd .15 .40
394 Mike G. Brown UER .08 .25
shown with record
of 31-104
395 Mark Clear .05 .15
396 Dennis Eckersley .30 .75
397 Dwight Evans .30 .75
398 Rich Gedman .05 .15
399 Glenn Hoffman .05 .15
400 Bruce Hurst .05 .15
401 John Henry Johnson .05 .15
402 Ed Jurak .05 .15
403 Rick Miller .05 .15
404 Jeff Newman .05 .15
405 Reid Nichols .05 .15
406 Bob Ojeda .05 .15
407 Jerry Remy .05 .15
408 Jim Rice .15 .40
409 Bob Stanley .05 .15
410 Dave Stapleton .05 .15
411 John Tudor .15 .40
412 Carl Yastrzemski .60 1.50
413 Buddy Bell .15 .40
414 Larry Biittner .05 .15
415 John Butcher .05 .15
416 Danny Darwin .05 .15
417 Bucky Dent .15 .40
418 Dave Hostetler .05 .15
419 Charlie Hough .15 .40
420 Bobby Johnson .05 .15
421 Odell Jones .05 .15
422 Jon Matlack .05 .15
423 Pete O'Brien RC* .20 .50
424 Larry Parrish .05 .15
425 Mickey Rivers .05 .15
426 Billy Sample .05 .15
427 Dave Schmidt .05 .15
428 Mike Smithson .05 .15
429 Bill Stein .05 .15
430 Dave Stewart .15 .40
431 Jim Sundberg .15 .40
432 Frank Tanana .15 .40
433 Dave Tobik .05 .15
434 Wayne Tolleson .05 .15
435 George Wright .05 .15
436 Bill Almon .05 .15
437 Keith Atherton .05 .15
438 Dave Beard .05 .15
439 Tom Burgmeier .05 .15
440 Jeff Burroughs .05 .15
441 Chris Codiroli .05 .15
442 Tim Conroy .05 .15
443 Mike Davis .05 .15
444 Wayne Gross .05 .15
445 Garry Hancock .05 .15
446 Mike Heath .05 .15
447 Rickey Henderson 1.00 2.50
448 Donnie Hill .05 .15
449 Bob Kearney .05 .15
450 Bill Krueger RC .08 .25
451 Rick Langford .05 .15
452 Carney Lansford .15 .40
453 Dave Lopes .15 .40
454 Steve McCatty .05 .15
455 Dan Meyer .05 .15
456 Dwayne Murphy .05 .15
457 Mike Norris .05 .15
458 Ricky Peters .05 .15
459 Tony Phillips RC .40 1.00
460 Tom Underwood .05 .15
461 Mike Warren .15 .40
462 Johnny Bench .60 1.50
463 Bruce Berenyi .15 .40
464 Dann Bilardello .05 .15
465 Cesar Cedeno .15 .40
466 Dave Concepcion .15 .40
467 Dan Driessen .05 .15
468 Nick Esasky .05 .15
469 Rich Gale .05 .15
470 Ben Hayes .05 .15
471 Paul Householder .05 .15
472 Tom Hume .05 .15
473 Alan Knicely .05 .15
474 Eddie Milner .05 .15
475 Ron Oester .05 .15
476 Kelly Paris .05 .15
477 Frank Pastore .05 .15
478 Ted Power .05 .15
479 Joe Price .05 .15
480 Charlie Puleo .05 .15
481 Gary Redus RC* .20 .50
482 Bill Scherrer .05 .15
483 Mario Soto .15 .40
484 Alex Trevino .05 .15
485 Duane Walker .05 .15
486 Larry Bowa .15 .40
487 Warren Brusstar .05 .15
488 Bill Buckner .15 .40
489 Bill Campbell .05 .15
490 Ron Cey .15 .40
491 Jody Davis .05 .15
492 Leon Durham .05 .15
493 Mel Hall .15 .40
494 Ferguson Jenkins .15 .40
495 Jay Johnstone .05 .15
496 Craig Lefferts RC .08 .25
497 Carmelo Martinez .05 .15
498 Jerry Morales .05 .15
499 Keith Moreland .05 .15
500 Dickie Noles .05 .15
501 Mike Proly .05 .15
502 Chuck Rainey .05 .15
503 Dick Ruthven .05 .15
504 Ryne Sandberg 2.50 6.00
505 Lee Smith .15 .40
506 Steve Trout .05 .15
507 Gary Woods .05 .15
508 Juan Beniquez .05 .15
509 Bob Boone .15 .40
510 Rick Burleson .05 .15
511 Rod Carew .30 .75
512 Bobby Clark .05 .15
513 John Curtis .05 .15
514 Doug DeCinces .05 .15
515 Brian Downing .15 .40
516 Tim Foli .05 .15
517 Ken Forsch .05 .15
518 Bobby Grich .15 .40
519 Andy Hassler .05 .15
520 Reggie Jackson .30 .75
521 Ron Jackson .05 .15
522 Tommy John .15 .40
523 Bruce Kison .05 .15
524 Steve Lubratich .05 .15
525 Fred Lynn .15 .40
526 Gary Pettis .05 .15
527 Luis Sanchez .05 .15
528 Daryl Sconiers .05 .15
529 Ellis Valentine .05 .15
530 Rob Wilfong .05 .15
531 Mike Witt .05 .15
532 Geoff Zahn .05 .15
533 Bud Anderson .05 .15
534 Chris Bando .05 .15
535 Alan Bannister .05 .15
536 Bert Blyleven .15 .40
537 Tom Brennan .05 .15
538 Jamie Easterly .05 .15
539 Juan Eichelberger .05 .15
540 Jim Essian .05 .15
541 Mike Fischlin .05 .15
542 Julio Franco .15 .40
543 Mike Hargrove .05 .15
544 Toby Harrah .15 .40
545 Ron Hassey .05 .15
546 Neal Heaton .05 .15
547 Bake McBride .15 .40
548 Broderick Perkins .05 .15
549 Larry Sorensen .05 .15
550 Dan Spillner .05 .15
551 Rick Sutcliffe .15 .40
552 Pat Tabler .05 .15
553 Gorman Thomas .15 .40
554 Andre Thornton .05 .15
555 George Vukovich .05 .15
556 Darrell Brown .05 .15
557 Tom Brunansky .05 .15
558 Randy Bush .05 .15
559 Bobby Castillo .05 .15
560 John Castino .05 .15
561 Ron Davis .05 .15
562 Dave Engle .05 .15
563 Lenny Faedo .05 .15
564 Pete Filson .05 .15
565 Gary Gaetti .30 .75
566 Mickey Hatcher .05 .15
567 Kent Hrbek .15 .40
568 Rusty Kuntz .05 .15
569 Tim Laudner .05 .15
570 Rick Lysander .05 .15
571 Bobby Mitchell .05 .15
572 Ken Schrom .05 .15
573 Ray Smith .05 .15
574 Tim Teufel RC .20 .50
575 Frank Viola .30 .75
576 Gary Ward .05 .15
577 Ron Washington .05 .15
578 Len Whitehouse .05 .15
579 Al Williams .05 .15
580 Bob Bailor .05 .15
581 Mark Bradley .05 .15
582 Hubie Brooks .05 .15

583 Carlos Diaz .05 .15
584 George Foster .15 .40
585 Brian Giles .05 .15
586 Danny Heep .05 .15
587 Keith Hernandez .15 .40
588 Ron Hodges .05 .15
589 Scott Holman .05 .15
590 Dave Kingman .15 .40
591 Ed Lynch .05 .15
592 Jose Oquendo RC .20 .50
593 Jesse Orosco .05 .15
594 Junior Ortiz .05 .15
595 Tom Seaver .60 1.50
596 Doug Sisk .05 .15
597 Rusty Staub .15 .40
598 John Stearns .05 .15
599 Darryl Strawberry RC 2.00 5.00
600 Craig Swan .05 .15
601 Walt Terrell .05 .15
602 Mike Torrez .05 .15
603 Mookie Wilson .15 .40
604 Jamie Allen .05 .15
605 Jim Beattie .05 .15
606 Tony Bernazard .05 .15
607 Manny Castillo .05 .15
608 Bill Caudill .05 .15
609 Bryan Clark .05 .15
610 Al Cowens .05 .15
611 Dave Henderson .15 .40
612 Steve Henderson .05 .15
613 Orlando Mercado .05 .15
614 Mike Moore .05 .15
615 Ricky Nelson UER .05 .15
Jamie Nelson's
stats on back
616 Spike Owen RC .20 .50
617 Pat Putnam .05 .15
618 Ron Roenicke .05 .15
619 Mike Stanton .05 .15
620 Bob Stoddard .05 .15
621 Rick Sweet .05 .15
622 Roy Thomas .05 .15
623 Ed VandeBerg .05 .15
624 Matt Young RC .20 .50
625 Richie Zisk .05 .15
626 Fred Lynn IA .15 .40
627 Manny Trillo IA .05 .15
628 Steve Garvey IA .05 .15
629 Rod Carew IA .15 .40
630 Wade Boggs IA .60 1.50
631 Tim Raines IA .05 .15
632 Al Oliver .15 .40
Double Trouble
633 Steve Sax IA .05 .15
634 Dickie Thon IA .05 .15
635 Dan Quisenberry .05 .15
Tippy Martinez
636 Joe Morgan .60 1.50
Pete Rose
Tony Perez
637 Lance Parrish .30 .75
Bob Boone
638 George Brett .75 2.00
Gaylord Perry
639 Dave Righetti .30 .75
Mike Warren
Bob Forsch
640 Johnny Bench .60 1.50
Carl Yastrzemski
641 Gaylord Perry IA .05 .15
642 Steve Carlton IA .15 .40
643 Joe Altobelli MG .05 .15
Paul Owens MG
644 Rick Dempsey WS .05 .15
645 Mike Boddicker WS .05 .15
646 Scott McGregor WS .05 .15
647 CL: Orioles .05 .15
Royals
Joe Altobelli MG
648 CL: Phillies .05 .15
Giants
Paul Owens MG
649 CL: White Sox .30 .75
Red Sox
Tony LaRussa MG
650 CL: Tigers .30 .75
Rangers
Sparky Anderson MG
651 CL: Dodgers .30 .75
A's
Tommy Lasorda MG
652 CL: Yankees .30 .75
Reds
Billy Martin MG
653 CL: Blue Jays .15 .40
Cubs
Bobby Cox MG
654 CL: Braves .30 .75
Angels
Joe Torre MG
655 CL: Brewers .05 .15
Indians
Rene Lachemann MG
656 CL: Astros .05 .15
Twins
Bob Lillis MG
657 CL: Pirates .05 .15
Mets
Chuck Tanner MG
658 CL: Expos .05 .15
Mariners
Bill Virdon MG
659 CL: Padres .15 .40
Specials
Dick Williams MG
660 CL: Cardinals .30 .75
Teams
Whitey Herzog MG

1984 Fleer Update

This set was Fleer's first update set and portrayed players with their proper team for the current year and rookies who were not in their regular issue. Like the Topps Traded sets of the time, the Fleer Update sets were distributed in factory set form through hobby dealers only. The set was quite popular with collectors, and, apparently, the print run was relatively short, as the set was quickly in short supply and exhibited a rapid and dramatic price increase in the mid to late 1980's. The cards are numbered on the back with a U prefix and placed in alphabetical order by player name. The key (extended) Rookie Cards in this set are Roger Clemens, John Franco, Dwight Gooden, Jimmy Key, Mark Langston, Kirby Puckett, and Bret Saberhagen. Collectors are urged to be careful if purchasing single cards of Clemens, Darling, Gooden, Puckett, Rose, or Saberhagen as these specific cards have been illegally reprinted. These fakes are blurry when compared to the real cards and have noticeably different printing dot patterns under 8X or greater magnification..

COMP.FACT.SET (132) 125.00 250.00
1 Willie Aikens .40 1.00
2 Luis Aponte .40 1.00
3 Mark Bailey .40 1.00
4 Bob Bailor .40 1.00
5 Dusty Baker .60 1.50
6 Steve Balboni .40 1.00
7 Alan Bannister .40 1.00
8 Marty Barrett XRC .75 2.00
9 Dave Beard .40 1.00
10 Joe Beckwith .40 1.00
11 Dave Bergman .40 1.00
12 Tony Bernazard .40 1.00
13 Bruce Bochte .40 1.00
14 Barry Bonnell .40 1.00
15 Phil Bradley .75 2.00
16 Fred Breining .40 1.00
17 Mike C. Brown .40 1.00
18 Bill Buckner .60 1.50
19 Ray Burris .40 1.00
20 John Butcher .40 1.00
21 Brett Butler .60 1.50
22 Enos Cabell .40 1.00
23 Bill Campbell .40 1.00
24 Bill Caudill .40 1.00
25 Bobby Clark .40 1.00
26 Bryan Clark .40 1.00
27 Roger Clemens XRC 60.00 150.00
28 Jaime Cocanower .40 1.00
29 Ron Darling XRC 2.00 5.00
30 Alvin Davis XRC .75 2.00
31 Bob Dernier .40 1.00
32 Carlos Diaz .40 1.00
33 Mike Easler .40 1.00
34 Dennis Eckersley 1.00 2.50
35 Jim Essian .40 1.00
36 Darrell Evans .60 1.50
37 Mike Fitzgerald .40 1.00
38 Tim Foli .40 1.00
39 John Franco XRC 2.00 5.00
40 George Frazier .40 1.00
41 Rich Gale .40 1.00
42 Barbaro Garbey .40 1.00
43 Dwight Gooden XRC 30.00 80.00
44 Rich Gossage .60 1.50
45 Wayne Gross .40 1.00
46 Mark Gubicza XRC .75 2.00
47 Jackie Gutierrez .40 1.00
48 Toby Harrah .60 1.50
49 Ron Hassey .40 1.00
50 Richie Hebner .40 1.00
51 Willie Hernandez .40 1.00
52 Ed Hodge .40 1.00
53 Ricky Horton .40 1.00
54 Art Howe .40 1.00
55 Dane Iorg .40 1.00
56 Brook Jacoby .75 2.00
57 Dion James XRC .40 1.00
58 Mike Jeffcoat XRC .40 1.00
59 Ruppert Jones .40 1.00
60 Bob Kearney .40 1.00
61 Jimmy Key XRC 2.00 5.00
62 Dave Kingman .60 1.50
63 Brad Komminsk XRC .40 1.00
64 Jerry Koosman .60 1.50
65 Wayne Krenchicki .40 1.00
66 Rusty Kuntz .40 1.00
67 Frank LaCorte .40 1.00
68 Dennis Lamp .40 1.00
69 Tito Landrum .40 1.00
70 Mark Langston XRC 2.00 5.00
71 Rick Leach .40 1.00
72 Craig Lefferts .40 1.00
73 Gary Lucas .40 1.00
74 Jerry Martin .40 1.00
75 Carmelo Martinez .40 1.00
76 Mike Mason XRC .40 1.00
77 Gary Matthews .60 1.50
78 Andy McGaffigan .40 1.00
79 Joey McLaughlin .40 1.00
80 Joe Morgan .60 1.50
81 Darryl Motley .40 1.00
82 Graig Nettles .60 1.50
83 Phil Niekro .60 1.50
84 Ken Oberkfell .40 1.00
85 Al Oliver .60 1.50
86 Jorge Orta .40 1.00
87 Amos Otis .60 1.50
88 Bob Owchinko .40 1.00
89 Dave Parker .60 1.50
90 Jack Perconte .40 1.00
91 Tony Perez 1.00 2.50
92 Gerald Perry .75 2.00
93 Kirby Puckett XRC 75.00 200.00
94 Shane Rawley .40 1.00
95 Floyd Rayford .40 1.00
96 Ron Reed .40 1.00
97 R.J. Reynolds .40 1.00
98 Gene Richards .40 1.00
99 Jose Rijo XRC 2.00 5.00
100 Jeff D. Robinson .40 1.00
101 Ron Romanick .40 1.00
102 Pete Rose 5.00 12.00
103 Bret Saberhagen XRC 4.00 10.00
104 Scott Sanderson .40 1.00
105 Dick Schofield XRC .75 2.00
106 Tom Seaver 1.50 4.00
107 Jim Slaton .40 1.00
108 Mike Smithson .40 1.00
109 Lary Sorensen .40 1.00
110 Tim Stoddard .40 1.00
111 Jeff Stone XRC .40 1.00
112 Champ Summers .40 1.00
113 Jim Sundberg .60 1.50
114 Rick Sutcliffe .60 1.50
115 Craig Swan .40 1.00
116 Derrel Thomas .40 1.00
117 Gorman Thomas .60 1.50
118 Alex Trevino .40 1.00
119 Manny Trillo .40 1.00
120 John Tudor .60 1.50
121 Tom Underwood .40 1.00
122 Mike Vail .40 1.00
123 Tom Waddell .40 1.00
124 Gary Ward .40 1.00
125 Terry Whitfield .40 1.00
126 Curtis Wilkerson .40 1.00
127 Frank Williams .40 1.00
128 Glenn Wilson .60 1.50
129 John Wockenfuss .40 1.00
130 Ned Yost .40 1.00
131 Mike Young XRC .40 1.00
132 Checklist 1-132 .40 1.00

1984 Fleer Stickers

The stickers in this 126-sticker set measure approximately 1 15/16" by 2 1/2". The 1984 Fleer sticker set is a very attractive set with a beige border. Many players are featured more than once in the set due to the fact that the album issued to house the set contains league leader categories in which to place the stickers. The checklist below is ordered by categories, e.g., Game Winning RBI's (1-5), Batting Average (6-15), Home Runs (16-23), Hits (24-31), Slugging Percentage (32-39), Pinch Hits (40-43), Designated Hitter's Hits (44-47), On Base Percentage (48-55), Won/Lost Percentage (56-64), Earned Run Average (65-66), Saves (67-77), Strikeouts (78-87), Stolen Bases (88-95), Future Hall of Famers (96-103), Rookie Stars (104-113), World Series Batting (114-122) and Playoff Managers (123-126). These stickers were originally issued in packs of six for 25 cents plus a team logo.

COMPLETE SET (126) 5.00 12.00
1 Dickie Thon .01 .05
2 Ken Landreaux .01 .05
3 Darrell Evans .05 .15
4 Harold Baines .05 .15
5 Dave Winfield .20 .50
6 Bill Madlock .01 .05
7 Lonnie Smith .01 .05
8 Jose Cruz .05 .15
9 George Hendrick .01 .05
10 Ray Knight .01 .05
11 Wade Boggs .25 .60
12 Rod Carew .20 .50
13 Lou Whitaker .08 .25
14 Alan Trammell .15 .40
15 Cal Ripken .75 2.00
16 Mike Schmidt .30 .75
17 Dale Murphy .15 .40
18 Andre Dawson .15 .40
19 Pedro Guerrero .05 .15
20 Jim Rice .05 .15
21 Tony Armas .01 .05
22 Ron Kittle .01 .05
23 Eddie Murray .20 .50
24 Jose Cruz .05 .15
25 Andre Dawson .15 .40
26 Rafael Ramirez .01 .05
27 Al Oliver .05 .15
28 Wade Boggs .30 .75
29 Cal Ripken .75 2.00
30 Lou Whitaker .05 .15
31 Cecil Cooper .05 .15
32 Dale Murphy .15 .40
33 Andre Dawson .15 .40
34 Pedro Guerrero .05 .15
35 Mike Schmidt .25 .60
36 George Brett .40 1.00
37 Jim Rice .05 .15
38 Eddie Murray .15 .40
39 Carlton Fisk .15 .40
40 Rusty Staub .05 .15
41 Duane Walker .01 .05
42 Steve Braun .01 .05
43 Kurt Bevacqua .01 .05
44 Hal McRae .05 .15
45 Don Baylor .05 .15
46 Ken Singleton .01 .05
47 Greg Luzinski .05 .15
48 Mike Schmidt .15 .40
49 Keith Hernandez .05 .15
50 Dale Murphy .15 .40
51 Tim Raines .08 .25
52 Wade Boggs .30 .75
53 Rickey Henderson .30 .75
54 Rod Carew .20 .50
55 Ken Singleton .01 .05
56 John Denny .01 .05
57 John Candelaria .01 .05
58 Larry McWilliams .01 .05
59 Pascual Perez .01 .05
60 Jesse Orosco .01 .05
61 Moose Haas .01 .05
62 Richard Dotson .01 .05
63 Mike Flanagan .01 .05
64 Scott McGregor .01 .05
65 Atlee Hammaker .01 .05
66 Rick Honeycutt .01 .05
67 Lee Smith .15 .40
68 Al Holland .01 .05
69 Greg Minton .01 .05
70 Bruce Sutter .05 .15
71 Jeff Reardon .05 .15
72 Frank DiPino .01 .05
73 Dan Quisenberry .05 .15
74 Bob Stanley .01 .05
75 Ron Davis .01 .05
76 Bill Caudill .01 .05
77 Peter Ladd .01 .05
78 Steve Carlton .15 .40
79 Mario Soto .01 .05
80 Larry McWilliams .01 .05
81 Fernando Valenzuela .05 .15
82 Nolan Ryan .75 2.00
83 Jack Morris .08 .25
84 Floyd Bannister .01 .05
85 Dave Stieb .01 .05
86 Dave Righetti .01 .05
87 Rick Sutcliffe .05 .15
88 Tim Raines .08 .25
89 Alan Wiggins .01 .05
90 Steve Sax .05 .15
91 Mookie Wilson .08 .25
92 Rickey Henderson .30 .75
93 Rudy Law .01 .05
94 Willie Wilson .05 .15
95 Julio Cruz .01 .05
96 Johnny Bench .20 .50
97 Carl Yastrzemski .20 .50
98 Gaylord Perry .15 .40
99 Pete Rose .30 .75
100 Joe Morgan .20 .50
101 Steve Carlton .20 .50
102 Jim Palmer .20 .50
103 Rod Carew .20 .50
104 Darryl Strawberry .25 .60
105 Craig McMurtry .01 .05
106 Mel Hall .01 .05
107 Lee Tunnell .01 .05
108 Bill Dawley .01 .05
109 Ron Kittle .01 .05
110 Mike Boddicker .01 .05
111 Julio Franco .15 .40
112 Daryl Sconiers .01 .05
113 Neal Heaton .01 .05
114 John Shelby .01 .05
115 Rick Dempsey .05 .15
116 John Lowenstein .01 .05
117 Jim Dwyer .01 .05
118 Bo Diaz .01 .05
119 Pete Rose .30 .75
120 Joe Morgan .20 .50
121 Gary Matthews .01 .05
122 Garry Maddox .01 .05
123 Paul Owens MG .01 .05
124 Tom Lasorda MG .08 .25
125 Joe Altobelli MG .01 .05
126 Tony LaRussa MG .05 .15

1985 Fleer

The 1985 Fleer set consists of 660 standard-size cards. Wax packs contained 15 cards plus logo stickers. Card fronts feature a full color photo, team logo along with the player's name and position. The borders enclosing the photo are color-coded to correspond to the player's team. The cards are ordered alphabetically within team. The teams are ordered based on their respective performance during the prior year. Subsets include Specials (626-643) and Major League Prospects (644-653). The black and white photo on the reverse is included for the third straight year. Rookie Cards include Roger Clemens, Eric Davis, Shawon Dunston, John Franco, Dwight Gooden, Orel Hershiser, Jimmy Key, Mark Langston, Terry Pendleton, Kirby Puckett and Bret Saberhagen

COMPLETE SET (660) 25.00 60.00
COMP.FACT.SET (660) 50.00 100.00
1 Doug Bair .05 .15
2 Juan Berenguer .05 .15
3 Dave Bergman .05 .15
4 Tom Brookens .05 .15
5 Marty Castillo .05 .15
6 Darrell Evans .15 .40
7 Barbaro Garbey .05 .15
8 Kirk Gibson .15 .40
9 John Grubb .05 .15
10 Willie Hernandez .05 .15
11 Larry Herndon .05 .15
12 Howard Johnson .15 .40
13 Ruppert Jones .05 .15
14 Rusty Kuntz .05 .15
15 Chet Lemon .15 .40
16 Aurelio Lopez .05 .15
17 Sid Monge .05 .15
18 Jack Morris .15 .40
19 Lance Parrish .15 .40
20 Dan Petry .05 .15
21 Dave Rozema .05 .15
22 Bill Scherrer .05 .15
23 Alan Trammell .15 .40
24 Lou Whitaker .15 .40
25 Milt Wilcox .05 .15
26 Kurt Bevacqua .05 .15
27 Greg Booker .05 .15
28 Bobby Brown .05 .15
29 Luis DeLeon .05 .15
30 Dave Dravecky .05 .15
31 Tim Flannery .05 .15
32 Steve Garvey .15 .40
33 Rich Gossage .15 .40
34 Tony Gwynn 1.00 2.50
35 Greg Harris .05 .15
36 Andy Hawkins .05 .15
37 Terry Kennedy .05 .15
38 Craig Lefferts .05 .15
39 Tim Lollar .05 .15
40 Carmelo Martinez .05 .15
41 Kevin McReynolds .15 .40
42 Graig Nettles .15 .40
43 Luis Salazar .05 .15
44 Eric Show .05 .15
45 Garry Templeton .15 .40
46 Mark Thurmond .05 .15
47 Ed Whitson .05 .15
48 Alan Wiggins .05 .15
49 Rich Bordi .05 .15
50 Larry Bowa .15 .40
51 Warren Brusstar .05 .15
52 Ron Cey .15 .40
53 Henry Cotto RC .08 .25
54 Jody Davis .05 .15
55 Bob Dernier .05 .15
56 Leon Durham .05 .15
57 Dennis Eckersley .30 .75
58 George Frazier .05 .15
59 Richie Hebner .05 .15
60 Dave Lopes .15 .40
61 Gary Matthews .15 .40
62 Keith Moreland .05 .15
63 Rick Reuschel .15 .40
64 Dick Ruthven .05 .15
65 Ryne Sandberg 1.00 2.50
66 Scott Sanderson .05 .15
67 Lee Smith .15 .40
68 Tim Stoddard .05 .15
69 Rick Sutcliffe .15 .40
70 Steve Trout .05 .15
71 Gary Woods .05 .15
72 Wally Backman .05 .15
73 Bruce Berenyi .05 .15
74 Hubie Brooks UER .05 .15
Kelvin Chapman's
stats on card back
75 Kelvin Chapman .05 .15
76 Ron Darling .15 .40
77 Sid Fernandez .15 .40
78 Mike Fitzgerald .05 .15
79 George Foster .15 .40
80 Brent Gaff .05 .15
81 Ron Gardenhire .05 .15
82 Dwight Gooden RC 1.25 3.00
83 Tom Gorman .05 .15
84 Danny Heep .05 .15
85 Keith Hernandez .15 .40
86 Ray Knight .15 .40
87 Ed Lynch .05 .15
88 Jose Oquendo .05 .15
89 Jesse Orosco .05 .15
90 Rafael Santana .05 .15
91 Doug Sisk .05 .15
92 Rusty Staub .15 .40
93 Darryl Strawberry .50 1.25
94 Walt Terrell .05 .15
95 Mookie Wilson .15 .40
96 Jim Acker .05 .15
97 Willie Aikens .05 .15
98 Doyle Alexander .05 .15
99 Jesse Barfield .15 .40
100 George Bell .15 .40
101 Jim Clancy .05 .15
102 Dave Collins .05 .15
103 Tony Fernandez .15 .40
104 Damaso Garcia .05 .15
105 Jim Gott .05 .15
106 Alfredo Griffin .05 .15
107 Garth Iorg .05 .15
108 Roy Lee Jackson .05 .15
109 Cliff Johnson .05 .15
110 Jimmy Key RC .40 1.00
111 Dennis Lamp .05 .15
112 Rick Leach .05 .15
113 Luis Leal .05 .15
114 Buck Martinez .05 .15
115 Lloyd Moseby .05 .15
116 Rance Mulliniks .05 .15
117 Dave Stieb .15 .40
118 Willie Upshaw .05 .15
119 Ernie Whitt .05 .15
120 Mike Armstrong .05 .15
121 Don Baylor .15 .40
122 Marty Bystrom .05 .15
123 Rick Cerone .05 .15
124 Joe Cowley .05 .15
125 Brian Dayett .05 .15
126 Tim Foli .05 .15
127 Ray Fontenot .05 .15
128 Ken Griffey .15 .40
129 Ron Guidry .15 .40
130 Toby Harrah .15 .40
131 Jay Howell .05 .15
132 Steve Kemp .05 .15
133 Don Mattingly 2.00 5.00
134 Bobby Meacham .05 .15
135 John Montefusco .05 .15
136 Omar Moreno .05 .15
137 Dale Murray .05 .15
138 Phil Niekro .15 .40
139 Mike Pagliarulo .05 .15
140 Willie Randolph .15 .40
141 Dennis Rasmussen .05 .15
142 Dave Righetti .15 .40
143 Jose Rijo RC .40 1.00
144 Andre Robertson .05 .15
145 Bob Shirley .05 .15
146 Dave Winfield .15 .40
147 Butch Wynegar .05 .15
148 Gary Allenson .05 .15
149 Tony Armas .15 .40
150 Marty Barrett .05 .15
151 Wade Boggs .50 1.25
152 Dennis Boyd .05 .15
153 Bill Buckner .15 .40
154 Mark Clear .05 .15
155 Roger Clemens RC 6.00 15.00
156 Steve Crawford .05 .15
157 Mike Easler .05 .15
158 Dwight Evans .30 .75
159 Rich Gedman .05 .15
160 Jackie Gutierrez .15 .40
Wade Boggs
shown on deck
161 Bruce Hurst .05 .15
162 John Henry Johnson .05 .15
163 Rick Miller .05 .15
164 Reid Nichols .05 .15
165 Al Nipper .05 .15
166 Bob Ojeda .05 .15
167 Jerry Remy .05 .15
168 Jim Rice .15 .40
169 Bob Stanley .05 .15
170 Mike Boddicker .05 .15
171 Al Bumbry .05 .15
172 Todd Cruz .05 .15
173 Rich Dauer .05 .15
174 Storm Davis .05 .15
175 Rick Dempsey .05 .15
176 Jim Dwyer .05 .15
177 Mike Flanagan .05 .15
178 Dan Ford .05 .15
179 Wayne Gross .05 .15
180 John Lowenstein .05 .15
181 Dennis Martinez .15 .40
182 Tippy Martinez .05 .15
183 Scott McGregor .05 .15
184 Eddie Murray .50 1.25
185 Joe Nolan .05 .15
186 Floyd Rayford .05 .15
187 Cal Ripken 2.00 5.00
188 Gary Roenicke .05 .15
189 Lenn Sakata .05 .15
190 John Shelby .05 .15
191 Ken Singleton .15 .40
192 Sammy Stewart .05 .15
193 Bill Swaggerty .05 .15
194 Tom Underwood .05 .15
195 Mike Young .05 .15
196 Steve Balboni .05 .15
197 Joe Beckwith .05 .15
198 Bud Black .05 .15
199 George Brett 1.25 3.00
200 Onix Concepcion .05 .15
201 Mark Gubicza RC .20 .50
202 Larry Gura .05 .15
203 Mark Huismann .05 .15
204 Dane Iorg .05 .15
205 Danny Jackson .05 .15
206 Charlie Leibrandt .05 .15
207 Hal McRae .15 .40
208 Darryl Motley .05 .15
209 Jorge Orta .05 .15
210 Greg Pryor .05 .15
211 Dan Quisenberry .05 .15
212 Bret Saberhagen RC .60 1.
213 Pat Sheridan .05
214 Don Slaught .05
215 U.L. Washington .05
216 John Wathan .05
217 Frank White .15
218 Willie Wilson .15
219 Neil Allen .05
220 Joaquin Andujar .15
221 Steve Braun .05
222 Danny Cox .05
223 Bob Forsch .05
224 David Green .05
225 George Hendrick .15
226 Tom Herr .05
227 Ricky Horton .05
228 Art Howe .05
229 Mike Jorgensen .05
230 Kurt Kepshire .05
231 Jeff Lahti .05
232 Tito Landrum .05
233 Dave LaPoint .05
234 Willie McGee .15
235 Tom Nieto .05
236 Terry Pendleton RC .40 1.
237 Darrell Porter .05
238 Dave Rucker .05
239 Lonnie Smith .05
240 Ozzie Smith .75 2.0
241 Bruce Sutter .15 .4
242 Andy Van Slyke UER .30
Bats Right,
Throws Left
243 Dave Von Ohlen .05
244 Larry Andersen .05
245 Bill Campbell .05
246 Steve Carlton .15 .4
247 Tim Corcoran .05
248 Ivan DeJesus .05 .1
249 John Denny .05
250 Bo Diaz .05
251 Greg Gross .05
252 Kevin Gross .05
253 Von Hayes .05
254 Al Holland .05
255 Charles Hudson .05 .1
256 Jerry Koosman .15 .4
257 Joe Lefebvre .05 .1
258 Sixto Lezcano .05 .1
259 Garry Maddox .05 .1
260 Len Matuszek .05 .1
261 Tug McGraw .15 .4
262 Al Oliver .15 .4
263 Shane Rawley .05 .15
264 Juan Samuel .05 .15
265 Mike Schmidt 1.25 3.0
266 Jeff Stone RC .05 .1
267 Ozzie Virgil .05 .15
268 Glenn Wilson .05 .15
269 John Wockenfuss .05 .15
270 Darrell Brown .05 .15
271 Tom Brunansky .05 .15
272 Randy Bush .05 .15
273 John Butcher .05 .15
274 Bobby Castillo .05 .15
275 Ron Davis .05 .15
276 Dave Engle .05 .15
277 Pete Filson .05 .15
278 Gary Gaetti .15 .40
279 Mickey Hatcher .05 .15
280 Ed Hodge .05 .15
281 Kent Hrbek .15 .40
282 Houston Jimenez .05 .15
283 Tim Laudner .05 .15
284 Rick Lysander .05 .15
285 Dave Meier .05 .15
286 Kirby Puckett RC 6.00 15.00
287 Pat Putnam .05 .15
288 Ken Schrom .05 .15
289 Mike Smithson .05 .15
290 Tim Teufel .05 .15
291 Frank Viola .15 .40
292 Ron Washington .05 .15
293 Don Aase .05 .15
294 Juan Beniquez .05 .15
295 Bob Boone .15 .40
296 Mike C. Brown .05 .15
297 Rod Carew .30 .75
298 Doug Corbett .05 .15
299 Doug DeCinces .05 .15
300 Brian Downing .15 .40
301 Ken Forsch .05 .15
302 Bobby Grich .15 .40
303 Reggie Jackson .30 .75
304 Tommy John .15 .40
305 Curt Kaufman .05 .15
306 Bruce Kison .05 .15
307 Fred Lynn .15 .40
308 Gary Pettis .05 .15
309 Ron Romanick .05 .15
310 Luis Sanchez .05 .15
311 Dick Schofield .05 .15
312 Daryl Sconiers .05 .15
313 Jim Slaton .05 .15
314 Derrel Thomas .05 .15
315 Rob Wilfong .05 .15
316 Mike Witt .05 .15
317 Geoff Zahn .05 .15
318 Len Barker .05 .15
319 Steve Bedrosian .05 .15
320 Bruce Benedict .05 .15
321 Rick Camp .05 .15
322 Chris Chambliss .15 .40

3 Jeff Dedmon .05 .15
4 Terry Forster .15 .40
5 Gene Garber .05 .15
6 Albert Hall .05 .15
7 Terry Harper .05 .15
8 Bob Horner .15 .40
9 Glenn Hubbard .05 .15
0 Randy Johnson .05 .15
1 Brad Komminsk .05 .15
2 Rick Mahler .05 .15
3 Craig McMurtry .05 .15
4 Donnie Moore .05 .15
5 Dale Murphy .30 .75
6 Ken Oberkfell .05 .15
7 Pascual Perez .05 .15
8 Gerald Perry .05 .15
9 Rafael Ramirez .05 .15
0 Jerry Royster .05 .15
1 Alex Trevino .05 .15
2 Claudell Washington .05 .15
3 Alan Ashby .05 .15
4 Mark Bailey .05 .15
5 Kevin Bass .05 .15
6 Enos Cabell .05 .15
7 Jose Cruz .15 .40
8 Bill Dawley .05 .15
9 Frank DiPino .05 .15
0 Bill Doran .05 .15
1 Phil Garner .15 .40
2 Bob Knepper .05 .15
3 Mike LaCoss .05 .15
4 Jerry Mumphrey .05 .15
55 Joe Niekro .05 .15
56 Terry Puhl .05 .15
57 Craig Reynolds .05 .15
58 Vern Ruhle .05 .15
59 Nolan Ryan 2.50 6.00
60 Joe Sambito .05 .15
61 Mike Scott .15 .40
62 Dave Smith .05 .15
63 Julio Solano .05 .15
64 Dickie Thon .05 .15
65 Denny Walling .05 .15
66 Dave Anderson .05 .15
67 Bob Bailor .05 .15
68 Greg Brock .05 .15
69 Carlos Diaz .05 .15
70 Pedro Guerrero .15 .40
71 Orel Hershiser RC 1.25 3.00
72 Rick Honeycutt .05 .15
73 Burt Hooton .05 .15
74 Ken Howell .05 .15
375 Ken Landreaux .05 .15
376 Candy Maldonado .05 .15
377 Mike Marshall .05 .15
378 Tom Niedenfuer .05 .15
379 Alejandro Pena .05 .15
380 Jerry Reuss UER .05 .15
381 R.J. Reynolds .05 .15
382 German Rivera .05 .15
383 Bill Russell .15 .40
384 Steve Sax .05 .15
385 Mike Scioscia .15 .40
386 Franklin Stubbs .05 .15
387 Fernando Valenzuela .15 .40
388 Bob Welch .15 .40
389 Terry Whitfield .05 .15
390 Steve Yeager .15 .40
391 Pat Zachry .05 .15
392 Fred Breining .05 .15
393 Gary Carter .15 .40
394 Andre Dawson .15 .40
395 Miguel Dilone .05 .15
396 Dan Driessen .05 .15
397 Doug Flynn .05 .15
398 Terry Francona .15 .40
399 Bill Gullickson .05 .15
400 Bob James .05 .15
401 Charlie Lea .05 .15
402 Bryan Little .05 .15
403 Gary Lucas .05 .15
404 David Palmer .05 .15
405 Tim Raines .15 .40
406 Mike Ramsey .05 .15
407 Jeff Reardon .15 .40
408 Steve Rogers .15 .40
409 Dan Schatzeder .05 .15
410 Bryn Smith .05 .15
411 Mike Stenhouse .05 .15
412 Tim Wallach .05 .15
413 Jim Wohlford .05 .15
414 Bill Almon .05 .15
415 Keith Atherton .05 .15
416 Bruce Bochte .05 .15
417 Tom Burgmeier .05 .15
418 Ray Burris .05 .15
419 Bill Caudill .05 .15
420 Chris Codiroli .05 .15
421 Tim Conroy .05 .15
422 Mike Davis .05 .15
423 Jim Essian .05 .15
424 Mike Heath .05 .15
425 Rickey Henderson .60 1.50
426 Donnie Hill .05 .15
427 Dave Kingman .15 .40
428 Bill Krueger .05 .15
429 Carney Lansford .15 .40
430 Steve McCatty .05 .15
431 Joe Morgan .15 .40
432 Dwayne Murphy .05 .15
433 Tony Phillips .05 .15
434 Lary Sorensen .05 .15
435 Mike Warren .05 .15
436 Curt Young .05 .15
437 Luis Aponte .05 .15
438 Chris Bando .05 .15
439 Tony Bernazard .05 .15
440 Bert Blyleven .15 .40
441 Brett Butler .15 .40
442 Ernie Camacho .05 .15
443 Joe Carter .50 1.25
444 Carmelo Castillo .05 .15
445 Jamie Easterly .05 .15
446 Steve Farr RC .20 .50
447 Mike Fischlin .05 .15
448 Julio Franco .15 .40
449 Mel Hall .05 .15
450 Mike Hargrove .05 .15
451 Neal Heaton .05 .15
452 Brook Jacoby .05 .15
453 Mike Jeffcoat .05 .15
454 Don Schulze .05 .15
455 Roy Smith .05 .15
456 Pat Tabler .05 .15
457 Andre Thornton .05 .15
458 George Vukovich .05 .15
459 Tom Waddell .05 .15
460 Jerry Willard .05 .15
461 Dale Berra .05 .15
462 John Candelaria .05 .15
463 Jose DeLeon .05 .15
464 Doug Frobel .05 .15
465 Cecilio Guante .05 .15
466 Brian Harper .05 .15
467 Lee Lacy .05 .15
468 Bill Madlock .15 .40
469 Lee Mazzilli .15 .40
470 Larry McWilliams .05 .15
471 Jim Morrison .05 .15
472 Tony Pena .05 .15
473 Johnny Ray .05 .15
474 Rick Rhoden .05 .15
475 Don Robinson .05 .15
476 Rod Scurry .05 .15
477 Kent Tekulve .05 .15
478 Jason Thompson .05 .15
479 John Tudor .15 .40
480 Lee Tunnell .05 .15
481 Marvell Wynne .05 .15
482 Salome Barojas .05 .15
483 Dave Beard .05 .15
484 Jim Beattie .05 .15
485 Barry Bonnell .05 .15
486 Phil Bradley .20 .50
487 Al Cowens .05 .15
488 Alvin Davis RC .20 .50
489 Dave Henderson .05 .15
490 Steve Henderson .05 .15
491 Bob Kearney .05 .15
492 Mark Langston RC .40 1.00
493 Larry Milbourne .05 .15
494 Paul Mirabella .05 .15
495 Mike Moore .05 .15
496 Edwin Nunez .05 .15
497 Spike Owen .05 .15
498 Jack Perconte .05 .15
499 Ken Phelps .05 .15
500 Jim Presley .20 .50
501 Mike Stanton .05 .15
502 Bob Stoddard .05 .15
503 Gorman Thomas .15 .40
504 Ed VandeBerg .05 .15
505 Matt Young .05 .15
506 Juan Agosto .05 .15
507 Harold Baines .15 .40
508 Floyd Bannister .05 .15
509 Britt Burns .05 .15
510 Julio Cruz .05 .15
511 Richard Dotson .05 .15
512 Jerry Dybzinski .05 .15
513 Carlton Fisk .30 .75
514 Scott Fletcher .05 .15
515 Jerry Hairston .05 .15
516 Marc Hill .05 .15
517 LaMarr Hoyt .05 .15
518 Ron Kittle .05 .15
519 Rudy Law .05 .15
520 Vance Law .05 .15
521 Greg Luzinski .15 .40
522 Gene Nelson .05 .15
523 Tom Paciorek .05 .15
524 Ron Reed .05 .15
525 Bert Roberge .05 .15
526 Tom Seaver .30 .75
527 Roy Smalley .05 .15
528 Dan Spillner .05 .15
529 Mike Squires .05 .15
530 Greg Walker .05 .15
531 Cesar Cedeno .15 .40
532 Dave Concepcion .15 .40
533 Eric Davis RC 1.25 3.00
534 Nick Esasky .05 .15
535 Tom Foley .05 .15
536 John Franco UER RC .40 1.00
Koufax misspelled
as Kofax on back
537 Brad Gulden .05 .15
538 Tom Hume .05 .15
539 Wayne Krenchicki .05 .15
540 Andy McGaffigan .05 .15
541 Eddie Milner .05 .15
542 Ron Oester .05 .15
543 Bob Owchinko .05 .15
544 Dave Parker .15 .40
545 Frank Pastore .05 .15
546 Tony Perez .30 .75
547 Ted Power .05 .15
548 Joe Price .05 .15
549 Gary Redus .05 .15
550 Pete Rose 1.50 4.00
551 Jeff Russell .05 .15
552 Mario Soto .15 .40
553 Jay Tibbs .05 .15
554 Duane Walker .05 .15
555 Alan Bannister .05 .15
556 Buddy Bell .15 .40
557 Danny Darwin .05 .15
558 Charlie Hough .15 .40
559 Bobby Jones .05 .15
560 Odell Jones .05 .15
561 Jeff Kunkel .05 .15
562 Mike Mason RC .08 .25
563 Pete O'Brien .05 .15
564 Larry Parrish .05 .15
565 Mickey Rivers .05 .15
566 Billy Sample .05 .15
567 Dave Schmidt .05 .15
568 Donnie Scott .05 .15
569 Dave Stewart .15 .40
570 Frank Tanana .15 .40
571 Wayne Tolleson .05 .15
572 Gary Ward .05 .15
573 Curtis Wilkerson .05 .15
574 George Wright .05 .15
575 Ned Yost .05 .15
576 Mark Brouhard .05 .15
577 Mike Caldwell .05 .15
578 Bobby Clark .05 .15
579 Jaime Cocanower .05 .15
580 Cecil Cooper .15 .40
581 Rollie Fingers .15 .40
582 Jim Gantner .05 .15
583 Moose Haas .05 .15
584 Dion James .05 .15
585 Pete Ladd .05 .15
586 Rick Manning .05 .15
587 Bob McClure .05 .15
588 Paul Molitor .15 .40
589 Charlie Moore .05 .15
590 Ben Oglivie .15 .40
591 Chuck Porter .05 .15
592 Randy Ready RC .08 .25
593 Ed Romero .05 .15
594 Bill Schroeder .05 .15
595 Ray Searage .05 .15
596 Ted Simmons .15 .40
597 Jim Sundberg .15 .40
598 Don Sutton .15 .40
599 Tom Tellmann .05 .15
600 Rick Waits .05 .15
601 Robin Yount .75 2.00
602 Dusty Baker .15 .40
603 Bob Brenly .05 .15
604 Jack Clark .15 .40
605 Chili Davis .15 .40
606 Mark Davis .05 .15
607 Dan Gladden RC .20 .50
608 Atlee Hammaker .05 .15
609 Mike Krukow .05 .15
610 Duane Kuiper .05 .15
611 Bob Lacey .05 .15
612 Bill Laskey .05 .15
613 Gary Lavelle .05 .15
614 Johnnie LeMaster .05 .15
615 Jeff Leonard .05 .15
616 Randy Lerch .05 .15
617 Greg Minton .05 .15
618 Steve Nicosia .05 .15
619 Gene Richards .05 .15
620 Jeff D. Robinson .05 .15
621 Scot Thompson .05 .15
622 Manny Trillo .05 .15
623 Brad Wellman .05 .15
624 Frank Williams .05 .15
625 Joel Youngblood .05 .15
626 Cal Ripken IA 1.25 3.00
627 Mike Schmidt IA .50 1.25
628 Sparky Anderson IA .15 .40
629 Dave Winfield .15 .40
Rickey Henderson
630 Mike Schmidt .75 2.00
Ryne Sandberg
631 Darryl Strawberry .50 1.25
Gary Carter
Steve Garvey
Ozzie Smith
632 Gary Carter .05 .15
Charlie Lea
633 Steve Garvey .15 .40
Rich Gossage
634 Dwight Gooden .50 1.25
Juan Samuel
635 Willie Upshaw IA .05 .15
636 Lloyd Moseby IA .05 .15
637 Al Holland .05 .15
638 Lee Tunnell .05 .15
639 Reggie Jackson IA .15 .40
640 Pete Rose .50 1.25
4000th Hit IA
641 Cal Ripken Jr. 1.25 3.00
Cal Ripken Sr.
642 Cubs Division Champs .15 .40
643 Two Perfect Games .15 .40
and One No-Hitter:
Mike Witt
David Palmer
Jack Morris
644 W.Lozado RC/V.Mata RC .05 .15
645 K.Gruber RC/R.O'Neal RC .20 .50
646 J.Roman RC/J.Skinner .05 .15
647 S.Kiefer RC/D.Tartabull RC .40 1.00
648 R.Deer RC/A.Sanchez RC .20 .50
649 B.Hatcher RC/S.Dunston RC .40 1.00
650 R.Robinson RC/M.Bielecki RC .05 .15
651 Z.Smith RC/P.Zuvella RC .20 .50
652 J.Hesketh RC/G.Davis RC .20 .50
653 J.Russell RC/S.Jeltz RC .05 .15
654 CL: Tigers .05 .15
Padres
and Cubs
Mets
655 CL: Blue Jays .05 .15
Yankees
and Red Sox
Orioles
656 CL: Royals .05 .15
Cardinals
and Phillies
Twins
657 CL: Angels .05 .15
Braves
and Astros
Dodgers
658 CL: Expos .05 .15
A's
and Indians
Pirates
659 CL: Mariners .05 .15
White Sox
and Reds
Rangers
660 CL: Brewers .05 .15
Giants
and Special Cards

1985 Fleer Update

This 132-card standard-size update set was issued in factory set form exclusively through hobby dealers. Design is identical to the regular-issue 1985 Fleer cards except for the U prefixed card numbers on back. Cards are ordered alphabetically by the player's name. This set features the extended Rookie Cards of Vince Coleman, Darren Daulton, Ozzie Guillen and Mickey Tettleton.

COMP.FACT.SET (132) 3.00 8.00
1 Don Aase .05 .15
2 Bill Almon .05 .15
3 Dusty Baker .15 .40
4 Dale Berra .05 .15
5 Karl Best .05 .15
6 Tim Birtsas .05 .15
7 Vida Blue .15 .40
8 Rich Bordi .05 .15
9 Daryl Boston XRC .08 .25
10 Hubie Brooks .05 .15
11 Chris Brown XRC .08 .25
12 Tom Browning XRC .20 .50
13 Al Bumbry .05 .15
14 Tim Burke .05 .15
15 Ray Burris .05 .15
16 Jeff Burroughs .05 .15
17 Ivan Calderon XRC .20 .50
18 Jeff Calhoun .05 .15
19 Bill Campbell .05 .15
20 Don Carman .05 .15
21 Gary Carter .15 .40
22 Bobby Castillo .05 .15
23 Bill Caudill .05 .15
24 Rick Cerone .05 .15
25 Jack Clark .15 .40
26 Pat Clements .05 .15
27 Stu Cliburn .05 .15
28 Vince Coleman XRC .40 1.00
29 Dave Collins .05 .15
30 Fritz Connally .05 .15
31 Henry Cotto .08 .25
32 Danny Darwin .05 .15
33 Darren Daulton XRC .40 1.00
34 Jerry Davis .05 .15
35 Brian Dayett .05 .15
36 Ken Dixon .05 .15
37 Tommy Dunbar .05 .15
38 Mariano Duncan XRC .20 .50
39 Bob Fallon .05 .15
40 Brian Fisher XRC .08 .25
41 Mike Fitzgerald .05 .15
42 Ray Fontenot .05 .15
43 Greg Gagne XRC .20 .50
44 Oscar Gamble .05 .15
45 Jim Gott .05 .15
46 David Green .05 .15
47 Alfredo Griffin .05 .15
48 Ozzie Guillen XRC 2.00 5.00
49 Toby Harrah .15 .40
50 Ron Hassey .05 .15
51 Rickey Henderson 1.00 2.50
52 Steve Henderson .05 .15
53 George Hendrick .15 .40
54 Teddy Higuera XRC .20 .50
55 Al Holland .05 .15
56 Burt Hooton .05 .15
57 Jay Howell .05 .15
58 LaMarr Hoyt .05 .15
59 Tim Hulett XRC .08 .25
60 Bob James .05 .15
61 Cliff Johnson .05 .15
62 Howard Johnson .15 .40
63 Ruppert Jones .05 .15
64 Steve Kemp .05 .15
65 Bruce Kison .05 .15
66 Mike LaCoss .05 .15
67 Lee Lacy .05 .15
68 Dave LaPoint .05 .15
69 Gary Lavelle .05 .15
70 Vance Law .05 .15
71 Manuel Lee XRC .08 .25
72 Sixto Lezcano .05 .15
73 Tim Lollar .05 .15
74 Urbano Lugo .05 .15
75 Fred Lynn .15 .40
76 Steve Lyons XRC .20 .50
77 Mickey Mahler .05 .15
78 Ron Mathis .05 .15
79 Len Matuszek .05 .15
80 Oddibe McDowell XRC .20 .50
81 Roger McDowell UER XRC .20 .50
82 Donnie Moore .05 .15
83 Ron Musselman .05 .15
84 Al Oliver .15 .40
85 Joe Orsulak XRC .20 .50
86 Dan Pasqua XRC .20 .50
87 Chris Pittaro .05 .15
88 Rick Reuschel .15 .40
89 Earnie Riles .05 .15
90 Jerry Royster .05 .15
91 Dave Rozema .05 .15
92 Dave Rucker .05 .15
93 Vern Ruhle .05 .15
94 Mark Salas .05 .15
95 Luis Salazar .05 .15
96 Joe Sambito .05 .15
97 Billy Sample .05 .15
98 Alejandro Sanchez XRC .08 .25
99 Calvin Schiraldi XRC .20 .50
100 Rick Schu .05 .15
101 Larry Sheets XRC .08 .25
102 Ron Shephard .05 .15
103 Nelson Simmons .05 .15
104 Don Slaught .05 .15
105 Roy Smalley .05 .15
106 Lonnie Smith .05 .15
107 Nate Snell .05 .15
108 Lary Sorensen .05 .15
109 Chris Speier .05 .15
110 Mike Stenhouse .05 .15
111 Tim Stoddard .05 .15
112 John Stuper .05 .15
113 Jim Sundberg .15 .40
114 Bruce Sutter .15 .40
115 Don Sutton .15 .40
116 Bruce Tanner .05 .15
117 Kent Tekulve .05 .15
118 Walt Terrell .05 .15
119 Mickey Tettleton XRC .20 .50
120 Rich Thompson .05 .15
121 Louis Thornton .05 .15
122 Alex Trevino .05 .15
123 John Tudor .15 .40
124 Jose Uribe .05 .15
125 Dave Valle XRC .20 .50
126 Dave Von Ohlen .05 .15
127 Curt Wardle .05 .15
128 U.L. Washington .05 .15
129 Ed Whitson .05 .15
130 Herm Winningham .05 .15
131 Rich Yett .05 .15
132 Checklist U1-U132 .05 .15

1985 Fleer Limited Edition

This 44-card set features standard size cards which were distributed in a colorful box as a complete set. The back of the box gives a complete checklist of the cards in the set. The cards are ordered alphabetically by the player's name. Backs of the cards are yellow and white whereas the fronts show a picture of the player inside a red banner-type border.

COMP. FACT. SET (44) 3.00 8.00
1 Buddy Bell .01 .05
2 Bert Blyleven .02 .10
3 Wade Boggs .20 .50
4 George Brett .50 1.25
5 Rod Carew .15 .40
6 Steve Carlton .15 .40
7 Alvin Davis .01 .05
8 Andre Dawson .08 .25
9 Steve Garvey .05 .15
10 Rich Gossage .02 .10
11 Tony Gwynn .60 1.50
12 Keith Hernandez .02 .10
13 Kent Hrbek .02 .10
14 Reggie Jackson .20 .50
15 Dave Kingman .02 .10
16 Ron Kittle .01 .05
17 Mark Langston .02 .10
18 Jeff Leonard .01 .05
19 Bill Madlock .01 .05
20 Don Mattingly .50 1.25
21 Jack Morris .02 .10
22 Dale Murphy .08 .25
23 Eddie Murray .20 .50
24 Tony Pena .02 .10
25 Dan Quisenberry .01 .05
26 Tim Raines .02 .10
27 Jim Rice .02 .10
28 Cal Ripken 1.00 2.50
29 Pete Rose .30 .75
30 Nolan Ryan 1.00 2.50
31 Ryne Sandberg .40 1.00
32 Steve Sax .01 .05
33 Mike Schmidt .20 .50
34 Tom Seaver .15 .40
35 Ozzie Smith .40 1.00
36 Mario Soto .01 .05
37 Dave Stieb .01 .05
38 Darryl Strawberry .02 .10
39 Rick Sutcliffe .01 .05
40 Alan Trammell .05 .15
41 Willie Upshaw .01 .05
42 Fernando Valenzuela .02 .10
43 Dave Winfield .10 .30
44 Robin Yount .20 .50

1985 Fleer Star Stickers

The stickers in this 126-sticker set measure approximately 1 15/16" by 2 1/2". The 1985 Fleer stickers set can be housed in a Fleer sticker album. Stickers are numbered on the fronts. A distinctive feature of the set is the inclusion of stop-action (designated SA in the checklist below) photos on cards 62 through 79. These photos are actually a series of six consecutive stickers which depict a player in action through the course of an activity; e.g., Eddie Murray's swing, Tom Seaver's wind-up and Mike Schmidt fielding. The backs of these stickers are blue and similar in design to past years. Player selection is highlighted by RC-year stickers of superstars Roger Clemens and Kirby Puckett.

COMPLETE SET (126) 20.00 50.00
1 Pete Rose 1.25 3.00
2 Pete Rose 1.25 3.00
3 Pete Rose 1.25 3.00
4 Don Mattingly 3.00 8.00
5 Dave Winfield .50 1.25
6 Wade Boggs 1.00 2.50
7 Buddy Bell .07 .20
8 Tony Gwynn 3.00 8.00
9 Lee Lacy .02 .10
10 Chili Davis .07 .20
11 Ryne Sandberg 1.50 4.00
12 Tony Armas .02 .10
13 Jim Rice .07 .20
14 Dave Kingman .07 .20
15 Alvin Davis .07 .20
16 Gary Carter 1.25
17 Mike Schmidt 1.00 2.50
18 Dale Murphy .20 .50
19 Ron Cey .07 .20
20 Eddie Murray .60 1.50
21 Harold Baines .07 .20
22 Kirk Gibson .07 .20
23 Jim Rice .07 .20
24 Gary Matthews .02 .10
25 Keith Hernandez .07 .20
26 Gary Carter 1.25
27 George Hendrick .02 .10
28 Tony Armas .02 .10
29 Dave Kingman .07 .20
30 Dwayne Murphy .02 .10
31 Lance Parrish .07 .20
32 Andre Thornton .02 .10
33 Dale Murphy .20 .50
34 Mike Schmidt 1.00 2.50
35 Gary Carter 1.25
36 Darryl Strawberry .07 .20
37 Don Mattingly 3.00 8.00
38 Larry Parrish .02 .10
39 George Bell .07 .20
40 Dwight Evans .07 .20
41 Cal Ripken 3.00 8.00
42 Tim Raines .07 .20
43 Johnny Ray .02 .10
44 Juan Samuel .02 .10
45 Ryne Sandberg 1.50 4.00
46 Mike Easler .02 .10
47 Andre Thornton .02 .10
48 Dave Kingman .07 .20
49 Don Baylor .07 .20
50 Rusty Staub .07 .20
51 Steve Braun .02 .10
52 Kevin Bass .02 .10
53 Greg Gross .02 .10
54 Rickey Henderson 2.00 5.00
55 Dave Collins .02 .10
56 Brett Butler .07 .20
57 Gary Pettis .02 .10
58 Tim Raines .07 .20
59 Juan Samuel .02 .10
60 Alan Wiggins .02 .10
61 Lonnie Smith .02 .10
62 Eddie Murray SA .30 .75
63 Eddie Murray SA .30 .75
64 Eddie Murray SA .30 .75
65 Eddie Murray SA .30 .75
66 Eddie Murray SA .30 .75
67 Eddie Murray SA .30 .75
68 Tom Seaver SA .40 1.00
69 Tom Seaver SA .40 1.00
70 Tom Seaver SA .40 1.00
71 Tom Seaver SA .40 1.00
72 Tom Seaver SA .40 1.00
73 Tom Seaver SA .40 1.00
74 Mike Schmidt SA .50 1.25
75 Mike Schmidt SA .50 1.25
76 Mike Schmidt SA .50 1.25
77 Mike Schmidt SA .50 1.25
78 Mike Schmidt SA .50 1.25
79 Mike Schmidt SA .50 1.25
80 Mike Boddicker .02 .10
81 Bert Blyleven .07 .20
82 Jack Morris .07 .20
83 Dan Petry .02 .10
84 Frank Viola .07 .20
85 Joaquin Andujar .02 .10
86 Mario Soto .02 .10
87 Dwight Gooden 1.00 2.50
88 Joe Niekro .02 .10
89 Rick Sutcliffe .02 .10
90 Mike Boddicker .02 .10
91 Dave Stieb .02 .10
92 Bert Blyleven .07 .20
93 Phil Niekro .25 .60
94 Alejandro Pena .02 .10
95 Dwight Gooden 1.00 2.50
96 Orel Hershiser 1.00 2.50
97 Rick Rhoden .02 .10
98 John Candelaria .02 .10
99 Dan Quisenberry .02 .10
100 Bill Caudill .02 .10
101 Willie Hernandez .02 .10
102 Dave Righetti .07 .20
103 Ron Davis .02 .10
104 Bruce Sutter .07 .20
105 Lee Smith .10 .30
106 Jesse Orosco .07 .20
107 Al Holland .02 .10
108 Goose Gossage .07 .20
109 Mark Langston .30 .75
110 Dave Stieb .07 .20
111 Mike Witt .02 .10
112 Bert Blyleven .07 .20
113 Dwight Gooden 1.00 2.50
114 Fernando Valenzuela .07 .20
115 Nolan Ryan 3.00 8.00
116 Mario Soto .02 .10
117 Ron Darling .07 .20
118 Dan Gladden .02 .10
119 Jeff Stone .02 .10
120 John Franco .30 .75
121 Barbaro Garbey .02 .10
122 Kirby Puckett 3.00 8.00
123 Roger Clemens 6.00 15.00
124 Bret Saberhagen .30 .75
125 Sparky Anderson MG .10 .30
126 Dick Williams MG .02 .10
NNO Sticker Album 4.00 10.00

1986 Fleer

The 1986 Fleer set consists of 660-card standard-size cards. Wax packs included 15 cards plus logo stickers. Card fronts feature dark blue borders (resulting in extremely condition sensitive cards commonly found with chipped edges), a team logo along with the player's name and position. The player cards are alphabetized within team and the teams are ordered by their 1985 season finish and won-lost record. Subsets include Specials (626-643) and Major League Prospects (644-653). The Dennis and Tippy Martinez cards were apparently switched in the set numbering, as their adjacent numbers (279 and 280) were reversed on the Orioles checklist card. The set includes the Rookie Cards of Rick Aguilera, Jose Canseco, Darren Daulton, Len Dykstra, Cecil Fielder, Andres Galarraga and Paul O'Neill.

COMPLETE SET (660) 15.00 40.00
COMP.FACT.SET (660) 15.00 40.00
1 Steve Balboni .05 .15
2 Joe Beckwith .05 .15
3 Buddy Biancalana .05 .15
4 Bud Black .05 .15
5 George Brett .75 2.00
6 Onix Concepcion .05 .15
7 Steve Farr .05 .15
8 Mark Gubicza .05 .15
9 Dane Iorg .05 .15
10 Danny Jackson .05 .15
11 Lynn Jones .05 .15
12 Mike Jones .05 .15
13 Charlie Leibrandt .05 .15
14 Hal McRae .08 .25
15 Omar Moreno .05 .15
16 Darryl Motley .05 .15
17 Jorge Orta .05 .15
18 Dan Quisenberry .05 .15
19 Bret Saberhagen .08 .25
20 Pat Sheridan .05 .15
21 Lonnie Smith .05 .15
22 Jim Sundberg .08 .25
23 John Wathan .05 .15

1986 Fleer

24 Frank White .08 .25
25 Willie Wilson .08 .25
26 Joaquin Andujar .08 .25
27 Steve Braun .05 .15
28 Bill Campbell .05 .15
29 Cesar Cedeno .08 .25
30 Jack Clark .08 .25
31 Vince Coleman RC .40 1.00
32 Danny Cox .05 .15
33 Ken Dayley .05 .15
34 Ivan DeJesus .05 .15
35 Bob Forsch .05 .15
36 Brian Harper .05 .15
37 Tom Herr .05 .15
38 Ricky Horton .05 .15
39 Kurt Kepshire .05 .15
40 Jeff Lahti .05 .15
41 Tito Landrum .05 .15
42 Willie McGee .08 .25
43 Tom Nieto .05 .15
44 Terry Pendleton .08 .25
45 Darrell Porter .05 .15
46 Ozzie Smith .50 1.25
47 John Tudor .08 .25
48 Andy Van Slyke .20 .50
49 Todd Worrell RC .20 .50
50 Jim Acker .05 .15
51 Doyle Alexander .05 .15
52 Jesse Barfield .08 .25
53 George Bell .08 .25
54 Jeff Burroughs .05 .15
55 Bill Caudill .05 .15
56 Jim Clancy .05 .15
57 Tony Fernandez .05 .15
58 Tom Filer .05 .15
59 Damaso Garcia .05 .15
60 Tom Henke .08 .25
61 Garth Iorg .05 .15
62 Cliff Johnson .05 .15
63 Jimmy Key .08 .25
64 Dennis Lamp .05 .15
65 Gary Lavelle .05 .15
66 Buck Martinez .05 .15
67 Lloyd Moseby .05 .15
68 Rance Mulliniks .05 .15
69 Al Oliver .08 .25
70 Dave Stieb .08 .25
71 Louis Thornton .05 .15
72 Willie Upshaw .05 .15
73 Ernie Whitt .05 .15
74 Rick Aguilera RC .20 .50
75 Wally Backman .05 .15
76 Gary Carter .08 .25
77 Ron Darling .08 .25
78 Len Dykstra RC .60 1.50
79 Sid Fernandez .05 .15
80 George Foster .08 .25
81 Dwight Gooden .30 .75
82 Tom Gorman .05 .15
83 Danny Heep .05 .15
84 Keith Hernandez .08 .25
85 Howard Johnson .08 .25
86 Ray Knight .08 .25
87 Terry Leach .05 .15
88 Ed Lynch .05 .15
89 Roger McDowell RC* .20 .50
90 Jesse Orosco .05 .15
91 Tom Paciorek .05 .15
92 Ronn Reynolds .05 .15
93 Rafael Santana .05 .15
94 Doug Sisk .05 .15
95 Rusty Staub .08 .25
96 Darryl Strawberry .20 .50
97 Mookie Wilson .08 .25
98 Neil Allen .05 .15
99 Don Baylor .08 .25
100 Dale Berra .05 .15
101 Rich Bordi .05 .15
102 Marty Bystrom .05 .15
103 Joe Cowley .05 .15
104 Brian Fisher RC .05 .15
105 Ken Griffey .08 .25
106 Ron Guidry .08 .25
107 Ron Hassey .05 .15
108 Rickey Henderson .30 .75
109 Don Mattingly 1.00 2.50
110 Bobby Meacham .05 .15
111 John Montefusco .05 .15
112 Phil Niekro .08 .25
113 Mike Pagliarulo .05 .15
114 Dan Pasqua .05 .15
115 Willie Randolph .08 .25
116 Dave Righetti .08 .25
117 Andre Robertson .05 .15
118 Billy Sample .05 .15
119 Bob Shirley .05 .15
120 Ed Whitson .05 .15
121 Dave Winfield .08 .25
122 Butch Wynegar .05 .15
123 Dave Anderson .05 .15
124 Bob Bailor .05 .15
125 Greg Brock .05 .15
126 Enos Cabell .05 .15
127 Bobby Castillo .05 .15
128 Carlos Diaz .05 .15
129 Mariano Duncan RC .20 .50
130 Pedro Guerrero .08 .25
131 Orel Hershiser .30 .75
132 Rick Honeycutt .05 .15
133 Ken Howell .05 .15
134 Ken Landreaux .05 .15
135 Bill Madlock .08 .25
136 Candy Maldonado .05 .15
137 Mike Marshall .05 .15
138 Len Matuszek .05 .15
139 Tom Niedenfuer .05 .15
140 Alejandro Pena .05 .15
141 Jerry Reuss .05 .15
142 Bill Russell .08 .25
143 Steve Sax .05 .15
144 Mike Scioscia .08 .25
145 Fernando Valenzuela .08 .25
146 Bob Welch .08 .25
147 Terry Whitfield .05 .15
148 Juan Beniquez .05 .15
149 Bob Boone .08 .25
150 John Candelaria .05 .15
151 Rod Carew .20 .50
152 Stu Cliburn .05 .15
153 Doug DeCinces .05 .15
154 Brian Downing .08 .25
155 Ken Forsch .05 .15
156 Craig Gerber .05 .15
157 Bobby Grich .08 .25
158 George Hendrick .08 .25
159 Al Holland .05 .15
160 Reggie Jackson .20 .50
161 Ruppert Jones .05 .15
162 Urbano Lugo .05 .15
163 Kirk McCaskill RC .20 .50
164 Donnie Moore .05 .15
165 Gary Pettis .05 .15
166 Ron Romanick .05 .15
167 Dick Schofield .05 .15
168 Daryl Sconiers .05 .15
169 Jim Slaton .05 .15
170 Don Sutton .08 .25
171 Mike Witt .05 .15
172 Buddy Bell .08 .25
173 Tom Browning .05 .15
174 Dave Concepcion .08 .25
175 Eric Davis .30 .75
176 Bo Diaz .05 .15
177 Nick Esasky .05 .15
178 John Franco .08 .25
179 Tom Hume .05 .15
180 Wayne Krenchicki .05 .15
181 Andy McGaffigan .05 .15
182 Eddie Milner .05 .15
183 Ron Oester .05 .15
184 Dave Parker .08 .25
185 Frank Pastore .05 .15
186 Tony Perez .20 .50
187 Ted Power .05 .15
188 Joe Price .05 .15
189 Gary Redus .05 .15
190 Ron Robinson .05 .15
191 Pete Rose 1.00 2.50
192 Mario Soto .08 .25
193 John Stuper .05 .15
194 Jay Tibbs .05 .15
195 Dave Van Gorder .05 .15
196 Max Venable .05 .15
197 Juan Agosto .05 .15
198 Harold Baines .08 .25
199 Floyd Bannister .05 .15
200 Britt Burns .05 .15
201 Julio Cruz .05 .15
202 Joel Davis .05 .15
203 Richard Dotson .05 .15
204 Carlton Fisk .20 .50
205 Scott Fletcher .05 .15
206 Ozzie Guillen RC .75 2.00
207 Jerry Hairston .05 .15
208 Tim Hulett .05 .15
209 Bob James .05 .15
210 Ron Kittle .05 .15
211 Rudy Law .05 .15
212 Bryan Little .05 .15
213 Gene Nelson .05 .15
214 Reid Nichols .05 .15
215 Luis Salazar .05 .15
216 Tom Seaver .20 .50
217 Dan Spillner .05 .15
218 Bruce Tanner .05 .15
219 Greg Walker .05 .15
220 Dave Wehrmeister .05 .15
221 Juan Berenguer .05 .15
222 Dave Bergman .05 .15
223 Tom Brookens .05 .15
224 Darrell Evans .08 .25
225 Barbaro Garbey .05 .15
226 Kirk Gibson .08 .25
227 John Grubb .05 .15
228 Willie Hernandez .05 .15
229 Larry Herndon .05 .15
230 Chet Lemon .08 .25
231 Aurelio Lopez .05 .15
232 Jack Morris .08 .25
233 Randy O'Neal .05 .15
234 Lance Parrish .08 .25
235 Dan Petry .05 .15
236 Alejandro Sanchez .05 .15
237 Bill Scherrer .05 .15
238 Nelson Simmons .05 .15
239 Frank Tanana .08 .25
240 Walt Terrell .05 .15
241 Alan Trammell .08 .25
242 Lou Whitaker .08 .25
243 Milt Wilcox .05 .15
244 Hubie Brooks .05 .15
245 Tim Burke .05 .15
246 Andre Dawson .08 .25
247 Mike Fitzgerald .05 .15
248 Terry Francona .08 .25
249 Bill Gullickson .05 .15
250 Joe Hesketh .05 .15
251 Bill Laskey .05 .15
252 Vance Law .05 .15
253 Charlie Lea .05 .15
254 Gary Lucas .05 .15
255 David Palmer .05 .15
256 Tim Raines .08 .25
257 Jeff Reardon .08 .25
258 Bert Roberge .05 .15
259 Dan Schatzeder .05 .15
260 Bryn Smith .05 .15
261 Randy St.Claire .05 .15
262 Scot Thompson .05 .15
263 Tim Wallach .05 .15
264 U.L. Washington .05 .15
265 Mitch Webster .05 .15
266 Herm Winningham .05 .15
267 Floyd Youmans .05 .15
268 Don Aase .05 .15
269 Mike Boddicker .05 .15
270 Rich Dauer .05 .15
271 Storm Davis .05 .15
272 Rick Dempsey .05 .15
273 Ken Dixon .05 .15
274 Jim Dwyer .05 .15
275 Mike Flanagan .05 .15
276 Wayne Gross .05 .15
277 Lee Lacy .05 .15
278 Fred Lynn .08 .25
279 Tippy Martinez .05 .15
280 Dennis Martinez .08 .25
281 Scott McGregor .05 .15
282 Eddie Murray .30 .75
283 Floyd Rayford .05 .15
284 Cal Ripken 1.25 3.00
285 Gary Roenicke .05 .15
286 Larry Sheets .05 .15
287 John Shelby .05 .15
288 Nate Snell .05 .15
289 Sammy Stewart .05 .15
290 Alan Wiggins .05 .15
291 Mike Young .05 .15
292 Alan Ashby .05 .15
293 Mark Bailey .05 .15
294 Kevin Bass .05 .15
295 Jeff Calhoun .05 .15
296 Jose Cruz .08 .25
297 Glenn Davis .05 .15
298 Bill Dawley .05 .15
299 Frank DiPino .05 .15
300 Bill Doran .05 .15
301 Phil Garner .08 .25
302 Jeff Heathcock .05 .15
303 Charlie Kerfeld .05 .15
304 Bob Knepper .05 .15
305 Ron Mathis .05 .15
306 Jerry Mumphrey .05 .15
307 Jim Pankovits .05 .15
308 Terry Puhl .05 .15
309 Craig Reynolds .05 .15
310 Nolan Ryan 1.50 4.00
311 Mike Scott .08 .25
312 Dave Smith .05 .15
313 Dickie Thon .05 .15
314 Denny Walling .05 .15
315 Kurt Bevacqua .05 .15
316 Al Bumbry .05 .15
317 Jerry Davis .05 .15
318 Luis DeLeon .05 .15
319 Dave Dravecky .05 .15
320 Tim Flannery .05 .15
321 Steve Garvey .08 .25
322 Rich Gossage .08 .25
323 Tony Gwynn .50 1.25
324 Andy Hawkins .05 .15
325 LaMarr Hoyt .05 .15
326 Roy Lee Jackson .05 .15
327 Terry Kennedy .05 .15
328 Craig Lefferts .05 .15
329 Carmelo Martinez .05 .15
330 Lance McCullers .05 .15
331 Kevin McReynolds .05 .15
332 Graig Nettles .08 .25
333 Jerry Royster .05 .15
334 Eric Show .05 .15
335 Tim Stoddard .05 .15
336 Garry Templeton .08 .25
337 Mark Thurmond .05 .15
338 Ed Wojna .05 .15
339 Tony Armas .08 .25
340 Marty Barrett .05 .15
341 Wade Boggs .20 .50
342 Dennis Boyd .05 .15
343 Bill Buckner .08 .25
344 Mark Clear .05 .15
345 Roger Clemens 2.00 5.00
346 Steve Crawford .05 .15
347 Mike Easler .05 .15
348 Dwight Evans .20 .50
349 Rich Gedman .05 .15
350 Jackie Gutierrez .05 .15
351 Glenn Hoffman .05 .15
352 Bruce Hurst .05 .15
353 Bruce Kison .05 .15
354 Tim Lollar .05 .15
355 Steve Lyons .05 .15
356 Al Nipper .05 .15
357 Bob Ojeda .05 .15
358 Jim Rice .08 .25
359 Bob Stanley .05 .15
360 Mike Trujillo .05 .15
361 Thad Bosley .05 .15
362 Warren Brusstar .05 .15
363 Ron Cey .08 .25
364 Jody Davis .05 .15
365 Bob Dernier .05 .15
366 Shawon Dunston .08 .25
367 Leon Durham .05 .15
368 Dennis Eckersley .20 .50
369 Ray Fontenot .05 .15
370 George Frazier .05 .15
371 Billy Hatcher .05 .15
372 Dave Lopes .08 .25
373 Gary Matthews .08 .25
374 Ron Meridith .05 .15
375 Keith Moreland .05 .15
376 Reggie Patterson .05 .15
377 Dick Ruthven .05 .15
378 Ryne Sandberg .60 1.50
379 Scott Sanderson .05 .15
380 Lee Smith .08 .25
381 Lary Sorensen .05 .15
382 Chris Speier .05 .15
383 Rick Sutcliffe .08 .25
384 Steve Trout .05 .15
385 Gary Woods .05 .15
386 Bert Blyleven .08 .25
387 Tom Brunansky .05 .15
388 Randy Bush .05 .15
389 John Butcher .05 .15
390 Ron Davis .05 .15
391 Dave Engle .05 .15
392 Frank Eufemia .05 .15
393 Pete Filson .05 .15
394 Gary Gaetti .08 .25
395 Greg Gagne .05 .15
396 Mickey Hatcher .05 .15
397 Kent Hrbek .08 .25
398 Tim Laudner .05 .15
399 Rick Lysander .05 .15
400 Dave Meier .05 .15
401 Kirby Puckett .75 2.00
402 Mark Salas .05 .15
403 Ken Schrom .05 .15
404 Roy Smalley .05 .15
405 Mike Smithson .05 .15
406 Mike Stenhouse .05 .15
407 Tim Teufel .05 .15
408 Frank Viola .08 .25
409 Ron Washington .05 .15
410 Keith Atherton .05 .15
411 Dusty Baker .08 .25
412 Tim Birtsas .05 .15
413 Bruce Bochte .05 .15
414 Chris Codiroli .05 .15
415 Dave Collins .05 .15
416 Mike Davis .05 .15
417 Alfredo Griffin .05 .15
418 Mike Heath .05 .15
419 Steve Henderson .05 .15
420 Donnie Hill .05 .15
421 Jay Howell .05 .15
422 Tommy John .08 .25
423 Dave Kingman .08 .25
424 Bill Krueger .05 .15
425 Rick Langford .05 .15
426 Carney Lansford .08 .25
427 Steve McCatty .05 .15
428 Dwayne Murphy .05 .15
429 Steve Ontiveros RC .05 .15
430 Tony Phillips .05 .15
431 Jose Rijo .08 .25
432 Mickey Tettleton RC .20 .50
433 Luis Aguayo .05 .15
434 Larry Andersen .05 .15
435 Steve Carlton .08 .25
436 Don Carman .05 .15
437 Tim Corcoran .05 .15
438 Darren Daulton RC .40 1.00
439 John Denny .05 .15
440 Tom Foley .05 .15
441 Greg Gross .05 .15
442 Kevin Gross .05 .15
443 Von Hayes .05 .15
444 Charles Hudson .05 .15
445 Garry Maddox .05 .15
446 Shane Rawley .05 .15
447 Dave Rucker .05 .15
448 John Russell .05 .15
449 Juan Samuel .05 .15
450 Mike Schmidt .75 2.00
451 Rick Schu .05 .15
452 Dave Shipanoff .05 .15
453 Dave Stewart .08 .25
454 Jeff Stone .05 .15
455 Kent Tekulve .05 .15
456 Ozzie Virgil .05 .15
457 Glenn Wilson .05 .15
458 Jim Beattie .05 .15
459 Karl Best .05 .15
460 Barry Bonnell .05 .15
461 Phil Bradley .05 .15
462 Ivan Calderon RC* .20 .50
463 Al Cowens .05 .15
464 Alvin Davis .05 .15
465 Dave Henderson .05 .15
466 Bob Kearney .05 .15
467 Mark Langston .08 .25
468 Bob Long .05 .15
469 Mike Moore .05 .15
470 Edwin Nunez .05 .15
471 Spike Owen .05 .15
472 Jack Perconte .05 .15
473 Jim Presley .05 .15
474 Donnie Scott .05 .15
475 Bill Swift .05 .15
476 Danny Tartabull .08 .25
477 Gorman Thomas .08 .25
478 Roy Thomas .05 .15
479 Ed VandeBerg .05 .15
480 Frank Wills .05 .15
481 Matt Young .05 .15
482 Ray Burris .05 .15
483 Jaime Cocanower .05 .15
484 Cecil Cooper .08 .25
485 Danny Darwin .05 .15
486 Rollie Fingers .08 .25
487 Jim Gantner .05 .15
488 Bob L. Gibson .05 .15
489 Moose Haas .05 .15
490 Teddy Higuera RC* .20 .50
491 Paul Householder .05 .15
492 Pete Ladd .05 .15
493 Rick Manning .05 .15
494 Bob McClure .05 .15
495 Paul Molitor .08 .25
496 Charlie Moore .05 .15
497 Ben Oglivie .08 .25
498 Randy Ready .05 .15
499 Earnie Riles .05 .15
500 Ed Romero .05 .15
501 Bill Schroeder .05 .15
502 Ray Searage .05 .15
503 Ted Simmons .08 .25
504 Pete Vuckovich .05 .15
505 Rick Waits .05 .15
506 Robin Yount .50 1.25
507 Len Barker .05 .15
508 Steve Bedrosian .05 .15
509 Bruce Benedict .05 .15
510 Rick Camp .05 .15
511 Rick Cerone .05 .15
512 Chris Chambliss .08 .25
513 Jeff Dedmon .05 .15
514 Terry Forster .08 .25
515 Gene Garber .05 .15
516 Terry Harper .05 .15
517 Bob Horner .08 .25
518 Glenn Hubbard .05 .15
519 Joe Johnson .05 .15
520 Brad Komminsk .05 .15
521 Rick Mahler .05 .15
522 Dale Murphy .20 .50
523 Ken Oberkfell .05 .15
524 Pascual Perez .05 .15
525 Gerald Perry .05 .15
526 Rafael Ramirez .05 .15
527 Steve Shields .05 .15
528 Zane Smith .05 .15
529 Bruce Sutter .08 .25
530 Milt Thompson RC .20 .50
531 Claudell Washington .05 .15
532 Paul Zuvella .05 .15
533 Vida Blue .08 .25
534 Bob Brenly .05 .15
535 Chris Brown RC .05 .15
536 Chili Davis .08 .25
537 Mark Davis .05 .15
538 Rob Deer .05 .15
539 Dan Driessen .05 .15
540 Scott Garrelts .05 .15
541 Dan Gladden .05 .15
542 Jim Gott .05 .15
543 David Green .05 .15
544 Atlee Hammaker .05 .15
545 Mike Jeffcoat .05 .15
546 Mike Krukow .05 .15
547 Dave LaPoint .05 .15
548 Jeff Leonard .05 .15
549 Greg Minton .05 .15
550 Alex Trevino .05 .15
551 Manny Trillo .05 .15
552 Jose Uribe .05 .15
553 Brad Wellman .05 .15
554 Frank Williams .05 .15
555 Joel Youngblood .05 .15
556 Alan Bannister .05 .15
557 Glenn Brummer .05 .15
558 Steve Buechele RC .20 .50
559 Jose Guzman RC .05 .15
560 Toby Harrah .08 .25
561 Greg Harris .05 .15
562 Dwayne Henry .05 .15
563 Burt Hooton .05 .15
564 Charlie Hough .08 .25
565 Mike Mason .05 .15
566 Oddibe McDowell .05 .15
567 Dickie Noles .05 .15
568 Pete O'Brien .05 .15
569 Larry Parrish .05 .15
570 Dave Rozema .05 .15
571 Dave Schmidt .05 .15
572 Don Slaught .05 .15
573 Wayne Tolleson .05 .15
574 Duane Walker .05 .15
575 Gary Ward .05 .15
576 Chris Welsh .05 .15
577 Curtis Wilkerson .05 .15
578 George Wright .05 .15
579 Chris Bando .05 .15
580 Tony Bernazard .05 .15
581 Brett Butler .08 .25
582 Ernie Camacho .05 .15
583 Joe Carter .08 .25
584 Carmen Castillo .05 .15
585 Jamie Easterly .05 .15
586 Julio Franco .08 .25
587 Mel Hall .05 .15
588 Mike Hargrove .05 .15
589 Neal Heaton .05 .15
590 Brook Jacoby .05 .15
591 Otis Nixon RC .40 1.00
592 Jerry Reed .05 .15
593 Vern Ruhle .05 .15
594 Pat Tabler .05 .15
595 Rich Thompson .05 .15
596 Andre Thornton .05 .15
597 Dave Von Ohlen .05 .15
598 George Vukovich .05 .15
599 Tom Waddell .05 .15
600 Curt Wardle .05 .15
601 Jerry Willard .05 .15
602 Bill Almon .05 .15
603 Mike Bielecki .05 .15
604 Sid Bream .05 .15
605 Mike C. Brown .05 .15
606 Pat Clements .05 .15
607 Jose DeLeon .05 .15
608 Denny Gonzalez .05 .15
609 Cecilio Guante .05 .15
610 Steve Kemp .05 .15
611 Sammy Khalifa .05 .15
612 Lee Mazzilli .08 .25
613 Larry McWilliams .05 .15
614 Jim Morrison .05 .15
615 Joe Orsulak RC* .20 .50
616 Tony Pena .05 .15
617 Johnny Ray .05 .15
618 Rick Reuschel .08 .25
619 R.J. Reynolds .05 .15
620 Rick Rhoden .05 .15
621 Don Robinson .05 .15
622 Jason Thompson .05 .15
623 Lee Tunnell .05 .15
624 Jim Winn .05 .15
625 Marvell Wynne .05 .15
626 Dwight Gooden IA .20 .50
627 Don Mattingly IA .50 1.25
628 Pete Rose 4192 .20 .50
629 Rod Carew 3000 Hits .08 .25
630 T.Seaver .08 .25
P.Niekro
631 Don Baylor Ouch .08 .25
632 Tim Raines .08 .25
Strawberry
633 C.Ripken .60 1.50
A.Trammell
634 Wade Boggs .40 1.00
G.Brett
635 B.Horner .20 .50
D.Murphy
636 W.McGee .08 .25
V.Coleman
637 Vince Coleman IA .08 .25
638 Pete Rose .30 .75
D.Gooden
639 Wade Boggs .50 1.25
D.Mattingly
640 Murphy .20 .50
Garvey
Parker
641 D.Gooden .20 .50
F.Valenzuela
642 Jimmy Key .08 .25
D.Stieb
643 C.Fisk .08 .25
R.Gedman
644 Benito Santiago RC .75 2.00
645 M.Woodard .05 .15
C.Ward RC
646 Paul O'Neill RC 1.50 4.00
647 Andres Galarraga RC .60 1.50
648 B.Kipper .05 .15
C.Ford RC
649 Jose Canseco RC 3.00 8.00
650 Mark McLemore RC .40 1.00
651 R.Woodward .05 .15
M.Brantley RC
652 B.Robidoux .05 .15
M.Funderburk RC
653 Cecil Fielder RC .75 2.00
654 CL: Royals .05 .15
Cardinals
Blue Jays
Mets
655 CL: Yankees .05 .15
Dodgers
Angels
Reds UER/(168 Darly S
656 CL: White Sox .05 .15
Tigers
Expos
Orioles/(279 Dennis&#
657 CL: Astros .05 .15
Padres
Red Sox
Cubs
658 CL: Twins .05 .15
A's
Phillies
Mariners
659 CL: Brewers .05 .15
Braves
Giants
Rangers
660 CL: Indians .05 .15
Pirates
Special Cards

1986 Fleer All-Stars

Randomly inserted in wax and cello packs, this 12-card standard-size set features top stars. The cards feature red backgrounds (American Leaguers) and blue backgrounds (National Leaguers). The 12 selections cover each position, left and right-handed starting pitchers, a reliever, and a designated hitter.

COMPLETE SET (12) 10.00 25.00
RANDOM INSERTS IN PACKS 1.25 2.50
1 Don Mattingly 3.00 8.00
2 Tom Herr .20 .50
3 George Brett 2.50 6.00
4 Gary Carter .30 .75
5 Cal Ripken 4.00 10.00
6 Dave Parker .30 .75
7 Rickey Henderson 1.00 2.50
8 Pedro Guerrero .30 .75
9 Dan Quisenberry .20 .50
10 Dwight Gooden 1.00 2.50
11 Gorman Thomas .30 .75
12 John Tudor .30 .75

1986 Fleer Future Hall of Famers

These six standard-size cards were issued one per Fleer three-packs. This set features players that Fleer predicts will be "Future Hall of Famers." The card backs describe career highlights, records, and honors won by the player.

COMPLETE SET (6) 6.00 15.00
SEMISTARS .25 .60
ONE PER RACK PACK
1 Pete Rose 2.50 6.00
2 Steve Carlton .25 .60
3 Tom Seaver .50 1.25
4 Rod Carew .50 1.25
5 Nolan Ryan 4.00 10.00
6 Reggie Jackson .50 1.25

1986 Fleer Wax Box Cards

The cards in this eight-card set measure the standard size and were found on the bottom of the Fleer regular issue wax pack and cello pack boxes as four-card panel. Cards have essentially the same design as the 1986 Fleer regular issue set. These eight cards (C1 to C8) are considered a separate set in their own right and are not typically included in a complete set of the regular issue 1986 Fleer cards. The value of the panel uncut is slightly greater, perhaps by 25 percent greater, than the value of the individual cards cut up carefully.

COMPLETE SET (8) 2.50 6.00
C1 Royals Logo .08 .25
C2 George Brett 1.25 3.00
C3 Ozzie Guillen .30 .75
C4 Dale Murphy .30 .75
C5 Cardinals Logo .08 .25
C6 Tom Browning .08 .25
C7 Gary Carter .40 1.00
C8 Carlton Fisk .40 1.00

1986 Fleer Update

This 132-card standard-size set was distributed in factory set form through hobby dealers. These sets were distributed in 50-set cases. In addition to the complete set of 132 cards, the box also contains 25 Team Logo Stickers.The card fronts look very similar to the 1986 Fleer regular issue. These cards are just as condition sensitive with most cards having chippled edges straight out of the box. The cards are numbered (with a U prefix) alphabetically according to player's last name. The extended Rookie Cards in this set include Barry Bonds, Bobby Bonilla, Will Clark, Wally Joyner and John Kruk.

COMP.FACT.SET (132) 12.50 30.00
1 Mike Aldrete XRC .05 .15
2 Andy Allanson XRC .05 .15
3 Neil Allen .05 .15
4 Joaquin Andujar .08 .25
5 Paul Assenmacher XRC .20 .50
6 Scott Bailes XRC .05 .15
7 Jay Baller XRC .05 .15
8 Scott Bankhead .05 .15
9 Bill Bathe XRC .05 .15
10 Don Baylor .08 .25
11 Billy Beane XRC .40 1.00
12 Steve Bedrosian .05 .15
13 Juan Beniquez .05 .15
14 Barry Bonds XRC 6.00 15.00
15 Bobby Bonilla XRC .40 1.00
16 Rich Bordi .05 .15
17 Bill Campbell .05 .15

Tom Candiotti .05 .15
John Cangelosi XRC .20 .50
Jose Canseco 1.50 4.00
Chuck Cary XRC .05 .15
Juan Castillo XRC .05 .15
Rick Cerone .05 .15
John Cerutti XRC .05 .15
Will Clark XRC .75 2.00
Mark Clear .05 .15
Darnell Coles .05 .15
Dave Collins .05 .15
Tim Conroy .05 .15
Ed Correa .05 .15
Joe Cowley .05 .15
Bill Dawley .05 .15
Rob Deer .05 .15
John Denny .05 .15
Jim Deshaies XRC .05 .15
Doug Drabek XRC .40 1.00
Mike Easler .05 .15
Mark Eichhorn .05 .15
Dave Engle .05 .15
Mike Fischlin .05 .15
Scott Fletcher .05 .15
Terry Forster .08 .25
Terry Francona .08 .25
Andres Galarraga .60 1.50
Lee Guetterman .05 .15
Bill Gullickson .05 .15
Jackie Gutierrez .05 .15
Moose Haas .05 .15
Billy Hatcher .05 .15
Mike Heath .05 .15
Guy Hoffman .05 .15
Tom Hume .05 .15
Pete Incaviglia XRC .20 .50
Dane Iorg .05 .15
Chris James XRC .05 .15
Stan Javier XRC* .20 .50
Tommy John .08 .25
Tracy Jones .05 .15
Wally Joyner XRC .40 1.00
Wayne Krenchicki .05 .15
John Kruk XRC .60 1.50
Mike LaCoss .05 .15
Pete Ladd .05 .15
Dave LaPoint .05 .15
Mike LaValliere XRC .20 .50
Rudy Law .05 .15
Dennis Leonard .05 .15
Steve Lombardozzi .05 .15
Aurelio Lopez .05 .15
Mickey Mahler .05 .15
Candy Maldonado .05 .15
Roger Mason XRC* .05 .15
Greg Mathews .05 .15
Andy McGaffigan .05 .15
Joel McKeon .05 .15
Kevin Mitchell XRC .40 1.00
Bill Mooneyham .05 .15
Omar Moreno .05 .15
Jerry Mumphrey .05 .15
Al Newman XRC .08 .25
Phil Niekro .08 .25
Randy Niemann .05 .15
Juan Nieves .05 .15
Bob Ojeda .05 .15
Rick Ownbey .05 .15
Tom Paciorek .05 .15
David Palmer .05 .15
Jeff Parrett XRC .05 .15
Pat Perry .05 .15
Dan Plesac .05 .15
Darrell Porter .05 .15
Luis Quinones .05 .15
Rey Quinones UER
(Misspelled Quinonez) .05 .15
Gary Redus .05 .15
5 Jeff Reed .05 .15
Bip Roberts XRC .20 .50
Billy Joe Robidoux .05 .15
Gary Roenicke .05 .15
Ron Roenicke .05 .15
00 Angel Salazar .05 .15
01 Joe Sambito .05 .15
02 Billy Sample .05 .15
03 Dave Schmidt .05 .15
04 Ken Schrom .05 .15
05 Ruben Sierra XRC .60 1.50
06 Ted Simmons .08 .25
07 Sammy Stewart .05 .15
08 Kurt Stillwell .05 .15
09 Dale Sveum .05 .15
10 Tim Teufel .05 .15
11 Bob Tewksbury XRC .20 .50
12 Andres Thomas .05 .15
13 Jason Thompson .05 .15
14 Milt Thompson .20 .50
15 Robby Thompson XRC .20 .50
16 Jay Tibbs .05 .15
17 Fred Toliver .05 .15
18 Wayne Tolleson .05 .15
19 Alex Trevino .05 .15
20 Manny Trillo .05 .15
21 Ed VandeBerg .05 .15
22 Ozzie Virgil .05 .15
23 Tony Walker .05 .15
24 Gene Walter .05 .15
25 Duane Ward XRC .20 .50
26 Jerry Willard .05 .15
27 Mitch Williams XRC .20 .50
28 Reggie Williams .05 .15
29 Bobby Witt XRC .20 .50

130 Marvell Wynne .05 .15
131 Steve Yeager .08 .25
132 Checklist 1-132 .05 .15

1986 Fleer League Leaders

This 44-card standard-size set is also sometimes referred to as the Walgreen's set. Although the set was distributed through Walgreen's, there is no mention on the cards or box of that fact. The cards are easily recognizable by the fact that they contain the phrase "Fleer League Leaders" at the top of the obverse. Both sides of the cards are designed with a blue stripe on white pattern. The checklist for the set is given on the outside of the red, white, blue, and gold box in which the set was packaged. A first year card of Jose Canseco highlights the set.

COMP.FACT. SET (44) 2.50 6.00
1 Wade Boggs .20 .50
2 George Brett .30 .75
3 Jose Canseco .75 2.00
4 Rod Carew .07 .20
5 Gary Carter .20 .50
6 Jack Clark .02 .10
7 Vince Coleman .02 .10
8 Jose Cruz .02 .10
9 Alvin Davis .01 .05
10 Mariano Duncan .01 .05
11 Leon Durham .01 .05
12 Carlton Fisk .15 .40
13 Julio Franco .02 .10
14 Scott Garrelts .01 .05
15 Steve Garvey .05 .15
16 Dwight Gooden .02 .10
17 Ozzie Guillen .01 .05
18 Willie Hernandez .01 .05
19 Bob Horner .01 .05
20 Kent Hrbek .02 .10
21 Charlie Leibrandt .01 .05
22 Don Mattingly .20 .50
23 Oddibe McDowell .01 .05
24 Willie McGee .02 .10
25 Keith Moreland .01 .05
26 Lloyd Moseby .01 .05
27 Dale Murphy .07 .20
28 Phil Niekro .15 .40
29 Joe Orsulak .01 .05
30 Dave Parker .02 .10
31 Lance Parrish .02 .10
32 Kirby Puckett .20 .50
33 Tim Raines .02 .10
34 Earnie Riles .01 .05
35 Cal Ripken .60 1.50
36 Pete Rose .20 .50
37 Bret Saberhagen .02 .10
38 Juan Samuel .01 .05
39 Ryne Sandberg .20 .50
40 Tom Seaver .15 .40
41 Lee Smith .05 .15
42 Ozzie Smith .30 .75
43 Dave Stieb .01 .05
44 Robin Yount .10 .30

1986 Fleer Limited Edition

The 44-card boxed standard-size set was produced by Fleer for McCrory's. The cards have green and yellow borders. Card backs are printed in red and black on white card stock. The back of the original box gives a complete checklist of the players in the set. The set box also contains six logo stickers.

COMP.FACT. SET (44) 2.50 6.00
1 Doyle Alexander .01 .05
2 Joaquin Andujar .01 .05
3 Harold Baines .05 .15
4 Wade Boggs .15 .40
5 Phil Bradley .01 .05
6 George Brett .20 .50
7 Hubie Brooks .01 .05
8 Chris Brown .01 .05
9 Tom Brunansky .01 .05
10 Gary Carter .15 .40
11 Vince Coleman .02 .10
12 Cecil Cooper .02 .10
13 Jose Cruz .02 .10
14 Mike Davis .01 .05
15 Carlton Fisk .15 .40
16 Julio Franco .02 .10
17 Damaso Garcia .01 .05
18 Rich Gedman .01 .05
19 Kirk Gibson .02 .10
20 Dwight Gooden .05 .15
21 Pedro Guerrero .02 .10
22 Tony Gwynn .30 .75
23 Rickey Henderson .30 .75
24 Orel Hershiser .05 .15
25 LaMarr Hoyt .01 .05
26 Reggie Jackson .20 .50
27 Don Mattingly .30 .75
28 Oddibe McDowell .01 .05
29 Willie McGee .02 .10
30 Paul Molitor .05 .15
31 Dale Murphy .07 .20
32 Eddie Murray .15 .40
33 Dave Parker .02 .10
34 Tony Pena .02 .10
35 Jeff Reardon .01 .05
36 Cal Ripken .60 1.50
37 Pete Rose .20 .50
38 Bret Saberhagen .02 .10
39 Juan Samuel .01 .05
40 Ryne Sandberg .20 .50
41 Mike Schmidt .20 .50
42 Lee Smith .05 .15
43 Don Sutton .15 .40
44 Lou Whitaker .02 .10

1986 Fleer Mini

The Fleer "Classic Miniatures" set consists of 120 small cards with all new pictures of the players as compared to the 1986 Fleer regular issue. The cards are only1 13/16" by 2 9/16", making them some of the smallest (in size) produced in the 1980's. Card backs provide career year-by-year statistics. The complete set was distributed in a red, white, and silver factory box along with 18 logo stickers. The card numbering is done in the same team order as the 1986 Fleer regular set. An early card of Jose Canseco is featured in this set.

COMP.FACT SET (120) 3.00 8.00
1 George Brett .30 .75
2 Dan Quisenberry .01 .05
3 Bret Saberhagen .02 .10
4 Lonnie Smith .01 .05
5 Willie Wilson .02 .10
6 Jack Clark .02 .10
7 Vince Coleman .02 .10
8 Tom Herr .01 .05
9 Willie McGee .02 .10
10 Ozzie Smith .30 .75
11 John Tudor .01 .05
12 Jesse Barfield .01 .05
13 George Bell .02 .10
14 Tony Fernandez .02 .10
15 Damaso Garcia .01 .05
16 Dave Stieb .01 .05
17 Gary Carter .15 .40
18 Ron Darling .01 .05
19A Dwight Gooden/(R on Mets logo) .10 .30
19B Dwight Gooden
(No R on Mets logo) .10 .30
20 Keith Hernandez .02 .10
21 Darryl Strawberry .02 .10
22 Ron Guidry .02 .10
23 Rickey Henderson .25 .60
24 Don Mattingly .30 .75
25 Dave Righetti .01 .05
26 Dave Winfield .15 .40
27 Mariano Duncan .01 .05
28 Pedro Guerrero .02 .10
29 Bill Madlock .02 .10
30 Mike Marshall .01 .05
31 Fernando Valenzuela .05 .15
32 Reggie Jackson .20 .50
33 Gary Pettis .01 .05
34 Ron Romanick .01 .05
35 Don Sutton .10 .30
36 Mike Witt .01 .05
37 Buddy Bell .02 .10
38 Tom Browning .01 .05
39 Dave Parker .02 .10
40 Pete Rose .20 .50
41 Mario Soto .01 .05
42 Harold Baines .05 .15
43 Carlton Fisk .16 .40
44 Ozzie Guillen .05 .15
45 Ron Kittle .01 .05
46 Tom Seaver .15 .40
47 Kirk Gibson .02 .10
48 Jack Morris .05 .15
49 Lance Parrish .02 .10
50 Alan Trammell .05 .15
51 Lou Whitaker .02 .10
52 Hubie Brooks .01 .05
53 Andre Dawson .15 .40
54 Tim Raines .02 .10
55 Bryn Smith .01 .05
56 Tim Wallach .01 .05
57 Mike Boddicker .01 .05
58 Eddie Murray .15 .40
59 Cal Ripken .60 1.50
60 John Shelby .01 .05
61 Mike Young .01 .05
62 Jose Cruz .02 .10
63 Glenn Davis .01 .05
64 Phil Garner .02 .10
65 Nolan Ryan .60 1.50
66 Mike Scott .01 .05
67 Steve Garvey .02 .10
68 Rich Gossage .02 .10
69 Tony Gwynn .40 1.00
70 Andy Hawkins .01 .05
71 Garry Templeton .01 .05
72 Wade Boggs .15 .40
73 Roger Clemens .40 1.00
74 Dwight Evans .02 .10
75 Rich Gedman .01 .05
76 Jim Rice .02 .10
77 Shawon Dunston .01 .05
78 Leon Durham .01 .05
79 Keith Moreland .01 .05
80 Ryne Sandberg .20 .50
81 Rick Sutcliffe .01 .05
82 Bert Blyleven .02 .10
83 Tom Brunansky .01 .05
84 Kent Hrbek .02 .10
85 Kirby Puckett .20 .50
86 Bruce Bochte .01 .05
87 Jose Canseco .30 .75
88 Mike Davis .01 .05
89 Jay Howell .01 .05
90 Dwayne Murphy .01 .05
91 Steve Carlton .15 .40
92 Von Hayes .01 .05
93 Juan Samuel .01 .05
94 Mike Schmidt .15 .40
95 Glenn Wilson .01 .05
96 Phil Bradley .01 .05
97 Alvin Davis .01 .05
98 Jim Presley .01 .05
99 Danny Tartabull .01 .05
100 Cecil Cooper .02 .10
101 Paul Molitor .15 .40
102 Ernie Riles .01 .05
103 Robin Yount .15 .40
104 Bob Horner .01 .05
105 Dale Murphy .07 .20
106 Bruce Sutter .02 .10
107 Claudell Washington .01 .05
108 Chris Brown .01 .05
109 Chili Davis .02 .10
110 Scott Garrelts .01 .05
111 Oddibe McDowell .01 .05
112 Pete O'Brien .01 .05
113 Gary Ward .01 .05
114 Brett Butler .02 .10
115 Julio Franco .02 .10
116 Brook Jacoby .01 .05
117 Mike C. Brown .01 .05
118 Joe Orsulak .01 .05
119 Tony Pena .02 .10
120 R.J. Reynolds .01 .05

1986 Fleer Sluggers/Pitchers

Fleer produced this 44-card boxed standard-size set although it was primarily distributed by Kress, McCrory, Newberry, T.G.Y., and other similar stores. The set features 22 sluggers and 22 pitchers and is subtitled "Baseball's Best". The set was packaged in a red, white, blue, and yellow custom box along with six logo stickers. The set checklist is given on the back of the box. The card numbering is in alphabetical order by the player's name. The Will Clark and Bobby Witt cards were the first major league cards produced of those players. In addition, an early card of Jose Canseco is featured in this set.

COMP.FACT.SET (44) 2.50 6.00
1 Bert Blyleven .02 .10
2 Wade Boggs .15 .40
3 George Brett .30 .75
4 Tom Browning .01 .05
5 Jose Canseco .40 1.00
6 Will Clark .40 1.00
7 Roger Clemens .30 .75
8 Alvin Davis .01 .05
9 Julio Franco .02 .10
10 Kirk Gibson .02 .10
11 Dwight Gooden .02 .10
12 Rich Gossage .02 .10
13 Pedro Guerrero .01 .05
14 Ron Guidry .02 .10
15 Tony Gwynn .30 .75
16 Orel Hershiser .07 .20
17 Kent Hrbek .02 .10
18 Reggie Jackson .15 .40
19 Wally Joyner .15 .40
20 Charlie Leibrandt .01 .05
21 Don Mattingly .30 .75
22 Willie McGee .02 .10
23 Jack Morris .02 .10
24 Dale Murphy .07 .20
25 Eddie Murray .15 .40
26 Jeff Reardon .01 .05
27 Rick Reuschel .01 .05
28 Cal Ripken .60 1.50
29 Pete Rose .20 .50
30 Nolan Ryan .60 1.50
31 Bret Saberhagen .02 .10
32 Ryne Sandberg .20 .50
33 Mike Schmidt .20 .50
34 Tom Seaver .15 .40
35 Bryn Smith .01 .05
36 Mario Soto .02 .10
37 Dave Stieb .01 .05
38 Darryl Strawberry .02 .10
39 Rick Sutcliffe .01 .05
40 John Tudor .01 .05
41 Fernando Valenzuela .02 .10
42 Bobby Witt .02 .10
43 Mike Witt .01 .05
44 Robin Yount .15 .40

1986 Fleer Sluggers/Pitchers Box Cards

The cards in this six-card set each measure the standard size. Cards have essentially the same design as the 1986 Fleer Sluggers vs. Pitchers set of Baseball's Best. The cards were printed on the bottom of the counter display box which held 24 small boxed sets; hence theoretically these box cards are 1/24 as plentiful as the regular boxed set cards. These six cards, numbered M1 to M5 with one blank-back (unnumbered) card, are considered a separate set in their own right and are not typically included in a complete set of the 1986 Fleer Sluggers vs. Pitchers set of 44. The value of the panels uncut is slightly greater, perhaps by 25 percent greater, than the value of the individual cards cut up carefully.

COMPLETE SET (6) 4.00 10.00
M1 Harold Baines .60 1.50
M2 Steve Carlton 1.50 4.00
M3 Gary Carter 1.25 3.00
M4 Vince Coleman .30 .75
M5 Kirby Puckett 2.50 6.00
NNO New York Mets .20 .50

1986 Fleer Star Stickers

The standard-size stickers (made of card stock) 132-card set were distributed in wax packs and feature card photos on the front surrounded by a yellow border and a cranberry frame. The backs are printed in blue and black on white card stock. The backs contain year-by-year statistical information. They are numbered on the back in the upper left-hand corner. The card numbering is in alphabetical order by the player's name. A first year card of slugger Jose Canseco is featured in this set.

COMPLETE SET (132) 6.00 15.00
1 Harold Baines .05 .15
2 Jesse Barfield .01 .05
3 Don Baylor .02 .10
4 Juan Beniquez .01 .05
5 Tim Birtsas .01 .05
6 Bert Blyleven .02 .10
7 Bruce Bochte .01 .05
8 Wade Boggs .20 .50
9 Dennis Boyd .01 .05
10 Phil Bradley .01 .05
11 George Brett .50 1.25
12 Hubie Brooks .01 .05
13 Chris Brown .01 .05
14 Tom Browning .01 .05
15 Tom Brunansky .01 .05
16 Bill Buckner .02 .10
17 Britt Burns .01 .05
18 Brett Butler .02 .10
19 Jose Canseco .75 2.00
20 Rod Carew .15 .40
21 Steve Carlton .15 .40
22 Don Carman .01 .05
23 Gary Carter .20 .50
24 Jack Clark .02 .10
25 Vince Coleman .02 .10
26 Cecil Cooper .02 .10
27 Jose Cruz .02 .10
28 Ron Darling .01 .05
29 Alvin Davis .01 .05
30 Jody Davis .01 .05
31 Mike Davis .01 .05
32 Andre Dawson .07 .20
33 Mariano Duncan .01 .05
34 Shawon Dunston .02 .10
35 Leon Durham .01 .05
36 Darrell Evans .02 .10
37 Tony Fernandez .02 .10
38 Carlton Fisk .15 .40
39 John Franco .07 .20
40 Julio Franco .02 .10
41 Damaso Garcia .01 .05
42 Scott Garrelts .01 .05
43 Steve Garvey .07 .20
44 Rich Gedman .01 .05
45 Kirk Gibson .02 .10
46 Dwight Gooden .05 .15
47 Pedro Guerrero .02 .10
48 Ron Guidry .02 .10
49 Ozzie Guillen .20 .50
50 Tony Gwynn .50 1.25
51 Andy Hawkins .01 .05
52 Von Hayes .01 .05
53 Rickey Henderson .30 1.00
54 Tom Henke .01 .05
55 Keith Hernandez .02 .10
56 Willie Hernandez .01 .05
57 Tommy Herr .01 .05
58 Orel Hershiser .05 .15
59 Teddy Higuera .01 .05
60 Bob Horner .01 .05
61 Charlie Hough .02 .10
62 Jay Howell .01 .05
63 LaMarr Hoyt .01 .05
64 Kent Hrbek .02 .10
65 Reggie Jackson .20 .50
66 Bob James .01 .05
67 Dave Kingman .02 .10
68 Ron Kittle .01 .05
69 Charlie Leibrandt .01 .05
70 Fred Lynn .02 .10
71 Mike Marshall .01 .05
72 Don Mattingly .50 1.25
73 Oddibe McDowell .01 .05
74 Willie McGee .02 .10
75 Scott McGregor .01 .05
76 Paul Molitor .20 .50
77 Donnie Moore .01 .05
78 Keith Moreland .01 .05
79 Jack Morris .02 .10
80 Dale Murphy .07 .20
81 Eddie Murray .20 .50
82 Phil Niekro .15 .40
83 Joe Orsulak .01 .05
84 Dave Parker .02 .10
85 Lance Parrish .02 .10
86 Larry Parrish .01 .05
87 Tony Pena .02 .10
88 Gary Pettis .01 .05
89 Jim Presley .01 .05
90 Kirby Puckett 1.00 1.00
91 Dan Quisenberry .01 .05
92 Tim Raines .02 .10
93 Johnny Ray .01 .05
94 Jeff Reardon .02 .10
95 Rick Reuschel .02 .10
96 Jim Rice .02 .10
97 Dave Righetti .01 .05
98 Earnie Riles .01 .05
99 Cal Ripken 1.00 2.50
100 Ron Romanick .01 .05
101 Pete Rose .30 .75
102 Nolan Ryan 1.00 2.50
103 Bret Saberhagen .02 .10
104 Mark Salas .01 .05
105 Juan Samuel .01 .05
106 Ryne Sandberg .30 .75
107 Mike Schmidt .20 .50
108 Mike Scott .01 .05
109 Tom Seaver .15 .40
110 Bryn Smith .01 .05
111 Dave Smith .02 .10
112 Lee Smith .05 .15
113 Ozzie Smith .30 .75
114 Mario Soto .01 .05
115 Dave Stieb .01 .05
116 Darryl Strawberry .02 .10
117 Bruce Sutter .02 .10
118 Garry Templeton .01 .05
119 Gorman Thomas .01 .05
120 Andre Thornton .01 .05
121 Alan Trammell .05 .15
122 John Tudor .01 .05
123 Fernando Valenzuela .07 .20
124 Frank Viola .02 .10
125 Gary Ward .01 .05
126 Lou Whitaker .02 .10
127 Frank White .02 .10
128 Glenn Wilson .01 .05
129 Willie Wilson .01 .05
130 Dave Winfield .15 .40
131 Robin Yount .15 .40
132 Checklist Card .07 .20
Dwight Gooden
Dale Murphy

1986 Fleer Stickers Wax Box Cards

The bottoms of the Star Sticker wax boxes contained a set of four cards done in a similar format to the stickers; these cards (they are not stickers but truly cards) are numbered with the prefix S and are considered a separate set. Each individual card measures 2 1/2" by 3 1/2". The value of the panel uncut is slightly greater, perhaps by 25 percent greater, than the value of the individual cards cut up carefully.

COMPLETE SET (4) 1.50 4.00
S1 Dodgers Team Logo/(Checklist back) .08 .25
S2 Wade Boggs .75 2.00
S3 Steve Garvey .30 .75
S4 Dave Winfield .60 1.50

1987 Fleer

This set consists of 660 standard-size cards. Cards were primarily issued in 17-card wax packs, rack packs and hobby and retail factory sets. The wax packs were packed 36 to a box and 20 boxes to a case. The rack packs were packed 24 to a box and 3 boxes to a case and had 51 regular cards and three sticker card per pack. Card fronts feature a distinctive light blue and white blended border encasing a color photo. Cards are again organized numerically by teams with team ordering based on the previous seasons record. The last 36 cards in the set consist of Specials (625-643), Rookie Pairs (644-653), and checklists (654-660). The key Rookie Cards in this set are Barry Bonds, Bobby Bonilla, Will Clark, Chuck Finley, Bo Jackson, Wally Joyner, John Kruk, Barry Larkin and Devon White.

COMPLETE SET (660) 12.50 30.00
COMP.FACT.SET (672) 15.00 40.00
1 Rick Aguilera .05 .15
2 Richard Anderson .05 .15
3 Wally Backman .05 .15
4 Gary Carter .08 .25
5 Ron Darling .08 .25
6 Len Dykstra .08 .25
7 Kevin Elster RC .20 .50
8 Sid Fernandez .05 .15
9 Dwight Gooden .15 .40
10 Ed Hearn RC .05 .15
11 Danny Heep .05 .15
12 Keith Hernandez .08 .25
13 Howard Johnson .08 .25
14 Ray Knight .08 .25
15 Lee Mazzilli .08 .25
16 Roger McDowell .05 .15
17 Kevin Mitchell RC .50 1.25
18 Randy Niemann .05 .15
19 Bob Ojeda .05 .15
20 Jesse Orosco .05 .15
21 Rafael Santana .05 .15
22 Doug Sisk .05 .15
23 Darryl Strawberry .08 .25
24 Tim Teufel .05 .15
25 Mookie Wilson .08 .25
26 Tony Armas .08 .25
27 Marty Barrett .05 .15
28 Don Baylor .08 .25
29 Wade Boggs .15 .40
30 Oil Can Boyd .05 .15
31 Bill Buckner .08 .25
32 Roger Clemens 1.25 3.00
33 Steve Crawford .05 .15
34 Dwight Evans .15 .40
35 Rich Gedman .05 .15
36 Dave Henderson .05 .15
37 Bruce Hurst .05 .15
38 Tim Lollar .05 .15
39 Al Nipper .05 .15
40 Spike Owen .05 .15
41 Jim Rice .08 .25
42 Ed Romero .05 .15
43 Joe Sambito .05 .15
44 Calvin Schiraldi .05 .15
45 Tom Seaver UER .15 .40
Lifetime saves total 0, should be 1
46 Jeff Sellers .05 .15
47 Bob Stanley .05 .15
48 Sammy Stewart .05 .15
49 Larry Andersen .05 .15
50 Alan Ashby .05 .15
51 Kevin Bass .05 .15
52 Jeff Calhoun .05 .15
53 Jose Cruz .08 .25
54 Danny Darwin .05 .15
55 Glenn Davis .05 .15
56 Jim Deshaies RC .08 .25
57 Bill Doran .05 .15
58 Phil Garner .08 .25
59 Billy Hatcher .05 .15
60 Charlie Kerfeld .05 .15
61 Bob Knepper .05 .15
62 Dave Lopes .08 .25
63 Aurelio Lopez .05 .15
64 Jim Pankovits .05 .15
65 Terry Puhl .05 .15
66 Craig Reynolds .05 .15
67 Nolan Ryan 1.25 3.00
68 Mike Scott .08 .25
69 Dave Smith .05 .15
70 Dickie Thon .05 .15
71 Tony Walker .05 .15
72 Denny Walling .05 .15
73 Bob Boone .08 .25
74 Rick Burleson .05 .15
75 John Candelaria .05 .15
76 Doug Corbett .05 .15
77 Doug DeCinces .05 .15
78 Brian Downing .08 .25
79 Chuck Finley RC .50 1.25
80 Terry Forster .08 .25
81 Bob Grich .08 .25
82 George Hendrick .08 .25
83 Jack Howell .05 .15
84 Reggie Jackson .15 .40
85 Ruppert Jones .05 .15
86 Wally Joyner RC .50 1.25
87 Gary Lucas .05 .15
88 Kirk McCaskill .05 .15
89 Donnie Moore .05 .15
90 Gary Pettis .05 .15
91 Vern Ruhle .05 .15
92 Dick Schofield .05 .15
93 Don Sutton .08 .25
94 Rob Wilfong .05 .15
95 Mike Witt .05 .15
96 Doug Drabek RC .50 1.25
97 Mike Easler .05 .15
98 Mike Fischlin .05 .15
99 Brian Fisher .05 .15

100 Ron Guidry .08 .25
101 Rickey Henderson .25 .60
102 Tommy John .08 .25
103 Ron Kittle .05 .15
104 Don Mattingly .75 2.00
105 Bobby Meacham .05 .15
106 Joe Niekro .05 .15
107 Mike Pagliarulo .05 .15
108 Dan Pasqua .05 .15
109 Willie Randolph .08 .25
110 Dennis Rasmussen .05 .15
111 Dave Righetti .08 .25
112 Gary Roenicke .05 .15
113 Rod Scurry .05 .15
114 Bob Shirley .05 .15
115 Joel Skinner .05 .15
116 Tim Stoddard .05 .15
117 Bob Tewksbury RC .20 .50
118 Wayne Tolleson .05 .15
119 Claudell Washington .05 .15
120 Dave Winfield .08 .25
121 Steve Buechele .05 .15
122 Ed Correa .05 .15
123 Scott Fletcher .05 .15
124 Jose Guzman .05 .15
125 Toby Harrah .08 .25
126 Greg Harris .05 .15
127 Charlie Hough .08 .25
128 Pete Incaviglia RC .20 .50
129 Mike Mason .05 .15
130 Oddibe McDowell .05 .15
131 Dale Mohorcic .05 .15
132 Pete O'Brien .05 .15
133 Tom Paciorek .05 .15
134 Larry Parrish .05 .15
135 Geno Petralli .05 .15
136 Darrell Porter .05 .15
137 Jeff Russell .05 .15
138 Ruben Sierra RC .75 2.00
139 Don Slaught .05 .15
140 Gary Ward .05 .15
141 Curtis Wilkerson .05 .15
142 Mitch Williams RC .20 .50
143 Bobby Witt RC UER .20 .50
Tulsa misspelled as Tusla; ERA should be 6.43, not .643
144 Dave Bergman .05 .15
145 Tom Brookens .05 .15
146 Bill Campbell .05 .15
147 Chuck Cary .05 .15
148 Darnell Coles .05 .15
149 Dave Collins .05 .15
150 Darrell Evans .08 .25
151 Kirk Gibson .08 .25
152 John Grubb .05 .15
153 Willie Hernandez .05 .15
154 Larry Herndon .05 .15
155 Eric King .05 .15
156 Chet Lemon .08 .25
157 Dwight Lowry .05 .15
158 Jack Morris .08 .25
159 Randy O'Neal .05 .15
160 Lance Parrish .08 .25
161 Dan Petry .05 .15
162 Pat Sheridan .05 .15
163 Jim Slaton .05 .15
164 Frank Tanana .08 .25
165 Walt Terrell .05 .15
166 Mark Thurmond .05 .15
167 Alan Trammell .08 .25
168 Lou Whitaker .08 .25
169 Luis Aguayo .05 .15
170 Steve Bedrosian .05 .15
171 Don Carman .05 .15
172 Darren Daulton .08 .25
173 Greg Gross .05 .15
174 Kevin Gross .05 .15
175 Von Hayes .05 .15
176 Charles Hudson .05 .15
177 Tom Hume .05 .15
178 Steve Jeltz .05 .15
179 Mike Maddux RC .05 .15
180 Shane Rawley .05 .15
181 Gary Redus .05 .15
182 Ron Roenicke .05 .15
183 Bruce Ruffin RC .08 .25
184 John Russell .05 .15
185 Juan Samuel .05 .15
186 Dan Schatzeder .05 .15
187 Mike Schmidt .60 1.50
188 Rick Schu .05 .15
189 Jeff Stone .05 .15
190 Kent Tekulve .05 .15
191 Milt Thompson .05 .15
192 Glenn Wilson .05 .15
193 Buddy Bell .08 .25
194 Tom Browning .05 .15
195 Sal Butera .05 .15
196 Dave Concepcion .08 .25
197 Kal Daniels .05 .15
198 Eric Davis .15 .40
199 John Denny .05 .15
200 Bo Diaz .05 .15
201 Nick Esasky .05 .15
202 John Franco .08 .25
203 Bill Gullickson .05 .15
204 Barry Larkin RC 3.00 8.00
205 Eddie Milner .05 .15
206 Rob Murphy .05 .15
207 Ron Oester .05 .15
208 Dave Parker .08 .25
209 Tony Perez .15 .40
210 Ted Power .05 .15
211 Joe Price .05 .15
212 Ron Robinson .05 .15
213 Pete Rose .75 2.00
214 Mario Soto .08 .25
215 Kurt Stillwell .05 .15
216 Max Venable .05 .15
217 Chris Welsh .05 .15
218 Carl Willis RC .05 .15
219 Jesse Barfield .08 .25
220 George Bell .08 .25
221 Bill Caudill .05 .15
222 John Cerutti .05 .15
223 Jim Clancy .05 .15
224 Mark Eichhorn .05 .15
225 Tony Fernandez .05 .15
226 Damaso Garcia .05 .15
227 Kelly Gruber ERR .05 .15
Wrong birth year
228 Tom Henke .05 .15
229 Garth Iorg .05 .15
230 Joe Johnson .05 .15
231 Cliff Johnson .05 .15
232 Jimmy Key .08 .25
233 Dennis Lamp .05 .15
234 Rick Leach .05 .15
235 Buck Martinez .05 .15
236 Lloyd Moseby .05 .15
237 Rance Mulliniks .05 .15
238 Dave Stieb .08 .25
239 Willie Upshaw .05 .15
240 Ernie Whitt .05 .15
241 Andy Allanson RC .05 .15
242 Scott Bailes .05 .15
243 Chris Bando .05 .15
244 Tony Bernazard .05 .15
245 John Butcher .05 .15
246 Brett Butler .08 .25
247 Ernie Camacho .05 .15
248 Tom Candiotti .05 .15
249 Joe Carter .08 .25
250 Carmen Castillo .05 .15
251 Julio Franco .08 .25
252 Mel Hall .05 .15
253 Brook Jacoby .05 .15
254 Phil Niekro .08 .25
255 Otis Nixon .05 .15
256 Dickie Noles .05 .15
257 Bryan Oelkers .05 .15
258 Ken Schrom .05 .15
259 Don Schulze .05 .15
260 Cory Snyder .05 .15
261 Pat Tabler .05 .15
262 Andre Thornton .05 .15
263 Rich Yett .05 .15
264 Mike Aldrete .05 .15
265 Juan Berenguer .05 .15
266 Vida Blue .08 .25
267 Bob Brenly .05 .15
268 Chris Brown .05 .15
269 Will Clark RC 1.25 3.00
270 Chili Davis .08 .25
271 Mark Davis .05 .15
272 Kelly Downs RC .08 .25
273 Scott Garrelts .05 .15
274 Dan Gladden .05 .15
275 Mike Krukow .05 .15
276 Randy Kutcher .05 .15
277 Mike LaCoss .05 .15
278 Jeff Leonard .05 .15
279 Candy Maldonado .05 .15
280 Roger Mason .05 .15
281 Bob Melvin .05 .15
282 Greg Minton .05 .15
283 Jeff D. Robinson .05 .15
284 Harry Spilman .05 .15
285 Robby Thompson RC .20 .50
286 Jose Uribe .05 .15
287 Frank Williams .05 .15
288 Joel Youngblood .05 .15
289 Jack Clark .08 .25
290 Vince Coleman .05 .15
291 Tim Conroy .05 .15
292 Danny Cox .05 .15
293 Ken Dayley .05 .15
294 Curt Ford .05 .15
295 Bob Forsch .05 .15
296 Tom Herr .05 .15
297 Ricky Horton .05 .15
298 Clint Hurdle .05 .15
299 Jeff Lahti .05 .15
300 Steve Lake .05 .15
301 Tito Landrum .05 .15
302 Mike LaValliere RC .20 .50
303 Greg Mathews .05 .15
304 Willie McGee .08 .25
305 Jose Oquendo .05 .15
306 Terry Pendleton .08 .25
307 Pat Perry .05 .15
308 Ozzie Smith .40 1.00
309 Ray Soff .05 .15
310 John Tudor .08 .25
311 Andy Van Slyke UER .15 .40
Bats R, Throws L
312 Todd Worrell .05 .15
313 Dann Bilardello .05 .15
314 Hubie Brooks .05 .15
315 Tim Burke .05 .15
316 Andre Dawson .08 .25
317 Mike Fitzgerald .05 .15
318 Tom Foley .05 .15
319 Andres Galarraga .08 .25
320 Joe Hesketh .05 .15
321 Wallace Johnson .05 .15
322 Wayne Krenchicki .05 .15
323 Vance Law .05 .15
324 Dennis Martinez .08 .25
325 Bob McClure .05 .15
326 Andy McGaffigan .05 .15
327 Al Newman RC .05 .15
328 Tim Raines .08 .25
329 Jeff Reardon .08 .25
330 Luis Rivera RC .08 .25
331 Bob Sebra .08 .25
332 Bryn Smith .05 .15
333 Jay Tibbs .05 .15
334 Tim Wallach .05 .15
335 Mitch Webster .05 .15
336 Jim Wohlford .05 .15
337 Floyd Youmans .05 .15
338 Chris Bosio RC .20 .50
339 Glenn Braggs RC .08 .25
340 Rick Cerone .05 .15
341 Mark Clear .05 .15
342 Bryan Clutterbuck .05 .15
343 Cecil Cooper .08 .25
344 Rob Deer .05 .15
345 Jim Gantner .05 .15
346 Ted Higuera .05 .15
347 John Henry Johnson .05 .15
348 Tim Leary .05 .15
349 Rick Manning .05 .15
350 Paul Molitor .08 .25
351 Charlie Moore .05 .15
352 Juan Nieves .05 .15
353 Ben Oglivie .08 .25
354 Dan Plesac .05 .15
355 Ernest Riles .05 .15
356 Billy Joe Robidoux .05 .15
357 Bill Schroeder .05 .15
358 Dale Sveum .05 .15
359 Gorman Thomas .08 .25
360 Bill Wegman .05 .15
361 Robin Yount .40 1.00
362 Steve Balboni .05 .15
363 Scott Bankhead .08 .25
364 Buddy Biancalana .05 .15
365 Bud Black .05 .15
366 George Brett .60 1.50
367 Steve Farr .05 .15
368 Mark Gubicza .05 .15
369 Bo Jackson RC 3.00 8.00
370 Danny Jackson .05 .15
371 Mike Kingery RC .08 .25
372 Rudy Law .05 .15
373 Charlie Leibrandt .05 .15
374 Dennis Leonard .05 .15
375 Hal McRae .08 .25
376 Jorge Orta .05 .15
377 Jamie Quirk .05 .15
378 Dan Quisenberry .08 .25
379 Bret Saberhagen .08 .25
380 Angel Salazar .05 .15
381 Lonnie Smith .05 .15
382 Jim Sundberg .08 .25
383 Frank White .08 .25
384 Willie Wilson .08 .25
385 Joaquin Andujar .08 .25
386 Doug Bair .05 .15
387 Dusty Baker .08 .25
388 Bruce Bochte .05 .15
389 Jose Canseco .60 1.50
390 Chris Codiroli .05 .15
391 Mike Davis .05 .15
392 Alfredo Griffin .05 .15
393 Moose Haas .05 .15
394 Donnie Hill .05 .15
395 Jay Howell .05 .15
396 Dave Kingman .08 .25
397 Carney Lansford .08 .25
398 Dave Leiper .05 .15
399 Bill Mooneyham .05 .15
400 Dwayne Murphy .05 .15
401 Steve Ontiveros .08 .25
402 Tony Phillips .05 .15
403 Eric Plunk .05 .15
404 Jose Rijo .08 .25
405 Terry Steinbach RC .50 1.25
406 Dave Stewart .08 .25
407 Mickey Tettleton .05 .15
408 Dave Von Ohlen .05 .15
409 Jerry Willard .05 .15
410 Curt Young .05 .15
411 Bruce Bochy .05 .15
412 Dave Dravecky .05 .15
413 Tim Flannery .05 .15
414 Steve Garvey .08 .25
415 Rich Gossage .08 .25
416 Tony Gwynn .40 1.00
417 Andy Hawkins .05 .15
418 LaMarr Hoyt .08 .25
419 Terry Kennedy .05 .15
420 John Kruk RC .75 2.00
421 Dave LaPoint .05 .15
422 Craig Lefferts .05 .15
423 Carmelo Martinez .05 .15
424 Lance McCullers .05 .15
425 Kevin McReynolds .05 .15
426 Graig Nettles .08 .25
427 Bip Roberts RC .20 .50
428 Jerry Royster .05 .15
429 Benito Santiago .08 .25
430 Eric Show .05 .15
431 Bob Stoddard .05 .15
432 Garry Templeton .08 .25
433 Gene Walter .05 .15
434 Ed Whitson .05 .15
435 Marvell Wynne .05 .15
436 Dave Anderson .05 .15
437 Greg Brock .05 .15
438 Enos Cabell .05 .15
439 Mariano Duncan .05 .15
440 Pedro Guerrero .08 .25
441 Orel Hershiser .15 .40
442 Rick Honeycutt .05 .15
443 Ken Howell .05 .15
444 Ken Landreaux .05 .15
445 Bill Madlock .08 .25
446 Mike Marshall .05 .15
447 Len Matuszek .05 .15
448 Tom Niedenfuer .05 .15
449 Alejandro Pena .05 .15
450 Dennis Powell .05 .15
451 Jerry Reuss .05 .15
452 Bill Russell .08 .25
453 Steve Sax .05 .15
454 Mike Scioscia .08 .25
455 Franklin Stubbs .05 .15
456 Alex Trevino .05 .15
457 Fernando Valenzuela .08 .25
458 Ed VandeBerg .05 .15
459 Bob Welch .08 .25
460 Reggie Williams .05 .15
461 Don Aase .05 .15
462 Juan Beniquez .05 .15
463 Mike Boddicker .05 .15
464 Juan Bonilla .05 .15
465 Rich Bordi .05 .15
466 Storm Davis .05 .15
467 Rick Dempsey .05 .15
468 Ken Dixon .05 .15
469 Jim Dwyer .05 .15
470 Mike Flanagan .05 .15
471 Jackie Gutierrez .05 .15
472 Brad Havens .05 .15
473 Lee Lacy .05 .15
474 Fred Lynn .08 .25
475 Scott McGregor .05 .15
476 Eddie Murray .25 .60
477 Tom O'Malley .05 .15
478 Cal Ripken Jr. 1.00 2.50
479 Larry Sheets .05 .15
480 John Shelby .05 .15
481 Nate Snell .05 .15
482 Jim Traber .05 .15
483 Mike Young .05 .15
484 Neil Allen .05 .15
485 Harold Baines .08 .25
486 Floyd Bannister .05 .15
487 Daryl Boston .05 .15
488 Ivan Calderon .08 .25
489 John Cangelosi .05 .15
490 Steve Carlton .08 .25
491 Joe Cowley .05 .15
492 Julio Cruz .05 .15
493 Bill Dawley .05 .15
494 Jose DeLeon .05 .15
495 Richard Dotson .05 .15
496 Carlton Fisk .15 .40
497 Ozzie Guillen .15 .40
498 Jerry Hairston .05 .15
499 Ron Hassey .05 .15
500 Tim Hulett .05 .15
501 Bob James .05 .15
502 Steve Lyons .05 .15
503 Joel McKeon .05 .15
504 Gene Nelson .05 .15
505 Dave Schmidt .05 .15
506 Ray Searage .05 .15
507 Bobby Thigpen RC .20 .50
508 Greg Walker .05 .15
509 Jim Acker .05 .15
510 Doyle Alexander .05 .15
511 Paul Assenmacher .20 .50
512 Bruce Benedict .05 .15
513 Chris Chambliss .08 .25
514 Jeff Dedmon .05 .15
515 Gene Garber .05 .15
516 Ken Griffey .08 .25
517 Terry Harper .05 .15
518 Bob Horner .08 .25
519 Glenn Hubbard .05 .15
520 Rick Mahler .05 .15
521 Omar Moreno .05 .15
522 Dale Murphy .15 .40
523 Ken Oberkfell .05 .15
524 Ed Olwine .05 .15
525 David Palmer .05 .15
526 Rafael Ramirez .05 .15
527 Billy Sample .05 .15
528 Ted Simmons .08 .25
529 Zane Smith .05 .15
530 Bruce Sutter .08 .25
531 Andres Thomas .05 .15
532 Ozzie Virgil .05 .15
533 Allan Anderson RC .05 .15
534 Keith Atherton .05 .15
535 Billy Beane .08 .25
536 Bert Blyleven .08 .25
537 Tom Brunansky .05 .15
538 Randy Bush .05 .15
539 George Frazier .05 .15
540 Gary Gaetti .08 .25
541 Greg Gagne .05 .15
542 Mickey Hatcher .05 .15
543 Neal Heaton .05 .15
544 Kent Hrbek .08 .25
545 Roy Lee Jackson .05 .15
546 Tim Laudner .05 .15
547 Steve Lombardozzi .05 .15
548 Mark Portugal RC .20 .50
549 Kirby Puckett .40 1.00
550 Jeff Reed .05 .15
551 Mark Salas .05 .15
552 Roy Smalley .05 .15
553 Mike Smithson .05 .15
554 Frank Viola .08 .25
555 Thad Bosley .05 .15
556 Ron Cey .08 .25
557 Jody Davis .05 .15
558 Ron Davis .05 .15
559 Bob Dernier .05 .15
560 Frank DiPino .05 .15
561 Shawon Dunston UER .05 .15
Wrong birth year listed on card back
562 Leon Durham .05 .15
563 Dennis Eckersley .15 .40
564 Terry Francona .08 .25
565 Dave Gumpert .05 .15
566 Guy Hoffman .05 .15
567 Ed Lynch .05 .15
568 Gary Matthews .08 .25
569 Keith Moreland .05 .15
570 Jamie Moyer RC .75 2.00
571 Jerry Mumphrey .05 .15
572 Ryne Sandberg .50 1.25
573 Scott Sanderson .05 .15
574 Lee Smith .08 .25
575 Chris Speier .05 .15
576 Rick Sutcliffe .08 .25
577 Manny Trillo .05 .15
578 Steve Trout .05 .15
579 Karl Best .05 .15
580 Scott Bradley .05 .15
581 Phil Bradley .05 .15
582 Mickey Brantley .05 .15
583 Mike G. Brown P .05 .15
584 Alvin Davis .05 .15
585 Lee Guetterman .05 .15
586 Mark Huismann .05 .15
587 Bob Kearney .05 .15
588 Pete Ladd .05 .15
589 Mark Langston .05 .15
590 Mike Moore .05 .15
591 Mike Morgan .05 .15
592 John Moses .05 .15
593 Ken Phelps .05 .15
594 Jim Presley .05 .15
595 Rey Quinones UER .05 .15
Quinonez on front
596 Harold Reynolds .08 .25
597 Billy Swift .05 .15
598 Danny Tartabull .05 .15
599 Steve Yeager .08 .25
600 Matt Young .05 .15
601 Bill Almon .05 .15
602 Rafael Belliard RC .20 .50
603 Mike Bielecki .05 .15
604 Barry Bonds RC 5.00 12.00
605 Bobby Bonilla RC .50 1.25
606 Sid Bream .05 .15
607 Mike C. Brown .05 .15
608 Pat Clements .05 .15
609 Mike Diaz .05 .15
610 Cecilio Guante .05 .15
611 Barry Jones .05 .15
612 Bob Kipper .05 .15
613 Larry McWilliams .05 .15
614 Jim Morrison .05 .15
615 Joe Orsulak .05 .15
616 Junior Ortiz .05 .15
617 Tony Pena .05 .15
618 Johnny Ray .05 .15
619 Rick Reuschel .08 .25
620 R.J. Reynolds .05 .15
621 Rick Rhoden .05 .15
622 Don Robinson .05 .15
623 Bob Walk .05 .15
624 Jim Winn .05 .15
625 P.Incaviglia/J.Canseco .30 .75
626 Don Sutton .08 .25
Phil Niekro
627 Dave Righetti .05 .15
Don Aase
628 W.Joyner/J.Canseco .30 .75
629 Gary Carter .15 .40
Sid Fernandez
Dwight Gooden
Keith Hernandez
Darryl Strawberry
630 Mike Scott .05 .15
Mike Krukow
631 Fernando Valenzuela .05 .15
John Franco
632 Count'Em .05 .15
Bob Horner
633 Canseco/Rice/Puckett .30 .75
634 Gary Carter .25 .60
Roger Clemens
635 Steve Carlton 4000K's .08 .25
636 Glenn Davis .25 .60
Eddie Murray
637 Wade Boggs .08 .25
Keith Hernandez
638 D.Mattingly/D.Strawberry .40 1.00
639 Dave Parker .25 .60
Ryne Sandberg
640 Dwight Gooden .25 .60
Roger Clemens
641 Mike Witt .05 .15
Charlie Hough
642 Juan Samuel .08 .25
Tim Raines
643 Harold Baines .08 .25
Jesse Barfield
644 Dave Clark RC .20 .50
Greg Swindell RC
645 Ron Karkovice RC .20 .50
Russ Morman RC
646 Devon White RC .50 1.25
Willie Fraser RC
647 Mike Stanley RC .20 .50
Jerry Browne RC
648 Dave Magadan RC .20 .50
Phil Lombardi RC
649 Jose Gonzalez RC .08 .25
Ralph Bryant RC
650 Jimmy Jones RC .08 .25
Randy Asadoor RC
651 Tracy Jones RC .08 .25
Marvin Freeman RC
652 John Stefero .20 .50
Kevin Seitzer RC
653 Rob Nelson RC .08 .25
Steve Fireovid RC
654 CL: Mets .05 .15
Red Sox
Astros
Angels
655 CL: Yankees .05 .15
Rangers
Tigers
Phillies
656 CL: Reds .05 .15
Blue Jays
Indians
Giants
ERR 230
231 wrong
657 CL: Cardinals .05 .15
Expos
Brewers
Royals
658 CL: A's .05 .15
Padres
Dodgers
Orioles
659 CL: White Sox .05 .15
Braves
Twins
Cubs
660 CL: Mariners .05 .15
Pirates
Special Cards
ER 580
581 wrong

1987 Fleer Glossy

COMP.FACT.SET (672) 15.00 40.00
*STARS: .5X TO 1.2X BASIC CARDS
*ROOKIES: .5X TO 1.2X BASIC CARDS
DISTRIBUTED ONLY IN FACTORY SET FORM
FACTORY SET PRICE IS FOR SEALED SETS
OPENED SETS SELL FOR 50-60% OF SEALED
604 Barry Bonds 5.00 12.00

1987 Fleer All-Stars

This 12-card standard-size set was distributed as an insert in packs of the Fleer regular issue. The cards are designed with a color player photo superimposed on a gray or black background with yellow stars. The player's name, team, and position are printed in orange on black or gray at the bottom of the obverse. The card backs are done predominantly in gray, red, and black and are numbered on the back in the upper right hand corner.

COMPLETE SET (12) 8.00 20.00
RANDOM INSERTS IN PACKS
1 Don Mattingly 2.50 6.00
2 Gary Carter .30 .75
3 Tony Fernandez .20 .50
4 Steve Sax .20 .50
5 Kirby Puckett 1.25 3.00
6 Mike Schmidt 2.00 5.00
7 Mike Easler .20 .50
8 Todd Worrell .20 .50
9 George Bell .30 .75
10 Fernando Valenzuela .30 .75
11 Roger Clemens 4.00 10.00
12 Tim Raines .30 .75

1987 Fleer Headliners

This six-card standard-size set was distributed one per rack pack as well as with three-pack wax pack rack packs. The obverse features the player photo against a beige background with irregular red strip[es]. The checklist below also lists each player's team affiliation. The set is sequenced in alphabetical ord[er].

COMPLETE SET (6) 2.50 6.0
ONE PER RACK PACK
1 Wade Boggs .25 [illegible]
2 Jose Canseco 1.00 2.5
3 Dwight Gooden .25 [illegible]
4 Rickey Henderson .40 1.0
5 Keith Hernandez .15 [illegible]
6 Jim Rice .15 [illegible]

1987 Fleer Wax Box Cards

The cards in this 16-card set measure the standard 1/2" by 3 1/2". Cards have essentially the same design as the 1987 Fleer regular issue set. The car[ds] were printed on the bottoms of the regular issue wa[x] pack boxes. These 16 cards (C1 to C16) are considered a separate set in their own right and are not typically included in a complete set of the regul[ar] issue 1987 Fleer cards. The value of the panel unc[ut] is slightly greater, perhaps by 25 percent greater, than the value of the individual cards cut up careful[ly].

COMPLETE SET (16) 4.00 10.0
C1 Mets Logo .02 .1
C2 Jesse Barfield .02 .1
C3 George Brett 1.25 3.0
C4 Dwight Gooden .20 .5
C5 Boston Logo .02 .1
C6 Keith Hernandez .08 .2
C7 Wally Joyner .30 .7
C8 Dale Murphy .30 .7
C9 Astros Logo .02 .1
C10 Dave Parker .08 .2
C11 Kirby Puckett .80 1.0
C12 Dave Righetti .02 .1
C13 Angels Logo .02 .1
C14 Ryne Sandberg .75 2.0
C15 Mike Schmidt .60 1.5
C16 Robin Yount .30 .7

1987 Fleer World Series

This 12-card standard-size set of features highlights of the previous year's World Series between the Me[ts] and the Red Sox. The sets were packaged as a complete set insert with the collated sets (of the 198[7] Fleer regular issue) which were sold by Fleer directl[y] to hobby card dealers; they were not available in the general retail candy store outlets.

COMPLETE SET (12) .75 2.0
ONE SET PER FACTORY SET
1 Bruce Hurst .05 .1
2 Keith Hernandez and .08 .2
Wade Boggs
3 Roger Clemens 1.25 3.0
4 Gary Carter .08 .2
5 Ron Darling .08 .2
6 Marty Barrett .05 .1
7 Dwight Gooden .15 .4
8 Strategy at Work/(Mets Conference) .08 .2
9 Dwight Evans .15 .4
Congratulated by Rich Gedman
10 Dave Henderson .05 .15
11 Ray Knight .08 .25
Darryl Strawberry
12 Ray Knight .08 .25

1987 Fleer World Series Glossy

*GLOSSY: .5X TO 1.2X BASIC WS
DISTRIBUTED ONLY IN FACTORY SET FORM

1987 Fleer Update

This 132-card standard-size set was distributed exclusively in factory set form through hobby dealers. In addition to the complete set of 132 cards, the box also contained 25 Team Logo stickers. The cards look very similar to the 1987 Fleer regular issue except for the U-prefixed numbering on back. Cards are ordered alphabetically according to player's last name. The key extended Rookie Cards i[n] this set are Ellis Burks, Greg Maddux, Fred McGriff and Matt Williams. In addition an early card of

endary slugger Mark McGwire highlights this set.
MP.FACT.SET (132) 5.00 12.00
cott Bankhead .02 .10
ric Bell .05 .15
uan Beniquez .02 .10
uan Berenguer .02 .10
ike Birkbeck .05 .15
andy Bockus .02 .10
od Booker .02 .10
had Bosley .02 .10
reg Brock .02 .10
Bob Brower .02 .10
Chris Brown .02 .10
Jerry Browne .05 .15
Ralph Bryant .02 .10
DeWayne Buice .02 .10
Ellis Burks XRC .30 .75
Casey Candaele .02 .10
Steve Carlton .05 .15
Juan Castillo .05 .15
Chuck Crim .02 .10
Mark Davidson .02 .10
Mark Davis .02 .10
Storm Davis .02 .10
Bill Dawley .02 .10
Andre Dawson .05 .15
Brian Dayett .02 .10
Rick Dempsey .02 .10
Ken Dowell .02 .10
Dave Dravecky .02 .10
Mike Dunne .02 .10
Dennis Eckersley .08 .25
Cecil Fielder .05 .15
Brian Fisher .02 .10
Willie Fraser .05 .15
Ken Gerhart .02 .10
Jim Gott .02 .10
Dan Gladden .02 .10
Mike Greenwell XRC .10 .30
Cecilio Guante .02 .10
Albert Hall .02 .10
Atlee Hammaker .02 .10
Mickey Hatcher .02 .10
Mike Heath .02 .10
Neal Heaton .02 .10
Mike Henneman XRC .10 .30
Guy Hoffman .02 .10
Charles Hudson .02 .10
Chuck Jackson .02 .10
Mike Jackson XRC .10 .30
Reggie Jackson .08 .25
Chris James .02 .10
Dion James .02 .10
Stan Javier .02 .10
Stan Jefferson .02 .10
Jimmy Jones .05 .15
Tracy Jones .02 .10
Terry Kennedy .02 .10
Mike Kingery .05 .15
Ray Knight .05 .15
Gene Larkin XRC .10 .30
Mike LaValliere .10 .30
Jack Lazorko .02 .10
Terry Leach .02 .10
Rick Leach .02 .10
Craig Lefferts .02 .10
Jim Lindeman .05 .15
Bill Long .02 .10
Mike Loynd XRC .05 .15
Greg Maddux XRC 5.00 12.00
Bill Madlock .05 .15
Dave Magadan .10 .30
Joe Magrane XRC .05 .15
Fred Manrique .02 .10
Mike Mason .02 .10
Lloyd McClendon XRC .10 .30
Fred McGriff .40 1.00
Mark McGwire 2.00 5.00
Mark McLemore .05 .15
Kevin McReynolds .02 .10
Dave Meads .02 .10
Greg Minton .02 .10
John Mitchell XRC .05 .15
Kevin Mitchell .08 .25
John Morris .02 .10
Jeff Musselman .02 .10
Randy Myers XRC .30 .75
Gene Nelson .02 .10
Joe Niekro .02 .10
Tom Nieto .02 .10
Reid Nichols .02 .10
Matt Nokes XRC .10 .30
Dickie Noles .02 .10
Edwin Nunez .02 .10
Jose Nunez XRC .02 .10
Paul O'Neill .15 .40
Jim Paciorek .02 .10
Lance Parrish .05 .15
Bill Pecota XRC .05 .15
Tony Pena .02 .10
Luis Polonia XRC .10 .30
Randy Ready .02 .10
Jeff Reardon .05 .15
Gary Redus .02 .10
Rick Rhoden .02 .10
Wally Ritchie .02 .10
Jeff M. Robinson UER/(Wrong Jeff's .02 .10
stats on back
Mark Salas .02 .10
Dave Schmidt .02 .10
Kevin Seitzer UER .10 .30
John Shelby .02 .10
John Smiley XRC .10 .30
111 Lary Sorensen .02 .10
112 Chris Speier .02 .10
113 Randy St.Claire .02 .10
114 Jim Sundberg .05 .15
115 B.J. Surhoff XRC .30 .75
116 Greg Swindell .10 .30
117 Danny Tartabull .02 .10
118 Dorn Taylor .02 .10
119 Lee Tunnell .02 .10
120 Ed VandeBerg .02 .10
121 Andy Van Slyke .08 .25
122 Gary Ward .02 .10
123 Devon White .30 .75
124 Alan Wiggins .02 .10
125 Bill Wilkinson .02 .10
126 Jim Winn .02 .10
127 Frank Williams .02 .10
128 Ken Williams .02 .10
129 Matt Williams XRC .60 1.50
130 Herm Winningham .02 .10
131 Matt Young .02 .10
132 Checklist 1-132 .02 .10

1987 Fleer Update Glossy

COMP.FACT.SET (132) 6.00 15.00
*STARS: .4X TO 1X BASIC CARDS
*ROOKIES: .4X TO 1X BASIC CARDS
DISTRIBUTED ONLY IN FACTORY SET FORM

1987 Fleer Award Winners

This small set of 44 standard-size cards was produced for 7-Eleven stores by Fleer. The cards feature full color fronts and yellow, white, and black backs. The card fronts are distinguished by their yellow frame around the player's full-color photo. The box for the cards describes the set as the "1987 Limited Edition Baseball's Award Winners." The checklist for the set is given on the back of the set box. The card numbering is in alphabetical order by player's name.

COMP.FACT.SET (44) 2.00 5.00
1 Marty Barrett .01 .05
2 George Bell .01 .05
3 Bert Blyleven .02 .10
4 Bob Boone .02 .10
5 John Candelaria .01 .05
6 Jose Canseco .20 .50
7 Gary Carter .05 .15
8 Joe Carter .07 .20
9 Roger Clemens .30 .75
10 Cecil Cooper .02 .10
11 Eric Davis .05 .15
12 Tony Fernandez .02 .10
13 Scott Fletcher .01 .05
14 Bob Forsch .01 .05
15 Dwight Gooden .05 .15
16 Ron Guidry .02 .10
17 Ozzie Guillen .02 .10
18 Bill Gullickson .01 .05
19 Tony Gwynn .30 .75
20 Bob Knepper .01 .05
21 Ray Knight .01 .05
22 Mark Langston .01 .05
23 Candy Maldonado .01 .05
24 Don Mattingly .30 .75
25 Roger McDowell .01 .05
26 Dale Murphy .07 .20
27 Dave Parker .02 .10
28 Lance Parrish .02 .10
29 Gary Pettis .01 .05
30 Kirby Puckett .20 .50
31 Johnny Ray .01 .05
32 Dave Righetti .01 .05
33 Cal Ripken .60 1.50
34 Bret Saberhagen .02 .10
35 Ryne Sandberg .20 .50
36 Mike Schmidt .20 .50
37 Mike Scott .01 .05
38 Ozzie Smith .30 .75
39 Robby Thompson .02 .10
40 Fernando Valenzuela .02 .10
41 Mitch Webster UER/(Mike on front) .01 .05
42 Frank White .02 .10
43 Mike Witt .01 .05
44 Todd Worrell .02 .10

1987 Fleer Baseball All-Stars

This small set of 44 standard-size cards was produced for Ben Franklin stores by Fleer. The cards feature full color fronts and red, white, and blue backs. The card fronts are easily distinguished by their white vertical stripes over a bright red background. The box for the cards proclaims "Limited Edition Baseball All-Stars" and is styled in the same manner and color scheme as the cards themselves. The checklist for the set is given on the back of the set box. The card numbering is in alphabetical order by player's name.

COMP. FACT. SET (44) 2.50 6.00
1 Harold Baines .05 .15
2 Jesse Barfield .01 .05
3 Wade Boggs .20 .50
4 Dennis Boyd .01 .05
5 Scott Bradley .01 .05
6 Jose Canseco .20 .50
7 Gary Carter .15 .40
8 Joe Carter .07 .20
9 Mark Clear .01 .05
10 Roger Clemens .30 .75
11 Jose Cruz .02 .10
12 Chili Davis .05 .15
13 Jody Davis .01 .05
14 Rob Deer .01 .05
15 Brian Downing .01 .05
16 Sid Fernandez .01 .05
17 John Franco .02 .10
18 Andres Galarraga .15 .40
19 Dwight Gooden .05 .15
20 Tony Gwynn .30 .75
21 Charlie Hough .01 .05
22 Bruce Hurst .01 .05
23 Wally Joyner .07 .20
24 Carney Lansford .02 .10
25 Fred Lynn .02 .10
26 Don Mattingly .30 .75
27 Willie McGee .02 .10
28 Jack Morris .02 .10
29 Dale Murphy .07 .20
30 Bob Ojeda .01 .05
31 Tony Pena .01 .05
32 Kirby Puckett .20 .50
33 Dan Quisenberry .01 .05
34 Tim Raines .02 .10
35 Willie Randolph .02 .10
36 Cal Ripken .60 1.50
37 Pete Rose .20 .50
38 Nolan Ryan .60 1.50
39 Juan Samuel .01 .05
40 Mike Schmidt .20 .50
41 Ozzie Smith .30 .75
42 Andres Thomas .01 .05
43 Fernando Valenzuela .02 .10
44 Mike Witt .01 .05

1987 Fleer Exciting Stars

This small 44-card boxed standard-size set was produced by Fleer for distribution by the Cumberland Farm stores. The cards feature full color fronts. The set is titled "Baseball's Exciting Stars." Each individual boxed set includes the 44 cards and six logo stickers. The checklist for the set is found on the back panel of the box. The card numbering is in alphabetical order by player's name.

COMP.FACT.SET (44) 2.00 5.00
1 Don Aase .01 .05
2 Rick Aguilera .02 .10
3 Jesse Barfield .01 .05
4 Wade Boggs .15 .40
5 Oil Can Boyd .01 .05
6 Sid Bream .01 .05
7 Jose Canseco .20 .50
8 Steve Carlton .15 .40
9 Gary Carter .15 .40
10 Will Clark .30 .75
11 Roger Clemens .30 .75
12 Danny Cox .01 .05
13 Alvin Davis .01 .05
14 Eric Davis .05 .15
15 Rob Deer .01 .05
16 Brian Downing .01 .05
17 Gene Garber .01 .05
18 Steve Garvey .05 .15
19 Dwight Gooden .05 .15
20 Mark Gubicza .01 .05
21 Mel Hall .01 .05
22 Terry Harper .01 .05
23 Von Hayes .01 .05
24 Rickey Henderson .25 .60
25 Tom Henke .01 .05
26 Willie Hernandez .01 .05
27 Ted Higuera .01 .05
28 Rick Honeycutt .01 .05
29 Kent Hrbek .02 .10
30 Wally Joyner .07 .20
31 Charlie Kerfeld .01 .05
32 Fred Lynn .02 .10
33 Don Mattingly .30 .75
34 Tim Raines .02 .10
35 Dennis Rasmussen .01 .05
36 Johnny Ray .01 .05
37 Jim Rice .02 .10
38 Pete Rose .20 .50
39 Lee Smith .05 .15
40 Cory Snyder .01 .05
41 Darryl Strawberry .02 .10
42 Kent Tekulve .01 .05
43 Willie Wilson .02 .10
44 Bobby Witt .01 .05

1987 Fleer Game Winners

This small 44-card boxed standard-size set was produced by Fleer for distribution by several store chains, including Bi-Mart, Pay'n'Save, Mott's, M.E.Moses, and Winn's. The cards feature full color fronts. The set is titled "Baseball's Game Winners." Each individual boxed set includes the 44 cards and six logo stickers. The checklist for the set is found on the back panel of the box. The card numbering is in alphabetical order by player's name.

COMP.FACT.SET (44) 2.50 6.00
1 Harold Baines .05 .15
2 Don Baylor .02 .10
3 George Bell .01 .05
4 Tony Bernazard .01 .05
5 Wade Boggs .20 .50
6 George Brett .30 .75
7 Hubie Brooks .01 .05
8 Jose Canseco .30 .75
9 Gary Carter .15 .40
10 Roger Clemens .30 .75
11 Eric Davis .02 .10
12 Glenn Davis .01 .05
13 Shawon Dunston .01 .05
14 Mark Eichhorn .01 .05
15 Gary Gaetti .02 .10
16 Steve Garvey .05 .15
17 Kirk Gibson .02 .10
18 Dwight Gooden .05 .15
19 Von Hayes .01 .05
20 Willie Hernandez .01 .05
21 Ted Higuera .01 .05
22 Wally Joyner .07 .20
23 Bob Knepper .01 .05
24 Mike Krukow .01 .05
25 Jeff Leonard .01 .05
26 Don Mattingly .30 .75
27 Kirk McCaskill .01 .05
28 Kevin McReynolds .01 .05
29 Jim Morrison .01 .05
30 Dale Murphy .07 .20
31 Pete O'Brien .01 .05
32 Bob Ojeda .01 .05
33 Larry Parrish .01 .05
34 Ken Phelps .01 .05
35 Dennis Rasmussen .01 .05
36 Ernest Riles .01 .05
37 Cal Ripken .60 1.50
38 Ron Robinson .01 .05
39 Steve Sax .01 .05
40 Mike Schmidt .20 .50
41 John Tudor .01 .05
42 Fernando Valenzuela .02 .10
43 Mike Witt .01 .05
44 Curt Young .01 .05

1987 Fleer Hottest Stars

This 44-card boxed standard-size set was produced by Fleer for distribution by Revco stores all over the country. The cards feature full color fronts and red, white, and black backs. The card fronts are easily distinguished by their solid red outside borders and and white and blue inner borders framing the player's picture. The box for the cards proclaims "1987 Limited Edition Baseball's Hottest Stars" and is styled in the same manner and color scheme as the cards themselves. The checklist for the set is given on the back of the set box. The card numbering is in alphabetical order by player's name. An early card of Barry Bonds highlights this set.

COMP.FACT.SET (44) 10.00 25.00
DISTRIBUTED IN FACTORY SET FORM
FACTORY SET PRICE IS FOR SEALED SETS
1 Joaquin Andujar .02 .10
2 Harold Baines .05 .15
3 Kevin Bass .02 .10
4 Don Baylor .05 .15
5 Barry Bonds 8.00 20.00
6 George Brett .40 1.00
7 Tom Brunansky .02 .10
8 Brett Butler .05 .15
9 Jose Canseco .40 1.00
10 Roger Clemens 1.25 3.00
11 Ron Darling .02 .10
12 Eric Davis .08 .25
13 Andre Dawson .05 .15
14 Doug DeCinces .02 .10
15 Leon Durham .02 .10
16 Mark Eichhorn .02 .10
17 Scott Garrelts .02 .10
18 Dwight Gooden .08 .25
19 Dave Henderson .02 .10
20 Rickey Henderson .15 .40
21 Keith Hernandez .05 .15
22 Ted Higuera .02 .10
23 Bob Horner .05 .15
24 Pete Incaviglia .05 .15
25 Wally Joyner .08 .25
26 Mark Langston .02 .10
27 Don Mattingly UER .50 1.25
28 Dale Murphy .08 .25
29 Kirk McCaskill .02 .10
30 Willie McGee .05 .15
31 Dave Righetti .05 .15
32 Pete Rose .50 1.25
33 Bruce Ruffin .02 .10
34 Steve Sax .02 .10
35 Mike Schmidt .40 1.00
36 Larry Sheets .02 .10
37 Eric Show .02 .10
38 Dave Smith .02 .10
39 Cory Snyder .02 .10
40 Frank Tanana .05 .15
41 Alan Trammell .05 .15
42 Reggie Williams .02 .10
43 Mookie Wilson .05 .15
44 Todd Worrell .05 .15

1987 Fleer League Leaders

This small set of 44 standard-size cards was produced for Walgreens by Fleer. The cards feature full color fronts and red, white, and blue backs. The card fronts are easily distinguished by their light blue vertical stripes over a white background. The box for the cards proclaims a "Walgreens Exclusive" and is styled in the same manner and color scheme as the cards themselves. The checklist for the set is given on the back of the set box. The card numbering is in alphabetical order by player's name.

COMP.FACT.SET (44) 2.50 6.00
1 Jesse Barfield .01 .05
2 Mike Boddicker .01 .05
3 Wade Boggs .20 .50
4 Phil Bradley .01 .05
5 George Brett .30 .75
6 Hubie Brooks .01 .05
7 Chris Brown .01 .05
8 Jose Canseco .30 .75
9 Joe Carter .07 .20
10 Roger Clemens .30 .75
11 Vince Coleman .01 .05
12 Joe Cowley .01 .05
13 Kal Daniels .01 .05
14 Glenn Davis .01 .05
15 Jody Davis .01 .05
16 Darrell Evans .02 .10
17 Dwight Evans .02 .10
18 John Franco .02 .10
19 Julio Franco .02 .10
20 Dwight Gooden .05 .15
21 Rich Gossage .02 .10
22 Tom Herr .01 .05
23 Ted Higuera .01 .05
24 Bob Horner .02 .10
25 Pete Incaviglia .02 .10
26 Wally Joyner .07 .20
27 Dave Kingman .02 .10
28 Don Mattingly .30 .75
29 Willie McGee .02 .10
30 Donnie Moore .01 .05
31 Keith Moreland .01 .05
32 Eddie Murray .20 .50
33 Mike Pagliarulo .01 .05
34 Larry Parrish .01 .05
35 Tony Pena .02 .10
36 Kirby Puckett .20 .50
37 Pete Rose .20 .50
38 Juan Samuel .01 .05
39 Ryne Sandberg .30 .75
40 Mike Schmidt .20 .50
41 Darryl Strawberry .02 .10
42 Greg Walker .01 .05
43 Bob Welch .01 .05
44 Todd Worrell .01 .05

1987 Fleer Limited Edition

This 44-card boxed standard-size set was (mass) produced by Fleer for distribution by McCrory's and is sometimes referred to as the McCrory's set. The numerical checklist on the back of the box shows that the set is numbered alphabetically.

COMP.FACT.SET (44) 2.00 5.00
1 Floyd Bannister .01 .05
2 Marty Barrett .01 .05
3 Steve Bedrosian .01 .05
4 George Bell .01 .05
5 George Brett .30 .75
6 Jose Canseco .20 .50
7 Joe Carter .07 .20
8 Will Clark .40 1.00
9 Roger Clemens .20 .50
10 Vince Coleman .01 .05
11 Glenn Davis .01 .05
12 Mike Davis .01 .05
13 Len Dykstra .05 .15
14 John Franco .02 .10
15 Julio Franco .02 .10
16 Steve Garvey .05 .15
17 Kirk Gibson .02 .10
18 Dwight Gooden .05 .15
19 Tony Gwynn .30 .75
20 Keith Hernandez .02 .10
21 Teddy Higuera .01 .05
22 Kent Hrbek .02 .10
23 Wally Joyner .07 .20
24 Mike Krukow .01 .05
25 Mike Marshall .01 .05
26 Don Mattingly .30 .75
27 Oddibe McDowell .01 .05
28 Jack Morris .02 .10
29 Lloyd Moseby .01 .05
30 Dale Murphy .07 .20
31 Eddie Murray .20 .50
32 Tony Pena .02 .10
33 Jim Presley .01 .05
34 Jeff Reardon .05 .15
35 Jim Rice .02 .10
36 Pete Rose .20 .50
37 Mike Schmidt .20 .50
38 Mike Scott .01 .05
39 Lee Smith .05 .15
40 Lonnie Smith .01 .05
41 Gary Ward .01 .05
42 Dave Winfield .15 .40
43 Todd Worrell .02 .10
44 Robin Yount .15 .40

1987 Fleer Limited Box Cards

The cards in this six-card set each measure the standard size. Cards have essentially the same design as the 1987 Fleer Limited Edition cards which were distributed by McCrory's. The cards were printed on the bottom of the counter display box which held 24 small boxed sets; hence theoretically these box cards are 1/24 as plentiful as the regular boxed set cards. These six cards, numbered C1 to C6, are considered a separate set in their own right and are not typically included in a complete set of the 1987 Fleer Limited Edition set of 44. The value of the panels uncut is slightly greater, perhaps by 25 percent greater, than the value of the individual cards cut up carefully.

COMPLETE SET (6) .75 2.00
C1 Ron Darling .08 .25
C2 Bill Buckner .20 .50
C3 John Candelaria .08 .25
C4 Jack Clark .20 .50
C5 Bret Saberhagen .20 .50
C6 Houston Astros .08 .25

1987 Fleer Mini

The 1987 Fleer "Classic Miniatures" set consists of 120 small cards with all new pictures of the players as compared to the 1987 Fleer regular issue. The cards are only 1 13/16" by 2 9/16", making them one of the smallest cards issued in the 1980's. Card backs provide career year-by-year statistics. The complete set was distributed in a blue, red, white, and silver factory box along with 18 logo stickers. The card numbering is by alphabetical order.

COMP.FACT.SET (120) 2.50 6.00
1 Don Aase .01 .05
2 Joaquin Andujar .01 .05
3 Harold Baines .05 .15
4 Jesse Barfield .01 .05
5 Kevin Bass .01 .05
6 Don Baylor .02 .10
7 George Bell .01 .05
8 Tony Bernazard .01 .05
9 Bert Blyleven .02 .10
10 Wade Boggs .15 .40
11 Phil Bradley .01 .05
12 Sid Bream .01 .05
13 George Brett .30 .75
14 Hubie Brooks .01 .05
15 Chris Brown .01 .05
16 Tom Candiotti .01 .05
17 Jose Canseco .20 .50
18 Gary Carter .05 .15
19 Joe Carter .07 .20
20 Roger Clemens .30 .75
21 Vince Coleman .01 .05
22 Cecil Cooper .02 .10
23 Ron Darling .01 .05
24 Alvin Davis .01 .05
25 Chili Davis .05 .15
26 Eric Davis .02 .10
27 Glenn Davis .01 .05
28 Mike Davis .01 .05
29 Doug DeCinces .01 .05
30 Rob Deer .01 .05
31 Jim Deshaies .01 .05
32 Bo Diaz .01 .05
33 Richard Dotson .01 .05
34 Brian Downing .01 .05
35 Shawon Dunston .01 .05
36 Mark Eichhorn .01 .05
37 Dwight Evans .02 .10
38 Tony Fernandez .02 .10
39 Julio Franco .02 .10
40 Gary Gaetti .02 .10
41 Andres Galarraga .15 .40
42 Scott Garrelts .01 .05
43 Steve Garvey .05 .15
44 Kirk Gibson .02 .10
45 Dwight Gooden .05 .15
46 Ken Griffey Sr. .02 .10
47 Mark Gubicza .01 .05
48 Ozzie Guillen .02 .10
49 Bill Gullickson .01 .05
50 Tony Gwynn .30 .75
51 Von Hayes .01 .05
52 Rickey Henderson .30 .75
53 Keith Hernandez .02 .10
54 Willie Hernandez .01 .05
55 Ted Higuera .01 .05
56 Charlie Hough .01 .05
57 Kent Hrbek .02 .10
58 Pete Incaviglia .02 .10
59 Wally Joyner .10 .30
60 Bob Knepper .01 .05
61 Mike Krukow .01 .05
62 Mark Langston .01 .05
63 Carney Lansford .02 .10
64 Jim Lindeman .01 .05
65 Bill Madlock .02 .10
66 Don Mattingly .30 .75
67 Kirk McCaskill .01 .05
68 Lance McCullers .01 .05
69 Keith Moreland .01 .05
70 Jack Morris .02 .10
71 Jim Morrison .01 .05
72 Lloyd Moseby .01 .05
73 Jerry Mumphrey .01 .05
74 Dale Murphy .07 .20
75 Eddie Murray .20 .50
76 Pete O'Brien .01 .05
77 Bob Ojeda .01 .05
78 Jesse Orosco .02 .10
79 Dan Pasqua .01 .05
80 Dave Parker .02 .10
81 Larry Parrish .01 .05
82 Jim Presley .01 .05
83 Kirby Puckett .20 .50
84 Dan Quisenberry .01 .05
85 Tim Raines .02 .10
86 Dennis Rasmussen .01 .05
87 Johnny Ray .01 .05
88 Jeff Reardon .02 .10
89 Jim Rice .02 .10
90 Dave Righetti .01 .05
91 Earnest Riles .01 .05
92 Cal Ripken .60 1.50
93 Ron Robinson .01 .05
94 Juan Samuel .01 .05
95 Ryne Sandberg .25 .60
96 Steve Sax .01 .05
97 Mike Schmidt .15 .40
98 Ken Schrom .01 .05
99 Mike Scott .01 .05
100 Ruben Sierra .15 .40
101 Lee Smith .05 .15
102 Ozzie Smith .30 .75
103 Cory Snyder .01 .05
104 Kent Tekulve .01 .05
105 Andres Thomas .01 .05
106 Robby Thompson .02 .10
107 Alan Trammell .05 .15
108 John Tudor .01 .05
109 Fernando Valenzuela .02 .10
110 Greg Walker .01 .05
111 Mitch Webster .01 .05
112 Lou Whitaker .02 .10
113 Frank White .02 .10
114 Reggie Williams .01 .05
115 Glenn Wilson .01 .05
116 Willie Wilson .02 .10
117 Dave Winfield .20 .50
118 Mike Witt .01 .05
119 Todd Worrell .02 .10
120 Floyd Youmans .01 .05

1987 Fleer Record Setters

This 44-card boxed standard-size set was produced by Fleer for distribution by Eckerd's Drug Stores and is sometimes referred to as the Eckerd's set. Six team logo stickers are included in the box with the complete set. The numerical checklist on the back of the box shows that the set is numbered alphabetically.

COMP.FACT.SET (44) 2.00 5.00
1 George Brett .20 .50
2 Chris Brown .01 .05
3 Jose Canseco UER/(3 of 444 on back) .20 .50
4 Roger Clemens .20 .50
5 Alvin Davis UER/(5 of 441 on back, .01 .05
upside down o
6 Shawon Dunston .01 .05
7 Tony Fernandez .02 .10
8 Carlton Fisk UER/(8 of 44' on back) .15 .40

9 Gary Gaetti UER/(9 of 444 on back) .02 .10
10 Gene Garber .01 .05
11 Rich Gedman .01 .05
12 Dwight Gooden .05 .15
13 Ozzie Guillen .02 .10
14 Bill Gullickson .01 .05
15 Billy Hatcher .01 .05
16 Orel Hershiser .02 .10
17 Wally Joyner .10 .30
18 Ray Knight .01 .05
19 Craig Lefferts .01 .05
20 Don Mattingly .30 .75
21 Kevin Mitchell .05 .15
22 Lloyd Moseby .01 .05
23 Dale Murphy .07 .20
24 Eddie Murray .15 .40
25 Phil Niekro .10 .30
26 Ben Oglivie .01 .05
27 Jesse Orosco .02 .10
28 Joe Orsulak .01 .05
29 Larry Parrish .01 .05
30 Tim Raines .02 .10
31 Shane Rawley .01 .05
32 Dave Righetti .01 .05
33 Pete Rose .20 .50
34 Steve Sax .01 .05
35 Mike Schmidt .20 .50
36 Mike Scott .01 .05
37 Don Sutton .10 .30
38 Alan Trammell .05 .15
39 John Tudor .01 .05
40 Gary Ward .01 .05
41 Lou Whitaker .02 .10
42 Willie Wilson .02 .10
43 Todd Worrell .02 .10
44 Floyd Youmans .01 .05

1987 Fleer Sluggers/Pitchers

Fleer produced this 44-card boxed standard-size set although it was primarily distributed by McCrory, McLellan, Newberry, H.L.Green, T.G.Y., and other similar stores. The set features 28 sluggers and 16 pitchers and is subtitled "Baseball's Best". The set was packaged in a red, white, blue, and yellow custom box along with six logo stickers. The set checklist is given on the back of the box. The checklist on the back of the set box misspells McGwire as McGuire. The card numbering is in alphabetical order by player's name.

COMP.FACT. SET (44) 4.00 10.00
1 Kevin Bass .01 .05
2 Jesse Barfield .01 .05
3 George Bell .01 .05
4 Wade Boggs .20 .50
5 Sid Bream .01 .05
6 George Brett .30 .75
7 Ivan Calderon .01 .05
8 Jose Canseco .20 .50
9 Jack Clark .02 .10
10 Roger Clemens .40 1.00
11 Eric Davis .02 .10
12 Andre Dawson .08 .25
13 Sid Fernandez .01 .05
14 John Franco .02 .10
15 Dwight Gooden .05 .15
16 Pedro Guerrero .01 .05
17 Tony Gwynn .30 .75
18 Rickey Henderson .30 .75
19 Tom Henke .01 .05
20 Ted Higuera .01 .05
21 Pete Incaviglia .02 .10
22 Wally Joyner .10 .30
23 Jeff Leonard .01 .05
24 Joe Magrane .01 .05
25 Don Mattingly .30 .75
26 Mark McGwire 1.00 2.50
27 Jack Morris .02 .10
28 Dale Murphy .08 .25
29 Dave Parker .02 .10
30 Ken Phelps .01 .05
31 Kirby Puckett .20 .50
32 Tim Raines .02 .10
33 Jeff Reardon .02 .10
34 Dave Righetti .01 .05
35 Cal Ripken .75 2.00
36 Bret Saberhagen .02 .10
37 Mike Schmidt .20 .50
38 Mike Scott .01 .05
39 Kevin Seitzer .08 .25
40 Darryl Strawberry .02 .10
41 Rick Sutcliffe .01 .05
42 Pat Tabler .01 .05
43 Fernando Valenzuela .02 .10
44 Mike Witt .01 .05

1987 Fleer Sluggers/Pitchers Box Cards

The cards in this six-card set each measure the standard size. Cards have essentially the same design as the 1987 Fleer Sluggers vs. Pitchers set of Baseball's Best. The cards were printed on the bottom of the counter display box which held 24 small boxed sets; hence theoretically these box cards are 1/24 as plentiful as the regular boxed set cards. These six cards, numbered M1 to M5 with one blank-back (unnumbered) card, are considered a separate set in their own right and are not typically included in a complete set of the 1987 Fleer Sluggers vs. Pitchers set of 44. The value of the panels uncut is slightly greater, perhaps by 25 percent greater, than the value of the individual cards cut up carefully.

COMPLETE SET (6) 8.00 20.00
M1 Steve Bedrosian .40 1.00
M2 Will Clark 4.00 10.00
M3 Vince Coleman .40 1.00
M4 Bo Jackson 3.00 8.00
M5 Cory Snyder .40 1.00
NNO Team Logo/(Blank back) .40 1.00

1987 Fleer Star Stickers

These Star Stickers were distributed as a separate issue by Fleer with five star stickers and a logo sticker in each wax pack. The 132-card (sticker) set features 2 1/2" by 3 1/2" full-color fronts and even statistics on the sticker back, which is an indication that the Fleer Company understands that these stickers are rarely used as stickers but more like traditional cards. The fronts are surrounded by a green border and the backs are printed in green and yellow on white card stock. The numbering is in alphabetical order by player's name.

COMPLETE SET (132) 6.00 15.00
1 Don Aase .01 .05
2 Harold Baines .07 .20
3 Floyd Bannister .01 .05
4 Jesse Barfield .01 .05
5 Marty Barrett .01 .05
6 Kevin Bass .01 .05
7 Don Baylor .02 .10
8 Steve Bedrosian .01 .05
9 George Bell .01 .05
10 Bert Blyleven .02 .10
11 Mike Boddicker .01 .05
12 Wade Boggs .15 .40
13 Phil Bradley .01 .05
14 Sid Bream .01 .05
15 George Brett .50 1.25
16 Hubie Brooks .01 .05
17 Tom Brunansky .01 .05
18 Tom Candiotti .01 .05
19 Jose Canseco .30 .75
20 Gary Carter .15 .40
21 Joe Carter .10 .30
22 Will Clark .50 1.25
23 Mark Clear .01 .05
24 Roger Clemens .40 1.00
25 Vince Coleman .01 .05
26 Jose Cruz .02 .10
27 Ron Darling .01 .05
28 Alvin Davis .01 .05
29 Chili Davis .07 .20
30 Eric Davis .07 .20
31 Glenn Davis .01 .05
32 Mike Davis .01 .05
33 Andre Dawson .10 .30
34 Doug DeCinces .01 .05
35 Brian Downing .01 .05
36 Shawon Dunston .01 .05
37 Mark Eichhorn .01 .05
38 Dwight Evans .02 .10
39 Tony Fernandez .02 .10
40 Bob Forsch .01 .05
41 John Franco .02 .10
42 Julio Franco .02 .10
43 Gary Gaetti .02 .10
44 Gene Garber .01 .05
45 Scott Garrelts .01 .05
46 Steve Garvey .07 .20
47 Kirk Gibson .02 .10
48 Dwight Gooden .07 .20
49 Ken Griffey Sr. .02 .10
50 Ozzie Guillen .02 .10
51 Bill Gullickson .01 .05
52 Tony Gwynn .50 1.25
53 Mel Hall .01 .05
54 Greg A. Harris .01 .05
55 Von Hayes .01 .05
56 Rickey Henderson .30 .75
57 Tom Henke .01 .05
58 Keith Hernandez .02 .10
59 Willie Hernandez .01 .05
60 Ted Higuera .01 .05
61 Bob Horner .01 .05
62 Charlie Hough .01 .05
63 Jay Howell .01 .05
64 Kent Hrbek .02 .10
65 Bruce Hurst .01 .05
66 Pete Incaviglia .02 .10
67 Bob James .01 .05
68 Wally Joyner .15 .40
69 Mike Krukow .01 .05
70 Mark Langston .01 .05
71 Carney Lansford .02 .10
72 Fred Lynn .02 .10
73 Bill Madlock .02 .10
74 Don Mattingly .50 1.25
75 Kirk McCaskill .01 .05
76 Lance McCullers .01 .05
77 Oddibe McDowell .01 .05
78 Paul Molitor .20 .50
79 Keith Moreland .01 .05
80 Jack Morris .02 .10
81 Jim Morrison .01 .05
82 Jerry Mumphrey .01 .05
83 Dale Murphy .10 .30
84 Eddie Murray .20 .50
85 Ben Oglivie .01 .05
86 Bob Ojeda .01 .05
87 Jesse Orosco .02 .10
88 Dave Parker .02 .10
89 Larry Parrish .01 .05
90 Tony Pena .02 .10
91 Jim Presley .01 .05
92 Kirby Puckett .20 .50
93 Dan Quisenberry .01 .05
94 Tim Raines .02 .10
95 Dennis Rasmussen .01 .05
96 Shane Rawley .01 .05
97 Johnny Ray .01 .05
98 Jeff Reardon .02 .10
99 Jim Rice .02 .10
100 Dave Righetti .01 .05
101 Cal Ripken 1.00 2.50
102 Pete Rose .40 1.00
103 Nolan Ryan 1.00 2.50
104 Juan Samuel .01 .05
105 Ryne Sandberg .40 1.00
106 Steve Sax .01 .05
107 Mike Schmidt .20 .50
108 Mike Scott .01 .05
109 Dave Smith .01 .05
110 Lee Smith .07 .20
111 Lonnie Smith .01 .05
112 Ozzie Smith .40 1.00
113 Cory Snyder .01 .05
114 Darryl Strawberry .02 .10
115 Don Sutton .20 .50
116 Kent Tekulve .01 .05
117 Andres Thomas .01 .05
118 Alan Trammell .07 .20
119 John Tudor .01 .05
120 Fernando Valenzuela .02 .10
121 Bob Welch .02 .10
122 Lou Whitaker .02 .10
123 Frank White .02 .10
124 Reggie Williams .01 .05
125 Willie Wilson .02 .10
126 Dave Winfield .15 .40
127 Mike Witt .01 .05
128 Todd Worrell .02 .10
129 Curt Young .01 .05
130 Robin Yount .15 .40
131 Jose Canseco CL .30 .75
Don Mattingly
132 Bo Jackson CL .10 .30
Eric Davis

1987 Fleer Stickers Wax Box Cards

The bottoms of the Star Sticker wax boxes contained two different sets of four cards done in a similar format to the stickers; these cards (they are not stickers but truly cards) are numbered with the prefix S and are considered a separate set. The value of the panels uncut is slightly greater, perhaps by 25 percent greater, than the value of the individual cards cut up carefully. When cut properly, the individual cards measure standard size, 2 1/2" by 3 1/2".

COMPLETE SET (8) 2.50 6.00
S1 Detroit Logo .02 .10
S2 Wade Boggs .60 1.50
S3 Bert Blyleven .08 .25
S4 Jose Cruz .08 .25
S5 Glenn Davis .02 .10
S6 Phillies Logo .02 .10
S7 Bob Horner .02 .10
S8 Don Mattingly 1.50 4.00

1988 Fleer

This set consists of 660 standard-size cards. Cards were primarily issued in 15-card wax packs and hobby and retail factory sets. Each wax pack contained one of 26 different "Stadium Card" stickers. Card fronts feature a distinctive white background with red and blue diagonal stripes across the card. As in years past cards are organized numerically by teams and team order is based upon the previous season's record. Subsets include Specials (622-640), Rookie Pairs (641-653), and checklists (654-660). Rookie Cards in this set include Jay Bell, Ellis Burks, Ken Caminiti, Ron Gant, Tom Glavine, Mark Grace, Edgar Martinez, Jack McDowell and Matt Williams.

COMPLETE SET (660) 6.00 15.00
COMP.RETAIL SET (660) 6.00 15.00
COMP.HOBBY SET (672) 6.00 15.00
1 Keith Atherton .02 .10
2 Don Baylor .05 .15
3 Juan Berenguer .02 .10
4 Bert Blyleven .05 .15
5 Tom Brunansky .02 .10
6 Randy Bush .02 .10
7 Steve Carlton .05 .15
8 Mark Davidson .02 .10
9 George Frazier .02 .10
10 Gary Gaetti .05 .15
11 Greg Gagne .02 .10
12 Dan Gladden .02 .10
13 Kent Hrbek .05 .15
14 Gene Larkin RC .15 .40
15 Tim Laudner .02 .10
16 Steve Lombardozzi .02 .10
17 Al Newman .02 .10
18 Joe Niekro .02 .10
19 Kirby Puckett .10 .30
20 Jeff Reardon .05 .15
21A Dan Schatzeder ERR .05 .15
21B Dan Schatzeder COR .02 .10
22 Roy Smalley .02 .10
23 Mike Smithson .02 .10
24 Les Straker .02 .10
25 Frank Viola .05 .15
26 Jack Clark .05 .15
27 Vince Coleman .02 .10
28 Danny Cox .02 .10
29 Bill Dawley .02 .10
30 Ken Dayley .02 .10
31 Doug DeCinces .02 .10
32 Curt Ford .02 .10
33 Bob Forsch .02 .10
34 David Green .02 .10
35 Tom Herr .02 .10
36 Ricky Horton .02 .10
37 Lance Johnson RC .15 .40
38 Steve Lake .02 .10
39 Jim Lindeman .02 .10
40 Joe Magrane RC .15 .40
41 Greg Mathews .02 .10
42 Willie McGee .05 .15
43 John Morris .02 .10
44 Jose Oquendo .02 .10
45 Tony Pena .02 .10
46 Terry Pendleton .05 .15
47 Ozzie Smith .20 .50
48 John Tudor .05 .15
49 Lee Tunnell .02 .10
50 Todd Worrell .02 .10
51 Doyle Alexander .02 .10
52 Dave Bergman .02 .10
53 Tom Brookens .02 .10
54 Darrell Evans .05 .15
55 Kirk Gibson .10 .30
56 Mike Heath .02 .10
57 Mike Henneman RC .15 .40
58 Willie Hernandez .02 .10
59 Larry Herndon .02 .10
60 Eric King .02 .10
61 Chet Lemon .05 .15
62 Scott Lusader .02 .10
63 Bill Madlock .05 .15
64 Jack Morris .05 .15
65 Jim Morrison .02 .10
66 Matt Nokes RC .15 .40
67 Dan Petry .02 .10
68A Jeff M. Robinson .07 .20
ERR, Stats for Jeff D. Robinson
on card back
Born 12-13-60
68B Jeff M. Robinson .02 .10
COR, Born 12-14-61
69 Pat Sheridan .02 .10
70 Nate Snell .02 .10
71 Frank Tanana .05 .15
72 Walt Terrell .02 .10
73 Mark Thurmond .02 .10
74 Alan Trammell .05 .15
75 Lou Whitaker .05 .15
76 Mike Aldrete .02 .10
77 Bob Brenly .02 .10
78 Will Clark .10 .30
79 Chili Davis .05 .15
80 Kelly Downs .02 .10
81 Dave Dravecky .02 .10
82 Scott Garrelts .02 .10
83 Atlee Hammaker .02 .10
84 Dave Henderson .02 .10
85 Mike Krukow .02 .10
86 Mike LaCoss .02 .10
87 Craig Lefferts .02 .10
88 Jeff Leonard .02 .10
89 Candy Maldonado .02 .10
90 Eddie Milner .02 .10
91 Bob Melvin .02 .10
92 Kevin Mitchell .05 .15
93 Jon Perlman RC .02 .10
94 Rick Reuschel .05 .15
95 Don Robinson .02 .10
96 Chris Speier .02 .10
97 Harry Spilman .02 .10
98 Robby Thompson .02 .10
99 Jose Uribe .02 .10
100 Mark Wasinger .02 .10
101 Matt Williams RC .60 1.50
102 Jesse Barfield .05 .15
103 George Bell .05 .15
104 Juan Beniquez .02 .10
105 John Cerutti .02 .10
106 Jim Clancy .02 .10
107 Rob Ducey RC .02 .10
108 Mark Eichhorn .02 .10
109 Tony Fernandez .02 .10
110 Cecil Fielder .05 .15
111 Kelly Gruber .02 .10
112 Tom Henke .02 .10
113A Garth Iorg ERR .07 .20
Misspelled Iorq
on card front
113B Garth Iorg COR .02 .10
114 Jimmy Key .05 .15
115 Rick Leach .02 .10
116 Manny Lee .02 .10
117 Nelson Liriano RC .02 .10
118 Fred McGriff .10 .30
119 Lloyd Moseby .02 .10
120 Rance Mulliniks .02 .10
121 Jeff Musselman .02 .10
122 Jose Nunez .02 .10
123 Dave Stieb .05 .15
124 Willie Upshaw .02 .10
125 Duane Ward .02 .10
126 Ernie Whitt .02 .10
127 Rick Aguilera .02 .10
128 Wally Backman .02 .10
129 Mark Carreon RC .05 .15
130 Gary Carter .05 .15
131 David Cone .05 .15
132 Ron Darling .05 .15
133 Len Dykstra .05 .15
134 Sid Fernandez .02 .10
135 Dwight Gooden .05 .15
136 Keith Hernandez .05 .15
137 Gregg Jefferies RC .15 .40
138 Howard Johnson .05 .15
139 Terry Leach .02 .10
140 Barry Lyons .02 .10
141 Dave Magadan .02 .10
142 Roger McDowell .02 .10
143 Kevin McReynolds .02 .10
144 Keith A. Miller RC .15 .40
145 John Mitchell RC .05 .15
146 Randy Myers .05 .15
147 Bob Ojeda .02 .10
148 Jesse Orosco .02 .10
149 Rafael Santana .02 .10
150 Doug Sisk .02 .10
151 Darryl Strawberry .05 .15
152 Tim Teufel .02 .10
153 Gene Walter .02 .10
154 Mookie Wilson .05 .15
155 Jay Aldrich .02 .10
156 Chris Bosio .02 .10
157 Glenn Braggs .02 .10
158 Greg Brock .02 .10
159 Juan Castillo .02 .10
160 Mark Clear .02 .10
161 Cecil Cooper .05 .15
162 Chuck Crim .02 .10
163 Rob Deer .02 .10
164 Mike Felder .02 .10
165 Jim Gantner .02 .10
166 Ted Higuera .02 .10
167 Steve Kiefer .02 .10
168 Rick Manning .02 .10
169 Paul Molitor .05 .15
170 Juan Nieves .02 .10
171 Dan Plesac .02 .10
172 Earnest Riles .02 .10
173 Bill Schroeder .02 .10
174 Steve Stanicek .02 .10
175 B.J. Surhoff .05 .15
176 Dale Sveum .02 .10
177 Bill Wegman .02 .10
178 Robin Yount .20 .50
179 Hubie Brooks .02 .10
180 Tim Burke .02 .10
181 Casey Candaele .02 .10
182 Mike Fitzgerald .02 .10
183 Tom Foley .02 .10
184 Andres Galarraga .05 .15
185 Neal Heaton .02 .10
186 Wallace Johnson .02 .10
187 Vance Law .02 .10
188 Dennis Martinez .05 .15
189 Bob McClure .02 .10
190 Andy McGaffigan .02 .10
191 Reid Nichols .02 .10
192 Pascual Perez .02 .10
193 Tim Raines .05 .15
194 Jeff Reed .02 .10
195 Bob Sebra .02 .10
196 Bryn Smith .02 .10
197 Randy St.Claire .02 .10
198 Tim Wallach .02 .10
199 Mitch Webster .02 .10
200 Herm Winningham .02 .10
201 Floyd Youmans .02 .10
202 Brad Arnsberg .02 .10
203 Rick Cerone .02 .10
204 Pat Clements .02 .10
205 Henry Cotto .02 .10
206 Mike Easler .02 .10
207 Ron Guidry .05 .15
208 Bill Gullickson .02 .10
209 Rickey Henderson .10 .30
210 Charles Hudson .02 .10
211 Tommy John .05 .15
212 Roberto Kelly RC .15 .40
213 Ron Kittle .02 .10
214 Don Mattingly .40 1.00
215 Bobby Meacham .02 .10
216 Mike Pagliarulo .02 .10
217 Dan Pasqua .02 .10
218 Willie Randolph .05 .15
219 Rick Rhoden .02 .10
220 Dave Righetti .05 .15
221 Jerry Royster .02 .10
222 Tim Stoddard .02 .10
223 Wayne Tolleson .02 .10
224 Gary Ward .02 .10
225 Claudell Washington .02 .10
226 Dave Winfield .05 .15
227 Buddy Bell .05 .15
228 Tom Browning .02 .10
229 Dave Concepcion .05 .15
230 Kal Daniels .02 .10
231 Eric Davis .05 .15
232 Bo Diaz .02 .10
233 Nick Esasky .02 .10
Has a dollar sign
before '87 SB totals
234 John Franco .05 .15
235 Guy Hoffman .02 .10
236 Tom Hume .02 .10
237 Tracy Jones .02 .10
238 Bill Landrum .02 .10
239 Barry Larkin .07 .20
240 Terry McGriff .02 .10
241 Rob Murphy .02 .10
242 Ron Oester .02 .10
243 Dave Parker .05 .15
244 Pat Perry .02 .10
245 Ted Power .02 .10
246 Dennis Rasmussen .02 .10
247 Ron Robinson .02 .10
248 Kurt Stillwell .02 .10
249 Jeff Treadway RC .15 .40
250 Frank Williams .02 .10
251 Steve Balboni .02 .10
252 Bud Black .02 .10
253 Thad Bosley .02 .10
254 George Brett .30 .75
255 John Davis RC .02 .10
256 Steve Farr .02 .10
257 Gene Garber .02 .10
258 Jerry Don Gleaton .02 .10
259 Mark Gubicza .02 .10
260 Bo Jackson .10 .30
261 Danny Jackson .02 .10
262 Ross Jones .02 .10
263 Charlie Leibrandt .02 .10
264 Bill Pecota RC .05 .15
265 Melido Perez RC .15 .40
266 Jamie Quirk .02 .10
267 Dan Quisenberry .02 .10
268 Bret Saberhagen .05 .15
269 Angel Salazar .02 .10
270 Kevin Seitzer UER .05 .15
Wrong birth year
271 Danny Tartabull .02 .10
272 Gary Thurman RC .02 .10
273 Frank White .05 .15
274 Willie Wilson .05 .15
275 Tony Bernazard .02 .10
276 Jose Canseco .30 .75
277 Mike Davis .02 .10
278 Storm Davis .02 .10
279 Dennis Eckersley .07 .20
280 Alfredo Griffin .02 .10
281 Rick Honeycutt .02 .10
282 Jay Howell .02 .10
283 Reggie Jackson .07 .20
284 Dennis Lamp .02 .10
285 Carney Lansford .05 .15
286 Mark McGwire 1.00 2.50
287 Dwayne Murphy .02 .10
288 Gene Nelson .02 .10
289 Steve Ontiveros .02 .10
290 Tony Phillips .02 .10
291 Eric Plunk .02 .10
292 Luis Polonia RC .15 .40
293 Rick Rodriguez .02 .10
294 Terry Steinbach .05 .15
295 Dave Stewart .05 .15
296 Curt Young .02 .10
297 Luis Aguayo .02 .10
298 Steve Bedrosian .02 .10
299 Jeff Calhoun .02 .10
300 Don Carman .02 .10
301 Todd Frohwirth .02 .10
302 Greg Gross .02 .10
303 Kevin Gross .02 .10
304 Von Hayes .02 .10
305 Keith Hughes RC .02 .10
306 Mike Jackson RC .15 .40
307 Chris James .02 .10
308 Steve Jeltz .02 .10
309 Mike Maddux .02 .10
310 Lance Parrish .05 .15
311 Shane Rawley .02 .10
312 Wally Ritchie .02 .10
313 Bruce Ruffin .02 .10
314 Juan Samuel .02 .10
315 Mike Schmidt .30 .75
316 Rick Schu .02 .10
317 Jeff Stone .02 .10
318 Kent Tekulve .02 .10
319 Milt Thompson .02 .10
320 Glenn Wilson .02 .10
321 Rafael Belliard .02 .10
322 Barry Bonds 1.00 2
323 Bobby Bonilla UER .05
Wrong birth year
324 Sid Bream .02
325 John Cangelosi .02
326 Mike Diaz .02
327 Doug Drabek .02
328 Mike Dunne .02
329 Brian Fisher .02
330 Brett Gideon .02
331 Terry Harper .02
332 Bob Kipper .02
333 Mike LaValliere .02
334 Jose Lind RC .15
335 Junior Ortiz .02
336 Vicente Palacios RC .02
337 Bob Patterson .02
338 Al Pedrique .02
339 R.J. Reynolds .02
340 John Smiley RC .15
341 Andy Van Slyke UER .07
Wrong batting and
throwing listed
342 Bob Walk .02
343 Marty Barrett .02
344 Todd Benzinger RC .15
345 Wade Boggs .07
346 Tom Bolton .02
347 Oil Can Boyd .02
348 Ellis Burks RC .20
349 Roger Clemens .60 1
350 Steve Crawford .02
351 Dwight Evans .07
352 Wes Gardner .02
353 Rich Gedman .02
354 Mike Greenwell .02
355 Sam Horn RC .05
356 Bruce Hurst .02
357 John Marzano .02
358 Al Nipper .02
359 Spike Owen .02
360 Jody Reed RC .15
361 Jim Rice .05
362 Ed Romero .02
363 Kevin Romine RC .02
364 Joe Sambito .02
365 Calvin Schiraldi .02
366 Jeff Sellers .02
367 Bob Stanley .02
368 Scott Bankhead .02
369 Phil Bradley .02
370 Scott Bradley .02
371 Mickey Brantley .02
372 Mike Campbell RC .02
373 Alvin Davis .02
374 Lee Guetterman .02
375 Dave Hengel .02
376 Mike Kingery .02
377 Mark Langston .02
378 Edgar Martinez RC 2.50 6
379 Mike Moore .02
380 Mike Morgan .02
381 John Moses .02
382 Donell Nixon .02
383 Edwin Nunez .02
384 Ken Phelps .02
385 Jim Presley .02
386 Rey Quinones .02
387 Jerry Reed .02
388 Harold Reynolds .05
389 Dave Valle .02
390 Bill Wilkinson .02
391 Harold Baines .05
392 Floyd Bannister .02
393 Daryl Boston .02
394 Ivan Calderon .02
395 Jose DeLeon .02
396 Richard Dotson .02
397 Carlton Fisk .07
398 Ozzie Guillen .05
399 Ron Hassey .02
400 Donnie Hill .02
401 Bob James .02
402 Dave LaPoint .02
403 Bill Lindsey .02
404 Bill Long .02
405 Steve Lyons .02
406 Fred Manrique .02
407 Jack McDowell RC .20
408 Gary Redus .02
409 Ray Searage .02
410 Bobby Thigpen .02
411 Greg Walker .02
412 Ken Williams RC .02
413 Jim Winn .02
414 Jody Davis .02
415 Andre Dawson .05
416 Brian Dayett .02
417 Bob Dernier .02
418 Frank DiPino .02
419 Shawon Dunston .02
420 Leon Durham .02
421 Les Lancaster .02
422 Ed Lynch .02
423 Greg Maddux .60 1.
424 Dave Martinez .02
425A Keith Moreland ERR .60 1.
425B Keith Moreland COR .05
Bat on shoulder
426 Jamie Moyer .05
427 Jerry Mumphrey .02
428 Paul Noce .02
429 Rafael Palmeiro .25

Card	Low	High
430 Wade Rowdon	.02	.10
431 Ryne Sandberg	.25	.60
432 Scott Sanderson	.02	.10
433 Lee Smith	.05	.15
434 Jim Sundberg	.05	.15
435 Rick Sutcliffe	.05	.15
436 Manny Trillo	.02	.10
437 Juan Agosto	.02	.10
438 Larry Andersen	.02	.10
439 Alan Ashby	.02	.10
440 Kevin Bass	.02	.10
441 Ken Caminiti RC	1.25	3.00
442 Rocky Childress	.02	.10
443 Jose Cruz	.05	.15
444 Danny Darwin	.02	.10
445 Glenn Davis	.02	.10
446 Jim Deshaies	.02	.10
447 Bill Doran	.02	.10
448 Ty Gainey	.02	.10
449 Billy Hatcher	.02	.10
450 Jeff Heathcock	.02	.10
451 Bob Knepper	.02	.10
452 Rob Mallicoat	.02	.10
453 Dave Meads	.02	.10
454 Craig Reynolds	.02	.10
455 Nolan Ryan	.60	1.50
456 Mike Scott	.05	.15
457 Dave Smith	.02	.10
458 Denny Walling	.02	.10
459 Robbie Wine	.02	.10
460 Gerald Young	.02	.10
461 Bob Brower	.02	.10
462A Jerry Browne ERR	.60	1.50
462B Jerry Browne COR	.05	.15
Posed with bat		
463 Steve Buechele	.02	.10
464 Edwin Correa	.02	.10
465 Cecil Espy RC	.02	.10
466 Scott Fletcher	.02	.10
467 Jose Guzman	.02	.10
468 Greg Harris	.02	.10
469 Charlie Hough	.05	.15
470 Pete Incaviglia	.02	.10
471 Paul Kilgus	.02	.10
472 Mike Loynd	.02	.10
473 Oddibe McDowell	.02	.10
474 Dale Mohorcic	.02	.10
475 Pete O'Brien	.02	.10
476 Larry Parrish	.02	.10
477 Geno Petralli	.02	.10
478 Jeff Russell	.02	.10
479 Ruben Sierra	.05	.15
480 Mike Stanley	.02	.10
481 Curtis Wilkerson	.02	.10
482 Mitch Williams	.02	.10
483 Bobby Witt	.02	.10
484 Tony Armas	.05	.15
485 Bob Boone	.05	.15
486 Bill Buckner	.05	.15
487 DeWayne Buice	.02	.10
488 Brian Downing	.05	.15
489 Chuck Finley	.05	.15
490 Willie Fraser UER	.02	.10
Wrong bio stats,		
for George Hendrick		
491 Jack Howell	.02	.10
492 Ruppert Jones	.02	.10
493 Wally Joyner	.05	.15
494 Jack Lazorko	.02	.10
495 Gary Lucas	.02	.10
496 Kirk McCaskill	.02	.10
497 Mark McLemore	.02	.10
498 Darrell Miller	.02	.10
499 Greg Minton	.02	.10
500 Donnie Moore	.02	.10
501 Gus Polidor	.02	.10
502 Johnny Ray	.02	.10
503 Mark Ryal	.02	.10
504 Dick Schofield	.02	.10
505 Don Sutton	.05	.15
506 Devon White	.05	.15
507 Mike Witt	.02	.10
508 Dave Anderson	.02	.10
509 Tim Belcher	.02	.10
510 Ralph Bryant	.02	.10
511 Tim Crews RC	.15	.40
512 Mike Devereaux RC	.15	.40
513 Mariano Duncan	.02	.10
514 Pedro Guerrero	.05	.15
515 Jeff Hamilton	.02	.10
516 Mickey Hatcher	.02	.10
517 Brad Havens	.02	.10
518 Orel Hershiser	.05	.15
519 Shawn Hillegas RC	.02	.10
520 Ken Howell	.02	.10
521 Tim Leary	.02	.10
522 Mike Marshall	.02	.10
523 Steve Sax	.02	.10
524 Mike Scioscia	.05	.15
525 Mike Sharperson	.02	.10
526 John Shelby	.02	.10
527 Franklin Stubbs	.02	.10
528 Fernando Valenzuela	.05	.15
529 Bob Welch	.05	.15
530 Matt Young	.02	.10
531 Jim Acker	.02	.10
532 Paul Assenmacher	.02	.10
533 Jeff Blauser RC	.15	.40
534 Joe Boever	.02	.10
535 Martin Clary	.02	.10
536 Kevin Coffman	.02	.10
537 Jeff Dedmon	.02	.10
538 Ron Gant RC	.20	.50
539 Tom Glavine RC	1.25	3.00
540 Ken Griffey	.05	.15
541 Albert Hall	.02	.10
542 Glenn Hubbard	.02	.10
543 Dion James	.02	.10
544 Dale Murphy	.07	.20
545 Ken Oberkfell	.02	.10
546 David Palmer	.02	.10
547 Gerald Perry	.02	.10
548 Charlie Puleo	.02	.10
549 Ted Simmons	.05	.15
550 Zane Smith	.02	.10
551 Andres Thomas	.02	.10
552 Ozzie Virgil	.02	.10
553 Don Aase	.02	.10
554 Jeff Ballard RC	.02	.10
555 Eric Bell	.02	.10
556 Mike Boddicker	.02	.10
557 Ken Dixon	.02	.10
558 Jim Dwyer	.02	.10
559 Ken Gerhart	.02	.10
560 Rene Gonzales RC	.05	.15
561 Mike Griffin	.02	.10
562 John Habyan UER	.02	.10
Misspelled Hayban on		
both sides of card		
563 Terry Kennedy	.02	.10
564 Ray Knight	.05	.15
565 Lee Lacy	.02	.10
566 Fred Lynn	.05	.15
567 Eddie Murray	.10	.30
568 Tom Niedenfuer	.02	.10
569 Bill Ripken RC	.15	.40
570 Cal Ripken	.50	1.25
571 Dave Schmidt	.02	.10
572 Larry Sheets	.02	.10
573 Pete Stanicek RC	.02	.10
574 Mark Williamson	.02	.10
575 Mike Young	.02	.10
576 Shawn Abner	.02	.10
577 Greg Booker	.02	.10
578 Chris Brown	.02	.10
579 Keith Comstock	.02	.10
580 Joey Cora RC	.15	.40
581 Mark Davis	.02	.10
582 Tim Flannery	.07	.20
With surfboard		
583 Goose Gossage	.05	.15
584 Mark Grant	.02	.10
585 Tony Gwynn	.20	.50
586 Andy Hawkins	.02	.10
587 Stan Jefferson	.02	.10
588 Jimmy Jones	.02	.10
589 John Kruk	.05	.15
590 Shane Mack	.02	.10
591 Carmelo Martinez	.02	.10
592 Lance McCullers UER	.02	.10
6'11 tall		
593 Eric Nolte	.02	.10
594 Randy Ready	.02	.10
595 Luis Salazar	.02	.10
596 Benito Santiago	.05	.15
597 Eric Show	.02	.10
598 Garry Templeton	.05	.15
599 Ed Whitson	.02	.10
600 Scott Bailes	.02	.10
601 Chris Bando	.02	.10
602 Jay Bell RC	.20	.50
603 Brett Butler	.05	.15
604 Tom Candiotti	.02	.10
605 Joe Carter	.05	.15
606 Carmen Castillo	.02	.10
607 Brian Dorsett	.02	.10
608 John Farrell RC	.05	.15
609 Julio Franco	.05	.15
610 Mel Hall	.02	.10
611 Tommy Hinzo	.02	.10
612 Brook Jacoby	.02	.10
613 Doug Jones RC	.15	.40
614 Ken Schrom	.02	.10
615 Cory Snyder	.02	.10
616 Sammy Stewart	.02	.10
617 Greg Swindell	.02	.10
618 Pat Tabler	.02	.10
619 Ed VandeBerg	.02	.10
620 Eddie Williams RC	.05	.15
621 Rich Yett	.02	.10
622 Wally Joyner	.05	.15
Cory Snyder		
623 George Bell	.02	.10
Pedro Guerrero		
624 M.McGwire/J.Canseco	.60	1.50
625 Dave Righetti	.02	.10
Dan Plesac		
626 Bret Saberhagen	.05	.15
Mike Witt		
Jack Morris		
627 John Franco	.02	.10
Steve Bedrosian		
628 Ozzie Smith	.10	.30
Ryne Sandberg		
629 Mark McGwire HL	.50	1.25
630 Mike Greenwell	.10	.30
Ellis Burks		
Todd Benzinger		
631 Tony Gwynn	.07	.20
Tim Raines		
632 Mike Scott	.05	.15
Orel Hershiser		
633 P.Tabler/M.McGwire	.50	1.25
634 Tony Gwynn	.07	.20
Vince Coleman		
635 Fernandez/Ripken/Trammell	.20	.50
636 Mike Schmidt	.10	.30
Gary Carter		
637 Darryl Strawberry	.05	.15
Eric Davis		
638 Matt Nokes	.07	.20
Kirby Puckett		
639 Keith Hernandez	.05	.15
Dale Murphy		
640 B.Ripken/C.Ripken	.30	.75
641 M.Grace RC	1.25	3.00
D.Jackson		
642 Damon Berryhill RC	.15	.40
Jeff Montgomery RC		
643 Felix Fermin	.05	.15
Jesse Reid RC		
644 Greg Myers	.15	.40
Greg Tabor RC		
645 Joey Meyer	.05	.15
Jim Eppard RC		
646 Adam Peterson RC	.15	.40
Randy Velarde RC		
647 Pete Smith RC	.15	.40
Chris Gwynn RC		
648 Tom Newell	.05	.15
Greg Jelks RC		
649 Mario Diaz	.05	.15
Clay Parker RC		
650 Jack Savage	.05	.15
Todd Simmons RC		
651 John Burkett	.15	.40
Kirt Manwaring RC		
652 Dave Otto	.20	.50
Walt Weiss RC		
653 Jeff King	.15	.40
Randell Byers RC		
654 CL: Twins/Cards	.02	.10
Tigers/Giants UER		
90 Bob Melvin,		
91 Eddie Milner		
655 CL: Blue Jays/Mets	.02	.10
Brewers/Expos UER		
Mets listed before		
Blue Jays on card		
656 CL: Yankees/Reds	.02	.10
Royals/A's		
657 CL: Phillies/Pirates	.02	.10
Red Sox/Mariners		
658 CL: White Sox/Cubs	.02	.10
Astros/Rangers		
659 CL: Angels/Dodgers	.02	.10
Braves/Orioles		
660 CL: Padres/Indians	.02	.10
Rookies/Specials		

1988 Fleer Glossy

Card	Low	High
COMP.FACT.SET (672)	8.00	25.00
*STARS: .6X TO 1.5X BASIC CARDS		
*ROOKIES: .75X TO 2X BASIC CARDS		
DISTRIBUTED ONLY IN FACTORY SET FORM		
378 Edgar Martinez	12.00	30.00

1988 Fleer All-Stars

These 12 standard-size cards were inserted randomly in wax and cello packs of the 1988 Fleer set. The cards show the player silhouetted against a light green background with dark green stripes. The player's name, team, and position are printed in yellow at the bottom of the obverse. The card backs are done predominantly in green, white, and black. The players are the "best" at each position, three pitchers, eight position players, and a designated hitter.

Card	Low	High
COMPLETE SET (12)	2.50	6.00
RANDOM INSERTS IN PACKS	.40	.75
1 Matt Nokes	.60	1.50
2 Tom Henke	.15	.40
3 Ted Higuera	.15	.40
4 Roger Clemens	2.50	6.00
5 George Bell	.25	.60
6 Andre Dawson	.25	.60
7 Eric Davis	.25	.60
8 Wade Boggs	.30	.75
9 Alan Trammell	.25	.60
10 Juan Samuel	.15	.40
11 Jack Clark	.25	.60
12 Paul Molitor	.25	.60

1988 Fleer Headliners

This six-card standard-size set was distributed one per rack pack. The obverse features the player photo superimposed on a gray newsprint background. The cards are printed in red, black, and white on the back describing why that particular player made headlines the previous season. The set is sequenced in alphabetical order.

Card	Low	High
COMPLETE SET (6)	2.50	6.00
ONE PER RACK PACK	.10	.20
1 Don Mattingly	.50	1.25
2 Mark McGwire	1.50	4.00
3 Jack Morris	.07	.20
4 Darryl Strawberry	.07	.20
5 Dwight Gooden	.10	.20
6 Tim Raines	.07	.20

1988 Fleer Wax Box Cards

The cards in this 16-card set measure the standard size. Cards have essentially the same design as the 1988 Fleer regular issue set. The cards were printed on the bottoms of the regular issue wax pack boxes. These 16 cards (C1 to C16) are considered a separate set in their own right and are not typically included in a complete set of the regular issue 1988 Fleer cards. The value of the panel uncut is slightly greater, perhaps by 25 percent greater, than the value of the individual cards cut up carefully.

Card	Low	High
COMPLETE SET (16)	3.00	8.00
C1 Cardinals Logo	.02	.10
C2 Dwight Evans	.08	.25
C3 Andres Galarraga	.40	1.00
C4 Wally Joyner	.08	.25
C5 Twins Logo	.02	.10
C6 Dale Murphy	.40	1.00
C7 Kirby Puckett	.50	1.25
C8 Shane Rawley	.02	.10
C9 Giants Logo	.02	.10
C10 Ryne Sandberg	1.00	2.50
C11 Mike Schmidt	.50	1.25
C12 Kevin Seitzer	.02	.10
C13 Tigers Logo	.02	.10
C14 Dave Stewart	.08	.25
C15 Tim Wallach	.02	.10
C16 Todd Worrell	.08	.25

1988 Fleer World Series

This 12-card standard-size set features highlights of the previous year's World Series between the Minnesota Twins and the St. Louis Cardinals. The sets were packaged as a complete set insert with the collated sets (of the 1988 Fleer regular issue) which were sold by Fleer directly to hobby card dealers; they were not available in the general retail candy store outlets. The set numbering is essentially in chronological order of the events from the immediate past World Series.

Card	Low	High
COMPLETE SET (12)	.75	2.00
ONE SET PER FACTORY SET		
1 Dan Gladden	.02	.10
2 Randy Bush	.02	.10
3 John Tudor	.05	.15
4 Ozzie Smith	.20	.50
5 T.Worrell	.02	.10
T.Pena		
6 Vince Coleman	.02	.10
7 T.Herr	.02	.10
D.Driessen		
8 Kirby Puckett	.10	.30
9 Kent Hrbek	.05	.15
10 Tom Herr	.02	.10
11 Don Baylor	.05	.15
12 Frank Viola	.05	.15

1988 Fleer World Series Glossy

*GLOSSY: .5X TO 1.2X BASIC WS
DISTRIBUTED ONLY IN FACTORY SET FORM

1988 Fleer Update

This 132-card standard-size set was distributed exclusively in factory set form in a red, white and blue, cellophane-wrapped box through hobby dealers. In addition to the complete set of 132 cards, the box also contained 25 Team Logo stickers. The cards look very similar to the 1988 Fleer regular issue except for the U-prefixed numbering on back. Cards are ordered alphabetically by player's last name. This was the first Fleer Update set to adopt the Fleer "alphabetical within team" numbering system. The key extended Rookie Cards in this set are Roberto Alomar, Craig Biggio Al Leiter, John Smoltz and David Wells.

Card	Low	High
COMP.FACT.SET (132)	4.00	10.00
1 Jose Bautista XRC	.08	.25
2 Joe Orsulak	.02	.10
3 Doug Sisk	.02	.10
4 Craig Worthington	.02	.10
5 Mike Boddicker	.02	.10
6 Rick Cerone	.02	.10
7 Larry Parrish	.02	.10
8 Lee Smith	.07	.20
9 Mike Smithson	.02	.10
10 John Trautwein	.02	.10
11 Sherman Corbett XRC	.02	.10
12 Chili Davis	.07	.20
13 Jim Eppard	.02	.10
14 Bryan Harvey XRC	.20	.50
15 John Davis	.02	.10
16 Dave Gallagher	.02	.10
17 Ricky Horton	.02	.10
18 Dan Pasqua	.02	.10
19 Melido Perez	.02	.10
20 Jose Segura	.02	.10
21 Andy Allanson	.02	.10
22 Jon Perlman XRC	.02	.10
23 Domingo Ramos	.02	.10
24 Rick Rodriguez	.02	.10
25 Willie Upshaw	.02	.10
26 Paul Gibson	.02	.10
27 Don Heinkel	.02	.10
28 Ray Knight	.07	.20
29 Gary Pettis	.02	.10
30 Luis Salazar	.02	.10
31 Mike Macfarlane XRC	.20	.50
32 Jeff Montgomery	.20	.50
33 Ted Power	.02	.10
34 Israel Sanchez	.02	.10
35 Kurt Stillwell	.02	.10
36 Pat Tabler	.02	.10
37 Don August	.02	.10
38 Darryl Hamilton XRC	.20	.50
39 Jeff Leonard	.02	.10
40 Joey Meyer	.02	.10
41 Allan Anderson	.02	.10
42 Brian Harper	.02	.10
43 Tom Herr	.02	.10
44 Charlie Lea	.02	.10
45 John Moses	.02	.10
Listed as Hohn on		
checklist card		
46 John Candelaria	.02	.10
47 Jack Clark	.07	.20
48 Richard Dotson	.02	.10
49 Al Leiter XRC	.40	1.00
50 Rafael Santana	.02	.10
51 Don Slaught	.02	.10
52 Todd Burns	.02	.10
53 Dave Henderson	.02	.10
54 Doug Jennings XRC	.02	.10
55 Dave Parker	.07	.20
56 Walt Weiss	.30	.75
57 Bob Welch	.07	.20
58 Henry Cotto	.02	.10
59 Mario Diaz UER	.02	.10
Listed as Marion		
on card front		
60 Mike Jackson	.07	.20
61 Bill Swift	.02	.10
62 Jose Cecena	.02	.10
63 Ray Hayward	.02	.10
64 Jim Steels UER	.02	.10
Listed as Jim Steele		
on card back		
65 Pat Borders XRC	.20	.50
66 Sil Campusano	.02	.10
67 Mike Flanagan	.02	.10
68 Todd Stottlemyre XRC	.20	.50
69 David Wells XRC	.60	1.50
70 Jose Alvarez XRC	.08	.25
71 Paul Runge	.02	.10
72 Cesar Jimenez	.02	.10
Card was intended		
for German Jiminez&		
it's his photo		
73 Pete Smith	.02	.10
74 John Smoltz XRC	1.50	4.00
75 Damon Berryhill	.08	.25
76 Goose Gossage	.07	.20
77 Mark Grace	.75	2.00
78 Darrin Jackson	.08	.25
79 Vance Law	.02	.10
80 Jeff Pico	.02	.10
81 Gary Varsho	.02	.10
82 Tim Birtsas	.02	.10
83 Rob Dibble XRC	.30	.75
84 Danny Jackson	.02	.10
85 Paul O'Neill	.10	.30
86 Jose Rijo	.07	.20
87 Chris Sabo XRC	.30	.75
88 John Fishel XRC	.02	.10
89 Craig Biggio XRC	2.00	5.00
90 Terry Puhl	.02	.10
91 Rafael Ramirez	.02	.10
92 Louie Meadows XRC	.02	.10
93 Kirk Gibson	.20	.50
94 Alfredo Griffin	.02	.10
95 Jay Howell	.02	.10
96 Jesse Orosco	.02	.10
97 Alejandro Pena	.02	.10
98 Tracy Woodson XRC	.08	.25
99 John Dopson	.02	.10
100 Brian Holman XRC	.08	.25
101 Rex Hudler	.02	.10
102 Jeff Parrett	.02	.10
103 Nelson Santovenia	.02	.10
104 Kevin Elster	.02	.10
105 Jeff Innis	.02	.10
106 Mackey Sasser XRC	.20	.50
107 Phil Bradley	.02	.10
108 Danny Clay XRC	.02	.10
109 Greg A.Harris	.02	.10
110 Ricky Jordan XRC	.20	.50
111 David Palmer	.02	.10
112 Jim Gott	.02	.10
113 Tommy Gregg UER	.02	.10
Photo actually		
Randy Milligan		
114 Barry Jones	.02	.10
115 Randy Milligan XRC	.08	.25
116 Luis Alicea XRC	.20	.50
117 Tom Brunansky	.02	.10
118 John Costello XRC	.02	.10
119 Jose DeLeon	.02	.10
120 Bob Horner	.07	.20
121 Scott Terry	.02	.10
122 Roberto Alomar XRC	.75	2.00
123 Dave Leiper	.02	.10
124 Keith Moreland	.02	.10
125 Mark Parent XRC	.02	.10
126 Dennis Rasmussen	.02	.10
127 Randy Bockus	.02	.10
128 Brett Butler	.07	.20
129 Donell Nixon	.02	.10
130 Earnest Riles	.02	.10
131 Roger Samuels	.02	.10
132 Checklist U1-U132	.02	.10

1988 Fleer Update Glossy

Card	Low	High
COMP.FACT.SET (132)	10.00	25.00
*STARS: .75X TO 2X BASIC CARDS		
*ROOKIES: .75X TO 2X BASIC CARDS		
DISTRIBUTED ONLY IN FACTORY SET FORM		

1988 Fleer Award Winners

This small set of 44 standard-size cards was produced for 7-Eleven stores by Fleer. The cards feature full color fronts and red, white, and blue backs. The card fronts are distinguished by the red, white, and blue frame around the player's full-color photo. The box for the cards describes the set as the "1988 Limited Edition Baseball Award Winners." The checklist for the set is given on the back of the set box. The card numbering is in alphabetical order by player's name.

Card	Low	High
COMP.FACT.SET (44)	3.00	8.00
1 Steve Bedrosian	.01	.05
2 George Bell	.01	.05
3 Wade Boggs	.15	.40
4 Jose Canseco	.15	.40
5 Will Clark	.20	.50
6 Roger Clemens	.25	.60
7 Kal Daniels	.01	.05
8 Eric Davis	.02	.10
9 Andre Dawson	.10	.30
10 Mike Dunne	.01	.05
11 Dwight Evans	.02	.10
12 Carlton Fisk	.15	.40
13 Julio Franco	.01	.05
14 Dwight Gooden	.02	.10
15 Pedro Guerrero	.01	.05
16 Tony Gwynn	.30	.75
17 Orel Hershiser	.02	.10
18 Tom Henke	.01	.05
19 Ted Higuera	.01	.05
20 Charlie Hough	.02	.10
21 Wally Joyner	.02	.10
22 Jimmy Key	.02	.10
23 Don Mattingly	.30	.75
24 Mark McGwire	.40	1.00
25 Paul Molitor	.20	.50
26 Jack Morris	.02	.10
27 Dale Murphy	.10	.30
28 Terry Pendleton	.02	.10
29 Kirby Puckett	.15	.40
30 Tim Raines	.02	.10
31 Jeff Reardon	.02	.10
32 Harold Reynolds	.02	.10
33 Dave Righetti	.01	.05
34 Benito Santiago	.02	.10
35 Mike Schmidt	.20	.50
36 Mike Scott	.01	.05
37 Kevin Seitzer	.02	.10
38 Larry Sheets	.01	.05
39 Ozzie Smith	.30	.75
40 Darryl Strawberry	.02	.10
41 Rick Sutcliffe	.01	.05
42 Danny Tartabull	.01	.05
43 Alan Trammell	.07	.20
44 Tim Wallach	.01	.05

1988 Fleer Baseball All-Stars

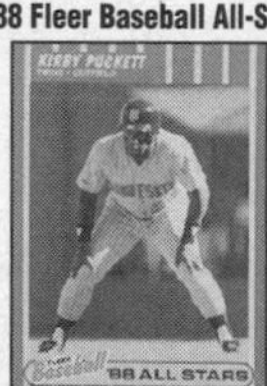

This small boxed set of 44 standard-size cards was produced exclusively for Ben Franklin Stores. The cards feature full color fronts and white and blue backs. The card fronts are distinguished by the yellow and blue striped background behind the player's full-color photo. The box for the cards describes the set as the "1988 Fleer Baseball All-Stars." The checklist for the set is given on the back of the set box. The card numbering is in alphabetical order by player's name.

Card	Low	High
COMP.FACT.SET (44)	2.50	6.00
1 George Bell	.01	.05
2 Wade Boggs	.15	.40
3 Bobby Bonilla	.02	.10
4 George Brett	.20	.50
5 Jose Canseco	.15	.40
6 Jack Clark	.02	.10
7 Will Clark	.20	.50
8 Roger Clemens	.30	.75
9 Eric Davis	.02	.10
10 Andre Dawson	.07	.20
11 Julio Franco	.01	.05
12 Dwight Gooden	.02	.10
13 Tony Gwynn	.30	.75
14 Orel Hershiser	.02	.10
15 Teddy Higuera	.01	.05
16 Charlie Hough	.02	.10
17 Kent Hrbek	.02	.10
18 Bruce Hurst	.01	.05
19 Wally Joyner	.02	.10
20 Mark Langston	.01	.05
21 Dave LaPoint	.01	.05
22 Candy Maldonado	.01	.05
23 Don Mattingly	.30	.75
24 Roger McDowell	.01	.05
25 Mark McGwire	.40	1.00
26 Jack Morris	.02	.10
27 Dale Murphy	.07	.20
28 Eddie Murray	.15	.40
29 Matt Nokes	.01	.05
30 Kirby Puckett	.15	.40
31 Tim Raines	.02	.10
32 Willie Randolph	.02	.10
33 Jeff Reardon	.02	.10
34 Nolan Ryan	.60	1.50
35 Juan Samuel	.01	.05
36 Mike Schmidt	.15	.40
37 Mike Scott	.01	.05
38 Kevin Seitzer	.02	.10
39 Ozzie Smith	.30	.75
40 Darryl Strawberry	.02	.10
41 Rick Sutcliffe	.01	.05
42 Alan Trammell	.05	.15
43 Tim Wallach	.01	.05
44 Dave Winfield	.15	.40

1988 Fleer Baseball MVP's

This small 44-card boxed standard-size set was produced by Fleer for distribution by the Toys'r'Us stores. The cards feature full color fronts. The set is titled "Baseball MVP." Each individual boxed set includes the 44 cards and six logo stickers. The checklist for the set is found on the back panel of the box. The card fronts have a vanilla-yellow and blue border. The box refers to Toys'r'Us but there is no mention of Toys'r'Us anywhere on the cards themselves. The card numbering is in alphabetical order by player's name.

Card	Low	High
COMP.FACT.SET (44)	3.00	8.00
1 George Bell	.01	.05
2 Wade Boggs	.15	.40
3 Jose Canseco	.15	.40
4 Ivan Calderon	.01	.05
5 Will Clark	.20	.50
6 Roger Clemens	.30	.75
7 Vince Coleman	.01	.05
8 Eric Davis	.02	.10
9 Andre Dawson	.07	.20
10 Dave Dravecky	.02	.10
11 Mike Dunne	.01	.05
12 Dwight Evans	.02	.10
13 Sid Fernandez	.01	.05
14 Tony Fernandez	.01	.05
15 Julio Franco	.02	.10
16 Dwight Gooden	.02	.10
17 Tony Gwynn	.30	.75
18 Ted Higuera	.01	.05
19 Charlie Hough	.02	.10
20 Wally Joyner	.05	.15
21 Mark Langston	.01	.05
22 Don Mattingly	.30	.75
23 Mark McGwire	.40	1.00
24 Jack Morris	.02	.10
25 Dale Murphy	.07	.20
26 Kirby Puckett	.10	.30
27 Tim Raines	.02	.10
28 Willie Randolph	.02	.10
29 Ryne Sandberg	.20	.50
30 Benito Santiago	.02	.10
31 Mike Schmidt	.20	.50
32 Mike Scott	.01	.05
33 Kevin Seitzer	.01	.05
34 Larry Sheets	.01	.05
35 Ozzie Smith	.30	.75
36 Dave Stewart	.02	.10
37 Darryl Strawberry	.02	.10
38 Rick Sutcliffe	.01	.05
39 Alan Trammell	.05	.15
40 Fernando Valenzuela	.02	.10
41 Frank Viola	.01	.05
42 Tim Wallach	.01	.05
43 Dave Winfield	.20	.50
44 Robin Yount	.15	.40

1988 Fleer Exciting Stars

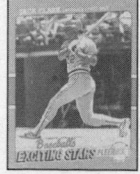

This small boxed set of 44 standard-size cards was produced exclusively for Cumberland Farm Stores.

The cards feature full color fronts and red, white, and blue backs. The card fronts are distinguished by the framing of the player's full-color photo with a blue border with a red and white bar stripe across the middle. The box for the cards describes the set as the "1988 Fleer Baseball's Exciting Stars." The checklist for the set is given on the back of the set box. The card numbering is in alphabetical order by player's name.

COMP.FACT SET (44) 2.00 5.00
1 Harold Baines .05 .15
2 Kevin Bass .01 .05
3 George Bell .01 .05
4 Wade Boggs .15 .40
5 Mickey Brantley .01 .05
6 Sid Bream .01 .05
7 Jose Canseco .10 .30
8 Jack Clark .02 .10
9 Will Clark .20 .50
10 Roger Clemens .30 .75
11 Vince Coleman .01 .05
12 Eric Davis .02 .10
13 Andre Dawson .07 .20
14 Julio Franco .02 .10
15 Dwight Gooden .02 .10
16 Mike Greenwell .01 .05
17 Tony Gwynn .30 .75
18 Von Hayes .01 .05
19 Tom Henke .01 .05
20 Orel Hershiser .02 .10
21 Teddy Higuera .01 .05
22 Brook Jacoby .01 .05
23 Wally Joyner .05 .15
24 Jimmy Key .02 .10
25 Don Mattingly .30 .75
26 Mark McGwire .40 1.00
27 Jack Morris .02 .10
28 Dale Murphy .07 .20
29 Matt Nokes .01 .05
30 Kirby Puckett .10 .30
31 Tim Raines .02 .10
32 Ryne Sandberg .20 .50
33 Benito Santiago .02 .10
34 Mike Schmidt .20 .50
35 Mike Scott .01 .05
36 Kevin Seitzer .02 .10
37 Larry Sheets .01 .05
38 Ruben Sierra .02 .10
39 Darryl Strawberry .02 .10
40 Rick Sutcliffe .01 .05
41 Danny Tartabull .01 .05
42 Alan Trammell .05 .15
43 Fernando Valenzuela .02 .10
44 Devon White .01 .05

1988 Fleer Hottest Stars

This 44-card boxed standard-size set was produced by Fleer for exclusive distribution by Revco Discount Drug stores all over the country. The cards feature full color fronts and red, white, and blue backs. The card fronts are easily distinguished by the flaming baseball in the lower right corner which says "Fleer Baseball's Hottest Stars." The player's picture is framed in red fading from orange down to yellow. The box for the cards proclaims "1988 Limited Edition Baseball's Hottest Stars" and is styled in blue, red, and yellow. The checklist for the set is given on the back of the set box. The box refers to Revco but there is no mention of Revco anywhere on the cards themselves. The card numbering is in alphabetical order by player's name.

COMP.FACT SET (44) 2.00 5.00
1 George Bell .01 .05
2 Wade Boggs .15 .40
3 Bobby Bonilla .02 .10
4 George Brett .20 .50
5 Jose Canseco .10 .30
6 Will Clark .20 .50
7 Roger Clemens .30 .75
8 Eric Davis .02 .10
9 Andre Dawson .07 .20
10 Tony Fernandez .02 .10
11 Julio Franco .02 .10
12 Gary Gaetti .02 .10
13 Dwight Gooden .02 .10
14 Mike Greenwell .01 .05
15 Tony Gwynn .30 .75
16 Rickey Henderson .25 .60
17 Keith Hernandez .02 .10
18 Tom Herr .01 .05
19 Orel Hershiser .02 .10
20 Ted Higuera .01 .05
21 Wally Joyner .02 .10
22 Jimmy Key .02 .10
23 Mark Langston .01 .05
24 Don Mattingly .30 .75
25 Jack McDowell .05 .15
26 Mark McGwire .40 1.00
27 Kevin Mitchell .02 .10
28 Jack Morris .02 .10
29 Dale Murphy .07 .20
30 Kirby Puckett .10 .30
31 Tim Raines .02 .10
32 Shane Rawley .01 .05
33 Benito Santiago .02 .10
34 Mike Schmidt .20 .50
35 Mike Scott .01 .05
36 Kevin Seitzer .01 .05
37 Larry Sheets .01 .05
38 Ruben Sierra .02 .10
39 Dave Smith .01 .05
40 Ozzie Smith .30 .75
41 Darryl Strawberry .02 .10
42 Rick Sutcliffe .01 .05
43 Pat Tabler .01 .05
44 Alan Trammell .05 .15

1988 Fleer League Leaders

This small boxed set of 44 standard-size cards was produced exclusively for Walgreen Drug Stores. The cards feature full color fronts and pink, white, and blue backs. The card fronts are distinguished by the blue solid and striped background behind the player's full-color photo. The box for the cards describes the set as the "1988 Fleer Baseball's League Leaders." The checklist for the set is given on the back of the set box. The card numbering is in alphabetical order by player's name.

COMP.FACT SET (44) 2.00 5.00
1 George Bell .01 .05
2 Wade Boggs .15 .40
3 Ivan Calderon .01 .05
4 Jose Canseco .15 .40
5 Will Clark .20 .50
6 Roger Clemens .30 .75
7 Vince Coleman .01 .05
8 Eric Davis .02 .10
9 Andre Dawson .10 .30
10 Bill Doran .01 .05
11 Dwight Evans .02 .10
12 Julio Franco .02 .10
13 Gary Gaetti .02 .10
14 Andres Galarraga .10 .30
15 Dwight Gooden .02 .10
16 Tony Gwynn .30 .75
17 Tom Henke .01 .05
18 Keith Hernandez .02 .10
19 Orel Hershiser .02 .10
20 Ted Higuera .01 .05
21 Kent Hrbek .02 .10
22 Wally Joyner .07 .20
23 Jimmy Key .02 .10
24 Mark Langston .01 .05
25 Don Mattingly .30 .75
26 Mark McGwire .40 1.00
27 Paul Molitor .20 .50
28 Jack Morris .02 .10
29 Dale Murphy .10 .30
30 Kirby Puckett .15 .40
31 Tim Raines .02 .10
32 Rick Reuschel .01 .05
33 Bret Saberhagen .02 .10
34 Benito Santiago .02 .10
35 Mike Schmidt .20 .50
36 Mike Scott .01 .05
37 Kevin Seitzer .02 .10
38 Larry Sheets .01 .05
39 Ruben Sierra .02 .10
40 Darryl Strawberry .02 .10
41 Rick Sutcliffe .01 .05
42 Alan Trammell .07 .20
43 Andy Van Slyke .02 .10
44 Todd Worrell .02 .10

1988 Fleer Mini

The 1988 Fleer "Classic Miniatures" set consists of 120 small cards with all new pictures of the players as compared to the 1988 Fleer regular issue. The cards are only 1 13/16" by 2 9/16", making them one of the smallest cards issued in the 1980's. Card backs provide career year-by-year statistics. The complete set was distributed in a green, red, white, and silver box along with 18 logo stickers. The card numbering is by alphabetical team order within league and alphabetically within each team. A rookie year card of Mark Grace highlights the set.

COMP.FACT SET (120) 4.00 10.00
1 Eddie Murray .20 .50
2 Dave Schmidt .01 .05
3 Larry Sheets .01 .05
4 Wade Boggs .20 .50
5 Roger Clemens .30 .75
6 Dwight Evans .02 .10
7 Mike Greenwell .01 .05
8 Sam Horn .01 .05
9 Lee Smith .02 .10
10 Brian Downing .01 .05
11 Wally Joyner .02 .10
12 Devon White .01 .05
13 Mike Witt .01 .05
14 Ivan Calderon .01 .05
15 Ozzie Guillen .02 .10
16 Jack McDowell .05 .15
17 Kenny Williams .08 .25
18 Joe Carter .07 .20
19 Julio Franco .02 .10
20 Pat Tabler .01 .05
21 Doyle Alexander .01 .05
22 Jack Morris .02 .10
23 Matt Nokes .01 .05
24 Walt Terrell .01 .05
25 Alan Trammell .05 .15
26 Bret Saberhagen .02 .10
27 Kevin Seitzer .02 .10
28 Danny Tartabull .01 .05
29 Gary Thurman .01 .05
30 Ted Higuera .01 .05
31 Paul Molitor .20 .50
32 Dan Plesac .01 .05
33 Robin Yount .10 .30
34 Gary Gaetti .02 .10
35 Kent Hrbek .02 .10
36 Kirby Puckett .10 .30
37 Jeff Reardon .02 .10
38 Frank Viola .01 .05
39 Jack Clark .02 .10
40 Rickey Henderson .25 .60
41 Don Mattingly .30 .75
42 Willie Randolph .02 .10
43 Dave Righetti .01 .05
44 Dave Winfield .15 .40
45 Jose Canseco .15 .40
46 Mark McGwire .40 1.00
47 Dave Parker .02 .10
48 Dave Stewart .02 .10
49 Walt Weiss .07 .20
50 Bob Welch .01 .05
51 Mickey Brantley .01 .05
52 Mark Langston .01 .05
53 Harold Reynolds .02 .10
54 Scott Fletcher .01 .05
55 Charlie Hough .02 .10
56 Pete Incaviglia .01 .05
57 Larry Parrish .01 .05
58 Ruben Sierra .02 .10
59 George Bell .01 .05
60 Mark Eichhorn .01 .05
61 Tony Fernandez .02 .10
62 Tom Henke .01 .05
63 Jimmy Key .02 .10
64 Dion James .01 .05
65 Dale Murphy .07 .20
66 Zane Smith .01 .05
67 Andre Dawson .07 .20
68 Mark Grace .60 1.50
69 Jerry Mumphrey .01 .05
70 Ryne Sandberg .30 .75
71 Rick Sutcliffe .01 .05
72 Kal Daniels .01 .05
73 Eric Davis .02 .10
74 John Franco .02 .10
75 Ron Robinson .01 .05
76 Jeff Treadway .01 .05
77 Kevin Bass .01 .05
78 Glenn Davis .01 .05
79 Nolan Ryan .60 1.50
80 Mike Scott .01 .05
81 Dave Smith .01 .05
82 Kirk Gibson .02 .10
83 Pedro Guerrero .01 .05
84 Orel Hershiser .02 .10
85 Steve Sax .01 .05
86 Fernando Valenzuela .02 .10
87 Tim Burke .01 .05
88 Andres Galarraga .07 .20
89 Neal Heaton .01 .05
90 Tim Raines .02 .10
91 Tim Wallach .01 .05
92 Dwight Gooden .02 .10
93 Keith Hernandez .02 .10
94 Gregg Jefferies .05 .15
95 Howard Johnson .01 .05
96 Roger McDowell .01 .05
97 Darryl Strawberry .02 .10
98 Steve Bedrosian .01 .05
99 Von Hayes .01 .05
100 Shane Rawley .01 .05
101 Juan Samuel .01 .05
102 Mike Schmidt .10 .30
103 Bobby Bonilla .02 .10
104 Mike Dunne .01 .05
105 Andy Van Slyke .02 .10
106 Vince Coleman .01 .05
107 Bob Horner .01 .05
108 Willie McGee .02 .10
109 Ozzie Smith .30 .75
110 John Tudor .01 .05
111 Todd Worrell .02 .10
112 Tony Gwynn .30 .75
113 John Kruk .02 .10
114 Lance McCullers .01 .05
115 Benito Santiago .02 .10
116 Will Clark .20 .50
117 Jeff Leonard .01 .05
118 Candy Maldonado .01 .05
119 Kirt Manwaring .01 .05
120 Don Robinson .01 .05

1988 Fleer Record Setters

This small boxed set of 44 standard-size cards was produced exclusively for Eckerd's Drug Stores. The cards feature full color fronts and red, white, and blue backs. The card fronts are distinguished by the red and blue frame around the player's full-color photo. The box for the cards describes the set as the "1988 Baseball Record Setters." The checklist for the set is given on the back of the set box. The card numbering is in alphabetical order by player's name.

COMP.FACT SET (44) 2.50 6.00
1 Jesse Barfield .01 .05
2 George Bell .01 .05
3 Wade Boggs .15 .40
4 Jose Canseco .10 .30
5 Jack Clark .02 .10
6 Will Clark .20 .50
7 Roger Clemens .30 .75
8 Alvin Davis .01 .05
9 Eric Davis .02 .10
10 Andre Dawson .07 .20
11 Mike Dunne .01 .05
12 John Franco .02 .10
13 Julio Franco .02 .10
14 Dwight Gooden .02 .10
15 Mark Gubicza .01 .05
Listed as Gubicko on box checklist
16 Ozzie Guillen .02 .10
17 Tony Gwynn .30 .75
18 Orel Hershiser .02 .10
19 Teddy Higuera .01 .05
20 Howard Johnson UER .01 .05
Missing '87 stats on card back
21 Wally Joyner .05 .15
22 Jimmy Key .02 .10
23 Jeff Leonard .01 .05
24 Don Mattingly .30 .75
25 Mark McGwire .40 1.00
26 Jack Morris .02 .10
27 Dale Murphy .07 .20
28 Larry Parrish .01 .05
29 Kirby Puckett .10 .30
30 Tim Raines .02 .10
31 Harold Reynolds .02 .10
32 Dave Righetti .01 .05
33 Cal Ripken .60 1.50
34 Benito Santiago .02 .10
35 Mike Schmidt .20 .50
36 Mike Scott .01 .05
37 Kevin Seitzer .02 .10
38 Ozzie Smith .30 .75
39 Darryl Strawberry .02 .10
40 Rick Sutcliffe .01 .05
41 Alan Trammell .05 .15
42 Frank Viola .01 .05
43 Mitch Williams .01 .05
44 Todd Worrell .02 .10

1988 Fleer Sluggers/Pitchers

Fleer produced this 44-card boxed standard-size set although it was primarily distributed by McCrory, McLellan, J.J Newberry, H.L.Green, T.G.Y., and other similar stores. The set is subtitled "Baseball's Best". The set was packaged in a green custom box along with six logo stickers. The set checklist is given on the back of the box. The bottoms of the boxes which held the individual set boxes also contained a panel of six cards; these box bottom cards were numbered C1 through C6. The card numbering is in alphabetical order by player's name.

COMP.FACT SET (44) 2.50 6.00
1 George Bell .01 .05
2 Wade Boggs .15 .40
3 Bobby Bonilla .02 .10
4 Tom Brunansky .01 .05
5 Ellis Burks .15 .40
6 Jose Canseco .10 .30
7 Joe Carter .07 .20
8 Will Clark .20 .50
9 Roger Clemens .30 .75
10 Eric Davis .02 .10
11 Glenn Davis .01 .05
12 Andre Dawson .07 .20
13 Dennis Eckersley .15 .40
14 Andres Galarraga .07 .20
15 Dwight Gooden .02 .10
16 Pedro Guerrero .01 .05
17 Tony Gwynn .30 .75
18 Orel Hershiser .02 .10
19 Ted Higuera .01 .05
20 Pete Incaviglia .01 .05
21 Danny Jackson .01 .05
22 Doug Jennings .01 .05
23 Mark Langston .01 .05
24 Dave LaPoint .01 .05
25 Mike LaValliere .01 .05
26 Don Mattingly .30 .75
27 Mark McGwire .40 1.00
28 Dale Murphy .07 .20
29 Ken Phelps .01 .05
30 Kirby Puckett .10 .30
31 Johnny Ray .01 .05
32 Jeff Reardon .02 .10
33 Dave Righetti .01 .05
34 Cal Ripken UER/(Misspelled Ripkin on card front) .60 1.50
35 Chris Sabo .02 .10
36 Mike Schmidt .20 .50
37 Mike Scott .02 .05
38 Kevin Seitzer .02 .10
39 Dave Stewart .02 .10
40 Darryl Strawberry .02 .10
41 Greg Swindell .01 .05
42 Frank Tanana .01 .05
43 Dave Winfield .20 .50
44 Todd Worrell .02 .10

1988 Fleer Sluggers/Pitchers Box Cards

The cards in this six-card set each measure the standard size. Cards have essentially the same design as the 1988 Fleer Sluggers vs. Pitchers set of Baseball's Best. The cards were printed on the bottom of the counter display box which held 24 small boxed sets; hence theoretically these box cards are 1/24 as plentiful as the regular boxed set cards. These six cards, numbered C1 to C6 are considered a separate set in their own right and are not typically included in a complete set of the 1988 Fleer Sluggers vs. Pitchers set of 44. The value of the panels uncut is slightly greater, perhaps by 25 percent greater, than the value of the individual cards cut up carefully.

COMPLETE SET (6) 3.00 8.00
C1 Ron Darling .40 1.00
C2 Rickey Henderson 1.25 3.00
C3 Carney Lansford .40 1.00
C4 Rafael Palmeiro 1.25 3.00
C5 Frank Viola .40 1.00
C6 Twins Logo/(Checklist back) .40 1.00

1988 Fleer Star Stickers

These Star Stickers were distributed as a separate issue by Fleer, with five star stickers and a logo sticker in each wax pack. The 132-card (sticker) set features 2 1/2" by 3 1/2" full-color fronts and even statistics on the sticker back, which is an indication that the Fleer Company understands that these stickers are rarely used as stickers but more like traditional cards. The fronts are surrounded by a silver-gray border and the backs are printed in red and black on white card stock. The set numbering is in alphabetical order within team and alphabetically by team within each league.

COMPLETE SET (132) 6.00 15.00
1 Mike Boddicker .01 .05
2 Eddie Murray .20 .50
3 Cal Ripken 1.00 2.50
4 Larry Sheets .01 .05
5 Wade Boggs .20 .50
6 Ellis Burks .20 1.00
7 Roger Clemens .40 1.25
8 Dwight Evans .02 .10
9 Mike Greenwell .01 .05
10 Bruce Hurst .01 .05
11 Brian Downing .01 .05
12 Wally Joyner .02 .10
13 Mike Witt .01 .05
14 Ivan Calderon .01 .05
15 Jose DeLeon .01 .05
16 Ozzie Guillen .60 1.50
17 Bobby Thigpen .01 .05
18 Joe Carter .07 .20
19 Julio Franco .02 .10
20 Brook Jacoby .01 .05
21 Cory Snyder .01 .05
22 Pat Tabler .01 .05
23 Doyle Alexander .01 .05
24 Kirk Gibson .02 .10
25 Mike Henneman .02 .10
26 Jack Morris .02 .10
27 Matt Nokes .01 .05
28 Walt Terrell .01 .05
29 Alan Trammell .05 .15
30 George Brett .40 1.25
31 Charlie Leibrandt .01 .05
32 Bret Saberhagen .02 .10
33 Kevin Seitzer .01 .05
34 Danny Tartabull .01 .05
35 Frank White .02 .10
36 Rob Deer .01 .05
37 Ted Higuera .01 .05
38 Paul Molitor .20 .50
39 Dan Plesac .01 .05
40 Robin Yount .15 .40
41 Bert Blyleven .02 .10
42 Tom Brunansky .01 .05
43 Gary Gaetti .02 .10
44 Kent Hrbek .02 .10
45 Kirby Puckett .20 .50
46 Jeff Reardon .02 .10
47 Frank Viola .01 .05
48 Don Mattingly .50 1.25
49 Mike Pagliarulo .01 .05
50 Willie Randolph .02 .10
51 Rick Rhoden .01 .05
52 Dave Righetti .01 .05
53 Dave Winfield .15 .40
54 Jose Canseco .15 .40
55 Carney Lansford .02 .10
56 Mark McGwire .60 1.50
57 Dave Stewart .02 .10
58 Curt Young .01 .05
59 Alvin Davis .01 .05
60 Mark Langston .01 .05
61 Ken Phelps .01 .05
62 Harold Reynolds .02 .10
63 Scott Fletcher .01 .05
64 Charlie Hough .02 .10
65 Pete Incaviglia .01 .05
66 Oddibe McDowell .01 .05
67 Pete O'Brien .01 .05
68 Larry Parrish .01 .05
69 Ruben Sierra .02 .10
70 Jesse Barfield .01 .05
71 George Bell .01 .05
72 Tony Fernandez .02 .10
73 Tom Henke .01 .05
74 Jimmy Key .01 .05
75 Lloyd Moseby .01 .05
76 Dion James .01 .05
77 Dale Murphy .07 .20
78 Zane Smith .01 .05
79 Andre Dawson .07 .20
80 Ryne Sandberg .40 1.00
81 Rick Sutcliffe .01 .05
82 Kal Daniels .01 .05
83 Eric Davis .02 .10
84 John Franco .02 .10
85 Kevin Bass .01 .05
86 Glenn Davis .01 .05
87 Bill Doran .01 .05
88 Nolan Ryan 1.00 2.50
89 Mike Scott .01 .05
90 Dave Smith .01 .05
91 Pedro Guerrero .01 .05
92 Orel Hershiser .02 .10
93 Steve Sax .01 .05
94 Fernando Valenzuela .02 .10
95 Tim Burke .01 .05
96 Andres Galarraga .07 .20
97 Tim Raines .02 .10
98 Tim Wallach .01 .05
99 Mitch Webster .01 .05
100 Ron Darling .01 .05
101 Sid Fernandez .01 .05
102 Dwight Gooden .02 .10
103 Keith Hernandez .02 .10
104 Howard Johnson .01 .05
105 Roger McDowell .01 .05
106 Darryl Strawberry .02 .10
107 Steve Bedrosian .01 .05
108 Von Hayes .01 .05
109 Shane Rawley .01 .05
110 Juan Samuel .01 .05
111 Mike Schmidt .20 .50
112 Milt Thompson .01 .05
113 Sid Bream .01 .05
114 Bobby Bonilla .02 .10
115 Mike Dunne .01 .05
116 Andy Van Slyke .02 .10
117 Vince Coleman .01 .05
118 Willie McGee .02 .10
119 Terry Pendleton .02 .10
120 Ozzie Smith .40 1.00
121 John Tudor .01 .05
122 Todd Worrell .02 .10
123 Tony Gwynn .50 1.25
124 John Kruk .08 .25
125 Benito Santiago .02 .10
126 Will Clark .20 .50
127 Dave Dravecky .02 .10
128 Jeff Leonard .01 .05
129 Candy Maldonado .01 .05
130 Rick Reuschel .01 .05
131 Don Robinson .01 .05
132 Checklist Card .01 .05

1988 Fleer Stickers Wax Box Cards

The bottoms of the Star Sticker wax boxes contained two different sets of four cards done in a similar format to the stickers; these cards (they are not stickers but truly cards) are numbered with the prefix S and are considered a separate set. The value of the panels uncut is slightly greater, perhaps by 25 percent greater, than the value of the individual cards cut up carefully.

COMPLETE SET (8) 1.50 4.00
S1 Mark McGwire 1.50 4.00
Eric Davis
S2 Gary Carter .40 1.00
S3 Kevin Mitchell .30 .75
S4 Ron Guidry .30 .75
S5 Rickey Henderson .75 2.00
S6 Don Baylor .30 .75
S7 Giants Logo .20 .50
S8 Detroit Logo .20 .50

1988 Fleer Superstars

Fleer produced this 44-card boxed standard-size s although it was primarily distributed by McCrory, McLellan, J.J Newberry, H.L.Green, T.G.Y., and oth similar stores. The set is subtitled "Fleer Superstars". The set was packaged in a red, white, blue, and yellow custom box along with six logo stickers. Th set checklist is given on the back of the box. The bottoms of the boxes which held the individual set boxes also contained a panel of six cards; these bo bottom cards were numbered C1 through C6. The card numbering is in alphabetical order by player's name.

COMP.FACT SET (44) 2.50 6.0
1 Steve Bedrosian .01 .0
2 George Bell .01 .0
3 Wade Boggs .15 .4
4 Barry Bonds .30 1.0
5 Jose Canseco .10 .3
6 Joe Carter .07 .2
7 Jack Clark .02 .1
8 Will Clark .20 .5
9 Roger Clemens .30 .7
10 Alvin Davis .01 .0
11 Eric Davis .02 .
12 Glenn Davis .01 .0
13 Andre Dawson .07 .2
14 Dwight Gooden .02 .1
15 Orel Hershiser .02 .1
16 Teddy Higuera .01 .0
17 Kent Hrbek .02 .1
18 Wally Joyner .02 .1
19 Jimmy Key .01 .0
20 John Kruk .02 .1
21 Jeff Leonard .01 .0
22 Don Mattingly .30 .7
23 Mark McGwire .40 1.0
24 Kevin McReynolds .01 .0
25 Dale Murphy .07 .2
26 Matt Nokes .01 .0
27 Terry Pendleton .02 .1
28 Kirby Puckett .15 .4
29 Tim Raines .02 .1
30 Rick Rhoden .01 .0
31 Cal Ripken .60 1.5
32 Benito Santiago .02 .1
33 Mike Schmidt .15 .4
34 Mike Scott .01 .0
35 Kevin Seitzer .02 .1
36 Ruben Sierra .02 .1
37 Cory Snyder .01 .0
38 Darryl Strawberry .02 .1
39 Rick Sutcliffe .01 .0
40 Danny Tartabull .01 .0
41 Alan Trammell .05 .1
42 Kenny Williams .08 .2
43 Mike Witt .01 .0
44 Robin Yount .15 .4

1988 Fleer Superstars Box Cards

The cards in this six-card set each measure the standard size. Cards have essentially the same design as the 1988 Fleer Superstars set. The cards were printed on the bottom of the counter display b which held 24 small boxed sets; hence theoretically these box cards are 1/24 as plentiful as the regular boxed set cards. These six cards, numbered C1 to C are considered a separate set in their own right and are not typically included in a complete set of the 1988 Fleer Superstars set of 44. The value of the panels uncut is slightly greater, perhaps by 25 percent greater, than the value of the individual car cut up carefully.

COMPLETE SET (6) 4.00 10.0
C1 Pete Incaviglia .20 .5
C2 Rickey Henderson 2.00 5.0
C3 Tony Fernandez .20 .5
C4 Shane Rawley .20 .5
C5 Ryne Sandberg 2.00 5.0
C6 Cardinals Logo/(Checklist back) .20 .5

1988 Fleer Team Leaders

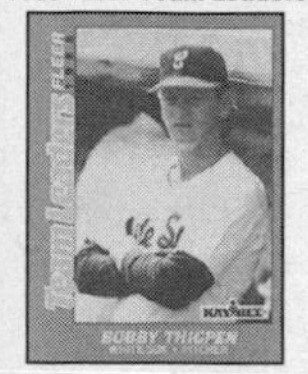

44-card boxed standard-size set was produced leer for exclusive distribution by Kay Bee Toys is sometimes referred to as the Fleer Kay Bee set. team logo stickers are included in the box with complete set. The numerical checklist on the back ne box shows that the set is numbered nabetically. The cards have a distinctive red der on the fronts. The Kay Bee logo is printed in ower right corner of the obverse of each card.

MP.FACT SET (44) 3.00 8.00
eorge Bell .01 .05
ade Boggs .20 .50
se Canseco .15 .40
ill Clark .25 .60
oger Clemens .30 .75
ic Davis .02 .10
ndre Dawson .10 .30
ilio Franco .02 .10
ndres Galarraga .10 .30
Dwight Gooden .02 .10
Tony Gwynn .30 .75
Tom Henke .01 .05
Orel Hershiser .02 .10
Kent Hrbek .02 .10
Ted Higuera .01 .05
Wally Joyner .07 .20
Jimmy Key .01 .05
Mark Langston .01 .05
Don Mattingly .30 .75
Willie McGee .02 .10
Mark McGwire .40 1.00
Paul Molitor .20 .50
Jack Morris .02 .10
Dale Murphy .10 .30
Larry Parrish .01 .05
Kirby Puckett .15 .40
Tim Raines .02 .10
Jeff Reardon .02 .10
Dave Righetti .01 .05
Cal Ripken .60 1.50
Don Robinson .01 .05
Bret Saberhagen .02 .10
Juan Samuel .01 .05
Mike Schmidt .20 .50
Mike Scott .01 .05
Kevin Seitzer .02 .10
Dave Smith .01 .05
Ozzie Smith .30 .75
Zane Smith .01 .05
Darryl Strawberry .02 .10
Rick Sutcliffe .01 .05
Bobby Thigpen .01 .05
Alan Trammell .07 .20
Andy Van Slyke .01 .05

1989 Fleer

s set consists of 660 standard-size cards. Cards e primarily issued in 15-card wax packs, rack ks and hobby and retail factory sets. Card fronts ture a distinctive gray border background with ite and yellow trim. Cards are again organized habetically within teams and teams ordered by vious season record. The last 33 cards in the set nsist of Specials (628-639), Rookie Pairs (640-), and checklists (654-660). Approximately half the California Angels players have white rather n yellow halos. Certain Oakland A's player cards e red instead of green lines for front photo ders. Checklist cards are available either with or hout positions listed for each player. Rookie rds in this set include Craig Biggio, Ken Griffey Randy Johnson, Gary Sheffield, and John Smoltz. interesting variation was discovered in late 1999 Beckett Grading Services on the Randy Johnson (card number 381). It seems the most common sion features a crudely-blacked out image of an field billboard. A scarcer version clearly reveals words "Marlboro" on the billboard. One of the bby's most notorious errors and variations hails m this product. Card number 616, Billy Ripken, s originally published with a four-letter word printed on the bat. Needless to say, this caused te a stir in 1989 and the card was quickly rinted. Because of this, several different variations re printed with the final solution (and the most mmon version of this card) being a black box ering the bat knob. The first variation is still ively sought after in the hobby and the other sions are still sought after by collectors seeking a aster" set.

COMPLETE SET (660) 6.00 15.00
COMP.FACT.SET (672) 6.00 15.00
1 Don Baylor .02 .10
2 Lance Blankenship RC .02 .10
3 Todd Burns UER .01 .05
Wrong birthdate;
before
after All-Star
stats missing
4 Greg Cadaret UER .01 .05
All-Star Break stats
show 3 losses, should be 2
5 Jose Canseco .08 .25
6 Storm Davis .01 .05
7 Dennis Eckersley .05 .15
8 Mike Gallego .01 .05
9 Ron Hassey .01 .05
10 Dave Henderson .01 .05
11 Rick Honeycutt .01 .05
12 Glenn Hubbard .01 .05
13 Stan Javier .01 .05
14 Doug Jennings RC .01 .05
15 Felix Jose RC .02 .10
16 Carney Lansford .02 .10
17 Mark McGwire .40 1.00
18 Gene Nelson .01 .05
19 Dave Parker .02 .10
20 Eric Plunk .01 .05
21 Luis Polonia .01 .05
22 Terry Steinbach .02 .10
23 Dave Stewart .02 .10
24 Walt Weiss .01 .05
25 Bob Welch .02 .10
26 Curt Young .01 .05
27 Rick Aguilera .01 .05
28 Wally Backman .01 .05
29 Mark Carreon UER .01 .05
After All-Star Break
batting 7.14
30 Gary Carter .02 .10
31 David Cone .02 .10
32 Ron Darling .02 .10
33 Len Dykstra .02 .10
34 Kevin Elster .01 .05
35 Sid Fernandez .01 .05
36 Dwight Gooden .02 .10
37 Keith Hernandez .02 .10
38 Gregg Jefferies .01 .05
39 Howard Johnson .02 .10
40 Terry Leach .01 .05
41 Dave Magadan UER .01 .05
Bio says 15 doubles,
should be 13
42 Bob McClure .01 .05
43 Roger McDowell UER .01 .05
Led Mets with 58
should be 62
44 Kevin McReynolds .01 .05
45 Keith A. Miller .01 .05
46 Randy Myers .02 .10
47 Bob Ojeda .01 .05
48 Mackey Sasser .01 .05
49 Darryl Strawberry .02 .10
50 Tim Teufel .01 .05
51 Dave West RC .02 .10
52 Mookie Wilson .02 .10
53 Dave Anderson .01 .05
54 Tim Belcher .01 .05
55 Mike Davis .01 .05
56 Mike Devereaux .01 .05
57 Kirk Gibson .02 .10
58 Alfredo Griffin .01 .05
59 Chris Gwynn .01 .05
60 Jeff Hamilton .01 .05
61A Danny Heep ERR .08 .25
Lake Hills
61B Danny Heep COR .01 .05
San Antonio
62 Orel Hershiser .02 .10
63 Brian Holton .01 .05
64 Jay Howell .01 .05
65 Tim Leary .01 .05
66 Mike Marshall .01 .05
67 Ramon Martinez RC .08 .25
68 Jesse Orosco .01 .05
69 Alejandro Pena .01 .05
70 Steve Sax .01 .05
71 Mike Scioscia .02 .10
72 Mike Sharperson .01 .05
73 John Shelby .01 .05
74 Franklin Stubbs .01 .05
75 John Tudor .02 .10
76 Fernando Valenzuela .02 .10
77 Tracy Woodson .01 .05
78 Marty Barrett .01 .05
79 Todd Benzinger .01 .05
80 Mike Boddicker UER .01 .05
Rochester in '76,
should be '78
81 Wade Boggs .05 .15
82 Oil Can Boyd .01 .05
83 Ellis Burks .02 .10
84 Rick Cerone .01 .05
85 Roger Clemens .40 1.00
86 Steve Curry .01 .05
87 Dwight Evans .05 .15
88 Wes Gardner .01 .05
89 Rich Gedman .01 .05
90 Mike Greenwell .01 .05
91 Bruce Hurst .01 .05
92 Dennis Lamp .01 .05
93 Spike Owen .01 .05
94 Larry Parrish UER .01 .05
Before All-Star Break
batting 1.90
95 Carlos Quintana RC .02 .10
96 Jody Reed .01 .05
97 Jim Rice .02 .10
98A Kevin Romine ERR .08 .25
Photo actually
Randy Kutcher batting
98B Kevin Romine COR .01 .05
Arms folded
99 Lee Smith .02 .10
100 Mike Smithson .01 .05
101 Bob Stanley .01 .05
102 Allan Anderson .01 .05
103 Keith Atherton .01 .05
104 Juan Berenguer .01 .05
105 Bert Blyleven .02 .10
106 Eric Bullock UER .01 .05
Bats
Throws Right,
should be Left
107 Randy Bush .01 .05
108 John Christensen .01 .05
109 Mark Davidson .01 .05
110 Gary Gaetti .02 .10
111 Greg Gagne .01 .05
112 Dan Gladden .01 .05
113 German Gonzalez .01 .05
114 Brian Harper .01 .05
115 Tom Herr .01 .05
116 Kent Hrbek .02 .10
117 Gene Larkin .01 .05
118 Tim Laudner .01 .05
119 Charlie Lea .01 .05
120 Steve Lombardozzi .01 .05
121A John Moses ERR .08 .25
Tempe
121B John Moses COR .01 .05
Phoenix
122 Al Newman .01 .05
123 Mark Portugal .01 .05
124 Kirby Puckett .08 .25
125 Jeff Reardon .02 .10
126 Fred Toliver .01 .05
127 Frank Viola .02 .10
128 Doyle Alexander .01 .05
129 Dave Bergman .01 .05
130A Tom Brookens ERR .30 .75
130B Tom Brookens COR .01 .05
131 Paul Gibson .01 .05
132A Mike Heath ERR .30 .75
132B Mike Heath COR .01 .05
133 Don Heinkel .01 .05
134 Mike Henneman .01 .05
135 Guillermo Hernandez .01 .05
136 Eric King .01 .05
137 Chet Lemon .02 .10
138 Fred Lynn UER .02 .10
'74 and '75 stats missing
139 Jack Morris .02 .10
140 Matt Nokes .01 .05
141 Gary Pettis .01 .05
142 Ted Power .01 .05
143 Jeff M. Robinson .01 .05
144 Luis Salazar .01 .05
145 Steve Searcy .01 .05
146 Pat Sheridan .01 .05
147 Frank Tanana .02 .10
148 Alan Trammell .02 .10
149 Walt Terrell .01 .05
150 Jim Walewander .01 .05
151 Lou Whitaker .02 .10
152 Tim Birtsas .01 .05
153 Tom Browning .01 .05
154 Keith Brown .01 .05
155 Norm Charlton RC .08 .25
156 Dave Concepcion .02 .10
157 Kal Daniels .01 .05
158 Eric Davis .02 .10
159 Bo Diaz .01 .05
160 Rob Dibble RC .15 .40
161 Nick Esasky .01 .05
162 John Franco .02 .10
163 Danny Jackson .01 .05
164 Barry Larkin .05 .15
165 Rob Murphy .01 .05
166 Paul O'Neill .05 .15
167 Jeff Reed .01 .05
168 Jose Rijo .02 .10
169 Ron Robinson .01 .05
170 Chris Sabo RC .15 .40
171 Candy Sierra .01 .05
172 Van Snider .01 .05
173A Jeff Treadway 10.00 25.00
173B Jeff Treadway .01 .05
No target on front
174 Frank Williams UER .01 .05
After All-Star Break
stats are jumbled
175 Herm Winningham .01 .05
176 Jim Adduci .01 .05
177 Don August .01 .05
178 Mike Birkbeck .01 .05
179 Chris Bosio .01 .05
180 Glenn Braggs .01 .05
181 Greg Brock .01 .05
182 Mark Clear .01 .05
183 Chuck Crim .01 .05
184 Rob Deer .01 .05
185 Tom Filer .01 .05
186 Jim Gantner .01 .05
187 Darryl Hamilton RC .08 .25
188 Ted Higuera .01 .05
189 Odell Jones .01 .05
190 Jeffrey Leonard .01 .05
191 Joey Meyer .01 .05
192 Paul Mirabella .01 .05
193 Paul Molitor .02 .10
194 Charlie O'Brien .01 .05
195 Dan Plesac .01 .05
196 Gary Sheffield RC .60 1.50
197 B.J. Surhoff .02 .10
198 Dale Sveum .01 .05
199 Bill Wegman .01 .05
200 Robin Yount .15 .40
201 Rafael Belliard .01 .05
202 Barry Bonds .60 1.50
203 Bobby Bonilla .02 .10
204 Sid Bream .01 .05
205 Benny Distefano .01 .05
206 Doug Drabek .01 .05
207 Mike Dunne .01 .05
208 Felix Fermin .01 .05
209 Brian Fisher .01 .05
210 Jim Gott .01 .05
211 Bob Kipper .01 .05
212 Dave LaPoint .01 .05
213 Mike LaValliere .01 .05
214 Jose Lind .01 .05
215 Junior Ortiz .01 .05
216 Vicente Palacios .01 .05
217 Tom Prince .01 .05
218 Gary Redus .01 .05
219 R.J. Reynolds .01 .05
220 Jeff D. Robinson .01 .05
221 John Smiley .01 .05
222 Andy Van Slyke .05 .15
223 Bob Walk .01 .05
224 Glenn Wilson .01 .05
225 Jesse Barfield .02 .10
226 George Bell .02 .10
227 Pat Borders RC .08 .25
228 John Cerutti .01 .05
229 Jim Clancy .01 .05
230 Mark Eichhorn .01 .05
231 Tony Fernandez .02 .10
232 Cecil Fielder .02 .10
233 Mike Flanagan .01 .05
234 Kelly Gruber .01 .05
235 Tom Henke .01 .05
236 Jimmy Key .02 .10
237 Rick Leach .01 .05
238 Manny Lee UER .01 .05
Bio says regular
shortstop, sic,
Tony Fernandez
239 Nelson Liriano .01 .05
240 Fred McGriff .05 .15
241 Lloyd Moseby .01 .05
242 Rance Mulliniks .01 .05
243 Jeff Musselman .01 .05
244 Dave Stieb .02 .10
245 Todd Stottlemyre .01 .05
246 Duane Ward .01 .05
247 David Wells .02 .10
248 Ernie Whitt UER .01 .05
HR total 21,
should be 121
249 Luis Aguayo .01 .05
250A Neil Allen ERR .30 .75
250B Neil Allen COR .02 .10
Syosset, NY
251 John Candelaria .01 .05
252 Jack Clark .02 .10
253 Richard Dotson .01 .05
254 Rickey Henderson .08 .25
255 Tommy John .02 .10
256 Roberto Kelly .01 .05
257 Al Leiter .08 .25
258 Don Mattingly .25 .60
259 Dale Mohorcic .01 .05
260 Hal Morris RC .08 .25
261 Scott Nielsen .01 .05
262 Mike Pagliarulo UER .01 .05
Wrong birthdate
263 Hipolito Pena .01 .05
264 Ken Phelps .01 .05
265 Willie Randolph .02 .10
266 Rick Rhoden .01 .05
267 Dave Righetti .02 .10
268 Rafael Santana .01 .05
269 Steve Shields .01 .05
270 Joel Skinner .01 .05
271 Don Slaught .01 .05
272 Claudell Washington .01 .05
273 Gary Ward .01 .05
274 Dave Winfield .02 .10
275 Luis Aquino .01 .05
276 Floyd Bannister .01 .05
277 George Brett .25 .60
278 Bill Buckner .02 .10
279 Nick Capra .01 .05
280 Jose DeJesus .01 .05
281 Steve Farr .01 .05
282 Jerry Don Gleaton .01 .05
283 Mark Gubicza .01 .05
284 T.Gordon RC UER .20 .50
285 Bo Jackson .08 .25
286 Charlie Leibrandt .01 .05
287 Mike Macfarlane RC .08 .25
288 Jeff Montgomery .01 .05
289 Bill Pecota UER .01 .05
Photo actually
Brad Wellman
290 Jamie Quirk .01 .05
291 Bret Saberhagen .02 .10
292 Kevin Seitzer .01 .05
293 Kurt Stillwell .01 .05
294 Pat Tabler .01 .05
295 Danny Tartabull .01 .05
296 Gary Thurman .01 .05
297 Frank White .01 .05
298 Willie Wilson .02 .10
299 Roberto Alomar .08 .25
300 S.Alomar Jr. RC UER .15 .40
Wrong birthdate, says
6/16/66, should say
6/18/66
301 Chris Brown .01 .05
302 Mike Brumley UER .01 .05
133 hits in '88,
should be 134
303 Mark Davis .01 .05
304 Mark Grant .01 .05
305 Tony Gwynn .10 .30
306 Greg W. Harris RC .02 .10
307 Andy Hawkins .01 .05
308 Jimmy Jones .01 .05
309 John Kruk .02 .10
310 Dave Leiper .01 .05
311 Carmelo Martinez .01 .05
312 Lance McCullers .01 .05
313 Keith Moreland .01 .05
314 Dennis Rasmussen .01 .05
315 Randy Ready UER .01 .05
1214 games in '88,
should be 114
316 Benito Santiago .02 .10
317 Eric Show .01 .05
318 Todd Simmons .01 .05
319 Garry Templeton .02 .10
320 Dickie Thon .01 .05
321 Ed Whitson .01 .05
322 Marvell Wynne .01 .05
323 Mike Aldrete .01 .05
324 Brett Butler .02 .10
325 Will Clark UER .05 .15
Three consecutive
100 RBI seasons
326 Kelly Downs UER .01 .05
'88 stats missing
327 Dave Dravecky .01 .05
328 Scott Garrelts .01 .05
329 Atlee Hammaker .01 .05
330 Charlie Hayes RC .08 .25
331 Mike Krukow .01 .05
332 Craig Lefferts .01 .05
333 Candy Maldonado .01 .05
334 Kirt Manwaring UER .01 .05
Bats Rights
335 Bob Melvin .01 .05
336 Kevin Mitchell .02 .10
337 Donell Nixon .01 .05
338 Tony Perezchica .01 .05
339 Joe Price .01 .05
340 Rick Reuschel .02 .10
341 Earnest Riles .01 .05
342 Don Robinson .01 .05
343 Chris Speier .01 .05
344 Robby Thompson UER .01 .05
West Plam Beach
345 Jose Uribe .01 .05
346 Matt Williams .08 .25
347 Trevor Wilson RC .02 .10
348 Juan Agosto .01 .05
349 Larry Andersen .01 .05
350A Alan Ashby ERR .75 2.00
350B Alan Ashby COR .01 .05
351 Kevin Bass .01 .05
352 Buddy Bell .02 .10
353 Craig Biggio RC 1.00 2.50
354 Danny Darwin .01 .05
355 Glenn Davis .01 .05
356 Jim Deshaies .01 .05
357 Bill Doran .01 .05
358 John Fishel RC .01 .05
359 Billy Hatcher .01 .05
360 Bob Knepper .01 .05
361 Louie Meadows UER RC .01 .05
Bio says 10 EBH's
and 6 SB's in '88,
should be 3 and 4
362 Dave Meads .01 .05
363 Jim Pankovits .01 .05
364 Terry Puhl .01 .05
365 Rafael Ramirez .01 .05
366 Craig Reynolds .01 .05
367 Mike Scott .02 .10
Card number listed
as 368 on Astros CL
368 Nolan Ryan .40 1.00
369 Dave Smith .01 .05
370 Gerald Young .01 .05
371 Hubie Brooks .01 .05
372 Tim Burke .01 .05
373 John Dopson .01 .05
374 Mike R. Fitzgerald .01 .05
375 Tom Foley .01 .05
376 Andres Galarraga UER .02 .10
Home: Caracus
377 Neal Heaton .01 .05
378 Joe Hesketh .01 .05
379 Brian Holman RC .02 .10
380 Rex Hudler .01 .05
381 Randy Johnson RC UER .75 2.00
381B R.Johnson Marlboro ERR 12.50 30.00
381C R.Johnson Red Tint
381D R.Johnson Black Box
381E R.Johnson Green Tint
382 Wallace Johnson .01 .05
383 Tracy Jones .01 .05
384 Dave Martinez .01 .05
385 Dennis Martinez .02 .10
386 Andy McGaffigan .01 .05
387 Otis Nixon .01 .05
388 Johnny Paredes .01 .05
389 Jeff Parrett .01 .05
390 Pascual Perez .01 .05
391 Tim Raines .02 .10
392 Luis Rivera .01 .05
393 Nelson Santovenia .01 .05
394 Bryn Smith .01 .05
395 Tim Wallach .01 .05
396 Andy Allanson UER .01 .05
1214 hits in '88,
should be 114
397 Rod Allen RC .01 .05
398 Scott Bailes .01 .05
399 Tom Candiotti .01 .05
400 Joe Carter .02 .10
401 Carmen Castillo UER .01 .05
After All-Star Break
batting 2.50
402 Dave Clark UER .01 .05
Card front shows
position as Rookie;
after All-Star Break
batting 3.14
403 John Farrell UER .01 .05
Typo in runs
allowed in '88
404 Julio Franco .02 .10
405 Don Gordon .01 .05
406 Mel Hall .01 .05
407 Brad Havens .01 .05
408 Brook Jacoby .01 .05
409 Doug Jones .01 .05
410 Jeff Kaiser .01 .05
411 Luis Medina .01 .05
412 Cory Snyder .01 .05
413 Greg Swindell .01 .05
414 Ron Tingley UER .01 .05
Hit HR in first ML
at-bat, should be
first AL at-bat
415 Willie Upshaw .01 .05
416 Ron Washington .01 .05
417 Rich Yett .01 .05
418 Damon Berryhill .01 .05
419 Mike Bielecki .01 .05
420 Doug Dascenzo .01 .05
421 Jody Davis UER .01 .05
Braves stats for
'88 missing
422 Andre Dawson .02 .10
423 Frank DiPino .01 .05
424 Shawon Dunston .01 .05
425 Rich Gossage .02 .10
426 Mark Grace UER .08 .25
Minor League stats
for '88 missing
427 Mike Harkey RC .02 .10
428 Darrin Jackson .02 .10
429 Les Lancaster .01 .05
430 Vance Law .01 .05
431 Greg Maddux .20 .50
432 Jamie Moyer .02 .10
433 Al Nipper .01 .05
434 Rafael Palmeiro UER .08 .25
170 hits in '88,
should be 178
435 Pat Perry .01 .05
436 Jeff Pico .01 .05
437 Ryne Sandberg .15 .40
438 Calvin Schiraldi .01 .05
439 Rick Sutcliffe .02 .10
440A Manny Trillo ERR .75 2.00
440B Manny Trillo COR .01 .05
441 Gary Varsho UER .01 .05
Wrong birthdate;
.303 should be .302;
11/28 should be 9/19
442 Mitch Webster .01 .05
443 Luis Alicea RC .08 .25
444 Tom Brunansky .01 .05
445 Vince Coleman UER .01 .05
Third straight with 83
should be fourth straight with 81
446 John Costello UER RC .01 .05
Home California,
should be New York
447 Danny Cox .01 .05
448 Ken Dayley .01 .05
449 Jose DeLeon .01 .05
450 Curt Ford .01 .05
451 Pedro Guerrero .02 .10
452 Bob Horner .02 .10
453 Tim Jones .01 .05
454 Steve Lake .01 .05
455 Joe Magrane UER .01 .05
Des Moines,IO
456 Greg Mathews .01 .05
457 Willie McGee .02 .10
458 Larry McWilliams .01 .05
459 Jose Oquendo .01 .05
460 Tony Pena .01 .05
461 Terry Pendleton .02 .10
462 Steve Peters UER .01 .05
Lives in Harrah,
not Harah
463 Ozzie Smith .15 .40
464 Scott Terry .01 .05
465 Denny Walling .01 .05
466 Todd Worrell .01 .05
467 Tony Armas UER .02 .10
Before All-Star Break
batting 2.39
468 Dante Bichette RC .15 .40
469 Bob Boone .02 .10
470 Terry Clark .01 .05
471 Stu Cliburn .01 .05
472 Mike Cook UER .01 .05
TM near Angels logo
missing from front
473 Sherman Corbett RC .01 .05
474 Chili Davis .02 .10
475 Brian Downing .02 .10
476 Jim Eppard .01 .05
477 Chuck Finley .02 .10
478 Willie Fraser .01 .05
479 Bryan Harvey UER RC .08 .25
ML record shows 0-0,
should be 7-5
480 Jack Howell .01 .05
481 Wally Joyner UER .02 .10
Yorba Linda, GA
482 Jack Lazorko .01 .05
483 Kirk McCaskill .01 .05
484 Mark McLemore .01 .05
485 Greg Minton .01 .05
486 Dan Petry .01 .05
487 Johnny Ray .01 .05
488 Dick Schofield .01 .05
489 Devon White .02 .10
490 Mike Witt .01 .05
491 Harold Baines .02 .10
492 Daryl Boston .01 .05
493 Ivan Calderon UER .01 .05
'80 stats shifted
494 Mike Diaz .01 .05
495 Carlton Fisk .05 .15
496 Dave Gallagher .01 .05
497 Ozzie Guillen .02 .10
498 Shawn Hillegas .01 .05
499 Lance Johnson .01 .05
500 Barry Jones .01 .05
501 Bill Long .01 .05
502 Steve Lyons .01 .05
503 Fred Manrique .01 .05
504 Jack McDowell .02 .10
505 Donn Pall .01 .05
506 Kelly Paris .01 .05
507 Dan Pasqua .01 .05
508 Ken Patterson .01 .05
509 Melido Perez .01 .05
510 Jerry Reuss .01 .05
511 Mark Salas .01 .05
512 Bobby Thigpen UER .01 .05
'86 ERA 4.69,
should be 4.68
513 Mike Woodard .01 .05
514 Bob Brower .01 .05
515 Steve Buechele .01 .05
516 Jose Cecena .01 .05
517 Cecil Espy .01 .05
518 Scott Fletcher .01 .05
519 Cecilio Guante .01 .05
'87 Yankee stats
are off-centered
520 Jose Guzman .01 .05
521 Ray Hayward .01 .05
522 Charlie Hough .02 .10
523 Pete Incaviglia .01 .05
524 Mike Jeffcoat .01 .05
525 Paul Kilgus .01 .05
526 Chad Kreuter RC .08 .25
527 Jeff Kunkel .01 .05
528 Oddibe McDowell .01 .05
529 Pete O'Brien .01 .05
530 Geno Petralli .01 .05
531 Jeff Russell .01 .05
532 Ruben Sierra .02 .10
533 Mike Stanley .01 .05
534A Ed VandeBerg ERR .75 2.00
534B Ed VandeBerg COR .01 .05
535 Curtis Wilkerson ERR .01 .05
Pitcher headings
at bottom
536 Mitch Williams .01 .05
537 Bobby Witt UER .01 .05
'85 ERA .643,
should be 6.43
538 Steve Balboni .01 .05
539 Scott Bankhead .01 .05
540 Scott Bradley .01 .05
541 Mickey Brantley .01 .05
542 Jay Buhner .02 .10
543 Mike Campbell .01 .05
544 Darnell Coles .01 .05
545 Henry Cotto .01 .05
546 Alvin Davis .01 .05
547 Mario Diaz .01 .05
548 Ken Griffey Jr. RC 5.00 12.00
549 Erik Hanson RC .08 .25
550 Mike Jackson UER .01 .05
Lifetime ERA 3.345,
should be 3.45
551 Mark Langston .01 .05
552 Edgar Martinez .08 .25
553 Bill McGuire .01 .05
554 Mike Moore .01 .05
555 Jim Presley .01 .05
556 Rey Quinones .01 .05
557 Jerry Reed .01 .05
558 Harold Reynolds .02 .10

559 Mike Schooler .01 .05
560 Bill Swift .01 .05
561 Dave Valle .01 .05
562 Steve Bedrosian .01 .05
563 Phil Bradley .01 .05
564 Don Carman .01 .05
565 Bob Dernier .01 .05
566 Marvin Freeman .01 .05
567 Todd Frohwirth .01 .05
568 Greg Gross .01 .05
569 Kevin Gross .01 .05
570 Greg A. Harris .01 .05
571 Von Hayes .01 .05
572 Chris James .01 .05
573 Steve Jeltz .01 .05
574 Ron Jones UER .02 .10
Led IL in '88 with 85, should be 75
575 Ricky Jordan RC .08 .25
576 Mike Maddux .01 .05
577 David Palmer .01 .05
578 Lance Parrish .02 .10
579 Shane Rawley .01 .05
580 Bruce Ruffin .01 .05
581 Juan Samuel .01 .05
582 Mike Schmidt .20 .50
583 Kent Tekulve .01 .05
584 Milt Thompson UER .01 .05
19 hits in '88, should be 109
585 Jose Alvarez RC .02 .10
586 Paul Assenmacher .01 .05
587 Bruce Benedict .01 .05
588 Jeff Blauser .01 .05
589 Terry Blocker .01 .05
590 Ron Gant .02 .10
591 Tom Glavine .08 .25
592 Tommy Gregg .01 .05
593 Albert Hall .01 .05
594 Dion James .01 .05
595 Rick Mahler .01 .05
596 Dale Murphy .05 .15
597 Gerald Perry .01 .05
598 Charlie Puleo .01 .05
599 Ted Simmons .02 .10
600 Pete Smith .01 .05
601 Zane Smith .01 .05
602 John Smoltz RC .60 1.50
603 Bruce Sutter .02 .10
604 Andres Thomas .01 .05
605 Ozzie Virgil .01 .05
606 Brady Anderson RC .15 .40
607 Jeff Ballard .01 .05
608 Jose Bautista RC .02 .10
609 Ken Gerhart .01 .05
610 Terry Kennedy .01 .05
611 Eddie Murray .08 .25
612 Carl Nichols UER .01 .05
Before All-Star Break batting 1.88
613 Tom Niedenfuer .01 .05
614 Joe Orsulak .01 .05
615 Oswald Peraza UER .01 .05
(Shown as Oswaldo
616A B.Ripken Rick Face 8.00 20.00
616B B.Ripken White Out 60.00 120.00
616C Ripken Wht Sribble 40.00 100.00
616D Ripken Blk Sribble 3.00 8.00
616E B.Ripken Blk Box 2.50 6.00
617 Cal Ripken .30 .75
618 Dave Schmidt .01 .05
619 Rick Schu .01 .05
620 Larry Sheets .01 .05
621 Doug Sisk .01 .05
622 Pete Stanicek .01 .05
623 Mickey Tettleton .01 .05
624 Jay Tibbs .01 .05
625 Jim Traber .01 .05
626 Mark Williamson .01 .05
627 Craig Worthington .01 .05
628 Jose Canseco 40 40 .08 .25
629 Tom Browning Perfect .01 .05
630 R.Alomar/S.Alomar .08 .25
631 W.Clark/R.Palmeiro .05 .15
632 D.Strawberry/W.Clark .02 .10
633 W.Boggs/C.Lansford .02 .10
634 McGwire/Cans/Stein .30 .75
635 M.Davis/D.Gooden .01 .05
636 D.Jackson/D.Cone UER .01 .05
637 C.Sabo/B.Bonilla UER .02 .10
638 A.Galarraga/G.Perry UER .01 .05
639 K.Puckett/E.Davis .05 .15
640 S.Wilson/C.Drew .01 .05
641 K.Brown/K.Reimer .08 .25
642 B.Pounders RC/J.Clark .02 .10
643 M.Capel/D.Hall .01 .05
644 J.Girardi RC/R.Roomes .15 .40
645 L.Harris RC/M.Brown .08 .25
646 L.De Los Santos/J.Campbell .01 .05
647 R.Kramer/M.Garcia .01 .05
648 T.Lovullo RC/R.Palacios .02 .10
649 J.Corsi/B.Milacki .01 .05
650 G.Hall/M.Rochford .01 .05
651 T.Taylor/V.Lovelace RC .02 .10
652 K.Hill RC/D.Cook .08 .25
653 S.Service/S.Turner .01 .05
654 CL: Oakland .01 .05
Mets
Dodgers
Red Sox
10 Henderson;
68 Jess Orosco
655A CL: Twins .01 .05
Tigers ERR
Reds
Brewers
179 Boslo and
Twins
Tigers positions
listed
655B CL: Twins .01 .05
Tigers COR
Reds
Brewers
179 Boslo but
Twins
Tigers positions
not listed
656 CL: Pirates .01 .05
Blue Jays
Yankees
Royals
225 Jess Barfield
657 CL: Padres .01 .05
Giants
Astros
Expos
367
368 wrong
658 CL: Indians .01 .05
Cubs
Cardinals
Angels
449 Deleon
659 CL: White Sox .01 .05
Rangers
Mariners
Phillies
660 CL: Braves .01 .05
Orioles
Specials
Checklists
632 hyphenated differently and 650 Hall;
595 Rich Mahler;
619 Rich Schu

1989 Fleer Glossy

COMP.FACT.SET (672) 40.00 100.00
*STARS: 2X TO 5X BASIC CARDS
*ROOKIES: 2X TO 5X BASIC CARDS
DISTRIBUTED ONLY IN FACTORY SET FORM

1989 Fleer All-Stars

This twelve-card standard-size subset was randomly inserted in Fleer wax and cello packs. The players selected are the 1989 Fleer Major League All-Star team. One player has been selected for each position along with a DH and three pitchers. The cards feature a distinctive green background on the card fronts. The set is sequenced in alphabetical order.

COMPLETE SET (12) 2.00 5.00
RANDOM INSERTS IN PACKS 1.00 2.00
1 Bobby Bonilla .30 .75
2 Jose Canseco .75 2.00
3 Will Clark .50 1.25
4 Dennis Eckersley .50 1.25
5 Julio Franco .30 .75
6 Mike Greenwell .15 .40
7 Orel Hershiser .30 .75
8 Paul Molitor .30 .75
9 Mike Scioscia .30 .75
10 Darryl Strawberry .30 .75
11 Alan Trammell .30 .75
12 Frank Viola .30 .75

1989 Fleer For The Record

This six-card standard-size insert set was distributed one per rack pack. The set is subtitled "For The Record" and commemorates record-breaking events for those players from the previous season. The card backs are printed in red, black, and gray on white card stock. The set is sequenced in alphabetical order.

COMPLETE SET (6) 3.00 8.00
ONE PER RACK PACK .50 1.00
1 Wade Boggs .40 1.00
2 Roger Clemens 2.50 6.00
3 Andres Galarraga .25 .60
4 Kirk Gibson .25 .60
5 Greg Maddux 1.25 3.00
6 Don Mattingly 1.50 4.00

1989 Fleer Wax Box Cards

The cards in this 28-card set measure the standard 2 1/2" by 3 1/2". Cards have essentially the same design as the 1989 Fleer regular issue set. The cards were printed on the bottoms of the regular issue wax pack boxes. These 28 cards (C1 to C28) are considered a separate set in their own right and are not typically included in a complete set of the regular issue 1989 Fleer cards. The value of the panel uncut is slightly greater, perhaps by 25 percent greater, than the value of the individual cards cut up carefully. The wax box cards are further distinguished by the gray card stock used.

COMPLETE SET (28) 4.00 10.00
C1 Mets Logo .05 .15
C2 Wade Boggs .30 .75
C3 George Brett .60 1.50
C4 Jose Canseco UER .60 1.50
'88 strikeouts 121 and career strikeouts 49, should be 128 and 491
C5 A's Logo .05 .15
C6 Will Clark .40 1.00
C7 David Cone .25 .60
C8 Andres Galarraga UER .25 .60
Career average .289 should be .269
C9 Dodgers Logo .05 .15
C10 Kirk Gibson .08 .25
C11 Mike Greenwell .05 .15
C12 Tony Gwynn 1.00 2.50
C13 Tigers Logo .05 .15
C14 Orel Hershiser .08 .25
C15 Danny Jackson .05 .15
C16 Wally Joyner .08 .25
C17 Red Sox Logo .05 .15
C18 Yankees Logo .05 .15
C19 Fred McGriff UER .40 1.00
Career BA of .289 should be .269
C20 Kirby Puckett .75 2.00
C21 Chris Sabo .05 .15
C22 Kevin Seitzer .05 .15
C23 Pirates Logo .05 .15
C24 Astros Logo .05 .15
C25 Darryl Strawberry .08 .25
C26 Alan Trammell .15 .40
C27 Andy Van Slyke .05 .15
C28 Frank Viola .05 .15

1989 Fleer World Series

This 12-card standard-size set features highlights of the previous year's World Series between the Dodgers and the Athletics. The sets were packaged as a complete set insert with the collated sets (of the 1989 Fleer regular issue) which were sold by Fleer directly to hobby card dealers; they were not available in the general retail candy store outlets. The Kirk Gibson card from this set highlights one of the most famous home runs in World Series history.

COMPLETE SET (12) .75 2.00
ONE SET PER FACTORY SET
1 Mickey Hatcher .01 .05
2 Tim Belcher .01 .05
3 Jose Canseco .08 .25
4 Mike Scioscia .02 .10
5 Kirk Gibson .02 .10
6 Orel Hershiser .02 .10
7 Mike Marshall .01 .05
8 Mark McGwire .40 1.00
9 Steve Sax .01 .05
10 Walt Weiss .01 .05
11 Orel Hershiser .02 .10
12 Dodger Blue World Champs .02 .10

1989 Fleer Glossy World Series

*GLOSSY: .5X TO 1.2X BASIC WS
DISTRIBUTED ONLY IN FACTORY SET FORM

1989 Fleer Update

The 1989 Fleer Update set contains 132 standard-size cards. The cards were distributed exclusively in factory set form in grey and white, cellophane wrapped boxes through hobby dealers. The cards are identical in design to regular issue 1989 Fleer cards except for the U-prefixed numbering on back. The set numbering is in team order with players within teams ordered alphabetically. The set includes special cards for Nolan Ryan's 5,000th strikeout and Mike Schmidt's retirement. Rookie Cards include Kevin Appier, Joey (Albert) Belle, Deion Sanders, Greg Vaughn, Robin Ventura and Todd Zeile.

COMP.FACT.SET (132) 2.00 5.00
1 Phil Bradley .01 .05
2 Mike Devereaux .01 .05
3 Steve Finley RC .30 .75
4 Kevin Hickey .01 .05
5 Brian Holton .01 .05
6 Bob Milacki .01 .05
7 Randy Milligan .01 .05
8 John Dopson .01 .05
9 Nick Esasky .01 .05
10 Rob Murphy .01 .05
11 Jim Abbott RC .40 1.00
12 Bert Blyleven .02 .10
13 Jeff Manto RC .02 .10
14 Bob McClure .01 .05
15 Lance Parrish .02 .10
16 Lee Stevens RC .08 .25
17 Claudell Washington .01 .05
18 Mark Davis RC .08 .25
19 Eric King .01 .05
20 Ron Kittle .01 .05
21 Matt Merullo .01 .05
22 Steve Rosenberg .01 .05
23 Robin Ventura RC .30 .75
24 Keith Atherton .01 .05
25 Albert Belle RC .40 1.00
26 Jerry Browne .01 .05
27 Felix Fermin .01 .05
28 Brad Komminsk .01 .05
29 Pete O'Brien .01 .05
30 Mike Brumley .01 .05
31 Tracy Jones .01 .05
32 Mike Schwabe .01 .05
33 Gary Ward .01 .05
34 Frank Williams .01 .05
35 Kevin Appier RC .20 .50
36 Bob Boone .02 .10
37 Luis DeLosSantos .01 .05
38 Jim Eisenreich .01 .05
39 Jaime Navarro RC .02 .10
40 Billy Spiers RC .08 .25
41 Greg Vaughn RC .15 .40
42 Randy Veres .01 .05
43 Wally Backman .01 .05
44 Shane Rawley .01 .05
45 Steve Balboni .01 .05
46 Jesse Barfield .02 .10
47 Alvaro Espinoza .01 .05
48 Bob Geren RC .01 .05
49 Mel Hall .01 .05
50 Andy Hawkins .01 .05
51 Hensley Meulens RC .02 .10
52 Steve Sax .01 .05
53 Deion Sanders RC .60 1.50
54 Rickey Henderson .08 .25
55 Mike Moore .01 .05
56 Tony Phillips .01 .05
57 Greg Briley .02 .10
58 Gene Harris RC .02 .10
59 Randy Johnson 1.00 2.50
60 Jeffrey Leonard .01 .05
61 Dennis Powell .01 .05
62 Omar Vizquel RC .40 1.00
63 Kevin Brown .08 .25
64 Julio Franco .02 .10
65 Jamie Moyer .02 .10
66 Rafael Palmeiro .08 .25
67 Nolan Ryan .60 1.50
68 Francisco Cabrera RC .02 .10
69 Junior Felix RC .02 .10
70 Al Leiter .08 .25
71 Alex Sanchez RC .01 .05
72 Geronimo Berroa .01 .05
73 Derek Lilliquist RC .02 .10
74 Lonnie Smith .01 .05
75 Jeff Treadway .01 .05
76 Paul Kilgus .01 .05
77 Lloyd McClendon .01 .05
78 Scott Sanderson .01 .05
79 Dwight Smith RC .08 .25
80 Jerome Walton RC .08 .25
81 Mitch Williams .01 .05
82 Steve Wilson .02 .10
83 Todd Benzinger .01 .05
84 Ken Griffey Sr. .02 .10
85 Rick Mahler .01 .05
86 Rolando Roomes .01 .05
87 Scott Scudder RC .02 .10
88 Jim Clancy .01 .05
89 Rick Rhoden .01 .05
90 Dan Schatzeder .01 .05
91 Mike Morgan .01 .05
92 Eddie Murray .08 .25
93 Willie Randolph .02 .10
94 Ray Searage .01 .05
95 Mike Aldrete .01 .05
96 Kevin Gross .01 .05
97 Mark Langston .01 .05
98 Spike Owen .01 .05
99 Zane Smith .01 .05
100 Don Aase .01 .05
101 Barry Lyons .01 .05
102 Juan Samuel .01 .05
103 Wally Whitehurst RC .02 .10
104 Dennis Cook .01 .05
105 Len Dykstra .02 .10
106 Charlie Hayes .08 .25
107 Tommy Herr .01 .05
108 Ken Howell .01 .05
109 John Kruk .02 .10
110 Roger McDowell .01 .05
111 Terry Mulholland .01 .05
112 Jeff Parrett .01 .05
113 Neal Heaton .01 .05
114 Jeff King .01 .05
115 Randy Kramer .01 .05
116 Bill Landrum .01 .05
117 Cris Carpenter RC * .02 .10
118 Frank DiPino .01 .05
119 Ken Hill .08 .25
120 Dan Quisenberry .01 .05
121 Milt Thompson .01 .05
122 Todd Zeile RC .15 .40
123 Jack Clark .02 .10
124 Bruce Hurst .01 .05
125 Mark Parent RC .01 .05
126 Bip Roberts .01 .05
127 Jeff Brantley UER RC .08 .25
128 Terry Kennedy .01 .05
129 Mike LaCoss .01 .05
130 Greg Litton .01 .05
131 Mike Schmidt SPEC .30 .75
132 Checklist 1-132 .01 .05

1989 Fleer Baseball All-Stars

The 1989 Fleer Baseball All-Stars set contains 44 standard-size cards. The fronts are yellowish beige with salmon pinstripes; the vertically oriented backs are red, white and pink and feature career stats. The card numbering of this set is ordered alphabetically by player's name. The cards were distributed through Ben Franklin stores as a boxed set.

COMP.FACT.SET (44) 2.50 6.00
1 Doyle Alexander .01 .05
2 George Bell .01 .05
3 Wade Boggs .15 .40
4 Bobby Bonilla .02 .10
5 Jose Canseco .15 .40
6 Will Clark .30 .75
7 Roger Clemens .30 .75
8 Vince Coleman .01 .05
9 David Cone .07 .20
10 Mark Davis .01 .05
11 Andre Dawson .07 .20
12 Dennis Eckersley .15 .40
13 Andres Galarraga .07 .20
14 Kirk Gibson .02 .10
15 Dwight Gooden .02 .10
16 Mike Greenwell .01 .05
17 Mark Gubicza .01 .05
18 Ozzie Guillen .01 .05
19 Tony Gwynn .30 .75
20 Rickey Henderson .25 .60
21 Orel Hershiser .02 .10
22 Danny Jackson .01 .05
23 Doug Jones .01 .05
24 Ricky Jordan .01 .05
25 Bob Knepper .01 .05
26 Barry Larkin .20 .50
27 Vance Law .01 .05
28 Don Mattingly .30 .75
29 Mark McGwire .40 1.00
30 Paul Molitor .15 .40
31 Gerald Perry .01 .05
32 Kirby Puckett .15 .40
33 Johnny Ray .01 .05
34 Harold Reynolds .02 .10
35 Cal Ripken .60 1.50
36 Don Robinson .01 .05
37 Ruben Sierra .02 .10
38 Dave Smith .01 .05
39 Darryl Strawberry .02 .10
40 Dave Stieb .01 .05
41 Alan Trammell .05 .15
42 Andy Van Slyke .01 .05
43 Frank Viola .01 .05
44 Dave Winfield .15 .40

1989 Fleer Baseball MVP's

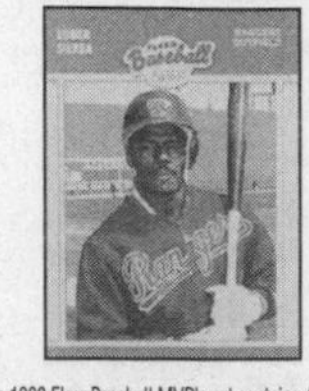

The 1989 Fleer Baseball MVP's set contains 44 standard-size cards. The fronts and backs are green and yellow. The horizontally oriented backs feature career stats. The card numbering of this set is ordered alphabetically by player's name. The cards were distributed through Toys 'R' Us stores as a boxed set.

COMP.FACT.SET (44) 3.00 8.00
1 Steve Bedrosian .01 .05
2 George Bell .01 .05
3 Wade Boggs .15 .40
4 George Brett .20 .50
5 Hubie Brooks .01 .05
6 Jose Canseco .10 .30
7 Will Clark .20 .50
8 Roger Clemens .20 .50
9 Eric Davis .02 .10
10 Glenn Davis .01 .05
11 Andre Dawson .07 .20
12 Andres Galarraga .07 .20
13 Kirk Gibson .02 .10
14 Dwight Gooden .02 .10
15 Mark Grace .20 .50
16 Mike Greenwell .01 .05
17 Tony Gwynn .30 .75
18 Bryan Harvey .01 .05
19 Orel Hershiser .02 .10
20 Ted Higuera .01 .05
21 Danny Jackson .01 .05
22 Mike Jackson .02 .10
23 Doug Jones .01 .05
24 Greg Maddux .60 1.00
25 Mike Marshall .01 .05
26 Don Mattingly .30 .75
27 Fred McGriff .20 .50
28 Mark McGwire .40 1.00
29 Kevin McReynolds .01 .05
30 Jack Morris .02 .10
31 Gerald Perry .01 .05
32 Kirby Puckett .15 .40
33 Chris Sabo .01 .05
34 Mike Scott .01 .05
35 Ruben Sierra .02 .10
36 Darryl Strawberry .02 .10
37 Danny Tartabull .01 .05
38 Bobby Thigpen .01 .05
39 Alan Trammell .05 .15
40 Andy Van Slyke .02 .10
41 Frank Viola .01 .05
42 Walt Weiss .01 .05
43 Dave Winfield .15 .40
44 Todd Worrell .02 .10

1989 Fleer Exciting Stars

The 1989 Fleer Exciting Stars set contains 44 standard-size cards. The fronts have baby blue borders; the backs are pink and blue. The vertically oriented backs feature career stats. The card numbering of this set is ordered alphabetically by player's name. The cards were distributed as a boxed set.

COMP.FACT.SET (44) 2.50 6.00
1 Harold Baines .05 .15
2 Wade Boggs .15 .40
3 Jose Canseco .10 .30
4 Joe Carter .05 .15
5 Will Clark .20 .50
6 Roger Clemens .30 .75
7 Vince Coleman .01 .05
8 David Cone .07 .20
9 Eric Davis .02 .10
10 Glenn Davis .01 .05
11 Andre Dawson .07 .20
12 Dwight Evans .02 .10
13 Andres Galarraga .07 .20
14 Kirk Gibson .02 .10
15 Dwight Gooden .02 .10
16 Jim Gott .01 .05
17 Mark Grace .30 .75
18 Mike Greenwell .01 .05
19 Mark Gubicza .01 .05
20 Tony Gwynn .30 .75
21 Rickey Henderson .25 .60
22 Tom Henke .01 .05
23 Mike Henneman .01 .05
24 Orel Hershiser .02 .10
25 Danny Jackson .01 .05
26 Gregg Jefferies .01 .05
27 Ricky Jordan .01 .05
28 Wally Joyner .02 .10
29 Mark Langston .01
30 Tim Leary .01
31 Don Mattingly .30
32 Mark McGwire .40 1
33 Dale Murphy .07
34 Kirby Puckett .15
35 Chris Sabo .01
36 Kevin Seitzer .01
37 Ruben Sierra .02
38 Ozzie Smith .30
39 Dave Stewart .02
40 Darryl Strawberry .02
41 Alan Trammell .05
42 Frank Viola .01
43 Dave Winfield .15
44 Robin Yount .15

1989 Fleer Heroes of Baseba

The 1989 Fleer Heroes of Baseball set contains 4 standard-size cards. The fronts and backs are red white and blue. The vertically oriented backs feat career stats. The card numbering of this set is ordered alphabetically by player's name. The car were distributed through Woolworth stores as a boxed set.

COMP.FACT.SET (44) 2.50 6
1 George Bell .01
2 Wade Boggs .20
3 Barry Bonds .40
4 Tom Brunansky .01
5 Jose Canseco .15
6 Joe Carter .05
7 Will Clark .20
8 Roger Clemens .40 1
9 David Cone .07
10 Eric Davis .02
11 Glenn Davis .01
12 Andre Dawson .07
13 Dennis Eckersley .15
14 John Franco .02
15 Gary Gaetti .02
16 Andres Galarraga .07
17 Kirk Gibson .02
18 Dwight Gooden .02
19 Mike Greenwell .01
20 Tony Gwynn .30
21 Bryan Harvey .01
22 Orel Hershiser .02
23 Ted Higuera .01
24 Danny Jackson .01
25 Ricky Jordan .01
26 Don Mattingly .30
27 Fred McGriff .15
28 Mark McGwire .40 1
29 Kevin McReynolds .01
30 Gerald Perry .01
31 Kirby Puckett .20
32 Johnny Ray .01
33 Harold Reynolds .02
34 Cal Ripken .60 1
35 Ryne Sandberg .20
36 Kevin Seitzer .01
37 Ruben Sierra .02
38 Darryl Strawberry .02
39 Bobby Thigpen .01
40 Alan Trammell .05
41 Andy Van Slyke .02
42 Frank Viola .01
43 Dave Winfield .15
44 Robin Yount .20

1989 Fleer League Leaders

The 1989 Fleer League Leaders set contains 44 standard-size cards. The fronts are red and yellow the horizontally oriented backs are light blue and and feature career stats. The card numbering of th set is ordered alphabetically by player's name. The cards were distributed through Woolworth stores as a boxed set.

COMP.FACT.SET (44) 2.50 6
1 Allan Anderson .01
2 Wade Boggs .15
3 Jose Canseco .10
4 Will Clark .20
5 Roger Clemens .30
6 Vince Coleman .01
7 David Cone .07
8 Kal Daniels .01
9 Chili Davis .02
10 Eric Davis .02
11 Glenn Davis .01
12 Andre Dawson .07

3 John Franco .02 .10
4 Andres Galarraga .07 .20
5 Kirk Gibson .02 .10
5 Dwight Gooden .02 .10
7 Mark Grace .30 .75
3 Mike Greenwell .01 .05
9 Tony Gwynn .30 .75
0 Orel Hershiser .02 .10
1 Pete Incaviglia .01 .05
2 Danny Jackson .01 .05
3 Gregg Jefferies .01 .05
4 Joe Magrane .01 .05
5 Don Mattingly .30 .75
6 Fred McGriff .15 .40
7 Mark McGwire .40 1.00
3 Dale Murphy .07 .20
9 Dan Plesac .01 .05
0 Kirby Puckett .20 .50
1 Harold Reynolds .02 .10
2 Cal Ripken .60 1.50
3 Jeff M. Robinson .01 .05
4 Mike Scott .01 .05
5 Ozzie Smith .30 .75
6 Dave Stewart .02 .10
7 Darryl Strawberry .02 .10
8 Greg Swindell .01 .05
9 Bobby Thigpen .01 .05
0 Alan Trammell .05 .15
1 Andy Van Slyke .01 .05
2 Frank Viola .01 .05
3 Dave Winfield .15 .40
4 Robin Yount .20 .50

1989 Fleer Superstars

he 1989 Fleer Superstars set contains 44 standard-ize cards. The fronts are red and beige; the orizontally oriented backs are yellow, and feature areer stats. The card numbering of this set is rdered alphabetically by player's name. The cards ere distributed as a boxed set. The back panel of the ox contains the complete set checklist.

OMP.FACT SET (44) 2.50 6.00
Roberto Alomar .30 .75
Harold Baines .02 .10
Tim Belcher .01 .05
Wade Boggs .15 .40
George Brett .30 .75
Jose Canseco .10 .30
Gary Carter .05 .15
Will Clark .20 .50
Roger Clemens .30 .75
0 Kal Daniels UER/(Reverse negative .01 .05
photo on front
1 Eric Davis .02 .10
2 Andre Dawson .07 .20
3 Tony Fernandez .02 .10
4 Scott Fletcher .01 .05
5 Andres Galarraga .07 .20
6 Kirk Gibson .02 .10
7 Dwight Gooden .02 .10
8 Jim Gott .01 .05
9 Mark Grace .30 .75
0 Mike Greenwell .01 .05
1 Tony Gwynn .30 .75
2 Rickey Henderson .25 .60
3 Orel Hershiser .02 .10
4 Ted Higuera .01 .05
5 Gregg Jefferies .01 .05
6 Wally Joyner .02 .10
7 Mark Langston .01 .05
8 Greg Maddux .60 1.50
9 Don Mattingly .30 .75
0 Fred McGriff .15 .40
1 Mark McGwire .40 1.00
2 Dan Plesac .01 .05
3 Kirby Puckett .15 .40
4 Jeff Reardon .02 .10
5 Chris Sabo .01 .05
6 Mike Schmidt .20 .50
7 Mike Scott .01 .05
8 Cory Snyder .01 .05
9 Darryl Strawberry .02 .10
0 Alan Trammell .05 .15
1 Frank Viola .01 .05
2 Walt Weiss .01 .05
3 Dave Winfield .20 .50
4 Todd Worrell UER
(Statistical headings .01 .05
on back f

1990 Fleer

he 1990 Fleer set contains 660 standard-size cards. ards were primarily issued in wax packs, cello packs, rack packs and hobby and retail factory sets. Card fronts feature white outer borders with ribbon-like, colored inner borders. The set is again ordered numerically by teams based upon the previous season's record. Subsets include Decade Greats (621-630), Superstar Combinations (631-639), Rookie Prospects (640-653) and checklists (654-660). Rookie Cards of note include Moises Alou, Juan Gonzalez, David Justice, Sammy Sosa and Larry Walker.

COMPLETE SET (660) 6.00 15.00
COMP.RETAIL SET (660) 6.00 15.00
COMP.HOBBY SET (672) 6.00 15.00
1 Lance Blankenship .01 .05
2 Todd Burns .01 .05
3 Jose Canseco .05 .15
4 Jim Corsi .01 .05
5 Storm Davis .01 .05
6 Dennis Eckersley .02 .10
7 Mike Gallego .01 .05
8 Ron Hassey .01 .05
9 Dave Henderson .01 .05
10 Rickey Henderson .08 .25
11 Rick Honeycutt .01 .05
12 Stan Javier .01 .05
13 Felix Jose .01 .05
14 Carney Lansford .02 .10
15 Mark McGwire .40 1.00
16 Mike Moore .01 .05
17 Gene Nelson .01 .05
18 Dave Parker .02 .10
19 Tony Phillips .01 .05
20 Terry Steinbach .01 .05
21 Dave Stewart .02 .10
22 Walt Weiss .01 .05
23 Bob Welch .01 .05
24 Curt Young .01 .05
25 Paul Assenmacher .01 .05
26 Damon Berryhill .01 .05
27 Mike Bielecki .01 .05
28 Kevin Blankenship .01 .05
29 Andre Dawson .02 .10
30 Shawon Dunston .01 .05
31 Joe Girardi .05 .15
32 Mark Grace .05 .15
33 Mike Harkey .01 .05
34 Paul Kilgus .01 .05
35 Les Lancaster .01 .05
36 Vance Law .01 .05
37 Greg Maddux .15 .40
38 Lloyd McClendon .01 .05
39 Jeff Pico .01 .05
40 Ryne Sandberg .15 .40
41 Scott Sanderson .01 .05
42 Dwight Smith .01 .05
43 Rick Sutcliffe .02 .10
44 Jerome Walton .01 .05
45 Mitch Webster .01 .05
46 Curt Wilkerson .01 .05
47 Dean Wilkins RC .01 .05
48 Mitch Williams .01 .05
49 Steve Wilson .01 .05
50 Steve Bedrosian .01 .05
51 Mike Benjamin RC .02 .10
52 Jeff Brantley .01 .05
53 Brett Butler .02 .10
54 Will Clark UER .02 .10
55 Kelly Downs .01 .05
56 Scott Garrelts .01 .05
57 Atlee Hammaker .01 .05
58 Terry Kennedy .01 .05
59 Mike LaCoss .01 .05
60 Craig Lefferts .01 .05
61 Greg Litton .01 .05
62 Candy Maldonado .01 .05
63 Kirt Manwaring UER
(No '88 Phoenix stats/as note .01 .05
64 Randy McCament RC .01 .05
65 Kevin Mitchell .01 .05
66 Donell Nixon .01 .05
67 Ken Oberkfell .01 .05
68 Rick Reuschel .01 .05
69 Ernest Riles .01 .05
70 Don Robinson .01 .05
71 Pat Sheridan .01 .05
72 Chris Speier .01 .05
73 Robby Thompson .01 .05
74 Jose Uribe .01 .05
75 Matt Williams .02 .10
76 George Bell .01 .05
77 Pat Borders .01 .05
78 John Cerutti .01 .05
79 Junior Felix .01 .05
80 Tony Fernandez .01 .05
81 Mike Flanagan .01 .05
82 Mauro Gozzo RC .01 .05
83 Kelly Gruber .01 .05
84 Tom Henke .01 .05
85 Jimmy Key .02 .10
86 Manny Lee .01 .05
87 Nelson Liriano UER .01 .05
88 Lee Mazzilli .01 .05
89 Fred McGriff .08 .25
90 Lloyd Moseby .01 .05
91 Rance Mulliniks .01 .05
92 Alex Sanchez .01 .05
93 Dave Stieb .02 .10
94 Todd Stottlemyre .02 .10
95 Duane Ward UER .01 .05
96 David Wells .02 .10
97 Ernie Whitt .01 .05
98 Frank Wills .01 .05
99 Mookie Wilson .02 .10
100 Kevin Appier .02 .10
101 Luis Aquino .01 .05
102 Bob Boone .02 .10
103 George Brett .25 .60
104 Jose DeJesus .01 .05
105 Luis De Los Santos .01 .05
106 Jim Eisenreich .01 .05
107 Steve Farr .01 .05
108 Tom Gordon .02 .10
109 Mark Gubicza .01 .05
110 Bo Jackson .08 .25
111 Terry Leach .01 .05
112 Charlie Leibrandt .01 .05
113 Rick Luecken RC .01 .05
114 Mike Macfarlane .01 .05
115 Jeff Montgomery .02 .10
116 Bret Saberhagen .02 .10
117 Kevin Seitzer .01 .05
118 Kurt Stillwell .01 .05
119 Pat Tabler .01 .05
120 Danny Tartabull .01 .05
121 Gary Thurman .01 .05
122 Frank White .02 .10
123 Willie Wilson .01 .05
124 Matt Winters RC .01 .05
125 Jim Abbott .05 .15
126 Tony Armas .01 .05
127 Dante Bichette .02 .10
128 Bert Blyleven .02 .10
129 Chili Davis .02 .10
130 Brian Downing .01 .05
131 Mike Fetters RC .08 .25
132 Chuck Finley .02 .10
133 Willie Fraser .01 .05
134 Bryan Harvey .01 .05
135 Jack Howell .01 .05
136 Wally Joyner .02 .10
137 Jeff Manto .01 .05
138 Kirk McCaskill .01 .05
139 Bob McClure .01 .05
140 Greg Minton .01 .05
141 Lance Parrish .01 .05
142 Dan Petry .01 .05
143 Johnny Ray .01 .05
144 Dick Schofield .01 .05
145 Lee Stevens .02 .10
146 Claudell Washington .01 .05
147 Devon White .02 .10
148 Mike Witt .01 .05
149 Roberto Alomar .05 .15
150 Sandy Alomar Jr. .02 .10
151 Andy Benes .02 .10
152 Jack Clark .02 .10
153 Pat Clements .01 .05
154 Joey Cora .02 .10
155 Mark Davis .01 .05
156 Mark Grant .01 .05
157 Tony Gwynn .10 .30
158 Greg W. Harris .01 .05
159 Bruce Hurst .01 .05
160 Darrin Jackson .01 .05
161 Chris James .01 .05
162 Carmelo Martinez .01 .05
163 Mike Pagliarulo .01 .05
164 Mark Parent .01 .05
165 Dennis Rasmussen .01 .05
166 Bip Roberts .01 .05
167 Benito Santiago .02 .10
168 Calvin Schiraldi .01 .05
169 Eric Show .01 .05
170 Garry Templeton .01 .05
171 Ed Whitson .01 .05
172 Brady Anderson .02 .10
173 Jeff Ballard .01 .05
174 Phil Bradley .01 .05
175 Mike Devereaux .01 .05
176 Steve Finley .02 .10
177 Pete Harnisch .01 .05
178 Kevin Hickey .01 .05
179 Brian Holton .01 .05
180 Ben McDonald RC .08 .25
181 Bob Melvin .01 .05
182 Bob Milacki .01 .05
183 Randy Milligan UER .01 .05
184 Gregg Olson .02 .10
185 Joe Orsulak .01 .05
186 Bill Ripken .01 .05
187 Cal Ripken .30 .75
188 Dave Schmidt .01 .05
189 Larry Sheets .01 .05
190 Mickey Tettleton .01 .05
191 Mark Thurmond .01 .05
192 Jay Tibbs .01 .05
193 Jim Traber .01 .05
194 Mark Williamson .01 .05
195 Craig Worthington .01 .05
196 Don Aase .01 .05
197 Blaine Beatty RC .01 .05
198 Mark Carreon .01 .05
199 Gary Carter .02 .10
200 David Cone .02 .10
201 Ron Darling .01 .05
202 Kevin Elster .01 .05
203 Sid Fernandez .01 .05
204 Dwight Gooden .02 .10
205 Keith Hernandez .02 .10
206 Jeff Innis RC .01 .05
207 Gregg Jefferies .02 .10
208 Howard Johnson .01 .05
209 Barry Lyons UER .01 .05
210 Dave Magadan .01 .05
211 Kevin McReynolds .01 .05
212 Jeff Musselman .01 .05
213 Randy Myers .02 .10
214 Bob Ojeda .01 .05
215 Juan Samuel .01 .05
216 Mackey Sasser .01 .05
217 Darryl Strawberry .02 .10
218 Tim Teufel .01 .05
219 Frank Viola .01 .05
220 Juan Agosto .01 .05
221 Larry Andersen .01 .05
222 Eric Anthony RC .02 .10
223 Kevin Bass .01 .05
224 Craig Biggio .08 .25
225 Ken Caminiti .02 .10
226 Jim Clancy .01 .05
227 Danny Darwin .01 .05
228 Glenn Davis .01 .05
229 Jim Deshaies .01 .05
230 Bill Doran .01 .05
231 Bob Forsch .01 .05
232 Brian Meyer .01 .05
233 Terry Puhl .01 .05
234 Rafael Ramirez .01 .05
235 Rick Rhoden .01 .05
236 Dan Schatzeder .01 .05
237 Mike Scott .01 .05
238 Dave Smith .01 .05
239 Alex Trevino .01 .05
240 Glenn Wilson .01 .05
241 Gerald Young .01 .05
242 Tom Brunansky .01 .05
243 Cris Carpenter .01 .05
244 Alex Cole RC .02 .10
245 Vince Coleman .01 .05
246 John Costello .01 .05
247 Ken Dayley .01 .05
248 Jose DeLeon .01 .05
249 Frank DiPino .01 .05
250 Pedro Guerrero .01 .05
251 Ken Hill .02 .10
252 Joe Magrane .01 .05
253 Willie McGee UER .02 .10
254 John Morris .01 .05
255 Jose Oquendo .01 .05
256 Tony Pena .01 .05
257 Terry Pendleton .02 .10
258 Ted Power .01 .05
259 Dan Quisenberry .01 .05
260 Ozzie Smith .15 .40
261 Scott Terry .01 .05
262 Milt Thompson .01 .05
263 Denny Walling .01 .05
264 Todd Worrell .01 .05
265 Todd Zeile .02 .10
266 Marty Barrett .01 .05
267 Mike Boddicker .01 .05
268 Wade Boggs .05 .15
269 Ellis Burks .05 .15
270 Rick Cerone .01 .05
271 Roger Clemens .40 1.00
272 John Dopson .01 .05
273 Nick Esasky .01 .05
274 Dwight Evans .05 .15
275 Wes Gardner .01 .05
276 Rich Gedman .01 .05
277 Mike Greenwell .01 .05
278 Danny Heep .01 .05
279 Eric Hetzel .01 .05
280 Dennis Lamp .01 .05
281 Rob Murphy UER .01 .05
282 Joe Price .01 .05
283 Carlos Quintana .01 .05
284 Jody Reed .01 .05
285 Luis Rivera .01 .05
286 Kevin Romine .01 .05
287 Lee Smith .02 .10
288 Mike Smithson .01 .05
289 Bob Stanley .01 .05
290 Harold Baines .02 .10
291 Kevin Brown .02 .10
292 Steve Buechele .01 .05
293 Scott Coolbaugh RC .01 .05
294 Jack Daugherty RC .01 .05
295 Cecil Espy .01 .05
296 Julio Franco .02 .10
297 Juan Gonzalez RC .40 1.00
298 Cecilio Guante .01 .05
299 Drew Hall .01 .05
300 Charlie Hough .02 .10
301 Pete Incaviglia .01 .05
302 Mike Jeffcoat .01 .05
303 Chad Kreuter .01 .05
304 Jeff Kunkel .01 .05
305 Rick Leach .01 .05
306 Fred Manrique .01 .05
307 Jamie Moyer .02 .10
308 Rafael Palmeiro .05 .15
309 Geno Petralli .01 .05
310 Kevin Reimer .01 .05
311 Kenny Rogers .02 .10
312 Jeff Russell .01 .05
313 Nolan Ryan .40 1.00
314 Ruben Sierra .02 .10
315 Bobby Witt .01 .05
316 Chris Bosio .01 .05
317 Glenn Braggs UER .01 .05
318 Greg Brock .01 .05
319 Chuck Crim .01 .05
320 Rob Deer .01 .05
321 Mike Felder .01 .05
322 Tom Filer .01 .05
323 Tony Fossas RC .01 .05
324 Jim Gantner .01 .05
325 Darryl Hamilton .01 .05
326 Teddy Higuera .01 .05
327 Mark Knudson .01 .05
328 Bill Krueger UER .01 .05
329 Tim McIntosh RC .02 .10
330 Paul Molitor .02 .10
331 Jaime Navarro .01 .05
332 Charlie O'Brien .01 .05
333 Jeff Peterek RC .01 .05
334 Dan Plesac .01 .05
335 Jerry Reuss .01 .05
336 Gary Sheffield UER .08 .25
337 Bill Spiers .01 .05
338 B.J. Surhoff .02 .10
339 Greg Vaughn .01 .05
340 Robin Yount .15 .40
341 Hubie Brooks .01 .05
342 Tim Burke .01 .05
343 Mike Fitzgerald .01 .05
344 Tom Foley .01 .05
345 Andres Galarraga .02 .10
346 Damaso Garcia .01 .05
347 Marquis Grissom RC .15 .40
348 Kevin Gross .01 .05
349 Joe Hesketh .01 .05
350 Jeff Huson RC .01 .05
351 Wallace Johnson .01 .05
352 Mark Langston .01 .05
353A Dave Martinez Yellow .75 2.00
353B Dave Martinez .01 .05
Red on front
354 Dennis Martinez UER .02 .10
355 Andy McGaffigan .01 .05
356 Otis Nixon .01 .05
357 Spike Owen .01 .05
358 Pascual Perez .01 .05
359 Tim Raines .02 .10
360 Nelson Santovenia .01 .05
361 Bryn Smith .01 .05
362 Zane Smith .01 .05
363 Larry Walker RC .40 1.00
364 Tim Wallach .01 .05
365 Rick Aguilera .02 .10
366 Allan Anderson .01 .05
367 Wally Backman .01 .05
368 Doug Baker .01 .05
369 Juan Berenguer .01 .05
370 Randy Bush .01 .05
371 Carmelo Castillo .01 .05
372 Mike Dyer RC .01 .05
373 Gary Gaetti .02 .10
374 Greg Gagne .01 .05
375 Dan Gladden .01 .05
376 German Gonzalez UER .01 .05
377 Brian Harper .01 .05
378 Kent Hrbek .02 .10
379 Gene Larkin .01 .05
380 Tim Laudner UER .01 .05
381 John Moses .01 .05
382 Al Newman .01 .05
383 Kirby Puckett .08 .25
384 Shane Rawley .01 .05
385 Jeff Reardon .02 .10
386 Roy Smith .01 .05
387 Gary Wayne .01 .05
388 Dave West .01 .05
389 Tim Belcher .01 .05
390 Tim Crews UER .01 .05
391 Mike Davis .01 .05
392 Rick Dempsey .01 .05
393 Kirk Gibson .02 .10
394 Jose Gonzalez .01 .05
395 Alfredo Griffin .01 .05
396 Jeff Hamilton .01 .05
397 Lenny Harris .01 .05
398 Mickey Hatcher .01 .05
399 Orel Hershiser .02 .10
400 Jay Howell .01 .05
401 Mike Marshall .01 .05
402 Ramon Martinez .01 .05
403 Mike Morgan .01 .05
404 Eddie Murray .08 .25
405 Alejandro Pena .01 .05
406 Willie Randolph .02 .10
407 Mike Scioscia .01 .05
408 Ray Searage .01 .05
409 Fernando Valenzuela .02 .10
410 Jose Vizcaino RC .08 .25
411 John Wetteland .08 .25
412 Jack Armstrong .01 .05
413 Todd Benzinger UER .01 .05
414 Tim Birtsas .01 .05
415 Tom Browning .01 .05
416 Norm Charlton .01 .05
417 Eric Davis .02 .10
418 Rob Dibble .02 .10
419 John Franco .02 .10
420 Ken Griffey Sr. .02 .10
421 Chris Hammond RC .02 .10
422 Danny Jackson .01 .05
423 Barry Larkin .05 .15
424 Tim Leary .01 .05
425 Rick Mahler .01 .05
426 Joe Oliver .01 .05
427 Paul O'Neill .05 .15
428 Luis Quinones UER .01 .05
429 Jeff Reed .01 .05
430 Jose Rijo .01 .05
431 Ron Robinson .01 .05
432 Rolando Roomes .01 .05
433 Chris Sabo .01 .05
434 Scott Scudder .01 .05
435 Herm Winningham .01 .05
436 Steve Balboni .01 .05
437 Jesse Barfield .01 .05
438 Mike Blowers RC .02 .10
439 Tom Brookens .01 .05
440 Greg Cadaret .01 .05
441 Alvaro Espinoza UER .01 .05
442 Bob Geren .01 .05
443 Lee Guetterman .01 .05
444 Mel Hall .01 .05
445 Andy Hawkins .01 .05
446 Roberto Kelly .01 .05
447 Don Mattingly .25 .60
448 Lance McCullers .01 .05
449 Hensley Meulens .01 .05
450 Dale Mohorcic .01 .05
451 Clay Parker .01 .05
452 Eric Plunk .01 .05
453 Dave Righetti .01 .05
454 Deion Sanders .08 .25
455 Steve Sax .01 .05
456 Don Slaught .01 .05
457 Walt Terrell .01 .05
458 Dave Winfield .02 .10
459 Jay Bell .02 .10
460 Rafael Belliard .01 .05
461 Barry Bonds .40 1.00
462 Bobby Bonilla .02 .10
463 Sid Bream .01 .05
464 Benny Distefano .01 .05
465 Doug Drabek .01 .05
466 Jim Gott .01 .05
467 Billy Hatcher UER .01 .05
468 Neal Heaton .01 .05
469 Jeff King .01 .05
470 Bob Kipper .01 .05
471 Randy Kramer .01 .05
472 Bill Landrum .01 .05
473 Mike LaValliere .01 .05
474 Jose Lind .01 .05
475 Junior Ortiz .01 .05
476 Gary Redus .01 .05
477 Rick Reed RC .08 .25
478 R.J. Reynolds .01 .05
479 Jeff D. Robinson .01 .05
480 John Smiley .01 .05
481 Andy Van Slyke .05 .15
482 Bob Walk .01 .05
483 Andy Allanson .01 .05
484 Scott Bailes .01 .05
485 Albert Belle .08 .25
486 Bud Black .01 .05
487 Jerry Browne .01 .05
488 Tom Candiotti .01 .05
489 Joe Carter .02 .10
490 Dave Clark .01 .05
No '84 stats
491 John Farrell .01 .05
492 Felix Fermin .01 .05
493 Brook Jacoby .01 .05
494 Dion James .01 .05
495 Doug Jones .01 .05
496 Brad Komminsk .01 .05
497 Rod Nichols .01 .05
498 Pete O'Brien .01 .05
499 Steve Olin RC .02 .10
500 Jesse Orosco .01 .05
501 Joel Skinner .01 .05
502 Cory Snyder .01 .05
503 Greg Swindell .01 .05
504 Rich Yett .01 .05
505 Scott Bankhead .01 .05
506 Scott Bradley .01 .05
507 Greg Briley UER .01 .05
508 Jay Buhner .02 .10
509 Darnell Coles .01 .05
510 Keith Comstock .01 .05
511 Henry Cotto .01 .05
512 Alvin Davis .01 .05
513 Ken Griffey Jr. .40 1.00
514 Erik Hanson .01 .05
515 Gene Harris .01 .05
516 Brian Holman .01 .05
517 Mike Jackson .01 .05
518 Randy Johnson .20 .50
519 Jeffrey Leonard .01 .05
520 Edgar Martinez .05 .15
521 Dennis Powell .01 .05
522 Jim Presley .01 .05
523 Jerry Reed .01 .05
524 Harold Reynolds .02 .10
525 Mike Schooler .01 .05
526 Bill Swift .01 .05
527 Dave Valle .01 .05
528 Omar Vizquel .08 .25
529 Ivan Calderon .01 .05
530 Carlton Fisk UER .05 .15
531 Scott Fletcher .01 .05
532 Dave Gallagher .01 .05
533 Ozzie Guillen .02 .10
534 Greg Hibbard RC .01 .05
535 Shawn Hillegas .01 .05
536 Lance Johnson .01 .05
537 Eric King .01 .05
538 Ron Kittle .01 .05
539 Steve Lyons .01 .05
540 Carlos Martinez .01 .05
541 Tom McCarthy .01 .05
542 Matt Merullo .01 .05
543 Donn Pall UER .01 .05
544 Dan Pasqua .01 .05
545 Ken Patterson .01 .05
546 Melido Perez .01 .05
547 Steve Rosenberg .01 .05
548 Sammy Sosa RC 1.00 2.50
549 Bobby Thigpen .01 .05
550 Robin Ventura .08 .25
551 Greg Walker .01 .05
552 Don Carman .01 .05
553 Pat Combs .01 .05
554 Dennis Cook .01 .05
555 Darren Daulton .02 .10
556 Len Dykstra .02 .10
557 Curt Ford .01 .05
558 Charlie Hayes .01 .05
559 Von Hayes .01 .05
560 Tommy Herr .01 .05
561 Ken Howell .01 .05
562 Steve Jeltz .01 .05
563 Ron Jones .01 .05
564 Ricky Jordan UER .01 .05
565 John Kruk .02 .10
566 Steve Lake .01 .05
567 Roger McDowell .01 .05
568 Terry Mulholland UER .01 .05
569 Dwayne Murphy .01 .05
570 Jeff Parrett .01 .05
571 Randy Ready .01 .05
572 Bruce Ruffin .01 .05
573 Dickie Thon .01 .05
574 Jose Alvarez UER .01 .05
575 Geronimo Berroa .01 .05
576 Jeff Blauser .01 .05
577 Joe Boever .01 .05
578 Marty Clary UER .01 .05
579 Jody Davis .01 .05
580 Mark Eichhorn .01 .05
581 Darrell Evans .02 .10
582 Ron Gant .02 .10
583 Tom Glavine .05 .15
584 Tommy Greene RC .02 .10
585 Tommy Gregg .01 .05
586 David Justice RC .20 .50
587 Mark Lemke .01 .05
588 Derek Lilliquist .01 .05
589 Oddibe McDowell .01 .05
590 Kent Mercker RC .01 .05
591 Dale Murphy .05 .15
592 Gerald Perry .01 .05
593 Lonnie Smith .01 .05
594 Pete Smith .01 .05
595 John Smoltz .08 .25
596 Mike Stanton UER RC .08 .25
597 Andres Thomas .01 .05
598 Jeff Treadway .01 .05
599 Doyle Alexander .01 .05
600 Dave Bergman .01 .05
601 Brian DuBois RC .01 .05
602 Paul Gibson .01 .05
603 Mike Heath .01 .05
604 Mike Henneman .01 .05
605 Guillermo Hernandez .01 .05
606 Shawn Holman RC .01 .05
607 Tracy Jones .01 .05
608 Chet Lemon .01 .05
609 Fred Lynn .01 .05
610 Jack Morris .02 .10
611 Matt Nokes .01 .05
612 Gary Pettis .01 .05
613 Kevin Ritz RC .01 .05
614 Jeff M. Robinson .01 .05
615 Steve Searcy .01 .05
616 Frank Tanana .01 .05
617 Alan Trammell .02 .10
618 Gary Ward .01 .05
619 Lou Whitaker .02 .10
620 Frank Williams .01 .05
621A George Brett '80 ERR .75 2.00
621B George Brett '80 .10 .30
622 Fern.Valenzuela '81 .01 .05
623 Dale Murphy '82 .05 .15
624A Cal Ripken '83 ERR 2.00 5.00
624B Cal Ripken '83 COR .15 .40
625 Ryne Sandberg '84 .08 .25
626 Don Mattingly '85 .07 .20
627 Roger Clemens '86 .20 .50
628 George Bell '87 .01 .05
629 Jose Canseco '88 UER .02 .10
630A Will Clark '89 ERR 32 .40 1.00
630B Will Clark '89 COR 321 .05 .15
631 M.Davis/M.Williams .01 .05
632 W.Boggs/M.Greenwell .02 .10
633 M.Gubicza/J.Russell .01 .05
634 C.Ripken/T.Fernandez .08 .25
635 K.Puckett/Bo Jackson .05 .15
636 N.Ryan/M.Scott .15 .40
637 W.Clark/K.Mitchell .02 .10
638 M.McGwire/D.Mattingly .10 .30
639 R.Sandberg/H.Johnson .08 .25
640 R.Seañez RC/C.Charland RC .02 .10
641 G.Canale RC/K.Maas RC .08 .25
642 Kelly Mann RC/D.Hansen RC .08 .25
643 G.Smith RC/S.Tate RC .02 .10
644 T.Drees RC/D.Howitt RC .02 .10
645 M.Roesler RC/D.May RC .02 .10
646 S.Hemond RC/M.Gardner RC .02 .10
647 John Orton RC/S.Leius RC .02 .10
648 R.Monteleone RC/D.Williams RC .02 .10
649 M.Huff RC/S.Frey RC .02 .10
650 C.McElroy RC/M.Alou RC .30 .75
651 B.Rose RC/M.Hartley RC .08 .25
652 M.Kinzer RC/W.Edwards RC .02 .10
653 D.DeShields RC/J.Grimsley RC .08 .25
654 CL: A's .01 .05
Cubs
Giants
Blue Jays
655 CL: Royals .01 .05

Angels
Padres
Orioles
656 CL: Mets .01 .05
Astros
Cards
Red Sox
657 CL: Rangers .01 .05
Brewers
Expos
Twins
658 CL: Dodgers .01 .05
Reds
Yankees
Pirates
659 CL: Indians .01 .05
Mariners
White Sox
Phillies
660A CL: Braves/Tigers/Specials
Checklists/(Checklist .01 .05
660B CL: Braves/Tigers/Specials
Checklists/(Checklist .01 .05
NNO 10th Anniversary Pin .75 2.00

1990 Fleer Canadian

STARS: 4X to 10X BASIC CARDS
YOUNG STARS: 4X to 10X BASIC CARDS
*ROOKIES: 4X to 10X BASIC CARDS

1990 Fleer All-Stars

The 1990 Fleer All-Star insert set includes 12 standard-size cards. The set was randomly inserted in 33-card cellos and wax packs. The set is sequenced in alphabetical order. The fronts are white with a light gray screen and bright red stripes. The player selection for the set is Fleer's opinion of the best Major Leaguer at each position.

COMPLETE SET (12) 1.25 3.00
RANDOM INSERTS IN PACKS
1 Harold Baines .08 .25
2 Will Clark .08 .25
3 Mark Davis .05 .15
4 Howard Johnson UER .05 .15
5 Joe Magrane .05 .15
6 Kevin Mitchell .05 .15
7 Kirby Puckett .25 .60
8 Cal Ripken .75 2.00
9 Ryne Sandberg .40 1.00
10 Mike Scott .05 .15
11 Ruben Sierra .08 .25
12 Mickey Tettleton .05 .15

1990 Fleer League Standouts

This six-card standard-size insert set was distributed one per 45-card rack pack. The set is subtitled "Standouts" and commemorates outstanding events for those players from the previous season.

COMPLETE SET (6) 3.00 8.00
ONE PER RACK PACK .60 1.25
1 Barry Larkin .50 1.25
2 Don Mattingly 2.00 5.00
3 Darryl Strawberry .30 .75
4 Jose Canseco .50 1.25
5 Wade Boggs .50 1.25
6 Mark Grace .50 1.25

1990 Fleer Soaring Stars

The 1990 Fleer Soaring Stars set was issued exclusively in jumbo cello packs. This 12-card, standard-size set features some of the most popular young players entering the 1990 season. The set gives the visual impression of rockets exploding in the air to honor these young players.

COMPLETE SET (12) 6.00 15.00
RANDOM INSERTS IN JUMBO PACKS
1 Todd Zeile .40 1.00
2 Mike Stanton .20 .50
3 Larry Walker .75 2.00
4 Robin Ventura .75 2.00
5 Scott Coolbaugh .20 .50
6 Ken Griffey Jr. 2.50 6.00
7 Tom Gordon .40 1.00
8 Jerome Walton .20 .50
9 Junior Felix .20 .50
10 Jim Abbott .60 1.50
11 Ricky Jordan .20 .50
12 Dwight Smith .20 .50

1990 Fleer Wax Box Cards

The 1990 Fleer wax box cards comprise seven different box bottoms with four cards each, for a total of 28 standard-size cards. The outer front borders are white; the inner, ribbon-like borders are different depending on the team. The vertically oriented backs are gray. The cards are numbered with a "C" prefix.

COMPLETE SET (28) 5.00 12.00
C1 Giants Logo .02 .10
C2 Tim Belcher .02 .10
C3 Roger Clemens 1.00 2.50
C4 Eric Davis .08 .25
C5 Glenn Davis .02 .10
C6 Cubs Logo .02 .10
C7 John Franco .08 .25
C8 Mike Greenwell .02 .10
C9 A's Logo .02 .10
C10 Ken Griffey Jr. 1.50 4.00
C11 Pedro Guerrero .02 .10
C12 Tony Gwynn 1.00 2.50
C13 Blue Jays Logo .02 .10
C14 Orel Hershiser .08 .25
C15 Bo Jackson .30 .75
C16 Howard Johnson .02 .10
C17 Mets Logo .02 .10
C18 Cardinals Logo .02 .10
C19 Don Mattingly 1.00 2.50
C20 Mark McGwire .75 2.00
C21 Kevin Mitchell .02 .10
C22 Kirby Puckett .40 1.00
C23 Royals Logo .02 .10
C24 Orioles Logo .02 .10
C25 Ruben Sierra .08 .25
C26 Dave Stewart .08 .25
C27 Jerome Walton .02 .10
C28 Robin Yount .50 1.25

1990 Fleer World Series

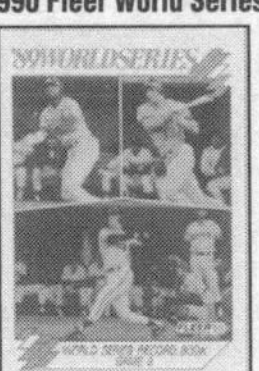

This 12-card standard-size set was issued as an insert in with the Fleer factory sets, celebrating the 1989 World Series. This set marked the fourth year that Fleer issued a special World Series set in their factory (or vend) set. The design of these cards are different from the regular Fleer issue as the photo is framed by a white border with red and blue World Series cards and the player description in black.

COMPLETE SET (12) .40 1.00
ONE SET PER FACTORY SET
1 Mike Moore .01 .05
2 Kevin Mitchell .01 .05
3 Terry Steinbach .01 .05
4 Will Clark .02 .10
5 Jose Canseco .05 .15
6 Walt Weiss .01 .05
7 Terry Steinbach .01 .05
8 Dave Stewart .02 .10
9 Dave Parker .02 .10
10 D.Parker/J.Canseco/W.Clark .02 .10
11 Rickey Henderson .08 .25
12 Oakland A's Celebrate .02 .10

1990 Fleer Update

The 1990 Fleer Update set contains 132 standard-size cards. This set marked the seventh consecutive year Fleer issued an end of season Update set. The set was issued exclusively as a boxed set through hobby dealers. The set is checklisted alphabetically by team for each league and then alphabetically within each team. The fronts are styled the same as the 1990 Fleer regular issue set. The backs are numbered with the prefix "U" for Update. Rookie Cards in this set include Travis Fryman, Todd Hundley, John Olerud and Frank Thomas.

COMP.FACT.SET (132) 1.50 4.00
U PREFIX ON CARD NUMBERS
1 Steve Avery .01 .05
2 Francisco Cabrera .01 .05
3 Nick Esasky .01 .05
4 Jim Kremers RC .01 .05
5 Greg Olson (C) RC .02 .10
6 Jim Presley .01 .05
7 Shawn Boskie RC .02 .10
8 Joe Kraemer RC .01 .05
9 Luis Salazar .01 .05
10 Hector Villanueva RC .01 .05
11 Glenn Braggs .01 .05
12 Mariano Duncan .01 .05
13 Billy Hatcher .01 .05
14 Tim Layana RC .01 .05
15 Hal Morris .01 .05
16 Javier Ortiz RC .01 .05
17 Dave Rohde RC .01 .05
18 Eric Yelding RC .01 .05
19 Hubie Brooks .01 .05
20 Kal Daniels .01 .05
21 Dave Hansen RC .01 .05
22 Mike Hartley .01 .05
23 Stan Javier .01 .05
24 Jose Offerman RC .08 .25
25 Juan Samuel .01 .05
26 Dennis Boyd .01 .05
27 Delino DeShields .08 .25
28 Steve Frey .01 .05
29 Mark Gardner .01 .05
30 Chris Nabholz RC .02 .10
31 Bill Sampen RC .01 .05
32 Dave Schmidt .01 .05
33 Daryl Boston .01 .05
34 Chuck Carr RC .02 .10
35 John Franco .02 .10
36 Todd Hundley RC .08 .25
37 Julio Machado RC .01 .05
38 Alejandro Pena .01 .05
39 Darren Reed RC .01 .05
40 Kelvin Torve .01 .05
41 Darrel Akerfelds .01 .05
42 Jose DeJesus .01 .05
43 Dave Hollins UER RC .08 .25
44 Carmelo Martinez .01 .05
45 Brad Moore .01 .05
46 Dale Murphy .05 .15
47 Wally Backman .01 .05
48 Stan Belinda RC .02 .10
49 Bob Patterson .01 .05
50 Ted Power .01 .05
51 Don Slaught .01 .05
52 Geronimo Pena RC .02 .10
53 Lee Smith .02 .10
54 John Tudor .01 .05
55 Joe Carter .02 .10
56 Thomas Howard .01 .05
57 Craig Lefferts .01 .05
58 Rafael Valdez RC .01 .05
59 Dave Anderson .01 .05
60 Kevin Bass .01 .05
61 John Burkett .01 .05
62 Gary Carter .02 .10
63 Rick Parker RC .01 .05
64 Trevor Wilson .01 .05
65 Chris Hoiles RC .08 .25
66 Tim Hulett .01 .05
67 Dave Wayne Johnson RC .01 .05
68 Curt Schilling .40 1.00
69 David Segui RC .15 .40
70 Tom Brunansky .01 .05
71 Greg A. Harris .01 .05
72 Dana Kiecker RC .01 .05
73 Tim Naehring RC .02 .10
74 Tony Pena .01 .05
75 Jeff Reardon .02 .10
76 Jerry Reed .01 .05
77 Mark Eichhorn .01 .05
78 Mark Langston .01 .05
79 John Orton .01 .05
80 Luis Polonia .01 .05
81 Dave Winfield .02 .10
82 Cliff Young RC .01 .05
83 Wayne Edwards RC .01 .05
84 Alex Fernandez RC .08 .25
85 Craig Grebeck RC .02 .10
86 Scott Radinsky RC .02 .10
87 Frank Thomas RC .75 2.00
88 Beau Allred RC .01 .05
89 Sandy Alomar Jr. .02 .10
90 Carlos Baerga RC .08 .25
91 Kevin Bearse RC .01 .05
92 Chris James .01 .05
93 Candy Maldonado .01 .05
94 Jeff Manto .01 .05
95 Cecil Fielder .02 .10
96 Travis Fryman RC .15 .40
97 Lloyd Moseby .01 .05
98 Edwin Nunez .01 .05
99 Tony Phillips .01 .05
100 Larry Sheets .01 .05
101 Mark Davis .01 .05
102 Storm Davis .01 .05
103 Gerald Perry .01 .05
104 Terry Shumpert RC .01 .05
105 Edgar Diaz RC .01 .05
106 Dave Parker .02 .10
107 Tim Drummond RC .01 .05
108 Junior Ortiz .01 .05
109 Park Pittman RC .01 .05
110 Kevin Tapani RC .08 .25
111 Oscar Azocar RC .01 .05
112 Jim Leyritz RC .08 .25
113 Kevin Maas .02 .10
114 Alan Mills RC .02 .10
115 Matt Nokes .01 .05
116 Pascual Perez .01 .05
117 Ozzie Canseco .01 .05
118 Scott Sanderson .01 .05
119 Tino Martinez .20 .50
120 Jeff Schaefer RC .01 .05
121 Matt Young .01 .05
122 Brian Bohanon RC .02 .10
123 Jeff Huson .01 .05
124 Ramon Manon RC .01 .05
125 Gary Mielke RC .01 .05
126 Willie Blair RC .02 .10
127 Glenallen Hill .01 .05
128 John Olerud RC .20 .50
129 Luis Sojo RC .01 .05
130 Mark Whiten RC .08 .25
131 Nolan Ryan SPEC .40 1.00
132 Checklist U1-U132 .01 .05

1990 Fleer Award Winners

The 1990 Fleer Award Winners set was printed by Fleer for Hills stores (as well as for some 7/Eleven's) and released early in the summer of 1990. The original suggested retail price for the set at Hills was 2.49. The set features a player photo within a trophy design with the player's name, team and position at the base. This 44-card standard-size set is numbered in alphabetical order, although Will Clark erroneously precedes Jack Clark. Card number 10 is listed on the box checklist as being Ron Darling, but Darling is not in the set. Consequently the numbers on the box checklist between 10 and 37 are off by one. Darryl Strawberry (38) is not listed on the box, but is included in the set.

COMP.FACT SET (44) 5.00 12.00
1 Jeff Ballard .01 .05
2 Tim Belcher .01 .05
3 Bert Blyleven .02 .10
4 Wade Boggs .15 .40
5 Bob Boone .02 .10
6 Jose Canseco .15 .40
7 Will Clark .20 .50
8 Jack Clark .02 .10
9 Vince Coleman .01 .05
10 Eric Davis .02 .10
11 Jose DeLeon .01 .05
12 Tony Fernandez .02 .10
13 Carlton Fisk .15 .40
14 Scott Garrelts .01 .05
15 Tom Gordon .05 .15
16 Ken Griffey Jr. 1.50 4.00
17 Von Hayes .01 .05
18 Rickey Henderson .30 .75
19 Bo Jackson .25 .60
20 Howard Johnson .01 .05
21 Don Mattingly .40 1.00
22 Fred McGriff .15 .40
23 Kevin Mitchell .01 .05
24 Gregg Olson .01 .05
25 Gary Pettis .01 .05
26 Kirby Puckett .20 .50
27 Harold Reynolds .02 .10
28 Jeff Russell .01 .05
29 Nolan Ryan .75 2.00
30 Bret Saberhagen .02 .10
31 Ryne Sandberg .30 .75
32 Benito Santiago .02 .10
33 Mike Scott .01 .05
34 Ruben Sierra .02 .10
35 Lonnie Smith .01 .05
36 Ozzie Smith .40 1.00
37 Dave Stewart .02 .10
38 Darryl Strawberry .02 .10
39 Greg Swindell .01 .05
40 Andy Van Slyke .01 .05
41 Tim Wallach .01 .05
42 Jerome Walton .01 .05
43 Mitch Williams .01 .05
44 Robin Yount .15 .40

1990 Fleer Baseball All-Stars

The 1990 Fleer Baseball All-Stars Set was produced by Fleer for the Ben Franklin chain and released early in the summer of 1990. This standard-size 44-card set features some of the best of today's players in alphabetical order. The design of the cards has vertical stripes on the front of the card. The set's custom box gives the set checklist on the back panel. The box also includes six peel-off team logo stickers each with a trivia quiz on back.

COMP.FACT SET (44) 5.00 12.00
1 Wade Boggs .15 .40
2 Bobby Bonilla .01 .05
3 Tim Burke .01 .05
4 Jose Canseco .15 .40
5 Will Clark .20 .50
6 Eric Davis .02 .10
7 Glenn Davis .01 .05
8 Julio Franco .02 .10
9 Tony Fernandez .02 .10
10 Gary Gaetti .02 .10
11 Scott Garrelts .01 .05
12 Mark Grace .20 .50
13 Mike Greenwell .01 .05
14 Ken Griffey Jr. 1.50 4.00
15 Mark Gubicza .01 .05
16 Pedro Guerrero .01 .05
17 Von Hayes .01 .05
18 Orel Hershiser .02 .10
19 Bruce Hurst .01 .05
20 Bo Jackson .20 .50
21 Howard Johnson .01 .05
22 Doug Jones .01 .05
23 Barry Larkin .20 .50
24 Don Mattingly .40 1.00
25 Mark McGwire .50 1.25
26 Kevin McReynolds .01 .05
27 Kevin Mitchell .01 .05
28 Dan Plesac .01 .05
29 Kirby Puckett .20 .50
30 Cal Ripken .75 2.00
31 Bret Saberhagen .02 .10
32 Ryne Sandberg .40 1.00
33 Steve Sax .01 .05
34 Ruben Sierra .02 .10
35 Ozzie Smith .40 1.00
36 John Smoltz .05 .15
37 Darryl Strawberry .02 .10
38 Terry Steinbach .01 .05
39 Dave Stewart .02 .10
40 Bobby Thigpen .01 .05
41 Alan Trammell .05 .15
42 Devon White .01 .05
43 Mitch Williams .01 .05
44 Robin Yount .15 .40

1990 Fleer Baseball MVP's

The 1990 Fleer Baseball MVP's were produced by Fleer exclusively for the Toys'R'Us chain and released early in the summer of 1990. This set has a multi-colored border, is standard size, and has 44 players arranged in alphabetical order. The set's custom box gives the set checklist on the back panel. The box also includes six peel-off team logo stickers.

COMP.FACT SET (44) 5.00 12.00
1 George Bell .01 .05
2 Bert Blyleven .02 .10
3 Wade Boggs .15 .40
4 Bobby Bonilla .01 .05
5 George Brett .40 1.00
6 Jose Canseco .15 .40
7 Will Clark .20 .50
8 Roger Clemens .40 1.00
9 Eric Davis .02 .10
10 Glenn Davis .01 .05
11 Tony Fernandez .02 .10
12 Dwight Gooden .02 .10
13 Mike Greenwell .01 .05
14 Ken Griffey Jr. 1.25 3.00
15 Pedro Guerrero .01 .05
16 Tony Gwynn .40 1.00
17 Rickey Henderson .25 .60
18 Tom Herr .01 .05
19 Orel Hershiser .02 .10
20 Kent Hrbek .02 .10
21 Bo Jackson .20 .50
22 Howard Johnson .01 .05
23 Don Mattingly .40 1.00
24 Fred McGriff .15 .40
25 Mark McGwire .50 1.25
26 Kevin Mitchell .01 .05
27 Paul Molitor .15 .40
28 Dale Murphy .07 .20
29 Kirby Puckett .20 .50
30 Tim Raines .02 .10
31 Cal Ripken .75 2.00
32 Bret Saberhagen .02 .10
33 Ryne Sandberg .30 .75
34 Ruben Sierra .02 .10
35 Dwight Smith .01 .05
36 Ozzie Smith .40 1.00
37 Darryl Strawberry .02 .10
38 Dave Stewart .02 .10
39 Greg Swindell .01 .05
40 Bobby Thigpen .01 .05
41 Alan Trammell .05 .15
42 Jerome Walton .01 .05
43 Mitch Williams .01 .05
44 Robin Yount .15 .40

1990 Fleer League Leaders

The 1990 Fleer League Leader set was issued by Fleer for Walgreen stores. This set design features solid blue borders with the players photo inset within the middle of the card. This 44-card, standard-size set is numbered in alphabetical order. The set's custom box gives the set checklist on the back panel. The box also includes six peel-off team logo stickers. The original suggested retail price for the set at Walgreen's was 2.49.

COMP.FACT SET (44) 5.00 12.00
1 Roberto Alomar .30 .75
2 Tim Belcher .01 .05
3 George Bell .01 .05
4 Wade Boggs .15 .40
5 Jose Canseco .20 .50
6 Will Clark .20 .50
7 David Cone .07 .20
8 Eric Davis .02 .10
9 Glenn Davis .01 .05
10 Nick Esasky .01 .05
11 Dennis Eckersley .15 .40
12 Mark Grace .20 .50
13 Mike Greenwell .01 .05
14 Ken Griffey Jr. 1.50 4.00
15 Mark Gubicza .01 .05
16 Pedro Guerrero .01 .05
17 Tony Gwynn .40 1.00
18 Rickey Henderson .25 .60
19 Bo Jackson .20 .50
20 Doug Jones .01 .05
21 Ricky Jordan .01 .05
22 Barry Larkin .20 .50
23 Don Mattingly .40 1.00
24 Fred McGriff .15 .40
25 Mark McGwire .50 1.25
26 Kevin Mitchell .01 .05
27 Jack Morris .02 .10
28 Gregg Olson .01 .05
29 Dan Plesac .01 .05
30 Kirby Puckett .20 .50
31 Nolan Ryan .75 2.00
32 Bret Saberhagen .02 .10
33 Ryne Sandberg .40 1.00
34 Steve Sax .01 .05
35 Mike Scott .01 .05
36 Ruben Sierra .02 .10
37 Lonnie Smith .01 .05
38 Darryl Strawberry .02 .10
39 Bobby Thigpen .01 .05
40 Andy Van Slyke .02 .10
41 Tim Wallach .01 .05
42 Jerome Walton UER/(Photo actually .01 .05
Eric Yelding)
43 Devon White .01 .05
44 Robin Yount .15 .40

1991 Fleer

The 1991 Fleer set consists of 720 standard-size cards. Cards were primarily issued in wax packs, cello packs and factory sets. This set does not have what had been a Fleer tradition in prior years, the two-player Rookie Cards and there are less two-player special cards than in prior years. The design features bright yellow borders with the information in black indicating name, position, and team. The set is again ordered numerically by teams, followed by combination cards, rookie prospect pairs, and checklists. There are no notable Rookie Cards in this set. A number of the cards in the set can be found with photos cropped (very slightly) differently as Fleer used two separate printers in their attempt to maximize production.

COMPLETE SET (720) 3.00 8.00
COMP.RETAIL SET (732) 4.00 10.00
COMP.HOBBY SET (732) 4.00 10.00
1 Troy Afenir RC .01 .05
2 Harold Baines .02 .10
3 Lance Blankenship .01 .05
4 Todd Burns .01 .05
5 Jose Canseco .05 .15
6 Dennis Eckersley .02 .10
7 Mike Gallego .01 .05
8 Ron Hassey .01 .05
9 Dave Henderson .01 .05
10 Rickey Henderson .08 .25
11 Rick Honeycutt .01 .05
12 Doug Jennings .01 .05
13 Joe Klink .01 .05
14 Carney Lansford .02 .10
15 Darren Lewis .01 .05
16 Willie McGee UER .02 .1
17 Mark McGwire UER .30 .7
18 Mike Moore .01 .0
19 Gene Nelson .01 .0
20 Dave Otto .01 .0
21 Jamie Quirk .01 .0
22 Willie Randolph .02 .1
23 Scott Sanderson .01 .0
24 Terry Steinbach .01 .0
25 Dave Stewart .02 .1
26 Walt Weiss .01 .0
27 Bob Welch .01 .0
28 Curt Young .01 .0
29 Wally Backman .01 .0
30 Stan Belinda UER .01 .0
31 Jay Bell .02 .1
32 Rafael Belliard .01 .0
33 Barry Bonds .40 1.0
34 Bobby Bonilla .02 .1
35 Sid Bream .01 .0
36 Doug Drabek .01 .0
37 Carlos Garcia RC .02 .1
38 Neal Heaton .01 .0
39 Jeff King .01 .0
40 Bob Kipper .01 .0
41 Bill Landrum .01 .0
42 Mike LaValliere .01 .0
43 Jose Lind .01 .0
44 Carmelo Martinez .01 .0
45 Bob Patterson .01 .0
46 Ted Power .01 .0
47 Gary Redus .01 .0
48 R.J. Reynolds .01 .0
49 Don Slaught .01 .0
50 John Smiley .01 .0
51 Zane Smith .01 .0
52 Randy Tomlin RC .02 .1
53 Andy Van Slyke .05 .1
54 Bob Walk .01 .0
55 Jack Armstrong .01 .0
56 Todd Benzinger .01 .0
57 Glenn Braggs .01 .0
58 Keith Brown .01 .0
59 Tom Browning .01 .0
60 Norm Charlton .01 .0
61 Eric Davis .02 .1
62 Rob Dibble .02 .1
63 Bill Doran .01 .0
64 Mariano Duncan .01 .0
65 Chris Hammond .01 .0
66 Billy Hatcher .01 .0
67 Danny Jackson .01 .0
68 Barry Larkin .05 .1
69 Tim Layana UER .01 .0
70 Terry Lee RC .01 .0
71 Rick Mahler .01 .0
72 Hal Morris .01 .0
73 Randy Myers .01 .0
74 Ron Oester .01 .0
75 Joe Oliver .01 .0
76 Paul O'Neill .05 .1
77 Luis Quinones .01 .0
78 Jeff Reed .01 .0
79 Jose Rijo .01 .0
80 Chris Sabo .01 .0
81 Scott Scudder .01 .0
82 Herm Winningham .01 .0
83 Larry Andersen .01 .0
84 Marty Barrett .01 .0
85 Mike Boddicker .01 .0
86 Wade Boggs .05 .1
87 Tom Bolton .01 .0
88 Tom Brunansky .01 .0
89 Ellis Burks .02 .1
90 Roger Clemens .30 .7
91 Scott Cooper .01 .0
92 John Dopson .01 .0
93 Dwight Evans .05 .1
94 Wes Gardner .01 .0
95 Jeff Gray .01 .0
96 Mike Greenwell .01 .0
97 Greg A. Harris .01 .0
98 Daryl Irvine RC .01 .0
99 Dana Kiecker .01 .0
100 Randy Kutcher .01 .0
101 Dennis Lamp .01 .0
102 Mike Marshall .01 .0
103 John Marzano .01 .0
104 Rob Murphy .01 .0
105 Tim Naehring .01 .0
106 Tony Pena .01 .0
107 Phil Plantier RC .08 .2
108 Carlos Quintana .01 .0
109 Jeff Reardon .02 .1
110 Jerry Reed .01 .0
111 Jody Reed .01 .0
112 Luis Rivera UER .01 .0
Born 1/3/84
113 Kevin Romine .01 .0
114 Phil Bradley .01 .0
115 Ivan Calderon .01 .0
116 Wayne Edwards .01 .0
117 Alex Fernandez .01 .0
118 Carlton Fisk .05 .1
119 Scott Fletcher .01 .0
120 Craig Grebeck .01 .0
121 Ozzie Guillen .02 .1
122 Greg Hibbard .01 .0
123 Lance Johnson UER .01 .0
Born Cincinnati, should
be Lincoln Heights
124 Barry Jones .01 .0
125 Ron Karkovice .01 .0

126 Eric King .01 .05
127 Steve Lyons .01 .05
128 Carlos Martinez .01 .05
129 Jack McDowell UER .01 .05
Stanford misspelled
as Standford on back
130 Donn Pall .01 .05
No dots over any
i's in text
131 Dan Pasqua .01 .05
132 Ken Patterson .01 .05
133 Melido Perez .01 .05
134 Adam Peterson .01 .05
135 Scott Radinsky .01 .05
136 Sammy Sosa .08 .25
137 Bobby Thigpen .01 .05
138 Frank Thomas .08 .25
139 Robin Ventura .02 .10
140 Daryl Boston .01 .05
141 Chuck Carr .01 .05
142 Mark Carreon .01 .05
143 David Cone .02 .10
144 Ron Darling .01 .05
145 Kevin Elster .01 .05
146 Sid Fernandez .01 .05
147 John Franco .02 .10
148 Dwight Gooden .02 .10
149 Tom Herr .01 .05
150 Todd Hundley .01 .05
151 Gregg Jefferies .01 .05
152 Howard Johnson .01 .05
153 Dave Magadan .01 .05
154 Kevin McReynolds .01 .05
155 Keith Miller UER .01 .05
Text says Rochester in
'87, stats say Tide-
water, mixed up with
other Keith Miller
156 Bob Ojeda .01 .05
157 Tom O'Malley .01 .05
158 Alejandro Pena .01 .05
159 Darren Reed .01 .05
160 Mackey Sasser .01 .05
161 Darryl Strawberry .02 .10
162 Tim Teufel .01 .05
163 Kelvin Torve .01 .05
164 Julio Valera .01 .05
165 Frank Viola .02 .10
166 Wally Whitehurst .01 .05
167 Jim Acker .01 .05
168 Derek Bell .02 .10
169 George Bell .01 .05
170 Willie Blair .01 .05
171 Pat Borders .01 .05
172 John Cerutti .01 .05
173 Junior Felix .01 .05
174 Tony Fernandez .01 .05
175 Kelly Gruber UER .01 .05
Born in Houston,
should be Bellaire
176 Tom Henke .01 .05
177 Glenallen Hill .01 .05
178 Jimmy Key .02 .10
179 Manny Lee .01 .05
180 Fred McGriff .05 .15
181 Rance Mulliniks .01 .05
182 Greg Myers .01 .05
183 John Olerud UER .02 .10
Listed as throwing
right, should be left
184 Luis Sojo .01 .05
185 Dave Stieb .01 .05
186 Todd Stottlemyre .01 .05
187 Duane Ward .01 .05
188 David Wells .02 .10
189 Mark Whiten .01 .05
190 Ken Williams .01 .05
191 Frank Wills .01 .05
192 Mookie Wilson .02 .10
193 Don Aase .01 .05
194 Tim Belcher UER .01 .05
Born Sparta, Ohio,
should say Mt. Gilead
195 Hubie Brooks .01 .05
196 Dennis Cook .01 .05
197 Tim Crews .01 .05
198 Kal Daniels .01 .05
199 Kirk Gibson .02 .10
200 Jim Gott .01 .05
201 Alfredo Griffin .01 .05
202 Chris Gwynn .01 .05
203 Dave Hansen .01 .05
204 Lenny Harris .01 .05
205 Mike Hartley .01 .05
206 Mickey Hatcher .01 .05
207 Carlos Hernandez .01 .05
208 Orel Hershiser .02 .10
209 Jay Howell UER .01 .05
No 1982 Yankee stats
210 Mike Huff .01 .05
211 Stan Javier .01 .05
212 Ramon Martinez .01 .05
213 Mike Morgan .01 .05
214 Eddie Murray .08 .25
215 Jim Neidlinger RC .01 .05
216 Jose Offerman .01 .05
217 Jim Poole .01 .05
218 Juan Samuel .01 .05
219 Mike Scioscia .01 .05
220 Ray Searage .01 .05
221 Mike Sharperson .01 .05
222 Fernando Valenzuela .02 .10
223 Jose Vizcaino .01 .05
224 Mike Aldrete .01 .05
225 Scott Anderson RC .01 .05
226 Dennis Boyd .01 .05
227 Tim Burke .01 .05
228 Delino DeShields .02 .10
229 Mike Fitzgerald .01 .05
230 Tom Foley .01 .05
231 Steve Frey .01 .05
232 Andres Galarraga .02 .10
233 Mark Gardner .01 .05
234 Marquis Grissom .02 .10
235 Kevin Gross .01 .05
No date given for
first Expos win
236 Drew Hall .01 .05
237 Dave Martinez .01 .05
238 Dennis Martinez .02 .10
239 Dale Mohorcic .01 .05
240 Chris Nabholz .01 .05
241 Otis Nixon .01 .05
242 Junior Noboa .01 .05
243 Spike Owen .01 .05
244 Tim Raines .02 .10
245 Mel Rojas UER .01 .05
Stats show 3.60 ERA,
bio says 3.19 ERA
246 Scott Ruskin .01 .05
247 Bill Sampen .01 .05
248 Nelson Santovenia .01 .05
249 Dave Schmidt .01 .05
250 Larry Walker .08 .25
251 Tim Wallach .01 .05
252 Dave Anderson .01 .05
253 Kevin Bass .01 .05
254 Steve Bedrosian .01 .05
255 Jeff Brantley .01 .05
256 John Burkett .01 .05
257 Brett Butler .02 .10
258 Gary Carter .02 .10
259 Will Clark .05 .15
260 Steve Decker RC .02 .10
261 Kelly Downs .01 .05
262 Scott Garrelts .01 .05
263 Terry Kennedy .01 .05
264 Mike LaCoss .01 .05
265 Mark Leonard RC .01 .05
266 Greg Litton .01 .05
267 Kevin Mitchell .01 .05
268 Randy O'Neal .01 .05
269 Rick Parker .01 .05
270 Rick Reuschel .01 .05
271 Ernest Riles .01 .05
272 Don Robinson .01 .05
273 Robby Thompson .01 .05
274 Mark Thurmond .01 .05
275 Jose Uribe .01 .05
276 Matt Williams .02 .10
277 Trevor Wilson .01 .05
278 Gerald Alexander RC .01 .05
279 Brad Arnsberg .01 .05
280 Kevin Belcher RC .01 .05
281 Joe Bitker RC .01 .05
282 Kevin Brown .02 .10
283 Steve Buechele .01 .05
284 Jack Daugherty .01 .05
285 Julio Franco .02 .10
286 Juan Gonzalez .08 .25
287 Bill Haselman RC .01 .05
288 Charlie Hough .02 .10
289 Jeff Huson .01 .05
290 Pete Incaviglia .01 .05
291 Mike Jeffcoat .01 .05
292 Jeff Kunkel .01 .05
293 Gary Mielke .01 .05
294 Jamie Moyer .02 .10
295 Rafael Palmeiro .05 .15
296 Geno Petralli .01 .05
297 Gary Pettis .01 .05
298 Kevin Reimer .01 .05
299 Kenny Rogers .02 .10
300 Jeff Russell .01 .05
301 John Russell .01 .05
302 Nolan Ryan .40 1.00
303 Ruben Sierra .02 .10
304 Bobby Witt .01 .05
305 Jim Abbott UER .05 .15
Text on back states he won
Sullivan Award outstanding amateur
athlete in 1989;should be '88
306 Kent Anderson .01 .05
307 Dante Bichette .02 .10
308 Bert Blyleven .02 .10
309 Chili Davis .02 .10
310 Brian Downing .01 .05
311 Mark Eichhorn .01 .05
312 Mike Fetters .01 .05
313 Chuck Finley .02 .10
314 Willie Fraser .01 .05
315 Bryan Harvey .01 .05
316 Donnie Hill .01 .05
317 Wally Joyner .02 .10
318 Mark Langston .01 .05
319 Kirk McCaskill .01 .05
320 John Orton .01 .05
321 Lance Parrish .02 .10
322 Luis Polonia UER .01 .05
1984 Madfison,
should be Madison
323 Johnny Ray .01 .05
324 Bobby Rose .01 .05
325 Dick Schofield .01 .05
326 Rick Schu .01 .05
327 Lee Stevens .01 .05
328 Devon White .02 .10
329 Dave Winfield .02 .10
330 Cliff Young .01 .05
331 Dave Bergman .01 .05
332 Phil Clark RC .02 .10
333 Darnell Coles .01 .05
334 Milt Cuyler .01 .05
335 Cecil Fielder .02 .10
336 Travis Fryman .02 .10
337 Paul Gibson .01 .05
338 Jerry Don Gleaton .01 .05
339 Mike Heath .01 .05
340 Mike Henneman .01 .05
341 Chet Lemon .01 .05
342 Lance McCullers .01 .05
343 Jack Morris .02 .10
344 Lloyd Moseby .01 .05
345 Edwin Nunez .01 .05
346 Clay Parker .01 .05
347 Dan Petry .01 .05
348 Tony Phillips .01 .05
349 Jeff M. Robinson .01 .05
350 Mark Salas .01 .05
351 Mike Schwabe .01 .05
352 Larry Sheets .01 .05
353 John Shelby .01 .05
354 Frank Tanana .01 .05
355 Alan Trammell .02 .10
356 Gary Ward .01 .05
357 Lou Whitaker .02 .10
358 Beau Allred .01 .05
359 Sandy Alomar Jr. .01 .05
360 Carlos Baerga .01 .05
361 Kevin Bearse .01 .05
362 Tom Brookens .01 .05
363 Jerry Browne UER .01 .05
No dot over i in
first text line
364 Tom Candiotti .01 .05
365 Alex Cole .01 .05
366 John Farrell UER .01 .05
Born in Neptune,
should be Monmouth
367 Felix Fermin .01 .05
368 Keith Hernandez .02 .10
369 Brook Jacoby .01 .05
370 Chris James .01 .05
371 Dion James .01 .05
372 Doug Jones .01 .05
373 Candy Maldonado .01 .05
374 Steve Olin .01 .05
375 Jesse Orosco .01 .05
376 Rudy Seanez .01 .05
377 Joel Skinner .01 .05
378 Cory Snyder .01 .05
379 Greg Swindell .01 .05
380 Sergio Valdez .01 .05
381 Mike Walker .01 .05
382 Colby Ward RC .01 .05
383 Turner Ward RC .08 .25
384 Mitch Webster .01 .05
385 Kevin Wickander .01 .05
386 Darrel Akerfelds .01 .05
387 Joe Boever .01 .05
388 Rod Booker .01 .05
389 Sil Campusano .01 .05
390 Don Carman .01 .05
391 Wes Chamberlain RC .08 .25
392 Pat Combs .01 .05
393 Darren Daulton .02 .10
394 Jose DeJesus .01 .05
395A Len Dykstra .02 .10
Name spelled Lenny on back
395B Len Dykstra .02 .10
Name spelled Len on back
396 Jason Grimsley .01 .05
397 Charlie Hayes .01 .05
398 Von Hayes .01 .05
399 David Hollins UER .01 .05
At-bats& should
say at-bats
400 Ken Howell .01 .05
401 Ricky Jordan .01 .05
402 John Kruk .02 .10
403 Steve Lake .01 .05
404 Chuck Malone .01 .05
405 Roger McDowell UER .01 .05
Says Phillies is
saves, should say in
406 Chuck McElroy .01 .05
407 Mickey Morandini .01 .05
408 Terry Mulholland .01 .05
409 Dale Murphy .05 .15
410A Randy Ready ERR .01 .05
No Brewers stats
listed for 1983
410B Randy Ready COR .01 .05
411 Bruce Ruffin .01 .05
412 Dickie Thon .01 .05
413 Paul Assenmacher .01 .05
414 Damon Berryhill .01 .05
415 Mike Bielecki .01 .05
416 Shawn Boskie .01 .05
417 Dave Clark .01 .05
418 Doug Dascenzo .01 .05
419A Andre Dawson ERR .02 .10
No stats for 1976
419B Andre Dawson COR .02 .10
420 Shawon Dunston .01 .05
421 Joe Girardi .01 .05
422 Mark Grace .05 .15
423 Mike Harkey .01 .05
424 Les Lancaster .01 .05
425 Bill Long .01 .05
426 Greg Maddux .15 .40
427 Derrick May .01 .05
428 Jeff Pico .01 .05
429 Domingo Ramos .01 .05
430 Luis Salazar .01 .05
431 Ryne Sandberg .15 .40
432 Dwight Smith .01 .05
433 Greg Smith .01 .05
434 Rick Sutcliffe .02 .10
435 Gary Varsho .01 .05
436 Hector Villanueva .01 .05
437 Jerome Walton .01 .05
438 Curtis Wilkerson .01 .05
439 Mitch Williams .01 .05
440 Steve Wilson .01 .05
441 Marvell Wynne .01 .05
442 Scott Bankhead .01 .05
443 Scott Bradley .01 .05
444 Greg Briley .01 .05
445 Mike Brumley UER .01 .05
Text 40 SB's in 1988,
stats say 41
446 Jay Buhner .02 .10
447 Dave Burba RC .08 .25
448 Henry Cotto .01 .05
449 Alvin Davis .01 .05
450 Ken Griffey Jr. .25 .60
Bat around .300
450A Ken Griffey Jr. .50 1.25
Bat .300
451 Erik Hanson .01 .05
452 Gene Harris UER .01 .05
63 career runs,
should be 73
453 Brian Holman .01 .05
454 Mike Jackson .01 .05
455 Randy Johnson .10 .30
456 Jeffrey Leonard .01 .05
457 Edgar Martinez .05 .15
458 Tino Martinez .08 .25
459 Pete O'Brien UER .01 .05
1987 BA .266,
should be .286
460 Harold Reynolds .02 .10
461 Mike Schooler .01 .05
462 Bill Swift .01 .05
463 David Valle .01 .05
464 Omar Vizquel .05 .15
465 Matt Young .01 .05
466 Brady Anderson .02 .10
467 Jeff Ballard UER .01 .05
Missing top of right
parenthesis after
Saberhagen in last
text line
468 Juan Bell .01 .05
469A Mike Devereaux .02 .10
First line of text
ends with six
469B Mike Devereaux .02 .10
First line of text
ends with runs
470 Steve Finley .02 .10
471 Dave Gallagher .01 .05
472 Leo Gomez .01 .05
473 Rene Gonzales .01 .05
474 Pete Harnisch .01 .05
475 Kevin Hickey .01 .05
476 Chris Hoiles .01 .05
477 Sam Horn .01 .05
478 Tim Hulett .01 .05
Photo shows National
Leaguer sliding into
second base
479 Dave Johnson .01 .05
480 Ron Kittle UER .01 .05
Edmonton misspelled
as Edmundton
481 Ben McDonald .01 .05
482 Bob Melvin .01 .05
483 Bob Milacki .01 .05
484 Randy Milligan .01 .05
485 John Mitchell .01 .05
486 Gregg Olson .01 .05
487 Joe Orsulak .01 .05
488 Joe Price .01 .05
489 Bill Ripken .01 .05
490 Cal Ripken .30 .75
491 Curt Schilling .08 .25
492 David Segui .01 .05
493 Anthony Telford RC .01 .05
494 Mickey Tettleton .01 .05
495 Mark Williamson .01 .05
496 Craig Worthington .01 .05
497 Juan Agosto .01 .05
498 Eric Anthony .01 .05
499 Craig Biggio .05 .15
500 Ken Caminiti UER .02 .10
Born 4
4, should
be 4
21
501 Casey Candaele .01 .05
502 Andujar Cedeno .01 .05
503 Danny Darwin .01 .05
504 Mark Davidson .01 .05
505 Glenn Davis .01 .05
506 Jim Deshaies .01 .05
507 Luis Gonzalez RC .20 .50
508 Bill Gullickson .01 .05
509 Xavier Hernandez .01 .05
510 Brian Meyer .01 .05
511 Ken Oberkfell .01 .05
512 Mark Portugal .01 .05
513 Rafael Ramirez .01 .05
514 Karl Rhodes .01 .05
515 Mike Scott .01 .05
516 Mike Simms RC .01 .05
517 Dave Smith .01 .05
518 Franklin Stubbs .01 .05
519 Glenn Wilson .01 .05
520 Eric Yelding UER .01 .05
Text has 63 steals,
stats have 64,
which is correct
521 Gerald Young .01 .05
522 Shawn Abner .01 .05
523 Roberto Alomar .05 .15
524 Andy Benes .01 .05
525 Joe Carter .02 .10
526 Jack Clark .02 .10
527 Joey Cora .01 .05
528 Paul Faries RC .01 .05
529 Tony Gwynn .10 .30
530 Atlee Hammaker .01 .05
531 Greg W. Harris .01 .05
532 Thomas Howard .01 .05
533 Bruce Hurst .01 .05
534 Craig Lefferts .01 .05
535 Derek Lilliquist .01 .05
536 Fred Lynn .01 .05
537 Mike Pagliarulo .01 .05
538 Mark Parent .01 .05
539 Dennis Rasmussen .01 .05
540 Bip Roberts .01 .05
541 Richard Rodriguez RC .01 .05
542 Benito Santiago .02 .10
543 Calvin Schiraldi .01 .05
544 Eric Show .01 .05
545 Phil Stephenson .01 .05
546 Garry Templeton UER .01 .05
Born 3/24/57,
should be 3/24/56
547 Ed Whitson .01 .05
548 Eddie Williams .01 .05
549 Kevin Appier .02 .10
550 Luis Aquino .01 .05
551 Bob Boone .02 .10
552 George Brett .25 .60
553 Jeff Conine RC .15 .40
554 Steve Crawford .01 .05
555 Mark Davis .01 .05
556 Storm Davis .01 .05
557 Jim Eisenreich .01 .05
558 Steve Farr .01 .05
559 Tom Gordon .01 .05
560 Mark Gubicza .01 .05
561 Bo Jackson .08 .25
562 Mike Macfarlane .01 .05
563 Brian McRae RC .08 .25
564 Jeff Montgomery .01 .05
565 Bill Pecota .01 .05
566 Gerald Perry .01 .05
567 Bret Saberhagen .02 .10
568 Jeff Schulz RC .01 .05
569 Kevin Seitzer .01 .05
570 Terry Shumpert .01 .05
571 Kurt Stillwell .01 .05
572 Danny Tartabull .01 .05
573 Gary Thurman .01 .05
574 Frank White .02 .10
575 Willie Wilson .01 .05
576 Chris Bosio .01 .05
577 Greg Brock .01 .05
578 George Canale .01 .05
579 Chuck Crim .01 .05
580 Rob Deer .01 .05
581 Edgar Diaz .01 .05
582 Tom Edens RC .01 .05
583 Mike Felder .01 .05
584 Jim Gantner .01 .05
585 Darryl Hamilton .01 .05
586 Ted Higuera .01 .05
587 Mark Knudson .01 .05
588 Bill Krueger .01 .05
589 Tim McIntosh .01 .05
590 Paul Mirabella .01 .05
591 Paul Molitor .02 .10
592 Jaime Navarro .01 .05
593 Dave Parker .02 .10
594 Dan Plesac .01 .05
595 Ron Robinson .01 .05
596 Gary Sheffield .02 .10
597 Bill Spiers .01 .05
598 B.J. Surhoff .02 .10
599 Greg Vaughn .01 .05
600 Randy Veres .01 .05
601 Robin Yount .15 .40
602 Rick Aguilera .02 .10
603 Allan Anderson .01 .05
604 Juan Berenguer .01 .05
605 Randy Bush .01 .05
606 Carmelo Castillo .01 .05
607 Tim Drummond .01 .05
608 Scott Erickson .01 .05
609 Gary Gaetti .02 .10
610 Greg Gagne .01 .05
611 Dan Gladden .01 .05
612 Mark Guthrie .01 .05
613 Brian Harper .01 .05
614 Kent Hrbek .02 .10
615 Gene Larkin .01 .05
616 Terry Leach .01 .05
617 Nelson Liriano .01 .05
618 Shane Mack .01 .05
619 John Moses .01 .05
620 Pedro Munoz RC .02 .10
621 Al Newman .01 .05
622 Junior Ortiz .01 .05
623 Kirby Puckett .08 .25
624 Roy Smith .01 .05
625 Kevin Tapani .01 .05
626 Gary Wayne .01 .05
627 David West .01 .05
628 Cris Carpenter .01 .05
629 Vince Coleman .01 .05
630 Ken Dayley .01 .05
631A Jose DeLeon ERR .01 .05
(missing '79 Bradenton stats
631B Jose DeLeon COR .01 .05
(with '79 Bradenton stats
632 Frank DiPino .01 .05
633 Bernard Gilkey .02 .10
634A Pedro Guerrero ERR .02 .10
634B Pedro Guerrero COR .02 .10
635 Ken Hill .01 .05
636 Felix Jose .01 .05
637 Ray Lankford .02 .10
638 Joe Magrane .01 .05
639 Tom Niedenfuer .01 .05
640 Jose Oquendo .01 .05
641 Tom Pagnozzi .01 .05
642 Terry Pendleton .02 .10
643 Mike Perez RC .02 .10
644 Bryn Smith .01 .05
645 Lee Smith .02 .10
646 Ozzie Smith .15 .40
647 Scott Terry .01 .05
648 Bob Tewksbury .01 .05
649 Milt Thompson .01 .05
650 John Tudor .01 .05
651 Denny Walling .01 .05
652 Craig Wilson RC .01 .05
653 Todd Worrell .01 .05
654 Todd Zeile .01 .05
655 Oscar Azocar .01 .05
656 Steve Balboni UER .01 .05
Born 1/5/57,
should be 1/16
657 Jesse Barfield .01 .05
658 Greg Cadaret .01 .05
659 Chuck Cary .01 .05
660 Rick Cerone .01 .05
661 Dave Eiland .01 .05
662 Alvaro Espinoza .01 .05
663 Bob Geren .01 .05
664 Lee Guetterman .01 .05
665 Mel Hall .01 .05
666 Andy Hawkins .01 .05
667 Jimmy Jones .01 .05
668 Roberto Kelly .01 .05
669 Dave LaPoint UER .01 .05
No '81 Brewers stats,
totals also are wrong
670 Tim Leary .01 .05
671 Jim Leyritz .01 .05
672 Kevin Maas .01 .05
673 Don Mattingly .25 .60
674 Matt Nokes .01 .05
675 Pascual Perez .01 .05
676 Eric Plunk .01 .05
677 Dave Righetti .02 .10
678 Jeff D. Robinson .01 .05
679 Steve Sax .01 .05
680 Mike Witt .01 .05
681 Steve Avery UER .01 .05
Born in New Jersey,
should say Michigan
682 Mike Bell RC .01 .05
683 Jeff Blauser .01 .05
684 Francisco Cabrera UER .01 .05
Born 10/16,
should say 10/10
685 Tony Castillo .01 .05
686 Marty Clary UER .01 .05
Shown pitching righty,
but bio has left
687 Nick Esasky .01 .05
688 Ron Gant .02 .10
689 Tom Glavine .05 .15
690 Mark Grant .01 .05
691 Tommy Gregg .01 .05
692 Dwayne Henry .01 .05
693 Dave Justice .02 .10
694 Jimmy Kremers .01 .05
695 Charlie Leibrandt .01 .05
696 Mark Lemke .01 .05
697 Oddibe McDowell .01 .05
698 Greg Olson .01 .05
699 Jeff Parrett .01 .05
700 Jim Presley .01 .05
701 Victor Rosario RC .01 .05
702 Lonnie Smith .01 .05
703 Pete Smith .01 .05
704 John Smoltz .05 .15
705 Mike Stanton .01 .05
706 Andres Thomas .01 .05
707 Jeff Treadway .01 .05
708 Jim Vatcher RC .01 .05
709 Ryne Sandberg .08 .25
Cecil Fielder
710 Barry Bonds .50 1.25
Ken Griffey Jr.
711 Bobby Bonilla .02 .10
Barry Larkin
712 Bobby Thigpen .01 .05
John Franco
713 Andre Dawson .08 .25
Ryne Sandberg UER
Ryno misspelled Rhino
714 CL:A's .01 .05
Pirates
Reds
Red Sox
715 CL:White Sox .01 .05
Mets
Blue Jays
Dodgers
716 CL:Expos .01 .05
Giants
Rangers
Angels
717 CL:Tigers .01 .05
Indians
Phillies
Cubs
718 CL:Mariners .01 .05
Orioles
Astros
Padres
719 CL:Royals .01 .05
Brewers
Twins
Cardinals
720 CL:Yankees .01 .05
Braves
Superstars
Specials

1991 Fleer All-Stars

For the sixth consecutive year Fleer issued an All-Star insert set. This year the cards were only available as random inserts in Fleer cello packs. This ten-card standard-size set is reminiscent of the 1971 Topps Greatest Moments set with two pictures on the (black-bordered) front as well as a photo on the back.

COMPLETE SET (10) 6.00 15.00
RANDOM INSERTS IN CELLO PACKS
1 Ryne Sandberg 1.25 3.00
2 Barry Larkin .50 1.25
3 Matt Williams .30 .75
4 Cecil Fielder .30 .75
5 Barry Bonds 3.00 8.00
6 Rickey Henderson .75 2.00
7 Ken Griffey Jr. 2.00 5.00
8 Jose Canseco .50 1.25
9 Benito Santiago .30 .75
10 Roger Clemens 2.50 6.00

1991 Fleer Pro-Visions

This 12-card standard-size insert set features paintings by artist Terry Smith framed by distinctive black borders on each card front. The cards were randomly inserted in wax and rack packs. An additional four-card set was issued only in 1991 Fleer factory sets. Those cards are numbered 1-4. Unlike the 12 cards inserted in packs, these factory set cards feature white borders on front.

COMP.WAX SET (12) 1.50 4.00
COMP.FACT.SET (4) 1.00 2.00
1-12: RANDOM INSERTS IN PACKS
F1-F4: ONE SET PER FACT.SET
1 Kirby Puckett UER .30 .75
.326 average,
should be .328
2 Will Clark UER .20 .50
On tenth line, pennant
misspelled pennent
3 Ruben Sierra UER .10 .30
No apostrophe
in hasn't
4 Mark McGwire UER 1.00 2.50
Fisk won ROY in
'72, not '82
5 Bo Jackson .30 .75
Bio says 6', others
have him at 6'1"
6 Jose Canseco UER .20 .50
Bio 6'3", 230
text has 6'4", 240
7 Dwight Gooden UER .10 .30
2.80 ERA in Lynchburg,
should be 2.50
8 Mike Greenwell UER .05 .15
.328 BA and 87 RBI,
should be .325 and 95
9 Roger Clemens 1.00 2.50
10 Eric Davis .10 .30
11 Don Mattingly .75 2.00
12 Darryl Strawberry .10 .30

1 Barry Bonds 1.25 3.00
Factory set exclusive
2 Rickey Henderson .30 .75
Factory set exclusive
3 Ryne Sandberg .50 1.25
Factory set exclusive
4 Dave Stewart .10 .30
Factory set exclusive

1991 Fleer Wax Box Cards

These cards were issued on the bottom of 1991 Fleer wax boxes. This set celebrated the spate of no-hitters in 1990 and were printed on three different boxes. These standard size cards, come four to a box, three about the no-hitters and one team logo card on each box. The cards are blank backed and are numbered on the front in a subtle way. They are ordered below as they are numbered, which is by chronological order of their no-hitters. Only the player cards are listed below since there was a different team logo card on each box.

COMPLETE SET (9) 1.50 4.00
1 Mark Langston .02 .10
and Mike Witt
2 Randy Johnson .40 1.00
3 Nolan Ryan 1.25 3.00
4 Dave Stewart .07 .20
5 Fernando Valenzuela .07 .20
6 Andy Hawkins .02 .10
7 Melido Perez .02 .10
8 Terry Mulholland .02 .10
9 Dave Stieb .07 .20

1991 Fleer World Series

This eight-card set captures highlights from the 1990 World Series between the Cincinnati Reds and the Oakland Athletics. The set was only available as an insert with the 1991 Fleer factory sets. The standard-size cards have on the fronts color action photos, bordered in blue on a white card face. The words "World Series '90" appears in red and blue lettering above the pictures. The backs have a similar design, only with a summary of an aspect of the Series on a yellow background.

COMPLETE SET (8) .30 .75
ONE COMPLETE SET PER FACTORY SET
1 Eric Davis .02 .10
2 Billy Hatcher .01 .05
3 Jose Canseco .05 .15
4 Rickey Henderson .08 .25
5 Chris Sabo .01 .05
6 Dave Stewart .02 .10
7 Jose Rijo .01 .05
8 Reds Celebrate .01 .05

1991 Fleer Update

The 1991 Fleer Update set contains 132 standard-size cards. The cards were distributed exclusively in factory set form through hobby dealers. Card design is identical to regular issue 1991 Fleer cards with the notable bright yellow borders except for the U-prefixed numbering on back. The cards are ordered alphabetically by team. The key Rookie Cards in this set are Jeff Bagwell and Ivan Rodriguez.

COMP.FACT.SET (132) 2.00 5.00
1 Glenn Davis .01 .05
2 Dwight Evans .05 .15
3 Jose Mesa .01 .05
4 Jack Clark .02 .10
5 Danny Darwin .01 .05
6 Steve Lyons .01 .05
7 Mo Vaughn .02 .10
8 Floyd Bannister .01 .05
9 Gary Gaetti .02 .10
10 Dave Parker .02 .10
11 Joey Cora .01 .05
12 Charlie Hough .02 .10
13 Matt Merullo .01 .05
14 Warren Newson RC .01 .05
15 Tim Raines .02 .10
16 Albert Belle .02 .10
17 Glenallen Hill .01 .05
18 Shawn Hillegas .01 .05
19 Mark Lewis .01 .05
20 Charles Nagy .01 .05
21 Mark Whiten .01 .05
22 John Cerutti .01 .05
23 Rob Deer .01 .05
24 Mickey Tettleton .01 .05
25 Warren Cromartie .01 .05
26 Kirk Gibson .02 .10
27 David Howard RC .01 .05
28 Brent Mayne .01 .05
29 Dante Bichette .02 .10
30 Mark Lee RC .01 .05
31 Julio Machado .01 .05
32 Edwin Nunez .01 .05
33 Willie Randolph .02 .10
34 Franklin Stubbs .01 .05
35 Bill Wegman .01 .05
36 Chili Davis .02 .10
37 Chuck Knoblauch .02 .10
38 Scott Leius .01 .05
39 Jack Morris .02 .10
40 Mike Pagliarulo .01 .05
41 Lenny Webster .01 .05
42 John Habyan .01 .05
43 Steve Howe .01 .05
44 Jeff Johnson RC .01 .05
45 Scott Kamieniecki RC .01 .05
46 Pat Kelly RC .01 .05
47 Hensley Meulens .01 .05
48 Wade Taylor RC .01 .05
49 Bernie Williams .08 .25
50 Kirk Dressendorfer RC .01 .05
51 Ernest Riles .01 .05
52 Rich DeLucia RC .01 .05
53 Tracy Jones .01 .05
54 Bill Krueger .01 .05
55 Alonzo Powell RC .01 .05
56 Jeff Schaefer .01 .05
57 Russ Swan .01 .05
58 John Barfield .01 .05
59 Rich Gossage .02 .10
60 Jose Guzman .01 .05
61 Dean Palmer .02 .10
62 Ivan Rodriguez RC .75 2.00
63 Roberto Alomar .05 .15
64 Tom Candiotti .01 .05
65 Joe Carter .02 .10
66 Ed Sprague .01 .05
67 Pat Tabler .01 .05
68 Mike Timlin RC .02 .10
69 Devon White .02 .10
70 Rafael Belliard .01 .05
71 Juan Berenguer .01 .05
72 Sid Bream .01 .05
73 Marvin Freeman .01 .05
74 Kent Mercker .01 .05
75 Otis Nixon .01 .05
76 Terry Pendleton .02 .10
77 George Bell .01 .05
78 Danny Jackson .01 .05
79 Chuck McElroy .01 .05
80 Gary Scott RC .01 .05
81 Heathcliff Slocumb RC .02 .10
82 Dave Smith .01 .05
83 Rick Wilkins RC .01 .05
84 Freddie Benavides RC .01 .05
85 Ted Power .01 .05
86 Mo Sanford RC .01 .05
87 Jeff Bagwell RC .60 1.50
88 Steve Finley .02 .10
89 Pete Harnisch .01 .05
90 Darryl Kile .02 .10
91 Brett Butler .02 .10
92 John Candelaria .01 .05
93 Gary Carter .02 .10
94 Kevin Gross .01 .05
95 Bob Ojeda .01 .05
96 Darryl Strawberry .02 .10
97 Ivan Calderon .01 .05
98 Ron Hassey .01 .05
99 Gilberto Reyes .01 .05
100 Hubie Brooks .01 .05
101 Rick Cerone .01 .05
102 Vince Coleman .01 .05
103 Jeff Innis .01 .05
104 Pete Schourek RC .01 .05
105 Andy Ashby RC .08 .25
106 Wally Backman .01 .05
107 Darrin Fletcher .01 .05
108 Tommy Greene .01 .05
109 John Morris .01 .05
110 Mitch Williams .01 .05
111 Lloyd McClendon .01 .05
112 Orlando Merced RC .01 .05
113 Vicente Palacios .01 .05
114 Gary Varsho .01 .05
115 John Wehner RC .01 .05
116 Rex Hudler .01 .05
117 Tim Jones .01 .05
118 Geronimo Pena .01 .05
119 Gerald Perry .01 .05
120 Larry Andersen .01 .05
121 Jerald Clark .01 .05
122 Scott Coolbaugh .01 .05
123 Tony Fernandez .01 .05
124 Darrin Jackson .01 .05
125 Fred McGriff .05 .15
126 Jose Mota RC .01 .05
127 Tim Teufel .01 .05
128 Bud Black .01 .05
129 Mike Felder .01 .05
130 Willie McGee .02 .10
131 Dave Righetti .02 .10
132 Checklist U1-U132 .01 .05

1992 Fleer

The 1992 Fleer set contains 720 standard-size cards issued in one comprehensive series. The cards were distributed in plastic wrapped packs, 35-card cello packs, 42-card rack packs and factory sets. The card fronts shade from metallic pale green to white as one moves down the face. The team logo and player's name appear to the right of the picture, running the length of the card. The cards are ordered alphabetically within and according to teams for each league with AL preceding NL. Topical subsets feature Major League Prospects (652-680), Record Setters (681-687), League Leaders (688-697), Super Star Specials (698-707) and Pro Visions (708-713). Rookie Cards include Scott Brosius and Vinny Castilla.

COMPLETE SET (720) 4.00 10.00
COMP.HOBBY SET (732) 8.00 20.00
COMP.RETAIL SET (732) 8.00 20.00
1 Brady Anderson .02 .10
2 Jose Bautista .02 .10
3 Juan Bell .02 .10
4 Glenn Davis .02 .10
5 Mike Devereaux .02 .10
6 Dwight Evans .05 .15
7 Mike Flanagan .02 .10
8 Leo Gomez .02 .10
9 Chris Hoiles .02 .10
10 Sam Horn .02 .10
11 Tim Hulett .02 .10
12 Dave Johnson .02 .10
13 Chito Martinez .02 .10
14 Ben McDonald .02 .10
15 Bob Melvin .02 .10
16 Luis Mercedes .02 .10
17 Jose Mesa .02 .10
18 Bob Milacki .02 .10
19 Randy Milligan .02 .10
20 Mike Mussina UER .08 .25
Card back refers
to him as Jeff
21 Gregg Olson .02 .10
22 Joe Orsulak .02 .10
23 Jim Poole .02 .10
24 Arthur Rhodes .02 .10
25 Billy Ripken .02 .10
26 Cal Ripken .30 .75
27 David Segui .02 .10
28 Roy Smith .02 .10
29 Anthony Telford .02 .10
30 Mark Williamson .02 .10
31 Craig Worthington .02 .10
32 Wade Boggs .05 .15
33 Tom Bolton .02 .10
34 Tom Brunansky .02 .10
35 Ellis Burks .02 .10
36 Jack Clark .02 .10
37 Roger Clemens .20 .50
38 Danny Darwin .02 .10
39 Mike Greenwell .02 .10
40 Joe Hesketh .02 .10
41 Daryl Irvine .02 .10
42 Dennis Lamp .02 .10
43 Tony Pena .02 .10
44 Phil Plantier .02 .10
45 Carlos Quintana .02 .10
46 Jeff Reardon .02 .10
47 Jody Reed .02 .10
48 Luis Rivera .02 .10
49 Mo Vaughn .02 .10
50 Jim Abbott .05 .15
51 Kyle Abbott .02 .10
52 Ruben Amaro .02 .10
53 Scott Bailes .02 .10
54 Chris Beasley .02 .10
55 Mark Eichhorn .02 .10
56 Mike Fetters .02 .10
57 Chuck Finley .02 .10
58 Gary Gaetti .02 .10
59 Dave Gallagher .02 .10
60 Donnie Hill .02 .10
61 Bryan Harvey UER .02 .10
Lee Smith led the
Majors with 47 saves
62 Wally Joyner .02 .10
63 Mark Langston .02 .10
64 Kirk McCaskill .02 .10
65 John Orton .02 .10
66 Lance Parrish .02 .10
67 Luis Polonia .02 .10
68 Bobby Rose .02 .10
69 Dick Schofield .02 .10
70 Luis Sojo .02 .10
71 Lee Stevens .02 .10
72 Dave Winfield .02 .10
73 Cliff Young .02 .10
74 Wilson Alvarez .02 .10
75 Esteban Beltre .02 .10
76 Joey Cora .02 .10
77 Brian Drahman .02 .10
78 Alex Fernandez .02 .10
79 Carlton Fisk .05 .15
80 Scott Fletcher .02 .10
81 Craig Grebeck .02 .10
82 Ozzie Guillen .02 .10
83 Greg Hibbard .02 .10
84 Charlie Hough .02 .10
85 Mike Huff .02 .10
86 Bo Jackson .08 .25
87 Lance Johnson .02 .10
88 Ron Karkovice .02 .10
89 Jack McDowell .02 .10
90 Matt Merullo .02 .10
91 Warren Newson .02 .10
92 Donn Pall UER .02 .10
Called Dunn on
card back
93 Dan Pasqua .02 .10
94 Ken Patterson .02 .10
95 Melido Perez .02 .10
96 Scott Radinsky .02 .10
97 Tim Raines .02 .10
98 Sammy Sosa .08 .25
99 Bobby Thigpen .02 .10
100 Frank Thomas .08 .25
101 Robin Ventura .02 .10
102 Mike Aldrete .02 .10
103 Sandy Alomar Jr. .02 .10
104 Carlos Baerga .02 .10
105 Albert Belle .02 .10
106 Willie Blair .02 .10
107 Jerry Browne .02 .10
108 Alex Cole .02 .10
109 Felix Fermin .02 .10
110 Glenallen Hill .02 .10
111 Shawn Hillegas .02 .10
112 Chris James .02 .10
113 Reggie Jefferson .02 .10
114 Doug Jones .02 .10
115 Eric King .02 .10
116 Mark Lewis .02 .10
117 Carlos Martinez .02 .10
118 Charles Nagy UER .02 .10
Throws right, but
card says left
119 Rod Nichols .02 .10
120 Steve Olin .02 .10
121 Jesse Orosco .02 .10
122 Rudy Seanez .02 .10
123 Joel Skinner .02 .10
124 Greg Swindell .02 .10
125 Jim Thome .08 .25
126 Mark Whiten .02 .10
127 Scott Aldred .02 .10
128 Andy Allanson .02 .10
129 John Cerutti .02 .10
130 Milt Cuyler .02 .10
131 Mike Dalton .02 .10
132 Rob Deer .02 .10
133 Cecil Fielder .02 .10
134 Travis Fryman .02 .10
135 Dan Gakeler .02 .10
136 Paul Gibson .02 .10
137 Bill Gullickson .02 .10
138 Mike Henneman .02 .10
139 Pete Incaviglia .02 .10
140 Mark Leiter .02 .10
141 Scott Livingstone .02 .10
142 Lloyd Moseby .02 .10
143 Tony Phillips .02 .10
144 Mark Salas .02 .10
145 Frank Tanana .02 .10
146 Walt Terrell .02 .10
147 Mickey Tettleton .02 .10
148 Alan Trammell .02 .10
149 Lou Whitaker .02 .10
150 Kevin Appier .02 .10
151 Luis Aquino .02 .10
152 Todd Benzinger .02 .10
153 Mike Boddicker .02 .10
154 George Brett .25 .60
155 Storm Davis .02 .10
156 Jim Eisenreich .02 .10
157 Kirk Gibson .02 .10
158 Tom Gordon .02 .10
159 Mark Gubicza .02 .10
160 David Howard .02 .10
161 Mike Macfarlane .02 .10
162 Brent Mayne .02 .10
163 Brian McRae .02 .10
164 Jeff Montgomery .02 .10
165 Bill Pecota .02 .10
166 Harvey Pulliam .02 .10
167 Bret Saberhagen .02 .10
168 Kevin Seitzer .02 .10
169 Terry Shumpert .02 .10
170 Kurt Stillwell .02 .10
171 Danny Tartabull .02 .10
172 Gary Thurman .02 .10
173 Dante Bichette .02 .10
174 Kevin D. Brown .02 .10
175 Chuck Crim .02 .10
176 Jim Gantner .02 .10
177 Darryl Hamilton .02 .10
178 Ted Higuera .02 .10
179 Darren Holmes .02 .10
180 Mark Lee .02 .10
181 Julio Machado .02 .10
182 Paul Molitor .02 .10
183 Jaime Navarro .02 .10
184 Edwin Nunez .02 .10
185 Dan Plesac .02 .10
186 Willie Randolph .02 .10
187 Ron Robinson .02 .10
188 Gary Sheffield .02 .10
189 Bill Spiers .02 .10
190 B.J. Surhoff .02 .10
191 Dale Sveum .02 .10
192 Greg Vaughn .02 .10
193 Bill Wegman .02 .10
194 Robin Yount .15 .40
195 Rick Aguilera .02 .10
196 Allan Anderson .02 .10
197 Steve Bedrosian .02 .10
198 Randy Bush .02 .10
199 Larry Casian .02 .10
200 Chili Davis .02 .10
201 Scott Erickson .02 .10
202 Greg Gagne .02 .10
203 Dan Gladden .02 .10
204 Brian Harper .02 .10
205 Kent Hrbek .02 .10
206 Chuck Knoblauch UER .02 .10
Career hit total
of 59 is wrong
207 Gene Larkin .02 .10
208 Terry Leach .02 .10
209 Scott Leius .02 .10
210 Shane Mack .02 .10
211 Jack Morris .02 .10
212 Pedro Munoz .02 .10
213 Denny Neagle .02 .10
214 Al Newman .02 .10
215 Junior Ortiz .02 .10
216 Mike Pagliarulo .02 .10
217 Kirby Puckett .08 .25
218 Paul Sorrento .02 .10
219 Kevin Tapani .02 .10
220 Lenny Webster .02 .10
221 Jesse Barfield .02 .10
222 Greg Cadaret .02 .10
223 Dave Eiland .02 .10
224 Alvaro Espinoza .02 .10
225 Steve Farr .02 .10
226 Bob Geren .02 .10
227 Lee Guetterman .02 .10
228 John Habyan .02 .10
229 Mel Hall .02 .10
230 Steve Howe .02 .10
231 Mike Humphreys .02 .10
232 Scott Kamieniecki .02 .10
233 Pat Kelly .02 .10
234 Roberto Kelly .02 .10
235 Tim Leary .02 .10
236 Kevin Maas .02 .10
237 Don Mattingly .25 .60
238 Hensley Meulens .02 .10
239 Matt Nokes .02 .10
240 Pascual Perez .02 .10
241 Eric Plunk .02 .10
242 John Ramos .02 .10
243 Scott Sanderson .02 .10
244 Steve Sax .02 .10
245 Wade Taylor .02 .10
246 Randy Velarde .02 .10
247 Bernie Williams .05 .15
248 Troy Afenir .02 .10
249 Harold Baines .02 .10
250 Lance Blankenship .02 .10
251 Mike Bordick .02 .10
252 Jose Canseco .05 .15
253 Steve Chitren .02 .10
254 Ron Darling .02 .10
255 Dennis Eckersley .02 .10
256 Mike Gallego .02 .10
257 Dave Henderson .02 .10
258 Rickey Henderson UER .08 .25
Wearing 24 on front
and 22 on back
259 Rick Honeycutt .02 .10
260 Brook Jacoby .02 .10
261 Carney Lansford .02 .10
262 Mark McGwire .25 .60
263 Mike Moore .02 .10
264 Gene Nelson .02 .10
265 Jamie Quirk .02 .10
266 Joe Slusarski .02 .10
267 Terry Steinbach .02 .10
268 Dave Stewart .02 .10
269 Todd Van Poppel .02 .10
270 Walt Weiss .02 .10
271 Bob Welch .02 .10
272 Curt Young .02 .10
273 Scott Bradley .02 .10
274 Greg Briley .02 .10
275 Jay Buhner .02 .10
276 Henry Cotto .02 .10
277 Alvin Davis .02 .10
278 Rich DeLucia .02 .10
279 Ken Griffey Jr. .20 .50
280 Erik Hanson .02 .10
281 Brian Holman .02 .10
282 Mike Jackson .02 .10
283 Randy Johnson .08 .25
284 Tracy Jones .02 .10
285 Bill Krueger .02 .10
286 Edgar Martinez .05 .15
287 Tino Martinez .05 .15
288 Rob Murphy .02 .10
289 Pete O'Brien .02 .10
290 Alonzo Powell .02 .10
291 Harold Reynolds .02 .10
292 Mike Schooler .02 .10
293 Russ Swan .02 .10
294 Bill Swift .02 .10
295 Dave Valle .02 .10
296 Omar Vizquel .05 .15
297 Gerald Alexander .02 .10
298 Brad Arnsberg .02 .10
299 Kevin Brown .02 .10
300 Jack Daugherty .02 .10
301 Mario Diaz .02 .10
302 Brian Downing .02 .10
303 Julio Franco .02 .10
304 Juan Gonzalez .05 .15
305 Rich Gossage .02 .10
306 Jose Guzman .02 .10
307 Jose Hernandez RC .08 .25
308 Jeff Huson .02 .10
309 Mike Jeffcoat .02 .10
310 Terry Mathews .02 .10
311 Rafael Palmeiro .05 .15
312 Dean Palmer .02 .10
313 Geno Petralli .02 .10
314 Gary Pettis .02 .10
315 Kevin Reimer .02 .10
316 Ivan Rodriguez .08 .25
317 Kenny Rogers .02 .10
318 Wayne Rosenthal .02 .10
319 Jeff Russell .02 .10
320 Nolan Ryan .40 1.00
321 Ruben Sierra .02 .10
322 Jim Acker .02 .10
323 Roberto Alomar .05 .15
324 Derek Bell .02 .10
325 Pat Borders .02 .10
326 Tom Candiotti .02 .10
327 Joe Carter .02 .10
328 Rob Ducey .02 .10
329 Kelly Gruber .02 .10
330 Juan Guzman .02 .10
331 Tom Henke .02 .10
332 Jimmy Key .02 .10
333 Manny Lee .02 .10
334 Al Leiter .02 .10
335 Bob MacDonald .02 .10
336 Candy Maldonado .02 .10
337 Rance Mulliniks .02 .10
338 Greg Myers .02 .10
339 John Olerud UER .02 .10
1991 BA has .256,
but text says .258
340 Ed Sprague .02 .10
341 Dave Stieb .02 .10
342 Todd Stottlemyre .02 .10
343 Mike Timlin .02 .10
344 Duane Ward .02 .10
345 David Wells .02 .10
346 Devon White .02 .10
347 Mookie Wilson .02 .10
348 Eddie Zosky .02 .10
349 Steve Avery .02 .10
350 Mike Bell .02 .10
351 Rafael Belliard .02 .10
352 Juan Berenguer .02 .10
353 Jeff Blauser .02 .10
354 Sid Bream .02 .10
355 Francisco Cabrera .02 .10
356 Marvin Freeman .02 .10
357 Ron Gant .02 .10
358 Tom Glavine .05 .15
359 Brian Hunter .02 .10
360 Dave Justice .02 .10
361 Charlie Leibrandt .02 .10
362 Mark Lemke .02 .10
363 Kent Mercker .02 .10
364 Keith Mitchell .02 .10
365 Greg Olson .02 .10
366 Terry Pendleton .02 .10
367 Armando Reynoso RC .08 .25
368 Deion Sanders .05 .15
369 Lonnie Smith .02 .10
370 Pete Smith .02 .10
371 John Smoltz .05 .15
372 Mike Stanton .02 .10
373 Jeff Treadway .02 .10
374 Mark Wohlers .02 .10
375 Paul Assenmacher .02 .10
376 George Bell .02 .10
377 Shawn Boskie .02 .10
378 Frank Castillo .02 .10
379 Andre Dawson .02 .10
380 Shawon Dunston .02 .10
381 Mark Grace .05 .15
382 Mike Harkey .02 .10
383 Danny Jackson .02 .10
384 Les Lancaster .02 .10
385 Ced Landrum .02 .10
386 Greg Maddux .15 .40
387 Derrick May .02 .10
388 Chuck McElroy .02 .10
389 Ryne Sandberg .15 .40
390 Heathcliff Slocumb .02 .10
391 Dave Smith .02 .10
392 Dwight Smith .02 .10
393 Rick Sutcliffe .02 .10
394 Hector Villanueva .02 .10
395 Chico Walker .02 .10
396 Jerome Walton .02 .10
397 Rick Wilkins .02 .10
398 Jack Armstrong .02 .10
399 Freddie Benavides .02 .10
400 Glenn Braggs .02 .10
401 Tom Browning .02 .10
402 Norm Charlton .02 .10
403 Eric Davis .02 .10
404 Rob Dibble .02 .10
405 Bill Doran .02 .10
406 Mariano Duncan .02 .10
407 Kip Gross .02 .10
408 Chris Hammond .02 .10
409 Billy Hatcher .02 .10
410 Chris Jones .02 .10
411 Barry Larkin .05 .15
412 Hal Morris .02 .10
413 Randy Myers .02 .10
414 Joe Oliver .02 .10
415 Paul O'Neill .05 .15
416 Ted Power .02 .10
417 Luis Quinones .02 .10
418 Jeff Reed .02 .10
419 Jose Rijo .02 .10
420 Chris Sabo .02 .10
421 Reggie Sanders .02 .10
422 Scott Scudder .02 .10
423 Glenn Sutko .02 .10
424 Eric Anthony .02 .10
425 Jeff Bagwell .08 .25
426 Craig Biggio .05 .15
427 Ken Caminiti .02 .10
428 Casey Candaele .02 .10
429 Mike Capel .02 .10
430 Andujar Cedeno .02 .10
431 Jim Corsi .02 .10
432 Mark Davidson .02 .10
433 Steve Finley .02 .10
434 Luis Gonzalez .02 .10
435 Pete Harnisch .02 .10
436 Dwayne Henry .02 .10
437 Xavier Hernandez .02 .10
438 Jimmy Jones .02 .10
439 Darryl Kile .02 .10
440 Rob Mallicoat .02 .10
441 Andy Mota .02 .10
442 Al Osuna .02 .10
443 Mark Portugal .02 .10
444 Scott Servais .02 .10
445 Mike Simms .02 .10
446 Gerald Young .02 .10
447 Tim Belcher .02 .10
448 Brett Butler .02 .10
449 John Candelaria .02 .10
450 Gary Carter .02 .10
451 Dennis Cook .02 .10
452 Tim Crews .02 .10
453 Kal Daniels .02 .10
454 Jim Gott .02 .10
455 Alfredo Griffin .02 .10
456 Kevin Gross .02 .10
457 Chris Gwynn .02 .10
458 Lenny Harris .02 .10
459 Orel Hershiser .02 .10
460 Jay Howell .02 .10
461 Stan Javier .02 .10
462 Eric Karros .02 .10
463 Ramon Martinez UER .02 .10
Card says bats right,
should be left
464 Roger McDowell UER .02 .10
Wins add up to 54,
totals have 51
465 Mike Morgan .02 .10
466 Eddie Murray .08 .25
467 Jose Offerman .02 .10
468 Bob Ojeda .02 .10
469 Juan Samuel .02 .10
470 Mike Scioscia .02 .10
471 Darryl Strawberry .02 .10
472 Bret Barberie .02 .10
473 Brian Barnes .02 .10
474 Eric Bullock .02 .10
475 Ivan Calderon .02 .10
476 Delino DeShields .02 .10
477 Jeff Fassero .02 .10
478 Mike Fitzgerald .02 .10
479 Steve Frey .02 .10
480 Andres Galarraga .02 .10
481 Mark Gardner .02 .10
482 Marquis Grissom .02 .10
483 Chris Haney .02 .10
484 Barry Jones .02 .10
485 Dave Martinez .02 .10
486 Dennis Martinez .02 .10
487 Chris Nabholz .02 .10
488 Spike Owen .02 .10
489 Gilberto Reyes .02 .10
490 Mel Rojas .02 .10
491 Scott Ruskin .02 .10
492 Bill Sampen .02 .10
493 Larry Walker .05 .15
494 Tim Wallach .02 .10
495 Daryl Boston .02 .10
496 Hubie Brooks .02 .10
497 Tim Burke .02 .10
498 Mark Carreon .02 .10
499 Tony Castillo .02 .10
500 Vince Coleman .02 .10
501 David Cone .02 .10
502 Kevin Elster .02 .10
503 Sid Fernandez .02 .10
504 John Franco .02 .10
505 Dwight Gooden .02 .10
506 Todd Hundley .02 .10
507 Jeff Innis .02 .10
508 Gregg Jefferies .02 .10
509 Howard Johnson .02 .10
510 Dave Magadan .02 .10
511 Terry McDaniel .02 .10
512 Kevin McReynolds .02 .10
513 Keith Miller .02 .10

14 Charlie O'Brien .02 .10
15 Mackey Sasser .02 .10
16 Pete Schourek .02 .10
17 Julio Valera .02 .10
18 Frank Viola .02 .10
19 Wally Whitehurst .02 .10
20 Anthony Young .02 .10
21 Andy Ashby .02 .10
22 Kim Batiste .02 .10
23 Joe Boever .02 .10
24 Wes Chamberlain .02 .10
25 Pat Combs .02 .10
26 Danny Cox .02 .10
27 Darren Daulton .02 .10
28 Jose DeJesus .02 .10
29 Len Dykstra .02 .10
30 Darrin Fletcher .02 .10
31 Tommy Greene .02 .10
32 Jason Grimsley .02 .10
33 Charlie Hayes .02 .10
34 Von Hayes .02 .10
35 Dave Hollins .02 .10
36 Ricky Jordan .02 .10
37 John Kruk .02 .10
38 Jim Lindeman .02 .10
39 Mickey Morandini .02 .10
40 Terry Mulholland .02 .10
41 Dale Murphy .05 .15
42 Randy Ready .02 .10
43 Wally Ritchie UER .02 .10
Letters in data are
cut off on card
44 Bruce Ruffin .02 .10
45 Steve Searcy .02 .10
46 Dickie Thon .02 .10
47 Mitch Williams .02 .10
48 Stan Belinda .02 .10
49 Jay Bell .02 .10
50 Barry Bonds .40 1.00
51 Bobby Bonilla .02 .10
52 Steve Buechele .02 .10
53 Doug Drabek .02 .10
54 Neal Heaton .02 .10
55 Jeff King .02 .10
56 Bob Kipper .02 .10
57 Bill Landrum .02 .10
58 Mike LaValliere .02 .10
59 Jose Lind .02 .10
60 Lloyd McClendon .02 .10
61 Orlando Merced .02 .10
62 Bob Patterson .02 .10
63 Joe Redfield .02 .10
64 Gary Redus .02 .10
65 Rosario Rodriguez .02 .10
66 Don Slaught .02 .10
67 John Smiley .02 .10
68 Zane Smith .02 .10
69 Randy Tomlin .02 .10
70 Andy Van Slyke .05 .15
71 Gary Varsho .02 .10
72 Bob Walk .02 .10
73 John Wehner UER .02 .10
Actually played for
Carolina in 1991,
not Cards
74 Juan Agosto .02 .10
75 Cris Carpenter .02 .10
76 Jose DeLeon .02 .10
77 Rich Gedman .02 .10
78 Bernard Gilkey .02 .10
79 Pedro Guerrero .02 .10
80 Ken Hill .02 .10
81 Rex Hudler .02 .10
82 Felix Jose .02 .10
83 Ray Lankford .02 .10
84 Omar Olivares .02 .10
85 Jose Oquendo .02 .10
86 Tom Pagnozzi .02 .10
87 Geronimo Pena .02 .10
88 Mike Perez .02 .10
89 Gerald Perry .02 .10
90 Bryn Smith .02 .10
91 Lee Smith .02 .10
92 Ozzie Smith .15 .40
93 Scott Terry .02 .10
94 Bob Tewksbury .02 .10
95 Milt Thompson .02 .10
96 Todd Zeile .02 .10
97 Larry Andersen .02 .10
98 Oscar Azocar .02 .10
99 Andy Benes .02 .10
00 Ricky Bones .02 .10
01 Jerald Clark .02 .10
02 Pat Clements .02 .10
03 Paul Faries .02 .10
04 Tony Fernandez .02 .10
05 Tony Gwynn .10 .30
06 Greg W. Harris .02 .10
07 Thomas Howard .02 .10
08 Bruce Hurst .02 .10
09 Darrin Jackson .02 .10
10 Tom Lampkin .02 .10
11 Craig Lefferts .02 .10
12 Jim Lewis RC .02 .10
13 Mike Maddux .02 .10
14 Fred McGriff .05 .15
15 Jose Melendez .02 .10
16 Jose Mota .02 .10
17 Dennis Rasmussen .02 .10
18 Bip Roberts .02 .10
19 Rich Rodriguez .02 .10
20 Benito Santiago .02 .10
21 Craig Shipley .02 .10

622 Tim Teufel .02 .10
623 Kevin Ward .02 .10
624 Ed Whitson .02 .10
625 Dave Anderson .02 .10
626 Kevin Bass .02 .10
627 Rod Beck RC .15 .40
628 Bud Black .02 .10
629 Jeff Brantley .02 .10
630 John Burkett .02 .10
631 Will Clark .05 .15
632 Royce Clayton .02 .10
633 Steve Decker .02 .10
634 Kelly Downs .02 .10
635 Mike Felder .02 .10
636 Scott Garrelts .02 .10
637 Eric Gunderson .02 .10
638 Bryan Hickerson RC .02 .10
639 Darren Lewis .02 .10
640 Greg Litton .02 .10
641 Kirt Manwaring .02 .10
642 Paul McClellan .02 .10
643 Willie McGee .02 .10
644 Kevin Mitchell .02 .10
645 Francisco Oliveras .02 .10
646 Mike Remlinger .02 .10
647 Dave Righetti .02 .10
648 Robby Thompson .02 .10
649 Jose Uribe .02 .10
650 Matt Williams .02 .10
651 Trevor Wilson .02 .10
652 Tom Goodwin MLP UER .02 .10
Timed in 3.5,
should be be timed
653 Terry Bross MLP .02 .10
654 Mike Christopher MLP .02 .10
655 Kenny Lofton MLP .05 .15
656 Chris Cron MLP .02 .10
657 Willie Banks MLP .02 .10
658 Pat Rice MLP .02 .10
659A R.Maurer MLP ERR RC .30 .75
659B Rob Maurer MLP COR RC .02 .10
660 Don Harris MLP .02 .10
661 Henry Rodriguez MLP .02 .10
662 Cliff Brantley MLP .02 .10
663 Mike Linskey MLP UER .02 .10
220 pounds in data,
200 in text
664 Gary DiSarcina MLP .02 .10
665 Gil Heredia RC .08 .25
666 Vinny Castilla RC .40 1.00
667 Paul Abbott MLP .02 .10
668 Monty Fariss MLP UER .02 .10
Called Paul on back
669 Jarvis Brown MLP .02 .10
670 Wayne Kirby RC .02 .10
671 Scott Brosius RC .15 .40
672 Bob Hamelin MLP .02 .10
673 Joel Johnston MLP .02 .10
674 Tim Spehr MLP .02 .10
675A J.Gardner MLP ERR .30 .75
675B Jeff Gardner MLP COR .02 .10
676 Rico Rossy MLP .02 .10
677 Roberto Hernandez MLP RC .02 .10
678 Ted Wood MLP .02 .10
679 Cal Eldred MLP .02 .10
680 Sean Berry MLP .02 .10
681 Rickey Henderson RS .05 .15
682 Nolan Ryan RS .20 .50
683 Dennis Martinez RS .02 .10
684 Wilson Alvarez RS .02 .10
685 Joe Carter RS .02 .10
686 Dave Winfield RS .02 .10
687 David Cone RS .02 .10
688 Jose Canseco LL UER .02 .10
Text on back has 42 stolen
bases in 88; should be 40
689 Howard Johnson LL .02 .10
690 Julio Franco LL .02 .10
691 Terry Pendleton LL .02 .10
692 Cecil Fielder LL .02 .10
693 Scott Erickson LL .02 .10
694 Tom Glavine LL .02 .10
695 Dennis Martinez LL .02 .10
696 Bryan Harvey LL .02 .10
697 Lee Smith LL .02 .10
698 Roberto Alomar .02 .10
Sandy Alomar Jr.
699 Bobby Bonilla .02 .10
Will Clark
700 Wohlers/Mercker/Pena .02 .10
701 B.Jackson/F.Thomas .05 .15
702 Paul Molitor .02 .10
Brett Butler
703 C.Ripken/J.Carter .15 .40
704 Barry Larkin .05 .15
Kirby Puckett
705 M.Vaughn/C.Fielder .02 .10
706 Ramon Martinez .02 .10
Ozzie Guillen
707 Harold Baines .02 .10
Wade Boggs
708 Robin Yount PV .08 .25
709 Ken Griffey Jr. PV UER .10 .30
Missing quotations on
back; BA has .322, but
was actually .327
710 Nolan Ryan PV .20 .50
711 Cal Ripken PV .15 .40
712 Frank Thomas PV .05 .15
713 Dave Justice PV .02 .10
714 Checklist 1-101 .02 .10
715 Checklist 102-194 .02 .10
716 Checklist 195-296 .02 .10
717 Checklist 297-397 .02 .10
718 Checklist 398-494 .02 .10
719 Checklist 495-596 .02 .10
720A CL 597-720 ERR .02 .10
659 Rob Mauer
720B CL 597-720 COR .02 .10
659 Rob Maurer

1992 Fleer All-Stars

Cards from this 24-card standard-size set were randomly inserted in plastic wrap packs. Selected members of the American and National League 1991 All-Star squads comprise this set.

COMPLETE SET (24) 12.50 30.00
RANDOM INSERTS IN WAX PACKS
1 Felix Jose .30 .75
2 Tony Gwynn 1.00 2.50
3 Barry Bonds 3.00 8.00
4 Bobby Bonilla .30 .75
5 Mike LaValliere .30 .75
6 Tom Glavine .50 1.25
7 Ramon Martinez .30 .75
8 Lee Smith .30 .75
9 Mickey Tettleton .30 .75
10 Scott Erickson .30 .75
11 Frank Thomas .75 2.00
12 Danny Tartabull .30 .75
13 Will Clark .50 1.25
14 Ryne Sandberg 1.25 3.00
15 Terry Pendleton .30 .75
16 Barry Larkin .50 1.25
17 Rafael Palmeiro .50 1.25
18 Julio Franco .30 .75
19 Robin Ventura .30 .75
20 Cal Ripken 2.50 6.00
21 Joe Carter .30 .75
22 Kirby Puckett .75 2.00
23 Ken Griffey Jr. 1.50 4.00
24 Jose Canseco .50 1.25

1992 Fleer Clemens

Roger Clemens served as a spokesperson for Fleer during 1992 and was the exclusive subject of this 15-card standard-size set. The first 12-card Clemens "Career Highlights" subseries was randomly inserted in 1992 Fleer packs. Two-thousand signed cards were randomly inserted in wax packs and could also be won by entering a drawing. However, these cards are uncertifiable as they do not have any distinguishable marks. Moreover, a three-card Clemens subset (13-15) was available through a special mail-in offer. The glossy color photos on the fronts are bordered in black and accented with gold stripes and lettering on the top of the card.

COMPLETE SET (12) 5.00 12.00
COMMON CLEMENS (1-12) .40 1.00
RANDOM INSERTS IN PACKS
COMMON MAIL-IN (13-15) .40 1.00
MAIL-IN CARDS DIST.VIA WRAPPER EXCH.
AU CARD RANDOM INSERT IN PACKS
AUTOGRAPH CARD IS NOT CERTIFIED
AU Roger Clemens AU/2000 30.00 60.00
NNO R.Clemens 2.50 6.00
P.Mullan Promo

1992 Fleer Lumber Company

The 1992 Fleer Lumber Company standard-size set features nine outstanding hitters in Major League Baseball. This set was only available as a bonus in Fleer hobby factory sets.

COMPLETE SET (9) 4.00 10.00
ONE SET PER HOBBY FACTORY SET
L1 Cecil Fielder .30 .75
L2 Mickey Tettleton .30 .75
L3 Darryl Strawberry .30 .75
L4 Ryne Sandberg 1.25 3.00
L5 Jose Canseco .50 1.25
L6 Matt Williams .30 .75
L7 Cal Ripken 2.50 6.00
L8 Barry Bonds 3.00 8.00
L9 Ron Gant .30 .75

1992 Fleer Rookie Sensations

Cards from the 20-card Fleer Rookie Sensations set were randomly inserted in 1992 Fleer 35-card cello packs. The cards were extremely popular upon release resulting in packs selling for levels far above suggested retail levels. The glossy color photos on the fronts have a white border on a royal blue card face. The words "Rookie Sensations" appear above the picture in gold foil lettering, while the player's name appears on a gold foil plaque beneath the picture. Through a mail-in offer for ten Fleer baseball card wrappers and 1.00 for postage and handling, Fleer offered an uncut 8 1/2" by 11" numbered promo sheet picturing ten of the 20-card set on each side in a reduced-size front-only format. The offer indicated an expiration date of July 31, 1992, or whenever the production quantity of 250,000 sheets was exhausted.

COMPLETE SET (20) 10.00 25.00
RANDOM INSERTS IN CELLO PACKS
1 Frank Thomas 10.00 25.00
2 Todd Van Poppel .60 1.50
3 Orlando Merced .60 1.50
4 Jeff Bagwell 3.00 8.00
5 Jeff Fassero .60 1.50
6 Darren Lewis .60 1.50
7 Milt Cuyler .60 1.50
8 Mike Timlin .60 1.50
9 Brian McRae .60 1.50
10 Chuck Knoblauch .75 2.00
11 Rich DeLucia .60 1.50
12 Ivan Rodriguez 2.00 5.00
13 Juan Guzman .60 1.50
14 Steve Chitren .60 1.50
15 Mark Wohlers .60 1.50
16 Wes Chamberlain .60 1.50
17 Ray Lankford .75 2.00
18 Chito Martinez .60 1.50
19 Phil Plantier .60 1.50
20 Scott Leius UER .60 1.50

1992 Fleer Smoke 'n Heat

This 12-card standard-size set features outstanding major league pitchers, especially the premier fastball pitchers in both leagues. These cards were only available in Fleer's 1992 Christmas factory set.

COMPLETE SET (12) 4.00 10.00
ONE SET PER RETAIL FACTORY SET
S1 Lee Smith .30 .75
S2 Jack McDowell .30 .75
S3 David Cone .30 .75
S4 Roger Clemens 1.50 4.00
S5 Nolan Ryan 3.00 8.00
S6 Scott Erickson .30 .75
S7 Tom Glavine .50 1.25
S9 Andy Benes .30 .75
S10 Steve Avery .30 .75
S11 Randy Johnson .75 2.00
S12 Jim Abbott .50 1.25

1992 Fleer Team Leaders

Cards from the 20-card Fleer Team Leaders set were randomly inserted in 1992 Fleer 42-card rack packs.

COMPLETE SET (20) 10.00 25.00
ONE TL OR CLEMENS PER RACK PACK
1 Don Mattingly 4.00 10.00
2 Howard Johnson .60 1.50
3 Chris Sabo UER .60 1.50
4 Carlton Fisk 1.00 2.50
5 Kirby Puckett 1.50 4.00
6 Cecil Fielder .60 1.50
7 Tony Gwynn 2.00 5.00
8 Will Clark 1.00 2.50
9 Bobby Bonilla .60 1.50
10 Len Dykstra .60 1.50
11 Tom Glavine 1.00 2.50
12 Rafael Palmeiro 1.00 2.50
13 Wade Boggs 1.00 2.50
14 Joe Carter .60 1.50
15 Ken Griffey Jr. 3.00 8.00
16 Darryl Strawberry .60 1.50
17 Cal Ripken 5.00 12.00
18 Danny Tartabull .60 1.50
19 Jose Canseco 1.00 2.50
20 Andre Dawson .60 1.50

1992 Fleer Update

The 1992 Fleer Update set contains 132 standard-size cards. Cards were distributed exclusively in factory sets through hobby dealers. Factory sets included a four-card, black-bordered "92 Headliners" insert set for a total of 136 cards. Due to lackluster retail response for previous Fleer Update sets, wholesale orders for this product were low, resulting in a short print run. As word got out that the cards were in short supply, the secondary market prices soared soon after release. The basic card design is identical to the regular issue 1992 Fleer cards except for the U-prefixed numbering on back. The cards are checklisted alphabetically within and according to teams for each league with AL preceding NL. Rookie Cards in this set include Jeff Kent and Mike Piazza. The Piazza card is widely recognized as one of the more desirable singles issued in the 1990's.

COMP.FACT.SET (136) 30.00 60.00
COMPLETE SET (132) 30.00 60.00
U PREFIX ON REG.CARD NUMBERS
1 Todd Frohwirth .20 .50
2 Alan Mills .20 .50
3 Rick Sutcliffe .40 1.00
4 John Valentin RC .60 1.50
5 Frank Viola .40 1.00
6 Bob Zupcic RC .20 .50
7 Mike Butcher .20 .50
8 Chad Curtis RC .60 1.50
9 Damion Easley RC .60 1.50
10 Tim Salmon .60 1.50
11 Julio Valera .20 .50
12 George Bell .20 .50
13 Roberto Hernandez .20 .50
14 Shawn Jeter RC .20 .50
15 Thomas Howard .20 .50
16 Jesse Levis .20 .50
17 Kenny Lofton .60 1.50
18 Paul Sorrento .20 .50
19 Rico Brogna .20 .50
20 John Doherty RC .20 .50
21 Dan Gladden .20 .50
22 Buddy Groom RC .20 .50
23 Shawn Hare RC .20 .50
24 John Kiely .20 .50
25 Kurt Knudsen .20 .50
26 Gregg Jefferies .20 .50
27 Wally Joyner .40 1.00
28 Kevin Koslofski .20 .50
29 Kevin McReynolds .20 .50
30 Rusty Meacham .20 .50
31 Keith Miller .20 .50
32 Hipolito Pichardo RC .20 .50
33 Jim Austin .20 .50
34 Scott Fletcher .20 .50
35 John Jaha RC .60 1.50
36 Pat Listach RC .60 1.50
37 Dave Nilsson .20 .50
38 Kevin Seitzer .20 .50
39 Tom Edens .20 .50
40 Pat Mahomes RC .60 1.50
41 John Smiley .20 .50
42 Charlie Hayes .20 .50
43 Sam Militello .20 .50
44 Andy Stankiewicz .20 .50
45 Danny Tartabull .20 .50
46 Bob Wickman 1.00 2.50
47 Jerry Browne .20 .50
48 Kevin Campbell .20 .50
49 Vince Horsman .20 .50
50 Troy Neel RC .20 .50
51 Ruben Sierra .40 1.00
52 Bruce Walton .20 .50
53 Willie Wilson .20 .50
54 Bret Boone .60 1.50
55 Dave Fleming .20 .50
56 Kevin Mitchell .20 .50
57 Jeff Nelson RC 1.00 2.50
58 Shane Turner .20 .50
59 Jose Canseco .60 1.50
60 Jeff Frye RC .20 .50
61 Danny Leon .20 .50
62 Roger Pavlik RC .20 .50
63 David Cone .40 1.00
64 Pat Hentgen .20 .50
65 Randy Knorr .20 .50
66 Jack Morris .40 1.00
67 Dave Winfield .40 1.00
68 David Nied RC .20 .50
69 Otis Nixon .20 .50
70 Alejandro Pena .20 .50
71 Jeff Reardon .40 1.00
72 Alex Arias RC .20 .50
73 Jim Bullinger .20 .50
74 Mike Morgan .20 .50
75 Rey Sanchez RC .60 1.50
76 Bob Scanlan .20 .50
77 Sammy Sosa Cubs 1.50 4.00
78 Scott Bankhead .20 .50
79 Tim Belcher .20 .50
80 Steve Foster .20 .50
81 Willie Greene .20 .50
82 Bip Roberts .20 .50
83 Scott Ruskin .20 .50
84 Greg Swindell .20 .50
85 Juan Guerrero .20 .50
86 Butch Henry .20 .50
87 Doug Jones .20 .50
88 Brian Williams RC .20 .50
89 Tom Candiotti .20 .50
90 Eric Davis .40 1.00
91 Carlos Hernandez .20 .50
92 Mike Piazza RC 30.00 80.00
93 Mike Sharperson .20 .50
94 Eric Young RC .60 1.50
95 Moises Alou .40 1.00
96 Greg Colbrunn .20 .50
97 Wil Cordero .20 .50
98 Ken Hill .20 .50
99 John Vander Wal RC .60 1.50
100 John Wetteland .40 1.00
101 Bobby Bonilla .40 1.00
102 Eric Hillman RC .20 .50
103 Pat Howell .20 .50
104 Jeff Kent RC 10.00 25.00
105 Dick Schofield .20 .50
106 Ryan Thompson RC .20 .50
107 Chico Walker .20 .50
108 Juan Bell .20 .50
109 Mariano Duncan .20 .50
110 Jeff Grotewold .20 .50
111 Ben Rivera .20 .50
112 Curt Schilling .60 1.50
113 Victor Cole RC .20 .50
114 Al Martin RC .60 1.50
115 Roger Mason .20 .50
116 Blas Minor .20 .50
117 Tim Wakefield RC 4.00 10.00
118 Mark Clark RC .20 .50
119 Rheal Cormier .20 .50
120 Donovan Osborne .20 .50
121 Todd Worrell .20 .50
122 Jeremy Hernandez RC .20 .50
123 Randy Myers .20 .50
124 Frank Seminara RC .20 .50
125 Gary Sheffield .40 1.00
126 Dan Walters .20 .50
127 Steve Hosey .20 .50
128 Mike Jackson .20 .50
129 Jim Pena .20 .50
130 Cory Snyder .20 .50
131 Bill Swift .20 .50
132 Checklist U1-U132 .20 .50

1992 Fleer Update Headliners

Each 1992 Fleer Update factory set included a four-card set of Headliner inserts. The cards are numbered separately and have a completely different design to the base cards. Each Headliner features UV coating and black borders. The set features a selection of stars that made headlines in the 1991 season. Cards are numbered on back X of 4.

COMPLETE SET (4) 3.00 8.00
ONE SET PER FACTORY SET
1 Ken Griffey Jr. 1.50 4.00
2 Robin Yount 1.25 3.00
3 Jeff Reardon .30 .75
4 Cecil Fielder .30 .75

1992 Fleer Citgo The Performer

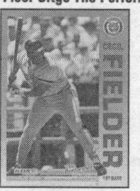

This 24-card standard-size set was produced by Fleer for 7-Eleven. During April and May at any of the 1,600 participating 7-Eleven stores, customers who purchased eight gallons or more of mid-grade or premium Citgo-brand gasoline received a packet of five trading cards. During June or while supplies last, customers who wanted additional cards could receive three trading cards of their choice per eight gallon or more fill-up by sending in a self-addressed envelope with 1.00 to cover postage and handling. The front design has color action player photos, with a metallic blue-green border that fades to white as one moves down the card face. The card front prominently features "The Performer". The team logo, player's name, and his position appear in the wider right border. The top half of the backs have close-up photos, while the bottom half carry biography and complete career statistics.

COMPLETE SET (24) 3.00 8.00
1 Nolan Ryan .50 1.25
2 Frank Thomas .15 .40
3 Ryne Sandberg .20 .50
4 Ken Griffey Jr. .50 1.25
5 Cal Ripken .50 1.25
6 Roger Clemens .30 .75
7 Cecil Fielder .05 .15
8 Dave Justice .10 .30
9 Wade Boggs .15 .40
10 Tony Gwynn .30 .75
11 Kirby Puckett .15 .40
12 Darryl Strawberry .05 .15
13 Jose Canseco .15 .40
14 Barry Larkin .10 .30
15 Terry Pendleton .02 .10
16 Don Mattingly .25 .60
17 Rickey Henderson .25 .60
18 Ruben Sierra .05 .15
19 Jeff Bagwell .30 .75
20 Tom Glavine .10 .30
21 Ramon Martinez .05 .15
22 Will Clark .10 .30
23 Barry Bonds .25 .60
24 Roberto Alomar .10 .30

1992 Fleer Gwynn Casa de Amparo

This one card set was produced by the Fleer Corporation for Casa de Amparo (Spanish for house of refuge) which provided care for over 600 children each year. Tony Gwynn served as a spokesperson for the house. The front features a color picture of Tony Gwynn hold Casa's Poster Child for 1992. The back displays information about Casa de Amparo.

1 Tony Gwynn 2.00 5.00

1993 Fleer

The 720-card 1993 Fleer baseball set contains two series of 360 standard-size cards. Cards were distributed in plastic wrapped packs, cello packs, jumbo packs and rack packs. For the first time in years, Fleer did not issue a factory set. In fact, Fleer discontinued issuing factory sets from 1993 through 1998. The cards are checklisted below alphabetically within and according to teams for each league with NL preceding AL. Topical subsets include League Leaders (344-348/704-708), Round Trippers (349-353/709-713), and Super Star Specials (354-357/714-717). Each series concludes with checklists (358-360/718-720). There are no key Rookie Cards in this set.

COMPLETE SET (720) 15.00 40.00
COMPLETE SERIES 1 (360) 8.00 20.00
COMPLETE SERIES 2 (360) 8.00 20.00
1 Steve Avery .02 .10
2 Sid Bream .02 .10
3 Ron Gant .07 .20
4 Tom Glavine .10 .30
5 Brian Hunter .02 .10
6 Ryan Klesko .07 .20
7 Charlie Leibrandt .02 .10
8 Kent Mercker .02 .10
9 David Nied .02 .10
10 Otis Nixon .02 .10
11 Greg Olson .02 .10
12 Terry Pendleton .07 .20
13 Deion Sanders .10 .30
14 John Smoltz .10 .30
15 Mike Stanton .02 .10
16 Mark Wohlers .02 .10
17 Paul Assenmacher .02 .10
18 Steve Buechele .02 .10
19 Shawon Dunston .02 .10
20 Mark Grace .10 .30
21 Derrick May .02 .10
22 Chuck McElroy .02 .10
23 Mike Morgan .02 .10
24 Rey Sanchez .02 .10
25 Ryne Sandberg .30 .75
26 Bob Scanlan .02 .10
27 Sammy Sosa .20 .50
28 Rick Wilkins .02 .10
29 Bobby Ayala RC .02 .10
30 Tim Belcher .02 .10
31 Jeff Branson .02 .10
32 Norm Charlton .02 .10
33 Steve Foster .02 .10
34 Willie Greene .02 .10
35 Chris Hammond .02 .10
36 Milt Hill .02 .10
37 Hal Morris .02 .10
38 Joe Oliver .02 .10
39 Paul O'Neill .10 .30
40 Tim Pugh RC .02 .10
41 Jose Rijo .02 .10
42 Bip Roberts .02 .10
43 Chris Sabo .02 .10
44 Reggie Sanders .07 .20
45 Eric Anthony .02 .10
46 Jeff Bagwell .10 .30
47 Craig Biggio .10 .30
48 Joe Boever .02 .10

Card	Low	High
49 Casey Candaele	.02	.10
50 Steve Finley	.07	.20
51 Luis Gonzalez	.07	.20
52 Pete Harnisch	.02	.10
53 Xavier Hernandez	.02	.10
54 Doug Jones	.02	.10
55 Eddie Taubensee	.02	.10
56 Brian Williams	.02	.10
57 Pedro Astacio	.02	.10
58 Todd Benzinger	.02	.10
59 Brett Butler	.07	.20
60 Tom Candiotti	.02	.10
61 Lenny Harris	.02	.10
62 Carlos Hernandez	.02	.10
63 Orel Hershiser	.07	.20
64 Eric Karros	.07	.20
65 Ramon Martinez	.02	.10
66 Jose Offerman	.02	.10
67 Mike Scioscia	.02	.10
68 Mike Sharperson	.02	.10
69 Eric Young	.02	.10
70 Moises Alou	.07	.20
71 Ivan Calderon	.02	.10
72 Archi Cianfrocco	.02	.10
73 Wil Cordero	.02	.10
74 Delino DeShields	.02	.10
75 Mark Gardner	.02	.10
76 Ken Hill	.02	.10
77 Tim Laker RC	.02	.10
78 Chris Nabholz	.02	.10
79 Mel Rojas	.02	.10
80 John Vander Wal UER (Misspelled Vander Wall in I	.02	.10
81 Larry Walker	.07	.20
82 Tim Wallach	.02	.10
83 John Wetteland	.07	.20
84 Bobby Bonilla	.07	.20
85 Daryl Boston	.02	.10
86 Sid Fernandez	.02	.10
87 Eric Hillman	.02	.10
88 Todd Hundley	.02	.10
89 Howard Johnson	.02	.10
90 Jeff Kent	.20	.50
91 Eddie Murray	.20	.50
92 Bill Pecota	.02	.10
93 Bret Saberhagen	.07	.20
94 Dick Schofield	.02	.10
95 Pete Schourek	.02	.10
96 Anthony Young	.02	.10
97 Ruben Amaro	.02	.10
98 Juan Bell	.02	.10
99 Wes Chamberlain	.02	.10
100 Darren Daulton	.07	.20
101 Mariano Duncan	.02	.10
102 Mike Hartley	.02	.10
103 Ricky Jordan	.02	.10
104 John Kruk	.07	.20
105 Mickey Morandini	.02	.10
106 Terry Mulholland	.02	.10
107 Ben Rivera	.02	.10
108 Curt Schilling	.07	.20
109 Keith Shepherd RC	.02	.10
110 Stan Belinda	.02	.10
111 Jay Bell	.07	.20
112 Barry Bonds	.60	1.50
113 Jeff King	.02	.10
114 Mike LaValliere	.02	.10
115 Jose Lind	.02	.10
116 Roger Mason	.02	.10
117 Orlando Merced	.02	.10
118 Bob Patterson	.02	.10
119 Don Slaught	.02	.10
120 Zane Smith	.02	.10
121 Randy Tomlin	.02	.10
122 Andy Van Slyke	.10	.30
123 Tim Wakefield	.20	.50
124 Rheal Cormier	.02	.10
125 Bernard Gilkey	.02	.10
126 Felix Jose	.02	.10
127 Ray Lankford	.07	.20
128 Bob McClure	.02	.10
129 Donovan Osborne	.02	.10
130 Tom Pagnozzi	.02	.10
131 Geronimo Pena	.02	.10
132 Mike Perez	.02	.10
133 Lee Smith	.07	.20
134 Bob Tewksbury	.02	.10
135 Todd Worrell	.02	.10
136 Todd Zeile	.02	.10
137 Jerald Clark	.02	.10
138 Tony Gwynn	.25	.60
139 Greg W. Harris	.02	.10
140 Jeremy Hernandez	.02	.10
141 Darrin Jackson	.02	.10
142 Mike Maddux	.02	.10
143 Fred McGriff	.10	.30
144 Jose Melendez	.02	.10
145 Rich Rodriguez	.02	.10
146 Frank Seminara	.02	.10
147 Gary Sheffield	.07	.20
148 Kurt Stillwell	.02	.10
149 Dan Walters	.02	.10
150 Rod Beck	.02	.10
151 Bud Black	.02	.10
152 Jeff Brantley	.02	.10
153 John Burkett	.02	.10
154 Will Clark	.10	.30
155 Royce Clayton	.02	.10
156 Mike Jackson	.02	.10
157 Darren Lewis	.02	.10
158 Kirt Manwaring	.02	.10
159 Willie McGee	.07	.20
160 Cory Snyder	.02	.10
161 Bill Swift	.02	.10
162 Trevor Wilson	.02	.10
163 Brady Anderson	.07	.20
164 Glenn Davis	.02	.10
165 Mike Devereaux	.02	.10
166 Todd Frohwirth	.02	.10
167 Leo Gomez	.02	.10
168 Chris Hoiles	.02	.10
169 Ben McDonald	.02	.10
170 Randy Milligan	.02	.10
171 Alan Mills	.02	.10
172 Mike Mussina	.10	.30
173 Gregg Olson	.02	.10
174 Arthur Rhodes	.02	.10
175 David Segui	.02	.10
176 Ellis Burks	.07	.20
177 Roger Clemens	.40	1.00
178 Scott Cooper	.02	.10
179 Danny Darwin	.02	.10
180 Tony Fossas	.02	.10
181 Paul Quantrill	.02	.10
182 Jody Reed	.02	.10
183 John Valentin	.02	.10
184 Mo Vaughn	.07	.20
185 Frank Viola	.07	.20
186 Bob Zupcic	.02	.10
187 Jim Abbott	.10	.30
188 Gary DiSarcina	.02	.10
189 Damion Easley	.02	.10
190 Junior Felix	.02	.10
191 Chuck Finley	.07	.20
192 Joe Grahe	.02	.10
193 Bryan Harvey	.02	.10
194 Mark Langston	.02	.10
195 John Orton	.02	.10
196 Luis Polonia	.02	.10
197 Tim Salmon	.10	.30
198 Luis Sojo	.02	.10
199 Wilson Alvarez	.02	.10
200 George Bell	.02	.10
201 Alex Fernandez	.02	.10
202 Craig Grebeck	.02	.10
203 Ozzie Guillen	.07	.20
204 Lance Johnson	.02	.10
205 Ron Karkovice	.02	.10
206 Kirk McCaskill	.02	.10
207 Jack McDowell	.02	.10
208 Scott Radinsky	.02	.10
209 Tim Raines	.07	.20
210 Frank Thomas	.20	.50
211 Robin Ventura	.07	.20
212 Sandy Alomar Jr.	.02	.10
213 Carlos Baerga	.02	.10
214 Dennis Cook	.02	.10
215 Thomas Howard	.02	.10
216 Mark Lewis	.02	.10
217 Derek Lilliquist	.02	.10
218 Kenny Lofton	.07	.20
219 Charles Nagy	.02	.10
220 Steve Olin	.02	.10
221 Paul Sorrento	.02	.10
222 Jim Thome	.10	.30
223 Mark Whiten	.02	.10
224 Milt Cuyler	.02	.10
225 Rob Deer	.02	.10
226 John Doherty	.02	.10
227 Cecil Fielder	.07	.20
228 Travis Fryman	.07	.20
229 Mike Henneman	.02	.10
230 John Kiely UER/(Card has batting stats of Pat Ke	.02	.10
231 Kurt Knudsen	.02	.10
232 Scott Livingstone	.02	.10
233 Tony Phillips	.02	.10
234 Mickey Tettleton	.02	.10
235 Kevin Appier	.07	.20
236 George Brett	.50	1.25
237 Tom Gordon	.02	.10
238 Gregg Jefferies	.02	.10
239 Wally Joyner	.07	.20
240 Kevin Koslofski	.02	.10
241 Mike Macfarlane	.02	.10
242 Brian McRae	.02	.10
243 Rusty Meacham	.02	.10
244 Keith Miller	.02	.10
245 Jeff Montgomery	.02	.10
246 Hipolito Pichardo	.02	.10
247 Ricky Bones	.02	.10
248 Cal Eldred	.02	.10
249 Mike Fetters	.02	.10
250 Darryl Hamilton	.02	.10
251 Doug Henry	.02	.10
252 John Jaha	.02	.10
253 Pat Listach	.02	.10
254 Paul Molitor	.07	.20
255 Jaime Navarro	.02	.10
256 Kevin Seitzer	.02	.10
257 B.J. Surhoff	.07	.20
258 Greg Vaughn	.02	.10
259 Bill Wegman	.02	.10
260 Robin Yount	.30	.75
261 Rick Aguilera	.02	.10
262 Chili Davis	.07	.20
263 Scott Erickson	.02	.10
264 Greg Gagne	.02	.10
265 Mark Guthrie	.02	.10
266 Brian Harper	.02	.10
267 Kent Hrbek	.07	.20
268 Terry Jorgensen	.02	.10
269 Gene Larkin	.02	.10
270 Scott Leius	.02	.10
271 Pat Mahomes	.02	.10
272 Pedro Munoz	.02	.10
273 Kirby Puckett	.20	.50
274 Kevin Tapani	.02	.10
275 Carl Willis	.02	.10
276 Steve Farr	.02	.10
277 John Habyan	.02	.10
278 Mel Hall	.02	.10
279 Charlie Hayes	.02	.10
280 Pat Kelly	.02	.10
281 Don Mattingly	.50	1.25
282 Sam Militello	.02	.10
283 Matt Nokes	.02	.10
284 Melido Perez	.02	.10
285 Andy Stankiewicz	.02	.10
286 Danny Tartabull	.02	.10
287 Randy Velarde	.02	.10
288 Bob Wickman	.02	.10
289 Bernie Williams	.10	.30
290 Lance Blankenship	.02	.10
291 Mike Bordick	.02	.10
292 Jerry Browne	.02	.10
293 Dennis Eckersley	.07	.20
294 Rickey Henderson	.20	.50
295 Vince Horsman	.02	.10
296 Mark McGwire	.50	1.25
297 Jeff Parrett	.02	.10
298 Ruben Sierra	.07	.20
299 Terry Steinbach	.02	.10
300 Walt Weiss	.02	.10
301 Bob Welch	.02	.10
302 Willie Wilson	.02	.10
303 Bobby Witt	.02	.10
304 Bret Boone	.07	.20
305 Jay Buhner	.07	.20
306 Dave Fleming	.02	.10
307 Ken Griffey Jr.	.40	1.00
308 Erik Hanson	.02	.10
309 Edgar Martinez	.10	.30
310 Tino Martinez	.10	.30
311 Jeff Nelson	.02	.10
312 Dennis Powell	.02	.10
313 Mike Schooler	.02	.10
314 Russ Swan	.02	.10
315 Dave Valle	.02	.10
316 Omar Vizquel	.10	.30
317 Kevin Brown	.07	.20
318 Todd Burns	.02	.10
319 Jose Canseco	.10	.30
320 Julio Franco	.07	.20
321 Jeff Frye	.02	.10
322 Juan Gonzalez	.07	.20
323 Jose Guzman	.02	.10
324 Jeff Huson	.02	.10
325 Dean Palmer	.07	.20
326 Kevin Reimer	.02	.10
327 Ivan Rodriguez	.10	.30
328 Kenny Rogers	.07	.20
329 Dan Smith	.02	.10
330 Roberto Alomar	.10	.30
331 Derek Bell	.02	.10
332 Pat Borders	.02	.10
333 Joe Carter	.07	.20
334 Kelly Gruber	.02	.10
335 Tom Henke	.02	.10
336 Jimmy Key	.07	.20
337 Manuel Lee	.02	.10
338 Candy Maldonado	.02	.10
339 John Olerud	.07	.20
340 Todd Stottlemyre	.02	.10
341 Duane Ward	.02	.10
342 Devon White	.07	.20
343 Dave Winfield	.07	.20
344 Edgar Martinez LL	.07	.20
345 Cecil Fielder LL	.02	.10
346 Kenny Lofton LL	.02	.10
347 Jack Morris LL	.02	.10
348 Roger Clemens LL	.20	.50
349 Fred McGriff RT	.07	.20
350 Barry Bonds RT	.30	.75
351 Gary Sheffield RT	.02	.10
352 Darren Daulton RT	.02	.10
353 Dave Hollins RT	.02	.10
354 P.Martinez R.Martinez	.20	.50
355 K.Puckett I.Rodriguez	.10	.30
356 Sandberg Sheffield	.20	.50
357 R.Alomar Knoblauch Baerg	.07	.20
358 Checklist 1-120	.02	.10
359 Checklist 121-240	.02	.10
360 Checklist 241-360	.02	.10
361 Rafael Belliard	.02	.10
362 Damon Berryhill	.02	.10
363 Mike Bielecki	.02	.10
364 Jeff Blauser	.02	.10
365 Francisco Cabrera	.02	.10
366 Marvin Freeman	.02	.10
367 David Justice	.07	.20
368 Mark Lemke	.02	.10
369 Alejandro Pena	.02	.10
370 Jeff Reardon	.07	.20
371 Lonnie Smith	.02	.10
372 Pete Smith	.02	.10
373 Shawn Boskie	.02	.10
374 Jim Bullinger	.02	.10
375 Frank Castillo	.02	.10
376 Doug Dascenzo	.02	.10
377 Andre Dawson	.07	.20
378 Mike Harkey	.02	.10
379 Greg Hibbard	.02	.10
380 Greg Maddux	.30	.75
381 Ken Patterson	.02	.10
382 Jeff D. Robinson	.02	.10
383 Luis Salazar	.02	.10
384 Dwight Smith	.02	.10
385 Jose Vizcaino	.02	.10
386 Scott Bankhead	.02	.10
387 Tom Browning	.02	.10
388 Darnell Coles	.02	.10
389 Rob Dibble	.07	.20
390 Bill Doran	.02	.10
391 Dwayne Henry	.02	.10
392 Cesar Hernandez	.02	.10
393 Roberto Kelly	.02	.10
394 Barry Larkin	.10	.30
395 Dave Martinez	.02	.10
396 Kevin Mitchell	.02	.10
397 Jeff Reed	.02	.10
398 Scott Ruskin	.02	.10
399 Greg Swindell	.02	.10
400 Dan Wilson	.07	.20
401 Andy Ashby	.02	.10
402 Freddie Benavides	.02	.10
403 Dante Bichette	.07	.20
404 Willie Blair	.02	.10
405 Denis Boucher	.02	.10
406 Vinny Castilla	.20	.50
407 Braulio Castillo	.02	.10
408 Alex Cole	.02	.10
409 Andres Galarraga	.07	.20
410 Joe Girardi	.02	.10
411 Butch Henry	.02	.10
412 Darren Holmes	.02	.10
413 Calvin Jones	.02	.10
414 Steve Reed RC	.02	.10
415 Kevin Ritz	.02	.10
416 Jim Tatum RC	.02	.10
417 Jack Armstrong	.02	.10
418 Bret Barberie	.02	.10
419 Ryan Bowen	.02	.10
420 Cris Carpenter	.02	.10
421 Chuck Carr	.02	.10
422 Scott Chiamparino	.02	.10
423 Jeff Conine	.07	.20
424 Jim Corsi	.02	.10
425 Steve Decker	.02	.10
426 Chris Donnels	.02	.10
427 Monty Fariss	.02	.10
428 Bob Natal	.02	.10
429 Pat Rapp	.02	.10
430 Dave Weathers	.02	.10
431 Nigel Wilson	.02	.10
432 Ken Caminiti	.07	.20
433 Andujar Cedeno	.02	.10
434 Tom Edens	.02	.10
435 Juan Guerrero	.02	.10
436 Pete Incaviglia	.02	.10
437 Jimmy Jones	.02	.10
438 Darryl Kile	.07	.20
439 Rob Murphy	.02	.10
440 Al Osuna	.02	.10
441 Mark Portugal	.02	.10
442 Scott Servais	.02	.10
443 John Candelaria	.02	.10
444 Tim Crews	.02	.10
445 Eric Davis	.07	.20
446 Tom Goodwin	.02	.10
447 Jim Gott	.02	.10
448 Kevin Gross	.02	.10
449 Dave Hansen	.02	.10
450 Jay Howell	.02	.10
451 Roger McDowell	.02	.10
452 Bob Ojeda	.02	.10
453 Henry Rodriguez	.02	.10
454 Darryl Strawberry	.07	.20
455 Mitch Webster	.02	.10
456 Steve Wilson	.02	.10
457 Brian Barnes	.02	.10
458 Sean Berry	.02	.10
459 Jeff Fassero	.02	.10
460 Darrin Fletcher	.02	.10
461 Marquis Grissom	.07	.20
462 Dennis Martinez	.07	.20
463 Spike Owen	.02	.10
464 Matt Stairs	.02	.10
465 Sergio Valdez	.02	.10
466 Kevin Bass	.02	.10
467 Vince Coleman	.02	.10
468 Mark Dewey	.02	.10
469 Kevin Elster	.02	.10
470 Tony Fernandez	.02	.10
471 John Franco	.07	.20
472 Dave Gallagher	.02	.10
473 Paul Gibson	.02	.10
474 Dwight Gooden	.07	.20
475 Lee Guetterman	.02	.10
476 Jeff Innis	.02	.10
477 Dave Magadan	.02	.10
478 Charlie O'Brien	.02	.10
479 Willie Randolph	.07	.20
480 Mackey Sasser	.02	.10
481 Ryan Thompson	.02	.10
482 Chico Walker	.02	.10
483 Kyle Abbott	.02	.10
484 Bob Ayrault	.02	.10
485 Kim Batiste	.02	.10
486 Cliff Brantley	.02	.10
487 Jose DeLeon	.02	.10
488 Len Dykstra	.07	.20
489 Tommy Greene	.02	.10
490 Jeff Grotewold	.02	.10
491 Dave Hollins	.02	.10
492 Danny Jackson	.02	.10
493 Stan Javier	.02	.10
494 Tom Marsh	.02	.10
495 Greg Mathews	.02	.10
496 Dale Murphy	.10	.30
497 Todd Pratt RC	.07	.20
498 Mitch Williams	.02	.10
499 Danny Cox	.02	.10
500 Doug Drabek	.02	.10
501 Carlos Garcia	.02	.10
502 Lloyd McClendon	.02	.10
503 Denny Neagle	.07	.20
504 Gary Redus	.02	.10
505 Bob Walk	.02	.10
506 John Wehner	.02	.10
507 Luis Alicea	.02	.10
508 Mark Clark	.02	.10
509 Pedro Guerrero	.07	.20
510 Rex Hudler	.02	.10
511 Brian Jordan	.07	.20
512 Omar Olivares	.02	.10
513 Jose Oquendo	.02	.10
514 Gerald Perry	.02	.10
515 Bryn Smith	.02	.10
516 Craig Wilson	.02	.10
517 Tracy Woodson	.02	.10
518 Larry Andersen	.02	.10
519 Andy Benes	.02	.10
520 Jim Deshaies	.02	.10
521 Bruce Hurst	.02	.10
522 Randy Myers	.02	.10
523 Benito Santiago	.07	.20
524 Tim Scott	.02	.10
525 Tim Teufel	.02	.10
526 Mike Benjamin	.02	.10
527 Dave Burba	.02	.10
528 Craig Colbert	.02	.10
529 Mike Felder	.02	.10
530 Bryan Hickerson	.02	.10
531 Chris James	.02	.10
532 Mark Leonard	.02	.10
533 Greg Litton	.02	.10
534 Francisco Oliveras	.02	.10
535 John Patterson	.02	.10
536 Jim Pena	.02	.10
537 Dave Righetti	.07	.20
538 Robby Thompson	.02	.10
539 Jose Uribe	.02	.10
540 Matt Williams	.07	.20
541 Storm Davis	.02	.10
542 Sam Horn	.02	.10
543 Tim Hulett	.02	.10
544 Craig Lefferts	.02	.10
545 Chito Martinez	.02	.10
546 Mark McLemore	.02	.10
547 Luis Mercedes	.02	.10
548 Bob Milacki	.02	.10
549 Joe Orsulak	.02	.10
550 Billy Ripken	.02	.10
551 Cal Ripken	.60	1.50
552 Rick Sutcliffe	.07	.20
553 Jeff Tackett	.02	.10
554 Wade Boggs	.10	.30
555 Tom Brunansky	.02	.10
556 Jack Clark	.07	.20
557 John Dopson	.02	.10
558 Mike Gardiner	.02	.10
559 Mike Greenwell	.02	.10
560 Greg A. Harris	.02	.10
561 Billy Hatcher	.02	.10
562 Joe Hesketh	.02	.10
563 Tony Pena	.02	.10
564 Phil Plantier	.02	.10
565 Luis Rivera	.02	.10
566 Herm Winningham	.02	.10
567 Matt Young	.02	.10
568 Bert Blyleven	.07	.20
569 Mike Butcher	.02	.10
570 Chuck Crim	.02	.10
571 Chad Curtis	.02	.10
572 Tim Fortugno	.02	.10
573 Steve Frey	.02	.10
574 Gary Gaetti	.07	.20
575 Scott Lewis	.02	.10
576 Lee Stevens	.02	.10
577 Ron Tingley	.02	.10
578 Julio Valera	.02	.10
579 Shawn Abner	.02	.10
580 Joey Cora	.02	.10
581 Chris Cron	.02	.10
582 Carlton Fisk	.10	.30
583 Roberto Hernandez	.02	.10
584 Charlie Hough	.07	.20
585 Terry Leach	.02	.10
586 Donn Pall	.02	.10
587 Dan Pasqua	.02	.10
588 Steve Sax	.02	.10
589 Bobby Thigpen	.02	.10
590 Albert Belle	.07	.20
591 Felix Fermin	.02	.10
592 Glenallen Hill	.02	.10
593 Brook Jacoby	.02	.10
594 Reggie Jefferson	.02	.10
595 Carlos Martinez	.02	.10
596 Jose Mesa	.02	.10
597 Rod Nichols	.02	.10
598 Junior Ortiz	.02	.10
599 Eric Plunk	.02	.10
600 Ted Power	.02	.10
601 Scott Scudder	.02	.10
602 Kevin Wickander	.02	.10
603 Skeeter Barnes	.02	.10
604 Mark Carreon	.02	.10
605 Dan Gladden	.02	.10
606 Bill Gullickson	.02	.10
607 Chad Kreuter	.02	.10
608 Mark Leiter	.02	.10
609 Mike Munoz	.02	.10
610 Rich Rowland	.02	.10
611 Frank Tanana	.02	.10
612 Walt Terrell	.02	.10
613 Alan Trammell	.07	.20
614 Lou Whitaker	.07	.20
615 Luis Aquino	.02	.10
616 Mike Boddicker	.02	.10
617 Jim Eisenreich	.02	.10
618 Mark Gubicza	.02	.10
619 David Howard	.02	.10
620 Mike Magnante	.02	.10
621 Brent Mayne	.02	.10
622 Kevin McReynolds	.02	.10
623 Eddie Pierce RC	.02	.10
624 Bill Sampen	.02	.10
625 Steve Shifflett	.02	.10
626 Gary Thurman	.02	.10
627 Curt Wilkerson	.02	.10
628 Chris Bosio	.02	.10
629 Scott Fletcher	.02	.10
630 Jim Gantner	.02	.10
631 Dave Nilsson	.02	.10
632 Jesse Orosco	.02	.10
633 Dan Plesac	.02	.10
634 Ron Robinson	.02	.10
635 Bill Spiers	.02	.10
636 Franklin Stubbs	.02	.10
637 Willie Banks	.02	.10
638 Randy Bush	.02	.10
639 Chuck Knoblauch	.07	.20
640 Shane Mack	.02	.10
641 Mike Pagliarulo	.02	.10
642 Jeff Reboulet	.02	.10
643 John Smiley	.02	.10
644 Mike Trombley	.02	.10
645 Gary Wayne	.02	.10
646 Lenny Webster	.02	.10
647 Tim Burke	.02	.10
648 Mike Gallego	.02	.10
649 Dion James	.02	.10
650 Jeff Johnson	.02	.10
651 Scott Kamieniecki	.02	.10
652 Kevin Maas	.02	.10
653 Rich Monteleone	.02	.10
654 Jerry Nielsen	.02	.10
655 Scott Sanderson	.02	.10
656 Mike Stanley	.02	.10
657 Gerald Williams	.02	.10
658 Curt Young	.02	.10
659 Harold Baines	.07	.20
660 Kevin Campbell	.02	.10
661 Ron Darling	.02	.10
662 Kelly Downs	.02	.10
663 Eric Fox	.02	.10
664 Dave Henderson	.02	.10
665 Rick Honeycutt	.02	.10
666 Mike Moore	.02	.10
667 Jamie Quirk	.02	.10
668 Jeff Russell	.02	.10
669 Dave Stewart	.07	.20
670 Greg Briley	.02	.10
671 Dave Cochrane	.02	.10
672 Henry Cotto	.02	.10
673 Rich DeLucia	.02	.10
674 Brian Fisher	.02	.10
675 Mark Grant	.02	.10
676 Randy Johnson	.20	.50
677 Tim Leary	.02	.10
678 Pete O'Brien	.02	.10
679 Lance Parrish	.07	.20
680 Harold Reynolds	.07	.20
681 Shane Turner	.02	.10
682 Jack Daugherty	.02	.10
683 David Hulse RC	.02	.10
684 Terry Mathews	.02	.10
685 Al Newman	.02	.10
686 Edwin Nunez	.02	.10
687 Rafael Palmeiro	.10	.30
688 Roger Pavlik	.02	.10
689 Geno Petralli	.02	.10
690 Nolan Ryan	.75	2.00
691 David Cone	.07	.20
692 Alfredo Griffin	.02	.10
693 Juan Guzman	.02	.10
694 Pat Hentgen	.02	.10
695 Randy Knorr	.02	.10
696 Bob MacDonald	.02	.10
697 Jack Morris	.07	.20
698 Ed Sprague	.02	.10
699 Dave Stieb	.02	.10
700 Pat Tabler	.02	.10
701 Mike Timlin	.02	.10
702 David Wells	.07	.20
703 Eddie Zosky	.02	.10
704 Gary Sheffield LL	.02	.10
705 Darren Daulton LL	.02	.10
706 Marquis Grissom LL	.02	.10
707 Greg Maddux LL	.20	.50
708 Bill Swift LL	.02	.10
709 Juan Gonzalez RT	.02	.10
710 Mark McGwire RT	.25	.60
711 Cecil Fielder RT	.02	.10
712 Albert Belle RT	.07	.20
713 Joe Carter RT	.02	.10
714 F.Thomas C.Fielder	.10	.30
715 L.Walker D.Daulton SS	.07	.20
716 E.Martinez R.Ventura SS	.07	.20
717 R.Clemens D.Eckersley	.20	.5
718 Checklist 361-480	.02	.1
719 Checklist 481-600	.02	.1
720 Checklist 601-720	.02	.

1993 Fleer All-Stars

This 24-card standard-size set featuring members of the American and National league All-Star squads, was randomly inserted in wax packs. 12 American League players were seeded in series 1 packs and National League players in series 2.

COMPLETE SET (24)	15.00	40.0
COMPLETE SERIES 1 (12)	10.00	25.0
COMPLETE SERIES 2 (12)	6.00	15.0
AL: RANDOM INSERTS IN SER.1 PACKS		
NL: RANDOM INSERTS IN SER.2 PACKS		
AL1 Frank Thomas AL	1.25	3.0
AL2 Roberto Alomar AL	.75	2.0
AL3 Edgar Martinez AL	.75	2.
AL4 Pat Listach AL	.25	.
AL5 Cecil Fielder AL	.50	1.
AL6 Juan Gonzalez AL	.50	1.2
AL7 Ken Griffey Jr. AL	2.50	6.0
AL8 Joe Carter AL	.50	1.2
AL9 Kirby Puckett AL	1.25	3.0
AL10 Brian Harper AL	.25	.
AL11 Dave Fleming AL	.25	.
AL12 Jack McDowell AL	.25	.
NL1 Fred McGriff NL	.75	2.0
NL2 Delino DeShields NL	.25	.
NL3 Gary Sheffield NL	.50	1.
NL4 Barry Larkin NL	.75	2.
NL5 Felix Jose NL	.25	.
NL6 Larry Walker NL	.50	1.
NL7 Barry Bonds NL	4.00	10.
NL8 Andy Van Slyke NL	.75	2.
NL9 Darren Daulton NL	.50	1.
NL10 Greg Maddux NL	2.00	5.
NL11 Tom Glavine NL	.75	2.
NL12 Lee Smith NL	.50	1.

1993 Fleer Glavine

As part of the Signature Series, this 12-card standard-size set spotlights Tom Glavine. An additional three cards (13-15) were available via a mail-in offer and are generally considered to be a separate set. The mail-in offer expired on Septemb 30, 1993. Reportedly, a filmmaking problem durin production resulted in eight variations in this 12-c insert set. Different backs appear on eight of the 12 cards. Cards 1-4 and 7-10 in wax packs feature ca back text variations from those included in the rack and jumbo magazine packs. The text differences occur in the first few words of text on the card back. No corrections were made in Series I. The correct Glavine cards appeared in Series II wax, rack, and jumbo magazine packs. In addition, Tom Glavine signed cards for this set. Unlike some of the previ autograph cards from Fleer, these cards were certified as authentic by the manufacturer.

COMPLETE SET (12)	1.50	4.
COMMON GLAVINE (1-12)	.20	.
RANDOM INSERTS IN ALL PACKS		
COMMON MAIL-IN (13-15)	.75	2.
MAIL-IN CARDS DIST.VIA WRAPPER EXCH.		
AU Tom Glavine AU	30.00	60.

1993 Fleer Golden Moments

Cards from this six-card standard-size set, featuri memorable moments from the previous season, w randomly inserted in 1993 Fleer wax packs, three each in series 1 and 2.

COMPLETE SET (6)	5.00	12.
COMPLETE SERIES 1 (3)	1.50	4.
COMPLETE SERIES 2 (3)	3.00	8.
RANDOM INSERTS IN WAX PACKS		
A1 George Brett	2.50	6.
A2 Mickey Morandini	.20	.
A3 Dave Winfield	.40	1.

nnis Eckersley .40 1.00
Roberts .20 .50
Gonzalez 1.00 2.50
homas

1993 Fleer Major League Prospects

from this 36-card standard-size set, featuring a ion of prospects, were randomly inserted in acks, 18 in each series. Early Cards of Pedro nez and Mike Piazza are featured within this set.

PLETE SET (36) 12.50 30.00
PLETE SERIES 1 (18) 8.00 20.00
PLETE SERIES 2 (18) 4.00 10.00
OM INSERTS IN WAX PACKS
vin Nieves .20 .50
es 1
ling Hitchcock .30 .75
es 1
Costo .20 .50
es 1
ny Alexander .20 .50
es 1
Embree .20 .50
es 1
in Young .30 .75
es 1
Snow .50 1.25
es 1
s Springer .20 .50
es 1
Ashley .20 .50
es 1
vin Rogers .20 .50
es 1
eve Hosey .20 .50
es 1
c Wedge .20 .50
es 1
Piazza Ser 1 3.00 8.00
sse Levis .20 .50
es 1
o Brogna .20 .50
es 1
x Arias .20 .50
es 1
d Brewer .20 .50
es 1
y Neel .20 .50
es 1
ter Tucker .20 .50
es 2
y Woodson .20 .50
es 2
Colbrunn .20 .50
es 2
artinez Ser.2 2.50 6.00
e Silvestri .20 .50
es 2
Bottenfield .20 .50
es 2
el Bournigal .20 .50
es 2
Bruett .20 .50
es 2
e Mlicki .20 .50
es 2
l Wagner .20 .50
es 2
ke Williams .20 .50
es 2
nry Mercedes .20 .50
es 2
tt Taylor .20 .50
es 2
nnis Moeller .20 .50
es 2
y Lopez .50 1.25
es 2
ve Cooke .20 .50
es 2
e Young .20 .50
es 2
Ryan .20 .50
es 2

1993 Fleer Pro-Visions

from this six-card standard-size set, featuring tion of superstars in fantasy paintings, were nly inserted in poly packs, three each in series d series two.

LETE SET (6) 2.00 5.00
COMPLETE SERIES 1 (3) 1.25 3.00
COMPLETE SERIES 2 (3) .75 2.00
RANDOM INSERTS IN WAX PACKS
A1 Roberto Alomar .75 2.00
A2 Dennis Eckersley .50 1.25
A3 Gary Sheffield .50 1.25
B1 Andy Van Slyke .75 2.00
B2 Tom Glavine .75 2.00
B3 Cecil Fielder .50 1.25

1993 Fleer Rookie Sensations

Cards from this 20-card standard-size set, featuring a selection of 1993's top rookies, were randomly inserted in cello packs, 10 in each series.

COMPLETE SET (20) 8.00 20.00
COMPLETE SERIES 1 (10) 4.00 10.00
COMPLETE SERIES 2 (10) 4.00 10.00
RANDOM INSERTS IN CELLO PACKS
RSA1 Kenny Lofton .75 2.00
RSA2 Cal Eldred .40 1.00
RSA3 Pat Listach .40 1.00
RSA4 Roberto Hernandez .40 1.00
RSA5 Dave Fleming .40 1.00
RSA6 Eric Karros .75 2.00
RSA7 Reggie Sanders .75 2.00
RSA8 Derrick May .40 1.00
RSA9 Mike Perez .40 1.00
RSA10 Donovan Osborne .40 1.00
RSB1 Moises Alou .75 2.00
RSB2 Pedro Astacio .40 1.00
RSB3 Jim Austin .40 1.00
RSB4 Chad Curtis .40 1.00
RSB5 Gary DiSarcina .40 1.00
RSB6 Scott Livingstone .40 1.00
RSB7 Sam Militello .40 1.00
RSB8 Arthur Rhodes .40 1.00
RSB9 Tim Wakefield 2.00 5.00
RSB10 Bob Zupcic .40 1.00

1993 Fleer Team Leaders

One Team Leader or Tom Glavine insert was seeded into each Fleer rack pack. Series 1 racks included 10 American League players, while series 2 racks included 10 National League players.

COMPLETE SET (20) 30.00 80.00
COMPLETE SERIES 1 (10) 20.00 50.00
COMPLETE SERIES 2 (10) 8.00 20.00
ONE TL OR GLAVINE PER RACK PACK
AL: RANDOM INSERTS IN SER.1 PACKS
NL: RANDOM INSERTS IN SER.2 PACKS
AL1 Kirby Puckett 2.00 5.00
AL2 Mark McGwire 5.00 12.00
AL3 Pat Listach .40 1.00
AL4 Roger Clemens 4.00 10.00
AL5 Frank Thomas 2.00 5.00
AL6 Carlos Baerga .40 1.00
AL7 Brady Anderson .75 2.00
AL8 Juan Gonzalez .75 2.00
AL9 Roberto Alomar 1.25 3.00
AL10 Ken Griffey Jr. 4.00 10.00
NL1 Will Clark 1.25 3.00
NL2 Terry Pendleton .75 2.00
NL3 Ray Lankford .75 2.00
NL4 Eric Karros .75 2.00
NL5 Gary Sheffield .75 2.00
NL6 Ryne Sandberg 3.00 8.00
NL7 Marquis Grissom .75 2.00
NL8 John Kruk .75 2.00
NL9 Jeff Bagwell 1.25 3.00
NL10 Andy Van Slyke 1.25 3.00

1993 Fleer Final Edition

This 300-card standard-size set was issued exclusively in factory set form (along with ten Diamond Tribute inserts) to update and feature rookies not in the regular 1993 Fleer set. The cards are identical in design to regular issue 1993 Fleer cards except for the F-prefixed numbering. Cards are ordered alphabetically within teams with NL preceding AL. The set closes with checklist cards (298-300). The only key Rookie Card in this set features Jim Edmonds.

COMP.FACT.SET (310) 4.00 10.00
COMPLETE SET (300) 3.00 8.00
F PREFIX ON REG.CARD NUMBERS
1 Steve Bedrosian .02 .10
2 Jay Howell .02 .10
3 Greg Maddux .30 .75
4 Greg McMichael RC .05 .15
5 Tony Tarasco RC .05 .15
6 Jose Bautista .02 .10
7 Jose Guzman .02 .10
8 Greg Hibbard .02 .10
9 Candy Maldonado .02 .10
10 Randy Myers .02 .10
11 Matt Walbeck RC .15 .40
12 Turk Wendell .02 .10
13 Willie Wilson .02 .10
14 Greg Cadaret .02 .10
15 Roberto Kelly .02 .10
16 Randy Milligan .02 .10
17 Kevin Mitchell .02 .10
18 Jeff Reardon .07 .20
19 John Roper .02 .10
20 John Smiley .02 .10
21 Andy Ashby .02 .10
22 Dante Bichette .07 .20
23 Willie Blair .02 .10
24 Pedro Castellano .02 .10
25 Vinny Castilla .20 .50
26 Jerald Clark .02 .10
27 Alex Cole .02 .10
28 Scott Fredrickson RC .05 .15
29 Jay Gainer RC .05 .15
30 Andres Galarraga .07 .20
31 Joe Girardi .02 .10
32 Ryan Hawblitzel .02 .10
33 Charlie Hayes .02 .10
34 Darren Holmes .02 .10
35 Chris Jones .02 .10
36 David Nied .02 .10
37 Jayhawk Owens RC .05 .15
38 Lance Painter RC .15 .40
39 Jeff Parrett .02 .10
40 Steve Reed .02 .10
41 Armando Reynoso .02 .10
42 Bruce Ruffin .02 .10
43 Danny Sheaffer RC .05 .15
44 Keith Shepherd .02 .10
45 Jim Tatum .02 .10
46 Gary Wayne .02 .10
47 Eric Young .02 .10
48 Luis Aquino .02 .10
49 Alex Arias .02 .10
50 Jack Armstrong .02 .10
51 Bret Barberie .02 .10
52 Geronimo Berroa .02 .10
53 Ryan Bowen .02 .10
54 Greg Briley .02 .10
55 Cris Carpenter .02 .10
56 Chuck Carr .02 .10
57 Jeff Conine .07 .20
58 Jim Corsi .02 .10
59 Orestes Destrade .02 .10
60 Junior Felix .02 .10
61 Chris Hammond .02 .10
62 Bryan Harvey .02 .10
63 Charlie Hough .07 .20
64 Joe Klink .02 .10
65 Richie Lewis RC UER .05 .15
Refers to place of birth and residence as Illinois instead of Indiana
66 Mitch Lyden RC .05 .15
67 Bob Natal .02 .10
68 Scott Pose RC .05 .15
69 Rich Renteria .02 .10
70 Benito Santiago .07 .20
71 Gary Sheffield .07 .20
72 Matt Turner RC .05 .15
73 Walt Weiss .02 .10
74 Darrell Whitmore RC .05 .15
75 Nigel Wilson .02 .10
76 Kevin Bass .02 .10
77 Doug Drabek .02 .10
78 Tom Edens .02 .10
79 Chris James .02 .10
80 Greg Swindell .02 .10
81 Omar Daal RC .05 .15
82 Raul Mondesi .07 .20
83 Jody Reed .02 .10
84 Cory Snyder .02 .10
85 Rick Trlicek .02 .10
86 Tim Wallach .02 .10
87 Todd Worrell .02 .10
88 Tavo Alvarez .02 .10
89 Frank Bolick .02 .10
90 Kent Bottenfield .02 .10
91 Greg Colbrunn .02 .10
92 Cliff Floyd .07 .20
93 Lou Frazier RC .05 .15
94 Mike Gardiner .02 .10
95 Mike Lansing RC .15 .40
96 Bill Risley .02 .10
97 Jeff Shaw .02 .10
98 Kevin Baez .02 .10
99 Tim Bogar RC .05 .15
100 Jeromy Burnitz .07 .20
101 Mike Draper .02 .10
102 Darrin Jackson .02 .10
103 Mike Maddux .02 .10
104 Joe Orsulak .02 .10
105 Doug Saunders RC .05 .15
106 Frank Tanana .02 .10
107 Dave Telgheder RC .05 .15
108 Larry Andersen .02 .10
109 Jim Eisenreich .02 .10
110 Pete Incaviglia .02 .10
111 Danny Jackson .02 .10
112 David West .02 .10
113 Al Martin .02 .10
114 Blas Minor .02 .10
115 Dennis Moeller .02 .10
116 William Pennyfeather .02 .10
117 Rich Robertson RC .05 .15
118 Ben Shelton .02 .10
119 Lonnie Smith .02 .10
120 Freddie Toliver .02 .10
121 Paul Wagner .02 .10
122 Kevin Young .07 .20
123 Rene Arocha RC .15 .40
124 Gregg Jefferies .02 .10
125 Paul Kilgus .02 .10
126 Les Lancaster .02 .10
127 Joe Magrane .02 .10
128 Rob Murphy .02 .10
129 Erik Pappas .02 .10
130 Stan Royer .02 .10
131 Ozzie Smith .30 .75
132 Tom Urbani RC .05 .15
133 Mark Whiten .02 .10
134 Derek Bell .02 .10
135 Doug Brocail .02 .10
136 Phil Clark .02 .10
137 Mark Ettles RC .05 .15
138 Jeff Gardner .02 .10
139 Pat Gomez RC .05 .15
140 Ricky Gutierrez .02 .10
141 Gene Harris .02 .10
142 Kevin Higgins .02 .10
143 Trevor Hoffman .20 .50
144 Phil Plantier .02 .10
145 Kerry Taylor RC .05 .15
146 Guillermo Velasquez .02 .10
147 Wally Whitehurst .02 .10
148 Tim Worrell RC .15 .40
149 Todd Benzinger .02 .10
150 Barry Bonds .60 1.50
151 Greg Brummett RC .05 .15
152 Mark Carreon .02 .10
153 Dave Martinez .02 .10
154 Jeff Reed .02 .10
155 Kevin Rogers .02 .10
156 Harold Baines .07 .20
157 Damon Buford .02 .10
158 Paul Carey RC .05 .15
159 Jeffrey Hammonds .02 .10
160 Jamie Moyer .07 .20
161 Sherman Obando RC .05 .15
162 John O'Donoghue RC .05 .15
163 Brad Pennington .02 .10
164 Jim Poole .02 .10
165 Harold Reynolds .07 .20
166 Fernando Valenzuela .07 .20
167 Jack Voigt RC .05 .15
168 Mark Williamson .02 .10
169 Scott Bankhead .02 .10
170 Greg Blosser .02 .10
171 Jim Byrd RC .05 .15
172 Ivan Calderon .02 .10
173 Andre Dawson .07 .20
174 Scott Fletcher .02 .10
175 Jose Melendez .02 .10
176 Carlos Quintana .02 .10
177 Jeff Russell .02 .10
178 Aaron Sele .02 .10
179 Rod Correia RC .05 .15
180 Chili Davis .07 .20
181 Jim Edmonds RC 1.25 3.00
182 Rene Gonzales .02 .10
183 Hilly Hathaway RC .05 .15
184 Torey Lovullo .02 .10
185 Greg Myers .02 .10
186 Gene Nelson .02 .10
187 Troy Percival .10 .30
188 Scott Sanderson .02 .10
189 Darryl Scott RC .05 .15
190 J.T.Snow RC .25 .60
191 Russ Springer .02 .10
192 Jason Bere .02 .10
193 Rodney Bolton .02 .10
194 Ellis Burks .07 .20
195 Bo Jackson .20 .50
196 Mike LaValliere .02 .10
197 Scott Ruffcorn .02 .10
198 Jeff Schwarz .02 .10
199 Jerry DiPoto .02 .10
200 Alvaro Espinoza .02 .10
201 Wayne Kirby .02 .10
202 Tom Kramer RC .05 .15
203 Jesse Levis .02 .10
204 Manny Ramirez .30 .75
205 Jeff Treadway .02 .10
206 Bill Wertz RC .05 .15
207 Cliff Young .02 .10
208 Matt Young .02 .10
209 Kirk Gibson .07 .20
210 Greg Gohr .02 .10
211 Bill Krueger .02 .10
212 Bob MacDonald .02 .10
213 Mike Moore .02 .10
214 David Wells .07 .20
215 Billy Brewer .02 .10
216 David Cone .07 .20
217 Greg Gagne .02 .10
218 Mark Gardner .02 .10
219 Chris Haney .02 .10
220 Phil Hiatt .02 .10
221 Jose Lind .02 .10
222 Juan Bell .02 .10
223 Tom Brunansky .02 .10
224 Mike Ignasiak .02 .10
225 Joe Kmak .02 .10
226 Tom Lampkin .02 .10
227 Graeme Lloyd RC .15 .40
228 Carlos Maldonado .02 .10
229 Matt Mieske .02 .10
230 Angel Miranda .02 .10
231 Troy O'Leary RC .15 .40
232 Kevin Reimer .02 .10
233 Larry Casian .02 .10
234 Jim Deshaies .02 .10
235 Eddie Guardado RC .25 .60
236 Chip Hale .02 .10
237 Mike Maksudian RC .05 .15
238 David McCarty .02 .10
239 Pat Meares RC .15 .40
240 George Tsamis RC .05 .15
241 Dave Winfield .07 .20
242 Jim Abbott .10 .30
243 Wade Boggs .10 .30
244 Andy Cook RC .05 .15
245 Russ Davis RC .05 .15
246 Mike Humphreys .02 .10
247 Jimmy Key .07 .20
248 Jim Leyritz .02 .10
249 Bobby Munoz .02 .10
250 Paul O'Neill .10 .30
251 Spike Owen .02 .10
252 Dave Silvestri .02 .10
253 Marcos Armas RC .05 .15
254 Brent Gates .02 .10
255 Rich Gossage .07 .20
256 Scott Lydy RC .05 .15
257 Henry Mercedes .02 .10
258 Mike Mohler RC .15 .40
259 Troy Neel .02 .10
260 Edwin Nunez .02 .10
261 Craig Paquette .02 .10
262 Kevin Seitzer .02 .10
263 Rich Amaral .02 .10
264 Mike Blowers .02 .10
265 Chris Bosio .02 .10
266 Norm Charlton .02 .10
267 Jim Converse RC .05 .15
268 John Cummings RC .05 .15
269 Mike Felder .02 .10
270 Mike Hampton .07 .20
271 Bill Haselman .02 .10
272 Dwayne Henry .02 .10
273 Greg Litton .02 .10
274 Mackey Sasser .02 .10
275 Lee Tinsley .02 .10
276 David Wainhouse .02 .10
277 Jeff Bronkey .02 .10
278 Benji Gil .02 .10
279 Tom Henke .02 .10
280 Charlie Leibrandt .02 .10
281 Robb Nen .07 .20
282 Bill Ripken .02 .10
283 Jon Shave RC .05 .15
284 Doug Strange .02 .10
285 Matt Whiteside RC .05 .15
286 Scott Brow RC .05 .15
287 Willie Canate RC .05 .15
288 Tony Castillo .02 .10
289 Domingo Cedeno RC .05 .15
290 Darnell Coles .02 .10
291 Danny Cox .02 .10
292 Mark Eichhorn .02 .10
293 Tony Fernandez .02 .10
294 Al Leiter .07 .20
295 Paul Molitor .07 .20
296 Dave Stewart .07 .20
297 Woody Williams RC .25 .60
298 Checklist F1-F100 .02 .10
299 Checklist F101-F200 .02 .10
300 Checklist F201-F300 .02 .10

1993 Fleer Final Edition Diamond Tribute

Each Fleer Final Edition factory set contained a complete 10-card set of Diamond Tribute inserts. These cards are numbered separately and feature a totally different design from the base cards. Each card is numbered "X" of 10 on back.

COMPLETE SET (10) 1.50 4.00
ONE SET PER FINAL EDITION FACTORY SET
1 Wade Boggs .20 .50
2 George Brett .75 2.00
3 Andre Dawson .10 .30
4 Carlton Fisk .20 .50
5 Paul Molitor .10 .30
6 Nolan Ryan 1.25 3.00
7 Lee Smith .10 .30
8 Ozzie Smith .50 1.25
9 Dave Winfield .10 .30
10 Robin Yount .50 1.25

1993 Fleer Atlantic

This standard-size set of 25 cards features 24 high-profile players plus a checklist and was offered free in packs of five cards with a minimum purchase of eight gallons of Atlantic gasoline. The cards were available from June 14 to July 25, 1993, at participating Atlantic retailers in New York and Pennsylvania. The Atlantic Collector's Edition logo appears in the lower left. The cards are sequenced in alphabetical order. This set features one of the earliest cards picturing Barry Bonds as a member of the San Francisco Giants.

COMPLETE SET (25) 3.00 8.00
1 Roberto Alomar .15 .40
2 Barry Bonds .50 1.25
3 Bobby Bonilla .02 .10
4 Will Clark .20 .50
5 Roger Clemens .50 1.25
6 Darren Daulton .07 .20
7 Dennis Eckersley .20 .50
8 Cecil Fielder .07 .20
9 Tom Glavine .20 .50
10 Juan Gonzalez .15 .40
11 Ken Griffey Jr. .75 2.00
12 John Kruk .07 .20
13 Greg Maddux .50 1.25
14 Don Mattingly .50 1.25
15 Fred McGriff .10 .30
16 Mark McGwire .60 1.50
17 Terry Pendleton .02 .10
18 Kirby Puckett .20 .50
19 Cal Ripken 1.00 2.50
20 Nolan Ryan 1.00 2.50
21 Ryne Sandberg .40 1.00
22 Gary Sheffield .20 .50
23 Frank Thomas .20 .50
24 Andy Van Slyke .02 .10
25 Checklist 1-25 .02 .10

1993 Fleer Fruit of the Loom

The 1993 Fleer Fruit of the Loom set consists of 66 cards measuring the standard size. Six-card packs were inserted in three-packs of Fruit of the Loom boys briefs. The cards have the same design as the regular issue 1993 Fleer. The only exception is the Fruit of the Loom logo which appears on the front. The cards are numbered on the back ordered alphabetically by player's name.

COMPLETE SET (66) 60.00 120.00
1 Roberto Alomar .60 1.50
2 Brady Anderson .30 .75
3 Jeff Bagwell 1.50 4.00
4 Albert Belle .30 .75
5 Craig Biggio .40 1.00
6 Barry Bonds 3.00 8.00
7 George Brett 3.00 8.00
8 Brett Butler .30 .75
9 Jose Canseco 1.00 2.50
10 Joe Carter .30 .75
11 Will Clark .60 1.50
12 Roger Clemens 3.00 8.00
13 Darren Daulton .30 .75
14 Andre Dawson .60 1.50
15 Delino DeShields .20 .50
16 Rob Dibble .30 .75
17 Doug Drabek .20 .50
18 Dennis Eckersley 1.00 2.50
19 Cecil Fielder .20 .50
20 Travis Fryman .30 .75
21 Tom Glavine .60 1.50
22 Juan Gonzalez .60 1.50
23 Dwight Gooden .30 .75
24 Mark Grace .40 1.00
25 Ken Griffey Jr. 4.00 10.00
26 Marquis Grissom .30 .75
27 Juan Guzman .20 .50
28 Tony Gwynn 3.00 8.00
29 Rickey Henderson 2.00 5.00
30 David Justice .60 1.50
31 Eric Karros .40 1.00
32 Chuck Knoblauch .60 1.50
33 John Kruk .30 .75
34 Ray Lankford .30 .75
35 Barry Larkin .60 1.50
36 Pat Listach .20 .50
37 Kenny Lofton .40 1.00
38 Shane Mack .20 .50
39 Greg Maddux 3.00 8.00
40 Dennis Martinez .30 .75
41 Edgar Martinez .40 1.00
42 Ramon Martinez .20 .50
43 Don Mattingly 3.00 8.00
44 Jack McDowell .20 .50
45 Fred McGriff .40 1.00
46 Mark McGwire 4.00 10.00
47 Jeff Montgomery .30 .75
48 Eddie Murray 1.25 3.00
49 Charles Nagy .20 .50
50 Tom Pagnozzi .20 .50
51 Terry Pendleton .20 .50
52 Kirby Puckett 1.50 4.00
53 Jose Rijo .20 .50
54 Cal Ripken 6.00 15.00
55 Nolan Ryan 6.00 15.00
56 Ryne Sandberg 2.00 5.00
57 Gary Sheffield 1.25 3.00
58 Bill Swift .20 .50
59 Danny Tartabull .20 .50
60 Mickey Tettleton .20 .50
61 Frank Thomas 1.00 2.50
62 Andy Van Slyke .20 .50
63 Robin Ventura .40 1.00
64 Larry Walker .60 1.50
65 Robin Yount 1.00 2.50
66 Checklist 1-66 .20 .50

1994 Fleer

The 1994 Fleer baseball set consists of 720 standard-size cards. Cards were distributed in hobby, retail, and jumbo packs. The cards are numbered on the back, grouped alphabetically within teams, and checklisted below alphabetically according to teams for each league with AL preceding NL. The set closes with a Superstar Specials (706-713) subset. There are no key Rookie Cards in this set.

COMPLETE SET (720) 20.00 50.00
1 Brady Anderson .10 .30
2 Harold Baines .10 .30
3 Mike Devereaux .05 .15
4 Todd Frohwirth .05 .15
5 Jeffrey Hammonds .05 .15
6 Chris Hoiles .05 .15
7 Tim Hulett .05 .15
8 Ben McDonald .05 .15
9 Mark McLemore .05 .15
10 Alan Mills .05 .15
11 Jamie Moyer .10 .30
12 Mike Mussina .20 .50
13 Gregg Olson .05 .15
14 Mike Pagliarulo .05 .15
15 Brad Pennington .05 .15
16 Jim Poole .05 .15
17 Harold Reynolds .10 .30
18 Arthur Rhodes .05 .15
19 Cal Ripken Jr. 1.00 2.50
20 David Segui .05 .15
21 Rick Sutcliffe .10 .30
22 Fernando Valenzuela .10 .30
23 Jack Voigt .05 .15
24 Mark Williamson .05 .15
25 Scott Bankhead .05 .15
26 Roger Clemens .60 1.50
27 Scott Cooper .05 .15
28 Danny Darwin .05 .15
29 Andre Dawson .10 .30
30 Rob Deer .05 .15
31 John Dopson .05 .15
32 Scott Fletcher .05 .15
33 Mike Greenwell .05 .15
34 Greg A. Harris .05 .15
35 Billy Hatcher .05 .15
36 Bob Melvin .05 .15
37 Tony Pena .05 .15
38 Paul Quantrill .05 .15
39 Carlos Quintana .05 .15
40 Ernest Riles .05 .15
41 Jeff Russell .05 .15
42 Ken Ryan .05 .15
43 Aaron Sele .05 .15
44 John Valentin .05 .15
45 Mo Vaughn .10 .30
46 Frank Viola .10 .30
47 Bob Zupcic .05 .15
48 Mike Butcher .05 .15
49 Rod Correia .05 .15
50 Chad Curtis .05 .15
51 Chili Davis .10 .30
52 Gary DiSarcina .05 .15
53 Damion Easley .05 .15
54 Jim Edmonds .30 .75
55 Chuck Finley .10 .30
56 Steve Frey .05 .15
57 Rene Gonzales .05 .15
58 Joe Grahe .05 .15
59 Hilly Hathaway .05 .15
60 Stan Javier .05 .15
61 Mark Langston .05 .15
62 Phil Leftwich RC .05 .15
63 Torey Lovullo .05 .15
64 Joe Magrane .05 .15
65 Greg Myers .05 .15
66 Ken Patterson .05 .15
67 Eduardo Perez .05 .15

68 Luis Polonia .05 .15
69 Tim Salmon .20 .50
70 J.T.Snow .10 .30
71 Ron Tingley .05 .15
72 Julio Valera .05 .15
73 Wilson Alvarez .05 .15
74 Tim Belcher .05 .15
75 George Bell .05 .15
76 Jason Bere .05 .15
77 Rod Bolton .05 .15
78 Ellis Burks .10 .30
79 Joey Cora .05 .15
80 Alex Fernandez .05 .15
81 Craig Grebeck .05 .15
82 Ozzie Guillen .10 .30
83 Roberto Hernandez .05 .15
84 Bo Jackson .30 .75
85 Lance Johnson .05 .15
86 Ron Karkovice .05 .15
87 Mike LaValliere .05 .15
88 Kirk McCaskill .05 .15
89 Jack McDowell .05 .15
90 Warren Newson .05 .15
91 Dan Pasqua .05 .15
92 Scott Radinsky .05 .15
93 Tim Raines .10 .30
94 Steve Sax .05 .15
95 Jeff Schwarz .05 .15
96 Frank Thomas .30 .75
97 Robin Ventura .10 .30
98 Sandy Alomar Jr. .05 .15
99 Carlos Baerga .05 .15
100 Albert Belle .10 .30
101 Mark Clark .05 .15
102 Jerry DiPoto .05 .15
103 Alvaro Espinoza .05 .15
104 Felix Fermin .05 .15
105 Jeremy Hernandez .05 .15
106 Reggie Jefferson .05 .15
107 Wayne Kirby .05 .15
108 Tom Kramer .05 .15
109 Mark Lewis .05 .15
110 Derek Lilliquist .05 .15
111 Kenny Lofton .10 .30
112 Candy Maldonado .05 .15
113 Jose Mesa .05 .15
114 Jeff Mutis .05 .15
115 Charles Nagy .05 .15
116 Bob Ojeda .05 .15
117 Junior Ortiz .05 .15
118 Eric Plunk .05 .15
119 Manny Ramirez .30 .75
120 Paul Sorrento .05 .15
121 Jim Thome .20 .50
122 Jeff Treadway .05 .15
123 Bill Wertz .05 .15
124 Skeeter Barnes .05 .15
125 Milt Cuyler .05 .15
126 Eric Davis .10 .30
127 John Doherty .05 .15
128 Cecil Fielder .10 .30
129 Travis Fryman .10 .30
130 Kirk Gibson .10 .30
131 Dan Gladden .05 .15
132 Greg Gohr .05 .15
133 Chris Gomez .05 .15
134 Bill Gullickson .05 .15
135 Mike Henneman .05 .15
136 Kurt Knudsen .05 .15
137 Chad Kreuter .05 .15
138 Bill Krueger .05 .15
139 Scott Livingstone .05 .15
140 Bob MacDonald .05 .15
141 Mike Moore .05 .15
142 Tony Phillips .05 .15
143 Mickey Tettleton .05 .15
144 Alan Trammell .10 .30
145 David Wells .10 .30
146 Lou Whitaker .10 .30
147 Kevin Appier .10 .30
148 Stan Belinda .05 .15
149 George Brett .75 2.00
150 Billy Brewer .05 .15
151 Hubie Brooks .05 .15
152 David Cone .10 .30
153 Gary Gaetti .10 .30
154 Greg Gagne .05 .15
155 Tom Gordon .05 .15
156 Mark Gubicza .05 .15
157 Chris Gwynn .05 .15
158 John Habyan .05 .15
159 Chris Haney .05 .15
160 Phil Hiatt .05 .15
161 Felix Jose .05 .15
162 Wally Joyner .10 .30
163 Jose Lind .05 .15
164 Mike Macfarlane .05 .15
165 Mike Magnante .05 .15
166 Brent Mayne .05 .15
167 Brian McRae .05 .15
168 Kevin McReynolds .05 .15
169 Keith Miller .05 .15
170 Jeff Montgomery .05 .15
171 Hipolito Pichardo .05 .15
172 Rico Rossy .05 .15
173 Juan Bell .05 .15
174 Ricky Bones .05 .15
175 Cal Eldred .05 .15
176 Mike Fetters .05 .15
177 Darryl Hamilton .05 .15
178 Doug Henry .05 .15
179 Mike Ignasiak .05 .15
180 John Jaha .05 .15
181 Pat Listach .05 .15
182 Graeme Lloyd .05 .15
183 Matt Mieske .05 .15
184 Angel Miranda .05 .15
185 Jaime Navarro .05 .15
186 Dave Nilsson .05 .15
187 Troy O'Leary .05 .15
188 Jesse Orosco .05 .15
189 Kevin Reimer .05 .15
190 Kevin Seitzer .05 .15
191 Bill Spiers .05 .15
192 B.J. Surhoff .10 .30
193 Dickie Thon .05 .15
194 Jose Valentin .05 .15
195 Greg Vaughn .05 .15
196 Bill Wegman .05 .15
197 Robin Yount .50 1.25
198 Rick Aguilera .05 .15
199 Willie Banks .05 .15
200 Bernardo Brito .05 .15
201 Larry Casian .05 .15
202 Scott Erickson .05 .15
203 Eddie Guardado .10 .30
204 Mark Guthrie .05 .15
205 Chip Hale .05 .15
206 Brian Harper .05 .15
207 Mike Hartley .05 .15
208 Kent Hrbek .10 .30
209 Terry Jorgensen .05 .15
210 Chuck Knoblauch .10 .30
211 Gene Larkin .05 .15
212 Shane Mack .05 .15
213 David McCarty .05 .15
214 Pat Meares .05 .15
215 Pedro Munoz .05 .15
216 Derek Parks .05 .15
217 Kirby Puckett .30 .75
218 Jeff Reboulet .05 .15
219 Kevin Tapani .05 .15
220 Mike Trombley .05 .15
221 George Tsamis .05 .15
222 Carl Willis .05 .15
223 Dave Winfield .10 .30
224 Jim Abbott .20 .50
225 Paul Assenmacher .05 .15
226 Wade Boggs .20 .50
227 Russ Davis .05 .15
228 Steve Farr .05 .15
229 Mike Gallego .05 .15
230 Paul Gibson .05 .15
231 Steve Howe .05 .15
232 Dion James .05 .15
233 Domingo Jean .05 .15
234 Scott Kamieniecki .05 .15
235 Pat Kelly .05 .15
236 Jimmy Key .10 .30
237 Jim Leyritz .05 .15
238 Kevin Maas .05 .15
239 Don Mattingly .75 2.00
240 Rich Monteleone .05 .15
241 Bobby Munoz .05 .15
242 Matt Nokes .05 .15
243 Paul O'Neill .20 .50
244 Spike Owen .05 .15
245 Melido Perez .05 .15
246 Lee Smith .10 .30
247 Mike Stanley .05 .15
248 Danny Tartabull .05 .15
249 Randy Velarde .05 .15
250 Bob Wickman .05 .15
251 Bernie Williams .20 .50
252 Mike Aldrete .05 .15
253 Marcos Armas .05 .15
254 Lance Blankenship .05 .15
255 Mike Bordick .05 .15
256 Scott Brosius .10 .30
257 Jerry Browne .05 .15
258 Ron Darling .05 .15
259 Kelly Downs .05 .15
260 Dennis Eckersley .10 .30
261 Brent Gates .05 .15
262 Rich Gossage .10 .30
263 Scott Hemond .05 .15
264 Dave Henderson .05 .15
265 Rick Honeycutt .05 .15
266 Vince Horsman .05 .15
267 Scott Lydy .05 .15
268 Mark McGwire .75 2.00
269 Mike Mohler .05 .15
270 Troy Neel .05 .15
271 Edwin Nunez .05 .15
272 Craig Paquette .05 .15
273 Ruben Sierra .10 .30
274 Terry Steinbach .05 .15
275 Todd Van Poppel .05 .15
276 Bob Welch .05 .15
277 Bobby Witt .05 .15
278 Rich Amaral .05 .15
279 Mike Blowers .05 .15
280 Bret Boone UER .10 .30
Name spelled Brett on front
281 Chris Bosio .05 .15
282 Jay Buhner .10 .30
283 Norm Charlton .05 .15
284 Mike Felder .05 .15
285 Dave Fleming .05 .15
286 Ken Griffey Jr. .60 1.50
287 Erik Hanson .05 .15
288 Bill Haselman .05 .15
289 Brad Holman RC .05 .15
290 Randy Johnson .30 .75
291 Tim Leary .05 .15
292 Greg Litton .05 .15
293 Dave Magadan .05 .15
294 Edgar Martinez .20 .50
295 Tino Martinez .20 .50
296 Jeff Nelson .05 .15
297 Erik Plantenberg RC .05 .15
298 Mackey Sasser .05 .15
299 Brian Turang RC .05 .15
300 Dave Valle .05 .15
301 Omar Vizquel .20 .50
302 Brian Bohanon .05 .15
303 Kevin Brown .10 .30
304 Jose Canseco UER .20 .50
Back mentions 1991 as his
40
40 MVP season; should be '88
305 Mario Diaz .05 .15
306 Julio Franco .10 .30
307 Juan Gonzalez .10 .30
308 Tom Henke .05 .15
309 David Hulse .05 .15
310 Manuel Lee .05 .15
311 Craig Lefferts .05 .15
312 Charlie Leibrandt .05 .15
313 Rafael Palmeiro .20 .50
314 Dean Palmer .10 .30
315 Roger Pavlik .05 .15
316 Dan Peltier .05 .15
317 Gene Petralli .05 .15
318 Gary Redus .05 .15
319 Ivan Rodriguez .20 .50
320 Kenny Rogers .10 .30
321 Nolan Ryan 1.25 3.00
322 Doug Strange .05 .15
323 Matt Whiteside .05 .15
324 Roberto Alomar .20 .50
325 Pat Borders .05 .15
326 Joe Carter .10 .30
327 Tony Castillo .05 .15
328 Darnell Coles .05 .15
329 Danny Cox .05 .15
330 Mark Eichhorn .05 .15
331 Tony Fernandez .05 .15
332 Alfredo Griffin .05 .15
333 Juan Guzman .05 .15
334 Rickey Henderson .30 .75
335 Pat Hentgen .05 .15
336 Randy Knorr .05 .15
337 Al Leiter .10 .30
338 Paul Molitor .10 .30
339 Jack Morris .10 .30
340 John Olerud .10 .30
341 Dick Schofield .05 .15
342 Ed Sprague .05 .15
343 Dave Stewart .10 .30
344 Todd Stottlemyre .05 .15
345 Mike Timlin .05 .15
346 Duane Ward .05 .15
347 Turner Ward .05 .15
348 Devon White .10 .30
349 Woody Williams .10 .30
350 Steve Avery .05 .15
351 Steve Bedrosian .05 .15
352 Rafael Belliard .05 .15
353 Damon Berryhill .05 .15
354 Jeff Blauser .05 .15
355 Sid Bream .05 .15
356 Francisco Cabrera .05 .15
357 Marvin Freeman .05 .15
358 Ron Gant .10 .30
359 Tom Glavine .20 .50
360 Jay Howell .05 .15
361 David Justice .10 .30
362 Ryan Klesko .10 .30
363 Mark Lemke .05 .15
364 Javier Lopez .10 .30
365 Greg Maddux .50 1.25
366 Fred McGriff .20 .50
367 Greg McMichael .05 .15
368 Kent Mercker .05 .15
369 Otis Nixon .05 .15
370 Greg Olson .05 .15
371 Bill Pecota .05 .15
372 Terry Pendleton .10 .30
373 Deion Sanders .20 .50
374 Pete Smith .05 .15
375 John Smoltz .20 .50
376 Mike Stanton .05 .15
377 Tony Tarasco .05 .15
378 Mark Wohlers .05 .15
379 Jose Bautista .05 .15
380 Shawn Boskie .05 .15
381 Steve Buechele .05 .15
382 Frank Castillo .05 .15
383 Mark Grace .20 .50
384 Jose Guzman .05 .15
385 Mike Harkey .05 .15
386 Greg Hibbard .05 .15
387 Glenallen Hill .05 .15
388 Steve Lake .05 .15
389 Derrick May .05 .15
390 Chuck McElroy .05 .15
391 Mike Morgan .05 .15
392 Randy Myers .05 .15
393 Dan Plesac .05 .15
394 Kevin Roberson .05 .15
395 Rey Sanchez .05 .15
396 Ryne Sandberg .50 1.25
397 Bob Scanlan .05 .15
398 Dwight Smith .05 .15
399 Sammy Sosa .30 .75
400 Jose Vizcaino .05 .15
401 Rick Wilkins .05 .15
402 Willie Wilson .05 .15
403 Eric Yelding .05 .15
404 Bobby Ayala .05 .15
405 Jeff Branson .05 .15
406 Tom Browning .05 .15
407 Jacob Brumfield .05 .15
408 Tim Costo .05 .15
409 Rob Dibble .10 .30
410 Willie Greene .05 .15
411 Thomas Howard .05 .15
412 Roberto Kelly .05 .15
413 Bill Landrum .05 .15
414 Barry Larkin .20 .50
415 Larry Luebbers RC .05 .15
416 Kevin Mitchell .05 .15
417 Hal Morris .05 .15
418 Joe Oliver .05 .15
419 Tim Pugh .05 .15
420 Jeff Reardon .10 .30
421 Jose Rijo .05 .15
422 Bip Roberts .05 .15
423 John Roper .05 .15
424 Johnny Ruffin .05 .15
425 Chris Sabo .05 .15
426 Juan Samuel .05 .15
427 Reggie Sanders .10 .30
428 Scott Service .05 .15
429 John Smiley .05 .15
430 Jerry Spradlin RC .05 .15
431 Kevin Wickander .05 .15
432 Freddie Benavides .05 .15
433 Dante Bichette .10 .30
434 Willie Blair .05 .15
435 Daryl Boston .05 .15
436 Kent Bottenfield .05 .15
437 Vinny Castilla .10 .30
438 Jerald Clark .05 .15
439 Alex Cole .05 .15
440 Andres Galarraga .10 .30
441 Joe Girardi .05 .15
442 Greg W. Harris .05 .15
443 Charlie Hayes .05 .15
444 Darren Holmes .05 .15
445 Chris Jones .05 .15
446 Roberto Mejia .05 .15
447 David Nied .05 .15
448 Jayhawk Owens .05 .15
449 Jeff Parrett .05 .15
450 Steve Reed .05 .15
451 Armando Reynoso .05 .15
452 Bruce Ruffin .05 .15
453 Mo Sanford .05 .15
454 Danny Sheaffer .05 .15
455 Jim Tatum .05 .15
456 Gary Wayne .05 .15
457 Eric Young .05 .15
458 Luis Aquino .05 .15
459 Alex Arias .05 .15
460 Jack Armstrong .05 .15
461 Bret Barberie .05 .15
462 Ryan Bowen .05 .15
463 Chuck Carr .05 .15
464 Jeff Conine .10 .30
465 Henry Cotto .05 .15
466 Orestes Destrade .05 .15
467 Chris Hammond .05 .15
468 Bryan Harvey .05 .15
469 Charlie Hough .10 .30
470 Joe Klink .05 .15
471 Richie Lewis .05 .15
472 Bob Natal .05 .15
473 Pat Rapp .05 .15
474 Rich Renteria .05 .15
475 Rich Rodriguez .05 .15
476 Benito Santiago .10 .30
477 Gary Sheffield .10 .30
478 Matt Turner .05 .15
479 David Weathers .05 .15
480 Walt Weiss .05 .15
481 Darrell Whitmore .05 .15
482 Eric Anthony .05 .15
483 Jeff Bagwell .20 .50
484 Kevin Bass .05 .15
485 Craig Biggio .20 .50
486 Ken Caminiti .10 .30
487 Andujar Cedeno .05 .15
488 Chris Donnels .05 .15
489 Doug Drabek .05 .15
490 Steve Finley .10 .30
491 Luis Gonzalez .10 .30
492 Pete Harnisch .05 .15
493 Xavier Hernandez .05 .15
494 Doug Jones .05 .15
495 Todd Jones .05 .15
496 Darryl Kile .10 .30
497 Al Osuna .05 .15
498 Mark Portugal .05 .15
499 Scott Servais .05 .15
500 Greg Swindell .05 .15
501 Eddie Taubensee .05 .15
502 Jose Uribe .05 .15
503 Brian Williams .05 .15
504 Billy Ashley .05 .15
505 Pedro Astacio .05 .15
506 Brett Butler .10 .30
507 Tom Candiotti .05 .15
508 Omar Daal .05 .15
509 Jim Gott .05 .15
510 Kevin Gross .05 .15
511 Dave Hansen .05 .15
512 Carlos Hernandez .05 .15
513 Orel Hershiser .10 .30
514 Eric Karros .10 .30
515 Pedro Martinez .30 .75
516 Ramon Martinez .05 .15
517 Roger McDowell .05 .15
518 Raul Mondesi .10 .30
519 Jose Offerman .05 .15
520 Mike Piazza .60 1.50
521 Jody Reed .05 .15
522 Henry Rodriguez .05 .15
523 Mike Sharperson .05 .15
524 Cory Snyder .05 .15
525 Darryl Strawberry .10 .30
526 Rick Trlicek .05 .15
527 Tim Wallach .05 .15
528 Mitch Webster .05 .15
529 Steve Wilson .05 .15
530 Todd Worrell .05 .15
531 Moises Alou .10 .30
532 Brian Barnes .05 .15
533 Sean Berry .05 .15
534 Greg Colbrunn .05 .15
535 Delino DeShields .05 .15
536 Jeff Fassero .05 .15
537 Darrin Fletcher .05 .15
538 Cliff Floyd .10 .30
539 Lou Frazier .05 .15
540 Marquis Grissom .10 .30
541 Butch Henry .05 .15
542 Ken Hill .05 .15
543 Mike Lansing .05 .15
544 Brian Looney RC .05 .15
545 Dennis Martinez .10 .30
546 Chris Nabholz .05 .15
547 Randy Ready .05 .15
548 Mel Rojas .05 .15
549 Kirk Rueter .05 .15
550 Tim Scott .05 .15
551 Jeff Shaw .05 .15
552 Tim Spehr .05 .15
553 John Vander Wal .05 .15
554 Larry Walker .10 .30
555 John Wetteland .10 .30
556 Rondell White .10 .30
557 Tim Bogar .05 .15
558 Bobby Bonilla .10 .30
559 Jeromy Burnitz .10 .30
560 Sid Fernandez .05 .15
561 John Franco .10 .30
562 Dave Gallagher .05 .15
563 Dwight Gooden .10 .30
564 Eric Hillman .05 .15
565 Todd Hundley .05 .15
566 Jeff Innis .05 .15
567 Darrin Jackson .05 .15
568 Howard Johnson .05 .15
569 Bobby Jones .05 .15
570 Jeff Kent .20 .50
571 Mike Maddux .05 .15
572 Jeff McKnight .05 .15
573 Eddie Murray .30 .75
574 Charlie O'Brien .05 .15
575 Joe Orsulak .05 .15
576 Bret Saberhagen .10 .30
577 Pete Schourek .05 .15
578 Dave Telgheder .05 .15
579 Ryan Thompson .05 .15
580 Anthony Young .05 .15
581 Ruben Amaro .05 .15
582 Larry Andersen .05 .15
583 Kim Batiste .05 .15
584 Wes Chamberlain .05 .15
585 Darren Daulton .10 .30
586 Mariano Duncan .05 .15
587 Lenny Dykstra .10 .30
588 Jim Eisenreich .05 .15
589 Tommy Greene .05 .15
590 Dave Hollins .05 .15
591 Pete Incaviglia .05 .15
592 Danny Jackson .05 .15
593 Ricky Jordan .05 .15
594 John Kruk .10 .30
595 Roger Mason .05 .15
596 Mickey Morandini .05 .15
597 Terry Mulholland .05 .15
598 Todd Pratt .05 .15
599 Ben Rivera .05 .15
600 Curt Schilling .10 .30
601 Kevin Stocker .05 .15
602 Milt Thompson .05 .15
603 David West .05 .15
604 Mitch Williams .05 .15
605 Jay Bell .10 .30
606 Dave Clark .05 .15
607 Steve Cooke .05 .15
608 Tom Foley .05 .15
609 Carlos Garcia .05 .15
610 Joel Johnston .05 .15
611 Jeff King .05 .15
612 Al Martin .05 .15
613 Lloyd McClendon .05 .15
614 Orlando Merced .05 .15
615 Blas Minor .05 .15
616 Denny Neagle .10 .30
617 Mark Petkovsek RC .05 .15
618 Tom Prince .05 .15
619 Don Slaught .05 .15
620 Zane Smith .05 .15
621 Randy Tomlin .05 .15
622 Andy Van Slyke .20 .50
623 Paul Wagner .05 .15
624 Tim Wakefield .20 .50
625 Bob Walk .05 .15
626 Kevin Young .05 .15
627 Luis Alicea .05 .15
628 Rene Arocha .05 .15
629 Rod Brewer .05 .15
630 Rheal Cormier .05 .15
631 Bernard Gilkey .05 .15
632 Lee Guetterman .05 .15
633 Gregg Jefferies .05 .15
634 Brian Jordan .10 .30
635 Les Lancaster .05 .15
636 Ray Lankford .10 .30
637 Rob Murphy .05 .15
638 Omar Olivares .05 .15
639 Jose Oquendo .05 .15
640 Donovan Osborne .05 .15
641 Tom Pagnozzi .05 .15
642 Erik Pappas .05 .15
643 Geronimo Pena .05 .15
644 Mike Perez .05 .15
645 Gerald Perry .05 .15
646 Ozzie Smith .50 1.25
647 Bob Tewksbury .05 .15
648 Allen Watson .05 .15
649 Mark Whiten .05 .15
650 Tracy Woodson .05 .15
651 Todd Zeile .05 .15
652 Andy Ashby .05 .15
653 Brad Ausmus .20 .50
654 Billy Bean .05 .15
655 Derek Bell .05 .15
656 Andy Benes .05 .15
657 Doug Brocail .05 .15
658 Jarvis Brown .05 .15
659 Archi Cianfrocco .05 .15
660 Phil Clark .05 .15
661 Mark Davis .05 .15
662 Jeff Gardner .05 .15
663 Pat Gomez .05 .15
664 Ricky Gutierrez .05 .15
665 Tony Gwynn .40 1.00
666 Gene Harris .05 .15
667 Kevin Higgins .05 .15
668 Trevor Hoffman .20 .50
669 Pedro Martinez RC .05 .15
670 Tim Mauser .05 .15
671 Melvin Nieves .05 .15
672 Phil Plantier .05 .15
673 Frank Seminara .05 .15
674 Craig Shipley .05 .15
675 Kerry Taylor .05 .15
676 Tim Teufel .05 .15
677 Guillermo Velasquez .05 .15
678 Wally Whitehurst .05 .15
679 Tim Worrell .05 .15
680 Rod Beck .05 .15
681 Mike Benjamin .05 .15
682 Todd Benzinger .05 .15
683 Bud Black .05 .15
684 Barry Bonds .75 2.00
685 Jeff Brantley .05 .15
686 Dave Burba .05 .15
687 John Burkett .05 .15
688 Mark Carreon .05 .15
689 Will Clark .20 .50
690 Royce Clayton .05 .15
691 Bryan Hickerson .05 .15
692 Mike Jackson .05 .15
693 Darren Lewis .05 .15
694 Kirt Manwaring .05 .15
695 Dave Martinez .05 .15
696 Willie McGee .10 .30
697 John Patterson .05 .15
698 Jeff Reed .05 .15
699 Kevin Rogers .05 .15
700 Scott Sanderson .05 .15
701 Steve Scarsone .05 .15
702 Billy Swift .05 .15
703 Robby Thompson .05 .15
704 Matt Williams .10 .30
705 Trevor Wilson .05 .15
706 Fred McGriff .10 .30
Ron Gant
David Justice
707 John Olerud .10 .30
Paul Molitor
708 Mike Mussina .10 .30
Jack McDowell
709 Lou Whitaker .10 .30
Alan Trammell
710 Rafael Palmeiro .10 .30
Juan Gonzalez
711 Brett Butler .20 .50
Tony Gwynn
712 Kirby Puckett .20 .50
Chuck Knoblauch
713 Mike Piazza .30 .75
Eric Karros
714 Checklist 1 .05 .15
715 Checklist 2 .05 .15
716 Checklist 3 .05 .15
717 Checklist 4 .05 .15
718 Checklist 5 .05 .15
719 Checklist 6 .05 .15
720 Checklist 7 .05 .15
P69 Tim Salmon Promo .40 1.00

1994 Fleer All-Rookies

Collectors could redeem an All-Rookie Team Exchange card by mail for this nine-card set of 1994 rookies at each position as chosen by Fleer. The expiration date to remeem this set was September 30, 1994. None of these players were in the basic 1994 Fleer set. The exchange card was randomly inserted into all 1994 Fleer packs.

COMPLETE SET (9) 3.00
ONE SET PER EXCHANGE CARD VIA MAIL
M1 Kurt Abbott .20
M2 Rich Becker .20
M3 Carlos Delgado .60
M4 Jorge Fabregas .20
M5 Bob Hamelin .20
M6 John Hudek .20
M7 Tim Hyers .20
M8 Luis Lopez .20
M9 James Mouton .20
NNO Expired All-Rookie Exch. .20

1994 Fleer All-Stars

Fleer issued this 50-card standard-size set in 1994 to commemorate the All-Stars of the 1993 season. The cards were exclusively available in the Fleer packs at a rate of one in two. The set features 25 American League (1-25) and 25 National League (26-50) All-Stars. Each league's all-stars are sequenced in alphabetical order.

COMPLETE SET (50) 10.00
STATED ODDS 1:2
1 Roberto Alomar .25
2 Carlos Baerga .07
3 Albert Belle .15
4 Wade Boggs .25
5 Joe Carter .15
6 Scott Cooper .07
7 Cecil Fielder .15
8 Travis Fryman .15
9 Juan Gonzalez .15
10 Ken Griffey Jr. .75
11 Pat Hentgen .07
12 Randy Johnson .40
13 Jimmy Key .15
14 Mark Langston .07
15 Jack McDowell .07
16 Paul Molitor .15
17 Jeff Montgomery .07
18 Mike Mussina .25
19 John Olerud .15
20 Kirby Puckett .40
21 Cal Ripken 1.25
22 Ivan Rodriguez .25
23 Frank Thomas .40
24 Greg Vaughn .07
25 Duane Ward .07
26 Steve Avery .10
27 Rod Beck .07
28 Jay Bell .15
29 Andy Benes .07
30 Jeff Blauser .07
31 Barry Bonds 1.00
32 Bobby Bonilla .15
33 John Burkett .07
34 Darren Daulton .15
35 Andres Galarraga .15
36 Tom Glavine .25
37 Mark Grace .25
38 Marquis Grissom .15
39 Tony Gwynn .50
40 Bryan Harvey .07
41 Dave Hollins .07
42 David Justice .15
43 Darryl Kile .15
44 John Kruk .15
45 Barry Larkin .25
46 Terry Mulholland .07
47 Mike Piazza .75
48 Ryne Sandberg .60
49 Gary Sheffield .15
50 John Smoltz .25

1994 Fleer Award Winners

Randomly inserted in foil packs at a rate of one in this six-card standard-size set spotlights six outstanding players who received awards.

COMPLETE SET (6) 3.00
STATED ODDS 1:37
1 Frank Thomas .50
2 Barry Bonds 1.25
3 Jack McDowell .08
4 Greg Maddux .75

Salmon .30 .75
e Piazza 1.00 2.50

994 Fleer Golden Moments

e standard-size cards were issued one per blue jumbo pack. The fronts feature borderless color r action photos. A shrink-wrapped package ining a jumbo set was issued one per Fleer y case. Jumbos were later issued for retail oses with a production number of 10,000. The ard-size cards are not individually numbered.

PLETE SET (10) 12.50 30.00
PER BLUE RETAIL JUMBO PACK
MBOS: .4X TO 1X BASIC GM
JUMBO SET PER HOBBY CASE
BOS ALSO REPACKAGED FOR RETAIL
rk Whiten .25 .60
rlos Baerga .25 .60
ve Winfield .50 1.25
n Griffey Jr. 2.50 6.00
Jackson 1.25 3.00
orge Brett 3.00 8.00
lan Ryan 5.00 12.00
ed McGriff .75 2.00
ank Thomas 1.25 3.00
osio .25 .60
bott
e

1994 Fleer League Leaders

domly inserted in all pack types at a rate of one in this 28-card set features six statistical leaders n for the American (1-6) and the National (7-12) gues.

MPLETE SET (12) 2.00 5.00
TED ODDS 1:17
hn Olerud .15 .40
bert Belle .15 .40
fael Palmeiro .20 .50
enny Lofton .15 .40
ck McDowell .08 .25
evin Appier .15 .40
ndres Galarraga .15 .40
arry Bonds .60 1.50
en Dykstra .15 .40
Chuck Carr .08 .25
Tom Glavine UER NNO .20 .50
Greg Maddux 1.00 2.50

1994 Fleer Lumber Company

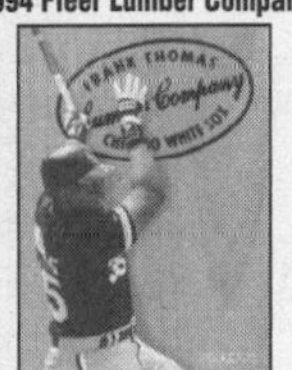

ndomly inserted in jumbo packs at a rate of one in , this ten-card standard-size set features the best ers in the game. The cards are numbered habetically.

MPLETE SET (10) 4.00 10.00
ATED ODDS 1:5 JUMBO
lbert Belle .20 .50
arry Bonds 1.25 3.00
on Gant .20 .50
uan Gonzalez .20 .50
Ken Griffey Jr. 1.00 2.50
avid Justice .20 .50
red McGriff .30 .75
afael Palmeiro .30 .75
rank Thomas .50 1.25
Matt Williams .20 .50

1994 Fleer Major League Prospects

ndomly inserted in all pack types at a rate of one in , this 35-card standard-size set showcases some of the outstanding young players in Major League Baseball. The cards are numbered on the back "X of 35" and are sequenced in alphabetical order.

COMPLETE SET (35) 6.00 15.00
STATED ODDS 1:6
1 Kurt Abbott .08 .25
2 Brian Anderson .30 .75
3 Rich Aude .08 .25
4 Cory Bailey .08 .25
5 Danny Bautista .08 .25
6 Marty Cordova .08 .25
7 Tripp Cromer .08 .25
8 Midre Cummings .08 .25
9 Carlos Delgado .50 1.25
10 Steve Dreyer .08 .25
11 Steve Dunn .08 .25
12 Jeff Granger .08 .25
13 Tyrone Hill .08 .25
14 Denny Hocking .08 .25
15 John Hope .08 .25
16 Butch Huskey .08 .25
17 Miguel Jimenez .08 .25
18 Chipper Jones .75 2.00
19 Steve Karsay .08 .25
20 Mike Kelly .08 .25
21 Mike Lieberthal .30 .75
22 Albie Lopez .08 .25
23 Jeff McNeely .08 .25
24 Danny Miceli .08 .25
25 Nate Minchey .08 .25
26 Marc Newfield .08 .25
27 Darren Oliver .30 .75
28 Luis Ortiz .08 .25
29 Curtis Pride .30 .75
30 Roger Salkeld .08 .25
31 Scott Sanders .08 .25
32 Dave Staton .08 .25
33 Salomon Torres .08 .25
34 Steve Trachsel .08 .25
35 Chris Turner .08 .25

1994 Fleer Pro-Visions

Randomly inserted in all pack types at a rate of one in 12, this nine-card standard-size set features on its fronts colorful artistic player caricatures with surrealistic backgrounds drawn by illustrator Wayne Still. When all nine cards are placed in order in a collector sheet, the backgrounds fit together to form a composite. The cards are numbered on the back "X of 9."

COMPLETE SET (9) 1.50 4.00
STATED ODDS 1:12
1 Darren Daulton .15 .40
2 John Olerud .15 .40
3 Matt Williams .15 .40
4 Carlos Baerga .07 .20
5 Ozzie Smith .60 1.50
6 Juan Gonzalez .15 .40
7 Jack McDowell .07 .20
8 Mike Piazza .75 2.00
9 Tony Gwynn .50 1.25

1994 Fleer Rookie Sensations

Randomly inserted in jumbo packs at a rate of one in four, this 20-card standard-size set features outstanding rookies. The fronts are "double exposed," with a player action cutout superimposed over a second photo. The cards are numbered on the back "X of 20" and are sequenced in alphabetical order.

COMPLETE SET (20) 8.00 20.00
STATED ODDS 1:4 JUMBO
1 Rene Arocha .40 1.00
2 Jason Bere .40 1.00
3 Jeromy Burnitz .75 2.00
4 Chuck Carr .40 1.00
5 Jeff Conine .75 2.00
6 Steve Cooke .40 1.00
7 Cliff Floyd .75 2.00
8 Jeffrey Hammonds .40 1.00
9 Wayne Kirby .40 1.00
10 Mike Lansing .40 1.00
11 Al Martin .40 1.00
12 Greg McMichael .40 1.00
13 Troy Neel .40 1.00
14 Mike Piazza 3.00 8.00
15 Armando Reynoso .40 1.00
16 Kirk Rueter .40 1.00
17 Tim Salmon 1.25 3.00
18 Aaron Sele .40 1.00
19 J.T.Snow .75 2.00
20 Kevin Stocker .40 1.00

1994 Fleer Salmon

Spotlighting American League Rookie of the Year Tim Salmon, this 15-card standard size set was issued in two forms. Cards 1-12 were randomly inserted in packs (one in eight) and 13-15 were available through a mail-in offer. Ten wrappers and 1.50 were necessary to acquire the mail-ins. The mail-in expiration date was September 30, 1994. Salmon autographed more than 2,000 of his cards.

COMPLETE SET (12) 6.00 15.00
COMMON CARD (1-12) .40 1.00
1-12 STATED ODDS 1:8
COMMON MAIL-IN (13-15) .40 1.00
13-15 DISTRIBUTED VIA WRAPPER EXCH.
AU Tim Salmon AU/2000 6.00 15.00

1994 Fleer Smoke 'n Heat

Randomly inserted in wax packs at a rate of one in 36, this 12-card standard-size set showcases the best pitchers in the game. The cards are numbered on the back "X of 12." and are sequenced in alphabetical order.

COMPLETE SET (12) 25.00 60.00
STATED ODDS 1:36
1 Roger Clemens 4.00 10.00
2 David Cone .75 2.00
3 Juan Guzman .40 1.00
4 Pete Harnisch .40 1.00
5 Randy Johnson 2.00 5.00
6 Mark Langston .40 1.00
7 Greg Maddux 3.00 8.00
8 Mike Mussina 1.25 3.00
9 Jose Rijo .40 1.00
10 Nolan Ryan 8.00 20.00
11 Curt Schilling .75 2.00
12 John Smoltz 1.25 3.00

1994 Fleer Team Leaders

Randomly inserted in all pack types, this 28-card standard-size set features Fleer's selected top player from each of the 28 major league teams. The card numbering is arranged alphabetically by city according to the American (1-14) and the National (15-28) Leagues.

COMPLETE SET (28) 10.00 25.00
RANDOM INSERTS IN ALL PACKS
1 Cal Ripken 1.50 4.00
2 Mo Vaughn .20 .50
3 Tim Salmon .30 .75
4 Frank Thomas .50 1.25
5 Carlos Baerga .08 .25
6 Cecil Fielder .08 .25
7 Brian McRae .08 .25
8 Greg Vaughn .08 .25
9 Kirby Puckett .50 1.25
10 Don Mattingly 1.25 3.00
11 Mark McGwire 1.25 3.00
12 Ken Griffey Jr. 1.00 2.50
13 Juan Gonzalez .20 .50
14 Paul Molitor .20 .50
15 David Justice .20 .50
16 Ryne Sandberg .75 2.00
17 Barry Larkin .30 .75
18 Andres Galarraga .20 .50
19 Gary Sheffield .20 .50
20 Jeff Bagwell .30 .75
21 Mike Piazza 1.00 2.50
22 Marquis Grissom .20 .50
23 Bobby Bonilla .20 .50
24 Len Dykstra .20 .50
25 Jay Bell .20 .50
26 Gregg Jefferies .08 .25
27 Tony Gwynn .60 1.50
28 Will Clark .30 .75

1994 Fleer Update

This 200-card standard-size set highlights traded players in their new uniforms and promising young rookies. The Update set was exclusively distributed in factory set form through hobby dealers. Each hobby case contained 20 cases. A ten card Diamond Tribute set was included in each factory set for a total of 210 cards. The cards are numbered on the back, grouped alphabetically by team by league with AL preceding NL. Key Rookie Cards include Chan Ho Park and Alex Rodriguez.

COMP.FACT.SET (210) 12.50 30.00
U PREFIX ON REG.CARD NUMBERS
1 Mark Eichhorn .08 .25
2 Sid Fernandez .08 .25
3 Leo Gomez .08 .25
4 Mike Oquist .08 .25
5 Rafael Palmeiro .30 .75
6 Chris Sabo .08 .25
7 Dwight Smith .08 .25
8 Lee Smith .20 .50
9 Damon Berryhill .08 .25
10 Wes Chamberlain .08 .25
11 Gar Finnvold .08 .25
12 Chris Howard .08 .25
13 Tim Naehring .08 .25
14 Otis Nixon .08 .25
15 Brian Anderson RC .20 .50
16 Jorge Fabregas .08 .25
17 Rex Hudler .08 .25
18 Bo Jackson .50 1.25
19 Mark Leiter .08 .25
20 Spike Owen .08 .25
21 Harold Reynolds .20 .50
22 Chris Turner .08 .25
23 Dennis Cook .08 .25
24 Jose DeLeon .08 .25
25 Julio Franco .20 .50
26 Joe Hall .08 .25
27 Darrin Jackson .08 .25
28 Dane Johnson .08 .25
29 Norberto Martin .08 .25
30 Scott Sanderson .08 .25
31 Jason Grimsley .08 .25
32 Dennis Martinez .20 .50
33 Jack Morris .20 .50
34 Eddie Murray .50 1.25
35 Chad Ogea .08 .25
36 Tony Pena .08 .25
37 Paul Shuey .08 .25
38 Omar Vizquel .30 .75
39 Danny Bautista .08 .25
40 Tim Belcher .08 .25
41 Joe Boever .08 .25
42 Storm Davis .08 .25
43 Junior Felix .08 .25
44 Mike Gardiner .08 .25
45 Buddy Groom .08 .25
46 Juan Samuel .08 .25
47 Vince Coleman .08 .25
48 Bob Hamelin .08 .25
49 Dave Henderson .08 .25
50 Rusty Meacham .08 .25
51 Terry Shumpert .08 .25
52 Jeff Bronkey .08 .25
53 Alex Diaz .08 .25
54 Brian Harper .08 .25
55 Jose Mercedes .08 .25
56 Jody Reed .08 .25
57 Bob Scanlan .08 .25
58 Turner Ward .08 .25
59 Rich Becker .08 .25
60 Alex Cole .08 .25
61 Denny Hocking .08 .25
62 Scott Leius .08 .25
63 Pat Mahomes .08 .25
64 Carlos Pulido .08 .25
65 Dave Stevens .08 .25
66 Matt Walbeck .08 .25
67 Xavier Hernandez .08 .25
68 Sterling Hitchcock .08 .25
69 Terry Mulholland .08 .25
70 Luis Polonia .08 .25
71 Gerald Williams .08 .25
72 Mark Acre RC .08 .25
73 Geronimo Berroa .08 .25
74 Rickey Henderson .50 1.25
75 Stan Javier .08 .25
76 Steve Karsay .08 .25
77 Carlos Reyes .08 .25
78 Bill Taylor RC .20 .50
79 Eric Anthony .08 .25
80 Bobby Ayala .08 .25
81 Tim Davis .08 .25
82 Felix Fermin .08 .25
83 Reggie Jefferson .08 .25
84 Keith Mitchell .08 .25
85 Bill Risley .08 .25
86 Alex Rodriguez RC ! 5.00 12.00
87 Roger Salkeld .08 .25
88 Dan Wilson .08 .25
89 Cris Carpenter .08 .25
90 Will Clark .30 .75
91 Jeff Frye .08 .25
92 Rick Helling .08 .25
93 Chris James .08 .25
94 Oddibe McDowell .08 .25
95 Billy Ripken .08 .25
96 Carlos Delgado .30 .75
97 Alex Gonzalez .08 .25
98 Shawn Green .50 1.25
99 Darren Hall .08 .25
100 Mike Huff .08 .25
101 Mike Kelly .08 .25
102 Roberto Kelly .08 .25
103 Charlie O'Brien .08 .25
104 Jose Oliva .08 .25
105 Gregg Olson .08 .25
106 Willie Banks .08 .25
107 Jim Bullinger .08 .25
108 Chuck Crim .08 .25
109 Shawon Dunston .08 .25
110 Karl Rhodes .08 .25
111 Steve Trachsel .08 .25
112 Anthony Young .08 .25
113 Eddie Zambrano .08 .25
114 Bret Boone .20 .50
115 Jeff Brantley .08 .25
116 Hector Carrasco .08 .25
117 Tony Fernandez .08 .25
118 Tim Fortugno .08 .25
119 Erik Hanson .08 .25
120 Chuck McElroy .08 .25
121 Deion Sanders .30 .75
122 Ellis Burks .20 .50
123 Marvin Freeman .08 .25
124 Mike Harkey .08 .25
125 Howard Johnson .08 .25
126 Mike Kingery .08 .25
127 Nelson Liriano .08 .25
128 Marcus Moore .08 .25
129 Mike Munoz .08 .25
130 Kevin Ritz .08 .25
131 Walt Weiss .08 .25
132 Kurt Abbott RC .08 .25
133 Jerry Browne .08 .25
134 Greg Colbrunn .08 .25
135 Jeremy Hernandez .08 .25
136 Dave Magadan .08 .25
137 Kurt Miller .08 .25
138 Robb Nen .20 .50
139 Jesus Tavarez RC .08 .25
140 Sid Bream .08 .25
141 Tom Edens .08 .25
142 Tony Eusebio .08 .25
143 John Hudek RC .08 .25
144 Brian L.Hunter .08 .25
145 Orlando Miller .08 .25
146 James Mouton .08 .25
147 Shane Reynolds .08 .25
148 Rafael Bournigal .08 .25
149 Delino DeShields .08 .25
150 Garey Ingram RC .08 .25
151 Chan Ho Park RC .30 .75
152 Wil Cordero .08 .25
153 Pedro Martinez .50 1.25
154 Randy Milligan .08 .25
155 Lenny Webster .08 .25
156 Rico Brogna .08 .25
157 Josias Manzanillo .08 .25
158 Kevin McReynolds .08 .25
159 Mike Remlinger .08 .25
160 David Segui .08 .25
161 Pete Smith .08 .25
162 Kelly Stinnett RC .20 .50
163 Jose Vizcaino .08 .25
164 Billy Hatcher .08 .25
165 Doug Jones .08 .25
166 Mike Lieberthal .20 .50
167 Tony Longmire .08 .25
168 Bobby Munoz .08 .25
169 Paul Quantrill .08 .25
170 Heathcliff Slocumb .08 .25
171 Fernando Valenzuela .20 .50
172 Mark Dewey .08 .25
173 Brian R. Hunter .08 .25
174 Jon Lieber .20 .50
175 Ravelo Manzanillo .08 .25
176 Dan Miceli .08 .25
177 Rick White .08 .25
178 Bryan Eversgerd .08 .25
179 John Habyan .08 .25
180 Terry McGriff .08 .25
181 Vicente Palacios .08 .25
182 Rich Rodriguez .08 .25
183 Rick Sutcliffe .20 .50
184 Donnie Elliott .08 .25
185 Joey Hamilton .08 .25
186 Tim Hyers RC .08 .25
187 Luis Lopez .08 .25
188 Ray McDavid .08 .25
189 Bip Roberts .08 .25
190 Scott Sanders .08 .25
191 Eddie Williams .08 .25
192 Steve Frey .08 .25
193 Pat Gomez .08 .25
194 Rich Monteleone .08 .25
195 Mark Portugal .08 .25
196 Darryl Strawberry .20 .50
197 Salomon Torres .08 .25
198 W.VanLandingham RC .08 .25
199 Checklist .08 .25
200 Checklist .08 .25

1994 Fleer Update Diamond Tribute

Each 1994 Fleer Update factory set contained a complete 10-card set of Diamond Tribute inserts. This was the third and final year that Fleer included an insert set in their factory boxed update sets. The 1994 Diamond Tribute inserts feature a player action shot cut out against a backdrop of clouds and baseballs. The selection once again focuses on the game's top veterans. Cards are numbered "X" of 10 on the back.

COMPLETE SET (10) .75 2.00
ONE SET PER UPDATE FACTORY SET
1 Barry Bonds .40 1.00
2 Joe Carter .05 .15
3 Will Clark .08 .25
4 Roger Clemens .30 .75
5 Tony Gwynn .20 .50
6 Don Mattingly .40 1.00
7 Fred McGriff .08 .25
8 Eddie Murray .15 .40
9 Kirby Puckett .15 .40
10 Cal Ripken .50 1.25

1994 Fleer Sunoco

These 25 standard-size cards feature white-bordered color player action shots on their fronts. The cards are numbered on the back as "X of 25."

COMPLETE SET (25) 2.50 6.00
1 Roberto Alomar .08 .25
2 Carlos Baerga .02 .10
3 Jeff Bagwell .20 .50
4 Jay Bell .02 .10
5 Barry Bonds .40 1.00
6 Joe Carter .05 .15
7 Roger Clemens .40 1.00
8 Darren Daulton .05 .15
9 Len Dykstra .05 .15
10 Cecil Fielder .05 .15
11 Tom Glavine .08 .25
12 Juan Gonzalez .15 .40
13 Ken Griffey Jr. .50 1.25
14 David Justice .08 .25
15 John Kruk .05 .15
16 Greg Maddux .50 1.25
17 Don Mattingly .40 1.00
18 Jack McDowell .02 .10
19 John Olerud .05 .15
20 Mike Piazza .60 1.50
21 Kirby Puckett .15 .40
22 Tim Salmon .08 .25
23 Frank Thomas .20 .50
24 Andy Van Slyke .02 .10
25 Checklist .02 .10

1995 Fleer

The 1995 Fleer set consists of 600 standard-size cards issued as one series. Each pack contained at least one insert card with some 'Hot Packs' containing nothing but insert cards. Full-bleed fronts have two player photos and, atypical of baseball cards fronts, biographical information such as height, weight, etc. The backgrounds are multi-colored. The backs are horizontal and contain year-by-year statistics along with a photo. There was a different design for each of baseball's six divisions. The checklist is arranged alphabetically by teams within each league with AL preceding NL. To preview the product prior to it's public release, Fleer printed up additional quantities of cards 26, 78, 155, 235, 285, 351, 509 and 514 and mailed them to dealers and hobby media.

COMPLETE SET (600) 20.00 50.00
1 Brady Anderson .10 .30
2 Harold Baines .10 .30
3 Damon Buford .05 .15
4 Mike Devereaux .05 .15
5 Mark Eichhorn .05 .15
6 Sid Fernandez .05 .15
7 Leo Gomez .05 .15
8 Jeffrey Hammonds .05 .15
9 Chris Hoiles .05 .15
10 Rick Krivda .05 .15
11 Ben McDonald .05 .15
12 Mark McLemore .05 .15
13 Alan Mills .05 .15
14 Jamie Moyer .10 .30
15 Mike Mussina .20 .50
16 Mike Oquist .05 .15
17 Rafael Palmeiro .20 .50
18 Arthur Rhodes .05 .15
19 Cal Ripken 1.00 2.50
20 Chris Sabo .05 .15
21 Lee Smith .10 .30
22 Jack Voigt .05 .15
23 Damon Berryhill .05 .15
24 Tom Brunansky .05 .15
25 Wes Chamberlain .05 .15
26 Roger Clemens .60 1.50
27 Scott Cooper .05 .15
28 Andre Dawson .10 .30
29 Gar Finnvold .05 .15
30 Tony Fossas .05 .15
31 Mike Greenwell .05 .15
32 Joe Hesketh .05 .15
33 Chris Howard .05 .15
34 Chris Nabholz .05 .15
35 Tim Naehring .05 .15
36 Otis Nixon .05 .15
37 Carlos Rodriguez .05 .15
38 Rich Rowland .05 .15
39 Ken Ryan .05 .15
40 Aaron Sele .05 .15
41 John Valentin .05 .15
42 Mo Vaughn .10 .30
43 Frank Viola .10 .30
44 Danny Bautista .05 .15
45 Joe Boever .05 .15
46 Milt Cuyler .05 .15
47 Storm Davis .05 .15
48 John Doherty .05 .15
49 Junior Felix .05 .15
50 Cecil Fielder .10 .30
51 Travis Fryman .10 .30
52 Mike Gardiner .05 .15
53 Kirk Gibson .10 .30
54 Chris Gomez .05 .15
55 Buddy Groom .05 .15
56 Mike Henneman .05 .15
57 Chad Kreuter .05 .15
58 Mike Moore .05 .15
59 Tony Phillips .05 .15
60 Juan Samuel .05 .15
61 Mickey Tettleton .05 .15
62 Alan Trammell .10 .30
63 David Wells .10 .30
64 Lou Whitaker .10 .30
65 Jim Abbott .20 .50
66 Joe Ausanio .05 .15
67 Wade Boggs .20 .50
68 Mike Gallego .05 .15
69 Xavier Hernandez .05 .15
70 Sterling Hitchcock .05 .15
71 Steve Howe .05 .15
72 Scott Kamieniecki .05 .15
73 Pat Kelly .05 .15
74 Jimmy Key .10 .30
75 Jim Leyritz .05 .15
76 Don Mattingly .75 2.00
77 Terry Mulholland .05 .15
78 Paul O'Neill .20 .50
79 Melido Perez .05 .15
80 Luis Polonia .05 .15
81 Mike Stanley .05 .15
82 Danny Tartabull .05 .15
83 Randy Velarde .05 .15
84 Bob Wickman .05 .15
85 Bernie Williams .20 .50
86 Gerald Williams .05 .15
87 Roberto Alomar .20 .50
88 Pat Borders .05 .15
89 Joe Carter .10 .30
90 Tony Castillo .05 .15
91 Brad Cornett RC .05 .15
92 Carlos Delgado .10 .30
93 Alex Gonzalez .05 .15
94 Shawn Green .10 .30
95 Juan Guzman .05 .15
96 Darren Hall .05 .15
97 Pat Hentgen .05 .15
98 Mike Huff .05 .15
99 Randy Knorr .05 .15
100 Al Leiter .10 .30
101 Paul Molitor .10 .30
102 John Olerud .10 .30
103 Dick Schofield .05 .15
104 Ed Sprague .05 .15
105 Dave Stewart .10 .30
106 Todd Stottlemyre .05 .15
107 Devon White .10 .30
108 Woody Williams .05 .15
109 Wilson Alvarez .05 .15
110 Paul Assenmacher .05 .15
111 Jason Bere .05 .15
112 Dennis Cook .05 .15
113 Joey Cora .05 .15
114 Jose DeLeon .05 .15
115 Alex Fernandez .05 .15
116 Julio Franco .10 .30
117 Craig Grebeck .05 .15
118 Ozzie Guillen .10 .30
119 Roberto Hernandez .05 .15
120 Darrin Jackson .05 .15

121 Lance Johnson .05 .15
122 Ron Karkovice .05 .15
123 Mike LaValliere .05 .15
124 Norberto Martin .05 .15
125 Kirk McCaskill .05 .15
126 Jack McDowell .05 .15
127 Tim Raines .10 .30
128 Frank Thomas .30 .75
129 Robin Ventura .10 .30
130 Sandy Alomar Jr. .05 .15
131 Carlos Baerga .05 .15
132 Albert Belle .10 .30
133 Mark Clark .05 .15
134 Alvaro Espinoza .05 .15
135 Jason Grimsley .05 .15
136 Wayne Kirby .05 .15
137 Kenny Lofton .10 .30
138 Albie Lopez .05 .15
139 Dennis Martinez .10 .30
140 Jose Mesa .05 .15
141 Eddie Murray .30 .75
142 Charles Nagy .05 .15
143 Tony Pena .05 .15
144 Eric Plunk .05 .15
145 Manny Ramirez .20 .50
146 Jeff Russell .05 .15
147 Paul Shuey .05 .15
148 Paul Sorrento .05 .15
149 Jim Thome .20 .50
150 Omar Vizquel .20 .50
151 Dave Winfield .10 .30
152 Kevin Appier .10 .30
153 Billy Brewer .05 .15
154 Vince Coleman .05 .15
155 David Cone .10 .30
156 Gary Gaetti .10 .30
157 Greg Gagne .05 .15
158 Tom Gordon .05 .15
159 Mark Gubicza .05 .15
160 Bob Hamelin .05 .15
161 Dave Henderson .05 .15
162 Felix Jose .05 .15
163 Wally Joyner .10 .30
164 Jose Lind .05 .15
165 Mike Macfarlane .05 .15
166 Mike Magnante .05 .15
167 Brent Mayne .05 .15
168 Brian McRae .05 .15
169 Rusty Meacham .05 .15
170 Jeff Montgomery .05 .15
171 Hipolito Pichardo .05 .15
172 Terry Shumpert .05 .15
173 Michael Tucker .05 .15
174 Ricky Bones .05 .15
175 Jeff Cirillo .05 .15
176 Alex Diaz .05 .15
177 Cal Eldred .05 .15
178 Mike Fetters .05 .15
179 Darryl Hamilton .05 .15
180 Brian Harper .05 .15
181 John Jaha .05 .15
182 Pat Listach .05 .15
183 Graeme Lloyd .05 .15
184 Jose Mercedes .05 .15
185 Matt Mieske .05 .15
186 Dave Nilsson .05 .15
187 Jody Reed .05 .15
188 Bob Scanlan .05 .15
189 Kevin Seitzer .05 .15
190 Bill Spiers .05 .15
191 B.J. Surhoff .10 .30
192 Jose Valentin .05 .15
193 Greg Vaughn .05 .15
194 Turner Ward .05 .15
195 Bill Wegman .05 .15
196 Rick Aguilera .05 .15
197 Rich Becker .05 .15
198 Alex Cole .05 .15
199 Marty Cordova .05 .15
200 Steve Dunn .05 .15
201 Scott Erickson .05 .15
202 Mark Guthrie .05 .15
203 Chip Hale .05 .15
204 LaTroy Hawkins .05 .15
205 Denny Hocking .05 .15
206 Chuck Knoblauch .10 .30
207 Scott Leius .05 .15
208 Shane Mack .05 .15
209 Pat Mahomes .05 .15
210 Pat Meares .05 .15
211 Pedro Munoz .05 .15
212 Kirby Puckett .30 .75
213 Jeff Reboulet .05 .15
214 Dave Stevens .05 .15
215 Kevin Tapani .05 .15
216 Matt Walbeck .05 .15
217 Carl Willis .05 .15
218 Brian Anderson .05 .15
219 Chad Curtis .05 .15
220 Chili Davis .10 .30
221 Gary DiSarcina .05 .15
222 Damion Easley .05 .15
223 Jim Edmonds .20 .50
224 Chuck Finley .10 .30
225 Joe Grahe .05 .15
226 Rex Hudler .05 .15
227 Bo Jackson .30 .75
228 Mark Langston .05 .15
229 Phil Leftwich .05 .15
230 Mark Leiter .05 .15
231 Spike Owen .05 .15
232 Bob Patterson .05 .15
233 Troy Percival .10 .30
234 Eduardo Perez .05 .15
235 Tim Salmon .20 .50
236 J.T. Snow .10 .30
237 Chris Turner .05 .15
238 Mark Acre .05 .15
239 Geronimo Berroa .05 .15
240 Mike Bordick .05 .15
241 John Briscoe .05 .15
242 Scott Brosius .10 .30
243 Ron Darling .05 .15
244 Dennis Eckersley .10 .30
245 Brent Gates .05 .15
246 Rickey Henderson .30 .75
247 Stan Javier .05 .15
248 Steve Karsay .05 .15
249 Mark McGwire .75 2.00
250 Troy Neel .05 .15
251 Steve Ontiveros .05 .15
252 Carlos Reyes .05 .15
253 Ruben Sierra .10 .30
254 Terry Steinbach .05 .15
255 Bill Taylor .05 .15
256 Todd Van Poppel .05 .15
257 Bobby Witt .05 .15
258 Rich Amaral .05 .15
259 Eric Anthony .05 .15
260 Bobby Ayala .05 .15
261 Mike Blowers .05 .15
262 Chris Bosio .05 .15
263 Jay Buhner .10 .30
264 John Cummings .05 .15
265 Tim Davis .05 .15
266 Felix Fermin .05 .15
267 Dave Fleming .05 .15
268 Goose Gossage .10 .30
269 Ken Griffey Jr. .60 1.50
270 Reggie Jefferson .05 .15
271 Randy Johnson .30 .75
272 Edgar Martinez .20 .50
273 Tino Martinez .20 .50
274 Greg Pirkl .05 .15
275 Bill Risley .05 .15
276 Roger Salkeld .05 .15
277 Luis Sojo .05 .15
278 Mac Suzuki .05 .15
279 Dan Wilson .05 .15
280 Kevin Brown .10 .30
281 Jose Canseco .20 .50
282 Cris Carpenter .05 .15
283 Will Clark .20 .50
284 Jeff Frye .05 .15
285 Juan Gonzalez .10 .30
286 Rick Helling .05 .15
287 Tom Henke .05 .15
288 David Hulse .05 .15
289 Chris James .05 .15
290 Manuel Lee .05 .15
291 Oddibe McDowell .05 .15
292 Dean Palmer .10 .30
293 Roger Pavlik .05 .15
294 Bill Ripken .05 .15
295 Ivan Rodriguez .20 .50
296 Kenny Rogers .10 .30
297 Doug Strange .05 .15
298 Matt Whiteside .05 .15
299 Steve Avery .05 .15
300 Steve Bedrosian .05 .15
301 Rafael Belliard .05 .15
302 Jeff Blauser .05 .15
303 Dave Gallagher .05 .15
304 Tom Glavine .20 .50
305 David Justice .10 .30
306 Mike Kelly .05 .15
307 Roberto Kelly .05 .15
308 Ryan Klesko .10 .30
309 Mark Lemke .05 .15
310 Javier Lopez .10 .30
311 Greg Maddux .50 1.25
312 Fred McGriff .20 .50
313 Greg McMichael .05 .15
314 Kent Mercker .05 .15
315 Charlie O'Brien .05 .15
316 Jose Oliva .05 .15
317 Terry Pendleton .10 .30
318 John Smoltz .20 .50
319 Mike Stanton .05 .15
320 Tony Tarasco .05 .15
321 Terrell Wade .05 .15
322 Mark Wohlers .05 .15
323 Kurt Abbott .05 .15
324 Luis Aquino .05 .15
325 Bret Barberie .05 .15
326 Ryan Bowen .05 .15
327 Jerry Browne .05 .15
328 Chuck Carr .05 .15
329 Matias Carrillo .05 .15
330 Greg Colbrunn .05 .15
331 Jeff Conine .10 .30
332 Mark Gardner .05 .15
333 Chris Hammond .05 .15
334 Bryan Harvey .05 .15
335 Richie Lewis .05 .15
336 Dave Magadan .05 .15
337 Terry Mathews .05 .15
338 Robb Nen .10 .30
339 Yorkis Perez .05 .15
340 Pat Rapp .05 .15
341 Benito Santiago .10 .30
342 Gary Sheffield .10 .30
343 Dave Weathers .05 .15
344 Moises Alou .10 .30
345 Sean Berry .05 .15
346 Wil Cordero .05 .15
347 Joey Eischen .05 .15
348 Jeff Fassero .05 .15
349 Darrin Fletcher .05 .15
350 Cliff Floyd .10 .30
351 Marquis Grissom .10 .30
352 Butch Henry .05 .15
353 Gil Heredia .05 .15
354 Ken Hill .05 .15
355 Mike Lansing .05 .15
356 Pedro Martinez .20 .50
357 Mel Rojas .05 .15
358 Kirk Rueter .05 .15
359 Tim Scott .05 .15
360 Jeff Shaw .05 .15
361 Larry Walker .10 .30
362 Lenny Webster .05 .15
363 John Wetteland .10 .30
364 Rondell White .10 .30
365 Bobby Bonilla .10 .30
366 Rico Brogna .05 .15
367 Jeromy Burnitz .10 .30
368 John Franco .10 .30
369 Dwight Gooden .10 .30
370 Todd Hundley .05 .15
371 Jason Jacome .05 .15
372 Bobby Jones .05 .15
373 Jeff Kent .10 .30
374 Jim Lindeman .05 .15
375 Josias Manzanillo .05 .15
376 Roger Mason .05 .15
377 Kevin McReynolds .05 .15
378 Joe Orsulak .05 .15
379 Bill Pulsipher .05 .15
380 Bret Saberhagen .10 .30
381 David Segui .05 .15
382 Pete Smith .05 .15
383 Kelly Stinnett .05 .15
384 Ryan Thompson .05 .15
385 Jose Vizcaino .05 .15
386 Toby Borland .05 .15
387 Ricky Bottalico .05 .15
388 Darren Daulton .10 .30
389 Mariano Duncan .05 .15
390 Lenny Dykstra .10 .30
391 Jim Eisenreich .05 .15
392 Tommy Greene .05 .15
393 Dave Hollins .05 .15
394 Pete Incaviglia .05 .15
395 Danny Jackson .05 .15
396 Doug Jones .05 .15
397 Ricky Jordan .05 .15
398 John Kruk .10 .30
399 Mike Lieberthal .10 .30
400 Tony Longmire .05 .15
401 Mickey Morandini .05 .15
402 Bobby Munoz .05 .15
403 Curt Schilling .10 .30
404 Heathcliff Slocumb .05 .15
405 Kevin Stocker .05 .15
406 Fernando Valenzuela .10 .30
407 David West .05 .15
408 Willie Banks .05 .15
409 Jose Bautista .05 .15
410 Steve Buechele .05 .15
411 Jim Bullinger .05 .15
412 Chuck Crim .05 .15
413 Shawon Dunston .05 .15
414 Kevin Foster .05 .15
415 Mark Grace .20 .50
416 Jose Hernandez .05 .15
417 Glenallen Hill .05 .15
418 Brooks Kieschnick .05 .15
419 Derrick May .05 .15
420 Randy Myers .05 .15
421 Dan Plesac .05 .15
422 Karl Rhodes .05 .15
423 Rey Sanchez .05 .15
424 Sammy Sosa .30 .75
425 Steve Trachsel .05 .15
426 Rick Wilkins .05 .15
427 Anthony Young .05 .15
428 Eddie Zambrano .05 .15
429 Bret Boone .10 .30
430 Jeff Branson .05 .15
431 Jeff Brantley .05 .15
432 Hector Carrasco .05 .15
433 Brian Dorsett .05 .15
434 Tony Fernandez .05 .15
435 Tim Fortugno .05 .15
436 Erik Hanson .05 .15
437 Thomas Howard .05 .15
438 Kevin Jarvis .05 .15
439 Barry Larkin .20 .50
440 Chuck McElroy .05 .15
441 Kevin Mitchell .05 .15
442 Hal Morris .05 .15
443 Jose Rijo .05 .15
444 John Roper .05 .15
445 Johnny Ruffin .05 .15
446 Deion Sanders .20 .50
447 Reggie Sanders .10 .30
448 Pete Schourek .05 .15
449 John Smiley .05 .15
450 Eddie Taubensee .05 .15
451 Jeff Bagwell .20 .50
452 Kevin Bass .05 .15
453 Craig Biggio .20 .50
454 Ken Caminiti .10 .30
455 Andujar Cedeno .05 .15
456 Doug Drabek .05 .15
457 Tony Eusebio .05 .15
458 Mike Felder .05 .15
459 Steve Finley .10 .30
460 Luis Gonzalez .10 .30
461 Mike Hampton .10 .30
462 Pete Harnisch .05 .15
463 John Hudek .05 .15
464 Todd Jones .05 .15
465 Darryl Kile .10 .30
466 James Mouton .05 .15
467 Shane Reynolds .05 .15
468 Scott Servais .05 .15
469 Greg Swindell .05 .15
470 Dave Veres RC .15 .40
471 Brian Williams .05 .15
472 Jay Bell .10 .30
473 Jacob Brumfield .05 .15
474 Dave Clark .05 .15
475 Steve Cooke .05 .15
476 Midre Cummings .05 .15
477 Mark Dewey .05 .15
478 Tom Foley .05 .15
479 Carlos Garcia .05 .15
480 Jeff King .05 .15
481 Jon Lieber .05 .15
482 Ravelo Manzanillo .05 .15
483 Al Martin .05 .15
484 Orlando Merced .05 .15
485 Danny Miceli .05 .15
486 Denny Neagle .10 .30
487 Lance Parrish .10 .30
488 Don Slaught .05 .15
489 Zane Smith .05 .15
490 Andy Van Slyke .20 .50
491 Paul Wagner .05 .15
492 Rick White .05 .15
493 Luis Alicea .05 .15
494 Rene Arocha .05 .15
495 Rheal Cormier .05 .15
496 Bryan Eversgerd .05 .15
497 Bernard Gilkey .05 .15
498 John Habyan .05 .15
499 Gregg Jefferies .05 .15
500 Brian Jordan .10 .30
501 Ray Lankford .10 .30
502 John Mabry .05 .15
503 Terry McGriff .05 .15
504 Tom Pagnozzi .05 .15
505 Vicente Palacios .05 .15
506 Geronimo Pena .05 .15
507 Gerald Perry .05 .15
508 Rich Rodriguez .05 .15
509 Ozzie Smith .50 1.25
510 Bob Tewksbury .05 .15
511 Allen Watson .05 .15
512 Mark Whiten .05 .15
513 Todd Zeile .05 .15
514 Dante Bichette .10 .30
515 Willie Blair .05 .15
516 Ellis Burks .10 .30
517 Marvin Freeman .05 .15
518 Andres Galarraga .10 .30
519 Joe Girardi .05 .15
520 Greg W. Harris .05 .15
521 Charlie Hayes .05 .15
522 Mike Kingery .05 .15
523 Nelson Liriano .05 .15
524 Mike Munoz .05 .15
525 David Nied .05 .15
526 Steve Reed .05 .15
527 Kevin Ritz .05 .15
528 Bruce Ruffin .05 .15
529 John Vander Wal .05 .15
530 Walt Weiss .05 .15
531 Eric Young .05 .15
532 Billy Ashley .05 .15
533 Pedro Astacio .05 .15
534 Rafael Bournigal .05 .15
535 Brett Butler .10 .30
536 Tom Candiotti .05 .15
537 Omar Daal .05 .15
538 Delino DeShields .05 .15
539 Darren Dreifort .05 .15
540 Kevin Gross .05 .15
541 Orel Hershiser .10 .30
542 Garey Ingram .05 .15
543 Eric Karros .10 .30
544 Ramon Martinez .05 .15
545 Raul Mondesi .10 .30
546 Chan Ho Park .10 .30
547 Mike Piazza .50 1.25
548 Henry Rodriguez .05 .15
549 Rudy Seanez .05 .15
550 Ismael Valdes .05 .15
551 Tim Wallach .05 .15
552 Todd Worrell .05 .15
553 Andy Ashby .05 .15
554 Brad Ausmus .10 .30
555 Derek Bell .05 .15
556 Andy Benes .05 .15
557 Phil Clark .05 .15
558 Donnie Elliott .05 .15
559 Ricky Gutierrez .05 .15
560 Tony Gwynn .40 1.00
561 Joey Hamilton .05 .15
562 Trevor Hoffman .10 .30
563 Luis Lopez .05 .15
564 Pedro A. Martinez .05 .15
565 Tim Mauser .05 .15
566 Phil Plantier .05 .15
567 Bip Roberts .05 .15
568 Scott Sanders .05 .15
569 Craig Shipley .05 .15
570 Jeff Tabaka .05 .15
571 Eddie Williams .05 .15
572 Rod Beck .05 .15
573 Mike Benjamin .05 .15
574 Barry Bonds .75 2.00
575 Dave Burba .05 .15
576 John Burkett .05 .15
577 Mark Carreon .05 .15
578 Royce Clayton .05 .15
579 Steve Frey .05 .15
580 Bryan Hickerson .05 .15
581 Mike Jackson .05 .15
582 Darren Lewis .05 .15
583 Kirt Manwaring .05 .15
584 Rich Monteleone .05 .15
585 John Patterson .05 .15
586 J.R. Phillips .05 .15
587 Mark Portugal .05 .15
588 Joe Rosselli .05 .15
589 Darryl Strawberry .10 .30
590 Bill Swift .05 .15
591 Robby Thompson .05 .15
592 William VanLandingham .05 .15
593 Matt Williams .10 .30
594 Checklist .05 .15
595 Checklist .05 .15
596 Checklist .05 .15
597 Checklist .05 .15
598 Checklist .05 .15
599 Checklist .05 .15
600 Checklist .05 .15

1995 Fleer All-Fleer

This nine-card standard-size set was available through a 1995 Fleer wrapper offer. Nine of the leading players for each position are featured in this set. The wrapper redemption offer expired on September 30, 1995. The fronts feature the player's photo covering most of the card with a small section on the right set off for the words "All Fleer 9" along with the player's name. The backs feature player information as to why they are among the best in the game.

COMPLETE SET (9) 4.00 10.00
SETS WERE AVAILABLE VIA WRAPPER OFFER
1 Mike Piazza .50 1.25
2 Frank Thomas .30 .75
3 Roberto Alomar .20 .50
4 Cal Ripken 1.00 2.50
5 Matt Williams .10 .30
6 Barry Bonds .75 2.00
7 Ken Griffey Jr. .60 1.50
8 Tony Gwynn .40 1.00
9 Greg Maddux .50 1.25

1995 Fleer All-Rookies

This nine-card standard-size set was available through a Rookie Exchange redemption card randomly inserted in packs. The redemption deadline was 9/30/95. This set features players who made their major league debut in 1995. The fronts have an action photo with a grainy background. The player's name and team are in gold foil at the bottom. Horizontal backs have a player photo the left and minor league highlights to the right.

COMPLETE SET (9) 1.25 3.00
ONE SET PER EXCHANGE CARD VIA MAIL
M1 Edgardo Alfonzo .08 .25
M2 Jason Bates .08 .25
M3 Brian Boehringer .08 .25
M4 Darren Bragg .08 .25
M5 Brad Clontz .08 .25
M6 Jim Dougherty .08 .25
M7 Todd Hollandsworth .08 .25
M8 Rudy Pemberton .08 .25
M9 Frank Rodriguez .08 .25
NNO Expired All-Rookie Exch. .08 .25

1995 Fleer All-Stars

Randomly inserted in all pack types at a rate of one in three, this 25-card standard-size set showcases those that participated in the 1994 mid-season classic held in Pittsburgh. Horizontally designed, the fronts contain photos of American League stars with the back protraying the National League player from the same position. On each side, the 1994 All-Star Game logo appears in gold foil as does either the A.L. or N.L. logo in silver foil.

COMPLETE SET (25) 4.00 10.00
STATED ODDS 1:3
1 M.Piazza .60 1.50
I.Rodriguez
2 F.Thomas .40 1.00
G.Jefferies
3 R.Alomar .25 .60
M.Duncan
4 W.Boggs .25 .60
M.Williams
5 C.Ripken 1.25 3.00
O.Smith
6 B.Bonds 1.00 2.50
J.Carter
7 K.Griffey .75 2.00
T.Gwynn
8 K.Puckett .40 1.00
D.Justice
9 G.Maddux .60 1.50
J.Key
10 C.Knoblauch .15 .40
W.Cordero
11 S.Cooper .15 .40
K.Caminiti
12 W.Clark .25 .60
C.Garcia
13 J.Bagwell .25 .60
P.Molitor
14 T.Fryman .25 .60
C.Biggio
15 M.Tettleton .25 .60
F.McGriff
16 K.Lofton .15 .40
M.Alou
17 A.Belle .15 .40
M.Grissom
18 P.O'Neill .25 .60
D.Bichette
19 D.Cone .15 .40
K.Hill
20 M.Mussina .25 .60
D.Drabek
21 R.Johnson .40 1.00
J.Hudek
22 P.Hentgen .07 .20
D.Jackson
23 W.Alvarez .07 .20
R.Beck
24 L.Smith .15 .40
R.Myers
25 J.Bere .07 .20
D.Jones

1995 Fleer Award Winners

Randomly inserted in all pack types at a rate of one in 24, this six card standard-size set highlights the major award winners of 1994. Card fronts feature action photos that are full-bleed on the right border and have gold border on the left. Within the gold border are the player's name and Fleer Award Winner. The backs contain a photo with text that references 1994 accomplishments.

COMPLETE SET (6) 2.00 5.00
STATED ODDS 1:24
1 Frank Thomas .50 1.25
2 Jeff Bagwell .30 .75
3 David Cone .20 .50
4 Greg Maddux .75 2.00
5 Bob Hamelin .08 .25
6 Raul Mondesi .20 .50

1995 Fleer League Leaders

Randomly inserted in all pack types at a rate of one in 12, this 10-card standard-size set features 1994 American and National League leaders in various categories. The horizontal cards have player photos on front and back. The back also has a brief write-up concerning the accomplishment.

COMPLETE SET (10) 3.00 8.00
STATED ODDS 1:12
1 Paul O'Neill .30 .75
2 Ken Griffey Jr. 1.00 2.50
3 Kirby Puckett .50 1.25
4 Jimmy Key .20 .50
5 Randy Johnson .50 1.25
6 Tony Gwynn .60 1.50
7 Matt Williams .20 .50
8 Jeff Bagwell .30 .75
9 G.Maddux .75 2.00
K.Hill
10 Andy Benes .08 .25

1995 Fleer Lumber Company

Randomly inserted in retail packs at a rate of one in 24, this standard-size set highlights 10 of the game's top sluggers. Full-bleed card fronts feature an action photo with the Lumber Company logo, which includes the player's name, toward the bottom of the photo. Card backs have a player photo and woodgrain background with a write-up that highlights individual achievements.

COMPLETE SET (10) 12.50
STATED ODDS 1:24 RETAIL
1 Jeff Bagwell 1.00
2 Albert Belle .60
3 Barry Bonds 4.00
4 Jose Canseco 1.00
5 Joe Carter .60
6 Ken Griffey Jr. 3.00
7 Fred McGriff 1.00
8 Kevin Mitchell .30
9 Frank Thomas 1.50
10 Matt Williams .60

1995 Fleer Major League Prospects

Randomly inserted in all pack types at a rate of one in six, this 10-card standard-size set spotlights major league hopefuls. Card fronts feature a player photo with the words "Major League Prospects" serving as part of the background. The player's name and team appear in silver foil at the bottom. The backs have a photo and a write-up on his minor league career.

COMPLETE SET (10) 4.00
STATED ODDS 1:6
1 Garret Anderson .20
2 James Baldwin .08
3 Alan Benes .08
4 Armando Benitez .08
5 Ray Durham .20
6 Brian L.Hunter .08
7 Derek Jeter 1.50
8 Charles Johnson .20
9 Orlando Miller .08
10 Alex Rodriguez 1.50

1995 Fleer Pro-Visions

Randomly inserted in all pack types at a rate of one in nine, this six card standard-size set features top players illustrated by Wayne Anthony Still. The colorful artwork on front features the player in a surrealistic setting. The backs offer write-up on the player's previous season.

COMPLETE SET (6) 1.25
STATED ODDS 1:9
1 Mike Mussina .20
2 Raul Mondesi .10
3 Jeff Bagwell .20
4 Greg Maddux .50
5 Tim Salmon .20
6 Manny Ramirez .20

1995 Fleer Rookie Sensations

Randomly inserted in 18-card packs, this 20-card standard-size set features top rookies from the 1994 season. The fronts have full-bleed color photos with the team and player's name in gold foil along the right edge. The backs also have full-bleed color photos along with player information.

COMPLETE SET (20) 15.00
RANDOM INSERTS IN JUMBO PACKS
1 Kurt Abbott .75
2 Rico Brogna .75
3 Hector Carrasco .75
4 Kevin Foster .75
5 Chris Gomez .75
6 Darren Hall .75
7 Bob Hamelin .75
8 Joey Hamilton .75
9 John Hudek .75
10 Ryan Klesko 1.50
11 Javier Lopez 1.50
12 Matt Mieske .75
13 Raul Mondesi 1.50
14 Manny Ramirez 2.00
15 Shane Reynolds .75
16 Bill Risley .75
17 Johnny Ruffin .75
18 Steve Trachsel .75
19 William VanLandingham .75
20 Rondell White 1.50

1995 Fleer Team Leaders

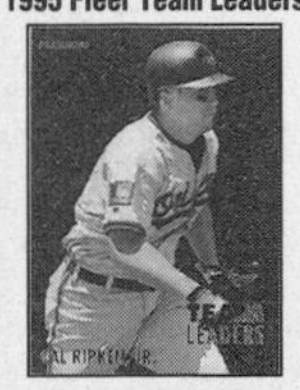

ndomly inserted in 12-card hobby packs at a rate one in 24, this 28-card standard-size set features players from each team. Each team is represented h card the has the team's leading hitter on one e with the leading pitcher on the other side. The m logo, "Team Leaders" and the player's name are d foil stamped on front and back.

MPLETE SET (28) 40.00 100.00
ATED ODDS 1:24 HOBBY
C.Ripken 10.00 25.00
M.Mussina
R.Clemens 6.00 15.00
M.Vaughn
T.Salmon 2.00 5.00
C.Finley
F.Thomas 3.00 8.00
J.McDowell
A.Belle 1.25 3.00
D.Martinez
C.Fielder 1.25 3.00
M.Moore
B.Hamelin 1.25 3.00
D.Cone
G.Vaughn .60 1.50
R.Bones
K.Puckett 3.00 8.00
R.Aguilera
D.Mattingly 8.00 20.00
J.Key
R.Sierra 1.25 3.00
D.Eckersley
K.Griffey 6.00 15.00
R.Johnson
J.Canseco 2.00 5.00
K.Rogers
J.Carter 1.25 3.00
P.Hentgen
G.Maddux 5.00 12.00
D.Justice
S.Sosa 3.00 8.00
S.Trachsel
K.Mitchell .60 1.50
J.Rijo
D.Bichette 1.25 3.00
B.Ruffin
J.Conine 1.25 3.00
R.Nen
J.Bagwell 2.00 5.00
D.Drabek
1 M.Piazza 5.00 12.00
R.Martinez
2 M.Alou 1.25 3.00
K.Hill
3 B.Bonilla 1.25 3.00
B.Saberhagen
4 D.Daulton 1.25 3.00
D.Jackson
5 J.Bell 1.25 3.00
Z.Smith
6 G.Jefferies .60 1.50
B.Tewksbury
7 T.Gwynn 4.00 10.00
A.Benes
8 M.Williams 1.25 3.00
R.Beck

1995 Fleer Update

This 200-card standard-size set features many players who were either rookies in 1995 or played for new teams. These cards were issued in either 12-card packs with a suggested retail price of $1.49 or 18-card packs that had a suggested retail price of $2.29. Each Fleer Update pack included one card from several insert sets produced with this product. Hot packs featuring only these insert cards were included one every 72 packs. The full-bleed fronts have two player photos and, atypical of baseball card fronts, biographical information such as height, weight, etc. The backgrounds are multi-colored. The backs are horizontal, have yearly statistics, a photo, and are numbered with the prefix "U". The checklist is arranged alphabetically by team within each league's divisions. Key Rookie Cards in this set include Bobby Higginson and Hideo Nomo.

COMPLETE SET (200) 6.00 15.00
ONE INSERT PER PACK
U PREFIX ON CARD NUMBERS
1 Manny Alexander .02 .10
2 Bret Barberie .02 .10
3 Armando Benitez .02 .10
4 Kevin Brown .07 .20
5 Doug Jones .02 .10
6 Sherman Obando .02 .10
7 Andy Van Slyke .10 .30
8 Stan Belinda .02 .10
9 Jose Canseco .10 .30
10 Vaughn Eshelman .02 .10
11 Mike Macfarlane .02 .10
12 Troy O'Leary .02 .10
13 Steve Rodriguez .02 .10
14 Lee Tinsley .02 .10
15 Tim Vanegmond .02 .10
16 Mark Whiten .02 .10
17 Sean Bergman .02 .10
18 Chad Curtis .02 .10
19 John Flaherty .02 .10
20 Bob Higginson RC .30 .75
21 Felipe Lira .02 .10
22 Shannon Penn .02 .10
23 Todd Steverson .02 .10
24 Sean Whiteside .02 .10
25 Tony Fernandez .02 .10
26 Jack McDowell .02 .10
27 Andy Pettitte .10 .30
28 John Wetteland .07 .20
29 David Cone .07 .20
30 Mike Timlin .02 .10
31 Duane Ward .02 .10
32 Jim Abbott .10 .30
33 James Baldwin .02 .10
34 Mike Devereaux .02 .10
35 Ray Durham .07 .20
36 Tim Fortugno .02 .10
37 Scott Ruffcorn .02 .10
38 Chris Sabo .02 .10
39 Paul Assenmacher .02 .10
40 Bud Black .02 .10
41 Orel Hershiser .07 .20
42 Julian Tavarez .02 .10
43 Dave Winfield .07 .20
44 Pat Borders .02 .10
45 Melvin Bunch RC .02 .10
46 Tom Goodwin .02 .10
47 Jon Nunnally .02 .10
48 Joe Randa .07 .20
49 Dilson Torres RC .02 .10
50 Joe Vitiello .02 .10
51 David Hulse .02 .10
52 Scott Karl .02 .10
53 Mark Kiefer .02 .10
54 Derrick May .02 .10
55 Joe Oliver .02 .10
56 Al Reyes RC .02 .10
57 Steve Sparks RC .15 .40
58 Jerald Clark .02 .10
59 Eddie Guardado .02 .10
60 Kevin Maas .02 .10
61 David McCarty .02 .10
62 Brad Radke RC .30 .75
63 Scott Stahoviak .02 .10
64 Garret Anderson .07 .20
65 Shawn Boskie .02 .10
66 Mike James .02 .10
67 Tony Phillips .02 .10
68 Lee Smith .07 .20
69 Mitch Williams .02 .10
70 Jim Corsi .02 .10
71 Mike Harkey .02 .10
72 Dave Stewart .07 .20
73 Todd Stottlemyre .02 .10
74 Joey Cora .02 .10
75 Chad Kreuter .02 .10
76 Jeff Nelson .02 .10
77 Alex Rodriguez .50 1.25
78 Ron Villone .02 .10
79 Bob Wells RC .15 .40
80 Jose Alberro RC .02 .10
81 Terry Burrows .02 .10
82 Kevin Gross .02 .10
83 Wilson Heredia .02 .10
84 Mark McLemore .02 .10
85 Otis Nixon .02 .10
86 Jeff Russell .02 .10
87 Mickey Tettleton .02 .10
88 Bob Tewksbury .02 .10
89 Pedro Borbon .02 .10
90 Marquis Grissom .07 .20
91 Chipper Jones .20 .50
92 Mike Mordecai .02 .10
93 Jason Schmidt .20 .50
94 John Burkett .02 .10
95 Andre Dawson .07 .20
96 Matt Dunbar RC .02 .10
97 Charles Johnson .07 .20
98 Terry Pendleton .07 .20
99 Rich Scheid .02 .10
100 Quilvio Veras .02 .10
101 Bobby Witt .02 .10
102 Eddie Zosky .02 .10
103 Shane Andrews .02 .10
104 Reid Cornelius .02 .10
105 Chad Fonville RC .02 .10
106 Mark Grudzielanek RC .30 .75
107 Roberto Kelly .02 .10
108 Carlos Perez RC .15 .40
109 Tony Tarasco .02 .10
110 Brett Butler .07 .20
111 Carl Everett .07 .20
112 Pete Harnisch .02 .10
113 Doug Henry .02 .10
114 Kevin Lomon RC .02 .10
115 Blas Minor .02 .10
116 Dave Mlicki .02 .10
117 Ricky Otero RC .02 .10
118 Norm Charlton .02 .10
119 Tyler Green .02 .10
120 Gene Harris .02 .10
121 Charlie Hayes .02 .10
122 Gregg Jefferies .02 .10
123 Michael Mimbs RC .02 .10
124 Paul Quantrill .02 .10
125 Frank Castillo .02 .10
126 Brian McRae .02 .10
127 Jaime Navarro .02 .10
128 Mike Perez .02 .10
129 Tanyon Sturtze .02 .10
130 Ozzie Timmons .02 .10
131 John Courtright .02 .10
132 Ron Gant .07 .20
133 Xavier Hernandez .02 .10
134 Brian Hunter .02 .10
135 Benito Santiago .07 .20
136 Pete Smith .02 .10
137 Scott Sullivan .02 .10
138 Derek Bell .02 .10
139 Doug Brocail .02 .10
140 Ricky Gutierrez .02 .10
141 Pedro A.Martinez .02 .10
142 Orlando Miller .02 .10
143 Phil Plantier .02 .10
144 Craig Shipley .02 .10
145 Rich Aude .02 .10
146 Jason Christiansen RC .02 .10
147 Freddy Adrian Garcia RC .02 .10
148 Jim Gott .02 .10
149 Mark Johnson RC .15 .40
150 Esteban Loaiza .02 .10
151 Dan Plesac .02 .10
152 Gary Wilson RC .02 .10
153 Allen Battle .02 .10
154 Terry Bradshaw .02 .10
155 Scott Cooper .02 .10
156 Tripp Cromer .02 .10
157 John Frascatore RC .02 .10
158 John Habyan .02 .10
159 Tom Henke .02 .10
160 Ken Hill .02 .10
161 Danny Jackson .02 .10
162 Donovan Osborne .02 .10
163 Tom Urbani .02 .10
164 Roger Bailey .02 .10
165 Jorge Brito RC .02 .10
166 Vinny Castilla .07 .20
167 Darren Holmes .02 .10
168 Roberto Mejia .02 .10
169 Bill Swift .02 .10
170 Mark Thompson .02 .10
171 Larry Walker .07 .20
172 Greg Hansell .02 .10
173 Dave Hansen .02 .10
174 Carlos Hernandez .02 .10
175 Hideo Nomo RC .75 2.00
176 Jose Offerman .02 .10
177 Antonio Osuna .02 .10
178 Reggie Williams .02 .10
179 Todd Williams .02 .10
180 Andres Berumen .02 .10
181 Ken Caminiti .07 .20
182 Andujar Cedeno .02 .10
183 Steve Finley .07 .20
184 Bryce Florie .02 .10
185 Dustin Hermanson .02 .10
186 Ray Holbert .02 .10
187 Melvin Nieves .02 .10
188 Roberto Petagine .02 .10
189 Jody Reed .02 .10
190 Fernando Valenzuela .07 .20
191 Brian Williams .02 .10
192 Mark Dewey .02 .10
193 Glenallen Hill .02 .10
194 Chris Hook RC .02 .10
195 Terry Mulholland .02 .10
196 Steve Scarsone .02 .10
197 Trevor Wilson .02 .10
198 Checklist .02 .10
199 Checklist .02 .10
200 Checklist .02 .10

1995 Fleer Update Diamond Tribute

This 10-card standard-size set featuring some of baseball's leading stars were inserted at a stated rate of one in five packs. The cards are numbered in the lower right with an "X" of 10.

COMPLETE SET (10) 3.00 8.00
STATED ODDS 1:5 HOB/RET
1 Jeff Bagwell .20 .50
2 Albert Belle .10 .30
3 Barry Bonds .75 2.00
4 David Cone .10 .30
5 Dennis Eckersley .10 .30
6 Ken Griffey Jr. .60 1.50
7 Rickey Henderson .30 .75
8 Greg Maddux .50 1.25
9 Frank Thomas .30 .75
10 Matt Williams .10 .30

1995 Fleer Update Headliners

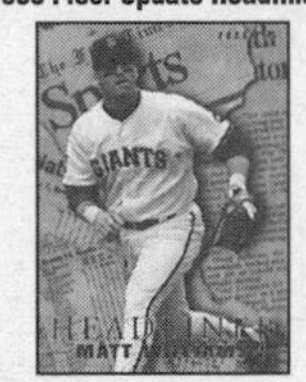

Inserted one every three packs, this 20-card standard-size set features various major league stars. The cards are numbered in the lower left as "X" of 20.

COMPLETE SET (20) 5.00 12.00
STATED ODDS 1:3
1 Jeff Bagwell .20 .50
2 Albert Belle .10 .30
3 Barry Bonds .75 2.00
4 Jose Canseco .20 .50
5 Joe Carter .10 .30
6 Will Clark .20 .50
7 Roger Clemens .60 1.50
8 Lenny Dykstra .10 .30
9 Cecil Fielder .10 .30
10 Juan Gonzalez .10 .30
11 Ken Griffey Jr. .60 1.50
12 Kenny Lofton .10 .30
13 Greg Maddux .50 1.25
14 Fred McGriff .20 .50
15 Mike Piazza .50 1.25
16 Kirby Puckett .30 .75
17 Tim Salmon .20 .50
18 Frank Thomas .30 .75
19 Mo Vaughn .10 .30
20 Matt Williams .10 .30

1995 Fleer Update Rookie Update

Inserted one in every four packs, this 10-card standard-size set features some of 1995's best rookies. The cards are numbered as "X of 10". Chipper Jones and Hideo Nomo are among the players included in this set.

COMPLETE SET (10) 4.00 10.00
STATED ODDS 1:4
1 Shane Andrews .08 .25
2 Ray Durham .20 .50
3 Shawn Green .20 .50
4 Charles Johnson .20 .50
5 Chipper Jones .60 1.50
6 Esteban Loaiza .08 .25
7 Hideo Nomo .75 2.00
8 Jon Nunnally .08 .25
9 Alex Rodriguez 1.50 4.00
10 Julian Tavarez .08 .25

1995 Fleer Update Smooth Leather

Inserted one every five jumbo packs, this 10-card standard-size set features many leading defensive wizards. The card fronts feature a player photo. Underneath the player photo, is his name along with the words "smooth leather" on the bottom. The right corner features a glove. All of this information as well as the "Fleer 95" logo is in gold print. All of this is on a card with a special leather-like coating. The back features a photo as well as fielding information. The cards are numbered in the lower left as "X of 10" and are sequenced in alphabetical order.

COMPLETE SET (10) 10.00 25.00
STATED ODDS 1:5 JUMBO
1 Roberto Alomar .60 1.50
2 Barry Bonds 2.50 6.00
3 Ken Griffey Jr. 2.00 5.00
4 Marquis Grissom .40 1.00
5 Darren Lewis .20 .50
6 Kenny Lofton .40 1.00
7 Don Mattingly 2.50 6.00
8 Cal Ripken 3.00 8.00
9 Ivan Rodriguez .60 1.50
10 Matt Williams .40 1.00

1995 Fleer Update Soaring Stars

This nine-card standard-size set was inserted one every 36 packs. The fronts feature the player's photo set against a prismatic background of baseballs. The player's name, the "Soaring Stars" logo as well as a star are all printed in gold foil at the bottom. The back has a player photo, his name as well as some career information. The cards are numbered in the upper right "X of 9" and are sequenced in alphabetical order.

COMPLETE SET (10) 10.00 25.00
STATED ODDS 1:36
1 Moises Alou 1.00 2.50
2 Jason Bere .50 1.25
3 Jeff Conine 1.00 2.50
4 Cliff Floyd 1.00 2.50
5 Pat Hentgen .50 1.25
6 Kenny Lofton 1.00 2.50
7 Raul Mondesi 1.00 2.50
8 Mike Piazza 4.00 10.00
9 Tim Salmon 1.50 4.00

1996 Fleer

The 1996 Fleer baseball set consists of 600 standard-size cards issued in one series. Cards were issued in 11-card packs with a suggested retail price of $1.49. Borderless fronts are matte-finished and have full-color action shots with the player's name, team and position stamped in gold foil. Backs contain a biography and career stats on the top and a full-color head shot with a 1995 synopsis on the bottom. The matte finish on the cards was designed so collectors could have an easier surface for cards to be autographed. Fleer included in each pack a "Thanks a Million" scratch-off game card redeemable for instant-win prizes and a chance to bat for a million-dollar prize in a Major League park. Rookie Cards in this set include Matt Lawton and Mike Sweeney. A Cal Ripken promo was distributed to dealers and hobby media to preview the set.

COMPLETE SET (600) 20.00 50.00
1 Manny Alexander .10 .30
2 Brady Anderson .10 .30
3 Harold Baines .10 .30
4 Armando Benitez .10 .30
5 Bobby Bonilla .10 .30
6 Kevin Brown .10 .30
7 Scott Erickson .10 .30
8 Curtis Goodwin .10 .30
9 Jeffrey Hammonds .10 .30
10 Jimmy Haynes .10 .30
11 Chris Hoiles .10 .30
12 Doug Jones .10 .30
13 Rick Krivda .10 .30
14 Jeff Manto .10 .30
15 Ben McDonald .10 .30
16 Jamie Moyer .10 .30
17 Mike Mussina .20 .50
18 Jesse Orosco .10 .30
19 Rafael Palmeiro .20 .50
20 Cal Ripken 1.00 2.50
21 Rick Aguilera .10 .30
22 Luis Alicea .10 .30
23 Stan Belinda .10 .30
24 Jose Canseco .20 .50
25 Roger Clemens .60 1.50
26 Vaughn Eshelman .10 .30
27 Mike Greenwell .10 .30
28 Erik Hanson .10 .30
29 Dwayne Hosey .10 .30
30 Mike Macfarlane UER .10 .30
31 Tim Naehring .10 .30
32 Troy O'Leary .10 .30
33 Aaron Sele .10 .30
34 Zane Smith .10 .30
35 Jeff Suppan .10 .30
36 Lee Tinsley .10 .30
37 John Valentin .10 .30
38 Mo Vaughn .10 .30
39 Tim Wakefield .10 .30
40 Jim Abbott .20 .50
41 Brian Anderson .10 .30
42 Garret Anderson .10 .30
43 Chili Davis .10 .30
44 Gary DiSarcina .10 .30
45 Damion Easley .10 .30
46 Jim Edmonds .10 .30
47 Chuck Finley .10 .30
48 Todd Greene .10 .30
49 Mike Harkey .10 .30
50 Mike James .10 .30
51 Mark Langston .10 .30
52 Greg Myers .10 .30
53 Orlando Palmeiro .10 .30
54 Bob Patterson .10 .30
55 Troy Percival .10 .30
56 Tony Phillips .10 .30
57 Tim Salmon .20 .50
58 Lee Smith .10 .30
59 J.T. Snow .10 .30
60 Randy Velarde .10 .30
61 Wilson Alvarez .10 .30
62 Luis Andujar .10 .30
63 Jason Bere .10 .30
64 Ray Durham .10 .30
65 Alex Fernandez .10 .30
66 Ozzie Guillen .10 .30
67 Roberto Hernandez .10 .30
68 Lance Johnson .10 .30
69 Matt Karchner .10 .30
70 Ron Karkovice .10 .30
71 Norberto Martin .10 .30
72 Dave Martinez .10 .30
73 Kirk McCaskill .10 .30
74 Lyle Mouton .10 .30
75 Tim Raines .10 .30
76 Mike Sirotka RC .10 .30
77 Frank Thomas .30 .75
78 Larry Thomas .10 .30
79 Robin Ventura .10 .30
80 Sandy Alomar Jr. .10 .30
81 Paul Assenmacher .10 .30
82 Carlos Baerga .10 .30
83 Albert Belle .10 .30
84 Mark Clark .10 .30
85 Alan Embree .10 .30
86 Alvaro Espinoza .10 .30
87 Orel Hershiser .10 .30
88 Ken Hill .10 .30
89 Kenny Lofton .10 .30
90 Dennis Martinez .10 .30
91 Jose Mesa .10 .30
92 Eddie Murray .30 .75
93 Charles Nagy .10 .30
94 Chad Ogea .10 .30
95 Tony Pena .10 .30
96 Herb Perry .10 .30
97 Eric Plunk .10 .30
98 Jim Poole .10 .30
99 Manny Ramirez .20 .50
100 Paul Sorrento .10 .30
101 Julian Tavarez .10 .30
102 Jim Thome .20 .50
103 Omar Vizquel .20 .50
104 Dave Winfield .10 .30
105 Danny Bautista .10 .30
106 Joe Boever .10 .30
107 Chad Curtis .10 .30
108 John Doherty .10 .30
109 Cecil Fielder .10 .30
110 John Flaherty .10 .30
111 Travis Fryman .10 .30
112 Chris Gomez .10 .30
113 Bob Higginson .10 .30
114 Mark Lewis .10 .30
115 Jose Lima .10 .30
116 Felipe Lira .10 .30
117 Brian Maxcy .10 .30
118 C.J. Nitkowski .10 .30
119 Phil Plantier .10 .30
120 Clint Sodowsky .10 .30
121 Alan Trammell .10 .30
122 Lou Whitaker .10 .30
123 Kevin Appier .10 .30
124 Johnny Damon .20 .50
125 Gary Gaetti .10 .30
126 Tom Goodwin .10 .30
127 Tom Gordon .10 .30
128 Mark Gubicza .10 .30
129 Bob Hamelin .10 .30
130 David Howard .10 .30
131 Jason Jacome .10 .30
132 Wally Joyner .10 .30
133 Keith Lockhart .10 .30
134 Brent Mayne .10 .30
135 Jeff Montgomery .10 .30
136 Jon Nunnally .10 .30
137 Juan Samuel .10 .30
138 Mike Sweeney RC .40 1.00
139 Michael Tucker .10 .30
140 Joe Vitiello .10 .30
141 Ricky Bones .10 .30
142 Chuck Carr .10 .30
143 Jeff Cirillo .10 .30
144 Mike Fetters .10 .30
145 Darryl Hamilton .10 .30
146 David Hulse .10 .30
147 John Jaha .10 .30
148 Scott Karl .10 .30
149 Mark Kiefer .10 .30
150 Pat Listach .10 .30
151 Mark Loretta .10 .30
152 Mike Matheny .10 .30
153 Matt Mieske .10 .30
154 Dave Nilsson .10 .30
155 Joe Oliver .10 .30
156 Al Reyes .10 .30
157 Kevin Seitzer .10 .30
158 Steve Sparks .10 .30
159 B.J. Surhoff .10 .30
160 Jose Valentin .10 .30
161 Greg Vaughn .10 .30
162 Fernando Vina .10 .30
163 Rich Becker .10 .30
164 Ron Coomer .10 .30
165 Marty Cordova .10 .30
166 Chuck Knoblauch .10 .30
167 Matt Lawton RC .20 .50
168 Pat Meares .10 .30
169 Paul Molitor .10 .30
170 Pedro Munoz .10 .30
171 Jose Parra .10 .30
172 Kirby Puckett .30 .75
173 Brad Radke .10 .30
174 Jeff Reboulet .10 .30
175 Rich Robertson .10 .30
176 Frank Rodriguez .10 .30
177 Scott Stahoviak .10 .30
178 Dave Stevens .10 .30
179 Matt Walbeck .10 .30
180 Wade Boggs .20 .50
181 David Cone .10 .30
182 Tony Fernandez .10 .30
183 Joe Girardi .10 .30
184 Derek Jeter 1.25 3.00
185 Scott Kamieniecki .10 .30
186 Pat Kelly .10 .30
187 Jim Leyritz .10 .30
188 Tino Martinez .20 .50
189 Don Mattingly .75 2.00
190 Jack McDowell .10 .30
191 Jeff Nelson .10 .30
192 Paul O'Neill .20 .50
193 Melido Perez .10 .30
194 Andy Pettitte .20 .50
195 Mariano Rivera .60 1.50
196 Ruben Sierra .10 .30
197 Mike Stanley .10 .30
198 Darryl Strawberry .10 .30
199 John Wetteland .10 .30
200 Bob Wickman .10 .30
201 Bernie Williams .20 .50
202 Mark Acre .10 .30
203 Geronimo Berroa .10 .30
204 Mike Bordick .10 .30
205 Scott Brosius .10 .30
206 Dennis Eckersley .10 .30
207 Brent Gates .10 .30
208 Jason Giambi .10 .30
209 Rickey Henderson .30 .75
210 Jose Herrera .10 .30
211 Stan Javier .10 .30
212 Doug Johns .10 .30
213 Mark McGwire .75 2.00
214 Steve Ontiveros .10 .30
215 Craig Paquette .10 .30
216 Ariel Prieto .10 .30
217 Carlos Reyes .10 .30
218 Terry Steinbach .10 .30
219 Todd Stottlemyre .10 .30
220 Danny Tartabull .10 .30
221 Todd Van Poppel .10 .30
222 John Wasdin .10 .30
223 George Williams .10 .30
224 Steve Wojciechowski .10 .30
225 Rich Amaral .10 .30
226 Bobby Ayala .10 .30
227 Tim Belcher .10 .30
228 Andy Benes .10 .30
229 Chris Bosio .10 .30
230 Darren Bragg .10 .30
231 Jay Buhner .10 .30
232 Norm Charlton .10 .30
233 Vince Coleman .10 .30
234 Joey Cora .10 .30
235 Russ Davis .10 .30
236 Alex Diaz .10 .30
237 Felix Fermin .10 .30
238 Ken Griffey Jr. .60 1.50
239 Sterling Hitchcock .10 .30
240 Randy Johnson .30 .75
241 Edgar Martinez .20 .50
242 Bill Risley .10 .30
243 Alex Rodriguez .60 1.50
244 Luis Sojo .10 .30
245 Dan Wilson .10 .30
246 Bob Wolcott .10 .30
247 Will Clark .20 .50
248 Jeff Frye .10 .30
249 Benji Gil .10 .30
250 Juan Gonzalez .10 .30
251 Rusty Greer .10 .30
252 Kevin Gross .10 .30
253 Roger McDowell .10 .30
254 Mark McLemore .10 .30
255 Otis Nixon .10 .30
256 Luis Ortiz .10 .30
257 Mike Pagliarulo .10 .30
258 Dean Palmer .10 .30
259 Roger Pavlik .10 .30
260 Ivan Rodriguez .20 .50
261 Kenny Rogers .10 .30
262 Jeff Russell .10 .30
263 Mickey Tettleton .10 .30
264 Bob Tewksbury .10 .30
265 Dave Valle .10 .30
266 Matt Whiteside .10 .30
267 Roberto Alomar .20 .50
268 Joe Carter .10 .30
269 Tony Castillo .10 .30
270 Domingo Cedeno .10 .30
271 Tim Crabtree UER .10 .30
272 Carlos Delgado .10 .30
273 Alex Gonzalez .10 .30
274 Shawn Green .10 .30
275 Juan Guzman .10 .30
276 Pat Hentgen .10 .30

277 Al Leiter .10 .30
278 Sandy Martinez .10 .30
279 Paul Menhart .10 .30
280 John Olerud .10 .30
281 Paul Quantrill .10 .30
282 Ken Robinson .10 .30
283 Ed Sprague .10 .30
284 Mike Timlin .10 .30
285 Steve Avery .10 .30
286 Rafael Belliard .10 .30
287 Jeff Blauser .10 .30
288 Pedro Borbon .10 .30
289 Brad Clontz .10 .30
290 Mike Devereaux .10 .30
291 Tom Glavine .20 .50
292 Marquis Grissom .10 .30
293 Chipper Jones .30 .75
294 David Justice .10 .30
295 Mike Kelly .10 .30
296 Ryan Klesko .10 .30
297 Mark Lemke .10 .30
298 Javier Lopez .10 .30
299 Greg Maddux .50 1.25
300 Fred McGriff .20 .50
301 Greg McMichael .10 .30
302 Kent Mercker .10 .30
303 Mike Mordecai .10 .30
304 Charlie O'Brien .10 .30
305 Eduardo Perez .10 .30
306 Luis Polonia .10 .30
307 Jason Schmidt .20 .50
308 John Smoltz .20 .50
309 Terrell Wade .10 .30
310 Mark Wohlers .10 .30
311 Scott Bullett .10 .30
312 Jim Bullinger .10 .30
313 Larry Casian .10 .30
314 Frank Castillo .10 .30
315 Shawon Dunston .10 .30
316 Kevin Foster .10 .30
317 Matt Franco RC .10 .30
318 Luis Gonzalez .10 .30
319 Mark Grace .20 .50
320 Jose Hernandez .10 .30
321 Mike Hubbard .10 .30
322 Brian McRae .10 .30
323 Randy Myers .10 .30
324 Jaime Navarro .10 .30
325 Mark Parent .10 .30
326 Mike Perez .10 .30
327 Rey Sanchez .10 .30
328 Ryne Sandberg .50 1.25
329 Scott Servais .10 .30
330 Sammy Sosa .30 .75
331 Ozzie Timmons .10 .30
332 Steve Trachsel .10 .30
333 Todd Zeile .10 .30
334 Bret Boone .10 .30
335 Jeff Branson .10 .30
336 Jeff Brantley .10 .30
337 Dave Burba .10 .30
338 Hector Carrasco .10 .30
339 Mariano Duncan .10 .30
340 Ron Gant .10 .30
341 Lenny Harris .10 .30
342 Xavier Hernandez .10 .30
343 Thomas Howard .10 .30
344 Mike Jackson .10 .30
345 Barry Larkin .20 .50
346 Darren Lewis .10 .30
347 Hal Morris .10 .30
348 Eric Owens .10 .30
349 Mark Portugal .10 .30
350 Jose Rijo .10 .30
351 Reggie Sanders .10 .30
352 Benito Santiago .10 .30
353 Pete Schourek .10 .30
354 John Smiley .10 .30
355 Eddie Taubensee .10 .30
356 Jerome Walton .10 .30
357 David Wells .10 .30
358 Roger Bailey .10 .30
359 Jason Bates .10 .30
360 Dante Bichette .10 .30
361 Ellis Burks .10 .30
362 Vinny Castilla .10 .30
363 Andres Galarraga .10 .30
364 Darren Holmes .10 .30
365 Mike Kingery .10 .30
366 Curt Leskanic .10 .30
367 Quinton McCracken .10 .30
368 Mike Munoz .10 .30
369 David Nied .10 .30
370 Steve Reed .10 .30
371 Bryan Rekar .10 .30
372 Kevin Ritz .10 .30
373 Bruce Ruffin .10 .30
374 Bret Saberhagen .10 .30
375 Bill Swift .10 .30
376 John Vander Wal .10 .30
377 Larry Walker .10 .30
378 Walt Weiss .10 .30
379 Eric Young .10 .30
380 Kurt Abbott .10 .30
381 Alex Arias .10 .30
382 Jerry Browne .10 .30
383 John Burkett .10 .30
384 Greg Colbrunn .10 .30
385 Jeff Conine .10 .30
386 Andre Dawson .10 .30
387 Chris Hammond .10 .30
388 Charles Johnson .10 .30
389 Terry Mathews .10 .30
390 Robb Nen .10 .30
391 Joe Orsulak .10 .30
392 Terry Pendleton .10 .30
393 Pat Rapp .10 .30
394 Gary Sheffield .10 .30
395 Jesus Tavarez .10 .30
396 Marc Valdes .10 .30
397 Quilvio Veras .10 .30
398 Randy Veres .10 .30
399 Devon White .10 .30
400 Jeff Bagwell .20 .50
401 Derek Bell .10 .30
402 Craig Biggio .20 .50
403 John Cangelosi .10 .30
404 Jim Dougherty .10 .30
405 Doug Drabek .10 .30
406 Tony Eusebio .10 .30
407 Ricky Gutierrez .10 .30
408 Mike Hampton .10 .30
409 Dean Hartgraves .10 .30
410 John Hudek .10 .30
411 Brian Hunter .10 .30
412 Todd Jones .10 .30
413 Darryl Kile .10 .30
414 Dave Magadan .10 .30
415 Derrick May .10 .30
416 Orlando Miller .10 .30
417 James Mouton .10 .30
418 Shane Reynolds .10 .30
419 Greg Swindell .10 .30
420 Jeff Tabaka .10 .30
421 Dave Veres .10 .30
422 Billy Wagner .10 .30
423 Donne Wall .10 .30
424 Rick Wilkins .10 .30
425 Billy Ashley .10 .30
426 Mike Blowers .10 .30
427 Brett Butler .10 .30
428 Tom Candiotti .10 .30
429 Juan Castro .10 .30
430 John Cummings .10 .30
431 Delino DeShields .10 .30
432 Joey Eischen .10 .30
433 Chad Fonville .10 .30
434 Greg Gagne .10 .30
435 Dave Hansen .10 .30
436 Carlos Hernandez .10 .30
437 Todd Hollandsworth .10 .30
438 Eric Karros .10 .30
439 Roberto Kelly .10 .30
440 Ramon Martinez .10 .30
441 Raul Mondesi .10 .30
442 Hideo Nomo .30 .75
443 Antonio Osuna .10 .30
444 Chan Ho Park .10 .30
445 Mike Piazza .50 1.25
446 Felix Rodriguez .10 .30
447 Kevin Tapani .10 .30
448 Ismael Valdes .10 .30
449 Todd Worrell .10 .30
450 Moises Alou .10 .30
451 Shane Andrews .10 .30
452 Yamil Benitez .10 .30
453 Sean Berry .10 .30
454 Wil Cordero .10 .30
455 Jeff Fassero .10 .30
456 Darrin Fletcher .10 .30
457 Cliff Floyd .10 .30
458 Mark Grudzielanek .10 .30
459 Gil Heredia .10 .30
460 Tim Laker .10 .30
461 Mike Lansing .10 .30
462 Pedro Martinez .20 .50
463 Carlos Perez .10 .30
464 Curtis Pride .10 .30
465 Mel Rojas .10 .30
466 Kirk Rueter .10 .30
467 F.P. Santangelo .10 .30
468 Tim Scott .10 .30
469 David Segui .10 .30
470 Tony Tarasco .10 .30
471 Rondell White .10 .30
472 Edgardo Alfonzo .10 .30
473 Tim Bogar .10 .30
474 Rico Brogna .10 .30
475 Damon Buford .10 .30
476 Paul Byrd .10 .30
477 Carl Everett .10 .30
478 John Franco .10 .30
479 Todd Hundley .10 .30
480 Butch Huskey .10 .30
481 Jason Isringhausen .10 .30
482 Bobby Jones .10 .30
483 Chris Jones .10 .30
484 Jeff Kent .10 .30
485 Dave Mlicki .10 .30
486 Robert Person .10 .30
487 Bill Pulsipher .10 .30
488 Kelly Stinnett .10 .30
489 Ryan Thompson .10 .30
490 Jose Vizcaino .10 .30
491 Howard Battle .10 .30
492 Toby Borland .10 .30
493 Ricky Bottalico .10 .30
494 Darren Daulton .10 .30
495 Lenny Dykstra .10 .30
496 Jim Eisenreich .10 .30
497 Sid Fernandez .10 .30
498 Tyler Green .10 .30
499 Charlie Hayes .10 .30
500 Gregg Jefferies .10 .30
501 Kevin Jordan .10 .30
502 Tony Longmire .10 .30
503 Tom Marsh .10 .30
504 Michael Mimbs .10 .30
505 Mickey Morandini .10 .30
506 Gene Schall .10 .30
507 Curt Schilling .10 .30
508 Heathcliff Slocumb .10 .30
509 Kevin Stocker .10 .30
510 Andy Van Slyke .20 .50
511 Lenny Webster .10 .30
512 Mark Whiten .10 .30
513 Mike Williams .10 .30
514 Jay Bell .10 .30
515 Jacob Brumfield .10 .30
516 Jason Christiansen .10 .30
517 Dave Clark .10 .30
518 Midre Cummings .10 .30
519 Angelo Encarnacion .10 .30
520 John Ericks .10 .30
521 Carlos Garcia .10 .30
522 Mark Johnson .10 .30
523 Jeff King .10 .30
524 Nelson Liriano .10 .30
525 Esteban Loaiza .10 .30
526 Al Martin .10 .30
527 Orlando Merced .10 .30
528 Dan Miceli .10 .30
529 Ramon Morel .10 .30
530 Denny Neagle .10 .30
531 Steve Parris .10 .30
532 Dan Plesac .10 .30
533 Don Slaught .10 .30
534 Paul Wagner .10 .30
535 John Wehner .10 .30
536 Kevin Young .10 .30
537 Allen Battle .10 .30
538 David Bell .10 .30
539 Alan Benes .10 .30
540 Scott Cooper .10 .30
541 Tripp Cromer .10 .30
542 Tony Fossas .10 .30
543 Bernard Gilkey .10 .30
544 Tom Henke .10 .30
545 Brian Jordan .10 .30
546 Ray Lankford .10 .30
547 John Mabry .10 .30
548 T.J. Mathews .10 .30
549 Mike Morgan .10 .30
550 Jose Oliva .10 .30
551 Jose Oquendo .10 .30
552 Donovan Osborne .10 .30
553 Tom Pagnozzi .10 .30
554 Mark Petkovsek .10 .30
555 Danny Sheaffer .10 .30
556 Ozzie Smith .50 1.25
557 Mark Sweeney .10 .30
558 Allen Watson .10 .30
559 Andy Ashby .10 .30
560 Brad Ausmus .10 .30
561 Willie Blair .10 .30
562 Ken Caminiti .10 .30
563 Andujar Cedeno .10 .30
564 Glenn Dishman .10 .30
565 Steve Finley .10 .30
566 Bryce Florie .10 .30
567 Tony Gwynn .40 1.00
568 Joey Hamilton .10 .30
569 Dustin Hermanson UER .10 .30
570 Trevor Hoffman .10 .30
571 Brian Johnson .10 .30
572 Marc Kroon .10 .30
573 Scott Livingstone .10 .30
574 Marc Newfield .10 .30
575 Melvin Nieves .10 .30
576 Jody Reed .10 .30
577 Bip Roberts .10 .30
578 Scott Sanders .10 .30
579 Fernando Valenzuela .10 .30
580 Eddie Williams .10 .30
581 Rod Beck .10 .30
582 Marvin Benard RC .10 .30
583 Barry Bonds .75 2.00
584 Jamie Brewington RC .10 .30
585 Mark Carreon .10 .30
586 Royce Clayton .10 .30
587 Shawn Estes .10 .30
588 Glenallen Hill .10 .30
589 Mark Leiter .10 .30
590 Kirt Manwaring .10 .30
591 David McCarty .10 .30
592 Terry Mulholland .10 .30
593 John Patterson .10 .30
594 J.R. Phillips .10 .30
595 Deion Sanders .20 .50
596 Steve Scarsone .10 .30
597 Robby Thompson .10 .30
598 Sergio Valdez .10 .30
599 William Van Landingham .10 .30
600 Matt Williams .10 .30
P20 Cal Ripken 1.25 3.00
Promo

1996 Fleer Tiffany

COMPLETE SET (600) 75.00 150.00
*STARS: 2X TO 5X BASIC CARDS
*ROOKIES: 4X TO 10X BASIC CARDS
ONE PER PACK

1996 Fleer Checklists

Checklist cards were seeded one per six regular packs and have glossy, borderless fronts with full-color shots of the Major League's best. "Checklist" and the player's name are stamped in gold foil. Backs list the entire rundown of '96 Fleer cards printed in black type on a white background.

COMPLETE SET (10) 1.50 4.00
STATED ODDS 1:6
1 Barry Bonds .40 1.00
2 Ken Griffey Jr. .30 .75
3 Chipper Jones .15 .40
4 Greg Maddux .25 .60
5 Mike Piazza .25 .60
6 Manny Ramirez .08 .25
7 Cal Ripken .50 1.25
8 Frank Thomas .15 .40
9 Mo Vaughn .05 .15
10 Matt Williams .05 .15

1996 Fleer Golden Memories

Randomly inserted at a rate of one in 10 regular packs, this 10-card standard-size set features important highlights of the 1995 season. Fronts have two action shots, one serving as a background, the other a full-color cutout. "Golden Memories" and player's name are printed vertically in white type. Backs contain a biography, player close-up and career statistics.

COMPLETE SET (10) 3.00 8.00
STATED ODDS 1:10
1 Albert Belle .15 .40
2 B.Bonds .40 1.00
S.Sosa
3 Greg Maddux .60 1.50
4 Edgar Martinez .25 .60
5 Ramon Martinez .15 .40
6 Mark McGwire 1.00 2.50
7 Eddie Murray .40 1.00
8 Cal Ripken 1.25 3.00
9 Frank Thomas .40 1.00
10 A.Trammell .15 .40
L.Whitaker

1996 Fleer Lumber Company

This retail-exclusive 12-card set was inserted one in every nine packs and features RBI and HR power hitters. The fronts display a color action player cut-out on a wood background with embossed printing. The backs carry a player photo and information about the player.

COMPLETE SET (12) 10.00 25.00
STATED ODDS 1:9 RETAIL
1 Albert Belle .40 1.00
2 Dante Bichette .40 1.00
3 Barry Bonds 2.50 6.00
4 Ken Griffey Jr. 2.00 5.00
5 Mark McGwire 2.50 6.00
6 Mike Piazza 1.50 4.00
7 Manny Ramirez .60 1.50
8 Tim Salmon .60 1.50
9 Sammy Sosa 1.00 2.50
10 Frank Thomas 1.00 2.50
11 Mo Vaughn .40 1.00
12 Matt Williams .40 1.00

1996 Fleer Postseason Glory

Randomly inserted in regular packs at a rate of one in five, this five-card standard-size set highlights great moments of the 1996 Divisional, League Championship and World Series games. Horizontal, white-bordered fronts feature a player in three full-color action cutouts with black strips on top and bottom. "Post-Season Glory" appears on top and the player's name is printed in silver hologram foil. White-bordered backs are split between a full-color player close-up and a description of his post-season play printed in white type on a black background.

COMPLETE SET (5) .75 2.00
STATED ODDS 1:5
1 Tom Glavine .08 .25
2 Ken Griffey Jr. .30 .75
3 Orel Hershiser .05 .15
4 Randy Johnson .15 .40
5 Jim Thome .08 .25

1996 Fleer Prospects

Randomly inserted at a rate of one in six regular packs, this ten-card standard-size set focuses on players moving up through the farm system. Borderless fronts have full-color head shots on one-color backgrounds. "Prospect" and the player's name are stamped in silver hologram foil. Backs feature a full-color action shot with a synopsis of talent printed in a green box.

COMPLETE SET (10) 1.50 4.00
STATED ODDS 1:6
1 Yamil Benitez .20 .50
2 Roger Cedeno .20 .50
3 Tony Clark .20 .50
4 Micah Franklin .20 .50
5 Karim Garcia .20 .50
6 Todd Greene .20 .50
7 Alex Ochoa .20 .50
8 Ruben Rivera .20 .50
9 Chris Snopek .20 .50
10 Shannon Stewart .40 1.00

1996 Fleer Road Warriors

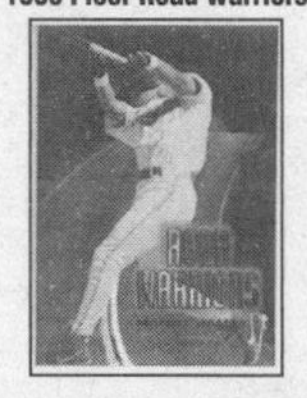

Randomly inserted in regular packs at a rate of one in 13, this 10-card standard-size set focuses on players who thrive on the road. Fronts feature a full-color player cutout set against a winding rural highway background. "Road Warriors" is printed in reverse type with a hazy white border and the player's name is printed in white type underneath. Backs include the player's road stats, biography and a close-up shot.

COMPLETE SET (10) 5.00 12.00
STATED ODDS 1:13
1 Derek Bell .20 .50
2 Tony Gwynn .60 1.50
3 Greg Maddux .75 2.00
4 Mark McGwire 1.25 3.00
5 Mike Piazza .75 2.00
6 Manny Ramirez .30 .75
7 Tim Salmon .30 .75
8 Frank Thomas .50 1.25
9 Mo Vaughn .20 .50
10 Matt Williams .20 .50

1996 Fleer Rookie Sensations

Randomly inserted at a rate of one in 11 regular packs, this 15-card standard-size set highlights 1995's best rookies. Borderless, horizontal fronts have a full-color action shot and a silver hologram strip containing the player's name and team logo. Horizontal backs have full-color head shots with a player profile all printed on a white background.

COMPLETE SET (15) 6.00 15.00
STATED ODDS 1:11
1 Garret Anderson .50 1.25
2 Marty Cordova .50 1.25
3 Johnny Damon .75 2.00
4 Ray Durham .50 1.25
5 Carl Everett .50 1.25
6 Shawn Green .50 1.25
7 Brian L.Hunter .50 1.25
8 Jason Isringhausen .50 1.25
9 Charles Johnson .50 1.25
10 Chipper Jones 1.25 3.00
11 John Mabry .50 1.25
12 Hideo Nomo 1.25 3.00
13 Troy Percival .50 1.25
14 Andy Pettitte .75 2.00
15 Quilvio Veras .50 1.25

1996 Fleer Smoke 'n Heat

Randomly inserted at a rate of one in nine regular packs, this 10-card standard-size set celebrates the pitchers with rifle arms and a high strikeout count. Fronts feature a full-color player cutout set against a red flame background. "Smoke 'n Heat" and the player's name are printed in gold type. Backs feature the pitcher's 1995 numbers, a biography and career stats along with a full-color close-up.

COMPLETE SET (10) 2.50 6.00
STATED ODDS 1:9
1 Kevin Appier .20 .50
2 Roger Clemens 1.00 2.50
3 David Cone .20 .50
4 Chuck Finley .20 .50
5 Randy Johnson .50 1.25
6 Greg Maddux .75 2.00
7 Pedro Martinez .30 .75
8 Hideo Nomo .50 1.25
9 John Smoltz .30 .75
10 Todd Stottlemyre .20 .50

1996 Fleer Team Leaders

This hobby-exclusive 28-card set was randomly inserted one in every nine packs and features statistical and inspirational leaders. The fronts display color action player cut-out on a foil background of the team name and logo. The backs carry a player portrait and player information.

COMPLETE SET (28) 25.00 60.00
STATED ODDS 1:9 HOBBY
1 Cal Ripken 4.00 10.00
2 Mo Vaughn .50 1.25
3 Jim Edmonds .50 1.25
4 Frank Thomas 1.25 3.00
5 Kenny Lofton .50 1.25
6 Travis Fryman .50 1.25
7 Gary Gaetti .50 1.25
8 B.J. Surhoff .50 1.25
9 Kirby Puckett 1.25 3.00
10 Don Mattingly 3.00 8.00
11 Mark McGwire 3.00 8.00
12 Ken Griffey Jr. 2.50 6.00
13 Juan Gonzalez .50 1.25
14 Joe Carter .50 1.25
15 Greg Maddux 2.00 5.00
16 Sammy Sosa 1.25 3.00
17 Barry Larkin .75 2.00
18 Dante Bichette .50 1.25
19 Jeff Conine .50 1.25
20 Jeff Bagwell .75 2.00
21 Mike Piazza 2.00 5.00
22 Rondell White .50 1.25
23 Rico Brogna .50 1.25
24 Darren Daulton .50 1.25
25 Jeff King .50 1.25
26 Ray Lankford .50 1.25
27 Tony Gwynn 1.50 4.00
28 Barry Bonds 3.00 8.00

1996 Fleer Tomorrow's Legends

Randomly inserted in regular packs at a rate of one in 13, this 10-card set focuses on young talent with bright futures. Multicolored fronts have four panels of art that serve as a background and a full-color player cutout. "Tomorrow's Legends" and player's name are printed in white type at the bottom. Backs include the player's '95 stats, biography and a full-color close-up shot.

COMPLETE SET (10) 4.00 10.00
STATED ODDS 1:13
1 Garret Anderson .30 .75
2 Jim Edmonds .30 .75
3 Brian L.Hunter .30 .75
4 Jason Isringhausen .30 .75
5 Charles Johnson .30 .75
6 Chipper Jones .75 2.00
7 Ryan Klesko .30 .75
8 Hideo Nomo .75 2.00
9 Manny Ramirez .50 1.25
10 Rondell White .30 .75

1996 Fleer Zone

This 12-card set was randomly inserted one in every 90 packs and features "unstoppable" hitters and "unhittable" pitchers. The fronts display a color action player cut-out printed on holographic foil. The backs carry a player portrait with information as to why they were selected for this set.

COMPLETE SET (12) 15.00 40.00
STATED ODDS 1:90
1 Albert Belle 1.00 2.50
2 Barry Bonds 4.00 10.00
3 Ken Griffey Jr. 5.00 12.00
4 Tony Gwynn 2.50 6.00
5 Randy Johnson 2.50 6.00
6 Kenny Lofton 1.00 2.50
7 Greg Maddux 4.00 10.00
8 Edgar Martinez 1.50 4.00
9 Mike Piazza 2.50 6.00
10 Frank Thomas 2.50 6.00
11 Mo Vaughn 1.00 2.50
12 Matt Williams 1.00 2.50

1996 Fleer Update

The 1996 Fleer Update set was issued in one series totalling 250 cards. The 11-card packs retailed for $1.49 each. The fronts feature color action player photos. The backs carry complete player stats and "Did you know?" fact. The cards are grouped alphabetically within teams and checklisted below alphabetically according to teams for each league with AL preceding NL. The set contains the subset Encore (U211-U245). Notable Rookie Cards inclu[de] Tony Batista, Mike Cameron, Matt Mantei and Ch[ris] Singleton.

COMPLETE SET (250) 12.50 30.
U1 Roberto Alomar .20
U2 Mike Devereaux .10
U3 Scott McClain RC .10
U4 Roger McDowell .10
U5 Kent Mercker .10
U6 Jimmy Myers RC .10
U7 Randy Myers .10
U8 B.J. Surhoff .10
U9 Tony Tarasco .10
U10 David Wells .10
U11 Wil Cordero .10
U12 Tom Gordon .10
U13 Reggie Jefferson .10
U14 Jose Malave .10
U15 Kevin Mitchell .10
U16 Jamie Moyer .10
U17 Heathcliff Slocumb .10
U18 Mike Stanley .10
U19 George Arias .10
U20 Jorge Fabregas .10
U21 Don Slaught .10
U22 Randy Velarde .10
U23 Harold Baines .10
U24 Mike Cameron RC .30
U25 Darren Lewis .10
U26 Tony Phillips .10
U27 Bill Simas .10
U28 Chris Snopek .10
U29 Kevin Tapani .10
U30 Danny Tartabull .10
U31 Julio Franco .10
U32 Jack McDowell .10
U33 Kimera Bartee .10
U34 Mark Lewis .10
U35 Melvin Nieves .10
U36 Mark Parent .10
U37 Eddie Williams .10
U38 Tim Belcher .10
U39 Sal Fasano .10
U40 Chris Haney .10
U41 Mike Macfarlane .10
U42 Jose Offerman .10
U43 Joe Randa .10
U44 Bip Roberts .10
U45 Chuck Carr .10
U46 Bobby Hughes .10
U47 Graeme Lloyd .10
U48 Ben McDonald .10
U49 Kevin Wickander .10
U50 Rick Aguilera .10
U51 Mike Durant .10
U52 Chip Hale .10
U53 LaTroy Hawkins .10
U54 Dave Hollins .10
U55 Roberto Kelly .10
U56 Paul Molitor .10
U57 Dan Naulty RC .10
U58 Mariano Duncan .10
U59 Andy Fox .10
U60 Joe Girardi .10
U61 Dwight Gooden .10
U62 Jimmy Key .10
U63 Matt Luke .10
U64 Tino Martinez .20 .50
U65 Jeff Nelson .10 .30
U66 Tim Raines .10 .30
U67 Ruben Rivera .10 .30
U68 Kenny Rogers .10 .30
U69 Gerald Williams .10 .30
U70 Tony Batista RC .30 .75
U71 Allen Battle .10 .30
U72 Jim Corsi .10 .30
U73 Steve Cox .10 .30
U74 Pedro Munoz .10 .30
U75 Phil Plantier .10 .30
U76 Scott Spiezio .10 .30
U77 Ernie Young .10 .30
U78 Russ Davis .10 .30
U79 Sterling Hitchcock .10 .30
U80 Edwin Hurtado .10 .30
U81 Raul Ibanez RC 1.00 2.50
U82 Mike Jackson .10 .30
U83 Ricky Jordan .10 .30
U84 Paul Sorrento .10 .30
U85 Doug Strange .10 .30
U86 Mark Brandenberg RC .10 .30
U87 Damon Buford .10 .30
U88 Kevin Elster .10 .30
U89 Darryl Hamilton .10 .30
U90 Ken Hill .10 .30
U91 Ed Vosberg .10 .30
U92 Craig Worthington .10 .30
U93 Tilson Brito RC .10 .30
U94 Giovanni Carrara RC .10 .30
U95 Felipe Crespo .10 .30
U96 Erik Hanson .10 .30
U97 Marty Janzen RC .10 .30
U98 Otis Nixon .10 .30
U99 Charlie O'Brien .10 .30
U100 Robert Perez .10 .30
U101 Paul Quantrill .10 .30
U102 Bill Risley .10 .30
U103 Juan Samuel .10 .30

104 Jermaine Dye .10 .30
105 Wonderful Monds RC .10 .30
106 Dwight Smith .10 .30
107 Jerome Walton .10 .30
108 Terry Adams .10 .30
109 Leo Gomez .10 .30
110 Robin Jennings .10 .30
111 Doug Jones .10 .30
112 Brooks Kieschnick .10 .30
113 Dave Magadan .10 .30
U114 Jason Maxwell RC .10 .30
U115 Rodney Myers RC .10 .30
U116 Eric Anthony .10 .30
U117 Vince Coleman .10 .30
U118 Eric Davis .10 .30
U119 Steve Gibralter .10 .30
U120 Curtis Goodwin .10 .30
U121 Willie Greene .10 .30
U122 Mike Kelly .10 .30
U123 Marcus Moore .10 .30
U124 Chad Mottola .10 .30
U125 Chris Sabo .10 .30
U126 Roger Salkeld .10 .30
U127 Pedro Castellano .10 .30
U128 Trenidad Hubbard .10 .30
U129 Jayhawk Owens .10 .30
U130 Jeff Reed .10 .30
U131 Kevin Brown .10 .30
U132 Al Leiter .10 .30
U133 Matt Mantei RC .20 .50
U134 Dave Weathers .10 .30
U135 Devon White .10 .30
U136 Bob Abreu .30 .75
U137 Sean Berry .10 .30
U138 Doug Brocail .10 .30
U139 Richard Hidalgo .10 .30
U140 Alvin Morman .10 .30
U141 Mike Blowers .10 .30
U142 Roger Cedeno .10 .30
U143 Greg Gagne .10 .30
U144 Karim Garcia .10 .30
U145 Wilton Guerrero RC .10 .30
U146 Israel Alcantara RC .10 .30
U147 Omar Daal .10 .30
U148 Ryan McGuire .10 .30
U149 Sherman Obando .10 .30
U150 Jose Paniagua .10 .30
U151 Henry Rodriguez .10 .30
U152 Andy Stankiewicz .10 .30
U153 Dave Veres .10 .30
U154 Juan Acevedo .10 .30
U155 Mark Clark .10 .30
U156 Bernard Gilkey .10 .30
U157 Pete Harnisch .10 .30
U158 Lance Johnson .10 .30
U159 Brent Mayne .10 .30
U160 Rey Ordonez .10 .30
U161 Kevin Roberson .10 .30
U162 Paul Wilson .10 .30
U163 David Doster RC .10 .30
U164 Mike Grace RC .10 .30
U165 Rich Hunter RC .10 .30
U166 Pete Incaviglia .10 .30
U167 Mike Lieberthal .10 .30
U168 Terry Mulholland .10 .30
U169 Ken Ryan .10 .30
U170 Benito Santiago .10 .30
U171 Kevin Sefcik RC .10 .30
U172 Lee Tinsley .10 .30
U173 Todd Zeile .10 .30
U174 Francisco Cordova RC .20 .50
U175 Danny Darwin .10 .30
U176 Charlie Hayes .10 .30
U177 Jason Kendall .10 .30
U178 Mike Kingery .10 .30
U179 Jon Lieber .10 .30
U180 Zane Smith .10 .30
U181 Luis Alicea .10 .30
U182 Cory Bailey .10 .30
U183 Andy Benes .10 .30
U184 Pat Borders .10 .30
U185 Mike Busby RC .10 .30
U186 Royce Clayton .10 .30
U187 Dennis Eckersley .10 .30
U188 Gary Gaetti .10 .30
U189 Ron Gant .10 .30
U190 Aaron Holbert .10 .30
U191 Willie McGee .10 .30
U192 Miguel Mejia RC .10 .30
U193 Jeff Parrett .10 .30
U194 Todd Stottlemyre .10 .30
U195 Sean Bergman .10 .30
U196 Archi Cianfrocco .10 .30
U197 Rickey Henderson .30 .75
U198 Wally Joyner .10 .30
U199 Craig Shipley .10 .30
U200 Bob Tewksbury .10 .30
U201 Tim Worrell .10 .30
U202 Rich Aurilia RC .20 .50
U203 Doug Creek .10 .30
U204 Shawon Dunston .10 .30
U205 Osvaldo Fernandez RC .10 .30
U206 Mark Gardner .10 .30
U207 Stan Javier .10 .30
U208 Marcus Jensen .10 .30
U209 Chris Singleton RC .20 .50
U210 Allen Watson .10 .30
U211 Jeff Bagwell ENC .20 .50
U212 Derek Bell ENC .10 .30
U213 Albert Belle ENC .10 .30
U214 Wade Boggs ENC .20 .50
U215 Barry Bonds ENC .75 2.00
U216 Jose Canseco ENC .20 .50
U217 Marty Cordova ENC .10 .30
U218 Jim Edmonds ENC .10 .30
U219 Cecil Fielder ENC .10 .30
U220 Andres Galarraga ENC .10 .30
U221 Juan Gonzalez ENC .10 .30
U222 Mark Grace ENC .20 .50
U223 Ken Griffey Jr. ENC .60 1.50
U224 Tony Gwynn ENC .40 1.00
U225 Jason Isringhausen ENC .10 .30
U226 Derek Jeter ENC .75 2.00
U227 Randy Johnson ENC .30 .75
U228 Chipper Jones ENC .30 .75
U229 Ryan Klesko ENC .10 .30
U230 Barry Larkin ENC .20 .50
U231 Kenny Lofton ENC .10 .30
U232 Greg Maddux ENC .50 1.25
U233 Raul Mondesi ENC .10 .30
U234 Hideo Nomo ENC .30 .75
U235 Mike Piazza ENC .50 1.25
U236 Manny Ramirez ENC .20 .50
U237 Cal Ripken ENC .60 1.50
U238 Tim Salmon ENC .20 .50
U239 Ryne Sandberg ENC .50 1.25
U240 Reggie Sanders ENC .10 .30
U241 Gary Sheffield ENC .10 .30
U242 Sammy Sosa ENC .30 .75
U243 Frank Thomas ENC .30 .75
U244 Mo Vaughn ENC .10 .30
U245 Matt Williams ENC .10 .30
U246 Barry Bonds CL .40 1.00
U247 Ken Griffey Jr. CL .40 1.00
U248 Rey Ordonez CL .10 .30
U249 Ryne Sandberg CL .30 .75
U250 Frank Thomas CL .20 .50

1996 Fleer Update Tiffany

COMPLETE SET (250) 60.00 120.00
*STARS: 1.25X TO 3X BASIC CARDS
*ROOKIES: 2X TO 5X BASIC CARDS
ONE TIFFANY PER PACK

1996 Fleer Update Diamond Tribute

Randomly inserted in packs at a rate of one in 100, this 10-card set spotlights future Hall of Famers with holographic foils in a diamond design.

COMPLETE SET (10) 75.00 150.00
STATED ODDS 1:100
1 Wade Boggs 2.50 6.00
2 Barry Bonds 10.00 25.00
3 Ken Griffey Jr. 8.00 20.00
4 Tony Gwynn 5.00 12.00
5 Rickey Henderson 4.00 10.00
6 Greg Maddux 6.00 15.00
7 Eddie Murray 4.00 10.00
8 Cal Ripken 12.50 30.00
9 Ozzie Smith 6.00 15.00
10 Frank Thomas 4.00 10.00

1996 Fleer Update Headliners

Randomly inserted exclusively in retail packs at a rate of one in 20, cards from this 20-card set feature raised textured printing. The fronts carry color action player photos with the word "headliner" running continuously across the background.

COMPLETE SET (20) 15.00 40.00
STATED ODDS 1:5 RETAIL
1 Roberto Alomar .50 1.25
2 Jeff Bagwell .50 1.25
3 Albert Belle .30 .75
4 Barry Bonds 2.00 5.00
5 Cecil Fielder .30 .75
6 Juan Gonzalez .30 .75
7 Ken Griffey Jr. 1.50 4.00
8 Tony Gwynn 1.00 2.50
9 Randy Johnson .75 2.00
10 Chipper Jones .75 2.00
11 Ryan Klesko .30 .75
12 Kenny Lofton .30 .75
13 Greg Maddux 1.25 3.00
14 Hideo Nomo .75 2.00
15 Mike Piazza 1.25 3.00
16 Manny Ramirez .50 1.25
17 Cal Ripken 2.50 6.00
18 Tim Salmon .50 1.25
19 Frank Thomas .75 2.00
20 Matt Williams .30 .75

1996 Fleer Update New Horizons

Randomly inserted in hobby packs only at a rate of one in five, this 20-card set features 1996 rookies and prospects. The fronts carry player action color photos printed on foil cards. The backs display a player portrait and information about the player.

COMPLETE SET (20) 6.00 15.00
STATED ODDS 1:5 HOBBY
1 Bob Abreu .60 1.50
2 George Arias .20 .50
3 Tony Batista .40 1.00
4 Steve Cox .20 .50
5 Jermaine Dye .20 .50
6 Andy Fox .20 .50
7 Mike Grace .20 .50
8 Todd Greene .20 .50
9 Wilton Guerrero .20 .50
10 Richard Hidalgo .20 .50
11 Raul Ibanez .50 1.25
12 Robin Jennings .20 .50
13 Marcus Jensen .20 .50
14 Jason Kendall .20 .50
15 Jason Maxwell .20 .50
16 Ryan McGuire .20 .50
17 Miguel Mejia .20 .50
18 Wonderful Monds .20 .50
19 Rey Ordonez .20 .50
20 Paul Wilson .20 .50

1996 Fleer Update Smooth Leather

Randomly inserted in packs at a rate of one in five, this 10-card set features defensive stars. The fronts display color player photos and gold foil printing. The backs carry a player portrait and information about why the player was selected for this set.

COMPLETE SET (10) 4.00 10.00
STATED ODDS 1:5
1 Roberto Alomar .25 .60
2 Barry Bonds 1.00 2.50
3 Will Clark .25 .60
4 Ken Griffey Jr. .75 2.00
5 Kenny Lofton .15 .40
6 Greg Maddux .60 1.50
7 Raul Mondesi .15 .40
8 Rey Ordonez .15 .40
9 Cal Ripken 1.25 3.00
10 Matt Williams .15 .40

1996 Fleer Update Soaring Stars

Randomly inserted in packs at a rate of one in 11, this 10-card set features 10 of the hottest young players. The fronts carry color player cut-outs on a background of soaring baseballs in etched foil. The backs display another player photo on the same background with player information.

COMPLETE SET (10) 10.00 25.00
STATED ODDS 1:11
1 Jeff Bagwell .50 1.25
2 Barry Bonds 2.00 5.00
3 Juan Gonzalez .30 .75
4 Ken Griffey Jr. 1.50 4.00
5 Chipper Jones .75 2.00
6 Greg Maddux 1.25 3.00
7 Mike Piazza 1.25 3.00
8 Manny Ramirez .50 1.25
9 Frank Thomas .75 2.00
10 Matt Williams .30 .75

1997 Fleer

The 1997 Fleer set was issued in two series totaling 761 cards and distributed in 10-card packs with a suggested retail price of $1.49. The fronts feature color action player photos with a matte finish and gold foil printing. The backs carry another player photo with player information and career statistics. Cards 491-500 are a Checklist subset of Series one and feature black-and-white or sepia tone photos of big-name players. Series two contains the following subsets: Encore (696-720) which are redesigned cards of the big-name players from Series one, and Checklists (721-748). Cards 749 and 750 are expansion team logo cards with the insert checklists on the backs. Many dealers believe that cards numbered 751-761 were shortprinted. An Andruw Jones autographed Circa card numbered to 200 was also randomly inserted into packs. Rookie Cards in this set include Jose Cruz Jr., Brian Giles and Fernando Tatis.

COMPLETE SET (761) 30.00 80.00
COMPLETE SERIES 1 (500) 12.50 30.00
COMPLETE SERIES 2 (261) 15.00 40.00
COMMON CARD (1-750) .10 .30
COMMON CARD (751-761) .20 .50
751-761 BELIEVED TO BE SHORT-PRINTED
A.JONES CIRCA AU RANDOM IN PACKS
SUBSET CARDS HALF VALUE OF BASE CARDS
1 Roberto Alomar .20 .50
2 Brady Anderson .10 .30
3 Bobby Bonilla .10 .30
4 Rocky Coppinger .10 .30
5 Cesar Devarez .10 .30
6 Scott Erickson .10 .30
7 Jeffrey Hammonds .10 .30
8 Chris Hoiles .10 .30
9 Eddie Murray .30 .75
10 Mike Mussina .20 .50
11 Randy Myers .10 .30
12 Rafael Palmeiro .20 .50
13 Cal Ripken 1.00 2.50
14 B.J. Surhoff .10 .30
15 David Wells .10 .30
16 Todd Zeile .10 .30
17 Darren Bragg .10 .30
18 Jose Canseco .20 .50
19 Roger Clemens .60 1.50
20 Wil Cordero .10 .30
21 Jeff Frye .10 .30
22 Nomar Garciaparra .50 1.25
23 Tom Gordon .10 .30
24 Mike Greenwell .10 .30
25 Reggie Jefferson .10 .30
26 Jose Malave .10 .30
27 Tim Naehring .10 .30
28 Troy O'Leary .10 .30
29 Heathcliff Slocumb .10 .30
30 Mike Stanley .10 .30
31 John Valentin .10 .30
32 Mo Vaughn .10 .30
33 Tim Wakefield .10 .30
34 Garret Anderson .10 .30
35 George Arias .10 .30
36 Shawn Boskie .10 .30
37 Chili Davis .10 .30
38 Jason Dickson .10 .30
39 Gary DiSarcina .10 .30
40 Jim Edmonds .10 .30
41 Darin Erstad .10 .30
42 Jorge Fabregas .10 .30
43 Chuck Finley .10 .30
44 Todd Greene .10 .30
45 Mike Holtz .10 .30
46 Rex Hudler .10 .30
47 Mike James .10 .30
48 Mark Langston .10 .30
49 Troy Percival .10 .30
50 Tim Salmon .20 .50
51 Jeff Schmidt .10 .30
52 J.T. Snow .10 .30
53 Randy Velarde .10 .30
54 Wilson Alvarez .10 .30
55 Harold Baines .10 .30
56 James Baldwin .10 .30
57 Jason Bere .10 .30
58 Mike Cameron .10 .30
59 Ray Durham .10 .30
60 Alex Fernandez .10 .30
61 Ozzie Guillen .10 .30
62 Roberto Hernandez .10 .30
63 Ron Karkovice .10 .30
64 Darren Lewis .10 .30
65 Dave Martinez .10 .30
66 Lyle Mouton .10 .30
67 Greg Norton .10 .30
68 Tony Phillips .10 .30
69 Chris Snopek .10 .30
70 Kevin Tapani .10 .30
71 Danny Tartabull .10 .30
72 Frank Thomas .30 .75
73 Robin Ventura .10 .30
74 Sandy Alomar Jr. .10 .30
75 Albert Belle .10 .30
76 Mark Carreon .10 .30
77 Julio Franco .10 .30
78 Brian Giles RC .60 1.50
79 Orel Hershiser .10 .30
80 Kenny Lofton .10 .30
81 Dennis Martinez .10 .30
82 Jack McDowell .10 .30
83 Jose Mesa .10 .30
84 Charles Nagy .10 .30
85 Chad Ogea .10 .30
86 Eric Plunk .10 .30
87 Manny Ramirez .20 .50
88 Kevin Seitzer .10 .30
89 Julian Tavarez .10 .30
90 Jim Thome .20 .50
91 Jose Vizcaino .10 .30
92 Omar Vizquel .20 .50
93 Brad Ausmus .10 .30
94 Kimera Bartee .10 .30
95 Raul Casanova .10 .30
96 Tony Clark .10 .30
97 John Cummings .10 .30
98 Travis Fryman .10 .30
99 Bob Higginson .10 .30
100 Mark Lewis .10 .30
101 Felipe Lira .10 .30
102 Phil Nevin .10 .30
103 Melvin Nieves .10 .30
104 Curtis Pride .10 .30
105 A.J. Sager .10 .30
106 Ruben Sierra .10 .30
107 Justin Thompson .10 .30
108 Alan Trammell .10 .30
109 Kevin Appier .10 .30
110 Tim Belcher .10 .30
111 Jaime Bluma .10 .30
112 Johnny Damon .20 .50
113 Tom Goodwin .10 .30
114 Chris Haney .10 .30
115 Keith Lockhart .10 .30
116 Mike Macfarlane .10 .30
117 Jeff Montgomery .10 .30
118 Jose Offerman .10 .30
119 Craig Paquette .10 .30
120 Joe Randa .10 .30
121 Bip Roberts .10 .30
122 Jose Rosado .10 .30
123 Mike Sweeney .10 .30
124 Michael Tucker .10 .30
125 Jeromy Burnitz .10 .30
126 Jeff Cirillo .10 .30
127 Jeff D'Amico .10 .30
128 Mike Fetters .10 .30
129 John Jaha .10 .30
130 Scott Karl .10 .30
131 Jesse Levis .10 .30
132 Mark Loretta .10 .30
133 Mike Matheny .10 .30
134 Ben McDonald .10 .30
135 Matt Mieske .10 .30
136 Marc Newfield .10 .30
137 Dave Nilsson .10 .30
138 Jose Valentin .10 .30
139 Fernando Vina .10 .30
140 Bob Wickman .10 .30
141 Gerald Williams .10 .30
142 Rick Aguilera .10 .30
143 Rich Becker .10 .30
144 Ron Coomer .10 .30
145 Marty Cordova .10 .30
146 Roberto Kelly .10 .30
147 Chuck Knoblauch .10 .30
148 Matt Lawton .10 .30
149 Pat Meares .10 .30
150 Travis Miller .10 .30
151 Paul Molitor .10 .30
152 Greg Myers .10 .30
153 Dan Naulty .10 .30
154 Kirby Puckett .30 .75
155 Brad Radke .10 .30
156 Frank Rodriguez .10 .30
157 Scott Stahoviak .10 .30
158 Dave Stevens .10 .30
159 Matt Walbeck .10 .30
160 Todd Walker .10 .30
161 Wade Boggs .20 .50
162 David Cone .10 .30
163 Mariano Duncan .10 .30
164 Cecil Fielder .10 .30
165 Joe Girardi .10 .30
166 Dwight Gooden .10 .30
167 Charlie Hayes .10 .30
168 Derek Jeter .75 2.00
169 Jimmy Key .10 .30
170 Jim Leyritz .10 .30
171 Tino Martinez .20 .50
172 Ramiro Mendoza RC .10 .30
173 Jeff Nelson .10 .30
174 Paul O'Neill .20 .50
175 Andy Pettitte .20 .50
176 Mariano Rivera .30 .75
177 Ruben Rivera .10 .30
178 Kenny Rogers .10 .30
179 Darryl Strawberry .10 .30
180 John Wetteland .10 .30
181 Bernie Williams .20 .50
182 Willie Adams .10 .30
183 Tony Batista .10 .30
184 Geronimo Berroa .10 .30
185 Mike Bordick .10 .30
186 Scott Brosius .10 .30
187 Bobby Chouinard .10 .30
188 Jim Corsi .10 .30
189 Brent Gates .10 .30
190 Jason Giambi .10 .30
191 Jose Herrera .10 .30
192 Damon Mashore .10 .30
193 Mark McGwire .75 2.00
194 Mike Mohler .10 .30
195 Scott Spiezio .10 .30
196 Terry Steinbach .10 .30
197 Bill Taylor .10 .30
198 John Wasdin .10 .30
199 Steve Wojciechowski .10 .30
200 Ernie Young .10 .30
201 Rich Amaral .10 .30
202 Jay Buhner .10 .30
203 Norm Charlton .10 .30
204 Joey Cora .10 .30
205 Russ Davis .10 .30
206 Ken Griffey Jr. .60 1.50
207 Sterling Hitchcock .10 .30
208 Brian Hunter .10 .30
209 Raul Ibanez .10 .30
210 Randy Johnson .30 .75
211 Edgar Martinez .20 .50
212 Jamie Moyer .10 .30
213 Alex Rodriguez .50 1.25
214 Paul Sorrento .10 .30
215 Matt Wagner .10 .30
216 Bob Wells .10 .30
217 Dan Wilson .10 .30
218 Damon Buford .10 .30
219 Will Clark .20 .50
220 Kevin Elster .10 .30
221 Juan Gonzalez .10 .30
222 Rusty Greer .10 .30
223 Kevin Gross .10 .30
224 Darryl Hamilton .10 .30
225 Mike Henneman .10 .30
226 Ken Hill .10 .30
227 Mark McLemore .10 .30
228 Darren Oliver .10 .30
229 Dean Palmer .10 .30
230 Roger Pavlik .10 .30
231 Ivan Rodriguez .20 .50
232 Mickey Tettleton .10 .30
233 Bobby Witt .10 .30
234 Jacob Brumfield .10 .30
235 Joe Carter .10 .30
236 Tim Crabtree .10 .30
237 Carlos Delgado .10 .30
238 Huck Flener .10 .30
239 Alex Gonzalez .10 .30
240 Shawn Green .10 .30
241 Juan Guzman .10 .30
242 Pat Hentgen .10 .30
243 Marty Janzen .10 .30
244 Sandy Martinez .10 .30
245 Otis Nixon .10 .30
246 Charlie O'Brien .10 .30
247 John Olerud .10 .30
248 Robert Perez .10 .30
249 Ed Sprague .10 .30
250 Mike Timlin .10 .30
251 Steve Avery .10 .30
252 Jeff Blauser .10 .30
253 Brad Clontz .10 .30
254 Jermaine Dye .10 .30
255 Tom Glavine .20 .50
256 Marquis Grissom .10 .30
257 Andruw Jones .20 .50
258 Chipper Jones .30 .75
259 David Justice .10 .30
260 Ryan Klesko .10 .30
261 Mark Lemke .10 .30
262 Javier Lopez .10 .30
263 Greg Maddux .50 1.25
264 Fred McGriff .20 .50
265 Greg McMichael .10 .30
266 Denny Neagle .10 .30
267 Terry Pendleton .10 .30
268 Eddie Perez .10 .30
269 John Smoltz .20 .50
270 Terrell Wade .10 .30
271 Mark Wohlers .10 .30
272 Terry Adams .10 .30
273 Brant Brown .10 .30
274 Leo Gomez .10 .30
275 Luis Gonzalez .10 .30
276 Mark Grace .20 .50
277 Tyler Houston .10 .30
278 Robin Jennings .10 .30
279 Brooks Kieschnick .10 .30
280 Brian McRae .10 .30
281 Jaime Navarro .10 .30
282 Ryne Sandberg .50 1.25
283 Scott Servais .10 .30
284 Sammy Sosa .30 .75
285 Dave Swartzbaugh .10 .30
286 Amaury Telemaco .10 .30
287 Steve Trachsel .10 .30
288 Pedro Valdes .10 .30
289 Turk Wendell .10 .30
290 Bret Boone .10 .30
291 Jeff Branson .10 .30
292 Jeff Brantley .10 .30
293 Eric Davis .10 .30
294 Willie Greene .10 .30
295 Thomas Howard .10 .30
296 Barry Larkin .20 .50
297 Kevin Mitchell .10 .30
298 Hal Morris .10 .30
299 Chad Mottola .10 .30
300 Joe Oliver .10 .30
301 Mark Portugal .10 .30
302 Roger Salkeld .10 .30
303 Reggie Sanders .10 .30
304 Pete Schourek .10 .30
305 John Smiley .10 .30
306 Eddie Taubensee .10 .30
307 Dante Bichette .10 .30
308 Ellis Burks .10 .30
309 Vinny Castilla .10 .30
310 Andres Galarraga .10 .30
311 Curt Leskanic .10 .30
312 Quinton McCracken .10 .30
313 Neifi Perez .10 .30
314 Jeff Reed .10 .30
315 Steve Reed .10 .30
316 Armando Reynoso .10 .30
317 Kevin Ritz .10 .30
318 Bruce Ruffin .10 .30
319 Larry Walker .10 .30
320 Walt Weiss .10 .30
321 Jamey Wright .10 .30
322 Eric Young .10 .30
323 Kurt Abbott .10 .30
324 Alex Arias .10 .30
325 Kevin Brown .10 .30
326 Luis Castillo .10 .30
327 Greg Colbrunn .10 .30
328 Jeff Conine .10 .30
329 Andre Dawson .10 .30
330 Charles Johnson .10 .30
331 Al Leiter .10 .30
332 Ralph Milliard .10 .30
333 Robb Nen .10 .30
334 Pat Rapp .10 .30
335 Edgar Renteria .10 .30
336 Gary Sheffield .10 .30
337 Devon White .10 .30
338 Bob Abreu .20 .50
339 Jeff Bagwell .20 .50
340 Derek Bell .10 .30
341 Sean Berry .10 .30
342 Craig Biggio .20 .50
343 Doug Drabek .10 .30
344 Tony Eusebio .10 .30
345 Ricky Gutierrez .10 .30
346 Mike Hampton .10 .30
347 Brian Hunter .10 .30
348 Todd Jones .10 .30
349 Darryl Kile .10 .30
350 Derrick May .10 .30
351 Orlando Miller .10 .30
352 James Mouton .10 .30
353 Shane Reynolds .10 .30
354 Billy Wagner .10 .30
355 Donne Wall .10 .30
356 Mike Blowers .10 .30
357 Brett Butler .10 .30
358 Roger Cedeno .10 .30
359 Chad Curtis .10 .30
360 Delino DeShields .10 .30
361 Greg Gagne .10 .30
362 Karim Garcia .10 .30
363 Wilton Guerrero .10 .30
364 Todd Hollandsworth .10 .30
365 Eric Karros .10 .30
366 Ramon Martinez .10 .30
367 Raul Mondesi .10 .30
368 Hideo Nomo .30 .75
369 Antonio Osuna .10 .30
370 Chan Ho Park .10 .30
371 Mike Piazza .50 1.25
372 Ismael Valdes .10 .30
373 Todd Worrell .10 .30
374 Moises Alou .10 .30
375 Shane Andrews .10 .30
376 Yamil Benitez .10 .30
377 Jeff Fassero .10 .30
378 Darrin Fletcher .10 .30
379 Cliff Floyd .10 .30
380 Mark Grudzielanek .10 .30
381 Mike Lansing .10 .30
382 Barry Manuel .10 .30
383 Pedro Martinez .20 .50
384 Henry Rodriguez .10 .30
385 Mel Rojas .10 .30
386 F.P. Santangelo .10 .30
387 David Segui .10 .30
388 Ugueth Urbina .10 .30
389 Rondell White .10 .30
390 Edgardo Alfonzo .10 .30
391 Carlos Baerga .10 .30
392 Mark Clark .10 .30
393 Alvaro Espinoza .10 .30
394 John Franco .10 .30
395 Bernard Gilkey .10 .30
396 Pete Harnisch .10 .30
397 Todd Hundley .10 .30
398 Butch Huskey .10 .30
399 Jason Isringhausen .10 .30
400 Lance Johnson .10 .30
401 Bobby Jones .10 .30
402 Alex Ochoa .10 .30
403 Rey Ordonez .10 .30
404 Robert Person .10 .30
405 Paul Wilson .10 .30
406 Matt Beech .10 .30
407 Ron Blazier .10 .30
408 Ricky Bottalico .10 .30
409 Lenny Dykstra .20 .50
410 Jim Eisenreich .10 .30
411 Bobby Estalella .10 .30
412 Mike Grace .10 .30
413 Gregg Jefferies .10 .30
414 Mike Lieberthal .10 .30
415 Wendell Magee .10 .30
416 Mickey Morandini .10 .30
417 Ricky Otero .10 .30
418 Scott Rolen .20 .50
419 Ken Ryan .10 .30
420 Benito Santiago .10 .30
421 Curt Schilling .10 .30
422 Kevin Sefcik .10 .30
423 Jermaine Allensworth .10 .30
424 Trey Beamon .10 .30
425 Jay Bell .10 .30
426 Francisco Cordova .10 .30
427 Carlos Garcia .10 .30
428 Mark Johnson .10 .30
429 Jason Kendall .10 .30
430 Jeff King .10 .30
431 Jon Lieber .10 .30
432 Al Martin .10 .30
433 Orlando Merced .10 .30
434 Ramon Morel .10 .30
435 Matt Ruebel .10 .30
436 Jason Schmidt .10 .30

437 Marc Wilkins .10 .30
438 Alan Benes .10 .30
439 Andy Benes .10 .30
440 Royce Clayton .10 .30
441 Dennis Eckersley .10 .30
442 Gary Gaetti .10 .30
443 Ron Gant .10 .30
444 Aaron Holbert .10 .30
445 Brian Jordan .10 .30
446 Ray Lankford .10 .30
447 John Mabry .10 .30
448 T.J. Mathews .10 .30
449 Willie McGee .10 .30
450 Donovan Osborne .10 .30
451 Tom Pagnozzi .10 .30
452 Ozzie Smith .50 1.25
453 Todd Stottlemyre .10 .30
454 Mark Sweeney .10 .30
455 Dmitri Young .10 .30
456 Andy Ashby .10 .30
457 Ken Caminiti .10 .30
458 Archi Cianfrocco .10 .30
459 Steve Finley .10 .30
460 John Flaherty .10 .30
461 Chris Gomez .10 .30
462 Tony Gwynn .40 1.00
463 Joey Hamilton .10 .30
464 Rickey Henderson .30 .75
465 Trevor Hoffman .10 .30
466 Brian Johnson .10 .30
467 Wally Joyner .10 .30
468 Jody Reed .10 .30
469 Scott Sanders .10 .30
470 Bob Tewksbury .10 .30
471 Fernando Valenzuela .10 .30
472 Greg Vaughn .10 .30
473 Tim Worrell .10 .30
474 Rich Aurilia .10 .30
475 Rod Beck .10 .30
476 Marvin Benard .10 .30
477 Barry Bonds .75 2.00
478 Jay Canizaro .10 .30
479 Shawon Dunston .10 .30
480 Shawn Estes .10 .30
481 Mark Gardner .10 .30
482 Glenallen Hill .10 .30
483 Stan Javier .10 .30
484 Marcus Jensen .10 .30
485 Bill Mueller RC .50 1.25
486 Wm. VanLandingham .10 .30
487 Allen Watson .10 .30
488 Rick Wilkins .10 .30
489 Matt Williams .10 .30
490 Desi Wilson .10 .30
491 Albert Belle CL .10 .30
492 Ken Griffey Jr. CL .40 1.00
493 Andruw Jones CL .10 .30
494 Chipper Jones CL .20 .50
495 Mark McGwire CL .40 1.00
496 Paul Molitor CL .10 .30
497 Mike Piazza CL .30 .75
498 Cal Ripken CL .50 1.25
499 Alex Rodriguez CL .30 .75
500 Frank Thomas CL .20 .50
501 Kenny Lofton .10 .30
502 Carlos Perez .10 .30
503 Tim Raines .10 .30
504 Danny Patterson .10 .30
505 Derrick May .10 .30
506 Dave Hollins .10 .30
507 Felipe Crespo .10 .30
508 Brian Banks .10 .30
509 Jeff Kent .10 .30
510 Bubba Trammell RC .15 .40
511 Robert Person .10 .30
512 David Arias-Ortiz RC 30.00 80.00
513 Ryan Jones .10 .30
514 David Justice .10 .30
515 Will Cunnane .10 .30
516 Russ Johnson .10 .30
517 John Burkett .10 .30
518 Robinson Checo RC .10 .30
519 Ricardo Rincon RC .10 .30
520 Woody Williams .10 .30
521 Rick Helling .10 .30
522 Jorge Posada .20 .50
523 Kevin Orie .10 .30
524 Fernando Tatis RC .10 .30
525 Jermaine Dye .10 .30
526 Brian Hunter .10 .30
527 Greg McMichael .10 .30
528 Matt Wagner .10 .30
529 Richie Sexson .10 .30
530 Scott Ruffcorn .10 .30
531 Luis Gonzalez .10 .30
532 Mike Johnson RC .10 .30
533 Mark Petkovsek .10 .30
534 Doug Drabek .10 .30
535 Jose Canseco .20 .50
536 Bobby Bonilla .10 .30
537 J.T. Snow .10 .30
538 Shawon Dunston .10 .30
539 John Ericks .10 .30
540 Terry Steinbach .10 .30
541 Jay Bell .10 .30
542 Joe Borowski RC .15 .40
543 David Wells .10 .30
544 Justin Towle RC .10 .30
545 Mike Blowers .10 .30
546 Shannon Stewart .10 .30
547 Rudy Pemberton .10 .30
548 Bill Swift .10 .30
549 Osvaldo Fernandez .10 .30
550 Eddie Murray .30 .75
551 Don Wengert .10 .30
552 Brad Ausmus .10 .30
553 Carlos Garcia .10 .30
554 Jose Guillen .10 .30
555 Rheal Cormier .10 .30
556 Doug Brocail .10 .30
557 Rex Hudler .10 .30
558 Armando Benitez .10 .30
559 Eli Marrero .10 .30
560 Ricky Ledee RC .15 .40
561 Bartolo Colon .10 .30
562 Quilvio Veras .10 .30
563 Alex Fernandez .10 .30
564 Darren Dreifort .10 .30
565 Benji Gil .10 .30
566 Kent Mercker .10 .30
567 Glendon Rusch .10 .30
568 Ramon Tatis RC .10 .30
569 Roger Clemens .60 1.50
570 Mark Lewis .10 .30
571 Emil Brown RC .10 .30
572 Jaime Navarro .10 .30
573 Sherman Obando .10 .30
574 John Wasdin .10 .30
575 Calvin Maduro .10 .30
576 Todd Jones .10 .30
577 Orlando Merced .10 .30
578 Cal Eldred .10 .30
579 Mark Gubicza .10 .30
580 Michael Tucker .10 .30
581 Tony Saunders RC .10 .30
582 Garvin Alston .10 .30
583 Joe Roa .10 .30
584 Brady Raggio RC .10 .30
585 Jimmy Key .10 .30
586 Marc Sagmoen RC .10 .30
587 Jim Bullinger .10 .30
588 Yorkis Perez .10 .30
589 Jose Cruz Jr. RC .15 .40
590 Mike Stanton .10 .30
591 Delvi Cruz RC .15 .40
592 Steve Karsay .10 .30
593 Mike Trombley .10 .30
594 Doug Glanville .10 .30
595 Scott Sanders .10 .30
596 Thomas Howard .10 .30
597 T.J. Staton RC .10 .30
598 Garrett Stephenson .10 .30
599 Rico Brogna .10 .30
600 Albert Belle .10 .30
601 Jose Vizcaino .10 .30
602 Chili Davis .10 .30
603 Shane Mack .10 .30
604 Jim Eisenreich .10 .30
605 Todd Zeile .10 .30
606 Brian Boehringer RC .10 .30
607 Paul Shuey .10 .30
608 Kevin Tapani .10 .30
609 John Wetteland .10 .30
610 Jim Leyritz .10 .30
611 Ray Montgomery RC .10 .30
612 Doug Bochtler .10 .30
613 Wady Almonte RC .10 .30
614 Danny Tartabull .10 .30
615 Orlando Miller .10 .30
616 Bobby Ayala .10 .30
617 Tony Graffanino .10 .30
618 Marc Valdes .10 .30
619 Ron Villone .10 .30
620 Derrek Lee .20 .50
621 Greg Colbrunn .10 .30
622 Felix Heredia RC .15 .40
623 Carl Everett .10 .30
624 Mark Thompson .10 .30
625 Jeff Granger .10 .30
626 Damian Jackson .10 .30
627 Mark Leiter .10 .30
628 Chris Holt .10 .30
629 Dario Veras RC .10 .30
630 Dave Burba .10 .30
631 Darryl Hamilton .10 .30
632 Mark Acre .10 .30
633 Fernando Hernandez RC .10 .30
634 Terry Mulholland .10 .30
635 Dustin Hermanson .10 .30
636 Delino DeShields .10 .30
637 Steve Avery .10 .30
638 Tony Womack RC .15 .40
639 Mark Whiten .10 .30
640 Marquis Grissom .10 .30
641 Xavier Hernandez .10 .30
642 Eric Davis .10 .30
643 Bob Tewksbury .10 .30
644 Dante Powell .10 .30
645 Carlos Castillo RC .10 .30
646 Chris Widger .10 .30
647 Moises Alou .10 .30
648 Pat Listach .10 .30
649 Edgar Ramos RC .10 .30
650 Deion Sanders .20 .50
651 John Olerud .10 .30
652 Todd Dunwoody .10 .30
653 Randall Simon RC .15 .40
654 Dan Carlson .10 .30
655 Matt Williams .10 .30
656 Jeff King .10 .30
657 Luis Alicea .10 .30
658 Brian Moehler RC .15 .40
659 Ariel Prieto .10 .30
660 Kevin Elster .10 .30
661 Mark Hutton .10 .30
662 Aaron Sele .10 .30
663 Graeme Lloyd .10 .30
664 John Burke .10 .30
665 Mel Rojas .10 .30
666 Sid Fernandez .10 .30
667 Pedro Astacio .10 .30
668 Jeff Abbott .10 .30
669 Darren Daulton .10 .30
670 Mike Bordick .10 .30
671 Sterling Hitchcock .10 .30
672 Damion Easley .10 .30
673 Armando Reynoso .10 .30
674 Pat Cline .10 .30
675 Orlando Cabrera RC .30 .75
676 Alan Embree .10 .30
677 Brian Bevil .10 .30
678 David Weathers .10 .30
679 Cliff Floyd .10 .30
680 Joe Randa .10 .30
681 Bill Haselman .10 .30
682 Jeff Fassero .10 .30
683 Matt Morris .10 .30
684 Mark Portugal .10 .30
685 Lee Smith .10 .30
686 Pokey Reese .10 .30
687 Benito Santiago .10 .30
688 Brian Johnson .10 .30
689 Brent Brede RC .10 .30
690 Shigetoshi Hasegawa RC .20 .50
691 Julio Santana .10 .30
692 Steve Kline .10 .30
693 Julian Tavarez .10 .30
694 John Hudek .10 .30
695 Manny Alexander .10 .30
696 Roberto Alomar ENC .10 .30
697 Jeff Bagwell ENC .10 .30
698 Barry Bonds ENC .40 1.00
699 Ken Caminiti ENC .10 .30
700 Juan Gonzalez ENC .10 .30
701 Ken Griffey Jr. ENC .40 1.00
702 Tony Gwynn ENC .20 .50
703 Derek Jeter ENC .40 1.00
704 Andruw Jones ENC .20 .50
705 Chipper Jones ENC .20 .50
706 Barry Larkin ENC .10 .30
707 Greg Maddux ENC .30 .75
708 Mark McGwire ENC .40 1.00
709 Paul Molitor ENC .10 .30
710 Hideo Nomo ENC .10 .30
711 Andy Pettitte ENC .10 .30
712 Mike Piazza ENC .30 .75
713 Manny Ramirez ENC .20 .50
714 Cal Ripken ENC .50 1.25
715 Alex Rodriguez ENC .30 .75
716 Ryne Sandberg ENC .30 .75
717 John Smoltz ENC .10 .30
718 Frank Thomas ENC .20 .50
719 Mo Vaughn ENC .10 .30
720 Bernie Williams ENC .10 .30
721 Tim Salmon CL .10 .30
722 Greg Maddux CL .30 .75
723 Cal Ripken CL .50 1.25
724 Mo Vaughn CL .10 .30
725 Ryne Sandberg CL .30 .75
726 Frank Thomas CL .20 .50
727 Barry Larkin CL .10 .30
728 Manny Ramirez CL .10 .30
729 Andres Galarraga CL .10 .30
730 Tony Clark CL .10 .30
731 Gary Sheffield CL .10 .30
732 Jeff Bagwell CL .10 .30
733 Kevin Appier CL .10 .30
734 Mike Piazza CL .30 .75
735 Jeff Cirillo CL .10 .30
736 Paul Molitor CL .10 .30
737 Henry Rodriguez CL .10 .30
738 Todd Hundley CL .10 .30
739 Derek Jeter CL .40 1.00
740 Mark McGwire CL .40 1.00
741 Curt Schilling CL .10 .30
742 Jason Kendall CL .10 .30
743 Tony Gwynn CL .20 .50
744 Barry Bonds CL .40 1.00
745 Ken Griffey Jr. CL .40 1.00
746 Brian Jordan CL .10 .30
747 Juan Gonzalez CL .10 .30
748 Joe Carter CL .10 .30
749 Arizona Diamondbacks CL .10 .30
750 Tampa Bay Devil Rays CL .10 .30
751 Hideki Irabu RC .30 .75
752 Jeremi Gonzalez RC .20 .50
753 Mario Valdez RC .20 .50
754 Aaron Boone .30 .75
755 Brett Tomko .20 .50
756 Jaret Wright RC .30 .75
757 Ryan McGuire .20 .50
758 Jason McDonald .20 .50
759 Adrian Brown RC .20 .50
760 Keith Foulke RC .75 2.00
761 Bonus Checklist (751-761) .20 .50
P489 Matt Williams Promo .40 1.00
NNO A.Jones Circa AU/200 10.00 25.00

1997 Fleer Tiffany

*TIFFANY 1-750: 10X TO 25X BASIC CARDS
*TIFFANY RC's 1-750: 6X TO 15X BASIC
*TIFFANY 751-761: 4X TO 10X BASIC
*TIFFANY 751-761: 3X TO 8X BASIC RC'S
STATED ODDS 1:20
512 David Arias-Ortiz 200.00 400.00
675 Orlando Cabrera 5.00 12.00
760 Keith Foulke 6.00 15.00

1997 Fleer Bleacher Blasters

Randomly inserted in Fleer series two retail packs only at a rate of one in 36, this 10-card set features color action photos of power hitters who reach the bleachers with great frequency.
COMPLETE SET (10) 20.00 50.00
SER.2 STATED ODDS 1:36 RETAIL
1 Albert Belle 1.25 3.00
2 Barry Bonds 5.00 12.00
3 Juan Gonzalez 1.25 3.00
4 Ken Griffey Jr. 12.00 30.00
5 Mark McGwire 5.00 12.00
6 Mike Piazza 3.00 8.00
7 Alex Rodriguez 4.00 10.00
8 Frank Thomas 3.00 8.00
9 Mo Vaughn 1.25 3.00
10 Matt Williams 1.25 3.00

1997 Fleer Decade of Excellence

Randomly inserted in Fleer Series two hobby packs only at a rate of one in 36, this 12-card set spotlights players who started their major league careers no later than 1987. The set features photos of these players from the 1987 season in the 1987 Fleer Baseball card design.
COMPLETE SET (12) 10.00 25.00
SER.2 STATED ODDS 1:36 HOBBY
*RARE TRAD: 2X TO 5X BASIC DECADE
RARE TRAD STATED ODDS 1:360 HOBBY
1 Wade Boggs .60 1.50
2 Barry Bonds 1.50 4.00
3 Roger Clemens 1.25 3.00
4 Tony Gwynn 1.00 2.50
5 Rickey Henderson 1.00 2.50
6 Greg Maddux 1.50 4.00
7 Mark McGwire 1.50 4.00
8 Paul Molitor 1.00 2.50
9 Eddie Murray .60 1.50
10 Cal Ripken 3.00 8.00
11 Ryne Sandberg 1.50 4.00
12 Matt Williams .40 1.00

1997 Fleer Diamond Tribute

Randomly inserted in Fleer Series two packs at a rate of one in 288, this 12-card set features color action images of Baseball's top players on a dazzling foil background.
SER.2 STATED ODDS 1:288
1 Albert Belle 1.00 2.50
2 Barry Bonds 4.00 10.00
3 Juan Gonzalez 1.00 2.50
4 Ken Griffey Jr. 20.00 50.00
5 Tony Gwynn 2.50 6.00
6 Greg Maddux 4.00 10.00
7 Mark McGwire 4.00 10.00
8 Eddie Murray 1.50 4.00
9 Mike Piazza 2.50 6.00
10 Cal Ripken 8.00 20.00
11 Alex Rodriguez 3.00 8.00
12 Frank Thomas 2.50 6.00

1997 Fleer Golden Memories

Randomly inserted in first series packs at a rate of one in 16, this ten-card set commemorates major achievements by individual players from the 1996 season. The fronts feature color player images on a background of the top portion of the sun and its rays. The backs carry player information.
COMPLETE SET (10) 4.00 10.00
SER.1 STATED ODDS 1:16 HOBBY
1 Barry Bonds 1.25 3.00
2 Dwight Gooden .20 .50
3 Todd Hundley .20 .50
4 Mark McGwire 1.25 3.00
5 Paul Molitor .20 .50
6 Eddie Murray .50 1.25
7 Hideo Nomo .50 1.25
8 Mike Piazza .75 2.00
9 Cal Ripken 1.50 4.00
10 Ozzie Smith w kids .75 2.00

1997 Fleer Goudey Greats

Randomly inserted in Fleer Series two packs at a rate of one in eight, this 15-card set features color player photos of today's stars on cards styled and sized to resemble the 1933 Goudey Baseball card set.
COMPLETE SET (15) 6.00 15.00
SER.2 STATED ODDS 1:8
*FOIL CARDS: 6X TO 15X BASIC GOUDEY
FOIL SER.2 STATED ODDS 1:800
1 Barry Bonds 1.25 3.00
2 Ken Griffey Jr. 1.00 2.50
3 Tony Gwynn .60 1.50
4 Derek Jeter 1.25 3.00
5 Chipper Jones .50 1.25
6 Kenny Lofton .20 .50
7 Greg Maddux .75 2.00
8 Mark McGwire 1.25 3.00
9 Eddie Murray .50 1.25
10 Mike Piazza .75 2.00
11 Cal Ripken 1.50 4.00
12 Alex Rodriguez .75 2.00
13 Ryne Sandberg .75 2.00
14 Frank Thomas .50 1.25
15 Mo Vaughn .20 .50

1997 Fleer Headliners

Randomly inserted in Fleer Series two packs at a rate of one in two, this 20-card set features color action photos of top players who make headlines for their teams. The backs carry player information.
COMPLETE SET (20) 4.00 10.00
SER.2 STATED ODDS 1:2
1 Jeff Bagwell .10 .30
2 Albert Belle .07 .20
3 Barry Bonds .50 1.25
4 Ken Caminiti .07 .20
5 Juan Gonzalez .07 .20
6 Ken Griffey Jr. .40 1.00
7 Tony Gwynn .25 .60
8 Derek Jeter .50 1.25
9 Andruw Jones .10 .30
10 Chipper Jones .20 .50
11 Greg Maddux .30 .75
12 Mark McGwire .50 1.25
13 Paul Molitor .07 .20
14 Eddie Murray .20 .50
15 Mike Piazza .30 .75
16 Cal Ripken .60 1.50
17 Alex Rodriguez .30 .75
18 Ryne Sandberg .30 .75
19 John Smoltz .10 .30
20 Frank Thomas .20 .50

1997 Fleer Lumber Company

Randomly inserted exclusively in Fleer Series one retail packs, this 18-card set features a selection of the game's top sluggers. The innovative design displays pure die-cut circular borders, simulating the effect of a cut tree.
COMPLETE SET (18) 25.00 60.00
SER.1 STATED ODDS 1:48 RETAIL
1 Brady Anderson 1.00 2.50
2 Jeff Bagwell 1.50 4.00
3 Albert Belle 1.00 2.50
4 Barry Bonds 4.00 10.00
5 Jay Buhner 1.00 2.50
6 Ellis Burks 1.00 2.50
7 Andres Galarraga 1.50 4.00
8 Juan Gonzalez 1.00 2.50
9 Ken Griffey Jr. 5.00 12.00
10 Todd Hundley 1.00 2.50
11 Ryan Klesko 1.00 2.50
12 Mark McGwire 4.00 10.00
13 Mike Piazza 2.50 6.00
14 Alex Rodriguez 3.00 8.00
15 Gary Sheffield 1.00 2.50
16 Sammy Sosa 1.50 4.00
17 Frank Thomas 2.50 6.00
18 Mo Vaughn 1.00 2.50

1997-98 Fleer Million Dollar Moments

Inserted one per pack into 1997 Fleer 2, 1997 Flair Showcase, 1998 Fleer 1 and 1998 Ultra 1; these 50 cards mix a selection of retired legends with today's stars, highlighting key moments in baseball history. The first 45 cards in the set are common to find. Cards 46-50 are extremely shortprinted with each card being tougher to find than the next as you work your way up to card number 50. Prior to the July 31st, 1998 deadline, collectors could mail in their 45-card sets (plus $5.99 for postage and handling) and receive a complete 50-card exchange set. The lucky collectors that managed to obtain one or more of the shortprinted cards could receive a shopping spree at card shops nationwide selected by Fleer. Each shortprinted card had to be mailed in along with a complete 45-card set to receive the following shopping allowances: number 46/$100, number 47/$250, number 48/$500, number 49/$1000. A grand prize of $1,000,000 cash (payable in increments of $50,000 annually over 20 years) was available for one collector that could obtain and redeem all five shortprint cards (numbers 46-50). This set was actually a part of a multi-sport promotion (baseball, basketball and football) for Fleer with each sport offering a separate $1,000,000 grand prize. In addition, 10,000 instant winner cards per sport (good for an assortment of material including shopping sprees, video games and various Fleer sets) were randomly seeded into packs. We are listing cards numbered from 46-50, however no prices are assigned for these cards.
COMPLETE SET (45) 3.00 8.00
1-45 SET REDEEMABLE FOR 1-50 EXCH.SET
EXCHANGE DEADLINE: 7/31/98
1 Checklist .02 .10
2 Derek Jeter .25 .60
3 Babe Ruth .60 1.50
4 Barry Bonds .25 .60
5 Brooks Robinson .08 .25
6 Todd Hundley .02 .10
7 Johnny Vander Meer .02 .10
8 Cal Ripken .30 .75
9 Bill Mazeroski .05 .15
10 Chipper Jones .08 .25
11 Frank Robinson .05 .15
12 Roger Clemens .20 .50
13 Bob Feller .05 .15
14 Mike Piazza .15 .40
15 Joe Nuxhall .02 .10
16 Hideo Nomo .08 .25
17 Jackie Robinson .08 .25
18 Orel Hershiser .02 .10
19 Bobby Thomson .02 .10
20 Joe Carter .02 .10
21 Al Kaline .08 .25
22 Bernie Williams .05 .15
23 Don Larsen .05 .15
24 Rickey Henderson .08 .25
25 Maury Wills .02 .10
26 Andruw Jones .05 .15
27 Bobby Richardson .05 .15
28 Alex Rodriguez .15 .40
29 Jim Bunning .05 .15
30 Ken Caminiti .02 .10
31 Bob Gibson .05 .15
32 Frank Thomas .08 .25
33 Mickey Lolich .02 .10
34 John Smoltz .05 .15
35 Ron Swoboda .02 .10
36 Albert Belle .02 .10
37 Chris Chambliss .02 .10
38 Juan Gonzalez .02 .10
39 Ron Blomberg .02 .10
40 John Wetteland .02 .10
41 Carlton Fisk .08 .25
42 Mo Vaughn .02 .10
43 Bucky Dent .02 .10
44 Greg Maddux .15 .40
45 Willie Stargell .02 .10
46 Tony Gwynn SP
47 Joel Youngblood SP
48 Andy Pettitte SP
49 Mookie Wilson SP
50 Jeff Bagwell SP

1997-98 Fleer Million Dollar Moments Redemption

COMPLETE SET (45) 3.00 8.00
1 Checklist .25 .60
2 Derek Jeter 1.50 4.00
3 Babe Ruth 1.50 4.00
4 Barry Bonds 1.25 3.00
5 Brooks Robinson .40 1.00
6 Todd Hundley .25 .60
7 Johnny Vander Meer .25 .60
8 Cal Ripken 2.00 5.00
9 Bill Mazeroski .40 1.00
10 Chipper Jones .60 1.50
11 Frank Robinson .40 1.00
12 Roger Clemens .75 2.00
13 Bob Feller .40 1.00
14 Mike Piazza .60 1.50
15 Joe Nuxhall .25 .60
16 Hideo Nomo .60 1.50
17 Jackie Robinson .60 1.50
18 Orel Hershiser .25 .60
19 Bobby Thomson .40 1.00
20 Joe Carter .25 .60
21 Al Kaline .60 1.50
22 Bernie Williams .40 1.00
23 Don Larsen .25 .60
24 Rickey Henderson .60 1.50
25 Maury Wills .25 .60
26 Andruw Jones .25 .60
27 Bobby Richardson .25 .60
28 Alex Rodriguez 1.00 2.50
29 Jim Bunning .40 1.00
30 Ken Caminiti .25 .60
31 Bob Gibson .40 1.00
32 Frank Thomas .60 1.50
33 Mickey Lolich .25 .60
34 John Smoltz .60 1.50
35 Ron Swoboda .25 .60
36 Albert Belle .25 .60
37 Chris Chambliss .25 .60
38 Juan Gonzalez .25 .60
39 Ron Blomberg .25 .60
40 John Wetteland .25 .60
41 Carlton Fisk .40 1.00
42 Mo Vaughn .25 .60
43 Bucky Dent .25 .60
44 Greg Maddux .75 2.00
45 Willie Stargell .40 1.00
46 Tony Gwynn .60 1.50
47 Joel Youngblood .25 .60
48 Andy Pettitte .40 1.00
49 Mookie Wilson .25 .60
50 Jeff Bagwell .40 1.00

1997 Fleer New Horizons

Randomly inserted in Fleer Series two packs at a rate of one in four, this 15-card set features borderless color action photos of Rookies and prospects. The backs carry player information.
COMPLETE SET (15) 3.00 8.00
SER.2 STATED ODDS 1:4
1 Bob Abreu .30 .75
2 Jose Cruz Jr. .25 .60
3 Darin Erstad .20 .50
4 Nomar Garciaparra .75 2.00
5 Vladimir Guerrero .50 1.25
6 Wilton Guerrero .20 .50
7 Jose Guillen .20 .50
8 Hideki Irabu .50 1.25
9 Andruw Jones .30 .75
10 Kevin Orie .20 .50
11 Scott Rolen .30 .75
12 Scott Spiezio .20 .50
13 Bubba Trammell .25 .60
14 Todd Walker .20 .50
15 Dmitri Young .20 .50

1997 Fleer Night and Day

Randomly inserted in Fleer Series one packs at a rate of one in 240, this ten-card set features color action player photos of superstars who excel in day games, night games, or both and are printed on lenticular 3D cards. The backs carry player information.
COMPLETE SET (10) 25.00 60.00
SER.1 STATED ODDS 1:240
1 Barry Bonds 4.00 10.00
2 Ellis Burks 1.00 2.50
3 Juan Gonzalez 1.00 2.50
4 Ken Griffey Jr. 10.00 25.00
5 Mark McGwire 4.00 10.00
6 Mike Piazza 2.50 6.00
7 Manny Ramirez 1.50 4.00

Alex Rodriguez 3.00 8.00
John Smoltz 1.50 4.00
10 Frank Thomas 5.00 12.00

1997 Fleer Rookie Sensations

Randomly inserted in Fleer Series one packs at a rate of one in six, this 20-card set honors the top rookies from the 1996 season and the 1997 season rookies/prospects. The fronts freature color action player images on a multi-color swirling background. The backs carry a paragraph with information about the player.

COMPLETE SET (20) 8.00 20.00
SER.1 STATED ODDS 1:6
1 Jermaine Allensworth .30 .75
2 James Baldwin .30 .75
3 Alan Benes .30 .75
4 Jermaine Dye .30 .75
5 Darin Erstad .30 .75
6 Todd Hollandsworth .30 .75
7 Derek Jeter 2.00 5.00
8 Jason Kendall .30 .75
9 Alex Ochoa .30 .75
10 Rey Ordonez .30 .75
11 Edgar Renteria .30 .75
12 Bob Abreu .50 1.25
13 Nomar Garciaparra 1.25 3.00
14 Wilton Guerrero .30 .75
15 Andruw Jones .50 1.25
16 Wendell Magee .30 .75
17 Neifi Perez .30 .75
18 Scott Rolen .50 1.25
19 Scott Spiezio .30 .75
20 Todd Walker .30 .75

1997 Fleer Soaring Stars

Randomly inserted in Fleer Series two packs at a rate of one in 12, this 12-card set features color action photos of players who enjoyed a meteoric rise to stardom and have all the skills to stay there. The player's image is set on a background of twinkling stars.

COMPLETE SET (12) 12.50 30.00
SER.2 STATED ODDS 1:12
*GLOWING: 4X TO 10X BASIC SOARING
GLOWING: RANDOM INS.IN SER.2 PACKS
LAST 20% OF PRINT RUN WAS GLOWING
1 Albert Belle .25 .60
2 Barry Bonds 1.50 4.00
3 Juan Gonzalez .25 .60
4 Ken Griffey Jr. 1.25 3.00
5 Derek Jeter 1.50 4.00
6 Andruw Jones .40 1.00
7 Chipper Jones .60 1.50
8 Greg Maddux 1.00 2.50
9 Mark McGwire 1.50 4.00
10 Mike Piazza 1.00 2.50
11 Alex Rodriguez 1.00 2.50
12 Frank Thomas .60 1.50

1997 Fleer Team Leaders

Randomly inserted in Fleer Series one packs at a rate of one in 20, this 28-card set honors statistical or inspirational leaders from each team on a die-cut card. The fronts feature color action player images with the player's face in the background. The backs carry a paragraph with information about the player.

COMPLETE SET (28) 15.00 40.00
SER.1 STATED ODDS 1:20
1 Cal Ripken 3.00 8.00
2 Mo Vaughn .40 1.00
3 Jim Edmonds .40 1.00
4 Frank Thomas 1.00 2.50
5 Albert Belle .40 1.00
6 Bob Higginson .40 1.00
7 Kevin Appier .40 1.00
8 John Jaha .40 1.00
9 Paul Molitor 1.00 2.50
10 Andy Pettitte .60 1.50
11 Mark McGwire 1.50 4.00
12 Ken Griffey Jr. 2.00 5.00
13 Juan Gonzalez .40 1.00
14 Pat Hentgen .40 1.00
15 Chipper Jones 1.00 2.50
16 Mark Grace .60 1.50
17 Barry Larkin .60 1.50
18 Ellis Burks .40 1.00
19 Gary Sheffield .40 1.00
20 Jeff Bagwell .60 1.50
21 Mike Piazza 1.00 2.50
22 Henry Rodriguez .40 1.00
23 Todd Hundley .40 1.00
24 Curt Schilling .40 1.00
25 Jeff King .40 1.00
26 Brian Jordan .40 1.00
27 Tony Gwynn 1.00 2.50
28 Barry Bonds 1.50 4.00

1997 Fleer Zone

Randomly inserted in Fleer Series one hobby packs only at a rate of one in 80, this 20-card set features color player images of some of the 1996 season's unstoppable hitters and unhittable pitchers on a holographic card. The backs carry another color photo with a paragraph about the player.

COMPLETE SET (20) 100.00 200.00
SER.1 STATED ODDS 1:80 HOBBY
1 Jeff Bagwell 2.50 6.00
2 Albert Belle 1.50 4.00
3 Barry Bonds 10.00 25.00
4 Ken Caminiti 1.50 4.00
5 Andres Galarraga 1.50 4.00
6 Juan Gonzalez 1.50 4.00
7 Ken Griffey Jr. 8.00 20.00
8 Tony Gwynn 5.00 12.00
9 Chipper Jones 4.00 10.00
10 Greg Maddux 6.00 15.00
11 Mark McGwire 10.00 25.00
12 Dean Palmer 1.50 4.00
13 Andy Pettitte 2.50 6.00
14 Mike Piazza 6.00 15.00
15 Alex Rodriguez 6.00 15.00
16 Gary Sheffield 1.50 4.00
17 John Smoltz 2.50 6.00
18 Frank Thomas 4.00 10.00
19 Jim Thome 2.50 6.00
20 Matt Williams 1.50 4.00

1997 Fleer Firestone

This one-card set features a color portrait with gold foil printing of Roy Firestone, the host of ESPN's "Up Close Prime Time." The back displays information about the interviewer.

1 Roy Firestone .75 2.00

1998 Fleer Diamond Skills Commemorative Sheet

This attractive eight-card unperforated sheet was distributed nationwide by hobby shops that participated in Fleer's Diamond Skills youth baseball program. Each shop that enrolled with Fleer in early April, 1998 received 25 sheets to give away to young baseball fans participating in the contest. From April 1st through June 30th, 1998, MLB and Fleer/SkyBox distributed more than 600,000 questionaire surveys. Each survey was then filled out and brought into an a local card shop, where the participating youth had to buy two packs of Fleer/SkyBox trading cards. In exchange for the two wrappers from those packs and the completed survey, the youth received one of these commemorative sheets.

NNO Commemorative Sheet 2.00 5.00

1998 Fleer Mantle and Sons

This special one-shot standard-sized card was distributed at Fleer's booth at the Sportsfest '98 show in Philadelphia as well as the National Convention in Chicago in the Summer of 1998. In conjunction with their licensing agreement with the Mantle family and accompanying 1998 Mantle promotions, Fleer brought Mantle's sons Danny and David to the aforementioned trade shows to sign this special card for collectors. The back of the card outlines Mickey Mantle's various card appearances in Fleer's 1998 products. Pricing is provided below for both signed and unsigned versions of this card.

NNO Mickey Mantle w sons AU 4.00 10.00
NNO Mickey Mantle w sons 1.25 3.00

1998 Fleer National Promos

NC1 Mickey Mantle 2.00 5.00
NC2 Mickey Mantle 2.00 5.00
David Mantle
Danny Mantle

1998 Fleer Postcard Mantle Promo

This one-card set features a color photo of Mickey Mantle as the A.L. Most Valuable Player in 1962 with a white border and measuring approximately 4 1/4" by 5 1/2". The white back has a date of August 5, 1998, and the words "Isn't it about time your customers complete their '63 set?" Only 3,500 of the cards were printed and are serially numbered.

1 Mickey Mantle 2.00 5.00

1998 Fleer/SkyBox Player's Choice Sheet

This one-card set was given out at stadiums during the final weekend of the 1998 season and measures approximately 8 1/2" by 11". The card features color action player images of nominees for Outstanding Player, Pitcher and Rookie, Comeback Player of the Year, Man of the Year, and Player of the Year. One side displays the NL nominees and the other the AL ones. The players are checklisted below in alphabetical order.

NNO Player's Choice AL/NL 2.00 5.00

1999 Fleer Stan Musial NSCC Commemorative

This five-card over-sized (3 1/2" by 5") set was distributed to attendees of the 20th Annual National Sports Collectors Convention held in Atlanta in July, 1999. The cards were packaged in complete set form within a sealed clear plastic cello wrapper. An unnumbered Cover Card (bereft of any player images) displays the 20th National Convention logo on front and a checklist on back. This was the top card in each cello wrapped set. Card NC1 was a straight parallel of the basic issue 1999 Fleer Stan Musial card (number 6 within the basic Fleer set, but renumbered as NC1 for this set) and is the only standard-sized card in the set. Cards NC2-NC4 are quasi-reprints of selected cards from the 1999 Fleer Stan Musial Monumental Moments set - taking those standard sized cards and incorporating them into an over-sized card format with the famous Arch of St.Louis in the background.

COMPLETE SET (5) 10.00 25.00
COMMON CARD (NC1-NC4) 2.00 5.00

1999 Fleer 23K McGwire

This card was issued by Fleer and commemorated the breaking of the single season homer record by Mark McGwire. The front has a relief photo of McGwire and a fascimile autograph. The back has information about the homer as well as the date listed on top. The card is also serial numbered on the back. However, it is possible that more of these cards were issued so any further information about this set is appreciated.

1 Mark McGwire 4.00 10.00

1999 Fleer Diamond Skills Commemorative Sheet

For the second year running, Fleer issued an attractive eight-card unperforated sheet. The sheet was distributed nationwide by hobby shops that participated in Fleer's Diamond Skills youth baseball program.

NNO Diamond Skills Sheet 2.00 5.00

1999 Fleer Spectra Star

These six cards of baseball's leading superstars were issued by Fleer along with a kite. These cards are in the design of the 1999 Fleer set but are numbered "x" of 6. The kites were issued by Spectra Star.

COMPLETE SET (6) 12.50 30.00
1 Mark McGwire 2.50 6.00
2 Ken Griffey Jr. 3.00 8.00
3 Derek Jeter 4.00 10.00
4 Greg Maddux 2.00 5.00
5 Mike Piazza 2.50 6.00
6 Sammy Sosa 1.50 4.00

1999 Fleer White Rose

These 30 cards were issued along with a special truck in a combo package. The cards are sequenced thusly: Cards 1-14 are American League teams in alphabetical order; 15-26 are National League teams in alpha order, 27 and 28 are 1993 Expansion teams and 29 and 30 and 1998 Expansion team. The cards have the 1999 Fleer fronts and are specially numbered for this set. We are only pricing the cards here.

COMPLETE SET (30) 30.00 80.00
1 Cal Ripken Jr 4.00 10.00
2 Nomar Garciaparra 2.00 5.00
3 Tim Salmon .60 1.50
4 Frank Thomas 1.25 3.00
5 Jim Thome 1.00 2.50
6 Tony Clark .40 1.00
7 Johnny Damon 1.00 2.50
8 Jeromy Burnitz .60 1.50
9 Brad Radke .40 1.00
10 Derek Jeter 4.00 10.00
11 Ben Grieve .60 1.50
12 Ken Griffey Jr. 3.00 8.00
13 Ivan Rodriguez 1.25 3.00
14 Carlos Delgado 1.00 2.50
15 Greg Maddux 2.50 6.00
16 Sammy Sosa 1.50 4.00
17 Sean Casey .60 1.50
18 Jeff Bagwell 1.25 3.00
19 Raul Mondesi .40 1.00
20 Vladimir Guerrero 1.50 4.00
21 Mike Piazza 2.50 6.00
22 Scott Rolen .60 1.50
23 Jose Guillen .75 2.00
24 Mark McGwire 2.50 6.00
25 Tony Gwynn 2.00 5.00
26 Barry Bonds 2.00 5.00
27 Larry Walker 1.00 2.50
28 Livan Hernandez .40 1.00
29 Matt Williams .60 1.50
30 Wade Boggs 1.25 3.00

2000 Fleer Club 3000

This set honors batters who have collected 3,000 hits and pitchers who have collected 3,000 strikeouts in their careers. The cards were seeded across all 2000 Fleer brands and each card in our checklist is marked with an abbreviation for the product it hails from. Pack odds are as follows - Fleer-distributed cards 1:36, Fleer Focus-distributed cards 1:36, Fleer Mystique-distributed cards 1:32, Fleer Showcase-distributed cards 1:24, and Ultra-distributed cards 1:24. These cards are unnumbered so we have sequenced them in alphabetical order by player initials.

COMPLETE SET (14) 15.00 40.00
COMP.FLEER SET (3) 3.00 8.00
COMP.FOCUS SET (3) 2.50 6.00
COMP.MYSTIQUE SET (3) 4.00 10.00
COMP.SHOWCASE SET (2) 3.00 8.00
COMP.ULTRA SET (3) 2.50 6.00
FLEER STATED ODDS 1:36
FOCUS STATED ODDS 1:36
MYSTIQUE STATED ODDS 1:20
SHOWCASE STATED ODDS 1:24
ULTRA STATED ODDS 1:24
SHOW SUFFIX ON SHOWCASE DISTRIBUTION
ACTUAL CARDS ARE ALL UNNUMBERED
BG Bob Gibson MYST .75 2.00
CR Cal Ripken MYST 4.00 10.00
CY Carl Yastrzemski ULT 2.00 5.00
DW Dave Winfield MYST .75 2.00
GB George Brett FLE 2.50 6.00
LB Lou Brock SHOW .75 2.00
NR Nolan Ryan SHOW 4.00 10.00
PM Paul Molitor FOCUS 1.25 3.00
RC Rod Carew FLE .75 2.00
RY Robin Yount FLE 1.25 3.00
SC Steve Carlton FOCUS .50 1.25
SM Stan Musial FOCUS 2.00 5.00
TG Tony Gwynn ULT 1.25 3.00
WB Wade Boggs ULT .75 2.00

2000 Fleer Club 3000 Memorabilia

Randomly inserted into all 2000 Fleer products, these cards feature game used memorabilia from legends of the game that have either collected 3,000 hits or struck out 3,000 batters during their career. The cards (and patterns of distribution) parallel the more common Club 3000 cards that lack the memorabilia elements. Each player has five different cards: A bat, a hat, a jersey, a combo of bat and jersey and a combo of bat, hat and jersey. Each card is sequentially numbered and detailed within our checklist. Please see the Fleer Club 3000 listing for specific information on which Fleer product each card was distributed in.

B/WN 225-335 OF EACH BAT PRODUCED
B/WN 55-115 OF EACH HAT PRODUCED
700-1000 OF EACH JSY UNLESS STATED
100 #'d COPIES OF EACH BAT-JSY MADE
25 #'d COPIES OF EACH BAT-HAT-JSY MADE
PRINT RUNS LISTED BELOW
ACTUAL CARDS ARE ALL UNNUMBERED
NO PRICING ON QTY OF 25 OR LESS
BG1 B.Gibson Bat/265 10.00 25.00
BG2 B.Gibson Hat/55 30.00 60.00
BG3 B.Gibson Jersey/825 6.00 15.00
BG4 B.Gibson Bat-Jersey/100 20.00 50.00
CR1 C.Ripken Bat/265 30.00 80.00
CR2 C.Ripken Hat/55 60.00 150.00
CR3 C.Ripken Jersey/825 10.00 25.00
CR4 C.Ripken Bat-Jersey/100 20.00 50.00
CY1 C.Yaz Bat/250 15.00 40.00
CY2 C.Yaz Hat/100 20.00 50.00
CY3 C.Yaz Jersey/440 10.00 25.00
CY4 C.Yaz Bat-Jersey/100 10.00 25.00
DW1 D.Winfield Bat/270 6.00 15.00
DW2 D.Winfield Hat/55 20.00 50.00
DW3 D.Winfield Jersey/825 8.00 20.00
DW4 D.Winfield Bat-Jersey/100 15.00 40.00
GB1 G.Brett Bat/240 12.00 30.00
GB2 G.Brett Hat/105 30.00 60.00
GB3 G.Brett Jersey/445 10.00 25.00
GB4 G.Brett Bat-Jersey/100 30.00 60.00
LB1 L.Brock Bat/270 10.00 25.00
LB2 L.Brock Hat/60 30.00 60.00
LB3 L.Brock Jersey/680 6.00 15.00
LB4 L.Brock Bat-Jersey/100 15.00 40.00
NR1 N.Ryan Bat/265 10.00 25.00
NR2 N.Ryan Hat/65 60.00 120.00
NR3 N.Ryan Jersey/780 10.00 25.00
NR4 N.Ryan Bat-Jersey/100 60.00 150.00
PM1 P.Molitor Bat/335 10.00 25.00
PM2 P.Molitor Hat/65 15.00 40.00
PM3 P.Molitor Jersey/975 10.00 25.00
PM4 P.Molitor Bat-Jersey/100 10.00 25.00
RC1 R.Carew Bat/225 10.00 25.00
RC2 R.Carew Hat/105 30.00 60.00
RC3 R.Carew Jersey/395 6.00 15.00
RC4 R.Carew Bat-Jersey/100 15.00 40.00
RY1 R.Yount Bat/230 12.50 30.00
RY2 R.Yount Hat/105 40.00 80.00
RY3 R.Yount Jersey/445 6.00 15.00
RY4 R.Yount Bat-Jersey/100 40.00 80.00
SC1 S.Carlton Bat/325 6.00 15.00
SC2 S.Carlton Hat/65 20.00 50.00
SC3 S.Carlton Jersey/750 10.00 25.00
SC4 S.Carlton Bat-Jersey/100 20.00 50.00
SM1 S.Musial Bat/325 10.00 25.00
SM2 S.Musial Hat/65 50.00 100.00
SM3 S.Musial Jersey/975 12.00 30.00
SM4 S.Musial Bat-Jersey/100 30.00 60.00
TG1 T.Gwynn Bat/260 10.00 25.00
TG2 T.Gwynn Hat/115 40.00 80.00
TG3 T.Gwynn Jersey/450 10.00 25.00
TG4 T.Gwynn Bat-Jersey/100 40.00 80.00
WB1 W.Boggs Bat/250 10.00 25.00
WB2 W.Boggs Hat/100 10.00 25.00
WB3 W.Boggs Jersey/440 8.00 20.00
WB4 W.Boggs Bat-Jersey/100 10.00 25.00

2000 Fleer Japan Sheet

This sheet featured eight of the leading players in baseball. The cards feature the design of the Fleer 2000 set. These sheets were given away at the 2000 season-opening series between the Mets and Cubs in Japan.

1 Sammy Sosa 2.00 5.00
Mike Piazza
Chipper Jones
Ivan Rodri

2000 Fleer Oreo

These two standard-size cards were issued by Fleer in conjunction with the "Oreo Stacking Contest 2000". These cards were given away to each youngster who attempted to pile Oreo cookies as high as they could. Both cards have special poses not in the regular Fleer sets. These cards are not numbered so we have placed them in alphabetical order.

COMPLETE SET (2) 2.50 6.00
1 Ken Griffey Jr. 2.00 5.00
2 Derek Jeter 2.50 6.00

2000 Fleer Twizzlers

These 12 cards, designed in the style of 2000 Fleer, were inserted in packs of Twizzlers. These cards are different from the regular Fleer cards as they are glossy on both sides and have a "team twizzler" logo on the back. The first six cards were issued to coincinide with the start of the 2000 season while the final six cards were issued approximately two months later.

COMPLETE SET (12) 6.00 15.00
1 Mark McGwire 1.00 2.50
2 Cal Ripken Jr. 2.00 5.00
3 Chipper Jones .60 1.50
4 Bernie Williams .40 1.00
5 Alex Rodriguez .75 2.00
6 Curt Schilling .40 1.00
7 Ken Griffey Jr. 1.25 3.00
8 Sammy Sosa .60 1.50
9 Mike Piazza .60 1.50
10 Pedro Martinez .40 1.00
11 Kenny Lofton .25 .60
12 Larry Walker .40 1.00

2001 Fleer Autographics

Randomly inserted into packs of Fleer Focus (1:72 w/memorabilia), Fleer Triple Crown (1:72 w/memorabilia cards), Ultra (1:48 w/memorabilia cards), 2002 Fleer Platinum Rack Packs (on average 1:6 racks contains an Autographics card) and 2002 Fleer Genuine (1:18 Hobby Direct box and 1:30 Hobby Distributor box), this insert set features authentic autographs from modern stars and prospects. The cards are designed horizontally with a full color player image at the side allowing plenty of room for the player's autograph. Card backs are unnumbered and feature Fleer's certificate of authenticity. Cards are checklisted alphabetically by player's last name and abbreviations indicating which brands each card was distributed in follows the player name. The brand legend is as follows: FC = Fleer Focus, TC = Fleer Triple Crown, UL = Ultra.

FOCUS: AUTO OR FEEL GAME 1:72
GENUINE: STATED ODDS 1:24
PREMIUM: STATED ODDS 1:96 RETAIL
SHOWCASE: STATED ODDS 1:96 RETAIL
'02 PLATINUM: AUTO OR BAT 1:1 RACK
'02 GENUINE: 1:18 HOB.DIR., 1:30 HOB.DIST.
FC SUFFIX ON FOCUS DISTRIBUTION
FS SUFFIX ON SHOWCASE DISTRIBUTION
FP'02 SUFFIX ON ULTRA DISTRIBUTION
GN SUFFIX ON GENUINE DISTRIBUTION
PM SUFFIX ON PREMIUM DISTRIBUTION
TC SUFFIX ON TRIPLE CROWN DISTRIBUTION
UL SUFFIX ON ULTRA DISTRIBUTION
1 Roberto Alomar 10.00 25.00
2 Jimmy Anderson 3.00 8.00
3 Ryan Anderson 3.00 8.00
4 Rick Ankiel 3.00 8.00
6 Carlos Beltran 12.00 30.00
7 Adrian Beltre 6.00 15.00
8 Peter Bergeron 3.00 8.00
9 Lance Berkman 3.00 8.00
10 Barry Bonds 25.00 60.00
11 Milton Bradley 3.00 8.00
12 Ryan Bradley 3.00 8.00
13 Dee Brown 3.00 8.00
14 Roosevelt Brown 3.00 8.00
15 Jeromy Burnitz 3.00 8.00
16 Pat Burrell 3.00 8.00
17 Alex Cabrera 10.00 25.00
18 Sean Casey 3.00 8.00
19 Eric Chavez 3.00 8.00
20 Giuseppe Chiaramonte 3.00 8.00
21 Joe Crede 3.00 8.00
22 Jose Cruz Jr. 3.00 8.00
23 Johnny Damon 5.00 12.00
24 Carlos Delgado 3.00 8.00
25 Ryan Dempster 3.00 8.00
26 J.D. Drew 3.00 8.00
27 Adam Dunn 5.00 12.00
28 Erubiel Durazo 3.00 8.00
29 Jermaine Dye 3.00 8.00
30 David Eckstein 3.00 8.00
31 Jim Edmonds 5.00 12.00
32 Alex Escobar 3.00 8.00
33 Seth Etherton 3.00 8.00
34 Adam Everett 3.00 8.00
35 Carlos Febles 3.00 8.00
36 Troy Glaus 10.00 25.00
37 Chad Green 3.00 8.00
38 Ben Grieve 3.00 8.00
39 Wilton Guerrero 3.00 8.00
40 Tony Gwynn 20.00 50.00
41 Toby Hall 3.00 8.00
42 Todd Helton 5.00 12.00
43 Chad Hermansen 3.00 8.00
44 Dustin Hermanson 3.00 8.00
45 Shea Hillenbrand 3.00 8.00
46 Aubrey Huff 3.00 8.00
47 Derek Jeter 150.00 300.00
48 D'Angelo Jimenez 3.00 8.00
49 Randy Johnson 40.00 100.00
50 Chipper Jones 20.00 50.00
51 Cesar King 3.00 8.00
52 Paul Konerko 5.00 12.00
53 Corey Koskie 3.00 8.00
54 Mike Lamb 3.00 8.00
55 Matt Lawton 3.00 8.00
56 Corey Lee 3.00 8.00
57 Derrek Lee 3.00 8.00
58 Mike Lieberthal 3.00 8.00
59 Cole Liniak 3.00 8.00
60 Steve Lomasney 3.00 8.00
61 Terrence Long 3.00 8.00
62 Mike Lowell 3.00 8.00
63 Julio Lugo 3.00 8.00
64 Greg Maddux 40.00 100.00
65 Jason Marquis 3.00 8.00
66 Edgar Martinez 5.00 12.00
67 Justin Miller 3.00 8.00
68 Kevin Millwood 3.00 8.00
69 Eric Milton 3.00 8.00
70 Bengie Molina 3.00 8.00
71 Mike Mussina 5.00 12.00
72 David Ortiz 20.00 50.00
73 Russ Ortiz 3.00 8.00
74 Pablo Ozuna 3.00 8.00
75 Corey Patterson 3.00 8.00
76 Carl Pavano 3.00 8.00
77 Jay Payton 3.00 8.00
78 Wily Pena 3.00 8.00
79 Josh Phelps 3.00 8.00
80 Adam Platt 3.00 8.00
81 Juan Pierre 3.00 8.00
82 Brad Radke 3.00 8.00
83 Mark Redman 3.00 8.00
84 Matt Riley 3.00 8.00
85 Cal Ripken 50.00 120.00
86 John Rocker 10.00 25.00
87 Alex Rodriguez 40.00 100.00
88 Scott Rolen 5.00 12.00
89 Alex Sanchez 3.00 8.00
90 Fernando Seguignol 3.00 8.00
91 Richie Sexson 3.00 8.00
92 Gary Sheffield 3.00 8.00
93 Alfonso Soriano 5.00 12.00
94 Dernell Stenson 3.00 8.00
95 Garrett Stephenson 3.00 8.00
96 Shannon Stewart 3.00 8.00
97 Fernando Tatis 3.00 8.00
98 Miguel Tejada 10.00 25.00
99 Jorge Toca 3.00 8.00
100 Robin Ventura 3.00 8.00
101 Jose Vidro 3.00 8.00
102 Billy Wagner 3.00 8.00
103 Kip Wells 3.00 8.00
104 Vernon Wells 3.00 8.00
105 Rondell White 3.00 8.00
106 Bernie Williams 30.00 80.00
107 Scott Williamson 3.00 8.00
108 Preston Wilson 3.00 8.00
109 Kerry Wood 3.00 8.00
110 Jamey Wright 3.00 8.00
111 Julio Zuleta 3.00 8.00

2001 Fleer Autographics Gold

*GOLD: .75X TO 2X BASIC AUTOS
STATED PRINT RUN 50 SERIAL #'d SETS

2001 Fleer Autographics Silver

*SILVER: .6X TO 1.5X BASIC AUTOS
STATED PRINT RUN 250 SERIAL #'d SETS

2001 Fleer Feel the Game

This insert set features game-used bat cards of major league stars. The cards were distributed across several different Fleer products issued in 2001. Please note that the cards are listed below in alphabetical order for convience. Cards with "FC" listed after the players name were inserted into Fleer Focus packs (one Autographic or Feel Game in every 72 packs), "TC" listed after the players name were inserted into packs of Fleer Triple Crown (one Feel Game, Autographic or Crown of Gold in every 72 packs), while cards with "UL" after their name were inserted into Ultra packs (one Autographic or Feel Game in every 48 packs).

*GOLD: 1.25X TO 2.5X BASIC FEEL GAME
GOLD PRINT RUN 50 SERIAL #'d SETS
1 Moises Alou Bat 2.00 5.00
2 Brady Anderson Bat 2.00 5.00
3 Adrian Beltre Bat 5.00 12.00
4 Dante Bichette Bat 2.00 5.00
5 Roger Cedeno Bat 2.00 5.00
6 Ben Davis Bat 2.00 5.00
7 Carlos Delgado Bat 2.00 5.00
8 J.D. Drew Bat 2.00 5.00
9 Jermaine Dye Bat 2.00 5.00
10 Jason Giambi Bat 2.00 5.00
11 Brian Giles Bat 2.00 5.00
12 Juan Gonzalez Bat 2.00 5.00
13 Rickey Henderson Bat 5.00 12.00
14 Richard Hidalgo Bat 2.00 5.00
15 Chipper Jones Bat 5.00 12.00
16 Eric Karros Bat 2.00 5.00
17 Javy Lopez Bat 2.00 5.00
18 Tino Martinez Bat 3.00 8.00
19 Raul Mondesi Bat 2.00 5.00
20 Phil Nevin Bat 2.00 5.00
21 Chan Ho Park Bat 3.00 8.00
22 Ivan Rodriguez Bat 3.00 8.00
23 Matt Stairs Bat 2.00 5.00
24 Shannon Stewart Bat 2.00 5.00
25 Frank Thomas Bat 5.00 12.00
26 Jose Vidro Bat 2.00 5.00
27 Matt Williams Bat 2.00 5.00
28 Preston Wilson Bat 2.00 5.00

2001 Fleer Season Pass

Randomly inserted into various 2001 Fleer products, these exchange cards allow collectors to receive every Fleer card made of this player in 2001 (minus any one of one's). Each season pass exchange card is a one of one. Each exchange card must have been redeemed no later than 12/01/01.

2001 Fleer Bonds Home Run King Jumbo

This one card set, features three different images of Bonds on the front along with a large "Home Run King 73" logo. The top of the card features the words Barry Bonds on the top. The back of the card features a blurb detailing Bonds' amazing 2001 season. There is also a career batting line. On the bottom, the cards are serial numbered.

BBHRK Barry Bonds 1.50 4.00

2001 Fleer Ripken Cal to Greatness Jumbo

This one card set, features four different images of Ripken on front along with a large "8" on the right side. The top of the card features the words "8/10/81 -10-6/01" and "Cal to Greatness" on the top. The back of the card features various honors and records that Ripken owns. There is also a career batting line. On the bottom, the cards are serial numbered out of 2632, which was the number of games in Ripken's consecutive game hitting streak.

NNO Cal Ripken 4.00 10.00

2001 Fleer Ripken Commemorative 50000

This set was issued by Fleer's and features highlights of the career of Cal Ripken Jr. Unlike the other set with a print run of 2632 sets, this set was issued to a print run of 50,000 sets and does not feature memorabilia cards. The set was issued in the following subsets: Career Highlights (1-12); The Streak (13-24); Final Season (25-35); Last Game (36-40) and Fleer Reprints (41-60).

COMPLETE SET 4.00 10.00
COMMON CARD .20 .50

2001 Fleer Cal Ripken Career Highlights 2632

Issued as a special boxed set, this set featured 60 base cards, 20 Fleer Reprint Cards, 10 Career Highlight cards, 13 Streak Cards, 17 Final Season Cards and a Jersey and a Bat Card. These sets with memorabilia cards were numbered to 2632 to match the consecutive game streak of Ripken.

COMP.FACT SET
COMMON CARD

2002 Fleer

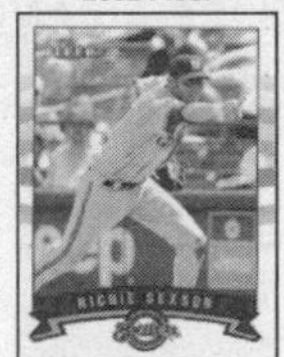

This 540 card set was issued in May, 2002. These cards were issued in 10 card packs which came packed 24 packs to a box and 10 boxes to a case and had an SRP of $2 per pack. Cards number 432 through 491 featured players who switched teams in the off season while cards 492 through 531 featured leading prospects and cards numbered 532 through 540 feature photos of important ballparks along with checklists on the back.

COMPLETE SET (540) 15.00 40.00
COMMON CARD (1-540) .08 .25
COMMON CARD (492-531) .20 .50

Card	Low	High
1 Darin Erstad FP	.08	.25
2 Randy Johnson FP	.25	.60
3 Chipper Jones FP	.25	.60
4 Jay Gibbons FP	.08	.25
5 Nomar Garciaparra FP	.40	1.00
6 Sammy Sosa FP	.25	.60
7 Frank Thomas FP	.25	.60
8 Ken Griffey Jr. FP	.50	1.25
9 Jim Thome FP	.15	.40
10 Todd Helton FP	.15	.40
11 Jeff Weaver FP	.08	.25
12 Cliff Floyd FP	.08	.25
13 Jeff Bagwell FP	.15	.40
14 Mike Sweeney FP	.08	.25
15 Adrian Beltre FP	.08	.25
16 Richie Sexson FP	.08	.25
17 Brad Radke FP	.08	.25
18 Vladimir Guerrero FP	.25	.60
19 Mike Piazza FP	.40	1.00
20 Derek Jeter FP	.50	1.25
21 Eric Chavez FP	.08	.25
22 Pat Burrell FP	.08	.25
23 Brian Giles FP	.08	.25
24 Trevor Hoffman FP	.08	.25
25 Barry Bonds FP	.40	1.00
26 Ichiro Suzuki FP	.40	1.00
27 Albert Pujols FP	.40	1.00
28 Ben Grieve FP	.08	.25
29 Alex Rodriguez FP	.30	.75
30 Carlos Delgado FP	.08	.25
31 Miguel Tejada	.15	.40
32 Todd Hollandsworth	.08	.25
33 Marlon Anderson	.08	.25
34 Kerry Robinson	.08	.25
35 Chris Richard	.08	.25
36 Jamey Wright	.08	.25
37 Ray Lankford	.15	.40
38 Mike Bordick	.15	.40
39 Danny Graves	.08	.25
40 A.J. Pierzynski	.15	.40
41 Shannon Stewart	.15	.40
42 Tony Armas Jr.	.08	.25
43 Brad Ausmus	.15	.40
44 Alfonso Soriano	.15	.40
45 Junior Spivey	.08	.25
46 Brent Mayne	.08	.25
47 Jim Thome	.25	.60
48 Dan Wilson	.08	.25
49 Geoff Jenkins	.08	.25
50 Kris Benson	.08	.25
51 Rafael Furcal	.15	.40
52 Wiki Gonzalez	.08	.25
53 Jeff Kent	.15	.40
54 Curt Schilling	.15	.40
55 Ken Harvey	.08	.25
56 Roosevelt Brown	.08	.25
57 David Segui	.08	.25
58 Mario Valdez	.08	.25
59 Adam Dunn	.15	.40
60 Bob Howry	.08	.25
61 Michael Barrett	.08	.25
62 Garret Anderson	.15	.40
63 Kelvim Escobar	.08	.25
64 Ben Grieve	.08	.25
65 Randy Johnson	.40	1.00
66 Jose Offerman	.08	.25
67 Jason Kendall	.15	.40
68 Joel Pineiro	.08	.25
69 Alex Escobar	.08	.25
70 Chris George	.08	.25
71 Bobby Higginson	.15	.40
72 Nomar Garciaparra	.60	1.50
73 Pat Burrell	.15	.40
74 Lee Stevens	.08	.25
75 Felipe Lopez	.08	.25
76 Al Leiter	.15	.40
77 Jim Edmonds	.15	.40
78 Al Levine	.08	.25
79 Raul Mondesi	.15	.40
80 Jose Valentin	.08	.25
81 Matt Clement	.15	.40
82 Richard Hidalgo	.15	.40
83 Jamie Moyer	.15	.40
84 Brian Schneider	.08	.25
85 John Franco	.15	.40
86 Brian Buchanan	.08	.25
87 Roy Oswalt	.15	.40
88 Johnny Estrada	.08	.25
89 Marcus Giles	.15	.40
90 Carlos Valderrama	.08	.25
91 Mark Mulder	.15	.40
92 Mark Grace	.25	.60
93 Andy Ashby	.08	.25
94 Woody Williams	.08	.25
95 Ben Petrick	.08	.25
96 Roy Halladay	.15	.40
97 Fred McGriff	.25	.60
98 Shawn Green	.15	.40
99 Todd Hundley	.08	.25
100 Carlos Febles	.08	.25
101 Jason Marquis	.08	.25
102 Mike Redmond	.08	.25
103 Shane Halter	.08	.25
104 Trot Nixon	.15	.40
105 Jeremy Giambi	.08	.25
106 Carlos Delgado	.15	.40
107 Richie Sexson	.15	.40
108 Russ Ortiz	.08	.25
109 David Ortiz	.40	1.00
110 Curtis Leskanic	.08	.25
111 Jay Payton	.08	.25
112 Travis Phelps	.08	.25
113 J.T. Snow	.15	.40
114 Edgar Renteria	.15	.40
115 Freddy Garcia	.15	.40
116 Cliff Floyd	.15	.40
117 Charles Nagy	.08	.25
118 Tony Batista	.08	.25
119 Rafael Palmeiro	.25	.60
120 Darren Dreifort	.08	.25
121 Warren Morris	.08	.25
122 Augie Ojeda	.08	.25
123 Rusty Greer	.15	.40
124 Esteban Yan	.08	.25
125 Corey Patterson	.08	.25
126 Matt Ginter	.08	.25
127 Matt Lawton	.08	.25
128 Miguel Batista	.08	.25
129 Randy Winn	.08	.25
130 Eric Milton	.08	.25
131 Jack Wilson	.08	.25
132 Sean Casey	.15	.40
133 Mike Sweeney	.15	.40
134 Jason Tyner	.08	.25
135 Carlos Hernandez	.08	.25
136 Shea Hillenbrand	.15	.40
137 Shawn Wooten	.08	.25
138 Peter Bergeron	.08	.25
139 Travis Lee	.08	.25
140 Craig Wilson	.08	.25
141 Carlos Guillen	.15	.40
142 Chipper Jones	.40	1.00
143 Gabe Kapler	.15	.40
144 Raul Ibanez	.08	.25
145 Eric Chavez	.15	.40
146 D'Angelo Jimenez	.08	.25
147 Chad Hermansen	.08	.25
148 Joe Kennedy	.08	.25
149 Mariano Rivera	.40	1.00
150 Jeff Bagwell	.25	.60
151 Joe McEwing	.08	.25
152 Ronnie Belliard	.08	.25
153 Desi Relaford	.08	.25
154 Vinny Castilla	.15	.40
155 Tim Hudson	.15	.40
156 Wilton Guerrero	.08	.25
157 Raul Casanova	.08	.25
158 Edgardo Alfonzo	.08	.25
159 Derrek Lee	.25	.60
160 Phil Nevin	.15	.40
161 Roger Clemens	.75	2.00
162 Jason LaRue	.08	.25
163 Brian Lawrence	.08	.25
164 Adrian Beltre	.15	.40
165 Troy Glaus	.15	.40
166 Jeff Weaver	.08	.25
167 B.J. Surhoff	.15	.40
168 Eric Byrnes	.08	.25
169 Mike Sirotka	.08	.25
170 Bill Haselman	.08	.25
171 Javier Vazquez	.15	.40
172 Sidney Ponson	.08	.25
173 Adam Everett	.08	.25
174 Bubba Trammell	.08	.25
175 Robb Nen	.15	.40
176 Barry Larkin	.25	.60
177 Tony Graffanino	.08	.25
178 Rich Garces	.08	.25
179 Juan Uribe	.08	.25
180 Tom Glavine	.25	.60
181 Eric Karros	.15	.40
182 Michael Cuddyer	.08	.25
183 Wade Miller	.08	.25
184 Matt Williams	.15	.40
185 Matt Morris	.15	.40
186 Rickey Henderson	.40	1.00
187 Trevor Hoffman	.15	.40
188 Wilson Betemit	.08	.25
189 Steve Karsay	.08	.25
190 Frank Catalanotto	.08	.25
191 Jason Schmidt	.15	.40
192 Roger Cedeno	.08	.25
193 Magglio Ordonez	.15	.40
194 Pat Hentgen	.08	.25
195 Mike Lieberthal	.15	.40
196 Andy Pettitte	.25	.60
197 Jay Gibbons	.08	.25
198 Rolando Arrojo	.08	.25
199 Joe Mays	.08	.25
200 Aubrey Huff	.15	.40
201 Nelson Figueroa	.08	.25
202 Paul Konerko	.15	.40
203 Ken Griffey Jr.	.75	2.00
204 Brandon Duckworth	.08	.25
205 Sammy Sosa	.40	1.00
206 Carl Everett	.15	.40
207 Scott Rolen	.25	.60
208 Orlando Hernandez	.15	.40
209 Todd Helton	.25	.60
210 Preston Wilson	.15	.40
211 Gil Meche	.08	.25
212 Bill Mueller	.15	.40
213 Craig Biggio	.25	.60
214 Dean Palmer	.15	.40
215 Randy Wolf	.08	.25
216 Jeff Suppan	.08	.25
217 Jimmy Rollins	.15	.40
218 Alexis Gomez	.08	.25
219 Ellis Burks	.15	.40
220 Ramon E. Martinez	.08	.25
221 Ramiro Mendoza	.08	.25
222 Einar Diaz	.08	.25
223 Brent Abernathy	.08	.25
224 Darin Erstad	.15	.40
225 Reggie Taylor	.08	.25
226 Jason Jennings	.08	.25
227 Ray Durham	.15	.40
228 John Parrish	.08	.25
229 Kevin Young	.08	.25
230 Xavier Nady	.08	.25
231 Juan Cruz	.08	.25
232 Greg Norton	.08	.25
233 Barry Bonds	1.00	2.50
234 Kip Wells	.08	.25
235 Paul LoDuca	.15	.40
236 Javy Lopez	.15	.40
237 Luis Castillo	.08	.25
238 Tom Gordon	.08	.25
239 Mike Mordecai	.08	.25
240 Damian Rolls	.08	.25
241 Julio Lugo	.08	.25
242 Ichiro Suzuki	.75	2.00
243 Tony Womack	.08	.25
244 Matt Anderson	.08	.25
245 Carlos Lee	.15	.40
246 Alex Rodriguez	.50	1.50
247 Bernie Williams	.25	.60
248 Scott Sullivan	.08	.25
249 Mike Hampton	.15	.40
250 Orlando Cabrera	.15	.40
251 Benito Santiago	.15	.40
252 Steve Finley	.15	.40
253 Dave Williams	.08	.25
254 Adam Kennedy	.08	.25
255 Omar Vizquel	.25	.60
256 Garrett Stephenson	.08	.25
257 Fernando Tatis	.08	.25
258 Mike Piazza	.60	1.50
259 Scott Spiezio	.08	.25
260 Jacque Jones	.15	.40
261 Russell Branyan	.08	.25
262 Mark McLemore	.08	.25
263 Mitch Meluskey	.08	.25
264 Marlon Byrd	.08	.25
265 Kyle Farnsworth	.08	.25
266 Billy Sylvester	.08	.25
267 C.C. Sabathia	.15	.40
268 Mark Buehrle	.15	.40
269 Geoff Blum	.08	.25
270 Bret Prinz	.08	.25
271 Placido Polanco	.08	.25
272 John Olerud	.15	.40
273 Pedro Martinez	.25	.60
274 Doug Mientkiewicz	.15	.40
275 Jason Bere	.08	.25
276 Bud Smith	.08	.25
277 Terrence Long	.08	.25
278 Troy Percival	.15	.40
279 Derek Jeter	1.00	2.50
280 Eric Owens	.08	.25
281 Jay Bell	.15	.40
282 Mike Cameron	.08	.25
283 Joe Randa	.08	.25
284 Brian Roberts	.15	.40
285 Ryan Klesko	.15	.40
286 Ryan Dempster	.08	.25
287 Cristian Guzman	.08	.25
288 Tim Salmon	.25	.60
289 Mark Johnson	.08	.25
290 Brian Giles	.15	.40
291 Jon Lieber	.08	.25
292 Fernando Vina	.08	.25
293 Mike Mussina	.25	.60
294 Juan Pierre	.15	.40
295 Carlos Beltran	.15	.40
296 Vladimir Guerrero	.40	1.00
297 Orlando Merced	.08	.25
298 Jose Hernandez	.08	.25
299 Mike Lamb	.08	.25
300 David Eckstein	.15	.40
301 Mark Loretta	.08	.25
302 Greg Vaughn	.08	.25
303 Jose Vidro	.08	.25
304 Jose Ortiz	.08	.25
305 Mark Grudzielanek	.08	.25
306 Rob Bell	.08	.25
307 Elmer Dessens	.08	.25
308 Tomas Perez	.08	.25
309 Jerry Hairston Jr.	.08	.25
310 Mike Stanton	.08	.25
311 Todd Walker	.08	.25
312 Jason Varitek	.40	1.00
313 Masato Yoshii	.08	.25
314 Ben Sheets	.15	.40
315 Roberto Hernandez	.08	.25
316 Eli Marrero	.08	.25
317 Josh Beckett	.15	.40
318 Robert Fick	.08	.25
319 Aramis Ramirez	.15	.40
320 Bartolo Colon	.15	.40
321 Kenny Kelly	.08	.25
322 Luis Gonzalez	.15	.40
323 John Smoltz	.25	.60
324 Homer Bush	.08	.25
325 Kevin Millwood	.15	.40
326 Manny Ramirez	.25	.60
327 Armando Benitez	.08	.25
328 Luis Alicea	.08	.25
329 Mark Kotsay	.15	.40
330 Felix Rodriguez	.08	.25
331 Eddie Taubensee	.08	.25
332 John Burkett	.08	.25
333 Ramon Ortiz	.08	.25
334 Daryle Ward	.08	.25
335 Jarrod Washburn	.08	.25
336 Benji Gil	.08	.25
337 Mike Lowell	.15	.40
338 Larry Walker	.15	.40
339 Andruw Jones	.25	.60
340 Scott Elarton	.08	.25
341 Tony McKnight	.08	.25
342 Frank Thomas	.40	1.00
343 Kevin Brown	.15	.40
344 Jermaine Dye	.15	.40
345 Luis Rivas	.08	.25
346 Jeff Conine	.15	.40
347 Bobby Kielty	.08	.25
348 Jeffrey Hammonds	.08	.25
349 Keith Foulke	.15	.40
350 Dave Martinez	.08	.25
351 Adam Eaton	.08	.25
352 Brandon Inge	.08	.25
353 Tyler Houston	.08	.25
354 Bobby Abreu	.15	.40
355 Ivan Rodriguez	.25	.60
356 Doug Glanville	.08	.25
357 Jorge Julio	.08	.25
358 Kerry Wood	.15	.40
359 Eric Munson	.08	.25
360 Joe Crede	.15	.40
361 Denny Neagle	.08	.25
362 Vance Wilson	.08	.25
363 Neifi Perez	.08	.25
364 Darryl Kile	.15	.40
365 Jose Macias	.08	.25
366 Michael Coleman	.08	.25
367 Erubiel Durazo	.08	.25
368 Darrin Fletcher	.08	.25
369 Matt White	.08	.25
370 Marvin Benard	.08	.25
371 Brad Penny	.08	.25
372 Chuck Finley	.15	.40
373 Delino DeShields	.08	.25
374 Adrian Brown	.08	.25
375 Corey Koskie	.08	.25
376 Kazuhiro Sasaki	.15	.40
377 Brent Butler	.08	.25
378 Paul Wilson	.08	.25
379 Scott Williamson	.08	.25
380 Mike Young	.40	1.00
381 Toby Hall	.08	.25
382 Shane Reynolds	.08	.25
383 Tom Goodwin	.08	.25
384 Seth Etherton	.08	.25
385 Billy Wagner	.15	.40
386 Josh Phelps	.08	.25
387 Kyle Lohse	.08	.25
388 Jeremy Fikac	.08	.25
389 Jorge Posada	.25	.60
390 Bret Boone	.15	.40
391 Angel Berroa	.08	.25
392 Matt Mantei	.08	.25
393 Alex Gonzalez	.08	.25
394 Scott Strickland	.08	.25
395 Charles Johnson	.15	.40
396 Ramon Hernandez	.08	.25
397 Damian Jackson	.08	.25
398 Albert Pujols	.75	2.00
399 Gary Bennett	.08	.25
400 Edgar Martinez	.25	.60
401 Carl Pavano	.15	.40
402 Chris Gomez	.08	.25
403 Jaret Wright	.08	.25
404 Lance Berkman	.15	.40
405 Robert Person	.08	.25
406 Brook Fordyce	.08	.25
407 Adam Pettyjohn	.08	.25
408 Chris Carpenter	.15	.40
409 Rey Ordonez	.08	.25
410 Eric Gagne	.15	.40
411 Damion Easley	.08	.25
412 A.J. Burnett	.15	.40
413 Aaron Boone	.15	.40
414 J.D. Drew	.15	.40
415 Kelly Stinnett	.08	.25
416 Mark Quinn	.08	.25
417 Brad Radke	.15	.40
418 Jose Cruz Jr.	.08	.25
419 Greg Maddux	.60	1.50
420 Steve Cox	.08	.25
421 Torii Hunter	.15	.40
422 Sandy Alomar Jr.	.08	.25
423 Barry Zito	.15	.40
424 Bill Hall	.15	.40
425 Marquis Grissom	.15	.40
426 Rich Aurilia	.08	.25
427 Royce Clayton	.08	.25
428 Travis Fryman	.15	.40
429 Pablo Ozuna	.08	.25
430 David Dellucci	.08	.25
431 Vernon Wells	.15	.40
432 Gregg Zaun CP	.08	.25
433 Alex Gonzalez CP	.08	.25
434 Hideo Nomo CP	.40	1.00
435 Jeromy Burnitz CP	.15	.40
436 Gary Sheffield CP	.15	.40
437 Tino Martinez CP	.25	.60
438 Tsuyoshi Shinjo CP	.15	.40
439 Chan Ho Park CP	.15	.40
440 Tony Clark CP	.08	.25
441 Brad Fullmer CP	.08	.25
442 Jason Giambi CP	.15	.40
443 Billy Koch CP	.08	.25
444 Mo Vaughn CP	.15	.40
445 Alex Ochoa CP	.08	.25
446 Darren Lewis CP	.08	.25
447 John Rocker CP	.15	.40
448 Scott Hatteberg CP	.08	.25
449 Brady Anderson CP	.15	.40
450 Chuck Knoblauch CP	.15	.40
451 Pokey Reese CP	.08	.25
452 Brian Jordan CP	.15	.40
453 Albie Lopez CP	.08	.25
454 David Bell CP	.08	.25
455 Juan Gonzalez CP	.15	.40
456 Terry Adams CP	.08	.25
457 Kenny Lofton CP	.15	.40
458 Shawn Estes CP	.08	.25
459 Josh Fogg CP	.08	.25
460 Dmitri Young CP	.15	.40
461 Johnny Damon Sox CP	.25	.60
462 Chris Singleton CP	.08	.25
463 Ricky Ledee CP	.08	.25
464 Dustin Hermanson CP	.08	.25
465 Aaron Sele CP	.08	.25
466 Chris Stynes CP	.08	.25
467 Matt Stairs CP	.08	.25
468 Kevin Appier CP	.15	.40
469 Omar Daal CP	.08	.25
470 Moises Alou CP	.15	.40
471 Juan Encarnacion CP	.08	.25
472 Robin Ventura CP	.15	.40
473 Eric Hinske CP	.08	.25
474 Rondell White CP	.15	.40
475 Carlos Pena CP	.08	.25
476 Craig Paquette CP	.08	.25
477 Marty Cordova CP	.08	.25
478 Brett Tomko CP	.08	.25
479 Reggie Sanders CP	.08	.25
480 Roberto Alomar CP	.25	.60
481 Jeff Cirillo CP	.08	.25
482 Todd Zeile CP	.15	.40
483 John Vander Wal CP	.08	.25
484 Rick Helling CP	.08	.25
485 Jeff D'Amico CP	.08	.25
486 David Justice CP	.15	.40
487 Jason Isringhausen CP	.15	.40
488 Shigetoshi Hasegawa CP	.15	.40
489 Eric Young CP	.08	.25
490 David Wells CP	.15	.40
491 Ruben Sierra CP	.08	.25
492 Aaron Cook FF RC	.30	.75
493 Takahito Nomura FF RC	.30	.75
494 Austin Kearns FF	.20	.50
495 Kazuhisa Ishii FF RC	.50	1.25
496 Mark Teixeira FF	.75	2.00
497 Rene Reyes FF RC	.30	.75
498 Tim Spooneybarger FF	.20	.50
499 Ben Broussard FF	.20	.50
500 Eric Cyr FF	.20	.50
501 Anastacio Martinez FF RC	.30	.75
502 Morgan Ensberg FF	.30	.75
503 Steve Kent FF RC	.30	.75
504 Franklin Nunez FF RC	.30	.75
505 Adam Walker FF RC	.30	.75
506 Anderson Machado FF RC	.30	.75
507 Ryan Drese FF	.20	.50
508 Luis Ugueto FF RC	.30	.75
509 Jorge Nunez FF RC	.30	.75
510 Colby Lewis FF	.20	.50
511 Ron Calloway FF RC	.30	.75
512 Hansel Izquierdo FF RC	.30	.75
513 Jason Lane FF	.30	.75
514 Rafael Soriano FF	.20	.50
515 Jackson Melian FF	.20	.50
516 Edwin Almonte FF RC	.30	.75
517 Satoru Komiyama FF RC	.30	.75
518 Corey Thurman FF RC	.30	.75
519 Jorge De La Rosa FF RC	.30	.75
520 Victor Martinez FF	.75	2.00
521 Dewon Brazelton FF	.20	.50
522 Marlon Byrd FF	.20	.50
523 Jae Seo FF	.20	.50
524 Orlando Hudson FF	.20	.50
525 Sean Burroughs FF	.20	.50
526 Ryan Langerhans FF	.30	.75
527 David Kelton FF	.20	.50
528 So Taguchi FF RC	.50	1.25
529 Tyler Walker FF	.20	.50
530 Hank Blalock FF	.50	1.25
531 Mark Prior FF	.50	1.25
532 Yankee Stadium CL	.15	.40
533 Fenway Park CL	.15	.40
534 Wrigley Field CL	.15	.40
535 Dodger Stadium CL	.15	.40
536 Camden Yards CL	.15	.40
537 PacBell Park CL	.08	.25
538 Jacobs Field CL	.08	.25
539 SAFECO Field CL	.08	.25
540 Miller Field CL	.08	.25

2002 Fleer Gold Backs

*GOLD BACK: .75X TO 2X BASIC
*GOLD BACK 492-531: .75X TO 2X BASIC
RANDOM INSERTS IN PACKS
15% OF PRINT RUN ARE GOLD BACKS

2002 Fleer Mini

*MINI: 10X TO 25X BASIC
*MINI 492-531: 5X TO 12X BASIC
RANDOM INSERTS IN RETAIL PACKS
STATED PRINT RUN 50 SERIAL #'d SETS

2002 Fleer Tiffany

*TIFFANY: 4X TO 10X BASIC
*TIFFANY 492-531: 2X TO 5X BASIC
RANDOM INSERTS IN HOBBY PACKS
STATED PRINT RUN 200 SERIAL #'d SETS

2002 Fleer Barry Bonds Career Highlights

Issued at overall odds of one in 12 hobby packs and one in 36 retail packs, these 10 cards feature highlights from Barry Bonds career. These cards were issued in different rates depending on which card number it was.

COMPLETE SET (10)	15.00	40.00
COMMON CARD (1-3)	1.50	4.00
COMMON CARD (4-6)	2.00	5.00
COMMON CARD (7-9)	3.00	8.00
COMMON CARD (10)	2.00	5.00

1-3 ODDS 1:65 HOBBY, 1:225 RETAIL
4-6 ODDS 1:125 HOBBY, 1:400 RETAIL
7-9 ODDS 1:250 HOBBY, 1:500 RETAIL
10 ODDS 1:383 HOBBY, 1:800 RETAIL
OVERALL ODDS 1:12 HOBBY, 1:36 RETAIL

2002 Fleer Barry Bonds Career Highlights Autographs

Randomly inserted in packs, these 10 cards not only parallel the Bonds Career Highlight set but also include an autograph from Barry Bonds on the card. Each card was issued to a stated print run of 25 serial numbered sets and due to market scarcity no pricing is provided.

COMMON CARD (1-10) 125.00 200.00
RANDOM INSERTS IN ALL PACKS
STATED PRINT RUN 25 SERIAL #'d SETS

2002 Fleer Classic Cuts Autographs

Inserted in packs at a stated rate of one in 432 hobby packs, these nine cards feature autographs from a retired legend. A few cards were issued to a smaller quantity and we have notated that information along with their stated print run next to their name in our checklist.

STATED ODDS 1:432 HOBBY
SP PRINT RUNS PROVIDED BY FLEER
SP'S ARE NOT SERIAL NUMBERED

Card	Low	High
BRA Brooks Robinson SP/200	10.00	25.00
GPA Gaylord Perry SP/225	6.00	15.00
HKA Harmon Killebrew	15.00	40.00
JMA Juan Marichal	8.00	20.00
LAA Luis Aparicio	6.00	15.00
PRA Phil Rizzuto SP/125	20.00	50.00
RCA Ron Cey	6.00	15.00
RFA Rollie Fingers SP/35	6.00	15.00
TLA Tommy Lasorda SP/35	30.00	60.00

2002 Fleer Classic Cuts Game Used

Inserted at stated odds of one in 24, these 94 cards feature retired players along with an authentic game-used memorabilia piece of that player. Some cards were issued in shorter quantites and we have provided the stated print run next to the player's name in our checklist.

STATED ODDS 1:24 HOBBY
SP PRINT RUNS PROVIDED BY FLEER
SP'S ARE NOT SERIAL NUMBERED
NO PRICING ON QTY OF 110 OR LESS

Card	Low	High
ADJ Andre Dawson Jsy	4.00	10.00
ATB Alan Trammell Bat	4.00	10.00
BBB Bobby Bonds Bat	4.00	10.00
BBJ Bobby Bonds Jsy	4.00	10.00
BDB Bill Dickey Bat/200 *	6.00	15.00
BJJ Bo Jackson Jsy	4.00	10.00
BMB Billy Martin Bat/65 *	10.00	25.00
BRB Brooks Robinson Bat/250 *	6.00	15.00
BTB Bill Terry Bat/65 *	15.00	40.00
CFB Carlton Fisk Bat	6.00	15.00
CFJ Carlton Fisk Jsy/150 *	6.00	15.00
CHJ Jim Hunter Jsy	6.00	15.00
CRBG Cal Ripken Btg Glv/100 *	12.00	30.00
CRFG Cal Ripken Fld Glv/60 *	12.00	30.00
CRJ Cal Ripken Jsy	8.00	20.00
CRP Cal Ripken Pants/200 *	10.00	25.00
DEB Dwight Evans Bat/250 *	6.00	15.00
DEJ Dwight Evans Jsy	6.00	15.00
DMB Don Mattingly Bat/200 *	10.00	25.00
DMJ Don Mattingly Jsy	10.00	25.00
DPB Dave Parker Bat	4.00	10.00
DWB Dave Winfield Bat	4.00	10.00
DWJ Dave Winfield Jsy/231 *	4.00	10.00
DWP Dave Winfield Pants	4.00	10.00
DZJ Don Zimmer Jsy/90 *	6.00	15.00
EMB Eddie Mathews Bat/200 *	4.00	10.00
EMB Eddie Murray Bat	6.00	15.00
EMJ Eddie Murray Jsy	6.00	15.00
EMP Eddie Murray Patch/45 *	15.00	40.00
EWJ Earl Weaver Jsy	4.00	10.00
GBB George Brett Bat/250 *	10.00	25.00
GBJ George Brett Jsy/250 *	10.00	25.00
GHB Gil Hodges Bat/200 *	6.00	15.00
GKB George Kell Bat/150 *	6.00	15.00
HBB Hank Bauer Bat	6.00	15.00
HWP Hoyt Wilhelm Pants/150 *	4.00	10.00
JBB Johnny Bench Bat/100 *	10.00	25.00
JBJ Johnny Bench Jsy	6.00	15.00
JMB Joe Morgan Bat/250 *	4.00	10.00
JPJ Jim Palmer Jsy/273 *	4.00	10.00
JRB Jim Rice Bat/225 *	4.00	10.00
JRJ Jim Rice Jsy/90 *	6.00	15.00
JTJ Joe Torre Jsy/125 *	6.00	15.00
KGB Kirk Gibson Bat	4.00	10.00
KPJ Kirby Puckett Jsy	6.00	15.00
LDB Larry Doby Bat/250 *	10.00	25.00
LPP Lou Piniella Pants	4.00	10.00
NFB Nellie Fox Bat/200 *	6.00	15.00
NRJ Nolan Ryan Jsy	15.00	40.00
NRP Nolan Ryan Pants/200 *	15.00	40.00
OCB Orlando Cepeda Bat/45 *	6.00	15.00
OCP Orlando Cepeda Pants	4.00	10.00
OSJ Ozzie Smith Jsy/250 *	10.00	25.00
PBB Paul Blair Bat	4.00	10.00
PMB Paul Molitor Bat/250 *	4.00	10.00
PMP Paul Molitor Patch/110 *	6.00	15.00
RFJ Rollie Fingers Jsy	4.00	10.00
RJB Reggie Jackson Bat/50 *	12.50	30.00
RJP Reggie Jackson Pants	6.00	15.00
RKB Ralph Kiner Bat/47 *	6.00	15.00
RMP Roger Maris Pants/200 *	12.00	50.00
RSB Ryne Sandberg Bat	6.00	15.00
RYB Robin Yount Bat	4.00	10.00
SAP Sparky Anderson Pants	4.00	10.00
SCP Steve Carlton Pants	4.00	10.00
SGB Steve Garvey Bat	4.00	10.00
TJJ Tommy John Jsy/55 *	6.00	15.00
TKB Ted Kluszewski Bat/200 *	6.00	15.00
TKP Ted Kluszewski Pants	6.00	15.00
TPB Tony Perez Bat/250 *	4.00	10.00
TPJ Tony Perez Jsy	4.00	10.00
TWB Ted Williams Bat	20.00	50.00
TWP Ted Williams Pants	12.50	30.00
WBB Wade Boggs Bat/99 *	10.00	25.00
WBJ Wade Boggs Jsy	4.00	10.00
WBP Wade Boggs Patch/50 *	15.00	40.00
WMJ Willie McCovey Jsy/300 *	4.00	10.00
WSB Willie Stargell Bat/250 *	6.00	15.00
YBB Yogi Berra Bat/72 *	10.00	25.00
RCCB Rod Carew Bat	4.00	10.00

2002 Fleer Classic Cuts Game Used Autographs

Randomly inserted in packs, these three cards feature not only a game-used piece from a retired player but also an authentic autograph. The stated print run for each player is listed next to their name in our checklist.

RANDOM INSERTS IN HOBBY PACKS
STATED PRINT RUNS LISTED BELOW

Card	Low	High
BRB Brooks Robinson Bat/45	30.00	60.00
LAB Luis Aparicio Bat/45	15.00	40.00
RFJ Rollie Fingers Jsy/35	5.00	12.00

2002 Fleer Diamond Standouts

Randomly inserted in packs, these 10 cards have a stated print run of 1200 serial numbered sets. These cards feature players who most fans would consider the top 10 stars in Baseball.

COMPLETE SET (10) 30.00 80.00
RANDOM INSERTS IN HOBBY PACKS
STATED PRINT RUN 1200 SERIAL #'d SETS

Card	Low	High
1 Mike Piazza	3.00	8.00
2 Derek Jeter	5.00	12.00
3 Ken Griffey Jr.	4.00	10.00
4 Barry Bonds	5.00	12.00
5 Sammy Sosa	3.00	8.00
6 Alex Rodriguez	2.50	6.00
7 Ichiro Suzuki	4.00	10.00
8 Greg Maddux	3.00	8.00
9 Jason Giambi	3.00	8.00
10 Nomar Garciaparra	3.00	8.00

2002 Fleer Golden Memories

Issued in packs at a stated rate of one in 24 packs, these 15 cards feature players who have earned many honors during their playing career.
COMPLETE SET (15) 15.00 40.00
STATED ODDS 1:24 HOBBY/RETAIL
1 Frank Thomas 1.00 2.50
2 Derek Jeter 2.50 6.00
3 Albert Pujols 2.00 5.00
4 Barry Bonds 2.50 6.00
5 Alex Rodriguez 1.25 3.00
6 Randy Johnson 1.00 2.50
7 Jeff Bagwell .60 1.50
8 Greg Maddux 1.50 4.00
9 Ivan Rodriguez .60 1.50
10 Ichiro Suzuki 2.00 5.00
11 Mike Piazza 1.50 4.00
12 Pat Burrell .60 1.50
13 Rickey Henderson 1.00 2.50
14 Vladimir Guerrero 1.00 2.50
15 Sammy Sosa 1.00 2.50

2002 Fleer Headliners

Issued at a stated rate of one in eight hobby packs and one in 12 retail packs, these 20 cards feature players who achieved noteworthy feats during the 2001 season.
COMPLETE SET (20) 10.00 25.00
STATED ODDS 1:8 HOBBY, 1:12 RETAIL
1 Randy Johnson .50 1.25
2 Alex Rodriguez .60 1.50
3 Todd Helton .40 1.00
4 Pedro Martinez .40 1.00
5 Ichiro Suzuki 1.00 2.50
6 Vladimir Guerrero .50 1.25
7 Derek Jeter 1.25 3.00
8 Adam Dunn .40 1.00
9 Luis Gonzalez .40 1.00
10 Kazuhiro Sasaki .40 1.00
11 Sammy Sosa .50 1.25
12 Jason Giambi .40 1.00
13 Ken Griffey Jr. 1.00 2.50
14 Roger Clemens 1.00 2.50
15 Brandon Duckworth .40 1.00
16 Nomar Garciaparra .75 2.00
17 Bud Smith .40 1.00
18 Juan Gonzalez .40 1.00
19 Chipper Jones .50 1.25
20 Barry Bonds 1.25 3.00

2002 Fleer Rookie Flashbacks

Issued at a stated rate of one in three retail packs, these 20 cards feature players who made their major league debut in 2001.
COMPLETE SET (20) 10.00 25.00
STATED ODDS 1:3 RETAIL
1 Bret Prinz .40 1.00
2 Albert Pujols 1.50 4.00
3 C.C. Sabathia .40 1.00
4 Ichiro Suzuki 1.50 4.00
5 Juan Cruz .40 1.00
6 Jay Gibbons .40 1.00
7 Bud Smith .40 1.00
8 Johnny Estrada .40 1.00
9 Roy Oswalt .40 1.00
10 Tsuyoshi Shinjo .40 1.00
11 Brandon Duckworth .40 1.00
12 Jackson Melian .40 1.00
13 Josh Beckett .40 1.00
14 Morgan Ensberg .40 1.00
15 Brian Lawrence .40 1.00
16 Eric Hinske .40 1.00
17 Juan Uribe .40 1.00
18 Matt White .40 1.00
19 Junior Spivey .40 1.00
20 Wilson Betemit .40 1.00

2002 Fleer Rookie Sensations

Randomly inserted in hobby packs and printed to a stated print run of 1500 serial numbered sets, these 20 cards feature players who made their major league debut in 2001.
COMPLETE SET (20) 20.00 50.00
RANDOM INSERTS IN HOBBY PACKS
STATED PRINT RUN 1500 SERIAL #'d SETS
1 Bret Prinz 2.00 5.00
2 Albert Pujols 6.00 15.00
3 C.C. Sabathia 2.00 5.00
4 Ichiro Suzuki 6.00 15.00
5 Juan Cruz 2.00 5.00
6 Jay Gibbons 2.00 5.00
7 Bud Smith 2.00 5.00
8 Johnny Estrada 2.00 5.00
9 Roy Oswalt 2.00 5.00
10 Tsuyoshi Shinjo 2.00 5.00
11 Brandon Duckworth 2.00 5.00
12 Jackson Melian 2.00 5.00
13 Josh Beckett 2.00 5.00
14 Morgan Ensberg 2.00 5.00
15 Brian Lawrence 2.00 5.00
16 Eric Hinske 2.00 5.00
17 Juan Uribe 2.00 5.00
18 Matt White 2.00 5.00
19 Junior Spivey 2.00 5.00
20 Wilson Betemit 2.00 5.00

2002 Fleer Then and Now

Randomly inserted in hobby packs, these 10 cards feature a player from the past who compares with one of today's stars. These cards are printed to a stated print run of 275 serial numbered sets.
COMPLETE SET (10) 60.00 150.00
RANDOM INSERTS IN HOBBY PACKS
STATED PRINT RUN 275 SERIAL #'d SETS
1 E.Mathews 6.00 15.00
C.Jones
2 W.McCovey 12.50 30.00
B.Bonds
3 J.Bench 8.00 20.00
M.Piazza
4 E.Banks 6.00 15.00
A.Rodriguez
5 R.Henderson 10.00 25.00
I.Suzuki
6 T.Seaver 10.00 25.00
R.Clemens
7 J.Marichal 6.00 15.00
P.Martinez
8 R.Jackson 12.50 30.00
D.Jeter
9 N.Ryan 20.00 50.00
K.Wood
10 J.Morgan 10.00 25.00
K.Griffey Jr.

2002 Fleer Collection

This set, which combined a photo of a die cast car along with an Ultra card of the featured player was produced by Fleer and featured one player from each team. This set was issued by the Fleer Collectibles division of Fleer. We are pricing both the car and the card here.
COMPLETE SET 40.00 100.00
1 Troy Glaus 1.00 2.50
2 Luis Gonzalez 1.00 2.50
3 Chipper Jones 2.00 5.00
4 Cal Ripken Jr. 4.00 10.00
5 Nomar Garciaparra 2.00 5.00
6 Sammy Sosa 1.50 4.00
7 Frank Thomas 1.25 3.00
8 Ken Griffey Jr. 3.00 8.00
9 Jim Thome 1.00 2.50
10 Todd Helton 1.00 2.50
11 Tony Clark .40 1.00
12 A.J. Burnett .40 1.00
13 Jeff Bagwell 1.25 3.00
14 Mike Sweeney 1.00 2.50
15 Shawn Green 1.00 2.50
16 Ben Sheets .60 1.50
17 Doug Mientkiewicz .40 1.00
18 Vladimir Guerrero 1.50 4.00
19 Mike Piazza 2.00 5.00
20 Derek Jeter 4.00 10.00
21 Tim Hudson 1.00 2.50
22 Pat Burrell .60 1.50
23 Jason Kendall .60 1.50
24 Phil Nevin .60 1.50
25 Barry Bonds 2.00 5.00
26 Ichiro Suzuki 4.00 10.00
27 Albert Pujols 3.00 8.00
28 Ben Grieve .40 1.00
29 Alex Rodriguez 1.50 4.00
30 Carlos Delgado 1.25 3.00

2002 Fleer Bonds 4X MVP Jumbo

This one card jumbo set was made specifically for Shop at Home by Fleer. The card honors Barry Bonds as the only player ever to win 4 Most Valuable Player awards.
NNO Barry Bonds 6.00 15.00

2002 Fleer Barry Bonds 600 Home Run Chasing History

This one card set, which measures 3 1/2" by 2 1/2" honors Barry Bonds 600th career homer. This card was issued to a stated print run of 600 serial numbered sets. This card has the bat piece used as part of the 600 on the left side of the card while the right side is used for both a portrait and action shot of Bonds along with an autograph. The back of the card gives congratulations for receiving this card as well as the individual serial numbering.
1 Barry Bonds 75.00 150.00

2002 Fleer Barry Bonds 600 Home Run Jumbo

BB600 Barry Bonds 2.00 5.00

2002 Fleer Barry Bonds 600 Home Run Jumbo Game Used Autographed

This one card set, serial numbered to 600 and measuring 5 1/4" by 3 1/2", features a authentic game used bat piece and an autograph of Bonds. The left features a head shot was well as an action shot of Bonds. While the right side of the card features the bat piece as well as the autograph. The back has information about the 600th homer blast as well as serial numbering on the back. In addition, these cards come with certificates of authenticity which were issued by Goldin Sports Marketing.
1 Barry Bonds 40.00 80.00

2002 Fleer Jeter Turn 2

This three-card standard-size set feature Yankee superstar Derek Jeter and honors his work with his Turn 2 foundation. These three cards were originally distributed at a special banquet to raise money for the foundation. In addition, these cards were sent to every youngster who entered an essay contest at more than 100 after-school recreation centers in New York City.
COMPLETE SET 2.00 5.00
COMMON CARD .75 2.00

2003 Fleer 3D

This 72 "card" set was issued by Fleer late during the 2003 season and featured puzzle pieces which could be put together into a little statue of the player. The pieces came four "cards" and one statue to a package which had an $1.99 SRP. Please note that we are pricing the unassembled "cards" here. The set is broken up into 6 subsets: Sliding (1-12); Fielding (13-24); Diving Fielder (25-36); Left-Handed Batter (37-48); Right-Handed Batter (49-60); Pitching (61-72).
COMPLETE SET 10.00 20.00
1 Derek Jeter 1.00 2.50
2 Barry Bonds .60 1.50
3 Ichiro Suzuki .50 1.25
4 Jason Giambi .15 .40
5 Chipper Jones .40 1.00
6 Alfonso Soriano .25 .60
7 Miguel Tejada .25 .60
8 Nomar Garciaparra .25 .60
9 Alex Rodriguez .50 1.25
10 Ken Griffey Jr .75 2.00
11 Sammy Sosa .40 1.00
12 Albert Pujols .50 1.25
13 Nomar Garciaparra H .25 .60
14 Nomar Garciaparra A .25 .60
15 Derek Jeter H 1.00 2.50
16 Derek Jeter A 1.00 2.50
17 Sammy Sosa .40 1.00
18 Chipper Jones .40 1.00
19 Alfonso Soriano H .25 .60
20 Alfonso Soriano A .25 .60
21 Alex Rodriguez H .50 1.25
22 Alex Rodriguez A .50 1.25
23 Miguel Tejada .25 .60
24 Albert Pujols .50 1.25
25 Derek Jeter H 1.00 2.50
26 Derek Jeter A 1.00 2.50
27 Sammy Sosa H .40 1.00
28 Sammy Sosa A .40 1.00
29 Chipper Jones .40 1.00
30 Alfonso Soriano H .25 .60
31 Alfonso Soriano A .25 .60
32 Miguel Tejada .25 .60
33 Nomar Garciaparra .25 .60
34 Alex Rodriguez .50 1.25
35 Albert Pujols H .50 1.25
36 Albert Pujols A .50 1.25
37 Jason Giambi H .15 .40
38 Jason Giambi A .15 .40
39 Jason Giambi ALT .15 .40
40 Ken Griffey Jr H .75 2.00
41 Ken Griffey Jr A .75 2.00
42 Ken Griffey Jr ALT .75 2.00
43 Barry Bonds H .60 1.50
44 Barry Bonds A .60 1.50
45 Barry Bonds ALT .60 1.50
46 Ichiro Suzuki H .50 1.25
47 Ichiro Suzuki A .50 1.25
48 Ichiro Suzuki ALT .50 1.25
49 Derek Jeter H 1.00 2.50
50 Derek Jeter A 1.00 2.50
51 Sammy Sosa H .40 1.00
52 Sammy Sosa A .40 1.00
53 Chipper Jones .40 1.00
54 Alfonso Soriano H .25 .60
55 Alfonso Soriano A .25 .60
56 Miguel Tejada .25 .60
57 Nomar Garciaparra .25 .60
58 Alex Rodriguez .50 1.25
59 Albert Pujols H .50 1.25
60 Albert Pujols A .50 1.25
61 Roger Clemens H .50 1.25
62 Roger Clemens A .50 1.25
63 Curt Schilling H .25 .60
64 Curt Schilling A .25 .60
65 Pedro Martinez H .25 .60
66 Pedro Martinez A .25 .60
67 Greg Maddux H .50 1.25
68 Greg Maddux A .50 1.25
69 Mark Prior H .25 .60
70 Mark Prior A .25 .60
71 Mariano Rivera H .50 1.25
72 Mariano Rivera A .50 1.25

2003 Fleer Barry Bonds 5 Time MVP

This one card set, features a bat chip and authentic autograph of Barry Bonds on the front and the card is serial numbered to 613 on the back.
1 Barry Bonds AU/613 50.00 100.00

2003 Fleer Cub Foods

This 10 card set, which measures 2" by 2 3/4" were inserted as individual cards in 24-ct cases of Pepsi and released through the Cub Foods Chain located primarily in Minnesota. The busy fronts have a player photo, the team logo in the background and logos for both cub foods and pepsi. The backs have biographical information, recent seasonal and career stats and an informational blurb.
COMPLETE SET (10) 6.00 15.00
1 Ichiro Suzuki .60 1.50
2 Kerry Wood .20 .50
3 Mike Piazza .50 1.25
4 Randy Johnson .50 1.25
5 Magglio Ordonez .30 .75
6 Brad Radke .20 .50
7 Omar Vizquel .30 .75
8 Ben Sheets .20 .50
9 Barry Zito .30 .75
10 Ken Griffey Jr 1.00 2.50

2003 Fleer Die Cast

This 33 item set was issued as a combination card/die-cast card by Fleer. The car is set to a 1:64 scale while there is an also an Ultra card issued as part of the package. We are pricing the combination car/card here. Please note that these items are checklisted in alphabetical order.
COMPLETE SET 15.00 40.00
1 Josh Beckett .40 1.00
2 Lance Berkman .60 1.50
3 Barry Bonds 1.50 4.00
4 Pat Burrell .40 1.00
5 Carlos Delgado .40 1.00
6 Adam Dunn .60 1.50
7 Robert Fick .40 1.00
8 Jason Giambi .40 1.00
9 Nomar Garciaparra .60 1.50
10 Jay Gibbons .40 1.00
11 Brian Giles .40 1.00
12 Troy Glaus .40 1.00
13 Tom Glavine .60 1.50
14 Shawn Green .40 1.00
15 Ben Grieve .40 1.00
16 Vladimir Guerrero .60 1.50
17 Todd Helton .60 1.50
18 Trevor Hoffman .60 1.50
19 Torii Hunter .40 1.00
20 Derek Jeter 2.50 6.00
21 Randy Johnson 1.00 2.50
22 Chipper Jones 1.00 2.50
23 Magglio Ordonez .60 1.50
24 Mike Piazza 1.00 2.50
25 Albert Pujols 1.25 3.00
26 Alex Rodriguez 1.25 3.00
27 Richie Sexson .40 1.00
28 Sammy Sosa 1.00 2.50
29 Ichiro Suzuki 1.25 3.00
30 Mike Sweeney .40 1.00
31 Miguel Tejada .60 1.50
32 Jim Thome .60 1.50
33 Omar Vizquel .60 1.50

2006 Fleer

This 400-card set was released in April, 2006. The set was issued in 10-card hobby or retail packs. Both the hobby and retail packs had an $1.59 SRP and came 36 packs to a box and 10 boxes to a case. Cards numbered 401-430 featured 2006 rookies and were only available in the Fleer factory sets.
COMP.FACT.SET (430) 20.00 50.00
COMPLETE SET (400) 15.00 40.00
COMMON CARD (1-400) .15 .40
COMMON ROOKIE .20 .50
COMMON ROOKIE (401-430) .25 .60
401-430 AVAIL. IN FLEER FACT.SET
1 Adam Kennedy .15 .40
2 Bartolo Colon .15 .40
3 Bengie Molina .15 .40
4 Chone Figgins .15 .40
5 Dallas McPherson .15 .40
6 Darin Erstad .15 .40
7 Francisco Rodriguez .25 .60
8 Garret Anderson .15 .40
9 Jarrod Washburn .15 .40
10 John Lackey .25 .60
11 Orlando Cabrera .15 .40
12 Ryan Theriot RC .60 1.50
13 Steve Finley .15 .40
14 Vladimir Guerrero .25 .60
15 Adam Everett .15 .40
16 Andy Pettitte .25 .60
17 Charlton Jimerson (RC) .20 .50
18 Brad Lidge .15 .40
19 Chris Burke .15 .40
20 Craig Biggio .25 .60
21 Jason Lane .15 .40
22 Jeff Bagwell .25 .60
23 Lance Berkman .25 .60
24 Morgan Ensberg .15 .40
25 Roger Clemens .50 1.25
26 Roy Oswalt .25 .60
27 Willy Taveras .15 .40
28 Barry Zito .25 .60
29 Bobby Crosby .15 .40
30 Bobby Kielty .15 .40
31 Dan Johnson .15 .40
32 Danny Haren .15 .40
33 Eric Chavez .15 .40
34 Huston Street .15 .40
35 Jason Kendall .15 .40
36 Jay Payton .15 .40
37 Joe Blanton .15 .40
38 Mark Kotsay .15 .40
39 Nick Swisher .25 .60
40 Rich Harden .15 .40
41 Ron Flores RC .20 .50
42 Alex Rios .15 .40
43 John-Ford Griffin (RC) .20 .50
44 Dave Bush .15 .40
45 Eric Hinske .15 .40
46 Frank Catalanotto .15 .40
47 Gustavo Chacin .15 .40
48 Josh Towers .15 .40
49 Miguel Batista .15 .40
50 Orlando Hudson .15 .40
51 Roy Halladay .25 .60
52 Shea Hillenbrand .15 .40
53 Shaun Marcum (RC) .20 .50
54 Vernon Wells .15 .40
55 Adam LaRoche .15 .40
56 Andruw Jones .15 .40
57 Chipper Jones .40 1.00
58 Anthony Lerew (RC) .20 .50
59 Jeff Francoeur .40 1.00
60 John Smoltz .40 1.00
61 Johnny Estrada .15 .40
62 Julio Franco .15 .40
63 Joey Devine RC .20 .50
64 Marcus Giles .15 .40
65 Mike Hampton .15 .40
66 Rafael Furcal .15 .40
67 Chuck James (RC) .20 .50
68 Tim Hudson .25 .60
69 Ben Sheets .15 .40
70 Bill Hall .15 .40
71 Brady Clark .15 .40
72 Carlos Lee .15 .40
73 Chris Capuano .15 .40
74 Nelson Cruz (RC) .75 2.00
75 Derrick Turnbow .15 .40
76 Doug Davis .15 .40
77 Geoff Jenkins .15 .40
78 J.J. Hardy .15 .40
79 Lyle Overbay .15 .40
80 Prince Fielder .75 2.00
81 Rickie Weeks .15 .40
82 Albert Pujols .50 1.25
83 Chris Carpenter .25 .60
84 David Eckstein .15 .40
85 Jason Isringhausen .15 .40
86 Tyler Johnson (RC) .20 .50
87 Adam Wainwright (RC) .30 .75
88 Jim Edmonds .25 .60
89 Chris Duncan (RC) .30 .75
90 Mark Grudzielanek .15 .40
91 Mark Mulder .15 .40
92 Matt Morris .15 .40
93 Reggie Sanders .15 .40
94 Scott Rolen .25 .60
95 Yadier Molina .40 1.00
96 Aramis Ramirez .15 .40
97 Carlos Zambrano .25 .60
98 Corey Patterson .15 .40
99 Derrek Lee .15 .40
100 Glendon Rusch .15 .40
101 Greg Maddux .50 1.25
102 Jeromy Burnitz .15 .40
103 Kerry Wood .15 .40
104 Mark Prior .25 .60
105 Michael Barrett .15 .40
106 Geovany Soto (RC) .50 1.25
107 Nomar Garciaparra .25 .60
108 Ryan Dempster .15 .40
109 Todd Walker .15 .40
110 Alex S. Gonzalez .15 .40
111 Aubrey Huff .15 .40
112 Victor Diaz .15 .40
113 Carl Crawford .25 .60
114 Danys Baez .15 .40
115 Joey Gathright .15 .40
116 Jonny Gomes .15 .40
117 Jorge Cantu .15 .40
118 Julio Lugo .15 .40
119 Rocco Baldelli .15 .40
120 Scott Kazmir .25 .60
121 Toby Hall .15 .40
122 Tim Corcoran RC .20 .50
123 Alex Cintron .15 .40
124 Brandon Webb .25 .60
125 Chad Tracy .15 .40
126 Dustin Nippert (RC) .20 .50
127 Claudio Vargas .15 .40
128 Craig Counsell .15 .40
129 Javier Vazquez .15 .40
130 Jose Valverde .15 .40
131 Luis Gonzalez .15 .40
132 Royce Clayton .15 .40
133 Russ Ortiz .15 .40
134 Shawn Green .15 .40
135 Tony Clark .15 .40
136 Troy Glaus .15 .40
137 Brad Penny .15 .40
138 Cesar Izturis .15 .40
139 Derek Lowe .15 .40
140 Eric Gagne .15 .40
141 Hee Seop Choi .15 .40
142 J.D. Drew .15 .40
143 Jason Phillips .15 .40
144 Jayson Werth .25 .60
145 Jeff Kent .15 .40
146 Jeff Weaver .15 .40
147 Milton Bradley .15 .40
148 Odalis Perez .15 .40
149 Hong-Chih Kuo (RC) .50 1.25
150 Brian Myrow RC .20 .50
151 Armando Benitez .15 .40
152 Edgardo Alfonzo .15 .40
153 J.T. Snow .15 .40
154 Jason Schmidt .15 .40
155 Lance Niekro .15 .40
156 Doug Clark (RC) .20 .50
157 Dan Ortmeier (RC) .20 .50
158 Moises Alou .15 .40
159 Noah Lowry .15 .40
160 Omar Vizquel .25 .60
161 Pedro Feliz .15 .40
162 Randy Winn .15 .40
163 Jeremy Accardo RC .20 .50
164 Aaron Boone .15 .40
165 Ryan Garko (RC) .20 .50
166 C.C. Sabathia .25 .60
167 Casey Blake .15 .40
168 Cliff Lee .25 .60
169 Coco Crisp .15 .40
170 Grady Sizemore .25 .60
171 Jake Westbrook .15 .40
172 Jhonny Peralta .15 .40
173 Kevin Millwood .15 .40
174 Scott Elarton .15 .40
175 Travis Hafner .15 .40
176 Victor Martinez .25 .60
177 Adrian Beltre .40 1.00
178 Eddie Guardado .15 .40
179 Felix Hernandez .25 .60
180 Gil Meche .15 .40
181 Ichiro Suzuki .50 1.25
182 Jamie Moyer .15 .40
183 Jeremy Reed .15 .40
184 Jaime Bubela (RC) .20 .50
185 Raul Ibanez .25 .60
186 Richie Sexson .15 .40
187 Ryan Franklin .15 .40
188 Jeff Harris RC .15 .40
189 A.J. Burnett .15 .40
190 Josh Wilson (RC) .20 .50
191 Josh Johnson (RC) .50 1.25
192 Carlos Delgado .15 .40
193 Dontrelle Willis .15 .40
194 Bernie Castro (RC) .20 .50
195 Josh Beckett .15 .40
196 Juan Encarnacion .15 .40
197 Juan Pierre .15 .40
198 Robert Andino RC .20 .50
199 Miguel Cabrera .40 1.00
200 Ryan Jorgensen RC .20 .50
201 Paul Lo Duca .15 .40
202 Todd Jones .15 .40
203 Braden Looper .15 .40
204 Carlos Beltran .25 .60
205 Cliff Floyd .15 .40
206 David Wright .30 .75
207 Doug Mientkiewicz .15 .40
208 Jae Seo .15 .40
209 Jose Reyes .25 .60
210 Anderson Hernandez (RC) .20 .50
211 Miguel Cairo .15 .40
212 Mike Cameron .15 .40
213 Mike Piazza .40 1.00
214 Pedro Martinez .25 .60
215 Tom Glavine .25 .60
216 Tim Hamulack (RC) .20 .50
217 Brad Wilkerson .15 .40
218 Darrell Rasner (RC) .20 .50
219 Chad Cordero .15 .40
220 Cristian Guzman .15 .40
221 Jason Bergmann RC .20 .50
222 John Patterson .15 .40
223 Jose Guillen .15 .40
224 Jose Vidro .15 .40
225 Livan Hernandez .15 .40
226 Nick Johnson .15 .40
227 Preston Wilson .15 .40
228 Ryan Zimmerman (RC) .60 1.50
229 Vinny Castilla .15 .40
230 B.J. Ryan .15 .40
231 B.J. Surhoff .15 .40
232 Brian Roberts .15 .40
233 Walter Young (RC) .20 .50
234 Daniel Cabrera .15 .40
235 Erik Bedard .15 .40
236 Javy Lopez .15 .40
237 Jay Gibbons .15 .40
238 Luis Matos .15 .40
239 Melvin Mora .15 .40
240 Miguel Tejada .25 .60
241 Rafael Palmeiro .25 .60
242 Alejandro Freire RC .20 .50
243 Sammy Sosa .40 1.00
244 Adam Eaton .15 .40
245 Brian Giles .15 .40
246 Brian Lawrence .15 .40
247 Dave Roberts .25 .60
248 Jake Peavy .15 .40
249 Khalil Greene .15 .40
250 Mark Loretta .15 .40
251 Ramon Hernandez .15 .40
252 Ryan Klesko .15 .40
253 Trevor Hoffman .25 .60
254 Woody Williams .15 .40
255 Craig Breslow RC .20 .50
256 Billy Wagner .15 .40
257 Bobby Abreu .15 .40
258 Brett Myers .15 .40
259 Chase Utley .25 .60
260 David Bell .15 .40
261 Jim Thome .25 .60
262 Jimmy Rollins .25 .60
263 Jon Lieber .15 .40
264 Danny Sandoval RC .20 .50
265 Mike Lieberthal .15 .40
266 Pat Burrell .15 .40
267 Randy Wolf .15 .40
268 Ryan Howard .30 .75
269 J.J. Furmaniak (RC) .20 .50
270 Ronny Paulino (RC) .20 .50
271 Craig Wilson .15 .40
272 Bryan Bullington (RC) .20 .50
273 Jack Wilson .15 .40
274 Jason Bay .15 .40
275 Matt Capps (RC) .20 .50
276 Oliver Perez .15 .40
277 Rob Mackowiak .15 .40
278 Tom Gorzelanny (RC) .20 .50
279 Zach Duke .15 .40
280 Alfonso Soriano .25 .60
281 Chris R. Young .15 .40
282 David Dellucci .15 .40
283 Francisco Cordero .15 .40
284 Jason Botts (RC) UER .20 .50
285 Hank Blalock .15 .40
286 Josh Rupe (RC) .20 .50
287 Kevin Mench .15 .40
288 Laynce Nix .15 .40
289 Mark Teixeira .25 .60
290 Michael Young .15 .40
291 Richard Hidalgo .15 .40
292 Scott Feldman RC .20 .50
293 Bill Mueller .15 .40
294 Hanley Ramirez (RC) .30 .75
295 Curt Schilling .25 .60
296 David Ortiz .40 1.00
297 Alejandro Machado (RC) .20 .50
298 Edgar Renteria .15 .40
299 Jason Varitek .40 1.00
300 Johnny Damon .25 .60
301 Keith Foulke .15 .40
302 Manny Ramirez .40 1.00
303 Matt Clement .15 .40
304 Craig Hansen RC .50 1.25
305 Tim Wakefield .25 .60
306 Trot Nixon .15 .40
307 Aaron Harang .15 .40
308 Adam Dunn .25 .60
309 Austin Kearns .15 .40
310 Brandon Claussen .15 .40
311 Chris Booker (RC) .20 .50
312 Edwin Encarnacion .40 1.00
313 Chris Denorfia (RC) .20 .50
314 Felipe Lopez .15 .40
315 Miguel Perez (RC) .20 .50
316 Ken Griffey Jr. .75 2.00
317 Ryan Freel .15 .40
318 Sean Casey .15 .40
319 Wily Mo Pena .15 .40
320 Mike Esposito (RC) .20 .50
321 Aaron Miles .15 .40
322 Brad Hawpe .15 .40
323 Brian Fuentes .15 .40
324 Clint Barmes .15 .40
325 Cory Sullivan .15 .40
326 Garrett Atkins .15 .40
327 J.D. Closser .15 .40
328 Jeff Francis .15 .40
329 Luis Gonzalez .15 .40
330 Matt Holliday .40 1.00
331 Todd Helton .25 .60
332 Angel Berroa .15 .40
333 David DeJesus .15 .40
334 Emil Brown .15 .40
335 Jeremy Affeldt .15 .40
336 Chris Demaria RC .20 .50
337 Mark Teahen .15 .40

338 Matt Stairs .15 .40
339 Steve Stemle RC .20 .50
340 Mike Sweeney .15 .40
341 Runelvys Hernandez .15 .40
342 Jonah Bayliss RC .20 .50
343 Zack Greinke .25 .60
344 Brandon Inge .15 .40
345 Carlos Guillen .15 .40
346 Carlos Pena .25 .60
347 Chris Shelton .15 .40
348 Craig Monroe .15 .40
349 Dmitri Young .15 .40
350 Ivan Rodriguez .25 .60
351 Jeremy Bonderman .15 .40
352 Magglio Ordonez .25 .60
353 Mark Woodyard (RC) .20 .50
354 Omar Infante .15 .40
355 Placido Polanco .15 .40
356 Rondell White .15 .40
357 Brad Radke .15 .40
358 Carlos Silva .15 .40
359 Jacque Jones .15 .40
360 Joe Mauer .25 .60
361 Chris Heintz RC .20 .50
362 Joe Nathan .15 .40
363 Johan Santana .25 .60
364 Justin Morneau .25 .60
365 Francisco Liriano (RC) .50 1.25
366 Travis Bowyer (RC) .20 .50
367 Michael Cuddyer .15 .40
368 Scott Baker .15 .40
369 Shannon Stewart .15 .40
370 Torii Hunter .15 .40
371 A.J. Pierzynski .15 .40
372 Aaron Rowand .15 .40
373 Carl Everett .15 .40
374 Dustin Hermanson .15 .40
375 Frank Thomas .40 1.00
376 Freddy Garcia .15 .40
377 Jermaine Dye .15 .40
378 Joe Crede .15 .40
379 Jon Garland .15 .40
380 Jose Contreras .15 .40
381 Juan Uribe .15 .40
382 Mark Buehrle .25 .60
383 Orlando Hernandez .15 .40
384 Paul Konerko .25 .60
385 Scott Podsednik .15 .40
386 Tadahito Iguchi .15 .40
387 Alex Rodriguez .50 1.25
388 Bernie Williams .25 .60
389 Chien-Ming Wang .25 .60
390 Derek Jeter 1.00 2.50
391 Gary Sheffield .15 .40
392 Hideki Matsui .40 1.00
393 Jason Giambi .15 .40
394 Jorge Posada .25 .60
395 Mike Vento (RC) .20 .50
396 Mariano Rivera .50 1.25
397 Mike Mussina .25 .60
398 Randy Johnson .40 1.00
399 Robinson Cano .25 .60
400 Tino Martinez .15 .40
401 Alay Soler RC .25 .60
402 Boof Bonser (RC) .40 1.00
403 Cole Hamels (RC) .75 2.00
404 Ian Kinsler (RC) .75 2.00
405 Jason Kubel (RC) .25 .60
406 Joel Zumaya (RC) .60 1.50
407 Jonathan Papelbon (RC) 1.25 3.00
408 Jered Weaver (RC) .75 2.00
409 Kendry Morales (RC) .60 1.50
410 Lastings Milledge (RC) .25 .60
411 Matt Kemp (RC) .60 1.50
412 Taylor Buchholz (RC) .25 .60
413 Andre Ethier (RC) .75 2.00
414 Dan Uggla (RC) .40 1.00
415 Jeremy Sowers (RC) .25 .60
416 Chad Billingsley (RC) .40 1.00
417 Josh Barfield (RC) .25 .60
418 Matt Cain (RC) 1.50 4.00
419 Fausto Carmona (RC) .25 .60
420 Josh Willingham (RC) .40 1.00
421 Jeremy Hermida (RC) .25 .60
422 Conor Jackson (RC) .40 1.00
423 Dave Gassner (RC) .25 .60
424 Brian Bannister (RC) .25 .60
425 Fernando Nieve (RC) .25 .60
426 Justin Verlander (RC) 2.00 5.00
427 Scott Olsen (RC) .25 .60
428 Takashi Saito RC .40 1.00
429 Willie Eyre (RC) .25 .60
430 Travis Ishikawa (RC) .40 1.00

2006 Fleer Glossy Gold

STATED ODDS 1:144 HOBBY, 1:144 RETAIL
NO PRICING DUE TO SCARCITY

2006 Fleer Glossy Silver

*GLOSSY SILVER: 2X TO 5X BASIC
*GLOSSY SILVER: 1.5X TO 4X BASIC RC
STATED ODDS 1:12 HOBBY, 1:24 RETAIL

2006 Fleer Autographics

STATED ODDS 1:432 HOBBY, 1:432 RETAIL
SP PRINT RUNS PROVIDED BY UD
SP'S ARE NOT SERIAL-NUMBERED
NO SP PRICING ON QTY OF 25 OR LESS
AN Garret Anderson 6.00 15.00
CS Chris Shelton 6.00 15.00
EC Eric Chavez 6.00 15.00
GA Garrett Atkins 6.00 15.00
JB Joe Blanton 6.00 15.00
KG Ken Griffey Jr.SP/150 * 50.00 120.00
KY Kevin Youkilis 6.00 15.00
NS Nick Swisher 6.00 15.00
TI Tadahito Iguchi 6.00 15.00

2006 Fleer Award Winners

COMPLETE SET (6) 6.00 15.00
OVERALL INSERT ODDS ONE PER PACK
AW1 Albert Pujols 1.25 3.00
AW2 Alex Rodriguez 1.25 3.00
AW3 Chris Carpenter .60 1.50
AW4 Bartolo Colon .40 1.00
AW5 Ryan Howard .75 2.00
AW6 Huston Street .40 1.00

2006 Fleer Fabrics

STATED ODDS 1:36 HOBBY, 1:72 RETAIL
SP INFO PROVIDED BY UPPER DECK
AJ Andruw Jones Jsy 3.00 8.00
AP Albert Pujols Jsy 6.00 15.00
AR Aramis Ramirez Jsy 3.00 8.00
AS Alfonso Soriano Jsy 3.00 8.00
BA Bobby Abreu Jsy 3.00 8.00
CB Carlos Beltran Jsy 3.00 8.00
CJ Chipper Jones Jsy 4.00 10.00
CS Curt Schilling Jsy 3.00 8.00
DJ Derek Jeter Jsy 10.00 25.00
DL Derrek Lee Jsy 3.00 8.00
DO David Ortiz Pants 4.00 10.00
DW Dontrelle Willis Jsy SP 4.00 10.00
EC Eric Chavez Jsy 3.00 8.00
EG Eric Gagne Jsy 3.00 8.00
GM Greg Maddux Jsy 4.00 10.00
GR Khalil Greene Jsy 4.00 10.00
GS Gary Sheffield Jsy SP 4.00 10.00
IR Ivan Rodriguez Jsy 3.00 8.00
JE Jim Edmonds Jsy 3.00 8.00
JM Joe Mauer Jsy 4.00 10.00
JP Jake Peavy Jsy 3.00 8.00
JS Johan Santana Jsy 4.00 10.00
JT Jim Thome Jsy 4.00 10.00
KG Ken Griffey Jr. Jsy 6.00 15.00
LG Luis Gonzalez Jsy 3.00 8.00
MC Miguel Cabrera Jsy 4.00 10.00
MP Mark Prior Jsy 4.00 10.00
MR Manny Ramirez Jsy 4.00 10.00
MT Mark Teixeira Jsy 4.00 10.00
MY Michael Young Jsy 3.00 8.00
PM Pedro Martinez Jsy 4.00 10.00
RC Roger Clemens Jsy 6.00 15.00
RH Roy Halladay Jsy 3.00 8.00
RJ Randy Johnson Jsy 4.00 10.00
RW Rickie Weeks Jsy 3.00 8.00
SM John Smoltz Jsy 4.00 10.00
TE Miguel Tejada Jsy 3.00 8.00
TH Todd Helton Jsy 4.00 10.00
VG Vladimir Guerrero Jsy 4.00 10.00
WR David Wright Jsy 4.00 10.00

2006 Fleer Lumber Company

COMPLETE SET (25) 10.00 25.00
OVERALL INSERT ODDS ONE PER PACK
LC1 Adam Dunn .60 1.50
LC2 Albert Pujols 1.25 3.00
LC3 Alex Rodriguez 1.25 3.00
LC4 Alfonso Soriano .60 1.50
LC5 Andruw Jones .40 1.00
LC6 Aramis Ramirez .40 1.00
LC7 Bobby Abreu .40 1.00
LC8 Carlos Delgado .40 1.00
LC9 Carlos Lee .40 1.00
LC10 David Ortiz 1.00 2.50
LC11 David Wright .75 2.00
LC12 Derrek Lee .40 1.00
LC13 Eric Chavez .40 1.00
LC14 Gary Sheffield .40 1.00
LC15 Jeff Kent .40 1.00
LC16 Ken Griffey Jr. 2.00 5.00
LC17 Manny Ramirez 1.00 2.50
LC18 Mark Teixeira .60 1.50
LC19 Miguel Cabrera 1.00 2.50
LC20 Miguel Tejada .60 1.50
LC21 Paul Konerko .60 1.50
LC22 Richie Sexson .40 1.00
LC23 Todd Helton .60 1.50
LC24 Troy Glaus .40 1.00
LC25 Vladimir Guerrero .60 1.50

2006 Fleer Smoke 'n Heat

COMPLETE SET (15) 8.00 20.00
OVERALL INSERT ODDS ONE PER PACK
SH1 Carlos Zambrano .60 1.50
SH2 Chris Carpenter .60 1.50
SH3 Curt Schilling .60 1.50
SH4 Dontrelle Willis .40 1.00
SH5 Felix Hernandez .60 1.50
SH6 Jake Peavy .40 1.00
SH7 Johan Santana .60 1.50
SH8 John Smoltz 1.00 2.50
SH9 Mark Prior .60 1.50
SH10 Pedro Martinez .60 1.50
SH11 Randy Johnson 1.00 2.50
SH12 Roger Clemens 1.25 3.00
SH13 Roy Halladay .60 1.50
SH14 Roy Oswalt .60 1.50
SH15 Scott Kazmir .60 1.50

2006 Fleer Smooth Leather

COMPLETE SET (14) 10.00 25.00
OVERALL INSERT ODDS ONE PER PACK
SL1 Alex Rodriguez 1.25 3.00
SL2 Andruw Jones .40 1.00
SL3 Derek Jeter 2.50 6.00
SL4 Derrek Lee .40 1.00
SL5 Eric Chavez .40 1.00
SL6 Greg Maddux 1.25 3.00
SL7 Ichiro Suzuki 1.25 3.00
SL8 Ivan Rodriguez .60 1.50
SL9 Jim Edmonds .60 1.50
SL10 Mike Mussina .60 1.50
SL11 Omar Vizquel .60 1.50
SL12 Scott Rolen .60 1.50
SL13 Todd Helton .60 1.50
SL14 Torii Hunter .40 1.00

2006 Fleer Stars of Tomorrow

COMPLETE SET (10) 6.00 15.00
OVERALL INSERT ODDS ONE PER PACK
ST1 David Wright .75 2.00
ST2 Ryan Howard .75 2.00
ST3 Felix Hernandez .60 1.50
ST4 Jeff Francoeur 1.00 2.50
ST5 Joe Mauer .60 1.50
ST6 Mark Prior .60 1.50
ST7 Mark Teixeira .60 1.50
ST8 Miguel Cabrera 1.00 2.50
ST9 Prince Fielder 2.00 5.00
ST10 Rickie Weeks .40 1.00

2006 Fleer Team Fleer

OVERALL INSERT ODDS ONE PER PACK
TF1 Albert Pujols 6.00 15.00
TF2 Alex Rodriguez 6.00 15.00
TF3 Alfonso Soriano 3.00 8.00
TF4 Andruw Jones 2.00 5.00
TF5 Bobby Abreu 2.00 5.00
TF6 David Ortiz 5.00 12.00
TF7 David Wright 4.00 10.00
TF8 Eric Gagne 2.00 5.00
TF9 Ichiro Suzuki 6.00 15.00
TF10 Jason Varitek 5.00 12.00
TF11 Jeff Kent 2.00 5.00
TF12 Johan Santana 3.00 8.00
TF13 Jose Reyes 3.00 8.00
TF14 Manny Ramirez 5.00 12.00
TF15 Mariano Rivera 6.00 15.00
TF16 Miguel Cabrera 5.00 12.00
TF17 Miguel Tejada 3.00 8.00
TF18 Mike Piazza 5.00 12.00
TF19 Roger Clemens 6.00 15.00
TF20 Torii Hunter 2.00 5.00

2006 Fleer Team Leaders

COMPLETE SET (30) 15.00 40.00
OVERALL INSERT ODDS ONE PER PACK
TL1 Troy Glaus .60 1.50
Brandon Webb
TL2 Andruw Jones 1.00 2.50
John Smoltz
TL3 Miguel Tejada .60 1.50
Erik Bedard
TL4 David Ortiz 1.00 2.50
Curt Schilling
TL5 Derrek Lee .60 1.50
Mark Prior
TL6 Paul Konerko .60 1.50
Mark Buehrle
TL7 Ken Griffey Jr. 2.00 5.00
Aaron Harang
TL8 Travis Hafner .60 1.50
Cliff Lee
TL9 Todd Helton .60 1.50
Jeff Francis
TL10 Ivan Rodriguez .60 1.50
Jeremy Bonderman
TL11 Miguel Cabrera 1.00 2.50
Dontrelle Willis
TL12 Lance Berkman 1.25 3.00
Roger Clemens
TL13 Mike Sweeney .60 1.50
Zack Greinke
TL14 Jeff Kent .40 1.00
Derek Lowe
TL15 Carlos Lee .40 1.00
Ben Sheets
TL16 Torii Hunter .60 1.50
Johan Santana
TL17 David Wright .75 2.00
Pedro Martinez
TL18 Derek Jeter 2.50 6.00
Randy Johnson
TL19 Eric Chavez .60 1.50
Barry Zito
TL20 Bobby Abreu .40 1.00
Brett Myers
TL21 Jason Bay .40 1.00
Zach Duke
TL22 Brian Giles .40 1.00
Jake Peavy
TL23 Moises Alou .40 1.00
Jason Schmidt
TL24 Ichiro Suzuki 1.25 3.00
Felix Hernandez
TL25 Albert Pujols 1.25 3.00
Chris Carpenter
TL26 Carl Crawford .60 1.50
Scott Kazmir
TL27 Mark Teixeira .60 1.50
Kenny Rogers
TL28 Vernon Wells .60 1.50
Roy Halladay
TL29 Jose Guillen .40 1.00
Livan Hernandez
TL30 Vladimir Guerrero .60 1.50
Bartolo Colon

2006 Fleer Top 40

STATED ODDS 2:1 FAT PACKS
1 Ken Griffey Jr. 2.00 5.00
2 Derek Jeter 2.50 6.00
3 Albert Pujols 1.25 3.00
4 Alex Rodriguez 1.25 3.00
5 Vladimir Guerrero .60 1.50
6 Roger Clemens 1.25 3.00
7 Derrek Lee .40 1.00
8 David Ortiz 1.00 2.50
9 Miguel Cabrera 1.00 2.50
10 Bobby Abreu .40 1.00
11 Mark Teixeira .60 1.50
12 Johan Santana .60 1.50
13 Hideki Matsui 1.00 2.50
14 Ichiro Suzuki 1.25 3.00
15 Andruw Jones .40 1.00
16 Eric Chavez .40 1.00
17 Roy Oswalt .60 1.50
18 Curt Schilling .60 1.50
19 Randy Johnson 1.00 2.50
20 Ivan Rodriguez .60 1.50
21 Chipper Jones 1.00 2.50
22 Mark Prior .60 1.50
23 Jason Bay .40 1.00
24 Pedro Martinez .60 1.50
25 David Wright .75 2.00
26 Carlos Beltran .60 1.50
27 Jim Edmonds .60 1.50
28 Chris Carpenter .60 1.50
29 Roy Halladay .60 1.50
30 Jake Peavy .40 1.00
31 Paul Konerko .60 1.50
32 Travis Hafner .40 1.00
33 Barry Zito .60 1.50
34 Miguel Tejada .60 1.50
35 Josh Beckett .40 1.00
36 Todd Helton .60 1.50
37 Dontrelle Willis .40 1.00
38 Manny Ramirez 1.00 2.50
39 Mariano Rivera 1.25 3.00
40 Jeff Kent .40 1.00

2007 Fleer

COMPLETE SET (400) 30.00 60.00
COMP.FACT.SET (430) 30.00 60.00
COMMON CARD (1-430) .12 .30
COMMON RC .25 .60
401-430 ISSUED IN FACT.SET
OVERALL PRINTING PLATE ODDS 1:720
PLATE PRINT RUN 1 SET PER COLOR
BLACK-CYAN-MAGENTA-YELLOW ISSUED
NO PLATE PRICING DUE TO SCARCITY
1 Chad Cordero .12 .30
2 Alfonso Soriano .20 .50
3 Nick Johnson .12 .30
4 Austin Kearns .12 .30
5 Ramon Ortiz .12 .30
6 Brian Schneider .12 .30
7 Ryan Zimmerman .20 .50
8 Jose Vidro .12 .30
9 Felipe Lopez .12 .30
10 Cristian Guzman .12 .30
11 B.J. Ryan .12 .30
12 Alex Rios .12 .30
13 Vernon Wells .12 .30
14 Roy Halladay .20 .50
15 A.J. Burnett .12 .30
16 Lyle Overbay .12 .30
17 Troy Glaus .12 .30
18 Bengie Molina .12 .30
19 Gustavo Chacin .12 .30
20 Aaron Hill .12 .30
21 Vicente Padilla .12 .30
22 Kevin Millwood .12 .30
23 Akinori Otsuka .12 .30
24 Adam Eaton .12 .30
25 Hank Blalock .12 .30
26 Mark Teixeira .20 .50
27 Michael Young .12 .30
28 Mark DeRosa .12 .30
29 Gary Matthews .12 .30
30 Ian Kinsler .20 .50
31 Carlos Lee .12 .30
32 James Shields .12 .30
33 Scott Kazmir .20 .50
34 Carl Crawford .20 .50
35 Jonny Gomes .12 .30
36 Tim Corcoran .12 .30
37 B.J. Upton .12 .30
38 Rocco Baldelli .12 .30
39 Jae Seo .12 .30
40 Jorge Cantu .12 .30
41 Ty Wigginton .12 .30
42 Chris Carpenter .20 .50
43 Albert Pujols .40 1.00
44 Scott Rolen .20 .50
45 Jim Edmonds .20 .50
46 Jason Isringhausen .12 .30
47 Yadier Molina .30 .75
48 Adam Wainwright .20 .50
49 Mark Mulder .12 .30
50 Jason Marquis .12 .30
51 Juan Encarnacion .12 .30
52 Aaron Miles .12 .30
53 Ichiro Suzuki .40 1.00
54 Felix Hernandez .20 .50
55 Kenji Johjima .30 .75
56 Richie Sexson .12 .30
57 Yuniesky Betancourt .12 .30
58 J.J. Putz .12 .30
59 Jarrod Washburn .12 .30
60 Ben Broussard .12 .30
61 Adrian Beltre .30 .75
62 Raul Ibanez .20 .50
63 Jose Lopez .12 .30
64 Matt Cain .20 .50
65 Noah Lowry .12 .30
66 Jason Schmidt .12 .30
67 Pedro Feliz .12 .30
68 Matt Morris .12 .30
69 Ray Durham .12 .30
70 Steve Finley .12 .30
71 Randy Winn .12 .30
72 Moises Alou .12 .30
73 Eliezer Alfonzo .12 .30
74 Armando Benitez .12 .30
75 Omar Vizquel .20 .50
76 Chris R. Young .12 .30
77 Adrian Gonzalez .25 .60
78 Khalil Greene .12 .30
79 Mike Piazza .30 .75
80 Josh Barfield .12 .30
81 Brian Giles .12 .30
82 Jake Peavy .12 .30
83 Trevor Hoffman .20 .50
84 Mike Cameron .12 .30
85 Dave Roberts .20 .50
86 David Wells .12 .30
87 Zach Duke .12 .30
88 Ian Snell .12 .30
89 Jason Bay .20 .50
90 Freddy Sanchez .12 .30
91 Jack Wilson .12 .30
92 Tom Gorzelanny .12 .30
93 Chris Duffy .12 .30
94 Jose Castillo .12 .30
95 Matt Capps .12 .30
96 Mike Gonzalez .12 .30
97 Chase Utley .20 .50
98 Jimmy Rollins .20 .50
99 Aaron Rowand .12 .30
100 Ryan Howard .25 .60
101 Cole Hamels .25 .60
102 Pat Burrell .12 .30
103 Shane Victorino .12 .30
104 Jamie Moyer .12 .30
105 Mike Lieberthal .12 .30
106 Tom Gordon .12 .30
107 Brett Myers .12 .30
108 Nick Swisher .20 .50
109 Barry Zito .20 .50
110 Jason Kendall .12 .30
111 Milton Bradley .12 .30
112 Bobby Crosby .12 .30
113 Huston Street .12 .30
114 Eric Chavez .12 .30
115 Frank Thomas .30 .75
116 Dan Haren .12 .30
117 Jay Payton .12 .30
118 Randy Johnson .30 .75
119 Mike Mussina .20 .50
120 Bobby Abreu .12 .30
121 Jason Giambi .12 .30
122 Derek Jeter .75 2.00
123 Alex Rodriguez .40 1.00
124 Jorge Posada .20 .50
125 Robinson Cano .20 .50
126 Mariano Rivera .40 1.00
127 Chien-Ming Wang .20 .50
128 Hideki Matsui .30 .75
129 Gary Sheffield .12 .30
130 Lastings Milledge .20 .50
131 Tom Glavine .20 .50
132 Billy Wagner .12 .30
133 Pedro Martinez .20 .50
134 Paul LoDuca .12 .30
135 Carlos Delgado .12 .30
136 Carlos Beltran .20 .50
137 David Wright .25 .60
138 Jose Reyes .20 .50
139 Julio Franco .12 .30
140 Michael Cuddyer .12 .30
141 Justin Morneau .20 .50
142 Johan Santana .20 .50
143 Francisco Liriano .12 .30
144 Joe Mauer .25 .60
145 Torii Hunter .12 .30
146 Luis Castillo .12 .30
147 Joe Nathan .12 .30
148 Carlos Silva .12 .30
149 Boof Bonser .12 .30
150 Ben Sheets .12 .30
151 Prince Fielder .20 .50
152 Bill Hall .12 .30
153 Rickie Weeks .12 .30
154 Geoff Jenkins .12 .30
155 Kevin Mench .12 .30
156 Francisco Cordero .12 .30
157 Chris Capuano .12 .30
158 Brady Clark .12 .30
159 Tony Gwynn Jr. .12 .30
160 Chad Billingsley .20 .50
161 Russell Martin .12 .30
162 Wilson Betemit .12 .30
163 Nomar Garciaparra .20 .50
164 Kenny Lofton .12 .30
165 Rafael Furcal .12 .30
166 Julio Lugo .12 .30
167 Brad Penny .12 .30
168 Jeff Kent .12 .30
169 Greg Maddux .40 1.00
170 Derek Lowe .12 .30
171 Andre Ethier .20 .50
172 Chone Figgins .12 .30
173 Francisco Rodriguez .20 .50
174 Garret Anderson .12 .30
175 Orlando Cabrera .12 .30
176 Adam Kennedy .12 .30
177 John Lackey .20 .50
178 Vladimir Guerrero .20 .50
179 Bartolo Colon .12 .30
180 Jered Weaver .20 .50
181 Juan Rivera .12 .30
182 Howie Kendrick .12 .30
183 Ervin Santana .12 .30
184 Mark Redman .12 .30
185 David DeJesus .12 .30
186 Joey Gathright .12 .30
187 Mike Sweeney .12 .30
188 Mark Teahen .12 .30
189 Angel Berroa .12 .30
190 Ambiorix Burgos .12 .30
191 Luke Hudson .12 .30
192 Mark Grudzielanek .12 .30
193 Roger Clemens .40 1.00
194 Willy Taveras .12 .30
195 Craig Biggio .20 .50
196 Andy Pettitte .20 .50
197 Roy Oswalt .20 .50
198 Lance Berkman .20 .50
199 Morgan Ensberg .12 .30
200 Brad Lidge .12 .30
201 Chris Burke .12 .30
202 Miguel Cabrera .30 .75
203 Dontrelle Willis .12 .30
204 Josh Johnson .30 .75
205 Ricky Nolasco .12 .30
206 Dan Uggla .12 .30
207 Jeremy Hermida .12 .30
208 Scott Olsen .12 .30
209 Josh Willingham .20 .50
210 Joe Borowski .12 .30
211 Hanley Ramirez .20 .50
212 Mike Jacobs .12 .30
213 Kenny Rogers .12 .30
214 Justin Verlander .30 .75
215 Ivan Rodriguez .20 .50
216 Magglio Ordonez .20 .50
217 Todd Jones .12 .30
218 Joel Zumaya .12 .30
219 Jeremy Bonderman .12 .30
220 Nate Robertson .12 .30
221 Brandon Inge .12 .30
222 Craig Monroe .12 .30
223 Carlos Guillen .12 .30
224 Jeff Francis .12 .30
225 Brian Fuentes .12 .30
226 Todd Helton .20 .50
227 Matt Holliday .30 .75
228 Garrett Atkins .12 .30
229 Clint Barmes .12 .30
230 Jason Jennings .12 .30
231 Aaron Cook .12 .30
232 Brad Hawpe .12 .30
233 Cory Sullivan .12 .30
234 Aaron Boone .12 .30
235 C.C. Sabathia .20 .50
236 Grady Sizemore .20 .50
237 Travis Hafner .12 .30
238 Jhonny Peralta .12 .30
239 Jake Westbrook .12 .30
240 Jeremy Sowers .12 .30
241 Andy Marte .12 .30
242 Victor Martinez .20 .50
243 Jason Michaels .12 .30
244 Cliff Lee .20 .50
245 Bronson Arroyo .12 .30
246 Aaron Harang .12 .30
247 Ken Griffey Jr. .60 1.50
248 Adam Dunn .20 .50
249 Rich Aurilia .12 .30
250 Eric Milton .12 .30
251 David Ross .12 .30
252 Brandon Phillips .12 .30
253 Ryan Freel .12 .30
254 Eddie Guardado .12 .30
255 Jose Contreras .12 .30
256 Freddy Garcia .12 .30
257 Jon Garland .12 .30
258 Mark Buehrle .20 .50
259 Bobby Jenks .12 .30
260 Paul Konerko .20 .50
261 Jermaine Dye .12 .30
262 Joe Crede .12 .30
263 Jim Thome .20 .50
264 Javier Vazquez .12 .30
265 A.J. Pierzynski .12 .30
266 Tadahito Iguchi .12 .30
267 Carlos Zambrano .20 .50
268 Derrek Lee .12 .30
269 Aramis Ramirez .12 .30
270 Ryan Theriot .12 .30
271 Juan Pierre .12 .30
272 Rich Hill .12 .30
273 Ryan Dempster .12 .30
274 Jacque Jones .12 .30
275 Mark Prior .20 .50
276 Kerry Wood .12 .30
277 Josh Beckett .12 .30
278 David Ortiz .30 .75
279 Kevin Youkilis .12 .30
280 Jason Varitek .30 .75
281 Manny Ramirez .30 .75
282 Curt Schilling .20 .50
283 Jon Lester .20 .50
284 Jonathan Papelbon .30 .75
285 Alex Gonzalez .12 .30
286 Mike Lowell .12 .30
287 Kyle Snyder .12 .30
288 Miguel Tejada .20 .50
289 Erik Bedard .12 .30
290 Ramon Hernandez .12 .30
291 Melvin Mora .12 .30
292 Nick Markakis .25 .60
293 Brian Roberts .12 .30
294 Corey Patterson .12 .30
295 Kris Benson .12 .30
296 Jay Gibbons .12 .30
297 Rodrigo Lopez .12 .30
298 Chris Ray .12 .30
299 Andruw Jones .12 .30
300 Brian McCann .12 .30
301 Jeff Francoeur .30 .75
302 Chuck James .12 .30
303 John Smoltz .30 .75
304 Bob Wickman .12 .30
305 Edgar Renteria .12 .30
306 Adam LaRoche .12 .30
307 Marcus Giles .12 .30
308 Tim Hudson .20 .50
309 Chipper Jones .30 .75
310 Miguel Batista .12 .30
311 Claudio Vargas .12 .30
312 Brandon Webb .20 .50
313 Luis Gonzalez .12 .30
314 Livan Hernandez .12 .30
315 Stephen Drew .12 .30
316 Johnny Estrada .12 .30
317 Orlando Hudson .12 .30

18 Conor Jackson .12 .30
19 Chad Tracy .12 .30
20 Carlos Quentin .12 .30
21 Alvin Colina RC .60 1.50
22 Miguel Montero (RC) .25 .60
23 Jeff Fiorentino (RC) .25 .60
24 Jeff Baker (RC) .25 .60
25 Brian Burres (RC) .25 .60
26 David Murphy (RC) .25 .60
27 Francisco Cruceta (RC) .25 .60
28 Beltran Perez (RC) .25 .60
29 Scott Moore (RC) .25 .60
330 Sean Henn (RC) .25 .60
331 Ryan Sweeney (RC) .25 .60
332 Josh Fields (RC) .25 .60
333 Jerry Owens (RC) .25 .60
334 Vinny Rottino (RC) .25 .60
335 Kevin Kouzmanoff (RC) .25 .60
336 Alexi Casilla RC .40 1.00
337 Justin Hampson (RC) .25 .60
338 Troy Tulowitzki (RC) .75 2.00
339 Jose Garcia RC .25 .60
340 Andrew Miller RC 1.00 2.50
341 Glen Perkins (RC) .25 .60
342 Ubaldo Jimenez (RC) .75 2.00
343 Doug Slaten RC .25 .60
344 Angel Sanchez RC .25 .60
345 Mitch Maier RC .25 .60
346 Ryan Braun RC .25 .60
347 Joselo Diaz (RC) .25 .60
348 Delwyn Young (RC) .25 .60
349 Kevin Hooper (RC) .25 .60
350 Dennis Sarfate (RC) .25 .60
351 Andy Cannizaro RC .25 .60
352 Devern Hansack RC .25 .60
353 Michael Bourn (RC) .40 1.00
354 Carlos Maldonado (RC) .25 .60
355 Shane Youman RC .25 .60
356 Philip Humber (RC) .25 .60
357 Hector Gimenez (RC) .25 .60
358 Fred Lewis (RC) .40 1.00
359 Ryan Feierabend (RC) .25 .60
360 Juan Morillo (RC) .25 .60
361 Travis Chick (RC) .25 .60
362 Oswaldo Navarro RC .25 .60
363 Cesar Jimenez RC .25 .60
364 Brian Stokes (RC) .25 .60
365 Delmon Young (RC) .40 1.00
366 Juan Salas (RC) .25 .60
367 Shawn Riggans (RC) .25 .60
368 Adam Lind (RC) .25 .60
369 Joaquin Arias (RC) .25 .60
370 Eric Stults RC .25 .60
371 Brandon Webb CL .20 .50
372 John Smoltz CL .30 .75
373 Miguel Tejada CL .20 .50
374 David Ortiz CL .30 .75
375 Carlos Zambrano CL .20 .50
376 Jermaine Dye CL .12 .30
377 Ken Griffey Jr. CL .60 1.50
378 Victor Martinez CL .20 .50
379 Todd Helton CL .20 .50
380 Ivan Rodriguez CL .20 .50
381 Miguel Cabrera CL .30 .75
382 Lance Berkman CL .20 .50
383 Mike Sweeney CL .12 .30
384 Vladimir Guerrero CL .20 .50
385 Derek Lowe CL .12 .30
386 Bill Hall CL .12 .30
387 Johan Santana CL .20 .50
388 Carlos Beltran CL .20 .50
389 Derek Jeter CL .75 2.00
390 Nick Swisher CL .20 .50
391 Ryan Howard CL .25 .60
392 Jason Bay CL .20 .50
393 Trevor Hoffman CL .20 .50
394 Omar Vizquel CL .20 .50
395 Ichiro Suzuki CL .40 1.00
396 Albert Pujols CL .40 1.00
397 Carl Crawford CL .20 .50
398 Mark Teixeira CL .20 .50
399 Roy Halladay CL .20 .50
400 Ryan Zimmerman CL .20 .50
401 Mark Reynolds RC .75 2.00
402 Micah Owings (RC) .25 .60
403 Jarrod Saltalamacchia (RC) .40 1.00
404 Daisuke Matsuzaka RC 1.00 2.50
405 Hideki Okajima RC 1.25 3.00
406 Felix Pie (RC) .25 .60
407 Mike Fontenot (RC) .25 .60
408 John Danks RC .40 1.00
409 Josh Hamilton (RC) .75 2.00
410 Homer Bailey (RC) .40 1.00
411 Alejandro De Aza RC .40 1.00
412 Matt Lindstrom (RC) .25 .60
413 Hunter Pence (RC) .75 2.00
414 Alex Gordon RC .75 2.00
415 Billy Butler (RC) .40 1.00
416 Brandon Wood (RC) .25 .60
417 Andy LaRoche (RC) .25 .60
418 Ryan Bruan (RC) 1.25 3.00
419 Joe Smith RC .25 .60
420 Carlos Gomez RC .50 1.25
421 Tyler Clippard (RC) .40 1.00
422 Matt DeSalvo (RC) .25 .60
423 Phil Hughes (RC) .60 1.50
424 Kei Igawa RC .60 1.50
425 Chase Wright RC .60 1.50
426 Travis Buck (RC) .25 .60
427 Zack Segovia (RC) .25 .60
428 Tim Lincecum RC 1.25 3.00
429 Elijah Dukes RC .40 1.00
430 Akinori Iwamura RC .60 1.50

2007 Fleer Mini Die Cuts

*MINI: 1.25X TO 3X BASIC
*MINI RC: .6X TO 1.5X BASIC RC
STATED ODDS 1:2 HOBBY, 1:2 RETAIL

2007 Fleer Mini Die Cuts Gold

STATED ODDS 1:576 HOBBY, 1:576 RETAIL
NO PRICING DUE TO SCARCITY

2007 Fleer Autographics

STATED ODDS 1:720
NO PRICING ON MOST DUE TO SCARCITY
BH Bill Hall 20.00 50.00
CB Chris Booker 6.00 15.00
CK Casey Kotchman 6.00 15.00
DJ Dan Johnson 6.00 15.00
JJ Jorge Julio 6.00 15.00
KH Koyie Hill 6.00 15.00
NS Nick Swisher 6.00 15.00

2007 Fleer Crowning Achievement

COMPLETE SET (20) 6.00 15.00
STATED ODDS 1:5
OVERALL PRINTING PLATE ODDS 1:720
PLATE PRINT RUN 1 SET PER COLOR
BLACK-CYAN-MAGENTA-YELLOW ISSUED
NO PLATE PRICING DUE TO SCARCITY
AP Albert Pujols 1.25 3.00
BZ Barry Zito .60 1.50
CD Carlos Delgado .40 1.00
CS Curt Schilling .60 1.50
DJ Derek Jetcr 2.50 6.00
DO David Ortiz 1.00 2.50
FT Frank Thomas 1.00 2.50
GM Greg Maddux 1.25 3.00
IS Ichiro Suzuki 1.25 3.00
JS Johan Santana .60 1.50
JT Jim Thome .60 1.50
KG Ken Griffey Jr. 2.00 5.00
MC Miguel Cabrera 1.00 2.50
MP Mike Piazza 1.00 2.50
MR Manny Ramirez 1.00 2.50
PM Pedro Martinez .60 1.50
RC Roger Clemens 1.25 3.00
RH Ryan Howard .75 2.00
TG Tom Glavine .60 1.50
TH Trevor Hoffman .60 1.50

2007 Fleer Fresh Ink

STATED ODDS 1:720
NO PRICING ON MOST DUE TO SCARCITY
CC Craig Counsell 6.00 15.00
GQ Guillermo Quiroz 6.00 15.00
JB Joe Blanton 6.00 15.00
KG Khalil Greene 10.00 25.00
LN Leo Nunez 6.00 15.00
MM Matt Murton 15.00 40.00
SD Scott Dunn 6.00 15.00
SR Saul Rivera 6.00 15.00

2007 Fleer Genuine Coverage

STATED ODDS 1:720
MANY NOT PRICED DUE TO SCARCITY
AP Albert Pujols 8.00 20.00
AR Aramis Ramirez 4.00 10.00
BE Adrian Beltre 4.00 10.00
BR Brian Roberts 4.00 10.00
BS Ben Sheets 4.00 10.00
CB Carlos Beltran 6.00 15.00
CS C.C. Sabathia 4.00 10.00
DJ Derek Jeter 10.00 25.00
DW Dontrelle Willis 4.00 10.00
GJ Geoff Jenkins 4.00 10.00
HA Rich Harden 4.00 10.00
IS Ian Snell 4.00 10.00
JM Justin Morneau 5.00 12.00
JP Jake Peavy 4.00 10.00
KG Ken Griffey Jr. 8.00 20.00
MR Manny Ramirez 6.00 15.00
PK Paul Konerko 4.00 10.00
RS Richie Sexson 4.00 10.00
TH Torii Hunter 4.00 10.00

2007 Fleer In the Zone

COMPLETE SET (10) 5.00 12.00
STATED ODDS 1:10 HOBBY, 1:10 RETAIL
OVERALL PRINTING PLATE ODDS 1:720
PLATE PRINT RUN 1 SET PER COLOR
BLACK-CYAN-MAGENTA-YELLOW ISSUED
NO PLATE PRICING DUE TO SCARCITY
AJ Andruw Jones .40 1.00
AP Albert Pujols 1.25 3.00
AR Alex Rodriguez 1.25 3.00
DO David Ortiz 1.00 2.50
DW David Wright .75 2.00
KG Ken Griffey Jr. 2.00 5.00
MC Miguel Cabrera 1.00 2.50
MT Mark Teixeira .60 1.50
RH Ryan Howard .75 2.00
VG Vladimir Guerrero .60 1.50

2007 Fleer Perfect 10

COMPLETE SET (20) 6.00 15.00
STATED ODDS 1:5
OVERALL PRINTING PLATE ODDS 1:720
PLATE PRINT RUN 1 SET PER COLOR
BLACK-CYAN-MAGENTA-YELLOW ISSUED
NO PLATE PRICING DUE TO SCARCITY
AP Albert Pujols 1.25 3.00
AS Alfonso Sorlano .60 1.50
BH Bill Hall .40 1.00
CB Carlos Beltran .60 1.50
CC Carl Crawford .60 1.50
CJ Chipper Jones 1.00 2.50
CU Chase Utley .60 1.50
DJ Derek Jeter 2.50 6.00
DO David Ortiz 1.00 2.50
IR Ivan Rodriguez .60 1.50
JB Jason Bay .60 1.50
JD Jermaine Dye .40 1.00
JS Johan Santana .60 1.50
MC Miguel Cabrera 1.00 2.50
MM Mike Mussina .60 1.50
MY Michael Young .40 1.00
RC Roger Clemens 1.25 3.00
RH Roy Halladay .60 1.50
RH Ryan Howard .75 2.00
VG Vladimir Guerrero .60 1.50

2007 Fleer Rookie Sensations

COMPLETE SET (25) 6.00 15.00
STATED ODDS APPX 1:1 HOBBY, 1:1 RETAIL
OVERALL PRINTING PLATE ODDS 1:720
PLATE PRINT RUN 1 SET PER COLOR
BLACK-CYAN-MAGENTA-YELLOW ISSUED
NO PLATE PRICING DUE TO SCARCITY
BB Boof Bonser .40 1.00
CB Chad Billingsley .60 1.50
CH Cole Hamels .75 2.00
CJ Conor Jackson .40 1.00
DU Dan Uggla .40 1.00
FL Francisco Liriano .40 1.00
HR Hanley Ramirez .60 1.50
IK Ian Kinsler .60 1.50
JB Josh Barfield .40 1.00
JH Jeremy Hermida .40 1.00
JJ Josh Johnson 1.00 2.50
JL Jon Lester .60 1.50
JP Jonathan Papelbon 1.00 2.50
JS Jeremy Sowers .40 1.00
JV Justin Verlander 1.00 2.50
JW Jered Weaver .60 1.50
KJ Kenji Johjima 1.00 2.50
LO James Loney .40 1.00
MK Matt Kemp .75 2.00
NM Nick Markakis .75 2.00
PF Prince Fielder .60 1.50
RG Matt Garza .40 1.00
RN Ricky Nolasco .40 1.00
RZ Ryan Zimmerman .60 1.50
SO Scott Olsen .40 1.00

2007 Fleer Soaring Stars

STATED ODDS 1:2 FAT PACKS
OVERALL PRINTING PLATE ODDS 1:720
PLATE PRINT RUN 1 SET PER COLOR
BLACK-CYAN-MAGENTA-YELLOW ISSUED
NO PLATE PRICING DUE TO SCARCITY
AD Adam Dunn .60 1.50
AJ Andruw Jones .40 1.00
AL Alex Rodriguez 1.25 3.00
AP Albert Pujols 1.25 3.00
AR Alex Rios .40 1.00
AS Alfonso Soriano .60 1.50
BW Brandon Webb .60 1.50
BZ Barry Zito .60 1.50
CB Carlos Beltran .60 1.50
CJ Chipper Jones 1.00 2.50
CU Chase Utley .60 1.50
DA Johnny Damon .60 1.50
DJ Derek Jeter 2.50 6.00
DL Derrek Lee .40 1.00
DO David Ortiz 1.00 2.50
DW David Wright .75 2.00
HA Roy Halladay .60 1.50
IR Ivan Rodriguez .60 1.50
IS Ichiro Suzuki 1.25 3.00
JB Jason Bay .40 1.00
JD Jermaine Dye .40 1.00
JG Jon Garland .40 1.00
JM Joe Mauer .75 2.00
JS Johan Santana .60 1.50
JV Justin Verlander 1.00 2.50
KG Ken Griffey Jr. 2.00 5.00
LB Lance Berkman .60 1.50
MC Miguel Cabrera 1.00 2.50
MP Mike Piazza 1.00 2.50
MR Manny Ramirez 1.00 2.50
MT Mark Teixeira .60 1.50
NG Nomar Garciaparra .60 1.50
PF Prince Fielder .60 1.50
PM Pedro Martinez .60 1.50
RH Ryan Howard .75 2.00
RI Mariano Rivera 1.25 3.00
RO Roy Oswalt .60 1.50
TE Miguel Tejada .60 1.50
TG Tom Glavine .60 1.50
TH Travis Hafner .40 1.00
VG Vladimir Guerrero .60 1.50
WI Dontrelle Willis .40 1.00

2007 Fleer Year in Review

COMPLETE SET (20) 6.00 15.00
STATED ODDS 1:5
OVERALL PRINTING PLATE ODDS 1:720
PLATE PRINT RUN 1 SET PER COLOR
BLACK-CYAN-MAGENTA-YELLOW ISSUED
NO PLATE PRICING DUE TO SCARCITY
AP Albert Pujols 1.25 3.00
AR Alex Rodriguez 1.25 3.00
AS Alfonso Soriáno .60 1.50
BA Bobby Abreu .40 1.00
CU Chase Utley .60 1.50
DJ Derek Jeter 2.50 6.00
DO David Ortiz 1.00 2.50
FL Francisco Liriano .40 1.00
FS Freddy Sanchez .40 1.00
HO Ryan Howard .75 2.00
JD Jermaine Dye .40 1.00
JM Joe Mauer .75 2.00
JR Jose Reyes .60 1.50
JV Justin Verlander 1.00 2.50
JW Jered Weaver .60 1.50
KG Ken Griffey Jr. 2.00 5.00
MD Mark DeRosa .40 1.00
MO Justin Morneau .60 1.50
RH Roy Halladay .60 1.50
TH Travis Hafner .40 1.00

1933 Goudey

The cards in this 240-card set measure approximately 2 3/8" by 2 7/8". The 1933 Goudey set, was that company's first baseball issue. The four Babe Ruth and two Lou Gehrig cards in the set are extremely popular with collectors. Card number 106, Napoleon Lajoie, was not printed in 1933, and was circulated to a limited number of collectors in 1934 upon request (it was printed along with the 1934 Goudey cards). An album was offered to house the 1933 set. Several minor leaguers are depicted. Card number 1 (Bengough) is very rarely found in mint condition; in fact, as a general rule all the first series cards are more difficult to find in Mint condition. Players with more than one card are also sometimes differentiated below by their pose: BAT (Batting), FIELD (Fielding), PIT (Pitching), THROW (Throwing). One of the Babe Ruth cards was double printed (DP) apparently in place of the Lajoie and hence is easier to obtain than the others. Due to the scarcity of the Lajoie card, the set is considered complete at 239 cards and is priced as such below. One copy of card number 106 as Leo Durocher is known to exist. The card was apparently cut from a proof sheet and is the only known copy to exist. A large window display poster which measured 5 3/8" by 11 1/4" was sent to stores and used the same Babe Ruth photo as in the Goudey Premium set. The gum used was approximately the same dimension as the actual card. At the factory each piece was scored twice so it could be snapped into three pieces. The gum had a spearmint flavor and according to collectors who remember chewing said gum, the flavor did not last very long.

COMPLETE SET (239) 40000.00 80000.00
COMMON CARD (1-52) 30.00 80.00
COMMON (41/43/53-240) 50.00 120.00
WRAPPER (1-CENT, BAT.) 40.00 100.00
WRAPPER (1-CENT, AD) 50.00 120.00
1 Benny Bengough RC 1000.00 2000.00
2 Dazzy Vance RC 500.00 1000.00
3 Hugh Critz BAT RC 60.00 150.00
4 Heinie Schuble RC 60.00 150.00
5 Babe Herman RC 125.00 300.00
6 Jimmy Dykes RC 40.00 100.00
7 Ted Lyons RC 150.00 400.00
8 Roy Johnson RC 40.00 100.00
9 Dave Harris RC 50.00 120.00
10 Glenn Myatt RC 100.00 250.00
11 Billy Rogell RC 60.00 150.00
12 George Pipgras RC 60.00 150.00
13 Fresco Thompson RC 50.00 120.00
14 Henry Johnson RC 60.00 150.00
15 Victor Sorrell RC 50.00 120.00
16 George Blaeholder RC 60.00 150.00
17 Watson Clark RC 50.00 120.00
18 Muddy Ruel RC 50.00 120.00
19 Bill Dickey RC 400.00 800.00
20 Bill Terry THROW RC 150.00 400.00
21 Phil Collins RC 40.00 100.00
22 Pie Traynor RC 300.00 600.00
23 Kiki Cuyler RC 250.00 500.00
24 Horace Ford RC 75.00 200.00
25 Paul Waner RC 400.00 800.00
26 Bill Cissell RC 40.00 100.00
27 George Connally RC 60.00 150.00
28 Dick Bartell RC 50.00 120.00
29 Jimmie Foxx RC 600.00 1200.00
30 Frank Hogan RC 50.00 120.00
31 Tony Lazzeri RC 400.00 800.00
32 Bud Clancy RC 50.00 120.00
33 Ralph Kress RC 40.00 100.00
34 Bob O'Farrell RC 60.00 150.00
35 Al Simmons RC 150.00 400.00
36 Tommy Thevenow RC 40.00 100.00
37 Jimmy Wilson RC 50.00 120.00
38 Fred Brickell RC 60.00 150.00
39 Mark Koenig RC 40.00 100.00
40 Taylor Douthit RC 50.00 120.00
41 Gus Mancuso CATCH 40.00 100.00
42 Eddie Collins RC 125.00 300.00
43 Lew Fonseca RC 60.00 150.00
44 Jim Bottomley RC 125.00 300.00
45 Larry Benton RC 40.00 100.00
46 Ethan Allen RC 60.00 150.00
47 Heinie Manush BAT RC 125.00 300.00
48 Marty McManus RC 60.00 150.00
49 Frankie Frisch RC 250.00 500.00
50 Ed Brandt RC 40.00 100.00
51 Charlie Grimm RC 60.00 150.00
52 Andy Cohen RC 40.00 100.00
53 Babe Ruth RC 10000.00 20000.00
54 Ray Kremer RC 30.00 80.00
55 Pat Malone RC 40.00 100.00
56 Red Ruffing RC 150.00 400.00
57 Earl Clark RC 30.00 80.00
58 Lefty O'Doul RC 60.00 150.00
59 Bing Miller RC 50.00 120.00
60 Waite Hoyt RC 150.00 400.00
61 Max Bishop RC 50.00 120.00
62 Pepper Martin RC 60.00 150.00
63 Joe Cronin BAT RC 100.00 250.00
64 Burleigh Grimes RC 125.00 300.00
65 Milt Gaston RC 40.00 100.00
66 George Grantham RC 30.00 80.00
67 Guy Bush RC 40.00 100.00
68 Horace Lisenbee RC 30.00 80.00
69 Randy Moore RC 40.00 100.00
70 Floyd (Pete) Scott RC 40.00 100.00
71 Robert J. Burke RC 40.00 100.00
72 Owen Carroll RC 40.00 100.00
73 Jesse Haines RC 75.00 200.00
74 Eppa Rixey RC 100.00 250.00
75 Willie Kamm RC 40.00 100.00
76 Mickey Cochrane RC 125.00 300.00
77 Adam Comorosky RC 50.00 120.00
78 Jack Quinn RC 40.00 100.00
79 Red Faber RC 125.00 300.00
80 Clyde Manion RC 40.00 100.00
81 Sam Jones RC 40.00 100.00
82 Dib Williams RC 30.00 80.00
83 Pete Jablonowski RC 40.00 100.00
84 Glenn Spencer RC 50.00 120.00
85 Heinie Sand RC 40.00 100.00
86 Phil Todt RC 50.00 120.00
87 Frank O'Rourke RC 40.00 100.00
88 Russell Rollings RC 30.00 80.00
89 Tris Speaker RET 400.00 800.00
90 Jess Petty RC 40.00 100.00
91 Tom Zachary RC 30.00 80.00
92 Lou Gehrig RC 3000.00 6000.00
93 John Welch RC 60.00 150.00
94 Bill Walker RC 50.00 120.00
95 Alvin Crowder RC 50.00 120.00
96 Willis Hudlin RC 40.00 100.00
97 Joe Morrissey RC 30.00 80.00
98 Wally Berger RC 50.00 120.00
99 Tony Cuccinello RC 30.00 80.00
100 George Uhle RC 40.00 100.00
101 Richard Coffman RC 30.00 80.00
102 Travis Jackson RC 75.00 200.00
103 Earle Combs RC 100.00 250.00
104 Fred Marberry RC 40.00 100.00
105 Bernie Friberg RC 40.00 100.00
106 Napoleon Lajoie SP 20000.00 40000.00
107 Heinie Manush RC 100.00 250.00
108 Joe Kuhel RC 40.00 100.00
109 Joe Cronin RC 75.00 200.00
110 Goose Goslin RC 75.00 200.00
111 Monte Weaver RC 50.00 120.00
112 Fred Schulte RC 40.00 100.00
113 Oswald Bluege POR RC 50.00 120.00
114 Luke Sewell FIELD RC 50.00 120.00
115 Cliff Heathcote RC 40.00 100.00
116 Eddie Morgan RC 40.00 100.00
117 Rabbit Maranville RC 125.00 300.00
118 Val Picinich RC 40.00 100.00
119 Rogers Hornsby Field RC 500.00 1000.00
120 Carl Reynolds RC 50.00 120.00
121 Walter Stewart RC 30.00 80.00
122 Alvin Crowder RC 40.00 100.00
123 Jack Russell RC 40.00 100.00
124 Earl Whitehill RC 50.00 120.00
125 Bill Terry RC 100.00 250.00
126 Joe Moore BAT RC 50.00 120.00
127 Mel Ott RC 500.00 1000.00
128 Chuck Klein RC 150.00 400.00
129 Hal Schumacher PIT RC 50.00 120.00
130 Fred Fitzsimmons POR RC 40.00 100.00
131 Fred Frankhouse RC 50.00 120.00
132 Jim Elliott RC 40.00 100.00
133 Fred Lindstrom RC 125.00 300.00
134 Sam Rice RC 125.00 300.00
135 Woody English RC 40.00 100.00
136 Flint Rhem RC 40.00 100.00
137 Red Lucas RC 50.00 120.00
138 Herb Pennock RC 125.00 300.00
139 Ben Cantwell RC 40.00 100.00
140 Bump Hadley RC 40.00 100.00
141 Ray Benge RC 30.00 80.00
142 Paul Richards RC 30.00 80.00
143 Glenn Wright RC 60.00 150.00
144 Babe Ruth Bat DP RC 6000.00 12000.00
145 Rube Walberg RC 40.00 100.00
146 Walter Stewart PIT RC 40.00 100.00
147 Leo Durocher RC 100.00 250.00
148 Eddie Farrell RC 40.00 100.00
149 Babe Ruth RC 6000.00 12000.00
150 Ray Kolp RC 50.00 120.00
151 Jake Flowers RC 50.00 120.00
152 Zack Taylor RC 40.00 100.00
153 Buddy Myer RC 40.00 100.00
154 Jimmie Foxx RC 800.00 1500.00
155 Joe Judge RC 40.00 100.00
156 Danny MacFayden RC 40.00 100.00
157 Sam Byrd RC 50.00 120.00
158 Moe Berg RC 500.00 1000.00
159 Oswald Bluege FIELD RC 40.00 100.00
160 Lou Gehrig RC 3000.00 6000.00
161 Al Spohrer RC 50.00 120.00
162 Leo Mangum RC 50.00 120.00
163 Luke Sewell POR RC 40.00 100.00
164 Lloyd Waner RC 300.00 600.00
165 Joe Sewell RC 100.00 250.00
166 Sam West RC 50.00 120.00
167 Jack Russell RC 40.00 100.00
168 Goose Goslin RC 125.00 300.00
169 Al Thomas RC 30.00 80.00
170 Harry McCurdy RC 40.00 100.00
171 Charlie Jamieson RC 30.00 80.00
172 Billy Hargrave RC 30.00 80.00
173 Roscoe Holm RC 40.00 100.00
174 Warren (Curly) Ogden RC 30.00 80.00
175 Dan Howley MG RC 40.00 100.00
176 John Ogden RC 30.00 80.00
177 Walter French RC 40.00 100.00
178 Jackie Warner RC 30.00 80.00
179 Fred Leach RC 30.00 80.00
180 Eddie Moore RC 40.00 100.00
181 Babe Ruth RC 6000.00 12000.00
182 Andy High RC 30.00 80.00
183 Rube Walberg RC 30.00 80.00
184 Charley Berry RC 60.00 150.00
185 Bob Smith RC 40.00 100.00
186 John Schulte RC 40.00 100.00
187 Heinie Manush RC 75.00 200.00
188 Rogers Hornsby RC 300.00 600.00
189 Joe Cronin RC 100.00 250.00
190 Fred Schulte RC 30.00 80.00
191 Ben Chapman RC 40.00 100.00
192 Walter Brown RC 40.00 100.00
193 Lynford Lary RC 50.00 120.00
194 Earl Averill RC 150.00 400.00
195 Evar Swanson RC 40.00 100.00
196 Leroy Mahaffey RC 30.00 80.00
197 Rick Ferrell RC 125.00 300.00
198 Jack Burns RC 40.00 100.00
199 Tom Bridges RC 40.00 100.00
200 Bill Hallahan RC 50.00 120.00
201 Ernie Orsatti RC 40.00 100.00
202 Gabby Hartnett RC 125.00 300.00
203 Lon Warneke RC 30.00 80.00
204 Riggs Stephenson RC 40.00 100.00
205 Heinie Meine RC 40.00 100.00
206 Gus Suhr RC 30.00 80.00
207 Mel Ott Bat RC 300.00 600.00
208 Bernie James RC 50.00 120.00
209 Adolfo Luque RC 30.00 80.00
210 Spud Davis RC 40.00 100.00
211 Hack Wilson RC 600.00 1200.00
212 Billy Urbanski RC 40.00 100.00
213 Earl Adams RC 50.00 120.00
214 John Kerr RC 40.00 100.00
215 Russ Van Atta RC 40.00 100.00
216 Lefty Gomez RC 150.00 400.00
217 Frank Crosetti RC 100.00 250.00
218 Wes Ferrell RC 60.00 150.00
219 Mule Haas UER RC 60.00 150.00
220 Lefty Grove RC 300.00 600.00
221 Dale Alexander RC 40.00 100.00
222 Charley Gehringer RC 400.00 800.00
223 Dizzy Dean RC 500.00 1000.00
224 Frank Demaree RC 50.00 120.00
225 Bill Jurges RC 40.00 100.00
226 Charley Root RC 75.00 200.00
227 Billy Herman RC 150.00 400.00
228 Tony Piet RC 30.00 80.00
229 Arky Vaughan RC 100.00 250.00
230 Carl Hubbell PIT RC 250.00 500.00
231 Joe Moore FIELD RC 40.00 100.00
232 Lefty O'Doul RC 60.00 150.00
233 Johnny Vergez RC 50.00 120.00
234 Carl Hubbell RC 300.00 600.00
235 Fred Fitzsimmons PIT RC 40.00 100.00
236 George Davis RC 40.00 100.00
237 Gus Mancuso FIELD RC 60.00 150.00
238 Hugh Critz FIELD RC 40.00 100.00
239 Leroy Parmelee RC 40.00 100.00
240 Hal Schumacher RC 50.00 120.00

1934 Goudey

The cards in this 96-card color set measure approximately 2 3/8" by 2 7/8". Cards 1-48 are considered to be the easiest to find (although card number 1, Foxx, is very scarce in mint condition) while 73-96 are much more difficult to find. Cards of this 1934 Goudey series are slightly less abundant than cards of the 1933 Goudey set. Of the 96 cards, 84 contain a "Lou Gehrig Says" line on the front in a blue design, while 12 of the high series (80-91) contain a "Chuck Klein Says" line in a red design. These Chuck Klein cards are indicated in the checklist below by CK and are in fact the 12 National Leaguers in the high series.

COMPLETE SET (96) 9000.00 16000.00
COMMON CARD (1-48) 30.00 50.00
COMMON CARD (49-72) 40.00 75.00
COMMON CARD (73-96) 100.00 175.00
WRAPPER (1-CENT, WHT.) 75.00 100.00
WRAPPER (1-CENT, CLR.) 75.00 100.00
1 Jimmie Foxx 450.00 750.00
2 Mickey Cochrane 100.00 175.00
3 Charlie Grimm 35.00 60.00
4 Woody English 30.00 50.00
5 Ed Brandt 30.00 50.00
6 Dizzy Dean 500.00 1000.00
7 Leo Durocher 125.00 250.00
8 Tony Piet 30.00 50.00
9 Ben Chapman 35.00 60.00
10 Chuck Klein 125.00 250.00
11 Paul Waner 125.00 250.00
12 Carl Hubbell 100.00 175.00
13 Frankie Frisch 125.00 250.00
14 Willie Kamm 30.00 50.00
15 Alvin Crowder 30.00 50.00
16 Joe Kuhel 30.00 50.00
17 Hugh Critz 30.00 50.00
18 Heinie Manush 75.00 125.00
19 Lefty Grove 250.00 500.00
20 Frank Hogan 30.00 50.00
21 Bill Terry 150.00 300.00
22 Arky Vaughan 125.00 250.00
23 Charley Gehringer 200.00 400.00
24 Ray Benge 30.00 50.00
25 Roger Cramer RC 35.00 60.00
26 Gerald Walker RC 30.00 50.00
27 Luke Appling RC 150.00 300.00
28 Ed Coleman RC 30.00 50.00
29 Larry French RC 30.00 50.00
30 Julius Solters RC 30.00 50.00
31 Buck Jordan RC 30.00 50.00
32 Blondy Ryan RC 30.00 50.00
33 Don Hurst RC 30.00 50.00

34 Chick Hafey RC 75.00 125.00
35 Ernie Lombardi RC 90.00 150.00
36 Walter Betts RC 30.00 50.00
37 Lou Gehrig 4000.00 8000.00
38 Oral Hildebrand RC 30.00 50.00
39 Fred Walker RC 30.00 50.00
40 John Stone 30.00 50.00
41 George Earnshaw RC 30.00 50.00
42 John Allen RC 30.00 50.00
43 Dick Porter RC 30.00 50.00
44 Tom Bridges 35.00 60.00
45 Oscar Melillo RC 30.00 50.00
46 Joe Stripp RC 30.00 50.00
47 John Frederick RC 30.00 50.00
48 Tex Carleton RC 30.00 50.00
49 Sam Leslie RC 40.00 75.00
50 Walter Beck RC 40.00 75.00
51 Rip Collins RC 40.00 75.00
52 Herman Bell RC 40.00 75.00
53 George Watkins RC 40.00 75.00
54 Wesley Schulmerich RC 40.00 75.00
55 Ed Holley RC 40.00 75.00
56 Mark Koenig 60.00 100.00
57 Bill Swift RC 40.00 75.00
58 Earl Grace RC 40.00 75.00
59 Joe Mowry RC 40.00 75.00
60 Lynn Nelson RC 40.00 75.00
61 Lou Gehrig 3000.00 6000.00
62 Hank Greenberg RC 600.00 1200.00
63 Minter Hayes RC 40.00 75.00
64 Frank Grube RC 40.00 75.00
65 Cliff Bolton RC 40.00 75.00
66 Mel Harder RC 60.00 100.00
67 Bob Weiland RC 40.00 75.00
68 Bob Johnson RC 60.00 100.00
69 John Marcum RC 40.00 75.00
70 Pete Fox RC 40.00 75.00
71 Lyle Tinning RC 40.00 75.00
72 Arndt Jorgens RC 40.00 75.00
73 Ed Wells RC 100.00 175.00
74 Bob Boken RC 100.00 175.00
75 Bill Werber RC 100.00 175.00
76 Hal Trosky RC 125.00 200.00
77 Joe Vosmik RC 100.00 175.00
78 Pinky Higgins RC 125.00 200.00
79 Eddie Durham RC 100.00 175.00
80 Marty McManus CK 100.00 175.00
81 Bob Brown CK RC 100.00 175.00
82 Bill Hallahan CK 100.00 175.00
83 Jim Mooney CK RC 100.00 175.00
84 Paul Derringer CK RC 125.00 225.00
85 Adam Comorosky CK 100.00 175.00
86 Lloyd Johnson CK RC 100.00 175.00
87 George Darrow CK RC 100.00 175.00
88 Homer Peel CK RC 100.00 175.00
89 Linus Frey CK RC 100.00 175.00
90 KiKi Cuyler CK 200.00 400.00
91 Dolph Camilli CK RC 125.00 200.00
92 Steve Larkin RC 100.00 175.00
93 Fred Ostermueller RC 100.00 175.00
94 Red Rolfe RC 150.00 300.00
95 Myril Hoag RC 100.00 175.00
96 James DeShong RC 300.00 500.00

2014 Immaculate Collection

1-100 PRINT RUN 99 SER.#'d SETS
101-127/154 PRINT RUN 49 SER.#'d SETS
128-152/155 PRINT RUN 99 SER.#'d SETS
EXCHANGE DEADLINE 3/3/2016
1 Mike Trout 10.00 25.00
2 Derek Jeter 10.00 25.00
3 Albert Pujols 2.50 6.00
4 Ichiro Suzuki 3.00 8.00
5 Clayton Kershaw 4.00 10.00
6 David Ortiz 2.00 5.00
7 Miguel Cabrera 2.00 5.00
8 Buster Posey 6.00 15.00
9 Joe Mauer 1.50 4.00
10 Jose Fernandez 2.00 5.00
11 Bryce Harper 3.00 8.00
12 Andrew McCutchen 2.00 5.00
13 Yu Darvish 2.00 5.00
14 Manny Machado 2.00 5.00
15 David Wright 1.50 4.00
16 Robinson Cano 1.50 4.00
17 Yadier Molina 2.00 5.00
18 Dustin Pedroia 2.00 5.00
19 Evan Longoria 1.50 4.00
20 Stephen Strasburg 2.00 5.00
21 Freddie Freeman 2.50 6.00
22 Paul Goldschmidt 2.00 5.00
23 Giancarlo Stanton 2.00 5.00
24 Matt Kemp 1.50 4.00
25 Yoenis Cespedes 2.00 5.00
26 Joey Votto 2.00 5.00
27 Chris Sale 2.00 5.00
28 Josh Hamilton 1.50 4.00
29 Ryan Braun 1.50 4.00
30 Jacoby Ellsbury 1.50 4.00
31 Matt Harvey 1.50 4.00
32 Wil Myers 1.25 3.00
33 Yasiel Puig 2.00 5.00
34 Ryan Howard 1.50 4.00
35 Jason Heyward 1.50 4.00
36 Troy Tulowitzki 2.00 5.00
37 Justin Verlander 2.00 5.00
38 Pedro Alvarez 1.25 3.00
39 Michael Wacha 1.50 4.00
40 Gerrit Cole 2.00 5.00
41 Matt Holliday 2.00 5.00
42 Jose Bautista 1.50 4.00
43 Adrian Gonzalez 1.50 4.00
44 Jimmy Rollins 1.50 4.00
45 Paul Konerko 1.50 4.00
46 Mark Trumbo 1.25 3.00
47 Shelby Miller 1.50 4.00
48 Zack Wheeler 1.50 4.00
49 Josh Donaldson 1.50 4.00
50 Jean Segura 1.50 4.00
51 Prince Fielder 1.50 4.00
52 Alex Rodriguez 2.50 6.00
53 Eric Hosmer 1.50 4.00
54 Adrian Beltre 2.00 5.00
55 Jose Reyes 1.50 4.00
56 Madison Bumgarner 5.00 12.00
57 Max Scherzer 2.00 5.00
58 Chris Davis 1.25 3.00
59 Adam Wainwright 1.50 4.00
60 Carlos Beltran 1.50 4.00
61 Adam Jones 1.50 4.00
62 Cliff Lee 1.50 4.00
63 David Price 1.50 4.00
64 Sonny Gray 1.50 4.00
65 Tyler Skaggs 1.25 3.00
66 Pablo Sandoval 1.50 4.00
67 Felix Hernandez 1.50 4.00
68 Hyun-Jin Ryu 1.50 4.00
69 Jose Altuve 1.50 4.00
70 Alex Gordon 1.50 4.00
71 Edwin Encarnacion 2.00 5.00
72 Alex Wood 1.25 3.00
73 Salvador Perez 1.50 4.00
74 Zack Greinke 1.50 4.00
75 Matt Carpenter 2.00 5.00
76 Chase Utley 1.50 4.00
77 Justin Upton 1.50 4.00
78 Shin-Soo Choo 1.50 4.00
79 Anthony Rendon 2.00 5.00
80 Mike Napoli 1.25 3.00
81 Starling Marte 1.50 4.00
82 Carlos Gonzalez 1.50 4.00
83 Craig Kimbrel 1.50 4.00
84 Hanley Ramirez 1.50 4.00
85 Andrelton Simmons 1.25 3.00
86 Hisashi Iwakuma 1.50 4.00
87 Brian McCann 1.50 4.00
88 Cole Hamels 1.50 4.00
89 Carlos Santana 1.50 4.00
90 Everth Cabrera 1.25 3.00
91 Aramis Ramirez 1.25 3.00
92 Brandon Phillips 1.25 3.00
93 Matt Adams 1.25 3.00
94 Mariano Rivera 2.50 6.00
95 Frank Thomas 2.00 5.00
96 Ken Griffey Jr. 6.00 15.00
97 Cal Ripken Jr. 5.00 12.00
98 George Brett 6.00 15.00
99 Nolan Ryan 6.00 15.00
100 Pete Rose 6.00 15.00
101 Kolten Wong JSY AU/49 10.00 25.00
104 Juan Centeno JSY AU/49 RC 3.00 8.00
105 Enny Romero JSY AU/49 RC 3.00 8.00
106 Josmil Pinto JSY AU/49 RC 3.00 8.00
107 G.Polanco JSY AU/49 RC 5.00 12.00
108 Cameron Rupp JSY AU/49 RC 3.00 8.00
109 Ryan Goins JSY AU/49 RC 4.00 10.00
110 Abraham Almonte JSY AU/49 RC 3.00 8.00
111 Billy Hamilton JSY AU/49 RC 6.00 15.00
113 Oscar Taveras JSY AU/49 6.00 15.00
114 Jimmy Nelson JSY AU/49 RC 3.00 8.00
115 Jose Ramirez JSY AU/49 RC 15.00 40.00
116 Marcus Semien JSY AU/49 RC 3.00 8.00
117 Matt Davidson JSY AU/49 4.00 10.00
118 Matt Shoemaker JSY AU/49 5.00 12.00
119 Michael Choice JSY AU/49 3.00 8.00
120 Reymond Fuentes JSY AU/49 RC 3.00 8.00
121 Taijuan Walker JSY AU/49 3.00 8.00
122 Yordano Ventura JSY AU/49 12.00 30.00
123 Chad Bettis JSY AU/49 3.00 8.00
124 Matt den Dekker JSY AU/49 6.00 15.00
125 J.R. Murphy JSY AU/49 3.00 8.00
126 Xander Bogaerts JSY AU/49 15.00 40.00
127 N.Castellanos JSY AU/49 RC 8.00 20.00
128 Masahiro Tanaka JSY/99 RC 8.00 20.00
129 Taijuan Walker AU/99 RC 8.00 20.00
130 Jose Abreu AU/99 RC 20.00 50.00
131 Xander Bogaerts AU/99 RC 15.00 40.00
132 Kolten Wong AU/99 RC 4.00 10.00
133 Matt den Dekker AU/99 RC 4.00 10.00
134 Michael Choice AU/99 RC 3.00 8.00
135 Jimmy Nelson AU/99 RC 3.00 8.00
136 Matt Davidson AU/99 RC 4.00 10.00
137 J.R. Murphy AU/80 RC 3.00 8.00
140 Yordano Ventura AU/99 RC 8.00 20.00
141 Tanner Roark AU/99 RC 3.00 8.00
143 James Paxton AU/99 RC 10.00 25.00
144 Matt Shoemaker AU/99 RC 3.00 8.00
145 Enny Romero AU/99 RC 3.00 8.00
146 Kris Johnson AU/99 RC 3.00 8.00
147 Stolmy Pimentel AU/99 RC 3.00 8.00
148 Chad Bettis AU/99 RC 3.00 8.00
149 Ehire Adrianza AU/99 RC 3.00 8.00
150 G.Springer AU/99 RC 20.00 50.00
151 Chris Owings AU/99 RC
152 O.Taveras AU/99 RC EXCH 4.00 10.00
154 Jose Abreu JSY AU/49 25.00 60.00
155 Jose Abreu JSY/99 RC 15.00 40.00

2014 Immaculate Collection Accolades Materials

RANDOM INSERTS IN PACKS
PRINT RUNS B/WN 5-99 COPIES PER
NO PRICING ON QTY 10 OR LESS
1 Honus Wagner/20 50.00 120.00
3 Joe Jackson/79 50.00 120.00
5 Ty Cobb/99 25.00 60.00
6 Pee Wee Reese/99 5.00 12.00
7 Burleigh Grimes/20 40.00 100.00
8 Jimmie Foxx/99 10.00 25.00
9 Mel Ott/99 15.00 40.00
10 Rogers Hornsby/99 20.00 50.00
11 Tris Speaker/99 12.00 30.00
12 Gil Hodges/99 5.00 12.00
13 Lou Gehrig/99 40.00 100.00
14 Jackie Robinson/99 20.00 50.00
15 Leo Durocher/49 10.00 25.00
16 Joe DiMaggio/49 30.00 80.00
17 Nolan Ryan/99 10.00 25.00
18 Greg Maddux/49 8.00 20.00
19 Lou Brock/99 5.00 12.00
20 Cal Ripken Jr./99 8.00 20.00
21 Reggie Jackson/99 5.00 12.00
22 Mike Schmidt/49 10.00 25.00
23 Rod Carew/25 8.00 20.00
24 Willie McCovey/49 5.00 12.00
25 Tony Gwynn/99 6.00 15.00

2014 Immaculate Collection Accolades Materials Prime

*PRIME: 1X TO 2.5X BASIC
RANDOM INSERTS IN PACKS
PRINT RUNS B/WN 1-25 COPIES PER
NO PRICING ON QTY 10 OR LESS

2014 Immaculate Collection All-Star Autographs

RANDOM INSERTS IN PACKS
PRINT RUNS B/WN 15-99 COPIES PER
EXCHANGE DEADLINE 3/3/2016
5 Adam Jones/25 12.00 30.00
6 Max Scherzer/25 15.00 40.00
7 David Wright/25 15.00 40.00
8 Matt Harvey/25 EXCH 30.00 80.00
9 Salvador Perez/99 EXCH 15.00 40.00
11 Carlos Gomez/99 6.00 15.00
12 Freddie Freeman/49 12.00 30.00
13 Jose Fernandez/49 EXCH 12.00 30.00
15 Chris Sale/25 10.00 25.00

2014 Immaculate Collection Clubhouse Material

RANDOM INSERTS IN PACKS
PRINT RUNS B/WN 15-99 COPIES PER
NO PRICING ON QTY 15 OR LESS
1 Jim Palmer/49 6.00 15.00
2 Alex Rodriguez/25 10.00 25.00
3 Tony Gwynn/99 4.00 10.00
4 Jose Bautista/49 3.00 8.00
5 Ken Griffey Jr./25 30.00 80.00
6 Alan Trammell/99 5.00 12.00
7 Josh Hamilton/49 3.00 8.00
9 Kirby Puckett/20 20.00 50.00
10 Rickey Henderson/99 4.00 10.00
11 Pete Rose/49 8.00 20.00
12 Miguel Cabrera/49 4.00 10.00
13 Justin Verlander/49 4.00 10.00
14 Nick Swisher/99 3.00 8.00
15 A.J. Burnett/25 2.50 6.00
17 Yu Darvish/25 10.00 25.00
18 Evan Longoria/25 3.00 8.00
19 Tony Gwynn/99 4.00 10.00
20 Prince Fielder/99 3.00 8.00
21 Robinson Cano/25 3.00 8.00
22 CC Sabathia/49 3.00 8.00
23 Derek Jeter/25 12.00 30.00
24 Mike Schmidt/49 6.00 15.00
25 Victor Martinez/25 5.00 12.00
28 Drew Smyly/99 2.50 6.00
29 Albert Pujols/99 5.00 12.00
30 Yasiel Puig/99 6.00 15.00

2014 Immaculate Collection Clubhouse Signatures

RANDOM INSERTS IN PACKS
PRINT RUNS B/WN 15-99 COPIES PER
NO PRICING ON QTY 15 OR LESS
EXCHANGE DEADLINE 3/3/2016
1 Matt Carpenter/25 15.00 40.00
4 Chris Davis/25 6.00 15.00
6 Evan Gattis/99 4.00 10.00
10 Mark Grace/25 10.00 25.00
11 Norichika Aoki/99 6.00 15.00
12 Reymond Fuentes/99 4.00 10.00
14 Justin Upton/25 8.00 20.00
15 R.A. Dickey/25 8.00 20.00
16 Roy Halladay/25 15.00 40.00
17 Hisashi Iwakuma/99 6.00 15.00
18 Josh Donaldson/99 12.00 30.00
19 Miguel Sano/99 12.00 30.00
20 Darryl Strawberry/25 12.00 30.00
21 Shelby Miller/99 5.00 12.00
22 Shane Victorino/49 5.00 12.00
23 David Freese/25 5.00 12.00
24 Rafael Palmeiro/25 8.00 20.00
25 Adrian Beltre/25 6.00 15.00
27 George Springer/99 10.00 25.00
28 Dan Petry/99 4.00 10.00
29 Garry Templeton/99 4.00 10.00
30 Glenn Hubbard/99 4.00 10.00
31 Mark Langston/99 4.00 10.00
32 Shawon Dunston/99 4.00 10.00
33 Ellis Burks/99 4.00 10.00
34 Jose Abreu/99 25.00 60.00
35 Michael Wacha/49 10.00 25.00
36 Billy Hamilton/99 5.00 12.00
37 J.R. Murphy/99 4.00 10.00
38 Michael Choice/99 4.00 10.00
40 Eric Hosmer/25 10.00 25.00
41 Xander Bogaerts/75 15.00 40.00
42 Gerrit Cole/25 6.00 15.00
43 John Kruk/25 8.00 20.00
44 Taijuan Walker/99 4.00 10.00
45 Oscar Taveras/99 8.00 20.00
46 Carlos Gonzalez/25 8.00 20.00
47 Darin Ruf/99 5.00 12.00
48 Gregory Polanco/99 4.00 10.00
49 Raul Ibanez/49 5.00 12.00
50 Paul Konerko/49 12.00 30.00
51 Matt den Dekker/99 5.00 12.00
52 Andre Thornton/99 4.00 10.00
53 Jose Fernandez/25 12.00 30.00
54 Victor Martinez/25 15.00 40.00
55 Frank White/99 4.00 10.00
57 Bret Saberhagen/99 4.00 10.00
58 Jay Bruce/49 10.00 25.00
59 Zack Wheeler/49 5.00 12.00
60 Gary Gaetti/99 4.00 10.00

2014 Immaculate Collection Derek Jeter Tribute All-Star

RANDOM INSERTS IN PACKS
STATED PRINT RUN 14 SER.#'d SETS
1 Derek Jeter 10.00 25.00
2 Derek Jeter 10.00 25.00
3 Derek Jeter 10.00 25.00
4 Derek Jeter 10.00 25.00
5 Derek Jeter 10.00 25.00
6 Derek Jeter 10.00 25.00
7 Derek Jeter 10.00 25.00
8 Derek Jeter 10.00 25.00
9 Derek Jeter 10.00 25.00
10 Derek Jeter 10.00 25.00
11 Derek Jeter 10.00 25.00
12 Derek Jeter 10.00 25.00
13 Derek Jeter 10.00 25.00
14 Derek Jeter 10.00 25.00

2014 Immaculate Collection Derek Jeter Tribute All-Star Jersey Number

*JSY NUM: 1.5X TO 4X BASIC
RANDOM INSERTS IN PACKS
STATED PRINT RUN 2 SER.#'d SETS

2014 Immaculate Collection Diamond Fabric

RANDOM INSERTS IN PACKS
PRINT RUNS B/WN 45-99 COPIES PER
1 Austin Jackson/99 2.50 6.00
2 Andrew McCutchen/99 20.00 50.00
3 Stephen Strasburg/49 4.00 10.00
4 Eric Hosmer/99 3.00 8.00
5 Yoenis Cespedes/49 4.00 10.00
6 Dustin Pedroia/99 4.00 10.00
7 Adrian Beltre/99 4.00 10.00
8 Edwin Encarnacion/99 4.00 10.00
9 Madison Bumgarner/99 3.00 8.00
10 Rick Porcello/99 3.00 8.00
11 Matt Kemp/49 3.00 8.00
12 Manny Machado/49 4.00 10.00
13 Nick Swisher/99 3.00 8.00
14 Bryce Harper/49 10.00 25.00
15 Wil Myers/49 2.50 6.00

2014 Immaculate Collection Immaculate Autograph Materials

RANDOM INSERTS IN PACKS
PRINT RUNS B/WN 10-99 COPIES PER
NO PRICING ON QTY 10
EXCHANGE DEADLINE 3/3/2016
1 Stephen Strasburg/99 12.00 30.00
2 Troy Tulowitzki/99 10.00 25.00
3 Evan Longoria/99 6.00 15.00
4 Brandon Phillips/49 4.00 10.00
5 David Wright/99 12.00 30.00
6 Alan Trammell/49 10.00 25.00
7 Darryl Strawberry/99 8.00 20.00
8 Craig Biggio/49 15.00 40.00
9 Mark Grace/99 6.00 15.00
10 Evan Gattis/49 4.00 10.00
11 Fred McGriff/49 8.00 20.00
12 Edgar Martinez/49 5.00 12.00
13 Miguel Cabrera/49 40.00 100.00
14 Wade Boggs/49 15.00 40.00
15 Bo Jackson/49 30.00 80.00
16 Gary Sheffield/49 4.00 10.00
17 Barry Larkin/49 20.00 50.00
18 Joe Girardi/49 10.00 25.00
19 Jose Canseco/49 15.00 40.00
20 Tom Glavine/49 12.00 30.00
21 David Justice/49 10.00 25.00
22 Ken Griffey Jr./25 125.00 250.00
23 Will Clark/25 20.00 50.00
24 Pat Corbin/99 5.00 12.00
26 Ellis Burks/25 8.00 20.00
27 Luis Gonzalez/25 6.00 15.00
28 Nomar Garciaparra/49 15.00 40.00
29 Mike Trout/49 125.00 250.00
30 Clayton Kershaw/49 40.00 100.00
31 Wil Myers/99 4.00 10.00
32 Dennis Eckersley/49 8.00 20.00
33 Jose Fernandez/49 10.00 25.00
34 Gerrit Cole/99 8.00 20.00
35 Yoenis Cespedes/49 8.00 20.00
36 Mike Schmidt/25 20.00 50.00
37 Michael Morse/49 4.00 10.00
38 Shane Victorino/99 5.00 12.00
39 Shelby Miller/99 5.00 12.00
40 Nolan Ryan/20 40.00 100.00
41 Frank Thomas/25 40.00 100.00
42 Jay Bruce/99 8.00 20.00
43 Rafael Palmeiro/99 5.00 12.00
44 Adam Jones/99 10.00 25.00
45 Carlos Gonzalez/99 5.00 12.00
46 Eric Hosmer/99 10.00 25.00
47 Adrian Beltre/49 12.00 30.00

2014 Immaculate Collection Immaculate Autograph Materials Prime

*PRIME: .6X TO 1.5X BASIC
RANDOM INSERTS IN PACKS
PRINT RUNS B/WN 1-20 COPIES PER
NO PRICING ON QTY 15 OR LESS
EXCHANGE DEADLINE 3/3/2016
6 Alan Trammell/20 25.00 60.00

2014 Immaculate Collection Immaculate Autographs

RANDOM INSERTS IN PACKS
PRINT RUNS B/WN 15-99 COPIES PER
NO PRICING ON QTY 15
EXCHANGE DEADLINE 3/3/2016
1 Stephen Strasburg/25 15.00 40.00
2 Josh Donaldson/99 8.00 20.00
3 Carlos Gomez/99 6.00 15.00
4 Matt Carpenter/49 10.00 25.00
5 Jeff Bagwell/25 20.00 50.00
6 Shane Victorino/99 4.00 10.00
7 Matt Harvey/25 25.00 60.00
8 Brian McCann/25 8.00 20.00
9 David Freese/25 3.00 8.00
10 Evan Gattis/49 3.00 8.00
11 Victor Martinez/49 12.00 30.00
12 Shelby Miller/49 4.00 10.00
13 Paul Konerko/49 6.00 15.00
14 Pablo Sandoval/25 8.00 20.00
15 Paul Molitor/25 12.00 30.00
18 Joe Girardi/49 6.00 15.00
19 Robinson Cano/25 15.00 40.00
20 Wil Myers/25 10.00 25.00
21 Wally Joyner/49 3.00 8.00
22 Roy Halladay/25 15.00 40.00
23 Prince Fielder/25 8.00 20.00
24 David Wright/25 15.00 40.00
25 Dustin Pedroia/25 25.00 60.00
30 Bo Jackson/25 50.00 120.00
34 Brooks Robinson/25 15.00 40.00
35 Willie McCovey/25 20.00 50.00
36 Rickey Henderson/25 25.00 60.00
39 Giancarlo Stanton/25 25.00 60.00
42 Eric Davis/99 8.00 20.00
43 Joe Carter/25 10.00 25.00
45 Andres Galarraga/99 8.00 20.00
46 Bob Dernier/99 3.00 8.00
47 Starling Marte/99 10.00 25.00
48 Zoilo Almonte/99 4.00 10.00
49 Michael Wacha/25 12.00 30.00
50 Jarrod Parker/49 3.00 8.00
51 Junior Lake/99 3.00 8.00
53 Chris Sale/49 10.00 25.00
54 Kerry Wood/49 6.00 15.00
55 Adrian Gonzalez/25 10.00 25.00
56 Manny Machado/49 15.00 40.00
57 Bret Saberhagen/99 3.00 8.00
58 Jean Segura EXCH 4.00 10.00
59 Joe Mauer/25 15.00 40.00
60 Jose Canseco/99 6.00 15.00
61 Jay Bruce/49 6.00 15.00
62 Patrick Corbin/99 4.00 10.00
64 Carlos Martinez/99 4.00 10.00
65 Ivan Nova/99 4.00 10.00
66 Adam Eaton/99 3.00 8.00
67 Adam Jones/25 8.00 20.00
68 Gerardo Parra/99 3.00 8.00
69 Freddie Freeman/49 8.00 20.00
70 Gerrit Cole/49 8.00 20.00
71 Jose Fernandez/49 10.00 25.00
72 Justin Upton/25 4.00 10.00
73 Norichika Aoki/99 12.00 30.00
74 Wilin Rosario/99 3.00 8.00
75 Salvador Perez/99 8.00 20.00
76 Jered Weaver/25 10.00 25.00
77 Fred McGriff/25 12.00 30.00
78 Alan Trammell/25 10.00 25.00
79 Andre Thornton/99 3.00 8.00
80 Carlos Gonzalez/25 6.00 15.00
84 Max Scherzer/25 15.00 40.00
85 Raul Ibanez/49 4.00 10.00
86 Steve Finley/25 3.00 8.00
88 Bobby Witt/99 3.00 8.00
89 Zack Wheeler/49 3.00 8.00
90 Tony Pena/99 3.00 8.00
91 Yoenis Cespedes/25 6.00 15.00
92 Mookie Wilson/99 8.00 20.00
94 Ellis Burks/99 3.00 8.00
95 Anthony Rizzo/49 20.00 50.00
96 Brandon Barnes/99 3.00 8.00
97 Clayton Kershaw/25 40.00 100.00
98 Felix Hernandez/25 20.00 50.00
99 R.A. Dickey/25 6.00 15.00
100 Alex Wood/99 3.00 8.00

2014 Immaculate Collection Immaculate Dual Players Memorabilia

RANDOM INSERTS IN PACKS
PRINT RUNS B/WN 10-49 COPIES PER
NO PRICING ON QTY 10
1 D.Mattingly/K.Griffey Jr./49 6.00 15.00
2 E.Gattis/H.Pence/49 4.00 10.00
3 M.McGwire/R.Palmeiro/49 10.00 25.00
4 R.Howard/A.Beltre/49 5.00 12.00
5 A.Pujols/M.McGwire/49 10.00 25.00
7 E.Encarnacion/J.Bautista/49 5.00 12.00
8 D.Ortiz/D.Pedroia/49 8.00 20.00
9 G.Cole/H.Ryu/25 5.00 12.00
10 E.Gattis/M.Zunino/25 3.00 8.00
11 Z.Wheeler/T.Skaggs/25 4.00 10.00
12 T.Cobb/H.Wagner/20 100.00 200.00
13 L.Gehrig/P.Reese/49 50.00 120.00
14 M.Ott/R.Hornsby/25 40.00 100.00

2014 Immaculate Collection Immaculate Dual Players Memorabilia Prime

*PRIME: .75X TO 2X BASIC
RANDOM INSERTS IN PACKS
PRINT RUNS B/WN 1-25 COPIES PER
NO PRICING ON QTY 15 OR LESS

2014 Immaculate Collection Immaculate Duals Memorabilia

RANDOM INSERTS IN PACKS
PRINT RUNS B/WN 25-99 COPIES PER
1 Giancarlo Stanton/99 4.00 10.00
2 Matt Cain/49 3.00 8.00
3 Evan Longoria/99 3.00 8.00
4 Aroldis Chapman/99 4.00 10.00
5 Devin Mesoraco/99 2.50 6.00
6 Yoenis Cespedes/49 4.00 10.00
7 Matt Kemp/49 3.00 8.00
8 Miguel Cabrera/99 4.00 10.00
9 Torii Hunter/99 2.50 6.00
10 Neftali Feliz/99 2.50 6.00
11 Will Middlebrooks/49 2.50 6.00
12 Drew Smyly/99 2.50 6.00
13 Tyler Skaggs/25 2.50 6.00
14 Brett Lawrie/49 3.00 8.00
15 Jacoby Ellsbury/99 3.00 8.00

2014 Immaculate Collection Immaculate Duals Memorabilia Prime

*PRIME: .75X TO 2X BASIC
RANDOM INSERTS IN PACKS
PRINT RUNS B/WN 10-49 COPIES PER
NO PRICING ON QTY 10

2014 Immaculate Collection Immaculate Heroes Autographs

RANDOM INSERTS IN PACKS
PRINT RUNS B/WN 15-75 COPIES PER
NO PRICING ON QTY 15
EXCHANGE DEADLINE 3/3/2016
2 Nolan Ryan/25 90.00 150.00
3 Mariano Rivera/25 75.00 200.00
4 Gaylord Perry/25 6.00 15.00
5 Jeff Bagwell/49 15.00 40.00
6 Shane Victorino/49 5.00 12.00
7 Tim Wakefield/49 20.00 50.00
8 Andy Pettitte/25 15.00 40.00
9 David Freese/25 4.00 10.00
10 Tom Glavine/49 15.00 40.00
11 Victor Martinez/49 12.00 30.00
13 Paul Konerko/75 12.00 30.00
14 Pablo Sandoval/25 12.00 30.00
18 Joe Girardi/49 6.00 15.00
20 Wil Myers/25 8.00 20.00
21 Wally Joyner/75 4.00 10.00

2014 Immaculate Collection Immaculate Heroes Materials

RANDOM INSERTS IN PACKS
PRINT RUNS B/WN 10-99 COPIES PER
NO PRICING ON QTY 15 OR LESS
1 Frank Thomas/49 6.00 15.00
2 Nolan Ryan/49 20.00 50.00
3 Roy Halladay/20 5.00 12.00
4 Tom Glavine/49 5.00 12.00
6 Mark McGwire/49 10.00 25.00
7 Roger Clemens/49 6.00 15.00
8 Andy Pettitte/49 5.00 12.00
9 Tommy Lasorda/49 5.00 12.00
10 Nomar Garciaparra/49 5.00 12.00
11 Rollie Fingers/49 6.00 15.00
12 Mariano Rivera/25 10.00 25.00
13 Don Mattingly/49 10.00 25.00
14 Fred McGriff/20 5.00 12.00
15 Ryne Sandberg/49 8.00 20.00
16 Goose Gossage/49 5.00 12.00
17 Lenny Dykstra/49 4.00 10.00
18 Michael Young/49 4.00 10.00
19 Carlton Fisk/20 10.00 25.00
20 Todd Helton/49 5.00 12.00
21 Tony Perez/20 15.00 40.00
23 Harold Baines/49 5.00 12.00
24 Andre Dawson/49 5.00 12.00
26 Bo Jackson/49 10.00 25.00
27 Bob Horner/49 4.00 10.00
29 Tim Hudson/49 5.00 12.00
30 Derek Jeter/99 10.00 25.00

2014 Immaculate Collection Immaculate Heroes Materials Prime

*PRIME: .75X TO 2X BASIC
RANDOM INSERTS IN PACKS
PRINT RUNS B/WN 2-25 COPIES PER
NO PRICING ON QTY 15 OR LESS
5 Alan Trammell/25 10.00 25.00
25 Bert Blyleven/25 10.00 25.00

2014 Immaculate Collection Immaculate Hitters Memorabilia

RANDOM INSERTS IN PACKS
PRINT RUNS B/WN 10-99 COPIES PER
NO PRICING ON QTY 10
1 Brandon Phillips/49 2.50 6.00
2 Jay Bruce/99 3.00 8.00
3 Adam Jones/79 3.00 8.00
4 Paul Goldschmidt/49 4.00 10.00
5 Yoenis Cespedes/49 4.00 10.00
6 Chris Davis/99 2.50 6.00
7 Alfonso Soriano/99 3.00 8.00
8 Chase Utley/79 3.00 8.00
9 Carlos Gonzalez/79 3.00 8.00
10 Miguel Cabrera/99 4.00 10.00
11 Dustin Pedroia/79 4.00 10.00
12 Evan Longoria/99 3.00 8.00
13 David Wright/49 3.00 8.00
14 Jacoby Ellsbury/79 3.00 8.00
15 Bryce Harper/49 6.00 15.00
16 Prince Fielder/79 3.00 8.00
17 Nick Swisher/79 3.00 8.00
18 Eric Hosmer/25 3.00 8.00
19 Adrian Beltre/49 4.00 10.00
20 Jean Segura/99 3.00 8.00
21 Evan Gattis/49 2.50 6.00
22 Mike Napoli/79 2.50 6.00
24 Pablo Sandoval/99 8.00 20.00
25 Mark Teixeira/79 3.00 8.00

2014 Immaculate Collection Immaculate Hitters Memorabilia Prime

*PRIME: .75X TO 2X BASIC
RANDOM INSERTS IN PACKS
PRINT RUNS B/WN 5-25 COPIES PER
NO PRICING ON QTY 15 OR LESS

2014 Immaculate Collection Immaculate Ink

RANDOM INSERTS IN PACKS
PRINT RUNS B/WN 15-99 COPIES PER
NO PRICING ON QTY 15 OR LESS
EXCHANGE DEADLINE 3/3/2016
1 Jim Palmer/25 10.00 25.00
2 Jorge Posada/25 10.00 25.00
3 Craig Biggio/25 12.00 30.00
4 Mark Grace/25 10.00 25.00
5 Jose Canseco/49 10.00 25.00
6 Rafael Palmeiro/25 12.00 30.00
9 Gaylord Perry/49 10.00 25.00
11 Roy Halladay/49 12.00 30.00
12 Pablo Sandoval/49 5.00 12.00
13 Freddie Freeman/99 6.00 15.00
14 Giancarlo Stanton/25 20.00 50.00
18 Jay Bruce/99 6.00 15.00
20 Adam Jones/25 5.00 12.00
22 Carlos Gomez/99 6.00 15.00
23 Jose Fernandez/49 40.00 100.00
24 Oscar Taveras/99 10.00 25.00
25 Shelby Miller/99 5.00 12.00
26 Wil Myers/25 4.00 10.00
27 David Wright/25 10.00 25.00
28 Dustin Pedroia/25 20.00 50.00
34 Paul Konerko/49 12.00 30.00
35 Jay Buhner/99 10.00 25.00
36 Edgar Martinez/49 8.00 20.00
38 Felix Hernandez/25 15.00 40.00
39 Matt Harvey/25 20.00 50.00
41 Darryl Strawberry/25 10.00 25.00
43 Clayton Kershaw/25 30.00 80.00
44 Chris Sale/25 6.00 15.00
46 Manny Machado/25 20.00 50.00
47 Jered Weaver/25 10.00 25.00
48 Harold Baines/79 6.00 15.00
49 Steve Garvey/49 12.00 30.00
50 Al Kaline/25 25.00 50.00
51 Carlos Gonzalez/25 8.00 20.00
52 Eric Hosmer/25 20.00 50.00
56 Brian McCann/25 5.00 12.00
57 Carlos Correa/99 60.00 150.00
58 Javier Baez/99 10.00 25.00
59 Jameson Taillon/99 5.00 12.00
60 Archie Bradley/99 4.00 10.00

2014 Immaculate Collection Immaculate Pitchers Memorabilia

RANDOM INSERTS IN PACKS
PRINT RUNS B/WN 49-99 COPIES PER
1 Justin Verlander/79 4.00 10.00
2 Felix Hernandez/49 3.00 8.00
3 Max Scherzer/99 4.00 10.00
4 Gerrit Cole/49 4.00 10.00
5 Hisashi Iwakuma/79 3.00 8.00
6 Stephen Strasburg/49 4.00 10.00
7 Aroldis Chapman/99 4.00 10.00
8 Dillon Gee/99 2.50 6.00
9 Madison Bumgarner/49 6.00 15.00
10 Pat Corbin/79 3.00 8.00
11 Cliff Lee/49 3.00 8.00
12 Johan Santana/49 3.00 8.00
13 Hyun-Jin Ryu/49 3.00 8.00
14 Yovani Gallardo/99 2.50 6.00
15 Jon Lester/79 3.00 8.00

2014 Immaculate Collection Immaculate Pitchers Memorabilia Prime

*PRIME: .75X TO 2X BASIC
RANDOM INSERTS IN PACKS
PRINT RUNS B/WN 10-25 COPIES PER
NO PRICING ON QTY 15 OR LESS

2014 Immaculate Collection Immaculate Quad Players Memorabilia

RANDOM INSERTS IN PACKS
PRINT RUNS B/WN 25-49 COPIES PER
1 Mchd/Frnndz/Myrs/Puig/25 15.00 40.00
2 Rpkn/Thms/Grffy/Pzz/49 25.00 60.00
3 Sndbrg/Brtt/Schmdt/Hndrsn/49 20.00 50.00
4 Brock/Rose/Jackson/Carew/25 20.00 50.00
5 Ortiz/Pujols/Jeter/Ichiro/49 30.00 80.00

2014 Immaculate Collection Immaculate Quads Memorabilia

RANDOM INSERTS IN PACKS
STATED PRINT RUN 25 SER.#'d SETS
1 Adam Dunn 10.00 25.00
2 Jose Reyes 10.00 25.00
3 Nelson Cruz 5.00 12.00

Curtis Granderson 4.00 10.00
Troy Tulowitzki 5.00 12.00

2014 Immaculate Collection Immaculate Singles Memorabilia

ANDOM INSERTS IN PACKS
RINT RUNS B/WN 25-99 COPIES PER
Jay Bruce/99 3.00 8.00
Adrian Gonzalez/99 3.00 8.00
Logan Morrison/99 2.50 6.00
Josh Hamilton/99 3.00 8.00
Justin Upton/99 3.00 8.00
Shelby Miller/99 3.00 8.00
Carl Crawford/99 3.00 8.00
David Freese/99 2.50 6.00
Matt Kemp/99 3.00 8.00
Mark Teixeira/99 3.00 8.00
B.J. Upton/99 3.00 8.00
Michael Bourn/99 2.50 6.00
Starlin Castro/99 2.50 6.00
Ryan Braun/99 3.00 8.00
Nelson Cruz/99 4.00 10.00
Mike Napoli/99 2.50 6.00
17 Pablo Sandoval/99 3.00 8.00
18 Matt Holliday/99 4.00 10.00
19 Ryan Howard/99 3.00 8.00
20 Neftali Feliz/99 2.50 6.00
21 Bryce Harper/99 6.00 15.00
22 Stephen Strasburg/99 4.00 10.00
23 Prince Fielder/99 3.00 8.00
24 Felix Hernandez/99 3.00 8.00
25 Tom Seaver/25 10.00 25.00
26 Reggie Jackson/99 3.00 8.00
27 George Brett/99 10.00 25.00
28 Pete Rose/99 10.00 25.00
29 Cal Ripken Jr./99 12.00 30.00
30 Taijuan Walker/99 2.50 6.00
31 Travis d'Arnaud/99 3.00 8.00
32 Kolten Wong/99 5.00 12.00
33 Yordano Ventura/99 3.00 8.00
34 Nick Castellanos/49 8.00 20.00
35 Michael Choice/99 2.50 6.00
36 Cameron Rupp/99 2.50 6.00
37 J.R. Murphy/99 2.50 6.00
38 Ryan Goins/99 3.00 8.00
39 Wilmer Flores/99 3.00 8.00
40 Reymond Fuentes/99 2.50 6.00

2014 Immaculate Collection Immaculate Singles Memorabilia Prime

*PRIME: .6X TO 1.5X BASIC
RANDOM INSERTS IN PACKS
PRINT RUNS B/WN 1-99 COPIES PER
NO PRICING ON QTY 15 OR LESS

2014 Immaculate Collection Immaculate Swatches

RANDOM INSERTS IN PACKS
PRINT RUNS B/WN 15-99 COPIES PER
NO PRICING ON QTY 15
2 Justin Verlander/99 4.00 10.00
3 Alex Rodriguez/99 6.00 15.00
4 Mark Teixeira/99 3.00 8.00
5 Bryce Harper/49 6.00 15.00
6 Mike Trout/49 10.00 25.00
7 Manny Machado/49 4.00 10.00
8 Jose Fernandez/49 4.00 10.00
9 Wil Myers/99 2.50 6.00
10 Stephen Strasburg/99 4.00 10.00
11 Miguel Cabrera/99 5.00 12.00
12 Prince Fielder/99 3.00 8.00
13 Matt Harvey/99 3.00 8.00
14 Robinson Cano/99 3.00 8.00
15 Jay Bruce/99 3.00 8.00
16 Ichiro Suzuki/49 10.00 25.00
17 Brandon Phillips/99 2.50 6.00
18 Paul Goldschmidt/99 4.00 10.00
19 Matt Cain/99 3.00 8.00
20 Yoenis Cespedes/99 4.00 10.00
21 Derek Jeter/99 10.00 25.00
22 Albert Pujols/99 5.00 12.00
23 Chris Davis/99 2.50 6.00
24 Troy Tulowitzki/99 4.00 10.00
25 Evan Longoria/99 3.00 8.00
26 Andrew McCutchen/99 8.00 20.00
27 Josh Hamilton/99 3.00 8.00
28 Jose Bautista/99 3.00 8.00
29 Adam Jones/99 3.00 8.00
30 David Ortiz/99 4.00 10.00
31 Dustin Pedroia/99 4.00 10.00
32 Carlos Gonzalez/99 3.00 8.00
33 Adrian Beltre/99 4.00 10.00
34 Edwin Encarnacion/99 4.00 10.00
35 Ryan Howard/99 3.00 8.00
36 Shin-Soo Choo/99 3.00 8.00
37 Max Scherzer/99 4.00 10.00
38 Joey Votto/99 4.00 10.00
39 David Wright/99 3.00 8.00
40 Carlos Beltran/99 3.00 8.00
41 Cliff Lee/99 3.00 8.00
42 Buster Posey/99 6.00 15.00
43 CC Sabathia/99 3.00 8.00
44 Pete Rose/49 8.00 20.00
45 Darryl Strawberry/99 2.50 6.00
46 Kirby Puckett/99 4.00 10.00
47 Tom Glavine/99 3.00 8.00
48 Craig Biggio/49 3.00 8.00
49 Jeff Bagwell/99 3.00 8.00
50 Jose Canseco/49 6.00 15.00
51 Joe Girardi/99 3.00 8.00
52 Paul Molitor/99 4.00 10.00
53 Bernie Williams/49 3.00 8.00
54 Ozzie Smith/99 5.00 12.00
55 George Brett/49 8.00 20.00
56 Bo Jackson/99 10.00 25.00
57 Ryne Sandberg/25 10.00 25.00
58 Rickey Henderson/99 5.00 12.00
59 Tony Gwynn/99 4.00 10.00
60 Chipper Jones/99 4.00 10.00
61 Frank Thomas/25 12.00 30.00
62 Cal Ripken Jr./99 8.00 20.00
63 Nolan Ryan/99 12.00 30.00
64 Roberto Alomar/99 3.00 8.00
65 Ken Griffey Jr./49 12.00 30.00
66 Kolten Wong/99 3.00 8.00
67 Travis d'Arnaud/99 3.00 8.00
68 Wilmer Flores/99 3.00 8.00
69 Juan Centeno/99 2.50 6.00
70 Enny Romero/99 2.50 6.00
71 Josmil Pinto/99 2.50 6.00
72 Kris Johnson/99 2.50 6.00
73 Cameron Rupp/99 2.50 6.00
74 Ryan Goins/99 3.00 8.00
75 Abraham Almonte/99 2.50 6.00
76 Billy Hamilton/99 4.00 10.00
77 Charlie Leesman/99 2.50 6.00
78 David Holmberg/99 2.50 6.00
79 Jimmy Nelson/99 2.50 6.00
80 Jose Ramirez/99 20.00 50.00
81 Marcus Semien/99 2.50 6.00
82 Matt Davidson/99 3.00 8.00
83 Matt Shoemaker/99 4.00 10.00
84 Michael Choice/99 2.50 6.00
85 Reymond Fuentes/99 2.50 6.00
86 Taijuan Walker/99 2.50 6.00
87 Yordano Ventura/99 3.00 8.00
88 Nick Castellanos/99 4.00 10.00
89 Byron Buxton/99 6.00 15.00
90 Oscar Taveras/99 10.00 25.00
91 Xander Bogaerts/99 5.00 12.00
92 Chad Bettis/99 2.50 6.00
93 Matt den Dekker/99 3.00 8.00
94 J.R. Murphy/99 2.50 6.00
95 Masahiro Tanaka/99 12.00 30.00

2014 Immaculate Collection Immaculate Swatches Premium

*PREMIUM: 2X TO 5X BASIC
RANDOM INSERTS IN PACKS
PRINT RUNS B/WN 1-20 COPIES PER
NO PRICING ON QTY 15 OR LESS

2014 Immaculate Collection Immaculate Swatches Prime

*PRIME: .75X TO 2X BASIC
RANDOM INSERTS IN PACKS
PRINT RUNS B/WN 1-99 COPIES PER
NO PRICING ON QTY 15 OR LESS
1 Yasiel Puig/25 8.00 20.00
5 Bryce Harper/25 20.00 50.00
63 Nolan Ryan/25 30.00 80.00
95 Masahiro Tanaka/25 40.00 100.00

2014 Immaculate Collection Immaculate Trios Memorabilia

RANDOM INSERTS IN PACKS
PRINT RUNS B/WN 25-49 COPIES PER
1 Josh Hamilton/49 4.00 10.00
2 Tim Hudson/49 4.00 10.00
3 Johnny Cueto/49 4.00 10.00
4 Nick Markakis/49 4.00 10.00
5 Jeff Samardzija/49 3.00 8.00
6 Christian Yelich/49 6.00 15.00
7 Hisashi Iwakuma/25 6.00 15.00
8 Wellington Castillo/49 3.00 8.00
9 Alex Avila/49 4.00 10.00
10 Jason Heyward/49 4.00 10.00

2014 Immaculate Collection Immaculate Trios Players Memorabilia

RANDOM INSERTS IN PACKS
PRINT RUNS B/WN 25-79 COPIES PER
1 Vott/Cbrra/.McCtchn/49 15.00 40.00
2 Sbha/Lee/Schrzr/79 8.00 20.00
3 Psy/Hmltn/Cbrr/49 6.00 15.00
4 Myrs/Hrpr/Trout/49 20.00 50.00
5 Dvis/Gldschmdt/Cbrra/79 6.00 15.00
6 Phillips/Gonzalez/Goldschmidt/49 5.00 12.00
7 Jones/Hunter/Cano/79 4.00 10.00
8 Bltrn/Pjls/Ortz/79 6.00 15.00
9 Cnsco/Rdrguz/Smo/49 10.00 25.00
10 Mrry/Bnks/Schmdt/25 15.00 40.00

2014 Immaculate Collection Premium Material

RANDOM INSERTS IN PACKS
PRINT RUNS B/WN 25-99 COPIES PER
1 Alex Rodriguez/49 10.00 25.00
2 Adam Jones/49 4.00 10.00
3 Julio Teheran/25 4.00 10.00
4 Jose Fernandez/49 5.00 12.00
5 Michael Morse/49 3.00 8.00
6 Matt Harvey/79 4.00 10.00
7 Jose Bautista/25 8.00 20.00
8 Adam Eaton/49 3.00 8.00
9 Hisashi Iwakuma/49 3.00 8.00
10 Albert Pujols/25 6.00 15.00
11 Torii Hunter/79 3.00 8.00
12 Derek Jeter/79 30.00 60.00
13 Yasiel Puig/99 5.00 12.00
14 Anthony Rizzo/79 8.00 20.00
15 Justin Upton/49 4.00 10.00
16 Jacoby Ellsbury/49 4.00 10.00
17 Prince Fielder/49 4.00 10.00
18 Aramis Ramirez/49 3.00 8.00
19 David Wright/49 4.00 10.00
20 Pat Corbin/49 4.00 10.00
21 Justin Verlander/79 5.00 12.00
22 Yovani Gallardo/79 3.00 8.00
23 Miguel Cabrera/49 5.00 12.00
24 Xander Bogaerts/99 8.00 20.00
25 Jon Lester/49 4.00 10.00
26 Jeff Samardzija/49 3.00 8.00
27 Chase Utley/49 4.00 10.00
28 Drew Smyly/79 3.00 8.00
29 Pete Rose/25 12.00 30.00
30 Mike Piazza/49 5.00 12.00
31 Dennis Eckersley/79 5.00 12.00
32 Wilmer Flores/99 4.00 10.00
33 Cameron Rupp/99 3.00 8.00
34 Jose Ramirez/99 25.00 60.00
35 Reymond Fuentes/99 3.00 8.00
36 Yordano Ventura/99 4.00 10.00
37 Michael Choice/99 3.00 8.00
38 Travis d'Arnaud/99 4.00 10.00
39 Billy Hamilton/99 4.00 10.00
40 Taijuan Walker/99 3.00 8.00
41 Kolten Wong/99 6.00 15.00

2014 Immaculate Collection Rookie Autographs Materials Prime

*PRIME: .6X TO 1.5X BASIC
RANDOM INSERTS IN PACKS
PRINT RUNS B/WN 10-99 COPIES PER
NO PRICING ON QTY 10
EXCHANGE DEADLINE 3/3/2016
155 Jose Abreu JSY/25 100.00 250.00

2014 Immaculate Collection The Greatest Materials

RANDOM INSERTS IN PACKS
PRINT RUNS B/WN 10-49 COPIES PER
NO PRICING ON QTY 10 OR LESS
1 Mark McGwire/49 12.00 30.00
2 Pete Rose/49 12.00 30.00
3 George Brett/49 15.00 40.00
4 Mike Schmidt/25 12.00 30.00
5 Nolan Ryan/25 30.00 80.00
6 Reggie Jackson/49 6.00 15.00
7 Lou Brock/49 6.00 15.00
9 Robin Yount/49 8.00 20.00
10 Ozzie Smith/49 8.00 20.00
11 Jim Rice/49 6.00 15.00
12 Dale Murphy/49 8.00 20.00
13 Eddie Murray/49 6.00 15.00
14 Gaylord Perry/49 6.00 15.00
15 Carlton Fisk/25 8.00 20.00
16 Mike Piazza/49 10.00 25.00
17 Paul Molitor/49 6.00 15.00
18 Dennis Eckersley/49 6.00 15.00
19 Wade Boggs/49 6.00 15.00
20 Orlando Cepeda/25 8.00 20.00
22 Carl Yastrzemski/49 8.00 20.00
23 John Smoltz/49 8.00 20.00
24 Will Clark/49 6.00 15.00
25 Rod Carew/25 6.00 15.00
26 Gil Hodges/49 10.00 25.00
27 Ty Cobb/49 25.00 60.00
28 Lou Gehrig/49 40.00 100.00
29 Pee Wee Reese/49 10.00 25.00
30 Joe DiMaggio/49 30.00 80.00

2014 Immaculate Collection The Greatest Materials Prime

*PRIME: .6X TO 1.5X BASIC
RANDOM INSERTS IN PACKS
PRINT RUNS B/WN 1-25 COPIES PER
NO PRICING ON QTY 15 OR LESS

2014 Immaculate Collection The Greatest Signatures

RANDOM INSERTS IN PACKS
STATED PRINT RUN 20 SER.#'d SETS
EXCHANGE DEADLINE 3/3/2016
1 Ken Griffey Jr. 75.00 150.00
2 Cal Ripken Jr. 30.00 80.00
3 George Brett 50.00 120.00
4 Bo Jackson 40.00 100.00
5 Mariano Rivera 60.00 150.00
6 Ryne Sandberg 30.00 80.00
7 Nolan Ryan 50.00 125.00
8 Brooks Robinson 12.00 30.00
9 Willie McCovey 12.00 30.00
10 Rickey Henderson 30.00 80.00
11 Bob Gibson EXCH 12.00 30.00
12 Tony Gwynn 15.00 40.00
13 Johnny Bench 15.00 40.00
14 Chipper Jones 50.00 120.00
15 Frank Thomas 30.00 80.00

2015 Immaculate Collection

1-100 PRINT RUN 99 SER.#'d SETS
JSY AU PRINT RUN 99 SER.#'d SETS
AU PRINT RUNS B/WN 49-99 COPIES PER
EXCHANGE DEADLINE 2/26/2017
1 Mike Trout 8.00 20.00
2 Clayton Kershaw 3.00 8.00
3 Babe Ruth 4.00 10.00
4 Jose Abreu 1.50 4.00
5 Ichiro Suzuki 2.00 5.00
6 Giancarlo Stanton 1.50 4.00
7 Jose Bautista 1.25 3.00
8 David Wright 1.25 3.00
9 Bryce Harper 2.50 6.00
10 Robinson Cano 1.25 3.00
11 David Price 1.25 3.00
12 Miguel Cabrera 1.50 4.00
13 Troy Tulowitzki 1.50 4.00
14 Evan Longoria 1.25 3.00
15 Stephen Strasburg 1.50 4.00
16 Masahiro Tanaka 1.25 3.00
17 Yasiel Puig 1.50 4.00
18 Buster Posey 2.00 5.00
19 Madison Bumgarner 1.25 3.00
20 Felix Hernandez 1.25 3.00
21 Albert Pujols 2.00 5.00
22 Ryan Howard 1.25 3.00
23 Adam Jones 1.25 3.00
24 Yu Darvish 1.50 4.00
25 Alex Rodriguez 2.00 5.00
26 Chase Utley 1.25 3.00
27 Chris Davis 1.00 2.50
28 Yadier Molina 1.50 4.00
29 Alex Gordon 1.25 3.00
30 David Ortiz 1.50 4.00
31 Joey Votto 1.50 4.00
32 Matt Kemp 1.25 3.00
33 Carlos Gonzalez 1.25 3.00
34 Ryan Braun 1.25 3.00
35 Adrian Beltre 1.50 4.00
36 Wil Myers 1.00 2.50
37 Andrew McCutchen 1.50 4.00
38 Salvador Perez 1.25 3.00
39 Adam Wainwright 1.25 3.00
40 Eric Hosmer 1.25 3.00
41 Nelson Cruz 1.50 4.00
42 Chris Sale 1.50 4.00
43 Corey Kluber 1.25 3.00
44 Jacob deGrom 1.50 4.00
45 Matt Harvey 1.25 3.00
46 Yoenis Cespedes 1.25 3.00
47 Freddie Freeman 2.00 5.00
48 Jose Fernandez 1.50 4.00
49 Justin Verlander 1.50 4.00
50 Paul Goldschmidt 1.50 4.00
51 Wei-Yin Chen 1.00 2.50
52 Jose Altuve 1.50 4.00
53 Torii Hunter 1.00 2.50
54 Max Scherzer 1.50 4.00
55 Jon Lester 1.25 3.00
56 Anthony Rizzo 2.50 6.00
57 Sonny Gray 1.25 3.00
58 Victor Martinez 1.25 3.00
59 Yordano Ventura 1.25 3.00
60 Kennys Vargas 1.00 2.50
61 Joe Mauer 1.25 3.00
62 Zack Greinke 1.50 4.00
63 Hunter Pence 1.25 3.00
64 Johnny Cueto 1.25 3.00
65 Jered Weaver 1.25 3.00
66 James Shields 1.00 2.50
67 Chris Carter 1.00 2.50
68 Michael Brantley 1.25 3.00
69 Carlos Gomez 1.00 2.50
70 Josh Donaldson 1.25 3.00
71 Jonathan Lucroy 1.25 3.00
72 Josh Harrison 1.00 2.50
73 Edwin Encarnacion 1.50 4.00
74 Todd Frazier 1.25 3.00
75 Justin Upton 1.25 3.00
76 Jordan Zimmermann 1.25 3.00
77 Kyle Seager 1.00 2.50
78 Adrian Gonzalez 1.25 3.00
79 Matt Carpenter 1.50 4.00
80 Anthony Rendon 1.50 4.00
81 Manny Machado 1.50 4.00
82 Hanley Ramirez 1.25 3.00
83 Dustin Pedroia 1.50 4.00
84 Jason Heyward 1.25 3.00
85 CC Sabathia 1.25 3.00
86 Nolan Arenado 2.00 5.00
87 Mookie Betts 2.50 6.00
88 Taijuan Walker 1.00 2.50
89 Julio Teheran 1.25 3.00
90 Gregory Polanco 1.25 3.00
91 Kirby Puckett 1.50 4.00
92 Bo Jackson 1.50 4.00
93 Pete Rose 3.00 8.00
94 Nolan Ryan 5.00 12.00
95 Ken Griffey Jr. 3.00 8.00
96 Stan Musial 2.50 6.00
97 Ty Cobb 2.50 6.00
98 Lou Gehrig 3.00 8.00
99 Roberto Clemente 4.00 10.00
100 Babe Ruth 4.00 10.00
101 Archie Bradley JSY AU/49 RC 4.00 10.00
102 Rusney Castillo JSY AU/49 RC 5.00 12.00
103 Yasmany Tomas JSY AU/49 RC 5.00 12.00
104 Matt Barnes JSY AU/49 RC 4.00 10.00
105 Brandon Finnegan JSY AU/49 RC 4.00 10.00
106 Kris Bryant JSY AU/49 100.00 200.00
107 Kendall Graveman JSY AU/49 RC 4.00 10.00
108 Yorman Rodriguez JSY AU/49 RC 4.00 10.00
109 Gary Brown JSY AU/49 RC 4.00 10.00
110 R.J. Alvarez JSY AU/49 RC 4.00 10.00
111 Jorge Soler JSY AU/49 10.00 25.00
112 Maikel Franco JSY AU/49 RC 5.00 12.00
113 Addison Russell JSY AU/49 RC 15.00 40.00
114 Lane Adams JSY AU/49 RC 4.00 10.00
115 Joc Pederson JSY AU/49 RC 8.00 20.00
116 Steven Moya JSY AU/49 RC 5.00 12.00
117 Cory Spangenberg JSY AU/49 RC 4.00 10.00
118 Francisco Lindor JSY AU/49 RC 20.00 50.00
119 Raisel Iglesias JSY AU/49 RC 5.00 12.00
120 Ryan Rua JSY AU/49 RC 4.00 10.00
121 Dilson Herrera JSY AU/49 RC 5.00 12.00
122 Edwin Escobar JSY AU/49 RC 4.00 10.00
123 Javier Baez JSY AU/49 RC 20.00 50.00
124 Matt Szczur JSY AU/49 RC 5.00 12.00
125 Jake Lamb JSY AU/49 RC 10.00 25.00
126 Michael Taylor JSY AU/49 RC 4.00 10.00
127 Rymer Liriano JSY AU/49 RC 4.00 10.00
128 Trevor May JSY AU/49 RC 4.00 10.00
129 Joey Gallo JSY AU/25 12.00 30.00
130 Carlos Correa JSY AU/49 30.00 80.00
132 Devon Travis AU/99 RC 3.00 8.00
133 Daniel Norris AU/99 RC 3.00 8.00
134 Odubel Herrera AU/99 RC 15.00 40.00
135 Roberto Osuna AU/99 RC 3.00 8.00
136 Daniel Muno AU/99 RC 3.00 8.00
137 James McCann AU/99 RC 10.00 25.00
138 Matt Clark AU/99 RC 3.00 8.00
139 Dalton Pompey AU/99 RC 6.00 15.00
140 Terrance Gore AU/99 RC 3.00 8.00
141 Jorge Soler AU/99 RC 3.00 8.00
142 Buck Farmer AU/99 RC 3.00 8.00
143 Mike Foltynewicz AU/99 RC 3.00 8.00
144 Anthony Ranaudo AU/99 RC 3.00 8.00
145 Miguel Castro AU/99 RC 3.00 8.00
147 Christian Walker AU/99 RC 6.00 15.00
148 Kris Bryant AU/99 RC 60.00 150.00
149 A.J. Cole AU/99 RC 3.00 8.00
150 Blake Swihart AU/99 RC 4.00 10.00
151 Dalier Hinojosa AU/99 RC 3.00 8.00
152 Austin Hedges AU/99 RC 3.00 8.00
153 Noah Syndergaard AU/99 RC 6.00 15.00
154 Lance McCullers AU/99 RC 6.00 15.00
155 Carlos Rodon AU/99 RC 5.00 12.00
156 Joey Gallo AU/49 RC 12.00 30.00
157 Jung-Ho Kang AU/99 RC 15.00 40.00
158 Carlos Correa AU/99 RC 30.00 80.00
159 Kevin Plawecki AU/99 RC 3.00 8.00

2015 Immaculate Collection Blue

*BLUE 132-159: .5X TO 1.2X BASIC
RANDOM INSERTS IN PACKS
1-100 PRINT RUN 10 SER.#'d SETS
132-159 PRINT RUNS B/WN 25-49 COPIES PER
NO 1-100 PRICING DUE TO SCARCITY
EXCHANGE DEADLINE 2/26/2017

2015 Immaculate Collection Red

*RED: .6X TO 1.5X BASIC
RANDOM INSERTS IN PACKS
STATED PRINT RUN 25 SER.#'d SETS
1 Mike Trout 15.00 40.00
91 Kirby Puckett 30.00 80.00
92 Bo Jackson 10.00 25.00
94 Nolan Ryan 15.00 40.00
95 Ken Griffey Jr. 15.00 40.00
99 Roberto Clemente 10.00 25.00

2015 Immaculate Collection Accolades Materials

RANDOM INSERTS IN PACKS
STATED PRINT RUN B/WN 5-99 COPIES PER
NO PRICING ON QTY 10 OR LESS
2 Lou Gehrig/25 50.00 120.00
3 Ty Cobb/15 30.00 80.00
5 Herb Pennock/20 8.00 20.00
6 Don Drysdale/99 3.00 8.00
7 Bob Feller/99 5.00 12.00
8 Harmon Killebrew/25 4.00 10.00
9 Luke Appling/49 5.00 12.00
10 Bill Dickey/25 5.00 12.00
11 Ken Boyer/20 4.00 10.00
12 Charlie Gehringer/15 12.00 30.00
13 Joe Cronin/25 5.00 12.00
14 Stan Musial/25 6.00 15.00
15 Ted Williams/25 20.00 50.00
17 Miller Huggins/25 5.00 12.00
19 Frankie Frisch/15 10.00 25.00
21 Gabby Hartnett/49 8.00 20.00
22 Gil McDougald/49 5.00 12.00
23 Lou Gehrig/25 50.00 120.00
25 Eddie Mathews/99 5.00 12.00

2015 Immaculate Collection All-Star Autographs

RANDOM INSERTS IN PACKS
PRINT RUNS B/WN 15-99 COPIES PER
EXCHANGE DEADLINE 2/26/2017
1 Paul Goldschmidt/15 15.00 40.00
2 Troy Tulowitzki/15 10.00 25.00
3 Jonathan Lucroy/15 8.00 20.00
4 Josh Donaldson/15 30.00 80.00
5 Jose Abreu/99 20.00 50.00
6 Yadier Molina/15 60.00 150.00
7 Yoenis Cespedes/15 5.00 12.00
8 Anthony Rizzo/15 20.00 50.00
9 Todd Frazier/15 15.00 40.00
10 Chris Sale/15 15.00 40.00

2015 Immaculate Collection Collegiate Autographs Materials

RANDOM INSERTS IN PACKS
PRINT RUNS B/WN 49-99 COPIES PER
EXCHANGE DEADLINE 2/26/2017
*PRIME/25: .75X TO 2X BASIC
1 Deven Marrero/99 4.00 10.00
2 Christian Walker/99 8.00 20.00
3 Andy Wilkins/99 4.00 10.00
4 Tyler Naquin/99 5.00 12.00
5 Luke Weaver/99 6.00 15.00
6 Michael Conforto/49 20.00 50.00
7 Peter O'Brien/99 6.00 15.00
8 Robert Refsnyder/99 5.00 12.00

2015 Immaculate Collection Collegiate Ink

RANDOM INSERTS IN PACKS
PRINT RUNS B/WN 25-79 COPIES PER
EXCHANGE DEADLINE 2/26/2017
12 James McCann/49 8.00 20.00
13 Andy Wilkins/79 6.00 15.00
14 Anthony Ranaudo/49 4.00 10.00
15 Kendall Graveman/49 4.00 10.00
16 Christian Walker/79 8.00 20.00
17 Brandon Finnegan/49 4.00 10.00
19 Jake Lamb/79 6.00 15.00
20 George Springer/25 8.00 20.00
21 Trea Turner/25 15.00 40.00
22 Carlos Rodon/25 10.00 25.00
38 Kyle Schwarber/49 30.00 80.00
39 Matt Szczur/79 5.00 12.00
40 Stephen Piscotty/79 5.00 12.00

2015 Immaculate Collection Collegiate Ink Red

*RED INK: .5X TO 1.2X BASIC
RANDOM INSERTS IN PACKS
PRINT RUNS B/WN 15-25 COPIES PER
EXCHANGE DEADLINE 2/26/2017
11 Fred Lynn/25 5.00 12.00
23 Stephen Strasburg/15 20.00 50.00
24 Troy Tulowitzki/15 12.00 30.00
25 Evan Longoria/15 10.00 25.00
26 Ryan Braun/15 8.00 20.00
27 Max Scherzer/15 25.00 60.00
28 Alex Gordon/15 20.00 50.00
29 Kyle Seager/15 10.00 25.00
30 Garrett Richards/15 10.00 25.00
31 Sonny Gray/15 15.00 40.00
32 Josh Donaldson/15 25.00 60.00
33 Dallas Keuchel/15 6.00 15.00
34 Dustin Pedroia/15 15.00 40.00
35 Charlie Blackmon/15 8.00 20.00
36 Jake Arrieta/15 30.00 80.00
37 Pedro Alvarez/15 10.00 25.00

2015 Immaculate Collection Collegiate Materials

RANDOM INSERTS IN PACKS
STATED PRINT RUN B/WN 25-99 COPIES PER
*JUMBO/25-99: .4X TO 1X BASIC
*PRIME/25: .5X TO 1.2X BASIC
1 Deven Marrero/99 2.50 6.00
2 Christian Walker/99 5.00 12.00
3 Andy Wilkins/25 2.50 6.00
4 Tyler Naquin/99 3.00 8.00
5 Luke Weaver/99 4.00 10.00
6 Michael Conforto/99 6.00 15.00
7 Peter O'Brien/99 4.00 10.00
8 Robert Refsnyder/99 3.00 8.00

2015 Immaculate Collection Diamond Signatures

RANDOM INSERTS IN PACKS
PRINT RUNS B/WN 10-99 COPIES PER
NO PRICING ON QTY 10
EXCHANGE DEADLINE 2/26/2017
1 Jose Abreu/99 15.00 40.00
2 Jose Altuve/49 20.00 50.00
3 Kris Bryant/25 75.00 200.00
4 Rusney Castillo/25 5.00 12.00
5 Yasmany Tomas/25 15.00 40.00
6 Jung-Ho Kang/99 25.00 60.00
7 Felix Hernandez/25 15.00 40.00
8 David Ortiz/15 30.00 80.00
10 Salvador Perez/48 20.00 50.00

2015 Immaculate Collection Diamond Signatures Holo Gold

*HOLO GOLD: .5X TO 1.2X BASIC
RANDOM INSERTS IN PACKS
PRINT RUNS B/WN 10-25 COPIES PER
NO PRICING ON QTY 10
EXCHANGE DEADLINE 2/26/2017
9 Adam Jones/15 20.00 50.00

2015 Immaculate Collection Immaculate Autograph Dual Materials

RANDOM INSERTS IN PACKS
PRINT RUNS B/WN 10-25 COPIES PER
NO PRICING ON QTY 10
EXCHANGE DEADLINE 2/26/2017
2 Jose Canseco/25 15.00 40.00
3 Byron Buxton/25 15.00 40.00
4 Andre Dawson/25 10.00 25.00
5 Adam Jones/25 8.00 20.00
6 Taijuan Walker/25 5.00 12.00
7 Yordano Ventura/25 10.00 25.00
8 Jose Abreu/25 12.00 30.00
9 Yoan Moncada/25 50.00 120.00
12 George Springer/25 6.00 15.00
14 Evan Gattis/25 5.00 12.00
15 Tom Glavine/25 12.00 30.00
16 Troy Tulowitzki/25 10.00 25.00
17 Evan Longoria/25 8.00 20.00
18 Jim Rice/25 10.00 25.00
19 Dave Winfield/15 15.00 40.00
20 Jameson Taillon/20 6.00 15.00
21 Billy Butler/20 5.00 12.00
22 Dallas Keuchel/20 12.00 30.00
23 Danny Santana/20 5.00 12.00
24 David Wright/20 12.00 30.00
25 Kyle Seager/20 12.00 30.00
26 Michael Brantley/20 10.00 25.00
27 Robinson Cano/20 10.00 25.00
28 Yadier Molina/20 40.00 100.00
29 Jacob deGrom/20 20.00 50.00
30 Kennys Vargas/20 5.00 12.00

2015 Immaculate Collection Immaculate Autograph Jumbo Materials

RANDOM INSERTS IN PACKS
PRINT RUNS B/WN 15-25 COPIES PER
EXCHANGE DEADLINE 2/26/2017
1 Joe Panik/25 6.00 15.00
2 Eric Hosmer/15 15.00 40.00
3 Dale Murphy/15 20.00 50.00
4 Devin Mesoraco/25 5.00 12.00
5 Matt Adams/25 5.00 12.00
6 Paul Goldschmidt/15 12.00 30.00
7 Starling Marte/25 10.00 25.00
8 Francisco Lindor/25 15.00 40.00
9 Josh Harrison/25 8.00 20.00
10 Yoan Moncada/25 40.00 100.00
11 Kennys Vargas/25 5.00 12.00
12 Chris Sale/25 10.00 25.00
13 Josh Donaldson/25 12.00 30.00
14 Freddie Freeman/25 8.00 20.00
15 Sonny Gray/25 6.00 15.00
16 Anthony Rendon/25 10.00 25.00
17 Kyle Schwarber/25 40.00 100.00
18 Evan Gattis/25 5.00 12.00
19 Joe Mauer/15 10.00 25.00
20 Matt Szczur/25 6.00 15.00
21 Yasmany Tomas/25 6.00 15.00
22 Gary Brown/25 5.00 12.00
23 Rusney Castillo/25 6.00 15.00
24 Kris Bryant/25 100.00 200.00
25 Addison Russell/25 20.00 50.00
26 Archie Bradley/25 5.00 12.00
27 Michael Taylor/25 10.00 25.00
28 Javier Baez/25 10.00 25.00
29 Maikel Franco/25 6.00 15.00
30 Jorge Soler/25 10.00 25.00

2015 Immaculate Collection Immaculate Autograph Materials

RANDOM INSERTS IN PACKS
PRINT RUNS B/WN 5-25 COPIES PER
NO PRICING ON QTY 10 OR LESS
EXCHANGE DEADLINE 2/26/2017
1 Vladimir Guerrero/15 10.00 25.00
6 Jose Fernandez/25 30.00 80.00
7 Evan Gattis/25 5.00 12.00
8 Mike Napoli/25 5.00 12.00
9 Sonny Gray/25 6.00 15.00
10 Byron Buxton/25 15.00 40.00
11 Adrian Beltre/15 10.00 25.00
12 Jameson Taillon/25 6.00 15.00
13 Salvador Perez/25 12.00 30.00
14 Anthony Rendon/25 10.00 25.00
15 Troy Tulowitzki/15 10.00 25.00
16 Evan Longoria/15 10.00 25.00
18 David Ortiz/15 30.00 80.00
19 Yoenis Cespedes/15 10.00 25.00
20 Eric Hosmer/15 15.00 40.00
21 Jose Altuve/15 25.00 60.00
22 Justin Upton/15 6.00 15.00
23 Andy Pettitte/15 20.00 50.00
24 Wei-Chung Wang/20 10.00 25.00
25 Tim Raines/20 6.00 15.00
26 Max Scherzer/20 15.00 40.00
27 Jose Abreu/20 12.00 30.00
28 Manny Machado/20 25.00 60.00
29 Pablo Sandoval/20 10.00 25.00
31 Adrian Gonzalez/20 6.00 15.00
32 Adam Jones/20 10.00 25.00
33 Freddie Freeman/20 10.00 25.00
34 Dustin Pedroia/20 12.00 30.00
36 Don Sutton/20 6.00 15.00
37 Edwin Encarnacion/20 8.00 20.00
38 Josh Donaldson/20 12.00 30.00
39 Paul Molitor/20 10.00 25.00
40 Andre Dawson/20 10.00 25.00
41 Yoan Moncada/20 50.00 120.00

2015 Immaculate Collection Immaculate Autograph Quad Materials

RANDOM INSERTS IN PACKS
PRINT RUNS B/WN 10-20 COPIES PER
NO PRICING ON QTY 15 OR LESS
EXCHANGE DEADLINE 2/26/2017
4 Kennys Vargas/20 8.00 20.00

2015 Immaculate Collection Immaculate Dual Autograph Materials

RANDOM INSERTS IN PACKS
PRINT RUNS B/WN 5-20 COPIES PER
NO PRICING ON QTY 10 OR LESS
EXCHANGE DEADLINE 2/26/2017
1 D.Ortiz/K.Vargas/20 25.00 60.00

2015 Immaculate Collection Immaculate Dual Players Memorabilia

RANDOM INSERTS IN PACKS
STATED PRINT RUN B/WN 15-99 COPIES PER
*PRIME/15-25: .6X TO 1.5X BASIC
1 Chance/Cobb/15 40.00 100.00
2 Ruth/Gehrig/20 150.00 250.00
3 P.Molitor/R.Carew/99 4.00 10.00
4 A.Bradley/Y.Tomas/99 3.00 8.00
5 Russell/Lindor/99 5.00 12.00
6 Thomas/Griffey Jr./99 10.00 25.00
7 Cabrera/Martinez/99 4.00 10.00
8 Rodriguez/Griffey Jr./99 10.00 25.00
9 Puig/Pederson/25 5.00 12.00
10 Fernandez/Stanton/49 4.00 10.00
11 K.Vargas/D.Ortiz/99 4.00 10.00
12 J.Abreu/R.Castillo/49 4.00 10.00
13 M.Tanaka/Y.Darvish/49 4.00 10.00
14 P.Martinez/V.Guerrero/99 3.00 8.00
15 Martinez/Clemens/49 8.00 20.00
16 McCutchen/Stanton/49 4.00 10.00
17 Canseco/McGwire/15 40.00 100.00
18 Harper/Strasburg/49 6.00 15.00
19 Taillon/Glasnow/99 5.00 12.00
20 Soler/Bryant/99 12.00 30.00

2015 Immaculate Collection Immaculate Duals Memorabilia

RANDOM INSERTS IN PACKS
STATED PRINT RUN B/WN 49-99 COPIES PER
1 Kris Bryant/99 12.00 30.00
2 Adrian Beltre/49 4.00 10.00
3 Aramis Ramirez/99 2.50 6.00
4 Brian McCann/99 3.00 8.00

5 Don Mattingly/99 8.00 20.00
6 Jeff Bagwell/99 3.00 8.00
7 Jose Bautista/99 3.00 8.00
8 Matt Carpenter/49 4.00 10.00
9 Billy Butler/99 2.50 6.00
10 Mookie Betts/49 5.00 12.00
11 Salvador Perez/99 3.00 8.00
12 Yasmany Tomas/99 3.00 8.00
13 Christian Yelich/99 5.00 12.00
14 Mike Napoli/49 2.50 6.00
15 Johnny Bench/49 10.00 25.00
16 Bo Jackson/49 8.00 20.00
17 Andy Pettitte/49 3.00 8.00
18 Yu Darvish/49 4.00 10.00
19 Ken Griffey Jr./49 12.00 30.00
20 Rickey Henderson/49 8.00 20.00

2015 Immaculate Collection Immaculate Equipment

RANDOM INSERTS IN PACKS
STATED PRINT RUN B/WN 10-49 COPIES PER
NO PRICING ON QTY 10
1 Lou Gehrig/15 200.00 400.00
3 Kirby Puckett/15 60.00 150.00
4 Rod Carew/25 6.00 15.00
5 Kris Bryant/49 15.00 40.00
6 Barry Bonds/49 8.00 20.00
7 Ken Griffey Jr./20 20.00 50.00
8 Tony Gwynn/25 15.00 40.00
9 Vladimir Guerrero/49 5.00 12.00
10 Javier Baez/20 8.00 20.00
11 Miguel Sano/20 8.00 20.00
12 Francisco Lindor/49 10.00 25.00
13 Kyle Schwarber/20 10.00 25.00
14 Michael Taylor/20 2.50 6.00
15 Yasmany Tomas/49 3.00 8.00
16 Byron Buxton/49 6.00 15.00
17 Addison Russell/49 10.00 25.00
18 Jose Bautista/15 5.00 12.00
19 Rickey Henderson/20 15.00 40.00
20 Albert Pujols/20 10.00 25.00

2015 Immaculate Collection Immaculate Heroes Materials

RANDOM INSERTS IN PACKS
STATED PRINT RUN B/WN 15-99 COPIES PER
1 Babe Ruth/15 200.00 400.00
2 Roberto Clemente/15 40.00 100.00
3 Wade Boggs/99 3.00 8.00
4 George Brett/49 8.00 20.00
5 Ozzie Smith/79 5.00 12.00
6 Bo Jackson/49 6.00 15.00
7 Barry Bonds/99 6.00 15.00
8 Red Schoendienst/99 3.00 8.00
9 Cal Ripken/99 6.00 15.00
10 Vladimir Guerrero/99 3.00 8.00
11 Mike Schmidt/49 5.00 12.00
12 Fred Lynn/99 2.50 6.00
13 Pete Rose/49 6.00 15.00
14 Greg Maddux/99 5.00 12.00
15 Robin Yount/25 10.00 25.00
16 Tony Gwynn/99 4.00 10.00
17 Reggie Jackson/79 3.00 8.00
18 Mark McGwire/99 5.00 12.00
19 Dave Winfield/99 3.00 8.00
20 Harmon Killebrew/49 4.00 10.00

2015 Immaculate Collection Immaculate Hitters Materials

RANDOM INSERTS IN PACKS
STATED PRINT RUN B/WN 15-99 COPIES PER
1 Pete Rose/25 12.00 30.00
2 Tony Gwynn/49 4.00 10.00
3 Adrian Gonzalez/49 3.00 8.00
4 Freddie Freeman/25 5.00 12.00
5 Nelson Cruz/99 4.00 10.00
6 Adrian Beltre/49 4.00 10.00
7 Giancarlo Stanton/25 4.00 10.00
8 Mike Trout/15 15.00 40.00
9 Jose Altuve/49 3.00 8.00
10 Kris Bryant/99 15.00 40.00
11 Jose Abreu/49 4.00 10.00
12 Miguel Cabrera/25 6.00 15.00
13 Corey Seager/99 5.00 12.00
14 Adam Jones/49 3.00 8.00
15 Robinson Cano/49 3.00 8.00
16 Josh Donaldson/99 3.00 8.00
17 Andrew McCutchen/20 8.00 20.00
18 Paul Goldschmidt/99 4.00 10.00
19 Evan Longoria/99 3.00 8.00
20 Jacoby Ellsbury/49 3.00 8.00

2015 Immaculate Collection Immaculate Ink

RANDOM INSERTS IN PACKS
PRINT RUNS B/WN 10-99 COPIES PER
NO PRICING ON QTY 10 OR LESS
EXCHANGE DEADLINE 2/26/2017
*HOLOGLD/15-25: .5X TO 1.2X BASIC
1 Jose Abreu/99 8.00 20.00
4 Charlie Blackmon/49 6.00 15.00
5 Anthony Rizzo/25 20.00 50.00
6 Andres Galarraga/25 10.00 25.00
7 Paul Goldschmidt/25 8.00 20.00
8 Josh Donaldson/25 20.00 50.00
9 Troy Tulowitzki/25 10.00 25.00
10 Evan Longoria/25 10.00 25.00
11 Roberto Alomar/25 12.00 30.00
12 Corey Kluber/49 5.00 12.00
15 Starling Marte/49 10.00 25.00
16 Justin Upton/25 10.00 25.00
19 Luis Severino/49 20.00 50.00
20 Kyle Seager/49 4.00 10.00
21 Miguel Sano/49 10.00 25.00
22 Jose Altuve/49 20.00 50.00
24 Frank Howard/49 4.00 10.00
27 Tim Raines/49 6.00 15.00
29 Rusney Castillo/25 5.00 12.00
32 Salvador Perez/49 12.00 30.00
33 Orlando Cepeda/25 20.00 50.00
35 Matt Adams/49 5.00 12.00
36 Mookie Betts/49 50.00 120.00
38 Kris Bryant/49 75.00 200.00
39 Wei-Yin Chen/25 30.00 80.00
42 Noah Syndergaard/49 20.00 50.00
43 Gregory Polanco/49 5.00 12.00
44 Yordano Ventura/49 8.00 20.00
45 Anthony Rendon/49 8.00 20.00
46 Victor Martinez/25 12.00 30.00
48 Sonny Gray/25 5.00 12.00
49 Chris Davis/15 10.00 25.00
51 Dennis Eckersley/25 6.00 15.00
52 Paul Molitor/25 6.00 15.00
53 Brooks Robinson/15 15.00 40.00
54 Bert Blyleven/25 10.00 25.00
56 Tony La Russa/25 10.00 25.00
57 Willie Horton/49 4.00 10.00
58 Dave Kingman/49 4.00 10.00
59 Kennys Vargas/49 4.00 10.00
60 Andre Thornton/49 4.00 10.00

2015 Immaculate Collection Immaculate Jumbo

RANDOM INSERTS IN PACKS
STATED PRINT RUN B/WN 5-99 COPIES PER
NO PRICING ON QTY 10 OR LESS
1 Kendall Graveman/49 2.50 6.00
2 Yasmany Tomas/49 3.00 8.00
3 Matt Barnes/49 2.50 6.00
4 Brandon Finnegan/49 2.50 6.00
5 Raisel Iglesias/49 3.00 8.00
6 Aaron Judge/49 30.00 80.00
7 Yorman Rodriguez/49 2.50 6.00
8 Tony Gwynn/25 12.00 30.00
9 Luis Severino/49 3.00 8.00
10 Maikel Franco/49 3.00 8.00
11 Michael Conforto/49 6.00 15.00
12 Daniel Carbonell/49 3.00 8.00
13 Daniel Robertson/49 2.50 6.00
14 Steven Moya/49 3.00 8.00
15 Cory Spangenberg/49 2.50 6.00
16 Andy Wilkins/49 2.50 6.00
17 Stephen Piscotty/25 8.00 20.00
18 Ryan Rua/49 2.50 6.00
19 Dilson Herrera/49 2.50 6.00
20 Edwin Escobar/49 2.50 6.00
21 D.J. Peterson/49 2.50 6.00
22 Matt Szczur/49 3.00 8.00
23 Peter O'Brien/49 4.00 10.00
24 Michael Taylor/49 2.50 6.00
25 Tyler Beede/49 3.00 8.00
26 Trevor May/49 2.50 6.00
27 Alex Rodriguez/20 8.00 20.00
28 Javier Baez/49 20.00 50.00
29 Christian Walker/49 5.00 12.00
30 Addison Russell/49 6.00 15.00
31 Corey Seager/49 8.00 20.00
32 Kris Bryant/49 20.00 50.00
33 Archie Bradley/49 2.50 6.00
34 Yoan Moncada/49 10.00 25.00
35 Kyle Zimmer/49 2.50 6.00
36 Willy Adames/49 4.00 10.00
37 Deven Marrero/49 2.50 6.00
38 Byron Buxton/49 4.00 10.00
39 Luis Encarnacion/49 2.50 6.00
40 Francisco Lindor/49 15.00 40.00
41 Kennys Vargas/49 4.00 10.00
42 Kyle Schwarber/49 8.00 20.00
43 Miguel Sano/49 5.00 12.00
45 Robert Refsnyder/49 3.00 8.00
46 Trea Turner/49 15.00 40.00
47 Tyler Glasnow/49 3.00 8.00
48 Manuel Margot/49 2.50 6.00
49 Jameson Taillon/49 3.00 8.00
50 R.J. Alvarez/49 2.50 6.00
53 Prince Fielder/49 3.00 8.00
55 Eric Hosmer/20 4.00 10.00
57 Rymer Liriano/49 2.50 6.00
59 Hanley Ramirez/49 3.00 8.00
61 Adrian Gonzalez/15 3.00 8.00
62 Mark McGwire/20 12.00 30.00
66 Barry Bonds/20 20.00 50.00
67 Justin Upton/49 3.00 8.00
69 Yu Darvish/20 4.00 10.00
70 Lane Adams/49 2.50 6.00
71 Carlos Beltran/49 3.00 8.00
73 Aramis Ramirez/49 2.50 6.00
74 Billy Butler/49 2.50 6.00
77 Matt Harvey/20 10.00 25.00
79 Brian McCann/49 3.00 8.00
82 Carlos Gonzalez/15 3.00 8.00
83 Luke Appling/20 10.00 25.00
84 Johnny Cueto/20 3.00 8.00
86 Mark Trumbo/49 2.50 6.00
87 Yadier Molina/20 10.00 25.00
88 Nelson Cruz/20 4.00 10.00
90 Pablo Sandoval/25 3.00 8.00
93 Mike Trout/20 15.00 40.00
95 Felix Hernandez/15 3.00 8.00
96 Clayton Kershaw/15 10.00 25.00
97 Adam Jones/15 3.00 8.00

2015 Immaculate Collection Immaculate Pitchers Materials

SEMISTARS 3.00 8.00
RANDOM INSERTS IN PACKS
STATED PRINT RUN B/WN 20-99 COPIES PER
1 Johnny Cueto/99 3.00 8.00
2 Clayton Kershaw/25 8.00 20.00
3 Yu Darvish/49 4.00 10.00
4 Masahiro Tanaka/25 3.00 8.00
5 Chris Sale/25 4.00 10.00
6 Jose Fernandez/20 4.00 10.00
7 Jon Lester/99 3.00 8.00
8 Madison Bumgarner/49 3.00 8.00
9 Nolan Ryan/49 8.00 20.00
10 Roger Clemens/99 5.00 12.00
11 Max Scherzer/99 4.00 10.00
12 Sonny Gray/99 3.00 8.00
13 Matt Harvey/99 3.00 8.00
14 Felix Hernandez/25 3.00 8.00
15 Archie Bradley/99 2.50 6.00
16 Jeff Samardzija/99 2.50 6.00
17 John Smoltz/49 4.00 10.00

2015 Immaculate Collection Immaculate Quad Players Memorabilia

RANDOM INSERTS IN PACKS
STATED PRINT RUN B/WN 10-99 COPIES PER
NO PRICING ON QTY 10
1 Ghrg/Clmnte/Wllms/Msl/49 125.00 250.00
2 Pnnck/Applng/Dcky/Byr/25 20.00 50.00
3 Ghrngr/Chnce/Cobb/Crnn/20 60.00 150.00
5 Fllr/Drysdle/Sttn/Jnkns/99 10.00 25.00
6 Brynt/Rssll/Baez/Schwrbr/99 40.00 100.00
7 Rssll/Bxtn/Lndr/Brnt/99 25.00 60.00
8 Uhra/Tnka/Drvsh/Szki/49 15.00 40.00
9 Tms/Abru/Cstllo/Puig/99 4.00 10.00
10 Pnce/Bmgrnr/Sndvl/Blt/99 10.00 25.00
11 Tiant/Crw/Ryn/Jcksn/49 20.00 50.00
12 Trre/Rse/Rbnsn/Cpda/99 12.00 30.00
13 McCtchn/Krshw/Trt/Stntn/49 20.00 50.00
14 Hndrsn/Hndrsn/Hndrsn/Hndrsn/49 15.00 40.00
15 Bggo/Smltz/Mrtnz/Jhnsn/99 12.00 30.00

2015 Immaculate Collection Immaculate Quads Memorabilia

RANDOM INSERTS IN PACKS
STATED PRINT RUN 99 SER.#'d SETS
1 Byron Buxton 6.00 15.00
2 Kennys Vargas 2.50 6.00
3 Kris Bryant 15.00 40.00
4 Addison Russell 8.00 20.00
5 Javier Baez 20.00 50.00
6 Corey Seager 6.00 15.00
7 Francisco Lindor 15.00 40.00
8 Kyle Schwarber 10.00 25.00
9 Yasmany Tomas 3.00 8.00
10 Archie Bradley 2.50 6.00
11 Miguel Sano 5.00 12.00
12 Raisel Iglesias 3.00 8.00
13 Maikel Franco 3.00 8.00
14 Michael Taylor 2.50 6.00
15 Michael Conforto 6.00 15.00

2015 Immaculate Collection Immaculate Swatches

RANDOM INSERTS IN PACKS
STATED PRINT RUN B/WN 15-99 COPIES PER
*PRIME/15-99: .5X TO 1.2X BASIC
1 Miguel Cabrera/79 4.00 10.00
2 Felix Hernandez/49 3.00 8.00
3 Andrew McCutchen/49 4.00 10.00
4 Clayton Kershaw/25 8.00 20.00
5 Mike Trout/49 20.00 50.00
6 Jose Abreu/25 4.00 10.00
7 Yu Darvish/99 4.00 10.00
8 Yasiel Puig/99 4.00 10.00
9 Giancarlo Stanton/49 4.00 10.00
10 Troy Tulowitzki/25 4.00 10.00
11 Yadier Molina/20 4.00 10.00
12 Alex Gordon/25 4.00 10.00
13 Robinson Cano/99 3.00 8.00
14 Bryce Harper/25 6.00 15.00
15 Prince Fielder/99 3.00 8.00
16 Anthony Rendon/25 4.00 10.00
17 Johnny Cueto/99 3.00 8.00
18 Ichiro Suzuki/25 5.00 12.00
19 Jose Bautista/49 3.00 8.00
20 Hyun-Jin Ryu/99 3.00 8.00
21 Cliff Lee/99 3.00 8.00
22 Max Scherzer/99 4.00 10.00
23 Carlos Gomez/49 2.50 6.00
24 Buster Posey/49 5.00 12.00
25 Paul Goldschmidt/49 4.00 10.00
26 Stephen Strasburg/49 4.00 10.00
27 Anthony Rizzo/49 6.00 15.00
28 Masahiro Tanaka/25 3.00 8.00
29 Billy Hamilton/99 3.00 8.00
30 Adrian Beltre/49 4.00 10.00
31 Jose Altuve/99 3.00 8.00
32 Madison Bumgarner/99 3.00 8.00
33 Hanley Ramirez/99 3.00 8.00
34 Adrian Gonzalez/99 3.00 8.00
35 Kris Bryant/99 12.00 30.00
36 Kendall Graveman/99 2.50 6.00
37 Yasmany Tomas/99 3.00 8.00
38 Matt Barnes/99 2.50 6.00
39 Brandon Finnegan/99 2.50 6.00
40 Raisel Iglesias/99 3.00 8.00
41 Aaron Judge/99 20.00 50.00
42 Yorman Rodriguez/99 2.50 6.00
43 Gary Brown/25 2.50 6.00
44 Luis Severino/99 3.00 8.00
45 Maikel Franco/99 3.00 8.00
46 Michael Conforto/99 4.00 15.00
47 Daniel Carbonell/99 3.00 8.00
48 Daniel Robertson/99 2.50 6.00
49 Steven Moya/99 3.00 8.00
50 Cory Spangenberg/99 2.50 6.00
51 Andy Wilkins/99 2.50 6.00
52 Stephen Piscotty/99 3.00 8.00
53 Ryan Rua/99 2.50 6.00
54 Dilson Herrera/99 3.00 8.00
55 Edwin Escobar/99 2.50 6.00
56 D.J. Peterson/99 2.50 6.00
57 Matt Szczur/99 3.00 8.00
58 Peter O'Brien/99 4.00 10.00
59 Michael Taylor/99 2.50 6.00
60 Tyler Beede/99 3.00 8.00
61 Trevor May/99 2.50 6.00
62 Jake Lamb/25 4.00 10.00
63 Javier Baez/99 20.00 50.00
64 Christian Walker/99 5.00 12.00
65 Jorge Soler/99 4.00 10.00
66 Addison Russell/99 5.00 12.00
67 Corey Seager/99 6.00 15.00
68 Archie Bradley/99 2.50 6.00
69 Yoan Moncada/99 6.00 15.00
70 Kyle Zimmer/99 2.50 6.00
71 Willy Adames/99 4.00 10.00
72 Deven Marrero/99 2.50 6.00
73 Byron Buxton/99 4.00 10.00
74 Luis Encarnacion/99 2.50 6.00
75 Francisco Lindor/99 15.00 40.00
76 Kennys Vargas/99 2.50 6.00
77 Kyle Schwarber/99 8.00 20.00
78 Miguel Sano/99 3.00 8.00
80 Robert Refsnyder/99 3.00 8.00
81 Trea Turner/99 8.00 20.00
82 Tyler Glasnow/99 3.00 8.00
83 Manuel Margot/99 2.50 6.00
84 Jameson Taillon/99 3.00 8.00
85 Bo Jackson/49 6.00 15.00
86 Ken Griffey Jr./99 8.00 20.00
87 George Brett/49 8.00 20.00
88 Barry Bonds/99 6.00 15.00
89 Frank Thomas/49 4.00 10.00
90 Craig Biggio/49 3.00 8.00
91 Cal Ripken/99 6.00 15.00
92 Nolan Ryan/99 6.00 15.00
93 Roberto Alomar/25 6.00 15.00
94 Pete Rose/99 8.00 20.00
95 Rickey Henderson/49 6.00 15.00
96 Ryne Sandberg/99 5.00 12.00
97 Mark McGwire/99 5.00 12.00
98 Pedro Martinez/79 3.00 8.00
99 Babe Ruth/15 150.00 300.00
100 Stan Musial/25 10.00 25.00
101 Roberto Clemente/15 40.00 100.00
102 Lou Gehrig/20 60.00 150.00
104 Herb Pennock/49 5.00 12.00
105 Don Drysdale/79 5.00 12.00
106 Bob Feller/49 4.00 10.00
107 Harmon Killebrew/49 5.00 12.00
108 Luke Appling/25 5.00 12.00
111 Charlie Gehringer/25 10.00 25.00
113 Ted Williams/99 25.00 60.00
115 Gabby Hartnett/99 6.00 15.00
116 Gil McDougald/49 6.00 15.00
117 Gary Carter/49 3.00 8.00
118 Kirby Puckett/79 8.00 20.00
119 Tony Gwynn/99 4.00 10.00

2015 Immaculate Collection Immaculate Trios Memorabilia

RANDOM INSERTS IN PACKS
STATED PRINT RUN 99 SER.#'d SETS
1 Byron Buxton 4.00 10.00
2 Kris Bryant 20.00 50.00
3 Yasmany Tomas 3.00 8.00
4 Archie Bradley 2.50 6.00
5 Kennys Vargas 2.50 6.00
6 Michael Taylor 2.50 6.00
7 Addison Russell 5.00 12.00
8 Cory Spangenberg 2.50 6.00
9 Maikel Franco 3.00 8.00
10 Lane Adams 2.50 6.00
11 Yorman Rodriguez 2.50 6.00
12 Steven Moya 3.00 8.00
13 Trevor May 2.50 6.00
14 R.J. Alvarez 2.50 6.00
15 Francisco Lindor 15.00 40.00

2015 Immaculate Collection Immaculate Trios Players Memorabilia

RANDOM INSERTS IN PACKS
STATED PRINT RUN B/WN 25-99 COPIES PER
1 Kllbrw/Clmnte/Msl/49 25.00 60.00
2 Ruth/Gehrig/Cobb/25 400.00 600.00
3 Applng/Ghrngr/Crnn/49 12.00 30.00
4 Marichal/Hunter/Drysdale/25 3.00 8.00
5 Rssll/Baez/Brynt/99 15.00 30.00
6 Szki/Tnka/Drvsh/25 12.00 30.00
7 Abru/Cstllo/Puig/49 4.00 10.00
8 Beltre/Ortiz/Cano/99 4.00 10.00
9 Lynn/Rice/Fisk/49 10.00 25.00
10 Rssll/Sgr/Lndr/99 6.00 15.00
11 Spngnbrg/Trnr/Baez/99 20.00 50.00
12 Jdge/Svrno/Rfsndr/99 20.00 50.00
13 Escobar/Margot/Marrero/99 2.50 6.00
14 Peterson/Franco/Sano/49 3.00 8.00
15 Soler/Iglesias/Tomas/99 4.00 10.00

2015 Immaculate Collection Multisport Autographs

RANDOM INSERTS IN PACKS
PRINT RUNS B/WN 5-25 COPIES PER
NO PRICING ON QTY 10 OR LESS
EXCHANGE DEADLINE 2/26/2017
1 Andrew Wiggins/15 150.00 250.00
2 Jabari Parker/15 100.00 200.00
5 Dante Exum/25 12.00 30.00
9 Kevin White/25 12.00 30.00
10 DeVante Parker/25 12.00 30.00

2015 Immaculate Collection Recollection Collection Autographs

RANDOM INSERTS IN PACKS
PRINT RUNS B/WN 1-99 COPIES PER
NO PRICING ON QTY 10 OR LESS
EXCHANGE DEADLINE 2/26/2017
1 Bill Buckner/99 5.00 12.00
2 Billy Hamilton/99 5.00 12.00
3 Bob Horner/99 4.00 10.00
7 Chris Owings/99 4.00 10.00
11 Fergie Jenkins/25 10.00 25.00
15 Jean Segura/98 5.00 12.00
19 Jean Segura/99 5.00 12.00
20 Jean Segura/99 5.00 12.00
24 Jonathan Schoop/99 4.00 10.00
28 Marcus Semien/99 4.00 10.00
32 Michael Young/25 8.00 20.00
36 Travis d'Arnaud/99 8.00 20.00

2015 Immaculate Collection Shadowbox Material Signatures

RANDOM INSERTS IN PACKS
PRINT RUNS B/WN 10-99 COPIES PER
NO PRICING ON QTY 10
EXCHANGE DEADLINE 2/26/2017
1 Robinson Cano/15 15.00 40.00
2 Jose Abreu/99 30.00 80.00
3 Todd Frazier/49 6.00 15.00
4 Byron Buxton/49 12.00 30.00
6 Adrian Gonzalez/25 8.00 20.00
7 Adrian Beltre/25 20.00 50.00
8 Devin Mesoraco/49 5.00 12.00
9 Jason Heyward/25 8.00 20.00
10 Jorge Soler/49 8.00 20.00
11 Kris Bryant/49 75.00 200.00
12 Felix Hernandez/25 20.00 50.00
13 Chris Sale/49 10.00 25.00
14 Victor Martinez/49 10.00 25.00
15 David Wright/15 10.00 25.00
16 Dustin Pedroia/15 20.00 50.00
17 Edwin Encarnacion/49 8.00 20.00
18 Eric Hosmer/49 15.00 40.00
19 Josh Donaldson/25 15.00 40.00
20 Manny Machado/25 25.00 60.00
21 Evan Longoria/25 8.00 20.00

2015 Immaculate Collection Shadowbox Signatures

RANDOM INSERTS IN PACKS
PRINT RUNS B/WN 7-99 COPIES PER
NO PRICING ON QTY 10 OR LESS
EXCHANGE DEADLINE 2/26/2017
*HOLOGLD/15-25: .5X TO 1.2X BASIC
2 Rusney Castillo/49 5.00 12.00
3 Yasmany Tomas/49 15.00 40.00
4 Matt Barnes/49 4.00 10.00
5 Brandon Finnegan/49 4.00 10.00
6 Daniel Norris/49 4.00 10.00
7 Kendall Graveman/49 4.00 10.00
8 Yorman Rodriguez/79 4.00 10.00
9 Gary Brown/49 4.00 10.00
10 R.J. Alvarez/78 4.00 10.00
11 Dalton Pompey/49 5.00 12.00
12 Maikel Franco/49 10.00 25.00
13 James McCann/49 10.00 25.00
14 Lane Adams/79 4.00 10.00
15 Joc Pederson/49 15.00 40.00
16 Steven Moya/49 5.00 12.00
17 Cory Spangenberg/49 4.00 10.00
18 Andy Wilkins/79 4.00 10.00
19 Terrance Gore/79 4.00 10.00
20 Ryan Rua/79 4.00 10.00
21 Dilson Herrera/79 5.00 12.00
22 Edwin Escobar/79 4.00 10.00
23 Jorge Soler/49 6.00 15.00
24 Matt Szczur/49 5.00 12.00
25 Buck Farmer/49 4.00 10.00
26 Michael Taylor/49 4.00 10.00
27 Rymer Liriano/49 4.00 10.00
28 Trevor May/49 4.00 10.00
29 Jake Lamb/49 6.00 15.00
30 Javier Baez/49 8.00 20.00
31 Mike Foltynewicz/49 4.00 10.00
32 Kennys Vargas/49 4.00 10.00
33 Anthony Ranaudo/49 4.00 10.00
34 Jung-Ho Kang/49 20.00 50.00
35 Jose Abreu/99 30.00 80.00
36 Jason Heyward/25 10.00 25.00
37 Edwin Encarnacion/25 6.00 15.00
38 Jacob deGrom/25 20.00 50.00
39 David Ortiz/15 30.00 80.00
40 Carlos Rodon/25 10.00 25.00
41 Tyler Glasnow/49 5.00 12.00
42 Anthony Rendon/49 8.00 20.00
43 Corey Seager/49 25.00 60.00
44 Max Scherzer/25 20.00 50.00
45 Omar Vizquel/49 8.00 20.00
46 Francisco Lindor/49 30.00 80.00
47 Addison Russell/48 20.00 50.00
48 Chris Sale/49 10.00 25.00
49 Freddie Freeman/25 8.00 20.00
50 Dustin Pedroia/25 15.00 40.00
51 David Wright/25 10.00 25.00
52 Kris Bryant/25 75.00 200.00
53 Wei-Yin Chen/25 30.00 80.00
54 Adam Jones/25 6.00 15.00
55 Jose Fernandez/25 12.00 30.00
56 Manny Machado/25 20.00 50.00
57 Pablo Sandoval/25 6.00 15.00
59 Josh Harrison/99 6.00 15.00
60 Evan Gattis/49 4.00 10.00
61 Matt Adams/49 4.00 10.00
62 Michael Brantley/25 5.00 12.00
63 Ryan Braun/25 6.00 15.00
64 Corey Kluber/25 6.00 15.00

2015 Immaculate Collection The Greatest Materials

RANDOM INSERTS IN PACKS
STATED PRINT RUN B/WN 5-99 COPIES PER
NO PRICING ON QTY 5
3 Barry Bonds/99 5.00 12.00
4 Duke Snider/99 5.00 12.00
5 Tony Perez/15 3.00 8.00
6 Joe Morgan/15 3.00 8.00
7 Rod Carew/49 3.00 8.00
8 Mark McGwire/49 6.00 15.00
9 Roberto Alomar/25 3.00 8.00
10 Mariano Rivera/20 5.00 12.00
11 Ryne Sandberg/20 8.00 20.00
12 Tommy Lasorda/99 3.00 8.00
13 Bob Feller/49 6.00 15.00
14 Goose Gossage/49 3.00 8.00
15 Rollie Fingers/49 3.00 8.00

2016 Immaculate Collection

1-100 PRINT RUN 99 SER.#'d SETS
JSY AU PRINT RUN 99 SER.#'d SETS
EXCHANGE DEADLINE 2/17/2018
1 Babe Ruth 4.00 10.00
2 Bill Dickey 1.00 2.50
3 Charlie Gehringer 1.00 2.50
4 Frank Chance 1.25 3.00
5 George Case 1.00 2.50
6 George Kelly 1.00 2.50
7 Gil Hodges 1.25 3.00
8 Honus Wagner 1.50 4.00
9 Jimmie Foxx 1.50 4.00
10 Joe Jackson 2.00 5.00
11 Leo Durocher 1.00 2.50
12 Lou Gehrig 3.00 8.00
13 Mel Ott 1.50 4.00
14 Miller Huggins 1.00 2.50
15 Nap Lajoie 1.50 4.00
16 Pee Wee Reese 1.25 3.00
17 Roger Maris 1.50 4.00
18 Rogers Hornsby 1.25 3.00
19 Stan Musial 2.50 6.00
20 Ted Kluszewski 1.25 3.00
21 Tommy Henrich 1.00 2.50
22 Ty Cobb 2.50 6.00
23 Mike Trout 8.00 20.00
24 Bryce Harper 2.50 6.00
25 Carlos Correa 1.50 4.00
26 Josh Donaldson 1.25 3.00
27 Andrew McCutchen 1.50 4.00
28 Ichiro Suzuki 2.00 5.00
29 Clayton Kershaw 3.00 8.00
30 Jake Arrieta 1.25 3.00
31 Dallas Keuchel 1.25 3.00
32 Jose Bautista 1.25 3.00
33 Joey Votto 1.50 4.00
34 Kris Bryant 6.00 15.00
35 Zack Greinke 1.25 3.00
36 Anthony Rizzo 2.50 6.00
37 Paul Goldschmidt 1.50 4.00
38 Chris Davis 1.00 2.50
39 Adrian Beltre 1.50 4.00
40 Albert Pujols 2.00 5.00
41 Buster Posey 2.00 5.00
42 David Wright 1.25 3.00
43 Jacob deGrom 1.50 4.00
44 Jose Abreu 1.50 4.00
45 Xander Bogaerts 1.50 4.00
46 Joc Pederson 1.25 3.00
47 Sonny Gray 1.25 3.00
48 Todd Frazier 1.25 3.00
49 Yadier Molina 1.50 4.00
50 Noah Syndergaard 1.25 3.00
51 Felix Hernandez 1.25 3.00
52 Chris Sale 1.50 4.00
53 David Price 1.25 3.00
54 Francisco Lindor 1.50 4.00
55 Alex Gordon 1.25 3.00
56 Brandon Crawford 1.25 3.00
57 Miguel Cabrera 1.50 4.00
58 A.J. Pollock 1.00 2.50
59 Jose Altuve 1.25 3.00
60 Troy Tulowitzki 1.50 4.00
61 Lorenzo Cain 1.00 2.50
62 Robinson Cano 1.25 3.00
63 Jonathan Lucroy 1.25 3.00
64 Matt Carpenter 1.50 4.00
65 Madison Bumgarner 1.25 3.00
66 Adam Wainwright 1.25 3.00
67 Nelson Cruz 1.50 4.00
68 Pete Rose 3.00 8.00
69 Nolan Arenado 2.00 5.00
70 Manny Machado 1.50 4.00
71 Yoenis Cespedes 1.50 4.00
72 Giancarlo Stanton 1.50 4.00
73 Max Scherzer 1.50 4.00
74 Gerrit Cole 1.50 4.00
75 Corey Kluber 1.25 3.00
76 George Springer 1.25 3.00
77 Mookie Betts 2.50 6.00
78 Charlie Blackmon 1.50 4.00
79 Maikel Franco 1.25 3.00
80 Wil Myers 1.00 2.50
81 Brian McCann 1.25 3.00
82 Salvador Perez 1.25 3.00
83 Alex Rodriguez 2.00 5.00
84 David Ortiz 1.50 4.00
85 Prince Fielder 1.25 3.00
86 Adrian Gonzalez 1.25 3.00
87 Eric Hosmer 1.25 3.00
88 Jason Kipnis 1.25 3.00
89 Michael Brantley 1.25 3.00
90 Anthony Rendon 1.50 4.00
91 Evan Longoria 1.25 3.00
92 Carlos Gonzalez 1.25 3.00
93 Jung-Ho Kang 1.00 2.50
94 J.D. Martinez 1.50 4.00
95 Adam Eaton 1.00 2.50
96 Starling Marte 1.25 3.00
97 Hunter Pence 1.25 3.00
98 Joe Panik 1.25 3.00
99 Yu Darvish 1.50 4.00
100 Matt Harvey 1.25 3.00
101 Brian Ellington JSY AU RC 4.00 10.00
103 Elias Diaz JSY AU RC 4.00 10.00
104 Carl Edwards Jr. JSY AU RC 6.00 15.00
105 Corey Seager JSY AU RC 40.00 100.00
106 Tyler Duffey JSY AU RC 4.00 10.00
108 Frankie Montas JSY AU RC 5.00 12.00
109 Jonathan Gray JSY AU RC 4.00 10.00
110 Jorge Lopez JSY AU RC 4.00 10.00
111 Jose Peraza JSY AU RC 6.00 15.00
112 John Lamb JSY AU RC 4.00 10.00
113 Kelby Tomlinson JSY AU RC 6.00 15.00
114 Travis Jankowski JSY AU RC 4.00 10.00
115 Ketel Marte JSY AU RC 8.00 20.00
116 Kyle Schwarber JSY AU RC 12.00 30.00
117 Luis Severino JSY AU RC 10.00 25.00
118 Mac Williamson JSY AU RC 5.00 12.00
119 Max Kepler JSY AU RC 6.00 15.00
120 Michael Conforto JSY AU RC EXCH 20.0050.00
121 Michael Reed JSY AU RC 4.00 10.00
122 Miguel Sano JSY AU RC 10.00 25.00
123 Peter O'Brien JSY AU RC 4.00 10.00
124 Raul Mondesi JSY AU RC 8.00 20.00
125 Trevor Story JSY AU RC 10.00 25.00
126 Rob Refsnyder JSY AU RC 5.00 12.00
127 Stephen Piscotty JSY AU RC 6.00 15.00
128 Tom Murphy JSY AU RC 4.00 10.00
129 Trayce Thompson JSY AU RC 6.00 15.00
130 Trea Turner JSY AU RC 12.00 30.00
131 Alex Dickerson JSY AU RC 4.00 10.00
132 Brian Johnson JSY AU RC 4.00 10.00
133 Colin Rea JSY AU RC 4.00 10.00
134 Dariel Alvarez JSY AU RC 4.00 10.00
135 Jerad Eickhoff JSY AU RC 6.00 15.00
136 Kyle Waldrop JSY AU RC 5.00 12.00
137 Luke Jackson JSY AU RC 4.00 10.00
138 Pedro Severino JSY AU RC 4.00 10.00
139 Socrates Brito JSY AU RC 4.00 10.00
140 Zack Godley JSY AU RC 6.00 15.00

2016 Immaculate Collection Red

*RED 1-100: .6X TO 1.5X BASIC
*RED JSY AU/49: .5X TO 1.2X BASIC p/r 99
*RED JSY AU/25: .6X TO 1.5X BASIC p/r 99
RANDOM INSERTS IN PACKS
1-100 PRINT RUN 25 SER.#'d SETS
101-140 PRINT RUNS B/WN 25-49 COPIES PER
EXCHANGE DEADLINE 2/17/2018
102 Brandon Drury JSY AU/49 EXCH 8.00 20.00
107 Greg Bird JSY AU/49 6.00 15.00

2016 Immaculate Collection Diamond Inscriptions

RANDOM INSERTS IN PACKS
PRINT RUNS B/WN 25-99 COPIES PER
*RED/25: .5X TO 1.2X p/r 99
*RED/25: .4X TO 1X p/r 25
EXCHANGE DEADLINE 2/17/2018
1 Aaron Nola/25 12.00 30.00
2 Alex Dickerson/25 4.00 10.00
3 Byung-ho Park/25 12.00 30.00
4 Carl Edwards Jr./25 5.00 12.00
5 Colin Rea/25 4.00 10.00
6 Corey Seager/25 40.00 100.00
8 Jerad Eickhoff/25 12.00 30.00
10 Ketel Marte/25 8.00 20.00
11 Kyle Schwarber/25 10.00 25.00
12 Kyle Waldrop/25 5.00 12.00
14 Mac Williamson/25 4.00 10.00
15 Michael Reed/25 4.00 10.00
16 Miguel Sano/25 12.00 30.00
17 Raul Mondesi/25
18 Socrates Brito/25
19 Stephen Piscotty/25 6.00 15.00
20 Tom Murphy/25 4.00 10.00
21 Jose Abreu/99 10.00 25.00
22 Starling Marte/99 10.00 25.00
23 Joe Panik/99 4.00 10.00
24 Omar Vizquel/99 4.00 10.00
25 Kris Bryant/99 40.00 100.00
26 Josh Donaldson/99 12.00 30.00
27 Manny Machado/99 20.00 50.00
28 Fernando Rodney/99 3.00 8.00
29 Billy Burns/99 3.00 8.00
30 Yasmany Tomas/25 4.00 10.00
31 James McCann/25 5.00 12.00
32 Jorge Soler/25 6.00 15.00
33 Daniel Norris/25 4.00 10.00
34 Brandon Finnegan/25 10.00 25.00
35 Maikel Franco/25
36 Eddie Rosario/25 5.00 12.00
37 Odubel Herrera/25
38 Kevin Plawecki/25 4.00 10.00
39 Carlos Rodon/25 6.00 15.00
40 Steven Matz/25 6.00 15.00
41 Joc Pederson/99 8.00 20.00
42 Andres Galarraga/99 6.00 15.00
43 Byron Buxton/25
44 Devon Travis/25 4.00 10.00
45 Dilson Herrera/25
46 Adrian Gonzalez/99 5.00 12.00
47 Albert Pujols/25 50.00 120.00

8 Jason Heyward/99 12.00 30.00
9 Jose Altuve/99
0 Kolten Wong/99 4.00 10.00
1 Lorenzo Cain/99
2 Edgar Martinez/99 15.00 40.00
3 Robinson Cano/99 10.00 25.00
4 Xander Bogaerts/99 20.00 50.00
5 Yadier Molina/99 25.00 60.00

2016 Immaculate Collection Dual Diamond Inscriptions

RANDOM INSERTS IN PACKS
PRINT RUNS B/WN 25-99 COPIES PER
EXCHANGE DEADLINE 2/17/2018
*RED/25: .5X TO 1.2X BASIC
1 Bryant/Schwarber/49
2 Fisk/Rice/49 25.00 60.00
4 Keuchel/Arrieta/49
5 dGrm/Syndrgrd/49 40.00 100.00
6 Griffey Jr./Piazza/49 125.00 300.00
7 Park/Sano/99 10.00 25.00
9 Henderson/Brock/25 50.00 120.00

2016 Immaculate Collection Dugout Collection Ink

RANDOM INSERTS IN PACKS
PRINT RUNS B/WN 15-25 COPIES PER
NO PRICING ON QTY 15
EXCHANGE DEADLINE 2/17/2018
1 Julio Urias/25 10.00 25.00
2 Willson Contreras/25
3 Yoan Moncada/25 10.00 25.00
4 Clint Frazier/25 10.00 25.00
5 Trevor Story/25 15.00 40.00
6 Mike Gerber/25 4.00 10.00
7 A.J. Reed/25 4.00 10.00
8 Orlando Arcia/25 10.00 25.00
9 Aaron Judge/25 60.00 150.00
10 Javier Guerra/25 4.00 10.00
11 Brandon Nimmo/25 6.00 15.00
13 Lucas Giolito/25 6.00 15.00
14 Aaron Blair/25 4.00 10.00
15 Rafael Devers/25 30.00 80.00
16 Lewis Brinson/25 6.00 15.00
17 Jose Berrios/25
18 Jorge Mateo/25 5.00 12.00

2016 Immaculate Collection Hitters Ink

RANDOM INSERTS IN PACKS
PRINT RUNS B/WN 10-25 COPIES PER
NO PRICING ON QTY 15 OR LESS
EXCHANGE DEADLINE 2/17/2018
1 Ken Griffey Jr./25 75.00 200.00
2 Mike Piazza/25 25.00 60.00
3 Josh Donaldson/25 12.00 30.00
5 Jose Abreu/25 8.00 20.00
6 Frank Thomas/25 25.00 60.00
7 Reggie Jackson/25 15.00 40.00
8 Mark McGwire/25 40.00 100.00
9 Barry Bonds/25 60.00 150.00
11 Jose Bautista/25 12.00 30.00
13 Paul Goldschmidt/25 15.00 40.00
14 David Ortiz/25 30.00 80.00
15 George Brett/25 40.00 100.00
16 Johnny Bench/25 20.00 50.00
18 Roberto Alomar/25 12.00 30.00
19 Edgar Martinez/25 5.00 12.00
20 Paul Molitor/25 6.00 15.00
21 Craig Biggio/25 12.00 30.00
22 Vladimir Guerrero/25 8.00 20.00
23 Chipper Jones/25 40.00 100.00
24 Rod Carew/25 10.00 25.00
25 Pete Rose/25 20.00 50.00

2016 Immaculate Collection Immaculate Autograph Dual Materials

RANDOM INSERTS IN PACKS
PRINT RUNS B/WN 10-49 COPIES PER
NO PRICING ON QTY 15 OR LESS
EXCHANGE DEADLINE 2/17/2018
*RED/25: .5X TO 1.2X BASIC
1 Josh Donaldson/25 15.00 40.00
2 Clayton Kershaw/25 40.00 100.00
3 Carlos Gomez/25 6.00 15.00
4 Jose Abreu/25 10.00 25.00
5 Anthony Rizzo/25
6 David Price/25 10.00 25.00
8 Edwin Encarnacion/25 10.00 25.00
9 Freddie Freeman/25 8.00 20.00
10 Michael Brantley/25 4.00 10.00
11 Todd Frazier/25
12 Matt Carpenter/49 5.00 12.00
13 Xander Bogaerts/49 15.00 40.00
15 Billy Hamilton/20
16 Lorenzo Cain/49
17 Brandon Phillips/49 10.00 25.00
18 Kyle Seager/25 3.00 8.00
19 Brett Gardner/25 4.00 10.00
20 Mookie Betts/25 30.00 80.00
22 Brandon Belt/25 4.00 10.00
25 Eric Hosmer/25 10.00 25.00

2016 Immaculate Collection Immaculate Autograph Materials

RANDOM INSERTS IN PACKS
PRINT RUNS B/WN 15-99 COPIES PER
NO PRICING ON QTY 15 OR LESS
EXCHANGE DEADLINE 2/17/2018
*RED/25: .5X TO 1.2X BASIC
1 Kris Bryant/49 40.00 100.00
2 David Wright/25 15.00 40.00
3 Don Mattingly/25 30.00 80.00
5 David Ortiz/25 25.00 60.00
6 Todd Helton/25 8.00 20.00
7 Edgar Martinez/99 6.00 15.00
8 Prince Fielder/25 6.00 15.00
14 Brian McCann/25 4.00 10.00
16 Gerrit Cole/49 5.00 12.00
17 Joe Mauer/25 10.00 25.00
18 Wil Myers/25 3.00 8.00
19 Frank Thomas/49 25.00 60.00
20 Anthony Rendon/49 6.00 15.00
21 Pete Rose/25 25.00 60.00
22 Evan Longoria/25 6.00 15.00
23 Troy Tulowitzki/25
25 Bob Gibson/25 12.00 30.00
26 Matt Carpenter/49 5.00 12.00
27 Clayton Kershaw/25 40.00 100.00
28 Max Scherzer/25 25.00 60.00
29 Jose Canseco/25 15.00 40.00
30 Will Clark/25 20.00 50.00

2016 Immaculate Collection Immaculate Autograph Quad Materials

RANDOM INSERTS IN PACKS
PRINT RUNS B/WN 25-49 COPIES PER
EXCHANGE DEADLINE 2/17/2018
*RED/25: .5X TO 1.2X BASIC
1 Barry Bonds/25 100.00 250.00
2 Mark McGwire/25 60.00 150.00
3 Joe Mauer/49 10.00 25.00
4 Joe Panik/49 8.00 20.00
5 Rusney Castillo/25 3.00 8.00
6 Edgar Martinez/49 6.00 15.00
7 Dale Murphy/49 8.00 20.00
8 Will Clark/49 20.00 50.00
9 Ron Guidry/49 20.00 50.00
10 Maikel Franco/25 8.00 20.00
11 Jose Peraza/25 12.00 30.00
12 Lucas Giolito/25 5.00 12.00
13 Aaron Blair/25 5.00 12.00
14 Yoan Moncada/25 40.00 100.00
15 Dansby Swanson/25 15.00 40.00
16 Steven Matz/25 8.00 20.00
17 Alex Bregman/25 20.00 50.00
18 Blake Snell/25 4.00 10.00
19 Alex Reyes/25
20 Rafael Devers/25 30.00 80.00

2016 Immaculate Collection Immaculate Autograph Triple Materials

RANDOM INSERTS IN PACKS
STATED PRINT RUN 25 SER.#'d SETS
EXCHANGE DEADLINE 2/17/2018
1 Evan Longoria 6.00 15.00
2 Evan Gattis
3 Jose Canseco 15.00 40.00
4 Frank Thomas 25.00 60.00
5 David Wright 15.00 40.00
6 Manny Machado 30.00 80.00
7 Prince Fielder 6.00 15.00
8 Kris Bryant 60.00 150.00
9 Kyle Schwarber 15.00 40.00
10 Corey Seager
11 Miguel Sano 12.00 30.00
12 Ketel Marte 6.00 15.00
13 Trea Turner 20.00 50.00
14 Max Kepler 12.00 30.00
15 Tom Murphy 3.00 8.00
16 Tyler White 3.00 8.00
17 Byung-ho Park EXCH 12.00 30.00
18 Aaron Nola 6.00 15.00
19 Henry Owens
20 Stephen Piscotty 10.00 25.00

2016 Immaculate Collection Immaculate Autographs

RANDOM INSERTS IN PACKS
PRINT RUNS B/WN 10-49 COPIES PER
NO PRICING ON QTY 10
*RED/25: .5X TO 1.2X p/r 49
*RED/25: .4X TO 1X p/r 25
EXCHANGE DEADLINE 2/17/2018
2 Yoenis Cespedes/25 12.00 30.00
3 Adam Eaton/49 3.00 8.00
4 Kevin Pillar/49 6.00 15.00
5 Michael Wacha/25 5.00 12.00
7 Max Scherzer/25 20.00 50.00
8 Jered Weaver/25 5.00 12.00
9 R.A. Dickey/25 5.00 12.00
10 Shane Victorino/25 5.00 12.00
11 Wil Myers/25 4.00 10.00
12 Jonathan Lucroy/49 5.00 12.00
13 Fernando Rodney/25 4.00 10.00
14 Norichika Aoki/49 3.00 8.00
15 Jean Segura/49 4.00 10.00

2016 Immaculate Collection Immaculate Dual Players Memorabilia

RANDOM INSERTS IN PACKS
PRINT RUNS B/WN 5-99 COPIES PER
NO PRICING ON QTY 15 OR LESS
*RED/25: .5X TO 1.2X BASIC
10 Correa/Bryant/99 6.00 15.00
11 Harper/Dnldsn/99 8.00 20.00
12 D.Keuchel/J.Arrieta/49 4.00 10.00
13 J.Bautista/J.Donaldson/49 4.00 10.00
14 Syndrgrd/dGrm/99 6.00 15.00
15 Gordon/Perez/49 6.00 15.00
16 Ripken/Brett/49 15.00 40.00
17 Posey/Trout/99 10.00 25.00
18 N.Cruz/C.Davis/49 5.00 12.00
19 Altuve/Bogaerts/99 10.00 25.00
20 Schrzr/Krshw/99 6.00 15.00

2016 Immaculate Collection Immaculate Duals Memorabilia

RANDOM INSERTS IN PACKS
PRINT RUNS B/WN 5-99 COPIES PER
NO PRICING ON QTY 5
*RED/25: .5X TO 1.2X BASIC
1 Kyle Schwarber/99 6.00 15.00
2 Ichiro Suzuki/25 5.00 12.00
3 Adam Jones/20 6.00 15.00
4 Adrian Gonzalez/99 3.00 8.00
5 Albert Pujols/99 5.00 12.00
6 Yadier Molina/99 6.00 15.00
7 Andrew McCutchen/99 6.00 15.00
8 Jung-Ho Kang/99 5.00 12.00
9 Jose Altuve/99 5.00 12.00
10 David Price/99 3.00 8.00
11 Anthony Rizzo/99 6.00 15.00
12 Miguel Sano/99 4.00 10.00
13 Corey Seager/99 20.00 50.00
14 David Ortiz/25 6.00 15.00
15 Mookie Betts/49 8.00 20.00
16 Freddie Freeman/49 5.00 12.00
17 Yu Darvish/25 5.00 12.00
18 Frank Thomas/49 4.00 10.00
19 George Brett/99 8.00 20.00

2016 Immaculate Collection Immaculate Heroes Autographs

RANDOM INSERTS IN PACKS
PRINT RUNS B/WN 15-99 COPIES PER
NO PRICING ON QTY 15
*RED/25: .5X TO 1.2X p/r 49-99
*RED/25: .4X TO 1X p/r 25
EXCHANGE DEADLINE 2/17/2018
1 Andre Dawson/99 10.00 25.00
2 Paul Molitor/49 10.00 25.00
3 Roberto Alomar/49 4.00 10.00
4 Will Clark/49 12.00 30.00
5 Dave Winfield/25 10.00 25.00
6 Ron Guidry/25 6.00 15.00
7 Craig Biggio/25 12.00 30.00
8 Bert Blyleven/25 8.00 20.00
9 Bo Jackson/25 40.00 100.00
10 Bob Gibson/49 20.00 50.00
11 Brooks Robinson/25 15.00 40.00
12 Jim Rice/25 5.00 12.00
13 John Smoltz/25 15.00 40.00
14 Juan Gonzalez/25 10.00 25.00
15 Ken Griffey Jr./25
16 Mike Schmidt/25 25.00 60.00
17 Ozzie Smith/25 20.00 50.00
18 Phil Niekro/25
19 Rollie Fingers/25 10.00 25.00
20 Mariano Rivera/25 40.00 100.00
21 Tom Glavine/25 12.00 30.00
24 Ryne Sandberg/25 20.00 50.00

2016 Immaculate Collection Immaculate Initiations Jumbo Materials

RANDOM INSERTS IN PACKS
PRINT RUNS B/WN 15-99 COPIES PER
NO PRICING ON QTY 15 OR LESS
1 Kris Bryant/99 5.00 12.00
2 Francisco Lindor/99 4.00 10.00
3 Javier Baez/99 5.00 12.00
4 Addison Russell/99 4.00 10.00
5 Yasmany Tomas/99 2.50 6.00
6 Maikel Franco/99 3.00 8.00
7 Carlos Correa/25 5.00 12.00
8 Jacob deGrom/99 4.00 10.00
9 Kolten Wong/99 3.00 8.00
10 Nolan Arenado/99 5.00 12.00
12 Mike Trout/25 15.00 40.00
13 Manny Machado/99 4.00 10.00
14 Sonny Gray/49 3.00 8.00
15 Jose Fernandez/25 4.00 10.00
16 Gerrit Cole/99 4.00 10.00
17 Kyle Schwarber/99 5.00 12.00
18 Corey Seager/99 8.00 20.00
19 Masahiro Tanaka/49 3.00 8.00
20 Yasiel Puig/25 4.00 10.00
22 Aaron Nola/49 5.00 12.00
23 Miguel Sano/99 4.00 10.00
24 Mookie Betts/25 6.00 15.00
25 Chris Heston/25 2.50 6.00
26 Dallas Keuchel/99 3.00 8.00
27 Noah Syndergaard/49 3.00 8.00
28 Yordano Ventura/99 3.00 8.00
29 Taijuan Walker/99 2.50 6.00
30 Michael Conforto/99 3.00 8.00
31 Stephen Piscotty/99 4.00 10.00
32 Trea Turner/99 5.00 12.00
33 Raul Mondesi/99 3.00 8.00
34 Byron Buxton/99 3.00 8.00
35 George Springer/99 3.00 8.00
36 Joc Pederson/25 3.00 8.00
37 Xander Bogaerts/25 4.00 10.00
38 Rougned Odor/99 3.00 8.00
39 Steven Matz/25 3.00 8.00
40 Joe Panik/49 3.00 8.00

2016 Immaculate Collection Immaculate Ink

RANDOM INSERTS IN PACKS
PRINT RUNS B/WN 25-49 COPIES PER
*RED/25: .5X TO 1.2X p/r 49
*RED/25: .4X TO 1X p/r 25
EXCHANGE DEADLINE 2/17/2018
1 Kris Bryant/49 60.00 150.00
2 Rusney Castillo/25 4.00 10.00
3 Jonathan Lucroy/49 4.00 10.00
4 Jung-Ho Kang/25 10.00 25.00
5 Sonny Gray/49 8.00 20.00
6 Yasmany Tomas/25 4.00 10.00
7 Adrian Gonzalez/25 6.00 15.00
8 Chris Sale/25 6.00 15.00
9 Corey Kluber/25 10.00 25.00
10 Dallas Keuchel/25 10.00 25.00
11 David Ortiz/25 30.00 80.00
12 Joc Pederson/25 10.00 25.00
13 Jose Altuve/25 25.00 60.00
14 Jose Fernandez/25 20.00 50.00
15 Max Scherzer/25 20.00 50.00
16 Robinson Cano/25 12.00 30.00
17 Yadier Molina/25 30.00 80.00
18 Adam Jones/25 10.00 25.00
19 Wei-Yin Chen/25 40.00 100.00
23 Evan Gattis/25
24 Paul Goldschmidt/25 12.00 30.00
25 Michael Brantley/25 5.00 12.00

2016 Immaculate Collection Immaculate Jumbo Material Autographs

RANDOM INSERTS IN PACKS
PRINT RUNS B/WN 10-25 COPIES PER
NO PRICING ON QTY 10
EXCHANGE DEADLINE 2/17/2018
1 Chipper Jones/25 30.00 80.00
2 Robin Ventura/25 10.00 25.00
3 Joe Girardi/25 8.00 20.00
4 Brandon Belt/25 5.00 12.00
6 Matt Adams/25
7 Yordano Ventura/25
8 Cal Ripken/25 50.00 120.00
9 Frank Thomas/25 40.00 100.00
10 Jose Abreu/25 15.00 40.00
11 Dennis Eckersley/25 8.00 20.00
13 Josh Donaldson/25 15.00 40.00
14 Carl Edwards Jr./25 6.00 15.00
15 Socrates Brito/25
16 Colin Rea/25 4.00 10.00
17 Kyle Waldrop/25 6.00 15.00
18 Alex Dickerson/25
19 Jerad Eickhoff/25 6.00 15.00
20 Luke Jackson/25

2016 Immaculate Collection Immaculate Jumbo Materials

RANDOM INSERTS IN PACKS
PRINT RUNS B/WN 1-99 COPIES PER
NO PRICING ON QTY 15 OR LESS
1 Aaron Nola/25 5.00 12.00
2 Brandon Drury/99 4.00 10.00
3 Byung-ho Park/49 3.00 8.00
4 Carl Edwards Jr./99 3.00 8.00
5 Corey Seager/99 8.00 20.00
6 Frankie Montas/99 3.00 8.00
7 Greg Bird/99 3.00 8.00
8 Henry Owens/25 3.00 8.00
9 Jonathan Gray/99 2.50 6.00
10 Jorge Lopez/99 2.50 6.00
11 Jose Peraza/99 3.00 8.00
12 Kaleb Cowart/99 2.50 6.00
13 Kelby Tomlinson/99 2.50 6.00
15 Ketel Marte/99 5.00 12.00
16 Kyle Schwarber/99 5.00 12.00
17 Luis Severino/99 3.00 8.00
18 Mac Williamson/99 2.50 6.00
19 Max Kepler/99 4.00 10.00
20 Michael Conforto/99 3.00 8.00
21 Michael Reed/99 2.50 6.00
22 Miguel Sano/99 4.00 10.00
23 Peter O'Brien/99 2.50 6.00
24 Raul Mondesi/99 3.00 8.00
25 Richie Shaffer/99 2.50 6.00
26 Rob Refsnyder/99 3.00 8.00
27 Stephen Piscotty/99 4.00 10.00
28 Tom Murphy/99 2.50 6.00
29 Trayce Thompson/99 4.00 10.00
30 Trea Turner/99 8.00 20.00
31 Zack Godley/99 2.50 6.00
32 Socrates Brito/99 2.50 6.00
33 Dariel Alvarez/99 2.50 6.00
34 Brian Johnson/99 2.50 6.00
35 John Lamb/99 2.50 6.00
36 Kyle Waldrop/99 3.00 8.00
37 Brian Ellington/99 2.50 6.00
39 Tyler Duffey/99 2.50 6.00
40 Elias Diaz/99 2.50 6.00
41 Jerad Eickhoff/99 4.00 10.00
42 Travis Jankowski/99 2.50 6.00
43 Colin Rea/99 2.50 6.00
44 Alex Dickerson/99 2.50 6.00
45 Luke Jackson/99 2.50 6.00
46 Pedro Severino/99 2.50 6.00
47 Yoan Moncada/99 6.00 15.00
48 Yoan Lopez/99 2.50 6.00
49 Clint Frazier/99 10.00 25.00
50 Lucas Giolito/99 4.00 10.00
51 Aaron Judge/99 25.00 60.00
52 A.J. Reed/99 2.50 6.00
53 Orlando Arcia/99 3.00 8.00
54 Willson Contreras/99 6.00 15.00
55 Nomar Mazara/99 4.00 10.00
56 Blake Snell/99 3.00 8.00
57 Sean Manaea/99 2.50 6.00
58 Matt Olson/99 5.00 121.00
59 Jose Berrios/99 3.00 8.00
60 Byron Buxton/99 2.50 6.00
61 Mallex Smith/99 2.50 6.00
63 Alex Reyes/99 3.00 8.00
64 Tyler Naquin/99 3.00 8.00
65 Trevor Story/99 10.00 25.00
66 Aaron Blair/99 2.50 6.00
67 J.P. Crawford/25 2.50 6.00
68 Tyler Glasnow/99 3.00 8.00
69 Lewis Brinson/25 4.00 10.00
70 Kris Bryant/99 5.00 12.00
71 Francisco Lindor/99 5.00 12.00
72 Maikel Franco/99 3.00 8.00
76 Vladimir Guerrero/25 6.00 15.00
77 Don Mattingly/25 15.00 40.00
78 Josh Hamilton/49 3.00 8.00
79 Addison Russell/99 4.00 10.00
80 Barry Bonds/25 12.00 30.00
82 Ken Griffey Jr./49 15.00 40.00
83 Mike Piazza/99 4.00 10.00
85 Jim Rice/25 8.00 20.00
87 Mark McGwire/25 10.00 25.00
88 Albert Pujols/25 5.00 12.00
89 Miguel Cabrera/99 4.00 10.00
90 Mike Trout/25 15.00 40.00
91 Yu Darvish/25 4.00 10.00
92 Sonny Gray/99 3.00 8.00
94 Kirby Puckett/25 50.00 120.00
95 Tyler Beede/99 3.00 8.00
96 Luis Encarnacion/99 2.50 6.00
97 Matt Moore/99 3.00 8.00
98 Matt Wieters/25 4.00 10.00
99 Manny Machado/25 4.00 10.00
100 Brian Dozier/25 3.00 8.00

2016 Immaculate Collection Immaculate Marks

RANDOM INSERTS IN PACKS
PRINT RUNS B/WN 25-99 COPIES PER
*RED/25: .5X TO 1.2X p/r 49
*RED/25: .4X TO 1X p/r 25
EXCHANGE DEADLINE 2/17/2018
1 Chipper Jones/49 20.00 50.00
2 Barry Bonds/25 60.00 150.00
3 Don Mattingly/49 20.00 50.00
4 Brooks Robinson/49 12.00 30.00
5 Al Kaline/49 15.00 40.00
6 Bruce Sutter/49 6.00 15.00
7 Wade Boggs/49 20.00 50.00
8 Ryne Sandberg/49 15.00 40.00
9 Dave Winfield/49 8.00 20.00
10 Tom Glavine/49 10.00 25.00
11 Rickey Henderson/49 25.00 60.00
12 Dale Murphy/49 6.00 15.00
14 Whitey Herzog/49
15 Cal Ripken/49 25.00 60.00
16 Roberto Alomar/49 10.00 25.00
17 Rollie Fingers/99 5.00 12.00
18 Fergie Jenkins/99 10.00 25.00
19 Roger Clemens/49 20.00 50.00
20 Billy Williams/99 8.00 20.00
21 John Smoltz/49 10.00 25.00
22 Mike Piazza/49 40.00 100.00
23 Reggie Jackson/49 20.00 50.00
24 Andre Dawson/49 4.00 10.00
25 Will Clark/49 10.00 25.00

2016 Immaculate Collection Immaculate Quad Players Memorabilia

RANDOM INSERTS IN PACKS
PRINT RUNS B/WN 5-99 COPIES PER
NO PRICING ON QTY 15
*RED/25: .5X TO 1.2X BASIC
1 Case/Brck/Cobb/Hndrsn/25 40.00 100.00
5 deGrm/Crra/Abreu/Brnt/49 6.00 15.00
6 Brtt/Grffy Jr./Rpkn/Thms/25 50.00 120.00
8 Fisk/Rdrgz/Bnch/Pzza/49 20.00 50.00
9 Ryan/Clmns/Bllw/Crltn/49 20.00 50.00
10 Rose/Bnch/Schmdt/Jcksn/49 25.00 60.00
11 Park/Sgr/Mda/Schwrbr/99 6.00 15.00
12 Trnr/Stry/Sano/Psctty/99 12.00 30.00
13 Owns/Svrno/Nola/Gray/99 6.00 15.00
14 Marte/Rfsndr/Stry/Prza/99 12.00 30.00
15 Hrpr/Psy/Stntn/Trt/25 20.00 50.00

2016 Immaculate Collection Immaculate Quads Memorabilia

RANDOM INSERTS IN PACKS
PRINT RUNS B/WN 25-99 COPIES PER
*RED/25: .5X TO 1.2X BASIC
1 Yoan Moncada/99 10.00 25.00
2 Lucas Giolito/99 4.00 10.00
3 Jose Peraza/99 3.00 8.00
4 Willson Contreras/99 8.00 20.00
5 Dansby Swanson/25 8.00 20.00
6 Kyle Schwarber/99 6.00 15.00
7 Corey Seager/99 20.00 50.00
8 Aaron Nola/25 5.00 12.00
9 Miguel Sano/99 4.00 10.00
10 Kenta Maeda/25 5.00 12.00
11 Byung-ho Park/99 3.00 8.00
12 Trea Turner/99 8.00 20.00
13 Stephen Piscotty/99 4.00 10.00
14 Raul Mondesi/99 5.00 12.00
15 Henry Owens/99 3.00 8.00

2016 Immaculate Collection Immaculate Standard Materials

RANDOM INSERTS IN PACKS
PRINT RUNS B/WN 10-99 COPIES PER
NO PRICING ON QTY 15 OR LESS
*RED/49: .5X TO 1.2X BASIC p/r 99
*RED/25: .6X TO 1.5X BASIC p/r 99
1 Cal Ripken/49 12.00 30.00
2 Mark McGwire/49 10.00 25.00
3 Don Mattingly/49 8.00 20.00
4 Barry Bonds/49 8.00 20.00
5 Joe Torre/49 6.00 15.00
6 Kris Bryant/99 5.00 12.00
7 Frank Robinson/49 8.00 20.00
8 A.J. Reed/99 2.50 6.00
9 Vladimir Guerrero/49 6.00 15.00
10 Gregory Polanco/99 3.00 8.00
12 Steve Carlton/99 3.00 8.00
13 Jameson Taillon/99 6.00 15.00
14 Archie Bradley/99 2.50 6.00
15 Yasmany Tomas/99 2.50 6.00
16 Javier Baez/99 5.00 12.00
17 Hanley Ramirez/99 3.00 8.00
18 Taijuan Walker/99 2.50 6.00
19 Francisco Lindor/99 4.00 10.00
20 Maikel Franco/99 3.00 8.00
21 Addison Russell/99 4.00 10.00
23 Michael Taylor/99 2.50 6.00
24 Jimmy Wynn/99 6.00 15.00
25 Mike Piazza/99 4.00 10.00
26 Fergie Jenkins/49 10.00 25.00
28 Tyler Glasnow/99 3.00 8.00
29 Tyler Beede/99 3.00 8.00
30 Brett Phillips/99 2.50 6.00
31 Yordano Ventura/99 3.00 8.00
32 Wei-Chieh Huang/99 2.50 6.00
34 Ron Guidry/49 3.00 8.00
35 Matt Olson/99 5.00 12.00
37 Carlos Beltran/99 3.00 8.00
38 Evan Gattis/49 2.50 6.00
39 Curtis Granderson/99 3.00 8.00
40 Max Scherzer/49 4.00 10.00
41 Prince Fielder/99 3.00 8.00
46 Mark Trumbo/49 2.50 6.00
49 Lucas Giolito/99 4.00 10.00
50 Josh Hamilton/99 3.00 8.00
51 Nelson Cruz/99 4.00 10.00
52 Jake Arrieta/20 3.00 8.00
55 Wil Myers/49 2.50 6.00
59 Aroldis Chapman/20 4.00 10.00
62 Jose Reyes/49 3.00 8.00
63 Pablo Sandoval/49 3.00 8.00
65 Nick Swisher/49 3.00 8.00
70 Jon Lester/49 3.00 8.00
73 Jimmy Rollins/49 3.00 8.00
74 Johnny Cueto/20 3.00 8.00
75 Hanley Ramirez/49 3.00 8.00
80 David Freese/20 2.50 6.00
84 Daniel Murphy/49 3.00 8.00
85 Dexter Fowler/49 3.00 8.00
87 Dansby Swanson/99 6.00 15.00
88 Billy Butler/49 2.50 6.00
89 Nick Markakis/25 3.00 8.00
90 Russell Martin/49 2.50 6.00
96 Byron Buxton/99 3.00 8.00
97 Rickey Henderson/25 12.00 30.00

2016 Immaculate Collection Immaculate Swatches

RANDOM INSERTS IN PACKS
PRINT RUNS B/WN 5-99 COPIES PER
NO PRICING ON QTY 10 OR LESS
*PRIME/49: .5X TO 1.2X BASIC p/r 99
*PRIME/25: .6X TO 1.5X BASIC p/r 99
4 Gil Hodges/25 10.00 25.00
5 Leo Durocher/99 2.50 6.00
8 Pee Wee Reese/25 3.00 8.00
11 Stan Musial/25
12 Tommy Henrich/99 2.50 6.00
14 Kenta Maeda/99 5.00 12.00
15 Ketel Marte/99 5.00 12.00
16 Kyle Schwarber/99 5.00 12.00
17 Luis Severino/99 3.00 8.00
18 Mac Williamson/99 2.50 6.00
19 Max Kepler/99 4.00 10.00
20 Michael Conforto/99 3.00 8.00
21 Michael Reed/99 2.50 6.00
22 Miguel Sano/99 4.00 10.00
23 Peter O'Brien/99 2.50 6.00
24 Raul Mondesi/99 3.00 8.00
25 Richie Shaffer/99 2.50 6.00
26 Rob Refsnyder/99 3.00 8.00
27 Stephen Piscotty/99 4.00 10.00
28 Tom Murphy/99 2.50 6.00
29 Trayce Thompson/99 4.00 10.00
30 Trea Turner/99 5.00 12.00
31 Zack Godley/99 2.50 6.00
32 Socrates Brito/99 2.50 6.00
33 Dariel Alvarez/99 2.50 6.00
34 Brian Johnson/99 2.50 6.00
35 John Lamb/99 2.50 6.00
36 Kyle Waldrop/99 2.50 6.00
37 Brian Ellington/99 2.50 6.00
38 Zach Davies/25 3.00 8.00
39 Tyler Duffey/99 3.00 8.00
40 Elias Diaz/99 2.50 6.00
41 Jerad Eickhoff/99 4.00 10.00
42 Travis Jankowski/99 2.50 6.00
43 Colin Rea/99 2.50 6.00
44 Alex Dickerson/99 2.50 6.00
45 Luke Jackson/99 2.50 6.00
46 Pedro Severino/99 2.50 6.00
47 Aaron Nola/49 5.00 12.00
48 Brandon Drury/99 4.00 10.00
49 Byung-ho Park/99 3.00 8.00
50 Carl Edwards Jr./99 3.00 8.00
51 Corey Seager/99 8.00 20.00
52 Frankie Montas/99 3.00 8.00
53 Greg Bird/99 3.00 8.00
54 Henry Owens/99 3.00 8.00
55 Jonathan Gray/99 2.50 6.00
56 Jorge Lopez/99 2.50 6.00
57 Jose Peraza/99 3.00 8.00
58 Kaleb Cowart/99 2.50 6.00
59 Kelby Tomlinson/99 2.50 6.00
60 Mike Trout/25 20.00 50.00
61 Josh Donaldson/99 3.00 8.00
62 Bryce Harper/49 6.00 15.00
63 Clayton Kershaw/99 5.00 12.00
64 Buster Posey/99 5.00 12.00
65 Dallas Keuchel/99 3.00 8.00
66 Carlos Correa/99 4.00 10.00
67 Kris Bryant/99 8.00 20.00
68 Nelson Cruz/99 4.00 10.00
69 Carlos Gonzalez/99 3.00 8.00
70 Albert Pujols/99 5.00 12.00
71 Edwin Encarnacion/99 4.00 10.00
72 David Ortiz/99 4.00 10.00
73 Anthony Rizzo/99 6.00 15.00
74 Alex Rodriguez/99 5.00 12.00
75 Joe Mauer/99 3.00 8.00
76 Joey Votto/99 4.00 10.00
77 Ryan Howard/99 3.00 8.00
78 Ryan Braun/99 3.00 8.00
79 Kyle Seager/99 2.50 6.00
80 Jake Arrieta/99 3.00 8.00
81 Gerrit Cole/99 4.00 10.00
82 David Price/99 3.00 8.00
83 Adam Wainwright/99 3.00 8.00
84 Sonny Gray/99 3.00 8.00
85 Chris Sale/99 4.00 10.00
86 Chris Archer/20 2.50 6.00
87 Jacob deGrom/99 4.00 10.00
88 Johnny Bench/99 4.00 10.00
89 Barry Bonds/99 5.00 12.00
90 Nolan Ryan/49 15.00 40.00
91 Rickey Henderson/99 5.00 12.00
92 Mark McGwire/99 6.00 15.00
93 Ken Griffey Jr./99 8.00 20.00
94 Mike Piazza/99 4.00 10.00
95 Trevor Story/99 10.00 25.00
96 Reggie Jackson/99 5.00 12.00
97 Eddie Murray/25 8.00 20.00
98 Bert Blyleven/99 3.00 8.00
99 Ernie Banks/99 8.00 20.00

2016 Immaculate Collection Immaculate Trio Players Memorabilia

RANDOM INSERTS IN PACKS
PRINT RUNS B/WN 15-99 COPIES PER
NO PRICING ON QTY 15
*RED/25: .5X TO 1.2X BASIC
1 Brtt/Rpkn/Grffy/49 20.00 50.00
2 Bggo/Ryan/Clmns/99 15.00 40.00
3 Schwrbr/Sgr/Sano/99 6.00 15.00
6 Hdgs/Drchr/Reese/49 12.00 30.00
7 Svrno/Bird/Rfsndr/99 4.00 10.00
8 Park/Sano/Kplr/99 5.00 12.00
10 Encrncn/Btsta/Dnldsn/49 8.00 20.00
11 Crra/Spingr/Altve/99 10.00 25.00
12 Grdn/Prz/Hsmr/49 6.00 15.00
13 Gnzlz/Pdrsn/Puig/49 8.00 20.00
14 Gnzlz/Arndo/Stry/49 12.00 30.00
15 Rzzo/Brynt/Schwrbr/99 15.00 40.00

2016 Immaculate Collection Immaculate Trios Memorabilia

RANDOM INSERTS IN PACKS
PRINT RUNS B/WN 25-99 COPIES PER
*RED/25: .5X TO 1.2X BASIC
1 Kyle Schwarber/49 6.00 15.00
2 Corey Seager/49 20.00 50.00
3 Miguel Sano/49 4.00 10.00
4 Trea Turner/49 8.00 20.00
5 Stephen Piscotty/49 4.00 10.00
6 Jonathan Gray/49 2.50 6.00
7 Byung-ho Park/99 3.00 8.00
8 Kenta Maeda/25 5.00 12.00
9 Aaron Nola/25 5.00 12.00
10 Jose Peraza/49 3.00 8.00
11 Raul Mondesi/25 5.00 12.00
12 Rob Refsnyder/25 3.00 8.00
13 Ketel Marte/49 5.00 12.00
14 Luis Severino/49 3.00 8.00
15 Henry Owens/25 3.00 8.00

2016 Immaculate Collection Jersey Numbers

RANDOM INSERTS IN PACKS
PRINT RUNS B/WN 1-60 COPIES PER
NO PRICING ON QTY 19 OR LESS
1 Mike Trout/27 20.00 50.00
4 Bryce Harper/34 8.00 20.00
5 Clayton Kershaw/22 10.00 25.00
6 Miguel Cabrera/24 5.00 12.00
7 Josh Donaldson/20 4.00 10.00
8 Adrian Beltre/29 5.00 12.00
9 Chris Sale/49 5.00 12.00
10 Madison Bumgarner/40 4.00 10.00
11 Nelson Cruz/23 5.00 12.00
13 David Ortiz/34 5.00 12.00
15 Anthony Rizzo/44 6.00 15.00
17 Buster Posey/28 6.00 15.00
18 Giancarlo Stanton/27 5.00 12.00
20 Paul Goldschmidt/44 5.00 12.00
21 Andrew McCutchen/22 10.00 25.00
23 Dallas Keuchel/60 4.00 10.00
24 Justin Verlander/35 5.00 12.00
25 Nolan Arenado/28 6.00 15.00

2016 Immaculate Collection Past and Present Autographs

RANDOM INSERTS IN PACKS
PRINT RUNS B/WN 25-99 COPIES PER
EXCHANGE DEADLINE 2/17/2018
1 Josh Donaldson/99 12.00 30.00
2 Anthony Rizzo/99 12.00 30.00
3 David Price/25 20.00 50.00
4 Jake Arrieta/49
5 Jason Heyward/49 12.00 30.00
6 Albert Pujols/25 50.00 120.00
8 Don Mattingly/25 25.00 60.00
10 Paul Molitor/49 10.00 25.00

2016 Immaculate Collection Past and Present Autographs Red

*RED/25: .5X TO 1.2X p/r 99
*RED/25: .4X TO 1X p/r 25
RANDOM INSERTS IN PACKS
PRINT RUNS B/WN 10-25 COPIES PER
NO PRICING ON QTY 10
EXCHANGE DEADLINE 2/17/2018
7 Daniel Murphy/25 20.00 50.00

2016 Immaculate Collection Rookie Autographs

RANDOM INSERTS IN PACKS
STATED PRINT RUN 49 SER.#'d SETS
*RED/25: .5X TO 1.2X BASIC
EXCHANGE DEADLINE 2/17/2018
1 Aaron Nola 10.00 25.00
2 Alex Dickerson 3.00 8.00
3 Brian Johnson 3.00 8.00
4 Byung-ho Park 6.00 15.00
5 Carl Edwards Jr. 4.00 10.00
6 Colin Rea 3.00 8.00
7 Corey Seager 25.00 60.00
8 Dariel Alvarez 3.00 8.00
9 Henry Owens 4.00 10.00
10 Jerad Eickhoff 10.00 25.00
11 Jorge Lopez 3.00 8.00
12 Jose Peraza 5.00 12.00
13 Ross Stripling 3.00 8.00
14 Ketel Marte 6.00 15.00
15 Kyle Schwarber 12.00 30.00
16 Kyle Waldrop 4.00 10.00
17 Luis Severino 4.00 10.00
18 Luke Jackson 3.00 8.00
19 Mac Williamson 3.00 8.00
20 Max Kepler 5.00 12.00
21 Michael Reed 3.00 8.00
22 Miguel Sano 10.00 25.00
23 Pedro Severino 3.00 8.00
24 Raul Mondesi 4.00 10.00
25 Socrates Brito 3.00 8.00
26 Stephen Piscotty 8.00 20.00
27 Tom Murphy 3.00 8.00
28 Trea Turner 12.00 30.00
29 Tyler Duffey 3.00 8.00
30 Zack Godley 3.00 8.00
31 Robert Stephenson 3.00 8.00
32 Mallex Smith 3.00 8.00

2016 Immaculate Collection Rookie Premium Patch Autographs

RANDOM INSERTS IN PACKS
PRINT RUNS B/WN 10-25 COPIES PER
NO PRICING ON QTY 10
EXCHANGE DEADLINE 2/17/2018
1 Brian Ellington/25 5.00 12.00
3 Elias Diaz/25 5.00 12.00
4 Carl Edwards Jr./25 6.00 15.00
5 Corey Seager/25 EXCH 40.00 100.00
6 Tyler Duffey/25 5.00 12.00
8 Frankie Montas/25 6.00 15.00
9 Jonathan Gray/25 5.00 12.00
10 Jorge Lopez/25 5.00 12.00
11 Jose Peraza/25 10.00 25.00
13 Kelby Tomlinson/25 6.00 15.00
14 Travis Jankowski/25 10.00 25.00
15 Ketel Marte/25 10.00 25.00
16 Kyle Schwarber/25
17 Luis Severino/25 10.00 25.00
18 Mac Williamson/25 12.00 30.00
19 Max Kepler/25 30.00 80.00
20 Michael Conforto/25 EXCH 20.00 50.00
21 Michael Reed/25 5.00 12.00
22 Miguel Sano/25 12.00 30.00
23 Peter O'Brien/25
25 Trevor Story/25 30.00 80.00
27 Stephen Piscotty/25 15.00 40.00
28 Tom Murphy/25 5.00 12.00
29 Trayce Thompson/25 6.00 15.00
30 Trea Turner/25 20.00 50.00

2016 Immaculate Collection USA Jersey Signatures

RANDOM INSERTS IN PACKS
STATED PRINT RUN 25 SER.#'d SETS
EXCHANGE DEADLINE 2/17/2018
1 Buster Posey
2 Kris Bryant 60.00 150.00
3 Alex Bregman 20.00 50.00
4 Gerrit Cole 6.00 15.00
5 George Springer 12.00 30.00
6 Michael Conforto EXCH 25.00 60.00
7 Michael Wacha 5.00 12.00
8 Sonny Gray 5.00 12.00
9 Trea Turner 25.00 60.00
10 Carlos Rodon 6.00 15.00

2017 Immaculate Collection

1-100 PRINT RUN 99 SER.#'d SETS
JSY AU PRINT RUN 99 SER.#'d SETS
EXCHANGE DEADLINE 2/16/2019
1 Babe Ruth 4.00 10.00
2 Bill Dickey 1.00 2.50
3 Billy Martin 1.25 3.00
4 George Kelly 1.00 2.50
5 Harry Hooper 1.00 2.50
6 Honus Wagner 1.50 4.00
7 Mickey Mantle 5.00 12.00
8 Joe DiMaggio 3.00 8.00
9 Kiki Cuyler 1.25 3.00
10 Lefty Gomez 1.00 2.50
11 Lloyd Waner 1.25 3.00
12 Luke Appling 1.25 3.00
13 Max Carey 1.00 2.50
14 Joe Cronin 1.00 2.50
15 Nellie Fox 1.25 3.00
16 Paul Waner 1.25 3.00
17 Roberto Clemente 8.00 20.00
18 Roger Maris 1.50 4.00
19 Stan Musial 2.50 6.00
20 Ted Lyons 1.00 2.50
21 Ted Williams 4.00 10.00
22 Tommy Henrich 1.00 2.50
23 Ernie Banks 3.00 8.00
24 Herb Pennock 1.25 3.00
25 Jackie Robinson 1.50 4.00
26 Leo Durocher 1.00 2.50
27 Lou Gehrig 3.00 8.00
28 Pee Wee Reese 1.25 3.00
29 Paul Goldschmidt 1.50 4.00
30 A.J. Pollock 1.00 2.50
31 Jean Segura 1.25 3.00
32 Freddie Freeman 2.00 5.00
33 Manny Machado 1.50 4.00
34 Mookie Betts 2.50 6.00
35 Xander Bogaerts 1.50 4.00
36 Chris Sale 1.50 4.00
37 Jackie Bradley Jr. 1.50 4.00
38 David Price 1.25 3.00
39 Rick Porcello 1.25 3.00
40 Kris Bryant 2.00 5.00
41 Anthony Rizzo 2.50 6.00
42 Jon Lester 1.25 3.00
43 Addison Russell 1.50 4.00
44 Jake Arrieta 1.25 3.00
45 Kyle Schwarber 1.50 4.00
46 Joey Votto 1.50 4.00
47 Francisco Lindor 1.50 4.00
48 Corey Kluber 1.25 3.00
49 Edwin Encarnacion 1.50 4.00
50 Carlos Santana 1.25 3.00
51 Jose Ramirez 1.25 3.00
52 Nolan Arenado 2.00 5.00
53 Charlie Blackmon 1.50 4.00
54 Trevor Story 1.50 4.00
55 Miguel Cabrera 1.50 4.00
56 Ian Kinsler 1.25 3.00
57 Justin Verlander 1.50 4.00
58 Michael Fulmer 1.00 2.50
59 Jose Altuve 1.25 3.00
60 Carlos Correa 1.50 4.00
61 Eric Hosmer 1.25 3.00
62 Salvador Perez 1.25 3.00
63 Mike Trout 6.00 15.00
64 Albert Pujols 2.00 5.00
65 Corey Seager 1.50 4.00
66 Clayton Kershaw 3.00 8.00
67 Justin Turner 1.25 3.00
68 Giancarlo Stanton 1.50 4.00
69 Christian Yelich 2.00 5.00
70 Ichiro 2.00 5.00
71 Ryan Braun 1.25 3.00
72 Jonathan Villar 1.00 2.50
73 Brian Dozier 1.50 4.00
74 Noah Syndergaard 1.25 3.00
75 Yoenis Cespedes 1.50 4.00
76 Masahiro Tanaka 1.25 3.00
77 Gary Sanchez 1.50 4.00
78 Andrew McCutchen 3.00 8.00
79 Starling Marte 1.25 3.00
80 Madison Bumgarner 1.25 3.00
81 Buster Posey 2.00 5.00
82 Robinson Cano 1.25 3.00
83 Felix Hernandez 1.25 3.00
84 Nelson Cruz 1.50 4.00
85 Matt Carpenter 1.50 4.00
86 Yadier Molina 2.50 6.00
87 Evan Longoria 1.25 3.00
88 Adrian Beltre 1.50 4.00
89 Josh Donaldson 1.25 3.00
90 Jose Bautista 1.25 3.00
91 J.A. Happ 1.25 3.00
92 Bryce Harper 5.00 12.00
93 Max Scherzer 1.50 4.00
94 Daniel Murphy 1.25 3.00
95 Trea Turner 1.25 3.00
96 George Brett 6.00 15.00
97 Cal Ripken 8.00 20.00
98 Kirby Puckett 8.00 20.00
99 Ken Griffey Jr. 3.00 8.00
100 Nolan Ryan 6.00 15.00
101 Yoan Moncada JSY AU RC 15.00 40.00
102 Bnntndi JSY AU RC 25.00 60.00
103 Swnsn JSY AU RC EXCH 15.00 40.00
104 Alex Bregman JSY AU RC 25.00 60.00
105 David Dahl JSY AU RC 6.00 15.00
106 Tyler Glasnow JSY AU RC 5.00 12.00
107 Josh Bell JSY AU RC 12.00 30.00
108 Alex Reyes JSY AU RC 5.00 12.00
109 Orlando Arcia JSY AU RC 8.00 20.00
110 Jose De Leon JSY AU RC 4.00 10.00
111 Joe Musgrove JSY AU RC 4.00 10.00
112 Manuel Margot JSY AU RC 4.00 10.00
113 Aaron Judge JSY AU RC 100.00 250.00
114 David Paulino JSY AU RC 5.00 12.00
115 Reynaldo Lopez JSY AU RC 4.00 10.00
116 Jeff Hoffman JSY AU RC EXCH 4.00 10.00
117 Braden Shipley JSY AU RC 4.00 10.00
118 Hunter Renfroe JSY AU RC 5.00 12.00
119 Jorge Alfaro JSY AU RC 8.00 20.00
120 Carson Fulmer JSY AU RC 4.00 10.00
121 Luke Weaver JSY AU RC 5.00 12.00
122 Raimel Tapia JSY AU RC 5.00 12.00
123 Adalberto Mejia JSY AU RC EXCH 6.00 15.00
124 Gavin Cecchini JSY AU RC EXCH 6.00 15.00
125 Jacoby Jones JSY AU RC 5.00 12.00
126 Yohander Mendez JSY AU RC 4.00 10.00
127 Chad Pinder JSY AU RC 5.00 12.00
128 Carson Kelly JSY AU RC 5.00 12.00
129 Trey Mancini JSY AU RC 8.00 20.00
130 Teoscar Hernandez JSY AU RC 12.00 30.00
131 Ryon Healy JSY AU RC 6.00 15.00
132 Erik Gonzalez JSY AU RC 4.00 10.00
133 Roman Quinn JSY AU RC 5.00 12.00
134 Matt Olson JSY AU RC 6.00 15.00
135 Jharel Cotton JSY AU RC 6.00 15.00
136 Jake Thompson JSY AU RC EXCH 5.00 12.00
137 Renato Nunez JSY AU RC 5.00 12.00
138 Jose Rondon JSY AU RC 4.00 10.00

2017 Immaculate Collection Gold

*GOLD JSY AU: .5X TO 1.2X BASIC
RANDOM INSERTS IN PACKS
1-100 PRINT RUN 5 SER.#'d SETS
101-138 PRINT RUNS 49 SER.#'d SETS
NO 1-100 PRICING DUE TO SCARCITY
EXCHANGE DEADLINE 2/16/2019

2017 Immaculate Collection Red

*RED: .6X TO 1.5X BASIC
RANDOM INSERTS IN PACKS
STATED PRINT RUN 25 SER.#'d SETS
EXCHANGE DEADLINE 2/16/2019
7 Mickey Mantle 12.00 30.00
17 Roberto Clemente 30.00 80.00
27 Lou Gehrig 10.00 25.00
41 Anthony Rizzo 8.00 20.00
77 Gary Sanchez 12.00 30.00
81 Buster Posey 10.00 25.00
98 Kirby Puckett 20.00 50.00
99 Ken Griffey Jr. 10.00 25.00

2017 Immaculate Collection Immaculate Autographs

RANDOM INSERTS IN PACKS
PRINT RUNS B/WN 10-99 COPIES PER
NO PRICING ON QTY 16 OR LESS
EXCHANGE DEADLINE 2/16/2019
*BLUE/25: .5X TO 1.2X p/r 49-99
3 Carlton Fisk/25 10.00 25.00
4 Darryl Strawberry/25 10.00 25.00
6 George Springer/49 6.00 15.00
8 Jeff Bagwell/25 20.00 50.00
9 Jose Abreu/25 8.00 20.00
11 Ozzie Smith/25 20.00 50.00
13 Mark Prior/99 4.00 10.00
14 Roberto Alomar/25 10.00 25.00
15 Tom Glavine/25 10.00 25.00
16 Wade Boggs/49 15.00 40.00
17 Tyler Naquin/25 5.00 12.00
19 Bob Gibson/25 15.00 40.00
20 Jose Altuve/25 25.00 60.00
21 Jason Kipnis/25 5.00 12.00
24 Jose Canseco/99 10.00 25.00

2017 Immaculate Collection Immaculate Bats Autographs

RANDOM INSERTS IN PACKS
PRINT RUNS B/WN 5-99 COPIES PER
NO PRICING ON QTY 5
EXCHANGE DEADLINE 2/16/2019
1 Yoan Moncada/99 20.00 50.00
4 Dansby Swanson/99 15.00 40.00
5 Josh Bell/99 20.00 50.00
6 Trey Mancini/99 12.00 30.00
7 Aaron Judge/99 100.00 250.00
8 Jacoby Jones/99 6.00 15.00
9 David Dahl/99 6.00 15.00
11 Nolan Arenado/25 25.00 60.00
12 Paul Goldschmidt/25 25.00 60.00
14 Josh Donaldson/25 15.00 40.00
15 Jackie Bradley Jr./25 12.00 30.00
16 Jose Altuve/25 40.00 100.00

2017 Immaculate Collection Immaculate Carbon Material Signatures

RANDOM INSERTS IN PACKS
PRINT RUNS B/WN 5-49 COPIES PER
NO PRICING ON QTY 5
EXCHANGE DEADLINE 2/16/2019
3 Jackie Bradley Jr./25 12.00 30.00
4 Trea Turner/25 15.00 40.00
5 Corey Seager/25 20.00 50.00
6 Starling Marte/25 25.00 60.00
8 Gary Sanchez/25 40.00 100.00
9 Eric Hosmer/25 12.00 30.00
10 Jose Altuve/25
11 Andrew Benintendi/49 30.00 80.00
12 Yoan Moncada/49 20.00 50.00
13 Alex Bregman/49 15.00 40.00
14 Dansby Swanson/49 15.00 40.00
15 Josh Bell/49 12.00 30.00
16 David Dahl/49 6.00 15.00
17 Hunter Renfroe/49 8.00 20.00
18 Aaron Judge/49
19 Trey Mancini/49 20.00 50.00
20 Ryon Healy/49 8.00 20.00
21 Orlando Arcia/49 8.00 20.00
22 Jacoby Jones/49 5.00 12.00
23 Manuel Margot/49 4.00 10.00
24 Nomar Mazara/25 5.00 12.00
26 Tyler Naquin/25 8.00 20.00
27 Stephen Piscotty/25 15.00 40.00

2017 Immaculate Collection Immaculate Carbon Signatures

RANDOM INSERTS IN PACKS
PRINT RUNS B/WN 5-99 COPIES PER
NO PRICING ON QTY 15 OR LESS
EXCHANGE DEADLINE 2/16/2019
*BLUE/25: .5X TO 1.2X p/r 49-99
3 Jackie Bradley Jr./49 12.00 30.00
6 Trea Turner/25 8.00 20.00
7 Corey Seager/25 25.00 60.00
9 Vladimir Guerrero Jr./25 200.00 500.00
10 Andre Dawson/25 15.00 40.00
11 Starling Marte/25 8.00 20.00
13 Gary Sanchez/49 25.00 60.00
14 Nomar Mazara/25 8.00 20.00
15 Eric Hosmer/25 10.00 25.00
16 Frank Thomas/25 20.00 50.00
18 Tyler Naquin/25 5.00 12.00
19 J.P. Crawford/99 10.00 25.00
21 Stephen Piscotty/25 5.00 12.00
25 Cody Bellinger/25 40.00 100.00
26 Jose Abreu/25 10.00 25.00

2017 Immaculate Collection Immaculate Dual Autographs

RANDOM INSERTS IN PACKS
PRINT RUNS B/WN 10-25 COPIES PER
NO PRICING ON QTY 10
EXCHANGE DEADLINE 2/16/2019
*BLUE/25:.5X TO 1.2X BASIC
1 Dawson/Sandberg 60.00 150.00
2 Bagwell/Biggio 50.00 120.00
3 Rodriguez/Bench 50.00 125.00
5 Benintendi/Moncada 30.00 80.00
6 Ortiz/Francona 75.00 200.00
7 Swanson/Bregman 25.00 60.00
8 Seager/Seager 15.00 40.00
9 Griffey Jr./Martinez 75.00 200.00
12 Molitor/Yount 30.00 80.00
13 Strawberry/Gooden 30.00 80.00
14 Thomas/Sandberg 60.00 150.00

2017 Immaculate Collection Immaculate Dual Material Autographs

RANDOM INSERTS IN PACKS
PRINT RUNS B/W 15-99 COPIES PER
NO PRICING ON QTY 15
EXCHANGE DEADLINE 2/16/2019
*BLUE/25: .5X TO 1.2X p/r 49-99
1 Alan Trammell/49 12.00 30.00
2 Bo Jackson/25 40.00 100.00
3 Darryl Strawberry/25 15.00 40.00
4 Dwight Gooden/25 12.00 30.00
5 David Price/25 6.00 15.00
7 Nelson Cruz/24 12.00 30.00
8 Luis Severino/25 15.00 40.00
10 Kyle Schwarber/25 15.00 40.00
11 Trea Turner/25 6.00 15.00
12 Corey Seager/99 20.00 50.00
13 Jose Abreu/25 10.00 25.00
14 Matt Adams/25 5.00 12.00
15 Mike Napoli/25 15.00 40.00
16 Max Scherzer/25 40.00 100.00
17 Cody Bellinger/49 40.00 100.00
18 Yasmany Tomas/25 5.00 12.00
19 Adrian Gonzalez/25 10.00 25.00
20 Jackie Bradley Jr./25 12.00 30.00
21 Kyle Seager/25 5.00 12.00
22 Xander Bogaerts/25 15.00 40.00
23 Jose Altuve/25 20.00 50.00
24 Lorenzo Cain/25 10.00 25.00
25 Ian Happ/99 8.00 20.00

2017 Immaculate Collection Immaculate Dual Players Memorabilia

RANDOM INSERTS IN PACKS
PRINT RUNS B/WN 5-99 COPIES PER
NO PRICING ON QTY 15 OR LESS
*BLUE/25: .6X TO 1.5X BASIC
3 Robinson/Reese/25 20.00 50.00
4 Banks/Cuyler/25 10.00 25.00
5 Fox/Lyons/25 20.00 50.00
8 Carey/Waner/25 15.00 40.00
9 Robinson/Clemente/25 50.00 120.00
10 Maris/Henrich/99 10.00 25.00
11 Bryant/Trout/99 20.00 50.00
12 Wee Reese/Seager/99 4.00 10.00
13 Maris/Mantle/25 60.00 150.00
15 Murphy/Altuve/99 3.00 8.00
16 Beltre/Arenado/99 5.00 12.00
17 Killebrew/Puckett/99 12.00 30.00
18 Ichiro/Rodriguez/49 8.00 20.00
19 Betts/Bogaerts/99 6.00 15.00
20 Pujols/Trout/99 20.00 50.00

2017 Immaculate Collection Immaculate Duals Memorabilia

RANDOM INSERTS IN PACKS
PRINT RUNS B/WN 25-99 COPIES PER
*PRIME/25: .6X TO 1.5X BASIC
1 Kris Bryant/49 8.00 20.00
2 Mike Trout/25 25.00 60.00
3 Buster Posey/99 5.00 12.00
4 Carlos Correa/99 4.00 10.00
5 Frank Thomas/99 6.00 15.00
6 Yu Darvish/25 4.00 10.00
7 Giancarlo Stanton/99 6.00 15.00
8 Yadier Molina/99 4.00 10.00
9 Francisco Lindor/99 4.00 10.00
10 Javier Baez/99 5.00 12.00
11 Alex Gordon/99 5.00 12.00
12 Jose Abreu/99 4.00 10.00
13 Chris Davis/99 2.50 6.00
14 Justin Verlander/99 4.00 10.00
15 Rick Porcello/99 3.00 8.00
16 Daniel Murphy/99 3.00 8.00
17 Charlie Blackmon/99 4.00 10.00
18 Mookie Betts/99 6.00 15.00
19 Robinson Cano/99 3.00 8.00
20 Jake Arrieta/25 3.00 8.00

2017 Immaculate Collection Immaculate Home Plate Signatures

RANDOM INSERTS IN PACKS
PRINT RUNS B/WN 25-99 COPIES PER
EXCHANGE DEADLINE 2/16/2019
*BLUE/25: .5X TO 1.2X p/r 99
1 Alex Reyes/99 4.00 10.00
2 Carson Fulmer/99 3.00 8.00
3 Jose De Leon/99 3.00 8.00
4 Tyler Glasnow/99 5.00 12.00
5 Reynaldo Lopez/99 3.00 8.00
6 Luke Weaver/99 5.00 12.00
7 Jake Thompson/99 3.00 8.00
8 Yadier Molina/25 30.00 80.00
9 Marcus Stroman/25 5.00 12.00
10 Yasmany Tomas/25 4.00 10.00
11 Joe Panik/25 10.00 25.00
12 Justin Turner/25 12.00 30.00
13 Charlie Blackmon/25 12.00 30.00
14 Corey Kluber/25 8.00 20.00
15 Anthony Rizzo/25 50.00 120.00

2017 Immaculate Collection Immaculate Jumbo Materials

RANDOM INSERTS IN PACKS
PRINT RUNS B/WN 1-99 COPIES PER
NO PRICING ON QTY 15 OR LESS
1 Yoan Moncada/99 5.00 12.00
2 Andrew Benintendi/99 6.00 15.00
3 Dansby Swanson/99 5.00 12.00
4 Alex Bregman/99 5.00 12.00
5 David Dahl/99 3.00 8.00
6 Tyler Glasnow/99 3.00 8.00
7 Mickey Mantle/20 150.00 300.00
8 Alex Reyes/99 3.00 8.00
9 Orlando Arcia/99 4.00 10.00
10 Jose De Leon/99 2.50 6.00
11 Joe Musgrove/99 2.50 6.00
12 Manuel Margot/99 2.50 6.00
13 Aaron Judge/99 30.00 80.00
14 David Paulino/99 3.00 8.00
15 Reynaldo Lopez/99 2.50 6.00
16 Jeff Hoffman/99 2.50 6.00
17 Braden Shipley/99 2.50 6.00
18 Hunter Renfroe/99 3.00 8.00
19 Jorge Alfaro/99 3.00 8.00
20 Carson Fulmer/99 2.50 6.00
21 Luke Weaver/99 3.00 8.00
22 Raimel Tapia/99 3.00 8.00
23 Adalberto Mejia/99 2.50 6.00
24 Gavin Cecchini/99 2.50 6.00
25 Jacoby Jones/99 3.00 8.00
26 Yohander Mendez/99 2.50 6.00
27 Chad Pinder/99 2.50 6.00
28 Carson Kelly/99 3.00 8.00
29 Trey Mancini/99 6.00 15.00
30 Teoscar Hernandez/99 8.00 20.00
31 Ryon Healy/99 3.00 8.00
32 Erik Gonzalez/99 2.50 6.00
33 Roman Quinn/99 2.50 6.00
34 Matt Olson/99 5.00 12.00
35 Jharel Cotton/99 2.50 6.00
36 Jake Thompson/99 2.50 6.00
37 Renato Nunez/99 5.00 12.00
38 Jose Rondon/99 2.50 6.00
39 Clayton Kershaw/25 12.00 30.00
40 Goose Gossage/25 3.00 8.00
41 Buster Posey/25 5.00 12.00
42 Brandon Phillips/99 2.50 6.00
43 Adam Duvall/99 4.00 10.00
44 Kyle Schwarber/99 4.00 10.00
45 Corey Seager/99 4.00 10.00
46 Johnny Cueto/25 3.00 8.00
47 Hanley Ramirez/25 3.00 8.00
48 Marcell Ozuna/49 4.00 10.00
49 Ken Griffey Jr./25 12.00 30.00
50 Cody Bellinger/99 12.00 30.00
52 Troy Tulowitzki/25 4.00 10.00
53 Gary Sanchez/49 12.00 30.00
54 Lorenzo Cain/49 2.50 6.00
55 Addison Russell/49 4.00 10.00
56 Kris Bryant/49 6.00 15.00
57 Francisco Lindor/49 4.00 10.00
58 Noah Syndergaard/49 3.00 8.00
65 Paul Molitor/20 12.00 30.00
67 Ryne Sandberg/25 12.00 30.00
69 Stephen Piscotty/99 3.00 8.00
70 Edwin Encarnacion/20 4.00 10.00
71 Greg Maddux/25 15.00 40.00
72 Ivan Rodriguez/25 6.00 15.00
73 Byron Buxton/99 3.00 8.00
74 Willson Contreras/99 4.00 10.00
75 Rickey Henderson/25 12.00 30.00
76 Tony Gwynn/25 20.00 50.00
77 Miguel Sano/99 3.00 8.00
78 A.J. Reed/99 2.50 6.00
79 David Wright/99 3.00 8.00
81 Don Mattingly/25 12.00 30.00
85 Vladimir Guerrero/25 10.00 25.00
87 Bert Blyleven/25 5.00 12.00
88 David Price/25 3.00 8.00
89 Tim Tebow/99 13.00 30.00
92 Jason Heyward/25 3.00 8.00
95 Kirby Puckett/20 25.00 60.00
98 Pete Rose/25 20.00 50.00
99 Rickey Henderson/25 12.00 30.00
100 Yoenis Cespedes/25 4.00 10.00

2017 Immaculate Collection Immaculate Legends Memorabilia

RANDOM INSERTS IN PACKS
PRINT RUNS B/WN 5-99 COPIES PER
NO PRICING ON QTY 15 OR LESS
3 George Kelly/25 12.00 30.00
6 Joe Cronin/25 8.00 20.00
8 Kiki Cuyler/25 12.00 30.00
11 Luke Appling/99 5.00 12.00
12 Max Carey/25 20.00 50.00
17 Stan Musial/25 12.00 30.00
20 Ernie Banks/25 8.00 20.00
21 Herb Pennock/25 8.00 20.00
23 Leo Durocher/99 4.00 10.00
25 Pee Wee Reese/25 12.00 30.00
26 Bob Feller/99 5.00 12.00
27 Duke Snider/99 5.00 12.00
28 Al Kaline/49 6.00 15.00
29 Harmon Killebrew/25 8.00 20.00
30 Bobby Doerr/49 5.00 12.00
32 Eddie Mathews/25 6.00 15.00
34 Rick Ferrell/25 8.00 20.00

2017 Immaculate Collection Immaculate Material

RANDOM INSERTS IN PACKS
PRINT RUNS B/WN 5-99 COPIES PER
NO PRICING ON QTY 15 OR LESS
*GOLD/25-49: .6X TO 1.5X BASIC
1 Yoan Moncada/99 5.00 12.00
2 Andrew Benintendi/99 8.00 20.00
3 Dansby Swanson/99 6.00 15.00
4 Alex Bregman/99 6.00 15.00
5 David Dahl/99 3.00 8.00
6 Tyler Glasnow/99 3.00 8.00
8 Alex Reyes/99 3.00 8.00
9 Orlando Arcia/99 4.00 10.00
10 Jose De Leon/99 2.50 6.00
11 Joe Musgrove/99 2.50 6.00
12 Manuel Margot/99 2.50 6.00
13 Aaron Judge/99 25.00 60.00
14 David Paulino/99 3.00 8.00
15 Josh Bell/49 6.00 15.00
16 Reynaldo Lopez/99 2.50 6.00
17 Jeff Hoffman/99 2.50 6.00
18 Braden Shipley/99 2.50 6.00
19 Hunter Renfroe/99 3.00 8.00
20 Jorge Alfaro/99 3.00 8.00
21 Carson Fulmer/99 2.50 6.00
22 Luke Weaver/99 3.00 8.00
23 Raimel Tapia/99 3.00 8.00
24 Adalberto Mejia/99 2.50 6.00
25 Gavin Cecchini/99 2.50 6.00
26 Jacoby Jones/99 3.00 8.00
27 Yohander Mendez/99 2.50 6.00
28 Chad Pinder/99 2.50 6.00
29 Carson Kelly/99 3.00 8.00
30 Trey Mancini/99 5.00 12.00
31 Teoscar Hernandez/99 8.00 20.00
32 Ryon Healy/99 3.00 8.00
33 Erik Gonzalez/99 2.50 6.00
34 Roman Quinn/99 2.50 6.00
35 Matt Olson/99 5.00 12.00
36 Jharel Cotton/99 2.50 6.00
37 Jake Thompson/99 2.50 6.00
38 Renato Nunez/99 5.00 12.00
39 Jose Rondon/99 2.50 6.00
40 Miguel Sano/99 3.00 8.00
41 George Springer/99 3.00 8.00
42 Javier Baez/99 5.00 12.00
43 Kyle Schwarber/99 4.00 10.00
44 Stephen Piscotty/99 3.00 8.00
45 A.J. Reed/99 2.50 6.00
46 Blake Snell/99 3.00 8.00
47 Brandon Nimmo/99 3.00 8.00
48 Byron Buxton/99 3.00 8.00
49 Greg Bird/99 3.00 8.00
50 Jacob deGrom/99 4.00 10.00
51 Jose Peraza/99 3.00 8.00
52 Ketel Marte/99 3.00 8.00
53 Lucas Giolito/99 3.00 8.00
54 Luis Severino/99 3.00 8.00
55 Raul A. Mondesi/99 2.50 6.00
56 Tim Anderson/99 4.00 10.00
57 Kevin Kiermaier/99 3.00 8.00
58 Tom Murphy/99 2.50 6.00
59 Willson Contreras/99 4.00 10.00
60 Kris Bryant/99 5.00 12.00
61 Roger Maris/25 30.00 80.00
65 Stan Musial/99 15.00 40.00
66 Jose Bautista/99 3.00 8.00
67 Rougned Odor/99 3.00 8.00
68 Victor Martinez/99 3.00 8.00
69 Brandon Phillips/99 2.50 6.00
70 Jay Bruce/99 3.00 8.00
72 Mike Piazza/99 8.00 20.00
73 Bo Jackson/99 12.00 30.00
74 Cole Hamels/99 3.00 8.00
75 Kenta Maeda/99 3.00 8.00
76 Giancarlo Stanton/49 10.00 25.00
77 Elvis Andrus/99 3.00 8.00
78 Don Mattingly/99 12.00 30.00
79 Jorge Posada/99 4.00 10.00
80 Matt Carpenter/99 4.00 10.00
81 Andrew McCutchen/99 4.00 10.00
82 Bryce Harper/49 6.00 15.00
83 Mike Trout/25 30.00 80.00
84 Adam Wainwright/99 3.00 8.00
85 Johnny Cueto/99 3.00 8.00
86 Ian Kinsler/99 3.00 8.00
87 Joey Votto/99 4.00 10.00
88 Yu Darvish/25 4.00 10.00
89 Tim Tebow/99 12.00 30.00
91 Vladimir Guerrero/99 6.00 15.00
92 Jeff Bagwell/99 5.00 12.00
93 Adrian Gonzalez/99 3.00 8.00
94 Maikel Franco/49 5.00 12.00
95 Trevor Story/99 4.00 10.00
96 Michael Taylor/99 2.50 6.00
97 Cal Ripken/99 25.00 60.00
98 Chipper Jones/99 8.00 20.00
100 Reggie Jackson/99 6.00 15.00

2017 Immaculate Collection Immaculate Material Signatures

RANDOM INSERTS IN PACKS
PRINT RUNS B/W 5-99 COPIES PER
NO PRICING ON QTY 15 OR LESS
EXCHANGE DEADLINE 2/16/2019
*BLUE/25: .5X TO 1.2X p/r 49-99
3 Jason Kipnis/49 6.00 15.00
4 Noah Syndergaard/25 12.00 30.00
5 Jacob deGrom/25 15.00 40.00
6 Jim Rice/25 8.00 20.00
7 Steve Finley/49 4.00 10.00
9 Francisco Lindor/99 15.00 40.00
10 Kyle Seager/25 5.00 12.00
11 Dennis Eckersley/25 10.00 25.00
12 Javier Baez/25 20.00 50.00
14 Trea Turner/99 10.00 25.00
16 Corey Seager/49 20.00 50.00
17 Yadier Molina/25 30.00 80.00
18 Joe Panik/25 8.00 20.00
20 Stephen Piscotty/25 6.00 15.00
22 Eric Hosmer/25 15.00 40.00
23 Corey Kluber/25 10.00 25.00
24 Jose Altuve/25 25.00 60.00
26 Dwight Gooden/49 6.00 15.00
27 Chipper Jones/25 40.00 100.00
28 Paul Goldschmidt/25 12.00 30.00
31 Nolan Arenado/25

2017 Immaculate Collection Immaculate Parchment Signatures

RANDOM INSERTS IN PACKS
PRINT RUNS B/WN 7-35 COPIES PER
NO PRICING ON QTY 15 OR LESS
EXCHANGE DEADLINE 2/16/2019
2 Pete Rose/25
3 Goose Gossage/35 12.00 30.00
4 Whitey Ford/25 30.00 80.00
5 Luis Aparicio/20 15.00 40.00

2017 Immaculate Collection Immaculate Quad Autograph Materials Rookie

RANDOM INSERTS IN PACKS
PRINT RUNS B/W 49-99 COPIES PER
EXCHANGE DEADLINE 2/16/2019
*GOLD/49: .4X TO 1X p/r 49-99
*GOLD/25: .5X TO 1.2X p/r 49-99
1 Yoan Moncada/99 15.00 40.00
2 Andrew Benintendi/99 40.00 100.00
3 Dansby Swanson/99 15.00 40.00
4 Alex Bregman/99 20.00 50.00
5 David Dahl/99 5.00 12.00
6 Tyler Glasnow/99 6.00 15.00
7 Josh Bell/49 15.00 40.00
8 Alex Reyes/99 8.00 20.00
9 Orlando Arcia/99 6.00 15.00
10 Jose De Leon/99 4.00 10.00
11 Manuel Margot/99 4.00 10.00
12 Aaron Judge/99 100.00 250.00
14 Hunter Renfroe/99 5.00 12.00
15 Jorge Alfaro/99 5.00 12.00

2017 Immaculate Collection Immaculate Quad Material Autographs

RANDOM INSERTS IN PACKS
PRINT RUNS B/WN 5-25 COPIES PER
NO PRICING ON QTY 15 OR LESS
EXCHANGE DEADLINE 2/16/2019
3 Phil Niekro/25 12.00 30.00
7 Andre Dawson/25 15.00 40.00
8 Bob Feller/25 25.00 60.00
11 Dennis Eckersley/25 8.00 20.00
12 David Ortiz/25 40.00 100.00
14 Jeff Bagwell/25 20.00 50.00
16 Roberto Alomar/25 20.00 50.00
17 Cody Bellinger/25 75.00 200.00
18 Al Kaline/25 30.00 80.00
19 Bobby Doerr/25 25.00 60.00

2017 Immaculate Collection Immaculate Quad Players Memorabilia

RANDOM INSERTS IN PACKS
PRINT RUNS B/WN 5-99 COPIES PER
NO PRICING ON QTY 10 OR LESS
*BLUE/20-25: .6X TO 1.5X BASIC
1 Brtt/Grffy/Rpkn/Thms/49 30.00 80.00
2 Hrpr/Psy/Trt/Brynt/99 30.00 80.00
6 Crnn/Bnks/Drchr/Rse/25 20.00 50.00
8 Mncda/Brgmn/Bnntndi/Swnsn/99 10.00 25.00
9 Jdge/Rnfoe/Dahl/Bell/99 12.00 30.00
10 Josh Donaldson 8.00 20.00
Adrian Beltre
Manny Machado
Nolan Arenado/49
11 Cbrra/McCtchn/Vtto/Altve/99 6.00 15.00
12 Fllr/Clmns/Gbsn/Ryan/49 20.00 50.00
13 Crtr/Rdrgz/Bnch/Pzza/49 10.00 25.00
14 Jmnz/Mtn/Rbls/Grrro/99 10.00 25.00
15 Pujols/Ichiro/25 20.00 50.00

2017 Immaculate Collection Immaculate Quads

RANDOM INSERTS IN PACKS
PRINT RUNS B/WN 3-99 COPIES PER
NO PRICING ON QTY 10 OR LESS
*BLUE/25: .6X TO 1.5X BASIC
1 Mike Trout/25 20.00 50.00
4 Clayton Kershaw/99 8.00 20.00

Tony Gwynn/99 6.00 15.00
Francisco Lindor/99 4.00 10.00
Kris Bryant/49 5.00 12.00
Yoan Moncada/99 6.00 15.00

2017 Immaculate Collection Immaculate Rookie Carbon Signatures

RANDOM INSERTS IN PACKS
STATED PRINT RUN 49 SER.#'d SETS
EXCHANGE DEADLINE 2/16/2019
Andrew Benintendi 30.00 80.00
Yoan Moncada 15.00 40.00
Alex Bregman 12.00 30.00
Dansby Swanson 10.00 25.00
Josh Bell 12.00 30.00
David Dahl 8.00 20.00
Hunter Renfroe 6.00 15.00
Aaron Judge 100.00 250.00
Trey Mancini 6.00 15.00
0 Ryon Healy 4.00 10.00
1 Orlando Arcia 6.00 15.00
2 Jacoby Jones 8.00 20.00
3 Manuel Margot 3.00 8.00

2017 Immaculate Collection Immaculate Signatures

RANDOM INSERTS IN PACKS
PRINT RUNS B/WN 5-99 COPIES PER
NO PRICING ON QTY 15 OR LESS
EXCHANGE DEADLINE 2/16/2019
*BLUE/25: .5X TO 1.2X p/r 49-99
1 Eloy Jimenez/99 20.00 50.00
3 Nolan Arenado/25 20.00 50.00
4 Yadier Molina/25 30.00 80.00
5 Corey Seager/49 10.00 25.00
9 Gary Sanchez/99 15.00 40.00
10 Francisco Lindor/99 12.00 30.00
11 Justin Turner/99 10.00 25.00
12 Chris Sale/99 8.00 20.00
13 Josh Donaldson/25 10.00 25.00
14 Corey Kluber/25 8.00 20.00
15 Charlie Blackmon/49 10.00 25.00
18 Terry Francona/25 12.00 30.00
19 Roy Oswalt/25 5.00 12.00
20 Edgar Renteria/49 5.00 12.00
23 Andres Galarraga/99 5.00 12.00
24 Cole Hamels/25 6.00 15.00
25 Jason Giambi/49 5.00 12.00
26 Rafael Palmeiro/25 5.00 12.00
27 Jose Canseco/49 10.00 25.00
31 Willie McGee/99 8.00 20.00
32 Tom Glavine/25 10.00 25.00
33 Craig Biggio/49 10.00 25.00
35 Frank Howard/99 3.00 8.00
36 Paul Goldschmidt/25 15.00 40.00
39 Billy Wagner/99 3.00 8.00
43 Boog Powell/49 6.00 15.00
44 Bo Jackson/25 6.00 15.00
47 Ken Griffey Sr./99 4.00 10.00
49 Mark Grace/25 10.00 25.00

2017 Immaculate Collection Immaculate Signatures Patches Rookie

RANDOM INSERTS IN PACKS
PRINT RUNS B/W 49-99 COPIES PER
EXCHANGE DEADLINE 2/16/2019
*GOLD/49: .4X TO 1X p/r 49-99
*GOLD/25: .5X TO 1.2X p/r 49-99
1 Yoan Moncada/49 15.00 40.00
2 Andrew Benintendi/49 40.00 100.00
3 Dansby Swanson/99 15.00 40.00
4 Alex Bregman/49 20.00 50.00
5 David Dahl/99 5.00 12.00
6 Tyler Glasnow/99 8.00 20.00
7 Josh Bell/49 15.00 40.00
8 Alex Reyes/99 6.00 15.00
9 Orlando Arcia/99 6.00 15.00
10 Jose De Leon/99 4.00 10.00
11 Joe Musgrove/99 4.00 10.00
12 Manuel Margot/99 4.00 10.00
13 Aaron Judge/49 100.00 250.00
14 David Paulino/99 5.00 12.00
15 Reynaldo Lopez/99 4.00 10.00
17 Hunter Renfroe/99 5.00 12.00
18 Jorge Alfaro/99 8.00 20.00
19 Carson Fulmer/99 4.00 10.00
20 Luke Weaver/99 8.00 20.00
22 Jacoby Jones/99 5.00 12.00
23 Yohander Mendez/99 4.00 10.00
24 Carson Kelly/99 5.00 12.00
25 Ryon Healy/99 8.00 20.00
26 Erik Gonzalez/99 4.00 10.00
27 Roman Quinn/99 6.00 15.00
28 Teoscar Hernandez/99 6.00 15.00
29 Raimel Tapia/99 5.00 12.00
30 Matt Olson/99 8.00 20.00

2017 Immaculate Collection Immaculate Swatches

RANDOM INSERTS IN PACKS
PRINT RUNS B/WN 5-99 COPIES PER
NO PRICING ON QTY 15 OR LESS
*PRIME/25-49: .6X TO 1.5X BASIC
3 Billy Martin/99 3.00 8.00
4 George Kelly/25 10.00 25.00
9 Kiki Cuyler/25 10.00 25.00
12 Luke Appling/49 5.00 12.00
13 Max Carey/25 15.00 40.00
14 Joe Cronin/25 6.00 15.00
15 Nellie Fox/49 12.00 30.00
18 Roger Maris/49 10.00 25.00
19 Stan Musial/25 6.00 15.00
20 Ted Lyons/25 10.00 25.00
22 Tommy Henrich/99 2.50 6.00
23 Ernie Banks/25 12.00 30.00
24 Herb Pennock/25 5.00 12.00
25 Jackie Robinson/25 25.00 60.00
26 Leo Durocher/49 2.50 6.00
28 Pee Wee Reese/25 5.00 12.00
29 Yoan Moncada/99 5.00 12.00
30 Andrew Benintendi/99 5.00 12.00
31 Dansby Swanson/99 5.00 12.00
32 Alex Bregman/99 5.00 12.00
33 David Dahl/99 3.00 8.00
34 Tyler Glasnow/99 3.00 8.00
35 Josh Bell/99 6.00 15.00
36 Alex Reyes/99 3.00 8.00
37 Orlando Arcia/99 4.00 10.00
38 Jose De Leon/99 2.50 6.00
39 Joe Musgrove/99 2.50 6.00
40 Manuel Margot/99 2.50 6.00
41 Aaron Judge/99 12.00 30.00
42 David Paulino/99 3.00 8.00
43 Reynaldo Lopez/99 2.50 6.00
44 Jeff Hoffman/99 2.50 6.00
45 Braden Shipley/99 2.50 6.00
46 Hunter Renfroe/99 3.00 8.00
47 Jorge Alfaro/99 3.00 8.00
48 Carson Fulmer/99 2.50 6.00
49 Luke Weaver/99 2.50 6.00
50 Raimel Tapia/99 3.00 8.00
51 Adalberto Mejia/99 2.50 6.00
52 Gavin Cecchini/99 2.50 6.00
53 Jacoby Jones/99 3.00 8.00
54 Yohander Mendez/99 2.50 6.00
55 Chad Pinder/99 2.50 6.00
56 Carson Kelly/99 3.00 8.00
57 Trey Mancini/99 5.00 12.00
58 Teoscar Hernandez/99 8.00 20.00
59 Ryon Healy/99 3.00 8.00
60 Erik Gonzalez/99 2.50 6.00
61 Roman Quinn/99 2.50 6.00
62 Matt Olson/99 5.00 12.00
63 Jharel Cotton/99 2.50 6.00
64 Jake Thompson/99 2.50 6.00
65 Renato Nunez/99 5.00 12.00
66 Jose Rondon/99 2.50 6.00
67 Brendan Rodgers/99 3.00 8.00
68 Kevin Maitan/99 5.00 12.00
69 Victor Robles/99 6.00 15.00
70 Cody Bellinger/99 8.00 20.00
71 Gleyber Torres/99 5.00 12.00
72 Jake Arrieta/25 3.00 8.00
73 Brandon Crawford/99 3.00 8.00
74 Alex Gordon/99 3.00 8.00
75 Eric Hosmer/99 3.00 8.00
76 Adam Duvall/99 4.00 10.00
77 Buster Posey/99 5.00 12.00
78 Yoenis Cespedes/99 4.00 10.00
79 Rick Porcello/99 3.00 8.00
80 Mookie Betts/99 6.00 15.00
81 Cole Hamels/99 3.00 8.00
82 Salvador Perez/99 3.00 8.00
83 Joey Votto/99 4.00 10.00
84 Josh Donaldson/99 3.00 8.00
85 Kris Bryant/99 8.00 20.00
87 Clayton Kershaw/49 8.00 20.00
88 Yadier Molina/99 4.00 10.00
89 Tim Tebow/99 10.00 25.00
90 Corey Seager/99 4.00 10.00
91 Kenta Maeda/99 3.00 8.00
92 Carlos Gonzalez/99 3.00 8.00
93 Josh Tomlin/99 2.50 6.00
94 Felix Hernandez/99 3.00 8.00
95 Jackie Bradley Jr./99 4.00 10.00
96 Manny Machado/99 4.00 10.00
97 Ken Griffey Jr./49 6.00 15.00
98 George Brett/99 8.00 20.00
99 Cal Ripken/99 8.00 20.00
100 Kirby Puckett/99 6.00 15.00

2017 Immaculate Collection Immaculate Trio Players Memorabilia

RANDOM INSERTS IN PACKS
PRINT RUNS B/WN 5-99 COPIES PER
NO PRICING ON QTY 5
*BLUE/25: .6X TO 1.5X BASIC
1 Benintendi/Swanson/Moncada/99 8.00 20.00
2 Judge/Bregman/Dahl/99 12.00 30.00
3 Jones/Bell/Renfroe/99 6.00 15.00
4 Reyes/Fulmer/Glasnow/99 3.00 8.00
5 Trout/Posey/Bryant/49 15.00 40.00
6 Dawson/Sandberg/Banks/99 12.00 30.00
8 Arrieta/Kershaw/Price/25 8.00 20.00
9 Mauer/Sano/Dozier/25 4.00 10.00
10 Thomas/Abreu/Moncada/99 8.00 20.00
11 Benintendi/Pedroia/Ortiz/99 8.00 20.00
12 Jones/Swnsn/Frman/99 6.00 15.00
13 Helton/Pujols/Delgado/99 5.00 12.00
14 Ripken/Brett/Griffey Jr./25 30.00 80.00

2017 Immaculate Collection Immaculate Trios Memorabilia

RANDOM INSERTS IN PACKS
PRINT RUNS B/WN 7-99 COPIES PER
NO PRICING ON QTY 7
*BLUE/25: .6X TO 1.5X BASIC
1 Mike Napoli/99 2.50 6.00
2 Kris Bryant/49 8.00 20.00
3 Eric Hosmer/99 3.00 8.00
4 Troy Tulowitzki/99 4.00 10.00
5 Adam Duvall/99 3.00 8.00
6 Mike Trout/49 20.00 50.00
8 Madison Bumgarner/99 3.00 8.00
9 Jose Bautista/99 3.00 8.00
10 Cole Hamels/99 3.00 8.00
11 Jacob deGrom/99 4.00 10.00
12 Jean Segura/49 3.00 8.00
13 Dustin Pedroia/99 6.00 15.00
14 Trea Turner/99 3.00 8.00
15 Joey Votto/99 6.00 15.00

2017 Immaculate Collection Immaculate Triple Material Autographs

RANDOM INSERTS IN PACKS
PRINT RUNS B/WN 10-99 COPIES PER
NO PRICING ON QTY 10
EXCHANGE DEADLINE 2/16/2019
1 Trea Turner/25 15.00 40.00
2 Joe Panik/25 12.00 30.00
3 Yadier Molina/25 40.00 100.00
4 Freddie Freeman/25
6 Cody Bellinger/25 50.00 120.00
7 Kyle Schwarber/25 15.00 40.00
8 Stephen Piscotty/25 8.00 20.00
9 Gary Sanchez/99 15.00 40.00
10 Ian Happ/99 12.00 30.00
11 Marcus Stroman/25
12 Xander Bogaerts/25 20.00 50.00
13 Justin Turner/25
14 Charlie Blackmon/49 10.00 25.00
15 Corey Kluber/25 8.00 20.00
16 Chris Sale/99 15.00 40.00
18 Anthony Rizzo/25 20.00 50.00
19 Noah Syndergaard/25 12.00 30.00
20 Jason Kipnis/25 10.00 25.00

2017 Immaculate Collection Immaculate Triple Material Autographs Blue

*BLUE/25: .5X TO 1.2X p/r 49-99
RANDOM INSERTS IN PACKS
PRINT RUNS B/WN 5-25 COPIES PER
NO PRICING ON QTY 10 OR LESS
EXCHANGE DEADLINE 2/16/2019
9 Gary Sanchez/25 25.00 60.00

2017 Immaculate Collection Immaculate Triple Signatures

RANDOM INSERTS IN PACKS
PRINT RUNS B/WN 10-25 COPIES PER
NO PRICING ON QTY 10
EXCHANGE DEADLINE 2/16/2019
1 Bnntndi/Swnsn/Mncda 60.00 150.00
2 Bnntndi/Rice/Brdly Jr. 60.00 150.00
3 Rdgrs/Hltn/Arndo 50.00 120.00
4 Dnldsn/Mchdo/Bltre 40.00 100.00
5 Dzr/Pdra/Altve 40.00 100.00
6 Rssll/Rzzo/Baez 50.00 120.00
7 Klbr/Lndr/Rmrz 75.00 200.00

2017 Immaculate Collection Immaculate Tweed Weave Signatures

RANDOM INSERTS IN PACKS
PRINT RUNS B/WN 10-99 COPIES PER
NO PRICING ON QTY 15 OR LESS
EXCHANGE DEADLINE 2/16/2019
*BLUE/25: .5X TO 1.2X p/r 49-99
2 Nelson Cruz/99 6.00 15.00
3 Don Sutton/49 4.00 10.00
4 Goose Gossage/49 10.00 25.00
5 Nomar Mazara/49 6.00 15.00
6 Addison Russell/49 10.00 25.00
8 Paul Molitor/25 12.00 30.00
9 Freddie Freeman/25 12.00 30.00
10 Gerrit Cole/25 8.00 20.00
11 Orlando Cepeda/25 20.00 50.00
13 Yoan Moncada/25 20.00 50.00
16 George Springer/25 8.00 20.00
17 Brooks Robinson/25 12.00 30.00
18 Edgar Renteria/25 6.00 15.00
19 Phil Niekro/25 8.00 20.00
20 Yasmany Tomas/25 4.00 10.00
22 Will Clark/25 12.00 30.00
24 Bob Gibson/25 15.00 40.00
25 Edwin Encarnacion/20 20.00 50.00
26 Manny Machado/20 20.00 50.00
27 Yoenis Cespedes/20 10.00 25.00
36 Cody Bellinger/99 60.00 150.00
37 Aaron Judge/25 125.00 300.00

2017 Immaculate Collection Rookie Autograph Premium Patch

RANDOM INSERTS IN PACKS
STATED PRINT RUN 25 SER.#'d SETS
EXCHANGE DEADLINE 2/16/2019
1 Yoan Moncada 25.00 60.00
2 Andrew Benintendi 50.00 120.00
3 Dansby Swanson EXCH 20.00 50.00
4 Alex Bregman 25.00 60.00
5 David Dahl 8.00 20.00
6 Tyler Glasnow 30.00 80.00
8 Alex Reyes 15.00 40.00
9 Orlando Arcia 20.00 50.00
10 Jose De Leon 6.00 15.00
11 Manuel Margot 6.00 15.00
12 Aaron Judge 150.00 400.00
14 Hunter Renfroe 10.00 25.00
15 Jorge Alfaro 15.00 40.00
16 Carson Fulmer 10.00 25.00
17 Ryon Healy 15.00 40.00

2017 Immaculate Collection Shadowbox Materials

RANDOM INSERTS IN PACKS
PRINT RUNS B/WN 1-25 COPIES PER
NO PRICING ON QTY 15 OR LESS
3 Ichiro/25 20.00 50.00
5 Buster Posey/25 15.00 40.00
6 Manny Machado/25 15.00 40.00
7 Mickey Mantle/25 60.00 120.00
13 Corey Seager/25 10.00 25.00
14 Kyle Schwarber/25 5.00 12.00
15 Miguel Sano/25 10.00 25.00
16 Mike Napoli/25 6.00 15.00
25 Miguel Cabrera/25 5.00 12.00
26 Alex Gordon/25 4.00 10.00
27 Felix Hernandez/25 4.00 10.00
28 Robinson Cano/25 4.00 10.00
29 Dallas Keuchel/25 4.00 10.00
30 Jackie Bradley Jr./25 12.00 30.00
31 Yoenis Cespedes/25 10.00 25.00
32 Salvador Perez/25 4.00 10.00
33 Adrian Gonzalez/25 4.00 10.00
34 Matt Carpenter/25 5.00 12.00
37 Kyle Seager/25 3.00 8.00
38 Rollie Fingers/25 10.00 25.00
40 Barry Larkin/25 10.00 25.00
41 Gary Carter/25 15.00 40.00
48 Todd Frazier/25 4.00 10.00
53 Javier Baez/25 6.00 15.00
54 Addison Russell/25 5.00 12.00
55 Adam Duvall/25 15.00 40.00
56 Billy Hamilton/25 4.00 10.00
57 Brandon Crawford/25 12.00 30.00
62 George Springer/25 4.00 10.00

2018 Immaculate Collection

48-147 PRINT RUN 99 SER.#'d SETS
EXCHANGE DEADLINE 2/1/2020
1 Anthony Banda/99 JSY AU RC 3.00 8.00
2 Luiz Gohara/99 JSY AU RC 3.00 8.00
3 Max Fried/99 JSY AU RC 12.00 30.00
4 O.Albies/99 JSY AU RC 12.00 30.00
5 Lucas Sims/99 JSY AU RC 3.00 8.00
6 A.Hays/99 JSY AU RC 10.00 25.00
7 Chance Sisco/99 JSY AU RC 4.00 10.00
8 Anthony Santander/99 JSY AU RC 3.00 8.00
9 Victor Caratini/99 JSY AU RC 4.00 10.00
10 Nicky Delmonico/99 JSY AU RC 3.00 8.00
11 Tyler Mahle/99 JSY AU RC 4.00 10.00
12 F.Mejia/99 JSY AU RC 6.00 15.00
13 G.Allen/99 JSY AU RC 8.00 20.00
14 R.McMahon/99 JSY AU RC 8.00 20.00
15 J.D. Davis/99 JSY AU RC 4.00 10.00
16 Cameron Gallagher/99 JSY AU RC 3.00 8.00
18 A.Verdugo/49 JSY AU RC 10.00 25.00
19 Kyle Farmer/99 JSY AU RC 3.00 8.00
20 B.Anderson/99 JSY AU RC 12.00 30.00
21 Dillon Peters/99 JSY AU RC 3.00 8.00
22 Brandon Woodruff/99 JSY AU RC 4.00 10.00
23 M.Garver/99 JSY AU RC 3.00 8.00
24 Zack Granite/99 JSY AU RC 3.00 8.00
25 Felix Jorge/99 JSY AU RC 3.00 8.00
26 Tomas Nido/99 JSY AU RC 3.00 8.00
27 R.Hoskins/99 JSY AU RC 25.00 60.00
28 Chris Flexen/99 JSY AU RC 3.00 8.00
29 A.Rosario/99 JSY AU RC 4.00 10.00
30 C.Frazier/99 JSY AU RC 6.00 15.00
31 M.Andujar/99 JSY AU RC 20.00 50.00
32 Tyler Wade/99 JSY AU RC 4.00 10.00
33 Dustin Fowler/99 JSY AU RC 3.00 8.00
34 Paul Blackburn/99 JSY AU RC 3.00 8.00
35 J.P. Crawford/99 JSY AU RC 5.00 12.00
36 Nick Williams/99 JSY AU RC 4.00 10.00
37 S.Ohtani/99 JSY AU RC 250.00 400.00
38 Thyago Vieira/99 JSY AU RC 3.00 8.00
39 Reyes Moronta/99 JSY AU RC 3.00 8.00
40 J.Flaherty/99 JSY AU RC 5.00 12.00
41 H.Bader/99 JSY AU RC 5.00 12.00
42 Willie Calhoun/99 JSY AU RC 4.00 10.00
43 Richard Urena/99 JSY AU RC 3.00 8.00
44 V.Robles/99 JSY AU RC 6.00 15.00
45 Erick Fedde/99 JSY AU RC 3.00 8.00
46 Andrew Stevenson/99 JSY AU RC 3.00 8.00
47 R.Devers/99 JSY AU RC 12.00 30.00
48 Mike Trout 5.00 12.00
49 Miguel Cabrera 1.00 2.50
50 Clayton Kershaw 2.00 5.00
51 Buster Posey 1.25 3.00
52 Jose Altuve .75 2.00
53 Aaron Judge 2.50 6.00
54 Adrian Beltre 1.00 2.50
55 Yadier Molina 1.00 2.50
56 Giancarlo Stanton 1.00 2.50
57 Cody Bellinger 2.00 5.00
58 Nolan Arenado 1.25 3.00
59 Paul Goldschmidt 1.00 2.50
60 Max Scherzer 1.00 2.50
61 Corey Kluber .75 2.00
62 Gary Sanchez 1.00 2.50
63 Andrew McCutchen 1.00 2.50
64 Francisco Lindor 1.00 2.50
65 Marcell Ozuna 1.00 2.50
66 Corey Seager 1.00 2.50
67 Eric Hosmer .75 2.00
68 George Springer .75 2.00
69 Charlie Blackmon 1.00 2.50
70 Chris Sale 1.00 2.50
71 Noah Syndergaard .75 2.00
72 Madison Bumgarner .75 2.00
73 Jose Ramirez .75 2.00
74 Josh Donaldson .75 2.00
75 Trea Turner .75 2.00
76 Mookie Betts 1.50 4.00
77 Yu Darvish 1.00 2.50
78 Luis Severino .75 2.00
79 Robinson Cano .75 2.00
80 Miguel Sano .75 2.00
81 Bryce Harper 1.50 4.00
82 Joey Votto 1.00 2.50
83 Justin Turner 1.00 2.50
84 Albert Pujols 1.25 3.00
85 Xander Bogaerts 1.00 2.50
86 Kris Bryant 1.25 3.00
87 Anthony Rizzo 1.50 4.00
88 Daniel Murphy .75 2.00
89 Carlos Correa 1.00 2.50
90 Salvador Perez .75 2.00
91 Byron Buxton .75 2.00
92 Didi Gregorius .75 2.00
93 J.D. Martinez 1.00 2.50
94 Yoan Moncada 1.00 2.50
95 Joey Gallo .75 2.00
96 Andrew Benintendi 1.00 2.50
97 Dansby Swanson 1.00 2.50
98 Freddie Freeman 1.25 3.00
99 Jose Abreu 1.00 2.50
100 Dee Gordon .60 1.50
101 Nelson Cruz 1.00 2.50
102 Khris Davis 1.00 2.50
103 Ernie Banks 1.00 2.50
104 Lou Gehrig 2.00 5.00
105 Joe Jackson 1.25 3.00
106 Babe Ruth 2.00 5.00
107 Honus Wagner 1.00 2.50
108 Joe DiMaggio 2.00 5.00
109 Mickey Mantle 3.00 8.00
110 Roberto Clemente 6.00 15.00
111 Roger Maris 1.00 2.50
112 Stan Musial 1.50 4.00
113 Ted Williams 2.00 5.00
114 Jackie Robinson 1.00 2.50
115 Babe Ruth 2.00 5.00
116 Ken Griffey Jr. 2.50 6.00
117 Nolan Ryan 4.00 10.00
118 Masahiro Tanaka .75 2.00
119 Ender Inciarte .60 1.50
120 DJ LeMahieu 1.00 2.50
121 Manny Machado 1.00 2.50
122 Nomar Mazara .60 1.50
123 Jonathan Schoop .60 1.50
124 Mitch Haniger .75 2.00
125 Matt Chapman 1.00 2.50
126 Hunter Renfroe .60 1.50
127 Nick Castellanos 1.00 2.50
128 Christian Yelich 1.25 3.00
129 A.J. Pollock .60 1.50
130 Matt Olson .60 1.50
131 Manuel Margot .60 1.50
132 Josh Bell .75 2.00
133 Paul DeJong 1.00 2.50
134 Trey Mancini .75 2.00
135 Addison Russell .75 2.00
136 Lewis Brinson .60 1.50
137 Bradley Zimmer .60 1.50
138 Jose Berrios .75 2.00
139 Dallas Keuchel .75 2.00
140 Corey Dickerson .60 1.50
141 Ian Happ .75 2.00
142 David Dahl .60 1.50
143 Lance McCullers .60 1.50
144 Gerrit Cole 1.00 2.50
145 Michael Conforto .75 2.00
146 Odubel Herrera .75 2.00
147 Kevin Kiermaier .75 2.00

2018 Immaculate Collection Gold

*GOLD JSY AU: .4X TO 1X BASIC
RANDOM INSERTS IN PACKS
PRINT RUNS B/WN 5-49 COPIES PER
NO PRICING ON QTY 5
EXCHANGE DEADLINE 2/1/2020
17 Walker Buehler JSY AU/49 12.00 30.00
30 Clint Frazier JSY AU/25 6.00 15.00

2018 Immaculate Collection Red

*RED: 1X TO 2.5X BASIC
RANDOM INSERTS IN PACKS
STATED PRINT RUN 25 SER.#'d SETS

2018 Immaculate Collection Dugout Collection Autographs

RANDOM INSERTS IN PACKS
PRINT RUNS B/WN 5-99 COPIES PER
NO PRICING ON QTY 15 OR LESS
EXCHANGE DEADLINE 2/1/2020
*BLUE/25: .6X TO 1.5X p/r 99
*BLUE/25: .5X TO 1.2X p/r 49
*BLUE/25: .4X TO 1X p/r 25
1 Clint Frazier/99 8.00 20.00
4 Victor Robles/99 15.00 40.00
5 Jim Rice/99 4.00 10.00
6 Stephen Piscotty/99 4.00 10.00
8 David Ortiz/25 20.00 50.00
9 Nick Williams/99 3.00 8.00
10 Josh Bell/99 3.00 8.00
11 Erick Fedde/99 2.50 6.00
12 Luiz Gohara/99 2.50 6.00
13 Mitch Keller/99 3.00 8.00
14 Andrew Stevenson/99 2.50 6.00
15 Kyle Lewis/99 5.00 12.00
16 Kyle Tucker/99 6.00 15.00
17 Justus Sheffield/99 8.00 20.00
18 Leody Taveras/99 3.00 8.00
19 Carson Fulmer/99 2.50 6.00
20 Max Fried/99 10.00 25.00
26 Carlos Correa/49 15.00 40.00
27 Robin Yount/99 12.00 30.00
28 Tyler Glasnow/99 2.50 6.00
34 Xander Bogaerts/20 15.00 40.00
37 Keith Hernandez/20 10.00 25.00
41 Rickey Henderson/25 20.00 50.00
52 Ted Simmons/49 20.00 50.00
53 Anthony Rizzo/49 15.00 40.00

2018 Immaculate Collection Immaculate Autographs

RANDOM INSERTS IN PACKS
PRINT RUNS B/WN 5-99 COPIES PER
NO PRICING ON QTY 15 OR LESS
EXCHANGE DEADLINE 2/1/2020
*BLUE/25: .6X TO 1.5X p/r 70-99
*BLUE/25: .5X TO 1.2X p/r 49
*BLUE/25: .4X TO 1X p/r 25
3 Carlos Martinez/70 3.00 8.00
4 Darryl Strawberry/70 5.00 12.00
6 George Springer/99 8.00 20.00
7 Gerrit Cole/25 8.00 20.00
8 Joey Gallo/25 8.00 20.00
9 Jose Abreu/25 8.00 20.00
10 Manny Machado/49 12.00 50.00
12 Nelson Cruz/25 6.00 15.00
14 Trea Turner/25 10.00 25.00
20 Adam Jones/25 6.00 15.00
21 Addison Russell/25 5.00 12.00
23 Byron Buxton/25 5.00 12.00
24 Evan Gattis/99 3.00 8.00

2018 Immaculate Collection Immaculate Carbon Material Signatures

RANDOM INSERTS IN PACKS
PRINT RUNS B/WN 5-25 COPIES PER
NO PRICING ON QTY 15 OR LESS
EXCHANGE DEADLINE 2/1/2020
3 Andres Galarraga/25 6.00 15.00
4 Andrew Benintendi/25 8.00 20.00
15 Juan Gonzalez/25 8.00 20.00
19 Starling Marte/25 6.00 15.00

2018 Immaculate Collection Immaculate Carbon Signatures

RANDOM INSERTS IN PACKS
PRINT RUNS B/WN 5-99 COPIES PER
NO PRICING ON QTY 15 OR LESS
EXCHANGE DEADLINE 2/1/2020
*BLUE/25: .6X TO 1.5X p/r 99
*BLUE/25: .5X TO 1.2X p/r 49
*BLUE/25: .4X TO 1X p/r 20-25
3 Andres Galarraga/49 5.00 12.00
4 Andrew Benintendi/25 25.00 60.00
6 Cody Bellinger/20
7 Jose Abreu/20 8.00 20.00
8 Darryl Strawberry/49 6.00 15.00
10 Edwin Encarnacion/25 8.00 20.00
12 Eric Thames/49 4.00 10.00
13 Gary Sanchez/20 20.00 50.00
17 Jim Rice/25 6.00 15.00
18 Jonathan Lucroy/25 5.00 12.00
19 Juan Gonzalez/99 5.00 12.00
21 Nomar Mazara/20 4.00 10.00
25 Starling Marte/25 5.00 12.00
26 Barry Larkin/20 15.00 40.00
27 Trey Mancini/49 4.00 10.00
28 Xander Bogaerts/25 15.00 40.00
29 Fernando Tatis Jr./49 40.00 100.00
30 Bo Bichette/49 15.00 40.00

2018 Immaculate Collection Immaculate Dual Autographs

RANDOM INSERTS IN PACKS
PRINT RUNS B/WN 7-49 COPIES PER
NO PRICING ON QTY 7
EXCHANGE DEADLINE 2/1/2020
*GOLD/25: .5X TO 1.2X p/r 49
1 Williams/Hoskins/49 30.00 80.00
2 Sims/Albies/49 15.00 40.00
3 Hays/Sisco/49 20.00 50.00
5 Frazier/Andujar/49 60.00 150.00
6 Rosario/Crawford/49 8.00 20.00
7 Mejia/Caratini/49 4.00 10.00
8 Albies/Robles/49 30.00 80.00
9 Frazier/Hoskins/49 25.00 60.00
11 Jimenez/Robert/49 100.00 250.00
12 Springer/Altuve/25 25.00 60.00
13 Bellinger/Turner/25 25.00 60.00

2018 Immaculate Collection Immaculate Dual Material Autographs

RANDOM INSERTS IN PACKS
PRINT RUNS B/WN 10-99 COPIES PER
NO PRICING ON QTY 15 OR LESS
EXCHANGE DEADLINE 2/1/2020
*BLUE/25: .6X TO 1.5X p/r 49-99
*BLUE/25: .4X TO 1X p/r 20-25
148 Scott Kingery/99 10.00 25.00
149 Ronald Guzman/99 3.00 8.00
150 Christian Villanueva/99 6.00 15.00
151 Ronald Acuna Jr./99 75.00 200.00
152 Gleyber Torres/99 30.00 80.00
DMAAG Adrian Gonzalez/25 6.00 15.00
DMABB Byron Buxton/25 6.00 15.00
DMACC Carlos Correa/49 20.00 50.00
DMACS Chris Sale/25 12.00 30.00
DMAHP Hunter Pence/25 10.00 25.00
DMAJA Jose Abreu/20 10.00 25.00
DMAJT Justin Turner/25 15.00 40.00
DMAJV Jonathan Villar/99 3.00 8.00
DMANM Nomar Mazara/25 5.00 12.00
DMAOC Orlando Cepeda/25 12.00 30.00
DMASM Starling Marte/49 4.00 10.00

2018 Immaculate Collection Immaculate Jumbo

RANDOM INSERTS IN PACKS
PRINT RUNS B/WN 4-99 COPIES PER
NO PRICING ON QTY 15 OR LESS
1 Anthony Banda/99 2.00 5.00
2 Luiz Gohara/99 2.00 5.00
3 Max Fried/99 8.00 20.00
4 Ozzie Albies/99 5.00 12.00
5 Lucas Sims/99 2.00 5.00
6 Austin Hays/99 3.00 8.00
7 Chance Sisco/99 2.50 6.00
8 Anthony Santander/99 2.00 5.00
9 Victor Caratini/99 2.50 6.00
10 Nicky Delmonico/99 2.00 5.00
11 Tyler Mahle/99 2.50 6.00
12 Francisco Mejia/99 2.50 6.00
13 Greg Allen/99 2.00 5.00
14 Ryan McMahon/99 2.50 6.00
15 J.D. Davis/99 2.50 6.00
16 Cameron Gallagher/99 2.00 5.00
17 Walker Buehler/99 4.00 10.00
18 Alex Verdugo/99 3.00 8.00
19 Kyle Farmer/99 2.00 5.00
20 Brian Anderson/99 2.50 6.00
21 Dillon Peters/99 2.00 5.00
22 Brandon Woodruff/99 2.50 6.00
23 Mitch Garver/99 2.00 5.00
24 Zack Granite/99 2.00 5.00
25 Felix Jorge/99 2.00 5.00
26 Tomas Nido/99 2.00 5.00
27 Rhys Hoskins/99 6.00 15.00
28 Chris Flexen/99 2.00 5.00
29 Amed Rosario/99 2.50 6.00
30 Clint Frazier/99 4.00 10.00
31 Miguel Andujar/99 6.00 15.00
32 Tyler Wade/99 2.50 6.00
33 Dustin Fowler/99 2.00 5.00
34 Paul Blackburn/99 2.00 5.00
35 J.P. Crawford/99 2.00 5.00
36 Nick Williams/99 2.50 6.00
37 Shohei Ohtani/99 12.00 30.00
38 Thyago Vieira/99 2.00 5.00
39 Reyes Moronta/99 2.00 5.00
40 Jack Flaherty/99 3.00 8.00
41 Harrison Bader/99 3.00 8.00
42 Willie Calhoun/99 2.50 6.00
43 Richard Urena/99 2.00 5.00
44 Victor Robles/99 4.00 10.00
45 Erick Fedde/99 2.00 5.00
46 Andrew Stevenson/99 2.00 5.00
47 Rafael Devers/99 6.00 15.00
48 Shohei Ohtani/99 12.00 30.00
50 Vladimir Guerrero Jr./99 12.00 30.00
51 Brendan Rodgers/99 2.50 6.00
52 Gleyber Torres/99 8.00 20.00
53 Eloy Jimenez/99 6.00 15.00
54 Lazaro Armenteros/99 4.00 10.00
55 Kevin Maitan/99 2.50 6.00
63 Eric Thames/25 4.00 10.00
64 Stephen Piscotty/99 2.00 5.00
69 Corey Seager/99 3.00 8.00
70 Miguel Sano/99 2.50 6.00
71 Andrew Benintendi/99 3.00 8.00
72 Francisco Lindor/20 8.00 20.00
73 Franklin Barreto/99 2.00 5.00
74 Lewis Brinson/99 2.00 5.00
75 Michael Kopech/99 4.00 10.00
77 Aaron Judge/99 10.00 25.00
78 Nick Senzel/99 5.00 12.00
82 Ronald Acuna Jr./99 12.00 30.00
98 Bo Bichette/99 8.00 20.00
99 Fernando Tatis Jr./99 15.00 40.00
100 Juan Soto/99 15.00 40.00

2018 Immaculate Collection Immaculate Jumbo Bats

RANDOM INSERTS IN PACKS
PRINT RUNS B/WN 5-99 COPIES PER
NO PRICING ON QTY 10 OR LESS
*RED/25: .6X TO 1.5X p/r 99
*RED/25: .5X TO 1.2X p/r 49
*RED/25: .4X TO 1X p/r 25
1 Adrian Beltre/49 4.00 10.00
2 Albert Pujols/25 8.00 20.00
3 Anthony Rizzo/49 5.00 12.00
5 Barry Larkin/49 3.00 8.00
6 Shohei Ohtani/49 15.00 40.00
7 Carlos Correa/49 4.00 10.00
8 Carlos Delgado/25 3.00 8.00
9 Eddie Murray/49 6.00 15.00
10 Evan Longoria/25 4.00 10.00
11 Gary Sheffield/25 8.00 20.00
13 Giancarlo Stanton/25 10.00 25.00
14 Ivan Rodriguez/49 3.00 8.00
15 Joe Torre/25 10.00 25.00
16 Joey Votto/25 6.00 15.00
17 Jose Canseco/49 8.00 20.00
18 Jose Ramirez/49 3.00 8.00
20 Omar Vizquel/49 3.00 8.00
21 Rafael Palmeiro/49 3.00 8.00
22 Roberto Alomar/49 8.00 20.00
23 Robin Yount/25 10.00 25.00
25 Yasiel Puig/49 4.00 10.00

2018 Immaculate Collection Immaculate Legend Relics

RANDOM INSERTS IN PACKS
PRINT RUNS B/WN 5-49 COPIES PER
NO PRICING ON QTY 15 OR LESS
*RED/25: .5X TO 1.2X p/r 49
*RED/25: .4X TO 1X p/r 25
3 Billy Martin/49 20.00 50.00
4 Ernie Banks/49 6.00 15.00
7 Herb Pennock/25 10.00 25.00
9 Jackie Robinson/25 20.00 50.00
10 Joe Cronin/25 8.00 20.00
13 Kiki Cuyler/25 4.00 10.00
16 Lloyd Waner/25 5.00 12.00
18 Luke Appling/25 4.00 10.00
19 Max Carey/25 8.00 20.00
20 Mickey Mantle/25 60.00 150.00
22 Paul Waner/25 6.00 15.00

23 Pee Wee Reese/25 10.00 25.00
26 Stan Musial/25 8.00 20.00
29 Tommy Henrich/49 2.50 6.00

2018 Immaculate Collection Immaculate Material Signatures

RANDOM INSERTS IN PACKS
PRINT RUNS B/WN 10-99 COPIES PER
NO PRICING ON QTY 15 OR LESS
EXCHANGE DEADLINE 2/1/2020
1 Jose Abreu/25 10.00 25.00
2 Josh Donaldson/25 10.00 25.00
3 Aaron Judge/49 60.00 150.00
6 Freddie Freeman/25 12.00 30.00
7 Jim Rice/25 12.00 30.00
8 Cody Bellinger/35 25.00 60.00
9 Manny Machado/25 15.00 40.00
11 Wil Myers/25 5.00 12.00
12 Matt Olson/99 4.00 10.00
13 Salvador Perez/25 12.00 30.00
15 Trevor Story/49 5.00 12.00
16 Starling Marte/49 4.00 10.00
17 Nolan Arenado/25 20.00 50.00
18 Marcell Ozuna/35 8.00 20.00
20 Justin Turner/49 10.00 25.00
21 Juan Gonzalez/99 5.00 12.00
23 Andrew Benintendi/25 8.00 20.00
24 Trey Mancini/49 4.00 10.00
25 Gary Sheffield/20 12.00 30.00
26 Gary Sanchez/25 15.00 40.00
28 Cole Hamels/35 8.00 20.00
29 Yoenis Cespedes/25 12.00 30.00
30 Don Mattingly/25 30.00 80.00
31 Barry Larkin/25 6.00 15.00
32 Jeff Bagwell/20 6.00 15.00
33 Bo Jackson/25 40.00 100.00
34 Adrian Beltre/35 15.00 40.00
35 Luis Robert/99 20.00 50.00
36 Carlos Gonzalez/25 6.00 15.00
37 Dustin Pedroia/25 12.00 30.00
38 Noah Syndergaard/25
39 Alan Trammell/25 20.00 50.00
43 Andy Pettitte/25 12.00 30.00
44 Bernie Williams/25 12.00 30.00
45 Byron Buxton/35 5.00 12.00
48 Dwight Gooden/25 12.00 30.00
49 Hunter Pence/35 8.00 20.00
50 Joe Panik/49 4.00 10.00
51 Kyle Seager/49 3.00 8.00
52 Marcus Stroman/49 6.00 15.00
53 Mike Napoli/49 3.00 8.00

2018 Immaculate Collection Immaculate Material Signatures Gold

*GOLD/49: .4X TO 1X p/r 49-99
*GOLD/20-25: .4X TO 1X p/r 20-25
*GOLD/20-25: .5X TO 1.2X p/r 35
*GOLD/20-25: .6X TO 1.5X p/r 49-99
RANDOM INSERTS IN PACKS
PRINT RUNS B/WN 5-49 COPIES PER
NO PRICING ON QTY 15 OR LESS
EXCHANGE DEADLINE 2/1/2020
46 Corey Seager/20 15.00 40.00

2018 Immaculate Collection Immaculate Parchment Signatures

RANDOM INSERTS IN PACKS
PRINT RUNS B/WN 5-99 COPIES PER
NO PRICING ON QTY 15 OR LESS
EXCHANGE DEADLINE 2/1/2020
*BLUE/25: .6X TO 1.5X p/r 79-99
*BLUE/25: .5X TO 1.2X p/r 35-49
*BLUE/25: .4X TO 1X p/r 20-25
3 Carlos Gonzalez/79 3.00 8.00
5 Charles Johnson/99 2.50 6.00
6 Darrell Evans/99 2.50 6.00
8 Dwight Gooden/24 10.00 25.00
10 Gaylord Perry/35 6.00 15.00
11 Ian Kinsler/25 5.00 12.00
12 Jeff Bagwell/25 5.00 12.00
15 Fernando Tatis Jr./99 40.00 100.00
16 Keith Hernandez/49 8.00 20.00
17 Lee Smith/99 5.00 12.00
18 Kyle Tucker/99 6.00 15.00
19 Luis Tiant/79 6.00 15.00
22 Salvador Perez/25 10.00 25.00
23 Tony Oliva/25 15.00 40.00
24 Forrest Whitley/99 6.00 15.00
25 Yoenis Cespedes/20 6.00 15.00

2018 Immaculate Collection Immaculate Quad Material Autographs

RANDOM INSERTS IN PACKS
PRINT RUNS B/WN 5-99 COPIES PER
NO PRICING ON QTY 10 OR LESS
EXCHANGE DEADLINE 2/1/2020
*BLUE/25: .6X TO 1.5X p/r 49-99
*BLUE/25: .4X TO 1X p/r 20-25
2 Victor Robles/25 15.00 40.00
3 Chance Sisco/99 4.00 10.00
4 Michael Kopech/49 15.00 40.00
7 Brendan Rodgers/49 8.00 20.00
9 Mitch Keller/99 8.00 20.00
11 Estevan Florial/99 25.00 60.00
12 Ryan McMahon/49 6.00 15.00
13 Alex Verdugo/99 6.00 15.00
15 Paul Molitor/25 10.00 25.00
18 Nick Williams/99 4.00 10.00
19 Tyler Wade/99 4.00 10.00
20 Cody Bellinger/20 30.00 80.00

2018 Immaculate Collection Immaculate Rookie Bat Autographs

RANDOM INSERTS IN PACKS
PRINT RUNS B/WN 10-99 COPIES PER
NO PRICING ON QTY 10
EXCHANGE DEADLINE 2/1/2020
2 Amed Rosario/99 8.00 20.00
3 Andrew Stevenson/99 2.50 6.00
4 Austin Hays/99 4.00 10.00
6 Chance Sisco/99 4.00 10.00
7 Clint Frazier/25 12.00 30.00
8 Dustin Fowler/99 2.50 6.00
9 Francisco Mejia/37 4.00 10.00
12 Max Fried/99 10.00 25.00
14 Mitch Garver/99 2.50 6.00
16 Nicky Delmonico/99 2.50 6.00
18 Rafael Devers/49 10.00 25.00
19 Rhys Hoskins/25 30.00 80.00
20 Ryan McMahon/99 3.00 8.00
22 Victor Caratini/99 3.00 8.00
23 Victor Robles/47 12.00 30.00
24 Willie Calhoun/99 3.00 8.00
25 Zack Granite/99 2.50 6.00

2018 Immaculate Collection Immaculate Rookie Bat Autographs Red

*RED/49: .5X TO 1.2X p/r 99
*RED/49: .4X TO 1X p/r 37-49
*RED/25: .6X TO 1.5X p/r 99
*RED/25: .5X TO 1.2X p/r 37-49
RANDOM INSERTS IN PACKS
PRINT RUNS B/WN 5-49 COPIES PER
NO PRICING ON QTY 15 OR LESS
EXCHANGE DEADLINE 2/1/2020
15 Nick Williams/49 4.00 10.00

2018 Immaculate Collection Immaculate Rookie Carbon Signatures

RANDOM INSERTS IN PACKS
PRINT RUNS B/WN 5-99 COPIES PER
NO PRICING ON QTY 15 OR LESS
EXCHANGE DEADLINE 2/1/2020
*BLUE/25: .6X TO 1.5X p/r 99
*BLUE/25: .5X TO 1.2X p/r 35-49
*BLUE/25: .4X TO 1X p/r 25
1 Ozzie Albies/25 15.00 40.00
2 Austin Hays/99 4.00 10.00
3 Chance Sisco/99 4.00 10.00
4 Rafael Devers/46 10.00 25.00
5 Victor Caratini/99 3.00 8.00
6 Nicky Delmonico/99 2.50 6.00
7 Francisco Mejia/35 4.00 10.00
8 Ryan McMahon/99 3.00 8.00
10 Alex Verdugo/99 6.00 15.00
11 Mitch Garver/99 2.50 6.00
12 Amed Rosario/49 5.00 12.00
13 Clint Frazier/25 12.00 30.00
14 Dustin Fowler/99 2.50 6.00
17 Rhys Hoskins/25 30.00 80.00
19 Willie Calhoun/99 3.00 8.00
20 Victor Robles/35 12.00 30.00

2018 Immaculate Collection Immaculate Signatures

RANDOM INSERTS IN PACKS
PRINT RUNS B/WN 10-99 COPIES PER
NO PRICING ON QTY 15 OR LESS
EXCHANGE DEADLINE 2/1/2020
*GOLD/49: .5X TO 1.2X p/r 99
*GOLD/25: .5X TO 1.2X p/r 49
1 Willie McGee/99 6.00 15.00
3 Gary Sheffield/25 4.00 10.00
4 Shohei Ohtani/99 125.00 300.00
5 Buddy Bell/99 4.00 10.00
6 Lee Smith/99 5.00 12.00
9 Fred Lynn/25 6.00 15.00
10 Don Sutton/49 4.00 10.00
12 Joe Carter/25 5.00 12.00
14 Terry Francona/49 10.00 25.00
15 Darryl Strawberry/49 6.00 15.00
18 Chris Sale/25 15.00 40.00
19 Charles Johnson/99 2.50 6.00
20 Paul Goldschmidt/25 10.00 25.00
21 Jose Abreu/25 8.00 20.00
24 Eric Thames/99 3.00 8.00

2018 Immaculate Collection Immaculate Swatches

RANDOM INSERTS IN PACKS
PRINT RUNS B/WN 10-99 COPIES PER
NO PRICING ON QTY 10 OR LESS
1 Anthony Banda/99 2.00 5.00
2 Luiz Gohara/99 2.00 5.00
3 Max Fried/99 8.00 20.00
4 Ozzie Albies/99 5.00 12.00
5 Lucas Sims/99 2.00 5.00
6 Austin Hays/99 3.00 8.00
7 Chance Sisco/99 2.50 6.00
8 Anthony Santander/99 2.00 5.00
9 Victor Caratini/99 2.50 6.00
10 Nicky Delmonico/99 2.00 5.00
11 Tyler Mahle/99 2.50 6.00
12 Francisco Mejia/99 2.50 6.00
13 Greg Allen/99 2.00 5.00
14 Ryan McMahon/99 2.50 6.00
15 J.D. Davis/99 2.50 6.00
16 Cameron Gallagher/99 2.00 5.00
17 Walker Buehler/99 4.00 10.00
18 Alex Verdugo/99 3.00 8.00
19 Kyle Farmer/99 2.00 5.00
20 Brian Anderson/99 2.50 6.00
21 Dillon Peters/99 2.00 5.00
22 Brandon Woodruff/99 2.50 6.00
23 Mitch Garver/99 2.00 5.00
24 Zack Granite/99 2.00 5.00
25 Felix Jorge/99 2.00 5.00
26 Tomas Nido/99 2.00 5.00
27 Rhys Hoskins/99 6.00 15.00
28 Chris Flexen/99 2.00 5.00
29 Amed Rosario/99 2.50 6.00
30 Clint Frazier/99 4.00 10.00
31 Miguel Andujar/99 6.00 15.00
32 Tyler Wade/99 2.50 6.00
33 Dustin Fowler/99 2.00 5.00
34 Paul Blackburn/99 2.00 5.00
35 J.P. Crawford/99 2.00 5.00
36 Nick Williams/99 2.50 6.00
37 Shohei Ohtani/99 12.00 30.00
38 Thyago Vieira/99 2.00 5.00
39 Reyes Moronta/99 2.00 5.00
40 Jack Flaherty/99 3.00 8.00
41 Harrison Bader/99 3.00 8.00
42 Willie Calhoun/99 2.50 6.00
43 Richard Urena/99 2.00 5.00
44 Victor Robles/99 4.00 10.00
45 Erick Fedde/99 2.00 5.00
46 Andrew Stevenson/99 2.00 5.00
47 Rafael Devers/99 6.00 15.00
48 Kris Bryant/25 6.00 15.00
49 Bryce Harper/25 6.00 15.00
50 Mike Trout/25 10.00 25.00
51 Salvador Perez/99 2.50 6.00
52 Marcell Ozuna/99 3.00 8.00
53 Evan Longoria/99 2.50 6.00
55 J.D. Martinez/25 5.00 12.00
56 Miguel Cabrera/49 4.00 10.00
57 Adrian Beltre/25 4.00 10.00
58 Jose Altuve/49 3.00 8.00
59 Ronald Acuna Jr./99 12.00 30.00
60 Gleyber Torres/99 8.00 20.00
61 David Price/49 3.00 8.00
62 Noah Syndergaard/49 3.00 8.00
63 Yu Darvish/25 5.00 12.00
64 Vladimir Guerrero Jr./99 12.00 30.00
65 Jason Kipnis/25 4.00 10.00
66 Kirby Puckett/49 8.00 20.00
67 Anthony Rendon/49 4.00 10.00
68 Whit Merrifield/99 3.00 8.00
69 Buster Posey/49 5.00 12.00
70 Todd Frazier/99 2.50 6.00
71 Corey Seager/99 3.00 8.00
72 Andrew Benintendi/99 3.00 8.00
73 Jonathan Schoop/49 2.50 6.00
74 Manny Machado/49 4.00 10.00
76 Dustin Pedroia/49 4.00 10.00
77 Luis Severino/99 2.50 6.00
78 Mariano Rivera/99 4.00 10.00
79 Bernie Williams/99 2.50 6.00
80 Bo Jackson/49 8.00 20.00
81 David Ortiz/49 4.00 10.00
82 Eddie Murray/49 6.00 15.00
83 Frank Howard/49 5.00 12.00
84 George Brett/25 10.00 25.00
85 Greg Maddux/49 5.00 12.00
86 Keith Hernandez/25 3.00 8.00
87 Barry Larkin/49 3.00 8.00
88 Aaron Judge/99 10.00 25.00
89 Shohei Ohtani/99 12.00 30.00
90 Trea Turner/99 2.50 6.00
91 Gary Sanchez/99 3.00 8.00
92 Paul Goldschmidt/25 5.00 12.00
93 Ken Griffey Jr./25 10.00 25.00
94 Cal Ripken/25 12.00 30.00
95 Nolan Ryan/25 15.00 40.00
96 Joe Mauer/25 4.00 10.00

2018 Immaculate Collection Immaculate Swatches Jersey Number

*JSY NUM/20-25: .6X TO 1.5X p/r 99
*JSY NUM/20-25: .5X TO 1.2X p/r 49
*JSY NUM/20-25: .4X TO 1X p/r 25
RANDOM INSERTS IN PACKS
PRINT RUNS B/WN 1-25 COPIES PER
NO PRICING ON QTY 10 OR LESS
54 Jake Arrieta/25 4.00 10.00

2018 Immaculate Collection Immaculate Triple Material Autographs

RANDOM INSERTS IN PACKS
PRINT RUNS B/WN 5-99 COPIES PER
NO PRICING ON QTY 15 OR LESS
EXCHANGE DEADLINE 2/1/2020
*BLUE/25: .6X TO 1.5X p/r 49-99
*BLUE/25: .4X TO 1X p/r 25
2 Vladimir Guerrero Jr./25 200.00 500.00
4 Lou Brock/25 12.00 30.00
6 Don Sutton/25 10.00 25.00
12 Goose Gossage/25 5.00 12.00
14 Clint Frazier/25 15.00 40.00
15 Rhys Hoskins/25 30.00 80.00
16 Ozzie Albies/49 30.00 80.00
17 Rafael Devers/25 20.00 50.00
20 Miguel Andujar/99 40.00 100.00

2018 Immaculate Collection Immaculate Triple Signatures

RANDOM INSERTS IN PACKS
PRINT RUNS B/WN 3-25 COPIES PER
NO PRICING ON QTY 15 OR LESS
EXCHANGE DEADLINE 2/1/2020
5 Torres/Jimenez/Acuna/25 200.00 400.00
6 Tatis/Vlad Jr./Senzel/25 200.00 500.00
8 Tucker/Bichette/Rodgers/25 40.00 100.00

2018 Immaculate Collection Immaculate Tweed Weave Signatures

RANDOM INSERTS IN PACKS
PRINT RUNS B/WN 5-99 COPIES PER
NO PRICING ON QTY 15 OR LESS
EXCHANGE DEADLINE 2/1/2020
*BLUE/25: .6X TO 1.5X p/r 99
4 Andres Galarraga/99 4.00 10.00
6 Boog Powell/25 10.00 25.00
9 Dave Concepcion/40 20.00 50.00
15 Jose Abreu/20 8.00 20.00
16 Juan Gonzalez/70 5.00 12.00
22 Nomar Mazara/25 4.00 10.00
23 Omar Vizquel/20 6.00 15.00

2018 Immaculate Collection Rookie Debut Signatures

RANDOM INSERTS IN PACKS
PRINT RUNS B/WN 5-99 COPIES PER
NO PRICING ON QTY 6 OR LESS
EXCHANGE DEADLINE 2/1/2020
*JSY NUM/50-77: .4X TO 1X p/r 99
*JSY NUM/50-77: .3X TO .8X p/r 49
*JSY NUM/50-77: .25X TO .6X p/r 25
*JSY NUM/30-48: .5X TO 1.2X p/r 99
*JSY NUM/30-48: .4X TO 1X p/r 49
*JSY NUM/30-48: .3X TO .8X p/r 25
*JSY NUM/23-28: .6X TO 1.5X p/r 99
*JSY NUM/23-28: .5X TO 1.2X p/r 49
*JSY NUM/23-25: .4X TO 1X p/r 25
1 Anthony Banda/99 2.50 6.00
2 Luiz Gohara/99 2.50 6.00
3 Max Fried/99 10.00 25.00
4 Ozzie Albies/49 20.00 50.00
5 Lucas Sims/99 2.50 6.00
6 Austin Hays/99 4.00 10.00
7 Chance Sisco/99 4.00 10.00
8 Anthony Santander/99 2.50 6.00
9 Victor Caratini/99 3.00 8.00
10 Nicky Delmonico/99 2.50 6.00
11 Tyler Mahle/99 3.00 8.00
12 Francisco Mejia/99 3.00 8.00
13 Greg Allen/99 5.00 12.00
14 Ryan McMahon/99 3.00 8.00
15 J.D. Davis/99 3.00 8.00
16 Cameron Gallagher/99 2.50 6.00
17 Walker Buehler/99 12.00 30.00
18 Alex Verdugo/99 6.00 15.00
20 Brian Anderson/99 3.00 8.00
21 Dillon Peters/99 2.50 6.00
22 Brandon Woodruff/99 3.00 8.00
23 Mitch Garver/99 2.50 6.00
24 Zack Granite/99 2.50 6.00
25 Felix Jorge/99 2.50 6.00
26 Tomas Nido/99 2.50 6.00
27 Rhys Hoskins/99 25.00 60.00
28 Chris Flexen/99 2.50 6.00
29 Amed Rosario/25 12.00 30.00
30 Clint Frazier/99 6.00 15.00
31 Miguel Andujar/99 15.00 40.00
32 Tyler Wade/99 3.00 8.00
33 Dustin Fowler/99 2.50 6.00
34 Paul Blackburn/99 2.50 6.00
35 J.P. Crawford/25 4.00 10.00
36 Nick Williams/99 3.00 8.00
38 Thyago Vieira/99 2.50 6.00
39 Reyes Moronta/99 2.50 6.00
40 Jack Flaherty/99 4.00 10.00
41 Harrison Bader/99 4.00 10.00
42 Willie Calhoun/99 3.00 8.00
43 Richard Urena/99 2.50 6.00
44 Victor Robles/99 12.00 30.00
45 Erick Fedde/99 2.50 6.00
46 Andrew Stevenson/99 2.50 6.00
47 Rafael Devers/25 12.00 30.00

2018 Immaculate Collection Rookie Dual Material Autographs

RANDOM INSERTS IN PACKS
PRINT RUNS B/WN 49-99 COPIES PER
EXCHANGE DEADLINE 2/1/2020
*GOLD/49: .4X TO 1X BASIC
1 Max Fried/99 12.00 30.00
2 Ozzie Albies/99 20.00 50.00
3 Lucas Sims/99 3.00 8.00
4 Austin Hays/99 5.00 12.00
5 Chance Sisco/99 4.00 10.00
6 Victor Caratini/99 4.00 10.00
7 Nicky Delmonico/99 3.00 8.00
8 Francisco Mejia/99 6.00 15.00
9 Greg Allen/99 3.00 8.00
10 Ryan McMahon/99 6.00 15.00
11 Shohei Ohtani/49 200.00 400.00
12 Walker Buehler/99 15.00 40.00
13 Alex Verdugo/99 10.00 25.00
14 Kyle Farmer/99 3.00 8.00
15 Zack Granite/99 3.00 8.00
16 Jack Flaherty/99 5.00 12.00
17 Chris Flexen/99 3.00 8.00
18 Amed Rosario/99 4.00 10.00
19 Clint Frazier/99 10.00 25.00
20 Miguel Andujar/99 40.00 100.00
21 Tyler Wade/99 4.00 10.00
22 J.P. Crawford/99 3.00 8.00
23 Nick Williams/99 4.00 10.00
25 Harrison Bader/99 5.00 12.00
26 Willie Calhoun/99 4.00 10.00
27 Richard Urena/99 3.00 8.00
28 Victor Robles/99 10.00 25.00
29 Erick Fedde/99 3.00 8.00
30 Rafael Devers/99 12.00 30.00

2018 Immaculate Collection Rookie Premium Patch Autographs

RANDOM INSERTS IN PACKS
PRINT RUNS B/WN 10-25 COPIES PER
NO PRICING ON QTY 15 OR LESS
EXCHANGE DEADLINE 2/1/2020
1 Ozzie Albies/25 30.00 80.00
2 Chance Sisco/25 10.00 25.00
3 Francisco Mejia/25 12.00 30.00
5 Shohei Ohtani/25 150.00 400.00
6 Jack Flaherty/25 8.00 20.00
7 Amed Rosario/25 20.00 50.00
10 J.P. Crawford/25 5.00 12.00
12 Rhys Hoskins/25 50.00 120.00
13 Willie Calhoun/25 6.00 15.00
14 Victor Robles/25 40.00 100.00
15 Rafael Devers/25 20.00 50.00

2018 Immaculate Collection Rookie Quad Material Autographs

RANDOM INSERTS IN PACKS
PRINT RUNS B/WN 49-99 COPIES PER
EXCHANGE DEADLINE 2/1/2020
*GOLD/49: .4X TO 1X BASIC
1 Ozzie Albies/99 20.00 50.00
2 Chance Sisco/99 4.00 10.00
3 Francisco Mejia/99 6.00 15.00
4 Alex Verdugo/99 6.00 15.00
5 Shohei Ohtani/49 200.00 400.00
6 Jack Flaherty/99 5.00 12.00
7 Amed Rosario/99 4.00 10.00
8 Clint Frazier/99 10.00 25.00
9 Miguel Andujar/99 40.00 100.00
10 J.P. Crawford/99 3.00 8.00
11 Nick Williams/99 4.00 10.00
12 Rhys Hoskins/99 20.00 50.00
13 Willie Calhoun/99 4.00 10.00
14 Victor Robles/99 10.00 25.00
15 Rafael Devers/99 12.00 30.00

2018 Immaculate Collection Shadowbox Dual Materials

RANDOM INSERTS IN PACKS
PRINT RUNS B/WN 5-99 COPIES PER
NO PRICING ON QTY 15 OR LESS
3 Marcell Ozuna/49 4.00 10.00
6 Jose Altuve/49 4.00 10.00
7 Aaron Judge/25 15.00 40.00
8 Max Scherzer/25 10.00 25.00
9 Charlie Blackmon/25 5.00 12.00
15 Ichiro/20 12.00 30.00
16 Shohei Ohtani/99 12.00 30.00
17 Edwin Encarnacion/49 4.00 10.00
18 Nelson Cruz/49 4.00 10.00
20 Giancarlo Stanton/99 6.00 15.00
23 Miguel Cabrera/49 4.00 10.00
26 Francisco Lindor/25 8.00 20.00
29 Jose Ramirez/49 3.00 8.00
30 Marcus Stroman/49 3.00 8.00
31 Buster Posey/25 6.00 15.00
33 Gary Sanchez/25 5.00 12.00
34 Stan Musial/25 8.00 20.00
35 Roger Maris/25 20.00 50.00
36 Mickey Mantle/49 30.00 80.00
37 Ernie Banks/49 6.00 15.00
38 Andrew Benintendi/25 5.00 12.00
41 Trea Turner/25 4.00 10.00
43 Madison Bumgarner/49 3.00 8.00
46 Rickey Henderson/25 25.00 60.00
47 Rod Carew/25 8.00 20.00
48 Tom Glavine/49 5.00 12.00

2018 Immaculate Collection Shadowbox Dual Materials Jumbo

RANDOM INSERTS IN PACKS
PRINT RUNS B/WN 1-99 COPIES PER
NO PRICING ON QTY 15 OR LESS
1 Jeff Bagwell/25 4.00 10.00
2 Shohei Ohtani/99 12.00 30.00
3 Ivan Rodriguez/25 4.00 10.00
5 Frank Thomas/25 8.00 20.00
7 Eddie Murray/25 8.00 20.00
8 Don Mattingly/49 10.00 25.00
9 Juan Gonzalez/25 10.00 25.00
11 Rafael Devers/25 10.00 25.00
12 Amed Rosario/99 2.50 6.00
13 Shohei Ohtani/99 12.00 30.00
14 Rhys Hoskins/99 6.00 15.00
15 Clint Frazier/99 4.00 10.00
16 Victor Robles/99 3.00 8.00
19 Mike Piazza/25 8.00 20.00
20 Nolan Ryan/25 15.00 40.00
21 Orel Hershiser/25 12.00 30.00
22 Ryne Sandberg/25 12.00 30.00
23 Buster Posey/25 6.00 15.00
24 Aaron Judge/99 10.00 25.00
25 Nomar Mazara/99 2.00 5.00
26 Salvador Perez/99 2.50 6.00
27 Mickey Mantle/25 60.00 150.00
28 Clayton Kershaw/25 10.00 25.00
29 Ronald Acuna Jr./99 12.00 30.00
30 Vladimir Guerrero Jr./99 12.00 30.00
31 Nick Senzel/99 5.00 12.00
32 Eloy Jimenez/99 6.00 15.00
34 Ted Williams/25 75.00 200.00
40 Robinson Cano/25 4.00 10.00
41 Evan Longoria/49 3.00 8.00
42 Noah Syndergaard/25 4.00 10.00
43 Barry Larkin/25 4.00 10.00
45 Lee Smith/25 3.00 8.00

2019 Immaculate Collection

RANDOM INSERTS IN PACKS
NO PRICING QTY 3
1-50 PRINT RUN B/TW 20-99 COPIES PER
51-150 PRINT RUN B/TW 3-99 COPIES PER
EXCHANGE DEADLINE 2/21/2021
1 Cedric Mullins JSY AU/99 RC 5.00 12.00
2 Enyel De Los Santos JSY AU/99 RC 3.00 8.00
3 Daniel Ponce de Leon JSY AU/99 RC 5.00 12.00
4 Jonathan Davis JSY AU/99 RC 4.00 10.00
5 Kevin Newman JSY AU/99 RC 5.00 12.00
6 Sean Reid-Foley JSY AU/99 RC 3.00 8.00
7 Garrett Hampson JSY AU/99 RC 3.00 8.00
8 Brad Keller JSY AU/99 RC 3.00 8.00
9 Chris Shaw JSY AU/99 RC 5.00 12.00
10 Kevin Kramer JSY AU/99 RC 4.00 10.00
11 Myles Straw JSY AU/99 RC 5.00 12.00
12 Ryan O'Hearn JSY AU/99 RC 3.00 8.00
13 Michael Kopech JSY AU/99 RC 6.00 15.00
14 Jake Cave JSY AU/99 RC 4.00 10.00
15 Corbin Burnes JSY AU/99 RC 5.00 12.00
16 Luis Urias JSY AU/99 RC 5.00 12.00
17 Justus Sheffield JSY AU/99 RC 5.00 12.00
18 Kyle Wright JSY AU/99 RC 5.00 12.00
19 Christin Stewart JSY AU/99 RC 4.00 10.00
20 Vladimir Guerrero Jr. JSY AU/99 RC 50.00 120.00
21 Touki Toussaint JSY AU/99 RC 4.00 10.00
22 Jake Bauers JSY AU/99 RC 5.00 12.00
23 Chance Adams JSY AU/99 RC 3.00 8.00
24 Stephen Gonsalves JSY AU/99 RC 3.00 8.00
25 Caleb Ferguson JSY AU/99 RC 4.00 10.00
26 Danny Jansen JSY AU/99 RC 3.00 8.00
27 Dennis Santana JSY AU/99 RC 3.00 8.00
28 Kyle Tucker JSY AU/99 RC 15.00 40.00
29 Rowdy Tellez JSY AU/99 RC 5.00 12.00
30 Jonathan Loaisiga JSY AU/49 RC 5.00 12.00
31 Eloy Jimenez JSY AU/99 RC 20.00 50.00
32 Cionel Perez JSY AU/99 RC 3.00 8.00
33 Steven Duggar JSY AU/99 RC 4.00 10.00
34 Taylor Ward JSY AU/99 RC 3.00 8.00
35 Jacob Nix JSY AU/99 RC 4.00 10.00
36 Patrick Wisdom JSY AU/99 RC 3.00 8.00
37 Dakota Hudson JSY AU/99 RC 4.00 10.00
38 Fernando Tatis Jr. JSY AU/99 RC 75.00 200.00
39 Framber Valdez JSY AU/99 RC 3.00 8.00
40 Bryse Wilson JSY AU/99 RC 4.00 10.00
41 Luis Ortiz JSY AU/99 RC 3.00 8.00
42 Ramon Laureano JSY AU/99 RC 8.00 20.00
43 Reese McGuire JSY AU/99 RC 5.00 12.00
44 Ryan Borucki JSY AU/99 RC 3.00 8.00
45 Jeff McNeil JSY AU/99 RC 8.00 20.00
46 Kolby Allard JSY AU/99 RC 5.00 12.00
47 David Fletcher JSY AU/99 RC 10.00 25.00
48 Nick Senzel JSY AU/20 RC 15.00 40.00
49 Brandon Lowe JSY AU/99 RC 8.00 20.00
50 Josh James JSY AU/99 RC 5.00 12.00
51 Mike Trout JSY/99 20.00 50.00
52 Kris Bryant JSY/99 4.00 10.00
53 Bryce Harper JSY/99 5.00 12.00
54 Jose Altuve JSY/99 2.50 6.00
55 Christian Yelich JSY/99 4.00 10.00
56 Mookie Betts JSY/99 5.00 12.00
57 Clayton Kershaw JSY/99 6.00 15.00
58 Joey Gallo JSY/99 2.50 6.00
59 Ronald Acuna Jr. JSY/99 8.00 20.00
60 Gleyber Torres JSY/99 5.00 12.00
61 Juan Soto JSY/99 10.00 25.00
62 Walker Buehler JSY/99 4.00 10.00
63 Joey Votto JSY/99 3.00 8.00
64 Nolan Arenado JSY/99 4.00 10.00
65 Whit Merrifield JSY/99 3.00 8.00
66 Brian Anderson JSY/99 2.00 5.00
67 Jacob deGrom JSY/99 3.00 8.00
68 Khris Davis JSY/25 5.00 12.00
69 Starling Marte JSY/99 2.50 6.00
70 Buster Posey JSY/99 4.00 10.00
71 Blake Snell JSY/49 3.00 8.00
72 Jose Berrios JSY/99 2.50 6.00
73 Albert Pujols JSY/99 4.00 10.00
74 Miguel Cabrera JSY/99 4.00 10.00
75 Jose Abreu JSY/99 3.00 8.00
76 David Peralta JSY/99 2.00 5.00
77 Jose Ramirez JSY/99 2.50 6.00
78 Felix Hernandez JSY/99 2.50 6.00
79 Trey Mancini JSY/99 2.50 6.00
80 Yadier Molina JSY/99 3.00 8.00
81 Marcus Stroman JSY/99 2.50 6.00
82 Manny Machado JSY/99 3.00 8.00
83 Max Scherzer JSY/99 3.00 8.00
84 Anthony Rizzo JSY/99 5.00 12.00
85 Shohei Ohtani JSY/99 4.00 10.00
86 Miguel Andujar JSY/99 3.00 8.00
87 Aaron Judge JSY/99 8.00 20.00
88 Javier Baez JSY/99 4.00 10.00
89 Giancarlo Stanton JSY/99 3.00 8.00
90 Freddie Freeman JSY/99 4.00 10.00
91 Carlos Correa JSY/99 3.00 8.00
92 Andrew Benintendi JSY/99 3.00 8.00
93 Cody Bellinger JSY/99 6.00 15.00
94 George Springer JSY/99 2.50 6.00
95 Maikel Franco JSY/99 2.50 6.00
96 Justin Turner JSY/49 3.00 8.00
97 Corey Kluber JSY/99 2.50 6.00
98 Scooter Gennett JSY/99 2.50 6.00
99 Alex Bregman JSY/99 3.00 8.00
101 Francisco Lindor JSY/49 4.00 10.00
102 Josh Hader JSY/99 2.00 5.00
103 Noah Syndergaard JSY/99 2.50 6.00
104 Jameson Taillon JSY/99 2.50 6.00
105 Brandon Crawford JSY/99 2.50 6.00
106 Willson Contreras JSY/99 2.50 6.00
107 Charlie Blackmon JSY/99 3.00 8.00
108 Mitch Haniger JSY/99 2.50 6.00
109 Ozzie Albies JSY/99 3.00 8.00
110 Chris Sale JSY/99 3.00 8.00
111 Justin Verlander JSY/99 3.00 8.00
112 Patrick Corbin JSY/99 2.50 6.00
113 Matt Carpenter JSY/99 3.00 8.00
114 Xander Bogaerts JSY/99 3.00 8.00
115 Trevor Story JSY/62 3.00 8.00
116 Miguel Sano JSY/99 2.50 6.00
117 Matt Olson JSY/99 2.00 5.00
118 Rhys Hoskins JSY/99 4.00 10.00
119 Teoscar Hernandez JSY/99 3.00 8.00
120 Victor Robles JSY/99 4.00 10.00
121 Yoan Moncada JSY/99 3.00 8.00
122 Edwin Encarnacion JSY/99 3.00 8.00
123 Robinson Cano JSY/99 2.50 6.00
124 Nelson Cruz JSY/99 3.00 8.00
125 Marcell Ozuna JSY/99 3.00 8.00
126 Paul Goldschmidt JSY/99 3.00 8.00
127 Jordan Hicks JSY/99 2.50 6.00
128 Edwin Diaz JSY/99 2.50 6.00
129 Stephen Strasburg JSY/99 3.00 8.00
130 Gerrit Cole JSY/99 3.00 8.00
131 Luis Severino JSY/99 2.50 6.00
132 Gary Sanchez JSY/99 3.00 8.00
133 Jon Lester JSY/99 2.50 6.00
134 Rick Porcello JSY/99 2.50 6.00
135 David Price JSY/99 2.50 6.00
136 Ichiro JSY/99 4.00 10.00
137 Joc Pederson JSY/99 2.50 6.00
138 Ryan Braun JSY/99 2.50 6.00
139 Adalberto Mondesi JSY/99 2.50 6.00
140 Amed Rosario JSY/99 2.50 6.00
141 Kyle Schwarber JSY/99 3.00 8.00
142 Trea Turner JSY/99 2.50 6.00
143 Andrew McCutchen JSY/49 4.00 10.00
144 David Dahl JSY/99 2.00 5.00
145 Yasiel Puig JSY/99 3.00 8.00
146 Nicholas Castellanos JSY/99 3.00 8.00
147 Eugenio Suarez JSY/99 2.50 6.00
148 Hunter Renfroe JSY/99 2.00 5.00
149 Michael Conforto JSY/99 2.50 6.00
150 Daniel Murphy JSY/60 2.50 6.00

2019 Immaculate Collection Batting Stance Memorabilia Autographs

RANDOM INSERTS IN PACKS
STATED PRINT RUN 25 SER.#'d SETS
EXCHANGE DEADLINE 2/21/2021
1 Jake Bauers 8.00 20.00
2 Kyle Tucker 10.00 25.00
3 Ryan O'Hearn 5.00 12.00
4 Jeff McNeil 12.00 30.00
5 Jake Cave 6.00 15.00
6 Kevin Kramer 6.00 15.00
7 Cedric Mullins 8.00 20.00
8 Garrett Hampson 5.00 12.00
9 Christin Stewart 6.00 15.00
10 Kevin Newman 8.00 20.00
11 Chris Shaw 8.00 20.00
12 David Fletcher 15.00 40.00
13 Ramon Laureano 12.00 30.00
15 Brandon Lowe 12.00 30.00
16 Taylor Ward 5.00 12.00
17 Rowdy Tellez 8.00 20.00
18 Myles Straw 8.00 20.00
20 Danny Jansen 5.00 12.00

2019 Immaculate Collection Clutch Dual Memorabilia Autographs

RANDOM INSERTS IN PACKS
PRINT RUNS B/WN 4-49 COPIES PER
NO PRICING QTY 15 OR LESS
EXCHANGE DEADLINE 2/21/2021
*RED/25: .5X TO 1.2X p/r 49
3 Cody Bellinger/25 60.00 150.00
4 Marcus Stroman/49 5.00 12.00
5 Trevor Story/25 8.00 20.00
16 Gary Sanchez/25 15.00 40.00
17 Goose Gossage/25 6.00 15.00
19 Matt Carpenter/34 8.00 20.00

2019 Immaculate Collection Clutch Rookies Dual Memorabilia Autographs

RANDOM INSERTS IN PACKS
PRINT RUNS B/WN 25-49 COPIES PER
EXCHANGE DEADLINE 2/21/2021
1 Jake Bauers/25 8.00 20.00
2 Kyle Tucker/49 8.00 20.00
3 Ryan O'Hearn/49 4.00 10.00
4 Myles Straw/25 8.00 20.00
5 Garrett Hampson/25 5.00 12.00
6 Jake Cave/25 6.00 15.00
7 Yusei Kikuchi/49 6.00 15.00
8 Michael Kopech/49 8.00 20.00
9 Luis Urias/49 6.00 15.00
10 Jacob Nix/25 6.00 15.00
11 Cedric Mullins/25 8.00 20.00
12 Brandon Lowe/49 10.00 25.00
13 Rowdy Tellez/49 6.00 15.00
14 Vladimir Guerrero Jr./49 60.00 150.00
15 Fernando Tatis Jr./49 75.00 200.00

2019 Immaculate Collection Complete Quad Memorabilia Autographs

RANDOM INSERTS IN PACKS
STATED PRINT RUN 25 SER.#'d SETS
EXCHANGE DEADLINE 2/21/2021

ys Hoskins 15.00 40.00
on Judge 50.00 120.00
dimir Guerrero Jr. 60.00 150.00
nsby Swanson 8.00 20.00
vid Dahl 5.00 12.00
tor Robles 15.00 40.00
x Reyes 6.00 15.00
sh Bell 6.00 15.00
ncisco Mejia 6.00 15.00
Walker Buehler 10.00 25.00

2019 Immaculate Collection Cowhide Memorabilia Autographs

DOM INSERTS IN PACKS
NT RUNS B/WN 5-25 COPIES PER
PRICING QTY 15 OR LESS
CHANGE DEADLINE 2/21/2021
lando Arcia/25 5.00 12.00
P. Crawford/25 5.00 12.00
ex Reyes/25 6.00 15.00
ake Bauers/25 8.00 20.00
ergie Jenkins/20 15.00 40.00
erry Wood/25 12.00 30.00
Pete Alonso/25 60.00 150.00
Luis Severino/25 6.00 15.00
Michael Taylor/25 5.00 12.00
Nolan Ryan/25 50.00 120.00

2019 Immaculate Collection Dual Material Autographs

NDOM INSERTS IN PACKS
NT RUNS B/WN 20-99 COPIES PER
CHANGE DEADLINE 2/21/2021
OLD/49: .5X TO 1.2X p/r 99
OLD/20-25: .5X TO 1.2X p/r 49
OLD/20-25: .4X TO 1X p/r 25
Cody Bellinger/49 50.00 120.00
Aaron Judge/25 60.00 150.00
Shohei Ohtani/25 75.00 200.00
Pedro Martinez/25 6.00 15.00
Frank Robinson/25 20.00 50.00
Steve Garvey/49 12.00 30.00
Larry Walker/25 25.00 60.00
Dale Murphy/49 15.00 40.00
Whit Merrifield/99 5.00 12.00
Trea Turner/49 5.00 12.00
Ken Griffey Jr./20 75.00 200.00
Ronald Acuna Jr./49 75.00 200.00
Jason Giambi/49 4.00 10.00
Miguel Andujar/49 6.00 15.00
Jose Abreu/25 8.00 20.00
Mitch Haniger/49 5.00 12.00

2019 Immaculate Collection Dugout Collection Dual Memorabilia Autographs

RANDOM INSERTS IN PACKS
PRINT RUNS B/WN 10-25 COPIES PER
NO PRICING QTY 15 OR LESS
EXCHANGE DEADLINE 2/21/2021
Stephen Gonsalves/25 5.00 12.00
2 Jonathan Loaisiga/25 6.00 15.00
3 Ramon Laureano/20 12.00 30.00
4 Kevin Kramer/25 6.00 15.00
5 Danny Jansen/25 5.00 12.00
6 Luis Urias/25 8.00 20.00
7 Steven Duggar/25 6.00 15.00
8 Jonathan Davis/25 6.00 15.00
9 Dakota Hudson/25 6.00 15.00
10 Patrick Wisdom/20 5.00 12.00
11 Kevin Newman/25 8.00 20.00
12 Reese McGuire/25 8.00 20.00
13 Justus Sheffield/25 8.00 20.00
14 Michael Kopech/25 10.00 25.00
15 Ryan Borucki/25 5.00 12.00
16 Sean Reid-Foley/25 5.00 12.00
17 Cionel Perez/25 5.00 12.00
18 Kyle Tucker/25 10.00 25.00
19 Caleb Ferguson/25 6.00 15.00
20 Carlos Correa/25 20.00 50.00
21 Edgar Martinez/25 10.00 25.00
23 Ivan Rodriguez/25 15.00 40.00
24 Yusei Kikuchi/25 8.00 20.00
25 Victor Robles/20 10.00 25.00
26 Ryan McMahon/25 5.00 12.00
27 Rhys Hoskins/25 10.00 25.00
28 Harrison Bader/25 6.00 15.00
29 David Dahl/25 5.00 12.00
30 Clint Frazier/25 6.00 15.00
31 Chance Sisco/25 5.00 12.00
32 Alex Reyes/20 6.00 15.00
33 Carson Fulmer/25 5.00 12.00
34 Dustin Fowler/25 5.00 12.00
35 Vladimir Guerrero Jr./20 60.00 150.00
36 Eloy Jimenez/25 20.00 50.00
37 Fernando Tatis Jr./25 60.00 150.00
38 Willie Calhoun/25 5.00 12.00
39 Zack Granite/20 5.00 12.00
40 Rowdy Tellez/25 8.00 20.00

2019 Immaculate Collection Extra Bases Triple Memorabilia Autographs

RANDOM INSERTS IN PACKS
PRINT RUNS B/WN 7-25 COPIES PER
NO PRICING QTY 15 OR LESS
EXCHANGE DEADLINE 2/21/2021
1 Jose Abreu/25 6.00 15.00
2 Miguel Andujar/25 8.00 20.00
3 Xander Bogaerts/25 25.00 60.00
4 Whit Merrifield/25 8.00 20.00
6 Rhys Hoskins/25 10.00 25.00
7 Nolan Arenado/49 20.00 50.00
8 Freddie Freeman/25 10.00 25.00
9 Pete Rose/25 15.00 40.00
10 Craig Biggio/25 15.00 40.00
13 Jose Ramirez/25 6.00 15.00
14 Matt Carpenter/25 8.00 20.00
15 Edgar Martinez/25 6.00 15.00
16 Jim Rice/25 6.00 15.00
18 Francisco Lindor/25 8.00 20.00
19 Juan Gonzalez/25 12.00 30.00
20 Vladimir Guerrero/25 12.00 30.00

2019 Immaculate Collection Hats Off Memorabilia Autographs

RANDOM INSERTS IN PACKS
PRINT RUNS B/WN 10-25 COPIES PER
NO PRICING QTY 15 OR LESS
EXCHANGE DEADLINE 2/21/2021
1 Carson Fulmer/25 5.00 12.00
2 Brendan Rodgers/25 8.00 20.00
3 Lewis Brinson/25 5.00 12.00
4 Yandy Diaz/25 6.00 15.00
5 Sean Newcomb/25 5.00 12.00
6 Lazaro Armenteros/25 6.00 15.00
7 Vladimir Guerrero Jr./25 30.00 80.00
8 Adrian Beltre/25 8.00 20.00
10 Craig Biggio/25 6.00 15.00
11 Robin Yount/25 8.00 20.00
15 Luis Severino/25 6.00 15.00
17 Estevan Florial/25 8.00 20.00
18 Luis Robert/25 60.00 150.00
19 Jo Adell/25 EXCH 25.00 60.00
20 Victor Victor Mesa/25 10.00 25.00

2019 Immaculate Collection Immaculate Doubles Memorabilia Autographs

RANDOM INSERTS IN PACKS
STATED PRINT RUN 99 SER.#'d SETS
EXCHANGE DEADLINE 2/21/2021
*GOLD: .5X TO 1.2X
1 Cedric Mullins 5.00 12.00
2 Enyel De Los Santos 3.00 8.00
3 Daniel Ponce de Leon 5.00 12.00
4 Jonathan Davis 4.00 10.00
5 Kevin Newman 5.00 12.00
6 Sean Reid-Foley 3.00 8.00
7 Garrett Hampson 3.00 8.00
8 Brad Keller 3.00 8.00
9 Chris Shaw 5.00 12.00
10 Kevin Kramer 4.00 10.00
11 Myles Straw 5.00 12.00
12 Ryan O'Hearn 3.00 8.00
13 Michael Kopech 6.00 15.00
14 Jake Cave 4.00 10.00
15 Corbin Burnes 5.00 12.00
16 Luis Urias 5.00 12.00
17 Justus Sheffield 5.00 12.00
18 Kyle Wright 5.00 12.00
19 Christin Stewart 4.00 10.00
20 Vladimir Guerrero Jr. 40.00 100.00
21 Touki Toussaint 4.00 10.00
22 Jake Bauers 5.00 12.00
23 Chance Adams 3.00 8.00
24 Stephen Gonsalves 3.00 8.00
25 Caleb Ferguson 4.00 10.00
26 Danny Jansen 3.00 8.00
27 Dennis Santana 3.00 8.00
28 Kyle Tucker 6.00 15.00
29 Rowdy Tellez 5.00 12.00
30 Jonathan Loaisiga 4.00 10.00
31 Eloy Jimenez 12.00 30.00
32 Cionel Perez 3.00 8.00
33 Steven Duggar 4.00 10.00
34 Taylor Ward 3.00 8.00
35 Jacob Nix 4.00 10.00
36 Patrick Wisdom 3.00 8.00
37 Dakota Hudson 4.00 10.00
38 Fernando Tatis Jr. 50.00 120.00
39 Framber Valdez 3.00 8.00
40 Bryse Wilson 4.00 10.00
41 Luis Ortiz 3.00 8.00
42 Ramon Laureano 8.00 20.00
43 Reese McGuire 5.00 12.00
44 Ryan Borucki 3.00 8.00
45 Jeff McNeil 8.00 20.00
46 Kolby Allard 5.00 12.00
47 David Fletcher 10.00 25.00
49 Brandon Lowe 8.00 20.00
50 Josh James 5.00 12.00

2019 Immaculate Collection Immaculate Duals Memorabilia

1 Mike Trout 15.00 40.00
2 Jose Altuve 2.50 6.00
3 Mookie Betts 8.00 20.00
4 Christian Yelich 4.00 10.00
5 Clayton Kershaw 6.00 15.00
6 Ronald Acuna Jr. 8.00 20.00
7 Nolan Arenado 4.00 10.00
8 Alex Bregman 3.00 8.00
9 Jose Ramirez 2.50 6.00
10 Freddie Freeman 4.00 10.00
11 Miguel Cabrera 3.00 8.00
12 Andrew Benintendi 3.00 8.00
13 Kris Bryant 6.00 15.00
14 Javier Baez 4.00 10.00
15 Aaron Judge 8.00 20.00
16 Shohei Ohtani 4.00 10.00
17 Max Scherzer 3.00 8.00
18 Jacob deGrom 3.00 8.00
19 Blake Snell 2.50 6.00
20 Chris Sale 3.00 8.00
21 Bryce Harper 5.00 12.00
22 Manny Machado 3.00 8.00
23 Juan Soto 10.00 25.00
24 Cody Bellinger 8.00 20.00
25 Gleyber Torres 6.00 15.00

2019 Immaculate Collection Immaculate Fives Memorabilia Autographs

RANDOM INSERTS IN PACKS
STATED PRINT RUN 99 SER.#'d SETS
EXCHANGE DEADLINE 2/21/2021
*GOLD: .5X TO 1.5X
1 Cedric Mullins 5.00 12.00
2 Brad Keller 3.00 8.00
3 Ryan O'Hearn 3.00 8.00
4 Michael Kopech 6.00 15.00
5 Corbin Burnes 5.00 12.00
6 Luis Urias 5.00 12.00
7 Justus Sheffield 5.00 12.00
8 Christin Stewart 4.00 10.00
9 Vladimir Guerrero Jr. 50.00 120.00
10 Jake Bauers 5.00 12.00
11 Danny Jansen 3.00 8.00
12 Kyle Tucker 6.00 15.00
13 Eloy Jimenez 12.00 30.00
14 Steven Duggar 4.00 10.00
15 Dakota Hudson 4.00 10.00
16 Fernando Tatis Jr. 60.00 150.00
17 Ramon Laureano 8.00 20.00
18 Jeff McNeil 8.00 20.00
19 David Fletcher 10.00 25.00
20 Nick Senzel 20.00 50.00

2019 Immaculate Collection Immaculate Jumbo

RANDOM INSERTS IN PACKS
PRINT RUNS B/WN 3-49 COPIES PER
NO PRICING QTY 15 OR LESS
1 Cedric Mullins/49 3.00 8.00
2 Enyel De Los Santos/49 2.00 5.00
3 Daniel Ponce de Leon/49 3.00 8.00
4 Jonathan Davis/49 2.50 6.00
5 Kevin Newman/49 3.00 8.00
6 Sean Reid-Foley/49 2.00 5.00
7 Garrett Hampson/49 2.00 5.00
8 Brad Keller/49 2.00 5.00
9 Chris Shaw/49 3.00 8.00
10 Kevin Kramer/49 2.50 6.00
11 Myles Straw/49 3.00 8.00
12 Ryan O'Hearn/49 2.00 5.00
13 Michael Kopech/49 4.00 10.00
14 Jake Cave/49 2.50 6.00
15 Corbin Burnes/49 3.00 8.00
16 Luis Urias/49 3.00 8.00
17 Justus Sheffield/49 3.00 8.00
18 Kyle Wright/49 3.00 8.00
19 Christin Stewart/49 2.50 6.00
20 Vladimir Guerrero Jr./49 12.00 30.00
21 Touki Toussaint/49 2.50 6.00
22 Jake Bauers/49 3.00 8.00
23 Chance Adams/49 2.00 5.00
24 Stephen Gonsalves/49 2.00 5.00
25 Caleb Ferguson/49 2.50 6.00
26 Danny Jansen/49 2.00 5.00
27 Dennis Santana/49 2.00 5.00
28 Kyle Tucker/49 4.00 10.00
29 Rowdy Tellez/49 3.00 8.00
30 Jonathan Loaisiga/49 2.50 6.00
31 Eloy Jimenez/49 8.00 20.00
32 Cionel Perez/49 2.00 5.00
33 Steven Duggar/49 2.50 6.00
34 Taylor Ward/49 2.00 5.00
35 Jacob Nix/49 2.50 6.00
36 Patrick Wisdom/49 2.00 5.00
37 Dakota Hudson/49 2.50 6.00
38 Fernando Tatis Jr./49 20.00 50.00
39 Framber Valdez/49 2.00 5.00
40 Bryse Wilson/49 2.50 6.00
41 Luis Ortiz/49 2.00 5.00
42 Ramon Laureano/49 4.00 10.00
43 Reese McGuire/49 3.00 8.00
44 Ryan Borucki/49 2.00 5.00
45 Jeff McNeil/49 5.00 12.00
46 Kolby Allard/49 3.00 8.00
47 David Fletcher/49 6.00 15.00
48 Nick Senzel/49 6.00 15.00
49 Brandon Lowe/49 3.00 8.00
50 Josh James/49 3.00 8.00
51 Wander Franco/49 30.00 80.00
52 Brendan McKay/49 3.00 8.00
53 Bo Bichette/49 20.00 50.00
54 Royce Lewis/49 8.00 20.00
56 Jo Adell/49 6.00 15.00
57 Estevan Florial/49 3.00 8.00
62 Gil Hodges/25 4.00 10.00
66 Adalberto Mondesi/49 2.50 6.00
67 Aaron Judge/49 15.00 40.00
68 Shohei Ohtani/49 12.00 30.00
69 Corey Seager/49 3.00 8.00
70 Rhys Hoskins/49 8.00 20.00
71 Rafael Devers/49 4.00 10.00
72 Eric Thames/49 2.00 5.00
76 Mike Piazza/31 5.00 12.00
77 Paul Molitor/49 3.00 8.00
79 Willie Stargell/49 2.50 6.00
80 Adrian Beltre/49 3.00 8.00
82 Ronald Acuna Jr./49 15.00 40.00
84 Don Mattingly/23 10.00 25.00
85 Mookie Betts/25 8.00 20.00
87 Tony Gwynn/49 15.00 40.00
88 Vladimir Guerrero/49 2.50 6.00
89 Carlos Correa/25 12.00 30.00
90 George Brett/25 10.00 25.00
91 Roberto Alomar/25 4.00 10.00
92 Gleyber Torres/49 6.00 15.00
93 Tyler O'Neill/49 2.50 6.00
94 Forrest Whitley/49 3.00 8.00
95 Victor Victor Mesa/49 4.00 10.00
96 Victor Mesa Jr./49 5.00 12.00
97 Yusei Kikuchi/49 3.00 8.00
98 Jesus Sanchez/49 2.00 5.00

2019 Immaculate Collection Immaculate Quads Memorabilia

RANDOM INSERTS IN PACKS
PRINT RUNS B/WN 5-49 COPIES PER
NO PRICING QTY 15 OR LESS
*RED/25: .6X TO 1.5X p/r 49
1 Matt Chapman/49 3.00 8.00
2 Ozzie Albies/49 3.00 8.00
3 Corbin Burnes/49 3.00 8.00
7 Mickey Mantle/49 25.00 60.00
9 Juan Soto/49 10.00 25.00
10 Corey Ray/49 2.00 5.00
11 Joey Gallo/49 2.50 6.00
12 Christian Yelich/49 8.00 20.00
13 Giancarlo Stanton/49 3.00 8.00
14 Jesus Aguilar/49 2.00 5.00
15 Bryce Harper/49 15.00 40.00
16 Eugenio Suarez/49 2.50 6.00
17 Miguel Andujar/49 3.00 8.00
18 Shohei Ohtani/49 12.00 30.00
19 Salvador Perez/49 2.50 6.00
20 Paul Goldschmidt/49 3.00 8.00
21 Corey Kluber/49 2.50 6.00
22 Jose Berrios/49 2.50 6.00
23 Edwin Diaz/49 2.50 6.00
24 Adalberto Mondesi/49 2.50 6.00
25 Gary Sanchez/49 3.00 8.00

2019 Immaculate Collection Immaculate Swatches

RANDOM INSERTS IN PACKS
STATED PRINT RUN 49 SER.#'d SETS
*BSBLLS: .6X TO 1.5X
1 Cedric Mullins 3.00 8.00
2 Enyel De Los Santos 2.00 5.00
3 Daniel Ponce de Leon 3.00 8.00
4 Jonathan Davis 2.50 6.00
5 Kevin Newman 3.00 8.00
6 Sean Reid-Foley 2.00 5.00
7 Garrett Hampson 2.00 5.00
8 Brad Keller 2.00 5.00
9 Chris Shaw 3.00 8.00
10 Kevin Kramer 2.50 6.00
11 Myles Straw 3.00 8.00
12 Ryan O'Hearn 2.00 5.00
13 Michael Kopech 4.00 10.00
14 Jake Cave 2.50 6.00
15 Corbin Burnes 3.00 8.00
16 Luis Urias 3.00 8.00
17 Justus Sheffield 3.00 8.00
18 Kyle Wright 3.00 8.00
19 Christin Stewart 2.50 6.00
20 Vladimir Guerrero Jr. 12.00 30.00
21 Touki Toussaint 2.50 6.00
22 Jake Bauers 3.00 8.00
23 Chance Adams 2.00 5.00
24 Stephen Gonsalves 2.00 5.00
25 Caleb Ferguson 2.50 6.00
26 Danny Jansen 2.00 5.00
27 Dennis Santana 2.00 5.00
28 Kyle Tucker 4.00 10.00
29 Rowdy Tellez 3.00 8.00
30 Jonathan Loaisiga 2.50 6.00
31 Eloy Jimenez 8.00 20.00
32 Cionel Perez 2.00 5.00
33 Steven Duggar 2.50 6.00
34 Taylor Ward 2.00 5.00
35 Jacob Nix 2.50 6.00
36 Patrick Wisdom 2.00 5.00
37 Dakota Hudson 2.50 6.00
38 Fernando Tatis Jr. 20.00 50.00
39 Framber Valdez 2.00 5.00
40 Bryse Wilson 2.50 6.00
41 Luis Ortiz 2.00 5.00
42 Ramon Laureano 4.00 10.00
43 Reese McGuire 3.00 8.00
44 Ryan Borucki 2.00 5.00
45 Jeff McNeil 5.00 12.00
46 Kolby Allard 3.00 8.00
47 David Fletcher 6.00 15.00
48 Nick Senzel 6.00 15.00
49 Brandon Lowe 3.00 8.00
50 Josh James 3.00 8.00
51 Jonathan Villar 2.00 5.00
52 Ketel Marte 2.00 5.00
53 Aaron Judge 8.00 20.00
54 Shohei Ohtani 4.00 10.00
55 Dee Gordon 2.00 5.00
56 Kevin Kiermaier 2.50 6.00
57 Charlie Blackmon 3.00 8.00
58 Brett Gardner 4.00 10.00
59 Marcus Semien 2.00 5.00
60 Kris Bryant 4.00 10.00
61 Francisco Lindor 3.00 8.00
62 Tim Anderson 3.00 8.00
63 Eric Hosmer 2.50 6.00
64 Starling Marte 2.50 6.00
65 George Springer 2.50 6.00
66 Jose Altuve 2.00 5.00
67 Lorenzo Cain 2.00 5.00
68 Francisco Mejia 2.50 6.00
69 Harrison Bader 2.50 6.00
70 Victor Robles 4.00 10.00
71 Willy Adames 2.00 5.00
72 Austin Meadows 2.50 6.00
73 Walker Buehler 4.00 10.00
74 Amed Rosario 2.50 6.00
75 Mike Trout 15.00 40.00

2019 Immaculate Collection Immaculate Triples Memorabilia

RANDOM INSERTS IN PACKS
PRINT RUNS B/WN 20-49 COPIES PER
*RED/25: .6X TO 1.5X p/r 49
1 Ken Griffey Jr./49 15.00 40.00
2 Vladimir Guerrero Jr./49 12.00 30.00
3 Fernando Tatis Jr./49 20.00 50.00
4 Eloy Jimenez/49 8.00 20.00
5 Jesus Luzardo/49 3.00 8.00
6 David Ortiz/49 6.00 15.00
7 Dale Murphy/49 3.00 8.00
8 Larry Walker/49 2.50 6.00
9 Mike Trout/49 20.00 50.00
10 Yusei Kikuchi/49 3.00 8.00
11 Randy Johnson/49 5.00 12.00
12 Dave Concepcion/20 3.00 8.00
13 Mike Mussina/49 2.50 6.00
14 Jose Abreu/49 3.00 8.00
15 John Smoltz/49 3.00 8.00
16 Pedro Martinez/49 2.50 6.00
17 Craig Biggio/49 2.50 6.00
18 Frank Robinson/49 10.00 25.00
19 Kyle Tucker/49 4.00 10.00
20 Mitch Haniger/49 2.50 6.00
21 Roberto Alomar/49 2.50 6.00
22 Mike Piazza/49 3.00 8.00
23 Michael Kopech/49 4.00 10.00
24 Cal Ripken/49 10.00 25.00
25 Luis Severino/49 2.50 6.00

2019 Immaculate Collection Jackets Autographs

RANDOM INSERTS IN PACKS
PRINT RUNS B/WN 20-49 COPIES PER
EXCHANGE DEADLINE 2/21/2021
1 Don Mattingly/25 25.00 60.00
2 Alex Reyes/25 6.00 15.00
3 Joe Morgan/20 6.00 15.00
4 Vladimir Guerrero/25 20.00 50.00
5 Amed Rosario/25 6.00 15.00
6 Chance Sisco/25 6.00 15.00
7 Dansby Swanson/25 8.00 20.00
8 David Dahl/25 5.00 12.00
9 Dustin Fowler/25 5.00 12.00
10 Harrison Bader/25 6.00 15.00
11 Walker Buehler/25 8.00 20.00
12 Willie Calhoun/25 5.00 12.00
13 Yoan Moncada/25 8.00 20.00
14 Carson Fulmer/25 5.00 12.00
15 Clint Frazier/49 8.00 20.00
16 Framber Valdez/25 5.00 12.00
17 Touki Toussaint/25 6.00 15.00
18 Luis Ortiz/25 5.00 12.00
19 Myles Straw/25 8.00 20.00
20 Taylor Ward/25 5.00 12.00

2019 Immaculate Collection Jumbo Jersey Autographs

RANDOM INSERTS IN PACKS
PRINT RUNS B/WN 5-25 COPIES PER
NO PRICING QTY 15 OR LESS
EXCHANGE DEADLINE 2/21/2021
1 Andrew Stevenson/25 5.00 12.00
2 Brandon Nimmo/25 6.00 15.00
3 Brandon Woodruff/25 5.00 12.00
7 Jackie Bradley Jr./25 8.00 20.00
10 Marcell Ozuna/25 8.00 20.00
11 Nelson Cruz/25 10.00 25.00
25 Scooter Gennett/25 6.00 15.00
32 Kerry Wood/25 8.00 20.00
38 Michael Chavis/25 8.00 20.00

2019 Immaculate Collection Legends Dual Materials

RANDOM INSERTS IN PACKS
PRINT RUNS B/WN 10-49 COPIES PER
NO PRICING QTY 15 OR LESS
*RED/25: .6X TO 1.5X p/r 49
3 Mickey Mantle/49 25.00 60.00
5 Yogi Berra/25 5.00 12.00
6 Ted Williams/25 25.00 60.00
7 Bob Turley/49 2.00 5.00
8 Reggie Jackson/49 2.50 6.00
9 Harmon Killebrew/25 5.00 12.00
10 Billy Williams/49 2.50 6.00
11 Orlando Cepeda/25 4.00 10.00
12 Tony Gwynn/49 8.00 20.00
13 Rod Carew/49 2.50 6.00
14 Nolan Ryan/49 10.00 25.00
15 Johnny Bench/49 10.00 25.00
16 Willie McCovey/49 8.00 20.00
17 Bobby Doerr/49 2.50 6.00
18 Larry Doby/49 2.50 6.00
19 Pete Rose/49 15.00 40.00
20 Mariano Rivera/49 4.00 10.00
21 Frank Robinson/49 8.00 20.00
22 George Brett/49 10.00 25.00
23 Bill Mazeroski/49 2.50 6.00
24 Cal Ripken/49 15.00 40.00
25 Ichiro/49 8.00 20.00

2019 Immaculate Collection Legends Materials

RANDOM INSERTS IN PACKS
PRINT RUNS B/WN 7-49 COPIES PER
NO PRICING QTY 15 OR LESS
*RED/25: .6X TO 1.5X
2 Billy Martin/49 2.50 6.00
3 Casey Stengel/49 2.50 6.00
4 Don Drysdale/49 2.50 6.00
5 Edd Roush/49 2.50 6.00
6 Gil Hodges/49 2.50 6.00
7 Herb Pennock/49 2.50 6.00
8 Leo Durocher/49 2.00 5.00
9 Mickey Mantle/49 25.00 60.00
12 Ted Williams/49 15.00 40.00
13 Yogi Berra/49 3.00 8.00
14 Richie Ashburn/49 2.50 6.00
15 Dom DiMaggio/49 2.00 5.00
16 Bob Lemon/49 2.50 6.00
17 Ralph Kiner/49 2.50 6.00
18 Duke Snider/49 2.50 6.00
19 Al Kaline/49 3.00 8.00
20 Nolan Ryan/49 10.00 25.00
21 Rod Carew/49 2.50 6.00
22 Al Simmons/25 4.00 10.00
23 Bob Meusel/49 2.00 5.00
25 Whitey Ford/49 2.50 6.00

2019 Immaculate Collection Matinee Dual Memorabilia Autographs

RANDOM INSERTS IN PACKS
PRINT RUNS B/WN 10-35 COPIES PER
NO PRICING QTY 15 OR LESS
EXCHANGE DEADLINE 2/21/2021
*RED/25: .4X TO 1X
1 Aaron Judge/20 50.00 120.00
2 Nomar Mazara/35 4.00 10.00
6 Barry Larkin/20 20.00 50.00
7 Amed Rosario/20 6.00 15.00
8 Rhys Hoskins/35 12.00 30.00
9 Adrian Beltre/20 8.00 20.00
10 Manny Machado/25 25.00 60.00

2019 Immaculate Collection Moments Memorabilia Autographs

RANDOM INSERTS IN PACKS
PRINT RUNS B/WN 5-25 COPIES PER
NO PRICING QTY 15 OR LESS
EXCHANGE DEADLINE 2/21/2021
6 Juan Marichal/25 15.00 40.00
7 Don Mattingly/25 25.00 60.00
13 John Smoltz/25 8.00 20.00
15 Vladimir Guerrero/25 10.00 25.00
16 Larry Walker/25 25.00 60.00
17 Carlton Fisk/25 15.00 40.00
19 Tommy Lasorda/25 15.00 40.00
20 Dave Winfield/25 12.00 30.00

2019 Immaculate Collection Old English Memorabilia Autographs

RANDOM INSERTS IN PACKS
PRINT RUNS B/WN 3-49 COPIES PER
NO PRICING QTY 17 OR LESS
EXCHANGE DEADLINE 2/21/2021
*RED/20-25: .5X TO 1.2X p/r 34-49
1 Andrew Benintendi/49 15.00 40.00
2 Miguel Andujar/49 10.00 25.00
3 Alex Verdugo/49 8.00 20.00
4 Harrison Bader/49 5.00 12.00
5 Rhys Hoskins/49 15.00 40.00
6 Shohei Ohtani/35 75.00 200.00
8 Josh Donaldson/34 15.00 40.00
9 Clint Frazier/49 5.00 12.00
12 Marcell Ozuna/49 10.00 25.00
13 Kyle Schwarber/17 8.00 20.00
15 Orlando Arcia/49 6.00 15.00
19 Shohei Ohtani/35 75.00 200.00

2019 Immaculate Collection Past and Present Dual Memorabilia Autographs

RANDOM INSERTS IN PACKS
PRINT RUNS B/WN 5-25 COPIES PER
NO PRICING QTY 15 OR LESS
EXCHANGE DEADLINE 2/21/2021
3 Eloy Jimenez/25 25.00 60.00
5 Justus Sheffield/25 10.00 25.00

2019 Immaculate Collection Premium Memorabilia Autographs

RANDOM INSERTS IN PACKS
PRINT RUNS B/WN 25-49 COPIES PER
EXCHANGE DEADLINE 2/21/2021
1 Joey Lucchesi/25 5.00 12.00
2 Francisco Mejia/25 6.00 15.00
3 Austin Riley/49 20.00 50.00
4 Bo Bichette/49 50.00 120.00
5 Ryan McMahon/25 5.00 12.00
6 Brian Anderson/49 4.00 10.00
7 Pete Alonso/25 100.00 250.00
8 Clint Frazier/25 10.00 25.00
9 Adalberto Mondesi/49 5.00 12.00
10 German Marquez/25 5.00 12.00
11 Brandon Woodruff/25 5.00 12.00
12 Lewis Brinson/25 5.00 12.00
13 Jose Berrios/49 5.00 12.00
14 Sean Manaea/25 5.00 12.00
15 Max Fried/25 8.00 20.00

2019 Immaculate Collection Prospect Patch Autographs

RANDOM INSERTS IN PACKS
PRINT RUNS B/WN 20-99 COPIES PER
EXCHANGE DEADLINE 2/21/2021
*GOLD/49: .5X TO 1.2X p/r 99
*GOLD/25: .5X TO 1.2X p/r 49
*GOLD/25: .4X TO 1X p/r 20-30
1 Corey Ray/30 5.00 12.00
3 Jon Duplantier/49 4.00 10.00
6 Mitch Keller/20 6.00 15.00
7 Ke'Bryan Hayes/25 5.00 12.00
8 Leody Taveras/49 4.00 10.00
10 Wander Franco/99 60.00 150.00
11 Sean Murphy/25 6.00 15.00
12 Ian Anderson/49 10.00 25.00
13 Austin Riley/20 25.00 60.00
14 Adbert Alzolay/49 4.00 10.00
15 Kyle Lewis/49 30.00 80.00
16 Julio Pablo Martinez/49 4.00 10.00
17 Khalil Lee/30 5.00 12.00
18 Bo Bichette/25 75.00 200.00
19 Forrest Whitley/25 8.00 20.00
20 Brent Honeywell/49 5.00 12.00

2019 Immaculate Collection Pure Memorabilia Autographs

RANDOM INSERTS IN PACKS
PRINT RUNS B/WN 10-49 COPIES PER
NO PRICING QTY 15 OR LESS
EXCHANGE DEADLINE 2/21/2021
1 Carlos Martinez/25 6.00 15.00
2 Forrest Whitley/25 8.00 20.00
3 Joey Votto/25 8.00 20.00
4 Ken Griffey Sr./25 5.00 12.00
5 Alan Trammell/25 20.00 50.00
6 Pete Alonso/49 50.00 120.00
7 Rafael Devers/25 15.00 40.00
8 Reggie Jackson/25 15.00 40.00
9 Ronald Acuna Jr./49 50.00 120.00
10 Sean Manaea/25 5.00 12.00
11 Trey Mancini/25 6.00 15.00
13 Keston Hiura/49 15.00 40.00
14 Fernando Tatis Jr./49 50.00 120.00
15 Vladimir Guerrero Jr./25 60.00 150.00

2019 Immaculate Collection Rookie Debut Dual Memorabilia Autographs

RANDOM INSERTS IN PACKS
PRINT RUNS B/WN 10-25 COPIES PER
NO PRICING QTY 15 OR LESS
EXCHANGE DEADLINE 2/21/2021
1 Ranger Suarez/25 5.00 12.00
2 Justin Williams/25 5.00 12.00
6 Victor Reyes/25 8.00 20.00
7 Jon Duplantier/25 5.00 12.00
10 Nick Margevicius/25 5.00 12.00
11 Kyle Zimmer/25 5.00 12.00
12 Jake Cave/25 6.00 15.00
13 Josh James/25 8.00 20.00
16 Jake Bauers/25 8.00 20.00
17 Corbin Burnes/25 8.00 20.00
18 Christin Stewart/25 6.00 15.00
22 Chance Adams/25 5.00 12.00
23 Touki Toussaint/25 6.00 15.00
24 Luis Urias/25 8.00 20.00
26 Ryan O'Hearn/25 5.00 12.00
27 Jonathan Loaisiga/25 6.00 15.00
28 Caleb Ferguson/25 6.00 15.00
29 Chris Paddack/25 15.00 40.00

2019 Immaculate Collection Rookie Matinee Dual Memorabilia Autographs

RANDOM INSERTS IN PACKS
PRINT RUNS B/WN 25-49 COPIES PER
EXCHANGE DEADLINE 2/21/2021
1 Jake Bauers/49 6.00 15.00
2 Reese McGuire/25 8.00 20.00
3 Luis Urias/49 6.00 15.00
4 Kyle Tucker/49 12.00 30.00
5 Cedric Mullins/25 8.00 20.00
6 Christin Stewart/49 5.00 12.00
7 Vladimir Guerrero Jr./49 60.00 150.00
8 Danny Jansen/49 4.00 10.00
9 Kevin Newman/25 8.00 20.00
10 Fernando Tatis Jr./49 75.00 200.00
11 Rowdy Tellez/49 6.00 15.00
12 Ryan O'Hearn/49 4.00 10.00
13 Steven Duggar/25 6.00 15.00
14 Brandon Lowe/49 10.00 25.00
15 David Fletcher/49 12.00 30.00
16 Jake Cave/25 6.00 15.00
17 Kevin Kramer/25 6.00 15.00
18 Myles Straw/25 8.00 20.00
19 Taylor Ward/25 5.00 12.00
20 Garrett Hampson/25 5.00 12.00

2019 Immaculate Collection Signatures

RANDOM INSERTS IN PACKS
PRINT RUNS B/WN 7-99 COPIES PER
NO PRICING QTY 15 OR LESS
EXCHANGE DEADLINE 2/21/2021
*GOLD/49: .5X TO 1.2X p/r 99
*GOLD/25: .5X TO 1.2X p/r 49
2 Cesar Hernandez/99 2.50 6.00
3 Whit Merrifield/99 8.00 20.00
4 David Ross/25 15.00 40.00
5 Mike Mussina/49 4.00 10.00
7 Pete Rose/25 20.00 50.00
8 Ted Simmons/49 20.00 50.00
9 Xander Bogaerts/49 12.00 30.00
10 Adrian Gonzalez/25 5.00 12.00
11 Alex Wood/99 2.50 6.00
12 Carlton Fisk/25 15.00 40.00
13 Fergie Jenkins/49 4.00 10.00
14 Carlos Martinez/49 4.00 10.00
15 Jose Berrios/49 4.00 10.00
17 Nomar Mazara/49 8.00 20.00
18 Tim Wakefield/49 8.00 20.00
21 Charlie Blackmon/49 8.00 20.00
22 Darryl Strawberry/49 3.00 8.00
23 Jose Ramirez/49 4.00 10.00
25 Omar Vizquel/49 6.00 15.00
26 Yadier Molina/25 6.00 15.00
27 Dale Murphy/49 10.00 25.00
30 Trea Turner/49 8.00 20.00
32 Francisco Lindor/25 12.00 30.00

33 Steve Garvey/49 12.00 30.00
34 Keith Hernandez/49 10.00 25.00
35 Rafael Devers/49 10.00 25.00
36 Rhys Hoskins/49 10.00 25.00
38 Jason Giambi/25 4.00 10.00
39 Kevin Mitchell/49 12.00 30.00
40 Ozzie Albies/49 12.00 30.00

2019 Immaculate Collection Team Heroes Dual Memorabilia Autographs

RANDOM INSERTS IN PACKS
PRINT RUNS B/WN 10-49 COPIES PER
NO PRICING QTY 15 OR LESS
EXCHANGE DEADLINE 2/21/2021
2 Scooter Gennett/20 6.00 15.00
3 Freddie Freeman/25 15.00 40.00
5 Nolan Arenado/20 20.00 50.00
6 Max Muncy/25 6.00 15.00
7 Eddie Rosario/20 6.00 15.00
8 Luis Severino/20 6.00 15.00
9 Jacob deGrom/25 8.00 20.00
10 George Springer/25 15.00 40.00
11 Anthony Rizzo/20 12.00 30.00
12 Mitch Haniger/49 5.00 12.00
13 Matt Olson/25 10.00 25.00
14 Jose Ramirez/25 6.00 15.00
15 Chris Sale/25 8.00 20.00

2019 Immaculate Collection Winter Collection Triple Memorabilia Autographs

RANDOM INSERTS IN PACKS
STATED PRINT RUN 25 SER.#'d SETS
EXCHANGE DEADLINE 2/21/2021
1 Bryse Wilson 6.00 15.00
2 Kolby Allard 8.00 20.00
3 Cedric Mullins 10.00 25.00
4 Jake Bauers 8.00 20.00
5 Garrett Hampson 5.00 12.00
6 Christin Stewart 6.00 15.00
7 Josh James 8.00 20.00
8 Brad Keller 5.00 12.00
9 Ryan O'Hearn 5.00 12.00
10 David Fletcher 15.00 40.00
11 Dennis Santana 5.00 12.00
12 Corbin Burnes 8.00 20.00
13 Jake Cave 6.00 15.00
14 Jeff McNeil 12.00 30.00
15 Chance Adams 5.00 12.00
16 Enyel De Los Santos 5.00 12.00
17 Jacob Nix 6.00 15.00
18 Chris Shaw 8.00 20.00
19 Daniel Ponce de Leon 8.00 20.00
20 Brandon Lowe 12.00 30.00

2020 Immaculate Collection

RANDOM INSERTS IN PACKS
NO PRICING QTY 15 OR LESS
1-100 PRINT RUN B/TW 10-99 COPIES PER
101-161 STATED PRINT RUN 99 SER.#'d SETS
1 Max Fried JSY/99 3.00 8.00
2 Yogi Berra JSY/25 10.00 25.00
3 Michael Brantley JSY/99 2.50 6.00
4 Vladimir Guerrero Jr. JSY/99 6.00 15.00
5 Juan Soto JSY/99 6.00 15.00
6 Cody Bellinger JSY/99 6.00 15.00
7 Mickey Mantle JSY/49 20.00 50.00
8 Freddie Freeman JSY/99 4.00 10.00
9 Josh Donaldson JSY/99 2.50 6.00
10 Bryce Harper JSY/99 5.00 12.00
11 Josh Bell JSY/99 2.50 6.00
12 Aaron Nola JSY/49 4.00 10.00
13 Ronald Acuna Jr. JSY/99 6.00 15.00
14 Ted Williams JSY/49 20.00 50.00
15 Rafael Devers JSY/99 4.00 10.00
16 Jim Thome JSY/99 2.50 6.00
17 Leo Durocher JSY/99 2.00 5.00
18 Andrew Benintendi JSY/99 3.00 8.00
19 Herb Pennock JSY/49 8.00 20.00
20 Nelson Cruz JSY/99 3.00 8.00
21 Giancarlo Stanton JSY/99 3.00 8.00
22 Anthony Rizzo JSY/99 5.00 12.00
23 Justin Verlander JSY/99 3.00 8.00
24 Rhys Hoskins JSY/99 4.00 10.00
26 Pete Alonso JSY/49 10.00 25.00
27 Alex Bregman JSY/99 3.00 8.00
28 Max Scherzer JSY/25 5.00 12.00
29 Chris Sale JSY/99 3.00 8.00
30 Yoan Moncada JSY/99 3.00 8.00
31 Edd Roush JSY/25 12.00 30.00
32 Shohei Ohtani JSY/99 4.00 10.00
33 Tim Anderson JSY/99 3.00 8.00
34 Roy Campanella JSY/49 6.00 15.00
35 Stephen Strasburg JSY/99 3.00 8.00
36 Jeff Bagwell JSY/99 5.00 12.00
37 Josh Hader JSY/99 2.00 5.00
38 Matt Chapman JSY/99 3.00 8.00
39 Albert Pujols JSY/99 4.00 10.00
41 Mookie Betts JSY/99 8.00 20.00
42 Noah Syndergaard JSY/99 2.50 6.00
44 Matt Olson JSY/99 2.00 5.00
45 Jonathan Villar JSY/49 2.50 6.00
47 Jack Flaherty JSY/99 2.50 6.00
49 Tony Lazzeri JSY/25 12.00 30.00
50 Alan Trammell JSY/99 8.00 20.00
51 Jose Altuve JSY/99 2.50 6.00
53 Eloy Jimenez JSY/99 4.00 10.00
54 Tim Raines JSY/99 2.50 6.00
55 Charlie Blackmon JSY/25 5.00 12.00
56 Chris Paddack JSY/99 3.00 8.00
57 Keston Hiura JSY/99 4.00 10.00
59 Joey Gallo JSY/99 3.00 8.00
60 Nolan Arenado JSY/99 4.00 10.00
61 Mike Trout JSY/99 15.00 40.00
62 Jacob deGrom JSY/49 4.00 10.00
63 Adalberto Mondesi JSY/99 3.00 8.00
64 Walker Buehler JSY/99 4.00 10.00
65 Gary Sanchez JSY/99 3.00 8.00
66 Ozzie Albies JSY/99 3.00 8.00
67 Aaron Judge JSY/99 6.00 15.00
68 Starling Marte JSY/99 2.50 6.00
69 Roberto Clemente JSY/49 30.00 80.00
70 Ron Santo JSY/49 10.00 25.00
71 Marcell Ozuna JSY/99 3.00 8.00
72 Fernando Tatis Jr. JSY/99 8.00 20.00
73 George Springer JSY/99 2.50 6.00
74 Kris Bryant JSY/99 4.00 10.00
75 Trea Turner JSY/99 2.50 6.00
76 Christian Yelich JSY/49 5.00 12.00
77 Ken Boyer JSY/25 6.00 15.00
78 Whit Merrifield JSY/99 3.00 8.00
79 Trevor Story JSY/99 3.00 8.00
80 George Brett JSY/49 12.00 30.00
81 Jose Berrios JSY/99 2.50 6.00
82 Trey Mancini JSY/99 3.00 8.00
83 Gil Hodges JSY/49 5.00 12.00
84 Jose Ramirez JSY/99 2.50 6.00
85 Eddie Rosario JSY/99 2.50 6.00
86 Paul Goldschmidt JSY/99 3.00 8.00
87 Clayton Kershaw JSY/99 6.00 15.00
88 Manny Machado JSY/99 3.00 8.00
89 Gleyber Torres JSY/99 6.00 15.00
90 Stan Musial JSY/49 10.00 25.00
91 Xander Bogaerts JSY/99 3.00 8.00
92 Craig Biggio JSY/99 2.50 6.00
93 Blake Snell JSY/49 3.00 8.00
94 Gerrit Cole JSY/99 5.00 12.00
95 Frank Chance JSY/25 12.00 30.00
96 Javier Baez JSY/99 4.00 10.00
97 Jorge Soler JSY/99 3.00 8.00
98 Austin Meadows JSY/99 2.50 6.00
99 Ramon Laureano JSY/99 3.00 8.00
100 J.D. Martinez JSY/99 3.00 8.00
101 Matt Thaiss JSY AU/99 RC 4.00 10.00
102 Jonathan Hernandez JSY AU/99 RC 3.00 8.00
103 Deivy Grullon JSY AU/99 RC 3.00 8.00
104 Jordan Yamamoto JSY AU/99 RC 4.00 10.00
105 Edwin Rios JSY AU/99 RC 8.00 20.00
106 Lewis Thorpe JSY AU/99 RC 3.00 8.00
107 Nick Solak JSY AU/99 RC 5.00 12.00
108 Zac Gallen JSY AU/99 RC 8.00 20.00
109 Jake Fraley JSY AU/99 RC 4.00 10.00
110 Tyrone Taylor JSY AU/99 RC 3.00 8.00
111 A.J. Puk JSY AU/99 RC 6.00 15.00
112 Patrick Sandoval JSY AU/99 RC 5.00 12.00
113 Randy Arozarena JSY AU/99 RC 40.00 100.00
114 Domingo Leyba JSY AU/99 RC 4.00 10.00
115 Dylan Cease JSY AU/99 RC 6.00 15.00
116 Anthony Kay JSY AU/99 RC 3.00 8.00
117 Gavin Lux JSY AU/99 RC 20.00 50.00
118 Michael King JSY AU/99 RC 5.00 12.00
119 Joe Palumbo JSY AU/99 RC 3.00 8.00
120 Jake Rogers JSY AU/99 RC 3.00 8.00
121 Danny Mendick JSY AU/99 RC 4.00 10.00
122 Sean Murphy JSY AU/99 RC 5.00 12.00
123 Isan Diaz JSY AU/99 RC 5.00 12.00
124 Bobby Bradley JSY AU/99 RC 4.00 10.00
126 Bo Bichette JSY AU/99 RC 40.00 100.00
127 Dustin May JSY AU/99 RC 20.00 50.00
128 Andres Munoz JSY AU/99 RC 4.00 10.00
129 Josh Rojas JSY AU/99 RC 3.00 8.00
130 Kyle Lewis JSY AU/99 RC 25.00 60.00
131 Logan Webb JSY AU/99 RC 4.00 10.00
132 Brusdar Graterol JSY AU/99 RC 5.00 12.00
133 Bryan Abreu JSY AU/99 RC 3.00 8.00
134 Aristides Aquino JSY AU/99 RC 10.00 25.00
135 Tony Gonsolin JSY AU/99 RC 12.00 30.00
136 Sheldon Neuse JSY AU/99 RC 4.00 10.00
137 Brendan McKay JSY AU/99 RC 5.00 12.00
138 Logan Allen JSY AU/99 RC 3.00 8.00
139 Zack Collins JSY AU/99 RC 4.00 10.00
140 Abraham Toro JSY AU/99 RC 4.00 10.00
141 Adbert Alzolay JSY AU/99 RC 4.00 10.00
142 Donnie Walton JSY AU/99 RC 8.00 20.00
143 Jesus Luzardo JSY AU/99 RC 6.00 15.00
144 Aaron Civale JSY AU/99 RC 5.00 12.00
145 Nico Hoerner JSY AU/99 RC 15.00 40.00
146 Michel Baez JSY AU/99 RC 3.00 8.00
147 Justin Dunn JSY AU/99 RC 4.00 10.00
148 Mauricio Dubon JSY AU/99 RC 4.00 10.00
149 T.J. Zeuch JSY AU/99 RC 3.00 8.00
150 Sam Hilliard JSY AU/99 RC 5.00 12.00
151 Rico Garcia JSY AU/99 RC 5.00 12.00
152 Willi Castro JSY AU/99 RC 5.00 12.00
153 Tres Barrera JSY AU/99 RC 6.00 15.00
154 Yordan Alvarez JSY AU/99 RC 25.00 60.00
155 Ronald Bolanos JSY AU/99 RC 5.00 12.00
156 Jaylin Davis JSY AU/99 RC 5.00 12.00
157 Trent Grisham JSY AU/99 RC 12.00 30.00
158 Adrian Morejon JSY AU/99 RC 3.00 8.00
159 Travis Demeritte JSY AU/99 RC 4.00 10.00
160 Brock Burke JSY AU/99 RC 3.00 8.00
161 Yonathan Daza JSY AU/99 RC 4.00 10.00

2020 Immaculate Collection Red

*RED 1-100/49: .5X TO 1.2X
*RED 1-100/25: .6X TO 1.5X
*RED 101-161/49: .6X TO 1.2X
RANDOM INSERTS IN PACKS
PRINT RUNS B/WN 10-49 COPIES PER
NO PRICING QTY 15 OR LESS
7 Mickey Mantle JSY/25 30.00 80.00
14 Ted Williams JSY/25 30.00 80.00
83 Gil Hodges JSY/25 10.00 25.00
90 Stan Musial JSY/25 20.00 50.00

2020 Immaculate Collection Batting Stance Memorabilia Autographs

RANDOM INSERTS IN PACKS
PRINT RUNS B/WN 10-25 COPIES PER
NO PRICING QTY 15 OR LESS
EXCHANGE DEADLINE 2/21/2022
4 Deivy Grullon/25 5.00 12.00
6 Randy Arozarena/25 60.00 150.00
7 Nick Solak/25 8.00 20.00
8 Sheldon Neuse/25 6.00 15.00
9 Jaylin Davis/25 8.00 20.00
10 Mauricio Dubon/25 6.00 15.00
12 Jake Fraley/25 6.00 15.00
14 Bo Bichette/25 60.00 150.00
15 Isan Diaz/25 8.00 20.00
16 Sean Murphy/25 8.00 20.00

2020 Immaculate Collection Clearly Clutch Rookies Dual Memorabilia Autographs

RANDOM INSERTS IN PACKS
STATED PRINT RUN 25 SER.#'d SETS
EXCHANGE DEADLINE 2/21/2022
1 Bobby Bradley 4.00 10.00
2 Travis Demeritte 4.00 10.00
3 Nick Solak 5.00 12.00
4 Yonathan Daza 4.00 10.00
5 Zack Collins 4.00 10.00
6 Jake Rogers 3.00 8.00
7 Sean Murphy 5.00 12.00
8 Aristides Aquino 8.00 20.00
9 Sam Hilliard 5.00 12.00
10 Yordan Alvarez 25.00 60.00
12 Kyle Lewis 25.00 60.00
13 Randy Arozarena 40.00 100.00
14 Nico Hoerner 15.00 40.00
15 Willi Castro 5.00 12.00
16 Gavin Lux 20.00 50.00
17 Mauricio Dubon 4.00 10.00
18 Bo Bichette 40.00 100.00
19 Isan Diaz 5.00 12.00
20 Yu Chang 5.00 12.00

2020 Immaculate Collection Clutch Dual Memorabilia Autographs

RANDOM INSERTS IN PACKS
PRINT RUNS B/WN 10-49 COPIES PER
NO PRICING QTY 15 OR LESS
*BLUE/25: .5X TO 1.2X p/r 49
1 Aaron Judge/25 60.00 150.00
2 Billy Williams/15
3 Alex Rodriguez/15
4 Roberto Alomar/24 15.00 40.00
5 Gerrit Cole/15
6 Ryan Braun/15
7 Dallas Keuchel/10
8 Robinson Cano/10
9 Dennis Eckersley/15
10 Rickey Henderson/25 50.00 120.00
11 Dylan Carlson/49 15.00 40.00
12 Reggie Jackson/15
13 Evan Longoria/15
14 Orlando Cepeda/10
15 Fergie Jenkins/49 6.00 15.00
16 Nelson Cruz/22 8.00 20.00
17 Jim Palmer/14
18 Marcell Ozuna/15
19 Jorge Soler/49 6.00 15.00
20 Josh Donaldson/26 12.00 30.00

2020 Immaculate Collection Clutch Rookies Dual Memorabilia Autographs

RANDOM INSERTS IN PACKS
STATED PRINT RUN 49 SER.#'d SETS
EXCHANGE DEADLINE 2/21/2022
*BLUE/25: .5X TO 1.2X
1 Bobby Bradley 5.00 12.00
2 Travis Demeritte 5.00 12.00
3 Nick Solak 6.00 15.00
4 Yonathan Daza 5.00 12.00
5 Zack Collins 5.00 12.00
6 Jake Rogers 4.00 10.00
7 Sean Murphy 6.00 15.00
8 Aristides Aquino 10.00 25.00
9 Sam Hilliard 6.00 15.00
10 Yordan Alvarez 30.00 80.00
12 Kyle Lewis 30.00 80.00
13 Randy Arozarena 50.00 120.00
14 Nico Hoerner 20.00 50.00
15 Willi Castro 6.00 15.00
16 Gavin Lux 25.00 60.00
17 Mauricio Dubon 5.00 12.00
18 Bo Bichette 50.00 120.00
19 Isan Diaz 6.00 15.00
20 Yu Chang 6.00 15.00

2020 Immaculate Collection Debut Jumbo Material Autographs

RANDOM INSERTS IN PACKS
STATED PRINT RUN 99 SER.#'d SETS
EXCHANGE DEADLINE 2/21/2022
*HOLO GOLD/50-73: .4X TO 1X
*HOLO GOLD/39-49: .5X TO 1.2X
*HOLO GOLD/19-31: .6X TO 1.5X
*RED/35-49: .5X TO 1.2X
*HOLO SLVR/25: .6X TO 1.5X
1 Adbert Alzolay 4.00 10.00
2 Tres Barrera 6.00 15.00
3 Andres Munoz 4.00 10.00
4 Tyrone Taylor 3.00 8.00
5 Danny Mendick 4.00 10.00
6 Lewis Thorpe 3.00 8.00
7 Deivy Grullon 3.00 8.00
8 Travis Demeritte 4.00 10.00
9 Domingo Leyba 4.00 10.00
10 T.J. Zeuch 3.00 8.00
11 Donnie Walton 8.00 20.00
12 Ronald Bolanos 5.00 12.00
13 Edwin Rios 8.00 20.00
14 Rico Garcia 5.00 12.00
15 Jaylin Davis 5.00 12.00
16 Randy Arozarena 40.00 100.00
17 Jonathan Hernandez 3.00 8.00
18 Josh Rojas 3.00 8.00
19 Patrick Sandoval 5.00 12.00

2020 Immaculate Collection Debut Moments Memorabilia Autographs

RANDOM INSERTS IN PACKS
STATED PRINT RUN 49 SER.#'d SETS
EXCHANGE DEADLINE 2/21/2022
*BLUE/25: .5X TO 1.2X
1 Matt Thaiss 5.00 12.00
2 Jonathan Hernandez 4.00 10.00
3 Edwin Rios 10.00 25.00
4 Nick Solak 6.00 15.00
5 Jake Fraley 5.00 12.00
6 A.J. Puk 8.00 20.00
7 Randy Arozarena 50.00 120.00
8 Dylan Cease 8.00 20.00
9 Gavin Lux 25.00 60.00
10 Joe Palumbo 4.00 10.00
11 Danny Mendick 5.00 12.00
12 Isan Diaz 6.00 15.00
13 Yu Chang 6.00 15.00
14 Dustin May 25.00 60.00
15 Josh Rojas 4.00 10.00
16 Logan Webb 5.00 12.00
17 Bryan Abreu 4.00 10.00
18 Tony Gonsolin 15.00 40.00
19 Brendan McKay 6.00 15.00
20 Zack Collins 5.00 12.00
21 Adbert Alzolay 5.00 12.00
22 Jesus Luzardo 8.00 20.00
23 Nico Hoerner 20.00 50.00
24 Justin Dunn 5.00 12.00
25 T.J. Zeuch 4.00 10.00
26 Rico Garcia 6.00 15.00
27 Tres Barrera 8.00 20.00
28 Ronald Bolanos 6.00 15.00
30 Travis Demeritte 5.00 12.00
31 Yonathan Daza 5.00 12.00
32 Brock Burke 4.00 10.00
33 Adrian Morejon 4.00 10.00
34 Jaylin Davis 6.00 15.00
35 Yordan Alvarez 30.00 80.00
36 Willi Castro 6.00 15.00
37 Sam Hilliard 6.00 15.00
38 Mauricio Dubon 5.00 12.00
39 Michel Baez 4.00 10.00
40 Aaron Civale 6.00 15.00
41 Donnie Walton 10.00 25.00
42 Abraham Toro 5.00 12.00
43 Logan Allen 4.00 10.00
44 Sheldon Neuse 5.00 12.00
45 Aristides Aquino 10.00 25.00
46 Brusdar Graterol 6.00 15.00
47 Kyle Lewis 30.00 80.00
48 Andres Munoz 5.00 12.00
49 Bo Bichette 50.00 120.00
50 Bobby Bradley 5.00 12.00
51 Sean Murphy 6.00 15.00
52 Jake Rogers 4.00 10.00
53 Michael King 6.00 15.00
54 Anthony Kay 4.00 10.00
55 Domingo Leyba 5.00 12.00
56 Patrick Sandoval 6.00 15.00
57 Tyrone Taylor 4.00 10.00
58 Zac Gallen 10.00 25.00
59 Deivy Grullon 4.00 10.00
60 Jordan Yamamoto 5.00 12.00

2020 Immaculate Collection Debut Moments Memorabilia Leather Autographs

RANDOM INSERTS IN PACKS
STATED PRINT RUN 99 SER.#'d SETS
EXCHANGE DEADLINE 2/21/2022
*BROWN/49: .5X TO 1.2X
1 Matt Thaiss 4.00 10.00
2 Jonathan Hernandez 3.00 8.00
3 Edwin Rios 8.00 20.00
4 Nick Solak 5.00 12.00
5 Jake Fraley 4.00 10.00
6 A.J. Puk 6.00 15.00
7 Randy Arozarena 40.00 100.00
8 Dylan Cease 6.00 15.00
9 Gavin Lux 20.00 50.00
10 Joe Palumbo 3.00 8.00
11 Danny Mendick 4.00 10.00
12 Isan Diaz 5.00 12.00
13 Yu Chang 5.00 12.00
15 Josh Rojas 3.00 8.00
16 Logan Webb 4.00 10.00
17 Bryan Abreu 3.00 8.00
18 Tony Gonsolin 12.00 30.00
19 Brendan McKay 5.00 12.00
20 Zack Collins 4.00 10.00
21 Adbert Alzolay 4.00 10.00
22 Jesus Luzardo 6.00 15.00
23 Nico Hoerner 15.00 40.00
24 Justin Dunn 4.00 10.00
25 T.J. Zeuch 3.00 8.00
26 Rico Garcia 5.00 12.00
27 Tres Barrera 6.00 15.00
28 Ronald Bolanos 5.00 12.00
30 Travis Demeritte 4.00 10.00
31 Yonathan Daza 4.00 10.00
32 Brock Burke 3.00 8.00
33 Adrian Morejon 3.00 8.00
34 Jaylin Davis 5.00 12.00
35 Yordan Alvarez 25.00 60.00
36 Willi Castro 5.00 12.00
37 Sam Hilliard 5.00 12.00
38 Mauricio Dubon 4.00 10.00
39 Michel Baez 3.00 8.00
40 Aaron Civale 5.00 12.00
41 Donnie Walton 8.00 20.00
42 Abraham Toro 4.00 10.00
43 Logan Allen 3.00 8.00
44 Sheldon Neuse 4.00 10.00
45 Aristides Aquino 8.00 20.00
46 Brusdar Graterol 5.00 12.00
47 Kyle Lewis 25.00 60.00
48 Andres Munoz 4.00 10.00
49 Bo Bichette 40.00 100.00
50 Bobby Bradley 4.00 10.00
51 Sean Murphy 5.00 12.00
52 Jake Rogers 3.00 8.00
53 Michael King 5.00 12.00
54 Anthony Kay 3.00 8.00
55 Domingo Leyba 4.00 10.00
56 Patrick Sandoval 5.00 12.00
57 Tyrone Taylor 3.00 8.00
58 Zac Gallen 8.00 20.00
59 Deivy Grullon 3.00 8.00
60 Jordan Yamamoto 4.00 10.00

2020 Immaculate Collection Dugout Collection Dual Memorabilia Autographs

RANDOM INSERTS IN PACKS
STATED PRINT RUN 25 SER.#'d SETS
EXCHANGE DEADLINE 2/21/2022
1 Bobby Bradley 6.00 15.00
2 Domingo Leyba 6.00 15.00
6 Jake Fraley 6.00 15.00
8 Rico Garcia 8.00 20.00
9 Jonathan Hernandez 5.00 12.00
10 Justin Dunn 6.00 15.00
11 Matt Thaiss 6.00 15.00
12 Tony Gonsolin 20.00 50.00
13 Yonathan Daza 6.00 15.00
14 Jordan Yamamoto 6.00 15.00
18 T.J. Zeuch 5.00 12.00
19 Anthony Kay 5.00 12.00
20 Adrian Morejon 5.00 12.00

2020 Immaculate Collection Extra Bases Triple Memorabilia Autographs

RANDOM INSERTS IN PACKS
PRINT RUNS B/WN 10-25 COPIES PER
NO PRICING QTY 15 OR LESS
EXCHANGE DEADLINE 2/21/2022
1 Brandon Lowe/25 12.00 30.00
2 Dakota Hudson/25 15.00 40.00
3 Victor Mesa Jr./25 12.00 30.00
4 Evan White/25 12.00 30.00
5 Kyle Tucker/25 20.00 50.00
6 Kevin Newman/25 10.00 25.00
7 Ryan Mountcastle/25 8.00 20.00
8 Jonathan Loaisiga/25 6.00 15.00
9 Estevan Florial/25 20.00 50.00
10 Mike Soroka/25 30.00 80.00
11 Ryan O'Hearn/25 8.00 20.00
12 Jordan Hicks/25 6.00 15.00
13 Garrett Hampson/25 5.00 12.00
14 Cavan Biggio/25 20.00 50.00
15 Daniel Ponce de Leon/25 8.00 20.00
16 Christin Stewart/25 5.00 12.00
17 Ian Anderson/25 25.00 60.00
18 David Fletcher/25 12.00 30.00
19 Josh James/25 8.00 20.00
20 Alex Reyes/25 6.00 15.00
21 Vladimir Guerrero Jr./25 25.00 60.00
22 Michael Chavis/25 15.00 40.00
23 Alex Kirilloff/25 20.00 50.00
24 Yadier Molina/25 40.00 100.00
25 Austin Riley/25 12.00 30.00
28 Dylan Carlson/25 20.00 50.00
29 Andy Pettitte/25 12.00 30.00

2020 Immaculate Collection Flannel Sigs

RANDOM INSERTS IN PACKS
STATED PRINT RUN 25 SER.#'d SETS
EXCHANGE DEADLINE 2/21/2022
1 Adbert Alzolay 6.00 15.00
2 Nico Hoerner 25.00 60.00
3 Willi Castro 8.00 20.00
4 Brusdar Graterol 8.00 20.00
6 Deivi Garcia 40.00 100.00
7 Estevan Florial 20.00 50.00
8 Jasson Dominguez EXCH 125.00 300.00
9 Michael King 8.00 20.00
10 Adonis Medina 8.00 20.00
12 Deivy Grullon 5.00 12.00
13 Johan Rojas 10.00 25.00

2020 Immaculate Collection Hats Off Memorabilia Autographs

RANDOM INSERTS IN PACKS
PRINT RUNS B/WN 10-25 COPIES PER
NO PRICING QTY 15 OR LESS
EXCHANGE DEADLINE 2/21/2022
4 Joey Bart/25 25.00 60.00
11 Casey Mize/25 25.00 60.00

2020 Immaculate Collection Ichiro Tribute

RANDOM INSERTS IN PACKS
STATED PRINT RUN 51 SER.#'d SETS
1 Ichiro 8.00 20.00

2020 Immaculate Collection Immaculate Duals Memorabilia

RANDOM INSERTS IN PACKS
PRINT RUNS B/WN 10-49 COPIES PER
NO PRICING QTY 15 OR LESS
1 Tim Anderson/49 4.00 10.00
2 Rafael Devers/49 5.00 12.00
3 Mike Trout/49 20.00 50.00
4 Nelson Cruz/49 4.00 10.00
5 Alex Bregman/49 4.00 10.00
6 George Springer/49 3.00 8.00
7 Jose Abreu/49 4.00 10.00
8 Greg Maddux/49 5.00 12.00
9 Lou Brock/49 8.00 20.00
10 Ozzie Smith/49 5.00 12.00
11 Richie Ashburn/10
12 Bert Blyleven/49 3.00 8.00
13 Fergie Jenkins/49 3.00 8.00
14 Brooks Robinson/10
15 Craig Biggio/49 3.00 8.00
16 Pete Alonso/49 10.00 25.00
17 Ronald Acuna Jr./49 8.00 20.00
18 Juan Soto/49 8.00 20.00
19 Christian Yelich/49 5.00 12.00
20 Nolan Arenado/49 5.00 12.00
21 Cody Bellinger/49 8.00 20.00
22 Keston Hiura/49 5.00 12.00
23 Vladimir Guerrero Jr./49 8.00 20.00
24 Gleyber Torres/49 8.00 20.00
25 Joey Votto/49 4.00 10.00
26 Buster Posey/49 5.00 12.00
27 Jose Ramirez/49 3.00 8.00
28 Starling Marte/49 3.00 8.00
29 Marcell Ozuna/49 4.00 10.00
30 Chris Paddack/49 4.00 10.00
32 Xander Bogaerts/49 4.00 10.00
33 Brandon Lowe/49 4.00 10.00
34 Larry Walker/49 3.00 8.00
35 Mookie Betts/49 10.00 25.00

2020 Immaculate Collection Immaculate Duals Memorabilia Blue

*RED/25: .5X TO 1.2X p/r 49
RANDOM INSERTS IN PACKS
PRINT RUNS B/WN 5-25 COPIES PER
NO PRICING QTY 15 OR LESS
9 Lou Brock/25 12.00 30.00

2020 Immaculate Collection Immaculate Signatures

RANDOM INSERTS IN PACKS
PRINT RUNS B/WN 10-99 COPIES PER
NO PRICING QTY 15 OR LESS
EXCHANGE DEADLINE 2/21/2022
*HOLO SLVR/25: .5X TO 1.5X p/r 99
7 Aaron Judge/25 60.00 150.00
8 Yoshitomo Tsutsugo/99 12.00 30.00
9 Dale Murphy/49 8.00 20.00
10 Eloy Jimenez/49 10.00 25.00
11 Andre Dawson/25 12.00 30.00
12 Fernando Tatis Jr./99 60.00 150.00
13 Frank Thomas/49 25.00 60.00
14 J.D. Martinez/49 10.00 25.00
16 Kenny Lofton/49 8.00 20.00
17 Matt Chapman/25 10.00 25.00
19 Pete Alonso/99 30.00 80.00
21 Reggie Jackson/25 EXCH 15.00 40.00
22 Ronald Acuna Jr./49 50.00 120.00
23 Wade Boggs/25 15.00 40.00
24 Tony Perez/25 15.00 40.00
25 Trevor Hoffman/25 5.00 12.00
27 Pete Rose/25 50.00 120.00
28 Elroy Face/25 8.00 20.00
30 Matt Carpenter/25 6.00 15.00
31 Mark Grace/25 12.00 30.00
32 Jose Ramirez/25 15.00 40.00
33 Jose Canseco/49 10.00 25.00
34 John Smoltz/25 12.00 30.00
35 Gleyber Torres/49 20.00 50.00
37 Adrian Beltre/25 20.00 50.00
38 Alan Trammell/49 15.00 40.00
39 Austin Riley/49 8.00 20.00
40 Clayton Kershaw/25 60.00 150.00

2020 Immaculate Collection Immaculate Signatures Red

*RED/49: .5X TO 1.2X p/r 99
*RED/25: .5X TO 1.2X p/r 49
RANDOM INSERTS IN PACKS
PRINT RUNS B/WN 5-49 COPIES PER
NO PRICING QTY 15 OR LESS
EXCHANGE DEADLINE 2/21/2022
38 Alan Trammell/25 30.00 80.00

2020 Immaculate Collection Immaculate Triples Memorabilia

RANDOM INSERTS IN PACKS
PRINT RUNS B/WN 25-49 COPIES PER
1 Wade Boggs/49 5.00 12.00
2 Vladimir Guerrero/49 3.00 8.00
3 Robin Yount/49 10.00 25.00
4 Willie McCovey/25 4.00 10.00
5 Jeff Bagwell/49 6.00 15.00
6 Dakota Hudson/49 3.00 8.00
7 Mike Soroka/49 4.00 10.00
8 Jeff McNeil/49 3.00 8.00
9 Josh Hader/49 2.50 6.00
10 Eloy Jimenez/49 5.00 12.00
11 Fernando Tatis Jr./49 10.00 25.00
12 Anthony Rizzo/49 6.00 15
13 John Smoltz/49 4.00 10
14 Clayton Kershaw/49 8.00 20
15 Alex Rodriguez/49 5.00 12
16 Jose Altuve/49 3.00 8
17 Brian Anderson/49 2.50 6
18 Josh Bell/49 3.00 8
19 Freddie Freeman/49 5.00 12.
20 Nathaniel Lowe /49 2.50 6.
21 Luis Arraez/49 5.00 12.
22 Brendan Rodgers/49 4.00 10.
23 Gary Carter/25 4.00 10.
24 Reggie Jackson/49 8.00 20.
25 Ken Griffey Jr./49 20.00 50.

2020 Immaculate Collection Immaculate Triples Memorabilia Blue

*RED/25: .5X TO 1.2X p/r 49
RANDOM INSERTS IN PACKS
PRINT RUNS B/WN 10-25 COPIES PER
NO PRICING QTY 15 OR LESS
1 Wade Boggs/25 12.00 30.0
3 Robin Yount/25 15.00 40.0

2020 Immaculate Collection Jackets Autographs

RANDOM INSERTS IN PACKS
PRINT RUNS B/WN 5-25 COPIES PER
NO PRICING QTY 15 OR LESS
EXCHANGE DEADLINE 2/21/2022
6 Steve Garvey/25 40.00 100.0
8 Anthony Kay/25 5.00 12.0
12 Nathaniel Lowe /25 5.00 12.0
15 Ryne Sandberg/25 25.00 60.0
16 Aristides Aquino/25 15.00 40.0
17 Nico Hoerner/25 25.00 60.0
18 Zac Gallen/25 12.00 30.0
19 Dylan Cease/25 10.00 25.0
20 Jesus Luzardo/25 10.00 25.0
21 Kyle Lewis/25 60.00 150.0
22 Logan Allen/25 5.00 12.0
23 Trent Grisham/25 20.00 50.0

2020 Immaculate Collection Jumbo

RANDOM INSERTS IN PACKS
PRINT RUNS B/WN 5-49 COPIES PER
NO PRICING QTY 15 OR LESS
1 Jasson Dominguez/49 40.00 100.00
2 Matt Thaiss/49 3.00 8.00
3 Triston McKenzie/49 4.00 10.00
4 Logan Allen/49 2.50 6.00
5 Michel Baez/49 2.50 6.00
6 Yu Chang/49 4.00 10.00
7 Tony Gonsolin/49 10.00 25.00
8 Danny Mendick/49 3.00 8.00
9 Domingo Leyba/49 3.00 8.00
10 Dustin Pedroia/25 5.00 12.00
11 Pete Alonso/25 12.00 30.00
12 Ke'Bryan Hayes/49 2.50 6.00
13 Justin Dunn/49 3.00 8.00
14 Nico Hoerner/49 10.00 25.00
15 Kyle Lewis/49 12.00 30.00
16 Lewis Thorpe/49 2.50 6.00
17 Ken Griffey Jr./25 25.00 60.00
18 Mark McGwire/25 12.00 30.00
19 Tony Lazzeri/5
20 Nick Solak/49 4.00 10.00
21 Abraham Toro/49 3.00 8.00
22 Aristides Aquino/49 5.00 12.00
23 Patrick Sandoval/49 4.00 10.00
24 Kirby Puckett/10
25 Wander Franco/49 8.00 20.00
26 Bobby Bradley/49 3.00 8.00
27 Sean Murphy/49 4.00 10.00
28 Alex Rodriguez/25 6.00 15.00
29 Adrian Morejon/49 2.50 6.00
30 Logan Webb/49 3.00 8.00
31 Jonathan Hernandez/49 2.50 6.00
32 Dwight Gooden/15
33 Yonathan Daza/49 3.00 8.00
34 Tres Barrera/49 5.00 12.00
35 Yordan Alvarez/49 5.00 12.00
36 A.J. Puk/49 5.00 12.00
37 Rico Garcia/49 4.00 10.00
38 Sheldon Neuse/49 3.00 8.00
39 Gavin Lux/49 6.00 15.00
40 Jesus Sanchez/49 2.50 6.00
41 Donnie Walton/49 6.00 15.00
42 Dylan Carlson/49 10.00 25.00
43 Jake Rogers/49 2.50 6.00
44 Ron Santo/10
45 Josh Rojas/49 2.50 6.00
46 Adbert Alzolay/49 3.00 8.00
47 Dustin May/49 10.00 25.00
48 Aaron Civale/49 4.00 10.00
49 Travis Demeritte/49 3.00 8.00
50 Brendan McKay/49 4.00 10.00
51 Zack Collins/49 3.00 8.00
52 Casey Mize/49 8.00 20.00
53 Willie McCovey/49 3.00 8.00
54 Dylan Cease/49 5.00 12.00
55 Herb Pennock/10
56 Bobby Dalbec/49 6.00 15.00
58 Starlin Castro/49 2.50 6.00
59 Luis Robert/49 25.00 60.00
60 Randy Johnson/49 4.00 10.00
61 Trent Grisham/49 10.00 25.00
62 Tyrone Taylor/49 2.50 6.00
63 Ronald Acuna Jr./49 8.00 20.00
64 Leo Durocher/15
65 Jordan Yamamoto /49 3.00 8.00
66 Randy Arozarena/49 8.00 20.00
67 Jo Adell/49 5.00 12.00

ickey Mantle/7
uis Aparicio/5
ryan Abreu/49 2.50 6.00
ac Gallen/49 6.00 15.00
ladimir Guerrero Jr./49 8.00 20.00
im Thome/5
eivy Grullon/49 2.50 6.00
ed Williams/15
etel Marte/49 3.00 8.00
aylin Davis/49 4.00 10.00
en Boyer/5
nthony Kay/49 2.50 6.00
ndres Munoz/49 3.00 8.00
.J. Zeuch/49 2.50 6.00
ake Fraley/49 3.00 8.00
dwin Rios/49 6.00 15.00
o Bichette/49 20.00 50.00
Alex Kirilloff/49 5.00 12.00
Nate Pearson/49 5.00 12.00
Ronald Bolanos/49 4.00 10.00
Brock Burke/49 2.50 6.00
Sixto Sanchez/49 4.00 10.00
Jesus Luzardo/49 5.00 12.00
Sam Hilliard/49 4.00 10.00
Taylor Trammell/25 4.00 10.00
Isan Diaz/49 4.00 10.00
Albert Pujols/25 6.00 15.00
Mauricio Dubon/49 3.00 8.00
Brusdar Graterol/49 4.00 10.00
Joe Palumbo/49 2.50 6.00
Willi Castro/49 4.00 10.00
0 Michael King/49 4.00 10.00

2020 Immaculate Collection Legends Dual Materials

ANDOM INSERTS IN PACKS
RINT RUNS B/WN 10-49 COPIES PER
O PRICING QTY 15 OR LESS
Edd Roush/10
Frank Chance/25 12.00 30.00
Herb Pennock/10
Leo Durocher/49 2.50 6.00
Mickey Mantle/49 20.00 50.00
Luis Aparicio/49 6.00 15.00
Randy Johnson/49 4.00 10.00
Alex Rodriguez/49 5.00 12.00
Albert Pujols/49 5.00 12.00
0 Pete Rose/49 10.00 25.00

2020 Immaculate Collection Legends Dual Materials Blue

RED/25: .5X TO 1.2X p/r 49
ANDOM INSERTS IN PACKS
RINT RUNS B/WN 5-25 COPIES PER
O PRICING QTY 15 OR LESS
0 Pete Rose/25 15.00 40.00

2020 Immaculate Collection Legends Material

RANDOM INSERTS IN PACKS
PRINT RUNS B/WN 7-49 COPIES PER
NO PRICING QTY 15 OR LESS
1 Billy Martin/10
2 Casey Stengel/10
3 Don Drysdale/10
4 Gil Hodges/49 5.00 12.00
5 Joe Jackson/15
6 Roy Campanella/49 6.00 15.00
7 Tony Lazzeri/25 12.00 30.00
8 Babe Ruth/7
9 Joe DiMaggio/10
10 Joe Sewell/10
11 Ken Boyer/25 6.00 15.00
12 Roberto Clemente/25 40.00 100.00
13 Ron Santo/49 10.00 25.00
14 Stan Musial/49 10.00 25.00
15 Ted Williams/49 20.00 50.00
16 Yogi Berra/10
17 Tony Gwynn/49 4.00 10.00
18 Tim Raines/49 3.00 8.00
19 Cal Ripken/49 12.00 30.00
20 Jim Thome/49 3.00 8.00
21 Harold Baines/49 6.00 15.00
22 Frank Thomas/49 4.00 10.00
23 Johnny Bench/49 6.00 15.00
24 Willie McCovey/49 3.00 8.00
25 Trevor Hoffman/49 3.00 8.00
26 Tom Glavine/49 3.00 8.00
27 Greg Maddux/49 5.00 12.00
28 George Brett/49 12.00 30.00
29 Chipper Jones/49 4.00 10.00
30 Rickey Henderson/49 4.00 10.00

2020 Immaculate Collection Legends Material Blue

*RED/25: .5X TO 1.2X p/r 49
RANDOM INSERTS IN PACKS
PRINT RUNS B/WN 5-25 COPIES PER
NO PRICING QTY 15 OR LESS
4 Gil Hodges/25 10.00 25.00
15 Ted Williams/25 30.00 80.00
23 Johnny Bench/25 15.00 40.00

2020 Immaculate Collection Materials

RANDOM INSERTS IN PACKS
PRINT RUNS B/WN 25-49 COPIES PER
1 Jacob deGrom/49 4.00 10.00
2 Craig Biggio/49 3.00 8.00
3 Eddie Murray/49 3.00 8.00
4 James Paxton/49 3.00 8.00
5 Daniel Murphy/49 3.00 8.00
6 Adrian Beltre/49 4.00 10.00
7 Alex Rodriguez/49 5.00 12.00
8 Adam Wainwright/49 3.00 8.00
9 Amed Rosario/49 3.00 8.00
10 Chris Paddack/49 4.00 10.00
11 Marcell Ozuna/49 4.00 10.00
12 Freddie Freeman/49 5.00 12.00
13 Miguel Sano/49 3.00 8.00
14 J.D. Davis/49 2.50 6.00
15 Sean Manaea/49 2.50 6.00
16 Enos Slaughter/25 8.00 20.00
17 A.J. Puk/49 5.00 12.00
18 Tim Anderson/49 4.00 10.00
19 Wander Franco/49 8.00 20.00
20 Joe Morgan/49 3.00 8.00
21 Keston Hiura/49 5.00 12.00
22 Lucas Giolito/49 3.00 8.00
23 Kyle Seager/49 2.50 6.00
24 Kevin Newman/49 3.00 8.00
25 Isan Diaz/49 4.00 10.00
26 Chris Davis/49 2.50 6.00
27 Bryce Harper/49 6.00 15.00
28 Ken Griffey Jr./49 20.00 50.00
29 Alex Verdugo/49 3.00 8.00
30 Cody Bellinger/49 8.00 20.00
31 Josh Hader/49 2.50 6.00
32 Mike Trout/27 25.00 60.00
33 Willy Adames/49 2.50 6.00
34 Craig Kimbrel/49 3.00 8.00
35 Yordan Alvarez/49 5.00 12.00
36 Forrest Whitley/49 2.50 6.00
37 Gary Carter/49 3.00 8.00
38 Catfish Hunter/49 3.00 8.00
39 Nelson Cruz/49 4.00 10.00
40 Joey Votto/49 4.00 10.00
41 Andrew McCutchen/49 4.00 10.00
42 Zack Wheeler/49 3.00 8.00
43 Brandon Lowe/49 4.00 10.00
44 Rickey Henderson/49 4.00 10.00
45 Anthony Santander/49 2.50 6.00
46 Aaron Nola/49 4.00 10.00
47 Roberto Alomar/49 3.00 8.00
48 Gavin Lux/49 6.00 15.00
49 Adalberto Mondesi/49 4.00 10.00
50 Masahiro Tanaka/49 4.00 10.00
51 Kirby Puckett/49 15.00 40.00
52 CC Sabathia/49 3.00 8.00
53 George Springer/49 3.00 8.00
54 Johnny Cueto/49 3.00 8.00
55 Brendan McKay/49 4.00 10.00

2020 Immaculate Collection Matinee Dual Memorabilia Autographs

RANDOM INSERTS IN PACKS
PRINT RUNS B/WN 10-49 COPIES PER
NO PRICING QTY 15 OR LESS
*BLUE/2-25: .5X TO 1.2X p/r 49
1 Ian Desmond/49 4.00 10.00
2 Josh Donaldson/49 10.00 25.00
3 Clint Frazier/49 12.00 30.00
4 Stephen Gonsalves/49 4.00 10.00
5 Shohei Ohtani/24 60.00 150.00
6 Xander Bogaerts/31 8.00 20.00
7 Barry Larkin/29 20.00 50.00
8 Gary Sanchez/25 8.00 20.00
9 Edwin Encarnacion/28 8.00 20.00
10 Jonathan Lucroy/23 6.00 15.00
11 Cedric Mullins/17 8.00 20.00
12 Garrett Hampson/17 5.00 12.00
13 Jake Cave/21 6.00 15.00
14 Kevin Kramer/14
15 Kevin Newman/14
16 Byron Buxton/18 6.00 15.00
17 Andres Galarraga/14
18 Fernando Tatis Jr./10

2020 Immaculate Collection Mike Trout MVP

RANDOM INSERTS IN PACKS
STATED PRINT RUN 27 SER.#'d SETS
1 Mike Trout 50.00 120.00

2020 Immaculate Collection Moments Memorabilia Autographs

RANDOM INSERTS IN PACKS
PRINT RUNS B/WN 15-20 COPIES PER
NO PRICING QTY 15 OR LESS
EXCHANGE DEADLINE 2/21/2022
13 Jose Canseco/20 15.00 40.00

2020 Immaculate Collection Monochrome Memorabilia Autographs

RANDOM INSERTS IN PACKS
STATED PRINT RUN 49 SER.#'d SETS
EXCHANGE DEADLINE 2/21/2022
*BLUE/25: .5X TO 1.2X
1 Matt Thaiss 5.00 12.00
2 Jonathan Hernandez 4.00 10.00
3 Edwin Rios 10.00 25.00
4 Nick Solak 6.00 15.00
5 Jake Fraley 5.00 12.00
6 A.J. Puk 8.00 20.00
7 Randy Arozarena 50.00 120.00
8 Dylan Cease 8.00 20.00
9 Gavin Lux 25.00 60.00
10 Joe Palumbo 4.00 10.00
11 Danny Mendick 5.00 12.00
12 Isan Diaz 6.00 15.00
13 Yu Chang 6.00 15.00
14 Dustin May 20.00 50.00
15 Josh Rojas 4.00 10.00
16 Logan Webb 5.00 12.00
17 Bryan Abreu 4.00 10.00
18 Tony Gonsolin 15.00 40.00
19 Brendan McKay 6.00 15.00
20 Zack Collins 5.00 12.00
21 Adbert Alzolay 5.00 12.00
22 Jesus Luzardo 8.00 20.00
23 Nico Hoerner 20.00 50.00
24 Justin Dunn 5.00 12.00
25 T.J. Zeuch 4.00 10.00
26 Rico Garcia 6.00 15.00
27 Tres Barrera 8.00 20.00
28 Ronald Bolanos 6.00 15.00
30 Travis Demeritte 5.00 12.00
31 Yonathan Daza 5.00 12.00
32 Brock Burke 4.00 10.00
33 Adrian Morejon 4.00 10.00
34 Jaylin Davis 6.00 15.00
35 Yordan Alvarez 30.00 80.00
36 Willi Castro 6.00 15.00
37 Sam Hilliard 6.00 15.00
38 Mauricio Dubon 5.00 12.00
39 Michel Baez 4.00 10.00
40 Aaron Civale 6.00 15.00
41 Donnie Walton 10.00 25.00
42 Abraham Toro 5.00 12.00
43 Logan Allen 4.00 10.00
44 Sheldon Neuse 5.00 12.00
45 Aristides Aquino 10.00 25.00
46 Brusdar Graterol 6.00 15.00
47 Kyle Lewis 30.00 80.00
48 Andres Munoz 5.00 12.00
49 Bo Bichette 50.00 120.00
50 Bobby Bradley 5.00 12.00
51 Sean Murphy 6.00 15.00
52 Jake Rogers 4.00 10.00
53 Michael King 6.00 15.00
54 Anthony Kay 4.00 10.00
55 Domingo Leyba 5.00 12.00
56 Patrick Sandoval 6.00 15.00
57 Tyrone Taylor 4.00 10.00
58 Zac Gallen 10.00 25.00
59 Lewis Thorpe 4.00 10.00
60 Jordan Yamamoto 5.00 12.00

2020 Immaculate Collection Monuments

RANDOM INSERTS IN PACKS
PRINT RUNS B/WN 15-25 COPIES PER
NO PRICING QTY 15 OR LESS
1 DMagio/Mntle/Brra/Ruth/25 250.00 600.00
2 Clmnte/Musl/Jcksn/Wllms/25 100.00 250.00
4 Ryn/Jhnson/Clmens/Seavr/20 75.00 200.00
5 Snders/Tebw/Jckson/Wilsn/25 75.00 200.00
6 Bichette/Robert/Alvarez/Lux/25 75.00 200.00
7 Rtschmn/Domnguz/Adll/Frnco/25 75.00 200.00
8 deGrm/Snll/Vrlndr/Schrzr/25 20.00 50.00
9 Trout/Bellngr/Btts/Ylch/25 75.00 200.00
11 Chipper/Ichiro/Pujols/ARod/25 50.00 120.00
12 Cabrra/Posy/Trout/Beltre/25 30.00 80.00
13 Brett/Hendrsn/CRJ/Mttngly/25 40.00 100.00
14 Bnch/Strgell/Torre/Jcksn/25 25.00 60.00
15 Ryan/Ford/Gibsn/Seavr/25 30.00 80.00
16 Sndbrg/Robnsn/Smith/Hrnndz/25 40.00 100.00
17 Rose/Perez/Morgan/Bench/25 30.00 80.00
18 Sparky/Weaver/Torre/Lasorda/25 50.00 120.00
19 Snto/Wllms/Maddx/Sndbrg/25 25.00 60.00
20 Alnso/Acna/Ohtni/Alvarz/25 60.00 150.00

2020 Immaculate Collection Premium Memorabilia Autographs

RANDOM INSERTS IN PACKS
PRINT RUNS B/WN 10-25 COPIES PER
NO PRICING QTY 15 OR LESS
EXCHANGE DEADLINE 2/21/2022
4 J.D. Davis/25 5.00 12.00
6 Tristen Lutz/25 6.00 15.00
9 Chris Paddack/25 8.00 20.00
16 Brandon Lowe/25 12.00 30.00
19 Jeff McNeil/25 10.00 25.00

2020 Immaculate Collection Premium Patch Autographs

RANDOM INSERTS IN PACKS
STATED PRINT RUN 25 SER.#'d SETS
EXCHANGE DEADLINE 2/21/2022
1 Yordan Alvarez 40.00 100.00
2 Bo Bichette 60.00 150.00
3 Gavin Lux 30.00 80.00
4 Aristides Aquino 15.00 40.00
5 Kyle Lewis 60.00 150.00
7 Brusdar Graterol 8.00 20.00
8 Jesus Luzardo 10.00 25.00
9 Brendan McKay 8.00 20.00
10 A.J. Puk 10.00 25.00
11 Nico Hoerner 25.00 60.00
12 Dylan Cease 10.00 25.00
13 Dustin May 25.00 60.00
14 Zac Gallen 12.00 30.00
15 Trent Grisham 20.00 50.00
16 Sean Murphy 8.00 20.00
17 Justin Dunn 6.00 15.00
18 Mauricio Dubon 6.00 15.00
19 Willi Castro 8.00 20.00
20 Yonathan Daza 6.00 15.00

2020 Immaculate Collection Prospect Patch Autographs

RANDOM INSERTS IN PACKS
PRINT RUNS B/WN 23-99 COPIES PER
EXCHANGE DEADLINE 2/21/2022
*HOLO GOLD/45: .4X TO 1X p/r 45
*HOLO GOLD/17-26: .6X TO 1.5X p/r 99
*HOLO GOLD/17-26: .5X TO 1.2X p/r 49
1 Adley Rutschman/23 30.00 80.00
2 Bobby Witt Jr./49 40.00 100.00
3 CJ Abrams/49 40.00 100.00
6 Andrew Vaughn/25 20.00 50.00
9 Wander Franco/49 EXCH 40.00 100.00
10 Ryan Mountcastle/49 6.00 15.00
12 Sixto Sanchez/49 6.00 15.00
13 Jo Adell/99 25.00 60.00
17 Alec Bohm/49 40.00 100.00
18 Alex Kirilloff/49 15.00 40.00
19 Forrest Whitley/99 6.00 15.00

2020 Immaculate Collection Prospect Patch Autographs Red

*RED/25: .6X TO 1.5X p/r 99
RANDOM INSERTS IN PACKS
PRINT RUNS B/WN 15-25 COPIES PER
NO PRICING QTY 15 OR LESS
EXCHANGE DEADLINE 2/21/2022
4 Jasson Dominguez/25 125.00 300.00
14 Luis Robert/25 150.00 400.00

2020 Immaculate Collection Rookie Dual Memorabilia Signatures

RANDOM INSERTS IN PACKS
STATED PRINT RUN 49 SER.#'d SETS
EXCHANGE DEADLINE 2/21/2022
*RED/25: .5X TO 1.2X
1 Matt Thaiss 5.00 12.00
2 Yordan Alvarez 30.00 80.00
3 Adrian Morejon 4.00 10.00
4 Jordan Yamamoto 5.00 12.00
5 Trent Grisham 15.00 40.00
6 Michel Baez 4.00 10.00
7 Sam Hilliard 6.00 15.00
8 Zac Gallen 10.00 25.00
9 Jake Fraley 5.00 12.00
10 Willi Castro 6.00 15.00
11 A.J. Puk 8.00 20.00
12 Brock Burke 4.00 10.00
13 Jesus Luzardo 8.00 20.00
14 Justin Dunn 5.00 12.00
15 Dylan Cease 8.00 20.00
16 Anthony Kay 4.00 10.00
17 Gavin Lux 25.00 60.00
18 Michael King 6.00 15.00
19 Joe Palumbo 4.00 10.00
20 Jake Rogers 4.00 10.00
21 Mauricio Dubon 5.00 12.00
22 Sean Murphy 6.00 15.00
24 Bobby Bradley 5.00 12.00
26 Bo Bichette 50.00 120.00
27 Dustin May 25.00 60.00
28 Aaron Civale 6.00 15.00
29 Nico Hoerner 20.00 50.00
30 Kyle Lewis 30.00 80.00
31 Logan Webb 5.00 12.00
32 Brusdar Graterol 6.00 15.00
33 Bryan Abreu 4.00 10.00
34 Aristides Aquino 10.00 25.00
35 Tony Gonsolin 15.00 40.00
36 Sheldon Neuse 5.00 12.00
37 Brendan McKay 6.00 15.00
38 Logan Allen 4.00 10.00
39 Zack Collins 5.00 12.00
40 Abraham Toro 5.00 12.00

2020 Immaculate Collection Rookie Patch Autographs Holo Gold

*HOLO GOLD/50-85: .4X TO 1X
*HOLO GOLD/30-49: .5X TO 1.2X
*HOLO GOLD/19-23: .6X TO 1.5X
RANDOM INSERTS IN PACKS
PRINT RUNS B/WN 1-85 COPIES PER
NO PRICING QTY 15 OR LESS
EXCHANGE DEADLINE 2/21/2022
130 Kyle Lewis/30 50.00 120.00
134 Aristides Aquino/44 40.00 100.00

2020 Immaculate Collection Rookie Patch Autographs Holo Silver

*HOLO SLVR/25: .6X TO 1.5X
RANDOM INSERTS IN PACKS
STATED PRINT RUN 25 SER.#'d SETS
EXCHANGE DEADLINE 2/21/2022
130 Kyle Lewis 50.00 120.00
134 Aristides Aquino 40.00 100.00
154 Yordan Alvarez 50.00 120.00

2020 Immaculate Collection Rookie Reserve Memorabilia

RANDOM INSERTS IN PACKS
PRINT RUNS B/WN 10-25 COPIES PER
NO PRICING QTY 15 OR LESS
1 Luis Robert/25 60.00 150.00
2 Yordan Alvarez/25 40.00 100.00
3 Aristides Aquino/25 20.00 50.00
6 Brendan McKay/25 5.00 12.00
7 Dustin May/25 12.00 30.00
8 Nico Hoerner/25 20.00 50.00
10 Jesus Luzardo/25 15.00 40.00
11 A.J. Puk/25 6.00 15.00
12 Sean Murphy/25 10.00 25.00
13 Dylan Cease/25 6.00 15.00
14 Kwang-Hyun Kim/25 75.00 200.00
15 Shun Yamaguchi/25 12.00 30.00
16 Trent Grisham/25 12.00 30.00
17 Kyle Lewis/25 30.00 80.00
18 Adbert Alzolay/25 12.00 30.00
19 Zac Gallen/25 8.00 20.00
20 Isan Diaz/25 15.00 40.00

2020 Immaculate Collection Team Heroes Dual Memorabilia Autographs

RANDOM INSERTS IN PACKS
PRINT RUNS B/WN 5-25 COPIES PER
NO PRICING QTY 15 OR LESS
EXCHANGE DEADLINE 2/21/2022
1 Harold Baines/25 10.00 25.00
8 Kerry Wood/25 15.00 40.00
15 Jose Canseco/20 15.00 40.00
16 Andres Galarraga/25 12.00 30.00

2020 Immaculate Collection Winter Collection Triple Memorabilia Autographs

RANDOM INSERTS IN PACKS
STATED PRINT RUN 25 SER.#'d SETS
EXCHANGE DEADLINE 2/21/2022
1 Yordan Alvarez 40.00 100.00
2 Luis Robert EXCH 150.00 400.00
3 Casey Mize 25.00 60.00
4 Bobby Witt Jr. 50.00 120.00
5 Joey Bart 25.00 60.00
6 Dylan Carlson 20.00 50.00
7 Alec Bohm 40.00 100.00
8 Jasson Dominguez 125.00 300.00
9 Andres Gimenez 6.00 15.00
10 Brady Singer 12.00 30.00
14 Travis Demeritte 6.00 15.00
15 Logan Webb 6.00 15.00
16 Zack Collins 6.00 15.00
17 Deivy Grullon 5.00 12.00
18 Bryan Abreu 5.00 12.00
19 Aaron Civale 8.00 20.00
20 Adbert Alzolay 6.00 15.00

2020 Immaculate Collection Yordan Alvarez Rookie of the Year

RANDOM INSERTS IN PACKS
STATED PRINT RUN 44 SER.#'d SETS
1 Yordan Alvarez 10.00 25.00

1949 Leaf

The cards in this 98-card set measure 2 3/8" by 2 7/8". The 1949 Leaf set was the first post-war baseball series issued in color. This effort was not entirely successful due to a lack of refinement which resulted in many color variations and cards out of register. In addition, the set was skip numbered from 1-168, with 49 of the 98 cards printed in limited quantities (marked with SP in the checklist). Cards 102 and 136 have variations, and cards are sometimes found with overprinted, incorrect or blank backs. Some cards were produced with a 1948 copyright date but overwhelming evidence seemed to indicate that this set was not actually released until early in 1949. An album to hold these cards was available as a premium. The album could only be obtained by sending in five wrappers and 25 cents. Since so few albums appear on the secondary market, no value is attached to them. Notable Rookie Cards in this set include Stan Musial, Satchel Paige, and Jackie Robinson. A proof card of Hal Newhouser; with a different photo and back biography recently surfaced. So far; there is only one known copy of this card.

COMPLETE SET (98) 25000.00 40000.00
COMMON CARD (1-168) 15.00 25.00
COMMON SP's 200.00 300.00
WRAPPER (1-CENT) 120.00 160.00
1 Joe DiMaggio 1000.00 2000.00
3 Babe Ruth 2000.00 4000.00
4 Stan Musial 1500.00 3000.00
5 Virgil Trucks SP RC 250.00 400.00
8 S.Paige SP RC 9000.00 15000.00
10 Dizzy Trout 25.00 40.00
11 Phil Rizzuto 150.00 300.00
13 Cass Michaels SP RC 200.00 300.00
14 Billy Johnson 25.00 40.00
17 Frank Overmire RC 15.00 25.00
19 Johnny Wyrostek SP 200.00 300.00
20 Hank Sauer SP 250.00 400.00
22 Al Evans RC 15.00 25.00
26 Sam Chapman 25.00 40.00
27 Mickey Harris RC 15.00 25.00
28 Jim Hegan RC 25.00 40.00
29 Elmer Valo RC 25.00 40.00
30 Billy Goodman SP RC 250.00 400.00
31 Lou Brissie RC 15.00 25.00
32 Warren Spahn 400.00 800.00
33 Peanuts Lowrey SP RC 200.00 300.00
36 Al Zarilla SP 200.00 300.00
38 Ted Kluszewski RC 125.00 200.00
39 Ewell Blackwell 35.00 60.00
42A Kent Peterson RC 15.00 25.00
42B Kent Peterson Red Cap
43 Ed Stevens SP RC 200.00 300.00
45 Ken Keltner SP RC 200.00 300.00
46 Johnny Mize 60.00 100.00
47 George Vico RC 15.00 25.00
48 Johnny Schmitz SP RC 200.00 300.00
49 Del Ennis RC 35.00 60.00
50 Dick Wakefield RC 15.00 25.00
51 Alvin Dark SP RC 300.00 500.00
53 Johnny VanderMeer 60.00 100.00
54 Bobby Adams SP RC 200.00 300.00
55 Tommy Henrich SP 300.00 500.00
56 Larry Jansen 25.00 40.00
57 Bob McCall RC 15.00 25.00
59 Luke Appling 60.00 100.00
61 Jake Early RC 15.00 25.00
62 Eddie Joost SP 200.00 300.00
63 Barney McCosky SP 200.00 300.00
65 Bob Elliott UER 60.00 100.00
66 Orval Grove SP RC 200.00 300.00
68 Eddie Miller SP 200.00 300.00
70 Honus Wagner 250.00 500.00
72 Hank Edwards RC 15.00 25.00
73 Pat Seerey RC 15.00 25.00
75 Dom DiMaggio SP 350.00 600.00
76 Ted Williams 800.00 1500.00
77 Roy Smalley RC 15.00 25.00
78 Hoot Evers SP RC 200.00 300.00
79 Jackie Robinson RC 6000.00 12000.00
81 Whitey Kurowski SP RC 200.00 300.00
82 Johnny Lindell 25.00 40.00
83 Bobby Doerr 60.00 100.00
84 Sid Hudson 15.00 25.00
85 Dave Philley SP RC 250.00 400.00
86 Ralph Weigel RC 15.00 25.00
88 Frank Gustine SP RC 200.00 300.00
91 Ralph Kiner 125.00 250.00
93 Bob Feller SP 1400.00 2000.00
95 Snuffy Stirnweiss 25.00 40.00
97 Marty Marion 35.00 60.00
98 Hal Newhouser SP RC 350.00 600.00
98A Hal Newhouser Proof
102A G.Hermansk ERR 150.00 250.00
102B Gene Hermanski COR RC 25.00 40.00
104 Eddie Stewart SP RC 200.00 300.00
106 Lou Boudreau MG RC 60.00 100.00
108 Matt Batts SP RC 200.00 300.00
111 Jerry Priddy RC 15.00 25.00
113 Dutch Leonard SP 200.00 300.00
117 Joe Gordon RC 25.00 40.00
120 George Kell SP RC 350.00 600.00
121 Johnny Pesky SP RC 250.00 400.00
123 Cliff Fannin SP RC 200.00 300.00
125 Andy Pafko RC 15.00 25.00
127 Enos Slaughter SP 500.00 800.00
128 Buddy Rosar 15.00 25.00
129 Kirby Higbe SP 200.00 300.00
131 Sid Gordon SP 200.00 300.00
133 Tommy Holmes SP RC 300.00 500.00
136A C.Aberson Full Slv RC 15.00 25.00
136B C.Aberson Short Slv 150.00 250.00
137 Harry Walker SP RC 250.00 400.00
138 Larry Doby SP RC 400.00 700.00
139 Johnny Hopp RC 15.00 25.00
142 D.Murtaugh SP RC 250.00 400.00
143 Dick Sisler SP RC 200.00 300.00
144 Bob Dillinger SP RC 200.00 300.00
146 Pete Reiser SP 300.00 500.00
149 Hank Majeski SP RC 200.00 300.00
153 Floyd Baker SP RC 200.00 300.00
158 H.Brecheen SP RC 250.00 400.00
159 Mizell Platt RC 15.00 25.00
160 Bob Scheffing SP RC 200.00 300.00
161 V.Stephens SP RC 250.00 400.00
163 F.Hutchinson SP RC 250.00 400.00
165 Dale Mitchell SP RC 250.00 400.00
168 Phil Cavarretta SP RC 300.00 500.00
NNO Album

1949 Leaf Premiums

This set of eight large, blank-backed premiums is rather scarce. They were issued as premiums with the 1949 Leaf Gum set. The catalog designation is R401-4. The set is subtitled "Baseball's Immortals" and there is no reference anywhere on the premium to Leaf, the issuing company. These large photos measure approximately 5 1/2" x 7 3/16" and are printed on thin paper.

COMPLETE SET (8) 2500.00 5000.00
1 Grover C. Alexander 200.00 400.00
2 Mickey Cochrane 200.00 400.00
3 Lou Gehrig 500.00 1000.00
4 Walter Johnson 300.00 600.00
5 Christy Mathewson 300.00 600.00
6 John McGraw 200.00 400.00
7 Babe Ruth 750.00 1500.00
8 Ed Walsh 150.00 300.00

1960 Leaf

The cards in this 144-card set measure the standard size. The 1960 Leaf set was issued in a regular gum package style but with a marble instead of gum. This set was issued in five card nickel packs which came 24 to a box. The series was a joint production by Sports Novelties, Inc., and Leaf, two Chicago-based companies. Cards 73-144 are more difficult to find than the lower numbers. Photo variations exist (probably proof cards) for the eight cards listed with an asterisk and there is a well-known error card, number 25 showing Brooks Lawrence (in a Reds uniform) with Jim Grant's name on front, and Grant's biography and record on back. The corrected version with Grant's photo is the more difficult variety. The only notable Rookie Card in this set is Dallas Green. The complete set price below includes both versions of Jim Grant.

COMPLETE SET (144) 1000.00 2000.00
COMMON CARD (1-72) 1.25 3.00
COMMON CARD (73-144) 12.50 30.00
WRAPPER (5-CENT) 20.00 50.00
1 Luis Aparicio * 10.00 25.00
2 Woody Held 1.25 3.00
3 Frank Lary 1.50 4.00
4 Camilo Pascual 2.00 5.00
5 Pancho Herrera 1.25 3.00
6 Felipe Alou 3.00 8.00
7 Benjamin Daniels 1.25 3.00
8 Roger Craig 2.00 5.00
9 Eddie Kasko 1.25 3.00
10 Bob Grim 1.50 4.00
11 Jim Busby 1.50 4.00
12 Ken Boyer* 3.00 8.00
13 Bob Boyd 1.25 3.00
14 Sam Jones 1.50 4.00
15 Larry Jackson 1.50 4.00
16 Roy Face 1.50 4.00
17 Walt Moryn * 1.25 3.00
18 Jim Gilliam 2.00 5.00
19 Don Newcombe 2.00 5.00
20 Glen Hobbie 1.25 3.00
21 Pedro Ramos 1.50 4.00
22 Ryne Duren 1.25 3.00
23 Joey Jay * 1.50 4.00
24 Lou Berberet 1.25 3.00
25A Jim Grant ERR 6.00 15.00
25B Jim Grant COR 10.00 25.00
26 Tom Borland RC 1.25 3.00
27 Brooks Robinson 25.00 60.00
28 Jerry Adair RC 1.25 3.00
29 Ron Jackson 1.25 3.00
30 George Strickland 1.25 3.00
31 Rocky Bridges 1.25 3.00
32 Bill Tuttle 1.50 4.00
33 Ken Hunt RC 1.25 3.00
34 Hal Griggs 1.25 3.00
35 Jim Coates * 1.25 3.00
36 Brooks Lawrence 1.25 3.00
37 Duke Snider 15.00 40.00
38 Al Spangler RC 1.25 3.00
39 Jim Owens 1.25 3.00
40 Bill Virdon 2.00 5.00
41 Ernie Broglio 1.25 3.00
42 Andre Rodgers 1.25 3.00
43 Julio Becquer 1.50 4.00
44 Tony Taylor 1.50 4.00
45 Jerry Lynch 1.50 4.00
46 Clete Boyer 3.00 8.00
47 Jerry Lumpe 1.25 3.00
48 Charlie Maxwell 1.50 4.00
49 Jim Perry 1.50 4.00
50 Danny McDevitt 1.25 3.00
51 Juan Pizarro 1.25 3.00
52 Dallas Green RC 3.00 8.00
53 Bob Friend 1.50 4.00
54 Jack Sanford 1.50 4.00
55 Jim Rivera 1.25 3.00
56 Ted Wills RC 1.25 3.00
57 Milt Pappas 1.50 4.00
58A Hal Smith * 1.25 3.00
58B Hal Smith
Blacked out team
58C Hal Smith 75.00 200.00
No team on back
59 Bobby Avila 1.25 3.00
60 Clem Labine 2.00 5.00
61 Norman Rehm RC * 1.25 3.00
62 John Gabler RC 1.50 4.00
63 John Tsitouris RC 1.25 3.00
64 Dave Sisler 1.25 3.00
65 Vic Power 1.50 4.00
66 Earl Battey 1.25 3.00
67 Bob Purkey 1.25 3.00
68 Moe Drabowsky 1.50 4.00
69 Hoyt Wilhelm 6.00 15.00
70 Humberto Robinson 1.25 3.00
71 Whitey Herzog 3.00 8.00
72 Dick Donovan * 1.25 3.00
73 Gordon Jones 12.50 30.00
74 Joe Hicks RC 12.50 30.00
75 Ray Culp RC 15.00 40.00
76 Dick Drott 12.50 30.00
77 Bob Duliba RC 12.50 30.00
78 Art Ditmar 12.50 30.00
79 Steve Korcheck 12.50 30.00
80 Henry Mason RC 12.50 30.00
81 Harry Simpson 12.50 30.00
82 Gene Green 12.50 30.00
83 Bob Shaw 12.50 30.00
84 Howard Reed 12.50 30.00
85 Dick Stigman 12.50 30.00
86 Rip Repulski 12.50 30.00
87 Seth Morehead 12.50 30.00
88 Camilo Carreon RC 12.50 30.00
89 Johnny Blanchard 15.00 40.00
90 Billy Hoeft 12.50 30.00
91 Fred Hopke RC 12.50 30.00
92 Joe Martin RC 12.50 30.00
93 Wally Shannon RC 12.50 30.00
94 Hal R. 15.00 40.00
Hal W. Smith
95 Al Schroll 12.50 30.00
96 John Kucks 12.50 30.00
97 Tom Morgan 12.50 30.00
98 Willie Jones 12.50 30.00
99 Marshall Renfroe RC 12.50 30.00
100 Willie Tasby 12.50 30.00
101 Irv Noren 12.50 30.00
102 Russ Snyder RC 12.50 30.00
103 Bob Turley 15.00 40.00
104 Jim Woods RC 12.50 30.00
105 Ronnie Kline 12.50 30.00
106 Steve Bilko 12.50 30.00
107 Elmer Valo 12.50 30.00
108 Tom McAvoy RC 12.50 30.00
109 Stan Williams 12.50 30.00
110 Earl Averill Jr. 12.50 30.00
111 Lee Walls 12.50 30.00
112 Paul Richards MG 12.50 30.00

113 Ed Sadowski 12.50 30.00
114 Stover McIlwain RC 12.50 30.00
115 Chuck Tanner UER 15.00 40.00
116 Lou Klimchock RC 12.50 30.00
117 Neil Chrisley 12.50 30.00
118 Johnny Callison 20.00 50.00
119 Hal Smith 12.50 30.00
120 Carl Sawatski 12.50 30.00
121 Frank Leja 12.50 30.00
122 Earl Torgeson 12.50 30.00
123 Art Schult 12.50 30.00
124 Jim Brosnan 12.50 30.00
125 Sparky Anderson 30.00 60.00
126 Joe Pignatano 12.50 30.00
127 Rocky Nelson 12.50 30.00
128 Orlando Cepeda 40.00 80.00
129 Daryl Spencer 12.50 30.00
130 Ralph Lumenti 12.50 30.00
131 Sam Taylor 12.50 30.00
132 Harry Brecheen CO 15.00 40.00
133 Johnny Groth 12.50 30.00
134 Wayne Terwilliger 12.50 30.00
135 Kent Hadley 12.50 30.00
136 Faye Throneberry 12.50 30.00
137 Jack Meyer 12.50 30.00
138 Chuck Cottier RC 12.50 30.00
139 Joe DeMaestri 12.50 30.00
140 Gene Freese 12.50 30.00
141 Curt Flood 20.00 50.00
142 Gino Cimoli 12.50 30.00
143 Clay Dalrymple RC 12.50 30.00
144 Jim Bunning 40.00 80.00

1990 Leaf

The 1990 Leaf set was the first premium set introduced by Donruss and represents one of the more significant products issued in the 1990's. The cards were issued in 15-card foil wrapped packs and were not available in factory sets. Each pack also contained one three-piece puzzle panel of a 63-piece Yogi Berra "Donruss Hall of Fame Diamond King" puzzle. This set, which was produced on high quality paper stock, was issued in two separate series of 264 standard-size cards each. The second series was issued approximately six weeks after the release of the first series. The cards feature full-color photos on both the front and back. Rookie Cards in the set include David Justice, John Olerud, Sammy Sosa, Frank Thomas and Larry Walker.

COMPLETE SET (528) 20.00 50.00
COMPLETE SERIES 1 (264) 12.50 30.00
COMPLETE SERIES 2 (264) 6.00 15.00
BEWARE THOMAS COUNTERFEIT
COMP. BERRA PUZZLE .40 1.00
1 Introductory Card .15 .40
2 Mike Henneman .15 .40
3 Steve Bedrosian .15 .40
4 Mike Scott .15 .40
5 Allan Anderson .15 .40
6 Rick Sutcliffe .25 .60
7 Gregg Olson .25 .60
8 Kevin Elster .15 .40
9 Pete O'Brien .15 .40
10 Carlton Fisk .40 1.00
11 Joe Magrane .15 .40
12 Roger Clemens 1.50 4.00
13 Tom Glavine .40 1.00
14 Tom Gordon .25 .60
15 Todd Benzinger .15 .40
16 Hubie Brooks .15 .40
17 Roberto Kelly .15 .40
18 Barry Larkin .40 1.00
19 Mike Boddicker .15 .40
20 Roger McDowell .15 .40
21 Nolan Ryan 2.00 5.00
22 John Farrell .15 .40
23 Bruce Hurst .15 .40
24 Wally Joyner .25 .60
25 Greg Maddux 2.00 5.00
26 Chris Bosio .15 .40
27 John Cerutti .15 .40
28 Tim Burke .15 .40
29 Dennis Eckersley .25 .60
30 Glenn Davis .15 .40
31 Jim Abbott .40 1.00
32 Mike LaValliere .15 .40
33 Andres Thomas .15 .40
34 Lou Whitaker .25 .60
35 Alvin Davis .15 .40
36 Melido Perez .15 .40
37 Craig Biggio .60 1.50
38 Rick Aguilera .25 .60
39 Pete Harnisch .15 .40
40 David Cone .25 .60
41 Scott Garrelts .15 .40
42 Jay Howell .15 .40
43 Eric King .15 .40
44 Pedro Guerrero .15 .40
45 Mike Bielecki .15 .40
46 Bob Boone .25 .60
47 Kevin Brown .25 .60
48 Jerry Browne .15 .40
49 Mike Scioscia .15 .40
50 Chuck Cary .15 .40
51 Wade Boggs .40 1.00
52 Von Hayes .15 .40
53 Tony Fernandez .15 .40
54 Dennis Martinez .25 .60
55 Tom Candiotti .15 .40
56 Andy Benes .25 .60
57 Rob Dibble .25 .60
58 Chuck Crim .15 .40
59 John Smoltz .60 1.50
60 Mike Heath .15 .40
61 Kevin Gross .15 .40
62 Mark McGwire 1.50 4.00
63 Bert Blyleven .25 .60
64 Bob Walk .15 .40
65 Mickey Tettleton .15 .40
66 Sid Fernandez .15 .40
67 Terry Kennedy .15 .40
68 Fernando Valenzuela .25 .60
69 Don Mattingly 1.50 4.00
70 Paul O'Neill .40 1.00
71 Robin Yount 1.00 2.50
72 Bret Saberhagen .25 .60
73 Geno Petralli .15 .40
74 Brook Jacoby .15 .40
75 Roberto Alomar .40 1.00
76 Devon White .25 .60
77 Jose Lind .15 .40
78 Pat Combs .15 .40
79 Dave Stieb .25 .60
80 Tim Wallach .15 .40
81 Dave Stewart .25 .60
82 Eric Anthony RC .15 .40
83 Randy Bush .15 .40
84 Rickey Henderson CL .25 .60
85 Jaime Navarro .15 .40
86 Tommy Gregg .15 .40
87 Frank Tanana .15 .40
88 Omar Vizquel .60 1.50
89 Ivan Calderon .15 .40
90 Vince Coleman .15 .40
91 Barry Bonds 2.00 5.00
92 Randy Milligan .15 .40
93 Frank Viola .15 .40
94 Matt Williams .25 .60
95 Alfredo Griffin .15 .40
96 Steve Sax .15 .40
97 Gary Gaetti .25 .60
98 Ryne Sandberg 1.25 3.00
99 Danny Tartabull .15 .40
100 Rafael Palmeiro .40 1.00
101 Jesse Orosco .15 .40
102 Garry Templeton .15 .40
103 Frank DiPino .15 .40
104 Tony Pena .15 .40
105 Dickie Thon .15 .40
106 Kelly Gruber .15 .40
107 Marquis Grissom RC .75 2.00
108 Jose Canseco .40 1.00
109 Mike Blowers RC .15 .40
110 Tom Browning .15 .40
111 Greg Vaughn .15 .40
112 Oddibe McDowell .15 .40
113 Gary Ward .15 .40
114 Jay Buhner .25 .60
115 Eric Show .15 .40
116 Bryan Harvey .15 .40
117 Andy Van Slyke .40 1.00
118 Jeff Ballard .15 .40
119 Barry Lyons .15 .40
120 Kevin Mitchell .15 .40
121 Mike Gallego .15 .40
122 Dave Smith .15 .40
123 Kirby Puckett .60 1.50
124 Jerome Walton .15 .40
125 Bo Jackson .60 1.50
126 Harold Baines .25 .60
127 Scott Bankhead .15 .40
128 Ozzie Guillen .25 .60
129 Jose Oquendo UER .15 .40
League misspelled
as Legue
130 John Dopson .15 .40
131 Charlie Hayes .15 .40
132 Fred McGriff .60 1.50
133 Chet Lemon .15 .40
134 Gary Carter .25 .60
135 Rafael Ramirez .15 .40
136 Shane Mack .15 .40
137 Mark Grace .40 1.00
138 Phil Bradley .15 .40
139 Dwight Gooden .25 .60
140 Harold Reynolds .25 .60
141 Scott Fletcher .15 .40
142 Ozzie Smith 1.00 2.50
143 Mike Greenwell .15 .40
144 Pete Smith .15 .40
145 Mark Gubicza .15 .40
146 Chris Sabo .15 .40
147 Ramon Martinez .15 .40
148 Tim Leary .15 .40
149 Randy Myers .25 .60
150 Jody Reed .15 .40
151 Bruce Ruffin .15 .40
152 Jeff Russell .15 .40
153 Doug Jones .15 .40
154 Tony Gwynn .75 2.00
155 Mark Langston .15 .40
156 Mitch Williams .15 .40
157 Gary Sheffield .60 1.50
158 Tom Henke .15 .40
159 Oil Can Boyd .15 .40
160 Rickey Henderson .60 1.50
161 Bill Doran .15 .40
162 Chuck Finley .25 .60
163 Jeff King .15 .40
164 Nick Esasky .15 .40
165 Cecil Fielder .25 .60
166 Dave Valle .15 .40
167 Robin Ventura .60 1.50
168 Jim Deshaies .15 .40
169 Juan Berenguer .15 .40
170 Craig Worthington .15 .40
171 Gregg Jefferies .25 .60
172 Will Clark .40 1.00
173 Kirk Gibson .25 .60
174 Checklist 89-176 .25 .60
Carlton Fisk
175 Bobby Thigpen .15 .40
176 John Tudor .15 .40
177 Andre Dawson .25 .60
178 George Brett 1.50 4.00
179 Steve Buechele .15 .40
180 Albert Belle .60 1.50
181 Eddie Murray .60 1.50
182 Bob Geren .15 .40
183 Rob Murphy .15 .40
184 Tom Herr .15 .40
185 George Bell .15 .40
186 Spike Owen .15 .40
187 Cory Snyder .15 .40
188 Fred Lynn .15 .40
189 Eric Davis .25 .60
190 Dave Parker .25 .60
191 Jeff Blauser .15 .40
192 Matt Nokes .15 .40
193 Delino DeShields RC .40 1.00
194 Scott Sanderson .15 .40
195 Lance Parrish .15 .40
196 Bobby Bonilla .25 .60
197 Cal Ripken 2.00 5.00
198 Kevin McReynolds .15 .40
199 Robby Thompson .15 .40
200 Tim Belcher .15 .40
201 Jesse Barfield .15 .40
202 Mariano Duncan .15 .40
203 Bill Spiers .15 .40
204 Frank White .25 .60
205 Julio Franco .25 .60
206 Greg Swindell .15 .40
207 Benito Santiago .25 .60
208 Johnny Ray .15 .40
209 Gary Redus .15 .40
210 Jeff Parrett .15 .40
211 Jimmy Key .25 .60
212 Tim Raines .25 .60
213 Carney Lansford .25 .60
214 Gerald Young .15 .40
215 Gene Larkin .15 .40
216 Dan Plesac .15 .40
217 Lonnie Smith .15 .40
218 Alan Trammell .25 .60
219 Jeffrey Leonard .15 .40
220 Sammy Sosa RC 4.00 10.00
221 Todd Zeile .25 .60
222 Bill Landrum .15 .40
223 Mike Devereaux .15 .40
224 Mike Marshall .15 .40
225 Jose Uribe .15 .40
226 Juan Samuel .15 .40
227 Mel Hall .15 .40
228 Kent Hrbek .25 .60
229 Shawon Dunston .15 .40
230 Kevin Seitzer .15 .40
231 Pete Incaviglia .15 .40
232 Sandy Alomar Jr. .25 .60
233 Bip Roberts .15 .40
234 Scott Terry .15 .40
235 Dwight Evans .40 1.00
236 Ricky Jordan .15 .40
237 John Olerud RC 1.25 3.00
238 Zane Smith .15 .40
239 Walt Weiss .15 .40
240 Alvaro Espinoza .15 .40
241 Billy Hatcher .15 .40
242 Paul Molitor .25 .60
243 Dale Murphy .40 1.00
244 Dave Bergman .15 .40
245 Ken Griffey Jr. 4.00 10.00
246 Ed Whitson .15 .40
247 Kirk McCaskill .15 .40
248 Jay Bell .25 .60
249 Ben McDonald RC .40 1.00
250 Darryl Strawberry .25 .60
251 Brett Butler .25 .60
252 Terry Steinbach .15 .40
253 Ken Caminiti .25 .60
254 Dan Gladden .15 .40
255 Dwight Smith .15 .40
256 Kurt Stillwell .15 .40
257 Ruben Sierra .25 .60
258 Mike Schooler .15 .40
259 Lance Johnson .15 .40
260 Terry Pendleton .25 .60
261 Ellis Burks .40 1.00
262 Len Dykstra .25 .60
263 Mookie Wilson .25 .60
264 Nolan Ryan CL UER .60 1.50
265 Nolan Ryan SPEC 1.00 2.50
266 Brian DuBois RC .15 .40
267 Don Robinson .15 .40
268 Glenn Wilson .15 .40
269 Kevin Tapani RC .40 1.00
270 Marvell Wynne .15 .40
271 Bill Ripken .15 .40
272 Howard Johnson .15 .40
273 Brian Holman .15 .40
274 Dan Pasqua .15 .40
275 Ken Dayley .15 .40
276 Jeff Reardon .25 .60
277 Jim Presley .15 .40
278 Jim Eisenreich .15 .40
279 Danny Jackson .15 .40
280 Orel Hershiser .25 .60
281 Andy Hawkins .15 .40
282 Jose Rijo .15 .40
283 Luis Rivera .15 .40
284 John Kruk .25 .60
285 Jeff Huson RC .15 .40
286 Joel Skinner .15 .40
287 Jack Clark .25 .60
288 Chili Davis .25 .60
289 Joe Girardi .40 1.00
290 B.J. Surhoff .25 .60
291 Luis Sojo RC .15 .40
292 Tom Foley .15 .40
293 Mike Moore .15 .40
294 Ken Oberkfell .15 .40
295 Luis Polonia .15 .40
296 Doug Drabek .15 .40
297 David Justice RC 1.25 3.00
298 Paul Gibson .15 .40
299 Edgar Martinez .40 1.00
300 Frank Thomas RC 10.00 25.00
301 Eric Yelding RC .15 .40
302 Greg Gagne .15 .40
303 Brad Komminsk .15 .40
304 Ron Darling .15 .40
305 Kevin Bass .15 .40
306 Jeff Hamilton .15 .40
307 Ron Karkovice .15 .40
308 M.Thompson UER Lankford .40 1.00
309 Mike Harkey .15 .40
310 Mel Stottlemyre Jr. .15 .40
311 Kenny Rogers .25 .60
312 Mitch Webster .15 .40
313 Kal Daniels .15 .40
314 Matt Nokes .15 .40
315 Dennis Lamp .15 .40
316 Ken Howell .15 .40
317 Glenallen Hill .15 .40
318 Dave Martinez .15 .40
319 Chris James .15 .40
320 Mike Pagliarulo .15 .40
321 Hal Morris .15 .40
322 Rob Deer .15 .40
323 Greg Olson C RC .15 .40
324 Tony Phillips .15 .40
325 Larry Walker RC 4.00 10.00
326 Ron Hassey .15 .40
327 Jack Howell .15 .40
328 John Smiley .15 .40
329 Steve Finley .25 .60
330 Dave Magadan .15 .40
331 Greg Litton .15 .40
332 Mickey Hatcher .15 .40
333 Lee Guetterman .15 .40
334 Norm Charlton .15 .40
335 Edgar Diaz RC .15 .40
336 Willie Wilson .15 .40
337 Bobby Witt .15 .40
338 Candy Maldonado .15 .40
339 Craig Lefferts .15 .40
340 Dante Bichette .25 .60
341 Wally Backman .15 .40
342 Dennis Cook .15 .40
343 Pat Borders .15 .40
344 Wallace Johnson .15 .40
345 Willie Randolph .25 .60
346 Danny Darwin .15 .40
347 Al Newman .15 .40
348 Mark Knudson .15 .40
349 Joe Boever .15 .40
350 Larry Sheets .15 .40
351 Mike Jackson .15 .40
352 Wayne Edwards RC .15 .40
353 Bernard Gilkey RC .40 1.00
354 Don Slaught .15 .40
355 Joe Orsulak .15 .40
356 John Franco .25 .60
357 Jeff Brantley .15 .40
358 Mike Morgan .15 .40
359 Deion Sanders .60 1.50
360 Terry Leach .15 .40
361 Les Lancaster .15 .40
362 Storm Davis .15 .40
363 Scott Coolbaugh RC .15 .40
364 Checklist 265-352 .40 1.00
Ozzie Smith
365 Cecilio Guante .15 .40
366 Joey Cora .25 .60
367 Willie McGee .25 .60
368 Jerry Reed .15 .40
369 Darren Daulton .25 .60
370 Manny Lee .15 .40
371 Mark Gardner RC .15 .40
372 Rick Honeycutt .15 .40
373 Steve Balboni .15 .40
374 Jack Armstrong .15 .40
375 Charlie O'Brien .15 .40
376 Ron Gant .25 .60
377 Lloyd Moseby .15 .40
378 Gene Harris .15 .40
379 Joe Carter .25 .60
380 Scott Bailes .15 .40
381 R.J. Reynolds .15 .40
382 Bob Melvin .15 .40
383 Tim Teufel .15 .40
384 John Burkett .15 .40
385 Felix Jose .15 .40
386 Larry Andersen .15 .40
387 David West .15 .40
388 Luis Salazar .15 .40
389 Mike Macfarlane .15 .40
390 Charlie Hough .25 .60
391 Greg Briley .15 .40
392 Donn Pall .15 .40
393 Bryn Smith .15 .40
394 Carlos Quintana .15 .40
395 Steve Lake .15 .40
396 Mark Whiten RC .40 1.00
397 Edwin Nunez .15 .40
398 Rick Parker RC .15 .40
399 Mark Portugal .15 .40
400 Roy Smith .15 .40
401 Hector Villanueva RC .15 .40
402 Bob Milacki .15 .40
403 Alejandro Pena .15 .40
404 Scott Bradley .15 .40
405 Ron Kittle .15 .40
406 Bob Tewksbury .15 .40
407 Wes Gardner .15 .40
408 Ernie Whitt .15 .40
409 Terry Shumpert RC .15 .40
410 Tim Layana RC .15 .40
411 Chris Gwynn .15 .40
412 Jeff D. Robinson .15 .40
413 Scott Scudder .15 .40
414 Kevin Romine .15 .40
415 Jose DeJesus .15 .40
416 Mike Jeffcoat .15 .40
417 Rudy Seanez RC .15 .40
418 Mike Dunne .15 .40
419 Dick Schofield .15 .40
420 Steve Wilson .15 .40
421 Bill Krueger .15 .40
422 Junior Felix .15 .40
423 Drew Hall .15 .40
424 Curt Young .15 .40
425 Franklin Stubbs .15 .40
426 Dave Winfield .25 .60
427 Rick Reed RC .40 1.00
428 Charlie Leibrandt .15 .40
429 Jeff M. Robinson .15 .40
430 Erik Hanson .15 .40
431 Barry Jones .15 .40
432 Alex Trevino .15 .40
433 John Moses .15 .40
434 Dave Wayne Johnson RC .15 .40
435 Mackey Sasser .15 .40
436 Rick Leach .15 .40
437 Lenny Harris .15 .40
438 Carlos Martinez .15 .40
439 Rex Hudler .15 .40
440 Domingo Ramos .15 .40
441 Gerald Perry .15 .40
442 Jeff Russell .15 .40
443 Carlos Baerga RC .40 1.00
444 Will Clark CL .25 .60
445 Stan Javier .15 .40
446 Kevin Maas RC .40 1.00
447 Tom Brunansky .15 .40
448 Carmelo Martinez .15 .40
449 Willie Blair RC .15 .40
450 Andres Galarraga .25 .60
451 Bud Black .15 .40
452 Greg W. Harris .15 .40
453 Joe Oliver .15 .40
454 Greg Brock .15 .40
455 Jeff Treadway .15 .40
456 Lance McCullers .15 .40
457 Dave Schmidt .15 .40
458 Todd Burns .15 .40
459 Max Venable .15 .40
460 Neal Heaton .15 .40
461 Mark Williamson .15 .40
462 Keith Miller .15 .40
463 Mike LaCoss .15 .40
464 Jose Offerman RC .40 1.00
465 Jim Leyritz RC .75 2.00
466 Glenn Braggs .15 .40
467 Ron Robinson .15 .40
468 Mark Davis .15 .40
469 Gary Pettis .15 .40
470 Keith Hernandez .25 .60
471 Dennis Rasmussen .15 .40
472 Mark Eichhorn .15 .40
473 Ted Power .15 .40
474 Terry Mulholland .15 .40
475 Todd Stottlemyre .25 .60
476 Jerry Goff RC .15 .40
477 Gene Nelson .15 .40
478 Rich Gedman .15 .40
479 Brian Harper .15 .40
480 Mike Felder .15 .40
481 Steve Avery .15 .40
482 Jack Morris .25 .60
483 Randy Johnson 1.25 3.00
484 Scott Radinsky RC .15 .40
485 Jose DeLeon .15 .40
486 Stan Belinda RC .15 .40
487 Brian Holton .15 .40
488 Mark Carreon .15 .40
489 Trevor Wilson .15 .40
490 Mike Sharperson .15 .40
491 Alan Mills RC .15 .40
492 John Candelaria .15 .40
493 Paul Assenmacher .15 .40
494 Steve Crawford .15 .40
495 Brad Arnsberg .15 .40
496 Sergio Valdez RC .15 .40
497 Mark Parent .15 .40
498 Tom Pagnozzi .15 .40
499 Greg A. Harris .15 .40
500 Randy Ready .15 .40
501 Duane Ward .15 .40
502 Nelson Santovenia .15 .40
503 Joe Klink RC .15 .40
504 Eric Plunk .15 .40
505 Jeff Reed .15 .40
506 Ted Higuera .15 .40
507 Joe Hesketh .15 .40
508 Dan Petry .15 .40
509 Matt Young .15 .40
510 Jerald Clark .15 .40
511 John Orton RC .15 .40
512 Scott Ruskin RC .15 .40
513 Chris Hoiles RC .40 1.00
514 Daryl Boston .15 .40
515 Francisco Oliveras .15 .40
516 Ozzie Canseco .15 .40
517 Xavier Hernandez RC .15 .40
518 Fred Manrique .15 .40
519 Shawn Boskie RC .15 .40
520 Jeff Montgomery .25 .60
521 Jack Daugherty RC .15 .40
522 Keith Comstock .15 .40
523 Greg Hibbard RC .15 .40
524 Lee Smith .25 .60
525 Dana Kiecker RC .15 .40
526 Darrel Akerfelds .15 .40
527 Greg Myers .15 .40
528 Ryne Sandberg CL .60 1.50

1991 Leaf Previews

The 1991 Leaf Previews set consists of 26 standard-size cards. Cards from this set were issued as inserts (four at a time) inside specially marked 1991 Donruss hobby factory sets. The front design has color action player photos, with white and silver borders.

COMPLETE SET (26) 12.00 30.00
FOUR PER DONRUSS HOBBY FACT.SET
1 David Justice .40 1.00
2 Ryne Sandberg 1.50 4.00
3 Barry Larkin .60 1.50
4 Craig Biggio .60 1.50
5 Ramon Martinez .20 .50
6 Tim Wallach .20 .50
7 Dwight Gooden .40 1.00
8 Len Dykstra .40 1.00
9 Barry Bonds 3.00 8.00
10 Ray Lankford .40 1.00
11 Tony Gwynn 1.25 3.00
12 Will Clark .60 1.50
13 Leo Gomez .20 .50
14 Wade Boggs .60 1.50
15 Chuck Finley UER .40 1.00
16 Carlton Fisk .60 1.50
17 Sandy Alomar Jr. .20 .50
18 Cecil Fielder .40 1.00
19 Bo Jackson .40 1.00
20 Paul Molitor .40 1.00
21 Kirby Puckett 1.00 2.50
22 Don Mattingly 2.50 6.00
23 Rickey Henderson 1.00 2.50
24 Tino Martinez .40 1.00
25 Nolan Ryan 4.00 10.00
26 Dave Stieb .20 .50

2018 Limited

INSERTED IN '18 CHRONICLES PACKS
*SLVR/199: 1X TO 2.5X BASE
*SLVR RC/199: .6X TO 1.5X BASE RC
*GOLD/99: 1.2X TO 3X BASE
*GOLD RC/99: .75X TO 2X BASE RC
1 Aaron Judge .60 1.50
2 Rhys Hoskins RC 1.00 2.50
3 Kris Bryant .30 .75
4 Adrian Beltre .25 .60
5 Cody Bellinger .50 1.25
6 Rafael Devers RC .75 2.00
7 Clint Frazier RC .50 1.25
8 Miguel Andujar RC 1.00 2.50
9 Ronald Acuna Jr. RC 5.00 12.00
10 Nolan Arenado .30 .75
11 Amed Rosario RC .30 .75
12 Gleyber Torres RC 2.50 6.00
13 Austin Hays RC .40 1.00
14 Manny Machado .25 .60
15 Ozzie Albies RC .75 2.00
16 Mike Trout 1.25 3.00
17 Paul Goldschmidt .25 .60
18 Shohei Ohtani RC 1.50 4.00
19 Bryce Harper .40 1.00
20 Clayton Kershaw .50 1.25

2018 Limited Ruby

*RUBY: 3X TO 8X BASIC
*RUBY RC: 2X TO 5X BASIC RC
INSERTED IN '18 CHRONICLES PACKS
STATED PRINT RUN 25 SER.#'d SETS
16 Mike Trout 15.00 40.00

2019 Limited

RANDOM INSERTS IN PACKS
*GOLD/199: 1.2X TO 3X
*BLUE/99: 1.5X TO 4X
*RED/50: 2X TO 5X
*HOLO SLVR/25: 3X TO 8X
1 Pete Alonso RC 4.00 10.00
2 Eloy Jimenez RC 1.50 4.00
3 Fernando Tatis Jr. RC 2.00 5.00
4 Michael Kopech RC .30 .75
5 Carter Kieboom RC .25 .60
6 Yusei Kikuchi RC .25 .60
7 Chris Paddack RC .30 .75
8 Mike Trout 1.25 3.
9 Cole Tucker RC .25
10 Mookie Betts .40 1.
11 Bryan Reynolds RC .50 1.
12 Shohei Ohtani .30
13 Vladimir Guerrero Jr. RC 2.50 6.
14 Paul DeJong .25
15 Anthony Rizzo .40 1.
16 Darwinzon Hernandez RC .15
17 Brandon Nimmo .20
18 Matt Olson .15
19 Josh Naylor .20 .5
20 Kyle Schwarber .25 .6

2020 Limited

RANDOM INSERTS IN PACKS
1 Shogo Akiyama RC .40 1.0
2 Yordan Alvarez RC 1.25 3.0
3 Bo Bichette RC 3.00 8.0
4 Aristides Aquino RC .50 1.2
5 Gavin Lux RC 1.50 4.0
6 Yoshitomo Tsutsugo RC .30 .7
7 Brendan McKay RC .40 1.0
8 Luis Robert RC 4.00 10.0
9 Dylan Cease RC .50 1.2
10 Sheldon Neuse RC .30 .75
11 Trent Grisham RC 1.00 2.50
12 Yonathan Daza RC .30 .75
13 Michel Baez RC .25 .60
14 Nico Hoerner RC 1.00 2.50
15 Jesus Luzardo RC .50 1.25
16 Brusdar Graterol RC .40 1.00
17 Nolan Arenado .30 .75
18 Jacob deGrom .25 .60
19 Trea Turner .20 .50
20 Alex Bregman .25 .60

2020 Limited Signatures

RANDOM INSERTS IN PACKS
PRINT RUNS B/WN 5-99 COPIES PER
NO PRICING QTY 15 OR LESS
EXCHANGE DEADLINE 3/18/2022
1 Shogo Akiyama/49 6.00 15.00
2 Yordan Alvarez/50 20.00 50.00
3 Bo Bichette/30 30.00 80.00
4 Aristides Aquino/60 8.00 20.00
6 Yoshitomo Tsutsugo/99 10.00 25.00
8 Luis Robert EXCH/99 75.00 200.00
9 Dylan Cease/90 6.00 15.00
10 Sheldon Neuse/97 4.00 10.00
11 Trent Grisham/96 12.00 30.00
12 Yonathan Daza/99 4.00 10.00
13 Michel Baez/99 3.00 8.00
14 Nico Hoerner/99 12.00 30.00
16 Brusdar Graterol/99 5.00 12.00
19 Trea Turner/25

1965 O-Pee-Chee

The cards in this 283-card set measure the standard size. This set is essentially the same as the regular 1965 Topps set, except that the words "Printed in Canada" appear on the bottom of the back. On a white border, the fronts feature color player photos with rounded corners. The team name appears within a pennant design below the photo. The player's name and position are also printed on the front. On a blue background, the horizontal backs carry player biography and statistics on a gray card stock. Remember the prices below apply only to the O-Pee-Chee cards -- NOT to the 1965 Topps cards which are much more plentiful. Notable Rookie Cards include Bert Campaneris, Denny McLain, Joe Morgan and Luis Tiant.

COMPLETE SET (283) 1250.00 2500.00
COMMON PLAYER (1-198) 1.50 4.00
COMMON PLAYER (199-283) 2.50 6.00
1 Oliva 12.50 30.00
Howard
Brooks LL !
2 Clemente 15.00 40.00
Aaron
Carty LL
3 Kill 40.00 80.00
Mantle
Powell LL
4 Mays 10.00 25.00
Will
Cepeda
LL
5 Brooks 30.00 60.00
Kill
Mantle
LL
6 Boyer 8.00 20.00
Mays
Santo LL
7 Dean Chance 4.00 10.00
Joel Horlen LL
8 Koufax 12.50 30.00
Drysdale LL
9 AL Pitching Leaders 4.00 10.00
Dean Chance
Gary Peters
Dav

Card	Low	High
10 NL Pitching Leaders	4.00	10.00
Larry Jackson		
Ray Sadecki		
J		
11 AL Strikeout Leaders	4.00	10.00
Al Downing		
Dean Chance		
Cam		
12 Veale	4.00	10.00
Drysdale		
Gibson LL		
13 Pedro Ramos	2.50	6.00
14 Len Gabrielson	1.50	4.00
15 Robin Roberts	6.00	15.00
16 Joe Morgan RC DP !	50.00	100.00
17 John Romano	1.50	4.00
18 Bill McCool	1.50	4.00
19 Gates Brown	2.50	6.00
20 Jim Bunning	6.00	15.00
21 Don Blasingame	1.50	4.00
22 Charlie Smith	1.50	4.00
23 Bob Tiefenauer	1.50	4.00
24 Twins Team	4.00	10.00
25 Al McBean	1.50	4.00
26 Bob Knoop	1.50	4.00
27 Dick Bertell	1.50	4.00
28 Barney Schultz	1.50	4.00
29 Felix Mantilla	1.50	4.00
30 Jim Bouton	4.00	10.00
31 Mike White	1.50	4.00
32 Herman Franks MG	1.50	4.00
33 Jackie Brandt	1.50	4.00
34 Cal Koonce	1.50	4.00
35 Ed Charles	1.50	4.00
36 Bob Wine	1.50	4.00
37 Fred Gladding	1.50	4.00
38 Jim King	1.50	4.00
39 Gerry Arrigo	1.50	4.00
40 Frank Howard	3.00	8.00
41 Bruce Howard	1.50	4.00
Marv Staehle		
42 Earl Wilson	2.50	6.00
43 Mike Shannon	2.50	6.00
44 Wade Blasingame	1.50	4.00
45 Roy McMillan	2.50	6.00
46 Bob Lee	1.50	4.00
47 Tommy Harper	2.50	6.00
48 Claude Raymond	2.50	6.00
49 Curt Blefary RC	2.50	6.00
50 Juan Marichal	6.00	15.00
51 Bill Bryan	1.50	4.00
52 Ed Roebuck	1.50	4.00
53 Dick McAuliffe	2.50	6.00
54 Joe Gibbon	1.50	4.00
55 Tony Conigliaro	8.00	20.00
56 Ron Kline	1.50	4.00
57 Cardinals Team	4.00	10.00
58 Fred Talbot	1.50	4.00
59 Nate Oliver	1.50	4.00
60 Jim O'Toole	2.50	6.00
61 Chris Cannizzaro	1.50	4.00
62 Jim Kaat UER/(Misspelled Katt)	3.00	8.00
63 Ty Cline	1.50	4.00
64 Lou Burdette	2.50	6.00
65 Tony Kubek	6.00	15.00
66 Bill Rigney MG	1.50	4.00
67 Harvey Haddix	2.50	6.00
68 Del Crandall	2.50	6.00
69 Bill Virdon	2.50	6.00
70 Bill Skowron	3.00	8.00
71 John O'Donoghue	1.50	4.00
72 Tony Gonzalez	1.50	4.00
73 Dennis Ribant	1.50	4.00
74 Rico Petrocelli RC	6.00	15.00
75 Deron Johnson	2.50	6.00
76 Sam McDowell	3.00	8.00
77 Doug Camilli	1.50	4.00
78 Dal Maxvill	2.50	6.00
79 Checklist 1-88	4.00	10.00
80 Turk Farrell	1.50	4.00
81 Don Buford	2.50	6.00
82 Sandy Alomar RC	3.00	8.00
83 George Thomas	1.50	4.00
84 Ron Herbel	1.50	4.00
85 Willie Smith	1.50	4.00
86 Buster Narum	1.50	4.00
87 Nelson Mathews	1.50	4.00
88 Jack Lamabe	1.50	4.00
89 Mike Hershberger	1.50	4.00
90 Rich Rollins	2.50	6.00
91 Cubs Team	4.00	10.00
92 Dick Howser	2.50	6.00
93 Jack Fisher	1.50	4.00
94 Charlie Lau	2.50	6.00
95 Bill Mazeroski	6.00	15.00
96 Sonny Siebert	2.50	6.00
97 Pedro Gonzalez	1.50	4.00
98 Bob Miller	1.50	4.00
99 Gil Hodges MG	4.00	10.00
100 Ken Boyer	6.00	15.00
101 Fred Newman	1.50	4.00
102 Steve Boros	1.50	4.00
103 Harvey Kuenn	2.50	6.00
104 Checklist 89-176	4.00	10.00
105 Chico Salmon	1.50	4.00
106 Gene Oliver	1.50	4.00
107 Pat Corrales RC	2.50	6.00
108 Don Mincher	1.50	4.00
109 Walt Bond	1.50	4.00
110 Ron Santo	3.00	8.00
111 Lee Thomas	2.50	6.00
112 Derrell Griffith	1.50	4.00
113 Steve Barber	1.50	4.00
114 Jim Hickman	2.50	6.00
115 Bobby Richardson	6.00	15.00
116 Bob Tolan RC	2.50	6.00
117 Wes Stock	1.50	4.00
118 Hal Lanier	2.50	6.00
119 John Kennedy	1.50	4.00
120 Frank Robinson	30.00	60.00
121 Gene Alley	2.50	6.00
122 Bill Pleis	1.50	4.00
123 Frank Thomas	2.50	6.00
124 Tom Satriano	1.50	4.00
125 Juan Pizarro	1.50	4.00
126 Dodgers Team	4.00	10.00
127 Frank Lary	1.50	4.00
128 Vic Davalillo	1.50	4.00
129 Bennie Daniels	1.50	4.00
130 Al Kaline	30.00	60.00
131 Johnny Keane MG	1.50	4.00
132 World Series Game 1	4.00	10.00
Cards take opener/(Mike Shan		
133 Mel Stottlemyre WS	4.00	10.00
134 Mickey Mantle WS3	60.00	120.00
135 Ken Boyer WS	6.00	15.00
136 Tim McCarver WS	4.00	10.00
137 Jim Bouton WS	4.00	10.00
138 Bob Gibson WS7	8.00	20.00
139 World Series Summary	4.00	10.00
Cards celebrate		
140 Dean Chance	2.50	6.00
141 Charlie James	1.50	4.00
142 Bill Monbouquette	1.50	4.00
143 John Gelnar	1.50	4.00
Jerry May		
144 Ed Kranepool	2.50	6.00
145 Luis Tiant RC	8.00	20.00
146 Ron Hansen	1.50	4.00
147 Dennis Bennett	1.50	4.00
148 Willie Kirkland	1.50	4.00
149 Wayne Schurr	1.50	4.00
150 Brooks Robinson	30.00	60.00
151 Athletics Team	4.00	10.00
152 Phil Ortega	1.50	4.00
153 Norm Cash	4.00	10.00
154 Bob Humphreys	1.50	4.00
155 Roger Maris	50.00	100.00
156 Bob Sadowski	1.50	4.00
157 Zoilo Versalles	2.50	6.00
158 Dick Sisler MG	1.50	4.00
159 Jim Duffalo	1.50	4.00
160 Roberto Clemente !	125.00	250.00
161 Frank Baumann	1.50	4.00
162 Russ Nixon	1.50	4.00
163 John Briggs	1.50	4.00
164 Al Spangler	1.50	4.00
165 Dick Ellsworth	1.50	4.00
166 Tommie Agee RC	3.00	8.00
167 Bill Wakefield	1.50	4.00
168 Dick Green	2.50	6.00
169 Dave Vineyard	1.50	4.00
170 Hank Aaron	100.00	200.00
171 Jim Roland	1.50	4.00
172 Jim Piersall	3.00	8.00
173 Tigers Team	4.00	10.00
174 Joe Jay	1.50	4.00
175 Bob Aspromonte	1.50	4.00
176 Willie McCovey	12.50	30.00
177 Pete Mikkelsen	1.50	4.00
178 Dalton Jones	1.50	4.00
179 Hal Woodeshick	1.50	4.00
180 Bob Allison	2.50	6.00
181 Don Loun	1.50	4.00
Joe McCabe		
182 Mike de la Hoz	1.50	4.00
183 Dave Nicholson	1.50	4.00
184 John Boozer	1.50	4.00
185 Max Alvis	1.50	4.00
186 Bill Cowan	1.50	4.00
187 Casey Stengel MG	10.00	25.00
188 Sam Bowens	1.50	4.00
189 Checklist 177-264	4.00	10.00
190 Bill White	3.00	8.00
191 Phil Regan	2.50	6.00
192 Jim Coker	1.50	4.00
193 Gaylord Perry	10.00	25.00
194 Bill Kelso	2.50	6.00
Rick Reichardt		
195 Bob Veale	2.50	6.00
196 Ron Fairly	2.50	6.00
197 Diego Segui	1.50	4.00
198 Smoky Burgess	2.50	6.00
199 Bob Heffner	2.50	6.00
200 Joe Torre	4.00	10.00
201 Cesar Tovar RC	2.50	6.00
202 Leo Burke	2.50	6.00
203 Dallas Green	2.50	6.00
204 Russ Snyder	2.50	6.00
205 Warren Spahn	20.00	50.00
206 Willie Horton	4.00	10.00
207 Pete Rose	125.00	250.00
208 Tommy John	4.00	10.00
209 Pirates Team	4.00	10.00
210 Jim Fregosi	3.00	8.00
211 Steve Ridzik	2.50	6.00
212 Ron Brand	2.50	6.00
213 Jim Davenport	2.50	6.00
214 Bob Purkey	2.50	6.00
215 Pete Ward	2.50	6.00
216 Al Worthington	2.50	6.00
217 Walt Alston MG	4.00	10.00
218 Dick Schofield	2.50	6.00
219 Bob Meyer	2.50	6.00
220 Billy Williams	6.00	15.00
221 John Tsitouris	2.50	6.00
222 Bob Tillman	2.50	6.00
223 Dan Osinski	2.50	6.00
224 Bob Chance	2.50	6.00
225 Bo Belinsky	3.00	8.00
226 Elvio Jimenez	3.00	8.00
Jake Gibbs		
227 Bobby Klaus	2.50	6.00
228 Jack Sanford	2.50	6.00
229 Lou Clinton	2.50	6.00
230 Ray Sadecki	2.50	6.00
231 Jerry Adair	2.50	6.00
232 Steve Blass	2.50	6.00
233 Don Zimmer	3.00	8.00
234 White Sox Team	4.00	10.00
235 Chuck Hinton	2.50	6.00
236 Denny McLain RC	15.00	40.00
237 Bernie Allen	2.50	6.00
238 Joe Moeller	2.50	6.00
239 Doc Edwards	2.50	6.00
240 Bob Bruce	2.50	6.00
241 Mack Jones	2.50	6.00
242 George Brunet	2.50	6.00
243 Tommy Helms RC	3.00	8.00
244 Lindy McDaniel	3.00	8.00
245 Joe Pepitone	3.00	8.00
246 Tom Butters	3.00	8.00
247 Wally Moon	3.00	8.00
248 Gus Triandos	2.50	6.00
249 Dave McNally	3.00	8.00
250 Willie Mays	100.00	200.00
251 Billy Herman MG	3.00	8.00
252 Pete Richert	2.50	6.00
253 Danny Cater	2.50	6.00
254 Roland Sheldon	2.50	6.00
255 Camilo Pascual	3.00	8.00
256 Tito Francona	2.50	6.00
257 Jim Wynn	3.00	8.00
258 Larry Bearnarth	2.50	6.00
259 Jim Northrup RC	4.00	10.00
260 Don Drysdale	12.50	30.00
261 Duke Carmel	2.50	6.00
262 Bud Daley	2.50	6.00
263 Marty Keough	2.50	6.00
264 Bob Buhl	2.50	6.00
265 Jim Pagliaroni	2.50	6.00
266 Bert Campaneris RC	5.00	12.00
267 Senators Team	4.00	10.00
268 Ken McBride	2.50	6.00
269 Frank Bolling	2.50	6.00
270 Milt Pappas	2.50	6.00
271 Don Wert	2.50	6.00
272 Chuck Schilling	2.50	6.00
273 4th Series Checklist	5.00	12.00
274 Lum Harris MG	2.50	6.00
275 Dick Groat	4.00	10.00
276 Hoyt Wilhelm	6.00	15.00
277 Johnny Lewis	2.50	6.00
278 Ken Retzer	2.50	6.00
279 Dick Tracewski	2.50	6.00
280 Dick Stuart	3.00	8.00
281 Bill Stafford	2.50	6.00
282 Masanori Murakami RC	30.00	60.00
283 Fred Whitfield	3.00	8.00

1966 O-Pee-Chee

The cards in this 196-card set measure 2 1/2" by 3 1/2". This set is essentially the same as the regular 1966 Topps set, except that the words "Printed In Canada" appear on the bottom of the back, and the background colors are slightly different. On a white border, the fronts feature color player photos. The team name appears within a tilted bar in the top right corner, while the player's name and position are printed inside a bar under the photo. The horizontal backs carry player biography and statistics. The set was issued in five-card nickel packs which came 36 to a box. Remember the prices below apply only to the O-Pee- Chee cards -- NOT to the 1966 Topps cards which are much more plentiful. Notable Rookie Cards include Jim Palmer.

Card	Low	High
COMPLETE SET (196)	750.00	1500.00
1 Willie Mays	200.00	400.00
2 Ted Abernathy	1.25	3.00
3 Sam Mele MG	1.25	3.00
4 Ray Culp	1.25	3.00
5 Jim Fregosi	1.50	4.00
6 Chuck Schilling	1.25	3.00
7 Tracy Stallard	1.25	3.00
8 Floyd Robinson	1.25	3.00
9 Clete Boyer	1.50	4.00
10 Tony Cloninger	1.25	3.00
11 Brant Alyea	1.50	4.00
Pete Craig		
12 John Tsitouris	1.25	3.00
13 Lou Johnson	1.50	4.00
14 Norm Siebern	1.25	3.00
15 Vern Law	1.50	4.00
16 Larry Brown	1.25	3.00
17 John Stephenson	1.25	3.00
18 Roland Sheldon	1.25	3.00
19 Giants Team	2.50	6.00
20 Willie Horton	1.50	4.00
21 Don Nottebart	1.25	3.00
22 Joe Nossek	1.25	3.00
23 Jack Sanford	1.25	3.00
24 Don Kessinger RC	2.50	6.00
25 Pete Ward	1.50	4.00
26 Ray Sadecki	1.25	3.00
27 Darold Knowles	1.25	3.00
Andy Etchebarren		
28 Phil Niekro	12.50	30.00
29 Mike Brumley	1.25	3.00
30 Pete Rose	75.00	150.00
31 Jack Cullen	1.50	4.00
32 Adolfo Phillips	1.25	3.00
33 Jim Pagliaroni	1.25	3.00
34 Checklist 1-88	5.00	12.00
35 Ron Swoboda	2.50	6.00
36 Jim Hunter	12.50	30.00
37 Billy Herman MG	1.50	4.00
38 Ron Nischwitz	1.25	3.00
39 Ken Henderson	1.25	3.00
40 Jim Grant	1.25	3.00
41 Don LeJohn	1.25	3.00
42 Aubrey Gatewood	1.25	3.00
43 Don Landrum	1.25	3.00
44 Bill Davis	1.25	3.00
Tom Kelley		
45 Jim Gentile	1.50	4.00
46 Howie Koplitz	1.25	3.00
47 J.C. Martin	1.25	3.00
48 Paul Blair	1.50	4.00
49 Woody Woodward	1.25	3.00
50 Mickey Mantle	250.00	500.00
51 Gordon Richardson	1.25	3.00
52 Wes Covington	2.50	6.00
Johnny Callison		
53 Bob Duliba	1.25	3.00
54 Jose Pagan	1.25	3.00
55 Ken Harrelson	1.50	4.00
56 Sandy Valdespino	1.25	3.00
57 Jim Lefebvre	1.50	4.00
58 Dave Wickersham	1.25	3.00
59 Reds Team	2.50	6.00
60 Curt Flood	3.00	8.00
61 Bob Bolin	1.25	3.00
62 Merritt Ranew/(with sold line)	1.25	3.00
63 Jim Stewart	1.25	3.00
64 Bob Bruce	1.25	3.00
65 Leon Wagner	1.25	3.00
66 Al Weis	1.25	3.00
67 Cleon Jones	2.50	6.00
Dick Selma		
68 Hal Reniff	1.25	3.00
69 Ken Hamlin	1.25	3.00
70 Carl Yastrzemski	20.00	50.00
71 Frank Carpin	1.25	3.00
72 Tony Perez	15.00	40.00
73 Jerry Zimmerman	1.25	3.00
74 Don Mossi	1.50	4.00
75 Tommy Davis	1.50	4.00
76 Red Schoendienst MG	2.50	6.00
77 Johnny Orsino	1.25	3.00
78 Frank Linzy	1.25	3.00
79 Joe Pepitone	2.50	6.00
80 Richie Allen	3.00	8.00
81 Ray Oyler	1.25	3.00
82 Bob Hendley	1.25	3.00
83 Albie Pearson	1.50	4.00
84 Jim Beauchamp	1.25	3.00
Dick Kelley		
85 Eddie Fisher	1.25	3.00
86 John Bateman	1.25	3.00
87 Dan Napoleon	1.25	3.00
88 Fred Whitfield	1.25	3.00
89 Ted Davidson	1.25	3.00
90 Luis Aparicio	5.00	12.00
91 Bob Uecker/(with traded line)	6.00	15.00
92 Yankees Team	10.00	25.00
93 Jim Lonborg	1.50	4.00
94 Matty Alou	1.50	4.00
95 Pete Richert	1.25	3.00
96 Felipe Alou	2.50	6.00
97 Jim Merritt	1.25	3.00
98 Don Demeter	1.25	3.00
99 W.Stargell	3.00	8.00
Clendenon		
100 Sandy Koufax	75.00	150.00
101 Checklist 89-176	5.00	12.00
102 Ed Kirkpatrick	1.25	3.00
103 Dick Groat/(with traded line)	1.50	4.00
104 Alex Johnson/(with traded line)	1.50	4.00
105 Milt Pappas	1.50	4.00
106 Rusty Staub	2.50	6.00
107 Larry Stahl	1.25	3.00
Ron Tompkins		
108 Bobby Klaus	1.25	3.00
109 Ralph Terry	1.50	4.00
110 Ernie Banks	20.00	50.00
111 Gary Peters	1.25	3.00
112 Manny Mota	1.50	4.00
113 Hank Aguirre	1.25	3.00
114 Jim Gosger	1.25	3.00
115 Bill Henry	1.25	3.00
116 Walt Alston MG	2.50	6.00
117 Jake Gibbs	1.25	3.00
118 Mike McCormick	1.25	3.00
119 Art Shamsky	1.25	3.00
120 Harmon Killebrew	10.00	25.00
121 Ray Herbert	1.25	3.00
122 Joe Gaines	1.25	3.00
123 Frank Bork	1.25	3.00
Jerry May		
124 Tug McGraw	2.50	6.00
125 Lou Brock	12.50	30.00
126 Jim Palmer RC	75.00	150.00
127 Ken Berry	1.25	3.00
128 Jim Landis	1.25	3.00
129 Jack Kralick	1.25	3.00
130 Joe Torre	3.00	8.00
131 Angels Team	3.00	8.00
132 Orlando Cepeda	5.00	12.00
133 Don McMahon	1.25	3.00
134 Wes Parker	1.50	4.00
135 Dave Morehead	1.25	3.00
136 Woody Held	1.25	3.00
137 Pat Corrales	1.25	3.00
138 Roger Repoz	1.25	3.00
139 Byron Browne	1.25	3.00
Don Young		
140 Jim Maloney	1.50	4.00
141 Tom McCraw	1.25	3.00
142 Don Dennis	1.25	3.00
143 Jose Tartabull	1.50	4.00
144 Don Schwall	1.25	3.00
145 Bill Freehan	1.50	4.00
146 George Altman	1.25	3.00
147 Lum Harris MG	1.25	3.00
148 Bob Johnson	1.25	3.00
149 Dick Nen	1.25	3.00
150 Rocky Colavito	5.00	12.00
151 Gary Wagner	1.25	3.00
152 Frank Malzone	1.50	4.00
153 Rico Carty	1.50	4.00
154 Chuck Hiller	1.25	3.00
155 Marcelino Lopez	1.25	3.00
156 Dick Schofield	1.25	3.00
Hal Lanier		
157 Rene Lachemann	1.50	4.00
158 Jim Brewer	1.25	3.00
159 Chico Ruiz	1.25	3.00
160 Whitey Ford	20.00	50.00
161 Jerry Lumpe	1.25	3.00
162 Lee Maye	1.25	3.00
163 Tito Francona	1.25	3.00
164 Tommie Agee	1.50	4.00
Marv Staehle		
165 Don Lock	1.25	3.00
166 Chris Krug	1.25	3.00
167 Boog Powell	3.00	8.00
168 Dan Osinski	1.25	3.00
169 Duke Sims	1.25	3.00
170 Cookie Rojas	1.50	4.00
171 Nick Willhite	1.25	3.00
172 Mets Team	3.00	8.00
173 Al Spangler	1.25	3.00
174 Ron Taylor	1.50	4.00
175 Bert Campaneris	2.50	6.00
176 Jim Davenport	1.25	3.00
177 Hector Lopez	1.25	3.00
178 Bob Tillman	1.25	3.00
179 Dennis Aust	1.50	4.00
Bob Tolan		
180 Vada Pinson	2.50	6.00
181 Al Worthington	1.25	3.00
182 Jerry Lynch	1.25	3.00
183 Checklist 177-264	5.00	12.00
184 Denis Menke	1.25	3.00
185 Bob Buhl	1.50	4.00
186 Ruben Amaro	1.25	3.00
187 Chuck Dressen MG	1.50	4.00
188 Al Luplow	1.25	3.00
189 John Roseboro	1.50	4.00
190 Jimmie Hall	1.25	3.00
191 Darrell Sutherland	1.25	3.00
192 Vic Power	1.50	4.00
193 Dave McNally	1.50	4.00
194 Senators Team	3.00	8.00
195 Joe Morgan	10.00	25.00
196 Don Pavletich	1.50	4.00

1967 O-Pee-Chee

The cards in this 196-card set measure 2 1/2" by 3 1/2". This set is essentially the same as the regular 1967 Topps set, except that the words "Printed in Canada" appear on the bottom right corner of the back. On a white border, fronts feature color player photos with a thin black border. The player's name and position appear in the top part, while the team name is printed in big letters in the bottom part of the photo. On a green background, the backs carry player biography and statistics and two cartoon-like facts. Each checklist card features a small circular picture of a popular player included in that series. The set was issued in five card nickel packs which came 36 packs to a box. Remember the prices below apply only to the O-Pee-Chee cards -- NOT to the 1967 Topps cards which are much more plentiful.

Card	Low	High
COMPLETE SET (196)	600.00	1200.00
1 The Champs	12.50	30.00
Frank Robinson		
Hank Bauer		
Brooks Rob		
2 Jack Hamilton	1.25	3.00
3 Duke Sims	1.25	3.00
4 Hal Lanier	1.25	3.00
5 Whitey Ford	10.00	25.00
6 Dick Simpson	1.25	3.00
7 Don McMahon	1.25	3.00
8 Chuck Harrison	1.25	3.00
9 Ron Hansen	1.25	3.00
10 Matty Alou	1.50	4.00
11 Barry Moore	1.25	3.00
12 Jim Campanis	1.50	4.00
Bill Singer		
13 Joe Sparma	1.25	3.00
14 Phil Linz	1.50	4.00
15 Earl Battey	1.25	3.00
16 Bill Hands	1.25	3.00
17 Jim Gosger	1.25	3.00
18 Gene Oliver	1.25	3.00
19 Jim McGlothlin	1.25	3.00
20 Orlando Cepeda	4.00	10.00
21 Dave Bristol MG	1.25	3.00
22 Gene Brabender	1.25	3.00
23 Larry Elliot	1.25	3.00
24 Bob Allen	1.25	3.00
25 Elston Howard	2.50	6.00
26 Bob Priddy/(with traded line)	1.25	3.00
27 Bob Saverine	1.25	3.00
28 Barry Latman	1.25	3.00
29 Tommy McCraw	1.25	3.00
30 Al Kaline	10.00	25.00
31 Jim Brewer	1.25	3.00
32 Bob Bailey	1.50	4.00
33 Sal Bando RC	3.00	8.00
34 Pete Cimino	1.25	3.00
35 Rico Carty	1.50	4.00
36 Bob Tillman	1.25	3.00
37 Rick Wise	1.50	4.00
38 Bob Johnson	1.25	3.00
39 Curt Simmons	1.50	4.00
40 Rick Reichardt	1.25	3.00
41 Joe Hoerner	1.25	3.00
42 Mets Team	5.00	12.00
43 Chico Salmon	1.25	3.00
44 Joe Nuxhall	1.50	4.00
45 Roger Maris	30.00	60.00
46 Lindy McDaniel	1.50	4.00
47 Ken McMullen	1.25	3.00
48 Bill Freehan	1.50	4.00
49 Roy Face	1.50	4.00
50 Tony Oliva	3.00	8.00
51 Dave Adlesh	1.25	3.00
Wes Bales		
52 Dennis Higgins	1.25	3.00
53 Clay Dalrymple	1.25	3.00
54 Dick Green	1.25	3.00
55 Don Drysdale	8.00	20.00
56 Jose Tartabull	1.50	4.00
57 Pat Jarvis	1.50	4.00
58 Paul Schaal	1.25	3.00
59 Ralph Terry	1.50	4.00
60 Luis Aparicio	4.00	10.00
61 Gordy Coleman	1.25	3.00
62 Checklist 1-109	5.00	12.00
Frank Robinson		
63 Lou Brock	3.00	8.00
Curt Flood		
64 Fred Valentine	1.25	3.00
65 Tom Haller	1.50	4.00
66 Manny Mota	1.50	4.00
67 Ken Berry	1.25	3.00
68 Bob Buhl	1.50	4.00
69 Vic Davalillo	1.25	3.00
70 Ron Santo	3.00	8.00
71 Camilo Pascual	1.50	4.00
72 Tigers Rookies	1.50	4.00
George Korince/(photo actually		
J		
73 Rusty Staub	3.00	8.00
74 Wes Stock	1.25	3.00
75 George Scott	1.50	4.00
76 Jim Barbieri	1.25	3.00
77 Dooley Womack	1.25	3.00
78 Pat Corrales	1.25	3.00
79 Bubba Morton	1.25	3.00
80 Jim Maloney	1.50	4.00
81 Eddie Stanky MG	1.50	4.00
82 Steve Barber	1.25	3.00
83 Ollie Brown	1.25	3.00
84 Tommie Sisk	1.25	3.00
85 Johnny Callison	1.50	4.00
86 Mike McCormick/(with traded line)	1.50	4.00
87 George Altman	1.25	3.00
88 Mickey Lolich	2.50	6.00
89 Felix Millan	1.50	4.00
90 Jim Nash	1.25	3.00
91 Johnny Lewis	1.25	3.00
92 Ray Washburn	1.25	3.00
93 S.Bahnsen RC	2.50	6.00
B.Murcer		
94 Ron Fairly	1.50	4.00
95 Sonny Siebert	1.25	3.00
96 Art Shamsky	1.25	3.00
97 Mike Cuellar	2.50	6.00
98 Rich Rollins	1.25	3.00
99 Lee Stange	1.25	3.00
100 Frank Robinson	8.00	20.00
101 Ken Johnson	1.25	3.00
102 Phillies Team	2.50	6.00
103 Mickey Mantle CL2 DP	10.00	25.00
104 Minnie Rojas	1.25	3.00
105 Ken Boyer	3.00	8.00
106 Randy Hundley	1.50	4.00
107 Joel Horlen	1.25	3.00
108 Alex Johnson	1.50	4.00
109 R.Colavito	3.00	8.00
L.Wagner		
110 Jack Aker	1.25	3.00
111 John Kennedy	1.25	3.00
112 Dave Wickersham	1.25	3.00
113 Dave Nicholson	1.25	3.00
114 Jack Baldschun	1.25	3.00
115 Paul Casanova	1.25	3.00
116 Herman Franks MG	1.25	3.00
117 Darrell Brandon	1.25	3.00
118 Bernie Allen	1.25	3.00
119 Wade Blasingame	1.25	3.00
120 Floyd Robinson	1.25	3.00
121 Ed Bressoud	1.25	3.00
122 George Brunet	1.25	3.00
123 Jim Price	1.50	4.00
Luke Walker		
124 Jim Stewart	1.25	3.00
125 Moe Drabowsky	1.50	4.00
126 Tony Taylor	1.25	3.00
127 John O'Donoghue	1.25	3.00
128 Ed Spiezio	1.25	3.00
129 Phil Roof	1.25	3.00
130 Phil Regan	1.50	4.00
131 Yankees Team	5.00	12.00
132 Ozzie Virgil	1.25	3.00
133 Ron Kline	1.25	3.00
134 Gates Brown	1.25	3.00
135 Deron Johnson	1.50	4.00
136 Carroll Sembera	1.25	3.00
137 Ron Clark RC	1.25	3.00
Jim Ollom RC		
138 Dick Kelley	1.25	3.00
139 Dalton Jones	1.25	3.00
140 Willie Stargell	10.00	25.00
141 John Miller	1.25	3.00
142 Jackie Brandt	1.25	3.00
143 Pete Ward	2.50	6.00
Don Buford		
144 Bill Hepler	1.25	3.00
145 Larry Brown	1.25	3.00
146 Steve Carlton	30.00	60.00
147 Tom Egan	1.25	3.00
148 Adolfo Phillips	1.25	3.00
149 Joe Moeller	1.25	3.00
150 Mickey Mantle	200.00	400.00
151 World Series Game 1	2.50	6.00
Moe mows down 11/(Moe Drabow		
152 Jim Palmer WS2	4.00	10.00
153 World Series Game 3	2.50	6.00
Paul Blair's homer		
defeats L		
154 World Series Game 4	2.50	6.00
Orioles four straight/(Brook		
155 World Series Summary	2.50	6.00
Winners celebrate		
156 Ron Herbel	1.25	3.00
157 Danny Cater	1.25	3.00
158 Jimmie Coker	1.25	3.00
159 Bruce Howard	1.25	3.00
160 Willie Davis	1.50	4.00
161 Dick Williams MG	1.50	4.00
162 Billy O'Dell	1.25	3.00
163 Vic Roznovsky	1.25	3.00
164 Dwight Siebler	1.25	3.00
165 Cleon Jones	1.50	4.00
166 Eddie Mathews	8.00	20.00
167 Joe Coleman	1.25	3.00
Tim Cullen		
168 Ray Culp	1.25	3.00
169 Horace Clarke	1.25	3.00
170 Dick McAuliffe	1.50	4.00
171 Calvin Koonce	1.25	3.00
172 Bill Heath	1.25	3.00
173 Cardinals Team	2.50	6.00
174 Dick Radatz	1.50	4.00
175 Bobby Knoop	1.25	3.00
176 Sammy Ellis	1.25	3.00
177 Tito Fuentes	1.25	3.00
178 John Buzhardt	1.25	3.00
179 Charles Vaughan	1.50	4.00
Cecil Upshaw		
180 Curt Blefary	1.25	3.00
181 Terry Fox	1.25	3.00
182 Ed Charles	1.25	3.00
183 Jim Pagliaroni	1.25	3.00
184 George Thomas	1.25	3.00
185 Ken Holtzman RC	2.50	6.00
186 Ed Kranepool	2.50	6.00
Ron Swoboda		
187 Pedro Ramos	1.25	3.00
188 Ken Harrelson	1.50	4.00
189 Chuck Hinton	1.25	3.00
190 Turk Farrell	1.25	3.00
191 Checklist 197-283/(Willie Mays)	6.00	15.00
192 Fred Gladding	1.25	3.00
193 Jose Cardenal	1.50	4.00
194 Bob Allison	1.50	4.00
195 Al Jackson	1.25	3.00
196 Johnny Romano	1.25	3.00

1967 O-Pee-Chee Paper Inserts

These posters measure approximately 5" by 7" and are very similar to the American Topps poster (paper insert) issue, except that they say "Ptd. in Canada" on the bottom. The fronts feature color player photos with thin borders. The player's name and position, team name, and the card number appear inside a circle in the lower right. A facsimile player autograph rounds out the front. The backs are blank. This Canadian version is much more difficult to find than the American version. These numbered "All-Star" inserts have fold lines which are generally not very noticeable when stored carefully. There is some confusion as to whether these posters were issued in 1967 or 1968.

Card	Low	High
COMPLETE SET (32)	175.00	350.00
1 Boog Powell	2.00	5.00
2 Bert Campaneris	1.25	3.00
3 Brooks Robinson	8.00	20.00
4 Tommie Agee	1.00	2.50
5 Carl Yastrzemski	10.00	25.00
6 Mickey Mantle	50.00	100.00
7 Frank Howard	1.50	4.00
8 Sam McDowell	1.25	3.00
9 Orlando Cepeda	3.00	8.00
10 Chico Cardenas	1.00	2.50

11 Bob Clemente 75.00 150.00
12 Willie Mays 15.00 40.00
13 Cleon Jones 1.00 2.50
14 John Callison 1.00 2.50
15 Hank Aaron 12.50 30.00
16 Don Drysdale 6.00 15.00
17 Bobby Knoop 1.00 2.50
18 Tony Oliva 2.00 5.00
19 Frank Robinson 6.00 15.00
20 Denny McLain 2.00 5.00
21 Al Kaline 10.00 25.00
22 Joe Pepitone 1.25 3.00
23 Harmon Killebrew 8.00 20.00
24 Leon Wagner 1.00 2.50
25 Joe Morgan 6.00 15.00
26 Ron Santo 2.00 5.00
27 Joe Torre 2.00 5.00
28 Juan Marichal 5.00 12.00
29 Matty Alou 1.25 3.00
30 Felipe Alou 1.50 4.00
31 Ron Hunt 1.00 2.50
32 Willie McCovey 6.00 15.00

1968 O-Pee-Chee

The cards in this 196-card set measure 2 1/2" by 3 1/2". This set is essentially the same as the regular 1968 Topps set, except that the words "Printed in Canada" appear on the bottom of the back and the backgrounds have a different color. The fronts feature color player photos with rounded corners. The player's name is printed under the photo, while his position and team name appear in a circle in the lower right. On a light brown background, the backs carry player biography and statistics and a cartoon-like trivia question. Each checklist card features a small circular picture of a popular player included in that series. Remember the prices below apply only to the O-Pee-Chee cards -- NOT to the 1968 Topps cards which are much more plentiful. The key card in the set is Nolan Ryan in his Rookie Card year. The first OPC cards of Hall of Famers Rod Carew and Tom Seaver also appear in this set.

COMPLETE SET (196) 1000.00 2000.00
1 Clemente 15.00 40.00
Gon
M.Alou LL !
2 Yaz 8.00 20.00
F.Rob
Kaline LL
3 Cepeda 10.00 25.00
Clemente
Aar LL
4 Yaz 8.00 20.00
Killebrew
F.Rob LL
5 Aaron 4.00 10.00
Santo
McCovey LL
6 Yaz 4.00 10.00
Killebrew
Howard LL
7 NL ERA Leaders 2.50 6.00
Phil Niekro
Jim Bunning
Chris Sh
8 AL ERA Leaders 2.50 6.00
Joel Horlen
Gary Peters
Sonny Si
9 McCorm 2.50 6.00
Jenk
Bunn
Ost LL
10 AL Pitching Leaders 2.50 6.00
Jim Lonborg
Earl Wilson
Dea
11 Bunning 3.00 8.00
Jenkins
Perry LL
12 AL Strikeout Leaders 2.50 6.00
Jim Lonborg
Sam McDowell
D
13 Chuck Hartenstein 1.25 3.00
14 Jerry McNertney 1.25 3.00
15 Ron Hunt 1.25 3.00
16 Lou Piniella 3.00 8.00
17 Dick Hall 1.25 3.00
18 Mike Hershberger 1.25 3.00
19 Juan Pizarro 1.25 3.00
20 Brooks Robinson 12.50 30.00
21 Ron Davis 1.25 3.00
22 Pat Dobson 1.50 4.00
23 Chico Cardenas 1.50 4.00
24 Bobby Locke 1.25 3.00
25 Julian Javier 1.50 4.00
26 Darrell Brandon 1.25 3.00
27 Gil Hodges MG 4.00 10.00
28 Ted Uhlaender 1.25 3.00
29 Joe Verbanic 1.25 3.00
30 Joe Torre 3.00 8.00
31 Ed Stroud 1.25 3.00
32 Joe Gibbon 1.25 3.00
33 Pete Ward 1.50 4.00
34 Al Ferrara 1.25 3.00
35 Steve Hargan 1.25 3.00
36 Bob Moose 1.50 4.00
Bob Robertson
37 Billy Williams 4.00 10.00
38 Tony Pierce 1.25 3.00
39 Cookie Rojas 1.25 3.00
40 Denny McLain 4.00 10.00
41 Julio Gotay 1.25 3.00
42 Larry Haney 1.25 3.00
43 Gary Bell 1.25 3.00
44 Frank Kostro 1.25 3.00
45 Tom Seaver 30.00 60.00
46 Dave Ricketts 1.25 3.00
47 Ralph Houk MG 1.50 4.00
48 Ted Davidson 1.25 3.00
49 Ed Brinkman 1.25 3.00
50 Willie Mays 40.00 80.00
51 Bob Locker 1.25 3.00
52 Hawk Taylor 1.25 3.00
53 Gene Alley 1.50 4.00
54 Stan Williams 1.25 3.00
55 Felipe Alou 2.50 6.00
56 Dave May RC 1.25 3.00
57 Dan Schneider 1.25 3.00
58 Eddie Mathews 8.00 20.00
59 Don Lock 1.25 3.00
60 Ken Holtzman 1.50 4.00
61 Reggie Smith 2.50 6.00
62 Chuck Dobson 1.25 3.00
63 Dick Kenworthy 1.25 3.00
64 Jim Merritt 1.25 3.00
65 John Roseboro 1.50 4.00
66 Casey Cox 1.25 3.00
67 Checklist 1-109 3.00 8.00
Jim Kaat
68 Ron Willis 1.25 3.00
69 Tom Tresh 1.50 4.00
70 Bob Veale 1.50 4.00
71 Vern Fuller 1.25 3.00
72 Tommy John 3.00 8.00
73 Jim Ray Hart 1.50 4.00
74 Milt Pappas 1.50 4.00
75 Don Mincher 1.25 3.00
76 Jim Britton 1.50 4.00
Ron Reed
77 Don Wilson 1.50 4.00
78 Jim Northrup 3.00 8.00
79 Ted Kubiak 1.25 3.00
80 Rod Carew 30.00 60.00
81 Larry Jackson 1.25 3.00
82 Sam Bowens 1.25 3.00
83 John Stephenson 1.25 3.00
84 Bob Tolan 1.25 3.00
85 Gaylord Perry 4.00 10.00
86 Willie Stargell 4.00 10.00
87 Dick Williams MG 1.50 4.00
88 Phil Regan 1.50 4.00
89 Jake Gibbs 1.50 4.00
90 Vada Pinson 2.50 6.00
91 Jim Ollom 1.25 3.00
92 Ed Kranepool 1.50 4.00
93 Tony Cloninger 1.25 3.00
94 Lee Maye 1.25 3.00
95 Bob Aspromonte 1.25 3.00
96 Frank Coggins 1.25 3.00
Dick Nold
97 Tom Phoebus 1.25 3.00
98 Gary Sutherland 1.25 3.00
99 Rocky Colavito 4.00 10.00
100 Bob Gibson 12.50 30.00
101 Glenn Beckert 1.50 4.00
102 Jose Cardenal 1.50 4.00
103 Don Sutton 4.00 10.00
104 Dick Dietz 1.25 3.00
105 Al Downing 1.50 4.00
106 Dalton Jones 1.25 3.00
107 Checklist 110-196 3.00 8.00
Juan Marichal
108 Don Pavletich 1.25 3.00
109 Bert Campaneris 1.50 4.00
110 Hank Aaron 40.00 80.00
111 Rich Reese 1.25 3.00
112 Woody Fryman 1.25 3.00
113 Tom Matchick 1.50 4.00
Daryl Patterson
114 Ron Swoboda 1.50 4.00
115 Sam McDowell 1.50 4.00
116 Ken McMullen 1.25 3.00
117 Larry Jaster 1.25 3.00
118 Mark Belanger 1.50 4.00
119 Ted Savage 1.25 3.00
120 Mel Stottlemyre 2.50 6.00
121 Jimmie Hall 1.25 3.00
122 Gene Mauch MG 1.50 4.00
123 Jose Santiago 1.25 3.00
124 Nate Oliver 1.25 3.00
125 Joel Horlen 1.25 3.00
126 Bobby Etheridge 1.25 3.00
127 Paul Lindblad 1.25 3.00
128 Tom Dukes 1.25 3.00
Alonzo Harris
129 Mickey Stanley 3.00 8.00
130 Tony Perez 4.00 10.00
131 Frank Bertaina 1.25 3.00
132 Bud Harrelson 1.50 4.00
133 Fred Whitfield 1.25 3.00
134 Pat Jarvis 1.25 3.00
135 Paul Blair 1.50 4.00
136 Randy Hundley 1.50 4.00
137 Twins Team 2.50 6.00
138 Ruben Amaro 1.25 3.00
139 Chris Short 1.25 3.00
140 Tony Conigliaro 4.00 10.00
141 Dal Maxvill 1.25 3.00
142 Buddy Bradford 1.25 3.00
Bill Voss
143 Pete Cimino 1.25 3.00
144 Joe Morgan 6.00 15.00
145 Don Drysdale 6.00 15.00
146 Sal Bando 1.50 4.00
147 Frank Linzy 1.25 3.00
148 Dave Bristol MG 1.25 3.00
149 Bob Saverine 1.25 3.00
150 Roberto Clemente 50.00 100.00
151 Lou Brock WS1 5.00 12.00
152 Carl Yastrzemski WS2 5.00 12.00
153 Nellie Briles WS 2.50 6.00
154 Bob Gibson WS4 5.00 12.00
155 Jim Lonborg WS 2.50 6.00
156 Rico Petrocelli WS 2.50 6.00
157 World Series Game 7 2.50 6.00
St. Louis wins it
158 World Series Summary 2.50 6.00
Cardinals celebrate
159 Don Kessinger 1.50 4.00
160 Earl Wilson 1.50 4.00
161 Norm Miller 1.25 3.00
162 Hal Gilson 1.50 4.00
Mike Torrez
163 Gene Brabender 1.25 3.00
164 Ramon Webster 1.25 3.00
165 Tony Oliva 3.00 8.00
166 Claude Raymond 1.50 4.00
167 Elston Howard 3.00 8.00
168 Dodgers Team 2.50 6.00
169 Bob Bolin 1.25 3.00
170 Jim Fregosi 1.50 4.00
171 Don Nottebart 1.25 3.00
172 Walt Williams 1.25 3.00
173 John Boozer 1.25 3.00
174 Bob Tillman 1.25 3.00
175 Maury Wills 3.00 8.00
176 Bob Allen 1.25 3.00
177 N.Ryan 300.00 600.00
J.Koosman RC !
178 Don Wert 1.50 4.00
179 Bill Stoneman 1.25 3.00
180 Curt Flood 2.50 6.00
181 Jerry Zimmerman 1.25 3.00
182 Dave Giusti 1.25 3.00
183 Bob Kennedy MG 1.50 4.00
184 Lou Johnson 1.25 3.00
185 Tom Haller 1.25 3.00
186 Eddie Watt 1.25 3.00
187 Sonny Jackson 1.25 3.00
188 Cap Peterson 1.25 3.00
189 Bill Landis 1.25 3.00
190 Bill White 1.50 4.00
191 Dan Frisella 1.25 3.00
192 Checklist 3 4.00 10.00
Carl Yastrzemski
193 Jack Hamilton 1.25 3.00
194 Don Buford 1.25 3.00
195 Joe Pepitone 1.50 4.00
196 Gary Nolan 1.50 4.00

1969 O-Pee-Chee

The cards in this 218-card set measure 2 1/2" by 3 1/2". This set is essentially the same as the regular 1969 Topps set, except that the words "Printed in Canada" appear on the bottom of the back and the backgrounds have a purple color. The fronts feature color player photos with rounded corners and thin black borders. The player's name and position are printed inside a circle in the top right corner, while the team name appears in the lower part of the photo. On a magenta background, the backs carry player biography and statistics. Each checklist card features a small circular picture of a popular player included in that series. Remember the prices below apply only to the O-Pee-Chee cards -- NOT to the 1969 Topps cards which are much more plentiful. Notable Rookie Cards include Graig Nettles.

COMPLETE SET (218) 500.00 1000.00
1 Yaz 8.00 20.00
Cater
Oliva LL DP!
2 Rose 4.00 10.00
M.Alou
F.Alou LL
3 AL RBI Leaders 2.50 6.00
Ken Harrelson
Frank Howard
Jim N
4 McCov 3.00 8.00
Santo
B.Will LL
5 AL Home Run Leaders 2.50 6.00
Frank Howard
Willie Horton/
6 McCov 3.00 8.00
R.Allen
Banks LL
7 AL ERA Leaders 2.50 6.00
Luis Tiant
Sam McDowell
Dave McN
8 Gibson 3.00 8.00
Bolin
Veale LL
9 AL Pitching Leaders 2.50 6.00
Denny McLain
Dave McNally
L
10 Marich 4.00 10.00
Gibson
Jenk LL
11 AL Strikeout Leaders 3.00 8.00
Sam McDowell
Denny McLain/
12 Gibson 2.50 6.00
Jenkins
LL DP
13 Mickey Stanley 1.50 4.00
14 Al McBean .75 2.00
15 Boog Powell 2.50 6.00
16 Cesar Gutierrez .75 2.00
Rich Robertson
17 Mike Marshall 1.50 4.00
18 Dick Schofield .75 2.00
19 Ken Suarez .75 2.00
20 Ernie Banks 10.00 25.00
21 Jose Santiago .75 2.00
22 Jesus Alou 1.50 4.00
23 Lew Krausse .75 2.00
24 Walt Alston MG 2.50 6.00
25 Roy White 1.50 4.00
26 Clay Carroll 1.50 4.00
27 Bernie Allen .75 2.00
28 Mike Ryan .75 2.00
29 Dave Morehead .75 2.00
30 Bob Allison 1.50 4.00
31 Amos Otis 2.50 6.00
G.Gentry RC
32 Sammy Ellis .75 2.00
33 Wayne Causey .75 2.00
34 Gary Peters .75 2.00
35 Joe Morgan 5.00 12.00
36 Luke Walker .75 2.00
37 Curt Motton .75 2.00
38 Zoilo Versalles 1.50 4.00
39 Dick Hughes .75 2.00
40 Mayo Smith MG .75 2.00
41 Bob Barton .75 2.00
42 Tommy Harper 1.50 4.00
43 Joe Niekro 1.50 4.00
44 Danny Cater .75 2.00
45 Maury Wills 2.50 6.00
46 Fritz Peterson 1.50 4.00
47 Paul Popovich .75 2.00
48 Brant Alyea .75 2.00
49 Steve Jones .75 2.00
Ellie Rodriguez
50 Roberto Clemente/(Bob on card) 40.00 80.00
51 Woody Fryman 1.50 4.00
52 Mike Andrews .75 2.00
53 Sonny Jackson .75 2.00
54 Cisco Carlos .75 2.00
55 Jerry Grote 1.50 4.00
56 Rich Reese .75 2.00
57 Denny McLain CL 3.00 8.00
58 Fred Gladding .75 2.00
59 Jay Johnstone 1.50 4.00
60 Nelson Briles 1.50 4.00
61 Jimmie Hall .75 2.00
62 Chico Salmon .75 2.00
63 Jim Hickman .75 2.00
64 Bill Monbouquette .75 2.00
65 Willie Davis 1.50 4.00
66 Mike Adamson .75 2.00
Merv Rettenmund
67 Bill Stoneman 1.50 4.00
68 Dave Duncan 1.50 4.00
69 Steve Hamilton 1.50 4.00
70 Tommy Helms 1.50 4.00
71 Steve Whitaker 1.50 4.00
72 Ron Taylor 1.50 4.00
73 Johnny Briggs .75 2.00
74 Preston Gomez MG .75 2.00
75 Luis Aparicio 3.00 8.00
76 Norm Miller .75 2.00
77 Ron Perranoski .75 2.00
78 Tom Satriano .75 2.00
79 Milt Pappas 1.50 4.00
80 Norm Cash 1.50 4.00
81 Mel Queen .75 2.00
82 Al Oliver RC 4.00 10.00
83 Mike Ferraro 1.50 4.00
84 Bob Humphreys .75 2.00
85 Lou Brock 10.00 25.00
86 Pete Richert .75 2.00
87 Horace Clarke 1.50 4.00
88 Rich Nye .75 2.00
89 Russ Gibson .75 2.00
90 Jerry Koosman 2.50 6.00
91 Al Dark MG 1.50 4.00
92 Jack Billingham 1.50 4.00
93 Joe Foy .75 2.00
94 Hank Aguirre .75 2.00
95 Johnny Bench 30.00 60.00
96 Denver LeMaster .75 2.00
97 Buddy Bradford .75 2.00
98 Dave Giusti .75 2.00
99 Twins Rookies 8.00 20.00
Danny Morris
Graig Nettles
100 Hank Aaron 30.00 60.00
101 Daryl Patterson .75 2.00
102 Jim Davenport .75 2.00
103 Roger Repoz .75 2.00
104 Steve Blass .75 2.00
105 Rick Monday 1.50 4.00
106 Jim Hannan .75 2.00
107 Checklist 110-218 3.00 8.00
Bob Gibson
108 Tony Taylor 1.50 4.00
109 Jim Lonborg 1.50 4.00
110 Mike Shannon 1.50 4.00
111 John Morris .75 2.00
112 J.C. Martin 1.50 4.00
113 Dave May .75 2.00
114 Alan Closter 1.50 4.00
John Cumberland
115 Bill Hands .75 2.00
116 Chuck Harrison .75 2.00
117 Jim Fairey 1.50 4.00
118 Stan Williams .75 2.00
119 Doug Rader 1.50 4.00
120 Pete Rose 30.00 60.00
121 Joe Grzenda .75 2.00
122 Ron Fairly 1.50 4.00
123 Wilbur Wood 1.50 4.00
124 Hank Bauer MG 1.50 4.00
125 Ray Sadecki .75 2.00
126 Dick Tracewski .75 2.00
127 Kevin Collins 1.50 4.00
128 Tommie Aaron 1.50 4.00
129 Bill McCool .75 2.00
130 Carl Yastrzemski 10.00 25.00
131 Chris Cannizzaro .75 2.00
132 Dave Baldwin .75 2.00
133 Johnny Callison 1.50 4.00
134 Jim Weaver .75 2.00
135 Tommy Davis 1.50 4.00
136 Steve Huntz .75 2.00
Mike Torrez
137 Wally Bunker .75 2.00
138 John Bateman .75 2.00
139 Andy Kosco .75 2.00
140 Jim Lefebvre 1.50 4.00
141 Bill Dillman .75 2.00
142 Woody Woodward .75 2.00
143 Joe Nossek .75 2.00
144 Bob Hendley .75 2.00
145 Max Alvis .75 2.00
146 Jim Perry 1.50 4.00
147 Leo Durocher MG 2.50 6.00
148 Lee Stange .75 2.00
149 Ollie Brown .75 2.00
150 Denny McLain 2.50 6.00
151 Clay Dalrymple/(Catching, Phillies) 1.50 4.00
152 Tommie Sisk .75 2.00
153 Ed Brinkman .75 2.00
154 Jim Britton .75 2.00
155 Pete Ward 1.50 4.00
156 Hal Gilson .75 2.00
Leon McFadden
157 Bob Rodgers 1.50 4.00
158 Joe Gibbon .75 2.00
159 Jerry Adair .75 2.00
160 Vada Pinson 2.50 6.00
161 John Purdin .75 2.00
162 Bob Gibson WS1 4.00 10.00
163 World Series Game 2 3.00 8.00
Tiger homers
deck the Cards#
164 T.McCarver 6.00 15.00
Maris WS3 DP
165 Lou Brock WS4 4.00 10.00
166 Al Kaline WS5 4.00 10.00
167 Jim Northrup WS 3.00 8.00
168 M.Lolich 4.00 10.00
B.Gibson WS7
169 World Series Summary 3.00 8.00
Tigers celebrate/(Dick McAu
170 Frank Howard 1.50 4.00
171 Glenn Beckert 1.50 4.00
172 Jerry Stephenson .75 2.00
173 Bob Christian .75 2.00
Gerry Nyman
174 Grant Jackson .75 2.00
175 Jim Bunning 3.00 8.00
176 Joe Azcue .75 2.00
177 Ron Reed .75 2.00
178 Ray Oyler .75 2.00
179 Don Pavletich .75 2.00
180 Willie Horton 1.50 4.00
181 Mel Nelson .75 2.00
182 Bill Rigney MG .75 2.00
183 Don Shaw 1.50 4.00
184 Roberto Pena .75 2.00
185 Tom Phoebus .75 2.00
186 John Edwards .75 2.00
187 Leon Wagner .75 2.00
188 Rick Wise 1.50 4.00
189 Joe Lahoud .75 2.00
John Thibodeau
190 Willie Mays 50.00 100.00
191 Lindy McDaniel 1.50 4.00
192 Jose Pagan .75 2.00
193 Don Cardwell 1.50 4.00
194 Ted Uhlaender .75 2.00
195 John Odom .75 2.00
196 Lum Harris MG .75 2.00
197 Dick Selma .75 2.00
198 Willie Smith .75 2.00
199 Jim French .75 2.00
200 Bob Gibson 6.00 15.00
201 Russ Snyder .75 2.00
202 Don Wilson 1.50 4.00
203 Dave Johnson 1.50 4.00
204 Jack Hiatt .75 2.00
205 Rick Reichardt .75 2.00
206 Larry Hisle 1.50 4.00
Barry Lersch
207 Roy Face 1.50 4.00
208 Donn Clendenon/(Montreal Expos) 1.50 4.00
209 Larry Haney UER
(Reversed negative) .75 2.00
210 Felix Millan .75 2.00
211 Galen Cisco .75 2.00
212 Tom Tresh 1.50 4.00
213 Gerry Arrigo .75 2.00
214 Checklist 3 3.00 8.00
With 69T deckle CL
on back (no playe
215 Rico Petrocelli 1.50 4.00
216 Don Sutton 3.00 8.00
217 John Donaldson .75 2.00
218 John Roseboro 1.50 4.00

1969 O-Pee-Chee Deckle

This set is very similar to the U.S. deckle version produced by Topps. The cards measure approximately 2 1/8" by 3 1/8" (slightly smaller than the American issue) and are cut with deckle edges. The fronts feature black-and-white player photos with white borders and facsimile autographs in black ink (instead of blue ink like the Topps issue). The backs are blank. The cards are unnumbered and checklisted below in alphabetical order. Remember the prices below apply only to the O-Pee-Chee Deckle cards -- NOT to the 1969 Topps Deckle cards which are much more plentiful.

COMPLETE SET (24) 125.00 250.00
1 Richie Allen 2.00 5.00
2 Luis Aparicio 3.00 8.00
3 Rod Carew 4.00 10.00
4 Roberto Clemente 75.00 150.00
5 Curt Flood 1.50 4.00
6 Bill Freehan 1.50 4.00
7 Bob Gibson 4.00 10.00
8 Ken Harrelson 1.50 4.00
9 Tommy Helms 1.25 3.00
10 Tom Haller 1.25 3.00
11 Willie Horton 1.50 4.00
12 Frank Howard 2.00 5.00
13 Willie McCovey 4.00 10.00
14 Denny McLain 2.00 5.00
15 Juan Marichal 4.00 10.00
16 Willie Mays 40.00 80.00
17 Boog Powell 2.00 5.00
18 Brooks Robinson 6.00 15.00
19 Ron Santo 2.50 6.00
20 Rusty Staub 1.50 4.00
21 Mel Stottlemyre 1.25 3.00
22 Luis Tiant 1.25 3.00
23 Maury Wills 1.50 4.00
24 Carl Yastrzemski 8.00 20.00

1970 O-Pee-Chee

The cards in this 546-card set measure 2 1/2" by 3 1/2". This set is essentially the same as the regular 1970 Topps set, except that the words "Printed in Canada" appear on the backs and the backs are bilingual. On a gray border, the fronts feature color player photos with thin white borders. The player's name and position are printed under the photo, while the team name appears in the upper part of the picture. The horizontal backs carry player biography and statistics in French and English. The card stock is a deeper shade of yellow on the reverse for the O-Pee-Chee cards. The set was issued in eight-card dime packs which came 36 packs to a box. Remember the prices below apply only to the O-Pee-Chee cards -- NOT to the 1970 Topps cards which are much more plentiful. Notable Rookie Cards include Thurman Munson.

COMPLETE SET (546) 750.00 1500.00
COMMON PLAYER (1-459) .60 1.50
COMMON PLAYER (460-546) 1.00 2.50
1 Mets Team ! 12.50 40.00
2 Diego Segui .75 2.00
3 Darrel Chaney .60 1.50
4 Tom Egan .60 1.50
5 Wes Parker .75 2.00
6 Grant Jackson .60 1.50
7 Gary Boyd .60 1.50
Russ Nagelson
8 Jose Martinez .60 1.50
9 Checklist 1-132 6.00 15.00
10 Carl Yastrzemski 10.00 25.00
11 Nate Colbert .60 1.50
12 John Hiller .75 2.00
13 Jack Hiatt .60 1.50
14 Hank Allen .60 1.50
15 Larry Dierker .60 1.50
16 Charlie Metro MG .60 1.50
17 Hoyt Wilhelm 2.50 6.00
18 Carlos May .75 2.00
19 John Boccabella .60 1.50
20 Dave McNally .75 2.00
21 Vida Blue 2.50 6.00
G.Tenace RC
22 Ray Washburn .60 1.50
23 Bill Robinson .75 2.00
24 Dick Selma .60 1.50
25 Cesar Tovar .60 1.50
26 Tug McGraw 1.50 4.00
27 Chuck Hinton .60 1.50
28 Billy Wilson .60 1.50
29 Sandy Alomar .75 2.00
30 Matty Alou .75 2.00
31 Marty Pattin .75 2.00
32 Harry Walker MG .60 1.50
33 Don Wert .60 1.50
34 Willie Crawford .60 1.50
35 Joel Horlen .60 1.50
36 Danny Breeden .75 2.00
Bernie Carbo
37 Dick Drago .60 1.50
38 Mack Jones .60 1.50
39 Mike Nagy .60 1.50
40 Richie Allen 1.50 4.00
41 George Lauzerique .60 1.50
42 Tito Fuentes .60 1.50
43 Jack Aker .60 1.50
44 Roberto Pena .60 1.50
45 Dave Johnson .75 2.00
46 Ken Rudolph .60 1.50
47 Bob Miller .60 1.50
48 Gil Garrido .60 1.50
49 Tim Cullen .60 1.50
50 Tommie Agee .75 2.00
51 Bob Christian .60 1.50
52 Bruce Dal Canton .60 1.50
53 John Kennedy .60 1.50
54 Jeff Torborg .75 2.00
55 John Odom .60 1.50
56 Joe Lis .60 1.50
Scott Reid
57 Pat Kelly .60 1.50
58 Dave Marshall .60 1.50
59 Dick Ellsworth .60 1.50
60 Jim Wynn .75 2.00
61 Rose 6.00 15.00
Clemente
Jones LL
62 R.Carew 1.25 3.00
T.Oliva
LL
63 McCovey 1.25 3.00
Santo
Perez LL
64 Kill 2.50 6.00
Powell
Reggie LL
65 McCovey 2.50 6.00
Aaron
May LL
66 Kill 2.50 6.00
Howard
Reggie LL
67 Marich 3.00 8.00
Carlton
Gibs LL
68 Bosm .75 2.00
Palmer
Cuellar LL
69 Seav 3.00 8.00
Niek
Jenk
Mar LL
70 AL Pitching Leaders .75 2.00
Dennis McLain
Mike Cuellar/
71 F.Jenkins 1.25 3.00
B.Gibson
LL
72 AL Strikeout Leaders .75 2.00
Sam McDowell
Mickey Lolich#
73 Wayne Granger .60 1.50
74 Greg Washburn .60 1.50
Wally Wolf
75 Jim Kaat .75 2.00
76 Carl Taylor .60 1.50
77 Frank Linzy .60 1.50
78 Joe Lahoud .60 1.50
79 Clay Kirby .60 1.50
80 Don Kessinger .75 2.00
81 Dave May .60 1.50
82 Frank Fernandez .60 1.50
83 Don Cardwell .60 1.50
84 Paul Casanova .60 1.50
85 Max Alvis .60 1.50
86 Lum Harris MG .60 1.50
87 Steve Renko .75 2.00
88 Miguel Fuentes .75 2.00
Dick Baney
89 Juan Rios .60 1.50
90 Tim McCarver 1.25 3.00
91 Rich Morales .60 1.50
92 George Culver .60 1.50
93 Rick Renick .60 1.50
94 Fred Patek .75 2.00
95 Earl Wilson .75 2.00
96 Jerry Reuss RC 1.25 3.00
97 Joe Moeller .60 1.50
98 Gates Brown .75 2.00
99 Bobby Pfeil .60 1.50
100 Mel Stottlemyre .75 2.00
101 Bobby Floyd .60 1.50

102 Joe Rudi .75 2.00
103 Frank Reberger .60 1.50
104 Gerry Moses .60 1.50
105 Tony Gonzalez .60 1.50
106 Darold Knowles .60 1.50
107 Bobby Etheridge .60 1.50
108 Tom Burgmeier .60 1.50
109 Garry Jestadt .75 2.00
Carl Morton
110 Bob Moose .60 1.50
111 Mike Hegan .75 2.00
112 Dave Nelson .60 1.50
113 Jim Ray .60 1.50
114 Gene Michael .75 2.00
115 Alex Johnson .75 2.00
116 Sparky Lyle 1.25 3.00
117 Don Young .60 1.50
118 George Mitterwald .60 1.50
119 Chuck Taylor .60 1.50
120 Sal Bando .75 2.00
121 Fred Beene .60 1.50
Terry Crowley
122 George Stone .60 1.50
123 Don Gutteridge MG .60 1.50
124 Larry Jaster .60 1.50
125 Deron Johnson .60 1.50
126 Marty Martinez .60 1.50
127 Joe Coleman .60 1.50
128 Checklist 133-263 3.00 8.00
129 Jimmie Price .60 1.50
130 Ollie Brown .60 1.50
131 Ray Lamb .60 1.50
Bob Stinson
132 Jim McGlothlin .60 1.50
133 Clay Carroll .60 1.50
134 Danny Walton .60 1.50
135 Dick Dietz .60 1.50
136 Steve Hargan .60 1.50
137 Art Shamsky .60 1.50
138 Joe Foy .60 1.50
139 Rich Nye .60 1.50
140 Reggie Jackson 30.00 60.00
141 Dave Cash .75 2.00
Johnny Jeter
142 Fritz Peterson .60 1.50
143 Phil Gagliano .60 1.50
144 Ray Culp .60 1.50
145 Rico Carty .75 2.00
146 Danny Murphy .60 1.50
147 Angel Hermoso .60 1.50
148 Earl Weaver MG 2.00 5.00
149 Billy Champion .60 1.50
150 Harmon Killebrew 4.00 10.00
151 Dave Roberts .60 1.50
152 Ike Brown .60 1.50
153 Gary Gentry .60 1.50
154 Jim Miles .60 1.50
Jan Dukes
155 Denis Menke .60 1.50
156 Eddie Fisher .60 1.50
157 Manny Mota 1.25 3.00
158 Jerry McNertney .75 2.00
159 Tommy Helms .75 2.00
160 Phil Niekro 2.50 6.00
161 Richie Scheinblum .60 1.50
162 Jerry Johnson .60 1.50
163 Syd O'Brien .60 1.50
164 Ty Cline .60 1.50
165 Ed Kirkpatrick .60 1.50
166 Al Oliver 1.50 4.00
167 Bill Burbach .60 1.50
168 Dave Watkins .60 1.50
169 Tom Hall .60 1.50
170 Billy Williams 3.00 8.00
171 Jim Nash .60 1.50
172 Ralph Garr RC 1.25 3.00
173 Jim Hicks .60 1.50
174 Ted Sizemore .75 2.00
175 Dick Bosman .60 1.50
176 Jim Ray Hart .75 2.00
177 Jim Northrup .75 2.00
178 Denny LeMaster .60 1.50
179 Ivan Murrell .60 1.50
180 Tommy John 1.25 3.00
181 Sparky Anderson MG 3.00 8.00
182 Dick Hall .60 1.50
183 Jerry Grote .75 2.00
184 Ray Fosse .60 1.50
185 Don Mincher .75 2.00
186 Rick Joseph .60 1.50
187 Mike Hedlund .60 1.50
188 Manny Sanguillen .75 2.00
189 Thurman Munson RC .50.00 100.00
190 Joe Torre 1.50 4.00
191 Vicente Romo .60 1.50
192 Jim Qualls .60 1.50
193 Mike Wegener .60 1.50
194 Chuck Manuel RC 1.50 4.00
195 Tom Seaver NLCS1 8.00 20.00
196 Ken Boswell NLCS 1.50 4.00
197 Nolan Ryan NLCS3 12.50 40.00
198 Mets Celebrate 8.00 20.00
N.Ryan
199 AL Playoff Game 1 1.50 4.00
Orioles win squeaker/(Mike Cue
200 Boog Powell ALCS 1.50 4.00
201 AL Playoff Game 3 1.50 4.00
Birds wrap it up/(Boog Powell
202 AL Playoff Summary 1.50 4.00
Orioles celebrate
203 Rudy May .60 1.50
204 Len Gabrielson .60 1.50
205 Bert Campaneris .75 2.00
206 Clete Boyer .75 2.00
207 Norman McRae .60 1.50
Bob Reed
208 Fred Gladding .60 1.50
209 Ken Suarez .60 1.50
210 Juan Marichal 3.00 8.00
211 Ted Williams MG 8.00 20.00
212 Al Santorini .60 1.50
213 Andy Etchebarren .60 1.50
214 Ken Boswell .60 1.50
215 Reggie Smith 1.25 3.00
216 Chuck Hartenstein .60 1.50
217 Ron Hansen .60 1.50
218 Ron Stone .60 1.50
219 Jerry Kenney .60 1.50
220 Steve Carlton 8.00 20.00
221 Ron Brand .60 1.50
222 Jim Rooker .60 1.50
223 Nate Oliver .60 1.50
224 Steve Barber .75 2.00
225 Lee May .75 2.00
226 Ron Perranoski .60 1.50
227 John Mayberry RC .75 2.00
228 Aurelio Rodriguez .60 1.50
229 Rich Robertson .60 1.50
230 Brooks Robinson 8.00 20.00
231 Luis Tiant 1.25 3.00
232 Bob Didier .60 1.50
233 Lew Krausse .60 1.50
234 Tommy Dean .60 1.50
235 Mike Epstein .60 1.50
236 Bob Veale .60 1.50
237 Russ Gibson .60 1.50
238 Jose Laboy .75 2.00
239 Ken Berry .60 1.50
240 Fergie Jenkins 3.00 8.00
241 Al Fitzmorris .60 1.50
Scott Northey
242 Walt Alston MG 1.50 4.00
243 Joe Sparma .75 2.00
244 Checklist 264-372 3.00 8.00
245 Leo Cardenas .60 1.50
246 Jim McAndrew .60 1.50
247 Lou Klimchock .60 1.50
248 Jesus Alou .60 1.50
249 Bob Locker .60 1.50
250 Willie McCovey 5.00 12.00
251 Dick Schofield .60 1.50
252 Lowell Palmer .60 1.50
253 Ron Woods .60 1.50
254 Camilo Pascual .60 1.50
255 Jim Spencer .60 1.50
256 Vic Davalillo .60 1.50
257 Dennis Higgins .60 1.50
258 Paul Popovich .60 1.50
259 Tommie Reynolds .60 1.50
260 Claude Osteen .75 2.00
261 Curt Motton .60 1.50
262 Jerry Morales .60 1.50
Jim Williams
263 Duane Josephson .60 1.50
264 Rich Hebner .60 1.50
265 Randy Hundley .60 1.50
266 Wally Bunker .60 1.50
267 Herman Hill .60 1.50
Paul Ratliff
268 Claude Raymond .75 2.00
269 Cesar Gutierrez .60 1.50
270 Chris Short .60 1.50
271 Greg Goossen .75 2.00
272 Hector Torres .60 1.50
273 Ralph Houk MG .75 2.00
274 Gerry Arrigo .60 1.50
275 Duke Sims .60 1.50
276 Ron Hunt .60 1.50
277 Paul Doyle .60 1.50
278 Tommie Aaron .60 1.50
279 Bill Lee 1.25 3.00
280 Donn Clendenon .75 2.00
281 Casey Cox .60 1.50
282 Steve Huntz .60 1.50
283 Angel Bravo .60 1.50
284 Jack Baldschun .60 1.50
285 Paul Blair .75 2.00
286 Bill Buckner RC 3.00 8.00
287 Fred Talbot .60 1.50
288 Larry Hisle .75 2.00
289 Gene Brabender .60 1.50
290 Rod Carew 10.00 25.00
291 Leo Durocher MG 1.50 4.00
292 Eddie Leon .60 1.50
293 Bob Bailey .75 2.00
294 Jose Azcue .60 1.50
295 Cecil Upshaw .60 1.50
296 Woody Woodward .60 1.50
297 Curt Blefary .60 1.50
298 Ken Henderson .60 1.50
299 Buddy Bradford .60 1.50
300 Tom Seaver 12.50 40.00
301 Chico Salmon .60 1.50
302 Jeff James .60 1.50
303 Brant Alyea .60 1.50
304 Bill Russell RC 3.00 8.00
305 Don Buford WS 1.50 4.00
306 World Series Game 2 1.50 4.00
Donn Clendenon's homer
break
307 World Series Game 3 1.50 4.00
Tommie Agee's catch
saves th
308 World Series Game 4 1.50 4.00
J.C. Martin's bunt
ends dead
309 Jerry Koosman WS 1.50 4.00
310 WS Celebration Mets 3.00 8.00
311 Dick Green .60 1.50
312 Mike Torrez .60 1.50
313 Mayo Smith MG .60 1.50
314 Bill McCool .60 1.50
315 Luis Aparicio 3.00 8.00
316 Skip Guinn .60 1.50
317 Billy Conigliaro .75 2.00
Luis Alvarado
318 Willie Smith .60 1.50
319 Clay Dalrymple .60 1.50
320 Jim Maloney .75 2.00
321 Lou Piniella 1.25 3.00
322 Luke Walker .60 1.50
323 Wayne Comer .60 1.50
324 Tony Taylor .75 2.00
325 Dave Boswell .60 1.50
326 Bill Voss .60 1.50
327 Hal King RC .60 1.50
328 George Brunet .60 1.50
329 Chris Cannizzaro .60 1.50
330 Lou Brock 5.00 12.00
331 Chuck Dobson .60 1.50
332 Bobby Wine .75 2.00
333 Bobby Murcer 1.25 3.00
334 Phil Regan .60 1.50
335 Bill Freehan .75 2.00
336 Del Unser .60 1.50
337 Mike McCormick .75 2.00
338 Paul Schaal .60 1.50
339 Johnny Edwards .60 1.50
340 Tony Conigliaro 1.50 4.00
341 Bill Sudakis .60 1.50
342 Wilbur Wood .75 2.00
343 Checklist 373-459 3.00 8.00
344 Marcelino Lopez .60 1.50
345 Al Ferrara .60 1.50
346 Red Schoendienst MG .75 2.00
347 Russ Snyder .60 1.50
348 Mike Jorgensen .75 2.00
Jesse Hudson
349 Steve Hamilton .60 1.50
350 Roberto Clemente 40.00 80.00
351 Tom Murphy .60 1.50
352 Bob Barton .60 1.50
353 Stan Williams .60 1.50
354 Amos Otis .75 2.00
355 Doug Rader .60 1.50
356 Fred Lasher .60 1.50
357 Bob Burda .60 1.50
358 Pedro Borbon RC .75 2.00
359 Phil Roof .60 1.50
360 Curt Flood 1.25 3.00
361 Ray Jarvis .60 1.50
362 Joe Hague .60 1.50
363 Tom Shopay .60 1.50
364 Dan McGinn .75 2.00
365 Zoilo Versalles .60 1.50
366 Barry Moore .60 1.50
367 Mike Lum .60 1.50
368 Ed Herrmann .60 1.50
369 Alan Foster .60 1.50
370 Tommy Harper .75 2.00
371 Rod Gaspar .60 1.50
372 Dave Giusti .60 1.50
373 Roy White .75 2.00
374 Tommie Sisk .60 1.50
375 Johnny Callison 1.25 3.00
376 Lefty Phillips MG .60 1.50
377 Bill Butler .60 1.50
378 Jim Davenport .60 1.50
379 Tom Tischinski .60 1.50
380 Tony Perez 3.00 8.00
381 Bobby Brooks .60 1.50
Mike Olivo
382 Jack DiLauro .60 1.50
383 Mickey Stanley .75 2.00
384 Gary Neibauer .60 1.50
385 George Scott .75 2.00
386 Bill Dillman .60 1.50
387 Orioles Team 1.50 4.00
388 Byron Browne .60 1.50
389 Jim Shellenback .60 1.50
390 Willie Davis 1.25 3.00
391 Larry Brown .60 1.50
392 Walt Hriniak .75 2.00
393 John Gelnar .60 1.50
394 Gil Hodges MG 1.50 4.00
395 Walt Williams .60 1.50
396 Steve Blass .75 2.00
397 Roger Repoz .60 1.50
398 Bill Stoneman .60 1.50
399 Yankees Team 1.50 4.00
400 Denny McLain 1.50 4.00
401 John Harrell .60 1.50
Bernie Williams
402 Ellie Rodriguez .60 1.50
403 Jim Bunning 3.00 8.00
404 Rich Reese .60 1.50
405 Bill Hands .60 1.50
406 Mike Andrews .60 1.50
407 Bob Watson .75 2.00
408 Paul Lindblad .60 1.50
409 Bob Tolan .60 1.50
410 Boog Powell 1.50 4.00
411 Dodgers Team 1.50 4.00
412 Larry Burchart .60 1.50
413 Sonny Jackson .60 1.50
414 Paul Edmondson .60 1.50
415 Julian Javier .75 2.00
416 Joe Verbanic .60 1.50
417 John Bateman .60 1.50
418 John Donaldson .60 1.50
419 Ron Taylor .75 2.00
420 Ken McMullen .75 2.00
421 Pat Dobson .75 2.00
422 Royals Team 1.50 4.00
423 Jerry May .60 1.50
424 Mike Kilkenny .75 2.00
425 Bobby Bonds 3.00 8.00
426 Bill Rigney MG .60 1.50
427 Fred Norman .60 1.50
428 Don Buford .60 1.50
429 Randy Bobb .60 1.50
Jim Cosman
430 Andy Messersmith .75 2.00
431 Ron Swoboda .75 2.00
432 Checklist 460-546 3.00 8.00
433 Ron Bryant .60 1.50
434 Felipe Alou 1.25 3.00
435 Nelson Briles .75 2.00
436 Phillies Team 1.50 4.00
437 Danny Cater .60 1.50
438 Pat Jarvis .60 1.50
439 Lee Maye .60 1.50
440 Bill Mazeroski 3.00 8.00
441 John O'Donoghue .60 1.50
442 Gene Mauch MG .75 2.00
443 Al Jackson .60 1.50
444 Billy Farmer .60 1.50
John Matias
445 Vada Pinson 1.25 3.00
446 Billy Grabarkewitz .60 1.50
447 Lee Stange .60 1.50
448 Astros Team 1.50 4.00
449 Jim Palmer 6.00 15.00
450 Willie McCovey AS 3.00 8.00
451 Boog Powell AS 1.50 4.00
452 Felix Millan AS 1.25 3.00
453 Rod Carew AS 3.00 8.00
454 Ron Santo AS 1.50 4.00
455 Brooks Robinson AS 3.00 8.00
456 Don Kessinger AS 1.25 3.00
457 Rico Petrocelli AS 1.50 4.00
458 Pete Rose AS 8.00 20.00
459 Reggie Jackson AS 6.00 15.00
460 Matty Alou AS 1.50 4.00
461 Carl Yastrzemski AS 5.00 12.00
462 Hank Aaron AS 8.00 20.00
463 Frank Robinson AS 4.00 10.00
464 Johnny Bench AS 8.00 20.00
465 Bill Freehan AS 1.50 4.00
466 Juan Marichal AS 2.50 6.00
467 Denny McLain AS 2.50 6.00
468 Jerry Koosman AS 1.50 4.00
469 Sam McDowell AS 1.50 4.00
470 Willie Stargell 5.00 12.00
471 Chris Zachary 1.00 2.50
472 Braves Team 1.50 4.00
473 Don Bryant 1.00 2.50
474 Dick Kelley 1.00 2.50
475 Dick McAuliffe 1.50 4.00
476 Don Shaw 1.00 2.50
477 Al Severinsen 1.00 2.50
Roger Freed
478 Bob Heise 1.00 2.50
479 Dick Woodson 1.00 2.50
480 Glenn Deckert 1.50 4.00
481 Jose Tartabull 1.00 2.50
482 Tom Hilgendorf 1.00 2.50
483 Gail Hopkins 1.00 2.50
484 Gary Nolan 1.50 4.00
485 Jay Johnstone 1.50 4.00
486 Terry Harmon 1.00 2.50
487 Cisco Carlos 1.00 2.50
488 J.C. Martin 1.00 2.50
489 Eddie Kasko MG 1.00 2.50
490 Bill Singer 1.50 4.00
491 Graig Nettles 2.50 6.00
492 Keith Lampard 1.00 2.50
Scipio Spinks
493 Lindy McDaniel 1.50 4.00
494 Larry Stahl 1.00 2.50
495 Dave Morehead 1.00 2.50
496 Steve Whitaker 1.00 2.50
497 Eddie Watt 1.00 2.50
498 Al Weis 1.00 2.50
499 Skip Lockwood 1.00 2.50
500 Hank Aaron 30.00 60.00
501 White Sox Team 1.50 4.00
502 Rollie Fingers 5.00 12.00
503 Dal Maxvill 1.00 2.50
504 Don Pavletich 1.00 2.50
505 Ken Holtzman 1.50 4.00
506 Ed Stroud 1.00 2.50
507 Pat Corrales 1.00 2.50
508 Joe Niekro 1.50 4.00
509 Expos Team 2.50 6.00
510 Tony Oliva 2.50 6.00
511 Joe Hoerner 1.00 2.50
512 Billy Harris 1.00 2.50
513 Preston Gomez MG 1.00 2.50
514 Steve Hovley 1.00 2.50
515 Don Wilson 1.50 4.00
516 John Ellis 1.00 2.50
Jim Lyttle
517 Joe Gibbon 1.00 2.50
518 Bill Melton 1.00 2.50
519 Don McMahon 1.00 2.50
520 Willie Horton 1.50 4.00
521 Cal Koonce 1.00 2.50
522 Angels Team 1.50 4.00
523 Jose Pena 1.00 2.50
524 Alvin Dark MG 1.50 4.00
525 Jerry Adair 1.00 2.50
526 Ron Herbel 1.00 2.50
527 Don Bosch 1.50 4.00
528 Elrod Hendricks 1.00 2.50
529 Bob Aspromonte 1.00 2.50
530 Bob Gibson 8.00 20.00
531 Ron Clark 1.00 2.50
532 Danny Murtaugh MG 1.50 4.00
533 Buzz Stephen 1.00 2.50
534 Twins Team 1.50 4.00
535 Andy Kosco 1.00 2.50
536 Mike Kekich 1.00 2.50
537 Joe Morgan 5.00 12.00
538 Bob Humphreys 1.00 2.50
539 Larry Bowa RC 4.00 10.00
540 Gary Peters 1.00 2.50
541 Bill Heath 1.00 2.50
542 Checklist 547-633 3.00 8.00
543 Clyde Wright 1.00 2.50
544 Reds Team 2.50 6.00
545 Ken Harrelson 1.50 4.00
546 Ron Reed 1.50 4.00

1971 O-Pee-Chee

The cards in this 752-card set measure 2 1/2" by 3 1/2". The 1971 O-Pee-Chee set is a challenge to complete in "Mint" condition because the black borders are easily scratched and damaged. The O-Pee-Chee cards seem to have been cut (into individual cards) not as sharply as the Topps cards; the borders frequently appear slightly frayed. The players are also pictured in black and white on the back of the card. The next-to-last series (524-643) and the last series (644-752) are somewhat scarce. The O-Pee-Chee cards can be distinguished from Topps cards by the "Printed in Canada" on the bottom of the reverse. The reverse color is yellow instead of the green found on the backs of the 1971 Topps cards. The card backs are written in both French and English, except for cards 524-752 which were printed in English only. There are several cards which are different from the corresponding Topps card with a different pose or different team noted in bold type, i.e. "Recently Traded to ..." These changed cards are numbers 31, 32, 73, 144, 151, 161, 172, 182, 191, 202, 207, 248, 289 and 578. These cards were issued in eight-card dime packs which came 36 packs to a box. Remember, the prices below apply only to the 1971 O-Pee-Chee cards -- NOT Topps cards which are much more plentiful. Notable Rookie Cards include Dusty Baker and Don Baylor (Sharing the same card), Bert Blyleven, Dave Concepcion and Steve Garvey.

COMPLETE SET (752) 1250.00 2500.00
COMMON PLAYER (1-393) .60 1.50
COMMON PLAYER (394-523) 1.25 3.00
COMMON PLAYER (524-643) 1.50 4.00
COMMON PLAYER (644-752) 4.00 10.00
1 Orioles Team 10.00 25.00
2 Dock Ellis .60 1.50
3 Dick McAuliffe .75 2.00
4 Vic Davalillo .60 1.50
5 Thurman Munson 75.00 150.00
6 Ed Spiezio .60 1.50
7 Jim Holt .60 1.50
8 Mike McQueen .60 1.50
9 George Scott .75 2.00
10 Claude Osteen .75 2.00
11 Elliott Maddox .60 1.50
12 Johnny Callison .75 2.00
13 Charlie Brinkman .60 1.50
Dick Moloney
14 Dave Concepcion RC 10.00 25.00
15 Andy Messersmith .75 2.00
16 Ken Singleton RC 1.25 3.00
17 Billy Sorrell .60 1.50
18 Norm Miller .60 1.50
19 Skip Pitlock .60 1.50
20 Reggie Jackson 30.00 60.00
21 Dan McGinn .75 2.00
22 Phil Roof .60 1.50
23 Oscar Gamble .60 1.50
24 Rich Hand .60 1.50
25 Cito Gaston .75 2.00
26 Bert Blyleven RC 10.00 25.00
27 Fred Cambria .60 1.50
Gene Clines
28 Ron Klimkowski .60 1.50
29 Don Buford .60 1.50
30 Phil Niekro 3.00 8.00
31 John Bateman/(different pose) 1.25 3.00
32 Jerry DeVanon .75 2.00
Recently Traded To Orioles
33 Del Unser .60 1.50
34 Sandy Vance .60 1.50
35 Lou Piniella 1.25 3.00
36 Dean Chance .75 2.00
37 Rich McKinney .60 1.50
38 Jim Colborn .60 1.50
39 Gene Lamont RC .75 2.00
40 Lee May .75 2.00
41 Rick Austin .60 1.50
42 Boots Day .75 2.00
43 Steve Kealey .60 1.50
44 Johnny Edwards .60 1.50
45 Jim Hunter 3.00 8.00
46 Dave Campbell .75 2.00
47 Johnny Jeter .60 1.50
48 Dave Baldwin .60 1.50
49 Don Money .60 1.50
50 Willie McCovey 5.00 12.00
51 Steve Kline .60 1.50
52 Earl Williams RC .60 1.50
53 Paul Blair .75 2.00
54 Checklist 1-132 4.00 10.00
55 Steve Carlton 10.00 25.00
56 Duane Josephson .60 1.50
57 Von Joshua .60 1.50
58 Bill Lee .75 2.00
59 Gene Mauch MG .75 2.00
60 Dick Bosman .60 1.50
61 A.Johnson 1.25 3.00
Yaz
Oliva LL
62 NL Batting Leaders .75 2.00
Rico Carty
Joe Torre
Manny S
63 AL RBI Leaders 1.25 3.00
Frank Howard
Tony Conigliaro
B
64 Bench 3.00 8.00
Perez
B.Will LL
65 F.Howard 1.25 3.00
Kill
Yaz LL
66 Bench 3.00 8.00
B.Will
Perez LL
67 Segui 1.25 3.00
Palmer
Wright LL
68 Seaver 1.25 3.00
Simpson
Walker LL
69 AL Pitching Leaders .75 2.00
Mike Cuellar
Dave McNally
J
70 Gibson 3.00 8.00
Perry
Jenk LL
71 AL Strikeout Leaders .75 2.00
Sam McDowell
Mickey Lolich#
72 Seaver 3.00 8.00
Gibson
Jenk LL
73 George Brunet/(St. Louis Cardinals).60 1.50
74 Pete Hamm .60 1.50
Jim Nettles
75 Gary Nolan .75 2.00
76 Ted Savage .60 1.50
77 Mike Compton .60 1.50
78 Jim Spencer .60 1.50
79 Wade Blasingame .60 1.50
80 Bill Melton .60 1.50
81 Felix Millan .60 1.50
82 Casey Cox .60 1.50
83 Tim Foli RC .75 2.00
84 Marcel Lachemann RC .60 1.50
85 Bill Grabarkewitz .60 1.50
86 Mike Kilkenny .75 2.00
87 Jack Heidemann .60 1.50
88 Hal King .60 1.50
89 Ken Brett .60 1.50
90 Joe Pepitone .75 2.00
91 Bob Lemon MG .75 2.00
92 Fred Wenz .60 1.50
93 Norm McRae .60 1.50
Denny Riddleberger
94 Don Hahn .75 2.00
95 Luis Tiant .75 2.00
96 Joe Hague .60 1.50
97 Floyd Wicker .60 1.50
98 Joe Decker .60 1.50
99 Mark Belanger .75 2.00
100 Pete Rose 50.00 100.00
101 Les Cain .60 1.50
102 Ken Forsch .75 2.00
Larry Howard
103 Rich Severson .60 1.50
104 Dan Frisella .60 1.50
105 Tony Conigliaro .75 2.00
106 Tom Dukes .60 1.50
107 Roy Foster .60 1.50
108 John Cumberland .60 1.50
109 Steve Hovley .60 1.50
110 Bill Mazeroski 3.00 8.00
111 Loyd Colson .60 1.50
Bobby Mitchell
112 Manny Mota .75 2.00
113 Jerry Crider .60 1.50
114 Billy Conigliaro .75 2.00
115 Donn Clendenon .75 2.00
116 Ken Sanders .60 1.50
117 Ted Simmons RC 4.00 10.00
118 Cookie Rojas .75 2.00
119 Frank Lucchesi MG .60 1.50
120 Willie Horton .75 2.00
121 Jim Dunegan .60 1.50
Roe Skidmore
122 Eddie Watt .60 1.50
123 Checklist 133-263 4.00 10.00
124 Don Gullett RC .75 2.00
125 Ray Fosse .60 1.50
126 Danny Coombs .60 1.50
127 Danny Thompson .75 2.00
128 Frank Johnson .60 1.50
129 Aurelio Monteagudo .60 1.50
130 Denis Menke .60 1.50
131 Curt Blefary .60 1.50
132 Jose Laboy .75 2.00
133 Mickey Lolich .75 2.00
134 Jose Arcia .60 1.50
135 Rick Monday .75 2.00
136 Duffy Dyer .60 1.50
137 Marcelino Lopez .60 1.50
138 Joe Lis .75 2.00
Willie Montanez
139 Paul Casanova .60 1.50
140 Gaylord Perry 3.00 8.00
141 Frank Quilici MG .60 1.50
142 Mack Jones .75 2.00
143 Steve Blass .75 2.00
144 Jackie Hernandez .75 2.00
145 Bill Singer .75 2.00
146 Ralph Houk MG .75 2.00
147 Bob Priddy .60 1.50
148 John Mayberry .75 2.00
149 Mike Hershberger .60 1.50
150 Sam McDowell .75 2.00
151 Tommy Davis/(Oakland A's) 1.25 3.00
152 Lloyd Allen .60 1.50
Winston Llenas
153 Gary Ross .60 1.50
154 Cesar Gutierrez .60 1.50
155 Ken Henderson .60 1.50
156 Bart Johnson .60 1.50
157 Bob Bailey 1.25 3.00
158 Jerry Reuss .75 2.00
159 Jarvis Tatum .60 1.50
160 Tom Seaver 12.50 40.00
161 Ron Hunt/(different pose) 2.50 6.00
162 Jack Billingham .60 1.50
163 Buck Martinez .75 2.00
164 Frank Duffy .75 2.00
Milt Wilcox
165 Cesar Tovar .60 1.50
166 Joe Hoerner .60 1.50
167 Tom Grieve RC .75 2.00
168 Bruce Dal Canton .60 1.50
169 Ed Herrmann .60 1.50
170 Mike Cuellar .75 2.00
171 Bobby Wine .75 2.00
172 Duke Sims/(Los Angeles Dodgers).75 2.00
173 Gil Garrido .60 1.50
174 Dave LaRoche .60 1.50
175 Jim Hickman .60 1.50
176 Bob Montgomery RC .75 2.00
177 Hal McRae .75 2.00
178 Dave Duncan .75 2.00
179 Mike Corkins .60 1.50
180 Al Kaline 10.00 25.00
181 Hal Lanier .60 1.50
182 Al Downing/(Los Angeles Dodgers).75 2.00
183 Gil Hodges MG 1.25 3.00
184 Stan Bahnsen .60 1.50
185 Julian Javier .60 1.50
186 Bob Spence .60 1.50
187 Ted Abernathy .60 1.50
188 Bobby Valentino RC 3.00 8.00
189 George Mitterwald .60 1.50
190 Bob Tolan .60 1.50
191 Mike Andrews/(Chicago White Sox).75 2.00
192 Billy Wilson .60 1.50
193 Bob Grich RC 1.25 3.00
194 Mike Lum .60 1.50
195 Boog Powell ALCS .75 2.00
196 AL Playoff Game 2 .75 2.00
Dave McNally makes it
two stra
197 Jim Palmer ALCS2 1.25 3.00
198 AL Playoff Summary .75 2.00
Orioles Celebrate
199 NL Playoff Game 1 .75 2.00
Ty Cline pinch-triple
decides
200 NL Playoff Game 2 .75 2.00
Bobby Tolan scores for
third t
201 Ty Cline NLCS .75 2.00
202 Claude Raymond/(different pose) 2.50 6.00
203 Larry Gura .75 2.00
204 Bernie Smith .60 1.50
George Kopacz
205 Gerry Moses .60 1.50
206 Checklist 264-393 5.00 12.00
207 Alan Foster/(Cleveland Indians) .75 2.00
208 Billy Martin MG 1.25 3.00
209 Steve Renko .75 2.00
210 Rod Carew 8.00 20.00
211 Phil Hennigan .60 1.50
212 Rich Hebner .75 2.00
213 Frank Baker .60 1.50
214 Al Ferrara .60 1.50
215 Diego Segui .60 1.50
216 Reggie Cleveland .75 2.00
Luis Melendez
217 Ed Stroud .60 1.50
218 Tony Cloninger .60 1.50
219 Elrod Hendricks .60 1.50
220 Ron Santo 1.25 3.00
221 Dave Morehead .60 1.50
222 Bob Watson .75 2.00
223 Cecil Upshaw .60 1.50
224 Alan Gallagher .60 1.50

225 Gary Peters .60 1.50
226 Bill Russell .75 2.00
227 Floyd Weaver .60 1.50
228 Wayne Garrett .60 1.50
229 Jim Hannan .60 1.50
230 Willie Stargell 8.00 20.00
231 John Lowenstein RC .75 2.00
232 John Strohmayer .75 2.00
233 Larry Bowa .75 2.00
234 Jim Lyttle .60 1.50
235 Nate Colbert .60 1.50
236 Bob Humphreys .60 1.50
237 Cesar Cedeno RC .75 2.00
238 Chuck Dobson .60 1.50
239 Red Schoendienst MG .75 2.00
240 Clyde Wright .60 1.50
241 Dave Nelson .60 1.50
242 Jim Ray .60 1.50
243 Carlos May .60 1.50
244 Bob Tillman .60 1.50
245 Jim Kaat .75 2.00
246 Tony Taylor .60 1.50
247 Jerry Cram .75 2.00
Paul Splittorff
248 Hoyt Wilhelm/(Atlanta Braves) 4.00 10.00
249 Chico Salmon .60 1.50
250 Johnny Bench 30.00 60.00
251 Frank Reberger .60 1.50
252 Eddie Leon .60 1.50
253 Bill Sudakis .60 1.50
254 Cal Koonce .60 1.50
255 Bob Robertson .75 2.00
256 Tony Gonzalez .60 1.50
257 Nelson Briles .75 2.00
258 Dick Green .60 1.50
259 Dave Marshall .60 1.50
260 Tommy Harper .75 2.00
261 Darold Knowles .60 1.50
262 Jim Williams .60 1.50
Dave Robinson
263 John Ellis .60 1.50
264 Joe Morgan 4.00 10.00
265 Jim Northrup .75 2.00
266 Bill Stoneman .75 2.00
267 Rich Morales .60 1.50
268 Phillies Team 1.25 3.00
269 Gail Hopkins .60 1.50
270 Rico Carty .75 2.00
271 Bill Zepp .60 1.50
272 Tommy Helms .75 2.00
273 Pete Richert .60 1.50
274 Ron Slocum .60 1.50
275 Vada Pinson .75 2.00
276 George Foster RC 4.00 10.00
277 Gary Waslewski .60 1.50
278 Jerry Grote .75 2.00
279 Lefty Phillips MG .60 1.50
280 Fergie Jenkins 3.00 8.00
281 Danny Walton .60 1.50
282 Jose Pagan .60 1.50
283 Dick Such .60 1.50
284 Jim Gosger .75 2.00
285 Sal Bando .75 2.00
286 Jerry McNertney .60 1.50
287 Mike Fiore .60 1.50
288 Joe Moeller .60 1.50
289 Rusty Staub/(Different pose) 4.00 10.00
290 Tony Oliva 1.25 3.00
291 George Culver .60 1.50
292 Jay Johnstone .75 2.00
293 Pat Corrales .75 2.00
294 Steve Dunning .75 2.00
295 Bobby Bonds 2.50 6.00
296 Tom Timmermann .60 1.50
297 Johnny Briggs .60 1.50
298 Jim Nelson .60 1.50
299 Ed Kirkpatrick .60 1.50
300 Brooks Robinson 10.00 25.00
301 Earl Wilson .60 1.50
302 Phil Gagliano .60 1.50
303 Lindy McDaniel .75 2.00
304 Ron Brand .75 2.00
305 Reggie Smith .75 2.00
306 Jim Nash .60 1.50
307 Don Wert .60 1.50
308 Cardinals Team 1.25 3.00
309 Dick Ellsworth .60 1.50
310 Tommie Agee .75 2.00
311 Lee Stange .60 1.50
312 Harry Walker MG .60 1.50
313 Tom Hall .60 1.50
314 Jeff Torborg .75 2.00
315 Ron Fairly 1.25 3.00
316 Fred Scherman .60 1.50
317 Jim Driscoll .60 1.50
Angel Mangual
318 Rudy May .60 1.50
319 Ty Cline .60 1.50
320 Dave McNally .75 2.00
321 Tom Matchick .60 1.50
322 Jim Beauchamp .60 1.50
323 Billy Champion .60 1.50
324 Graig Nettles 1.25 3.00
325 Juan Marichal 4.00 10.00
326 Richie Scheinblum .60 1.50
327 World Series Game 1 .75 2.00
Boog Powell homers to
opposi
328 Don Buford WS .75 2.00
329 Frank Robinson WS3 1.25 3.00
330 World Series Game 4 .75 2.00
Reds stay alive
331 Brooks Robinson WS5 3.00 8.00
332 World Series Summary .75 2.00
Orioles Celebrate
333 Clay Kirby .60 1.50
334 Roberto Pena .60 1.50
335 Jerry Koosman .75 2.00
336 Tigers Team 1.25 3.00
337 Jesus Alou .60 1.50
338 Gene Tenace .75 2.00
339 Wayne Simpson .60 1.50
340 Rico Petrocelli .75 2.00
341 Steve Garvey RC 20.00 50.00
342 Frank Tepedino .75 2.00
343 Milt May RC .75 2.00
344 Ellie Rodriguez .60 1.50
345 Joel Horlen .60 1.50
346 Lum Harris MG .60 1.50
347 Ted Uhlaender .60 1.50
348 Fred Norman .60 1.50
349 Rich Reese .60 1.50
350 Billy Williams 3.00 8.00
351 Jim Shellenback .60 1.50
352 Denny Doyle .60 1.50
353 Carl Taylor .60 1.50
354 Don McMahon .60 1.50
355 Bud Harrelson 1.25 3.00
356 Bob Locker .60 1.50
357 Reds Team 1.25 3.00
358 Danny Carver .60 1.50
359 Ron Reed .60 1.50
360 Jim Fregosi .75 2.00
361 Don Sutton 3.00 8.00
362 Mike Adamson .60 1.50
Roger Freed
363 Mike Nagy .60 1.50
364 Tommy Dean .60 1.50
365 Bob Johnson .60 1.50
366 Ron Stone .60 1.50
367 Dalton Jones .60 1.50
368 Bob Veale .75 2.00
369 Checklist 394-523 4.00 10.00
370 Joe Torre 2.50 6.00
371 Jack Hiatt .60 1.50
372 Lew Krausse .60 1.50
373 Tom McCraw .60 1.50
374 Clete Boyer .75 2.00
375 Steve Hargan .60 1.50
376 Clyde Mashore .75 2.00
Ernie McAnally
377 Greg Garrett .60 1.50
378 Tito Fuentes .60 1.50
379 Wayne Granger .60 1.50
380 Ted Williams MG 6.00 15.00
381 Fred Gladding .60 1.50
382 Jake Gibbs .60 1.50
383 Rod Gaspar .60 1.50
384 Rollie Fingers 3.00 8.00
385 Maury Wills 2.50 6.00
386 Red Sox Team 1.25 3.00
387 Ron Herbel .60 1.50
388 Al Oliver 1.25 3.00
389 Ed Brinkman .60 1.50
390 Glenn Beckert .75 2.00
391 Steve Brye .75 2.00
Cotton Nash
392 Grant Jackson .60 1.50
393 Merv Rettenmund .75 2.00
394 Clay Carroll 1.25 3.00
395 Roy White 1.50 4.00
396 Dick Schofield 1.25 3.00
397 Alvin Dark MG 1.50 4.00
398 Howie Reed 1.25 3.00
399 Jim French 1.25 3.00
400 Hank Aaron 40.00 80.00
401 Tom Murphy 1.25 3.00
402 Dodgers Team 2.50 6.00
403 Joe Coleman 1.25 3.00
404 Buddy Harris 1.25 3.00
Roger Metzger
405 Leo Cardenas 1.25 3.00
406 Ray Sadecki 1.25 3.00
407 Joe Rudi 1.50 4.00
408 Rafael Robles 1.25 3.00
409 Don Pavletich 1.25 3.00
410 Ken Holtzman 1.50 4.00
411 George Spriggs 1.25 3.00
412 Jerry Johnson 1.25 3.00
413 Pat Kelly 1.25 3.00
414 Woodie Fryman 1.25 3.00
415 Mike Hegan 1.25 3.00
416 Gene Alley 1.25 3.00
417 Dick Hall 1.25 3.00
418 Adolfo Phillips 1.50 4.00
419 Ron Hansen 1.25 3.00
420 Jim Merritt 1.25 3.00
421 John Stephenson 1.25 3.00
422 Frank Bertaina 1.25 3.00
423 Dennis Saunders 1.25 3.00
Tim Marting
424 Roberto Rodriquez 1.25 3.00
425 Doug Rader 1.50 4.00
426 Chris Cannizzaro 1.25 3.00
427 Bernie Allen 1.25 3.00
428 Jim McAndrew 1.25 3.00
429 Chuck Hinton 1.25 3.00
430 Wes Parker 1.50 4.00
431 Tom Burgmeier 1.25 3.00
432 Bob Didier 1.25 3.00
433 Skip Lockwood 1.25 3.00
434 Gary Sutherland 1.50 4.00
435 Jose Cardenal 1.50 4.00
436 Wilbur Wood 1.50 4.00
437 Danny Murtaugh MG 1.50 4.00
438 Mike McCormick 1.50 4.00
439 Greg Luzinski RC 2.50 6.00
440 Bert Campaneris 1.50 4.00
441 Milt Pappas 1.50 4.00
442 Angels Team 2.50 6.00
443 Rich Robertson 1.25 3.00
444 Jimmie Price 1.25 3.00
445 Art Shamsky 1.25 3.00
446 Bobby Bolin 1.25 3.00
447 Cesar Geronimo 1.50 4.00
448 Dave Roberts 1.25 3.00
449 Brant Alyea 1.25 3.00
450 Bob Gibson 8.00 20.00
451 Joe Keough 1.25 3.00
452 John Boccabella 1.50 4.00
453 Terry Crowley 1.25 3.00
454 Mike Paul 1.25 3.00
455 Don Kessinger 1.50 4.00
456 Bob Meyer 1.25 3.00
457 Willie Smith 1.25 3.00
458 Ron Lolich 1.25 3.00
Dave Lemonds
459 Jim Lefebvre 1.25 3.00
460 Fritz Peterson 1.25 3.00
461 Jim Ray Hart 1.25 3.00
462 Senators Team 2.50 6.00
463 Tom Kelley 1.25 3.00
464 Aurelio Rodriguez 1.25 3.00
465 Tim McCarver 2.50 6.00
466 Ken Berry 1.25 3.00
467 Al Santorini 1.25 3.00
468 Frank Fernandez 1.25 3.00
469 Bob Aspromonte 1.25 3.00
470 Bob Oliver 1.25 3.00
471 Tom Griffin 1.25 3.00
472 Ken Rudolph 1.25 3.00
473 Gary Wagner 1.25 3.00
474 Jim Fairey 1.50 4.00
475 Ron Perranoski 1.25 3.00
476 Dal Maxvill 1.25 3.00
477 Earl Weaver MG 3.00 8.00
478 Bernie Carbo 1.25 3.00
479 Dennis Higgins 1.25 3.00
480 Manny Sanguillen 1.50 4.00
481 Daryl Patterson 1.25 3.00
482 Padres Team 2.50 6.00
483 Gene Michael 1.25 3.00
484 Don Wilson 1.25 3.00
485 Ken McMullen 1.25 3.00
486 Steve Huntz 1.25 3.00
487 Paul Schaal 1.25 3.00
488 Jerry Stephenson 1.25 3.00
489 Luis Alvarado 1.25 3.00
490 Deron Johnson 1.25 3.00
491 Jim Hardin 1.25 3.00
492 Ken Boswell 1.25 3.00
493 Dave May 1.25 3.00
494 Ralph Garr 1.50 4.00
Rick Kester
495 Felipe Alou 1.50 4.00
496 Woody Woodward 1.25 3.00
497 Horacio Pina 1.25 3.00
498 John Kennedy 1.25 3.00
499 Checklist 524-643 3.00 8.00
500 Jim Perry 1.50 4.00
501 Andy Etchebarren 1.25 3.00
502 Cubs Team 2.50 6.00
503 Gates Brown 1.50 4.00
504 Ken Wright 1.25 3.00
505 Ollie Brown 1.25 3.00
506 Bobby Knoop 1.25 3.00
507 George Stone 1.25 3.00
508 Roger Repoz 1.25 3.00
509 Jim Grant 1.25 3.00
510 Ken Harrelson 1.50 4.00
511 Chris Short 1.50 4.00
512 Dick Mills 1.25 3.00
Mike Garman
513 Nolan Ryan 100.00 200.00
514 Ron Woods 1.25 3.00
515 Carl Morton 1.50 4.00
516 Ted Kubiak 1.25 3.00
517 Charlie Fox MG 1.25 3.00
518 Joe Grzenda 1.25 3.00
519 Willie Crawford 1.25 3.00
520 Tommy John 2.50 6.00
521 Leron Lee 1.25 3.00
522 Twins Team 2.50 6.00
523 John Odom 1.25 3.00
524 Mickey Stanley 2.50 6.00
525 Ernie Banks 40.00 80.00
526 Ray Jarvis 1.50 4.00
527 Cleon Jones 2.50 6.00
528 Wally Bunker 1.50 4.00
529 Bill Buckner 2.50 6.00
530 Carl Yastrzemski 20.00 50.00
531 Mike Torrez 1.50 4.00
532 Bill Rigney MG 1.50 4.00
533 Mike Ryan 1.50 4.00
534 Luke Walker 1.50 4.00
535 Curt Flood 2.50 6.00
536 Claude Raymond 2.50 6.00
537 Tom Egan 1.50 4.00
538 Angel Bravo 1.50 4.00
539 Larry Brown 1.50 4.00
540 Larry Dierker 2.50 6.00
541 Bob Burda 1.50 4.00
542 Bob Miller 1.50 4.00
543 Yankees Team 6.00 15.00
544 Vida Blue 2.50 6.00
545 Dick Dietz 1.50 4.00
546 John Matias 1.50 4.00
547 Pat Dobson 1.50 4.00
548 Don Mason 1.50 4.00
549 Jim Brewer 1.50 4.00
550 Harmon Killebrew 12.50 40.00
551 Frank Linzy 1.50 4.00
552 Buddy Bradford 1.50 4.00
553 Kevin Collins 1.50 4.00
554 Lowell Palmer 1.50 4.00
555 Walt Williams 1.50 4.00
556 Jim McGlothlin 1.50 4.00
557 Tom Satriano 1.50 4.00
558 Hector Torres 1.50 4.00
559 AL Rookie Pitchers 1.50 4.00
Terry Cox
Bill Gogolewski
Ga
560 Rusty Staub 3.00 8.00
561 Syd O'Brien 1.50 4.00
562 Dave Giusti 1.50 4.00
563 Giants Team 3.00 8.00
564 Al Fitzmorris 1.50 4.00
565 Jim Wynn 2.50 6.00
566 Tim Cullen 1.50 4.00
567 Walt Alston MG 4.00 10.00
568 Sal Campisi 1.50 4.00
569 Ivan Murrell 1.50 4.00
570 Jim Palmer 20.00 50.00
571 Ted Sizemore 1.50 4.00
572 Jerry Kenney 1.50 4.00
573 Ed Kranepool 2.50 6.00
574 Jim Bunning 4.00 10.00
575 Bill Freehan 2.50 6.00
576 Cubs Rookies 1.50 4.00
Adrian Garrett
Brock Davis
Garry J
577 Jim Lonborg 2.50 6.00
578 Eddie Kasko/(Topps 578 is 2.50 6.00
Ron Hunt)
579 Marty Pattin 1.50 4.00
580 Tony Perez 12.50 30.00
581 Roger Nelson 1.50 4.00
582 Dave Cash 2.50 6.00
583 Ron Cook 1.50 4.00
584 Indians Team 3.00 8.00
585 Willie Davis 2.50 6.00
586 Dick Woodson 1.50 4.00
587 Sonny Jackson 1.50 4.00
588 Tom Bradley 1.50 4.00
589 Bob Barton 1.50 4.00
590 Alex Johnson 2.50 6.00
591 Jackie Brown 1.50 4.00
592 Randy Hundley 2.50 6.00
593 Jack Aker 1.50 4.00
594 Al Hrabosky RC 2.50 6.00
595 Dave Johnson 2.50 6.00
596 Mike Jorgensen 1.50 4.00
597 Ken Suarez 1.50 4.00
598 Rick Wise 2.50 6.00
599 Norm Cash 2.50 6.00
600 Willie Mays 75.00 150.00
601 Ken Tatum 1.50 4.00
602 Marty Martinez 1.50 4.00
603 Pirates Team 3.00 8.00
604 John Gelnar 1.50 4.00
605 Orlando Cepeda 4.00 10.00
606 Chuck Taylor 1.50 4.00
607 Paul Ratliff 1.50 4.00
608 Mike Wegener 2.50 6.00
609 Leo Durocher MG 3.00 8.00
610 Amos Otis 2.50 6.00
611 Tom Phoebus 1.50 4.00
612 Indians Rookies 1.50 4.00
Lou Camilli
Ted Ford
Steve Ming
613 Pedro Borbon 1.50 4.00
614 Billy Cowan 1.50 4.00
615 Mel Stottlemyre 2.50 6.00
616 Larry Hisle 2.50 6.00
617 Clay Dalrymple 1.50 4.00
618 Tug McGraw 2.50 6.00
619 Checklist 644-752 4.00 10.00
620 Frank Howard 2.50 6.00
621 Ron Bryant 1.50 4.00
622 Joe Lahoud 1.50 4.00
623 Pat Jarvis 1.50 4.00
624 Athletics Team 3.00 8.00
625 Lou Brock 20.00 50.00
626 Freddie Patek 2.50 6.00
627 Steve Hamilton 1.50 4.00
628 John Bateman 2.50 6.00
629 John Hiller 3.00 8.00
630 Roberto Clemente 100.00 200.00
631 Eddie Fisher 1.50 4.00
632 Darrel Chaney 1.50 4.00
633 AL Rookie Outfielders 1.50 4.00
Bobby Brooks
Pete Koegel/
634 Phil Regan 1.50 4.00
635 Bobby Murcer 2.50 6.00
636 Denny LeMaster 1.50 4.00
637 Dave Bristol MG 1.50 4.00
638 Stan Williams 1.50 4.00
639 Tom Haller 1.50 4.00
640 Frank Robinson 30.00 60.00
641 Mets Team 10.00 25.00
642 Jim Roland 1.50 4.00
643 Rick Reichardt 1.50 4.00
644 Jim Stewart 4.00 10.00
645 Jim Maloney 5.00 12.00
646 Bobby Floyd 4.00 10.00
647 Juan Pizarro 4.00 10.00
648 Jon Matlack RC SP 8.00 20.00
649 Sparky Lyle 6.00 15.00
650 Richie Allen SP ! 20.00 50.00
651 Jerry Robertson 4.00 10.00
652 Braves Team 6.00 15.00
653 Russ Snyder 4.00 10.00
654 Don Shaw 4.00 10.00
655 Mike Epstein 4.00 10.00
656 Gerry Nyman 4.00 10.00
657 Jose Azcue 4.00 10.00
658 Paul Lindblad 4.00 10.00
659 Byron Browne 4.00 10.00
660 Ray Culp 4.00 10.00
661 Chuck Tanner MG 6.00 15.00
662 Mike Hedlund 4.00 10.00
663 Marv Staehle 4.00 10.00
664 Rookie Pitchers 6.00 15.00
Archie Reynolds
Bob Reynolds
Ke
665 Ron Swoboda 6.00 15.00
666 Gene Brabender 4.00 10.00
667 Pete Ward 5.00 12.00
668 Gary Neibauer 4.00 10.00
669 Ike Brown 4.00 10.00
670 Bill Hands 4.00 10.00
671 Bill Voss 4.00 10.00
672 Ed Crosby 4.00 10.00
673 Gerry Janeski 4.00 10.00
674 Expos Team 6.00 15.00
675 Dave Boswell 4.00 10.00
676 Tommie Reynolds 4.00 10.00
677 Jack DiLauro 4.00 10.00
678 George Thomas 4.00 10.00
679 Don O'Riley 4.00 10.00
680 Don Mincher 4.00 10.00
681 Bill Butler 4.00 10.00
682 Terry Harmon 4.00 10.00
683 Bill Burbach 4.00 10.00
684 Curt Motton 4.00 10.00
685 Moe Drabowsky 4.00 10.00
686 Chico Ruiz 4.00 10.00
687 Ron Taylor 5.00 12.00
688 Sparky Anderson MG 20.00 50.00
689 Frank Baker 4.00 10.00
690 Bob Moose 4.00 10.00
691 Bob Heise 4.00 10.00
692 AL Rookie Pitchers 4.00 10.00
Hal Haydel
Rogelio Moret
Way
693 Jose Pena 4.00 10.00
694 Rick Renick 4.00 10.00
695 Joe Niekro 5.00 12.00
696 Jerry Morales 4.00 10.00
697 Rickey Clark 4.00 10.00
698 Brewers Team 8.00 20.00
699 Jim Britton 5.00 12.00
700 Boog Powell 12.50 40.00
701 Bob Garibaldi 4.00 10.00
702 Milt Ramirez 4.00 10.00
703 Mike Kekich 4.00 10.00
704 J.C. Martin 4.00 10.00
705 Dick Selma 4.00 10.00
706 Joe Foy 4.00 10.00
707 Fred Lasher 4.00 10.00
708 Russ Nagelson 4.00 10.00
709 D.Baylor 60.00 120.00
D.Baker RC SP !
710 Sonny Siebert 4.00 10.00
711 Larry Stahl 4.00 10.00
712 Jose Martinez 4.00 10.00
713 Mike Marshall 8.00 20.00
714 Dick Williams MG 6.00 15.00
715 Horace Clarke 4.00 10.00
716 Dave Leonhard 4.00 10.00
717 Tommie Aaron 5.00 12.00
718 Billy Wynne 4.00 10.00
719 Jerry May 4.00 10.00
720 Matty Alou 5.00 12.00
721 John Morris 4.00 10.00
722 Astros Team 8.00 20.00
723 Vicente Romo 4.00 10.00
724 Tom Tischinski 4.00 10.00
725 Gary Gentry 4.00 10.00
726 Paul Popovich 4.00 10.00
727 Ray Lamb 4.00 10.00
728 NL Rookie Outfielders 4.00 10.00
Wayne Redmond
Keith Lampar
729 Dick Billings 4.00 10.00
730 Jim Rooker 4.00 10.00
731 Jim Qualls 4.00 10.00
732 Bob Reed 4.00 10.00
733 Lee Maye 4.00 10.00
734 Rob Gardner 4.00 10.00
735 Mike Shannon 6.00 15.00
736 Mel Queen 4.00 10.00
737 Preston Gomez MG 4.00 10.00
738 Russ Gibson 4.00 10.00
739 Barry Lersch 4.00 10.00
740 Luis Aparicio 20.00 50.00
741 Skip Guinn 4.00 10.00
742 Royals Team 6.00 15.00
743 John O'Donoghue 5.00 12.00
744 Chuck Manuel 4.00 10.00
745 Sandy Alomar 5.00 12.00
746 Andy Kosco 4.00 10.00
747 NL Rookie Pitchers 4.00 10.00
Al Severinsen
Scipio Spinks/
748 John Purdin 4.00 10.00
749 Ken Szotkiewicz 4.00 10.00
750 Denny McLain 12.50 40.00
751 Al Weis 6.00 15.00
752 Dick Drago 5.00 12.00

1972 O-Pee-Chee

The cards in this 525-card set measure 2 1/2" by 3 1/2". The 1972 O-Pee-Chee set is very similar to the 1972 Topps set. On a white background, the fronts feature color player photos with multicolored frames, rounded bottom corners and the top part of the photo also rounded. The player's name and team name appear on the front. The horizontal backs carry player biography and statistics in French and English and have a different color than the 1972 Topps cards. Features appearing for the first time were "Boyhood Photos" (KP: 341-348 and 491-498) and "In Action" cards. The O-Pee-Chee cards can be distinguished from Topps cards by the "Printed in Canada" on the bottom of the back. This was the first year the cards denoted O.P.C. in the copyright line rather than T.C.G. There is one card in the set which is notably different from the corresponding Topps number on the back, No. 465 Gil Hodges, which notes his death in April of 1972. Remember, the prices below apply only to the O-Pee-Chee cards -- NOT Topps cards which are much more plentiful. The cards were packaged in 36 count boxes with eight cards per pack which cost ten cents each. Notable Rookie Cards include Carlton Fisk.

COMPLETE SET (525) 1000.00 2000.00
COMMON PLAYER (1-132) .40 1.00
COMMON PLAYER (133-263) .60 1.50
COMMON PLAYER (264-394) .75 2.00
COMMON PLAYER (395-525) 1.00 2.50
1 Pirates Team 5.00 12.00
2 Ray Culp .40 1.00
3 Bob Tolan .40 1.00
4 Checklist 1-132 2.50 6.00
5 John Bateman .75 2.00
6 Fred Scherman .40 1.00
7 Enzo Hernandez .40 1.00
8 Ron Swoboda .75 2.00
9 Stan Williams .40 1.00
10 Amos Otis .75 2.00
11 Bobby Valentine .75 2.00
12 Jose Cardenal .40 1.00
13 Joe Grzenda .40 1.00
14 Phillies Rookies .40 1.00
Pete Koegel
Mike Anderson
Wayn
15 Walt Williams .40 1.00
16 Mike Jorgensen .40 1.00
17 Dave Duncan .75 2.00
18 Juan Pizarro .40 1.00
19 Billy Cowan .40 1.00
20 Don Wilson .40 1.00
21 Braves Team .75 2.00
22 Rob Gardner .40 1.00
23 Ted Kubiak .40 1.00
24 Ted Ford .40 1.00
25 Bill Singer .40 1.00
26 Andy Etchebarren .40 1.00
27 Bob Johnson .40 1.00
28 Bob Gebhard .40 1.00
Steve Brye
Hal Haydel
29 Bill Bonham .40 1.00
30 Rico Petrocelli .75 2.00
31 Cleon Jones .75 2.00
32 Cleon Jones IA .40 1.00
33 Billy Martin MG 2.50 6.00
34 Billy Martin IA 1.50 4.00
35 Jerry Johnson .40 1.00
36 Jerry Johnson IA .40 1.00
37 Carl Yastrzemski 8.00 20.00
38 Carl Yastrzemski IA 3.00 8.00
39 Bob Barton .40 1.00
40 Bob Barton IA .40 1.00
41 Tommy Davis .75 2.00
42 Tommy Davis IA .40 1.00
43 Rick Wise .75 2.00
44 Rick Wise IA .40 1.00
45 Glenn Beckert .75 2.00
46 Glenn Beckert IA .40 1.00
47 John Ellis .40 1.00
48 John Ellis IA .40 1.00
49 Willie Mays 30.00 60.00
50 Willie Mays IA ! 12.50 30.00
51 Harmon Killebrew 5.00 12.00
52 Harmon Killebrew IA 2.50 6.00
53 Bud Harrelson .75 2.00
54 Bud Harrelson IA .40 1.00
55 Clyde Wright .40 1.00
56 Rich Chiles .40 1.00
57 Bob Oliver .40 1.00
58 Ernie McAnally .75 2.00
59 Fred Stanley .40 1.00
60 Manny Sanguillen .75 2.00
61 Burt Hooton RC .75 2.00
62 Angel Mangual .40 1.00
63 Duke Sims .40 1.00
64 Pete Broberg .40 1.00
65 Cesar Cedeno .75 2.00
66 Ray Corbin .40 1.00
67 Red Schoendienst MG 1.50 4.00
68 Jim York .40 1.00
69 Roger Freed .40 1.00
70 Mike Cuellar .75 2.00
71 Angels Team .75 2.00
72 Bruce Kison .40 1.00
73 Steve Huntz .40 1.00
74 Cecil Upshaw .40 1.00
75 Bert Campaneris .75 2.00
76 Don Carrithers .40 1.00
77 Ron Theobald .40 1.00
78 Steve Arlin .40 1.00
79 Carlton Fisk 40.00 80.00
Cooper RC !
80 Tony Perez 3.00 8.00
81 Mike Hedlund .40 1.00
82 Ron Woods .75 2.00
83 Dalton Jones .40 1.00
84 Vince Colbert .40 1.00
85 NL Batting Leaders 1.50 4.00
Joe Torre
Ralph Garr
Glenn B
86 AL Batting Leaders 1.50 4.00
Tony Oliva
Bobby Murcer
Merv
87 Torre 2.50 6.00
Starg
Aaron LL
88 Kill 2.50 6.00
F.Rob
R.Smith LL
89 Stargell 1.50 4.00
Aaron
May LL
90 Melton 1.50 4.00
Cash
Reggie LL
91 Seaver 1.50 4.00
Roberts
Wilson LL
92 Blue 1.50 4.00
Wood
Palmer LL
93 Jenk 2.50 6.00
Carlton
Seaver LL
94 AL Pitching Leaders 1.50 4.00
Mickey Lolich
Vida Blue
Wil
95 Seaver 2.50 6.00
Jenkins
Stone LL
96 AL Strikeout Leaders 1.50 4.00
Mickey Lolich
Vida Blue
Jo
97 Tom Kelley .40 1.00
98 Chuck Tanner MG .75 2.00
99 Ross Grimsley .40 1.00
100 Frank Robinson 4.00 10.00
101 J.R.Richard RC 1.50 4.00
102 Lloyd Allen .40 1.00
103 Checklist 133-263 2.50 6.00
104 Toby Harrah RC .75 2.00
105 Gary Gentry .40 1.00
106 Brewers Team .75 2.00
107 Jose Cruz RC .75 2.00
108 Gary Waslewski .40 1.00
109 Jerry May .40 1.00
110 Ron Hunt .75 2.00
111 Jim Grant .40 1.00
112 Greg Luzinski .75 2.00
113 Rogelio Moret .40 1.00
114 Bill Buckner .75 2.00
115 Jim Fregosi .75 2.00
116 Ed Farmer .40 1.00
117 Cleo James .40 1.00
118 Skip Lockwood .40 1.00
119 Marty Perez .40 1.00
120 Bill Freehan .75 2.00
121 Ed Sprague .40 1.00
122 Larry Biittner .40 1.00
123 Ed Acosta .40 1.00
124 Yankees Rookies .40 1.00
Alan Closter
Rusty Torres
Roger
125 Dave Cash .75 2.00
126 Bart Johnson .40 1.00
127 Duffy Dyer .40 1.00
128 Eddie Watt .40 1.00
129 Charlie Fox MG .40 1.00
130 Bob Gibson 4.00 10.00
131 Jim Nettles .40 1.00
132 Joe Morgan 3.00 8.00
133 Joe Keough .60 1.50
134 Carl Morton 1.00 2.50
135 Vada Pinson 1.00 2.50
136 Darrel Chaney .60 1.50
137 Dick Williams MG 1.00 2.50
138 Mike Kekich .60 1.50
139 Tim McCarver 1.00 2.50
140 Pat Dobson 1.00 2.50
141 Mets Rookies 1.00 2.50
Buzz Capra
Leroy Stanton
Jon Matla
142 Chris Chambliss RC 2.00 5.00

143 Garry Jestadt .60 1.50
144 Marty Pattin .60 1.50
145 Don Kessinger 1.00 2.50
146 Steve Kealey .60 1.50
147 Dave Kingman RC 3.00 8.00
148 Dick Billings .60 1.50
149 Gary Neibauer .60 1.50
150 Norm Cash 1.00 2.50
151 Jim Brewer .60 1.50
152 Gene Clines .60 1.50
153 Rick Auerbach .60 1.50
154 Ted Simmons 2.00 5.00
155 Larry Dierker 1.00 2.50
156 Twins Team 1.00 2.50
157 Don Gullett .60 1.50
158 Jerry Kenney .60 1.50
159 John Boccabella 1.00 2.50
160 Andy Messersmith 1.00 2.50
161 Brock Davis .60 1.50
162 Darrell Porter RC UER 1.00 2.50
163 Tug McGraw 2.00 5.00
164 Tug McGraw IA 1.00 2.50
165 Chris Speier RC 1.00 2.50
166 Chris Speier IA .60 1.50
167 Deron Johnson .60 1.50
168 Deron Johnson IA .60 1.50
169 Vida Blue 2.00 5.00
170 Vida Blue IA 1.00 2.50
171 Darrell Evans 2.00 5.00
172 Darrell Evans IA 1.00 2.50
173 Clay Kirby .60 1.50
174 Clay Kirby IA .60 1.50
175 Tom Haller .60 1.50
176 Tom Haller IA .60 1.50
177 Paul Schaal .60 1.50
178 Paul Schaal IA .60 1.50
179 Dock Ellis .60 1.50
180 Dock Ellis IA .60 1.50
181 Ed Kranepool 1.00 2.50
182 Ed Kranepool IA .60 1.50
183 Bill Melton .60 1.50
184 Bill Melton IA .60 1.50
185 Ron Bryant .60 1.50
186 Ron Bryant IA .60 1.50
187 Gates Brown .60 1.50
188 Frank Lucchesi MG .60 1.50
189 Gene Tenace 1.00 2.50
190 Dave Giusti .60 1.50
191 Jeff Burroughs RC 2.00 5.00
192 Cubs Team 1.00 2.50
193 Kurt Bevacqua .60 1.50
194 Fred Norman .60 1.50
195 Orlando Cepeda 3.00 8.00
196 Mel Queen .60 1.50
197 Johnny Briggs .60 1.50
198 Charlie Hough RC 3.00 8.00
199 Mike Fiore .60 1.50
200 Lou Brock 4.00 10.00
201 Phil Roof .60 1.50
202 Scipio Spinks .60 1.50
203 Ron Blomberg .60 1.50
204 Tommy Helms .60 1.50
205 Dick Drago .60 1.50
206 Dal Maxvill .60 1.50
207 Tom Egan .60 1.50
208 Milt Pappas 1.00 2.50
209 Joe Rudi 1.00 2.50
210 Denny McLain 1.00 2.50
211 Gary Sutherland 1.00 2.50
212 Grant Jackson .60 1.50
213 Angels Rookies .60 1.50
Billy Parker
Art Kusnyer
Tom Sil
214 Mike McQueen .60 1.50
215 Alex Johnson 1.00 2.50
216 Joe Niekro 1.00 2.50
217 Roger Metzger .60 1.50
218 Eddie Kasko MG .60 1.50
219 Rennie Stennett 1.00 2.50
220 Jim Perry 1.00 2.50
221 NL Playoffs 1.00 2.50
Bucs champs
222 Brooks Robinson ALCS 2.00 5.00
223 Dave McNally WS 1.00 2.50
224 World Series Game 2
(Dave Johnson 1.00 2.50
and Mark Belan
225 Manny Sanguillen WS 1.00 2.50
226 Roberto Clemente WS4 4.00 10.00
227 Nellie Briles WS 1.00 2.50
228 World Series Game 6
(Frank Robinson and 2.00 5.00
Manny Sa
229 Steve Blass WS 1.00 2.50
230 World Series Summary 1.00 2.50
Pirates celebrate
231 Casey Cox .60 1.50
232 Chris Arnold .60 1.50
Jim Barr
Dave Rader
233 Jay Johnstone 1.00 2.50
234 Ron Taylor 2.00 5.00
235 Merv Rettenmund .60 1.50
236 Jim McGlothlin .60 1.50
237 Yankees Team 1.00 2.50
238 Leron Lee .60 1.50
239 Tom Timmermann .60 1.50
240 Richie Allen 1.00 2.50
241 Rollie Fingers 3.00 8.00
242 Don Mincher .60 1.50
243 Frank Linzy .60 1.50
244 Steve Braun .60 1.50
245 Tommie Agee 1.00 2.50
246 Tom Burgmeier .60 1.50
247 Milt May .60 1.50
248 Tom Bradley .60 1.50
249 Harry Walker MG .60 1.50
250 Boog Powell 1.00 2.50
251 Checklist 264-394 2.50 6.00
252 Ken Reynolds .60 1.50
253 Sandy Alomar 1.00 2.50
254 Boots Day 1.00 2.50
255 Jim Lonborg 1.00 2.50
256 George Foster 1.00 2.50
257 Jim Foor .60 1.50
Tim Hosley
Paul Jata
258 Randy Hundley .60 1.50
259 Sparky Lyle 1.00 2.50
260 Ralph Garr 1.00 2.50
261 Steve Mingori .60 1.50
262 Padres Team 1.00 2.50
263 Felipe Alou 1.00 2.50
264 Tommy John 1.25 3.00
265 Wes Parker 1.25 3.00
266 Bobby Bolin .75 2.00
267 Dave Concepcion 2.50 6.00
268 Dwain Anderson .75 2.00
Chris Floethe
269 Don Hahn .75 2.00
270 Jim Palmer 4.00 10.00
271 Ken Rudolph .75 2.00
272 Mickey Rivers RC 1.25 3.00
273 Bobby Floyd .75 2.00
274 Al Severinsen .75 2.00
275 Cesar Tovar .75 2.00
276 Gene Mauch MG 1.25 3.00
277 Elliott Maddox .75 2.00
278 Dennis Higgins .75 2.00
279 Larry Brown .75 2.00
280 Willie McCovey 3.00 8.00
281 Bill Parsons .75 2.00
282 Astros Team 1.25 3.00
283 Darrell Brandon .75 2.00
284 Ike Brown .75 2.00
285 Gaylord Perry 4.00 10.00
286 Gene Alley .75 2.00
287 Jim Hardin .75 2.00
288 Johnny Jeter .75 2.00
289 Syd O'Brien .75 2.00
290 Sonny Siebert .75 2.00
291 Hal McRae 1.25 3.00
292 Hal McRae IA .75 2.00
293 Danny Frisella .75 2.00
294 Danny Frisella IA .75 2.00
295 Dick Dietz .75 2.00
296 Dick Dietz IA .75 2.00
297 Claude Osteen 1.25 3.00
298 Claude Osteen IA .75 2.00
299 Hank Aaron 30.00 60.00
300 Hank Aaron IA 12.50 30.00
301 George Mitterwald .75 2.00
302 George Mitterwald IA .75 2.00
303 Joe Pepitone 1.25 3.00
304 Joe Pepitone IA .75 2.00
305 Ken Boswell .75 2.00
306 Ken Boswell IA .75 2.00
307 Steve Renko 1.25 3.00
308 Steve Renko IA .75 2.00
309 Roberto Clemente 40.00 80.00
310 Roberto Clemente IA 12.50 40.00
311 Clay Carroll .75 2.00
312 Clay Carroll IA .75 2.00
313 Luis Aparicio 4.00 10.00
314 Luis Aparicio IA 2.50 6.00
315 Paul Splittorff .75 2.00
316 Cardinals Rookies 1.25 3.00
Jim Bibby
Jorge Roque
Santiag
317 Rich Hand .75 2.00
318 Sonny Jackson .75 2.00
319 Aurelio Rodriguez .75 2.00
320 Steve Blass 1.25 3.00
321 Joe Lahoud .75 2.00
322 Jose Pena .75 2.00
323 Earl Weaver MG 3.00 8.00
324 Mike Ryan .75 2.00
325 Mel Stottlemyre 1.25 3.00
326 Pat Kelly .75 2.00
327 Steve Stone RC 1.25 3.00
328 Red Sox Team 1.25 3.00
329 Roy Foster .75 2.00
330 Jim Hunter 4.00 10.00
331 Stan Swanson 1.25 3.00
332 Buck Martinez .75 2.00
333 Steve Barber .75 2.00
334 Rangers Rookies .75 2.00
Bill Fahey
Jim Mason
Tom Raglan
335 Bill Hands .75 2.00
336 Marty Martinez .75 2.00
337 Mike Kilkenny 1.25 3.00
338 Bob Grich 1.25 3.00
339 Ron Cook .75 2.00
340 Roy White 1.25 3.00
341 Joe Torre KP 1.25 3.00
342 Wilbur Wood KP .75 2.00
343 Willie Stargell KP 1.25 3.00
344 Dave McNally KP .75 2.00
345 Rick Wise KP .75 2.00
346 Jim Fregosi KP .75 2.00
347 Tom Seaver KP 3.00 8.00
348 Sal Bando KP .75 2.00
349 Al Fitzmorris .75 2.00
350 Frank Howard 1.25 3.00
351 Braves Rookies 1.25 3.00
Tom House
Rick Kester
Jimmy Brit
352 Dave LaRoche .75 2.00
353 Art Shamsky .75 2.00
354 Tom Murphy .75 2.00
355 Bob Watson 1.25 3.00
356 Gerry Moses .75 2.00
357 Woodie Fryman .75 2.00
358 Sparky Anderson MG 3.00 8.00
359 Don Pavletich .75 2.00
360 Dave Roberts .75 2.00
361 Mike Andrews .75 2.00
362 Mets Team 2.50 6.00
363 Ron Klimkowski .75 2.00
364 Johnny Callison 1.25 3.00
365 Dick Bosman 1.25 3.00
366 Jimmy Rosario .75 2.00
367 Ron Perranoski .75 2.00
368 Danny Thompson .75 2.00
369 Jim LeFebvre 1.25 3.00
370 Don Buford .75 2.00
371 Denny LeMaster .75 2.00
372 Lance Clemons .75 2.00
Monty Montgomery
373 John Mayberry 1.25 3.00
374 Jack Heidemann .75 2.00
375 Reggie Cleveland 1.25 3.00
376 Andy Kosco .75 2.00
377 Terry Harmon .75 2.00
378 Checklist 395-525 3.00 8.00
379 Ken Berry .75 2.00
380 Earl Williams .75 2.00
381 White Sox Team 1.25 3.00
382 Joe Gibbon .75 2.00
383 Brant Alyea .75 2.00
384 Dave Campbell 1.25 3.00
385 Mickey Stanley 1.25 3.00
386 Jim Colborn .75 2.00
387 Horace Clarke 1.25 3.00
388 Charlie Williams .75 2.00
389 Bill Rigney MG .75 2.00
390 Willie Davis 1.25 3.00
391 Ken Sanders .75 2.00
392 Fred Cambria 1.25 3.00
Richie Zisk RC
393 Curt Motton .75 2.00
394 Ken Forsch 1.25 3.00
395 Matty Alou 1.25 3.00
396 Paul Lindblad 1.00 2.50
397 Phillies Team 2.50 6.00
398 Larry Hisle 1.25 3.00
399 Milt Wilcox 1.25 3.00
400 Tony Oliva 2.50 6.00
401 Jim Nash 1.00 2.50
402 Bobby Heise 1.00 2.50
403 John Cumberland 1.00 2.50
404 Jeff Torborg 1.25 3.00
405 Ron Fairly 1.25 3.00
406 George Hendrick RC 1.25 3.00
407 Chuck Taylor 1.00 2.50
408 Jim Northrup 1.25 3.00
409 Frank Baker 1.00 2.50
410 Fergie Jenkins 4.00 10.00
411 Bob Montgomery 1.00 2.50
412 Dick Kelley 1.00 2.50
413 Don Eddy 1.00 2.50
Dave Lemonds
414 Bob Miller 1.00 2.50
415 Cookie Rojas 1.00 2.50
416 Johnny Edwards 1.00 2.50
417 Tom Hall 1.00 2.50
418 Tom Shopay 1.00 2.50
419 Jim Spencer 1.00 2.50
420 Steve Carlton 12.50 30.00
421 Ellie Rodriguez 1.00 2.50
422 Ray Lamb 1.00 2.50
423 Oscar Gamble 1.25 3.00
424 Bill Gogolewski 1.00 2.50
425 Ken Singleton 1.25 3.00
426 Ken Singleton IA 1.00 2.50
427 Tito Fuentes 1.00 2.50
428 Tito Fuentes IA 1.00 2.50
429 Bob Robertson 1.00 2.50
430 Bob Robertson IA 1.00 2.50
431 Cito Gaston 1.25 3.00
432 Cito Gaston IA 1.00 2.50
433 Johnny Bench 12.50 40.00
434 Johnny Bench IA 8.00 20.00
435 Reggie Jackson 20.00 50.00
436 Reggie Jackson IA ! 10.00 25.00
437 Maury Wills 2.50 6.00
438 Maury Wills IA 1.25 3.00
439 Billy Williams 3.00 8.00
440 Billy Williams IA 2.50 6.00
441 Thurman Munson 10.00 25.00
442 Thurman Munson IA 5.00 12.00
443 Ken Henderson 1.00 2.50
444 Ken Henderson IA 1.00 2.50
445 Tom Seaver 20.00 50.00
446 Tom Seaver IA 10.00 25.00
447 Willie Stargell 4.00 10.00
448 Willie Stargell IA 2.50 6.00
449 Bob Lemon MG 1.25 3.00
450 Mickey Lolich 1.25 3.00
451 Tony LaRussa 3.00 8.00
452 Ed Herrmann 1.00 2.50
453 Barry Lersch 1.00 2.50
454 A's Team 2.50 6.00
455 Tommy Harper 1.25 3.00
456 Mark Belanger 1.25 3.00
457 Padres Rookies 1.00 2.50
Darcy Fast
Derrel Thomas
Mike Iv
458 Aurelio Monteagudo 1.00 2.50
459 Rick Renick 1.00 2.50
460 Al Downing 1.00 2.50
461 Tim Cullen 1.00 2.50
462 Rickey Clark 1.00 2.50
463 Bernie Carbo 1.00 2.50
464 Jim Roland 1.00 2.50
465 Gil Hodges MG/(Mentions his 12.50 40.00
death on 4/2/72)
466 Norm Miller 1.00 2.50
467 Steve Kline 1.00 2.50
468 Richie Scheinblum 1.00 2.50
469 Ron Herbel 1.00 2.50
470 Ray Fosse 1.00 2.50
471 Luke Walker 1.00 2.50
472 Phil Gagliano 1.00 2.50
473 Dan McGinn 1.00 2.50
474 J.Oates RC 10.00 25.00
Don Baylor
475 Gary Nolan 1.00 2.50
476 Lee Richard 1.00 2.50
477 Tom Phoebus 1.00 2.50
478 Checklist 5th Series 3.00 8.00
479 Don Shaw 1.00 2.50
480 Lee May 1.25 3.00
481 Billy Conigliaro 1.00 2.50
482 Joe Hoerner 1.00 2.50
483 Ken Suarez 1.00 2.50
484 Lum Harris MG 1.00 2.50
485 Phil Regan 1.00 2.50
486 John Lowenstein 1.00 2.50
487 Tigers Team 2.50 6.00
488 Mike Nagy 1.00 2.50
489 Terry Humphrey 1.00 2.50
Keith Lampard
490 Dave McNally 1.25 3.00
491 Lou Piniella KP 1.25 3.00
492 Mel Stottlemyre KP 1.25 3.00
493 Bob Bailey KP 1.25 3.00
494 Willie Horton KP 1.25 3.00
495 Bill Melton KP 1.00 2.50
496 Bud Harrelson KP 1.25 3.00
497 Jim Perry KP 1.25 3.00
498 Brooks Robinson KP 2.50 6.00
499 Vicente Romo 1.00 2.50
500 Joe Torre 3.00 8.00
501 Pete Hamm 1.00 2.50
502 Jackie Hernandez 1.00 2.50
503 Gary Peters 1.00 2.50
504 Ed Spiezio 1.00 2.50
505 Mike Marshall 1.25 3.00
506 Terry Ley 1.25 3.00
Jim Moyer
Dick Tidrow
507 Fred Gladding 1.00 2.50
508 Ellie Hendricks 1.00 2.50
509 Don McMahon 1.00 2.50
510 Ted Williams MG 8.00 20.00
511 Tony Taylor 1.00 2.50
512 Paul Popovich 1.00 2.50
513 Lindy McDaniel 1.25 3.00
514 Ted Sizemore 1.00 2.50
515 Bert Blyleven 2.50 6.00
516 Oscar Brown 1.00 2.50
517 Ken Brett 1.00 2.50
518 Wayne Garrett 1.00 2.50
519 Ted Abernathy 1.00 2.50
520 Larry Bowa 1.25 3.00
521 Alan Foster 1.00 2.50
522 Dodgers Team 2.50 6.00
523 Chuck Dobson 1.00 2.50
524 Ed Armbrister 1.00 2.50
Mel Behney
525 Carlos May 1.25 3.00

1973 O-Pee-Chee

The cards in this 660-card set measure 2 1/2" by 3 1/2". This set is essentially the same as the regular 1973 Topps set, except that the words "Printed in Canada" appear on the backs and the backs are bilingual. On a white border, the fronts feature color player photos with rounded corners and thin black borders. The player's name and position and the team name are also printed on the front. An "All-Time Leaders" series (471-478) appears in this set. Kid pictures appeared again for the second year in a row (341-346). The backs carry player biography and statistics in French and English. The cards are numbered on the back. The backs appear to be more "yellow" than the Topps backs. Remember, the prices below apply only to the O-Pee-Chee cards -- NOT Topps cards which are more plentiful. Unlike the 1973 Topps set, all cards in this set were issued equally and at the same time, i.e., there were no scarce series with the O-Pee-Chee cards. Although there are no scarce series, cards 529-660 attract a slight premium. Because of the premium that high series Topps cards attract, there is a perception that O-Pee-Chee cards of the same number sequence are less available. The key card in this set is the Mike Schmidt Rookie Card. The cards were packaged in 10 count packs with 36 cards in a box which cost 10 cents. Other Rookie Cards of note in this set include Bob Boone and Dwight Evans.

COMPLETE SET (660) 500.00 1000.00
COMMON PLAYER (1-528) .30 .75
COMMON PLAYER (529-660) 1.25 3.00
1 Aaron 20.00 50.00
Ruth
Mays !
2 Rich Hebner .60 1.50
3 Jim Lonborg .60 1.50
4 John Milner .30 .75
5 Ed Brinkman .30 .75
6 Mac Scarce .30 .75
7 Texas Rangers Team .60 1.50
8 Tom Hall .30 .75
9 Johnny Oates .30 .75
10 Don Sutton 2.50 6.00
11 Chris Chambliss .60 1.50
12 Padres Leaders .60 1.50
Don Zimmer MG
Dave Garcia CO
Joh
13 George Hendrick .60 1.50
14 Sonny Siebert .30 .75
15 Ralph Garr .60 1.50
16 Steve Braun .30 .75
17 Fred Gladding .30 .75
18 Leroy Stanton .30 .75
19 Tim Foli .30 .75
20 Stan Bahnsen .30 .75
21 Randy Hundley .60 1.50
22 Ted Abernathy .30 .75
23 Dave Kingman .60 1.50
24 Al Santorini .30 .75
25 Roy White .60 1.50
26 Pirates Team .60 1.50
27 Bill Gogolewski .30 .75
28 Hal McRae .60 1.50
29 Tony Taylor .60 1.50
30 Tug McGraw .60 1.50
31 Buddy Bell RC 1.00 2.50
32 Fred Norman .30 .75
33 Jim Breazeale .30 .75
34 Pat Dobson .30 .75
35 Willie Davis .60 1.50
36 Steve Barber .30 .75
37 Bill Robinson .60 1.50
38 Mike Epstein .30 .75
39 Dave Roberts .30 .75
40 Reggie Smith .60 1.50
41 Tom Walker .30 .75
42 Mike Andrews .30 .75
43 Randy Moffitt .30 .75
44 Rick Monday .60 1.50
45 Ellie Rodriguez/(photo actually .30 .75
John Felske)
46 Lindy McDaniel .60 1.50
47 Luis Melendez .30 .75
48 Paul Splittorff .30 .75
49 Twins Leaders .60 1.50
Frank Quilici MG
Vern Morgan CO
B
50 Roberto Clemente 20.00 50.00
51 Chuck Seelbach .30 .75
52 Denis Menke .30 .75
53 Steve Dunning .30 .75
54 Checklist 1-132 1.25 3.00
55 Jon Matlack .60 1.50
56 Merv Rettenmund .30 .75
57 Derrel Thomas .30 .75
58 Mike Paul .30 .75
59 Steve Yeager RC .60 1.50
60 Ken Holtzman .60 1.50
61 B.Williams 1.50 4.00
R.Carew LL
62 J.Bench 1.00 2.50
D.Allen LL
63 J.Bench 1.00 2.50
D.Allen LL
64 L.Brock .60 1.50
Campaneris LL
65 S.Carlton .60 1.50
L.Tiant LL
66 Carlton .60 1.50
Perry
Wood LL
67 S.Carlton 12.50 40.00
N.Ryan LL
68 C.Carroll .60 1.50
S.Lyle LL
69 Phil Gagliano .30 .75
70 Milt Pappas .60 1.50
71 Johnny Briggs .30 .75
72 Ron Reed .30 .75
73 Ed Herrmann .30 .75
74 Billy Champion .30 .75
75 Vada Pinson .60 1.50
76 Doug Rader .30 .75
77 Mike Torrez .60 1.50
78 Richie Scheinblum .30 .75
79 Jim Willoughby .30 .75
80 Tony Oliva 1.50 4.00
81 Chicago Cubs Leaders .60 1.50
Whitey Lockman MG
Hank Agui
82 Fritz Peterson .30 .75
83 Leron Lee .30 .75
84 Rollie Fingers 2.50 6.00
85 Ted Simmons .60 1.50
86 Tom McCraw .30 .75
87 Ken Boswell .30 .75
88 Mickey Stanley .60 1.50
89 Jack Billingham .30 .75
90 Brooks Robinson 4.00 10.00
91 Dodgers Team .60 1.50
92 Jerry Bell .30 .75
93 Jesus Alou .30 .75
94 Dick Billings .30 .75
95 Steve Blass .60 1.50
96 Doug Griffin .30 .75
97 Willie Montanez .60 1.50
98 Dick Woodson .30 .75
99 Carl Taylor .30 .75
100 Hank Aaron 20.00 50.00
101 Ken Henderson .30 .75
102 Rudy May .30 .75
103 Celerino Sanchez .30 .75
104 Reggie Cleveland .60 1.50
105 Carlos May .30 .75
106 Terry Humphrey .30 .75
107 Phil Hennigan .30 .75
108 Bill Russell .60 1.50
109 Doyle Alexander .60 1.50
110 Bob Watson .60 1.50
111 Dave Nelson .30 .75
112 Gary Ross .30 .75
113 Jerry Grote .60 1.50
114 Lynn McGlothen .30 .75
115 Ron Santo 1.50 4.00
116 Yankees Leaders .60 1.50
Ralph Houk MG
Jim Hegan CO
Elst
117 Ramon Hernandez .30 .75
118 John Mayberry .60 1.50
119 Larry Bowa .60 1.50
120 Joe Coleman .30 .75
121 Dave Rader .30 .75
122 Jim Strickland .30 .75
123 Sandy Alomar .60 1.50
124 Jim Hardin .30 .75
125 Ron Fairly .60 1.50
126 Jim Brewer .30 .75
127 Brewers Team .60 1.50
128 Ted Sizemore .30 .75
129 Terry Forster .60 1.50
130 Pete Rose 12.50 40.00
131 Red Sox Leaders .60 1.50
Eddie Kasko MG
Doug Camilli CO/
132 Matty Alou .60 1.50
133 Dave Roberts .30 .75
134 Milt Wilcox .30 .75
135 Lee May .60 1.50
136 Orioles Leaders 1.50 4.00
Earl Weaver MG
George Bamberger
137 Jim Beauchamp .30 .75
138 Horacio Pina .30 .75
139 Carmen Fanzone .30 .75
140 Lou Piniella 1.00 2.50
141 Bruce Kison .30 .75
142 Thurman Munson 4.00 10.00
143 John Curtis .30 .75
144 Marty Perez .30 .75
145 Bobby Bonds 1.50 4.00
146 Woodie Fryman .30 .75
147 Mike Anderson .30 .75
148 Dave Goltz .30 .75
149 Ron Hunt .30 .75
150 Wilbur Wood .60 1.50
151 Wes Parker .60 1.50
152 Dave May .30 .75
153 Al Hrabosky .60 1.50
154 Jeff Torborg .60 1.50
155 Sal Bando .60 1.50
156 Cesar Geronimo .30 .75
157 Denny Riddleberger .30 .75
158 Astros Team .60 1.50
159 Cito Gaston .60 1.50
160 Jim Palmer 3.00 8.00
161 Ted Martinez .30 .75
162 Pete Broberg .30 .75
163 Vic Davalillo .30 .75
164 Monty Montgomery .30 .75
165 Luis Aparicio 2.50 6.00
166 Terry Harmon .30 .75
167 Steve Stone .60 1.50
168 Jim Northrup .60 1.50
169 Ron Schueler RC .60 1.50
170 Harmon Killebrew 2.50 6.00
171 Bernie Carbo .30 .75
172 Steve Kline .30 .75
173 Hal Breeden .60 1.50
174 Goose Gossage RC 3.00 8.00
175 Frank Robinson 3.00 8.00
176 Chuck Taylor .30 .75
177 Bill Plummer .30 .75
178 Don Rose .30 .75
179 Oakland A's Leaders .60 1.50
Dick Williams MG
Jerry Adair
180 Fergie Jenkins 2.00 5.00
181 Jack Brohamer .30 .75
182 Mike Caldwell RC .60 1.50
183 Don Buford .30 .75
184 Jerry Koosman .60 1.50
185 Jim Wynn .60 1.50
186 Bill Fahey .30 .75
187 Luke Walker .30 .75
188 Cookie Rojas .60 1.50
189 Greg Luzinski 1.00 2.50
190 Bob Gibson 4.00 10.00
191 Tigers Team .60 1.50
192 Pat Jarvis .30 .75
193 Carlton Fisk 5.00 12.00
194 Jorge Orta .30 .75
195 Clay Carroll .30 .75
196 Ken McMullen .30 .75
197 Ed Goodson .30 .75
198 Horace Clarke .30 .75
199 Bert Blyleven 1.50 4.00
200 Billy Williams 2.50 6.00
201 A.L. Playoffs .60 1.50
A's over Tigers;
George Hendrick s
202 N.L. Playoffs .60 1.50
Reds over Pirates
George Foster's#
203 Gene Tenace WS .60 1.50
204 World Series Game 2 .60 1.50
A's two straight
205 World Series Game 3 1.00 2.50
Reds win squeeker/(Tony Pere
206 Gene Tenace WS .60 1.50
207 Blue Moon Odom WS .60 1.50
208 World Series Game 6 2.50 6.00
Reds' slugging
ties series/
209 World Series Game 7 .60 1.50
Bert Campaneris stars
winnin
210 World Series Summary .60 1.50
World champions:
A's Win
211 Balor Moore .30 .75
212 Joe Lahoud .30 .75
213 Steve Garvey 2.50 6.00
214 Dave Hamilton .30 .75
215 Dusty Baker 1.50 4.00
216 Toby Harrah .60 1.50
217 Don Wilson .30 .75
218 Aurelio Rodriguez .30 .75
219 Cardinals Team .60 1.50
220 Nolan Ryan 50.00 100.00
221 Fred Kendall .30 .75
222 Rob Gardner .30 .75
223 Bud Harrelson .60 1.50
224 Bill Lee .60 1.50
225 Al Oliver .60 1.50
226 Ray Fosse .30 .75
227 Wayne Twitchell .30 .75
228 Bobby Darwin .30 .75
229 Roric Harrison .30 .75
230 Joe Morgan 3.00 8.00
231 Bill Parsons .30 .75
232 Ken Singleton .60 1.50
233 Ed Kirkpatrick .30 .75
234 Bill North .30 .75
235 Jim Hunter 2.50 6.00
236 Tito Fuentes .30 .75
237 Braves Leaders 1.50 4.00
Eddie Mathews MG
Lew Burdette CO#
238 Tony Muser .30 .75
239 Pete Richert .30 .75
240 Bobby Murcer 1.00 2.50
241 Dwain Anderson .30 .75
242 George Culver .30 .75
243 Angels Team .60 1.50
244 Ed Acosta .30 .75
245 Carl Yastrzemski 5.00 12.00
246 Ken Sanders .30 .75
247 Del Unser .30 .75
248 Jerry Johnson .30 .75
249 Larry Biittner .30 .75
250 Manny Sanguillen .60 1.50
251 Roger Nelson .30 .75
252 Giants Leaders .60 1.50
Charlie Fox MG
Joe Amalfitano CO#
253 Mark Belanger .60 1.50
254 Bill Stoneman .60 1.50
255 Reggie Jackson 8.00 20.00
256 Chris Zachary .30 .75
257 N.Y. Mets Leaders 1.50 4.00
Yogi Berra MG
Roy McMillan CO#
258 Tommy John 1.00 2.50
259 Jim Holt .30 .75
260 Gary Nolan .60 1.50
261 Pat Kelly .30 .75
262 Jack Aker .30 .75
263 George Scott .60 1.50
264 Checklist 133-264 1.00 2.50
265 Gene Michael .60 1.50
266 Mike Lum .30 .75
267 Lloyd Allen .30 .75
268 Jerry Morales .30 .75
269 Tim McCarver 1.00 2.50
270 Luis Tiant 1.00 2.50
271 Tom Hutton .30 .75
272 Ed Farmer .30 .75
273 Chris Speier .30 .75
274 Darold Knowles .30 .75
275 Tony Perez 2.50 6.00
276 Joe Lovitto .30 .75
277 Bob Miller .30 .75
278 Orioles Team .60 1.50
279 Mike Strahler .30 .75
280 Al Kaline 4.00 10.00
281 Mike Jorgensen .30 .75
282 Steve Hovley .30 .75

283 Ray Sadecki .30 .75
284 Glenn Borgmann .30 .75
285 Don Kessinger .60 1.50
286 Frank Linzy .30 .75
287 Eddie Leon .30 .75
288 Gary Gentry .30 .75
289 Bob Oliver .30 .75
290 Cesar Cedeno .60 1.50
291 Rogelio Moret .30 .75
292 Jose Cruz .60 1.50
293 Bernie Allen .30 .75
294 Steve Arlin .30 .75
295 Bert Campaneris .60 1.50
296 Sparky Anderson MG 1.50 4.00
297 Walt Williams .30 .75
298 Ron Bryant .30 .75
299 Ted Ford .30 .75
300 Steve Carlton 5.00 12.00
301 Billy Grabarkewitz .30 .75
302 Terry Crowley .30 .75
303 Nelson Briles .30 .75
304 Duke Sims .30 .75
305 Willie Mays 20.00 50.00
306 Tom Burgmeier .30 .75
307 Boots Day .30 .75
308 Skip Lockwood .30 .75
309 Paul Popovich .30 .75
310 Dick Allen 1.00 2.50
311 Joe Decker .30 .75
312 Oscar Brown .30 .75
313 Jim Ray .30 .75
314 Ron Swoboda .60 1.50
315 John Odom .30 .75
316 Padres Team .60 1.50
317 Danny Cater .30 .75
318 Jim McGlothlin .30 .75
319 Jim Spencer .30 .75
320 Lou Brock 4.00 10.00
321 Rich Hinton .30 .75
322 Garry Maddox RC .60 1.50
323 Billy Martin MG 1.00 2.50
324 Al Downing .30 .75
325 Boog Powell .60 1.50
326 Darrell Brandon .30 .75
327 John Lowenstein .30 .75
328 Bill Bonham .30 .75
329 Ed Kranepool .60 1.50
330 Rod Carew 4.00 10.00
331 Carl Morton .30 .75
332 John Felske .30 .75
333 Gene Clines .30 .75
334 Freddie Patek .30 .75
335 Bob Tolan .30 .75
336 Tom Bradley .30 .75
337 Dave Duncan .60 1.50
338 Checklist 265-396 1.00 2.50
339 Dick Tidrow .30 .75
340 Nate Colbert .30 .75
341 Jim Palmer KP 1.00 2.50
342 Sam McDowell KP .60 1.50
343 Bobby Murcer KP .60 1.50
344 Jim Hunter KP 1.00 2.50
345 Chris Speier KP .30 .75
346 Gaylord Perry KP .60 1.50
347 Royals Team .60 1.50
348 Rennie Stennett .30 .75
349 Dick McAuliffe .30 .75
350 Tom Seaver 6.00 15.00
351 Jimmy Stewart .30 .75
352 Don Stanhouse .30 .75
353 Steve Brye .30 .75
354 Billy Parker .30 .75
355 Mike Marshall .60 1.50
356 White Sox Leaders .60 1.50
Chuck Tanner MG
Joe Lonnett CO
357 Ross Grimsley .30 .75
358 Jim Nettles .30 .75
359 Cecil Upshaw .30 .75
360 Joe Rudi/(photo actually .60 1.50
Gene Tenace)
361 Fran Healy .30 .75
362 Eddie Watt .30 .75
363 Jackie Hernandez .30 .75
364 Rick Wise .30 .75
365 Rico Petrocelli .60 1.50
366 Brock Davis .30 .75
367 Burt Hooton .60 1.50
368 Bill Buckner .60 1.50
369 Lerrin LaGrow .30 .75
370 Willie Stargell 2.50 6.00
371 Mike Kekich .30 .75
372 Oscar Gamble .30 .75
373 Clyde Wright .30 .75
374 Darrell Evans 1.00 2.50
375 Larry Dierker .60 1.50
376 Frank Duffy .30 .75
377 Expos Leaders 1.00 2.50
Gene Mauch MG
Dave Bristol CO
Lar
378 Lenny Randle .30 .75
379 Cy Acosta .30 .75
380 Johnny Bench 6.00 15.00
381 Vicente Romo .30 .75
382 Mike Hegan .30 .75
383 Diego Segui .30 .75
384 Don Baylor 1.50 4.00
385 Jim Perry .60 1.50
386 Don Money .30 .75
387 Jim Barr .30 .75
388 Ben Oglivie .60 1.50
389 Mets Team 2.00 5.00
390 Mickey Lolich .60 1.50
391 Lee Lacy RC .60 1.50
392 Dick Drago .30 .75
393 Jose Cardenal .30 .75
394 Sparky Lyle .60 1.50
395 Roger Metzger .30 .75
396 Grant Jackson .30 .75
397 Dave Cash .60 1.50
398 Rich Hand .30 .75
399 George Foster .60 1.50
400 Gaylord Perry 2.50 6.00
401 Clyde Mashore .30 .75
402 Jack Hiatt .30 .75
403 Sonny Jackson .30 .75
404 Chuck Brinkman .30 .75
405 Cesar Tovar .30 .75
406 Paul Lindblad .30 .75
407 Felix Millan .30 .75
408 Jim Colborn .30 .75
409 Ivan Murrell .30 .75
410 Willie McCovey 3.00 8.00
411 Ray Corbin .30 .75
412 Manny Mota .60 1.50
413 Tom Timmerman .30 .75
414 Ken Rudolph .30 .75
415 Marty Pattin .30 .75
416 Paul Schaal .30 .75
417 Scipio Spinks .30 .75
418 Bobby Grich .60 1.50
419 Casey Cox .30 .75
420 Tommie Agee .30 .75
421 Angels Leaders .60 1.50
Bobby Winkles MG
Tom Morgan CO
S
422 Bob Robertson .30 .75
423 Johnny Jeter .30 .75
424 Denny Doyle .30 .75
425 Alex Johnson .30 .75
426 Dave LaRoche .30 .75
427 Rick Auerbach .30 .75
428 Wayne Simpson .30 .75
429 Jim Fairey .30 .75
430 Vida Blue .60 1.50
431 Gerry Moses .30 .75
432 Dan Frisella .30 .75
433 Willie Horton .60 1.50
434 Giants Team 1.00 2.50
435 Rico Carty .60 1.50
436 Jim McAndrew .30 .75
437 John Kennedy .30 .75
438 Enzo Hernandez .30 .75
439 Eddie Fisher .30 .75
440 Glenn Beckert .30 .75
441 Gail Hopkins .30 .75
442 Dick Dietz .30 .75
443 Danny Thompson .30 .75
444 Ken Brett .30 .75
445 Ken Berry .30 .75
446 Jerry Reuss .60 1.50
447 Joe Hague .30 .75
448 John Hiller .60 1.50
449 Indians Leaders 2.00 5.00
Ken Aspromonte MG
Rocky Colavito
450 Joe Torre 1.00 2.50
451 John Vuckovich .30 .75
452 Paul Casanova .30 .75
453 Checklist 397-528 1.00 2.50
454 Tom Haller .30 .75
455 Bill Melton .30 .75
456 Dick Green .30 .75
457 John Strohmayer .30 .75
458 Jim Mason .30 .75
459 Jimmy Howarth .30 .75
460 Bill Freehan .60 1.50
461 Mike Corkins .30 .75
462 Ron Blomberg .30 .75
463 Ken Tatum .30 .75
464 Chicago Cubs Team 1.00 2.50
465 Dave Giusti .30 .75
466 Jose Arcia .30 .75
467 Mike Ryan .30 .75
468 Tom Griffin .30 .75
469 Dan Monzon .30 .75
470 Mike Cuellar .60 1.50
471 Ty Cobb LDR 5.00 12.00
472 Lou Gehrig LDR 8.00 20.00
473 Hank Aaron LDR 5.00 12.00
474 Babe Ruth LDR 10.00 25.00
475 Ty Cobb LDR 4.00 10.00
476 Walter Johnson ATL/113 Shutouts 1.00 2.50
477 Cy Young ATL/511 Wins 1.00 2.50
478 Walter Johnson ATL
3508 Strikeouts 1.00 2.50
479 Hal Lanier .30 .75
480 Juan Marichal 2.50 6.00
481 White Sox Team Card 1.00 2.50
482 Rick Reuschel RC 1.00 2.50
483 Dal Maxvill .30 .75
484 Ernie McAnally .30 .75
485 Norm Cash .60 1.50
486 Phillies Leaders .60 1.50
Danny Ozark MG
Carroll Beringer
487 Bruce Dal Canton .30 .75
488 Dave Campbell .60 1.50
489 Jeff Burroughs .60 1.50
490 Claude Osteen .60 1.50
491 Bob Montgomery .30 .75
492 Pedro Borbon .30 .75
493 Duffy Dyer .30 .75
494 Rich Morales .30 .75
495 Tommy Helms .30 .75
496 Ray Lamb .30 .75
497 Cardinals Leaders 1.00 2.50
Red Schoendienst MG
Vern Benso
498 Graig Nettles 1.50 4.00
499 Bob Moose .30 .75
500 Oakland A's Team 1.00 2.50
501 Larry Gura .30 .75
502 Bobby Valentine 1.00 2.50
503 Phil Niekro 2.50 6.00
504 Earl Williams .30 .75
505 Bob Bailey .30 .75
506 Bart Johnson .30 .75
507 Darrel Chaney .30 .75
508 Gates Brown .30 .75
509 Jim Nash .30 .75
510 Amos Otis .60 1.50
511 Sam McDowell .60 1.50
512 Dalton Jones .30 .75
513 Dave Marshall .30 .75
514 Jerry Kenney .30 .75
515 Andy Messersmith .60 1.50
516 Danny Walton .30 .75
517 Pirates Leaders 1.00 2.50
Bill Virdon MG
Don Leppert CO
B
518 Bob Veale .30 .75
519 John Edwards .30 .75
520 Mel Stottlemyre .60 1.50
521 Atlanta Braves Team 1.00 2.50
522 Leo Cardenas .30 .75
523 Wayne Granger .30 .75
524 Gene Tenace .60 1.50
525 Jim Fregosi .60 1.50
526 Ollie Brown .30 .75
527 Dan McGinn .30 .75
528 Paul Blair .60 1.50
529 Milt May 1.25 3.00
530 Jim Kaat 1.50 4.00
531 Ron Woods 1.25 3.00
532 Steve Mingori 1.25 3.00
533 Larry Stahl 1.25 3.00
534 Dave Lemonds 1.25 3.00
535 John Callison 1.50 4.00
536 Phillies Team 2.50 6.00
537 Bill Slayback 1.25 3.00
538 Jim Ray Hart 1.50 4.00
539 Tom Murphy 1.25 3.00
540 Cleon Jones 1.50 4.00
541 Bob Bolin 1.25 3.00
542 Pat Corrales 1.50 4.00
543 Alan Foster 1.25 3.00
544 Von Joshua 1.25 3.00
545 Orlando Cepeda 4.00 10.00
546 Jim York 1.25 3.00
547 Bobby Heise 1.25 3.00
548 Don Durham 1.25 3.00
549 Whitey Herzog MG 1.50 4.00
550 Dave Johnson 1.50 4.00
551 Mike Kilkenny 1.50 4.00
552 J.C. Martin 1.25 3.00
553 Mickey Scott 1.25 3.00
554 Dave Concepcion 2.50 6.00
555 Bill Hands 1.25 3.00
556 Yankees Team 2.50 6.00
557 Bernie Williams 1.25 3.00
558 Jerry May 1.25 3.00
559 Barry Lersch 1.25 3.00
560 Frank Howard 1.50 4.00
561 Jim Geddes 1.25 3.00
562 Wayne Garrett 1.25 3.00
563 Larry Haney 1.25 3.00
564 Mike Thompson 1.25 3.00
565 Jim Hickman 1.25 3.00
566 Lew Krausse 1.25 3.00
567 Bob Fenwick 1.25 3.00
568 Ray Newman 1.25 3.00
569 Walt Alston MG 3.00 8.00
570 Bill Singer 1.50 4.00
571 Rusty Torres 1.25 3.00
572 Gary Sutherland 1.25 3.00
573 Fred Beene 1.25 3.00
574 Bob Didier 1.25 3.00
575 Dock Ellis 1.25 3.00
576 Expos Team 3.00 8.00
577 Eric Soderholm 1.25 3.00
578 Ken Wright 1.25 3.00
579 Tom Grieve 1.50 4.00
580 Joe Pepitone 1.50 4.00
581 Steve Kealey 1.25 3.00
582 Darrell Porter 1.50 4.00
583 Bill Greif 1.25 3.00
584 Chris Arnold 1.25 3.00
585 Joe Niekro 1.50 4.00
586 Bill Sudakis 1.25 3.00
587 Rich McKinney 1.25 3.00
588 Checklist 529-660 8.00 20.00
589 Ken Forsch 1.25 3.00
590 Deron Johnson 1.25 3.00
591 Mike Hedlund 1.25 3.00
592 John Boccabella 1.25 3.00
593 Royals Leaders 1.25 3.00
Jack McKeon MG
Galen Cisco CO
Ha
594 Vic Harris 1.25 3.00
595 Don Gullett 1.50 4.00
596 Red Sox Team 2.50 6.00
597 Mickey Rivers 1.50 4.00
598 Phil Roof 1.25 3.00
599 Ed Crosby 1.25 3.00
600 Dave McNally 1.50 4.00
601 Rookie Catchers 1.50 4.00
Sergio Robles
George Pena
Rick
602 Rookie Pitchers 1.50 4.00
Mel Behney
Ralph Garcia
Doug Ra
603 Rookie 3rd Basemen 1.50 4.00
Terry Hughes
Bill McNulty
Ke
604 Rookie Pitchers 1.50 4.00
Jesse Jefferson
Dennis O'Toole/
605 Enos Cabell RC 1.50 4.00
606 Gary Matthews RC 2.50 6.00
607 Rookie Shortstops 1.50 4.00
Pepe Frias
Ray Busse
Mario Gu
608 Steve Busby RC 2.50 6.00
609 Davey Lopes RC 2.50 6.00
610 Charlie Hough 1.50 4.00
611 Rookie Outfielders 1.50 4.00
Rich Coggins
Jim Wohlford
Ri
612 Rookie Pitchers 1.50 4.00
Steve Lawson
Bob Reynolds
Brent
613 Bob Boone RC 6.00 15.00
614 Dwight Evans RC 8.00 20.00
615 Mike Schmidt RC 100.00 250.00
Cey !
616 Rookie Pitchers 1.50 4.00
Norm Angelini
Steve Blateric
Mi
617 Rich Chiles 1.25 3.00
618 Andy Etchebarren 1.25 3.00
619 Billy Wilson 1.25 3.00
620 Tommy Harper 1.50 4.00
621 Joe Ferguson 1.50 4.00
622 Larry Hisle 1.50 4.00
623 Steve Renko 1.25 3.00
624 Leo Durocher MG 3.00 8.00
625 Angel Mangual 1.25 3.00
626 Bob Barton 1.25 3.00
627 Luis Alvarado 1.25 3.00
628 Jim Slaton 1.25 3.00
629 Indians Team 2.50 6.00
630 Denny McLain 2.50 6.00
631 Tom Matchick 1.25 3.00
632 Dick Selma 1.25 3.00
633 Ike Brown 1.25 3.00
634 Alan Closter 1.25 3.00
635 Gene Alley 1.50 4.00
636 Rickey Clark 1.25 3.00
637 Norm Miller 1.25 3.00
638 Ken Reynolds 1.25 3.00
639 Willie Crawford 1.25 3.00
640 Dick Bosman 1.25 3.00
641 Reds Team 2.50 6.00
642 Jose Laboy 1.25 3.00
643 Al Fitzmorris 1.25 3.00
644 Jack Heidemann 1.25 3.00
645 Bob Locker 1.25 3.00
646 Brewers Leaders 1.50 4.00
Del Crandall MG
Harvey Kuenn CO#
647 George Stone 1.25 3.00
648 Tom Egan 1.25 3.00
649 Rich Folkers 1.25 3.00
650 Felipe Alou 2.50 6.00
651 Don Carrithers 1.25 3.00
652 Ted Kubiak 1.25 3.00
653 Joe Hoerner 1.25 3.00
654 Twins Team 2.50 6.00
655 Clay Kirby 1.25 3.00
656 John Ellis 1.25 3.00
657 Bob Johnson 1.25 3.00
658 Elliott Maddox 1.25 3.00
659 Jose Pagan 1.25 3.00
660 Fred Scherman 2.50 6.00

1973 O-Pee-Chee Blue Team Checklists

This 24-card standard-size set is somewhat difficult to find. These blue-bordered team checklist cards are very similar in design to the mass produced red trim team checklist cards issued by O-Pee-Chee the next year and obviously very similar to the Topps issue. The primary difference compared to the Topps issue is the existence of a little French language on the reverse of the O-Pee-Chee. The fronts feature facsimile autographs on a white background. On an orange background, the backs carry the team checklists. The words "Team Checklist" are printed in French and English. The cards are unnumbered and checklisted below in alphabetical order.

COMPLETE SET (24) 60.00 120.00
COMMON TEAM (1-24) 2.50 6.00

1974 O-Pee-Chee

The cards in this 660-card set measure 2 1/2" by 3 1/2". The 1974 O-Pee-Chee cards are very similar to the 1974 Topps cards. Since the O-Pee-Chee cards were printed substantially later than the Topps cards, there was no "San Diego rumored moving to Washington" problem in the O-Pee-Chee set. On a white background, the fronts feature color player photos with rounded corners and blue borders. The player's name and position and the team name also appear on the front. The horizontal backs are golden yellow instead of green like the 1974 Topps and carry player biography and statistics in French and English. There are a number of obverse differences between the two sets as well; they are numbers 3, 4, 5, 6, 7, 8, 9, 99, 166 and 196. The Aaron Specials generally feature two past cards per card instead of four as in the Topps. Remember, the prices below apply only to O-Pee-Chee cards -- they are NOT prices for Topps cards as the Topps cards are generally much more available. The cards were issued in eight card packs with 36 packs to a box. Notable Rookie Cards include Dave Parker and Dave Winfield.

COMPLETE SET (660) 600.00 1000.00
1 Hank Aaron 30.00 60.00
Complete ML record
2 Aaron Special 54-57 5.00 12.00
Special 54-57
Records on back
3 Aaron Special 58-59 5.00 12.00
Special 58-59
4 Aaron Special 60-61 5.00 12.00
Special 60-61
5 Aaron Special 62-63 5.00 12.00
Special 62-63
6 Aaron Special 64-65 5.00 12.00
Special 64-65
7 Aaron Special 66-67 5.00 12.00
Special 66-67
8 Aaron Special 68-69 5.00 12.00
Special 68-69
9 Aaron Special 70-73 5.00 12.00
Special 70-73
Milestone homers
10 Johnny Bench 10.00 25.00
11 Jim Bibby .40 1.00
12 Dave May .40 1.00
13 Tom Hilgendorf .40 1.00
14 Paul Popovich .40 1.00
15 Joe Torre 1.50 4.00
16 Orioles Team .75 2.00
17 Doug Bird .40 1.00
18 Gary Thomasson .40 1.00
19 Gerry Moses .40 1.00
20 Nolan Ryan 40.00 80.00
21 Bob Gallagher .40 1.00
22 Cy Acosta .40 1.00
23 Craig Robinson .40 1.00
24 John Hiller .75 2.00
25 Ken Singleton .75 2.00
26 Bill Campbell .40 1.00
27 George Scott .75 2.00
28 Manny Sanguillen .75 2.00
29 Phil Niekro 2.50 6.00
30 Bobby Bonds 1.50 4.00
31 Astros Leaders .75 2.00
Preston Gomez MG
Roger Craig CO/
32 Johnny Grubb .40 1.00
33 Don Newhauser .40 1.00
34 Andy Kosco .40 1.00
35 Gaylord Perry 2.50 6.00
36 Cardinals Team .75 2.00
37 Dave Sells .40 1.00
38 Don Kessinger .75 2.00
39 Ken Suarez .40 1.00
40 Jim Palmer 5.00 12.00
41 Bobby Floyd .40 1.00
42 Claude Osteen .75 2.00
43 Jim Wynn .75 2.00
44 Mel Stottlemyre .75 2.00
45 Dave Johnson .75 2.00
46 Pat Kelly .40 1.00
47 Dick Ruthven .40 1.00
48 Dick Sharon .40 1.00
49 Steve Renko .75 2.00
50 Rod Carew 5.00 12.00
51 Bob Heise .40 1.00
52 Al Oliver .75 2.00
53 Fred Kendall .40 1.00
54 Elias Sosa .40 1.00
55 Frank Robinson 5.00 12.00
56 New York Mets Team .75 2.00
57 Darold Knowles .40 1.00
58 Charlie Spikes .40 1.00
59 Ross Grimsley .40 1.00
60 Lou Brock 4.00 10.00
61 Luis Aparicio 2.50 6.00
62 Bob Locker .40 1.00
63 Bill Sudakis .40 1.00
64 Doug Rau .40 1.00
65 Amos Otis .75 2.00
66 Sparky Lyle .75 2.00
67 Tommy Helms .40 1.00
68 Grant Jackson .40 1.00
69 Del Unser .40 1.00
70 Dick Allen 1.25 3.00
71 Dan Frisella .40 1.00
72 Aurelio Rodriguez .40 1.00
73 Mike Marshall 1.25 3.00
74 Twins Team .75 2.00
75 Jim Colborn .40 1.00
76 Mickey Rivers .75 2.00
77 Rich Troedson .40 1.00
78 Giants Leaders .75 2.00
Charlie Fox MG
John McNamara CO/
79 Gene Tenace .75 2.00
80 Tom Seaver 8.00 20.00
81 Frank Duffy .40 1.00
82 Dave Giusti .40 1.00
83 Orlando Cepeda 2.50 6.00
84 Rick Wise .40 1.00
85 Joe Morgan 5.00 12.00
86 Joe Ferguson .75 2.00
87 Fergie Jenkins 2.50 6.00
88 Fred Patek .75 2.00
89 Jackie Brown .40 1.00
90 Bobby Murcer .75 2.00
91 Ken Forsch .40 1.00
92 Paul Blair .75 2.00
93 Rod Gilbreath .40 1.00
94 Tigers Team .75 2.00
95 Steve Carlton 5.00 12.00
96 Jerry Hairston .40 1.00
97 Bob Bailey .75 2.00
98 Bert Blyleven 1.50 4.00
99 George Theodore/(Topps 99 is 1.25 3.00
Brewers Leaders)
100 Willie Stargell 5.00 12.00
101 Bobby Valentine .75 2.00
102 Bill Greif .40 1.00
103 Sal Bando .75 2.00
104 Ron Bryant .40 1.00
105 Carlton Fisk 8.00 20.00
106 Harry Parker .40 1.00
107 Alex Johnson .40 1.00
108 Al Hrabosky .75 2.00
109 Bobby Grich .75 2.00
110 Billy Williams 2.50 6.00
111 Clay Carroll .40 1.00
112 Davey Lopes 1.25 3.00
113 Dick Drago .40 1.00
114 Angels Team .75 2.00
115 Willie Horton .75 2.00
116 Jerry Reuss .75 2.00
117 Ron Blomberg .40 1.00
118 Bill Lee .75 2.00
119 Phillies Leaders .75 2.00
Danny Ozark MG
Ray Rippelmeyer
120 Wilbur Wood .40 1.00
121 Larry Lintz .40 1.00
122 Jim Holt .40 1.00
123 Nellie Briles .75 2.00
124 Bobby Coluccio .40 1.00
125 Nate Colbert .40 1.00
126 Checklist 1-132 2.00 5.00
127 Tom Paciorek .75 2.00
128 John Ellis .40 1.00
129 Chris Speier .40 1.00
130 Reggie Jackson 10.00 25.00
131 Bob Boone 1.25 3.00
132 Felix Millan .40 1.00
133 David Clyde .40 1.00
134 Denis Menke .40 1.00
135 Roy White .75 2.00
136 Rick Reuschel .75 2.00
137 Al Bumbry .75 2.00
138 Eddie Brinkman .40 1.00
139 Aurelio Monteagudo .40 1.00
140 Darrell Evans 1.25 3.00
141 Pat Bourque .40 1.00
142 Pedro Garcia .40 1.00
143 Dick Woodson .40 1.00
144 Walt Alston MG 1.50 4.00
145 Dock Ellis .40 1.00
146 Ron Fairly .75 2.00
147 Bart Johnson .40 1.00
148 Dave Hilton .40 1.00
149 Mac Scarce .40 1.00
150 John Mayberry .75 2.00
151 Diego Segui .40 1.00
152 Oscar Gamble .75 2.00
153 Jon Matlack .75 2.00
154 Astros Team .75 2.00
155 Bert Campaneris .75 2.00
156 Randy Moffitt .40 1.00
157 Vic Harris .40 1.00
158 Jack Billingham .40 1.00
159 Jim Ray Hart .40 1.00
160 Brooks Robinson 5.00 12.00
161 Ray Burris .75 2.00
162 Bill Freehan .75 2.00
163 Ken Berry .40 1.00
164 Tom House .40 1.00
165 Willie Davis .75 2.00
166 Mickey Lolich/(Topps 166 is 1.50 4.00
Royals Leaders)
167 Luis Tiant 1.25 3.00
168 Danny Thompson .40 1.00
169 Steve Rogers RC 1.25 3.00
170 Bill Melton .40 1.00
171 Eduardo Rodriguez .40 1.00
172 Gene Clines .40 1.00
173 Randy Jones RC 1.25 3.00
174 Bill Robinson .75 2.00
175 Reggie Cleveland .75 2.00
176 John Lowenstein .40 1.00
177 Dave Roberts .40 1.00
178 Garry Maddox .75 2.00
179 Yogi Berra MG 3.00 8.00
180 Ken Holtzman .75 2.00
181 Cesar Geronimo .40 1.00
182 Lindy McDaniel .75 2.00
183 Johnny Oates .40 1.00
184 Rangers Team .75 2.00
185 Jose Cardenal .40 1.00
186 Fred Scherman .40 1.00
187 Don Baylor 1.25 3.00
188 Rudy Meoli .40 1.00
189 Jim Brewer .40 1.00
190 Tony Oliva 1.25 3.00
191 Al Fitzmorris .40 1.00
192 Mario Guerrero .40 1.00
193 Tom Walker .40 1.00
194 Darrell Porter .75 2.00
195 Carlos May .40 1.00
196 Jim Hunter/(Topps 196 is 2.50 6.00
Jim Fregosi)
197 Vicente Romo .40 1.00
198 Dave Cash .40 1.00
199 Mike Kekich .40 1.00
200 Cesar Cedeno .75 2.00
201 Rod Carew 3.00 8.00
Pete Rose LL
202 Reggie 3.00 8.00
W.Stargell LL
203 Reggie 3.00 8.00
W.Stargell LL
204 T.Harper 1.25 3.00
Lou Brock LL
205 Wilbur Wood .75 2.00
Ron Bryant LL
206 Jim Palmer 2.50 6.00
T.Seaver LL
207 Nolan Ryan 8.00 20.00
T.Seaver LL
208 John Hiller .75 2.00
Mike Marshall LL
209 Ted Sizemore .40 1.00
210 Bill Singer .40 1.00
211 Chicago Cubs Team .75 2.00
212 Rollie Fingers 2.50 6.00
213 Dave Rader .40 1.00
214 Bill Grabarkewitz .40 1.00
215 Al Kaline 6.00 15.00
216 Ray Sadecki .40 1.00
217 Tim Foli .40 1.00
218 John Briggs .40 1.00
219 Doug Griffin .40 1.00
220 Don Sutton 2.50 6.00
221 White Sox Leaders .75 2.00
Chuck Tanner MG
Jim Mahoney CO
222 Ramon Hernandez .40 1.00
223 Jeff Burroughs 1.25 3.00
224 Roger Metzger .40 1.00
225 Paul Splittorff .40 1.00
226 Padres Team Card 1.25 3.00
227 Mike Lum .40 1.00
228 Ted Kubiak .40 1.00
229 Fritz Peterson .40 1.00
230 Tony Perez 2.50 6.00
231 Dick Tidrow .40 1.00
232 Steve Brye .40 1.00
233 Jim Barr .40 1.00
234 John Milner .40 1.00
235 Dave McNally .75 2.00
236 Red Schoendienst MG 1.50 4.00
237 Ken Brett .40 1.00
238 Fran Healy .40 1.00
239 Bill Russell .75 2.00
240 Joe Coleman .40 1.00
241 Glenn Beckert .40 1.00
242 Bill Gogolewski .40 1.00
243 Bob Oliver .40 1.00
244 Carl Morton .40 1.00
245 Cleon Jones .40 1.00
246 A's Team 1.25 3.00
247 Rick Miller .40 1.00
248 Tom Hall .40 1.00
249 George Mitterwald .40 1.00
250 Willie McCovey 4.00 10.00
251 Graig Nettles 1.25 3.00
252 Dave Parker RC 6.00 15.00
253 John Boccabella .40 1.00
254 Stan Bahnsen .40 1.00
255 Larry Bowa .75 2.00
256 Tom Griffin .40 1.00
257 Buddy Bell 1.25 3.00
258 Jerry Morales .40 1.00
259 Bob Reynolds .40 1.00
260 Ted Simmons 1.50 4.00
261 Jerry Bell .40 1.00
262 Ed Kirkpatrick .40 1.00
263 Checklist 133-264 1.50 4.00
264 Joe Rudi .75 2.00
265 Tug McGraw 1.50 4.00
266 Jim Northrup .75 2.00
267 Andy Messersmith .75 2.00
268 Tom Grieve .75 2.00
269 Bob Johnson .40 1.00

270 Ron Santo 1.50 4.00
271 Bill Hands .40 1.00
272 Paul Casanova .40 1.00
273 Checklist 265-396 1.50 4.00
274 Fred Beene .40 1.00
275 Ron Hunt .40 1.00
276 Angels Leaders .75 2.00
Bobby Winkles MG
John Roseboro CO
277 Gary Nolan .75 2.00
278 Cookie Rojas .75 2.00
279 Jim Crawford .40 1.00
280 Carl Yastrzemski 8.00 20.00
281 Giants Team .75 2.00
282 Doyle Alexander .75 2.00
283 Mike Schmidt 12.50 40.00
284 Dave Duncan .75 2.00
285 Reggie Smith .75 2.00
286 Tony Muser .40 1.00
287 Clay Kirby .40 1.00
288 Gorman Thomas 1.25 3.00
289 Rick Auerbach .40 1.00
290 Vida Blue .75 2.00
291 Don Hahn .40 1.00
292 Chuck Seelbach .40 1.00
293 Milt May .40 1.00
294 Steve Foucault .40 1.00
295 Rick Monday .75 2.00
296 Ray Corbin .40 1.00
297 Hal Breeden .40 1.00
298 Roric Harrison .40 1.00
299 Gene Michael .40 1.00
300 Pete Rose 12.50 30.00
301 Bob Montgomery .40 1.00
302 Rudy May .40 1.00
303 George Hendrick .75 2.00
304 Don Wilson .40 1.00
305 Tito Fuentes .40 1.00
306 Earl Weaver MG 1.50 4.00
307 Luis Melendez .40 1.00
308 Bruce Dal Canton .40 1.00
309 Dave Roberts .40 1.00
310 Terry Forster .75 2.00
311 Jerry Grote .75 2.00
312 Deron Johnson .40 1.00
313 Barry Lersch .40 1.00
314 Brewers Team .40 1.00
315 Ron Cey 1.25 3.00
316 Jim Perry .75 2.00
317 Richie Zisk .75 2.00
318 Jim Merritt .40 1.00
319 Randy Hundley .40 1.00
320 Dusty Baker 1.25 3.00
321 Steve Braun .40 1.00
322 Ernie McAnally .40 1.00
323 Richie Scheinblum .40 1.00
324 Steve Kline .40 1.00
325 Tommy Harper .75 2.00
326 Sparky Anderson MG 1.50 4.00
327 Tom Timmermann .40 1.00
328 Skip Jutze .40 1.00
329 Mark Belanger .75 2.00
330 Juan Marichal 2.50 6.00
331 Carlton Fisk 3.00 8.00
J.Bench AS
332 Dick Allen 4.00 10.00
H.Aaron AS
333 Rod Carew 2.00 5.00
J.Morgan AS
334 B.Robinson 1.50 4.00
R.Santo AS
335 Bert Campaneris .75 2.00
Chris Speier AS
336 Bobby Murcer 2.50 6.00
P.Rose AS
337 Amos Otis .75 2.00
Cesar Cedeno AS
338 R.Jackson 3.00 8.00
B.Williams AS
339 Jim Hunter 1.50 4.00
R.Wise AS
340 Thurman Munson 5.00 12.00
341 Dan Driessen RC .75 2.00
342 Jim Lonborg .75 2.00
343 Royals Team .75 2.00
344 Mike Caldwell .40 1.00
345 Bill North .40 1.00
346 Ron Reed .40 1.00
347 Sandy Alomar .75 2.00
348 Pete Richert .40 1.00
349 John Vukovich .40 1.00
350 Bob Gibson 4.00 10.00
351 Dwight Evans 1.50 4.00
352 Bill Stoneman .40 1.00
353 Rich Coggins .40 1.00
354 Chicago Cubs Leaders .75 2.00
Whitey Lockman MG
J.C. Mart
355 Dave Nelson .40 1.00
356 Jerry Koosman .75 2.00
357 Buddy Bradford .40 1.00
358 Dal Maxvill .40 1.00
359 Brent Strom .40 1.00
360 Greg Luzinski 1.25 3.00
361 Don Carrithers .40 1.00
362 Hal King .40 1.00
363 Yankees Team 1.25 3.00
364 Cito Gaston .75 2.00
365 Steve Busby .75 2.00
366 Larry Hisle .75 2.00
367 Norm Cash 1.25 3.00
368 Manny Mota .75 2.00
369 Paul Lindblad .40 1.00
370 Bob Watson .75 2.00
371 Jim Slaton .40 1.00
372 Ken Reitz .40 1.00
373 John Curtis .40 1.00
374 Marty Perez .40 1.00
375 Earl Williams .40 1.00
376 Jorge Orta .40 1.00
377 Ron Woods .40 1.00
378 Burt Hooton .75 2.00
379 Billy Martin MG 1.25 3.00
380 Bud Harrelson .75 2.00
381 Charlie Sands .40 1.00
382 Bob Moose .40 1.00
383 Phillies Team .75 2.00
384 Chris Chambliss .75 2.00
385 Don Gullett .75 2.00
386 Gary Matthews 1.25 3.00
387 Rich Morales .40 1.00
388 Phil Roof .40 1.00
389 Gates Brown .40 1.00
390 Lou Piniella 1.25 3.00
391 Billy Champion .40 1.00
392 Dick Green .40 1.00
393 Orlando Pena .40 1.00
394 Ken Henderson .40 1.00
395 Doug Rader .40 1.00
396 Tommy Davis .75 2.00
397 George Stone .40 1.00
398 Duke Sims .40 1.00
399 Mike Paul .40 1.00
400 Harmon Killebrew 4.00 10.00
401 Elliott Maddox .40 1.00
402 Jim Rooker .40 1.00
403 Red Sox Leaders .75 2.00
Darrell Johnson MG
Eddie Popowsk
404 Jim Howarth .40 1.00
405 Ellie Rodriguez .40 1.00
406 Steve Arlin .40 1.00
407 Jim Wohlford .40 1.00
408 Charlie Hough .75 2.00
409 Ike Brown .40 1.00
410 Pedro Borbon .40 1.00
411 Frank Baker .40 1.00
412 Chuck Taylor .40 1.00
413 Don Money .75 2.00
414 Checklist 397-528 1.50 4.00
415 Gary Gentry .40 1.00
416 White Sox Team .75 2.00
417 Rich Folkers .40 1.00
418 Walt Williams .40 1.00
419 Wayne Twitchell .40 1.00
420 Ray Fosse .40 1.00
421 Dan Fife .40 1.00
422 Gonzalo Marquez .40 1.00
423 Fred Stanley .40 1.00
424 Jim Beauchamp .40 1.00
425 Pete Broberg .40 1.00
426 Rennie Stennett .40 1.00
427 Bobby Bolin .40 1.00
428 Gary Sutherland .40 1.00
429 Dick Lange .40 1.00
430 Matty Alou .75 2.00
431 Gene Garber RC .75 2.00
432 Chris Arnold .40 1.00
433 Lerrin LaGrow .40 1.00
434 Ken McMullen .40 1.00
435 Dave Concepcion 1.25 3.00
436 Don Hood .40 1.00
437 Jim Lyttle .40 1.00
438 Ed Herrmann .40 1.00
439 Norm Miller .40 1.00
440 Jim Kaat 1.50 4.00
441 Tom Ragland .40 1.00
442 Alan Foster .40 1.00
443 Tom Hutton .40 1.00
444 Vic Davalillo .40 1.00
445 George Medich .40 1.00
446 Len Randle .40 1.00
447 Twins Leaders .75 2.00
Frank Quilici MG
Ralph Rowe CO
Bo
448 Ron Hodges .40 1.00
449 Tom McCraw .40 1.00
450 Rich Hebner .75 2.00
451 Tommy John 1.50 4.00
452 Gene Hiser .40 1.00
453 Balor Moore .40 1.00
454 Kurt Bevacqua .40 1.00
455 Tom Bradley .40 1.00
456 Dave Winfield RC 30.00 60.00
457 Chuck Goggin .40 1.00
458 Jim Ray .40 1.00
459 Reds Team 1.25 3.00
460 Boog Powell 1.25 3.00
461 John Odom .40 1.00
462 Luis Alvarado .40 1.00
463 Pat Dobson .40 1.00
464 Jose Cruz 1.25 3.00
465 Dick Bosman .40 1.00
466 Dick Billings .40 1.00
467 Winston Llenas .40 1.00
468 Pepe Frias .40 1.00
469 Joe Decker .40 1.00
470 Reggie Jackson ALCS 3.00 8.00
471 N.L. Playoffs .75 2.00
Mets over Reds/(Jon Matlack pitchi
472 Darold Knowles WS .75 2.00
473 Willie Mays WS2 5.00 12.00
474 Bert Campaneris WS .75 2.00
475 Rusty Staub WS .75 2.00
476 Cleon Jones WS .75 2.00
477 Reggie Jackson WS6 3.00 8.00
478 Bert Campaneris WS .75 2.00
479 World Series Summary .75 2.00
A's Celebrate; Win/2nd cons
480 Willie Crawford .40 1.00
481 Jerry Terrell .40 1.00
482 Bob Didier .40 1.00
483 Braves Team .75 2.00
484 Carmen Fanzone .40 1.00
485 Felipe Alou 1.25 3.00
486 Steve Stone .75 2.00
487 Ted Martinez .40 1.00
488 Andy Etchebarren .40 1.00
489 Pirates Leaders .75 2.00
Danny Murtaugh MG
Don Osborn CO#
490 Vada Pinson 1.25 3.00
491 Roger Nelson .40 1.00
492 Mike Rogodzinski .40 1.00
493 Joe Hoerner .40 1.00
494 Ed Goodson .40 1.00
495 Dick McAuliffe .75 2.00
496 Tom Murphy .40 1.00
497 Bobby Mitchell .40 1.00
498 Pat Corrales .40 1.00
499 Rusty Torres .40 1.00
500 Lee May .75 2.00
501 Eddie Leon .40 1.00
502 Dave LaRoche .40 1.00
503 Eric Soderholm .40 1.00
504 Joe Niekro .75 2.00
505 Bill Buckner .75 2.00
506 Ed Farmer .40 1.00
507 Larry Stahl .40 1.00
508 Expos Team 1.25 3.00
509 Jesse Jefferson .40 1.00
510 Wayne Garrett .40 1.00
511 Toby Harrah .75 2.00
512 Joe Lahoud .40 1.00
513 Jim Campanis .40 1.00
514 Paul Schaal .40 1.00
515 Willie Montanez .40 1.00
516 Horacio Pina .40 1.00
517 Mike Hegan .40 1.00
518 Derrel Thomas .40 1.00
519 Bill Sharp .40 1.00
520 Tim McCarver 1.25 3.00
521 Indians Leaders .75 2.00
Ken Aspromonte MG
Clay Bryant CO
522 J.R. Richard 1.25 3.00
523 Cecil Cooper 1.25 3.00
524 Bill Plummer .40 1.00
525 Clyde Wright .40 1.00
526 Frank Tepedino .75 2.00
527 Bobby Darwin .40 1.00
528 Bill Bonham .40 1.00
529 Horace Clarke .75 2.00
530 Mickey Stanley .75 2.00
531 Expos Leaders 1.25 3.00
Gene Mauch MG
Dave Bristol CO
Cal
532 Skip Lockwood .40 1.00
533 Mike Phillips .40 1.00
534 Eddie Watt .40 1.00
535 Bob Tolan .40 1.00
536 Duffy Dyer .40 1.00
537 Steve Mingori .40 1.00
538 Cesar Tovar .40 1.00
539 Lloyd Allen .40 1.00
540 Bob Robertson .40 1.00
541 Indians Team .75 2.00
542 Goose Gossage 1.25 3.00
543 Danny Cater .40 1.00
544 Ron Schueler .40 1.00
545 Billy Conigliaro .75 2.00
546 Mike Corkins .40 1.00
547 Glenn Borgmann .40 1.00
548 Sonny Siebert .40 1.00
549 Mike Jorgensen .40 1.00
550 Sam McDowell .75 2.00
551 Von Joshua .40 1.00
552 Denny Doyle .40 1.00
553 Jim Willoughby .40 1.00
554 Tim Johnson .40 1.00
555 Woody Fryman .40 1.00
556 Dave Campbell .75 2.00
557 Jim McGlothlin .40 1.00
558 Bill Fahey .40 1.00
559 Darrell Chaney .40 1.00
560 Mike Cuellar .75 2.00
561 Ed Kranepool .75 2.00
562 Jack Aker .40 1.00
563 Hal McRae .75 2.00
564 Mike Ryan .40 1.00
565 Milt Wilcox .40 1.00
566 Jackie Hernandez .40 1.00
567 Red Sox Team .75 2.00
568 Mike Torrez .75 2.00
569 Rick Dempsey .75 2.00
570 Ralph Garr .75 2.00
571 Rich Hand .40 1.00
572 Enzo Hernandez .40 1.00
573 Mike Adams .40 1.00
574 Bill Parsons .40 1.00
575 Steve Garvey 1.50 4.00
576 Scipio Spinks .40 1.00
577 Mike Sadek .40 1.00
578 Ralph Houk MG .75 2.00
579 Cecil Upshaw .40 1.00
580 Jim Spencer .40 1.00
581 Fred Norman .40 1.00
582 Bucky Dent RC 2.50 6.00
583 Marty Pattin .40 1.00
584 Ken Rudolph .40 1.00
585 Merv Rettenmund .40 1.00
586 Jack Brohamer .40 1.00
587 Larry Christenson .40 1.00
588 Hal Lanier .40 1.00
589 Boots Day .75 2.00
590 Rogelio Moret .40 1.00
591 Sonny Jackson .40 1.00
592 Ed Bane .40 1.00
593 Steve Yeager .75 2.00
594 Leroy Stanton .40 1.00
595 Steve Blass .75 2.00
596 Rookie Pitchers .40 1.00
Wayne Garland
Fred Holdsworth
M
597 Rookie Shortstops .75 2.00
Dave Chalk
John Gamble
Pete M
598 Ken Griffey Sr. RC 6.00 15.00
599 Rookie Pitchers 1.25 3.00
Ron Diorio
Dave Freisleben
Fran
600 Bill Madlock RC 3.00 8.00
601 Brian Downing RC 1.50 4.00
602 Rookie Pitchers .75 2.00
Glenn Abbott
Rick Henninger
Cra
603 Rookie Catchers .75 2.00
Barry Foote
Tom Lundstedt
Charl
604 A.Thornton 3.00 8.00
F.White RC
605 Frank Tanana RC 2.00 5.00
606 Rookie Outfielders .75 2.00
Jim Fuller
Wilbur Howard
Tom
607 Rookie Shortstops .75 2.00
Leo Foster
Tom Heintzelman
Da
608 Rookie Pitchers 1.25 3.00
Bob Apodaca
Dick Baney
John D'A
609 Rico Petrocelli .75 2.00
610 Dave Kingman 1.50 4.00
611 Rich Stelmaszek .40 1.00
612 Luke Walker .40 1.00
613 Dan Monzon .40 1.00
614 Adrian Devine .40 1.00
615 John Jeter .40 1.00
616 Larry Gura .40 1.00
617 Ted Ford .40 1.00
618 Jim Mason .40 1.00
619 Mike Anderson .40 1.00
620 Al Downing .40 1.00
621 Bernie Carbo .40 1.00
622 Phil Gagliano .40 1.00
623 Celerino Sanchez .40 1.00
624 Bob Miller .40 1.00
625 Ollie Brown .40 1.00
626 Pirates Team .75 2.00
627 Carl Taylor .40 1.00
628 Ivan Murrell .40 1.00
629 Rusty Staub 1.25 3.00
630 Tommy Agee .75 2.00
631 Steve Barber .40 1.00
632 George Culver .40 1.00
633 Dave Hamilton .40 1.00
634 Eddie Mathews MG 1.50 4.00
635 John Edwards .40 1.00
636 Dave Goltz .40 1.00
637 Checklist 529-660 1.50 4.00
638 Ken Sanders .40 1.00
639 Joe Lovitto .40 1.00
640 Milt Pappas .75 2.00
641 Chuck Brinkman .40 1.00
642 Terry Harmon .40 1.00
643 Dodgers Team .75 2.00
644 Wayne Granger .40 1.00
645 Ken Boswell .40 1.00
646 George Foster 1.25 3.00
647 Juan Beniquez .75 2.00
648 Terry Crowley .40 1.00
649 Fernando Gonzalez .40 1.00
650 Mike Epstein .40 1.00
651 Leron Lee .40 1.00
652 Gail Hopkins .40 1.00
653 Bob Stinson .75 2.00
654 Jesus Alou .75 2.00
655 Mike Tyson .40 1.00
656 Adrian Garrett .40 1.00
657 Jim Shellenback .40 1.00
658 Lee Lacy .40 1.00
659 Joe Lis .40 1.00
660 Larry Dierker 1.25 3.00

1974 O-Pee-Chee Team Checklists

The cards in this 24-card set measure 2 1/2" by 3 1/2". The fronts have red borders and feature the year and team name in a green panel decorated by a crossed bats design, below which is a white area containing facsimile autographs of various players. On a light yellow background, the backs list team members alphabetically, along with their card number, uniform number and position. The words "Team Checklist" appear in French and English. The cards are unnumbered and checklisted below in alphabetical order.

COMPLETE SET (24) 20.00 50.00
COMMON TEAM (1-24) 1.00 2.50

1975 O-Pee-Chee

The cards in this 660-card set measure 2 1/2" by 3 1/2". The 1975 O Pee Chee cards are very similar to the 1975 Topps cards, yet rather different from previous years' issues. The most prominent change for the fronts is the use of a two-color fram colors surrounding the picture area rather than a single, subdued color. The fronts feature color player photos with rounded corners. The player's name and position, the team name and a facsimile autograph round out the front. The backs are printed in red and green on a yellow-vanilla card stock and carry player biography and statistics in French and English. Cards 189-212 depict the MVPs of both leagues from 1951 through 1974. The first six cards (1-6) feature players breaking records or achieving milestones during the previous season. Cards 306-313 picture league leaders in various statistical categories. Cards 459-466 depict the results of post-season action. Team cards feature a checklist back for players on that team. Remember, the prices below apply only to O-Pee-Chee cards -- they are NOT prices for Topps cards as the Topps cards are generally much more available. The cards were issued in eight card packs which cost 10 cents and came 48 packs to a box. Notable Rookie Cards include George Brett, Fred Lynn, Keith Hernandez, Jim Rice and Robin Yount.

COMPLETE SET (660) 500.00 1000.00
1 Hank Aaron HL 12.50 40.00
2 Lou Brock HL 1.50 4.00
3 Bob Gibson HL 1.50 4.00
4 Al Kaline HL 3.00 8.00
5 Nolan Ryan HL 12.50 30.00
6 Mike Marshall RB .60 1.50
Hurls 106 Games
7 S.Busby 5.00 12.00
Bosman
N.Ryan HL
8 Rogelio Moret .30 .75
9 Frank Tepedino .60 1.50
10 Willie Davis .60 1.50
11 Bill Melton .30 .75
12 David Clyde .30 .75
13 Gene Locklear .60 1.50
14 Milt Wilcox .30 .75
15 Jose Cardenal .60 1.50
16 Frank Tanana 1.00 2.50
17 Dave Concepcion 1.00 2.50
18 Tigers Team CL 1.00 2.50
Ralph Houk MG
19 Jerry Koosman .60 1.50
20 Thurman Munson 4.00 10.00
21 Rollie Fingers 2.00 5.00
22 Dave Cash .30 .75
23 Bill Russell .60 1.50
24 Al Fitzmorris .30 .75
25 Lee May .60 1.50
26 Dave McNally .60 1.50
27 Ken Reitz .30 .75
28 Tom Murphy .30 .75
29 Dave Parker 1.50 4.00
30 Bert Blyleven 1.00 2.50
31 Dave Rader .30 .75
32 Reggie Cleveland .60 1.50
33 Dusty Baker 1.00 2.50
34 Steve Renko .30 .75
35 Ron Santo .60 1.50
36 Joe Lovitto .30 .75
37 Dave Freisleben .30 .75
38 Buddy Bell 1.00 2.50
39 Andre Thornton .60 1.50
40 Bill Singer .30 .75
41 Cesar Geronimo .60 1.50
42 Joe Coleman .30 .75
43 Cleon Jones .60 1.50
44 Pat Dobson .30 .75
45 Joe Rudi .60 1.50
46 Phillies Team CL(Danny Ozark MG 1.00 2.50
47 Tommy John 1.00 2.50
48 Freddie Patek .60 1.50
49 Larry Dierker .60 1.50
50 Brooks Robinson 4.00 10.00
51 Bob Forsch .60 1.50
52 Darrell Porter .60 1.50
53 Dave Giusti .30 .75
54 Eric Soderholm .30 .75
55 Bobby Bonds 1.50 4.00
56 Rick Wise .60 1.50
57 Dave Johnson .60 1.50
58 Chuck Taylor .30 .75
59 Ken Henderson .30 .75
60 Fergie Jenkins 2.00 5.00
61 Dave Winfield 10.00 25.00
62 Fritz Peterson .30 .75
63 Steve Swisher .30 .75
64 Dave Chalk .30 .75
65 Don Gullett .60 1.50
66 Willie Horton .60 1.50
67 Tug McGraw 1.00 2.50
68 Ron Blomberg .30 .75
69 John Odom .30 .75
70 Mike Schmidt 12.50 30.00
71 Charlie Hough .60 1.50
72 Royals Team CL(Jack McKeon MG 1.00 2.50
73 J.R. Richard .60 1.50
74 Mark Belanger .60 1.50
75 Ted Simmons 1.00 2.50
76 Ed Sprague .30 .75
77 Richie Zisk .60 1.50
78 Ray Corbin .30 .75
79 Gary Matthews .60 1.50
80 Carlton Fisk 4.00 10.00
81 Ron Reed .30 .75
82 Pat Kelly .30 .75
83 Jim Merritt .30 .75
84 Enzo Hernandez .30 .75
85 Bill Bonham .30 .75
86 Joe Lis .30 .75
87 George Foster 1.00 2.50
88 Tom Egan .30 .75
89 Jim Ray .30 .75
90 Rusty Staub 1.00 2.50
91 Dick Green .30 .75
92 Cecil Upshaw .30 .75
93 Davey Lopes 1.00 2.50
94 Jim Lonborg .60 1.50
95 John Mayberry .60 1.50
96 Mike Cosgrove .30 .75
97 Earl Williams .30 .75
98 Rich Folkers .30 .75
99 Mike Hegan .30 .75
100 Willie Stargell 2.50 6.00
101 Expos Team CL(Gene Mauch MG 1.00 2.50
102 Joe Decker .30 .75
103 Rick Miller .30 .75
104 Bill Madlock 1.00 2.50
105 Buzz Capra .30 .75
106 Mike Hargrove RC 1.50 4.00
107 Jim Barr .30 .75
108 Tom Hall .30 .75
109 George Hendrick .60 1.50
110 Wilbur Wood .30 .75
111 Wayne Garrett .30 .75
112 Larry Hardy .30 .75
113 Elliott Maddox .30 .75
114 Dick Lange .30 .75
115 Joe Ferguson .30 .75
116 Lerrin LaGrow .30 .75
117 Orioles Team CL 1.50 4.00
Earl Weaver MG
118 Mike Anderson .30 .75
119 Tommy Helms .30 .75
120 Steve Busby/(photo actually .60 1.50
Fran Healy)
121 Bill North .30 .75
122 Al Hrabosky .60 1.50
123 Johnny Briggs .30 .75
124 Jerry Reuss .60 1.50
125 Ken Singleton .60 1.50
126 Checklist 1-132 1.50 4.00
127 Glenn Borgmann .30 .75
128 Bill Lee .60 1.50
129 Rick Monday .60 1.50
130 Phil Niekro 1.50 4.00
131 Toby Harrah .60 1.50
132 Randy Moffitt .30 .75
133 Dan Driessen .60 1.50
134 Ron Hodges .30 .75
135 Charlie Spikes .30 .75
136 Jim Mason .30 .75
137 Terry Forster .60 1.50
138 Del Unser .30 .75
139 Horacio Pina .30 .75
140 Steve Garvey 1.50 4.00
141 Mickey Stanley .60 1.50
142 Bob Reynolds .30 .75
143 Cliff Johnson RC .60 1.50
144 Jim Wohlford .30 .75
145 Ken Holtzman .60 1.50
146 Padres Team CL 1.00 2.50
John McNamara MG
147 Pedro Garcia .30 .75
148 Jim Rooker .30 .75
149 Tim Foli .30 .75
150 Bob Gibson 3.00 8.00
151 Steve Brye .30 .75
152 Mario Guerrero .30 .75
153 Rick Reuschel .60 1.50
154 Mike Lum .30 .75
155 Jim Bibby .30 .75
156 Dave Kingman 1.00 2.50
157 Pedro Borbon .60 1.50
158 Jerry Grote .30 .75
159 Steve Arlin .30 .75
160 Graig Nettles 1.00 2.50
161 Stan Bahnsen .30 .75
162 Willie Montanez .30 .75
163 Jim Brewer .30 .75
164 Mickey Rivers .60 1.50
165 Doug Rader .60 1.50
166 Woodie Fryman .30 .75
167 Rich Coggins .30 .75
168 Bill Greif .30 .75
169 Cookie Rojas .30 .75
170 Bert Campaneris .60 1.50
171 Ed Kirkpatrick .30 .75
172 Red Sox Team CL(Darrell
Johnson MG 1.50 4.00
173 Steve Rogers .60 1.50
174 Bake McBride .60 1.50
175 Don Money .60 1.50
176 Burt Hooton .60 1.50
177 Vic Correll .30 .75
178 Cesar Tovar .30 .75
179 Tom Bradley .30 .75
180 Joe Morgan 3.00 8.00
181 Fred Beene .30 .75
182 Don Hahn .30 .75
183 Mel Stottlemyre .60 1.50
184 Jorge Orta .30 .75
185 Steve Carlton 4.00 10.00
186 Willie Crawford .30 .75
187 Denny Doyle .30 .75
188 Tom Griffin .30 .75
189 Y.Berra 2.50 6.00
R.Campanella MVP
190 Bobby Shantz 1.00 2.50
Hank Sauer MVP
191 Al Rosen 1.00 2.50
R.Campanella MV
192 Yogi Berra 2.50 6.00
W.Mays MVP
193 Y.Berra 1.50 4.00
R.Campanella MVP
194 M.Mantle 6.00 15.00
D.Newcombe MVP
195 Mickey Mantle 8.00 20.00
H.Aaron MV
196 Jackie Jensen 1.00 2.50
Ernie Banks MVP
197 Nellie Fox 1.50 4.00
E.Banks MVP
198 Roger Maris 1.00 2.50
Dick Groat MVP
199 Rog.Maris 1.50 4.00
F.Robinson MVP
200 Mickey Mantle 6.00 15.00
M.Wills MV
201 Els.Howard 1.00 2.50
S.Koufax MVP
202 B.Robinson 1.00 2.50
K.Boyer MVP
203 Zoilo Versalles 1.00 2.50
W.Mays M
204 R.Clemente 3.00 8.00
F.Robinson MV
205 C.Yastrzemski 1.00 2.50
Cepeda MVP
206 Denny McLain 1.00 2.50
B.Gibson MV
207 H.Killebrew 1.00 2.50
W.McCovey MV
208 Boog Powell 1.00 2.50
J.Bench MVP
209 Vida Blue 1.00 2.50
Joe Torre MVP
210 Dick Allen 1.00 2.50
J.Bench MVP
211 Reggie Jackson 3.00 8.00
P.Rose MV
212 Jeff Burroughs 1.00 2.50
Steve Garvey MVP
213 Oscar Gamble .60 1.50
214 Harry Parker .30 .75
215 Bobby Valentine .60 1.50
216 Giants Team CL 1.00 2.50
Wes Westrum MG
217 Lou Piniella 1.00 2.50
218 Jerry Johnson .30 .75
219 Ed Herrmann .30 .75
220 Don Sutton 1.50 4.00
221 Aurelio Rodriguez .30 .75
222 Dan Spillner .30 .75
223 Robin Yount RC 30.00 60.00
224 Ramon Hernandez .30 .75
225 Bob Grich .60 1.50
226 Bill Campbell .30 .75
227 Bob Watson .60 1.50
228 George Brett RC 50.00 100.00
229 Barry Foote .60 1.50
230 Jim Hunter 2.00 5.00
231 Mike Tyson .30 .75
232 Diego Segui .30 .75
233 Billy Grabarkewitz .30 .75
234 Tom Grieve .60 1.50
235 Jack Billingham .60 1.50
236 Angels Team CL 1.00 2.50
Willie Williams MG
237 Carl Morton .30 .75
238 Dave Duncan .60 1.50

239 George Stone .30 .75
240 Garry Maddox .60 1.50
241 Dick Tidrow .30 .75
242 Jay Johnstone .60 1.50
243 Jim Kaat 1.00 2.50
244 Bill Buckner .60 1.50
245 Mickey Lolich 1.00 2.50
246 Cardinals Team CL 1.00 2.50
Red Schoendienst MG
247 Enos Cabell .30 .75
248 Randy Jones 1.00 2.50
249 Danny Thompson .30 .75
250 Ken Brett .30 .75
251 Fran Healy .30 .75
252 Fred Scherman .30 .75
253 Jesus Alou .30 .75
254 Mike Torrez .60 1.50
255 Dwight Evans 1.00 2.50
256 Billy Champion .30 .75
257 Checklist 133-264 1.50 4.00
258 Dave LaRoche .30 .75
259 Len Randle .30 .75
260 Johnny Bench 8.00 20.00
261 Andy Hassler .30 .75
262 Rowland Office .30 .75
263 Jim Perry .60 1.50
264 John Milner .30 .75
265 Ron Bryant .30 .75
266 Sandy Alomar .60 1.50
267 Dick Ruthven .30 .75
268 Hal McRae .60 1.50
269 Doug Rau .30 .75
270 Ron Fairly .60 1.50
271 Jerry Moses .30 .75
272 Lynn McGlothen .30 .75
273 Steve Braun .30 .75
274 Vicente Romo .30 .75
275 Paul Blair .60 1.50
276 White Sox Team CL 1.00 2.50
Chuck Tanner MG
277 Frank Taveras .30 .75
278 Paul Lindblad .30 .75
279 Milt May .30 .75
280 Carl Yastrzemski 6.00 15.00
281 Jim Slaton .30 .75
282 Jerry Morales .30 .75
283 Steve Foucault .30 .75
284 Ken Griffey Sr. 2.00 5.00
285 Ellie Rodriguez .30 .75
286 Mike Jorgensen .30 .75
287 Roric Harrison .30 .75
288 Bruce Ellingsen .30 .75
289 Ken Rudolph .30 .75
290 Jon Matlack .30 .75
291 Bill Sudakis .30 .75
292 Ron Schueler .30 .75
293 Dick Sharon .30 .75
294 Geoff Zahn .30 .75
295 Vada Pinson 1.00 2.50
296 Alan Foster .30 .75
297 Craig Kusick .30 .75
298 Johnny Grubb .30 .75
299 Bucky Dent 1.00 2.50
300 Reggie Jackson 8.00 20.00
301 Dave Roberts .30 .75
302 Rick Burleson .60 1.50
303 Grant Jackson .30 .75
304 Pirates Team CL 1.00 2.50
Danny Murtaugh MG
305 Jim Colborn .30 .75
306 Rod Carew 1.00 2.50
R.Garr LL
307 Dick Allen 2.00 5.00
M.Schmidt LL
308 Jeff Burroughs 1.00 2.50
Bench LL
309 Billy North 1.00 2.50
Brock LL
310 Hunter 1.00 2.50
Jenk
Niekro LL
311 Jim Hunter 1.00 2.50
B.Capra LL
312 Nolan Ryan 8.00 20.00
S.Carlton LL
313 Terry Forster .60 1.50
Mike Marshall LL
314 Buck Martinez .30 .75
315 Don Kessinger .60 1.50
316 Jackie Brown .30 .75
317 Joe Lahoud .30 .75
318 Ernie McAnally .30 .75
319 Johnny Oates .30 .75
320 Pete Rose 12.50 40.00
321 Rudy May .30 .75
322 Ed Goodson .30 .75
323 Fred Holdsworth .30 .75
324 Ed Kranepool .60 1.50
325 Tony Oliva 1.00 2.50
326 Wayne Twitchell .30 .75
327 Jerry Hairston .30 .75
328 Sonny Siebert .30 .75
329 Ted Kubiak .30 .75
330 Mike Marshall .60 1.50
331 Indians Team CL(Frank
Robinson MG 1.00 2.50
332 Fred Kendall .30 .75
333 Dick Drago .30 .75
334 Greg Gross .30 .75
335 Jim Palmer 3.00 8.00
336 Rennie Stennett .30 .75
337 Kevin Kobel .30 .75
338 Rick Stelmaszek .30 .75
339 Jim Fregosi .60 1.50
340 Paul Splittorff .30 .75
341 Hal Breeden .30 .75
342 Leroy Stanton .30 .75
343 Danny Frisella .30 .75
344 Ben Oglivie .60 1.50
345 Clay Carroll .60 1.50
346 Bobby Darwin .30 .75
347 Mike Caldwell .30 .75
348 Tony Muser .30 .75
349 Ray Sadecki .30 .75
350 Bobby Murcer .60 1.50
351 Bob Boone 1.00 2.50
352 Darold Knowles .30 .75
353 Luis Melendez .30 .75
354 Dick Bosman .30 .75
355 Chris Cannizzaro .30 .75
356 Rico Petrocelli .60 1.50
357 Ken Forsch .30 .75
358 Al Bumbry .60 1.50
359 Paul Popovich .30 .75
360 George Scott .60 1.50
361 Dodgers Team CL 1.00 2.50
Walter Alston MG
362 Steve Hargan .30 .75
363 Carmen Fanzone .30 .75
364 Doug Bird .30 .75
365 Bob Bailey .30 .75
366 Ken Sanders .30 .75
367 Craig Robinson .30 .75
368 Vic Albury .30 .75
369 Merv Rettenmund .30 .75
370 Tom Seaver 6.00 15.00
371 Gates Brown .30 .75
372 John D'Acquisto .30 .75
373 Bill Sharp .30 .75
374 Eddie Watt .30 .75
375 Roy White .60 1.50
376 Steve Yeager .60 1.50
377 Tom Hilgendorf .30 .75
378 Derrel Thomas .30 .75
379 Bernie Carbo .30 .75
380 Sal Bando .60 1.50
381 John Curtis .30 .75
382 Don Baylor 1.00 2.50
383 Jim York .30 .75
384 Brewers Team CL 1.00 2.50
Del Crandall MG
385 Dock Ellis .30 .75
386 Checklist 265-396 1.50 4.00
387 Jim Spencer .30 .75
388 Steve Stone .60 1.50
389 Tony Solaita .30 .75
390 Ron Cey 1.00 2.50
391 Don DeMola .30 .75
392 Bruce Bochte RC .60 1.50
393 Gary Gentry .30 .75
394 Larvell Blanks .30 .75
395 Bud Harrelson .60 1.50
396 Fred Norman .60 1.50
397 Bill Freehan .60 1.50
398 Elias Sosa .30 .75
399 Terry Harmon .30 .75
400 Dick Allen 1.00 2.50
401 Mike Wallace .30 .75
402 Bob Tolan .30 .75
403 Tom Buskey .30 .75
404 Ted Sizemore .30 .75
405 John Montague .30 .75
406 Bob Gallagher .30 .75
407 Herb Washington RC 1.00 2.50
408 Clyde Wright .30 .75
409 Bob Robertson .30 .75
410 Mike Cueller .60 1.50
sic, Cuellar
411 George Mitterwald .30 .75
412 Bill Hands .30 .75
413 Marty Pattin .30 .75
414 Manny Mota .60 1.50
415 John Hiller .60 1.50
416 Larry Lintz .30 .75
417 Skip Lockwood .30 .75
418 Leo Foster .30 .75
419 Dave Goltz .30 .75
420 Larry Bowa 1.00 2.50
421 Mets Team CL 1.50 4.00
Yogi Berra MG
422 Brian Downing .60 1.50
423 Clay Kirby .30 .75
424 John Lowenstein .30 .75
425 Tito Fuentes .30 .75
426 George Medich .30 .75
427 Clarence Gaston .60 1.50
428 Dave Hamilton .30 .75
429 Jim Dwyer .30 .75
430 Luis Tiant 1.00 2.50
431 Rod Gilbreath .30 .75
432 Ken Berry .30 .75
433 Larry Demery .30 .75
434 Bob Locker .30 .75
435 Dave Nelson .30 .75
436 Ken Frailing .30 .75
437 Al Cowens .60 1.50
438 Don Carrithers .30 .75
439 Ed Brinkman .30 .75
440 Andy Messersmith .60 1.50
441 Bobby Heise .30 .75
442 Maximino Leon .30 .75
443 Twins Team 1.00 2.50
Frank Quilici MG
444 Gene Garber .60 1.50
445 Felix Millan .30 .75
446 Bart Johnson .30 .75
447 Terry Crowley .30 .75
448 Frank Duffy .30 .75
449 Charlie Williams .30 .75
450 Willie McCovey 3.00 8.00
451 Rick Dempsey .60 1.50
452 Angel Mangual .30 .75
453 Claude Osteen .60 1.50
454 Doug Griffin .30 .75
455 Don Wilson .30 .75
456 Bob Coluccio .30 .75
457 Mario Mendoza .30 .75
458 Ross Grimsley .30 .75
459 1974 AL Champs .60 1.50
A's over Orioles/(Second base
ac
460 Steve Garvey NLCS 1.00 2.50
461 Reggie Jackson WS1 2.50 6.00
462 World Series Game 2
(Dodger dugout) .60 1.50
463 Rollie Fingers WS3 1.00 2.50
464 World Series Game 4/(A's batter) .60 1.50
465 Joe Rudi WS .60 1.50
466 WS Summary 1.00 2.50
A's
467 Ed Halicki .30 .75
468 Bobby Mitchell .30 .75
469 Tom Dettore .30 .75
470 Jeff Burroughs .60 1.50
471 Bob Stinson .30 .75
472 Bruce Dal Canton .30 .75
473 Ken McMullen .30 .75
474 Luke Walker .30 .75
475 Darrell Evans .60 1.50
476 Ed Figueroa .30 .75
477 Tom Hutton .30 .75
478 Tom Burgmeier .30 .75
479 Ken Boswell .30 .75
480 Carlos May .30 .75
481 Will McEnaney .60 1.50
482 Tom McCraw .30 .75
483 Steve Ontiveros .30 .75
484 Glenn Beckert .60 1.50
485 Sparky Lyle .60 1.50
486 Ray Fosse .30 .75
487 Astros Team CL 1.00 2.50
Preston Gomez MG
488 Bill Travers .30 .75
489 Cecil Cooper 1.00 2.50
490 Reggie Smith .60 1.50
491 Doyle Alexander .60 1.50
492 Rich Hebner .60 1.50
493 Don Stanhouse .30 .75
494 Pete LaCock .30 .75
495 Nelson Briles .60 1.50
496 Pepe Frias .30 .75
497 Jim Nettles .30 .75
498 Al Downing .30 .75
499 Marty Perez .30 .75
500 Nolan Ryan 40.00 80.00
501 Bill Robinson .60 1.50
502 Pat Bourque .30 .75
503 Fred Stanley .30 .75
504 Buddy Bradford .30 .75
505 Chris Speier .30 .75
506 Leron Lee .30 .75
507 Tom Carroll .30 .75
508 Bob Hansen .30 .75
509 Dave Hilton .30 .75
510 Vida Blue .60 1.50
511 Rangers Team CL 1.00 2.50
Billy Martin MG
512 Larry Milbourne .30 .75
513 Dick Pole .30 .75
514 Jose Cruz 1.00 2.50
515 Manny Sanguillen .60 1.50
516 Don Hood .30 .75
517 Checklist 397-528 1.50 4.00
518 Leo Cardenas .30 .75
519 Jim Todd .30 .75
520 Amos Otis .60 1.50
521 Dennis Blair .30 .75
522 Gary Sutherland .30 .75
523 Tom Paciorek .60 1.50
524 John Doherty .30 .75
525 Tom House .30 .75
526 Larry Hisle .60 1.50
527 Mac Scarce .30 .75
528 Eddie Leon .30 .75
529 Gary Thomasson .30 .75
530 Gaylord Perry 1.50 4.00
531 Reds Team 2.50 6.00
532 Gorman Thomas .60 1.50
533 Rudy Meoli .30 .75
534 Alex Johnson .30 .75
535 Gene Tenace .60 1.50
536 Bob Moose .30 .75
537 Tommy Harper .60 1.50
538 Duffy Dyer .30 .75
539 Jesse Jefferson .30 .75
540 Lou Brock 3.00 8.00
541 Roger Metzger .30 .75
542 Pete Broberg .30 .75
543 Larry Biittner .30 .75
544 Steve Mingori .30 .75
545 Billy Williams 1.50 4.00
546 John Knox .30 .75
547 Von Joshua .30 .75
548 Charlie Sands .30 .75
549 Bill Butler .30 .75
550 Ralph Garr .60 1.50
551 Larry Christenson .30 .75
552 Jack Brohamer .30 .75
553 John Boccabella .30 .75
554 Goose Gossage 1.00 2.50
555 Al Oliver 1.00 2.50
556 Tim Johnson .30 .75
557 Larry Gura .30 .75
558 Dave Roberts .30 .75
559 Bob Montgomery .30 .75
560 Tony Perez 2.00 5.00
561 A's Team CL 1.00 2.50
Alvin Dark MG
562 Gary Nolan .60 1.50
563 Wilbur Howard .30 .75
564 Tommy Davis .60 1.50
565 Joe Torre 1.00 2.50
566 Ray Burris .30 .75
567 Jim Sundberg RC 1.00 2.50
568 Dale Murray .30 .75
569 Frank White .60 1.50
570 Jim Wynn .60 1.50
571 Dave Lemanczyk .30 .75
572 Roger Nelson .30 .75
573 Orlando Pena .30 .75
574 Tony Taylor .30 .75
575 Gene Clines .30 .75
576 Phil Roof .30 .75
577 John Morris .30 .75
578 Dave Tomlin .30 .75
579 Skip Pitlock .30 .75
580 Frank Robinson 3.00 8.00
581 Darrel Chaney .30 .75
582 Eduardo Rodriguez .30 .75
583 Andy Etchebarren .30 .75
584 Mike Garman .30 .75
585 Chris Chambliss .60 1.50
586 Tim McCarver 1.00 2.50
587 Chris Ward .30 .75
588 Rick Auerbach .30 .75
589 Braves Team CL 1.00 2.50
Clyde King MG
590 Cesar Cedeno .60 1.50
591 Glenn Abbott .30 .75
592 Balor Moore .30 .75
593 Gene Lamont .30 .75
594 Jim Fuller .30 .75
595 Joe Niekro .60 1.50
596 Ollie Brown .30 .75
597 Winston Llenas .30 .75
598 Bruce Kison .30 .75
599 Nate Colbert .30 .75
600 Rod Carew 4.00 10.00
601 Juan Beniquez .30 .75
602 John Vukovich .30 .75
603 Lew Krausse .30 .75
604 Oscar Zamora .30 .75
605 John Ellis .30 .75
606 Bruce Miller .30 .75
607 Jim Holt .30 .75
608 Gene Michael .30 .75
609 Elrod Hendricks .30 .75
610 Ron Hunt .30 .75
611 Yankees: Team 1.00 2.50
MG
Bill Virdon
612 Terry Hughes .30 .75
613 Bill Parsons .30 .75
614 Rookie Pitchers .60 1.50
Jack Kucek
Dyar Miller
Vern Ruh
615 Dennis Leonard RC 1.00 2.50
616 Jim Rice RC 8.00 20.00
617 Doug DeCinces RC 1.00 2.50
618 Rick Rhoden .60 1.50
McGregor RC
619 Rookie Outfielders .60 1.50
Benny Ayala
Nyls Nyman
Tommy
620 Gary Carter RC 10.00 25.00
621 John Denny RC 1.00 2.50
622 Fred Lynn RC 4.00 10.00
623 K.Hernandez 5.00 12.00
P.Garner RC
624 Rookie Pitchers .60 1.50
Doug Konieczny
Gary Lavelle
Jim
625 Boog Powell 1.00 2.50
626 Larry Haney/(photo actually .30 .75
Dave Duncan)
627 Tom Walker .30 .75
628 Ron LeFlore RC .60 1.50
629 Joe Hoerner .30 .75
630 Greg Luzinski 1.00 2.50
631 Lee Lacy .30 .75
632 Morris Nettles .30 .75
633 Paul Casanova .30 .75
634 Cy Acosta .30 .75
635 Chuck Dobson .30 .75
636 Charlie Moore .30 .75
637 Ted Martinez .30 .75
638 Cubs Team CL 1.00 2.50
Jim Marshall MG
639 Steve Kline .30 .75
640 Harmon Killebrew 3.00 8.00
641 Jim Northrup .60 1.50
642 Mike Phillips .30 .75
643 Brent Strom .30 .75
644 Bill Fahey .30 .75
645 Danny Cater .30 .75
646 Checklist 529-660 1.50 4.00
647 Claudell Washington RC 1.00 2.50
648 Dave Pagan .60 1.50
649 Jack Heidemann .30 .75
650 Dave May .30 .75
651 John Morlan .30 .75
652 Lindy McDaniel .60 1.50
653 Lee Richard .30 .75
654 Jerry Terrell .30 .75
655 Rico Carty .60 1.50
656 Bill Plummer .30 .75
657 Bob Oliver .30 .75
658 Vic Harris .30 .75
659 Bob Apodaca .30 .75
660 Hank Aaron 12.50 40.00

1976 O-Pee-Chee

This is a 660-card standard-size set. The 1976 O-Pee-Chee cards are very similar to the 1976 Topps cards, yet rather different from previous years' issues. The most prominent change is that the backs are much brighter than their American counterparts. The cards parallel the American issue and it is a challenge to find well centered examples of these cards. Notable Rookie Cards include Dennis Eckersley and Ron Guidry.

COMPLETE SET (660) 400.00 800.00
1 Hank Aaron RB 10.00 25.00
Most RBI's, 2262
2 Bobby Bonds RB 1.25 3.00
Most leadoff
homers& 32;
Plus 3
3 Mickey Lolich RB .60 1.50
Lefthander& Most
Strikeouts 267
4 Dave Lopes RB .60 1.50
Most consecutive
SB attempts& 38
5 Tom Seaver RB 3.00 8.00
Most cons. seasons
with 200 SO's&
6 Rennie Stennett RB .60 1.50
Most hits in a 9
inning game&
7 Jim Umbarger .30 .75
8 Tito Fuentes .30 .75
9 Paul Lindblad .30 .75
10 Lou Brock 3.00 8.00
11 Jim Hughes .30 .75
12 Richie Zisk .60 1.50
13 John Wockenfuss .30 .75
14 Gene Garber .60 1.50
15 George Scott .60 1.50
16 Bob Apodaca .30 .75
17 New York Yankees 1.25 3.00
Team Card
18 Dale Murray .30 .75
19 George Brett 30.00 60.00
20 Bob Watson .60 1.50
21 Dave LaRoche .30 .75
22 Bill Russell .60 1.50
23 Brian Downing .30 .75
24 Cesar Geronimo .60 1.50
25 Mike Torrez .60 1.50
26 Andre Thornton .60 1.50
27 Ed Figueroa .30 .75
28 Dusty Baker 1.25 3.00
29 Rick Burleson .60 1.50
30 John Montefusco RC .60 1.50
31 Len Randle .30 .75
32 Danny Frisella .30 .75
33 Bill North .30 .75
34 Mike Garman .30 .75
35 Tony Oliva 1.25 3.00
36 Frank Taveras .30 .75
37 John Hiller .60 1.50
38 Garry Maddox .60 1.50
39 Pete Broberg .30 .75
40 Dave Kingman 1.25 3.00
41 Tippy Martinez .60 1.50
42 Barry Foote .60 1.50
43 Paul Splittorff .30 .75
44 Doug Rader .60 1.50
45 Boog Powell 1.25 3.00
46 Los Angeles Dodgers 1.25 3.00
Team Card
Walt Alston MG/(C
47 Jesse Jefferson .30 .75
48 Dave Concepcion 1.25 3.00
49 Dave Duncan .60 1.50
50 Fred Lynn 1.25 3.00
51 Ray Burris .30 .75
52 Dave Chalk .30 .75
53 Mike Beard RC .30 .75
54 Dave Rader .30 .75
55 Gaylord Perry 2.00 5.00
56 Bob Tolan .30 .75
57 Phil Garner .60 1.50
58 Ron Reed .60 1.50
59 Larry Hisle .60 1.50
60 Jerry Reuss .60 1.50
61 Ron LeFlore .60 1.50
62 Johnny Oates .60 1.50
63 Bobby Darwin .30 .75
64 Jerry Koosman .60 1.50
65 Chris Chambliss .60 1.50
66 Father and Son .60 1.50
Gus
Buddy Bell
67 Bob .60 1.50
Ray Boone FS
68 Father and Son .30 .75
Joe Coleman
Joe Coleman Jr.
69 Father and Son .30 .75
Jim
Mike Hegan
70 Father and Son .60 1.50
Roy Smalley
Roy Smalley Jr.
71 Steve Rogers 1.25 3.00
72 Hal McRae .60 1.50
73 Baltimore Orioles 1.25 3.00
Team Card
Earl Weaver MG/(Che
74 Oscar Gamble .60 1.50
75 Larry Dierker .60 1.50
76 Willie Crawford .30 .75
77 Pedro Borbon .60 1.50
78 Cecil Cooper .60 1.50
79 Jerry Morales .30 .75
80 Jim Kaat 1.50 4.00
81 Darrell Evans .60 1.50
82 Von Joshua .30 .75
83 Jim Spencer .30 .75
84 Brent Strom .30 .75
85 Mickey Rivers .60 1.50
86 Mike Tyson .30 .75
87 Tom Burgmeier .30 .75
88 Duffy Dyer .30 .75
89 Vern Ruhle .30 .75
90 Sal Bando .60 1.50
91 Tom Hutton .30 .75
92 Eduardo Rodriguez .30 .75
93 Mike Phillips .30 .75
94 Jim Dwyer .30 .75
95 Brooks Robinson 4.00 10.00
96 Doug Bird .30 .75
97 Wilbur Howard .30 .75
98 Dennis Eckersley RC 20.00 50.00
99 Lee Lacy .30 .75
100 Jim Hunter 2.00 5.00
101 Pete LaCock .30 .75
102 Jim Willoughby .30 .75
103 Biff Pocoroba RC .30 .75
104 Reds Team 1.50 4.00
105 Gary Lavelle .30 .75
106 Tom Grieve .60 1.50
107 Dave Roberts .30 .75
108 Don Kirkwood .30 .75
109 Larry Lintz .30 .75
110 Carlos May .30 .75
111 Danny Thompson .30 .75
112 Kent Tekulve RC 1.25 3.00
113 Gary Sutherland .30 .75
114 Jay Johnstone .60 1.50
115 Ken Holtzman .60 1.50
116 Charlie Moore .30 .75
117 Mike Jorgensen .30 .75
118 Boston Red Sox 1.25 3.00
Team Card
Darrell Johnson/(Check
119 Checklist 1-132 1.25 3.00
120 Rusty Staub .60 1.50
121 Tony Solaita .30 .75
122 Mike Cosgrove .30 .75
123 Walt Williams .30 .75
124 Doug Rau .30 .75
125 Don Baylor 1.50 4.00
126 Tom Dettore .30 .75
127 Larvell Blanks .30 .75
128 Ken Griffey Sr. 1.50 4.00
129 Andy Etchebarren .30 .75
130 Luis Tiant 1.25 3.00
131 Bill Stein .30 .75
132 Don Hood .30 .75
133 Gary Matthews .60 1.50
134 Mike Ivie .30 .75
135 Bake McBride .60 1.50
136 Dave Goltz .30 .75
137 Bill Robinson .60 1.50
138 Lerrin LaGrow .30 .75
139 Gorman Thomas .60 1.50
140 Vida Blue .60 1.50
141 Larry Parrish RC 1.25 3.00
142 Dick Drago .30 .75
143 Jerry Grote .30 .75
144 Al Fitzmorris .30 .75
145 Larry Bowa .60 1.50
146 George Medich .30 .75
147 Houston Astros 1.25 3.00
Team Card
Bill Virdon MG/(Checkl
148 Stan Thomas .30 .75
149 Tommy Davis .60 1.50
150 Steve Garvey 1.50 4.00
151 Bill Bonham .30 .75
152 Leroy Stanton .30 .75
153 Buzz Capra .30 .75
154 Bucky Dent .60 1.50
155 Jack Billingham .60 1.50
156 Rico Carty .60 1.50
157 Mike Caldwell .30 .75
158 Ken Reitz .30 .75
159 Jerry Terrell .30 .75
160 Dave Winfield 8.00 20.00
161 Bruce Kison .30 .75
162 Jack Pierce .30 .75
163 Jim Slaton .30 .75
164 Pepe Mangual .30 .75
165 Gene Tenace .60 1.50
166 Skip Lockwood .30 .75
167 Freddie Patek .60 1.50
168 Tom Hilgendorf .30 .75
169 Graig Nettles 1.25 3.00
170 Rick Wise .30 .75
171 Greg Gross .30 .75
172 Texas Rangers 1.25 3.00
Team Card
Frank Lucchesi MG/(Chec
173 Steve Swisher .30 .75
174 Charlie Hough .60 1.50
175 Ken Singleton .60 1.50
176 Dick Lange .30 .75
177 Marty Perez .30 .75
178 Tom Buskey .30 .75
179 George Foster 1.25 3.00
180 Goose Gossage 1.50 4.00
181 Willie Montanez .30 .75
182 Harry Rasmussen .30 .75
183 Steve Braun .30 .75
184 Bill Greif .30 .75
185 Dave Parker 1.50 4.00
186 Tom Walker .30 .75
187 Pedro Garcia .30 .75
188 Fred Scherman .30 .75
189 Claudell Washington .60 1.50
190 Jon Matlack .30 .75
191 NL Batting Leaders .60 1.50
Bill Madlock
Ted Simmons
Man
192 R.Carew 1.50 4.00
Lynn
T.Munson LL
193 Schmidt 2.00 5.00
Kingman
Luz LL
194 Reggie 2.00 5.00
Scott
Mayb LL
195 Luzin 1.25 3.00
Bench
Perez LL
196 AL RBI Leaders .60 1.50
George Scott
John Mayberry
Fred
197 Lopes 1.25 3.00
Morgan
Brock LL
198 AL Steals Leaders .60 1.50
Mickey Rivers
Claudell Washing
199 Seaver 1.50 4.00
Jones
Messers LL
200 Hunter 1.25 3.00
Palmer
Blue LL
201 R.Jones 1.25 3.00
Messer
Seaver LL
202 Palmer 2.00 5.00
Hunter
Eck LL
203 Seaver 1.50 4.00
Montef
Messer LL
204 Tanana .60 1.50
Blylev
Perry LL
205 Leading Firemen .60 1.50
Al Hrabosky
Rich Gossage
206 Manny Trillo .30 .75
207 Andy Hassler .30 .75
208 Mike Lum .30 .75
209 Alan Ashby .60 1.50
210 Lee May .60 1.50
211 Clay Carroll .60 1.50
212 Pat Kelly .30 .75
213 Dave Heaverlo .30 .75
214 Eric Soderholm .30 .75
215 Reggie Smith .60 1.50
216 Montreal Expos 1.25 3.00
Team Card
Karl Kuehl MG/(Checkli
217 Dave Freisleben .30 .75
218 John Knox .30 .75
219 Tom Murphy .30 .75
220 Manny Sanguillen .60 1.50
221 Jim Todd .30 .75
222 Wayne Garrett .30 .75
223 Ollie Brown .30 .75
224 Jim York .30 .75
225 Roy White .60 1.50
226 Jim Sundberg .60 1.50
227 Oscar Zamora .30 .75
228 John Hale .30 .75
229 Jerry Remy .30 .75
230 Carl Yastrzemski 6.00 15.00
231 Tom House .30 .75
232 Frank Duffy .30 .75
233 Grant Jackson .30 .75
234 Mike Sadek .30 .75
235 Bert Blyleven 1.50 4.00
236 Kansas City Royals 1.25 3.00
Team Card
Whitey Herzog MG/(
237 Dave Hamilton .30 .75

238 Larry Biittner .30 .75
239 John Curtis .30 .75
240 Pete Rose 12.50 40.00
241 Hector Torres .30 .75
242 Dan Meyer .30 .75
243 Jim Rooker .30 .75
244 Bill Sharp .30 .75
245 Felix Millan .30 .75
246 Cesar Tovar .30 .75
247 Terry Harmon .30 .75
248 Dick Tidrow .30 .75
249 Cliff Johnson .60 1.50
250 Fergie Jenkins 2.00 5.00
251 Rick Monday .60 1.50
252 Tim Nordbrook .30 .75
253 Bill Buckner .60 1.50
254 Rudy Meoli .30 .75
255 Fritz Peterson .30 .75
256 Rowland Office .30 .75
257 Ross Grimsley .30 .75
258 Nyls Nyman .30 .75
259 Darrel Chaney .30 .75
260 Steve Busby .30 .75
261 Gary Thomasson .30 .75
262 Checklist 133-264 1.25 3.00
263 Lyman Bostock RC 1.25 3.00
264 Steve Renko .30 .75
265 Willie Davis .60 1.50
266 Alan Foster .30 .75
267 Aurelio Rodriguez .30 .75
268 Del Unser .30 .75
269 Rick Austin .30 .75
270 Willie Stargell 2.00 5.00
271 Jim Lonborg .60 1.50
272 Rick Dempsey .60 1.50
273 Joe Niekro .60 1.50
274 Tommy Harper .60 1.50
275 Rick Manning .30 .75
276 Mickey Scott .30 .75
277 Chicago Cubs 1.25 3.00
Team Card
Jim Marshall MG/(Checkli
278 Bernie Carbo .30 .75
279 Roy Howell .30 .75
280 Burt Hooton .60 1.50
281 Dave May .30 .75
282 Dan Osborn .30 .75
283 Merv Rettenmund .30 .75
284 Steve Ontiveros .30 .75
285 Mike Cuellar .60 1.50
286 Jim Wohlford .30 .75
287 Pete Mackanin .30 .75
288 Bill Campbell .30 .75
289 Enzo Hernandez .30 .75
290 Ted Simmons .60 1.50
291 Ken Sanders .30 .75
292 Leon Roberts .30 .75
293 Bill Castro .30 .75
294 Ed Kirkpatrick .30 .75
295 Dave Cash .30 .75
296 Pat Dobson .30 .75
297 Roger Metzger .30 .75
298 Dick Bosman .30 .75
299 Champ Summers .30 .75
300 Johnny Bench 8.00 20.00
301 Jackie Brown .30 .75
302 Rick Miller .30 .75
303 Steve Foucault .30 .75
304 California Angels 1.25 3.00
Team Card
Dick Williams MG/(C
305 Andy Messersmith .60 1.50
306 Rod Gilbreath .30 .75
307 Al Bumbry .60 1.50
308 Jim Barr .30 .75
309 Bill Melton .30 .75
310 Randy Jones .60 1.50
311 Cookie Rojas .30 .75
312 Don Carrithers .30 .75
313 Dan Ford .30 .75
314 Ed Kranepool .30 .75
315 Al Hrabosky .60 1.50
316 Robin Yount 10.00 25.00
317 John Candelaria RC 1.25 3.00
318 Bob Boone 1.25 3.00
319 Larry Gura .30 .75
320 Willie Horton .60 1.50
321 Jose Cruz 1.25 3.00
322 Glenn Abbott .30 .75
323 Rob Sperring .30 .75
324 Jim Bibby .30 .75
325 Tony Perez 2.00 5.00
326 Dick Pole .30 .75
327 Dave Moates .30 .75
328 Carl Morton .30 .75
329 Joe Ferguson .30 .75
330 Nolan Ryan 20.00 50.00
331 San Diego Padres 1.25 3.00
Team Card
John McNamara MG/(Ch
332 Charlie Williams .30 .75
333 Bob Coluccio .30 .75
334 Dennis Leonard .60 1.50
335 Bob Grich .60 1.50
336 Vic Albury .60 1.50
337 Bud Harrelson .60 1.50
338 Bob Bailey .30 .75
339 John Denny .60 1.50
340 Jim Rice 2.50 6.00
341 Lou Gehrig ATG 8.00 20.00
342 Rogers Hornsby ATG 1.50 4.00
343 Pie Traynor ATG 1.25 3.00
344 Honus Wagner ATG 3.00 8.00
345 Babe Ruth ATG 10.00 25.00
346 Ty Cobb ATG 8.00 20.00
347 Ted Williams ATG 8.00 20.00
348 Mickey Cochrane ATG 1.25 3.00
349 Walter Johnson ATG 3.00 8.00
350 Lefty Grove ATG 1.25 3.00
351 Randy Hundley .60 1.50
352 Dave Giusti .30 .75
353 Sixto Lezcano .60 1.50
354 Ron Blomberg .30 .75
355 Steve Carlton 4.00 10.00
356 Ted Martinez .30 .75
357 Ken Forsch .30 .75
358 Buddy Bell .60 1.50
359 Rick Reuschel .60 1.50
360 Jeff Burroughs .60 1.50
361 Detroit Tigers 1.25 3.00
Team Card
Ralph Houk MG/(Checkli
362 Will McEnaney .60 1.50
363 Dave Collins RC .60 1.50
364 Elias Sosa .30 .75
365 Carlton Fisk 3.00 8.00
366 Bobby Valentine .60 1.50
367 Bruce Miller .30 .75
368 Wilbur Wood .30 .75
369 Frank White .60 1.50
370 Ron Cey .60 1.50
371 Ellie Hendricks .30 .75
372 Rick Baldwin .30 .75
373 Johnny Briggs .30 .75
374 Dan Warthen .30 .75
375 Ron Fairly .60 1.50
376 Rich Hebner .60 1.50
377 Mike Hegan .30 .75
378 Steve Stone .60 1.50
379 Ken Boswell .30 .75
380 Bobby Bonds 1.50 4.00
381 Denny Doyle .30 .75
382 Matt Alexander .30 .75
383 John Ellis .30 .75
384 Philadelphia Phillies 1.25 3.00
Team Card
Danny Ozark MG/
385 Mickey Lolich .60 1.50
386 Ed Goodson .30 .75
387 Mike Miley .30 .75
388 Stan Perzanowski .30 .75
389 Glenn Adams .30 .75
390 Don Gullett .60 1.50
391 Jerry Hairston .30 .75
392 Checklist 265-396 1.25 3.00
393 Paul Mitchell .30 .75
394 Fran Healy .30 .75
395 Jim Wynn .60 1.50
396 Bill Lee .30 .75
397 Tim Foli .30 .75
398 Dave Tomlin .30 .75
399 Luis Melendez .30 .75
400 Rod Carew 3.00 8.00
401 Ken Brett .30 .75
402 Don Money .60 1.50
403 Geoff Zahn .30 .75
404 Enos Cabell .30 .75
405 Rollie Fingers 2.00 5.00
406 Ed Herrmann .30 .75
407 Tom Underwood .30 .75
408 Charlie Spikes .30 .75
409 Dave Lemanczyk .30 .75
410 Ralph Garr .60 1.50
411 Bill Singer .30 .75
412 Toby Harrah .60 1.50
413 Pete Varney .30 .75
414 Wayne Garland .30 .75
415 Vada Pinson 1.50 4.00
416 Tommy John 1.50 4.00
417 Gene Clines .30 .75
418 Jose Morales RC .60 1.50
419 Reggie Cleveland .30 .75
420 Joe Morgan 3.00 8.00
421 Oakland A's 1.25 3.00
Team Card/(No MG on front;
checklis
422 Johnny Grubb .30 .75
423 Ed Halicki .30 .75
424 Phil Roof .30 .75
425 Rennie Stennett .30 .75
426 Bob Forsch .30 .75
427 Kurt Bevacqua .30 .75
428 Jim Crawford .30 .75
429 Fred Stanley .30 .75
430 Jose Cardenal .60 1.50
431 Dick Ruthven .30 .75
432 Tom Veryzer .30 .75
433 Rick Waits .30 .75
434 Morris Nettles .30 .75
435 Phil Niekro 2.00 5.00
436 Bill Fahey .30 .75
437 Terry Forster .30 .75
438 Doug DeCinces .60 1.50
439 Rick Rhoden .60 1.50
440 John Mayberry .60 1.50
441 Gary Carter 3.00 8.00
442 Hank Webb .30 .75
443 San Francisco Giants 1.25 3.00
Team Card/(No MG on front;#
444 Gary Nolan .60 1.50
445 Rico Petrocelli .60 1.50
446 Larry Haney .30 .75
447 Gene Locklear .60 1.50
448 Tom Johnson .30 .75
449 Bob Robertson .30 .75
450 Jim Palmer 3.00 8.00
451 Buddy Bradford .30 .75
452 Tom Hausman .30 .75
453 Lou Piniella 1.25 3.00
454 Tom Griffin .30 .75
455 Dick Allen 1.25 3.00
456 Joe Coleman .30 .75
457 Ed Crosby .30 .75
458 Earl Williams .30 .75
459 Jim Brewer .30 .75
460 Cesar Cedeno .60 1.50
461 NL and AL Champs .60 1.50
Reds sweep Bucs;
Bosox surprise
462 World Series .60 1.50
Reds Champs
463 Steve Hargan .30 .75
464 Ken Henderson .30 .75
465 Mike Marshall .60 1.50
466 Bob Stinson .30 .75
467 Woodie Fryman .30 .75
468 Jesus Alou .30 .75
469 Rawly Eastwick .60 1.50
470 Bobby Murcer .60 1.50
471 Jim Burton .30 .75
472 Bob Davis .30 .75
473 Paul Blair .60 1.50
474 Ray Corbin .30 .75
475 Joe Rudi .60 1.50
476 Bob Moose .30 .75
477 Cleveland Indians 1.25 3.00
Team Card
Frank Robinson MG/(
478 Lynn McGlothen .30 .75
479 Bobby Mitchell .30 .75
480 Mike Schmidt 10.00 25.00
481 Rudy May .30 .75
482 Tim Hosley .30 .75
483 Mickey Stanley .30 .75
484 Eric Raich .30 .75
485 Mike Hargrove .60 1.50
486 Bruce Dal Canton .30 .75
487 Leron Lee .30 .75
488 Claude Osteen .60 1.50
489 Skip Jutze .30 .75
490 Frank Tanana .60 1.50
491 Terry Crowley .30 .75
492 Martin Pattin .30 .75
493 Derrel Thomas .30 .75
494 Craig Swan .60 1.50
495 Nate Colbert .30 .75
496 Juan Beniquez .30 .75
497 Joe McIntosh .30 .75
498 Glenn Borgmann .30 .75
499 Mario Guerrero .30 .75
500 Reggie Jackson 8.00 20.00
501 Billy Champion .30 .75
502 Tim McCarver 1.25 3.00
503 Elliott Maddox .30 .75
504 Pittsburgh Pirates 1.25 3.00
Team Card
Danny Murtaugh MG/
505 Mark Belanger .60 1.50
506 George Mitterwald .30 .75
507 Ray Bare .30 .75
508 Duane Kuiper .30 .75
509 Bill Hands .30 .75
510 Amos Otis .60 1.50
511 Jamie Easterley .30 .75
512 Ellie Rodriguez .30 .75
513 Bart Johnson .30 .75
514 Dan Driessen .60 1.50
515 Steve Yeager .60 1.50
516 Wayne Granger .30 .75
517 John Milner .30 .75
518 Doug Flynn .30 .75
519 Steve Brye .30 .75
520 Willie McCovey 3.00 8.00
521 Jim Colborn .30 .75
522 Ted Sizemore .30 .75
523 Bob Montgomery .30 .75
524 Pete Falcone .30 .75
525 Billy Williams 2.00 5.00
526 Checklist 397-528 1.25 3.00
527 Mike Anderson .30 .75
528 Dock Ellis .30 .75
529 Deron Johnson .30 .75
530 Don Sutton 2.00 5.00
531 New York Mets 1.25 3.00
Team Card
Joe Frazier MG/(Checkli
532 Milt May .30 .75
533 Lee Richard .30 .75
534 Stan Bahnsen .30 .75
535 Dave Nelson .30 .75
536 Mike Thompson .30 .75
537 Tony Muser .30 .75
538 Pat Darcy .30 .75
539 John Balaz .30 .75
540 Bill Freehan .60 1.50
541 Steve Mingori .30 .75
542 Keith Hernandez 1.25 3.00
543 Wayne Twitchell .30 .75
544 Pepe Frias .30 .75
545 Sparky Lyle .60 1.50
546 Dave Rosello .30 .75
547 Roric Harrison .30 .75
548 Manny Mota .60 1.50
549 Randy Tate .30 .75
550 Hank Aaron 12.50 40.00
551 Jerry DaVanon .30 .75
552 Terry Humphrey .30 .75
553 Randy Moffitt .30 .75
554 Ray Fosse .30 .75
555 Dyar Miller .30 .75
556 Minnesota Twins 1.25 3.00
Team Card
Gene Mauch MG/(Checkl
557 Dan Spillner .30 .75
558 Clarence Gaston .60 1.50
559 Clyde Wright .30 .75
560 Jorge Orta .30 .75
561 Tom Carroll .30 .75
562 Adrian Garrett .30 .75
563 Larry Demery .30 .75
564 Kurt Bevacqua Gum 1.25 3.00
565 Tug McGraw 1.25 3.00
566 Ken McMullen .30 .75
567 George Stone .30 .75
568 Rob Andrews .30 .75
569 Nelson Briles .60 1.50
570 George Hendrick .60 1.50
571 Don DeMola .30 .75
572 Rich Coggins .30 .75
573 Bill Travers .30 .75
574 Don Kessinger .60 1.50
575 Dwight Evans 1.25 3.00
576 Maximino Leon .30 .75
577 Marc Hill .30 .75
578 Ted Kubiak .30 .75
579 Clay Kirby .30 .75
580 Bert Campaneris .60 1.50
581 St. Louis Cardinals 1.25 3.00
Team Card
Red Schoendienst M
582 Mike Kekich .30 .75
583 Tommy Helms .30 .75
584 Stan Wall .30 .75
585 Joe Torre 1.50 4.00
586 Ron Schueler .30 .75
587 Leo Cardenas .30 .75
588 Kevin Kobel .30 .75
589 Mike Flanagan RC 1.25 3.00
590 Chet Lemon RC .60 1.50
591 Rookie Pitchers .60 1.50
Steve Grilli
Craig Mitchell
Jos
592 Willie Randolph RC 4.00 10.00
593 Rookie Pitchers .60 1.50
Larry Anderson
Ken Crosby
Mark
594 Rookie Catchers .60 1.50
OF
Andy Merchant
Ed Ott
Royle S
595 Rookie Pitchers .60 1.50
Art DeFillipis
Randy Lerch
Sid
596 Rookie Infielders .60 1.50
Craig Reynolds
Lamar Johnson/
597 Rookie Pitchers .60 1.50
Don Aase
Jack Kucek
Frank LaCor
598 Rookie Outfielders .60 1.50
Hector Cruz
Jamie Quirk
Jerr
599 Ron Guidry RC ! 5.00 12.00
600 Tom Seaver 6.00 15.00
601 Ken Rudolph .30 .75
602 Doug Konieczny .30 .75
603 Jim Holt .30 .75
604 Joe Lovitto .30 .75
605 Al Downing .30 .75
606 Milwaukee Brewers 1.25 3.00
Team Card
Alex Grammas MG/(Ch
607 Rich Hinton .30 .75
608 Vic Correll .30 .75
609 Fred Norman .30 .75
610 Greg Luzinski 1.25 3.00
611 Rich Folkers .30 .75
612 Joe Lahoud .30 .75
613 Tim Johnson .30 .75
614 Fernando Arroyo .30 .75
615 Mike Cubbage .30 .75
616 Buck Martinez .60 1.50
617 Darold Knowles .30 .75
618 Jack Brohamer .30 .75
619 Bill Butler .30 .75
620 Al Oliver .60 1.50
621 Tom Hall .30 .75
622 Rick Auerbach .30 .75
623 Bob Allietta .30 .75
624 Tony Taylor .30 .75
625 J.R. Richard .60 1.50
626 Bob Sheldon .30 .75
627 Bill Plummer .30 .75
628 John D'Acquisto .30 .75
629 Sandy Alomar .60 1.50
630 Chris Speier .30 .75
631 Atlanta Braves 1.25 3.00
Team Card
Dave Bristol MG/(Check
632 Rogelio Moret .30 .75
633 John Stearns RC .60 1.50
634 Larry Christenson .30 .75
635 Jim Fregosi .60 1.50
636 Joe Decker .30 .75
637 Bruce Bochte .30 .75
638 Doyle Alexander .60 1.50
639 Fred Kendall .30 .75
640 Bill Madlock 1.25 3.00
641 Tom Paciorek .60 1.50
642 Dennis Blair .30 .75
643 Checklist 529-660 1.25 3.00
644 Tom Bradley .30 .75
645 Darrell Porter .60 1.50
646 John Lowenstein .30 .75
647 Ramon Hernandez .30 .75
648 Al Cowens .30 .75
649 Dave Roberts .30 .75
650 Thurman Munson 4.00 10.00
651 John Odom .30 .75
652 Ed Armbrister .30 .75
653 Mike Norris RC .60 1.50
654 Doug Griffin .30 .75
655 Mike Vail .30 .75
656 Chicago White Sox 1.25 3.00
Team Card
Chuck Tanner MG/(Ch
657 Roy Smalley RC .60 1.50
658 Jerry Johnson .30 .75
659 Ben Oglivie .60 1.50
660 Davey Lopes ! 1.25 3.00

1977 O-Pee-Chee

The 1977 O-Pee-Chee set of 264 standard-size cards is not only much smaller numerically than its American counterpart, but also contains many different poses and is loaded with players from the two Canadian teams, including many players from the inaugural year of the Blue Jays and many single cards of players who were on multiplayer rookie cards. On a white background, the fronts feature color player photos with thin black borders. The player's name and position, a facsimile autograph, and the team name also appear on the front. The horizontal backs carry player biography and statistics in French and English. The numbering of this set is different than the U.S. issue, the backs have different colors and the words "O-Pee-Chee Printed in Canada" are printed on the back.

COMPLETE SET (264) 150.00 300.00
1 George Brett 4.00 10.00
Bill Madlock LL
2 Graig Nettles .75 2.00
Mike Schmidt LL
3 Lee May .60 1.50
George Foster LL
4 Bill North .30 .75
Dave Lopes LL
5 Jim Palmer .60 1.50
Randy Jones LL
6 Nolan Ryan 8.00 20.00
Tom Seaver LL
7 Mark Fidrych .30 .75
John Denny LL
8 Bill Campbell .30 .75
Rawly Eastwick LL
9 Mike Jorgensen .30 .75
10 Jim Hunter 1.00 2.50
11 Ken Griffey Sr. .60 1.50
12 Bill Campbell .12 .30
13 Otto Velez .30 .75
14 Milt May .12 .30
15 Dennis Eckersley 2.00 5.00
16 John Mayberry .30 .75
17 Larry Bowa .30 .75
18 Don Carrithers .30 .75
19 Ken Singleton .30 .75
20 Bill Stein .12 .30
21 Ken Brett .12 .30
22 Gary Woods .12 .30
23 Steve Swisher .12 .30
24 Don Sutton 1.00 2.50
25 Willie Stargell 1.00 2.50
26 Jerry Koosman .30 .75
27 Del Unser .30 .75
28 Bob Grich .30 .75
29 Jim Slaton .12 .30
30 Thurman Munson 2.00 5.00
31 Dan Driessen .12 .30
32 Tom Bruno .30 .75
33 Larry Hisle .30 .75
34 Phil Garner .12 .30
35 Mike Hargrove .30 .75
36 Jackie Brown .30 .75
37 Carl Yastrzemski 3.00 8.00
38 Dave Roberts .12 .30
39 Ray Fosse .12 .30
40 Dave McKay .12 .30
41 Paul Splittorff .12 .30
42 Garry Maddox .12 .30
43 Phil Niekro 1.00 2.50
44 Roger Metzger .12 .30
45 Gary Carter 1.00 2.50
46 Jim Spencer .12 .30
47 Ross Grimsley .12 .30
48 Bob Bailor .30 .75
49 Chris Chambliss .30 .75
50 Will McEnaney .30 .75
51 Lou Brock 1.50 4.00
52 Rollie Fingers 1.00 2.50
53 Chris Speier .12 .30
54 Bombo Rivera .30 .75
55 Pete Broberg .12 .30
56 Bill Madlock .75 2.00
57 Rick Rhoden .30 .75
58 Blue Jays Coaches .30 .75
Don Leppert
Bob Miller
Jackie
59 John Candelaria .12 .30
60 Ed Kranepool .12 .30
61 Dave LaRoche .12 .30
62 Jim Rice .75 2.00
63 Don Stanhouse .30 .75
64 Jason Thompson RC .30 .75
65 Nolan Ryan 12.50 40.00
66 Tom Poquette .12 .30
67 Leon Hooten .30 .75
68 Bob Boone .30 .75
69 Mickey Rivers .30 .75
70 Gary Nolan .12 .30
71 Sixto Lezcano .12 .30
72 Larry Parrish .30 .75
73 Dave Goltz .12 .30
74 Bert Campaneris .30 .75
75 Vida Blue .30 .75
76 Rick Cerone .30 .75
77 Ralph Garr .30 .75
78 Ken Forsch .12 .30
79 Willie Montanez .12 .30
80 Jim Palmer 1.50 4.00
81 Jerry White .30 .75
82 Gene Tenace .30 .75
83 Bobby Murcer .30 .75
84 Garry Templeton .60 1.50
85 Bill Singer .30 .75
86 Buddy Bell .30 .75
87 Luis Tiant .30 .75
88 Rusty Staub .60 1.50
89 Sparky Lyle .30 .75
90 Jose Morales .30 .75
91 Dennis Leonard .30 .75
92 Tommy Smith .12 .30
93 Steve Carlton 2.00 5.00
94 John Scott .30 .75
95 Bill Bonham .12 .30
96 Dave Lopes .30 .75
97 Jerry Reuss .30 .75
98 Dave Kingman .60 1.50
99 Dan Warthen .30 .75
100 Johnny Bench 4.00 10.00
101 Bert Blyleven .60 1.50
102 Cecil Cooper .30 .75
103 Mike Willis .30 .75
104 Dan Ford .12 .30
105 Frank Tanana .30 .75
106 Bill North .12 .30
107 Joe Ferguson .12 .30
108 Dick Williams MG .12 .30
109 John Denny .30 .75
110 Willie Randolph .60 1.50
111 Reggie Cleveland .30 .75
112 Doug Howard .30 .75
113 Randy Jones .12 .30
114 Rico Carty .30 .75
115 Mark Fidrych RC 2.00 5.00
116 Darrell Porter .30 .75
117 Wayne Garrett .30 .75
118 Greg Luzinski .60 1.50
119 Jim Barr .12 .30
120 George Foster .60 1.50
121 Phil Roof .30 .75
122 Bucky Dent .30 .75
123 Steve Braun .12 .30
124 Checklist 1-132 .60 1.50
125 Lee May .30 .75
126 Woodie Fryman .30 .75
127 Jose Cardenal .30 .75
128 Doug Rau .12 .30
129 Rennie Stennett .12 .30
130 Pete Vuckovich RC .30 .75
131 Cesar Cedeno .30 .75
132 Jon Matlack .12 .30
133 Don Baylor .60 1.50
134 Darrel Chaney .12 .30
135 Tony Perez 1.00 2.50
136 Aurelio Rodriguez .12 .30
137 Carlton Fisk 2.50 6.00
138 Wayne Garland .12 .30
139 Dave Hilton .30 .75
140 Rawly Eastwick .12 .30
141 Amos Otis .30 .75
142 Tug McGraw .30 .75
143 Rod Carew 2.50 6.00
144 Mike Torrez .30 .75
145 Sal Bando .30 .75
146 Dock Ellis .12 .30
147 Jose Cruz .30 .75
148 Alan Ashby .30 .75
149 Gaylord Perry 1.00 2.50
150 Keith Hernandez .30 .75
151 Dave Pagan .12 .30
152 Richie Zisk .12 .30
153 Steve Rogers .30 .75
154 Mark Belanger .30 .75
155 Andy Messersmith .30 .75
156 Dave Winfield 6.00 15.00
157 Chuck Hartenstein .30 .75
158 Manny Trillo .12 .30
159 Steve Yeager .30 .75
160 Cesar Geronimo .12 .30
161 Jim Rooker .12 .30
162 Tim Foli .30 .75
163 Fred Lynn .30 .75
164 Ed Figueroa .12 .30
165 Johnny Grubb .12 .30
166 Pedro Garcia .30 .75
167 Ron LeFlore .30 .75
168 Rich Hebner .30 .75
169 Larry Herndon RC .30 .75
170 George Brett 12.50 30.00
171 Joe Kerrigan .30 .75
172 Bud Harrelson .30 .75
173 Bobby Bonds .75 2.00
174 Bill Travers .12 .30
175 John Lowenstein .30 .75
176 Butch Wynegar RC .30 .75
177 Pete Falcone .12 .30
178 Claudell Washington .30 .75
179 Checklist 133-264 .60 1.50
180 Dave Cash .30 .75
181 Fred Norman .12 .30
182 Roy White .30 .75
183 Marty Perez .12 .30
184 Jesse Jefferson .30 .75
185 Jim Sundberg .30 .75
186 Dan Meyer .30 .75
187 Fergie Jenkins 1.00 2.50
188 Tom Veryzer .12 .30
189 Dennis Blair .30 .75
190 Rick Manning .12 .30
191 Doug Bird .12 .30
192 Al Bumbry .30 .75
193 Dave Roberts .12 .30
194 Larry Christenson .12 .30
195 Chet Lemon .30 .75
196 Ted Simmons .30 .75
197 Ray Burris .12 .30
198 Expos Coaches .30 .75
Jim Brewer
Billy Gardner
Mickey V
199 Ron Cey .30 .75
200 Reggie Jackson 4.00 10.00
201 Pat Zachry .12 .30
202 Doug Ault .30 .75
203 Al Oliver .30 .75
204 Robin Yount 4.00 10.00
205 Tom Seaver 3.00 8.00
206 Joe Rudi .30 .75
207 Barry Foote .30 .75
208 Toby Harrah .30 .75
209 Jeff Burroughs .30 .75
210 George Scott .30 .75
211 Jim Mason .30 .75
212 Vern Ruhle .12 .30
213 Fred Kendall .12 .30
214 Rick Reuschel .30 .75
215 Hal McRae .30 .75
216 Chip Lang .30 .75
217 Graig Nettles .60 1.50
218 George Hendrick .30 .75
219 Glenn Abbott .12 .30
220 Joe Morgan 2.00 5.00
221 Sam Ewing .30 .75
222 George Medich .12 .30
223 Reggie Smith .30 .75
224 Dave Hamilton .12 .30
225 Pepe Frias .30 .75
226 Jay Johnstone .30 .75
227 J.R. Richard .30 .75
228 Doug DeCinces .30 .75
229 Dave Lemanczyk .30 .75
230 Rick Monday .30 .75
231 Manny Sanguillen .30 .75
232 John Montefusco .12 .30
233 Duane Kuiper .12 .30
234 Ellis Valentine .12 .30
235 Dick Tidrow .12 .30
236 Ben Oglivie .30 .75
237 Rick Burleson .30 .75
238 Roy Hartsfield MG .30 .75
239 Lyman Bostock .30 .75
240 Pete Rose 8.00 20.00
241 Mike Ivie .12 .30
242 Dave Parker .60 1.50
243 Bill Greif .30 .75
244 Freddie Patek .30 .75
245 Mike Schmidt 6.00 15.00
246 Brian Downing .30 .75
247 Steve Hargan .12 .30
248 Dave Collins .30 .75
249 Felix Millan .30 .75
250 Don Gullett .30 .75
251 Jerry Royster .12 .30
252 Earl Williams .30 .75
253 Frank Duffy .12 .30
254 Tippy Martinez .12 .30
255 Steve Garvey .75 2.00
256 Alvis Woods .30 .75
257 John Hiller .30 .75
258 Dave Concepcion .60 1.50
259 Dwight Evans .60 1.50
260 Pete MacKanin .30 .75
261 George Brett RB 5.00 12.00
Most Consec. Games
Three Or More
262 Minnie Minoso RB .30 .75
Oldest Player To
Hit Safely
263 Jose Morales RB .30 .75
Most Pinch-hits, Season
264 Nolan Ryan RB 6.00 15.00
Most Seasons 300
Or More Strikeout

1978 O-Pee-Chee

The 242 standard-size cards comprising the 1978 O-Pee-Chee set differ from the cards of the 1978 Topps set by having a higher ratio of cards of players from the two Canadian teams, a practice begun by O-Pee-Chee in 1977 and continued to 1988. The fronts feature white-bordered color player photos, each framed by a colored line. The player's name appears in black lettering at the right of lower white margin. His team name appears in colored cursive lettering, interrupting the framing line at the bottom left of the photo; his position appears within a white baseball icon in an upper corner. The tan and brown horizontal backs carry the player's name, team and position in the brown border at the bottom. Biography, major league statistics, career highlights in both French and English and a bilingual result of an "at bat" in the "Play Ball" game also appear. The asterisked cards have an extra line on the front indicating team change. Double-printed (DP) cards are also noted below. The key card in this set is the Eddie Murray Rookie Card.

COMPLETE SET (242)	100.00	200.00
COMMON PLAYER (1-242)	.10	.25
COMMON PLAYER DP (1-242)	.08	.20
1 Dave Parker	.60	1.50
Rod Carew LL		
2 George Foster	.25	.60
Jim Rice LL DP		
3 George Foster	.25	.60
Larry Hisle LL		
4 Stolen Base Leaders DP	.10	.25
Frank Taveras		
Freddie Pat		
5 Victory Leaders	1.00	2.50
Steve Carlton		
Dave Goltz		
Dennis		
6 Phil Niekro	2.50	6.00
Nolan Ryan LL DP		
7 John Candelaria	.25	.60
Frank Tanana LL DP		
8 Rollie Fingers	.50	1.25
Bill Campbell LL		
9 Steve Rogers DP	.12	.30
10 Graig Nettles DP	.30	.75
11 Doug Capilla	.10	.25
12 George Scott	.25	.60
13 Gary Woods	.25	.60
14 Tom Veryzer	.25	.60
Now with Cleveland as of 12-9-77		
15 Wayne Garland	.10	.25
16 Amos Otis	.25	.60
17 Larry Christenson	.10	.25
18 Dave Cash	.25	.60
19 Jim Barr	.10	.25
20 Ruppert Jones	.10	.25
21 Eric Soderholm	.10	.25
22 Jesse Jefferson	.25	.60
23 Jerry Morales	.10	.25
24 Doug Rau	.10	.25
25 Rennie Stennett	.10	.25
26 Lee Mazzilli	.10	.25
27 Dick Williams MG	.25	.60
28 Joe Rudi	.25	.60
29 Robin Yount	4.00	10.00
30 Don Gullett DP	.10	.25
31 Roy Howell DP	.08	.20
32 Cesar Geronimo	.10	.25
33 Rick Langford DP	.08	.20
34 Dan Ford	.10	.25
35 Gene Tenace	.25	.60
36 Santo Alcala	.25	.60
37 Rick Burleson	.25	.60
38 Dave Rozema	.10	.25
39 Duane Kuiper	.10	.25
40 Ron Fairly	.25	.60
Now with California as of 12-8-77		
41 Dennis Leonard	.25	.60
42 Greg Luzinski	.50	1.25
43 Willie Montanez	.25	.60
Now with N.Y. Mets as of 12-8-77		
44 Enos Cabell	.10	.25
45 Ellis Valentine	.25	.60
46 Steve Stone	.25	.60
47 Lee May DP	.12	.30
48 Roy White	.25	.60
49 Jerry Garvin	.10	.25
50 Johnny Bench	3.00	8.00
51 Garry Templeton	.25	.60
52 Doyle Alexander	.25	.60
53 Steve Henderson	.10	.25
54 Stan Bahnsen	.10	.25
55 Dan Meyer	.10	.25
56 Rick Reuschel	.25	.60
57 Reggie Smith	.25	.60
58 Blue Jays Team DP CL	.30	.75
59 John Montefusco	.10	.25
60 Dave Parker	.50	1.25
61 Jim Bibby	.10	.25
62 Fred Lynn	.25	.60
63 Jose Morales	.25	.60
64 Aurelio Rodriguez	.10	.25
65 Frank Tanana	.25	.60
66 Darrell Porter	.25	.60
67 Otto Velez	.10	.25
68 Larry Bowa	.50	1.25
69 Jim Hunter	1.00	2.50
70 George Foster	.50	1.25
71 Cecil Cooper DP	.12	.30
72 Gary Alexander DP	.08	.20
73 Paul Thormodsgard	.10	.25
74 Toby Harrah	.25	.60
75 Mitchell Page	.10	.25
76 Alan Ashby	.10	.25
77 Jorge Orta	.10	.25
78 Dave Winfield	4.00	10.00
79 Andy Messersmith	.25	.60
Now with N.Y. Yankees as of 12-8-		
80 Ken Singleton	.25	.60
81 Will McEnaney	.25	.60
82 Lou Piniella	.25	.60
83 Bob Forsch	.10	.25
84 Dan Driessen	.10	.25
85 Dave Lemanczyk	.10	.25
86 Paul Dade	.10	.25
87 Bill Campbell	.10	.25
88 Ron LeFlore	.25	.60
89 Bill Madlock	.25	.60
90 Tony Perez DP	.50	1.25
91 Freddie Patek	.25	.60
92 Glenn Abbott	.10	.25
93 Garry Maddox	.25	.60
94 Steve Staggs	.10	.25
95 Bobby Murcer	.25	.60
96 Don Sutton	1.00	2.50
97 Al Oliver	1.00	2.50
Now with Texas Rangers as of 12-8-77		
98 Jon Matlack	.25	.60
Now with Texas Rangers as of 12-8-77		
99 Sam Mejias	.25	.60
100 Pete Rose DP	5.00	12.00
101 Randy Jones	.10	.25
102 Sixto Lezcano	.10	.25
103 Jim Clancy DP	.12	.30
104 Butch Wynegar	.10	.25
105 Nolan Ryan	12.50	40.00
106 Wayne Gross	.10	.25
107 Bob Watson	.25	.60
108 Joe Kerrigan	.25	.60
Now with Baltimore as of 12-8-77		
109 Keith Hernandez	.25	.60
110 Reggie Jackson	3.00	8.00
111 Denny Doyle	.10	.25
112 Sam Ewing	.25	.60
113 Bert Blyleven	1.00	2.50
Now with Pittsburgh as of 12-8-77		
114 Andre Thornton	.25	.60
115 Milt May	.10	.25
116 Jim Colborn	.10	.25
117 Warren Cromartie RC	.50	1.25
118 Ted Sizemore	.10	.25
119 Checklist 1-121	.50	1.25
120 Tom Seaver	2.50	6.00
121 Luis Gomez	.25	.60
122 Jim Spencer	.25	.60
Now with N.Y. Yankees as of 12-12-77		
123 Leroy Stanton	.10	.25
124 Luis Tiant	.25	.60
125 Mark Belanger	.25	.60
126 Jackie Brown	.10	.25
127 Bill Buckner	.25	.60
128 Bill Robinson	.25	.60
129 Rick Cerone	.25	.60
130 Ron Cey	.50	1.25
131 Jose Cruz	.25	.60
132 Len Randle DP	.08	.20
133 Bob Grich	.25	.60
134 Jeff Burroughs	.25	.60
135 Gary Carter	1.00	2.50
136 Milt Wilcox	.10	.25
137 Carl Yastrzemski	2.50	6.00
138 Dennis Eckersley	1.25	3.00
139 Tim Nordbrook	.10	.25
140 Ken Griffey Sr.	.50	1.25
141 Bob Boone	.50	1.25
142 Dave Goltz DP	.08	.20
143 Al Cowens	.10	.25
144 Bill Atkinson	.10	.25
145 Chris Chambliss	.25	.60
146 Jim Slaton	.25	.60
Now with Detroit Tigers as of 12-9-77		
147 Bill Stein	.10	.25
148 Bob Bailor	.25	.60
149 J.R. Richard	.25	.60
150 Ted Simmons	.25	.60
151 Rick Manning	.10	.25
152 Lerrin LaGrow	.10	.25
153 Larry Parrish	.50	1.25
154 Eddie Murray RC!	30.00	60.00
155 Phil Niekro	1.00	2.50
156 Bake McBride	.25	.60
157 Pete Vuckovich	.25	.60
158 Ivan DeJesus	.10	.25
159 Rick Rhoden	.25	.60
160 Joe Morgan	1.25	3.00
161 Ed Ott	.10	.25
162 Don Stanhouse	.25	.60
163 Jim Rice	.50	1.25
164 Bucky Dent	.25	.60
165 Jim Kern	.10	.25
166 Doug Rader	.10	.25
167 Steve Kemp	.10	.25
168 John Mayberry	.25	.60
169 Tim Foli	.25	.60
Now with N.Y. Mets as of 12-7-77		
170 Steve Carlton	1.50	4.00
171 Pepe Frias	.25	.60
172 Pat Zachry	.10	.25
173 Don Baylor	.50	1.25
174 Sal Bando DP	.12	.30
175 Alvis Woods	.25	.60
176 Mike Hargrove	.25	.60
177 Vida Blue	.25	.60
178 George Hendrick	.25	.60
179 Jim Palmer	1.25	3.00
180 Andre Dawson	5.00	12.00
181 Paul Moskau	.10	.25
182 Mickey Rivers	.25	.60
183 Checklist 122-242	.50	1.25
184 Jerry Johnson	.25	.60
185 Willie McCovey	1.25	3.00
186 Enrique Romo	.10	.25
187 Butch Hobson	.10	.25
188 Rusty Staub	.50	1.25
189 Wayne Twitchell	.25	.60
190 Steve Garvey	1.00	2.50
191 Rick Waits	.10	.25
192 Doug DeCinces	.25	.60
193 Tom Murphy	.10	.25
194 Rich Hebner	.25	.60
195 Ralph Garr	.25	.60
196 Bruce Sutter	.50	1.25
197 Tom Poquette	.10	.25
198 Wayne Garrett	.10	.25
199 Pedro Borbon	.10	.25
200 Thurman Munson	1.50	4.00
201 Rollie Fingers	1.00	2.50
202 Doug Ault	.25	.60
203 Phil Garner DP	.08	.20
204 Lou Brock	1.25	3.00
205 Ed Kranepool	.25	.60
206 Bobby Bonds	.50	1.25
Now with White Sox as of 12-15-77		
207 Expos Team DP	.50	1.25
208 Bump Wills	.10	.25
209 Gary Matthews	.25	.60
210 Carlton Fisk	1.50	4.00
211 Jeff Byrd	.25	.60
212 Jason Thompson	.25	.60
213 Larvell Blanks	.10	.25
214 Sparky Lyle	.25	.60
215 George Brett	8.00	20.00
216 Del Unser	.10	.25
217 Manny Trillo	.10	.25
218 Roy Hartsfield MG	.25	.60
219 Carlos Lopez	.25	.60
Now with Baltimore as of 12-7-77		
220 Dave Concepcion	.50	1.25
221 John Candelaria	.25	.60
222 Dave Lopes	.25	.60
223 Tim Blackwell DP	.12	.30
Now with Chicago Cubs as of 2-1-7		
224 Chet Lemon	.25	.60
225 Mike Schmidt	5.00	12.00
226 Cesar Cedeno	.25	.60
227 Mike Willis	.25	.60
228 Willie Randolph	.50	1.25
229 Doug Bair	.10	.25
230 Rod Carew	1.50	4.00
231 Mike Flanagan	.25	.60
232 Chris Speier	.10	.25
233 Don Aase	.25	.60
Now with California as of 12-8-77		
234 Buddy Bell	.25	.60
235 Mark Fidrych	1.00	2.50
236 Lou Brock RB	1.25	3.00
Most Steals& Lifetime		
237 Sparky Lyle RB	.25	.60
Most Games Pure		
Relief& Lifetime		
238 Willie McCovey RB	1.00	2.50
Most Times 2 HR's		
in Inning& L		
239 Brooks Robinson RB	1.00	2.50
Most Consecutive		
Seasons with		
240 Pete Rose RB	3.00	8.00
Most Hits& Switch-		
hitter& Lifetime		
241 Nolan Ryan RB	6.00	15.00
Most games 10 or More		
Strikeouts&		
242 Reggie Jackson RB	1.50	4.00
Most Homers& One		
World Series		

1979 O-Pee-Chee

This set is an abridgement of the 1979 Topps set. The 374 standard-size cards comprising the 1979 O-Pee-Chee set differ from the cards of the 1979 Topps set by having a higher ratio of cards of players from the two Canadian teams, a practice begun by O-Pee-Chee in 1977 and continued to 1988. The 1979 O-Pee-Chee set was the largest (374) original baseball card set issued (up to that time) by O-Pee-Chee. The fronts feature white-bordered color player photos. The player's name, position, and team appear in colored lettering within the lower white margin. The green and white horizontal backs carry the player's name, team and position at the top. Biography, major league statistics, career highlights in both French and English and a bilingual trivia question and answer also appear. The asterisked cards have an extra line on the front indicating team change. Double-printed (DP) cards are also noted below. The fronts have an O-Pee-Chee logo in the lower left corner comparable to the Topps logo on the 1979 American Set. The cards are sequenced in the same order as the Topps cards; the O-Pee-Chee cards are in effect a compressed version of the Topps set. The key card in this set is the Ozzie Smith Rookie Card. This set was issued in 15 cent wax packs which came 24 boxes to a case.

COMPLETE SET (374)	100.00	200.00
COMMON PLAYER (1-374)	.10	.25
COMMON PLAYER DP (1-374)	.08	.20
1 Lee May	.40	1.00
2 Dick Drago	.10	.25
3 Paul Dade	.10	.25
4 Ross Grimsley	.10	.25
5 Joe Morgan DP	1.00	2.50
6 Kevin Kobel	.10	.25
7 Terry Forster	.10	.25
8 Paul Molitor	6.00	15.00
9 Steve Carlton	1.50	4.00
10 Dave Goltz	.10	.25
11 Dave Winfield	2.50	6.00
12 Dave Rozema	.10	.25
13 Ed Figueroa	.10	.25
14 Alan Ashby	.20	.50
Trade with Blue Jays 11-28-78		
15 Dale Murphy	1.50	4.00
16 Dennis Eckersley	.75	2.00
17 Ron Blomberg	.10	.25
18 Wayne Twitchell	.20	.50
Free Agent as of 3-1-79		
19 Al Hrabosky	.10	.25
20 Fred Norman	.10	.25
21 Steve Garvey DP	.40	1.00
22 Willie Stargell	.75	2.00
23 John Hale	.10	.25
24 Mickey Rivers	.20	.50
25 Jack Brohamer	.10	.25
26 Tom Underwood	.10	.25
27 Mark Belanger	.20	.50
28 Elliott Maddox	.10	.25
29 John Candelaria	.20	.50
30 Shane Rawley	.10	.25
31 Steve Yeager	.20	.50
32 Warren Cromartie	.40	1.00
33 Jason Thompson	.20	.50
34 Roger Erickson	.10	.25
35 Gary Matthews	.20	.50
36 Pete Falcone	.20	.50
Traded 12-5-78		
37 Dick Tidrow	.10	.25
38 Bob Boone	.40	1.00
39 Jim Bibby	.10	.25
40 Len Barker	.20	.50
Trade with Rangers 10-3-78		
41 Robin Yount	2.50	6.00
42 Sam Mejias	.20	.50
Traded 12-14-78		
43 Ray Burris	.10	.25
44 Tom Seaver DP	2.00	5.00
45 Roy Howell	.10	.25
46 Jim Todd	.20	.50
Free Agent 3-1-79		
47 Frank Duffy	.10	.25
48 Joel Youngblood	.10	.25
49 Vida Blue	.20	.50
50 Cliff Johnson	.10	.25
51 Nolan Ryan	12.50	30.00
52 Ozzie Smith RC	40.00	80.00
53 Jim Sundberg	.20	.50
54 Mike Paxton	.10	.25
55 Lou Whitaker	2.50	6.00
56 Dan Schatzeder	.10	.25
57 Rick Burleson	.10	.25
58 Doug Bair	.10	.25
59 Ted Martinez	.10	.25
60 Bob Watson	.20	.50
61 Jim Clancy	.20	.50
62 Rowland Office	.10	.25
63 Bobby Murcer	.20	.50
64 Don Gullett	.20	.50
65 Tom Paciorek	.10	.25
66 Rick Rhoden	.10	.25
67 Duane Kuiper	.10	.25
68 Bruce Boisclair	.10	.25
69 Manny Sarmiento	.10	.25
70 Wayne Cage	.10	.25
71 John Hiller	.20	.50
72 Rick Cerone	.10	.25
73 Dwight Evans	.40	1.00
74 Buddy Solomon	.10	.25
75 Roy White	.20	.50
76 Mike Flanagan	.40	1.00
77 Tom Johnson	.10	.25
78 Glenn Burke	.10	.25
79 Frank Taveras	.10	.25
80 Don Sutton	.75	2.00
81 Leon Roberts	.10	.25
82 George Hendrick	.40	1.00
83 Aurelio Rodriguez	.10	.25
84 Ron Reed	.10	.25
85 Alvis Woods	.10	.25
86 Jim Beattie DP	.08	.20
87 Larry Hisle	.10	.25
88 Mike Garman	.10	.25
89 Tim Johnson	.10	.25
90 Paul Splittorff	.10	.25
91 Darrel Chaney	.10	.25
92 Mike Torrez	.20	.50
93 Eric Soderholm	.10	.25
94 Ron Cey	.20	.50
95 Randy Jones	.10	.25
96 Bill Madlock	.20	.50
97 Steve Kemp DP	.08	.20
98 Bob Apodaca	.10	.25
99 Johnny Grubb	.10	.25
100 Larry Milbourne	.10	.25
101 Johnny Bench DP	2.50	6.00
102 Dave Lemanczyk	.10	.25
103 Reggie Cleveland	.10	.25
104 Larry Bowa	.20	.50
105 Denny Martinez	.60	1.50
106 Bill Travers	.10	.25
107 Willie McCovey	1.00	2.50
108 Wilbur Wood	.10	.25
109 Dennis Leonard	.20	.50
110 Roy Smalley	.20	.50
111 Cesar Geronimo	.10	.25
112 Jesse Jefferson	.20	.50
113 Dave Revering	.10	.25
114 Goose Gossage	.40	1.00
115 Steve Stone	.20	.50
Free Agent 11-25-78		
116 Doug Flynn	.10	.25
117 Bob Forsch	.10	.25
118 Paul Mitchell	.10	.25
119 Toby Harrah	.20	.50
Traded 12-8-78		
120 Steve Rogers	.20	.50
121 Checklist 1-125 DP	.08	.20
122 Balor Moore	.10	.25
123 Rick Reuschel	.20	.50
124 Jeff Burroughs	.20	.50
125 Willie Randolph	.20	.50
126 Bob Stinson	.10	.25
127 Rick Wise	.10	.25
128 Luis Gomez	.20	.50
129 Tommy John	.60	1.50
Signed as Free Agent 11-22-78		
130 Richie Zisk	.10	.25
131 Mario Guerrero	.10	.25
132 Oscar Gamble	.20	.50
Trade with Padres 10-25-78		
133 Don Money	.10	.25
134 Joe Rudi	.20	.50
135 Woodie Fryman	.10	.25
136 Butch Hobson	.20	.50
137 Jim Colborn	.10	.25
138 Tom Grieve	.20	.50
Traded 12-5-78		
139 Andy Messersmith	.20	.50
Free Agent 2-7-79		
140 Andre Thornton	.20	.50
141 Ken Kravec	.10	.25
142 Bobby Bonds	.60	1.50
Trade with Rangers 10-3-78		
143 Jose Cruz	.40	1.00
144 Dave Lopes	.20	.50
145 Jerry Garvin	.10	.25
146 Pepe Frias	.10	.25
147 Mitchell Page	.10	.25
148 Ted Sizemore	.20	.50
Traded 2-23-79		
149 Rich Gale	.10	.25
150 Steve Ontiveros	.10	.25
151 Rod Carew	1.50	4.00
Traded 2-5-79		
152 Lary Sorensen DP	.08	.20
153 Willie Montanez	.10	.25
154 Floyd Bannister	.20	.50
Traded 12-8-78		
155 Bert Blyleven	.40	1.00
156 Ralph Garr	.20	.50
157 Thurman Munson	1.50	4.00
158 Bob Robertson	.20	.50
Free Agent 3-1-79		
159 Jon Matlack	.10	.25
160 Carl Yastrzemski	2.50	6.00
161 Gaylord Perry	.75	2.00
162 Mike Tyson	.10	.25
163 Cecil Cooper	.20	.50
164 Pedro Borbon	.10	.25
165 Art Howe DP	.08	.20
166 Joe Coleman	.20	.50
Free Agent 3-1-79		
167 George Brett	8.00	20.00
168 Gary Alexander	.10	.25
169 Chet Lemon	.20	.50
170 Craig Swan	.10	.25
171 Chris Chambliss	.20	.50
172 John Montague	.10	.25
173 Ron Jackson	.20	.50
Traded 12-4-78		
174 Jim Palmer	1.25	3.00
175 Willie Upshaw	.40	1.00
176 Tug McGraw	.20	.50
177 Bill Buckner	.20	.50
178 Doug Rau	.10	.25
179 Andre Dawson	2.50	6.00
180 Jim Wright	.10	.25
181 Garry Templeton	.20	.50
182 Bill Bonham	.10	.25
183 Lee Mazzilli	.10	.25
184 Alan Trammell	3.00	8.00
185 Amos Otis	.20	.50
186 Tom Dixon	.10	.25
187 Mike Cubbage	.10	.25
188 Sparky Lyle	.40	1.00
Traded 11-10-78		
189 Juan Bernhardt	.10	.25
190 Bump Wills/(Texas Rangers)	.40	1.00
191 Dave Kingman	.40	1.00
192 Lamar Johnson	.10	.25
193 Lance Rautzhan	.10	.25
194 Ed Herrmann	.10	.25
195 Bill Campbell	.10	.25
196 Gorman Thomas	.20	.50
197 Paul Moskau	.10	.25
198 Dale Murray	.10	.25
199 John Mayberry	.20	.50
200 Phil Garner	.10	.25
201 Dan Ford	.20	.50
Traded 12-4-78		
202 Gary Thomasson	.20	.50
Traded 2-15-79		
203 Rollie Fingers	.75	2.00
204 Al Oliver	.20	.50
205 Doug Ault	.20	.50
206 Scott McGregor	.20	.50
207 Dave Cash	.10	.25
208 Bill Plummer	.10	.25
209 Ivan DeJesus	.10	.25
210 Jim Rice	.40	1.00
211 Ray Knight	.20	.50
212 Paul Hartzell	.20	.50
Traded 2-5-79		
213 Tim Foli	.10	.25
214 Butch Wynegar DP	.08	.20
215 Darrell Evans	.40	1.00
216 Ken Griffey Sr.	.20	.50
217 Doug DeCinces	.20	.50
218 Ruppert Jones	.10	.25
219 Bob Montgomery	.10	.25
220 Rick Manning	.10	.25
221 Chris Speier	.10	.25
222 Bobby Valentine	.20	.50
223 Dave Parker	.20	.50
224 Larry Biittner	.10	.25
225 Ken Clay	.10	.25
226 Gene Tenace	.20	.50
227 Frank White	.20	.50
228 Rusty Staub	.40	1.00
229 Lee Lacy	.10	.25
230 Doyle Alexander	.10	.25
231 Bruce Bochte	.10	.25
232 Steve Henderson	.10	.25
233 Jim Lonborg	.20	.50
234 Dave Concepcion	.40	1.00
235 Jerry Morales	.20	.50
Traded 12-4-78		
236 Len Randle	.10	.25
237 Bill Lee DP	.12	.30
Traded 12-7-78		
238 Bruce Sutter	.75	2.00
239 Jim Essian	.10	.25
240 Graig Nettles	.40	1.00
241 Otto Velez	.10	.25
242 Checklist 126-250 DP	.08	.20
243 Reggie Smith	.20	.50
244 Stan Bahnsen DP	.08	.20
245 Garry Maddox DP	.08	.20
246 Joaquin Andujar	.20	.50
247 Dan Driessen	.10	.25
248 Bob Grich	.20	.50
249 Fred Lynn	.20	.50
250 Skip Lockwood	.10	.25
251 Craig Reynolds	.20	.50
Traded 12-5-78		
252 Willie Horton	.20	.50
253 Rick Waits	.10	.25
254 Bucky Dent	.20	.50
255 Bob Knepper	.10	.25
256 Miguel Dilone	.10	.25
257 Bob Owchinko	.10	.25
258 Al Cowens	.10	.25
259 Bob Bailor	.10	.25
260 Larry Christenson	.10	.25
261 Tony Perez	.75	2.00
262 Blue Jays Team	.60	1.50
Roy Hartsfield MG/(Team checklist		
263 Glenn Abbott	.10	.25
264 Ron Guidry	.20	.50
265 Ed Kranepool	.10	.25
266 Charlie Hough	.20	.50
267 Ted Simmons	.40	1.00
268 Jack Clark	.20	.50
269 Enos Cabell	.10	.25
270 Gary Carter	.75	2.00
271 Sam Ewing	.10	.25
272 Tom Burgmeier	.10	.25
273 Freddie Patek	.10	.25
274 Frank Tanana	.20	.50
275 Leroy Stanton	.10	.25
276 Ken Forsch	.10	.25
277 Ellis Valentine	.10	.25
278 Greg Luzinski	.20	.50
279 Rick Bosetti	.10	.25
280 John Stearns	.10	.25
281 Enrique Romo	.20	.50
Traded 12-5-78		
282 Bob Bailey	.10	.25
283 Sal Bando	.20	.50
284 Matt Keough	.10	.25
285 Biff Pocoroba	.10	.25
286 Mike Lum	.20	.50
Free Agent 3-1-79		
287 Jay Johnstone	.20	.50
288 John Montefusco	.10	.25
289 Ed Ott	.10	.25
290 Dusty Baker	.40	1.00
291 Rico Carty	.40	1.00
Waivers from A's 10-2-78		
292 Nino Espinosa	.10	.25
293 Rich Hebner	.20	.50
294 Cesar Cedeno	.20	.50
295 Darrell Porter	.20	.50
296 Rod Gilbreath	.10	.25
297 Jim Kern	.20	.50
Trade with Indians 10-3-78		
298 Claudell Washington	.20	.50
299 Luis Tiant	.40	1.00
Signed as Free Agent 11-14-78		
300 Mike Parrott	.10	.25
301 Pete Broberg	.20	.50
Free Agent 3-1-79		
302 Greg Gross	.20	.50
Traded 2-23-79		
303 Darold Knowles	.20	.50
Free Agent 2-12-79		
304 Paul Blair	.20	.50
305 Julio Cruz	.10	.25
306 Hal McRae	.40	1.00
307 Ken Reitz	.10	.25
308 Tom Murphy	.10	.25
309 Terry Whitfield	.10	.25
310 J.R. Richard	.20	.50
311 Mike Hargrove	.40	1.00
Trade with Rangers 10-25-78		
312 Rick Dempsey	.20	.50
313 Phil Niekro	.75	2.00
314 Bob Stanley	.10	.25
315 Jim Spencer	.10	.25
316 George Foster	.20	.50
317 Dave LaRoche	.10	.25
318 Rudy May	.10	.25
319 Jeff Newman	.10	.25
320 Rick Monday DP	.08	.20
321 Omar Moreno	.10	.25
322 Dave McKay	.20	.50
323 Mike Schmidt	4.00	10.00
324 Ken Singleton	.20	.50
325 Jerry Remy	.10	.25
326 Bert Campaneris	.20	.50
327 Pat Zachry	.10	.25
328 Larry Herndon	.10	.25
329 Mark Fidrych	.60	1.50
330 Del Unser	.10	.25
331 Gene Garber	.20	.50
332 Bake McBride	.20	.50
333 Jorge Orta	.10	.25
334 Don Kirkwood	.10	.25
335 Don Baylor	.40	1.00
336 Bill Robinson	.20	.50
337 Manny Trillo	.20	.50
Traded 2-23-79		
338 Eddie Murray	10.00	25.00
339 Tom Hausman	.10	.25
340 George Scott DP	.08	.20
341 Rick Sweet	.10	.25
342 Lou Piniella	.20	.50
343 Pete Rose	6.00	15.00
Free Agent 12-5-79		
344 Stan Papi	.20	.50
Traded 12-7-78		
345 Jerry Koosman	.40	1.00
Traded 12-8-78		
346 Hosken Powell	.10	.25
347 George Medich	.10	.25
348 Ron LeFlore DP	.08	.20
349 Montreal Expos Team	.60	1.50
Dick Williams MG/(Team check		
350 Lou Brock	1.25	3.00
351 Bill North	.10	.25
352 Jim Hunter DP	.60	1.50
353 Checklist 251-374 DP	.12	.30
354 Ed Halicki	.10	.25
355 Tom Hutton	.10	.25
356 Mike Caldwell	.10	.25
357 Larry Parrish	.40	1.00
358 Geoff Zahn	.10	.25
359 Derrel Thomas	.20	.50
Signed as Free Agent 11-14-78		
360 Carlton Fisk	1.25	3.00
361 John Henry Johnson	.10	.25
362 Dave Chalk	.10	.25
363 Dan Meyer DP	.08	.20
364 Sixto Lezcano	.10	.25
365 Rennie Stennett	.10	.25
366 Mike Willis	.20	.50
367 Buddy Bell DP	.08	.20
Traded 12-8-78		
368 Mickey Stanley	.10	.25
369 Dave Rader	.20	.50
Traded 2-23-79		
370 Burt Hooton	.20	.50
371 Keith Hernandez	.40	1.00
372 Bill Stein	.10	.25
373 Hal Dues	.10	.25
374 Reggie Jackson DP	2.50	6.00

1980 O-Pee-Chee

This set is an abridgement of the 1980 Topps set. The cards are printed on white stock rather than the gray stock used by Topps. The 374 standard-size cards also differ from their Topps counterparts by ving a higher ratio of cards of players from the two anadian teams, a practice begun by O-Pee-Chee in 977 and continued to 1988. The fronts feature hite-bordered color player photos framed by a lored line. The player's name appears in the white rder at the top and also as a simulated autograph ross the photo. The player's position appears thin a colored banner at the upper left; his team me appears within a colored banner at the lower ght. The blue and white horizontal backs carry the ayer's name, team and position at the top. ography, major league statistics and career ghlights in both French and English also appear. e cards are numbered on the back. The asterisked rds have an extra line, "Now with (new team ame)" on the front indicating team change. Color hanges, to correspond to the new team, are apparent the pennant name and frame on the front. Double- inted (DP) cards are also noted below. The cards in is set were produced in lower quantities than other -Pee-Chee sets of this era reportedly due to the mpany being on strike. The cards are sequenced in e same order as the Topps cards.

OMPLETE SET (374) 75.00 150.00
OMMON PLAYER (1-374) .08 .25
OMMON CARD DP (1-374) .02 .10
Craig Swan .08 .25
Dennis Martinez .40 1.00
Dave Cash (Now With Padres) .15 .40
Bruce Sutter .60 1.50
Ron Jackson .08 .25
Balor Moore .15 .40
Dan Ford .08 .25
Pat Putnam .08 .25
Derrel Thomas .08 .25
0 Jim Slaton .08 .25
1 Lee Mazzilli .15 .40
2 Del Unser .08 .25
3 Mark Wagner .08 .25
4 Vida Blue .30 .75
5 Jay Johnstone .15 .40
6 Julio Cruz DP .02 .10
7 Tony Scott .08 .25
8 Jeff Newman DP .02 .10
9 Luis Tiant .15 .40
0 Carlton Fisk 1.25 3.00
1 Dave Palmer .08 .25
2 Bombo Rivera .08 .25
3 Bill Fahey .08 .25
4 Frank White .30 .75
5 Rico Carty .15 .40
6 Bill Bonham DP .02 .10
7 Rick Miller .08 .25
8 J.R. Richard .15 .40
9 Joe Ferguson DP .02 .10
0 Bill Madlock .15 .40
1 Pete Vuckovich .08 .25
2 Doug Flynn .08 .25
3 Bucky Dent .15 .40
4 Mike Ivie .08 .25
5 Bob Stanley .08 .25
6 Al Bumbry .15 .40
7 Gary Carter .75 2.00
8 John Milner DP .02 .10
9 Sid Monge .08 .25
0 Bill Russell .15 .40
1 John Stearns .08 .25
2 Dave Stieb .40 1.00
3 .15 .40
4 Bob Owchinko .08 .25
5 Ron LeFlore .30 .75
Now with Expos
6 Ted Sizemore .08 .25
7 Ted Simmons .15 .40
8 Pepe Frias .15 .40
Now with Rangers
9 Ken Landreaux .08 .25
0 Manny Trillo .15 .40
1 Rick Dempsey .15 .40
2 Cecil Cooper .15 .40
3 Bill Lee .15 .40
4 Victor Cruz .08 .25
5 Johnny Bench 2.00 5.00
6 Rich Dauer .08 .25
7 Frank Tanana .15 .40
8 Francisco Barrios .08 .25
9 Bob Horner .15 .40
0 Fred Lynn DP .07 .20
1 Bob Knepper .08 .25
2 Sparky Lyle .15 .40
3 Larry Cox .08 .25
4 Dock Ellis .15 .40
Now with Pirates
5 Phil Garner .15 .40
6 Greg Luzinski .15 .40
7 Checklist 1-125 .30 .75
8 Dave Lemanczyk .08 .25
9 Tony Perez .60 1.50
Now with Red Sox
70 Gary Thomasson .08 .25
71 Craig Reynolds .08 .25
72 Amos Otis .15 .40
73 Biff Pocoroba .08 .25
74 Matt Keough .08 .25
75 Bill Buckner .15 .40
76 John Castino .08 .25
77 Goose Gossage .40 1.00
78 Gary Alexander .08 .25
79 Phil Huffman .08 .25
80 Bruce Bochte .08 .25
81 Darrell Evans .15 .40
82 Terry Puhl .15 .40
83 Jason Thompson .08 .25
84 Lary Sorensen .08 .25
85 Jerry Remy .08 .25
86 Tony Brizzolara .08 .25
87 Willie Wilson DP .07 .20
88 Eddie Murray 6.00 12.00
89 Larry Christenson .08 .25
90 Bob Randall .08 .25
91 Greg Pryor .08 .25
92 Glenn Abbott .08 .25
93 Jack Clark .15 .40
94 Rick Waits .08 .25
95 Luis Gomez .15 .40
Now with Braves
96 Burt Hooton .15 .40
97 John Henry Johnson .08 .25
98 Ray Knight .15 .40
99 Rick Reuschel .15 .40
100 Champ Summers .08 .25
101 Ron Davis .08 .25
102 Warren Cromartie .15 .40
103 Ken Reitz .08 .25
104 Hal McRae .15 .40
105 Alan Ashby .08 .25
106 Kevin Kobel .08 .25
107 Buddy Bell .15 .40
108 Dave Goltz .15 .40
Now with Dodgers
109 John Montefusco .08 .25
110 Lance Parrish .15 .40
111 Mike LaCoss .08 .25
112 Jim Rice .15 .40
113 Steve Carlton 1.25 3.00
114 Sixto Lezcano .08 .25
115 Ed Halicki .08 .25
116 Jose Morales .08 .25
117 Dave Concepcion .30 .75
118 Joe Cannon .08 .25
119 Willie Montanez .15 .40
Now with Padres
120 Lou Piniella .30 .75
121 Bill Stein .08 .25
122 Dave Winfield 2.00 5.00
123 Alan Trammell .75 2.00
124 Andre Dawson 1.25 3.00
125 Marc Hill .08 .25
126 Don Aase .08 .25
127 Dave Kingman .30 .75
128 Checklist 126-250 .30 .75
129 Dennis Lamp .08 .25
130 Phil Niekro .75 2.00
131 Tim Foli DP .02 .10
132 Jim Clancy .15 .40
133 Bill Atkinson .15 .40
Now with White Sox
134 Paul Dade DP .02 .10
135 Dusty Baker .15 .40
136 Al Oliver .30 .75
137 Dave Chalk .08 .25
138 Bill Robinson .08 .25
139 Robin Yount 2.50 6.00
140 Dan Schatzeder .15 .40
Now with Tigers
141 Mike Schmidt DP 2.00 5.00
142 Ralph Garr .15 .40
Now with Angels
143 Dale Murphy .75 2.00
144 Jerry Koosman .15 .40
145 Tom Veryzer .08 .25
146 Rick Bosetti .08 .25
147 Jim Spencer .08 .25
148 Gaylord Perry .75 2.00
Now with Rangers
149 Paul Blair .15 .40
150 Don Baylor .30 .75
151 Dave Rozema .08 .25
152 Steve Garvey .40 1.00
153 Elias Sosa .08 .25
154 Larry Gura .08 .25
155 Tim Johnson .08 .25
156 Steve Henderson .08 .25
157 Ron Guidry .15 .40
158 Mike Edwards .08 .25
159 Butch Wynegar .08 .25
160 Randy Jones .08 .25
161 Denny Walling .08 .25
162 Mike Hargrove .15 .40
163 Dave Parker .40 1.00
164 Roger Metzger .08 .25
165 Johnny Grubb .08 .25
166 Steve Kemp .08 .25
167 Bob Lacey .08 .25
168 Chris Speier .08 .25
169 Dennis Eckersley .60 1.50
170 Keith Hernandez .15 .40
171 Claudell Washington .15 .40
172 Tom Underwood .15 .40
Now with Yankees
173 Dan Driessen .08 .25
174 Al Cowens .15 .40
Now with Angels
175 Rich Hebner .15 .40
Now with Tigers
176 Willie McCovey .75 2.00
177 Carney Lansford .15 .40
178 Ken Singleton .15 .40
179 Jim Essian .08 .25
180 Mike Vail .08 .25
181 Randy Lerch .08 .25
182 Larry Parrish .30 .75
183 Checklist 251-374 .30 .75
184 George Hendrick .15 .40
185 Bob Davis .08 .25
186 Gary Matthews .15 .40
187 Lou Whitaker .75 2.00
188 Darrell Porter DP .07 .20
189 Wayne Gross .08 .25
190 Bobby Murcer .15 .40
191 Willie Aikens .15 .40
Now with Royals
192 Jim Kern .08 .25
193 Cesar Cedeno .15 .40
194 Joel Youngblood .08 .25
195 Ross Grimsley .08 .25
196 Jerry Mumphrey .15 .40
Now with Padres
197 Kevin Bell .08 .25
198 Garry Maddox .15 .40
199 Dave Freisleben .08 .25
200 Ed Ott .08 .25
201 Enos Cabell .08 .25
202 Pete LaCock .08 .25
203 Fergie Jenkins .75 2.00
204 Milt Wilcox .08 .25
205 Ozzie Smith 7.50 15.00
206 Ellis Valentine .15 .40
207 Dan Meyer .08 .25
208 Barry Foote .08 .25
209 George Foster .15 .40
210 Dwight Evans .15 .40
211 Paul Molitor 5.00 10.00
212 Tony Solaita .08 .25
213 Bill North .08 .25
214 Paul Splittorff .08 .25
215 Bobby Bonds .40 1.00
Now with Cardinals
216 Butch Hobson .08 .25
217 Mark Belanger .15 .40
218 Grant Jackson .08 .25
219 Tom Hutton DP .02 .10
220 Pat Zachry .08 .25
221 Duane Kuiper .08 .25
222 Larry Hisle DP .02 .10
223 Mike Krukow .08 .25
224 Johnnie LeMaster .08 .25
225 Billy Almon .15 .40
Now with Expos
226 Joe Niekro .15 .40
227 Dave Revering .08 .25
228 Don Sutton .60 1.50
229 John Hiller .15 .40
230 Alvis Woods .08 .25
231 Mark Fidrych .40 1.00
232 Duffy Dyer .08 .25
233 Nino Espinosa .08 .25
234 Doug Bair .08 .25
235 George Brett 7.50 16.00
236 Mike Torrez .08 .25
237 Frank Taveras .08 .25
238 Bert Blyleven .40 1.00
239 Willie Randolph .15 .40
240 Mike Sadek DP .02 .10
241 Jerry Royster .08 .25
242 John Denny .15 .40
Now with Indians
243 Rick Monday .08 .25
244 Jesse Jefferson .15 .40
245 Aurelio Rodriguez .15 .40
Now with Padres
246 Bob Boone .30 .75
247 Cesar Geronimo .08 .25
248 Bob Shirley .08 .25
249 Expos Checklist .40 1.00
250 Bob Watson .30 .75
Now with Yankees
251 Mickey Rivers .15 .40
252 Mike Tyson DP .07 .20
Now with Cubs
253 Wayne Nordhagen .08 .25
254 Roy Howell .08 .25
255 Lee May .15 .40
256 Jerry Martin .08 .25
257 Bake McBride .08 .25
258 Silvio Martinez .08 .25
259 Jim Mason .08 .25
260 Tom Seaver 2.00 5.00
261 Rich Wortham DP .02 .10
262 Mike Cubbage .08 .25
263 Gene Garber .15 .40
264 Bert Campaneris .15 .40
265 Tom Buskey .08 .25
266 Leon Roberts .08 .25
267 Ron Cey .30 .75
268 Steve Ontiveros .08 .25
269 Mike Caldwell .08 .25
270 Nelson Norman .08 .25
271 Steve Rogers .15 .40
272 Jim Morrison .08 .25
273 Clint Hurdle .15 .40
274 Dale Murray .08 .25
275 Jim Barr .08 .25
276 Jim Sundberg DP .07 .20
277 Willie Horton .15 .40
278 Andre Thornton .15 .40
279 Bob Forsch .08 .25
280 Joe Strain .08 .25
281 Rudy May .15 .40
Now with Yankees
282 Pete Rose 6.00 12.00
283 Jeff Burroughs .15 .40
284 Rick Langford .08 .25
285 Ken Griffey Sr. .30 .75
286 Bill Nahorodny .15 .40
Now with Braves
287 Art Howe .15 .40
288 Ed Figueroa .08 .25
289 Joe Rudi .15 .40
290 Alfredo Griffin .15 .40
291 Dave Lopes .15 .40
292 Rick Manning .08 .25
293 Dennis Leonard .15 .40
294 Bud Harrelson .15 .40
295 Skip Lockwood .15 .40
Now with Red Sox
296 Roy Smalley .08 .25
297 Kent Tekulve .15 .40
298 Scot Thompson .08 .25
299 Ken Kravec .08 .25
300 Blue Jays Checklist .40 1.00
301 Scott Sanderson .15 .40
302 Charlie Moore .08 .25
303 Nolan Ryan 12.50 25.00
Now with Astros
304 Bob Bailor .15 .40
305 Bob Stinson .08 .25
306 Al Hrabosky .15 .40
Now with Braves
307 Mitchell Page .08 .25
308 Garry Templeton .08 .25
309 Chet Lemon .15 .40
310 Jim Palmer .75 2.00
311 Rick Cerone .15 .40
Now with Yankees
312 Jon Matlack .08 .25
313 Don Money .08 .25
314 Reggie Jackson 2.50 6.00
315 Brian Downing .08 .25
316 Woodie Fryman .08 .25
317 Alan Bannister .08 .25
318 Ron Reed .08 .25
319 Willie Stargell .75 2.00
320 Jerry Garvin DP .02 .10
321 Cliff Johnson .00 .25
322 Doug DeCinces .15 .40
323 Gene Richards .08 .25
324 Joaquin Andujar .15 .40
325 Richie Zisk .08 .25
326 Bob Grich .15 .40
327 Gorman Thomas .15 .40
328 Chris Chambliss .30 .75
Now with Braves
329 Blue Jays Prospects .30 .75
Butch Edge
Pat Kelly
Ted Wi
330 Larry Bowa .15 .40
331 Barry Bonnell .15 .40
Now with Blue Jays
332 John Candelaria .15 .40
333 Toby Harrah .15 .40
334 Larry Biittner .08 .25
335 Mike Flanagan .15 .40
336 Ed Kranepool .08 .25
337 Ken Forsch DP .02 .10
338 John Mayberry .15 .40
339 Rick Burleson .08 .25
340 Milt May .15 .40
Now with Giants
341 Roy White .15 .40
342 Joe Morgan .75 2.00
343 Rollie Fingers .75 2.00
344 Mario Mendoza .08 .25
345 Stan Bahnsen .08 .25
346 Tug McGraw .15 .40
347 Rusty Staub .15 .40
348 Tommy John .30 .75
349 Ivan DeJesus .08 .25
350 Reggie Smith .15 .40
351 Expos Prospects .40 1.00
Tony Bernazard
Randy Miller
Joh
352 Floyd Bannister .08 .25
353 Rod Carew DP .60 1.50
354 Otto Velez .08 .25
355 Gene Tenace .15 .40
356 Freddie Patek .15 .40
Now with Angels
357 Elliott Maddox .08 .25
358 Pat Underwood .08 .25
359 Graig Nettles .30 .75
360 Rodney Scott .08 .25
361 Terry Whitfield .08 .25
362 Fred Norman .15 .40
Now with Expos
363 Sal Bando .15 .40
364 Greg Gross .08 .25
365 Carl Yastrzemski DP .75 2.00
366 Paul Hartzell .08 .25
367 Jose Cruz .15 .40
368 Shane Rawley .08 .25
369 Jerry White .08 .25
370 Rick Wise .15 .40
Now with Padres
371 Steve Yeager .30 .75
372 Omar Moreno .08 .25
373 Bump Wills .08 .25
374 Craig Kusick .15 .40
Now with Padres

1981 O-Pee-Chee

This set is an abridgement of the 1981 Topps set. The 374 standard-size cards comprising the 1981 O-Pee-Chee set differ from the cards of the 1981 Topps set by having a higher ratio of cards of players from the two Canadian teams, a practice begun by O-Pee-Chee in 1977 and continued to 1988. The fronts feature white-bordered color player photos framed by a colored line that is wider at the bottom. The player's name appears in that wider colored area. The player's position and team appear within a colored baseball cap icon at the lower left. The red and white horizontal backs carry the player's name and position at the top. Biography, major league statistics, and career highlights in both French and English also appear. In cases where a player changed teams or was traded before press time, a small line of print on the obverse makes note of the change. Double-printed (DP) cards are also noted below. The card backs are typically found printed on white card stock. There is, however, a "variation" set printed on gray card stock; gray backs are worth 50 percent more than corresponding white backs listed below. Notable Rookie Cards include Harold Baines, Kirk Gibson and Tim Raines.

COMPLETE SET (374) 25.00 60.00
COMMON PLAYER (1-374) .04 .10
COMMON PLAYER DP (1-374) .02 .05
1 Frank Pastore .02 .10
2 Phil Huffman .02 .10
3 Len Barker .02 .10
4 Robin Yount .75 2.00
5 Dave Stieb .08 .25
6 Gary Carter .40 1.00
7 Butch Hobson .02 .10
Now with Angels
8 Lance Parrish .08 .25
9 Bruce Sutter .40 1.00
Now with Cardinals
10 Mike Flanagan .08 .25
11 Paul Mirabella .02 .10
12 Craig Reynolds .02 .10
13 Joe Charboneau .20 .50
14 Dan Driessen .02 .10
15 Larry Parrish .02 .10
16 Ron Davis .02 .10
17 Cliff Johnson .02 .10
Now with Athletics
18 Bruce Bochte .02 .10
19 Jim Clancy .02 .10
20 Bill Russell .02 .10
21 Ron Oester .02 .10
22 Danny Darwin .02 .10
23 Willie Aikens .02 .10
24 Don Stanhouse .02 .10
25 Sixto Lezcano .02 .10
Now with Cardinals
26 U.L. Washington .02 .10
27 Champ Summers DP .01 .05
28 Enrique Romo .02 .10
29 Gene Tenace .08 .25
30 Jack Clark .08 .25
31 Checklist 1-125 DP .01 .05
32 Ken Oberkfell .02 .10
33 Rick Honeycutt .02 .10
Now with Rangers
34 Al Bumbry .02 .10
35 John Tamargo DP .01 .05
36 Ed Farmer .02 .10
37 Gary Roenicke .02 .10
38 Tim Foli DP .01 .05
39 Eddie Murray 2.50 6.00
40 Roy Howell .02 .10
Now with Brewers
41 Bill Gullickson .20 .50
42 Jerry White DP .01 .05
43 Tim Blackwell .02 .10
44 Steve Henderson .02 .10
45 Enos Cabell .02 .10
Now with Giants
46 Rick Bosetti .02 .10
47 Bill North .02 .10
48 Rich Gossage .20 .50
49 Bob Shirley .02 .10
Now with Cardinals
50 Dave Lopes .08 .25
51 Shane Rawley .02 .10
52 Lloyd Moseby .08 .25
53 Burt Hooton .02 .10
54 Ivan DeJesus .02 .10
55 Mike Norris .02 .10
56 Del Unser .02 .10
57 Dave Revering .02 .10
58 Joel Youngblood .02 .10
59 Steve McCatty .02 .10
60 Willie Randolph .08 .25
61 Butch Wynegar .02 .10
62 Gary Lavelle .02 .10
63 Willie Montanez .02 .10
64 Terry Puhl .02 .10
65 Scott McGregor .02 .10
66 Buddy Bell .08 .25
67 Toby Harrah .08 .25
68 Jim Rice .08 .25
69 Darrell Evans .08 .25
70 Al Oliver DP .07 .20
71 Hal Dues .02 .10
72 Barry Evans DP .01 .05
73 Doug Bair .02 .10
74 Mike Hargrove .08 .25
75 Reggie Smith .08 .25
76 Mario Mendoza .02 .10
Now with Rangers
77 Mike Barlow .02 .10
78 Garth Iorg .02 .10
79 Jeff Reardon RC .40 1.00
80 Roger Erickson .02 .10
81 Dave Stapleton .02 .10
82 Barry Bonnell .02 .10
83 Dave Concepcion .08 .25
84 Johnnie LeMaster .02 .10
85 Mike Caldwell .02 .10
86 Wayne Gross .02 .10
87 Rick Camp .02 .10
88 Joe Lefebvre .02 .10
89 Darrell Jackson .02 .10
90 Bake McBride .02 .10
91 Tim Stoddard DP .01 .05
92 Mike Easler .02 .10
93 Jim Bibby .02 .10
94 Kent Tekulve .08 .25
95 Jim Sundberg .08 .25
96 Tommy John .20 .50
97 Chris Speier .02 .10
98 Clint Hurdle .08 .25
99 Phil Garner .08 .25
100 Rod Carew .60 1.50
101 Steve Stone .02 .10
102 Joe Niekro .02 .10
103 Jerry Martin .02 .10
Now with Giants
104 Ron LeFlore DP .02 .10
Now with White Sox
105 Jose Cruz .08 .25
106 Don Money .02 .10
107 Bobby Brown .02 .10
108 Larry Herndon .02 .10
109 Dennis Eckersley .40 1.00
110 Carl Yastrzemski .60 1.50
111 Greg Minton .02 .10
112 Dan Schatzeder .02 .10
113 George Brett 3.00 8.00
114 Tom Underwood .02 .10
115 Roy Smalley .02 .10
116 Carlton Fisk .75 2.00
Now with White Sox
117 Pete Falcone .02 .10
118 Dale Murphy .60 1.50
119 Tippy Martinez .02 .10
120 Larry Bowa .08 .25
121 Julio Cruz .02 .10
122 Jim Gantner .08 .25
123 Al Cowens .02 .10
124 Jerry Garvin .02 .10
125 Andre Dawson .75 2.00
126 Charlie Leibrandt RC .20 .50
127 Willie Stargell .30 .75
128 Andre Thornton .08 .25
129 Art Howe .02 .10
130 Larry Gura .02 .10
131 Jerry Remy .02 .10
132 Rick Dempsey .08 .25
133 Alan Trammell DP .30 .75
134 Mike LaCoss .02 .10
135 Gorman Thomas .02 .10
136 Expos Future Stars 2.50 6.00
Tim Raines
Roberto Ramos
Bob
137 Bill Madlock .08 .25
138 Rich Dotson DP .02 .10
139 Oscar Gamble .02 .10
140 Bob Forsch .02 .10
141 Miguel Dilone .02 .10
142 Jackson Todd .02 .10
143 Dan Meyer .02 .10
144 Garry Templeton .02 .10
145 Mickey Rivers .08 .25
146 Alan Ashby .02 .10
147 Dale Berra .02 .10
148 Randy Jones .02 .10
Now with Mets
149 Joe Nolan .02 .10
150 Mark Fidrych .20 .50
151 Tony Armas .02 .10
152 Steve Kemp .02 .10
153 Jerry Reuss .08 .25
154 Rick Langford .02 .10
155 Chris Chambliss .08 .25
156 Bob McClure .02 .10
157 John Wathan .02 .10
158 John Curtis .02 .10
159 Steve Howe .08 .25
160 Garry Maddox .02 .10
161 Dan Graham .02 .10
162 Doug Corbett .02 .10
163 Rob Dressler .02 .10
164 Bucky Dent .08 .25
165 Alvis Woods .02 .10
166 Floyd Bannister .02 .10
167 Lee Mazzilli .02 .10
168 Don Robinson DP .01 .05
169 John Mayberry .02 .10
170 Woodie Fryman .02 .10
171 Gene Richards .02 .10
172 Rick Burleson .02 .10
Now with Angels
173 Bump Wills .02 .10
174 Glenn Abbott .02 .10
175 Dave Collins .02 .10
176 Mike Krukow .02 .10
177 Rick Monday .08 .25
178 Dave Parker .20 .50
179 Rudy May .02 .10
180 Pete Rose 1.25 3.00
181 Elias Sosa .02 .10
182 Bob Grich .08 .25
183 Fred Norman .02 .10
184 Jim Dwyer .02 .10
Now with Orioles
185 Dennis Leonard .02 .10
186 Gary Matthews .02 .10
187 Ron Hassey DP .01 .05
188 Doug DeCinces .08 .25
189 Craig Swan .02 .10
190 Cesar Cedeno .08 .25
191 Rick Sutcliffe .08 .25
192 Kiko Garcia .02 .10
193 Pete Vuckovich .02 .10
Now with Brewers
194 Tony Bernazard .02 .10
Now with White Sox
195 Keith Hernandez .08 .25
196 Jerry Mumphrey .02 .10
197 Jim Kern .02 .10
198 Jerry Dybzinski .02 .10
199 John Lowenstein .02 .10
200 George Foster .08 .25
201 Phil Niekro .30 .75
202 Bill Buckner .08 .25
203 Steve Carlton .60 1.50
204 John D'Acquisto .02 .10
Now with Angels
205 Rick Reuschel .08 .25
206 Dan Quisenberry .08 .25
207 Mike Schmidt DP .75 2.00
208 Bob Watson .08 .25
209 Jim Spencer .02 .10
210 Jim Palmer .30 .75
211 Derrel Thomas .02 .10
212 Steve Nicosia .02 .10
213 Omar Moreno .02 .10
214 Richie Zisk .02 .10
Now with Mariners
215 Larry Hisle .02 .10
216 Mike Torrez .02 .10
217 Rich Hebner .02 .10
218 Britt Burns RC .08 .25
219 Ken Landreaux .02 .10
220 Tom Seaver .75 2.00
221 Bob Davis .02 .10
Now with Angels
222 Jorge Orta .02 .10
223 Bobby Bonds .08 .25
224 Pat Zachry .02 .10
225 Ruppert Jones .02 .10
226 Duane Kuiper .02 .10
227 Rodney Scott .02 .10
228 Tom Paciorek .08 .25
229 Rollie Fingers .30 .75
Now with Brewers
230 George Hendrick .02 .10
231 Tony Perez .30 .75
232 Grant Jackson .02 .10
233 Damaso Garcia .02 .10
234 Lou Whitaker .50 1.25
235 Scott Sanderson .02 .10
236 Mike Ivie .02 .10
237 Charlie Moore .02 .10
238 Blue Jays Rookies .02 .10
Luis Leal
Brian Milner
Ken Sc
239 Rick Miller DP .01 .05
Now with Red Sox
240 Nolan Ryan 4.00 10.00
241 Checklist 126-250 DP .01 .05
242 Chet Lemon .02 .10
243 Dave Palmer .02 .10
244 Ellis Valentine .02 .10
245 Carney Lansford .08 .25
Now with Red Sox
246 Ed Ott DP .01 .05
247 Glenn Hubbard DP .01 .05
248 Joey McLaughlin .02 .10
249 Jerry Narron .02 .10
250 Ron Guidry .08 .25
251 Steve Garvey .20 .50
252 Victor Cruz .02 .10
253 Bobby Murcer .08 .25
254 Ozzie Smith 3.00 8.00
255 John Stearns .02 .10
256 Bill Campbell .02 .10
257 Rennie Stennett .02 .10
258 Rick Waits .02 .10
259 Gary Lucas .02 .10
260 Ron Cey .08 .25
261 Rickey Henderson 5.00 12.00
262 Sammy Stewart .02 .10
263 Brian Downing .02 .10
264 Mark Bomback .02 .10
265 John Candelaria .08 .25
266 Renie Martin .02 .10
267 Stan Bahnsen .02 .10
268 Montreal Expos CL .20 .50
269 Ken Forsch .02 .10
270 Greg Luzinski .08 .25

271 Ron Jackson .02 .10
272 Wayne Garland .02 .10
273 Milt May .02 .10
274 Rick Wise .02 .10
275 Dwight Evans .20 .50
276 Sal Bando .08 .25
277 Alfredo Griffin .02 .10
278 Rick Sofield .02 .10
279 Bob Knepper .02 .10
Now with Astros
280 Ken Griffey .08 .25
281 Ken Singleton .08 .25
282 Ernie Whitt .08 .25
283 Billy Sample .02 .10
284 Jack Morris .30 .75
285 Dick Ruthven .02 .10
286 Johnny Bench .75 2.00
287 Dave Smith .08 .25
288 Amos Otis .08 .25
289 Dave Goltz .02 .10
290 Bob Boone DP .07 .20
291 Aurelio Lopez .02 .10
292 Tom Hume .02 .10
293 Charlie Lea .02 .10
294 Bert Blyleven .20 .50
Now with Indians
295 Hal McRae .08 .25
296 Bob Stanley .02 .10
297 Bob Bailor .02 .10
Now with Mets
298 Jerry Koosman .08 .25
299 Elliott Maddox .02 .10
Now with Yankees
300 Paul Molitor 2.00 5.00
301 Matt Keough .02 .10
302 Pat Putnam .02 .10
303 Dan Ford .02 .10
304 John Castino .02 .10
305 Barry Foote .02 .10
306 Lou Piniella .08 .25
307 Gene Garber .02 .10
308 Rick Manning .02 .10
309 Don Baylor .20 .50
310 Vida Blue DP .07 .20
311 Doug Flynn .02 .10
312 Rick Rhoden .02 .10
313 Fred Lynn .08 .25
Now with Angels
314 Rich Dauer .02 .10
315 Kirk Gibson RC 2.00 5.00
316 Ken Reitz .02 .10
Now with Cubs
317 Lonnie Smith .08 .25
318 Steve Yeager .02 .10
319 Rowland Office .02 .10
320 Tom Burgmeier .02 .10
321 Leon Durham RC .08 .25
Now with Cubs
322 Neil Allen .02 .10
323 Ray Burris .02 .10
Now with Expos
324 Mike Willis .02 .10
325 Ray Knight .08 .25
326 Rafael Landestoy .02 .10
327 Moose Haas .02 .10
328 Ross Baumgarten .02 .10
329 Joaquin Andujar .08 .25
330 Frank White .08 .25
331 Toronto Blue Jays CL .08 .25
332 Dick Drago .02 .10
333 Sid Monge .02 .10
334 Joe Sambito .02 .10
335 Rick Cerone .02 .10
336 Eddie Whitson .02 .10
337 Sparky Lyle .08 .25
338 Checklist 251-374 .08 .25
339 Jon Matlack .02 .10
340 Ben Oglivie .02 .10
341 Dwayne Murphy .02 .10
342 Terry Crowley .02 .10
343 Frank Taveras .02 .10
344 Steve Rogers .02 .10
345 Warren Cromartie .02 .10
346 Bill Caudill .02 .10
347 Harold Baines RC 4.00 10.00
348 Frank LaCorte .02 .10
349 Glenn Hoffman .02 .10
350 J.R. Richard .02 .10
351 Otto Velez .02 .10
352 Ted Simmons .08 .25
Now with Brewers
353 Terry Kennedy .02 .10
Now with Padres
354 Al Hrabosky .02 .10
355 Bob Horner .08 .25
356 Cecil Cooper .08 .25
357 Bob Welch .08 .25
358 Paul Moskau .02 .10
359 Dave Rader .02 .10
Now with Angels
360 Willie Wilson .08 .25
361 Dave Kingman DP .08 .25
362 Joe Rudi .02 .10
Now with Red Sox
363 Rich Gale .02 .10
364 Steve Trout .02 .10
365 Graig Nettles DP .10 .30
366 Lamar Johnson .08 .25
367 Denny Martinez .30 .75
368 Manny Trillo .02 .10
369 Frank Tanana/Now with Red Sox .08 .25
370 Reggie Jackson .75 2.00
371 Bill Lee .08 .25
372 Jay Johnstone .08 .25
373 Jason Thompson .02 .10
374 Tom Hutton .02 .10

1981 O-Pee-Chee Posters

The 24 full-color posters comprising the 1981 O-Pee-Chee poster insert set were inserted one per regular wax pack and feature players of the Montreal Expos (numbered 1-12) and the Toronto Blue Jays (numbered 13-24). These posters are typically found with two folds and measure approximately 4 7/8" by 6 7/8". The posters are blank-backed and are numbered at the bottom in French and English. A distinctive red (Expos) or blue (Blue Jays) border surrounds the player photo.

COMPLETE SET (24) 8.00 20.00
1 Willie Montanez .08 .25
2 Rodney Scott .08 .25
3 Chris Speier .08 .25
4 Larry Parrish .20 .50
5 Warren Cromartie .20 .50
6 Andre Dawson .75 2.00
7 Ellis Valentine .08 .25
8 Gary Carter .60 1.50
9 Steve Rogers .08 .25
10 Woodie Fryman .08 .25
11 Jerry White .08 .25
12 Scott Sanderson .08 .25
13 John Mayberry .20 .50
14 Damaso Garcia UER
(Misspelled Damasa) .08 .25
15 Alfredo Griffin .08 .25
16 Garth Iorg .08 .25
17 Alvis Woods .08 .25
18 Rick Bosetti .08 .25
19 Barry Bonnell .08 .25
20 Ernie Whitt .08 .25
21 Jim Clancy .08 .25
22 Dave Stieb .30 .75
23 Otto Velez .08 .25
24 Lloyd Moseby .20 .50

1982 O-Pee-Chee

This set is an abridgement of the 1982 Topps set. The 396 standard-size cards comprising the 1982 O-Pee-Chee set differ from the cards of the 1982 Topps set by having a higher ratio of cards of players from the two Canadian teams, a practice begun by O-Pee-Chee in 1977 and continued to 1988. The set contains virtually the same pictures for the players also featured in the 1982 Topps issue, but the O-Pee-Chee photos appear brighter. The fronts feature white-bordered color player photos with colored lines within the wide white margin on the left. The player's name, team and position appear in colored lettering within the wide bottom margin. The player's name also appears as a simulated autograph across the photo. The blue print on green horizontal backs carry the player's name, bilingual position and biography at the top. The player's major league statistics follow below. The cards are numbered on the back. The asterisked cards have an extra line on the front inside the picture area indicating team change. In Action (IA) and All-Star (AS) cards are indicated in the checklist below; these are included in the set in addition to the player's regular card. The 396 cards in the set were the largest "original" or distinct set total printed up to that time by O-Pee-Chee; the previous high had been 374 in 1979, 1980 and 1981.

COMPLETE SET (396) 20.00 50.00
1 Dan Spillner .02 .10
2 Ken Singleton AS .02 .10
3 John Candelaria .02 .10
4 Frank Tanana .08 .25
Traded to Rangers Jan. 15/82
5 Reggie Smith .08 .25
6 Rick Monday .02 .10
7 Scott Sanderson .02 .10
8 Rich Dauer .02 .10
9 Ron Guidry .08 .25
10 Ron Guidry IA .02 .10
11 Tom Brookens .02 .10
12 Moose Haas .02 .10
13 Chet Lemon .08 .25
Traded to Tigers Nov. 27/81
14 Steve Howe .02 .10
15 Ellis Valentine .02 .10
16 Toby Harrah .08 .25
17 Darrell Evans .08 .25
18 Johnny Bench .75 2.00
19 Ernie Whitt .08 .25
20 Garry Maddox .02 .10
21 Graig Nettles IA .08 .25
22 Al Oliver IA .08 .25
23 Bob Boone .08 .25
Traded to Angels Dec. 9/81
24 Pete Rose IA .60 1.50
25 Jerry Remy .02 .10
26 Jorge Orta .08 .25
Traded to Dodgers Dec 9/81
27 Bobby Bonds .08 .25
28 Jim Clancy .02 .10
29 Dwayne Murphy .02 .10
30 Tom Seaver .75 2.00
31 Tom Seaver IA .40 1.00
32 Claudell Washington .02 .10
33 Bob Shirley .02 .10
34 Bob Forsch .02 .10
35 Willie Aikens .02 .10
36 Rod Carew AS .30 .75
37 Willie Randolph .08 .25
38 Charlie Lea .02 .10
39 Lou Whitaker .30 .75
40 Dave Parker .08 .25
41 Dave Parker IA .02 .10
42 Mark Belanger .08 .25
Traded to Dodgers Dec. 24/81
43 Rick Langford .02 .10
44 Rollie Fingers IA .20 .50
45 Rick Cerone .02 .10
46 Johnny Wockenfuss .02 .10
47 Jack Morris AS .08 .25
48 Cesar Cedeno .02 .10
Traded to Reds Dec. 18/81
49 Alvis Woods .02 .10
50 Buddy Bell .08 .25
51 Mickey Rivers IA .02 .10
52 Steve Rogers .02 .10
53 Blue Jays Leaders .08 .25
John Mayberry
Dave Stieb/(Tea
54 Ron Hassey .02 .10
55 Rick Burleson .02 .10
56 Harold Baines .20 .50
57 Craig Reynolds .02 .10
58 Carlton Fisk AS .30 .75
59 Jim Kern .02 .10
Traded to Reds Feb. 10/82
60 Tony Armas .02 .10
61 Warren Cromartie .02 .10
62 Graig Nettles .08 .25
63 Jerry Koosman .08 .25
64 Pat Zachry .02 .10
65 Terry Kennedy .02 .10
66 Richie Zisk .02 .10
67 Rich Gale .08 .25
Traded to Giants Dec. 10/81
68 Steve Carlton .60 1.50
69 Greg Luzinski IA .08 .25
70 Tim Raines .75 2.00
71 Roy Lee Jackson .02 .10
72 Carl Yastrzemski .60 1.50
73 John Castino .02 .10
74 Joe Niekro .08 .25
75 Tommy John .20 .50
76 Dave Winfield AS .30 .75
77 Miguel Dilone .02 .10
78 Gary Gray .02 .10
79 Tom Hume .02 .10
80 Jim Palmer .50 1.25
81 Jim Palmer IA .30 .75
82 Vida Blue IA .08 .25
83 Garth Iorg .02 .10
84 Rennie Stennett .02 .10
85 Dave Lopes IA .08 .25
Traded to A's Feb. 8/82
86 Dave Concepcion .08 .25
87 Matt Keough .02 .10
88 Jim Spencer .02 .10
89 Steve Henderson .02 .10
90 Nolan Ryan 4.00 10.00
91 Carney Lansford .08 .25
92 Bake McBride .02 .10
93 Dave Stapleton .02 .10
94 Expos Team Leaders .08 .25
Warren Cromartie
Bill Gullick
95 Ozzie Smith 4.00 10.00
Traded to Cardinals Feb. 11/82
96 Rich Hebner .02 .10
97 Tim Foli .02 .10
Traded to Angels Dec. 11/82
98 Darrell Porter .02 .10
99 Barry Bonnell .02 .10
100 Mike Schmidt 1.25 3.00
101 Mike Schmidt IA .60 1.50
102 Dan Briggs .02 .10
103 Al Cowens .02 .10
104 Grant Jackson .08 .25
Traded to Royals Jan. 19/82
105 Kirk Gibson .30 .75
106 Dan Schatzeder .08 .25
Traded to Giants Dec. 9/81
107 Juan Berenguer .02 .10
108 Jack Morris .20 .50
109 Dave Revering .02 .10
110 Carlton Fisk .60 1.50
111 Carlton Fisk IA .30 .75
112 Billy Sample .02 .10
113 Steve McCatty .02 .10
114 Ken Landreaux .02 .10
115 Gaylord Perry .40 1.00
116 Elias Sosa .02 .10
117 Rich Gossage IA .08 .25
118 Expos Future Stars 2.00 5.00
Terry Francona
Brad Mills
Br
119 Billy Almon .02 .10
120 Gary Lucas .02 .10
121 Ken Oberkfell .02 .10
122 Steve Carlton IA .30 .75
123 Jeff Reardon .20 .50
124 Bill Buckner .08 .25
125 Danny Ainge .60 1.50
Voluntarily Retired Nov. 30/81
126 Paul Splittorff .02 .10
127 Lonnie Smith .02 .10
Traded to Cardinals Nov. 19/81
128 Rudy May .02 .10
129 Checklist 1-132 .02 .10
130 Julio Cruz .02 .10
131 Stan Bahnsen .02 .10
132 Pete Vuckovich .02 .10
133 Luis Salazar .02 .10
134 Dan Ford .08 .25
Traded to Orioles Jan. 28/82
135 Denny Martinez .30 .75
136 Lary Sorensen .02 .10
137 Fergie Jenkins .40 1.00
Traded to Cubs Dec. 15/81
138 Rick Camp .02 .10
139 Wayne Nordhagen .02 .10
140 Ron LeFlore .08 .25
141 Rick Sutcliffe .08 .25
142 Rick Waits .02 .10
143 Mookie Wilson .30 .75
144 Greg Minton .02 .10
145 Bob Horner .08 .25
146 Joe Morgan IA .30 .75
147 Larry Gura .02 .10
148 Alfredo Griffin .02 .10
149 Pat Putnam .02 .10
150 Ted Simmons .08 .25
151 Gary Matthews .08 .25
152 Greg Luzinski .08 .25
153 Mike Flanagan .08 .25
154 Jim Morrison .02 .10
155 Otto Velez .02 .10
156 Frank White .08 .25
157 Doug Corbett .02 .10
158 Brian Downing .02 .10
159 Willie Randolph IA .08 .25
160 Luis Tiant .08 .25
161 Andre Thornton .02 .10
162 Amos Otis .08 .25
163 Paul Mirabella .02 .10
164 Bert Blyleven .20 .50
165 Rowland Office .02 .10
166 Gene Tenace .08 .25
167 Cecil Cooper .08 .25
168 Bruce Benedict .02 .10
169 Mark Clear .02 .10
170 Jim Bibby .02 .10
171 Ken Griffey IA .08 .25
Traded to Yankees Nov 4/81
172 Bill Gullickson .02 .10
173 Mike Scioscia .02 .10
174 Doug DeCinces .08 .25
Traded to Angels Jan 28/82
175 Jerry Mumphrey .02 .10
176 Rollie Fingers .40 1.00
177 George Foster IA .08 .25
Traded to Mets Feb 10/82
178 Mitchell Page .02 .10
179 Steve Garvey .30 .75
180 Steve Garvey IA .08 .25
181 Woodie Fryman .02 .10
182 Larry Herndon .02 .10
Traded to Tigers Dec. 9/81
183 Frank White IA .08 .25
184 Alan Ashby .02 .10
185 Phil Niekro .40 1.00
186 Leon Roberts .02 .10
187 Rod Carew .60 1.50
188 Willie Stargell IA .30 .75
189 Joel Youngblood .02 .10
190 J.R. Richard .02 .10
191 Tim Wallach .30 .75
192 Broderick Perkins .02 .10
193 Johnny Grubb .02 .10
194 Larry Bowa .08 .25
Traded to Cubs Jan. 27/82
195 Paul Molitor 1.25 3.00
196 Willie Upshaw .02 .10
197 Roy Smalley .02 .10
198 Chris Speier .02 .10
199 Don Aase .02 .10
200 George Brett 2.50 6.00
201 George Brett IA 1.25 3.00
202 Rick Manning .02 .10
203 Blue Jays Prospects .30 .75
Jesse Barfield
Brian Milner#
204 Rick Reuschel .08 .25
205 Neil Allen .02 .10
206 Leon Durham .02 .10
207 Jim Gantner .08 .25
208 Joe Morgan .30 .75
209 Gary Lavelle .02 .10
210 Keith Hernandez .08 .25
211 Joe Charboneau .02 .10
212 Mario Mendoza .02 .10
213 Willie Randolph AS .08 .25
214 Lance Parrish .20 .50
215 Mike Krukow .02 .10
Traded to Phillies Dec. 8/81
216 Ron Cey .08 .25
217 Ruppert Jones .02 .10
218 Dave Lopes .08 .25
Traded to A's Feb. 8/82
219 Steve Yeager .02 .10
220 Manny Trillo .02 .10
221 Dave Concepcion IA .08 .25
222 Butch Wynegar .02 .10
223 Lloyd Moseby .02 .10
224 Bruce Bochte .02 .10
225 Ed Ott .02 .10
226 Checklist 133-264 .02 .10
227 Ray Burris .02 .10
228 Reggie Smith IA .08 .25
229 Oscar Gamble .02 .10
230 Willie Wilson .02 .10
231 Brian Kingman .02 .10
232 John Stearns .02 .10
233 Duane Kuiper .02 .10
Traded to Giants Nov. 16/81
234 Don Baylor .08 .25
235 Mike Easler .02 .10
236 Lou Piniella .08 .25
237 Robin Yount .60 1.50
238 Kevin Saucier .02 .10
239 Jon Matlack .02 .10
240 Bucky Dent .08 .25
241 Bucky Dent IA .02 .10
242 Milt May .02 .10
243 Lee Mazzilli .02 .10
244 Gary Carter .40 1.00
245 Ken Reitz .02 .10
246 Scott McGregor AS .02 .10
247 Pedro Guerrero .08 .25
248 Art Howe .02 .10
249 Dick Tidrow .02 .10
250 Tug McGraw .08 .25
251 Fred Lynn .08 .25
252 Fred Lynn IA .02 .10
253 Gene Richards .02 .10
254 Jorge Bell RC .40 1.00
George Bell
255 Tony Perez .40 1.00
256 Tony Perez IA .20 .50
257 Rich Dotson .02 .10
258 Bo Diaz .02 .10
Traded to Phillies Nov. 19/81
259 Rodney Scott .02 .10
260 Bruce Sutter .40 1.00
261 George Brett AS 1.25 3.00
262 Rick Dempsey .08 .25
263 Mike Phillips .02 .10
264 Jerry Garvin .02 .10
265 Al Bumbry .20 .50
266 Hubie Brooks .02 .10
267 Vida Blue .08 .25
268 Rickey Henderson 2.00 5.00
269 Rick Peters .02 .10
270 Rusty Staub .08 .25
271 Sixto Lezcano .02 .10
Traded to Padres Dec. 10/81
272 Bump Wills .02 .10
273 Gary Allenson .02 .10
274 Randy Jones .02 .10
275 Bob Watson .08 .25
276 Dave Kingman .08 .25
277 Terry Puhl .02 .10
278 Jerry Reuss .08 .25
279 Sammy Stewart .02 .10
280 Ben Oglivie .02 .10
281 Kent Tekulve .08 .25
282 Ken Macha .08 .25
283 Ron Davis .02 .10
284 Bob Grich .08 .25
285 Sparky Lyle .08 .25
286 Rich Gossage AS .08 .25
287 Dennis Eckersley .40 1.00
288 Garry Templeton .02 .10
Traded to Padres Dec. 10/81
289 Bob Stanley .02 .10
290 Ken Singleton .02 .10
291 Mickey Hatcher .02 .10
292 Dave Palmer .02 .10
293 Damaso Garcia .02 .10
294 Don Money .02 .10
295 George Hendrick .02 .10
296 Steve Kemp .02 .10
Traded to White Sox Nov. 27/81
297 Dave Smith .02 .10
298 Bucky Dent AS .02 .10
299 Steve Trout .02 .10
300 Reggie Jackson 1.25 3.00
Traded to Angels Jan. 26/82
301 Reggie Jackson IA .60 1.50
Traded to Angels Jan. 26/82
302 Doug Flynn .08 .25
Traded to Rangers Dec. 14/81
303 Wayne Gross .02 .10
304 Johnny Bench IA .30 .75
305 Don Sutton .40 1.00
306 Don Sutton IA .30 .75
307 Mark Bomback .02 .10
308 Charlie Moore .02 .10
309 Jeff Burroughs .02 .10
310 Mike Hargrove .08 .25
311 Enos Cabell .02 .10
312 Lenny Randle .02 .10
313 Ivan DeJesus .02 .10
Traded to Phillies Jan. 27/82
314 Buck Martinez .02 .10
315 Burt Hooton .02 .10
316 Scott McGregor .02 .10
317 Dick Ruthven .02 .10
318 Mike Heath .02 .10
319 Ray Knight .08 .25
Traded to Astros Dec. 18/81
320 Chris Chambliss .02 .10
321 Chris Chambliss IA .02 .10
322 Ross Baumgarten .02 .10
323 Bill Lee .08 .25
324 Gorman Thomas .02 .10
325 Jose Cruz .08 .25
326 Al Oliver .08 .25
327 Jackson Todd .02 .10
328 Ed Farmer .02 .10
Traded to Phillies Jan. 28/82
329 U.L. Washington .02 .10
330 Ken Griffey .08 .25
Traded to Yankees Nov. 4/81
331 John Milner .02 .10
332 Don Robinson .02 .10
333 Cliff Johnson .02 .10
334 Fernando Valenzuela .30 .75
335 Jim Sundberg .08 .25
336 George Foster .08 .25
Traded to Mets Feb. 10/82
337 Pete Rose AS .60 1.50
338 Dave Lopes AS .08 .25
Traded to A's Feb. 8/82
339 Mike Schmidt AS .60 1.50
340 Dave Concepcion AS .02 .10
341 Andre Dawson AS .30 .75
342 George Foster AS .08 .25
Traded to Mets Feb. 10/82
343 Dave Parker AS .08 .25
344 Gary Carter AS .08 .25
345 Fernando Valenzuela AS .20 .50
346 Tom Seaver AS .30 .75
347 Bruce Sutter AS .20 .50
348 Darrell Porter IA .02 .10
349 Dave Collins .02 .10
Traded to Yankees Dec. 23/81
350 Amos Otis IA .02 .10
351 Frank Taveras .02 .10
Traded to Expos Dec. 14/81
352 Dave Winfield .60 1.50
353 Larry Parrish .02 .10
354 Roberto Ramos .02 .10
355 Dwight Evans .08 .25
356 Mickey Rivers .02 .10
357 Butch Hobson .02 .10
358 Carl Yastrzemski IA .30 .75
359 Ron Jackson .02 .10
360 Len Barker .02 .10
361 Pete Rose 1.25 3.00
362 Kevin Hickey RC .02 .10
363 Rod Carew IA .30 .75
364 Hector Cruz .02 .10
365 Bill Madlock .08 .25
366 Jim Rice .08 .25
367 Ron Cey IA .08 .25
368 Luis Leal .04 .10
369 Dennis Leonard .02 .10
370 Mike Norris .02 .10
371 Tom Paciorek .08 .25
Traded to White Sox Dec. 11/81
372 Willie Stargell .40 1.00
373 Dan Driessen .02 .10
374 Larry Bowa IA .08 .25
Traded to Cubs Jan. 27/82
375 Dusty Baker .08 .25
376 Joey McLaughlin .02 .10
377 Reggie Jackson AS .60 1.50
Traded to Angels Jan. 26/82
378 Mike Caldwell .02 .10
379 Andre Dawson .60 1.50
380 Dave Stieb .02 .10
381 Alan Trammell .30 .75
382 John Mayberry .02 .10
383 John Wathan .02 .10
384 Hal McRae .08 .25
385 Ken Forsch .02 .10
386 Jerry White .02 .10
387 Tom Veryzer .02 .10
Traded to Mets Jan. 8/82
388 Joe Rudi .02 .10
Traded to A's Dec. 4/81
389 Bob Knepper .02 .10
390 Eddie Murray 1.50 4.00
391 Dale Murphy .30 .75
392 Bob Boone IA .08 .25
Traded to Angels Dec. 6/81
393 Al Hrabosky .02 .10
394 Checklist 265-396 .02 .10
395 Omar Moreno .02 .10
396 Rich Gossage .30 .75

1982 O-Pee-Chee Posters

These 24 full-color posters comprising the 1982 O-Pee-Chee poster insert set were inserted one per regular wax pack and feature players of the Montreal Expos (numbered 13-24) and the Toronto Blue Jays (numbered 1-12). These posters are typically found with two folds and measure approximately 4 7/8" by 6 7/8". The posters are blank-backed and are numbered at the bottom in French and English. A distinctive red (Blue Jays) or blue (Expos) border surrounds the player photo.

COMPLETE SET (24) 3.00 8.00
1 John Mayberry .20 .50
2 Damaso Garcia .08 .25
3 Ernie Whitt .08 .25
4 Lloyd Moseby .08 .25
5 Alvis Woods .08 .25
6 Dave Stieb .30 .75
7 Roy Lee Jackson .08 .25
8 Joey McLaughlin .08 .25
9 Luis Leal .08 .25
10 Aurelio Rodriguez .08 .25
11 Otto Velez .08 .25
12 Juan Berenguer UER
(Misspelled Berenger) .08 .25
13 Warren Cromartie .08 .25
14 Rodney Scott .08 .25
15 Larry Parrish .20 .50
16 Gary Carter 1.00 2.50
17 Tim Raines .40 1.00
18 Andre Dawson .75 2.00
19 Terry Francona .30 .75
20 Steve Rogers .08 .25
21 Bill Gullickson .08 .25
22 Scott Sanderson .08 .25
23 Jeff Reardon .40 1.00
24 Jerry White .08 .25

1983 O-Pee-Chee

This set is an abridgement of the 1983 Topps set. The 396 standard-size cards comprising the 1983 O-Pee-Chee set differ from the cards of the 1983 Topps set by having a higher ratio of cards of players from the two Canadian teams, a practice begun by O-Pee-Chee in 1977 and continued to 1988. The set contains virtually the same pictures for the players also featured in the 1983 Topps issue. The fronts feature white-bordered color player action photos framed by a colored line. A circular color player head shot also appears on the front at the lower right. The player's name, team and bilingual position appear at the lower left. The pink and white horizontal backs carry the player's name and biography at the top. The player's major league statistics and bilingual career highlights follow below. The asterisked cards have an extra line on the front inside the picture area indicating team change. The O-Pee-Chee logo appears on the front of every card. Super Veteran (SV) and All-Star (AS) cards are indicated in the checklist below; these are included in the set in addition to the player's regular card. The 1983 O-Pee-Chee set was issued in nine-card packs which cost 25 cents Canadian at time of issue. The set features Rookie Cards of Tony Gwynn and Ryne Sandberg.

COMPLETE SET (396) 25.00 60.00
1 Rusty Staub .07 .20
2 Larry Parrish .02 .10
3 George Brett 1.50 4.00
4 Carl Yastrzemski .50 1.25
5 Al Oliver SV .07 .20
6 Bill Virdon MG .02 .10
7 Gene Richards .02 .10
8 Steve Balboni .02 .10
9 Joey McLaughlin .02 .10
10 Gorman Thomas .02 .10
11 Chris Chambliss .07 .20
12 Ray Burris .02 .10
13 Larry Herndon .02 .10
14 Ozzie Smith 1.00 2.50
15 Ron Cey .07 .20
Now with Cubs
16 Willie Wilson .07 .20
17 Kent Tekulve .02 .10
18 Kent Tekulve SV .02 .10
19 Oscar Gamble .02 .10
20 Carlton Fisk .40 1.00
21 Dale Murphy AS .20 .50
22 Randy Lerch .02 .10
23 Dale Murphy .20 .50
24 Steve Mura .07 .20
Now with White Sox
25 Hal McRae .07 .20
26 Dennis Lamp .02 .10
27 Ron Washington .02 .10
28 Bruce Bochte .02 .10
29 Randy Jones .07 .20
Now with Pirates
30 Jim Rice .07 .20
31 Bill Gullickson .07 .20
32 Dave Concepcion AS .07 .20
33 Ted Simmons SV .07 .20
34 Bobby Cox MG .02 .10
35 Rollie Fingers .20 .50
36 Rollie Fingers SV .10 .30
37 Mike Hargrove .07 .20
38 Roy Smalley .02 .10
39 Terry Puhl .02 .10
40 Fernando Valenzuela .20 .50
41 Garry Maddox .02 .10

Card	Low	High
42 Dale Murray	.07	.20
Now with Yankees		
43 Bob Dernier	.02	.10
44 Don Robinson	.02	.10
45 John Mayberry	.02	.10
46 Richard Dotson	.02	.10
47 Wayne Nordhagen	.02	.10
Now with Cubs		
48 Lary Sorensen	.02	.10
49 Willie McGee RC	1.25	3.00
50 Bob Horner	.02	.10
51 Rusty Staub SV	.07	.20
52 Tom Seaver	1.00	2.50
Now with Mets		
53 Chet Lemon	.02	.10
54 Scott Sanderson	.02	.10
55 Mookie Wilson	.07	.20
56 Reggie Jackson	.60	1.50
57 Tim Blackwell	.02	.10
58 Keith Moreland	.02	.10
59 Alvis Woods	.07	.20
Now with Athletics		
60 Johnny Bench	.60	1.50
61 Johnny Bench SV	.30	.75
62 Jim Gott	.02	.10
63 Rick Monday	.02	.10
64 Gary Matthews	.07	.20
65 Jack Morris	.07	.20
66 Lou Whitaker	.20	.50
67 U.L. Washington	.02	.10
68 Eric Show	.02	.10
69 Lee Lacy	.02	.10
70 Steve Carlton	.40	1.00
71 Steve Carlton SV	.30	.75
72 Tom Paciorek	.02	.10
73 Manny Trillo	.07	.20
Now with Indians		
74 Tony Perez SV	.10	.30
75 Amos Otis	.07	.20
76 Rick Mahler	.02	.10
77 Hosken Powell	.02	.10
78 Bill Caudill	.02	.10
79 Dan Petry	.02	.10
80 George Foster	.07	.20
81 Joe Morgan	.20	.50
Now with Phillies		
82 Burt Hooton	.02	.10
83 Ryne Sandberg RC	6.00	15.00
84 Alan Ashby	.02	.10
85 Ken Singleton	.07	.20
86 Tom Hume	.02	.10
87 Dennis Leonard	.02	.10
88 Jim Gantner	.07	.20
89 Leon Roberts	.07	.20
Now with Royals		
90 Jerry Reuss	.07	.20
91 Ben Oglivie	.02	.10
92 Sparky Lyle SV	.07	.20
93 John Castino	.02	.10
94 Phil Niekro	.20	.50
95 Alan Trammell	.20	.50
96 Gaylord Perry	.20	.50
97 Tom Herr	.02	.10
98 Vance Law	.02	.10
99 Dickie Noles	.02	.10
100 Pete Rose	1.00	2.50
101 Pete Rose SV	.50	1.25
102 Dave Concepcion	.07	.20
103 Darrell Porter	.02	.10
104 Ron Guidry	.07	.20
105 Don Baylor	.07	.20
Now with Yankees		
106 Steve Rogers AS	.02	.10
107 Greg Minton	.02	.10
108 Glenn Hoffman	.02	.10
109 Luis Leal	.02	.10
110 Ken Griffey	.07	.20
111 Expos Leaders	.07	.20
Al Oliver		
Steve Rogers/(Team chec		
112 Luis Pujols	.02	.10
113 Julio Cruz	.02	.10
114 Jim Slaton	.02	.10
115 Chili Davis	.20	.50
116 Pedro Guerrero	.07	.20
117 Mike Ivie	.02	.10
118 Chris Welsh	.02	.10
119 Frank Pastore	.02	.10
120 Len Barker	.02	.10
121 Chris Speier	.02	.10
122 Bobby Murcer	.07	.20
123 Bill Russell	.02	.10
124 Lloyd Moseby	.02	.10
125 Leon Durham	.02	.10
126 Carl Yastrzemski SV	.20	.50
127 John Candelaria	.02	.10
128 Phil Garner	.07	.20
129 Checklist 1-132	.02	.10
130 Dave Stieb	.02	.10
131 Geoff Zahn	.02	.10
132 Todd Cruz	.02	.10
133 Tony Pena	.02	.10
134 Hubie Brooks	.02	.10
135 Dwight Evans	.07	.20
136 Willie Aikens	.02	.10
137 Woodie Fryman	.02	.10
138 Rick Dempsey	.07	.20
139 Bruce Berenyi	.02	.10
140 Willie Randolph	.07	.20
141 Eddie Murray	1.00	2.50
142 Mike Caldwell	.02	.10
143 Tony Gwynn RC	10.00	25.00
144 Tommy John SV	.07	.20
145 Don Sutton	.40	1.00
146 Don Sutton SV	.20	.50
147 Rick Manning	.02	.10
148 George Hendrick	.02	.10
149 Johnny Ray	.02	.10
150 Bruce Sutter	.07	.20
151 Bruce Sutter SV	.07	.20
152 Jay Johnstone	.07	.20
153 Jerry Koosman	.07	.20
154 Johnnie LeMaster	.02	.10
155 Dan Quisenberry	.07	.20
156 Luis Salazar	.02	.10
157 Steve Bedrosian	.07	.20
158 Jim Sundberg	.02	.10
159 Gaylord Perry SV	.10	.30
160 Dave Kingman	.10	.30
161 Dave Kingman SV	.02	.10
162 Mark Clear	.02	.10
163 Cal Ripken	4.00	10.00
164 Dave Palmer	.02	.10
165 Dan Driessen	.02	.10
166 Tug McGraw	.10	.30
167 Dennis Martinez	.07	.20
168 Juan Eichelberger	.07	.20
Now with Indians		
169 Doug Flynn	.02	.10
170 Steve Howe	.02	.10
171 Frank White	.07	.20
172 Mike Flanagan	.07	.20
173 Andre Dawson AS	.10	.30
174 Manny Trillo AS	.07	.20
Now with Indians		
175 Bo Diaz	.02	.10
176 Dave Righetti	.07	.20
177 Harold Baines	.20	.50
178 Vida Blue	.07	.20
179 Luis Tiant SV	.07	.20
180 Rickey Henderson	1.00	2.50
181 Rick Rhoden	.02	.10
182 Fred Lynn	.07	.20
183 Ed VandeBerg	.02	.10
184 Dwayne Murphy	.02	.10
185 Tim Lollar	.02	.10
186 Dave Tobik	.02	.10
187 Tug McGraw SV	.07	.20
188 Rick Miller	.02	.10
189 Dan Schatzeder	.02	.10
190 Cecil Cooper	.07	.20
191 Jim Beattie	.02	.10
192 Rich Dauer	.02	.10
193 Al Cowens	.02	.10
194 Roy Lee Jackson	.02	.10
195 Mike Gates	.02	.10
196 Tommy John	.20	.50
197 Bob Forsch	.02	.10
198 Steve Garvey	.20	.50
Now with Padres		
199 Brad Mills	.02	.10
200 Rod Carew	.40	1.00
201 Rod Carew SV	.20	.50
202 Blue Jays Leaders	.07	.20
Dave Stieb		
Damaso Garcia/(Tea		
203 Floyd Bannister	.07	.20
Now with White Sox		
204 Bruce Benedict	.02	.10
205 Dave Parker	.07	.20
206 Ken Oberkfell	.02	.10
207 Graig Nettles SV	.07	.20
208 Sparky Lyle	.07	.20
209 Jason Thompson	.02	.10
210 Jack Clark	.07	.20
211 Jim Kaat	.07	.20
212 John Stearns	.02	.10
213 Tom Burgmeier	.02	.10
214 Jerry White	.02	.10
215 Mario Soto	.02	.10
216 Scott McGregor	.02	.10
217 Tim Stoddard	.02	.10
218 Bill Laskey	.02	.10
219 Reggie Jackson SV	.20	.50
220 Dusty Baker	.07	.20
221 Joe Niekro	.07	.20
222 Damaso Garcia	.02	.10
223 John Montefusco	.02	.10
224 Mickey Rivers	.02	.10
225 Enos Cabell	.02	.10
226 LaMarr Hoyt	.02	.10
227 Tim Raines	.20	.50
228 Joaquin Andujar	.02	.10
229 Tim Wallach	.07	.20
230 Fergie Jenkins	.40	1.00
231 Fergie Jenkins SV	.20	.50
232 Tom Brunansky	.07	.20
233 Ivan DeJesus	.02	.10
234 Bryn Smith	.02	.10
235 Claudell Washington	.02	.10
236 Steve Renko	.02	.10
237 Dan Norman	.02	.10
238 Cesar Cedeno	.07	.20
239 Dave Stapleton	.02	.10
240 Rich Gossage	.20	.50
241 Rich Gossage SV	.10	.30
242 Bob Stanley	.02	.10
243 Rich Gale	.07	.20
Now with Reds		
244 Sixto Lezcano	.02	.10
245 Steve Sax	.07	.20
246 Jerry Mumphrey	.02	.10
247 Dave Smith	.02	.10
248 Bake McBride	.02	.10
249 Checklist 133-264	.02	.10
250 Bill Buckner	.07	.20
251 Kent Hrbek	.20	.50
252 Gene Tenace	.02	.10
Now with Pirates		
253 Charlie Lea	.02	.10
254 Rick Cerone	.02	.10
255 Gene Garber	.02	.10
256 Gene Garber SV	.02	.10
257 Jesse Barfield	.07	.20
258 Dave Winfield	.40	1.00
259 Don Money	.02	.10
260 Steve Kemp	.02	.10
Now with Yankees		
261 Steve Yeager	.02	.10
262 Keith Hernandez	.07	.20
263 Tippy Martinez	.02	.10
264 Joe Morgan SV	.20	.50
Now with Phillies		
265 Joel Youngblood	.02	.10
Now with Giants		
266 Bruce Sutter AS	.20	.50
267 Terry Francona	.07	.20
268 Neil Allen	.02	.10
269 Ron Oester	.02	.10
270 Dennis Eckersley	.40	1.00
271 Dale Berra	.02	.10
272 Al Bumbry	.02	.10
273 Lonnie Smith	.02	.10
274 Terry Kennedy	.02	.10
275 Ray Knight	.02	.10
276 Mike Norris	.02	.10
277 Rance Mulliniks	.02	.10
278 Dan Spillner	.02	.10
279 Bucky Dent	.07	.20
280 Bert Blyleven	.20	.50
281 Barry Bonnell	.02	.10
282 Reggie Smith	.07	.20
283 Reggie Smith SV	.07	.20
284 Ted Simmons	.07	.20
285 Lance Parrish	.07	.20
286 Larry Christenson	.02	.10
287 Ruppert Jones	.02	.10
288 Bob Welch	.07	.20
289 John Wathan	.02	.10
290 Jeff Reardon	.07	.20
291 Dave Revering	.02	.10
292 Craig Swan	.02	.10
293 Graig Nettles	.07	.20
294 Alfredo Griffin	.02	.10
295 Jerry Remy	.02	.10
296 Joe Sambito	.02	.10
297 Ron LeFlore	.02	.10
298 Brian Downing	.02	.10
299 Jim Palmer	.20	.50
300 Mike Schmidt	.75	2.00
301 Mike Schmidt SV	.40	1.00
302 Ernie Whitt	.02	.10
303 Andre Dawson	.20	.50
304 Bobby Murcer SV	.07	.20
305 Larry Bowa	.07	.20
306 Lee Mazzilli	.02	.10
Now with Pirates		
307 Lou Piniella	.07	.20
308 Buck Martinez	.07	.20
309 Jerry Martin	.02	.10
310 Greg Luzinski	.07	.20
311 Al Oliver	.07	.20
312 Mike Torrez	.02	.10
Now with Mets		
313 Dick Ruthven	.02	.10
314 Gary Carter AS	.20	.50
315 Rick Burleson	.02	.10
316 Phil Niekro SV	.10	.30
317 Moose Haas	.02	.10
318 Carney Lansford	.07	.20
Now with Athletics		
319 Tim Foli	.02	.10
320 Steve Rogers	.02	.10
321 Kirk Gibson	.20	.50
322 Glenn Hubbard	.02	.10
323 Luis DeLeon	.02	.10
324 Mike Marshall	.02	.10
325 Von Hayes	.02	.10
Now with Phillies		
326 Garth Iorg	.02	.10
327 Jose Cruz	.07	.20
328 Jim Palmer SV	.10	.30
329 Darrell Evans	.07	.20
330 Buddy Bell	.07	.20
331 Mike Krukow	.02	.10
Now with Giants		
332 Omar Moreno	.02	.10
Now with Astros		
333 Dave LaRoche	.02	.10
334 Dave LaRoche SV	.02	.10
335 Bill Madlock	.07	.20
336 Garry Templeton	.02	.10
337 John Lowenstein	.02	.10
338 Willie Upshaw	.02	.10
339 Dave Hostetler RC	.02	.10
340 Larry Gura	.02	.10
341 Doug DeCinces	.07	.20
342 Mike Schmidt AS	.40	1.00
343 Charlie Hough	.07	.20
344 Andre Thornton	.02	.10
345 Jim Clancy	.02	.10
346 Ken Forsch	.02	.10
347 Sammy Stewart	.02	.10
348 Alan Bannister	.02	.10
349 Checklist 265-396	.02	.10
350 Robin Yount	.40	1.00
351 Warren Cromartie	.02	.10
352 Tim Raines AS	.20	.50
353 Tony Armas	.02	.10
Now with Red Sox		
354 Tom Seaver SV	.50	1.25
Now with Mets		
355 Tony Perez	.30	.75
Now with Phillies		
356 Toby Harrah	.02	.10
357 Dan Ford	.02	.10
358 Charlie Puleo	.02	.10
Now with Reds		
359 Dave Collins	.02	.10
Now with Blue Jays		
360 Nolan Ryan	3.00	8.00
361 Nolan Ryan SV	1.50	4.00
362 Bill Almon	.02	.10
Now with Athletics		
363 Eddie Milner	.02	.10
364 Gary Lucas	.02	.10
365 Dave Lopes	.07	.20
366 Bob Boone	.07	.20
367 Biff Pocoroba	.02	.10
368 Richie Zisk	.02	.10
369 Tony Bernazard	.02	.10
370 Gary Carter	.40	1.00
371 Paul Molitor	.50	1.25
372 Art Howe	.02	.10
373 Pete Rose AS	.50	1.25
374 Glenn Adams	.02	.10
375 Pete Vuckovich	.02	.10
376 Gary Lavelle	.02	.10
377 Lee May	.07	.20
378 Lee May SV	.07	.20
379 Butch Wynegar	.02	.10
380 Ron Davis	.02	.10
381 Bob Grich	.07	.20
382 Gary Roenicke	.02	.10
383 Jim Kaat SV	.07	.20
384 Steve Carlton AS	.20	.50
385 Mike Easler	.02	.10
386 Rod Carew AS	.20	.50
387 Bob Grich AS	.07	.20
388 George Brett AS	.75	2.00
389 Robin Yount AS	.20	.50
390 Reggie Jackson AS	.20	.50
391 Rickey Henderson AS	.20	.50
392 Fred Lynn AS	.07	.20
393 Carlton Fisk AS	.20	.50
394 Pete Vuckovich AS	.02	.10
395 Larry Gura AS	.02	.10
396 Dan Quisenberry AS	.02	.10

1984 O-Pee-Chee

This set is an abridgement of the 1984 Topps set. The 396 standard-size cards comprising the 1984 O-Pee-Chee set differ from the cards of the 1984 Topps set by having a higher ratio of cards of players from the two Canadian teams, a practice begun by O-Pee-Chee in 1977 and continued to 1988. The set contains virtually the same pictures for the players also featured in the 1984 Topps issue. The fronts feature white-bordered color player action photos. A color player head shot also appears on the front at the lower left. The player's name and position appear in colored lettering within the white margin at the lower right. His team name appears in vertical colored lettering within the white margin on the left. The red, white and blue horizontal backs carry the player's name and biography at the top. The player's major league statistics and bilingual career highlights follow below. The asterisked cards have an extra line on the front inside the picture area indicating team change. The O-Pee-Chee logo appears on the front of every card. All-Star (AS) cards are indicated in the checklist below; they are included in the set in addition to the player's regular card. The O-Pee-Chee set came in 12-card packs which cost 35 cents Canadian at time of issue. Notable Rookie Cards include Don Mattingly and Darryl Strawberry.

Card	Low	High
COMPLETE SET (396)	15.00	40.00
1 Pascual Perez	.01	.05
2 Cal Ripken AS	1.25	3.00
3 Lloyd Moseby AS	.01	.05
4 Mel Hall	.01	.05
5 Willie Wilson	.01	.05
6 Mike Morgan	.01	.05
7 Gary Lucas	.02	.10
Now with Expos		
8 Don Mattingly RC	6.00	15.00
9 Jim Gott	.01	.05
10 Robin Yount	.20	.50
11 Joey McLaughlin	.01	.05
12 Billy Sample	.01	.05
13 Oscar Gamble	.01	.05
14 Bill Russell	.01	.05
15 Burt Hooton	.01	.05
16 Omar Moreno	.01	.05
17 Dave Lopes	.02	.10
18 Dale Berra	.01	.05
19 Rance Mulliniks	.01	.05
20 Greg Luzinski	.02	.10
21 Doug Sisk	.01	.05
22 Don Robinson	.01	.05
23 Keith Moreland	.01	.05
24 Richard Dotson	.01	.05
25 Glenn Hubbard	.01	.05
26 Rod Carew	.40	1.00
27 Alan Wiggins	.01	.05
28 Frank Viola	.20	.50
29 Phil Niekro	.40	1.00
Now with Yankees		
30 Wade Boggs	1.25	3.00
31 Dave Parker	.08	.25
Now with Reds		
32 Bobby Ramos	.01	.05
33 Tom Burgmeier	.01	.05
34 Eddie Milner	.01	.05
35 Don Sutton	.30	.75
36 Glenn Wilson	.01	.05
37 Mike Krukow	.01	.05
38 Dave Collins	.01	.05
39 Garth Iorg	.01	.05
40 Dusty Baker	.08	.25
41 Tony Bernazard	.02	.10
Now with Indians		
42 Claudell Washington	.01	.05
43 Cecil Cooper	.02	.10
44 Dan Driessen	.01	.05
45 Jerry Mumphrey	.01	.05
46 Rick Rhoden	.01	.05
47 Rudy Law	.01	.05
48 Julio Franco	.20	.50
49 Mike Norris	.01	.05
50 Chris Chambliss	.01	.05
51 Pete Falcone	.01	.05
52 Mike Marshall	.01	.05
53 Amos Otis	.02	.10
Now with Pirates		
54 Jesse Orosco	.02	.10
55 Dave Concepcion	.02	.10
56 Gary Allenson	.01	.05
57 Dan Schatzeder	.01	.05
58 Jerry Remy	.01	.05
59 Carney Lansford	.02	.10
60 Paul Molitor	.40	1.00
61 Chris Codiroli	.01	.05
62 Dave Hostetler	.01	.05
63 Ed VandeBerg	.01	.05
64 Ryne Sandberg	1.50	4.00
65 Kirk Gibson	.20	.50
66 Nolan Ryan	2.50	6.00
67 Gary Ward	.01	.05
Now with Rangers		
68 Luis Salazar	.01	.05
69 Dan Quisenberry AS	.01	.05
70 Gary Matthews	.01	.05
71 Pete O'Brien	.02	.10
72 John Wathan	.01	.05
73 Jody Davis	.01	.05
74 Kent Tekulve	.01	.05
75 Bob Forsch	.01	.05
76 Alfredo Griffin	.01	.05
77 Bryn Smith	.01	.05
78 Mike Torrez	.01	.05
79 Mike Hargrove	.02	.10
80 Steve Rogers	.01	.05
81 Bake McBride	.01	.05
82 Doug DeCinces	.01	.05
83 Richie Zisk	.01	.05
84 Randy Bush	.01	.05
85 Atlee Hammaker	.01	.05
86 Chet Lemon	.01	.05
87 Frank Pastore	.01	.05
88 Alan Trammell	.20	.50
89 Terry Francona	.02	.10
90 Pedro Guerrero	.02	.10
91 Dan Spillner	.01	.05
92 Lloyd Moseby	.01	.05
93 Bob Knepper	.01	.05
94 Ted Simmons AS	.02	.10
95 Aurelio Lopez	.01	.05
96 Bill Buckner	.02	.10
97 LaMarr Hoyt	.01	.05
98 Tom Brunansky	.02	.10
99 Ron Oester	.01	.05
100 Reggie Jackson	.50	1.25
101 Ron Davis	.01	.05
102 Ken Oberkfell	.01	.05
103 Dwayne Murphy	.01	.05
104 Jim Slaton	.01	.05
Now with Angels		
105 Tony Armas	.01	.05
106 Ernie Whitt	.02	.10
107 Johnnie LeMaster	.01	.05
108 Randy Moffitt	.01	.05
109 Terry Forster	.01	.05
110 Ron Guidry	.02	.10
111 Bill Virdon MG	.01	.05
112 Doyle Alexander	.01	.05
113 Lonnie Smith	.01	.05
114 Checklist 1-132	.01	.05
115 Andre Thornton	.01	.05
116 Jeff Reardon	.02	.10
117 Tom Herr	.02	.10
118 Charlie Hough	.02	.10
119 Phil Garner	.02	.10
120 Keith Hernandez	.08	.25
121 Rich Gossage	.20	.50
Now with Padres		
122 Ted Simmons	.02	.10
123 Butch Wynegar	.01	.05
124 Damaso Garcia	.01	.05
125 Britt Burns	.01	.05
126 Bert Blyleven	.02	.10
127 Carlton Fisk	.20	.50
128 Rick Manning	.01	.05
129 Bill Laskey	.01	.05
130 Ozzie Smith	.75	2.00
131 Bo Diaz	.01	.05
132 Tom Paciorek	.01	.05
133 Dave Rozema	.01	.05
134 Dave Stieb	.01	.05
135 Brian Downing	.01	.05
136 Rick Camp	.01	.05
137 Willie Aikens	.02	.10
Now with Blue Jays		
138 Charlie Moore	.01	.05
139 George Frazier	.02	.10
Now with Indians		
140 Storm Davis	.01	.05
141 Glenn Hoffman	.01	.05
142 Charlie Lea	.01	.05
143 Mike Vail	.01	.05
144 Steve Sax	.02	.10
145 Gary Lavelle	.01	.05
146 Gorman Thomas	.02	.10
Now with Mariners		
147 Dan Petry	.01	.05
148 Mark Clear	.01	.05
149 Dave Beard	.02	.10
Now with Mariners		
150 Dale Murphy	.20	.50
151 Steve Trout	.01	.05
152 Tony Pena	.02	.10
153 Geoff Zahn	.01	.05
154 Dave Henderson	.01	.05
155 Frank White	.02	.10
156 Dick Ruthven	.01	.05
157 Gary Gaetti	.08	.25
158 Lance Parrish	.02	.10
159 Joe Price	.01	.05
160 Mario Soto	.01	.05
161 Tug McGraw	.08	.25
162 Bob Ojeda	.01	.05
163 George Hendrick	.01	.05
164 Scott Sanderson	.01	.05
Now with Cubs		
165 Ken Singleton	.01	.05
166 Terry Kennedy	.01	.05
167 Gene Garber	.01	.05
168 Juan Bonilla	.01	.05
169 Larry Parrish	.02	.10
170 Jerry Reuss	.02	.10
171 John Tudor	.02	.10
Now with Pirates		
172 Dave Kingman	.02	.10
173 Garry Templeton	.01	.05
174 Bob Boone	.02	.10
175 Graig Nettles	.02	.10
176 Lee Smith	.20	.50
177 LaMarr Hoyt AS	.01	.05
178 Bill Krueger	.01	.05
179 Buck Martinez	.01	.05
180 Manny Trillo	.02	.10
Now with Giants		
181 Lou Whitaker AS	.02	.10
182 Darryl Strawberry RC	1.25	3.00
183 Neil Allen	.01	.05
184 Jim Rice AS	.02	.10
185 Sixto Lezcano	.01	.05
186 Tom Hume	.01	.05
187 Garry Maddox	.01	.05
188 Bryan Little	.01	.05
189 Jose Cruz	.02	.10
190 Ben Oglivie	.01	.05
191 Cesar Cedeno	.02	.10
192 Nick Esasky	.01	.05
193 Ken Forsch	.01	.05
194 Jim Palmer	.20	.50
195 Jack Morris	.02	.10
196 Steve Howe	.01	.05
197 Harold Baines	.02	.10
198 Bill Doran	.02	.10
199 Willie Hernandez	.02	.10
200 Andre Dawson	.20	.50
201 Bruce Kison	.01	.05
202 Bobby Cox MG	.02	.10
203 Matt Keough	.01	.05
204 Ron Guidry AS	.02	.10
205 Greg Minton	.01	.05
206 Al Holland	.01	.05
207 Luis Leal	.01	.05
208 Jose Oquendo RC	.01	.05
209 Leon Durham	.01	.05
210 Joe Morgan	.30	.75
Now with Athletics		
211 Lou Whitaker	.02	.10
212 George Brett	1.25	3.00
213 Bruce Hurst	.01	.05
214 Steve Carlton	.40	1.00
215 Tippy Martinez	.01	.05
216 Ken Landreaux	.01	.05
217 Alan Ashby	.01	.05
218 Dennis Eckersley	.20	.50
219 Craig McMurtry	.01	.05
220 Fernando Valenzuela	.02	.10
221 Cliff Johnson	.01	.05
222 Rick Honeycutt	.01	.05
223 George Brett AS	.60	1.50
224 Rusty Staub	.02	.10
225 Lee Mazzilli	.01	.05
226 Pat Putnam	.01	.05
227 Bob Welch	.02	.10
228 Rick Cerone	.01	.05
229 Lee Lacy	.01	.05
230 Rickey Henderson	.75	2.00
231 Gary Redus	.01	.05
232 Tim Wallach	.02	.10
233 Checklist 133-264	.01	.05
234 Rafael Ramirez	.01	.05
235 Matt Young RC	.01	.05
236 Ellis Valentine	.01	.05
237 John Castino	.01	.05
238 Eric Show	.01	.05
239 Bob Horner	.01	.05
240 Eddie Murray	.50	1.25
241 Billy Almon	.01	.05
242 Greg Brock	.01	.05
243 Bruce Sutter	.02	.10
244 Dwight Evans	.02	.10
245 Rick Sutcliffe	.02	.10
246 Terry Crowley	.01	.05
247 Fred Lynn	.02	.10
248 Bill Dawley	.01	.05
249 Dave Stapleton	.01	.05
250 Bill Madlock	.01	.05
251 Jim Sundberg	.02	.10
Now with Brewers		
252 Steve Yeager	.01	.05
253 Jim Wohlford	.01	.05
254 Shane Rawley	.01	.05
255 Bruce Benedict	.01	.05
256 Dave Geisel	.01	.05
Now with Mariners		
257 Julio Cruz	.01	.05
258 Luis Sanchez	.01	.05
259 Von Hayes	.01	.05
260 Scott McGregor	.01	.05
261 Tom Seaver	.75	2.00
Now with White Sox		
262 Doug Flynn	.01	.05
263 Wayne Gross	.01	.05
Now with Orioles		
264 Larry Gura	.01	.05
265 John Montefusco	.01	.05
266 Dave Winfield AS	.20	.50
267 Tim Lollar	.01	.05
268 Ron Washington	.01	.05
269 Mickey Rivers	.01	.05
270 Mookie Wilson	.02	.10
271 Moose Haas	.01	.05
272 Rick Dempsey	.02	.10
273 Dan Quisenberry	.01	.05
274 Steve Henderson	.01	.05
275 Len Matuszek	.01	.05
276 Frank Tanana	.02	.10
277 Dave Righetti	.01	.05
278 Jorge Bell	.08	.25
279 Ivan DeJesus	.01	.05
280 Floyd Bannister	.01	.05
281 Dale Murray	.01	.05
282 Andre Robertson	.01	.05
283 Rollie Fingers	.20	.50
284 Tommy John	.08	.25
285 Darrell Porter	.01	.05
286 Lary Sorensen	.02	.10
Now with Athletics		
287 Warren Cromartie	.02	.10
Now playing in Japan		
288 Jim Beattie	.01	.05
289 Blue Jays Leaders	.02	.10
Lloyd Moseby		
Dave Stieb/(Team		
290 Dave Dravecky	.02	.10
291 Eddie Murray AS	.20	.50
292 Greg Bargar	.01	.05
293 Tom Underwood	.02	.10
Now with Orioles		
294 U.L. Washington	.01	.05
295 Mike Flanagan	.01	.05
296 Rich Gedman	.01	.05
297 Bruce Berenyi	.01	.05
298 Jim Gantner	.02	.10
299 Bill Caudill	.02	.10
Now with Athletics		
300 Pete Rose	1.00	2.50
Now with Expos		
301 Steve Kemp	.01	.05
302 Barry Bonnell	.02	.10
Now with Mariners		
303 Joel Youngblood	.01	.05
304 Rick Langford	.01	.05
305 Roy Smalley	.01	.05
306 Ken Griffey	.02	.10
307 Al Oliver	.02	.10
308 Ron Hassey	.01	.05
309 Len Barker	.01	.05
310 Willie McGee	.08	.25
311 Jerry Koosman	.02	.10
Now with Phillies		
312 Jorge Orta	.02	.10
Now with Royals		
313 Pete Vuckovich	.01	.05
314 George Wright	.01	.05
315 Bob Grich	.02	.10
316 Jesse Barfield	.02	.10
317 Willie Upshaw	.01	.05
318 Bill Gullickson	.01	.05
319 Ray Burris	.02	.10
Now with Athletics		
320 Bob Stanley	.01	.05
321 Ray Knight	.01	.05
322 Ken Schrom	.01	.05
323 Johnny Ray	.01	.05
324 Brian Giles	.01	.05
325 Darrell Evans	.02	.10
Now with Tigers		
326 Mike Caldwell	.01	.05
327 Ruppert Jones	.01	.05
328 Chris Speier	.01	.05
329 Bobby Castillo	.01	.05
330 John Candelaria	.01	.05

331 Bucky Dent .02 .10
332 Expos Leaders .02 .10
Al Oliver
Charlie Lea/(Team check
333 Larry Herndon .01 .05
334 Chuck Rainey .01 .05
335 Don Baylor .02 .10
336 Bob James .01 .05
337 Jim Clancy .01 .05
338 Duane Kuiper .01 .05
339 Roy Lee Jackson .01 .05
340 Hal McRae .02 .10
341 Larry McWilliams .01 .05
342 Tim Foli .02 .10
Now with Yankees
343 Fergie Jenkins .20 .50
344 Dickie Thon .01 .05
345 Kent Hrbek .08 .25
346 Larry Bowa .02 .10
347 Buddy Bell .02 .10
348 Toby Harrah .02 .10
Now with Yankees
349 Dan Ford .01 .05
350 George Foster .02 .10
351 Lou Piniella .02 .10
352 Dave Stewart .20 .50
353 Mike Easler .02 .10
Now with Red Sox
354 Jeff Burroughs .01 .05
355 Jason Thompson .01 .05
356 Glenn Abbott .01 .05
357 Ron Cey .02 .10
358 Bob Dernier .01 .05
359 Jim Acker .01 .05
360 Willie Randolph .02 .10
361 Mike Schmidt .60 1.50
362 David Green .01 .05
363 Cal Ripken 2.50 6.00
364 Jim Rice .02 .10
365 Steve Bedrosian .01 .05
366 Gary Carter .20 .50
367 Chili Davis .02 .10
368 Hubie Brooks .01 .05
369 Steve McCatty .01 .05
370 Tim Raines .20 .50
371 Joaquin Andujar .01 .05
372 Gary Roenicke .01 .05
373 Ron Kittle .01 .05
374 Rich Dauer .01 .05
375 Dennis Leonard .01 .05
376 Rick Burleson .01 .05
377 Eric Rasmussen .01 .05
378 Dave Winfield .20 .50
379 Checklist 265-396 .01 .05
380 Steve Garvey .08 .25
381 Jack Clark .02 .10
382 Odell Jones .01 .05
383 Terry Puhl .01 .05
384 Joe Niekro .02 .10
385 Tony Perez .30 .75
Now with Reds
386 George Hendrick AS .01 .05
387 Johnny Ray AS .01 .05
388 Mike Schmidt AS .20 .50
389 Ozzie Smith AS .40 1.00
390 Tim Raines AS .08 .25
391 Dale Murphy AS .08 .25
392 Andre Dawson AS .08 .25
393 Gary Carter AS .02 .10
394 Steve Rogers AS .01 .05
395 Steve Carlton AS .20 .50
396 Jesse Orosco AS .01 .05

1985 O-Pee-Chee

This set is an abridgement of the 1985 Topps set. The 396 standard-size cards comprising the 1985 O-Pee-Chee set differ from the cards of the 1985 Topps set by having a higher ratio of cards of players from the two Canadian teams, a practice begun by O-Pee-Chee in 1977 and continued to 1988. The set contains virtually the same pictures for the players also featured in the 1985 Topps issue. The fronts feature white-bordered color player photos. The player's name, position and team name and logo appear at the bottom of the photo. The green and white horizontal backs carry the player's name and biography at the top. The player's major league statistics and bilingual profile follow below. A bilingual trivia question and answer round out the back. The O-Pee-Chee logo appears on the front of every card. Notable Rookie Cards include Dwight Gooden and Kirby Puckett.

COMPLETE SET (396) 15.00 40.00
1 Tom Seaver .20 .50
2 Gary Lavelle .02 .10
Traded to Blue Jays 1-26-85
3 Tim Wallach .02 .10
4 Jim Wohlford .01 .05
5 Jeff Robinson .01 .05
6 Willie Wilson .01 .05
7 Cliff Johnson .02 .10
Free Agent with Rangers 12-20-84
8 Willie Randolph .02 .10
9 Larry Herndon .01 .05
10 Kirby Puckett RC 3.00 8.00
11 Mookie Wilson .02 .10
12 Dave Lopes .02 .10
Traded to Cubs 8-31-84
13 Tim Lollar .02 .10
Traded to White Sox 12-6-84
14 Chris Bando .01 .05
15 Jerry Koosman .02 .10
16 Bobby Meacham .01 .05
17 Mike Scott .01 .05
18 Rich Gedman .01 .05
19 George Frazier .01 .05
20 Chet Lemon .01 .05
21 Dave Concepcion .02 .10
22 Jason Thompson .01 .05
23 Bret Saberhagen RC* .40 1.00
24 Jesse Barfield .01 .05
25 Steve Bedrosian .01 .05
26 Roy Smalley .02 .10
Traded to Twins 2-19-85
27 Bruce Berenyi .01 .05
28 Butch Wynegar .01 .05
29 Alan Ashby .01 .05
30 Cal Ripken 1.50 4.00
31 Luis Leal .01 .05
32 Dave Dravecky .02 .10
33 Tito Landrum .01 .05
34 Pedro Guerrero .02 .10
35 Graig Nettles .02 .10
36 Fred Breining .01 .05
37 Roy Lee Jackson .01 .05
38 Steve Henderson .01 .05
39 Gary Pettis UER/(Photo actually .02 .10
Gary's little
b
40 Phil Niekro .20 .50
41 Dwight Gooden RC 1.25 3.00
42 Luis Sanchez .01 .05
43 Lee Smith .20 .50
44 Dickie Thon .01 .05
45 Greg Minton .01 .05
46 Mike Flanagan .01 .05
47 Bud Black .01 .05
48 Tony Fernandez .20 .50
49 Carlton Fisk .20 .50
50 John Candelaria .01 .05
51 Bob Watson .02 .10
Announced his Retirement
52 Rick Leach .01 .05
53 Rick Rhoden .01 .05
54 Cesar Cedeno .02 .10
55 Frank Tanana .01 .05
56 Larry Bowa .02 .10
57 Willie McGee .02 .10
58 Rich Dauer .01 .05
59 Jorge Bell .02 .10
60 George Hendrick .02 .10
Traded to Pirates 12-12-84
61 Donnie Moore .02 .10
Drafted by Angels 1-24-85
62 Mike Ramsey .01 .05
63 Nolan Ryan 1.25 3.00
64 Mark Bailey .01 .05
65 Bill Buckner .02 .10
66 Jerry Reuss .01 .05
67 Mike Schmidt .40 1.00
68 Von Hayes .01 .05
69 Phil Bradley .02 .10
70 Don Baylor .02 .10
71 Julio Cruz .01 .05
72 Rick Sutcliffe .01 .05
73 Storm Davis .01 .05
74 Mike Krukow .01 .05
75 Willie Upshaw .01 .05
76 Craig Lefferts .01 .05
77 Lloyd Moseby .01 .05
78 Ron Davis .01 .05
79 Rick Mahler .01 .05
80 Keith Hernandez .02 .10
81 Vance Law .02 .10
Traded to Expos 12-7-84
82 Joe Price .01 .05
83 Dennis Lamp .01 .05
84 Gary Ward .01 .05
85 Mike Marshall .01 .05
86 Marvell Wynne .01 .05
87 David Green .01 .05
88 Bryn Smith .01 .05
89 Sixto Lezcano .01 .05
Free Agent with Pirates 1-26-85
90 Rich Gossage .02 .10
91 Jeff Burroughs .02 .10
Purchased by Blue Jays 12-22-84
92 Bobby Brown .01 .05
93 Oscar Gamble .01 .05
94 Rick Dempsey .02 .10
95 Jose Cruz .02 .10
96 Johnny Ray .01 .05
97 Joel Youngblood .01 .05
98 Eddie Whitson .02 .10
Free Agent with 12-28-84
99 Milt Wilcox .01 .05
100 George Brett 1.25 3.00
101 Jim Acker .01 .05
102 Jim Sundberg .02 .10
Traded to Royals 1-18-85
103 Ozzie Virgil .01 .05
104 Mike Fitzgerald .02 .10
Traded to Expos 12-10-84
105 Ron Kittle .01 .05
106 Pascual Perez .01 .05
107 Barry Bonnell .01 .05
108 Lou Whitaker .08 .25
109 Gary Roenicke .01 .05
110 Alejandro Pena .01 .05
111 Doug DeCinces .01 .05
112 Doug Flynn .01 .05
113 Tom Herr .02 .10
114 Bob James .02 .10
Traded to White Sox 12-7-84
115 Rickey Henderson 1.25 3.00
Traded to Yankees 12-8-84
116 Pete Rose .20 .50
117 Greg Gross .01 .05
118 Eric Show .01 .05
119 Buck Martinez .02 .10
120 Steve Kemp .01 .05
Traded to Pirates 12-20-84
121 Checklist 1-132 .01 .05
122 Tom Brunansky .02 .10
123 Dave Kingman .02 .10
124 Garry Templeton .01 .05
125 Kent Tekulve .01 .05
126 Darryl Strawberry .20 .50
127 Mark Gubicza RC .02 .10
128 Ernie Whitt .01 .05
129 Don Robinson .01 .05
130 Al Oliver .02 .10
Traded to Dodgers 2-4-85
131 Mario Soto .01 .05
132 Jeff Leonard .01 .05
133 Andre Dawson .20 .50
134 Bruce Hurst .01 .05
135 Bobby Cox MG
(Team checklist back) .02 .10
136 Matt Young .01 .05
137 Bob Forsch .01 .05
138 Ron Darling .02 .10
139 Steve Trout .01 .05
140 Geoff Zahn .01 .05
141 Ken Forsch .01 .05
142 Jerry Willard .01 .05
143 Bill Gullickson .01 .05
144 Mike Mason .01 .05
145 Alvin Davis .02 .10
146 Gary Redus .01 .05
147 Willie Aikens .01 .05
148 Steve Yeager .01 .05
149 Dickie Noles .01 .05
150 Jim Rice .02 .10
151 Moose Haas .01 .05
152 Steve Balboni .01 .05
153 Frank LaCorte .01 .05
154 Angel Salazar .02 .10
Drafted by Cardinals 1-24-85
155 Bob Grich .02 .10
156 Craig Reynolds .01 .05
157 Bill Madlock .02 .10
158 Pat Tabler .01 .05
159 Don Slaught .02 .10
Traded to Rangers 1-18-85
160 Lance Parrish .02 .10
161 Ken Schrom .01 .05
162 Wally Backman .01 .05
163 Dennis Eckersley .20 .50
164 Dave Collins .02 .10
Traded to A's 12-8-84
165 Dusty Baker .08 .25
166 Claudell Washington .01 .05
167 Rick Camp .01 .05
168 Garth Iorg .01 .05
169 Shane Rawley .01 .05
170 George Foster .02 .10
171 Tony Bernazard .01 .05
172 Don Sutton .30 .75
Traded to A's 12-8-84
173 Jerry Remy .01 .05
174 Rick Honeycutt .01 .05
175 Dave Parker .02 .10
176 Buddy Bell .02 .10
177 Steve Garvey .08 .25
178 Miguel Dilone .01 .05
179 Tommy John .08 .25
180 Dave Winfield .20 .50
181 Alan Trammell .08 .25
182 Rollie Fingers .08 .25
183 Larry McWilliams .01 .05
184 Carmen Castillo .01 .05
185 Al Holland .01 .05
186 Jerry Mumphrey .01 .05
187 Chris Chambliss .02 .10
188 Jim Clancy .01 .05
189 Glenn Wilson .01 .05
190 Rusty Staub .02 .10
191 Ozzie Smith .75 2.00
192 Howard Johnson .08 .25
Traded to Mets 12-7-84
193 Jimmy Key RC .20 .50
194 Terry Kennedy .01 .05
195 Glenn Hubbard .01 .05
196 Pete O'Brien .01 .05
197 Keith Moreland .01 .05
198 Eddie Milner .01 .05
199 Dave Engle .01 .05
200 Reggie Jackson .20 .50
201 Burt Hooton .02 .10
Free Agent with Rangers 1-3-85
202 Gorman Thomas .01 .05
203 Larry Parrish .01 .05
204 Bob Stanley .01 .05
205 Steve Rogers .01 .05
206 Phil Garner .01 .05
207 Ed VandeBerg .01 .05
208 Jack Clark .08 .25
Traded to Cardinals 2-1-85
209 Bill Campbell .01 .05
210 Gary Matthews .01 .05
211 Dave Palmer .01 .05
212 Tony Perez .20 .50
213 Sammy Stewart .01 .05
214 John Tudor .02 .10
Traded to Cardinals 12-12-84
215 Bob Brenly .02 .10
216 Jim Gantner .01 .05
217 Bryan Clark .01 .05
218 Doyle Alexander .01 .05
219 Bo Diaz .01 .05
220 Fred Lynn .02 .10
Free Agent with Orioles 12-11-84
221 Eddie Murray .20 .50
222 Hubie Brooks .01 .05
Traded to Expos 12-10-84
223 Tom Hume .01 .05
224 Al Cowens .01 .05
225 Mike Boddicker .01 .05
226 Len Matuszek .01 .05
227 Danny Darwin .02 .10
Traded to Brewers 1-18-85
228 Scott McGregor .01 .05
229 Dave LaPoint .02 .10
Traded to Giants 2-1-85
230 Gary Carter .30 .75
Traded to Mets 12-10-84
231 Joaquin Andujar .01 .05
232 Rafael Ramirez .01 .05
233 Wayne Gross .01 .05
234 Neil Allen .01 .05
235 Gary Maddox .01 .05
236 Mark Thurmond .01 .05
237 Julio Franco .08 .25
238 Ray Burris .02 .10
Traded to Brewers 12-8-84
239 Tim Teufel .01 .05
240 Dave Stieb .01 .05
241 Brett Butler .02 .10
242 Greg Brock .01 .05
243 Barbaro Garbey .01 .05
244 Greg Walker .01 .05
245 Chili Davis .02 .10
246 Darrell Porter .01 .05
247 Tippy Martinez .01 .05
248 Terry Forster .01 .05
249 Harold Baines .08 .25
250 Jesse Orosco .02 .10
251 Brad Gulden .01 .05
252 Mike Hargrove .02 .10
253 Nick Esasky .01 .05
254 Frank Williams .01 .05
255 Lonnie Smith .01 .05
256 Daryl Sconiers .01 .05
257 Bryan Little .02 .10
Traded to White Sox 12-7-84
258 Terry Francona .02 .10
259 Mark Langston RC .20 .50
260 Dave Righetti .02 .10
261 Checklist 133-264 .01 .05
262 Bob Horner .01 .05
263 Mel Hall .01 .05
264 John Shelby .01 .05
265 Juan Samuel .01 .05
266 Frank Viola .02 .10
267 Jim Fanning MG#Now Vice President
Player#Developme .01 .05
268 Dick Ruthven .01 .05
269 Bobby Ramos .01 .05
270 Dan Quisenberry .01 .05
271 Dwight Evans .02 .10
272 Andre Thornton .01 .05
273 Orel Hershiser .75 2.00
274 Ray Knight .01 .05
275 Bill Caudill .02 .10
Traded to Blue Jays 12-8-84
276 Charlie Hough .02 .10
277 Tim Raines .08 .25
278 Mike Squires .01 .05
279 Alex Trevino .01 .05
280 Ron Romanick .01 .05
281 Tom Niedenfuer .01 .05
282 Mike Stenhouse .02 .10
Traded to Twins 1-9-85
283 Terry Puhl .01 .05
284 Hal McRae .01 .05
285 Dan Driessen .01 .05
286 Rudy Law .01 .05
287 Walt Terrell .02 .10
Traded to Tigers 12-7-84
288 Jeff Kunkel .01 .05
289 Bob Knepper .01 .05
290 Cecil Cooper .02 .10
291 Bob Welch .01 .05
292 Frank Pastore .01 .05
293 Dan Schatzeder .01 .05
294 Tom Nieto .01 .05
295 Joe Niekro .02 .10
296 Ryne Sandberg .75 2.00
297 Gary Lucas .01 .05
298 John Castino .01 .05
299 Bill Doran .01 .05
300 Rod Carew .20 .50
301 John Montefusco .01 .05
302 Johnnie LeMaster .01 .05
303 Jim Beattie .01 .05
304 Gary Gaetti .02 .10
305 Dale Berra .02 .10
Traded to Yankees 12-20-84
306 Rick Reuschel .02 .10
307 Ken Oberkfell .01 .05
308 Kent Hrbek .02 .10
309 Mike Witt .01 .05
310 Manny Trillo .01 .05
311 Jim Gott .02 .10
Traded to Giants 1-26-85
312 LaMarr Hoyt .02 .10
Traded to Padres 12-6-84
313 Dave Schmidt .01 .05
314 Ron Oester .01 .05
315 Doug Sisk .01 .05
316 John Lowenstein .01 .05
317 Derrel Thomas .02 .10
Traded to Angels 9-6-84
318 Ted Simmons .02 .10
319 Darrell Evans .02 .10
320 Dale Murphy .08 .25
321 Ricky Horton .01 .05
322 Ken Phelps .01 .05
323 Lee Mazzilli .02 .10
324 Don Mattingly 1.50 4.00
325 John Denny .01 .05
326 Ken Singleton .01 .05
327 Brook Jacoby .01 .05
328 Greg Luzinski .02 .10
Announced his Retirement
329 Bob Ojeda .01 .05
330 Leon Durham .01 .05
331 Bill Laskey .01 .05
332 Ben Oglivie .01 .05
333 Willie Hernandez .01 .05
334 Bob Dernier .01 .05
335 Bruce Benedict .01 .05
336 Rance Mulliniks .01 .05
337 Rick Cerone .02 .10
Traded to Braves 12-6-84
338 Britt Burns .01 .05
339 Danny Heep .01 .05
340 Robin Yount .20 .50
341 Andy Van Slyke .08 .25
342 Curt Wilkerson .01 .05
343 Bill Russell .02 .10
344 Dave Henderson .01 .05
345 Charlie Lea .01 .05
346 Terry Pendleton RC .20 .50
347 Carney Lansford .01 .05
348 Bob Boone .02 .10
349 Mike Easler .02 .10
350 Wade Boggs .40 1.00
351 Atlee Hammaker .01 .05
352 Joe Morgan .20 .50
353 Damaso Garcia .01 .05
354 Floyd Bannister .01 .05
355 Bert Blyleven .02 .10
356 John Butcher .01 .05
357 Fernando Valenzuela .02 .10
358 Tony Pena .02 .10
359 Mike Smithson .01 .05
360 Steve Carlton .20 .50
361 Alfredo Griffin .02 .10
Traded to A's 12-8-84
362 Craig McMurtry .01 .05
363 Bill Dawley .01 .05
364 Richard Dotson .01 .05
365 Carmelo Martinez .01 .05
366 Ron Cey .02 .10
367 Tony Scott .01 .05
368 Dave Bergman .01 .05
369 Steve Sax .01 .05
370 Bruce Sutter .02 .10
371 Mickey Rivers .01 .05
372 Kirk Gibson .02 .10
373 Scott Sanderson .01 .05
374 Brian Downing .01 .05
375 Jeff Reardon .02 .10
376 Frank DiPino .01 .05
377 Checklist 265-396 .01 .05
378 Alan Wiggins .01 .05
379 Charles Hudson .01 .05
380 Ken Griffey .02 .10
381 Tom Paciorek .01 .05
382 Jack Morris .02 .10
383 Tony Gwynn 1.25 3.00
384 Jody Davis .01 .05
385 Jose DeLeon .01 .05
386 Bob Kearney .01 .05
387 George Wright .01 .05
388 Ron Guidry .02 .10
389 Rick Manning .01 .05
390 Sid Fernandez .02 .10
391 Bruce Bochte .01 .05
392 Dan Petry .01 .05
393 Tim Stoddard .02 .10
Free Agent with Padres 1-2-85
394 Tony Armas .01 .05
395 Paul Molitor .20 .50
396 Mike Heath .01 .05

1985 O-Pee-Chee Posters

The 24 full-color posters in the 1985 O-Pee-Chee poster insert set were inserted one per regular wax pack and feature players of the Montreal Expos (numbered 1-12) and the Toronto Blue Jays (numbered 13-24). These posters are typically found with two folds and measure approximately 4 7/8" by 6 7/8". The posters are blank-backed and are numbered at the bottom in French and English. A distinctive blue (Blue Jays) or red (Expos) border surrounds the player photo.

COMPLETE SET (24) 2.50 6.00
1 Mike Fitzgerald .08 .25
2 Dan Driessen .08 .25
3 Dave Palmer .08 .25
4 U.L. Washington .08 .25
5 Hubie Brooks .08 .25
6 Tim Wallach .20 .50
7 Tim Raines .30 .75
8 Herm Winningham .08 .25
9 Andre Dawson .40 1.00
10 Charlie Lea .08 .25
11 Steve Rogers .08 .25
12 Jeff Reardon .20 .50
13 Buck Martinez .20 .50
14 Willie Upshaw .08 .25
15 Damaso Garcia UER .08 .25
(Misspelled Domaso)
16 Tony Fernandez .30 .75
17 Rance Mulliniks .08 .25
18 George Bell .20 .50
19 Lloyd Moseby .08 .25
20 Jesse Barfield .20 .50
21 Doyle Alexander .08 .25
22 Dave Stieb .20 .50
23 Bill Caudill .08 .25
24 Gary Lavelle .08 .25

1986 O-Pee-Chee

This set is an abridgement of the 1986 Topps set. The 396 standard-size cards comprising the 1986 O-Pee-Chee set differ from the cards of the 1986 Topps set by having a higher ratio of cards of players from the two Canadian teams, a practice begun by O-Pee-Chee in 1977 and continued to 1988. The fronts feature black-and-white-bordered color player photos. The player's name appears within the white margin at the bottom. His team name appears within the black margin at the top and his position appears within a colored circle at the photo's lower left. The red horizontal backs carry the player's name and biography at the top. The player's major league statistics follow below. Some backs also have bilingual career highlights, some have bilingual baseball facts and still others have neither. The asterisked cards have an extra line on the front inside the picture area indicating team change. The O-Pee-Chee logo appears on the front of every card.

COMPLETE SET (396) 10.00 25.00
1 Pete Rose .75 2.00
2 Ken Landreaux .01 .05
3 Rob Picciolo .01 .05
4 Steve Garvey .05 .15
5 Andy Hawkins .01 .05
6 Rudy Law .01 .05
7 Lonnie Smith .01 .05
8 Dwayne Murphy .01 .05
9 Moose Haas .01 .05
10 Tony Gwynn .60 1.50
11 Bob Ojeda .02 .10
Now with Mets
12 Jose Uribe .01 .05
13 Bob Kearney .01 .05
14 Julio Cruz .01 .05
15 Eddie Whitson .01 .05
16 Rick Schu .01 .05
17 Mike Stenhouse .02 .10
Now with Red Sox
18 Lou Thornton .01 .05
19 Ryne Sandberg .30 .75
20 Lou Whitaker .02 .10
21 Mark Brouhard .01 .05
22 Gary Lavelle .01 .05
23 Manny Lee .01 .05
24 Don Slaught .01 .05
25 Willie Wilson .01 .05
26 Mike Marshall .01 .05
27 Ray Knight .01 .05
28 Mario Soto .01 .05
29 Dave Anderson .01 .05
30 Eddie Murray .30 .75
31 Dusty Baker .02 .10
32 Steve Yeager .02 .10
Now with Mariners
33 Andy Van Slyke .02 .10
34 Dave Righetti .02 .10
35 Jeff Reardon .02 .10
36 Burt Hooton .01 .05
37 Johnny Ray .01 .05
38 Glenn Hoffman .01 .05
39 Rick Mahler .01 .05
40 Ken Griffey .02 .10
41 Brad Wellman .01 .05
42 Joe Hesketh .01 .05
43 Mark Salas .01 .05
44 Jorge Orta .01 .05
45 Damaso Garcia .01 .05
46 Jim Acker .01 .0
47 Bill Madlock .02 .1
48 Bill Almon .01 .0
49 Rick Manning .01 .0
50 Dan Quisenberry .01 .0
51 Jim Gantner .01 .0
52 Kevin Bass .01 .0
53 Len Dykstra RC .40 1.0
54 John Franco .05 .1
55 Fred Lynn .02 .1
56 Jim Morrison .01 .0
57 Bill Doran .01 .0
58 Leon Durham .01 .0
59 Andre Thornton .01 .0
60 Dwight Evans .02 .1
61 Larry Herndon .01 .0
62 Bob Boone .02 .1
63 Kent Hrbek .05 .1
64 Floyd Bannister .01 .0
65 Harold Baines .05 .1
66 Pat Tabler .01 .0
67 Carmelo Martinez .01 .0
68 Ed Lynch .01 .0
69 George Foster .02 .1
70 Dave Winfield .15 .4
71 Ken Schrom .01 .0
Now with Indians
72 Toby Harrah .01 .0
73 Jackie Gutierrez .01 .0
Now with Orioles
74 Rance Mulliniks .01 .0
75 Jose DeLeon .01 .0
76 Ron Romanick .01 .0
77 Charlie Leibrandt .01 .0
78 Bruce Benedict .01 .0
79 Dave Schmidt .01 .0
Now with White Sox
80 Darryl Strawberry .05 .1
81 Wayne Krenchicki .01 .0
82 Tippy Martinez .01 .0
83 Phil Garner .02 .1
84 Darrell Porter .02 .1
Now with Rangers
85 Tony Perez .15 .4
Eric Davis also
shown in photo
86 Tom Waddell .01 .0
87 Tim Hulett .01 .0
88 Barbaro Garbey .01 .0
Now with A's
89 Randy St. Claire .01 .0
90 Garry Templeton .01 .0
91 Tim Teufel .02 .1
Now with Mets
92 Al Cowens .01 .0
93 Scot Thompson .01 .0
94 Tom Herr .01 .0
95 Ozzie Virgil .02 .1
Now with Braves
96 Jose Cruz .01 .0
97 Gary Gaetti .02 .1
98 Roger Clemens 2.00 5.0
99 Vance Law .01 .0
100 Nolan Ryan .60 1.5
101 Mike Smithson .01 .0
102 Rafael Santana .01 .0
103 Darrell Evans .02 .1
104 Rich Gossage .08 .2
105 Gary Ward .01 .0
106 Jim Gott .01 .0
107 Rafael Ramirez .01 .0
108 Ted Power .01 .0
109 Ron Guidry .02 .1
110 Scott McGregor .01 .0
111 Mike Scioscia .02 .1
112 Glenn Hubbard .01 .0
113 U.L. Washington .01 .0
114 Al Oliver .02 .1
115 Jay Howell .01 .0
116 Brook Jacoby .01 .0
117 Willie McGee .02 .1
118 Jerry Royster .01 .0
119 Barry Bonnell .01 .0
120 Steve Carlton .15 .4
121 Alfredo Griffin .01 .0
122 David Green .02 .1
Now with Brewers
123 Greg Walker .01 .0
124 Frank Tanana .01 .0
125 Dave Lopes .02 .1
126 Mike Krukow .01 .0
127 Jack Howell .01 .0
128 Greg Harris .01 .0
129 Herm Winningham .01 .0
130 Alan Trammell .05 .1
131 Checklist 1-132 .01 .0
132 Razor Shines .01 .0
133 Bruce Sutter .15 .4
134 Carney Lansford .01 .0
135 Joe Niekro .02 .1
136 Ernie Whitt .01 .0
137 Charlie Moore .01 .0
138 Mel Hall .01 .0
139 Roger McDowell .01 .0
140 John Candelaria .01 .0
141 Bob Rodgers MG CL .01 .0
142 Manny Trillo .02 .1
Now with Cubs
143 Dave Palmer .02 .1
Now with Braves
144 Robin Yount .08 .2
145 Pedro Guerrero .02 .1
146 Von Hayes .01 .0

147 Lance Parrish .02 .10
148 Mike Heath .02 .10
Now with Cardinals
149 Brett Butler .02 .10
150 Joaquin Andujar .02 .10
Now with A's
151 Graig Nettles .02 .10
152 Pete Vuckovich .01 .05
153 Jason Thompson .01 .05
154 Bert Roberge .01 .05
155 Bob Grich .02 .10
156 Roy Smalley .01 .05
157 Ron Hassey .01 .05
158 Bob Stanley .01 .05
159 Orel Hershiser .15 .40
160 Chet Lemon .01 .05
161 Terry Puhl .01 .05
162 Dave LaPoint .02 .10
Now with Tigers
163 Onix Concepcion .01 .05
164 Steve Balboni .01 .05
165 Mike Davis .01 .05
166 Dickie Thon .01 .05
167 Zane Smith .01 .05
168 Jeff Burroughs .01 .05
169 Alex Trevino .02 .10
Now with Dodgers
170 Gary Carter .15 .40
171 Tito Landrum .01 .05
172 Sammy Stewart .02 .10
Now with Red Sox
173 Wayne Gross .01 .05
174 Britt Burns .02 .10
Now with Yankees
175 Steve Sax .01 .05
176 Jody Davis .01 .05
177 Joel Youngblood .01 .05
178 Fernando Valenzuela .02 .10
179 Storm Davis .01 .05
180 Don Mattingly .50 1.25
181 Steve Bedrosian .02 .10
Now with Phillies
182 Jesse Orosco .02 .10
183 Gary Roenicke .02 .10
Now with Yankees
184 Don Baylor .02 .10
185 Rollie Fingers .15 .40
186 Ruppert Jones .01 .05
187 Scott Fletcher .02 .10
Now with Rangers
188 Bob Dernier .01 .05
189 Mike Mason .01 .05
190 George Hendrick .01 .05
191 Wally Backman .01 .05
192 Oddibe McDowell .01 .05
193 Bruce Hurst .01 .05
194 Ron Cey .02 .10
195 Dave Concepcion .02 .10
196 Doyle Alexander .01 .05
197 Dale Murphy .20 .50
198 Mark Langston .02 .10
199 Dennis Eckersley .15 .40
200 Mike Schmidt .15 .40
201 Nick Esasky .01 .05
202 Ken Dayley .01 .05
203 Rick Cerone .01 .05
204 Larry McWilliams .01 .05
205 Brian Downing .01 .05
206 Danny Darwin .01 .05
207 Bill Caudill .01 .05
208 Dave Rozema .01 .05
209 Eric Show .01 .05
210 Brad Komminsk .01 .05
211 Chris Bando .01 .05
212 Chris Speier .01 .05
213 Jim Clancy .01 .05
214 Randy Bush .01 .05
215 Frank White .02 .10
216 Dan Petry .01 .05
217 Tim Wallach .01 .05
218 Mitch Webster .01 .05
219 Dennis Lamp .01 .05
220 Bob Horner .01 .05
221 Dave Henderson .01 .05
222 Dave Smith .01 .05
223 Willie Upshaw .01 .05
224 Cesar Cedeno .02 .10
225 Ron Darling .01 .05
226 Lee Lacy .01 .05
227 John Tudor .01 .05
228 Jim Presley .01 .05
229 Bill Gullickson .02 .10
Now with Reds
230 Terry Kennedy .01 .05
231 Bob Knepper .01 .05
232 Rick Rhoden .01 .05
233 Richard Dotson .01 .05
234 Jesse Barfield .01 .05
235 Butch Wynegar .01 .05
236 Jerry Reuss .02 .10
237 Juan Samuel .01 .05
238 Larry Parrish .01 .05
239 Bill Buckner .02 .10
240 Pat Sheridan .01 .05
241 Tony Fernandez .05 .15
242 Rich Thompson .01 .05
Now with Brewers
243 Rickey Henderson .20 .50
244 Craig Lefferts .01 .05
245 Jim Sundberg .01 .05
246 Phil Niekro .15 .40
247 Terry Harper .01 .05
248 Spike Owen .01 .05
249 Bret Saberhagen .08 .25
250 Dwight Gooden .08 .25
251 Rich Dauer .01 .05
252 Keith Hernandez .02 .10
253 Bo Diaz .01 .05
254 Ozzie Guillen RC .60 1.50
255 Tony Armas .01 .05
256 Andre Dawson .08 .25
257 Doug DeCinces .01 .05
258 Tim Burke .01 .05
259 Dennis Boyd .01 .05
260 Tony Pena .01 .05
261 Sal Butera .02 .10
Now with Reds
262 Wade Boggs .30 .75
263 Checklist 133-264 .01 .05
264 Ron Oester .01 .05
265 Ron Davis .01 .05
266 Keith Moreland .01 .05
267 Paul Molitor .20 .50
268 John Denny .02 .10
Now with Reds
269 Frank Viola .02 .10
270 Jack Morris .02 .10
271 Dave Collins .02 .10
Now with Tigers
272 Bert Blyleven .02 .10
273 Jerry Willard .01 .05
274 Matt Young .01 .05
275 Charlie Hough .02 .10
276 Dave Dravecky .02 .10
277 Garth Iorg .01 .05
278 Hal McRae .01 .05
279 Curt Wilkerson .01 .05
280 Tim Raines .02 .10
281 Bill Laskey .02 .10
Now with Giants
282 Jerry Mumphrey .02 .10
Now with Cubs
283 Pat Clements .01 .05
284 Bob James .01 .05
285 Buddy Bell .02 .10
286 Tom Brookens .01 .05
287 Dave Parker .02 .10
288 Ron Kittle .01 .05
289 Johnnie LeMaster .01 .05
290 Carlton Fisk .15 .40
291 Jimmy Key .05 .15
292 Gary Matthews .01 .05
293 Marvell Wynne .01 .05
294 Danny Cox .01 .05
295 Kirk Gibson .02 .10
296 Mariano Duncan RC .05 .15
297 Ozzie Smith .40 1.00
298 Craig Reynolds .01 .05
299 Bryn Smith .01 .05
300 George Brett .40 1.00
301 Walt Terrell .01 .05
302 Greg Gross .01 .05
303 Claudell Washington .01 .05
304 Howard Johnson .02 .10
305 Phil Bradley .01 .05
306 R.J. Reynolds .01 .05
307 Bob Brenly .01 .05
308 Hubie Brooks .01 .05
309 Alvin Davis .01 .05
310 Donnie Hill .01 .05
311 Dick Schofield .01 .05
312 Tom Filer .01 .05
313 Mike Fitzgerald .01 .05
314 Marty Barrett .01 .05
315 Mookie Wilson .02 .10
316 Alan Knicely .01 .05
317 Ed Romero .01 .05
Now with Red Sox
318 Glenn Wilson .01 .05
319 Bud Black .01 .05
320 Jim Rice .02 .10
321 Terry Pendleton .05 .15
322 Dave Kingman .02 .10
323 Gary Pettis .01 .05
324 Dan Schatzeder .01 .05
325 Juan Beniquez .02 .10
Now with Orioles
326 Kent Tekulve .01 .05
327 Mike Pagliarulo .01 .05
328 Pete O'Brien .01 .05
329 Kirby Puckett .75 2.00
330 Rick Sutcliffe .01 .05
331 Alan Ashby .01 .05
332 Willie Randolph .02 .10
333 Tom Henke .02 .10
334 Ken Oberkfell .01 .05
335 Don Sutton .15 .40
336 Dan Gladden .01 .05
337 George Vukovich .01 .05
338 Jorge Bell .02 .10
339 Jim Dwyer .01 .05
340 Cal Ripken .60 1.50
341 Willie Hernandez .01 .05
342 Gary Redus .02 .10
Now with Phillies
343 Jerry Koosman .02 .10
344 Jim Wohlford .01 .05
345 Donnie Moore .01 .05
346 Floyd Youmans .01 .05
347 Gorman Thomas .01 .05
348 Cliff Johnson .01 .05
349 Ken Howell .01 .05
350 Jack Clark .02 .10
351 Gary Lucas .02 .10
Now with Angels
352 Bob Clark .01 .05
353 Dave Stieb .01 .05
354 Tony Bernazard .01 .05
355 Lee Smith .08 .25
356 Mickey Hatcher .01 .05
357 Ed VandeBerg .02 .10
Now with Dodgers
358 Rick Dempsey .01 .05
359 Bobby Cox MG .02 .10
360 Lloyd Moseby .01 .05
361 Shane Rawley .01 .05
362 Garry Maddox .01 .05
363 Buck Martinez .01 .05
364 Ed Nunez .01 .05
365 Luis Leal .01 .05
366 Dale Berra .01 .05
367 Mike Boddicker .01 .05
368 Greg Brock .01 .05
369 Al Holland .01 .05
370 Vince Coleman RC .08 .25
371 Rod Carew .15 .40
372 Ben Oglivie .01 .05
373 Lee Mazzilli .01 .05
374 Terry Francona .02 .10
375 Rich Gedman .01 .05
376 Charlie Lea .01 .05
377 Joe Carter .40 1.00
378 Bruce Bochte .01 .05
379 Bobby Meacham .01 .05
380 LaMarr Hoyt .01 .05
381 Jeff Leonard .01 .05
382 Ivan Calderon RC .02 .10
383 Chris Brown RC .01 .05
384 Steve Trout .01 .05
385 Cecil Cooper .02 .10
386 Cecil Fielder RC .60 1.50
387 Tim Flannery .01 .05
388 Chris Codiroli .01 .05
389 Glenn Davis .01 .05
390 Tom Seaver .15 .40
391 Julio Franco .05 .15
392 Tom Brunansky .01 .05
393 Rob Wilfong .01 .05
394 Reggie Jackson .15 .40
395 Scott Garrelts .01 .05
396 Checklist 265-396 .01 .05

1986 O-Pee-Chee Box Bottoms

O-Pee-Chee printed four different four-card panels on the bottoms of its 1986 wax pack boxes. If cut, each card would measure approximately the standard size. These 16 cards, in alphabetical order and designated A through P, are considered a separate set from the regular issue, but are styled almost exactly the same, differing only in the player photo and colors for the team name, borders and position on the front. The backs are identical, except for the letter designations instead of numbers.

COMPLETE SET (16) 6.00 15.00
A George Bell .08 .25
B Wade Boggs .60 1.50
C George Brett 1.50 4.00
D Vince Coleman .08 .25
E Carlton Fisk .60 1.50
F Dwight Gooden .30 .75
G Pedro Guerrero .08 .25
H Ron Guidry .20 .50
I Reggie Jackson .60 1.50
J Don Mattingly 1.50 4.00
K Oddibe McDowell .08 .25
L Willie McGee .20 .50
M Dale Murphy .40 1.00
N Pete Rose .60 1.50
O Bret Saberhagen .20 .50
P Fernando Valenzuela .20 .50

1987 O-Pee-Chee

This set is an abridgement of the 1987 Topps set. The 396 standard-size cards comprising the 1987 O-Pee-Chee set differ from the cards of the 1987 Topps set by having a higher ratio of cards of players from the two Canadian teams, a practice begun by O-Pee-Chee in 1977 and continued to 1988. The fronts feature wood grain bordered color player photos. The player's name appears in the colored rectangle at the lower right. His team logo appears at the upper left. The yellow, white and blue horizontal backs carry the player's name and bilingual position at the top. The player's major league statistics follow below. Some backs also have bilingual career highlights, some have bilingual baseball facts and still others have both or neither. The asterisked cards have an extra line on the front inside the picture area indicating team change. The O-Pee-Chee logo appears on the front of every card. Notable Rookie Cards include Barry Bonds.

COMPLETE SET (396) 6.00 15.00
1 Ken Oberkfell .01 .05
2 Jack Howell .01 .05
3 Hubie Brooks .01 .05
4 Bob Grich .02 .10
5 Rick Leach .01 .05
6 Phil Niekro .15 .40
7 Rickey Henderson .20 .50
8 Terry Pendleton .02 .10
9 Jay Tibbs .01 .05
10 Cecil Cooper .02 .10
11 Mario Soto .01 .05
12 George Bell .01 .05
13 Nick Esasky .01 .05
14 Larry McWilliams .01 .05
15 Dan Quisenberry .01 .05
16 Ed Lynch .01 .05
17 Pete O'Brien .01 .05
18 Luis Aguayo .01 .05
19 Matt Young .02 .10
Now with Dodgers
20 Gary Carter .15 .40
21 Tom Paciorek .01 .05
22 Doug DeCinces .01 .05
23 Lee Smith .05 .15
24 Jesse Barfield .01 .05
25 Bert Blyleven .02 .10
26 Greg Brock .02 .10
Now with Brewers
27 Dan Petry .01 .05
28 Rick Dempsey .02 .10
Now with Indians
29 Jimmy Key .05 .15
30 Tim Raines .02 .10
31 Bruce Hurst .01 .05
32 Manny Trillo .01 .05
33 Andy Van Slyke .02 .10
34 Ed VandeBerg .02 .10
Now with Indians
35 Sid Bream .01 .05
36 Dave Winfield .15 .40
37 Scott Garrelts .01 .05
38 Dennis Leonard .01 .05
39 Marty Barrett .01 .05
40 Dave Righetti .01 .05
41 Bo Diaz .01 .05
42 Gary Redus .01 .05
43 Tom Niedenfuer .01 .05
44 Greg Harris .01 .05
45 Jim Presley .01 .05
46 Danny Gladden .01 .05
47 Roy Smalley .01 .05
48 Wally Backman .01 .05
49 Tom Seaver .15 .40
50 Dave Smith .01 .05
51 Mel Hall .01 .05
52 Tim Flannery .01 .05
53 Julio Cruz .01 .05
54 Dick Schofield .01 .05
55 Tim Wallach .01 .05
56 Glenn Davis .01 .05
57 Darren Daulton .05 .15
58 Chico Walker .01 .05
59 Garth Iorg .01 .05
60 Tony Pena .01 .05
61 Ron Hassey .01 .05
62 Dave Dravecky .01 .05
63 Jorge Orta .01 .05
64 Al Nipper .01 .05
65 Tom Browning .01 .05
66 Marc Sullivan .01 .05
67 Todd Worrell .02 .10
68 Glenn Hubbard .01 .05
69 Carney Lansford .02 .10
70 Charlie Hough .02 .10
71 Lance McCullers .01 .05
72 Walt Terrell .01 .05
73 Bob Kearney .01 .05
74 Dan Pasqua .01 .05
75 Ron Darling .01 .05
76 Robin Yount .15 .40
77 Pat Tabler .01 .05
78 Tom Foley .01 .05
79 Juan Nieves .01 .05
80 Wally Joyner RC .20 .50
81 Wayne Krenchicki .01 .05
82 Kirby Puckett .30 .75
83 Bob Ojeda .01 .05
84 Mookie Wilson .02 .10
85 Kevin Bass .01 .05
86 Kent Tekulve .01 .05
87 Mark Salas .01 .05
88 Brian Downing .01 .05
89 Ozzie Guillen .02 .10
90 Dave Stieb .01 .05
91 Rance Mulliniks .01 .05
92 Mike Witt .01 .05
93 Charlie Moore .01 .05
94 Jose Uribe .01 .05
95 Oddibe McDowell .01 .05
96 Ray Soff .01 .05
97 Glenn Wilson .01 .05
98 Brook Jacoby .01 .05
99 Darryl Motley .02 .10
Now with Braves
100 Steve Garvey .05 .15
101 Frank White .02 .10
102 Mike Moore .01 .05
103 Rick Aguilera .02 .10
104 Buddy Bell .02 .10
105 Floyd Youmans .01 .05
106 Lou Whitaker .02 .10
107 Ozzie Smith .30 .75
108 Jim Gantner .01 .05
109 R.J. Reynolds .01 .05
110 John Tudor .01 .05
111 Alfredo Griffin .01 .05
112 Mike Flanagan .01 .05
113 Neil Allen .01 .05
114 Ken Griffey .02 .10
115 Donnie Moore .01 .05
116 Bob Horner .01 .05
117 Ron Shepherd .01 .05
118 Cliff Johnson .01 .05
119 Vince Coleman .01 .05
120 Eddie Murray .15 .40
121 Dwayne Murphy .01 .05
122 Jim Clancy .01 .05
123 Ken Landreaux .01 .05
124 Tom Nieto .02 .10
Now with Twins
125 Bob Brenly .01 .05
126 George Brett .30 .75
127 Vance Law .01 .05
128 Checklist 1-132 .01 .05
129 Bob Knepper .01 .05
130 Dwight Gooden .05 .15
131 Juan Bonilla .01 .05
132 Tim Burke .01 .05
133 Bob McClure .01 .05
134 Scott Bailes .01 .05
135 Mike Easler .02 .10
Now with Phillies
136 Ron Romanick .02 .10
Now with Yankees
137 Rich Gedman .01 .05
138 Bob Dernier .01 .05
139 John Denny .01 .05
140 Bret Saberhagen .02 .10
141 Herm Winningham .01 .05
142 Rick Sutcliffe .01 .05
143 Ryne Sandberg .15 .40
144 Mike Scioscia .02 .10
145 Charlie Kerfeld .01 .05
146 Jim Rice .02 .10
147 Steve Trout .01 .05
148 Jesse Orosco .02 .10
149 Mike Boddicker .01 .05
150 Wade Boggs .15 .40
151 Dane Iorg .01 .05
152 Rick Burleson .02 .10
Now with Orioles
153 Duane Ward RC .02 .10
154 Rick Reuschel .01 .05
155 Nolan Ryan .60 1.50
156 Bill Caudill .01 .05
157 Danny Darwin .01 .05
158 Ed Romero .01 .05
159 Bill Almon .01 .05
160 Julio Franco .02 .10
161 Kent Hrbek .02 .10
162 Chili Davis .05 .15
163 Kevin Gross .01 .05
164 Carlton Fisk .15 .40
165 Jeff Reardon .05 .15
Now with Twins
166 Bob Boone .02 .10
167 Rick Honeycutt .01 .05
168 Dan Schatzeder .01 .05
169 Jim Wohlford .01 .05
170 Phil Bradley .01 .05
171 Ken Schrom .01 .05
172 Ron Oester .01 .05
173 Juan Beniquez .02 .10
Now with Royals
174 Tony Armas .01 .05
175 Bob Stanley .01 .05
176 Steve Buechele .01 .05
177 Keith Moreland .01 .05
178 Cecil Fielder .05 .15
179 Gary Gaetti .02 .10
180 Chris Brown .01 .05
181 Tom Herr .01 .05
182 Lee Lacy .01 .05
183 Ozzie Virgil .01 .05
184 Paul Molitor .15 .40
185 Roger McDowell .01 .05
186 Mike Marshall .01 .05
187 Ken Howell .01 .05
188 Rob Deer .01 .05
189 Joe Hesketh .01 .05
190 Jim Sundberg .01 .05
191 Kelly Gruber .01 .05
192 Cory Snyder .01 .05
193 Dave Concepcion .02 .10
194 Kirk McCaskill .01 .05
195 Mike Pagliarulo .01 .05
196 Rick Manning .01 .05
197 Brett Butler .02 .10
198 Tony Gwynn .50 1.25
199 Mariano Duncan .01 .05
200 Pete Rose .15 .40
201 John Cangelosi .01 .05
202 Danny Cox .01 .05
203 Butch Wynegar .02 .10
Now with Yankees
204 Chris Chambliss .02 .10
205 Graig Nettles .02 .10
206 Chet Lemon .01 .05
207 Don Aase .01 .05
208 Mike Mason .01 .05
209 Alan Trammell .05 .15
210 Lloyd Moseby .01 .05
211 Richard Dotson .01 .05
212 Mike Fitzgerald .01 .05
213 Darrell Porter .01 .05
214 Checklist 265-396 .01 .05
215 Mark Langston .01 .05
216 Steve Farr .01 .05
217 Dann Bilardello .01 .05
218 Gary Ward .02 .10
Now with Yankees
219 Cecilio Guante .02 .10
Now with Yankees
220 Joe Carter .08 .25
221 Ernie Whitt .01 .05
222 Denny Walling .01 .05
223 Charlie Leibrandt .01 .05
224 Wayne Tolleson .01 .05
225 Mike Smithson .01 .05
226 Zane Smith .01 .05
227 Terry Puhl .01 .05
228 Eric Davis .05 .15
229 Don Mattingly .30 .75
230 Don Baylor .02 .10
231 Frank Tanana .01 .05
232 Tom Brookens .01 .05
233 Steve Bedrosian .01 .05
234 Wallace Johnson .01 .05
235 Alvin Davis .01 .05
236 Tommy John .02 .10
237 Jim Morrison .01 .05
238 Ricky Horton .01 .05
239 Shane Rawley .01 .05
240 Steve Balboni .01 .05
241 Mike Krukow .01 .05
242 Rick Mahler .01 .05
243 Bill Doran .01 .05
244 Mark Clear .01 .05
245 Willie Upshaw .01 .05
246 Hal McRae .01 .05
247 Jose Canseco .60 1.50
248 George Hendrick .01 .05
249 Doyle Alexander .01 .05
250 Teddy Higuera .01 .05
251 Tom Hume .01 .05
252 Denny Martinez .02 .10
253 Eddie Milner .02 .10
Now with Giants
254 Steve Sax .01 .05
255 Juan Samuel .01 .05
256 Dave Bergman .01 .05
257 Bob Forsch .01 .05
258 Steve Yeager .01 .05
259 Don Sutton .15 .40
260 Vida Blue .05 .15
Now with A's
261 Tom Brunansky .01 .05
262 Joe Sambito .01 .05
263 Mitch Webster .01 .05
264 Checklist 133-264 .01 .05
265 Darrell Evans .02 .10
266 Dave Kingman .02 .10
267 Howard Johnson .02 .10
268 Greg Pryor .01 .05
269 Tippy Martinez .01 .05
270 Jody Davis .01 .05
271 Steve Carlton .15 .40
272 Andres Galarraga .20 .50
273 Fernando Valenzuela .02 .10
274 Jeff Hearron .01 .05
275 Ray Knight .02 .10
Now with Orioles
276 Bill Madlock .02 .10
277 Tom Henke .01 .05
278 Gary Pettis .01 .05
279 Jimy Williams MG CL .01 .05
280 Jeffrey Leonard .01 .05
281 Bryn Smith .01 .05
282 John Cerutti .01 .05
283 Gary Roenicke .02 .10
Now with Braves
284 Joaquin Andujar .01 .05
285 Dennis Boyd .01 .05
286 Tim Hulett .01 .05
287 Craig Lefferts .01 .05
288 Tito Landrum .01 .05
289 Manny Lee .01 .05
290 Leon Durham .01 .05
291 Johnny Ray .01 .05
292 Franklin Stubbs .01 .05
293 Bob Rodgers MG CL .01 .05
294 Terry Francona .02 .10
295 Len Dykstra .05 .15
296 Tom Candiotti .01 .05
297 Frank DiPino .01 .05
298 Craig Reynolds .01 .05
299 Jerry Hairston .01 .05
300 Reggie Jackson .20 .50
Now with A's
301 Luis Aquino .01 .05
302 Greg Walker .01 .05
303 Terry Kennedy .02 .10
Now with Orioles
304 Phil Garner .02 .10
305 John Franco .02 .10
306 Bill Buckner .02 .10
307 Kevin Mitchell RC .08 .25
Now with Padres
308 Don Slaught .01 .05
309 Harold Baines .02 .10
310 Frank Viola .01 .05
311 Dave Lopes .02 .10
312 Cal Ripken .60 1.50
313 John Candelaria .01 .05
314 Bob Sebra .01 .05
315 Bud Black .01 .05
316 Brian Fisher .02 .10
Now with Pirates
317 Clint Hurdle .02 .10
318 Earnest Riles .01 .05
319 Dave LaPoint .02 .10
Now with Cardinals
320 Barry Bonds RC 4.00 10.00
321 Tim Stoddard .01 .05
322 Ron Cey .05 .15
Now with A's
323 Al Newman .01 .05
324 Jerry Royster .02 .10
Now with White Sox
325 Garry Templeton .01 .05
326 Mark Gubicza .01 .05
327 Andre Thornton .01 .05
328 Bob Welch .02 .10
329 Tony Fernandez .02 .10
330 Mike Scott .01 .05
331 Jack Clark .02 .10
332 Danny Tartabull .02 .10
Now with Royals
333 Greg Minton .01 .05
334 Ed Correa .01 .05
335 Candy Maldonado .01 .05
336 Dennis Lamp .02 .10
Now with Indians
337 Sid Fernandez .01 .05
338 Greg Gross .01 .05
339 Willie Hernandez .01 .05
340 Roger Clemens .50 1.25
341 Mickey Hatcher .01 .05
342 Bob James .01 .05
343 Jose Cruz .02 .10
344 Bruce Sutter .15 .40
345 Andre Dawson .08 .25
346 Shawon Dunston .01 .05
347 Scott McGregor .01 .05
348 Carmelo Martinez .01 .05
349 Storm Davis .02 .10
Now with Padres
350 Keith Hernandez .02 .10
351 Andy McGaffigan .01 .05
352 Dave Parker .02 .10
353 Ernie Camacho .01 .05
354 Eric Show .01 .05
355 Don Carman .01 .05
356 Floyd Bannister .01 .05
357 Willie McGee .02 .10
358 Atlee Hammaker .01 .05
359 Dale Murphy .08 .25
360 Pedro Guerrero .01 .05
361 Will Clark RC .40 1.00
362 Bill Campbell .01 .05
363 Alejandro Pena .01 .05
364 Dennis Rasmussen .01 .05
365 Rick Rhoden .02 .10
Now with Yankees
366 Randy St. Claire .01 .05
367 Willie Wilson .02 .10
368 Dwight Evans .02 .10
369 Moose Haas .01 .05
370 Fred Lynn .02 .10
371 Mark Eichhorn .01 .05
372 Dave Schmidt .02 .10
Now with Orioles
373 Jerry Reuss .01 .05
374 Lance Parrish .02 .10
375 Ron Guidry .02 .10
376 Jack Morris .02 .10
377 Willie Randolph .02 .10
378 Joel Youngblood .01 .05
379 Darryl Strawberry .05 .15
380 Rich Gossage .08 .25
381 Dennis Eckersley .15 .40
382 Gary Lucas .01 .05
383 Ron Davis .01 .05
384 Pete Incaviglia .02 .10
385 Orel Hershiser .02 .10
386 Kirk Gibson .02 .10
387 Don Robinson .01 .05
388 Darnell Coles .01 .05
389 Von Hayes .01 .05
390 Gary Matthews .01 .05
391 Jay Howell .01 .05
392 Tim Laudner .01 .05
393 Rod Scurry .01 .05
394 Tony Bernazard .01 .05
395 Damaso Garcia .02 .10
Now with Braves
396 Mike Schmidt .15 .40

1987 O-Pee-Chee Box Bottoms

O-Pee-Chee printed two different four-card panels on the bottoms of its 1987 wax pack boxes. If cut, each card would measure approximately 2 1/8" by 3". These eight cards, in alphabetical order and designated A through H, are considered a separate set from the regular issue, but are styled almost exactly the same, differing only in the player photo and colors for the team name, borders and position on the front. On the horizontal backs, purple borders frame a yellow panel that presents bilingual text describing an outstanding achievement or milestone in the player's career.

COMPLETE SET (8) 2.50 6.00
A Don Baylor .30 .75
B Steve Carlton .60 1.50
C Ron Cey .30 .75
D Cecil Cooper .30 .75
E Rickey Henderson .60 1.50
F Jim Rice .30 .75
G Don Sutton .60 1.50
H Dave Winfield .60 1.50

1988 O-Pee-Chee

This set is an abridgement of the 1988 Topps set. The 396 standard-size cards comprising the 1988 O-Pee-Chee set differ from the cards of the 1988 Topps set by having a higher ratio of cards of players from the two Canadian teams, a practice begun by O-Pee-Chee in 1977 and continued to 1988. The fronts feature white-bordered color player photos framed by a colored line. The player's name appears in the colored diagonal stripe at the lower right. His team name appears at the top. The orange horizontal backs carry the player's name, position and biography printed across the row of baseball icons at the top. The player's major league statistics follow below. Some backs also have bilingual career highlights, some have bilingual baseball facts and still others have both or neither. The asterisked cards have an extra line on the front inside the picture area indicating team change. They are styled like the 1988 Topps regular issue cards. The O-Pee-Chee logo appears on the front of every card. This set includes the first two 1987 draft picks of both the Montreal Expos and the Toronto Blue Jays.

COMPLETE SET (396) 4.00 10.00
1 Chris James .01 .05
2 Steve Buechele .01 .05
3 Mike Henneman .02 .10
4 Eddie Murray .15 .40
5 Bret Saberhagen .02 .10
6 Nathan Minchey .01 .05
Expos' second
draft choice
7 Harold Reynolds .02 .10
8 Bo Jackson .08 .25
9 Mike Easler .01 .05
10 Ryne Sandberg .15 .40
11 Mike Young .01 .05
12 Tony Phillips .01 .05
13 Andres Thomas .01 .05
14 Tim Burke .01 .05
15 Chili Davis .05 .15
Now with Angels
16 Jim Lindeman .01 .05
17 Ron Oester .01 .05
18 Craig Reynolds .01 .05
19 Juan Samuel .01 .05
20 Kevin Gross .01 .05
21 Cecil Fielder .02 .10
22 Greg Swindell .01 .05
23 Jose DeLeon .01 .05
24 Jim Deshaies .01 .05
25 Andres Galarraga .08 .25
26 Mitch Williams .01 .05
27 R.J. Reynolds .01 .05
28 Jose Nunez .01 .05
29 Angel Salazar .01 .05
30 Sid Fernandez .01 .05
31 Keith Moreland .01 .05
32 John Kruk .02 .10
33 Rob Deer .01 .05
34 Ricky Horton .01 .05
35 Harold Baines .05 .15
36 Jamie Moyer .02 .10
37 Kevin McReynolds .01 .05
38 Ron Darling .01 .05
39 Ozzie Smith .20 .50
40 Orel Hershiser .02 .10
41 Bob Melvin .02 .10
42 Alfredo Griffin .02 .10
Now with Dodgers
43 Dick Schofield .01 .05
44 Terry Steinbach .01 .05
45 Kent Hrbek .02 .10
46 Darnell Coles .01 .05
47 Jimmy Key .02 .10
48 Alan Ashby .01 .05
49 Julio Franco .02 .10
50 Hubie Brooks .01 .05
51 Chris Bando .01 .05
52 Fernando Valenzuela .02 .10
53 Kal Daniels .01 .05
54 Jim Clancy .01 .05
55 Phil Bradley .02 .10
Now with Phillies
56 Andy McGaffigan .01 .05
57 Mike LaValliere .01 .05
58 Dave Magadan .01 .05
59 Danny Cox .01 .05
60 Rickey Henderson .15 .40
61 Jim Rice .02 .10
62 Calvin Schiraldi .02 .10
Now with Cubs
63 Jerry Mumphrey .01 .05
64 Ken Caminiti RC .75 2.00
65 Leon Durham .01 .05
66 Shane Rawley .01 .05
67 Ken Oberkfell .01 .05
68 Keith Hernandez .02 .10
69 Bob Brenly .01 .05
70 Roger Clemens .40 1.00
71 Gary Pettis .02 .10
Now with Tigers
72 Dennis Eckersley .15 .40
73 Dave Smith .01 .05
74 Cal Ripken .60 1.50
75 Joe Carter .08 .25
76 Denny Martinez .02 .10
77 Juan Beniquez .01 .05
78 Tim Laudner .01 .05
79 Ernie Whitt .01 .05
80 Mark Langston .01 .05
81 Dale Sveum .01 .05
82 Dion James .01 .05
83 Dave Valle .01 .05
84 Bill Wegman .01 .05
85 Howard Johnson .01 .05
86 Benito Santiago .01 .05
87 Casey Candaele .01 .05
88 Delino DeShields XRC .20 .50
Expos' first
draft choice
89 Dave Winfield .15 .40
90 Dale Murphy .08 .25
91 Jay Howell .02 .10
Now with Dodgers
92 Ken Williams RC .05 .15
93 Bob Sebra .01 .05
94 Tim Wallach .01 .05
95 Lance Parrish .01 .05
96 Todd Benzinger .01 .05
97 Scott Garrelts .01 .05
98 Jose Guzman .01 .05
99 Jeff Reardon .02 .10
100 Jack Clark .02 .10
101 Tracy Jones .01 .05
102 Barry Larkin .30 .75
103 Curt Young .01 .05
104 Juan Nieves .01 .05
105 Terry Pendleton .02 .10
106 Rob Ducey RC .01 .05
107 Scott Bailes .01 .05
108 Eric King .01 .05
109 Mike Pagliarulo .01 .05
110 Teddy Higuera .01 .05
111 Pedro Guerrero .01 .05
112 Chris Brown .01 .05
113 Kelly Gruber .01 .05
114 Jack Howell .01 .05
115 Johnny Ray .01 .05
116 Mark Eichhorn .01 .05
117 Tony Pena .01 .05
118 Bob Welch .02 .10
Now with Athletics
119 Mike Kingery .01 .05
120 Kirby Puckett .30 .75
121 Charlie Hough .02 .10
122 Tony Bernazard .01 .05
123 Tom Candiotti .01 .05
124 Ray Knight .01 .05
125 Bruce Hurst .01 .05
126 Steve Jeltz .01 .05
127 Ron Guidry .02 .10
128 Duane Ward .01 .05
129 Greg Minton .01 .05
130 Buddy Bell .02 .10
131 Denny Walling .01 .05
132 Donnie Hill .01 .05
133 Wayne Tolleson .01 .05
134 Bob Rodgers MG CL .01 .05
135 Todd Worrell .02 .10
136 Brian Dayett .01 .05
137 Chris Bosio .01 .05
138 Mitch Webster .01 .05
139 Jerry Browne .01 .05
140 Jesse Barfield .01 .05
141 Doug DeCinces .02 .10
Now with Cardinals
142 Andy Van Slyke .02 .10
143 Doug Drabek .02 .10
144 Jeff Parrett .01 .05
145 Bill Madlock .02 .10
146 Larry Herndon .01 .05
147 Bill Buckner .02 .10
148 Carmelo Martinez .01 .05
149 Ken Howell .01 .05
150 Eric Davis .02 .10
151 Randy Ready .01 .05
152 Jeffrey Leonard .01 .05
153 Dave Stieb .02 .10
154 Jeff Stone .01 .05
155 Dave Righetti .01 .05
156 Gary Matthews .02 .10
157 Gary Carter .15 .40
158 Bob Boone .02 .10
159 Glenn Davis .01 .05
160 Willie McGee .02 .10
161 Bryn Smith .01 .05
162 Mark McLemore RC .02 .10
163 Dale Mohorcic .01 .05
164 Mike Flanagan .01 .05
165 Robin Yount .15 .40
166 Bill Doran .01 .05
167 Rance Mulliniks .01 .05
168 Wally Joyner .05 .15
169 Cory Snyder .01 .05
170 Rich Gossage .08 .25
171 Rick Mahler .01 .05
172 Henry Cotto .01 .05
173 George Bell .01 .05
174 B.J. Surhoff .02 .10
175 Kevin Bass .01 .05
176 Jeff Reed .01 .05
177 Frank Tanana .01 .05
178 Darryl Strawberry .02 .10
179 Lou Whitaker .02 .10
180 Terry Kennedy .01 .05
181 Mariano Duncan .01 .05
182 Ken Phelps .01 .05
183 Bob Dernier .02 .10
Now with Phillies
184 Ivan Calderon .01 .05
185 Rick Rhoden .01 .05
186 Rafael Palmeiro .20 .50
187 Kelly Downs .01 .05
188 Spike Owen .01 .05
189 Bobby Bonilla .02 .10
190 Candy Maldonado .01 .05
191 John Cerutti .01 .05
192 Devon White .02 .10
193 Brian Fisher .01 .05
194 Alex Sanchez 1st Draft .01 .05
195 Dan Quisenberry .01 .05
196 Dave Engle .01 .05
197 Lance McCullers .01 .05
198 Franklin Stubbs .01 .05
199 Scott Bradley .01 .05
200 Wade Boggs .15 .40
201 Kirk Gibson .02 .10
202 Brett Butler .02 .10
Now with Giants
203 Dave Anderson .01 .05
204 Donnie Moore .01 .05
205 Nelson Liriano RC .01 .05
206 Danny Gladden .01 .05
207 Dan Pasqua .02 .10
Now with White Sox
208 Robby Thompson .01 .05
209 Richard Dotson .02 .10
Now with Yankees
210 Willie Randolph .02 .10
211 Danny Tartabull .01 .05
212 Greg Brock .01 .05
213 Albert Hall .01 .05
214 Dave Schmidt .01 .05
215 Von Hayes .01 .05
216 Herm Winningham .01 .05
217 Mike Davis .02 .10
Now with Dodgers
218 Charlie Leibrandt .01 .05
219 Mike Stanley .02 .10
220 Tom Henke .01 .05
221 Dwight Evans .02 .10
222 Willie Wilson .01 .05
223 Stan Jefferson .01 .05
224 Mike Dunne .01 .05
225 Mike Scioscia .02 .10
226 Larry Parrish .01 .05
227 Mike Scott .01 .05
228 Wallace Johnson .01 .05
229 Jeff Musselman .01 .05
230 Pat Tabler .01 .05
231 Paul Molitor .15 .40
232 Bob James .01 .05
233 Joe Niekro .01 .05
234 Oddibe McDowell .01 .05
235 Gary Ward .01 .05
236 Ted Power .02 .10
Now with Royals
237 Pascual Perez .01 .05
238 Luis Polonia .01 .05
239 Mike Diaz .01 .05
240 Lee Smith .02 .10
Now with Red Sox
241 Willie Upshaw .01 .05
242 Tom Niedenfuer .01 .05
243 Tim Raines .02 .10
244 Jeff D. Robinson .01 .05
245 Rich Gedman .01 .05
246 Scott Bankhead .01 .05
247 Andre Dawson .08 .25
248 Brook Jacoby .01 .05
249 Mike Marshall .01 .05
250 Nolan Ryan .60 1.50
251 Tom Foley .01 .05
252 Bob Brower .01 .05
253 Checklist .01 .05
254 Scott McGregor .01 .05
255 Ken Griffey .02 .10
256 Ken Schrom .01 .05
257 Gary Gaetti .02 .10
258 Ed Nunez .01 .05
259 Frank Viola .01 .05
260 Vince Coleman .01 .05
261 Reid Nichols .01 .05
262 Tim Flannery .01 .05
263 Glenn Braggs .01 .05
264 Garry Templeton .01 .05
265 Bo Diaz .01 .05
266 Matt Nokes .01 .05
267 Barry Bonds .60 1.50
268 Bruce Ruffin .01 .05
269 Ellis Burks RC .20 .50
270 Mike Witt .01 .05
271 Ken Gerhart .01 .05
272 Lloyd Moseby .01 .05
273 Garth Iorg .01 .05
274 Mike Greenwell .01 .05
275 Kevin Seitzer .02 .10
276 Luis Salazar .01 .05
277 Shawon Dunston .01 .05
278 Rick Reuschel .01 .05
279 Randy St.Claire .01 .05
280 Pete Incaviglia .01 .05
281 Mike Boddicker .01 .05
282 Jay Tibbs .01 .05
283 Shane Mack .01 .05
284 Walt Terrell .01 .05
285 Jim Presley .01 .05
286 Greg Walker .01 .05
287 Dwight Gooden .02 .10
288 Jim Morrison .01 .05
289 Gene Garber .01 .05
290 Tony Fernandez .05 .15
291 Ozzie Virgil .01 .05
292 Carney Lansford .02 .10
293 Jim Acker .01 .05
294 Tommy Hinzo .01 .05
295 Bert Blyleven .08 .25
296 Ozzie Guillen .05 .15
297 Zane Smith .01 .05
298 Milt Thompson .01 .05
299 Len Dykstra .02 .10
300 Don Mattingly .30 .75
301 Bud Black .01 .05
302 Jose Uribe .01 .05
303 Manny Lee .01 .05
304 Sid Bream .01 .05
305 Steve Sax .01 .05
306 Billy Hatcher .01 .05
307 John Shelby .01 .05
308 Lee Mazzilli .01 .05
309 Bill Long .01 .05
310 Tom Herr .01 .05
311 Derek Bell XRC .15 .40
Blue Jays' second
draft choice
312 George Brett .30 .75
313 Bob McClure .01 .05
314 Jimy Williams MG CL .01 .05
315 Dave Parker .02 .10
Now with Athletics
316 Doyle Alexander .01 .05
317 Dan Plesac .01 .05
318 Mel Hall .01 .05
319 Ruben Sierra .01 .05
320 Alan Trammell .05 .15
321 Mike Schmidt .15 .40
322 Wally Ritchie .01 .05
323 Rick Leach .01 .05
324 Danny Jackson .01 .05
Now with Reds
325 Glenn Hubbard .01 .05
326 Frank White .02 .10
327 Larry Sheets .01 .05
328 John Cangelosi .01 .05
329 Bill Gullickson .01 .05
330 Eddie Whitson .01 .05
331 Brian Downing .01 .05
332 Gary Redus .01 .05
333 Wally Backman .01 .05
334 Dwayne Murphy .01 .05
335 Claudell Washington .01 .05
336 Dave Concepcion .02 .10
337 Jim Gantner .01 .05
338 Marty Barrett .01 .05
339 Mickey Hatcher .01 .05
340 Jack Morris .02 .10
341 John Franco .02 .10
342 Ron Robinson .01 .05
343 Greg Gagne .01 .05
344 Steve Bedrosian .01 .05
345 Scott Fletcher .01 .05
346 Vance Law .02 .10
Now with Cubs
347 Joe Johnson .02 .10
Now with Angels
348 Jim Eisenreich .08 .25
349 Alvin Davis .01 .05
350 Will Clark .20 .50
351 Mike Aldrete .01 .05
352 Billy Ripken .01 .05
353 Dave Stewart .02 .10
354 Neal Heaton .01 .05
355 Roger McDowell .01 .05
356 John Tudor .01 .05
357 Floyd Bannister .02 .10
Now with Royals
358 Rey Quinones .01 .05
359 Glenn Wilson .02 .10
Now with Mariners
360 Tony Gwynn .30 .75
361 Greg Maddux 1.00 2.50
362 Juan Castillo .01 .05
363 Willie Fraser .01 .05
364 Nick Esasky .01 .05
365 Floyd Youmans .01 .05
366 Chet Lemon .01 .05
367 Matt Young .02 .10
Now with A's
368 Gerald Young .01 .05
369 Bob Stanley .01 .05
370 Jose Canseco .15 .40
371 Joe Hesketh .01 .05
372 Rick Sutcliffe .02 .10
373 Checklist 133-264 .01 .05
374 Checklist 265-396 .01 .05
375 Tom Brunansky .01 .05
376 Jody Davis .01 .05
377 Sam Horn RC .01 .05
378 Mark Gubicza .01 .05
379 Rafael Ramirez .02 .10
Now with Astros
380 Joe Magrane .01 .05
381 Pete O'Brien .01 .05
382 Lee Guetterman .01 .05
383 Eric Bell .01 .05
384 Gene Larkin .02 .10
385 Carlton Fisk .15 .40
386 Mike Fitzgerald .01 .05
387 Kevin Mitchell .02 .10
388 Jim Winn .01 .05
389 Mike Smithson .01 .05
390 Darrell Evans .02 .10
391 Terry Leach .01 .05
392 Charlie Kerfeld .01 .05
393 Mike Krukow .01 .05
394 Mark McGwire 1.25 3.00
395 Fred McGriff .20 .50
396 DeWayne Buice .01 .05

1988 O-Pee-Chee Box Bottoms

O-Pee-Chee printed four different four-card panels on the bottoms of its 1988 wax pack boxes. If cut, each card would measure approximately the standard size. These 16 cards, in alphabetical order and designated A through P, are considered a separate set from the regular issue but are styled almost exactly the same, differing only in the player photo and colors for the team name, borders and position on the front. The backs are identical, except for the letter designations instead of numbers.

COMPLETE SET (16) 6.00 15.00
A Don Baylor .08 .25
B Steve Bedrosian .02 .10
C Juan Beniquez .02 .10
D Bob Boone .08 .25
E Darrell Evans .08 .25
F Tony Gwynn 2.50 6.00
G John Kruk .08 .25
H Marvell Wynne .02 .10
I Joe Carter .30 .75
J Eric Davis .08 .25
K Howard Johnson .02 .10
L Darryl Strawberry .08 .25
M Rickey Henderson .75 2.00
N Nolan Ryan 4.00 10.00
O Mike Schmidt .60 1.50
P Kent Tekulve .02 .10

1989 O-Pee-Chee

The 1989 O-Pee-Chee baseball set contains 396 standard-size cards that feature white bordered color player photos framed by colored lines. The player's name and team appear at the lower right. The bilingual pinkish horizontal backs are bordered in black and carry the player's biography and statistics.

COMPLETE SET (396) 8.00 20.00
COMPLETE FACT. SET (396) 8.00 20.00
1 Brook Jacoby .01 .05
2 Atlee Hammaker .05 .15
3 Jack Clark .01 .05
4 Dave Stieb .02 .10
5 Bud Black .01 .05
6 Damon Berryhill .01 .05
7 Mike Scioscia .02 .10
8 Jose Uribe .01 .05
9 Mike Aldrete .01 .05
10 Andre Dawson .08 .25
11 Bruce Sutter .15 .40
12 Dale Sveum .01 .05
13 Dan Quisenberry .01 .05
14 Tom Niedenfuer .01 .05
15 Robby Thompson .01 .05
16 Ron Robinson .01 .05
17 Brian Downing .01 .05
18 Rick Rhoden .01 .05
19 Greg Gagne .01 .05
20 Allan Anderson .01 .05
21 Eddie Whitson .01 .05
22 Billy Ripken .01 .05
23 Mike Fitzgerald .01 .05
24 Shane Rawley .01 .05
25 Frank White .02 .10
26 Don Mattingly .40 1.00
27 Fred Lynn .01 .05
28 Mike Moore .01 .05
29 Kelly Gruber .01 .05
30 Dwight Gooden .02 .10
31 Dan Pasqua .01 .05
32 Dennis Rasmussen .01 .05
33 B.J. Surhoff .02 .10
34 Sid Fernandez .01 .05
35 John Tudor .01 .05
36 Mitch Webster .01 .05
37 Doug Drabek .01 .05
38 Bobby Witt .01 .05
39 Mike Maddux .01 .05
40 Steve Sax .01 .05
41 Orel Hershiser .02 .10
42 Pete Incaviglia .01 .05
43 Guillermo Hernandez .01 .05
44 Kevin Coffman .01 .05
45 Kal Daniels .01 .05
46 Carlton Fisk .15 .40
47 Carney Lansford .02 .10
48 Tim Burke .01 .05
49 Alan Trammell .60 1.50
50 George Bell .01 .05
51 Tony Gwynn .50 1.25
52 Bob Brenly .01 .05
53 Ruben Sierra .02 .10
54 Otis Nixon .01 .05
55 Julio Franco .02 .10
56 Pat Tabler .01 .05
57 Alvin Davis .01 .05
58 Kevin Seitzer .01 .05
59 Mark Davis .01 .05
60 Tom Brunansky .01 .05
61 Jeff Treadway .01 .05
62 Alfredo Griffin .01 .05
63 Keith Hernandez .02 .10
64 Alex Trevino .01 .05
65 Rick Reuschel .01 .05
66 Bob Walk .01 .05
67 Dave Palmer .01 .05
68 Pedro Guerrero .01 .05
69 Jose Oquendo .01 .05
70 Mark McGwire .60 1.50
71 Mike Boddicker .01 .05
72 Wally Backman .01 .05
73 Pascual Perez .01 .05
74 Joe Hesketh .01 .05
75 Tom Henke .01 .05
76 Nelson Liriano .01 .05
77 Doyle Alexander .01 .05
78 Tim Wallach .01 .05
79 Scott Bankhead .01 .05
80 Cory Snyder .01 .05
81 Dave Magadan .01 .05
82 Randy Ready .01 .05
83 Steve Buechele .01 .05
84 Bo Jackson .08 .25
85 Kevin McReynolds .01 .05
86 Jeff Reardon .02 .10
87 Tim Raines/(Named Rock on card) .02 .10
88 Melido Perez .01 .05
89 Dave LaPoint .01 .05
90 Vince Coleman .01 .05
91 Floyd Youmans .01 .05
92 Buddy Bell .02 .10
93 Andres Galarraga .08 .25
94 Tony Pena .01 .05
95 Gerald Young .01 .05
96 Rick Cerone .01 .05
97 Ken Oberkfell .01 .05
98 Larry Sheets .01 .05
99 Chuck Crim .01 .05
100 Mike Schmidt .15 .40
101 Ivan Calderon .01 .05
102 Kevin Bass .01 .05
103 Chili Davis .02 .10
104 Randy Myers .02 .10
105 Ron Darling .01 .05
106 Willie Upshaw .01 .05
107 Jose DeLeon .01 .05
108 Fred Manrique .01 .05
109 Johnny Ray .01 .05
110 Paul Molitor .15 .40
111 Rance Mulliniks .01 .05
112 Jim Presley .01 .05
113 Lloyd Moseby .01 .05
114 Lance Parrish .01 .05
115 Jody Davis .01 .05
116 Matt Nokes .01 .05
117 Dave Anderson .01 .05
118 Checklist 1-132 .01 .05
119 Rafael Belliard .01 .05
120 Frank Viola .01 .05
121 Roger Clemens .40 1.00
122 Luis Salazar .01 .05
123 Mike Stanley .01 .05
124 Jim Traber .01 .05
125 Mike Krukow .01 .05
126 Sid Bream .01 .05
127 Joel Skinner .01 .05
128 Milt Thompson .01 .05
129 Terry Clark .01 .05
130 Gerald Perry .01 .05
131 Bryn Smith .01 .05
132 Kirby Puckett .40 1.00
133 Bill Long .01 .05
134 Jim Gantner .01 .05
135 Jose Rijo .01 .05
136 Joey Meyer .01 .05
137 Geno Petralli .01 .05
138 Wallace Johnson .01 .05
139 Mike Flanagan .01 .05
140 Shawon Dunston .01 .05
141 Eric Plunk .01 .05
142 Bobby Bonilla .02 .10
143 Jack McDowell .15 .40
144 Mookie Wilson .01 .05
145 Dave Stewart .02 .10
146 Gary Pettis .01 .05
147 Eric Show .01 .05
148 Eddie Murray .15 .40
149 Lee Smith .02 .10
150 Fernando Valenzuela .02 .10
151 Bob Welch .01 .05
152 Harold Baines .05 .15
153 Albert Hall .01 .05
154 Don Carman .01 .05
155 Marty Barrett .01 .05
156 Chris Sabo .01 .05
157 Bret Saberhagen .15 .40
158 Danny Cox .01 .05
159 Tom Foley .01 .05
160 Jeffrey Leonard .01 .05
161 Brady Anderson RC .30 .75
162 Rich Gossage .02 .10
163 Greg Brock .01 .05
164 Joe Carter .05 .15
165 Mike Dunne .01 .05
166 Jeff Russell .01 .05
167 Dan Plesac .01 .05
168 Willie Wilson .01 .05
169 Mike Jackson .02 .10
170 Tony Fernandez .05 .15
171 Jamie Moyer .05 .15
172 Jim Gott .01 .05
173 Mel Hall .01 .05
174 Mark McGwire .60 1.50
175 John Shelby .01 .05
176 Jeff Parrett .01 .05
177 Tim Belcher .01 .05
178 Rich Gedman .01 .05
179 Ozzie Virgil .01 .05
180 Mike Scott .01 .05
181 Dickie Thon .01 .05
182 Rob Murphy .01 .05
183 Oddibe McDowell .01 .05
184 Wade Boggs .15 .40
185 Claudell Washington .01 .05
186 Randy Johnson RC 1.25 3.00
187 Paul O'Neill .02 .10
188 Todd Benzinger .01 .05
189 Kevin Mitchell .02 .10
190 Mike Witt .01 .05
191 Sil Campusano .01 .05
192 Ken Gerhart .01 .05
193 Bob Rodgers MG .01 .05
194 Floyd Bannister .01 .05
195 Ozzie Guillen .05 .15
196 Ron Gant .02 .10
197 Neal Heaton .01 .05
198 Bill Swift .01 .05
199 Dave Parker .02 .10
200 George Brett .30 .75
201 Bo Diaz .01 .05
202 Brad Moore .01 .05
203 Rob Ducey .01 .05
204 Bert Blyleven .08 .25
205 Dwight Evans .02 .10
206 Roberto Alomar .30 .75
207 Henry Cotto .01 .05
208 Harold Reynolds .02 .10
209 Jose Guzman .01 .05
210 Dale Murphy .08 .25
211 Mike Pagliarulo .01 .05
212 Jay Howell .01 .05
213 Rene Gonzales .01 .05
214 Scott Garrelts .01 .05
215 Kevin Gross .01 .05
216 Jack Howell .01 .05
217 Kurt Stillwell .01 .05
218 Mike LaValliere .01 .05
219 Jim Clancy .01 .05
220 Gary Gaetti .02 .10
221 Hubie Brooks .01 .05
222 Bruce Ruffin .01 .05
223 Jay Buhner .08 .25
224 Cecil Fielder .02 .10
225 Willie McGee .02 .10
226 Bill Doran .01 .05
227 John Farrell .01 .05
228 Nelson Santovenia .01 .05
229 Jimmy Key .02 .10
230 Ozzie Smith .30 .75
231 Dave Schmidt .02 .10
232 Jody Reed .01 .05
233 Gregg Jefferies .01 .05
234 Tom Browning .01 .05
235 John Kruk .02 .10
236 Charles Hudson .01 .05
237 Todd Stottlemyre .02 .10
238 Don Slaught .01 .05
239 Tim Laudner .01 .05
240 Greg Maddux .50 1.25
241 Brett Butler .02 .10
242 Checklist 133-264 .01 .05
243 Bob Boone .02 .10
244 Willie Randolph .02 .10
245 Jim Rice .02 .10
246 Rey Quinones .01 .05
247 Checklist 265-396 .01 .05
248 Stan Javier .01 .05
249 Tim Leary .01 .05
250 Cal Ripken .60 1.50
251 John Dopson .01 .05
252 Billy Hatcher .01 .05
253 Robin Yount .15 .40
254 Mickey Hatcher .01 .05
255 Bob Horner .01 .05
256 Benny Santiago .02 .10
257 Luis Rivera .01 .05

58 Fred McGriff .08 .25
59 Dave Wells .01 .05
60 Dave Winfield .15 .40
61 Rafael Ramirez .01 .05
62 Nick Esasky .01 .05
63 Barry Bonds .40 1.00
64 Joe Magrane .05 .15
65 Kent Hrbek .02 .10
66 Jack Morris .02 .10
67 Jeff M. Robinson .01 .05
68 Ron Kittle .01 .05
69 Candy Maldonado .01 .05
70 Wally Joyner .02 .10
71 Glenn Braggs .01 .05
72 Ron Hassey .01 .05
73 Jose Lind .01 .05
74 Mark Eichhorn .01 .05
75 Danny Tartabull .01 .05
76 Paul Kilgus .01 .05
77 Mike Davis .01 .05
78 Andy McGaffigan .01 .05
79 Scott Bradley .01 .05
80 Bob Knepper .01 .05
81 Gary Redus .01 .05
82 Rickey Henderson .08 .25
83 Andy Allanson .01 .05
84 Rick Leach .01 .05
85 John Candelaria .01 .05
86 Dick Schofield .01 .05
87 Bryan Harvey .01 .05
88 Randy Bush .01 .05
89 Ernie Whitt .01 .05
90 John Franco .02 .10
91 Todd Worrell .01 .05
92 Teddy Higuera .01 .05
93 Keith Moreland .01 .05
94 Juan Berenguer .01 .05
95 Scott Fletcher .01 .05
96 Roger McDowell .02 .10
Now with Indians 12-6-88
97 Mark Grace .30 .75
98 Chris James .01 .05
99 Frank Tanana .01 .05
00 Darryl Strawberry .02 .10
01 Charlie Leibrandt .01 .05
02 Gary Ward .01 .05
03 Brian Fisher .01 .05
04 Terry Steinbach .01 .05
05 Dave Smith .01 .05
06 Greg Minton .01 .05
07 Lance McCullers .01 .05
08 Phil Bradley .01 .05
09 Terry Kennedy .01 .05
10 Rafael Palmeiro .08 .25
11 Ellis Burks .05 .15
12 Doug Jones .01 .05
13 Denny Martinez .02 .10
14 Pete O'Brien .01 .05
15 Greg Swindell .01 .05
16 Walt Weiss .01 .05
17 Pete Stanicek .01 .05
18 Gene Nelson .01 .05
19 Danny Jackson .01 .05
20 Lou Whitaker .02 .10
21 Will Clark .08 .25
22 John Smiley .01 .05
23 Mike Marshall .01 .05
24 Gary Carter .15 .40
25 Jesse Barfield .01 .05
26 Dennis Boyd .01 .05
27 Dave Henderson .01 .05
28 Chet Lemon .01 .05
29 Bob Melvin .02 .10
30 Eric Davis .02 .10
31 Ted Power .01 .05
32 Carmelo Martinez .01 .05
33 Bob Ojeda .01 .05
34 Steve Lyons .02 .10
35 Dave Righetti .02 .10
36 Steve Balboni .01 .05
37 Calvin Schiraldi .01 .05
38 Vance Law .01 .05
39 Zane Smith .01 .05
40 Kirk Gibson .02 .10
41 Jim Deshaies .01 .05
42 Tom Brookens .01 .05
43 Pat Borders .75 2.00
44 Devon White .02 .10
45 Charlie Hough .02 .10
46 Rex Hudler .01 .05
47 John Cerutti .01 .05
48 Kirk McCaskill .01 .05
49 Len Dykstra .02 .10
50 Andy Van Slyke .02 .10
51 Jeff D. Robinson .01 .05
52 Rick Schu .01 .05
53 Bruce Benedict .01 .05
54 Bill Wegman .01 .05
55 Mark Langston .01 .05
56 Steve Farr .01 .05
57 Richard Dotson .01 .05
58 Andres Thomas .01 .05
59 Alan Ashby .01 .05
60 Ryne Sandberg .30 .75
61 Kelly Downs .01 .05
62 Jeff Musselman .01 .05
63 Barry Larkin .08 .25
64 Rob Deer .01 .05
65 Mike Henneman .01 .05
66 Nolan Ryan .60 1.50
67 Johnny Paredes .01 .05
68 Bobby Thigpen .01 .05
69 Mickey Brantley .01 .05
370 Dennis Eckersley .15 .40
371 Manny Lee .01 .05
372 Juan Samuel .01 .05
373 Tracy Jones .01 .05
374 Mike Greenwell .01 .05
375 Terry Pendleton .02 .10
376 Steve Lombardozzi .01 .05
377 Mitch Williams .01 .05
378 Glenn Davis .01 .05
379 Mark Gubicza .01 .05
380 Orel Hershiser WS .20 .50
381 Jimy Williams MG .01 .05
382 Kirk Gibson WS .75 2.00
383 Howard Johnson .01 .05
384 David Cone .08 .25
385 Von Hayes .01 .05
386 Luis Polonia .01 .05
387 Danny Gladden .01 .05
388 Pete Smith .01 .05
389 Jose Canseco .20 .50
390 Mickey Hatcher .01 .05
391 Wil Tejada .01 .05
392 Duane Ward .01 .05
393 Rick Mahler .01 .05
394 Rick Sutcliffe .02 .10
395 Dave Martinez .01 .05
396 Ken Dayley .01 .05

1989 O-Pee-Chee Box Bottoms

These standard-size box bottom cards feature on their fronts blue-bordered color player photos. The player's name and team appear at the bottom right. The horizontal black back carries bilingual career highlights within a purple panel. The value of the panels uncut is slightly greater, perhaps by 25 percent greater, than the value of the individual cards cut up carefully. The sixteen cards in this set honor players (and one manager) who reached career milestones during the 1988 season.The cards are lettered on the back.

COMPLETE SET (16) 5.00 12.00
A George Brett 1.00 2.50
B Bill Buckner .08 .25
C Darrell Evans .08 .25
D Rich Gossage .08 .25
E Greg Gross .02 .10
F Rickey Henderson .50 1.25
G Keith Hernandez .08 .25
H Tom Lasorda MG .08 .25
I Jim Rice .08 .25
J Cal Ripken 1.50 4.00
K Nolan Ryan 1.50 4.00
L Mike Schmidt .50 1.25
M Bruce Sutter .40 1.00
N Don Sutton .40 1.00
O Kent Tekulve .02 .10
P Dave Winfield .40 1.00

1990 O-Pee-Chee

The 1990 O-Pee-Chee baseball set was a 792-card standard-size set. For the first time since 1976, O-Pee-Chee issued the exact same set as Topps. The only distinctions are the bilingual text and the O-Pee-Chee copyright on the backs. The fronts feature color player photos bordered in various colors. The player's name appears at the bottom and his team name is printed at the top. The yellow horizontal backs carry the player's name, biography and position at the top, followed below by major league statistics. Cards 385-407 feature All-Stars, while cards 661-665 are Turn Back the Clock cards. Notable Rookie Cards include Juan Gonzalez, Sammy Sosa, Frank Thomas and Bernie Williams.

COMPLETE SET (792) 8.00 20.00
COMPLETE FACT.SET (792) 10.00 25.00
1 Nolan Ryan .75 2.00
2 Nolan Ryan Salute .40 1.00
3 Nolan Ryan Salute .40 1.00
4 Nolan Ryan Salute .40 1.00
5 Nolan Ryan Salute UER .40 1.00
Says Texas Stadium
rather than
Arlington Stadium
6 Vince Coleman RB .01 .05
7 Rickey Henderson RB .08 .25
8 Cal Ripken RB .30 .75
9 Eric Plunk .01 .05
10 Barry Larkin .08 .25
11 Paul Gibson .01 .05
12 Joe Girardi .02 .10
13 Mark Williamson .01 .05
14 Mike Fetters .01 .05
15 Teddy Higuera .01 .05
16 Kent Anderson .01 .05
17 Kelly Downs .01 .05
18 Carlos Quintana .01 .05
19 Al Newman .01 .05
20 Mark Gubicza .01 .05
21 Jeff Torborg MG .01 .05
22 Bruce Ruffin .01 .05
23 Randy Velarde .01 .05
24 Joe Hesketh .01 .05
25 Willie Randolph .02 .10
26 Don Slaught .02 .10
Now with Pirates
12
4
89
27 Rick Leach .01 .05
28 Duane Ward .01 .05
29 John Cangelosi .01 .05
30 David Cone .08 .25
31 Henry Cotto .01 .05
32 John Farrell .01 .05
33 Greg Walker .01 .05
34 Tony Fossas .01 .05
35 Benito Santiago .02 .10
36 John Costello .01 .05
37 Domingo Ramos .01 .05
38 Wes Gardner .01 .05
39 Curt Ford .01 .05
40 Jay Howell .01 .05
41 Matt Williams .05 .15
42 Jeff M. Robinson .01 .05
43 Dante Bichette .02 .10
44 Roger Salkeld FDP RC .01 .05
45 Dave Parker UER .05 .15
Born in Jackson
not Calhoun
46 Rob Dibble .01 .05
47 Brian Harper .01 .05
48 Zane Smith .01 .05
49 Tom Lawless .01 .05
50 Glenn Davis .01 .05
51 Doug Rader MG .01 .05
52 Jack Daugherty .01 .05
53 Mike LaCoss .01 .05
54 Joel Skinner .01 .05
55 Darrell Evans UER .02 .10
HR total should be
414, not 424
56 Franklin Stubbs .01 .05
57 Greg Vaughn .08 .25
58 Keith Miller .01 .05
59 Ted Power .02 .10
Now with Pirates
11/21/89
60 George Brett .30 .75
61 Deion Sanders .08 .25
62 Ramon Martinez .02 .10
63 Mike Pagliarulo .01 .05
64 Danny Darwin .01 .05
65 Devon White .01 .05
66 Greg Litton .01 .05
67 Scott Sanderson .02 .10
Now with Athletics
12/13/89
68 Dave Henderson .01 .05
69 Todd Frohwirth .01 .05
70 Mike Greenwell .01 .05
71 Allan Anderson .01 .05
72 Jeff Huson .01 .05
73 Bob Milacki .01 .05
74 Jeff Jackson FDP RC .01 .05
75 Doug Jones .01 .05
76 Dave Valle .01 .05
77 Dave Bergman .01 .05
78 Mike Flanagan .01 .05
79 Ron Kittle .01 .05
80 Jeff Russell .01 .05
81 Bob Rodgers MG .01 .05
82 Scott Terry .01 .05
83 Hensley Meulens .01 .05
84 Ray Searage .01 .05
85 Juan Samuel .02 .10
Now with Dodgers
12/20/89
86 Paul Kilgus .02 .10
Now with Blue Jays
12/7/89
87 Rick Luecken .02 .10
Now with Braves
12/17/89
88 Glenn Braggs .01 .05
89 Clint Zavaras .01 .05
90 Jack Clark .02 .10
91 Steve Frey .01 .05
92 Mike Stanley .01 .05
93 Shawn Hillegas .01 .05
94 Herm Winningham .01 .05
95 Todd Worrell .01 .05
96 Jody Reed .01 .05
97 Curt Schilling .60 1.50
98 Jose Gonzalez .01 .05
99 Rich Monteleone .01 .05
100 Will Clark .08 .25
101 Shane Rawley .01 .05
Now with Red Sox
1/9/90
102 Stan Javier .01 .05
103 Marvin Freeman .01 .05
104 Bob Knepper .01 .05
105 Randy Myers .02 .10
Now with Reds
12/8/89
106 Charlie O'Brien .01 .05
107 Fred Lynn .02 .10
Now with Padres
12/7/89
108 Rod Nichols .01 .05
109 Roberto Kelly .01 .05
110 Tommy Helms MG .01 .05
111 Ed Whited .01 .05
112 Glenn Wilson .01 .05
113 Manny Lee .01 .05
114 Mike Bielecki .01 .05
115 Tony Pena .02 .10
Now with Red Sox
11/28/89
116 Floyd Bannister .01 .05
117 Mike Sharperson .01 .05
118 Erik Hanson .01 .05
119 Billy Hatcher .01 .05
120 John Franco .05 .15
Now with Mets
12/8/89
121 Robin Ventura .08 .25
122 Shawn Abner .01 .05
123 Rich Gedman .01 .05
124 Dave Dravecky .01 .05
125 Kent Hrbek .02 .10
126 Randy Kramer .01 .05
127 Mike Devereaux .01 .05
128 Checklist 1 .01 .05
129 Ron Jones .01 .05
130 Bert Blyleven .08 .25
131 Matt Nokes .01 .05
132 Lance Blankenship .01 .05
133 Ricky Horton .01 .05
134 Earl Cunningham RC .01 .05
135 Dave Magadan .01 .05
136 Kevin Brown .08 .25
137 Marty Pevey .01 .05
138 Al Leiter .08 .25
139 Greg Brock .01 .05
140 Andre Dawson .08 .25
141 John Hart MG .01 .05
142 Jeff Wetherby .01 .05
143 Rafael Belliard .01 .05
144 Bud Black .01 .05
145 Terry Steinbach .01 .05
146 Rob Richie .01 .05
147 Chuck Finley .02 .10
148 Edgar Martinez .05 .15
149 Steve Farr .01 .05
150 Kirk Gibson .02 .10
151 Rick Mahler .01 .05
152 Lonnie Smith .01 .05
153 Randy Milligan .01 .05
154 Mike Maddux .02 .10
Now with Dodgers
12/21/89
155 Ellis Burks .05 .15
156 Ken Patterson .01 .05
157 Craig Biggio .08 .25
158 Craig Lefferts .02 .10
Now with Padres
12/7/89
159 Mike Felder .01 .05
160 Dave Righetti .01 .05
161 Harold Reynolds .02 .10
162 Todd Zeile .05 .15
163 Phil Bradley .01 .05
164 Jeff Juden FDP RC .01 .05
165 Walt Weiss .01 .05
166 Bobby Witt .01 .05
167 Kevin Appier .05 .15
168 Jose Lind .01 .05
169 Richard Dotson .02 .10
Now with Royals
12/6/89
170 George Bell .01 .05
171 Russ Nixon MG .01 .05
172 Tom Lampkin .01 .05
173 Tim Belcher .01 .05
174 Jeff Kunkel .01 .05
175 Mike Moore .01 .05
176 Luis Quinones .01 .05
177 Mike Henneman .01 .05
178 Chris James .01 .05
Now with Indians
12/6/89
179 Brian Holton .01 .05
180 Tim Raines .02 .10
181 Juan Agosto .01 .05
182 Mookie Wilson .02 .10
183 Steve Lake .01 .05
184 Danny Cox .01 .05
185 Ruben Sierra .02 .10
186 Dave LaPoint .01 .05
187 Rick Wrona .01 .05
188 Mike Smithson .02 .10
Now with Angels
12/19/89
189 Dick Schofield .01 .05
190 Rick Reuschel .01 .05
191 Pat Borders .01 .05
192 Don August .01 .05
193 Andy Benes .02 .10
194 Glenallen Hill .01 .05
195 Tim Burke .01 .05
196 Gerald Young .01 .05
197 Doug Drabek .01 .05
198 Mike Marshall .02 .10
Now with Mets
12/20/89
199 Sergio Valdez .01 .05
200 Don Mattingly .40 1.00
201 Cito Gaston MG .01 .05
202 Mike Macfarlane .01 .05
203 Mike Roesler .01 .05
204 Bob Dernier .01 .05
205 Mark Davis .02 .10
Now with Royals
12/11/89
206 Nick Esasky .02 .10
Now with Braves
11/17/89
207 Bob Ojeda .01 .05
208 Brook Jacoby .01 .05
209 Greg Mathews .01 .05
210 Ryne Sandberg .20 .50
211 John Cerutti .01 .05
212 Joe Orsulak .01 .05
213 Scott Bankhead .01 .05
214 Terry Francona .02 .10
215 Kirk McCaskill .01 .05
216 Ricky Jordan .01 .05
217 Don Robinson .01 .05
218 Wally Backman .01 .05
219 Donn Pall .01 .05
220 Barry Bonds .40 1.00
221 Gary Mielke .01 .05
222 Kurt Stillwell UER .01 .05
Graduate misspelled
as gradute
223 Tommy Gregg .01 .05
224 Delino DeShields RC .08 .25
225 Jim Deshaies .01 .05
226 Mickey Hatcher .01 .05
227 Kevin Tapani RC .08 .25
228 Dave Martinez .01 .05
229 David Wells .08 .25
230 Keith Hernandez .05 .15
Now with Indians
12/7/89
231 Jack McKeon MG .02 .10
232 Darnell Coles .01 .05
233 Ken Hill .02 .10
234 Mariano Duncan .01 .05
235 Jeff Reardon .02 .10
Now with Red Sox
12/6/89
236 Hal Morris .01 .05
Now with Reds
12/12/89
237 Kevin Ritz .01 .05
238 Felix Jose .01 .05
239 Eric Show .01 .05
240 Mark Grace .08 .25
241 Mike Krukow .01 .05
242 Fred Manrique .01 .05
243 Barry Jones .01 .05
244 Bill Schroeder .01 .05
245 Roger Clemens .40 1.00
246 Jim Eisenreich .01 .05
247 Jerry Reed .01 .05
248 Dave Anderson .02 .10
Now with Giants
11/29/89
249 MikeTexas Smith .01 .05
250 Jose Canseco .15 .40
251 Jeff Blauser .01 .05
252 Otis Nixon .01 .05
253 Mark Portugal .01 .05
254 Francisco Cabrera .01 .05
255 Bobby Thigpen .01 .05
256 Marvell Wynne .01 .05
257 Jose DeLeon .01 .05
258 Barry Lyons .01 .05
259 Lance McCullers .01 .05
260 Eric Davis .02 .10
261 Whitey Herzog MG .02 .10
262 Checklist 2 .01 .05
263 Mel Stottlemyre Jr. .01 .05
264 Bryan Clutterbuck .01 .05
265 Pete O'Brien .02 .10
Now with Mariners
12/7/89
266 German Gonzalez .01 .05
267 Mark Davidson .01 .05
268 Rob Murphy .01 .05
269 Dickie Thon .01 .05
270 Dave Stewart .02 .10
271 Chet Lemon .01 .05
272 Bryan Harvey .01 .05
273 Bobby Bonilla .01 .05
274 Mauro Gozzo .01 .05
275 Mickey Tettleton .02 .10
276 Gary Thurman .01 .05
277 Lenny Harris .01 .05
278 Pascual Perez .02 .10
Now with Yankees
11/27/89
279 Steve Buechele .01 .05
280 Lou Whitaker .02 .10
281 Kevin Bass .02 .10
Now with Giants
11/20/89
282 Derek Lilliquist .01 .05
283 Joey Belle .08 .25
284 Mark Gardner .01 .05
285 Willie McGee .02 .10
286 Lee Guetterman .01 .05
287 Vance Law .01 .05
288 Greg Briley .01 .05
289 Norm Charlton .01 .05
290 Robin Yount .20 .50
291 Dave Johnson MG .02 .10
292 Jim Gott .02 .10
Now with Dodgers
12/7/89
293 Mike Gallego .01 .05
294 Craig McMurtry .01 .05
295 Fred McGriff .08 .25
296 Jeff Ballard .01 .05
297 Tom Herr .01 .05
298 Dan Gladden .01 .05
299 Adam Peterson .01 .05
300 Bo Jackson .08 .25
301 Don Aase .01 .05
302 Marcus Lawton .01 .05
303 Rick Cerone .02 .10
Now with Yankees
12/19/89
304 Marty Clary .01 .05
305 Eddie Murray .15 .40
306 Tom Niedenfuer .01 .05
307 Bip Roberts .01 .05
308 Jose Guzman .01 .05
309 Eric Yelding .01 .05
310 Steve Bedrosian .01 .05
311 Dwight Smith .01 .05
312 Dan Quisenberry .01 .05
313 Gus Polidor .01 .05
314 Donald Harris FDP .01 .05
315 Bruce Hurst .01 .05
316 Carney Lansford .02 .10
317 Mark Guthrie .01 .05
318 Wallace Johnson .01 .05
319 Dion James .01 .05
320 Dave Stieb .02 .10
321 Joe Morgan MG .01 .05
322 Junior Ortiz .01 .05
323 Willie Wilson .01 .05
324 Pete Harnisch .01 .05
325 Robby Thompson .01 .05
326 Tom McCarthy .01 .05
327 Ken Williams .02 .10
328 Curt Young .01 .05
329 Oddibe McDowell .01 .05
330 Ron Darling .01 .05
331 Juan Gonzalez RC .60 1.50
332 Paul O'Neill .08 .25
333 Bill Wegman .01 .05
334 Johnny Ray .01 .05
335 Andy Hawkins .01 .05
336 Ken Griffey Jr. .75 2.00
337 Lloyd McClendon .01 .05
338 Dennis Lamp .01 .05
339 Dave Clark .02 .10
Now with Cubs
11/20/89
340 Fernando Valenzuela .02 .10
341 Tom Foley .01 .05
342 Alex Trevino .01 .05
343 Frank Tanana .01 .05
344 George Canale .01 .05
345 Harold Baines .05 .15
346 Jim Presley .01 .05
347 Junior Felix .01 .05
348 Gary Wayne .01 .05
349 Steve Finley .08 .25
350 Bret Saberhagen .02 .10
351 Roger Craig MG .01 .05
352 Bryn Smith .02 .10
Now with Cardinals
11/29/89
353 Sandy Alomar Jr. .05 .15
Now with Indians
12/6/89
354 Stan Belinda .01 .05
355 Marty Barrett .01 .05
356 Randy Ready .01 .05
357 Dave West .01 .05
358 Andres Thomas .01 .05
359 Jimmy Jones .01 .05
360 Paul Molitor .15 .40
361 Randy McCament .01 .05
362 Damon Berryhill .01 .05
363 Dan Petry .01 .05
364 Rolando Roomes .01 .05
365 Ozzie Guillen .02 .10
366 Mike Heath .01 .05
367 Mike Morgan .01 .05
368 Bill Doran .01 .05
369 Todd Burns .01 .05
370 Tim Wallach .01 .05
371 Jimmy Key .02 .10
372 Terry Kennedy .01 .05
373 Alvin Davis .01 .05
374 Steve Cummings RC .01 .05
375 Dwight Evans .02 .10
376 Checklist 3 UER .01 .05
Higuera misalphabet-
ized in Brewer list
377 Mickey Weston .01 .05
378 Luis Salazar .01 .05
379 Steve Rosenberg .01 .05
380 Dave Winfield .15 .40
381 Frank Robinson MG .05 .15
382 Jeff Musselman .01 .05
383 John Morris .01 .05
384 Pat Combs .01 .05
385 Fred McGriff AS .02 .10
386 Julio Franco AS .01 .05
387 Wade Boggs AS .08 .25
388 Cal Ripken AS .30 .75
389 Robin Yount AS .08 .25
390 Ruben Sierra AS .01 .05
391 Kirby Puckett AS .08 .25
392 Carlton Fisk AS .08 .25
393 Bret Saberhagen AS .01 .05
394 Jeff Ballard AS .01 .05
395 Jeff Russell AS .01 .05
396 Bart Giamatti RC MEM .08 .25
397 Will Clark AS .02 .10
398 Ryne Sandberg AS .08 .25
399 Howard Johnson AS .01 .05
400 Ozzie Smith AS .08 .25
401 Kevin Mitchell AS .01 .05
402 Eric Davis AS .01 .05
403 Tony Gwynn AS .08 .25
404 Craig Biggio AS .05 .15
405 Mike Scott AS .01 .05
406 Joe Magrane AS .01 .05
407 Mark Davis AS .01 .05
Now with Royals
12/11/89
408 Trevor Wilson .01 .05
409 Tom Brunansky .01 .05
410 Joe Boever .01 .05
411 Ken Phelps .01 .05
412 Jamie Moyer .01 .05
413 Brian DuBois .01 .05
414 Frank Thomas RC 1.25 3.00
415 Shawon Dunston .01 .05
416 Dave Johnson P .01 .05
417 Jim Gantner .01 .05
418 Tom Browning .01 .05
419 Beau Allred RC .01 .05
420 Carlton Fisk .15 .40
421 Greg Minton .01 .05
422 Pat Sheridan .01 .05
423 Fred Toliver .02 .10
Now with Yankees
9
27/89
424 Jerry Reuss .01 .05
425 Bill Landrum .01 .05
426 Jeff Hamilton UER .01 .05
Stats say he fanned
197 times in 1987
but he only had 147 at bats
427 Carmen Castillo .01 .05
428 Steve Davis .02 .10
Now with Dodgers
12/12/89
429 Tom Kelly MG .01 .05
430 Pete Incaviglia .01 .05
431 Randy Johnson .30 .75
432 Damaso Garcia .02 .10
Now with Yankees
12/22/89
433 Steve Olin .02 .10
434 Mark Carreon .01 .05
435 Kevin Seitzer .01 .05
436 Mel Hall .01 .05
437 Les Lancaster .01 .05
438 Greg Myers .01 .05
439 Jeff Parrett .01 .05
440 Alan Trammell .05 .15
441 Bob Kipper .01 .05
442 Jerry Browne .01 .05
443 Cris Carpenter .01 .05
444 Kyle Abbott FDP .01 .05
445 Danny Jackson .01 .05
446 Dan Pasqua .01 .05
447 Atlee Hammaker .01 .05
448 Greg Gagne .01 .05
449 Dennis Rasmussen .01 .05
450 Rickey Henderson .30 .75
451 Mark Lemke .01 .05
452 Luis DeLosSantos .01 .05
453 Jody Davis .01 .05
454 Jeff King .01 .05
455 Jeffrey Leonard .01 .05
456 Chris Gwynn .01 .05
457 Gregg Jefferies .01 .05
458 Bob McClure .01 .05
459 Jim Lefebvre MG .01 .05
460 Mike Scott .01 .05
461 Carlos Martinez .01 .05
462 Denny Walling .01 .05
463 Drew Hall .01 .05
464 Jerome Walton .01 .05
465 Kevin Gross .01 .05
466 Rance Mulliniks .01 .05
467 Juan Nieves .01 .05
468 Bill Ripken .01 .05
469 John Kruk .02 .10
470 Frank Viola .01 .05
471 Mike Brumley .02 .10
Now with Orioles
1
10/90
472 Jose Uribe .01 .05
473 Joe Price .01 .05
474 Rich Thompson .01 .05
475 Bob Welch .01 .05
476 Brad Komminsk .01 .05
477 Willie Fraser .01 .05
478 Mike LaValliere .01 .05
479 Frank White .02 .10
480 Sid Fernandez .01 .05
481 Garry Templeton .01 .05
482 Steve Carter .01 .05
483 Alejandro Pena .02 .10
Now with Mets
12/20/89
484 Mike Fitzgerald .01 .05
485 John Candelaria .01 .05
486 Jeff Treadway .01 .05
487 Steve Searcy .01 .05

Card	Low	High
488 Ken Oberkfell	.02	.10
Now with Astros		
12/6/89		
489 Nick Leyva MG	.01	.05
490 Dan Plesac	.01	.05
491 Dave Cochrane RC	.01	.05
492 Ron Oester	.01	.05
493 Jason Grimsley	.01	.05
494 Terry Puhl	.01	.05
495 Lee Smith	.02	.10
496 Cecil Espy UER	.01	.05
'88 stats have 3 SB's		
should be 33		
497 Dave Schmidt	.02	.10
Now with Expos		
12/13/89		
498 Rick Schu	.01	.05
499 Bill Long	.01	.05
500 Kevin Mitchell	.01	.05
501 Matt Young	.02	.10
Now with Mariners		
12/8/89		
502 Mitch Webster	.02	.10
Now with Indians		
11/20/89		
503 Randy St.Claire	.01	.05
504 Tom O'Malley	.01	.05
505 Kelly Gruber	.01	.05
506 Tom Glavine	.08	.25
507 Gary Redus	.01	.05
508 Terry Leach	.01	.05
509 Tom Pagnozzi	.01	.05
510 Dwight Gooden	.02	.10
511 Clay Parker	.01	.05
512 Gary Pettis	.02	.10
Now with Rangers		
11/24/89		
513 Mark Eichhorn	.02	.10
Now with Angels		
12/13/89		
514 Andy Allanson	.01	.05
515 Len Dykstra	.02	.10
516 Tim Leary	.01	.05
517 Roberto Alomar	.08	.25
518 Bill Krueger	.01	.05
519 Bucky Dent MG	.01	.05
520 Mitch Williams	.01	.05
521 Craig Worthington	.01	.05
522 Mike Dunne	.02	.10
Now with Padres		
12/4/89		
523 Jay Bell	.01	.05
524 Daryl Boston	.01	.05
525 Wally Joyner	.02	.10
526 Checklist 4	.01	.05
527 Ron Hassey	.01	.05
528 Kevin Wickander UER	.02	.10
Monthly scoreboard		
strikeout total was 2.2		
that was his innings		
pitched total		
529 Greg A. Harris	.01	.05
530 Mark Langston	.02	.10
Now with Angels		
12/4/89		
531 Ken Caminiti	.08	.25
532 Cecilio Guante	.02	.10
Now with Indians		
11/21/89		
533 Tim Jones	.01	.05
534 Louie Meadows	.01	.05
535 John Smoltz	.08	.25
536 Bob Geren	.01	.05
537 Mark Grant	.01	.05
538 Bill Spiers UER	.01	.05
Photo actually George Canale		
539 Neal Heaton	.01	.05
540 Danny Tartabull	.01	.05
541 Pat Perry	.01	.05
542 Darren Daulton	.02	.10
543 Nelson Liriano	.01	.05
544 Dennis Boyd	.02	.10
Now with Expos		
12/7/89		
545 Kevin McReynolds	.01	.05
546 Kevin Hickey	.01	.05
547 Jack Howell	.01	.05
548 Pat Clements	.01	.05
549 Don Zimmer MG	.01	.05
550 Julio Franco	.02	.10
551 Tim Crews	.01	.05
552 MikeMiss. Smith	.01	.05
553 Scott Scudder UER	.01	.05
Cedar Rapids		
554 Jay Buhner	.08	.25
555 Jack Morris	.02	.10
556 Gene Larkin	.01	.05
557 Jeff Innis	.01	.05
558 Rafael Ramirez	.01	.05
559 Andy McGaffigan	.01	.05
560 Steve Sax	.01	.05
561 Ken Dayley	.01	.05
562 Chad Kreuter	.01	.05
563 Alex Sanchez	.01	.05
564 Tyler Houston FDP RC	.01	.05
565 Scott Fletcher	.01	.05
566 Mark Knudson	.01	.05
567 Ron Gant	.02	.10
568 John Smiley	.01	.05
569 Ivan Calderon	.01	.05
570 Cal Ripken	.60	1.50
571 Brett Butler	.02	.10
572 Greg W. Harris	.01	.05
573 Danny Heep	.01	.05
574 Bill Swift	.01	.05
575 Lance Parrish	.01	.05
576 Mike Dyer RC	.01	.05
577 Charlie Hayes	.01	.05
578 Joe Magrane	.01	.05
579 Art Howe MG	.01	.05
580 Joe Carter	.02	.10
581 Ken Griffey Sr.	.02	.10
582 Rick Honeycutt	.01	.05
583 Bruce Benedict	.01	.05
584 Phil Stephenson	.01	.05
585 Kal Daniels	.01	.05
586 Edwin Nunez	.01	.05
587 Lance Johnson	.01	.05
588 Rick Rhoden	.01	.05
589 Mike Aldrete	.01	.05
590 Ozzie Smith	.20	.50
591 Todd Stottlemyre	.02	.10
592 R.J. Reynolds	.01	.05
593 Scott Bradley	.01	.05
594 Luis Sojo	.01	.05
595 Greg Swindell	.01	.05
596 Jose DeJesus	.01	.05
597 Chris Bosio	.01	.05
598 Brady Anderson	.08	.25
599 Frank Williams	.01	.05
600 Darryl Strawberry	.02	.10
601 Luis Rivera	.01	.05
602 Scott Garrelts	.01	.05
603 Tony Armas	.01	.05
604 Ron Robinson	.01	.05
605 Mike Scioscia	.02	.10
606 Storm Davis	.02	.10
Now with Royals		
12/7/89		
607 Steve Jeltz	.01	.05
608 Eric Anthony	.01	.05
609 Sparky Anderson MG	.02	.10
610 Pedro Guerrero	.01	.05
611 Walt Terrell	.02	.10
Now with Pirates		
11/29/89		
612 Dave Gallagher	.01	.05
613 Jeff Pico	.01	.05
614 Nelson Santovenia	.01	.05
615 Rob Deer	.01	.05
616 Brian Holman	.01	.05
617 Geronimo Berroa	.01	.05
618 Ed Whitson	.01	.05
619 Rob Ducey	.01	.05
620 Tony Castillo	.01	.05
621 Melido Perez	.01	.05
622 Sid Bream	.01	.05
623 Jim Corsi	.01	.05
624 Darrin Jackson	.01	.05
625 Roger McDowell	.01	.05
626 Bob Melvin	.02	.10
627 Jose Rijo	.01	.05
628 Candy Maldonado	.02	.10
Now with Indians		
11/28/89		
629 Eric Hetzel	.01	.05
630 Gary Gaetti	.02	.10
631 John Wetteland	.08	.25
632 Scott Lusader	.01	.05
633 Dennis Cook	.01	.05
634 Luis Polonia	.01	.05
635 Brian Downing	.01	.05
636 Jesse Orosco	.02	.10
637 Craig Reynolds	.01	.05
638 Jeff Montgomery	.02	.10
639 Tony LaRussa MG	.02	.10
640 Rick Sutcliffe	.02	.10
641 Doug Strange	.01	.05
642 Jack Armstrong	.01	.05
643 Alfredo Griffin	.01	.05
644 Paul Assenmacher	.01	.05
645 Jose Oquendo	.01	.05
646 Checklist 5	.01	.05
647 Rex Hudler	.02	.10
648 Jim Clancy	.01	.05
649 Dan Murphy	.01	.05
650 Mike Witt	.01	.05
651 Rafael Santana	.02	.10
Now with Indians		
1/10/90		
652 Mike Boddicker	.01	.05
653 John Moses	.01	.05
654 Paul Coleman FDP RC	.01	.05
655 Gregg Olson	.01	.05
656 Mackey Sasser	.01	.05
657 Terry Mulholland	.01	.05
658 Donell Nixon	.01	.05
659 Greg Cadaret	.01	.05
660 Vince Coleman	.01	.05
661 Dick Howser TBC'85	.01	.05
UER		
Seaver's 300th on 7/11/85		
should be 8/4/85		
662 Mike Schmidt TBC'80	.08	.25
663 Fred Lynn TBC'75	.01	.05
664 Johnny Bench TBC'70	.08	.25
665 Sandy Koufax TBC'65	.20	.50
666 Brian Fisher	.01	.05
667 Curt Wilkerson	.01	.05
668 Joe Oliver	.01	.05
669 Tom Lasorda MG	.08	.25
670 Dennis Eckersley	.15	.40
671 Bob Boone	.02	.10
672 Roy Smith	.01	.05
673 Joey Meyer	.01	.05
674 Spike Owen	.01	.05
675 Jim Abbott	.05	.15
676 Randy Kutcher	.01	.05
677 Jay Tibbs	.01	.05
678 Kirt Manwaring UER	.01	.05
88 Phoenix stats repeated		
679 Gary Ward	.01	.05
680 Howard Johnson	.01	.05
681 Mike Schooler	.01	.05
682 Dann Bilardello	.01	.05
683 Kenny Rogers	.02	.10
684 Julio Machado	.01	.05
685 Tony Fernandez	.01	.05
686 Carmelo Martinez	.02	.10
Now with Phillies		
12/4/89		
687 Tim Birtsas	.01	.05
688 Milt Thompson	.01	.05
689 Rich Yett	.02	.10
Now with Twins		
12/26/89		
690 Mark McGwire	.30	.75
691 Chuck Cary	.01	.05
692 Sammy Sosa RC	1.50	4.00
693 Calvin Schiraldi	.01	.05
694 Mike Stanton	.01	.05
695 Tom Henke	.01	.05
696 B.J. Surhoff	.02	.10
697 Mike Davis	.01	.05
698 Omar Vizquel	.08	.25
699 Jim Leyland MG	.01	.05
700 Kirby Puckett	.30	.75
701 Bernie Williams RC	.60	1.50
702 Tony Phillips	.01	.05
Now with Tigers		
12/5/89		
703 Jeff Brantley	.01	.05
704 Chip Hale	.01	.05
705 Claudell Washington	.01	.05
706 Geno Petralli	.01	.05
707 Luis Aquino	.01	.05
708 Larry Sheets	.02	.10
Now with Tigers		
1/10/90		
709 Juan Berenguer	.01	.05
710 Von Hayes	.01	.05
711 Rick Aguilera	.04	.10
712 Todd Benzinger	.01	.05
713 Tim Drummond	.01	.05
714 Marquis Grissom RC	.20	.50
715 Greg Maddux	.40	1.00
716 Steve Balboni	.01	.05
717 Ron Karkovice	.01	.05
718 Gary Sheffield	.20	.50
719 Wally Whitehurst	.01	.05
720 Andres Galarraga	.08	.25
721 Lee Mazzilli	.01	.05
722 Felix Fermin	.01	.05
723 Jeff D. Robinson	.01	.05
Now with Yankees		
12/4/89		
724 Juan Bell	.01	.05
725 Terry Pendleton	.02	.10
726 Gene Nelson	.01	.05
727 Pat Tabler	.01	.05
728 Jim Acker	.01	.05
729 Bobby Valentine MG	.01	.05
730 Tony Gwynn	.30	.75
731 Don Carman	.01	.05
732 Ernest Riles	.01	.05
733 John Dopson	.01	.05
734 Kevin Elster	.01	.05
735 Charlie Hough	.02	.10
736 Rick Dempsey	.01	.05
737 Chris Sabo	.01	.05
738 Gene Harris	.01	.05
739 Dale Sveum	.01	.05
740 Jesse Barfield	.01	.05
741 Steve Wilson	.01	.05
742 Ernie Whitt	.01	.05
743 Tom Candiotti	.01	.05
744 Kelly Mann	.01	.05
745 Hubie Brooks	.01	.05
746 Dave Smith	.01	.05
747 Randy Bush	.01	.05
748 Doyle Alexander	.01	.05
749 Mark Parent UER	.01	.05
'87 BA .80, should be .080		
750 Dale Murphy	.08	.25
751 Steve Lyons	.02	.10
752 Tom Gordon	.05	.15
753 Chris Speier	.01	.05
754 Bob Walk	.01	.05
755 Rafael Palmeiro	.08	.25
756 Ken Howell	.01	.05
757 Larry Walker RC	.60	1.50
758 Mark Thurmond	.01	.05
759 Tom Trebelhorn MG	.01	.05
760 Wade Boggs	.15	.40
761 Mike Jackson	.02	.10
762 Doug Dascenzo	.01	.05
763 Dennis Martinez	.02	.10
764 Tim Teufel	.01	.05
765 Chili Davis	.02	.10
766 Brian Meyer	.01	.05
767 Tracy Jones	.01	.05
768 Chuck Crim	.01	.05
769 Greg Hibbard	.01	.05
770 Cory Snyder	.01	.05
771 Pete Smith	.01	.05
772 Jeff Reed	.01	.05
773 Dave Leiper	.01	.05
774 Ben McDonald	.01	.05
775 Andy Van Slyke	.02	.10
776 Charlie Leibrandt	.02	.10
Now with Braves		
12/17/89		
777 Tim Laudner	.01	.05
778 Mike Jeffcoat	.01	.05
779 Lloyd Moseby	.02	.10
Now with Tigers		
12/7/89		
780 Orel Hershiser	.02	.10
781 Mario Diaz	.01	.05
782 Jose Alvarez	.02	.10
Now with Giants		
12/4/89		
783 Checklist 6	.01	.05
784 Scott Bailes	.02	.10
Now with Angels		
1/9/90		
785 Jim Rice	.02	.10
786 Eric King	.01	.05
787 Rene Gonzales	.01	.05
788 Frank DiPino	.01	.05
789 John Wathan MG	.01	.05
790 Gary Carter	.15	.40
791 Alvaro Espinoza	.01	.05
792 Gerald Perry	.01	.05

1990 O-Pee-Chee Box Bottoms

The 1990 O-Pee-Chee box bottom cards comprise four different box bottoms from the bottoms of wax pack boxes, with four cards each, for a total of 16 standard-size cards. The cards are nearly identical to the 1990 Topps Box Bottom cards. The fronts feature green-bordered color player action shots. The player's name appears at the bottom and his team name appears at the upper left. The yellow-green horizontal backs carry player career highlights in both English and French. The cards are lettered (A-P) rather than numbered on the back.

Card	Low	High
COMPLETE SET (16)	4.00	10.00
A Wade Boggs	.40	1.00
B George Brett	.75	2.00
C Andre Dawson	.20	.50
D Darrell Evans	.07	.20
E Dwight Gooden	.07	.20
F Rickey Henderson	.50	1.25
G Tom Lasorda MG	.20	.50
H Fred Lynn	.02	.10
I Mark McGwire	1.00	2.50
J Dave Parker	.07	.20
K Jeff Reardon	.07	.20
L Rick Reuschel	.02	.10
M Jim Rice	.07	.20
N Cal Ripken	1.50	4.00
O Nolan Ryan	1.50	4.00
P Ryne Sandberg	.75	2.00

1991 O-Pee-Chee

The 1991 O-Pee-Chee baseball set contains 792 standard-size cards. For the second time since 1976, O-Pee-Chee issued the exact same set as Topps. The only distinctions are the bilingual text and the O-Pee-Chee copyright on the backs. The fronts feature white-bordered color action player photos framed by two different colored lines. The player's name and position appear at the bottom of the photo, with his team name appearing just above. The Topps 40th anniversary logo appears in the upper left corner. The traded players have their new teams and dates of trade printed on the photo. The pinkish horizontal backs present player biography, statistics and bilingual career highlights. Cards 386-407 are an All-Star subset. Notable Rookie Cards include Carl Everett and Chipper Jones.

Card	Low	High
COMPLETE SET (792)	6.00	15.00
COMPLETE FACT.SET (792)	8.00	20.00
1 Nolan Ryan	.75	2.00
2 George Brett RB	.15	.40
3 Carlton Fisk RB	.08	.25
4 Kevin Maas RB	.01	.05
5 Cal Ripken RB	.30	.75
6 Nolan Ryan RB	.40	1.00
7 Ryne Sandberg RB	.08	.25
8 Bobby Thigpen RB	.01	.05
9 Darrin Fletcher	.01	.05
10 Gregg Olson	.01	.05
11 Roberto Kelly	.01	.05
12 Paul Assenmacher	.01	.05
13 Mariano Duncan	.01	.05
14 Dennis Lamp	.01	.05
15 Von Hayes	.01	.05
16 Mike Heath	.01	.05
17 Jeff Brantley	.01	.05
18 Nelson Liriano	.01	.05
19 Jeff D. Robinson	.01	.05
20 Pedro Guerrero	.01	.05
21 Joe Morgan MG	.01	.05
22 Storm Davis	.01	.05
23 Jim Gantner	.01	.05
24 Dave Martinez	.01	.05
25 Tim Belcher	.01	.05
26 Luis Sojo UER		
(Born in Barquisimeto&	.01	.05
not Caracas		
27 Bobby Witt	.01	.05
28 Alvaro Espinoza	.01	.05
29 Bob Walk	.01	.05
30 Gregg Jefferies	.01	.05
31 Colby Ward	.01	.05
32 Mike Simms	.01	.05
33 Barry Jones	.01	.05
34 Atlee Hammaker	.01	.05
35 Greg Maddux	.40	1.00
36 Donnie Hill	.01	.05
37 Tom Bolton	.01	.05
38 Scott Bradley	.01	.05
39 Jim Neidlinger	.01	.05
40 Kevin Mitchell	.01	.05
41 Ken Dayley	.02	.10
Now with Blue Jays/11/26/90		
42 Chris Hoiles	.01	.05
43 Roger McDowell	.01	.05
44 Mike Felder	.01	.05
45 Chris Sabo	.01	.05
46 Tim Drummond	.01	.05
47 Brook Jacoby	.01	.05
48 Dennis Boyd	.01	.05
49 Pat Borders	.01	.05
50 Bob Welch	.01	.05
51 Art Howe MG	.01	.05
52 Francisco Oliveras	.01	.05
53 Mike Sharperson UER	.01	.05
Born in 1961, not 1960		
54 Gary Mielke	.01	.05
55 Jeffrey Leonard	.01	.05
56 Jeff Parrett	.01	.05
57 Jack Howell	.01	.05
58 Mel Stottlemyre Jr.	.01	.05
59 Eric Yelding	.01	.05
60 Frank Viola	.01	.05
61 Stan Javier	.01	.05
62 Lee Guetterman	.01	.05
63 Milt Thompson	.01	.05
64 Tom Herr	.01	.05
65 Bruce Hurst	.01	.05
66 Terry Kennedy	.01	.05
67 Rick Honeycutt	.01	.05
68 Gary Sheffield	.20	.50
69 Steve Wilson	.01	.05
70 Ellis Burks	.02	.10
71 Jim Acker	.01	.05
72 Junior Ortiz	.01	.05
73 Craig Worthington	.01	.05
74 Shane Andrews RC	.01	.05
75 Jack Morris	.02	.10
76 Jerry Browne	.01	.05
77 Drew Hall	.01	.05
78 Geno Petralli	.01	.05
79 Frank Thomas	.25	.60
80 Fernando Valenzuela	.02	.10
81 Cito Gaston MG	.01	.05
82 Tom Glavine	.15	.40
83 Daryl Boston	.01	.05
84 Bob McClure	.01	.05
85 Jesse Barfield	.01	.05
86 Les Lancaster	.01	.05
87 Tracy Jones	.01	.05
88 Bob Tewksbury	.01	.05
89 Darren Daulton	.02	.10
90 Danny Tartabull	.01	.05
91 Greg Colbrunn	.01	.05
92 Danny Jackson	.02	.10
Now with Cubs/11/21/90		
93 Ivan Calderon	.01	.05
94 John Dopson	.01	.05
95 Paul Molitor	.15	.40
96 Trevor Wilson	.01	.05
97 Brady Anderson	.08	.25
98 Sergio Valdez	.01	.05
99 Chris Gwynn	.01	.05
100 Don Mattingly	.40	1.00
101 Rob Ducey	.01	.05
102 Gene Larkin	.01	.05
103 Tim Costo	.01	.05
104 Don Robinson	.01	.05
105 Kevin McReynolds	.01	.05
106 Ed Nunez	.02	.10
Now with Brewers/12/4/90		
107 Luis Polonia	.01	.05
108 Matt Young	.02	.10
Now with Red Sox/12/4/90		
109 Greg Riddoch MG	.01	.05
110 Tom Henke	.01	.05
111 Andres Thomas	.01	.05
112 Frank DiPino	.01	.05
113 Carl Everett RC	.40	1.00
114 Lance Dickson	.01	.05
115 Hubie Brooks	.02	.10
Now with Mets/12/15/90		
116 Mark Davis	.01	.05
117 Dion James	.01	.05
118 Tom Edens	.01	.05
119 Carl Nichols	.01	.05
120 Joe Carter	.05	.15
Now with Blue Jays/12/5/90		
121 Eric King	.02	.10
Now with Indians/12/4/90		
122 Paul O'Neill	.15	.40
123 Greg A. Harris	.01	.05
124 Randy Bush	.01	.05
125 Steve Bedrosian	.02	.10
Now with Twins/12/5/90		
126 Bernard Gilkey	.02	.10
127 Joe Price	.01	.05
128 Travis Fryman	.08	.25
Front has SS, back has SS-3B		
129 Mark Eichhorn	.01	.05
130 Ozzie Smith	.20	.50
131 Checklist 1	.01	.05
132 Jamie Quirk	.01	.05
133 Greg Briley	.01	.05
134 Kevin Elster	.01	.05
135 Jerome Walton	.01	.05
136 Dave Schmidt	.01	.05
137 Randy Ready	.01	.05
138 Jamie Moyer	.05	.15
Now with Cardinals/1/10/91		
139 Jeff Treadway	.01	.05
140 Fred McGriff	.08	.25
Now with Padres/12/5/90		
141 Nick Leyva MG	.01	.05
142 Curt Wilkerson	.02	.10
Now with Pirates/1/9/91		
143 John Smiley	.01	.05
144 Dave Henderson	.01	.05
145 Lou Whitaker	.02	.10
146 Dan Plesac	.01	.05
147 Carlos Baerga	.01	.05
148 Rey Palacios	.01	.05
149 Al Osuna UER/(Shown with glove on	.01	.05
right hand& bi		
150 Cal Ripken	.60	1.50
151 Tom Browning	.01	.05
152 Mickey Hatcher	.01	.05
153 Bryan Harvey	.01	.05
154 Jay Buhner	.02	.10
155 Dwight Evans	.05	.15
Now with Orioles/12/6/90		
156 Carlos Martinez	.01	.05
157 John Smoltz	.08	.25
158 Jose Uribe	.01	.05
159 Joe Boever	.01	.05
160 Vince Coleman	.01	.05
161 Tim Leary	.01	.05
162 Ozzie Canseco	.01	.05
163 Dave Johnson	.01	.05
164 Edgar Diaz	.01	.05
165 Sandy Alomar Jr.	.02	.10
166 Harold Baines	.05	.15
167 Randy Tomlin	.01	.05
168 John Olerud	.08	.25
169 Luis Aquino	.01	.05
170 Carlton Fisk	.15	.40
171 Tony LaRussa MG	.02	.10
172 Pete Incaviglia	.01	.05
173 Jason Grimsley	.01	.05
174 Ken Caminiti	.08	.25
175 Jack Armstrong	.01	.05
176 John Orton	.01	.05
177 Reggie Harris	.01	.05
178 Dave Valle	.01	.05
179 Pete Harnisch	.01	.05
Now with Astros/1/10/91		
180 Tony Gwynn	.30	.75
181 Duane Ward	.01	.05
182 Junior Noboa	.01	.05
183 Clay Parker	.01	.05
184 Gary Green	.01	.05
185 Joe Magrane	.01	.05
186 Rod Booker	.01	.05
187 Greg Cadaret	.01	.05
188 Damon Berryhill	.01	.05
189 Daryl Irvine	.01	.05
190 Matt Williams	.05	.15
191 Willie Blair	.02	.10
Now with Indians/11/6/90		
192 Rob Deer	.02	.10
Now with Tigers/11/21/90		
193 Felix Fermin	.01	.05
194 Xavier Hernandez	.01	.05
195 Wally Joyner	.02	.10
196 Jim Vatcher	.01	.05
197 Chris Nabholz	.01	.05
198 R.J. Reynolds	.01	.05
199 Mike Hartley	.01	.05
200 Darryl Strawberry	.05	.15
Now with Dodgers/11/8/90		
201 Tom Kelly MG	.01	.05
202 Jim Leyritz	.01	.05
203 Gene Harris	.01	.05
204 Herm Winningham	.01	.05
205 Mike Perez	.01	.05
206 Carlos Quintana	.01	.05
207 Gary Wayne	.01	.05
208 Willie Wilson	.01	.05
209 Ken Howell	.01	.05
210 Lance Parrish	.01	.05
211 Brian Barnes	.01	.05
212 Steve Finley	.08	.25
Now with Astros/1/10/91		
213 Frank Wills	.01	.05
214 Joe Girardi	.02	.10
215 Dave Smith	.02	.10
Now with Cubs/12/17/90		
216 Greg Gagne	.01	.05
217 Chris Bosio	.01	.05
218 Rick Parker	.01	.05
219 Jack McDowell	.01	.05
220 Tim Wallach	.01	.05
221 Don Slaught	.01	.05
222 Brian McRae RC	.08	.25
223 Allan Anderson	.01	.05
224 Juan Gonzalez	.08	.25
225 Randy Johnson	.25	.60
226 Alfredo Griffin	.01	.05
227 Steve Avery UER		
(Pitched 13 games for	.01	.05
Durham in		
228 Rex Hudler	.01	.05
229 Rance Mulliniks	.01	.05
230 Sid Fernandez	.01	.05
231 Doug Rader MG	.01	.05
232 Jose DeJesus	.01	.05
233 Al Leiter	.01	.05
234 Scott Erickson	.01	.05
235 Dave Parker	.02	.10
236 Frank Tanana	.01	.05
237 Rick Cerone	.01	.05
238 Mike Dunne	.01	.05
239 Darren Lewis	.02	.10
Now with Giants/12/4/90		
240 Mike Scott	.01	.05
241 Dave Clark UER		
(Career totals 19 HR	.01	.05
and 5 3B& sh		
242 Mike LaCoss	.01	.05
243 Lance Johnson	.01	.05
244 Mike Jeffcoat	.01	.05
245 Kal Daniels	.01	.05
246 Kevin Wickander	.01	.05
247 Jody Reed	.01	.05
248 Tom Gordon	.02	.10
249 Bob Melvin	.02	.10
250 Dennis Eckersley	.15	.40
251 Mark Lemke	.01	.05
252 Mel Rojas	.02	.10
253 Garry Templeton	.01	.05
254 Shawn Boskie	.01	.05
255 Brian Downing	.01	.05
256 Greg Hibbard	.01	.05
257 Tom O'Malley	.01	.05
258 Chris Hammond	.01	.05
259 Hensley Meulens	.01	.05
260 Harold Reynolds	.02	.10
261 Bud Harrelson MG	.01	.05
262 Tim Jones	.01	.05
263 Checklist 2	.01	.05
264 Dave Hollins	.01	.05
265 Mark Gubicza	.01	.05
266 Carmelo Castillo	.01	.05
267 Mark Knudson	.01	.05
268 Tom Brookens	.01	.05
269 Joe Hesketh	.01	.05
270 Mark McGwire	.30	.75
271 Omar Olivares	.01	.05
272 Jeff King	.01	.05
273 Johnny Ray	.01	.05
274 Ken Williams	.02	.10
275 Alan Trammell	.05	.15
276 Bill Swift	.01	.05
277 Scott Coolbaugh	.02	.10
Now with Padres/12/12/90		
278 Alex Fernandez UER	.01	.05
No '90 White Sox stats		
279 Jose Gonzalez	.01	.05
280 Bret Saberhagen	.02	.10
281 Larry Sheets	.01	.05
282 Don Carman	.01	.05
283 Marquis Grissom	.02	.10
284 Billy Spiers	.01	.05
285 Jim Abbott	.02	.10
286 Ken Oberkfell	.01	.05
287 Mark Grant	.01	.05
288 Derrick May	.01	.05
289 Tim Birtsas	.01	.05
290 Steve Sax	.01	.05
291 John Wathan MG	.01	.05
292 Bud Black	.01	.05
293 Jay Bell	.01	.05
294 Mike Moore	.01	.05
295 Rafael Palmeiro	.08	.25
296 Mark Williamson	.01	.05
297 Manny Lee	.01	.05
298 Omar Vizquel	.08	.25
299 Scott Radinsky	.01	.05
300 Kirby Puckett	.25	.60
301 Steve Farr	.02	.10
Now with Yankees/11/26/90		
302 Tim Teufel	.01	.05
303 Mike Boddicker	.02	.10
Now with Royals/11/21/90		
304 Kevin Reimer	.01	.05
305 Mike Scioscia	.02	.10
306 Lonnie Smith	.01	.05
307 Andy Benes	.01	.05
308 Tom Pagnozzi	.01	.05
309 Norm Charlton	.01	.05
310 Gary Carter	.15	.40
311 Jeff Pico	.01	.05
312 Charlie Hayes	.01	.05
313 Ron Robinson	.01	.05
314 Gary Pettis	.01	.05
315 Roberto Alomar	.15	.40
316 Gene Nelson	.01	.05
317 Mike Fitzgerald	.01	.05
318 Rick Aguilera	.02	.10
319 Jeff McKnight	.01	.05
320 Tony Fernandez	.02	.10
Now with Padres/12/5/90		
321 Bob Rodgers MG	.01	.05
322 Terry Shumpert	.01	.05
323 Cory Snyder	.01	.05

Card	Low	High
324 Ron Kittle	.01	.05
325 Brett Butler	.02	.10
Now with Dodgers/12/15/90		
326 Ken Patterson	.01	.05
327 Ron Hassey	.01	.05
328 Walt Terrell	.01	.05
329 David Justice UER	.15	.40
330 Dwight Gooden	.02	.10
331 Eric Anthony	.01	.05
332 Kenny Rogers	.05	.15
Now with White Sox/12/4/90		
333 Chipper Jones RC	15.00	40.00
334 Todd Benzinger	.01	.05
335 Mitch Williams	.01	.05
336 Matt Nokes	.01	.05
337 Keith Comstock	.01	.05
338 Luis Rivera	.01	.05
339 Larry Walker	.08	.25
340 Ramon Martinez	.01	.05
341 John Moses	.01	.05
342 Mickey Morandini	.01	.05
343 Jose Oquendo	.01	.05
344 Jeff Russell	.01	.05
345 Len Dykstra	.02	.10
346 Jesse Orosco	.02	.10
347 Greg Vaughn	.08	.25
348 Todd Stottlemyre	.02	.10
349 Dave Gallagher	.02	.10
Now with Angels/12/4/90		
350 Glenn Davis	.01	.05
351 Joe Torre MG	.02	.10
352 Frank White	.02	.10
353 Tony Castillo	.01	.05
354 Sid Bream	.02	.10
Now with Braves/12/5/90		
355 Chili Davis	.02	.10
356 Mike Marshall	.01	.05
357 Jack Savage	.01	.05
358 Mark Parent	.02	.10
Now with Rangers/12/12/90		
359 Chuck Cary	.01	.05
360 Tim Raines	.05	.15
Now with White Sox/12/23/90		
361 Scott Garrelts	.01	.05
362 Hector Villanueva	.01	.05
363 Rick Mahler	.01	.05
364 Dan Pasqua	.01	.05
365 Mike Schooler	.01	.05
366 Checklist 3	.01	.05
367 Dave Walsh RC	.01	.05
368 Felix Jose	.01	.05
369 Steve Searcy	.01	.05
370 Kelly Gruber	.01	.05
371 Jeff Montgomery	.01	.05
372 Spike Owen	.01	.05
373 Darrin Jackson	.01	.05
374 Larry Casian	.01	.05
375 Tony Pena	.01	.05
376 Mike Harkey	.01	.05
377 Rene Gonzales	.01	.05
378 Wilson Alvarez	.08	.25
379 Randy Velarde	.01	.05
380 Willie McGee	.05	.15
Now with Giants/12/3/90		
381 Jim Leyland MG	.01	.05
382 Mackey Sasser	.01	.05
383 Pete Smith	.01	.05
384 Gerald Perry	.02	.10
Now with Cardinals/12/13/90		
385 Mickey Tettleton	.02	.10
Now with Tigers/1/12/90		
386 Cecil Fielder AS	.02	.10
387 Julio Franco AS	.01	.05
388 Kelly Gruber AS	.01	.05
389 Alan Trammell AS	.02	.10
390 Jose Canseco AS	.08	.25
391 Rickey Henderson AS	.15	.40
392 Ken Griffey Jr. AS	.40	1.00
393 Carlton Fisk AS	.02	.10
394 Bob Welch AS	.01	.05
395 Chuck Finley AS	.01	.05
396 Bobby Thigpen AS	.01	.05
397 Eddie Murray AS	.02	.10
398 Ryne Sandberg AS	.05	.15
399 Matt Williams AS	.05	.15
400 Barry Larkin AS	.02	.10
401 Barry Bonds AS	.20	.50
402 Darryl Strawbery AS	.02	.10
403 Bobby Bonilla AS	.01	.05
404 Mike Scioscia AS	.01	.05
405 Doug Drabek AS	.01	.05
406 Frank Viola AS	.01	.05
407 John Franco AS	.01	.05
408 Earnie Riles	.02	.10
Now with Athletics/12/4/90		
409 Mike Stanley	.01	.05
410 Dave Righetti	.02	.10
Now with Giants/12/4/90		
411 Lance Blankenship	.01	.05
412 Dave Bergman	.01	.05
413 Terry Mulholland	.01	.05
414 Sammy Sosa	.15	.40
415 Rick Sutcliffe	.02	.10
416 Randy Milligan	.01	.05
417 Bill Krueger	.01	.05
418 Nick Esasky	.01	.05
419 Jeff Reed	.01	.05
420 Bobby Thigpen	.01	.05
421 Alex Cole	.01	.05
422 Rick Reuschel	.01	.05
423 Rafael Ramirez UER	.01	.05
Born 1959, not 1958		
424 Calvin Schiraldi	.01	.05
425 Andy Van Slyke	.01	.05
426 Joe Grahe	.01	.05
427 Rick Dempsey	.01	.05
428 John Barfield	.01	.05
429 Stump Merrill MG	.01	.05
430 Gary Gaetti	.02	.10
431 Paul Gibson	.01	.05
432 Delino DeShields	.02	.10
433 Pat Tabler	.01	.05
Now with Blue Jays/12/5/90		
434 Julio Machado	.01	.05
435 Kevin Maas	.01	.05
436 Scott Bankhead	.01	.05
437 Doug Dascenzo	.01	.05
438 Vicente Palacios	.01	.05
439 Dickie Thon	.01	.05
440 George Bell	.01	.05
Now with Cubs/12/6/90		
441 Zane Smith	.01	.05
442 Charlie O'Brien	.01	.05
443 Jeff Innis	.01	.05
444 Glenn Braggs	.01	.05
445 Greg Swindell	.01	.05
446 Craig Grebeck	.01	.05
447 John Burkett	.01	.05
448 Craig Lefferts	.01	.05
449 Juan Berenguer	.01	.05
450 Wade Boggs	.15	.40
451 Neal Heaton	.01	.05
452 Bill Schroeder	.01	.05
453 Lenny Harris	.01	.05
454 Kevin Appier	.02	.10
455 Walt Weiss	.01	.05
456 Charlie Leibrandt	.01	.05
457 Todd Hundley	.08	.25
458 Brian Holman	.01	.05
459 Tom Trebelhorn MG	.01	.05
460 Dave Stieb	.02	.10
461 Robin Ventura	.08	.25
462 Steve Frey	.01	.05
463 Dwight Smith	.01	.05
464 Steve Buechele	.01	.05
465 Ken Griffey Sr.	.02	.10
466 Charles Nagy	.02	.10
467 Dennis Cook	.01	.05
468 Tim Hulett	.01	.05
469 Chet Lemon	.01	.05
470 Howard Johnson	.01	.05
471 Mike Lieberthal RC	.20	.50
472 Kirt Manwaring	.01	.05
473 Curt Young	.01	.05
474 Phil Plantier	.01	.05
475 Teddy Higuera	.01	.05
476 Glenn Wilson	.01	.05
477 Mike Fetters	.01	.05
478 Kurt Stillwell	.01	.05
479 Bob Patterson	.01	.05
480 Dave Magadan	.01	.05
481 Eddie Whitson	.01	.05
482 Tino Martinez	.08	.25
483 Mike Aldrete	.01	.05
484 Dave LaPoint	.01	.05
485 Terry Pendleton	.05	.15
Now with Braves/12/3/90		
486 Tommy Greene	.01	.05
487 Rafael Belliard	.02	.10
Now with Braves/12/18/90		
488 Jeff Manto	.01	.05
489 Bobby Valentine MG	.01	.05
490 Kirk Gibson	.05	.15
Now with Royals/12/1/90		
491 Kurt Miller	.01	.05
492 Ernie Whitt	.01	.05
493 Jose Rijo	.01	.05
494 Chris James	.01	.05
495 Charlie Hough	.05	.15
Now with White Sox/12/20/90		
496 Marty Barrett	.01	.05
497 Ben McDonald	.01	.05
498 Mark Salas	.01	.05
499 Melido Perez	.01	.05
500 Will Clark	.15	.40
501 Mike Bielecki	.01	.05
502 Carney Lansford	.02	.10
503 Roy Smith	.01	.05
504 Julio Valera	.01	.05
505 Chuck Finley	.02	.10
506 Darnell Coles	.01	.05
507 Steve Jeltz	.01	.05
508 Mike York	.01	.05
509 Glenallen Hill	.01	.05
510 John Franco	.02	.10
511 Steve Balboni	.01	.05
512 Jose Mesa	.01	.05
513 Jerald Clark	.01	.05
514 Mike Stanton	.01	.05
515 Alvin Davis	.01	.05
516 Karl Rhodes	.01	.05
517 Joe Oliver	.01	.05
518 Cris Carpenter	.01	.05
519 Sparky Anderson MG	.02	.10
520 Mark Grace	.15	.40
521 Joe Orsulak	.01	.05
522 Stan Belinda	.01	.05
523 Rodney McCray	.01	.05
524 Darrel Akerfelds	.01	.05
525 Willie Randolph	.02	.10
526 Moises Alou	.02	.10
527 Checklist 4	.01	.05
528 Denny Martinez	.02	.10
529 Marc Newfield	.01	.05
530 Roger Clemens	.40	1.00
531 Dave Rohde	.01	.05
532 Kirk McCaskill	.01	.05
533 Oddibe McDowell	.01	.05
534 Mike Jackson	.02	.10
535 Ruben Sierra	.02	.10
536 Mike Witt	.01	.05
537 Jose Lind	.01	.05
538 Bip Roberts	.01	.05
539 Scott Terry	.01	.05
540 George Brett	.30	.75
541 Domingo Ramos	.01	.05
542 Rob Murphy	.01	.05
543 Junior Felix	.01	.05
544 Alejandro Pena	.01	.05
545 Dale Murphy	.15	.40
546 Jeff Ballard	.01	.05
547 Mike Pagliarulo	.01	.05
548 Jaime Navarro	.01	.05
549 John McNamara MG	.01	.05
550 Eric Davis	.02	.10
551 Bob Kipper	.01	.05
552 Jeff Hamilton	.01	.05
553 Joe Klink	.01	.05
554 Brian Harper	.01	.05
555 Turner Ward	.01	.05
556 Gary Ward	.01	.05
557 Wally Whitehurst	.01	.05
558 Otis Nixon	.02	.10
559 Adam Peterson	.01	.05
560 Greg Smith	.02	.10
Now with Dodgers/12/14/90		
561 Tim McIntosh	.01	.05
562 Jeff Kunkel	.01	.05
563 Brent Knackert	.01	.05
564 Dante Bichette	.02	.10
565 Craig Biggio	.05	.15
566 Craig Wilson	.01	.05
567 Dwayne Henry	.01	.05
568 Ron Karkovice	.01	.05
569 Curt Schilling	.25	.60
Now with Astros/1/10/91		
570 Barry Bonds	.30	.75
571 Pat Combs	.01	.05
572 Dave Anderson	.01	.05
573 Rich Rodriguez UER		
(Stats say drafted 4th&	.01	.05
but b		
574 John Marzano	.01	.05
575 Robin Yount	.15	.40
576 Jeff Kaiser	.01	.05
577 Bill Doran	.01	.05
578 Dave West	.01	.05
579 Roger Craig MG	.01	.05
580 Dave Stewart	.02	.10
581 Luis Quinones	.01	.05
582 Marty Clary	.01	.05
583 Tony Phillips	.01	.05
584 Kevin Brown	.05	.15
585 Pete O'Brien	.01	.05
586 Fred Lynn	.01	.05
587 Jose Offerman UER	.01	.05
588 Mark Whiten	.01	.05
589 Scott Ruskin	.01	.05
590 Eddie Murray	.15	.40
591 Ken Hill	.01	.05
592 B.J. Surhoff	.02	.10
593 Mike Walker	.01	.05
594 Rich Garces	.01	.05
595 Bill Landrum	.01	.05
596 Ronnie Walden	.01	.05
597 Jerry Don Gleaton	.01	.05
598 Sam Horn	.01	.05
599 Greg Myers	.01	.05
600 Bo Jackson	.08	.25
601 Bob Ojeda	.02	.10
Now with Dodgers/12/15/90		
602 Casey Candaele	.01	.05
603 Wes Chamberlain	.01	.05
604 Billy Hatcher	.01	.05
605 Jeff Reardon	.02	.10
606 Jim Gott	.01	.05
607 Edgar Martinez	.05	.15
608 Todd Burns	.01	.05
609 Jeff Torborg MG	.01	.05
610 Andres Galarraga	.08	.25
611 Dave Eiland	.01	.05
612 Steve Lyons	.02	.10
613 Eric Show	.02	.10
Now with Athletics/12/10/90		
614 Luis Salazar	.01	.05
615 Bert Blyleven	.02	.10
616 Todd Zeile	.02	.10
617 Bill Wegman	.01	.05
618 Sil Campusano	.01	.05
619 David Wells	.05	.15
620 Ozzie Guillen	.02	.10
621 Ted Power	.02	.10
Now with Reds/12/14/90		
622 Jack Daugherty	.01	.05
623 Jeff Blauser	.01	.05
624 Tom Candiotti	.01	.05
625 Terry Steinbach	.01	.05
626 Gerald Young	.01	.05
627 Tim Layana	.01	.05
628 Greg Litton	.01	.05
629 Wes Gardner	.02	.10
Now with Padres/12/15/90		
630 Dave Winfield	.15	.40
631 Mike Morgan	.01	.05
632 Lloyd Moseby	.01	.05
633 Kevin Tapani	.01	.05
634 Henry Cotto	.01	.05
635 Andy Hawkins	.01	.05
636 Geronimo Pena	.01	.05
637 Bruce Ruffin	.01	.05
638 Mike Macfarlane	.01	.05
639 Frank Robinson MG	.08	.25
640 Andre Dawson	.08	.25
641 Mike Henneman	.01	.05
642 Hal Morris	.01	.05
643 Jim Presley	.01	.05
644 Chuck Crim	.01	.05
645 Juan Samuel	.01	.05
646 Andujar Cedeno	.01	.05
647 Mark Portugal	.01	.05
648 Lee Stevens	.01	.05
649 Bill Sampen	.01	.05
650 Jack Clark	.05	.15
Now with Red Sox/12/15/90		
651 Alan Mills	.01	.05
652 Kevin Romine	.01	.05
653 Anthony Telford	.01	.05
654 Paul Sorrento	.02	.10
655 Erik Hanson	.01	.05
656 Checklist 5	.01	.05
657 Mike Kingery	.01	.05
658 Scott Aldred	.01	.05
659 Oscar Azocar	.01	.05
660 Lee Smith	.02	.10
661 Steve Lake	.01	.05
662 Rob Dibble	.01	.05
663 Greg Brock	.01	.05
664 John Farrell	.01	.05
665 Mike LaValliere	.01	.05
666 Danny Darwin	.01	.05
Now with Red Sox/12/19/90		
667 Kent Anderson	.01	.05
668 Bill Long	.01	.05
669 Lou Piniella MG	.02	.10
670 Rickey Henderson	.30	.75
671 Andy McGaffigan	.01	.05
672 Shane Mack	.01	.05
673 Greg Olson UER		
(6 RBI in '88 at Tide-	.01	.05
water and		
674 Kevin Gross	.02	.10
Now with Dodgers/12/3/90		
675 Tom Brunansky	.01	.05
676 Scott Chiamparino	.01	.05
677 Billy Ripken	.01	.05
678 Mark Davidson	.01	.05
679 Bill Bathe	.01	.05
680 David Cone	.08	.25
681 Jeff Schaefer	.01	.05
682 Ray Lankford	.08	.25
683 Derek Lilliquist	.01	.05
684 Milt Cuyler	.01	.05
685 Doug Drabek	.01	.05
686 Mike Gallego	.01	.05
687 John Cerutti	.01	.05
688 Rosario Rodriguez	.02	.10
Now with Pirates/12/20/90		
689 John Kruk	.02	.10
690 Orel Hershiser	.02	.10
691 Mike Blowers	.01	.05
692 Efrain Valdez	.01	.05
693 Francisco Cabrera	.01	.05
694 Randy Veres	.01	.05
695 Kevin Seitzer	.01	.05
696 Steve Olin	.01	.05
697 Shawn Abner	.01	.05
698 Mark Guthrie	.01	.05
699 Jim Lefebvre MG	.01	.05
700 Jose Canseco	.15	.40
701 Pascual Perez	.01	.05
702 Tim Naehring	.01	.05
703 Juan Agosto	.02	.10
Now with Cardinals/12/14/90		
704 Devon White	.05	.15
Now with Blue Jays/12/2/90		
705 Robby Thompson	.01	.05
706 Brad Arnsberg	.01	.05
707 Jim Eisenreich	.01	.05
708 John Mitchell	.01	.05
709 Matt Sinatro	.01	.05
710 Kent Hrbek	.02	.10
711 Jose DeLeon	.01	.05
712 Ricky Jordan	.01	.05
713 Scott Scudder	.01	.05
714 Marvell Wynne	.01	.05
715 Tim Burke	.01	.05
716 Bob Geren	.01	.05
717 Phil Bradley	.01	.05
718 Steve Crawford	.01	.05
719 Keith Miller	.01	.05
720 Cecil Fielder	.02	.10
721 Mark Lee	.01	.05
722 Wally Backman	.01	.05
723 Candy Maldonado	.01	.05
724 David Segui	.01	.05
725 Ron Gant	.02	.10
726 Phil Stephenson	.01	.05
727 Mookie Wilson	.02	.10
728 Scott Sanderson	.02	.10
Now with Yankees/12/31/90		
729 Don Zimmer MG	.01	.05
730 Barry Larkin	.15	.40
731 Jeff Gray	.01	.05
732 Franklin Stubbs	.02	.10
Now with Brewers/12/5/90		
733 Kelly Downs	.01	.05
734 John Russell	.01	.05
735 Ron Darling	.01	.05
736 Dick Schofield	.01	.05
737 Tim Crews	.01	.05
738 Mel Hall	.01	.05
739 Russ Swan	.01	.05
740 Ryne Sandberg	.20	.50
741 Jimmy Key	.02	.10
742 Tommy Gregg	.01	.05
743 Bryn Smith	.01	.05
744 Nelson Santovenia	.01	.05
745 Doug Jones	.01	.05
746 John Shelby	.01	.05
747 Tony Fossas	.01	.05
748 Al Newman	.01	.05
749 Greg W. Harris	.01	.05
750 Bobby Bonilla	.01	.05
751 Wayne Edwards	.01	.05
752 Kevin Bass	.01	.05
753 Paul Marak UER		
(Stats say drafted in	.01	.05
May& but bi		
754 Bill Pecota	.01	.05
755 Mark Langston	.01	.05
756 Jeff Huson	.01	.05
757 Mark Gardner	.01	.05
758 Mike Devereaux	.01	.05
759 Bobby Cox MG	.02	.10
760 Benny Santiago	.02	.10
761 Larry Andersen	.02	.10
Now with Padres/12/21/90		
762 Mitch Webster	.01	.05
763 Dana Kiecker	.01	.05
764 Mark Carreon	.01	.05
765 Shawon Dunston	.01	.05
766 Jeff M. Robinson	.02	.10
Now with Orioles/1/12/91		
767 Dan Wilson RC	.08	.25
768 Donn Pall	.01	.05
769 Tim Sherrill	.01	.05
770 Jay Howell	.01	.05
771 Gary Redus UER/(Born in Tanner&	.01	.05
should say Athen		
772 Kent Mercker UER		
(Born in Indianapolis&	.01	.05
should s		
773 Tom Foley	.01	.05
774 Dennis Rasmussen	.01	.05
775 Julio Franco	.02	.10
776 Brent Mayne	.01	.05
777 John Candelaria	.01	.05
778 Dan Gladden	.01	.05
779 Carmelo Martinez	.01	.05
780 Randy Myers	.02	.10
781 Darryl Hamilton	.01	.05
782 Jim Deshaies	.01	.05
783 Joel Skinner	.01	.05
784 Willie Fraser	.02	.10
Now with Blue Jays/12/2/90		
785 Scott Fletcher	.01	.05
786 Eric Plunk	.01	.05
787 Checklist 6	.01	.05
788 Bob Milacki	.01	.05
789 Tom Lasorda MG	.15	.40
790 Ken Griffey Jr.	.75	2.00
791 Mike Benjamin	.01	.05
792 Mike Greenwell	.01	.05

1991 O-Pee-Chee Box Bottoms

The 1991 O-Pee-Chee Box Bottom cards comprise four different box bottoms from the bottoms of wax pack boxes, with four cards each, for a total of 16 standard-size cards. The cards are nearly identical to the 1991 Topps Box Bottom cards. The fronts feature yellow-bordered color player action shots. The player's name and position appear at the bottom and his team name appears just above. The traded players have their new teams and dates of trade printed on the photo. The pink and blue horizontal backs carry player career highlights in both English and French. The cards are lettered (A-P) rather than numbered on the back.

Card	Low	High
COMPLETE SET (16)	4.00	10.00
A Bert Blyleven	.30	.75
B George Brett	.75	2.00
C Brett Butler	.08	.25
D Andre Dawson	.30	.75
E Dwight Evans	.08	.25
F Carlton Fisk	.50	1.25
G Alfredo Griffin	.02	.10
H Rickey Henderson	.50	1.25
I Willie McGee	.08	.25
J Dale Murphy	.30	.75
K Eddie Murray	.50	1.25
L Dave Parker	.08	.25
M Jeff Reardon	.08	.25
N Nolan Ryan	1.50	4.00
O Juan Samuel	.02	.10
P Robin Yount	.50	1.25

1992 O-Pee-Chee

The 1992 O-Pee-Chee set contains 792 standard-size cards. These cards were sold in ten-card wax packs with a stick of bubble gum. The fronts have either posed or action color player photos on a white card face. Different color stripes frame the pictures, and the player's name and team name appear in two short color stripes respectively at the bottom. In English and French, the horizontally oriented backs have biography and complete career batting or pitching record. In addition, some of the cards have a picture of a baseball field and stadium on the back. Special subsets included are Record Breakers (2-5), Prospects (58, 126, 179, 473, 551, 591, 618, 656, 676) and a five-card tribute to Gary Carter (45, 387, 389, 399, 402). Each wax pack wrapper served as an entry blank offering each collector the chance to win one of 1,000 complete factory sets of 1992 O-Pee-Chee Premier baseball cards.

Card	Low	High
COMPLETE SET (792)	10.00	25.00
COMPLETE FACT.SET (792)	12.50	30.00
1 Nolan Ryan	.75	2.00
2 Rickey Henderson RB	.15	.40
Some cards have print		
marks that show 1.991		
on the front		
3 Jeff Reardon RB	.01	.05
4 Nolan Ryan RB	.40	1.00
5 Dave Winfield RB	.05	.15
6 Brien Taylor RC	.01	.05
7 Jim Olander	.01	.05
8 Bryan Hickerson	.01	.05
9 Jon Farrell	.01	.05
10 Wade Boggs	.15	.40
11 Jack McDowell	.01	.05
12 Luis Gonzalez	.15	.40
13 Mike Scioscia	.02	.10
14 Wes Chamberlain	.01	.05
15 Dennis Martinez	.02	.10
16 Jeff Montgomery	.02	.10
17 Randy Milligan	.01	.05
18 Greg Cadaret	.01	.05
19 Jamie Quirk	.01	.05
20 Bip Roberts	.01	.05
21 Buck Rodgers MG	.01	.05
22 Bill Wegman	.01	.05
23 Chuck Knoblauch	.08	.25
24 Randy Myers	.02	.10
25 Ron Gant	.01	.05
26 Mike Bielecki	.01	.05
27 Juan Gonzalez	.08	.25
28 Mike Schooler	.01	.05
29 Mickey Tettleton	.01	.05
30 John Kruk	.02	.10
31 Bryn Smith	.01	.05
32 Chris Nabholz	.01	.05
33 Carlos Baerga	.01	.05
34 Jeff Juden	.01	.05
35 Dave Righetti	.01	.05
36 Scott Ruffcorn	.01	.05
37 Luis Polonia	.01	.05
38 Tom Candiotti	.02	.10
Now with Dodgers		
12-3-91		
39 Greg Olson	.01	.05
40 Cal Ripken	1.50	4.00
Lou Gehrig		
41 Craig Lefferts	.01	.05
42 Mike Macfarlane	.01	.05
43 Jose Lind	.01	.05
44 Rick Aguilera	.02	.10
45 Gary Carter	.20	.50
46 Steve Farr	.01	.05
47 Rex Hudler	.02	.10
48 Scott Scudder	.01	.05
49 Damon Berryhill	.01	.05
50 Ken Griffey Jr.	.50	1.25
51 Tom Runnells MG	.01	.05
52 Juan Bell	.01	.05
53 Tommy Gregg	.01	.05
54 David Wells	.05	.15
55 Rafael Palmeiro	.15	.40
56 Charlie O'Brien	.01	.05
57 Donn Pall	.01	.05
58 Brad Ausmus RC	.60	1.50
Jim Campanis Jr.		
Dave Nilsson		
Doug Robbins		
59 Mo Vaughn	.08	.25
60 Tony Fernandez	.01	.05
61 Paul O'Neill	.15	.40
62 Gene Nelson	.01	.05
63 Randy Ready	.01	.05
64 Bob Kipper	.02	.10
Now with Twins		
12-17-91		
65 Willie McGee	.02	.10
66 Scott Stahoviak	.01	.05
67 Luis Salazar	.01	.05
68 Marvin Freeman	.01	.05
69 Kenny Lofton	.15	.40
Now with Indians		
12-10-91		
70 Gary Gaetti	.02	.10
71 Erik Hanson	.01	.05
72 Eddie Zosky	.01	.05
73 Brian Barnes	.01	.05
74 Scott Leius	.01	.05
75 Bret Saberhagen	.02	.10
76 Mike Gallego	.01	.05
77 Jack Armstrong	.02	.10
Now with Indians		
11-15-91		
78 Ivan Rodriguez	.20	.50
79 Jesse Orosco	.02	.10
80 David Justice	.05	.15
81 Ced Landrum	.01	.05
82 Doug Simons	.01	.05
83 Tommy Greene	.01	.05
84 Leo Gomez	.01	.05
85 Jose DeLeon	.01	.05
86 Steve Finley	.02	.10
87 Bob MacDonald	.01	.05
88 Darrin Jackson	.01	.05
89 Neal Heaton	.01	.05
90 Robin-Yount	.15	.40
91 Jeff Reed	.01	.05
92 Lenny Harris	.01	.05
93 Reggie Jefferson	.01	.05
94 Sammy Sosa	.15	.40
95 Scott Bailes	.01	.05
96 Tom McKinnon	.01	.05
97 Luis Rivera	.01	.05
98 Mike Harkey	.01	.05
99 Jeff Treadway	.01	.05
100 Jose Canseco	.15	.40
101 Omar Vizquel	.02	.10
102 Scott Kamieniecki	.01	.05
103 Ricky Jordan	.01	.05
104 Jeff Ballard	.01	.05
105 Felix Jose	.01	.05
106 Mike Boddicker	.01	.05
107 Dan Pasqua	.01	.05
108 Mike Timlin	.01	.05
109 Roger Craig MG	.01	.05
110 Ryne Sandberg	.20	.50
111 Mark Carreon	.01	.05
112 Oscar Azocar	.01	.05
113 Mike Greenwell	.01	.05
114 Mark Portugal	.01	.05
115 Terry Pendleton	.01	.05
116 Willie Randolph	.02	.10
Now with Mets		
12-20-91		
117 Scott Terry	.01	.05
118 Chili Davis	.02	.10
119 Mark Gardner	.01	.05
120 Alan Trammell	.05	.15
121 Derek Bell	.02	.10
122 Gary Varsho	.01	.05
123 Bob Ojeda	.01	.05
124 Shawn Livsey	.01	.05
125 Chris Hoiles	.01	.05
126 Ryan Klesko	.08	.25
John Jaha		
Rico Brogna		
Dave Staton		
127 Carlos Quintana	.01	.05
128 Kurt Stillwell	.01	.05
129 Melido Perez	.01	.05
130 Alvin Davis	.01	.05
131 Checklist 1-132	.01	.05
132 Eric Show	.01	.05
133 Rance Mulliniks	.01	.05
134 Darryl Kile	.01	.05
135 Von Hayes	.02	.10
Now with Angels		
12-8-91		
136 Bill Doran	.01	.05
137 Jeff D. Robinson	.01	.05
138 Monty Fariss	.01	.05
139 Jeff Innis	.01	.05
140 Mark Grace UER	.15	.40
Home Calie., should be Calif.		
141 Jim Leyland MG UER	.01	.05
No closed parenthesis		
after East in 1991		
142 Todd Van Poppel	.01	.05
143 Paul Gibson	.01	.05
144 Bill Swift	.01	.05
145 Danny Tartabull	.02	.10
Now with Yankees		
1-6-92		
146 Al Newman	.01	.05
147 Cris Carpenter	.01	.05
148 Anthony Young	.01	.05
149 Brian Bohanon	.01	.05
150 Roger Clemens UER	.40	1.00
League leading ERA in		
1990 not italicized		
151 Jeff Hamilton	.01	.05
152 Charlie Leibrandt	.01	.05
153 Ron Karkovice	.01	.05
154 Hensley Meulens	.01	.05
155 Scott Bankhead	.01	.05
156 Manny Ramirez RC	2.00	5.00
157 Keith Miller	.02	.10
Now with Royals		
12-11-91		
158 Todd Frohwirth	.01	.05
159 Darrin Fletcher	.02	.10
Now with Expos		
12-9-91		
160 Bobby Bonilla	.01	.05

161 Casey Candaele .01 .05
162 Paul Faries .01 .05
163 Dana Kiecker .01 .05
164 Shane Mack .01 .05
165 Mark Langston .01 .05
166 Geronimo Pena .01 .05
167 Andy Allanson .01 .05
168 Dwight Smith .01 .05
169 Chuck Crim .02 .10
Now with Angels
12-10-91
170 Alex Cole .01 .05
171 Bill Plummer MG .01 .05
172 Juan Berenguer .01 .05
173 Brian Downing .01 .05
174 Steve Frey .01 .05
175 Orel Hershiser .02 .10
176 Ramon Garcia .01 .05
177 Dan Gladden .02 .10
Now with Tigers
12-19-91
178 Jim Acker .01 .05
179 Bobby DeJardin .01 .05
Cesar Bernhardt
Armando Moreno
Andy Stankiewicz
180 Kevin Mitchell .02 .10
181 Hector Villanueva .01 .05
182 Jeff Reardon .02 .10
183 Brent Mayne .01 .05
184 Jimmy Jones .01 .05
185 Benito Santiago .02 .10
186 Cliff Floyd .40 1.00
187 Ernie Riles .01 .05
188 Jose Guzman .01 .05
189 Junior Felix .01 .05
190 Glenn Davis .01 .05
191 Charlie Hough .02 .10
192 Dave Fleming .01 .05
193 Omar Olivares .01 .05
194 Eric Karros .08 .25
195 David Cone .08 .25
196 Frank Castillo .01 .05
197 Glenn Braggs .01 .05
198 Scott Aldred .01 .05
199 Jeff Blauser .01 .05
200 Len Dykstra .02 .10
201 Buck Showalter MG RC .08 .25
202 Rick Honeycutt .01 .05
203 Greg Myers .01 .05
204 Trevor Wilson .01 .05
205 Jay Howell .01 .05
206 Luis Sojo .01 .05
207 Jack Clark .02 .10
208 Julio Machado .01 .05
209 Lloyd McClendon .01 .05
210 Ozzie Guillen .02 .10
211 Jeremy Hernandez .01 .05
212 Randy Velarde .01 .05
213 Les Lancaster .01 .05
214 Andy Mota .01 .05
215 Rich Gossage .02 .10
216 Brent Gates .01 .05
217 Brian Harper .01 .05
218 Mike Flanagan .01 .05
219 Jerry Browne .01 .05
220 Jose Rijo .01 .05
221 Skeeter Barnes .01 .05
222 Jaime Navarro .01 .05
223 Mel Hall .01 .05
224 Bret Barberie .01 .05
225 Roberto Alomar .15 .40
226 Pete Smith .01 .05
227 Daryl Boston .01 .05
228 Eddie Whitson .01 .05
229 Shawn Boskie .01 .05
230 Dick Schofield .01 .05
231 Brian Drahman .01 .05
232 John Smiley .01 .05
233 Mitch Webster .01 .05
234 Terry Steinbach .01 .05
235 Jack Morris .05 .15
Now with Blue Jays
12-18-91
236 Bill Pecota .02 .10
Now with Mets
12-11-91
237 Jose Hernandez .01 .05
238 Greg Litton .01 .05
239 Brian Holman .01 .05
240 Andres Galarraga .08 .25
241 Gerald Young .01 .05
242 Mike Mussina .25 .60
243 Alvaro Espinoza .01 .05
244 Darren Daulton .02 .10
245 John Smoltz .08 .25
246 Jason Pruitt .01 .05
247 Chuck Finley .02 .10
248 Jim Gantner .01 .05
249 Tony Fossas .01 .05
250 Ken Griffey Sr. .02 .10
251 Kevin Elster .01 .05
252 Dennis Rasmussen .01 .05
253 Terry Kennedy .01 .05
254 Ryan Bowen .01 .05
255 Robin Ventura .02 .10
256 Mike Aldrete .01 .05
257 Jeff Russell .01 .05
258 Jim Lindeman .01 .05
259 Ron Darling .01 .05
260 Devon White .02 .10
261 Tom Lasorda MG .08 .25
262 Terry Lee .01 .05
263 Bob Patterson .01 .05
264 Checklist 133-264 .01 .05
265 Teddy Higuera .01 .05
266 Roberto Kelly .01 .05
267 Steve Bedrosian .01 .05
268 Brady Anderson .05 .15
269 Ruben Amaro Jr. .01 .05
270 Tony Gwynn .30 .75
271 Tracy Jones .01 .05
272 Jerry Don Gleaton .01 .05
273 Craig Grebeck .01 .05
274 Bob Scanlan .01 .05
275 Todd Zeile .02 .10
276 Shawn Green RC 1.50 4.00
277 Scott Chiamparino .01 .05
278 Darryl Hamilton .01 .05
279 Jim Clancy .01 .05
280 Carlos Martinez .01 .05
281 Kevin Appier .02 .10
282 John Wehner .01 .05
283 Reggie Sanders .02 .10
284 Gene Larkin .01 .05
285 Bob Welch .01 .05
286 Gilberto Reyes .01 .05
287 Pete Schourek .01 .05
288 Andujar Cedeno .01 .05
289 Mike Morgan .02 .10
Now with Cubs
12-3-91
290 Bo Jackson .02 .10
291 Phil Garner MG .01 .05
292 Ray Lankford .08 .25
293 Mike Henneman .01 .05
294 Dave Valle .01 .05
295 Alonzo Powell .01 .05
296 Tom Brunansky .01 .05
297 Kevin Brown .05 .15
298 Kelly Gruber .01 .05
299 Charles Nagy .01 .05
300 Don Mattingly .40 1.00
301 Kirk McCaskill .02 .10
Now with White Sox
12-28-91
302 Joey Cora .01 .05
303 Dan Plesac .01 .05
304 Joe Oliver .01 .05
305 Tom Glavine .15 .40
306 Al Shirley .01 .05
307 Bruce Ruffin .01 .05
308 Craig Shipley .01 .05
309 Dave Martinez .02 .10
Now with Reds
12-11-91
310 Jose Mesa .01 .05
311 Henry Cotto .01 .05
312 Mike LaValliere .01 .05
313 Kevin Tapani .01 .05
314 Jeff Huson .01 .05
315 Juan Samuel .01 .05
316 Curt Schilling .15 .40
317 Mike Bordick .02 .10
318 Steve Howe .01 .05
319 Tony Phillips .01 .05
320 George Bell .01 .05
321 Lou Piniella MG .02 .10
322 Tim Burke .01 .05
323 Milt Thompson .01 .05
324 Danny Darwin .01 .05
325 Joe Orsulak .01 .05
326 Eric King .01 .05
327 Jay Buhner .05 .15
328 Joel Johnston .01 .05
329 Franklin Stubbs .01 .05
330 Will Clark .15 .40
331 Steve Lake .01 .05
332 Chris Jones .02 .10
Now with Astros
12-19-91
333 Pat Tabler .01 .05
334 Kevin Gross .01 .05
335 Dave Henderson .01 .05
336 Greg Anthony .01 .05
337 Alejandro Pena .01 .05
338 Shawn Abner .01 .05
339 Tom Browning .01 .05
340 Otis Nixon .01 .05
341 Bob Geren .02 .10
Now with Reds
12-2-91
342 Tim Spehr .01 .05
343 John Vander Wal .01 .05
344 Jack Daugherty .01 .05
345 Zane Smith .01 .05
346 Rheal Cormier .01 .05
347 Kent Hrbek .02 .10
348 Rick Wilkins .01 .05
349 Steve Lyons .02 .10
350 Gregg Olson .01 .05
351 Greg Riddoch MG .01 .05
352 Ed Nunez .01 .05
353 Braulio Castillo .01 .05
354 Dave Bergman .01 .05
355 Warren Newson .01 .05
356 Luis Quinones .01 .05
Now with Twins
1-9-92
357 Mike Witt .01 .05
358 Ted Wood .01 .05
359 Mike Moore .01 .05
360 Lance Parrish .01 .05
361 Barry Jones .01 .05
362 Javier Ortiz .01 .05
363 John Candelaria .01 .05
364 Glenallen Hill .01 .05
365 Duane Ward .01 .05
366 Checklist 265-396 .01 .05
367 Rafael Belliard .01 .05
368 Bill Krueger .01 .05
369 Steve Whitaker .01 .05
370 Shawon Dunston .01 .05
371 Dante Bichette .02 .10
372 Kip Gross .02 .10
Now with Dodgers
11-27-91
373 Don Robinson .01 .05
374 Bernie Williams .15 .40
375 Bert Blyleven .02 .10
376 Chris Donnels .01 .05
377 Bob Zupcic .01 .05
378 Joel Skinner .01 .05
379 Steve Chitren .01 .05
380 Barry Bonds .40 1.00
381 Sparky Anderson MG .02 .10
382 Sid Fernandez .01 .05
383 Dave Hollins .01 .05
384 Mark Lee .01 .05
385 Tim Wallach .01 .05
386 Lance Blankenship .01 .05
387 Gary Carter TRIB .08 .25
388 Ron Tingley .01 .05
389 Gary Carter TRIB .08 .25
390 Gene Harris .01 .05
391 Jeff Schaefer .01 .05
392 Mark Grant .01 .05
393 Carl Willis .01 .05
394 Al Leiter .02 .10
395 Ron Robinson .01 .05
396 Tim Hulett .01 .05
397 Craig Worthington .01 .05
398 John Orton .01 .05
399 Gary Carter TRIB .08 .25
400 John Dopson .01 .05
401 Moises Alou .08 .25
402 Gary Carter TRIB .08 .25
403 Matt Young .01 .05
404 Wayne Edwards .01 .05
405 Nick Esasky .01 .05
406 Dave Eiland .01 .05
407 Mike Brumley .01 .05
408 Bob Milacki .01 .05
409 Geno Petralli .01 .05
410 Dave Stewart .02 .10
411 Mike Jackson .02 .10
412 Luis Aquino .01 .05
413 Tim Teufel .01 .05
414 Jeff Ware .01 .05
415 Jim Deshaies .01 .05
416 Ellis Burks .02 .10
417 Allan Anderson .01 .05
418 Alfredo Griffin .01 .05
419 Wally Whitehurst .01 .05
420 Sandy Alomar Jr. .02 .10
421 Juan Agosto .01 .05
422 Sam Horn .01 .05
423 Jeff Fassero .01 .05
424 Paul McClellan .01 .05
425 Cecil Fielder .02 .10
426 Tim Raines .02 .10
427 Eddie Taubensee .02 .10
428 Dennis Boyd .01 .05
429 Tony LaRussa MG .02 .10
430 Steve Sax .01 .05
431 Tom Gordon .02 .10
432 Billy Hatcher .01 .05
433 Cal Eldred .01 .05
434 Wally Backman .01 .05
435 Mark Eichhorn .01 .05
436 Mookie Wilson .02 .10
437 Scott Servais .01 .05
438 Mike Maddux .01 .05
439 Chico Walker .01 .05
440 Doug Drabek .01 .05
441 Rob Deer .01 .05
442 Dave West .01 .05
443 Spike Owen .01 .05
444 Tyrone Hill .01 .05
445 Matt Williams .05 .15
446 Mark Lewis .01 .05
447 David Segui .01 .05
448 Tom Pagnozzi .01 .05
449 Jeff Johnson .01 .05
450 Mark McGwire .40 1.00
451 Tom Henke .01 .05
452 Wilson Alvarez .02 .10
453 Gary Redus .01 .05
454 Darren Holmes .01 .05
455 Pete O'Brien .01 .05
456 Pat Combs .01 .05
457 Hubie Brooks .01 .05
Now with Angels
12-10-91
458 Frank Tanana .01 .05
459 Tom Kelly MG .01 .05
460 Andre Dawson .05 .15
461 Doug Jones .01 .05
462 Rich Rodriguez .01 .05
463 Mike Simms .01 .05
464 Mike Jeffcoat .01 .05
465 Barry Larkin .15 .40
466 Stan Belinda .01 .05
467 Lonnie Smith .01 .05
468 Greg A. Harris .01 .05
469 Jim Eisenreich .01 .05
470 Pedro Guerrero .01 .05
471 Jose DeJesus .01 .05
472 Rich Rowland .01 .05
473 Frank Bolick .15 .40
Craig Paquette
Tom Redington
Paul Russo UER
Line around top border
474 Mike Rossiter .01 .05
475 Robby Thompson .01 .05
476 Randy Bush .01 .05
477 Greg Hibbard .01 .05
478 Dale Sveum .02 .10
Now with Phillies
12-11-91
479 Chito Martinez .01 .05
480 Scott Sanderson .01 .05
481 Tino Martinez .08 .25
482 Jimmy Key .02 .10
483 Terry Shumpert .01 .05
484 Mike Hartley .01 .05
485 Chris Sabo .01 .05
486 Bob Walk .01 .05
487 John Cerutti .01 .05
488 Scott Cooper .01 .05
489 Bobby Cox MG .02 .10
490 Julio Franco .02 .10
491 Jeff Brantley .02 .10
492 Mike Devereaux .01 .05
493 Jose Offerman .01 .05
494 Gary Thurman .01 .05
495 Carney Lansford .02 .10
496 Joe Grahe .01 .05
497 Andy Ashby .02 .10
498 Gerald Perry .01 .05
499 Dave Otto .01 .05
500 Vince Coleman .01 .05
501 Rob Mallicoat .01 .05
502 Greg Briley .01 .05
503 Pascual Perez .01 .05
504 Aaron Sele RC .40 1.00
505 Bobby Thigpen .01 .05
506 Todd Benzinger .01 .05
507 Candy Maldonado .01 .05
508 Bill Gullickson .01 .05
509 Doug Dascenzo .01 .05
510 Frank Viola .01 .05
511 Kenny Rogers .01 .05
512 Mike Heath .01 .05
513 Kevin Bass .01 .05
514 Kim Batiste .01 .05
515 Delino DeShields .02 .10
516 Ed Sprague .01 .05
517 Jim Gott .01 .05
518 Jose Melendez .01 .05
519 Hal McRae MG .01 .05
520 Jeff Bagwell .30 .75
521 Joe Hesketh .01 .05
522 Milt Cuyler .01 .05
523 Shawn Hillegas .01 .05
524 Don Slaught .01 .05
525 Randy Johnson .20 .50
526 Doug Platt .01 .05
527 Checklist 397-528 .01 .05
528 Steve Foster .01 .05
529 Joe Girardi .02 .10
530 Jim Abbott .02 .10
531 Larry Walker .05 .15
532 Mike Huff .01 .05
533 Mackey Sasser .01 .05
534 Benji Gil .01 .05
535 Dave Stieb .01 .05
536 Willie Wilson .01 .05
537 Mark Leiter .01 .05
538 Jose Uribe .01 .05
539 Thomas Howard .01 .05
540 Ben McDonald .01 .05
541 Jose Tolentino .01 .05
542 Keith Mitchell .01 .05
543 Jerome Walton .01 .05
544 Cliff Brantley .01 .05
545 Andy Van Slyke .02 .10
546 Paul Sorrento .01 .05
547 Herm Winningham .01 .05
548 Mark Guthrie .01 .05
549 Joe Torre MG .02 .10
550 Darryl Strawberry .02 .10
551 Wilfredo Cordero .75 2.00
Chipper Jones
Manny Alexander
Alex Arias UER
No line around top border
552 Dave Gallagher .01 .05
553 Edgar Martinez .05 .15
554 Donald Harris .01 .05
555 Frank Thomas .20 .50
556 Storm Davis .01 .05
557 Dickie Thon .01 .05
558 Scott Garrelts .01 .05
559 Steve Olin .01 .05
560 Rickey Henderson .30 .75
561 Jose Vizcaino .01 .05
562 Wade Taylor .01 .05
563 Pat Borders .01 .05
564 Jimmy Gonzalez .01 .05
565 Lee Smith .02 .10
566 Bill Sampen .01 .05
567 Dean Palmer .02 .10
568 Bryan Harvey .01 .05
569 Tony Pena .01 .05
570 Lou Whitaker .02 .10
571 Randy Tomlin .01 .05
572 Greg Vaughn .02 .10
573 Kelly Downs .01 .05
574 Steve Avery UER .01 .05
Should be 13 games
for Durham in 1989
575 Kirby Puckett .40 1.00
576 Heathcliff Slocumb .01 .05
577 Kevin Seitzer .01 .05
578 Lee Guetterman .01 .05
579 Johnny Oates MG .01 .05
580 Greg Maddux .40 1.00
581 Stan Javier .01 .05
582 Vicente Palacios .01 .05
583 Mel Rojas .01 .05
584 Wayne Rosenthal .01 .05
585 Lenny Webster .01 .05
586 Rod Nichols .01 .05
587 Mickey Morandini .01 .05
588 Russ Swan .01 .05
589 Mariano Duncan .01 .05
Now with Phillies
12-10-91
590 Howard Johnson .01 .05
591 Jeromy Burnitz .08 .25
Jacob Brumfield
Alan Cockrell
D.J. Dozier
592 Denny Neagle .02 .10
593 Steve Decker .01 .05
594 Brian Barber .01 .05
595 Bruce Hurst .01 .05
596 Kent Mercker .01 .05
597 Mike Magnante .01 .05
598 Jody Reed .01 .05
599 Steve Searcy .01 .05
600 Paul Molitor .15 .40
601 Dave Smith .01 .05
602 Mike Fetters .01 .05
603 Luis Mercedes .01 .05
604 Chris Gwynn .02 .10
Now with Royals
12-11-91
605 Scott Erickson .01 .05
606 Brook Jacoby .01 .05
607 Todd Stottlemyre .01 .05
608 Scott Bradley .01 .05
609 Mike Hargrove MG .02 .10
610 Eric Davis .02 .10
611 Brian Hunter .01 .05
612 Pat Kelly .01 .05
613 Pedro Munoz .01 .05
614 Al Osuna .01 .05
615 Matt Merullo .01 .05
616 Larry Andersen .01 .05
617 Junior Ortiz .01 .05
618 Cesar Hernandez .01 .05
Steve Hosey
Jeff McNeely
Dan Peltier
619 Danny Jackson .01 .05
620 George Brett .30 .75
621 Dan Gakeler .01 .05
622 Steve Buechele .01 .05
623 Bob Tewksbury .01 .05
624 Shawn Estes RC .40 1.00
625 Kevin McReynolds .01 .05
626 Chris Haney .01 .05
627 Mike Sharperson .01 .05
628 Mark Williamson .01 .05
629 Wally Joyner .02 .10
630 Carlton Fisk .15 .40
631 Armando Reynoso .01 .05
632 Felix Fermin .01 .05
633 Mitch Williams .01 .05
634 Manuel Lee .01 .05
635 Harold Baines .05 .15
636 Greg W. Harris .01 .05
637 Orlando Merced .01 .05
638 Chris Bosio .01 .05
639 Wayne Housie .01 .05
640 Xavier Hernandez .01 .05
641 David Howard .01 .05
642 Tim Crews .01 .05
643 Rick Cerone .01 .05
644 Terry Leach .01 .05
645 Deion Sanders .08 .25
646 Craig Wilson .01 .05
647 Marquis Grissom .02 .10
648 Scott Fletcher .01 .05
649 Norm Charlton .01 .05
650 Jesse Barfield .01 .05
651 Joe Slusarski .01 .05
652 Bobby Rose .01 .05
653 Dennis Lamp .01 .05
654 Allen Watson .01 .05
655 Brett Butler .02 .10
656 1992 Prospects OF .05 .15
Rudy Pemberton
Henry Rodriguez
657 Dave Johnson .01 .05
658 Checklist 529-660 .01 .05
659 Brian McRae .01 .05
660 Fred McGriff .05 .15
661 Bill Landrum .01 .05
662 Juan Guzman .01 .05
663 Greg Gagne .01 .05
664 Ken Hill .02 .10
Now with Expos
11-25-91
665 Dave Haas .01 .05
666 Tom Foley .01 .05
667 Roberto Hernandez .02 .10
668 Dwayne Henry .01 .05
669 Jim Fregosi MG .01 .05
670 Harold Reynolds .02 .10
671 Mark Whiten .01 .05
672 Eric Plunk .01 .05
673 Todd Hundley .02 .10
674 Mo Sanford .01 .05
675 Bobby Witt .01 .05
676 Sam Militello .01 .05
Pat Mahomes
Turk Wendell
Roger Salkeld
677 John Marzano .01 .05
678 Joe Klink .01 .05
679 Pete Incaviglia .01 .05
680 Dale Murphy .15 .40
681 Rene Gonzales .01 .05
682 Andy Benes .01 .05
683 Jim Poole .01 .05
684 Trever Miller .01 .05
685 Scott Livingstone .01 .05
686 Rich DeLucia .01 .05
687 Harvey Pulliam .01 .05
688 Tim Belcher .01 .05
689 Mark Lemke .01 .05
690 John Franco .02 .10
691 Walt Weiss .01 .05
692 Scott Ruskin .02 .10
Now with Reds
12-11-91
693 Jeff King .01 .05
694 Mike Gardiner .01 .05
695 Gary Sheffield .20 .50
696 Joe Boever .01 .05
697 Mike Felder .01 .05
698 John Habyan .01 .05
699 Cito Gaston MG .01 .05
700 Ruben Sierra .02 .10
701 Scott Radinsky .01 .05
702 Lee Stevens .01 .05
703 Mark Wohlers .01 .05
704 Curt Young .01 .05
705 Dwight Evans .02 .10
706 Rob Murphy .01 .05
707 Gregg Jefferies .02 .10
Now with Royals
12-11-91
708 Tom Bolton .01 .05
709 Chris James .01 .05
710 Kevin Maas .01 .05
711 Ricky Bones .01 .05
712 Curt Wilkerson .01 .05
713 Roger McDowell .01 .05
714 Pokey Reese RC .15 .40
715 Craig Biggio .05 .15
716 Kirk Dressendorfer .01 .05
717 Ken Dayley .01 .05
718 B.J. Surhoff .02 .10
719 Terry Mulholland .01 .05
720 Kirk Gibson .02 .10
721 Mike Pagliarulo .01 .05
722 Walt Terrell .01 .05
723 Jose Oquendo .01 .05
724 Kevin Morton .01 .05
725 Dwight Gooden .02 .10
726 Kirt Manwaring .01 .05
727 Chuck McElroy .01 .05
728 Dave Burba .01 .05
729 Art Howe MG .01 .05
730 Ramon Martinez .01 .05
731 Donnie Hill .01 .05
732 Nelson Santovenia .01 .05
733 Bob Melvin .02 .10
734 Scott Hatteberg .01 .05
735 Greg Swindell .02 .10
Now with Reds
11-15-91
736 Lance Johnson .01 .05
737 Kevin Reimer .01 .05
738 Dennis Eckersley .15 .40
739 Rob Ducey .01 .05
740 Ken Caminiti .05 .15
741 Mark Gubicza .01 .05
742 Billy Spiers .01 .05
743 Darren Lewis .01 .05
744 Chris Hammond .01 .05
745 Dave Magadan .01 .05
746 Bernard Gilkey .02 .10
747 Willie Banks .01 .05
748 Matt Nokes .01 .05
749 Jerald Clark .01 .05
750 Travis Fryman .02 .10
751 Steve Wilson .01 .05
752 Billy Ripken .01 .05
753 Paul Assenmacher .01 .05
754 Charlie Hayes .01 .05
755 Alex Fernandez .01 .05
756 Gary Pettis .01 .05
757 Rob Dibble .01 .05
758 Tim Naehring .01 .05
759 Jeff Torborg MG .01 .05
760 Ozzie Smith .20 .50
761 Mike Fitzgerald .01 .05
762 John Burkett .01 .05
763 Kyle Abbott .01 .05
764 Tyler Green .01 .05
765 Pete Harnisch .01 .05
766 Mark Davis .01 .05
767 Kal Daniels .01 .05
768 Jim Thome .15 .40
769 Jack Howell .01 .05
770 Sid Bream .01 .05
771 Arthur Rhodes .01 .05
772 Garry Templeton .01 .05
773 Hal Morris .01 .05
774 Bud Black .01 .05
775 Ivan Calderon .01 .05
776 Doug Henry .01 .05
777 John Olerud .05 .15
778 Tim Leary .01 .05
779 Jay Bell .01 .05
780 Eddie Murray .20 .50
Now with Mets
11-27-91
781 Paul Abbott .01 .05
782 Phil Plantier .01 .05
783 Joe Magrane .01 .05
784 Ken Patterson .01 .05
785 Albert Belle .05 .15
786 Royce Clayton .01 .05
787 Checklist 661-792 .01 .05
788 Mike Stanton .01 .05
789 Bobby Valentine MG .01 .05
790 Joe Carter .02 .10
791 Danny Cox .01 .05
792 Dave Winfield .20 .50
Now with Blue Jays
12-19-91

1992 O-Pee-Chee Box Bottoms

This set consists of four display box bottoms, each featuring one of four team photos of the divisional champions from the 1991 season. The oversized cards measure approximately 5" by 7" and the card's title appears within a ghosted rectangle near the bottom of the white-bordered color photo. The unnumbered horizontal plain-cardboard backs carry the team's season highlights in both English and French in blue lettering.

COMPLETE SET (4) 1.25 3.00
1 Pirates Prevail .20 .50
2 Braves Beat Bucs .30 .75
3 Blue Jays Claim Crown .40 1.00
4 Kirby Puckett .75 2.00
Twins Tally in Tenth

1993 O-Pee-Chee

The 1993 O-Pee-Chee baseball set consists of 396 standard-size cards. This is the first year that the regular series does not parallel in design the series that Topps issued. The set was sold in wax packs with eight cards plus a random insert card from either a four-card World Series Heroes subset or an 18-card World Series Champions subset. The fronts features color action player photos with white borders. The player's name appears in a silver stripe across the bottom that overlaps the O-Pee-Chee logo. The backs display color close-ups next to a panel containing biographical data. The panel and a stripe at the bottom reflect the team colors. A white box in the center of the card contains statistics and bilingual (English and French) career highlights.

COMPLETE SET (396) 20.00 50.00
1 Jim Abbott .15 .40
Now with Yankees/12/6/92
2 Eric Anthony .02 .10
3 Harold Baines .07 .20
4 Roberto Alomar .25 .60
5 Steve Avery .02 .10
6 Jim Austin .02 .10
7 Mark Wohlers .02 .10
8 Steve Buechele .02 .10
9 Pedro Astacio .02 .10
10 Moises Alou .07 .20
11 Rod Beck .02 .10
12 Sandy Alomar .07 .20
13 Bret Boone .15 .40
14 Bryan Harvey .02 .10
15 Bobby Bonilla .07 .20
16 Brady Anderson .07 .20
17 Andy Benes .02 .10
18 Ruben Amaro Jr. .02 .10
19 Jay Bell .02 .10
20 Kevin Brown .15 .40
21 Scott Bankhead .07 .20
Now with Red Sox/12/8/92
22 Denis Boucher .02 .10
23 Kevin Appier .07 .20
24 Pat Kelly .02 .10
25 Rick Aguilera .02 .10
26 George Bell .02 .10
27 Steve Farr .02 .10
28 Chad Curtis .02 .10
29 Jeff Bagwell .60 1.50
30 Lance Blankenship .02 .10
31 Derek Bell .02 .10
32 Damon Berryhill .02 .10
33 Ricky Bones .02 .10
34 Rheal Cormier .02 .10
35 Andre Dawson .25 .60

Now with Red Sox/12/2/92
36 Brett Butler .07 .20
37 Sean Berry .02 .10
38 Bud Black .02 .10
39 Carlos Baerga .07 .20
40 Jay Buhner .15 .40
41 Charlie Hough .07 .20
42 Sid Fernandez .02 .10
43 Luis Mercedes .02 .10
44 Jerald Clark .07 .20
Now with Rockies/11/17/92
45 Wes Chamberlain .02 .10
46 Barry Bonds .75 2.00
Now with Giants/12/8/92
47 Jose Canseco .30 .75
48 Tim Belcher .02 .10
49 David Nied .02 .10
50 George Brett .60 1.50
51 Cecil Fielder .07 .20
52 Chili Davis .07 .20
Now with Angels/12/11/92
53 Alex Fernandez .02 .10
54 Charlie Hayes .07 .20
Now with Rockies/11/17/92
55 Rob Ducey .02 .10
56 Craig Biggio .25 .60
57 Mike Bordick .02 .10
58 Pat Borders .02 .10
59 Jeff Blauser .02 .10
60 Chris Bosio .07 .20
Now with Mariners/12/3/92
61 Bernard Gilkey .02 .10
62 Shawon Dunston .02 .10
63 Tom Candiotti .02 .10
64 Darrin Fletcher .02 .10
65 Jeff Brantley .07 .20
66 Albert Belle .07 .20
67 Dave Fleming .02 .10
68 John Franco .07 .20
69 Glenn Davis .02 .10
70 Tony Fernandez .07 .20
Now with Mets/10/26/92
71 Darren Daulton .07 .20
72 Doug Drabek .07 .20
Now with Astros/12/1/92
73 Julio Franco .07 .20
74 Tom Browning .02 .10
75 Tom Gordon .07 .20
76 Travis Fryman .07 .20
77 Scott Erickson .02 .10
78 Carlton Fisk .25 .60
79 Roberto Kelly .07 .20
Now with Reds/11/3/92
80 Gary DiSarcina .02 .10
81 Ken Caminiti .15 .40
82 Ron Darling .02 .10
83 Joe Carter .07 .20
84 Sid Bream .02 .10
85 Cal Eldred .02 .10
86 Mark Grace .15 .40
87 Eric Davis .07 .20
88 Ivan Calderon .07 .20
Now with Red Sox/12/8/92
89 John Burkett .02 .10
90 Felix Fermin .02 .10
91 Ken Griffey Jr. 1.00 2.50
92 Dwight Gooden .07 .20
93 Mike Devereaux .02 .10
94 Tony Gwynn .75 2.00
95 Mariano Duncan .02 .10
96 Jeff King .02 .10
97 Juan Gonzalez .25 .60
98 Norm Charlton .07 .20
Now with Mariners/11/17/92
99 Mark Gubicza .02 .10
100 Danny Gladden .02 .10
101 Greg Gagne .07 .20
Now with Royals/12/8/92
102 Ozzie Guillen .07 .20
103 Don Mattingly .75 2.00
104 Damion Easley .02 .10
105 Casey Candaele .02 .10
106 Dennis Eckersley .30 .75
107 David Cone .15 .40
Now with Royals/12/8/92
108 Ron Gant .02 .10
109 Mike Fetters .02 .10
110 Mike Harkey .02 .10
111 Kevin Gross .02 .10
112 Archi Cianfrocco .02 .10
113 Will Clark .25 .60
114 Glenallen Hill .02 .10
115 Erik Hanson .02 .10
116 Todd Hundley .07 .20
117 Leo Gomez .02 .10
118 Bruce Hurst .02 .10
119 Len Dykstra .07 .20
120 Jose Lind .07 .20
Now with Royals/11/19/92
121 Jose Guzman .07 .20
Now with Cubs/12/1/92
122 Rob Dibble .02 .10
123 Gregg Jefferies .02 .10
124 Bill Gullickson .02 .10
125 Brian Harper .02 .10
126 Roberto Hernandez .07 .20
127 Sam Militello .02 .10
128 Junior Felix .07 .20
Now with Marlins/11/17/92
129 Andujar Cedeno .02 .10
130 Rickey Henderson .40 1.00
131 Bob MacDonald .02 .10
132 Tom Glavine .30 .75
133 Scott Fletcher .07 .20
Now with Red Sox/11/30/92
134 Brian Jordan .07 .20
135 Greg Maddux 1.00 2.50
Now with Braves/12/9/92
136 Orel Hershiser .07 .20
137 Greg Colbrunn .02 .10
138 Royce Clayton .02 .10
139 Thomas Howard .02 .10
140 Randy Johnson .40 1.00
141 Jeff Innis .02 .10
142 Chris Hoiles .02 .10
143 Darrin Jackson .02 .10
144 Tommy Greene .02 .10
145 Mike LaValliere .02 .10
146 David Hulse .02 .10
147 Barry Larkin .15 .40
148 Wally Joyner .07 .20
149 Mike Henneman .02 .10
150 Kent Hrbek .07 .20
151 Bo Jackson .25 .60
152 Rich Monteleone .02 .10
153 Chuck Finley .07 .20
154 Steve Finley .07 .20
155 Dave Henderson .02 .10
156 Kelly Gruber .07 .20
Now with Angels/12/8/92
157 Brian Hunter .02 .10
158 Darryl Hamilton .02 .10
159 Derrick May .02 .10
160 Jay Howell .02 .10
161 Wil Cordero .02 .10
162 Bryan Hickerson .02 .10
163 Reggie Jefferson .02 .10
164 Edgar Martinez .15 .40
165 Nigel Wilson .02 .10
166 Howard Johnson .02 .10
167 Tim Hulett .02 .10
168 Mike Maddux .07 .20
Now with Mets/12/17/92
169 Dave Hollins .02 .10
170 Zane Smith .02 .10
171 Rafael Palmeiro .25 .60
172 Dave Martinez .07 .20
Now with Giants/12/9/92
173 Rusty Meacham .02 .10
174 Mark Leiter .02 .10
175 Chuck Knoblauch .25 .60
176 Lance Johnson .02 .10
177 Matt Nokes .02 .10
178 Luis Gonzalez .25 .60
179 Jack Morris .07 .20
180 David Justice .25 .60
181 Doug Henry .02 .10
182 Felix Jose .02 .10
183 Delino DeShields .02 .10
184 Rene Gonzales .02 .10
185 Pete Harnisch .02 .10
186 Mike Moore .07 .20
Now with Tigers/12/9/92
187 Juan Guzman .02 .10
188 John Olerud .15 .40
189 Ryan Klesko .07 .20
190 John Jaha .02 .10
191 Ray Lankford .07 .20
192 Jeff Fassero .02 .10
193 Darren Lewis .02 .10
194 Mark Lewis .02 .10
195 Alan Mills .02 .10
196 Wade Boggs .40 1.00
Now with Yankees/12/15/92
197 Hal Morris .02 .10
198 Ron Karkovice .02 .10
199 Joe Grahe .02 .10
200 Butch Henry .07 .20
Now with Rockies/11/17/92
201 Mark McGwire 1.00 2.50
202 Tom Henke .07 .20
Now with Rangers/12/15/92
203 Ed Sprague .02 .10
204 Charlie Leibrandt .07 .20
Now with Rangers/12/9/92
205 Pat Listach .02 .10
206 Omar Olivares .02 .10
207 Mike Morgan .02 .10
208 Eric Karros .15 .40
209 Marquis Grissom .07 .20
210 Willie McGee .07 .20
211 Derek Lilliquist .02 .10
212 Tino Martinez .25 .60
213 Jeff Kent .15 .40
214 Mike Mussina .25 .60
215 Randy Myers .07 .20
Now with Cubs/12/9/92
216 John Kruk .07 .20
217 Tom Brunansky .02 .10
218 Paul O'Neill .15 .40
Now with Yankees/11/3/92
219 Scott Livingstone .02 .10
220 John Valentin .02 .10
221 Eddie Zosky .02 .10
222 Pete Smith .02 .10
223 Bill Wegman .02 .10
224 Todd Zeile .07 .20
225 Tim Wallach .07 .20
Now with Dodgers/12/24/92
226 Mitch Williams .02 .10
227 Tim Wakefield .15 .40
228 Frank Viola .02 .10
229 Nolan Ryan 1.25 3.00
230 Kirk McCaskill .02 .10
231 Melido Perez .02 .10
232 Mark Langston .02 .10
233 Xavier Hernandez .02 .10
234 Jerry Browne .02 .10
235 Dave Stieb .07 .20
Now with White Sox/12/8/92
236 Mark Lemke .02 .10
237 Paul Molitor .25 .60
Now with Blue Jays/12/7/92
238 Geronimo Pena .02 .10
239 Ken Hill .02 .10
240 Jack Clark .02 .10
241 Greg Myers .02 .10
242 Pete Incaviglia .07 .20
Now with Phillies/12/8/92
243 Ruben Sierra .07 .20
244 Todd Stottlemyre .02 .10
245 Pat Hentgen .07 .20
246 Melvin Nieves .02 .10
247 Jaime Navarro .02 .10
248 Donovan Osborne .02 .10
249 Brian Barnes .02 .10
250 Cory Snyder .07 .20
Now with Dodgers/12/5/92
251 Kenny Lofton .15 .40
252 Kevin Mitchell .07 .20
Now with Reds/11/17/92
253 Dave Magadan .07 .20
Now with Marlins/12/8/92
254 Ben McDonald .02 .10
255 Fred McGriff .15 .40
256 Mickey Morandini .02 .10
257 Randy Tomlin .02 .10
258 Dean Palmer .07 .20
259 Roger Clemens .75 2.00
260 Joe Oliver .02 .10
261 Jeff Montgomery .07 .20
262 Tony Phillips .02 .10
263 Shane Mack .02 .10
264 Jack McDowell .02 .10
265 Mike Macfarlane .02 .10
266 Luis Polonia .02 .10
267 Doug Jones .02 .10
268 Terry Steinbach .02 .10
269 Jimmy Key .07 .20
Now with Yankees/12/10/92
270 Pat Tabler .02 .10
271 Otis Nixon .02 .10
272 Dave Nilsson .02 .10
273 Tom Pagnozzi .02 .10
274 Ryne Sandberg .60 1.50
275 Ramon Martinez .02 .10
276 Tim Laker .02 .10
277 Bill Swift .02 .10
278 Charles Nagy .02 .10
279 Harold Reynolds .15 .40
Now with Orioles/12/11/92
280 Eddie Murray .30 .75
281 Gregg Olson .02 .10
282 Frank Seminara .02 .10
283 Terry Mulholland .02 .10
284 Kevin Reimer .07 .20
Now with Brewers/11/17/92
285 Mike Greenwell .02 .10
286 Jose Rijo .02 .10
287 Brian McRae .02 .10
288 Frank Tanana .07 .20
Now with Mets/12/10/92
289 Pedro Munoz .02 .10
290 Tim Raines .07 .20
291 Andy Stankiewicz .02 .10
292 Tim Salmon .25 .60
293 Jimmy Jones .02 .10
294 Dave Stewart .07 .20
Now with Blue Jays/12/8/92
295 Mike Timlin .02 .10
296 Greg Olson .02 .10
297 Dan Plesac .07 .20
Now with Cubs/12/8/92
298 Mike Perez .02 .10
299 Jose Offerman .02 .10
300 Denny Martinez .07 .20
301 Robby Thompson .02 .10
302 Bret Saberhagen .07 .20
303 Joe Orsulak .07 .20
Now with Mets/12/18/92
304 Tim Naehring .02 .10
305 Bip Roberts .02 .10
306 Kirby Puckett .60 1.50
307 Steve Sax .02 .10
308 Danny Tartabull .02 .10
309 Jeff Juden .02 .10
310 Duane Ward .02 .10
311 Alejandro Pena .07 .20
Now with Pirates/12/10/92
312 Kevin Seitzer .02 .10
313 Ozzie Smith .40 1.00
314 Mike Piazza 1.25 3.00
315 Chris Nabholz .02 .10
316 Tony Pena .07 .20
317 Gary Sheffield .40 1.00
318 Mark Portugal .02 .10
319 Walt Weiss .07 .20
Now with Marlins/11/17/92
320 Manuel Lee .07 .20
Now with Rangers/12/19/92
321 David Wells .15 .40
322 Terry Pendleton .02 .10
323 Billy Spiers .02 .10
324 Lee Smith .07 .20
325 Bob Scanlan .02 .10
326 Mike Scioscia .07 .20
327 Spike Owen .07 .20
Now with Yankees/12/4/92
328 Mackey Sasser .07 .20
Now with Mariners/12/23/92
329 Arthur Rhodes .02 .10
330 Ben Rivera .02 .10
331 Ivan Rodriguez .40 1.00
332 Phil Plantier .07 .20
Now with Padres/12/10/92
333 Chris Sabo .02 .10
334 Mickey Tettleton .02 .10
335 John Smiley .07 .20
Now with Reds/11/30/92
336 Bobby Thigpen .02 .10
337 Randy Velarde .02 .10
338 Luis Sojo .07 .20
Now with Blue Jays/12/8/92
339 Scott Servais .02 .10
340 Bob Welch .02 .10
341 Devon White .02 .10
342 Jeff Reardon .07 .20
343 B.J. Surhoff .07 .20
344 Bob Tewksbury .02 .10
345 Jose Vizcaino .02 .10
346 Mike Sharperson .02 .10
347 Mel Rojas .02 .10
348 Matt Williams .15 .40
349 Steve Olin .02 .10
350 Mike Schooler .02 .10
351 Ryan Thompson .02 .10
352 Cal Ripken 1.25 3.00
353 Benito Santiago .15 .40
Now with Marlins/12/16/92
354 Curt Schilling .30 .75
355 Andy Van Slyke .02 .10
356 Kenny Rogers .02 .10
357 Jody Reed .07 .20
Now with Dodgers/11/17/92
358 Reggie Sanders .15 .40
359 Kevin McReynolds .02 .10
360 Alan Trammell .15 .40
361 Kevin Tapani .02 .10
362 Frank Thomas .30 .75
363 Bernie Williams .25 .60
364 John Smoltz .07 .20
365 Robin Yount .40 1.00
366 John Wetteland .07 .20
367 Bob Zupcic .02 .10
368 Julio Valera .02 .10
369 Brian Williams .02 .10
370 Willie Wilson .02 .10
Now with Cubs/12/18/92
371 Dave Winfield .40 1.00
Now with Twins/12/17/92
372 Deion Sanders .15 .40
373 Greg Vaughn .07 .20
374 Todd Worrell .07 .20
Now with Dodgers/12/9/92
375 Darryl Strawberry .07 .20
376 John Vander Wal .02 .10
377 Mike Benjamin .02 .10
378 Mark Whiten .02 .10
379 Omar Vizquel .07 .20
380 Anthony Young .02 .10
381 Rick Sutcliffe .02 .10
382 Candy Maldonado .07 .20
Now with Cubs/12/11/92
383 Francisco Cabrera .02 .10
384 Larry Walker .15 .40
385 Scott Cooper .02 .10
386 Gerald Williams .02 .10
387 Robin Ventura .15 .40
388 Carl Willis .02 .10
389 Lou Whitaker .07 .20
390 Hipolito Pichardo .02 .10
391 Rudy Seanez .02 .10
392 Greg Swindell .07 .20
Now with Astros/12/4/92
393 Mo Vaughn .25 .60
394 Checklist 1-132 .02 .10
395 Checklist 133-264 .02 .10
396 Checklist 265-396 .02 .10

1993 O-Pee-Chee World Champions

This 18-card standard-size set was randomly inserted in 1993 O-Pee-Chee wax packs and features the Toronto Blue Jays, the 1992 World Series Champions. The standard-size cards are similar to the regular issue, with glossy color action player photos with white borders on the fronts. They differ in having a gold (rather than silver) stripe across the bottom, which intersects a 1992 World Champions logo. The backs carry statistics on a burnt orange box against a light blue panel with bilingual (English and French) career highlights.

COMPLETE SET (18) 2.00 5.00
1 Roberto Alomar .60 1.50
2 Pat Borders .02 .10
3 Joe Carter .08 .25
4 David Cone .40 1.00
5 Kelly Gruber .02 .10
6 Juan Guzman .02 .10
7 Tom Henke .02 .10
8 Jimmy Key .08 .25
9 Manuel Lee .02 .10
10 Candy Maldonado .02 .10
11 Jack Morris .08 .25
12 John Olerud .20 .50
13 Ed Sprague .08 .25
14 Todd Stottlemyre .08 .25
15 Duane Ward .02 .10
16 Devon White .02 .10
17 Dave Winfield .75 2.00
18 Cito Gaston MG .02 .10

1993 O-Pee-Chee World Series Heroes

This four-card standard-size set was randomly inserted in 1993 O-Pee-Chee wax packs. These cards were more difficult to find than the 18-card World Series Champions insert set. The fronts feature color action player photos with white borders. The words "World Series Heroes" appear in a dark blue stripe above the picture, while the player's name is printed in the bottom white border. A 1992 World Series logo overlays the picture at the lower right corner. Over a ghosted version of the 1992 World Series logo, the backs summarize, in English and French, the player's outstanding performance in the 1992 World Series. The cards are numbered on the back in alphabetical order by player's name.

COMPLETE SET (4) .75 2.00
1 Pat Borders .08 .25
2 Jimmy Key .20 .50
3 Ed Sprague .08 .25
4 Dave Winfield .60 1.50

1994 O-Pee-Chee

The 1994 O-Pee-Chee baseball set consists of 270 standard-size cards. Production was limited to 2,500 individually numbered cases. Each display box contained 36 packs and one 5" by 7" All-Star Jumbo card. Each foil pack contained 14 regular cards plus either one chase card or one redemption card.

COMPLETE SET (270) 6.00 15.00
1 Paul Molitor .15 .40
2 Kirt Manwaring .01 .05
3 Brady Anderson .02 .10
4 Scott Cooper .01 .05
5 Kevin Stocker .01 .05
6 Alex Fernandez .01 .05
7 Jeff Montgomery .02 .10
8 Danny Tartabull .01 .05
9 Damion Easley .01 .05
10 Andujar Cedeno .01 .05
11 Steve Karsay .01 .05
12 Dave Stewart .02 .10
13 Fred McGriff .05 .15
14 Jaime Navarro .01 .05
15 Allen Watson .01 .05
16 Ryne Sandberg .30 .75
17 Arthur Rhodes .01 .05
18 Marquis Grissom .02 .10
19 John Burkett .01 .05
20 Robby Thompson .01 .05
21 Denny Martinez .02 .10
22 Ken Griffey Jr. .75 2.00
23 Orestes Destrade .01 .05
24 Dwight Gooden .02 .10
25 Rafael Palmeiro .08 .25
26 Pedro A.Martinez .01 .05
27 Wes Chamberlain .01 .05
28 Juan Gonzalez .08 .25
29 Kevin Mitchell .01 .05
30 Dante Bichette .02 .10
31 Howard Johnson .01 .05
32 Mickey Tettleton .01 .05
33 Robin Ventura .05 .15
34 Terry Mulholland .01 .05
35 Bernie Williams .08 .25
36 Eduardo Perez .01 .05
37 Rickey Henderson .20 .50
38 Terry Pendleton .01 .05
39 John Smoltz .08 .25
40 Derrick May .01 .05
41 Pedro Martinez .20 .50
42 Mark Portugal .01 .05
43 Albert Belle .04 .10
44 Edgar Martinez .05 .15
45 Gary Sheffield .20 .50
46 Bret Saberhagen .02 .10
47 Ricky Gutierrez .01 .05
48 Orlando Merced .01 .05
49 Mike Greenwell .01 .05
50 Jose Rijo .01 .05
51 Jeff Granger .01 .05
52 Mike Henneman .01 .05
53 Dave Winfield .15 .40
54 Don Mattingly .40 1.00
55 J.T. Snow .02 .10
56 Todd Van Poppel .01 .05
57 Chipper Jones .30 .75
58 Darryl Hamilton .01 .05
59 Delino DeShields .01 .05
60 Rondell White .02 .10
61 Eric Anthony .01 .05
62 Charlie Hough .01 .05
63 Sid Fernandez .01 .05
64 Derek Bell .01 .05
65 Phil Plantier .01 .05
66 Curt Schilling .15 .40
67 Roger Clemens .40 1.00
68 Jose Lind .01 .05
69 Andres Galarraga .08 .25
70 Tim Belcher .01 .05
71 Ron Karkovice .01 .05
72 Alan Trammell .05 .15
73 Pete Harnisch .01 .05
74 Mark McGwire .50 1.25
75 Ryan Klesko .02 .10
76 Ramon Martinez .01 .05
77 Gregg Jefferies .01 .05
78 Steve Buechele .01 .05
79 Bill Swift .01 .05
80 Matt Williams .05 .15
81 Randy Johnson .20 .50
82 Mike Mussina .08 .25
83 Andy Benes .01 .05
84 Dave Staton .01 .05
85 Steve Cooke .01 .05
86 Andy Van Slyke .01 .05
87 Ivan Rodriguez .20 .50
88 Frank Viola .02 .10
89 Aaron Sele .02 .10
90 Ellis Burks .02 .10
91 Wally Joyner .02 .10
92 Rick Aguilera .01 .05
93 Kirby Puckett .40 1.00
94 Roberto Hernandez .01 .05
95 Mike Stanley .01 .05
96 Roberto Alomar .08 .25
97 James Mouton .01 .05
98 Chad Curtis .01 .05
99 Mitch Williams .01 .05
100 Carlos Delgado .20 .50
101 Greg Maddux .40 1.00
102 Brian Harper .01 .05
103 Tom Pagnozzi .01 .05
104 Jose Offerman .01 .05
105 John Wetteland .02 .10
106 Carlos Baerga .02 .10
107 Dave Magadan .01 .05
108 Bobby Jones .01 .05
109 Tony Gwynn .40 1.00
110 Jeromy Burnitz .05 .15
111 Bip Roberts .01 .05
112 Carlos Garcia .01 .05
113 Jeff Russell .01 .05
114 Armando Reynoso .01 .05
115 Ozzie Guillen .02 .10
116 Bo Jackson .05 .15
117 Terry Steinbach .01 .05
118 Deion Sanders .08 .25
119 Randy Myers .01 .05
120 Mark Whiten .01 .05
121 Manny Ramirez .20 .50
122 Ben McDonald .01 .05
123 Darren Daulton .02 .10
124 Kevin Young .01 .05
125 Barry Larkin .08 .25
126 Cecil Fielder .02 .10
127 Frank Thomas .20 .50
128 Luis Polonia .01 .05
129 Steve Finley .02 .10
130 John Olerud .02 .10
131 John Jaha .01 .05
132 Darren Lewis .01 .05
133 Orel Hershiser .02 .10
134 Chris Bosio .01 .05
135 Ryan Thompson .01 .05
136 Chris Sabo .01 .05
137 Tommy Greene .01 .05
138 Andre Dawson .08 .25
139 Roberto Kelly .01 .05
140 Ken Hill .01 .05
141 Greg Gagne .01 .05
142 Julio Franco .02 .10
143 Chili Davis .02 .10
144 Dennis Eckersley .15 .40
145 Joe Carter .02 .10
146 Mark Grace .05 .15
147 Mike Piazza .40 1.00
148 J.R. Phillips .01 .05
149 Rich Amaral .01 .05
150 Benny Santiago .02 .10
151 Jeff King .01 .05
152 Dean Palmer .02 .10
153 Hal Morris .01 .05
154 Mike Macfarlane .01 .05
155 Chuck Knoblauch .02 .10
156 Pat Kelly .01 .05
157 Greg Swindell .01 .05
158 Chuck Finley .02 .10
159 Devon White .02 .10
160 Duane Ward .01 .05
161 Sammy Sosa .25 .60
162 Javy Lopez .05 .15
163 Eric Karros .02 .10
164 Royce Clayton .01 .05
165 Salomon Torres .01 .05
166 Jeff Kent .02 .10
167 Chris Hoiles .01 .05
168 Len Dykstra .02 .10
169 Jose Canseco .15 .40
170 Bret Boone .02 .10
171 Charlie Hayes .01 .05
172 Lou Whitaker .02 .10
173 Jack McDowell .01 .05
174 Jimmy Key .02 .10
175 Mark Langston .01 .05
176 Darryl Kile .01 .05
177 Juan Guzman .01 .05
178 Pat Borders .01 .05
179 Cal Eldred .01 .05
180 Jose Guzman .01 .05
181 Ozzie Smith .25 .60
182 Rod Beck .01 .05
183 Dave Fleming .01 .05
184 Eddie Murray .15 .40
185 Cal Ripken .75 2.00
186 Dave Hollins .01 .05
187 Will Clark .08 .25
188 Otis Nixon .01 .05
189 Joe Oliver .01 .05
190 Roberto Mejia .01 .05
191 Felix Jose .01 .05
192 Tony Phillips .01 .05
193 Wade Boggs .20 .50
194 Tim Salmon .05 .15
195 Ruben Sierra .02 .10
196 Steve Avery .01 .05
197 B.J. Surhoff .02 .10
198 Todd Zeile .02 .10
199 Raul Mondesi .08 .25
200 Barry Bonds .40 1.00
201 Sandy Alomar .02 .10
202 Bobby Bonilla .01 .05
203 Mike Devereaux .01 .05
204 Ricky Bottalico RC .01 .05
205 Kevin Brown .05 .15
206 Jason Bere .01 .05
207 Reggie Sanders .02 .10
208 David Nied .01 .05
209 Travis Fryman .02 .10
210 James Baldwin .01 .05
211 Jim Abbott .02 .10
212 Jeff Bagwell .30 .75
213 Bob Welch .02 .10
214 Jeff Blauser .02 .10
215 Brett Butler .02 .10
216 Pat Listach .01 .05
217 Bob Tewksbury .01 .05
218 Mike Lansing .01 .05
219 Wayne Kirby .01 .05
220 Chuck Carr .01 .05
221 Harold Baines .02 .10
222 Jay Bell .01 .05
223 Cliff Floyd .05 .15
224 Rob Dibble .01 .05
225 Kevin Appier .02 .10
226 Eric Davis .02 .10
227 Matt Walbeck .01 .05
228 Tim Raines .02 .10
229 Paul O'Neill .02 .10
230 Craig Biggio .08 .25
231 Brent Gates .01 .05
232 Rob Butler .01 .05
233 David Justice .05 .15
234 Rene Arocha .01 .05
235 Mike Morgan .01 .05
236 Denis Boucher .01 .05
237 Kenny Lofton .02 .10
238 Jeff Conine .02 .10
239 Bryan Harvey .01 .05
240 Danny Jackson .01 .05
241 Al Martin .01 .05
242 Tom Henke .01 .05
243 Erik Hanson .01 .05
244 Walt Weiss .01 .05
245 Brian McRae .01 .05
246 Kevin Tapani .01 .05
247 David McCarty .01 .05
248 Doug Drabek .01 .05
249 Troy Neel .01 .05
250 Tom Glavine .08 .25
251 Ray Lankford .02 .10
252 Wil Cordero .01 .05
253 Larry Walker .05 .15
254 Charles Nagy .01 .05
255 Kirk Rueter .01 .05
256 John Franco .02 .10
257 John Kruk .02 .10
258 Alex Gonzalez .01 .05
259 Mo Vaughn .08 .25
260 David Cone .05 .15
261 Kent Hrbek .02 .10
262 Lance Johnson .01 .05
263 Luis Gonzalez .08 .25
264 Mike Bordick .01 .05
265 Ed Sprague .01 .05
266 Moises Alou .05 .15
267 Omar Vizquel .02 .10
268 Jay Buhner .02 .10
269 Checklist .01 .05
270 Checklist .01 .05

1994 O-Pee-Chee All-Star Redemptions

Inserted one per pack, this standard-size, 25-card redemption set features some of the game's top stars. White borders surround a color player photo on front. The backs contain redemption information. Any five cards from this set and $20 CDN could be redeemed for a foil version of the jumbo set that was issued one per wax box. The redemption deadline was September 30, 1994.

COMPLETE SET (25)	5.00	12.00
1 Frank Thomas	.30	.75
2 Paul Molitor	.40	1.00
3 Barry Bonds	.60	1.50
4 Juan Gonzalez	.25	.60
5 Jeff Bagwell	.50	1.25
6 Carlos Baerga	.07	.20
7 Ryne Sandberg	.40	1.00
8 Ken Griffey Jr.	1.00	2.50
9 Mike Piazza	.75	2.00
10 Tim Salmon	.10	.30
11 Marquis Grissom	.10	.30
12 Albert Belle	.10	.30
13 Fred McGriff	.15	.40
14 Jack McDowell	.07	.20
15 Cal Ripken	1.25	3.00
16 John Olerud	.10	.30
17 Kirby Puckett	.50	1.25
18 Roger Clemens	.75	2.00
19 Larry Walker	.10	.30
20 Cecil Fielder	.10	.30
21 Roberto Alomar	.25	.60
22 Greg Maddux	1.00	2.50
23 Joe Carter	.10	.30
24 David Justice	.10	.30
25 Kenny Lofton	.15	.40

1994 O-Pee-Chee Jumbo All-Stars

COMPLETE SET (25)	15.00	40.00
FOIL: SAME VALUE AS BASIC JUMBOS		
1 Frank Thomas	.75	2.00
2 Paul Molitor	.60	1.50
3 Barry Bonds	1.50	4.00
4 Juan Gonzalez	.40	1.00
5 Jeff Bagwell	.75	2.00
6 Carlos Baerga	.08	.25
7 Ryne Sandberg	1.25	3.00
8 Ken Griffey Jr.	2.50	6.00
9 Mike Piazza	2.00	5.00
10 Tim Salmon	.40	1.00
11 Marquis Grissom	.20	.50
12 Albert Belle	.20	.50
13 Fred McGriff	.30	.75
14 Jack McDowell	.08	.25
15 Cal Ripken	3.00	8.00
16 John Olerud	.20	.50
17 Kirby Puckett	1.00	2.50
18 Roger Clemens	1.50	4.00
19 Larry Walker	.30	.75
20 Cecil Fielder	.20	.50
21 Roberto Alomar	.40	1.00
22 Greg Maddux	2.00	5.00
23 Joe Carter	.20	.50
24 David Justice	.20	.50
25 Kenny Lofton	.30	.75

1994 O-Pee-Chee Jumbo All-Stars Foil

These cards, parallel to the Jumbo All-Stars a collector received when buying a 1994 O-Pee-Chee Box were given a foil treatment. These cards were available by a collector accumulating five cards from the All-Star redemption set and sending in $20 Canadian. These cards were to be available to collectors by early October, 1994.

COMPLETE SET (25)	8.00	20.00
*SAME PRICE AS REGULAR JUMBO ALL-STAR		

1994 O-Pee-Chee Diamond Dynamos

This 18-card standard-size set was randomly inserted into 1994 OPC packs. According to the company approximately 5,000 sets were produced. The fronts feature player photos as well as red foil lettering while the backs have gold foil stamping. Between one or two cards from this set was included in each box.

COMPLETE SET (18)	10.00	25.00
1 Mike Piazza	8.00	20.00
2 Robert Mejia	.40	1.00
3 Wayne Kirby	.40	1.00
4 Kevin Stocker	.40	1.00
5 Chris Gomez	.40	1.00
6 Bobby Jones	.40	1.00
7 David McCarty	.40	1.00
8 Kirk Rueter	.40	1.00
9 J.T. Snow	.60	1.50
10 Wil Cordero	.40	1.00
11 Tim Salmon	2.50	6.00
12 Jeff Conine	.75	2.00
13 Jason Bere	.40	1.00
14 Greg McMichael	.40	1.00
15 Brent Gates	.40	1.00
16 Allen Watson	.40	1.00
17 Aaron Sele	.60	1.50
18 Carlos Garcia	.40	1.00

1994 O-Pee-Chee Hot Prospects

This nine-card standard-size insert set features some of 1994's leading prospects. According to the manufacturer, approximately 6,666 sets were produced. The cards features gold and red foil stamping, player photos on both sides and complete minor league stats. An average of one card was included in each display box.

COMPLETE SET (9)	8.00	20.00
1 Cliff Floyd	.75	2.00
2 James Mouton	.20	.50
3 Salomon Torres	.20	.50
4 Raul Mondesi	.40	1.00
5 Carlos Delgado	2.00	5.00
6 Manny Ramirez	2.50	6.00
7 Javy Lopez	1.00	2.50
8 Alex Gonzalez	.20	.50
9 Ryan Klesko	1.50	4.00

1994 O-Pee-Chee World Champions

This nine card insert set features members of the 1993 World Series champion Toronto Blue Jays. Randomly inserted in packs at a rate of one in 36, the player is superimposed over a background containing the phrase, "1993 World Series Champions". The backs contain World Series statistics from 1992 and 1993 and highlights.

COMPLETE SET (9)	6.00	15.00
1 Rickey Henderson	3.00	8.00
2 Devon White	.60	1.50
3 Paul Molitor	1.25	3.00
4 Joe Carter	.60	1.50
5 John Olerud	.75	2.00
6 Roberto Alomar	1.00	2.50
7 Ed Sprague	.40	1.00
8 Pat Borders	.40	1.00
9 Tony Fernandez	.75	2.00

2009 O-Pee-Chee

COMPLETE SET (600)	60.00	120.00
COMMON CARD (1-560)	.15	.40
COMMON RC (561-600)	.40	1.00
RC ODDS 1:3 HOBBY/RETAIL		
CL ODDS 1:3 HOBBY/RETAIL		
MOMENT ODDS 1:6 HOBBY/RETAIL		
LL ODDS 1:8 HOBBY/RETAIL		
1 Melvin Mora	.15	.40
2 Jim Thome	.25	.60
3 Jonathan Sanchez	.15	.40
4 Cesar Izturis	.15	.40
5 A.J. Pierzynski	.15	.40
6 Adam LaRoche	.15	.40
7 J.D. Drew	.15	.40
8 Brian Schneider	.15	.40
9 John Grabow	.15	.40
10 Jimmy Rollins	.25	.60
11 Jeff Baker	.15	.40
12 Daniel Cabrera	.15	.40
13 Kyle Lohse	.15	.40
14 Jason Giambi	.15	.40
15 Nate McLouth	.15	.40
16 Gary Matthews	.15	.40
17 Cody Ross	.15	.40
18 Justin Masterson	.15	.40
19 Jose Lopez	.15	.40
20 Brian Roberts	.15	.40
21 Cla Meredith	.15	.40
22 Ben Francisco	.15	.40
23 Brian McCann	.25	.60
24 Carlos Guillen	.15	.40
25 Chien-Ming Wang	.25	.60
26 Brandon Phillips	.15	.40
27 Saul Rivera	.15	.40
28 Torii Hunter	.15	.40
29 Jamie Moyer	.15	.40
30 Kevin Youkilis	.15	.40
31 Martin Prado	.15	.40
32 Magglio Ordonez	.25	.60
33 Nomar Garciaparra	.25	.60
34 Takashi Saito	.15	.40
35 Chase Headley	.15	.40
36 Mike Pelfrey	.15	.40
37 Ronny Cedeno	.15	.40
38 Dallas McPherson	.15	.40
39 Zack Greinke	.25	.60
40 Matt Cain	.25	.60
41 Xavier Nady	.15	.40
42 Willie Aybar	.15	.40
43 Edgar Gonzalez	.15	.40
44 Gabe Gross	.15	.40
45 Joey Votto	.40	1.00
46 Jason Michaels	.15	.40
47 Eric Chavez	.15	.40
48 Jason Bartlett	.15	.40
49 Jeremy Guthrie	.15	.40
50 Matt Holliday	.40	1.00
51 Ross Ohlendorf	.15	.40
52 Gil Meche	.15	.40
53 B.J. Upton	.25	.60
54 Ryan Doumit	.15	.40
55 Jay Bruce	.25	.60
56 Huston Street	.15	.40
57 Bobby Crosby	.15	.40
58 Jose Valverde	.15	.40
59 Brian Tallet	.15	.40
60 Adam Dunn	.25	.60
61 Victor Martinez	.25	.60
62 Jeff Francoeur	.25	.60
63 Emilio Bonifacio	.15	.40
64 Chone Figgins	.15	.40
65 Alexei Ramirez	.25	.60
66 Brian Giles	.15	.40
67 Khalil Greene	.15	.40
68 Phil Hughes	.15	.40
69 Mike Aviles	.15	.40
70 Ryan Braun	.25	.60
71 Braden Looper	.15	.40
72 Jhonny Peralta	.15	.40
73 Ian Stewart	.15	.40
74 James Loney	.15	.40
75 Chase Utley	.25	.60
76 Reed Johnson	.15	.40
77 Jorge Cantu	.15	.40
78 Julio Lugo	.15	.40
79 Raul Ibanez	.25	.60
80 Lance Berkman	.25	.60
81 Joel Peralta	.15	.40
82 Mark Hendrickson	.15	.40
83 Jeff Suppan	.15	.40
84 Scott Olsen	.15	.40
85 Joba Chamberlain	.15	.40
86 Fausto Carmona	.15	.40
87 Andy Pettitte	.25	.60
88 Jim Johnson	.15	.40
89 Chris Snyder	.15	.40
90 Nick Swisher	.25	.60
91 Edgar Renteria	.15	.40
92 Brandon Inge	.15	.40
93 Aubrey Huff	.15	.40
94 Stephen Drew	.15	.40
95 Denard Span	.15	.40
96 Carl Crawford	.25	.60
97 Felix Pie	.15	.40
98 Jeremy Sowers	.15	.40
99 Trevor Hoffman	.25	.60
100 Albert Pujols	.50	1.25
101 Radhames Liz	.15	.40
102 Doug Davis	.15	.40
103 Joel Hanrahan	.25	.60
104 Seth Smith	.15	.40
105 Francisco Liriano	.15	.40
106 Bobby Abreu	.15	.40
107 Willie Harris	.15	.40
108 Travis Ishikawa	.20	.50
109 Travis Hafner	.15	.40
110 Adrian Gonzalez	.30	.75
111 Shin-Soo Choo	.25	.60
112 Robinson Cano	.25	.60
113 Matt Capps	.15	.40
114 Gerald Laird	.15	.40
115 Max Scherzer	.40	1.00
116 Mike Jacobs	.15	.40
117 Asdrubal Cabrera	.25	.60
118 J.J. Hardy	.15	.40
119 Justin Upton	.25	.60
120 Mariano Rivera	.50	1.25
121 Jack Cust	.15	.40
122 Orlando Hudson	.15	.40
123 Brian Wilson	.40	1.00
124 Heath Bell	.15	.40
125 Chipper Jones	.40	1.00
126 Jason Marquis	.15	.40
127 Rocco Baldelli	.15	.40
128 Rafael Perez	.15	.40
129 Carlos Gomez	.15	.40
130 Kerry Wood	.15	.40
131 Adam Wainwright	.25	.60
132 Michael Bourn	.15	.40
133 Cristian Guzman	.15	.40
134 Dustin McGowan	.15	.40
135 James Shields	.15	.40
136 Matt Lindstrom	.15	.40
137 Rick Ankiel	.15	.40
138 J.P. Howell	.15	.40
139 Ben Zobrist	.25	.60
140 Tim Hudson	.25	.60
141 Clayton Kershaw	.75	2.00
142 Edwin Encarnacion	.40	1.00
143 Kevin Millwood	.15	.40
144 Jack Hannahan	.15	.40
145 Alex Gordon	.25	.60
146 Chad Durbin	.15	.40
147 Derrek Lee	.15	.40
148 Kevin Gregg	.15	.40
149 Clint Barmes	.15	.40
150 Dustin Pedroia	.30	.75
151 Brad Hawpe	.15	.40
152 Steven Shell	.15	.40
153 Jesse Crain	.15	.40
154 Edwar Ramirez	.15	.40
155 Jair Jurrjens	.15	.40
156 Matt Albers	.15	.40
157 Endy Chavez	.15	.40
158 Steve Pearce	.40	1.00
159 John Maine	.15	.40
160 Ryan Theriot	.15	.40
161 Eric Stults	.15	.40
162 Cha-Seung Baek	.15	.40
163 Alex Gonzalez	.15	.40
164 Dan Haren	.15	.40
165 Edwin Jackson	.15	.40
166 Felipe Lopez	.15	.40
167 David DeJesus	.15	.40
168 Todd Wellemeyer	.15	.40
169 Joey Gathright	.15	.40
170 Roy Oswalt	.25	.60
171 Carlos Pena	.25	.60
172 Nick Hundley	.15	.40
173 Adrian Beltre	.40	1.00
174 Omar Vizquel	.25	.60
175 Cole Hamels	.30	.75
176 Jarrod Saltalamacchia	.15	.40
177 Yuniesky Betancourt	.15	.40
178 Placido Polanco	.15	.40
179 Ryan Spilborghs	.15	.40
180 Josh Beckett	.15	.40
181 Cory Wade	.15	.40
182 Aaron Laffey	.15	.40
183 Kosuke Fukudome	.25	.60
184 Miguel Montero	.15	.40
185 Edinson Volquez	.15	.40
186 Jon Garland	.15	.40
187 Andruw Jones	.15	.40
188 Vernon Wells	.15	.40
189 Zach Duke	.15	.40
190 David Wright	.30	.75
191 Ryan Madson	.15	.40
192 Hideki Okajima	.15	.40
193 Ryan Church	.15	.40
194 Adam Jones	.25	.60
195 Geovany Soto	.25	.60
196 Jeremy Hermida	.15	.40
197 Juan Rivera	.15	.40
198 David Weathers	.15	.40
199 Jorge Campillo	.15	.40
200 Derek Jeter	1.00	2.50
201 Brett Myers	.15	.40
202 Brett Gardner	.25	.60
203 Rafael Furcal	.15	.40
204 Wandy Rodriguez	.15	.40
205 Ricky Nolasco	.15	.40
206 Ryan Freel	.15	.40
207 Jeremy Bonderman	.15	.40
208 Michael Wuertz	.15	.40
209 Hank Blalock	.15	.40
210 Alfonso Soriano	.25	.60
211 Jeff Clement	.15	.40
212 Garrett Atkins	.15	.40
213 Luis Vizcaino	.15	.40
214 Tim Redding	.15	.40
215 Ryan Ludwick	.25	.60
216 Mark Teahen	.15	.40
217 Chris Young	.15	.40
218 David Aardsma	.15	.40
219 Ubaldo Jimenez	.15	.40
220 Ryan Howard	.30	.75
221 Skip Schumaker	.15	.40
222 Craig Counsell	.15	.40
223 Chris Iannetta	.15	.40
224 Jason Kubel	.15	.40
225 Johan Santana	.25	.60
226 Luke Hochevar	.15	.40
227 Jason Bay	.25	.60
228 Alex Hinshaw	.15	.40
229 Jon Rauch	.15	.40
230 Carlos Quentin	.15	.40
231 Coco Crisp	.15	.40
232 Casey Blake	.15	.40
233 Carlos Marmol	.25	.60
234 Fernando Rodney	.15	.40
235 Jed Lowrie	.15	.40
236 Brad Penny	.15	.40
237 Reggie Willits	.15	.40
238 Mike Hampton	.15	.40
239 Mike Lowell	.15	.40
240 Randy Johnson	.40	1.00
241 Jarrod Washburn	.15	.40
242 B.J. Ryan	.15	.40
243 Javier Vazquez	.15	.40
244 Todd Helton	.25	.60
245 Matt Garza	.15	.40
246 Ramon Hernandez	.15	.40
247 Johnny Cueto	.25	.60
248 Willy Taveras	.15	.40
249 Carlos Silva	.15	.40
250 Manny Ramirez	.40	1.00
251 A.J. Burnett	.15	.40
252 Aaron Cook	.15	.40
253 Josh Bard	.15	.40
254 Aaron Harang	.15	.40
255 Jeff Samardzija	.25	.60
256 Brad Lidge	.15	.40
257 Pedro Feliz	.15	.40
258 Kazuo Matsui	.15	.40
259 Joe Blanton	.15	.40
260 Ian Kinsler	.25	.60
261 Rich Harden	.15	.40
262 Kelly Johnson	.15	.40
263 Anibal Sanchez	.15	.40
264 Mike Adams	.15	.40
265 Chad Billingsley	.25	.60
266 Chris Davis	.25	.60
267 Brandon Moss	.15	.40
268 Matt Kemp	.30	.75
269 Jose Arredondo	.15	.40
270 Mark Teixeira	.25	.60
271 Glen Perkins	.15	.40
272 Pat Burrell	.15	.40
273 Luke Scott	.15	.40
274 Scott Feldman	.25	.60
275 Ichiro Suzuki	.50	1.25
276 Cliff Floyd	.15	.40
277 Bill Hall	.15	.40
278 Bronson Arroyo	.15	.40
279 Lyle Overbay	.15	.40
280 Aramis Ramirez	.15	.40
281 Jeff Keppinger	.15	.40
282 Brandon Morrow	.15	.40
283 Ryan Shealy	.15	.40
284 Andy Sonnanstine	.15	.40
285 Josh Johnson	.25	.60
286 Carlos Ruiz	.15	.40
287 Gregg Zaun	.15	.40
288 Kenji Johjima	.25	.60
289 Mike Gonzalez	.15	.40
290 Carlos Delgado	.15	.40
291 Gary Sheffield	.15	.40
292 Brian Anderson	.15	.40
293 Josh Hamilton	.25	.60
294 Tom Gorzelanny	.15	.40
295 Yunel Escobar	.15	.40
296 Scott Hairston	.15	.40
297 Luis Castillo	.15	.40
298 Gabe Kapler	.15	.40
299 Nelson Cruz	.40	1.00
300 Tim Lincecum	.25	.60
301 Brian Bannister	.15	.40
302 Frank Francisco	.15	.40
303 Jose Guillen	.15	.40
304 Erick Aybar	.15	.40
305 Brad Ziegler	.15	.40
306 John Baker	.15	.40
307 Hong-Chih Kuo	.15	.40
308 Jo Jo Reyes	.15	.40
309 Josh Willingham	.25	.60
310 Billy Wagner	.15	.40
311 Nick Blackburn	.15	.40
312 David Purcey	.15	.40
313 Rafael Soriano	.15	.40
314 Zach Miner	.15	.40
315 Andre Ethier	.25	.60
316 Rickie Weeks	.15	.40
317 Akinori Iwamura	.15	.40
318 Hideki Matsui	.40	1.00
319 Ryan Rowland-Smith	.15	.40
320 Miguel Cabrera	.40	1.00
321 Manny Parra	.15	.40
322 Jack Wilson	.15	.40
323 Jeremy Reed	.15	.40
324 Chris Coste	.15	.40
325 Grady Sizemore	.25	.60
326 Andy LaRoche	.15	.40
327 Joel Pineiro	.15	.40
328 Brian Buscher	.15	.40
329 Randy Wolf	.15	.40
330 Jake Peavy	.15	.40
331 Curtis Granderson	.30	.75
332 Kyle Kendrick	.15	.40
333 Joe Saunders	.15	.40
334 Russell Martin	.15	.40
335 Conor Jackson	.15	.40
336 Paul Konerko	.25	.60
337 Kevin Slowey	.25	.60
338 Mark DeRosa	.25	.60
339 Garret Anderson	.15	.40
340 Michael Young	.15	.40
341 Greg Dobbs	.15	.40
342 Brian Moehler	.15	.40
343 Alex Rios	.15	.40
344 Mike Napoli	.15	.40
345 Bobby Jenks	.15	.40
346 Daric Barton	.15	.40
347 Jason Kendall	.15	.40
348 Chad Qualls	.15	.40
349 Milton Bradley	.15	.40
350 Joe Mauer	.30	.75
351 Livan Hernandez	.15	.40
352 Chris Ray	.15	.40
353 Bob Howry	.15	.40
354 Manny Corpas	.15	.40
355 Ervin Santana	.15	.40
356 Billy Butler	.15	.40
357 Russ Springer	.15	.40
358 Micah Owings	.15	.40
359 Corey Hart	.15	.40
360 Francisco Rodriguez	.25	.60
361 Ted Lilly	.15	.40
362 Adam Everett	.15	.40
363 Scott Rolen	.25	.60
364 Troy Tulowitzki	.40	1.00
365 Jacoby Ellsbury	.30	.75
366 Jayson Werth	.25	.60
367 Gio Gonzalez	.25	.60
368 Mark Ellis	.15	.40
369 Brendan Harris	.15	.40
370 David Ortiz	.40	1.00
371 Carlos Lee	.15	.40
372 Jonathan Broxton	.15	.40
373 Jesse Litsch	.15	.40
374 Barry Zito	.25	.60
375 Daisuke Matsuzaka	.25	.60
376 Kevin Kouzmanoff	.15	.40
377 Jesse Carlson	.15	.40
378 Brian Fuentes	.15	.40
379 Mark Reynolds	.15	.40
380 Brandon Webb	.25	.60
381 Scott Kazmir	.15	.40
382 Blake DeWitt	.15	.40
383 Kurt Suzuki	.15	.40
384 Chris Volstad	.15	.40
385 Gavin Floyd	.15	.40
386 Paul Maholm	.15	.40
387 Freddy Sanchez	.15	.40
388 Scott Baker	.15	.40
389 John Danks	.15	.40
390 CC Sabathia	.25	.60
391 Ryan Dempster	.15	.40
392 Tim Wakefield	.25	.60
393 Mike Cameron	.15	.40
394 Aaron Rowand	.15	.40
395 Howie Kendrick	.15	.40
396 Marlon Byrd	.15	.40
397 Dave Bush	.15	.40
398 George Sherrill	.15	.40
399 Francisco Cordero	.15	.40
400 Evan Longoria	.25	.60
401 Hiroki Kuroda	.15	.40
402 Sean Gallagher	.15	.40
403 Yovani Gallardo	.15	.40
404 Ryan Sweeney	.15	.40
405 Chris Dickerson	.15	.40
406 Jason Varitek	.40	1.00
407 Erik Bedard	.15	.40
408 J.J. Putz	.15	.40
409 Wily Mo Pena	.15	.40
410 Rich Hill	.15	.40
411 Delmon Young	.25	.60
412 David Eckstein	.15	.40
413 Marcus Thames	.15	.40
414 Dontrelle Willis	.15	.40
415 Joakim Soria	.15	.40
416 Chan Ho Park	.25	.60
417 Jered Weaver	.25	.60
418 Justin Duchscherer	.15	.40
419 Casey Kotchman	.15	.40
420 John Lackey	.25	.60
421 Peter Moylan	.15	.40
422 Bengie Molina	.15	.40
423 Mark Loretta	.15	.40
424 Dan Wheeler	.15	.40
425 Ken Griffey Jr.	.75	2.00
426 Justin Verlander	.40	1.00
427 Troy Glaus	.15	.40
428 Daniel Murphy RC	1.50	4.00
429 Brandon Backe	.15	.40
430 Nick Markakis	.30	.75
431 Travis Metcalf	.15	.40
432 Austin Kearns	.15	.40
433 Adam Lind	.15	.40
434 Jody Gerut	.15	.40
435 Jonathan Papelbon	.25	.60
436 Duaner Sanchez	.15	.40
437 David Murphy	.15	.40
438 Eddie Guardado	.15	.40
439 Johnny Damon	.25	.60
440 Derek Lowe	.15	.40
441 Miguel Olivo	.15	.40
442 Shaun Marcum	.15	.40
443 Ty Wigginton	.25	.60
444 Elijah Dukes	.15	.40
445 Felix Hernandez	.25	.60
446 Joe Inglett	.15	.40
447 Kelly Shoppach	.15	.40
448 Eric Hinske	.15	.40
449 Fred Lewis	.15	.40
450 Cliff Lee	.25	.60
451 Miguel Tejada	.25	.60
452 Jensen Lewis	.15	.40
453 Ryan Zimmerman	.25	.60
454 Jon Lester	.25	.60
455 Justin Morneau	.25	.60
456 John Smoltz	.40	1.00
457 Emmanuel Burriss	.15	.40
458 Joe Nathan	.15	.40
459 Jeff Niemann	.15	.40
460 Roy Halladay	.25	.60
461 Matt Diaz	.15	.40
462 Oscar Salazar	.15	.40
463 Chris Perez	.15	.40
464 Matt Joyce	.15	.40
465 Dan Uggla	.15	.40
466 Jermaine Dye	.15	.40
467 Shane Victorino	.15	.40
468 Chris Getz	.15	.40
469 Chris B. Young	.15	.40
470 Prince Fielder	.25	.60
471 Juan Pierre	.15	.40
472 Travis Buck	.15	.40
473 Dioner Navarro	.15	.40
474 Mark Buehrle	.25	.60
475 Hanley Ramirez	.25	.60
476 John Lannan	.15	.40
477 Lastings Milledge	.15	.40
478 Dallas Braden	.25	.60
479 Orlando Cabrera	.15	.40
480 Jose Reyes	.25	.60
481 Jorge Posada	.25	.60
482 Jason Isringhausen	.15	.40
483 Rich Aurilia	.15	.40
484 Hunter Pence	.25	.60
485 Carlos Zambrano	.25	.60
486 Randy Winn	.15	.40
487 Carlos Beltran	.25	.60
488 Armando Galarraga	.15	.40
489 Wilson Betemit	.15	.40
490 Vladimir Guerrero	.25	.60
491 Ryan Garko	.15	.40
492 Ian Snell	.15	.40
493 Yadier Molina	.40	1.00
494 Tom Glavine	.25	.60
495 Cameron Maybin	.15	.40
496 Vicente Padilla	.15	.40
497 Keiichi Yabu	.15	.40
498 Oliver Perez	.15	.40
499 Carlos Villanueva	.15	.40
500 Alex Rodriguez	.50	1:25
501 Baltimore Orioles CL	.15	.40
502 Boston Red Sox CL	.25	.60
503 Chicago White Sox CL	.15	.40
504 Houston Astros CL	.15	.40
505 Oakland Athletics CL	.15	.40
506 Toronto Blue Jays CL	.15	.40
507 Atlanta Braves CL	.15	.40
508 Milwaukee Brewers CL	.15	.40
509 St. Louis Cardinals CL	.25	.60
510 Chicago Cubs CL	.25	.60
511 Arizona Diamondbacks CL	.15	.40
512 Los Angeles Dodgers CL	.25	.60
513 San Francisco Giants CL	.15	.40
514 Cleveland Indians CL	.15	.40
515 Seattle Mariners CL	.15	.40
516 Florida Marlins CL	.15	.40
517 New York Mets CL	.25	.60
518 Washington Nationals CL	.15	.40
519 San Diego Padres CL	.15	.40
520 Pittsburgh Pirates CL	.15	.40
521 Tampa Bay Rays CL	.15	.40
522 Cincinnati Reds CL	.15	.40
523 Colorado Rockies CL	.15	.40
524 Kansas City Royals CL	.15	.40
525 Detroit Tigers CL	.15	.40
526 Minnesota Twins CL	.15	.40
527 New York Yankees CL	.25	.60
528 Philadelphia Phillies CL	.15	.40
529 Los Angeles Angels CL	.15	.40
530 Texas Rangers CL	.15	.40
531 Bradley/Mauer/Pedroia	.30	.75
532 Chipper/Holliday/Pujols	.50	1.25
533 M.Cabrera/ARod/Quentin	.50	1.25
534 Delgado/Dunn/Howard	.30	.75
535 Morneau/Hamilton/Cabrera	.40	1.00
536 Howard/Wright/A.Gon	.30	.75
537 C.Lee/D.Matsu/Halladay	.25	.60
538 Santana/Peavy/Lince	.25	.60
539 C.Lee/D.Matsu/Halladay	.25	.60
540 Lince/Dempster/Webb	.25	.60
541 Ervin Santana Roy Halladay/A.J. Burnett	.25	.60
542 Santana/Lince/Haren	.25	.60
543 Grady Sizemore	.25	.60
544 Ichiro Suzuki	.50	1.25
545 Hanley Ramirez	.25	.60
546 Jose Reyes	.25	.60
547 Johan Santana	.25	.60
548 Adrian Gonzalez	.30	.75
549 Carlos Zambrano	.25	.60
550 Jonathan Papelbon	.25	.60
551 Josh Hamilton	.25	.60
552 Derek Jeter	1.00	2.50
553 Kevin Youkilis	.15	.40
554 Joe Mauer	.30	.75
555 Kosuke Fukudome Ryan Theriot	.25	.60
556 Chipper Jones	.40	1.00
557 Lance Berkman	.25	.60
558 Michael Young	.15	.40
559 Evan Longoria	.25	.60
560 Alex Rodriguez	.50	1.25
561 Travis Snider RC	.60	1.50
562 James McDonald RC	1.00	2.50
563 Brian Duensing RC	.60	1.50
564 Josh Outman RC	.60	1.50
565 Josh Geer (RC)	.40	1.00
566 Kevin Jepsen (RC)	.40	1.00
567 Scott Lewis (RC)	.40	1.00
568 Jason Motte (RC)	.60	1.50
569 Ricky Romero (RC)	.60	1.50
570 Landon Powell (RC)	.40	1.00
571 Scott Elbert (RC)	.40	1.00
572 Bobby Parnell RC	.60	1.50
573 Ryan Perry RC	1.00	2.50
574 Phil Coke RC	.60	1.50
575 Trevor Cahill RC	1.00	2.50
576 Jesse Chavez RC	.40	1.00
577 George Kottaras (RC)	.40	1.00
578 Trevor Crowe RC	.40	1.00
579 David Freese RC	1.25	3.00
580 Matt Tuiasosopo (RC)	.40	1.00
581 Brett Anderson RC	.60	1.50
582 Casey McGehee (RC)	.40	1.00
583 Elvis Andrus RC	1.00	2.50
584 Shawn Kelley RC	.60	1.50
585 Mike Hinckley (RC)	.40	1.00
586 Donald Veal RC	.60	1.50
587 Colby Rasmus (RC)	.60	1.50
588 Shairon Martis RC	.60	1.50
589 Walter Silva RC	.60	1.50
590 Chris Jakubauskas RC	.60	1.50
591 Brad Nelson (RC)	.40	1.00
592 Alfredo Simon (RC)	.40	1.00
593 Koji Uehara RC	1.00	2.50
594 Rick Porcello RC	1.25	3.00

595 Kenshin Kawakami RC .60 1.50
596 Dexter Fowler (RC) .60 1.50
597 Jordan Schafer (RC) .60 1.50
598 David Patton RC .60 1.50
599 Luis Cruz RC .40 1.00
600 Joe Martinez RC .60 1.50

2009 O-Pee-Chee Black

*BLACK VET: 1X TO 2.5X BASIC
*BLACK RC: .75X TO 2X BASIC
STATED ODDS 1:6 HOBBY/RETAIL

2009 O-Pee-Chee Black Blank Back

RANDOM INSERTS IN PACKS
NO PRICING DUE TO SCARCITY

2009 O-Pee-Chee Black Mini

*BLK MINI VET: 4X TO 10X BASIC
*BLK MINI RC: 1.5X TO 4X BASIC
STATED ODDS 1:216 HOBBY/RETAIL

2009 O-Pee-Chee All-Rookie Team

STATED ODDS 1:40 HOBBY/RETAIL
AR1 Geovany Soto .60 1.50
AR2 Joey Votto 1.00 2.50
AR3 Alexei Ramirez .60 1.50
AR4 Evan Longoria .60 1.50
AR5 Mike Aviles .40 1.00
AR6 Jacoby Ellsbury .75 2.00
AR7 Jay Bruce .60 1.50
AR8 Kosuke Fukudome .60 1.50
AR9 Jair Jurrjens .40 1.00
AR10 Denard Span .40 1.00

2009 O-Pee-Chee Box Bottoms

CARDS LISTED ALPHABETICALLY
1 Ryan Braun .60 1.50
2 Miguel Cabrera 1.00 2.50
3 Adrian Gonzalez .75 2.00
4 Vladimir Guerrero .60 1.50
5 Josh Hamilton .60 1.50
6 Derek Jeter 2.50 6.00
7 Chipper Jones 1.00 2.50
8 Clayton Kershaw 2.00 5.00
9 Evan Longoria .60 1.50
10 Dustin Pedroia .75 2.00
11 Albert Pujols 1.25 3.00
12 Hanley Ramirez .60 1.50
13 Grady Sizemore .60 1.50
14 Alfonso Soriano .60 1.50
15 Ichiro Suzuki 1.25 3.00
16 Chase Utley .60 1.50

2009 O-Pee-Chee Face of the Franchise

STATED ODDS 1:13 HOBBY/RETAIL
FF1 Vladimir Guerrero .60 1.50
FF2 Roy Oswalt .60 1.50
FF3 Eric Chavez .40 1.00
FF4 Roy Halladay .60 1.50
FF5 Chipper Jones 1.00 2.50
FF6 Ryan Braun .60 1.50
FF7 Albert Pujols 1.25 3.00
FF8 Carlos Zambrano .60 1.50
FF9 Brandon Webb .60 1.50
FF10 Russell Martin .40 1.00
FF11 Tim Lincecum .60 1.50
FF12 Grady Sizemore .60 1.50
FF13 Ichiro Suzuki 1.25 3.00
FF14 Hanley Ramirez .60 1.50
FF15 David Wright .75 2.00
FF16 Ryan Zimmerman .60 1.50
FF17 Brian Roberts .40 1.00
FF18 Adrian Gonzalez .75 2.00
FF19 Jimmy Rollins .60 1.50
FF20 Nate McLouth .40 1.00
FF21 Michael Young .40 1.00
FF22 Evan Longoria .60 1.50
FF23 David Ortiz 1.00 2.50
FF24 Jay Bruce .60 1.50
FF25 Troy Tulowitzki 1.00 2.50
FF26 Alex Gordon .60 1.50
FF27 Miguel Cabrera 1.00 2.50
FF28 Joe Mauer .75 2.00
FF29 Carlos Quentin .40 1.00
FF30 Derek Jeter 2.50 6.00

2009 O-Pee-Chee Highlights and Milestones

STATED ODDS 1:27 HOBBY/RETAIL
HM1 Brad Lidge .40 1.00
HM2 Ken Griffey Jr. 2.00 5.00
HM3 Melvin Mora .40 1.00
HM4 Derek Jeter 2.50 6.00
HM5 Josh Hamilton .60 1.50
HM6 Alfonso Soriano .60 1.50
HM7 Francisco Rodriguez .60 1.50
HM8 Jon Lester .60 1.50
HM9 Carlos Zambrano .60 1.50
HM10 Adrian Beltre 1.00 2.50
HM11 Carlos Gomez .40 1.00
HM12 Kelly Shoppach .40 1.00
HM13 Manny Ramirez 1.00 2.50
HM14 Carlos Delgado .40 1.00
HM15 CC Sabathia .60 1.50

2009 O-Pee-Chee Materials

STATED ODDS 1:108 HOBBY
STATED ODDS 1:216 RETAIL
BBP Brad Penny/Josh Beckett/A.J. Burnett 4.00 10.00
BHH Rocco Baldelli/Corey Hart Jeremy Hermida 4.00 10.00
BMY Youkilis/Beltre/Mora 8.00 20.00
BYP Jonathan Papelbon Kevin Youkilis/Josh Beckett 6.00 15.00
CBG Chad Billingsley Fausto Carmona/Zack Greinke 4.00 10.00
CFM Nick Markakis/Jeff Francoeur Michael Cuddyer 6.00 15.00
CKR Ian Kinsler/Brian Roberts Robinson Cano 5.00 12.00
CSW Nick Swisher/Michael Cuddyer Josh Willingham 6.00 15.00
DLO Magglio Ordonez/Carlos Lee Jermaine Dye 6.00 15.00
EFG Jacoby Ellsbury Curtis Granderson/Chone Figgins 6.00 15.00
ELK Kemp/Ethier/Loney 8.00 20.00
FOD David Ortiz/Carlos Delgado Prince Fielder 5.00 12.00
GDH J.J. Hardy/Stephen Drew Khalil Greene 4.00 10.00
HAG Garrett Atkins/Carlos Gonzalez Todd Helton 4.00 10.00
HMC Justin Morneau Miguel Cabrera/Travis Hafner 6.00 15.00
HML Long/Morn/Hamil 8.00 20.00
HMW Jake Westbrook Travis Hafner/Victor Martinez 4.00 10.00
HRR Halladay/Rios/Rolen 8.00 20.00
JCP Posada/Cano/Jeter 10.00 25.00
KJN Jayson Nix/Kelly Johnson Howie Kendrick 4.00 10.00
LRF Kosuke Fukudome/Derrek Lee Aramis Ramirez 4.00 10.00
LWS Brad Lidge/Takashi Saito Billy Wagner 4.00 10.00
MFJ Kelly Johnson/Jeff Francoeur Brian McCann 4.00 10.00
MMM Russell Martin/Victor Martinez Joe Mauer 6.00 15.00
NMC Mauer/Nathan/Cuddyer 8.00 20.00
OHG Hafner/Ortiz/Giambi 4.00 10.00
OHP Roy Halladay Brad Penny/Roy Oswalt 5.00 12.00
PBO Ortiz/Pap/Buchholz 5.00 12.00
PCF Pujols/Fielder/M.Cabrera 10.00 25.00
PHB Cole Hamels/Erik Bedard Andy Pettitte 5.00 12.00
RPV Ivan Rodriguez/Jorge Posada Jason Varitek 5.00 12.00
VWB Clay Buchholz Justin Verlander/Jered Weaver 4.00 10.00
YDR Chris B. Young/Mark Reynolds Stephen Drew 5.00 12.00
YKM Michael Young/Ian Kinsler Kevin Millwood 4.00 10.00

2009 O-Pee-Chee Midsummer Memories

STATED ODDS 1:27 HOBBY/RETAIL
MM1 Ken Griffey Jr. 2.00 5.00
MM2 Hank Blalock .40 1.00
MM3 Michael Young .40 1.00
MM4 Ichiro Suzuki 1.25 3.00
MM5 Miguel Tejada .60 1.50
MM6 Alfonso Soriano .60 1.50
MM7 Jimmy Rollins .60 1.50
MM8 Derek Jeter 2.50 6.00
MM9 Justin Morneau .60 1.50
MM10 J.D. Drew .40 1.00
MM11 Carl Crawford .60 1.50
MM12 Vladimir Guerrero .60 1.50
MM13 Mark Teixeira .60 1.50
MM14 David Ortiz 1.00 2.50
MM15 Manny Ramirez 1.00 2.50

2009 O-Pee-Chee New York New York

STATED ODDS 1:40 HOBBY/RETAIL
NY1 CC Sabathia 1.00 2.50
NY2 Jorge Posada 1.00 2.50
NY3 Derek Jeter 4.00 10.00
NY4 Alex Rodriguez 2.00 5.00
NY5 Chien-Ming Wang 1.00 2.50
NY6 Joba Chamberlain .60 1.50
NY7 A.J. Burnett .60 1.50
NY8 Mariano Rivera 2.00 5.00
NY9 Nick Swisher 1.00 2.50
NY10 Robinson Cano 1.00 2.50
NY11 Mark Teixeira 1.00 2.50
NY12 Johnny Damon 1.00 2.50
NY13 Hideki Matsui 1.50 4.00
NY14 Andy Pettitte 1.00 2.50
NY15 Xavier Nady .60 1.50
NY16 Jose Reyes 1.00 2.50
NY17 David Wright 1.25 3.00
NY18 John Maine .60 1.50
NY19 Daniel Murphy 2.50 6.00
NY20 Francisco Rodriguez 1.00 2.50
NY21 Carlos Delgado .60 1.50
NY22 Luis Castillo .60 1.50
NY23 Ryan Church .60 1.50
NY24 Brian Schneider .60 1.50
NY25 J.J. Putz .60 1.50
NY26 Mike Pelfrey .60 1.50
NY27 Oliver Perez .60 1.50
NY28 Jeremy Reed .60 1.50
NY29 Johan Santana 1.00 2.50
NY30 Carlos Beltran 1.00 2.50

2009 O-Pee-Chee New York New York Multi Sport

RANDOM INSERTS IN PACKS
MS1 CC Sabathia 1.50 4.00
MS2 Henrik Lundqvist 4.00 10.00
MS3 Jose Reyes 1.50 4.00
MS4 Derek Jeter 6.00 15.00
MS5 David Wright 2.00 5.00
MS6 Rick DiPietro 2.50 6.00
MS7 Joba Chamberlain 1.00 2.50
MS8 Alex Rodriguez 3.00 8.00
MS9 Johan Santana 1.50 4.00
MS10 Carlos Beltran 1.50 4.00

2009 O-Pee-Chee Retro

RM1 Sidney Crosby 6.00 15.00
RM2 Alexander Ovechkin 6.00 15.00
RM3 Carey Price 3.00 8.00
RM4 Henrik Lundqvist 2.50 6.00
RM5 Jonathan Toews 3.00 8.00
RM6 Martin Brodeur 3.00 8.00
RM7 Evgeni Malkin 5.00 12.00
RM8 Jarome Iginla 2.50 6.00
RM9 Henrik Zetterberg 2.50 6.00
RM10 Roberto Luongo 2.50 6.00
RM11 Travis Snider 1.25 3.00
RM12 Russell Martin .75 2.00
RM13 Justin Morneau 1.25 3.00
RM14 Joey Votto 2.00 5.00
RM15 Alex Rios .75 2.00
RM16 Jon Lester 1.25 3.00
RM17 Ryan Howard 1.50 4.00
RM18 Johan Santana 1.25 3.00
RM19 CC Sabathia 1.25 3.00
RM20 Roy Halladay 1.25 3.00
RM21 Chase Utley 1.25 3.00
RM22 Chipper Jones 2.00 5.00
RM23 Ryan Braun 1.25 3.00
RM24 Ken Griffey Jr. 4.00 10.00
RM25 B.J. Upton 1.25 3.00
RM26 Hanley Ramirez 1.25 3.00
RM27 Alex Rodriguez 2.50 6.00
RM28 Cole Hamels 1.50 4.00
RM29 Albert Pujols 2.50 6.00
RM30 Derek Jeter 5.00 12.00
RM31 Manny Ramirez 2.00 5.00
RM32 David Wright 1.50 4.00
RM33 Evan Longoria 1.25 3.00

2009 O-Pee-Chee Signatures

STATED ODDS 1:216 HOBBY
STATED ODDS 1:1080 RETAIL
SAJ Joaquin Arias 4.00 10.00
SAL Aaron Laffey 6.00 15.00
SAR Alexei Ramirez 10.00 25.00
SBJ Brandon Jones 3.00 8.00
SBR Brian Barton 3.00 8.00
SCD Chris Duncan 10.00 25.00
SCH Corey Hart 5.00 12.00
SCS Clint Sammons 3.00 8.00
SCW Cory Wade 5.00 12.00
SDM David Murphy 3.00 8.00
SED Elijah Dukes 4.00 10.00
SEV Edinson Volquez 6.00 15.00
SFC Fausto Carmona 3.00 8.00
SHE Chase Headley 6.00 15.00
SHJ J.A. Happ 8.00 20.00
SIK Ian Kennedy 4.00 10.00
SJA Jonathan Albaladejo 4.00 10.00
SJB Jeremy Bonderman 15.00 40.00
SJC Jeff Clement 6.00 15.00
SJH Justin Hampson 3.00 8.00
SJL Jed Lowrie 4.00 10.00
SKJ Kelly Johnson 3.00 8.00
SKK Kevin Kouzmanoff 3.00 8.00
SKM Kyle McClellan 6.00 15.00
SKS Kurt Suzuki 6.00 15.00
SMB Michael Bourn 8.00 20.00
SMH Micah Hoffpauir 8.00 20.00
SMR Mike Rabelo 10.00 25.00
SNB Nick Blackburn 3.00 8.00
SRO Ross Ohlendorf 6.00 15.00
SSA Jarrod Saltalamacchia 6.00 15.00
SSM Sean Marshall 5.00 12.00
SSP Steve Pearce 5.00 12.00

2009 O-Pee-Chee The Award Show

STATED ODDS 1:20 HOBBY/RETAIL
AW1 Yadier Molina 1.00 2.50
AW2 Adrian Gonzalez .75 2.00
AW3 Brandon Phillips .40 1.00
AW4 David Wright .75 2.00
AW5 Jimmy Rollins .60 1.50
AW6 Carlos Beltran .60 1.50
AW7 Shane Victorino .40 1.00
AW8 Geovany Soto .60 1.50
AW9 Tim Lincecum .60 1.50
AW10 Albert Pujols 1.25 3.00
AW11 Joe Mauer .75 2.00
AW12 Carlos Pena .60 1.50
AW13 Dustin Pedroia .75 2.00
AW14 Adrian Beltre 1.00 2.50
AW15 Torii Hunter .40 1.00
AW16 Grady Sizemore .60 1.50
AW17 Ichiro Suzuki 1.25 3.00
AW18 Evan Longoria .60 1.50
AW19 Cliff Lee .60 1.50
AW20 Dustin Pedroia .75 2.00

2009 O-Pee-Chee Walk-Off Winners

STATED ODDS 1:40 HOBBY/RETAIL
WK1 Ryan Braun .60 1.50
WK2 Ryan Zimmerman .60 1.50
WK3 Michael Young .40 1.00
WK4 J.D. Drew .40 1.00
WK5 Carlos Ruiz .40 1.00
WK6 Dan Uggla .40 1.00
WK7 Johnny Damon .60 1.50
WK8 Jose Reyes .40 1.00
WK9 Ryan Ludwick .60 1.50
WK10 Dioner Navarro .40 1.00

2019 Panini America's Pastime Autographs

RANDOM INSERTS IN PACKS
STATED PRINT RUN 99 SER.#'d SETS
EXCHANGE DEADLINE 2/21/2021
*GOLD: .6X TO 1.5X
1 Taylor Ward 3.00 8.00
2 Kevin Newman 5.00 12.00
3 Jeff McNeil 8.00 20.00
4 Michael Kopech 6.00 15.00
5 Jake Bauers 5.00 12.00
6 Stephen Gonsalves 3.00 8.00
7 Dennis Santana 3.00 8.00
8 Ryan O'Hearn 3.00 8.00
9 Sean Reid-Foley 3.00 8.00
10 Kevin Kramer 4.00 10.00
11 Nick Senzel 10.00 25.00
12 Jonathan Davis 4.00 10.00
13 Daniel Ponce de Leon 5.00 12.00
14 Vladimir Guerrero Jr. 40.00 100.00
15 Josh James 5.00 12.00
16 Garrett Hampson 3.00 8.00
17 Danny Jansen 3.00 8.00
18 Luis Urias 5.00 12.00
19 Jacob Nix 4.00 10.00
20 Patrick Wisdom 3.00 8.00
21 Justus Sheffield 5.00 12.00
22 Corbin Burnes 5.00 12.00
23 Brad Keller 3.00 8.00
25 Ryan Borucki 3.00 8.00
26 Luis Ortiz 3.00 8.00
27 Jake Cave 4.00 10.00
28 Eloy Jimenez 12.00 30.00
29 Touki Toussaint 4.00 10.00
30 Kyle Wright 5.00 12.00
31 Kolby Allard 5.00 12.00
32 Dakota Hudson 4.00 10.00
33 Framber Valdez 3.00 8.00
34 David Fletcher 10.00 25.00
35 Brandon Lowe 8.00 20.00
36 Ramon Laureano 8.00 20.00
37 Jonathan Loaisiga 4.00 10.00
38 Cionel Perez 3.00 8.00
39 Myles Straw 5.00 12.00
40 Reese McGuire 5.00 12.00
41 Enyel De Los Santos 3.00 8.00
42 Chris Shaw 5.00 12.00
43 Cedric Mullins 5.00 12.00
44 Bryse Wilson 4.00 10.00
45 Rowdy Tellez 5.00 12.00
46 Fernando Tatis Jr. 40.00 100.00
47 Kyle Tucker 6.00 15.00
48 Chance Adams 3.00 8.00
49 Christin Stewart 4.00 10.00
50 Caleb Ferguson 4.00 10.00

2019 Panini America's Pastime Boys of Summer Autographs

RANDOM INSERTS IN PACKS
PRINT RUNS B/WN 10-99 COPIES PER
NO PRICING QTY 15 OR LESS
EXCHANGE DEADLINE 2/21/2021
*GOLD/25: .6X TO 1.5X p/r 99
*GOLD/25: .5X TO 1.2X p/r 35
2 Harrison Bader/20 6.00 15.00
4 Cameron Gallagher/35 4.00 10.00
8 Juan Soto/35 20.00 50.00
12 Darrell Evans/20 5.00 12.00
15 Victor Victor Mesa/99 6.00 15.00
16 Pete Alonso/99 25.00 60.00
17 Dillon Peters/99 3.00 8.00
18 Zack Granite/99 3.00 8.00
20 Andrew Stevenson/99 3.00 8.00

2019 Panini America's Pastime Material Signatures

RANDOM INSERTS IN PACKS
STATED PRINT RUN 99 SER.#'d SETS
EXCHANGE DEADLINE 2/21/2021
*GOLD: .6X TO 1.5X
1 Kevin Newman 5.00 12.00
2 Jeff McNeil 8.00 20.00
3 Michael Kopech 6.00 15.00
4 Jake Bauers 5.00 12.00
5 Stephen Gonsalves 3.00 8.00
6 Dennis Santana 3.00 8.00
7 Ryan O'Hearn 3.00 8.00
8 Kevin Kramer 4.00 10.00
9 Nick Senzel 10.00 25.00
10 Vladimir Guerrero Jr. 20.00 50.00
11 Josh James 5.00 12.00
12 Danny Jansen 3.00 8.00
13 Luis Urias 5.00 12.00
14 Justus Sheffield 5.00 12.00
15 Corbin Burnes 5.00 12.00
16 Brad Keller 3.00 8.00
18 Jake Cave 4.00 10.00
19 Eloy Jimenez 12.00 30.00
20 Touki Toussaint 4.00 10.00
21 Kyle Tucker 6.00 15.00
22 Dakota Hudson 4.00 10.00
23 Christin Stewart 4.00 10.00
24 David Fletcher 10.00 25.00
25 Ramon Laureano 8.00 20.00
26 Framber Valdez 3.00 8.00
27 Cedric Mullins 5.00 12.00
28 Rowdy Tellez 5.00 12.00
29 Fernando Tatis Jr. 40.00 100.00
30 Kyle Wright 5.00 12.00

2020 Panini America's Pastime

RANDOM INSERTS IN PACKS
PRINT RUNS B/WN 25-99 COPIES PER
EXCHANGE DEADLINE 3/18/2022
1 Josh Rojas/99 3.00 8.00
2 Yordan Alvarez/25 25.00 60.00
3 Sean Murphy/25 8.00 20.00
4 Ronald Bolanos/99 5.00 12.00
5 Yu Chang/99 5.00 12.00
6 Anthony Kay/99 3.00 8.00
7 Andres Munoz/99 4.00 10.00
8 Domingo Leyba/99 4.00 10.00
9 Michael King/99 5.00 12.00
10 Gavin Lux/99 20.00 50.00
11 Jesus Luzardo/99 6.00 15.00
12 Bo Bichette/99 60.00 150.00
13 Brendan McKay/99 5.00 12.00
14 Logan Allen/99 3.00 8.00
15 Nico Hoerner/99 12.00 30.00
16 Mauricio Dubon/99 4.00 10.00
17 Deivy Grullon/99 3.00 8.00
18 Aaron Civale/99 5.00 12.00
19 Logan Webb/99 4.00 10.00
20 Danny Mendick/99 4.00 10.00
21 Brock Burke/99 3.00 8.00
22 Sheldon Neuse/99 4.00 10.00
23 Tres Barrera/99 6.00 15.00
24 Randy Arozarena/99 40.00 100.00
25 Adbert Alzolay/99 4.00 10.00
26 Zac Gallen/99 8.00 20.00
27 Matt Thaiss/49 5.00 12.00
28 Tyrone Taylor/99 3.00 8.00
29 Willi Castro/99 5.00 12.00
30 Dylan Cease/99 6.00 15.00
31 Jaylin Davis/99 5.00 12.00
32 Bryan Abreu/99 3.00 8.00
33 Aristides Aquino/99 6.00 15.00
34 Abraham Toro/99 4.00 10.00
35 Edwin Rios/99 8.00 20.00
36 Jonathan Hernandez/99 3.00 8.00
37 Nick Solak/99 5.00 12.00
39 Donnie Walton/99 8.00 20.00
40 Kyle Lewis/99 30.00 80.00
41 Bobby Bradley/99 4.00 10.00
42 Justin Dunn/99 4.00 10.00
43 Adrian Morejon/99 3.00 8.00
44 Travis Demeritte/99 4.00 10.00
45 A.J. Puk/99 6.00 15.00
46 Trent Grisham/99 12.00 30.00
47 Brusdar Graterol/99 5.00 12.00
48 Zack Collins/99 4.00 10.00
49 Jordan Yamamoto/99 4.00 10.00
50 Isan Diaz/99 5.00 12.00
51 Yoshitomo Tsutsugo/99 4.00 10.00

2020 Panini America's Pastime Boys of Summer

RANDOM INSERTS IN PACKS
PRINT RUNS B/WN 15-99 COPIES PER
NO PRICING QTY 15 OR LESS
EXCHANGE DEADLINE 3/18/2022
1 Ronald Acuna Jr./25
2 Steve Garvey/99 15.00 40.00
3 Jose Canseco/25 15.00 40.00
4 Blake Snell/49 5.00 12.00
5 Cavan Biggio EXCH/99 6.00 15.00
6 Corbin Burnes/99 6.00 15.00
7 Dennis Eckersley/25 6.00 15.00
8 Fernando Tatis Jr./49 75.00 200.00
9 Goose Gossage/25 6.00 15.00
10 J.D. Martinez/25
12 Jose Ramirez/25 6.00 15.00
13 Keith Hernandez/25 12.00 30.00
15 Pete Rose/25 25.00 60.00
16 Trevor Hoffman/25 15.00 40.00
17 Vladimir Guerrero Jr./25 30.00 80.00
18 Walker Buehler/49 20.00 50.00

2020 Panini America's Pastime Boys of Summer Gold

*GOLD/25: .6X TO 1.5X p/r 99
*GOLD/25: .5X TO 1.2X p/r 49
RANDOM INSERTS IN PACKS
PRINT RUNS B/WN 10-25 COPIES PER
NO PRICING QTY 15 OR LESS
EXCHANGE DEADLINE 3/18/2022
2 Steve Garvey/25 30.00 80.00

2020 Panini America's Pastime Material Signatures

RANDOM INSERTS IN PACKS
STATED PRINT RUN 99 SER.#'d SETS
EXCHANGE DEADLINE 3/18/2022
*GOLD/25: .6X TO 1.5X
1 Yordan Alvarez 15.00 40.00
2 Jake Rogers 3.00 8.00
3 Sean Murphy 5.00 12.00
4 Yu Chang 5.00 12.00
5 Gavin Lux 20.00 50.00
6 Bo Bichette 40.00 100.00
7 Jesus Luzardo 6.00 15.00
8 Brendan McKay 5.00 12.00
9 Logan Allen 3.00 8.00
10 Nico Hoerner 12.00 30.00
11 Mauricio Dubon 4.00 10.00
12 Logan Webb 4.00 10.00
13 Sheldon Neuse 4.00 10.00
14 Sam Hilliard 5.00 12.00
15 Zac Gallen 8.00 20.00
16 Matt Thaiss 4.00 10.00
17 Willi Castro 5.00 12.00
18 Dylan Cease 6.00 15.00
19 Aristides Aquino 6.00 15.00
21 Kyle Lewis 30.00 80.00
22 Bobby Bradley 4.00 10.00
23 Justin Dunn 4.00 10.00
24 Adrian Morejon 3.00 8.00
25 A.J. Puk 6.00 15.00
26 Trent Grisham 12.00 30.00
27 Brusdar Graterol 5.00 12.00
28 Zack Collins 4.00 10.00
29 Jordan Yamamoto 4.00 10.00
30 Isan Diaz 5.00 12.00

2019 Panini Ascension

RANDOM INSERTS IN PACKS
*GOLD/199: 1.2X TO 3X
*BLUE/99: 1.5X TO 4X
*RED/50: 2X TO 5X
*HOLO SLVR/25: 3X TO 8X
1 Pete Alonso RC 2.00 5.00
2 Eloy Jimenez RC .60 1.50
3 Fernando Tatis Jr. RC 4.00 10.00
4 Nathaniel Lowe RC .20 .50
5 Kyle Tucker RC .30 .75
6 Yusei Kikuchi RC .25 .60
7 Chris Paddack RC .30 .75
8 Mike Trout 2.50 6.00
9 Bryce Harper .40 1.00
10 Aaron Judge .60 1.50
11 Michael Chavis RC .25 .60
12 Shohei Ohtani .30 .75
13 Charlie Blackmon .25 .60
14 Taylor Hearn .15 .40
15 Vladimir Guerrero Jr. RC 2.50 6.00
16 Kyle Freeland .20 .50
17 Mark Zagunis .15 .40
18 Thairo Estrada RC .25 .60
19 Lorenzo Cain .15 .40
20 Elvis Andrus .20 .50

2020 Panini Ascension Autographs

RANDOM INSERTS IN PACKS
EXCHANGE DEADLINE 3/18/2022
*GOLD/75-99: .5X TO 1.2X BASIC
*GOLD/50: .6X TO 1.5X BASIC
*RED/50: .6X TO 1.5X BASIC
*RED/25: .8X TO 2X BASIC
*BLUE/25: .8X TO 2X BASIC
1 David Bote 3.00 8.00
2 Roman Quinn 2.50 6.00
3 Dylan Carlson 10.00 25.00
4 Aaron Judge
5 Zach Davies 2.50 6.00
6 Tyler Mahle 2.50 6.00
7 Billy McKinney 2.50 6.00
8 Kaleb Cowart 2.50 6.00
9 DJ Stewart 2.50 6.00
10 Michael Lorenzen 2.50 6.00
11 Luke Farrell 2.50 6.00
12 Tanner Rainey 2.50 6.00
13 Jason Martin 3.00 8.00
15 Mitch Moreland 2.50 6.00
16 Cameron Gallagher 2.50 6.00
17 Chance Adams 2.50 6.00
18 Garrett Hampson 2.50 6.00
19 Nathaniel Lowe 2.50 6.00
20 Huascar Ynoa 4.00 10.00
21 J.T. Realmuto 6.00 15.00
22 Anthony Banda 2.50 6.00
23 Jonathan Loaisiga 3.00 8.00
24 Pablo Reyes 2.50 6.00
25 Ronald Acuna Jr. EXCH 50.00 120.00

2017 Panini Chronicles

COMP.SET w/o RCs (100) 8.00 20.00
101-150 PRINT RUN 499 SER.#'d SETS
1 Bryce Harper .40 1.00
2 Robbie Ray .15 .40
3 Yonder Alonso .15 .40
4 Jay Bruce .20 .50
5 Andrew McCutchen .25 .60
6 Jacob deGrom .25 .60
7 Mickey Mantle .75 2.00
8 Joey Gallo .20 .50
9 George Springer .20 .50
10 Chris Sale .25 .60
11 Justin Verlander .25 .60
12 Hunter Pence .20 .50
13 Giancarlo Stanton .25 .60
14 Jason Kipnis .20 .50
15 Jose Altuve .20 .50
16 Josh Donaldson .20 .50
17 Ben Gamel .20 .50
18 Matt Carpenter .25 .60
19 Odubel Herrera .20 .50
20 Salvador Perez .20 .50
21 Ryan Zimmerman .20 .50
22 Corey Seager .25 .60
23 Gerrit Cole .25 .60
24 Freddie Freeman .30 .75
25 Adrian Beltre .25 .60
26 Matt Holliday .25 .60
27 Scott Schebler .20 .50
28 Max Scherzer .25 .60
29 Yoenis Cespedes .25 .60
30 Trevor Story .25 .60
31 Elvis Andrus .20 .50
32 Joe Mauer .20 .50
33 Francisco Lindor .25 .60
34 Khris Davis .25 .60
35 Justin Bour .20 .50
36 Rougned Odor .20 .50
37 Miguel Sano .20 .50
38 Ryne Sandberg .50 1.25
39 Kole Calhoun .15 .40
40 Ryan Braun .20 .50
41 Zack Greinke .20 .50
42 Mike Schmidt .40 1.00
43 Yangervis Solarte .15 .40
44 Adam Jones .20 .50
45 Logan Morrison .15 .40
46 Bo Jackson .25 .60
47 Mike Trout 1.25 3.00
48 Mike Moustakas .20 .50
49 Buster Posey .30 .75
50 Felix Hernandez .20 .50
51 Joey Votto .25 .60
52 Nolan Arenado .30 .75
53 Justin Smoak .15 .40
54 Lorenzo Cain .15 .40
55 Josh Harrison .15 .40
56 Nolan Ryan .75 2.00
57 Gary Sanchez .25 .60
58 Todd Frazier .20 .50
59 Edwin Encarnacion .25 .60
60 Corey Dickerson .15 .40
61 Pete Rose .50 1.25
62 Eric Thames .20 .50
63 Cal Ripken .75 2.00
64 Adam Duvall .25 .60
65 Paul Goldschmidt .25 .60
66 Corey Kluber .20 .50
67 Madison Bumgarner .20 .50
68 Billy Hamilton .20 .50
69 Clayton Kershaw .50 1.25
70 Chris Archer .15 .40
71 Kris Bryant .30 .75
72 Yadier Molina .25 .60
73 Charlie Blackmon .25 .60
74 Anthony Rizzo .40 1.00
75 Albert Pujols .30 .75
76 Roger Clemens .30 .75
77 Jake Lamb .20 .50
78 Miguel Cabrera .25 .60
79 Wil Myers .15 .40
80 Yu Darvish .25 .60
81 Mark Reynolds .15 .40
82 George Brett .50 1.25
83 Bartolo Colon .15 .40
84 Dexter Fowler .20 .50
85 Trea Turner .20 .50
86 Mookie Betts .40 1.00
87 Carlos Correa .25 .60
88 Matt Davidson .20 .50
89 Javier Baez .30 .75
90 Marcell Ozuna .25 .60
91 Brian Dozier .25 .60
92 Ken Griffey Jr. .50 1.25
93 Alex Rodriguez .30 .75
94 Manny Machado .25 .60
95 Evan Longoria .20 .50
96 Rickey Henderson .25 .60
97 Dee Gordon .15 .40
98 Jose Bautista .20 .50
99 Robinson Cano .20 .50
100 Matt Kemp .20 .50
101 Hunter Renfroe RC .50 1.25
102 Andrew Benintendi RC 1.00 2.50
103 Alex Reyes RC .40 1.00
104 Sam Travis RC .30 .75
105 Alex Bregman RC 1.25 3.00
106 Josh Hader RC .30 .75
107 Carson Fulmer RC .30 .75
108 Dansby Swanson RC .75 2.00
109 David Dahl RC .40 1.00
110 Aaron Judge RC 6.00 15.00
111 Jordan Montgomery RC .50 1.25
112 Josh Bell RC .75 2.00
113 Manuel Margot RC .30 .75
114 Mitch Haniger RC .50 1.25
115 Orlando Arcia RC .30 .75
116 Franklin Barreto RC .30 .75
117 Trey Mancini RC .60 1.50
118 Tyler Glasnow RC .40 1.00
119 Yoan Moncada RC 1.00 2.50
120 Cody Bellinger RC 5.00 12.00
121 Ian Happ RC .60 1.50
122 Antonio Senzatela RC .30 .75
123 Jesse Winker RC .30 .75
124 Andrew Toles RC .30 .75
125 Francis Martes RC .30 .75
126 Christian Arroyo RC .50 1.25
127 Bradley Zimmer RC .40 1.00
128 Anthony Alford RC .30 .75
129 German Marquez RC .50 1.25
130 Dinelson Lamet RC .30 .75
131 Magneuris Sierra RC .30 .75
132 Derek Fisher RC .40 1.00
133 Jorge Bonifacio RC .30 .75
134 Bruce Maxwell RC .30 .75
135 Adam Frazier RC .30 .75
136 Guillermo Heredia RC .30 .75
137 Jose De Leon RC .30 .75
138 J.T. Riddle RC .30 .75
139 Jeff Hoffman RC .30 .75
140 Luis Castillo RC 1.00 2.50
141 Chad Pinder RC .30 .75
142 Ryon Healy RC .40 1.00
143 Adam Engel RC .30 .75
144 Erik Gonzalez RC .30 .75
145 Jake Thompson RC .30 .75
146 Lewis Brinson RC .50 1.25
147 Jacoby Jones RC .40 1.00
148 Tzu-Wei Lin RC .30 .75
149 Raimel Tapia RC .40 1.00
150 Paul DeJong RC 1.00 2.50

2017 Panini Chronicles Blue

*BLUE/399: .75X TO 2X BASIC
*BLUE RC/299: .4X TO 1X BASIC RC
RANDOM INSERTS IN PACKS
PRINT RUNS B/WN 299-399 COPIES PER

2017 Panini Chronicles Gold

*GOLD/999: .6X TO 1.5X BASIC
*GOLD RC/399: .4X TO 1X BASIC RC

RANDOM INSERTS IN PACKS
PRINT RUNS B/WN 399-999 COPIES PER

2017 Panini Chronicles Green

*GREEN: .75X TO 2X BASIC
*GREEN RC: .5X TO 1.2X BASIC RC
RANDOM INSERTS IN PACKS
STATED PRINT RUN 199 SER.#'d SETS

2017 Panini Chronicles Purple

*PURPLE: 1.2X TO 3X BASIC
*PURPLE RC: .6X TO 1.5X BASIC RC
RANDOM INSERTS IN PACKS
STATED PRINT RUN 99 SER.#'d SETS

2017 Panini Chronicles Red

*RED: 5X TO 12X BASIC
*RED RC: 1.5X TO 4X BASIC RC
RANDOM INSERTS IN PACKS
STATED PRINT RUN 25 SER.#'d SETS

2017 Panini Chronicles Autographs

RANDOM INSERTS IN PACKS
EXCHANGE DEADLINE 5/22/2019
*GOLD/49-99: .5X TO 1.2X BASIC
*GOLD/25: .6X TO 1.5X BASIC
*BLUE/25: .6X TO 1.5X BASIC
1 Aaron Judge 60.00 150.00
2 Cody Bellinger 75.00 200.00
3 Yoan Moncada
4 Andrew Benintendi 10.00 25.00
5 Magneuris Sierra 4.00 10.00
6 Dansby Swanson 10.00 25.00
7 Ryon Healy 3.00 8.00
8 Mitch Haniger 4.00 10.00
9 Antonio Senzatela 2.50 6.00
10 Ian Happ 5.00 12.00
11 Trey Mancini 6.00 15.00
12 Jordan Montgomery 4.00 10.00
13 Bradley Zimmer 3.00 8.00
14 Hunter Renfroe 3.00 8.00
15 Lewis Brinson 4.00 10.00
16 Alex Bregman 12.00 30.00
17 Josh Bell 8.00 20.00
18 Derek Fisher 3.00 8.00
19 Sam Travis 2.50 6.00
20 Franklin Barreto 2.50 6.00
21 Dinelson Lamet 2.50 6.00
22 David Dahl 3.00 8.00
23 Orlando Arcia 4.00 10.00
24 John Farrell 4.00 10.00
25 Francis Martes 2.50 6.00
26 Jose Abreu 8.00 20.00
27 Yoenis Cespedes
28 Ryne Sandberg 15.00 40.00
29 Tom Glavine
30 Anthony Alford 2.50 6.00
31 Wade Boggs
32 German Marquez 4.00 10.00
33 Chad Pinder 2.50 6.00
34 Jorge Alfaro 3.00 8.00
35 Adalberto Mejia 2.50 6.00
36 Renato Nunez 5.00 12.00
37 Gabriel Ynoa 2.50 6.00
38 Jose Rondon 2.50 6.00
39 Theo Epstein
40 Robin Yount 15.00 40.00
41 Keith Hernandez
42 Roger Clemens 20.00 50.00
43 Andres Galarraga 3.00 8.00
44 Robert Gsellman 2.50 6.00
45 Corey Seager
46 Gerrit Cole 4.00 10.00
47 Jason Kipnis 3.00 8.00
48 Yandy Diaz 5.00 12.00
49 Joc Pederson 3.00 8.00
50 Roy Halladay

2017 Panini Chronicles Signature Swatches

RANDOM INSERTS IN PACKS
PRINT RUNS B/WN 5-299 COPIES PER
NO PRICING ON QTY 10 OR LESS
EXCHANGE DEADLINE 5/22/2019
1 Aaron Judge/99 EXCH 60.00 150.00
6 Ian Happ/299 6.00 15.00
7 Andrew Benintendi/199 15.00 40.00
10 Bradley Zimmer/99 4.00 10.00
15 Paul Molitor/25 15.00 40.00
16 Paul Molitor/25 15.00 40.00
17 Paul Molitor/25 15.00 40.00
21 Edgar Martinez/299 4.00 10.00
22 Corey Seager/25 12.00 30.00
24 Josh Donaldson/25
25 Dave Concepcion/25 15.00 40.00
26 Todd Helton/25 12.00 30.00
28 Starling Marte/299 4.00 10.00
29 Andres Galarraga/49 5.00 12.00
31 Pete Rose/49 15.00 40.00
33 Fred McGriff/49 10.00 25.00
34 Luis Gonzalez/25
37 Ozzie Smith/25 15.00 40.00

2017 Panini Chronicles Signature Swatches Purple

*PURPLE: .5X TO 1.2X p/r 199-299
RANDOM INSERTS IN PACKS
PRINT RUNS B/WN 49-99 COPIES PER
EXCHANGE DEADLINE 5/22/2019
4 Alex Bregman/49 15.00 40.00
8 Trey Mancini/99 8.00 20.00

2017 Panini Chronicles Signature Swatches Red

*RED: .6X TO 1.5X p/r 199-299
*RED: .5X TO 1.2X p/r 49-99
RANDOM INSERTS IN PACKS
PRINT RUNS B/WN 3-25 COPIES PER
NO PRICING ON QTY 15 OR LESS
EXCHANGE DEADLINE 5/22/2019
4 Alex Bregman/25 20.00 50.00
8 Trey Mancini/25 10.00 25.00

2017 Panini Chronicles Swatches

RANDOM INSERTS IN PACKS
PRINT RUNS B/WN 10-499 COPIES PER
NO PRICING ON QTY 10
*PURPLE/49-99: .5X TO 1.2X p/r 149-499
*PURPLE/49-99: .4X TO 1X p/r 49-99
*PURPLE/25: .6X TO 1.5X p/r 149-499
*PURPLE/25: .5X TO 1.2X p/r 49-99
*RED/25: .6X TO 1.5X p/r 149-499
*RED/25: .5X TO 1.2X p/r 49-99
1 Mike Trout/99 15.00 40.00
2 Kris Bryant/49 5.00 12.00
3 Adrian Beltre/99 3.00 8.00
4 Alex Rodriguez/499 3.00 8.00
5 Justin Verlander/499 2.50 6.00
6 Eddie Mathews/49 5.00 12.00
8 Andrew Benintendi/499 3.00 8.00
9 Don Sutton/149 2.00 5.00
10 Yoan Moncada/499 3.00 8.00
11 Cody Bellinger/49 8.00 20.00
12 Rollie Fingers/299 4.00 10.00
13 Rick Ferrell/25
14 Harmon Killebrew/25 10.00 25.00
15 Tony Gwynn/499 2.50 6.00
16 Craig Biggio/499 2.00 5.00
17 George Brett/199 10.00 25.00
18 Mike Piazza/499 2.50 6.00
20 Duke Snider/25 5.00 12.00
21 Jake Arrieta/499 2.00 5.00
22 Max Scherzer/49 3.00 8.00
23 Clayton Kershaw/49 6.00 15.00
24 Anthony Rizzo/299 4.00 10.00
25 Madison Bumgarner/299 2.00 5.00
26 Xander Bogaerts/499 2.50 6.00
27 Paul Goldschmidt/99 3.00 8.00
28 Dansby Swanson/499 3.00 8.00
29 Nolan Arenado/499 3.00 8.00
30 Marcell Ozuna/499 2.50 6.00
31 Miguel Cabrera/499 2.50 6.00
32 Jose Canseco/199 4.00 10.00
33 Carlos Delgado/499 1.50 4.00
34 Bill Buckner/49 2.00 5.00
35 Aaron Judge/499 12.00 30.00
36 Paul Konerko/499 2.00 5.00
37 Andruw Jones/499 1.50 4.00
38 Miguel Sano/499 2.00 5.00
39 George Springer/499 2.00 5.00
40 Andy Pettitte/299 2.00 5.00
41 Curt Schilling/99 2.50 6.00
42 Josh Bell/499 3.00 8.00
43 Dale Murphy/99 5.00 12.00
44 Bert Blyleven/49 6.00 15.00
45 Juan Gonzalez/499 2.50 6.00
46 Lewis Brinson/499 2.50 6.00
47 Chipper Jones/499 2.50 6.00
48 Ken Griffey Jr./499 4.00 10.00
49 Jose Altuve/49 2.50 6.00
50 Harold Baines/499 2.00 5.00
51 Gary Sheffield/49 2.00 5.00
52 Andre Dawson/99 2.50 6.00
53 Edgar Martinez/499 2.00 5.00
54 Sparky Anderson/25 10.00 25.00
55 Bryce Harper/25 5.00 12.00
56 Dustin Pedroia/199 3.00 8.00
57 Joe Torre/499 2.00 5.00
58 Hideki Matsui/499 2.50 6.00
59 John Farrell/499 1.50 4.00
60 Gary Sanchez/499 2.50 6.00

2018 Panini Chronicles

INSERTED IN '18 CHRONICLES PACKS
*SLVR VET/199: 1X TO 2.5X BASE
*SLVR RC/199: .6X TO 1.5X BASE RC
*GOLD VET/99: 1.2X TO 3X BASE
*GOLD RC/99: .75X TO 2X BASE RC
1 Shohei Ohtani RC 1.50 4.00
2 Austin Hays RC .40 1.00
3 Noah Syndergaard .20 .50
4 Freddie Freeman .30 .75
5 Justin Bour .15 .40
6 Khris Davis .25 .60
7 Miguel Cabrera .25 .60
8 Giancarlo Stanton .25 .60
9 Yadier Molina .25 .60
10 Mookie Betts .40 1.00
11 Starling Marte .20 .50
12 Walker Buehler RC 1.25 3.00
13 Rafael Devers RC .75 2.00
14 Robinson Cano .20 .50
15 Victor Robles RC .60 1.50
16 Eric Hosmer .20 .50
17 Joey Votto .25 .60
18 Max Scherzer .25 .60
19 Paul Goldschmidt .25 .60
20 Clint Frazier RC .50 1.25
21 Clayton Kershaw .50 1.25
22 Kris Bryant .30 .75
23 Dustin Fowler RC .25 .60
24 Willie Calhoun RC .30 .75
25 Chris Sale .25 .60
26 Dominic Smith RC .25 .60
27 Miguel Andujar RC 1.00 2.50
28 Nicky Delmonico RC .25 .60
29 Jake Arrieta .20 .50
30 Shohei Ohtani RC 1.50 4.00
31 Eric Thames .20 .50
32 Luiz Gohara RC .25 .60
33 Jose Altuve .20 .50
34 Adrian Beltre .25 .60
35 Nolan Arenado .30 .75
36 Corey Seager .25 .60
37 Ronald Acuna Jr. RC 5.00 12.00
38 Gary Sanchez .25 .60
39 Jose Abreu .25 .60
40 Manny Machado .25 .60
41 Ozzie Albies RC .75 2.00
42 Rhys Hoskins RC 1.00 2.50
43 Harrison Bader RC .40 1.00
44 J.P. Crawford RC .25 .60
45 Carlos Correa .25 .60
46 Corey Kluber .20 .50
47 Mike Trout 1.25 3.00
48 Anthony Rizzo .40 1.00
49 Alex Gordon .20 .50
50 Josh Donaldson .20 .50
51 Albert Pujols .30 .75
52 Amed Rosario RC .30 .75
53 Andrew McCutchen .25 .60
54 Aaron Judge .60 1.50
55 Francisco Lindor .25 .60
56 Cody Bellinger .50 1.25
57 Chance Sisco RC .30 .75
58 Miguel Sano .20 .50
59 Bryce Harper .40 1.00
60 Gleyber Torres RC 2.50 6.00

2018 Panini Chronicles Blue

*BLUE: 1.5X TO 4X BASIC
*BLUE RC: 1X TO 2.5X BASIC RC
INSERTED IN '18 CHRONICLES PACKS
STATED PRINT RUN 49 SER.#'d SETS

2018 Panini Chronicles Holo Gold

*GOLD: 1.2X TO 3X BASIC
*GOLD RC: .75X TO 2X BASIC RC
INSERTED IN '18 CHRONICLES PACKS
STATED PRINT RUN 99 SER.#'d SETS

2018 Panini Chronicles Pink

*PINK: 2.5X TO 6X BASIC
*PINK RC: 1.5X TO 4X BASIC RC
INSERTED IN '18 CHRONICLES PACKS
STATED PRINT RUN 25 SER.#'d SETS

2018 Panini Chronicles Press Proof

*PP: .75X TO 2X BASIC
*PP RC: .5X TO 1.2X BASIC RC
INSERTED IN '18 CHRONICLES PACKS
STATED PRINT RUN 299 SER.#'d SETS

2018 Panini Chronicles Teal

*TEAL: 1X TO 2.5X BASIC
*TEAL RC: .6X TO 1.5X BASIC RC
INSERTED IN '18 CHRONICLES PACKS
STATED PRINT RUN 199 SER.#'d SETS

2018 Panini Chronicles Autographs

RANDOM INSERTS IN PACKS
CAAH Austin Hays 3.00 8.00
CACG Cameron Gallagher 2.50 6.00
CACP Chad Pinder 2.50 6.00
CADP Dillon Peters 2.50 6.00
CAFP Freddy Peralta 2.50 6.00
CAFR Franmil Reyes 4.00 10.00
CAGM German Marquez 2.50 6.00
CAGY Gabriel Ynoa 2.50 6.00
CAJE Jeurys Familia 3.00 8.00
CAJG Javier Guerra 2.50 6.00
CAJP James Paxton 3.00 8.00
CAJR Jose Rondon 2.50 6.00
CAKF Kyle Farmer 2.50 6.00
CALG Luiz Gohara 2.50 6.00
CALS Lucas Sims 2.50 6.00
CAMA Miguel Andujar 12.00 30.00
CAMG Mitch Garver 2.50 6.00
CARR Robbie Ray 2.50 6.00
CATW Tyler Wade 3.00 8.00
CAVC Victor Caratini 3.00 8.00

2018 Panini Chronicles Autographs Holo Silver

*PURPLE/25: .75X TO 2X BASE
RANDOM INSERTS IN PACKS
PRINT RUNS B/WN 5-25 COPIES PER
NO PRICING ON QTY 5
CADF Dustin Fowler/25 5.00 12.00

2018 Panini Chronicles Autographs Purple

*PURPLE/99: .5X TO 1.2X BASE
*PURPLE/35-49: .6X TO 1.5X BASE
RANDOM INSERTS IN PACKS
PRINT RUNS B/WN 10-99 COPIES PER
NO PRICING ON QTY 10
CADF Dustin Fowler/99 3.00 8.00

2018 Panini Chronicles Autographs Red

*RED/75-199: .5X TO 1.2X BASE
*RED/49: .6X TO 1.5X BASE
RANDOM INSERTS IN PACKS
PRINT RUNS B/WN 15-199 COPIES PER
NO PRICING ON QTY 15
CADF Dustin Fowler/199 3.00 8.00

2018 Panini Chronicles Signature Swatches

RANDOM INSERTS IN PACKS
*GOLD/99-149: .5X TO 1.2X BASIC
*RED/25: .75X TO 2X BASIC
CCSDP DJ Peters 6.00 15.00
CCSJB Jaime Barria 3.00 8.00
CCSWA Willy Adames 3.00 8.00

2018 Panini Chronicles Signature Swatches Blue

*BLUE/99: .5X TO 1.2X BASIC
RANDOM INSERTS IN PACKS
PRINT RUNS B/WN 49-99 COPIES PER
CCSAM Austin Meadows/49 6.00 15.00

2018 Panini Chronicles Signature Swatches Holo Gold

*RED/49: .5X TO 1.2X BASIC
*RED/25: .75X TO 2X BASIC
RANDOM INSERTS IN PACKS
PRINT RUNS B/WN 25-49 COPIES PER
CCSAM Austin Meadows/25 8.00 20.00

2018 Panini Chronicles Swatches

INSERTED IN '18 CHRONICLES PACKS
CSSO Shohei Ohtani 10.00 25.00
CSAR Amed Rosario 2.00 5.00
CSAH Austin Hays 2.50 6.00
CSVR Victor Robles 4.00 10.00
CSOA Ozzie Albies 5.00 12.00
CSRM Ryan McMahon 2.00 5.00
CSRH Rhys Hoskins 4.00 10.00
CSRD Rafael Devers 5.00 12.00
CSMA Miguel Andujar 4.00 10.00
CSMT Mike Trout 8.00 20.00
CSAJ Aaron Judge
CSRA Ronald Acuna Jr. 8.00 20.00
CSFT Fernando Tatis Jr. 12.00 30.00
CSMB Mookie Betts 4.00 10.00
CSCK Clayton Kershaw 5.00 12.00
CSJA Jose Altuve 2.00 5.00
CSKG Ken Griffey Jr. 8.00 20.00
CSGT Gleyber Torres 5.00 12.00
CSKP Kirby Puckett
CSNA Nolan Arenado 3.00 8.00
CSBH Bryce Harper 4.00 10.00
CSFL Francisco Lindor 2.50 6.00
CSMM Manny Machado 2.50 6.00

2018 Panini Chronicles Swatches Holo Gold

*HOLO GOLD/49: .5X TO 1.2X BASIC
*HOLO GOLD/25: .6X TO 1.5X BASIC
INSERTED IN '18 CHRONICLES PACKS
PRINT RUNS B/WN 25-49 COPIES PER
CSCF Clint Frazier/49 4.00 10.00

2018 Panini Chronicles Swatches Red

*RED/25: .6X TO 1.5X BASIC
INSERTED IN '18 CHRONICLES PACKS
PRINT RUNS B/WN 10-25 COPIES PER
NO PRICING ON QTY 10
CSCF Clint Frazier/25 5.00 12.00

2019 Panini Chronicles

RANDOM INSERTS IN PACKS
*RED/99: 1.5X TO 4X
*BLUE/50: 2X TO 5X
*PINK/25: 3X TO 8X
1 Joey Votto .25 .60
2 Joey Gallo .20 .50
3 Cody Bellinger .50 1.25
4 Pete Alonso RC 2.00 5.00
5 Bryce Harper .40 1.00
6 Fernando Tatis Jr. RC 4.00 10.00
7 Clayton Kershaw .50 1.25
8 Max Scherzer .25 .60
9 Javier Baez .30 .75
10 Nolan Arenado .30 .75
11 Aaron Judge .60 1.50
12 Ryan O'Hearn RC .15 .40
13 Jose Altuve .20 .50
14 Madison Bumgarner .20 .50
15 Christian Yelich .30 .75
16 Adam Jones .20 .50
17 Chris Paddack RC .30 .75
18 Ichiro .30 .75
19 Kyle Tucker RC .30 .75
20 Noah Syndergaard .20 .50
21 Blake Snell .20 .50
22 Christin Stewart RC .20 .50
23 Yusei Kikuchi RC .25 .60
24 Ronald Acuna Jr. 1.25 3.00
25 Anthony Rizzo .40 1.00
26 Carlos Correa .25 .60
27 Giancarlo Stanton .25 .60
28 Michael Kopech RC .30 .75
29 Paul Goldschmidt .25 .60
30 Shohei Ohtani .30 .75
31 Mookie Betts .40 1.00
32 Austin Riley RC .75 2.00
33 Francisco Lindor .25 .60
34 Eloy Jimenez RC .60 1.50
35 Jose Ramirez .20 .50
36 Kris Bryant .30 .75
37 Mike Trout 1.25 3.00
38 David Fletcher RC .50 1.25
39 Brandon Lowe RC .25 .60
40 Jake Bauers RC .25 .60
41 Touki Toussaint RC .20 .50
42 Rowdy Tellez RC .25 .60
43 Justus Sheffield RC .25 .60
44 Jason Martin RC .20 .50
45 Bryan Reynolds RC .50 1.25
46 Michael Chavis RC .25 .60
47 Cole Tucker RC .25 .60
48 Carter Kieboom RC .25 .60
49 Vladimir Guerrero Jr. RC 2.50 6.00
50 Nathaniel Lowe RC .20 .50

2020 Panini Chronicles

RANDOM INSERTS IN PACKS
1 Mike Trout 2.00 5.00
2 Vladimir Guerrero Jr. .50 1.25
3 Ronald Acuna Jr. 1.50 4.00
4 Juan Soto .75 2.00
5 Pete Alonso .60 1.50
6 Gleyber Torres .50 1.25
7 Aaron Judge .60 1.50
8 Shohei Ohtani .30 .75
9 Anthony Rizzo .40 1.00
10 Fernando Tatis Jr. 2.00 5.00
11 Cody Bellinger .50 1.25
12 Christian Yelich .30 .75
13 Max Scherzer .25 .60
14 Jacob deGrom .50 1.25
15 Gerrit Cole .40 1.00
16 Nolan Arenado .30 .75
17 Mookie Betts .50 1.25
18 Francisco Lindor .25 .60
19 Alex Bregman .25 .60
20 Rafael Devers .30 .75
21 Xander Bogaerts .25 .60
22 Jonathan Villar .15 .40
23 Blake Snell .20 .50
24 Keston Hiura .30 .75
25 Trea Turner .20 .50
26 Starling Marte .20 .50
27 Kris Bryant .30 .75
28 Paul Goldschmidt .25 .60
29 Trevor Bauer .25 .60
30 Bryce Harper .40 1.00
31 Bo Bichette RC 3.00 8.00
32 Yordan Alvarez RC 1.25 3.00
33 Nico Hoerner RC 1.00 2.50
34 Aristides Aquino RC .50 1.25
35 Gavin Lux RC 1.50 4.00
36 Dustin May RC 1.00 2.50
37 Dylan Cease RC .50 1.25
38 Luis Robert RC 4.00 10.00
39 Zac Gallen RC .60 1.50
40 Brendan McKay RC .40 1.00
41 Yoshitomo Tsutsugo RC .30 .75
42 Shogo Akiyama RC .40 1.00
43 A.J. Puk RC .50 1.25
44 Jesus Luzardo RC .50 1.25
45 Shun Yamaguchi RC .30 .75

2020 Panini Chronicles Signatures

RANDOM INSERTS IN PACKS
PRINT RUNS B/WN 5-99 COPIES PER
NO PRICING QTY 15 OR LESS
EXCHANGE DEADLINE 3/18/2022
6 Gleyber Torres EXCH/25 20.00 50.00
18 Francisco Lindor/49 6.00 15.00
25 Trea Turner/25 6.00 15.00
31 Bo Bichette/30 30.00 80.00
32 Yordan Alvarez/50 20.00 50.00
33 Nico Hoerner/99 12.00 30.00
34 Aristides Aquino/60 6.00 15.00
37 Dylan Cease/90 6.00 15.00
38 Luis Robert EXCH/99 75.00 200.00
39 Zac Gallen/49 6.00 15.00
41 Yoshitomo Tsutsugo/99 8.00 20.00
42 Shogo Akiyama/49 6.00 15.00
43 A.J. Puk/99 6.00 15.00
45 Shun Yamaguchi/99 4.00 10.00

2015 Panini Contenders

COMPLETE SET (99) 15.00 40.00
PLATE PRINT RUN 1 SET PER COLOR
NO PLATE PRICING DUE TO SCARCITY
1 A.J. Minter .25 .60
2 Corey Seager .75 2.00
3 Aaron Judge 3.00 8.00
4 Aaron Nola .30 .75
5 Alex Bregman .75 2.00
6 Alex Young .20 .50
7 Trea Turner .60 1.50
8 Andrew Benintendi 1.00 2.50
9 Richie Martin .20 .50
10 Andrew Stevenson .20 .50
11 Anthony Hermelyn .20 .50
12 Mikey White .25 .60
13 Austin Rei .25 .60
14 Barry Larkin .25 .60
15 Blake Trahan .20 .50
16 Bo Jackson .30 .75
17 Bob Gibson .25 .60
18 Braden Bishop .20 .50
19 Braden Shipley .20 .50
20 Brandon Koch .20 .50
21 Brandon Lowe .30 .75
22 Breckin Williams .20 .50
23 Brett Lilek .20 .50
24 Carson Fulmer .20 .50
25 Casey Hughston .20 .50
26 Chris Shaw .40 1.00
27 J.P. Crawford .20 .50
28 Cody Poteet .20 .50
29 Craig Biggio .25 .60
30 D.J. Peterson .20 .50
31 Dansby Swanson 1.25 3.00
32 Dave Winfield .25 .60
33 David Thompson .25 .60
34 Matt Olson .25 .60
35 Zack Erwin .20 .50
36 Dillon Tate .25 .60
37 Andrew Suarez .25 .60
38 Donnie Dewees .30 .75
39 Drew Smith .20 .50
40 Erick Fedde .20 .50
41 Frank Howard .20 .50
42 Frank Thomas .30 .75
43 Fred Lynn .20 .50
44 Garrett Cleavinger .25 .60
45 Grayson Long .20 .50
46 Harrison Bader .30 .75
47 Hunter Dozier .20 .50
48 Hunter Renfroe .30 .75
49 Ian Happ .75 2.00
50 Jake Lemoine .20 .50
51 Matt Chapman .30 .75
52 Jeff Degano .25 .60
53 Jeff Hendrix .25 .60
54 Jeff Hoffman .25 .60
55 John Elway .50 1.25
56 Jon Harris .25 .60
57 Josh Graham .25 .60
58 Tyler Beede .25 .60
59 Kevin Kramer .25 .60
60 Kevin Newman .30 .75
61 Mike Schmidt .50 1.25
62 Ryan Burr .20 .50
63 Dansby Swanson 1.25 3.00
64 Alex Bregman .75 2.00
65 Luke Weaver .30 .75
66 Dillon Tate .25 .60
67 Mark Mathias .25 .60
68 Mark McGwire .50 1.25
69 Matt Chapman .30 .75
70 Michael Conforto .25 .60
71 Michael Matuella .25 .60
72 Mikey White .25 .60
73 Nathan Kirby .25 .60
74 Ozzie Smith .40 1.00
75 Paul Molitor .30 .75
76 Peter O'Brien .30 .75
77 Phil Bickford .20 .50
78 Philip Pfeifer .20 .50
79 Randy Johnson .30 .75
80 Reggie Jackson .25 .60
81 Rhett Wiseman .20 .50
82 Riley Ferrell .20 .50
83 Robert Refsnyder .25 .60
84 Roger Clemens .40 1.00
85 Scott Kingery .30 .75
86 Skye Bolt .25 .60
87 Stephen Piscotty .25 .60
88 Tate Matheny .20 .50
89 Taylor Ward .30 .75
90 Thomas Eshelman .20 .50
91 Tony Gwynn .30 .75
92 Trea Turner .60 1.50
93 Tyler Alexander .20 .50
94 Tyler Beede .25 .60
95 Tyler Jay .20 .50
96 Tyler Krieger .20 .50
97 Tyler Naquin .25 .60
98 Walker Buehler 1.25 3.00
99 Will Clark .25 .60

2015 Panini Contenders Cracked Ice

*CRACKED ICE: 6X TO 15X BASIC
RANDOM INSERTS IN PACKS
STATED PRINT RUN 23 SER.#'d SETS

2015 Panini Contenders Draft

*DRAFT: 3X TO 8X BASIC
RANDOM INSERTS IN PACKS
STATED PRINT RUN 99 SER.#'d SETS

2015 Panini Contenders Alumni Ink

OVERALL AUTO ODDS 1:4 HOBBY
2 Aaron Judge 25.00 60.00
4 Braden Shipley 3.00 8.00
5 D.J. Peterson 3.00 8.00
7 Erick Fedde 3.00 8.00
9 Hunter Renfroe 5.00 12.00
10 Kyle Schwarber 30.00 80.00
13 Peter O'Brien 5.00 12.00
16 Trea Turner 10.00 25.00
17 Tyler Naquin 4.00 10.00
24 Barry Larkin 12.00 30.00
25 Mike Schmidt 20.00 100.00

2015 Panini Contenders Class Reunion

COMPLETE SET (25) 6.00 15.00
APPX.ODDS 1:4 HOBBY
1 Dansby Swanson 2.00 5.00
2 Alex Bregman 1.25 3.00
3 Dillon Tate .40 1.00
4 Tyler Jay .30 .75
5 Andrew Benintendi 1.50 4.00
6 Carson Fulmer .30 .75
7 Ian Happ 1.25 3.00
8 Breckin Williams .30 .75
9 Phil Bickford .30 .75
10 Kevin Newman .50 1.25
11 Richie Martin .30 .75
12 Walker Buehler 2.00 5.00
13 Cody Poteet .30 .75
14 Taylor Ward .50 1.25
15 Jon Harris .40 1.00
16 Chris Shaw .60 1.50
17 Garrett Cleavinger .40 1.00
18 Ryan Burr .30 .75
19 Nathan Kirby .40 1.00
20 Alex Young .30 .75
21 Thomas Eshelman .30 .75
22 Donnie Dewees .50 1.25
23 Scott Kingery .50 1.25
24 Brett Lilek .30 .75
25 Jeff Degano .40 1.00

2015 Panini Contenders College Ticket Autographs

OVERALL AUTO ODDS 1:4 HOBBY
*BLUE FOIL: .4X TO 1X BASIC
*RED FOIL: .4X TO 1X BASIC
*DRAFT/99: .5X TO 1.2X BASIC
*CRACKED/23: 1.2X TO 3X BASIC
PLATE PRINT RUN 1 SET PER COLOR
BLACK-CYAN-MAGENTA-YELLOW ISSUED
NO PLATE PRICING DUE TO SCARCITY
1 Swanson Thrwng 12.00 30.00
2 Tate Arm back 4.00 10.00
3 Bregman Prple jsy 15.00 40.00
4 Fulmer Frnt leg up 10.00 25.00
5 Benintendi Wht jsy 15.00 40.00
6 W.Buehler Wht jrsy 6.00 15.00
7 Tyler Jay 3.00 8.00
Throwing
8 Drew Smith 3.00 8.00
9 Kaprielian Fcng rght 6.00 15.00
10 Michael Matuella 4.00 10.00
Black jersey
11 Happ Fldng 6.00 15.00
12 Jon Harris 4.00 10.00
Arm back
13 Nathan Kirby 4.00 10.00
Looking straight
14 Phil Bickford 3.00 8.00
Arm down
15 Kevin Newman 5.00 12.00
Batting
16 DJ Stewart 4.00 10.00
Fielding
17 Richie Martin 3.00 8.00
Batting
18 Alex Young 3.00 8.00
Pitching
19 Cody Ponce 3.00 8.00
Front leg down
20 Kingery Fldng 5.00 12.00
22 Thomas Eshelman 3.00 8.00
Facing forward
23 Riley Ferrell 3.00 8.00
Arm back
24 Blake Trahan 3.00 8.00
Ball visible
25 Donnie Dewees 3.00 8.00
Swinging
26 Mikey White 4.00 10.00
Fielding
27 Rei Gld jsy 4.00 10.00
28 Brett Lilek 3.00 8.00
Black jersey
29 Taylor Ward 5.00 12.00
Catching
30 Andrew Stevenson 3.00 8.00
Purple jersey
31 Andrew Suarez 4.00 10.00
White jersey
32 Kevin Kramer 4.00 10.00
Sunglasses
33 Braden Bishop 3.00 8.00
34 Jeff Degano 3.00 8.00
Facing left
35 Christin Stewart 4.00 10.00
Pinstripe jersey
36 Bader Fcng lft 5.00 12.00
37 Wiseman Fldng 6.00 15.00
38 Brandon Koch 3.00 8.00
Arm down
39 Brandon Lowe 8.00 20.00
Arm up
40 David Thompson 3.00 8.00
Fielding
41 Mark Mathias 4.00 10.00
Fielding
42 Casey Hughston 3.00 8.00
Batting
43 Skye Bolt 4.00 10.00
Batting
44 Tate Matheny 3.00 8.00
Maroon jersey
45 Tyler Alexander 3.00 8.00
Facing forward
46 Tyler Krieger 3.00 8.00
Orange jersey
47 Philip Pfeifer 3.00 8.00
Arm back
50 A.J. Minter 4.00 10.00
White jersey

2015 Panini Contenders College Ticket Autographs Photo Variation

OVERALL AUTO ODDS 1:4 HOBBY
*BLUE FOIL: .4X TO 1X BASIC
*RED FOIL: .4X TO 1X BASIC
*DRAFT/99: .5X TO 1.2X BASIC
*CRACKED/23: 1.2X TO 3X BASIC
PLATE PRINT RUN 1 SET PER COLOR
BLACK-CYAN-MAGENTA-YELLOW ISSUED
NO PLATE PRICING DUE TO SCARCITY
1 Swanson Undr-hnd 30.00 80.00
2 Tate Arm DOWN 4.00 10.00
3 Bregman Yllw jsy 12.00 30.00
4 Fulmer Frnt leg down 10.00 25.00
5 Benintendi Red jsy 25.00 60.00
6 Walker Buehler 20.00 50.00
7 Tyler Jay 3.00 8.00
Arm back
8 Drew Smith 3.00 8.00
9 Kaprielian Fcng left 6.00 15.00
10 Michael Matuella 4.00 10.00
Blue jersey
11 Happ Bttng 12.00 30.00
12 Jon Harris 4.00 10.00
Arm up

athan Kirby 4.00 10.00
oking down
hil Bickford 3.00 8.00
ands together
evin Newman 5.00 12.00
rowing
J Stewart 4.00 10.00
nning
ichie Martin 3.00 8.00
elding
lex Young 3.00 8.00
and on cap
Cody Ponce 3.00 8.00
ont leg up
Kingery Running 5.00 12.00
Thomas Eshelman 3.00 8.00
acing right
Riley Ferrell 3.00 8.00
m down
Blake Trahan 3.00 8.00
ball
Donnie Dewees 5.00 12.00
Bat
Mikey White 4.00 10.00
rowing
Rei Blue jsy 4.00 10.00
Brett Lilek 3.00 8.00
ed jersey
Taylor Ward 5.00 12.00
winging
Andrew Stevenson 3.00 8.00
hite jersey
Andrew Suarez 4.00 10.00
ack jersey
Kevin Kramer 4.00 10.00
rowing
Braden Bishop 3.00 8.00
Jeff Degano 4.00 10.00
acing forward
Christin Stewart 4.00 10.00
range jersey
Bader Fcng right 5.00 12.00
Wiseman Bttng 6.00 15.00
Brandon Koch 3.00 8.00
m up
Brandon Lowe 8.00 20.00
m back
David Thompson 4.00 10.00
atting
Mark Mathias 4.00 10.00
atting
Casey Hughston 3.00 8.00
elding
Skye Bolt 4.00 10.00
elding
Tate Matheny 3.00 8.00
White jersey
Tyler Alexander 3.00 8.00
acing right
Tyler Krieger 3.00 8.00
lue jersey
Philip Pfeifer 3.00 8.00
eg up
A.J. Minter 4.00 10.00
aroon jersey

2015 Panini Contenders Collegiate Connections

MPLETE SET (25) 6.00 15.00
PX.ODDS 1:4 HOBBY
afael Palmeiro .40 1.00
ill Clark
o Jackson .50 1.25
rank Thomas
.Fulmer/D.Swanson 2.00 5.00
ave Winfield .50 1.25
aul Molitor
ulmer/Buehler 2.00 5.00
.Swanson/R.Wiseman 2.00 5.00
.Bregman/A.Stevenson 1.25 3.00
ody Poteet .40 1.00
evin Kramer
on Harris .40 1.00
ate Matheny
Carson Fulmer .40 1.00
yler Beede
Phil Bickford .30 .75
homas Eshelman
Newman/Kingery .50 1.25
Winston/Weaver .50 1.25
.Bader/R.Martin .50 1.25
Alex Young .30 .75
iley Ferrell
Riley Ferrell .30 .75
yler Alexander
Alex Young .30 .75
yler Alexander
Casey Hughston .40 1.00
ikey White
A.Judge/T.Ward 5.00 12.00
Andrew Suarez .40 1.00
avid Thompson
R.Wilson/T.Turner 1.00 2.50
Tyler Krieger .30 .75
ack Erwin
Brandon Koch .30 .75
rew Smith
Austin Rei .40 1.00
raden Bishop
Philip Pfeifer .30 .75
hett Wiseman

2015 Panini Contenders Collegiate Connections Signatures

OVERALL AUTO ODDS 1:4 HOBBY
1 Palmeiro/Clark 30.00 80.00
7 Bregman/Stevenson 25.00 60.00
9 Harris/Matheny 5.00 12.00
15 Young/Ferrell 4.00 10.00
19 Judge/Ward 15.00 40.00
20 Suarez/Thompson 8.00 20.00
21 Wilson/Turner 30.00 80.00
24 Rei/Bishop 15.00 40.00

2015 Panini Contenders Draft Ticket Autographs

OVERALL AUTO ODDS 1:4 HOBBY
*BLUE FOIL: .4X TO 1X BASIC
*RED FOIL: .4X TO 1X BASIC
*DRAFT/99: .5X TO 1.2X BASIC
*CRACKED/23: 1.2X TO 3X BASIC
PLATE PRINT RUN 1 SET PER COLOR
BLACK-CYAN-MAGENTA-YELLOW ISSUED
NO PLATE PRICING DUE TO SCARCITY
1 Brendan Rodgers 6.00 15.00
2 Daz Cameron 4.00 10.00
3 Garrett Whitley 4.00 10.00
4 Kyle Tucker 10.00 25.00
5 Trenton Clark 2.50 6.00
6 Nick Plummer 3.00 8.00
7 Tyler Stephenson 3.00 8.00
8 Mike Nikorak 2.50 6.00
10 Kolby Allard 2.50 6.00
11 Cornelius Randolph 2.50 6.00
12 Ryan Mountcastle 6.00 15.00
14 Chris Betts 3.00 8.00
15 Beau Burrows 3.00 8.00
16 Dakota Chalmers 2.50 6.00
17 Jalen Miller 2.50 6.00
18 Jacob Nix 2.50 6.00
19 Austin Riley 25.00 60.00
20 Demi Orimoloye 3.00 8.00
21 Eric Jenkins 2.50 6.00
22 Mitchell Hansen 2.50 6.00
23 Austin Smith 2.50 6.00
24 Peter Lambert 2.50 6.00
25 Jake Woodford 2.50 6.00
26 Juan Hillman 2.50 6.00
27 Triston McKenzie 2.50 6.00
28 Lucas Herbert 2.50 6.00
30 Mac Marshall 2.50 6.00
31 Nick Neidert 2.50 6.00
32 Nolan Watson 2.50 6.00
33 Ke'Bryan Hayes 3.00 8.00
34 Desmond Lindsay 4.00 10.00
35 Bryce Denton 4.00 10.00
36 Josh Naylor 3.00 8.00
37 Thomas Szapucki 2.50 6.00
38 Blake Perkins 2.50 6.00
39 Javier Medina 2.50 6.00
40 Jahmai Jones 3.00 8.00
41 Travis Blankenhorn 3.00 8.00
45 Max Wotell 2.50 6.00
46 Jordan Hicks 6.00 15.00
47 Nash Walters 2.50 6.00
48 Tyler Nevin 4.00 10.00
49 Drew Finley 2.50 6.00
50 Mike Soroka 8.00 20.00

2015 Panini Contenders Game Day Tickets

COMPLETE SET (24) 6.00 15.00
OVERALL AUTO ODDS 1:4 HOBBY
1 Dansby Swanson 2.00 5.00
2 Alex Bregman 1.25 3.00
3 Dillon Tate .40 1.00
4 Tyler Jay .30 .75
5 Andrew Benintendi 1.50 4.00
6 Carson Fulmer .30 .75
7 Ian Happ 1.25 3.00
8 Breckin Williams .30 .75
9 Phil Bickford .30 .75
10 Kevin Newman .50 1.25
11 Richie Martin .30 .75
12 Walker Buehler 2.00 5.00
13 Cody Poteet .30 .75
14 Taylor Ward .50 1.25
15 Jon Harris .40 1.00
16 Chris Shaw .60 1.50
17 Jake Lemoine .30 .75
18 Drew Smith .30 .75
19 Nathan Kirby .40 1.00
20 Alex Young .30 .75
21 Thomas Eshelman .30 .75
22 Donnie Dewees .50 1.25
23 Scott Kingery .50 1.25
24 Brett Lilek .30 .75
25 Jeff Degano .30 .75

2015 Panini Contenders International Ticket Autographs

OVERALL AUTO ODDS 1:4 HOBBY
*BLUE FOIL: .4X TO 1X BASIC
*RED FOIL: .4X TO 1X BASIC
*CRACKED/23: 1.2X TO 3X BASIC
PLATE PRINT RUN 1 SET PER COLOR
BLACK-CYAN-MAGENTA-YELLOW ISSUED
NO PLATE PRICING DUE TO SCARCITY
2 Christian Pache 15.00 40.00
4 Yadier Alvarez 5.00 12.00
8 Lucius Fox 5.00 12.00
9 Jeison Guzman 4.00 10.00
10 Jonathan Arauz 3.00 8.00
12 Vladimir Guerrero Jr. 100.00 250.00
13 Orlando Arcia 4.00 10.00
15 Yoan Moncada 20.00 50.00
16 Aristides Aquino 40.00 100.00
20 Franklin Barreto 4.00 10.00
21 Gilbert Lara 4.00 10.00
23 Jairo Labourt 3.00 8.00
24 Jarlin Garcia 4.00 10.00
25 Wei-Chieh Huang 4.00 10.00
26 Jorge Mateo 12.00 30.00
27 Julian Leon 3.00 8.00
29 Yoan Lopez 3.00 8.00
30 Victor Robles 12.00 30.00

2015 Panini Contenders Old School Colors

COMPLETE SET (47) 8.00 20.00
RANDOM INSERTS IN PACKS
1 Roger Clemens .50 1.25
2 Reggie Jackson .30 .75
3 Randy Johnson .40 1.00
4 Craig Biggio .30 .75
5 Frank Thomas .40 1.00
6 Will Clark .30 .75
7 Barry Larkin .30 .75
8 Mike Schmidt .60 1.50
9 Dave Winfield .30 .75
10 Bo Jackson .40 1.00
11 Rafael Palmeiro .30 .75
12 Paul Molitor .40 1.00
13 Richie Martin .25 .60
14 Tony Gwynn .40 1.00
15 Frank Howard .25 .60
16 John Elway .75 2.00
17 Fred Lynn .25 .60
18 A.J. Reed .30 .75
19 Aaron Nola .40 1.00
20 Kevin Newman .40 1.00
21 Peter O'Brien .40 1.00
22 Stephen Piscotty .30 .75
23 Aaron Judge 4.00 10.00
24 Braden Shipley .25 .60
25 D.J. Peterson .25 .60
26 Erick Fedde .25 .60
27 Hunter Dozier .25 .60
28 Hunter Renfroe .40 1.00
29 Kyle Schwarber 1.00 2.50
30 Luke Weaver .40 1.00
31 Michael Conforto .30 .75
32 Robert Refsnyder .30 .75
33 Trea Turner .75 2.00
34 Tyler Naquin .30 .75
35 Alex Bregman 1.00 2.50
36 Andrew Benintendi 1.25 3.00
37 Carson Fulmer .25 .60
38 Dansby Swanson 1.50 4.00
39 Breckin Williams .25 .60
40 Dillon Tate .25 .60
41 Ian Happ 1.00 2.50
42 Andrew Suarez .30 .75
43 Mark McGwire .60 1.50
44 Ozzie Smith .50 1.25
45 Bob Gibson .30 .75
46 Tyler Jay .25 .60
47 Phil Bickford .25 .60

2015 Panini Contenders Old School Colors Signatures

OVERALL AUTO ODDS 1:4 HOBBY
2 Reggie Jackson 10.00 25.00
3 Randy Johnson 25.00 60.00
7 Barry Larkin 10.00 25.00
11 Rafael Palmeiro 10.00 25.00
14 Tony Gwynn 50.00 120.00
18 John Elway 40.00 100.00

2015 Panini Contenders Passports

COMPLETE SET (25) 6.00 15.00
APPX.ODDS 1:4 HOBBY
1 Yoan Moncada 1.50 4.00
2 Aristides Aquino 6.00 15.00
3 Domingo Leyba .30 .75
4 Edmundo Sosa .40 1.00
5 Francisco Mejia .75 2.00
6 Franklin Barreto .40 1.00
7 Gilbert Lara .40 1.00
8 Gleyber Torres 5.00 12.00
9 Yoan Lopez .30 .75
10 Jorge Mateo 1.00 2.50
11 Julian Leon .30 .75
12 Luis Encarnacion .30 .75
13 Magneuris Sierra .50 1.25
14 Manuel Margot .30 .75
15 Marcos Molina .30 .75
16 Ozhaino Albies 3.00 8.00
17 Rafael Devers 2.00 5.00
18 Reynaldo Lopez .40 1.00
19 Richard Urena .50 1.25
20 Sergio Alcantara .30 .75
21 Teoscar Hernandez 1.00 2.50
22 Willy Adames .50 1.25
23 Yairo Munoz .40 1.00
24 Julio Urias 1.00 2.50
25 Luis Severino .40 1.00

2015 Panini Contenders Prospect Ticket Autographs

OVERALL AUTO ODDS 1:4 HOBBY
*BLUE FOIL: .4X TO 1X BASIC
*RED FOIL: .4X TO 1X BASIC
*CRACKED/23: 1.2X TO 3X BASIC
PLATE PRINT RUN 1 SET PER COLOR
BLACK-CYAN-MAGENTA-YELLOW ISSUED
NO PLATE PRICING DUE TO SCARCITY
2 Adam Walker 2.50 6.00
3 Brett Phillips 2.50 6.00
4 Correlle Prime 2.50 6.00
5 D.J. Peterson 2.50 6.00
6 Kyle Schwarber 6.00 15.00
8 Nick Kingham 2.50 6.00
9 Trea Turner 10.00 25.00
10 Tyrone Taylor 2.50 6.00
12 Andrew Faulkner 2.50 6.00
13 Jace Fry 2.50 6.00
14 Yoan Moncada 10.00 25.00
15 Aristides Aquino 40.00 100.00
17 Edmundo Sosa 3.00 8.00
18 Francisco Mejia 5.00 12.00
19 Franklin Barreto 6.00 15.00
20 Gilbert Lara 3.00 8.00
21 Gleyber Torres 25.00 60.00
22 Jairo Labourt 2.50 6.00
24 Javier Guerra 10.00 25.00
25 Jorge Mateo 4.00 10.00
28 Magneuris Sierra 6.00 15.00
29 Manuel Margot 2.50 6.00
31 Ozhaino Albies 20.00 50.00
32 Rafael Devers 15.00 40.00
34 Richard Urena 4.00 10.00
37 Willy Adames 4.00 10.00
39 Julio Urias 8.00 20.00
40 Luis Severino 4.00 10.00
41 Brent Honeywell 4.00 10.00
42 Mauricio Dubon 3.00 8.00
43 Micker Adolfo 3.00 8.00
45 Antonio Senzatela 3.00 8.00
46 Jake Lemoine 2.50 6.00
47 Corey Seager 15.00 40.00
48 Garrett Cleavinger 3.00 8.00
49 Grayson Long 2.50 6.00

2015 Panini Contenders School Colors

COMPLETE SET (52) 8.00 20.00
RANDOM INSERTS IN PACKS
1 Dansby Swanson 1.50 4.00
2 Alex Bregman 1.00 2.50
3 Dillon Tate .30 .75
4 Tyler Jay .25 .60
5 Andrew Benintendi 1.25 3.00
6 Carson Fulmer .25 .60
7 Ian Happ 1.00 2.50
8 Breckin Williams .25 .60
9 Phil Bickford .25 .60
10 Kevin Newman .40 1.00
11 Richie Martin .25 .60
12 Walker Buehler 1.50 4.00
13 Cody Poteet .25 .60
14 Taylor Ward .40 1.00
15 Jon Harris .30 .75
16 Chris Shaw .50 1.25
17 Jake Lemoine .25 .60
18 Ryan Burr .25 .60
19 Nathan Kirby .30 .75
20 Alex Young .25 .60
21 Thomas Eshelman .25 .60
22 Donnie Dewees .40 1.00
23 Scott Kingery .40 1.00
24 Brett Lilek .25 .60
25 Jeff Degano .30 .75
26 Andrew Stevenson .25 .60
27 Andrew Suarez .30 .75
28 Kevin Kramer .30 .75
29 Mikey White .30 .75
30 Tyler Alexander .25 .60
31 Anthony Hermelyn .25 .60
32 Grayson Long .25 .60
33 Garrett Cleavinger .30 .75
34 A.J. Minter .30 .75
35 Michael Matuella .30 .75
36 Riley Ferrell .25 .60
37 Austin Rei .30 .75
38 Blake Trahan .30 .75
39 Brandon Lowe .40 1.00
40 Braden Bishop .25 .60
41 Casey Hughston .25 .60
42 Drew Smith .25 .60
43 Harrison Bader .40 1.00
44 Philip Pfeifer .25 .60
45 Rhett Wiseman .25 .60
46 Tate Matheny .25 .60
47 Zack Erwin .25 .60
48 Brandon Koch .25 .60
49 David Thompson .30 .75
50 Tyler Krieger .25 .60
51 Skye Bolt .30 .75
52 A.J. Reed .30 .75

2015 Panini Contenders School Colors Signatures

OVERALL AUTO ODDS 1:4 HOBBY
1 Aaron Judge 75.00 200.00
4 Erick Fedde 8.00 20.00
5 Hunter Dozier 3.00 8.00
7 Kyle Schwarber 10.00 25.00
8 Luke Weaver 5.00 12.00
9 Michael Conforto 20.00 50.00
10 Robert Refsnyder 4.00 10.00
12 Tyler Naquin 4.00 10.00
13 Dansby Swanson 10.00 25.00
14 Alex Bregman 10.00 25.00
15 Dillon Tate 4.00 10.00
17 Andrew Benintendi 10.00 25.00
18 Carson Fulmer 3.00 8.00
19 Ian Happ 15.00 40.00
20 James Kaprielian 5.00 12.00
21 Phil Bickford 3.00 8.00
22 Kevin Newman 5.00 12.00
23 Richie Martin 3.00 8.00
24 Walker Buehler 6.00 15.00
25 DJ Stewart 4.00 10.00

2015 Panini Contenders USA Baseball Ticket Autographs

*BLUE FOIL: .4X TO 1X BASIC
*RED FOIL: .4X TO 1X BASIC
*DRAFT/99: .5X TO 1.2X BASIC
*CRACKED/23: 1.2X TO 3X BASIC
PLATE PRINT RUN 1 SET PER COLOR
BLACK-CYAN-MAGENTA-YELLOW ISSUED
NO PLATE PRICING DUE TO SCARCITY
1 Corey Seager 20.00 50.00
2 D.J. Peterson 2.50 6.00
3 Kyle Schwarber 10.00 25.00
4 Matt Olson 6.00 15.00
5 Michael Conforto 25.00 60.00
7 Alex Bregman 12.00 30.00
9 Kevin Kramer 3.00 8.00
13 Carson Fulmer 2.50 6.00
14 Riley Ferrell 2.50 6.00
16 Christin Stewart 3.00 8.00
17 Matt Chapman 4.00 10.00
18 Dansby Swanson 12.00 30.00
19 Daz Cameron 4.00 10.00
21 DJ Stewart 4.00 10.00
24 James Kaprielian 4.00 10.00
25 Thomas Eshelman 3.00 8.00
26 Taylor Ward 4.00 10.00
27 Ke'Bryan Hayes 5.00 12.00
29 Kolby Allard 2.50 6.00
31 Trenton Clark 3.00 8.00
32 Kyle Tucker 15.00 40.00
33 Lucas Herbert 3.00 8.00
34 Tyler Jay 3.00 8.00
35 Tyler Beede 3.00 8.00
36 Mark Mathias 4.00 10.00
37 Mikey White 4.00 10.00
42 A.J. Minter 3.00 8.00
45 Buddy Reed 10.00 25.00
46 Nick Banks 8.00 20.00
47 Garrett Hampson 5.00 12.00
48 Corey Ray 10.00 25.00
50 Ryan Howard 4.00 10.00
51 Anfernee Grier 3.00 8.00
52 Daulton Jefferies 4.00 10.00
54 Stephen Nogosek 3.00 8.00
55 Mike Shawaryn 3.00 8.00
56 Matt Thaiss 5.00 12.00
57 JJ Schwarz 15.00 40.00
58 Robert Tyler 3.00 8.00
59 Anthony Kay 3.00 8.00
61 Chris Okey 3.00 8.00
63 A.J. Puk 5.00 12.00
64 Tanner Houck 12.00 30.00
65 Zach Jackson 4.00 10.00
66 KJ Harrison 5.00 12.00
67 Logan Shore 10.00 25.00
68 Brendan McKay 10.00 25.00

2017 Panini Contenders College Tickets

INSERTED IN '17 EEE PACKS
EXCHANGE DEADLINE 6/6/2019
*CRACKED ICE/24: .75X TO 2X BASIC
1 Jake Burger 8.00 20.00
2 Evan White 4.00 10.00
3 Alex Faedo 8.00 20.00
4 David Peterson 5.00 12.00
5 Logan Warmoth 4.00 10.00
6 Tanner Houck 5.00 12.00
7 Brian Miller 3.00 8.00
8 Stuart Fairchild 3.00 8.00
9 Gavin Sheets 4.00 10.00
10 Joseph Dunand 5.00 12.00
12 Wil Crowe 4.00 10.00
13 KJ Harrison 5.00 12.00
14 Trevor Stephan 4.00 10.00
15 A.J. Minter 3.00 8.00
16 Casey Gillaspie 2.50 6.00
17 Harrison Bader 4.00 10.00
18 Zack Collins 3.00 8.00
19 Greg Deichmann 5.00 12.00
20 Drew Ellis 4.00 10.00
22 Morgan Cooper 3.00 8.00
23 Jake Thompson 2.50 6.00
24 Tommy Doyle
25 Ernie Clement 3.00 8.00
26 J.J. Matijevic 3.00 8.00
27 Connor Seabold 2.50 6.00
28 Will Gaddis 2.50 6.00
29 Dylan Busby 2.50 6.00
30 Brendan McKay 10.00 25.00
31 Joey Morgan 3.00 8.00
32 Quinn Brodey 2.50 6.00
33 Cody Sedlock 2.50 6.00
34 Kyle Wright 8.00 20.00

2017 Panini Contenders Rookie Ticket

INSERTED IN '17 CHRONICLES PACKS
EXCHANGE DEADLINE 5/22/2019
*CHAMP/35-49: .6X TO 1.5X BASIC
*CHAMP/25: .75X TO 2X BASIC
*CRACKED ICE/24: .75X TO 2X BASIC
*PLAYOFF/99: .5X TO 1.2X BASIC
*PLAYOFF/49: .6X TO 1.5X BASIC
*PLAYOFF/25: .75X TO 2X BASIC
1 Aaron Judge 50.00 120.00
2 Cody Bellinger
3 Yoan Moncada
4 Andrew Benintendi 15.00 40.00
5 Reynaldo Lopez 2.50 6.00
6 Dansby Swanson
7 Carson Fulmer 2.50 6.00
8 Ryon Healy 3.00 8.00
9 Mitch Haniger 4.00 10.00
10 Antonio Senzatela 2.50 6.00
11 Ian Happ 6.00 15.00
12 Trey Mancini
13 Jordan Montgomery 4.00 10.00
14 Bradley Zimmer 3.00 8.00
15 Hunter Renfroe 3.00 8.00
16 Jorge Bonifacio 2.50 6.00
17 Renato Nunez 5.00 12.00
18 Jacoby Jones 3.00 8.00
19 Alex Bregman 12.00 30.00
20 Josh Bell 6.00 15.00
21 Derek Fisher 3.00 8.00
22 Erik Gonzalez 2.50 6.00
23 Sam Travis 2.50 6.00
24 Franklin Barreto 2.50 6.00
25 Dinelson Lamet 2.50 6.00
26 Andrew Toles
27 Lewis Brinson
28 Orlando Arcia 4.00 10.00
29 Kyle Freeland 3.00 8.00
30 Jose De Leon 2.50 6.00
31 David Dahl 3.00 8.00
32 Yandy Diaz 5.00 12.00
33 Jorge Alfaro 3.00 8.00
34 Magneuris Sierra 4.00 10.00
35 Luke Weaver 5.00 12.00
36 Alex Reyes 5.00 12.00
37 Anthony Alford 2.50 6.00
38 Brock Stewart 2.50 6.00
39 Tyler Glasnow 3.00 8.00
40 Carson Kelly 3.00 8.00
41 Adam Frazier 2.50 6.00
42 Gavin Cecchini 2.50 6.00
43 Guillermo Heredia 2.50 6.00
44 German Marquez 4.00 10.00
45 Francis Martes 2.50 6.00
46 Matt Chapman 8.00 20.00
47 Hunter Dozier 2.50 6.00
48 Josh Hader 2.50 6.00
49 Aaron Judge 50.00 120.00
50 Cody Bellinger

2017 Panini Contenders USA Baseball 15U and Collegiate National Team Tickets

INSERTED IN '17 EEE PACKS
EXCHANGE DEADLINE 6/6/2019
*CRACKED ICE/24: .75X TO 2X BASIC
1 Seth Beer 8.00 20.00
2 Steven Gingery 6.00 15.00
3 Nick Madrigal 5.00 12.00
4 Jake McCarthy 3.00 8.00
5 Nick Meyer 3.00 8.00
6 Casey Mize 15.00 40.00
7 Konnor Pilkington 5.00 12.00
8 Dallas Woolfolk 2.50 6.00
9 Tyler Frank 3.00 8.00
10 Cadyn Grenier 3.00 8.00
11 Gianluca Dalatri 2.50 6.00
12 Braden Shewmake 8.00 20.00
13 Bryce Tucker
14 Andrew Vaughn 12.00 30.00
15 Steele Walker 3.00 8.00
16 Jeremy Eierman 5.00 12.00
17 Patrick Raby 4.00 10.00
18 Grant Koch 2.50 6.00
19 Travis Swaggerty 6.00 15.00
20 Tim Cate 3.00 8.00
21 Nick Sprengel 2.50 6.00
22 Johnny Aiello 3.00 8.00
23 Ryley Gilliam 2.50 6.00
24 Jon Olsen 2.50 6.00
25 Tyler Holton 2.50 6.00
26 Sean Wymer 2.50 6.00
27 Nelson Berkwich 2.50 6.00
28 Alek Boychuk 2.50 6.00
29 Michael Brooks 2.50 6.00
30 Dylan Crews 4.00 10.00
31 Pete Crow-Armstrong 10.00 25.00
32 Davis Diaz 2.50 6.00
33 Michael Flores 4.00 10.00
34 Lucas Gordon 3.00 8.00
35 Mac Guscette 3.00 8.00
36 Petey Halpin 6.00 15.00
37 Joshua Hartle 3.00 8.00
38 Rawley Hector 4.00 10.00
39 Jackson Miller 2.50 6.00
40 Robert Moore 2.50 6.00
41 Roc Riggio 2.50 6.00
42 Alejandro Rosario 5.00 12.00
43 Grant Taylor 4.00 10.00
44 Masyn Winn 2.50 6.00
45 Tanner Witt 3.00 8.00
46 Giuseppe Ferraro 3.00 8.00

2017 Panini Contenders USA Baseball 18U Tickets

INSERTED IN '17 EEE PACKS
EXCHANGE DEADLINE 6/6/2019
*CRACKED ICE/24: .75X TO 2X BASIC
1 Will Banfield 4.00 10.00
2 Raynel Delgado 5.00 12.00
3 Triston Casas 3.00 8.00
4 Carter Young 4.00 10.00
5 Cole Wilcox 3.00 8.00
6 Ryan Weathers 2.50 6.00
7 Brice Turang 8.00 20.00
8 Mason Denaburg 4.00 10.00
9 Brandon Dieter 2.50 6.00
10 Alek Thomas 4.00 10.00
11 JT Ginn 3.00 8.00
12 Nolan Gorman 12.00 30.00
13 Michael Siani 3.00 8.00
14 Kumar Rocker 6.00 15.00
15 Joseph Menefee 3.00 8.00
16 Ethan Hankins 12.00 30.00
17 Anthony Seigler 6.00 15.00
18 Landon Marceaux 2.50 6.00
19 Jarred Kelenic 10.00 25.00
20 Matthew Liberatore 3.00 8.00

2018 Panini Contenders Playoff Ticket Autographs

RANDOM INSERTS IN PACKS
PRINT RUNS B/WN 10-99 COPIES PER
NO PRICING ON QTY 10
3 Lucas Sims/49 4.00 10.00
4 Austin Hays/25 8.00 20.00
6 Gleyber Torres/10
8 Nicky Delmonico/99 3.00 8.00
10 Greg Allen/99 3.00 8.00
15 Kyle Farmer/49 4.00 10.00
16 Brian Anderson/99 4.00 10.00
17 Brandon Woodruff/99 4.00 10.00
21 Tyler Wade/99 4.00 10.00
22 Dustin Fowler/99 3.00 8.00
30 David Bote/99 12.00 30.00
32 Juan Soto/49 75.00 200.00

2018 Panini Contenders Season Ticket Autographs

INSERTED IN '18 CHRONICLES PACKS
1 Max Fried
2 Ozzie Albies 15.00 40.00
3 Lucas Sims 2.50 6.00
4 Austin Hays 4.00 10.00
5 Chance Sisco
6 Gleyber Torres 40.00 100.00
7 Rafael Devers
8 Nicky Delmonico 2.50 6.00
9 Francisco Mejia 3.00 8.00
10 Greg Allen 2.50 6.00
11 Ryan McMahon 10.00 25.00
12 J.D. Davis 3.00 8.00
13 Walker Buehler
14 Alex Verdugo 4.00 10.00
15 Kyle Farmer 2.50 6.00
16 Brian Anderson 3.00 8.00
17 Brandon Woodruff 3.00 8.00
18 Amed Rosario
19 Clint Frazier
20 Miguel Andujar 20.00 50.00
23 J.P. Crawford
24 Nick Williams
25 Rhys Hoskins
26 Jack Flaherty 4.00 10.00
27 Ronald Acuna Jr. 60.00 150.00
28 Willie Calhoun
29 Victor Robles
30 David Bote 10.00 25.00
32 Juan Soto 50.00 120.00

2018 Panini Contenders Season Tickets Autographs Cracked Ice

RANDOM INSERTS IN PACKS
STATED PRINT RUN 24 SER.#'d SETS
1 Max Fried 20.00 50.00
2 Ozzie Albies 40.00 100.00
3 Lucas Sims 5.00 12.00
4 Austin Hays 8.00 20.00
5 Chance Sisco 6.00 15.00
6 Gleyber Torres 75.00 200.00
7 Rafael Devers 12.00 30.00
8 Nicky Delmonico 5.00 12.00
9 Francisco Mejia 6.00 15.00
10 Greg Allen 5.00 12.00
11 Ryan McMahon 15.00 40.00
12 J.D. Davis 6.00 15.00
13 Walker Buehler 25.00 60.00
14 Alex Verdugo 8.00 20.00
15 Kyle Farmer 5.00 12.00
16 Brian Anderson 6.00 15.00
17 Brandon Woodruff 6.00 15.00
18 Amed Rosario 6.00 15.00
19 Clint Frazier 15.00 40.00
20 Miguel Andujar 50.00 210.00
21 Tyler Wade 6.00 15.00
22 Dustin Fowler 5.00 12.00
23 J.P. Crawford 5.00 12.00
24 Nick Williams 6.00 15.00
25 Rhys Hoskins 40.00 100.00
26 Jack Flaherty 8.00 20.00
27 Ronald Acuna Jr. 250.00 600.00
28 Willie Calhoun 6.00 15.00
29 Victor Robles 12.00 30.00
30 David Bote 40.00 100.00
31 Austin Meadows 8.00 20.00
32 Juan Soto 125.00 300.00

2018 Panini Contenders Season Tickets Autographs Red

RANDOM INSERTS IN PACKS
PRINT RUNS B/WN 25-199 COPIES PER
3 Lucas Sims/99 3.00 8.00
4 Austin Hays/49 6.00 15.00
6 Gleyber Torres/25 75.00 200.00
8 Nicky Delmonico/199 3.00 8.00
10 Greg Allen/199 3.00 8.00
15 Kyle Farmer/99 3.00 8.00
16 Brian Anderson/199 4.00 10.00
17 Brandon Woodruff/199 4.00 10.00
21 Tyler Wade/199 4.00 10.00
22 Dustin Fowler/199 3.00 8.00
30 David Bote/199 12.00 30.00
32 Juan Soto/99 60.00 150.00

2019 Panini Contenders Season Ticket Autographs

RANDOM INSERTS IN PACKS
EXCHANGE DEADLINE 2/21/2021
*GOLD/99: .5X TO 1.2X

*GOLD/50: .6X TO 1.5X
*RED/50: .6X TO 1.5X
*RED/25: .75X TO 2X
*CRACKED ICE/23: .75X TO 2X
1 Pete Alonso 40.00 100.00
2 Michael Kopech 5.00 12.00
3 Eloy Jimenez 10.00 25.00
4 Fernando Tatis Jr. EXCH 50.00 120.00
5 Yusei Kikuchi 4.00 10.00
6 Cole Tucker 4.00 10.00
8 Jeff McNeil 6.00 15.00
9 Chris Paddack 5.00 12.00
10 Kyle Tucker 5.00 12.00
13 Corbin Burnes 4.00 10.00
14 Jake Bauers 4.00 10.00
15 Jon Duplantier 2.50 6.00
16 Cal Quantrill 2.50 6.00
17 Vladimir Guerrero Jr. 40.00 100.00
18 Ramon Laureano 6.00 15.00
19 Brandon Lowe 6.00 15.00
20 Carter Kieboom 4.00 10.00
21 Nick Senzel 8.00 20.00
22 Michael Chavis 10.00 25.00
23 Danny Jansen 2.50 6.00
24 Luis Urias 4.00 10.00
25 Nathaniel Lowe 3.00 8.00
26 Keston Hiura 10.00 25.00
27 Austin Riley 8.00 20.00
28 Brendan Rodgers 4.00 10.00
29 Corbin Martin 4.00 10.00
30 Cavan Biggio 12.00 30.00
31 Mitch Keller 3.00 8.00

2020 Panini Contenders

AUTOGRAPHS RANDOM INSERTS IN PACKS
EXCHANGE DEADLINE 4/30/22
1 Anthony Rendon .30 .75
2 Max Muncy .25 .60
3 Francisco Lindor .30 .75
4 Elvis Andrus .25 .60
5 Mike Soroka .30 .75
6 Josh Bell .25 .60
7 Justin Verlander .30 .75
8 Chris Paddack .30 .75
9 Cavan Biggio .40 1.00
10 Eugenio Suarez .25 .60
11 Hyun-Jin Ryu .25 .60
12 Kyle Seager .20 .50
13 Matt Olson .20 .50
14 Yadier Molina .30 .75
15 Xander Bogaerts .30 .75
16 Matt Boyd .20 .50
17 Gleyber Torres .60 1.50
18 Christian Yelich .40 1.00
19 Aaron Nola .30 .75
20 Trey Mancini .30 .75
21 Jonathan Villar .20 .50
22 George Springer .25 .60
23 Mike Clevinger .25 .60
24 Austin Meadows .25 .60
25 Bryce Harper .50 1.25
26 Lucas Giolito .25 .60
27 Joey Votto .30 .75
28 Charlie Morton .30 .75
29 Kyle Hendricks .30 .75
30 J.T. Realmuto .30 .75
31 Ozzie Albies .30 .75
32 Anthony Rizzo .50 1.25
33 John Means .20 .50
34 Shane Bieber .30 .75
35 Shohei Ohtani .40 1.00
36 Rafael Devers .40 1.00
37 Trevor Story .30 .75
38 Josh Hader .20 .50
39 Jose Berrios .25 .60
40 Jacob deGrom .30 .75
41 Jorge Soler .30 .75
42 Josh Donaldson .25 .60
43 Manny Machado .30 .75
44 Mike Moustakas .25 .60
45 Juan Soto 1.00 2.50
46 Freddie Freeman .40 1.00
47 Joey Gallo .30 .75
48 Kevin Newman .25 .60
49 Fernando Tatis Jr. 1.25 3.00
50 Matt Chapman .30 .75
51 Buster Posey .40 1.00
52 Miguel Cabrera .30 .75
53 Nelson Cruz .30 .75
54 Aaron Judge .75 2.00
55 DJ LeMahieu .30 .75
56 Yoan Moncada .30 .75
57 Whit Merrifield .30 .75
58 Alex Bregman .30 .75
59 Kris Bryant .40 1.00
60 Nolan Arenado .40 1.00
61 Jack Flaherty .25 .60
62 Jose Altuve .25 .60
63 Lance Lynn .20 .50
64 Ronald Acuna Jr. 1.25 3.00
65 Eduardo Escobar .20 .50
66 Cody Bellinger .60 1.50
67 Rhys Hoskins .40 1.00
68 Mike Minor .20 .50
69 Bryan Reynolds .25 .60
70 Paul Goldschmidt .30 .75
71 Ketel Marte .25 .60
72 Gerrit Cole .50 1.25
73 Vladimir Guerrero Jr. .60 1.50
74 Marco Gonzales .20 .50
75 Zack Greinke .25 .60
76 Tyler Glasnow .20 .50
77 Brandon Crawford .25 .60
78 J.D. Martinez .30 .75
79 Trea Turner .25 .60
80 Javier Baez .40 1.00
81 Eduardo Rodriguez .20 .50
82 Marcus Semien .20 .50
83 Jorge Polanco .25 .60
84 Tim Anderson .30 .75
85 Luis Castillo .25 .60
86 Mookie Betts .60 1.50
87 David Fletcher .30 .75
88 Clayton Kershaw .60 1.50
89 Pete Alonso .75 2.00
90 Sandy Alcantara .20 .50
91 Charlie Blackmon .30 .75
92 Brian Anderson .20 .50
93 Blake Snell .25 .60
94 Mike Trout 1.50 4.00
95 Albert Pujols .40 1.00
96 Jose Ramirez .25 .60
97 Hunter Dozier .20 .50
98 Eloy Jimenez .60 1.50
99 Max Scherzer .30 .75
100 Jeff McNeil .25 .60
101 A.J. Puk AU RC EXCH 8.00 20.00
102 Zac Gallen AU RC 6.00 15.00
103 Yoshitomo Tsutsugo AU RC 3.00 8.00
104 Aaron Civale AU RC 4.00 10.00
105 Yordan Alvarez AU RC 12.00 30.00
106 Shun Yamaguchi AU RC 3.00 8.00
107 Adbert Alzolay AU RC 3.00 8.00
108 Adrian Morejon AU RC 2.50 6.00
109 Aristides Aquino AU RC 10.00 25.00
110 Bo Bichette AU RC 25.00 60.00
111 Shogo Akiyama AU RC 6.00 15.00
112 Sheldon Neuse AU RC 3.00 8.00
113 Brendan McKay AU RC EXCG 4.00 10.00
114 Brusdar Graterol AU RC 4.00 10.00
115 Dustin May AU RC 10.00 25.00
116 Sean Murphy AU RC 4.00 10.00
117 Nico Hoerner AU RC 10.00 25.00
118 Nick Solak AU RC 4.00 10.00
119 Luis Robert AU RC 40.00 100.00
120 Kyle Lewis AU RC 25.00 60.00
121 Kwang-Hyun Kim AU RC 8.00 20.00
123 Isan Diaz AU RC 4.00 10.00
124 Dylan Cease AU RC EXCH
125 Gavin Lux AU RC 15.00 40.00
126 Brock Burke AU RC 2.50 6.00
127 Randy Arozarena AU RC 20.00 50.00
129 Edwin Rios AU RC 6.00 15.00
130 Jake Rogers AU RC 2.50 6.00
131 Tony Gonsolin AU RC 10.00 25.00
132 Trent Grisham AU RC 10.00 25.00
134 Deivy Grullon AU RC 2.50 6.00
135 Jose Urquidy AU RC 3.00 8.00
136 Andres Munoz AU RC 3.00 8.00
137 Yonathan Daza AU RC 3.00 8.00
138 Bobby Bradley AU RC 3.00 8.00
139 Jonathan Hernandez AU RC 2.50 6.00
140 Matt Thaiss AU RC 3.00 8.00
141 Tres Barrera AU RC 5.00 12.00
142 Abraham Toro AU RC 3.00 8.00
143 Ronald Bolanos AU RC 4.00 10.00
145 T.J. Zeuch AU RC 2.50 6.00
146 Logan Webb AU RC 3.00 8.00
147 Domingo Leyba AU RC 3.00 8.00
148 Rico Garcia AU RC 4.00 10.00
149 Mauricio Dubon AU RC 3.00 8.00
150 Willi Castro AU RC 4.00 10.00
151 Anthony Kay AU RC 2.50 6.00
152 Michel Baez AU RC 2.50 6.00
153 Danny Mendick AU RC 3.00 8.00
154 Sam Hilliard AU RC 4.00 10.00
155 Lewis Thorpe AU RC 2.50 6.00
156 Justin Dunn AU RC 3.00 8.00
157 Logan Allen AU RC 2.50 6.00
158 Michael King AU RC 4.00 10.00
159 Bryan Abreu AU RC 2.50 6.00
160 Travis Demeritte AU RC 3.00 8.00
161 Jake Fraley AU RC 3.00 8.00
162 Jaylin Davis AU RC 4.00 10.00
163 Yu Chang AU RC 4.00 10.00
165 Patrick Sandoval AU RC 4.00 10.00
166 Zack Collins AU RC 3.00 8.00
167 Jordan Yamamoto AU RC 3.00 8.00

2020 Panini Contenders Cracked Ice Ticket

*CRCKD ICE: 3X TO 8X BASIC
*CRCKD ICE AU: .8X TO 2X BASIC
RANDOM INSERTS IN PACKS
STATED PRINT RUN 23 SER.#'d SETS
EXCHANGE DEADLINE 4/30/22
17 Gleyber Torres 8.00 20.00
45 Juan Soto 12.00 30.00
49 Fernando Tatis Jr. 25.00 60.00
86 Mookie Betts 12.00 30.00
88 Clayton Kershaw 10.00 25.00
98 Eloy Jimenez 8.00 20.00
103 Yoshitomo Tsutsugo AU 15.00 40.00
105 Yordan Alvarez AU 50.00 120.00
109 Aristides Aquino AU 20.00 50.00
110 Bo Bichette AU 60.00 150.00
111 Shogo Akiyama AU 15.00 40.00
113 Brendan McKay AU EXCH 12.00 30.00
119 Luis Robert AU 125.00 300.00
120 Kyle Lewis AU 100.00 250.00
121 Kwang-Hyun Kim AU 25.00 60.00
124 Dylan Cease AU EXCH 12.00 30.00
149 Mauricio Dubon AU 10.00 25.00

2020 Panini Contenders Draft Ticket Blue

*DRAFT BLUE: 1.2X TO 3X BASIC
*DRAFT BLUE AU: .5X TO 1.2X BASIC
RANDOM INSERTS IN PACKS
1-100 PRINT RUN 149 SER.#'d SETS
101-167 PRINT RUN B/TW 15-99 COPIES PER
NO PRICING ON QTY 15
EXCHANGE DEADLINE 4/30/22
17 Gleyber Torres 3.00 8.00
86 Mookie Betts 5.00 12.00
88 Clayton Kershaw 4.00 10.00
98 Eloy Jimenez 3.00 8.00
110 Bo Bichette AU 40.00 100.00
119 Luis Robert AU 75.00 200.00
122 Jesus Luzardo AU EXCH

2020 Panini Contenders Draft Ticket Purple

*DRAFT PRPL: 1.5X TO 4X BASIC
RANDOM INSERTS IN PACKS
17 Gleyber Torres 4.00 10.00
86 Mookie Betts 6.00 15.00
88 Clayton Kershaw 5.00 12.00
98 Eloy Jimenez 4.00 10.00

2020 Panini Contenders Draft Ticket Red

*DRAFT RED: 1.5X TO 4X BASIC
*DRAFT RED AU: .5X TO 1.2X BASIC
RANDOM INSERTS IN PACKS
1-100 PRINT RUN 99 SER.#'d SETS
101-167 PRINT RUN B/TW 15-75 COPIES PER
NO PRICING ON QTY 15
EXCHANGE DEADLINE 4/30/22
17 Gleyber Torres 4.00 10.00
86 Mookie Betts 6.00 15.00
88 Clayton Kershaw 5.00 12.00
98 Eloy Jimenez 4.00 10.00
110 Bo Bichette AU 40.00 100.00
119 Luis Robert AU 75.00 200.00

2020 Panini Contenders Variations

*VAR.: .4X TO 1X BASIC
RANDOM INSERTS IN PACKS
EXCHANGE DEADLINE 4/30/22
101 A.J. Puk AU EXCH 8.00 20.00
102 Zac Gallen AU 6.00 15.00
105 Yordan Alvarez AU 12.00 30.00
109 Aristides Aquino AU 10.00 25.00
110 Bo Bichette AU 25.00 60.00
111 Shogo Akiyama AU 6.00 15.00
117 Nico Hoerner AU 10.00 25.00
119 Luis Robert AU 40.00 100.00
120 Kyle Lewis AU 25.00 60.00
121 Kwang-Hyun Kim AU 8.00 20.00
125 Gavin Lux AU 15.00 40.00
126 Trent Grisham AU 10.00 25.00
127 Randy Arozarena AU 20.00 50.00
129 Edwin Rios AU 6.00 15.00
132 Trent Grisham AU 10.00 25.00

2020 Panini Contenders Variations Cracked Ice Ticket

*VAR.CRCKD ICE: .8X TO 2X BASIC
RANDOM INSERTS IN PACKS
STATED PRINT RUN 23 SER.#'d SETS
EXCHANGE DEADLINE 4/30/22
103 Yoshitomo Tsutsugo AU 15.00 40.00
105 Yordan Alvarez AU 50.00 120.00
109 Aristides Aquino AU 20.00 50.00
110 Bo Bichette AU 60.00 150.00
111 Shogo Akiyama AU 15.00 40.00
113 Brendan McKay AU EXCH 12.00 30.00
119 Luis Robert AU 125.00 300.00
120 Kyle Lewis AU 100.00 250.00
121 Kwang-Hyun Kim AU 25.00 60.00
124 Dylan Cease AU EXCH 12.00 30.00
149 Mauricio Dubon AU 10.00 25.00

2020 Panini Contenders Variations Draft Ticket Blue

*VAR.DRAFT BLUE: .5X TO 1.2X BASIC
RANDOM INSERTS IN PACKS
PRINT RUN B/TW 35-99 COPIES PER
EXCHANGE DEADLINE 4/30/22
110 Bo Bichette AU 40.00 100.00
119 Luis Robert AU 75.00 200.00

2020 Panini Contenders Variations Draft Ticket Red

*VAR.DRAFT RED: .5X TO 1.2X BASIC
RANDOM INSERTS IN PACKS
STATED PRINT RUN 75 SER.#'d SETS
EXCHANGE DEADLINE 4/30/22
110 Bo Bichette AU 40.00 100.00
119 Luis Robert AU 75.00 200.00

2020 Panini Contenders Contenders Autographs

RANDOM INSERTS IN PACKS
EXCHANGE DEADLINE 4/30/22
*CRCKD ICE/23: .8X TO 2X BASIC
1 Miguel Amaya 3.00 8.00
2 Brandon Lowe 4.00 10.00
3 Jordan Romano 4.00 10.00
4 Colton Welker 2.50 6.00
5 Brennen Davis 5.00 12.00
6 Cionel Perez 2.50 6.00
7 Matthew Thompson 3.00 8.00
8 Evan White 2.50 6.00
9 Pablo Reyes 2.50 6.00
10 Malfrin Sosa 3.00 8.00
11 Kameron Misner 4.00 10.00
12 Joey Cantillo 2.50 6.00
13 Ryne Nelson 3.00 8.00
14 Seth Johnson 2.50 6.00
15 Drey Jameson 2.50 6.00
16 Nick Neidert 2.50 6.00
17 Sammy Siani 2.50 6.00
18 Adonis Rosa 4.00 10.00
19 Nick Maton 2.50 6.00
20 Je'Von Ward 2.50 6.00
21 Matt Mervis 2.50 6.00
22 Mason McCoy 2.50 6.00
23 Josh Fleming 3.00 8.00
24 Junior Martina 2.50 6.00
25 Victor Bericoto 5.00 12.00
26 Ronny Mauricio 6.00 15.00
27 Shay Whitcomb 3.00 8.00
28 Shed Long Jr. 3.00 8.00
29 Wander Franco 25.00 60.00
30 Bryce Elder 3.00 8.00
31 Brandon Williamson 4.00 10.00
32 Antoine Kelly 5.00 12.00
33 Austin Shenton 2.50 6.00
34 D'Shawn Knowles 2.50 6.00
35 Eddy Diaz 2.50 6.00
36 Evan Fitterer 5.00 12.00
37 Gilberto Jimenez 10.00 25.00
38 Ismael Mena 4.00 10.00
39 Austin Allen 3.00 8.00
40 Isaac Galloway 2.50 6.00
41 Yoan Lopez 2.50 6.00
42 A.J. Vukovich 5.00 12.00
43 Travis Blankenhorn 5.00 12.00
44 Sam Hentges 2.50 6.00
45 Chad Sobotka 2.50 6.00

2020 Panini Contenders Draft Pick Ticket Autographs

RANDOM INSERTS IN PACKS
EXCHANGE DEADLINE 4/30/22
1 Austin Martin 20.00 50.00
2 Spencer Torkelson 60.00 150.00
3 Emerson Hancock 10.00 25.00
4 Zac Veen 15.00 40.00
5 Asa Lacy 8.00 20.00
6 Nick Gonzales 15.00 40.00
7 Garrett Mitchell 8.00 20.00
8 Mick Abel 6.00 15.00
9 Austin Hendrick 10.00 25.00
10 Jared Kelley 6.00 15.00
11 Garrett Crochet 30.00 80.00
12 Casey Martin 10.00 25.00
13 Jordan Walker 8.00 20.00
14 Nick Bitsko 8.00 20.00
15 Ed Howard 15.00 40.00
16 Reid Detmers 6.00 15.00
18 Cade Cavalli 4.00 10.00
19 Daniel Cabrera 6.00 15.00
20 Max Meyer 10.00 25.00

2020 Panini Contenders Draft Pick Ticket Autographs Cracked Ice

*CRCKD ICE: .8X TO 2X BASIC
RANDOM INSERTS IN PACKS
STATED PRINT RUN 23 SER.#'d SETS
EXCHANGE DEADLINE 4/30/22
1 Austin Martin 50.00 120.00
6 Nick Gonzales 40.00 100.00
8 Mick Abel 25.00 60.00
9 Austin Hendrick 25.00 60.00
12 Casey Martin 25.00 60.00
13 Jordan Walker 15.00 40.00

2020 Panini Contenders Draft Pick Ticket Autographs Draft Blue

*DRAFT BLUE: .5X TO 1.2X BASIC
RANDOM INSERTS IN PACKS
PRINT RUN B/TW 49-99 COPIES PER
EXCHANGE DEADLINE 4/30/22
1 Austin Martin/49 30.00 80.00
12 Casey Martin/99 15.00 40.00

2020 Panini Contenders Draft Pick Ticket Autographs Draft Red

*DRAFT RED: .5X TO 1.2X BASIC
RANDOM INSERTS IN PACKS
STATED PRINT RUN 75 SER.#'d SETS
EXCHANGE DEADLINE 4/30/22
1 Austin Martin 30.00 80.00
6 Nick Gonzales 25.00 60.00
8 Mick Abel 15.00 40.00
12 Casey Martin 15.00 40.00

2020 Panini Contenders Draft Pick Ticket Autographs 2

RANDOM INSERTS IN PACKS
EXCHANGE DEADLINE 4/30/22
*DRAFT BLUE/99: .5X TO 1.2X BASIC
*DRAFT RED/75: .5X TO 1.2X BASIC
1 Patrick Bailey 6.00 15.00
2 Heston Kjerstad 15.00 40.00
4 Pete Crow-Armstrong 8.00 20.00
5 Tyler Soderstrom 10.00 25.00
6 Austin Wells 10.00 25.00
7 Jared Shuster 8.00 20.00
8 Carmen Mlodzinski 2.50 6.00
9 Tanner Burns 4.00 10.00
10 Bobby Miller 6.00 15.00
11 Nick Loftin 5.00 12.00
13 Alika Williams 3.00 8.00
14 Slade Cecconi 3.00 8.00
15 Jordan Westburg 6.00 15.00
16 Aaron Sabato 12.00 30.00
17 Bryce Jarvis 2.50 6.00
18 Dillon Dingler 6.00 15.00
19 Drew Romo 6.00 15.00
20 Justin Lange 2.50 6.00
21 Justin Foscue 6.00 15.00
22 Carson Tucker 6.00 15.00

2020 Panini Contenders Draft Pick Ticket Autographs 2 Cracked Ice

*CRCKD ICE: .8X TO 2X BASIC
RANDOM INSERTS IN PACKS
STATED PRINT RUN 23 SER.#'d SETS
EXCHANGE DEADLINE 4/30/22
4 Pete Crow-Armstrong 40.00 100.00
11 Nick Loftin 20.00 50.00

2020 Panini Contenders First Rounders

RANDOM INSERTS IN PACKS
*GOLD: .8X TO 2X BASIC
1 Garrett Mitchell 2.50 6.00
2 Robert Hassell 2.50 6.00
3 Pete Crow-Armstrong 1.00 2.50
4 Spencer Torkelson 3.00 8.00
5 Austin Martin 1.00 2.50
6 Asa Lacy 2.00 5.00
7 Nick Gonzales 1.50 4.00
8 Zac Veen 1.50 4.00
9 Emerson Hancock 1.25 3.00
10 Reid Detmers .75 2.00
11 Max Meyer 1.25 3.00
12 Heston Kjerstad 1.50 4.00
13 Patrick Bailey 1.00 2.50
14 Tyler Soderstrom 1.25 3.00
15 Austin Hendrick 3.00 8.00

2020 Panini Contenders First Rounders Cracked Ice

*CRCKD ICE: 1.5X TO 4X BASIC
RANDOM INSERTS IN PACKS
STATED PRINT RUN 23 SER.#'d SETS
8 Zac Veen 10.00 25.00

2020 Panini Contenders Future Stars

RANDOM INSERTS IN PACKS
1 Wander Franco 2.50 6.00
2 Jo Adell 1.25 3.00
3 Casey Mize 1.00 2.50
4 Nate Pearson .60 1.50
5 Drew Waters .75 2.00
6 Hunter Greene .50 1.25
7 Nick Madrigal 1.00 2.50
8 Andrew Vaughn 1.25 3.00
9 Bobby Dalbec .75 2.00
10 Sixto Sanchez .50 1.25
11 Tyler Freeman .40 1.00
12 Evan White .30 .75
13 Nolan Jones .50 1.25
14 Alex Kirilloff .60 1.50
15 Jasson Dominguez 4.00 10.00
16 MacKenzie Gore .60 1.50
17 Dylan Carlson 1.25 3.00
18 Brady Singer .40 1.00
19 Ryan Mountcastle .50 1.25
20 Joey Bart 1.00 2.50

2020 Panini Contenders Future Stars Cracked Ice

*CRCKD ICE: 1.5X TO 4X BASIC
RANDOM INSERTS IN PACKS
STATED PRINT RUN 23 SER.#'d SETS
5 Drew Waters 10.00 25.00
16 MacKenzie Gore 6.00 15.00

2020 Panini Contenders Future Stars Gold

*GOLD: .8X TO 2X BASIC
RANDOM INSERTS IN PACKS
STATED PRINT RUN 99 SER.#'d SETS
16 MacKenzie Gore 3.00 8.00

2020 Panini Contenders Game Day

RANDOM INSERTS IN PACKS
*GOLD: .8X TO 2X BASIC
1 Gleyber Torres 1.00 2.50
2 Alex Bregman .50 1.25
3 Javier Baez .60 1.50
4 Shohei Ohtani .60 1.50
5 Francisco Lindor .50 1.25
6 Justin Verlander .50 1.25
7 Bryce Harper .75 2.00
8 Manny Machado .50 1.25
9 Nolan Arenado .60 1.50
10 Jacob deGrom .50 1.25

2020 Panini Contenders Game Day Cracked Ice

*CRCKD ICE: 1.5X TO 4X BASIC
RANDOM INSERTS IN PACKS
STATED PRINT RUN 23 SER.#'d SETS
1 Gleyber Torres 12.00 30.00

2020 Panini Contenders Gold Rush

RANDOM INSERTS IN PACKS
1 Mike Trout 60.00 150.00
2 Pete Alonso 25.00 60.00
3 Yordan Alvarez 30.00 80.00
4 Juan Soto 40.00 100.00

2020 Panini Contenders Legacy

RANDOM INSERTS IN PACKS
1 Ken Griffey Jr. 1.00 2.50
2 Greg Maddux .60 1.50
3 Frank Thomas 1.00 2.50
4 Jim Thome .40 1.00
5 Cal Ripken 1.50 4.00
6 Reggie Jackson .40 1.00
7 Nolan Ryan 1.50 4.00
8 Randy Johnson 1.00 2.50
9 Mark McGwire .75 2.00
10 Pedro Martinez .40 1.00

2020 Panini Contenders Legacy Cracked Ice

*CRCKD ICE: 1.5X TO 4X BASIC
RANDOM INSERTS IN PACKS
STATED PRINT RUN 23 SER.#'d SETS
1 Ken Griffey Jr. 25.00 60.00
3 Frank Thomas 10.00 25.00
7 Nolan Ryan 12.00 30.00
8 Randy Johnson 12.00 30.00
9 Mark McGwire 10.00 25.00

2020 Panini Contenders Legacy Gold

*GOLD: .8X TO 2X BASIC
RANDOM INSERTS IN PACKS
STATED PRINT RUN 99 SER.#'d SETS
3 Frank Thomas 5.00 12.00
7 Nolan Ryan 6.00 15.00
8 Randy Johnson 6.00 15.00

2020 Panini Contenders Legendary

RANDOM INSERTS IN PACKS
1 Sandy Koufax 1.00 2.50
2 Ichiro .60 1.50
3 Tony Gwynn .50 1.25
4 Alex Rodriguez .60 1.50
5 George Brett 1.00 2.50
6 Vladimir Guerrero .40 1.00
7 Ryne Sandberg 1.00 2.50
8 Rickey Henderson .50 1.25

2020 Panini Contenders Legendary Cracked Ice

*CRCKD ICE: 1.5X TO 4X BASIC
RANDOM INSERTS IN PACKS
STATED PRINT RUN 23 SER.#'d SETS
3 Tony Gwynn 15.00 40.00
4 Alex Rodriguez 15.00 40.00
8 Rickey Henderson 12.00 30.00

2020 Panini Contenders Legendary Gold

*GOLD: .8X TO 2X BASIC
RANDOM INSERTS IN PACKS
STATED PRINT RUN 99 SER.#'d SETS
4 Alex Rodriguez 3.00 8.00
8 Rickey Henderson 4.00 10.00

2020 Panini Contenders Potential

RANDOM INSERTS IN PACKS
1 Luis Robert 3.00 8.00
2 Gilberto Jimenez 1.50 4.00
3 Roberto Campos 1.50 4.00
4 Erick Pena 1.00 2.50
5 Taylor Trammell .40 1.00
6 Logan Gilbert .40 1.00
7 CJ Abrams 1.25 3.00
8 Nate Pearson .60 1.50
9 Cristian Pache 1.00 2.50
10 Matthew Liberatore .40 1.00
11 Jarred Kelenic 2.00 5.00
12 Oscar Colas 1.00 2.50

2020 Panini Contenders Potential Cracked Ice

*CRCKD ICE: 1.5X TO 4X BASIC
RANDOM INSERTS IN PACKS
STATED PRINT RUN 23 SER.#'d SETS
1 Luis Robert 25.00 60.00
9 Cristian Pache 6.00 23.00
12 Oscar Colas 12.00 30.00

2020 Panini Contenders Potential Gold

*GOLD: .8X TO 2X BASIC
RANDOM INSERTS IN PACKS
STATED PRINT RUN 99 SER.#'d SETS
1 Luis Robert 12.00 30.00
12 Oscar Colas 6.00 15.00

2020 Panini Contenders Prospect Ticket Autographs

RANDOM INSERTS IN PACKS
EXCHANGE DEADLINE 4/30/22
1 Adley Rutschman 15.00 40.00
2 Evan White 5.00 12.00
3 Cristian Pache 10.00 25.00
4 Nick Madrigal 10.00 25.00
5 Hunter Greene 8.00 20.00

2020 Panini Contenders Prospect Ticket Autographs Cracked Ice

*CRCKD ICE: .8X TO 2X BASIC
RANDOM INSERTS IN PACKS
STATED PRINT RUN 23 SER.#'d SETS
EXCHANGE DEADLINE 4/30/22
1 Adley Rutschman 40.00 100.00

2020 Panini Contenders Prospect Ticket Autographs Draft Blue

*DRAFT BLUE: .5X TO 1.2X BASIC
RANDOM INSERTS IN PACKS
PRINT RUN B/TW 35-99 COPIES PER
EXCHANGE DEADLINE 4/30/22
1 Adley Rutschman/35 25.00 60.00

2020 Panini Contenders Prospect Ticket Autographs Draft Red

*DRAFT RED/75: .5X TO 1.2X BASIC
*DRAFT RED/25: .8X TO 2X BASIC
RANDOM INSERTS IN PACKS
PRINT RUN B/TW 25-75 COPIES PER
EXCHANGE DEADLINE 4/30/22
1 Adley Rutschman/25 40.00 100.00

2020 Panini Contenders Prospect Ticket Autographs

RANDOM INSERTS IN PACKS
EXCHANGE DEADLINE 4/30/22
*DRAFT BLUE/99: .5X TO 1.2X BASIC
*DRAFT RED/75: .5X TO 1.2X BASIC
*CRCKD ICE/23: .8X TO 2X BASIC
1 Jeremy Arocho 2.50 6
2 Malcom Nunez 5.00 12
3 Grant McCray 4.00 10
4 Norge Vera 3.00 8
5 Vaughn Grissom 4.00 10
6 Yiddi Cappe 5.00 12
7 Roberto Campos 20.00 50
8 Victor Vodnik 2.50 6
9 Yoelqui Cespedes 25.00 60
10 Oscar Colas 8.00 20

2020 Panini Contenders Retr '98 Rookie Ticket Autograph

RANDOM INSERTS IN PACKS
EXCHANGE DEADLINE 4/30/22
*DRAFT BLUE/30-99: .5X TO 1.2X BASIC
*DRAFT RED/75: .5X TO 1.2X BASIC
*CRCKD ICE/23: .8X TO 2X BASIC
1 Yordan Alvarez 15.00 40
2 Gavin Lux 15.00 40
3 A.J. Puk EXCH 8.00 20
4 Kyle Lewis 20.00 50
5 Nico Hoerner 8.00 20
6 Luis Robert EXCH 50.00 120
7 Sheldon Neuse 3.00 8
8 Zac Gallen 5.00 12
9 Adbert Alzolay 3.00 8
10 Isan Diaz 4.00 10
11 Matt Thaiss 3.00 8
12 Jordan Yamamoto 3.00 8
13 Lewis Thorpe 2.50 6
14 Sam Hilliard 4.00 10
15 Tony Gonsolin 10.00 25

2020 Panini Contenders Retr '99 Rookie Ticket Autograph

RANDOM INSERTS IN PACKS
EXCHANGE DEADLINE 4/30/22
1 Sean Murphy 4.00 10
2 Aristides Aquino 8.00 20
3 Shogo Akiyama 4.00 10
4 Yu Chang 4.00 10
5 Shun Yamaguchi 3.00 8
6 Jesus Luzardo EXCH 5.00 12
7 Dylan Cease 5.00 12
8 Brendan McKay EXCH 4.00 10
9 Yoshitomo Tsutsugo 8.00 20
10 Abraham Toro 3.00 8

2020 Panini Contenders Retr '99 Rookie Ticket Autograph Cracked Ice

*CRCKD ICE: .8X TO 2X BASIC
RANDOM INSERTS IN PACKS
STATED PRINT RUN 23 SER.#'d SETS
EXCHANGE DEADLINE 4/30/22
3 Shogo Akiyama 12.00 30
9 Yoshitomo Tsutsugo 30.00 80

2020 Panini Contenders Retr '99 Rookie Ticket Autographs Draft Blue

3 Shogo Akiyama/49 8.00 20
9 Yoshitomo Tsutsugo/33 10.00 25

2020 Panini Contenders Retr '99 Rookie Ticket Autographs Draft Red

*DRAFT RED: .5X TO 1.2X BASIC
RANDOM INSERTS IN PACKS
STATED PRINT RUN 75 SER.#'d SETS
EXCHANGE DEADLINE 4/30/22
3 Shogo Akiyama 8.00 20
9 Yoshitomo Tsutsugo 10.00 25

2020 Panini Contenders Rook of the Year Contenders Autographs

RANDOM INSERTS IN PACKS
EXCHANGE DEADLINE 4/30/22
1 A.J. Puk 5.00 12
3 Aristides Aquino 5.00 12
4 Bo Bichette
5 Brendan McKay 4.00 10.
6 Brusdar Graterol 4.00 10
7 Dylan Cease 5.00 12
8 Gavin Lux 15.00 40.
9 Isan Diaz 4.00 10.
10 Jesus Luzardo 5.00 12.
11 Kwang-Hyun Kim
12 Kyle Lewis
13 Luis Robert
14 Nico Hoerner 10.00 25.
15 Sean Murphy 6.00 15.
16 Shogo Akiyama 4.00 10.
17 Shun Yamaguchi 3.00 8.
18 Yordan Alvarez 12.00 30.
19 Yoshitomo Tsutsugo 3.00 8.
20 Zac Gallen 5.00 12.

2020 Panini Contenders Rook of the Year Contenders Autographs Cracked Ice

*CRCKD ICE: .8X TO 2X BASIC
RANDOM INSERTS IN PACKS
STATED PRINT RUN 23 SER.#'d SETS
EXCHANGE DEADLINE 4/30/22
11 Kwang-Hyun Kim 30.00 80.
13 Luis Robert 150.00 400

20 Panini Contenders Rookie Roundup Autographs
DOM INSERTS IN PACKS
HANGE DEADLINE 4/30/22
CKD ICE/23: .8X TO 2X BASIC
n Lopes 3.00 8.00
om Nunez 3.00 8.00
an Wong 3.00 8.00
ch Green 2.50 6.00
cob Waguespack 3.00 8.00
ike Brosseau 5.00 12.00
th Brown 2.50 6.00
orge Alcala 2.50 6.00
yan McBroom 6.00 15.00
evin Ginkel 2.50 6.00
Kyle Garlick 4.00 10.00
LaMonte Wade Jr. 4.00 10.00
Dillon Tate 2.50 6.00
Robel Garcia 2.50 6.00
Scott Heineman 2.50 6.00

020 Panini Contenders Round Numbers Dual Autographs
DOM INSERTS IN PACKS
HANGE DEADLINE 4/30/22
CKD ICE/23: .6X TO 1.5X BASIC
Martin/S.Torkelson 60.00 150.00
Bailey/T.Soderstrom
S.Beer/T.Casas 10.00 25.00
3.Baty/J.Jung 15.00 40.00

020 Panini Contenders Up and Coming
DOM INSERTS IN PACKS
LD: .8X TO 2X BASIC
CKD ICE: 1.5X TO 4X BASIC
ylan Carlson 1.25 3.00
is Matos .50 1.25
ailyn Marquez .75 2.00
ristian Robinson 1.00 2.50
rik Skubal 1.50 4.00
ulio Rodriguez 2.00 5.00
ndrew Vaughn 1.25 3.00
alcom Nunez .60 1.50
uis V. Garcia .50 1.25
Ji-Hwan Bae .50 1.25

2020 Panini Contenders Winning Tickets
NDOM INSERTS IN PACKS
asson Dominguez 5.00 12.00
o Bichette 2.50 6.00
ordan Alvarez 1.50 4.00
ete Alonso 1.25 3.00
ander Franco 3.00 8.00
ladimir Guerrero Jr. 1.00 2.50
Mike Trout 2.50 6.00
avier Baez .60 1.50
ody Bellinger 1.00 2.50
Christian Yelich .60 1.50
Ronald Acuna Jr. 2.00 5.00
Juan Soto 1.50 4.00
Rafael Devers .60 1.50
Aaron Judge 1.25 3.00
Fernando Tatis Jr. 2.00 5.00

2020 Panini Contenders Winning Tickets Cracked Ice
RCKD ICE: 1.5X TO 4X BASIC
NDOM INSERTS IN PACKS
ATED PRINT RUN 23 SER.#'d SETS
asson Dominguez 40.00 100.00
Bo Bichette 20.00 50.00
Ronald Acuna Jr. 12.00 30.00
Juan Soto 10.00 25.00
Fernando Tatis Jr. 25.00 60.00

2020 Panini Contenders Winning Tickets Gold
OLD: .8X TO 2X BASIC
NDOM INSERTS IN PACKS
ATED PRINT RUN 99 SER.#'d SETS
asson Dominguez 20.00 50.00
Ronald Acuna Jr. 6.00 15.00
Juan Soto 5.00 12.00

2017 Panini Contenders Draft Picks
L VERSIONS EQUALLY PRICED
CHANGE DEADLINE 03/06/2019
A.J. Puk .30 .75
Blue jersey
A.J. Puk .30 .75
White jersey
Barry Larkin .25 .60
Batting
Barry Larkin .25 .60
Running
Bo Jackson .30 .75
Black and white photo
Bo Jackson .30 .75
Color photo
Cal Quantrill .20 .50
Glove down
Cal Quantrill .20 .50
Glove up
Corey Ray .25 .60
Holding bat
Corey Ray .25 .60
Running
Craig Biggio .25 .60
Pirates jersey
Craig Biggio .25 .60
Seton Hall jersey
Dave Winfield .25 .60
Bierman Field on card back
Dave Winfield .25 .60
Siebert Field on card back
8A Frank Thomas .30 .75
Black and white photo
8B Frank Thomas .30 .75
Color photo
9A Fred Lynn .20 .50
Hat
9B Fred Lynn .20 .50
Helmet
10A John Elway .50 1.25
10B John Elway .50 1.25
11A Justin Dunn .20 .50
Number showing
11B Justin Dunn .20 .50
No number
12A Kyle Lewis .40 1.00
12B Kyle Lewis .40 1.00
13A Mark McGwire .50 1.25
13B Mark McGwire .50 1.25
14A Matt Thaiss .20 .50
Gray jersey
14B Matt Thaiss .20 .50
White jersey
15A Nick Senzel .60 1.50
15B Nick Senzel .60 1.50
16A Ozzie Smith .40 1.00
16B Ozzie Smith .40 1.00
17A Brent Rooker .50 1.25
17B Brent Rooker .50 1.25
18A Paul Molitor .30 .75
Bierman Field on card back
18B Paul Molitor .30 .75
Siebert Field on card back
19A Rafael Palmeiro .25 .60
Maroon jersey
19B Rafael Palmeiro .25 .60
White jersey
20A Reggie Jackson .25 .60
Full bat
20B Reggie Jackson .25 .60
Partial bat
21A Roger Clemens .40 1.00
21B Roger Clemens .40 1.00
22A T.J. Zeuch .20 .50
Ball showing
22B T.J. Zeuch .20 .50
No ball
23A Tony Gwynn .30 .75
Zoomed in
23B Tony Gwynn .30 .75
Zoomed out
24A Will Clark .25 .60
Batting gloves on both hands
24B Will Clark .25 .60
Batting gloves on one hand
25A Zack Collins .25 .60
Orange jersey
25B Zack Collins .25 .60
White jersey
27A Brendan McKay AU 12.00 30.00
27B Brendan McKay AU 12.00 30.00
28A Royce Lewis AU 25.00 60.00
28B Royce Lewis AU 25.00 60.00
29A Austin Beck AU 12.00 30.00
29B Austin Beck AU 12.00 30.00
30A Kendall AU Glass 6.00 15.00
30B Kendall AU No Glass 6.00 15.00
31A Faedo AU 5.00 12.00
31B Faedo AU 5.00 12.00
32A Kyle Wright AU 10.00 25.00
32B Kyle Wright AU 10.00 25.00
33A DL Hall AU 4.00 10.00
Glove up
33B DL Hall AU 4.00 10.00
Glove down
34A Keston Hiura AU 6.00 15.00
Blue jersey
34B Keston Hiura AU 6.00 15.00
Gray jersey
35A Jo Adell AU EXCH 25.00 60.00
35B Jo Adell AU EXCH 25.00 60.00
36A Shane Baz AU 5.00 12.00
Arm back
36B Shane Baz AU 5.00 12.00
Arm down
37A Seth Romero AU 3.00 8.00
Ball showing
37B Seth Romero AU 3.00 8.00
No ball
38A Alex Lange AU 5.00 12.00
Glove next to face
38B Alex Lange AU 5.00 12.00
Ball behind head
39A MacKenzie Gore AU 20.00 50.00
39B MacKenzie Gore AU 20.00 50.00
40A Clarke Schmidt AU 5.00 12.00
Gray jersey
40B Clarke Schmidt AU 5.00 12.00
White jersey
41A Griffin Canning AU 5.00 12.00
Pinstripe jersey
41B Griffin Canning AU 5.00 12.00
White jersey
42A Nick Pratto AU 5.00 12.00
42B Nick Pratto AU 5.00 12.00
43A Pavin Smith AU 10.00 25.00
43B Pavin Smith AU 10.00 25.00
44A J.B. Bukauskas AU 5.00 12.00
Side view
44B J.B. Bukauskas AU 5.00 12.00
Front view
45A Adam Haseley AU 6.00 15.00
Batting
45B Adam Haseley AU 6.00 15.00
Sunglasses on
46 Logan Warmoth AU 5.00 12.00
47 Jake Burger AU 6.00 15.00
48 Heliot Ramos AU 8.00 20.00
49 David Peterson AU 4.00 10.00
50 Tanner Houck AU 15.00 40.00
51 Mark Vientos AU 5.00 12.00
52 Trevor Rogers AU 5.00 12.00
53 Bubba Thompson AU 5.00 12.00
54 Christopher Seise AU 5.00 12.00
55 Matt Sauer AU 4.00 10.00
56 Evan White AU 5.00 12.00
57 Sam Carlson AU 4.00 10.00
58 Quentin Holmes AU 4.00 10.00
59 Brian Miller AU 3.00 8.00
60 Tristen Lutz AU 5.00 12.00

2017 Panini Contenders Draft Picks Cracked Ice Ticket
*ICE 1-25: 4X TO 10X BASIC
*ICE AU 27-60: 1X TO 2.5X BASIC
RANDOM INSERTS IN PACKS
STATED PRINT RUN 23 SER.#'d SETS
EXCHANGE DEADLINE 03/06/2019

2017 Panini Contenders Draft Picks Draft Ticket
*DRAFT 1-25: 2.5X TO 6X BASIC
*DRAFT AU 27-60: .5X TO 1.2X BASIC
RANDOM INSERTS IN PACKS
STATED PRINT RUN 99 SER.#'d SETS
EXCHANGE DEADLINE 03/06/2019

2017 Panini Contenders Draft Picks Game Day Tickets
RANDOM INSERTS IN PACKS
1 Brendan McKay 1.00 2.50
2 Brian Miller .25 .60
3 Alex Faedo .40 1.00
4 Kyle Wright .75 2.00
5 Keston Hiura 1.25 3.00
6 Evan White .40 1.00
7 Nick Senzel .75 2.00
8 Clarke Schmidt .40 1.00
9 Griffin Canning .40 1.00
10 Pavin Smith .75 2.00
11 David Peterson .30 .75
12 Adam Haseley .50 1.25
13 Jake Burger .50 1.25
14 Tanner Houck 1.25 3.00
15 Logan Warmoth .40 1.00

2017 Panini Contenders Draft Picks Alumni Ink
RANDOM INSERTS IN PACKS
EXCHANGE DEADLINE 03/06/2019
1 Reggie Jackson 15.00 40.00
2 Barry Bonds 60.00 150.00
3 Frank Thomas
4 John Elway
5 Bo Jackson 50.00 120.00
6 Mark McGwire
7 Barry Larkin
8 Roger Clemens
9 Ozzie Smith
10 Paul Molitor

2017 Panini Contenders Draft Picks Collegiate Connections Dual Signatures
RANDOM INSERTS IN PACKS
EXCHANGE DEADLINE 03/06/2019
1 Kendall/Wright 15.00 40.00
2 Schmidt/Crowe 15.00 40.00
3 Smith/Haseley
4 Bukauskas/Warmoth 6.00 15.00
5 Bo Jackson
Frank Thomas
7 Bonds/Jackson 100.00 250.00
8 Palmeiro/Clark 75.00 200.00
9 Winfield/Molitor 20.00 50.00
10 Miller/Warmoth 12.00 30.00

2017 Panini Contenders Draft Picks International Ticket Autographs
RANDOM INSERTS IN PACKS
EXCHANGE DEADLINE 03/06/2019
*DRAFT/99: .5X TO 1.2X BASIC
*ICE/23: .75X TO 2X BASIC
1 Luis Robert 40.00 100.00
2 Honny Mauricio 5.00 12.00
3 Julio Rodriguez 20.00 50.00
4 George Valera EXCH 6.00 15.00
6 Jelfry Marte 5.00 12.00
7 Adrian Hernandez 3.00 8.00
8 Larry Ernesto 3.00 8.00
9 Ynmanol Marinez 4.00 10.00
10 Ronny Rojas 3.00 8.00
11 Carlos Aguiar 4.00 10.00
12 Luis Garcia 5.00 12.00

2017 Panini Contenders Draft Picks Old School Colors
COMPLETE SET (10) 4.00 10.00
RANDOM INSERTS IN PACKS
1 Reggie Jackson .30 .75
2 Craig Biggio .30 .75
3 Frank Thomas .40 1.00
4 John Elway .60 1.50
5 Bo Jackson .60 1.50
6 Mark McGwire .60 1.50
7 Barry Larkin .30 .75
8 Roger Clemens .50 1.25
9 Ozzie Smith .50 1.25
10 Paul Molitor .40 1.00

2017 Panini Contenders Draft Picks Old School Colors Signatures
RANDOM INSERTS IN PACKS
EXCHANGE DEADLINE 03/06/2019
1 Reggie Jackson 15.00 40.00
2 Craig Biggio
3 Frank Thomas
4 John Elway 40.00 100.00
5 Bo Jackson 50.00 120.00
7 Barry Larkin
8 Roger Clemens 15.00 40.00
9 Ozzie Smith
10 Paul Molitor 10.00 25.00

2017 Panini Contenders Draft Picks Prospect Ticket Autographs
RANDOM INSERTS IN PACKS
EXCHANGE DEADLINE 03/06/2019
*DRAFT/99: .5X TO 1.2X BASIC
*ICE/23: .75X TO 2X BASIC
1 Nick Senzel 12.00 30.00
2 Eloy Jimenez 40.00 100.00
3 Carlos Rincon 3.00 8.00
4 Vladimir Guerrero Jr. 100.00 250.00
5 Kevin Maitan 10.00 25.00
6 Andres Gimenez 6.00 15.00
7 Ronald Acuna 60.00 150.00
8 Jomar Reyes 5.00 12.00
9 Willi Castro 5.00 12.00
10 Albert Abreu 4.00 10.00
11 Gleyber Torres 50.00 125.00
12 Amed Rosario 5.00 12.00
13 David Garcia 4.00 10.00
14 Luis Almanzar 3.00 8.00
15 Luis V. Garcia 4.00 10.00
16 Yoan Moncada
17 Cristian Pache
18 Willy Adames 4.00 10.00
19 Abraham Gutierrez 5.00 12.00
20 Victor Robles 6.00 15.00
21 Rafael Devers 12.00 30.00
22 Francisco Mejia 5.00 12.00
23 Blake Rutherford 5.00 12.00

2017 Panini Contenders Draft Picks School Colors
COMPLETE SET (15) 4.00 10.00
RANDOM INSERTS IN PACKS
1 Brendan McKay 1.00 2.50
2 Brian Miller .25 .60
3 Alex Faedo .40 1.00
4 Kyle Wright .75 2.00
5 Keston Hiura 1.25 3.00
6 Evan White .40 1.00
7 Nick Senzel .75 2.00
8 Clarke Schmidt .40 1.00
9 Griffin Canning .40 1.00
10 Pavin Smith .75 2.00
11 David Peterson .30 .75
12 Adam Haseley .50 1.25
13 Jake Burger .50 1.25
14 Tanner Houck 1.25 3.00
15 Logan Warmoth .40 1.00

2017 Panini Contenders Draft Picks School Colors Signatures
RANDOM INSERTS IN PACKS
EXCHANGE DEADLINE 03/06/2019
1 Brendan McKay 15.00 40.00
2 Jeren Kendall
3 Alex Faedo
4 Kyle Wright
5 Keston Hiura
6 Seth Romero
7 Alex Lange
8 Clarke Schmidt
9 Griffin Canning
10 Pavin Smith
11 J.B. Bukauskas
12 Adam Haseley 12.00 30.00
13 Jake Burger 12.00 30.00
14 Tanner Houck
15 Logan Warmoth
16 David Peterson 8.00 20.00
18 Evan White
19 Brian Miller
20 Wil Crowe

2018 Panini Contenders Draft Picks
1 A.J. Puk .25 .60
Puk...
2 Adam Haseley .30 .75
3 Alex Faedo .30 .75
Against...
4 Barry Larkin .25 .60
Larkin...
5 Bo Jackson .30 .75
Before...
6 Reggie Jackson .25 .60
While...
7 Brendan McKay .30 .75
McKay...
8 Brent Rooker .25 .60
By...
9 Chance Adams .30 .75
Transferring...
10 Clarke Schmidt .30 .75
Equally...
11 Craig Biggio .25 .60
As a...
12 Dave Winfield .25 .60
During...
13 David Peterson .25 .60
Peterson...
14 Evan White .30 .75
Kentucky...
15 Frank Thomas .30 .75
After...
16 Fred Lynn .20 .50
USC...
17 J.B. Bukauskas .20 .50
If...
18 Jake Burger .20 .50
Missouri...
19 Jon Duplantier .20 .50
After...
20 Keston Hiura .50 1.25
A...
21 Kyle Wright .50 1.25
22 Mark McGwire .50 1.25
23 Nick Senzel .60 1.50
24 Ozzie Smith .40 1.00
25 Paul Molitor .30 .75
Molitor...

2018 Panini Contenders Draft Picks Cracked Ice Ticket
*ICE: 4X TO 10X BASIC
RANDOM INSERTS IN PACKS
STATED PRINT RUN 23 SER.#'d SETS

2018 Panini Contenders Draft Picks Variations
*VAR: .4X TO 1X BASIC
RANDOM INSERTS IN PACKS

2018 Panini Contenders Draft Picks Variations Cracked Ice Ticket
*ICE: 4X TO 10X BASIC
RANDOM INSERTS IN PACKS
STATED PRINT RUN 23 SER.#'d SETS

2018 Panini Contenders Draft Picks Variations Draft Ticket
*DRAFT: 2.5X TO 6X BASIC
RANDOM INSERTS IN PACKS
STATED PRINT RUN 99 SER.#'d SETS

2018 Panini Contenders Draft Picks Collegiate Connections Signatures
RANDOM INSERTS IN PACKS
*ICE/23: .5X TO 1.2X BASIC
1 Singer/Kower 20.00 50.00
3 Bohm/Jenista
4 Knight/Cole 15.00 40.00
5 Grenier/Madrigal 15.00 40.00
6 Cortes/Hill 15.00 40.00
7 Tristan Beck 10.00 25.00
Kris Bubic
9 Singer/Faedo 12.00 30.00
10 Rooker/Pilkington 8.00 20.00

2018 Panini Contenders Draft Picks Draft Ticket
*DRAFT: 2.5X TO 6X BASIC
RANDOM INSERTS IN PACKS
STATED PRINT RUN 99 SER.#'d SETS

2018 Panini Contenders Draft Picks Draft Ticket Autographs
RANDOM INSERTS IN PACKS
*VAR DRFT/99: .5X TO 1.2X BASIC
*DRAFT/99: .5X TO 1.2X BASIC
1 Brady Singer 8.00 20.00
2 Shane McClanahan 5.00 12.00
3 Casey Mize 12.00 30.00
4 Matthew Liberatore 4.00 10.00
5 Brice Turang 10.00 25.00
6 Nolan Gorman 20.00 50.00
7 Joey Bart 25.00 60.00
8 Ryan Rolison 6.00 15.00
9 Travis Swaggerty 10.00 25.00
10 Jackson Kowar 6.00 15.00
11 Nick Madrigal 12.00 30.00
12 Steele Walker 4.00 10.00
13 Trevor Larnach 8.00 20.00
15 Jarred Kelenic 30.00 80.00
16 Seth Beer 15.00 40.00
18 Logan Gilbert 5.00 12.00
19 Jonathan India 8.00 20.00
20 Alec Bohm 10.00 25.00
21 Ryan Weathers 4.00 10.00
23 Tristan Beck 4.00 10.00
24 Griffin Conine 6.00 15.00
25 Will Banfield 3.00 8.00
26 Daniel Lynch 4.00 10.00
27 Triston Casas 8.00 20.00
30 Grant Lavigne 8.00 20.00
31 Kody Clemens 5.00 12.00
32 Cole Winn 4.00 10.00
33 Eric Cole 4.00 10.00
34 Jake McCarthy 5.00 12.00
36 Xavier Edwards 5.00 12.00
37 Tim Cate 5.00 12.00
38 Connor Scott 4.00 10.00
39 Luken Baker 5.00 12.00
40 Blaine Knight 4.00 10.00
41 Bo Naylor 4.00 10.00
42 Joe Gray 5.00 12.00
43 Parker Meadows 4.00 10.00
44 Lyon Richardson 5.00 12.00
45 Konnor Pilkington 4.00 10.00
46 Simeon Woods-Richardson 4.00 10.00
47 Tanner Dodson 4.00 10.00
48 Osiris Johnson 4.00 10.00
49 Braxton Ashcraft 5.00 12.00
50 Cadyn Grenier 4.00 10.00
51 Anthony Seigler 8.00 20.00
52 Josh Stowers 8.00 20.00
53 Colton Eastman 4.00 10.00
54 Jeremiah Jackson 4.00 10.00
55 Tristen Pompey 5.00 12.00
56 Tyler Frank 3.00 8.00
57 Jonathan Bowlan 3.00 8.00
58 Ryan Jeffers 6.00 15.00
59 Josh Breaux 4.00 10.00
60 Kris Bubic 5.00 12.00
61 Owen White 5.00 12.00
63 Jordan Groshans 6.00 15.00
64 Griffin Roberts 3.00 8.00
65 Greyson Jenista 6.00 15.00
66 Nico Hoerner 12.00 30.00
67 Brennen Davis 10.00 25.00
68 Adam Hill 3.00 8.00
69 Carlos Cortes 4.00 10.00
70 Alek Thomas 8.00 20.00
71 Jayson Schroeder 3.00 8.00
72 Grayson Rodriguez 6.00 15.00
73 Jameson Hannah 5.00 12.00
75 Nick Decker 6.00 15.00
76 Lenny Torres Jr. 4.00 10.00
77 Nick Schnell 4.00 10.00
78 Ethan Hankins 4.00 10.00
79 Nick Sandlin 3.00 8.00
80 Mason Denaburg 4.00 10.00

2018 Panini Contenders Draft Picks Draft Ticket Autographs Cracked Ice
ICE: .75X TO 2X BASIC
RANDOM INSERTS IN PACKS
STATED PRINT RUN 23 SER.#'d SETS
20 Alec Bohm 40.00 100.00

2018 Panini Contenders Draft Picks Draft Ticket Variation Autographs
*VAR: .4X TO 1X BASIC
RANDOM INSERTS IN PACKS
17 Joromy Eierman 4.00 10.00

2018 Panini Contenders Draft Picks Draft Ticket Variation Autographs Cracked Ice
*VAR ICE: .75X TO 2X BASIC
RANDOM INSERTS IN PACKS
STATED PRINT RUN 23 SER.#'d SETS
17 Jeremy Eierman 8.00 20.00
20 Alec Bohm 40.00 100.00

2018 Panini Contenders Draft Picks Game Day Tickets
RANDOM INSERTS IN PACKS
*ICE/23: 2.5X TO 6X BASIC
1 Brady Singer .50 1.25
2 Shane McClanahan .40 1.00
3 Casey Mize 2.00 5.00
4 Ryan Rolison .50 1.25
5 Travis Swaggerty .75 2.00
6 Jackson Kowar .25 .60
7 Nick Madrigal 1.50 4.00
8 Cadyn Grenier .30 .75
9 Logan Gilbert .40 1.00
10 Greyson Jenista .50 1.25
11 Alec Bohm 1.25 3.00
12 Joey Bart 2.50 6.00
13 Trevor Larnach 1.50 4.00
14 Nico Hoerner 1.25 3.00
15 Kris Bubic .40 1.00
16 Griffin Roberts .25 .60
17 Steele Walker .30 .75
18 Seth Beer 1.00 2.50
19 Jake McCarthy .40 1.00
20 Jonathan India .40 1.00

2018 Panini Contenders Draft Picks International Ticket Autographs
RANDOM INSERTS IN PACKS
*DRAFT/99: .5X TO 1.2X BASIC
*ICE/23: .75X TO 2X BASIC
1 Robert Puason 10.00 25.00
2 Jhon Diaz 5.00 12.00
3 Noelvi Marte 6.00 15.00
4 Frankely Hurtado 3.00 8.00
5 Jeffrey Diaz 3.00 8.00
6 Estanli Castillo 3.00 8.00
7 Julio Pablo Martinez 15.00 40.00

2018 Panini Contenders Draft Picks Old School Colors
RANDOM INSERTS IN PACKS
*ICE/23: 4X TO 10X BASIC
1 Reggie Jackson .30 .75
2 Frank Thomas .40 1.00
3 Bo Jackson .40 1.00
4 Mark McGwire .60 1.50
5 Barry Larkin .30 .75
6 Craig Biggio .30 .75
7 Paul Molitor .40 1.00
8 Roger Clemens .50 1.25
9 Ozzie Smith .50 1.25

2018 Panini Contenders Draft Picks Old School Colors Signatures
RANDOM INSERTS IN PACKS
*ICE/23: .6X TO 1.5X BASIC
1 Reggie Jackson 10.00 25.00
2 Dave Winfield
3 Frank Thomas 20.00 50.00
4 Bo Jackson 25.00 60.00
5 Mark McGwire 15.00 40.00
6 Barry Larkin 8.00 20.00
7 Will Clark 15.00 40.00
8 Paul Molitor 10.00 25.00
9 Roger Clemens 12.00 30.00
10 Ozzie Smith 15.00 40.00

2018 Panini Contenders Draft Picks Prospect Ticket Autographs
RANDOM INSERTS IN PACKS
*VAR: .4X TO 1X BASIC
*VAR DRFT/99: .5X TO 1.2X BASIC
*DRAFT/99: .5X TO 1.2X BASIC
1 Aramis Ademan 4.00 10.00
2 Yordan Alvarez 40.00 100.00
3 Keibert Ruiz 5.00 12.00
4 DJ Peters 6.00 15.00
5 Estevan Florial 5.00 12.00
6 Luis Robert 60.00 150.00
7 Fernando Tatis Jr. 40.00 100.00
8 Miguel Aparicio 3.00 8.00
9 Vladimir Guerrero Jr. 75.00 200.00
10 Eloy Jimenez 15.00 40.00
11 D.J. Wilson 3.00 8.00
12 Michael Kopech 6.00 15.00
13 Jose Siri 3.00 8.00
14 Brendan Rodgers 5.00 12.00
15 Jeisson Rosario 5.00 12.00
16 Sandro Fabian 3.00 8.00
17 Leody Taveras 4.00 10.00
18 Akil Baddoo 4.00 10.00
19 Brendan McKay 5.00 12.00
20 Jesus Sanchez 5.00 12.00
21 Kyle Tucker 6.00 15.00
22 James Nelson 3.00 8.00
23 Forrest Whitley 5.00 12.00
24 Carter Kieboom 8.00 20.00
25 Austin Riley 40.00 100.00
26 Mitch Keller 4.00 10.00
27 Franklin Perez 3.00 8.00
28 Chance Adams 5.00 12.00
29 Sixto Sanchez 4.00 10.00
30 Justus Sheffield 5.00 12.00
31 Bo Bichette 15.00 40.00
32 Brent Honeywell 5.00 12.00

2018 Panini Contenders Draft Picks Prospect Ticket Autographs Cracked Ice
*ICE: .75X TO 2X BASIC
RANDOM INSERTS IN PACKS
STATED PRINT RUN 23 SER.#'d SETS
3 Keibert Ruiz 25.00 60.00

2018 Panini Contenders Draft Picks School Colors
RANDOM INSERTS IN PACKS
*ICE/23: 2.5X TO 6X BASIC
1 Brady Singer .50 1.25
2 Shane McClanahan .40 1.00
3 Casey Mize 2.00 5.00
4 Ryan Rolison .50 1.25
5 Travis Swaggerty .75 2.00
6 Jackson Kowar .25 .60
7 Nick Madrigal 1.50 4.00
8 Cadyn Grenier .30 .75
9 Logan Gilbert .40 1.00
10 Greyson Jenista .50 1.25
11 Alec Bohm 1.25 3.00
12 Joey Bart 2.50 6.00
13 Trevor Larnach 1.50 4.00
14 Griffin Conine .50 1.25
15 Kris Bubic .40 1.00
16 Griffin Roberts .25 .60
17 Steele Walker .30 .75
18 Seth Beer 1.00 2.50
19 Jake McCarthy .40 1.00
20 Jonathan India .40 1.00
21 Nico Hoerner 1.25 3.00

2018 Panini Contenders Draft Picks School Colors Signatures
RANDOM INSERTS IN PACKS
*ICE/23: .6X TO 1.5X BASIC
1 Brady Singer 10.00 25.00
2 Shane McClanahan 5.00 12.00
3 Casey Mize 15.00 40.00
4 Ryan Rolison 6.00 15.00
5 Travis Swaggerty 10.00 25.00
6 Jackson Kowar 3.00 8.00
7 Nick Madrigal 20.00 50.00
8 Cadyn Grenier 4.00 10.00
9 Logan Gilbert 5.00 12.00
10 Trevor Larnach 20.00 50.00
13 Kris Bubic
14 Griffin Roberts 3.00 8.00
15 Jonathan India 10.00 25.00
17 Steele Walker 4.00 10.00
18 Seth Beer 12.00 30.00
19 Jake McCarthy 5.00 12.00
20 Nico Hoerner 15.00 40.00

2019 Panini Contenders Draft Picks
1 Adley Rutschman 1.25 3.00
2 Alek Manoah .40 1.00
3 Andrew Vaughn .60 1.50
4 Frank Thomas .30 .75
5 Reggie Jackson .25 .60
6 Braden Shewmake .60 1.50
7 Bryson Stott .60 1.50
8 Casey Mize .50 1.25
9 Hunter Bishop .60 1.50
10 JJ Bleday 1.00 2.50
11 Joey Bart .60 1.50
12 Jonathan India .25 .60
13 Josh Jung .60 1.50
14 Kameron Misner .50 1.25
15 Kody Hoese .60 1.50

16 Davis Wendzel .25 .60
17 Logan Davidson .20 .50
18 Logan Wyatt .30 .75
19 Michael Busch .60 1.50
20 Nick Lodolo .40 1.00
21 Nick Madrigal .60 1.50
22 Nico Hoerner .60 1.50
23 Shea Langeliers .40 1.00
24 Will Wilson .30 .75
25 Zack Thompson .30 .75

2019 Panini Contenders Draft Picks Cracked Ice Ticket

*CRCKD ICE: 2X TO 5X BASIC
RANDOM INSERTS IN PACKS
STATED PRINT RUN 23 SER.#'d SETS

2019 Panini Contenders Draft Picks Variations

*VAR: .4X TO 1X BASIC
RANDOM INSERTS IN PACKS

2019 Panini Contenders Draft Picks Variations Cracked Ice Ticket

*VAR CRCKD ICE: 2X TO 5X BASIC
RANDOM INSERTS IN PACKS
STATED PRINT RUN 23 SER.#'d SETS

2019 Panini Contenders Draft Picks Variations Draft Ticket

*VAR DRAFT: 1X TO 2.5X BASIC
RANDOM INSERTS IN PACKS
STATED PRINT RUN 99 SER.#'d SETS

2019 Panini Contenders Draft Picks Collegiate Connections Signatures

RANDOM INSERTS IN PACKS
EXCHANGE DEADLINE 10/24/2020
*CRCKD ICE/23: .5X TO 1.2X BASIC
1 Rutschman/Madrigal 50.00 120.00
2 Wendzel/Langeliers
4 Strumpf/Toglia 10.00 25.00
9 Fletcher/Campbell 12.00 30.00
10 Busch/Baum 20.00 50.00

2019 Panini Contenders Draft Picks Draft Ticket Autographs

RANDOM INSERTS IN PACKS
EXCHANGE DEADLINE 10/24/2020
*PRSPCT/99: .5X TO 1.2X BASIC
*CRCKD ICE/23: .75X TO 2X BASIC
1 Logan Davidson 2.50 6.00
2 Daniel Espino 3.00 8.00
3 Zack Thompson 4.00 10.00
4 Brennan Malone 2.50 6.00
5 Jackson Rutledge 5.00 12.00
6 George Kirby 4.00 10.00
7 Michael Busch 3.00 8.00
8 Rece Hinds 3.00 8.00
9 Logan Wyatt 4.00 10.00
11 Seth Johnson 2.50 6.00
14 J.J. Goss 3.00 8.00
15 Matt Canterino 3.00 8.00
16 Drey Jameson 2.50 6.00
17 Trejyn Fletcher 4.00 10.00
18 Chase Strumpf 5.00 12.00
21 Gunnar Henderson 5.00 12.00
22 Kyle Stowers 4.00 10.00
23 Kendall Williams 4.00 10.00
24 Nasim Nunez 2.50 6.00
25 Tyler Baum 3.00 8.00
26 Sammy Siani 3.00 8.00
27 Ethan Small 3.00 8.00
28 Josh Wolf 3.00 8.00
30 Logan Driscoll 4.00 10.00
31 T.J. Sikkema 4.00 10.00
32 Ryan Jensen 4.00 10.00
33 Anthony Volpe 10.00 25.00
34 Michael Toglia 4.00 10.00
35 Korey Lee 5.00 12.00
36 Kody Hoese 8.00 20.00
37 Davis Wendzel 3.00 8.00
38 John Doxakis 4.00 10.00
40 Matt Wallner 5.00 12.00
42 Ryan Garcia 2.50 6.00
43 Brady McConnell 4.00 10.00
44 Tommy Henry 3.00 8.00
45 Matt Gorski 4.00 10.00
47 Greg Jones 3.00 8.00
48 Aaron Schunk 5.00 12.00
51 Isaiah Campbell 5.00 12.00
52 Josh Smith 5.00 12.00
53 Karl Kauffmann 2.50 6.00
54 Kyren Paris 2.50 6.00
56 Yordys Valdes 5.00 12.00
58 Alec Marsh 3.00 8.00
59 Dominic Fletcher 2.50 6.00
60 Jared Triolo 4.00 10.00

2019 Panini Contenders Draft Picks Game Day Tickets

RANDOM INSERTS IN PACKS
*CRCKD ICE/23: 1.5X TO 4X BASIC
1 Adley Rutschman 1.50 4.00
2 Alek Manoah .50 1.25
3 Andrew Vaughn .75 2.00
4 Bobby Witt Jr. 1.00 2.50
5 Braden Shewmake .75 2.00
6 Bryson Stott .75 2.00
7 CJ Abrams 1.25 3.00
8 Riley Greene 1.00 2.50
9 Hunter Bishop .75 2.00
10 JJ Bleday 1.25 3.00
11 Josh Jung .75 2.00
12 Kameron Misner .60 1.50
13 Kody Hoese .75 2.00
14 Logan Davidson .25 .60
15 Logan Wyatt .40 1.00
16 Michael Busch .75 2.00
17 Nick Lodolo .50 1.25
18 Shea Langeliers .50 1.25
19 Will Wilson .40 1.00
20 Zack Thompson .40 1.00

2019 Panini Contenders Draft Picks International Ticket Autographs

RANDOM INSERTS IN PACKS
EXCHANGE DEADLINE 10/24/2020
*DRAFT/99: .5X TO 1.2X BASIC
*CRCKD ICE/23: .75X TO 2X BASIC
1 Noelvi Marte 6.00 15.00
2 Kevin Alcantara 5.00 12.00
3 Richard Gallardo 3.00 8.00
4 Diego Cartaya 5.00 12.00
5 Marco Luciano 10.00 25.00
6 Osiel Rodriguez 4.00 10.00
7 Orelvis Martinez 4.00 10.00

2019 Panini Contenders Draft Picks Legacy

RANDOM INSERTS IN PACKS
*CRCKD ICE/23: 1.5X TO 4X BASIC
1 Bobby Witt Jr. 1.00 2.50
2 Josh Jung .75 2.00
3 Shea Langeliers .50 1.25
4 Adley Rutschman 1.50 4.00
5 Andrew Vaughn .75 2.00
6 Will Wilson .40 1.00
7 Nolan Gorman .75 2.00
8 Adley Rutschman 1.50 4.00
9 Riley Greene 1.00 2.50
10 CJ Abrams 1.25 3.00

2019 Panini Contenders Draft Picks Legacy Signatures

RANDOM INSERTS IN PACKS
EXCHANGE DEADLINE 10/24/2020
*CRCKD ICE/23: .75X TO 2X
1 Bobby Witt Jr. 15.00 40.00
4 Adley Rutschman 25.00 60.00
5 Andrew Vaughn 10.00 25.00
7 Nolan Gorman 8.00 20.00
8 Adley Rutschman 25.00 60.00
9 Riley Greene 10.00 25.00
10 CJ Abrams 15.00 40.00

2019 Panini Contenders Draft Picks Prospect Ticket Autographs

RANDOM INSERTS IN PACKS
EXCHANGE DEADLINE 10/24/2020
*DRAFT/99: .5X TO 1.2X BASIC
*CRCKD ICE/23: .75X TO 2X BASIC
1 Wander Franco 25.00 60.00
2 Shervyen Newton 4.00 10.00
3 Royce Lewis 5.00 12.00
4 Casey Mize 6.00 15.00
5 Jhoan Duran 4.00 10.00
6 Moises Gomez 4.00 10.00
8 Carlos Rodriguez 2.50 6.00
9 Gavin Lux 15.00 40.00
10 Yordan Alvarez 40.00 100.00
11 Nick Madrigal 8.00 20.00
12 Jonathan India 3.00 8.00
13 Nolan Gorman 8.00 20.00
14 Luis Robert 25.00 60.00
15 Randy Florentino 2.50 6.00
16 Livan Soto 3.00 8.00
17 Victor Victor Mesa 5.00 12.00
18 Vidal Brujan 8.00 20.00
19 Nico Hoerner 8.00 20.00
20 Michael King 3.00 8.00
21 Miguel Vargas 12.00 30.00
22 Gabriel Maciel 2.50 6.00
23 Jarred Kelenic 10.00 25.00
24 Antonio Cabello 5.00 12.00
25 Luis Toribio 2.50 6.00

2019 Panini Contenders Draft Picks RPS Draft Ticket Autographs

RANDOM INSERTS IN PACKS
EXCHANGE DEADLINE 10/24/2020
*VAR: .4X TO 1X BASIC
*DRAFT/99: .5X TO 1.2X BASIC
*VAR DRAFT/99: .5X TO 1.2X BASIC
*CRCKD ICE/23: .75X TO 2X BASIC
*VAR CRCKD ICE/23: .75X TO 2X BASIC
1 Adley Rutschman 20.00 50.00
2 Bobby Witt Jr. EXCH 10.00 25.00
3 CJ Abrams 12.00 30.00
4 Andrew Vaughn 8.00 20.00
5 Riley Greene EXCH 15.00 40.00
6 Shea Langeliers 8.00 20.00
7 Corbin Carroll 4.00 10.00
8 Josh Jung 8.00 20.00
9 Hunter Bishop 8.00 20.00
10 Kameron Misner EXCH 6.00 15.00
11 Bryson Stott 4.00 10.00
12 Brett Baty 5.00 12.00
13 Nick Lodolo 5.00 12.00
14 JJ Bleday 12.00 30.00
15 Alek Manoah EXCH 5.00 12.00
16 Will Wilson 4.00 10.00

2019 Panini Contenders Draft Picks School Colors

RANDOM INSERTS IN PACKS
*CRCKD ICE/23: 1.5X TO 4X BASIC
1 Adley Rutschman 1.50 4.00
2 Alek Manoah .50 1.25
3 Andrew Vaughn .75 2.00
4 Bobby Witt Jr. 1.00 2.50
5 Braden Shewmake .75 2.00
6 Bryson Stott .75 2.00
7 CJ Abrams 1.25 3.00
8 Riley Greene 1.00 2.50
9 Hunter Bishop .75 2.00
10 JJ Bleday 1.25 3.00
11 Josh Jung .75 2.00
12 Kameron Misner .60 1.50
13 Kody Hoese .75 2.00
14 Logan Davidson .25 .60
15 Logan Wyatt .40 1.00
16 Michael Busch .75 2.00
17 Nick Lodolo .50 1.25
18 Shea Langeliers .50 1.25
19 Will Wilson .40 1.00
20 Zack Thompson .40 1.00

2019 Panini Contenders Draft Picks School Colors Signatures

RANDOM INSERTS IN PACKS
EXCHANGE DEADLINE 10/24/2020
*CRCKD ICE/23: .75X TO 2X
1 Adley Rutschman 25.00 60.00
2 Andrew Vaughn 10.00 25.00
3 Bobby Witt Jr. 20.00 50.00
4 Bryson Stott 10.00 25.00
5 CJ Abrams 15.00 40.00
6 Corbin Carroll 5.00 12.00
7 Kody Hoese 10.00 25.00
8 Hunter Bishop 10.00 25.00
9 JJ Bleday 15.00 40.00
10 Josh Jung 12.00 30.00
13 Logan Davidson 3.00 8.00
14 Logan Wyatt 5.00 12.00
15 Michael Busch 10.00 25.00
16 Nick Lodolo 6.00 15.00
17 Riley Greene 6.00 15.00
18 Shea Langeliers 6.00 15.00
19 Will Wilson 5.00 12.00
20 Zack Thompson 5.00 12.00

2018 Panini Contenders Optic

1 Amed Rosario .30 .75
2 Austin Hays .40 1.00
3 Clint Frazier .50 1.25
4 Ronald Acuna Jr. 5.00 12.00
5 Miguel Andujar 1.00 2.50
6 Ozzie Albies .75 2.00
7 Rafael Devers .75 2.00
8 Rhys Hoskins 1.00 2.50
9 Shohei Ohtani 1.50 4.00
10 Gleyber Torres RC 2.50 6.00

2019 Panini Contenders Optic

RANDOM INSERTS IN PACKS
*HOLO: .75X TO 2X
*HYPER/299: .75X TO 2X
*RUBY/199: 1X TO 2.5X
*BLUE/99: 1.2X TO 3X
*PURPLE/75: 1.2X TO 3X
*GREEN/50: 1.5X TO 4X
*PINK/25: 2.5X TO 6X
1 Pete Alonso RC 4.00 10.00
2 Eloy Jimenez RC .60 1.50
3 Fernando Tatis Jr. RC 3.00 8.00
4 Michael Kopech RC .30 .75
5 Kyle Tucker RC .30 .75
6 Yusei Kikuchi RC .25 .60
7 Chris Paddack RC .30 .75
8 Mike Trout 2.50 6.00
9 Nick Senzel RC .50 1.25
10 Aaron Judge .60 1.50
11 Kris Bryant .30 .75
12 Shohei Ohtani .30 .75
13 Ozzie Albies .25 .60
14 Andrew Benintendi .25 .60
15 Juan Soto .75 2.00
16 Felix Hernandez .20 .50
17 Jose Ramirez .20 .50
18 Ronald Acuna Jr. 2.50 6.00
19 Trea Turner .20 .50
20 Vladimir Guerrero Jr. RC 2.50 6.00
21 Corey Kluber .20 .50
22 Carter Kieboom RC .25 .60
23 Trevor Story .25 .60
24 Brandon Lowe RC .25 .60
25 Michael Chavis RC .25 .60

2019 Panini Contenders Optic Draft Picks Autographs

RANDOM INSERTS IN PACKS
EXCHANGE DEADLINE 10/24/2020
*HYPER/20: .75X TO 2X BASIC
1 Adley Rutschman 25.00 60.00
2 Bobby Witt Jr. EXCH 20.00 50.00
3 CJ Abrams 15.00 40.00
4 Andrew Vaughn 20.00 50.00
5 Riley Greene EXCH 12.00 30.00
6 Shea Langeliers 8.00 20.00
7 Corbin Carroll 5.00 12.00
8 Josh Jung 8.00 20.00
9 Hunter Bishop 10.00 25.00
10 Kameron Misner EXCH 6.00 15.00
11 Bryson Stott 10.00 25.00
12 Logan Davidson 3.00 8.00
13 Nick Lodolo 6.00 15.00
14 Michael Busch 10.00 25.00
15 Zack Thompson 5.00 12.00
16 Brett Baty 6.00 15.00
17 Will Wilson 5.00 12.00
18 Alek Manoah EXCH 10.00 25.00
19 JJ Bleday 15.00 40.00
20 Jackson Rutledge 6.00 15.00

2020 Panini Contenders Optic

RANDOM INSERTS IN '20 CHRONICLES
1 Bo Bichette RC 3.00 8.00
2 Yordan Alvarez RC 1.25 3.00
3 Gavin Lux RC 1.50 4.00
4 Brendan McKay RC .40 1.00
5 Aristides Aquino RC .50 1.25
6 Yoshitomo Tsutsugo RC .30 .75
7 Luis Robert RC 4.00 10.00
8 Aaron Judge .60 1.50
9 Mike Trout 2.00 5.00
10 Cody Bellinger .50 1.25
11 Fernando Tatis Jr. 2.00 5.00
12 Vladimir Guerrero Jr. .50 1.25
13 Shohei Ohtani .30 .75
14 Mookie Betts .50 1.25
15 Manny Machado .25 .60
16 Bryce Harper .40 1.00
17 Francisco Lindor .25 .60
18 Rafael Devers .30 .75
19 Alex Bregman .25 .60
20 Matt Chapman .25 .60
21 Ronald Acuna Jr. 1.50 4.00
22 Juan Soto .75 2.00
23 Pete Alonso .60 1.50
24 Christian Yelich .30 .75
25 Clayton Kershaw .50 1.25
26 Shogo Akiyama RC .40 1.00
27 Isan Diaz RC .40 1.00
28 Nico Hoerner RC 1.00 2.50
29 Xander Bogaerts .25 .60
30 Josh Bell .20 .50

2020 Panini Contenders Optic Blue Ice

*BLUE VET: 1.5X TO 4X BASIC
*BLUE RC: 1X TO 2.5X BASIC RC
RANDOM INSERTS IN '20 CHRONICLES
STATED PRINT RUN 99 SER.#'d SETS
1 Bo Bichette 20.00 50.00
2 Yordan Alvarez 10.00 25.00
7 Luis Robert 30.00 80.00
9 Mike Trout 12.00 30.00

2020 Panini Contenders Optic Green

*GREEN VET: 2.5X TO 6X BASIC
*GREEN RC: 1.5X TO 4X BASIC RC
RANDOM INSERTS IN '20 CHRONICLES
STATED PRINT RUN 50 SER.#'d SETS
1 Bo Bichette 30.00 80.00
2 Yordan Alvarez 25.00 60.00
7 Luis Robert 40.00 100.00
9 Mike Trout 25.00 60.00

2020 Panini Contenders Optic Holo

*HOLO VET: 1X TO 2.5X BASIC
*HOLO RC: .6X TO 1.5X BASIC RC
RANDOM INSERTS IN '20 CHRONICLES
7 Luis Robert 8.00 20.00

2020 Panini Contenders Optic Hyper

*HYPER VET: 1.2X TO 3X BASIC
*HYPER RC: .8X TO 2X BASIC RC
RANDOM INSERTS IN '20 CHRONICLES
STATED PRINT RUN 299 SER.#'d SETS
7 Luis Robert 15.00 40.00

2020 Panini Contenders Optic Pink

*PINK VET: 4X TO 10X BASIC
*PINK RC: 2.5X TO 6X BASIC RC
RANDOM INSERTS IN '20 CHRONICLES
STATED PRINT RUN 25 SER.#'d SETS
1 Bo Bichette 50.00 120.00
2 Yordan Alvarez 40.00 100.00
7 Luis Robert 60.00 150.00
9 Mike Trout 30.00 80.00

2020 Panini Contenders Optic Purple Mojo

*PURPLE VET: 1.5X TO 4X BASIC
*PURPLE RC: 1X TO 2.5X BASIC RC
RANDOM INSERTS IN '20 CHRONICLES
STATED PRINT RUN 75 SER.#'d SETS
1 Bo Bichette 20.00 50.00
2 Yordan Alvarez 15.00 40.00
7 Luis Robert 30.00 80.00
9 Mike Trout 20.00 50.00

2020 Panini Contenders Optic Ruby Wave

*RUBY VET: 1.2X TO 3X BASIC
*RUBY RC: .8X TO 2X BASIC RC
RANDOM INSERTS IN '20 CHRONICLES
STATED PRINT RUN 199 SER.#'d SETS
7 Luis Robert 15.00 40.00

2020 Panini Contenders Optic Draft Pick Ticket Autographs

RANDOM INSERTS IN '20 CONTENDERS
EXCHANGE DEADLINE 4/30/22
1 Austin Martin
2 Spencer Torkelson
3 Emerson Hancock 12.00 30.00
4 Zac Veen
5 Asa Lacy 20.00 50.00

2020 Panini Contenders Optic Draft Pick Ticket Autographs Cracked Ice

*CRCKD ICE: .8X TO 2X BASIC
RANDOM INSERTS IN '20 CONTENDERS
STATED PRINT RUN 23 SER.#'d SETS
EXCHANGE DEADLINE 4/30/22
2 Spencer Torkelson 400.00 800.00

2020 Panini Contenders Optic Rookie Ticket Autograph Variations

RANDOM INSERTS IN '20 CONTENDERS
EXCHANGE DEADLINE 4/30/22
1 Bo Bichette EXCH 30.00 80.00
2 Yordan Alvarez 20.00 50.00
3 Gavin Lux 20.00 50.00
4 Brendan McKay 5.00 12.00
5 Aristides Aquino 12.00 30.00
6 Yoshitomo Tsutsugo 8.00 20.00
7 Luis Robert EXCH 50.00 120.00
8 Dustin May 12.00 30.00
9 Dylan Cease EXCH 6.00 15.00
10 Zac Gallen 6.00 15.00
11 A.J. Puk EXCH 6.00 15.00
12 Brusdar Graterol 5.00 12.00
13 Adbert Alzolay 4.00 10.00
14 Aaron Civale 5.00 12.00
15 Tony Gonsolin 6.00 15.00
16 Sean Murphy 5.00 12.00
17 Kwang-Hyun Kim 15.00 40.00
18 Shun Yamaguchi 4.00 10.00
19 Jesus Luzardo
20 Bryan Abreu 3.00 8.00
21 Shogo Akiyama 8.00 20.00
22 Isan Diaz EXCH 5.00 12.00
23 Nico Hoerner 10.00 25.00
24 Brendan McKay 5.00 12.00
25 Mauricio Dubon 4.00 10.00

2020 Panini Contenders Optic Rookie Ticket Autograph Variations Cracked Ice

*CRCKD ICE: .8X TO 2X BASIC
RANDOM INSERTS IN '20 CONTENDERS
STATED PRINT RUN 23 SER.#'d SETS
EXCHANGE DEADLINE 4/30/22
2 Yordan Alvarez 60.00 150.00
8 Dustin May 30.00 80.00

2020 Panini Contenders Optic Rookie Ticket Autographs

RANDOM INSERTS IN '20 CONTENDERS
EXCHANGE DEADLINE 4/30/22
1 Bo Bichette EXCH 30.00 80.00
2 Yordan Alvarez 20.00 50.00
3 Gavin Lux 20.00 50.00
4 Brendan McKay 5.00 12.00
5 Aristides Aquino 12.00 30.00
6 Yoshitomo Tsutsugo 8.00 20.00
7 Luis Robert EXCH 50.00 120.00
8 Dustin May 12.00 30.00
9 Dylan Cease EXCH 6.00 15.00
10 Zac Gallen 6.00 15.00
11 A.J. Puk EXCH 6.00 15.00
12 Brusdar Graterol 5.00 12.00
13 Adbert Alzolay 4.00 10.00
14 Aaron Civale 5.00 12.00
15 Tony Gonsolin 6.00 15.00
16 Sean Murphy 5.00 12.00
17 Kwang-Hyun Kim 15.00 40.00
18 Shun Yamaguchi 4.00 10.00
19 Jesus Luzardo
20 Bryan Abreu 3.00 8.00
21 Shogo Akiyama 8.00 20.00
22 Isan Diaz EXCH 5.00 12.00
23 Nico Hoerner 10.00 25.00
24 Brendan McKay 5.00 12.00
25 Mauricio Dubon 4.00 10.00

2020 Panini Contenders Optic Rookie Ticket Autographs Cracked Ice

*CRCKD ICE: .8X TO 2X BASIC
RANDOM INSERTS IN '20 CONTENDERS
STATED PRINT RUN 23 SER.#'d SETS
EXCHANGE DEADLINE 4/30/22
2 Yordan Alvarez 60.00 150.00
8 Dustin May 30.00 80.00

2020 Panini Contenders Optic Season Ticket

RANDOM INSERTS IN PACKS
31 Trea Turner .60 1.50
32 Gerrit Cole 1.25 3.00
33 Jacob deGrom .75 2.00
34 Miguel Cabrera .75 2.00
35 Albert Pujols 1.00 2.50
36 Robinson Cano .60 1.50
37 Nolan Arenado 1.00 2.50
38 Walker Buehler 1.00 2.50
39 Jack Flaherty .60 1.50
40 Gleyber Torres 1.50 4.00
41 Kris Bryant 1.00 2.50
42 Whit Merrifield .75 2.00
43 Starling Marte .60 1.50
44 Ozzie Albies .75 2.00
45 Freddie Freeman 1.00 2.50
46 Trevor Story .75 2.00
47 Paul Goldschmidt .75 2.00
48 J.D. Martinez .75 2.00
49 Austin Meadows .60 1.50
50 Shane Bieber .75 2.00
51 Anthony Rendon .75 2.00
52 Alex Verdugo .60 1.50
53 Charlie Blackmon .75 2.00
54 Chris Paddack .75 2.00
55 Keston Hiura 1.00 2.50
56 Max Scherzer .75 2.00
57 Yoan Moncada .75 2.00
58 Max Muncy .60 1.50
59 Cavan Biggio 1.00 2.50
60 Victor Robles 1.00 2.50
61 Tommy Edman .75 2.00
62 Jose Ramirez .60 1.50
63 Amed Rosario .60 1.50
64 Adalberto Mondesi .75 2.00
65 Willy Adames .50 1.25
66 Mike Soroka .75 2.00
67 Eloy Jimenez 1.50 4.00
68 Justin Verlander .75 2.00
69 Nelson Cruz .75 2.00
70 Javier Baez 1.00 2.50
71 Stephen Strasburg .75 2.00

2020 Panini Contenders Optic Season Ticket Cracked Ice

*CRCKD ICE: 1.2X TO 3X BASIC
RANDOM INSERTS IN '20 CONTENDERS
STATED PRINT RUN 23 SER.#'d SETS
34 Miguel Cabrera 8.00 20.00
38 Walker Buehler 6.00 15.00
45 Freddie Freeman 8.00 20.00

2018 Panini Cornerstones

1 Jack Flaherty JSY AU RC 5.00 12.00
2 Rhys Hoskins JSY AU RC 20.00 50.00
3 Ozzie Albies JSY AU RC 15.00 40.00
4 Miguel Andujar JSY AU RC 25.00 60.00
5 Rafael Devers JSY AU RC 20.00 50.00
6 Chance Sisco JSY AU RC 4.00 10.00
7 Victor Caratini JSY AU RC 8.00 20.00
8 Francisco Mejia JSY AU RC 10.00 25.00
9 Kyle Farmer JSY AU RC 3.00 8.00
10 Austin Hays JSY AU RC 5.00 12.00
11 Alex Verdugo JSY AU RC 8.00 20.00
12 Zack Granite JSY AU RC 3.00 8.00
13 Clint Frazier JSY AU RC 8.00 20.00
14 Nick Williams JSY AU RC 4.00 10.00
15 Harrison Bader JSY AU RC 5.00 12.00
16 Willie Calhoun JSY AU RC 4.00 10.00
17 Victor Robles JSY AU RC 8.00 20.00
18 Max Fried JSY AU RC 12.00 30.00
19 Lucas Sims JSY AU RC 3.00 8.00
20 Walker Buehler JSY AU RC 12.00 30.00
21 Erick Fedde JSY AU RC 3.00 8.00
22 Amed Rosario JSY AU RC 5.00 12.00
23 Tyler Wade JSY AU RC 4.00 10.00
24 J.P. Crawford JSY AU RC 3.00 8.00
25 Shohei Ohtani JSY AU RC 150.00 300.00
26 Mike Trout 5.00 12.00
27 Bryce Harper 1.25 3.00
28 Aaron Judge 5.00 12.00
29 Cody Bellinger 1.50 4.00
30 Jose Altuve .60 1.50
31 Ichiro 1.00 2.50
32 Clayton Kershaw 1.50 4.00
33 Buster Posey 1.00 2.50
34 Giancarlo Stanton .75 2.00
35 Shohei Ohtani 3.00 8.00
36 J.D. Martinez .75 2.00
37 Paul Goldschmidt .75 2.00
38 Joey Votto .75 2.00
39 George Springer .60 1.50
40 Jose Ramirez .60 1.50
41 Max Scherzer .75 2.00
42 Albert Pujols 1.00 2.50
43 Francisco Lindor .75 2.00
44 Kris Bryant 1.00 2.50
45 Manny Machado .75 2.00
46 Gary Sanchez .75 2.00
47 Miguel Cabrera .75 2.00
48 Andrew McCutchen .75 2.00
49 Carlos Correa .75 2.00
50 Nolan Arenado 1.00 2.50

2018 Panini Cornerstones Reserve Materials

INSERTED IN '18 CHRONICLES PACKS
PRINT RUNS B/WN 49-99 COPIES PER
*QRTZ/49: .5X TO 1.2X p/r 99
*QRTZ/25: .6X TO 1.5X p/r 99
*GRANITE/25: .6X TO 1.5X p/r 99
*GRANITE/25: .5X TO 1.2X p/r 49
1 Ozzie Albies/99 4.00 10.00
2 Rafael Devers/99 6.00 15.00
3 Clint Frazier/99 4.00 10.00
4 Rhys Hoskins/99 4.00 10.00
5 Amed Rosario/99 2.50 6.00
6 Nick Williams/99 2.50 6.00
7 Francisco Mejia/99 2.50 6.00
8 Willie Calhoun/99 2.50 6.00
9 Victor Robles/99 4.00 10.00
10 J.P. Crawford/99 2.00 5.00
11 Kyle Farmer/99 2.00 5.00
12 Paul Blackburn/99 2.00 5.00
13 Miguel Andujar/99 5.00 12.00
14 Walker Buehler/99 4.00 10.00
15 Chance Sisco/99 2.50 6.00
16 Gary Sanchez/99 3.00 8.00
17 George Springer/99 2.50 6.00
18 Adrian Beltre/49 4.00 10.00
19 Andrew Benintendi/99 3.00 8.00
20 Buster Posey/49 4.00 10.00
21 Clayton Kershaw/49 4.00 10.00
22 Corey Seager/99 3.00 8.00
23 Giancarlo Stanton/99 4.00 10.00
24 Shohei Ohtani/99 10.00 25.00
25 Marcell Ozuna/99 3.00 8.00

2018 Panini Cornerstones Rookie Reserve Signatures

RANDOM INSERTS IN PACKS
STATED PRINT RUN 99 SER.#'d SETS
*QUARTZ/49: .5X TO 1.2X BASIC
*GRANITE/25: .75X TO 2X BASIC
1 Brandon Woodruff 4.00 10.00
2 Rhys Hoskins 12.00 30.00
3 Ozzie Albies 12.00 30.00
4 Miguel Andujar 6.00 15.00
5 Rafael Devers 8.00 20.00
6 Chance Sisco 4.00 10.00
7 Victor Caratini 4.00 10.00
8 Francisco Mejia 4.00 10.00
9 Kyle Farmer 3.00 8.00
10 Austin Hays 5.00
11 Alex Verdugo 5.00
12 Zack Granite 3.00
13 Clint Frazier 6.00
14 Nick Williams 4.00
15 Harrison Bader 5.00
16 Willie Calhoun 4.00
17 Victor Robles 8.00
18 Max Fried 12.00
20 Walker Buehler 15.00
21 Erick Fedde 3.00
22 Amed Rosario 4.00
23 Tyler Wade 4.00
24 J.P. Crawford 3.00
25 Richard Urena 3.00

2019 Panini Cornerstones

INSERTED IN '19 CHRONICLES PACKS
STATED PRINT RUN 99 SER.#'d SETS
26 Mike Trout 6.00
27 Shohei Ohtani 1.00
28 Aaron Judge 2.00
29 Mookie Betts 1.25
30 Alex Bregman .75
31 Christian Yelich 1.00
32 Francisco Lindor .75
33 Javier Baez 1.00
34 Nolan Arenado 1.00
35 Ronald Acuna Jr. 4.00

2019 Panini Cornerstones Prospect Quad Relic Autogra[phs]

INSERTED IN '19 CHRONICLES PACKS
PRINT RUNS B/WN 25-99 COPIES PER
EXCHANGE DEADLINE 2/21/2021
*CRYSTAL/49: .5X TO 1.2X p/r 99
*CRYSTAL/25: .5X TO 1.2X p/r 49
1 Forrest Whitley/49 6.00
2 Brendan Rodgers/49 6.00
3 Bo Bichette/99 30.00
4 Wander Franco/25 50.00
6 Ian Anderson/49 10.00
8 Mitch Keller/49 5.00
9 Leody Taveras/49 4.00
12 Sean Murphy/25 6.00
14 Adbert Alzolay/49 4.00
15 Kyle Lewis/49 8.00
16 Julio Pablo Martinez/49 4.00
17 Khalil Lee/49 4.00
18 Brent Honeywell/49 5.00
19 Yordan Alvarez/49 40.00
20 Corey Ray/49 4.00

2019 Panini Cornerstones Prospect Quad Relic Autogra[phs] Crystal

*CRYSTAL/49: .5X TO 1.2X p/r 99
*CRYSTAL/25: .5X TO 1.2X p/r 49
INSERTED IN '19 CHRONICLES PACKS
PRINT RUNS B/WN 25-49 COPIES PER
EXCHANGE DEADLINE 2/21/2021
1 Forrest Whitley/25 12.00

2019 Panini Cornerstones Qu[ad] Relic Autographs

INSERTED IN '19 CHRONICLES PACKS
PRINT RUNS B/WN 7-49 COPIES PER
NO PRICING QTY 15 OR LESS
EXCHANGE DEADLINE 2/21/2021
*CRYSTAL/25: .5X TO 1.2X p/r 49
2 Juan Soto/49 30.00
3 Jose Ramirez/25 6.00
4 Justin Turner/25 6.00
5 Jose Canseco/49 20.00
6 Rod Carew/15
7 Tom Glavine/15
8 Al Oliver/25 5.00
9 Mitch Haniger/25 6.00
10 Juan Gonzalez/49 4.00
11 Omar Vizquel/25 6.00
12 Whit Merrifield/25 8.00
13 Aaron Judge/10
14 Shohei Ohtani/7
15 Ichiro/7

2018 Panini Crusade

INSERTED IN '18 CHRONICLES PACKS
1 Gleyber Torres RC 2.50
2 Giancarlo Stanton .25
3 Rhys Hoskins RC 1.00
4 Jose Altuve .20
5 Manny Machado .25
6 Clint Frazier RC .50
7 Aaron Judge .60
8 Kris Bryant .30
9 Miguel Andujar RC 1.00
10 Rafael Devers RC .75
11 Alex Verdugo RC .40
12 Bryce Harper .40
13 Nick Williams RC .30
14 Shohei Ohtani RC 1.50
15 Ryan McMahon RC .30
16 Victor Robles RC .60
17 Austin Hays RC .40
18 Ronald Acuna Jr. RC 5.00
19 Mike Trout 1.25
20 Dominic Smith RC .25
21 Cody Bellinger .50
22 Nolan Arenado .30
23 Amed Rosario RC .30
24 J.P. Crawford RC .25
25 Ozzie Albies RC .75

2018 Panini Crusade Blue Ic[e]

*BLUE: 1X TO 2.5X BASIC
*BLUE RC: .6X TO 1.5X BASIC
INSERTED IN '18 CHRONICLES PACKS

ATED PRINT RUN 149 SER.#'d SETS
Rhys Hoskins 4.00 10.00
Shohei Ohtani 6.00 15.00
Ronald Acuna Jr. 6.00 15.00
Mike Trout 6.00 15.00

2018 Panini Crusade Green
GREEN: 1.5X TO 4X BASIC
GREEN RC: 1X TO 2.5X BASIC
SERTED IN '18 CHRONICLES PACKS
TATED PRINT RUN 50 SER.#'d SETS
Gleyber Torres 8.00 20.00
Rhys Hoskins 6.00 15.00
Aaron Judge 12.00 30.00
Miguel Andujar 10.00 25.00
Shohei Ohtani 10.00 25.00
Ronald Acuna Jr. 10.00 25.00
Mike Trout 10.00 25.00

2018 Panini Crusade Holo
HOLO: .75X TO 2X BASIC
HOLO RC: .5X TO 1.2X BASIC
SERTED IN '18 CHRONICLES PACKS
Rhys Hoskins 3.00 8.00
4 Shohei Ohtani 5.00 12.00
8 Ronald Acuna Jr. 5.00 12.00
9 Mike Trout 5.00 12.00

2018 Panini Crusade Hyper
HYPER: .75X TO 2X BASIC
HYPER RC: .5X TO 1.2X BASIC
SERTED IN '18 CHRONICLES PACKS
TATED PRINT RUN 299 SER.#'d SETS
Rhys Hoskins 3.00 8.00
4 Shohei Ohtani 5.00 12.00
8 Ronald Acuna Jr. 5.00 12.00
9 Mike Trout 5.00 12.00

2018 Panini Crusade Pink
PINK: 2.5X TO 6X BASIC
PINK RC: 1.5X TO 4X BASIC
SERTED IN '18 CHRONICLES PACKS
TATED PRINT RUN 25 SER.#'d SETS
Gleyber Torres 12.00 30.00
Rhys Hoskins 10.00 25.00
Aaron Judge 20.00 50.00
Miguel Andujar 15.00 40.00
4 Shohei Ohtani 15.00 40.00
8 Ronald Acuna Jr. 15.00 40.00
9 Mike Trout 15.00 40.00

2018 Panini Crusade Purple Mojo
PURPLE: 1.2X TO 3X BASIC
PURPLE RC: .75X TO 2X BASIC
SERTED IN '18 CHRONICLES PACKS
TATED PRINT RUN 99 SER.#'d SETS
Gleyber Torres 6.00 15.00
Rhys Hoskins 5.00 12.00
4 Shohei Ohtani 8.00 20.00
8 Ronald Acuna Jr. 8.00 20.00
9 Mike Trout 8.00 20.00

2018 Panini Crusade Ruby Wave
RUBY: 1X TO 2.5X BASIC
RUBY RC: .6X TO 1.5X BASIC
SERTED IN '18 CHRONICLES PACKS
TATED PRINT RUN 199 SER.#'d SETS
Rhys Hoskins 4.00 10.00
4 Shohei Ohtani 6.00 15.00
8 Ronald Acuna Jr. 6.00 15.00
9 Mike Trout 6.00 15.00

2018 Panini Crusade Signatures
RANDOM INSERTS IN PACKS
Felix Jorge 2.50 6.00
Andrew Stevenson 2.50 6.00
0 Jimmie Sherfy 2.50 6.00
5 Trevor Story 6.00 15.00
18 Franmil Reyes 4.00 10.00
20 Yairo Munoz 6.00 15.00

2019 Panini Crusade
RANDOM INSERTS IN PACKS
*HOLO: .75X TO 2X
*HYPER/299: .75X TO 2X
*RUBY/199: 1X TO 2.5X
*BLUE/99: 1.2X TO 3X
*PURPLE/75: 1.2X TO 3X
*GREEN/50: 1.5X TO 4X
*PINK/25: 2.5X TO 6X
1 Pete Alonso RC 5.00 12.00
2 Eloy Jimenez RC .60 1.50
3 Fernando Tatis Jr. RC 4.00 10.00
4 Michael Kopech RC .30 .75
5 Kyle Tucker RC .30 .75
6 Yusei Kikuchi RC .25 .60
7 Chris Paddack RC .30 .75
8 Mike Trout 1.25 3.00
9 Bryce Harper .40 1.00
10 Aaron Judge .60 1.50
11 Kris Bryant .30 .75
12 Shohei Ohtani .30 .75
13 Jacob deGrom .25 .60
14 Nick Senzel RC .50 1.25
15 Shaun Anderson RC .15 .40
16 Gleyber Torres .50 1.25
17 Juan Soto .75 2.00
18 Carter Kieboom RC .25 .60
19 Jose Altuve .20 .50
20 Brandon Lowe RC .25 .60
21 Vladimir Guerrero Jr. RC 4.00 10.00
22 Cody Bellinger .50 1.25
23 Rhys Hoskins .30 .75
24 Blake Snell .20 .50
25 Max Scherzer .25 .60

2020 Panini Crusade
RANDOM INSERTS IN PACKS
1 Bo Bichette RC 3.00 8.00
2 Yordan Alvarez RC 1.25 3.00
3 Gavin Lux RC 1.50 4.00
4 Brendan McKay RC .40 1.00
5 Aristides Aquino RC .50 1.25
6 Yoshitomo Tsutsugo RC .30 .75
7 Luis Robert RC 4.00 10.00
8 Aaron Judge .60 1.50
9 Mike Trout 2.00 5.00
10 Cody Bellinger .50 1.25
11 Fernando Tatis Jr. 2.00 5.00
12 Vladimir Guerrero Jr. .50 1.25
13 Kwang-Hyun Kim RC .75 2.00
14 Ketel Marte .20 .50
15 Blake Snell .20 .50
16 Pete Alonso .60 1.50
17 Kris Bryant .30 .75
18 Kyle Lewis RC 4.00 10.00
19 Nick Solak RC .40 1.00
20 A.J. Puk RC .50 1.25

2016 Panini Flawless
STATED PRINT RUN 20 SER.#'d SETS
1 Albert Pujols 25.00 60.00
2 Babe Ruth 60.00 150.00
3 Bill Dickey 12.00 30.00
4 Bryce Harper 75.00 200.00
5 Buster Posey 15.00 40.00
6 Cal Ripken 40.00 100.00
7 Carl Yastrzemski 25.00 60.00
8 Carlos Correa 50.00 120.00
9 Clayton Kershaw 25.00 60.00
10 Dizzy Dean 15.00 40.00
11 Eddie Collins 12.00 30.00
12 Frank Chance 12.00 30.00
13 Frank Thomas 30.00 80.00
14 George Brett 50.00 120.00
15 George Sisler 12.00 30.00
16 Greg Maddux 30.00 80.00
17 Herb Pennock 10.00 25.00
18 Honus Wagner 20.00 50.00
19 Ichiro Suzuki 60.00 150.00
20 Jackie Robinson 25.00 60.00
21 Jimmie Foxx 15.00 40.00
22 Joe DiMaggio 25.00 60.00
23 Joe Jackson 30.00 80.00
24 Jose Abreu 12.00 30.00
25 Josh Donaldson 12.00 30.00
26 Ken Griffey Jr. 75.00 200.00
27 Kirby Puckett 60.00 150.00
28 Kris Bryant 60.00 150.00
29 Lefty Gomez 10.00 25.00
30 Lou Gehrig 60.00 150.00
31 Mark McGwire 20.00 50.00
32 Masahiro Tanaka 20.00 50.00
33 Mel Ott 20.00 50.00
34 Miguel Cabrera 25.00 60.00
35 Mike Schmidt 20.00 50.00
36 Mike Trout 75.00 200.00
37 Nolan Ryan 50.00 120.00
38 Pete Rose 25.00 60.00
39 Roberto Clemente 40.00 100.00
40 Roger Maris 20.00 50.00
41 Rogers Hornsby 20.00 50.00
42 Ryne Sandberg 25.00 60.00
43 Stan Musial 20.00 50.00
44 Ted Williams 30.00 80.00
45 Tony Gwynn 40.00 100.00
46 Tony Lazzeri 15.00 40.00
47 Tris Speaker 10.00 25.00
48 Ty Cobb 30.00 80.00
49 Willie Keeler 20.00 50.00
50 Yadier Molina 30.00 80.00
51 Barry Bonds AM 30.00 80.00
52 Bo Jackson AM 25.00 60.00
53 Randy Johnson AM 20.00 50.00
54 Frank Thomas AM 30.00 80.00
55 Mark McGwire AM 20.00 50.00
56 Buster Posey AM 15.00 40.00
57 Dustin Pedroia AM 15.00 40.00
58 Kyle Schwarber AM 25.00 60.00
59 Jake Arrieta AM 20.00 50.00
60 Michael Conforto AM 20.00 50.00
61 Stephen Piscotty AM 15.00 40.00
62 Trea Turner AM 15.00 40.00
63 David Price AM 20.00 50.00
64 Max Scherzer AM 12.00 30.00
65 Will Clark AM 25.00 60.00
66 Jackie Robinson AM 25.00 60.00
67 Craig Biggio AM 15.00 40.00
68 Tony Gwynn AM 40.00 100.00
69 Josh Donaldson AM 12.00 30.00
70 Matt Harvey AM 15.00 40.00
71 Clayton Kershaw USA 60.00 150.00
72 Kris Bryant USA 125.00 300.00
73 Buster Posey USA 50.00 120.00
74 Manny Machado USA 40.00 100.00
75 Kyle Schwarber USA 40.00 100.00
76 Corey Seager USA 75.00 150.00
77 Michael Conforto USA 40.00 100.00
78 Trea Turner USA 40.00 100.00
79 Mark McGwire USA 60.00 150.00
80 Frank Thomas USA 50.00 120.00
81 Ken Griffey Jr. USA 100.00 250.00
82 Bryce Harper USA 75.00 200.00
83 Mike Trout USA 125.00 300.00
84 Andrew McCutchen USA 50.00 120.00
85 Alex Rodriguez USA 60.00 150.00
86 Kyle Schwarber RC 25.00 60.00
87 Corey Seager RC 40.00 100.00
88 Miguel Sano RC 12.00 30.00
89 Michael Conforto RC 20.00 50.00
90 Stephen Piscotty RC 15.00 40.00
91 Trea Turner RC 15.00 40.00
92 Luis Severino RC 10.00 25.00
93 Rob Refsnyder RC 10.00 25.00
94 Aaron Nola RC 15.00 40.00
95 Ketel Marte RC 12.00 30.00
96 Raul Mondesi RC 12.00 30.00
97 Henry Owens RC 10.00 25.00
98 Greg Bird RC 10.00 25.00
99 Jose Peraza RC 10.00 25.00
100 Hector Olivera RC 10.00 25.00
101 Trevor Story RC 30.00 80.00
102 Byung-ho Park RC 20.00 50.00
103 Kenta Maeda RC 20.00 50.00

2016 Panini Flawless Ruby
*RUBY: .4X TO 1X BASIC
RANDOM INSERTS IN PACKS
STATED PRINT RUN 15 SER.#'d SETS

2016 Panini Flawless Dual Diamond Memorabilia Ruby
RANDOM INSERTS IN PACKS
PRINT RUNS B/WN 15-20 COPIES PER
1 Adam Wainwright 20.00 50.00
Yadier Molina/20
4 Belt/Bumgarner/20 60.00 150.00
8 Chris Archer 15.00 40.00
Kevin Kiermaier/20
9 Ichiro/Gordon/15 25.00 60.00
20 Kyle Seager 20.00 50.00
Robinson Cano/20
22 Harvey/Syndrgrd/20 30.00 80.00

2016 Panini Flawless Dual Diamond Memorabilia Sapphire
RANDOM INSERTS IN PACKS
PRINT RUNS B/WN 10-20 COPIES PER
NO PRICING ON QTY 10
1 Wnwrght/Mlna/15 60.00 150.00
3 McCtchn/Marte/15 50.00 120.00
4 Belt/Bumgarner/15 75.00 200.00
7 Dallas Keuchel 15.00 40.00
Collin McHugh/15
8 Chris Archer 15.00 40.00
Kevin Kiermaier/15
12 Stanton/Fernandez/15 20.00 50.00
14 Velander/Martinez/15 20.00 50.00
15 McCann/Ellsbury/15 30.00 80.00
20 Seager/Cano/15 25.00 60.00
22 Harvey/Syndrgrd/15 40.00 100.00

2016 Panini Flawless Dual Patches
RANDOM INSERTS IN PACKS
STATED PRINT RUN 25 SER.#'d SETS
10 Dallas Keuchel 8.00 20.00

2016 Panini Flawless Dual Patches Ruby
*RUBY/15-20: .4X TO 1X BASIC
RANDOM INSERTS IN PACKS
PRINT RUNS B/WN 15-20 COPIES PER
3 Andrew McCutchen/15 50.00 120.00
38 Manny Machado/15 20.00 50.00

2016 Panini Flawless Dual Patches Sapphire
*SAPPHIRE/15: .4X TO 1X BASIC
RANDOM INSERTS IN PACKS
PRINT RUNS B/WN 10-15 COPIES PER
NO PRICING ON QTY 10
1 Adam Wainwright/15 10.00 25.00
3 Andrew McCutchen/15 50.00 120.00
11 Dee Gordon/15 6.00 15.00
17 J.D. Martinez/15 12.00 30.00
22 Jose Altuve/15 50.00 120.00
34 Jung-Ho Kang/15 20.00 50.00
37 Madison Bumgarner/15 15.00 40.00
38 Manny Machado/15 20.00 50.00

2016 Panini Flawless Dual Signatures
STATED PRINT RUN 25 SER.#'d SETS
*RUBY/20: .4X TO 1X BASIC
*SAPPHIRE/15: .4X TO 1X BASIC
FDAL A.Nola/L.Severino 10.00 25.00
FDCJ C.Seager/J.Peraza 25.00 60.00
FDCK C.Edwards Jr./K.Schwarber 8.00 20.00
FDJT J.Gray/T.Murphy 6.00 15.00
FDKS K.Schwarber/T.Murphy 20.00 50.00
FDMM M.Kepler/M.Sano 15.00 40.00
FDRG R.Refsnyder/G.Bird 8.00 20.00
FDTC T.Turner/C.Seager 60.00 150.00

2016 Panini Flawless Flawless Cuts
RANDOM INSERTS IN PACKS
PRINT RUNS B/WN 1-25 COPIES PER
NO PRICING ON QTY 10 OR LESS
2 Bob Meusel/25 60.00 150.00
21 Sam Rice/15 75.00 200.00
22 Stan Musial/25 40.00 100.00
23 Ted Williams/25 250.00 400.00

2016 Panini Flawless Flawless Cuts Memorabilia
RANDOM INSERTS IN PACKS
PRINT RUNS B/WN 1-25 COPIES PER
NO PRICING ON QTY 10 OR LESS
*PRIME/25: .5X TO 1.2X BASIC
2 Bob Meusel/25 60.00 150.00
7 George Sisler/15 250.00 400.00
13 Lefty Gomez/15 60.00 150.00
21 Sam Rice/25 100.00 250.00
22 Stan Musial/25 60.00 150.00
23 Ted Williams/25 400.00 600.00

2016 Panini Flawless Greats Autographs
RANDOM INSERTS IN PACKS
PRINT RUNS B/WN 5-25 COPIES PER
NO PRICING ON QTY 5
*RUBY/20: .4X TO 1X BASIC
*SAPPHIRE/15: .4X TO 1X BASIC
GAAG Andres Galarraga/25 10.00 25.00
GAAP Albert Pujols/15 60.00 150.00
GABB Barry Bonds/15 100.00 250.00
GABJ Bo Jackson/25 40.00 100.00
GACJ Chipper Jones/15 40.00 100.00
GACR Cal Ripken/15 50.00 120.00
GADM Dale Murphy/25 10.00 25.00
GADO David Ortiz/25 50.00 120.00
GAFT Frank Thomas/25 40.00 100.00
GAGB George Brett/15 100.00 250.00
GAIR Ivan Rodriguez/15 60.00 150.00
GAJC Jose Canseco/25 25.00 60.00
GAMM Mark McGwire/15 60.00 150.00
GAMP Mike Piazza/15 50.00 120.00
GAMR Mariano Rivera/15 75.00 200.00
GAMS Mike Schmidt/15 30.00 80.00
GANR Nolan Ryan/25 50.00 120.00
GAOV Omar Vizquel/25 10.00 25.00
GARS Ryne Sandberg/15 30.00 80.00
GATH Todd Helton/15 15.00 40.00
GAWC Will Clark/15 30.00 80.00
GAWM Willie McGee/25 15.00 40.00

2016 Panini Flawless Greats Dual Memorabilia Autographs
RANDOM INSERTS IN PACKS
PRINT RUNS B/WN 15-25 COPIES PER
GDBBP Barry Bonds/15 250.00 400.00
GDBBS Barry Bonds/15 250.00 400.00
GDBJ Bo Jackson/15 60.00 150.00
GDCB Craig Biggio/15 50.00 120.00
GDCF Carlton Fisk/15 50.00 120.00
GDCJ Chipper Jones/15 60.00 150.00
GDEM Eddie Murray/15 50.00 120.00
GDGB George Brett/15 250.00 500.00
GDGMA Greg Maddux/15 75.00 200.00
GDGMC Greg Maddux/15 75.00 200.00
GDJB Johnny Bench/15 75.00 200.00
GDJM Joe Morgan/15 40.00 100.00
GDJS John Smoltz/15 60.00 150.00
GDMMO Mark McGwire/15 150.00 300.00
GDMMS Mark McGwire/15 150.00 300.00
GDMR Mariano Rivera/15 150.00 300.00
GDPM Pedro Martinez/15 60.00 150.00
GDRC Rod Carew/15 60.00 150.00
GDRH Rickey Henderson/15
GDRJO Reggie Jackson/15 50.00 120.00
GDRJC Reggie Jackson/15 50.00 120.00
GDRP Rafael Palmeiro/25 25.00 60.00
GDRS Red Schoendienst/25 60.00 150.00
GDRS Ryne Sandberg/15 30.00 80.00
GDSC Steve Carlton/15 50.00 120.00

2016 Panini Flawless Greats Dual Memorabilia Autographs Ruby
*RUBY/20: .4X TO 1X BASIC
RANDOM INSERTS IN PACKS
PRINT RUNS B/WN 10-20 COPIES PER
NO PRICING ON QTY 10
GDGP Gaylord Perry/20 25.00 60.00
GDNR Nolan Ryan/20 125.00 300.00
GDPM Paul Molitor/20 30.00 80.00

2016 Panini Flawless Greats Dual Memorabilia Autographs Sapphire
*SAPPHIRE/15: .4X TO 1X BASIC
RANDOM INSERTS IN PACKS
PRINT RUNS B/WN 5-15 COPIES PER
NO PRICING ON QTY 5
GDDO David Ortiz/15 200.00 400.00
GDFTC Frank Thomas/15 75.00 200.00
GDFTT Frank Thomas/15 75.00 200.00
GDGP Gaylord Perry/15 25.00 60.00
GDNR Nolan Ryan/15 125.00 300.00
GDPM Paul Molitor/20 30.00 80.00

2016 Panini Flawless Hall of Fame Autographs
RANDOM INSERTS IN PACKS
PRINT RUNS B/WN 5-25 COPIES PER
NO PRICING ON QTY 10 OR LESS
*RUBY/15-20: .4X TO 1X BASIC
*SAPPHIRE/15: .4X TO 1X BASIC
HOFAD Andre Dawson/25 15.00 40.00
HOFBL Barry Larkin/15 30.00 80.00
HOFCB Craig Biggio/15 20.00 50.00
HOFCR Cal Ripken/15 50.00 120.00
HOFCY Carl Yastrzemski/15 60.00 150.00
HOFFT Frank Thomas/25 40.00 100.00
HOFGB George Brett/15 100.00 250.00
HOFJR Jim Rice/25 10.00 25.00
HOFJS John Smoltz/15 25.00 60.00
HOFLB Lou Brock/15 20.00 50.00
HOFMS Mike Schmidt/15 30.00 80.00
HOFNR Nolan Ryan/25 50.00 120.00
HOFRC Rod Carew/15 20.00 50.00
HOFRJ Reggie Jackson/15 20.00 50.00
HOFRS Ryne Sandberg/15 30.00 80.00
HOFSC Steve Carlton/15 15.00 40.00

2016 Panini Flawless Material Greats
RANDOM INSERTS IN PACKS
PRINT RUNS B/WN 5-25 COPIES PER
NO PRICING ON QTY 10 OR LESS
*RUBY/20: .4X TO 1X BASIC
*SAPPHIRE/15: .4X TO 1X BASIC
1 Babe Ruth/25 200.00 400.00
2 Bill Dickey/25 10.00 25.00
3 Bob Feller/25 10.00 25.00
4 Charlie Gehringer/25 12.00 30.00
5 Duke Snider/25 12.00 30.00
7 Herb Pennock/25 10.00 25.00
9 Jackie Robinson/25 40.00 100.00
10 John McGraw/25 25.00 60.00
11 Joe DiMaggio/25 50.00 120.00
12 Lefty O'Doul/25 12.00 30.00
13 Lefty Gomez/25 25.00 60.00
14 Lou Gehrig/25 100.00 250.00
15 Mel Ott/25 12.00 30.00
16 Roberto Clemente/25 30.00 80.00
18 Rogers Hornsby/25 12.00 30.00
19 Stan Musial/25 20.00 50.00
20 Ted Williams/25 25.00 60.00
21 Tony Gwynn/25 15.00 40.00
22 Tony Lazzeri/25 20.00 50.00
23 Sam Rice/25 25.00 60.00
25 Warren Spahn/25 12.00 30.00

2016 Panini Flawless Patch Autographs
RANDOM INSERTS IN PACKS
PRINT RUNS B/WN 10-25 COPIES PER
NO PRICING ON QTY 10
PAAR Addison Russell/25 25.00 60.00
PACS Chris Sale/25 25.00 60.00
PADA Dale Murphy/25 40.00 100.00
PADK Dallas Keuchel/25 15.00 40.00
PADW David Wright/25 30.00 80.00
PAEM Edgar Martinez/25 15.00 40.00
PAFH Felix Hernandez/25 30.00 80.00
PAFL Fred Lynn/25 12.00 30.00
PAFV Fernando Valenzuela/15
PAJD Jacob deGrom/25 30.00 80.00
PAKB Kris Bryant/25 150.00 300.00
PASG Sonny Gray/25 20.00 50.00
PAYM Yoan Moncada/25 150.00 300.00
PAYAM Yadier Molina/25 100.00 250.00

2016 Panini Flawless Patch Autographs Ruby
*RUBY/20: .4X TO 1X BASIC
RANDOM INSERTS IN PACKS
PRINT RUNS B/WN 5-20 COPIES PER
NO PRICING ON QTY 10 OR LESS
PATF Todd Frazier/20 12.00 30.00

2016 Panini Flawless Patch Autographs Sapphire
*SAPPHIRE/15: .4X TO 1X BASIC
RANDOM INSERTS IN PACKS
PRINT RUNS B/WN 5-15 COPIES PER
NO PRICING ON QTY 5
PADO David Ortiz/15 75.00 200.00
PAJP Joc Pederson/15 20.00 50.00
PATF Todd Frazier/15 12.00 30.00

2016 Panini Flawless Patches
RANDOM INSERTS IN PACKS
PRINT RUNS B/WN 15-25 COPIES PER
3 Andrew McCutchen/25 25.00 60.00
12 Devin Mesoraco/15 6.00 15.00
22 Jose Altuve/25 20.00 50.00

2016 Panini Flawless Patches Ruby
*RUBY/20: .4X TO 1X BASIC
RANDOM INSERTS IN PACKS
PRINT RUNS B/WN 10-20 COPIES PER
NO PRICING ON QTY 10 OR LESS
1 Adam Wainwright/20 10.00 25.00
14 Freddie Freeman/20 12.00 30.00
37 Madison Bumgarner/20 15.00 40.00

2016 Panini Flawless Patches Sapphire
*SAPPHIRE/15: .4X TO 1X BASIC
RANDOM INSERTS IN PACKS
PRINT RUNS B/WN 10-15 COPIES PER
NO PRICING ON QTY 10
1 Adam Wainwright/15 10.00 25.00
7 Carlos Gonzalez/15 8.00 20.00
10 Dallas Keuchel/15 8.00 20.00
11 Dee Gordon/15 6.00 15.00
14 Freddie Freeman/15 12.00 30.00
15 Giancarlo Stanton/15 12.00 30.00
17 J.D. Martinez/15 12.00 30.00
25 Prince Fielder/15
34 Jung-Ho Kang/15 20.00 50.00
36 Kevin Kiermaier/15 12.00 30.00
37 Madison Bumgarner/15 15.00 40.00
50 Yu Darvish/15 10.00 25.00

2016 Panini Flawless Players Collection
1 Al Simmons/25 15.00 40.00
4 Barry Bonds/25 20.00 50.00
5 Bill Dickey/25 20.00 50.00
7 Bob Meusel/25 15.00 40.00
8 Cal Ripken/25 30.00 80.00
9 Chuck Klein/25 20.00 50.00
10 Dave Bancroft/25 12.00 30.00
12 Earl Averill/25 40.00 100.00
14 Frank Chance/25 30.00 80.00
16 Gabby Hartnett/25 20.00 50.00
17 George Brett/25 20.00 50.00
18 George Sisler/25 20.00 50.00
19 Goose Goslin/25 15.00 40.00
21 Herb Pennock/25 15.00 40.00
22 Honus Wagner/25 75.00 200.00
24 Jim Bottomley/25 15.00 40.00
26 Joe DiMaggio/25 60.00 150.00
27 Joe Jackson/25 100.00 250.00
28 John McGraw/25 30.00 80.00
29 Ken Griffey Jr./25 30.00 80.00
30 Kirby Puckett/25 50.00 120.00
31 Lefty Gomez/25 40.00 100.00
32 Lefty O'Doul/25 20.00 50.00
33 Lou Gehrig/25 100.00 250.00
34 Mel Ott/25 30.00 80.00
35 Miller Huggins/25 20.00 50.00
36 Nap Lajoie/25 40.00 100.00
37 Roberto Clemente/25 75.00 200.00
38 Roger Bresnahan/25 20.00 50.00
39 Roger Maris/25 30.00 80.00
40 Rogers Hornsby/25 30.00 80.00
41 Sam Crawford/25 20.00 50.00
42 Sam Rice/25 30.00 80.00
43 Stan Musial/25 25.00 60.00
44 Ted Williams/25 60.00 150.00
45 Tom Yawkey/25 30.00 80.00
46 Tony Gwynn/25 25.00 60.00
47 Tony Lazzeri/25 30.00 80.00
48 Tris Speaker/25 30.00 80.00
49 Ty Cobb/25 100.00 250.00
50 Willie Keeler/25 40.00 100.00

2016 Panini Flawless Autographs Red
RANDOM INSERTS IN PACKS
STATED PRINT RUN 25 SER.#'d SETS
*BLUE/25: .4X TO 1X BASIC
*RED/25: .4X TO 1X BASIC
1 Addison Russell/25 15.00 40.00
2 Brian Johnson/25 6.00 15.00
6 Corey Seager/25 30.00 80.00
8 Frank Thomas/25 40.00 100.00
11 Kris Bryant/25 75.00 200.00
12 Kyle Schwarber/25 15.00 40.00
13 Mac Williamson/25 8.00 20.00
14 Manny Machado/25 60.00 150.00
16 Michael Conforto/25 12.00 30.00
17 Peter O'Brien/25 6.00 15.00
18 Richie Shaffer/25 6.00 15.00
19 Rob Refsnyder/25 10.00 25.00
20 Todd Frazier/25 10.00 25.00
22 Tom Murphy/25 6.00 15.00
23 Travis Jankowski/25 6.00 15.00
24 Trea Turner/25 20.00 50.00

2016 Panini Flawless Rookie Autographs
RANDOM INSERTS IN PACKS
STATED PRINT RUN 25 SER.#'d SETS
*RUBY/20: .4X TO 1X BASIC
*SAPPHIRE/15: .4X TO 1X BASIC
RAAN Aaron Nola 15.00 40.00
RABD Brandon Drury 10.00 25.00
RABJ Brian Johnson 6.00 15.00
RABP Byung-ho Park 30.00 80.00
RACE Carl Edwards Jr. 8.00 20.00
RACS Corey Seager 60.00 150.00
RAGB Greg Bird 8.00 20.00
RAJG Jonathan Gray 6.00 15.00
RAJP Jose Peraza 8.00 20.00
RAKM Ketel Marte 12.00 30.00
RAKS Kyle Schwarber 20.00 50.00
RAKW Kyle Waldrop 8.00 20.00
RALS Luis Severino 8.00 20.00
RAMC Michael Conforto 8.00 20.00
RAMK Max Kepler 25.00 60.00
RAMS Miguel Sano 20.00 50.00
RAMW Mac Williamson 8.00 20.00
RAPO Peter O'Brien 6.00 15.00
RARM Raul Mondesi 8.00 20.00
RARR Rob Refsnyder 8.00 20.00
RARS Richie Shaffer 6.00 15.00
RASP Stephen Piscotty 20.00 50.00
RATJ Travis Jankowski 6.00 15.00
RATM Tom Murphy 6.00 15.00
RATS Trevor Story 40.00 100.00
RATT Trea Turner 20.00 50.00

2016 Panini Flawless Rookie Patch Autographs
RANDOM INSERTS IN PACKS
STATED PRINT RUN 25 SER.#'d SETS
RPAAN Aaron Nola 25.00 60.00
RPABD Brandon Drury 12.00 30.00
RPACS Corey Seager 100.00 250.00
RPADA Daniel Alvarez 6.00 15.00
RPAKC Kaleb Cowart 10.00 25.00
RPAKM Ketel Marte 15.00 40.00
RPAKS Kyle Schwarber 60.00 150.00
RPAKS Kyle Schwarber 60.00 150.00
RPALS Luis Severino 8.00 20.00
RPAMC Michael Conforto 60.00 150.00
RPAMS Miguel Sano 30.00 80.00
RPAMW Mac Williamson 40.00 100.00
RPAPO Peter O'Brien 20.00 50.00
RPARM Raul Mondesi 20.00 50.00
RPARR Rob Refsnyder 15.00 40.00
RPARS Richie Shaffer 10.00 25.00
RPASP Stephen Piscotty 6.00 15.00
RPATS Trevor Story 25.00 60.00
RPATT Trea Turner 30.00 80.00
RPAZD Zach Davies 30.00 80.00

2016 Panini Flawless Rookie Patch Autographs Ruby
*RUBY: .4X TO 1X BASIC
RANDOM INSERTS IN PACKS
STATED PRINT RUN 20 SER.#'d SETS
RPAJG Jonathan Gray 10.00 25.00
RPAKW Kyle Waldrop 10.00 25.00

2016 Panini Flawless Rookie Patch Autographs Sapphire
*SAPPHIRE: .4X TO 1X BASIC
RANDOM INSERTS IN PACKS
STATED PRINT RUN 15 SER.#'d SETS
RPABJ Brian Johnson 10.00 25.00
RPAGB Greg Bird 8.00 20.00
RPAJG Jonathan Gray 10.00 25.00
RPAKW Kyle Waldrop 10.00 25.00

2016 Panini Flawless Rookie Patches
RANDOM INSERTS IN PACKS
STATED PRINT RUN 25 SER.#'d SETS
1 Kyle Schwarber 15.00 40.00
2 Corey Seager 20.00 50.00
3 Miguel Sano 10.00 25.00
4 Michael Conforto 8.00 20.00
5 Stephen Piscotty 15.00 40.00
6 Trea Turner 20.00 50.00
7 Luis Severino 8.00 20.00
8 Rob Refsnyder 8.00 20.00
9 Aaron Nola 12.00 30.00
10 Ketel Marte 12.00 30.00
11 Raul Mondesi 8.00 20.00
12 Jonathan Gray 6.00 15.00
13 Greg Bird 8.00 20.00
14 Richie Shaffer 6.00 15.00
15 Travis Jankowski 6.00 15.00
16 Mac Williamson 10.00 25.00
17 Brian Johnson 6.00 15.00
18 Peter O'Brien 6.00 15.00
19 Kyle Waldrop 8.00 20.00
20 Brandon Drury 10.00 25.00
21 Daniel Alvarez 6.00 15.00
24 Colin Rea 6.00 15.00

2016 Panini Flawless Rookie Patches Ruby
*RUBY: .4X TO 1X BASIC
RANDOM INSERTS IN PACKS
STATED PRINT RUN 20 SER.#'d SETS
23 Gary Sanchez 30.00 80.00

2016 Panini Flawless Rookie Patches Sapphire
*SAPPHIRE: .4X TO 1X BASIC
RANDOM INSERTS IN PACKS
STATED PRINT RUN 15 SER.#'d SETS
23 Gary Sanchez 30.00 80.00

2016 Panini Flawless Rookie Signatures
RANDOM INSERTS IN PACKS
STATED PRINT RUN 25 SER.#'d SETS
*RUBY/20: .4X TO 1X BASIC
*SAPPHIRE/15: .4X TO 1X BASIC
RFAN Aaron Nola 15.00 40.00
RFBD Brandon Drury 10.00 25.00
RFBJ Brian Johnson 6.00 15.00
RFBP Byung-ho Park 30.00 80.00
RFCE Carl Edwards Jr. 8.00 20.00
RFCS Corey Seager 60.00 150.00
RFGB Greg Bird 8.00 20.00
RFJG Jonathan Gray 6.00 15.00
RFJP Jose Peraza 8.00 20.00
RFKM Ketel Marte 12.00 30.00
RFKS Kyle Schwarber 20.00 50.00
RFKW Kyle Waldrop 8.00 20.00
RFLS Luis Severino 8.00 20.00
RFMC Michael Conforto 8.00 20.00
RFMK Max Kepler 25.00 60.00
RFMS Miguel Sano 20.00 50.00
RFPO Peter O'Brien 6.00 15.00
RFRM Raul Mondesi 8.00 20.00
RFRR Rob Refsnyder 8.00 20.00
RFRS Richie Shaffer 6.00 15.00
RFSP Stephen Piscotty 10.00 25.00
RFTJ Travis Jankowski 6.00 15.00
RFTM Tom Murphy 6.00 15.00
RFTT Trevor Story 40.00 100.00
RFTT Trea Turner 20.00 50.00
RFWM Mac Williamson 8.00 20.00

2016 Panini Flawless Signatures
RANDOM INSERTS IN PACKS
PRINT RUNS B/WN 5-25 COPIES PER
NO PRICING ON QTY 10 OR LESS
*RUBY/20: .4X TO 1X BASIC
*SAPPHIRE/15: .4X TO 1X BASIC
FSAG Andres Galarraga/25 10.00 25.00
FSAR Anthony Rizzo/25 30.00 80.00
FSBJ Bo Jackson/25 40.00 100.00
FSCJ Chipper Jones/15 40.00 100.00
FSCR Cal Ripken/15 50.00 120.00
FSDM Daniel Murphy/25
FSDM Don Mattingly/15 50.00 120.00
FSDO David Ortiz/25 50.00 120.00
FSFT Frank Thomas/25 40.00 100.00
FSGB George Brett/15 100.00 250.00
FSJA Jose Abreu/15 15.00 40.00
FSJC Jose Canseco/15 25.00 60.00
FSJD Josh Donaldson/15 15.00 40.00
FSJG Jacob deGrom/25 15.00 40.00
FSJS John Smoltz/15 15.00 40.00
FSKB Kris Bryant/25 75.00 200.00
FSNR Nolan Ryan/25 50.00 120.00
FSOV Omar Vizquel/25 15.00 40.00
FSRJ Reggie Jackson/15 20.00 50.00
FSRS Ryne Sandberg/15 30.00 80.00
FSSC Steve Carlton/15 15.00 40.00
FSWC Wei-Yin Chen/25 50.00 120.00
FSWM Willie McGee/25 15.00 40.00
FSYM Yoan Moncada/15 60.00 150.00
FSYAM Yadier Molina/25 50.00 120.00

2016 Panini Flawless Teammates Triple Relics
RANDOM INSERTS IN PACKS
PRINT RUNS B/WN 5-25 COPIES PER
NO PRICING ON QTY 5
*RUBY/20: .4X TO 1X BASIC
*SAPPHIRE/15: .4X TO 1X BASIC
1 Msl/Ghrg/Ruth/25 250.00 500.00
5 Dcky/DMggo/Gmz/25 40.00 100.00

6 Goslin/Rice/Sisler/25 20.00 50.00
8 Hggns/Ruth/Ghrg/25 250.00 500.00
9 Msl/Ghrg/Lzzri/25 75.00 200.00
10 Ruth/Pnnck/Ghrg/25 250.00 500.00
11 Ghrngr/Cobb/Hlmnn/25 40.00 100.00
12 Sthwrth/Bttmly/Hrnsby/15 30.00 80.00
13 Herman/Klein/Hartnett/25 20.00 50.00
14 Gehringer/Goslin/Greenberg/25 25.00 60.00
15 Greenberg/Herman/Kiner/25 25.00 60.00
18 Kelly/Bancroft/Frisch/25 20.00 50.00
20 Foxx/Wlams/DMggo/25 50.00 125.00
23 McGraw/Ott/Hornsby/25 25.00 60.00
25 Spahn/Sain/Waner/25 20.00 50.00

2016 Panini Flawless Transitions Signatures

RANDOM INSERTS IN PACKS
PRINT RUNS B/WN 15-25 COPIES PER
*RUBY/20: .4X TO 1X BASIC
*SAPPHIRE/15: .4X TO 1X BASIC
TAG Alex Gordon/25
TBJ Brian Johnson/25 6.00 15.00
TBL Barry Larkin/15 30.00 80.00
TDP David Price/25 20.00 50.00
TDPE Dustin Pedroia/15
TFT Frank Thomas/25 25.00 60.00
TGC Gerrit Cole/25 20.00 50.00
TKS Kyle Schwarber/25 20.00 50.00
TMC Michael Conforto/25 8.00 20.00
TMM Mark McGwire/15 60.00 150.00
TMW Mac Williamson/25 8.00 20.00
TPO Peter O'Brien/25 6.00 15.00
TRR Rob Refsnyder/25 8.00 20.00
TRS Richie Shaffer/25 6.00 15.00
TSG Sonny Gray/25
TTF Todd Frazier/25 10.00 25.00
TTH Todd Helton/15 15.00 40.00
TTJ Travis Jankowski/25 6.00 15.00
TTM Tom Murphy/25 6.00 15.00
TTT Trea Turner/25 20.00 50.00
TWC Will Clark/15 30.00 80.00

2017 Panini Flawless

RANDOM INSERTS IN PACKS
STATED PRINT RUN 20 SER.#'d SETS
1 Babe Ruth 60.00 150.00
2 Lou Gehrig 25.00 60.00
3 Ty Cobb 25.00 60.00
4 Roberto Clemente 60.00 150.00
5 Honus Wagner 25.00 60.00
6 Joe DiMaggio 30.00 80.00
7 Mickey Mantle 50.00 120.00
8 Ted Williams 40.00 100.00
9 Jackie Robinson 20.00 50.00
10 Stan Musial 20.00 50.00
11 Kirby Puckett 40.00 100.00
12 Joe Jackson 50.00 120.00
13 Roger Maris 30.00 80.00
14 Ken Griffey Jr. 40.00 100.00
15 Cal Ripken 25.00 60.00
16 George Brett 20.00 50.00
17 Nolan Ryan 25.00 60.00
18 Mike Trout 30.00 80.00
19 Kris Bryant 25.00 60.00
20 Clayton Kershaw 25.00 60.00
21 Buster Posey 15.00 40.00
22 Ichiro 30.00 80.00
23 Frank Thomas 20.00 50.00
24 Andrew Benintendi RC 25.00 60.00
25 Corey Seager 20.00 50.00
26 Gary Sanchez 25.00 60.00
27 David Ortiz 20.00 50.00
28 Dansby Swanson RC 15.00 40.00
29 Albert Pujols 20.00 50.00
30 Bryce Harper 60.00 150.00
31 Ken Griffey Jr. 40.00 100.00
32 Alex Bregman RC 15.00 40.00
33 Ichiro 30.00 80.00
34 Yoan Moncada RC 25.00 60.00
35 Bo Jackson 25.00 60.00
36 Jimmie Foxx 25.00 60.00
37 Rogers Hornsby 20.00 50.00
38 Tony Gwynn 30.00 80.00
39 Mike Piazza 25.00 60.00
40 Nolan Ryan 25.00 60.00
41 Nolan Ryan 25.00 60.00
42 Mel Ott 20.00 50.00
43 Thurman Munson 50.00 120.00
44 Carlos Correa 20.00 50.00
45 Pete Rose 25.00 60.00
46 Jackie Robinson AM 20.00 50.00
47 Bo Jackson AM 25.00 60.00
48 Tony Gwynn AM 30.00 80.00
50 George Sisler AM 10.00 25.00
51 Will Clark AM 15.00 40.00
52 Frank Thomas AM 20.00 50.00
53 Andrew Benintendi AM 25.00 60.00
54 Dansby Swanson AM 15.00 40.00
55 Alex Bregman AM 15.00 40.00
56 Kris Bryant USA 25.00 60.00
57 Corey Seager USA 20.00 50.00
58 Mike Trout USA 30.00 80.00
59 Ken Griffey Jr. USA 40.00 100.00
60 Manny Machado USA 15.00 40.00
61 Clayton Kershaw USA 25.00 60.00
62 Buster Posey USA 15.00 40.00
63 Dansby Swanson USA 15.00 40.00
64 Alex Bregman USA 15.00 40.00
65 Roger Clemens USA 15.00 40.00
66 Babe Ruth 30.00 80.00
67 Lou Gehrig 25.00 60.00
68 Joe DiMaggio 30.00 80.00
69 Ted Williams 40.00 100.00
70 Mickey Mantle 50.00 120.00
71 Jackie Robinson 20.00 50.00
72 Ken Griffey Jr. 40.00 100.00
73 Ty Cobb 25.00 60.00
74 Roberto Clemente 60.00 150.00
75 Honus Wagner 25.00 60.00
76 Babe Ruth 60.00 150.00
77 Ty Cobb 25.00 60.00
78 Ted Williams 40.00 100.00
79 Lou Gehrig 25.00 60.00
80 Roberto Clemente 60.00 150.00
81 Mike Trout 30.00 80.00
82 Mickey Mantle 50.00 120.00
83 Cal Ripken 25.00 60.00
84 Honus Wagner 25.00 60.00
85 Albert Pujols 20.00 50.00
86 Babe Ruth AS 60.00 150.00
87 Lou Gehrig AS 25.00 60.00
88 Joe DiMaggio AS 30.00 80.00
89 Ted Williams AS 40.00 100.00
90 Stan Musial AS 20.00 50.00
91 Roberto Clemente AS 60.00 150.00
92 Kirby Puckett AS 40.00 100.00
93 Ken Griffey Jr. AS 40.00 100.00
94 Bo Jackson AS 25.00 60.00
95 Kris Bryant AS 25.00 60.00
96 Cal Ripken AS 25.00 60.00
97 Reggie Jackson AS 20.00 50.00
98 Ichiro AS 30.00 80.00
99 Mike Trout AS 30.00 80.00
100 Mickey Mantle AS 25.00 60.00
101 Aaron Judge RC 75.00 200.00
102 Aaron Judge AM 75.00 200.00
103 Aaron Judge 75.00 200.00
104 Aaron Judge AS 75.00 200.00
105 Cody Bellinger RC 125.00 300.00
106 Cody Bellinger 125.00 300.00
107 Cody Bellinger AS 125.00 300.00

2017 Panini Flawless Ruby

*RUBY: .4X TO 1X BASIC
RANDOM INSERTS IN PACKS
STATED PRINT RUN 15 SER.#'d SETS

2017 Panini Flawless Cuts

RANDOM INSERTS IN PACKS
PRINT RUNS B/WN 1-25 COPIES PER
NO PRICING ON QTY 10 OR LESS
2 Stan Musial/25 40.00 100.00
3 Harmon Killebrew/25 25.00 60.00
8 Bobby Thomson/25 20.00 50.00
9 Carl Hubbell/15 30.00 80.00
12 Ed Barrow/15 150.00 400.00
13 Gary Carter/25 20.00 50.00
14 Ralph Kiner/25 20.00 50.00
15 Joe Medwick/15 40.00 100.00
16 Joe Sewell/25 20.00 50.00
17 Johnny Mize/25 40.00 100.00

2017 Panini Flawless Cuts Memorabilia

RANDOM INSERTS IN PACKS
PRINT RUNS B/WN 2-25 COPIES PER
NO PRICING ON QTY 10 OR LESS
7 Ted Williams/25 300.00 600.00

2017 Panini Flawless Dual Player Signatures

RANDOM INSERTS IN PACKS
PRINT RUNS B/WN 15-25 COPIES PER
*SAPPHIRE/15: .4X TO 1X BASIC
1 Naquin/Turner/25 10.00 25.00
2 Seager/Schwarber/25 30.00 80.00
5 Benintendi/Moncada/25 25.00 60.00
6 Sanchez/Story/25
7 Sale/Kluber/25 30.00 80.00
8 Lindor/Kluber/15 40.00 100.00
9 David Dahl
Raimel Tapia/25 10.00 25.00
10 Bell/Glasnow/25 15.00 40.00
11 Fulmer/Moncada/25 15.00 40.00
12 Alex Reyes
Jose De Leon/25 10.00 25.00
13 Henderson/Brock/25 40.00 100.00
14 ThomasySandberg/25 50.00 120.00
15 Dawson/Grace/15 40.00 100.00
16 Griffey Jr./Griffey Sr./25 100.00 250.00
17 Ryan/Clemens/20 100.00 250.00
18 Mattingly/McGee/15 40.00 100.00
19 Jimenez/Happ/25 30.00 80.00
20 Frazier/Torres/25 60.00 150.00

2017 Panini Flawless Dual Player Signatures Ruby

*RUBY/15-20: .4X TO 1X BASIC
RANDOM INSERTS IN PACKS
PRINT RUNS B/WN 10-20 COPIES PER
NO PRICING ON QTY 10
3 Machado/Beltre/15

2017 Panini Flawless USA Signatures

RANDOM INSERTS IN PACKS
PRINT RUNS B/WN 15-25 COPIES PER
*SAPPHIRE/15: .4X TO 1X BASIC
1 Francisco Lindor/15 30.00 80.00
3 Addison Russell/20 15.00 40.00
6 Dansby Swanson/25 20.00 50.00
7 Frank Thomas/15 40.00 100.00
8 Nomar Garciaparra/25 20.00 50.00
9 Jason Giambi/25 8.00 20.00

2017 Panini Flawless USA Signatures Ruby

*RUBY/15-20: .4X TO 1X BASIC
RANDOM INSERTS IN PACKS
PRINT RUNS B/WN 10-20 COPIES PER
NO PRICING ON QTY 10
10 Shawn Green/15 8.00 20.00

2019 Panini Flawless

STATED PRINT RUN 20 SER.#'d SETS
1 Mike Trout 75.00 200.00
2 Mookie Betts 40.00 100.00
3 Nolan Arenado 15.00 40.00
4 Christian Yelich 15.00 40.00
5 Aaron Judge 30.00 80.00
6 Bryce Harper 50.00 120.00
7 Ichiro 20.00 50.00
8 Albert Pujols 30.00 80.00
9 Ronald Acuna Jr. 60.00 150.00
10 Juan Soto 40.00 100.00
11 Gleyber Torres 25.00 60.00
12 Shohei Ohtani 30.00 80.00
13 Javier Baez 15.00 40.00
14 Cody Bellinger 30.00 80.00
15 Kris Bryant 15.00 40.00
16 Aaron Judge 30.00 80.00
17 Anthony Rizzo 20.00 50.00
18 Yadier Molina 12.00 30.00
19 Mike Trout 75.00 200.00
20 Aaron Judge 30.00 80.00
21 Johnny Bench LEG 12.00 30.00
22 Joe Jackson LEG 60.00 150.00
23 Al Kaline LEG 12.00 30.00
24 Christy Mathewson LEG 30.00 80.00
25 Lloyd Waner LEG 10.00 25.00
26 Harmon Killebrew LEG 12.00 30.00
27 Bob Feller LEG 15.00 40.00
28 Babe Ruth LEG 30.00 80.00
29 Joe Medwick LEG 8.00 20.00
30 Lefty Gomez LEG 15.00 40.00
31 Mickey Mantle LEG 40.00 100.00
32 Mule Suttles LEG 12.00 30.00
33 Cy Young LEG 20.00 50.00
34 Grover Alexander LEG 10.00 25.00
35 Hank Greenberg LEG 20.00 50.00
36 Yogi Berra LEG 20.00 50.00
37 Jackie Robinson LEG 25.00 60.00
38 Roberto Clemente LEG 60.00 150.00
39 Ty Cobb LEG
40 Honus Wagner LEG 50.00 120.00
41 Mike Trout AS 75.00 200.00
42 Aaron Judge AS 30.00 80.00
43 Cody Bellinger AS 30.00 80.00
44 Kirby Puckett AS 25.00 60.00
45 Mickey Mantle AS 40.00 100.00
46 Roger Maris AS 20.00 50.00
47 Roy Campanella AS 20.00 50.00
48 Pedro Martinez AS 20.00 50.00
49 Ken Griffey Jr. AS 40.00 100.00
50 Joe Cronin AS 8.00 20.00
51 Mariano Rivera AS 25.00 60.00
52 Randy Johnson AS 12.00 30.00
53 Ted Williams AS 25.00 60.00
54 Babe Ruth AS 30.00 80.00
55 Bob Gibson AS 15.00 40.00
56 Fernando Tatis Jr. RC 80.00 200.00
57 Pete Alonso RC 60.00 150.00
58 Vladimir Guerrero Jr. RC 50.00 125.00
59 Eloy Jimenez RC 40.00 100.00
60 Jeff McNeil RC 30.00 80.00
61 Yusei Kikuchi RC 12.00 30.00
62 Austin Riley RC 20.00 50.00
63 Vladimir Guerrero Jr. 50.00 125.00
64 Fernando Tatis Jr. 80.00 200.00
65 Pete Alonso 60.00 150.00

2019 Panini Flawless Autographs

RANDOM INSERTS IN PACKS
STATED PRINT RUN 25 SER.#'d SETS
*RUBY/20: .4X TO 1X BASIC
2 David Ross 15.00 40.00
3 Luis Severino 12.00 30.00
6 Blake Snell 12.00 30.00
7 J.T. Realmuto 30.00 80.00
8 Jason Giambi 10.00 25.00
10 Frank Thomas 40.00 100.00
11 Kyle Hendricks 50.00 120.00
12 David Wright 15.00 40.00
13 Lou Brock 20.00 50.00
14 Walker Buehler 20.00 50.00
15 Ronald Acuna Jr. 80.00 200.00
16 Corey Seager 15.00 40.00
17 Matt Carpenter 15.00 40.00
18 Andre Dawson 12.00 30.00
19 J.D. Martinez 15.00 40.00
20 Juan Soto 60.00 150.00
21 Tom Glavine 12.00 30.00
23 Keith Hernandez 10.00 25.00
24 Omar Vizquel 12.00 30.00
26 Juan Marichal 12.00 30.00
27 Josh Hader 10.00 25.00
28 Kyle Schwarber 15.00 40.00
30 Tony Perez 15.00 40.00
32 Pete Rose 25.00 60.00
33 Goose Gossage 12.00 30.00
36 Paul Molitor 15.00 40.00
37 Paul Molitor 15.00 40.00
38 Mark Grace 12.00 30.00

2019 Panini Flawless Dual Patch Autographs

RANDOM INSERTS IN PACKS
STATED PRINT RUN 25 SER.#'d SETS
*RUBY: .4X TO 1X BASIC
1 Pete Alonso 100.00 250.00
2 Jon Duplantier 10.00 25.00
4 Darwinzon Hernandez 10.00 25.00
5 Dylan Cease 15.00 40.00
7 Brendan Rodgers 15.00 40.00
9 Keston Hiura 30.00 80.00
12 Carter Kieboom 15.00 40.00
13 Yordan-Alvarez 75.00 200.00
14 Jonathan Loaisiga 12.00 30.00
16 Touki Toussaint 12.00 30.00
17 Bo Bichette 40.00 100.00
19 Willy Adames 10.00 25.00

2019 Panini Flawless Dual Patches

RANDOM INSERTS IN PACKS
PRINT RUNS B/WN 7-25 COPIES PER
NO PRICING ON QTY 15 OR LESS
*RUBY/20: .4X TO 1X BASIC
2 Gary Carter/25 15.00 40.00
17 Justin Verlander/25 8.00 20.00
19 Matt Chapman/25 8.00 20.00
20 Austin Riley/25 12.00 30.00

2019 Panini Flawless Dual Signature Patches

RANDOM INSERTS IN PACKS
PRINT RUNS B/WN 15-25 COPIES PER
NO PRICING ON QTY 15 OR LESS
*RUBY/20: .4X TO 1X BASIC
5 Hoskins/Alonso/25 80.00 200.00

2019 Panini Flawless Dual Signatures

RANDOM INSERTS IN PACKS
PRINT RUNS B/WN 15-25 COPIES PER
NO PRICING ON QTY 15 OR LESS
*RUBY/20: .4X TO 1X BASIC
4 Acuna Jr./Ohtani/25 125.00 300.00
5 Soto/Acuna Jr/25 200.00 500.00
7 Mesa/Franco/25 75.00 200.00
8 Tatis Jr/Vlad Jr./25 150.00 400.00
9 Whitley/Tucker/25 20.00 50.00
10 Jimenez/Kopech/25 40.00 100.00

2019 Panini Flawless Legendary Dual Materials

RANDOM INSERTS IN PACKS
PRINT RUNS B/WN 15-25 COPIES PER
NO PRICING ON QTY 15 OR LESS
*RUBY/20: .4X TO 1X BASIC
2 Mule Suttles/25 15.00 40.00
3 Stan Musial/25 15.00 40.00
4 Hank Greenberg/25 15.00 40.00
5 Roberto Clemente/25 40.00 100.00
6 Joe Cronin/25 10.00 25.00
7 Roger Maris/25 15.00 40.00
8 Tommy Henrich/25 10.00 25.00
9 Bill Dickey/25 12.00 30.00
11 Jimmie Foxx/25 25.00 60.00
12 Jackie Robinson/25 30.00 80.00
13 Joe Jackson/25 60.00 150.00
15 Joe McCarthy/25 10.00 25.00
18 Tony Lazzeri/25 12.00 30.00
19 Bob Meusel/25 15.00 40.00
20 Miller Huggins/25 10.00 25.00
23 Jackie Robinson/20 30.00 80.00

2019 Panini Flawless Legends Jumbo Material

RANDOM INSERTS IN PACKS
PRINT RUNS B/WN 7-25 COPIES PER
NO PRICING ON QTY 15 OR LESS
*RUBY/20: .4X TO 1X BASIC
8 Bill Dickey/25 15.00 40.00
10 Tommy Henrich/25 10.00 25.00
11 Elston Howard/25 10.00 25.00
15 Dom DiMaggio/25 10.00 25.00
18 Mule Suttles/25 15.00 40.00
19 Roberto Clemente/25 50.00 120.00

2019 Panini Flawless Legends Jumbo Material Ruby

*RUBY/20: .4X TO 1X BASIC
RANDOM INSERTS IN PACKS
PRINT RUNS B/WN 10-20 COPIES PER
NO PRICING ON QTY 15 OR LESS
5 Roger Bresnahan/20 25.00 60.00
13 Tom Yawkey/20 10.00 25.00
14 Ernie Lombardi/20 15.00 40.00
17 Carl Furillo/20 10.00 25.00

2019 Panini Flawless Memorable Marks Autographs

RANDOM INSERTS IN PACKS
PRINT RUNS B/WN 15-25 COPIES PER
NO PRICING ON QTY 15 OR LESS
*RUBY/20: .4X TO 1X BASIC
2 Adrian Beltre/25 15.00 40.00
3 Carlton Fisk/25 12.00 30.00
4 David Ross/25 15.00 40.00
5 Lou Whitaker/25 20.00 50.00
7 Charlie Blackmon/25 15.00 40.00
9 Joe Carter/25 10.00 25.00
12 Tim Wakefield/25 12.00 30.00
13 Ken Griffey Sr./25 10.00 25.00
14 Dennis Eckersley/25 12.00 30.00
15 Francisco Lindor/25 15.00 40.00
16 Matt Chapman/25 15.00 40.00
17 Austin Riley/25 20.00 50.00
18 Royce Lewis/25 20.00 50.00
20 Rod Carew/20 12.00 30.00

2019 Panini Flawless Milestones Jersey Autographs

RANDOM INSERTS IN PACKS
PRINT RUNS B/WN 15-25 COPIES PER
NO PRICING ON QTY 15 OR LESS
*RUBY/20: .4X TO 1X BASIC
2 Austin Riley/25 20.00 50.00
19 Blake Snell/25 12.00 30.00

2019 Panini Flawless Moments Jersey Autographs

RANDOM INSERTS IN PACKS
STATED PRINT RUN 25 SER.#'d SETS
*RUBY/20: .4X TO 1X BASIC
18 Jordan Hicks 15.00 40.00
20 Austin Riley 20.00 50.00

2019 Panini Flawless Patch Autographs

RANDOM INSERTS IN PACKS
PRINT RUNS B/WN 15-25 COPIES PER
NO PRICING ON QTY 15 OR LESS
*RUBY/20: .4X TO 1X BASIC
5 Jordan Hicks/25 15.00 40.00
12 Austin Riley/25 20.00 50.00
14 Blake Snell/25 12.00 30.00
17 Chris Paddack/25 20.00 50.00
19 Josh Naylor/25 12.00 30.00
21 Ronald Acuna Jr./25 100.00 250.00
24 Pete Alonso/25 60.00 150.00
26 Carter Kieboom/25 15.00 40.00
29 Rhys Hoskins/20 30.00 80.00

2019 Panini Flawless Patches

RANDOM INSERTS IN PACKS
PRINT RUNS B/WN 3-25 COPIES PER
NO PRICING ON QTY 15 OR LESS
*RUBY/20: .4X TO 1X BASIC
1 Yusei Kikuchi/25 12.00 30.00
6 Fernando Tatis Jr./25 50.00 125.00
23 Eloy Jimenez/20 50.00 120.00
31 Michael Kopech/20 10.00 25.00

2019 Panini Flawless Penmanship Materials Dual Patch Autographs

RANDOM INSERTS IN PACKS
STATED PRINT RUN 25 SER.#'d SETS
4 Oscar Mercado 25.00 60.00
9 Keston Hiura 40.00 100.00

2019 Panini Flawless Performances Patch Autographs

RANDOM INSERTS IN PACKS
PRINT RUNS B/WN 20-25 COPIES PER
*RUBY/20: .4X TO 1X BASIC
1 Rhys Hoskins/20 30.00 80.00
4 Juan Soto/25 75.00 200.00

2019 Panini Flawless Quad Patch Signatures

RANDOM INSERTS IN PACKS
STATED PRINT RUN 25 SER.#'d SETS
*RUBY/20: .4X TO 1X BASIC
4 Paul DeJong 25.00 60.00
9 Cal Quantrill 10.00 25.00

2019 Panini Flawless Rookie Dual Patch Autographs

RANDOM INSERTS IN PACKS
STATED PRINT RUN 25 SER.#'d SETS
*RUBY: .4X TO 1X BASIC
1 Vladimir Guerrero Jr. 75.00 200.00
2 Eloy Jimenez 40.00 100.00
3 Ryan O'Hearn 10.00 25.00
4 Fernando Tatis Jr. 125.00 300.00
5 Reese McGuire 15.00 40.00
6 Jake Bauers 15.00 40.00
8 Justus Sheffield 15.00 40.00
9 Michael Kopech 20.00 50.00
10 Kyle Tucker 20.00 50.00
11 Luis Urias 15.00 40.00
12 Jeff McNeil 25.00 60.00
13 Kyle Wright 15.00 40.00
14 Ramon Laureano 25.00 60.00
15 Steven Duggar 12.00 30.00
16 Josh James 15.00 40.00
17 Dennis Santana 10.00 25.00
18 Christin Stewart 12.00 30.00
19 Cedric Mullins 15.00 40.00
20 Corbin Burnes 15.00 40.00

2019 Panini Flawless Rookie Patch Autographs

RANDOM INSERTS IN PACKS
STATED PRINT RUN 25 SER.#'d SETS
*RUBY: .4X TO 1X BASIC
1 Vladimir Guerrero Jr. 75.00 200.00
2 Eloy Jimenez 40.00 100.00
3 Ryan O'Hearn 10.00 25.00
4 Fernando Tatis Jr. 125.00 300.00
5 Reese McGuire 15.00 40.00
6 Jake Bauers 15.00 40.00
8 Justus Sheffield 15.00 40.00
9 Michael Kopech 20.00 50.00
10 Kyle Tucker 20.00 50.00
11 Luis Urias 10.00 25.00
12 Jeff McNeil 30.00 80.00
13 Kyle Wright 15.00 40.00
14 Ramon Laureano 25.00 60.00
15 Steven Duggar 12.00 30.00
16 Josh James 15.00 40.00
17 Dennis Santana 10.00 25.00
18 Christin Stewart 12.00 30.00
19 Cedric Mullins 15.00 40.00
20 Corbin Burnes 15.00 40.00

2019 Panini Flawless Rookie Triple Patch Autographs

RANDOM INSERTS IN PACKS
STATED PRINT RUN 25 SER.#'d SETS
*RUBY: .4X TO 1X BASIC
1 Vladimir Guerrero Jr. 75.00 200.00
2 Eloy Jimenez 40.00 100.00
3 Ryan O'Hearn 10.00 25.00
4 Fernando Tatis Jr. 125.00 300.00
5 Reese McGuire 15.00 40.00
6 Jake Bauers 15.00 40.00
8 Justus Sheffield 15.00 40.00
9 Michael Kopech 20.00 50.00
10 Kyle Tucker 20.00 50.00
11 Luis Urias 15.00 40.00
12 Jeff McNeil 25.00 60.00
13 Kyle Wright 15.00 40.00
14 Ramon Laureano 25.00 60.00
15 Steven Duggar 12.00 30.00
16 Josh James 15.00 40.00
17 Dennis Santana 10.00 25.00
18 Christin Stewart 12.00 30.00
19 Cedric Mullins 15.00 40.00
20 Corbin Burnes 15.00 40.00

2019 Panini Flawless Signature Patches

RANDOM INSERTS IN PACKS
STATED PRINT RUN 25 SER.#'d SETS
*RUBY/20: .4X TO 1X BASIC
11 Nathaniel Lowe 12.00 30.00
19 Matt Chapman 20.00 50.00

2019 Panini Flawless Signatures

RANDOM INSERTS IN PACKS
PRINT RUNS B/WN 15-25 COPIES PER
NO PRICING ON QTY 15 OR LESS
*RUBY/20: .4X TO 1X BASIC
1 Vladimir Guerrero Jr./25 60.00 150.00
2 Aaron Judge/20 60.00 150.00
3 Shohei Ohtani/25 60.00 150.00
4 Ken Griffey Jr./20 100.00 250.00
5 Ken Griffey Jr./20 100.00 250.00
8 Frank Thomas/20 40.00 100.00
11 Shohei Ohtani/25 60.00 150.00
18 Jason Giambi/20 10.00 25.00

2019 Panini Flawless Signatures Ruby

*RUBY/20: .4X TO 1X BASIC
RANDOM INSERTS IN PACKS
PRINT RUNS B/WN 10-20 COPIES PER
NO PRICING ON QTY 15 OR LESS
14 Steve Garvey/20 40.00 100.00

2019 Panini Flawless Spikes

RANDOM INSERTS IN PACKS
PRINT RUNS B/WN 5-20 COPIES PER
NO PRICING ON QTY 15 OR LESS
2 Jeff McNeil/20 60.00 150.00
11 Jake Bauers/20 20.00 50.00
13 Albert Pujols/17 150.00 400.00
17 Carlos Correa/16 50.00 120.00

2019 Panini Flawless Triple Legends Relics

RANDOM INSERTS IN PACKS
STATED PRINT RUN 25 SER.#'d SETS
*RUBY/20: .4X TO 1X BASIC
2 Greenberg/Kaline/Cobb 40.00 100.00
3 Foxx/Williams/Cronin 25.00 60.00
4 Jackson/Wagner/Hornsby 75.00 200.00
5 DiMaggio/Clemente/Robinson 100.00 250.00
6 Ott/Maris/Musial 30.00 80.00
8 Sewell/Speaker/Lemon 15.00 40.00
9 Maris/Howard/Mantle 40.00 100.00

2019 Panini Flawless Triple Legends Relics Ruby

*RUBY/20: .4X TO 1X BASIC
RANDOM INSERTS IN PACKS
PRINT RUNS B/WN 10-20 COPIES PER
NO PRICING ON QTY 15 OR LESS
1 Gehrig/Mantle/Ruth/20 300.00 600.00
10 Wagner/Ruth/Cobb/20 150.00 400.00

2019 Panini Flawless Triple Patch Autographs

RANDOM INSERTS IN PACKS
PRINT RUNS B/WN 20-25 COPIES PER
*RUBY/20: .4X TO 1X BASIC
3 Juan Soto/20 75.00 200.00
5 Nathaniel Lowe /25 12.00 30.00
8 Luis Arraez/25 40.00 100.00

2019 Panini Flawless Triple Patch Signatures

RANDOM INSERTS IN PACKS
PRINT RUNS B/WN 15-25 COPIES PER
NO PRICING ON QTY 15 OR LESS
*RUBY/20: .4X TO 1X BASIC
6 Ronald Acuna Jr./25 100.00 250.00
9 David Fletcher/25 30.00 80.00
10 Corbin Martin/25 15.00 40.00

2019 Panini Flawless Two Player Dual Rookie Patch Autographs

RANDOM INSERTS IN PACKS
STATED PRINT RUN 25 SER.#'d SETS
*RUBY: .4X TO 1X BASIC
2 Tucker/Jimenez 40.00 100.00
3 Tatis Jr/Urias 75.00 200.00
4 Tucker/Mullins 10.00 25.00
5 Eloy/Vlad Jr 60.00 150.00
6 Kopech/Sheffield 15.00 40.00
7 Bauers/O'Hearn 10.00 25.00
9 Urias/McNeil 15.00 40.00

2017 Panini Gold Standard

1-25 PRINT RUN 269 SER.#'d SETS
INSERTED IN '17 CHRONICLES PACKS
JSY AU PRINT RUNS B/WN 99-199 COPIES PER
EXCHANGE DEADLINE 5/22/2019
1 Mike Trout/269 5.00 12.00
2 Ichiro/269 1.25 3.00
3 Kris Bryant/269 1.25 3.00
4 Bryce Harper/269 1.50 4.00
5 Carlos Correa/269 1.00 2.50
6 Buster Posey/269 1.25 3.00
7 Mickey Mantle/269 3.00 8.00
8 Clayton Kershaw/269 2.00 5.00
9 Anthony Rizzo/269 1.50 4.00
10 Francisco Lindor/269 1.00 2.50
11 Paul Goldschmidt/269 1.00 2.50
12 Nolan Arenado/269 1.25 3.00
13 Mookie Betts/269 1.50 4.0
14 Corey Seager/269 1.00 2.5
15 Albert Pujols/269 1.25 3.0
16 Noah Syndergaard/269 .75 2.0
17 Chris Sale/269 1.00 2.5
18 Justin Turner/269 .75 2.0
19 Xander Bogaerts/269 1.00 2.5
20 Gary Sanchez/269 1.00 2.5
21 Yadier Molina/269 1.00 2.5
22 Yoenis Cespedes/269 1.00 2.5
23 Josh Donaldson/269 .75 2.0
24 Jose Altuve/269 .75 2.0
25 Andrew McCutchen/269 1.00 2.5
26 Andrew Benintendi AU JSY/199 RC 15.00 40.0
27 Yoan Moncada AU JSY/99 RC 10.00 25.0
28 Alex Bregman AU JSY/199 RC 40.00 100.0
29 Dansby Swanson AU JSY/199 RC 6.00 15.0
30 Ian Happ AU JSY/199 RC 8.00 20.0
31 Cody Bellinger AU JSY/99 RC 30.00 80.0
32 Aaron Judge AU JSY/199 RC 60.00 150.0
33 Trey Mancini AU JSY/199 RC 8.00 20.0
34 Jordan Montgomery AU JSY/199 RC 10.00 25.0
35 Bradley Zimmer AU JSY/199 RC 4.00 10.0
36 Mitch Haniger AU JSY/199 RC 6.00 15.0
37 Andrew Toles AU JSY/199 RC 3.00 8.0
38 Alex Reyes AU JSY/99 RC 6.00 15.0
39 Tyler Glasnow AU JSY/199 RC 4.00 10.0
40 Manuel Margot AU JSY/99 RC 4.00 10.0
41 Hunter Renfroe AU JSY/99 RC 5.00 12.0
42 Jorge Bonifacio AU JSY/99 RC 4.00 10.0
43 Antonio Senzatela AU JSY/199 RC 3.00 8.0
44 Amir Garrett AU JSY/199 RC 5.00 12.0
45 David Dahl AU JSY/199 RC 4.00 10.0
46 Sam Travis AU JSY/199 RC 5.00 12.0
47 Ryon Healy AU JSY/199 RC 5.00 12.0
48 Carson Fulmer AU JSY/199 RC 3.00 8.0
49 Lewis Brinson AU JSY/99 RC 6.00 15.0
50 Jacoby Jones AU JSY/199 RC 4.00 10.0

2017 Panini Gold Standard Blue

*BLUE: .75X TO 2X BASIC
INSERTED IN '17 CHRONICLES PACKS
STATED PRINT RUN 79 SER.#'d SETS
1 Mike Trout 8.00 20.0

2017 Panini Gold Standard Newly Minted Memorabilia

INSERTED IN '17 CHRONICLES PACKS
STATED PRINT RUN 99 SER.#'d SETS
*BLUE/25: .5X TO 1.2X BASIC
1 Andrew Benintendi 6.00 15.00
2 Yoan Moncada 5.00 12.00
3 Alex Bregman 6.00 15.00
4 Dansby Swanson 5.00 12.00
5 Ian Happ 4.00 10.00
6 Cody Bellinger 5.00 12.00
7 Aaron Judge 15.00 40.00
8 Trey Mancini 4.00 10.00
9 Jordan Montgomery 3.00 8.00
10 Bradley Zimmer 2.50 6.00
11 Mitch Haniger 3.00 8.00
13 Alex Reyes 2.50 6.00
14 Tyler Glasnow 2.50 6.00
15 Manuel Margot 2.00 5.00
16 Hunter Renfroe 2.50 6.00
17 Jorge Bonifacio 2.00 5.00
18 Antonio Senzatela 2.00 5.00
19 Gleyber Torres 4.00 10.00
20 David Dahl 2.50 6.00
21 Sam Travis 2.00 5.00
22 Ryon Healy 2.50 6.00
24 Lewis Brinson 3.00 8.00
25 Jacoby Jones 2.50 6.00

2017 Panini Gold Standard Rookie Jersey Autographs Double

INSERTED IN '17 CHRONICLES PACKS
PRINT RUNS B/WN 99-199 COPIES PER
EXCHANGE DEADLINE 5/22/2019
*PRIME/25: .6X TO 1.5X p/r 199
*PRIME/25: .5X TO 1.2X p/r 99
1 Andrew Benintendi/199 15.00 40.00
2 Yoan Moncada/99 10.00 25.00
3 Alex Bregman/199 20.00 50.00
4 Dansby Swanson/199 12.00 30.00
5 Ian Happ/199 8.00 20.00
6 Cody Bellinger/99 25.00 60.00
7 Aaron Judge/199 75.00 200.00
8 Trey Mancini/199 8.00 20.00
9 Jordan Montgomery/199 10.00 25.00
10 Bradley Zimmer/199 4.00 10.00
11 Mitch Haniger/199 6.00 15.00
12 Raimel Tapia/199 4.00 10.00
13 Alex Reyes/99 6.00 15.00
14 Tyler Glasnow/99 5.00 12.00
15 Manuel Margot/99 4.00 10.00
16 Hunter Renfroe/99 5.00 12.00
17 Jorge Bonifacio/199 3.00 8.00
18 Antonio Senzatela/199 3.00 8.00
19 Amir Garrett/199 5.00 12.00
20 David Dahl/199 4.00 10.00
21 Sam Travis/199 5.00 12.00
22 Ryon Healy/199 5.00 12.00
23 Chad Pinder/199
24 Lewis Brinson/99 6.00 15.00
25 Jacoby Jones/199 4.00 10.00

2017 Panini Gold Standard Rookie Jersey Autographs Prime

*PRIME/25: .6X TO 1.5X p/r 199
*PRIME/25: .5X TO 1.2X p/r 99
INSERTED IN '17 CHRONICLES PACKS

PRINT RUNS B/WN 13-25 COPIES PER
NO PRICING ON QTY 13
EXCHANGE DEADLINE 5/22/2019

2018 Panini Illusions
INSERTED IN '18 CHRONICLES PACKS
1 Gleyber Torres RC 2.50 6.00
2 Mike Trout 1.25 3.00
3 Bryce Harper .40 1.00
4 Kris Bryant .30 .75
5 Aaron Judge .60 1.50
6 Ichiro .30 .75
7 Mickey Mantle .75 2.00
8 Joey Lucchesi RC .25 .60
9 Scott Kingery RC .40 1.00
10 Clint Frazier RC .50 1.25
11 Rafael Devers RC .75 2.00
12 Shohei Ohtani RC 1.50 4.00
13 Rhys Hoskins RC 1.00 2.50
14 Ronald Acuna Jr. RC 5.00 12.00
15 Amed Rosario RC .30 .75
16 Austin Hays RC .40 1.00
17 Ozzie Albies RC .75 2.00
18 Miguel Andujar RC 1.00 2.50
19 Jordan Hicks RC .50 1.25
20 Juan Soto RC 5.00 12.00
21 Victor Robles RC .60 1.50
22 Willie Calhoun RC .30 .75
23 Max Fried RC 1.00 2.50
24 Richard Urena RC .25 .60
25 Alex Verdugo RC .40 1.00
26 Chris Flexen RC .25 .60
27 Harrison Bader RC .40 1.00
28 Brandon Woodruff RC .30 .75
29 Zack Granite RC .25 .60
30 Giancarlo Stanton .25 .60

2018 Panini Illusions Trophy Collection Blue
*BLUE: 1.2X TO 3X BASIC
*BLUE RC: .75X TO 2X BASIC
INSERTED IN '18 CHRONICLES PACKS
STATED PRINT RUN 99 SER.#'d SETS
12 Shohei Ohtani 8.00 20.00

2018 Panini Illusions Trophy Collection Red
*RED: 2X TO 5X BASIC
*RED RC: 1.2X TO 3X BASIC
INSERTED IN '18 CHRONICLES PACKS
STATED PRINT RUN 25 SER.#'d SETS
2 Mike Trout 15.00 40.00
12 Shohei Ohtani 12.00 30.00

2018 Panini Illusions Autographs
RANDOM INSERTS IN PACKS
*GOLD/25: .75X TO 2X BASIC
8 Joey Lucchesi 2.50 6.00
9 Scott Kingery 4.00 10.00
18 Miguel Andujar 10.00 25.00
19 Jordan Hicks 5.00 12.00
20 Juan Soto 50.00 120.00
26 Chris Flexen 2.50 6.00
28 Brandon Woodruff 3.00 8.00
29 Zack Granite 2.50 6.00

2019 Panini Leather and Lumber
101-151 RANDOMLY INSERTED
101-151 PRINT RUN B/WN 99-175 PER
EXCHANGE DEADLINE 11/29/2020
1 Miles Mikolas .40 1.00
2 Brandon Crawford .30 .75
3 Noah Syndergaard .30 .75
4 Kevin Pillar .25 .60
5 Max Scherzer .40 1.00
6 Nolan Arenado .50 1.25
7 Felix Hernandez .30 .75
8 Jameson Taillon .30 .75
9 Francisco Lindor .40 1.00
10 Jacob deGrom .40 1.00
11 Andrelton Simmons .25 .60
12 Chris Sale .40 1.00
13 Lorenzo Cain .25 .60
14 Manny Machado .40 1.00
15 Blake Snell .30 .75
16 Javier Baez .50 1.25
17 Carlos Rodon .30 .75
18 Luis Severino .30 .75
19 Stephen Strasburg .40 1.00
20 Carlos Carrasco .25 .60
21 David Peralta .25 .60
22 Jose Urena .25 .60
23 Chris Archer .25 .60
24 Jackie Bradley Jr. .40 1.00
25 Madison Bumgarner .30 .75
26 Carlos Correa .40 1.00
27 James Paxton .30 .75
28 Paul Goldschmidt .40 1.00
29 Aaron Nola .30 .75
30 Gerrit Cole .40 1.00
31 Justin Smoak .25 .60
32 Justin Verlander .40 1.00
33 Anthony Rendon .40 1.00
34 Jose Berrios .30 .75
35 Matt Chapman .40 1.00
36 Kyle Freeland .30 .75
37 Clayton Kershaw .75 2.00
38 Corey Kluber .30 .75
39 Francisco Mejia .30 .75
40 Adam Jones .30 .75
41 Matt Carpenter .40 1.00
42 Gleyber Torres .75 2.00
43 Jose Ramirez .30 .75
44 Walker Buehler .50 1.25
45 Brandon Belt .30 .75
46 Miguel Andujar .40 1.00
47 Charlie Blackmon .40 1.00
48 Yadier Molina .40 1.00
49 Jon Lester .30 .75
50 Alex Bregman .40 1.00
51 Trey Mancini .30 .75
52 Eric Hosmer .30 .75
53 Starling Marte .30 .75
54 Joey Votto .40 1.00
55 J.T. Realmuto .40 1.00
56 Miguel Cabrera .40 1.00
57 Trea Turner .30 .75
58 Nicholas Castellanos .40 1.00
59 Wilson Ramos .25 .60
60 Harrison Bader .30 .75
61 Salvador Perez .30 .75
62 Kris Bryant .50 1.25
63 Aaron Judge 1.00 2.50
64 Anthony Rizzo .60 1.50
65 Matt Olson .25 .60
66 Freddie Freeman .50 1.25
67 Christian Yelich .50 1.25
68 Jesus Aguilar .25 .60
69 Trevor Story .40 1.00
70 Mike Trout 2.00 5.00
71 Albert Pujols .50 1.25
72 Khris Davis .40 1.00
73 Ronald Acuna Jr. 2.00 5.00
74 Rafael Devers .50 1.25
75 Mike Moustakas .30 .75
76 Joey Wendle .25 .60
77 Rhys Hoskins .50 1.25
78 Eugenio Suarez .30 .75
79 Willy Adames .25 .60
80 Eddie Rosario .30 .75
81 Shohei Ohtani .50 1.25
82 Joey Gallo .30 .75
83 Ozzie Albies .40 1.00
84 Mitch Haniger .30 .75
85 Austin Meadows .30 .75
86 Cody Bellinger .75 2.00
87 Mookie Betts .60 1.50
88 A.J. Pollock .25 .60
89 J.D. Martinez .40 1.00
90 Nomar Mazara .25 .60
91 Jose Abreu .40 1.00
92 Whit Merrifield .40 1.00
93 Jose Altuve .30 .75
94 Odubel Herrera .30 .75
95 Andrew Benintendi .40 1.00
96 Michael Conforto .30 .75
97 Juan Soto 1.25 3.00
98 Bryce Harper .60 1.50
99 Giancarlo Stanton .40 1.00
100 Nelson Cruz .40 1.00
101 Dakota Hudson AU/149 RC 4.00 10.00
102 Cedric Mullins AU/149 RC 5.00 12.00
103 Kyle Tucker AU/149 RC 8.00 20.00
104 Ramon Laureano AU/149 RC 5.00 12.00
105 Jake Cave AU/149 RC 4.00 10.00
106 Jake Bauers AU/149 RC 5.00 12.00
107 Rowdy Tellez AU/149 RC 5.00 12.00
108 Enyel De Los Santos AU/149 RC 3.00 8.00
109 Ryan Borucki AU/149 RC 3.00 8.00
110 Stephen Gonsalves AU/149 RC 3.00 8.00
111 Brandon Lowe AU/149 RC 8.00 20.00
112 Kevin Newman AU/149 RC 5.00 12.00
113 Luis Urias AU/149 RC 4.00 10.00
114 Framber Valdez AU/149 RC 3.00 8.00
115 Dennis Santana AU/149 RC
116 Jonathan Loaisiga AU/149 RC
117 Sean Reid-Foley AU/149 RC 3.00 8.00
118 Chris Shaw AU/99 RC 5.00 12.00
119 Justus Sheffield AU/149 RC 5.00 12.00
120 Danny Jansen AU/149 RC 3.00 8.00
121 Jeff McNeil AU/99 RC 8.00 20.00
122 Steven Duggar AU/149 RC 4.00 10.00
123 Corbin Burnes AU/149 RC 5.00 12.00
124 Kyle Wright AU/149 RC 5.00 12.00
125 Kolby Allard AU/149 RC 5.00 12.00
126 Kevin Kramer AU/149 RC 4.00 10.00
127 Brad Keller AU/149 RC 3.00 8.00
128 Ryan O'Hearn AU/149 RC 3.00 8.00
129 Touki Toussaint AU/149 RC 4.00 10.00
130 Chance Adams AU/149 RC 3.00 8.00
131 David Fletcher AU/149 RC 10.00 25.00
132 Michael Kopech AU/149 RC 6.00 15.00
133 Josh James AU/149 RC 5.00 12.00
134 Christin Stewart AU/149 RC 4.00 10.00
135 Caleb Ferguson AU/149 RC 4.00 10.00
136 Taylor Ward AU/149 RC 3.00 8.00
137 Vladimir Guerrero Jr. AU/149 RC 25.00 60.00
138 Garrett Hampson AU/149 RC 3.00 8.00
139 Eloy Jimenez AU/99 RC 20.00 50.00
140 Fernando Tatis Jr. AU/149 RC 50.00 120.00
141 Yusei Kikuchi AU/149 RC 12.00 30.00
142 Cionel Perez AU/175 RC 3.00 8.00
143 Daniel Ponce de Leon AU/175 RC 5.00 12.00
144 Bryse Wilson AU/175 RC 4.00 10.00
145 Jacob Nix AU/175 RC 4.00 10.00
146 Jonathan Davis AU/175 RC 4.00 10.00
147 Luis Ortiz AU/175 RC 3.00 8.00
148 Myles Straw AU/175 RC 6.00 15.00
149 Patrick Wisdom AU/175 RC 3.00 8.00
150 Reese McGuire AU/175 RC 5.00 12.00
151 Pete Alonso AU/149 RC 50.00 120.00

2019 Panini Leather and Lumber Die Cut
*DIE CUT: .5X TO 1.2X BASIC
RANDOM INSERTS IN PACKS

2019 Panini Leather and Lumber Die Cut Blue
*DIE CUT BLUE: 1.5X TO 4X BASIC
RANDOM INSERTS IN PACKS
STATED PRINT RUN 25 SER.#'d SETS

2019 Panini Leather and Lumber Die Cut Gold
*DIE CUT GOLD: 1X TO 2.5X BASIC
RANDOM INSERTS IN PACKS
STATED PRINT RUN 99 SER.#'d SETS

2019 Panini Leather and Lumber Embossed
*EMBOSSED: .5X TO 1.2X BASIC
RANDOM INSERTS IN PACKS

2019 Panini Leather and Lumber Embossed Gold Proof
*EMBOSSED GOLD: .6X TO 1.5X BASIC
RANDOM INSERTS IN PACKS

2019 Panini Leather and Lumber 500 HR Club Bats
RANDOM INSERTS IN PACKS
1 Eddie Murray 6.00 15.00
2 Ken Griffey Jr. 15.00 40.00
3 Frank Robinson 6.00 15.00
4 Willie McCovey 6.00 15.00
5 Harmon Killebrew 8.00 20.00
6 Reggie Jackson 6.00 15.00
7 Albert Pujols 12.00 30.00
8 Frank Thomas 8.00 20.00
9 Gary Sheffield 5.00 12.00
10 David Ortiz 8.00 20.00

2019 Panini Leather and Lumber Autographs
RANDOM INSERTS IN PACKS
EXCHANGE DEADLINE 11/29/2020
1 Yohander Mendez 2.50 6.00
4 Stephen Piscotty 2.50 6.00
5 Matt Barnes 2.50 6.00
7 Marcell Ozuna 4.00 10.00
9 Mitch Haniger 3.00 8.00
10 Marwin Gonzalez 2.50 6.00
11 Shohei Ohtani 100.00 250.00
12 Tom Glavine
14 Jackie Bradley Jr.
15 Mitch Garver 2.50 6.00
16 J.T. Realmuto 12.00 30.00
17 Jason Kipnis 3.00 8.00
18 Francisco Lindor 12.00 30.00
19 Sean Newcomb 2.50 6.00
20 Ryne Sandberg
21 Jedd Gyorko 2.50 6.00
22 Yadier Molina 25.00 60.00
24 Julio Urias 4.00 10.00
25 Nolan Arenado 20.00 50.00
26 Stephen Strasburg
27 Aaron Nola
29 Wilson Ramos 4.00 10.00
30 Edgar Martinez 8.00 20.00
32 Luis Severino 3.00 8.00
33 Mike Leake 2.50 6.00
34 Tony Kemp 2.50 6.00
36 Mike Mussina 8.00 20.00
39 John Smoltz
40 Max Muncy 6.00 15.00

2019 Panini Leather and Lumber Autographs Blue
*BLUE p/r 60-150: .5X TO 1.2X BASIC
*BLUE p/r 50: .6X TO 1.5X BASIC
*BLUE p/r 25: .75X TO 2X BASIC
RANDOM INSERTS IN PACKS
PRINT RUNS B/WN 5-150 COPIES PER
NO PRICING ON QTY 15 OR LESS
EXCHANGE DEADLINE 11/29/2020
2 J.D. Davis/50 4.00 10.00
23 Juan Soto/25 EXCH 20.00 50.00

2019 Panini Leather and Lumber Autographs Gold
*GOLD p/r 75-200: .5X TO 1.2X BASIC
*GOLD p/r 20-25: .75X TO 2X BASIC
RANDOM INSERTS IN PACKS
PRINT RUNS B/WN 7-200 COPIES PER
NO PRICING ON QTY 15 OR LESS
EXCHANGE DEADLINE 11/29/2020
23 Juan Soto/25 EXCH 20.00 50.00

2019 Panini Leather and Lumber Autographs Holo Gold
*HOLO GLD p/r 25: .75X TO 2X BASIC
RANDOM INSERTS IN PACKS
PRINT RUNS B/WN 2-25 COPIES PER
NO PRICING ON QTY 10 OR LESS
EXCHANGE DEADLINE 11/29/2020
3 Anthony Banda/25 10.00 25.00
8 Alex Reyes/25 6.00 15.00

2019 Panini Leather and Lumber Autographs Holo Silver
*HOLO SLV p/r 99: .5X TO 1.2X BASIC
*HOLO SLV p/r 49-50: .6X TO 1.5X BASIC
*HOLO SLV p/r 25: .75X TO 2X BASIC
RANDOM INSERTS IN PACKS
PRINT RUNS B/WN 3-99 COPIES PER
NO PRICING ON QTY 15 OR LESS
EXCHANGE DEADLINE 11/29/2020
2 J.D. Davis/25 5.00 12.00
3 Anthony Banda/50 8.00 20.00
8 Alex Reyes/50 5.00 12.00

2019 Panini Leather and Lumber Baseball Signatures
RANDOM INSERTS IN PACKS
EXCHANGE DEADLINE 11/29/2020
*BLK GLD p/r 22: .75X TO 2X BASIC
1 Aaron Judge 60.00 150.00
2 Adrian Beltre
3 Andres Galarraga 6.00 15.00
4 Don Mattingly 40.00 100.00
5 Dwight Gooden 4.00 10.00
6 Kerry Wood 5.00 12.00
8 Miguel Cabrera EXCH
9 Orlando Hernandez 2.50 6.00
11 Wade Boggs 20.00 50.00
13 Cesar Hernandez
16 Jim Rice
19 Gleyber Torres 8.00 20.00
20 Cody Bellinger EXCH
26 Tim Wakefield
27 Ronald Guzman 2.50 6.00
30 Cameron Gallagher
33 Amed Rosario 5.00 12.00
34 Jordan Hicks
35 Trey Mancini
38 Chance Sisco
39 Harrison Bader
41 Ronald Acuna Jr. EXCH 40.00 100.00
42 Andrew Stevenson 2.50 6.00
43 Omar Vizquel
44 Mike Mussina 8.00 20.00
45 Gary Sheffield
46 Chris Sale EXCH 6.00 15.00
47 Shohei Ohtani 100.00 250.00
48 George Brett 60.00 150.00
49 Kevin Mitchell

2019 Panini Leather and Lumber Baseball Signatures Black
*BLACK p/r 25: .75X TO 2X BASIC
RANDOM INSERTS IN PACKS
PRINT RUNS B/WN 5-25 COPIES PER
NO PRICING ON QTY 15 OR LESS
EXCHANGE DEADLINE 11/29/2020
36 Juan Soto/25 EXCH 20.00 50.00

2019 Panini Leather and Lumber Baseball Signatures Blue
*BLUE p/r 49: .6X TO 1.5X BASIC
*BLUE p/r 20-25: .75X TO 2X BASIC
RANDOM INSERTS IN PACKS
PRINT RUNS B/WN 5-49 COPIES PER
NO PRICING ON QTY 20 OR LESS
EXCHANGE DEADLINE 11/29/2020
36 Juan Soto/25 EXCH 20.00 50.00

2019 Panini Leather and Lumber Baseball Signatures Light Blue
*LGHT BLUE p/r 20-25: .75X TO 2X BASIC
RANDOM INSERTS IN PACKS
PRINT RUNS B/WN 5-25 COPIES PER
NO PRICING ON QTY 18 OR LESS
EXCHANGE DEADLINE 11/29/2020
25 David Bote/20
28 Freddy Peralta/20
36 Juan Soto/25 EXCH 20.00 50.00
37 Willy Adames/20 8.00 20.00

2019 Panini Leather and Lumber Baseball Signatures Pink
*PINK p/r 25: .75X TO 2X BASIC
RANDOM INSERTS IN PACKS
PRINT RUNS B/WN 5-25 COPIES PER
NO PRICING ON QTY 15 OR LESS
EXCHANGE DEADLINE 11/29/2020
36 Juan Soto/25 EXCH 20.00 50.00

2019 Panini Leather and Lumber Bat Patrol
RANDOM INSERTS IN PACKS
*GOLD/99: .75X TO 2X BASIC
*HOLO SILVER/25: 1.2X TO 3X BASIC
1 Joe Jackson .75 2.00
2 Tony Gwynn .60 1.50
3 Ichiro .75 2.00
4 Joe DiMaggio 1.25 3.00
5 Rod Carew .50 1.25
6 Edd Roush .50 1.25
7 Ken Griffey Jr. 1.25 3.00
8 Juan Soto 2.00 5.00
9 Robinson Cano .50 1.25
10 Tony Lazzeri .50 1.25
11 Wade Boggs .50 1.25
12 Paul Molitor .60 1.50
13 Jose Altuve .50 1.25
14 Christian Yelich .75 2.00
15 Dustin Pedroia .60 1.50

2019 Panini Leather and Lumber Benchmarks
RANDOM INSERTS IN PACKS
*GOLD/99: .75X TO 2X BASIC
*HOLO SILVER/25: 1.2X TO 3X BASIC
1 Frank Thomas .60 1.50
2 Shohei Ohtani .75 2.00
3 Mike Trout 3.00 8.00
4 Jacob deGrom .60 1.50
5 Greg Maddux .75 2.00
6 Jose Altuve .50 1.25
7 Ronald Acuna Jr. 3.00 8.00
8 Alex Rodriguez .75 2.00
9 Joey Votto .60 1.50
10 Yogi Berra .60 1.50
11 Tony Gwynn .60 1.50
12 Randy Johnson .60 1.50
13 Mookie Betts 1.00 2.50
14 Cal Ripken 2.00 5.00
15 Justin Verlander .60 1.50
16 Aaron Nola .50 1.25
17 Ichiro .75 2.00
18 Max Scherzer .60 1.50
19 Chris Sale .60 1.50
20 Vladimir Guerrero .50 1.25

2019 Panini Leather and Lumber Big Bats
RANDOM INSERTS IN PACKS
PRINT RUNS B/WN 35-199 COPIES PER
2 Bo Jackson/50 8.00 20.00
4 George Springer/84 4.00 10.00
5 Jorge Soler/71 5.00 12.00
7 Vladimir Guerrero Jr./199 15.00 40.00
8 Rickey Henderson/49 8.00 20.00
9 Fernando Tatis Jr./99 8.00 20.00
10 Kirby Puckett/35 25.00 60.00
11 Adam Jones/79 4.00 10.00
12 Mike Piazza/119 5.00 12.00
15 Yasmani Grandal/50 4.00 10.00

2019 Panini Leather and Lumber Big Bats Gold
*GOLD/99: .4X TO 1X p/r 199
*GOLD/35-49: .5X TO 1.2X p/r 71-199
*GOLD/35-49: .4X TO 1X p/r 35-49
*GOLD/25: .6X TO 1.5X p/r 71-199
*GOLD/25: .5X TO 1.2X p/r 35-49
RANDOM INSERTS IN PACKS
PRINT RUNS B/WN 25-99 COPIES PER
3 Kris Bryant/49 8.00 20.00
6 Eloy Jimenez/49 6.00 15.00
13 Jose Canseco/49 5.00 12.00
14 Miguel Andujar/49 6.00 15.00

2019 Panini Leather and Lumber Big Bats Holo Silver
*SILVR 20-25: .6X TO 1.5X p/r 71-199
*SILVR 20-25: .5X TO 1.2X p/r 35-50
RANDOM INSERTS IN PACKS
PRINT RUNS B/WN 10-25 COPIES PER
NO PRICING ON QTY 15 OR LESS
3 Kris Bryant/25 10.00 25.00
6 Eloy Jimenez/25 8.00 20.00
13 Jose Canseco/25 6.00 15.00
14 Miguel Andujar/25 8.00 20.00

2019 Panini Leather and Lumber Equalizers
RANDOM INSERTS IN PACKS
*GOLD/99: .75X TO 2X BASIC
*HOLO SILVER/25: 1.2X TO 3X BASIC
1 Nolan Arenado .75 2.00
2 Babe Ruth
3 Giancarlo Stanton .60 1.50
4 Mike Trout 3.00 8.00
5 Ken Griffey Jr. 1.25 3.00
6 Alex Rodriguez .75 2.00
7 Miguel Cabrera .60 1.50
8 Javier Baez .75 2.00
9 Joe DiMaggio 1.25 3.00
10 Joey Votto .60 1.50
11 Mookie Betts 1.00 2.50
12 Christian Yelich .75 2.00
13 Francisco Lindor .60 1.50
14 Alex Bregman .60 1.50
15 Anthony Rizzo 1.00 2.50
16 Bryce Harper 1.00 2.50
17 Aaron Judge 1.50 4.00
18 Manny Machado .60 1.50
19 Vladimir Guerrero .50 1.25
20 Trevor Story .60 1.50

2019 Panini Leather and Lumber Flashing the Leather
RANDOM INSERTS IN PACKS
PRINT RUNS B/WN 55-299 COPIES PER
*BLUE/49: .5X TO 1.2X BASIC
*GOLD/99: .4X TO 1X BASIC
*GOLD/25: .6X TO 1.5X BASIC
*SLVR/25: .6X TO 1.5X BASIC
1 Jose Peraza/299 3.00 8.00
2 Andrew Benintendi/299 5.00 12.00
3 Ozzie Albies/174 4.00 10.00
4 Shohei Ohtani/99 6.00 15.00
5 Francisco Lindor/55 4.00 10.00
6 Byron Buxton/125 3.00 8.00
7 J.P. Crawford/299 2.50 6.00
8 Cody Bellinger/199 5.00 12.00
9 Dansby Swanson/249 4.00 10.00
10 Billy Martin/99 8.00 20.00
11 Gil Hodges/99 10.00 25.00
12 Ken Griffey Jr./99 10.00 25.00
13 Clint Frazier/299 3.00 8.00
14 Jim Rice/199 3.00 8.00
15 Alex Bregman/125 4.00 10.00

2019 Panini Leather and Lumber Grip It 'n Rip It
RANDOM INSERTS IN PACKS
PRINT RUNS B/WN 25-99 COPIES PER
*GOLD/35-49: .5X TO 1.2X p/r 56-99
*GOLD/20: .4X TO 1X p/r 25
1 Kyle Tucker/99 5.00 12.00
2 Cedric Mullins/75 4.00 10.00
3 Jake Bauers/99 4.00 10.00
4 Garrett Hampson/72 2.50 6.00
5 Christin Stewart/50 4.00 10.00
6 Myles Straw/72 4.00 10.00
7 Ryan O'Hearn/99 2.50 6.00
8 David Fletcher/99 8.00 20.00
9 Taylor Ward/80 2.50 6.00
10 Jake Cave/56 3.00 8.00
11 Ramon Laureano/88 5.00 12.00
12 Shohei Ohtani/25 12.00 30.00
13 Brandon Lowe/77 4.00 10.00
14 Jonathan Davis/99 3.00 8.00

2019 Panini Leather and Lumber Grip It 'n Rip It Holo Silver
*SLVR/25: .6X TO 1.5X p/r 56-99
*SLVR/25: .5X TO 1.2X p/r 50
RANDOM INSERTS IN PACKS
PRINT RUNS B/WN 15-25 COPIES PER
NO PRICING ON QTY 15
15 Danny Jansen/25 4.00 10.00

2019 Panini Leather and Lumber Hit-N-Run
RANDOM INSERTS IN PACKS
*GOLD/99: .75X TO 2X BASIC
*HOLO SILVER/25: 1.2X TO 3X BASIC
1 Ichiro .75 2.00
2 Mookie Betts 1.00 2.50
3 Rickey Henderson .60 1.50
4 Charlie Blackmon .60 1.50
5 Mike Trout 3.00 8.00
6 Jose Altuve .50 1.25
7 Kevin Kiermaier .50 1.25
8 Alex Rodriguez .75 2.00
9 Lorenzo Cain .40 1.00
10 Jose Ramirez .50 1.25
11 Whit Merrifield .60 1.50
12 Trea Turner .50 1.25
13 Dee Gordon .40 1.00
14 Starling Marte .50 1.25
15 Vladimir Guerrero .50 1.25

2019 Panini Leather and Lumber Hitter Inc. Signatures Bat
RANDOM INSERTS IN PACKS
PRINT RUNS B/WN 5-25 COPIES PER
EXCHANGE DEADLINE 11/29/2020
1 Victor Robles/20 10.00 25.00
17 Alex Verdugo/25 6.00 15.00

2019 Panini Leather and Lumber Hitter Inc. Signatures Bat Gold
*GOLD/50: .25X TO .6X BASIC
RANDOM INSERTS IN PACKS
PRINT RUNS B/WN 7-50 COPIES PER
NO PRICING ON QTY 15 OR LESS
EXCHANGE DEADLINE 11/29/2020
5 Rafael Devers/25 10.00 25.00

2019 Panini Leather and Lumber Hitter Inc. Signatures Jersey
RANDOM INSERTS IN PACKS
PRINT RUN B/WN 5-25 COPIES PER
NO PRICING ON QTY 15 OR LESS
EXCHANGE DEADLINE 11/29/2020
16 Dontrelle Willis/25 5.00 12.00
17 Alex Verdugo/25 6.00 15.00
21 Dustin Fowler/25 5.00 12.00
22 Michael Taylor/25 5.00 12.00

2019 Panini Leather and Lumber Home Run Kings
RANDOM INSERTS IN PACKS
*GOLD/99: .75X TO 2X BASIC
*HOLO SILVER/25: 1.2X TO 3X BASIC
1 Babe Ruth 1.50 4.00
2 Jimmie Foxx .60 1.50
3 Willie McCovey .50 1.25
4 Harmon Killebrew .60 1.50
5 David Ortiz .60 1.50
6 Ken Griffey Jr. 1.25 3.00
7 Albert Pujols .75 2.00
8 Alex Rodriguez .75 2.00
9 Frank Thomas .60 1.50
10 Frank Robinson .50 1.25

2019 Panini Leather and Lumber Knothole Gang
RANDOM INSERTS IN PACKS
*GOLD/99: .75X TO 2X BASIC
*HOLO SILVER/25: 1.2X TO 3X BASIC
1 Roy Campanella .60 1.50
2 Shohei Ohtani .75 2.00
3 Ozzie Albies .60 1.50
4 Trevor Story .60 1.50
5 Christian Yelich .75 2.00
6 Mitch Haniger .50 1.25
7 Kris Bryant .75 2.00
8 Bryce Harper 1.00 2.50
9 Aaron Judge 1.50 4.00
10 Gleyber Torres 1.25 3.00
11 Starling Marte .50 1.25
12 Eugenio Suarez .50 1.25
13 Cody Bellinger 1.25 3.00
14 Anthony Rendon .60 1.50
15 Rhys Hoskins .75 2.00

2019 Panini Leather and Lumber Leather and Lace Signatures
RANDOM INSERTS IN PACKS
STATED PRINT RUN 25 SER.#'d SETS
EXCHANGE DEADLINE 11/29/2020
1 Jacob Nix 6.00 15.00
2 Francisco Mejia 6.00 15.00
3 Fernando Tatis Jr. 50.00 120.00
4 Enyel De Los Santos 5.00 12.00
5 Justus Sheffield 8.00 20.00
6 Dakota Hudson 6.00 15.00
7 Daniel Ponce de Leon 8.00 20.00
8 Reese McGuire 8.00 20.00
9 Vladimir Guerrero Jr. 30.00 80.00
11 Kyle Tucker 10.00 25.00
12 Jonathan Loaisiga 6.00 15.00
13 Chance Adams 5.00 12.00
14 Michael Kopech 10.00 25.00
15 Brad Keller 5.00 12.00

2019 Panini Leather and Lumber Leather and Lace Signatures Gold
*GOLD: .4X TO 1X BASIC
RANDOM INSERTS IN PACKS
STATED PRINT RUN 20 SER.#'d SETS
EXCHANGE DEADLINE 11/29/2020
10 Eloy Jimenez 20.00 50.00

2019 Panini Leather and Lumber Leather and Lumber
RANDOM INSERTS IN PACKS
*GOLD/99: .75X TO 2X BASIC
*HOLO SILVER/25: 1.2X TO 3X BASIC
1 Anthony Rizzo 1.00 2.50
2 Alex Bregman .60 1.50
3 Manny Machado .60 1.50
4 Mike Trout 3.00 8.00
5 Javier Baez .75 2.00
6 Nolan Arenado .75 2.00
7 Matt Chapman .60 1.50
8 Adrian Beltre .60 1.50
9 Francisco Lindor .60 1.50
10 Yadier Molina .60 1.50

2019 Panini Leather and Lumber Leather and Lumber Dual Bat Relics
RANDOM INSERTS IN PACKS
PRINT RUNS B/WN 49-299 COPIES PER
1 Adrian Beltre/49 5.00 12.00
3 Alex Verdugo/199 3.00 8.00
4 Carlos Correa/299 4.00 10.00
5 Corey Seager/199 4.00 10.00
6 David Dahl/199 2.50 6.00
7 Eddie Murray/299 3.00 8.00
8 Eric Thames/249 2.50 6.00
9 Gary Carter/199 3.00 8.00
10 J.P. Crawford/199 2.50 6.00
11 Miguel Andujar/125 4.00 10.00
12 Max Kepler/199 3.00 8.00
14 Nicky Delmonico/249 2.50 6.00
15 Rickey Henderson/199 8.00 20.00
16 Ryan McMahon/249 2.50 6.00
17 Shohei Ohtani/99 8.00 20.00
18 Stephen Piscotty/299 2.50 6.00
19 Yoan Moncada/30 5.00 12.00
20 Kirby Puckett/130 6.00 15.00
21 Harrison Bader/299 3.00 8.00
22 Francisco Mejia/99 3.00 8.00
23 Dustin Pedroia/99 4.00 10.00
24 Lewis Brinson/199 2.50 6.00
25 Rhys Hoskins/99 5.00 12.00
26 Tony Gwynn/199 4.00 10.00
27 Willson Contreras/299 3.00 8.00
28 Willie Stargell/149 3.00 8.00
29 Willie Calhoun/199 2.50 6.00
30 Hanley Ramirez/299 3.00 8.00

2019 Panini Leather and Lumber Leather and Lumber Dual Bat-Jersey Relics
RANDOM INSERTS IN PACKS
PRINT RUNS B/WN 35-99 COPIES PER
1 Adrian Beltre/35 5.00 12.00
2 Alex Bregman/99 4.00 10.00
3 Alex Verdugo/99 3.00 8.00
4 Carlos Correa/99 4.00 10.00
5 Corey Seager/99 4.00 10.00
6 David Dahl/99 2.50 6.00
7 Eddie Murray/99 3.00 8.00
8 Eric Thames/99 2.50 6.00
9 Gary Carter/99 3.00 8.00
10 J.P. Crawford/99 2.50 6.00
11 Miguel Andujar/99 4.00 10.00
12 Max Kepler/99 3.00 8.00
13 Miguel Sano/49 4.00 10.00
14 Nicky Delmonico/99 2.50 6.00
15 Rickey Henderson/49 10.00 25.00
16 Ryan McMahon/99 2.50 6.00
17 Shohei Ohtani/99 8.00 20.00
18 Stephen Piscotty/99 2.50 6.00
19 Yoan Moncada/50 5.00 12.00
20 Kirby Puckett/49 8.00 20.00
21 Harrison Bader/99 3.00 8.00
22 Francisco Mejia/49 4.00 10.00
23 Dustin Pedroia/49 5.00 12.00
24 Lewis Brinson/99 2.50 6.00
25 Rhys Hoskins/49 6.00 15.00
26 Tony Gwynn/49 5.00 12.00
27 Willson Contreras/99 3.00 8.00
28 Willie Stargell/99 3.00 8.00
29 Willie Calhoun/99 2.50 6.00
30 Hanley Ramirez/99 3.00 8.00

2019 Panini Leather and Lumber Leather and Lumber Dual Jersey Relics
RANDOM INSERTS IN PACKS
PRINT RUNS B/WN 49-349 COPIES PER
1 Adrian Beltre/349 4.00 10.00
2 Alex Bregman/349 4.00 10.00
3 Alex Verdugo/349 3.00 8.00
4 Carlos Correa/249 4.00 10.00
5 Corey Seager/349 4.00 10.00
6 David Dahl/349 2.50 6.00
7 Eddie Murray/249 3.00 8.00
8 Eric Thames/349 2.50 6.00
9 Gary Carter/49 4.00 10.00
10 J.P. Crawford/349 2.50 6.00
11 Miguel Andujar/349 4.00 10.00
12 Max Kepler/349 3.00 8.00
13 Miguel Sano/349 3.00 8.00
14 Nicky Delmonico/349 2.50 6.00
15 Rickey Henderson/99 8.00 20.00
16 Ryan McMahon/349 2.50 6.00
17 Shohei Ohtani/349 8.00 20.00
18 Stephen Piscotty/349 2.50 6.00
19 Yoan Moncada/349 4.00 10.00
21 Harrison Bader/349 3.00 8.00
22 Francisco Mejia/349 3.00 8.00
23 Dustin Pedroia/349 4.00 10.00
24 Lewis Brinson/349 2.50 6.00
25 Rhys Hoskins/349 5.00 12.00

26 Tony Gwynn/249 4.00 10.00
27 Willson Contreras/349 3.00 8.00
28 Willie Stargell/349 3.00 8.00
29 Willie Calhoun/349 2.50 6.00
30 Hanley Ramirez/349 3.00 8.00

2019 Panini Leather and Lumber Leather and Lumber Dual Jersey-Glove Relics

RANDOM INSERTS IN PACKS
STATED PRINT RUN 25 SER.#'d SETS
2 Alex Bregman 8.00 20.00
4 Carlos Correa 8.00 20.00
5 Corey Seager 8.00 20.00
6 David Dahl 5.00 12.00
8 Eric Thames 5.00 12.00
9 Gary Carter 6.00 15.00
10 J.P. Crawford 5.00 12.00
11 Miguel Andujar 8.00 20.00
12 Max Kepler 6.00 15.00
13 Miguel Sano 6.00 15.00
14 Nicky Delmonico 5.00 12.00
15 Rickey Henderson 5.00 40.00
16 Ryan McMahon 5.00 12.00
17 Shohei Ohtani 15.00 40.00
18 Stephen Piscotty 5.00 12.00
19 Yoan Moncada 8.00 20.00
20 Kirby Puckett 12.00 30.00
21 Harrison Bader 6.00 15.00
22 Francisco Mejia 6.00 15.00
23 Dustin Pedroia 8.00 20.00
24 Lewis Brinson 5.00 12.00
25 Rhys Hoskins 10.00 25.00
27 Willson Contreras 6.00 15.00
28 Willie Stargell 6.00 15.00
29 Willie Calhoun 5.00 12.00
30 Hanley Ramirez 6.00 15.00

2019 Panini Leather and Lumber Leather and Lumber Signatures

RANDOM INSERTS IN PACKS
PRINT RUNS B/WN 10-150 COPIES PER
NO PRICING ON QTY 10
EXCHANGE DEADLINE 11/29/2020
3 Jake Bauers/25 8.00 20.00
4 Kyle Tucker/25 10.00 25.00
6 Garrett Hampson/40 4.00 10.00
8 Myles Straw/99 5.00 12.00
10 David Fletcher/150 10.00 25.00
11 Jake Cave/99 4.00 10.00
14 Brandon Lowe/25 12.00 30.00
16 Kevin Kramer/99 4.00 10.00
18 Francisco Mejia/25 6.00 15.00
20 Patrick Wisdom/99 3.00 8.00

2019 Panini Leather and Lumber Leather and Lumber Signatures Blue

RANDOM INSERTS IN PACKS
PRINT RUNS B/WN 7-75 COPIES PER
NO PRICING ON QTY 15 OR LESS
EXCHANGE DEADLINE 11/29/2020
3 Jake Bauers/50 6.00 15.00
5 Cedric Mullins/50 6.00 15.00
6 Garrett Hampson/50 4.00 10.00
7 Christin Stewart/50 5.00 12.00
8 Myles Straw/50 6.00 15.00
9 Ryan O'Hearn/50 4.00 10.00
10 David Fletcher/75 10.00 25.00
11 Jake Cave/50 5.00 12.00
12 Jeff McNeil/50 10.00 25.00
13 Danny Jansen/25 5.00 12.00
15 Ramon Laureano/50 10.00 25.00
16 Kevin Kramer/50 5.00 12.00
17 Kevin Newman/50 6.00 15.00
18 Francisco Mejia/50 5.00 12.00
19 Chris Shaw/50 6.00 15.00
20 Patrick Wisdom/50 4.00 10.00

2019 Panini Leather and Lumber Leather and Lumber Signatures Gold

RANDOM INSERTS IN PACKS
PRINT RUNS B/WN 9-99 COPIES PER
NO PRICING ON QTY 9
EXCHANGE DEADLINE 11/29/2020
3 Jake Bauers/75 5.00 12.00
4 Kyle Tucker/20 10.00 25.00
5 Cedric Mullins/75 5.00 12.00
6 Garrett Hampson/75 3.00 8.00
8 Myles Straw/75 5.00 12.00
9 Ryan O'Hearn/75 3.00 8.00
10 David Fletcher/99 10.00 25.00
11 Jake Cave/75 4.00 10.00
12 Jeff McNeil/75 8.00 20.00
14 Brandon Lowe/20 12.00 30.00
15 Ramon Laureano/75 8.00 20.00
16 Kevin Kramer/75 4.00 10.00
17 Kevin Newman/75 5.00 12.00
18 Francisco Mejia/75 4.00 10.00
20 Patrick Wisdom/75 3.00 8.00

2019 Panini Leather and Lumber Leather and Lumber Signatures Holo Silver

RANDOM INSERTS IN PACKS
PRINT RUNS B/WN 5-25 COPIES PER
NO PRICING ON QTY 15 OR LESS
EXCHANGE DEADLINE 11/29/2020
3 Jake Bauers/25 8.00 20.00
5 Cedric Mullins/25 8.00 20.00
6 Garrett Hampson/25 5.00 12.00
7 Christin Stewart/25 6.00 15.00
8 Myles Straw/25 8.00 20.00
9 Ryan O'Hearn/25 5.00 12.00
10 David Fletcher/25 15.00 40.00
11 Jake Cave/25 6.00 15.00
12 Jeff McNeil/25 12.00 30.00
15 Ramon Laureano/25 12.00 30.00
16 Kevin Kramer/25 6.00 15.00
17 Kevin Newman/25 8.00 20.00
18 Francisco Mejia/25 6.00 15.00
19 Chris Shaw/25 8.00 20.00
20 Patrick Wisdom/25 5.00 12.00

2019 Panini Leather and Lumber Leather and Lumber Triple Bat-Jersey Relics

RANDOM INSERTS IN PACKS
*GOLD/75-299: .5X TO 1.2X BASIC
*GOLD/49: .6X TO 1.5X BASIC
*GOLD/25: .75X TO 2X BASIC
*HOLO GLD/25: .75X TO 2X BASIC
1 Eloy Jimenez 4.00 10.00
2 Kyle Tucker 3.00 8.00
3 Cedric Mullins 2.50 6.00
4 Jake Bauers 2.50 6.00
5 Christin Stewart 2.00 5.00
6 Ryan O'Hearn 1.50 4.00
7 Jeff McNeil 3.00 8.00
8 Ramon Laureano 3.00 8.00
9 Corey Seager 2.50 6.00
10 Brandon Lowe 2.50 6.00
11 Amed Rosario 2.00 5.00
12 Chance Sisco 1.50 4.00
13 J.P. Crawford 1.50 4.00
14 Jose Peraza 2.00 5.00
15 Shohei Ohtani 6.00 15.00
16 Max Kepler 2.00 5.00
17 Willson Contreras 2.00 5.00
18 Austin Hays 2.50 6.00
20 Bernie Williams 2.00 5.00
21 Carlton Fisk 2.00 5.00
22 Francisco Mejia 2.00 5.00
23 Delino DeShields Jr. 1.50 4.00
24 Gregory Polanco 2.00 5.00
25 Jake Cave 2.00 5.00
26 Craig Biggio 2.00 5.00
27 Jose Canseco 2.00 5.00
28 Jose Reyes 2.00 5.00
29 Kevin Kramer 2.00 5.00
30 Alex Verdugo 2.00 5.00
31 Taylor Ward 1.50 4.00
32 Omar Vizquel 2.00 5.00
33 Jose Canseco 2.00 5.00
34 Willie McCovey 3.00 8.00
35 Kevin Newman 2.50 6.00
36 David Fletcher 5.00 12.00
37 Chris Shaw 2.50 6.00
38 Patrick Wisdom 1.50 4.00
39 Danny Jansen 1.50 4.00
40 Rowdy Tellez 2.50 6.00

2019 Panini Leather and Lumber Leather and Lumber Triple Jersey Relics

RANDOM INSERTS IN PACKS
1 Eloy Jimenez 4.00 10.00
2 Kyle Tucker 3.00 8.00
3 Cedric Mullins 2.50 6.00
4 Jake Bauers 2.50 6.00
5 Christin Stewart 2.00 5.00
6 Ryan O'Hearn 1.50 4.00
7 Jeff McNeil 3.00 8.00
8 Ramon Laureano 3.00 8.00
9 Corey Seager 2.50 6.00
10 Brandon Lowe 2.50 6.00
11 Amed Rosario 2.00 5.00
12 Chance Sisco 1.50 4.00
13 J.P. Crawford 1.50 4.00
14 Jose Peraza 2.00 5.00
15 Shohei Ohtani 5.00 12.00
16 Max Kepler 2.00 5.00
17 Willson Contreras 2.00 5.00
18 Austin Hays 2.50 6.00
20 Bernie Williams 2.00 5.00
21 Carlton Fisk 2.00 5.00
22 Francisco Mejia 2.00 5.00
23 Delino DeShields Jr. 1.50 4.00
24 Gregory Polanco 2.00 5.00
25 Jake Cave 2.00 5.00
26 Craig Biggio 2.00 5.00
27 Jose Canseco 2.00 5.00
28 Jose Reyes 4.00 10.00
29 Kevin Kramer 2.00 5.00
30 Alex Verdugo 2.00 5.00
31 Taylor Ward 1.50 4.00
32 Omar Vizquel 2.00 5.00
33 Jose Canseco 2.00 5.00
35 Kevin Newman 2.50 6.00
36 David Fletcher 5.00 12.00
37 Chris Shaw 2.50 6.00
38 Patrick Wisdom 1.50 4.00
39 Danny Jansen 1.50 4.00
40 Rowdy Tellez 2.50 6.00

2019 Panini Leather and Lumber Leather and Lumber Triple Jersey Relics Holo Silver

*SLVR/75-99: .5X TO 1.5X BASIC
*SLVR/49: .6X TO 1.5X BASIC
RANDOM INSERTS IN PACKS
PRINT RUN B/WN 49-99 COPIES PER
19 Mike Piazza/49 4.00 10.00

2019 Panini Leather and Lumber Leather Signatures

RANDOM INSERTS IN PACKS
EXCHANGE DEADLINE 11/29/2020
*DRK BRWN/20: .75X TO 2X BASIC
1 Josh Donaldson 8.00 20.00
2 Omar Vizquel
3 Pete Rose EXCH 10.00 25.00
4 Jose Canseco EXCH 8.00 20.00
5 Steve Garvey
6 Don Mattingly 40.00 100.00
7 Ozzie Smith
8 Brooks Robinson
9 Ivan Rodriguez EXCH 12.00 30.00

2019 Panini Leather and Lumber Legendary Lumber

RANDOM INSERTS IN PACKS
PRINT RUNS B/WN 10-99 COPIES PER
NO PRICING ON QTY 15 OR LESS
*GOLD/49: .5X TO 1.2X p/r 99
*GOLD/25: .5X TO 1.2X p/r 49
*SLVR/25: .6X TO 1.5X p/r 99
2 Frank Chance/49 8.00 20.00
4 Edd Roush/49 8.00 20.00
8 Roy Campanella/25 8.00 20.00
9 Tony Lazzeri/99 5.00 12.00
10 Kirby Puckett/99 6.00 15.00

2019 Panini Leather and Lumber Life on the Edge

RANDOM INSERTS IN PACKS
*GOLD/99: .75X TO 2X BASIC
*HOLO SILVER/25: 1.2X TO 3X BASIC
1 Kyle Freeland .50 1.25
2 Chris Sale .60 1.50
3 Clayton Kershaw 1.25 3.00
4 Max Scherzer .60 1.50
5 Greg Maddux .75 2.00
6 Justin Verlander .60 1.50
7 Corey Kluber .50 1.25
8 Blake Snell .50 1.25
9 Aaron Nola .50 1.25
10 Jacob deGrom .60 1.50

2019 Panini Leather and Lumber Lumber Signatures

RANDOM INSERTS IN PACKS
EXCHANGE DEADLINE 11/29/2020
1 Don Mattingly 40.00 100.00
2 Wade Boggs 20.00 50.00
3 Ted Simmons 15.00 40.00
7 Andrew Benintendi EXCH 12.00 30.00
8 Jose Canseco EXCH 8.00 20.00
9 Andres Galarraga 6.00 15.00

2019 Panini Leather and Lumber Lumber Signatures Blue

*BLUE/20: .75X TO 2X BASIC
RANDOM INSERTS IN PACKS
PRINT RUNS B/WN 10-20 COPIES PER
NO PRICING ON QTY 15 OR LESS
EXCHANGE DEADLINE 11/29/2020
6 Kyle Schwarber/20

2019 Panini Leather and Lumber Lumberjacks

RANDOM INSERTS IN PACKS
*GOLD/99: .75X TO 2X BASIC
*HOLO SILVER/25: 1.2X TO 3X BASIC
1 Jose Abreu .60 1.50
2 David Ortiz .60 1.50
3 Khris Davis .60 1.50
4 Paul Goldschmidt .60 1.50
5 Nelson Cruz .60 1.50
6 Roy Campanella .60 1.50
7 Jose Ramirez .50 1.25
8 Edwin Encarnacion .60 1.50
9 Bryce Harper 1.00 2.50
10 J.D. Martinez .60 1.50
11 Joey Gallo .50 1.25
12 Miguel Cabrera .60 1.50
13 Kyle Schwarber .60 1.50
14 Rhys Hoskins .75 2.00
15 Aaron Judge 1.50 4.00

2019 Panini Leather and Lumber Maple and Ash

RANDOM INSERTS IN PACKS
*GOLD/99: .75X TO 2X BASIC
*HOLO SILVER/25: 1.2X TO 3X BASIC
1 Charlie Blackmon .60 1.50
2 Gleyber Torres 1.25 3.00
3 Ryne Sandberg 1.25 3.00
4 Joe Jackson .75 2.00
5 Joe DiMaggio 1.25 3.00
6 Cal Ripken 2.00 5.00
7 Shohei Ohtani .75 2.00
8 Matt Chapman .60 1.50
9 Yogi Berra .60 1.50
10 Cody Bellinger 1.25 3.00

2019 Panini Leather and Lumber Naturals

RANDOM INSERTS IN PACKS
*GOLD/99: .75X TO 2X BASIC
*HOLO SILVER/25: 1.2X TO 3X BASIC
1 Rickey Henderson .60 1.50
2 Chipper Jones .60 1.50
3 Ken Griffey Jr. 1.25 3.00
4 Barry Larkin .50 1.25
5 Robinson Cano .50 1.25
6 Miguel Cabrera .60 1.50
7 Mike Trout 3.00 8.00
8 Mookie Betts 1.00 2.50
9 Joe Jackson .75 2.00
10 Babe Ruth 1.50 4.00
11 Ichiro .75 2.00
12 Vladimir Guerrero .50 1.25
13 Ronald Acuna Jr. 3.00 8.00
14 Joe DiMaggio 1.25 3.00
15 Juan Soto 2.00 5.00

2019 Panini Leather and Lumber Power Alley

RANDOM INSERTS IN PACKS
*GOLD/99: .75X TO 2X BASIC
*HOLO SILVER/25: 1.2X TO 3X BASIC
1 Andrew McCutchen .60 1.50
2 Alex Bregman .60 1.50
3 Christian Yelich .75 2.00
4 Whit Merrifield .60 1.50
5 Barry Larkin .50 1.25
6 Lorenzo Cain .40 1.00
7 Juan Soto 2.00 5.00
8 Kris Bryant .75 2.00
9 Javier Baez .75 2.00
10 Ken Boyer .40 1.00
11 Joe DiMaggio 1.25 3.00
12 Gleyber Torres 1.25 3.00
13 Mike Trout 3.00 8.00
14 Miguel Cabrera .60 1.50
15 Gil Hodges .50 1.25

2019 Panini Leather and Lumber Rivals Materials

RANDOM INSERTS IN PACKS
PRINT RUNS B/WN 15-199 COPIES PER
NO PRICING ON QTY 15
*GOLD/99: .4X TO 1X p/r 99-199
*GOLD/35-49: .5X TO 1.2X p/r 99-199
*GOLD/25: .5X TO 1.2X p/r 49-50
1 Rodriguez/Ortiz/199 5.00 12.00
2 Piazza/Clemens/149 5.00 12.00
3 Jose Bautista 3.00 8.00
Rougned Odor/199
4 Madison Bumgarner 4.00 10.00
Yasiel Puig/199
5 Judge/Betts/199 10.00 25.00
6 Smith/Yount/199 5.00 12.00
8 Aaron Nola 5.00 12.00
Max Scherzer/50
10 Campy/Berra/49 12.00 30.00
11 Pujols/Ichiro/49 6.00 15.00
12 Soto/Acuna/199 6.00 15.00
13 Cabrera/Clemens/199 5.00 12.00
14 Adrian Beltre 4.00 10.00
Felix Hernandez/99
15 Bryant/Molina/199 5.00 12.00

2019 Panini Leather and Lumber Rivals Materials Holo Silver

*SLVR/25: .6X TO 1.5X p/r 99-199
*SLVR/25: .5X TO 1.2X p/r 49-50
RANDOM INSERTS IN PACKS
PRINT RUNS B/WN 5-25 COPIES PER
NO PRICING ON QTY 10 OR LESS
7 Snell/Sale/25 6.00 15.00

2019 Panini Leather and Lumber Rookie Baseball Signatures Black

*BLACK p/r 75-149: .4X TO 1X BASIC
*BLACK p/r 25: .6X TO 1.5X BASIC
RANDOM INSERTS IN PACKS
PRINT RUNS B/WN 1-149 COPIES PER
NO PRICING ON QTY 4 OR LESS
EXCHANGE DEADLINE 11/29/2020

2019 Panini Leather and Lumber Rookie Baseball Signatures Black Gold

*BLCK GLD: .6X TO 1.5X BASIC
RANDOM INSERTS IN PACKS
STATED PRINT RUN 25 SER.#'d SETS
EXCHANGE DEADLINE 11/29/2020

2019 Panini Leather and Lumber Rookie Baseball Signatures Blue

*BLUE p/r 60-99: .4X TO 1X BASIC
*BLUE p/r 25: .6X TO 1.5X BASIC
RANDOM INSERTS IN PACKS
PRINT RUNS B/WN 4-99 COPIES PER
NO PRICING ON QTY 4
EXCHANGE DEADLINE 11/29/2020

2019 Panini Leather and Lumber Rookie Baseball Signatures Light Blue

*LT BLUE p/r 49-50: .5X TO 1.2X BASIC
*LT BLUE p/r 35: .6X TO 1.5X BASIC
RANDOM INSERTS IN PACKS
PRINT RUNS B/WN 35-50 COPIES PER
EXCHANGE DEADLINE 11/29/2020

2019 Panini Leather and Lumber Rookie Baseball Signatures Pink

*PINK p/r 75-99: .4X TO 1X BASIC
*PINK p/r 50: .5X TO 1.2X BASIC
*PINK p/r 25: .6X TO 1.5X BASIC
RANDOM INSERTS IN PACKS
PRINT RUNS B/WN 1-75 COPIES PER
NO PRICING ON QTY 1
EXCHANGE DEADLINE 11/29/2020

2019 Panini Leather and Lumber Rookie Leather Signatures

*LEATHER p/r 99-149: .4X TO 1X BASIC
RANDOM INSERTS IN PACKS
PRINT RUNS B/WN 99-149 COPIES PER
EXCHANGE DEADLINE 11/29/2020

2019 Panini Leather and Lumber Rookie Leather Signatures Black and Silver

*BLK SLVR: .6X TO 1.5X BASIC
RANDOM INSERTS IN PACKS
STATED PRINT RUN 25 SER.#'d SETS
EXCHANGE DEADLINE 11/29/2020

2019 Panini Leather and Lumber Rookie Leather Signatures Dark Brown

*DRK BRWN p/r 75-99: .4X TO 1X BASIC
*DRK BRWN p/r 49: .5X TO 1.2X BASIC
RANDOM INSERTS IN PACKS
PRINT RUNS B/WN 49-99 COPIES PER
EXCHANGE DEADLINE 11/29/2020

2019 Panini Leather and Lumber Rookie Lumber Signatures

*LUMBER p/r 99-149: .4X TO 1X BASIC
RANDOM INSERTS IN PACKS
PRINT RUNS B/WN 99-149 COPIES PER
EXCHANGE DEADLINE 11/29/2020

2019 Panini Leather and Lumber Rookie Lumber Signatures Blue

*BLUE p/r 75-99: .4X TO 1X BASIC
*BLUE p/r 49: .5X TO 1.2X BASIC
RANDOM INSERTS IN PACKS
PRINT RUNS B/WN 49-99 COPIES PER
EXCHANGE DEADLINE 11/29/2020

2019 Panini Leather and Lumber Rookie Lumber Signatures Holo Silver

*HOLO SLVR: .6X TO 1.5X BASIC
RANDOM INSERTS IN PACKS
STATED PRINT RUN 25 SER.#'d SETS
EXCHANGE DEADLINE 11/29/2020

2019 Panini Leather and Lumber Slugfest

RANDOM INSERTS IN PACKS
*GOLD/99: .75X TO 2X BASIC
*HOLO SILVER/25: 1.2X TO 3X BASIC
1 Jose Abreu .60 1.50
2 Adrian Beltre .60 1.50
3 Albert Pujols .75 2.00
4 Rhys Hoskins .75 2.00
5 Ronald Acuna Jr. 3.00 8.00
6 Jimmie Foxx .60 1.50
7 Bryce Harper 1.00 2.50
8 J.D. Martinez .60 1.50
9 Ken Boyer .40 1.00
10 Paul Goldschmidt .60 1.50
11 Giancarlo Stanton .60 1.50
12 Babe Ruth 1.50 4.00
13 Alex Rodriguez .75 2.00
14 Shohei Ohtani .75 2.00
15 Aaron Judge 1.50 4.00
16 Josh Donaldson .50 1.25
17 Kris Bryant .75 2.00
18 Frank Thomas .60 1.50
19 Roy Campanella .60 1.50
20 Khris Davis .60 1.50

2019 Panini Leather and Lumber Sweet Feet

RANDOM INSERTS IN PACKS
PRINT RUNS B/WN 50-194 COPIES PER
5 Corey Seager/50 5.00 12.00
6 Darryl Strawberry/99 4.00 10.00
10 Joc Pederson/194 3.00 8.00
15 Vladimir Guerrero/99 6.00 15.00

2019 Panini Leather and Lumber Sweet Feet Blue

*BLUE/49: .5X TO 1.2X p/r 99-194
RANDOM INSERTS IN PACKS
PRINT RUNS B/WN 15-99 COPIES PER
NO PRICING ON QTY 15
1 Myles Straw/23 6.00 15.00
2 Amed Rosario/30 4.00 10.00
3 Austin Hays/48 5.00 12.00
4 Victor Robles/25 8.00 20.00
7 Gleyber Torres/49 6.00 15.00
8 Ichiro/49 12.00 30.00
11 Manuel Margot/49 3.00 8.00
12 Mike Trout/25 40.00 100.00
13 Nick Williams/25 4.00 10.00
14 Shohei Ohtani/99 8.00 20.00
16 Paul Molitor/95 8.00 20.00
17 Juan Soto/25 10.00 25.00
19 Orlando Arcia/25 4.00 10.00
20 Javier Baez/25 8.00 20.00

2019 Panini Leather and Lumber Sweet Feet Gold

*GOLD/75-99: .4X TO 1X p/r 99-194
*GOLD/20: .6X TO 1.5X p/r 99
*GOLD/20: .5X TO 1.2X p/r 50
RANDOM INSERTS IN PACKS
PRINT RUNS B/WN 20-199 COPIES PER
2 Amed Rosario/50 4.00 10.00
7 Gleyber Torres/50 6.00 15.00
8 Ichiro/70 10.00 25.00
12 Mike Trout/49 30.00 80.00
13 Nick Williams/49 3.00 8.00
14 Shohei Ohtani/199 8.00 20.00
17 Juan Soto/42 8.00 20.00

2019 Panini Leather and Lumber Sweet Feet Holo Silver

*SLVR/25: .6X TO 1.5X p/r 99-194
RANDOM INSERTS IN PACKS
PRINT RUNS B/WN 10-25 COPIES PER
NO PRICING ON QTY 10
2 Amed Rosario/25 5.00 12.00
3 Austin Hays/25 6.00 15.00
7 Gleyber Torres/25 8.00 20.00
8 Ichiro/25 15.00 40.00
11 Manuel Margot/25 4.00 10.00
14 Shohei Ohtani/25 12.00 30.00
16 Paul Molitor/25 12.00 30.00
18 Ronald Acuna Jr./25 10.00 25.00

2019 Panini Leather and Lumber W.A.R. Daddys

RANDOM INSERTS IN PACKS
*GOLD/99: .75X TO 2X BASIC
*HOLO SILVER/25: 1.2X TO 3X BASIC
1 Jimmie Foxx .60 1.50
2 J.D. Martinez .60 1.50
3 Alex Rodriguez .75 2.00
4 Frank Robinson .50 1.25
5 Randy Johnson .60 1.50
6 Ken Griffey Jr. 1.25 3.00
7 Giancarlo Stanton .60 1.50
8 Babe Ruth 1.50 4.00
9 Clayton Kershaw 1.25 3.00
10 Nolan Ryan 2.00 5.00

2020 Panini Legacy

RANDOM INSERTS IN PACKS
1 Shogo Akiyama RC .40 1.00
2 Yordan Alvarez RC 1.25 3.00
3 Bo Bichette RC 3.00 8.00
4 Aristides Aquino RC .50 1.25
5 Gavin Lux RC 1.50 4.00
6 Yoshitomo Tsutsugo RC .30 .75
7 Brendan McKay RC .40 1.00
8 Luis Robert RC 4.00 10.00
9 Adrian Morejon RC .25 .60
10 Michael King RC .40 1.00
11 Rafael Devers .30 .75
12 Justin Verlander .25 .60
13 Anthony Rendon .25 .60
14 Jose Ramirez .20 .50
15 Clayton Kershaw .50 1.25

2020 Panini Legacy Signatures

RANDOM INSERTS IN PACKS
PRINT RUNS B/WN 10-99 COPIES PER
NO PRICING QTY 15 OR LESS
EXCHANGE DEADLINE 3/18/2022
1 Shogo Akiyama/49 6.00 15.00
2 Yordan Alvarez/50 20.00 50.00
3 Bo Bichette/30 30.00 80.00
4 Aristides Aquino/60 8.00 20.00
6 Yoshitomo Tsutsugo/99 8.00 20.00
8 Luis Robert EXCH/99 75.00 200.00
9 Adrian Morejon/96 3.00 8.00
10 Michael King/99 5.00 12.00
14 Jose Ramirez/25 6.00 15.00

2020 Panini Luminance Autographs

RANDOM INSERTS IN PACKS
EXCHANGE DEADLINE 3/18/2022
*GOLD/75-99: .5X TO 1.2X BASIC
*GOLD/50: .6X TO 1.5X BASIC
*GOLD/25: .8X TO 2X BASIC
*RED/50: .6X TO 1.5X BASIC
*RED/25: .8X TO 2X BASIC
*BLUE/25: .8X TO 2X BASIC
1 Kyle Wright 4.00 10.00
2 Evan White 2.50 6.00
3 J.D. Davis 2.50 6.00
4 Myles Straw 4.00 10.00
5 Jeff McNeil 3.00 8.00
6 Stephen Piscotty 2.50 6.00
7 Daniel Robertson 2.50 6.00
8 Andrew Stevenson 2.50 6.00
9 Odubel Herrera 3.00 8.00
10 Jose Ramirez 6.00 15.00
11 Jonathan Davis 3.00 8.00
12 Luis Ortiz 2.50 6.00
13 Austin Voth 2.50 6.00
14 Josh Hader 2.50 6.00
15 Tyler Glasnow 2.50 6.00
16 Derek Fisher 2.50 6.00
17 Jake Cave 3.00 8.00
18 Yohander Mendez 2.50 6.00
19 Cesar Hernandez 2.50 6.00
20 Brian Anderson 2.50 6.00
21 Rio Ruiz 2.50 6.00
22 Josh James 4.00 10.00
23 Carlos Martinez 3.00 8.00
24 Michael Chavis 6.00 15.00
25 Connor Sadzeck 2.50 6.00

2020 Panini Magnitude

RANDOM INSERTS IN PACKS
1 Mike Trout 2.00 5.00
2 Aaron Judge .60 1.50
3 Shohei Ohtani .30 .75
4 Cody Bellinger .50 1.25
5 Christian Yelich .30 .75
6 Juan Soto .75 2.00
7 Ronald Acuna Jr. 1.50 4.00
8 Vladimir Guerrero Jr. .50 1.25
9 Pete Alonso .40 1.00
10 Fernando Tatis Jr. 2.00 5.00
11 Yordan Alvarez RC 1.25 3.00
12 Gavin Lux RC 1.50 4.00
13 Luis Robert RC 4.00 10.00
14 Aristides Aquino RC .50 1.25
15 Bo Bichette RC 3.00 8.00
16 Brendan McKay RC .40 1.00
17 Dustin May RC 1.00 2.50
18 Kris Bryant .30 .75
19 Francisco Lindor .25 .60
20 Bryce Harper .40 1.00
21 Javier Baez .30 .75
22 Shogo Akiyama RC .40 1.00
23 Gerrit Cole .40 1.00
24 Mookie Betts .50 1.25
25 Yoshitomo Tsutsugo RC .30 .75

2020 Panini Mosaic

RANDOM INSERTS IN PACKS
1 Josh Rojas RC .25 .60
2 Rico Garcia RC .40 1.00
3 Yordan Alvarez RC 1.25 3.00
4 Jesus Luzardo RC .50 1.25
5 Jake Rogers RC .25 .60
6 Sean Murphy RC .40 1.00
7 Ronald Bolanos RC .40 1.00
8 Yu Chang RC .40 1.00
9 Anthony Kay RC .25 .60
10 Andres Munoz RC .30 .75
11 Domingo Leyba RC .30 .75
12 Michael King RC .40 1.00
13 Gavin Lux RC 1.50 4.00
14 Bo Bichette RC 3.00 8.00
15 Brendan McKay RC .40 1.00
16 Logan Allen RC .25 .60
17 Nico Hoerner RC 1.00 2.50
18 Mauricio Dubon RC .30 .75
19 Joe Palumbo RC .25 .60
20 Deivy Grullon RC .25 .60
21 Aaron Civale RC .40 1.00
22 Tony Gonsolin RC 1.00 2.50
23 Logan Webb RC .30 .75
24 Danny Mendick RC .30 .75
25 Brock Burke RC .25 .60
26 Sheldon Neuse RC .30 .75
27 Tres Barrera RC .50 1.25
28 Randy Arozarena RC 2.00 5.00
29 Adbert Alzolay RC .30 .75
30 Sam Hilliard RC .40 1.00
31 Zac Gallen RC .60 1.50
32 Matt Thaiss RC .30 .75
33 Tyrone Taylor RC .25 .60
34 Patrick Sandoval RC .40 1.00
35 Willi Castro RC .40 1.00
36 Lewis Thorpe RC .25 .60
37 Dylan Cease RC .50 1.25
38 Jaylin Davis RC .40 1.00
39 Bryan Abreu RC .25 .60
40 Aristides Aquino RC .50 1.25
41 Abraham Toro RC .30 .75
42 Edwin Rios RC .60 1.50
43 Jonathan Hernandez RC .25 .60
44 Michel Baez RC .25 .60
45 Nick Solak RC .40 1.00
46 Dustin May RC 1.00 2.50
47 Donnie Walton RC .60 1.50
48 Jake Fraley RC .30 .75
49 Kyle Lewis RC 4.00 10.00
50 Bobby Bradley RC .30 .75
51 Justin Dunn RC .30 .75
52 Adrian Morejon RC .25 .60
53 Travis Demeritte RC .30 .75
54 A.J. Puk RC .50 1.25
55 Trent Grisham RC 1.00 2.50
56 Brusdar Graterol RC .40 1.00
57 Zack Collins RC .30 .75
58 Jordan Yamamoto RC .30 .75
59 Isan Diaz RC .40 1.00
60 T.J. Zeuch RC .25 .60
61 Yonathan Daza RC .30 .75
62 Shun Yamaguchi RC .30 .75
63 Kwang-Hyun Kim RC .75 2.00
64 Shogo Akiyama RC .40 1.00
65 Yoshitomo Tsutsugo RC .30 .75
66 Luis Robert RC 4.00 10.00
67 Trey Mancini .25 .60
68 Rafael Devers .30 .75
69 J.D. Martinez .25 .60
70 Aaron Judge .60 1.50
71 Gleyber Torres .50 1.25
72 Vladimir Guerrero Jr. .50 1.25
73 Josh Bell .20 .50
74 Blake Snell .20 .50
75 Eloy Jimenez .50 1.25
76 Jose Ramirez .20 .50
77 Francisco Lindor .25 .60
78 Miguel Cabrera .25 .60
79 Whit Merrifield .25 .60
80 Nelson Cruz .25 .60
81 Nolan Arenado .30 .75
82 Mike Trout 2.00 5.00
83 Shohei Ohtani .30 .75
84 Cody Bellinger .50 1.25
85 Manny Machado .25 .60
86 Alex Bregman .25 .60
87 Jose Altuve .20 .50
88 Gerrit Cole .40 1.00
89 Ronald Acuna Jr. 1.50 4.00
90 Ozzie Albies .25 .60
91 Juan Soto .75 2.00
92 Max Scherzer .25 .60
93 Fernando Tatis Jr. 2.00 5.00
94 Pete Alonso .60 1.50
95 Bryce Harper .40 1.00
96 Javier Baez .30 .75
97 Christian Yelich .30 .75
98 Keston Hiura .30 .75
99 Paul Goldschmidt .25 .60
100 Joey Votto .25 .60

2020 Panini Mosaic Blue

*BLUE VET: 2X TO 5X BASIC
*BLUE RC: 1.2X TO 3X BASIC RC
RANDOM INSERTS IN PACKS
STATED PRINT RUN 99 SER.#'d SETS
3 Yordan Alvarez 12.00 30.00
14 Bo Bichette 40.00 100.00
28 Randy Arozarena 30.00 80.00
49 Kyle Lewis 25.00 60.00
63 Kwang-Hyun Kim 12.00 30.00
66 Luis Robert 40.00 100.00
70 Aaron Judge 10.00 25.00
71 Gleyber Torres 6.00 15.00
82 Mike Trout 25.00 60.00
84 Cody Bellinger 10.00 25.00
89 Ronald Acuna Jr. 15.00 40.00
93 Fernando Tatis Jr. 20.00 50.00

2020 Panini Mosaic Mosaic

*MOSAIC VET: 1X TO 2.5X BASIC
*MOSAIC RC: .6X TO 1.5X BASIC RC
RANDOM INSERTS IN PACKS

3 Yordan Alvarez 3.00 8.00
14 Bo Bichette 8.00 20.00
28 Randy Arozarena 15.00 40.00
49 Kyle Lewis 8.00 20.00
66 Luis Robert 15.00 40.00
82 Mike Trout 12.00 30.00
93 Fernando Tatis Jr. 6.00 15.00

2020 Panini Mosaic Purple

*PURPLE VET: 2.5X TO 6X BASIC
*PURPLE RC: 1.5X TO 4X BASIC RC
RANDOM INSERTS IN PACKS
STATED PRINT RUN 49 SER.#'d SETS
3 Yordan Alvarez 15.00 40.00
14 Bo Bichette 50.00 120.00
17 Nico Hoerner 15.00 40.00
28 Randy Arozarena 40.00 100.00
49 Kyle Lewis 30.00 80.00
63 Kwang-Hyun Kim 15.00 40.00
66 Luis Robert 50.00 120.00
70 Aaron Judge 12.00 30.00
71 Gleyber Torres 8.00 20.00
82 Mike Trout 40.00 100.00
84 Cody Bellinger 12.00 30.00
89 Ronald Acuna Jr. 20.00 50.00
93 Fernando Tatis Jr. 25.00 60.00

2020 Panini Mosaic Silver

3 Yordan Alvarez 3.00 8.00
14 Bo Bichette 8.00 20.00
28 Randy Arozarena 15.00 40.00
49 Kyle Lewis 8.00 20.00
66 Luis Robert 15.00 40.00
82 Mike Trout 12.00 30.00
93 Fernando Tatis Jr. 6.00 15.00

2020 Panini Mosaic White

*WHITE VET: 10X TO 25X BASIC
*WHITE RC: 6X TO 15X BASIC RC
RANDOM INSERTS IN PACKS
STATED PRINT RUN 25 SER.#'d SETS
3 Yordan Alvarez 30.00 80.00
13 Gavin Lux 25.00 60.00
14 Bo Bichette 150.00 400.00
17 Nico Hoerner 30.00 80.00
28 Randy Arozarena 125.00 300.00
49 Kyle Lewis 40.00 100.00
55 Trent Grisham 20.00 50.00
63 Kwang-Hyun Kim 30.00 80.00
66 Luis Robert 125.00 300.00
70 Aaron Judge 25.00 60.00
71 Gleyber Torres 15.00 40.00
82 Mike Trout 200.00 500.00
84 Cody Bellinger 25.00 60.00
89 Ronald Acuna Jr. 50.00 120.00
91 Juan Soto 125.00 300.00
93 Fernando Tatis Jr. 50.00 120.00

2019 Panini National Treasures

RANDOMLY INSERTED IN PACKS
PRINT RUNS B/WN 1-99 COPIES PER
NO PRICING ON QTY 15 OR LESS
EXCHANGE DEADLINE 3/25/21
1 Bryse Wilson JSY AU/99 RC 5.00 12.00
2 Touki Toussaint JSY AU/99 RC 5.00 12.00
3 M.Kopech JSY AU/99 RC 10.00 25.00
4 R.Laureano JSY AU/99 RC 15.00 40.00
5 Garrett Hampson JSY AU/99 RC 4.00 10.00
6 Dennis Santana JSY AU/99 RC 4.00 10.00
7 Ryan O'Hearn JSY AU/99 RC 6.00 15.00
8 Jonathan Loaisiga JSY AU/99 RC 5.00 12.00
9 E.Jimenez JSY AU/99 RC 25.00 60.00
10 Reese McGuire JSY AU/99 RC 6.00 15.00
11 Corbin Burnes JSY AU/99 RC 6.00 15.00
12 Jake Cave JSY AU/99 RC 5.00 12.00
13 Luis Ortiz JSY AU/99 RC 4.00 10.00
14 Kyle Wright JSY AU/99 RC 6.00 15.00
15 Chris Shaw JSY AU/99 RC 6.00 15.00
16 Kevin Kramer JSY AU/99 RC 6.00 15.00
17 Framber Valdez JSY AU/99 RC 4.00 10.00
18 D.Hudson JSY AU/99 RC 12.00 30.00
19 K.Newman JSY AU/99 RC 15.00 40.00
20 Danny Jansen JSY AU/99 RC 4.00 10.00
21 Brad Keller JSY AU/99 RC 4.00 10.00
22 Chance Adams JSY AU/99 RC 4.00 10.00
23 Enyel De Los Santos JSY AU/99 RC 4.00 10.00
24 Taylor Ward JSY AU/99 RC 4.00 10.00
26 K.Tucker JSY AU/99 RC 15.00 40.00
27 Patrick Wisdom JSY AU/99 RC 4.00 10.00
28 J.McNeil JSY AU/99 RC 20.00 50.00
29 Guerrero Jr. JSY AU/99 RC 100.00 250.00
30 Cionel Perez JSY AU/99 RC 4.00 10.00
31 Kolby Allard JSY AU/99 RC 6.00 15.00
32 Stephen Gonsalves JSY AU/99 RC 6.00 15.00
33 B.Lowe JSY AU/99 RC 8.00 20.00
34 Myles Straw JSY AU/99 RC 6.00 15.00
35 Tatis Jr. JSY AU/99 RC 125.00 300.00
36 Sean Reid-Foley JSY AU/99 RC 4.00 10.00
37 Jonathan Davis JSY AU/99 RC 5.00 12.00
38 Ryan Borucki JSY AU/99 RC 4.00 10.00
39 Christin Stewart JSY AU/99 RC 5.00 12.00
40 Cedric Mullins JSY AU/99 RC 6.00 15.00
41 Justus Sheffield JSY AU/99 RC 6.00 15.00
42 Caleb Ferguson JSY AU/99 RC 5.00 12.00
43 Jacob Nix JSY AU/99 RC 5.00 12.00
44 Daniel Ponce de Leon JSY AU/99 RC 6.00 15.00
45 Josh James JSY AU/99 RC 6.00 15.00
46 David Fletcher JSY AU/99 RC 8.00 20.00
47 Steven Duggar JSY AU/99 RC 5.00 12.00
48 Rowdy Tellez JSY AU/99 RC 6.00 15.00
49 Luis Urias JSY AU/99 RC 6.00 15.00
50 Jake Bauers JSY AU/99 RC 6.00 15.00
51 P.Alonso JSY AU/49 RC 125.00 300.00
53 C.Paddack JSY AU/75 RC 15.00 40.00
54 B.Reynolds JSY AU/99 RC 40.00 100.00
55 C.Tucker JSY AU/99 RC 20.00 50.00
56 M.Chavis JSY AU/99 RC 15.00 40.00
57 Y.Kikuchi JSY AU/99 RC 10.00 25.00
58 D.Hernandez JSY AU/66 RC 4.00 10.00
59 Ty France JSY AU/99 RC 15.00 40.00
60 Taylor Hearn JSY AU/99 RC 4.00 10.00
61 C.Kieboom JSY AU/99 RC 15.00 40.00
63 Cal Quantrill JSY AU/25 RC 6.00 15.00
64 Nathaniel Lowe JSY AU/99 RC 5.00 12.00
66 A.Riley JSY AU/99 RC 20.00 50.00
67 Shaun Anderson JSY AU/99 RC 4.00 10.00
68 K.Hiura JSY AU/99 RC 15.00 40.00
69 Nicky Lopez JSY AU/49 RC 8.00 20.00
71 Brendan Rodgers JSY AU/99 RC 6.00 15.00
72 L.Arraez JSY AU/99 RC 25.00 60.00
73 O.Mercado JSY AU/79 RC 20.00 50.00
74 Addie Joss JSY/25 25.00 60.00
75 Mitch Haniger JSY/99 2.50 6.00
76 Rafael Devers JSY/99 4.00 10.00
77 Franmil Reyes JSY/99 2.00 5.00
78 Roger Maris JSY/25
79 Tommy Pham JSY/99 2.00 5.00
80 Juan Soto JSY/99 10.00 25.00
81 Adrian Beltre JSY/99 3.00 8.00
82 Nicholas Castellanos JSY/99 3.00 8.00
83 Jose Urena JSY/99 2.00 5.00
84 Rhys Hoskins JSY/99 4.00 10.00
85 David Peralta JSY/99 2.00 5.00
86 Joey Gallo JSY/99 2.50 6.00
87 Ichiro Suzuki JSY/99 4.00 10.00
88 Felix Hernandez JSY/99 2.50 6.00
89 Marcell Ozuna JSY/99 3.00 8.00
90 Ron Santo JSY/49 10.00 25.00
91 Mookie Betts JSY/49 6.00 15.00
92 Evan Longoria JSY/99 2.50 6.00
93 Eugenio Suarez JSY/99 2.50 6.00
94 Justin Verlander JSY/99 3.00 8.00
95 Luke Weaver JSY/99 2.00 5.00
96 Roberto Clemente JSY/99 25.00 60.00
97 Tommy Henrich JSY/49 2.50 6.00
98 Bobby Thomson JSY/25
99 Gleyber Torres JSY/99 12.00 30.00
100 Josh Bell JSY/99 3.00 8.00
101 Trevor Story JSY/99 3.00 8.00
102 Jose Altuve JSY/49 3.00 8.00
103 Shohei Ohtani JSY/99 15.00 40.00
104 Gerrit Cole JSY/99 3.00 8.00
105 David Price JSY/99 2.50 6.00
106 Bryce Harper JSY/99 10.00 25.00
107 Hunter Dozier JSY/99 2.00 5.00
108 German Marquez JSY/99 2.00 5.00
109 Xander Bogaerts JSY/99 6.00 15.00
110 Michael Conforto JSY/99 2.50 6.00
111 Paul Goldschmidt JSY/91 3.00 8.00
112 Freddie Freeman JSY/49 5.00 12.00
113 Mike Trout JSY/99 12.00 30.00
114 Lucas Giolito JSY/99 2.50 6.00
115 Chris Sale JSY/99 3.00 8.00
116 Trey Mancini JSY/99 2.50 6.00
117 Corey Kluber JSY/99 2.50 6.00
118 Jake Arrieta JSY/99 2.50 6.00
119 Mickey Mantle JSY/99 25.00 60.00
120 Eddie Stanky JSY/99 4.00 10.00
121 Aaron Nola JSY/99 2.50 6.00
122 Manny Machado JSY/99 3.00 8.00
123 Billy Martin JSY/49 12.00 30.00
124 Giancarlo Stanton JSY/99 3.00 8.00
125 Francisco Lindor JSY/99 3.00 8.00
126 Christian Yelich JSY/99 4.00 10.00
127 Stephen Strasburg JSY/99 3.00 8.00
128 Edwin Diaz JSY/49 3.00 8.00
129 Masahiro Tanaka JSY/49 3.00 8.00
131 Marcus Stroman JSY/99 2.50 6.00
132 Patrick Corbin JSY/99 2.50 6.00
133 Adalberto Mondesi JSY/99 2.50 6.00
134 Noah Syndergaard JSY/99 2.50 6.00
135 Anthony Rizzo JSY/99 5.00 12.00
136 Miguel Cabrera JSY/99 3.00 8.00
137 Jacob deGrom JSY/49 4.00 10.00
138 Javier Baez JSY/99 4.00 10.00
139 Max Scherzer JSY/99 3.00 8.00
140 Albert Pujols JSY/49 5.00 12.00
141 Starling Marte JSY/99 2.50 6.00
142 Harvey Kuenn JSY/99 2.00 5.00
143 Jose Abreu JSY/99 3.00 8.00
144 Mike Soroka JSY/99 3.00 8.00
145 George Springer JSY/99 2.50 6.00
146 Aaron Judge JSY/99 8.00 20.00
147 Lorenzo Cain JSY/99 2.00 5.00
149 Austin Meadows JSY/49 3.00 8.00
150 J.D. Martinez JSY/99 3.00 8.00
151 Ronald Acuna Jr. JSY/99 12.00 30.00
152 Clayton Kershaw JSY/99 6.00 15.00
153 Buster Posey JSY/49 5.00 12.00
154 Matt Chapman JSY/99 3.00 8.00
155 Ken Boyer JSY/49 6.00 15.00
156 Alex Bregman JSY/99 3.00 8.00
157 Jose Berrios JSY/99 2.50 6.00
159 Michael Brantley JSY/99 2.50 6.00
160 Jack Flaherty JSY/99 2.50 6.00
161 Nolan Arenado JSY/99 4.00 10.00
162 Madison Bumgarner JSY/99 2.50 6.00
163 Carl Furillo JSY/49 2.50 6.00
164 Cody Bellinger JSY/49 8.00 20.00
165 Ozzie Albies JSY/99 3.00 8.00
166 Eddie Rosario JSY/99 2.50 6.00
167 Andrew Benintendi JSY/99 3.00 8.00
168 Whit Merrifield JSY/99 3.00 8.00
169 J.T. Realmuto JSY/99 3.00 8.00
170 Max Fried JSY/99 3.00 8.00
171 Jose Ramirez JSY/99 2.50 6.00
172 Kris Bryant JSY/99 12.00 30.00
173 Paul DeJong JSY/99 3.00 8.00
174 Herb Pennock JSY/49 3.00 8.00
175 Rogers Hornsby JSY/25 10.00 25.00
176 Luke Appling JSY/99 3.00 8.00
177 Leo Durocher JSY/99 3.00 8.00
178 Mule Suttles JSY/99 20.00 50.00
181 Tom Seaver JSY/49 4.00 10.00
182 Charlie Keller JSY/99 2.00 5.00
183 Yogi Berra JSY/99 15.00 40.00
184 Ted Williams JSY/25 20.00 50.00
185 Bill Dickey JSY/25 12.00 30.00
186 Joe Cronin JSY/25 3.00 8.00
188 Paul Waner JSY/99 6.00 15.00
189 Walter Alston JSY/99 2.50 6.00
191 Don Drysdale JSY/99 2.50 6.00
192 Satchel Paige JSY/25 30.00 80.00
193 Billy Herman JSY/25 3.00 8.00
194 Lloyd Waner JSY/25
195 Willie Keeler JSY/99 10.00 25.00
196 Tony Lazzeri JSY/49 6.00 15.00
197 Casey Stengel JSY/49 3.00 8.00
198 Johnny Mize JSY/49 5.00 12.00
200 Ted Lyons JSY/49 6.00 15.00
201 Jimmie Foxx JSY/25 15.00 40.00
202 Honus Wagner JSY/25 50.00 120.00
203 Joe Jackson JSY/49 40.00 100.00
204 Harry Hooper JSY/25 3.00 8.00
205 Hank Greenberg JSY/99 10.00 25.00
206 Jackie Robinson JSY/99 25.00 60.00
209 Roy Campanella JSY/25
210 Gil Hodges JSY/99 4.00 10.00
212 Ty Cobb JSY/25
214 Joe Sewell JSY/49 8.00 20.00
215 Stan Musial JSY/49 10.00 25.00
216 Joe McCarthy JSY/25 15.00 40.00
218 Frank Chance JSY/99 8.00 20.00
220 Max Carey JSY/49 2.50 6.00
222 Tris Speaker JSY/25 15.00 40.00
223 Edd Roush JSY/99 6.00 15.00

2019 Panini National Treasures Gold

*GOLD/49: .5X TO 1.2X p/r 79-99
*GOLD/25: .8X TO 2X p/r 79-99
*GOLD/25: .6X TO 1.5X p/r 49
RANDOM INSERTS IN PACKS
PRINT RUNS B/WN 25-49 COPIES PER
EXCHANGE DEADLINE 3/25/21
51 Pete Alonso JSY AU/25 200.00 500.00
68 Keston Hiura JSY AU/49 30.00 80.00

2019 Panini National Treasures Holo Gold

*HOLO GOLD/20-25: .8X TO 2X p/r 49
*HOLO GOLD/20-25: .6X TO 1.5X p/r 49
RANDOM INSERTS IN PACKS
PRINT RUNS B/WN 15-25 COPIES PER
NO PRICING ON QTY 15 OR LESS
EXCHANGE DEADLINE 3/25/21
51 Pete Alonso JSY AU/20 200.00 500.00
56 Michael Chavis JSY AU/25 40.00 100.00
68 Keston Hiura JSY AU/25 40.00 100.00

2019 Panini National Treasures Cleats

RANDOM INSERTS IN PACKS
PRINT RUNS B/WN 7-25 COPIES PER
NO PRICING ON QTY 15 OR LESS
1 Mike Piazza/25 5.00 12.00
2 Starlin Castro/22 6.00 15.00
3 Brendan Rodgers/25 5.00 12.00
4 Nick Senzel/22 10.00 25.00
5 Fernando Tatis Jr./25 10.00 25.00
6 Brandon Lowe/25 5.00 12.00
7 Michael Kopech/25 6.00 15.00
8 Kyle Schwarber/25 5.00 12.00
9 Eloy Jimenez/25 12.00 30.00
12 Kyle Tucker/25 6.00 15.00
13 Ken Griffey Jr./20 25.00 60.00
14 Vladimir Guerrero Jr./25 15.00 40.00
15 Pete Alonso/25 30.00 80.00

2019 Panini National Treasures Colossal Material Signatures

RANDOM INSERTS IN PACKS
PRINT RUNS B/WN 5-99 COPIES PER
NO PRICING ON QTY 15 OR LESS
EXCHANGE DEADLINE 3/25/21
4 George Springer/25 6.00 15.00
5 Xander Bogaerts/25 15.00 40.00
6 Stephen Strasburg/25 12.00 30.00
7 Michael Brantley/99 8.00 20.00
8 Jonathan Villar/75 3.00 8.00
9 Adalberto Mondesi/99 6.00 15.00
10 Miguel Cabrera/25 25.00 60.00
11 Hunter Dozier/99 3.00 8.00
12 Cal Ripken/25 50.00 120.00
13 Ronald Acuna Jr./25 50.00 120.00
14 Dick Williams/25 5.00 12.00
15 Ralph Kiner/25 15.00 40.00
16 Luis Aparicio/25 20.00 50.00
17 Ozzie Smith/25 15.00 40.00
18 Fernando Tatis Jr./99 50.00 120.00
19 Eloy Jimenez/25 EXCH 25.00 60.00
20 Jose Canseco/99 10.00 25.00

2019 Panini National Treasures Colossal Materials

RANDOM INSERTS IN PACKS
PRINT RUNS B/WN 5-49 COPIES PER
NO PRICING ON QTY 15 OR LESS
*HOLO GOLD/25: .6X TO 1.5X p/r 66-99
*HOLO GOLD/25: .5X TO 1.2X p/r 49
1 Mike Trout/49 20.00 50.00
2 Kris Bryant/25 6.00 15.00
3 Anthony Rizzo/49 6.00 15.00
4 Jose Altuve/25 4.00 10.00
5 Rafael Devers/99 4.00 10.00
6 Franmil Reyes/99 2.00 5.00
7 Matt Chapman/99 3.00 8.00
8 Josh Bell/99 2.50 6.00
9 Justin Verlander/99 3.00 8.00
10 Aaron Judge/99 8.00 20.00
11 Shohei Ohtani/49 4.00 10.00
12 Miguel Cabrera/49 4.00 10.00
13 Noah Syndergaard/49 3.00 8.00
14 Gerrit Cole/99 3.00 8.00
15 German Marquez/99 2.00 5.00
16 Patrick Corbin/66 2.50 6.00
17 Marcell Ozuna/99 3.00 8.00
18 Tommy Pham/99 2.00 5.00
19 Adrian Beltre/49 4.00 10.00
20 Albert Pujols/49 5.00 12.00
21 Brandon Woodruff/99 2.00 5.00
23 Clayton Kershaw/49 8.00 20.00
24 Clint Frazier/99 2.50 6.00
25 David Bote/99 2.50 6.00
26 David Ortiz/49 4.00 10.00
27 David Wright/99 2.50 6.00
28 Evan Longoria/99 2.50 6.00
29 Felix Hernandez/99 2.50 6.00
30 Frank Thomas/49 4.00 10.00
31 Freddie Freeman/49 5.00 12.00
32 Giancarlo Stanton/49 4.00 10.00
33 Ivan Rodriguez/49 3.00 8.00
34 Joey Votto/99 3.00 8.00
35 Jose Abreu/99 3.00 8.00
36 Larry Walker/99 2.50 6.00
37 Ozzie Albies/99 5.00 12.00
38 Victor Robles/99 4.00 10.00
39 Walker Buehler/99 4.00 10.00
40 Miguel Andujar/99 3.00 8.00

2019 Panini National Treasures Cut Signature Booklets

RANDOM INSERTS IN PACKS
PRINT RUNS B/WN 5-49 COPIES PER
NO PRICING ON QTY 15 OR LESS
EXCHANGE DEADLINE 3/25/21
*NAMES/20-25: .5X TO 1.2X p/r 49
*NAMES/20-25: .5X TO 1.2X p/r 25
*STAT./20-25: .5X TO 1.2X p/r 49
*STAT./20-25: .4X TO 1X p/r 25
*STAT.VAR./20-25: .5X TO 1.2X p/r 49
*STAT.VAR./20-25: .4X TO 1X p/r 25
4 Bobby Thomson/49 12.00 30.00
5 Gary Carter/49 12.00 30.00
6 Harmon Killebrew/49 25.00 60.00
11 Stan Musial/25 30.00 80.00
15 Ryne Sandberg/25 40.00 100.00
16 Vladimir Guerrero/25 15.00 40.00
18 Harmon Killebrew/25 30.00 80.00
19 Gary Carter/25 15.00 40.00
20 John Smoltz/25 30.00 80.00
22 Cal Ripken/25 EXCH 25.00 60.00
31 Aaron Judge/49 60.00 150.00
33 Roger Clemens/25 30.00 80.00

2019 Panini National Treasures Cut Signature Material Booklets

RANDOM INSERTS IN PACKS
PRINT RUNS B/WN 3-30 COPIES PER
NO PRICING ON QTY 15 OR LESS
EXCHANGE DEADLINE 3/25/21
*NAMES/20: .4X TO 1X BASIC
*STAT./20: .4X TO 1X BASIC
3 Adrian Beltre/30 20.00 50.00
9 Craig Biggio/20
15 Paul Molitor/20
25 Pete Rose/20 30.00 80.00
30 Gary Carter/25 20.00 50.00

2019 Panini National Treasures Debut Material Signature Booklets

RANDOM INSERTS IN PACKS
PRINT RUNS B/WN 25-99 COPIES PER
EXCHANGE DEADLINE 3/25/21
*HOLO GOLD: .6X TO 1.5X p/r 99
1 Pete Alonso/99 60.00 150.00
2 Jon Duplantier/99 3.00 8.00
3 Chris Paddack/25
4 Cole Tucker/99 10.00 25.00
6 Carter Kieboom/25 15.00 40.00
7 Cal Quantrill/25 5.00 12.00
8 Nathaniel Lowe/99 4.00 10.00
10 Vladimir Guerrero Jr./99 50.00 120.00
11 Fernando Tatis Jr./49 60.00 150.00
12 Eloy Jimenez/49 15.00 40.00
13 Michael Kopech/25 10.00 25.00
14 Jonathan Loaisiga/99 4.00 10.00
15 Jake Bauers/25 8.00 20.00
16 Brendan Rodgers/25 EXCH 10.00 25.00

2019 Panini National Treasures Decades Signatures Booklets

RANDOM INSERTS IN PACKS
PRINT RUNS B/WN 5-25 COPIES PER
NO PRICING ON QTY 15 OR LESS
EXCHANGE DEADLINE 3/25/21
6 Andres Galarraga 100.00 250.00
Joey Votto
Jose Ramirez
Mark Grace
Roberto Alomar
Trevor Story/25

2019 Panini National Treasures Game Gear

RANDOM INSERTS IN PACKS
PRINT RUNS B/WN 25-99 COPIES PER
*HOLO GOLD/25: .6X TO 1.5X p/r 99
*HOLO GOLD/25: .5X TO 1.2X p/r 49
1 Alex Rodriguez/99 4.00 10.00
2 Eric Thames/99 2.00 5.00
3 Albert Pujols/49 5.00 12.00
4 Rafael Devers/99 4.00 10.00
5 Tony Gwynn/99 3.00 8.00
6 Mike Trout/49 15.00 40.00
7 CC Sabathia/99 2.50 6.00
8 Don Mattingly/49 8.00 20.00
9 Frank Robinson/99 8.00 20.00
10 George Brett/49 8.00 20.00
11 Leo Durocher/49 5.00 12.00
12 Nolan Ryan/99 12.00 30.00
13 Rod Carew/49 3.00 8.00
14 Ryne Sandberg/49 8.00 20.00
15 Steve Garvey/99 15.00 40.00
16 Lou Gehrig/25 50.00 120.00
17 Edwin Encarnacion/49 4.00 10.00
18 Carl Furillo/99 2.00 5.00
19 Mark Grace/99 2.50 6.00
20 Joe Jackson/49 40.00 100.00
21 Harmon Killebrew/49 6.00 15.00
22 Mike Piazza/49 4.00 10.00
23 Mickey Mantle/49 25.00 60.00
24 Roberto Alomar/49 3.00 8.00
25 Buster Posey/49 5.00 12.00

2019 Panini National Treasures Game Gear Holo Gold

*HOLO GOLD/25: .6X TO 1.5X p/r 99
*HOLO GOLD/25: .5X TO 1.2X p/r 49
RANDOM INSERTS IN PACKS
PRINT RUNS B/WN 10-25 COPIES PER
NO PRICING ON QTY 15 OR LESS
20 Joe Jackson/25 100.00 250.00

2019 Panini National Treasures Game Gear Duals

RANDOM INSERTS IN PACKS
PRINT RUNS B/WN 25-99 COPIES PER
*HOLO GOLD/25: .6X TO 1.5X p/r 99
*HOLO GOLD/25: .5X TO 1.2X p/r 49
1 Alex Rodriguez/99 4.00 10.00
2 Eric Thames/99 2.00 5.00
3 Albert Pujols/99 4.00 10.00
4 Rafael Devers/99 4.00 10.00
5 Tony Gwynn/49 4.00 10.00
6 Mike Trout/27 20.00 50.00
7 CC Sabathia/99 2.50 6.00
8 Don Mattingly/49 8.00 20.00
9 Frank Robinson/99 3.00 8.00
10 George Brett/25 10.00 25.00
11 Leo Durocher/49 5.00 12.00
12 Nolan Ryan/99 10.00 25.00
13 Rod Carew/49 3.00 8.00
14 Ryne Sandberg/99 6.00 15.00
15 Steve Garvey/99 15.00 40.00
17 Edwin Encarnacion/99 3.00 8.00
18 Carl Furillo/99 2.00 5.00
19 Mark Grace/99 2.50 6.00
20 Joe Jackson/25 100.00 250.00
21 Harmon Killebrew/25 8.00 20.00
22 Mike Piazza/99 3.00 8.00
23 Mickey Mantle/49 25.00 60.00
24 Roberto Alomar/99 2.50 6.00
25 Buster Posey/99 4.00 10.00

2019 Panini National Treasures Game Gear Eights

RANDOM INSERTS IN PACKS
PRINT RUNS B/WN 25-99 COPIES PER
*HOLO GOLD/25: .6X TO 1.5X p/r 99
*HOLO GOLD/25: .5X TO 1.2X p/r 49
1 Vladimir Guerrero Jr./99 10.00 25.00
2 Eloy Jimenez/99 8.00 20.00
3 Fernando Tatis Jr./99 8.00 80.00
4 Shohei Ohtani/99 4.00 10.00
5 Aaron Judge/99 8.00 20.00
6 Justus Sheffield/99 3.00 8.00
7 Pete Alonso/99 15.00 40.00
8 Michael Kopech/99 4.00 10.00
9 Wander Franco/99 8.00 20.00
10 Victor Victor Mesa/99 4.00 10.00
11 Brendan Rodgers/99 3.00 8.00
12 Jeff McNeil/99 5.00 12.00
13 Bo Bichette/99 6.00 15.00
15 Keston Hiura/99 6.00 15.00
16 Nick Senzel/99 6.00 15.00
17 Kyle Wright/99 3.00 8.00
18 Christin Stewart/99 2.50 6.00
19 Ryan O'Hearn/99 2.00 5.00
20 Dennis Santana/99 2.00 5.00
21 Jonathan Loaisiga/99 2.50 6.00
22 Touki Toussaint/99 2.50 6.00
23 Chance Adams/99 2.00 5.00
24 Bryse Wilson/99 2.50 6.00
25 Garrett Hampson/99 2.00 5.00
26 Enyel De Los Santos/99 2.00 5.00
27 Danny Jansen/99 2.00 5.00
29 Mike Trout/27 20.00 50.00
30 Dakota Hudson/99 2.50 6.00
31 Jonathan Davis/99 2.50 6.00
32 Adrian Beltre/49 4.00 10.00
35 Ronald Acuna Jr./99 15.00 40.00
36 Juan Soto/99 10.00 25.00
37 Jo Adell/99 6.00 15.00
38 Rafael Devers/99 4.00 10.00
44 Ivan Rodriguez/99 2.50 6.00
47 Estevan Florial/99 3.00 8.00
48 Forrest Whitley/99 3.00 8.00
49 Nathaniel Lowe/99 2.50 6.00
50 Corbin Burnes/99 3.00 8.00

2019 Panini National Treasures Game Gear Sevens

RANDOM INSERTS IN PACKS
PRINT RUNS B/WN 25-99 COPIES PER
*HOLO GOLD/25: .6X TO 1.5X p/r 99
*HOLO GOLD/25: .5X TO 1.2X p/r 49
1 Vladimir Guerrero Jr./99 10.00 25.00
2 Eloy Jimenez/99 8.00 20.00
3 Fernando Tatis Jr./99 8.00 20.00
4 Shohei Ohtani/99 4.00 10.00
5 Aaron Judge/99 8.00 20.00
6 Justus Sheffield/99 3.00 8.00
7 Pete Alonso/99 15.00 40.00
8 Michael Kopech/99 4.00 10.00
9 Wander Franco/99 8.00 20.00
10 Victor Victor Mesa/99 4.00 10.00
11 Brendan Rodgers/99 3.00 8.00
12 Jeff McNeil/99 5.00 12.00
13 Bo Bichette/99 6.00 15.00
15 Keston Hiura/99 6.00 15.00
16 Nick Senzel/99 6.00 15.00
17 Kyle Wright/99 3.00 8.00
18 Christin Stewart/99 2.50 6.00
19 Ryan O'Hearn/99 2.00 5.00
20 Dennis Santana/99 2.00 5.00
21 Jonathan Loaisiga/99 2.50 6.00
22 Touki Toussaint/99 2.50 6.00
23 Chance Adams/99 2.00 5.00
24 Bryse Wilson/99 2.50 6.00
25 Garrett Hampson/99 2.00 5.00
26 Enyel De Los Santos/99 2.00 5.00
27 Danny Jansen/99 2.00 5.00
29 Mike Trout/27 20.00 50.00
30 Dakota Hudson/99 2.50 6.00
31 Jonathan Davis/99 2.50 6.00
32 Adrian Beltre/49 4.00 10.00
35 Ronald Acuna Jr./99 15.00 40.00
36 Juan Soto/99 10.00 25.00
37 Jo Adell/99 6.00 15.00
38 Rafael Devers/99 4.00 10.00
42 Christian Yelich/49 5.00 12.00
44 Ivan Rodriguez/25 8.00 20.00
46 Ken Griffey Jr./25 15.00 40.00
47 Estevan Florial/99 3.00 8.00
48 Forrest Whitley/99 3.00 8.00
49 Nathaniel Lowe/99 2.50 6.00
50 Corbin Burnes/99 3.00 8.00

2019 Panini National Treasures Game Gear Signatures

RANDOM INSERTS IN PACKS
PRINT RUNS B/WN 49-99 COPIES PER
EXCHANGE DEADLINE 3/25/21
*HOLO GOLD: .6X TO 1.5X p/r 99
*HOLO GOLD: .5X TO 1.2X p/r 49
1 Vladimir Guerrero Jr./49 25.00 60.00
2 Eloy Jimenez/49 15.00 40.00
3 Fernando Tatis Jr./49 50.00 120.00
4 Pete Alonso/99 60.00 150.00
6 Kyle Tucker/49 8.00 20.00
8 Justus Sheffield/99 5.00 12.00
9 Christin Stewart/49 5.00 12.00
10 Ramon Laureano/99 8.00 20.00
11 Michael Kopech/99 6.00 15.00
13 Jonathan Loaisiga/99 4.00 10.00
14 Luis Ortiz/99 3.00 8.00
15 Kevin Newman/99 5.00 12.00
16 Jon Duplantier/99 3.00 8.00
18 Bryan Reynolds/99 8.00 20.00
19 Michael Chavis/99 12.00 30.00
21 Austin Riley/49 20.00 50.00
22 Keston Hiura/99 15.00 40.00
24 Nathaniel Lowe/99 5.00 12.00

2019 Panini National Treasures Game Gear Signatures Dual

RANDOM INSERTS IN PACKS
PRINT RUNS B/WN 25-99 COPIES PER
EXCHANGE DEADLINE 3/25/21
1 Vladimir Guerrero Jr./25 30.00 80.00
2 Eloy Jimenez/25 20.00 50.00
3 Fernando Tatis Jr./49 50.00 120.00
4 Pete Alonso/99 60.00 150.00
6 Kyle Tucker/25 10.00 25.00
8 Justus Sheffield/99 5.00 12.00
9 Christin Stewart/25 6.00 15.00
10 Ramon Laureano/99 8.00 20.00
11 Michael Kopech/99 6.00 15.00
13 Jonathan Loaisiga/99 4.00 10.00
14 Luis Ortiz/99 3.00 8.00
15 Kevin Newman/99 5.00 12.00
16 Jon Duplantier/99 3.00 8.00
17 Chris Paddack/99 6.00 15.00
18 Bryan Reynolds/99 8.00 20.00
19 Michael Chavis/99 12.00 30.00
21 Austin Riley/25 25.00 60.00
22 Keston Hiura/99 15.00 40.00
24 Nathaniel Lowe/99 5.00 12.00

2019 Panini National Treasures Game Gear Signatures Trio

RANDOM INSERTS IN PACKS
PRINT RUNS B/WN 25-99 COPIES PER
EXCHANGE DEADLINE 3/25/21
1 Vladimir Guerrero Jr./25 30.00 80.00
2 Eloy Jimenez/25 20.00 50.00
3 Fernando Tatis Jr./49 50.00 120.00
4 Pete Alonso/99 60.00 150.00
6 Kyle Tucker/25 10.00 25.00
8 Justus Sheffield/99 5.00 12.00
9 Christin Stewart/25 6.00 15.00
10 Ramon Laureano/99 8.00 20.00
11 Michael Kopech/99 6.00 15.00
13 Jonathan Loaisiga/99 4.00 10.00
14 Luis Ortiz/99 3.00 8.00
15 Kevin Newman/99 5.00 12.00
16 Jon Duplantier/99 3.00 8.00
17 Chris Paddack/99 6.00 15.00
18 Bryan Reynolds/99 8.00 20.00
19 Michael Chavis/99 12.00 30.00
21 Austin Riley/25 25.00 60.00
22 Keston Hiura/25 15.00 40.00
24 Nathaniel Lowe/99 5.00 12.00

2019 Panini National Treasures Game Gear Sixes

RANDOM INSERTS IN PACKS
PRINT RUNS B/WN 10-99 COPIES PER
NO PRICING ON QTY 15 OR LESS
*HOLO GOLD/25: .6X TO 1.5X p/r 99
*HOLO GOLD/25: .5X TO 1.2X p/r 49
1 Vladimir Guerrero Jr./99 8.00 20.00
2 Eloy Jimenez/99 8.00 20.00
3 Fernando Tatis Jr./99 8.00 20.00
4 Shohei Ohtani/99 4.00 10.00
5 Aaron Judge/99 8.00 20.00
6 Justus Sheffield/99 5.00 12.00
7 Pete Alonso/99 15.00 40.00
8 Michael Kopech/99 4.00 10.00
9 Wander Franco/99 8.00 20.00
10 Victor Victor Mesa/99 4.00 10.00
11 Brendan Rodgers/99 3.00 8.00
12 Jeff McNeil/99 5.00 12.00
13 Bo Bichette/99 12.00 30.00
15 Keston Hiura/99 6.00 15.00
16 Nick Senzel/99 6.00 15.00
17 Kyle Wright/99 3.00 8.00
18 Christin Stewart/99 2.50 6.00
19 Ryan O'Hearn/99 2.00 5.00
20 Dennis Santana/99 2.00 5.00
21 Jonathan Loaisiga/99 2.50 6.00
22 Touki Toussaint/99 6.00 15.00
23 Chance Adams/99 2.00 5.00
24 Bryse Wilson/99 2.50 6.00
25 Garrett Hampson/99 2.00 5.00
26 Enyel De Los Santos/99 2.00 5.00
27 Danny Jansen/99 2.00 5.00
29 Mike Trout/27 20.00 50.00
30 Dakota Hudson/99 2.50 6.00
31 Jonathan Davis/99 2.50 6.00
32 Adrian Beltre/49 4.00 10.00
33 Carlos Correa/49 4.00 10.00
35 Ronald Acuna Jr./99 15.00 40.00
36 Juan Soto/99 10.00 25.00
37 Jo Adell/99 6.00 15.00
38 Rafael Devers/99 4.00 10.00
42 Christian Yelich/99 4.00 10.00
44 Ivan Rodriguez/25 8.00 20.00
46 Ken Griffey Jr./25 15.00 40.00
47 Estevan Florial/99 3.00 8.00
48 Forrest Whitley/99 3.00 8.00
49 Nathaniel Lowe/99 2.50 6.00
50 Corbin Burnes/99 3.00 8.00

2019 Panini National Treasures Game Gear Trios

RANDOM INSERTS IN PACKS
PRINT RUNS B/WN 10-99 COPIES PER
NO PRICING ON QTY 15 OR LESS
*HOLO GOLD/25: .6X TO 1.5X p/r 99
*HOLO GOLD/25: .5X TO 1.2X p/r 49
1 Alex Rodriguez/99 4.00 10.00
2 Eric Thames/99 2.00 5.00
3 Albert Pujols/49 5.00 12.00
4 Rafael Devers/99 4.00 10.00
5 Tony Gwynn/49 4.00 10.00
6 Mike Trout/27 20.00 50.00
7 CC Sabathia/99 2.50 6.00
8 Don Mattingly/49 8.00 20.00
9 Frank Robinson/49 3.00 8.00
10 George Brett/25 10.00 25.00
11 Leo Durocher/49 5.00 12.00
12 Nolan Ryan/99 10.00 25.00
13 Rod Carew/25 4.00 10.00
14 Ryne Sandberg/49 6.00 15.00
15 Steve Garvey/99 15.00 40.00
17 Edwin Encarnacion/99 3.00 8.00
18 Carl Furillo/49 2.50 6.00
19 Mark Grace/99 2.50 6.00
22 Mike Piazza/49 4.00 10.00
23 Mickey Mantle/49 25.00 60.00
24 Roberto Alomar/99 2.50 6.00
25 Buster Posey/99 4.00 10.00

2019 Panini National Treasures Hall of Fame Materials

RANDOM INSERTS IN PACKS
PRINT RUNS B/WN 25-99 COPIES PER
*PRIME/25: .6X TO 1.5X p/r 99
*PRIME/25: .5X TO 1.2X p/r 49
1 Eddie Murray/99 2.50 6.00
2 Catfish Hunter/49 3.00 8.00
3 Ivan Rodriguez/99 2.50 6.00
4 Mike Piazza/99 3.00 8.00
5 Greg Maddux/99 4.00 10.00
6 Cal Ripken/99 10.00 25.00
7 Pedro Martinez/99 2.50 6.00
8 Fergie Jenkins/99 2.50 6.00
9 Joe Morgan/99 2.50 6.00
10 Wade Boggs/99 2.50 6.00
11 Goose Gossage/99 2.50 6.00
12 Rollie Fingers/99 2.50 6.00
13 Dave Winfield/99 2.50 6.00
14 Tony Gwynn/99 5.00 12.00
15 Barry Larkin/99 2.50 6.00
16 Tom Seaver/49 3.00 8.00
17 Andre Dawson/99 2.50 6.00
18 Johnny Bench/99 6.00 15.00
19 Craig Biggio/99 2.50 6.00
20 Bert Blyleven/99 2.50 6.00
21 Frank Robinson/99 2.50 6.00
22 Duke Snider/25 4.00 10.00
23 Rickey Henderson/49 6.00 15.00
24 George Brett/49 8.00 20.00
25 Robin Yount/99 3.00 8.00

26 Harmon Killebrew/25 5.00 12.00
27 Randy Johnson/99 3.00 8.00
28 Brooks Robinson/99 2.50 6.00
29 Orlando Cepeda/99 2.50 6.00
30 Mule Suttles/99 20.00 50.00
31 Ryne Sandberg/99 6.00 15.00
32 Ozzie Smith/99 4.00 10.00
33 Ken Griffey Jr./99 6.00 15.00
34 Roberto Alomar/99 2.50 6.00
35 John Smoltz/99 3.00 8.00
36 Frank Thomas/49 6.00 15.00
37 Rod Carew/99 6.00 15.00
38 Jim Palmer/25 4.00 10.00
39 Paul Molitor/99 5.00 12.00
40 Kirby Puckett/49 20.00 50.00
41 Lou Brock/49 8.00 20.00
42 Gary Carter/99 2.50 6.00
43 Willie McCovey/99 2.50 6.00
44 Nolan Ryan/99 10.00 25.00
45 Al Kaline/49 4.00 10.00
46 Reggie Jackson/99 2.50 6.00
47 Alan Trammell/99 2.50 6.00
48 Juan Marichal/20 4.00 10.00
49 Vladimir Guerrero/99 2.50 6.00
50 Tom Glavine/99 2.50 6.00

2019 Panini National Treasures Hall of Fame Signatures

RANDOM INSERTS IN PACKS
PRINT RUNS B/WN 10-49 COPIES PER
NO PRICING ON QTY 18 OR LESS
EXCHANGE DEADLINE 3/25/21
12 Monte Irvin/49 5.00 12.00

2019 Panini National Treasures Legendary Jumbo Materials Booklets

RANDOM INSERTS IN PACKS
PRINT RUNS B/WN 10-49 COPIES PER
NO PRICING ON QTY 15 OR LESS
*HOLO GOLD/25: .5X TO 1.2X p/r 49
1 Bill Mazeroski/49 6.00 15.00
2 Mike Trout/49 25.00 60.00
3 Ichiro Suzuki/49 10.00 25.00
6 Leo Durocher/25 3.00 8.00
7 Joe Cronin/25 3.00 8.00
8 Tom Yawkey/49 12.00 30.00
9 Paul Molitor/49 4.00 10.00
10 Eddie Stanky/49 2.50 6.00
11 Tommy Lasorda/49 3.00 8.00
12 Tommy Henrich/49 8.00 20.00
15 Ron Santo/21 15.00 40.00

2019 Panini National Treasures Legendary Jumbo Materials Booklets Holo Gold

*HOLO GOLD/25: .5X TO 1.2X p/r 49
RANDOM INSERTS IN PACKS
PRINT RUNS B/WN 7-25 COPIES PER
NO PRICING ON QTY 15 OR LESS
1 Bill Mazeroski/25 15.00 40.00
3 Ichiro Suzuki/25 15.00 40.00

2019 Panini National Treasures Legendary Silhouette Duals Booklets

RANDOM INSERTS IN PACKS
PRINT RUNS B/WN 5-49 COPIES PER
NO PRICING ON QTY 15 OR LESS
*HOLO GOLD/25: .5X TO 1.2X p/r 49
1 A.Pujols/I.Suzuki 20.00 50.00
3 H.Pennock/J.Cronin 12.00 30.00
4 B.Lemon/T.Speaker
5 M.Mantle/R.Maris 125.00 400.00
6 H.Killebrew/K.Puckett 30.00 80.00
7 E.Sawyer/J.McCarthy 25.00 60.00
8 A.Kaline/H.Kuenn 20.00 50.00

2019 Panini National Treasures Legends Materials Booklets

RANDOM INSERTS IN PACKS
PRINT RUNS B/WN 10-49 COPIES PER
NO PRICING ON QTY 15 OR LESS
*HOLO GOLD/25: .5X TO 1.2X p/r 49
2 Babe Ruth/25 75.00 200.00
4 Red Schoendienst/49 3.00 8.00
5 Miller Huggins/49 8.00 20.00
6 Ty Cobb/25 50.00 120.00
7 Tom Yawkey/49 12.00 30.00
8 Heinie Groh/49 2.50 6.00
9 Tris Speaker/49 15.00 40.00
10 Max Carey/49 5.00 12.00
11 Joe Dugan/49 6.00 15.00
12 Mule Suttles/49 25.00 60.00
13 Doc Cramer/49 8.00 20.00
14 Dom DiMaggio/49 20.00 50.00
15 Carl Furillo/49 2.50 6.00
16 Richie Ashburn/49 20.00 50.00

2019 Panini National Treasures Legends Materials Booklets Duals Holo Gold

*HOLO GOLD/25: .5X TO 1.2X p/r 49
RANDOM INSERTS IN PACKS
PRINT RUNS B/WN 10-25 COPIES PER
NO PRICING ON QTY 15 OR LESS
16 Richie Ashburn/25 75.00 200.00

2019 Panini National Treasures Player's Weekend Signatures

RANDOM INSERTS IN PACKS
STATED PRINT RUN 99 SER.#'d SETS
EXCHANGE DEADLINE 3/25/21
1 Dennis Santana 3.00 8.00
2 Ryan O'Hearn 3.00 8.00
3 Corbin Burnes 5.00 12.00
4 Jake Cave 4.00 10.00
5 Dakota Hudson 4.00 10.00
6 Brad Keller 3.00 8.00
7 Jeff McNeil 8.00 20.00
8 David Fletcher 10.00 25.00
9 Steven Duggar 4.00 10.00

2019 Panini National Treasures Retro Materials

RANDOM INSERTS IN PACKS
PRINT RUNS B/WN 5-99 COPIES PER
NO PRICING ON QTY 15 OR LESS
*HOLO GOLD/25: .6X TO 1.5X p/r 99
*HOLO GOLD/25: .5X TO 1.2X p/r 49
1 Ron Santo/49 10.00 25.00
2 Ken Griffey Jr./99 20.00 50.00
3 Cal Ripken/49 12.00 30.00
4 Kirby Puckett/49 20.00 50.00
5 Frank Robinson/49 3.00 8.00
6 Jose Canseco/49 3.00 8.00
7 Ichiro Suzuki/99 4.00 10.00
8 Orlando Cepeda/25 4.00 10.00
11 Gary Carter/49 3.00 8.00
12 Mariano Rivera/49 8.00 20.00
13 Frank Thomas/99 3.00 8.00
14 Goose Gossage/99 2.50 6.00
15 Ivan Rodriguez/99 2.50 6.00
16 Mark McGwire/49 6.00 15.00
17 Rollie Fingers/49 3.00 8.00
19 Eddie Murray/49 3.00 8.00
21 Red Schoendienst/25 10.00 25.00
22 Steve Garvey/99 8.00 20.00
23 Larry Walker/99 2.50 6.00
24 John Smoltz/49 4.00 10.00
25 Tommy Henrich/25 10.00 25.00
26 Eddie Sawyer/49 2.50 6.00
27 Casey Stengel/25 6.00 15.00
28 Roberto Alomar/49 3.00 8.00
29 Ted Williams/25 50.00

2019 Panini National Treasures Retro Signatures

RANDOM INSERTS IN PACKS
PRINT RUNS B/WN 10-99 COPIES PER
NO PRICING ON QTY 15 OR LESS
EXCHANGE DEADLINE 3/25/21
1 Ken Griffey Jr./49 75.00 200.00
2 Frank Thomas/49 25.00 60.00
3 Juan Soto/99 30.00 80.00
4 Max Muncy/49 EXCH 5.00 12.00
5 Walker Buehler/49 25.00 60.00
6 Jose Canseco/49 8.00 20.00
7 Vladimir Guerrero/25 15.00 40.00
8 Ronald Acuna Jr./99 50.00 120.00
9 Gleyber Torres/99 30.00 80.00
11 Willie McGee/25 10.00 25.00
12 Roger Clemens/25 30.00 80.00
13 Whit Merrifield/49 6.00 15.00
14 Joey Votto/25 EXCH 20.00 50.00
15 Roger Clemens/25 30.00 80.00
16 Craig Biggio/25 EXCH 10.00 25.00
17 Alex Rodriguez/25 30.00 80.00
18 Chris Sale/49 10.00 25.00
19 Ichiro Suzuki/25
20 Ivan Rodriguez/25 15.00 40.00
21 Nolan Arenado/49 25.00 60.00
22 Lou Whitaker/49 12.00 30.00
23 Bob Gibson/25 20.00 50.00
26 Ken Griffey Jr./25 100.00 250.00
28 Cal Ripken/25 30.00 80.00
30 Nolan Ryan/25 50.00 120.00
31 Nolan Ryan/25 50.00 120.00
32 Nolan Ryan/25 50.00 120.00
33 Nolan Ryan/25 50.00 120.00
34 Rickey Henderson/25 30.00 80.00
35 Alan Trammell/49 25.00 60.00
36 Shohei Ohtani/99 50.00 120.00
37 Aaron Judge/99 50.00 120.00
38 David Ross/25 25.00 60.00
39 Frank Robinson/25 15.00 40.00
40 Frank Robinson/25 15.00 40.00

2019 Panini National Treasures Rookie Signature Jumbo Material Booklets

RANDOM INSERTS IN PACKS
STATED PRINT RUN 99 SER.#'d SETS
EXCHANGE DEADLINE 3/25/21
1 Michael Kopech 6.00 15.00
2 Ramon Laureano 15.00 40.00
3 Ryan O'Hearn 3.00 8.00
4 Eloy Jimenez 20.00 50.00
5 Corbin Burnes 8.00 20.00
6 Kyle Wright 5.00 12.00
7 Nick Senzel EXCH 20.00 50.00
8 Kyle Tucker 6.00 15.00
9 Jeff McNeil 15.00 20.00
10 Vladimir Guerrero Jr. 50.00 120.00
11 Fernando Tatis Jr. 50.00 120.00
12 Christin Stewart 4.00 10.00
13 Cedric Mullins 5.00 12.00
14 Justus Sheffield 5.00 12.00
16 Jake Bauers 5.00 12.00

2019 Panini National Treasures Rookie Signature Material Names

RANDOM INSERTS IN PACKS
STATED PRINT RUN 99 SER.#'d SETS
EXCHANGE DEADLINE 3/25/21
*GOLD: .5X TO 1.2X BASIC
*HOLO GOLD: .6X TO 1.5X BASIC
1 Kyle Tucker 10.00 25.00
2 Patrick Wisdom 3.00 8.00
3 Jeff McNeil 10.00 25.00
4 Vladimir Guerrero Jr. 50.00 120.00
5 Cionel Perez 3.00 8.00
6 Kolby Allard 5.00 12.00
7 Stephen Gonsalves 3.00 8.00
8 Brandon Lowe 8.00 20.00
9 Eloy Jimenez 15.00 40.00
10 Fernando Tatis Jr. 60.00 150.00
11 Sean Reid-Foley 3.00 8.00
12 Jonathan Davis 4.00 10.00
13 Ryan Borucki 3.00 8.00
14 Christin Stewart 4.00 10.00
15 Cedric Mullins 5.00 12.00
16 Justus Sheffield 5.00 12.00
17 Caleb Ferguson 4.00 10.00
18 Jacob Nix 4.00 10.00
19 Daniel Ponce de Leon 5.00 12.00
20 Josh James 5.00 12.00
21 David Fletcher 10.00 25.00
22 Steven Duggar 4.00 10.00
23 Rowdy Tellez 5.00 12.00
24 Luis Urias 5.00 12.00
25 Jake Bauers 5.00 12.00

2019 Panini National Treasures Rookie Signature Material Names Holo Gold

*HOLO GOLD: .6X TO 1.5X BASIC
RANDOM INSERTS IN PACKS
STATED PRINT RUN 25 SER.#'d SETS
EXCHANGE DEADLINE 3/25/21
1 Kyle Tucker 25.00 60.00
3 Jeff McNeil 30.00 80.00

2019 Panini National Treasures Rookie Signatures

RANDOM INSERTS IN PACKS
STATED PRINT RUN 99 SER.#'d SETS
EXCHANGE DEADLINE 3/25/21
1 Touki Toussaint 4.00 10.00
2 Michael Kopech 6.00 15.00
3 Ramon Laureano 8.00 20.00
4 Ryan O'Hearn 3.00 8.00
5 Eloy Jimenez 15.00 40.00
6 Corbin Burnes 5.00 12.00
7 Kyle Wright 5.00 12.00
8 Dakota Hudson 4.00 10.00
9 Danny Jansen 3.00 8.00
11 Kyle Tucker 6.00 15.00
12 Jeff McNeil 8.00 20.00
13 Vladimir Guerrero Jr. 50.00 120.00
14 Fernando Tatis Jr. 40.00 100.00
15 Christin Stewart 4.00 10.00
16 Cedric Mullins 5.00 12.00
17 Justus Sheffield 5.00 12.00
18 David Fletcher 6.00 15.00
19 Luis Urias EXCH 8.00 20.00
20 Jake Bauers EXCH 5.00 12.00

2019 Panini National Treasures Rookie Silhouette Signatures

RANDOM INSERTS IN PACKS
PRINT RUNS B/WN 10-25 COPIES PER
NO PRICING ON QTY 15 OR LESS
EXCHANGE DEADLINE 3/25/21
1 Yusei Kikuchi/25 EXCH 8.00 20.00
2 Ramon Laureano/25 20.00 50.00
3 Ryan O'Hearn/25 5.00 12.00
4 Eloy Jimenez/25 20.00 50.00
5 Corbin Burnes/25 8.00 20.00
6 Kyle Wright/25 8.00 20.00
7 Dakota Hudson/25 6.00 15.00
9 Brad Keller/25 5.00 12.00
10 Kyle Tucker/25 15.00 40.00
12 Vladimir Guerrero Jr./25 60.00 150.00
13 Brandon Lowe/25 12.00 30.00
14 Fernando Tatis Jr./25 100.00 250.00
16 Cedric Mullins/25 8.00 20.00
17 Justus Sheffield/25 8.00 20.00
18 Luis Urias/25 8.00 20.00
19 Jake Bauers/25 8.00 20.00
20 Jon Duplantier/25 5.00 12.00
21 Chris Paddack/25 12.00 30.00
22 Pete Alonso/25 60.00 150.00
23 Michael Chavis/25 20.00 50.00
24 Cole Tucker/25 8.00 20.00
25 Bryan Reynolds/25 15.00 40.00

2019 Panini National Treasures Rookie Triple Material Ink

RANDOM INSERTS IN PACKS
STATED PRINT RUN 99 SER.#'d SETS
EXCHANGE DEADLINE 3/25/21
*GOLD: .5X TO 1.2X BASIC
*HOLO GOLD: .6X TO 1.5X BASIC
1 Bryse Wilson 4.00 10.00
2 Touki Toussaint 4.00 10.00
3 Michael Kopech 6.00 15.00
4 Ramon Laureano 10.00 25.00
5 Garrett Hampson 3.00 8.00
6 Dennis Santana 3.00 8.00
7 Ryan O'Hearn 3.00 8.00
8 Jonathan Loaisiga 4.00 10.00
9 Eloy Jimenez 15.00 40.00
10 Reese McGuire 5.00 12.00
11 Corbin Burnes 5.00 12.00
12 Jake Cave 10.00 25.00
13 Luis Ortiz 3.00 8.00
14 Kyle Wright 5.00 12.00
15 Chris Shaw 5.00 12.00
16 Kevin Kramer 4.00 10.00
17 Framber Valdez 3.00 8.00
18 Dakota Hudson 4.00 10.00
19 Kevin Newman 5.00 12.00
20 Danny Jansen 3.00 8.00
21 Vladimir Guerrero Jr. 50.00 120.00
22 Chance Adams 3.00 8.00
23 Enyel De Los Santos 3.00 8.00
24 Taylor Ward 3.00 8.00

2019 Panini National Treasures Shadowbox Material Signatures

RANDOM INSERTS IN PACKS
PRINT RUNS B/WN 5-49 COPIES PER
NO PRICING ON QTY 15 OR LESS
EXCHANGE DEADLINE 3/25/21
2 Pete Alonso/25 75.00 200.00
3 Chris Paddack/25 25.00 60.00
4 Yusei Kikuchi/25 EXCH 8.00 20.00
5 Jon Duplantier/25 5.00 12.00
6 Mitch Moreland/25 5.00 12.00
7 Andres Galarraga/25 15.00 40.00
8 Kerry Wood/25 5.00 12.00
9 Scooter Gennett/35 5.00 12.00
10 Miguel Cabrera/25 30.00 80.00
11 Vladimir Guerrero/25 15.00 40.00
12 Rhys Hoskins/25
14 Ozzie Albies/25 EXCH
15 Rafael Devers/25 EXCH 20.00 50.00
16 Ozzie Smith/25 15.00 40.00
17 Keith Hernandez/25 10.00 25.00
18 Larry Walker/25 15.00 40.00
19 Jason Giambi/25 5.00 12.00
20 Max Muncy/25
22 Whit Merrifield/35 8.00 20.00
23 Nolan Arenado/25
24 Omar Vizquel/25 EXCH 6.00 15.00
25 Patrick Corbin/25 8.00 20.00
26 Yandy Diaz/35 5.00 12.00
27 David Bote/25 6.00 15.00
28 Jose Berrios/25 6.00 15.00
29 Alex Verdugo/25 6.00 15.00
30 Juan Soto/25 60.00 150.00
33 Walker Buehler/25 20.00 50.00
34 Corey Seager/25 EXCH 12.00 30.00
36 Luis Severino/25 15.00 40.00
38 Shohei Ohtani/20 60.00 150.00
41 Ronald Acuna Jr./25 75.00 200.00
43 Charlie Blackmon/25 8.00 20.00
44 Mitch Haniger/49 6.00 15.00
45 Trey Mancini/25 6.00 15.00
46 Adrian Beltre/25
47 Joey Votto/25 EXCH
49 Blake Snell/25 10.00 25.00

2019 Panini National Treasures Signature Jumbo Material Booklets

RANDOM INSERTS IN PACKS
PRINT RUNS B/WN 15-99 COPIES PER
NO PRICING ON QTY 15 OR LESS
EXCHANGE DEADLINE 3/25/21
1 Shohei Ohtani/25 75.00 200.00
2 Aaron Judge/49 100.00 250.00
4 Forrest Whitley/99 8.00 20.00
5 Kyle Lewis/99 50.00 120.00
8 Wander Franco/99 75.00 200.00
10 Nolan Ryan/25 60.00 150.00

2019 Panini National Treasures Signatures

RANDOM INSERTS IN PACKS
PRINT RUNS B/WN 10-99 COPIES PER
NO PRICING ON QTY 15 OR LESS
EXCHANGE DEADLINE 3/25/21
2 Charlie Blackmon/49 6.00 15.00
5 Max Muncy/99 12.00 30.00
6 Odubel Herrera/99 4.00 10.00
9 Shane Bieber/34 40.00 100.00
10 Trevor Story/99 5.00 12.00
11 Walker Buehler/99 40.00 100.00
13 Alex Verdugo/99 4.00 10.00
14 Chris Sale/25 8.00 20.00
18 Dansby Swanson/49 6.00 15.00
20 J.T. Realmuto/99 10.00 25.00
22 Orlando Hernandez/25 5.00 12.00
24 Ozzie Guillen/99 3.00 8.00
25 Goose Gossage/99 6.00 15.00
26 Jim Rice/99 4.00 10.00
27 Kerry Wood/99 3.00 8.00
28 Omar Vizquel/99 4.00 10.00
29 Ted Simmons/25 10.00 25.00
32 Andres Galarraga/99 4.00 10.00
36 Mitch Haniger/99 4.00 10.00

2019 Panini National Treasures Six Pack Material Signatures Booklets

RANDOM INSERTS IN PACKS
STATED PRINT RUN 99 SER.#'d SETS
EXCHANGE DEADLINE 3/25/21
1 Michael Kopech 10.00 25.00
2 Ryan O'Hearn 3.00 8.00
3 Eloy Jimenez 20.00 50.00
5 Kyle Tucker 12.00 30.00
6 Jeff McNeil 12.00 30.00
7 Vladimir Guerrero Jr. 50.00 120.00
8 Fernando Tatis Jr. 75.00 200.00
9 Justus Sheffield 5.00 12.00

2019 Panini National Treasures Social Signatures

RANDOM INSERTS IN PACKS
STATED PRINT RUN 99 SER.#'d SETS
EXCHANGE DEADLINE 3/25/21
1 Vladimir Guerrero Jr. 20.00 50.00
2 Eloy Jimenez 15.00 40.00
3 Kyle Tucker 10.00 25.00
4 Michael Kopech 6.00 15.00
5 Fernando Tatis Jr. 100.00 250.00
6 Bo Bichette 30.00 80.00
8 Justus Sheffield 5.00 12.00
10 Jonathan Loaisiga 5.00 12.00
11 Kyle Wright 5.00 12.00
12 Garrett Hampson 3.00 8.00
13 Christin Stewart 4.00 10.00
14 Kevin Newman 5.00 12.00
15 Kevin Kramer 4.00 10.00
16 Dakota Hudson 4.00 10.00
17 Keston Hiura 12.00 30.00
18 Jo Adell 40.00 100.00
19 Cavan Biggio 20.00 50.00
20 Leody Taveras 3.00 8.00

2019 Panini National Treasures Treasured Material Signatures

RANDOM INSERTS IN PACKS
PRINT RUNS B/WN 5-49 COPIES PER
NO PRICING ON QTY 15 OR LESS
EXCHANGE DEADLINE 3/25/21
*GOLD: .5X TO 1.2X p/r 49
1 Corey Kluber/25 6.00 15.00
2 Kerry Wood/25 5.00 12.00
3 Ronald Acuna Jr./25 60.00 150.00
4 Whit Merrifield/35 6.00 15.00
5 Yoshihisa Hirano/25
6 J.T. Realmuto/25 10.00 25.00
7 Rhys Hoskins/25 15.00 40.00
8 Jordan Hicks/49 EXCH 10.00 25.00
9 Keith Hernandez/25 10.00 25.00
10 Nolan Arenado/25 25.00 60.00
15 Andres Galarraga/25 6.00 15.00
16 Omar Vizquel/25 EXCH 6.00 15.00
18 Xander Bogaerts/25
21 Francisco Lindor/25 EXCH
22 Darryl Strawberry/25 5.00 12.00
23 Jose Abreu/25 8.00 20.00
24 Carlton Fisk/25
27 David Wright/49 12.00 30.00
28 Max Muncy/25 6.00 15.00
30 Charlie Blackmon/25 8.00 20.00
31 Reggie Jackson/49 12.00 30.00
33 Larry Walker/25
34 Mitch Moreland/25 5.00 12.00
35 Vladimir Guerrero/25
36 Yadier Molina/49 50.00 120.00
38 Mitch Haniger/25 6.00 15.00
39 David Bote/25 6.00 15.00
40 Jose Ramirez/25 6.00 15.00
43 Joe Carter/25 EXCH 5.00 12.00
44 Gleyber Torres/25 EXCH 30.00 80.00
45 Dennis Eckersley/25 12.00 30.00
46 Rod Carew/25 12.00 30.00
49 Jose Berrios/25 6.00 15.00
50 Nomar Mazara/25 5.00 12.00
51 Jason Giambi/20 5.00 12.00
53 John Smoltz/25 20.00 50.00
55 Chris Sale/25
56 Scooter Gennett/49 5.00 12.00
57 Tom Glavine/25 20.00 50.00
59 Craig Biggio/20 EXCH 15.00 40.00
60 Fergie Jenkins/25 6.00 15.00
61 Miguel Cabrera/20 25.00 60.00
63 Alex Wood/49 4.00 10.00
64 Charles Johnson/25 5.00 12.00
67 Trey Mancini/25 10.00 25.00
68 Ozzie Albies/25 EXCH 15.00 40.00
70 Yandy Diaz/49 5.00 12.00
71 Adrian Beltre/25
72 Mike Soroka/49 15.00 40.00
73 Rafael Devers/25 EXCH 20.00 50.00
75 Walker Buehler/25 20.00 50.00
76 Joey Votto/25 EXCH 25.00 60.00
77 Dale Murphy/20

2019 Panini National Treasures Treasured Signatures

RANDOM INSERTS IN PACKS
PRINT RUNS B/WN 25-49 COPIES PER
EXCHANGE DEADLINE 3/25/21
1 Rod Carew/25 12.00 30.00
2 Reggie Jackson/25 EXCH 12.00 30.00
3 Rickey Henderson/25 20.00 50.00
4 Ken Griffey Jr./49 100.00 250.00
5 Pedro Martinez/25 30.00 80.00
7 Clayton Kershaw/49 30.00 80.00
8 Cal Ripken/25 40.00 100.00
9 George Brett/25 40.00 100.00
10 Alan Trammell/49 5.00 12.00

2019 Panini National Treasures Treasured Threads Autographs

RANDOM INSERTS IN PACKS
PRINT RUNS B/WN 10-20 COPIES PER
NO PRICING ON QTY 15 OR LESS
EXCHANGE DEADLINE 3/25/21
6 Rickey Henderson/20 40.00 100.00
9 Jose Ramirez/20
10 Roger Clemens/20 40.00 100.00

2019 Panini National Treasures Triple Legend Duos Material Booklets

RANDOM INSERTS IN PACKS
PRINT RUNS B/WN 10-25 COPIES PER
NO PRICING ON QTY 15 OR LESS
2 Vaughan/Lombardi/O'Doul/25 25.00 60.00
3 Heilmann/Rice/Kamm/25 20.00 50.00
4 Frisch/Brecheen/Groh/25 15.00 40.00
6 Pujols/Cabrera/Trout/25 40.00 100.00
7 Drysdale/Pennock/Ryan/25
8 Stanky/Hodges/Campanella/25
9 Suttles/Henrich/Keeler/25 20.00 50.00
10 Robinson/Gehrig/Clemente/25

2019 Panini National Treasures Triple Legend Trios Material Booklets

RANDOM INSERTS IN PACKS
STATED PRINT RUN 25 SER.#'d SETS
1 Griffey Jr./Puckett/Mantle
2 Brett/Boyer/Santo 40.00 100.00
3 Alomar/Carew/Hornsby 25.00 60.00
4 Pujols/Mize/Gehrig
5 Ryan/Martinez/Johnson 30.00 80.00
6 Ripken/Cronin/Smith 15.00 40.00
7 Fisk/Rodriguez/Bench 30.00 80.00
8 Keller/Kiner/Musial 30.00 80.00
9 Waner/Jackson/Gwynn 60.00 150.00
10 Beltre/Rodriguez/Suzuki 15.00 40.00
11 Jackson/Winfield/Sanders 40.00 100.00

2019 Panini National Treasures Twelve Signature Booklets

RANDOM INSERTS IN PACKS
STATED PRINT RUN 25 SER.#'d SETS
EXCHANGE DEADLINE 3/25/21
1 Austin Riley 500.00 1200.00
Bryan Reynolds
Cal Quantrill
Chris Paddack
Eloy Jimenez
Fernando Tatis Jr.
Griffin Canning
Michael Chavis
Mitch Keller
Pete Alonso
Vladimir Guerrero Jr.
Yusei Kikuchi
2 Brendan Rodgers 600.00 1500.00
Carter Kieboom
Cavan Biggio
Eloy Jimenez
Fernando Tatis Jr.
Justus Sheffield
Keston Hiura
Kyle Tucker
Michael Kopech
Nick Senzel
Thairo Estrada
Vladimir Guerrero Jr. EXCH

2019 Panini Obsidian

RANDOM INSERTS IN PACKS
*PURPLE: 1X TO 2.5X
*ORANGE: 1.2X TO 3X
*RED: 2X TO 5X
1 Yadier Molina .40 1.00
2 Nick Senzel RC .75 2.00
3 Danny Jansen RC .25 .60
4 Blake Snell .30 .75
5 Bryce Harper .60 1.50
6 Aaron Nola .30 .75
7 Vladimir Guerrero Jr. RC 1.50 4.00
8 Ichiro .50 1.25
9 Alex Bregman .40 1.00
10 Cody Bellinger .75 2.00
11 Christian Yelich .50 1.25
12 Jeff McNeil RC .60 1.50
13 Oscar Mercado RC .60 1.50
14 Aaron Judge 1.00 2.50
15 Mike Trout 2.00 5.00
16 Yusei Kikuchi RC .40 1.00
17 Kyle Wright RC .40 1.00
18 Khris Davis .40 1.00
19 Ronald Acuna Jr. 2.00 5.00
20 Juan Soto 1.25 3.00
21 J.D. Martinez .40 1.00
22 Manny Machado .40 1.00
23 Keston Hiura RC .75 2.00
24 Whit Merrifield .40 1.00
25 Jose Ramirez .30 .75
26 Carter Kieboom RC .40 1.00
27 Jon Duplantier RC .25 .60
28 Corbin Burnes RC .40 1.00
29 Paul Goldschmidt .40 1.00
30 Gleyber Torres .75 2.00
31 Joey Votto .40 1.00
32 Kris Bryant .50 1.25
33 Javier Baez .50 1.25
34 Brad Keller RC .25 .60
35 Fernando Tatis Jr. RC 2.50 6.00
36 Jose Altuve .30 .75
37 Andrew Benintendi .40 1.00
38 Max Scherzer .40 1.00
39 Brandon Lowe RC .40 1.00
40 Ryan O'Hearn RC .25 .60
41 Justin Verlander .40 1.00
42 Trevor Story .40 1.00
43 Anthony Rizzo .60 1.50
44 Christin Stewart RC .30 .75
45 Pete Alonso RC 2.00 5.00
46 Cavan Biggio RC 1.25 3.00
47 Shohei Ohtani .50 1.25
48 Eloy Jimenez RC 1.00 2.50
49 Rhys Hoskins .50 1.25
50 Francisco Lindor .40 1.00
51 Mookie Betts .60 1.50
52 Jake Bauers RC .40 1.00
53 Freddie Freeman .50 1.25
54 Luis Urias RC .40 1.00
55 Jacob deGrom .40 1.00
56 Nolan Arenado .50 1.25
57 Kyle Tucker RC .50 1.25
58 Justus Sheffield RC .40 1.00
59 Chris Paddack RC .50 1.25
60 Peter Lambert RC .40 1.00

2019 Panini Obsidian Autographs

RANDOM INSERTS IN PACKS
EXCHANGE DEADLINE 2/21/2021
*PURPLE/75-99: .5X TO 1.2X
*PURPLE/35-50: .6X TO 1.5X
*PURPLE/25: .75X TO 2X
*ORANGE/50: .6X TO 1.5X
*ORANGE/25: .75X TO 2X
*RED/25: .75X TO 2X
1 Jonathan Loaisiga 3.00 8.00
3 Yusei Kikuchi 8.00 20.00
4 Chris Paddack 8.00 20.00
5 Luis Urias 4.00 10.00
6 Kyle Wright 4.00 10.00
7 Jake Bauers 4.00 10.00
8 Jon Duplantier 2.50 6.00
10 Cedric Mullins 4.00 10.00
11 Kyle Tucker 5.00 12.00
13 Pete Alonso 40.00 100.00
14 Jeff McNeil 6.00 15.00
15 Yordan Alvarez 40.00 100.00
16 Justus Sheffield 4.00 10.00
17 Danny Jansen 2.50 6.00
18 Eloy Jimenez 10.00 25.00
19 Vladimir Guerrero Jr. 50.00 120.00
20 Fernando Tatis Jr. 75.00 200.00
21 Corbin Burnes 4.00 10.00
22 Nathaniel Lowe 3.00 8.00
23 Michael Chavis 10.00 25.00
24 Keston Hiura 12.00 30.00
25 Ramon Laureano 6.00 15.00
26 Steven Duggar 3.00 8.00
28 Brandon Lowe 10.00 25.00
29 Rowdy Tellez 4.00 10.00
30 Kevin Newman 4.00 10.00
31 Cole Tucker 4.00 10.00
32 Bryan Reynolds 6.00 15.00
33 David Fletcher 8.00 20.00
34 Bryse Wilson 3.00 8.00
35 Shaun Anderson 2.50 6.00
36 Jake Cave 3.00 8.00
37 Carter Kieboom 4.00 10.00
38 Kevin Kramer 3.00 8.00
39 Cal Quantrill 2.50 6.00
40 Ty France 8.00 20.00

2020 Panini Obsidian

RANDOM INSERTS IN PACKS
1 Yordan Alvarez RC 2.00 5.00
2 Jake Rogers RC .40 1.00
3 Gavin Lux RC 2.50 6.00
4 Brendan McKay RC .60 1.50
5 Mauricio Dubon RC .50 1.25
6 Tony Gonsolin RC 1.50 4.00
7 Bryce Harper .60 1.50
8 Randy Arozarena RC 8.00 20.00
9 Sam Hilliard RC .60 1.50
10 Sean Murphy RC .60 1.50
11 Bryan Abreu RC .40 1.00
12 Nick Solak RC .60 1.50
13 Kyle Lewis RC 3.00 8.00
14 Jesus Luzardo RC .75 2.00
15 Justin Dunn RC .50 1.25
16 Travis Demeritte RC .50 1.25
17 Bo Bichette RC 3.00 8.00
18 Zack Collins RC .50 1.25
19 Isan Diaz RC .60 1.50
20 Kwang-Hyun Kim RC 1.25 3.00
21 Yoshitomo Tsutsugo RC .50 1.25
22 Luis Robert RC 6.00 15.00
23 Shogo Akiyama RC .60 1.50
24 Shun Yamaguchi RC .50 1.25
25 Jordan Yamamoto RC .50 1.25
26 Brusdar Graterol RC .60 1.50
27 A.J. Puk RC .75 2.00
28 Nico Hoerner RC 1.50 4.00
29 Bobby Bradley RC .50 1.25
30 Dustin May RC 1.50 4.00
31 Aristides Aquino RC .75 2.00
32 Dylan Cease RC .75 2.00
33 Zac Gallen RC 1.00 2.50
34 Sheldon Neuse RC .50 1.25
35 Josh Bell .30 .75
36 Eloy Jimenez .75 2.00
37 Francisco Lindor .40 1.00
38 Juan Soto 1.25 3.00
39 Nolan Arenado .50 1.25
40 Shohei Ohtani .50 1.25
41 Ronald Acuna Jr. 1.50 4.00
42 Rafael Devers .50 1.25
43 Aaron Judge 1.00 2.50
44 Vladimir Guerrero Jr. .75 2.00
45 Blake Snell .30 .75
46 Kris Bryant .50 1.25
47 Gleyber Torres .75 2.00
48 Mookie Betts .75 2.00
49 Mike Trout 2.00 5.00
50 Cody Bellinger .75 2.00
51 Alex Bregman .40 1.00
52 Trevor Story .40 1.00
53 Freddie Freeman .50 1.25
54 Rhys Hoskins .50 1.25
55 Pete Alonso 1.00 2.50
56 Javier Baez .50 1.25
57 Fernando Tatis Jr. 1.50 4.00
58 Trea Turner .30 .75
59 Clayton Kershaw .75 2.00
60 Starling Marte .30 .75

2020 Panini Obsidian Electric Etch Orange

*ORANGE VET: 1.5X TO 4X BASIC
*ORANGE RC: 1X TO 2.5X BASIC RC
RANDOM INSERTS IN PACKS
STATED PRINT RUN 50 SER.#'d SETS
8 Randy Arozarena 40.00 100.00
17 Bo Bichette 10.00 25.00
22 Luis Robert 30.00 80.00

2020 Panini Obsidian Electric Etch Purple

*PURPLE VET: 1X TO 2.5X BASIC
*PURPLE RC: .6X TO 1.5X BASIC RC
RANDOM INSERTS IN PACKS

STATED PRINT RUN 99 SER.#'d SETS
8 Randy Arozarena 25.00 60.00
22 Luis Robert 20.00 50.00

2020 Panini Obsidian Electric Etch Red

*RED VET: 2.5X TO 6X BASIC
*RED RC: 1.5X TO 4X BASIC RC
RANDOM INSERTS IN PACKS
STATED PRINT RUN 25 SER.#'d SETS
8 Randy Arozarena 60.00 150.00
17 Bo Bichette 15.00 40.00
22 Luis Robert 50.00 120.00

2020 Panini Obsidian Autographs

RANDOM INSERTS IN PACKS
EXCHANGE DEADLINE 3/18/2022
1 Adbert Alzolay 3.00 8.00
2 Anthony Kay 2.50 6.00
3 Brendan McKay 4.00 10.00
4 Deivy Grullon 2.50 6.00
5 Edwin Rios 6.00 15.00
6 Gavin Lux 15.00 40.00
7 Isan Diaz 4.00 10.00
8 Jaylin Davis 4.00 10.00
10 Kyle Lewis 25.00 60.00
11 Matt Thaiss 3.00 8.00
12 Nick Solak 4.00 10.00
13 Randy Arozarena 40.00 100.00
14 Sean Murphy 4.00 10.00
15 Shogo Akiyama 4.00 10.00
16 T.J. Zeuch 2.50 6.00
17 Travis Demeritte 3.00 8.00
19 Yordan Alvarez 12.00 30.00
20 Yu Chang 4.00 10.00
21 Zac Gallen 6.00 15.00
22 Yoshitomo Tsutsugo 3.00 8.00
23 Willi Castro 4.00 10.00
25 Tony Gonsolin 10.00 25.00
26 Shun Yamaguchi 3.00 8.00
27 Sheldon Neuse 3.00 8.00
30 Michael King 4.00 10.00
31 Luis Robert EXCH 60.00 150.00
32 Kwang-Hyun Kim 12.00 30.00
33 Jonathan Hernandez 2.50 6.00
34 Jake Rogers 2.50 6.00
35 Hunter Greene 4.00 10.00
36 Evan White 2.50 6.00
37 Dylan Carlson 10.00 25.00
39 Aristides Aquino 5.00 12.00
40 Andres Munoz 3.00 8.00

2020 Panini Obsidian Autographs Electric Etch Blue Crystals

RANDOM INSERTS IN PACKS
PRINT RUNS B/WN 21-25 COPIES PER
EXCHANGE DEADLINE 3/18/2022
13 Randy Arozarena/25 125.00 300.00

2020 Panini Obsidian Autographs Electric Etch Purple

*BLUE/75: .5X TO 1.2X
*BLUE/49: .6X TO 1.5X
*BLUE/25: .8X TO 2X
RANDOM INSERTS IN PACKS
PRINT RUNS B/WN 25-75 COPIES PER
EXCHANGE DEADLINE 3/18/2022
13 Randy Arozarena/75 75.00 200.00

2020 Panini Origins Autographs Gold Ink

*GOLD INK/25: .5X TO 1.2X p/r 49
RANDOM INSERTS IN PACKS
PRINT RUNS B/WN 3-25 COPIES PER
NO PRICING QTY 15 OR LESS
EXCHANGE DEADLINE 3/18/2022
18 Jasson Dominguez/25 150.00 400.00

2020 Panini Origins Autographs Silver Ink

RANDOM INSERTS IN PACKS
PRINT RUNS B/WN 5-49 COPIES PER
NO PRICING QTY 15 OR LESS
EXCHANGE DEADLINE 3/18/2022
1 Bo Bichette/49 50.00 120.00
2 Gavin Lux/49 25.00 60.00
3 Yordan Alvarez/25 30.00 80.00
4 A.J. Puk/49 8.00 20.00
5 Nico Hoerner/49 15.00 40.00
7 Isan Diaz/49 6.00 15.00
8 Dustin May/25 20.00 50.00
9 Zac Gallen/49 10.00 25.00
10 Dylan Cease/49 8.00 20.00
11 Brendan McKay/25 8.00 20.00
12 Alec Bohm/25
13 Estevan Florial/49 6.00 15.00
14 Fernando Tatis Jr./49 75.00 200.00
15 Pete Alonso/49 25.00 60.00
16 Forrest Whitley/49 4.00 10.00
17 Luis Robert/49 100.00 250.00
18 Jasson Dominguez/49 75.00 200.00
19 Jo Adell/49 40.00 100.00
20 Vladimir Guerrero Jr./25 15.00 40.00
21 Walker Buehler/49 8.00 20.00
22 Adley Rutschman/25 30.00 80.00
23 Cavan Biggio/49 8.00 20.00
24 Eloy Jimenez/25 15.00 40.00
25 Royce Lewis/25 15.00 40.00
26 Bobby Witt Jr./49 30.00 80.00
27 Austin Riley/25 12.00 30.00
28 Keston Hiura/49 8.00 20.00
29 Bryan Reynolds/49 5.00 12.00
30 Jon Duplantier/49 4.00 10.00
31 Cole Tucker/49 6.00 15.00
33 Joey Bart/25 30.00 80.00
35 Ozzie Smith/25
36 Victor Mesa Jr./49 10.00 25.00
38 Paul Molitor/25 8.00 20.00

2020 Panini Origins Rookie Jumbo Material Autographs

RANDOM INSERTS IN PACKS
PRINT RUNS B/WN 49-99 COPIES PER
EXCHANGE DEADLINE 3/18/2022
*BLUE/25: .6X TO 1.5X p/r 99
*BLUE/25: .5X TO 1.2X p/r 49
1 Yordan Alvarez/99 20.00 50.00
2 Bo Bichette/99 40.00 100.00
3 Gavin Lux/99 20.00 50.00
4 Brendan McKay/99 5.00 12.00
5 Dylan Cease/99 6.00 15.00
6 A.J. Puk/99 6.00 15.00
7 Jesus Luzardo/99 6.00 15.00
8 Nico Hoerner/99 12.00 30.00
9 Sean Murphy/99 5.00 12.00
10 Dustin May/49 15.00 40.00
11 Aristides Aquino/99 6.00 15.00
12 Kyle Lewis/99 40.00 100.00
13 Isan Diaz/99 5.00 12.00
14 Justin Dunn/99 4.00 10.00
15 Brusdar Graterol/99 5.00 12.00
16 Edwin Rios/99 8.00 20.00
17 Jaylin Davis/99 5.00 12.00
18 Josh Rojas/99 3.00 8.00
19 Mauricio Dubon/99 4.00 10.00
20 Yu Chang/99 5.00 12.00
21 Yonathan Daza/99 4.00 10.00

2020 Panini Origins Signatures

RANDOM INSERTS IN PACKS
EXCHANGE DEADLINE 3/18/2022
*RED/99: .5X TO 1.2X
*RED/49: .6X TO 1.5X
*RED/25: .8X TO 2X
*BLUE/25: .8X TO 2X
1 Trent Grisham 10.00 25.00
3 Sean Murphy 4.00 10.00
4 Bobby Bradley 3.00 8.00
5 Zac Gallen 6.00 15.00
6 Tony Gonsolin 10.00 25.00
7 Bryan Abreu 2.50 6.00
8 Gavin Lux 15.00 40.00
9 Sheldon Neuse 3.00 8.00
10 Yordan Alvarez 15.00 40.00
11 Isan Diaz 4.00 10.00
12 Dylan Cease 5.00 12.00
13 Yu Chang 4.00 10.00
14 Brendan McKay 4.00 10.00
15 Logan Allen 2.50 6.00
16 Michael King 4.00 10.00
17 Brusdar Graterol 4.00 10.00
18 Sam Hilliard 4.00 10.00
19 Kyle Lewis 30.00 80.00
20 Mauricio Dubon 3.00 8.00
21 A.J. Puk 5.00 12.00
22 Brock Burke 2.50 6.00
23 Aristides Aquino 5.00 12.00
24 Aaron Civale 4.00 10.00
25 Jesus Luzardo 5.00 12.00
26 Logan Webb 3.00 8.00
27 Jake Rogers 2.50 6.00
28 Jake Fraley 3.00 8.00
29 Willi Castro 4.00 10.00
30 Jordan Yamamoto 3.00 8.00
31 Justin Dunn 3.00 8.00
32 Bo Bichette 30.00 80.00
33 Anthony Kay 2.50 6.00
34 Zack Collins 3.00 8.00
35 Abraham Toro 3.00 8.00
36 Adrian Morejon 2.50 6.00
37 Matt Thaiss 3.00 8.00
38 Nico Hoerner 10.00 25.00
39 Michel Baez 2.50 6.00
40 Yoshitomo Tsutsugo 3.00 8.00

2018 Panini Phoenix

1 Alex Verdugo RC .40 1.00
2 Clint Frazier RC .50 1.25
3 Miguel Andujar RC 1.00 2.50
4 Max Scherzer .25 .60
5 Rhys Hoskins RC 1.00 2.50
6 Austin Hays RC .40 1.00
7 Mike Trout 1.25 3.00
8 Aaron Judge .60 1.50
9 Carlos Correa .25 .60
10 Kris Bryant .30 .75
11 Ozzie Albies RC .75 2.00
12 Gleyber Torres RC 2.50 6.00
13 Ryan McMahon RC .30 .75
14 Francisco Lindor .25 .60
15 Amed Rosario RC .30 .75
16 Paul Goldschmidt .25 .60
17 Bryce Harper .40 1.00
18 Cody Bellinger .50 1.25
19 J.P. Crawford RC .25 .60
20 Shohei Ohtani RC 1.50 4.00
21 Ronald Acuna Jr. RC 5.00 12.00
22 Rafael Devers RC .75 2.00
23 Giancarlo Stanton .25 .60
24 Victor Robles RC .60 1.50
25 Dominic Smith RC .25 .60

2018 Panini Phoenix Signatures

RANDOM INSERTS IN PACKS
8 Brian Anderson 3.00 8.00
9 Dillon Peters 2.50 6.00
10 Mitch Garver 2.50 6.00
11 Tomas Nido 2.50 6.00
12 Paul Blackburn 2.50 6.00
13 Christian Walker 3.00 8.00
16 Scott Kingery 4.00 10.00
17 Chris Taylor 3.00 8.00
20 Mark Zagunis 2.50 6.00

2019 Panini Phoenix

RANDOM INSERTS IN PACKS
*HOLO: .75X TO 2X
*HYPER/299: .75X TO 2X
*RUBY/199: 1X TO 2.5X
*BLUE/99: 1.2X TO 3X
*PURPLE/75: 1.2X TO 3X
*GREEN/50: 1.5X TO 4X
*PINK/25: 2.5X TO 6X
1 Pete Alonso RC 3.00 8.00
2 Eloy Jimenez RC .60 1.50
3 Fernando Tatis Jr. RC 4.00 10.00
4 Michael Kopech RC .30 .75
5 Kyle Tucker RC .30 .75
6 Yusei Kikuchi RC .25 .60
7 Chris Paddack RC .30 .75
8 Mike Trout 1.25 3.00
9 Bryce Harper .40 1.00
10 Aaron Judge .60 1.50
11 Kris Bryant .30 .75
12 Shohei Ohtani .30 .75
13 Aaron Nola .20 .50
14 Vladimir Guerrero Jr. RC 2.50 6.00
15 Michael Chavis RC .25 .60
16 Giancarlo Stanton .25 .60
17 Alex Bregman .25 .60
18 Matt Chapman .25 .60
19 Justin Verlander .25 .60
20 Jordan Hicks .20 .50
21 Brandon Lowe RC .25 .60
22 Miguel Andujar .25 .60
23 Whit Merrifield .25 .60
24 Freddie Freeman .30 .75
25 Christian Yelich .30 .75

2019 Panini Prime Swatches

RANDOM INSERTS IN PACKS
*GOLD/99: .5X TO 1.2X
*GOLD/50: .6X TO 1.5X
*GOLD/25-28: .75X TO 2X
*BLUE/25: .75X TO 2X
1 Brett Gardner 2.00 5.00
2 Starling Marte 2.00 5.00
3 Paul DeJong 2.50 6.00
4 Dallas Keuchel 2.00 5.00
5 Max Kepler 2.00 5.00
6 Willson Contreras 2.00 5.00
7 Ender Inciarte 1.50 4.00
8 Tim Anderson 2.50 6.00
9 Trey Mancini 2.00 5.00
10 Jose Peraza 2.00 5.00
11 Buster Posey 3.00 8.00
12 Eloy Jimenez 6.00 15.00
13 Fernando Tatis Jr. 10.00 25.00
14 Vladimir Guerrero Jr. 10.00 25.00
15 Pete Alonso 12.00 30.00
16 Luis Urias 2.50 6.00
17 Gerrit Cole 2.50 6.00
18 Evan Longoria 2.00 5.00
19 Edwin Diaz 2.00 5.00
20 Lorenzo Cain 1.50 4.00
21 Odubel Herrera 2.00 5.00
22 Brandon Belt 2.00 5.00
23 Jacob deGrom 2.50 6.00
24 Mike Trout 12.00 30.00
25 Mookie Betts 4.00 10.00

2020 Panini Phoenix

RANDOM INSERTS IN PACKS
1 Bo Bichette RC 3.00 8.00
2 Yordan Alvarez RC 1.25 3.00
3 Gavin Lux RC 1.50 4.00
4 Brendan McKay RC .40 1.00
5 Aristides Aquino RC .50 1.25
6 Yoshitomo Tsutsugo RC .30 .75
7 Luis Robert RC 4.00 10.00
8 Aaron Judge .60 1.50
9 Mike Trout 2.00 5.00
10 Cody Bellinger .50 1.25
11 Fernando Tatis Jr. 2.00 5.00
12 Vladimir Guerrero Jr. .50 1.25
13 Corey Kluber .20 .50
14 Dustin May RC 1.00 2.50
15 Gleyber Torres .50 1.25
16 Freddie Freeman .30 .75
17 Shohei Ohtani .30 .75
18 Nico Hoerner RC 1.00 2.50
19 Jake Rogers RC .25 .60
20 Jesus Luzardo RC .50 1.25

2020 Panini Playbook Autographs

RANDOM INSERTS IN PACKS
EXCHANGE DEADLINE 3/18/2022
*GOLD/99: .5X TO 1.2X BASIC
*GOLD/50: .6X TO 1.5X BASIC
*RED/50: .6X TO 1.5X BASIC
*RED/25: .8X TO 2X BASIC
*BLUE/25: .8X TO 2X BASIC
2 Enyel De Los Santos 2.50 6.00
3 Ryan O'Hearn 2.50 6.00
5 Kyle Tucker 3.00 8.00
6 Byron Buxton 3.00 8.00
7 Adley Rutschman 15.00 40.00
8 Daniel Ponce de Leon 2.50 6.00
9 Jake Bauers 3.00 8.00
10 Jose Suarez 2.50 6.00
11 Yoan Lopez 2.50 6.00
12 Kolby Allard 2.50 6.00
13 Joey Lucchesi 2.50 6.00
14 Domingo German 3.00 8.00
15 Harold Castro 3.00 8.00
16 Nick Senzel 4.00 10.00
17 Dawel Lugo 2.50 6.00
18 Reese McGuire 3.00 8.00
19 Brandon Lowe 5.00 12.00
21 A.J. Minter 3.00 8.00
22 Thyago Vieira 2.50 6.00
23 Mike Soroka 4.00 10.00
24 Matt Davidson 3.00 8.00
25 Brian O'Grady 2.50 6.00

2012 Panini Prizm

COMPLETE SET (200) 20.00 50.00
1 Buster Posey .50 1.25
2 Cameron Maybin .25 .60
3 Matt Kemp .30 .75
4 Eric Hosmer .30 .75
5 Adrian Beltre .40 1.00
6 Troy Tulowitzki .40 1.00
7 Robinson Cano .30 .75
8 Albert Pujols .50 1.25
9 Blake Beavan .25 .60
10 Evan Longoria .30 .75
11 Jason Heyward .30 .75
12 Pablo Sandoval .30 .75
13 Aroldis Chapman .40 1.00
14 David Price .30 .75
15 Hanley Ramirez .30 .75
16 Jose Bautista .30 .75
17 Matt Wieters .40 1.00
18 Alex Gordon .30 .75
19 Michael Bourn .25 .60
20 David Wright .30 .75
21 Elvis Andrus .30 .75
22 Derek Jeter 10.00 25.00
23 Andrew McCutchen .40 1.00
24 Miguel Cabrera .40 1.00
25 Ichiro Suzuki .50 1.25
26 Dustin Pedroia .30 .75
27 Gio Gonzalez .30 .75
28 Anthony Rizzo .60 1.50
29 Clayton Kershaw .75 2.00
30 Jacoby Ellsbury .30 .75
31 Prince Fielder .30 .75
32 Mariano Rivera .50 1.25
33 Adam Jones .30 .75
34 James Shields .25 .60
35 R.A. Dickey .30 .75
36 Colby Rasmus .30 .75
37 Hunter Pence .30 .75
38 Paul Konerko .25 .60
39 Adrian Gonzalez .30 .75
40 David Ortiz .40 1.00
41 Starlin Castro .30 .75
42 Dustin Ackley .25 .60
43 Austin Jackson .30 .75
44 David Freese .25 .60
45 Ryan Braun .25 .60
46 Ian Kennedy .25 .60
47 Curtis Granderson .30 .75
48 Josh Hamilton .30 .75
49 Stephen Strasburg .40 1.00
50 Mike Trout 50.00 120.00
51 Felix Hernandez .30 .75
52 Joey Votto .40 1.00
53 Justin Verlander .40 1.00
54 Freddie Freeman .50 1.25
55 Jose Altuve .30 .75
56 Mike Moustakas .30 .75
57 Giancarlo Stanton .40 1.00
58 Jason Kipnis .30 .75
59 Roy Halladay .30 .75
60 Jered Weaver .30 .75
61 Josh Roddick .25 .60
62 Yovani Gallardo .30 .75
63 Carlos Gonzalez .30 .75
64 Jimmy Rollins .30 .75
65 Ryan Howard .30 .75
66 Joe Mauer .30 .75
67 Alex Rodriguez .50 1.25
68 Jon Lester .25 .60
69 Jose Reyes .25 .60
70 Justin Upton .30 .75
71 Doug Fister .25 .60
72 Josh Willingham .30 .75
73 Yadier Molina .40 1.00
74 Edwin Encarnacion .40 1.00
75 Aramis Ramirez .25 .60
76 Ike Davis .25 .60
77 Jim Johnson .25 .60
78 Billy Butler .25 .60
79 Lance Lynn .25 .60
80 Max Scherzer .40 1.00
81 Johnny Cueto .30 .75
82 Zack Greinke .30 .75
83 Matt Cain .30 .75
84 B.J. Upton .30 .75
85 Kyle Lohse .25 .60
86 Cole Hamels .30 .75
87 Jay Bruce .30 .75
88 Darwin Barney .25 .60
89 Craig Kimbrel .30 .75
90 Matt Holliday .40 1.00
91 Allen Craig .30 .75
92 Jason Motte .25 .60
93 Kris Medlen .25 .60
94 Chris Sale .40 1.00
95 Tony Campana .25 .60
96 Matt Harrison .25 .60
97 Cliff Lee .30 .75
98 Kevin Youkilis .40 1.00
99 Paul Goldschmidt .40 1.00
100 Chipper Jones 1.00 2.50
101 Dayan Viciedo .25 .60
102 Alex Rios .30 .75
103 Shin-Soo Choo .30 .75
104 Brandon Phillips .25 .60
105 Justin Morneau .30 .75
106 Ryan Roberts .25 .60
107 Coco Crisp .25 .60
108 Nelson Cruz .40 1.00
109 Chase Utley .30 .75
110 Andre Ethier .30 .75
111 Ryan Zimmerman .30 .75
112 James Loney .25 .60
113 Carl Crawford .30 .75
114 Mark Trumbo .25 .60
115 Chase Headley .25 .60
116 Jed Lowrie .25 .60
117 Garrett Jones .25 .60
118 Todd Helton .30 .75
119 Michael Young .25 .60
120 Chris Perez .25 .60
121 Frank Thomas .40 1.00
122 Greg Maddux .50 1.25
123 Ozzie Smith .50 1.25
124 Ernie Banks .40 1.00
125 Stan Musial .60 1.50
126 Paul O'Neill .25 .60
127 Ken Griffey Jr. 10.00 25.00
128 Fernando Valenzuela .15 .40
129 Deion Sanders .25 .60
130 Bo Jackson .40 1.00
131 Don Mattingly .75 2.00
132 Al Kaline .40 1.00
133 Nolan Ryan 1.25 3.00
134 Brooks Robinson .25 .60
135 Will Clark .25 .60
136 Frank Robinson .25 .60
137 Bob Gibson .25 .60
138 Carl Yastrzemski .60 1.50
139 Ivan Rodriguez .25 .60
140 Tony Gwynn .40 1.00
141 Johnny Bench .40 1.00
142 Tom Seaver .25 .60
143 Paul Molitor .40 1.00
144 George Brett .75 2.00
145 Pete Rose .75 2.00
146 Reggie Jackson .25 .60
147 Robin Yount .40 1.00
148 Cal Ripken Jr. 1.25 3.00
149 Rickey Henderson .40 1.00
150 Ryne Sandberg .75 2.00
151 Yu Darvish RC 1.50 4.00
152 Bryce Harper RC 12.00 30.00
153 Wei-Yin Chen RC 1.50 4.00
154 Jarrod Parker RC .75 2.00
155 Brett Lawrie RC .75 2.00
156 Matt Moore RC 1.00 2.50
157 Wade Miley RC .75 2.00
158 Jesus Montero RC .60 1.50
159 Yoenis Cespedes RC 1.50 4.00
160 Sergio Romo RC .75 2.00
161 Scott Diamond RC .60 1.50
162 Jordan Pacheco RC .60 1.50
163 Tom Milone RC .60 1.50
164 Tyler Pastornicky RC .60 1.50
165 Dellin Betances RC 1.00 2.50
166 Trevor Bauer RC 2.00 5.00
167 Quintin Berry RC 1.00 2.50
168 Will Middlebrooks RC .75 2.00
169 Liam Hendriks RC .60 1.50
170 Drew Pomeranz RC .60 1.50
171 David Phelps RC .40 1.00
172 Hector Sanchez RC 1.00 2.50
173 Tyler Moore RC .60 1.50
174 Steve Lombardozzi RC .60 1.50
175 Adron Chambers RC 1.00 2.50
176 Eric Surkamp RC 1.00 2.50
177 Norichika Aoki RC .75 2.00
178 Brett Jackson RC 1.00 2.50
179 Matt Harvey RC 4.00 10.00
180 A.J. Griffin RC .75 2.00
181 Starling Marte RC .75 2.00
182 Andrelton Simmons RC 1.00 2.50
183 Elian Herrera RC 1.00 2.50
184 Drew Smyly RC .60 1.50
185 Hisashi Iwakuma RC 1.25 3.00
186 Matt Adams RC .75 2.00
187 Josh Vitters RC .75 2.00
188 Chris Archer RC .60 1.50
189 Michael Taylor RC .60 1.50
190 Ryan Cook RC .60 1.50
191 Joe Kelly RC 1.00 2.50
192 Zach McAllister RC .75 2.00
193 Jose Quintana RC .60 1.50
194 Addison Reed RC .60 1.50
195 Hector Santiago RC .75 2.00
196 Dale Thayer RC .40 1.00
197 Joe Wieland RC .60 1.50
198 Martin Maldonado RC 1.00 2.50
199 Wilin Rosario RC .60 1.50
200 Kirk Nieuwenhuis RC .60 1.50

2012 Panini Prizm 2013 National Convention Cracked Ice

*CRACKED ICE 1-150: 3X TO 8X BASIC
*CRACKED ICE 151-200: 1.2X TO 3X BASIC
ISSUED AT 2013 NATIONAL CONVENTION
ANNOUNCED PRINT RUN OF 25 COPIES

2012 Panini Prizm Prizms

*PRIZMS: 2X TO 5X BASIC
*PRIZMS RC: .75X TO 2X BASIC RC
22 Derek Jeter 250.00 600.00
50 Mike Trout 500.00 1200.00
127 Ken Griffey Jr. 200.00 500.00
152 Bryce Harper 40.00 100.00

2012 Panini Prizm Prizms Green

*GREEN VET: 2.5X TO 6X BASIC
*GREEN RC: 1X TO 2.5X BASIC RC
22 Derek Jeter 60.00 150.00
50 Mike Trout 750.00 2000.00
152 Bryce Harper 60.00 150.00

2012 Panini Prizm Prizms Red

*RED VET: 4X TO 10X BASIC
*RED RC: 1.5X TO 4X BASIC RC
22 Derek Jeter 100.00 250.00
50 Mike Trout 1250.00 3000.00
152 Bryce Harper 100.00 200.00

2012 Panini Prizm Autographs

EXCHANGE DEADLINE 10/17/2014
AC Allen Craig 6.00 15.00
AL Adam LaRoche 3.00 8.00
AR Alex Rios 4.00 10.00
BM Brandon McCarthy 3.00 8.00
BO Bo Jackson 40.00 100.00
BW Bernie Williams 15.00 40.00
CP Chris Perez 3.00 8.00
CR Clayton Richard 3.00 8.00
CR Cal Ripken Jr. 25.00 60.00
17 Cody Ross 3.00 8.00
CR Carlos Ruiz 4.00 10.00
CS Chris Sale 6.00 15.00
DB Darwin Barney 4.00 10.00
DF Doug Fister 3.00 8.00
DF Dexter Fowler 3.00 8.00
DH Derek Holland 3.00 8.00
DM Don Mattingly 20.00 50.00
DS Denard Span 3.00 8.00
DS Deion Sanders 15.00 40.00
DW Dave Winfield 10.00 25.00
DW David Wright 12.50 30.00
GB George Brett 40.00 80.00
GB Grant Balfour 3.00 8.00
JB Jonathan Broxton 3.00 8.00
JD Jarrod Dyson 12.00 30.00
JD J.D. Martinez 8.00 20.00
JG Joe Girardi 8.00 20.00
JJ Jim Johnson 5.00 12.00
JK Jason Kipnis 3.00 8.00
JN Joe Nathan 3.00 8.00
JR Ken Griffey Jr. 90.00 150.00
JS Jarrod Saltalamacchia 3.00 8.00
JT Josh Thole 3.00 8.00
JU Julio Teheran 4.00 10.00
JW Josh Willingham 4.00 10.00
KJ Kelly Johnson 3.00 8.00
LD Lucas Duda 5.00 12.00
MH Matt Harrison 3.00 8.00
MM Miguel Montero 3.00 8.00
MR Marc Rzepczynski 4.00 10.00
MR Mark Reynolds 3.00 8.00
MU David Murphy 3.00 8.00
PK Paul Konerko 4.00 10.00
RA R.A. Dickey 3.00 8.00
RH Rickey Henderson 40.00 80.00
RJ Reggie Jackson 20.00 50.00
RR Ryan Roberts 3.00 8.00
RS Ryne Sandberg 15.00 40.00
SS Sergio Santos 3.00 8.00
SS Skip Schumaker 3.00 8.00
TA Jose Tabata 3.00 8.00
TG Tony Gwynn 15.00 40.00
TP Trevor Plouffe 3.00 8.00
WD Wade Davis 3.00 8.00

2012 Panini Prizm Brilliance

*PRIZMS: 1X TO 2.5X BASIC
B1 Felix Hernandez .50 1.25
B2 Miguel Cabrera .60 1.50
B3 Josh Hamilton .50 1.25
B4 Johan Santana .50 1.25
B5 Pablo Sandoval .50 1.25
B6 Mike Trout 20.00 50.00
B7 Ryan Braun .40 1.00
B8 Matt Cain .50 1.25
B9 Adrian Beltre .60 1.50
B10 Philip Humber .40 1.00

2012 Panini Prizm Brilliance Prizms Green

*GREEN: 1.2X TO 3X BASIC

2012 Panini Prizm Dominance

*PRIZMS: 1X TO 2.5X BASIC
D1 Nolan Ryan 2.00 5.00
D2 Bob Gibson .40 1.00
D3 Tom Seaver .40 1.00
D4 Greg Maddux .75 2.00
D5 Justin Verlander .60 1.50
D6 Rickey Henderson .60 1.50
D7 George Brett 1.25 3.00
D8 Derek Jeter 1.50 4.00
D9 Albert Pujols .75 2.00
D10 Miguel Cabrera .60 1.50

2012 Panini Prizm Dominance Prizms

*PRIZMS: 1.5X TO 4X BASIC

2012 Panini Prizm Dominance Prizms Green

*GREEN: 1.2X TO 3X BASIC

2012 Panini Prizm Elite Extra Edition

*PRIZMS: 1X TO 2.5X BASIC
EEE1 Carlos Correa 2.50 6.00
EEE2 Byron Buxton 1.00 2.50
EEE3 Marcus Stroman .60 1.50
EEE4 Max Fried 1.50 4.00
EEE5 Jesse Winker .50 1.25
EEE6 Ty Hensley .50 1.25
EEE7 Kevin Plawecki .50 1.25
EEE8 Jeremy Baltz .25 .60
EEE9 Albert Almora 1.00 2.50
EEE10 Damion Carroll .25 .60

2012 Panini Prizm Elite Extra Edition Prizms Green

*GREEN: 1.2X TO 3X BASIC

2012 Panini Prizm Elite Extra Edition Autographs

STATED PRINT RUN 200 SER.#'d SETS
EXCHANGE DEADLINE 10/17/2014
EEEAR Addison Russell/200 12.00 30.00
EEEAS Austin Schotts/200 6.00 15.00
EEEAY Alex Yarbrough/200 3.00 8.00
EEECC Clint Coulter/200 5.00 12.00
EEECH Courtney Hawkins/200 6.00 15.00
EEECS Corey Seager/200 25.00 60.00
EEEDD David Dahl/200 8.00 20.00
EEEGC Gavin Cecchini/200 4.00 10.00
EEEJG Joey Gallo/200 25.00 60.00
EEEJO J.O. Berrios/200 12.00 30.00
EEEKB Keon Barnum/200 3.00 8.00
EEEKZ Kyle Zimmer/200 5.00 12.00
EEELG Lucas Giolito/68 10.00 25.00
EEELM Lance McCullers/200 5.00 12.00
EEEMM Max Muncy/200 12.00 30.00
EEEMO Matt Olson/200 8.00 20.00
EEEMS Matt Smoral/200 3.00 8.00
EEEMZ Mike Zunino/200 8.00 20.00
EEEPB Preston Beck/200 3.00 8.00
EEEPL Pat Light/200 3.00 8.00
EEEPO Peter O'Brien/200 3.00 8.00
EEEST Stryker Trahan/200 4.00 10.00
EEESW Shane Watson/200 6.00 15.00
EEETN Tyler Naquin/200 4.00 10.00
EEEWW Walker Weickel/200 3.00 8.00

2012 Panini Prizm Rookie Autographs

EXCHANGE DEADLINE 10/17/2014
RBJ Brett Jackson 3.00 8.00
RBL Brett Lawrie 6.00 15.00
RDB Dellin Betances 3.00 8.00
RJP Jarrod Parker 3.00 8.00
RMH Matt Harvey 12.00 30.00
RNA Norichika Aoki 12.50 30.00
RQB Quintin Berry 4.00 10.00
RSD Scott Diamond 4.00 10.00
RTB Trevor Bauer 6.00 15.00
RTF Todd Frazier 3.00 8.00
RTM Tom Milone 3.00 8.00
RYC Yoenis Cespedes 12.00 30.00

2012 Panini Prizm Rookie Relevance

COMPLETE SET (12) 8.00 20.00
RR1 Mike Trout 25.00 60.00
RR2 Bryce Harper 6.00 15.00
RR3 Yoenis Cespedes 1.00 2.50
RR4 Wade Miley .50 1.25
RR5 Wilin Rosario .40 1.00
RR6 Yu Darvish 1.00 2.50
RR7 Wei-Yin Chen 1.00 2.50
RR8 Todd Frazier .50 1.25
RR9 Brett Lawrie .50 1.25
RR10 Jesus Montero .40 1.00
RR11 Norichika Aoki .50 1.25
RR12 Jarrod Parker .50 1.25

2012 Panini Prizm Rookie Relevance Prizms

*PRIZMS: 1X TO 2.5X BASIC
RR2 Bryce Harper 4.00 10.00

2012 Panini Prizm Rookie Relevance Prizms Green

*GREEN: 1.2X TO 3X BASIC
RR2 Bryce Harper 5.00 12.00

2012 Panini Prizm Team MVP

MVP1 Craig Kimbrel .50 1.25
MVP2 Aaron Hill .40 1.00
MVP3 Jim Johnson .40 1.00
MVP4 Dustin Pedroia .50 1.25
MVP5 Starlin Castro .50 1.25
MVP6 Paul Konerko .40 1.00
MVP7 Jay Bruce .50 1.25
MVP8 Jason Kipnis .50 1.25
MVP9 Carlos Gonzalez .50 1.25
MVP10 Miguel Cabrera .60 1.50
MVP11 Jose Altuve .50 1.25
MVP12 Billy Butler .40 1.00
MVP13 Mike Trout 30.00 80.00
MVP14 Matt Kemp .50 1.25
MVP15 Giancarlo Stanton .60 1.50
MVP16 Ryan Braun .40 1.00
MVP17 Joe Mauer .50 1.25
MVP18 David Wright .50 1.25
MVP19 Derek Jeter 1.50 4.00
MVP20 Yoenis Cespedes 1.00 2.50
MVP21 Cole Hamels .50 1.25
MVP22 Andrew McCutchen .60 1.50
MVP23 Yadier Molina .60 1.50
MVP24 Chase Headley .40 1.00
MVP25 Buster Posey .75 2.00
MVP26 Felix Hernandez .50 1.25
MVP27 David Price .50 1.25
MVP28 Adrian Beltre .60 1.50
MVP29 Edwin Encarnacion .60 1.50
MVP30 Bryce Harper 6.00 15.00

2012 Panini Prizm Team MVP Prizms

*PRIZMS: 1X TO 2.5X BASIC
MVP30 Bryce Harper 10.00 25.00

2012 Panini Prizm Team MVP Prizms Green

*GREEN: 1.2X TO 3X BASIC

2012 Panini Prizm Top Prospects
*PRIZMS: 1X TO 2.5X BASIC
TP1 Jurickson Profar .50 1.25
TP2 Dylan Bundy .75 2.00
TP3 Shelby Miller .75 2.00
TP4 Gerrit Cole 2.50 6.00
TP5 Wil Myers .50 1.25
TP6 Zach Lee .40 1.00
TP7 Manny Machado 2.50 6.00
TP8 Mike Olt .50 1.25

2012 Panini Prizm Top Prospects Prizms Green
*GREEN: 1.2X TO 3X BASIC
TP7 Manny Machado 8.00 20.00

2012 Panini Prizm USA Baseball
USA1 Mike Trout 30.00 80.00
USA2 Buster Posey .75 2.00
USA3 Justin Verlander .60 1.50
USA4 Stephen Strasburg .60 1.50
USA5 Andrew McCutchen .60 1.50
USA6 Clayton Kershaw 1.25 3.00
USA7 Bryce Harper 6.00 15.00
USA8 Derek Jeter 1.50 4.00
USA9 Justin Upton .50 1.25
USA10 Austin Jackson .50 1.25

2012 Panini Prizm USA Baseball Prizms
*PRIZMS: 1.2X TO 3X BASIC

2013 Panini Prizm
1 Gio Gonzalez .20 .50
2 Alex Gordon .20 .50
3 Clayton Kershaw .50 1.25
4 Desmond Jennings .20 .50
5 Alfonso Soriano .20 .50
6 Tom Milone .15 .40
7 Prince Fielder .20 .50
8 David Freese .15 .40
9 Wellington Castillo .15 .40
10 Josh Reddick .15 .40
11 Dayan Viciedo .15 .40
12 Rickie Weeks .15 .40
13 Martin Prado .15 .40
14 Juan Pierre .15 .40
15 Yadier Molina .25 .60
16 Kris Medlen .20 .50
17 Jed Lowrie .15 .40
18 Zack Cozart .15 .40
19 Paul Goldschmidt .25 .60
20 Michael Bourn .15 .40
21 J.D. Martinez .25 .60
22 Matt Harvey .20 .50
23 Trevor Plouffe .15 .40
24 Victor Martinez .20 .50
25 Miguel Cabrera .25 .60
26 Matt Holliday .25 .60
27 A.J. Burnett .15 .40
28 Max Scherzer .25 .60
29 David Ortiz .25 .60
30 Chris Perez .15 .40
31 Fernando Rodney .15 .40
32 Yoenis Cespedes .25 .60
33 Jeff Samardzija .15 .40
34 Giancarlo Stanton .25 .60
35 James Shields .15 .40
36 Andre Ethier .20 .50
37 Madison Bumgarner .20 .50
38 Jarrod Parker .15 .40
39 Adam Dunn .20 .50
40 Justin Verlander .25 .60
41 Nick Swisher .20 .50
42 Matt Kemp .20 .50
43 Austin Jackson .15 .40
44 Derek Jeter 2.00 5.00
45 Ben Zobrist .20 .50
46 Melky Cabrera .15 .40
47 Hanley Ramirez .20 .50
48 Johan Santana .20 .50
49 Ian Desmond .15 .40
50 Shin-Soo Choo .20 .50
51 Daniel Murphy .20 .50
52 Freddie Freeman .30 .75
53 Coco Crisp .15 .40
54 Lance Berkman .20 .50
55 Carlos Quentin .15 .40
56 Lucas Duda .20 .50
57 Jay Bruce .20 .50
58 Cameron Maybin .15 .40
59 Ian Kinsler .20 .50
60 Jose Reyes .20 .50
61 Wade Miley .15 .40
62 Jordan Zimmermann .20 .50
63 Andy Pettitte .20 .50
64 Aramis Ramirez .15 .40
65 Adam Jones .20 .50
66 Ike Davis .15 .40
67 Cody Ross .15 .40
68 Johnny Cueto .20 .50
69 Scott Diamond .15 .40
70 Andrew McCutchen .25 .60
71 Dexter Fowler .20 .50
72 Michael Morse .15 .40
73 Bryce Harper .40 1.00
74 Evan Longoria .20 .50
75 Neil Walker .20 .50
76 Elvis Andrus .20 .50
77 David Price .20 .50
78 Pedro Alvarez .15 .40
79 Todd Helton .20 .50
80 Craig Kimbrel .20 .50
81 Dustin Pedroia .20 .50
82 Shane Victorino .20 .50
83 Dustin Ackley .15 .40
84 Will Middlebrooks .15 .40
85 Tim Lincecum .20 .50
86 David Wright .20 .50
87 Anthony Rizzo .40 1.00
88 Hunter Pence .20 .50
89 Michael Young .15 .40
90 CC Sabathia .20 .50
91 Troy Tulowitzki .25 .60
92 Carlos Santana .20 .50
93 Adam Wainwright .20 .50
94 Carl Crawford .20 .50
95 Joey Votto .25 .60
96 Jesus Montero .15 .40
97 Jason Grilli .15 .40
98 Brett Lawrie .20 .50
99 Adrian Gonzalez .20 .50
100 Yu Darvish .25 .60
101 B.J. Upton .20 .50
102 Curtis Granderson .20 .50
103 Jose Bautista .20 .50
104 Adrian Beltre .25 .60
105 Chris Sale .25 .60
106 Ichiro .30 .75
107 Nelson Cruz .25 .60
108 Norichika Aoki .15 .40
109 Justin Morneau .20 .50
110 Jered Weaver .20 .50
111 Brandon Phillips .15 .40
112 Ryan Braun .20 .50
113 Jose Altuve .20 .50
114 Yonder Alonso .15 .40
115 Ryan Howard .20 .50
116 Justin Upton .20 .50
117 Jeff Francoeur .20 .50
118 Felix Hernandez .20 .50
119 Chase Utley .20 .50
120 Jason Motte .15 .40
121 Robinson Cano .20 .50
122 Huston Street .15 .40
123 Josh Willingham .20 .50
124 Edwin Encarnacion .25 .60
125 Jason Heyward .20 .50
126 Jimmy Rollins .20 .50
127 Trevor Cahill .15 .40
128 Carlos Gonzalez .20 .50
129 Ryan Zimmerman .20 .50
130 Alex Rodriguez .30 .75
131 Billy Butler .15 .40
132 Nick Markakis .20 .50
133 Yovani Gallardo .15 .40
134 Stephen Strasburg .25 .60
135 Zack Greinke .20 .50
136 Wilin Rosario .15 .40
137 Pablo Sandoval .20 .50
138 Vinnie Pestano .15 .40
139 Mike Moustakas .20 .50
140 Torii Hunter .15 .40
141 Jacoby Ellsbury .20 .50
142 Logan Morrison .15 .40
143 Justin Ruggiano .15 .40
144 Matt Garza .15 .40
145 R.A. Dickey .20 .50
146 Starling Marte .20 .50
147 Chase Headley .15 .40
148 Marco Scutaro .20 .50
149 Roy Halladay .20 .50
150 Mark Trumbo .20 .50
151 Josh Hamilton .20 .50
152 Aroldis Chapman .25 .60
153 Wei-Yin Chen .15 .40
154 Asdrubal Cabrera .20 .50
155 Starlin Castro .15 .40
156 Carlos Beltran .20 .50
157 C.J. Wilson .15 .40
158 Mike Napoli .15 .40
159 Mike Trout 3.00 8.00
160 Cole Hamels .20 .50
161 Mariano Rivera .30 .75
162 Allen Craig .20 .50
163 Matt Moore .20 .50
164 Hisashi Iwakuma .20 .50
165 Ian Kennedy .15 .40
166 Buster Posey .30 .75
167 Albert Pujols .30 .75
168 Matt Cain .20 .50
169 Eric Hosmer .20 .50
170 Paul Konerko .20 .50
171 Matt Wieters .25 .60
172 Josh Johnson .20 .50
173 Joe Mauer .20 .50
174 Jim Johnson .15 .40
175 Alex Rios .20 .50
176 Tony Gwynn .25 .60
177 George Brett .50 1.25
178 Jeff Bagwell .20 .50
179 Bernie Williams .20 .50
180 Yogi Berra .25 .60
181 Craig Biggio .20 .50
182 Whitey Ford .20 .50
183 Ken Griffey Jr. 2.00 5.00
184 Pedro Martinez .20 .50
185 Will Clark .20 .50
186 Ryne Sandberg .50 1.25
187 Rickey Henderson .25 .60
188 Carlton Fisk .20 .50
189 Barry Larkin .20 .50
190 Don Mattingly .50 1.25
191 Andre Dawson .20 .50
192 Mike Piazza .25 .60
193 Nomar Garciaparra .20 .50
194 Pete Rose .50 1.25
195 Joe Carter .15 .40
196 Nolan Ryan .75 2.00
197 Willie McCovey .20 .50
198 Bo Jackson .25 .60
199 Cal Ripken Jr. .75 2.00
200 Chipper Jones .25 .60
201 Alfredo Marte RC .25 .60
202 Hyun-Jin Ryu RC .60 1.50
203 Evan Gattis RC .50 1.25
204 Hector Rondon RC .30 .75
205 Nate Freiman RC .25 .60
206 Nick Noonan RC .30 .75
207 Brandon Maurer RC .30 .75
208 Ryan Pressly RC .30 .75
209 Derrick Robinson RC .25 .60
210 Josh Prince RC .25 .60
211 Leury Garcia RC .25 .60
212 T.J. McFarland RC .25 .60
213 Paul Clemens RC .25 .60
214 Alex Wilson RC .25 .60
215 Luis D. Jimenez RC .25 .60
216 Zack Wheeler RC .50 1.25
217 Collin McHugh RC .25 .60
218 Chad Jenkins RC .25 .60
219 Melky Mesa RC .30 .75
220 Nolan Arenado RC 1.25 3.00
221 Khris Davis RC .75 2.00
222 Rob Scahill RC .25 .60
223 Kyuji Fujikawa RC .40 1.00
224 Mike Zunino RC .40 1.00
225 Andrew Taylor RC .25 .60
226 Joe Ortiz RC .25 .60
227 Anthony Rendon RC 1.25 3.00
228 Bruce Rondon RC .25 .60
229 Michael Wacha RC .30 .75
230 Andrew Werner RC .25 .60
231 Justin Grimm RC .25 .60
232 Dylan Bundy RC .60 1.50
233 Manny Machado RC 1.50 4.00
234 Carter Capps RC .25 .60
235 Kyle Gibson RC .40 1.00
236 Tom Koehler RC .25 .60
237 Jaye Chapman RC .25 .60
238 Ryan Jackson RC .25 .60
239 Gerrit Cole RC 1.50 4.00
240 Pedro Villarreal RC .25 .60
241 Zoilo Almonte RC .30 .75
242 Didi Gregorius RC 1.00 2.50
243 David Lough RC .25 .60
244 Chris Herrmann RC .25 .60
245 Rafael Ortega RC .25 .60
246 Bryan Morris RC .25 .60
247 Munenori Kawasaki RC .40 1.00
248 Tyler Cloyd RC .30 .75
249 Adam Eaton RC .40 1.00
250 Hiram Burgos RC .25 .60
251 Mickey Storey RC .25 .60
252 Nathan Karns RC .25 .60
253 Jackie Bradley Jr. RC .60 1.50
254 Brandon Barnes RC .25 .60
255 Yan Gomes RC .30 .75
256 Rob Brantly RC .25 .60
257 Aaron Hicks RC .40 1.00
258 Aaron Loup RC .25 .60
259 Nick Maronde RC .30 .75
260 Yasiel Puig RC 1.00 2.50
261 Brooks Raley RC .25 .60
262 Brock Holt RC .30 .75
263 Francisco Peguero RC .25 .60
264 Paco Rodriguez RC .40 1.00
265 Tyler Skaggs RC .40 1.00
266 Scott Rice RC .40 1.00
267 Wil Myers RC .30 .75
268 Jake Odorizzi RC .30 .75
269 Mike Olt RC .30 .75
270 Neftali Soto RC .30 .75
271 Tony Cingrani RC .50 1.25
272 Steven Lerud RC .25 .60
273 Deunte Heath RC .25 .60
274 Avisail Garcia RC .30 .75
275 Jurickson Profar RC .30 .75
276 Shelby Miller RC .60 1.50
277 Kevin Gausman RC .40 1.00
278 Carlos Martinez RC .40 1.00
279 L.J. Hoes RC .30 .75
280 Phillippe Aumont RC .25 .60
281 Sean Doolittle RC .25 .60
282 Nick Tepesch RC .30 .75
283 Jose Fernandez RC .60 1.50
284 Marcell Ozuna RC .60 1.50
285 Henry M. Rodriguez RC .25 .60
286 Eury Perez RC .25 .60
287 Matt Magill RC .25 .60
288 Adam Warren RC .25 .60
289 Jake Elmore RC .25 .60
290 Darin Ruf RC .50 1.25
291 Oswaldo Arcia RC .25 .60
292 Robbie Grossman RC .25 .60
293 J.J. Ramos RC .30 .75
294 Casey Kelly RC .30 .75
295 Jedd Gyorko RC .30 .75
296 Jean Machi RC .25 .60
297 Justin Wilson RC .25 .60
298 Jeurys Familia RC .40 1.00
299 Nick Franklin RC .30 .75
300 Allen Webster RC .30 .75
301 Mike Trout SP 12.00 30.00
302 Bryce Harper SP 2.00 5.00
303 Derek Jeter SP 3.00 8.00
304 Stephen Strasburg SP 1.25 3.00
305 Miguel Cabrera SP 1.25 3.00

2013 Panini Prizm Prizms
*PRIZMS 1-200: 1.2X TO 3X BASIC
*PRIZMS 201-300: .75X TO 2X BASIC RC
*PRIZMS 301-305: .4X TO 1X BASIC SP

2013 Panini Prizm Prizms Blue
*BLUE 1-200: 3X TO 8X BASIC
*BLUE 201-300: 2X TO 5X BASIC RC
*BLUE 301-305: .75X TO 2X BASIC SP
159 Mike Trout 60.00 150.00
301 Mike Trout 60.00 150.00

2013 Panini Prizm Prizms Blue Pulsar
*BLUE PULSAR 1-200: 3X TO 8X BASIC
*BLUE PULSAR 201-300: 2X TO 5X BASIC RC
*BLUE PULSAR 301-305: .75X TO 2X BASIC SP
159 Mike Trout 60.00 150.00
301 Mike Trout 60.00 150.00

2013 Panini Prizm Prizms Green
*GREEN 1-200: 4X TO 10X BASIC
*GREEN 201-300: 2.5X TO 6X BASIC RC
*GREEN 301-305: 1X TO 2.5X BASIC SP

2013 Panini Prizm Prizms Orange Die-Cut
*ORANGE 1-200: 8X TO 20X BASIC
*ORANGE 201-300: 5X TO 12X BASIC RC
STATED PRINT RUN 60 SER.#'d SETS
44 Derek Jeter 60.00 150.00
159 Mike Trout 100.00 250.00

2013 Panini Prizm Prizms Red
*RED 1-200: 2.5X TO 6X BASIC
*RED 201-300: 1.5X TO 4X BASIC RC
*RED 301-305: .6X TO 1.5X BASIC SP
159 Mike Trout 50.00 120.00
301 Mike Trout 50.00 120.00

2013 Panini Prizm Prizms Red Pulsar
*RED PULSAR 1-200: 3X TO 8X BASIC
*RED PULSAR 201-300: 2X TO 5X BASIC RC
*RED PULSAR 301-305: .75X TO 2X BASIC SP
159 Mike Trout 60.00 150.00
301 Mike Trout 60.00 150.00

2013 Panini Prizm Autographs
EXCHANGE DEADLINE 03/18/2015
AB Adrian Beltre 12.00 30.00
AC Asdrubal Cabrera 3.00 8.00
AE Andre Ethier 5.00 12.00
AR Aramis Ramirez 3.00 8.00
AT Alan Trammell 6.00 15.00
AZ Anthony Rizzo 10.00 25.00
BM Brandon McCarthy 3.00 8.00
BZ Ben Zobrist 5.00 12.00
CB Craig Biggio 6.00 15.00
CC Carl Crawford 6.00 15.00
CJ Cal Ripken Jr. 20.00 50.00
CL Cliff Lee 3.00 8.00
CR Carlos Ruiz 3.00 8.00
CS Chris Sale 5.00 12.00
DW David Wright 4.00 10.00
FT Frank Thomas 20.00 50.00
GP Glen Perkins 3.00 8.00
GS Gary Sheffield 4.00 10.00
HR Henry A. Rodriguez 3.00 8.00
ID Ike Davis 3.00 8.00
IN Ivan Nova 3.00 8.00
IR Ivan Rodriguez 8.00 20.00
JB Jay Bruce 3.00 8.00
JH J.J. Hardy 3.00 8.00
JJ Josh Johnson 4.00 10.00
JK Jason Kipnis 3.00 8.00
JM Jason Motte 3.00 8.00
JN Joe Nathan 3.00 8.00
JT Julio Teheran 5.00 12.00
JW Josh Willingham 3.00 8.00
JZ Jordan Zimmermann 3.00 8.00
KM Kris Medlen 3.00 8.00
MC James McDonald 3.00 8.00
MM Miguel Montero 3.00 8.00
MP Mike Piazza 20.00 50.00
MR Mariano Rivera 50.00 100.00
MT Mike Trout 60.00 120.00
PB Peter Bourjos 3.00 8.00
PK Pete Kozma 3.00 8.00
PO Paul O'Neill 5.00 12.00
RAE Adam Eaton 3.00 8.00
RAG Avisail Garcia 6.00 15.00
RAH Adeiny Hechavarria 3.00 8.00
RBC Billy Hamilton 3.00 8.00
RBH Brock Holt 3.00 8.00
RCK Casey Kelly 3.00 8.00
RCM Collin McHugh 3.00 8.00
RDB Dylan Bundy 3.00 8.00
RDG Didi Gregorius 3.00 8.00
RDL David Lough 3.00 8.00
RDR Darin Ruf 5.00 12.00
REP Eury Perez 3.00 8.00
RHR Henry M. Rodriguez 3.00 8.00
RJC Jaye Chapman 3.00 8.00
RJF Jeurys Familia 3.00 8.00
RJO Jake Odorizzi 3.00 8.00
RJP Jurickson Profar 4.00 10.00
RK Roger Clemens 15.00 40.00
RLJ L.J. Hoes 3.00 8.00
RMH Mike Olt 4.00 10.00
RMM Manny Machado 15.00 40.00
RMM Melky Mesa 3.00 8.00
RNM Nick Maronde 3.00 8.00
ROS Oscar Taveras 4.00 10.00
RPR Paco Rodriguez 3.00 8.00
RRB Rob Brantly 3.00 8.00
RRS Rob Scahill 3.00 8.00
RS Ryne Sandberg 12.00 30.00
RSM Shelby Miller 4.00 25.00
RST Shawn Tolleson 3.00 8.00
RTB Trevor Bauer 10.00 25.00
RTC Tony Cingrani 8.00 20.00
RTS Tyler Skaggs 3.00 8.00
RTY Tyler Cloyd 10.00 25.00
RWM Wil Myers 4.00 10.00
SM Sean Marshall 3.00 8.00
SR Sergio Romo 5.00 12.00
SS Stephen Strasburg 15.00 40.00
TC Tyler Clippard 3.00 8.00
TF Tyler Flowers 3.00 8.00
TM Tom Milone 3.00 8.00
WC Wei-Yin Chen 20.00 50.00
WE Willie Randolph 3.00 8.00
WI Wilin Rosario 3.00 8.00
WR Wandy Rodriguez 3.00 8.00
ZM Zach McAllister 3.00 8.00

2013 Panini Prizm Band of Brothers
1 Pjols/Hmltn/Trout 10.00 25.00
2 A.Burnett/A.McCutchen 1.25 3.00
3 Gnzlz/Ethier/Kemp 1.00 2.50
4 G.Stanton/L.Morrison 1.25 3.00
5 Hill/Gldschmdt/Mley 1.25 3.00
6 A.Soriano/A.Rizzo 2.00 5.00
7 Gnzlz/Tlwtzki/Rsrio 1.25 3.00
8 Cabrera/Bourn/Swisher 1.00 2.50
9 Ortz/Pdria/Ellsbry 1.25 3.00
10 A.Dunn/P.Konerko 1.00 2.50
11 Btler/Hsmr/Shlds 1.00 2.50
12 Rmrez/Braun/Gllrdo 1.00 2.50
13 D.Wright/I.Davis 1.00 2.50
14 Utly/Hlldy/Hwrd 1.00 2.50
15 C.Quentin/C.Headley .75 2.00
16 J.Mauer/J.Willingham 1.00 2.50
17 F.Hernandez/M.Morse 1.00 2.50
18 Lwrie/Encrncn/Btsta 1.25 3.00
19 Zbrst/Prce/Lngria 1.00 2.50
20 J.Castro/J.Altuve 1.00 2.50
21 C.Beltran/D.Freese SP 1.25 3.00
22 Jnes/Jhnsn/Mrkkis SP 1.25 3.00
23 Bltre/Knsler/Drvsh SP 1.50 4.00
24 Uptn/Hywrd/Uptn SP 1.25 3.00
25 Hrper/Gnzlez/Strsbrg SP 2.50 6.00
26 Phllps/Vtto/Cueto SP 1.50 4.00
27 Psey/Cain/Lnccm SP 2.00 5.00
28 Sbthia/Jter/Cano SP 4.00 10.00
29 Prkr/Rddck/Cspdes SP 1.50 4.00
30 Vrlndr/Cbrra/Fldr SP 1.50 4.00

2013 Panini Prizm Band of Brothers Prizms
*PRIZMS 1-20: .6X TO 1.5X BASIC
*PRIZMS 21-30: .5X TO 1.2X BASIC

2013 Panini Prizm Band of Brothers Prizms Blue
*BLUE 1-20: .75X TO 2X BASIC

2013 Panini Prizm Band of Brothers Prizms Blue Pulsar
*BLUE PULSAR: 1.2X TO 3X BASIC

2013 Panini Prizm Band of Brothers Prizms Green
*GREEN 1-20: .75X TO 2X BASIC
*GREEN 21-30: .6X TO 1.5X BASIC

2013 Panini Prizm Band of Brothers Prizms Red
*RED 1-20: .75X TO 2X BASIC
*RED 21-30: .6X TO 1.5X BASIC

2013 Panini Prizm Band of Brothers Prizms Red Pulsar
*RED PULSAR: 1.2X TO 3X BASIC

2013 Panini Prizm Father's Day
B6 Mike Trout BRIL 8.00 20.00
127 Ken Griffey Jr. (Rainbow Parallel) 2.00 5.00
149 Rickey Henderson (Rainbow Parallel) 1.00 2.50
152 Bryce Harper (Rainbow Parallel) 1.50 4.00
156 Matt Moore (Rainbowm Parallel) .75 2.00
159 Yoenis Cespedes (Rainbow Parallel) 1.00 2.50
179 Matt Harvey (Rainbow Parallel) .75 2.00
181 Starling Marte (Rainbow Parallel) .75 2.00
RR6 Yu Darvish RR 1.00 2.50
TP4 Gerrit Cole TP 4.00 10.00
MVP13 Mike Trout MVP 8.00 20.00

2013 Panini Prizm Fearless
1 Buster Posey 1.25 3.00
2 Yadier Molina 1.00 2.50
3 Derek Jeter 2.50 6.00
4 Mike Trout 8.00 20.00
5 Bryce Harper 1.50 4.00
6 Justin Verlander 1.00 2.50
7 Adrian Beltre 1.00 2.50
8 Jose Altuve .75 2.00
9 Felix Hernandez .75 2.00
10 Matt Cain .75 2.00
11 Giancarlo Stanton 1.00 2.50
12 Troy Tulowitzki 1.00 2.50
13 Michael Bourn .60 1.50
14 Dustin Pedroia .75 2.00
15 Brian McCann .75 2.00
16 Adam Jones .75 2.00
17 Stephen Strasburg 1.00 2.50
18 Michael Young .60 1.50
19 Brandon Phillips .60 1.50
20 Jose Bautista .75 2.00

2013 Panini Prizm Fearless Prizms
*PRIZMS: .75X TO 2X BASIC

2013 Panini Prizm Fearless Prizms Blue
*BLUE: 1X TO 2.5X BASIC

2013 Panini Prizm Fearless Prizms Blue Pulsar
*BLUE PULSAR: 1.2X TO 3X BASIC

2013 Panini Prizm Fearless Prizms Green
*GREEN: 1X TO 2.5X BASIC

2013 Panini Prizm Fearless Prizms Red
*RED: 1X TO 2.5X BASIC

2013 Panini Prizm Fearless Prizms Red Pulsar
*RED PULSAR: 1.2X TO 3X BASIC

2013 Panini Prizm Rookie Challengers
1 Yasiel Puig 2.00 5.00
2 Dylan Bundy 1.25 3.00
3 Evan Gattis 1.00 2.50
4 Jurickson Profar .60 1.50
5 Darin Ruf 1.00 2.50
6 Manny Machado 3.00 8.00
7 Tyler Skaggs .75 2.00
8 Shelby Miller 1.25 3.00
9 Gerrit Cole 3.00 8.00
10 Jake Odorizzi .60 1.50
11 Anthony Rendon 2.50 6.00
12 Michael Wacha .60 1.50
13 Nick Franklin .60 1.50
14 Zack Wheeler 1.00 2.50
15 Jedd Gyorko .60 1.50
16 Kevin Gausman .75 2.00
17 Didi Gregorius 2.00 5.00
18 Hyun-Jin Ryu 1.25 3.00

2013 Panini Prizm Rookie Challengers Prizms
*PRIZMS: .75X TO 2X BASIC
1 Yasiel Puig 15.00 40.00

2013 Panini Prizm Rookie Challengers Prizms Blue
*BLUE: 1.2X TO 3X BASIC

2013 Panini Prizm Rookie Challengers Prizms Green
*GREEN: 1.2X TO 3X BASIC

2013 Panini Prizm Rookie Challengers Prizms Red
*RED: 1.2X TO 3X BASIC

2013 Panini Prizm Superstar Spotlight
1 Albert Pujols 1.25 3.00
2 Matt Cain .75 2.00
3 Andrew McCutchen 1.00 2.50
4 Ryan Braun .75 2.00
5 Justin Verlander 1.00 2.50
6 David Wright .75 2.00
7 Giancarlo Stanton 1.00 2.50
8 Clayton Kershaw 2.00 5.00
9 Stephen Strasburg 1.00 2.50
10 Matt Kemp .75 2.00
11 Robinson Cano .75 2.00
12 Joey Votto 1.00 2.50
13 Felix Hernandez .75 2.00
14 Miguel Cabrera 1.00 2.50
15 Joe Mauer .75 2.00

2013 Panini Prizm Superstar Spotlight Prizms
*PRIZMS: .75X TO 2X BASIC

2013 Panini Prizm Superstar Spotlight Prizms Blue
*BLUE: 1X TO 2.5X BASIC

2013 Panini Prizm Superstar Spotlight Prizms Blue Pulsar
*BLUE PULSAR: 1.2X TO 3X BASIC

2013 Panini Prizm Superstar Spotlight Prizms Green
*GREEN: 1X TO 2.5X BASIC

2013 Panini Prizm Superstar Spotlight Prizms Red
*RED: 1X TO 2.5X BASIC

2013 Panini Prizm Top Prospects
1 Carlos Correa 5.00 12.00
2 Nick Castellanos 1.50 4.00
3 Bubba Starling .60 1.50
4 Jameson Taillon .60 1.50
5 Oscar Taveras .60 1.50
6 Miguel Sano .60 1.50
7 Billy Hamilton .60 1.50
8 Addison Russell .75 2.00
9 Javier Baez 2.00 5.00
10 Taijuan Walker .60 1.50
11 Travis d'Arnaud .60 1.50
12 Francisco Lindor 3.00 8.00

2013 Panini Prizm Top Prospects Prizms
*PRIZMS: .75X TO 2X BASIC

2013 Panini Prizm Top Prospects Prizms Blue
*BLUE: 1.2X TO 3X BASIC

2013 Panini Prizm Top Prospects Prizms Green
*GREEN: 1.2X TO 3X BASIC

2013 Panini Prizm Top Prospects Prizms Red
*RED: 1.2X TO 3X BASIC

2013 Panini Prizm USA Baseball
1 Dustin Pedroia .75 2.00
2 Joe Mauer .75 2.00
3 Troy Tulowitzki 1.00 2.50
4 Stephen Strasburg 1.00 2.50
5 Matt Harvey .75 2.00
6 R.A. Dickey .75 2.00
7 Alex Gordon .75 2.00
8 David Price .75 2.00
9 Jered Weaver .75 2.00
10 Mike Trout 8.00 20.00

2013 Panini Prizm USA Baseball Prizms
*PRIZMS: .75X TO 2X BASIC

2013 Panini Prizm USA Baseball Prizms Signatures
STATED PRINT RUN 25 SER.#'d SETS
EXCHANGE DEADLINE 03/18/2015
1 Dustin Pedroia 30.00 60.00
3 Troy Tulowitzki 40.00 80.00
4 Stephen Strasburg 60.00 120.00
7 Alex Gordon 15.00 40.00
10 Mike Trout 100.00 200.00

2014 Panini Prizm
COMP.SET w/o SP's (200) 20.00 50.00
1 Stephen Strasburg .25 .60
2 Starling Marte .20 .50
3 Mike Trout 1.25 3.00
4 Shin-Soo Choo .20 .50
5 Miguel Cabrera .25 .60
6 Yoenis Cespedes .25 .60
7 Michael Wacha .20 .50
8 Michael Cuddyer .15 .40
9 Max Scherzer .25 .60
10 Matt Wieters .25 .60
11 Matt Moore .20 .50
12 Robinson Cano .20 .50
13 Miguel Montero .15 .40
14 Shane Victorino .20 .50
15 Salvador Perez .20 .50
16 Ryan Zimmerman .20 .50
17 Ryan Howard .20 .50
18 Ryan Braun .20 .50
19 Matt Kemp .20 .50
20 Matt Holliday .25 .60
21 Matt Harvey .20 .50
22 Matt Carpenter .25 .60
23 Mat Latos .20 .50
24 Zack Greinke .20 .50
25 Yunel Escobar .15 .40
26 Yu Darvish .25 .60
27 Hyun-Jin Ryu .20 .50
28 Yasiel Puig .25 .60
29 Yadier Molina .25 .60
30 Will Venable .15 .40
31 Troy Tulowitzki .25 .60
32 Kris Medlen .20 .50
33 Koji Uehara .15 .40
34 Justin Verlander .25 .60
35 Justin Upton .20 .50
36 Justin Ruggiano .15 .40
37 Victor Martinez .20 .50
38 Justin Masterson .15 .40
39 Jurickson Profar .20 .50
40 Felix Hernandez .20 .50
41 Everth Cabrera .15 .40
42 Alex Gordon .20 .50
43 Albert Pujols .30 .75
44 Manny Machado .25 .60
45 Adrian Beltre .25 .60
46 Adam Wainwright .20 .50
47 Wil Myers .15 .40
48 Adam Dunn .20 .50
49 A.J. Burnett .15 .40
50 Martin Prado .15 .40
51 Marlon Byrd .15 .40
52 Mark Trumbo .15 .40
53 Mark Teixeira .20 .50
54 Adrian Gonzalez .20 .50
55 Justin Morneau .20 .50
56 Adam Jones .20 .50
57 Matt Cain .20 .50
58 Torii Hunter .15 .40
59 Tim Lincecum .20 .50
60 Andrew McCutchen .25 .60
61 Andrelton Simmons .20 .50
62 Allen Craig .20 .50
63 Alfonso Soriano .20 .50
64 Alex Rios .20 .50
65 Evan Longoria .20 .50
66 Eric Hosmer .20 .50
67 Elvis Andrus .20 .50
68 Edwin Encarnacion .20 .50
69 Dustin Pedroia .25 .60
70 David Wright .20 .50
71 Derek Holland .15 .40
72 Chase Headley .15 .40
73 David Price .20 .50
74 David Ortiz .25 .60
75 Chase Utley .20 .50
76 Derek Jeter .60 1.50
77 CC Sabathia .20 .50
78 Carlos Santana .20 .50
79 Bryce Harper .40 1.00
80 Carlos Gomez .15 .40
81 Austin Jackson .15 .40
82 Carl Crawford .20 .50
83 C.J. Wilson .15 .40

84 Buster Posey .30 .75
85 Carlos Gonzalez .20 .50
86 Brian Dozier .20 .50
87 Brandon Phillips .15 .40
88 Billy Butler .15 .40
89 Ben Zobrist .20 .50
90 B.J. Upton .20 .50
91 Carlos Beltran .20 .50
92 Anthony Rizzo .40 1.00
93 Francisco Liriano .15 .40
94 Josh Hamilton .20 .50
95 Josh Donaldson .20 .50
96 Jose Reyes .20 .50
97 David DeJesus .15 .40
98 Jose Bautista .20 .50
99 Clayton Kershaw .50 1.25
100 Jorge De La Rosa .15 .40
101 Jordan Zimmerman .20 .50
102 Jon Lester .20 .50
103 Joey Votto .25 .60
104 Joe Mauer .20 .50
105 Jimmy Rollins .20 .50
106 Jim Johnson .15 .40
107 Jose Fernandez .25 .60
108 Curtis Granderson .20 .50
109 Craig Kimbrel .20 .50
110 Colby Rasmus .20 .50
111 Coco Crisp .15 .40
112 Cliff Lee .20 .50
113 Jose Altuve .20 .50
114 Chris Tillman .15 .40
115 Chris Sale .25 .60
116 Jay Bruce .20 .50
117 Chris Davis .15 .40
118 Ichiro Suzuki .40 1.00
119 Jedd Gyorko .15 .40
120 Jean Segura .20 .50
121 Chris Johnson .15 .40
122 Jason Kipnis .20 .50
123 Hanley Ramirez .20 .50
124 Mike Napoli .15 .40
125 Jarrod Parker .15 .40
126 Paul Goldschmidt .25 .60
127 James Shields .15 .40
128 Jacoby Ellsbury .20 .50
129 J.J. Hardy .15 .40
130 Chris Carter .15 .40
131 Hunter Pence .20 .50
132 Hisashi Iwakuma .20 .50
133 Hiroki Kuroda .15 .40
134 Jason Grilli .15 .40
135 Greg Holland .15 .40
136 Giancarlo Stanton .25 .60
137 Freddie Freeman .30 .75
138 Jered Weaver .20 .50
139 Prince Fielder .20 .50
140 Pedro Alvarez .15 .40
141 Paul Konerko .20 .50
142 R.A. Dickey .20 .50
143 Pablo Sandoval .20 .50
144 Nick Swisher .20 .50
145 Nate Schierholtz .15 .40
146 Mitch Moreland .15 .40
147 Starlin Castro .15 .40
148 Gerrit Cole .25 .60
149 Chris Archer .15 .40
150 Julio Teheran .20 .50
151 Rickey Henderson .25 .60
152 Reggie Jackson .20 .50
153 Mike Schmidt .40 1.00
154 Ryne Sandberg .50 1.25
155 Ken Griffey Jr. .50 1.25
156 Alan Trammell .20 .50
157 Tony Gwynn .25 .60
158 Eddie Murray .20 .50
159 Cal Ripken Jr. .75 2.00
160 Bill Mazeroski .20 .50
161 Mariano Rivera .30 .75
162 Frank Thomas .25 .60
163 Don Mattingly .50 1.25
164 Chipper Jones .25 .60
165 Jeff Bagwell .20 .50
166 George Brett .50 1.25
167 Pete Rose .50 1.25
168 Pedro Martinez .20 .50
169 Ozzie Smith .30 .75
170 Nolan Ryan .75 2.00
171 Chad Bettis RC .25 .60
172 Xander Bogaerts RC .75 2.00
173 Ethan Martin RC .25 .60
174 Tim Beckham RC .40 1.00
175 Reymond Fuentes RC .25 .60
176 Taijuan Walker RC .25 .60
177 J.R. Murphy RC .25 .60
178 Chris Owings RC .25 .60
179 James Paxton RC .40 1.00
180 Cameron Rupp RC .25 .60
181 Wilmer Flores RC .30 .75
182 Travis D'Arnaud RC .30 .75
183 Kolten Wong RC .30 .75
184 Michael Choice RC .25 .60
185 Masahiro Tanaka RC .75 2.00
186 Ehire Adrianza RC .25 .60
187 Jimmy Nelson RC .25 .60
188 Charlie Leesman RC .25 .60
189 Brian Flynn RC .25 .60
190 Matt Davidson RC .30 .75
191 Logan Watkins RC .25 .60
192 Ryan Goins RC .30 .75
193 Max Stassi RC .25 .60
194 Marcus Semien RC .25 .60
195 Andrew Lambo RC .25 .60
196 David Holmberg RC .25 .60
197 Matt Den Dekker RC .30 .75
198 Kevin Pillar RC .25 .60
199 Jose Abreu RC 2.00 5.00
200 Billy Hamilton RC .30 .75
201 Miguel Cabrera SP 2.00 5.00
202 Andrew McCutchen SP 2.00 5.00
203 Wil Myers SP 1.25 3.00
204 Jose Fernandez SP 2.00 5.00
205 Max Scherzer SP 2.00 5.00
206 Clayton Kershaw SP 4.00 10.00
207 David Ortiz SP 2.00 5.00
208 Mariano Rivera SP 2.50 6.00
209 Yadier Molina SP 2.00 5.00
210 Chris Davis SP 1.25 3.00

2014 Panini Prizm Prizms

*PRIZMS 1-170: 1.5X TO 4X BASIC
*PRIZMS 171-200: 1X TO 2.5X BASIC RC
*PRIZMS 201-210: .4X TO 1X BASIC SP

2014 Panini Prizm Prizms Blue 42

*BLUE 42 1-170: 8X TO 20X BASIC
*BLUE 42 171-200: 5X TO 12X BASIC RC
STATED PRINT RUN 42 SER.#'d SETS
3 Mike Trout 30.00 80.00
5 Miguel Cabrera 15.00 40.00
28 Yasiel Puig 30.00 80.00
76 Derek Jeter 30.00 80.00
155 Ken Griffey Jr. 25.00 60.00
169 Ozzie Smith 12.00 30.00
199 Jose Abreu 60.00 120.00

2014 Panini Prizm Prizms Blue Mojo

*BLUE MOJO 1-170: 5X TO 12X BASIC
*BLUE MOJO 171-200: 3X TO 8X BASIC RC
*BLUE MOJO 201-210: .6X TO 1.5X BASIC SP
STATED PRINT RUN 75 SER.#'d SETS
76 Derek Jeter 12.00 30.00
199 Jose Abreu 12.00 30.00

2014 Panini Prizm Prizms Camo

*CAMO 1-170: 5X TO 12X BASIC
*CAMO 171-200: 3X TO 8X BASIC RC
199 Jose Abreu 12.00 30.00

2014 Panini Prizm Prizms Orange Die Cut

*ORANGE 1-170: 6X TO 15X BASIC
*ORANGE 171-200: 4X TO 10X BASIC RC
STATED PRINT RUN 60 SER.#'d SETS
3 Mike Trout 25.00 60.00
5 Miguel Cabrera 12.00 30.00
28 Yasiel Puig 25.00 60.00
76 Derek Jeter 25.00 60.00
155 Ken Griffey Jr. 20.00 50.00
169 Ozzie Smith 10.00 25.00
170 Nolan Ryan 20.00 50.00
199 Jose Abreu 30.00 80.00

2014 Panini Prizm Prizms Purple

*PURPLE 1-170: 4X TO 10X BASIC
*PURPLE 171-200: 2.5X TO 6X BASIC RC
*PURPLE 201-210: .5X TO 1.2X BASIC SP
STATED PRINT RUN 99 SER.#'d SETS
76 Derek Jeter 10.00 25.00
199 Jose Abreu 25.00 60.00

2014 Panini Prizm Prizms Red

*RED 1-170: 10X TO 25X BASIC
*RED 171-200: 6X TO 15X BASIC RC
*RED 201-210: 1.2X TO 3X BASIC SP
STATED PRINT RUN 25 SER.#'d SETS
5 Miguel Cabrera 20.00 50.00
28 Yasiel Puig 40.00 100.00
76 Derek Jeter 40.00 100.00
155 Ken Griffey Jr. 30.00 80.00
169 Ozzie Smith 15.00 40.00
170 Nolan Ryan 30.00 80.00
199 Jose Abreu 75.00 200.00

2014 Panini Prizm Prizms Red White and Blue Pulsar

*RWB 1-170: 6X TO 15X BASIC
*RWB 171-200: 4X TO 10X BASIC RC
162 Frank Thomas 8.00 20.00
199 Jose Abreu 12.00 30.00

2014 Panini Prizm Autographs Prizms

EXCHANGE DEADLINE 11/21/2015
AB Archie Bradley 2.50 6.00
BY Byron Buxton 5.00 12.00
CF Clint Frazier 10.00 25.00
DN Daniel Nava 2.50 6.00
JA Jose Abreu 30.00 60.00
JG Jonathan Gray 3.00 8.00
JS Jean Segura 3.00 8.00
JT Jameson Taillon 3.00 8.00
KB Kris Bryant 50.00 120.00
MC Matt Carpenter 6.00 15.00
MN Mike Napoli 5.00 12.00
MO Mitch Moreland 2.50 6.00
MS Miguel Sano 3.00 8.00
NS Noah Syndergaard 6.00 15.00
OT Oscar Taveras 12.00 30.00
SM Starling Marte 6.00 15.00
SV Shane Victorino 6.00 15.00

2014 Panini Prizm Autographs Prizms Mojo

*MOJO: .6X TO 1.5X BASIC
STATED PRINT RUN 75 SER.#'d SETS
EXCHANGE DEADLINE 11/21/2015
BP Brandon Phillips 5.00 12.00
CB Craig Biggio 15.00 40.00
CD Chris Davis 12.00 30.00
CK Clayton Kershaw 25.00 60.00
CM Carlos Martinez 5.00 12.00
DO David Ortiz 20.00 50.00
DS Darryl Strawberry 12.00 30.00
EM Edgar Martinez 12.00 30.00
JB Jeff Bagwell 12.00 30.00
JD Josh Donaldson 10.00 25.00
JF Jose Fernandez 25.00 60.00
JO Jose Bautista 10.00 25.00
JP Jarrod Parker 4.00 10.00
MG Mark Grace 15.00 40.00
MM Manny Machado 20.00 50.00
MT Mike Trout/25 150.00 250.00
PK Paul Konerko 8.00 20.00
PO Paul O'Neill 10.00 25.00
PR Pete Rose 90.00 150.00
TG Tom Glavine 12.00 30.00
TR Mark Trumbo 4.00 10.00
YC Yoenis Cespedes 12.00 30.00

2014 Panini Prizm Autographs Prizms Purple

*PURPLE: .5X TO 1.2X BASIC
STATED PRINT RUN 99 SER.#'d SETS
EXCHANGE DEADLINE 11/21/2015
BP Brandon Phillips 4.00 10.00
DS Darryl Strawberry 10.00 25.00
EM Edgar Martinez 10.00 25.00
GS George Springer 20.00 50.00
JD Josh Donaldson 8.00 20.00
JF Jose Fernandez 20.00 50.00
JP Jarrod Parker 3.00 8.00
PK Paul Konerko 10.00 25.00
TG Tom Glavine 10.00 25.00
TR Mark Trumbo 3.00 8.00

2014 Panini Prizm Chasing the Hall

1 Derek Jeter 2.50 6.00
2 Ichiro Suzuki 1.50 4.00
3 Albert Pujols 1.25 3.00
4 Dustin Pedroia 1.00 2.50
5 Paul Konerko .75 2.00
6 David Ortiz 1.00 2.50
7 Prince Fielder .75 2.00
8 Robinson Cano .75 2.00
9 Adam Dunn .75 2.00
10 Miguel Cabrera 1.00 2.50
11 Adrian Beltre 1.00 2.50
12 Carlos Beltran .75 2.00
13 Roy Halladay .75 2.00
14 Todd Helton .75 2.00
15 Felix Hernandez .75 2.00
16 Joe Mauer .75 2.00
17 Justin Verlander 1.00 2.50
18 CC Sabathia .75 2.00
19 Joey Votto 1.00 2.50
20 David Wright .75 2.00

2014 Panini Prizm Chasing the Hall Prizms

*PRIZMS: .5X TO 1.2X BASIC

2014 Panini Prizm Chasing the Hall Prizms Blue Mojo

*BLUE MOJO: 1.2X TO 3X BASIC
STATED PRINT RUN 75 SER.#'d SETS

2014 Panini Prizm Chasing the Hall Prizms Purple

*PURPLE: 1X TO 2.5X BASIC
STATED PRINT RUN 99 SER.#'d SETS

2014 Panini Prizm Chasing the Hall Prizms Red

*RED: 2.5X TO 6X BASIC
STATED PRINT RUN 25 SER.#'d SETS
1 Derek Jeter 40.00 100.00

2014 Panini Prizm Diamond Dominance

1 Andrew McCutchen 1.00 2.50
2 Mike Trout 5.00 12.00
3 Miguel Cabrera 1.00 2.50
4 Yadier Molina 1.00 2.50
5 Evan Longoria .75 2.00
6 Joey Votto 1.00 2.50
7 Robinson Cano .75 2.00
8 Chris Davis .60 1.50
9 Paul Goldschmidt 1.00 2.50
10 Clayton Kershaw 2.00 5.00
11 Josh Donaldson .75 2.00
12 Carlos Gomez .60 1.50
13 Matt Carpenter 1.00 2.50
14 Max Scherzer 1.00 2.50
15 Manny Machado 1.00 2.50
16 Dustin Pedroia 1.00 2.50
17 David Wright .75 2.00
18 Felix Hernandez .75 2.00
19 Freddie Freeman 1.25 3.00
20 Wil Myers .60 1.50
21 Bryce Harper 1.50 4.00
22 Albert Pujols 1.25 3.00
23 Adrian Beltre 1.00 2.50
24 Buster Posey 1.25 3.00
25 Troy Tulowitzki 1.00 2.50
26 Pete Rose 2.00 5.00
27 Mike Piazza 1.00 2.50
28 George Brett 2.00 5.00
29 Ken Griffey Jr. 2.00 5.00
30 Cal Ripken Jr. 3.00 8.00

2014 Panini Prizm Diamond Dominance Prizms

*PRIZMS: .5X TO 1.2X BASIC

2014 Panini Prizm Diamond Dominance Prizms Blue Mojo

*BLUE MOJO: 1.2X TO 3X BASIC
STATED PRINT RUN 75 SER.#'d SETS

2014 Panini Prizm Diamond Dominance Prizms Purple

*PURPLE: 1X TO 2.5X BASIC
STATED PRINT RUN 99 SER.#'d SETS

2014 Panini Prizm Diamond Dominance Prizms Red

*RED: 2.5X TO 6X BASIC
STATED PRINT RUN 25 SER.#'d SETS

2014 Panini Prizm Fearless

1 Yasiel Puig 1.00 2.50
2 Buster Posey 1.25 3.00
3 Yadier Molina 1.00 2.50
4 Chris Davis .60 1.50
5 David Ortiz 1.00 2.50
6 Mike Trout 5.00 12.00
7 Andrew McCutchen 1.00 2.50
8 Michael Cuddyer .60 1.50
9 Adrian Beltre 1.00 2.50
10 Jason Kipnis .75 2.00
11 Xander Bogaerts 2.00 5.00
12 Edwin Encarnacion 1.00 2.50
13 Josh Donaldson .75 2.00
14 Jay Bruce .75 2.00
15 Bryce Harper 1.50 4.00
16 Paul Goldschmidt 1.00 2.50
17 Torii Hunter .60 1.50
18 Pedro Alvarez .60 1.50
19 Josh Hamilton .75 2.00
20 Hisashi Iwakuma .75 2.00
21 Cliff Lee .75 2.00
22 Yu Darvish 1.00 2.50
23 Jose Fernandez 1.00 2.50
24 David Price .75 2.00

2014 Panini Prizm Fearless Prizms

*PRIZMS: .5X TO 1.2X BASIC

2014 Panini Prizm Fearless Prizms Blue Mojo

*BLUE MOJO: 1.2X TO 3X BASIC
STATED PRINT RUN 75 SER.#'d SETS

2014 Panini Prizm Fearless Prizms Purple

*PURPLE: 1X TO 2.5X BASIC
STATED PRINT RUN 99 SER.#'d SETS

2014 Panini Prizm Fearless Prizms Red

*RED: 2.5X TO 6X BASIC
STATED PRINT RUN 25 SER.#'d SETS

2014 Panini Prizm Gold Leather Die Cut

1 Yadier Molina 1.00 2.50
2 Paul Goldschmidt 1.00 2.50
3 Brandon Phillips .60 1.50
4 Carlos Gonzalez .75 2.00
5 Carlos Gomez .60 1.50
6 Adam Wainwright .75 2.00
7 R.A. Dickey .75 2.00
8 Shane Victorino .75 2.00
9 Adam Jones .75 2.00
10 Alex Gordon .75 2.00
11 Eric Hosmer .75 2.00
12 Dustin Pedroia 1.00 2.50
13 Manny Machado 1.00 2.50
14 J.J. Hardy .60 1.50
15 Andrelton Simmons .60 1.50

2014 Panini Prizm Gold Leather Die Cut Prizms

*PRIZMS: .5X TO 1.2X BASIC

2014 Panini Prizm Gold Leather Die Cut Prizms Blue Mojo

*BLUE MOJO: 1.2X TO 3X BASIC
STATED PRINT RUN 75 SER.#'d SETS

2014 Panini Prizm Gold Leather Die Cut Prizms Purple

*PURPLE: 1X TO 2.5X BASIC
STATED PRINT RUN 99 SER.#'d SETS

2014 Panini Prizm Gold Leather Die Cut Prizms Red

*RED: 2.5X TO 6X BASIC
STATED PRINT RUN 25 SER.#'d SETS

2014 Panini Prizm Intuition

1 Clayton Kershaw 2.00 5.00
2 Max Scherzer 1.00 2.50
3 Yu Darvish 1.00 2.50
4 Jose Fernandez 1.00 2.50
5 Chris Sale 1.00 2.50
6 Hyun-Jin Ryu .75 2.00
7 Kris Medlen .75 2.00
8 Justin Verlander 1.00 2.50
9 Matt Moore .75 2.00
10 R.A. Dickey .75 2.00
11 Craig Kimbrel .75 2.00
12 Felix Hernandez .75 2.00
13 Stephen Strasburg 1.00 2.50
14 Tim Lincecum .75 2.00
15 Bartolo Colon .60 1.50
16 Matt Harvey .75 2.00
17 Zack Greinke 1.00 2.50
18 Adam Wainwright .75 2.00
19 Shelby Miller .75 2.00
20 Jordan Zimmerman .75 2.00

2014 Panini Prizm Intuition Prizms

*PRIZMS: .5X TO 1.2X BASIC

2014 Panini Prizm Intuition Prizms Blue Mojo

*BLUE MOJO: 1.2X TO 3X BASIC
STATED PRINT RUN 75 SER.#'d SETS

2014 Panini Prizm Intuition Prizms Purple

*PURPLE: 1X TO 2.5X BASIC
STATED PRINT RUN 99 SER.#'d SETS

2014 Panini Prizm Intuition Prizms Red

*RED: 2.5X TO 6X BASIC
STATED PRINT RUN 25 SER.#'d SETS

2014 Panini Prizm Next Era

1 George Springer 2.50 6.00
2 Kris Bryant 4.00 10.00
3 Clint Frazier 2.50 6.00
4 Byron Buxton .75 2.00
5 Miguel Sano .75 2.00
6 Carlos Correa 3.00 8.00
7 Oscar Taveras .75 2.00
8 Archie Bradley .60 1.50
9 Noah Syndergaard .75 2.00
10 Gregory Polanco 1.00 2.50
11 Gosuke Katoh 1.00 2.50
12 Kyle Zimmer .60 1.50
13 Javier Baez 2.50 6.00
14 Jameson Taillon .75 2.00
15 Mark Appel .75 2.00
16 Jose Abreu 5.00 12.00
17 Robert Stephenson .60 1.50
18 Addison Russell 1.00 2.50
19 Masahiro Tanaka 5.00 12.00
20 Fransisco Lindor 4.00 10.00

2014 Panini Prizm Next Era Prizms

*PRIZM: .5X TO 1.2X BASIC

2014 Panini Prizm Next Era Prizms Blue Mojo

*BLUE MOJO: 1.2X TO 3X BASIC
STATED PRINT RUN 75 SER.#'d SETS

2014 Panini Prizm Next Era Prizms Purple

*PURPLE: 1X TO 2.5X BASIC
STATED PRINT RUN 99 SER.#'d SETS

2014 Panini Prizm Next Era Prizms Red

*RED: 2.5X TO 6X BASIC
STATED PRINT RUN 25 SER.#'d SETS
2 Kris Bryant 25.00 60.00
16 Jose Abreu 30.00 80.00

2014 Panini Prizm Rookie Autographs Prizms

EXCHANGE DEADLINE 11/21/2015
BF Brian Flynn 2.50 6.00
BH Billy Hamilton 3.00 8.00
CB Chad Bettis 2.50 6.00
CL Charlie Leesman 2.50 6.00
CO Chris Owings 2.50 6.00
CR Cameron Rupp 2.50 6.00
DH David Hale 2.50 6.00
EA Ehire Adrianza 2.50 6.00
EM Ethan Martin 2.50 6.00
ER Enny Romero 2.50 6.00
JN Jimmy Nelson 2.50 6.00
JP James Paxton 4.00 10.00
JR J.R. Murphy 3.00 8.00
JS Jonathan Schoop 2.50 6.00
KW Kolten Wong 5.00 12.00
MA Marcus Semien 2.50 6.00
MC Michael Choice 2.50 6.00
MD Matt Davidson 3.00 8.00
MS Max Stassi 2.50 6.00
RF Reymond Fuentes 2.50 6.00
TB Tim Beckham 4.00 10.00
TD Travis D'Arnaud 3.00 8.00
TR Tanner Roark 6.00 15.00
TW Taijuan Walker 5.00 12.00
WF Wilmer Flores 3.00 8.00
XB Xander Bogaerts 15.00 40.00
YV Yordano Ventura 12.00 30.00

2014 Panini Prizm Rookie Autographs Prizms Mojo

*MOJO: .6X TO 1.5X BASIC
STATED PRINT RUN 75 SER.#'d SETS
EXCHANGE DEADLINE 11/21/2015

2014 Panini Prizm Rookie Autographs Prizms Purple

*PURPLE: .5X TO 1.2X BASIC
STATED PRINT RUN 99 SER.#'d SETS
EXCHANGE DEADLINE 11/21/2015

2014 Panini Prizm Rookie Reign

1 Travis D'Arnaud .75 2.00
2 Kolten Wong .75 2.00
3 Nick Castellanos 2.00 5.00
4 Billy Hamilton .75 2.00
5 Chris Owings .60 1.50
6 Xander Bogaerts 2.00 5.00
7 Matt Davidson .75 2.00
8 Taijuan Walker .60 1.50
9 Michael Choice .60 1.50
10 Reymond Fuentes .60 1.50
11 J.R. Murphy .60 1.50
12 Cameron Rupp .60 1.50
13 Masahiro Tanaka 5.00 12.00
14 Yordano Ventura .75 2.00
15 James Paxton 1.00 2.50
16 Wilmer Flores .75 2.00
17 Tim Beckham 1.00 2.50
18 Kris Johnson .60 1.50
19 Jose Abreu 5.00 12.00
20 Logan Watkins .60 1.50

2014 Panini Prizm Rookie Reign Prizms

*PRIZM: .5X TO 1.2X BASIC

2014 Panini Prizm Rookie Reign Prizms Blue Mojo

*BLUE MOJO: 1.2X TO 3X BASIC
STATED PRINT RUN 75 SER.#'d SETS

2014 Panini Prizm Rookie Reign Prizms Purple

*PURPLE: 1X TO 2.5X BASIC
STATED PRINT RUN 99 SER.#'d SETS

2014 Panini Prizm Rookie Reign Prizms Red

*RED: 2.5X TO 6X BASIC
STATED PRINT RUN 25 SER.#'d SETS
19 Jose Abreu 40.00 100.00

2014 Panini Prizm Signature Distinctions Die Cut Prizms Purple

STATED PRINT RUN 99 SER.#'d SETS
EXCHANGE DEADLINE 11/21/2015
4 Bo Jackson 30.00 80.00
6 Nolan Ryan 50.00 120.00

2014 Panini Prizm Signature Distinctions Die Cut Prizms Mojo

STATED PRINT RUN 25 SER.#'d SETS
EXCHANGE DEADLINE 11/21/2015
1 George Brett 75.00 200.00
2 Ken Griffey Jr. 125.00 250.00
3 Cal Ripken Jr. 100.00 200.00
4 Bo Jackson 50.00 120.00
5 Frank Thomas 150.00 250.00
6 Nolan Ryan 100.00 200.00
7 Pedro Martinez 50.00 120.00
8 Mariano Rivera 125.00 250.00
9 Greg Maddux 100.00 200.00
10 Chipper Jones 100.00 200.00

2014 Panini Prizm Signatures

EXCHANGE DEADLINE 11/21/2015
1 Rusty Greer 2.50 6.00
2 Jason Grilli 2.50 6.00
3 Brandon Phillips 2.50 6.00
4 Steve Finley 2.50 6.00
5 Ike Davis 2.50 6.00
6 Archie Bradley 2.50 6.00
7 Glen Perkins 2.50 6.00
8 Zach McAllister 2.50 6.00
9 Rick Monday 2.50 6.00
10 Kevin Seitzer 2.50 6.00
11 Kevin Millar 2.50 6.00
12 Steve Sax 2.50 6.00
13 Lee Smith 6.00 15.00
14 Alex Avila 3.00 8.00
15 Adeiny Hechavarria 2.50 6.00
16 Alex Wood 6.00 15.00
17 Scott Diamond 2.50 6.00
18 Rick Dempsey 2.50 6.00
19 Dexter Fowler 5.00 12.00
20 Ron Darling 4.00 10.00
21 Dwayne Murphy 2.50 6.00
22 Lee Mazzilli 2.50 6.00
23 Ron Gant 2.50 6.00
24 Fred Lynn 4.00 10.00
25 Allen Craig 3.00 8.00
27 Shawn Green 2.50 6.00
28 Logan Morrison 2.50 6.00
29 Jose Altuve 20.00 50.00
30 Jon Jay 2.50 6.00
31 Wei-Yin Chen 15.00 40.00
32 Yovani Gallardo 2.50 6.00
33 Evan Longoria 6.00 15.00
34 Troy Tulowitzki 4.00 10.00
35 Stephen Strasburg 15.00 40.00
36 Dave Stieb 4.00 10.00
37 Evan Gattis 2.50 6.00
38 Tony Pena 2.50 6.00
39 Chris Perez 2.50 6.00
41 Chad Billingsley 3.00 8.00
42 Adam Eaton 2.50 6.00
43 Darin Ruf 3.00 8.00
44 Zoilo Almonte 3.00 8.00
45 Elvis Andrus 3.00 8.00
46 Dave Righetti 4.00 10.00
47 Ellis Burks 2.50 6.00
50 Frank White 2.50 6.00

2014 Panini Prizm Top of the Order

1 Shin-Soo Choo 1.00 2.50
2 Matt Carpenter 1.25 3.00
3 Dexter Fowler 1.00 2.50
4 Norichika Aoki .75 2.00
5 Carl Crawford 1.00 2.50
6 Jacoby Ellsbury 1.00 2.50
7 David DeJesus .75 2.00
8 Jose Reyes 1.00 2.50
9 Mike Trout 6.00 15.00
10 Derek Jeter 3.00 8.00
11 Austin Jackson .75 2.00
12 Alex Gordon 1.00 2.50
13 Coco Crisp .75 2.00
14 Jean Segura 1.00 2.50
15 Nick Swisher 1.00 2.50
16 Carlos Beltran 1.00 2.50
17 Shane Victorino 1.00 2.50
18 Starling Marte 1.00 2.50
19 Jose Bautista 1.00 2.50
20 Manny Machado 1.25 3.00

2014 Panini Prizm Top of the Order Prizms

*PRIZMS: .5X TO 1.2X BASIC

2014 Panini Prizm Top of the Order Prizms Blue Mojo

*BLUE MOJO: 1X TO 2.5X BASIC
STATED PRINT RUN 75 SER.#'d SETS
10 Derek Jeter 12.00 30.00

2014 Panini Prizm Top of the Order Prizms Purple

*PURPLE: .75X TO 2X BASIC
STATED PRINT RUN 99 SER.#'d SETS

2014 Panini Prizm Top of the Order Prizms Red

*RED: 2X TO 5X BASIC
STATED PRINT RUN 25 SER.#'d SETS
10 Derek Jeter 40.00 100.00

2014 Panini Prizm USA Baseball

1 Max Scherzer .75 2.00
2 Manny Machado .75 2.00
3 Eric Hosmer .60 1.50
4 Evan Longoria .60 1.50
5 Dustin Pedroia .75 2.00
6 Pedro Alvarez .50 1.25
7 Michael Wacha .60 1.50
8 Paul Konerko .60 1.50
9 Clayton Kershaw 1.50 4.00
10 Buster Posey 1.00 2.50

2014 Panini Prizm USA Baseball Prizms

*PRIZMS: .5X TO 1.2X BASIC

2014 Panini Prizm USA Baseball Prizms Blue Mojo

*BLUE MOJO: 1.2X TO 3X BASIC
STATED PRINT RUN 75 SER.#'d SETS

2014 Panini Prizm USA Baseball Autographs Prizms

EXCHANGE DEADLINE 11/21/2015
1 Max Scherzer 15.00 40.00
2 Manny Machado 15.00 40.00
3 Eric Hosmer 20.00 50.00
4 Evan Longoria 20.00 50.00
5 Dustin Pedroia 20.00 50.00
6 Pedro Alvarez EXCH 15.00 40.00
7 Michael Wacha 30.00 60.00
9 Clayton Kershaw 30.00 80.00

2015 Panini Prizm

COMPLETE SET (200) 20.00 50.00
1 Buster Posey .30 .75
2 Hunter Pence .20 .50
3 Madison Bumgarner .20 .50
4 Tim Lincecum .20 .50
5 Brandon Belt .20 .50
6 Michael Morse .15 .40
7 Tim Hudson .20 .50
8 Lorenzo Cain .15 .40
9 Eric Hosmer .20 .50
10 Greg Holland .15 .40
11 Alex Gordon .20 .50
12 Yordano Ventura .20 .50
13 Salvador Perez .20 .50
14 Mike Moustakas .20 .50
15 Adam Eaton .15 .40
16 Adam Jones .20 .50
17 Adam Wainwright .20 .50
18 Adrian Beltre .25 .60
19 Adrian Gonzalez .20 .50
20 Albert Pujols .30 .75
21 Alex Cobb .15 .40
22 Alex Wood .15 .40
23 Alexei Ramirez .20 .50
24 Andrew Cashner .15 .40
25 Andrew McCutchen .25 .60
26 Anthony Rendon .25 .60
27 Anthony Rizzo .40 1.00
28 Arismendy Alcantara .15 .40
29 Aroldis Chapman .25 .60
30 Melvin Upton Jr. .20 .50
31 Bartolo Colon .15 .40
32 Ben Zobrist .20 .50
33 Billy Butler .15 .40
34 Billy Hamilton .20 .50
35 Brett Gardner .20 .50
36 Brian Dozier .20 .50
37 Bryce Harper .40 1.00
38 Carlos Gomez .15 .40
39 Carlos Santana .20 .50
40 Charlie Blackmon .25 .60
41 Chase Utley .20 .50
42 Chris Carter .15 .40
43 Chris Davis .15 .40
44 Chris Sale .25 .60
45 Chris Tillman .15 .40
46 Clayton Kershaw .50 1.25
47 Cliff Lee .20 .50
48 Cole Hamels .20 .50
49 Corey Dickerson .15 .40
50 Corey Kluber .20 .50
51 Dallas Keuchel .20 .50
52 Danny Santana .15 .40
53 David Ortiz .25 .60
54 David Price .20 .50
55 David Robertson .20 .50
56 David Wright .20 .50
57 Dee Gordon .15 .40
58 Devin Mesoraco .15 .40
59 Didi Gregorius .20 .50
60 Doug Fister .15 .40
61 Dustin Pedroia .25 .60
62 Edwin Encarnacion .25 .60
63 Evan Gattis .15 .40
64 Evan Longoria .20 .50
65 Everth Cabrera .15 .40
66 Felix Hernandez .20 .50

67 Francisco Rodriguez .20 .50
68 Freddie Freeman .30 .75
69 George Springer .20 .50
70 Gerrit Cole .25 .60
71 Giancarlo Stanton .25 .60
72 Gregory Polanco .20 .50
73 Hanley Ramirez .20 .50
74 Henderson Alvarez .15 .40
75 Hisashi Iwakuma .20 .50
76 Hyun-Jin Ryu .20 .50
77 Ichiro Suzuki .30 .75
78 Jacob deGrom .25 .60
79 Jacoby Ellsbury .20 .50
80 Jake Arrieta .20 .50
81 James Loney .15 .40
82 Jason Heyward .20 .50
83 Jered Weaver .20 .50
84 Jimmy Rollins .20 .50
85 Joe Mauer .20 .50
86 Joey Votto .25 .60
87 John Lackey .20 .50
88 Johnny Cueto .20 .50
89 Jon Lester .20 .50
90 Jonathan Lucroy .20 .50
91 Jordan Zimmermann .20 .50
92 Jose Abreu .25 .60
93 Jose Altuve .20 .50
94 Jose Bautista .20 .50
95 Jose Fernandez .25 .60
96 Jose Reyes .20 .50
97 Josh Donaldson .20 .50
98 Julio Teheran .20 .50
99 Junior Lake .15 .40
100 Justin Morneau .20 .50
101 Justin Upton .20 .50
102 Justin Verlander .25 .60
103 Kevin Kiermaier .20 .50
104 Kolten Wong .20 .50
105 Kyle Seager .15 .40
106 Manny Machado .25 .60
107 Marcell Ozuna .25 .60
108 Mark Trumbo .15 .40
109 Masahiro Tanaka .20 .50
110 Matt Adams .15 .40
111 Matt Carpenter .25 .60
112 Matt Harvey .20 .50
113 Matt Holliday .25 .60
114 Matt Kemp .20 .50
115 Matt Shoemaker .20 .50
116 Max Scherzer .25 .60
117 Melky Cabrera .15 .40
118 Michael Brantley .20 .50
119 Miguel Cabrera .25 .60
120 Mike Trout 1.25 3.00
121 Mike Zunino .15 .40
122 Mookie Betts .40 1.00
123 Neil Walker .20 .50
124 Nelson Cruz .25 .60
125 Nolan Arenado .30 .75
126 Pablo Sandoval .20 .50
127 Patrick Corbin .20 .50
128 Paul Goldschmidt .25 .60
129 Phil Hughes .15 .40
130 Prince Fielder .20 .50
131 R.A. Dickey .20 .50
132 Robinson Cano .20 .50
133 Ryan Braun .20 .50
134 Ryan Howard .20 .50
135 Scott Kazmir .15 .40
136 Shelby Miller .20 .50
137 Shin-Soo Choo .20 .50
138 Sonny Gray .20 .50
139 Starlin Castro .15 .40
140 Starling Marte .20 .50
141 Stephen Strasburg .25 .60
142 Todd Frazier .20 .50
143 Troy Tulowitzki .25 .60
144 Victor Martinez .20 .50
145 Wei-Yin Chen .15 .40
146 Wil Myers .15 .40
147 Xander Bogaerts .25 .60
148 Yadier Molina .25 .60
149 Yan Gomes .15 .40
150 Yasiel Puig .25 .60
151 Yoenis Cespedes .25 .60
152 Yu Darvish .25 .60
153 Zack Greinke .20 .50
154 Ken Griffey Jr. .50 1.25
155 Cal Ripken .75 2.00
156 Pedro Martinez .20 .50
157 Randy Johnson .25 .60
158 Craig Biggio .20 .50
159 Rickey Henderson .25 .60
160 Mike Piazza .25 .60
161 Mark McGwire .40 1.00
162 Frank Thomas .25 .60
163 Kirby Puckett .25 .60
164 Mariano Rivera .30 .75
165 George Brett .50 1.25
166 Ryne Sandberg .50 1.25
167 Barry Bonds .40 1.00
168 Tony Gwynn .25 .60
169 Brandon Finnegan RC .25 .60
170 Rusney Castillo RC .30 .75
171 Dalton Pompey RC .30 .75
172 Javier Baez RC 2.00 5.00
173 Kennys Vargas RC .25 .60
174 Joc Pederson RC .50 1.25
175 Jorge Soler RC .40 1.00
176 Michael Taylor RC .25 .60
177 Mike Foltynewicz RC .25 .60
178 Maikel Franco RC .30 .75
179 Yorman Rodriguez RC .25 .60
180 Christian Walker RC .50 1.25
181 Jake Lamb RC .40 1.00
182 Rymer Liriano RC .25 .60
183 Daniel Norris RC .25 .60
184 Andy Wilkins RC .25 .60
185 Anthony Ranaudo RC .25 .60
186 Buck Farmer RC .25 .60
187 Cory Spangenberg RC .25 .60
188 Dilson Herrera RC .30 .75
189 Edwin Escobar RC .25 .60
190 Gary Brown RC .25 .60
191 James McCann RC .40 1.00
192 Kendall Graveman RC .25 .60
193 Lane Adams RC .25 .60
194 Matt Barnes RC .25 .60
195 Matt Szczur RC .30 .75
196 Steven Moya RC .30 .75
197 Terrance Gore RC .25 .60
198 Trevor May RC .25 .60
199 R.J. Alvarez RC .25 .60
200 Ryan Rua RC .25 .60

2015 Panini Prizm Prizms

*PRIZMS: 1.5X TO 4X BASIC
*PRIZMS RC: 1X TO 2.5X BASIC RC
RANDOM INSERTS IN PACKS

2015 Panini Prizm Prizms Black and White Checker

*BW CHECK: 3X TO 8X BASIC
*BW CHECK RC: 2X TO 5X BASIC
RANDOM INSERTS IN PACKS
STATED PRINT RUN 149 SER.#'d SETS
77 Ichiro Suzuki 4.00 10.00
120 Mike Trout 10.00 25.00
154 Ken Griffey Jr. 4.00 10.00
162 Frank Thomas 5.00 12.00
167 Barry Bonds 10.00 25.00
174 Joc Pederson 4.00 10.00

2015 Panini Prizm Prizms Blue

*BLUE: 4X TO 10X BASIC
*BLUE RC: 2.5X TO 6X BASIC
RANDOM INSERTS IN PACKS
STATED PRINT RUN 75 SER.#'d SETS
77 Ichiro Suzuki 5.00 12.00
120 Mike Trout 12.00 30.00
154 Ken Griffey Jr. 5.00 12.00
162 Frank Thomas 6.00 15.00
167 Barry Bonds 12.00 30.00
174 Joc Pederson 5.00 12.00

2015 Panini Prizm Prizms Blue Baseball

*BLUE BSBLL: 2.5X TO 6X BASIC
*BLUE BSBLL RC: 1.5X TO 4X BASIC RC
RANDOM INSERTS IN PACKS

2015 Panini Prizm Prizms Camo

*CAMO: 3X TO 8X BASIC
*CAMO RC: 2X TO 5X BASIC
RANDOM INSERTS IN PACKS
STATED PRINT RUN 199 SER.#'d SETS
77 Ichiro Suzuki 4.00 10.00
120 Mike Trout 10.00 25.00
154 Ken Griffey Jr. 4.00 10.00
162 Frank Thomas 5.00 12.00
167 Barry Bonds 10.00 25.00
174 Joc Pederson 4.00 10.00

2015 Panini Prizm Prizms Jackie Robinson

*ROBINSON: 6X TO 15X BASIC
*ROBINSON RC: 4X TO 10X BASIC
RANDOM INSERTS IN PACKS
STATED PRINT RUN 42 SER.#'d SETS
77 Ichiro Suzuki 8.00 20.00
120 Mike Trout 20.00 50.00
154 Ken Griffey Jr. 8.00 20.00
162 Frank Thomas 10.00 25.00
167 Barry Bonds 20.00 50.00

2015 Panini Prizm Prizms Orange

*ORANGE: 5X TO 12X BASIC
*ORANGE RC: 3X TO 8X BASIC
RANDOM INSERTS IN PACKS
STATED PRINT RUN 60 SER.#'d SETS
77 Ichiro Suzuki 6.00 15.00
120 Mike Trout 15.00 40.00
154 Ken Griffey Jr. 6.00 15.00
162 Frank Thomas 8.00 20.00
167 Barry Bonds 15.00 40.00
174 Joc Pederson 6.00 15.00

2015 Panini Prizm Prizms Purple Flash

*PRPLE FLSH: 4X TO 10X BASIC
*PRPLE FLSH RC: 2.5X TO 6X BASIC
RANDOM INSERTS IN PACKS
STATED PRINT RUN 99 SER.#'d SETS
77 Ichiro Suzuki 5.00 121.00
120 Mike Trout 12.00 30.00
154 Ken Griffey Jr. 5.00 12.00
162 Frank Thomas 6.00 15.00
167 Barry Bonds 12.00 30.00
174 Joc Pederson 5.00 12.00

2015 Panini Prizm Prizms Red Baseball

*RED BSBLL: 2.5X TO 6X BASIC
*RED BSBLL RC: 1.5X TO 4X BASIC RC
RANDOM INSERTS IN PACKS

2015 Panini Prizm Prizms Red Power

*RED POWER: 4X TO 10X BASIC
*RED POWER RC: 2.5X TO 6X BASIC
RANDOM INSERTS IN PACKS
STATED PRINT RUN 125 SER.#'d SETS
77 Ichiro Suzuki 5.00 12.00
120 Mike Trout 12.00 30.00
154 Ken Griffey Jr. 5.00 12.00
162 Frank Thomas 6.00 15.00
167 Barry Bonds 12.00 30.00
174 Joc Pederson 5.00 12.00

2015 Panini Prizm Prizms Red White and Blue Mojo

*RWB MOJO: 2.5X TO 6X BASIC
*RWB MOJO RC: 1.5X TO 4X BASIC RC
RANDOM INSERTS IN PACKS

2015 Panini Prizm Prizms Tie Dyed

*TIE DYE: 6X TO 15X BASIC
*TIE DYE RC: 4X TO 10X BASIC
RANDOM INSERTS IN PACKS
STATED PRINT RUN 50 SER.#'d SETS
77 Ichiro Suzuki 8.00 20.00
120 Mike Trout 20.00 50.00
162 Frank Thomas 10.00 25.00
167 Barry Bonds 10.00 25.00
174 Joc Pederson 8.00 20.00

2015 Panini Prizm Autograph Prizms

RANDOM INSERTS IN PACKS
3 Carlos Gomez 3.00 8.00
9 Wei-Chung Wang 3.00 8.00
11 Tommy La Stella 3.00 8.00
12 Matt Shoemaker 4.00 10.00
13 Kolten Wong 4.00 10.00
18 Matt den Dekker 3.00 8.00
20 Norichika Aoki 3.00 8.00
21 Fernando Rodney 3.00 8.00
22 Jedd Gyorko 3.00 8.00
27 Tim Raines 4.00 10.00
28 Aaron Judge 100.00 250.00
29 Luis Severino 8.00 20.00
30 Corey Seager 15.00 40.00
31 Addison Russell 10.00 25.00
32 Miguel Sano 5.00 12.00
35 Kris Bryant 75.00 150.00
37 Yasmany Tomas 4.00 10.00
38 Brandon Finnegan 3.00 8.00
39 Rusney Castillo 4.00 10.00
40 Dalton Pompey 4.00 10.00
41 Javier Baez 12.00 30.00
42 Kennys Vargas 3.00 8.00
43 Joc Pederson 4.00 10.00
44 Jorge Soler 8.00 20.00
45 Michael Taylor 3.00 8.00
46 Mike Foltynewicz 3.00 8.00
47 Maikel Franco 4.00 10.00
48 Yorman Rodriguez 3.00 8.00
49 Christian Walker 6.00 15.00
50 Jake Lamb 5.00 12.00
51 Rymer Liriano 3.00 8.00
52 Daniel Norris 3.00 8.00
53 Andy Wilkins 3.00 8.00
54 Anthony Ranaudo 3.00 8.00
55 Buck Farmer 3.00 8.00
56 Cory Spangenberg 3.00 8.00
57 Dilson Herrera 4.00 10.00
58 Edwin Escobar 3.00 8.00
60 James McCann 5.00 12.00
61 Kendall Graveman 3.00 8.00
63 Matt Barnes 3.00 8.00
64 Matt Szczur 4.00 10.00
65 Steven Moya 4.00 10.00
66 Terrance Gore 3.00 8.00
67 Trevor May 3.00 8.00
68 R.J. Alvarez 3.00 8.00
69 Ryan Rua 3.00 8.00
70 Matt Clark 3.00 8.00

2015 Panini Prizm Autograph Prizms Blue

*BLUE p/r 75: .5X TO 1.2X BASIC
*BLUE p/r 20-49: .6X TO 1.5X BASIC
RANDOM INSERTS IN PACKS
PRINT RUNS B/WN 20-75 COPIES PER
1 Alex Gordon/25 12.00 30.00
2 Gregory Polanco/75 5.00 12.00
4 Anthony Rizzo/25 15.00 40.00
5 Jose Fernandez/25 25.00 60.00
6 Jacob deGrom/75 12.00 30.00
10 Matt Adams/75 3.00 8.00
14 Xander Bogaerts/49 12.00 30.00
15 Chris Sale/49 15.00 40.00
16 Felix Hernandez/20 12.00 30.00
19 Corey Kluber/75 10.00 25.00
23 Raul Ibanez/49 6.00 15.00
24 Starling Marte/75 8.00 20.00
25 Jim Rice/25 6.00 15.00
26 Andy Pettitte/20 20.00 50.00
34 Byron Buxton/75 6.00 15.00
36 Francisco Lindor/75 15.00 40.00

2015 Panini Prizm Autograph Prizms Purple Flash

*PURPLE p/r 75-99: .5X TO 1.2X BASIC
*PURPLE p/r 25-49: .6X TO 1.5X BASIC
RANDOM INSERTS IN PACKS
PRINT RUNS B/WN 25-99 COPIES PER
1 Alex Gordon/49 12.00 30.00
2 Gregory Polanco/99 5.00 12.00
4 Anthony Rizzo/49 15.00 40.00
5 Jose Fernandez/49 25.00 60.00
6 Jacob deGrom/99 12.00 30.00
10 Matt Adams/99 3.00 8.00
14 Xander Bogaerts/75 10.00 25.00
16 Felix Hernandez/25 12.00 30.00
19 Corey Kluber/99 10.00 25.00
23 Raul Ibanez/75 5.00 12.00
24 Starling Marte/99 8.00 20.00
25 Jim Rice/49 6.00 15.00
26 Andy Pettitte/25 20.00 50.00
34 Byron Buxton/99 6.00 15.00
36 Francisco Lindor/99 15.00 40.00

2015 Panini Prizm Autograph Prizms Red Power

*PURPLE p/r 75-125: .5X TO 1.2X BASIC
*PURPLE p/r 49: .6X TO 1.5X BASIC
RANDOM INSERTS IN PACKS
PRINT RUNS B/WN 49-125 COPIES PER
1 Alex Gordon/75 10.00 25.00
2 Gregory Polanco/125 5.00 12.00
14 Xander Bogaerts/99 10.00 25.00
16 Felix Hernandez/49 12.00 30.00
17 Hisashi Iwakuma/125 6.00 15.00
19 Corey Kluber/125 10.00 25.00
24 Starling Marte/125 8.00 20.00
25 Jim Rice/75 5.00 12.00
26 Andy Pettitte/49 20.00 50.00
34 Byron Buxton/125 6.00 15.00
36 Francisco Lindor/125 15.00 40.00

2015 Panini Prizm Autograph Prizms Tie Dyed

*PURPLE p/r 25-50: .6X TO 1.5X BASIC
RANDOM INSERTS IN PACKS
PRINT RUNS B/WN 15-50 COPIES PER
NO PRICING ON QTY 15
2 Gregory Polanco/50 6.00 15.00
6 Jacob deGrom/50 15.00 40.00
10 Matt Adams/50 4.00 10.00
14 Xander Bogaerts/25 12.00 30.00
15 Chris Sale/25 15.00 40.00
19 Corey Kluber/50 12.00 30.00
23 Raul Ibanez/25 6.00 15.00
24 Starling Marte/50 10.00 25.00
34 Byron Buxton/50 8.00 20.00
36 Francisco Lindor/50 20.00 50.00

2015 Panini Prizm Diamond Marshals

COMPLETE SET (20) 10.00 25.00
RANDOM INSERTS IN PACKS
*PRIZMS: .6X TO 1.5X BASIC
*PRZMS FLSH/100: 2X TO 5X BASIC
1 Mike Trout 4.00 10.00
2 Buster Posey 1.00 2.50
3 Clayton Kershaw 1.50 4.00
4 Jose Abreu .75 2.00
5 Giancarlo Stanton .60 1.50
6 Masahiro Tanaka .60 1.50
7 Andrew McCutchen .75 2.00
8 Albert Pujols 1.00 2.50
9 Yasiel Puig .75 2.00
10 Anthony Rizzo 1.25 3.00
11 Adam Wainwright .60 1.50
12 Yu Darvish .75 2.00
13 Alex Gordon .60 1.50
14 Madison Bumgarner .60 1.50
15 Cal Ripken 2.50 6.00
16 Randy Johnson .75 2.00
17 Pedro Martinez .60 1.50
18 Ken Griffey Jr. 1.50 4.00
19 Roger Clemens 1.00 2.50
20 George Brett 1.50 4.00

2015 Panini Prizm Field Pass

COMPLETE SET (15) 10.00 25.00
RANDOM INSERTS IN PACKS
*PRIZMS: .6X TO 1.5X BASIC
*PRZMS FLSH/100: 2X TO 5X BASIC
1 David Ortiz .75 2.00
2 Albert Pujols 1.00 2.50
3 Carlos Santana .60 1.50
4 Evan Longoria .60 1.50
5 Troy Tulowitzki .75 2.00
6 David Price .60 1.50
7 Kennys Vargas .50 1.25
8 Miguel Cabrera .75 2.00
9 Jose Altuve .60 1.50
10 Jose Abreu .75 2.00
11 Freddie Freeman 1.00 2.50
12 Don Mattingly 1.50 4.00
13 Frank Thomas .75 2.00
14 Dante Bichette .50 1.25
15 Will Clark .60 1.50

2015 Panini Prizm Fireworks

RANDOM INSERTS IN PACKS
*PRIZMS: .6X TO 1.5X BASIC
*PRZMS FLSH/100: 2X TO 5X BASIC
1 Giancarlo Stanton .75 2.00
2 Jose Bautista .60 1.50
3 Miguel Cabrera .75 2.00
4 Mike Trout 4.00 10.00
5 Nelson Cruz .75 2.00
6 Albert Pujols 1.00 2.50
7 Yasiel Puig .75 2.00
8 Bryce Harper 1.25 3.00
9 David Ortiz .75 2.00
10 Jose Abreu .75 2.00
11 Andrew McCutchen .75 2.00
12 Paul Goldschmidt .75 2.00
13 Manny Machado .75 2.00
14 Adrian Beltre .75 2.00
15 David Wright .60 1.50
16 George Brett 1.50 4.00
17 Frank Thomas .75 2.00
18 Ken Griffey Jr. 1.50 4.00
19 Barry Bonds 1.25 3.00
20 Mark McGwire 1.25 3.00

2015 Panini Prizm Fresh Faces

COMPLETE SET (15) 10.00 25.00
RANDOM INSERTS IN PACKS
*PRIZMS: .6X TO 1.5X BASIC
*PRZMS FLSH/100: 2X TO 5X BASIC
1 Rusney Castillo .50 1.25
2 Dalton Pompey .50 1.25
3 Brandon Finnegan .40 1.00
4 Daniel Norris .40 1.00
5 Joc Pederson .75 2.00
6 Jorge Soler .60 1.50
7 Javier Baez 3.00 8.00
8 Dilson Herrera .50 1.25
9 Maikel Franco .50 1.25
10 Edwin Escobar .40 1.00
11 Byron Buxton .60 1.50
12 Jung-Ho Kang .40 1.00
13 Carlos Rodon .60 1.50
14 Kris Bryant 4.00 10.00
15 Yasmany Tomas .50 1.25

2015 Panini Prizm Fresh Faces Signature Prizms

RANDOM INSERTS IN PACKS
1 Mookie Betts 25.00 60.00
5 Robert Stephenson 3.00 8.00
8 Heath Hembree 3.00 8.00
11 C.C. Lee 12.00 30.00
18 Matt den Dekker 3.00 8.00
23 Jung-Ho Kang 20.00 50.00
25 Nick Martinez 5.00 12.00

2015 Panini Prizm Fresh Faces Signature Prizms Black and White Checker

*BW p/r 75-149: .5X TO 1.2X BASIC
RANDOM INSERTS IN PACKS
PRINT RUNS B/WN 75-149 COPIES PER
2 Clint Frazier/75 10.00 25.00
3 Matt Shoemaker/75 5.00 12.00
24 Jacob deGrom/75 12.00 30.00

2015 Panini Prizm Fresh Faces Signature Prizms Camo

*CAMO: .5X TO 1.2X BASIC
RANDOM INSERTS IN PACKS
PRINT RUNS B/WN 99-199 COPIES PER
24 Jacob deGrom/99 12.00 30.00

2015 Panini Prizm Fresh Faces Signature Prizms Red White and Blue

*RWB: .6X TO 1.5X BASIC
RANDOM INSERTS IN PACKS
STATED PRINT RUN 25 SER.#'d SETS
2 Clint Frazier 12.00 30.00
3 Matt Shoemaker 6.00 15.00
24 Jacob deGrom 15.00 40.00

2015 Panini Prizm Fresh Faces Signature Prizms Tie Dyed

*TIE DYED: .6X TO 1.5X BASIC
RANDOM INSERTS IN PACKS
STATED PRINT RUN 50 SER.#'d SETS
2 Clint Frazier 12.00 30.00
3 Matt Shoemaker 6.00 15.00
24 Jacob deGrom 15.00 40.00

2015 Panini Prizm Passion

COMPLETE SET (15) 5.00 12.00
RANDOM INSERTS IN PACKS
*PRIZMS: .6X TO 1.5X BASIC
*PRZMS FLSH/100: 2X TO 5X BASIC
1 Jason Heyward .60 1.50
2 Joe Mauer .60 1.50
3 Joe Panik .60 1.50
4 Dustin Pedroia .75 2.00
5 Jose Reyes .60 1.50
6 Troy Tulowitzki .75 2.00
7 Jackie Bradley Jr. .75 2.00
8 Adam Eaton .50 1.25
9 Miguel Cabrera .75 2.00
10 Brian Dozier .60 1.50
11 Buster Posey 1.00 2.50
12 Rougned Odor .60 1.50
13 Ian Kinsler .60 1.50
14 J.J. Hardy .50 1.25
15 Ichiro Suzuki 1.00 2.50

2015 Panini Prizm Pink Ribbon Ink Prizms

RANDOM INSERTS IN PACKS
PRINT RUNS B/WN 13-100 COPIES PER
NO PRICING ON QTY 13
1 Eric Hosmer/25 10.00 25.00
2 Carlos Gomez/25 8.00 20.00
3 Adam Jones/25 10.00 25.00
4 George Springer/24 10.00 25.00
5 Wil Myers/49 8.00 20.00
8 Justin Upton/25 20.00 50.00
10 Javier Baez/100 60.00 150.00

2015 Panini Prizm Signature Distinctions Prizms Die Cut Red Power

RANDOM INSERTS IN PACKS
STATED PRINT RUN 49 SER.#'d SETS
*PRPLE FLSH/25: .5X TO 1.2X BASIC
2 Jose Canseco 15.00 40.00
3 Paul Goldschmidt 12.00 30.00
4 Manny Machado 15.00 40.00
5 Freddie Freeman 12.00 30.00
7 Jim Palmer 10.00 25.00
8 Paul Molitor 12.00 30.00
9 Orlando Cepeda 12.00 30.00
10 Goose Gossage 15.00 40.00

2015 Panini Prizm Baseball Signature Prizms

RANDOM INSERTS IN PACKS
3 Edgar Martinez 4.00 10.00
4 Andres Galarraga 4.00 10.00
5 Jose Canseco 10.00 25.00
9 Luis Tiant 5.00 12.00
10 Brock Holt 6.00 15.00
19 Alexi Ogando 3.00 8.00
20 Dante Bichette 3.00 8.00
21 Carlos Martinez 4.00 10.00
22 David Justice 6.00 15.00

2015 Panini Prizm Baseball Signature Prizms Black and White Checker

*BW p/r 99-149: .5X TO 1.2X BASIC
*BW p/r 49: .6X TO 1.5X BASIC
RANDOM INSERTS IN PACKS
PRINT RUNS B/WN 49-149 COPIES PER
1 Salvador Perez/49 10.00 25.00
2 Willie McGee/49 8.00 20.00
12 Ozzie Guillen/99 4.00 10.00
16 Gary Gaetti/149 6.00 15.00
17 Jay Buhner/99 5.00 12.00

2015 Panini Prizm Baseball Signature Prizms Camo

*CAMO: .5X TO 1.2X BASIC
RANDOM INSERTS IN PACKS
PRINT RUNS B/WN 99-199 COPIES PER
2 Willie McGee/99 6.00 15.00
16 Gary Gaetti/149 6.00 15.00

2015 Panini Prizm Baseball Signature Prizms Red White and Blue

*RWB p/r 25: .6X TO 1.5X BASIC
RANDOM INSERTS IN PACKS
PRINT RUNS B/WN 10-25 COPIES PER
NO PRICING ON QTY 15 OR LESS
12 Ozzie Guillen/25 5.00 12.00
16 Gary Gaetti/25 8.00 20.00
17 Jay Buhner/25 6.00 15.00

2015 Panini Prizm Baseball Signature Prizms Tie Dyed

*TIE DYED p/r 25-50: .6X TO 1.5X BASIC
RANDOM INSERTS IN PACKS
PRINT RUNS B/WN 25-50 COPIES PER
1 Salvador Perez/25 10.00 25.00
2 Willie McGee/25 8.00 20.00
6 Nolan Ryan/25 40.00 100.00
12 Ozzie Guillen/50 5.00 12.00
15 Josh Donaldson/47 6.00 15.00
16 Gary Gaetti/50 8.00 20.00
17 Jay Buhner/50 6.00 15.00

2015 Panini Prizm USA Baseball

COMPLETE SET (10) 6.00 15.00
RANDOM INSERTS IN PACKS
*CAMO/199: 2X TO 5X BASIC
*PRIZM RWB/50: 2.5X TO 6X BASIC
1 Brandon Finnegan .50 1.25
2 David Price .60 1.50
3 Kolten Wong .60 1.50
4 George Springer .60 1.50
5 Billy Butler .50 1.25
6 Nick Swisher .60 1.50
7 Alex Gordon .60 1.50
8 Todd Frazier .60 1.50
9 Will Clark .60 1.50
10 Freddie Freeman 1.00 2.50

2015 Panini Prizm USA Baseball Signature Prizms Camo

RANDOM INSERTS IN PACKS
STATED PRINT RUN 25 SER.#'d SETS
1 Brandon Finnegan 8.00 20.00
2 David Price 15.00 40.00
8 Todd Frazier 20.00 50.00
9 Will Clark 150.00 250.00
10 Freddie Freeman 15.00 40.00

2017 Panini Prizm

INSERTED IN '17 CHRONICLES PACKS
1 Aaron Judge RC 15.00 40.00
2 Cody Bellinger RC 8.00 20.00
3 Yoan Moncada RC 1.50 4.00
4 Andrew Benintendi RC 1.50 4.00
5 Christian Arroyo RC .75 2.00
6 Dansby Swanson RC 1.25 3.00
7 Mickey Mantle 1.25 3.00
8 Ryon Healy RC .60 1.50
9 Mitch Haniger RC .75 2.00
10 Antonio Senzatela RC .50 1.25
11 Ian Happ RC 1.00 2.50
12 Trey Mancini RC 1.00 2.50
13 Jordan Montgomery RC .75 2.00
14 Bradley Zimmer RC .60 1.50
15 Hunter Renfroe RC .60 1.50
16 Jorge Bonifacio RC .50 1.25
17 Lewis Brinson RC .75 2.00
18 Jacoby Jones RC .60 1.50
19 Alex Bregman RC 2.00 5.00
20 Josh Bell RC 1.25 3.00
21 Derek Fisher RC .60 1.50
22 Austin Slater RC .50 1.25
23 Paul DeJong RC 1.50 4.00
24 K.Bryant/A.Rizzo .60 1.50
25 Sam Travis RC .50 1.25
26 Mike Trout 2.00 5.00
27 Ken Griffey Jr. .75 2.00
28 Bryce Harper .60 1.50
29 Eric Thames .30 .75
30 Manny Machado .40 1.00
31 Kris Bryant .50 1.25
32 Clayton Kershaw .75 2.00
33 Carlos Correa .40 1.00
34 Anthony Rizzo .60 1.50
35 Buster Posey .50 1.25
36 Mookie Betts .60 1.50
37 Paul Goldschmidt .40 1.00
38 Ryan Zimmerman .30 .75
39 Max Scherzer .40 1.00
40 George Brett .75 2.00
41 Joey Votto .40 1.00
42 Dallas Keuchel .30 .75
43 Franklin Barreto RC .50 1.25
44 Noah Syndergaard .30 .75
45 Nolan Arenado .50 1.25
46 Marcell Ozuna .40 1.00
47 Miguel Cabrera .40 1.00
48 Adrian Beltre .40 1.00
49 Francisco Lindor .40 1.00
50 Gary Sanchez .40 1.00

2017 Panini Prizm Blue Wave

*BLUE WAVE: .75X TO 2X BASIC
*BLUE WAVE RC: .75X TO 2X BASIC RC
INSERTED IN '17 CHRONICLES PACKS
STATED PRINT RUN 199 SER.#'d SETS
40 George Brett 8.00 20.00

2017 Panini Prizm Camo

*CAMO: 2.5X TO 6X BASIC
*CAMO RC: 2.5X TO 6X BASIC
INSERTED IN '17 CHRONICLES PACKS
STATED PRINT RUN 25 SER.#'d SETS
24 K.Bryant/A.Rizzo 10.00 25.00
26 Mike Trout 15.00 40.00
27 Ken Griffey Jr. 10.00 2.00
31 Kris Bryant 10.00 25.00
40 George Brett 40.00 100.00

2017 Panini Prizm Flash

*FLASH: .6X TO 1.5X BASIC
*FLASH RC: .6X TO 1.5X BASIC RC
INSERTED IN '17 CHRONICLES PACKS

2017 Panini Prizm Green Power

*GRN POWER: 2X TO 5X BASIC
*GRN POWER RC: 2X TO 5X BASIC
INSERTED IN '17 CHRONICLES PACKS
STATED PRINT RUN 49 SER.#'d SETS
24 K.Bryant/A.Rizzo 8.00 20.00
26 Mike Trout 12.00 30.00
27 Ken Griffey Jr. 8.00 20.00
31 Kris Bryant 8.00 20.00
40 George Brett 30.00 80.00

2017 Panini Prizm Light Blue

*LIGHT BLUE: .75X TO 2X BASIC
*LIGHT BLUE RC: .75X TO 2X BASIC RC
INSERTED IN '17 CHRONICLES PACKS
STATED PRINT RUN 299 SER.#'d SETS
40 George Brett 4.00 10.00

2017 Panini Prizm Orange

*ORANGE: .75X TO 2X BASIC
*ORANGE RC: .75X TO 2X BASIC RC
INSERTED IN '17 CHRONICLES PACKS
STATED PRINT RUN 399 SER.#'d SETS
40 George Brett 4.00 10.00

2017 Panini Prizm Purple Scope

*PURPLE: 1.2X TO 3X BASIC
*PURPLE RC: 1.2X TO 3X BASIC RC
INSERTED IN '17 CHRONICLES PACKS
STATED PRINT RUN 99 SER.#'d SETS
24 K.Bryant/A.Rizzo 5.00 12.00
26 Mike Trout 8.00 20.00
27 Ken Griffey Jr. 5.00 12.00
31 Kris Bryant 5.00 12.00
40 George Brett 10.00 25.00

2017 Panini Prizm Red Crystals

*RED CRSTLS: 1.5X TO 4X BASIC
*RED CRSTLS RC: 1.5X TO 4X BASIC RC
INSERTED IN '17 CHRONICLES PACKS
STATED PRINT RUN 75 SER.#'d SETS
24 K.Bryant/A.Rizzo 6.00 15.00
26 Mike Trout 10.00 25.00
27 Ken Griffey Jr. 6.00 15.00
31 Kris Bryant 6.00 15.00
40 George Brett 25.00 60.00

2017 Panini Prizm Autographs

INSERTED IN '17 CHRONICLES PACKS
EXCHANGE DEADLINE 5/22/2019
1 Andrew Benintendi 15.00 40.00
3 Alex Bregman 12.00 30.00
4 Dansby Swanson
5 Ian Happ 6.00 15.00
6 Cody Bellinger
7 Aaron Judge 75.00 200.00
8 Trey Mancini 5.00 12.00
11 Mitch Haniger 5.00 12.00
12 Theo Epstein
13 Alex Reyes 4.00 10.00
14 Tyler Glasnow 3.00 8.00
15 Manuel Margot 2.50 6.00
16 Hunter Renfroe 3.00 8.00
17 Jorge Bonifacio 2.50 6.00
18 Antonio Senzatela 2.50 6.00
19 Amir Garrett 2.50 6.00
20 David Dahl 3.00 8.00
21 Sam Travis 2.50 6.00
22 Ryon Healy 3.00 8.00
23 Magneuris Sierra 4.00 10.00
24 Lewis Brinson 4.00 10.00
25 Jacoby Jones 3.00 8.00
26 Adam Frazier 2.50 6.00
27 Brock Stewart 2.50 6.00
28 Hunter Dozier 2.50 6.00
29 Daniel Robertson 2.50 6.00
30 Kyle Freeland
31 Anthony Alford 2.50 6.00
32 Dinelson Lamet 2.50 6.00
33 Yandy Diaz 5.00 12.00
34 Derek Fisher 3.00 8.00
35 Francis Martes 2.50 6.00
36 Carson Fulmer 2.50 6.00
37 Anthony Rizzo 12.00 30.00

38 Jose Abreu 6.00 15.00
39 Yasmany Tomas
40 Wade Boggs 10.00 25.00
41 Ivan Rodriguez 3.00 8.00
42 Bob Gibson
43 Tom Glavine
44 Joey Votto 20.00 50.00
45 Francisco Lindor 8.00 20.00
46 Corey Seager
47 Gary Sanchez 20.00 50.00
48 Andrew McCutchen 40.00 100.00
49 Josh Donaldson 15.00 40.00
50 Willie McCovey 15.00 40.00

2017 Panini Prizm Autographs Blue Wave

*BLUE WAVE: .6X TO 1.5X BASIC
INSERTED IN '17 CHRONICLES PACKS
PRINT RUNS B/WN 40-49 COPIES PER
EXCHANGE DEADLINE 5/22/2019
9 Jordan Montgomery/49 10.00 25.00
10 Bradley Zimmer/48 8.00 20.00

2017 Panini Prizm Autographs Green Power

*GREEN POWER/20: .75X TO 2X BASIC
INSERTED IN '17 CHRONICLES PACKS
PRINT RUNS B/WN 15-20 COPIES PER
NO PRICING ON QTY 15
EXCHANGE DEADLINE 5/22/2019
9 Jordan Montgomery/20 12.00 30.00
10 Bradley Zimmer/20 10.00 25.00

2017 Panini Prizm Autographs Purple Scope

*PURPLE SCOPE: .6X TO 1.5X BASIC
INSERTED IN '17 CHRONICLES PACKS
PRINT RUNS B/WN 30-35 COPIES PER
EXCHANGE DEADLINE 5/22/2019
9 Jordan Montgomery/35 10.00 25.00
10 Bradley Zimmer/35 8.00 20.00

2017 Panini Prizm Autographs Red Crystals

*RED CRYSTALS: .75X TO 2X BASIC
INSERTED IN '17 CHRONICLES PACKS
PRINT RUNS B/WN 20-25 COPIES PER
EXCHANGE DEADLINE 5/22/2019
9 Jordan Montgomery/25 12.00 30.00
10 Bradley Zimmer/25 10.00 25.00

2018 Panini Prizm

INSERTED IN '18 CHRONICLES PACKS
1 Aaron Judge 1.00 2.50
2 Ozzie Albies RC 1.25 3.00
3 Ryan McMahon RC .50 1.25
4 Clint Frazier RC .75 2.00
5 Mike Trout 2.00 5.00
6 Ronald Acuna Jr. RC 8.00 20.00
7 Bryce Harper .60 1.50
8 Gary Sanchez .40 1.00
9 Miguel Andujar RC 1.50 4.00
10 Austin Hays RC .60 1.50
11 Nicky Delmonico RC .40 1.00
12 Rhys Hoskins RC 1.50 4.00
13 Alex Verdugo RC .60 1.50
14 Juan Soto RC 8.00 20.00
15 Paul Goldschmidt .40 1.00
16 Gleyber Torres RC 4.00 10.00
17 J.P. Crawford RC .40 1.00
18 Rafael Devers RC 1.25 3.00
19 Buster Posey .50 1.25
20 Victor Robles RC 1.00 2.50
21 Anthony Rizzo .60 1.50
22 Jose Altuve .50 1.25
23 Shohei Ohtani RC 2.50 6.00
24 Amed Rosario RC .50 1.25
25 Corey Seager .25 .60

2018 Panini Prizm Blue Ice

*BLUE ICE: 1X TO 2.5X BASIC
*BLUE ICE RC: .6X TO 1.5X BASIC
INSERTED IN '18 CHRONICLES PACKS
STATED PRINT RUN 149 SER.#'d SETS
23 Shohei Ohtani 8.00 20.00

2018 Panini Prizm Green

*GREEN: 1.5X TO 4X BASIC
*GREEN RC: 1X TO 2.5X BASIC
INSERTED IN '18 CHRONICLES PACKS
STATED PRINT RUN 50 SER.#'d SETS
23 Shohei Ohtani 12.00 30.00

2018 Panini Prizm Holo

*HOLO: .75X TO 2X BASIC
*HOLO RC: .5X TO 1.2X BASIC
INSERTED IN '18 CHRONICLES PACKS
23 Shohei Ohtani 6.00 15.00

2018 Panini Prizm Hyper

*HYPER: .75X TO 2X BASIC
*HYPER RC: .5X TO 1.2X BASIC
INSERTED IN '18 CHRONICLES PACKS
STATED PRINT RUN 299 SER.#'d SETS
23 Shohei Ohtani 6.00 15.00

2018 Panini Prizm Pink

*PINK: 2.5X TO 6X BASIC
*PINK RC: 1.5X TO 4X BASIC
INSERTED IN '18 CHRONICLES PACKS
STATED PRINT RUN 25 SER.#'d SETS
5 Mike Trout 15.00 40.00
23 Shohei Ohtani 20.00 50.00

2018 Panini Prizm Purple Mojo

*PURPLE: 1.2X TO 3X BASIC
*PURPLE RC: .75X TO 2X BASIC
INSERTED IN '18 CHRONICLES PACKS
STATED PRINT RUN 99 SER.#'d SETS
23 Shohei Ohtani 10.00 25.00

2018 Panini Prizm Ruby Wave

*RUBY: 1X TO 2.5X BASIC
*RUBY RC: .6X TO 1.5X BASIC
INSERTED IN '18 CHRONICLES PACKS
STATED PRINT RUN 199 SER.#'d SETS
23 Shohei Ohtani 8.00 20.00

2018 Panini Prizm Signatures

RANDOM INSERTS IN PACKS
3 Miguel Andujar 10.00 25.00
4 Brandon Woodruff 3.00 8.00
6 Kyle Farmer 2.50 6.00
8 Zack Granite 2.50 6.00
9 Chris Flexen 2.50 6.00
10 Thyago Vieira 2.50 6.00
11 Reyes Moronta 2.50 6.00
13 Brent Honeywell 4.00 10.00
16 Juan Soto 60.00 150.00
19 Matt Barnes 2.50 6.00

2019 Panini Prizm

1 Adam Jones .25 .60
2 Jake Cave RC .40 1.00
3 Danny Jansen RC .30 .75
4 Matt Olson .20 .50
5 Sean Newcomb .20 .50
6 David Wright .25 .60
7 Justus Sheffield RC .50 1.25
8 Yadier Molina .30 .75
9 Edwin Diaz .25 .60
10 Rowdy Tellez RC .50 1.25
11 Justin Smoak .20 .50
12 Miguel Cabrera .30 .75
13 Manny Machado .30 .75
14 Kyle Schwarber .30 .75
15 George Springer .25 .60
16 Justin Turner .25 .60
17 Robinson Cano .25 .60
18 A.J. Pollock .20 .50
19 Joey Gallo .20 .50
20 Jacob deGrom .30 .75
21 Jose Ramirez .25 .60
22 Stephen Strasburg .30 .75
23 Kevin Newman RC .50 1.25
24 Nomar Mazara .20 .50
25 Kolby Allard RC .50 1.25
26 Miles Mikolas .30 .75
27 Albert Pujols .40 1.00
28 Hunter Renfroe .20 .50
29 Mallex Smith .20 .50
30 Miguel Sano .25 .60
31 Chris Sale .30 .75
32 Cedric Mullins RC .50 1.25
33 Brandon Belt .25 .60
34 Wade Davis .20 .50
35 Adrian Beltre .30 .75
36 Sean Reid-Foley RC .30 .75
37 Andrew Benintendi .30 .75
38 Bryse Wilson RC .40 1.00
39 Corey Kluber .25 .60
40 Jose Altuve .25 .60
41 Jaime Barria .20 .50
42 Trevor Williams .20 .50
43 Franmil Reyes .50 1.25
44 Daniel Ponce de Leon RC .50 1.25
45 Chris Archer .20 .50
46 Michael Kopech RC .60 1.50
47 Adalberto Mondesi .40 1.00
48 Luis Ortiz RC .30 .75
49 Jose Urena .20 .50
50 Kyle Wright RC .50 1.25
51 Michael Brantley .25 .60
52 Steven Duggar RC .40 1.00
53 Dakota Hudson RC .40 1.00
54 Kris Bryant .40 1.00
55 Eddie Rosario .25 .60
56 Yoan Moncada .30 .75
57 David Peralta .20 .50
58 Jon Lester .25 .60
59 Luis Castillo .25 .60
60 Trey Mancini .25 .60
61 Francisco Lindor .30 .75
62 Ryan Yarbrough .20 .50
63 Chris Shaw RC .50 1.25
64 Brandon Lowe RC .50 1.25
65 Reese McGuire RC .50 1.25
66 Brandon Nimmo .25 .60
67 Cody Bellinger .60 1.50
68 Max Scherzer .30 .75
69 Mike Minor .20 .50
70 Francisco Mejia RC .40 1.00
71 Josh Donaldson .25 .60
72 Patrick Wisdom RC .30 .75
73 Starling Marte .25 .60
74 Shane Bieber .30 .75
75 Scooter Gennett .25 .60
76 Sean Manaea .20 .50
77 Joey Wendle .20 .50
78 Felix Hernandez .25 .60
79 Eugenio Suarez .25 .60
80 Enyel De Los Santos RC .30 .75
81 Austin Meadows .30 .75
82 Framber Valdez RC .30 .75
83 Andrelton Simmons .20 .50
84 Luis Severino .25 .60
85 Carlos Correa .30 .75
86 Jeremy Jeffress .20 .50
87 Whit Merrifield .30 .75
88 Dereck Rodriguez .20 .50
89 J.T. Realmuto .30 .75
90 Jose Abreu .30 .75
91 J.D. Martinez .30 .75
92 Nick Williams .20 .50
93 Nicholas Castellanos .30 .75
94 Kevin Pillar .20 .50
95 Taylor Ward RC .30 .75
96 Myles Straw RC .50 1.25
97 Luis Urias RC .50 1.25
98 Clayton Kershaw .60 1.50
99 Odubel Herrera .25 .60
100 Blake Treinen RC .30 .75
101 Victor Robles .40 1.00
102 Khris Davis .30 .75
103 Corbin Burnes RC .50 1.25
104 Stephen Gonsalves RC .30 .75
105 Gleyber Torres .60 1.50
106 Charlie Blackmon .30 .75
107 David Fletcher RC 1.00 2.50
108 Wilson Ramos .20 .50
109 Gerrit Cole .30 .75
110 Miguel Andujar .30 .75
111 Nelson Cruz .30 .75
112 Sandy Alcantara .20 .50
113 Trevor Story .30 .75
114 Alex Bregman .30 .75
115 Corey Dickerson .20 .50
116 Christian Yelich .40 1.00
117 Jeimer Candelario .20 .50
118 Rafael Devers .40 1.00
119 Ji-Man Choi .20 .50
120 Madison Bumgarner .25 .60
121 Touki Toussaint RC .40 1.00
122 Christin Stewart RC .40 1.00
123 German Marquez .20 .50
124 Mike Moustakas .25 .60
125 Mitch Haniger .25 .60
126 Brad Keller RC .30 .75
127 Tyler O'Neill .25 .60
128 Caleb Ferguson RC .40 1.00
129 Brandon Crawford .25 .60
130 Jameson Taillon .25 .60
131 Michael Conforto .25 .60
132 Trea Turner .25 .60
133 Freddy Peralta .30 .75
134 Willie Calhoun .20 .50
135 Aaron Judge .75 2.00
136 Eric Hosmer .25 .60
137 Noah Syndergaard .25 .60
138 Anthony Rendon .30 .75
139 Teoscar Hernandez .30 .75
140 Matt Chapman .30 .75
141 Kyle Tucker RC .60 1.50
142 Amed Rosario .25 .60
143 Harrison Bader .25 .60
144 Edwin Encarnacion .30 .75
145 Jeff McNeil RC .75 2.00
146 Juan Soto 1.00 2.50
147 Carlos Carrasco .20 .50
148 Bryce Harper .50 1.25
149 James Paxton .25 .60
150 Rhys Hoskins .40 1.00
151 Andrew Heaney .20 .50
152 Willy Adames .20 .50
153 Shohei Ohtani .40 1.00
154 Giancarlo Stanton .30 .75
155 Carlos Rodon .25 .60
156 Ramon Laureano RC .60 1.50
157 Nolan Arenado .40 1.00
158 David Bote .25 .60
159 Jake Bauers RC .50 1.25
160 Josh James RC .50 1.25
161 Ozzie Albies .30 .75
162 Jonathan Davis RC .40 1.00
163 Joey Votto .30 .75
164 Justin Verlander .30 .75
165 Kyle Freeland .25 .60
166 Tim Anderson .30 .75
167 Walker Buehler .40 1.00
168 Ryan Borucki RC .30 .75
169 Ronald Acuna Jr. 1.50 4.00
170 Jose Martinez .20 .50
171 Blake Snell .25 .60
172 Javier Baez .40 1.00
173 Hunter Pence .25 .60
174 Matt Carpenter .30 .75
175 Jose Berrios .25 .60
176 Kevin Kramer RC .40 1.00
177 Nick Markakis .25 .60
178 Jacob Nix RC .40 1.00
179 Ryan O'Hearn RC .40 1.00
180 Mookie Betts .50 1.25
181 Dennis Santana RC .30 .75
182 Jack Flaherty .25 .60
183 Xander Bogaerts .30 .75
184 Zack Greinke .25 .60
185 Cionel Perez RC .30 .75
186 Mike Foltynewicz .20 .50
187 Jackie Bradley Jr. .30 .75
188 Jonathan Loaisiga RC .40 1.00
189 Paul Goldschmidt .30 .75
190 Brian Anderson .20 .50
191 Aaron Nola .25 .60
192 Mike Trout 1.50 4.00
193 Lorenzo Cain .20 .50
194 Freddie Freeman .40 1.00
195 Jesus Aguilar .20 .50
196 Garrett Hampson RC .40 1.00
197 Travis Shaw .20 .50
198 Chance Adams RC .30 .75
199 Anthony Rizzo .50 1.25
200 Salvador Perez .25 .60
201 Chipper Jones .30 .75
202 Isaac Galloway RC .30 .75
203 Willians Astudillo RC .30 .75
204 Wade Boggs .25 .60
205 Juan Gonzalez .20 .50
206 Meibrys Viloria RC .30 .75
207 Ketel Marte .25 .60
208 Ranger Suarez RC .30 .75
209 Heath Fillmyer RC .30 .75
210 Rosell Herrera .20 .50
211 Miguel Tejada .20 .50
212 Nick Ciuffo RC .30 .75
213 Dwight Gooden .20 .50
214 Andre Dawson .25 .60
215 Brett Kennedy RC .30 .75
216 Robin Yount .30 .75
217 Marcus Semien .20 .50
218 Max Muncy .25 .60
219 Mike Piazza .30 .75
220 Jalen Beeks RC .30 .75
221 Ryan Meisinger RC .30 .75
222 David Ortiz .30 .75
223 Barry Larkin .25 .60
224 Starlin Castro .20 .50
225 C.D. Pelham RC .30 .75
226 Adam Kolarek RC .30 .75
227 Fernando Romero .20 .50
228 Tom Seaver .25 .60
229 Jefry Rodriguez RC .30 .75
230 Pablo Lopez RC .30 .75
231 Abiatal Avelino RC .30 .75
232 Alex Rodriguez .40 1.00
233 Ryne Sandberg .60 1.50
234 Harold Castro RC .40 1.00
235 Scott Barlow RC .30 .75
236 Aaron Hicks .25 .60
237 Thomas Pannone RC .50 1.25
238 Victor Reyes RC .30 .75
239 Dean Deetz RC .30 .75
240 Diego Castillo RC .30 .75
241 Rickey Henderson .30 .75
242 Javier Guerra RC .30 .75
243 Daniel Murphy .25 .60
244 Justin Verlander .30 .75
245 James Norwood RC .30 .75
246 Randy Johnson .30 .75
247 DJ Stewart RC .40 1.00
248 Roger Clemens .40 1.00
249 Jose Peraza .25 .60
250 Ozzie Smith .40 1.00
251 Kirby Puckett .30 .75
252 Gary Carter .25 .60
253 Andrew Velazquez .20 .50
254 Cal Ripken 1.00 2.50
255 Troy Tulowitzki .30 .75
256 Mariano Rivera .40 1.00
257 Yasiel Puig .30 .75
258 Tyler Mahle .20 .50
259 Justin Williams RC .30 .75
260 Michael Perez RC .30 .75
261 Nolan Ryan 1.00 2.50
262 Gabriel Guerrero RC .30 .75
263 Duane Underwood RC .30 .75
264 Trevor Richards RC .30 .75
265 Austin Voth RC .30 .75
266 Albert Pujols .40 1.00
267 Dawel Lugo RC .50 1.25
268 Luke Voit .50 1.25
269 Kevin Mitchell .20 .50
270 Ty Buttrey RC .50 1.25
271 Roberto Alomar .25 .60
272 Pablo Reyes RC .30 .75
273 Johan Camargo .20 .50
274 Yency Almonte RC .30 .75
275 Austin Dean RC .30 .75
276 Vladimir Guerrero .25 .60
277 Manny Machado .30 .75
278 Austin Wynns RC .30 .75
279 George Brett .60 1.50
280 Nick Martini RC .30 .75
281 Andrew McCutchen .30 .75
282 Yusei Kikuchi RC .50 1.25
283 Chad Sobotka RC .30 .75
284 Tanner Rainey RC .30 .75
285 Eric Hosmer .25 .60
286 Edmundo Sosa RC .40 1.00
287 Pedro Martinez .25 .60
288 Dontrelle Willis .20 .50
289 Kohl Stewart RC .40 1.00
290 Tony Gwynn .30 .75
291 Evan Longoria .25 .60
292 Connor Sadzeck RC .30 .75
293 Patrick Corbin .25 .60
294 Eric Haase RC .30 .75
295 Craig Biggio .25 .60
296 Larry Walker .25 .60
297 Tim Lincecum .25 .60
298 Dale Murphy .30 .75
299 Frank Thomas .30 .75
300 Ken Griffey Jr. .60 1.50

2019 Panini Prizm Prizms Blue

*BLUE: 1X TO 2.5X BASIC
*BLUE RC: .6X TO 1.5X BASIC
RANDOM INSERTS IN PACKS

2019 Panini Prizm Prizms Blue Mojo

*BLUE MOJO: 2X TO 5X
*BLUE MOJO RC: 1.2X TO 3X
RANDOM INSERTS IN PACKS
STATED PRINT RUN 399 SER.#'d SETS
192 Mike Trout 10.00 25.00
290 Tony Gwynn 4.00 10.00
300 Ken Griffey Jr. 8.00 20.00

2019 Panini Prizm Prizms Blue Wave

*BLUE WAVE: 3X TO 8X
*BLUE WAVE RC: 2X TO 5X
RANDOM INSERTS IN PACKS
STATED PRINT RUN 60 SER.#'d SETS
192 Mike Trout 25.00 60.00
251 Kirby Puckett 15.00 40.00
261 Nolan Ryan 10.00 25.00
279 George Brett 8.00 20.00
290 Tony Gwynn 6.00 15.00
299 Frank Thomas 5.00 12.00
300 Ken Griffey Jr. 12.00 30.00

2019 Panini Prizm Prizms Burgandy Shimmer

*BURGUNDY: 5X TO 12X
*BURGUNDY RC: 3X TO 8X
RANDOM INSERTS IN PACKS
STATED PRINT RUN 25 SER.#'d SETS
192 Mike Trout 75.00 200.00
251 Kirby Puckett 25.00 60.00
261 Nolan Ryan 15.00 40.00
279 George Brett 12.00 30.00
290 Tony Gwynn 10.00 25.00
299 Frank Thomas 8.00 20.00
300 Ken Griffey Jr. 20.00 50.00

2019 Panini Prizm Prizms Carolina Blue

*CAR BLUE: 1.2X TO 3X BASIC
*CAR BLUE RC: .75X TO 2X BASIC
RANDOM INSERTS IN PACKS

2019 Panini Prizm Prizms Cosmic Haze

*COSMIC: 1.2X TO 3X BASIC
*COSMIC RC: .75X TO 2X BASIC
RANDOM INSERTS IN PACKS

2019 Panini Prizm Prizms Green

*GREEN: 1.2X TO 3X BASIC
*GREEN RC: .75X TO 2X BASIC
RANDOM INSERTS IN PACKS

2019 Panini Prizm Prizms Hyper Blue

*HYPER BLUE: 1.2X TO 3X BASIC
*HYPER BLUE RC: .75X TO 2X BASIC
RANDOM INSERTS IN PACKS

2019 Panini Prizm Prizms Hyper Green and Yellow

*HYPER GY: 1.2X TO 3X BASIC
*HYPER GY RC: .75X TO 2X BASIC
RANDOM INSERTS IN PACKS

2019 Panini Prizm Prizms Hyper Purple and Green

*HYPER PG: 1.2X TO 3X BASIC
*HYPER PG RC: .75X TO 2X BASIC
RANDOM INSERTS IN PACKS

2019 Panini Prizm Prizms Lime Green Donut Circles

*LIME GREEN: 2X TO 5X
*LIME GREEN RC: 1.2X TO 3X
RANDOM INSERTS IN PACKS
STATED PRINT RUN 199 SER.#'d SETS
192 Mike Trout 10.00 25.00
290 Tony Gwynn 4.00 10.00
300 Ken Griffey Jr. 8.00 20.00

2019 Panini Prizm Prizms Navy Blue Kaleidoscope

*NAVY BLUE: 4X TO 10X
*NAVY BLUE RC: 2.5X TO 6X
RANDOM INSERTS IN PACKS
STATED PRINT RUN 35 SER.#'d SETS
192 Mike Trout 60.00 150.00
251 Kirby Puckett 20.00 50.00
261 Nolan Ryan 12.00 30.00
279 George Brett 10.00 25.00
290 Tony Gwynn 8.00 20.00
299 Frank Thomas 6.00 15.00
300 Ken Griffey Jr. 15.00 40.00

2019 Panini Prizm Prizms Neon Orange Donut Circles

*NEON ORANGE: 2.5X TO 6X
*NEON ORANGE RC: 1.5X TO 4X
RANDOM INSERTS IN PACKS
STATED PRINT RUN 150 SER.#'d SETS
192 Mike Trout 15.00 40.00
251 Kirby Puckett 12.00 30.00
279 George Brett 6.00 15.00
290 Tony Gwynn 5.00 12.00
300 Ken Griffey Jr. 10.00 25.00

2019 Panini Prizm Prizms Pink

*PINK: 1.2X TO 3X BASIC
*PINK RC: .75X TO 2X BASIC
RANDOM INSERTS IN PACKS

2019 Panini Prizm Prizms Power Plaid

*PLAID: 3X TO 8X
*PLAID RC: 2X TO 5X
RANDOM INSERTS IN PACKS
STATED PRINT RUN 75 SER.#'d SETS
192 Mike Trout 25.00 60.00
251 Kirby Puckett 15.00 40.00
261 Nolan Ryan 10.00 25.00
279 George Brett 8.00 20.00
290 Tony Gwynn 6.00 15.00
299 Frank Thomas 5.00 12.00
300 Ken Griffey Jr. 12.00 30.00

2019 Panini Prizm Prizms Purple

*PURPLE: 1.2X TO 3X BASIC
*PURPLE RC: .75X TO 2X BASIC
RANDOM INSERTS IN PACKS

2019 Panini Prizm Prizms Red

*RED: 1X TO 2.5X BASIC
*RED RC: .6X TO 1.5X BASIC
RANDOM INSERTS IN PACKS

2019 Panini Prizm Prizms Red Mojo

*RED MOJO: 2X TO 5X
*RED MOJO RC: 1.2X TO 3X
RANDOM INSERTS IN PACKS
STATED PRINT RUN 299 SER.#'d SETS
192 Mike Trout 10.00 25.00
290 Tony Gwynn 4.00 10.00
300 Ken Griffey Jr. 8.00 20.00

2019 Panini Prizm Prizms Red White and Blue

*RED WHT BLUE: 1.2X TO 3X BASIC
*RED WHT BLUE RC: .75X TO 2X BASIC
RANDOM INSERTS IN PACKS

2019 Panini Prizm Prizms Silver

*SILVER: 1.5X TO 4X BASIC
*SILVER RC: 1X TO 2.5X BASIC
RANDOM INSERTS IN PACKS
192 Mike Trout 8.00 20.00

2019 Panini Prizm Prizms Snake Skin

*SNAKE SKIN: 4X TO 10X
*SNAKE SKIN RC: 2.5X TO 6X
RANDOM INSERTS IN PACKS
STATED PRINT RUN 50 SER.#'d SETS
192 Mike Trout 30.00 80.00
251 Kirby Puckett 20.00 50.00
261 Nolan Ryan 12.00 30.00
279 George Brett 10.00 25.00
290 Tony Gwynn 8.00 20.00
299 Frank Thomas 6.00 15.00
300 Ken Griffey Jr. 15.00 40.00

2019 Panini Prizm Prizms Zebra Stripes

*ZEBRA: 3X TO 8X
*ZEBRA RC: 2X TO 5X
RANDOM INSERTS IN PACKS
STATED PRINT RUN 99 SER.#'d SETS
192 Mike Trout 60.00 150.00
251 Kirby Puckett 15.00 40.00
261 Nolan Ryan 10.00 25.00
279 George Brett 8.00 20.00
290 Tony Gwynn 6.00 15.00
299 Frank Thomas 5.00 12.00
300 Ken Griffey Jr. 12.00 30.00

2019 Panini Prizm Brilliance

RANDOM INSERTS IN PACKS
*PRIZMS: .75X TO 2X BASIC
1 Blake Snell .40 1.00
2 Justin Verlander .50 1.25
3 Jacob deGrom .50 1.25
4 Corey Kluber .40 1.00
5 Aaron Nola .40 1.00
6 Chris Sale .50 1.25
7 Kyle Freeland .40 1.00
8 Max Scherzer .50 1.25
9 Luis Severino .40 1.00
10 Miles Mikolas .50 1.25

2019 Panini Prizm Color Blast

RANDOM INSERTS IN PACKS
1 Bryce Harper 75.00 200.00
2 Shohei Ohtani 75.00 200.00
3 Kris Bryant 30.00 80.00
4 Aaron Judge 100.00 250.00
5 Mike Trout 100.00 250.00
6 Ronald Acuna Jr. 75.00 200.00
7 Mookie Betts 50.00 120.00
8 Manny Machado 30.00 80.00
9 Javier Baez 40.00 100.00
10 Christian Yelich 40.00 100.00

2019 Panini Prizm Fireworks

RANDOM INSERTS IN PACKS
*PRIZMS: .75X TO 2X BASIC
1 Mike Trout 2.50 6.00
2 Mookie Betts .75 2.00
3 Jose Ramirez .40 1.00
4 Christian Yelich .60 1.50
5 Javier Baez .60 1.50
6 Nolan Arenado .60 1.50
7 J.D. Martinez .50 1.25
8 Alex Bregman .50 1.25
9 Freddie Freeman .60 1.50
10 Paul Goldschmidt .50 1.25
11 Francisco Lindor .50 1.25
12 Trevor Story .50 1.25
13 Aaron Judge 1.25 3.00
14 Jose Altuve .40 1.00
15 Shohei Ohtani .60 1.50

2019 Panini Prizm Game Ball Graphs

RANDOM INSERTS IN PACKS
EXCHANGE DEADLINE 11/15/2020
1 Anthony Banda 2.50 6.00
2 Stephen Piscotty 2.50 6.00
3 Shane Bieber 15.00 40.00
4 David Dahl 2.50 6.00
5 Josh Bell 10.00 25.00
6 Reynaldo Lopez 3.00 8.00
7 Raimel Tapia 2.50 6.00
8 Franmil Reyes 2.50 6.00
9 Jordan Luplow 2.50 6.00
10 Renato Nunez 3.00 8.00
11 Merandy Gonzalez 2.50 6.00
12 Max Fried 4.00 10.00
13 Aaron Judge EXCH 40.00 100.00
14 Richard Urena 2.50 6.00
15 Austin Slater 2.50 6.00
16 Jacoby Jones 3.00 8.00
17 Luke Weaver 2.50 6.00
19 Luiz Gohara 2.50 6.00
20 Brandon Belt 3.00 8.00
21 Teoscar Hernandez 4.00 10.00
22 Jeimer Candelario 2.50 6.00
23 Eduardo Nunez 2.50 6.00
24 Alex Verdugo 6.00 15.00
25 David Bote 10.00 25.00

2019 Panini Prizm Illumination

RANDOM INSERTS IN PACKS
*PRIZMS: .75X TO 2X BASIC
1 Aaron Judge 1.25 3.00
2 Bryce Harper .75 2.00
3 Kris Bryant .60 1.50
4 Manny Machado .50 1.25
5 Charlie Blackmon .50 1.25
6 Scooter Gennett .40 1.00
7 Clayton Kershaw 1.00 2.50
8 Giancarlo Stanton .50 1.25
9 Rhys Hoskins .60 1.50
10 Mike Trout 2.50 6.00
11 Whit Merrifield .50 1.25
12 Khris Davis .50 1.25

2019 Panini Prizm Instant Impact

RANDOM INSERTS IN PACKS
*PRIZMS: .75X TO 2X BASIC
1 Gleyber Torres 1.00 2.50
2 Ronald Acuna Jr. 2.50 6.00
3 Walker Buehler .60 1.50
4 Shohei Ohtani .60 1.50
5 Miguel Andujar .50 1.25
6 Ozzie Albies .50 1.25
7 Juan Soto 1.50 4.00
8 Harrison Bader .40 1.00
9 Jack Flaherty .40 1.00
10 Joey Wendle .30 .75

2019 Panini Prizm Lumber Inc.

RANDOM INSERTS IN PACKS
*PRIZMS: .75X TO 2X BASIC
1 Khris Davis .50 1.25
2 Joey Gallo .40 1.00
3 J.D. Martinez .50 1.25
4 Giancarlo Stanton .50 1.25
5 Bryce Harper .75 2.00
6 Aaron Judge 1.25 3.00
7 Trevor Story .50 1.25
8 Matt Olson .30 .75
9 Mike Trout 2.50 6.00
10 Gary Sanchez .50 1.25

2019 Panini Prizm Machines

RANDOM INSERTS IN PACKS
*PRIZMS: .75X TO 2X BASIC
1 Mike Trout 2.50 6.00
2 Mookie Betts .75 2.00
3 Jose Altuve .40 1.00
4 Aaron Judge 1.25 3.00
5 Javier Baez .60 1.50
6 Alex Bregman .50 1.25
7 Nolan Arenado .60 1.50
8 Christian Yelich .60 1.50
9 Jose Ramirez .40 1.00
10 Paul Goldschmidt .50 1.25

2019 Panini Prizm Numbers Game

RANDOM INSERTS IN PACKS
*PRIZMS: .75X TO 2X BASIC
1 Juan Soto 1.50 4.00
2 Mookie Betts .75 2.00
3 Ronald Acuna Jr. 2.50 6.00
4 Miguel Andujar .50 1.25
5 Mike Trout 2.50 6.00
6 J.D. Martinez .50 1.25
7 Christian Yelich .60 1.50
8 Javier Baez .60 1.50

2019 Panini Prizm Pro Penmanship

RANDOM INSERTS IN PACKS
EXCHANGE DEADLINE 11/15/2020
1 Carson Kelly 2.50 6.00
2 Jharel Cotton 2.50 6.00
3 J.D. Davis 2.50 6.00
4 Roman Quinn 2.50 6.00
5 Adalberto Mondesi 6.00 15.00
6 Matt Barnes 2.50 6.00
7 Luis Perdomo 2.50 6.00
8 Jake Thompson 2.50 6.00
9 Trevor May 2.50 6.00
10 Brian Anderson 2.50 6.00
11 Carson Fulmer 2.50 6.00
12 Austin Barnes 2.50 6.00
13 Hunter Dozier 2.50 6.00
14 David Paulino 2.50 6.00
15 Andrew Suarez 2.50 6.00
16 Ryan McMahon 2.50 6.00
17 Jose De Leon 2.50 6.00
18 Kendall Graveman 2.50 6.00
19 Chance Sisco 2.50 6.00
20 Tim Beckham 3.00 8.00
21 Ji-Man Choi 2.50 6.00
22 Freddy Peralta 4.00 10.00
23 Odubel Herrera 3.00 8.00
25 Joe Musgrove 2.50 6.00

2019 Panini Prizm Profiles

RANDOM INSERTS IN PACKS
1 Mike Trout 25.00 60.00
2 Miguel Cabrera 4.00 10.00
3 David Ortiz 4.00 10.00
4 Yasiel Puig 4.00 10.00
5 Jose Altuve 3.00 8.00
6 Nolan Arenado 5.00 12.00
7 Francisco Lindor 4.00 10.00
8 Matt Carpenter 4.00 10.00
9 Max Scherzer 4.00 10.00

10 Clayton Kershaw 8.00 20.00
11 Jacob deGrom 4.00 10.00
12 Rickey Henderson 4.00 10.00
13 Ken Griffey Jr. 8.00 20.00
14 Juan Soto 12.00 30.00
15 Alex Bregman 4.00 10.00

2019 Panini Prizm Rookie Autographs

RANDOM INSERTS IN PACKS
EXCHANGE DEADLINE 11/15/2020
*PRIZM: .5X TO 1.2X
*PRIZM BLUE: .5X TO 1.2X
*PRIZM RED: .5X TO 1.2X
1 Kyle Wright 4.00 10.00
2 Justus Sheffield 4.00 10.00
3 Steven Duggar 3.00 8.00
4 Michael Kopech 5.00 12.00
5 Kolby Allard 4.00 10.00
7 Sean Reid-Foley 2.50 6.00
8 Jake Cave 3.00 8.00
9 Patrick Wisdom 2.50 6.00
10 Myles Straw 4.00 10.00
11 Luis Ortiz 2.50 6.00
12 Dakota Hudson 3.00 8.00
13 Brandon Lowe 12.00 30.00
14 Cedric Mullins 4.00 10.00
15 Framber Valdez 2.50 6.00
16 Reese McGuire 4.00 10.00
17 Taylor Ward 2.50 6.00
18 Chris Shaw 4.00 10.00
19 Rowdy Tellez 4.00 10.00
20 Danny Jansen 2.50 6.00
21 Enyel De Los Santos 2.50 6.00
22 Kevin Newman 4.00 10.00
23 Luis Urias 4.00 10.00
24 Bryse Wilson 3.00 8.00
25 Daniel Ponce de Leon 4.00 10.00
26 Jonathan Loaisiga 3.00 8.00
27 Josh James 4.00 10.00
28 Kyle Tucker 5.00 12.00
29 David Fletcher 8.00 20.00
30 Jacob Nix 3.00 8.00
31 Stephen Gonsalves 2.50 6.00
32 Ramon Laureano 6.00 15.00
33 Fernando Tatis Jr. 60.00 150.00
34 Chance Adams 2.50 6.00
35 Jonathan Davis 3.00 8.00
36 Garrett Hampson 2.50 6.00
37 Caleb Ferguson 3.00 8.00
38 Jake Bauers 4.00 10.00
39 Christin Stewart 3.00 8.00
40 Corbin Burnes 4.00 10.00
41 Cionel Perez 2.50 6.00
42 Eloy Jimenez 20.00 50.00
43 Touki Toussaint 3.00 8.00
44 Kevin Kramer 3.00 8.00
45 Vladimir Guerrero Jr. 30.00 80.00
46 Ryan O'Hearn 2.50 6.00
47 Dennis Santana 2.50 6.00
48 Ryan Borucki 2.50 6.00
49 Brad Keller 2.50 6.00
50 Jeff McNeil 6.00 15.00
51 Trevor Richards 2.50 6.00
53 Javier Guerra 2.50 6.00
54 Ryan Meisinger 2.50 6.00
55 Brett Kennedy 2.50 6.00
56 Eric Haase 2.50 6.00
57 Scott Barlow 2.50 6.00
58 James Norwood 2.50 6.00
59 Victor Reyes 2.50 6.00
60 Andrew Velazquez 2.50 6.00
61 Chad Sobotka 2.50 6.00
62 Duane Underwood 2.50 6.00
63 Austin Voth 2.50 6.00
64 Kohl Stewart 3.00 8.00
65 Nick Ciuffo 2.50 6.00
66 Pablo Lopez 2.50 6.00
67 Edmundo Sosa 3.00 8.00
68 Justin Williams 2.50 6.00
72 Ranger Suarez 2.50 6.00
75 Dean Deetz 2.50 6.00
76 Yusei Kikuchi 6.00 15.00
77 Austin Wynns 2.50 6.00
78 C.D. Pelham 2.50 6.00
81 Adam Kolarek 2.50 6.00
82 Abiatal Avelino 2.50 6.00
83 Thomas Pannone 4.00 10.00
88 Yency Almonte 2.50 6.00
89 Meibrys Viloria 2.50 6.00
90 Jefry Rodriguez 2.50 6.00
91 Tanner Rainey 2.50 6.00
92 Ty Buttrey 4.00 10.00
93 Gabriel Guerrero 2.50 6.00
94 Jalen Beeks 2.50 6.00
95 Connor Joe 2.50 6.00
96 Riley Ferrell 2.50 6.00
97 Richie Martin 2.50 6.00
99 Chris Ellis 2.50 6.00
100 Roseli Herrera 2.50 6.00

2019 Panini Prizm Rookie Autographs Prizms Blue Wave

*BLUE WAVE p/r 60: .6X TO 1.5X
*BLUE WAVE p/r 25: .75X TO 2X
RANDOM INSERTS IN PACKS
PRINT RUNS B/WN 5-60 COPIES PER
NO PRICING ON QTY 5 OR LESS
EXCHANGE DEADLINE 11/15/2020
85 Harold Castro/60 5.00 12.00

2019 Panini Prizm Rookie Autographs Prizms Burgandy Shimmer

*BURGANDY p/r 25: .75X TO 2X
RANDOM INSERTS IN PACKS
PRINT RUNS B/WN 5-25 COPIES PER
NO PRICING ON QTY 5
EXCHANGE DEADLINE 11/15/2020
85 Harold Castro/25 6.00 15.00

2019 Panini Prizm Rookie Autographs Prizms Carolina Blue

*CAR.BLUE p/r 50-100: .6X TO 1.5X
*CAR.BLUE p/r 25: .75X TO 2X
RANDOM INSERTS IN PACKS
PRINT RUNS B/WN 5-100 COPIES PER
NO PRICING ON QTY 5
EXCHANGE DEADLINE 11/15/2020
70 Nick Martini/100 4.00 10.00
74 Michael Perez/100 4.00 10.00
80 Isaac Galloway/100 4.00 10.00
84 Austin Dean/100 4.00 10.00
85 Harold Castro/100 5.00 12.00
86 Connor Sadzeck/100 4.00 10.00

2019 Panini Prizm Rookie Autographs Prizms Navy Blue Kaleidoscope

*NAVY p/r 35: .75X TO 2X
RANDOM INSERTS IN PACKS
PRINT RUNS B/WN 5-35 COPIES PER
NO PRICING ON QTY 5
EXCHANGE DEADLINE 11/15/2020
85 Harold Castro/35 6.00 15.00

2019 Panini Prizm Rookie Autographs Prizms Power Plaid

*PLAID p/r 75: .6X TO 1.5X
*PLAID p/r 25: .75X TO 2X
RANDOM INSERTS IN PACKS
PRINT RUNS B/WN 5-75 COPIES PER
NO PRICING ON QTY 5 OR LESS
EXCHANGE DEADLINE 11/15/2020
85 Harold Castro/75 5.00 12.00

2019 Panini Prizm Rookie Autographs Prizms Purple

*PURPLE p/r 50: .6X TO 1.5X
RANDOM INSERTS IN PACKS
PRINT RUNS B/WN 5-50 COPIES PER
NO PRICING ON QTY 5 OR LESS
EXCHANGE DEADLINE 11/15/2020
85 Harold Castro/50 5.00 12.00

2019 Panini Prizm Rookie Autographs Prizms Red White and Blue

*RWB p/r 50: .6X TO 1.5X
*RWB p/r 25: .75X TO 2X
RANDOM INSERTS IN PACKS
PRINT RUNS B/WN 5-50 COPIES PER
NO PRICING ON QTY 5 OR LESS
EXCHANGE DEADLINE 11/15/2020
85 Harold Castro/50 5.00 12.00

2019 Panini Prizm Rookie Autographs Prizms Snake Skin

*SNAKE p/r 50: .6X TO 1.5X
*SNAKE p/r 25: .75X TO 2X
RANDOM INSERTS IN PACKS
PRINT RUNS B/WN 5-50 COPIES PER
NO PRICING ON QTY 5 OR LESS
EXCHANGE DEADLINE 11/15/2020
85 Harold Castro/50 5.00 12.00

2019 Panini Prizm Rookie Autographs Prizms Zebra Stripes

*ZEBRA p/r 50-99: .6X TO 1.5X
*ZEBRA p/r 25: .75X TO 2X
RANDOM INSERTS IN PACKS
PRINT RUNS B/WN 3-99 COPIES PER
NO PRICING ON QTY 5 OR LESS
EXCHANGE DEADLINE 11/15/2020
85 Harold Castro/99 5.00 12.00

2019 Panini Prizm Scorching

RANDOM INSERTS IN PACKS
*PRIZMS: .75X TO 2X BASIC
1 Max Scherzer .50 1.25
2 Justin Verlander .50 1.25
3 Gerrit Cole .50 1.25
4 Jacob deGrom .50 1.25
5 Jordan Hicks .40 1.00
6 Aroldis Chapman .50 1.25
7 Trea Turner .40 1.00
8 Whit Merrifield .50 1.25
9 Jose Ramirez .40 1.00
10 Billy Hamilton .40 1.00
11 Luis Severino .40 1.00
12 Blake Snell .40 1.00
13 Michael Kopech .60 1.50
14 Shohei Ohtani .60 1.50
15 Walker Buehler .60 1.50

2019 Panini Prizm Signatures

RANDOM INSERTS IN PACKS
EXCHANGE DEADLINE 11/15/2020
1 Matt Olson 2.50 6.00
2 Andres Galarraga 3.00 8.00
3 Mike Foltynewicz 4.00 10.00
4 Jonathan Lucroy 3.00 8.00
5 Trevor Story 4.00 10.00
6 Victor Robles 6.00 15.00
7 Max Muncy 6.00 15.00
8 Lewis Brinson 2.50 6.00
9 Rhys Hoskins 10.00 25.00
10 Shohei Ohtani EXCH 75.00 200.00
11 Garrett Richards 3.00 8.00
12 Byron Buxton 3.00 8.00
13 Aledmys Diaz 3.00 8.00
14 Roberto Osuna 2.50 6.00
15 Fernando Rodney 2.50 6.00
16 Francisco Mejia 3.00 8.00
17 Walker Buehler 12.00 30.00
18 Eric Thames 2.50 6.00
19 Nomar Mazara 2.50 6.00
20 Bert Blyleven 3.00 8.00
22 Brian McCann 6.00 15.00
23 Carlos Gonzalez
24 Carlton Fisk 10.00 25.00
25 Eddie Rosario 6.00 15.00

2019 Panini Prizm Star Gazing

RANDOM INSERTS IN PACKS
*PRIZMS: .75X TO 2X BASIC
1 Mike Trout 2.50 6.00
2 Mookie Betts .75 2.00
3 Bryce Harper .75 2.00
4 Kris Bryant .60 1.50
5 Aaron Judge 1.25 3.00
6 Francisco Lindor .50 1.25
7 Nolan Arenado .60 1.50
8 Ronald Acuna Jr. 2.50 6.00
9 Shohei Ohtani .60 1.50
10 Jose Altuve .40 1.00

2020 Panini Prizm

1 Anthony Rendon .30 .75
2 Keston Hiura .40 1.00
3 T.J. Zeuch RC .30 .75
4 Brandon Woodruff .20 .50
5 Willy Adames .20 .50
6 Shin-Soo Choo .25 .60
7 Eddie Rosario .25 .60
8 Jorge Soler .30 .75
9 Kris Bryant .40 1.00
10 Domingo Leyba RC .40 1.00
11 Howie Kendrick .20 .50
12 Yasmani Grandal .20 .50
13 Yonathan Daza RC .40 1.00
14 David Fletcher .30 .75
15 Ramon Laureano .30 .75
16 John Means .20 .50
17 Kyle Seager .20 .50
18 Eduardo Rodriguez .20 .50
19 Jake Fraley RC .40 1.00
20 Austin Meadows .25 .60
21 Kirby Yates .20 .50
22 Niko Goodrum .25 .60
23 Mike Moustakas .25 .60
24 Lourdes Gurriel .25 .60
25 Isan Diaz RC .50 1.25
26 Patrick Sandoval RC .50 1.25
27 Tony Gonsolin RC 1.25 3.00
28 Cody Bellinger .60 1.50
29 Tommy Pham .20 .50
30 Nico Hoerner RC 1.25 3.00
31 Lucas Giolito .25 .60
32 Lorenzo Cain .20 .50
33 Joey Votto .30 .75
34 Buster Posey .40 1.00
35 Jacob deGrom .30 .75
36 Shane Bieber .30 .75
37 Brandon Lowe .30 .75
38 Cole Hamels .25 .60
39 Bobby Bradley RC .40 1.00
40 Zac Gallen RC .75 2.00
41 Starling Marte .25 .60
42 Julio Teheran .25 .60
43 Clayton Kershaw .60 1.50
44 Justin Dunn RC .40 1.00
45 Marco Gonzales .20 .50
46 Sheldon Neuse RC .40 1.00
47 Juan Soto 1.00 2.50
48 Jonathan Gray .20 .50
49 Jake Odorizzi .20 .50
50 Kyle Hendricks .30 .75
51 Marcell Ozuna .30 .75
52 Luke Weaver .20 .50
53 Randy Arozarena RC 2.50 6.00
54 Kolten Wong .25 .60
55 Aaron Nola .30 .75
56 Brusdar Graterol RC .50 1.25
57 Michael Brantley .25 .60
58 Jack Flaherty .25 .60
59 Ken Giles .20 .50
60 Marcus Stroman .25 .60
61 Jose Abreu .30 .75
62 Andres Munoz RC .40 1.00
63 Bryce Harper .50 1.25
64 Aaron Judge .75 2.00
65 Liam Hendriks .20 .50
66 Pete Alonso .75 2.00
67 Michael King RC .50 1.25
68 Matt Thaiss RC .40 1.00
69 Tyrone Taylor RC .30 .75
70 Logan Allen RC .30 .75
71 Bo Bichette RC 2.50 6.00
72 Deivy Grullon RC .30 .75
73 Joe Palumbo RC .30 .75
74 Brad Keller .20 .50
75 Spencer Turnbull .20 .50
76 Manny Machado .30 .75
77 Josh Bell .25 .60
78 Dallas Keuchel .25 .60
79 Evan Longoria .25 .60
80 Trent Grisham RC 1.25 3.00
81 Charlie Blackmon .30 .75
82 Gary Sanchez .30 .75
83 DJ LeMahieu .30 .75
84 Sean Manaea .20 .50
85 Gio Urshela .30 .75
86 George Springer .25 .60
87 James Paxton .25 .60
88 Luis Castillo .25 .60
89 Bryan Abreu RC .30 .75
90 Michel Baez RC .30 .75
91 Michael Chavis .25 .60
92 Hyun-Jin Ryu .25 .60
93 Stephen Strasburg .30 .75
94 Kyle Lewis RC 2.00 5.00
95 Josh Rojas RC .30 .75
96 Jonathan Hernandez RC .30 .75
97 Abraham Toro RC .40 1.00
98 Justin Turner .25 .60
99 Adalberto Mondesi .30 .75
100 Gleyber Torres .60 1.50
101 Adbert Alzolay RC .40 1.00
102 Dakota Hudson .25 .60
103 Nelson Cruz .30 .75
104 Jesus Luzardo RC .60 1.50
105 Jorge Polanco .25 .60
106 Ronald Bolanos RC .50 1.25
107 Josh Hader .20 .50
108 Scott Kingery .25 .60
109 Miguel Sano .25 .60
110 Hanser Alberto .20 .50
111 German Marquez .30 .75
112 Kevin Newman .25 .60
113 Willi Castro RC .50 1.25
114 Travis Demeritte RC .40 1.00
115 Mitch Garver .20 .50
116 Jordan Yamamoto RC .40 1.00
117 Mookie Betts .60 1.50
118 Omar Narvaez .20 .50
119 Max Fried .30 .75
120 Cavan Biggio .40 1.00
121 Danny Duffy .20 .50
122 Brett Gardner .25 .60
123 Marcus Semien .20 .50
124 Eduardo Escobar .20 .50
125 Avisail Garcia .25 .60
126 Dustin May RC 1.25 3.00
127 Lance Lynn .20 .50
128 Dylan Cease RC .60 1.50
129 Mike Clevinger .25 .60
130 Masahiro Tanaka .30 .75
131 Christian Yelich .40 1.00
132 Yu Darvish .30 .75
133 Sandy Alcantara .20 .50
134 Sean Murphy RC .50 1.25
135 Trent Thornton .20 .50
136 Sonny Gray .25 .60
137 Jake Rogers RC .30 .75
138 Francisco Lindor .30 .75
139 Adrian Morejon RC .30 .75
140 Aristides Aquino RC .60 1.50
141 Danny Mendick RC .40 1.00
142 Ketel Marte .25 .60
143 Xander Bogaerts .30 .75
144 Starlin Castro .20 .50
145 Max Kepler .25 .60
146 Jose Berrios .25 .60
147 Carlos Santana .25 .60
148 Trea Turner .25 .60
149 Matt Chapman .30 .75
150 Yusei Kikuchi .25 .60
151 Justin Verlander .30 .75
152 Yadier Molina .30 .75
153 Brendan McKay RC .50 1.25
154 Bryan Reynolds .25 .60
155 Mauricio Dubon RC .40 1.00
156 Rico Garcia RC .50 1.25
157 Matt Carpenter .30 .75
158 Jeff McNeil .25 .60
159 Miguel Cabrera .30 .75
160 Eloy Jimenez .60 1.50
161 Tim Anderson .30 .75
162 Shohei Ohtani .40 1.00
163 Noah Syndergaard .25 .60
164 Giancarlo Stanton .30 .75
165 Vladimir Guerrero Jr. .60 1.50
166 Freddie Freeman .40 1.00
167 Corey Kluber .25 .60
168 Logan Webb RC .40 1.00
169 David Dahl .20 .50
170 Mike Soroka .30 .75
171 Yu Chang RC .50 1.25
172 J.T. Realmuto .30 .75
173 Rafael Devers .40 1.00
174 Trevor Bauer .30 .75
175 Hunter Dozier .20 .50
176 Tyler Glasnow .20 .50
177 Eugenio Suarez .25 .60
178 Michael Conforto .25 .60
179 Nick Ahmed .20 .50
180 Javier Baez .40 1.00
181 Yordan Alvarez RC 1.50 4.00
182 Victor Robles .40 1.00
183 Chris Paddack .30 .75
184 Ronald Acuna Jr. 1.25 3.00
185 Matt Olson .20 .50
186 Paul Goldschmidt .30 .75
187 Patrick Corbin .25 .60
188 Alex Bregman .30 .75
189 Max Muncy .25 .60
190 Chris Sale .30 .75
191 Max Scherzer .30 .75
192 Jaylin Davis RC .50 1.25
193 Fernando Tatis Jr. 1.25 3.00
194 A.J. Puk RC .60 1.50
195 Brock Burke RC .30 .75
196 Mike Trout 1.50 4.00
197 Gerrit Cole .50 1.25
198 Gavin Lux RC 2.00 5.00
199 Matt Boyd .20 .50
200 Walker Buehler .40 1.00
201 Donnie Walton RC .75 2.00
202 Jonathan Villar .20 .50
203 Anthony Kay RC .30 .75
204 Dan Vogelbach .20 .50
205 Nicholas Castellanos .30 .75
206 Tres Barrera RC .60 1.50
207 Blake Snell .25 .60
208 Yoan Moncada .30 .75
209 Lewis Thorpe RC .30 .75
210 Rhys Hoskins .40 1.00
211 Aaron Civale RC .50 1.25
212 Trevor Story .30 .75
213 Tommy Edman .30 .75
214 Albert Pujols .40 1.00
215 Joey Gallo .30 .75
216 Christian Vazquez .20 .50
217 Charlie Morton .30 .75
218 Jose Ramirez .25 .60
219 Mike Fiers .20 .50
220 Corey Seager .30 .75
221 Jose Altuve .25 .60
222 Merrill Kelly .20 .50
223 Mike Yastrzemski .50 1.25
224 Anthony Rizzo .50 1.25
225 Paul DeJong .30 .75
226 Brian Anderson .20 .50
227 Robbie Ray .20 .50
228 J.D. Davis .20 .50
229 Josh Donaldson .25 .60
230 Nolan Arenado .40 1.00
231 Ozzie Albies .30 .75
232 Nick Solak RC .50 1.25
233 Zack Collins RC .40 1.00
234 Mike Minor .20 .50
235 Will Smith .40 1.00
236 Caleb Smith .20 .50
237 Carlos Correa .30 .75
238 Willson Contreras .30 .75
239 Zack Greinke .25 .60
240 Sam Hilliard RC .50 1.25
241 Edwin Rios RC .75 2.00
242 Kyle Schwarber .25 .60
243 Danny Santana .20 .50
244 J.D. Martinez .30 .75
245 James McCann .25 .60
246 Whit Merrifield .30 .75
247 Madison Bumgarner .25 .60
248 Zack Wheeler .25 .60
249 Trey Mancini .30 .75
250 Mitch Haniger .25 .60

2020 Panini Prizm Prizms Blue

*BLUE: 1X TO 2.5X BASIC
*BLUE RC: .6X TO 1.5X BASIC
RANDOM INSERTS IN PACKS
71 Bo Bichette 6.00 15.00

2020 Panini Prizm Prizms Blue Donut Circles

*BLUE DONUT: 2X TO 5X BASIC
*BLUE DONUT RC: 1.2X TO 3X BASIC
RANDOM INSERTS IN PACKS
STATED PRINT RUN 199 SER.#'d SETS
15 Ramon Laureano 2.50 6.00
71 Bo Bichette 12.00 30.00
94 Kyle Lewis 12.00 30.00

2020 Panini Prizm Prizms Blue Mojo

*BLUE MOJO: 2X TO 5X BASIC
*BLUE MOJO RC: 1.2X TO 3X BASIC
RANDOM INSERTS IN PACKS
STATED PRINT RUN 175 SER.#'d SETS
15 Ramon Laureano 2.50 6.00
71 Bo Bichette 12.00 30.00
94 Kyle Lewis 12.00 30.00

2020 Panini Prizm Prizms Blue Wave

*BLUE WAVE: 3X TO 8X
*BLUE WAVE RC: 2X TO 5X
RANDOM INSERTS IN PACKS
STATED PRINT RUN 60 SER.#'d SETS
15 Ramon Laureano 4.00 10.00
30 Nico Hoerner 10.00 25.00
71 Bo Bichette 20.00 50.00
94 Kyle Lewis 30.00 80.00
126 Dustin May 8.00 20.00
138 Francisco Lindor 5.00 12.00
198 Gavin Lux 15.00 40.00

2020 Panini Prizm Prizms Bronze Donut Circles

*BRNZ DONUT: 5X TO 12X
*BRNZ DONUT RC: 3X TO 8X
RANDOM INSERTS IN PACKS
STATED PRINT RUN 25 SER.#'d SETS
15 Ramon Laureano 6.00 15.00
30 Nico Hoerner 20.00 50.00
47 Juan Soto 20.00 50.00
63 Bryce Harper 12.00 30.00
64 Aaron Judge 15.00 40.00
71 Bo Bichette 40.00 100.00
86 George Springer 10.00 25.00
94 Kyle Lewis 50.00 120.00
100 Gleyber Torres 12.00 30.00
126 Dustin May 12.00 30.00
138 Francisco Lindor 8.00 20.00
181 Yordan Alvarez 30.00 80.00
184 Ronald Acuna Jr. 30.00 80.00
198 Gavin Lux 40.00 100.00

2020 Panini Prizm Prizms Burgundy Cracked Ice

*BUR.CRKD ICE: 5X TO 12X
*BUR.CRKD ICE RC: 3X TO 8X
RANDOM INSERTS IN PACKS
STATED PRINT RUN 25 SER.#'d SETS
15 Ramon Laureano 6.00 15.00
30 Nico Hoerner 20.00 50.00
47 Juan Soto 20.00 50.00
63 Bryce Harper 12.00 30.00
64 Aaron Judge 15.00 40.00
71 Bo Bichette 40.00 100.00
86 George Springer 10.00 25.00
94 Kyle Lewis 50.00 120.00
100 Gleyber Torres 12.00 30.00
126 Dustin May 12.00 30.00
138 Francisco Lindor 8.00 20.00
181 Yordan Alvarez 30.00 80.00
184 Ronald Acuna Jr. 30.00 80.00
198 Gavin Lux 40.00 100.00

2020 Panini Prizm Prizms Carolina Blue

*CAR.BLUE: 1.2X TO 3X BASIC
*CAR.BLUE RC: .8X TO 2X BASIC
RANDOM INSERTS IN PACKS
71 Bo Bichette 8.00 20.00
94 Kyle Lewis 6.00 15.00

2020 Panini Prizm Prizms Cosmic Haze

*COSMIC: 1.2X TO 3X BASIC
*COSMIC RC: .8X TO 2X BASIC
RANDOM INSERTS IN PACKS
71 Bo Bichette 8.00 20.00
94 Kyle Lewis 6.00 15.00

2020 Panini Prizm Prizms Green

*GREEN: 1.2X TO 3X BASIC
*GREEN RC: .8X TO 2X BASIC
RANDOM INSERTS IN PACKS
71 Bo Bichette 8.00 20.00
94 Kyle Lewis 6.00 15.00

2020 Panini Prizm Prizms Lime Green

*LIME GRN: 2.5X TO 6X BASIC
*LIME GRN RC: 1.5X TO 4X BASIC
RANDOM INSERTS IN PACKS
STATED PRINT RUN 125 SER.#'d SETS
15 Ramon Laureano 3.00 8.00
71 Bo Bichette 15.00 40.00
94 Kyle Lewis 15.00 40.00
126 Dustin May 6.00 15.00

2020 Panini Prizm Prizms Navy Blue Kaleidoscope

*NVY.BL.KAL: 4X TO 10X
*NVY.BL.KAL RC: 2.5X TO 6X
RANDOM INSERTS IN PACKS
STATED PRINT RUN 35 SER.#'d SETS
15 Ramon Laureano 5.00 12.00
30 Nico Hoerner 15.00 40.00
63 Bryce Harper 10.00 25.00
64 Aaron Judge 12.00 30.00
71 Bo Bichette 30.00 80.00
86 George Springer 8.00 20.00
94 Kyle Lewis 40.00 100.00
100 Gleyber Torres 10.00 25.00
126 Dustin May 10.00 25.00
138 Francisco Lindor 6.00 15.00
181 Yordan Alvarez 25.00 60.00
184 Ronald Acuna Jr. 25.00 60.00
198 Gavin Lux 30.00 80.00

2020 Panini Prizm Prizms Neon Orange

*NEON ORNG: 3X TO 8X BASIC
*NEON ORNG RC: 2X TO 5X BASIC
RANDOM INSERTS IN PACKS
STATED PRINT RUN 100 SER.#'d SETS
15 Ramon Laureano 4.00 10.00
30 Nico Hoerner 10.00 25.00
71 Bo Bichette 20.00 50.00
94 Kyle Lewis 30.00 80.00
126 Dustin May 8.00 20.00
138 Francisco Lindor 5.00 12.00

2020 Panini Prizm Prizms Pink

*PINK: 1.2X TO 3X BASIC
*PINK RC: .8X TO 2X BASIC
RANDOM INSERTS IN PACKS
71 Bo Bichette 8.00 20.00
94 Kyle Lewis 6.00 15.00

2020 Panini Prizm Prizms Power Plaid

*PLAID: 3X TO 8X
*PLAID RC: 2X TO 5X
RANDOM INSERTS IN PACKS
STATED PRINT RUN 75 SER.#'d SETS
15 Ramon Laureano 4.00 10.00
30 Nico Hoerner 10.00 25.00
71 Bo Bichette 20.00 50.00
94 Kyle Lewis 30.00 80.00
126 Dustin May 8.00 20.00
138 Francisco Lindor 5.00 12.00
198 Gavin Lux 15.00 40.00

2020 Panini Prizm Prizms Purple

*PURPLE: 1.2X TO 3X BASIC
*PURPLE RC: .8X TO 2X BASIC
RANDOM INSERTS IN PACKS
71 Bo Bichette 8.00 20.00
94 Kyle Lewis 6.00 15.00

2020 Panini Prizm Prizms Red

*RED: 1X TO 2.5X BASIC
*RED RC: .6X TO 1.5X BASIC
RANDOM INSERTS IN PACKS
71 Bo Bichette 6.00 15.00

2020 Panini Prizm Prizms Red Donut Circles

*RED DONUT: 3X TO 8X BASIC
*RED DONUT RC: 2X TO 5X BASIC
RANDOM INSERTS IN PACKS
STATED PRINT RUN 99 SER.#'d SETS
15 Ramon Laureano 4.00 10.00
30 Nico Hoerner 10.00 25.00
71 Bo Bichette 20.00 50.00
94 Kyle Lewis 30.00 80.00
126 Dustin May 8.00 20.00
138 Francisco Lindor 5.00 12.00
198 Gavin Lux 12.00 30.00

2020 Panini Prizm Prizms Red Mojo

*RED MOJO: 2.5X TO 6X BASIC
*RED MOJO RC: 1.5X TO 4X BASIC
RANDOM INSERTS IN PACKS
STATED PRINT RUN 149 SER.#'d SETS
15 Ramon Laureano 3.00 8.00
71 Bo Bichette 15.00 40.00
94 Kyle Lewis 15.00 40.00
126 Dustin May 6.00 15.00

2020 Panini Prizm Prizms Red Orange

*RED ORNG: 1.2X TO 3X BASIC
*RED ORNG RC: .8X TO 2X BASIC
RANDOM INSERTS IN PACKS
71 Bo Bichette 8.00 20.00
94 Kyle Lewis 6.00 15.00

2020 Panini Prizm Prizms Red Wave

*RED WAVE: 3X TO 8X BASIC
*RED WAVE RC: 2X TO 5X BASIC
RANDOM INSERTS IN PACKS
STATED PRINT RUN 99 SER.#'d SETS
15 Ramon Laureano 4.00 10.00
30 Nico Hoerner 10.00 25.00
71 Bo Bichette 20.00 50.00
94 Kyle Lewis 30.00 80.00
126 Dustin May 8.00 20.00
138 Francisco Lindor 5.00 12.00
198 Gavin Lux 12.00 30.00

2020 Panini Prizm Prizms Red White and Blue

*RWB: 1.2X TO 3X BASIC
*RWB RC: .8X TO 2X BASIC
RANDOM INSERTS IN PACKS
71 Bo Bichette 8.00 20.00
94 Kyle Lewis 6.00 15.00

2020 Panini Prizm Prizms Silver

*SILVER: 1.5X TO 4X BASIC
*SILVER RC: 1X TO 2.5X BASIC
RANDOM INSERTS IN PACKS
71 Bo Bichette 10.00 25.00
94 Kyle Lewis 8.00 20.00

2020 Panini Prizm Prizms Snake Skin

*SNAKE SKIN: 4X TO 10X
*SNAKE SKIN RC: 2.5X TO 6X
RANDOM INSERTS IN PACKS
STATED PRINT RUN 50 SER.#'d SETS
15 Ramon Laureano 5.00 12.00
30 Nico Hoerner 15.00 40.00
63 Bryce Harper 10.00 25.00
64 Aaron Judge 12.00 30.00
71 Bo Bichette 30.00 80.00
86 George Springer 8.00 20.00
94 Kyle Lewis 40.00 100.00
100 Gleyber Torres 10.00 25.00
126 Dustin May 10.00 25.00
138 Francisco Lindor 6.00 15.00
181 Yordan Alvarez 25.00 60.00
184 Ronald Acuna Jr. 25.00 60.00
198 Gavin Lux 30.00 80.00

2020 Panini Prizm Prizms Teal Wave

*TEAL WAVE: 1.2X TO 3X BASIC
*TEAL WAVE RC: .8X TO 2X BASIC
RANDOM INSERTS IN PACKS
71 Bo Bichette 8.00 20.00
94 Kyle Lewis 6.00 15.00

2020 Panini Prizm Brilliance

RANDOM INSERTS IN PACKS
*BLUE: .6X TO 1.5X BASIC
*CAR.BLUE: .6X TO 1.5X BASIC
*COSMIC: .6X TO 1.5X BASIC
*GREEN: .6X TO 1.5X BASIC
*PINK: .6X TO 1.5X BASIC
*PURPLE: .6X TO 1.5X BASIC
*RED: .6X TO 1.5X BASIC
*RED ORNG: .6X TO 1.5X BASIC
*RWB: .6X TO 1.5X BASIC
*SILVER: .6X TO 1.5X BASIC
*TEAL WAVE: .6X TO 1.5X BASIC
*WHITE WAVE: .6X TO 1.5X BASIC
*BLUE DONUT/199: .8X TO 2X BASIC
*BLUE MOJO/175: .8X TO 2X BASIC
*RED MOJO/149: 1X TO 2.5X BASIC
*LIME GRN/125: 1X TO 2.5X BASIC
1 Jacob deGrom .50 1.25
2 Gerrit Cole .75 2.00
3 Pete Alonso 1.25 3.00
4 Vladimir Guerrero Jr. 1.00 2.50
5 Javier Baez .60 1.50
6 Christian Yelich .60 1.50
7 Jose Altuve .40 1.00
8 Rafael Devers .60 1.50
9 Manny Machado .50 1.25
10 Charlie Blackmon .50 1.25

2020 Panini Prizm Brilliance Prizms Blue Wave

*BLUE WAVE: 1.2X TO 3X BASIC
RANDOM INSERTS IN PACKS
STATED PRINT RUN 60 SER.#'d SETS
4 Vladimir Guerrero Jr. 5.00 12.00

2020 Panini Prizm Brilliance Prizms Bronze Donut Circles
*BRNZ DONUT: 2X TO 5X BASIC
RANDOM INSERTS IN PACKS
STATED PRINT RUN 25 SER.#'d SETS
4 Vladimir Guerrero Jr. 8.00 20.00

2020 Panini Prizm Brilliance Prizms Burgundy Cracked Ice
*BUR.CRKD ICE: 2X TO 5X BASIC
RANDOM INSERTS IN PACKS
STATED PRINT RUN 25 SER.#'d SETS
4 Vladimir Guerrero Jr. 8.00 20.00

2020 Panini Prizm Brilliance Prizms Navy Blue Kaleidoscope
*NVY BLU.KAL.: 1.5X TO 4X BASIC
RANDOM INSERTS IN PACKS
STATED PRINT RUN 35 SER.#'d SETS
4 Vladimir Guerrero Jr. 6.00 15.00

2020 Panini Prizm Brilliance Prizms Neon Orange
*NEON ORNG: 1.2X TO 3X BASIC
RANDOM INSERTS IN PACKS
STATED PRINT RUN 100 SER.#'d SETS
4 Vladimir Guerrero Jr. 5.00 12.00

2020 Panini Prizm Brilliance Prizms Power Plaid
*PLAID: 1.2X TO 3X BASIC
RANDOM INSERTS IN PACKS
STATED PRINT RUN 75 SER.#'d SETS
4 Vladimir Guerrero Jr. 5.00 12.00

2020 Panini Prizm Brilliance Prizms Red Donut Circles
*RED DONUT: 1.2X TO 3X BASIC
RANDOM INSERTS IN PACKS
STATED PRINT RUN 99 SER.#'d SETS
4 Vladimir Guerrero Jr. 5.00 12.00

2020 Panini Prizm Brilliance Prizms Red Wave
*RED WAVE: 1.2X TO 3X BASIC
RANDOM INSERTS IN PACKS
STATED PRINT RUN 99 SER.#'d SETS
4 Vladimir Guerrero Jr. 5.00 12.00

2020 Panini Prizm Brilliance Prizms Snake Skin
*SNAKE SKIN: 1.5X TO 4X BASIC
RANDOM INSERTS IN PACKS
STATED PRINT RUN 50 SER.#'d SETS
4 Vladimir Guerrero Jr. 6.00 15.00

2020 Panini Prizm Color Blast
RANDOM INSERTS IN PACKS
1 Fernando Tatis Jr. 125.00 300.00
2 Vladimir Guerrero Jr. 125.00 300.00
3 Pete Alonso 100.00 250.00
4 Ken Griffey Jr. 150.00 400.00
5 Yordan Alvarez 80.00 200.00
6 Cody Bellinger 100.00 250.00
7 Juan Soto 150.00 400.00
8 Rafael Devers 30.00 80.00
9 Alex Bregman 50.00 120.00
10 Francisco Lindor 50.00 120.00

2020 Panini Prizm Fireworks
RANDOM INSERTS IN PACKS
1 Christian Yelich .60 1.50
2 Pete Alonso 1.25 3.00
3 Nolan Arenado .60 1.50
4 Mookie Betts 1.00 2.50
5 Cody Bellinger 1.00 2.50
6 Mike Trout 2.50 6.00
7 Ronald Acuna Jr. 2.00 5.00
8 Juan Soto 1.50 4.00
9 Jose Altuve .40 1.00
10 Aaron Judge 1.25 3.00

2020 Panini Prizm Fireworks Prizms Silver
*SILVER: .6X TO 1.5X BASIC
RANDOM INSERTS IN PACKS
2 Pete Alonso 3.00 8.00

2020 Panini Prizm Game Ball Graphs Prizms Silver
*SILVER: .5X TO 1.2X BASIC
RANDOM INSERTS IN PACKS
EXCHANGE DEADLINE 12/17/2021
2 Manny Machado 15.00 40.00
3 Gleyber Torres 30.00 80.00

2020 Panini Prizm Gems
RANDOM INSERTS IN PACKS
1 Bryce Harper 15.00 40.00
2 Christian Yelich 15.00 40.00
3 Shohei Ohtani 12.00 30.00
4 Javier Baez 12.00 30.00
5 Kris Bryant 20.00 50.00
6 Manny Machado 12.00 30.00
7 Mookie Betts 15.00 40.00
8 Mike Trout 60.00 150.00
9 Ronald Acuna Jr. 40.00 100.00
10 Aaron Judge 20.00 50.00

2020 Panini Prizm Illumination
RANDOM INSERTS IN PACKS
*BLUE: .6X TO 1.5X BASIC
*CAR.BLUE: .6X TO 1.5X BASIC
*COSMIC: .6X TO 1.5X BASIC
*GREEN: .6X TO 1.5X BASIC
*PINK: .6X TO 1.5X BASIC
*PURPLE: .6X TO 1.5X BASIC
*RED: .6X TO 1.5X BASIC
*RED ORNG: .6X TO 1.5X BASIC
*RWB: .6X TO 1.5X BASIC
*SILVER: .6X TO 1.5X BASIC
*TEAL WAVE: .6X TO 1.5X BASIC
*WHITE WAVE: .6X TO 1.5X BASIC
*BLUE DONUT/199: .8X TO 2X BASIC
*BLUE MOJO/175: .8X TO 2X BASIC
*RED MOJO/149: 1X TO 2.5X BASIC
*LIME GRN/125: 1X TO 2.5X BASIC
1 Stephen Strasburg .50 1.25
2 Justin Verlander .50 1.25
3 Fernando Tatis Jr. 2.00 5.00
4 Nolan Arenado .60 1.50
5 Bryce Harper .75 2.00
6 Yordan Alvarez 1.50 4.00
7 Freddie Freeman .60 1.50
8 Yoan Moncada .60 1.50
9 Kris Bryant .60 1.50
10 Ketel Marte .40 1.00
11 Shohei Ohtani .60 1.50
12 Anthony Rendon .50 1.25

2020 Panini Prizm Illumination Prizms Blue Wave
*BLUE WAVE/60: 1.2X TO 3X BASIC
RANDOM INSERTS IN PACKS
STATED PRINT RUN 60 SER.#'d SETS
3 Fernando Tatis Jr. 6.00 15.00

2020 Panini Prizm Illumination Prizms Bronze Donut Circles
*BRNZ DONUT/25: 2X TO 5X BASIC
RANDOM INSERTS IN PACKS
STATED PRINT RUN 25 SER.#'d SETS
3 Fernando Tatis Jr. 25.00 60.00

2020 Panini Prizm Illumination Prizms Burgundy Cracked Ice
*BUR.CRKD ICE/25: 2X TO 5X BASIC
RANDOM INSERTS IN PACKS
STATED PRINT RUN 25 SER.#'d SETS
3 Fernando Tatis Jr. 25.00 60.00

2020 Panini Prizm Illumination Prizms Navy Blue Kaleidoscope
*NVY BLU.KAL/35: 1.5X TO 4X BASIC
RANDOM INSERTS IN PACKS
STATED PRINT RUN 35 SER.#'d SETS
3 Fernando Tatis Jr. 15.00 40.00

2020 Panini Prizm Illumination Prizms Neon Orange
*NEON ORNG/100: 1.2X TO 3X BASIC
RANDOM INSERTS IN PACKS
STATED PRINT RUN 100 SER.#'d SETS
3 Fernando Tatis Jr. 6.00 15.00

2020 Panini Prizm Illumination Prizms Power Plaid
*PLAID/75: 1.2X TO 3X BASIC
RANDOM INSERTS IN PACKS
STATED PRINT RUN 75 SER.#'d SETS
3 Fernando Tatis Jr. 6.00 15.00

2020 Panini Prizm Illumination Prizms Red Donut Circles
*RED DONUT/99: 1.2X TO 3X BASIC
RANDOM INSERTS IN PACKS
STATED PRINT RUN 99 SER.#'d SETS
3 Fernando Tatis Jr. 6.00 15.00

2020 Panini Prizm Illumination Prizms Red Wave
*RED WAVE/99: 1.2X TO 3X BASIC
RANDOM INSERTS IN PACKS
STATED PRINT RUN 99 SER.#'d SETS
3 Fernando Tatis Jr. 6.00 15.00

2020 Panini Prizm Illumination Prizms Snake Skin
*SNAKE SKIN/50: 1.5X TO 4X BASIC
RANDOM INSERTS IN PACKS
STATED PRINT RUN 50 SER.#'d SETS
3 Fernando Tatis Jr. 15.00 40.00

2020 Panini Prizm Instant Impact
RANDOM INSERTS IN PACKS
*BLUE: .6X TO 1.5X BASIC
*CAR.BLUE: .6X TO 1.5X BASIC
*COSMIC: .6X TO 1.5X BASIC
*GREEN: .6X TO 1.5X BASIC
*PINK: .6X TO 1.5X BASIC
*PURPLE: .6X TO 1.5X BASIC
*RED: .6X TO 1.5X BASIC
*RED ORNG: .6X TO 1.5X BASIC
*RWB: .6X TO 1.5X BASIC
*SILVER: .6X TO 1.5X BASIC
*TEAL WAVE: .6X TO 1.5X BASIC
*WHITE WAVE: .6X TO 1.5X BASIC
1 Ronald Acuna Jr. 2.00 5.00
2 Bryce Harper .75 2.00
3 Javier Baez .60 1.50
4 Mike Trout 2.50 6.00
5 Christian Yelich .60 1.50
6 Josh Bell .40 1.00
7 Juan Soto 1.50 4.00
8 Cody Bellinger 1.00 2.50
9 Whit Merrifield .50 1.25
10 Xander Bogaerts .50 1.25

2020 Panini Prizm Instant Impact Prizms Blue Donut Circles
*BLUE DONUT/199: .8X TO 2X BASIC
RANDOM INSERTS IN PACKS
STATED PRINT RUN 199 SER.#'d SETS
2 Bryce Harper 4.00 10.00
4 Mike Trout 10.00 25.00
7 Juan Soto 3.00 8.00

2020 Panini Prizm Instant Impact Prizms Blue Mojo
*BLUE MOJO/175: .8X TO 2X BASIC
RANDOM INSERTS IN PACKS
STATED PRINT RUN 175 SER.#'d SETS
2 Bryce Harper 4.00
4 Mike Trout 10.00 25.00
7 Juan Soto 3.00 8.00

2020 Panini Prizm Instant Impact Prizms Blue Wave
*BLUE WAVE/60: 1.2X TO 3X BASIC
RANDOM INSERTS IN PACKS
STATED PRINT RUN 60 SER.#'d SETS
2 Bryce Harper 6.00 15.00
4 Mike Trout 15.00 40.00
7 Juan Soto 5.00 12.00

2020 Panini Prizm Instant Impact Prizms Bronze Donut Circles
*BRNZ DONUT/25: 2X TO 5X BASIC
RANDOM INSERTS IN PACKS
STATED PRINT RUN 25 SER.#'d SETS
2 Bryce Harper 10.00 25.00
4 Mike Trout 30.00 80.00
7 Juan Soto 8.00 20.00

2020 Panini Prizm Instant Impact Prizms Burgundy Cracked Ice
*BUR.CRKD ICE/25: 2X TO 5X BASIC
RANDOM INSERTS IN PACKS
STATED PRINT RUN 25 SER.#'d SETS
2 Bryce Harper 10.00 25.00
4 Mike Trout 30.00 80.00
7 Juan Soto 8.00 20.00

2020 Panini Prizm Instant Impact Prizms Lime Green
*LIME GRN/125: 1X TO 2.5X BASIC
RANDOM INSERTS IN PACKS
STATED PRINT RUN 125 SER.#'d SETS
2 Bryce Harper 5.00 12.00
4 Mike Trout 12.00 30.00
7 Juan Soto 4.00 10.00

2020 Panini Prizm Instant Impact Prizms Navy Blue Kaleidoscope
*NVY BLU.KAL/35: 1.5X TO 4X BASIC
RANDOM INSERTS IN PACKS
STATED PRINT RUN 35 SER.#'d SETS
2 Bryce Harper 8.00 20.00
4 Mike Trout 25.00 60.00
7 Juan Soto 6.00 15.00

2020 Panini Prizm Instant Impact Prizms Neon Orange
*NEON ORNG/100: 1.2X TO 3X BASIC
RANDOM INSERTS IN PACKS
STATED PRINT RUN 100 SER.#'d SETS
2 Bryce Harper 6.00 15.00
4 Mike Trout 15.00 40.00
7 Juan Soto 5.00 12.00

2020 Panini Prizm Instant Impact Prizms Power Plaid
*PLAID/75: 1.2X TO 3X BASIC
RANDOM INSERTS IN PACKS
STATED PRINT RUN 75 SER.#'d SETS
2 Bryce Harper 6.00 15.00
4 Mike Trout 15.00 40.00
7 Juan Soto 5.00 12.00

2020 Panini Prizm Instant Impact Prizms Red Donut Circles
*RED DONUT/99: 1.2X TO 3X BASIC
RANDOM INSERTS IN PACKS
STATED PRINT RUN 99 SER.#'d SETS
2 Bryce Harper 6.00 15.00
4 Mike Trout 15.00 40.00
7 Juan Soto 5.00 12.00

2020 Panini Prizm Instant Impact Prizms Red Mojo
*RED MOJO/149: 1X TO 2.5X BASIC
RANDOM INSERTS IN PACKS
STATED PRINT RUN 149 SER.#'d SETS
2 Bryce Harper 5.00 12.00
4 Mike Trout 12.00 30.00
7 Juan Soto 4.00 10.00

2020 Panini Prizm Instant Impact Prizms Red Wave
*RED WAVE/99: 1.2X TO 3X BASIC
RANDOM INSERTS IN PACKS
STATED PRINT RUN 99 SER.#'d SETS
2 Bryce Harper 6.00 15.00
4 Mike Trout 15.00 40.00
7 Juan Soto 5.00 12.00

2020 Panini Prizm Instant Impact Prizms Snake Skin
*SNAKE SKIN/50: 1.5X TO 4X BASIC
RANDOM INSERTS IN PACKS
STATED PRINT RUN 50 SER.#'d SETS
2 Bryce Harper 8.00 20.00
4 Mike Trout 25.00 60.00
7 Juan Soto 6.00 15.00

2020 Panini Prizm Lumber Inc
RANDOM INSERTS IN PACKS
1 Vladimir Guerrero Jr. 1.00 2.50
2 Nelson Cruz .50 1.25
3 Alex Bregman .50 1.25
4 Gleyber Torres 1.00 2.50
5 J.D. Martinez .50 1.25
6 Matt Olson .30 .75
7 Trey Mancini .50 1.25
8 Bryce Harper .75 2.00
9 Eugenio Suarez .40 1.00
10 Kyle Schwarber .50 1.25

2020 Panini Prizm Lumber Inc Prizms Silver
*SILVER: .6X TO 1.5X BASIC
RANDOM INSERTS IN PACKS
8 Bryce Harper 4.00 10.00

2020 Panini Prizm Machines
RANDOM INSERTS IN PACKS
*SILVER: .6X TO 1.5X BASIC
1 George Springer .40 1.00
2 Freddie Freeman .60 1.50
3 Ronald Acuna Jr. 2.00 5.00
4 Mike Trout 3.00 8.00
5 Tim Anderson .50 1.25
6 Ketel Marte .40 1.00
7 DJ LeMahieu .50 1.25
8 Jeff McNeil .40 1.00
9 Whit Merrifield .50 1.25
10 Rafael Devers .60 1.50

2020 Panini Prizm Now On Deck
RANDOM INSERTS IN PACKS
*SILVER: .6X TO 1.5X BASIC
1 Wander Franco 3.00 8.00
2 Luis Robert 3.00 8.00
3 Jo Adell 1.25 3.00
4 Royce Lewis .75 2.00
5 Cristian Pache 1.00 2.50
6 Alex Kirilloff .60 1.50
7 Joey Bart 1.00 2.50
8 Drew Waters .75 2.00
9 Dylan Carlson 1.25 3.00
10 Julio Rodriguez 2.00 5.00
11 Taylor Trammell .40 1.00
12 Keibert Ruiz .75 2.00
13 Alec Bohm 2.00 5.00
14 Ke'Bryan Hayes .30 .75
15 Nolan Jones .50 1.25

2020 Panini Prizm Numbers Game
RANDOM INSERTS IN PACKS
*BLUE: .6X TO 1.5X BASIC
*CAR.BLUE: .6X TO 1.5X BASIC
*COSMIC: .6X TO 1.5X BASIC
*GREEN: .6X TO 1.5X BASIC
*PINK: .6X TO 1.5X BASIC
*PURPLE: .6X TO 1.5X BASIC
*RED: .6X TO 1.5X BASIC
*RED ORNG: .6X TO 1.5X BASIC
*RWB: .6X TO 1.5X BASIC
*SILVER: .6X TO 1.5X BASIC
*TEAL WAVE: .6X TO 1.5X BASIC
*WHITE WAVE: .6X TO 1.5X BASIC
1 Juan Soto 1.50 4.00
2 Kris Bryant .60 1.50
3 Cody Bellinger 1.00 2.50
4 Alex Bregman .50 1.25
5 Mookie Betts 1.00 2.50
6 Jose Abreu .50 1.25
7 Nelson Cruz .50 1.25
8 Shohei Ohtani .60 1.50

2020 Panini Prizm Numbers Game Prizms Blue Donut Circles
*BLUE DONUT/199: .8X TO 2X BASIC
RANDOM INSERTS IN PACKS
STATED PRINT RUN 199 SER.#'d SETS
5 Mookie Betts 6.00 15.00

2020 Panini Prizm Numbers Game Prizms Blue Mojo
*BLUE MOJO/175: .8X TO 2X BASIC
RANDOM INSERTS IN PACKS
STATED PRINT RUN 175 SER.#'d SETS
5 Mookie Betts 6.00 15.00

2020 Panini Prizm Numbers Game Prizms Blue Wave
*BLUE WAVE/60: 1.2X TO 3X BASIC
RANDOM INSERTS IN PACKS
STATED PRINT RUN 60 SER.#'d SETS
1 Juan Soto 4.00 10.00
5 Mookie Betts 10.00 25.00

2020 Panini Prizm Numbers Game Prizms Bronze Donut Circles
*BRNZ DONUT/25: 2X TO 5X BASIC
RANDOM INSERTS IN PACKS
STATED PRINT RUN 25 SER.#'d SETS
1 Juan Soto 8.00 20.00
5 Mookie Betts 15.00 40.00

2020 Panini Prizm Numbers Game Prizms Burgundy Cracked Ice
*BUR.CRKD ICE/25: 2X TO 5X BASIC
RANDOM INSERTS IN PACKS
STATED PRINT RUN 25 SER.#'d SETS
1 Juan Soto 8.00 20.00
5 Mookie Betts 15.00 40.00

2020 Panini Prizm Numbers Game Prizms Lime Green
*LIME GRN/125: 1X TO 2.5X BASIC
RANDOM INSERTS IN PACKS
STATED PRINT RUN 125 SER.#'d SETS
5 Mookie Betts 8.00 20.00

2020 Panini Prizm Numbers Game Prizms Navy Blue Kaleidoscope
*NVY BLU.KAL/35: 1.5X TO 4X BASIC
RANDOM INSERTS IN PACKS
STATED PRINT RUN 35 SER.#'d SETS
1 Juan Soto 6.00 15.00
5 Mookie Betts 12.00 30.00

2020 Panini Prizm Numbers Game Prizms Neon Orange
*NEON ORNG/100: 1.2X TO 3X BASIC
RANDOM INSERTS IN PACKS
STATED PRINT RUN 100 SER.#'d SETS
1 Juan Soto 4.00 10.00
5 Mookie Betts 10.00 25.00

2020 Panini Prizm Numbers Game Prizms Power Plaid
*PLAID/75: 1.2X TO 3X BASIC
RANDOM INSERTS IN PACKS
STATED PRINT RUN 75 SER.#'d SETS
1 Juan Soto 4.00 10.00
5 Mookie Betts 10.00 25.00

2020 Panini Prizm Numbers Game Prizms Red Donut Circles
*RED DONUT/99: 1.2X TO 3X BASIC
RANDOM INSERTS IN PACKS
STATED PRINT RUN 99 SER.#'d SETS
1 Juan Soto 4.00 10.00
5 Mookie Betts 10.00 25.00

2020 Panini Prizm Numbers Game Prizms Red Mojo
*RED MOJO/149: 1X TO 2.5X BASIC
RANDOM INSERTS IN PACKS
STATED PRINT RUN 149 SER.#'d SETS
5 Mookie Betts 8.00 20.00

2020 Panini Prizm Numbers Game Prizms Red Wave
*RED WAVE/99: 1.2X TO 3X BASIC
RANDOM INSERTS IN PACKS
STATED PRINT RUN 99 SER.#'d SETS
1 Juan Soto 4.00 10.00
5 Mookie Betts 10.00 25.00

2020 Panini Prizm Numbers Game Prizms Snake Skin
*SNAKE SKIN/50: 1.5X TO 4X BASIC
RANDOM INSERTS IN PACKS
STATED PRINT RUN 50 SER.#'d SETS
1 Juan Soto 6.00 15.00
5 Mookie Betts 12.00 30.00

2020 Panini Prizm Pro Penmanship
RANDOM INSERTS IN PACKS
EXCHANGE DEADLINE 12/17/2021
1 Aaron Judge EXCH 40.00 100.00
2 Shohei Ohtani EXCH
3 Juan Soto EXCH 30.00 80.00
4 Eloy Jimenez EXCH 12.00 30.00
5 Vladimir Guerrero Jr. 25.00 60.00
6 Fernando Tatis Jr. 60.00 150.00
7 Michael Chavis 3.00 8.00
8 Mike Soroka 8.00 20.00
9 Xander Bogaerts 12.00 30.00
10 Nolan Arenado 20.00 50.00
11 Jaime Barria 2.50 6.00
12 Ryan O'Hearn 2.50 6.00
13 Adam Haseley 4.00 10.00
14 Patrick Wisdom 2.50 6.00
15 Austin Barnes 2.50 6.00
16 Willy Adames 2.50 6.00
17 Justin Williams 2.50 6.00
18 Austin Dean 2.50 6.00
19 Trevor Richards 2.50 6.00
20 Taylor Clarke 2.50 6.00

2020 Panini Prizm Pro Penmanship Prizms Silver
*SILVER: .5X TO 1.2X BASIC
RANDOM INSERTS IN PACKS
EXCHANGE DEADLINE 12/17/2021
2 Shohei Ohtani EXCH 50.00 120.00

2020 Panini Prizm Prospect Signatures
RANDOM INSERTS IN PACKS
EXCHANGE DEADLINE 12/17/2021
1 Drew Waters 10.00 25.00
2 Bobby Dalbec 5.00 12.00
3 Nick Madrigal 8.00 20.00
4 Jo Adell 15.00 40.00
5 Alex Kirilloff 5.00 12.00
6 Jasson Dominguez EXCH 125.00 300.00
7 Joey Bart 12.00 30.00
8 Wander Franco EXCH 50.00 120.00
9 Nate Pearson 10.00 25.00
10 Taylor Trammell 3.00 8.00
11 Vidal Brujan 8.00 20.00
12 Marco Luciano 10.00 25.00
13 Dylan Carlson 15.00 40.00
14 Alec Bohm 15.00 40.00
15 Royce Lewis 8.00 20.00
16 Sixto Sanchez 6.00 15.00
18 Luis Robert 50.00 120.00
19 Ryan Mountcastle 4.00 10.00

2020 Panini Prizm Prospect Signatures Prizms Silver
*SILVER: .5X TO 1.2X BASIC
RANDOM INSERTS IN PACKS
EXCHANGE DEADLINE 12/17/2021
4 Jo Adell 40.00 100.00
6 Jasson Dominguez EXCH 200.00 500.00

2020 Panini Prizm Rookie Autographs
RANDOM INSERTS IN PACKS
EXCHANGE DEADLINE 12/17/2021
1 Abraham Toro 3.00 8.00
2 Adrian Morejon 2.50 6.00
3 Kyle Lewis 20.00 50.00
4 Aaron Civale 4.00 10.00
5 Tony Gonsolin 10.00 25.00
6 Jake Fraley 3.00 8.00
7 Jake Rogers 2.50 6.00
8 Isan Diaz 4.00 10.00
9 Michael King 4.00 10.00
10 Brock Burke 2.50 6.00
11 Zac Gallen 6.00 15.00
12 T.J. Zeuch 2.50 6.00
13 Yu Chang 4.00 10.00
14 Gavin Lux 20.00 50.00
15 Logan Webb 3.00 8.00
16 Sam Hilliard 4.00 10.00
17 Brendan McKay 4.00 10.00
18 Sean Murphy 4.00 10.00
19 Danny Mendick 3.00 8.00
20 Jaylin Davis 4.00 10.00
21 Dustin May 25.00 60.00
22 Travis Demeritte 3.00 8.00
23 Sheldon Neuse 3.00 8.00
24 Anthony Kay 2.50 6.00
25 A.J. Puk 5.00 12.00
26 Ronald Bolanos 4.00 10.00
27 Jesus Luzardo 12.00 30.00
28 Andres Munoz 3.00 8.00
29 Jordan Yamamoto 3.00 8.00
30 Lewis Thorpe 2.50 6.00
31 Trent Grisham 6.00 15.00
32 Domingo Leyba 3.00 8.00
33 Donnie Walton 6.00 15.00
34 Patrick Sandoval 4.00 10.00
35 Deivy Grullon 2.50 6.00
36 Yonathan Daza 3.00 8.00
37 Justin Dunn 3.00 8.00
38 Joe Palumbo 2.50 6.00
39 Michel Baez 2.50 6.00
40 Brusdar Graterol 4.00 10.00
41 Nico Hoerner 6.00 15.00
42 Rico Garcia 4.00 10.00
43 Mauricio Dubon 6.00 15.00
44 Zack Collins 3.00 8.00
45 Bo Bichette 30.00 80.00
46 Bryan Abreu 2.50 6.00
47 Edwin Rios 6.00 15.00
48 Matt Thaiss 3.00 8.00
49 Yordan Alvarez EXCH 25.00 60.00
50 Willi Castro 4.00 10.00
51 Jonathan Hernandez 2.50 6.00
52 Bobby Bradley 3.00 8.00
53 Randy Arozarena 40.00 100.00
54 Logan Allen 2.50 6.00
55 Nick Solak 4.00 10.00
56 Adbert Alzolay 3.00 8.00
57 Dylan Cease 5.00 12.00
58 Tyrone Taylor 2.50 6.00
59 Tres Barrera 5.00 12.00
60 Josh Rojas 2.50 6.00
61 Aristides Aquino 8.00 20.00
62 Scott Heineman 2.50 6.00
63 Edgar Garcia 2.50 6.00
64 Kyle Garlick 4.00 10.00
66 Alex Young 2.50 6.00
67 Tyler Alexander 4.00 10.00
69 Huascar Ynoa 4.00 10.00
70 Bubba Starling 5.00 12.00
73 Nick Dini 3.00 8.00
74 Yoshitomo Tsutsugo EXCH 15.00 40.00
75 Hunter Harvey 4.00 10.00
76 Dom Nunez 3.00 8.00
78 Zach Green 2.50 6.00
79 Kwang-Hyun Kim 12.00 30.00
80 LaMonte Wade Jr. 4.00 10.00
81 Jacob Waguespack 3.00 8.00
82 Shun Yamaguchi 5.00 12.00
83 Robel Garcia 2.50 6.00
84 Jose Urquidy 2.50 6.00
85 Randy Dobnak 5.00 12.00
86 Mike Brosseau 5.00 12.00
88 Seth Brown 2.50 6.00
89 Jorge Alcala 2.50 6.00
90 Shogo Akiyama EXCH 25.00 60.00
91 Ryan McBroom 3.00 8.00
92 Brian O'Grady 2.50 6.00
93 Kevin Ginkel 2.50 6.00
94 Luis Robert 60.00 150.00

2020 Panini Prizm Rookie Autographs Prizms Blue
*BLUE/50-99: .6X TO 1.5X BASIC
*BLUE/35: .8X TO 2X BASIC
RANDOM INSERTS IN PACKS
PRINT RUNS B/WN 15-99 COPIES PER
NO PRICING ON QTY 15 OR LESS
EXCHANGE DEADLINE 12/17/2021
13 Yu Chang/99 8.00 20.00
49 Yordan Alvarez/75 EXCH 50.00 120.00

2020 Panini Prizm Rookie Autographs Prizms Blue Donut Circles
*BLUE DONUT/50: .6X TO 1.5X BASIC
*BLUE DONUT/40: .8X TO 2X BASIC
RANDOM INSERTS IN PACKS
PRINT RUNS B/WN 5-50 COPIES PER
NO PRICING ON QTY 15 OR LESS
EXCHANGE DEADLINE 12/17/2021
13 Yu Chang/50 10.00 25.00
49 Yordan Alvarez/40 EXCH 60.00 150.00
94 Luis Robert/40 150.00 400.00

2020 Panini Prizm Rookie Autographs Prizms Blue Wave
*BLUE WAVE/50: .6X TO 1.5X BASIC
*BLUE WAVE/35: .8X TO 2X BASIC
RANDOM INSERTS IN PACKS
PRINT RUNS B/WN 10-50 COPIES PER
NO PRICING ON QTY 15 OR LESS
EXCHANGE DEADLINE 12/17/2021
13 Yu Chang/50 10.00 25.00
49 Yordan Alvarez/35 EXCH 60.00 150.00
94 Luis Robert/50 125.00 300.00

2020 Panini Prizm Rookie Autographs Prizms Bronze Donut Circles
*BRNZ DONUT/25: .8X TO 2X BASIC
RANDOM INSERTS IN PACKS
PRINT RUNS B/WN 5-25 COPIES PER
NO PRICING ON QTY 15 OR LESS
EXCHANGE DEADLINE 12/17/2021
13 Yu Chang/25 15.00 40.00
14 Gavin Lux/25 50.00 120.00
49 Yordan Alvarez/25 EXCH 75.00 200.00
94 Luis Robert/25 150.00 400.00

2020 Panini Prizm Rookie Autographs Prizms Burgundy Cracked Ice
*BUR.CRKD ICE/25: .8X TO 2X BASIC
RANDOM INSERTS IN PACKS
PRINT RUNS B/WN 10-25 COPIES PER
NO PRICING ON QTY 15 OR LESS
EXCHANGE DEADLINE 12/17/2021
13 Yu Chang/25 15.00 40.00
14 Gavin Lux/25 50.00 120.00
77 Kean Wong/25 10.00 25.00
94 Luis Robert/25 150.00 400.00

2020 Panini Prizm Rookie Autographs Prizms Cosmic Haze
*COSMIC/50: .6X TO 1.5X BASIC
*COSMIC/25-30: .8X TO 2X BASIC
RANDOM INSERTS IN PACKS
PRINT RUNS B/WN 15-50 COPIES PER
NO PRICING ON QTY 15 OR LESS
EXCHANGE DEADLINE 12/17/2021
13 Yu Chang/50 10.00 25.00
49 Yordan Alvarez/25 EXCH 75.00 200.00
65 Genesis Cabrera/50 6.00 15.00
68 Austin Nola/50 6.00 15.00
71 Tim Lopes/50 5.00 12.00
72 Dillon Tate/50 4.00 10.00
77 Kean Wong/50 8.00 20.00
94 Luis Robert/50 125.00 300.00

2020 Panini Prizm Rookie Autographs Prizms Pink
*PINK/50: .6X TO 1.5X BASIC
*PINK/25-30: .8X TO 2X BASIC
RANDOM INSERTS IN PACKS
PRINT RUNS B/WN 15-50 COPIES PER
NO PRICING ON QTY 15 OR LESS
EXCHANGE DEADLINE 12/17/2021
13 Yu Chang/50 10.00 25.00
49 Yordan Alvarez/25 EXCH 75.00 200.00
65 Genesis Cabrera/50 6.00 15.00
68 Austin Nola/50 6.00 15.00
71 Tim Lopes/50 5.00 12.00
72 Dillon Tate/50 4.00 10.00
77 Kean Wong/50 8.00 20.00
94 Luis Robert/50 125.00 300.00

2020 Panini Prizm Rookie Autographs Prizms Purple
*PURPLE/50: .6X TO 1.5X BASIC
*PURPLE/25: .8X TO 2X BASIC
RANDOM INSERTS IN PACKS
PRINT RUNS B/WN 15-50 COPIES PER
NO PRICING ON QTY 15 OR LESS
EXCHANGE DEADLINE 12/17/2021
13 Yu Chang/50 10.00 25.00
49 Yordan Alvarez/25 EXCH 75.00 200.00
65 Genesis Cabrera/50 6.00 15.00
68 Austin Nola/50 6.00 15.00
71 Tim Lopes/50 5.00 12.00
72 Dillon Tate/50 4.00 10.00
77 Kean Wong/50 8.00 20.00
94 Luis Robert/50 125.00 300.00

2020 Panini Prizm Rookie Autographs Prizms Red
*RED/50-75: .6X TO 1.5X BASIC
*RED/25-35: .8X TO 2X BASIC
RANDOM INSERTS IN PACKS
PRINT RUNS B/WN 8-75 COPIES PER
NO PRICING ON QTY 15 OR LESS
EXCHANGE DEADLINE 12/17/2021
13 Yu Chang/75 8.00 20.00
49 Yordan Alvarez/50 EXCH 50.00 120.00

2020 Panini Prizm Rookie Autographs Prizms Red Donut Circles
*RED DONUT/35: .8X TO 2X BASIC
RANDOM INSERTS IN PACKS
PRINT RUNS B/WN 5-35 COPIES PER
NO PRICING ON QTY 15 OR LESS
EXCHANGE DEADLINE 12/17/2021
13 Yu Chang/35 12.00 30.00
14 Gavin Lux/35 50.00 120.00
49 Yordan Alvarez/35 EXCH 60.00 150.00
94 Luis Robert/35 150.00 400.00

2020 Panini Prizm Rookie Autographs Prizms Red Orange
*RED ORNG/25: .8X TO 2X BASIC
RANDOM INSERTS IN PACKS
PRINT RUNS B/WN 5-25 COPIES PER
NO PRICING ON QTY 15 OR LESS
EXCHANGE DEADLINE 12/17/2021
13 Yu Chang/25 15.00 40.00
14 Gavin Lux/25 50.00 120.00
94 Luis Robert/25 150.00 400.00

2020 Panini Prizm Rookie Autographs Prizms Red Wave
*RED WAVE/49-75: .6X TO 1.5X BASIC
RANDOM INSERTS IN PACKS
PRINT RUNS B/WN 10-75 COPIES PER

NO PRICING ON QTY 15 OR LESS
EXCHANGE DEADLINE 12/17/2021
13 Yu Chang/75 8.00 20.00
49 Yordan Alvarez/60 EXCH 50.00 120.00

2020 Panini Prizm Rookie Autographs Prizms Red White and Blue

*RWB/50: .6X TO 1.5X BASIC
*RWB/25: .8X TO 2X BASIC
RANDOM INSERTS IN PACKS
PRINT RUNS B/WN 15-50 COPIES PER
NO PRICING ON QTY 15 OR LESS
EXCHANGE DEADLINE 12/17/2021
13 Yu Chang/50 10.00 25.00
94 Luis Robert/50 125.00 300.00

2020 Panini Prizm Rookie Autographs Prizms Silver

*SILVER: .5X TO 1.2X BASIC
RANDOM INSERTS IN PACKS
EXCHANGE DEADLINE 12/17/2021
49 Yordan Alvarez EXCH 40.00 100.00

2020 Panini Prizm Rookie Autographs Prizms Snake Skin

*SNAKE SKIN/25-35: .8X TO 2X BASIC
RANDOM INSERTS IN PACKS
PRINT RUNS B/WN 10-35 COPIES PER
NO PRICING ON QTY 15 OR LESS
EXCHANGE DEADLINE 12/17/2021
13 Yu Chang/35 12.00 30.00
14 Gavin Lux/35 50.00 120.00
49 Yordan Alvarez/20 EXCH 75.00 200.00
94 Luis Robert/35 150.00 400.00

2020 Panini Prizm Scorching

RANDOM INSERTS IN PACKS
*SILVER: .6X TO 1.5X BASIC
1 Adalberto Mondesi .50 1.25
2 Trea Turner .40 1.00
3 Christian Yelich .60 1.50
4 Xander Bogaerts .50 1.25
5 Anthony Rendon .50 1.25
6 Marcus Semien .30 .75
7 Juan Soto 1.50 4.00
8 Manny Machado .50 1.25
9 Javier Baez .60 1.50
10 Fernando Tatis Jr. 2.00 5.00

2020 Panini Prizm Signatures

RANDOM INSERTS IN PACKS
EXCHANGE DEADLINE 12/17/2021
*SILVER: .5X TO 1.2X BASIC
1 Cody Bellinger 40.00 100.00
2 Ronald Acuna Jr. 40.00 100.00
3 Gleyber Torres 20.00 50.00
4 Rickey Henderson 25.00 60.00
5 Chipper Jones 40.00 100.00
6 Jorge Polanco 3.00 8.00
7 Rafael Palmeiro 5.00 12.00
8 Adalberto Mondesi 4.00 10.00
9 Don Mattingly 20.00 50.00
10 Gary Sanchez 4.00 10.00
11 Luis Perdomo 2.50 6.00
12 Reynaldo Lopez 3.00 8.00
13 Jason Martin 3.00 8.00
14 Terrance Gore 2.50 6.00
15 Scooter Gennett 3.00 8.00
16 Pablo Lopez 2.50 6.00
17 Jarlin Garcia 2.50 6.00
18 Christian Walker 3.00 8.00
19 Nick Martini 2.50 6.00
20 Meibrys Viloria 2.50 6.00

2020 Panini Prizm Star Gazing

RANDOM INSERTS IN PACKS
*BLUE: .6X TO 1.5X BASIC
*CAR.BLUE: .6X TO 1.5X BASIC
*COSMIC: .6X TO 1.5X BASIC
*GREEN: .6X TO 1.5X BASIC
*PINK: .6X TO 1.5X BASIC
*PURPLE: .6X TO 1.5X BASIC
*RED: .6X TO 1.5X BASIC
*RED ORNG: .6X TO 1.5X BASIC
*RWB: .6X TO 1.5X BASIC
*SILVER: .6X TO 1.5X BASIC
*TEAL WAVE: .6X TO 1.5X BASIC
*WHITE WAVE: .6X TO 1.5X BASIC
1 Mike Trout 2.50 6.00
2 Max Scherzer .50 1.25
3 Ronald Acuna Jr. 2.00 5.00
4 Fernando Tatis Jr. 2.00 5.00
5 Jose Altuve .40 1.00
6 Bo Bichette 2.50 6.00
7 Paul Goldschmidt .50 1.25
8 Anthony Rizzo .75 2.00
9 Aaron Judge 1.25 3.00
10 Clayton Kershaw 1.00 2.50

2020 Panini Prizm Star Gazing Prizms Blue Donut Circles

*BLUE DONUT/199: .8X TO 2X BASIC
RANDOM INSERTS IN PACKS
STATED PRINT RUN 199 SER.#'d SETS
1 Mike Trout 10.00 25.00
4 Fernando Tatis Jr. 4.00 10.00
9 Aaron Judge 6.00 15.00

2020 Panini Prizm Star Gazing Prizms Blue Mojo

*BLUE MOJO/175: .8X TO 2X BASIC
RANDOM INSERTS IN PACKS
STATED PRINT RUN 175 SER.#'d SETS
1 Mike Trout 10.00 25.00
4 Fernando Tatis Jr. 4.00 10.00
9 Aaron Judge 6.00 15.00

2020 Panini Prizm Star Gazing Prizms Blue Wave

*BLUE WAVE/60: 1.2X TO 3X BASIC
RANDOM INSERTS IN PACKS
STATED PRINT RUN 60 SER.#'d SETS
1 Mike Trout 30.00 80.00
4 Fernando Tatis Jr. 6.00 15.00
9 Aaron Judge 10.00 25.00

2020 Panini Prizm Star Gazing Prizms Bronze Donut Circles

*BRNZ DONUT/25: 2X TO 5X BASIC
RANDOM INSERTS IN PACKS
STATED PRINT RUN 25 SER.#'d SETS
1 Mike Trout 50.00 120.00
4 Fernando Tatis Jr. 10.00 25.00
6 Bo Bichette 20.00 50.00
9 Aaron Judge 15.00 40.00

2020 Panini Prizm Star Gazing Prizms Burgundy Cracked Ice

*BUR.CRKD ICE/25: 2X TO 5X BASIC
RANDOM INSERTS IN PACKS
STATED PRINT RUN 25 SER.#'d SETS
1 Mike Trout 50.00 120.00
4 Fernando Tatis Jr. 10.00 25.00
6 Bo Bichette 20.00 50.00
9 Aaron Judge 15.00 40.00

2020 Panini Prizm Star Gazing Prizms Lime Green

*LIME GRN/125: 1X TO 2.5X BASIC
RANDOM INSERTS IN PACKS
STATED PRINT RUN 125 SER.#'d SETS
1 Mike Trout 12.00 30.00
4 Fernando Tatis Jr. 5.00 12.00
9 Aaron Judge 8.00 20.00

2020 Panini Prizm Star Gazing Prizms Navy Blue Kaleidoscope

*NVY BLU.KAL./35: 1.5X TO 4X BASIC
RANDOM INSERTS IN PACKS
STATED PRINT RUN 35 SER.#'d SETS
1 Mike Trout 40.00 100.00
4 Fernando Tatis Jr. 8.00 20.00
6 Bo Bichette 15.00 40.00
9 Aaron Judge 12.00 30.00

2020 Panini Prizm Star Gazing Prizms Neon Orange

*NEON ORNG/100: 1.2X TO 3X BASIC
RANDOM INSERTS IN PACKS
STATED PRINT RUN 100 SER.#'d SETS
1 Mike Trout 15.00 40.00
4 Fernando Tatis Jr. 6.00 15.00
9 Aaron Judge 10.00 25.00

2020 Panini Prizm Star Gazing Prizms Power Plaid

*PLAID/75: 1.2X TO 3X BASIC
RANDOM INSERTS IN PACKS
STATED PRINT RUN 75 SER.#'d SETS
1 Mike Trout 30.00 80.00
4 Fernando Tatis Jr. 6.00 15.00
9 Aaron Judge 10.00 25.00

2020 Panini Prizm Star Gazing Prizms Red Donut Circles

*RED DONUT/99: 1.2X TO 3X BASIC
RANDOM INSERTS IN PACKS
STATED PRINT RUN 99 SER.#'d SETS
1 Mike Trout 15.00 40.00
4 Fernando Tatis Jr. 6.00 15.00
9 Aaron Judge 10.00 25.00

2020 Panini Prizm Star Gazing Prizms Red Mojo

*RED MOJO/149: 1X TO 2.5X BASIC
RANDOM INSERTS IN PACKS
STATED PRINT RUN 149 SER.#'d SETS
1 Mike Trout 12.00 30.00
4 Fernando Tatis Jr. 5.00 12.00
9 Aaron Judge 8.00 20.00

2020 Panini Prizm Star Gazing Prizms Red Wave

*RED WAVE/99: 1.2X TO 3X BASIC
RANDOM INSERTS IN PACKS
STATED PRINT RUN 99 SER.#'d SETS
1 Mike Trout 15.00 40.00
4 Fernando Tatis Jr. 6.00 15.00
9 Aaron Judge 10.00 25.00

2020 Panini Prizm Star Gazing Prizms Snake Skin

*SNAKE SKIN/50: 1.5X TO 4X BASIC
RANDOM INSERTS IN PACKS
STATED PRINT RUN 50 SER.#'d SETS
1 Mike Trout 40.00 100.00
4 Fernando Tatis Jr. 8.00 20.00
6 Bo Bichette 15.00 40.00
9 Aaron Judge 12.00 30.00

2020 Panini Prizm Top of the Class

RANDOM INSERTS IN PACKS
*SILVER: .6X TO 1.5X BASIC
1 Adley Rutschman 2.00 5.00
2 Bobby Witt Jr. 4.00 10.00
3 Andrew Vaughn 1.25 3.00
4 JJ Bleday 1.00 2.50
5 Riley Greene 1.25 3.00
6 CJ Abrams 1.25 3.00
7 Nick Lodolo .50 *1.25
8 Josh Jung .75 2.00
9 Shea Langeliers .60 1.50
10 Hunter Bishop .60 1.50
11 Alek Manoah .40 1.00
12 Brett Baty 1.00 2.50
13 Keoni Cavaco .30 .75
14 Bryson Stott .75 2.00
15 Will Wilson .40 1.00
16 Corbin Carroll .50 1.25
17 Jackson Rutledge .50 1.25
18 Quinn Priester .50 1.25
19 Zack Thompson .30 .75
20 George Kirby .50 1.25
21 Braden Shewmake .50 1.25
22 Greg Jones .40 1.00
23 Michael Toglia .30 .75
24 Daniel Espino .40 1.00
25 Kody Hoese 1.00 2.50
26 Blake Walston .50 1.25
27 Ryan Jensen .40 1.00
28 Ethan Small .40 1.00
29 Logan Davidson .40 1.00
30 Anthony Volpe 1.25 3.00

2020 Panini Prizm Warming in the Pen

RANDOM INSERTS IN PACKS
*SILVER: .6X TO 1.5X BASIC
1 Nate Pearson .60 1.50
2 Forrest Whitley .30 .75
3 Sixto Sanchez .50 1.25
4 Matt Manning .40 1.00
5 Ian Anderson .75 2.00
6 Deivi Garcia 1.25 3.00
7 Brent Honeywell .40 1.00
8 Tarik Skubal 1.50 4.00
9 Triston McKenzie .50 1.25
10 Casey Mize 1.00 2.50
11 Matthew Liberatore .40 1.00
12 Logan Gilbert .40 1.00
13 Brady Singer .40 1.00
14 MacKenzie Gore .60 1.50
15 Daniel Lynch .30 .75

2019 Panini Prizm Draft Picks

COMPLETE SET (100) 30.00 80.00
1 Adley Rutschman 1.50 4.00
2 Bobby Witt Jr. 1.00 2.50
3 Andrew Vaughn .75 2.00
4 CJ Abrams 1.25 3.00
5 Riley Greene 1.00 2.50
6 Matt Wallner .50 1.25
7 Shea Langeliers .50 1.25
8 Zack Thompson .40 1.00
9 Corbin Carroll .40 1.00
10 Josh Jung .75 2.00
11 Ethan Small .30 .75
12 Hunter Bishop .75 2.00
13 Kameron Misner .60 1.50
14 Bryson Stott .75 2.00
15 Adley Rutschman 1.50 4.00
16 Brett Baty .50 1.25
17 Will Wilson .40 1.00
18 Nick Lodolo .50 1.25
19 JJ Bleday 1.25 3.00
20 Alek Manoah .50 1.25
21 Will Wilson .40 1.00
22 Kody Hoese .75 2.00
23 Logan Davidson .25 .60
24 Daniel Espino .30 .75
25 Bobby Witt Jr. 1.00 2.50
26 Shea Langeliers .50 1.25
27 Zack Thompson .40 1.00
28 Brennan Malone .25 .60
29 Jackson Rutledge .50 1.25
30 Andrew Vaughn .75 2.00
31 George Kirby .40 1.00
32 Michael Busch .75 2.00
33 Will Wilson .40 1.00
34 Rece Hinds .30 .75
35 Matt Wallner .50 1.25
36 Logan Wyatt .40 1.00
37 Bobby Witt Jr. 1.00 2.50
38 Seth Johnson .25 .60
39 Brandon Williamson
40 Braden Shewmake .75 2.00
41 J.J. Goss .30 .75
42 Matt Canterino .30 .75
43 Josh Jung .75 2.00
44 Brett Baty .50 1.25
45 JJ Bleday 1.25 3.00
46 Drey Jameson .25 .60
47 Trejyn Fletcher .40 1.00
48 Andrew Vaughn .75 2.00
49 Chase Strumpf .50 1.25
50 Keoni Cavaco .60 1.50
51 Quinn Priester .40 1.00
52 Gunnar Henderson .50 1.25
53 Corbin Carroll .40 1.00
54 Kyle Stowers .40 1.00
55 Alek Manoah .50 1.25
56 Kendall Williams .40 1.00
57 Nasim Nunez .25 .60
58 Aaron Schunk .50 1.25
59 Sammy Siani .30 .75
60 Riley Greene 1.00 2.50
61 Ethan Small .30 .75
62 CJ Abrams 1.25 3.00
63 Josh Wolf .30 .75
64 Matthew Thompson .30 .75
65 Cameron Cannon .50 1.25
66 Hunter Bishop .75 2.00
67 T.J. Sikkema .40 1.00
68 Ryan Jensen .40 1.00
69 Anthony Volpe .75 2.00
70 Bryson Stott .75 2.00
71 Michael Toglia .40 1.00
72 Korey Lee .50 1.25
73 Kody Hoese .75 2.00
74 Davis Wendzel .30 .75
75 CJ Abrams 1.25 3.00
76 John Doxakis .40 1.00
77 CJ Abrams 1.25 3.00
78 Cameron Cannon .50 1.25
79 Brennan Malone .25 .60
80 Matt Wallner .50 1.25
81 Ryan Garcia .25 .60
82 Adley Rutschman 1.50 4.00
83 Brady McConnell .40 1.00
84 Braden Shewmake .75 2.00
85 Greg Jones .30 .75
86 Riley Greene 1.00 2.50
87 Bobby Witt Jr. 1.00 2.50
88 Riley Greene 1.00 2.50
89 Andrew Vaughn .75 2.00
90 Hunter Bishop .75 2.00
91 Zach Watson .40 1.00
92 Tyler Callihan .30 .75
93 Adley Rutschman 1.50 4.00
94 Bobby Witt Jr. 1.00 2.50
95 Andrew Vaughn .75 2.00
96 JJ Bleday 1.25 3.00
97 Anthony Volpe .75 2.00
98 Josh Jung .75 2.00
99 JJ Bleday 1.25 3.00
100 Adley Rutschman 1.50 4.00

2019 Panini Prizm Draft Picks Prizms Blue

*PRIZMS BLUE: 5X TO 1.2X BASIC
RANDOM INSERTS IN PACKS

2019 Panini Prizm Draft Picks Prizms Camo

*PRIZMS CAMO: 2.5X TO 6X BASIC
RANDOM INSERTS IN PACKS
STATED PRINT RUN 25 SER.#'d SETS

2019 Panini Prizm Draft Picks Prizms Carolina Blue

*PRIZMS CAR.BLUE: 2X TO 5X BASIC
RANDOM INSERTS IN PACKS
STATED PRINT RUN 30 SER.#'d SETS

2019 Panini Prizm Draft Picks Prizms Green

*PRIZMS GRN: .5X TO 1.2X BASIC
RANDOM INSERTS IN PACKS

2019 Panini Prizm Draft Picks Prizms Hyper

*PRIZMS HYPER: 1.2X TO 3X BASIC
RANDOM INSERTS IN PACKS
STATED PRINT RUN 75 SER.#'d SETS

2019 Panini Prizm Draft Picks Prizms Mojo

*PRIZMS MOJO: 1.5X TO 4X BASIC
RANDOM INSERTS IN PACKS
STATED PRINT RUN 49 SER.#'d SETS

2019 Panini Prizm Draft Picks Prizms Orange

*PRIZMS ORNG: .5X TO 1.2X BASIC
RANDOM INSERTS IN PACKS

2019 Panini Prizm Draft Picks Prizms Red

*PRIZMS RED: .5X TO 1.2X BASIC
RANDOM INSERTS IN PACKS

2019 Panini Prizm Draft Picks Prizms Red and Black Snake Skin

*PRIZMS SNAKE SKN: 1X TO 2.5X BASIC
RANDOM INSERTS IN PACKS

2019 Panini Prizm Draft Picks Prizms Red White and Blue

*PRIZMS RWB: 1.2X TO 3X BASIC
RANDOM INSERTS IN PACKS
STATED PRINT RUN 99 SER.#'d SETS

2019 Panini Prizm Draft Picks Prizms Silver

*PRIZMS SLVR: .5X TO 1.2X BASIC
RANDOM INSERTS IN PACKS

2019 Panini Prizm Draft Picks Autographs Prizms

RANDOM INSERTS IN PACKS
EXCHANGE DEADLINE 4/16/2021
*GREEN: .5X TO 1.2X
*RWB p/r 75-99: .5X TO 1.2X
*HYPER p/r 49-75: .5X TO 1.2X
*MOJO p/r 49: .5X TO 1.2X
*MOJO p/r 30: .6X TO 1.5X
*CAR BLUE p/r 30: .6X TO 1.5X
*CAR BLUE p/r 25: .75X TO 2X
*CAMO p/r 20-25: .75X TO 2X
*RB SNK SKN: 1X TO 2.5X BASIC
1 Adley Rutschman 20.00 50.00
2 Adley Rutschman 20.00 50.00
3 Bobby Witt Jr. 20.00 50.00
4 Bobby Witt Jr. 20.00 50.00
5 Andrew Vaughn 10.00 25.00
6 Andrew Vaughn 10.00 25.00
7 CJ Abrams 10.00 25.00
8 CJ Abrams 10.00 25.00
9 Riley Greene 10.00 25.00
10 Riley Greene 10.00 25.00
11 Shea Langeliers 6.00 15.00
12 Shea Langeliers 6.00 15.00
13 Corbin Carroll 3.00 8.00
14 Corbin Carroll 3.00 8.00
15 Josh Jung 6.00 15.00
16 Josh Jung 6.00 15.00
17 Hunter Bishop 6.00 15.00
18 Kameron Misner 5.00 12.00
19 Bryson Stott 6.00 15.00
20 Bryson Stott 6.00 15.00
21 Brett Baty 8.00 20.00
22 Nick Lodolo 4.00 10.00
23 JJ Bleday 10.00 25.00
24 Alek Manoah 4.00 10.00
25 Will Wilson 3.00 8.00
26 Will Wilson 3.00 8.00
27 Logan Davidson 2.00 5.00
28 Daniel Espino 2.50 6.00
29 Zack Thompson 3.00 8.00
30 Zack Thompson 3.00 8.00
31 Brennan Malone 2.00 5.00
32 Brennan Malone 2.00 5.00
33 Jackson Rutledge 4.00 10.00
34 George Kirby 3.00 8.00
35 Michael Busch 6.00 15.00
36 Rece Hinds 2.50 6.00
37 Logan Wyatt 3.00 8.00
38 Seth Johnson 2.00 5.00
40 Braden Shewmake EXCH 6.00 15.00
41 J.J. Goss 2.50 6.00
42 Matt Canterino 2.50 6.00
43 Drey Jameson 2.00 5.00
44 Trejyn Fletcher 3.00 8.00
45 Chase Strumpf 4.00 10.00
46 Keoni Cavaco 6.00 15.00
48 Gunnar Henderson 4.00 10.00
49 Kyle Stowers 3.00 8.00
50 Kendall Williams 3.00 8.00
51 Nasim Nunez 2.00 5.00
52 Will Holland 3.00 8.00
53 Sammy Siani 2.50 6.00
54 Ethan Small 2.50 6.00
55 Josh Wolf 2.50 6.00
57 Fidel Montero 3.00 8.00
58 T.J. Sikkema 3.00 8.00
59 Ryan Jensen 3.00 8.00
60 Anthony Volpe 6.00 15.00
61 Anthony Volpe 6.00 15.00
62 Michael Toglia 3.00 8.00
63 Korey Lee 4.00 10.00
64 Kody Hoese 6.00 15.00
65 Davis Wendzel 2.50 6.00
66 John Doxakis 3.00 8.00
67 Cameron Cannon 4.00 10.00
68 Matt Wallner 4.00 10.00
69 Matt Wallner 4.00 10.00
70 Joshua Mears 4.00 10.00
71 Ryan Garcia 2.00 5.00
72 Brady McConnell 3.00 8.00
73 Tommy Henry 2.50 6.00
74 Matt Gorski 3.00 8.00
75 Beau Philip 3.00 8.00
76 Greg Jones 2.50 6.00
77 Aaron Schunk 4.00 10.00
78 Nick Quintana 4.00 10.00
79 Jimmy Lewis 2.00 5.00
80 Isaiah Campbell 4.00 10.00
81 Josh Smith 4.00 10.00
82 Bayron Lora EXCH 12.00 30.00
83 Kyren Paris 2.00 5.00
85 Yordys Valdes 4.00 10.00
86 Matthew Lugo 3.00 8.00
87 Alec Marsh 2.50 6.00
88 Dominic Fletcher 2.00 5.00
89 Jared Triolo 3.00 8.00
90 Tyler Baum 2.50 6.00
91 Logan Driscoll 3.00 8.00
92 Karl Kauffmann 2.00 5.00
93 Zach Watson 3.00 8.00
94 Tyler Callihan 2.50 6.00
95 Andrew Abbott 2.00 5.00
96 Logan Allen 2.00 5.00
97 Tanner Allen 2.00 5.00
98 Patrick Bailey 4.00 10.00
99 Tyler Brown 12.00 30.00
100 Alec Burleson 3.00 8.00
101 Burl Carraway 4.00 10.00
102 Cade Cavalli 4.00 10.00
103 Colton Cowser 2.50 6.00
104 Jeff Criswell 3.00 8.00
105 Reid Detmers 6.00 15.00
106 Lucas Dunn 2.00 5.00
107 Justin Foscue 5.00 12.00
108 Nick Frasso 2.00 5.00
109 Heston Kjerstad 40.00 100.00
110 Asa Lacy 5.00 12.00
111 Nick Loftin 2.00 5.00
112 Austin Martin 20.00 50.00
113 Chris McMahon 2.00 5.00
114 Max Meyer 10.00 25.00
115 Garrett Mitchell 10.00 25.00
116 Doug Nikhazy 2.00 5.00
117 Casey Opitz 3.00 8.00
118 Spencer Torkelson 100.00 250.00
119 Luke Waddell 6.00 15.00
120 Cole Wilcox 2.50 6.00
121 Alika Williams 3.00 8.00
122 Jasson Dominguez 150.00 400.00
123 Robert Puason 10.00 25.00

2019 Panini Prizm Draft Picks College Ties Autographs Prizms

RANDOM INSERTS IN PACKS
EXCHANGE DEADLINE 4/16/2021
*ORNGE PLSR/20: .6X TO 1.5X
2 Vaughn/Lee 25.00 60.00
3 Misner/Sikkema 20.00 50.00
4 Wendzel/Langeliers 10.00 25.00
5 Rutschman/Philip 40.00 100.00

2019 Panini Prizm Draft Picks Color Blast

RANDOM INSERTS IN PACKS
1 Adley Rutschman 50.00 120.00
2 Bobby Witt Jr. 40.00 100.00
3 Andrew Vaughn 40.00 100.00
4 JJ Bleday 25.00 60.00
5 Riley Greene 50.00 120.00
6 CJ Abrams 20.00 50.00
7 Adley Rutschman 50.00 120.00
8 Josh Jung
9 Shea Langeliers
10 Hunter Bishop 20.00 50.00
11 Bobby Witt Jr. 40.00 100.00
12 Brett Baty
13 Andrew Vaughn 40.00 100.00
14 CJ Abrams 20.00 50.00
15 Josh Jung
16 Riley Greene 50.00 120.00

2020 Panini Prizm Draft Picks

1 Spencer Torkelson 3.00 8.00
2 Heston Kjerstad 1.00 2.50
3 Max Meyer .75 2.00
4 Asa Lacy 1.25 3.00
5 Austin Martin .60 1.50
6 Emerson Hancock .75 2.00
7 Nick Gonzales 1.00 2.50
8 Robert Hassell 1.50 4.00
9 Zac Veen 1.00 2.50
10 Reid Detmers .50 1.25
11 Garrett Crochet .50 1.25
12 Austin Hendrick 2.00 5.00
13 Patrick Bailey .60 1.50
14 Justin Foscue .75 2.00
15 Mick Abel .30 .75
16 Ed Howard 1.50 4.00
17 Nick Yorke 1.00 2.50
18 Bryce Jarvis .20 .50
19 Pete Crow-Armstrong .60 1.50
20 Garrett Mitchell 1.50 4.00
21 Jordan Walker .60 1.50
22 Cade Cavalli .40 1.00
23 Carson Tucker .60 1.50
24 Nick Bitsko .60 1.50
25 Jared Shuster .40 1.00
26 Tyler Soderstrom .75 2.00
27 Aaron Sabato .40 1.00
28 Austin Wells .75 2.00
29 Bobby Miller .75 2.00
30 Jordan Westburg .50 1.25
31 Carmen Mlodzinski .20 .50
32 Nick Loftin .30 .75
33 Slade Cecconi .25 .60
34 Justin Lange .20 .50
35 Drew Romo .50 1.25
36 Tanner Burns .30 .75
37 Alika Williams .25 .60
38 Dillon Dingler .60 1.50
39 Hudson Haskin .75 2.00
40 Dax Fulton .40 1.00
41 Ben Hernandez .30 .75
42 CJ Van Eyk .30 .75
43 Zach DeLoach .75 2.00
44 Jared Jones .30 .75
45 Owen Caissie .75 2.00
46 Bradlee Beesley .30 .75
47 Jared Kelley .20 .50
48 Christian Roa .25 .60
49 Casey Schmitt .60 1.50
50 Evan Carter 1.00 2.50
51 Burl Carraway .50 1.25
52 Brady Singer .25 .60
53 Freddy Zamora .30 .75
54 Masyn Winn .75 2.00
55 Cole Henry .25 .60
56 Logan T. Allen .20 .50
57 Ian Seymour .20 .50
58 Jeff Criswell .30 .75
59 Alerick Soularie .30 .75
60 Landon Knack .60 1.50
61 Kyle Nicolas .25 .60
62 Daniel Cabrera .75 2.00
63 Markevian Hence .20 .50
64 Connor Phillips .30 .75
65 Jackson Miller .50 1.25
66 Clayton Beeter .50 1.25
67 Nick Swiney .40 1.00
68 Jimmy Glowenke .50 1.25
69 Isaiah Greene .75 2.00
70 Alec Burleson .30 .75
71 Sammy Infante .75 2.00
72 Alex Santos .50 1.25
73 Trei Cruz .75 2.00
74 Anthony Servideo .25 .60
75 Zach McCambley .20 .50
76 Tyler Gentry .40 1.00
77 Trent Palmer .25 .60
78 Kaden Polcovich .30 .75
79 Nick Garcia .30 .75
80 Joey Bart .60 1.50
81 Sam Weatherly .20 .50
82 David Calabrese .50 1.25
83 Adisyn Coffey .25 .60
84 Bryce Bonnin .30 .75
85 Dane Dunning .20 .50
86 Tekoah Roby .20 .50
87 Casey Martin .60 1.50
88 Jordan Nwogu .75 2.00
89 Jordan DiValerio .20 .50
90 Liam Norris .20 .50
91 Anthony Walters .25 .60
92 Zavier Warren .20 .50
93 Levi Prater .25 .60
94 Holden Powell .20 .50
95 Petey Halpin .50 1.25
96 Hunter Barnhart .30 .75
97 Jesse Franklin .75 2.00
98 Michael Guldberg .25 .60
99 Trevor Hauver .30 .75
100 Jake Vogel .25 .60
101 Tyler Brown .30 .75
102 Gage Workman 1.00 2.50
103 Justin Lavey .25 .60
104 Jake Eder .20 .50
105 Matt Scheffler .20 .50
106 Nick Frasso .20 .50
107 Tyler Keenan .30 .75
108 Jack Hartman .20 .50
109 Levi Thomas .20 .50
110 Case Williams .25 .60
111 Werner Blakely .25 .60
112 Kade Mechals .20 .50
113 Mac Wainwright .25 .60
114 R.J. Dabovich .20 .50
115 Dylan MacLean .30 .75
116 Wander Franco 2.00 5.00
117 Luke Little .30 .75
118 Jeremy Wu-Yelland .30 .75
119 A.J. Vukovich .40 1.00
120 Matthew Dyer .30 .75
121 Joey Wiemer .30 .75
122 Ian Bedell .30 .75
123 Brady Lindsly .30 .75
124 Milan Tolentino .30 .75
125 Tanner Murray .25 .60
126 Spencer Strider .30 .75
127 Dane Acker .25 .60
128 Marco Raya .40 1.00
129 Beck Way .20 .50
130 Carson Taylor .30 .75
131 Zach Daniels .30 .75
132 Colten Keith 1.00 2.50
133 Carter Baumler .30 .75
134 Kyle Hurt .20 .50
135 Will Klein .25 .60
136 Zach Britton .25 .60
137 Taylor Dollard .20 .50
138 Logan Hofmann .20 .50
139 Ian Anderson .50 1.25
140 Jack Blomgren .30 .75
141 Adam Seminaris .25 .60
142 Bailey Horn .25 .60
143 Joe Boyle .30 .75
144 Matt Manning .25 .60
145 Triston McKenzie .30 .75
146 Baron Radcliff .25 .60
147 Gus Steiger .20 .50
148 Shane Drohan .25 .60
149 Brandon Pfaadt .20 .50
150 Eric Orze .20 .50
151 Hayden Cantrelle .20 .50
152 LJ Jones IV .30 .75
153 Mitchell Parker .20 .50
154 Mason Hickman .25 .60
155 Jeff Hakanson .20 .50
156 Jackson Coutts .25 .60
157 Stevie Emanuels .20 .50
158 Kala'i Rosario .25 .60
159 Gavin Stone .40 1.00
160 Brett Auerbach .30 .75
161 Jordan Mikel .20 .50
162 Thomas Girard .20 .50
163 Chase Antle .20 .50
164 Kale Emshoff .20 .50

2020 Panini Prizm Draft Picks Prizms Blue Donut Circles

*BLUE DONUT: 3X TO 8X BASIC
RANDOM INSERTS IN PACKS
STATED PRINT RUN 25 SER.#'d SETS
1 Spencer Torkelson 40.00 100.00
116 Wander Franco 20.00 50.00

2020 Panini Prizm Draft Picks Prizms Burgundy Cracked Ice

*BRGNDY ICE: 3X TO 8X BASIC
RANDOM INSERTS IN PACKS
STATED PRINT RUN 23 SER.#'d SETS
1 Spencer Torkelson 40.00 100.00
116 Wander Franco 20.00 50.00

2020 Panini Prizm Draft Picks Prizms Lime Green

*LIME GRN: 1.5X TO 4X BASIC
RANDOM INSERTS IN PACKS
STATED PRINT RUN 75 SER.#'d SETS
1 Spencer Torkelson 20.00 50.00

2020 Panini Prizm Draft Picks Prizms Neon Orange

*NEON ORNG: 2X TO 5X BASIC
RANDOM INSERTS IN PACKS
STATED PRINT RUN 50 SER.#'d SETS
1 Spencer Torkelson 25.00 60.00

2020 Panini Prizm Draft Picks Prizms Power Plaid

*PLAID: 2.5X TO 6X BASIC
RANDOM INSERTS IN PACKS
STATED PRINT RUN 35 SER.#'d SETS
1 Spencer Torkelson 30.00 80.00

2020 Panini Prizm Draft Picks Prizms Red Donut Circles

*RED DONUT: 1.5X TO 4X BASIC
RANDOM INSERTS IN PACKS
STATED PRINT RUN 99 SER.#'d SETS
1 Spencer Torkelson 20.00 50.00

2020 Panini Prizm Draft Picks Prizms Snake Skin

*SNAKE SKN: 3X TO 8X BASIC
RANDOM INSERTS IN PACKS
STATED PRINT RUN 25 SER.#'d SETS
1 Spencer Torkelson 40.00 100.00
116 Wander Franco 20.00 50.00

2020 Panini Prizm Draft Picks Prizms Tiger Stripes
*TIGER: 1.5X TO 4X BASIC
RANDOM INSERTS IN PACKS
STATED PRINT RUN 99 SER.#'d SETS
1 Spencer Torkelson 20.00 50.00

2020 Panini Prizm Draft Picks Prizms White Donut Circles
*WHT DONUT: 2X TO 5X BASIC
RANDOM INSERTS IN PACKS
STATED PRINT RUN 50 SER.#'d SETS
1 Spencer Torkelson 25.00 60.00

2020 Panini Prizm Draft Picks Autographs
RANDOM INSERTS IN PACKS
EXCHANGE DEADLINE 6/2/22
1 Miguel Amaya 3.00 8.00
2 Riley Greene 10.00 25.00
4 Jarred Kelenic 20.00 50.00
5 Evan White 2.50 6.00
6 Drew Rasmussen 4.00 10.00
7 Clay Aguilar 4.00 10.00
8 Triston Casas 8.00 20.00
9 Tarik Skubal 12.00 30.00
10 Luis V. Garcia 4.00 10.00
11 Erick Pena 12.00 30.00
12 Nate Pearson 8.00 20.00
13 Ryan Mountcastle 10.00 25.00
14 Shane Baz 2.50 6.00
15 Heliot Ramos 6.00 15.00
16 Hunter Greene 4.00 10.00
17 Josh Jung 6.00 15.00
19 Bobby Witt Jr. 20.00 50.00
20 A.J. Block 2.50 6.00
21 Ji-Hwan Bae 8.00 20.00
22 Andres Gimenez 3.00 8.00
23 CJ Abrams 10.00 25.00
24 Matthew Liberatore 5.00 12.00
25 Luisangel Acuna 15.00 40.00
26 Brice Turang 4.00 10.00
27 Corbin Carroll 4.00 10.00
28 Bobby Dalbec 6.00 15.00
29 Oneil Cruz 6.00 15.00
30 Drew Waters 6.00 15.00
31 JJ Bleday 8.00 20.00
33 Jesus Sanchez 2.50 6.00
34 Andrew Vaughn 10.00 25.00
35 Estevan Florial 4.00 10.00
37 Bryan Mata 2.50 6.00
38 Cristian Pache 12.00 30.00
39 Daniel Lynch 2.50 6.00
40 MacKenzie Gore 10.00 25.00
41 Noelvi Marte 10.00 25.00
42 Nolan Gorman 5.00 12.00
43 Spencer Howard 5.00 12.00
44 Travis Blankenhorn 5.00 12.00
46 Freudis Nova 2.50 6.00
47 Johan Rojas 5.00 12.00
48 Isaac Paredes 6.00 15.00
49 Jose Salas 2.50 6.00
50 Tyler Freeman 3.00 8.00
51 Kristian Robinson 8.00 20.00
52 Luis Rodriguez (ex-LA) 15.00 40.00
53 Alex Kirilloff 10.00 25.00
54 Tanner Houck 10.00 25.00
55 Mason Martin 5.00 12.00
57 Julio Rodriguez 20.00 50.00
58 Luis Garcia 10.00 25.00
61 Nolan Jones 6.00 15.00
62 Rylan Bannon 3.00 8.00
63 Yoelqui Cespedes 30.00 80.00
64 Yiddi Cappe 5.00 12.00
65 Dylan Carlson 10.00 25.00
66 Norge Vera 3.00 8.00
67 Zion Bannister 3.00 8.00
68 Tristen Lutz 3.00 8.00
69 Hyun-Il Choi 4.00 10.00
70 Oscar Colas 20.00 50.00

2020 Panini Prizm Draft Picks Base Autographs Prizms Silver
RANDOM INSERTS IN PACKS
EXCHANGE DEADLINE 6/2/22
1 Spencer Torkelson 40.00 100.00
2 Heston Kjerstad 12.00 30.00
3 Max Meyer 8.00 20.00
4 Asa Lacy 10.00 25.00
5 Austin Martin 20.00 50.00
6 Emerson Hancock 8.00 20.00
7 Nick Gonzales 10.00 25.00
8 Robert Hassell 10.00 25.00
9 Zac Veen 15.00 40.00
10 Reid Detmers 6.00 15.00
11 Garrett Crochet 15.00 40.00
12 Austin Hendrick 12.00 30.00
13 Patrick Bailey 8.00 20.00
14 Justin Foscue 6.00 15.00
15 Mick Abel 8.00 20.00
16 Ed Howard 12.00 30.00
17 Nick Yorke 10.00 25.00
18 Bryce Jarvis 2.00 5.00
19 Pete Crow-Armstrong 10.00 25.00
20 Garrett Mitchell 12.00 30.00
21 Jordan Walker 6.00 15.00
22 Cade Cavalli 5.00 12.00
23 Carson Tucker 6.00 15.00
24 Nick Bitsko 3.00 8.00
25 Jared Shuster 4.00 10.00
26 Tyler Soderstrom 8.00 20.00
27 Aaron Sabato 10.00 25.00
28 Austin Wells 8.00 20.00
30 Jordan Westburg 4.00 10.00
31 Carmen Mlodzinski 2.00 5.00
32 Nick Loftin 3.00 8.00
33 Slade Cecconi 2.50 6.00
34 Justin Lange 2.00 5.00
35 Drew Romo 3.00 8.00
36 Tanner Burns 4.00 10.00
37 Alika Williams 2.50 6.00
38 Dillon Dingler 6.00 15.00
39 Hudson Haskin 3.00 8.00
40 Dax Fulton 4.00 10.00
41 Ben Hernandez 3.00 8.00
42 CJ Van Eyk 3.00 8.00
43 Zach DeLoach 6.00 15.00
44 Jared Jones 3.00 8.00
45 Owen Caissie 5.00 12.00
46 Bradlee Beesley 3.00 8.00
47 Jared Kelley 2.00 5.00
49 Casey Schmitt 6.00 15.00
50 Evan Carter 4.00 10.00
51 Burl Carraway 5.00 12.00
53 Freddy Zamora 3.00 8.00
54 Masyn Winn 8.00 20.00
55 Cole Henry 2.50 6.00
56 Logan T. Allen 3.00 8.00
57 Ian Seymour 2.00 5.00
58 Jeff Criswell 4.00 10.00
59 Alerick Soularie 3.00 8.00
60 Landon Knack 4.00 10.00
61 Kyle Nicolas 2.50 6.00
62 Daniel Cabrera 6.00 15.00
63 Markevian Hence 2.00 5.00
64 Connor Phillips 3.00 8.00
65 Jackson Miller 3.00 8.00
66 Clayton Beeter 3.00 8.00
67 Nick Swiney 4.00 10.00
68 Jimmy Glowenke 2.50 6.00
69 Isaiah Greene 5.00 12.00
70 Alec Burleson 3.00 8.00
71 Sammy Infante 5.00 12.00
72 Alex Santos 5.00 12.00
73 Trei Cruz 5.00 12.00
75 Zach McCambley 2.00 5.00
76 Tyler Gentry 4.00 10.00
77 Trent Palmer 2.50 6.00
78 Kaden Polcovich 3.00 8.00
79 Nick Garcia 3.00 8.00
80 Joey Bart 8.00 20.00
81 Sam Weatherly 2.00 5.00
82 David Calabrese 3.00 8.00
83 Adisyn Coffey 2.50 6.00
84 Bryce Bonnin 3.00 8.00
85 Dane Dunning 2.00 5.00
87 Casey Martin 10.00 25.00
88 Jordan Nwogu 8.00 20.00
89 Jordan DiValerio 2.00 5.00
90 Liam Norris 2.00 5.00
91 Anthony Walters 2.50 6.00
92 Zavier Warren 2.00 5.00
93 Levi Prater 2.50 6.00
94 Holden Powell 2.00 5.00
96 Hunter Barnhart 3.00 8.00
97 Jesse Franklin 5.00 12.00
98 Michael Guldberg 2.50 6.00
100 Jake Vogel 2.50 6.00
101 Tyler Brown 3.00 8.00
102 Gage Workman 4.00 10.00
103 Justin Lavey 2.50 6.00
104 Jake Eder 2.00 5.00
105 Matt Scheffler 2.00 5.00
106 Nick Frasso 2.00 5.00
107 Tyler Keenan 3.00 8.00
108 Jack Hartman 2.00 5.00
109 Levi Thomas 2.00 5.00
110 Case Williams 2.50 6.00
111 Werner Blakely 2.50 6.00
112 Kade Mechals 2.00 5.00
114 R.J. Dabovich 2.00 5.00
115 Dylan MacLean 3.00 8.00
116 Wander Franco EXCH 40.00 100.00
118 Jeremy Wu-Yelland 3.00 8.00
119 A.J. Vukovich
120 Matthew Dyer 3.00 8.00
122 Ian Bedell 3.00 8.00
123 Brady Lindsly 3.00 8.00
125 Tanner Murray 2.50 6.00
126 Spencer Strider 3.00 8.00
127 Dane Acker 5.00 12.00
128 Marco Raya 3.00 8.00
129 Beck Way 2.00 5.00
130 Carson Taylor 3.00 8.00
132 Colten Keith 4.00 10.00
133 Carter Baumler 3.00 8.00
134 Kyle Hurt 2.00 5.00
135 Will Klein 2.50 6.00
136 Zach Britton 4.00 10.00
137 Taylor Dollard 2.00 5.00
138 Logan Hofmann 2.00 5.00
139 Ian Anderson 8.00 20.00
140 Jack Blomgren 4.00 10.00
141 Adam Seminaris 2.50 6.00
142 Bailey Horn 2.50 6.00
143 Joe Boyle 3.00 8.00
144 Matt Manning 5.00 12.00
145 Triston McKenzie 8.00 20.00
146 Baron Radcliff 2.50 6.00
147 Gus Steiger 2.00 5.00
148 Shane Drohan 2.50 6.00
149 Brandon Pfaadt 2.00 5.00
151 Hayden Cantrelle 2.00 5.00
153 Mitchell Parker 2.00 5.00
154 Mason Hickman 2.50 6.00
155 Jeff Hakanson 2.00 5.00
156 Jackson Coutts 2.50 6.00
157 Stevie Emanuels 2.00 5.00
158 Kala'i Rosario 2.50 6.00
159 Gavin Stone 15.00 40.00
160 Brett Auerbach 3.00 8.00
161 Jordan Mikel 2.00 5.00
162 Thomas Girard 2.00 5.00
163 Chase Antle 2.00 5.00
164 Kale Emshoff 2.00 5.00

2020 Panini Prizm Draft Picks Base Autographs Prizms Blue
*BLUE/60: .5X TO 1.2X BASIC
*BLUE/35-50: .6X TO 1.5X BASIC
RANDOM INSERTS IN PACKS
PRINT RUNS B/WN 35-60 COPIES PER
EXCHANGE DEADLINE 6/2/22
1 Spencer Torkelson/60 75.00 200.00
7 Nick Gonzales/60 20.00 50.00
22 Cade Cavalli/60 8.00 20.00
140 Jack Blomgren/60 8.00 20.00

2020 Panini Prizm Draft Picks Base Autographs Prizms Blue Donut Circles
*BLUE DONUT: .8X TO 2X BASIC
RANDOM INSERTS IN PACKS
STATED PRINT RUN 25 SER.#'d SETS
EXCHANGE DEADLINE 6/2/22
1 Spencer Torkelson 125.00 300.00
7 Nick Gonzales 30.00 80.00
12 Austin Hendrick 30.00 80.00
21 Jordan Walker 15.00 40.00
22 Cade Cavalli 12.00 30.00
27 Aaron Sabato 25.00 60.00
29 Bobby Miller 25.00 60.00
51 Burl Carraway 12.00 30.00
131 Zach Daniels 12.00 30.00
140 Jack Blomgren 12.00 30.00

2020 Panini Prizm Draft Picks Base Autographs Prizms Lime Green
*LIME GRN: .8X TO 2X BASIC
RANDOM INSERTS IN PACKS
STATED PRINT RUN 23 SER.#'d SETS
EXCHANGE DEADLINE 6/2/22
1 Spencer Torkelson 125.00 300.00
7 Nick Gonzales 30.00 80.00
12 Austin Hendrick 30.00 80.00
21 Jordan Walker 15.00 40.00
22 Cade Cavalli 12.00 30.00
27 Aaron Sabato 25.00 60.00
39 Hudson Haskin 8.00 20.00
51 Burl Carraway 12.00 30.00
131 Zach Daniels 12.00 30.00
140 Jack Blomgren 12.00 30.00

2020 Panini Prizm Draft Picks Base Autographs Prizms Neon Orange
*NEON ORNG: .8X TO 2X BASIC
RANDOM INSERTS IN PACKS
STATED PRINT RUN 20 SER.#'d SETS
EXCHANGE DEADLINE 6/2/22
1 Spencer Torkelson 125.00 300.00
7 Nick Gonzales 30.00 80.00
12 Austin Hendrick 30.00 80.00
21 Jordan Walker 15.00 40.00
22 Cade Cavalli 12.00 30.00
27 Aaron Sabato 25.00 60.00
39 Hudson Haskin 8.00 20.00
51 Burl Carraway 12.00 30.00
131 Zach Daniels 12.00 30.00
140 Jack Blomgren 12.00 30.00

2020 Panini Prizm Draft Picks Base Autographs Prizms Red
*RED/30-50: .6X TO 1.5X BASIC
RANDOM INSERTS IN PACKS
PRINT RUNS B/WN 30-50 COPIES PER
EXCHANGE DEADLINE 6/2/22
1 Spencer Torkelson/50 100.00 250.00
7 Nick Gonzales/50 25.00 60.00
22 Cade Cavalli/50 10.00 25.00
27 Aaron Sabato/50 20.00 50.00
51 Burl Carraway/50 8.00 20.00
52 Brady Singer/50 4.00 10.00
131 Zach Daniels/50 5.00 12.00
140 Jack Blomgren/50 10.00 25.00

2020 Panini Prizm Draft Picks Base Autographs Prizms Red Donut Circles
*RED DONUT/75-99: .5X TO 1.2X BASIC
*RED DONUT/35-50: .6X TO 1.5X BASIC
*RED DONUT/25: .8X TO 2X BASIC
RANDOM INSERTS IN PACKS
PRINT RUNS B/WN 25-99 COPIES PER
EXCHANGE DEADLINE 6/2/22
1 Spencer Torkelson/99 75.00 200.00
7 Nick Gonzales/75 20.00 50.00
22 Cade Cavalli/99 8.00 20.00
95 Petey Halpin/99 6.00 15.00
99 Trevor Hauver/99 4.00 10.00
117 Luke Little/99 4.00 10.00
121 Joey Wiemer/99 4.00 10.00
124 Milan Tolentino/75 4.00 10.00
131 Zach Daniels/99 4.00 10.00
152 LJ Jones IV/75 4.00 10.00

2020 Panini Prizm Draft Picks Base Autographs Prizms Tiger Stripes
*TIGER .8X TO 2X BASIC
RANDOM INSERTS IN PACKS
STATED PRINT RUN 25 SER.#'d SETS
EXCHANGE DEADLINE 6/2/22
1 Spencer Torkelson 125.00 300.00
7 Nick Gonzales 30.00 80.00
12 Austin Hendrick 30.00 80.00
21 Jordan Walker 15.00 40.00
22 Cade Cavalli 12.00 30.00
27 Aaron Sabato 25.00 60.00
29 Bobby Miller 25.00 60.00
51 Burl Carraway 12.00 30.00
131 Zach Daniels 12.00 30.00
140 Jack Blomgren 12.00 30.00

2020 Panini Prizm Draft Picks Base Autographs Prizms White Donut Circles
*WHT DONUT/35-50: .6X TO 1.5X BASIC
RANDOM INSERTS IN PACKS
PRINT RUNS B/WN 35-50 COPIES PER
EXCHANGE DEADLINE 6/2/22
1 Spencer Torkelson/50 100.00 250.00
7 Nick Gonzales/50 25.00 60.00
22 Cade Cavalli/50 10.00 25.00
27 Aaron Sabato/50 20.00 50.00
51 Burl Carraway/50 8.00 20.00
52 Brady Singer/50 4.00 10.00
131 Zach Daniels/50 5.00 12.00
140 Jack Blomgren/50 10.00 25.00

2020 Panini Prizm Draft Picks College Ties Autographs
RANDOM INSERTS IN PACKS
EXCHANGE DEADLINE 6/2/22
1 H.Haskin/K.Hoese 12.00 30.00
2 H.Bishop/S.Torkelson 60.00 150.00
4 A.Lacy/B.Shewmake 20.00 50.00
5 A.Martin/J.Bleday 40.00 100.00
6 A.Wells/N.Quintana 10.00 25.00
7 A.Sabato/M.Busch 25.00 60.00
8 P.Bailey/W.Wilson 15.00 40.00
9 G.Mitchell/M.Togila 15.00 40.00
10 C.Mize/T.Burns 15.00 40.00

2020 Panini Prizm Draft Picks Color Blast
RANDOM INSERTS IN PACKS
1 Spencer Torkelson 300.00 600.00
2 Heston Kjerstad 125.00 300.00
3 Austin Martin 300.00 600.00
4 Nick Gonzales
5 Robert Hassell 75.00 200.00
6 Zac Veen 100.00 250.00
7 Oscar Colas 60.00 150.00
8 Jasson Dominguez 400.00 800.00

2020 Panini Prizm Draft Picks Electric College Stars
RANDOM INSERTS IN PACKS
1 Spencer Torkelson 50.00 120.00
2 Heston Kjerstad 20.00 50.00
3 Austin Martin 15.00 40.00
4 Nick Gonzales 20.00 50.00
5 Asa Lacy 8.00 20.00
6 Max Meyer 15.00 40.00

2020 Panini Prizm Draft Picks Electric Dominican Prospect League Stars
RANDOM INSERTS IN PACKS
1 Victor Acosta 10.00 25.00
2 Cristian Santana 8.00 20.00
3 Willy Fanas 8.00 20.00
4 Shalin Polanco 8.00 20.00
5 Ambioris Tavarez 10.00 25.00
6 Danny De Andrade 5.00 12.00

2020 Panini Prizm Draft Picks Fireworks
RANDOM INSERTS IN PACKS
*BLUE: .5X TO 1.2X BASIC
*BLUE MOJO: .5X TO 1.2X BASIC
*BLUE WAVE: .5X TO 1.2X BASIC
*RED: .5X TO 1.2X BASIC
*RED MOJO: .5X TO 1.2X BASIC
*RED WAVE: .5X TO 1.2X BASIC
*BL.CAR.BL.HYP.: .5X TO 1.2X BASIC
*GRN YLW HYP.: .5X TO 1.2X BASIC
*PRPL RED HYP.: .5X TO 1.2X BASIC
*GRN PLSR.: .5X TO 1.2X BASIC
*SILVER.: .5X TO 1.2X BASIC
*RED DONUT: 1.2X TO 3X BASIC
*TIGER: 1.2X TO 3X BASIC
*LIME GRN: 1.2X TO 3X BASIC
*NEON ORNG: 1.5X TO 4X BASIC
*WHT DONUT: 1.5X TO 4X BASIC
1 Heston Kjerstad 1.25 3.00
2 Austin Martin .75 2.00
3 Zac Veen 1.25 3.00
4 Zach Daniels .40 1.00
5 Ed Howard 2.00 5.00
6 Pete Crow-Armstrong .75 2.00
7 David Calabrese .60 1.50
8 Daniel Cabrera 1.00 2.50
9 Gus Steiger .25 .60
10 Petey Halpin .60 1.50
11 Masyn Winn 1.00 2.50
12 Luke Little .40 1.00

2020 Panini Prizm Draft Picks Fireworks Prizms Blue Donut Circles
1 Heston Kjerstad 12.00 30.00
3 Zac Veen 10.00 25.00

2020 Panini Prizm Draft Picks Fireworks Prizms Burgundy Cracked Ice
*BRGNDY ICE: 2.5X TO 6X BASIC
RANDOM INSERTS IN PACKS
STATED PRINT RUN 23 SER.#'d SETS
1 Heston Kjerstad 12.00 30.00
3 Zac Veen 10.00 25.00

2020 Panini Prizm Draft Picks Fireworks Prizms Neon Orange
1 Heston Kjerstad 8.00 20.00

2020 Panini Prizm Draft Picks Fireworks Prizms Power Plaid
1 Heston Kjerstad 10.00 25.00

2020 Panini Prizm Draft Picks Fireworks Prizms Snake Skin
*SNAKE SKN: 2.5X TO 6X BASIC
RANDOM INSERTS IN PACKS
STATED PRINT RUN 25 SER.#'d SETS
1 Heston Kjerstad 12.00 30.00
3 Zac Veen 10.00 25.00

2020 Panini Prizm Draft Picks Fireworks Prizms White Donut Circles
1 Heston Kjerstad 8.00 20.00

2020 Panini Prizm Draft Picks Fireworks Autographs Prizms Silver
RANDOM INSERTS IN PACKS
EXCHANGE DEADLINE 6/2/22
*BLUE/60: .5X TO 1.2X BASIC
*BLUE/35: .6X TO 1.5X BASIC
*RED/30-50: .6X TO 1.5X BASIC
*WHT DONUT/30-50: .6X TO 1.5X BASIC
1 Heston Kjerstad 12.00 30.00
2 Austin Martin 20.00 50.00
3 Zac Veen 15.00 40.00
5 Ed Howard 12.00 30.00
6 Pete Crow-Armstrong 10.00 25.00
7 David Calabrese 3.00 8.00
8 Daniel Cabrera 6.00 15.00
9 Gus Steiger 2.00 5.00
11 Masyn Winn 8.00 20.00

2020 Panini Prizm Draft Picks Fireworks Autographs Prizms Blue Donut Circles
*BLUE DONUT: .8X TO 2X BASIC
RANDOM INSERTS IN PACKS
STATED PRINT RUN 25 SER.#'d SETS
EXCHANGE DEADLINE 6/2/22
4 Zach Daniels 12.00 30.00

2020 Panini Prizm Draft Picks Fireworks Autographs Prizms Lime Green
*LIME GRN: .8X TO 2X BASIC
RANDOM INSERTS IN PACKS
STATED PRINT RUN 23 SER.#'d SETS
EXCHANGE DEADLINE 6/2/22
4 Zach Daniels 12.00 30.00

2020 Panini Prizm Draft Picks Fireworks Autographs Prizms Neon Orange
*NEON ORNG: .8X TO 2X BASIC
RANDOM INSERTS IN PACKS
STATED PRINT RUN 20 SER.#'d SETS
EXCHANGE DEADLINE 6/2/22
4 Zach Daniels 12.00 30.00

2020 Panini Prizm Draft Picks Fireworks Autographs Prizms Red Donut Circles
*RED DONUT/75-99: .5X TO 1.2X BASIC
*RED DONUT/35: .6X TO 1.5X BASIC
RANDOM INSERTS IN PACKS
PRINT RUNS B/WN 35-99 COPIES PER
EXCHANGE DEADLINE 6/2/22
10 Petey Halpin/99 6.00 15.00
12 Luke Little/99 4.00 10.00

2020 Panini Prizm Draft Picks Fireworks Autographs Prizms Tiger Stripes
4 Zach Daniels 12.00 30.00

2020 Panini Prizm Draft Picks Power Surge
RANDOM INSERTS IN PACKS
*BLUE: .5X TO 1.2X BASIC
*BLUE MOJO: .5X TO 1.2X BASIC
*BLUE WAVE: .5X TO 1.2X BASIC
*RED: .5X TO 1.2X BASIC
*RED MOJO: .5X TO 1.2X BASIC
*RED WAVE: .5X TO 1.2X BASIC
*BL.CAR.BL.HYP.: .5X TO 1.2X BASIC
*GRN YLW HYP.: .5X TO 1.2X BASIC
*PRPL RED HYP.: .5X TO 1.2X BASIC
*GRN PLSR.: .5X TO 1.2X BASIC
*SILVER.: .5X TO 1.2X BASIC
1 Spencer Torkelson 2.50 6.00
2 Nick Gonzales 1.25 3.00
3 Austin Hendrick 2.50 6.00
4 A.J. Vukovich .50 1.25
5 Jordan Walker .75 2.00
6 Garrett Mitchell 2.00 5.00
7 Aaron Sabato .50 1.25
8 Jordan Westburg .60 1.50
9 Alerick Soularie .40 1.00
10 Alec Burleson .40 1.00
11 Casey Martin .75 2.00
12 Austin Wells 1.00 2.50

2020 Panini Prizm Draft Picks Power Surge Prizms Blue Donut Circles
*BLUE DONUT: 2.5X TO 6X BASIC
RANDOM INSERTS IN PACKS
STATED PRINT RUN 25 SER.#'d SETS
1 Spencer Torkelson 20.00 50.00
2 Nick Gonzales 10.00 25.00

2020 Panini Prizm Draft Picks Power Surge Prizms Burgundy Cracked Ice
*BRGNDY ICE: 2.5X TO 6X BASIC
RANDOM INSERTS IN PACKS
STATED PRINT RUN 23 SER.#'d SETS
1 Spencer Torkelson 25.00 60.00
2 Nick Gonzales 10.00 25.00

2020 Panini Prizm Draft Picks Power Surge Prizms Lime Green
*LIME GRN: 1.2X TO 3X BASIC
RANDOM INSERTS IN PACKS
STATED PRINT RUN 75 SER.#'d SETS
1 Spencer Torkelson 10.00 25.00

2020 Panini Prizm Draft Picks Power Surge Prizms Neon Orange
*NEON ORNG: 1.5X TO 4X BASIC
RANDOM INSERTS IN PACKS
STATED PRINT RUN 50 SER.#'d SETS
1 Spencer Torkelson 12.00 30.00

2020 Panini Prizm Draft Picks Power Surge Prizms Power Plaid
*PLAID: 2X TO 5X BASIC
RANDOM INSERTS IN PACKS
STATED PRINT RUN 35 SER.#'d SETS
1 Spencer Torkelson 15.00 40.00
2 Nick Gonzales 8.00 20.00

2020 Panini Prizm Draft Picks Power Surge Prizms Red Donut Circles
*RED DONUT: 1.2X TO 3X BASIC
RANDOM INSERTS IN PACKS
STATED PRINT RUN 99 SER.#'d SETS
1 Spencer Torkelson 10.00 25.00

2020 Panini Prizm Draft Picks Power Surge Prizms Snake Skin
*SNAKE SKN: 2.5X TO 6X BASIC
RANDOM INSERTS IN PACKS
STATED PRINT RUN 25 SER.#'d SETS
1 Spencer Torkelson 20.00 50.00
2 Nick Gonzales 10.00 25.00

2020 Panini Prizm Draft Picks Power Surge Prizms Tiger Stripes
*TIGER: 1.2X TO 3X BASIC
RANDOM INSERTS IN PACKS
STATED PRINT RUN 99 SER.#'d SETS
1 Spencer Torkelson 10.00 25.00
2 Nick Gonzales 15.00 40.00

2020 Panini Prizm Draft Picks Power Surge Prizms White Donut Circles
*WHT DONUT: 1.5X TO 4X BASIC
RANDOM INSERTS IN PACKS
STATED PRINT RUN 50 SER.#'d SETS
1 Spencer Torkelson 12.00 30.00

2020 Panini Prizm Draft Picks Power Surge Autographs Prizms Silver
RANDOM INSERTS IN PACKS
EXCHANGE DEADLINE 6/2/22
1 Spencer Torkelson 40.00 100.00
2 Nick Gonzales 10.00 25.00
3 Austin Hendrick 12.00 30.00
4 A.J. Vukovich
5 Jordan Walker 6.00 15.00
6 Garrett Mitchell 12.00 30.00
7 Aaron Sabato 10.00 25.00
8 Jordan Westburg 4.00 10.00
9 Alerick Soularie 3.00 8.00
10 Alec Burleson 3.00 8.00
11 Casey Martin 10.00 25.00
12 Austin Wells 8.00 20.00

2020 Panini Prizm Draft Picks Power Surge Autographs Prizms Blue
*BLUE: .5X TO 1.2X BASIC
RANDOM INSERTS IN PACKS
STATED PRINT RUN 60 SER.#'d SETS
EXCHANGE DEADLINE 6/2/22
1 Spencer Torkelson 75.00 200.00
2 Nick Gonzales 20.00 50.00

2020 Panini Prizm Draft Picks Power Surge Autographs Prizms Blue Donut Circles
*BLUE DONUT: .8X TO 2X BASIC
RANDOM INSERTS IN PACKS
STATED PRINT RUN 25 SER.#'d SETS
EXCHANGE DEADLINE 6/2/22
1 Spencer Torkelson 125.00 300.00
2 Nick Gonzales 30.00 80.00

2020 Panini Prizm Draft Picks Power Surge Autographs Prizms Lime Green
*LIME GRN: .8X TO 2X BASIC
RANDOM INSERTS IN PACKS
STATED PRINT RUN 23 SER.#'d SETS
EXCHANGE DEADLINE 6/2/22
1 Spencer Torkelson 125.00 300.00
2 Nick Gonzales 30.00 80.00
5 Jordan Walker 15.00 40.00

2020 Panini Prizm Draft Picks Power Surge Autographs Prizms Neon Orange
*NEON ORNG: .8X TO 2X BASIC
RANDOM INSERTS IN PACKS
STATED PRINT RUN 20 SER.#'d SETS
EXCHANGE DEADLINE 6/2/22
1 Spencer Torkelson 125.00 300.00
2 Nick Gonzales 30.00 80.00
5 Jordan Walker 15.00 40.00

2020 Panini Prizm Draft Picks Power Surge Autographs Prizms Red
*RED: .6X TO 1.5X BASIC
RANDOM INSERTS IN PACKS
STATED PRINT RUN 50 SER.#'d SETS
EXCHANGE DEADLINE 6/2/22
1 Spencer Torkelson 100.00 250.00
2 Nick Gonzales 25.00 60.00

2020 Panini Prizm Draft Picks Power Surge Autographs Prizms Red Donut Circles
1 Spencer Torkelson/99 75.00 200.00
2 Nick Gonzales/75 20.00 50.00

2020 Panini Prizm Draft Picks Power Surge Autographs Prizms Tiger Stripes
*TIGER .8X TO 2X BASIC
RANDOM INSERTS IN PACKS
STATED PRINT RUN 25 SER.#'d SETS
EXCHANGE DEADLINE 6/2/22
1 Spencer Torkelson 125.00 300.00
2 Nick Gonzales 30.00 80.00
5 Jordan Walker 15.00 40.00

2020 Panini Prizm Draft Picks Power Surge Autographs Prizms White Donut Circles
*WHT DONUT: .6X TO 1.5X BASIC
RANDOM INSERTS IN PACKS
STATED PRINT RUN 50 SER.#'d SETS
EXCHANGE DEADLINE 6/2/22
1 Spencer Torkelson 100.00 250.00
2 Nick Gonzales 25.00 60.00

2020 Panini Prizm Draft Picks Thunderstruck
RANDOM INSERTS IN PACKS
*BLUE: .5X TO 1.2X BASIC
*BLUE MOJO: .5X TO 1.2X BASIC
*BLUE WAVE: .5X TO 1.2X BASIC
*RED: .5X TO 1.2X BASIC
*RED MOJO: .5X TO 1.2X BASIC
*RED WAVE: .5X TO 1.2X BASIC
*BL.CAR.BL.HYP.: .5X TO 1.2X BASIC
*GRN YLW HYP.: .5X TO 1.2X BASIC
*PRPL RED HYP.: .5X TO 1.2X BASIC
*GRN PLSR.: .5X TO 1.2X BASIC
*SILVER.: .5X TO 1.2X BASIC
*RED DONUT: 1.2X TO 3X BASIC
*TIGER: 1.2X TO 3X BASIC
*LIME GRN: 1.2X TO 3X BASIC
1 Max Meyer 1.00 2.50
2 Asa Lacy 1.50 4.00
3 LJ Jones IV .40 1.00
4 Robert Hassell 2.00 5.00
5 Nick Yorke 1.25 3.00
6 Hayden Cantrelle .25 .60
7 Joey Wiemer .40 1.00
8 Milan Tolentino .40 1.00
9 Nick Loftin .40 1.00
10 Alika Williams .30 .75
11 Trevor Hauver .40 1.00
12 Hudson Haskin 1.00 2.50

2020 Panini Prizm Draft Picks Thunderstruck Prizms Blue Donut Circles
*BLUE DONUT: 2.5X TO 6X BASIC
RANDOM INSERTS IN PACKS
STATED PRINT RUN 25 SER.#'d SETS
2 Asa Lacy 12.00 30.00

2020 Panini Prizm Draft Picks Thunderstruck Prizms Burgundy Cracked Ice
*BRGNDY ICE: 2.5X TO 6X BASIC
RANDOM INSERTS IN PACKS
STATED PRINT RUN 23 SER.#'d SETS
2 Asa Lacy 12.00 30.00

2020 Panini Prizm Draft Picks Thunderstruck Prizms Power Plaid
*PLAID: 2X TO 5X BASIC
RANDOM INSERTS IN PACKS
STATED PRINT RUN 35 SER.#'d SETS
2 Asa Lacy 10.00 25.00

2020 Panini Prizm Draft Picks Thunderstruck Prizms Snake Skin
*SNAKE SKN: 2.5X TO 6X BASIC
RANDOM INSERTS IN PACKS
STATED PRINT RUN 25 SER.#'d SETS
2 Asa Lacy 12.00 30.00

2020 Panini Prizm Draft Picks Thunderstruck Autographs Prizms Silver
RANDOM INSERTS IN PACKS
EXCHANGE DEADLINE 6/2/22
*RED DONUT/75-99: .5X TO 1.2X BASIC
*RED DONUT/25: .8X TO 2X BASIC
*BLUE/60: .5X TO 1.2X BASIC
*BLUE/50: .6X TO 1.5X BASIC
*RED/35-50: .6X TO 1.5X BASIC
*WHT DONUT/35-50: .6X TO 1.5X BASIC
*WHT DONUT/25: .8X TO 2X BASIC
*BLUE DONUT/25: .8X TO 2X BASIC
*TIGER/25: .8X TO 2X BASIC
*LIME GRN/23: .8X TO 2X BASIC
*NEON ORNG/20: .8X TO 2X BASIC
1 Max Meyer 8.00 20.00
2 Asa Lacy 10.00 25.00
4 Robert Hassell 10.00 25.00
5 Nick Yorke 10.00 25.00
6 Hayden Cantrelle 2.00 5.00
7 Joey Wiemer 3.00 8.00
8 Milan Tolentino 3.00 8.00
9 Nick Loftin 3.00 8.00
10 Alika Williams 2.50 6.00
12 Hudson Haskin 3.00 8.00

2018 Panini Revolution
1 Ken Griffey Jr. .50 1.25
2 Mike Trout 1.25 3.00
3 Giancarlo Stanton .25 .60
4 Rafael Devers RC .75 2.00
5 Anthony Rizzo .40 1.00
6 Shohei Ohtani RC 1.50 4.00
7 Mickey Mantle .75 2.00
8 Victor Robles RC .60 1.50

9 Miguel Andujar RC 1.00 2.50
10 Scott Kingery RC .40 1.00
11 J.P. Crawford RC .25 .60
12 Gleyber Torres RC 2.50 6.00
13 Kris Bryant .30 .75
14 Cal Ripken .75 2.00
15 Aaron Judge .60 1.50
16 Amed Rosario RC .30 .75
17 Mookie Betts .40 1.00
18 Clint Frazier RC .50 1.25
19 Jose Altuve .20 .50
20 Austin Hays RC .40 1.00
21 Bryce Harper .40 1.00
22 Ronald Acuna Jr. RC 5.00 12.00
23 Ozzie Albies RC .75 2.00
24 Rhys Hoskins RC 1.00 2.50
25 Cody Bellinger .50 1.25

2018 Panini Signatures
RANDOM INSERTS IN PACKS
*RED/199: .5X TO 1.2X BASIC
*PRPLE/99: .5X TO 1.2X
*HOLO SLVR/25: .75X TO 2X
*RED/25: .75X TO 2X BASIC
7 Brian Anderson 3.00 8.00
10 Nicky Delmonico 2.50 6.00
11 Zack Granite 2.50 6.00
12 Felix Jorge 2.50 6.00
13 Tomas Nido 2.50 6.00
14 Chris Flexen 2.50 6.00
15 Paul Blackburn 2.50 6.00
16 DJ Peters 6.00 15.00
19 Lane Adams 2.50 6.00
20 Freddy Peralta 2.50 6.00

2019 Panini Signatures
RANDOM INSERTS IN PACKS
EXCHANGE DEADLINE 2/21/2021
*GOLD/99: .5X TO 1.2X
*GOLD/49: .6X TO 1.5X
*RED/50: .6X TO 1.5X
*RED/25: .75X TO 2X
*HOLO SLVR/23: .75X TO 2X
1 Yusniel Diaz 4.00 10.00
2 Darwinzon Hernandez 2.50 6.00
3 Dylan Cease 6.00 15.00
5 Keston Hiura 10.00 25.00
6 Carter Kieboom 4.00 10.00
7 Mitch Keller 3.00 8.00
8 Forrest Whitley 4.00 10.00
9 Brendan Rodgers 4.00 10.00
10 Jesus Luzardo 4.00 10.00

2017 Panini Spectra Rookie Jersey Autographs
INSERTED IN '17 CHRONICLES PACKS
EXCHANGE DEADLINE 5/22/2019
*NEON BLUE/99: .5X TO 1.2X BASIC
*PINK/49: .6X TO 1.5X BASIC
*NEON GREEN: .75X TO 2X BASIC
1 Andrew Benintendi 20.00 50.00
2 Yoan Moncada 10.00 25.00
3 Alex Bregman 25.00 60.00
4 Dansby Swanson 10.00 25.00
5 Ian Happ 5.00 12.00
6 Cody Bellinger 50.00 120.00
7 Aaron Judge 60.00 150.00
8 Trey Mancini 6.00 15.00
9 Jordan Montgomery 8.00 20.00
10 Bradley Zimmer 6.00 15.00
11 Mitch Haniger 6.00 15.00
12 Orlando Arcia 4.00 10.00
13 Alex Reyes 6.00 15.00
14 Tyler Glasnow 3.00 8.00
15 Manuel Margot 2.50 6.00
16 Hunter Renfroe 3.00 8.00
17 Jorge Bonifacio 2.50 6.00
18 Antonio Senzatela 2.50 6.00
19 Amir Garrett 4.00 10.00
20 David Dahl 3.00 8.00
21 Jorge Alfaro
22 Ryon Healy 5.00 12.00
23 Josh Bell 15.00 40.00
24 Lewis Brinson 5.00 12.00
25 Jacoby Jones 3.00 8.00

2017 Panini Spectra Signatures
INSERTED IN '17 CHRONICLES PACKS
PRINT RUNS B/WN 10-199 COPIES PER
NO PRICING ON QTY 15 OR LESS
EXCHANGE DEADLINE 5/22/2019
*NEON BLUE/35-60: .5X TO 1.2X p/r 199
*NEON BLUE/35-60: .4X TO 1X p/r 49-96
*NEON BLUE/20-25: .5X TO 1.2X p/r 49-96
*NEON GREEN/25: .6X TO 1.5X p/r 199
2 Brandon Belt/199 4.00 10.00
3 Ian Kinsler/49 5.00 12.00
4 Aaron Judge/199 60.00 150.00
5 Edwin Encarnacion/49 6.00 15.00
6 Mike Napoli/49 4.00 10.00
7 Byron Buxton/49 10.00 25.00
8 Alfonso Soriano/49 5.00 12.00
9 Wil Myers/25 5.00 12.00
10 Adam Duvall/96 6.00 15.00
13 Manny Machado/25 20.00 50.00
16 Mark Grace/49 10.00 25.00
17 Paul Goldschmidt/25 12.00 30.00
18 Nomar Mazara/199 3.00 8.00
19 Francisco Lindor/25 12.00 30.00
20 Nolan Arenado/25
21 Marcus Stroman/199 4.00 10.00
22 Xander Bogaerts/25 15.00 40.00
23 Yasmany Tomas/25 5.00 12.00
24 Jose Abreu/20

2017 Panini Spectra Signatures Neon Pink
*NEON PINK/35: .5X TO 1.2X p/r 199
*NEON PINK/35: .4X TO 1X p/r 49-96
*NEON PINK/20-25: .5X TO 1.2X p/r 49-96
INSERTED IN '17 CHRONICLES PACKS
PRINT RUNS B/WN 10-35 COPIES PER
NO PRICING ON QTY 15 OR LESS
EXCHANGE DEADLINE 5/22/2019
1 Hunter Pence/25 15.00 40.00

2017 Panini Spectra Triple Threat Materials
INSERTED IN '17 CHRONICLES PACKS
*NEON BLUE/49-99: .5X TO 1.2X p/r 149
*NEON BLUE/49-99: .4X TO 1X p/r 49-99
*PINK/49: .5X TO 1.2X p/r 149
*PINK/49: .4X TO 1X p/r 49-99
*PINK/25: .5X TO 1.2X p/r 49-99
*NEON GREEN/25: .6X TO 1.5X p/r 149
*NEON GREEN/25: .5X TO 1.2X p/r 49-99
1 Yoan Moncada/149 4.00 10.00
2 Andrew Benintendi/149 5.00 12.00
3 Cody Bellinger/149 5.00 12.00
4 Ian Happ/149 3.00 8.00
5 Dansby Swanson/149 4.00 10.00
6 Aaron Judge/149 20.00 50.00
7 Mickey Mantle/25 60.00 150.00
8 Alex Bregman/149 6.00 15.00
9 Mitch Haniger/149 4.00 10.00
10 Trey Mancini/149 3.00 8.00
12 Anthony Alford/149 1.50 4.00
13 Jordan Montgomery/149 2.50 6.00
14 Alex Reyes/149 2.00 5.00
15 David Dahl/149 2.00 5.00
16 Hunter Renfroe/149 2.00 5.00
17 Carson Fulmer/149 1.50 4.00
18 Antonio Senzatela/149 1.50 4.00
19 Tyler Glasnow/149 2.00 5.00
20 Jacoby Jones/149 2.00 5.00
21 Josh Bell/99 5.00 12.00
22 Starlin Castro/149 1.50 4.00
23 Jorge Bonifacio/149 1.50 4.00
24 Javier Baez/149 3.00 8.00
25 Clayton Kershaw/99 6.00 15.00
26 Gleyber Torres/149 6.00 15.00
27 Manny Machado/99 6.00 15.00
28 Justin Turner/99 2.50 6.00
29 Michael Conforto/149 2.50 6.00
30 Freddie Freeman/149 3.00 8.00
31 Marcell Ozuna/149 2.50 6.00
TTMJG Joey Gallo/149 2.00 5.00
33 Miguel Sano/149 2.00 5.00
34 Chris Davis/149 1.50 4.00
35 Giancarlo Stanton/49 8.00 20.00
36 Jose Abreu/149 2.50 6.00
TTMCS Chris Sale/99 3.00 8.00
38 Daniel Murphy/49 2.50 6.00
39 George Springer/149 4.00 10.00
40 Jacob deGrom/149 2.50 6.00
41 Yu Darvish/49 3.00 8.00
42 Dallas Keuchel/149 2.00 5.00
43 Andrew McCutchen/149 5.00 12.00
44 Billy Hamilton/149 2.00 5.00
45 Trea Turner/99 2.50 6.00
46 Jose Bautista/49 2.50 6.00
47 Brian Dozier/99 3.00 8.00
48 Jon Lester/149 2.00 5.00
49 Todd Frazier/149 2.00 5.00
50 Madison Bumgarner/49 2.50 6.00

2018 Panini Spectra Holo
INSERTED IN '18 CHRONICLES PACKS
1 Nolan Arenado .50 1.25
2 Carlos Correa .40 1.00
3 Cody Bellinger .75 2.00
4 Manny Machado .40 1.00
5 Noah Syndergaard .30 .75
6 Eric Hosmer .30 .75
7 Mickey Mantle 1.00 2.50
8 Max Scherzer .40 1.00
9 Nolan Ryan 1.25 3.00
10 Francisco Mejia RC .50 1.25
11 Yadier Molina .40 1.00
12 Ryan Braun .30 .75
13 Albert Pujols .50 1.25
14 Khris Davis .40 1.00
15 Gary Sanchez .40 1.00
16 Corey Kluber .40 1.00
17 Whit Merrifield .40 1.00
18 Mitch Garver .25 .60
19 Aaron Judge 1.00 2.50
20 Gerrit Cole .40 1.00
21 Nicky Delmonico RC .40 1.00
22 Alex Gordon .30 .75
23 Jose Altuve .30 .75
24 Anthony Rizzo .60 1.50
25 Adrian Beltre .40 1.00
26 Carlos Gonzalez .30 .75
27 Jose Abreu .40 1.00
28 Nelson Cruz .40 1.00
29 Josh Bell .30 .75
30 Willie Calhoun RC .50 1.25
31 J.P. Crawford RC .40 1.00
32 Clayton Kershaw .75 2.00
33 Alex Verdugo RC .60 1.50
34 Mike Trout 2.00 5.00
35 Shohei Ohtani RC 2.50 6.00
36 Brandon Woodruff RC .50 1.25
37 Walker Buehler RC 1.25 3.00
38 Ryan McMahon RC .50 1.25
39 Jake Arrieta .30 .75
40 Giancarlo Stanton .40 1.00
41 Brian Dozier .30 .75
42 Yoenis Cespedes .40 1.00
43 Justin Bour .25 .60
44 Thyago Vieira RC .40 1.00
45 Kyle Farmer RC .40 1.00
46 Tyler Mahle RC .50 1.25
47 Max Fried RC 1.50 4.00
48 Freddie Freeman .50 1.25
49 Ozzie Albies RC 1.25 3.00
50 Andrew McCutchen .40 1.00
51 Wil Myers .25 .60
52 Bryce Harper .60 1.50
53 Paul Blackburn RC .40 1.00
54 Matt Carpenter .40 1.00
55 Rafael Devers RC 1.25 3.00
56 Joey Votto .40 1.00
57 Dominic Smith RC .40 1.00
58 Reggie Jackson .30 .75
59 Alex Rodriguez .50 1.25
60 Victor Caratini RC .50 1.25
61 Rhys Hoskins RC 1.50 4.00
62 Mookie Betts .60 1.50
63 Greg Allen RC .40 1.00
64 Miguel Cabrera .40 1.00
65 Paul Goldschmidt .40 1.00
66 Ken Griffey Jr. .75 2.00
67 Nick Williams RC .50 1.25
68 Chance Sisco RC .50 1.25
69 Jack Flaherty RC .60 1.50
70 Buster Posey .50 1.25
71 Cameron Gallagher RC .40 1.00
72 Francisco Lindor .40 1.00
73 Zack Granite RC .40 1.00
74 Victor Robles RC 1.00 2.50
75 Austin Hays RC .60 1.50
76 Shohei Ohtani RC 2.50 6.00
77 George Brett .75 2.00
78 Ronald Acuna Jr. RC 3.00 8.00
79 Harrison Bader RC .60 1.50
80 Luiz Gohara RC .40 1.00
81 Clint Frazier RC .75 2.00
82 Tomas Nido RC .40 1.00
83 Richard Urena RC .40 1.00
84 Amed Rosario RC .50 1.25
85 Cal Ripken 1.25 3.00
86 Javier Baez .50 1.25
87 Juan Soto RC 3.00 8.00
88 Dustin Pedroia .40 1.00
89 Gleyber Torres RC 2.00 5.00
90 Justin Verlander .40 1.00
91 Kris Bryant .50 1.25
92 Scott Kingery RC .60 1.50
93 Shane Bieber RC 5.00 12.00
94 Josh Donaldson .30 .75
95 Dustin Fowler RC .40 1.00
96 Robinson Cano .30 .75
97 Ryne Sandberg .75 2.00
98 Brian Anderson RC .50 1.25
99 Ichiro .50 1.25
100 Miguel Andujar RC 1.50 4.00

2018 Panini Spectra Green Mosiac
*MOSIAC: 4X TO 10X BASIC
*MOSIAC RC: 2.5X TO 6X BASIC
INSERTED IN '18 CHRONICLES PACKS
STATED PRINT RUN 25 SER.#'d SETS
9 Nolan Ryan 20.00 50.00
66 Ken Griffey Jr. 15.00 40.00
85 Cal Ripken 20.00 50.00

2018 Panini Spectra Neon Blue
*BLUE: 2X TO 5X BASIC
*BLUE RC: 1.2X TO 3X BASIC
INSERTED IN '18 CHRONICLES PACKS
STATED PRINT RUN 99 SER.#'d SETS
66 Ken Griffey Jr. 8.00 20.00

2018 Panini Spectra Neon Green
*GREEN: 2.5X TO 6X BASIC
*GREEN RC: 1.5X TO 4X BASIC
INSERTED IN '18 CHRONICLES PACKS
STATED PRINT RUN 49 SER.#'d SETS
66 Ken Griffey Jr. 10.00 25.00
85 Cal Ripken 12.00 30.00

2018 Panini Spectra Neon Pink
*PINK: 2X TO 5X BASIC
*PINK RC: 1.2X TO 3X BASIC
INSERTED IN '18 CHRONICLES PACKS
STATED PRINT RUN 75 SER.#'d SETS
66 Ken Griffey Jr. 8.00 20.00

2018 Panini Spectra Rookie Jersey Autographs
RANDOM INSERTS IN PACKS
RJAAH Austin Hays 4.00 10.00
RJAAR Amed Rosario 3.00 8.00
RJAAV Alex Verdugo 4.00 10.00
RJACF Clint Frazier 6.00 15.00
RJACS Chance Sisco 3.00 8.00
RJAEF Erick Fedde 2.50 6.00
RJAFM Francisco Mejia 6.00 15.00
RJAHB Harrison Bader 4.00 10.00
RJAJC J.P. Crawford 2.50 6.00
RJALS Lucas Sims 2.50 6.00
RJAMA Miguel Andujar 10.00 25.00
RJAMF Max Fried 10.00 25.00
RJANW Nick Williams 3.00 8.00
RJAOA Ozzie Albies 10.00 25.00
RJARD Rafael Devers 12.00 30.00
RJARH Rhys Hoskins 15.00 40.00
RJASO Shohei Ohtani 75.00 200.00
RJATW Tyler Wade 3.00 8.00
RJAVC Victor Caratini 3.00 8.00
RJAVR Victor Robles 8.00 20.00
RJAWB Walker Buehler 20.00 50.00
RJAWC Willie Calhoun 3.00 8.00
RJAZG Zack Granite 2.50 6.00

2018 Panini Spectra Rookie Jersey Autographs Neon Blue
*BLUE: .5X TO 1.2X BASIC
RANDOM INSERTS IN PACKS
PRINT RUNS B/WN 75-99 COPIES PER
RJAKF Kyle Farmer/99 3.00 8.00
RJARM Ryan McMahon/99 4.00 10.00
RJASO Shohei Ohtani/75 100.00 250.00

2018 Panini Spectra Rookie Jersey Autographs Neon Green
*GREEN: .75X TO 2X BASIC
RANDOM INSERTS IN PACKS
STATED PRINT RUN 25 SER.#'d SETS
RJAKF Kyle Farmer 5.00 12.00
RJASO Shohei Ohtani 200.00 400.00

2018 Panini Spectra Rookie Jersey Autographs Neon Pink
*PINK: .6X TO 1.5X BASIC
RANDOM INSERTS IN PACKS
STATED PRINT RUN 49 SER.#'d SETS
RJAKF Kyle Farmer 4.00 10.00
RJASO Shohei Ohtani 150.00 300.00

2018 Panini Spectra Signatures
RANDOM INSERTS IN PACKS
PRINT RUNS B/WN 15-199 COPIES PER
NO PRICING ON QTY 15
*PINK/35: .75X TO 2X p/r 99-199
1 Charles Johnson/99 3.00 8.00
2 Juan Gonzalez/199 3.00 8.00
3 Rhys Hoskins/49 15.00 40.00
4 Clint Frazier/49 8.00 20.00
6 Kevin Maitan/149 4.00 10.00
7 David Wright/25 6.00 15.00
8 Marcus Stroman/99 4.00 10.00
9 Starling Marte/99 4.00 10.00
10 Trea Turner/49 5.00 12.00
11 Jackie Bradley Jr./49 6.00 15.00
12 Gary Sanchez/25 8.00 20.00
13 Jason Kipnis/25 6.00 15.00
16 Jose Altuve/49 10.00 25.00
17 Yadier Molina/25 25.00 60.00
18 Freddie Freeman/25 20.00 50.00
21 Gleyber Torres/99 25.00 60.00
22 Kyle Schwarber/49 10.00 25.00
23 Josh Tomlin/49 4.00 10.00
24 Yoan Moncada/20
25 Lewis Brinson/199 3.00 8.00

2018 Panini Spectra Signatures Neon Blue
*BLUE/60: .4X TO 1X p/r 99-199
*BLUE/25: .6X TO 1.5X p/r 99-199
*BLUE/25: .5X TO 1.2X p/r 49
RANDOM INSERTS IN PACKS
PRINT RUNS B/WN 10-60 COPIES PER
NO PRICING ON QTY 15 OR LESS
5 Carlos Delgado/20 5.00 12.00

2018 Panini Spectra Triple Threat Materials
INSERTED IN '18 CHRONICLES PACKS
PRINT RUNS B/WN 75-199 COPIES PER
*GREEN/25: .75X TO 2X p/r 149-199
1 Ryan McMahon/199 2.50 6.00
2 Rhys Hoskins/199 4.00 10.00
3 Ozzie Albies/199 4.00 10.00
4 Miguel Andujar/199 5.00 12.00
5 Rafael Devers/199 6.00 15.00
6 Chance Sisco/199 2.50 6.00
7 Victor Caratini/199 2.50 6.00
8 Francisco Mejia/199 2.50 6.00
9 Kyle Farmer/199 2.00 5.00
10 Austin Hays/199 3.00 8.00
11 Alex Verdugo/199 3.00 8.00
12 Zack Granite/199 2.00 5.00
13 Clint Frazier/199 4.00 10.00
14 Nick Williams/199 2.50 6.00
15 Harrison Bader/199 3.00 8.00
16 Willie Calhoun/199 2.50 6.00
17 Victor Robles/199 4.00 10.00
18 Max Fried/199 8.00 20.00
19 Lucas Sims/199 2.00 5.00
20 Walker Buehler/199 4.00 10.00
21 Erick Fedde/199 2.00 5.00
22 Amed Rosario/199 2.50 6.00
23 Tyler Wade/199 2.50 6.00
24 J.P. Crawford/199 2.00 5.00
25 Richard Urena/199 2.00 5.00
26 Cameron Gallagher/199 2.00 5.00
27 Nicky Delmonico/199 2.00 5.00
28 Mitch Garver/199 2.00 5.00
29 Brian Anderson/199 2.50 6.00
30 Anthony Santander/199 2.50 6.00
31 Dustin Fowler/199 2.00 5.00
32 Tyler Mahle/199 2.50 6.00
33 Anthony Banda/199 2.00 5.00
34 Felix Jorge/199 2.00 5.00
35 Mike Trout/75 20.00 50.00
36 Manny Machado/99 4.00 10.00
37 Dustin Pedroia/99 4.00 10.00
38 Kris Bryant/75 5.00 12.00
39 Aaron Judge/199 10.00 25.00
40 Joey Gallo/149 2.50 6.00
41 Joey Votto/99 4.00 10.00
42 Edwin Encarnacion/99 2.50 6.00
43 Mookie Betts/99 6.00 15.00
44 Shohei Ohtani/199 12.00 30.00
45 Andrew McCutchen/99 4.00 10.00
46 Didi Gregorius/99 3.00 8.00
47 Evan Longoria/199 2.50 6.00
48 Dee Gordon/199 2.00 5.00
49 Jose Ramirez/199 2.50 6.00

2018 Panini Spectra Triple Threat Materials Neon Blue
*BLUE/75-99: .5X TO 1.2X p/r 149-199
*BLUE/75-99: .4X TO 1X p/r 75-99
*BLUE/49: .5X TO 1.2X p/r 75-99
INSERTED IN '18 CHRONICLES PACKS
PRINT RUNS B/WN 49-99 COPIES PER
50 Jonathan Schoop/99 2.50 6.00

2018 Panini Spectra Triple Threat Materials Neon Pink
*PINK/49: .6X TO 1.5X p/r 149-199
*PINK/49: .5X TO 1.2X p/r 75-99
INSERTED IN '18 CHRONICLES PACKS
STATED PRINT RUN 49 SER.#'d SETS
50 Jonathan Schoop 3.00 8.00

2019 Panini Spectra
INSERTED IN '19 CHRONICLES PACKS
JSY AU (101-150) PRINT RUN 199 SER.#'d SETS
EXCHANGE DEADLINE 2/21/2021
1 Alex Bregman .40 1.00
2 Ichiro .50 1.25
3 Dakota Hudson RC .30 .75
4 Cavan Biggio RC 1.25 3.00
5 Bryce Harper .60 1.50
6 Keston Hiura RC .75 2.00
7 Danny Jansen RC .25 .60
8 Robinson Cano .30 .75
9 Yadier Molina .40 1.00
10 Ronald Acuna Jr. 2.00 5.00
11 Khris Davis .40 1.00
12 Kyle Wright RC .40 1.00
13 Yusei Kikuchi RC .40 1.00
14 Mike Trout 2.00 5.00
15 Aaron Judge 1.00 2.50
16 Peter Lambert RC .40 1.00
17 Jeff McNeil RC .60 1.50
18 Christian Yelich .50 1.25
19 Cody Bellinger .75 2.00
20 Paul Goldschmidt .40 1.00
21 Corbin Burnes RC .40 1.00
22 Jon Duplantier RC .25 .60
23 Jonathan Loaisiga RC .30 .75
24 Jose Ramirez .30 .75
25 Whit Merrifield .40 1.00
26 Matt Chapman .40 1.00
27 Manny Machado .40 1.00
28 J.D. Martinez .40 1.00
29 Juan Soto 1.25 3.00
30 Charlie Blackmon .40 1.00
31 Max Scherzer .40 1.00
32 Andrew Benintendi .40 1.00
33 Jose Altuve .30 .75
34 Fernando Tatis Jr. RC 3.00 8.00
35 Brad Keller RC .25 .60
36 Javier Baez .50 1.25
37 Kris Bryant .50 1.25
38 Joey Votto .40 1.00
39 Gleyber Torres .75 2.00
40 Rhys Hoskins .50 1.25
41 Eloy Jimenez RC 1.50 4.00
42 Shohei Ohtani .50 1.25
43 Austin Riley RC 1.25 3.00
44 Christin Stewart RC .30 .75
45 Pete Alonso RC 1.50 4.00
46 Anthony Rizzo .60 1.50
47 Trevor Story .40 1.00
48 Justin Verlander .40 1.00
49 Ryan O'Hearn RC .25 .60
50 Luis Urias RC .40 1.00
51 Chris Paddack RC .50 1.25
52 Justus Sheffield RC .40 1.00
53 Kyle Tucker RC .50 1.25
54 Nolan Arenado .50 1.25
55 Cedric Mullins RC .40 1.00
56 Jacob deGrom .40 1.00
57 Corbin Martin RC .40 1.00
58 Jake Bauers RC .40 1.00
59 Mookie Betts .60 1.50
60 Francisco Lindor .40 1.00
61 Ramon Laureano RC .50 1.25
62 Chris Shaw RC .40 1.00
63 Ozzie Albies .40 1.00
64 Garrett Hampson RC .25 .60
65 Kolby Allard RC .40 1.00
66 Cole Tucker RC .40 1.00
67 Kevin Newman RC .40 1.00
68 Steven Duggar RC .30 .75
69 Bryan Reynolds RC .40 1.00
70 Michael Chavis RC .40 1.00
71 Daniel Ponce de Leon RC .40 1.00
72 Jonathan Davis RC .30 .75
73 Noah Syndergaard .30 .75
74 Chance Adams RC .25 .60
75 Kyle Freeland .30 .75
76 Starling Marte .30 .75
77 Griffin Canning RC .40 1.00
78 Michael Kopech RC .50 1.25
79 Enyel De Los Santos RC .25 .60
80 Brandon Lowe RC .40 1.00
81 Josh James RC .40 1.00
82 Luis Ortiz RC .25 .60
83 David Fletcher RC .75 2.00
84 Cal Quantrill RC .25 .60
85 Nathaniel Lowe RC .75 2.00
86 Luis Arraez RC 2.00 5.00
87 Reese McGuire RC .40 1.00
88 Jake Cave RC .30 .75
89 Carter Kieboom RC .40 1.00
90 Brendan Rodgers RC .40 1.00
91 Buster Posey .50 1.25
92 Myles Straw RC .40 1.00
93 Nick Margevicius .25 .60
94 Kevin Kramer RC .30 .75
95 Vladimir Guerrero Jr. RC 4.00 10.00
96 Nick Senzel RC .75 2.00
97 Lorenzo Cain .25 .60
98 Bryse Wilson RC .30 .75
99 Rowdy Tellez RC .40 1.00
100 Miguel Andujar .40 1.00
101 Taylor Ward JSY AU/199 RC 2.50 6.00
102 Kevin Newman JSY AU/199 4.00 10.00
103 Jeff McNeil JSY AU/199 10.00 25.00
104 Michael Kopech JSY AU/199 6.00 15.00
105 Jake Bauers JSY AU/199 4.00 10.00
106 Stephen Gonsalves JSY AU/199 RC 2.50 6.00
107 Dennis Santana JSY AU/199 RC 2.50 6.00
108 Ryan O'Hearn JSY AU/199 2.50 6.00
109 Sean Reid-Foley JSY AU/199 RC 2.50 6.00
110 Kevin Kramer JSY AU/199 3.00 8.00
111 Caleb Ferguson JSY AU/199 RC 3.00 8.00
112 Jonathan Davis JSY AU/199 3.00 8.00
113 Daniel Ponce de Leon JSY AU/199 4.00 10.00
114 Kyle Tucker JSY AU/199 5.00 12.00
115 Josh James JSY AU/199 4.00 10.00
116 Garrett Hampson JSY AU/199 2.50 6.00
117 Danny Jansen JSY AU/199 2.50 6.00
118 Luis Urias JSY AU/199 4.00 10.00
119 Jacob Nix JSY AU/199 RC 3.00 8.00
120 Patrick Wisdom JSY AU/199 RC 2.50 6.00
121 Justus Sheffield JSY AU/199 4.00 10.00
122 Corbin Burnes JSY AU/199 4.00 10.00
123 Brad Keller JSY AU/199 2.50 6.00
125 Ryan Borucki JSY AU/199 RC 2.50 6.00
126 Luis Ortiz JSY AU/199 2.50 6.00
127 Jake Cave JSY AU/199 5.00 12.00
128 Chance Adams JSY AU/199 2.50 6.00
129 Touki Toussaint JSY AU/199 RC 3.00 8.00
130 Kyle Wright JSY AU/199 4.00 10.00
131 Kolby Allard JSY AU/199 4.00 10.00
132 Dakota Hudson JSY AU/199 6.00 15.00
133 Framber Valdez JSY AU/199 RC 2.50 6.00
134 David Fletcher JSY AU/199 8.00 20.00
135 Brandon Lowe JSY AU/199 6.00 15.00
136 Ramon Laureano JSY AU/199 6.00 15.00
137 Jonathan Loaisiga JSY AU/199 3.00 8.00
138 Cionel Perez JSY AU/199 RC 2.50 6.00
139 Myles Straw JSY AU/199 4.00 10.00
140 Reese McGuire JSY AU/199 4.00 10.00
141 Enyel De Los Santos JSY AU/199 2.50 6.00
142 Chris Shaw JSY AU/199 4.00 10.00
143 Cedric Mullins JSY AU/199 4.00 10.00
144 Bryse Wilson JSY AU/199 3.00 8.00
145 Rowdy Tellez JSY AU/199 5.00 12.00
146 Christin Stewart JSY AU/199 3.00 8.00
147 Vladimir Guerrero Jr. JSY AU/199 50.00 120.00
148 Eloy Jimenez JSY AU/199 15.00 40.00
149 Fernando Tatis Jr. JSY AU/199 50.00 120.00
150 Nick Senzel JSY AU/199 8.00 20.00

2020 Panini Spectra Neon Blue
*NEON BLUE 1-100: 1.5X TO 4X
*NEON BLUE JSY AU: .5X TO 1.2X
RANDOM INSERTS IN PACKS
STATED PRINT RUN 99 SER.#'d SETS
EXCHANGE DEADLINE 2/21/2021
38 Luis Robert 20.00 50.00
128 Randy Arozarena AU JSY 75.00 200.00
140 Aristides Aquino AU JSY 15.00 40.00
149 Kyle Lewis AU JSY 40.00 100.00

2020 Panini Spectra Neon Green
38 Luis Robert 25.00 60.00
114 Bo Bichette AU JSY 60.00 150.00
115 Brendan McKay AU JSY 12.00 30.00
117 Nico Hoerner AU JSY 30.00 80.00
128 Randy Arozarena AU JSY 125.00 300.00
140 Aristides Aquino AU JSY 25.00 60.00
142 Edwin Rios AU JSY 20.00 50.00
145 Nick Solak AU JSY 15.00 40.00
149 Kyle Lewis AU JSY 60.00 150.00

2020 Panini Spectra Neon Pink
*NEON PNK 1-100: 1.5X TO 4X
*NEON PNK JSY AU: .6X TO 1.5X
RANDOM INSERTS IN PACKS
1-100 STATED PRINT RUN 75 SER.#'d SETS
JSY AU STATED PRINT RUN 49 SER.#'d SETS
EXCHANGE DEADLINE 2/21/2021
38 Luis Robert 20.00 50.00
114 Bo Bichette AU JSY 50.00 120.00
115 Brendan McKay AU JSY 10.00 25.00
117 Nico Hoerner AU JSY 15.00 40.00
128 Randy Arozarena AU JSY 100.00 250.00
140 Aristides Aquino AU JSY 20.00 50.00
145 Nick Solak AU JSY 10.00 25.00
146 Dustin May AU JSY 25.00 60.00
149 Kyle Lewis AU JSY 50.00 120.00

2020 Panini Spectra Red
38 Luis Robert 40.00 100.00

2020 Panini Spectra Prospect Jersey Autographs
RANDOM INSERTS IN PACKS
STATED PRINT RUN 199 SER.#'d SETS
EXCHANGE DEADLINE 7/31/22
1 Andres Gimenez 8.00 20.00
3 Tristen Lutz 3.00 8.00
7 Jonathan India 5.00 12.00
8 Alex Kirilloff 8.00 20.00
9 Jo Adell 12.00 30.00
11 Tyler Stephenson 2.50 6.00
12 Forrest Whitley 2.50 6.00
13 Nick Neidert 2.50 6.00
14 Luis Robert 50.00 120.00
15 Colton Welker 2.50 6.00

2020 Panini Spectra Prospect Jersey Autographs Neon Blue
*N.BLUE/99: .5X TO 1.2X BASIC
*N.BLUE/49: .6X TO 1.5X BASIC
RANDOM INSERTS IN PACKS
PRINT RUN B/WN 25-60 COPIES PER
EXCHANGE DEADLINE 7/31/22
6 Alec Bohm 30.00 80.00
9 Jo Adell 25.00 60.00
14 Luis Robert 75.00 200.00

2020 Panini Spectra Prospect Jersey Autographs Neon Green
*N.GREEN/25: .8X TO 2X BASIC
RANDOM INSERTS IN PACKS
PRINT RUN B/WN 10-25 COPIES PER
NO PRICING QTY 15 OR LESS
EXCHANGE DEADLINE 7/31/22
7 Jonathan India 12.00 30.00
9 Jo Adell 40.00 100.00
14 Luis Robert 100.00 250.00

2020 Panini Spectra Prospect Jersey Autographs Neon Pink
*N.PINK/49: .6X TO 1.5X BASIC
*N.PINK/25: .8X TO 2X BASIC
RANDOM INSERTS IN PACKS
PRINT RUN B/WN 25-49 COPIES PER
EXCHANGE DEADLINE 7/31/22
6 Alec Bohm 50.00 120.00
9 Jo Adell 30.00 80.00

2020 Panini Spectra Signatures
RANDOM INSERTS IN PACKS
PRINT RUN B/WN 49-199 COPIES PER
EXCHANGE DEADLINE 7/31/22
1 Garrett Hampson 2.50 6.00
2 Enyel De Los Santos 2.50 6.00
4 Yoshitomo Tsutsugo 8.00 20.00
5 Jonathan Davis 3.00 8.00
6 Michael Chavis 5.00 12.00
7 Myles Straw 4.00 10.00
10 Rowdy Tellez 3.00 8.00
11 Sean Reid-Foley 2.50 6.00
12 Taylor Hearn 2.50 6.00
13 Brad Keller 2.50 6.00
14 Bryse Wilson 5.00 12.00
15 Caleb Ferguson 2.50 6.00
16 Chris Paddack 5.00 12.00
17 Cole Tucker 4.00 10.00
18 Corbin Burnes 3.00 8.00
19 David Fletcher 4.00 10.00
20 Eloy Jimenez 12.00 30.00
23 Ty France 6.00 15.00
24 Stephen Gonsalves 2.50 6.00

2020 Panini Spectra Signatures Neon Blue
*N.BLUE/60: .5X TO 1.2X p/r 199
*N.BLUE/25: .5X TO 1.2X p/r 49
RANDOM INSERTS IN PACKS
PRINT RUN B/WN 25-60 COPIES PER
EXCHANGE DEADLINE 7/31/22
4 Yoshitomo Tsutsugo 12.00 30.00
6 Michael Chavis 8.00 20.00
16 Chris Paddack 8.00 20.00

2020 Panini Spectra Signatures Neon Green
*N.GRN/25: .6X TO 1.5X BASIC
RANDOM INSERTS IN PACKS
PRINT RUN B/WN 5-25 COPIES PER
NO PRICING QTY 15 OR LESS
EXCHANGE DEADLINE 7/31/22
4 Yoshitomo Tsutsugo 15.00 40.00
6 Michael Chavis 10.00 25.00
16 Chris Paddack 12.00 30.00
19 David Fletcher 10.00 25.00
23 Ty France 12.00 30.00

2020 Panini Spectra Signatures Neon Pink
*N.PNK/35: .5X TO 1.2X BASIC
RANDOM INSERTS IN PACKS
PRINT RUN B/WN 10-35 COPIES PER
NO PRICING QTY 15 OR LESS
EXCHANGE DEADLINE 7/31/22
4 Yoshitomo Tsutsugo 12.00 30.00
6 Michael Chavis 8.00 20.00
16 Chris Paddack 8.00 20.00
19 David Fletcher 8.00 20.00

2020 Panini Spectra Silhouettes
RANDOM INSERTS IN PACKS
1 Nelson Cruz 2.50 6.00
2 Eloy Jimenez 3.00 8.00
3 Alex Gordon 2.00 5.00
4 Brandon Belt 2.00 5.00
8 Trey Mancini 2.50 6.00
9 Dustin May 4.00 10.00
10 Alex Bregman 2.50 6.00
11 Yadier Molina 2.50 6.00
12 Albert Pujols 4.00 10.00
13 Rafael Devers 3.00 8.00
14 Jose Abreu 2.50 6.00
15 Mike Trout 12.00 30.00
16 Fernando Tatis Jr. 8.00 20.00
17 Robinson Cano 2.00 5.00
18 Stephen Strasburg 2.50 6.00
19 Shun Yamaguchi 2.00 5.00
20 Corey Seager 6.00 15.00
21 Justin Verlander 2.50 6.00
22 Jorge Soler 2.50 6.00
23 Aaron Nola 2.00 5.00
26 Freddie Freeman 3.00 8.00
27 Gerrit Cole 4.00 10.00
28 George Springer 2.00 5.00
29 Hunter Renfroe 1.50 4.00
30 J.P. Crawford 1.50 4.00
31 Javier Baez 3.00 8.00
33 Evan Longoria 2.00 5.00
35 Trevor Story 2.50 6.00
36 Tim Anderson 2.50 6.00
37 Gary Sanchez 4.00 10.00
38 Luis Robert 8.00 20.00
39 J.D. Martinez 2.50 6.00
42 Marcell Ozuna 2.50 6.00
43 Dan Vogelbach 1.50 4.00

eston Hiura 3.00 8.00
osh Bell 2.00 5.00
Buster Posey 3.00 8.00
Joey Votto 2.50 6.00
Elvis Andrus 2.00 5.00
Ozzie Albies 2.50 6.00
Cavan Biggio 3.00 8.00
Gleyber Torres 4.00 10.00
Juan Soto 5.00 12.00
Josh Donaldson 2.00 5.00
Jonathan Schoop 1.50 4.00
Byron Buxton 2.00 5.00
Stephen Piscotty 1.50 4.00
Giancarlo Stanton 2.50 6.00
Vladimir Guerrero Jr. 5.00 12.00
Jonathan Villar 1.50 4.00
Andrew Benintendi 2.50 6.00
Aaron Judge 6.00 15.00
Nick Senzel 2.50 6.00
Cody Bellinger 5.00 12.00
Max Scherzer 2.50 6.00
Austin Meadows 2.00 5.00
Clayton Kershaw 4.00 10.00
Mookie Betts 10.00 25.00
Nolan Arenado 3.00 8.00
Eugenio Suarez 2.00 5.00
Brian Anderson 1.50 4.00
Madison Bumgarner 2.00 5.00
Kyle Schwarber 2.50 6.00
Eric Hosmer 2.00 5.00
Whit Merrifield 2.50 6.00
Anthony Rizzo 4.00 10.00
Austin Hays 2.50 6.00
Miguel Cabrera 2.50 6.00
Starling Marte 2.00 5.00
Matt Chapman 2.50 6.00
Joey Gallo 2.50 6.00
Rougned Odor 2.00 5.00
9 Christian Yelich 3.00 8.00
2 Max Kepler 2.00 5.00
Bryan Reynolds 2.00 5.00
Justin Upton 2.00 5.00
5 Lorenzo Cain 1.50 4.00
6 Ronald Acuna Jr. 6.00 15.00
8 Ketel Marte 2.00 5.00

2020 Panini Spectra Silhouettes Neon Blue

N.BLUE/49-99: .5X TO 1.2X BASIC
N.BLUE/20-25: .6X TO 1.5X BASIC
ANDOM INSERTS IN PACKS
RINT RUN B/WN 6-99 COPIES PER
O PRICING QTY 15 OR LESS
6 Fernando Tatis Jr. 12.00 30.00
8 Luis Robert 15.00 40.00
2 Juan Soto 8.00 20.00
2 Mookie Betts 20.00 50.00

2020 Panini Spectra Silhouettes Red

RED/25: .6X TO 1.5X BASIC
RANDOM INSERTS IN PACKS
PRINT RUN B/WN 4-25 COPIES PER
NO PRICING QTY 15 OR LESS
16 Fernando Tatis Jr. 15.00 40.00
38 Luis Robert 30.00 80.00
52 Juan Soto 12.00 30.00
96 Ronald Acuna Jr 40.00 100.00

2020 Panini Spectra Swatches

RANDOM INSERTS IN PACKS
1 Nelson Cruz 2.50 6.00
2 Eloy Jimenez 3.00 8.00
3 Alex Gordon 2.00 5.00
4 Brandon Belt 2.00 5.00
8 Trey Mancini 2.50 6.00
9 Dustin May 4.00 10.00
10 Alex Bregman 2.50 6.00
11 Yadier Molina 2.50 6.00
12 Albert Pujols 4.00 10.00
13 Rafael Devers 3.00 8.00
14 Jose Abreu 2.50 6.00
15 Mike Trout 12.00 30.00
16 Fernando Tatis Jr. 8.00 20.00
17 Robinson Cano 2.00 5.00
18 Stephen Strasburg 2.50 6.00
19 Shun Yamaguchi 2.00 5.00
20 Corey Seager 6.00 15.00
21 Justin Verlander 2.50 6.00
22 Jorge Soler 2.50 6.00
23 Aaron Nola 2.50 6.00
24 Manny Machado 2.50 6.00
26 Freddie Freeman 3.00 8.00
27 Gerrit Cole 4.00 10.00
28 George Springer 2.00 5.00
29 Hunter Renfroe 1.50 4.00
30 J.P. Crawford 1.50 4.00
31 Javier Baez 3.00 8.00
32 Pete Alonso 5.00 12.00
33 Evan Longoria 2.00 5.00
35 Trevor Story 2.50 6.00
36 Tim Anderson 2.50 6.00
37 Gary Sanchez 4.00 10.00
38 Luis Robert 8.00 20.00
39 J.D. Martinez 2.50 6.00
40 Nicholas Castellanos 2.50 6.00
41 Jacob deGrom 2.50 6.00
42 Marcell Ozuna 2.50 6.00
43 Dan Vogelbach 1.50 4.00
44 Keston Hiura 3.00 8.00
45 Josh Bell 2.00 5.00
46 Buster Posey 3.00 8.00
47 Joey Votto 2.50 6.00
48 Elvis Andrus 2.00 5.00
49 Ozzie Albies 2.50 6.00
50 Cavan Biggio 3.00 8.00
51 Gleyber Torres 4.00 10.00
52 Juan Soto 5.00 12.00
54 Josh Donaldson 2.00 5.00
55 Jonathan Schoop 1.50 4.00
56 Byron Buxton 2.00 5.00
57 Stephen Piscotty 1.50 4.00
58 Giancarlo Stanton 2.50 6.00
59 Vladimir Guerrero Jr. 5.00 12.00
60 Jonathan Villar 1.50 4.00
61 Andrew Benintendi 2.50 6.00
62 Aaron Judge 6.00 15.00
63 Nick Senzel 2.50 6.00
65 Cody Bellinger 5.00 12.00
66 Max Scherzer 2.50 6.00
70 Austin Meadows 2.00 5.00
71 Clayton Kershaw 4.00 10.00
72 Mookie Betts 10.00 25.00
73 Nolan Arenado 3.00 8.00
74 Eugenio Suarez 2.00 5.00
76 Brian Anderson 1.50 4.00
77 Madison Bumgarner 2.00 5.00
78 Kyle Schwarber 2.50 6.00
79 Eric Hosmer 2.00 5.00
80 Todd Frazier 2.00 5.00
81 Whit Merrifield 2.50 6.00
82 Anthony Rizzo 5.00 12.00
83 Austin Hays 2.50 6.00
84 Miguel Cabrera 2.50 6.00
85 Starling Marte 2.00 5.00
86 Matt Chapman 2.50 6.00
87 Joey Gallo 2.50 6.00
88 Rougned Odor 2.00 5.00
89 Christian Yelich 3.00 8.00
92 Max Kepler 2.00 5.00
93 Bryan Reynolds 2.00 5.00
94 Justin Upton 2.00 5.00
95 Lorenzo Cain 1.50 4.00
96 Ronald Acuna Jr. 6.00 15.00
98 Ketel Marte 2.00 5.00

2020 Panini Spectra Swatches Neon Blue

*N.BLUE/49-99: .5X TO 1.2X BASIC
*N.BLUE/25: .6X TO 1.5X BASIC
RANDOM INSERTS IN PACKS
PRINT RUN B/WN 10-99 COPIES PER
NO PRICING QTY 15 OR LESS
16 Fernando Tatis Jr. 12.00 30.00
32 Pete Alonso 10.00 25.00
38 Luis Robert 15.00 40.00
52 Juan Soto 8.00 20.00
72 Mookie Betts 15.00 40.00

2020 Panini Spectra Swatches Red

*RED/25: .6X TO 1.5X BASIC
RANDOM INSERTS IN PACKS
PRINT RUN B/WN 5-25 COPIES PER
NO PRICING QTY 15 OR LESS
16 Fernando Tatis Jr. 15.00 40.00
32 Pete Alonso 15.00 40.00
38 Luis Robert 30.00 80.00
52 Juan Soto 15.00 40.00
72 Mookie Betts 20.00 50.00
96 Ronald Acuna Jr. 40.00 100.00

2018 Panini Status

1 Shohei Ohtani RC 1.50 4.00
2 Clint Frazier RC .50 1.25
3 Rafael Devers RC .75 2.00
4 Rhys Hoskins RC 1.00 2.50
5 Austin Hays RC .40 1.00
6 Amed Rosario RC .30 .75
7 Victor Robles RC .60 1.50
8 Nick Williams RC .30 .75
9 Ozzie Albies RC .75 2.00
10 Ryan McMahon RC .30 .75
11 Victor Caratini RC .30 .75
12 Scott Kingery RC .40 1.00
13 Greg Allen RC .25 .60
14 Jack Flaherty RC .40 1.00
15 Andrew Stevenson .15 .40
16 Anthony Rizzo .40 1.00
17 Francisco Lindor .25 .60
18 Ronald Guzman RC .25 .60
19 Willy Adames RC .30 .75
20 Paul Goldschmidt .25 .60
21 Ronald Acuna Jr. RC 5.00 12.00
22 Corey Seager .25 .60
23 Gleyber Torres RC 2.50 6.00
24 Erick Fedde RC .25 .60
25 Jimmie Sherfy RC .25 .60

2018 Panini Status Autographs

RANDOM INSERTS IN PACKS
12 Scott Kingery 4.00 10.00
15 Andrew Stevenson 2.50 6.00
19 Willy Adames 3.00 8.00
25 Jimmie Sherfy 2.50 6.00

2018 Panini Status Autographs Gold

*GOLD/25: .75X TO 2X BASIC
RANDOM INSERTS IN PACKS
PRINT RUNS B/WN 3-25 COPIES PER
NO PRICING ON QTY 10 OR LESS
5 Austin Hays/25 8.00 20.00
13 Greg Allen/25 5.00 12.00

2019 Panini Status

RANDOM INSERTS IN PACKS
*GREEN: 1X TO 2.5X
*BLUE/99: 1.2X TO 3X
*RED/25: 2.5X TO 6X
1 Keston Hiura RC .50 1.25
2 Chris Paddack RC .30 .75
3 Corey Kluber .20 .50
4 Trevor Story .25 .60
5 Ramon Laureano RC .30 .75
6 Yusei Kikuchi RC .25 .60
7 Pete Alonso RC 4.00 10.00
8 Aaron Judge .60 1.50
9 Ty France RC .50 1.25
10 Javier Baez .30 .75
11 Eloy Jimenez RC .60 1.50
12 Michael Kopech RC .30 .75
13 Mike Trout 1.25 3.00
14 Shohei Ohtani .30 .75
15 Mookie Betts .40 1.00
16 Ryan O'Hearn RC .15 .40
17 Ichiro .30 .75
18 Joey Votto .25 .60
19 Jeff McNeil RC .40 1.00
20 Brandon Lowe RC .25 .60
21 Albert Pujols .30 .75
22 Fernando Tatis Jr. RC 2.00 5.00
23 Kris Bryant .30 .75
24 Yadier Molina .25 .60
25 Kyle Tucker RC .30 .75
26 Nathaniel Lowe RC .20 .50
27 Bryce Harper .40 1.00
28 Justus Sheffield RC .25 .60
29 Jason Martin RC .20 .50
30 Bryan Reynolds RC .50 1.25
31 Michael Chavis RC .25 .60
32 Cole Tucker RC .25 .60
33 Darwinzon Hernandez RC .15 .40
34 Vladimir Guerrero Jr. RC 2.50 6.00
35 Carter Kieboom RC .25 .60

2020 Panini Status

RANDOM INSERTS IN PACKS
1 Sean Murphy RC .40 1.00
2 Aristides Aquino RC .50 1.25
3 Gavin Lux RC 1.50 4.00
4 Mike Trout 2.00 5.00
5 Shogo Akiyama RC .40 1.00
6 Bo Bichette RC 3.00 8.00
7 Danny Mendick RC .30 .75
8 Khris Davis .25 .60
9 Shun Yamaguchi RC .30 .75
10 Bryce Harper .40 1.00
11 Yordan Alvarez RC 1.25 3.00
12 Brendan McKay RC .40 1.00
13 Aaron Judge .60 1.50
14 Nico Hoerner RC 1.00 2.50
15 Michel Baez RC .25 .60
16 Bobby Bradley RC .30 .75
17 Yoshitomo Tsutsugo RC .30 .75
18 Kwang-Hyun Kim RC .75 2.00
19 A.J. Puk RC .50 1.25
20 Luis Robert RC 4.00 10.00

2018 Prestige

1 Clint Frazier RC .50 1.25
2 J.P. Crawford RC .25 .60
3 Shohei Ohtani RC 1.50 4.00
4 Carlos Correa .25 .60
5 Joey Votto .25 .60
6 Kris Bryant .30 .75
7 Miguel Andujar RC 1.00 2.50
8 Ronald Acuna Jr. RC 5.00 12.00
9 Austin Hays RC .40 1.00
10 Buster Posey .30 .75
11 Mike Trout 1.25 3.00
12 Anthony Rizzo .40 1.00
13 Bryce Harper .40 1.00
14 Nolan Arenado .30 .75
15 Paul Goldschmidt .25 .60
16 Aaron Judge .60 1.50
17 Ozzie Albies RC .75 2.00
18 Trea Turner .20 .50
19 Gleyber Torres RC 2.50 6.00
20 Cody Bellinger .50 1.25
21 Manny Machado .25 .60
22 Rafael Devers RC .75 2.00
23 Nick Williams RC .30 .75
24 Ryan McMahon RC .30 .75
25 Alex Verdugo RC .40 1.00
26 Amed Rosario RC .30 .75
27 Victor Robles RC .60 1.50
28 Shohei Ohtani RC 1.50 4.00
29 Jose Altuve .20 .50
30 Rhys Hoskins RC 1.00 2.50

2018 Prestige Autographs

RANDOM INSERTS IN PACKS
1 Erik Gonzalez 2.50 6.00
7 Brandon Woodruff 3.00 8.00
8 Anthony Santander 2.50 6.00
11 Thyago Vieira 2.50 6.00
12 Reyes Moronta 2.50 6.00
15 Andrew Stevenson 2.50 6.00
16 Jimmie Sherfy 2.50 6.00
17 Shane Bieber
18 Bobby Witt 2.50 6.00
19 Christian Villanueva 2.50 6.00

2018 Prestige Autographs Xtra Points Holo Silver

*HOLO SLVR/25: .75X TO 2X BASIC
RANDOM INSERTS IN PACKS
PRINTR RUNS B/WN 5-25 COPIES PER
NO PRICING ON QTY 5
5 Greg Allen/25 5.00 12.00

2018 Prestige Autographs Xtra Points Purple

*PURPLE/99: .5X TO 1.2X BASIC
RANDOM INSERTS IN PACKS
PRINTR RUNS B/WN 10-99 COPIES PER
NO PRICING ON QTY 10
5 Greg Allen/99 3.00 8.00

2018 Prestige Autographs Xtra Points Red

*RED: .5X TO 1.2X BASIC
RANDOM INSERTS IN PACKS
STATED PRINT RUN 199 SER.#'d SETS
5 Greg Allen 3.00 8.00

2019 Prestige Autographs

RANDOM INSERTS IN PACKS
EXCHANGE DEADLINE 2/21/2021
*GOLD/99: .5X TO 1.2X
*GOLD/35: .6X TO 1.5X
*RED/50: .6X TO 1.5X
*RED/25: .75X TO 2X
*HOLO SLVR/23: .75X TO 2X
1 J.T. Realmuto 8.00 20.00
2 Joey Bart 8.00 20.00
3 Patrick Corbin 3.00 8.00
5 German Marquez 2.50 6.00
6 Matt Olson 2.50 6.00
7 Tim Anderson 4.00 10.00
8 Asdrubal Cabrera 3.00 8.00
9 Austin Meadows 3.00 8.00
10 Dan Vogelbach 2.50 6.00
11 Jorge Polanco 2.50 6.00

2018 Rookies and Stars

1 Shohei Ohtani RC 1.50 4.00
2 Buster Posey .30 .75
3 Ronald Acuna Jr. RC 5.00 12.00
4 Miguel Andujar RC 1.00 2.50
5 Rhys Hoskins RC 1.00 2.50
6 Chris Sale .25 .60
7 Austin Hays RC .40 1.00
8 Ozzie Albies RC .75 2.00
9 Bryce Harper .40 1.00
10 Joey Votto .25 .60
11 Cody Bellinger .50 1.25
12 Giancarlo Stanton .25 .60
13 Nolan Arenado .30 .75
14 Kris Bryant .30 .75
15 Amed Rosario RC .30 .75
16 Gleyber Torres RC 2.50 6.00
17 Rafael Devers RC .75 2.00
18 Mike Trout 1.25 3.00
19 Clint Frazier RC .50 1.25
20 Marcell Ozuna .25 .60

2019 Rookies and Stars

RANDOM INSERTS IN PACKS
*GOLD/199: 1.2X TO 3X
*BLUE/99: 1.5X TO 4X
*RED/50: 2X TO 5X
*HOLO SLVR/25: 3X TO 8X
1 Pete Alonso RC 2.00 5.00
2 Eloy Jimenez RC .60 1.50
3 Fernando Tatis Jr. RC 2.00 5.00
4 Michael Kopech RC .30 .75
5 Kyle Tucker RC .30 .75
6 Yusei Kikuchi RC .25 .60
7 Chris Paddack RC .30 .75
8 Mike Trout 1.25 3.00
9 Bryce Harper .40 1.00
10 Aaron Judge .60 1.50
11 Kris Bryant .30 .75
12 Shohei Ohtani .30 .75
13 Vladimir Guerrero Jr. RC 2.50 6.00
14 Nick Senzel RC .50 1.25
15 Carter Kieboom RC .25 .60
16 Xander Bogaerts .25 .60
17 Anthony Rendon .25 .60
18 Griffin Canning RC .25 .60
19 Cal Quantrill RC .15 .40
20 Nicky Lopez RC .25 .60

2020 Rookies and Stars

RANDOM INSERTS IN PACKS
1 Shogo Akiyama RC .40 1.00
2 Yordan Alvarez RC 1.25 3.00
3 Bo Bichette RC 3.00 8.00
4 Aristides Aquino RC .50 1.25
5 Gavin Lux RC 1.50 4.00
6 Yoshitomo Tsutsugo RC .30 .75
7 Brendan McKay RC .40 1.00
8 Luis Robert RC 4.00 10.00
9 Sean Murphy RC .40 1.00
10 Yu Chang RC .40 1.00
11 Domingo Leyba RC .30 .75
12 Edwin Rios RC .60 1.50
13 Tony Gonsolin RC 1.00 2.50
14 Willi Castro RC .40 1.00
15 Tyrone Taylor RC .25 .60
16 Gleyber Torres .50 1.25
17 Stephen Strasburg .25 .60
18 Jose Altuve .20 .50
19 Ozzie Albies .25 .60
20 Shane Bieber .25 .60

2020 Rookies and Stars Signatures

RANDOM INSERTS IN PACKS
PRINT RUNS B/WN 10-99 COPIES PER
NO PRICING QTY 15 OR LESS
EXCHANGE DEADLINE 3/18/2022
1 Shogo Akiyama/49 6.00 15.00
2 Yordan Alvarez/50 20.00 50.00
3 Bo Bichette/30 30.00 80.00
4 Aristides Aquino/60 8.00 20.00
6 Yoshitomo Tsutsugo/99 8.00 20.00
8 Luis Robert EXCH/99 75.00 200.00
9 Sean Murphy/99 5.00 12.00
10 Yu Chang/99 5.00 12.00
11 Domingo Leyba/99 4.00 10.00
12 Edwin Rios/99 8.00 20.00
13 Tony Gonsolin/99 12.00 30.00
14 Willi Castro/99 5.00 12.00
16 Gleyber Torres EXCH/25 20.00 50.00

1988 Score

This set consists of 660 standard-size cards. The set was distributed by Major League Marketing and features six distinctive border colors on the front. Subsets include Reggie Jackson Tribute (500-504), Highlights (652-660) and Rookie Prospects (623-647). Card number 501, showing Reggie as a member of the Baltimore Orioles, is one of the few opportunities collectors have to visually remember Reggie's one-year stay with the Orioles. The set is distinguished by the fact that each card back shows a full-color picture of the player. Rookie Cards in this set include Ellis Burks, Ken Caminiti, Tom Glavine and Matt Williams.

COMPLETE SET (660) 5.00 12.00
COMP.FACT.SET (660) 8.00 20.00
1 Don Mattingly .25 .60
2 Wade Boggs .05 .15
3 Tim Raines .02 .10
4 Andre Dawson .02 .10
5 Mark McGwire .60 1.50
6 Kevin Seitzer .01 .05
7 Wally Joyner .02 .10
8 Jesse Barfield .02 .10
9 Pedro Guerrero .02 .10
10 Eric Davis .02 .10
11 George Brett .20 .50
12 Ozzie Smith .10 .30
13 Rickey Henderson .07 .20
14 Jim Rice .02 .10
15 Matt Nokes RC .08 .25
16 Mike Schmidt .20 .50
17 Dave Parker .02 .10
18 Eddie Murray .07 .20
19 Andres Galarraga .02 .10
20 Tony Fernandez .01 .05
21 Kevin McReynolds .01 .05
22 B.J. Surhoff .02 .10
23 Pat Tabler .01 .05
24 Kirby Puckett .07 .20
25 Benny Santiago .02 .10
26 Ryne Sandberg .15 .40
27 Kelly Downs .01 .05
28 Jose Cruz .02 .10
29 Pete O'Brien .01 .05
30 Mark Langston .01 .05
31 Lee Smith .02 .10
32 Juan Samuel .01 .05
33 Kevin Bass .01 .05
34 R.J. Reynolds .01 .05
35 Steve Sax .01 .05
36 John Kruk .02 .10
37 Alan Trammell .02 .10
38 Chris Bosio .01 .05
39 Brook Jacoby .01 .05
40 Willie McGee UER .02 .10
Excited misspelled
as excitd
41 Dave Magadan .01 .05
42 Fred Lynn .02 .10
43 Kent Hrbek .02 .10
44 Brian Downing .02 .10
45 Jose Canseco .20 .50
46 Jim Presley .01 .05
47 Mike Stanley .01 .05
48 Tony Pena .01 .05
49 David Cone .02 .10
50 Rick Sutcliffe .02 .10
51 Doug Drabek .01 .05
52 Bill Doran .01 .05
53 Mike Scioscia .02 .10
54 Candy Maldonado .01 .05
55 Dave Winfield .02 .10
56 Lou Whitaker .02 .10
57 Tom Henke .01 .05
58 Ken Gerhart .01 .05
59 Glenn Braggs .01 .05
60 Julio Franco .02 .10
61 Charlie Leibrandt .01 .05
62 Gary Gaetti .02 .10
63 Bob Boone .02 .10
64 Luis Polonia RC .08 .25
65 Dwight Evans .05 .15
66 Phil Bradley .01 .05
67 Mike Boddicker .01 .05
68 Vince Coleman .01 .05
69 Howard Johnson .02 .10
70 Tim Wallach .01 .05
71 Keith Moreland .01 .05
72 Barry Larkin .05 .15
73 Alan Ashby .01 .05
74 Rick Rhoden .01 .05
75 Darrell Evans .02 .10
76 Dave Stieb .02 .10
77 Dan Plesac .01 .05
78 Will Clark UER .07 .20
Born 3/17/64
should be 3/13/64
79 Frank White .02 .10
80 Joe Carter .02 .10
81 Mike Witt .01 .05
82 Terry Steinbach .02 .10
83 Alvin Davis .01 .05
84 Tommy Herr .02 .10
85 Vance Law .01 .05
86 Kal Daniels .01 .05
87 Rick Honeycutt UER .01 .05
Wrong years for
stats on back
88 Alfredo Griffin .01 .05
89 Bret Saberhagen .02 .10
90 Bert Blyleven .02 .10
91 Jeff Reardon .02 .10
92 Cory Snyder .01 .05
93A Greg Walker ERR .75 2.00
93B Greg Walker COR .01 .05
93 of 660
94 Joe Magrane RC .08 .25
95 Rob Deer .01 .05
96 Ray Knight .02 .10
97 Casey Candaele .01 .05
98 John Cerutti .01 .05
99 Buddy Bell .02 .10
100 Jack Clark .02 .10
101 Eric Bell .01 .05
102 Willie Wilson .02 .10
103 Dave Schmidt .01 .05
104 Dennis Eckersley UER .05 .15
Complete games stats
are wrong
105 Don Sutton .02 .10
106 Danny Tartabull .01 .05
107 Fred McGriff .07 .20
108 Les Straker .01 .05
109 Lloyd Moseby .01 .05
110 Roger Clemens .40 1.00
111 Glenn Hubbard .01 .05
112 Ken Williams RC .01 .05
113 Ruben Sierra .02 .10
114 Stan Jefferson .01 .05
115 Milt Thompson .01 .05
116 Bobby Bonilla .02 .10
117 Wayne Tolleson .01 .05
118 Matt Williams RC .30 .75
119 Chet Lemon .02 .10
120 Dale Sveum .01 .05
121 Dennis Boyd .01 .05
122 Brett Butler .02 .10
123 Terry Kennedy .01 .05
124 Jack Howell .01 .05
125 Curt Young .01 .05
126A Dave Valle ERR .02 .10
Misspelled Dale
on card front
126B Dave Valle COR .01 .05
127 Curt Wilkerson .01 .05
128 Tim Teufel .01 .05
129 Ozzie Virgil .01 .05
130 Brian Fisher .01 .05
131 Lance Parrish .02 .10
132 Tom Browning .01 .05
133A Larry Andersen ERR .02 .10
Misspelled Anderson
on card front
133B Larry Andersen COR .01 .05
134A Bob Brenly ERR .02 .10
Misspelled Brenley
on card front
134B Bob Brenly COR .01 .05
135 Mike Marshall .01 .05
136 Gerald Perry .01 .05
137 Bobby Meacham .01 .05
138 Larry Herndon .01 .05
139 Fred Manrique .01 .05
140 Charlie Hough .02 .10
141 Ron Darling .02 .10
142 Herm Winningham .01 .05
143 Mike Diaz .01 .05
144 Mike Jackson RC .08 .25
145 Denny Walling .01 .05
146 Robby Thompson .01 .05
147 Franklin Stubbs .01 .05
148 Albert Hall .01 .05
149 Bobby Witt .01 .05
150 Lance McCullers .01 .05
151 Scott Bradley .01 .05
152 Mark McLemore .01 .05
153 Tim Laudner .01 .05
154 Greg Swindell .01 .05
155 Marty Barrett .01 .05
156 Mike Heath .01 .05
157 Gary Ward .01 .05
158A Lee Mazzilli ERR .02 .10
Misspelled Mazilli
on card front
158B Lee Mazzilli COR .02 .10
159 Tom Foley .01 .05
160 Robin Yount .10 .30
161 Steve Bedrosian .01 .05
162 Bob Walk .01 .05
163 Nick Esasky .01 .05
164 Ken Caminiti RC .75 2.00
165 Jose Uribe .01 .05
166 Dave Anderson .01 .05
167 Ed Whitson .01 .05
168 Ernie Whitt .01 .05
169 Cecil Cooper .02 .10
170 Mike Pagliarulo .01 .05
171 Pat Sheridan .01 .05
172 Chris Bando .01 .05
173 Lee Lacy .01 .05
174 Steve Lombardozzi .01 .05
175 Mike Greenwell .01 .05
176 Greg Minton .01 .05
177 Moose Haas .01 .05
178 Mike Kingery .01 .05
179 Greg A. Harris .01 .05
180 Bo Jackson .07 .20
181 Carmelo Martinez .01 .05
182 Alex Trevino .01 .05
183 Ron Oester .01 .05
184 Danny Darwin .01 .05
185 Mike Krukow .01 .05
186 Rafael Palmeiro .15 .40
187 Tim Burke .01 .05
188 Roger McDowell .01 .05
189 Garry Templeton .02 .10
190 Terry Pendleton .02 .10
191 Larry Parrish .01 .05
192 Rey Quinones .01 .05
193 Joaquin Andujar .02 .10
194 Tom Brunansky .01 .05
195 Donnie Moore .01 .05
196 Dan Pasqua .01 .05
197 Jim Gantner .01 .05
198 Mark Eichhorn .01 .05
199 John Grubb .01 .05
200 Bill Ripken RC .08 .25
201 Sam Horn RC .02 .10
202 Todd Worrell .01 .05
203 Terry Leach .01 .05
204 Garth Iorg .01 .05
205 Brian Dayett .01 .05
206 Bo Diaz .01 .05
207 Craig Reynolds .01 .05
208 Brian Holton .01 .05
209 Marvell Wynne UER .01 .05
Misspelled Marvelle
on card front
210 Dave Concepcion .02 .10
211 Mike Davis .01 .05
212 Devon White .02 .10
213 Mickey Brantley .01 .05
214 Greg Gagne .01 .05
215 Oddibe McDowell .01 .05
216 Jimmy Key .02 .10
217 Dave Bergman .01 .05
218 Calvin Schiraldi .01 .05
219 Larry Sheets .01 .05
220 Mike Easler .01 .05
221 Kurt Stillwell .01 .05
222 Chuck Jackson .01 .05
223 Dave Martinez .01 .05
224 Tim Leary .01 .05
225 Steve Garvey .02 .10
226 Greg Mathews .01 .05
227 Doug Sisk .01 .05
228 Dave Henderson .01 .05
Wearing Red Sox uniform;
Red Sox logo on back
229 Jimmy Dwyer .01 .05
230 Larry Owen .01 .05
231 Andre Thornton .01 .05
232 Mark Salas .01 .05
233 Tom Brookens .01 .05
234 Greg Brock .01 .05
235 Rance Mulliniks .01 .05
236 Bob Brower .01 .05
237 Joe Niekro .01 .05
238 Scott Bankhead .01 .05
239 Doug DeCinces .01 .05
240 Tommy John .02 .10
241 Rich Gedman .01 .05
242 Ted Power .01 .05
243 Dave Meads .01 .05
244 Jim Sundberg .02 .10
245 Ken Oberkfell .01 .05
246 Jimmy Jones .01 .05
247 Ken Landreaux .01 .05
248 Jose Oquendo .01 .05
249 John Mitchell RC .02 .10
250 Don Baylor .02 .10
251 Scott Fletcher .01 .05
252 Al Newman .01 .05
253 Carney Lansford .02 .10
254 Johnny Ray .01 .05
255 Gary Pettis .01 .05
256 Ken Phelps .01 .05
257 Rick Leach .01 .05
258 Tim Stoddard .01 .05
259 Ed Romero .01 .05
260 Sid Bream .01 .05
261A Tom Niedenfuer ERR .02 .10
Misspelled Neidenfuer
on card front
261B Tom Niedenfuer COR .01 .05
262 Rick Dempsey .01 .05
263 Lonnie Smith .01 .05
264 Bob Forsch .01 .05
265 Barry Bonds .75 2.00
266 Willie Randolph .02 .10
267 Mike Ramsey .01 .05
268 Don Slaught .01 .05
269 Mickey Tettleton .01 .05
270 Jerry Reuss .01 .05
271 Marc Sullivan .01 .05
272 Jim Morrison .01 .05
273 Steve Balboni .01 .05
274 Dick Schofield .01 .05
275 John Tudor .02 .10
276 Gene Larkin RC .08 .25
277 Harold Reynolds .02 .10
278 Jerry Browne .01 .05
279 Willie Upshaw .01 .05
280 Ted Higuera .01 .05
281 Terry McGriff .01 .05
282 Terry Puhl .01 .05
283 Mark Wasinger .01 .05
284 Luis Salazar .01 .05
285 Ted Simmons .02 .10
286 John Shelby .01 .05
287 John Smiley RC .08 .25
288 Curt Ford .01 .05
289 Steve Crawford .01 .05
290 Dan Quisenberry .01 .05

291 Alan Wiggins .01 .05
292 Randy Bush .01 .05
293 John Candelaria .01 .05
294 Tony Phillips .01 .05
295 Mike Morgan .01 .05
296 Bill Wegman .01 .05
297A Terry Francona ERR .02 .10
Misspelled Franconia
on card front
297B Terry Francona COR .02 .10
298 Mickey Hatcher .01 .05
299 Andres Thomas .01 .05
300 Bob Stanley .01 .05
301 Al Pedrique .01 .05
302 Jim Lindeman .01 .05
303 Wally Backman .01 .05
304 Paul O'Neill .05 .15
305 Hubie Brooks .01 .05
306 Steve Buechele .01 .05
307 Bobby Thigpen .01 .05
308 George Hendrick .02 .10
309 John Moses .01 .05
310 Ron Guidry .02 .10
311 Bill Schroeder .01 .05
312 Jose Nunez .01 .05
313 Bud Black .01 .05
314 Joe Sambito .01 .05
315 Scott McGregor .01 .05
316 Rafael Santana .01 .05
317 Frank Williams .01 .05
318 Mike Fitzgerald .01 .05
319 Rick Mahler .01 .05
320 Jim Gott .01 .05
321 Mariano Duncan .01 .05
322 Jose Guzman .01 .05
323 Lee Guetterman .01 .05
324 Dan Gladden .01 .05
325 Gary Carter .02 .10
326 Tracy Jones .01 .05
327 Floyd Youmans .01 .05
328 Bill Dawley .01 .05
329 Paul Noce .01 .05
330 Angel Salazar .01 .05
331 Goose Gossage .02 .10
332 George Frazier .01 .05
333 Ruppert Jones .01 .05
334 Billy Joe Robidoux .01 .05
335 Mike Scott .02 .10
336 Randy Myers .02 .10
337 Bob Sebra .01 .05
338 Eric Show .01 .05
339 Mitch Williams .01 .05
340 Paul Molitor .02 .10
341 Gus Polidor .01 .05
342 Steve Trout .01 .05
343 Jerry Don Gleaton .01 .05
344 Bob Knepper .01 .05
345 Mitch Webster .01 .05
346 John Morris .01 .05
347 Andy Hawkins .01 .05
348 Dave Leiper .01 .05
349 Ernest Riles .01 .05
350 Dwight Gooden .02 .10
351 Dave Righetti .02 .10
352 Pat Dodson .01 .05
353 John Habyan .01 .05
354 Jim Deshaies .01 .05
355 Butch Wynegar .01 .05
356 Bryn Smith .01 .05
357 Matt Young .01 .05
358 Tom Pagnozzi RC .02 .10
359 Floyd Rayford .01 .05
360 Darryl Strawberry .02 .10
361 Sal Butera .01 .05
362 Domingo Ramos .01 .05
363 Chris Brown .01 .05
364 Jose Gonzalez .01 .05
365 Dave Smith .01 .05
366 Andy McGaffigan .01 .05
367 Stan Javier .01 .05
368 Henry Cotto .01 .05
369 Mike Birkbeck .01 .05
370 Len Dykstra .02 .10
371 Dave Collins .01 .05
372 Spike Owen .01 .05
373 Geno Petralli .01 .05
374 Ron Karkovice .01 .05
375 Shane Rawley .01 .05
376 DeWayne Buice .01 .05
377 Bill Pecota RC .02 .10
378 Leon Durham .01 .05
379 Ed Olwine .01 .05
380 Bruce Hurst .01 .05
381 Bob McClure .01 .05
382 Mark Thurmond .01 .05
383 Buddy Biancalana .01 .05
384 Tim Conroy .01 .05
385 Tony Gwynn .10 .30
386 Greg Gross .01 .05
387 Barry Lyons .01 .05
388 Mike Felder .01 .05
389 Pat Clements .01 .05
390 Ken Griffey .02 .10
391 Mark Davis .01 .05
392 Jose Rijo .02 .10
393 Mike Young .01 .05
394 Willie Fraser .01 .05
395 Dion James .01 .05
396 Steve Shields .01 .05
397 Randy St.Claire .01 .05
398 Danny Jackson .01 .05
399 Cecil Fielder .02 .10
400 Keith Hernandez .02 .10
401 Don Carman .01 .05
402 Chuck Crim .01 .05
403 Rob Woodward .01 .05
404 Junior Ortiz .01 .05
405 Glenn Wilson .01 .05
406 Ken Howell .01 .05
407 Jeff Kunkel .01 .05
408 Jeff Reed .01 .05
409 Chris James .01 .05
410 Zane Smith .01 .05
411 Ken Dixon .01 .05
412 Ricky Horton .01 .05
413 Frank DiPino .01 .05
414 Shane Mack .01 .05
415 Danny Cox .01 .05
416 Andy Van Slyke .05 .15
417 Danny Heep .01 .05
418 John Cangelosi .01 .05
419A John Christensen ERR .02 .10
Christiansen
on card front
419B John Christensen COR .01 .05
420 Joey Cora RC .08 .25
421 Mike LaValliere .01 .05
422 Kelly Gruber .01 .05
423 Bruce Benedict .01 .05
424 Len Matuszek .01 .05
425 Kent Tekulve .01 .05
426 Rafael Ramirez .01 .05
427 Mike Flanagan .01 .05
428 Mike Gallego .01 .05
429 Juan Castillo .01 .05
430 Neal Heaton .01 .05
431 Phil Garner .02 .10
432 Mike Dunne .01 .05
433 Wallace Johnson .01 .05
434 Jack O'Connor .01 .05
435 Steve Jeltz .01 .05
436 Donell Nixon .01 .05
437 Jack Lazorko .01 .05
438 Keith Comstock .01 .05
439 Jeff D. Robinson .01 .05
440 Graig Nettles .02 .10
441 Mel Hall .01 .05
442 Gerald Young .01 .05
443 Gary Redus .01 .05
444 Charlie Moore .01 .05
445 Bill Madlock .02 .10
446 Mark Clear .01 .05
447 Greg Booker .01 .05
448 Rick Schu .01 .05
449 Ron Kittle .01 .05
450 Dale Murphy .05 .15
451 Bob Dernier .01 .05
452 Dale Mohorcic .01 .05
453 Rafael Belliard .01 .05
454 Charlie Puleo .01 .05
455 Dwayne Murphy .01 .05
456 Jim Eisenreich .01 .05
457 David Palmer .01 .05
458 Dave Stewart .02 .10
459 Pascual Perez .01 .05
460 Glenn Davis .01 .05
461 Dan Petry .01 .05
462 Jim Winn .01 .05
463 Darrell Miller .01 .05
464 Mike Moore .01 .05
465 Mike LaCoss .01 .05
466 Steve Farr .01 .05
467 Jerry Mumphrey .01 .05
468 Kevin Gross .01 .05
469 Bruce Bochy .01 .05
470 Orel Hershiser .02 .10
471 Eric King .01 .05
472 Ellis Burks RC .15 .40
473 Darren Daulton .02 .10
474 Mookie Wilson .02 .10
475 Frank Viola .02 .10
476 Ron Robinson .01 .05
477 Bob Melvin .01 .05
478 Jeff Musselman .01 .05
479 Charlie Kerfeld .01 .05
480 Richard Dotson .01 .05
481 Kevin Mitchell .02 .10
482 Gary Roenicke .01 .05
483 Tim Flannery .01 .05
484 Rich Yett .01 .05
485 Pete Incaviglia .01 .05
486 Rick Cerone .01 .05
487 Tony Armas .02 .10
488 Jerry Reed .01 .05
489 Dave Lopes .02 .10
490 Frank Tanana .02 .10
491 Mike Loynd .01 .05
492 Bruce Ruffin .01 .05
493 Chris Speier .01 .05
494 Tom Hume .01 .05
495 Jesse Orosco .01 .05
496 Robbie Wine UER .01 .05
Misspelled Robby
on card front
497 Jeff Montgomery RC .08 .25
498 Jeff Dedmon .01 .05
499 Luis Aguayo .01 .05
500 Reggie Jackson A's .05 .15
501 Reggie Jackson O's .05 .15
502 Reggie Jackson Yanks .05 .15
503 Reggie Jackson Angels .05 .15
504 Reggie Jackson A's .05 .15
505 Billy Hatcher .01 .05
506 Ed Lynch .01 .05
507 Willie Hernandez .01 .05
508 Jose DeLeon .01 .05
509 Joel Youngblood .01 .05
510 Bob Welch .02 .10
511 Steve Ontiveros .01 .05
512 Randy Ready .01 .05
513 Juan Nieves .01 .05
514 Jeff Russell .01 .05
515 Von Hayes .01 .05
516 Mark Gubicza .01 .05
517 Ken Dayley .01 .05
518 Don Aase .01 .05
519 Rick Reuschel .02 .10
520 Mike Henneman RC .08 .25
521 Rick Aguilera .01 .05
522 Jay Howell .01 .05
523 Ed Correa .01 .05
524 Manny Trillo .01 .05
525 Kirk Gibson .07 .20
526 Wally Ritchie .01 .05
527 Al Nipper .01 .05
528 Atlee Hammaker .01 .05
529 Shawon Dunston .01 .05
530 Jim Clancy .01 .05
531 Tom Paciorek .01 .05
532 Joel Skinner .01 .05
533 Scott Garrelts .01 .05
534 Tom O'Malley .01 .05
535 John Franco .02 .10
536 Paul Kilgus .01 .05
537 Darrell Porter .01 .05
538 Walt Terrell .01 .05
539 Bill Long .01 .05
540 George Bell .02 .10
541 Jeff Sellers .01 .05
542 Joe Boever .01 .05
543 Steve Howe .01 .05
544 Scott Sanderson .01 .05
545 Jack Morris .02 .10
546 Todd Benzinger RC .08 .25
547 Steve Henderson .01 .05
548 Eddie Milner .01 .05
549 Jeff M. Robinson .01 .05
550 Cal Ripken .30 .75
551 Jody Davis .01 .05
552 Kirk McCaskill .01 .05
553 Craig Lefferts .01 .05
554 Darnell Coles .01 .05
555 Phil Niekro .02 .10
556 Mike Aldrete .01 .05
557 Pat Perry .01 .05
558 Juan Agosto .01 .05
559 Rob Murphy .01 .05
560 Dennis Rasmussen .01 .05
561 Manny Lee .01 .05
562 Jeff Blauser RC .08 .25
563 Bob Ojeda .01 .05
564 Dave Dravecky .01 .05
565 Gene Garber .01 .05
566 Ron Roenicke .01 .05
567 Tommy Hinzo .01 .05
568 Eric Nolte .01 .05
569 Ed Hearn .01 .05
570 Mark Davidson .01 .05
571 Jim Walewander .01 .05
572 Donnie Hill UER .01 .05
84 Stolen Base
total listed as 7
573 Jamie Moyer .02 .10
574 Ken Schrom .01 .05
575 Nolan Ryan .40 1.00
576 Jim Acker .01 .05
577 Jamie Quirk .01 .05
578 Jay Aldrich .01 .05
579 Claudell Washington .01 .05
580 Jeff Leonard .01 .05
581 Carmen Castillo .01 .05
582 Daryl Boston .01 .05
583 Jeff DeWillis .01 .05
584 John Marzano .01 .05
585 Bill Gullickson .01 .05
586 Andy Allanson .01 .05
587 Lee Tunnell UER .01 .05
1987 stat line
reads .4.84 ERA
588 Gene Nelson .01 .05
589 Dave LaPoint .01 .05
590 Harold Baines .02 .10
591 Bill Buckner .02 .10
592 Carlton Fisk .05 .15
593 Rick Manning .01 .05
594 Doug Jones RC .08 .25
595 Tom Candiotti .01 .05
596 Steve Lake .01 .05
597 Jose Lind RC .08 .25
598 Ross Jones .01 .05
599 Gary Matthews .02 .10
600 Fernando Valenzuela .02 .10
601 Dennis Martinez .02 .10
602 Les Lancaster .01 .05
603 Ozzie Guillen .02 .10
604 Tony Bernazard .01 .05
605 Chili Davis .02 .10
606 Roy Smalley .01 .05
607 Ivan Calderon .01 .05
608 Jay Tibbs .01 .05
609 Guy Hoffman .01 .05
610 Doyle Alexander .01 .05
611 Mike Bielecki .01 .05
612 Shawn Hillegas RC .01 .05
613 Keith Atherton .01 .05
614 Eric Plunk .01 .05
615 Sid Fernandez .01 .05
616 Dennis Lamp .01 .05
617 Dave Engle .01 .05
618 Harry Spilman .01 .05
619 Don Robinson .01 .05
620 John Farrell RC .02 .10
621 Nelson Liriano RC .01 .05
622 Floyd Bannister .01 .05
623 Randy Milligan RC .02 .10
624 Kevin Elster .01 .05
625 Jody Reed RC .08 .25
626 Shawn Abner .01 .05
627 Kirt Manwaring RC .08 .25
628 Pete Stanicek RC .01 .05
629 Rob Ducey RC .01 .05
630 Steve Kiefer .01 .05
631 Gary Thurman RC .01 .05
632 Darrel Akerfelds RC .01 .05
633 Dave Clark .01 .05
634 Roberto Kelly RC .08 .25
635 Keith Hughes RC .01 .05
636 John Davis RC .01 .05
637 Mike Devereaux RC .08 .25
638 Tom Glavine RC UER 1.25 3.00
Struck out 34 in 32 innings, not 31
639 Keith A. Miller RC .08 .25
640 Chris Gwynn UER RC .08 .25
Wrong batting and
throwing on back
641 Tim Crews RC .08 .25
642 Mackey Sasser RC .08 .25
643 Vicente Palacios RC .01 .05
644 Kevin Romine RC .01 .05
645 Gregg Jefferies RC .08 .25
646 Jeff Treadway RC .08 .25
647 Ron Gant RC .15 .40
648 M.McGwire/M.Nokes .30 .75
649 Eric Davis .02 .10
Tim Raines
650 D.Mattingly/J.Clark .10 .30
651 Fernandez/Trammell/Ripken .08 .25
652 Vince Coleman HL .01 .05
653 Kirby Puckett HL .05 .15
654 Benito Santiago HL .01 .05
655 Juan Nieves HL .01 .05
656 Steve Bedrosian HL .01 .05
657 Mike Schmidt HL .07 .20
658 Don Mattingly HL .10 .30
659 Mark McGwire HL .30 .75
660 Paul Molitor HL .01 .05

1988 Score Glossy

COMP.FACT.SET (660) 60.00 120.00
*STARS: 5X TO 12X BASIC CARDS
*ROOKIES: 5X TO 12X BASIC CARDS
DISTRIBUTED ONLY IN FACTORY SET FORM

1988 Score Box Cards

There are six different wax box bottom panels each featuring three players and a trivia (related to a particular stadium for a given year) question. The players and trivia question cards are individually numbered. The trivia are numbered below with the prefix T in order to avoid confusion. The trivia cards are very unpopular with collectors since they do not picture any players. When panels of four are cut into individuals, the cards are standard size. The card backs of the players feature the respective League logos most prominently.

COMPLETE SET (24) 4.00 10.00
1 Terry Kennedy .02 .10
2 Don Mattingly .60 1.50
3 Willie Randolph .07 .20
4 Wade Boggs .50 1.00
5 Cal Ripken 1.25 3.00
6 George Bell .02 .10
7 Rickey Henderson .50 1.25
8 Dave Winfield .30 .75
9 Bret Saberhagen .07 .20
10 Gary Carter .30 .75
11 Jack Clark .07 .20
12 Ryne Sandberg .60 1.50
13 Mike Schmidt .30 .75
14 Ozzie Smith .60 1.50
15 Eric Davis .07 .20
16 Andre Dawson .20 .50
17 Darryl Strawberry .07 .20
18 Mike Scott .02 .10
T1 Fenway Park '60 .75 2.00
Ted Williams Hits
To The End
T2 Comiskey Park '83 .07 .20
Grand Slam (Fred Lynn)
Breaks
T3 Anaheim Stadium '87 .75 2.00
Old Rookie Record
Falls (Mar
T4 Wrigley Field '38 .07 .20
Gabby (Hartnett) Gets
Pennant
T5 Comiskey Park '50 .07 .20
Red (Schoendienst)
Rips Winnin
T6 County Stadium '87 .20 .50
Rookie (John Farrell)
Stops H

1988 Score Rookie/Traded

This 110-card standard-size set issued exclusively in a boxes factory-set form features traded players (1-65) and rookies (66-110) for the 1988 season. The cards are distinguishable from the regular Score set by the orange borders and by the fact that the numbering on the back has a T suffix. Apparently Score's first attempt at a Rookie/Traded set was produced very conservatively, resulting in a set which is now recognized as being much tougher to find than the other Rookie/Traded sets from the other major companies of that year. Extended Rookie Cards in this set include Roberto Alomar, Brady Anderson, Craig Biggio, Jay Buhner and Mark Grace.

COMP.FACT.SET (110) 15.00 40.00
1T Jack Clark .30 .75
2T Danny Jackson .08 .25
3T Brett Butler .30 .75
4T Kurt Stillwell .08 .25
5T Tom Brunansky .08 .25
6T Dennis Lamp .08 .25
7T Jose DeLeon .08 .25
8T Tom Herr .08 .25
9T Keith Moreland .08 .25
10T Kirk Gibson .75 2.00
11T Bud Black .08 .25
12T Rafael Ramirez .08 .25
13T Luis Salazar .08 .25
14T Goose Gossage .30 .75
15T Bob Welch .30 .75
16T Vance Law .08 .25
17T Ray Knight .30 .75
18T Dan Quisenberry .08 .25
19T Don Slaught .08 .25
20T Lee Smith .30 .75
21T Rick Cerone .08 .25
22T Pat Tabler .08 .25
23T Larry McWilliams .08 .25
24T Ricky Horton .08 .25
25T Graig Nettles .30 .75
26T Dan Petry .08 .25
27T Jose Rijo .30 .75
28T Chili Davis .30 .75
29T Dickie Thon .08 .25
30T Mackey Sasser .08 .25
31T Mickey Tettleton .08 .25
32T Rick Dempsey .08 .25
33T Ron Hassey .08 .25
34T Phil Bradley .08 .25
35T Jay Howell .08 .25
36T Bill Buckner .30 .75
37T Alfredo Griffin .08 .25
38T Gary Pettis .08 .25
39T Calvin Schiraldi .08 .25
40T John Candelaria .08 .25
41T Joe Orsulak .08 .25
42T Willie Upshaw .08 .25
43T Herm Winningham .08 .25
44T Ron Kittle .08 .25
45T Bob Dernier .08 .25
46T Steve Balboni .08 .25
47T Steve Shields .08 .25
48T Henry Cotto .08 .25
49T Dave Henderson .08 .25
50T Dave Parker .30 .75
51T Mike Young .08 .25
52T Mark Salas .08 .25
53T Mike Davis .08 .25
54T Rafael Santana .08 .25
55T Don Baylor .30 .75
56T Dan Pasqua .08 .25
57T Ernest Riles .08 .25
58T Glenn Hubbard .08 .25
59T Mike Smithson .08 .25
60T Richard Dotson .08 .25
61T Jerry Reuss .08 .25
62T Mike Jackson .30 .75
63T Floyd Bannister .08 .25
64T Jesse Orosco .08 .25
65T Larry Parrish .08 .25
66T Jeff Bittiger .08 .25
67T Ray Hayward .08 .25
68T Ricky Jordan XRC .30 .75
69T Tommy Gregg .08 .25
70T Brady Anderson XRC .50 1.25
71T Jeff Montgomery .30 .75
72T Darryl Hamilton XRC .30 .75
73T Cecil Espy XRC .08 .25
74T Greg Briley XRC .08 .25
75T Joey Meyer .08 .25
76T Mike Macfarlane XRC .30 .75
77T Oswald Peraza XRC .08 .25
78T Jack Armstrong XRC .08 .25
79T Don Heinkel .08 .25
80T Mark Grace XRC 3.00 8.00
81T Steve Curry .08 .25
82T Damon Berryhill XRC* .30 .75
83T Steve Ellsworth .08 .25
84T Pete Smith XRC* .08 .25
85T Jack McDowell XRC .50 1.25
86T Rob Dibble XRC .50 1.25
87T Bryan Harvey XRC .30 .75
88T John Dopson .08 .25
89T Dave Gallagher .08 .25
90T Todd Stottlemyre XRC .30 .75
91T Mike Schooler .08 .25
92T Don Gordon .08 .25
93T Sil Campusano .08 .25
94T Jeff Pico .08 .25
95T Jay Buhner XRC .75 2.00
96T Nelson Santovenia .08 .25
97T Al Leiter XRC 1.25 3.00
98T Luis Alicea XRC .30 .75
99T Pat Borders XRC .30 .75
100T Chris Sabo XRC .50 1.25
101T Tim Belcher .08 .25
102T Walt Weiss XRC* .50 1.25
103T Craig Biggio XRC 5.00 12.00
104T Don August .08 .25
105T Roberto Alomar XRC 4.00 10.00
106T Todd Burns .08 .25
107T John Costello XRC .08 .25
108T Melido Perez XRC* .30 .75
109T Darrin Jackson XRC* .08 .25
110T Orestes Destrade XRC .08 .25

1988 Score Rookie/Traded Glossy

COMP.FACT.SET (110) 75.00 150.00
*STARS: 1X TO 2.5X BASIC CARDS
*ROOKIES: 1X TO 2.5X BASIC CARDS
DISTRIBUTED ONLY IN FACTORY SET FORM

1988 Score Young Superstars I

This attractive high-gloss 40-card standard-size set of "Young Superstars" was distributed in a small blue box which had the checklist of the set on a side panel of the box. These were also distributed as an insert, one per rack pack. These attractive cards are in full color on the front and also have a full-color small portrait on the card back. The cards in this series are distinguishable from the cards in Series II by the fact that this series has a blue and green border on the card front instead of the (Series II) blue and pink border.

COMPLETE SET (40) 3.00 8.00
1 Mark McGwire 1.00 2.50
2 Benito Santiago .02 .10
3 Sam Horn .01 .05
4 Chris Bosio .01 .05
5 Matt Nokes .01 .05
6 Ken Williams .05 .15
7 Dion James .01 .05
8 B.J. Surhoff .05 .15
9 Joe Magrane .01 .05
10 Kevin Seitzer .01 .05
11 Stanley Jefferson .01 .05
12 Devon White .02 .10
13 Nelson Liriano .01 .05
14 Chris James .01 .05
15 Mike Henneman .02 .10
16 Terry Steinbach .01 .05
17 John Kruk .02 .10
18 Matt Williams .40 1.00
19 Kelly Downs .01 .05
20 Bill Ripken .01 .05
21 Ozzie Guillen .05 .15
22 Luis Polonia .01 .05
23 Dave Magadan .01 .05
24 Mike Greenwell .01 .05
25 Will Clark .40 1.00
26 Mike Dunne .01 .05
27 Wally Joyner .02 .10
28 Robby Thompson .01 .05
29 Ken Caminiti .30 .75
30 Jose Canseco .40 1.00
31 Todd Benzinger .01 .05
32 Pete Incaviglia .01 .05
33 John Farrell .01 .05
34 Casey Candaele .01 .05
35 Mike Aldrete .01 .05
36 Ruben Sierra .05 .15
37 Ellis Burks .07 .20
38 Tracy Jones .01 .05
39 Kal Daniels .01 .05
40 Cory Snyder .01 .05

1988 Score Young Superstars

This attractive high-gloss 40-card standard-size se of "Young Superstars" was distributed in a small purple box which had the checklist of the set on a side panel of the box. The cards were not distribute as an insert with rak paks as the first series was, bu were only available as a complete set from hobby dealers or through a mail-in offer direct from the company. These attractive cards are in full color on the front and also have a full-color small portrait or the card back. The cards in this series are distinguishable from the cards in Series I by the fac that this series has a blue and pink border on the card front instead of the (Series I) blue and green border.

COMP.FACT SET (40) 2.00 5.00
1 Don Mattingly .40 1.00
2 Glenn Braggs .01 .05
3 Dwight Gooden .02 .10
4 Jose Lind .01 .05
5 Danny Tartabull .01 .05
6 Tony Fernandez .02 .10
7 Julio Franco .02 .10
8 Andres Galarraga .07 .20
9 Bobby Bonilla .01 .05
10 Eric Davis .02 .10
11 Gerald Young .01 .05
12 Barry Bonds .30 .75
13 Jerry Browne .01 .05
14 Jeff Blauser .02 .10
15 Mickey Brantley .01 .05
16 Floyd Youmans .01 .05
17 Bret Saberhagen .02 .10
18 Shawon Dunston .01 .05
19 Len Dykstra .02 .10
20 Darryl Strawberry .02 .10
21 Rick Aguilera .02 .10
22 Ivan Calderon .01 .05
23 Roger Clemens .40 1.00
24 Vince Coleman .01 .05
25 Gary Thurman .01 .05
26 Jeff Treadway .01 .05
27 Oddibe McDowell .01 .05
28 Fred McGriff .07 .20
29 Mark McLemore .01 .05
30 Jeff Musselman .01 .05
31 Mitch Williams .01 .05
32 Dan Plesac .01 .05
33 Juan Nieves .01 .05
34 Barry Larkin .07 .20
35 Greg Mathews .01 .05
36 Shane Mack .01 .05
37 Scott Bankhead .01 .05
38 Eric Bell .01 .05
39 Greg Swindell .01 .05
40 Kevin Elster .01 .05

1989 Score

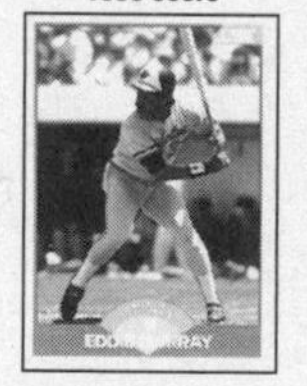

This 660-card standard-size set was distributed by Major League Marketing. Cards were issued primarily in fin-wrapped plastic packs and factory sets. Cards feature six distinctive inner border (inside a white outer border) colors on the front. Subsets include Highlights (652-660) and Rookie Prospects (621-651). Rookie Cards in this set include Brady Anderson, Craig Biggio, Randy Johnson, Gary Sheffield, and John Smoltz.

COMPLETE SET (660) 6.00 15.00
COMP.FACT.SET (660) 6.00 15.00
1 Jose Canseco .08 .25
2 Andre Dawson .02 .10
3 Mark McGwire UER .40 1.00
4 Benito Santiago .02 .10
5 Rick Reuschel .02 .10
6 Fred McGriff .05 .15
7 Kal Daniels .01 .05
8 Gary Gaetti .02 .10
9 Ellis Burks .02 .10
10 Darryl Strawberry .02 .10
11 Julio Franco .02 .10
12 Lloyd Moseby .01 .05
13 Jeff Pico .01 .05
14 Johnny Ray .01 .05
15 Cal Ripken .30 .75
16 Dick Schofield .01 .05
17 Mel Hall .01 .05
18 Bill Ripken .01 .05
19 Brook Jacoby .01 .05
20 Kirby Puckett .08 .25
21 Bill Doran .01 .05
22 Pete O'Brien .01 .05

Matt Nokes .01 .05
Brian Fisher .01 .05
Jack Clark .02 .10
Gary Pettis .01 .05
Dave Valle .01 .05
Willie Wilson .02 .10
Curt Young .01 .05
Dale Murphy .05 .15
Barry Larkin .05 .15
Dave Stewart .02 .10
Mike LaValliere .01 .05
Glenn Hubbard .01 .05
Ryne Sandberg .15 .40
Tony Pena .01 .05
Greg Walker .01 .05
Von Hayes .01 .05
Kevin Mitchell .02 .10
Tim Raines .02 .10
Keith Hernandez .02 .10
Keith Moreland .01 .05
Ruben Sierra .02 .10
Chet Lemon .02 .10
Willie Randolph .02 .10
Andy Allanson .01 .05
Candy Maldonado .01 .05
Sid Bream .01 .05
Denny Walling .01 .05
Dave Winfield .02 .10
1 Alvin Davis .01 .05
2 Cory Snyder .01 .05
3 Hubie Brooks .01 .05
4 Chili Davis .02 .10
5 Kevin Seitzer .01 .05
6 Jose Uribe .01 .05
7 Tony Fernandez .01 .05
8 Tim Teufel .01 .05
9 Oddibe McDowell .01 .05
0 Les Lancaster .01 .05
1 Billy Hatcher .01 .05
2 Dan Gladden .01 .05
3 Marty Barrett .01 .05
4 Nick Esasky .01 .05
5 Wally Joyner .02 .10
6 Mike Greenwell .01 .05
7 Ken Williams .01 .05
8 Bob Horner .02 .10
9 Steve Sax .01 .05
70 Rickey Henderson .08 .25
71 Mitch Webster .01 .05
72 Rob Deer .01 .05
73 Jim Presley .01 .05
74 Albert Hall .01 .05
75 George Brett COR .25 .60
75A George Brett ERR .40 1.00
76 Brian Downing .02 .10
77 Dave Martinez .01 .05
78 Scott Fletcher .01 .05
79 Phil Bradley .01 .05
80 Ozzie Smith .15 .40
81 Larry Sheets .01 .05
82 Mike Aldrete .01 .05
83 Darnell Coles .01 .05
84 Len Dykstra .02 .10
85 Jim Rice .02 .10
86 Jeff Treadway .01 .05
87 Jose Lind .01 .05
88 Willie McGee .02 .10
89 Mickey Brantley .01 .05
90 Tony Gwynn .10 .30
91 R.J. Reynolds .01 .05
92 Milt Thompson .01 .05
93 Kevin McReynolds .01 .05
94 Eddie Murray UER .08 .25
'86 batting .205,
should be .305
95 Lance Parrish .02 .10
96 Ron Kittle .01 .05
97 Gerald Young .01 .05
98 Ernie Whitt .01 .05
99 Jeff Reed .01 .05
100 Don Mattingly .25 .60
101 Gerald Perry .01 .05
102 Vance Law .01 .05
103 John Shelby .01 .05
104 Chris Sabo RC .15 .40
105 Danny Tartabull .01 .05
106 Glenn Wilson .01 .05
107 Mark Davidson .01 .05
108 Dave Parker .02 .10
109 Eric Davis .02 .10
110 Alan Trammell .02 .10
111 Ozzie Virgil .01 .05
112 Frank Tanana .02 .10
113 Rafael Ramirez .01 .05
114 Dennis Martinez .02 .10
115 Jose DeLeon .01 .05
116 Bob Ojeda .01 .05
117 Doug Drabek .01 .05
118 Andy Hawkins .01 .05
119 Greg Maddux .20 .50
120 Cecil Fielder UER .02 .10
Reversed Photo on back
121 Mike Scioscia .02 .10
122 Dan Petry .01 .05
123 Terry Kennedy .01 .05
124 Kelly Downs .01 .05
125 Greg Gross UER .01 .05
Gregg on back
126 Fred Lynn .02 .10
127 Barry Bonds .60 1.50
128 Harold Baines .02 .10
129 Doyle Alexander .01 .05
130 Kevin Elster .01 .05

131 Mike Heath .01 .05
132 Teddy Higuera .01 .05
133 Charlie Leibrandt .01 .05
134 Tim Laudner .01 .05
135A Ray Knight ERR .02 .10
Reverse negative
135B Ray Knight COR .02 .10
136 Howard Johnson .02 .10
137 Terry Pendleton .02 .10
138 Andy McGaffigan .01 .05
139 Ken Oberkfell .01 .05
140 Butch Wynegar .01 .05
141 Rob Murphy .01 .05
142 Rich Renteria .01 .05
143 Jose Guzman .01 .05
144 Andres Galarraga .02 .10
145 Ricky Horton .01 .05
146 Frank DiPino .01 .05
147 Glenn Braggs .01 .05
148 John Kruk .02 .10
149 Mike Schmidt .20 .50
150 Lee Smith .02 .10
151 Robin Yount .15 .40
152 Mark Eichhorn .01 .05
153 DeWayne Buice .01 .05
154 B.J. Surhoff .02 .10
155 Vince Coleman .01 .05
156 Tony Phillips .01 .05
157 Willie Fraser .01 .05
158 Lance McCullers .01 .05
159 Greg Gagne .01 .05
160 Jesse Barfield .02 .10
161 Mark Langston .01 .05
162 Kurt Stillwell .01 .05
163 Dion James .01 .05
164 Glenn Davis .01 .05
165 Walt Weiss .01 .05
166 Dave Concepcion .02 .10
167 Alfredo Griffin .01 .05
168 Don Heinkel .01 .05
169 Luis Rivera .01 .05
170 Shane Rawley .01 .05
171 Darrell Evans .02 .10
172 Robby Thompson .01 .05
173 Jody Davis .01 .05
174 Andy Van Slyke .05 .15
175 Wade Boggs UER .05 .15
Bio says .364,
should be .356
176 Garry Templeton .02 .10
'85 stats
off-centered
177 Gary Redus .01 .05
178 Craig Lefferts .01 .05
179 Carney Lansford .02 .10
180 Ron Darling .02 .10
181 Kirk McCaskill .01 .05
182 Tony Armas .02 .10
183 Steve Farr .01 .05
184 Tom Brunansky .01 .05
185 Bryan Harvey RC UER .08 .25
'87 games 47,
should be 3
186 Mike Marshall .01 .05
187 Bo Diaz .01 .05
188 Willie Upshaw .01 .05
189 Mike Pagliarulo .01 .05
190 Mike Krukow .01 .05
191 Tommy Herr .01 .05
192 Jim Pankovits .01 .05
193 Dwight Evans .05 .15
194 Kelly Gruber .01 .05
195 Bobby Bonilla .02 .10
196 Wallace Johnson .01 .05
197 Dave Stieb .02 .10
198 Pat Borders RC .08 .25
199 Rafael Palmeiro .08 .25
200 Dwight Gooden .02 .10
201 Pete Incaviglia .01 .05
202 Chris James .01 .05
203 Marvell Wynne .01 .05
204 Pat Sheridan .01 .05
205 Don Baylor .02 .10
206 Paul O'Neill .05 .15
207 Pete Smith .01 .05
208 Mark McLemore .01 .05
209 Henry Cotto .01 .05
210 Kirk Gibson .02 .10
211 Claudell Washington .01 .05
212 Randy Bush .01 .05
213 Joe Carter .02 .10
214 Bill Buckner .02 .10
215 Bert Blyleven UER .02 .10
216 Brett Butler .02 .10
217 Lee Mazzilli .02 .10
218 Spike Owen .01 .05
219 Bill Swift .01 .05
220 Tim Wallach .01 .05
221 David Cone .02 .10
222 Don Carman .01 .05
223 Rich Gossage .02 .10
224 Bob Walk .01 .05
225 Dave Righetti .02 .10
226 Kevin Bass .01 .05
227 Kevin Gross .01 .05
228 Tim Burke .01 .05
229 Rick Mahler .01 .05
230 Lou Whitaker UER .02 .10
252 games in '85,
should be 152
231 Luis Alicea RC .08 .25
232 Roberto Alomar .08 .25
233 Bob Boone .02 .10

234 Dickie Thon .01 .05
235 Shawon Dunston .01 .05
236 Pete Stanicek .01 .05
237 Craig Biggio RC 1.50 4.00
238 Dennis Boyd .01 .05
239 Tom Candiotti .01 .05
240 Gary Carter .02 .10
241 Mike Stanley .01 .05
242 Ken Phelps .01 .05
243 Chris Bosio .01 .05
244 Les Straker .01 .05
245 Dave Smith .01 .05
246 John Candelaria .01 .05
247 Joe Orsulak .01 .05
248 Storm Davis .01 .05
249 Floyd Bannister UER .01 .05
ML Batting Record
250 Jack Morris .02 .10
251 Bret Saberhagen .02 .10
252 Tom Niedenfuer .01 .05
253 Neal Heaton .01 .05
254 Eric Show .01 .05
255 Juan Samuel .01 .05
256 Dale Sveum .01 .05
257 Jim Gott .01 .05
258 Scott Garrelts .01 .05
259 Larry McWilliams .01 .05
260 Steve Bedrosian .01 .05
261 Jack Howell .01 .05
262 Jay Tibbs .01 .05
263 Jamie Moyer .02 .10
264 Doug Sisk .01 .05
265 Todd Worrell .01 .05
266 John Farrell .01 .05
267 Dave Collins .01 .05
268 Sid Fernandez .01 .05
269 Tom Brookens .01 .05
270 Shane Mack .01 .05
271 Paul Kilgus .01 .05
272 Chuck Crim .01 .05
273 Bob Knepper .01 .05
274 Mike Moore .01 .05
275 Guillermo Hernandez .01 .05
276 Dennis Eckersley .05 .15
277 Graig Nettles .02 .10
278 Rich Dotson .01 .05
279 Larry Herndon .01 .05
280 Gene Larkin .01 .05
281 Roger McDowell .01 .05
282 Greg Swindell .01 .05
283 Juan Agosto .01 .05
284 Jeff M. Robinson .01 .05
285 Mike Dunne .01 .05
286 Greg Mathews .01 .05
287 Kent Tekulve .01 .05
288 Jerry Mumphrey .01 .05
289 Jack McDowell .02 .10
290 Frank Viola .02 .10
291 Mark Gubicza .01 .05
292 Dave Schmidt .01 .05
293 Mike Henneman .01 .05
294 Jimmy Jones .01 .05
295 Charlie Hough .02 .10
296 Rafael Santana .01 .05
297 Chris Speier .01 .05
298 Mike Witt .01 .05
299 Pascual Perez .01 .05
300 Nolan Ryan .40 1.00
301 Mitch Williams .01 .05
302 Mookie Wilson .02 .10
303 Mackey Sasser .01 .05
304 John Cerutti .01 .05
305 Jeff Reardon .02 .10
306 Randy Myers UER .02 .10
6 hits in '87,
should be 61
307 Greg Brock .01 .05
308 Bob Welch .02 .10
309 Jeff D. Robinson .01 .05
310 Harold Reynolds .02 .10
311 Jim Walewander .01 .05
312 Dave Magadan .01 .05
313 Jim Gantner .01 .05
314 Walt Terrell .01 .05
315 Wally Backman .01 .05
316 Luis Salazar .01 .05
317 Rick Rhoden .01 .05
318 Tom Henke .01 .05
319 Mike Macfarlane RC .08 .25
320 Dan Plesac .01 .05
321 Calvin Schiraldi .01 .05
322 Stan Javier .01 .05
323 Devon White .02 .10
324 Scott Bradley .01 .05
325 Bruce Hurst .01 .05
326 Manny Lee .01 .05
327 Rick Aguilera .01 .05
328 Bruce Ruffin .01 .05
329 Ed Whitson .01 .05
330 Bo Jackson .08 .25
331 Ivan Calderon .01 .05
332 Mickey Hatcher .01 .05
333 Barry Jones .01 .05
334 Ron Hassey .01 .05
335 Bill Wegman .01 .05
336 Damon Berryhill .01 .05
337 Steve Ontiveros .01 .05
338 Dan Pasqua .01 .05
339 Bill Pecota .01 .05
340 Greg Cadaret .01 .05
341 Scott Bankhead .01 .05
342 Ron Guidry .02 .10
343 Danny Heep .01 .05

344 Bob Brower .01 .05
345 Rich Gedman .01 .05
346 Nelson Santovenia .01 .05
347 George Bell .02 .10
348 Ted Power .01 .05
349 Mark Grant .01 .05
350 Roger Clemens COR .40 1.00
350A Roger Clemens ERR .75 2.00
351 Bill Long .01 .05
352 Jay Bell .02 .10
353 Steve Balboni .01 .05
354 Bob Kipper .01 .05
355 Steve Jeltz .01 .05
356 Jesse Orosco .01 .05
357 Bob Dernier .01 .05
358 Mickey Tettleton .01 .05
359 Duane Ward .01 .05
360 Darrin Jackson .02 .10
361 Rey Quinones .01 .05
362 Mark Grace .08 .25
363 Steve Lake .01 .05
364 Pat Perry .01 .05
365 Terry Steinbach .02 .10
366 Alan Ashby .01 .05
367 Jeff Montgomery .01 .05
368 Steve Buechele .01 .05
369 Chris Brown .01 .05
370 Orel Hershiser .02 .10
371 Todd Benzinger .01 .05
372 Ron Gant .02 .10
373 Paul Assenmacher .01 .05
374 Joey Meyer .01 .05
375 Neil Allen .01 .05
376 Mike Davis .01 .05
377 Jeff Parrett .01 .05
378 Jay Howell .01 .05
379 Rafael Belliard .01 .05
380 Luis Polonia UER .01 .05
2 triples in '87,
should be 10
381 Keith Atherton .01 .05
382 Kent Hrbek .02 .10
383 Bob Stanley .01 .05
384 Dave LaPoint .01 .05
385 Rance Mulliniks .01 .05
386 Melido Perez .01 .05
387 Doug Jones .01 .05
388 Steve Lyons .01 .05
389 Alejandro Pena .01 .05
390 Frank White .02 .10
391 Pat Tabler .01 .05
392 Eric Plunk .01 .05
393 Mike Maddux .01 .05
394 Allan Anderson .01 .05
395 Bob Brenly .01 .05
396 Rick Cerone .01 .05
397 Scott Terry .01 .05
398 Mike Jackson .01 .05
399 Bobby Thigpen UER .01 .05
Bio says 37 saves in
'88, should be 34
400 Don Sutton .02 .10
401 Cecil Espy .01 .05
402 Junior Ortiz .01 .05
403 Mike Smithson .01 .05
404 Bud Black .01 .05
405 Tom Foley .01 .05
406 Andres Thomas .01 .05
407 Rick Sutcliffe .02 .10
408 Brian Harper .01 .05
409 John Smiley .01 .05
410 Juan Nieves .01 .05
411 Shawn Abner .01 .05
412 Wes Gardner .01 .05
413 Darren Daulton .02 .10
414 Juan Berenguer .01 .05
415 Charles Hudson .01 .05
416 Rick Honeycutt .01 .05
417 Greg Booker .01 .05
418 Tim Belcher .01 .05
419 Don August .01 .05
420 Dale Mohorcic .01 .05
421 Steve Lombardozzi .01 .05
422 Atlee Hammaker .01 .05
423 Jerry Don Gleaton .01 .05
424 Scott Bailes .01 .05
425 Bruce Sutter .02 .10
426 Randy Ready .01 .05
427 Jerry Reed .01 .05
428 Bryn Smith .01 .05
429 Tim Leary .01 .05
430 Mark Clear .01 .05
431 Terry Leach .01 .05
432 John Moses .01 .05
433 Ozzie Guillen .02 .10
434 Gene Nelson .01 .05
435 Gary Ward .01 .05
436 Luis Aguayo .01 .05
437 Fernando Valenzuela .02 .10
438 Jeff Russell UER .01 .05
Saves total does
not add up correctly
439 Cecilio Guante .01 .05
440 Don Robinson .01 .05
441 Rick Anderson .01 .05
442 Tom Glavine .08 .25
443 Daryl Boston .01 .05
444 Joe Price .01 .05
445 Stu Cliburn .01 .05
446 Manny Trillo .01 .05
447 Joel Skinner .01 .05
448 Charlie Puleo .01 .05
449 Carlton Fisk .05 .15

450 Will Clark .05 .15
451 Otis Nixon .01 .05
452 Rick Schu .01 .05
453 Todd Stottlemyre UER .01 .05
ML Batting Record
454 Tim Birtsas .01 .05
455 Dave Gallagher .01 .05
456 Barry Lyons .01 .05
457 Fred Manrique .01 .05
458 Ernest Riles .01 .05
459 Doug Jennings RC .01 .05
460 Joe Magrane .01 .05
461 Jamie Quirk .01 .05
462 Jack Armstrong RC .08 .25
463 Bobby Witt .01 .05
464 Keith A. Miller .01 .05
465 Todd Burns .01 .05
466 John Dopson .01 .05
467 Rich Yett .01 .05
468 Craig Reynolds .01 .05
469 Dave Bergman .01 .05
470 Rex Hudler .01 .05
471 Eric King .01 .05
472 Joaquin Andujar .02 .10
473 Sil Campusano .01 .05
474 Terry Mulholland .01 .05
475 Mike Flanagan .01 .05
476 Greg A. Harris .01 .05
477 Tommy John .02 .10
478 Dave Anderson .01 .05
479 Fred Toliver .01 .05
480 Jimmy Key .02 .10
481 Donell Nixon .01 .05
482 Mark Portugal .01 .05
483 Tom Pagnozzi .01 .05
484 Jeff Kunkel .01 .05
485 Frank Williams .01 .05
486 Jody Reed .01 .05
487 Roberto Kelly .01 .05
488 Shawn Hillegas UER .01 .05
165 innings in '87,
should be 165.2
489 Jerry Reuss .01 .05
490 Mark Davis .01 .05
491 Jeff Sellers .01 .05
492 Zane Smith .01 .05
493 Al Newman .01 .05
494 Mike Young .01 .05
495 Larry Parrish .01 .05
496 Herm Winningham .01 .05
497 Carmen Castillo .01 .05
498 Joe Hesketh .01 .05
499 Darrell Miller .01 .05
500 Mike LaCoss .01 .05
501 Charlie Lea .01 .05
502 Bruce Benedict .01 .05
503 Chuck Finley .02 .10
504 Brad Wellman .01 .05
505 Tim Crews .01 .05
506 Ken Gerhart .01 .05
507A Brian Holton ERR .01 .05
Born 1/25/65 Denver,
should be 11/29/59
in McKeesport
507B Brian Holton COR .75 2.00
508 Dennis Lamp .01 .05
509 Bobby Meacham UER .01 .05
'84 games 099
510 Tracy Jones .01 .05
511 Mike R. Fitzgerald .01 .05
512 Jeff Bittiger .01 .05
513 Tim Flannery .01 .05
514 Ray Hayward .01 .05
515 Dave Leiper .01 .05
516 Rod Scurry .01 .05
517 Carmelo Martinez .01 .05
518 Curtis Wilkerson .01 .05
519 Stan Jefferson .01 .05
520 Dan Quisenberry .01 .05
521 Lloyd McClendon .01 .05
522 Steve Trout .01 .05
523 Larry Andersen .01 .05
524 Don Aase .01 .05
525 Bob Forsch .01 .05
526 Geno Petralli .01 .05
527 Angel Salazar .01 .05
528 Mike Schooler .01 .05
529 Jose Oquendo .01 .05
530 Jay Buhner UER .02 .10
Wearing 43 on front,
listed as 34 on back
531 Tom Bolton .01 .05
532 Al Nipper .01 .05
533 Dave Henderson .01 .05
534 John Costello RC .01 .05
535 Donnie Moore .01 .05
536 Mike Laga .01 .05
537 Mike Gallego .01 .05
538 Jim Clancy .01 .05
539 Joel Youngblood .01 .05
540 Rick Leach .01 .05
541 Kevin Romine .01 .05
542 Mark Salas .01 .05
543 Greg Minton .01 .05
544 Dave Palmer .01 .05
545 Dwayne Murphy UER .01 .05
Game inning
546 Jim Deshaies .01 .05
547 Don Gordon .01 .05
548 Ricky Jordan RC .08 .25
549 Mike Boddicker .01 .05
550 Mike Scott .02 .10
551 Jeff Ballard .01 .05

552A Jose Rijo ERR .02 .10
Uniform listed as
24 on back
552B Jose Rijo COR .02 .10
Uniform listed as
27 on back
553 Danny Darwin .01 .05
554 Tom Browning .01 .05
555 Danny Jackson .01 .05
556 Rick Dempsey .01 .05
557 Jeffrey Leonard .01 .05
558 Jeff Musselman .01 .05
559 Ron Robinson .01 .05
560 John Tudor .02 .10
561 Don Slaught UER .01 .05
237 games in 1987
562 Dennis Rasmussen .01 .05
563 Brady Anderson RC .15 .40
564 Pedro Guerrero .02 .10
565 Paul Molitor .02 .10
566 Terry Clark .01 .05
567 Terry Puhl .01 .05
568 Mike Campbell .01 .05
569 Paul Mirabella .01 .05
570 Jeff Hamilton .01 .05
571 Oswald Peraza RC .01 .05
572 Bob McClure .01 .05
573 Jose Bautista RC .02 .10
574 Alex Trevino .01 .05
575 John Franco .02 .10
576 Mark Parent RC .01 .05
577 Nelson Liriano .01 .05
578 Steve Shields .01 .05
579 Odell Jones .01 .05
580 Al Leiter .08 .25
581 Dave Stapleton .01 .05
582 Orel Hershiser .08 .25
Jose Canseco
Kirk Gibson
Dave Stewart WS
583 Donnie Hill .01 .05
584 Chuck Jackson .01 .05
585 Rene Gonzales .01 .05
586 Tracy Woodson .01 .05
587 Jim Adduci .01 .05
588 Mario Soto .02 .10
589 Jeff Blauser .01 .05
590 Jim Traber .01 .05
591 Jon Perlman .01 .05
592 Mark Williamson .01 .05
593 Dave Meads .01 .05
594 Jim Eisenreich .01 .05
595A Paul Gibson P1 .40 1.00
595B Paul Gibson P2 .01 .05
Airbrushed leg on
player in background
596 Mike Birkbeck .01 .05
597 Terry Francona .02 .10
598 Paul Zuvella .01 .05
599 Franklin Stubbs .01 .05
600 Gregg Jefferies .01 .05
601 John Cangelosi .01 .05
602 Mike Sharperson .01 .05
603 Mike Diaz .01 .05
604 Gary Varsho .01 .05
605 Terry Blocker .01 .05
606 Charlie O'Brien .01 .05
607 Jim Eppard .01 .05
608 John Davis .01 .05
609 Ken Griffey Sr. .02 .10
610 Buddy Bell .02 .10
611 Ted Simmons UER .02 .10
'78 stats Cardinal
612 Matt Williams .08 .25
613 Danny Cox .01 .05
614 Al Pedrique .01 .05
615 Ron Oester .01 .05
616 John Smoltz RC .60 1.50
617 Bob Melvin .01 .05
618 Rob Dibble RC .15 .40
619 Kirt Manwaring .01 .05
620 Felix Fermin .01 .05
621 Doug Dascenzo .01 .05
622 Bill Brennan .01 .05
623 Carlos Quintana RC .02 .10
624 Mike Harkey RC UER .02 .10
13 and 31 walks in '88,
should be 35 and 33
625 Gary Sheffield RC .60 1.50
626 Tom Prince .01 .05
627 Steve Searcy .01 .05
628 Charlie Hayes RC .08 .25
Listed as outfielder
629 Felix Jose RC UER .02 .10
Modesto misspelled
as Modesta
630 Sandy Alomar Jr. RC .15 .40
Inconsistent design,
portrait on front
631 Derek Lilliquist RC .02 .10
632 Geronimo Berroa .01 .05
633 Luis Medina .01 .05
634 Tom Gordon RC UER .20 .50
635 Ramon Martinez RC .08 .25
636 Craig Worthington .01 .05
637 Edgar Martinez .08 .25
638 Chad Kreuter RC .08 .25
639 Ron Jones .02 .10
640 Van Snider RC .02 .10
641 Lance Blankenship RC .02 .10
642 Dwight Smith RC UER .08 .25
10 HR's in '87, should be 18
643 Cameron Drew .01 .05

644 Jerald Clark RC .02 .10
645 Randy Johnson RC 1.00 2.50
646 Norm Charlton RC .08 .25
647 Todd Frohwirth UER .01 .05
Southpaw on back
648 Luis De Los Santos .01 .05
649 Tim Jones .01 .05
650 Dave West RC UER .02 .10
ML hits 3
should be 6
651 Bob Milacki .01 .05
652 Wrigley Field HL .02 .10
653 Orel Hershiser HL .01 .05
654A Wade Boggs HL ERR .05 .15
'seaason' on back
654B Wade Boggs HL COR .02 .10
655 Jose Canseco HL .08 .25
656 Doug Jones HL .01 .05
657 Rickey Henderson HL .05 .15
658 Tom Browning HL .01 .05
659 Mike Greenwell HL .01 .05
660 Boston Red Sox HL .01 .05

1989 Score Rookie/Traded

The 1989 Score Rookie and Traded set contains 110 standard-size cards. The set was issued exclusively in factory set form through hobby dealers. The set was distributed in a blue box with 10 Magic Motion trivia cards. The fronts have coral green borders with pink diamonds at the bottom. Cards 1-80 feature traded players; cards 81-110 feature 1989 rookies. Rookie Cards in this set include Jim Abbott, Joey (Albert) Belle, Ken Griffey Jr. and John Wetteland.

COMP.FACT.SET (110) 6.00 15.00
1T Rafael Palmeiro .08 .25
2T Nolan Ryan .60 1.50
3T Jack Clark .02 .10
4T Dave LaPoint .01 .05
5T Mike Moore .01 .05
6T Pete O'Brien .01 .05
7T Jeffrey Leonard .01 .05
8T Rob Murphy .01 .05
9T Tom Herr .01 .05
10T Claudell Washington .01 .05
11T Mike Pagliarulo .01 .05
12T Steve Lake .01 .05
13T Spike Owen .01 .05
14T Andy Hawkins .01 .05
15T Todd Benzinger .01 .05
16T Mookie Wilson .02 .10
17T Bert Blyleven .02 .10
18T Jeff Treadway .01 .05
19T Bruce Hurst .01 .05
20T Steve Sax .01 .05
21T Juan Samuel .01 .05
22T Jesse Barfield .02 .10
23T Carmen Castillo .01 .05
24T Terry Leach .01 .05
25T Mark Langston .01 .05
26T Eric King .01 .05
27T Steve Balboni .01 .05
28T Len Dykstra .02 .10
29T Keith Moreland .01 .05
30T Terry Kennedy .01 .05
31T Eddie Murray .08 .25
32T Mitch Williams .01 .05
33T Jeff Parrett .01 .05
34T Wally Backman .01 .05
35T Julio Franco .02 .10
36T Lance Parrish .02 .10
37T Nick Esasky .01 .05
38T Luis Polonia .01 .05
39T Kevin Gross .01 .05
40T John Dopson .01 .05
41T Willie Randolph .02 .10
42T Jim Clancy .01 .05
43T Tracy Jones .01 .05
44T Phil Bradley .01 .05
45T Milt Thompson .01 .05
46T Chris James .01 .05
47T Scott Fletcher .01 .05
48T Kal Daniels .01 .05
49T Steve Bedrosian .01 .05
50T Rickey Henderson .08 .25
51T Dion James .01 .05
52T Tim Leary .01 .05
53T Roger McDowell .01 .05
54T Mel Hall .01 .05
55T Dickie Thon .01 .05
56T Zane Smith .01 .05
57T Danny Heep .01 .05
58T Bob McClure .01 .05
59T Brian Holton .01 .05
60T Randy Ready .01 .05
61T Bob Melvin .01 .05
62T Harold Baines .02 .10
63T Lance McCullers .01 .05
64T Jody Davis .01 .05
65T Darrell Evans .02 .10
66T Joel Youngblood .01 .05
67T Frank Viola .02 .10
68T Mike Aldrete .01 .05

69T Greg Cadaret .01 .05
70T John Kruk .02 .10
71T Pat Sheridan .01 .05
72T Oddibe McDowell .01 .05
73T Tom Brookens .01 .05
74T Bob Boone .02 .10
75T Walt Terrell .01 .05
76T Joel Skinner .01 .05
77T Randy Johnson .60 1.50
78T Felix Fermin .01 .05
79T Rick Mahler .01 .05
80T Richard Dotson .01 .05
81T Cris Carpenter RC * .02 .10
82T Billy Spiers RC .08 .25
83T Junior Felix RC .02 .10
84T Joe Girardi RC .15 .40
85T Jerome Walton RC .08 .25
86T Greg Litton .01 .05
87T Greg W.Harris RC .02 .10
88T Jim Abbott RC .40 1.00
89T Kevin Brown .08 .25
90T John Wetteland RC .15 .40
91T Gary Wayne .01 .05
92T Rich Monteleone .01 .05
93T Bob Geren RC .01 .05
94T Clay Parker .01 .05
95T Steve Finley RC .30 .75
96T Gregg Olson RC .08 .25
97T Ken Patterson .01 .05
98T Ken Hill RC .08 .25
99T Scott Scudder RC .02 .10
100T Ken Griffey Jr. RC 2.50 6.00
101T Jeff Brantley RC .08 .25
102T Donn Pall .01 .05
103T Carlos Martinez RC .02 .10
104T Joe Oliver RC .08 .25
105T Omar Vizquel RC .40 1.00
106T Albert Belle RC .40 1.00
107T Kenny Rogers RC .75 2.00
108T Mark Carreon .01 .05
109T Rolando Roomes .01 .05
110T Pete Harnisch RC .08 .25

1989 Score Hottest 100 Rookies

This set was distributed by Publications International in January 1989 through many retail stores and chains; the card set was packaged along with a colorful 48-page book for a suggested retail price of 12.95. Supposedly 225,000 sets were produced. The cards measure the standard size and show full color on both sides of the card. The cards were produced by Score as indicated on the card backs. The set is subtitled "Rising Star" on the reverse. The first six cards (1-6) of a 12-card set of Score's trivia cards, subtitled "Rookies to Remember" is included along with each set. This set is distinguished by the sharp blue borders and the player's first initial inside a yellow triangle in the lower left corner of the obverse. The set features Dave Justice appearing one year before his Rookie Card year.

COMP.FACT.SET (100) 4.00 10.00
1 Gregg Jefferies .01 .05
2 Vicente Palacios .01 .05
3 Cameron Drew .01 .05
4 Doug Dascenzo .01 .05
5 Luis Medina .01 .05
6 Craig Worthington .01 .05
7 Rob Ducey .01 .05
8 Hal Morris .05 .15
9 Bill Brennan .01 .05
10 Gary Sheffield .40 1.00
11 Mike Devereaux .01 .05
12 Hensley Meulens .01 .05
13 Carlos Quintana .01 .05
14 Todd Frohwirth .01 .05
15 Scott Lusader .01 .05
16 Mark Carreon .01 .05
17 Torey Lovullo .01 .05
18 Randy Velarde .05 .15
19 Billy Bean .05 .15
20 Lance Blankenship .01 .05
21 Chris Gwynn .01 .05
22 Felix Jose .01 .05
23 Derek Lilliquist .01 .05
24 Gary Thurman .01 .05
25 Ron Jones .01 .05
26 Dave Justice .75 2.00
27 Johnny Paredes .01 .05
28 Tim Jones .01 .05
29 Jose Gonzalez .01 .05
30 Geronimo Berroa .01 .05
31 Trevor Wilson .01 .05
32 Morris Madden .01 .05
33 Lance Johnson .01 .05
34 Marvin Freeman .01 .05
35 Jose Cecena .01 .05
36 Jim Corsi .01 .05
37 Rolando Roomes .01 .05
38 Scott Medvin .01 .05
39 Charlie Hayes .01 .05
40 Edgar Martinez .20 .50
41 Van Snider .01 .05
42 John Fishel .01 .05
43 Bruce Fields .01 .05
44 Darryl Hamilton .01 .05
45 Tom Prince .01 .05
46 Kirt Manwaring .01 .05
47 Steve Searcy .01 .05
48 Mike Harkey .01 .05
49 German Gonzalez .01 .05
50 Tony Perezchica .01 .05
51 Chad Kreuter .01 .05
52 Luis DeLosSantos .01 .05
53 Steve Curry .01 .05
54 Greg Briley .01 .05
55 Ramon Martinez .08 .25
56 Ron Tingley .01 .05
57 Randy Kramer .01 .05
58 Alex Madrid .01 .05
59 Kevin Reimer .01 .05
60 Dave Otto .01 .05
61 Ken Patterson .01 .05
62 Keith Miller .01 .05
63 Randy Johnson 1.50 4.00
64 Dwight Smith .05 .15
65 Eric Yelding .01 .05
66 Bob Geren .01 .05
67 Shane Turner .01 .05
68 Tom Gordon .15 .40
69 Jeff Huson .01 .05
70 Marty Brown .01 .05
71 Nelson Santovenia .01 .05
72 Roberto Alomar .40 1.00
73 Mike Schooler .01 .05
74 Pete Smith .01 .05
75 John Costello .01 .05
76 Chris Sabo .01 .05
77 Damon Berryhill .01 .05
78 Mark Grace .75 2.00
79 Melido Perez .01 .05
80 Al Leiter .15 .40
81 Todd Stottlemyre .01 .05
82 Mackey Sasser .01 .05
83 Don August .01 .05
84 Jeff Treadway .01 .05
85 Jody Reed .01 .05
86 Mike Campbell .01 .05
87 Ron Gant .05 .15
88 Ricky Jordan .01 .05
89 Terry Clark .01 .05
90 Roberto Kelly .01 .05
91 Pat Borders .05 .15
92 Bryan Harvey .01 .05
93 Joey Meyer .01 .05
94 Tim Belcher .01 .05
95 Walt Weiss .01 .05
96 Dave Gallagher .01 .05
97 Mike Macfarlane .01 .05
98 Craig Biggio 1.00 2.50
99 Jack Armstrong .01 .05
100 Todd Burns .01 .05

1989 Score Hottest 100 Stars

This set was distributed by Publications International in January 1989 through many retail stores and chains; the card set was packaged along with a colorful 48-page book for a suggested retail price of 12.95. Supposedly 225,000 sets were produced. The cards measure the standard size and show full color on both sides of the card. The cards were produced by Score as indicated on the card backs. The set is subtitled "Superstar" on the reverse. The last six cards (7-12) of a 12-card set of Score's trivia cards, subtitled "Rookies to Remember" is included along with each set. This set is distinguished by the sharp red borders and the player's first initial inside a yellow triangle in the upper left corner of the obverse.

COMP. FACT SET (100) 4.00 10.00
1 Jose Canseco .40 1.00
2 David Cone .20 .50
3 Dave Winfield .40 1.00
4 George Brett .75 2.00
5 Frank Viola .01 .05
6 Cory Snyder .01 .05
7 Alan Trammell .10 .30
8 Dwight Evans .05 .15
9 Tim Leary .01 .05
10 Don Mattingly .75 2.00
11 Kirby Puckett .40 1.00
12 Carney Lansford .05 .15
13 Dennis Martinez .05 .15
14 Kent Hrbek .05 .15
15 Dwight Gooden .05 .15
16 Dennis Eckersley .30 .75
17 Kevin Seitzer .01 .05
18 Lee Smith .05 .15
19 Danny Tartabull .01 .05
20 Gerald Perry .01 .05
21 Gary Gaetti .05 .15
22 Rick Reuschel .05 .15
23 Keith Hernandez .05 .15
24 Jeff Reardon .05 .15
25 Mark McGwire .60 1.50
26 Juan Samuel .01 .05
27 Jack Clark .01 .05
28 Robin Yount .40 1.00
29 Steve Bedrosian .01 .05
30 Kirk Gibson .05 .15
31 Barry Bonds .60 1.50
32 Dan Plesac .01 .05
33 Steve Sax .01 .05
34 Jeff M. Robinson .01 .05
35 Orel Hershiser .05 .15
36 Julio Franco .05 .15
37 Dave Righetti .01 .05
38 Bob Knepper .01 .05
39 Carlton Fisk .40 1.00
40 Tony Gwynn .75 2.00
41 Doug Jones .01 .05
42 Bobby Bonilla .05 .15
43 Ellis Burks .10 .30
44 Pedro Guerrero .01 .05
45 Rickey Henderson .60 1.50
46 Glenn Davis .01 .05
47 Benito Santiago .05 .15
48 Greg Maddux 1.00 2.50
49 Teddy Higuera .01 .05
50 Darryl Strawberry .05 .15
51 Ozzie Guillen .10 .30
52 Barry Larkin .20 .50
53 Tony Fernandez .05 .15
54 Ryne Sandberg .60 1.50
55 Joe Carter .10 .30
56 Rafael Palmeiro .30 .75
57 Paul Molitor .40 1.00
58 Eric Davis .05 .15
59 Mike Henneman .01 .05
60 Mike Scott .05 .15
61 Tom Browning .01 .05
62 Mark Davis .01 .05
63 Tom Henke .01 .05
64 Nolan Ryan 1.50 4.00
65 Fred McGriff .20 .50
66 Dale Murphy .20 .50
67 Mark Langston .01 .05
68 Bobby Thigpen .01 .05
69 Mark Gubicza .01 .05
70 Mike Greenwell .01 .05
71 Ron Darling .01 .05
72 Gerald Young .01 .05
73 Wally Joyner .05 .15
74 Andres Galarraga .20 .50
75 Danny Jackson .01 .05
76 Mike Schmidt .40 1.00
77 Cal Ripken 1.50 4.00
78 Alvin Davis .01 .05
79 Bruce Hurst .01 .05
80 Andre Dawson .20 .50
81 Bob Boone .05 .15
82 Harold Reynolds .05 .15
83 Eddie Murray .40 1.00
84 Robby Thompson .01 .05
85 Will Clark .20 .50
86 Vince Coleman .01 .05
87 Doug Drabek .01 .05
88 Ozzie Smith .60 1.50
89 Bob Welch .01 .05
90 Roger Clemens .75 2.00
91 George Bell .01 .05
92 Andy Van Slyke .05 .15
93 Willie McGee .05 .15
94 Todd Worrell .01 .05
95 Tim Raines .05 .15
96 Kevin McReynolds .01 .05
97 John Franco .05 .15
98 Jim Gott .01 .05
99 Johnny Ray .01 .05
100 Wade Boggs .40 1.00

1989 Scoremasters

The 1989 Scoremasters set contains 42 standard-size cards. The fronts are "pure" with attractively drawn action portraits. The backs feature write-ups of the players' careers. The set was issued in factory set form only. A first year card of Ken Griffey Jr. highlights the set.

COMP.FACT.SET (42) 4.00 10.00
DISTRIBUTED IN FACTORY SET FORM ONLY
1 Bo Jackson .08 .25
2 Jerome Walton .02 .10
3 Cal Ripken .30 .75
4 Mike Scott .01 .05
5 Nolan Ryan .40 1.00
6 Don Mattingly .25 .60
7 Tom Gordon .05 .15
8 Jack Morris .02 .10
9 Carlton Fisk .07 .20
10 Will Clark .05 .15
11 George Brett .25 .60
12 Kevin Mitchell .02 .10
13 Mark Langston .01 .05
14 Dave Stewart .02 .10
15 Dale Murphy .05 .15
16 Gary Gaetti .02 .10
17 Wade Boggs .05 .15
18 Eric Davis .02 .10
19 Kirby Puckett .08 .25
20 Roger Clemens .40 1.00
21 Orel Hershiser .02 .10
22 Mark Grace .08 .25
23 Ryne Sandberg .15 .40
24 Barry Larkin .05 .15
25 Ellis Burks .05 .15
26 Dwight Gooden .02 .10
27 Ozzie Smith .15 .40
28 Andre Dawson .02 .10
29 Julio Franco .02 .10
30 Ken Griffey Jr. 4.00 10.00
31 Ruben Sierra .02 .10
32 Mark McGwire .40 1.00
33 Andres Galarraga .02 .10
34 Joe Carter .02 .10
35 Vince Coleman .01 .05
36 Mike Greenwell .01 .05
37 Tony Gwynn .10 .30
38 Andy Van Slyke .05 .15
39 Gregg Jefferies .02 .10
40 Jose Canseco .08 .25
41 Dave Winfield .02 .10
42 Darryl Strawberry .02 .10
NNO Don Mattingly Promo 2.00 5.00
NNO Jose Canseco Sample

1989 Score Young Superstars I

The 1989 Score Young Superstars I set contains 42 standard-size cards. The fronts are pink, white and blue. The vertically oriented backs have color facial shots, 1988 and career stats, and biographical information. One card was included in each 1989 Score rack pack, and the cards were also distributed as a boxed set with five Magic Motion trivia cards.

COMPLETE SET (42) 3.00 8.00
ONE PER RACK PACK
1 Gregg Jefferies .15 .40
2 Jody Reed .08 .25
3 Mark Grace .40 1.00
4 Dave Gallagher .08 .25
5 Bo Jackson .40 1.00
6 Jay Buhner .15 .40
7 Melido Perez .08 .25
8 Bobby Witt .08 .25
9 David Cone .15 .40
10 Chris Sabo .08 .25
11 Pat Borders .08 .25
12 Mark Grant .08 .25
13 Mike Macfarlane .08 .25
14 Mike Jackson .08 .25
15 Ricky Jordan .08 .25
16 Ron Gant .15 .40
17 Al Leiter .40 1.00
18 Jeff Parrett .08 .25
19 Pete Smith .08 .25
20 Walt Weiss .15 .40
21 Doug Drabek .08 .25
22 Kirt Manwaring .08 .25
23 Keith Miller .08 .25
24 Damon Berryhill .08 .25
25 Gary Sheffield 2.00 5.00
26 Brady Anderson .25 .60
27 Mitch Williams .08 .25
28 Roberto Alomar .40 1.00
29 Bobby Thigpen .08 .25
30 Bryan Harvey UER .08 .25
31 Jose Rijo .08 .25
32 Dave West .08 .25
33 Joey Meyer .08 .25
34 Allan Anderson .08 .25
35 Rafael Palmeiro .40 1.00
36 Tim Belcher .08 .25
37 John Smiley .08 .25
38 Mackey Sasser .08 .25
39 Greg Maddux .75 2.00
40 Ramon Martinez .15 .40
41 Randy Myers .15 .40
42 Scott Bankhead .08 .25

1989 Score Young Superstars II

The 1989 Score Young Superstars II set contains 42 standard-size cards. The fronts are orange, white and purple. The vertically oriented backs have color facial shots, 1988 and career stats, and biographical information. The cards were distributed as a boxed set with five Magic Motion trivia cards. A first year card of Ken Griffey Jr. highlights the set.

COMP.FACT.SET (42) 10.00 25.00
DISTRIBUTED IN FACTORY SET FORM ONLY
1 Sandy Alomar Jr. .25 .60
2 Tom Gordon .25 .60
3 Ron Jones .08 .25
4 Todd Burns .08 .25
5 Paul O'Neill .25 .60
6 Gene Larkin .08 .25
7 Eric King .08 .25
8 Jeff M. Robinson .08 .25
9 Bill Wegman .08 .25
10 Cecil Espy .08 .25
11 Jose Guzman .08 .25
12 Kelly Gruber .08 .25
13 Duane Ward .08 .25
14 Mark Gubicza .08 .25
15 Norm Charlton .15 .40
16 Jose Oquendo .08 .25
17 Geronimo Berroa .08 .25
18 Ken Griffey Jr. 8.00 20.00
19 Lance McCullers .08 .25
20 Todd Stottlemyre .25 .60
21 Craig Worthington .08 .25
22 Mike Devereaux .08 .25
23 Tom Glavine .40 1.00
24 Dale Sveum .08 .25
25 Roberto Kelly .15 .40
26 Luis Medina .08 .25
27 Steve Searcy .08 .25
28 Don August .08 .25
29 Shawn Hillegas .08 .25
30 Mike Campbell .08 .25
31 Mike Harkey .08 .25
32 Randy Johnson 3.00 8.00
33 Craig Biggio 2.00 5.00
34 Mike Schooler .08 .25
35 Andres Thomas .08 .25
36 Jerome Walton .15 .40
37 Cris Carpenter .08 .25
38 Kevin Mitchell .15 .40
39 Eddie Williams .08 .25
40 Chad Kreuter .08 .25
41 Danny Jackson .08 .25
42 Kurt Stillwell .08 .25

1990 Score Promos

*PROMOS: 10X TO 20X BASIC CARDS

1990 Score

The 1990 Score set contains 704 standard-size cards. Cards were distributed in plastic-wrap packs and factory sets. The front borders are red, blue, green or white. The vertically oriented backs are white with borders that match the fronts, and feature color mugshots. Subsets include Draft Picks (661-682) and Dream Team (683-695). A special black and white horizontal-designed card of Bo Jackson in football pads holding a bat above his shoulders was a big hit in 1990. That card traded for as much as $10 but has since cooled off. Nevertheless, it remains one of the most noteworthy cards issued in the early 1990's. Rookie Cards of note include Juan Gonzalez, Dave Justice, Chuck Knoblauch, Dean Palmer, Sammy Sosa, Frank Thomas, Mo Vaughn, Larry Walker and Bernie Williams. A ten-card set of Dream Team Rookies was inserted into each hobby factory set, but was not included in retail factory sets.

COMPLETE SET (704) 6.00 15.00
COMP.RETAIL SET (704) 6.00 15.00
COMP.HOBBY SET (714) 6.00 15.00
1 Don Mattingly .25 .60
2 Cal Ripken .30 .75
3 Dwight Evans .05 .15
4 Barry Bonds .40 1.00
5 Kevin McReynolds .01 .05
6 Ozzie Guillen .02 .10
7 Terry Kennedy .01 .05
8 Bryan Harvey .01 .05
9 Alan Trammell .02 .10
10 Cory Snyder .01 .05
11 Jody Reed .01 .05
12 Roberto Alomar .05 .15
13 Pedro Guerrero .01 .05
14 Gary Redus .01 .05
15 Marty Barrett .01 .05
16 Ricky Jordan .01 .05
17 Joe Magrane .01 .05
18 Sid Fernandez .01 .05
19 Richard Dotson .01 .05
20 Jack Clark .02 .10
21 Bob Walk .01 .05
22 Ron Karkovice .01 .05
23 Lenny Harris .01 .05
24 Phil Bradley .01 .05
25 Andres Galarraga .02 .10
26 Brian Downing .01 .05
27 Dave Martinez .01 .05
28 Eric King .01 .05
29 Barry Lyons .01 .05
30 Dave Schmidt .01 .05
31 Mike Boddicker .01 .05
32 Tom Foley .01 .05
33 Brady Anderson .02 .10
34 Jim Presley .01 .05
35 Lance Parrish .01 .05
36 Von Hayes .01 .05
37 Lee Smith .02 .10
38 Herm Winningham .01 .05
39 Alejandro Pena .01 .05
40 Mike Scott .01 .05
41 Joe Orsulak .01 .05
42 Rafael Ramirez .01 .05
43 Gerald Young .01 .05
44 Dick Schofield .01 .05
45 Dave Smith .01 .05
46 Dave Magadan .01 .05
47 Dennis Martinez .02 .10
48 Greg Minton .01 .05
49 Milt Thompson .01 .05
50 Orel Hershiser .02 .10
51 Bip Roberts .01 .05
52 Jerry Browne .01 .05
53 Bob Ojeda .01 .05
54 Fernando Valenzuela .02 .10
55 Matt Nokes .01 .05
56 Brook Jacoby .01 .05
57 Frank Tanana .01 .05
58 Scott Fletcher .01 .05
59 Ron Oester .01 .05
60 Bob Boone .02 .10
61 Dan Gladden .01 .05
62 Darnell Coles .01 .05
63 Gregg Olson .02 .10
64 Todd Burns .01 .05
65 Todd Benzinger .01 .05
66 Dale Murphy .05 .15
67 Mike Flanagan .01 .05
68 Jose Oquendo .01 .05
69 Cecil Espy .01 .05
70 Chris Sabo .01 .05
71 Shane Rawley .01 .05
72 Tom Brunansky .01 .05
73 Vance Law .01 .05
74 B.J. Surhoff .02 .10
75 Lou Whitaker .02 .10
76 Ken Caminiti UER .02 .10
Euclid and Ohio should be
Hanford and California
77 Nelson Liriano .01 .05
78 Tommy Gregg .01 .05
79 Don Slaught .01 .05
80 Eddie Murray .08 .25
81 Joe Boever .01 .05
82 Charlie Leibrandt .01 .05
83 Jose Lind .01 .05
84 Tony Phillips .01 .05
85 Mitch Webster .01 .05
86 Dan Plesac .01 .05
87 Rick Mahler .01 .05
88 Steve Lyons .01 .05
89 Tony Fernandez .01 .05
90 Ryne Sandberg .15 .40
91 Nick Esasky .01 .05
92 Luis Salazar .01 .05
93 Pete Incaviglia .01 .05
94 Ivan Calderon .01 .05
95 Jeff Treadway .01 .05
96 Kurt Stillwell .01 .05
97 Gary Sheffield .08 .25
98 Jeffrey Leonard .01 .05
99 Andres Thomas .01 .05
100 Roberto Kelly .01 .05
101 Alvaro Espinoza .01 .05
102 Greg Gagne .01 .05
103 John Farrell .01 .05
104 Willie Wilson .01 .05
105 Glenn Braggs .01 .05
106 Chet Lemon .01 .05
107A Jamie Moyer ERR .02 .10
Scintilating
107B Jamie Moyer COR .20 .50
Scintillating
108 Chuck Crim .01 .05
109 Dave Valle .01 .05
110 Walt Weiss .01 .05
111 Larry Sheets .01 .05
112 Don Robinson .01 .05
113 Danny Heep .01 .05
114 Carmelo Martinez .01 .05
115 Dave Gallagher .01 .05
116 Mike LaValliere .01 .05
117 Bob McClure .01 .05
118 Rene Gonzales .01 .05
119 Mark Parent .01 .05
120 Wally Joyner .02 .10
121 Mark Gubicza .01 .05
122 Tony Pena .01 .05
123 Carmelo Castillo .01 .05
124 Howard Johnson .01 .05
125 Steve Sax .01 .05
126 Tim Belcher .01 .05
127 Tim Burke .01 .05
128 Al Newman .01 .05
129 Dennis Rasmussen .01 .05
130 Doug Jones .01 .05
131 Fred Lynn .01 .05
132 Jeff Hamilton .01 .05
133 German Gonzalez .01 .05
134 John Morris .01 .05
135 Dave Parker .02 .10
136 Gary Pettis .01 .05
137 Dennis Boyd .01 .05
138 Candy Maldonado .01 .05
139 Rick Cerone .01 .05
140 George Brett .25 .60
141 Dave Clark .01 .05
142 Dickie Thon .01 .05
143 Junior Ortiz .01 .05
144 Don August .01 .05
145 Gary Gaetti .02 .10
146 Kirt Manwaring .01 .05
147 Jeff Reed .01 .05
148 Jose Alvarez .01 .05
149 Mike Schooler .01 .05
150 Mark Grace .05 .15
151 Geronimo Berroa .01 .05
152 Barry Jones .01 .05
153 Geno Petralli .01 .05
154 Jim Deshaies .01 .05
155 Barry Larkin .05 .15
156 Alfredo Griffin .01 .05
157 Tom Henke .01 [illegible]
158 Mike Jeffcoat .01 [illegible]
159 Bob Welch .01 [illegible]
160 Julio Franco .02 [illegible]
161 Henry Cotto .01 [illegible]
162 Terry Steinbach .01 [illegible]
163 Damon Berryhill .01 [illegible]
164 Tim Crews .01 [illegible]
165 Tom Browning .01 [illegible]
166 Fred Manrique .01 [illegible]
167 Harold Reynolds .02 [illegible]
168A Ron Hassey ERR .01 [illegible]
27 on back
168B Ron Hassey COR .20 [illegible]
24 on back
169 Shawon Dunston .01 [illegible]
170 Bobby Bonilla .02 [illegible]
171 Tommy Herr .01 [illegible]
172 Mike Heath .01 [illegible]
173 Rich Gedman .01 [illegible]
174 Bill Ripken .01 [illegible]
175 Pete O'Brien .01 [illegible]
176A Lloyd McClendon ERR .01 [illegible]
Uniform number on
back listed as 1
176B Lloyd McClendon COR .20 [illegible]
Uniform number on
back listed as 10
177 Brian Holton .01 .05
178 Jeff Blauser .01 .05
179 Jim Eisenreich .01 .05
180 Bert Blyleven .02 .10
181 Rob Murphy .01 .05
182 Bill Doran .01 .05
183 Curt Ford .01 .05
184 Mike Henneman .01 .05
185 Eric Davis .02 .10
186 Lance McCullers .01 .05
187 Steve Davis RC .01 .05
188 Bill Wegman .01 .05
189 Brian Harper .01 .05
190 Mike Moore .01 .05
191 Dale Mohorcic .01 .05
192 Tim Wallach .01 .05
193 Keith Hernandez .02 .10
194 Dave Righetti .01 .05
195A Bret Saberhagen ERR .02 .10
Joke
195B Bret Saberhagen COR .20 .50
Joker
196 Paul Kilgus .01 .05
197 Bud Black .01 .05
198 Juan Samuel .01 .05
199 Kevin Seitzer .01 .05
200 Darryl Strawberry .02 .10
201 Dave Stieb .02 .10
202 Charlie Hough .02 .10
203 Jack Morris .02 .10
204 Rance Mulliniks .01 .05
205 Alvin Davis .01 .05
206 Jack Howell .01 .05
207 Ken Patterson .01 .05
208 Terry Pendleton .02 .10
209 Craig Lefferts .01 .05
210 Kevin Brown UER .02 .10
First mention of '89
Rangers should be '88
211 Dan Petry .01 .05
212 Dave Leiper .01 .05
213 Daryl Boston .01 .05
214 Kevin Hickey .01 .05
215 Mike Krukow .01 .05
216 Terry Francona .02 .10
217 Kirk McCaskill .01 .05
218 Scott Bailes .01 .05
219 Bob Forsch .01 .05
220A Mike Aldrete ERR .01 .05
25 on back
220B Mike Aldrete COR .20 .50
24 on back
221 Steve Buechele .01 .05
222 Jesse Barfield .01 .05
223 Juan Berenguer .01 .05
224 Andy McGaffigan .01 .05
225 Pete Smith .01 .05
226 Mike Witt .01 .05
227 Jay Howell .01 .05
228 Scott Bradley .01 .05
229 Jerome Walton .01 .05
230 Greg Swindell .01 .05
231 Atlee Hammaker .01 .05
232A Mike Devereaux ERR .01 .05
RF on front
232B Mike Devereaux COR .20 .50
CF on front
233 Ken Hill .02 .10
234 Craig Worthington .01 .05
235 Scott Terry .01 .05
236 Brett Butler .02 .10
237 Doyle Alexander .01 .05
238 Dave Anderson .01 .05
239 Bob Milacki .01 .05
240 Dwight Smith .01 .05
241 Otis Nixon .01 .05
242 Pat Tabler .01 .05
243 Derek Lilliquist .01 .05
244 Danny Tartabull .01 .05
245 Wade Boggs .05 .15
246 Scott Garrelts .01 .05
Should say Relief
Pitcher on front
247 Spike Owen .01 .05
248 Norm Charlton .01 .05

249 Gerald Perry .01 .05
250 Nolan Ryan .40 1.00
251 Kevin Gross .01 .05
252 Randy Milligan .01 .05
253 Mike LaCoss .01 .05
254 Dave Bergman .01 .05
255 Tony Gwynn .10 .30
256 Felix Fermin .01 .05
257 Greg W. Harris .01 .05
258 Junior Felix .01 .05
259 Mark Davis .01 .05
260 Vince Coleman .01 .05
261 Paul Gibson .01 .05
262 Mitch Williams .01 .05
263 Jeff Russell .01 .05
264 Omar Vizquel .08 .25
265 Andre Dawson .02 .10
266 Storm Davis .01 .05
267 Guillermo Hernandez .01 .05
268 Mike Felder .01 .05
269 Tom Candiotti .01 .05
270 Bruce Hurst .01 .05
271 Fred McGriff .08 .25
272 Glenn Davis .01 .05
273 John Franco .02 .10
274 Rich Yett .01 .05
275 Craig Biggio .08 .25
276 Gene Larkin .01 .05
277 Rob Dibble .02 .10
278 Randy Bush .01 .05
279 Kevin Bass .01 .05
280A Bo Jackson ERR .08 .25
Watham
280B Bo Jackson COR .30 .75
Wathan
281 Wally Backman .01 .05
282 Larry Andersen .01 .05
283 Chris Bosio .01 .05
284 Juan Agosto .01 .05
285 Ozzie Smith .15 .40
286 George Bell .01 .05
287 Rex Hudler .01 .05
288 Pat Borders .01 .05
289 Danny Jackson .01 .05
290 Carlton Fisk .05 .15
291 Tracy Jones .01 .05
292 Allan Anderson .01 .05
293 Johnny Ray .01 .05
294 Lee Guetterman .01 .05
295 Paul O'Neill .05 .15
296 Carney Lansford .02 .10
297 Tom Brookens .01 .05
298 Claudell Washington .01 .05
299 Hubie Brooks .01 .05
300 Will Clark .05 .15
301 Kenny Rogers .02 .10
302 Darrell Evans .02 .10
303 Greg Briley .01 .05
304 Donn Pall .01 .05
305 Teddy Higuera .01 .05
306 Dan Pasqua .01 .05
307 Dave Winfield .02 .10
308 Dennis Powell .01 .05
309 Jose DeLeon .01 .05
310 Roger Clemens UER .40 1.00
311 Melido Perez .01 .05
312 Devon White .02 .10
313 Dwight Gooden .02 .10
314 Carlos Martinez .01 .05
315 Dennis Eckersley .02 .10
316 Clay Parker UER .01 .05
Height 6'11-inch
317 Rick Honeycutt .01 .05
318 Tim Laudner .01 .05
319 Joe Carter .02 .10
320 Robin Yount .15 .40
321 Felix Jose .01 .05
322 Mickey Tettleton .01 .05
323 Mike Gallego .01 .05
324 Edgar Martinez .05 .15
325 Dave Henderson .01 .05
326 Chili Davis .02 .10
327 Steve Balboni .01 .05
328 Jody Davis .01 .05
329 Shawn Hillegas .01 .05
330 Jim Abbott .05 .15
331 John Dopson .01 .05
332 Mark Williamson .01 .05
333 Jeff D. Robinson .01 .05
334 John Smiley .01 .05
335 Bobby Thigpen .01 .05
336 Garry Templeton .01 .05
337 Marvell Wynne .01 .05
338A Ken Griffey Sr. ERR .02 .10
Uniform number on back listed as 25
338B Ken Griffey Sr. COR .20 .50
Uniform number on back listed as 30
339 Steve Finley .02 .10
340 Ellis Burks .05 .15
341 Frank Williams .01 .05
342 Mike Morgan .01 .05
343 Kevin Mitchell .01 .05
344 Joel Youngblood .01 .05
345 Mike Greenwell .01 .05
346 Glenn Wilson .01 .05
347 John Costello .01 .05
348 Wes Gardner .01 .05
349 Jeff Ballard .01 .05
350 Mark Thurmond UER .01 .05
ERA is 192, should be 1.92
351 Randy Myers .02 .10
352 Shawn Abner .01 .05
353 Jesse Orosco .01 .05
354 Greg Walker .01 .05
355 Pete Harnisch .01 .05
356 Steve Farr .01 .05
357 Dave LaPoint .01 .05
358 Willie Fraser .01 .05
359 Mickey Hatcher .01 .05
360 Rickey Henderson .08 .25
361 Mike Fitzgerald .01 .05
362 Bill Schroeder .01 .05
363 Mark Carreon .01 .05
364 Ron Jones .01 .05
365 Jeff Montgomery .02 .10
366 Bill Krueger .01 .05
367 John Cangelosi .01 .05
368 Jose Gonzalez .01 .05
369 Greg Hibbard RC .02 .10
370 John Smoltz .08 .25
371 Jeff Brantley .01 .05
372 Frank White .02 .10
373 Ed Whitson .01 .05
374 Willie McGee .02 .10
375 Jose Canseco .05 .15
376 Randy Ready .01 .05
377 Don Aase .01 .05
378 Tony Armas .01 .05
379 Steve Bedrosian .01 .05
380 Chuck Finley .02 .10
381 Kent Hrbek .02 .10
382 Jim Gantner .01 .05
383 Mel Hall .01 .05
384 Mike Marshall .01 .05
385 Mark McGwire .40 1.00
386 Wayne Tolleson .01 .05
387 Brian Holman .01 .05
388 John Wetteland .08 .25
389 Darren Daulton .02 .10
390 Rob Deer .01 .05
391 John Moses .01 .05
392 Todd Worrell .01 .05
393 Chuck Cary .01 .05
394 Stan Javier .01 .05
395 Willie Randolph .02 .10
396 Bill Buckner .01 .05
397 Robby Thompson .01 .05
398 Mike Scioscia .01 .05
399 Lonnie Smith .01 .05
400 Kirby Puckett .08 .25
401 Mark Langston .01 .05
402 Danny Darwin .01 .05
403 Greg Maddux .15 .40
404 Lloyd Moseby .01 .05
405 Rafael Palmeiro .05 .15
406 Chad Kreuter .01 .05
407 Jimmy Key .02 .10
408 Tim Birtsas .01 .05
409 Tim Raines .02 .10
410 Dave Stewart .02 .10
411 Eric Yelding RC .01 .05
412 Kent Anderson .01 .05
413 Les Lancaster .01 .05
414 Rick Dempsey .01 .05
415 Randy Johnson .20 .50
416 Gary Carter .02 .10
417 Rolando Roomes .01 .05
418 Dan Schatzeder .01 .05
419 Bryn Smith .01 .05
420 Ruben Sierra .02 .10
421 Steve Jeltz .01 .05
422 Ken Oberkfell .01 .05
423 Sid Bream .01 .05
424 Jim Clancy .01 .05
425 Kelly Gruber .01 .05
426 Rick Leach .01 .05
427 Len Dykstra .02 .10
428 Jeff Pico .01 .05
429 John Cerutti .01 .05
430 David Cone .02 .10
431 Jeff Kunkel .01 .05
432 Luis Aquino .01 .05
433 Ernie Whitt .01 .05
434 Bo Diaz .01 .05
435 Steve Lake .01 .05
436 Pat Perry .01 .05
437 Mike Davis .01 .05
438 Cecilio Guante .01 .05
439 Duane Ward .01 .05
440 Andy Van Slyke .05 .15
441 Gene Nelson .01 .05
442 Luis Polonia .01 .05
443 Kevin Elster .01 .05
444 Keith Moreland .01 .05
445 Roger McDowell .01 .05
446 Ron Darling .01 .05
447 Ernest Riles .01 .05
448 Mookie Wilson .02 .10
449A Billy Spiers ERR .01 .05
No birth year
449B Billy Spiers COR .20 .50
Born in 1966
450 Rick Sutcliffe .02 .10
451 Nelson Santovenia .01 .05
452 Andy Allanson .01 .05
453 Bob Melvin .01 .05
454 Benito Santiago .02 .10
455 Jose Uribe .01 .05
456 Bill Landrum .01 .05
457 Bobby Witt .01 .05
458 Kevin Romine .01 .05
459 Lee Mazzilli .01 .05
460 Paul Molitor .02 .10
461 Ramon Martinez .01 .05
462 Frank DiPino .01 .05
463 Walt Terrell .01 .05
464 Bob Geren .01 .05
465 Rick Reuschel .01 .05
466 Mark Grant .01 .05
467 John Kruk .02 .10
468 Gregg Jefferies .02 .10
469 R.J. Reynolds .01 .05
470 Harold Baines .02 .10
471 Dennis Lamp .01 .05
472 Tom Gordon .02 .10
473 Terry Puhl .01 .05
474 Curt Wilkerson .01 .05
475 Dan Quisenberry .02 .10
476 Oddibe McDowell .01 .05
477A Zane Smith ERR .01 .05
Career ERA .393
477B Zane Smith COR .20 .50
career ERA 3.93
478 Franklin Stubbs .01 .05
479 Wallace Johnson .01 .05
480 Jay Tibbs .01 .05
481 Tom Glavine .05 .15
482 Manny Lee .01 .05
483 Joe Hesketh UER .01 .05
Says Rookiess on back, should say Rookies
484 Mike Bielecki .01 .05
485 Greg Brock .01 .05
486 Pascual Perez .01 .05
487 Kirk Gibson .02 .10
488 Scott Sanderson .01 .05
489 Domingo Ramos .01 .05
490 Kal Daniels .01 .05
491A David Wells ERR .02 .10
Reverse negative photo on card back
491B David Wells COR .20 .50
492 Jerry Reed .01 .05
493 Eric Chow .01 .05
494 Mike Pagliarulo .01 .05
495 Ron Robinson .01 .05
496 Brad Komminsk .01 .05
497 Greg Litton .01 .05
498 Chris James .01 .05
499 Luis Quinones .01 .05
500 Frank Viola .01 .05
501 Tim Teufel UER .01 .05
Twins '85, the s is lower case, should be upper case
502 Terry Leach .01 .05
503 Matt Williams UER .02 .10
Wearing 10 on front, listed as 9 on back
504 Tim Leary .01 .05
505 Doug Drabek .01 .05
506 Mariano Duncan .01 .05
507 Charlie Hayes .01 .05
508 Joey Belle .08 .25
509 Pat Sheridan .01 .05
510 Mackey Sasser .01 .05
511 Jose Rijo .01 .05
512 Mike Smithson .01 .05
513 Gary Ward .01 .05
514 Dion James .01 .05
515 Jim Gott .01 .05
516 Drew Hall .01 .05
517 Doug Bair .01 .05
518 Scott Scudder .01 .05
519 Rick Aguilera .02 .10
520 Rafael Belliard .01 .05
521 Jay Buhner .02 .10
522 Jeff Reardon .02 .10
523 Steve Rosenberg .01 .05
524 Randy Velarde .01 .05
525 Jeff Musselman .01 .05
526 Bill Long .01 .05
527 Gary Wayne .01 .05
528 Dave Wayne Johnson RC .01 .05
529 Ron Kittle .01 .05
530 Erik Hanson UER .01 .05
5th line on back says seson, should say season
531 Steve Wilson .01 .05
532 Joey Meyer .01 .05
533 Curt Young .01 .05
534 Kelly Downs .01 .05
535 Joe Girardi .05 .15
536 Lance Blankenship .01 .05
537 Greg Mathews .01 .05
538 Donell Nixon .01 .05
539 Mark Knudson .01 .05
540 Jeff Wetherby RC .01 .05
541 Darrin Jackson .01 .05
542 Terry Mulholland .01 .05
543 Eric Hetzel .01 .05
544 Rick Reed RC .08 .25
545 Dennis Cook .01 .05
546 Mike Jackson .01 .05
547 Brian Fisher .01 .05
548 Gene Harris .01 .05
549 Jeff King .01 .05
550 Dave Dravecky .08 .25
551 Randy Kutcher .01 .05
552 Mark Portugal .01 .05
553 Jim Corsi .01 .05
554 Todd Stottlemyre .02 .10
555 Scott Bankhead .01 .05
556 Ken Dayley .01 .05
557 Rick Wrona .01 .05
558 Sammy Sosa RC 1.00 2.50
559 Keith Miller .01 .05
560 Ken Griffey Jr. .40 1.00
561A R.Sandberg HL ERR 3.00 8.00
561B R.Sandberg HL COR .08 .25
562 Billy Hatcher .01 .05
563 Jay Bell .02 .10
564 Jack Daugherty RC .01 .05
565 Rich Monteleone .01 .05
566 Bo Jackson AS-MVP .02 .10
567 Tony Fossas RC .01 .05
568 Roy Smith .01 .05
569 Jaime Navarro .01 .05
570 Lance Johnson .01 .05
571 Mike Dyer RC .01 .05
572 Kevin Ritz RC .01 .05
573 Dave West .01 .05
574 Gary Mielke RC .01 .05
575 Scott Lusader .01 .05
576 Joe Oliver .01 .05
577 Sandy Alomar Jr. .02 .10
578 Andy Benes UER .02 .10
Extra comma between day and year
579 Tim Jones .01 .05
580 Randy McCament RC .01 .05
581 Curt Schilling .40 1.00
582 John Orton RC .02 .10
583A Milt Cuyler ERR RC .02 .10
583B Milt Cuyler COR .20 .50
584 Eric Anthony RC .02 .10
585 Greg Vaughn .01 .05
586 Deion Sanders .08 .25
587 Jose DeJesus .01 .05
588 Chip Hale RC .01 .05
589 John Olerud RC .20 .50
590 Steve Olin RC .08 .25
591 Marquis Grissom RC .15 .40
592 Moises Alou RC .30 .75
593 Mark Lemke .01 .05
594 Dean Palmer RC .08 .25
595 Robin Ventura .08 .25
596 Tino Martinez .20 .50
597 Mike Huff RC .01 .05
598 Scott Hemond RC .01 .05
599 Wally Whitehurst .01 .05
600 Todd Zeile .02 .10
601 Glenallen Hill .01 .05
602 Hal Morris .01 .05
603 Juan Bell .01 .05
604 Bobby Rose .01 .05
605 Matt Merullo .01 .05
606 Kevin Maas RC .08 .25
607 Randy Nosek RC .01 .05
608A Billy Bates RC .01 .05
608B Billy Bates .01 .05
Text has no mention of triples
609 Mike Stanton RC .08 .25
610 Mauro Gozzo RC .01 .05
611 Charles Nagy .01 .05
612 Scott Coolbaugh RC .01 .05
613 Jose Vizcaino RC .08 .25
614 Greg Smith RC .01 .05
615 Jeff Huson RC .02 .10
616 Mickey Weston RC .01 .05
617 John Pawlowski .01 .05
618A Joe Skalski ERR .01 .05
27 on back
618B Joe Skalski COR .20 .50
67 on back
619 Bernie Williams RC .60 1.50
620 Shawn Holman RC .01 .05
621 Gary Eave RC .01 .05
622 Darrin Fletcher UER RC .02 .10
623 Pat Combs .01 .05
624 Mike Blowers RC .02 .10
625 Kevin Appier .02 .10
626 Pat Austin .01 .05
627 Kelly Mann RC .01 .05
628 Matt Kinzer RC .01 .05
629 Chris Hammond RC .02 .10
630 Dean Wilkins RC .01 .05
631 Larry Walker RC .40 1.00
632 Blaine Beatty RC .01 .05
633A Tommy Barrett ERR .01 .05
633B Tommy Barrett COR .20 .50
14 on back
634 Stan Belinda RC .02 .10
635 Mike Texas Smith RC .01 .05
636 Hensley Meulens .01 .05
637 Juan Gonzalez RC .40 1.00
638 Lenny Webster RC .02 .10
639 Mark Gardner RC .02 .10
640 Tommy Greene RC .02 .10
641 Mike Hartley RC .01 .05
642 Phil Stephenson .01 .05
643 Kevin Mmahat RC .01 .05
644 Ed Whited RC .01 .05
645 Delino DeShields RC .08 .25
646 Kevin Blankenship .01 .05
647 Paul Sorrento RC .08 .25
648 Mike Roesler RC .01 .05
649 Jason Grimsley RC .02 .10
650 Dave Justice RC .20 .50
651 Scott Cooper RC .02 .10
652 Dave Eiland .01 .05
653 Mike Munoz RC .01 .05
654 Jeff Fischer RC .01 .05
655 Terry Jorgensen RC .01 .05
656 George Canale RC .01 .05
657 Brian DuBois UER RC .01 .05
658 Carlos Quintana .01 .05
659 Luis de los Santos .01 .05
660 Jerald Clark .01 .05
661 Donald Harris RC .01 .05
662 Paul Coleman RC .02 .10
663 Frank Thomas RC .75 2.00
664 Brent Mayne DC RC .08 .25
665 Eddie Zosky RC .02 .10
666 Steve Hosey RC .02 .10
667 Scott Bryant RC .02 .10
668 Tom Goodwin RC .08 .25
669 Cal Eldred RC .08 .25
670 Earl Cunningham RC .02 .10
671 Alan Zinter DC RC .02 .10
672 Chuck Knoblauch RC .15 .40
673 Kyle Abbott RC .01 .05
674 Roger Salkeld RC .01 .05
675 Mo Vaughn RC .20 .50
676 Keith Kiki Jones RC .01 .05
677 Tyler Houston RC .08 .25
678 Jeff Jackson RC .01 .05
679 Greg Gohr RC .02 .10
680 Ben McDonald DC RC .08 .25
681 Greg Blosser RC .02 .10
682 Willie Greene RC .08 .25
683A Wade Boggs DT ERR .02 .10
Text says 215 hits in '89, should be 205
683B Wade Boggs DT COR .20 .50
Text says 205 hits in '89
684 Will Clark DT .02 .10
685 Tony Gwynn DT UER .05 .15
Text reads battling instead of batting
686 Rickey Henderson DT .05 .15
687 Bo Jackson DT .02 .10
688 Mark Langston DT .01 .05
689 Barry Larkin DT .02 .10
690 Kirby Puckett DT .05 .15
691 Ryne Sandberg DT .08 .25
692 Mike Scott DT .01 .05
693A Terry Steinbach DT .01 .05
ERR cathers
693B Terry Steinbach DT .01 .05
COR catchers
694 Bobby Thigpen DT .01 .05
695 Mitch Williams DT .01 .05
696 Nolan Ryan HL .15 .40
697 Bo Jackson FB 2.00 5.00
BB
698 Rickey Henderson .05 .15
ALCS-MVP
699 Will Clark .02 .10
NLCS-MVP
700 Dave Stewart .02 .10
Mike Moore WS
701 Lights Out .08 .25
702 Carney Lansford .05 .15
Rickey Henderson
Jose Canseco
Dave Henderson WS
703 WS Game 4 .01 .05
Wrap-up
704 Wade Boggs HL .02 .10

1990 Score Magic Motion Trivia

COMPLETE SET (56) 1.00 2.50
COMMON CARD .02 .10

1990 Score Rookie Dream Team

A ten-card set of Dream Team Rookies was inserted only into hobby factory sets. These standard size cards carry a B prefix on the card number and include a player at each position plus a commemorative card honoring the late Baseball Commissioner A. Bartlett Giamatti.

COMPLETE SET (10) 1.50 4.00
ONE SET PER HOBBY FACTORY SET
B1 Bart Giamatti MEM .40 1.00
B2 Pat Combs .07 .20
B3 Todd Zeile .15 .40
B4 Luis de los Santos .07 .20
B5 Mark Lemke .07 .20
B6 Robin Ventura .40 1.00
B7 Jeff Huson .15 .40
B8 Greg Vaughn .07 .20
B9 Marquis Grissom .60 1.50
B10 Eric Anthony .15 .40

1990 Score Rookie/Traded

The standard-size 110-card 1990 Score Rookie and Traded set marked the third consecutive year Score had issued an end of the year set to note trades and give rookies early cards. The set was issued through hobby accounts and only in factory set form. The first 66 cards are traded players while the last 44 cards are rookie cards. Hockey star Eric Lindros is included in this set. Rookie Cards in the set include Derek Bell, Todd Hundley and Ray Lankford.

COMP.FACT.SET (110) 1.25 3.00
1T Dave Winfield .02 .10
2T Kevin Bass .01 .05
3T Nick Esasky .01 .05
4T Mitch Webster .01 .05
5T Pascual Perez .01 .05
6T Gary Pettis .01 .05
7T Tony Pena .01 .05
8T Candy Maldonado .01 .05
9T Cecil Fielder .02 .10
10T Carmelo Martinez .01 .05
11T Mark Langston .01 .05
12T Dave Parker .02 .10
13T Don Slaught .01 .05
14T Tony Phillips .01 .05
15T John Franco .02 .10
16T Randy Myers .02 .10
17T Jeff Reardon .02 .10
18T Sandy Alomar Jr. .02 .10
19T Joe Carter .02 .10
20T Fred Lynn .01 .05
21T Storm Davis .01 .05
22T Craig Lefferts .01 .05
23T Pete O'Brien .01 .05
24T Dennis Boyd .01 .05
25T Lloyd Moseby .01 .05
26T Mark Davis .01 .05
27T Tim Leary .01 .05
28T Gerald Perry .01 .05
29T Don Aase .01 .05
30T Ernie Whitt .01 .05
31T Dale Murphy .05 .15
32T Alejandro Pena .01 .05
33T Juan Samuel .01 .05
34T Hubie Brooks .01 .05
35T Gary Carter .02 .10
36T Jim Presley .01 .05
37T Wally Backman .01 .05
38T Matt Nokes .01 .05
39T Dan Petry .01 .05
40T Franklin Stubbs .01 .05
41T Jeff Huson .01 .05
42T Billy Hatcher .01 .05
43T Terry Leach .01 .05
44T Phil Bradley .01 .05
45T Claudell Washington .01 .05
46T Luis Polonia .01 .05
47T Daryl Boston .01 .05
48T Lee Smith .02 .10
49T Tom Brunansky .01 .05
50T Mike Witt .01 .05
51T Willie Randolph .02 .10
52T Stan Javier .01 .05
53T Brad Komminsk .01 .05
54T John Candelaria .01 .05
55T Bryn Smith .01 .05
56T Glenn Braggs .01 .05
57T Keith Hernandez .02 .10
58T Ken Oberkfell .01 .05
59T Steve Jeltz .01 .05
60T Chris James .01 .05
61T Scott Sanderson .01 .05
62T Bill Long .01 .05
63T Rick Cerone .01 .05
64T Scott Bailes .01 .05
65T Larry Sheets .01 .05
66T Junior Ortiz .01 .05
67T Francisco Cabrera .01 .05
68T Gary DiSarcina RC .08 .25
69T Greg Olson (C) RC .01 .05
70T Beau Allred RC .01 .05
71T Oscar Azocar .01 .05
72T Kent Mercker RC .08 .25
73T John Burkett .01 .05
74T Carlos Baerga RC .08 .25
75T Dave Hollins RC .08 .25
76T Todd Hundley RC .08 .25
77T Rick Parker RC .01 .05
78T Steve Cummings RC .01 .05
79T Bill Sampen RC .01 .05
80T Jerry Kutzler RC .01 .05
81T Derek Bell RC .08 .25
82T Kevin Tapani RC .08 .25
83T Jim Leyritz RC .08 .25
84T Ray Lankford RC .15 .40
85T Wayne Edwards RC .01 .05
86T Frank Thomas .75 2.00
87T Tim Naehring RC .02 .10
88T Willie Blair RC .02 .10
89T Alan Mills RC .02 .10
90T Scott Radinsky RC .02 .10
91T Howard Farmer RC .01 .05
92T Julio Machado RC .01 .05
93T Rafael Valdez RC .01 .05
94T Shawn Boskie RC .02 .10
95T David Segui RC .15 .40
96T Chris Hoiles RC .08 .25
97T D.J.Dozier RC .02 .10
98T Hector Villanueva RC .01 .05
99T Eric Gunderson RC .01 .05
100T Eric Lindros .40 1.00
101T Dave Otto .01 .05
102T Dana Kiecker RC .01 .05
103T Tim Drummond RC .01 .05
104T Mickey Pina RC .01 .05
105T Craig Grebeck RC .02 .10
106T Bernard Gilkey RC .08 .25
107T Tim Layana RC .01 .05
108T Scott Chiamparino RC .01 .05
109T Steve Avery .01 .05
110T Terry Shumpert RC .01 .05

1990 Score 100 Superstars

The 1990 Score Superstars set contains 100 standard size cards. The fronts are red, white, blue and purple. The vertically oriented backs feature a large color facial shot and career highlights. The cards were distributed as a set in a blister pack, which also included a full color booklet with more information about each player.

COMP.FACT.SET (100) 4.00 10.00
1 Kirby Puckett .30 .75
2 Steve Sax .01 .05
3 Tony Gwynn .60 1.50
4 Willie Randolph .02 .10
5 Jose Canseco .30 .75
6 Ozzie Smith .50 1.25
7 Rick Reuschel .01 .05
8 Bill Doran .01 .05
9 Mickey Tettleton .02 .10
10 Don Mattingly .50 1.25
11 Greg Swindell .01 .05
12 Bert Blyleven .02 .10
13 Dave Stewart .02 .10
14 Andres Galarraga .10 .30
15 Darryl Strawberry .02 .10
16 Ellis Burks .07 .20
17 Paul O'Neill .02 .10
18 Bruce Hurst .01 .05
19 Dave Smith .01 .05
20 Carney Lansford .02 .10
21 Robby Thompson .01 .05
22 Gary Gaetti .02 .10
23 Jeff Russell .01 .05
24 Chuck Finley .02 .10
25 Mark McGwire .50 1.25
26 Alvin Davis .01 .05
27 George Bell .01 .05
28 Cory Snyder .01 .05
29 Keith Hernandez .02 .10
30 Will Clark .10 .30
31 Steve Bedrosian .01 .05
32 Ryne Sandberg .40 1.00
33 Tom Browning .01 .05
34 Tim Burke .01 .05
35 John Smoltz .10 .30
36 Phil Bradley .01 .05
37 Bobby Bonilla .02 .10
38 Kirk McCaskill .01 .05
39 Dave Righetti .01 .05
40 Bo Jackson .20 .50
41 Alan Trammell .07 .20
42 Mike Moore UER .01 .05
(Uniform number is 21& not 23 as
43 Harold Reynolds .02 .10
44 Nolan Ryan 1.25 3.00
45 Fred McGriff .07 .20
46 Brian Downing .01 .05
47 Brett Butler .02 .10
48 Mike Scioscia .02 .10
49 John Franco .02 .10
50 Kevin Mitchell .01 .05
51 Mark Davis .01 .05
52 Glenn Davis .01 .05
53 Barry Bonds .50 1.25
54 Dwight Evans .02 .10
55 Terry Steinbach .01 .05
56 Dave Gallagher .01 .05
57 Roberto Kelly .01 .05
58 Rafael Palmeiro .20 .50
59 Joe Carter .02 .10
60 Mark Grace .10 .30
61 Pedro Guerrero .01 .05
62 Von Hayes .01 .05
63 Benito Santiago .02 .10
64 Dale Murphy .10 .30
65 John Smiley .01 .05
66 Cal Ripken 1.25 3.00
67 Mike Greenwell .01 .05
68 Devon White .01 .05
69 Ed Whitson .01 .05
70 Carlton Fisk .20 .50
71 Lou Whitaker .02 .10
72 Danny Tartabull .01 .05
73 Vince Coleman .01 .05
74 Andre Dawson .20 .50
75 Tim Raines .02 .10
76 George Brett .40 1.00
77 Tom Herr .01 .05
78 Andy Van Slyke .02 .10
79 Roger Clemens .60 1.50
80 Wade Boggs .30 .75
81 Wally Joyner .02 .10
82 Lonnie Smith .01 .05
83 Howard Johnson .01 .05
84 Julio Franco .02 .10
85 Ruben Sierra .02 .10
86 Dan Plesac .01 .05
87 Bobby Thigpen .01 .05

88 Kevin Seltzer .01 .05
89 Dave Stieb .01 .05
90 Rickey Henderson .40 1.00
91 Jeffrey Leonard .01 .05
92 Robin Yount .20 .50
93 Mitch Williams .01 .05
94 Orel Hershiser .02 .10
95 Eric Davis .02 .10
96 Mark Langston .01 .05
97 Mike Scott .01 .05
98 Paul Molitor .30 .75
99 Dwight Gooden .02 .10
100 Kevin Bass .01 .05

1990 Score McDonald's

This 25-card standard-size set was produced by Score for McDonald's restaurants; included with the set were 15 World Series Trivia cards. The player cards were given away four to a pack and free with the purchase of fries and a drink, at only 11 McDonald's in the United States (in Idaho and Eastern Oregon) during a special promotion which lasted approximately three weeks. The front has color action player photos, with white and yellow borders on a purple card face that fades as one moves toward the middle of the card. The upper left corner of the picture is cut off to allow space for the McDonald's logo; the player's name and team logo at the bottom round out the card face. The backs have color mugshots, biography, statistics, and career summary.

COMPLETE SET (25) 400.00 800.00
1 Will Clark 12.50 30.00
2 Sandy Alomar Jr. 1.00 2.50
3 Julio Franco 3.00 8.00
4 Carlton Fisk 12.50 30.00
5 Rickey Henderson 15.00 40.00
6 Matt Williams 5.00 12.50
7 John Franco 3.00 8.00
8 Ryne Sandberg 15.00 40.00
9 Kelly Gruber 1.00 2.50
10 Andre Dawson 8.00 20.00
11 Barry Bonds 12.50 30.00
12 Gary Sheffield 12.50 30.00
13 Ramon Martinez 1.00 2.50
14 Len Dykstra 3.00 8.00
15 Benito Santiago 3.00 8.00
16 Cecil Fielder 3.00 8.00
17 John Olerud 5.00 12.50
18 Roger Clemens 20.00 50.00
19 George Brett 15.00 40.00
20 George Bell 1.00 2.50
21 Ozzie Guillen 5.00 12.50
22 Steve Sax 1.00 2.50
23 Dave Stewart 3.00 8.00
24 Ozzie Smith 15.00 40.00
25 Robin Yount 12.50 30.00

1990 Score Rising Stars

The 1990 Score Rising Stars set contains 100 standard size cards. The fronts are green, blue and white. The vertically oriented backs feature a large color facial shot and career highlights. The cards were distributed as a set in a blister pack, which also included a full color booklet with more information about each player.

COMP.FACT.SET (100) 6.00 15.00
DISTRIBUTED IN FACTORY SET FORM ONLY
1 Tom Gordon .08 .25
2 Jerome Walton .02 .10
3 Ken Griffey Jr. 1.00 2.50
4 Dwight Smith .02 .10
5 Jim Abbott .15 .40
6 Todd Zeile .08 .25
7 Donn Pall .02 .10
8 Rick Reed .25 .60
9 Albert Belle .25 .60
10 Gregg Jefferies .08 .25
11 Kevin Ritz .02 .10
12 Charlie Hayes .02 .10
13 Kevin Appier .08 .25
14 Jeff Huson .02 .10
15 Gary Wayne .02 .10
16 Eric Yelding .02 .10
17 Clay Parker .02 .10
18 Junior Felix .02 .10
19 Derek Lilliquist .02 .10
20 Gary Sheffield .25 .60
21 Craig Worthington .02 .10
22 Jeff Brantley .02 .10
23 Eric Hetzel .02 .10
24 Greg W.Harris .02 .10
25 John Wetteland .25 .60
26 Joe Oliver .02 .10
27 Kevin Maas .08 .25
28 Kevin Brown .08 .25
29 Mike Stanton .02 .10
30 Greg Vaughn .02 .10
31 Ron Jones .02 .10
32 Gregg Olson .08 .25
33 Joe Girardi .15 .40
34 Ken Hill .08 .25
35 Sammy Sosa 1.25 3.00
36 Geronimo Berroa .02 .10
37 Omar Vizquel .25 .60
38 Dean Palmer .25 .60
39 John Olerud .40 1.00
40 Deion Sanders .25 .60
41 Randy Kramer .02 .10
42 Scott Lusader .02 .10
43 Dave Wayne Johnson .02 .10
44 Jeff Wetherby .02 .10
45 Eric Anthony .02 .10
46 Kenny Rogers .08 .25
47 Matt Winters .02 .10
48 Mauro Gozzo .02 .10
49 Carlos Quintana .02 .10
50 Bob Geren .02 .10
51 Chad Kreuter .02 .10
52 Randy Johnson .60 1.50
53 Hensley Meulens .02 .10
54 Gene Harris .02 .10
55 Bill Spiers .02 .10
56 Kelly Mann .02 .10
57 Tom McCarthy .02 .10
58 Steve Finley .08 .25
59 Ramon Martinez .02 .10
60 Greg Briley .02 .10
61 Jack Daugherty .02 .10
62 Tim Jones .02 .10
63 Doug Strange .02 .10
64 John Orton .02 .10
65 Scott Scudder .02 .10
66 Mark Gardner .02 .10
67 Mark Carreon .02 .10
68 Bob Milacki .02 .10
69 Andy Benes .08 .25
70 Carlos Martinez .02 .10
71 Jeff King .02 .10
72 Brad Arnsberg .02 .10
73 Rick Wrona .02 .10
74 Cris Carpenter .02 .10
75 Dennis Cook .02 .10
76 Pete Harnisch .02 .10
77 Greg Hibbard .02 .10
78 Ed Whited .02 .10
79 Scott Coolbaugh .02 .10
80 Billy Bates .02 .10
81 German Gonzalez .02 .10
82 Lance Blankenship .02 .10
83 Lenny Harris .02 .10
84 Milt Cuyler .02 .10
85 Erik Hanson .02 .10
86 Kent Anderson .02 .10
87 Hal Morris .02 .10
88 Mike Brumley .02 .10
89 Ken Patterson .02 .10
90 Mike Devereaux .02 .10
91 Greg Litton .02 .10
92 Rolando Roomes .02 .10
93 Ben McDonald .02 .10
94 Curt Schilling .75 2.00
95 Jose DeJesus .02 .10
96 Robin Ventura .25 .60
97 Steve Searcy .02 .10
98 Chip Hale .02 .10
99 Marquis Grissom .25 .60
100 Luis de los Santos .02 .10

1990 Score Sportflics Ryan

This standard-size card was issued by Optigraphics (producer of Score and Sportflics) to commemorate the 11th National Sports Card Collectors Convention held in Arlington, Texas in July of 1990. This card featured a Score front similar to the Ryan 1990 Score highlight card except for the 11th National Convention Logo on the bottom right of the card. On the other side a Ryan Sportflics card was printed that stated (reflected) either Sportflics or 1990 National Sports Collectors Convention on the bottom of the card. This issue was limited to a printing of 600 cards with Ryan himself destroying the printing plates.

NNO Nolan Ryan
(No number on back; 125.00 300.00
card back is actu

1990 Score Young Superstars I

1990 Score Young Superstars I are glossy full color cards featuring 42 standard-size cards of popular young players. The first series was issued with 1990 Score baseball rack packs while the second series was available only via a mailaway from the company.

COMPLETE SET (42) 4.00 10.00
ONE PER RACK PACK
1 Bo Jackson .50 1.25
2 Dwight Smith .08 .25
3 Albert Belle .50 1.25
4 Gregg Olson .20 .50
5 Jim Abbott .30 .75
6 Felix Fermin .08 .25
7 Brian Holman .08 .25
8 Clay Parker .08 .25
9 Junior Felix .08 .25
10 Joe Oliver .08 .25
11 Steve Finley .20 .50
12 Greg Briley .08 .25
13 Greg Vaughn .08 .25
14 Bill Spiers .08 .25
15 Eric Yelding .08 .25
16 Jose Gonzalez .08 .25
17 Mark Carreon .08 .25
18 Greg W. Harris .08 .25
19 Felix Jose .08 .25
20 Bob Milacki .08 .25
21 Kenny Rogers .20 .50
22 Rolando Roomes .08 .25
23 Bip Roberts .08 .25
24 Jeff Brantley .08 .25
25 Jeff Ballard .08 .25
26 John Dopson .08 .25
27 Ken Patterson .08 .25
28 Omar Vizquel .50 1.25
29 Kevin Brown .20 .50
30 Derek Lilliquist .08 .25
31 David Wells .20 .50
32 Ken Hill .20 .50
33 Greg Litton .08 .25
34 Rob Ducey .08 .25
35 Carlos Martinez .08 .25
36 John Smoltz .50 1.25
37 Lenny Harris .08 .25
38 Charlie Hayes .08 .25
39 Tommy Gregg .08 .25
40 John Wetteland .50 1.25
41 Jeff Huson .08 .25
42 Eric Anthony .08 .25

1990 Score Young Superstars II

1990 Score Young Superstars II are glossy full color cards featuring 42 standard-size cards of popular young players. Whereas the first series was issued with 1990 Score baseball rack packs, this second series was available only via a mailaway from the company.

COMP.FACT.SET (42) 10.00 25.00
DISTRIBUTED ONLY IN FACTORY SET FORM
1 Todd Zeile .20 .50
2 Ben McDonald .08 .25
3 Delino DeShields .60 1.50
4 Pat Combs .08 .25
5 John Olerud 1.25 3.00
6 Marquis Grissom .60 1.50
7 Mike Stanton .08 .25
8 Robin Ventura .60 1.50
9 Larry Walker 1.50 4.00
10 Dante Bichette .20 .50
11 Jack Armstrong .08 .25
12 Jay Bell .20 .50
13 Andy Benes .20 .50
14 Joey Cora .20 .50
15 Rob Dibble .20 .50
16 Jeff King .08 .25
17 Jeff Hamilton .08 .25
18 Erik Hanson .08 .25
19 Pete Harnisch .08 .25
20 Greg Hibbard .08 .25
21 Stan Javier .08 .25
22 Mark Lemke .08 .25
23 Steve Olin .20 .50
24 Tommy Greene .08 .25
25 Sammy Sosa 2.50 6.00
26 Gary Wayne .08 .25
27 Deion Sanders .60 1.50
28 Steve Wilson .08 .25
29 Joe Girardi .20 .50
30 John Orton .08 .25
31 Kevin Tapani .60 1.50
32 Carlos Baerga .20 .50
33 Glenallen Hill .08 .25
34 Mike Blowers .20 .50
35 Dave Hollins .20 .50
36 Lance Blankenship .08 .25
37 Hal Morris .08 .25
38 Lance Johnson .08 .25
39 Chris Gwynn .08 .25
40 Doug Dascenzo .08 .25
41 Jerald Clark .08 .25
42 Carlos Quintana .08 .25

1991 Score Promos

*PROMOS: 50X TO 100X BASIC CARDS

1991 Score

The 1991 Score set contains 893 standard-size cards issued in two separate series of 441 and 452 cards each. This set marks the fourth consecutive year that Score issued a major set but the first time Score issued the set in two series. Cards were distributed in plastic-wrap packs, blister packs and factory sets. The card fronts feature one of four different solid color borders (black, blue, teal and white) framing the full-color photo of the cards. Subsets include Rookie Prospects (331-379), First Draft Picks (380-391, 671-682), AL All-Stars (392-401), Master Blasters (402-406, 689-693), K-Men (407-411, 684-688), Rifleman (412-416, 694-698), NL All-Stars (661-670), No-Hitters (699-707), Franchise (849-874), Award Winners (875-881) and Dream Team (882-893). An American Flag card (737) was issued to honor the American soldiers involved in Desert Storm. Rookie Cards in the set include Carl Everett, Jeff Conine, Chipper Jones, Mike Mussina and Rondell White. There are a number of pitchers whose card backs show Innings Pitched totals which do not equal the added year-by-year total; the following card numbers were affected, 4, 24, 29, 30, 51, 81, 109, 111, 118, 141, 150, 156, 177, 204, 218, 232, 235, 255, 287, 289, 311, and 328.

COMPLETE SET (893) 8.00 20.00
COMP.FACT.SET (900) 10.00 25.00
SUBSET CARDS HALF VALUE OF BASE CARDS
1 Jose Canseco .05 .15
2 Ken Griffey Jr. .25 .60
3 Ryne Sandberg .15 .40
4 Nolan Ryan .40 1.00
5 Bo Jackson .08 .25
6 Bret Saberhagen UER .01 .05
In bio, missed
misspelled as mised
7 Will Clark .05 .15
8 Ellis Burks .02 .10
9 Joe Carter .02 .10
10 Rickey Henderson .08 .25
11 Ozzie Guillen .02 .10
12 Wade Boggs .05 .15
13 Jerome Walton .01 .05
14 John Franco .02 .10
15 Ricky Jordan UER .01 .05
League misspelled
as legue
16 Wally Backman .01 .05
17 Rob Dibble .02 .10
18 Glenn Braggs .01 .05
19 Cory Snyder .01 .05
20 Kal Daniels .01 .05
21 Mark Langston .01 .05
22 Kevin Gross .01 .05
23 Don Mattingly UER .25 .60
24 Dave Righetti .02 .10
25 Roberto Alomar .05 .15
26 Robby Thompson .01 .05
27 Jack McDowell .01 .05
28 Bip Roberts UER .01 .05
Bio reads playd
29 Jay Howell .01 .05
30 Dave Stieb UER .01 .05
17 wins in bio,
18 in stats
31 Johnny Ray .01 .05
32 Steve Sax .01 .05
33 Terry Mulholland .01 .05
34 Lee Guetterman .01 .05
35 Tim Raines .02 .10
36 Scott Fletcher .01 .05
37 Lance Parrish .02 .10
38 Tony Phillips UER .01 .05
Born 4/15(should be 4/25
39 Todd Stottlemyre .01 .05
40 Alan Trammell .02 .10
41 Todd Burns .01 .05
42 Mookie Wilson .02 .10
43 Chris Bosio .01 .05
44 Jeffrey Leonard .01 .05
45 Doug Jones .01 .05
46 Mike Scott UER .01 .05
In first line,
dominate should
read dominating
47 Andy Hawkins .01 .05
48 Harold Reynolds .02 .10
49 Paul Molitor .02 .10
50 John Farrell .01 .05
51 Danny Darwin .01 .05
52 Jeff Blauser .01 .05
53 John Tudor UER .01 .05
41 wins in '81
54 Milt Thompson .01 .05
55 Dave Justice .02 .10
56 Greg Olson .01 .05
57 Willie Blair .01 .05
58 Rick Parker .01 .05
59 Shawn Boskie .01 .05
60 Kevin Tapani .01 .05
61 Dave Hollins .01 .05
62 Scott Radinsky .01 .05
63 Francisco Cabrera .01 .05
64 Tim Layana .01 .05
65 Jim Leyritz .01 .05
66 Wayne Edwards .01 .05
67 Lee Stevens .01 .05
68 Bill Sampen UER .01 .05
Fourth line, long is spelled along
69 Craig Grebeck UER .01 .05
Born in Cerritos, not Johnstown
70 John Burkett .01 .05
71 Hector Villanueva .01 .05
72 Oscar Azocar .01 .05
73 Alan Mills .01 .05
74 Carlos Baerga .01 .05
75 Charles Nagy .01 .05
76 Tim Drummond .01 .05
77 Dana Kiecker .01 .05
78 Tom Edens RC .01 .05
79 Kent Mercker .01 .05
80 Steve Avery .01 .05
81 Lee Smith .02 .10
82 Dave Martinez .01 .05
83 Dave Winfield .02 .10
84 Bill Spiers .01 .05
85 Dan Pasqua .01 .05
86 Randy Milligan .01 .05
87 Tracy Jones .01 .05
88 Greg Myers .01 .05
89 Keith Hernandez .02 .10
90 Todd Benzinger .01 .05
91 Mike Jackson .01 .05
92 Mike Stanley .01 .05
93 Candy Maldonado .01 .05
94 John Kruk UER .02 .10
No decimal point
before 1990 BA
95 Cal Ripken UER .30 .75
96 Willie Fraser .01 .05
97 Mike Felder .01 .05
98 Bill Landrum .01 .05
99 Chuck Crim .01 .05
100 Chuck Finley .02 .10
101 Kirt Manwaring .01 .05
102 Jaime Navarro .01 .05
103 Dickie Thon .01 .05
104 Brian Downing .01 .05
105 Jim Abbott .05 .15
106 Tom Brookens .01 .05
107 Darryl Hamilton UER .01 .05
Bio info is for
Jeff Hamilton
108 Bryan Harvey .01 .05
109 Greg A. Harris UER .01 .05
Shown pitching lefty, bio says righty
110 Greg Swindell .01 .05
111 Juan Berenguer .01 .05
112 Mike Heath .01 .05
113 Scott Bradley .01 .05
114 Jack Morris .02 .10
115 Barry Jones .01 .05
116 Kevin Romine .01 .05
117 Garry Templeton .01 .05
118 Scott Sanderson .01 .05
119 Roberto Kelly .01 .05
120 George Brett .25 .60
121 Oddibe McDowell .01 .05
122 Jim Acker .01 .05
123 Bill Swift UER .01 .05
Born 12/27/61,
should be 10/27
124 Eric King .01 .05
125 Jay Buhner .02 .10
126 Matt Young .01 .05
127 Alvaro Espinoza .01 .05
128 Greg Hibbard .01 .05
129 Jeff M. Robinson .01 .05
130 Mike Greenwell .01 .05
131 Dion James .01 .05
132 Donn Pall UER .01 .05
1988 ERA in stats 0.00
133 Lloyd Moseby .01 .05
134 Randy Velarde .01 .05
135 Allan Anderson .01 .05
136 Mark Davis .01 .05
137 Eric Davis .02 .10
138 Phil Stephenson .01 .05
139 Felix Fermin .01 .05
140 Pedro Guerrero .02 .10
141 Charlie Hough .02 .10
142 Mike Henneman .01 .05
143 Jeff Montgomery .01 .05
144 Lenny Harris .01 .05
145 Bruce Hurst .01 .05
146 Eric Anthony .01 .05
147 Paul Assenmacher .01 .05
148 Jesse Barfield .01 .05
149 Carlos Quintana .01 .05
150 Dave Stewart .02 .10
151 Roy Smith .01 .05
152 Paul Gibson .01 .05
153 Mickey Hatcher .01 .05
154 Jim Eisenreich .01 .05
155 Kenny Rogers .02 .10
156 Dave Schmidt .01 .05
157 Lance Johnson .01 .05
158 Dave West .01 .05
159 Steve Balboni .01 .05
160 Jeff Brantley .01 .05
161 Craig Biggio .05 .15
162 Brook Jacoby .01 .05
163 Dan Gladden .01 .05
164 Jeff Reardon UER .02 .10
Total IP shown as
943.2, should be 943.1
165 Mark Carreon .01 .05
166 Mel Hall .01 .05
167 Gary Mielke .01 .05
168 Cecil Fielder .02 .10
169 Darrin Jackson .01 .05
170 Rick Aguilera .02 .10
171 Walt Weiss .01 .05
172 Steve Farr .01 .05
173 Jody Reed .01 .05
174 Mike Jeffcoat .01 .05
175 Mark Grace .05 .15
176 Larry Sheets .01 .05
177 Bill Gullickson .01 .05
178 Chris Gwynn .01 .05
179 Melido Perez .01 .05
180 Sid Fernandez UER .01 .05
779 runs in 1990
181 Tim Burke .01 .05
182 Gary Pettis .01 .05
183 Rob Murphy .01 .05
184 Craig Lefferts .01 .05
185 Howard Johnson .01 .05
186 Ken Caminiti .02 .10
187 Tim Belcher .01 .05
188 Greg Cadaret .01 .05
189 Matt Williams .02 .10
190 Dave Magadan .01 .05
191 Geno Petralli .01 .05
192 Jeff D. Robinson .01 .05
193 Jim Deshaies .01 .05
194 Willie Randolph .02 .10
195 George Bell .01 .05
196 Hubie Brooks .01 .05
197 Tom Gordon .01 .05
198 Mike Fitzgerald .01 .05
199 Mike Pagliarulo .01 .05
200 Kirby Puckett .08 .25
201 Shawon Dunston .01 .05
202 Dennis Boyd .01 .05
203 Junior Felix UER .01 .05
Text has him in NL
204 Alejandro Pena .01 .05
205 Pete Smith .01 .05
206 Tom Glavine UER .05 .15
Lefty spelled leftie
207 Luis Salazar .01 .05
208 John Smoltz .05 .15
209 Doug Dascenzo .01 .05
210 Tim Wallach .01 .05
211 Greg Gagne .01 .05
212 Mark Gubicza .01 .05
213 Mark Parent .01 .05
214 Ken Oberkfell .01 .05
215 Gary Carter .02 .10
216 Rafael Palmeiro .05 .15
217 Tom Niedenfuer .01 .05
218 Dave LaPoint .01 .05
219 Jeff Treadway .01 .05
220 Mitch Williams UER .01 .05
'89 ERA shown as 2.76,
should be 2.64
221 Jose DeLeon .01 .05
222 Mike LaValliere .01 .05
223 Darrel Akerfelds .01 .05
224A Kent Anderson ERR .02 .10
First line& flachy
should read flashy
224B Kent Anderson COR .02 .10
Corrected in
factory sets
225 Dwight Evans .05 .15
226 Gary Redus .01 .05
227 Paul O'Neill .05 .15
228 Marty Barrett .01 .05
229 Tom Browning .01 .05
230 Terry Pendleton .02 .10
231 Jack Armstrong .01 .05
232 Mike Boddicker .01 .05
233 Neal Heaton .01 .05
234 Marquis Grissom .02 .10
235 Bert Blyleven .02 .10
236 Curt Young .01 .05
237 Don Carman .01 .05
238 Charlie Hayes .01 .05
239 Mark Knudson .01 .05
240 Todd Zeile .01 .05
241 Larry Walker UER .08 .25
Maple River, should
be Maple Ridge
242 Jerald Clark .01 .05
243 Jeff Ballard .01 .05
244 Jeff King .01 .05
245 Tom Brunansky .01 .05
246 Darren Daulton .02 .10
247 Scott Terry .01 .05
248 Rob Deer .01 .05
249 Brady Anderson UER .02 .10
1990 Hagerstown 1 hit,
should say 13 hits
250 Len Dykstra .02 .10
251 Greg W. Harris .01 .05
252 Mike Hartley .01 .05
253 Joey Cora .01 .05
254 Ivan Calderon .01 .05
255 Ted Power .01 .05
256 Sammy Sosa .08 .25
257 Steve Buechele .01 .05
258 Mike Devereaux UER .01 .05
No comma between
city and state
259 Brad Komminsk UER .01 .05
Last text line,
Ba should be BA
260 Ted Higuera .01 .05
261 Shawn Abner .01 .05
262 Dave Valle .01 .05
263 Jeff Huson .01 .05
264 Edgar Martinez .05 .15
265 Carlton Fisk .05 .15
266 Steve Finley .02 .10
267 John Wetteland .02 .10
268 Kevin Appier .02 .10
269 Steve Lyons .01 .05
270 Mickey Tettleton .01 .05
271 Luis Rivera .01 .05
272 Steve Jeltz .01 .05
273 R.J. Reynolds .01 .05
274 Carlos Martinez .01 .05
275 Dan Plesac .01 .05
276 Mike Morgan UER .01 .05
Total IP shown as
1149.1, should be 1149
277 Jeff Russell .01 .05
278 Pete Incaviglia .01 .05
279 Kevin Seitzer UER .01 .05
Bio has 200 hits twice
and .300 four times,
should be once and
three times
280 Bobby Thigpen .01 .05
281 Stan Javier UER .01 .05
Born 1/9,
should say 9/1
282 Henry Cotto .01 .05
283 Gary Wayne .01 .05
284 Shane Mack .01 .05
285 Brian Holman .01 .05
286 Gerald Perry .01 .05
287 Steve Crawford .01 .05
288 Nelson Liriano .01 .05
289 Don Aase .01 .05
290 Randy Johnson .10 .30
291 Harold Baines .02 .10
292 Kent Hrbek .02 .10
293A Les Lancaster ERR .01 .05
No comma between
Dallas and Texas
293B Les Lancaster COR .01 .05
Corrected in
factory sets
294 Jeff Musselman .01 .05
295 Kurt Stillwell .01 .05
296 Stan Belinda .01 .05
297 Lou Whitaker .02 .10
298 Glenn Wilson .01 .05
299 Omar Vizquel UER .05 .15
Born 5/15, should be
4/24, there is a decimal
before GP total for '90
300 Ramon Martinez .01 .05
301 Dwight Smith .01 .05
302 Tim Crews .01 .05
303 Lance Blankenship .01 .05
304 Sid Bream .01 .05
305 Rafael Ramirez .01 .05
306 Steve Wilson .01 .05
307 Mackey Sasser .01 .05
308 Franklin Stubbs .01 .05
309 Jack Daugherty UER .01 .05
Born 6/3/60,
should say July
310 Eddie Murray .08 .25
311 Bob Welch .01 .05
312 Brian Harper .01 .05
313 Lance McCullers .01 .05
314 Dave Smith .01 .05
315 Bobby Bonilla .02 .10
316 Jerry Don Gleaton .01 .05
317 Greg Maddux .15 .40
318 Keith Miller .01 .05
319 Mark Portugal .01 .05
320 Robin Ventura .02 .10
321 Bob Ojeda .01 .05
322 Mike Harkey .01 .05
323 Jay Bell .02 .10
324 Mark McGwire .30 .75
325 Gary Gaetti .02 .10
326 Jeff Pico .01 .05
327 Kevin McReynolds .01 .05
328 Frank Tanana .01 .05
329 Eric Yelding UER .01 .05
Listed as 6'3
should be 5'11
330 Barry Bonds .40 1.00
331 Brian McRae RC .08 .25
332 Pedro Munoz RC .02 .10
333 Daryl Irvine RC .01 .05
334 Chris Hoiles .01 .05
335 Thomas Howard .01 .05
336 Jeff Schulz RC .01 .05
337 Jeff Manto .01 .05
338 Beau Allred .01 .05
339 Mike Bordick RC .15 .40
340 Todd Hundley .01 .05
341 Jim Vatcher UER RC .01 .05
342 Luis Sojo .01 .05
343 Jose Offerman UER .01 .05
Born 1969, should
say 1968
344 Pete Coachman RC .01 .05
345 Mike Benjamin .01 .05
346 Ozzie Canseco .01 .05
347 Tim McIntosh .01 .05
348 Phil Plantier RC .02 .10
349 Terry Shumpert .01 .05
350 Darren Lewis .01 .05
351 David Walsh RC .01 .05
352A Scott Chiamparino .02 .10
ERR
Bats left, should be right
352B Scott Chiamparino .02 .10
COR
corrected in factory sets
353 Julio Valera .01 .05
UER Progressed mis-
spelled as progressed
354 Anthony Telford RC .01 .05
355 Kevin Wickander .01 .05
356 Tim Naehring .01 .05
357 Jim Poole .01 .05
358 Mark Whiten UER .01 .05
Shown hitting lefty, bio says righty
359 Terry Wells RC .01 .05
360 Rafael Valdez .01 .05
361 Mel Stottlemyre Jr. .01 .05
362 David Segui .01 .05
363 Paul Abbott RC .01 .05
364 Steve Howard .01 .05
365 Karl Rhodes .01 .05
366 Rafael Novoa RC .01 .05
367 Joe Grahe RC .01 .05
368 Darren Reed .01 .05

369 Jeff McKnight .01 .05
370 Scott Leius .01 .05
371 Mark Dewey RC .01 .05
372 Mark Lee UER RC .02 .10
373 Rosario Rodriguez UER RC .01 .05
374 Chuck McElroy .01 .05
375 Mike Bell RC .01 .05
376 Mickey Morandini .01 .05
377 Bill Haselman RC .01 .05
378 Dave Pavlas RC .01 .05
379 Derrick May .01 .05
380 Jeromy Burnitz RC .15 .40
381 Donald Peters RC .01 .05
382 Alex Fernandez FDP .01 .05
383 Mike Mussina RC 1.00 2.50
384 Dan Smith RC .02 .10
385 Lance Dickson RC .02 .10
386 Carl Everett RC .20 .50
387 Tom Nevers RC .02 .10
388 Adam Hyzdu RC .08 .25
389 Todd Van Poppel RC .08 .25
390 Rondell White RC .15 .40
391 Marc Newfield RC .02 .10
392 Julio Franco AS .01 .05
393 Wade Boggs AS .02 .10
394 Ozzie Guillen AS .01 .05
395 Cecil Fielder AS .01 .05
396 Ken Griffey Jr. AS .10 .30
397 Rickey Henderson AS .05 .15
398 Jose Canseco AS .02 .10
399 Roger Clemens AS .15 .40
400 Sandy Alomar Jr. AS .01 .05
401 Bobby Thigpen AS .01 .05
402 Bobby Bonilla MB .01 .05
403 Eric Davis MB .01 .05
404 Fred McGriff MB .02 .10
405 Glenn Davis MB .01 .05
406 Kevin Mitchell MB .01 .05
407 Rob Dibble KM .01 .05
408 Ramon Martinez KM .01 .05
409 David Cone KM .01 .05
410 Bobby Witt KM .01 .05
411 Mark Langston KM .01 .05
412 Bo Jackson RIF .02 .10
413 Shawon Dunston RIF .01 .05
UER
In the baseball, should say in baseball
414 Jesse Barfield RIF .01 .05
415 Ken Caminiti RIF .01 .05
416 Benito Santiago RIF .01 .05
417 Nolan Ryan HL .20 .50
418 Bobby Thigpen HL UER .01 .05
Back refers to Hal
McRae Jr., should
say Brian McRae
419 Ramon Martinez HL .01 .05
420 Bo Jackson HL .02 .10
421 Carlton Fisk HL .02 .10
422 Jimmy Key .02 .10
423 Junior Noboa .01 .05
424 Al Newman .01 .05
425 Pat Borders .01 .05
426 Von Hayes .01 .05
427 Tim Teufel .01 .05
428 Eric Plunk UER .01 .05
Text says Eric's had, no apostrophe needed
429 John Moses .01 .05
430 Mike Witt .01 .05
431 Otis Nixon .01 .05
432 Tony Fernandez .01 .05
433 Rance Mulliniks .01 .05
434 Dan Petry .01 .05
435 Bob Geren .01 .05
436 Steve Frey .01 .05
437 Jamie Moyer .02 .10
438 Junior Ortiz .01 .05
439 Tom O'Malley .01 .05
440 Pat Combs .01 .05
441 Jose Canseco DT .05 .15
442 Alfredo Griffin .01 .05
443 Andres Galarraga .02 .10
444 Bryn Smith .01 .05
445 Andre Dawson .02 .10
446 Juan Samuel .01 .05
447 Mike Aldrete .01 .05
448 Ron Gant .02 .10
449 Fernando Valenzuela .02 .10
450 Vince Coleman UER .01 .05
Should say topped
majors in steals four
times, not three times
451 Kevin Mitchell .01 .05
452 Spike Owen .01 .05
453 Mike Bielecki .01 .05
454 Dennis Martinez .02 .10
455 Brett Butler .02 .10
456 Ron Darling .01 .05
457 Dennis Rasmussen .01 .05
458 Ken Howell .01 .05
459 Steve Bedrosian .01 .05
460 Frank Viola .02 .10
461 Jose Lind .01 .05
462 Chris Sabo .01 .05
463 Dante Bichette .02 .10
464 Rick Mahler .01 .05
465 John Smiley .01 .05
466 Devon White .02 .10
467 John Orton .01 .05
468 Mike Stanton .01 .05
469 Billy Hatcher .01 .05
470 Wally Joyner .02 .10
471 Gene Larkin .01 .05
472 Doug Drabek .01 .05
473 Gary Sheffield .02 .10
474 David Wells .02 .10
475 Andy Van Slyke .05 .15
476 Mike Gallego .01 .05
477 B.J. Surhoff .02 .10
478 Gene Nelson .01 .05
479 Mariano Duncan .01 .05
480 Fred McGriff .05 .15
481 Jerry Browne .01 .05
482 Alvin Davis .01 .05
483 Bill Wegman .01 .05
484 Dave Parker .02 .10
485 Dennis Eckersley .02 .10
486 Erik Hanson UER .01 .05
Basketball misspelled
as baseketball
487 Bill Ripken .01 .05
488 Tom Candiotti .01 .05
489 Mike Schooler .01 .05
490 Gregg Olson .01 .05
491 Chris James .01 .05
492 Pete Harnisch .01 .05
493 Julio Franco .02 .10
494 Greg Briley .01 .05
495 Ruben Sierra .02 .10
496 Steve Olin .01 .05
497 Mike Fetters .01 .05
498 Mark Williamson .01 .05
499 Bob Tewksbury .01 .05
500 Tony Gwynn .10 .30
501 Randy Myers .01 .05
502 Keith Comstock .01 .05
503 Craig Worthington UER .01 .05
DeCinces misspelled
DiCinces on back
504 Mark Eichhorn UER .01 .05
Stats incomplete,
doesn't have '89 Braves stint
505 Barry Larkin .05 .15
506 Dave Johnson .01 .05
507 Bobby Witt .01 .05
508 Joe Orsulak .01 .05
509 Pete O'Brien .01 .05
510 Brad Arnsberg .01 .05
511 Storm Davis .01 .05
512 Bob Milacki .01 .05
513 Bill Pecota .01 .05
514 Glenallen Hill .01 .05
515 Danny Tartabull .01 .05
516 Mike Moore .01 .05
517 Ron Robinson UER .01 .05
577 K's in 1990
518 Mark Gardner .01 .05
519 Rick Wrona .01 .05
520 Mike Scioscia .01 .05
521 Frank Wills .01 .05
522 Greg Brock .01 .05
523 Jack Clark .02 .10
524 Bruce Ruffin .01 .05
525 Robin Yount .15 .40
526 Tom Foley .01 .05
527 Pat Perry .01 .05
528 Greg Vaughn .01 .05
529 Wally Whitehurst .01 .05
530 Norm Charlton .01 .05
531 Marvell Wynne .01 .05
532 Jim Gantner .01 .05
533 Greg Litton .01 .05
534 Manny Lee .01 .05
535 Scott Bailes .01 .05
536 Charlie Leibrandt .01 .05
537 Roger McDowell .01 .05
538 Andy Benes .01 .05
539 Rick Honeycutt .01 .05
540 Dwight Gooden .02 .10
541 Scott Garrelts .01 .05
542 Dave Clark .01 .05
543 Lonnie Smith .01 .05
544 Rick Reuschel .01 .05
545 Delino DeShields UER .02 .10
Rockford misspelled
as Rock Ford in '88
546 Mike Sharperson .01 .05
547 Mike Kingery .01 .05
548 Terry Kennedy .01 .05
549 David Cone .02 .10
550 Orel Hershiser .02 .10
551 Matt Nokes .01 .05
552 Eddie Williams .01 .05
553 Frank DiPino .01 .05
554 Fred Lynn .01 .05
555 Alex Cole .01 .05
556 Terry Leach .01 .05
557 Chet Lemon .01 .05
558 Paul Mirabella .01 .05
559 Bill Long .01 .05
560 Phil Bradley .01 .05
561 Duane Ward .01 .05
562 Dave Bergman .01 .05
563 Eric Show .01 .05
564 Xavier Hernandez .01 .05
565 Jeff Parrett .01 .05
566 Chuck Cary .01 .05
567 Ken Hill .01 .05
568 Bob Welch Hand .01 .05
Complement should be
compliment UER
569 John Mitchell .01 .05
570 Travis Fryman .02 .10
571 Derek Lilliquist .01 .05
572 Steve Lake .01 .05
573 John Barfield .01 .05
574 Randy Bush .01 .05
575 Joe Magrane .01 .05
576 Eddie Diaz .01 .05
577 Casey Candaele .01 .05
578 Jesse Orosco .01 .05
579 Tom Henke .01 .05
580 Rick Cerone UER .01 .05
Actually his third
go-round with Yankees
581 Drew Hall .01 .05
582 Tony Castillo .01 .05
583 Jimmy Jones .01 .05
584 Rick Reed .01 .05
585 Joe Girardi .01 .05
586 Jeff Gray RC .01 .05
587 Luis Polonia .01 .05
588 Joe Klink .01 .05
589 Rex Hudler .01 .05
590 Kirk McCaskill .01 .05
591 Juan Agosto .01 .05
592 Wes Gardner .01 .05
593 Rich Rodriguez RC .01 .05
594 Mitch Webster .01 .05
595 Kelly Gruber .01 .05
596 Dale Mohorcic .01 .05
597 Willie McGee .02 .10
598 Bill Krueger .01 .05
599 Bob Walk UER .01 .05
Cards says he's 33,
but actually he's 34
600 Kevin Maas .01 .05
601 Danny Jackson .01 .05
602 Craig McMurtry UER .01 .05
Anonymously misspelled
anonimously
603 Curtis Wilkerson .01 .05
604 Adam Peterson .01 .05
605 Sam Horn .01 .05
606 Tommy Gregg .01 .05
607 Ken Dayley .01 .05
608 Carmelo Castillo .01 .05
609 John Shelby .01 .05
610 Don Slaught .01 .05
611 Calvin Schiraldi .01 .05
612 Dennis Lamp .01 .05
613 Andres Thomas .01 .05
614 Jose Gonzalez .01 .05
615 Randy Ready .01 .05
616 Kevin Bass .01 .05
617 Mike Marshall .01 .05
618 Daryl Boston .01 .05
619 Andy McGaffigan .01 .05
620 Joe Oliver .01 .05
621 Jim Gott .01 .05
622 Jose Oquendo .01 .05
623 Jose DeJesus .01 .05
624 Mike Brumley .01 .05
625 John Olerud .02 .10
626 Ernest Riles .01 .05
627 Gene Harris .01 .05
628 Jose Uribe .01 .05
629 Darnell Coles .01 .05
630 Carney Lansford .02 .10
631 Tim Leary .01 .05
632 Tim Hulett .01 .05
633 Kevin Elster .01 .05
634 Tony Fossas .01 .05
635 Francisco Oliveras .01 .05
636 Bob Patterson .01 .05
637 Gary Ward .01 .05
638 Rene Gonzales .01 .05
639 Don Robinson .01 .05
640 Darryl Strawberry .02 .10
641 Dave Anderson .01 .05
642 Scott Scudder .01 .05
643 Reggie Harris UER .01 .05
Hepatitis misspelled
as hepititis
644 Dave Henderson .01 .05
645 Ben McDonald .01 .05
646 Bob Kipper .01 .05
647 Hal Morris UER .01 .05
It's should be its
648 Tim Birtsas .01 .05
649 Steve Searcy .01 .05
650 Dale Murphy .05 .15
651 Ron Oester .01 .05
652 Mike LaCoss .01 .05
653 Ron Jones .01 .05
654 Kelly Downs .01 .05
655 Roger Clemens .30 .75
656 Herm Winningham .01 .05
657 Trevor Wilson .01 .05
658 Jose Rijo .01 .05
659 Dann Bilardello UER .01 .05
Bio has 13 games, 1 hit,
and 32 AB, stats show 19, 2, and 37
660 Gregg Jefferies .01 .05
661 Doug Drabek AS UER .01 .05
Through is mis-
spelled though
662 Randy Myers AS .01 .05
663 Benny Santiago AS .01 .05
664 Will Clark AS .02 .10
665 Ryne Sandberg AS .08 .25
666 Barry Larkin AS UER .02 .10
Line 13, coolly misspelled cooly
667 Matt Williams AS .01 .05
668 Barry Bonds AS .20 .50
669 Eric Davis AS .01 .05
670 Bobby Bonilla AS .01 .05
671 Chipper Jones RC 2.00 5.00
672 Eric Christopherson RC .02 .10
673 Robbie Beckett RC .02 .10
674 Shane Andrews RC .08 .25
675 Steve Karsay RC .08 .25
676 Aaron Holbert RC .02 .10
677 Donovan Osborne RC .02 .10
678 Todd Ritchie RC .08 .25
679 Ronnie Walden RC .02 .10
680 Tim Costo RC .02 .10
681 Dan Wilson RC .08 .25
682 Kurt Miller RC .02 .10
683 Mike Lieberthal RC .15 .40
684 Roger Clemens KM .15 .40
685 Dwight Gooden KM .01 .05
686 Nolan Ryan KM .20 .50
687 Frank Viola KM .01 .05
688 Erik Hanson KM .01 .05
689 Matt Williams MB .01 .05
690 Jose Canseco MB UER .02 .10
Mammoth misspelled
as monmouth
691 Darryl Strawberry MB .01 .05
692 Bo Jackson MB .02 .10
693 Cecil Fielder MB .01 .05
694 Sandy Alomar Jr. RF .01 .05
695 Cory Snyder RF .01 .05
696 Eric Davis RF .01 .05
697 Ken Griffey Jr. RF .10 .30
698 Andy Van Slyke RF UER .02 .10
Line 2, outfielders
does not need
699 Mark Langston NH .01 .05
Mike Witt
700 Randy Johnson NH .05 .15
701 Nolan Ryan NH .20 .50
702 Dave Stewart NH .01 .05
703 Fernando Valenzuela NH .01 .05
704 Andy Hawkins NH .01 .05
705 Melido Perez NH .01 .05
706 Terry Mulholland NH .01 .05
707 Dave Stieb NH .01 .05
708 Brian Barnes RC .01 .05
709 Bernard Gilkey .01 .05
710 Steve Decker RC .01 .05
711 Paul Faries RC .01 .05
712 Paul Marak RC .01 .05
713 Wes Chamberlain RC .02 .10
714 Kevin Belcher RC .01 .05
715 Dan Boone UER .01 .05
IP adds up to 101,
but card has 101.2
716 Steve Adkins RC .01 .05
717 Geronimo Pena .01 .05
718 Howard Farmer .01 .05
719 Mark Leonard RC .01 .05
720 Tom Lampkin .01 .05
721 Mike Gardiner RC .01 .05
722 Jeff Conine RC .15 .40
723 Efrain Valdez RC .01 .05
724 Chuck Malone .01 .05
725 Leo Gomez .01 .05
726 Paul McClellan RC .01 .05
727 Mark Leiter RC .02 .10
728 Rich DeLucia UER RC .01 .05
729 Mel Rojas .01 .05
730 Hector Wagner RC .01 .05
731 Ray Lankford .02 .10
732 Turner Ward RC .02 .10
733 Gerald Alexander RC .01 .05
734 Scott Anderson RC .01 .05
735 Tony Perezchica .01 .05
736 Jimmy Kremers .01 .05
737 American Flag .08 .25
Pray for Peace
738 Mike York RC .01 .05
739 Mike Rochford .01 .05
740 Scott Aldred .01 .05
741 Rico Brogna .01 .05
742 Dave Burba RC .08 .25
743 Ray Stephens RC .01 .05
744 Eric Gunderson .01 .05
745 Troy Afenir RC .01 .05
746 Jeff Shaw .01 .05
747 Orlando Merced RC .02 .10
748 Omar Olivares UER RC .02 .10
749 Jerry Kutzler .01 .05
750 Mo Vaughn UER .02 .10
44 SB's in 1990
751 Matt Stark RC .01 .05
752 Randy Hennis RC .01 .05
753 Andujar Cedeno .01 .05
754 Kelvin Torve .01 .05
755 Joe Kraemer .01 .05
756 Phil Clark RC .02 .10
757 Ed Vosberg RC .01 .05
758 Mike Perez RC .02 .10
759 Scott Lewis RC .01 .05
760 Steve Chitren RC .01 .05
761 Ray Young RC .01 .05
762 Andres Santana .01 .05
763 Rodney McCray RC .01 .05
764 Sean Berry UER RC .02 .10
765 Brent Mayne .01 .05
766 Mike Simms RC .01 .05
767 Glenn Sutko RC .01 .05
768 Gary DiSarcina .01 .05
769 George Brett HL .08 .25
770 Cecil Fielder HL .01 .05
771 Jim Presley .01 .05
772 John Dopson .01 .05
773 Bo Jackson Breaker .02 .10
774 Brent Knackert UER .01 .05
Born in 1954,
shown throwing righty,
but bio says lefty
775 Bill Doran UER .01 .05
Reds in NL East
776 Dick Schofield .01 .05
777 Nelson Santovenia .01 .05
778 Mark Guthrie .01 .05
779 Mark Lemke .01 .05
780 Terry Steinbach .01 .05
781 Tom Bolton .01 .05
782 Randy Tomlin RC .02 .10
783 Jeff Kunkel .01 .05
784 Felix Jose .01 .05
785 Rick Sutcliffe .02 .10
786 John Cerutti .01 .05
787 Jose Vizcaino UER .01 .05
Offerman, not Opperman
788 Curt Schilling .08 .25
789 Ed Whitson .01 .05
790 Tony Pena .01 .05
791 John Candelaria .01 .05
792 Carmelo Martinez .01 .05
793 Sandy Alomar Jr. UER .01 .05
Indian's should
say Indians'
794 Jim Neidlinger RC .01 .05
795 Barry Larkin WS .02 .10
and Chris Sabo
796 Paul Sorrento .01 .05
797 Tom Pagnozzi .01 .05
798 Tino Martinez .08 .25
799 Scott Ruskin UER .01 .05
Text says first three
seasons but lists
averages for four
800 Kirk Gibson .02 .10
801 Walt Terrell .01 .05
802 John Russell .01 .05
803 Chili Davis .02 .10
804 Chris Nabholz .01 .05
805 Juan Gonzalez .08 .25
806 Ron Hassey .01 .05
807 Todd Worrell .01 .05
808 Tommy Greene .01 .05
809 Joel Skinner UER .01 .05
Joel, not Bob, was drafted in 1979
810 Benito Santiago .02 .10
811 Pat Tabler UER .01 .05
Line 3, always misspelled alway
812 Scott Erickson UER RC .01 .05
813 Moises Alou .02 .10
814 Dale Sveum .01 .05
815 Ryne Sandberg MANYR .08 .25
816 Rick Dempsey .01 .05
817 Scott Bankhead .01 .05
818 Jason Grimsley .01 .05
819 Doug Jennings .01 .05
820 Tom Herr .01 .05
821 Rob Ducey .01 .05
822 Luis Quinones .01 .05
823 Greg Minton .01 .05
824 Mark Grant .01 .05
825 Ozzie Smith UER .15 .40
826 Dave Eiland .01 .05
827 Danny Heep .01 .05
828 Hensley Meulens .01 .05
829 Charlie O'Brien .01 .05
830 Glenn Davis .01 .05
831 John Marzano UER .01 .05
International mis-
spelled Internaional
832 Steve Ontiveros .01 .05
833 Ron Karkovice .01 .05
834 Jerry Goff .01 .05
835 Ken Griffey Sr. .02 .10
836 Kevin Reimer .01 .05
837 Randy Kutcher UER .01 .05
Infectious mis-
spelled infectous
838 Mike Blowers .01 .05
839 Mike Macfarlane .01 .05
840 Frank Thomas UER .08 .25
1989 Sarasota stats,
15 games but 188 AB
841 K.Griffey Jr./K.Griffey Sr. .20 .50
842 Jack Howell .01 .05
843 Goose Gozzo .01 .05
844 Gerald Young .01 .05
845 Zane Smith .01 .05
846 Kevin Brown .02 .10
847 Sil Campusano .01 .05
848 Larry Andersen .01 .05
849 Cal Ripken FRAN .15 .40
850 Roger Clemens FRAN .15 .40
851 Sandy Alomar Jr. FRAN .01 .05
852 Alan Trammell FRAN .02 .10
853 George Brett FRAN .08 .25
854 Robin Yount FRAN .08 .25
855 Kirby Puckett FRAN .05 .15
856 Don Mattingly FRAN .10 .30
857 Rickey Henderson FRAN .05 .15
858 Ken Griffey Jr. FRAN .15 .40
859 Ruben Sierra FRAN .01 .05
860 John Olerud FRAN .01 .05
861 Dave Justice FRAN .01 .05
862 Ryne Sandberg FRAN .08 .25
863 Eric Davis FRAN .01 .05
864 Darryl Strawberry FRAN .01 .05
865 Tim Wallach FRAN .01 .05
866 Dwight Gooden FRAN .01 .05
867 Len Dykstra FRAN .01 .05
868 Barry Bonds FRAN .20 .50
869 Todd Zeile FRAN UER .01 .05
Powerful misspelled
as poweful
870 Benito Santiago FRAN .01 .05
871 Will Clark FRAN .02 .10
872 Craig Biggio FRAN .02 .10
873 Wally Joyner FRAN .01 .05
874 Frank Thomas FRAN .05 .15
875 Rickey Henderson MVP .05 .15
876 Barry Bonds MVP .20 .50
877 Bob Welch CY .01 .05
878 Doug Drabek CY .01 .05
879 Sandy Alomar Jr. ROY .01 .05
880 Dave Justice ROY .01 .05
881 Damon Berryhill .01 .05
882 Frank Viola DT .01 .05
883 Dave Stewart DT .01 .05
884 Doug Jones DT .01 .05
885 Randy Myers DT .01 .05
886 Will Clark DT .02 .10
887 Roberto Alomar DT .02 .10
888 Barry Larkin DT .02 .10
889 Wade Boggs DT .05 .15
890 Rickey Henderson DT .08 .25
891 Kirby Puckett DT .05 .15
892 Ken Griffey Jr DT .25 .60
893 Benny Santiago DT .02 .10

1991 Score Cooperstown

This seven-card standard-size set was available only in complete set form as an insert with 1991 Score factory sets. The card design is not like the regular 1991 Score cards. The card front features a portrait of the player in an oval on a white background. The words "Cooperstown Card" are prominently displayed on the front. The cards are numbered on the back with a B prefix.

COMPLETE SET (7) 2.50 6.00
ONE SET PER FACTORY SET
B1 Wade Boggs .25 .60
B2 Barry Larkin .25 .60
B3 Ken Griffey Jr. 1.00 2.50
B4 Rickey Henderson .40 1.00
B5 George Brett 1.00 2.50
B6 Will Clark .25 .60
B7 Nolan Ryan 1.50 4.00

1991 Score Hot Rookies

This ten-card standard-size set was inserted in the one per 1991 Score 100-card blister pack. The front features a color action player photo, with white borders and the words "Hot Rookie" in yellow above the picture. The card background shades from orange to yellow to orange as one moves down the card face. In a horizontal format, the left half of the back has a color head shot, while the right half has career summary.

COMPLETE SET (10) 3.00 8.00
ONE PER BLISTER PACK
1 David Justice .40 1.00
2 Kevin Maas .20 .50
3 Hal Morris .20 .50
4 Frank Thomas .75 2.00
5 Jeff Conine .40 1.00
6 Sandy Alomar Jr. .20 .50
7 Ray Lankford .40 1.00
8 Steve Decker .20 .50
9 Juan Gonzalez .75 2.00
10 Jose Offerman .20 .50

1991 Score Mantle

This seven-card standard-size set features Mickey Mantle at various points in his career. The fronts are full-color glossy shots of Mantle while the backs are in a horizontal format with a full-color photo and some narrative information. The cards were randomly inserted in second series packs. 2,500 serial numbered cards were actually signed by Mantle and stamped with certification press. A similar version of this set was also released to dealers and media members on Score's mailing list and was individually numbered to 5,000 on the back. The cards were sent in seven-card packs. The card number and the set serial number appear on the back.

COMPLETE SET (7) 20.00 50.00
COMMON MANTLE (1-7) 6.00 15.00
RANDOM INSERTS IN SER.2 PACKS
ONE PROMO SET SENT TO EACH DEALER
DEALER PROMOS NUMBERED OUT OF 5000
AU Mickey Mantle AU/2500 250.00 500.00

1991 Score Mantle Promos

COMPLETE SET (7) 20.00 50.00
COMMON MANTLE 4.00 10.00

1991 Score Rookie/Traded

The 1991 Score Rookie and Traded contains 110 standard-size player cards and was issued exclusively in factory set form along with 10 "World Series II" magic motion trivia cards through hobby dealers. The front design is identical to the regular issue 1991 Score set except for the distinctive mauve borders and T-suffixed numbering. Cards 1T-80T feature traded players, while cards 81T-110T focus on rookies. Rookie Cards in the set include Jeff Bagwell and Ivan Rodriguez.

COMP.FACT.SET (110) 2.00 5.00
1T Bo Jackson .20 .50
2T Mike Flanagan .02 .10
3T Pete Incaviglia .02 .10
4T Jack Clark .08 .25
5T Hubie Brooks .02 .10
6T Ivan Calderon .02 .10
7T Glenn Davis .02 .10
8T Wally Backman .02 .10
9T Dave Smith .02 .10
10T Tim Raines .08 .25
11T Joe Carter .08 .25
12T Sid Bream .02 .10
13T George Bell .02 .10
14T Steve Bedrosian .02 .10
15T Willie Wilson .02 .10
16T Darryl Strawberry .08 .25
17T Danny Jackson .02 .10
18T Kirk Gibson .08 .25
19T Willie McGee .08 .25
20T Junior Felix .02 .10
21T Steve Farr .02 .10
22T Pat Tabler .02 .10
23T Brett Butler .08 .25
24T Danny Darwin .02 .10
25T Mickey Tettleton .02 .10
26T Gary Carter .08 .25
27T Mitch Williams .02 .10
28T Candy Maldonado .02 .10
29T Otis Nixon .02 .10
30T Brian Downing .02 .10
31T Tom Candiotti .02 .10
32T John Candelaria .02 .10
33T Rob Murphy .02 .10
34T Deion Sanders .15 .40
35T Willie Randolph .08 .25
36T Pete Harnisch .02 .10
37T Dante Bichette .08 .25
38T Garry Templeton .02 .10
39T Gary Gaetti .08 .25
40T John Cerutti .02 .10
41T Rick Cerone .02 .10
42T Mike Pagliarulo .02 .10
43T Ron Hassey .02 .10
44T Roberto Alomar .15 .40
45T Mike Boddicker .02 .10
46T Bud Black .02 .10
47T Rob Deer .02 .10
48T Devon White .08 .25
49T Luis Sojo .02 .10
50T Terry Pendleton .08 .25
51T Kevin Gross .02 .10
52T Mike Huff .02 .10
53T Dave Righetti .08 .25
54T Matt Young .02 .10
55T Earnest Riles .02 .10
56T Bill Gullickson .02 .10
57T Vince Coleman .02 .10
58T Fred McGriff .15 .40
59T Franklin Stubbs .02 .10
60T Eric King .02 .10
61T Cory Snyder .02 .10
62T Dwight Evans .15 .40
63T Gerald Perry .02 .10
64T Eric Show .02 .10
65T Shawn Hillegas .02 .10
66T Tony Fernandez .02 .10
67T Tim Teufel .02 .10
68T Mitch Webster .02 .10
69T Mike Heath .02 .10
70T Chili Davis .08 .25
71T Larry Andersen .02 .10
72T Gary Varsho .02 .10
73T Juan Berenguer .02 .10
74T Jack Morris .08 .25
75T Barry Jones .02 .10
76T Rafael Belliard .02 .10
77T Steve Buechele .02 .10
78T Scott Sanderson .02 .10
79T Bob Ojeda .02 .10
80T Curt Schilling .20 .50
81T Brian Drahman RC .02 .10
82T Ivan Rodriguez RC .75 2.00
83T David Howard RC .02 .10
84T Heathcliff Slocumb RC .08 .25
85T Mike Timlin RC .08 .25
86T Darryl Kile .08 .25
87T Pete Schourek RC .02 .10
88T Bruce Walton RC .02 .10
89T Al Osuna RC .02 .10

90T Gary Scott RC .02 .10
91T Doug Simons RC .02 .10
92T Chris Jones RC .02 .10
93T Chuck Knoblauch .08 .25
94T Dana Allison RC .02 .10
95T Erik Pappas RC .02 .10
96T Jeff Bagwell RC .60 1.50
97T Kirk Dressendorfer RC .02 .10
98T Freddie Benavides RC .02 .10
99T Luis Gonzalez RC .20 .50
100T Wade Taylor RC .02 .10
101T Ed Sprague .02 .10
102T Bob Scanlan RC .02 .10
103T Rick Wilkins RC .02 .10
104T Chris Donnels RC .02 .10
105T Joe Slusarski RC .02 .10
106T Mark Lewis .02 .10
107T Pat Kelly RC .02 .10
108T John Briscoe RC .02 .10
109T Luis Lopez RC .02 .10
110T Jeff Johnson RC .02 .10

1991 Score All-Star Fanfest

This 11-card standard-size set was issued with a 3-D 1946 World Series trivia card. The cards feature on the fronts color action player photos, with red borders above and below the pictures. The card face is lime green with miniature yellow baseballs and blue player icons, and it can be seen at the top and bottom of the card front. The backs have a similar pattern on a white background and present biographical information as well as career highlights. The set features young players, who were apparently projected by Score to be future All-Stars. The cards are numbered on the back as "X of 10."

COMPLETE SET (10) 2.00 5.00
1 Ray Lankford .60 1.50
2 Steve Decker .08 .25
3 Gary Scott .08 .25
4 Hensley Meulens .08 .25
5 Tim Naehring .08 .25
6 Mark Whiten .08 .25
7 Ed Sprague .08 .25
8 Charles Nagy .08 .25
9 Terry Shumpert .08 .25
10 Chuck Knoblauch 1.00 2.50
NNO Title Card .08 .25

1991 Score 100 Rising Stars

The 1991 Score 100 Rising Stars sets were issued by Score with or without special books which goes with the cards. The standard-size cards feature 100 of the most popular rising stars. The sets (with the special book with brief biography on the players) are marketed for retail purposes at a suggested price of 12.95.

COMP. FACT SET (100) 3.00 8.00
1 Sandy Alomar Jr. .01 .05
2 Tom Edens .01 .05
3 Terry Shumpert .01 .05
4 Shawn Boskie .01 .05
5 Steve Avery .01 .05
6 Deion Sanders .08 .25
7 John Burkett .01 .05
8 Stan Belinda .01 .05
9 Thomas Howard .01 .05
10 Wayne Edwards .01 .05
11 Rick Parker .01 .05
12 Randy Veres .01 .05
13 Alex Cole .01 .05
14 Scott Chiamparino .01 .05
15 Greg Olson .01 .05
16 Jose DeJesus .01 .05
17 Mike Blowers .01 .05
18 Jeff Huson .01 .05
19 Willie Blair .01 .05
20 Howard Farmer .01 .05
21 Larry Walker .20 .50
22 Scott Hemond .01 .05
23 Mel Stottlemyre Jr. .01 .05
24 Mark Whiten .01 .05
25 Jeff Schulz .01 .05
26 Gary DiSarcina .01 .05
27 George Canale .01 .05
28 Dean Palmer .07 .20
29 Jim Leyritz .01 .05
30 Carlos Baerga .01 .05
31 Rafael Valdez .01 .05
32 Derek Bell .01 .05
33 Francisco Cabrera .01 .05
34 Chris Hoiles .01 .05
35 Craig Grebeck .01 .05
36 Scott Coolbaugh .01 .05
37 Kevin Wickander .01 .05
38 Marquis Grissom .07 .20
39 Chip Hale .01 .05
40 Kevin Maas .01 .05
41 Juan Gonzalez .25 .60
42 Eric Anthony .01 .05
43 Luis Sojo .01 .05
44 Paul Sorrento .01 .05
45 Dave Justice .07 .20
46 Oscar Azocar .01 .05
47 Charles Nagy .01 .05
48 Robin Ventura .07 .20
49 Reggie Harris .01 .05
50 Ben McDonald .01 .05
51 Hector Villanueva .01 .05
52 Kevin Tapani .01 .05
53 Brian Bohanon .01 .05
54 Tim Layana .01 .05
55 Delino DeShields .02 .10
56 Beau Allred .01 .05
57 Eric Gunderson .01 .05
58 Kent Mercker .01 .05
59 Juan Bell .01 .05
60 Glenallen Hill .01 .05
61 David Segui .01 .05
62 Alan Mills .01 .05
63 Mike Harkey .01 .05
64 Bill Sampen .01 .05
65 Greg Vaughn .07 .20
66 Alex Fernandez .01 .05
67 Mike Hartley .01 .05
68 Travis Fryman .07 .20
69 Dave Rohde .01 .05
70 Tom Lampkin .01 .05
71 Mark Gardner .01 .05
72 Pat Combs .01 .05
73 Kevin Appier .07 .20
74 Mike Fetters .01 .05
75 Greg Myers .01 .05
76 Steve Searcy .01 .05
77 Tim Naehring .01 .05
78 Frank Thomas .40 1.00
79 Todd Hundley .07 .20
80 Ed Vosberg .01 .05
81 Todd Zeile .02 .10
82 Lee Stevens .01 .05
83 Scott Radinsky .01 .05
84 Hensley Meulens .01 .05
85 Brian DuBois .01 .05
86 Steve Olin .01 .05
87 Julio Machado .01 .05
88 Jose Vizcaino .01 .05
89 Mark Lemke .01 .05
90 Felix Jose .01 .05
91 Wally Whitehurst .01 .05
92 Dana Kiecker .01 .05
93 Mike Munoz .01 .05
94 Adam Peterson .01 .05
95 Tim Drummond .01 .05
96 Dave Hollins .01 .05
97 Craig Wilson .01 .05
98 Hal Morris .01 .05
99 Jose Offerman .01 .05
100 John Olerud .07 .20

1991 Score 100 Superstars

The 1991 Score 100 Superstars sets were issued by Score with or without special books that came with the cards. The standard-size cards feature 100 of the most popular superstars. The sets (with the special book with brief biography on the players) are marketed for retail purposes at a suggested price of 12.95.

COMP. FACT SET (100) 3.00 8.00
1 Jose Canseco .20 .50
2 Bo Jackson .15 .40
3 Wade Boggs .20 .50
4 Will Clark .07 .20
5 Ken Griffey Jr. .60 1.50
6 Doug Drabek .01 .05
7 Kirby Puckett .25 .60
8 Joe Orsulak .01 .05
9 Eric Davis .02 .10
10 Rickey Henderson .30 .75
11 Len Dykstra .02 .10
12 Ruben Sierra .02 .10
13 Paul Molitor .20 .50
14 Ron Gant .02 .10
15 Ozzie Guillen .05 .15
16 Ramon Martinez .01 .05
17 Edgar Martinez .05 .15
18 Ozzie Smith .30 .75
19 Charlie Hayes .01 .05
20 Barry Larkin .07 .20
21 Cal Ripken .75 2.00
22 Andy Van Slyke .02 .10
23 Don Mattingly .40 1.00
24 Dave Stewart .02 .10
25 Nolan Ryan .75 2.00
26 Barry Bonds .30 .75
27 Gregg Olson .01 .05
28 Chris Sabo .01 .05
29 John Franco .02 .10
30 Gary Sheffield .20 .50
31 Jeff Treadway .01 .05
32 Tom Browning .01 .05
33 Jose Lind .01 .05
34 Dave Magadan .01 .05
35 Dale Murphy .07 .20
36 Tom Candiotti .01 .05
37 Willie McGee .02 .10
38 Robin Yount .20 .50
39 Mark McGwire .40 1.00
40 George Bell .02 .10
41 Carlton Fisk .20 .50
42 Bobby Bonilla .02 .10
43 Randy Milligan .01 .05
44 Dave Parker .02 .10
45 Shawon Dunston .01 .05
46 Brian Harper .01 .05
47 John Tudor .01 .05
48 Ellis Burks .02 .10
49 Bob Welch .01 .05
50 Roger Clemens .40 1.00
51 Mike Henneman .01 .05
52 Eddie Murray .15 .40
53 Kal Daniels .01 .05
54 Doug Jones .01 .05
55 Craig Biggio .05 .15
56 Rafael Palmeiro .15 .40
57 Wally Joyner .02 .10
58 Tim Wallach .01 .05
59 Bret Saberhagen .02 .10
60 Ryne Sandberg .30 .75
61 Benito Santiago .02 .10
62 Darryl Strawberry .02 .10
63 Alan Trammell .05 .15
64 Kelly Gruber .01 .05
65 Dwight Gooden .02 .10
66 Dave Winfield .20 .50
67 Rick Aguilera .02 .10
68 Dave Righetti .01 .05
69 Jim Abbott .02 .10
70 Frank Viola .01 .05
71 Fred McGriff .05 .15
72 Steve Sax .01 .05
73 Dennis Eckersley .15 .40
74 Cory Snyder .01 .05
75 Mackey Sasser .01 .05
76 Candy Maldonado .01 .05
77 Matt Williams .05 .15
78 Kent Hrbek .02 .10
79 Randy Myers .02 .10
80 Gregg Jefferies .01 .05
81 Joe Carter .02 .10
82 Mike Greenwell .01 .05
83 Jack Armstrong .01 .05
84 Julio Franco .02 .10
85 George Brett .30 .75
86 Howard Johnson .01 .05
87 Andre Dawson .07 .20
88 Cecil Fielder .02 .10
89 Tim Raines .02 .10
90 Chuck Finley .02 .10
91 Mark Grace .07 .20
92 Brook Jacoby .01 .05
93 Dave Stieb .01 .05
94 Tony Gwynn .40 1.00
95 Bobby Thigpen .01 .05
96 Roberto Kelly .01 .05
97 Kevin Seitzer .01 .05
98 Kevin Mitchell .01 .05
99 Dwight Evans .02 .10
100 Roberto Alomar .07 .20

1991 Score Rookies

This 40-card standard-sized set was distributed with five magic motion trivia cards. The fronts feature high glossy color action player photos, on a blue card face with meandering green lines.

COMP.FACT SET (40) 1.50 4.00
1 Mel Rojas .01 .05
2 Ray Lankford .10 .30
3 Scott Aldred .01 .05
4 Turner Ward .01 .05
5 Omar Olivares .01 .05
6 Mo Vaughn .60 1.50
7 Phil Clark .01 .05
8 Brent Mayne .01 .05
9 Scott Lewis .01 .05
10 Brian Barnes .01 .05
11 Bernard Gilkey .01 .05
12 Steve Decker .01 .05
13 Paul Marak .01 .05
14 Wes Chamberlain .01 .05
15 Kevin Belcher .01 .05
16 Steve Adkins .01 .05
17 Geronimo Pena .01 .05
18 Mark Leonard .01 .05
19 Jeff Conine .02 .10
20 Leo Gomez .01 .05
21 Chuck Malone .01 .05
22 Beau Allred .01 .05
23 Todd Hundley .10 .30
24 Lance Dickson .01 .05
25 Mike Benjamin .01 .05
26 Jose Offerman .01 .05
27 Terry Shumpert .01 .05
28 Darren Lewis .01 .05
29 Scott Chiamparino .01 .05
30 Tim Naehring .01 .05
31 David Segui .02 .10
32 Karl Rhodes .01 .05
33 Mickey Morandini .01 .05
34 Chuck McElroy .01 .05
35 Tim McIntosh .01 .05
36 Derrick May .01 .05
37 Rich DeLucia .01 .05
38 Tino Martinez .40 1.00
39 Hensley Meulens .01 .05
40 Andujar Cedeno .01 .05

1991 Score Ryan Life and Times

This four-card standard-size set was manufactured by Score to commemorate four significant milestones in Nolan Ryan's illustrious career beginning with his years growing up in Alvin, Texas, his years with the Mets and Angels, with the Astros and Rangers, and his career statistics. Each card commemorates a career milestone (all occur with the Rangers) and features Ryan's color photo on the front. They are part of "The Life and Times of Nolan Ryan," by Tarrant Printing, a special collector set that consists of four volumes (8 1/2" by 11" booklets) along with the cards packaged in a folder.

COMPLETE SET (4) 8.00 20.00
COMMON CARD (1-4) 2.00 5.00

1992 Score Samples

COMPLETE SET (6) 8.00 20.00
COMMON PLAYER (1-6) .20 .50
COMMON SP .50 1.00
1 Ken Griffey Jr. 4.00 10.00
2 Dave Justice .75 2.00
3 Robin Ventura .75 2.00
4 Steve Avery .20 .50
5 Ryne Sandberg SP 3.00 8.00
6 Shane Mack SP .40 1.00

1992 Score

The 1992 Score set marked the second year that Score released their set in two different series. The first series contains 442 cards while the second series contains 451 cards. Cards were distributed in plastic wrapped packs, blister packs, jumbo packs and factory sets. Each pack included a special "World Series II" trivia card. Topical subsets include Rookie Prospects (395-424/736-772/814-877), No-Hit Club (425-428/784-787), Highlights (429-430), AL All-Stars (431-440; with color montages displaying Chris Greco's player caricatures), Dream Team (441-442/883-893), NL All-Stars (773-782), Highlights (783, 795-797), Draft Picks (799-810), and Memorabilia (878-882). The memorabilia cards all feature items from the famed Barry Halper collection. Halper was a part-owner of Score at the time. All of the Rookie Prospects (736-772) can be found with or without the Rookie Prospect stripe. Rookie Cards in the set include Vinny Castilla and Manny Ramirez. Chuck Knoblauch, 1991 American League Rookie of the Year, autographed 3,000 of his own 1990 Score Draft Pick cards (card number 672) in gold ink, 2,989 were randomly inserted in Series two poly packs, while the other 11 were given away in a sweepstakes. The backs of these Knoblauch autograph cards have special holograms to differentiate them.

COMPLETE SET (893) 6.00 15.00
COMP.FACT.SET (910) 8.00 20.00
COMPLETE SERIES 1 (442) 3.00 8.00
COMPLETE SERIES 2 (451) 3.00 8.00
SUBSET CARDS HALF VALUE OF BASE CARDS
1 Ken Griffey Jr. .20 .50
2 Nolan Ryan .40 1.00
3 Will Clark .05 .15
4 Dave Justice .02 .10
5 Dave Henderson .01 .05
6 Bret Saberhagen .02 .10
7 Fred McGriff .05 .15
8 Erik Hanson .01 .05
9 Darryl Strawberry .02 .10
10 Dwight Gooden .02 .10
11 Juan Gonzalez .05 .15
12 Mark Langston .01 .05
13 Lonnie Smith .01 .05
14 Jeff Montgomery .01 .05
15 Roberto Alomar .05 .15
16 Delino DeShields .01 .05
17 Steve Bedrosian .01 .05
18 Terry Pendleton .02 .10
19 Mark Carreon .01 .05
20 Mark McGwire .25 .60
21 Roger Clemens .20 .50
22 Chuck Crim .01 .05
23 Don Mattingly .25 .60
24 Dickie Thon .01 .05
25 Ron Gant .02 .10
26 Milt Cuyler .01 .05
27 Mike Macfarlane .01 .05
28 Dan Gladden .01 .05
29 Melido Perez .01 .05
30 Willie Randolph .02 .10
31 Albert Belle .02 .10
32 Dave Winfield .02 .10
33 Jimmy Jones .01 .05
34 Kevin Gross .01 .05
35 Andres Galarraga .02 .10
36 Mike Devereaux .01 .05
37 Chris Bosio .01 .05
38 Mike LaValliere .01 .05
39 Gary Gaetti .02 .10
40 Felix Jose .01 .05
41 Alvaro Espinoza .01 .05
42 Rick Aguilera .02 .10
43 Mike Gallego .01 .05
44 Eric Davis .02 .10
45 George Bell .01 .05
46 Tom Brunansky .01 .05
47 Steve Farr .01 .05
48 Duane Ward .01 .05
49 David Wells .02 .10
50 Cecil Fielder .02 .10
51 Walt Weiss .01 .05
52 Todd Zeile .01 .05
53 Doug Jones .01 .05
54 Bob Walk .01 .05
55 Rafael Palmeiro .05 .15
56 Rob Deer .01 .05
57 Paul O'Neill .05 .15
58 Jeff Reardon .02 .10
59 Randy Ready .01 .05
60 Scott Erickson .01 .05
61 Paul Molitor .02 .10
62 Jack McDowell .01 .05
63 Jim Acker .01 .05
64 Jay Buhner .02 .10
65 Travis Fryman .02 .10
66 Marquis Grissom .02 .10
67 Mike Harkey .01 .05
68 Luis Polonia .01 .05
69 Ken Caminiti .02 .10
70 Chris Sabo .01 .05
71 Gregg Olson .01 .05
72 Carlton Fisk .05 .15
73 Juan Samuel .01 .05
74 Todd Stottlemyre .01 .05
75 Andre Dawson .02 .10
76 Alvin Davis .01 .05
77 Bill Doran .01 .05
78 B.J. Surhoff .02 .10
79 Kirk McCaskill .01 .05
80 Dale Murphy .05 .15
81 Jose DeLeon .01 .05
82 Alex Fernandez .01 .05
83 Ivan Calderon .01 .05
84 Brent Mayne .01 .05
85 Jody Reed .01 .05
86 Randy Tomlin .01 .05
87 Randy Milligan .01 .05
88 Pascual Perez .01 .05
89 Hensley Meulens .01 .05
90 Joe Carter .02 .10
91 Mike Moore .01 .05
92 Ozzie Guillen .02 .10
93 Shawn Hillegas .01 .05
94 Chili Davis .02 .10
95 Vince Coleman .01 .05
96 Jimmy Key .02 .10
97 Billy Ripken .01 .05
98 Dave Smith .01 .05
99 Tom Bolton .01 .05
100 Barry Larkin .05 .15
101 Kenny Rogers .02 .10
102 Mike Boddicker .01 .05
103 Kevin Elster .01 .05
104 Ken Hill .01 .05
105 Charlie Leibrandt .01 .05
106 Pat Combs .01 .05
107 Hubie Brooks .01 .05
108 Julio Franco .02 .10
109 Vicente Palacios .01 .05
110 Kal Daniels .01 .05
111 Bruce Hurst .01 .05
112 Willie McGee .02 .10
113 Ted Power .01 .05
114 Milt Thompson .01 .05
115 Doug Drabek .01 .05
116 Rafael Belliard .01 .05
117 Scott Garrelts .01 .05
118 Terry Mulholland .01 .05
119 Jay Howell .01 .05
120 Danny Jackson .01 .05
121 Scott Ruskin .01 .05
122 Robin Ventura .02 .10
123 Bip Roberts .01 .05
124 Jeff Russell .01 .05
125 Hal Morris .01 .05
126 Teddy Higuera .01 .05
127 Luis Sojo .01 .05
128 Carlos Baerga .01 .05
129 Jeff Ballard .01 .05
130 Tom Gordon .01 .05
131 Sid Bream .01 .05
132 Rance Mulliniks .01 .05
133 Andy Benes .01 .05
134 Mickey Tettleton .01 .05
135 Rich DeLucia .01 .05
136 Tom Pagnozzi .01 .05
137 Harold Baines .02 .10
138 Danny Darwin .01 .05
139 Kevin Bass .01 .05
140 Chris Nabholz .01 .05
141 Pete O'Brien .01 .05
142 Jeff Treadway .01 .05
143 Mickey Morandini .01 .05
144 Eric King .01 .05
145 Danny Tartabull .01 .05
146 Lance Johnson .01 .05
147 Casey Candaele .01 .05
148 Felix Fermin .01 .05
149 Rich Rodriguez .01 .05
150 Dwight Evans .05 .15
151 Joe Klink .01 .05
152 Kevin Reimer .01 .05
153 Orlando Merced .01 .05
154 Mel Hall .01 .05
155 Randy Myers .01 .05
156 Greg A. Harris .01 .05
157 Jeff Brantley .01 .05
158 Jim Eisenreich .01 .05
159 Luis Rivera .01 .05
160 Cris Carpenter .01 .05
161 Bruce Ruffin .01 .05
162 Omar Vizquel .05 .15
163 Gerald Alexander .01 .05
164 Mark Guthrie .01 .05
165 Scott Lewis .01 .05
166 Bill Sampen .01 .05
167 Dave Anderson .01 .05
168 Kevin McReynolds .01 .05
169 Jose Vizcaino .01 .05
170 Bob Geren .01 .05
171 Mike Morgan .01 .05
172 Jim Gott .01 .05
173 Mike Pagliarulo .01 .05
174 Mike Jeffcoat .01 .05
175 Craig Lefferts .01 .05
176 Steve Finley .02 .10
177 Wally Backman .01 .05
178 Kent Mercker .01 .05
179 John Cerutti .01 .05
180 Jay Bell .02 .10
181 Dale Sveum .01 .05
182 Greg Gagne .01 .05
183 Donnie Hill .01 .05
184 Rex Hudler .01 .05
185 Pat Kelly .01 .05
186 Jeff D. Robinson .01 .05
187 Jeff Gray .01 .05
188 Jerry Willard .01 .05
189 Carlos Quintana .01 .05
190 Dennis Eckersley .02 .10
191 Kelly Downs .01 .05
192 Gregg Jefferies .01 .05
193 Darrin Fletcher .01 .05
194 Mike Jackson .01 .05
195 Eddie Murray .08 .25
196 Bill Landrum .01 .05
197 Eric Yelding .01 .05
198 Devon White .02 .10
199 Larry Walker .05 .15
200 Ryne Sandberg .15 .40
201 Dave Magadan .01 .05
202 Steve Chitren .01 .05
203 Scott Fletcher .01 .05
204 Dwayne Henry .01 .05
205 Scott Coolbaugh .01 .05
206 Tracy Jones .01 .05
207 Von Hayes .01 .05
208 Bob Melvin .01 .05
209 Scott Scudder .01 .05
210 Luis Gonzalez .02 .10
211 Scott Sanderson .01 .05
212 Chris Donnels .01 .05
213 Heathcliff Slocumb .01 .05
214 Mike Timlin .01 .05
215 Brian Harper .01 .05
216 Juan Berenguer UER .01 .05
Decimal point missing
in IP total
217 Mike Henneman .01 .05
218 Bill Spiers .01 .05
219 Scott Terry .01 .05
220 Frank Viola .02 .10
221 Mark Eichhorn .01 .05
222 Ernest Riles .01 .05
223 Ray Lankford .02 .10
224 Pete Harnisch .01 .05
225 Bobby Bonilla .02 .10
226 Mike Scioscia .01 .05
227 Joel Skinner .01 .05
228 Brian Holman .01 .05
229 Gilberto Reyes .01 .05
230 Matt Williams .02 .10
231 Jaime Navarro .01 .05
232 Jose Rijo .01 .05
233 Atlee Hammaker .01 .05
234 Tim Teufel .01 .05
235 John Kruk .02 .10
236 Kurt Stillwell .01 .05
237 Dan Pasqua .01 .05
238 Tim Crews .01 .05
239 Dave Gallagher .01 .05
240 Leo Gomez .01 .05
241 Steve Avery .01 .05
242 Bill Gullickson .01 .05
243 Mark Portugal .01 .05
244 Lee Guetterman .01 .05
245 Benito Santiago .02 .10
246 Jim Gantner .01 .05
247 Robby Thompson .01 .05
248 Terry Shumpert .01 .05
249 Mike Bell .01 .05
250 Harold Reynolds .02 .10
251 Mike Felder .01 .05
252 Bill Pecota .01 .05
253 Bill Krueger .01 .05
254 Alfredo Griffin .01 .05
255 Lou Whitaker .02 .10
256 Roy Smith .01 .05
257 Jerald Clark .01 .05
258 Sammy Sosa .08 .25
259 Tim Naehring .01 .05
260 Dave Righetti .02 .10
261 Paul Gibson .01 .05
262 Chris James .01 .05
263 Larry Andersen .01 .05
264 Storm Davis .01 .05
265 Jose Lind .01 .05
266 Greg Hibbard .01 .05
267 Norm Charlton .01 .05
268 Paul Kilgus .01 .05
269 Greg Maddux .15 .40
270 Ellis Burks .02 .10
271 Frank Tanana .01 .05
272 Gene Larkin .01 .05
273 Ron Hassey .01 .05
274 Jeff M. Robinson .01 .05
275 Steve Howe .01 .05
276 Daryl Boston .01 .05
277 Mark Lee .01 .05
278 Jose Segura .01 .05
279 Lance Blankenship .01 .05
280 Don Slaught .01 .05
281 Russ Swan .01 .05
282 Bob Tewksbury .01 .05
283 Geno Petralli .01 .05
284 Shane Mack .01 .05
285 Bob Scanlan .01 .05
286 Tim Leary .01 .05
287 John Smoltz .05 .15
288 Pat Borders .01 .05
289 Mark Davidson .01 .05
290 Sam Horn .01 .05
291 Lenny Harris .01 .05
292 Franklin Stubbs .01 .05
293 Thomas Howard .01 .05
294 Steve Lyons .01 .05
295 Francisco Oliveras .01 .05
296 Terry Leach .01 .05
297 Barry Jones .01 .05
298 Lance Parrish .02 .10
299 Wally Whitehurst .01 .05
300 Bob Welch .01 .05
301 Charlie Hayes .01 .05
302 Charlie Hough .02 .10
303 Gary Redus .01 .05
304 Scott Bradley .01 .05
305 Jose Oquendo .01 .05
306 Pete Incaviglia .01 .05
307 Marvin Freeman .01 .05
308 Gary Pettis .01 .05
309 Joe Slusarski .01 .05
310 Kevin Seitzer .01 .05
311 Jeff Reed .01 .05
312 Pat Tabler .01 .05
313 Mike Maddux .01 .05
314 Bob Milacki .01 .05
315 Eric Anthony .01 .05
316 Dante Bichette .02 .10
317 Steve Decker .01 .05
318 Jack Clark .02 .10
319 Doug Dascenzo .01 .05
320 Scott Leius .01 .05
321 Jim Lindeman .01 .05
322 Bryan Harvey .01 .05
323 Spike Owen .01 .05
324 Roberto Kelly .01 .05
325 Stan Belinda .01 .05
326 Joey Cora .01 .05
327 Jeff Innis .01 .05
328 Willie Wilson .01 .05
329 Juan Agosto .01 .05
330 Charles Nagy .01 .05
331 Scott Bailes .01 .05
332 Pete Schourek .01 .05
333 Mike Flanagan .01 .05
334 Omar Olivares .01 .05
335 Dennis Lamp .01 .05
336 Tommy Greene .01 .05
337 Randy Velarde .01 .05
338 Tom Lampkin .01 .05
339 John Russell .01 .05

340 Bob Kipper .01 .05
341 Todd Burns .01 .05
342 Ron Jones .01 .05
343 Dave Valle .01 .05
344 Mike Heath .01 .05
345 John Olerud .02 .10
346 Gerald Young .01 .05
347 Ken Patterson .01 .05
348 Les Lancaster .01 .05
349 Steve Crawford .01 .05
350 John Candelaria .01 .05
351 Mike Aldrete .01 .05
352 Mariano Duncan .01 .05
353 Julio Machado .01 .05
354 Ken Williams .01 .05
355 Walt Terrell .01 .05
356 Mitch Williams .01 .05
357 Al Newman .01 .05
358 Bud Black .01 .05
359 Joe Hesketh .01 .05
360 Paul Assenmacher .01 .05
361 Bo Jackson .08 .25
362 Jeff Blauser .01 .05
363 Mike Brumley .01 .05
364 Jim Deshaies .01 .05
365 Brady Anderson .02 .10
366 Chuck McElroy .01 .05
367 Matt Merullo .01 .05
368 Tim Belcher .01 .05
369 Luis Aquino .01 .05
370 Joe Oliver .01 .05
371 Greg Swindell .01 .05
372 Lee Stevens .01 .05
373 Mark Knudson .01 .05
374 Bill Wegman .01 .05
375 Jerry Don Gleaton .01 .05
376 Pedro Guerrero .02 .10
377 Randy Bush .01 .05
378 Greg W. Harris .01 .05
379 Eric Plunk .01 .05
380 Jose DeJesus .01 .05
381 Bobby Witt .01 .05
382 Curtis Wilkerson .01 .05
383 Gene Nelson .01 .05
384 Wes Chamberlain .01 .05
385 Tom Henke .01 .05
386 Mark Lemke .01 .05
387 Greg Briley .01 .05
388 Rafael Ramirez .01 .05
389 Tony Fossas .01 .05
390 Henry Cotto .01 .05
391 Tim Hulett .01 .05
392 Dean Palmer .02 .10
393 Glenn Braggs .01 .05
394 Mark Salas .01 .05
395 Rusty Meacham .01 .05
396 Andy Ashby .01 .05
397 Jose Melendez .01 .05
398 Warren Newson .01 .05
399 Frank Castillo .01 .05
400 Chito Martinez .01 .05
401 Bernie Williams .05 .15
402 Derek Bell .02 .10
403 Javier Ortiz .01 .05
404 Tim Sherrill .01 .05
405 Rob MacDonald .01 .05
406 Phil Plantier .01 .05
407 Troy Afenir .01 .05
408 Gino Minutelli .01 .05
409 Reggie Jefferson .01 .05
410 Mike Remlinger .01 .05
411 Carlos Rodriguez .01 .05
412 Joe Redfield .01 .05
413 Alonzo Powell .01 .05
414 Scott Livingstone UER .01 .05
Travis Fryman,
not Woodie, should be
referenced on back
415 Scott Kamieniecki .01 .05
416 Tim Spehr .01 .05
417 Brian Hunter .01 .05
418 Ced Landrum .01 .05
419 Bret Barberie .01 .05
420 Kevin Morton .01 .05
421 Doug Henry RC .02 .10
422 Doug Piatt .01 .05
423 Pat Rice .01 .05
424 Juan Guzman .01 .05
425 Nolan Ryan NH .20 .50
426 Tommy Greene NH .01 .05
427 Bob Milacki and .01 .05
Mike Flanagan NH
Mark Williamson
and Gregg Olson
428 Wilson Alvarez NH .01 .05
429 Otis Nixon HL .01 .05
430 Rickey Henderson HL .05 .15
431 Cecil Fielder AS .01 .05
432 Julio Franco AS .01 .05
433 Cal Ripken AS .15 .40
434 Wade Boggs AS .02 .10
435 Joe Carter AS .01 .05
436 Ken Griffey Jr. AS .10 .30
437 Ruben Sierra AS .01 .05
438 Scott Erickson AS .01 .05
439 Tom Henke AS .01 .05
440 Terry Steinbach AS .01 .05
441 Rickey Henderson DT .08 .25
442 Ryne Sandberg DT .15 .40
443 Otis Nixon .01 .05
444 Scott Radinsky UER .01 .05
Photo on front is Tom Drees
445 Mark Grace .05 .15
446 Tony Pena .01 .05
447 Billy Hatcher .01 .05
448 Glenallen Hill .01 .05
449 Chris Gwynn .01 .05
450 Tom Glavine .05 .15
451 John Habyan .01 .05
452 Al Osuna .01 .05
453 Tony Phillips .01 .05
454 Greg Cadaret .01 .05
455 Rob Dibble .02 .10
456 Rick Honeycutt .01 .05
457 Jerome Walton .01 .05
458 Mookie Wilson .02 .10
459 Mark Gubicza .01 .05
460 Craig Biggio .05 .15
461 Dave Cochrane .01 .05
462 Keith Miller .01 .05
463 Alex Cole .01 .05
464 Pete Smith .01 .05
465 Brett Butler .02 .10
466 Jeff Huson .01 .05
467 Steve Lake .01 .05
468 Lloyd Moseby .01 .05
469 Tim McIntosh .01 .05
470 Dennis Martinez .02 .10
471 Greg Myers .01 .05
472 Mackey Sasser .01 .05
473 Junior Ortiz .01 .05
474 Greg Olson .01 .05
475 Steve Sax .01 .05
476 Ricky Jordan .01 .05
477 Max Venable .01 .05
478 Brian McRae .01 .05
479 Doug Simons .01 .05
480 Rickey Henderson .08 .25
481 Gary Varsho .01 .05
482 Carl Willis .01 .05
483 Rick Wilkins .01 .05
484 Donn Pall .01 .05
485 Edgar Martinez .05 .15
486 Tom Foley .01 .05
487 Mark Williamson .01 .05
488 Jack Armstrong .01 .05
489 Gary Carter .02 .10
490 Ruben Sierra .02 .10
491 Gerald Perry .01 .05
492 Rob Murphy .01 .05
493 Zane Smith .01 .05
494 Darryl Kile .02 .10
495 Kelly Gruber .01 .05
496 Jerry Browne .01 .05
497 Darryl Hamilton .01 .05
498 Mike Stanton .01 .05
499 Mark Leonard .01 .05
500 Jose Canseco .05 .15
501 Dave Martinez .01 .05
502 Jose Guzman .01 .05
503 Terry Kennedy .01 .05
504 Ed Sprague .01 .05
505 Frank Thomas UER .08 .25
His Gulf Coast League
stats are wrong
506 Darren Daulton .02 .10
507 Kevin Tapani .01 .05
508 Luis Salazar .01 .05
509 Paul Faries .01 .05
510 Sandy Alomar Jr. .01 .05
511 Jeff King .01 .05
512 Gary Thurman .01 .05
513 Chris Hammond .01 .05
514 Pedro Munoz .01 .05
515 Alan Trammell .02 .10
516 Geronimo Pena .01 .05
517 Rodney McCray UER .01 .05
Stole 6 bases in 1990, not 5;
career totals are correct at 7
518 Manny Lee .01 .05
519 Junior Felix .01 .05
520 Kirk Gibson .02 .10
521 Darrin Jackson .01 .05
522 John Burkett .01 .05
523 Jeff Johnson .01 .05
524 Jim Corsi .01 .05
525 Robin Yount .15 .40
526 Jamie Quirk .01 .05
527 Bob Ojeda .01 .05
528 Mark Lewis .01 .05
529 Bryn Smith .01 .05
530 Kent Hrbek .02 .10
531 Dennis Boyd .01 .05
532 Ron Karkovice .01 .05
533 Don August .01 .05
534 Todd Frohwirth .01 .05
535 Wally Joyner .02 .10
536 Dennis Rasmussen .01 .05
537 Andy Allanson .01 .05
538 Rich Gossage .02 .10
539 John Marzano .01 .05
540 Cal Ripken .30 .75
541 Bill Swift UER .01 .05
Brewers logo on front
542 Kevin Appier .02 .10
543 Dave Bergman .01 .05
544 Bernard Gilkey .01 .05
545 Mike Greenwell .01 .05
546 Jose Uribe .01 .05
547 Jesse Orosco .01 .05
548 Bob Patterson .01 .05
549 Mike Stanley .01 .05
550 Howard Johnson .01 .05
551 Joe Orsulak .01 .05
552 Dick Schofield .01 .05
553 Dave Hollins .01 .05
554 David Segui .01 .05
555 Barry Bonds .40 1.00
556 Mo Vaughn .02 .10
557 Craig Wilson .01 .05
558 Bobby Rose .01 .05
559 Rod Nichols .01 .05
560 Len Dykstra .02 .10
561 Craig Grebeck .01 .05
562 Darren Lewis .01 .05
563 Todd Benzinger .01 .05
564 Ed Whitson .01 .05
565 Jesse Barfield .01 .05
566 Lloyd McClendon .01 .05
567 Dan Plesac .01 .05
568 Danny Cox .01 .05
569 Skeeter Barnes .01 .05
570 Bobby Thigpen .01 .05
571 Deion Sanders .05 .15
572 Chuck Knoblauch .02 .10
573 Matt Nokes .01 .05
574 Herm Winningham .01 .05
575 Tom Candiotti .01 .05
576 Jeff Bagwell .08 .25
577 Brook Jacoby .01 .05
578 Chico Walker .01 .05
579 Brian Downing .01 .05
580 Dave Stewart .02 .10
581 Francisco Cabrera .01 .05
582 Rene Gonzales .01 .05
583 Stan Javier .01 .05
584 Randy Johnson .08 .25
585 Chuck Finley .02 .10
586 Mark Gardner .01 .05
587 Mark Whiten .01 .05
588 Garry Templeton .01 .05
589 Gary Sheffield .02 .10
590 Ozzie Smith .15 .40
591 Candy Maldonado .01 .05
592 Mike Sharperson .01 .05
593 Carlos Martinez .01 .05
594 Scott Bankhead .01 .05
595 Tim Wallach .01 .05
596 Tino Martinez .05 .15
597 Roger McDowell .01 .05
598 Cory Snyder .01 .05
599 Andujar Cedeno .01 .05
600 Kirby Puckett .08 .25
601 Rick Parker .01 .05
602 Todd Hundley .01 .05
603 Greg Litton .01 .05
604 Dave Johnson .01 .05
605 John Franco .02 .10
606 Mike Fetters .01 .05
607 Luis Alicea .01 .05
608 Trevor Wilson .01 .05
609 Rob Ducey .01 .05
610 Ramon Martinez .01 .05
611 Dave Burba .01 .05
612 Dwight Smith .01 .05
613 Kevin Maas .01 .05
614 John Costello .01 .05
615 Glenn Davis .01 .05
616 Shawn Abner .01 .05
617 Scott Hemond .01 .05
618 Tom Prince .01 .05
619 Wally Ritchie .01 .05
620 Jim Abbott .05 .15
621 Charlie O'Brien .01 .05
622 Jack Daugherty .01 .05
623 Tommy Gregg .01 .05
624 Jeff Shaw .01 .05
625 Tony Gwynn .10 .30
626 Mark Leiter .01 .05
627 Jim Clancy .01 .05
628 Tim Layana .01 .05
629 Jeff Schaefer .01 .05
630 Lee Smith .02 .10
631 Wade Taylor .01 .05
632 Mike Simms .01 .05
633 Terry Steinbach .01 .05
634 Shawon Dunston .01 .05
635 Tim Raines .02 .10
636 Kirt Manwaring .01 .05
637 Warren Cromartie .01 .05
638 Luis Quinones .01 .05
639 Greg Vaughn .01 .05
640 Kevin Mitchell .01 .05
641 Chris Hoiles .01 .05
642 Tom Browning .01 .05
643 Mitch Webster .01 .05
644 Steve Olin .01 .05
645 Tony Fernandez .01 .05
646 Juan Bell .01 .05
647 Joe Boever .01 .05
648 Carney Lansford .02 .10
649 Mike Benjamin .01 .05
650 George Brett .25 .60
651 Tim Burke .01 .05
652 Jack Morris .02 .10
653 Orel Hershiser .02 .10
654 Mike Schooler .01 .05
655 Andy Van Slyke .05 .15
656 Dave Stieb .01 .05
657 Dave Clark .01 .05
658 Ben McDonald .01 .05
659 John Smiley .01 .05
660 Wade Boggs .05 .15
661 Eric Bullock .01 .05
662 Eric Show .01 .05
663 Lenny Webster .01 .05
664 Mike Huff .01 .05
665 Rick Sutcliffe .02 .10
666 Jeff Manto .01 .05
667 Mike Fitzgerald .01 .05
668 Matt Young .01 .05
669 Dave West .01 .05
670 Mike Hartley .01 .05
671 Curt Schilling .05 .15
672 Brian Bohanon .01 .05
673 Cecil Espy .01 .05
674 Joe Grahe .01 .05
675 Sid Fernandez .01 .05
676 Edwin Nunez .01 .05
677 Hector Villanueva .01 .05
678 Sean Berry .01 .05
679 Dave Eiland .01 .05
680 David Cone .02 .10
681 Mike Bordick .01 .05
682 Tony Castillo .01 .05
683 John Barfield .01 .05
684 Jeff Hamilton .01 .05
685 Ken Dayley .01 .05
686 Carmelo Martinez .01 .05
687 Mike Capel .01 .05
688 Scott Chiamparino .01 .05
689 Rich Gedman .01 .05
690 Rich Monteleone .01 .05
691 Alejandro Pena .01 .05
692 Oscar Azocar .01 .05
693 Jim Poole .01 .05
694 Mike Gardiner .01 .05
695 Steve Buechele .01 .05
696 Rudy Seanez .01 .05
697 Paul Abbott .01 .05
698 Steve Searcy .01 .05
699 Jose Offerman .01 .05
700 Ivan Rodriguez .08 .25
701 Joe Girardi .01 .05
702 Tony Perezchica .01 .05
703 Paul McClellan .01 .05
704 David Howard .01 .05
705 Dan Petry .01 .05
706 Jack Howell .01 .05
707 Jose Mesa .01 .05
708 Randy St. Claire .01 .05
709 Kevin Brown .02 .10
710 Ron Darling .01 .05
711 Jason Grimsley .01 .05
712 John Orton .01 .05
713 Shawn Boskie .01 .05
714 Pat Clements .01 .05
715 Brian Barnes .01 .05
716 Luis Lopez .01 .05
717 Bob McClure .01 .05
718 Mark Davis .01 .05
719 Dann Bilardello .01 .05
720 Tom Edens .01 .05
721 Willie Fraser .01 .05
722 Curt Young .01 .05
723 Neal Heaton .01 .05
724 Craig Worthington .01 .05
725 Mel Rojas .01 .05
726 Daryl Irvine .01 .05
727 Roger Mason .01 .05
728 Kirk Dressendorfer .01 .05
729 Scott Aldred .01 .05
730 Willie Blair .01 .05
731 Allan Anderson .01 .05
732 Dana Kiecker .01 .05
733 Jose Gonzalez .01 .05
734 Brian Drahman .01 .05
735 Brad Komminsk .01 .05
736 Arthur Rhodes .01 .05
737 Terry Mathews .01 .05
738 Jeff Fassero .01 .05
739 Mike Magnante RC .02 .10
740 Kip Gross .01 .05
741 Jim Hunter .01 .05
742 Jose Mota .01 .05
743 Joe Bitker .01 .05
744 Tim Mauser .01 .05
745 Ramon Garcia .01 .05
746 Rod Beck RC .08 .25
747 Jim Austin RC .01 .05
748 Keith Mitchell .01 .05
749 Wayne Rosenthal .01 .05
750 Bryan Hickerson RC .02 .10
751 Bruce Egloff .01 .05
752 John Wehner .01 .05
753 Darren Holmes .01 .05
754 Dave Hansen .01 .05
755 Mike Mussina .08 .25
756 Anthony Young .01 .05
757 Ron Tingley .01 .05
758 Ricky Bones .01 .05
759 Mark Wohlers .01 .05
760 Wilson Alvarez .01 .05
761 Harvey Pulliam .01 .05
762 Ryan Bowen .01 .05
763 Terry Bross .01 .05
764 Joel Johnston .01 .05
765 Terry McDaniel .01 .05
766 Esteban Beltre .01 .05
767 Rob Maurer RC .01 .05
768 Ted Wood .01 .05
769 Mo Sanford .01 .05
770 Jeff Carter .01 .05
771 Gil Heredia RC .08 .25
772 Monty Fariss .01 .05
773 Will Clark AS .02 .10
774 Ryne Sandberg AS .08 .25
775 Barry Larkin AS .02 .10
776 Howard Johnson AS .01 .05
777 Barry Bonds AS .20 .50
778 Brett Butler AS .01 .05
779 Tony Gwynn AS .05 .15
780 Ramon Martinez AS .01 .05
781 Lee Smith AS .01 .05
782 Mike Scioscia AS .01 .05
783 Dennis Martinez HL UER .01 .05
Card has both 13th
and 15th perfect game
in Major League history
784 Dennis Martinez NH .01 .05
785 Mark Gardner NH .01 .05
786 Bret Saberhagen NH .01 .05
787 Kent Mercker NH .01 .05
Mark Wohlers
Alejandro Pena
788 Cal Ripken MVP .15 .40
789 Terry Pendleton MVP .01 .05
790 Roger Clemens CY .08 .25
791 Tom Glavine CY .02 .10
792 Chuck Knoblauch ROY .01 .05
793 Jeff Bagwell ROY .05 .15
794 Cal Ripken MANYR .15 .40
795 David Cone HL .01 .05
796 Kirby Puckett HL .05 .15
797 Steve Avery HL .01 .05
798 Jack Morris HL .01 .05
799 Allen Watson RC .02 .10
800 Manny Ramirez RC 1.50 4.00
801 Cliff Floyd RC .30 .75
802 Al Shirley RC .02 .10
803 Brian Barber RC .02 .10
804 Jon Farrell RC .02 .10
805 Brent Gates RC .02 .10
806 Scott Ruffcorn RC .02 .10
807 Tyrone Hill RC .02 .10
808 Benji Gil RC .08 .25
809 Aaron Sele RC .08 .25
810 Tyler Green RC .02 .10
811 Chris Jones .01 .05
812 Steve Wilson .01 .05
813 Freddie Benavides .01 .05
814 Don Wakamatsu RC .01 .05
815 Mike Humphreys .01 .05
816 Scott Servais .01 .05
817 Rico Rossy .01 .05
818 John Ramos .01 .05
819 Rob Mallicoat .01 .05
820 Milt Hill .01 .05
821 Carlos Garcia .01 .05
822 Stan Royer .01 .05
823 Jeff Plympton .01 .05
824 Braulio Castillo .01 .05
825 David Haas .01 .05
826 Luis Mercedes .01 .05
827 Eric Karros .02 .10
828 Shawn Hare RC .02 .10
829 Reggie Sanders .02 .10
830 Tom Goodwin .01 .05
831 Dan Gakeler .01 .05
832 Stacy Jones .01 .05
833 Kim Batiste .01 .05
834 Cal Eldred .01 .05
835 Chris George .01 .05
836 Wayne Housie .01 .05
837 Mike Ignasiak .01 .05
838 Josias Manzanillo RC .02 .10
839 Jim Olander .01 .05
840 Gary Cooper .01 .05
841 Royce Clayton .01 .05
842 Hector Fajardo RC .02 .10
843 Blaine Beatty .01 .05
844 Jorge Pedre .01 .05
845 Kenny Lofton .05 .15
846 Scott Brosius RC .20 .50
847 Chris Cron .01 .05
848 Denis Boucher .01 .05
849 Kyle Abbott .01 .05
850 Bob Zupcic RC .02 .10
851 Rheal Cormier .01 .05
852 Jimmy Lewis RC .01 .05
853 Anthony Telford .01 .05
854 Cliff Brantley .01 .05
855 Kevin Campbell .01 .05
856 Craig Shipley .01 .05
857 Chuck Carr .01 .05
858 Tony Eusebio .02 .10
859 Jim Thome .08 .25
860 Vinny Castilla RC .40 1.00
861 Dann Howitt .01 .05
862 Kevin Ward .01 .05
863 Steve Wapnick .01 .05
864 Rod Brewer RC .02 .10
865 Todd Van Poppel .01 .05
866 Jose Hernandez RC .08 .25
867 Amalio Carreno .01 .05
868 Calvin Jones .01 .05
869 Jeff Gardner .01 .05
870 Jarvis Brown .01 .05
871 Eddie Taubensee RC .08 .25
872 Andy Mota .01 .05
873 Chris Haney .01 .05
874 Roberto Hernandez .01 .05
875 Laddie Renfroe .01 .05
876 Scott Cooper .01 .05
877 Armando Reynoso RC .08 .25
878 Ty Cobb MEMO .08 .25
879 Babe Ruth MEMO .20 .50
880 Honus Wagner MEMO .08 .25
881 Lou Gehrig MEMO .15 .40
882 Satchel Paige MEMO .08 .25
883 Will Clark DT .02 .10
884 Cal Ripken DT .75 2.00
885 Wade Boggs DT .02 .10
886 Kirby Puckett DT .05 .15
887 Tony Gwynn DT .05 .15
888 Craig Biggio DT .02 .10
889 Scott Erickson DT .01 .05
890 Tom Glavine DT .02 .10
891 Rob Dibble DT .02 .10
892 Mitch Williams DT .01 .05
893 Frank Thomas DT .05 .15
X672 Knoblauch 90 Score AU/3000 12.50 30.00

1992 Score DiMaggio

This five-card standard-size insert set was issued in honor of one of baseball's all-time greats, Joe DiMaggio. These cards were randomly inserted in first series packs. According to sources at Score, 30,000 of each card were produced. On a white card face, the fronts have vintage photos that have been colorized and accented by red, white, and blue border stripes. DiMaggio autographed 2,500 cards for this promotion. 2,495 of these cards were inserted in packs while the other five were used as prizes in a mail-in sweepstakes. The autographed cards are individually numbered out of 2,500.

COMPLETE SET (5) 25.00 60.00
COMMON DIMAGGIO (1-5) 6.00 15.00
RANDOM INSERTS IN SER.1 PACKS
AU Joe DiMaggio AU/2500 200.00 400.00

1992 Score Factory Inserts

This 17-card insert standard-size set was distributed only in 1992 Score factory sets and consists of four topical subsets. Cards B1-B7 capture a moment from each game of the 1991 World Series. Cards B8-B11 are Cooperstown cards, honoring future Hall of Famers. Cards B12-B14 form a "Joe D" subset paying tribute to Joe DiMaggio. Cards B15-B17, subtitled "Yaz", conclude the set by commemorating Carl Yastrzemski's heroic feats twenty-five years ago in winning the Triple Crown and lifting the Red Sox to their first American League pennant in 21 years. Each subset displayed a different front design. The World Series cards carry full-bleed color action photos except for a blue stripe at the bottom, while the Cooperstown cards have a color portrait on a white card face. Both the DiMaggio and Yastrzemski subsets have action photos with silver borders; they differ in that the DiMaggio photos are black and white, the Yastrzemski photos color. The DiMaggio and Yastrzemski subsets are numbered on the back within each subset (e.g., "1 of 3") and as a part of the 17-card insert set (e.g., "B1"). In the DiMaggio and Yastrzemski subsets, Score varied the insert set slightly in retail versus hobby factory sets. In the hobby set, the DiMaggio cards display different black-and-white photos that are bordered beneath by a dark blue stripe (the stripe is green in the retail factory insert). On the backs, these hobby inserts have a red stripe at the bottom; the same stripe is dark blue on the retail inserts. The Yastrzemski cards in the hobby set have different color photos on their fronts than the retail inserts.

COMPLETE SET (17) 3.00 8.00
ONE SET PER FACTORY SET
B1 Greg Gagne WS .15 .40
B2 Scott Leius WS .15 .40
B3 Mark Lemke WS .15 .40
David Justice
B4 Lonnie Smith WS .15 .40
Brian Harper
B5 David Justice WS .30 .75
B6 Kirby Puckett WS .75 2.00
B7 Gene Larkin WS .15 .40
B8 Carlton Fisk COOP .50 1.25
B9 Ozzie Smith COOP 1.25 3.00
B10 Dave Winfield COOP .30 .75
B11 Robin Yount COOP 1.25 3.00
B12 Joe DiMaggio .40 1.00
B13 Joe DiMaggio .40 1.00
B14 Joe DiMaggio .40 1.00
B15 Carl Yastrzemski .20 .50
B16 Carl Yastrzemski .20 .50
B17 Carl Yastrzemski .20 .50

1992 Score Franchise

This four-card standard-size set features three all-time greats, Stan Musial, Mickey Mantle, and Carl Yastrzemski. Score produced 150,000 of each Franchise cardof which were randomly inserted in 1992 Score Series II poly packs, blister packs, and cello packs.

COMPLETE SET (4) 12.50 30.00
RANDOM INSERTS IN SER.2 PACKS
STATED PRINT RUN 150,000 SETS
1 Stan Musial 2.00 5.00
2 Mickey Mantle 4.00 10.00
3 Carl Yastrzemski 2.00 5.00
4 Musial 4.00 10.00
Mantle
Yaz

1992 Score Franchise Autographs

Randomly seeded into packs at an unspecified rate, this four card set is composed of legends Mickey Mantle, Stan Musial and Carl Yastrzemski (including a fourth card that combines all three players). The individually signed cards (each serial-numbered to 2,000 copies on back) are signed in blue ink of which is prone to fading. The triple-signed card (limited to only 500 serial-numbered copies) was signed in gold paint pen bvy each player and is recognized as one of the touchstone cards in the development of certified autograph trading cards within the modern era.

RANDOM INSERTS IN SER.2 PACKS
1-3 PRINT RUN 2000 SERIAL #'d SETS
COMBO CARD PRINT RUN 500 #'d COPIES
AU1 Stan Musial 60.00 120.00
AU2 Mickey Mantle 250.00 500.00
AU3 Carl Yastrzemski 50.00 100.00
AU4 Musial/Mantle/Yaz 450.00 900.00

1992 Score Hot Rookies

This ten-card standard-size set features color action player photos on a white face. These cards were inserted at a stated rate of one per blister pack.

COMPLETE SET (10) 3.00 8.00
ONE PER BLISTER PACK
1 Cal Eldred .20 .50
2 Royce Clayton .20 .50
3 Kenny Lofton .75 2.00
4 Todd Van Poppel .20 .50
5 Scott Cooper .20 .50
6 Todd Hundley .20 .50
7 Tino Martinez .75 2.00
8 Anthony Telford .20 .50
9 Derek Bell .20 .50
10 Reggie Jefferson .20 .50

1992 Score Impact Players

The 1992 Score Impact Players insert set was issued in two series each with 45 standard-size cards with the respective series of the 1992 regular issue Score cards. Five of these cards were inserted in each 1992 Score jumbo pack.

COMPLETE SET (90) 8.00 20.00
COMPLETE SERIES 1 (45) 5.00 12.00
COMPLETE SERIES 2 (45) 2.50 6.00
FIVE PER JUMBO PACK
1 Chuck Knoblauch .10 .30
2 Jeff Bagwell .30 .75
3 Juan Guzman .05 .15
4 Milt Cuyler .05 .15
5 Ivan Rodriguez .30 .75
6 Rich DeLucia .05 .15
7 Orlando Merced .05 .15
8 Ray Lankford .10 .30
9 Brian Hunter .05 .15
10 Roberto Alomar .20 .50
11 Wes Chamberlain .05 .15
12 Steve Avery .05 .15
13 Scott Erickson .05 .15
14 Jim Abbott .20 .50
15 Mark Whiten .05 .15
16 Leo Gomez .05 .15
17 Doug Henry .10 .30
18 Brent Mayne .05 .15
19 Charles Nagy .05 .15
20 Phil Plantier .05 .15
21 Mo Vaughn .10 .30
22 Craig Biggio .20 .50
23 Derek Bell .10 .30
24 Royce Clayton .05 .15
25 Gary Cooper .05 .15
26 Scott Cooper .05 .15
27 Juan Gonzalez .20 .50
28 Ken Griffey Jr. .60 1.50
29 Larry Walker .20 .50
30 John Smoltz .20 .50
31 Todd Hundley .05 .15
32 Kenny Lofton .20 .50
33 Andy Mota .05 .15
34 Todd Zeile .05 .15
35 Arthur Rhodes .05 .15
36 Jim Thome .30 .75
37 Todd Van Poppel .05 .15
38 Mark Wohlers .05 .15
39 Anthony Young .05 .15
40 Sandy Alomar Jr. .05 .15
41 John Olerud .10 .30
42 Robin Ventura .10 .30
43 Frank Thomas .30 .75
44 David Justice .10 .30
45 Hal Morris .05 .15
46 Ruben Sierra .10 .30
47 Travis Fryman .10 .30
48 Mike Mussina .30 .75
49 Tom Glavine .20 .50
50 Barry Larkin .20 .50

51 Will Clark	.20	.50
52 Jose Canseco	.20	.50
53 Bo Jackson	.30	.75
54 Dwight Gooden	.10	.30
55 Barry Bonds	1.25	3.00
56 Fred McGriff	.20	.50
57 Roger Clemens	.60	1.50
58 Benito Santiago	.10	.30
59 Darryl Strawberry	.10	.30
60 Cecil Fielder	.10	.30
61 John Franco	.10	.30
62 Matt Williams	.10	.30
63 Marquis Grissom	.10	.30
64 Danny Tartabull	.05	.15
65 Ron Gant	.10	.30
66 Paul O'Neill	.20	.50
67 Devon White	.10	.30
68 Rafael Palmeiro	.20	.50
69 Tom Gordon	.05	.15
70 Shawon Dunston	.05	.15
71 Rob Dibble	.10	.30
72 Eddie Zosky	.05	.15
73 Jack McDowell	.05	.15
74 Len Dykstra	.10	.30
75 Ramon Martinez	.05	.15
76 Reggie Sanders	.10	.30
77 Greg Maddux	.50	1.25
78 Ellis Burks	.10	.30
79 John Smiley	.05	.15
80 Roberto Kelly	.05	.15
81 Ben McDonald	.05	.15
82 Mark Lewis	.05	.15
83 Jose Rijo	.05	.15
84 Ozzie Guillen	.10	.30
85 Lance Dickson	.05	.15
86 Kim Batiste	.05	.15
87 Gregg Olson	.05	.15
88 Andy Benes	.05	.15
89 Cal Eldred	.05	.15
90 David Cone	.10	.30

1992 Score Rookie/Traded

The 1992 Score Rookie and Traded set contains 110 standard-size cards featuring traded veterans and rookies. This set was issued in complete set form and was released through hobby dealers. The set is arranged numerically such that cards 1T-79T are traded players and cards 80T-110T feature rookies. Notable Rookie Cards in this set include Brian Jordan and Jeff Kent.

COMP.FACT.SET (110)	3.00	8.00
1T Gary Sheffield	.10	.30
2T Kevin Seitzer	.07	.20
3T Danny Tartabull	.07	.20
4T Steve Sax	.07	.20
5T Bobby Bonilla	.10	.30
6T Frank Viola	.10	.30
7T Dave Winfield	.10	.30
8T Rick Sutcliffe	.10	.30
9T Jose Canseco	.20	.50
10T Greg Swindell	.07	.20
11T Eddie Murray	.30	.75
12T Randy Myers	.07	.20
13T Wally Joyner	.10	.30
14T Kenny Lofton	.20	.50
15T Jack Morris	.10	.30
16T Charlie Hayes	.07	.20
17T Pete Incaviglia	.07	.20
18T Kevin Mitchell	.07	.20
19T Kurt Stillwell	.07	.20
20T Bret Saberhagen	.10	.30
21T Steve Buechele	.07	.20
22T John Smiley	.07	.20
23T Sammy Sosa Cubs	.30	.75
24T George Bell	.07	.20
25T Curt Schilling	.20	.50
26T Dick Schofield	.07	.20
27T David Cone	.10	.30
28T Dan Gladden	.07	.20
29T Kirk McCaskill	.07	.20
30T Mike Gallego	.07	.20
31T Kevin McReynolds	.07	.20
32T Bill Swift	.07	.20
33T Dave Martinez	.07	.20
34T Storm Davis	.07	.20
35T Willie Randolph	.10	.30
36T Melido Perez	.07	.20
37T Mark Carreon	.07	.20
38T Doug Jones	.07	.20
39T Gregg Jefferies	.07	.20
40T Mike Jackson	.07	.20
41T Dickie Thon	.07	.20
42T Eric King	.07	.20
43T Herm Winningham	.07	.20
44T Derek Lilliquist	.07	.20
45T Dave Anderson	.07	.20
46T Jeff Reardon	.10	.30
47T Scott Bankhead	.07	.20
48T Cory Snyder	.07	.20
49T Al Newman	.07	.20
50T Keith Miller	.07	.20
51T Dave Burba	.07	.20
52T Bill Pecota	.07	.20
53T Chuck Crim	.07	.20
54T Mariano Duncan	.07	.20
55T Dave Gallagher	.07	.20
56T Chris Gwynn	.07	.20
57T Scott Ruskin	.07	.20
58T Jack Armstrong	.07	.20
59T Gary Carter	.10	.30
60T Andres Galarraga	.10	.30
61T Ken Hill	.07	.20
62T Eric Davis	.10	.30
63T Ruben Sierra	.10	.30
64T Darrin Fletcher	.07	.20
65T Tim Belcher	.07	.20
66T Mike Morgan	.07	.20
67T Scott Scudder	.07	.20
68T Tom Candiotti	.07	.20
69T Hubie Brooks	.07	.20
70T Kal Daniels	.07	.20
71T Bruce Ruffin	.07	.20
72T Billy Hatcher	.07	.20
73T Bob Melvin	.07	.20
74T Lee Guetterman	.07	.20
75T Rene Gonzales	.07	.20
76T Kevin Bass	.07	.20
77T Tom Bolton	.07	.20
78T John Wetteland	.10	.30
79T Bip Roberts	.07	.20
80T Pat Listach RC	.15	.40
81T John Doherty RC	.07	.20
82T Sam Militello	.07	.20
83T Brian Jordan RC	.25	.60
84T Jeff Kent RC	1.25	3.00
85T Dave Fleming	.07	.20
86T Jeff Tackett	.07	.20
87T Chad Curtis RC	.15	.40
88T Eric Fox RC	.07	.20
89T Denny Neagle	.10	.30
90T Donovan Osborne	.07	.20
91T Carlos Hernandez	.07	.20
92T Tim Wakefield RC	1.25	3.00
93T Tim Salmon	.20	.50
94T Dave Nilsson	.07	.20
95T Mike Perez	.07	.20
96T Pat Hentgen	.07	.20
97T Frank Seminara RC	.07	.20
98T Ruben Amaro	.07	.20
99T Archi Cianfrocco RC	.07	.20
100T Andy Stankiewicz	.07	.20
101T Jim Bullinger	.07	.20
102T Pat Mahomes RC	.15	.40
103T Hipolito Pichardo RC	.07	.20
104T Bret Boone	.20	.50
105T John Vander Wal	.07	.20
106T Vince Horsman	.07	.20
107T Jim Austin	.07	.20
108T Brian Williams RC	.07	.20
109T Dan Walters	.07	.20
110T Wil Cordero	.07	.20

1992 Score 100 Rising Stars

The 1992 Score Rising Stars set contains 100 standard size player cards and six "Magic Motion" trivia cards.

COMPLETE SET (100)	3.00	8.00
1 Milt Cuyler	.01	.05
2 David Howard	.01	.05
3 Brian R. Hunter	.01	.05
4 Darryl Kile	.02	.10
5 Pat Kelly	.01	.05
6 Luis Gonzalez	.08	.25
7 Mike Benjamin	.01	.05
8 Eric Anthony	.01	.05
9 Moises Alou	.05	.15
10 Darren Lewis	.01	.05
11 Chuck Knoblauch	.08	.25
12 Geronimo Pena	.01	.05
13 Jeff Plympton	.01	.05
14 Bret Barberie	.01	.05
15 Chris Haney	.01	.05
16 Rick Wilkins	.01	.05
17 Julio Valera	.01	.05
18 Joe Slusarski	.01	.05
19 Jose Melendez	.01	.05
20 Pete Schourek	.01	.05
21 Jeff Conine	.02	.10
22 Paul Faries	.01	.05
23 Scott Kamieniecki	.01	.05
24 Bernard Gilkey	.01	.05
25 Wes Chamberlain	.01	.05
26 Charles Nagy	.01	.05
27 Juan Guzman	.01	.05
28 Heath Slocumb	.01	.05
29 Eddie Taubensee	.02	.10
30 Cedric Landrum	.01	.05
31 Jose Offerman	.01	.05
32 Andres Santana	.01	.05
33 David Segui	.02	.10
34 Bernie Williams	.50	1.25
35 Jeff Bagwell	1.00	2.50
36 Kevin Morton	.01	.05
37 Kirk Dressendorfer	.01	.05
38 Mike Fetters	.01	.05
39 Darren Holmes	.01	.05
40 Jeff Johnson	.01	.05
41 Scott Aldred	.01	.05
42 Kevin Ward	.01	.05
43 Ray Lankford	.08	.25
44 Terry Shumpert	.01	.05
45 Wade Taylor	.01	.05
46 Rob MacDonald	.01	.05
47 Jose Mota	.01	.05
48 Reggie Harris	.01	.05
49 Mike Remlinger	.01	.05
50 Mark Lewis	.01	.05
51 Tino Martinez	.08	.25
52 Ed Sprague	.01	.05
53 Freddie Benavides	.01	.05
54 Rich DeLucia	.01	.05
55 Brian Drahman	.01	.05
56 Steve Decker	.01	.05
57 Scott Livingstone	.01	.05
58 Mike Timlin	.01	.05
59 Bob Scanlan	.01	.05
60 Dean Palmer	.05	.15
61 Frank Castillo	.01	.05
62 Mark Leonard	.01	.05
63 Chuck McElroy	.01	.05
64 Derek Bell	.01	.05
65 Andujar Cedeno	.01	.05
66 Leo Gomez	.01	.05
67 Rusty Meacham	.01	.05
68 Dann Howitt	.01	.05
69 Chris Jones	.01	.05
70 Dave Cochrane	.01	.05
71 Carlos Martinez	.01	.05
72 Hensley Meulens	.01	.05
73 Rich Reed	.01	.05
74 Pedro Munoz	.01	.05
75 Orlando Merced	.01	.05
76 Chito Martinez	.01	.05
77 Ivan Rodriguez	1.00	2.50
78 Brian Barnes	.01	.05
79 Chris Donnels	.01	.05
80 Todd Hundley	.02	.10
81 Gary Scott	.01	.05
82 John Wehner	.01	.05
83 Al Osuna	.01	.05
84 Luis Lopez	.01	.05
85 Brent Mayne	.01	.05
86 Phil Plantier	.01	.05
87 Joe Bitker	.01	.05
88 Scott Cooper	.01	.05
89 Chris Hammond	.02	.10
90 Tim Sherrill	.01	.05
91 Doug Simons	.01	.05
92 Kip Gross	.01	.05
93 Tim McIntosh	.01	.05
94 Larry Casian	.01	.05
95 Mike Dalton	.01	.05
96 Lance Dickson	.01	.05
97 Joe Grahe	.01	.05
98 Glenn Sutko	.01	.05
99 Gerald Alexander	.01	.05
100 Mo Vaughn	.08	.25

1992 Score 100 Superstars

The 1992 Score Superstars set contains 100 standard-size player cards and six "Magic Motion" trivia cards.

COMPLETE SET (100)	5.00	12.00
1 Ken Griffey Jr.	.75	2.00
2 Scott Erickson	.01	.05
3 John Smiley	.01	.05
4 Rick Aguilera	.02	.10
5 Jeff Reardon	.02	.10
6 Chuck Finley	.02	.10
7 Kirby Puckett	.25	.60
8 Paul Molitor	.15	.40
9 Dave Winfield	.15	.40
10 Mike Greenwell	.01	.05
11 Bret Saberhagen	.02	.10
12 Pete Harnisch	.01	.05
13 Ozzie Guillen	.05	.15
14 Hal Morris	.01	.05
15 Tom Glavine	.15	.40
16 David Cone	.05	.15
17 Edgar Martinez	.05	.15
18 Willie McGee	.02	.10
19 Jim Abbott	.02	.10
20 Mark Grace	.05	.15
21 George Brett	.50	1.25
22 Jack McDowell	.01	.05
23 Don Mattingly	.60	1.50
24 Will Clark	.08	.25
25 Dwight Gooden	.02	.10
26 Barry Bonds	.50	1.25
27 Rafael Palmeiro	.15	.40
28 Lee Smith	.02	.10
29 Wally Joyner	.02	.10
30 Wade Boggs	.30	.75
31 Tom Henke	.01	.05
32 Mark Langston	.01	.05
33 Robin Ventura	.08	.25
34 Steve Avery	.01	.05
35 Joe Carter	.02	.10
36 Benito Santiago	.02	.10
37 Dave Stieb	.01	.05
38 Julio Franco	.02	.10
39 Albert Belle	.02	.10
40 Dale Murphy	.08	.25
41 Rob Dibble	.01	.05
42 Dave Justice	.08	.25
43 Jose Rijo	.01	.05
44 Eric Davis	.02	.10
45 Terry Pendleton	.01	.05
46 Kevin Maas	.01	.05
47 Ozzie Smith	.40	1.00
48 Andre Dawson	.05	.15
49 Sandy Alomar Jr.	.02	.10
50 Nolan Ryan	1.25	3.00
51 Frank Thomas	.30	.75
52 Craig Biggio	.05	.15
53 Doug Drabek	.01	.05
54 Bobby Thigpen	.01	.05
55 Darryl Strawberry	.02	.10
56 Dennis Eckersley	.15	.40
57 John Franco	.02	.10
58 Paul O'Neill	.05	.15
59 Scott Sanderson	.01	.05
60 Dave Stewart	.02	.10
61 Ivan Calderon	.01	.05
62 Frank Viola	.01	.05
63 Mark McGwire	.60	1.50
64 Kelly Gruber	.01	.05
65 Fred McGriff	.05	.15
66 Cecil Fielder	.02	.10
67 Jose Canseco	.15	.40
68 Howard Johnson	.01	.05
69 Juan Gonzalez	.25	.60
70 Tim Wallach	.01	.05
71 John Olerud	.08	.25
72 Carlton Fisk	.15	.40
73 Otis Nixon	.01	.05
74 Roger Clemens	.60	1.50
75 Ramon Martinez	.02	.10
76 Ron Gant	.02	.10
77 Barry Larkin	.08	.25
78 Eddie Murray	.15	.40
79 Vince Coleman	.01	.05
80 Bobby Bonilla	.01	.05
81 Tony Gwynn	.50	1.25
82 Roberto Alomar	.08	.25
83 Ellis Burks	.02	.10
84 Robin Yount	.20	.50
85 Ryne Sandberg	.20	.50
86 Len Dykstra	.02	.10
87 Ruben Sierra	.02	.10
88 George Bell	.01	.05
89 Cal Ripken	1.25	3.00
90 Danny Tartabull	.01	.05
91 Gregg Olson	.01	.05
92 Dave Henderson	.01	.05
93 Kevin Mitchell	.01	.05
94 Ben McDonald	.01	.05
95 Matt Williams	.05	.15
96 Roberto Kelly	.01	.05
97 Dennis Martinez	.02	.10
98 Kent Hrbek	.02	.10
99 Felix Jose	.01	.05
100 Rickey Henderson	.30	.75

1992 Score/Pinnacle Promo Panels

COMPLETE SET (25)	20.00	50.00
1 Nolan Ryan	4.00	10.00
Terry Pendleton		
Willie McGee		
Lonnie		
2 Will Clark	.75	2.00
Mark Langston		
Paul Molitor		
Devon Whi		
3 Frank Thomas	3.00	8.00
David Justice		
Mark Carreon		
Dave He		
4 Kirby Puckett	2.50	6.00
Ryne Sandberg		
Roberto Alomar		
Davi		
5 Ozzie Smith	1.50	4.00
Darryl Strawberry		
Kevin Seitzer		
Jef		
6 Robin Yount	.75	2.00
Jay Buhner		
Chuck Crim		
Jimmy Jones		
7 Don Mattingly	1.50	4.00
Matt Williams		
Dave Winfield		
Georg		
8 Orel Hershisher	.40	1.00
Wes Chamberlain		
Gary Gaetti		
Dic		
9 Ron Gant	.75	2.00
Andres Galarraga		
Bruce Hurst		
Alex Fern		
10 Albert Belle	.60	1.50
Ellis Burks		
Melido Perez		
Kevin Gro		
11 Ivan Calderon	.40	1.00
Bill Doran		
Rick Aguilera		
Doug Jon		
12 Todd Zeile	.40	1.00
Mike Gallego		
Lenny Harris		
Jack Clark		
13 Harold Baines	.40	1.00
Walt Weiss		
Eric Davis		
Randy Ready		
14 N.Ryan	6.00	15.00
G.Brett		
G.Bell		
R.Palmeiro		
15 Chili Davis	.40	1.00
Phil Plantier		
David Wells		
Bob Walk		
16 John Olerud	.40	1.00
Dave Hollins		
Jack McDowell		
Juan Sam		
17 Carlton Fisk	.60	1.50
Kent Hrbek		
Denny Martinez		
Jim Acke		
18 Jay Buhner	.60	1.50
Gregg Olson		
Terry Steinbach		
Kirk McC		
19 Jeff Bagwell	1.50	4.00
Darryl Strawberry		
Travis Fryman		
An		
20 Alex Cole	.60	1.50
Jim Gantner		
Ken Caminiti		
Todd Stottle		
21 Alex Fernandez	.40	1.00
Bill Gullickson		
Jose Guzman		
Shaw		
22 Bernard Gilkey	.40	1.00
Omar Vizquel		
Ivan Calderon		
Ozzie		
23 Gary Gaetti	.40	1.00
Doug Drabek		
Brent Mayne		
Tom Bolton		
24 David Justice	.75	2.00
Kevin Maas		
Jody Reed		
Vince Colema		
25 Chili Davis	.40	1.00
Hensley Meulens		
David Howard		
Mark L		

1992 Score Proctor and Gamble

This 18-card standard-size set was produced by Score for Proctor and Gamble as a mail-in premium and contains 18 players from the 1992 All-Star Game line-up. The production run comprised 2,000,000 sets and 25 uncut sheets. A three-card sample set was also produced for sales representatives with a print run of 5,000,000 sets and 25 uncut sheets. The three sample cards, featuring Griffey, Sandberg, and Henderson, are stamped "sample" on the back. Collectors could obtain the set by sending in a required certificate, 99 cents, three UPC symbols from three different Proctor and Gamble products, and 50 cents for postage and handling. The certificate was published in a flyer inserted in Sunday, August 16 newspapers. The card fronts feature color action player cutouts superimposed on a diagonally striped background showing a large star behind the player. Card numbers 1-9 have a blue star on a graded magenta background, while card numbers 10-18 show a red star on blue-green. The backs display a close-up photo, biographical and statistical information, and career summary on a graded yellow-orange background. The cards are numbered "X/18" at the lower right corner.

COMPLETE SET (18)	2.00	5.00
1 Sandy Alomar Jr.	.05	.15
2 Mark McGwire	.40	1.00
3 Roberto Alomar	.08	.25
4 Wade Boggs	.15	.40
5 Cal Ripken	.75	2.00
6 Kirby Puckett	.20	.50
7 Ken Griffey Jr.	.60	1.50
8 Jose Canseco	.15	.40
9 Kevin Brown	.07	.20
10 Benito Santiago	.05	.15
11 Fred McGriff	.07	.20
12 Ryne Sandberg	.30	.75
13 Terry Pendleton	.02	.10
14 Ozzie Smith	.30	.75
15 Barry Bonds	.30	.75
16 Tony Gwynn	.40	1.00
17 Andy Van Slyke	.02	.10
18 Tom Glavine	.08	.25

1992 Score Rookies

This 40-card boxed set measures the standard size and features glossy color action player photos on a kelly green face with meandering purple stripes.

COMP.FACT SET (40)	1.50	4.00
1 Todd Van Poppel	.01	.05
2 Kyle Abbott	.01	.05
3 Derek Bell	.01	.05
4 Jim Thome	.60	1.50
5 Mark Wohlers	.01	.05
6 Todd Hundley	.08	.25
7 Arthur Lee Rhodes	.01	.05
8 John Ramos	.01	.05
9 Chris George	.01	.05
10 Kenny Lofton	.40	1.00
11 Ted Wood	.01	.05
12 Royce Clayton	.01	.05
13 Scott Cooper	.01	.05
14 Anthony Young	.01	.05
15 Joel Johnston	.01	.05
16 Andy Mota	.01	.05
17 Lenny Webster	.01	.05
18 Andy Ashby	.01	.05
19 Jose Mota	.01	.05
20 Tim McIntosh	.01	.05
21 Terry Bross	.01	.05
22 Harvey Pulliam	.01	.05
23 Hector Fajardo	.01	.05
24 Esteban Beltre	.01	.05
25 Gary DiSarcina	.01	.05
26 Mike Humphreys	.01	.05
27 Jarvis Brown	.01	.05
28 Gary Cooper	.01	.05
29 Chris Donnels	.01	.05
30 Monty Fariss	.01	.05
31 Eric Karros	.30	.75
32 Braulio Castillo	.01	.05
33 Cal Eldred	.01	.05
34 Tom Goodwin	.01	.05
35 Reggie Sanders	.20	.50
36 Scott Servais	.01	.05
37 Kim Batiste	.01	.05
38 Eric Wedge	.08	.25
39 Willie Banks	.01	.05
40 Mo Sanford	.01	.05

1993 Score

The 1993 Score baseball set consists of 660 standard-size cards issued in one single series. The cards were distributed in 16-card poly packs and 35-card jumbo superpacks. Topical subsets featured are Award Winners (481-486), Draft Picks (487-501), All-Star Caricature (502-512 [AL], 522-531 [NL]), Highlights (513-519), World Series Highlights (520-521), Dream Team (532-542) and Rookies (sprinkled throughout the set). Rookie Cards in this set include Derek Jeter, Jason Kendall and Shannon Stewart.

COMPLETE SET (660)	15.00	40.00
SUBSET CARDS HALF VALUE OF BASE CARDS		
1 Ken Griffey Jr.	.40	1.00
2 Gary Sheffield	.07	.20
3 Frank Thomas	.20	.50
4 Ryne Sandberg	.30	.75
5 Larry Walker	.07	.20
6 Cal Ripken	.60	1.50
7 Roger Clemens	.40	1.00
8 Bobby Bonilla	.07	.20
9 Carlos Baerga	.02	.10
10 Darren Daulton	.07	.20
11 Travis Fryman	.07	.20
12 Andy Van Slyke	.10	.30
13 Jose Canseco	.10	.30
14 Roberto Alomar	.10	.30
15 Tom Glavine	.10	.30
16 Barry Larkin	.10	.30
17 Gregg Jefferies	.02	.10
18 Craig Biggio	.10	.30
19 Shane Mack	.02	.10
20 Brett Butler	.07	.20
21 Dennis Eckersley	.07	.20
22 Will Clark	.10	.30
23 Don Mattingly	.50	1.25
24 Tony Gwynn	.25	.60
25 Ivan Rodriguez	.10	.30
26 Shawon Dunston	.02	.10
27 Mike Mussina	.10	.30
28 Marquis Grissom	.07	.20
29 Charles Nagy	.02	.10
30 Len Dykstra	.07	.20
31 Cecil Fielder	.07	.20
32 Jay Bell	.07	.20
33 B.J. Surhoff	.07	.20
34 Bob Tewksbury	.02	.10
35 Danny Tartabull	.02	.10
36 Terry Pendleton	.07	.20
37 Jack Morris	.07	.20
38 Hal Morris	.02	.10
39 Luis Polonia	.02	.10
40 Ken Caminiti	.07	.20
41 Robin Ventura	.07	.20
42 Darryl Strawberry	.07	.20
43 Wally Joyner	.07	.20
44 Fred McGriff	.10	.30
45 Kevin Tapani	.02	.10
46 Matt Williams	.07	.20
47 Robin Yount	.30	.75
48 Ken Hill	.02	.10
49 Edgar Martinez	.10	.30
50 Mark Grace	.10	.30
51 Juan Gonzalez	.07	.20
52 Curt Schilling	.07	.20
53 Dwight Gooden	.07	.20
54 Chris Hoiles	.02	.10
55 Frank Viola	.07	.20
56 Ray Lankford	.07	.20
57 George Brett	.50	1.25
58 Kenny Lofton	.07	.20
59 Nolan Ryan	.75	2.00
60 Mickey Tettleton	.02	.10
61 John Smoltz	.10	.30
62 Howard Johnson	.02	.10
63 Eric Karros	.07	.20
64 Rick Aguilera	.02	.10
65 Steve Finley	.07	.20
66 Mark Langston	.02	.10
67 Bill Swift	.02	.10
68 John Olerud	.07	.20
69 Kevin McReynolds	.02	.10
70 Jack McDowell	.02	.10
71 Rickey Henderson	.20	.50
72 Brian Harper	.02	.10
73 Mike Morgan	.02	.10
74 Rafael Palmeiro	.10	.30
75 Dennis Martinez	.07	.20
76 Tino Martinez	.10	.30
77 Eddie Murray	.20	.50
78 Ellis Burks	.07	.20
79 John Kruk	.07	.20
80 Gregg Olson	.02	.10
81 Bernard Gilkey	.02	.10
82 Milt Cuyler	.02	.10
83 Mike LaValliere	.02	.10
84 Albert Belle	.07	.20
85 Bip Roberts	.02	.10
86 Melido Perez	.02	.10
87 Otis Nixon	.02	.10
88 Bill Spiers	.02	.10
89 Jeff Bagwell	.10	.30
90 Orel Hershiser	.07	.20
91 Andy Benes	.02	.10
92 Devon White	.07	.20
93 Willie McGee	.07	.20
94 Ozzie Guillen	.07	.20
95 Ivan Calderon	.02	.10
96 Keith Miller	.02	.10
97 Steve Buechele	.02	.10
98 Kent Hrbek	.07	.20
99 Dave Hollins	.02	.10
100 Mike Bordick	.02	.10
101 Randy Tomlin	.02	.10
102 Omar Vizquel	.10	.30
103 Lee Smith	.07	.20
104 Leo Gomez	.02	.10
105 Jose Rijo	.02	.10
106 Mark Whiten	.02	.10
107 David Justice	.07	.20
108 Eddie Taubensee	.02	.10
109 Lance Johnson	.02	.10
110 Felix Jose	.02	.10
111 Mike Harkey	.02	.10
112 Randy Milligan	.02	.10
113 Anthony Young	.02	.10
114 Rico Brogna	.02	.10
115 Bret Saberhagen	.07	.20
116 Sandy Alomar Jr.	.02	.10
117 Terry Mulholland	.02	.10
118 Darryl Hamilton	.02	.10
119 Todd Zeile	.02	.10
120 Bernie Williams	.10	.30
121 Zane Smith	.02	.10
122 Derek Bell	.02	.10
123 Deion Sanders	.10	.30
124 Luis Sojo	.02	.10
125 Joe Oliver	.02	.10
126 Craig Grebeck	.02	.10
127 Andujar Cedeno	.02	.10
128 Brian McRae	.02	.10
129 Jose Offerman	.02	.10
130 Pedro Munoz	.02	.10
131 Bud Black	.02	.10
132 Mo Vaughn	.07	.20
133 Bruce Hurst	.02	.10
134 Dave Henderson	.02	.10
135 Tom Pagnozzi	.02	.10
136 Erik Hanson	.02	.10
137 Orlando Merced	.02	.10
138 Dean Palmer	.07	.20
139 John Franco	.07	.20
140 Brady Anderson	.07	.20
141 Ricky Jordan	.02	.10
142 Jeff Blauser	.02	.10
143 Sammy Sosa	.20	.50

144 Bob Walk .02 .10
145 Delino DeShields .02 .10
146 Kevin Brown .07 .20
147 Mark Lemke .02 .10
148 Chuck Knoblauch .07 .20
149 Chris Sabo .02 .10
150 Bobby Witt .02 .10
151 Luis Gonzalez .07 .20
152 Ron Karkovice .02 .10
153 Jeff Brantley .02 .10
154 Kevin Appier .07 .20
155 Darrin Jackson .02 .10
156 Kelly Gruber .02 .10
157 Royce Clayton .02 .10
158 Chuck Finley .07 .20
159 Jeff King .02 .10
160 Greg Vaughn .02 .10
161 Geronimo Pena .02 .10
162 Steve Farr .02 .10
163 Jose Oquendo .02 .10
164 Mark Lewis .02 .10
165 John Wetteland .07 .20
166 Mike Henneman .02 .10
167 Todd Hundley .02 .10
168 Wes Chamberlain .02 .10
169 Steve Avery .02 .10
170 Mike Devereaux .02 .10
171 Reggie Sanders .07 .20
172 Jay Buhner .07 .20
173 Eric Anthony .02 .10
174 John Burkett .02 .10
175 Tom Candiotti .02 .10
176 Phil Plantier .02 .10
177 Doug Henry .02 .10
178 Scott Leius .02 .10
179 Kirt Manwaring .02 .10
180 Jeff Parrett .02 .10
181 Don Slaught .02 .10
182 Scott Radinsky .02 .10
183 Luis Alicea .02 .10
184 Tom Gordon .02 .10
185 Rick Wilkins .02 .10
186 Todd Stottlemyre .02 .10
187 Moises Alou .07 .20
188 Joe Grahe .02 .10
189 Jeff Kent .20 .50
190 Bill Wegman .02 .10
191 Kim Batiste .02 .10
192 Matt Nokes .02 .10
193 Mark Wohlers .02 .10
194 Paul Sorrento .02 .10
195 Chris Hammond .02 .10
196 Scott Livingstone .02 .10
197 Doug Jones .02 .10
198 Scott Cooper .02 .10
199 Ramon Martinez .02 .10
200 Dave Valle .02 .10
201 Mariano Duncan .02 .10
202 Ben McDonald .02 .10
203 Darren Lewis .02 .10
204 Kenny Rogers .07 .20
205 Manuel Lee .02 .10
206 Scott Erickson .02 .10
207 Dan Gladden .02 .10
208 Bob Welch .02 .10
209 Greg Olson .02 .10
210 Dan Pasqua .02 .10
211 Tim Wallach .02 .10
212 Jeff Montgomery .02 .10
213 Derrick May .02 .10
214 Ed Sprague .02 .10
215 David Haas .02 .10
216 Darrin Fletcher .02 .10
217 Brian Jordan .07 .20
218 Jaime Navarro .02 .10
219 Randy Velarde .02 .10
220 Ron Gant .07 .20
221 Paul Quantrill .02 .10
222 Damion Easley .02 .10
223 Charlie Hough .07 .20
224 Brad Brink .02 .10
225 Barry Manuel .02 .10
226 Kevin Koslofski .02 .10
227 Ryan Thompson .02 .10
228 Mike Munoz .02 .10
229 Dan Wilson .07 .20
230 Peter Hoy .02 .10
231 Pedro Astacio .02 .10
232 Matt Stairs .02 .10
233 Jeff Reboulet .02 .10
234 Manny Alexander .02 .10
235 Willie Banks .02 .10
236 John Jaha .02 .10
237 Scooter Tucker .02 .10
238 Russ Springer .02 .10
239 Paul Miller .02 .10
240 Dan Peltier .02 .10
241 Ozzie Canseco .02 .10
242 Ben Rivera .02 .10
243 John Valentin .02 .10
244 Henry Rodriguez .02 .10
245 Derek Parks .02 .10
246 Carlos Garcia .02 .10
247 Tim Pugh RC .02 .10
248 Melvin Nieves .02 .10
249 Rich Amaral .02 .10
250 Willie Greene .02 .10
251 Tim Scott .02 .10
252 Dave Silvestri .02 .10
253 Rob Mallicoat .02 .10
254 Donald Harris .02 .10
255 Craig Colbert .02 .10
256 Jose Guzman .02 .10
257 Domingo Martinez RC .02 .10
258 William Suero .02 .10
259 Juan Guerrero .02 .10
260 J.T.Snow RC .20 .50
261 Tony Pena .02 .10
262 Tim Fortugno .02 .10
263 Tom Marsh .02 .10
264 Kurt Knudsen .02 .10
265 Tim Costo .02 .10
266 Steve Shifflett .02 .10
267 Billy Ashley .02 .10
268 Jerry Nielsen .02 .10
269 Pete Young .02 .10
270 Johnny Guzman .02 .10
271 Greg Colbrunn .02 .10
272 Jeff Nelson .02 .10
273 Kevin Young .07 .20
274 Jeff Frye .02 .10
275 J.T. Bruett .02 .10
276 Todd Pratt RC .08 .25
277 Mike Butcher .02 .10
278 John Flaherty .02 .10
279 John Patterson .02 .10
280 Eric Hillman .02 .10
281 Bien Figueroa .02 .10
282 Shane Reynolds .02 .10
283 Rich Rowland .02 .10
284 Steve Foster .02 .10
285 Dave Mlicki .02 .10
286 Mike Piazza 1.25 3.00
287 Mike Trombley .02 .10
288 Jim Pena .02 .10
289 Bob Ayrault .02 .10
290 Henry Mercedes .02 .10
291 Bob Wickman .02 .10
292 Jacob Brumfield .02 .10
293 David Hulse RC .02 .10
294 Ryan Klesko .07 .20
295 Doug Linton .02 .10
296 Steve Cooke .02 .10
297 Eddie Zosky .02 .10
298 Gerald Williams .02 .10
299 Jonathan Hurst .02 .10
300 Larry Carter RC .02 .10
301 William Pennyfeather .02 .10
302 Cesar Hernandez .02 .10
303 Steve Hosey .02 .10
304 Blas Minor .02 .10
305 Jeff Grotewald .02 .10
306 Bernardo Brito .02 .10
307 Rafael Bournigal .02 .10
308 Jeff Branson .02 .10
309 Tom Quinlan RC .02 .10
310 Pat Gomez RC .02 .10
311 Sterling Hitchcock RC .08 .25
312 Kent Bottenfield .02 .10
313 Alan Trammell .07 .20
314 Cris Colon .02 .10
315 Paul Wagner .02 .10
316 Matt Maysey .02 .10
317 Mike Stanton .02 .10
318 Rick Trlicek .02 .10
319 Kevin Rogers .02 .10
320 Mark Clark .02 .10
321 Pedro Martinez .40 1.00
322 Al Martin .02 .10
323 Mike Macfarlane .02 .10
324 Rey Sanchez .02 .10
325 Roger Pavlik .02 .10
326 Troy Neel .02 .10
327 Kerry Woodson .02 .10
328 Wayne Kirby .02 .10
329 Ken Ryan RC .08 .25
330 Jesse Levis .02 .10
331 Jim Austin .02 .10
332 Dan Walters .02 .10
333 Brian Williams .02 .10
334 Wil Cordero .02 .10
335 Bret Boone .07 .20
336 Hipolito Pichardo .02 .10
337 Pat Mahomes .02 .10
338 Andy Stankiewicz .02 .10
339 Jim Bullinger .02 .10
340 Archi Cianfrocco .02 .10
341 Ruben Amaro .02 .10
342 Frank Seminara .02 .10
343 Pat Hentgen .02 .10
344 Dave Nilsson .02 .10
345 Mike Perez .02 .10
346 Tim Salmon .10 .30
347 Tim Wakefield .20 .50
348 Carlos Hernandez .02 .10
349 Donovan Osborne .02 .10
350 Denny Neagle .07 .20
351 Sam Militello .02 .10
352 Eric Fox .02 .10
353 John Doherty .02 .10
354 Chad Curtis .02 .10
355 Jeff Tackett .02 .10
356 Dave Fleming .02 .10
357 Pat Listach .02 .10
358 Kevin Wickander .02 .10
359 John Vander Wal .02 .10
360 Arthur Rhodes .02 .10
361 Bob Scanlan .02 .10
362 Bob Zupcic .02 .10
363 Mel Rojas .02 .10
364 Jim Thome .10 .30
365 Bill Pecota .02 .10
366 Mark Carreon .02 .10
367 Mitch Williams .02 .10
368 Cal Eldred .02 .10
369 Stan Belinda .02 .10
370 Pat Kelly .02 .10
371 Rheal Cormier .02 .10
372 Juan Guzman .02 .10
373 Damon Berryhill .02 .10
374 Gary DiSarcina .02 .10
375 Norm Charlton .02 .10
376 Roberto Hernandez .02 .10
377 Scott Kamieniecki .02 .10
378 Rusty Meacham .02 .10
379 Kurt Stillwell .02 .10
380 Lloyd McClendon .02 .10
381 Mark Leonard .02 .10
382 Jerry Browne .02 .10
383 Glenn Davis .02 .10
384 Randy Johnson .20 .50
385 Mike Greenwell .02 .10
386 Scott Chiamparino .02 .10
387 George Bell .02 .10
388 Steve Olin .02 .10
389 Chuck McElroy .02 .10
390 Mark Gardner .02 .10
391 Rod Beck .02 .10
392 Dennis Rasmussen .02 .10
393 Charlie Leibrandt .02 .10
394 Julio Franco .07 .20
395 Pete Harnisch .02 .10
396 Sid Bream .02 .10
397 Milt Thompson .02 .10
398 Glenallen Hill .02 .10
399 Chico Walker .02 .10
400 Alex Cole .02 .10
401 Trevor Wilson .02 .10
402 Jeff Conine .07 .20
403 Kyle Abbott .02 .10
404 Tom Browning .02 .10
405 Jerald Clark .02 .10
406 Vince Horsman .02 .10
407 Kevin Mitchell .02 .10
408 Pete Smith .02 .10
409 Jeff Innis .02 .10
410 Mike Timlin .02 .10
411 Charlie Hayes .02 .10
412 Alex Fernandez .02 .10
413 Jeff Russell .02 .10
414 Jody Reed .02 .10
415 Mickey Morandini .02 .10
416 Darnell Coles .02 .10
417 Xavier Hernandez .02 .10
418 Steve Sax .02 .10
419 Joe Girardi .02 .10
420 Mike Fetters .02 .10
421 Danny Jackson .02 .10
422 Jim Gott .02 .10
423 Tim Belcher .02 .10
424 Jose Mesa .02 .10
425 Junior Felix .02 .10
426 Thomas Howard .02 .10
427 Julio Valera .02 .10
428 Dante Bichette .07 .20
429 Mike Sharperson .02 .10
430 Darryl Kile .07 .20
431 Lonnie Smith .02 .10
432 Monty Fariss .02 .10
433 Reggie Jefferson .02 .10
434 Bob McClure .02 .10
435 Craig Lefferts .02 .10
436 Duane Ward .02 .10
437 Shawn Abner .02 .10
438 Roberto Kelly .02 .10
439 Paul O'Neill .10 .30
440 Alan Mills .02 .10
441 Roger Mason .02 .10
442 Gary Pettis .02 .10
443 Steve Lake .02 .10
444 Gene Larkin .02 .10
445 Larry Andersen .02 .10
446 Doug Dascenzo .02 .10
447 Daryl Boston .02 .10
448 John Candelaria .02 .10
449 Storm Davis .02 .10
450 Tom Edens .02 .10
451 Mike Maddux .02 .10
452 Tim Naehring .02 .10
453 John Orton .02 .10
454 Joey Cora .02 .10
455 Chuck Crim .02 .10
456 Dan Plesac .02 .10
457 Mike Bielecki .02 .10
458 Terry Jorgensen .02 .10
459 John Habyan .02 .10
460 Pete O'Brien .02 .10
461 Jeff Treadway .02 .10
462 Frank Castillo .02 .10
463 Jimmy Jones .02 .10
464 Tommy Greene .02 .10
465 Tracy Woodson .02 .10
466 Rich Rodriguez .02 .10
467 Joe Hesketh .02 .10
468 Greg Myers .02 .10
469 Kirk McCaskill .02 .10
470 Ricky Bones .02 .10
471 Lenny Webster .02 .10
472 Francisco Cabrera .02 .10
473 Turner Ward .02 .10
474 Dwayne Henry .02 .10
475 Al Osuna .02 .10
476 Craig Wilson .02 .10
477 Chris Nabholz .02 .10
478 Rafael Belliard .02 .10
479 Terry Leach .02 .10
480 Tim Teufel .02 .10
481 Dennis Eckersley AW .07 .20
482 Barry Bonds MVP .30 .75
483 Dennis Eckersley AW .07 .20
484 Greg Maddux CY .20 .50
485 Pat Listach AW .02 .10
486 Eric Karros AW .02 .10
487 Jamie Arnold RC .02 .10
488 B.J.Wallace .02 .10
489 Derek Jeter RC 8.00 20.00
490 Jason Kendall RC .40 1.00
491 Rick Helling .02 .10
492 Derek Wallace RC .02 .10
493 Sean Lowe RC .02 .10
494 Shannon Stewart RC .30 .75
495 Benji Grigsby RC .02 .10
496 Todd Steverson RC .02 .10
497 Dan Serafini RC .02 .10
498 Michael Tucker .02 .10
499 Chris Roberts .02 .10
500 Pete Janicki RC .02 .10
501 Jeff Schmidt RC .02 .10
502 Edgar Martinez AS .07 .20
503 Omar Vizquel AS .07 .20
504 Ken Griffey Jr. AS .25 .60
505 Kirby Puckett AS .10 .30
506 Joe Carter AS .02 .10
507 Ivan Rodriguez AS .07 .20
508 Jack Morris AS .02 .10
509 Dennis Eckersley AS .07 .20
510 Frank Thomas AS .10 .30
511 Roberto Alomar AS .07 .20
512 Mickey Morandini AS .02 .10
513 Dennis Eckersley HL .07 .20
514 Jeff Reardon HL .02 .10
515 Danny Tartabull HL .02 .10
516 Bip Roberts HL .02 .10
517 George Brett HL .25 .60
518 Robin Yount HL .20 .50
519 Kevin Gross HL .02 .10
520 Ed Sprague WS .02 .10
521 Dave Winfield WS .02 .10
522 Ozzie Smith AS .20 .50
523 Barry Bonds AS .30 .75
524 Andy Van Slyke AS .07 .20
525 Tony Gwynn AS .10 .30
526 Darren Daulton AS .02 .10
527 Greg Maddux AS .20 .50
528 Fred McGriff AS .10 .30
529 Lee Smith AS .02 .10
530 Ryne Sandberg AS .20 .50
531 Gary Sheffield AS .02 .10
532 Ozzie Smith DT .20 .50
533 Kirby Puckett DT .10 .30
534 Gary Sheffield DT .02 .10
535 Andy Van Slyke DT .07 .20
536 Ken Griffey Jr. DT .25 .60
537 Ivan Rodriguez DT .07 .20
538 Charles Nagy DT .02 .10
539 Tom Glavine DT .07 .20
540 Dennis Eckersley DT .07 .20
541 Frank Thomas DT .10 .30
542 Roberto Alomar DT .07 .20
543 Sean Berry .02 .10
544 Mike Schooler .02 .10
545 Chuck Carr .02 .10
546 Lenny Harris .02 .10
547 Gary Scott .02 .10
548 Derek Lilliquist .02 .10
549 Brian Hunter .02 .10
550 Kirby Puckett MOY .10 .30
551 Jim Eisenreich .02 .10
552 Andre Dawson .07 .20
553 David Nied .02 .10
554 Spike Owen .02 .10
555 Greg Gagne .02 .10
556 Sid Fernandez .02 .10
557 Mark McGwire .50 1.25
558 Bryan Harvey .02 .10
559 Harold Reynolds .07 .20
560 Barry Bonds .60 1.50
561 Eric Wedge RC .08 .25
562 Ozzie Smith .30 .75
563 Rick Sutcliffe .07 .20
564 Jeff Reardon .07 .20
565 Alex Arias .02 .10
566 Greg Swindell .02 .10
567 Brook Jacoby .02 .10
568 Pete Incaviglia .02 .10
569 Butch Henry .02 .10
570 Eric Davis .07 .20
571 Kevin Seitzer .02 .10
572 Tony Fernandez .02 .10
573 Steve Reed RC .02 .10
574 Cory Snyder .02 .10
575 Joe Carter .07 .20
576 Greg Maddux .30 .75
577 Bert Blyleven UER .07 .20
578 Kevin Bass .02 .10
579 Carlton Fisk .10 .30
580 Doug Drabek .02 .10
581 Mark Gubicza .02 .10
582 Bobby Thigpen .02 .10
583 Chili Davis .07 .20
584 Scott Bankhead .02 .10
585 Harold Baines .07 .20
586 Eric Young .02 .10
587 Lance Parrish .07 .20
588 Juan Bell .02 .10
589 Bob Ojeda .02 .10
590 Joe Orsulak .02 .10
591 Benito Santiago .07 .20
592 Wade Boggs .10 .30
593 Robby Thompson .02 .10
594 Eric Plunk .02 .10
595 Hensley Meulens .02 .10
596 Lou Whitaker .07 .20
597 Dale Murphy .10 .30
598 Paul Molitor .07 .20
599 Greg W. Harris .02 .10
600 Darren Holmes .02 .10
601 Dave Martinez .02 .10
602 Tom Henke .02 .10
603 Mike Benjamin .02 .10
604 Rene Gonzales .02 .10
605 Roger McDowell .02 .10
606 Kirby Puckett .20 .50
607 Randy Myers .02 .10
608 Ruben Sierra .07 .20
609 Wilson Alvarez .02 .10
610 David Segui .02 .10
611 Juan Samuel .02 .10
612 Tom Brunansky .02 .10
613 Willie Randolph .07 .20
614 Tony Phillips .02 .10
615 Candy Maldonado .02 .10
616 Chris Bosio .02 .10
617 Bret Barberie .02 .10
618 Scott Sanderson .02 .10
619 Ron Darling .02 .10
620 Dave Winfield .07 .20
621 Mike Felder .02 .10
622 Greg Hibbard .02 .10
623 Mike Scioscia .02 .10
624 John Smiley .02 .10
625 Alejandro Pena .02 .10
626 Terry Steinbach .02 .10
627 Freddie Benavides .02 .10
628 Kevin Reimer .02 .10
629 Braulio Castillo .02 .10
630 Dave Stieb .02 .10
631 Dave Magadan .02 .10
632 Scott Fletcher .02 .10
633 Cris Carpenter .02 .10
634 Kevin Maas .02 .10
635 Todd Worrell .02 .10
636 Rob Deer .02 .10
637 Dwight Smith .02 .10
638 Chito Martinez .02 .10
639 Jimmy Key .07 .20
640 Greg A. Harris .02 .10
641 Mike Moore .02 .10
642 Pat Borders .02 .10
643 Bill Gullickson .02 .10
644 Gary Gaetti .07 .20
645 David Howard .02 .10
646 Jim Abbott .10 .30
647 Willie Wilson .02 .10
648 David Wells .07 .20
649 Andres Galarraga .07 .20
650 Vince Coleman .02 .10
651 Rob Dibble .07 .20
652 Frank Tanana .02 .10
653 Steve Decker .02 .10
654 David Cone .07 .20
655 Jack Armstrong .02 .10
656 Dave Stewart .07 .20
657 Billy Hatcher .02 .10
658 Tim Raines .07 .20
659 Walt Weiss .02 .10
660 Jose Lind .02 .10

1993 Score Boys of Summer

Randomly inserted exclusively into one in every four 1993 Score 35-card super packs, cards from this standard-size set feature 30 rookies expected to be the best in their class. Early cards of Pedro Martinez and Mike Piazza highlight this set.

COMPLETE SET (30) 20.00 50.00
RANDOM INSERTS IN JUMBO PACKS
1 Billy Ashley .60 1.50
2 Tim Salmon 1.25 3.00
3 Pedro Martinez 4.00 10.00
4 Luis Mercedes .60 1.50
5 Mike Piazza 4.00 10.00
6 Troy Neel .60 1.50
7 Melvin Nieves .60 1.50
8 Ryan Klesko .75 2.00
9 Ryan Thompson .60 1.50
10 Kevin Young .75 2.00
11 Gerald Williams .60 1.50
12 Willie Greene .60 1.50
13 John Patterson .60 1.50
14 Carlos Garcia .60 1.50
15 Ed Zosky .60 1.50
16 Sean Berry .60 1.50
17 Rico Brogna .60 1.50
18 Larry Carter .60 1.50
19 Bobby Ayala .60 1.50
20 Alan Embree .60 1.50
21 Donald Harris .60 1.50
22 Sterling Hitchcock .75 2.00
23 David Nied .60 1.50
24 Henry Mercedes .60 1.50
25 Ozzie Canseco .60 1.50
26 David Hulse .60 1.50
27 Al Martin .60 1.50
28 Dan Wilson .60 1.50
29 Paul Miller .60 1.50
30 Rich Rowland .60 1.50

1993 Score Franchise

This 28-card set honors the top player on each of the major league teams. These cards were randomly inserted into one in every 24 16-card packs. The set is arranged in alphabetical team order by league, with the exception of cards 29 and 30 which honor a player from the 1993 expansion teams.

COMPLETE SET (28) 60.00 120.00
STATED ODDS 1:24
1 Cal Ripken 10.00 25.00
2 Roger Clemens 6.00 15.00
3 Mark Langston .60 1.50
4 Frank Thomas 3.00 8.00
5 Carlos Baerga .60 1.50
6 Cecil Fielder 1.25 3.00
7 Gregg Jefferies .60 1.50
8 Robin Yount 5.00 12.00
9 Kirby Puckett 3.00 8.00
10 Don Mattingly 8.00 20.00
11 Dennis Eckersley 1.25 3.00
12 Ken Griffey Jr. 6.00 15.00
13 Juan Gonzalez 1.25 3.00
14 Roberto Alomar 2.00 5.00
15 Terry Pendleton 1.25 3.00
16 Ryne Sandberg 5.00 12.00
17 Barry Larkin 2.00 5.00
18 Jeff Bagwell 2.00 5.00
19 Brett Butler 1.25 3.00
20 Larry Walker 1.25 3.00
21 Bobby Bonilla 1.25 3.00
22 Darren Daulton 1.25 3.00
23 Andy Van Slyke 2.00 5.00
24 Ray Lankford 1.25 3.00
25 Gary Sheffield 1.25 3.00
26 Will Clark 2.00 5.00
27 Bryan Harvey .60 1.50
28 David Nied .60 1.50

1993 Score Gold Dream Team

Cards from this 12-card standard-size set feature Score's selection of the best players in baseball at each position. The cards were available only through a mail-in offer. Each card front features sepia tone photos of the players out of uniform, with the exception of Griffey's card (of whom is pictured in his Mariners togs). The photo edges are rounded with an airbrush effect.

COMPLETE SET (12) 2.00 5.00
SETS DISTRIBUTED VIA MAIL-IN OFFER
1 Ozzie Smith .30 .75
2 Kirby Puckett .20 .50
3 Gary Sheffield .07 .20
4 Andy Van Slyke .10 .30
5 Ken Griffey Jr. .40 1.00
6 Ivan Rodriguez .10 .30
7 Charles Nagy .02 .10
8 Tom Glavine .10 .30
9 Dennis Eckersley .07 .20
10 Frank Thomas .20 .50
11 Roberto Alomar .10 .30
NNO Header Card .02 .10

1993 Score Proctor and Gamble

This ten-card standard-size set was produced by Score as a promotion for Proctor and Gamble. The set was advertised through store displays; the set could be acquired by sending in three UPC symbols and money to cover postage and handling.

COMPLETE SET (10) 2.50 6.00
1 Wil Cordero .08 .25
2 Pedro Martinez 1.50 4.00
3 Bret Boone .75 2.00
4 Melvin Nieves .08 .25
5 Ryan Klesko .40 1.00
6 Ryan Thompson .08 .25
7 Kevin Young .08 .25
8 Willie Greene .08 .25
9 Eric Wedge .20 .50
10 David Nied .08 .25

1994 Score Samples

COMPLETE SET (19) 15.00 40.00
1 Barry Bonds .75 2.00
1GR Barry Bonds 1.25 3.00
2 John Olerud .20 .50
2GR John Olerud .60 1.50
3 Ken Griffey Jr. 1.25 3.00
3GR Ken Griffey Jr. 4.00 10.00
4 Jeff Bagwell .50 1.25
4GR Jeff Bagwell 2.00 5.00
5 John Burkett .08 .25
5GR John Burkett .40 1.00
6 Jack McDowell .08 .25
6GR Jack McDowell .40 1.00
7 Albert Belle .20 .50
7GR Albert Belle .60 1.50
8 Andres Galarraga .40 1.00
8GR Andres Galarraga 1.00 2.50
DT5 Barry Larkin 1.50 4.00
NNO Hobby Ad Card .08 .25
NNO Retail Ad Card .08 .25

1994 Score

The 1994 Score set of 660 standard-size cards was issued in two series of 330. Cards were distributed in 14-card hobby and retail packs. Each pack contained 13 basic cards plus one Gold Rush parallel card. Cards were also distributed in retail Jumbo packs. 4,875 cases of 1994 Score baseball were printed for the hobby. This figure does not take into account additional product printed for retail outlets. Among the subsets are American League stadiums (317-330) and National League stadiums (647-660). Rookie Cards include Trot Nixon and Billy Wagner.

COMPLETE SET (660) 10.00 25.00
COMPLETE SERIES 1 (330) 5.00 12.00
COMPLETE SERIES 2 (330) 5.00 12.00
SUBSET CARDS HALF VALUE OF BASE CARDS
1 Barry Bonds .60 1.50
2 John Olerud .07 .20
3 Ken Griffey Jr. .40 1.00
4 Jeff Bagwell .10 .30
5 John Burkett .02 .10
6 Jack McDowell .02 .10
7 Albert Belle .07 .20
8 Andres Galarraga .07 .20
9 Mike Mussina .10 .30
10 Will Clark .10 .30
11 Travis Fryman .07 .20
12 Tony Gwynn .25 .60
13 Robin Yount .30 .75
14 Dave Magadan .02 .10
15 Paul O'Neill .10 .30
16 Ray Lankford .07 .20
17 Damion Easley .02 .10
18 Andy Van Slyke .10 .30
19 Brian McRae .02 .10
20 Ryne Sandberg .30 .75
21 Kirby Puckett .20 .50
22 Dwight Gooden .07 .20
23 Don Mattingly .50 1.25
24 Kevin Mitchell .02 .10
25 Roger Clemens .40 1.00
26 Eric Karros .07 .20
27 Juan Gonzalez .07 .20
28 John Kruk .07 .20
29 Gregg Jefferies .02 .10
30 Tom Glavine .10 .30
31 Ivan Rodriguez .10 .30
32 Jay Bell .07 .20
33 Randy Johnson .20 .50
34 Darren Daulton .07 .20
35 Rickey Henderson .20 .50
36 Eddie Murray .20 .50
37 Brian Harper .02 .10
38 Delino DeShields .02 .10
39 Jose Lind .02 .10
40 Benito Santiago .07 .20
41 Frank Thomas .20 .50
42 Mark Grace .10 .30
43 Roberto Alomar .10 .30
44 Andy Benes .02 .10
45 Luis Polonia .02 .10
46 Brett Butler .07 .20
47 Terry Steinbach .02 .10
48 Craig Biggio .10 .30
49 Greg Vaughn .02 .10
50 Charlie Hayes .02 .10
51 Mickey Tettleton .02 .10
52 Jose Rijo .02 .10
53 Carlos Baerga .02 .10

54 Jeff Blauser .02 .10
55 Leo Gomez .02 .10
56 Bob Tewksbury .02 .10
57 Mo Vaughn .07 .20
58 Orlando Merced .02 .10
59 Tino Martinez .10 .30
60 Lenny Dykstra .07 .20
61 Jose Canseco .10 .30
62 Tony Fernandez .02 .10
63 Donovan Osborne .02 .10
64 Ken Hill .02 .10
65 Kent Hrbek .07 .20
66 Bryan Harvey .02 .10
67 Wally Joyner .07 .20
68 Derrick May .02 .10
69 Lance Johnson .02 .10
70 Willie McGee .07 .20
71 Mark Langston .02 .10
72 Terry Pendleton .07 .20
73 Joe Carter .07 .20
74 Barry Larkin .10 .30
75 Jimmy Key .07 .20
76 Joe Girardi .02 .10
77 B.J. Surhoff .07 .20
78 Pete Harnisch .02 .10
79 Lou Whitaker UER .07 .20
80 Cory Snyder .02 .10
81 Kenny Lofton .07 .20
82 Fred McGriff .10 .30
83 Mike Greenwell .02 .10
84 Mike Perez .02 .10
85 Cal Ripken .60 1.50
86 Don Slaught .02 .10
87 Omar Vizquel .10 .30
88 Curt Schilling .07 .20
89 Chuck Knoblauch .07 .20
90 Moises Alou .07 .20
91 Greg Gagne .02 .10
92 Bret Saberhagen .07 .20
93 Ozzie Guillen .07 .20
94 Matt Williams .07 .20
95 Chad Curtis .02 .10
96 Mike Harkey .02 .10
97 Devon White .07 .20
98 Walt Weiss .02 .10
99 Kevin Brown .07 .20
100 Gary Sheffield .07 .20
101 Wade Boggs .10 .30
102 Orel Hershiser .07 .20
103 Tony Phillips .02 .10
104 Andujar Cedeno .02 .10
105 Bill Spiers .02 .10
106 Otis Nixon .02 .10
107 Felix Fermin .02 .10
108 Bip Roberts .02 .10
109 Dennis Eckersley .07 .20
110 Dante Bichette .07 .20
111 Ben McDonald .02 .10
112 Jim Poole .02 .10
113 John Dopson .02 .10
114 Rob Dibble .07 .20
115 Jeff Treadway .02 .10
116 Ricky Jordan .02 .10
117 Mike Henneman .02 .10
118 Willie Blair .02 .10
119 Doug Henry .02 .10
120 Gerald Perry .02 .10
121 Greg Myers .02 .10
122 John Franco .07 .20
123 Roger Mason .02 .10
124 Chris Hammond .02 .10
125 Hubie Brooks .02 .10
126 Kent Mercker .02 .10
127 Jim Abbott .10 .30
128 Kevin Bass .02 .10
129 Rick Aguilera .02 .10
130 Mitch Webster .02 .10
131 Eric Plunk .02 .10
132 Mark Carreon .02 .10
133 Dave Stewart .07 .20
134 Willie Wilson .02 .10
135 Dave Fleming .02 .10
136 Jeff Tackett .02 .10
137 Geno Petralli .02 .10
138 Gene Harris .02 .10
139 Scott Bankhead .02 .10
140 Trevor Wilson .02 .10
141 Alvaro Espinoza .02 .10
142 Ryan Bowen .02 .10
143 Mike Moore .02 .10
144 Bill Pecota .02 .10
145 Jaime Navarro .02 .10
146 Jack Daugherty .02 .10
147 Bob Wickman .02 .10
148 Chris Jones .02 .10
149 Todd Stottlemyre .02 .10
150 Brian Williams .02 .10
151 Chuck Finley .07 .20
152 Lenny Harris .02 .10
153 Alex Fernandez .02 .10
154 Candy Maldonado .02 .10
155 Jeff Montgomery .02 .10
156 David West .02 .10
157 Mark Williamson .02 .10
158 Milt Thompson .02 .10
159 Ron Darling .02 .10
160 Stan Belinda .02 .10
161 Henry Cotto .02 .10
162 Mel Rojas .02 .10
163 Doug Strange .02 .10
164 Rene Arocha .02 .10
165 Tim Hulett .02 .10
166 Steve Avery .02 .10
167 Jim Thome .10 .30
168 Tom Browning .02 .10
169 Mario Diaz .02 .10
170 Steve Reed .02 .10
171 Scott Livingstone .02 .10
172 Chris Donnels .02 .10
173 John Jaha .02 .10
174 Carlos Hernandez .02 .10
175 Dion James .02 .10
176 Bud Black .02 .10
177 Tony Castillo .02 .10
178 Jose Guzman .02 .10
179 Torey Lovullo .02 .10
180 John Vander Wal .02 .10
181 Mike LaValliere .02 .10
182 Sid Fernandez .02 .10
183 Brent Mayne .02 .10
184 Terry Mulholland .02 .10
185 Willie Banks .02 .10
186 Steve Cooke .02 .10
187 Brent Gates .02 .10
188 Erik Pappas .02 .10
189 Bill Haselman .02 .10
190 Fernando Valenzuela .07 .20
191 Gary Redus .02 .10
192 Danny Darwin .02 .10
193 Mark Portugal .02 .10
194 Derek Lilliquist .02 .10
195 Charlie O'Brien .02 .10
196 Matt Nokes .02 .10
197 Danny Sheaffer .02 .10
198 Bill Gullickson .02 .10
199 Alex Arias .02 .10
200 Mike Fetters .02 .10
201 Brian Jordan .07 .20
202 Joe Grahe .02 .10
203 Tom Candiotti .02 .10
204 Jeremy Hernandez .02 .10
205 Mike Stanton .02 .10
206 David Howard .02 .10
207 Darren Holmes .02 .10
208 Rick Honeycutt .02 .10
209 Danny Jackson .02 .10
210 Rich Amaral .02 .10
211 Blas Minor .02 .10
212 Kenny Rogers .07 .20
213 Jim Leyritz .02 .10
214 Mike Morgan .02 .10
215 Dan Gladden .02 .10
216 Randy Velarde .02 .10
217 Mitch Williams .02 .10
218 Hipolito Pichardo .02 .10
219 Dave Burba .02 .10
220 Wilson Alvarez .02 .10
221 Bob Zupcic .02 .10
222 Francisco Cabrera .02 .10
223 Julio Valera .02 .10
224 Paul Assenmacher .02 .10
225 Jeff Branson .02 .10
226 Todd Frohwirth .02 .10
227 Armando Reynoso .02 .10
228 Rich Rowland .02 .10
229 Freddie Benavides .02 .10
230 Wayne Kirby .02 .10
231 Darryl Kile .07 .20
232 Skeeter Barnes .02 .10
233 Ramon Martinez .02 .10
234 Tom Gordon .02 .10
235 Dave Gallagher .02 .10
236 Ricky Bones .02 .10
237 Larry Andersen .02 .10
238 Pat Meares .02 .10
239 Zane Smith .02 .10
240 Tim Leary .02 .10
241 Phil Clark .02 .10
242 Danny Cox .02 .10
243 Mike Jackson .02 .10
244 Mike Gallego .02 .10
245 Lee Smith .07 .20
246 Todd Jones .02 .10
247 Steve Bedrosian .02 .10
248 Troy Neel .02 .10
249 Jose Bautista .02 .10
250 Steve Frey .02 .10
251 Jeff Reardon .07 .20
252 Stan Javier .02 .10
253 Mo Sanford .02 .10
254 Steve Sax .02 .10
255 Luis Aquino .02 .10
256 Domingo Jean .02 .10
257 Scott Servais .02 .10
258 Brad Pennington .02 .10
259 Dave Hansen .02 .10
260 Rich Gossage .07 .20
261 Jeff Fassero .02 .10
262 Junior Ortiz .02 .10
263 Anthony Young .02 .10
264 Chris Bosio .02 .10
265 Ruben Amaro .02 .10
266 Mark Eichhorn .02 .10
267 Dave Clark .02 .10
268 Gary Thurman .02 .10
269 Les Lancaster .02 .10
270 Jamie Moyer .07 .20
271 Ricky Gutierrez .02 .10
272 Greg A. Harris .02 .10
273 Mike Benjamin .02 .10
274 Gene Nelson .02 .10
275 Damon Berryhill .02 .10
276 Scott Radinsky .02 .10
277 Mike Aldrete .02 .10
278 Jerry DiPoto .02 .10
279 Chris Haney .02 .10
280 Richie Lewis .02 .10
281 Jarvis Brown .02 .10
282 Juan Bell .02 .10
283 Joe Klink .02 .10
284 Graeme Lloyd .02 .10
285 Casey Candaele .02 .10
286 Bob MacDonald .02 .10
287 Mike Sharperson .02 .10
288 Gene Larkin .02 .10
289 Brian Barnes .02 .10
290 David McCarty .02 .10
291 Jeff Innis .02 .10
292 Bob Patterson .02 .10
293 Ben Rivera .02 .10
294 John Habyan .02 .10
295 Rich Rodriguez .02 .10
296 Edwin Nunez .02 .10
297 Rod Brewer .02 .10
298 Mike Timlin .02 .10
299 Jesse Orosco .02 .10
300 Gary Gaetti .07 .20
301 Todd Benzinger .02 .10
302 Jeff Nelson .02 .10
303 Rafael Belliard .02 .10
304 Matt Whiteside .02 .10
305 Vinny Castilla .07 .20
306 Matt Turner .02 .10
307 Eduardo Perez .02 .10
308 Joel Johnston .02 .10
309 Chris Gomez .02 .10
310 Pat Rapp .02 .10
311 Jim Tatum .02 .10
312 Kirk Rueter .02 .10
313 John Flaherty .02 .10
314 Tom Kramer .02 .10
315 Mark Whiten .02 .10
316 Chris Bosio .02 .10
317 Baltimore Orioles CL .02 .10
318 Boston Red Sox CL UER
(Viola listed as 316; shoul .02 .10
319 California Angels CL .02 .10
320 Chicago White Sox CL .02 .10
321 Cleveland Indians CL .02 .10
322 Detroit Tigers CL .02 .10
323 Kansas City Royals CL .02 .10
324 Milwaukee Brewers CL .02 .10
325 Minnesota Twins CL .02 .10
326 New York Yankees CL .02 .10
327 Oakland Athletics CL .02 .10
328 Seattle Mariners CL .02 .10
329 Texas Rangers CL .02 .10
330 Toronto Blue Jays CL .02 .10
331 Frank Viola .07 .20
332 Ron Gant .07 .20
333 Charles Nagy .02 .10
334 Roberto Kelly .02 .10
335 Brady Anderson .07 .20
336 Alex Cole .02 .10
337 Alan Trammell .07 .20
338 Derek Bell .02 .10
339 Bernie Williams .10 .30
340 Jose Offerman .02 .10
341 Bill Wegman .02 .10
342 Ken Caminiti .07 .20
343 Pat Borders .02 .10
344 Kirt Manwaring .02 .10
345 Chili Davis .07 .20
346 Steve Buechele .02 .10
347 Robin Ventura .07 .20
348 Teddy Higuera .02 .10
349 Jerry Browne .02 .10
350 Scott Kamieniecki .02 .10
351 Kevin Tapani .02 .10
352 Marquis Grissom .07 .20
353 Jay Buhner .07 .20
354 Dave Hollins .02 .10
355 Dan Wilson .02 .10
356 Bob Walk .02 .10
357 Chris Hoiles .07 .20
358 Todd Zeile .02 .10
359 Kevin Appier .07 .20
360 Chris Sabo .02 .10
361 David Segui .02 .10
362 Jerald Clark .02 .10
363 Tony Pena .07 .20
364 Steve Finley .07 .20
365 Roger Pavlik .02 .10
366 John Smoltz .10 .30
367 Scott Fletcher .02 .10
368 Jody Reed .02 .10
369 David Wells .07 .20
370 Jose Vizcaino .02 .10
371 Pat Listach .02 .10
372 Orestes Destrade .07 .20
373 Danny Tartabull .02 .10
374 Greg W. Harris .02 .10
375 Juan Guzman .02 .10
376 Larry Walker .07 .20
377 Gary DiSarcina .02 .10
378 Bobby Bonilla .07 .20
379 Tim Raines .07 .20
380 Tommy Greene .02 .10
381 Chris Gwynn .02 .10
382 Jeff King .07 .20
383 Shane Mack .02 .10
384 Ozzie Smith .30 .75
385 Eddie Zambrano RC .02 .10
386 Mike Devereaux .02 .10
387 Erik Hanson .02 .10
388 Scott Cooper .02 .10
389 Dean Palmer .07 .20
390 John Wetteland .07 .20
391 Reggie Jefferson .02 .10
392 Mark Lemke .02 .10
393 Cecil Fielder .07 .20
394 Reggie Sanders .07 .20
395 Darryl Hamilton .02 .10
396 Daryl Boston .02 .10
397 Pat Kelly .02 .10
398 Joe Orsulak .02 .10
399 Ed Sprague .02 .10
400 Eric Anthony .02 .10
401 Scott Sanderson .02 .10
402 Jim Gott .02 .10
403 Ron Karkovice .02 .10
404 Phil Plantier .02 .10
405 David Cone .07 .20
406 Robby Thompson .02 .10
407 Dave Winfield .07 .20
408 Dwight Smith .02 .10
409 Ruben Sierra .07 .20
410 Jack Armstrong .02 .10
411 Mike Felder .02 .10
412 Wil Cordero .02 .10
413 Julio Franco .07 .20
414 Howard Johnson .02 .10
415 Mark McLemore .02 .10
416 Pete Incaviglia .02 .10
417 John Valentin .02 .10
418 Tim Wakefield .10 .30
419 Jose Mesa .02 .10
420 Bernard Gilkey .02 .10
421 Kirk Gibson .07 .20
422 David Justice .07 .20
423 Tom Brunansky .02 .10
424 John Smiley .02 .10
425 Kevin Maas .02 .10
426 Doug Drabek .02 .10
427 Paul Molitor .07 .20
428 Darryl Strawberry .07 .20
429 Tim Naehring .02 .10
430 Bill Swift .02 .10
431 Ellis Burks .07 .20
432 Greg Hibbard .02 .10
433 Felix Jose .02 .10
434 Bret Barberie .02 .10
435 Pedro Munoz .02 .10
436 Darrin Fletcher .02 .10
437 Bobby Witt .02 .10
438 Wes Chamberlain .02 .10
439 Mackey Sasser .02 .10
440 Mark Whiten .02 .10
441 Harold Reynolds .07 .20
442 Greg Olson .02 .10
443 Billy Hatcher .02 .10
444 Joe Oliver .02 .10
445 Sandy Alomar Jr. .02 .10
446 Tim Wallach .02 .10
447 Karl Rhodes .02 .10
448 Royce Clayton .02 .10
449 Cal Eldred .02 .10
450 Rick Wilkins .02 .10
451 Mike Stanley .02 .10
452 Charlie Hough .07 .20
453 Jack Morris .07 .20
454 Jon Ratliff RC .02 .10
455 Rene Gonzales .02 .10
456 Eddie Taubensee .02 .10
457 Roberto Hernandez .02 .10
458 Todd Hundley .02 .10
459 Mike Macfarlane .02 .10
460 Mickey Morandini .02 .10
461 Scott Erickson .02 .10
462 Lonnie Smith .02 .10
463 Dave Henderson .02 .10
464 Ryan Klesko .07 .20
465 Edgar Martinez .10 .30
466 Tom Pagnozzi .02 .10
467 Charlie Leibrandt .02 .10
468 Brian Anderson RC .08 .25
469 Harold Baines .07 .20
470 Tim Belcher .02 .10
471 Andre Dawson .07 .20
472 Eric Young .02 .10
473 Paul Sorrento .02 .10
474 Luis Gonzalez .07 .20
475 Rob Deer .02 .10
476 Mike Piazza .40 1.00
477 Kevin Reimer .02 .10
478 Jeff Gardner .02 .10
479 Melido Perez .02 .10
480 Darren Lewis .02 .10
481 Duane Ward .02 .10
482 Rey Sanchez .02 .10
483 Mark Lewis .02 .10
484 Jeff Conine .07 .20
485 Joey Cora .02 .10
486 Trot Nixon RC .40 1.00
487 Kevin McReynolds .02 .10
488 Mike Lansing .02 .10
489 Mike Pagliarulo .02 .10
490 Mariano Duncan .02 .10
491 Mike Bordick .02 .10
492 Kevin Young .02 .10
493 Dave Valle .02 .10
494 Wayne Gomes RC .02 .10
495 Rafael Palmeiro .10 .30
496 Deion Sanders .10 .30
497 Rick Sutcliffe .07 .20
498 Randy Milligan .02 .10
499 Carlos Quintana .02 .10
500 Chris Turner .02 .10
501 Thomas Howard .02 .10
502 Greg Swindell .02 .10
503 Chad Kreuter .02 .10
504 Eric Davis .07 .20
505 Dickie Thon .02 .10
506 Matt Drews RC .02 .10
507 Spike Owen .02 .10
508 Rod Beck .02 .10
509 Pat Hentgen .02 .10
510 Sammy Sosa .20 .50
511 J.T. Snow .07 .20
512 Chuck Carr .02 .10
513 Bo Jackson .20 .50
514 Dennis Martinez .07 .20
515 Phil Hiatt .02 .10
516 Jeff Kent .10 .30
517 Brooks Kieschnick RC .02 .10
518 Kirk Presley RC .02 .10
519 Kevin Seitzer .02 .10
520 Carlos Garcia .02 .10
521 Mike Blowers .02 .10
522 Luis Alicea .02 .10
523 David Hulse .02 .10
524 Greg Maddux .30 .75
525 Gregg Olson .02 .10
526 Hal Morris .02 .10
527 Daron Kirkreit .02 .10
528 David Nied .02 .10
529 Jeff Russell .02 .10
530 Kevin Gross .02 .10
531 John Doherty .02 .10
532 Matt Brunson RC .02 .10
533 Dave Nilsson .02 .10
534 Randy Myers .02 .10
535 Steve Farr .02 .10
536 Billy Wagner RC .50 1.25
537 Darnell Coles .02 .10
538 Frank Tanana .02 .10
539 Tim Salmon .10 .30
540 Kim Batiste .02 .10
541 George Bell .02 .10
542 Tom Henke .02 .10
543 Sam Horn .02 .10
544 Doug Jones .02 .10
545 Scott Leius .02 .10
546 Al Martin .02 .10
547 Bob Welch .02 .10
548 Scott Christman RC .02 .10
549 Norm Charlton .02 .10
550 Mark McGwire .50 1.25
551 Greg McMichael .02 .10
552 Tim Costo .02 .10
553 Rodney Bolton .02 .10
554 Pedro Martinez .20 .50
555 Marc Valdes .02 .10
556 Darrell Whitmore .02 .10
557 Tim Bogar .02 .10
558 Steve Karsay .02 .10
559 Danny Bautista .02 .10
560 Jeffrey Hammonds .02 .10
561 Aaron Sele .02 .10
562 Russ Springer .02 .10
563 Jason Bere .02 .10
564 Billy Brewer .02 .10
565 Sterling Hitchcock .02 .10
566 Bobby Munoz .02 .10
567 Craig Paquette .02 .10
568 Bret Boone .07 .20
569 Dan Peltier .02 .10
570 Jeromy Burnitz .07 .20
571 John Wasdin RC .02 .10
572 Chipper Jones .20 .50
573 Jamey Wright RC .02 .10
574 Jeff Granger .02 .10
575 Jay Powell RC .02 .10
576 Ryan Thompson .02 .10
577 Lou Frazier .02 .10
578 Paul Wagner .02 .10
579 Brad Ausmus .10 .30
580 Jack Voigt .02 .10
581 Kevin Rogers .02 .10
582 Damon Buford .02 .10
583 Paul Quantrill .02 .10
584 Marc Newfield .02 .10
585 Derrek Lee RC .60 1.50
586 Shane Reynolds .02 .10
587 Cliff Floyd .07 .20
588 Jeff Schwarz .02 .10
589 Ross Powell RC .02 .10
590 Gerald Williams .02 .10
591 Mike Trombley .02 .10
592 Ken Ryan .02 .10
593 John O'Donoghue .02 .10
594 Rod Correia .02 .10
595 Darrell Sherman .02 .10
596 Steve Scarsone .02 .10
597 Sherman Obando .02 .10
598 Kurt Abbott RC .02 .10
599 Dave Telgheder .02 .10
600 Rick Trlicek .02 .10
601 Carl Everett .07 .20
602 Luis Ortiz .02 .10
603 Larry Luebbers .02 .10
604 Kevin Roberson .02 .10
605 Butch Huskey .02 .10
606 Benji Gil .02 .10
607 Todd Van Poppel .02 .10
608 Mark Hutton .02 .10
609 Chip Hale .02 .10
610 Matt Maysey .02 .10
611 Scott Ruffcorn .02 .10
612 Hilly Hathaway .02 .10
613 Allen Watson .02 .10
614 Carlos Delgado .10 .30
615 Roberto Mejia .02 .10
616 Turk Wendell .02 .10
617 Tony Tarasco .02 .10
618 Raul Mondesi .07 .20
619 Kevin Stocker .02 .10
620 Javier Lopez .07 .20
621 Keith Kessinger .02 .10
622 Bob Hamelin .02 .10
623 John Roper .02 .10
624 Lenny Dykstra WS .02 .10
625 Joe Carter WS .02 .10
626 Jim Abbott HL .07 .20
627 Lee Smith HL .02 .10
628 Ken Griffey Jr. HL .25 .60
629 Dave Winfield HL .02 .10
630 Darryl Kile HL .02 .10
631 Frank Thomas MVP .10 .30
632 Barry Bonds MVP .30 .75
633 Jack McDowell AL CY .02 .10
634 Greg Maddux CY .20 .50
635 Tim Salmon ROY .07 .20
636 Mike Piazza ROY .20 .50
637 Brian Turang RC .02 .10
638 Rondell White .07 .20
639 Nigel Wilson .02 .10
640 Torii Hunter RC .40 1.00
641 Salomon Torres .02 .10
642 Kevin Higgins .02 .10
643 Eric Wedge .02 .10
644 Roger Salkeld .02 .10
645 Manny Ramirez .20 .50
646 Jeff McNeely .02 .10
647 Checklist .02 .10
Atlanta Braves
648 Checklist .02 .10
Chicago Cubs
649 Checklist .02 .10
Cincinnati Reds
650 Checklist .02 .10
Colorado Rockies
651 Checklist .02 .10
Florida Marlins
652 Checklist .02 .10
Houston Astros
653 Checklist .02 .10
Los Angeles Dodgers
654 Checklist .02 .10
Montreal Expos
655 Checklist .02 .10
New York Mets
656 Checklist .02 .10
Philadelphia Phillies
657 Checklist .02 .10
Pittsburgh Pirates
658 Checklist .02 .10
St. Louis Cardinals
659 Checklist .02 .10
San Diego Padres
660 Checklist .02 .10
San Francisco Giants

1994 Score Gold Rush

COMPLETE SET (660) 20.00 50.00
COMPLETE SERIES 1 (330) 10.00 25.00
COMPLETE SERIES 2 (330) 10.00 25.00
*STARS: 1.5X TO 4X BASIC CARDS
*ROOKIES: 1.25X TO 3X BASIC
ONE PER PACK
TWO PER JUMBO

1994 Score Boys of Summer

Randomly inserted in super packs at a rate of one in four, this 60-card set features top young stars and hopefuls. The set was issued in two series of 30 cards.

COMPLETE SET (60) 25.00 60.00
COMPLETE SERIES 1 (30) 10.00 25.00
COMPLETE SERIES 2 (30) 15.00 35.00
STATED ODDS 1:4 SUPER PACKS
1 Jeff Conine .75 2.00
2 Aaron Sele .40 1.00
3 Kevin Stocker .40 1.00
4 Pat Meares .40 1.00
5 Jeromy Burnitz .75 2.00
6 Mike Piazza 3.00 8.00
7 Allen Watson .40 1.00
8 Jeffrey Hammonds .40 1.00
9 Kevin Roberson .40 1.00
10 Hilly Hathaway .40 1.00
11 Kirk Rueter .40 1.00
12 Eduardo Perez .40 1.00
13 Ricky Gutierrez .40 1.00
14 Domingo Jean .40 1.00
15 David Nied .40 1.00
16 Wayne Kirby .40 1.00
17 Mike Lansing .40 1.00
18 Jason Bere .40 1.00
19 Brent Gates .40 1.00
20 Javier Lopez .75 2.00
21 Greg McMichael .40 1.00
22 David Hulse .40 1.00
23 Roberto Mejia .40 1.00
24 Tim Salmon 1.25 3.00
25 Rene Arocha .40 1.00
26 Bret Boone .75 2.00
27 David McCarty .40 1.00
28 Todd Van Poppel .40 1.00
29 Lance Painter .40 1.00
30 Erik Pappas .40 1.00
31 Chuck Carr .40 1.00
32 Mark Hutton .40 1.00
33 Jeff McNeely .40 1.00
34 Willie Greene .40 1.00
35 Nigel Wilson .40 1.00
36 Rondell White .75 2.00
37 Brian Turang .40 1.00
38 Manny Ramirez 2.00 5.00
39 Salomon Torres .40 1.00
40 Melvin Nieves .40 1.00
41 Ryan Klesko .75 2.00
42 Keith Kessinger .40 1.00
43 Brad Ausmus 1.25 3.00
44 Bob Hamelin .40 1.00
45 Carlos Delgado 1.25 3.00
46 Marc Newfield .40 1.00
47 Raul Mondesi .75 2.00
48 Tim Costo .40 1.00
49 Pedro Martinez 2.00 5.00
50 Steve Karsay .40 1.00
51 Danny Bautista .40 1.00
52 Butch Huskey .40 1.00
53 Kurt Abbott .40 1.00
54 Darrell Sherman .40 1.00
55 Damon Buford .40 1.00
56 Ross Powell .40 1.00
57 Darrell Whitmore .40 1.00
58 Chipper Jones 2.00 5.00
59 Jeff Granger .40 1.00
60 Cliff Floyd .75 2.00

1994 Score Cycle

This 20-card set was randomly inserted in second series foil at a rate of one in 72 and jumbo packs at a rate of one in 36. The set is arranged according to players with the most singles (1-5), doubles (6-10), triples (11-15) and home runs (16-20). The cards are number with a "TC" prefix.

COMPLETE SET (20) 20.00 50.00
SER.2 STATED ODDS 1:72, 1:36 JUM
TC1 Brett Butler 1.25 3.00
TC2 Kenny Lofton 1.25 3.00
TC3 Paul Molitor 3.00 8.00
TC4 Carlos Baerga 1.25 3.00
TC5 G.Jefferies 1.25 3.00
T.Phillips
TC6 John Olerud 1.25 3.00
TC7 Charlie Hayes 1.25 3.00
TC8 Lenny Dykstra 1.25 3.00
TC9 Dante Bichette 1.25 3.00
TC10 Devon White 1.25 3.00
TC11 Lance Johnson 1.25 3.00
TC12 J.Cora 1.25 3.00
S.Finley
TC13 Tony Fernandez 1.25 3.00
TC14 D.Hulse 1.25 3.00
B.Butler
TC15 Bell 1.25 3.00
McRae
Morandini
TC16 J.Gonzalez 6.00 15.00
B.Bonds
TC17 Ken Griffey Jr. 6.00 15.00
TC18 Frank Thomas 3.00 8.00
TC19 David Justice 1.25 3.00
TC20 M.Williams 1.25 3.00
A.Belle

1994 Score Dream Team

Randomly inserted in first series foil and jumbo packs at a rate of one in 72, this ten-card set feature's baseball's Dream Team as selected by Pinnacle Brands. Banded by forest green stripes above and below, the player photos on the fronts feature ten of baseball's best players sporting historical team uniforms from the 1930's. A Barry Larkin promo card was distributed to dealers and hobby media to preview the set.

COMPLETE SET (10) 25.00 60.00
SER.1 STATED ODDS 1:72, 1:36 JUM
1 Mike Mussina 3.00 8.00
2 Tom Glavine 3.00 8.00
3 Don Mattingly 12.50 30.00
4 Carlos Baerga 1.00 2.50
5 Barry Larkin 3.00 8.00
6 Matt Williams 2.00 5.00
7 Juan Gonzalez 2.00 5.00
8 Andy Van Slyke 3.00 8.00
9 Larry Walker 2.00 5.00
10 Mike Stanley 1.00 2.50
S5 Barry Larkin Sample .40 1.00

1994 Score Gold Stars

Randomly inserted at a rate of one in every 18 hobby packs, this 60-card set features National and American stars. Split into two series of 30 cards, the first series (1-30) comprises of National League players and the second series (31-60) American Leagues.

COMPLETE SET (60) 50.00 120.00
COMPLETE NL SERIES (30) 25.00 60.00
COMPLETE AL SERIES (30) 25.00 60.00
STATED ODDS 1:18 HOBBY
1 Barry Bonds 3.00 8.00
2 Orlando Merced .60 1.50
3 Mark Grace 1.00 2.50
4 Darren Daulton .60 1.50
5 Jeff Blauser .60 1.50
6 Deion Sanders 1.00 2.50
7 John Kruk .60 1.50
8 Jeff Bagwell 1.00 2.50
9 Gregg Jefferies .60 1.50

10 Matt Williams	.60	1.50
11 Andres Galarraga	1.00	2.50
12 Jay Bell	.60	1.50
13 Mike Piazza	1.50	4.00
14 Ron Gant	.60	1.50
15 Barry Larkin	1.00	2.50
16 Tom Glavine	1.00	2.50
17 Len Dykstra	.60	1.50
18 Fred McGriff	1.00	2.50
19 Andy Van Slyke	.60	1.50
20 Gary Sheffield	.60	1.50
21 John Burkett	.60	1.50
22 Dante Bichette	.60	1.50
23 Tony Gwynn	1.50	4.00
24 David Justice	.60	1.50
25 Marquis Grissom	.60	1.50
26 Bobby Bonilla	.60	1.50
27 Larry Walker	1.00	2.50
28 Brett Butler	.60	1.50
29 Robby Thompson	.60	1.50
30 Jeff Conine	.60	1.50
31 Joe Carter	1.00	2.50
32 Ken Griffey Jr.	3.00	8.00
33 Juan Gonzalez	1.00	2.50
34 Rickey Henderson	1.50	4.00
35 Bo Jackson	1.50	4.00
36 Cal Ripken	5.00	12.00
37 John Olerud	.60	1.50
38 Carlos Baerga	.60	1.50
39 Jack McDowell	.60	1.50
40 Cecil Fielder	.60	1.50
41 Kenny Lofton	.60	1.50
42 Roberto Alomar	1.00	2.50
43 Randy Johnson	1.50	4.00
44 Tim Salmon	.60	1.50
45 Frank Thomas	1.50	4.00
46 Albert Belle	.60	1.50
47 Greg Vaughn		
48 Travis Fryman	.60	1.50
49 Don Mattingly	3.00	8.00
50 Wade Boggs	1.00	2.50
51 Mo Vaughn	.60	1.50
52 Kirby Puckett	1.50	4.00
53 Devon White	.60	1.50
54 Tony Phillips	.60	1.50
55 Brian Harper	.60	1.50
56 Chad Curtis	.60	1.50
57 Paul Molitor	1.50	4.00
58 Ivan Rodriguez	1.00	2.50
59 Rafael Palmeiro	1.00	2.50
60 Brian McRae	.60	1.50

1994 Score Rookie/Traded Samples

COMPLETE SET (11)	5.00	12.00
CP2 Rafael Palmeiro	1.00	2.50
RT1 Will Clark	.75	2.00
RT2 Lee Smith	.30	.75
RT3 Bo Jackson	.75	2.00
RT4 Ellis Burks	.30	.75
RT5 Eddie Murray	1.00	2.50
RT6 Delino DeShields	.20	.50
RT102 Carlos Delgado	1.00	2.50
SU2 Manny Ramirez	1.00	2.50
NNO Title Card	.20	.50
NNO September Call-Up Redemption Sample	.20	.50

1994 Score Rookie/Traded

The 1994 Score Rookie and Traded set consists of 165 standard-size cards featuring rookie standouts, traded players, and new young prospects. The set is delineated by traded players (RT1-RT70) and rookies/young prospects (RT71-RT163). The set closes with checklists (RT164-RT165). Each foil pack contained one Gold Rush card. The cards are numbered on the back with an "RT" prefix. Several leading dealers are under the belief that Jose Lima's card (number RT158) was short-printed. Conversely, extra cards of John Mabry are typically found in place of the short Lima's. A special unnumbered September Call-Up Redemption card could be exchanged for an Alex Rodriguez card. The expiration date was January 31st, 1995. Odds of finding a redemption card were approximately one in 240 retail and hobby packs. Rookie Cards include Jose Lima and Chan Ho Park.

COMPLETE SET (165)	6.00	15.00
A.ROD CALL UP EXCH.STATED ODDS 1:240		
A.ROD CALL-UP VIA MAIL PER EXCH.CARD		
ACTUAL CARD REDEEMED IN 1995		
RT1 Will Clark	.20	.50
RT2 Lee Smith	.10	.30
RT3 Bo Jackson	.30	.75
RT4 Ellis Burks	.10	.30
RT5 Eddie Murray	.30	.75
RT6 Delino DeShields	.05	.15
RT7 Erik Hanson	.05	.15
RT8 Rafael Palmeiro	.20	.50
RT9 Luis Polonia	.05	.15
RT10 Omar Vizquel	.20	.50
RT11 Kurt Abbott	.05	.15
RT12 Vince Coleman	.05	.15
RT13 Rickey Henderson	.30	.75
RT14 Terry Mulholland	.05	.15
RT15 Greg Hibbard	.05	.15
RT16 Walt Weiss	.05	.15
RT17 Chris Sabo	.05	.15
RT18 Dave Henderson	.05	.15
RT19 Rick Sutcliffe	.10	.30
RT20 Harold Reynolds	.10	.30
RT21 Jack Morris	.10	.30
RT22 Dan Wilson	.05	.15
RT23 Dave Magadan	.05	.15
RT24 Dennis Martinez	.10	.30
RT25 Wes Chamberlain	.05	.15
RT26 Otis Nixon	.05	.15
RT27 Eric Anthony	.05	.15
RT28 Randy Milligan	.05	.15
RT29 Julio Franco	.10	.30
RT30 Kevin McReynolds	.05	.15
RT31 Anthony Young	.05	.15
RT32 Brian Harper	.05	.15
RT33 Gene Harris	.05	.15
RT34 Eddie Taubensee	.05	.15
RT35 David Segui	.05	.15
RT36 Stan Javier	.05	.15
RT37 Felix Fermin	.05	.15
RT38 Darrin Jackson	.05	.15
RT39 Tony Fernandez	.05	.15
RT40 Jose Vizcaino	.05	.15
RT41 Willie Banks	.05	.15
RT42 Brian Hunter	.05	.15
RT43 Reggie Jefferson	.05	.15
RT44 Junior Felix	.05	.15
RT45 Jack Armstrong	.05	.15
RT46 Bip Roberts	.05	.15
RT47 Jerry Browne	.05	.15
RT48 Marvin Freeman	.05	.15
RT49 Jody Reed	.05	.15
RT50 Alex Cole	.05	.15
RT51 Sid Fernandez	.05	.15
RT52 Pete Smith	.05	.15
RT53 Xavier Hernandez	.05	.15
RT54 Scott Sanderson	.05	.15
RT55 Turner Ward	.05	.15
RT56 Rex Hudler	.05	.15
RT57 Deion Sanders	.20	.50
RT58 Sid Bream	.05	.15
RT59 Tony Pena	.05	.15
RT60 Bret Boone	.10	.30
RT61 Bobby Ayala	.05	.15
RT62 Pedro Martinez	.30	.75
RT63 Howard Johnson	.05	.15
RT64 Mark Portugal	.05	.15
RT65 Roberto Kelly	.05	.15
RT66 Spike Owen	.05	.15
RT67 Jeff Treadway	.05	.15
RT68 Mike Harkey	.05	.15
RT69 Doug Jones	.05	.15
RT70 Steve Farr	.05	.15
RT71 Billy Taylor RC	.05	.15
RT72 Manny Ramirez	.30	.75
RT73 Bob Hamelin	.05	.15
RT74 Steve Karsay	.05	.15
RT75 Ryan Klesko	.10	.30
RT76 Cliff Floyd	.10	.30
RT77 Jeffrey Hammonds	.05	.15
RT78 Javier Lopez	.10	.30
RT79 Roger Salkeld	.05	.15
RT80 Hector Carrasco	.05	.15
RT81 Gerald Williams	.05	.15
RT82 Raul Mondesi	.10	.30
RT83 Sterling Hitchcock	.05	.15
RT84 Danny Bautista	.05	.15
RT85 Chris Turner	.05	.15
RT86 Shane Reynolds	.05	.15
RT87 Rondell White	.10	.30
RT88 Salomon Torres	.05	.15
RT89 Turk Wendell	.05	.15
RT90 Tony Tarasco	.05	.15
RT91 Shawn Green	.30	.75
RT92 Greg Colbrunn	.05	.15
RT93 Eddie Zambrano	.05	.15
RT94 Rich Becker	.05	.15
RT95 Chris Gomez	.05	.15
RT96 John Patterson	.05	.15
RT97 Derek Parks	.05	.15
RT98 Rich Rowland	.05	.15
RT99 James Mouton	.05	.15
RT100 Tim Hyers RC	.05	.15
RT101 Jose Valentin	.05	.15
RT102 Carlos Delgado	.20	.50
RT103 Robert Eenhoorn	.05	.15
RT104 John Hudek RC	.05	.15
RT105 Domingo Cedeno	.05	.15
RT106 Denny Hocking	.05	.15
RT107 Greg Pirkl	.05	.15
RT108 Mark Smith	.05	.15
RT109 Paul Shuey	.05	.15
RT110 Jorge Fabregas	.05	.15
RT111 Rikkert Faneyte RC	.05	.15
RT112 Rob Butler	.05	.15
RT113 Darren Oliver RC	.10	.30
RT114 Troy O'Leary	.05	.15
RT115 Scott Brow	.05	.15
RT116 Tony Eusebio	.05	.15
RT117 Carlos Reyes	.05	.15
RT118 J.R. Phillips	.05	.15
RT119 Alex Diaz	.05	.15
RT120 Charles Johnson	.10	.30
RT121 Nate Minchey	.05	.15
RT122 Scott Sanders	.05	.15
RT123 Daryl Boston	.05	.15
RT124 Joey Hamilton	.05	.15
RT125 Brian Anderson	.10	.30
RT126 Dan Miceli	.05	.15
RT127 Tom Brunansky	.05	.15
RT128 Dave Staton	.05	.15
RT129 Mike Oquist	.05	.15
RT130 John Mabry RC	.10	.30
RT131 Norberto Martin	.05	.15
RT132 Hector Fajardo	.05	.15
RT133 Mark Hutton	.05	.15
RT134 Fernando Vina	.05	.15
RT135 Lee Tinsley	.05	.15
RT136 Chan Ho Park RC	.20	.50
RT137 Paul Spoljaric	.05	.15
RT138 Matias Carrillo	.05	.15
RT139 Mark Kiefer	.05	.15
RT140 Stan Royer	.05	.15
RT141 Bryan Eversgerd	.05	.15
RT142 Brian L. Hunter	.05	.15
RT143 Joe Hall	.05	.15
RT144 Johnny Ruffin	.05	.15
RT145 Alex Gonzalez	.05	.15
RT146 Keith Lockhart RC	.10	.30
RT147 Tom Marsh	.05	.15
RT148 Tony Longmire	.05	.15
RT149 Keith Mitchell	.05	.15
RT150 Melvin Nieves	.05	.15
RT151 Kelly Stinnett RC	.05	.15
RT152 Miguel Jimenez	.05	.15
RT153 Jeff Juden	.05	.15
RT154 Matt Walbeck	.05	.15
RT155 Marc Newfield	.05	.15
RT156 Matt Mieske	.05	.15
RT157 Marcus Moore	.05	.15
RT158 Jose Lima SP RC	2.00	5.00
RT159 Mike Kelly	.05	.15
RT160 Jim Edmonds	.30	.75
RT161 Steve Trachsel	.05	.15
RT162 Greg Blosser	.05	.15
RT163 Mark Acre RC	.05	.15
RT164 AL Checklist	.05	.15
RT165 NL Checklist	.05	.15
HC1 Alex Rodriguez CU	50.00	120.00
NNO September Call-Up Trade EXP	.75	2.00

1994 Score Rookie/Traded Gold Rush

COMPLETE SET (165)	20.00	50.00
*STARS: 1X TO 2.5X BASIC CARDS		
*ROOKIES: 1X TO 2.5X BASIC CARDS		
ONE GOLD RUSH PER PACK		

1994 Score Rookie/Traded Changing Places

Randomly inserted in both retail and hobby packs at a rate of one in 36 Rookie/Traded packs, this 10-card standard-size set focuses on ten veteran superstar players who were traded prior to or during the 1994 season. Cards fronts feature a color photo with a slanted design. The backs have a short write-up and a distorted photo.

COMPLETE SET (10)	12.50	30.00
STATED ODDS 1:36 HOB/RET		
CP1 Will Clark	2.50	6.00
CP2 Rafael Palmeiro	2.50	6.00
CP3 Roberto Kelly	.75	2.00
CP4 Bo Jackson	4.00	10.00
CP5 Otis Nixon	.75	2.00
CP6 Rickey Henderson	4.00	10.00
CP7 Ellis Burks	1.50	4.00
CP8 Lee Smith	1.50	4.00
CP9 Delino DeShields	.75	2.00
CP10 Deion Sanders	2.50	6.00

1994 Score Rookie/Traded Super Rookies

Randomly inserted in hobby packs at a rate of one in 36, this 18-card standard-size set focuses on top rookies of 1994. Odds of finding one of these cards is approximately one in 36 hobby packs. Designed much like the Gold Rush, the cards have an all-foil design. The fronts have a player photo and the backs have a photo that serves as background to the Super Rookies logo and text.

COMPLETE SET (18)	10.00	25.00
STATED ODDS 1:36 HOBBY		
SU1 Carlos Delgado	1.50	4.00
SU2 Manny Ramirez	2.00	5.00
SU3 Ryan Klesko	1.00	2.50
SU4 Raul Mondesi	1.00	2.50
SU5 Bob Hamelin	.75	2.00
SU6 Steve Karsay	.75	2.00
SU7 Jeffrey Hammonds	.75	2.00
SU8 Cliff Floyd	1.00	2.50
SU9 Kurt Abbott	.75	2.00
SU10 Marc Newfield	.75	2.00
SU11 Javier Lopez	1.00	2.50
SU12 Rich Becker	.75	2.00
SU13 Greg Pirkl	.75	2.00
SU14 Rondell White	1.00	2.50
SU15 James Mouton	.75	2.00
SU16 Tony Tarasco	.75	2.00
SU17 Brian Anderson	1.00	2.50
SU18 Jim Edmonds	2.00	5.00

1995 Score Samples

COMPLETE SET (10)	4.00	10.00
2 Roberto Alomar	.40	1.00
4 Jose Canseco	.50	1.25
5 Matt Williams	.30	.75
221 Jeff Bagwell	.60	1.50
223 Albert Belle	.20	.50
224 Chuck Carr	.08	.25
288 Jorge Fabregas	.08	.25
DP8 McKay Christensen	.08	.25
HG5 Cal Ripken	2.00	5.00
NNO Title Card	.08	.25

1995 Score

The 1995 Score set consists of 605 standard-size cards issued in hobby, retail and jumbo packs. Hobby packs featured a special signed Ryan Klesko (RG1)card. Retail packs also had a Klesko card (SG1) but these were not signed.

COMPLETE SET (605)	10.00	25.00
COMPLETE SERIES 1 (330)	5.00	12.00
COMPLETE SERIES 2 (275)	5.00	12.00
SUBSET CARDS HALF VALUE OF BASE CARDS		
KLESKO RG1 SER.1 ODDS 1:720 RET		
KLESKO SG1 SER.1 ODDS 1:720 HOB		
1 Frank Thomas	.20	.50
2 Roberto Alomar	.10	.30
3 Cal Ripken	.60	1.50
4 Jose Canseco	.10	.30
5 Matt Williams	.07	.20
6 Esteban Beltre	.02	.10
7 Domingo Cedeno	.02	.10
8 John Valentin	.02	.10
9 Glenallen Hill	.02	.10
10 Rafael Belliard	.02	.10
11 Randy Myers	.02	.10
12 Mo Vaughn	.07	.20
13 Hector Carrasco	.02	.10
14 Chili Davis	.07	.20
15 Dante Bichette	.07	.20
16 Darrin Jackson	.02	.10
17 Mike Piazza	.30	.75
18 Junior Felix	.02	.10
19 Moises Alou	.07	.20
20 Mark Gubicza	.02	.10
21 Bret Saberhagen	.07	.20
22 Lenny Dykstra	.07	.20
23 Steve Howe	.02	.10
24 Mark Dewey	.02	.10
25 Brian Harper	.02	.10
26 Ozzie Smith	.30	.75
27 Scott Erickson	.02	.10
28 Tony Gwynn	.25	.60
29 Bob Welch	.02	.10
30 Barry Bonds	.60	1.50
31 Leo Gomez	.02	.10
32 Greg Maddux	.30	.75
33 Mike Greenwell	.02	.10
34 Sammy Sosa	.20	.50
35 Darnell Coles	.02	.10
36 Tommy Greene	.02	.10
37 Will Clark	.10	.30
38 Steve Ontiveros	.02	.10
39 Stan Javier	.02	.10
40 Bip Roberts	.02	.10
41 Paul O'Neill	.10	.30
42 Bill Haselman	.02	.10
43 Shane Mack	.02	.10
44 Orlando Merced	.02	.10
45 Kevin Seitzer	.02	.10
46 Trevor Hoffman	.07	.20
47 Greg Gagne	.02	.10
48 Jeff Kent	.07	.20
49 Tony Phillips	.02	.10
50 Ken Hill	.02	.10
51 Carlos Baerga	.02	.10
52 Henry Rodriguez	.02	.10
53 Scott Sanderson	.02	.10
54 Jeff Conine	.07	.20
55 Chris Turner	.02	.10
56 Ken Caminiti	.07	.20
57 Harold Baines	.07	.20
58 Charlie Hayes	.02	.10
59 Roberto Kelly	.02	.10
60 John Olerud	.07	.20
61 Tim Davis	.02	.10
62 Rich Rowland	.02	.10
63 Rey Sanchez	.02	.10
64 Junior Ortiz	.02	.10
65 Ricky Gutierrez	.02	.10
66 Rex Hudler	.02	.10
67 Johnny Ruffin	.02	.10
68 Jay Buhner	.07	.20
69 Tom Pagnozzi	.02	.10
70 Julio Franco	.07	.20
71 Eric Young	.02	.10
72 Mike Bordick	.02	.10
73 Don Slaught	.02	.10
74 Goose Gossage	.07	.20
75 Lonnie Smith	.02	.10
76 Jimmy Key	.07	.20
77 Dave Hollins	.02	.10
78 Mickey Tettleton	.02	.10
79 Luis Gonzalez	.07	.20
80 Dave Winfield	.07	.20
81 Ryan Thompson	.02	.10
82 Felix Jose	.02	.10
83 Rusty Meacham	.02	.10
84 Darryl Hamilton	.02	.10
85 John Wetteland	.07	.20
86 Tom Brunansky	.02	.10
87 Mark Lemke	.02	.10
88 Spike Owen	.02	.10
89 Shawon Dunston	.02	.10
90 Wilson Alvarez	.02	.10
91 Lee Smith	.07	.20
92 Scott Kamieniecki	.02	.10
93 Jacob Brumfield	.02	.10
94 Kirk Gibson	.07	.20
95 Joe Girardi	.02	.10
96 Mike Macfarlane	.02	.10
97 Greg Colbrunn	.02	.10
98 Ricky Bones	.02	.10
99 Delino DeShields	.02	.10
100 Pat Meares	.02	.10
101 Jeff Fassero	.02	.10
102 Jim Leyritz	.02	.10
103 Gary Redus	.02	.10
104 Terry Steinbach	.02	.10
105 Kevin McReynolds	.02	.10
106 Felix Fermin	.02	.10
107 Danny Jackson	.02	.10
108 Chris James	.02	.10
109 Jeff King	.02	.10
110 Pat Hentgen	.02	.10
111 Gerald Perry	.02	.10
112 Tim Raines	.07	.20
113 Eddie Williams	.02	.10
114 Jamie Moyer	.07	.20
115 Bud Black	.02	.10
116 Chris Gomez	.02	.10
117 Luis Lopez	.02	.10
118 Roger Clemens	.40	1.00
119 Javier Lopez	.07	.20
120 Dave Nilsson	.02	.10
121 Karl Rhodes	.02	.10
122 Rick Aguilera	.02	.10
123 Tony Fernandez	.02	.10
124 Bernie Williams	.10	.30
125 James Mouton	.02	.10
126 Mark Langston	.02	.10
127 Mike Lansing	.02	.10
128 Tino Martinez	.10	.30
129 Joe Orsulak	.02	.10
130 David Hulse	.02	.10
131 Pete Incaviglia	.02	.10
132 Mark Clark	.02	.10
133 Tony Eusebio	.02	.10
134 Chuck Finley	.07	.20
135 Lou Frazier	.02	.10
136 Craig Grebeck	.02	.10
137 Kelly Stinnett	.02	.10
138 Paul Shuey	.02	.10
139 David Nied	.02	.10
140 Billy Brewer	.02	.10
141 Dave Weathers	.02	.10
142 Scott Leius	.02	.10
143 Brian Jordan	.07	.20
144 Melido Perez	.02	.10
145 Tony Tarasco	.02	.10
146 Dan Wilson	.02	.10
147 Rondell White	.07	.20
148 Mike Henneman	.02	.10
149 Brian Johnson	.02	.10
150 Tom Henke	.02	.10
151 John Patterson	.02	.10
152 Bobby Witt	.02	.10
153 Eddie Taubensee	.02	.10
154 Pat Borders	.02	.10
155 Ramon Martinez	.02	.10
156 Mike Kingery	.02	.10
157 Zane Smith	.02	.10
158 Benito Santiago	.07	.20
159 Matias Carrillo	.02	.10
160 Scott Brosius	.07	.20
161 Dave Clark	.02	.10
162 Mark McLemore	.02	.10
163 Curt Schilling	.07	.20
164 J.T. Snow	.07	.20
165 Rod Beck	.02	.10
166 Scott Fletcher	.02	.10
167 Bob Tewksbury	.02	.10
168 Mike LaValliere	.02	.10
169 Dave Hansen	.02	.10
170 Pedro Martinez	.10	.30
171 Kirk Rueter	.02	.10
172 Jose Lind	.02	.10
173 Luis Alicea	.02	.10
174 Mike Moore	.02	.10
175 Andy Ashby	.02	.10
176 Jody Reed	.02	.10
177 Darryl Kile	.07	.20
178 Carl Willis	.02	.10
179 Jeromy Burnitz	.07	.20
180 Mike Gallego	.02	.10
181 Bill VanLandingham	.02	.10
182 Sid Fernandez	.02	.10
183 Kim Batiste	.02	.10
184 Greg Myers	.02	.10
185 Steve Avery	.02	.10
186 Steve Farr	.02	.10
187 Robb Nen	.07	.20
188 Dan Pasqua	.02	.10
189 Bruce Ruffin	.02	.10
190 Jose Valentin	.02	.10
191 Willie Banks	.02	.10
192 Mike Aldrete	.02	.10
193 Randy Milligan	.02	.10
194 Steve Karsay	.02	.10
195 Mike Stanley	.02	.10
196 Jose Mesa	.02	.10
197 Tom Browning	.02	.10
198 John Vander Wal	.02	.10
199 Kevin Brown	.07	.20
200 Mike Oquist	.02	.10
201 Greg Swindell	.02	.10
202 Eddie Zambrano	.02	.10
203 Joe Boever	.02	.10
204 Gary Varsho	.02	.10
205 Chris Gwynn	.02	.10
206 David Howard	.02	.10
207 Jerome Walton	.02	.10
208 Danny Darwin	.02	.10
209 Darryl Strawberry	.07	.20
210 Todd Van Poppel	.02	.10
211 Scott Livingstone	.02	.10
212 Dave Fleming	.02	.10
213 Todd Worrell	.02	.10
214 Carlos Delgado	.07	.20
215 Bill Pecota	.02	.10
216 Jim Lindeman	.02	.10
217 Rick White	.02	.10
218 Jose Oquendo	.02	.10
219 Tony Castillo	.02	.10
220 Fernando Vina	.02	.10
221 Jeff Bagwell	.10	.30
222 Randy Johnson	.20	.50
223 Albert Belle	.07	.20
224 Chuck Carr	.02	.10
225 Mark Leiter	.02	.10
226 Hal Morris	.02	.10
227 Robin Ventura	.07	.20
228 Mike Munoz	.02	.10
229 Jim Thome	.10	.30
230 Mario Diaz	.02	.10
231 John Doherty	.02	.10
232 Bobby Jones	.02	.10
233 Raul Mondesi	.07	.20
234 Ricky Jordan	.02	.10
235 John Jaha	.02	.10
236 Carlos Garcia	.02	.10
237 Kirby Puckett	.20	.50
238 Orel Hershiser	.07	.20
239 Don Mattingly	.50	1.25
240 Sid Bream	.02	.10
241 Brent Gates	.02	.10
242 Tony Longmire	.02	.10
243 Robby Thompson	.02	.10
244 Rick Sutcliffe	.07	.20
245 Dean Palmer	.07	.20
246 Marquis Grissom	.07	.20
247 Paul Molitor	.07	.20
248 Mark Carreon	.02	.10
249 Jack Voigt	.02	.10
250 Greg McMichael UER	.02	.10
251 Damon Berryhill	.02	.10
252 Brian Dorsett	.02	.10
253 Jim Edmonds	.10	.30
254 Barry Larkin	.10	.30
255 Jack McDowell	.02	.10
256 Wally Joyner	.07	.20
257 Eddie Murray	.20	.50
258 Lenny Webster	.02	.10
259 Milt Cuyler	.02	.10
260 Todd Benzinger	.02	.10
261 Vince Coleman	.02	.10
262 Todd Stottlemyre	.02	.10
263 Turner Ward	.02	.10
264 Ray Lankford	.07	.20
265 Matt Walbeck	.02	.10
266 Deion Sanders	.10	.30
267 Gerald Williams	.02	.10
268 Jim Gott	.02	.10
269 Jeff Frye	.02	.10
270 Jose Rijo	.02	.10
271 David Justice	.07	.20
272 Ismael Valdes	.02	.10
273 Ben McDonald	.02	.10
274 Darren Lewis	.02	.10
275 Graeme Lloyd	.02	.10
276 Luis Ortiz	.02	.10
277 Julian Tavarez	.02	.10
278 Mark Dalesandro	.02	.10
279 Brett Merriman	.02	.10
280 Ricky Bottalico	.02	.10
281 Robert Eenhoorn	.02	.10
282 Rikkert Faneyte	.02	.10
283 Mike Kelly	.02	.10
284 Mark Smith	.02	.10
285 Turk Wendell	.02	.10
286 Greg Blosser	.02	.10
287 Garey Ingram	.02	.10
288 Jorge Fabregas	.02	.10
289 Blaise Ilsley	.02	.10
290 Joe Hall	.02	.10
291 Orlando Miller	.02	.10
292 Jose Lima	.02	.10
293 Greg O'Halloran RC	.02	.10
294 Mark Kiefer	.02	.10
295 Jose Oliva	.02	.10
296 Rich Becker	.02	.10
297 Brian L.Hunter	.02	.10
298 Dave Silvestri	.02	.10
299 Armando Benitez	.02	.10
300 Darren Dreifort	.02	.10
301 John Mabry	.02	.10
302 Greg Pirkl	.02	.10
303 J.R. Phillips	.02	.10
304 Shawn Green	.07	.20
305 Roberto Petagine	.02	.10
306 Keith Lockhart	.02	.10
307 Jonathan Hurst	.02	.10
308 Paul Spoljaric	.02	.10
309 Mike Lieberthal	.07	.20
310 Garret Anderson	.07	.20
311 John Johnstone	.02	.10
312 Alex Rodriguez	.50	1.25
313 Kent Mercker	.02	.10
314 John Valentin	.02	.10
315 Kenny Rogers	.07	.20
316 Fred McGriff AS MVP	.07	.20
317 Team Checklists	.02	.10
318 Team Checklists	.02	.10
319 Team Checklists	.02	.10
320 Team Checklists	.02	.10
321 Team Checklists	.02	.10
322 Team Checklists	.02	.10
323 Team Checklists	.02	.10
324 Team Checklists	.02	.10
325 Team Checklists	.02	.10
326 Team Checklists	.02	.10
327 Team Checklists	.02	.10
328 Team Checklists	.02	.10
329 Team Checklists	.02	.10
330 Team Checklists	.02	.10
331 Pedro Munoz	.02	.10
332 Ryan Klesko	.07	.20
333 Andre Dawson	.07	.20
334 Derrick May	.02	.10
335 Aaron Sele	.02	.10
336 Kevin Mitchell	.02	.10
337 Steve Trachsel	.02	.10
338 Andres Galarraga	.07	.20
339 Terry Pendleton	.07	.20
340 Gary Sheffield	.07	.20
341 Travis Fryman	.07	.20
342 Bo Jackson	.20	.50
343 Gary Gaetti	.07	.20
344 Brett Butler	.07	.20
345 B.J. Surhoff	.07	.20
346 Larry Walker	.07	.20
347 Kevin Tapani	.02	.10
348 Rick Wilkins	.02	.10
349 Wade Boggs	.10	.30
350 Mariano Duncan	.02	.10
351 Ruben Sierra	.07	.20
352 Andy Van Slyke	.10	.30
353 Reggie Jefferson	.02	.10
354 Gregg Jefferies	.02	.10
355 Tim Naehring	.02	.10
356 John Roper	.02	.10
357 Joe Carter	.07	.20
358 Kurt Abbott	.02	.10
359 Lenny Harris	.02	.10
360 Lance Johnson	.02	.10
361 Brian Anderson	.02	.10
362 Jim Eisenreich	.02	.10
363 Jerry Browne	.02	.10
364 Mark Grace	.10	.30
365 Devon White	.07	.20
366 Reggie Sanders	.07	.20
367 Ivan Rodriguez	.10	.30
368 Kirt Manwaring	.02	.10
369 Pat Kelly	.02	.10
370 Ellis Burks	.07	.20
371 Charles Nagy	.02	.10
372 Kevin Bass	.02	.10
373 Lou Whitaker	.07	.20
374 Rene Arocha	.02	.10
375 Derek Parks	.02	.10
376 Mark Whiten	.02	.10
377 Mark McGwire	.50	1.25
378 Doug Drabek	.02	.10
379 Greg Vaughn	.02	.10
380 Al Martin	.02	.10
381 Ron Darling	.02	.10
382 Tim Wallach	.02	.10
383 Alan Trammell	.07	.20
384 Randy Velarde	.02	.10
385 Chris Sabo	.02	.10

386 Wil Cordero .02 .10
387 Darrin Fletcher .02 .10
388 David Segui .02 .10
389 Steve Buechele .02 .10
390 Dave Gallagher .02 .10
391 Thomas Howard .02 .10
392 Chad Curtis .02 .10
393 Cal Eldred .02 .10
394 Jason Bere .02 .10
395 Bret Barberie .02 .10
396 Paul Sorrento .02 .10
397 Steve Finley .07 .20
398 Cecil Fielder .07 .20
399 Eric Karros .07 .20
400 Jeff Montgomery .02 .10
401 Cliff Floyd .07 .20
402 Matt Mieske .02 .10
403 Brian Hunter .02 .10
404 Alex Cole .02 .10
405 Kevin Stocker .02 .10
406 Eric Davis .07 .20
407 Marvin Freeman .02 .10
408 Dennis Eckersley .07 .20
409 Todd Zeile .02 .10
410 Keith Mitchell .02 .10
411 Andy Benes .02 .10
412 Juan Bell .02 .10
413 Royce Clayton .02 .10
414 Ed Sprague .02 .10
415 Mike Mussina .10 .30
416 Todd Hundley .02 .10
417 Pat Listach .02 .10
418 Joe Oliver .02 .10
419 Rafael Palmeiro .10 .30
420 Tim Salmon .10 .30
421 Brady Anderson .07 .20
422 Kenny Lofton .07 .20
423 Craig Biggio .10 .30
424 Bobby Bonilla .07 .20
425 Kenny Rogers .07 .20
426 Derek Bell .02 .10
427 Scott Cooper .02 .10
428 Ozzie Guillen .07 .20
429 Omar Vizquel .10 .30
430 Phil Plantier .02 .10
431 Chuck Knoblauch .07 .20
432 Darren Daulton .07 .20
433 Bob Hamelin .02 .10
434 Tom Glavine .10 .30
435 Walt Weiss .02 .10
436 Jose Vizcaino .02 .10
437 Ken Griffey Jr. .40 1.00
438 Jay Bell .07 .20
439 Juan Gonzalez .07 .20
440 Jeff Blauser .02 .10
441 Rickey Henderson .20 .50
442 Bobby Ayala .02 .10
443 David Cone .07 .20
444 Pedro Martinez .10 .30
445 Manny Ramirez .10 .30
446 Mark Portugal .02 .10
447 Damion Easley .02 .10
448 Gary DiSarcina .02 .10
449 Roberto Hernandez .02 .10
450 Jeffrey Hammonds .02 .10
451 Jeff Treadway .02 .10
452 Jim Abbott .10 .30
453 Carlos Rodriguez .02 .10
454 Joey Cora .02 .10
455 Bret Boone .07 .20
456 Danny Tartabull .02 .10
457 John Franco .07 .20
458 Roger Salkeld .02 .10
459 Fred McGriff .10 .30
460 Pedro Astacio .02 .10
461 Jon Lieber .02 .10
462 Luis Polonia .02 .10
463 Geronimo Pena .02 .10
464 Tom Gordon .02 .10
465 Brad Ausmus .07 .20
466 Willie McGee .07 .20
467 Doug Jones .02 .10
468 John Smoltz .10 .30
469 Troy Neel .02 .10
470 Luis Sojo .02 .10
471 John Smiley .02 .10
472 Rafael Bournigal .02 .10
473 Bill Taylor .02 .10
474 Juan Guzman .02 .10
475 Dave Magadan .02 .10
476 Mike Devereaux .02 .10
477 Andujar Cedeno .02 .10
478 Edgar Martinez .10 .30
479 Milt Thompson .02 .10
480 Allen Watson .02 .10
481 Ron Karkovice .02 .10
482 Joey Hamilton .02 .10
483 Vinny Castilla .07 .20
484 Tim Belcher .02 .10
485 Bernard Gilkey .02 .10
486 Scott Servais .02 .10
487 Cory Snyder .02 .10
488 Mel Rojas .02 .10
489 Carlos Reyes .02 .10
490 Chip Hale .02 .10
491 Bill Swift .02 .10
492 Pat Rapp .02 .10
493 Brian McRae .02 .10
494 Mickey Morandini .02 .10
495 Tony Pena .02 .10
496 Danny Bautista .02 .10
497 Armando Reynoso .02 .10
498 Ken Ryan .02 .10
499 Billy Ripken .02 .10
500 Pat Mahomes .02 .10
501 Mark Acre .02 .10
502 Geronimo Berroa .02 .10
503 Norberto Martin .02 .10
504 Chad Kreuter .02 .10
505 Howard Johnson .02 .10
506 Eric Anthony .02 .10
507 Mark Wohlers .02 .10
508 Scott Sanders .02 .10
509 Pete Harnisch .02 .10
510 Wes Chamberlain .02 .10
511 Tom Candiotti .02 .10
512 Albie Lopez .02 .10
513 Denny Neagle .07 .20
514 Sean Berry .02 .10
515 Billy Hatcher .02 .10
516 Todd Jones .02 .10
517 Wayne Kirby .02 .10
518 Butch Henry .02 .10
519 Sandy Alomar Jr. .02 .10
520 Kevin Appier .07 .20
521 Roberto Mejia .02 .10
522 Steve Cooke .02 .10
523 Terry Shumpert .02 .10
524 Mike Jackson .02 .10
525 Kent Mercker .02 .10
526 David Wells .07 .20
527 Juan Samuel .02 .10
528 Salomon Torres .02 .10
529 Duane Ward .02 .10
530 Rob Dibble .07 .20
531 Mike Blowers .02 .10
532 Mark Eichhorn .02 .10
533 Alex Diaz .02 .10
534 Dan Miceli .02 .10
535 Jeff Branson .02 .10
536 Dave Stevens .02 .10
537 Charlie O'Brien .02 .10
538 Shane Reynolds .02 .10
539 Rich Amaral .02 .10
540 Rusty Greer .07 .20
541 Alex Arias .02 .10
542 Eric Plunk .02 .10
543 John Hudek .02 .10
544 Kirk McCaskill .02 .10
545 Jeff Reboulet .02 .10
546 Sterling Hitchcock .02 .10
547 Warren Newson .02 .10
548 Bryan Harvey .02 .10
549 Mike Huff .02 .10
550 Lance Parrish .07 .20
551 Ken Griffey Jr. HIT .25 .60
552 Matt Williams HIT .02 .10
553 Roberto Alomar HIT .02 .10
554 Jeff Bagwell HIT .07 .20
555 David Justice HIT .02 .10
556 Cal Ripken HIT .30 .75
557 Albert Belle HIT .02 .10
558 Mike Piazza HIT .15 .40
559 Kirby Puckett HIT .10 .30
560 Wade Boggs HIT .07 .20
561 Tony Gwynn HIT .10 .30
562 Barry Bonds HIT .30 .75
563 Mo Vaughn HIT .02 .10
564 Don Mattingly HIT .25 .60
565 Carlos Baerga HIT .02 .10
566 Paul Molitor HIT .02 .10
567 Raul Mondesi HIT .02 .10
568 Manny Ramirez HIT .07 .20
569 Alex Rodriguez HIT .20 .50
570 Will Clark HIT .07 .20
571 Frank Thomas HIT .10 .30
572 Moises Alou HIT .02 .10
573 Jeff Conine HIT .02 .10
574 Joe Ausanio .02 .10
575 Charles Johnson .07 .20
576 Ernie Young .02 .10
577 Jeff Granger .02 .10
578 Robert Perez .02 .10
579 Melvin Nieves .02 .10
580 Gar Finnvold .02 .10
581 Duane Singleton .02 .10
582 Chan Ho Park .07 .20
583 Fausto Cruz .02 .10
584 Dave Staton .02 .10
585 Denny Hocking .02 .10
586 Nate Minchey .02 .10
587 Marc Newfield .02 .10
588 Jayhawk Owens .02 .10
589 Darren Bragg .02 .10
590 Kevin King .02 .10
591 Kurt Miller .02 .10
592 Aaron Small .02 .10
593 Troy O'Leary .02 .10
594 Phil Stidham .02 .10
595 Steve Dunn .02 .10
596 Cory Bailey .02 .10
597 Alex Gonzalez .02 .10
598 Jim Bowie RC .02 .10
599 Jeff Cirillo .02 .10
600 Mark Hutton .02 .10
601 Russ Davis .02 .10
602 Checklist .02 .10
603 Checklist .02 .10
604 Checklist .02 .10
605 Checklist .02 .10
RG1 R.Klesko Rook.Great. .20 .50
SG1 Ryan Klesko AU/6100 4.00 10.00

1995 Score Gold Rush

COMPLETE SET (605) 20.00 50.00
COMPLETE SERIES 1 (330) 10.00 25.00
COMPLETE SERIES 2 (275) 10.00 25.00
*STARS: 2X TO 5X BASIC CARDS
ONE PER PACK

1995 Score Platinum Team Sets

*STARS: 5X TO 12X BASIC CARDS
ONE PLAT.TEAM VIA MAIL PER G.RUSH TEAM

1995 Score You Trade Em

COMPLETE SET (11) .60 1.50
ONE SET VIA MAIL PER REDEMPTION CARD
333T Andre Dawson .15 .40
339T Terry Pendleton .15 .40
344T Brett Butler .15 .40
346T Larry Walker .15 .40
352T Andy Van Slyke .25 .60
392T Chad Curtis .07 .20
427T Scott Cooper .07 .20
443T David Cone .15 .40
452T Jim Abbott .25 .60
493T Brian McRae .07 .20
530T Rob Dibble .15 .40
NNO Expired Trade Card .20 .50

1995 Score Airmail

This 18-card set was randomly inserted in series two jumbo packs at a rate of one in 24.

COMPLETE SET (18) 20.00 50.00
SER.2 STATED ODDS 1:24 JUMBO
AM1 Bob Hamelin .60 1.50
AM2 John Mabry .60 1.50
AM3 Marc Newfield .60 1.50
AM4 Jose Oliva .60 1.50
AM5 Charles Johnson 1.00 2.50
AM6 Russ Davis .60 1.50
AM7 Ernie Young .60 1.50
AM8 Billy Ashley .60 1.50
AM9 Ryan Klesko 1.00 2.50
AM10 J.R. Phillips .60 1.50
AM11 Cliff Floyd 1.00 2.50
AM12 Carlos Delgado 1.00 2.50
AM13 Melvin Nieves .60 1.50
AM14 Raul Mondesi 1.00 2.50
AM15 Manny Ramirez 1.50 4.00
AM16 Mike Kelly .60 1.50
AM17 Alex Rodriguez 6.00 15.00
AM18 Rusty Greer 1.00 2.50

1995 Score Contest Redemption

These cards were mailed to collectors who correctly identified intentional errors in two Pinnacle print ads depicting baseball scenes. The Alex Rodriguez card was the prize for the first ad, the Ivan Rodriguez card for the second ad.

COMPLETE SET 3.00 8.00
AD1 Alex Rodriguez 2.50 6.00
AD2 Ivan Rodriguez 1.25 3.00

1995 Score Double Gold Champs

This 12-card set was randomly inserted in second series hobby packs at a rate of one in 36.

COMPLETE SET (12) 30.00 80.00
SER.2 STATED ODDS 1:36 HOBBY
GC1 Frank Thomas 2.00 5.00
GC2 Ken Griffey Jr. 4.00 10.00
GC3 Barry Bonds 6.00 15.00
GC4 Tony Gwynn 2.50 6.00
GC5 Don Mattingly 5.00 12.00
GC6 Greg Maddux 3.00 8.00
GC7 Roger Clemens 4.00 10.00
GC8 Kenny Lofton .75 2.00
GC9 Jeff Bagwell 1.25 3.00
GC10 Matt Williams .75 2.00
GC11 Kirby Puckett 2.00 5.00
GC12 Cal Ripken 6.00 15.00

1995 Score Draft Picks

Randomly inserted in first series hobby packs at a rate of one in 36, this 18-card set takes a look at top picks selected in June of 1994. The cards are numbered with a "DP" prefix.

COMPLETE SET (18) 10.00 25.00
SER.1 STATED ODDS 1:36 HOBBY
DP1 McKay Christensen .40 1.00
DP2 Bret Wagner .40 1.00
DP3 Paul Wilson .40 1.00
DP4 C.J. Nitkowski .40 1.00
DP5 Josh Booty .40 1.00
DP6 Antone Williamson .40 1.00
DP7 Paul Konerko 2.00 5.00
DP8 Scott Elarton .60 1.50
DP9 Jacob Shumate .40 1.00
DP10 Terrence Long .40 1.00
DP11 Mark Johnson .60 1.50
DP12 Ben Grieve .40 1.00
DP13 Doug Million .40 1.00
DP14 Jayson Peterson .40 1.00
DP15 Dustin Hermanson .40 1.00
DP16 Matt Smith .40 1.00
DP17 Kevin Witt .40 1.00
DP18 Brian Buchanan .40 1.00

1995 Score Dream Team

Randomly inserted in first series hobby and retail packs at a rate of one in 72 packs, this 12-card hologram set showcases top performers from the 1994 season. The cards are numbered with a "DG" prefix.

COMPLETE SET (12) 10.00 25.00
SER.1 STATED ODDS 1:72
DG1 Frank Thomas 1.50 4.00
DG2 Roberto Alomar 1.00 2.50
DG3 Cal Ripken 5.00 12.00
DG4 Matt Williams .60 1.50
DG5 Mike Piazza 1.50 4.00
DG6 Albert Belle .60 1.50
DG7 Ken Griffey Jr. 3.00 8.00
DG8 Tony Gwynn 1.50 4.00
DG9 Paul Molitor 1.50 4.00
DG10 Jimmy Key .60 1.50
DG11 Greg Maddux 2.50 6.00
DG12 Lee Smith .60 1.50

1995 Score Hall of Gold

Randomly inserted in packs at a rate one in six, this 110-card multi-series set is a collection of top stars and young hopefuls. Cards numbered one through 55 were seeded in first series packs and cards 56-100 were seeded in second series packs.

COMPLETE SET (110) 12.50 30.00
COMPLETE SERIES 1 (55) 8.00 20.00
COMPLETE SERIES 2 (55) 5.00 12.00
STATED ODDS 1:6H/R, 1:4J, 1:3ANCO
*YTE CARDS: .4X TO 1X BASIC HALL
ONE YTE SET VIA MAIL PER YTE TRADE CARD
HG1 Ken Griffey Jr. 2.50 6.00
HG2 Matt Williams .50 1.25
HG3 Roberto Alomar .75 2.00
HG4 Jeff Bagwell .75 2.00
HG5 David Justice .50 1.25
HG6 Cal Ripken 4.00 10.00
HG7 Randy Johnson 1.25 3.00
HG8 Barry Larkin .75 2.00
HG9 Albert Belle .50 1.25
HG10 Mike Piazza 2.00 5.00
HG11 Kirby Puckett 1.25 3.00
HG12 Moises Alou .50 1.25
HG13 Jose Canseco .75 2.00
HG14 Tony Gwynn 1.50 4.00
HG15 Roger Clemens 2.50 6.00
HG16 Barry Bonds 4.00 10.00
HG17 Mo Vaughn .50 1.25
HG18 Greg Maddux 2.00 5.00
HG19 Dante Bichette .50 1.25
HG20 Will Clark .75 2.00
HG21 Lenny Dykstra .50 1.25
HG22 Don Mattingly 3.00 8.00
HG23 Carlos Baerga .25 .60
HG24 Ozzie Smith 2.00 5.00
HG25 Paul Molitor .50 1.25
HG26 Paul O'Neill .75 2.00
HG27 Deion Sanders .75 2.00
HG28 Jeff Conine .50 1.25
HG29 John Olerud .50 1.25
HG30 Jose Rijo .25 .60
HG31 Sammy Sosa 1.25 3.00
HG32 Robin Ventura .50 1.25
HG33 Raul Mondesi .50 1.25
HG34 Eddie Murray 1.25 3.00
HG35 Marquis Grissom .50 1.25
HG36 Darryl Strawberry .50 1.25
HG37 Dave Nilsson .25 .60
HG38 Manny Ramirez .75 2.00
HG39 Delino DeShields .25 .60
HG40 Lee Smith .50 1.25
HG41 Alex Rodriguez 3.00 8.00
HG42 Julio Franco .50 1.25
HG43 Bret Saberhagen .50 1.25
HG44 Ken Hill .25 .60
HG45 Roberto Kelly .25 .60
HG46 Hal Morris .25 .60
HG47 Jimmy Key .50 1.25
HG48 Terry Steinbach .25 .60
HG49 Mickey Tettleton .25 .60
HG50 Tony Phillips .25 .60
HG51 Carlos Garcia .25 .60
HG52 Jim Edmonds .75 2.00
HG53 Rod Beck .25 .60
HG54 Shane Mack .25 .60
HG55 Ken Caminiti .50 1.25
HG56 Frank Thomas 1.25 3.00
HG57 Kenny Lofton .50 1.25
HG58 Juan Gonzalez .50 1.25
HG59 Jason Bere .25 .60
HG60 Joe Carter .50 1.25
HG61 Gary Sheffield .50 1.25
HG62 Andres Galarraga .50 1.25
HG63 Ellis Burks .50 1.25
HG64 Bobby Bonilla .50 1.25
HG65 Tom Glavine .75 2.00
HG66 John Smoltz .75 2.00
HG67 Fred McGriff .75 2.00
HG68 Craig Biggio .75 2.00
HG69 Reggie Sanders .50 1.25
HG70 Kevin Mitchell .25 .60
HG71 Larry Walker .50 1.25
HG72 Carlos Delgado .50 1.25
HG73 Alex Gonzalez .25 .60
HG74 Ivan Rodriguez .75 2.00
HG75 Ryan Klesko .50 1.25
HG76 John Kruk .25 .60
HG77 Brian McRae .25 .60
HG78 Tim Salmon .75 2.00
HG79 Travis Fryman .50 1.25
HG80 Chuck Knoblauch .50 1.25
HG81 Jay Bell .50 1.25
HG82 Cecil Fielder .50 1.25
HG83 Cliff Floyd .50 1.25
HG84 Ruben Sierra .50 1.25
HG85 Mike Mussina .75 2.00
HG86 Mark Grace .75 2.00
HG87 Dennis Eckersley .50 1.25
HG88 Dennis Martinez .25 .60
HG89 Rafael Palmeiro .75 2.00
HG90 Ben McDonald .25 .60
HG91 Dave Hollins .25 .60
HG92 Steve Avery .25 .60
HG93 David Cone .50 1.25
HG94 Darren Daulton .50 1.25
HG95 Bret Boone .50 1.25
HG96 Wade Boggs .75 2.00
HG97 Doug Drabek .25 .60
HG98 Andy Benes .25 .60
HG99 Jim Thome .75 2.00
HG100 Chili Davis .50 1.25
HG101 Jeffrey Hammonds .25 .60
HG102 Rickey Henderson 1.25 3.00
HG103 Brett Butler .50 1.25
HG104 Tim Wallach .25 .60
HG105 Wil Cordero .25 .60
HG106 Mark Whiten .25 .60
HG107 Bob Hamelin .25 .60
HG108 Rondell White .50 1.25
HG109 Devon White .50 1.25
HG110 Tony Tarasco .25 .60

1995 Score Hall of Gold You Trade Em

COMPLETE SET (5) 1.25 3.00
ONE SET VIA MAIL PER GOLD TRADE CARD
HG71T Larry Walker .50 1.25
HG76T John Kruk .25 .60
HG77T Brian McRae .25 .60
HG93T David Cone .50 1.25
HG110T Tony Tarasco .25 .60
NNO Exp. Hall of Gold Trade Card .20 .50

1995 Score Rookie Dream Team

This 12-card set was randomly inserted in second series retail and hobby packs at a rate of one in 12. The cards are numbered with a "RDT" prefix.

COMPLETE SET (12) 25.00 60.00
SER.2 STAT.ODDS 1:72 HOB/RET, 1:43 ANCO
RDT PREFIX ON CARD NUMBERS
RDT1 J.R. Phillips 1.00 2.50
RDT2 Alex Gonzalez 1.00 2.50
RDT3 Alex Rodriguez 8.00 20.00
RDT4 Jose Oliva 1.00 2.50
RDT5 Charles Johnson 2.00 5.00
RDT6 Shawn Green 2.00 5.00
RDT7 Brian L.Hunter 1.00 2.50
RDT8 Garret Anderson 2.00 5.00
RDT9 Julian Tavarez 1.00 2.50
RDT10 Jose Lima 1.00 2.50
RDT11 Armando Benitez 1.00 2.50
RDT12 Ricky Bottalico 1.00 2.50

1995 Score Rules

Randomly inserted in first series jumbo packs, this 30-card standard-size set features top big league players. The cards are numbered with an "SR" prefix.

COMPLETE SET (30) 60.00 120.00
SER.1 STATED ODDS 1:8 JUMBO
*JUMBO'S: .5X TO 1.2X
JUMBOS ISSUED ONE PER COLLECTOR KIT
SR1 Ken Griffey Jr. 4.00 10.00
SR2 Frank Thomas 2.00 5.00
SR3 Mike Piazza 3.00 8.00
SR4 Jeff Bagwell 1.25 3.00
SR5 Alex Rodriguez 5.00 12.00
SR6 Albert Belle .75 2.00
SR7 Matt Williams .75 2.00
SR8 Roberto Alomar 1.25 3.00
SR9 Barry Bonds 6.00 15.00
SR10 Raul Mondesi .75 2.00
SR11 Jose Canseco 1.25 3.00
SR12 Kirby Puckett 2.00 5.00
SR13 Fred McGriff 1.25 3.00
SR14 Kenny Lofton .75 2.00
SR15 Greg Maddux 3.00 8.00
SR16 Juan Gonzalez .75 2.00
SR17 Cliff Floyd .75 2.00
SR18 Cal Ripken 6.00 15.00
SR19 Will Clark 1.25 3.00
SR20 Tim Salmon 1.25 3.00
SR21 Paul O'Neill 1.25 3.00
SR22 Jason Bere .40 1.00
SR23 Tony Gwynn 2.50 6.00
SR24 Manny Ramirez 1.25 3.00
SR25 Don Mattingly 5.00 12.00
SR26 David Justice .75 2.00
SR27 Javier Lopez .75 2.00
SR28 Ryan Klesko .75 2.00
SR29 Carlos Delgado .75 2.00
SR30 Mike Mussina 1.25 3.00

1995 Score Rules Jumbos

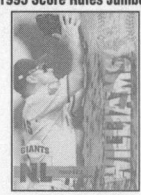

STATED PRINT RUN 3000 SER.#'d SETS
SR1 Ken Griffey Jr. 15.00 40.00
SR2 Frank Thomas 15.00 40.00
SR3 Mike Piazza 12.50 30.00
SR4 Jeff Bagwell 6.00 15.00
SR5 Alex Rodriguez 5.00 12.00
SR6 Albert Belle 6.00 15.00
SR7 Matt Williams 2.00 5.00
SR8 Roberto Alomar 4.00 10.00
SR9 Barry Bonds 3.00 8.00
SR10 Raul Mondesi 2.50 6.00
SR11 Jose Canseco 1.50 4.00
SR12 Kirby Puckett 40.00 80.00
SR13 Fred McGriff 1.50 4.00
SR14 Kenny Lofton 4.00 10.00
SR15 Greg Maddux 12.50 30.00
SR16 Juan Gonzalez 3.00 8.00
SR17 Cliff Floyd .60 1.50
SR18 Cal Ripken 20.00 50.00
SR19 Will Clark 20.00 50.00
SR20 Tim Salmon 2.50 6.00
SR21 Paul O'Neill 1.25 3.00
SR22 Jason Bere .60 1.50
SR23 Tony Gwynn 10.00 25.00
SR24 Manny Ramirez 5.00 12.00
SR25 Don Mattingly 6.00 15.00
SR26 David Justice 1.25 3.00
SR27 Javier Lopez 1.50 4.00
SR28 Ryan Klesko 3.00 8.00
SR29 Carlos Delgado 1.25 3.00
SR30 Mike Mussina 2.50 6.00

1996 Score Samples

COMPLETE SET (8) 3.00 8.00
3 Ryan Klesko .20 .50
4 Jim Edmonds .40 1.00
5 Barry Larkin .40 1.00
6 Jim Thome .50 1.25
7 Raul Mondesi .30 .75
110 Derek Bell .08 .25
240 Derek Jeter 2.00 5.00
241 Michael Tucker .20 .50

1996 Score

This set consists of 517 standard-size cards. These cards were issued in packs of 10 that retailed for 99 cents per pack. The fronts feature an action photo surrounded by white borders. The "Score 96" logo is in the upper left, while the player is identified on the bottom. The backs have season and career stats as well as a player photo and some text. A Cal Ripken tribute card was issued at a rate of 1 every 300 packs.

COMPLETE SET (517) 12.50 30.00
COMPLETE SERIES 1 (275) 6.00 15.00
COMPLETE SERIES 2 (242) 6.00 15.00
RIPKEN 2131 ODDS 1:300 H/R, 1:150 JUM
1 Will Clark .10 .30
2 Rich Becker .07 .20
3 Ryan Klesko .07 .20
4 Jim Edmonds .07 .20
5 Barry Larkin .10 .30
6 Jim Thome .10 .30
7 Raul Mondesi .07 .20
8 Don Mattingly .50 1.25
9 Jeff Conine .07 .20
10 Rickey Henderson .20 .50
11 Chad Curtis .07 .20
12 Darren Daulton .07 .20
13 Larry Walker .07 .20
14 Carlos Garcia .07 .20
15 Carlos Baerga .07 .20
16 Tony Gwynn .25 .60
17 Jon Nunnally .07 .20
18 Deion Sanders .10 .30
19 Mark Grace .10 .30
20 Alex Rodriguez .40 1.00
21 Frank Thomas .20 .50
22 Brian Jordan .07 .20
23 J.T. Snow .07 .20
24 Shawn Green .07 .20
25 Tim Wakefield .07 .20
26 Curtis Goodwin .07 .20
27 John Smoltz .10 .30
28 Devon White .07 .20
29 Brian L. Hunter .07 .20
30 Rusty Greer .07 .20
31 Rafael Palmeiro .10 .30
32 Bernard Gilkey .07 .20
33 John Valentin .07 .20
34 Randy Johnson .20 .50
35 Garret Anderson .07 .20
36 Rikkert Faneyte .07 .20
37 Ray Durham .07 .20
38 Bip Roberts .07 .20
39 Jaime Navarro .07 .20
40 Mark Johnson .07 .20
41 Darren Lewis .07 .20
42 Tyler Green .07 .20
43 Bill Pulsipher .07 .20
44 Jason Giambi .07 .20
45 Kevin Ritz .07 .20
46 Jack McDowell .07 .20
47 Felipe Lira .07 .20
48 Rico Brogna .07 .20
49 Terry Pendleton .07 .20
50 Rondell White .07 .20
51 Andre Dawson .07 .20
52 Kirby Puckett .20 .50
53 Wally Joyner .07 .20
54 B.J. Surhoff .07 .20
55 Randy Velarde .07 .20
56 Greg Vaughn .07 .20
57 Roberto Alomar .10 .30
58 David Justice .07 .20
59 Kevin Seitzer .07 .20
60 Cal Ripken .60 1.50
61 Ozzie Smith .30 .75
62 Mo Vaughn .07 .20
63 Ricky Bones .07 .20
64 Gary DiSarcina .07 .20

Card	Low	High
Matt Williams	.07	.20
Wilson Alvarez	.07	.20
Lenny Dykstra	.07	.20
Brian McRae	.07	.20
Todd Stottlemyre	.07	.20
Bret Boone	.07	.20
Sterling Hitchcock	.07	.20
Albert Belle	.07	.20
Todd Hundley	.07	.20
Vinny Castilla	.07	.20
Moises Alou	.07	.20
Cecil Fielder	.07	.20
Brad Radke	.07	.20
Quilvio Veras	.07	.20
Eddie Murray	.20	.50
James Mouton	.07	.20
Pat Listach	.07	.20
Mark Gubicza	.07	.20
Dave Winfield	.07	.20
Fred McGriff	.10	.30
Darryl Hamilton	.07	.20
Jeffrey Hammonds	.07	.20
Pedro Munoz	.07	.20
Craig Biggio	.10	.30
Cliff Floyd	.07	.20
Tim Naehring	.07	.20
Brett Butler	.07	.20
Kevin Foster	.07	.20
Pat Kelly	.07	.20
John Smiley	.07	.20
Terry Steinbach	.07	.20
Orel Hershiser	.07	.20
Darrin Fletcher	.07	.20
Walt Weiss	.07	.20
John Wetteland	.07	.20
Alan Trammell	.07	.20
Steve Avery	.07	.20
Tony Eusebio	.07	.20
Sandy Alomar Jr.	.07	.20
Joe Girardi	.07	.20
Rick Aguilera	.07	.20
Tony Tarasco	.07	.20
Chris Hammond	.07	.20
Mike Macfarlane	.07	.20
Doug Drabek	.07	.20
10 Derek Bell	.07	.20
11 Ed Sprague	.07	.20
12 Todd Hollandsworth	.07	.20
13 Otis Nixon	.07	.20
14 Keith Lockhart	.07	.20
15 Donovan Osborne	.07	.20
16 Dave Magadan	.07	.20
17 Edgar Martinez	.10	.30
18 Chuck Carr	.07	.20
19 J.R. Phillips	.07	.20
20 Sean Bergman	.07	.20
21 Andujar Cedeno	.07	.20
22 Eric Young	.07	.20
23 Al Martin	.07	.20
124 Mark Lemke	.07	.20
125 Jim Eisenreich	.07	.20
126 Benito Santiago	.07	.20
127 Ariel Prieto	.07	.20
128 Jim Bullinger	.07	.20
129 Russ Davis	.07	.20
130 Jim Abbott	.10	.30
131 Jason Isringhausen	.07	.20
132 Carlos Perez	.07	.20
133 David Segui	.07	.20
134 Troy O'Leary	.07	.20
135 Pat Meares	.07	.20
136 Chris Hoiles	.07	.20
137 Ismael Valdes	.07	.20
138 Jose Oliva	.07	.20
139 Carlos Delgado	.07	.20
140 Tom Goodwin	.07	.20
141 Bob Tewksbury	.07	.20
142 Chris Gomez	.07	.20
143 Jose Oquendo	.07	.20
144 Mark Lewis	.07	.20
145 Salomon Torres	.07	.20
146 Luis Gonzalez	.07	.20
147 Mark Carreon	.07	.20
148 Lance Johnson	.07	.20
149 Melvin Nieves	.07	.20
150 Lee Smith	.07	.20
151 Jacob Brumfield	.07	.20
152 Armando Benitez	.07	.20
153 Curt Schilling	.07	.20
154 Javier Lopez	.07	.20
155 Frank Rodriguez	.07	.20
156 Alex Gonzalez	.07	.20
157 Todd Worrell	.07	.20
158 Benji Gil	.07	.20
159 Greg Gagne	.07	.20
160 Tom Henke	.07	.20
161 Randy Myers	.07	.20
162 Joey Cora	.07	.20
163 Scott Ruffcorn	.07	.20
164 W. VanLandingham	.07	.20
165 Tony Phillips	.07	.20
166 Eddie Williams	.07	.20
167 Bobby Bonilla	.07	.20
168 Denny Neagle	.07	.20
169 Troy Percival	.07	.20
170 Billy Ashley	.07	.20
171 Andy Van Slyke	.10	.30
172 Jose Offerman	.07	.20
173 Mark Parent	.07	.20
174 Edgardo Alfonzo	.07	.20
175 Trevor Hoffman	.07	.20
176 David Cone	.07	.20
177 Dan Wilson	.07	.20
178 Steve Ontiveros	.07	.20
179 Dean Palmer	.07	.20
180 Mike Kelly	.07	.20
181 Jim Leyritz	.07	.20
182 Ron Karkovice	.07	.20
183 Kevin Brown	.07	.20
184 Jose Valentin	.07	.20
185 Jorge Fabregas	.07	.20
186 Jose Mesa	.07	.20
187 Brent Mayne	.07	.20
188 Carl Everett	.07	.20
189 Paul Sorrento	.07	.20
190 Pete Schourek	.07	.20
191 Scott Kamieniecki	.07	.20
192 Roberto Hernandez	.07	.20
193 Randy Johnson RR	.10	.30
194 Greg Maddux RR	.20	.50
195 Hideo Nomo RR	.10	.30
196 David Cone RR	.07	.20
197 Mike Mussina RR	.07	.20
198 Andy Benes RR	.07	.20
199 Kevin Appier RR	.07	.20
200 John Smoltz RR	.07	.20
201 John Wetteland RR	.07	.20
202 Mark Wohlers RR	.07	.20
203 Stan Belinda	.07	.20
204 Brian Anderson	.07	.20
205 Mike Devereaux	.07	.20
206 Mark Wohlers	.07	.20
207 Omar Vizquel	.10	.30
208 Jose Rijo	.07	.20
209 Willie Blair	.07	.20
210 Jamie Moyer	.07	.20
211 Craig Shipley	.07	.20
212 Shane Reynolds	.07	.20
213 Chad Fonville	.07	.20
214 Jose Vizcaino	.07	.20
215 Sid Fernandez	.07	.20
216 Andy Ashby	.07	.20
217 Frank Castillo	.07	.20
218 Kevin Tapani	.07	.20
219 Kent Mercker	.07	.20
220 Karim Garcia	.07	.20
221 Antonio Osuna	.07	.20
222 Tim Unroe	.07	.20
223 Johnny Damon	.10	.30
224 LaTroy Hawkins	.07	.20
225 Mariano Rivera	4.00	10.00
226 Jose Alberro	.07	.20
227 Angel Martinez	.07	.20
228 Jason Schmidt	.10	.30
229 Tony Clark	.07	.20
230 Kevin Jordan	.07	.20
231 Mark Thompson	.07	.20
232 Jim Dougherty	.07	.20
233 Roger Cedeno	.07	.20
234 Ugueth Urbina	.07	.20
235 Ricky Otero	.07	.20
236 Mark Smith	.07	.20
237 Brian Barber	.07	.20
238 Kevin Flora	.07	.20
239 Joe Rosselli	.07	.20
240 Derek Jeter	.50	1.25
241 Michael Tucker	.07	.20
242 Ben Blomdahl	.07	.20
243 Joe Vitiello	.07	.20
244 Todd Steverson	.07	.20
245 James Baldwin	.07	.20
246 Alan Embree	.07	.20
247 Shannon Penn	.07	.20
248 Chris Stynes	.07	.20
249 Oscar Munoz	.07	.20
250 Jose Herrera	.07	.20
251 Scott Sullivan	.07	.20
252 Reggie Williams	.07	.20
253 Mark Grudzielanek	.07	.20
254 Steve Rodriguez	.07	.20
255 Terry Bradshaw	.07	.20
256 F.P. Santangelo	.07	.20
257 Lyle Mouton	.07	.20
258 George Williams	.07	.20
259 Larry Thomas	.07	.20
260 Rudy Pemberton	.07	.20
261 Jim Pittsley	.07	.20
262 Les Norman	.07	.20
263 Ruben Rivera	.07	.20
264 Cesar Devarez	.07	.20
265 Greg Zaun	.07	.20
266 Dustin Hermanson	.07	.20
267 John Frascatore	.07	.20
268 Joe Randa	.07	.20
269 Jeff Bagwell CL	.07	.20
270 Mike Piazza CL	.20	.50
271 Dante Bichette CL	.07	.20
272 Frank Thomas CL	.10	.30
273 Ken Griffey Jr. CL	.25	.60
274 Cal Ripken CL	.30	.75
275 G.Maddux	.07	.20
A.Belle CL		
276 Greg Maddux	.30	.75
277 Pedro Martinez	.10	.30
278 Bobby Higginson	.07	.20
279 Ray Lankford	.07	.20
280 Shawon Dunston	.07	.20
281 Gary Sheffield	.07	.20
282 Ken Griffey Jr.	.40	1.00
283 Paul Molitor	.07	.20
284 Kevin Appier	.07	.20
285 Chuck Knoblauch	.07	.20
286 Alex Fernandez	.07	.20
287 Steve Finley	.07	.20
288 Jeff Blauser	.07	.20
289 Charles Johnson	.07	.20
290 John Franco	.07	.20
291 Mark Langston	.07	.20
292 Bret Saberhagen	.07	.20
293 John Mabry	.07	.20
294 Ramon Martinez	.07	.20
295 Mike Blowers	.07	.20
296 Paul O'Neill	.10	.30
297 Dave Nilsson	.07	.20
298 Dante Bichette	.07	.20
299 Marty Cordova	.07	.20
300 Jay Bell	.07	.20
301 Mike Mussina	.10	.30
302 Ivan Rodriguez	.10	.30
303 Jose Canseco	.10	.30
304 Jeff Bagwell	.10	.30
305 Manny Ramirez	.10	.30
306 Dennis Martinez	.07	.20
307 Charlie Hayes	.07	.20
308 Joe Carter	.07	.20
309 Travis Fryman	.07	.20
310 Mark McGwire	.50	1.25
311 Reggie Sanders	.07	.20
312 Julian Tavarez	.07	.20
313 Jeff Montgomery	.07	.20
314 Andy Benes	.07	.20
315 John Jaha	.07	.20
316 Jeff Kent	.07	.20
317 Mike Piazza	.30	.75
318 Erik Hanson	.07	.20
319 Kenny Rogers	.07	.20
320 Hideo Nomo	.20	.50
321 Gregg Jefferies	.07	.20
322 Chipper Jones	.20	.50
323 Jay Buhner	.07	.20
324 Dennis Eckersley	.07	.20
325 Kenny Lofton	.07	.20
326 Robin Ventura	.07	.20
327 Tom Glavine	.10	.30
328 Tim Salmon	.10	.30
329 Andres Galarraga	.07	.20
330 Hal Morris	.07	.20
331 Brady Anderson	.07	.20
332 Chili Davis	.07	.20
333 Roger Clemens	.40	1.00
334 Marquis Grissom	.07	.20
335 Mike Greenwell UER		
front reads Jeff Greenwell	.07	.20
336 Sammy Sosa	.20	.50
337 Ron Gant	.07	.20
338 Ken Caminiti	.07	.20
339 Danny Tartabull	.07	.20
340 Barry Bonds	.60	1.50
341 Ben McDonald	.07	.20
342 Ruben Sierra	.07	.20
343 Bernie Williams	.10	.30
344 Wil Cordero	.07	.20
345 Wade Boggs	.10	.30
346 Gary Gaetti	.07	.20
347 Greg Colbrunn	.07	.20
348 Juan Gonzalez	.07	.20
349 Marc Newfield	.07	.20
350 Charles Nagy	.07	.20
351 Robby Thompson	.07	.20
352 Roberto Petagine	.07	.20
353 Darryl Strawberry	.07	.20
354 Tino Martinez	.10	.30
355 Eric Karros	.07	.20
356 Cal Ripken SS	.30	.75
357 Cecil Fielder SS	.07	.20
358 Kirby Puckett SS	.10	.30
359 Jim Edmonds SS	.07	.20
360 Matt Williams SS	.07	.20
361 Alex Rodriguez SS	.20	.50
362 Barry Larkin SS	.07	.20
363 Rafael Palmeiro SS	.07	.20
364 David Cone SS	.07	.20
365 Roberto Alomar SS	.07	.20
366 Eddie Murray SS	.10	.30
367 Randy Johnson SS	.10	.30
368 Ryan Klesko SS	.07	.20
369 Raul Mondesi SS	.07	.20
370 Mo Vaughn SS	.07	.20
371 Will Clark SS	.07	.20
372 Carlos Baerga SS	.07	.20
373 Frank Thomas SS	.10	.30
374 Larry Walker SS	.07	.20
375 Garret Anderson SS	.07	.20
376 Edgar Martinez SS	.07	.20
377 Don Mattingly SS	.25	.60
378 Tony Gwynn SS	.10	.30
379 Albert Belle SS	.07	.20
380 Jason Isringhausen SS	.07	.20
381 Ruben Rivera SS	.07	.20
382 Johnny Damon SS	.07	.20
383 Karim Garcia SS	.07	.20
384 Derek Jeter SS	.25	.60
385 David Justice SS	.07	.20
386 Royce Clayton	.07	.20
387 Mark Whiten	.07	.20
388 Mickey Tettleton	.07	.20
389 Steve Trachsel	.07	.20
390 Danny Bautista	.07	.20
391 Midre Cummings	.07	.20
392 Scott Leius	.07	.20
393 Manny Alexander	.07	.20
394 Brent Gates	.07	.20
395 Rey Sanchez	.07	.20
396 Andy Pettitte	.10	.30
397 Jeff Cirillo	.07	.20
398 Kurt Abbott	.07	.20
399 Lee Tinsley	.07	.20
400 Paul Assenmacher	.07	.20
401 Scott Erickson	.07	.20
402 Todd Zeile	.07	.20
403 Tom Pagnozzi	.07	.20
404 Ozzie Guillen	.07	.20
405 Jeff Frye	.07	.20
406 Kirt Manwaring	.07	.20
407 Chad Ogea	.07	.20
408 Harold Baines	.07	.20
409 Jason Bere	.07	.20
410 Chuck Finley	.07	.20
411 Jeff Fassero	.07	.20
412 Joey Hamilton	.07	.20
413 John Olerud	.07	.20
414 Kevin Stocker	.07	.20
415 Eric Anthony	.07	.20
416 Aaron Sele	.07	.20
417 Chris Bosio	.07	.20
418 Michael Mimbs	.07	.20
419 Orlando Miller	.07	.20
420 Stan Javier	.07	.20
421 Matt Mieske	.07	.20
422 Jason Bates	.07	.20
423 Orlando Merced	.07	.20
424 John Flaherty	.07	.20
425 Reggie Jefferson	.07	.20
426 Scott Stahoviak	.07	.20
427 John Burkett	.07	.20
428 Rod Beck	.07	.20
429 Bill Swift	.07	.20
430 Scott Cooper	.07	.20
431 Mel Rojas	.07	.20
432 Todd Van Poppel	.07	.20
433 Bobby Jones	.07	.20
434 Mike Harkey	.07	.20
435 Sean Berry	.07	.20
436 Glenallen Hill	.07	.20
437 Ryan Thompson	.07	.20
438 Luis Alicea	.07	.20
439 Esteban Loaiza	.07	.20
440 Jeff Reboulet	.07	.20
441 Vince Coleman	.07	.20
442 Ellis Burks	.07	.20
443 Allen Battle	.07	.20
444 Jimmy Key	.07	.20
445 Ricky Bottalico	.07	.20
446 Delino DeShields	.07	.20
447 Albie Lopez	.07	.20
448 Mark Petkovsek	.07	.20
449 Tim Raines	.07	.20
450 Bryan Harvey	.07	.20
451 Pat Hentgen	.07	.20
452 Tim Laker	.07	.20
453 Tom Gordon	.07	.20
454 Phil Plantier	.07	.20
455 Ernie Young	.07	.20
456 Pete Harnisch	.07	.20
457 Roberto Kelly	.07	.20
458 Mark Portugal	.07	.20
459 Mark Leiter	.07	.20
460 Tony Pena	.07	.20
461 Roger Pavlik	.07	.20
462 Jeff King	.07	.20
463 Bryan Rekar	.07	.20
464 Al Leiter	.07	.20
465 Phil Nevin	.07	.20
466 Jose Lima	.07	.20
467 Mike Stanley	.07	.20
468 David McCarty	.07	.20
469 Herb Perry	.07	.20
470 Geronimo Berroa	.07	.20
471 David Wells	.07	.20
472 Vaughn Eshelman	.07	.20
473 Greg Swindell	.07	.20
474 Steve Sparks	.07	.20
475 Luis Sojo	.07	.20
476 Derrick May	.07	.20
477 Joe Oliver	.07	.20
478 Alex Arias	.07	.20
479 Brad Ausmus	.07	.20
480 Gabe White	.07	.20
481 Pat Rapp	.07	.20
482 Damon Buford	.07	.20
483 Turk Wendell	.07	.20
484 Jeff Brantley	.07	.20
485 Curtis Leskanic	.07	.20
486 Robb Nen	.07	.20
487 Lou Whitaker	.07	.20
488 Melido Perez	.07	.20
489 Luis Polonia	.07	.20
490 Scott Brosius	.07	.20
491 Robert Perez	.07	.20
492 Mike Sweeney RC	.30	.75
493 Mark Loretta	.07	.20
494 Alex Ochoa	.07	.20
495 Matt Lawton RC	.07	.20
496 Shawn Estes	.07	.20
497 John Wasdin	.07	.20
498 Marc Kroon	.07	.20
499 Chris Snopek	.07	.20
500 Jeff Suppan	.07	.20
501 Terrell Wade	.07	.20
502 Marvin Benard RC	.07	.20
503 Chris Widger	.07	.20
504 Quinton McCracken	.07	.20
505 Bob Wolcott	.07	.20
506 C.J. Nitkowski	.07	.20
507 Aaron Ledesma	.07	.20
508 Scott Hatteberg	.07	.20
509 Jimmy Haynes	.07	.20
510 Howard Battle	.07	.20
511 Marty Cordova CL	.07	.20
512 Randy Johnson CL	.10	.30
513 Mo Vaughn CL	.07	.20
514 Hideo Nomo CL	.07	.20
515 Greg Maddux CL	.20	.50
516 Barry Larkin CL	.07	.20
517 Tom Glavine CL	.07	.20
2131 Cal Ripken 2131	8.00	20.00

1996 Score All-Stars

Randomly inserted in second series jumbo packs at a rate of one in nine, this 20-card set was printed in rainbow holographic prismatic foil.

Card	Low	High
COMPLETE SET (20)	25.00	60.00
SER.2 STATED ODDS 1:9 JUMBO		
1 Frank Thomas	1.25	3.00
2 Albert Belle	.50	1.25
3 Ken Griffey Jr.	2.50	6.00
4 Cal Ripken	4.00	10.00
5 Mo Vaughn	.50	1.25
6 Matt Williams	.50	1.25
7 Barry Bonds	4.00	10.00
8 Dante Bichette	.50	1.25
9 Tony Gwynn	1.50	4.00
10 Greg Maddux	2.00	5.00
11 Randy Johnson	1.25	3.00
12 Hideo Nomo	1.25	3.00
13 Tim Salmon	.75	2.00
14 Jeff Bagwell	.75	2.00
15 Edgar Martinez	.75	2.00
16 Reggie Sanders	.50	1.25
17 Larry Walker	.50	1.25
18 Chipper Jones	1.25	3.00
19 Manny Ramirez	.75	2.00
20 Eddie Murray	1.25	3.00

1996 Score Big Bats

This 20-card set was randomly inserted in retail packs at a rate of approximately one in 31. The cards are numbered "X" of 20 in the upper left corner.

Card	Low	High
COMPLETE SET (20)	10.00	25.00
SER.1 STATED ODDS 1:31 RETAIL		
1 Cal Ripken	3.00	8.00
2 Ken Griffey Jr.	2.00	5.00
3 Frank Thomas	1.00	2.50
4 Jeff Bagwell	.60	1.50
5 Mike Piazza	1.00	2.50
6 Barry Bonds	1.50	4.00
7 Matt Williams	.40	1.00
8 Raul Mondesi	.40	1.00
9 Tony Gwynn	1.00	2.50
10 Albert Belle	.40	1.00
11 Manny Ramirez	.60	1.50
12 Carlos Baerga	.40	1.00
13 Mo Vaughn	.40	1.00
14 Dorok Boll	.40	1.00
15 Larry Walker	.60	1.50
16 Kenny Lofton	.40	1.00
17 Edgar Martinez	.60	1.50
18 Reggie Sanders	.40	1.00
19 Eddie Murray	.60	1.50
20 Chipper Jones	1.00	2.50

1996 Score Diamond Aces

This 30-card set features some of baseball's best players. These cards were inserted approximately one every eight jumbo packs.

Card	Low	High
COMPLETE SET (30)	60.00	120.00
SER.1 STATED ODDS 1:8 JUMBO		
1 Hideo Nomo	2.00	5.00
2 Brian L.Hunter	.75	2.00
3 Ray Durham	.75	2.00
4 Frank Thomas	2.00	5.00
5 Cal Ripken	3.00	8.00
6 Barry Bonds	6.00	15.00
7 Greg Maddux	3.00	8.00
8 Chipper Jones	2.00	5.00
9 Raul Mondesi	.75	2.00
10 Mike Piazza	3.00	8.00
11 Derek Jeter	5.00	12.00
12 Bill Pulsipher	.75	2.00
13 Larry Walker	.75	2.00
14 Ken Griffey Jr.	4.00	10.00
15 Alex Rodriguez	4.00	10.00
16 Manny Ramirez	1.25	3.00
17 Mo Vaughn	.75	2.00
18 Reggie Sanders	.75	2.00
19 Derek Bell	.75	2.00
20 Jim Edmonds	.75	2.00
21 Albert Belle	.75	2.00
22 Eddie Murray	2.00	5.00
23 Tony Gwynn	2.50	6.00
24 Jeff Bagwell	1.25	3.00
25 Carlos Baerga	.75	2.00
26 Matt Williams	.75	2.00
27 Garret Anderson	.75	2.00
28 Todd Hollandsworth	.75	2.00
29 Johnny Damon	.75	2.00
30 Tim Salmon	1.25	3.00

1996 Score Dream Team

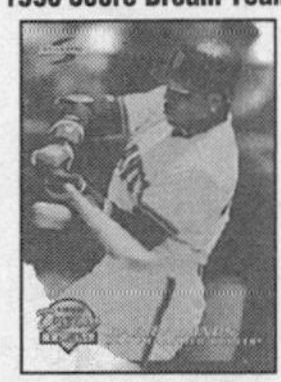

This nine-card set was randomly inserted in approximately one in 72 packs. This set features a leading player at each position. The cards are numbered in the upper right as "X" of nine.

Card	Low	High
COMPLETE SET (9)	25.00	60.00
SER.1 STATED ODDS 1:72 HOB/RET		
1 Cal Ripken	6.00	15.00
2 Frank Thomas	2.00	5.00
3 Carlos Baerga	.75	2.00
4 Matt Williams	.75	2.00
5 Mike Piazza	3.00	8.00
6 Barry Bonds	6.00	15.00
7 Ken Griffey Jr.	4.00	10.00
8 Manny Ramirez	1.25	3.00
9 Greg Maddux	3.00	8.00

1996 Score Dugout Collection

Card	Low	High
COMPLETE SERIES 1 (110)	20.00	50.00
COMPLETE SERIES 2 (110)	20.00	50.00

*DUGOUT: 1.5X TO 4X BASIC
STATED ODDS 1:3 HOB/RET
SUBSET CARDS HALF VALUE OF BASE CARDS
*AP DUGOUT: 10X TO 25X BASIC
AP STATED ODDS 1:36 HOB/RET

1996 Score Dugout Collection Artist's Proofs

*STARS: 2.5X TO 6X BASIC DUGOUT
STATED ODDS 1:36

1996 Score Future Franchise

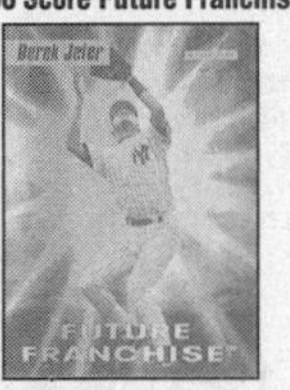

Randomly inserted in retail packs at a rate of one in 72, this 16-card set honors young stars of the game.

Card	Low	High
COMPLETE SET (16)	40.00	100.00
SER.2 STATED ODDS 1:72 HOB/RET		
1 Jason Isringhausen	1.50	4.00
2 Chipper Jones	4.00	10.00
3 Derek Jeter	10.00	25.00
4 Alex Rodriguez	8.00	20.00
5 Alex Ochoa	1.50	4.00
6 Manny Ramirez	2.50	6.00
7 Johnny Damon	1.50	4.00
8 Ruben Rivera	1.50	4.00
9 Karim Garcia	1.50	4.00
10 Garret Anderson	1.50	4.00
11 Marty Cordova	1.50	4.00
12 Bill Pulsipher	1.50	4.00
13 Hideo Nomo	4.00	10.00
14 Marc Newfield	1.50	4.00
15 Charles Johnson	1.50	4.00
16 Raul Mondesi	1.50	4.00

1996 Score Gold Stars

Randomly inserted in packs at a rate of one in 15, this 30-card set features borderless color action player photos with a special sepia player cutout inserted behind a gold foil stamp designating the star player.

Card	Low	High
COMPLETE SET (30)	20.00	50.00
SER.2 STATED ODDS 1:15 HOB/RET		
1 Ken Griffey Jr.	2.00	5.00
2 Frank Thomas	1.00	2.50
3 Reggie Sanders	.40	1.00
4 Tim Salmon	.60	1.50
5 Mike Piazza	1.50	4.00
6 Tony Gwynn	1.25	3.00
7 Gary Sheffield	.40	1.00
8 Matt Williams	.40	1.00
9 Bernie Williams	.60	1.50
10 Jason Isringhausen	.40	1.00
11 Albert Belle	.40	1.00
12 Chipper Jones	1.00	2.50
13 Edgar Martinez	.60	1.50
14 Barry Larkin	.60	1.50
15 Barry Bonds	3.00	8.00
16 Jeff Bagwell	.60	1.50
17 Greg Maddux	1.50	4.00
18 Mo Vaughn	.40	1.00
19 Ryan Klesko	.40	1.00
20 Sammy Sosa	1.00	2.50
21 Darren Daulton	.40	1.00
22 Ivan Rodriguez	.60	1.50
23 Dante Bichette	.40	1.00
24 Hideo Nomo	1.00	2.50
25 Cal Ripken	3.00	8.00
26 Rafael Palmeiro	.60	1.50
27 Larry Walker	.40	1.00
28 Carlos Baerga	.40	1.00
29 Randy Johnson	1.00	2.50
30 Manny Ramirez	.60	1.50

1996 Score Numbers Game

This 30-card set was inserted approximately one in every 15 packs. The cards are numbered as "X" of 30 in the upper left corner.

Card	Low	High
COMPLETE SET (30)	25.00	60.00
SER.1 STATED ODDS 1:15 HOB/RET		
1 Cal Ripken	3.00	8.00
2 Frank Thomas	1.00	2.50
3 Ken Griffey Jr.	2.00	5.00
4 Mike Piazza	1.00	2.50
5 Barry Bonds	1.50	4.00
6 Greg Maddux	1.50	4.00
7 Jeff Bagwell	.60	1.50
8 Derek Bell	.40	1.00
9 Tony Gwynn	1.00	2.50
10 Hideo Nomo	1.00	2.50
11 Raul Mondesi	.40	1.00
12 Manny Ramirez	.60	1.50
13 Albert Belle	.40	1.00
14 Matt Williams	.40	1.00
15 Jim Edmonds	.40	1.00
16 Edgar Martinez	.60	1.50
17 Mo Vaughn	.40	1.00
18 Reggie Sanders	.40	1.00
19 Chipper Jones	1.00	2.50
20 Larry Walker	.60	1.50
21 Juan Gonzalez	.40	1.00
22 Kenny Lofton	.40	1.00
23 Don Mattingly	2.00	5.00
24 Ivan Rodriguez	.60	1.50
25 Randy Johnson	1.00	2.50
26 Derek Jeter	2.50	6.00
27 J.T. Snow	.40	1.00
28 Will Clark	.60	1.50
29 Rafael Palmeiro	.60	1.50
30 Alex Rodriguez	1.25	3.00

1996 Score Power Pace

Randomly inserted in retail packs at a rate of one in 31, this 18-card set features homerun hitters.

Card	Low	High
COMPLETE SET (18)	25.00	60.00
SER.2 STATED ODDS 1:31 RETAIL		
1 Mark McGwire	4.00	10.00
2 Albert Belle	.60	1.50
3 Jay Buhner	.60	1.50
4 Frank Thomas	1.50	4.00
5 Matt Williams	.60	1.50
6 Gary Sheffield	.60	1.50
7 Mike Piazza	2.50	6.00
8 Larry Walker	.60	1.50
9 Mo Vaughn	.60	1.50
10 Rafael Palmeiro	1.00	2.50
11 Dante Bichette	.60	1.50
12 Ken Griffey Jr.	3.00	8.00
13 Barry Bonds	5.00	12.00
14 Manny Ramirez	1.00	2.50
15 Sammy Sosa	1.50	4.00
16 Tim Salmon	1.00	2.50
17 Dave Justice	.60	1.50
18 Eric Karros	.60	1.50

1996 Score Reflextions

This 20-card set was randomly inserted approximately one in every 31 hobby packs. Two players per card are featured, a veteran player and a younger star playing the same position.

Card	Low	High
COMPLETE SET (20)	40.00	100.00
SER.1 STATED ODDS 1:15 HOBBY		
1 C.Ripken	6.00	15.00
C.Jones		
2 K.Griffey Jr.	4.00	10.00
A.Rodriguez		
3 F.Thomas	2.00	5.00
M.Vaughn		
4 K.Lofton	.75	2.00
B.L.Hunter		
5 D.Mattingly	5.00	12.00
J.T.Snow		
6 M.Ramirez	1.25	3.00
R.Mondesi		
7 T.Gwynn	2.50	6.00
G.Anderson		
8 R.Alomar	1.25	3.00
C.Baerga		
9 A.Dawson	.75	2.00
L.Walker		
10 D.Jeter	5.00	12.00
B.Larkin		
11 B.Bonds	6.00	15.00
R.Sanders		
12 M.Piazza	3.00	8.00
A.Belle		

Card	Low	High
13 W.Boggs E.Martinez	1.25	3.00
14 D.Cone J.Smoltz	.75	2.00
15 J.Bagwell W.Clark	1.25	3.00
16 M.McGwire C.Fielder	5.00	12.00
17 G.Maddux M.Mussina	3.00	8.00
18 H.Nomo R.Johnson	2.00	5.00
19 J.Thome D.Palmer	1.25	3.00
20 C.Knoblauch C.Biggio	1.25	3.00

1996 Score Titanic Taters

Randomly inserted in hobby packs at a rate of one in 31, this 18-card set features long home run hitters.

Card	Low	High
COMPLETE SET (18)	30.00	80.00
SER.2 STATED ODDS 1:31 HOBBY		
1 Albert Belle	.75	2.00
2 Frank Thomas	2.00	5.00
3 Mo Vaughn	.75	2.00
4 Ken Griffey Jr.	4.00	10.00
5 Matt Williams	.75	2.00
6 Mark McGwire	5.00	12.00
7 Dante Bichette	.75	2.00
8 Tim Salmon	1.25	3.00
9 Jeff Bagwell	1.25	3.00
10 Rafael Palmeiro	1.25	3.00
11 Mike Piazza	3.00	8.00
12 Cecil Fielder	.75	2.00
13 Larry Walker	.75	2.00
14 Sammy Sosa	2.00	5.00
15 Manny Ramirez	1.25	3.00
16 Gary Sheffield	.75	2.00
17 Barry Bonds	6.00	15.00
18 Jay Buhner	.75	2.00

1997 Score

The 1997 Score set has a total of 550 cards. With cards 1-330 distributed in series one packs and cards 331-550 in series two packs. The 10-card Series one packs and the 12-card Series two packs carried a suggested retail price of $.99 each and were distributed exclusively to retail outlets. The fronts feature color player action photos in a white border. The backs carry player information and career statistics. The Hideki Irabu card (551A and B) is shortprinted (about twice as tough to pull as a basic card). One final note on the Irabu card, in the retail packs and factory sets, the card text is in English. In the Hobby Reserve packs, text is in Japanese. Notable Rookie Cards include Brian Giles.

Card	Low	High
COMPLETE SET (551)	15.00	40.00
COMP.FACT.SET (551)	15.00	40.00
COMPLETE SERIES 1 (330)	6.00	15.00
COMPLETE SERIES 2 (221)	10.00	25.00
IRABU ENGLISH IN FACT.SET/RETAIL PACKS		
1 Jeff Bagwell	.12	.30
2 Mickey Tettleton	.07	.20
3 Johnny Damon	.12	.30
4 Jeff Conine	.07	.20
5 Bernie Williams	.12	.30
6 Will Clark	.12	.30
7 Ryan Klesko	.07	.20
8 Cecil Fielder	.07	.20
9 Paul Wilson	.07	.20
10 Gregg Jefferies	.07	.20
11 Chili Davis	.07	.20
12 Albert Belle	.07	.20
13 Ken Hill	.07	.20
14 Cliff Floyd	.07	.20
15 Jaime Navarro	.07	.20
16 Ismael Valdes	.07	.20
17 Jeff King	.07	.20
18 Chris Bosio	.07	.20
19 Reggie Sanders	.07	.20
20 Darren Daulton	.07	.20
21 Ken Caminiti	.07	.20
22 Mike Piazza	.20	.50
23 Chad Mottola	.07	.20
24 Darin Erstad	.07	.20
25 Dante Bichette	.07	.20
26 Frank Thomas	.20	.50
27 Ben McDonald	.07	.20
28 Raul Casanova	.07	.20
29 Kevin Ritz	.07	.20
30 Garret Anderson	.07	.20
31 Jason Kendall	.07	.20
32 Billy Wagner	.07	.20
33 Dave Justice	.07	.20
34 Marty Cordova	.07	.20
35 Derek Jeter	.50	1.25
36 Trevor Hoffman	.07	.20
37 Geronimo Berroa	.07	.20
38 Walt Weiss	.07	.20
39 Kirt Manwaring	.07	.20
40 Alex Gonzalez	.07	.20
41 Sean Berry	.07	.20
42 Kevin Appier	.07	.20
43 Rusty Greer	.07	.20
44 Pete Incaviglia	.07	.20
45 Rafael Palmeiro	.07	.20
46 Eddie Murray	.12	.30
47 Moises Alou	.07	.20
48 Mark Lewis	.07	.20
49 Hal Morris	.07	.20
50 Edgar Renteria	.07	.20
51 Rickey Henderson	.20	.50
52 Pat Listach	.07	.20
53 John Wasdin	.07	.20
54 James Baldwin	.07	.20
55 Brian Jordan	.07	.20
56 Edgar Martinez	.12	.30
57 Wil Cordero	.07	.20
58 Danny Tartabull	.07	.20
59 Keith Lockhart	.07	.20
60 Rico Brogna	.07	.20
61 Ricky Bottalico	.07	.20
62 Terry Pendleton	.07	.20
63 Bret Boone	.07	.20
64 Charlie Hayes	.07	.20
65 Marc Newfield	.07	.20
66 Sterling Hitchcock	.07	.20
67 Roberto Alomar	.12	.30
68 John Jaha	.07	.20
69 Greg Colbrunn	.07	.20
70 Sal Fasano	.07	.20
71 Brooks Kieschnick	.07	.20
72 Pedro Martinez	.12	.30
73 Kevin Elster	.07	.20
74 Ellis Burks	.07	.20
75 Chuck Finley	.07	.20
76 John Olerud	.07	.20
77 Jay Bell	.07	.20
78 Allen Watson	.07	.20
79 Darryl Strawberry	.07	.20
80 Orlando Miller	.07	.20
81 Jose Herrera	.07	.20
82 Andy Pettitte	.12	.30
83 Juan Guzman	.07	.20
84 Alan Benes	.07	.20
85 Jack McDowell	.07	.20
86 Ugueth Urbina	.07	.20
87 Rocky Coppinger	.07	.20
88 Jeff Cirillo	.07	.20
89 Tom Glavine	.12	.30
90 Robby Thompson	.07	.20
91 Barry Bonds	.30	.75
92 Carlos Delgado	.07	.20
93 Mo Vaughn	.07	.20
94 Ryne Sandberg	.30	.75
95 Alex Rodriguez	.25	.60
96 Brady Anderson	.07	.20
97 Scott Brosius	.07	.20
98 Dennis Eckersley	.12	.30
99 Brian McRae	.07	.20
100 Rey Ordonez	.07	.20
101 John Valentin	.07	.20
102 Brett Butler	.07	.20
103 Eric Karros	.07	.20
104 Harold Baines	.12	.30
105 Javier Lopez	.07	.20
106 Alan Trammell	.12	.30
107 Jim Thome	.12	.30
108 Frank Rodriguez	.07	.20
109 Bernard Gilkey	.07	.20
110 Reggie Jefferson	.07	.20
111 Scott Stahoviak	.07	.20
112 Steve Gibralter	.07	.20
113 Todd Hollandsworth	.07	.20
114 Ruben Rivera	.07	.20
115 Dennis Martinez	.07	.20
116 Mariano Rivera	.25	.60
117 John Smoltz	.12	.30
118 John Mabry	.07	.20
119 Tom Gordon	.07	.20
120 Alex Ochoa	.07	.20
121 Jamey Wright	.07	.20
122 Dave Nilsson	.07	.20
123 Bobby Bonilla	.07	.20
124 Al Leiter	.07	.20
125 Rick Aguilera	.07	.20
126 Jeff Brantley	.07	.20
127 Kevin Brown	.07	.20
128 George Arias	.07	.20
129 Darren Oliver	.07	.20
130 Bill Pulsipher	.07	.20
131 Roberto Hernandez	.07	.20
132 Delino DeShields	.07	.20
133 Mark Grudzielanek	.07	.20
134 John Wetteland	.07	.20
135 Carlos Baerga	.07	.20
136 Paul Sorrento	.07	.20
137 Leo Gomez	.07	.20
138 Andy Ashby	.07	.20
139 Julio Franco	.07	.20
140 Brian Hunter	.07	.20
141 Jermaine Dye	.07	.20
142 Tony Clark	.07	.20
143 Ruben Sierra	.07	.20
144 Donovan Osborne	.07	.20
145 Mark McLemore	.07	.20
146 Terry Steinbach	.07	.20
147 Bob Wells	.07	.20
148 Chan Ho Park	.07	.20
149 Tim Salmon	.07	.20
150 Paul O'Neill	.12	.30
151 Cal Ripken	.60	1.50
152 Wally Joyner	.07	.20
153 Omar Vizquel	.12	.30
154 Mike Mussina	.12	.30
155 Andres Galarraga	.12	.30
156 Ken Griffey Jr.	.40	1.00
157 Kenny Lofton	.07	.20
158 Ray Durham	.07	.20
159 Hideo Nomo	.12	.30
160 Ozzie Guillen	.07	.20
161 Roger Pavlik	.07	.20
162 Manny Ramirez	.12	.30
163 Mark Lemke	.07	.20
164 Mike Stanley	.07	.20
165 Chuck Knoblauch	.07	.20
166 Kimera Bartee	.07	.20
167 Wade Boggs	.12	.30
168 Jay Buhner	.07	.20
169 Eric Young	.07	.20
170 Jose Canseco	.12	.30
171 Dwight Gooden	.07	.20
172 Fred McGriff	.12	.30
173 Sandy Alomar Jr.	.07	.20
174 Andy Benes	.07	.20
175 Dean Palmer	.07	.20
176 Larry Walker	.12	.30
177 Charles Nagy	.07	.20
178 David Cone	.07	.20
179 Mark Grace	.12	.30
180 Robin Ventura	.07	.20
181 Roger Clemens	.25	.60
182 Bobby Witt	.07	.20
183 Vinny Castilla	.07	.20
184 Gary Sheffield	.07	.20
185 Dan Wilson	.07	.20
186 Roger Cedeno	.07	.20
187 Mark McGwire	.30	.75
188 Darren Bragg	.07	.20
189 Quinton McCracken	.07	.20
190 Randy Myers	.07	.20
191 Jeromy Burnitz	.07	.20
192 Randy Johnson	.20	.50
193 Chipper Jones	.20	.50
194 Greg Vaughn	.07	.20
195 Travis Fryman	.07	.20
196 Tim Naehring	.07	.20
197 B.J. Surhoff	.07	.20
198 Juan Gonzalez	.07	.20
199 Terrell Wade	.07	.20
200 Jeff Frye	.07	.20
201 Joey Cora	.07	.20
202 Raul Mondesi	.07	.20
203 Ivan Rodriguez	.12	.30
204 Armando Reynoso	.07	.20
205 Jeffrey Hammonds	.07	.20
206 Darren Dreifort	.07	.20
207 Kevin Seitzer	.07	.20
208 Tino Martinez	.12	.30
209 Jim Bruske SP	.07	.20
210 Jeff Suppan	.07	.20
211 Mark Carreon	.07	.20
212 Wilson Alvarez	.07	.20
213 John Burkett	.07	.20
214 Tony Phillips	.07	.20
215 Greg Maddux	.30	.75
216 Mark Whiten	.07	.20
217 Curtis Pride	.07	.20
218 Lyle Mouton	.07	.20
219 Todd Hundley	.07	.20
220 Greg Gagne	.07	.20
221 Rich Amaral	.07	.20
222 Tom Goodwin	.07	.20
223 Chris Hoiles	.07	.20
224 Jayhawk Owens	.07	.20
225 Kenny Rogers	.07	.20
226 Mike Greenwell	.07	.20
227 Mark Wohlers	.07	.20
228 Henry Rodriguez	.07	.20
229 Robert Perez	.07	.20
230 Jeff Kent	.07	.20
231 Darryl Hamilton	.07	.20
232 Alex Fernandez	.07	.20
233 Ron Karkovice	.07	.20
234 Jimmy Haynes	.07	.20
235 Craig Biggio	.12	.30
236 Ray Lankford	.07	.20
237 Lance Johnson	.07	.20
238 Matt Williams	.07	.20
239 Chad Curtis	.07	.20
240 Mark Thompson	.07	.20
241 Jason Giambi	.07	.20
242 Barry Larkin	.12	.30
243 Paul Molitor	.20	.50
244 Sammy Sosa	.12	.30
245 Kevin Tapani	.07	.20
246 Marquis Grissom	.07	.20
247 Joe Carter	.07	.20
248 Ramon Martinez	.07	.20
249 Tony Gwynn	.20	.50
250 Andy Fox	.07	.20
251 Troy O'Leary	.07	.20
252 Warren Newson	.07	.20
253 Troy Percival	.07	.20
254 Jamie Moyer	.07	.20
255 Danny Graves	.07	.20
256 David Wells	.07	.20
257 Todd Zeile	.07	.20
258 Raul Ibanez	.12	.30
259 Tyler Houston	.07	.20
260 LaTroy Hawkins	.07	.20
261 Joey Hamilton	.07	.20
262 Mike Sweeney	.07	.20
263 Brant Brown	.07	.20
264 Pat Hentgen	.07	.20
265 Mark Johnson	.07	.20
266 Robb Nen	.07	.20
267 Justin Thompson	.07	.20
268 Ron Gant	.07	.20
269 Jeff D'Amico	.07	.20
270 Shawn Estes	.07	.20
271 Derek Bell	.07	.20
272 Fernando Valenzuela	.07	.20
273 Tom Pagnozzi	.07	.20
274 John Burke	.07	.20
275 Ed Sprague	.07	.20
276 F.P. Santangelo	.07	.20
277 Todd Greene	.07	.20
278 Butch Huskey	.07	.20
279 Steve Finley	.07	.20
280 Eric Davis	.07	.20
281 Shawn Green	.07	.20
282 Al Martin	.07	.20
283 Michael Tucker	.07	.20
284 Shane Reynolds	.07	.20
285 Matt Mieske	.07	.20
286 Jose Rosado	.07	.20
287 Mark Langston	.07	.20
288 Ralph Milliard	.07	.20
289 Mike Lansing	.07	.20
290 Scott Servais	.07	.20
291 Royce Clayton	.07	.20
292 Mike Grace	.07	.20
293 James Mouton	.07	.20
294 Charles Johnson	.07	.20
295 Gary Gaetti	.07	.20
296 Kevin Mitchell	.07	.20
297 Carlos Garcia	.07	.20
298 Desi Relaford	.07	.20
299 Jason Thompson	.07	.20
300 Osvaldo Fernandez	.07	.20
301 Fernando Vina	.07	.20
302 Jose Offerman	.07	.20
303 Yamil Benitez	.07	.20
304 J.T. Snow	.07	.20
305 Rafael Bournigal	.07	.20
306 Jason Isringhausen	.07	.20
307 Bobby Higginson	.07	.20
308 Nerio Rodriguez RC	.07	.20
309 Brian Giles RC	.40	1.00
310 Andruw Jones	.07	.20
311 Tony Graffanino	.07	.20
312 Arquimedez Pozo	.07	.20
313 Jermaine Allensworth	.07	.20
314 Jeff Darwin	.07	.20
315 George Williams	.07	.20
316 Karim Garcia	.07	.20
317 Trey Beamon	.07	.20
318 Mac Suzuki	.07	.20
319 Robin Jennings	.07	.20
320 Danny Patterson	.07	.20
321 Damon Mashore	.07	.20
322 Wendell Magee	.07	.20
323 Dax Jones	.07	.20
324 Todd Walker	.07	.20
325 Marvin Benard	.07	.20
326 Mike Cameron	.07	.20
327 Marcus Jensen	.07	.20
328 Eddie Murray CL	.12	.30
329 Paul Molitor CL	.20	.50
330 Todd Hundley CL	.07	.20
331 Norm Charlton	.07	.20
332 Bruce Ruffin	.07	.20
333 John Wetteland	.07	.20
334 Marquis Grissom	.07	.20
335 Sterling Hitchcock	.07	.20
336 John Olerud	.07	.20
337 David Wells	.07	.20
338 Chili Davis	.07	.20
339 Mark Lewis	.07	.20
340 Kenny Lofton	.07	.20
341 Alex Fernandez	.07	.20
342 Ruben Sierra	.07	.20
343 Delino DeShields	.07	.20
344 John Wasdin	.07	.20
345 Dennis Martinez	.07	.20
346 Kevin Elster	.07	.20
347 Bobby Bonilla	.07	.20
348 Jaime Navarro	.07	.20
349 Chad Curtis	.07	.20
350 Terry Steinbach	.07	.20
351 Ariel Prieto	.07	.20
352 Jeff Kent	.07	.20
353 Carlos Garcia	.07	.20
354 Mark Whiten	.07	.20
355 Todd Zeile	.07	.20
356 Eric Davis	.07	.20
357 Greg Colbrunn	.07	.20
358 Moises Alou	.07	.20
359 Allen Watson	.07	.20
360 Jose Canseco	.12	.30
361 Matt Williams	.07	.20
362 Jeff King	.07	.20
363 Darryl Hamilton	.07	.20
364 Mark Clark	.07	.20
365 J.T. Snow	.07	.20
366 Kevin Mitchell	.07	.20
367 Orlando Miller	.07	.20
368 Rico Brogna	.07	.20
369 Mike James	.07	.20
370 Brad Ausmus	.07	.20
371 Darryl Kile	.07	.20
372 Edgardo Alfonzo	.07	.20
373 Julian Tavarez	.07	.20
374 Darren Lewis	.07	.20
375 Steve Karsay	.07	.20
376 Lee Stevens	.07	.20
377 Albie Lopez	.07	.20
378 Orel Hershiser	.07	.20
379 Lee Smith	.07	.20
380 Rick Helling	.07	.20
381 Carlos Perez	.07	.20
382 Tony Tarasco	.07	.20
383 Melvin Nieves	.07	.20
384 Benji Gil	.07	.20
385 Devon White	.07	.20
386 Armando Benitez	.07	.20
387 Bill Swift	.07	.20
388 John Smiley	.07	.20
389 Midre Cummings	.07	.20
390 Tim Belcher	.07	.20
391 Tim Raines	.12	.30
392 Todd Worrell	.07	.20
393 Quilvio Veras	.07	.20
394 Matt Lawton	.07	.20
395 Aaron Sele	.07	.20
396 Bip Roberts	.07	.20
397 Denny Neagle	.07	.20
398 Tyler Green	.07	.20
399 Hipolito Pichardo	.07	.20
400 Scott Erickson	.07	.20
401 Bobby Jones	.07	.20
402 Jim Edmonds	.07	.20
403 Chad Ogea	.07	.20
404 Cal Eldred	.07	.20
405 Pat Listach	.07	.20
406 Todd Stottlemyre	.07	.20
407 Phil Nevin	.07	.20
408 Otis Nixon	.07	.20
409 Billy Ashley	.07	.20
410 Jimmy Key	.07	.20
411 Mike Timlin	.07	.20
412 Joe Vitiello	.07	.20
413 Rondell White	.07	.20
414 Jeff Fassero	.07	.20
415 Rex Hudler	.07	.20
416 Curt Schilling	.07	.20
417 Rich Becker	.07	.20
418 William Van Landingham	.07	.20
419 Chris Snopek	.07	.20
420 David Segui	.07	.20
421 Eddie Murray	.12	.30
422 Shane Andrews	.07	.20
423 Gary DiSarcina	.07	.20
424 Brian Hunter	.07	.20
425 Willie Greene	.07	.20
426 Felipe Crespo	.07	.20
427 Jason Bates	.07	.20
428 Albert Belle	.07	.20
429 Rey Sanchez	.07	.20
430 Roger Clemens	.25	.60
431 Deion Sanders	.12	.30
432 Ernie Young	.07	.20
433 Jay Bell	.07	.20
434 Jeff Blauser	.07	.20
435 Lenny Dykstra	.07	.20
436 Chuck Carr	.07	.20
437 Russ Davis	.07	.20
438 Carl Everett	.07	.20
439 Damion Easley	.07	.20
440 Pat Kelly	.07	.20
441 Pat Rapp	.07	.20
442 Dave Justice	.07	.20
443 Graeme Lloyd	.07	.20
444 Damon Buford	.07	.20
445 Jose Valentin	.07	.20
446 Jason Schmidt	.07	.20
447 Dave Martinez	.07	.20
448 Danny Tartabull	.07	.20
449 Jose Vizcaino	.07	.20
450 Steve Avery	.07	.20
451 Mike Devereaux	.07	.20
452 Jim Eisenreich	.07	.20
453 Mark Leiter	.07	.20
454 Roberto Kelly	.07	.20
455 Benito Santiago	.07	.20
456 Steve Trachsel	.07	.20
457 Gerald Williams	.07	.20
458 Pete Schourek	.07	.20
459 Esteban Loaiza	.07	.20
460 Mel Rojas	.07	.20
461 Tim Wakefield	.12	.30
462 Tony Fernandez	.07	.20
463 Doug Drabek	.07	.20
464 Joe Girardi	.07	.20
465 Mike Bordick	.07	.20
466 Jim Leyritz	.07	.20
467 Erik Hanson	.07	.20
468 Michael Tucker	.07	.20
469 Tony Womack RC	.07	.20
470 Doug Glanville	.07	.20
471 Rudy Pemberton	.07	.20
472 Keith Lockhart	.07	.20
473 Nomar Garciaparra	.12	.30
474 Scott Rolen	.12	.30
475 Jason Dickson	.07	.20
476 Glendon Rusch	.07	.20
477 Todd Walker	.07	.20
478 Dmitri Young	.07	.20
479 Rod Myers	.07	.20
480 Wilton Guerrero	.07	.20
481 Jorge Posada	.12	.30
482 Brant Brown	.07	.20
483 Bubba Trammell RC	.07	.20
484 Jose Guillen	.07	.20
485 Scott Spiezio	.07	.20
486 Bob Abreu	.12	.30
487 Chris Holt	.07	.20
488 Deivi Cruz RC	.07	.20
489 Vladimir Guerrero	.12	.30
490 Julio Santana	.07	.20
491 Ray Montgomery RC	.07	.20
492 Kevin Orie	.07	.20
493 Todd Hundley GY	.07	.20
494 Tim Salmon GY	.07	.20
495 Albert Belle GY	.07	.20
496 Manny Ramirez GY	.12	.30
497 Rafael Palmeiro GY	.07	.20
498 Juan Gonzalez GY	.07	.20
499 Ken Griffey Jr. GY	.40	1.00
500 Andruw Jones GY	.07	.20
501 Mike Piazza GY	.20	.50
502 Jeff Bagwell GY	.12	.30
503 Bernie Williams GY	.12	.30
504 Barry Bonds GY	.30	.75
505 Ken Caminiti GY	.07	.20
506 Darin Erstad GY	.07	.20
507 Alex Rodriguez GY	.25	.60
508 Frank Thomas GY	.20	.50
509 Chipper Jones GY	.20	.50
510 Mo Vaughn GY	.07	.20
511 Mark McGwire GY	.30	.75
512 Fred McGriff GY	.12	.30
513 Jay Buhner GY	.07	.20
515A Gary Sheffield GY	.07	.20
515B Jim Thome GY	.12	.30
516 Dean Palmer GY	.07	.20
517 Henry Rodriguez GY	.07	.20
518 Andy Pettitte RF	.12	.30
519 Mike Mussina RF	.12	.30
520 Greg Maddux RF	.30	.75
521 John Smoltz RF	.12	.30
522 Hideo Nomo RF	.12	.30
523 Troy Percival RF	.07	.20
524 John Wetteland RF	.07	.20
525 Roger Clemens RF	.25	.60
526 Charles Nagy RF	.07	.20
527 Mariano Rivera RF	.25	.60
528 Tom Glavine RF	.12	.30
529 Randy Johnson RF	.20	.50
530 Jason Isringhausen RF	.07	.20
531 Alex Fernandez RF	.07	.20
532 Kevin Brown RF	.07	.20
533 Chuck Knoblauch TG	.07	.20
534 Rusty Greer TG	.07	.20
535 Tony Gwynn TG	.20	.50
536 Ryan Klesko TG	.07	.20
537 Ryne Sandberg TG	.30	.75
538 Barry Larkin TG	.12	.30
539 Will Clark TG	.12	.30
540 Kenny Lofton TG	.07	.20
541 Paul Molitor TG	.20	.50
542 Roberto Alomar TG	.12	.30
543 Rey Ordonez TG	.07	.20
544 Jason Giambi TG	.07	.20
545 Derek Jeter TG	.50	1.25
546 Cal Ripken TG	.60	1.50
547 Ivan Rodriguez TG	.12	.30
548 Ken Griffey Jr. CL	.40	1.00
549 Frank Thomas CL	.20	.50
550 Mike Piazza CL	.20	.50
551A Hideki Irabu English SP	1.00	2.50
551B Hideki Irabu Japanese SP	1.00	2.50

1997 Score Artist's Proofs White Border

*STARS: 12.5X TO 30X BASIC CARDS
*ROOKIES: 4X TO 10X BASIC CARDS
RANDOM INSERTS IN RETAIL PACKS

1997 Score Hobby Reserve

*HOBBY RESERVE: .6X TO 1.5X

Card	Low	High
HR331 Norm Charlton	1.25	3.00
HR332 Bruce Ruffin	1.25	3.00
HR333 John Wetteland	1.25	3.00
HR334 Marquis Grissom	1.25	3.00
HR335 Sterling Hitchcock	1.25	3.00
HR336 John Olerud	1.25	3.00
HR337 David Wells	1.25	3.00
HR338 Chili Davis	1.25	3.00
HR339 Mark Lewis	1.25	3.00
HR340 Kenny Lofton	1.25	3.00
HR341 Alex Fernandez	1.25	3.00
HR342 Ruben Sierra	1.25	3.00
HR343 Delino DeShields	1.25	3.00
HR344 John Wasdin	1.25	3.00
HR345 Dennis Martinez	1.25	3.00
HR346 Kevin Elster	1.25	3.00
HR347 Bobby Bonilla	1.25	3.00
HR348 Jaime Navarro	1.25	3.00
HR349 Chad Curtis	1.25	3.00
HR350 Terry Steinbach	1.25	3.00
HR351 Ariel Prieto	1.25	3.00
HR352 Jeff Kent	1.25	3.00
HR353 Carlos Garcia	1.25	3.00
HR354 Mark Whiten	1.25	3.00
HR355 Todd Zeile	1.25	3.00
HR356 Eric Davis	1.25	3.00
HR357 Greg Colbrunn	1.25	3.00
HR358 Moises Alou	1.25	3.00
HR359 Allen Watson	1.25	3.00
HR360 Jose Canseco	2.00	5.00
HR361 Matt Williams	1.25	3.00
HR362 Jeff King	1.25	3.00
HR363 Darryl Hamilton	1.25	3.00
HR364 Mark Clark	1.25	3.00
HR365 J.T. Snow	1.25	3.00
HR366 Kevin Mitchell	1.25	3.00
HR367 Orlando Miller	1.25	3.00
HR368 Rico Brogna	1.25	3.00
HR369 Mike James	1.25	3.00
HR370 Brad Ausmus	1.25	3.00
HR371 Darryl Kile	1.25	3.00
HR372 Edgardo Alfonzo	1.25	3.00
HR373 Julian Tavarez	1.25	3.00
HR374 Darren Lewis	1.25	3.00
HR375 Steve Karsay	1.25	3.00
HR376 Lee Stevens	1.25	3.00
HR377 Albie Lopez	1.25	3.00
HR378 Orel Hershiser	1.25	3.00
HR379 Lee Smith	1.25	3.00
HR380 Rick Helling	1.25	3.00
HR381 Carlos Perez	1.25	3.00
HR382 Tony Tarasco	1.25	3.00
HR383 Melvin Nieves	1.25	3.00
HR384 Benji Gil	1.25	3.00
HR385 Devon White	1.25	3.00
HR386 Armando Benitez	1.25	3.00
HR387 Bill Swift	1.25	3.00
HR388 John Smiley	1.25	3.00
HR389 Midre Cummings	1.25	3.00
HR390 Tim Belcher	1.25	3.00
HR391 Tim Raines	2.00	5.00
HR392 Todd Worrell	1.25	3.00
HR393 Quilvio Veras	1.25	3.00
HR394 Matt Lawton	1.25	3.00
HR395 Aaron Sele	1.25	3.00
HR396 Bip Roberts	1.25	3.00
HR397 Denny Neagle	1.25	3.00
HR398 Tyler Green	1.25	3.00
HR399 Hipolito Pichardo	1.25	3.00
HR400 Scott Erickson	1.25	3.00
HR401 Bobby Jones	1.25	3.00
HR402 Jim Edmonds	1.25	3.00
HR403 Chad Ogea	1.25	3.00
HR404 Cal Eldred	1.25	3.00
HR405 Pat Listach	1.25	3.00
HR406 Todd Stottlemyre	1.25	3.00
HR407 Phil Nevin	1.25	3.00
HR408 Otis Nixon	1.25	3.00
HR409 Billy Ashley	1.25	3.00
HR410 Jimmy Key	1.25	3.00
HR411 Mike Timlin	1.25	3.00
HR412 Joe Vitiello	1.25	3.00
HR413 Rondell White	1.25	3.00
HR414 Jeff Fassero	1.25	3.00
HR415 Rex Hudler	1.25	3.00
HR416 Curt Schilling	1.25	3.00
HR417 Rich Becker	1.25	3.00
HR418 William Van Landingham	1.25	3.00
HR419 Chris Snopek	1.25	3.00
HR420 David Segui	1.25	3.00
HR421 Eddie Murray	2.00	5.00
HR422 Shane Andrews	1.25	3.00
HR423 Gary DiSarcina	1.25	3.00
HR424 Brian Hunter	1.25	3.00
HR425 Willie Greene	1.25	3.00
HR426 Felipe Crespo	1.25	3.00
HR427 Jason Bates	1.25	3.00
HR428 Albert Belle	1.25	3.00
HR429 Rey Sanchez	1.25	3.00
HR430 Roger Clemens	4.00	10.00
HR431 Deion Sanders	2.00	5.00
HR432 Ernie Young		
HR433 Jay Bell	1.25	3.00
HR434 Jeff Blauser	1.25	3.00
HR435 Lenny Dykstra	1.25	3.00
HR436 Chuck Carr	1.25	3.00
HR437 Russ Davis	1.25	3.00
HR438 Carl Everett	1.25	3.00
HR439 Damion Easley	1.25	3.00
HR440 Pat Kelly	1.25	3.00
HR441 Pat Rapp	1.25	3.00
HR442 Dave Justice	1.25	3.00
HR443 Graeme Lloyd	1.25	3.00
HR444 Damon Buford	1.25	3.00
HR445 Jose Valentin	1.25	3.00
HR446 Jason Schmidt	1.25	3.00
HR447 Dave Martinez	1.25	3.00
HR448 Danny Tartabull	1.25	3.00
HR449 Jose Vizcaino	1.25	3.00
HR450 Steve Avery	1.25	3.00
HR451 Mike Devereaux	1.25	3.00
HR452 Jim Eisenreich	1.25	3.00
HR453 Mark Leiter	1.25	3.00
HR454 Roberto Kelly	1.25	3.00
HR455 Benito Santiago	1.25	3.00
HR456 Steve Trachsel	1.25	3.00
HR457 Gerald Williams	1.25	3.00
HR458 Pete Schourek	1.25	3.00
HR459 Esteban Loaiza	1.25	3.00
HR460 Mel Rojas	1.25	3.00
HR461 Tim Wakefield	2.00	5.00
HR462 Tony Fernandez	1.25	3.00
HR463 Doug Drabek	1.25	3.00
HR464 Joe Girardi	1.25	3.00
HR465 Mike Bordick	1.25	3.00
HR466 Jim Leyritz	1.25	3.00
HR467 Erik Hanson	1.25	3.00
HR468 Michael Tucker	1.25	3.00
HR469 Tony Womack	1.25	3.00
HR470 Doug Glanville	1.25	3.00
HR471 Rudy Pemberton	1.25	3.00
HR472 Keith Lockhart	1.25	3.00
HR473 Nomar Garciaparra	2.00	5.00
HR474 Scott Rolen	2.00	5.00
HR475 Jason Dickson	1.25	3.00
HR476 Glendon Rusch	1.25	3.00
HR477 Todd Walker	1.25	3.00
HR478 Dmitri Young	1.25	3.00
HR479 Rod Myers	1.25	3.00

R480 Wilton Guerrero 1.25 3.00
R481 Jorge Posada 2.00 5.00
R482 Brant Brown 1.25 3.00
R483 Bubba Trammell 1.25 3.00
R484 Jose Guillen 1.25 3.00
R485 Scott Spiezio 1.25 3.00
R486 Bob Abreu 2.00 5.00
R487 Chris Holt 1.25 3.00
R488 Deivi Cruz 1.25 3.00
R489 Vladimir Guerrero 2.00 5.00
R490 Julio Santana 1.25 3.00
R491 Ray Montgomery 1.25 3.00
R492 Kevin Orie 1.25 3.00
R493 Todd Hundley GY 1.25 3.00
R494 Tim Salmon GY 1.25 3.00
R495 Albert Belle GY 1.25 3.00
R496 Manny Ramirez GY 2.00 5.00
R497 Rafael Palmeiro GY 1.25 3.00
R498 Juan Gonzalez GY 1.25 3.00
R499 Ken Griffey Jr. GY 6.00 15.00
R500 Andruw Jones GY 1.25 3.00
R501 Mike Piazza GY 3.00 8.00
R502 Jeff Bagwell GY 2.00 5.00
R503 Bernie Williams GY 2.00 5.00
R504 Barry Bonds GY 5.00 12.00
R505 Ken Caminiti GY 1.25 3.00
R506 Darin Erstad GY 1.25 3.00
R507 Alex Rodriguez GY 4.00 10.00
R508 Frank Thomas GY 3.00 8.00
R509 Chipper Jones GY 3.00 8.00
R510 Mo Vaughn GY 1.25 3.00
R511 Mark McGwire GY 5.00 12.00
R512 Fred McGriff GY 2.00 5.00
R513 Jay Buhner GY 1.25 3.00
R514 Jim Thome GY 2.00 5.00
R515 Gary Sheffield GY 1.25 3.00
R516 Dean Palmer GY 1.25 3.00
R517 Henry Rodriguez GY 1.25 3.00
R518 Andy Pettitte RF 2.00 5.00
R519 Mike Mussina RF 2.00 5.00
R520 Greg Maddux RF 5.00 12.00
R521 John Smoltz RF 2.00 5.00
R522 Hideo Nomo RF 2.00 5.00
R523 Troy Percival RF 1.25 3.00
R524 John Wetteland RF 1.25 3.00
R525 Roger Clemens RF 4.00 10.00
R526 Charles Nagy RF 1.25 3.00
R527 Mariano Rivera RF 4.00 10.00
R528 Tom Glavine RF 2.00 5.00
R529 Randy Johnson RF 3.00 8.00
R530 Jason Isringhausen RF 1.25 3.00
R531 Alex Fernandez RF 1.25 3.00
R532 Kevin Brown RF 1.25 3.00
R533 Chuck Knoblauch TG 1.25 3.00
R534 Rusty Greer TG 1.25 3.00
R535 Tony Gwynn TG 3.00 8.00
R536 Ryan Klesko TG 1.25 3.00
R537 Ryne Sandberg TG 5.00 12.00
R538 Barry Larkin TG 2.00 5.00
R539 Will Clark TG 2.00 5.00
R540 Kenny Lofton TG 1.25 3.00
R541 Paul Molitor TG 3.00 8.00
R542 Roberto Alomar TG 2.00 5.00
R543 Rey Ordonez TG 1.25 3.00
R544 Jason Giambi TG 1.25 3.00
R545 Derek Jeter TG 8.00 20.00
R546 Cal Ripken TG 10.00 25.00
R547 Ivan Rodriguez TG 2.00 5.00
R548 Ken Griffey Jr. CL 6.00 15.00
R549 Frank Thomas CL 3.00 8.00
R550 Mike Piazza CL 3.00 8.00

1997 Score Premium Stock

OMPLETE SET (330) 30.00 80.00
OMPLETE SERIES 1 (330) 15.00 40.00
STARS: .75X TO 2X BASIC CARDS
ROOKIES: .6X TO 1.5X BASIC CARDS
IRABU: .4X TO 1X BASIC IRABU
RM.STOCK DIST.ONLY IN HOBBY BOXES
RABU JAPANESE IN HOBBY RESERVE PACKS

1997 Score Reserve Collection

STARS: 5X TO 12X BASIC CARDS
ROOKIES: 2.5X TO 6X BASIC CARDS
RABU: 1.5X TO 3X BASIC IRABU
ER.2 ODDS 1:11 HOBBY

1997 Score Showcase Series

STARS: 3X TO 8X BASIC CARDS
ROOKIES: 1.5X TO 4X BASIC CARDS
RABU: .5X TO 1.2X BASIC IRABU
ER.1 ODDS 1:7 H/R, 1:2 JUM, 1:4 MAG
ER.2 ODDS 1:5 HOBBY, 1:7 RETAIL

1997 Score Showcase Series Artist's Proofs

*STARS: 10X TO 25X BASIC CARDS
*ROOKIES: 4X TO 10X BASIC CARDS
*IRABU: 2X TO 5X BASIC IRABU
SER.1 ODDS 1:35 H/R, 1:7 JUM, 1:17 MAG
SER.2 ODDS 1:23 HOBBY, 1:35 RETAIL

1997 Score All-Star Fanfest

This 20-card insert set features players that were involved in the 1996 All-Star game. The cards were available at a rate of 1:29 in special retail Score I boxes.

COMPLETE SET (20) 30.00 80.00
1 Frank Thomas 1.50 4.00
2 Jeff Bagwell 2.00 5.00
3 Chuck Knoblauch .75 2.00
4 Ryne Sandberg 2.00 5.00
5 Alex Rodriguez 4.00 10.00
6 Chipper Jones 3.00 8.00
7 Jim Thome 1.25 3.00
8 Ken Caminiti .60 1.50
9 Albert Belle .60 1.50
10 Tony Gwynn 3.00 8.00
11 Ken Griffey Jr. 5.00 12.00
12 Andruw Jones 2.50 6.00
13 Juan Gonzalez 1.25 3.00
14 Brian Jordan .60 1.50
15 Ivan Rodriguez 2.00 5.00
16 Mike Piazza 4.00 10.00
17 Andy Pettitte .75 2.00
18 John Smoltz 1.25 3.00
19 John Wetteland .60 1.50
20 Mark Wohlers .40 1.00

1997 Score Blast Masters

Randomly inserted in second series packs at a rate of 1:35 (retail) and 1:23 (hobby reserve), this 18-card set features color player photos on a gold prismatic foil card.

COMPLETE SET (18) 40.00 100.00
SER.2 ODDS 1:35 RETAIL, 1:23 HOBBY
1 Mo Vaughn .75 2.00
2 Mark McGwire 5.00 12.00
3 Juan Gonzalez .75 2.00
4 Albert Belle .75 2.00
5 Barry Bonds 6.00 15.00
6 Ken Griffey Jr. 4.00 10.00
7 Andruw Jones 1.25 3.00
8 Chipper Jones 2.00 5.00
9 Mike Piazza 3.00 8.00
10 Jeff Bagwell 1.25 3.00
11 Dante Bichette .75 2.00
12 Alex Rodriguez 3.00 8.00
13 Gary Sheffield .75 2.00
14 Ken Caminiti .75 2.00
15 Sammy Sosa 2.00 5.00
16 Vladimir Guerrero 2.00 5.00
17 Brian Jordan .75 2.00
18 Tim Salmon 1.25 3.00

1997 Score Franchise

Randomly inserted in series one hobby packs only at a rate of one in 72, this nine-card set honors superstar players for their irreplaceable contribution to their team. The fronts display sepia player portraits on a white baseball replica background. The backs carry an action player photo with a sentence about the player which explains why he was selected for this set.

COMPLETE SET (9) 8.00 20.00
SER.1 ODDS 1:72 H/R, 1:17 JUM, 1:35 MAG
*GLOWING: .6X TO 1.5X BASIC
GLOW.SER.1 ODDS 1:240H/R, 1:79J, 1:120M
1 Ken Griffey Jr. 2.00 5.00
2 John Smoltz .60 1.50
3 Cal Ripken 3.00 8.00
4 Chipper Jones 1.00 2.50
5 Mike Piazza 1.00 2.50
6 Albert Belle .40 1.00
7 Frank Thomas 1.00 2.50
8 Sammy Sosa .60 1.50
9 Roberto Alomar .60 1.50

1997 Score Heart of the Order

Randomly inserted in packs at a rate of 1:23 (retail) and 1:15 (hobby reserve), this 36-card set features color photos of players on six teams with a panorama of the stadium in the background. Each team's three cards form one collectible unit. Eighteen of these cards are found in retail packs, and eighteen in Hobby Reserve packs.

COMPLETE SET (36) 40.00 100.00
STATED ODDS 1:23 RETAIL, 1:15 HOBBY
1 Will Clark 1.00 2.50
2 Ivan Rodriguez 1.00 2.50
3 Juan Gonzalez .60 1.50
4 Frank Thomas 1.50 4.00
5 Albert Belle .60 1.50
6 Robin Ventura .60 1.50
7 Alex Rodriguez 2.50 6.00
8 Jay Buhner .60 1.50
9 Ken Griffey Jr. 3.00 8.00
10 Rafael Palmeiro 1.00 2.50
11 Roberto Alomar 1.00 2.50
12 Cal Ripken 5.00 12.00
13 Manny Ramirez 1.00 2.50
14 Matt Williams .60 1.50
15 Jim Thome 1.00 2.50
16 Derek Jeter 4.00 10.00
17 Wade Boggs 1.00 2.50
18 Bernie Williams 1.00 2.50
19 Chipper Jones 1.50 4.00
20 Andruw Jones 1.00 2.50
21 Ryan Klesko .60 1.50
22 Mike Piazza 2.50 6.00
23 Wilton Guerrero .60 1.50
24 Raul Mondesi .60 1.50
25 Tony Gwynn 2.00 5.00
26 Greg Vaughn .60 1.50
27 Ken Caminiti .60 1.50
28 Brian Jordan .60 1.50
29 Ron Gant .60 1.50
30 Dmitri Young .60 1.50
31 Darin Erstad .60 1.50
32 Tim Salmon 1.00 2.50
33 Jim Edmonds .60 1.50
34 Chuck Knoblauch .60 1.50
35 Paul Molitor .60 1.50
36 Todd Walker .60 1.50

1997 Score Highlight Zone

Randomly inserted in series one hobby packs only at a rate of one in 35, this 18-card set honors those mega-stars who have the incredible ability to consistently make the highlight films. The set is printed on thicker card stock with special foil stamping and a dot matrix holographic background.

COMPLETE SET (18) 75.00 150.00
SER.1 ODDS 1:35 HOBBY, 1:9 JUMBO PS
1 Frank Thomas 2.50 6.00
2 Ken Griffey Jr. 5.00 12.00
3 Mo Vaughn 1.00 2.50
4 Albert Belle 1.00 2.50
5 Mike Piazza 4.00 10.00
6 Barry Bonds 8.00 20.00
7 Greg Maddux 4.00 10.00
8 Sammy Sosa 2.50 6.00
9 Jeff Bagwell 1.50 4.00
10 Alex Rodriguez 4.00 10.00
11 Chipper Jones 2.50 6.00
12 Brady Anderson 1.00 2.50
13 Ozzie Smith 1.00 2.50
14 Edgar Martinez 1.50 4.00
15 Cal Ripken 8.00 20.00
16 Ryan Klesko 1.00 2.50
17 Randy Johnson 2.50 6.00
18 Eddie Murray 2.50 6.00

1997 Score Pitcher Perfect

Randomly inserted in series one packs at a rate of one in 23, this 15-card set features players photographed by Randy Johnson in unique poses and foil stamping. The backs carry player information.

COMPLETE SET (15) 2.00 5.00
SER.1 ODDS 1:23 H/R,1:11 MAG,1:15 JUM PS
1 Cal Ripken .60 1.50
2 Alex Rodriguez .30 .75
3 A.Rodriguez 1.25 3.00
C.Ripken
4 Edgar Martinez .10 .30
5 Ivan Rodriguez .10 .30
6 Mark McGwire .50 1.25
7 Tim Salmon .10 .30
8 Chili Davis .07 .20
9 Joe Carter .07 .20
10 Frank Thomas .10 .30
11 Will Clark .10 .30
12 Mo Vaughn .07 .20
13 Wade Boggs .10 .30
14 Ken Griffey Jr. .40 1.00
15 Randy Johnson .20 .50

1997 Score Stand and Deliver

Randomly inserted in series two packs at a rate of 1:71 (retail) and 1:47 (hobby reserve), this 24-card set features color player photos printed on silver foil card stock. The set is broken into six separate 4-card groupings. Groups contain players from the following teams: 1-4 (Braves), 5-8 (Mariners), 9-12 (Yankees), 13-16 (Dodgers), 17-20 (Indians) and 21-24 (Wild Card). The four players featured within the Wild Card group are from "lesser" teams not given a shot at winning the World Series. Each of these cards, unlike cards 1-20, has a "Wild Card" logo stamped on front. Collectors were then supposed to gather up the particular group that won the 1997 World Series, in this case - the Florida Marlins. Since none of the featured teams won, the 4-card Wild Card group was designated as the winner. The winning cards could then be mailed into Pinnacle for a special gold upgrade version of the set, framed in glass.

COMPLETE SET (24) 125.00 250.00
SER.2 ODDS 1:41 HOBBY, 1:71 RETAIL
1 Andruw Jones 2.50 6.00
2 Greg Maddux 6.00 15.00
3 Chipper Jones 4.00 10.00
4 John Smoltz 2.50 6.00
5 Ken Griffey Jr. 8.00 20.00
6 Alex Rodriguez 6.00 15.00
7 Jay Buhner 1.50 4.00
8 Randy Johnson 4.00 10.00
9 Derek Jeter 10.00 25.00
10 Andy Pettitte 2.50 6.00
11 Bernie Williams 2.50 6.00
12 Mariano Rivera 4.00 10.00
13 Mike Piazza 6.00 15.00
14 Hideo Nomo 4.00 10.00
15 Raul Mondesi 1.50 4.00
16 Todd Hollandsworth 1.50 4.00
17 Manny Ramirez 2.50 6.00
18 Jim Thome 2.50 6.00
19 Dave Justice 1.50 4.00
20 Matt Williams 1.50 4.00
21 Juan Gonzalez W 1.50 4.00
22 Jeff Bagwell W 2.50 6.00
23 Cal Ripken W 12.50 30.00
24 Frank Thomas W 4.00 10.00

1997 Score Stellar Season

Randomly inserted in series one pre-priced magazine packs only at a rate of one in 35, this 18-card set features players who had a star season. The cards are printed using dot matrix holographic printing.

COMPLETE SET (18) 25.00 60.00
SER.1 STATED ODDS 1:35 MAGAZINE
1 Juan Gonzalez .60 1.50
2 Chuck Knoblauch .60 1.50
3 Jeff Bagwell 1.00 2.50
4 John Smoltz 1.00 2.50
5 Mark McGwire 4.00 10.00
6 Ken Griffey Jr. 3.00 8.00
7 Frank Thomas 1.50 4.00
8 Alex Rodriguez 2.50 6.00
9 Mike Piazza 2.50 6.00
10 Albert Belle .60 1.50
11 Roberto Alomar 1.00 2.50
12 Sammy Sosa 1.50 4.00
13 Mo Vaughn .60 1.50
14 Brady Anderson .60 1.50
15 Henry Rodriguez .60 1.50
16 Eric Young .60 1.50
17 Gary Sheffield .60 1.50
18 Ryan Klesko .60 1.50

1997 Score Titanic Taters

Randomly inserted in series one retail packs only at a rate of one in 35, this 18-card set honors the long-ball ability of some of the league's top sluggers and uses dot matrix holographic printing.

COMPLETE SET (18) 60.00 120.00
SER.1 STATED ODDS 1:35 RETAIL
1 Mark McGwire 6.00 15.00
2 Mike Piazza 4.00 10.00
3 Ken Griffey Jr. 5.00 12.00
4 Juan Gonzalez 1.00 2.50
5 Frank Thomas 2.50 6.00
6 Albert Belle 1.00 2.50
7 Sammy Sosa 2.50 6.00
8 Jeff Bagwell 1.50 4.00
9 Todd Hundley 1.00 2.50
10 Ryan Klesko 1.00 2.50
11 Brady Anderson 1.00 2.50
12 Mo Vaughn 1.00 2.50
13 Jay Buhner 1.00 2.50
14 Chipper Jones 2.50 6.00
15 Barry Bonds 8.00 20.00
16 Gary Sheffield 1.00 2.50
17 Alex Rodriguez 4.00 10.00
18 Cecil Fielder 1.00 2.50

1997 Score Andruw Jones Blister Pack Special

This one-card set features a white bordered color photo of Andruw Jones batting with the distance of his home runs displayed in the background. The card was always inserted on the top of the prepriced 1997 Score Series II jumbo packs. The backs carry a "Thank you for buying Score Baseball Series II" sentence with a list and description of insert sets found in Score Series II. The rules for the Stand and Deliver Promotion rounded out the backs.

1 Andruw Jones .75 2.00

1997 Score Jumbos

Issued as box toppers in retail boxes
1 Frank Thomas 2.50 6.00
2 Ken Griffey Jr. 5.00 12.00
3 Cal Ripken 8.00 20.00
4 Chipper Jones 2.50 6.00
5 Mike Piazza 2.50 6.00
6 Juan Gonzalez 1.00 2.50
7 Derek Jeter 6.00 15.00
8 Andruw Jones 1.00 2.50
9 Alex Rodriguez 3.00 8.00

1998 Score Samples

COMPLETE SET (6) 5.00 12.00
10 Alex Rodriguez .75 2.00
24 Mike Piazza 1.00 2.50
34 Ken Griffey Jr. 1.25 3.00
43 Cal Ripken 1.50 4.00
51 Chipper Jones .75 2.00
60 Carlos Delgado .40 1.00

1998 Score

This 270-card set was distributed in 10-card packs exclusively to retail outlets with a suggested retail price of $.99. The fronts feature color player photos in a thin white border. The backs carry player information and statistics. In addition, two unnumbered checklist cards were created. The first card was available only in regular issue packs and provided listings for the standard 270-card set. A blank-backed checklist card was randomly seeded exclusively into All-Star Edition packs (released about three months after the regular packs went live). This checklist card provided listings only for the three insert sets exclusively distributed in All-Star Edition packs (First Pitch, Loaded Lineup and New Season).

COMPLETE SET (270) 15.00 40.00
1 Andruw Jones .10 .30
2 Dan Wilson .07 .20
3 Hideo Nomo .20 .50
4 Chuck Carr .07 .20
5 Barry Bonds .60 1.50
6 Jack McDowell .07 .20
7 Albert Belle .07 .20
8 Francisco Cordova .07 .20
9 Greg Maddux .30 .75
10 Alex Rodriguez .30 .75
11 Steve Avery .07 .20
12 Chuck McElroy .07 .20
13 Larry Walker .07 .20
14 Hideki Irabu .07 .20
15 Roberto Alomar .10 .30
16 Neifi Perez .07 .20
17 Jim Thome .10 .30
18 Rickey Henderson .20 .50
19 Andres Galarraga .07 .20
20 Jeff Fassero .07 .20
21 Kevin Young .07 .20
22 Derek Jeter .50 1.25
23 Andy Benes .07 .20
24 Mike Piazza .30 .75
25 Todd Stottlemyre .07 .20
26 Michael Tucker .07 .20
27 Denny Neagle .07 .20
28 Javier Lopez .07 .20
29 Aaron Sele .07 .20
30 Ryan Klesko .07 .20
31 Dennis Eckersley .07 .20
32 Quinton McCracken .07 .20
33 Brian Anderson .07 .20
34 Ken Griffey Jr. .40 1.00
35 Shawn Estes .07 .20
36 Tim Wakefield .07 .20
37 Jimmy Key .07 .20
38 Jeff Bagwell .10 .30
39 Edgardo Alfonzo .07 .20
40 Mike Cameron .07 .20
41 Mark McGwire .50 1.25
42 Tino Martinez .10 .30
43 Cal Ripken .60 1.50
44 Curtis Goodwin .07 .20
45 Bobby Ayala .07 .20
46 Sandy Alomar Jr. .07 .20
47 Bobby Jones .07 .20
48 Omar Vizquel .10 .30
49 Roger Clemens .40 1.00
50 Tony Gwynn .25 .60
51 Chipper Jones .20 .50
52 Ron Coomer .07 .20
53 Dmitri Young .07 .20
54 Brian Giles .07 .20
55 Steve Finley .07 .20
56 David Cone .07 .20
57 Andy Pettitte .10 .30
58 Wilton Guerrero .07 .20
59 Deion Sanders .10 .30
60 Carlos Delgado .07 .20
61 Jason Giambi .07 .20
62 Ozzie Guillen .07 .20
63 Jay Bell .07 .20
64 Barry Larkin .10 .30
65 Sammy Sosa .20 .50
66 Bernie Williams .10 .30
67 Terry Steinbach .07 .20
68 Scott Rolen .10 .30
69 Melvin Nieves .07 .20
70 Craig Biggio .10 .30
71 Todd Greene .07 .20
72 Greg Gagne .07 .20
73 Shigetoshi Hasegawa .07 .20
74 Mark McLemore .07 .20
75 Darren Bragg .07 .20
76 Brett Butler .07 .20
77 Ron Gant .07 .20
78 Mike Difelice RC .07 .20
79 Charles Nagy .07 .20
80 Scott Hatteberg .07 .20
81 Brady Anderson .07 .20
82 Jay Buhner .07 .20
83 Todd Hollandsworth .07 .20
84 Geronimo Berroa .07 .20
85 Jeff Suppan .07 .20
86 Pedro Martinez .10 .30
87 Roger Cedeno .07 .20
88 Ivan Rodriguez .10 .30
89 Jaime Navarro .07 .20
90 Chris Hoiles .07 .20
91 Nomar Garciaparra .30 .75
92 Rafael Palmeiro .10 .30
93 Darin Erstad .07 .20
94 Kenny Lofton .07 .20
95 Mike Timlin .07 .20
96 Chris Clemons .07 .20
97 Vinny Castilla .07 .20
98 Charlie Hayes .07 .20
99 Lyle Mouton .07 .20
100 Jason Dickson .07 .20
101 Justin Thompson .07 .20
102 Pat Kelly .07 .20
103 Chan Ho Park .07 .20
104 Ray Lankford .07 .20
105 Frank Thomas .20 .50
106 Jermaine Allensworth .07 .20
107 Doug Drabek .07 .20
108 Todd Hundley .07 .20
109 Carl Everett .07 .20
110 Edgar Martinez .10 .30
111 Robin Ventura .07 .20
112 John Wetteland .07 .20
113 Mariano Rivera .20 .50
114 Jose Rosado .07 .20
115 Ken Caminiti .07 .20
116 Paul O'Neill .10 .30
117 Tim Salmon .10 .30
118 Eduardo Perez .07 .20
119 Mike Jackson .07 .20
120 John Smoltz .10 .30
121 Brant Brown .07 .20
122 John Mabry .07 .20
123 Chuck Knoblauch .07 .20
124 Reggie Sanders .07 .20
125 Ken Hill .07 .20
126 Mike Mussina .10 .30
127 Chad Curtis .07 .20
128 Todd Worrell .07 .20
129 Chris Widger .07 .20
130 Damon Mashore .07 .20
131 Kevin Brown .10 .30
132 Bip Roberts .07 .20
133 Tim Naehring .07 .20
134 Dave Martinez .07 .20
135 Jeff Blauser .07 .20
136 David Justice .07 .20
137 Dave Hollins .07 .20
138 Pat Hentgen .07 .20
139 Darren Daulton .07 .20
140 Ramon Martinez .07 .20
141 Raul Casanova .07 .20
142 Tom Glavine .10 .30
143 J.T. Snow .07 .20
144 Tony Graffanino .07 .20
145 Randy Johnson .20 .50
146 Orlando Merced .07 .20
147 Jeff Juden .07 .20
148 Darryl Kile .07 .20
149 Ray Durham .07 .20
150 Alex Fernandez .07 .20
151 Joey Cora .07 .20
152 Royce Clayton .07 .20
153 Randy Myers .07 .20
154 Charles Johnson .07 .20
155 Alan Benes .07 .20
156 Mike Bordick .07 .20
157 Heathcliff Slocumb .07 .20
158 Roger Bailey .07 .20
159 Reggie Jefferson .07 .20
160 Ricky Bottalico .07 .20
161 Scott Erickson .07 .20
162 Matt Williams .07 .20
163 Robb Nen .07 .20
164 Matt Stairs .07 .20
165 Ismael Valdes .07 .20
166 Lee Stevens .07 .20
167 Gary DiSarcina .07 .20
168 Brad Radke .07 .20
169 Mike Lansing .07 .20
170 Armando Benitez .07 .20
171 Mike James .07 .20
172 Russ Davis .07 .20
173 Lance Johnson .07 .20
174 Joey Hamilton .07 .20
175 John Valentin .07 .20
176 David Segui .07 .20
177 David Wells .07 .20
178 Delino DeShields .07 .20
179 Eric Karros .07 .20
180 Jim Leyritz .07 .20
181 Raul Mondesi .07 .20
182 Travis Fryman .07 .20
183 Todd Zeile .07 .20
184 Brian Jordan .07 .20
185 Rey Ordonez .07 .20
186 Jim Edmonds .07 .20
187 Terrell Wade .07 .20
188 Marquis Grissom .07 .20
189 Chris Snopek .07 .20
190 Shane Reynolds .07 .20
191 Jeff Frye .07 .20
192 Paul Sorrento .07 .20
193 James Baldwin .07 .20
194 Brian McRae .07 .20
195 Fred McGriff .10 .30
196 Troy Percival .07 .20
197 Rich Amaral .07 .20
198 Juan Guzman .07 .20
199 Cecil Fielder .07 .20
200 Willie Blair .07 .20
201 Chili Davis .07 .20
202 Gary Gaetti .07 .20
203 B.J. Surhoff .07 .20
204 Steve Cooke .07 .20
205 Chuck Finley .07 .20
206 Jeff Kent .07 .20
207 Ben McDonald .07 .20
208 Jeffrey Hammonds .07 .20
209 Tom Goodwin .07 .20
210 Billy Ashley .07 .20
211 Wil Cordero .07 .20
212 Shawon Dunston .07 .20
213 Tony Phillips .07 .20
214 Jamie Moyer .07 .20
215 John Jaha .07 .20
216 Troy O'Leary .07 .20
217 Brad Ausmus .07 .20
218 Garret Anderson .07 .20
219 Wilson Alvarez .07 .20
220 Kent Mercker .07 .20
221 Wade Boggs .10 .30
222 Mark Wohlers .07 .20
223 Kevin Appier .07 .20
224 Tony Fernandez .07 .20
225 Ugueth Urbina .07 .20
226 Gregg Jefferies .07 .20
227 Mo Vaughn .07 .20
228 Arthur Rhodes .07 .20
229 Jorge Fabregas .07 .20
230 Mark Gardner .07 .20
231 Shane Mack .07 .20
232 Jorge Posada .10 .30
233 Jose Cruz Jr. .07 .20
234 Paul Konerko .07 .20
235 Derrek Lee .10 .30
236 Steve Woodard .07 .20
237 Todd Dunwoody .07 .20
238 Fernando Tatis .07 .20
239 Jacob Cruz .07 .20
240 Pokey Reese .07 .20
241 Mark Kotsay .07 .20
242 Matt Morris .07 .20
243 Antone Williamson .07 .20
244 Ben Grieve .07 .20
245 Ryan McGuire .07 .20
246 Lou Collier .07 .20
247 Shannon Stewart .07 .20
248 Brett Tomko .07 .20
249 Bobby Estalella .07 .20
250 Livan Hernandez .07 .20
251 Todd Helton .10 .30
252 Jaret Wright .07 .20
253 Darryl Hamilton IM .07 .20
254 Stan Javier IM .07 .20
255 Glenallen Hill IM .07 .20
256 Mark Gardner IM .07 .20
257 Cal Ripken IM .30 .75
258 Mike Mussina IM .07 .20
259 Mike Piazza IM .20 .50
260 Sammy Sosa IM .10 .30
261 Todd Hundley IM .07 .20
262 Eric Karros IM .07 .20
263 Denny Neagle IM .07 .20
264 Jeromy Burnitz IM .07 .20
265 Greg Maddux IM .20 .50
266 Tony Clark IM .07 .20
267 Vladimir Guerrero IM .10 .30

268 Cal Ripken CL UER .30 .75
269 Ken Griffey Jr. CL .25 .60
270 Mark McGwire CL .25 .60
NNO Checklist Regular Issue .07 .20
NNO Checklist All-Star Edition .10 .30

1998 Score Showcase Series

*SHOWCASE: 2X TO 5X BASIC CARDS
STATED ODDS 1:7

1998 Score Showcase Series Artist's Proofs

*SHOWCASE AP: 8X TO 20X BASIC CARDS
STATED ODDS 1:35

1998 Score All Score Team

Randomly inserted in packs at the rate of one in 35, this 20-card set features color player images on a metallic foil background. The backs carry a small player head photo with information stating why the player was selected to this appear in this set.

COMPLETE SET (20) 12.00 30.00
STATED ODDS 1:35
1 Mike Piazza 1.00 2.50
2 Ivan Rodriguez .60 1.50
3 Frank Thomas 1.00 2.50
4 Mark McGwire 1.50 4.00
5 Ryne Sandberg 1.50 4.00
6 Roberto Alomar .60 1.50
7 Cal Ripken 3.00 8.00
8 Barry Larkin .60 1.50
9 Paul Molitor 1.00 2.50
10 Travis Fryman .40 1.00
11 Kirby Puckett 1.00 2.50
12 Tony Gwynn 1.00 2.50
13 Ken Griffey Jr. 2.00 5.00
14 Juan Gonzalez .40 1.00
15 Barry Bonds 1.50 4.00
16 Andruw Jones .40 1.00
17 Roger Clemens 1.25 3.00
18 Randy Johnson 1.00 2.50
19 Greg Maddux 1.25 3.00
20 Dennis Eckersley .60 1.50

1998 Score All-Score Team Gold Jones Autograph

1 Andruw Jones Gold AU 10.00 25.00

1998 Score Complete Players

Randomly inserted in packs at the rate of one in 23, this 30-card set features three photos of each of the ten listed players with full holographic foil stamping.

COMPLETE SET (30) 75.00 150.00
STATED ODDS 1:23
THREE CARDS PER PLAYER
ALL 3 VARIETIES SAME PRICE
*GOLD: .4X TO 1X BASIC COMP.PLAY.
GOLD: RANDOM IN SCORE TEAM SETS
1A Ken Griffey Jr. 3.00 8.00
2A Mark McGwire 4.00 10.00
3A Derek Jeter 4.00 10.00
4A Cal Ripken 5.00 12.00
5A Mike Piazza 2.50 6.00
6A Darin Erstad .60 1.50
7A Frank Thomas 1.50 4.00
8A Andruw Jones 1.00 2.50
9A Nomar Garciaparra 2.50 6.00
10A Manny Ramirez 1.50 4.00

1998 Score First Pitch

This 20 card insert set features star players anxiously awaiting opening day. The player's name is at top with the "First Pitch" words on the bottom of the card. These cards were inserted one every 11 All-Star Edition packs.

COMPLETE SET (20) 25.00 60.00
STATED ODDS 1:11 AS EDIT.
1 Ken Griffey Jr. 2.00 5.00
2 Frank Thomas 1.00 2.50
3 Alex Rodriguez 1.50 4.00
4 Cal Ripken 3.00 8.00
5 Chipper Jones 1.00 2.50
6 Juan Gonzalez 1.00 2.50
7 Derek Jeter 2.50 6.00
8 Mike Piazza 1.50 4.00
9 Andruw Jones .60 1.50
10 Nomar Garciaparra 1.50 4.00
11 Barry Bonds 3.00 8.00
12 Jeff Bagwell .60 1.50
13 Scott Rolen .60 1.50
14 Hideo Nomo 1.00 2.50
15 Roger Clemens 2.00 5.00
16 Mark McGwire 2.50 6.00
17 Greg Maddux 1.50 4.00
18 Albert Belle .40 1.00
19 Ivan Rodriguez .60 1.50
20 Mo Vaughn .40 1.00

1998 Score Andruw Jones Icon Order Card

This one-card set features a white bordered color photo of Andruw Jones kneeling with his right arm resting on his bat. The card was always inserted on the top of the prepriced 1998 Score 27-card blister packs. The backs carry instructions on how to order a Pinnacle Icon display.

1 Andruw Jones .40 1.00

1998 Score Loaded Lineup

This 10-card set was inserted one every 45 Score All-Star Edition packs. The cards feature a player for each position and the cards are printed on all-foil micro etched cards.

COMPLETE SET (10) 25.00 60.00
STATED ODDS 1:45 AS EDIT.
LL1 Chuck Knoblauch .75 2.00
LL2 Tony Gwynn 2.50 6.00
LL3 Frank Thomas 2.00 5.00
LL4 Ken Griffey Jr. 4.00 10.00
LL5 Mike Piazza 3.00 8.00
LL6 Barry Bonds 6.00 15.00
LL7 Cal Ripken 6.00 15.00
LL8 Paul Molitor 2.00 5.00
LL9 Nomar Garciaparra 3.00 8.00
LL10 Greg Maddux 3.00 8.00

1998 Score New Season

This 15 card insert set features a mix of young and veteran players waiting for the new season to begin. The players photo take up most of the borderless cards with his name on top and the words "New Season" on the bottom.

COMPLETE SET (15) 20.00 50.00
STATED ODDS 1:23 AS EDIT.
NS1 Kenny Lofton .75 2.00
NS2 Nomar Garciaparra 2.50 6.00
NS3 Todd Helton 1.00 2.50
NS4 Miguel Tejada 1.25 3.00
NS5 Jaret Wright .60 1.50
NS6 Alex Rodriguez 2.50 6.00
NS7 Vladimir Guerrero 1.25 3.00
NS8 Ken Griffey Jr. 4.00 10.00
NS9 Ben Grieve .60 1.50
NS10 Travis Lee .60 1.50
NS11 Jose Cruz Jr. .60 1.50
NS12 Paul Konerko .75 2.00
NS13 Frank Thomas 1.25 3.00
NS14 Chipper Jones 1.25 3.00
NS15 Cal Ripken 5.00 12.00

1998 Score Rookie Traded

The 1998 Score Rookie and Traded set was issued in one series totalling 270 cards. The 10-card packs retail for $.99 each. The set contains the subset: Spring Training (253-267). Cards numbered one through 50 were inserted one per pack making them short prints compared to the other cards in the set. Paul Konerko signed 500 cards which were also randomly seeded into packs. Notable Rookie Cards include Magglio Ordonez.

COMPLETE SET (270) 15.00 40.00
COMMON SP (1-50) .10 .30
COMMON CARD (51-270) .07 .20
COMMON RC (51-270) .07 .20
KONERKO AU RANDOM INSERT IN PACKS
1 Tony Clark .10 .30
2 Juan Gonzalez .10 .30
3 Frank Thomas .30 .75
4 Greg Maddux .50 1.25
5 Barry Larkin .20 .50
6 Derek Jeter .75 2.00
7 Randy Johnson .30 .75
8 Roger Clemens .60 1.50
9 Tony Gwynn .40 1.00
10 Barry Bonds .75 2.00
11 Jim Edmonds .10 .30
12 Bernie Williams .20 .50
13 Ken Griffey Jr. .60 1.50
14 Tim Salmon .20 .50
15 Mo Vaughn .10 .30
16 David Justice .10 .30
17 Jose Cruz Jr. .10 .30
18 Andruw Jones .20 .50
19 Sammy Sosa .30 .75
20 Jeff Bagwell .20 .50
21 Scott Rolen .20 .50
22 Darin Erstad .10 .30
23 Andy Pettitte .20 .50
24 Mike Mussina .20 .50
25 Mark McGwire .75 2.00
26 Hideo Nomo .30 .75
27 Chipper Jones .30 .75
28 Cal Ripken 1.00 2.50
29 Chuck Knoblauch .10 .30
30 Alex Rodriguez .50 1.25
31 Jim Thome .20 .50
32 Mike Piazza .50 1.25
33 Ivan Rodriguez .20 .50
34 Roberto Alomar .20 .50
35 Nomar Garciaparra .50 1.25
36 Albert Belle .10 .30
37 Vladimir Guerrero .30 .75
38 Raul Mondesi .10 .30
39 Larry Walker .10 .30
40 Manny Ramirez .20 .50
41 Tino Martinez .20 .50
42 Craig Biggio .20 .50
43 Jay Buhner .10 .30
44 Kenny Lofton .10 .30
45 Pedro Martinez .20 .50
46 Edgar Martinez .20 .50
47 Gary Sheffield .10 .30
48 Jose Guillen .10 .30
49 Ken Caminiti .10 .30
50 Bobby Higginson .10 .30
51 Alan Benes .07 .20
52 Shawn Green .07 .20
53 Ron Coomer .07 .20
54 Charles Nagy .07 .20
55 Steve Karsay .07 .20
56 Matt Morris .07 .20
57 Bobby Jones .07 .20
58 Jason Kendall .07 .20
59 Jeff Conine .07 .20
60 Joe Girardi .07 .20
61 Mark Kotsay .07 .20
62 Eric Karros .07 .20
63 Bartolo Colon .07 .20
64 Mariano Rivera .20 .50
65 Alex Gonzalez .07 .20
66 Scott Spiezio .07 .20
67 Luis Castillo .07 .20
68 Joey Cora .07 .20
69 Mark McLemore .07 .20
70 Reggie Jefferson .07 .20
71 Lance Johnson .07 .20
72 Damian Jackson .07 .20
73 Jeff D'Amico .07 .20
74 David Ortiz .30 .75
75 J.T. Snow .07 .20
76 Todd Hundley .07 .20
77 Billy Wagner .07 .20
78 Vinny Castilla .07 .20
79 Ismael Valdes .07 .20
80 Neifi Perez .07 .20
81 Derek Bell .07 .20
82 Ryan Klesko .07 .20
83 Rey Ordonez .07 .20
84 Carlos Garcia .07 .20
85 Curt Schilling .07 .20
86 Robin Ventura .07 .20
87 Pat Hentgen .07 .20
88 Glendon Rusch .07 .20
89 Hideki Irabu .07 .20
90 Antone Williamson .07 .20
91 Denny Neagle .07 .20
92 Kevin Orie .07 .20
93 Reggie Sanders .07 .20
94 Brady Anderson .07 .20
95 Andy Benes .07 .20
96 John Valentin .07 .20
97 Bobby Bonilla .07 .20
98 Walt Weiss .07 .20
99 Robin Jennings .07 .20
100 Marty Cordova .07 .20
101 Brad Ausmus .07 .20
102 Brian Rose .07 .20
103 Calvin Maduro .07 .20
104 Raul Casanova .07 .20
105 Jeff King .07 .20
106 Sandy Alomar Jr. .07 .20
107 Tim Naehring .07 .20
108 Mike Cameron .07 .20
109 Omar Vizquel .10 .30
110 Brad Radke .07 .20
111 Jeff Fassero .07 .20
112 Deivi Cruz .07 .20
113 Dave Hollins .07 .20
114 Dean Palmer .07 .20
115 Esteban Loaiza .07 .20
116 Brian Giles .07 .20
117 Steve Finley .07 .20
118 Jose Canseco .10 .30
119 Al Martin .07 .20
120 Eric Young .07 .20
121 Curtis Goodwin .07 .20
122 Ellis Burks .07 .20
123 Mike Hampton .07 .20
124 Lou Collier .07 .20
125 John Olerud .07 .20
126 Ramon Martinez .07 .20
127 Todd Dunwoody .07 .20
128 Jermaine Allensworth .07 .20
129 Eduardo Perez .07 .20
130 Dante Bichette .07 .20
131 Edgar Renteria .07 .20
132 Bob Abreu .07 .20
133 Rondell White .07 .20
134 Michael Coleman .07 .20
135 Jason Giambi .07 .20
136 Brant Brown .07 .20
137 Michael Tucker .07 .20
138 Dave Nilsson .07 .20
139 Benito Santiago .07 .20
140 Ray Durham .07 .20
141 Jeff Kent .07 .20
142 Matt Stairs .07 .20
143 Kevin Young .07 .20
144 Eric Davis .07 .20
145 John Wetteland .07 .20
146 Esteban Yan RC .10 .30
147 Wilton Guerrero .07 .20
148 Moises Alou .07 .20
149 Edgardo Alfonzo .07 .20
150 Andy Ashby .07 .20
151 Todd Walker .07 .20
152 Jermaine Dye .07 .20
153 Brian Hunter .07 .20
154 Shawn Estes .07 .20
155 Bernard Gilkey .07 .20
156 Tony Womack .07 .20
157 John Smoltz .10 .30
158 Delino DeShields .07 .20
159 Jacob Cruz .07 .20
160 Javier Valentin .07 .20
161 Chris Hoiles .07 .20
162 Garret Anderson .07 .20
163 Dan Wilson .07 .20
164 Paul O'Neill .10 .30
165 Matt Williams .07 .20
166 Travis Fryman .07 .20
167 Javier Lopez .07 .20
168 Ray Lankford .07 .20
169 Bobby Estalella .07 .20
170 Henry Rodriguez .07 .20
171 Quinton McCracken .07 .20
172 Jaret Wright .07 .20
173 Darryl Kile .07 .20
174 Wade Boggs .10 .30
175 Orel Hershiser .07 .20
176 B.J. Surhoff .07 .20
177 Fernando Tatis .07 .20
178 Carlos Delgado .07 .20
179 Jorge Fabregas .07 .20
180 Tony Saunders .07 .20
181 Devon White .07 .20
182 Dmitri Young .07 .20
183 Ryan McGuire .07 .20
184 Mark Bellhorn .07 .20
185 Joe Carter .07 .20
186 Kevin Stocker .07 .20
187 Mike Lansing .07 .20
188 Jason Dickson .07 .20
189 Charles Johnson .07 .20
190 Will Clark .10 .30
191 Shannon Stewart .07 .20
192 Johnny Damon .10 .30
193 Todd Greene .07 .20
194 Carlos Baerga .07 .20
195 David Cone .07 .20
196 Pokey Reese .07 .20
197 Livan Hernandez .07 .20
198 Tom Glavine .10 .30
199 Geronimo Berroa .07 .20
200 Darryl Hamilton .07 .20
201 Terry Steinbach .07 .20
202 Robb Nen .07 .20
203 Ron Gant .07 .20
204 Rafael Palmeiro .10 .30
205 Rickey Henderson .20 .50
206 Justin Thompson .07 .20
207 Jeff Suppan .07 .20
208 Kevin Brown .10 .30
209 Jimmy Key .07 .20
210 Brian Jordan .07 .20
211 Aaron Sele .07 .20
212 Fred McGriff .10 .30
213 Jay Bell .07 .20
214 Andres Galarraga .07 .20
215 Mark Grace .10 .30
216 Brett Tomko .07 .20
217 Francisco Cordova .07 .20
218 Rusty Greer .07 .20
219 Bubba Trammell .07 .20
220 Derrek Lee .10 .30
221 Brian Anderson .07 .20
222 Mark Grudzielanek .07 .20
223 Marquis Grissom .07 .20
224 Gary DiSarcina .07 .20
225 Jim Leyritz .07 .20
226 Jeffrey Hammonds .07 .20
227 Karim Garcia .07 .20
228 Chan Ho Park .07 .20
229 Brooks Kieschnick .07 .20
230 Trey Beamon .07 .20
231 Kevin Appier .07 .20
232 Wally Joyner .07 .20
233 Richie Sexson .07 .20
234 Frank Catalanotto RC .20 .50
235 Rafael Medina .07 .20
236 Travis Lee .07 .20
237 Eli Marrero .07 .20
238 Carl Pavano .07 .20
239 Enrique Wilson .07 .20
240 Richard Hidalgo .07 .20
241 Todd Helton .10 .30
242 Ben Grieve .07 .20
243 Mario Valdez .07 .20
244 Magglio Ordonez RC .60 1.50
245 Juan Encarnacion .07 .20
246 Russell Branyan .07 .20
247 Sean Casey .07 .20
248 Abraham Nunez .07 .20
249 Brad Fullmer .07 .20
250 Paul Konerko .07 .20
251 Miguel Tejada .20 .50
252 Mike Lowell RC .40 1.00
253 Ken Griffey Jr. ST .25 .60
254 Frank Thomas ST .10 .30
255 Alex Rodriguez ST .20 .50
256 Jose Cruz Jr. ST .07 .20
257 Jeff Bagwell ST .20 .50
258 Chipper Jones ST .10 .30
259 Mo Vaughn ST .07 .20
260 Nomar Garciaparra ST .20 .50
261 Jim Thome ST .07 .20
262 Derek Jeter ST .25 .60
263 Mike Piazza ST .20 .50
264 Tony Gwynn ST .10 .30
265 Scott Rolen ST .10 .30
266 Andruw Jones ST .10 .30
267 Cal Ripken ST .30 .75
268 Checklist 1 .07 .20
269 Checklist 2 .07 .20
270 Checklist 3 .07 .20
S250 Paul Konerko AU/500 6.00 15.00

1998 Score Rookie Traded Showcase Series

*SHOWCASE 1-50: 1.25X TO 3X BASIC
*SHOWCASE 51-270: 2X TO 5X BASIC
*SHOWCASE RC'S 51-270: 1.5X TO 4X BASIC
STATED ODDS 1:7

1998 Score Rookie Traded Showcase Series Artist's Proofs

*SHOWCASE AP 1-50: 5X TO 12X BASIC
*SHOWCASE AP 51-270: 8X TO 20X BASIC
*SHOWCASE AP RC'S 51-270: 3X TO 8X BASIC
STATED ODDS 1:35

1998 Score Rookie Traded Showcase Series Artist's Proofs 1 of 1's

RANDOM INSERTS IN HOBBY PACKS
STATED PRINT RUN 1 SET
NO PRICING DUE TO SCARCITY

1998 Score Rookie Traded Complete Players Samples

COMPLETE SET (30) 20.00 50.00
THREE CARDS PER PLAYER
1A Ken Griffey Jr. 2.00 5.00
2A Larry Walker .40 1.00
3A Alex Rodriguez 1.00 2.50
4A Jose Cruz Jr. .20 .50
5A Jeff Bagwell .50 1.25
6A Greg Maddux 1.25 3.00
7A Ivan Rodriguez .50 1.25
8A Roger Clemens 1.00 2.50
9A Chipper Jones 1.00 2.50
10A Hideo Nomo .40 1.00

1998 Score Rookie Traded Complete Players

Randomly inserted in packs at a rate of one in 11, this 30-card set is an insert to the Score Rookie Traded base set. The card fronts feature special holographic foil stamping. Each player has three different cards highlighting his own power, speed and approach to the game. Put them together and form the Complete Player.

COMPLETE SET (30) 20.00 50.00
STATED ODDS 1:11
THREE CARDS PER PLAYER
ALL 3 VERSIONS SAME PRICE
1A Ken Griffey Jr. 1.50 4.00
2A Larry Walker .30 .75
3A Alex Rodriguez 1.25 3.00
4A Jose Cruz Jr. .30 .75
5A Jeff Bagwell .50 1.25
6A Greg Maddux 1.25 3.00
7A Ivan Rodriguez .50 1.25
8A Roger Clemens 1.50 4.00
9A Chipper Jones .75 2.00
10A Hideo Nomo .75 2.00

1998 Score Rookie Traded Star Gazing

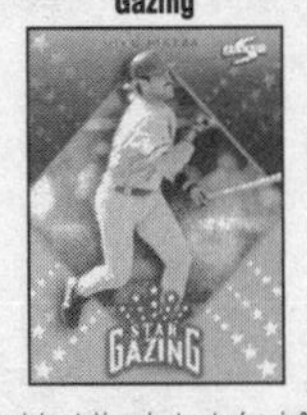

Randomly inserted in packs at a rate of one in 35, this 20-card set is an insert to the Score Rookie Traded base set. The fronts feature color action photos printed on a diamond-shaped star-gazing background. The player's name sits atop the player photo with the Score logo in the upper right corner.

COMPLETE SET (20) 10.00 25.00
STATED ODDS 1:35
1 Ken Griffey Jr. 1.25 3.00
2 Frank Thomas .60 1.50
3 Chipper Jones .60 1.50
4 Mark McGwire 1.50 4.00
5 Cal Ripken 2.00 5.00
6 Mike Piazza 1.00 2.50
7 Nomar Garciaparra 1.00 2.50
8 Derek Jeter 1.50 4.00
9 Juan Gonzalez .25 .60
10 Vladimir Guerrero .60 1.50
11 Alex Rodriguez 1.00 2.50
12 Tony Gwynn .75 2.00
13 Andruw Jones .40 1.00
14 Scott Rolen .40 1.00
15 Jose Cruz Jr. .25 .60
16 Mo Vaughn .25 .60
17 Bernie Williams .40 1.00
18 Greg Maddux 1.00 2.50
19 Tony Clark .25 .60
20 Ben Grieve .15 .40

2012 Score Hot Rookies Toronto Fall Expo

CRACKED ICE/25: 1.5X TO 4X BASE HI
13 Mike Trout 10.00 25.00
14 Brett Lawrie 2.00 5.00
15 Bryce Harper 5.00 12.00
16 Yu Darvish 4.00 10.00
17 Yoenis Cespedes 3.00 8.00
18 Drew Pomeranz .75 2.00

2018 Score

1 Mike Trout 1.25 3.00
2 Austin Hays RC .40 1.00
3 Amed Rosario RC .30 .75
4 Kris Bryant .30 .75
5 Aaron Judge .60 1.50
6 Bryce Harper .40 1.00
7 Yadier Molina .25 .60
8 Ozzie Albies RC .75 2.00
9 Chance Sisco RC .30 .75
10 Ronald Acuna Jr. RC 5.00 12.00
11 Shohei Ohtani RC 1.50 4.00
12 Rafael Devers RC .75 2.00
13 Nolan Arenado .30 .75
14 Manny Machado .25 .60
15 J.P. Crawford RC .25 .60
16 Shohei Ohtani RC 1.50 4.00
17 Max Scherzer .25 .60
18 Cody Bellinger .50 1.2
19 Alex Verdugo RC .40 1.0
20 Nick Williams RC .30 .7
21 Jose Altuve .20 .5
22 Giancarlo Stanton .25 .6
23 Rhys Hoskins RC 1.00 2.5
24 Clint Frazier RC .50 1.2
25 Ryan McMahon RC .30 .7
26 Victor Robles RC .60 1.5
27 Gleyber Torres RC 2.50 6.0
28 Dominic Smith RC .25 .6
29 Walker Buehler RC 1.25 3.0
30 Miguel Andujar RC 1.00 2.5

2019 Score

RANDOM INSERTS IN PACKS
*RED/99: 1.5X TO 4X
*BLUE/50: 2X TO 5X
*PINK/25: 3X TO 8X
1 Kyle Tucker .30 .7
2 Max Scherzer .25 .6
3 Aaron Judge .60 1.5
4 Pete Alonso RC 3.00 8.0
5 Michael Kopech RC .30 .7
6 Yusei Kikuchi RC .25 .6
7 Jacob deGrom .25 .6
8 Mookie Betts .40 1.0
9 Vladimir Guerrero Jr. RC 2.50 6.0
10 Christian Yelich .30 .7
11 Jose Altuve .20 .5
12 Kris Bryant .30 .7
13 Mike Trout 1.25 3.0
14 Bryce Harper .40 1.0
15 Eloy Jimenez RC .60 1.5
16 Fernando Tatis Jr. RC 4.00 10.0
17 Chris Paddack RC .30 .7
18 Cody Bellinger .50 1.2
19 Khris Davis .25 .6
20 Shohei Ohtani .30 .7

2020 Score

RANDOM INSERTS IN PACKS
1 Yordan Alvarez RC 1.25 3.0
2 Bo Bichette RC 3.00 8.0
3 Aristides Aquino RC .50 1.2
4 Gavin Lux RC 1.50 4.0
5 Luis Robert RC 4.00 10.0
6 Brendan McKay RC .40 1.0
7 Shogo Akiyama RC .40 1.0
8 Yoshitomo Tsutsugo RC .30 .7
9 Logan Webb RC .30 .7
10 Deivy Grullon RC .25 .6
11 Ronald Bolanos RC .40 1.0
12 Danny Mendick RC .30 .7
13 Kwang-Hyun Kim RC .75 2.0
14 Shun Yamaguchi RC .30 .7
15 Lewis Thorpe RC .25 .6
16 Luis Castillo .20 .5
17 Charlie Morton .25 .6
18 Manny Machado .25 .6
19 Chris Paddack .25 .6
20 Gary Sanchez .25 .6
21 Mike Trout 2.00 5.0
22 Nolan Arenado .30 .7
23 Ronald Acuna Jr. 1.50 4.0
24 Gerrit Cole .40 1.0
25 Walker Buehler .30 .7
26 Anthony Rendon .25 .6
27 Javier Baez .30 .7
28 Pete Alonso .60 1.5
29 Vladimir Guerrero Jr. .50 1.2
30 Ken Griffey Jr. .50 1.2

2020 Score Signatures

RANDOM INSERTS IN PACKS
PRINT RUNS B/WN 5-99 COPIES PER
NO PRICING QTY 15 OR LESS
EXCHANGE DEADLINE 3/18/2022
1 Yordan Alvarez/50 20.00 50.0
2 Bo Bichette/30 30.00 80.0
3 Aristides Aquino/60 8.00 20.0
5 Luis Robert EXCH/99 75.00 200.0
7 Shogo Akiyama/49 6.00 15.0
8 Yoshitomo Tsutsugo/99 8.00 20.0
9 Logan Webb/96 4.00 10.0
10 Deivy Grullon/99 3.00 8.0
13 Kwang-Hyun Kim/99 10.00 25.0
14 Shun Yamaguchi/99 4.00 10.0
18 Manny Machado/25

2018 Select

INSERTED IN '18 CHRONICLES PACKS
1 Dominic Smith RC .40 1.0
2 Ronald Acuna Jr. RC 10.00 25.0
3 Shohei Ohtani RC 2.50 6.0
4 Aaron Judge 1.00 2.5
5 Kris Bryant .50 1.2
6 Rhys Hoskins RC 1.50 4.0
7 Bryce Harper .60 1.5
8 Cody Bellinger .75 2.0
9 Victor Robles RC 1.00 2.5
10 Clint Frazier RC .50 1.2
11 Miguel Andujar RC 1.50 4.0
12 Manny Machado .40 1.0
13 Amed Rosario RC .50 1.2
14 Mookie Betts .60 1.5
15 Juan Soto RC 8.00 20.0
16 Jose Altuve .30 .7
17 Austin Hays RC .60 1.5
18 Mike Trout 2.00 5.0
19 Yadier Molina .40 1.0
20 Gleyber Torres RC 4.00 10.0
21 Ozzie Albies RC 1.25 3.0
22 Nolan Arenado .50 1.2
23 Rafael Devers RC 1.25 3.0

4 Willy Adames RC .50 1.25
5 Ryan McMahon RC .50 1.25

2018 Select Aqua
AQUA: .75X TO 2X BASIC
AQUA RC: .5X TO 1.2X BASIC
INSERTED IN '18 CHRONICLES PACKS
STATED PRINT RUN 299 SER.#'d SETS

2018 Select Black
BLACK: 2.5X TO 6X BASIC
BLACK RC:1.5X TO 4X BASIC
INSERTED IN '18 CHRONICLES PACKS
STATED PRINT RUN 25 SER.#'d SETS
5 Juan Soto 40.00 100.00

2018 Select Blue
BLUE: 1X TO 2.5X BASIC
BLUE RC: .6X TO 1.5X BASIC
INSERTED IN '18 CHRONICLES PACKS
STATED PRINT RUN 149 SER.#'d SETS

2018 Select Carolina Blue
CAR.BLUE: 1.5X TO 4X BASIC
CAR.BLUE RC: 1X TO 2.5X BASIC
INSERTED IN '18 CHRONICLES PACKS
STATED PRINT RUN 50 SER.#'d SETS
5 Juan Soto 25.00 60.00

2018 Select Orange
ORANGE: 1X TO 2.5X BASIC
ORANGE RC: .6X TO 1.5X BASIC
INSERTED IN '18 CHRONICLES PACKS
STATED PRINT RUN 199 SER.#'d SETS

2018 Select Prizm
PRIZM: .75X TO 2X BASIC
PRIZM RC: .5X TO 1.2X BASIC
INSERTED IN '18 CHRONICLES PACKS

2018 Select Red
RED: 1.2X TO 3X BASIC
RED RC: .75X TO 2X BASIC
INSERTED IN '18 CHRONICLES PACKS
STATED PRINT RUN 99 SER.#'d SETS

2018 Select Signatures
RANDOM INSERTS IN PACKS
Christian Villanueva 2.50 6.00
Luiz Gohara 2.50 6.00
Austin Hays 4.00 10.00
Lucas Sims 2.50 6.00
Anthony Santander 2.50 6.00
0 Cameron Gallagher 2.50 6.00
1 Nicky Delmonico 2.50 6.00
5 Dan Vogelbach 2.50 6.00
6 Daniel Norris 4.00 10.00
9 Tucker Barnhart 4.00 10.00
0 Jose Osuna 2.50 6.00

2020 Select
RANDOM INSERTS IN PACKS
1 Joe Palumbo RC .50 1.25
2 Brad Keller .25 .60
3 Yasmani Grandal .25 .60
4 Starling Marte .30 .75
5 Pete Alonso 1.00 2.50
6 Abraham Toro RC .60 1.50
7 Bo Bichette RC 4.00 10.00
8 Jake Fraley RC .60 1.50
9 Cody Bellinger .75 2.00
10 Michael Chavis .30 .75
11 Anthony Rendon .40 1.00
12 Shogo Akiyama RC .75 2.00
13 Andres Munoz RC .60 1.50
14 Sean Manaea .25 .60
15 Ramon Laureano .40 1.00
16 Kyle Lewis RC 4.00 10.00
17 Eddie Rosario .30 .75
18 Cole Hamels .30 .75
19 DJ LeMahieu .40 1.00
20 Tyrone Taylor RC .50 1.25
21 Jose Abreu .40 1.00
22 Josh Bell .30 .75
23 Liam Hendriks .25 .60
24 Justin Dunn RC .60 1.50
25 Mike Moustakas .30 .75
26 Kyle Hendricks .40 1.00
27 Nico Hoerner RC 2.00 5.00
28 Adalberto Mondesi .40 1.00
29 Sheldon Neuse RC .60 1.50
30 Josh Rojas RC .50 1.25
31 Bryce Harper .60 1.50
32 Kris Bryant .50 1.25
33 Kolten Wong .30 .75
34 Evan Longoria .30 .75
35 Juan Soto 1.25 3.00
36 Clayton Kershaw .75 2.00
37 Dallas Keuchel .30 .75
38 Lorenzo Cain .25 .60
39 Patrick Sandoval RC .75 2.00
40 Jonathan Hernandez RC .50 1.25
41 Deivy Grullon RC .50 1.25
42 Michael King RC .75 2.00
43 Marcell Ozuna .40 1.00
44 Kyle Seager .25 .60
45 Bobby Bradley RC .60 1.50
46 Julio Teheran .30 .75
47 Kirby Yates .25 .60
48 Marco Gonzales .25 .60
49 Stephen Strasburg .40 1.00
50 Hyun-Jin Ryu .30 .75
51 Joey Votto .40 1.00
52 Ken Giles .25 .60
53 John Means .25 .60
54 Zac Gallen RC 1.25 3.00
55 Spencer Turnbull .25 .60
56 Logan Allen RC .50 1.25
57 Tony Gonsolin RC 2.00 5.00
58 Michael Brantley .30 .75
59 Randy Arozarena RC 4.00 10.00
60 Lourdes Gurriel .30 .75
61 Howie Kendrick .25 .60
62 Tommy Pham .25 .60
63 George Springer .30 .75
64 Bryan Abreu RC .50 1.25
65 Buster Posey .50 1.25
66 Brusdar Graterol RC .75 2.00
67 Yonathan Daza RC .60 1.50
68 Jake Odorizzi .25 .60
69 Justin Turner .30 .75
70 Austin Meadows .30 .75
71 Charlie Blackmon .40 1.00
72 James Paxton .30 .75
73 Jorge Soler .40 1.00
74 T.J. Zeuch RC .50 1.25
75 Gleyber Torres .75 2.00
76 Isan Diaz RC .75 2.00
77 Marcus Stroman .30 .75
78 Jack Flaherty .30 .75
79 Michel Baez RC .50 1.25
80 Brandon Lowe .40 1.00
81 Luis Castillo .30 .75
82 David Fletcher .40 1.00
83 Willy Adames .25 .60
84 Matt Thaiss RC .60 1.50
85 Niko Goodrum .30 .75
86 Domingo Leyba RC .60 1.50
87 Trent Grisham RC 2.00 5.00
88 Aaron Nola .40 1.00
89 Brandon Woodruff .25 .60
90 Shin-Soo Choo .30 .75
91 Lucas Giolito .30 .75
92 Jacob deGrom .40 1.00
93 Gary Sanchez .40 1.00
94 Aaron Judge 1.00 2.50
95 Manny Machado .40 1.00
96 Eduardo Rodriguez .25 .60
97 Shane Bieber .40 1.00
98 Jonathan Gray .25 .60
99 Keston Hiura .50 1.25
100 Gio Urshela .40 1.00
101 Xander Bogaerts PRM .60 1.50
102 Jeff McNeil PRM .50 1.25
103 Corey Kluber PRM .50 1.25
104 Justin Verlander PRM .60 1.50
105 Omar Narvaez PRM .40 1.00
106 Ronald Acuna Jr. PRM 2.50 6.00
107 Miguel Cabrera PRM .60 1.50
108 Eloy Jimenez PRM 1.25 3.00
109 Javier Baez PRM .75 2.00
110 Josh Hader PRM .40 1.00
111 Sonny Gray PRM .40 1.00
112 Shohei Ohtani PRM .75 2.00
113 J.T. Realmuto PRM .60 1.50
114 A.J. Puk PRM RC 1.50 4.00
115 Carlos Santana PRM .50 1.25
116 Danny Mendick PRM RC 1.00 2.50
117 Mike Soroka PRM .60 1.50
118 Mookie Betts PRM 1.25 3.00
119 Max Fried PRM .60 1.50
120 Lance Lynn PRM .40 1.00
121 Vladimir Guerrero Jr. PRM 1.25 3.00
122 Noah Syndergaard PRM .50 1.25
123 Rafael Devers PRM .75 2.00
124 Masahiro Tanaka PRM .60 1.50
125 Logan Webb PRM RC 1.00 2.50
126 Mike Trout PRM 4.00 10.00
127 Yu Darvish PRM .60 1.50
128 Adrian Morejon PRM RC .75 2.00
129 Fernando Tatis Jr. PRM 2.00 5.00
130 Miguel Sano PRM .50 1.25
131 Matt Carpenter PRM .50 1.25
132 Jesus Luzardo PRM RC 1.50 4.00
133 Hanser Alberto PRM .40 1.00
134 Brendan McKay PRM RC 1.25 3.00
135 Sandy Alcantara PRM .40 1.00
136 Cavan Biggio PRM .75 2.00
137 Yusei Kikuchi PRM .50 1.25
138 Dustin May PRM RC 3.00 8.00
139 Adbert Alzolay PRM RC 1.00 2.50
140 Ketel Marte PRM .50 1.25
141 Luis Robert PRM RC 5.00 12.00
142 Hunter Dozier PRM .40 1.00
143 Gerrit Cole PRM 1.00 2.50
144 Dakota Hudson PRM .50 1.25
145 Trent Thornton PRM .40 1.00
146 Walker Buehler PRM .75 2.00
147 Kevin Newman PRM .50 1.25
148 Yu Chang PRM RC 1.25 3.00
149 Jordan Yamamoto PRM RC 1.00 2.50
150 Dylan Cease PRM RC 1.50 4.00
151 Max Scherzer PRM .60 1.50
152 Matt Olson PRM .40 1.00
153 Shun Yamaguchi PRM RC 1.00 2.50
154 Yordan Alvarez PRM RC 4.00 10.00
155 Max Kepler PRM .50 1.25
156 Jake Rogers PRM RC .75 2.00
157 Michael Conforto PRM .50 1.25
158 Brock Burke PRM RC .75 2.00
159 Aristides Aquino PRM RC 1.50 4.00
160 Travis Demeritte PRM RC 1.00 2.50
161 Mitch Garver PRM .40 1.00
162 Chris Sale PRM .60 1.50
163 Chris Paddack PRM .60 1.50
164 Ronald Bolanos PRM RC 1.25 3.00
165 Rico Garcia PRM RC 1.25 3.00
166 Paul Goldschmidt PRM .60 1.50
167 Jorge Polanco PRM .50 1.25
168 Nick Ahmed PRM .40 1.00
169 German Marquez PRM .60 1.50
170 Gavin Lux PRM RC 5.00 12.00
171 Marcus Semien PRM .40 1.00
172 Victor Robles PRM .75 2.00
173 Trea Turner PRM .50 1.25
174 Matt Chapman PRM .60 1.50
175 Yoshitomo Tsutsugo PRM RC 1.00 2.50
176 Bryan Reynolds PRM .50 1.25
177 Jaylin Davis PRM RC 1.25 3.00
178 Trevor Bauer PRM .60 1.50
179 Freddie Freeman PRM .75 2.00
180 Alex Bregman PRM .60 1.50
181 Christian Yelich PRM .75 2.00
182 Patrick Corbin PRM .50 1.25
183 Tyler Glasnow PRM .40 1.00
184 Tim Anderson PRM .60 1.50
185 Nelson Cruz PRM .60 1.50
186 Eduardo Escobar PRM .40 1.00
187 Mauricio Dubon PRM RC 1.00 2.50
188 Willi Castro PRM RC 1.25 3.00
189 Francisco Lindor PRM .60 1.50
190 Max Muncy PRM .50 1.25
191 Scott Kingery PRM .50 1.25
192 David Dahl PRM .40 1.00
193 Yadier Molina PRM .60 1.50
194 Eugenio Suarez PRM .50 1.25
195 Jose Berrios PRM .50 1.25
196 Matt Boyd PRM .40 1.00
197 Giancarlo Stanton PRM .60 1.50
198 Sean Murphy PRM RC 1.25 3.00
199 Danny Duffy PRM .40 1.00
200 Mike Clevinger PRM .50 1.25
201 Robbie Ray DMD .50 1.25
202 Tres Barrera DMD RC 2.00 5.00
203 Carlos Correa DMD .75 2.00
204 Albert Pujols DMD 1.00 2.50
205 Aaron Civale DMD RC 1.50 4.00
206 Kwang-Hyun Kim DMD RC 3.00 8.00
207 Caleb Smith DMD .50 1.25
208 Zack Greinke DMD .60 1.50
209 J.D. Martinez DMD .75 2.00
210 Trey Mancini DMD .75 2.00
211 Anthony Kay DMD RC 1.00 2.50
212 Willson Contreras DMD .75 2.00
213 Blake Snell DMD .60 1.50
214 Yoan Moncada DMD .75 2.00
215 Mike Minor DMD .50 1.25
216 Whit Merrifield DMD .75 2.00
217 Lewis Thorpe DMD RC 1.00 2.50
218 Danny Santana DMD .50 1.25
219 Nolan Arenado DMD 1.00 2.50
220 Christian Vazquez DMD .50 1.25
221 Mike Yastrzemski DMD 1.25 3.00
222 Jonathan Villar DMD .50 1.25
223 James McCann DMD .60 1.50
224 Rhys Hoskins DMD 1.00 2.50
225 J.D. Davis DMD .50 1.25
226 Ozzie Albies DMD .75 2.00
227 Nicholas Castellanos DMD .75 2.00
228 Edwin Rios DMD RC 2.50 6.00
229 Joey Gallo DMD .75 2.00
230 Brian Anderson DMD .50 1.25
231 Josh Donaldson DMD .60 1.50
232 Jose Altuve DMD .60 1.50
233 Donnie Walton DMD RC 2.50 6.00
234 Trevor Story DMD .75 2.00
235 Tommy Edman DMD .75 2.00
236 Anthony Rizzo DMD 1.25 3.00
237 Zack Collins DMD RC 1.25 3.00
238 Sam Hilliard DMD RC 1.50 4.00
239 Zack Wheeler DMD .60 1.50
240 Will Smith DMD 1.00 2.50
241 Kyle Schwarber DMD .75 2.00
242 Corey Seager DMD .75 2.00
243 Mitch Haniger DMD .60 1.50
244 Jose Ramirez DMD .60 1.50
245 Dan Vogelbach DMD .50 1.25
246 Madison Bumgarner DMD .60 1.50
247 Paul DeJong DMD .75 2.00
248 Nick Solak DMD RC 1.50 4.00
249 Charlie Morton DMD .75 2.00
250 Merrill Kelly DMD .50 1.25

2020 Select Prizms Blue
*BLUE 1-100: 1.5X TO 4X BASIC
*BLUE 1-100 RC: .8X TO 2X BASIC RC
*BLUE 101-200: 1X TO 2.5X BASIC
*BLUE 101-200 RC: .5X TO 1.2X BASIC
RANDOM INSERTS IN PACKS
STATED PRINT RUN 149 COPIES PER
7 Bo Bichette 15.00 40.00
9 Cody Bellinger 5.00 12.00
10 Michael Chavis 3.00 8.00
12 Shogo Akiyama 10.00 25.00
16 Kyle Lewis 10.00 25.00
75 Gleyber Torres 10.00 25.00
94 Aaron Judge 10.00 25.00
106 Ronald Acuna Jr. PRM 12.00 30.00
121 Vladimir Guerrero Jr. PRM 6.00 15.00
126 Mike Trout PRM 25.00 60.00
129 Fernando Tatis Jr. PRM 8.00 20.00
141 Luis Robert PRM 30.00 80.00
154 Yordan Alvarez PRM 15.00 40.00
155 Max Kepler PRM 8.00 20.00
159 Aristides Aquino PRM 12.00 30.00
170 Gavin Lux PRM 12.00 30.00
181 Christian Yelich PRM 10.00 25.00
189 Francisco Lindor PRM 4.00 10.00
193 Yadier Molina PRM 4.00 10.00

2020 Select Prizms Carolina Blue
RANDOM INSERTS IN PACKS
STATED PRINT RUN 35 COPIES PER
5 Pete Alonso 12.00 30.00
7 Bo Bichette 25.00 60.00
9 Cody Bellinger 10.00 25.00
10 Michael Chavis 5.00 12.00
12 Shogo Akiyama 15.00 40.00
16 Kyle Lewis 12.00 30.00
27 Nico Hoerner 15.00 40.00
75 Gleyber Torres 12.00 30.00
94 Aaron Judge 15.00 40.00
106 Ronald Acuna Jr. PRM 20.00 50.00
118 Mookie Betts PRM 8.00 20.00
121 Vladimir Guerrero Jr. PRM 12.00 30.00
126 Mike Trout PRM 50.00 120.00
129 Fernando Tatis Jr. PRM 12.00 30.00
132 Jesus Luzardo PRM 12.00 30.00
141 Luis Robert PRM 50.00 120.00
149 Jordan Yamamoto PRM 12.00 30.00
154 Yordan Alvarez PRM 25.00 60.00
155 Max Kepler PRM 12.00 30.00
156 Jake Rogers PRM 25.00 60.00
159 Aristides Aquino PRM 25.00 60.00
170 Gavin Lux PRM 30.00 80.00
181 Christian Yelich PRM 15.00 40.00
189 Francisco Lindor PRM 6.00 15.00
193 Yadier Molina PRM 10.00 25.00

2020 Select Prizms Cracked Ice
*CRKD ICE 1-100: 3X TO 8X BASIC
*CRKD ICE 1-100 RC: 1.5X TO 4X BASIC RC
*CRKD ICE 101-200: 2X TO 5X BASIC
*CRKD ICE 101-200 RC: 1X TO 2.5X BASIC
RANDOM INSERTS IN PACKS
STATED PRINT RUN 25 COPIES PER
5 Pete Alonso 15.00 40.00
7 Bo Bichette 30.00 80.00
9 Cody Bellinger 20.00 50.00
10 Michael Chavis 8.00 20.00
12 Shogo Akiyama 20.00 50.00
16 Kyle Lewis 15.00 40.00
27 Nico Hoerner 20.00 50.00
75 Gleyber Torres 25.00 60.00
94 Aaron Judge 20.00 50.00
106 Ronald Acuna Jr. PRM 25.00 60.00
118 Mookie Betts PRM 10.00 25.00
121 Vladimir Guerrero Jr. PRM 15.00 40.00
126 Mike Trout PRM 75.00 200.00
129 Fernando Tatis Jr. PRM 40.00 100.00
132 Jesus Luzardo PRM 20.00 50.00
141 Luis Robert PRM 60.00 150.00
149 Jordan Yamamoto PRM 15.00 40.00
154 Yordan Alvarez PRM 30.00 80.00
155 Max Kepler PRM 15.00 40.00
156 Jake Rogers PRM 30.00 80.00
159 Aristides Aquino PRM 30.00 80.00
170 Gavin Lux PRM 40.00 100.00
181 Christian Yelich PRM 20.00 50.00
189 Francisco Lindor PRM 8.00 20.00
193 Yadier Molina PRM 12.00 30.00

2020 Select Prizms Holo
RANDOM INSERTS IN PACKS
9 Cody Bellinger 5.00 12.00
10 Michael Chavis 3.00 8.00
12 Shogo Akiyama 10.00 25.00
16 Kyle Lewis 5.00 12.00
75 Gleyber Torres 10.00 25.00
94 Aaron Judge 10.00 25.00
106 Ronald Acuna Jr. PRM 15.00 40.00
121 Vladimir Guerrero Jr. PRM 10.00 25.00
126 Mike Trout PRM 30.00 80.00
129 Fernando Tatis Jr. PRM 10.00 25.00
132 Jesus Luzardo PRM 8.00 20.00
141 Luis Robert PRM 40.00 100.00
149 Jordan Yamamoto PRM 10.00 25.00
154 Yordan Alvarez PRM 20.00 50.00
155 Max Kepler PRM 10.00 25.00
159 Aristides Aquino PRM 20.00 50.00
170 Gavin Lux PRM 25.00 60.00
181 Christian Yelich PRM 12.00 30.00
189 Francisco Lindor PRM 5.00 12.00
193 Yadier Molina PRM 5.00 12.00

2020 Select Prizms Neon Green
*NEON GRN 1-100: 2X TO 5X BASIC
*NEON GRN 1-100 RC: 1X TO 2.5X BASIC RC
*NEON GRN 101-200: 1.2X TO 3X BASIC
*NEON GRN 101-200 RC: .6X TO 1.5X BASIC
RANDOM INSERTS IN PACKS
STATED PRINT RUN 99 COPIES PER
5 Pete Alonso 10.00 25.00
7 Bo Bichette 20.00 50.00
9 Cody Bellinger 8.00 20.00
10 Michael Chavis 4.00 10.00
12 Shogo Akiyama 12.00 30.00
16 Kyle Lewis 6.00 15.00
27 Nico Hoerner 12.00 30.00
75 Gleyber Torres 12.00 30.00
94 Aaron Judge 12.00 30.00
106 Ronald Acuna Jr. PRM 15.00 40.00
121 Vladimir Guerrero Jr. PRM 10.00 25.00
126 Mike Trout PRM 40.00 100.00
129 Fernando Tatis Jr. PRM 10.00 25.00
132 Jesus Luzardo PRM 10.00 25.00
141 Luis Robert PRM 40.00 100.00
149 Jordan Yamamoto PRM 10.00 25.00
154 Yordan Alvarez PRM 20.00 50.00
155 Max Kepler PRM 10.00 25.00
159 Aristides Aquino PRM 15.00 40.00
170 Gavin Lux PRM 25.00 60.00
181 Christian Yelich PRM 12.00 30.00
189 Francisco Lindor PRM 5.00 12.00
193 Yadier Molina PRM 5.00 12.00

2020 Select Prizms Red
*RED 1-100: 1.5X TO 4X BASIC
*RED 1-100 RC: .8X TO 2X BASIC RC
*RED 101-200: 1X TO 2.5X BASIC
*RED 101-200 RC: .5X TO 1.2X BASIC
RANDOM INSERTS IN PACKS
STATED PRINT RUN 199 COPIES PER
7 Bo Bichette 15.00 40.00
10 Michael Chavis 3.00 8.00
12 Shogo Akiyama 10.00 25.00
75 Gleyber Torres 10.00 25.00
94 Aaron Judge 10.00 25.00
106 Ronald Acuna Jr. PRM 12.00 30.00
121 Vladimir Guerrero Jr. PRM 6.00 15.00
126 Mike Trout PRM 25.00 60.00
129 Fernando Tatis Jr. PRM 8.00 20.00
141 Luis Robert PRM 30.00 80.00
154 Yordan Alvarez PRM 15.00 40.00
155 Max Kepler PRM 8.00 20.00
159 Aristides Aquino PRM 12.00 30.00
170 Gavin Lux PRM 12.00 30.00
181 Christian Yelich PRM 10.00 25.00
189 Francisco Lindor PRM 4.00 10.00

2020 Select Prizms Tie Dye
RANDOM INSERTS IN PACKS
STATED PRINT RUN 20 COPIES PER
5 Pete Alonso 40.00 100.00
7 Bo Bichette 30.00 80.00
9 Cody Bellinger 20.00 50.00
10 Michael Chavis 8.00 20.00
12 Shogo Akiyama 20.00 50.00
16 Kyle Lewis 15.00 40.00
27 Nico Hoerner 20.00 50.00
34 Evan Longoria 15.00 40.00
75 Gleyber Torres 25.00 60.00
94 Aaron Judge 20.00 50.00
104 Justin Verlander PRM 15.00 40.00
106 Ronald Acuna Jr. PRM 25.00 60.00
118 Mookie Betts PRM 10.00 25.00
121 Vladimir Guerrero Jr. PRM 15.00 40.00
126 Mike Trout PRM 150.00 400.00
129 Fernando Tatis Jr. PRM 40.00 100.00
132 Jesus Luzardo PRM 30.00 80.00
138 Dustin May PRM 10.00 25.00
141 Luis Robert PRM 60.00 150.00
149 Jordan Yamamoto PRM 15.00 40.00
154 Yordan Alvarez PRM 30.00 80.00
155 Max Kepler PRM 15.00 40.00
156 Jake Rogers PRM 30.00 80.00
159 Aristides Aquino PRM 30.00 80.00
170 Gavin Lux PRM 40.00 100.00
181 Christian Yelich PRM 20.00 50.00
189 Francisco Lindor PRM 8.00 20.00
193 Yadier Molina PRM 12.00 30.00

2020 Select Prizms Tri-Color
*TRI CLR 1-100: 1.2X TO 3X BASIC
*TRI CLR 1-100 RC: .6X TO 1.5X BASIC RC
*TRI CLR 101-200: .8X TO 2X BASIC
*TRI CLR 101-200 RC: .4X TO 1X BASIC
RANDOM INSERTS IN PACKS
12 Shogo Akiyama 5.00 12.00
75 Gleyber Torres 8.00 20.00
94 Aaron Judge 8.00 20.00
106 Ronald Acuna Jr. PRM 10.00 25.00
121 Vladimir Guerrero Jr. PRM 5.00 12.00
126 Mike Trout PRM 20.00 50.00
129 Fernando Tatis Jr. PRM 8.00 20.00
141 Luis Robert PRM 25.00 60.00
155 Max Kepler PRM 6.00 15.00
170 Gavin Lux PRM 12.00 30.00
181 Christian Yelich PRM 2.50 6.00

2020 Select Prizms White
*WHITE 1-100: 2X TO 5X BASIC
*WHITE 1-100 RC: 1X TO 2.5X BASIC RC
*WHITE 101-200: 1.2X TO 3X BASIC
*WHITE 101-200 RC: .6X TO 1.5X BASIC
RANDOM INSERTS IN PACKS
STATED PRINT RUN 50 COPIES PER
5 Pete Alonso 10.00 25.00
7 Bo Bichette 20.00 50.00
9 Cody Bellinger 8.00 20.00
10 Michael Chavis 4.00 10.00
12 Shogo Akiyama 12.00 30.00
16 Kyle Lewis 6.00 15.00
27 Nico Hoerner 12.00 30.00
75 Gleyber Torres 12.00 30.00
94 Aaron Judge 12.00 30.00
106 Ronald Acuna Jr. PRM 15.00 40.00
121 Vladimir Guerrero Jr. PRM 10.00 25.00
126 Mike Trout PRM 40.00 100.00
129 Fernando Tatis Jr. PRM 10.00 25.00
132 Jesus Luzardo PRM 8.00 20.00
141 Luis Robert PRM 40.00 100.00
149 Jordan Yamamoto PRM 10.00 25.00
154 Yordan Alvarez PRM 20.00 50.00
155 Max Kepler PRM 10.00 25.00
159 Aristides Aquino PRM 20.00 50.00
170 Gavin Lux PRM 25.00 60.00
181 Christian Yelich PRM 12.00 30.00
189 Francisco Lindor PRM 5.00 12.00
193 Yadier Molina PRM 5.00 12.00

2020 Select Artistic Impressions
1 Yordan Alvarez 30.00 80.00
2 Bo Bichette 20.00 50.00
3 Shohei Ohtani 10.00 25.00
4 Aaron Judge 20.00 50.00
5 Alex Bregman 12.00 30.00
6 Mookie Betts 10.00 25.00
7 Mike Trout 30.00 80.00
8 Juan Soto 15.00 40.00
9 Bryce Harper 12.00 30.00
10 Ronald Acuna Jr. 15.00 40.00

2020 Select '93 Retro Select Materials
RANDOM INSERTS IN PACKS
1 Cal Ripken 6.00 15.00
2 Ozzie Smith 6.00 15.00
3 Tony Gwynn 4.00 87.00
4 Roberto Alomar 4.00 10.00
5 Tom Glavine 2.50 6.00
6 Ivan Rodriguez 8.00 20.00
7 Greg Maddux 4.00 10.00
8 Paul Molitor 3.00 8.00
9 Roger Clemens 4.00 10.00
10 Dennis Eckersley 5.00 12.00
11 Ryne Sandberg 6.00 15.00
12 Barry Larkin 6.00 15.00
13 Mike Piazza 3.00 8.00
14 Wade Boggs 4.00 10.00
15 Randy Johnson 5.00 12.00
16 Frank Thomas 3.00 8.00
17 Juan Gonzalez 2.00 5.00
18 Kenny Lofton 10.00 25.00
19 Craig Biggio 2.50 6.00
20 Larry Walker 2.50 6.00

2020 Select '93 Retro Select Materials Prizms Holo
*HOLO: .5X TO 1.2X BASIC
RANDOM INSERTS IN PACKS
STATED PRINT RUN 75 COPIES PER
3 Tony Gwynn 6.00 15.00
14 Wade Boggs 8.00 20.00
19 Craig Biggio 5.00 12.00

2020 Select '93 Retro Select Materials Prizms Tri-Color
*TRI CLR: .5X TO 1.2X BASIC
RANDOM INSERTS IN PACKS
STATED PRINT RUN 49 COPIES PER
3 Tony Gwynn 6.00 15.00
14 Wade Boggs 8.00 20.00
19 Craig Biggio 5.00 12.00

2020 Select 25-Man
RANDOM INSERTS IN PACKS
1 J.T. Realmuto .75 2.00
2 Pete Alonso 2.00 5.00
3 DJ LeMahieu .75 2.00
4 Alex Bregman .75 2.00
5 Xander Bogaerts .75 2.00
6 Juan Soto 2.50 6.00
7 Mike Trout 4.00 10.00
8 Christian Yelich 1.00 2.50
9 Cody Bellinger 1.50 4.00
10 Justin Verlander .75 2.00
11 Jacob deGrom .75 2.00
12 Gerrit Cole 1.25 3.00
13 Max Scherzer .75 2.00
14 Stephen Strasburg .75 2.00
15 Liam Hendriks .50 1.25
16 Brandon Workman .50 1.25
17 Josh Hader .50 1.25
18 Ken Giles .50 1.25
19 Will Harris .75 2.00
20 Zack Britton .50 1.25
21 Kirby Yates .50 1.25
22 Mookie Betts 1.50 4.00
23 Jose Altuve .60 1.50
24 Anthony Rendon .75 2.00
25 Ronald Acuna Jr. 3.00 8.00

2020 Select 25-Man Prizms Holo
*HOLO: .6X TO 1.5X BASIC
RANDOM INSERTS IN PACKS
7 Mike Trout 8.00 20.00

2020 Select Hot Rookies
RANDOM INSERTS IN PACKS
*HOLO: .6X TO 1.5X BASIC
1 A.J. Puk 1.00 2.50
2 Bo Bichette 4.00 10.00
3 Brusdar Graterol .75 2.00
4 Gavin Lux 3.00 8.00
5 Yoshitomo Tsutsugo .60 1.50
6 Nick Solak .75 2.00
7 Sean Murphy .75 2.00
8 Yordan Alvarez 5.00 12.00
9 Zack Collins .60 1.50
10 Zac Gallen 1.25 3.00
11 Trent Grisham 2.00 5.00
12 Luis Robert 5.00 12.00
13 Mauricio Dubon .60 1.50
14 Jesus Luzardo 1.00 2.50
15 Dylan Cease 1.00 2.50
16 Brendan McKay .75 2.00
17 Aristides Aquino 1.00 2.50
18 Shun Yamaguchi .60 1.50
19 Kwang-Hyun Kim 1.50 4.00
20 Dustin May 2.00 5.00
21 Isan Diaz .75 2.00
22 Kyle Lewis 4.00 10.00
23 Nico Hoerner 2.00 5.00
24 Tony Gonsolin 2.00 5.00
25 Shogo Akiyama .75 2.00

2020 Select Launch Angle Autographs
6 Aristides Aquino 20.00 50.00
10 Yordan Alvarez 20.00 50.00

2020 Select Moon Shots
RANDOM INSERTS IN PACKS
1 Nomar Mazara .50 1.25
2 Ronald Acuna Jr. 3.00 8.00
3 Christian Yelich 1.00 2.50
4 Cody Bellinger 1.50 4.00
5 Josh Bell .60 1.50
6 Yordan Alvarez 5.00 12.00
7 Eugenio Suarez .60 1.50
8 Pete Alonso 2.00 5.00
9 Kyle Schwarber .75 2.00
10 Mike Trout 4.00 10.00
11 Nelson Cruz .75 2.00
12 Freddie Freeman 1.00 2.50
13 Aaron Judge 2.00 5.00
14 Shohei Ohtani 1.00 2.50
15 George Springer .60 1.50
16 Bryce Harper 1.25 3.00
17 Jorge Soler .75 2.00
18 Kris Bryant 1.00 2.50
19 Alex Bregman .75 2.00
20 Rhys Hoskins 1.00 2.50

2020 Select Moon Shots Prizms Holo
RANDOM INSERTS IN PACKS
4 Cody Bellinger 8.00 20.00
10 Mike Trout 8.00 20.00
14 Shohei Ohtani 6.00 15.00

2020 Select Phenomenon
RANDOM INSERTS IN PACKS
1 Rafael Devers 1.00 2.50
2 Juan Soto 2.50 6.00
3 Ronald Acuna Jr. 3.00 8.00
4 Vladimir Guerrero Jr. 1.50 4.00
5 Fernando Tatis Jr. 3.00 8.00
6 Eloy Jimenez 1.50 4.00
7 Gavin Lux 4.00 10.00
8 Jack Flaherty .60 1.50
9 Ozzie Albies .75 2.00
10 Yordan Alvarez 5.00 12.00
11 Bo Bichette 6.00 15.00
12 Luis Robert 5.00 12.00
13 Jo Adell 2.00 5.00
14 Wander Franco 5.00 12.00
15 Gleyber Torres 1.50 4.00

2020 Select Phenomenon Prizms Holo
RANDOM INSERTS IN PACKS
4 Vladimir Guerrero Jr. 10.00 25.00
7 Gavin Lux 10.00 25.00

2020 Select Phenoms
RANDOM INSERTS IN PACKS
*HOLO: .6X TO 1.5X BASIC
1 Wander Franco 5.00 12.00
2 Luis Robert 5.00 12.00
3 Jo Adell 2.00 5.00
4 Adley Rutschman 6.00 15.00
5 Casey Mize 1.50 4.00
6 Bobby Witt Jr. 2.50 6.00
7 Royce Lewis 1.25 3.00
8 Nate Pearson 1.00 2.50
9 Cristian Pache 1.50 4.00
10 Alex Kirilloff 1.00 2.50
11 Forrest Whitley .50 1.25
12 Jasson Dominguez 20.00 50.00
13 Joey Bart 1.50 4.00
14 Andrew Vaughn 2.00 5.00
15 Sixto Sanchez .75 2.00
16 Dylan Carlson 2.00 5.00
17 Julio Rodriguez 3.00 8.00
18 JJ Bleday 1.50 4.00
19 Ian Anderson 1.25 3.00
20 Alec Bohm 3.00 8.00
21 Keibert Ruiz 1.25 3.00
22 Nick Madrigal 1.50 4.00
23 CJ Abrams 2.00 5.00
24 Oneil Cruz .60 1.50
25 Tarik Skubal 2.50 6.00

2020 Select Rookie Jersey Autographs
RANDOM INSERTS IN PACKS
STATED PRINT RUN BTW 199-209 SER.#'d SET
EXCHANGE DEADLINE 10/15/2021
1 Randy Arozarena/209 25.00 60.00
2 Jordan Yamamoto /209 8.00 20.00
3 Adrian Morejon/209 3.00 8.00
4 Gavin Lux/209 20.00 50.00
5 Joe Palumbo/209 3.00 8.00
6 Isan Diaz/209 8.00 20.00
7 Adbert Alzolay/209 4.00 10.00
8 Mauricio Dubon/209 4.00 10.00
9 Jake Fraley/209 4.00 10.00
10 Matt Thaiss/209 4.00 10.00
11 Rico Garcia/209 5.00 12.00
12 Patrick Sandoval/209 5.00 12.00
13 T.J. Zeuch/209 3.00 8.00
14 Yu Chang/209 6.00 15.00
15 Sam Hilliard/209 5.00 12.00
16 Zack Collins/209 4.00 10.00
17 Ronald Bolanos/209 5.00 12.00
18 Danny Mendick/209 4.00 10.00
19 Aristides Aquino/209 15.00 40.00
20 Brock Burke/209 3.00 8.00
21 A.J. Puk/209 6.00 15.00
22 Tres Barrera/209 6.00 15.00
23 Kyle Lewis/209 25.00 60.00
24 Jaylin Davis/209 5.00 12.00
25 Logan Allen/209 3.00 8.00
26 Anthony Kay/209 3.00 8.00
27 Brendan McKay/209 8.00 20.00
28 Trent Grisham/209 12.00 30.00
29 Michel Baez/209 3.00 8.00
30 Bryan Abreu/209 3.00 8.00
31 Jonathan Hernandez/209 3.00 8.00
32 Domingo Leyba/209 4.00 10.00
33 Yordan Alvarez/209 30.00 80.00
34 Josh Rojas/209 3.00 8.00
35 Travis Demeritte/209 4.00 10.00
36 Bobby Bradley/209 4.00 10.00
37 Logan Webb/209 6.00 15.00
38 Andres Munoz/209 4.00 10.00
39 Justin Dunn/209 4.00 10.00
40 Yonathan Daza/209 4.00 10.00

41 Michael King/209 5.00 12.00
42 Jesus Luzardo/209 12.00 30.00
43 Nick Solak/209 5.00 12.00
44 Abraham Toro/209 8.00 20.00
45 Dustin May/199 20.00 50.00
46 Tony Gonsolin/209 4.00 10.00
47 Jake Rogers/209 10.00 25.00
48 Sean Murphy/209 5.00 12.00
49 Lewis Thorpe/209 3.00 8.00
50 Sheldon Neuse/209 4.00 10.00
51 Aaron Civale/209 5.00 12.00
52 Dylan Cease/209 6.00 15.00
53 Edwin Rios/209 8.00 20.00
54 Deivy Grullon/209 3.00 8.00
55 Donnie Walton/209 8.00 20.00
56 Zac Gallen/209 8.00 20.00
57 Bo Bichette/209 25.00 60.00
58 Nico Hoerner/209 12.00 30.00
59 Willi Castro/209 5.00 12.00
60 Brusdar Graterol/209 5.00 12.00
61 Tyrone Taylor/209 3.00 8.00
62 Luis Robert/199 EXCH 60.00 150.00

2020 Select Rookie Jersey Autographs Prizms Cracked Ice

*CRKD ICE: .6X TO 1.5X BASIC
RANDOM INSERTS IN PACKS
STATED PRINT RUN 25 SER.#'d SETS
NO PRICING DUE TO SCARCITY
EXCHANGE DEADLINE 10/15/2021
2 Jordan Yamamoto 15.00 40.00
6 Isan Diaz 25.00 60.00
8 Mauricio Dubon 15.00 40.00
9 Jake Fraley 20.00 50.00
10 Matt Thaiss 30.00 80.00
19 Aristides Aquino 125.00 300.00
23 Kyle Lewis 25.00 60.00
24 Jaylin Davis 40.00 100.00
31 Jonathan Hernandez 10.00 25.00
38 Andres Munoz 12.00 30.00
43 Nick Solak 15.00 40.00
50 Sheldon Neuse 15.00 40.00
56 Zac Gallen 30.00 80.00
57 Bo Bichette 75.00 200.00
60 Brusdar Graterol 15.00 40.00

2020 Select Rookie Jersey Autographs Prizms Holo

*HOLO: .5X TO 1.2X BASIC
RANDOM INSERTS IN PACKS
STATED PRINT RUN 99 SER.#'d SETS
EXCHANGE DEADLINE 10/15/2021
19 Aristides Aquino 50.00 120.00
23 Kyle Lewis 20.00 50.00
57 Bo Bichette 60.00 150.00

2020 Select Rookie Jersey Autographs Prizms Orange Pulsar

*ORNG PLSR/20: .6X TO 1.5X BASIC
RANDOM INSERTS IN PACKS
STATED PRINT RUN BTW 5-20 SER.#'d SET
NO PRICING QTY 15 OR LESS
EXCHANGE DEADLINE 10/15/2021
19 Aristides Aquino/20 125.00 300.00
33 Yordan Alvarez/20 125.00 300.00
57 Bo Bichette/20 75.00 200.00
62 Luis Robert/20 150.00 400.00

2020 Select Rookie Jersey Autographs Prizms Tri-Color

*TRI CLR: .5X TO 1.2X BASIC
RANDOM INSERTS IN PACKS
STATED PRINT RUN 49 SER.#'d SETS
EXCHANGE DEADLINE 10/15/2021
2 Jordan Yamamoto 12.00 30.00
6 Isan Diaz 15.00 40.00
8 Mauricio Dubon 12.00 30.00
10 Matt Thaiss 12.00 30.00
19 Aristides Aquino 100.00 250.00
23 Kyle Lewis 20.00 50.00
24 Jaylin Davis 30.00 80.00
31 Jonathan Hernandez 8.00 20.00
38 Andres Munoz 10.00 25.00
43 Nick Solak 12.00 30.00
56 Zac Gallen 15.00 40.00
57 Bo Bichette 60.00 150.00

2020 Select Rookie Jumbo Swatch

RANDOM INSERTS IN PACKS
*HOLO: .4X TO 1X BASIC
1 Jordan Yamamoto 2.50 6.00
2 Adrian Morejon 2.00 5.00
3 Gavin Lux 6.00 15.00
4 Isan Diaz 3.00 8.00
5 Adbert Alzolay 2.50 6.00
6 Mauricio Dubon 2.50 6.00
7 Jake Fraley 2.50 6.00
8 Matt Thaiss 2.50 6.00
9 Patrick Sandoval 3.00 8.00
11 Yu Chang 4.00 10.00
12 Sam Hilliard 3.00 8.00
13 Zack Collins 2.50 6.00
15 Aristides Aquino 5.00 12.00
16 A.J. Puk 4.00 10.00
17 Kyle Lewis 15.00 40.00
18 Jaylin Davis 3.00 8.00
19 Luis Robert 10.00 25.00
20 Anthony Kay 2.00 5.00
21 Brendan McKay 3.00 8.00
22 Trent Grisham 8.00 20.00
23 Michel Baez 2.00 5.00
24 Domingo Leyba 2.50 6.00
25 Yordan Alvarez 8.00 20.00
26 Travis Demeritte 2.50 6.00
27 Bobby Bradley 2.50 6.00
28 Logan Webb 2.50 6.00
29 Justin Dunn 2.50 6.00
30 Yonathan Daza 2.50 6.00
31 Jesus Luzardo 3.00 8.00
32 Nick Solak 3.00 8.00
33 Abraham Toro 2.50 6.00
34 Dustin May 6.00 15.00
35 Tony Gonsolin 8.00 20.00
36 Jake Rogers 2.00 5.00
37 Sean Murphy 3.00 8.00
38 Lewis Thorpe 2.00 5.00
39 Sheldon Neuse 4.00 10.00
40 Aaron Civale 3.00 8.00
41 Dylan Cease 4.00 10.00
42 Edwin Rios 5.00 12.00
43 Deivy Grullon 2.00 5.00
44 Donnie Walton 5.00 12.00
45 Zac Gallen 5.00 12.00
46 Bo Bichette 6.00 15.00
47 Nico Hoerner 5.00 12.00
48 Willi Castro 3.00 8.00
49 Brusdar Graterol 3.00 8.00
50 Tyrone Taylor 2.00 5.00

2020 Select Rookie Jumbo Swatch Prizms Cracked Ice

*CRKD ICE/25: .6X TO 1.5X BASIC
RANDOM INSERTS IN PACKS
STATED PRINT RUN 25 COPIES PER
3 Gavin Lux 30.00 80.00
9 Patrick Sandoval 10.00 25.00
15 Aristides Aquino 25.00 60.00
19 Luis Robert 20.00 50.00
25 Yordan Alvarez 30.00 80.00
46 Bo Bichette 40.00 100.00

2020 Select Rookie Jumbo Swatch Prizms Tri-Color

*TRI CLR: .5X TO 1.2X BASIC
RANDOM INSERTS IN PACKS
STATED PRINT RUN 99 COPIES PER
25 Yordan Alvarez 12.00 30.00

2020 Select Rookie Signatures

RANDOM INSERTS IN PACKS
STATED PRINT RUN 199 COPIES PER
EXCHANGE DEADLINE 10/15/2021
*HOLO: .5X TO 1.2X BASIC
*TRI CLR: .5X TO 1.2X BASIC
1 Nico Hoerner 10.00 25.00
2 Gavin Lux 30.00 80.00
3 Dylan Cease 5.00 12.00
4 Isan Diaz 8.00 20.00
5 Bo Bichette 40.00 100.00
6 Jesus Luzardo 5.00 12.00
7 Luis Robert 75.00 200.00
8 Brendan McKay 6.00 15.00
10 Sean Murphy 4.00 10.00

2020 Select Rookie Signatures Prizms Cracked Ice

*CRKD ICE: .6X TO 1.5X BASIC
RANDOM INSERTS IN PACKS
STATED PRINT RUN 25 SER.#'d SETS
NO PRICING DUE TO SCARCITY
EXCHANGE DEADLINE 10/15/2021
1 Nico Hoerner 25.00 60.00
2 Gavin Lux 100.00 250.00
10 Sean Murphy 12.00 30.00

2020 Select Select Stars

RANDOM INSERTS IN PACKS
1 Vladimir Guerrero Jr. 1.50 4.00
2 Anthony Rendon .75 2.00
3 Albert Pujols 1.00 2.50
4 Mike Trout 4.00 10.00
5 Yoan Moncada .75 2.00
6 Christian Yelich 1.00 2.50
7 Bryce Harper 1.25 3.00
8 Manny Machado .75 2.00
9 Justin Verlander .75 2.00
10 Jacob deGrom .75 2.00
11 Clayton Kershaw 1.50 4.00
12 Matt Chapman .75 2.00
13 Buster Posey 1.00 2.50
14 Anthony Rizzo 1.25 3.00
15 Max Scherzer .75 2.00

2020 Select Select Stars Prizms Holo

*HOLO: .6X TO 1.5X BASIC
RANDOM INSERTS IN PACKS
1 Vladimir Guerrero Jr. 10.00 25.00
4 Mike Trout 8.00 20.00
6 Christian Yelich 5.00 12.00

2020 Select Select Swatches

RANDOM INSERTS IN PACKS
1 Mike Trout 10.00 25.00
2 Aaron Judge 6.00 15.00
3 Pete Alonso 8.00 20.00
4 Rafael Devers 4.00 10.00
5 Cody Bellinger 6.00 15.00
6 Ronald Acuna Jr. 6.00 15.00
7 Freddie Freeman 4.00 10.00
8 Mookie Betts 6.00 15.00
9 Jose Altuve 2.50 6.00
10 Juan Soto 10.00 25.00
11 Ozzie Albies 3.00 8.00
12 Alex Bregman 3.00 8.00
13 Jose Abreu 3.00 8.00
14 Fernando Tatis Jr. 5.00 12.00
15 Justin Verlander 3.00 8.00
16 Shohei Ohtani 4.00 10.00
17 Anthony Rizzo 5.00 12.00
18 Javier Baez 4.00 10.00
19 Clayton Kershaw 6.00 15.00
20 Kris Bryant 4.00 10.00

2020 Select Select Swatches Prizms Cracked Ice

*CRKD ICE/24-25: .6X TO 1.5X BASIC
RANDOM INSERTS IN PACKS
PRINT RUN BTW 24-25 SER.#'d SETS
4 Rafael Devers/24 10.00 25.00
6 Ronald Acuna Jr./25 40.00 100.00
7 Freddie Freeman/25 10.00 25.00
13 Jose Abreu/25 10.00 25.00
14 Fernando Tatis Jr./25 20.00 50.00
19 Clayton Kershaw/25 10.00 25.00

2020 Select Select Swatches Prizms Holo

*HOLO: .4X TO 1X BASIC
RANDOM INSERTS IN PACKS
PRINT RUN BTW 149- 250 SER.#'d SETS
6 Ronald Acuna Jr./250 10.00 25.00
7 Freddie Freeman/149 5.00 12.00
13 Jose Abreu/250 6.00 15.00
19 Clayton Kershaw/149 6.00 15.00

2020 Select Select Swatches Prizms Tri-Color

*TRI CLR: .5X TO 1.2X BASIC
RANDOM INSERTS IN PACKS
STATED PRINT RUN 75 COPIES PER
4 Rafael Devers 8.00 20.00
6 Ronald Acuna Jr. 12.00 30.00
7 Freddie Freeman 6.00 15.00
13 Jose Abreu 8.00 20.00
19 Clayton Kershaw 8.00 20.00

2020 Select Sensations

RANDOM INSERTS IN PACKS
1 Aaron Judge 2.00 5.00
2 Javier Baez 1.00 2.50
3 Cody Bellinger 1.50 4.00
4 Gerrit Cole 1.25 3.00
5 Trevor Story .75 2.00
6 Jose Altuve .60 1.50
7 Christian Yelich 1.00 2.50
8 Mike Trout 4.00 10.00
9 Tim Anderson .75 2.00
10 Trea Turner .60 1.50
11 Francisco Lindor .75 2.00
12 Juan Soto 2.50 6.00
13 Adalberto Mondesi .75 2.00
14 Mookie Betts 1.50 4.00
15 Shohei Ohtani 1.00 2.50

2020 Select Sensations Prizms Holo

*HOLO: .6X TO 1.5X BASIC
RANDOM INSERTS IN PACKS
8 Mike Trout 8.00 20.00

2020 Select Signature Materials

RANDOM INSERTS IN PACKS
STATED PRINT RUN BTW 48-99 SER.#'d SET
EXCHANGE DEADLINE 10/15/2021
1 Brandon Woodruff/99 4.00 10.00
2 Carlos Correa/48 6.00 15.00
3 Paul Goldschmidt/49 12.00 30.00
4 Xander Bogaerts/99 25.00 60.00
10 Jorge Polanco/75 5.00 12.00
12 Anthony Rizzo/49 20.00 50.00
14 Curt Schilling/49 15.00 40.00
16 Rickey Henderson/75 40.00 100.00
18 Frank Thomas/75 30.00 80.00

2020 Select Signature Materials Prizms Holo

5 Jose Abreu/79 10.00 25.00
8 Manny Machado/75 15.00 40.00
9 Corey Seager/49 15.00 40.00
13 Ken Griffey Jr./25 150.00 400.00
15 John Smoltz/49 10.00 25.00
19 Mark McGwire/49 50.00 120.00

2020 Select Signature Materials Prizms Tri-Color

*TRI CLR/29-49: .5X TO 1.2X BASIC
*TRI CLR/25: .6X TO 1.5X BASIC
RANDOM INSERTS IN PACKS
STATED PRINT RUN BTW 10-49 SER.#'d SET
NO PRICING QTY 15 OR LESS
EXCHANGE DEADLINE 10/15/2021
5 Jose Abreu/35 10.00 25.00
6 Josh Bell/49 12.00 30.00
8 Manny Machado/49 15.00 40.00
9 Corey Seager/35 15.00 40.00
15 John Smoltz/29 10.00 25.00

2020 Select Signatures

RANDOM INSERTS IN PACKS
STATED PRINT RUN BTW 75-199 SER.#'d SET
EXCHANGE DEADLINE 10/15/2021
2 Josh Rojas/199 2.50 6.00
4 Michel Baez/199 2.50 6.00
6 Rico Garcia/199 4.00 10.00
7 Donnie Walton/199 6.00 15.00
8 Jake Fraley/199 8.00 20.00
9 Joe Palumbo/199 2.50 6.00
10 T.J. Zeuch/199 2.50 6.00
11 Jose Abreu/79 12.00 30.00
12 Ronald Bolanos/199 4.00 10.00
15 Fernando Tatis Jr./75 60.00 150.00
16 Vladimir Guerrero Jr./99 30.00 80.00
17 Kenny Lofton/99 12.00 30.00
18 Ben Zobrist/99 10.00 25.00
19 Jasson Dominguez/149 EXCH 200.00 500.00
22 Adalberto Mondesi/99 5.00 12.00
26 Michael Chavis/199 8.00 20.00
27 Jo Adell/199 EXCH 15.00 40.00
28 Nomar Mazara/99 6.00 15.00
29 Nick Senzel/199 8.00 20.00
30 Eloy Jimenez/99 15.00 40.00

2020 Select Signatures Prizms Cracked Ice

*CRKD ICE/25: .6X TO 1.5X BASIC p/r 149-199
*CRKD ICE/25: .5X TO 1.2X BASIC p/r 75-99
RANDOM INSERTS IN PACKS
STATED PRINT RUN BTW 15-25 SER.#'d SET
NO PRICING QTY 15 OR LESS
EXCHANGE DEADLINE 10/15/2021
1 Freddie Freeman/25 30.00 80.00
3 Ronald Acuna Jr./15
5 Josh Bell/25 15.00 40.00
10 T.J. Zeuch/25 6.00 15.00
13 Xander Bogaerts/25 50.00 120.00
14 Juan Soto/25 50.00 120.00
19 Jasson Dominguez/25 EXCH 400.00 800.00
21 Corey Seager/25 20.00 50.00
25 Shohei Ohtani/15
29 Nick Senzel/25 20.00 50.00

2020 Select Signatures Prizms Holo

*HOLO/35-99: .4X TO 1X BASIC p/r 75-99
*HOLO/35-99: .5X TO 1.2X BASIC p/r 149-199
RANDOM INSERTS IN PACKS
STATED PRINT RUN BTW 35-99 SER.#'d SET
EXCHANGE DEADLINE 10/15/2021
3 Ronald Acuna Jr./49 50.00 120.00
5 Josh Bell/49 12.00 30.00
24 Omar Vizquel/35 4.00 10.00
25 Shohei Ohtani/49 60.00 150.00

2020 Select Signatures Prizms Tri-Color

*TRI CLR/49: .5X TO 1.2X BASIC p/r 149-199
*TRI CLR/49: .4X TO 1X BASIC p/r 75-99
*TRI CLR/25: .6X TO 1.5X BASIC p/r 149-199
*TRI CLR/25: .5X TO 1.2X BASIC p/r 75-99
RANDOM INSERTS IN PACKS
STATED PRINT RUN BTW 25-49 SER.#'d SET
EXCHANGE DEADLINE 10/15/2021
1 Freddie Freeman/49 25.00 60.00
3 Ronald Acuna Jr./25 60.00 150.00
13 Xander Bogaerts/49 40.00 100.00
19 Jasson Dominguez/49 EXCH 300.00 600.00
21 Corey Seager/49 15.00 40.00
24 Omar Vizquel/25 5.00 12.00
25 Shohei Ohtani/25 75.00 200.00

2020 Select Sparks

RANDOM INSERTS IN PACKS
1 Mookie Betts 1.50 4.00
2 Francisco Lindor .75 2.00
3 Pete Alonso 2.00 5.00
4 Gleyber Torres 1.50 4.00
5 Mike Trout 4.00 10.00
6 Javier Baez 1.00 2.50
7 Fernando Tatis Jr. 3.00 8.00
8 Ketel Marte .60 1.50
9 Whit Merrifield .75 2.00
10 Jeff McNeil .60 1.50

2020 Select Sparks Prizms Holo

RANDOM INSERTS IN PACKS
5 Mike Trout 8.00 20.00

2020 Select Sparks Signatures

RANDOM INSERTS IN PACKS
STATED PRINT RUN 199 COPIES PER
EXCHANGE DEADLINE 10/15/2021
1 Zac Gallen 6.00 15.00
2 Zack Collins 3.00 8.00
3 Tony Gonsolin 10.00 25.00
4 Travis Demeritte 3.00 8.00
5 Bryan Abreu 2.50 6.00
6 Yu Chang 5.00 12.00
7 Brusdar Graterol 4.00 10.00
8 Trent Grisham 10.00 25.00
9 Logan Webb 3.00 8.00
10 Randy Arozarena 25.00 60.00
11 Anthony Kay 2.50 6.00
12 Jaylin Davis 4.00 10.00
13 Adbert Alzolay 3.00 8.00
14 Aaron Civale 6.00 15.00
15 Yonathan Daza 3.00 8.00
16 Patrick Sandoval 4.00 10.00
17 Tyrone Taylor 2.50 6.00
18 Andres Munoz 3.00 8.00
19 Jonathan Hernandez 2.50 6.00
20 Deivy Grullon 2.50 6.00
21 Tres Barrera 8.00 20.00
22 Michael King 4.00 10.00
23 Sheldon Neuse 3.00 8.00
24 Lewis Thorpe 2.50 6.00
25 Abraham Toro 3.00 8.00
26 Jake Rogers 8.00 20.00
27 Logan Allen 2.50 6.00
28 Danny Mendick 3.00 8.00
29 Domingo Leyba 3.00 8.00
30 Brock Burke 2.50 6.00
31 Justin Dunn 3.00 8.00
32 Mauricio Dubon 3.00 8.00
33 Adrian Morejon 2.50 6.00
34 Willi Castro 4.00 10.00
35 Jordan Yamamoto 3.00 8.00
36 Edwin Rios 6.00 15.00
37 A.J. Puk 5.00 12.00
38 Sam Hilliard 4.00 10.00
39 Bobby Bradley 3.00 8.00
40 Matt Thaiss 3.00 8.00

2020 Select Sparks Signatures Prizms Cracked Ice

*CRKD ICE: .6X TO 1.5X BASIC
RANDOM INSERTS IN PACKS
STATED PRINT RUN 25 SER.#'d SETS
EXCHANGE DEADLINE 10/15/2021
12 Jaylin Davis 20.00 50.00
27 Logan Allen 6.00 15.00
35 Jordan Yamamoto 20.00 50.00
37 A.J. Puk 15.00 40.00

2020 Select Sparks Signatures Prizms Holo

*HOLO: .5X TO 1.2X BASIC
RANDOM INSERTS IN PACKS
STATED PRINT RUN 99 SER.#'d SETS
EXCHANGE DEADLINE 10/15/2021
37 A.J. Puk 12.00 30.00

2020 Select Sparks Signatures Prizms Tri-Color

*TRI CLR: .5X TO 1.2X BASIC
RANDOM INSERTS IN PACKS
STATED PRINT RUN 49 SER.#'d SETS
EXCHANGE DEADLINE 10/15/2021
37 A.J. Puk 12.00 30.00

2020 Select X-Factor Material Signatures

RANDOM INSERTS IN PACKS
STATED PRINT RUN BTW 49-149 SER.#'d SET
EXCHANGE DEADLINE 10/15/2021
2 Byron Buxton/99 5.00 12.00
3 Fernando Tatis Jr./49 75.00 200.00
4 Gary Sanchez/149 12.00 30.00
6 Marcell Ozuna/99 6.00 15.00
12 Yoan Moncada/75 12.00 30.00
14 Ketel Marte/49 5.00 12.00
17 Jorge Polanco/75 5.00 12.00
20 Gleyber Torres/99 40.00 100.00

2020 Select X-Factor Material Signatures Prizms Cracked Ice

*CRKD ICE/25: .6X TO 1.5X BASIC p/r 149
*CRKD ICE/25: .5X TO 1.2X BASIC pr 49-99
RANDOM INSERTS IN PACKS
STATED PRINT RUN BTW 15-25 SER.#'d SET
NO PRICING QTY 15 OR LESS
EXCHANGE DEADLINE 10/15/2021
5 Gerrit Cole/20
10 Eloy Jimenez/25 EXCH 20.00 50.00
11 Juan Soto/25 50.00 120.00
15 Rafael Devers/15

2020 Select X-Factor Material Signatures Prizms Holo

RANDOM INSERTS IN PACKS
STATED PRINT RUN BTW 35-99 SER.#'d SET
EXCHANGE DEADLINE 10/15/2021
8 Ronald Acuna Jr./49 60.00 150.00
10 Eloy Jimenez/99 EXCH 15.00 40.00
15 Rafael Devers/75 10.00 25.00
18 Pete Alonso/75 50.00 120.00

2020 Select X-Factor Material Signatures Prizms Tri-Color

*TRI CLR/49: .5X TO 1.2X BASIC p/r 149
*TRI CLR/49: .4X TO 1X BASIC p/r 49-99
*TRI CLR/25: .5X TO 1.2X BASIC 49-99
RANDOM INSERTS IN PACKS
STATED PRINT RUN BTW 25-49 SER.#'d SET
EXCHANGE DEADLINE 10/15/2021
13 Stephen Strasburg/49
15 Rafael Devers/49 25.00 60.00
16 Whit Merrifield/49 12.00 30.00
18 Pete Alonso/49 50.00 120.00

1993 SP

This 290-card standard-size set, produced by Upper Deck, features fronts with action color player photos. Special subsets include All Star players (1-18) and Foil Prospects (271-290). Cards 19-270 are in alphabetical order by team nickname. Notable Rookie Cards include Johnny Damon and Derek Jeter.

COMPLETE SET (290) 150.00 400.00
COMMON CARD (1-270) .20 .50
FOIL PROSPECTS (271-290) .40 1.00
FOIL CARDS ARE CONDITION SENSITIVE
1 Roberto Alomar AS .50 1.25
2 Wade Boggs AS .50 1.25
3 Joe Carter AS .20 .50
4 Ken Griffey Jr. AS 1.50 4.00
5 Mark Langston AS .20 .50
6 John Olerud AS .30 .75
7 Kirby Puckett AS .75 2.00
8 Cal Ripken AS 2.50 6.00
9 Ivan Rodriguez AS .50 1.25
10 Barry Bonds AS 2.00 5.00
11 Darren Daulton AS .30 .75
12 Marquis Grissom AS .30 .75
13 David Justice AS .30 .75
14 John Kruk AS .30 .75
15 Barry Larkin AS .50 1.25
16 Terry Mulholland AS .20 .50
17 Ryne Sandberg AS 1.25 3.00
18 Gary Sheffield AS .30 .75
19 Chad Curtis .20 .50
20 Chili Davis .30 .75
21 Gary DiSarcina .20 .50
22 Damion Easley .20 .50
23 Chuck Finley .30 .75
24 Luis Polonia .20 .50
25 Tim Salmon .50 1.25
26 J.T.Snow RC .50 1.25
27 Russ Springer .20 .50
28 Jeff Bagwell .50 1.25
29 Craig Biggio .50 1.25
30 Ken Caminiti .30 .75
31 Andujar Cedeno .20 .50
32 Doug Drabek .20 .50
33 Steve Finley .30 .75
34 Luis Gonzalez .30 .75
35 Pete Harnisch .20 .50
36 Darryl Kile .30 .75
37 Mike Bordick .20 .50
38 Dennis Eckersley .30 .75
39 Brent Gates .20 .50
40 Rickey Henderson .75 2.00
41 Mark McGwire 2.00 5.00
42 Craig Paquette .20 .50
43 Ruben Sierra .30 .75
44 Terry Steinbach .20 .50
45 Todd Van Poppel .20 .50
46 Pat Borders .20 .50
47 Tony Fernandez .20 .50
48 Juan Guzman .20 .50
49 Pat Hentgen .20 .50
50 Paul Molitor .30 .75
51 Jack Morris .30 .75
52 Ed Sprague .20 .50
53 Duane Ward .20 .50
54 Devon White .30 .75
55 Steve Avery .20 .50
56 Jeff Blauser .20 .50
57 Ron Gant .30 .75
58 Tom Glavine .50 1.25
59 Greg Maddux 1.25 3.00
60 Fred McGriff .50 1.25
61 Terry Pendleton .30 .75
62 Deion Sanders .50 1.25
63 John Smoltz .50 1.25
64 Cal Eldred .20 .50
65 Darryl Hamilton .20 .50
66 John Jaha .20 .50
67 Pat Listach .20 .50
68 Jaime Navarro .20 .50
69 Kevin Reimer .20 .50
70 B.J. Surhoff .30 .75
71 Greg Vaughn .20 .50
72 Robin Yount 1.25 3.00
73 Rene Arocha RC .30 .75
74 Bernard Gilkey .20 .50
75 Gregg Jefferies .20 .50
76 Ray Lankford .30 .75
77 Tom Pagnozzi .20 .50
78 Lee Smith .30 .75
79 Ozzie Smith 1.25 3.00
80 Bob Tewksbury .20 .50
81 Mark Whiten .20 .50
82 Steve Buechele .20 .50
83 Mark Grace .50 1.25
84 Jose Guzman .20 .50
85 Derrick May .20 .50
86 Mike Morgan .20 .50
87 Randy Myers .20 .50
88 Kevin Roberson RC .20 .50
89 Sammy Sosa .75 2.00
90 Rick Wilkins .20 .50
91 Brett Butler .30 .75
92 Eric Davis .30 .75
93 Orel Hershiser .30 .75
94 Eric Karros .30 .75
95 Ramon Martinez .20 .50
96 Raul Mondesi .30 .75
97 Jose Offerman .20 .50
98 Mike Piazza 2.00 5.00
99 Darryl Strawberry .30 .75
100 Moises Alou .30 .75
101 Wil Cordero .20 .50
102 Delino DeShields .20 .50
103 Darrin Fletcher .20 .50
104 Ken Hill .20 .50
105 Mike Lansing RC .30 .75
106 Dennis Martinez .30 .75
107 Larry Walker .30 .75
108 John Wetteland .30 .75
109 Rod Beck .20 .50
110 John Burkett .20 .50
111 Will Clark .50 1.25
112 Royce Clayton .20 .50
113 Darren Lewis .20 .50
114 Willie McGee .30 .75
115 Bill Swift .20 .50
116 Robby Thompson .20 .50
117 Matt Williams .30 .75
118 Sandy Alomar Jr. .20 .50
119 Carlos Baerga .20 .50
120 Albert Belle .30 .75
121 Reggie Jefferson .20 .50
122 Wayne Kirby .20 .50
123 Kenny Lofton .30 .75
124 Carlos Martinez .20 .50
125 Charles Nagy .20 .50
126 Paul Sorrento .20 .50
127 Rich Amaral .20 .50
128 Jay Buhner .30 .75
129 Norm Charlton .20 .50
130 Dave Fleming .20 .50
131 Erik Hanson .20 .50
132 Randy Johnson .75 2.00
133 Edgar Martinez .50 1.25
134 Tino Martinez .50 1.25
135 Omar Vizquel .50 1.25
136 Bret Barberie .20 .50
137 Chuck Carr .20 .50
138 Jeff Conine .30 .75
139 Orestes Destrade .20 .50
140 Chris Hammond .20 .5
141 Bryan Harvey .20 .5
142 Benito Santiago .30 .7
143 Walt Weiss .20 .5
144 Darrell Whitmore RC .20 .5
145 Tim Bogar RC .20 .5
146 Bobby Bonilla .30 .7
147 Jeromy Burnitz .30 .7
148 Vince Coleman .20 .5
149 Dwight Gooden .30 .7
150 Todd Hundley .20 .5
151 Howard Johnson .20 .5
152 Eddie Murray .75 2.0
153 Bret Saberhagen .30 .7
154 Brady Anderson .30 .7
155 Mike Devereaux .20 .5
156 Jeffrey Hammonds .20 .5
157 Chris Hoiles .20 .5
158 Ben McDonald .20 .5
159 Mark McLemore .20 .5
160 Mike Mussina .50 1.2
161 Gregg Olson .20 .5
162 David Segui .20 .5
163 Derek Bell .20 .5
164 Andy Benes .20 .5
165 Archi Cianfrocco .20 .5
166 Ricky Gutierrez .20 .5
167 Tony Gwynn 1.00 2.5
168 Gene Harris .20 .5
169 Trevor Hoffman .75 2.0
170 Ray McDavid RC .20 .5
171 Phil Plantier .20 .5
172 Mariano Duncan .20 .5
173 Len Dykstra .30 .7
174 Tommy Greene .20 .5
175 Dave Hollins .20 .5
176 Pete Incaviglia .20 .5
177 Mickey Morandini .20 .5
178 Curt Schilling .30 .7
179 Kevin Stocker .20 .5
180 Mitch Williams .20 .5
181 Stan Belinda .20 .5
182 Jay Bell .30 .7
183 Steve Cooke .20 .5
184 Carlos Garcia .20 .5
185 Jeff King .20 .5
186 Orlando Merced .20 .5
187 Don Slaught .20 .5
188 Andy Van Slyke .50 1.2
189 Kevin Young .30 .7
190 Kevin Brown .30 .7
191 Jose Canseco .50 1.2
192 Julio Franco .30 .7
193 Benji Gil .20 .5
194 Juan Gonzalez .30 .7
195 Tom Henke .20 .5
196 Rafael Palmeiro .50 1.2
197 Dean Palmer .30 .7
198 Nolan Ryan 3.00 8.0
199 Roger Clemens 1.50 4.0
200 Scott Cooper .20 .5
201 Andre Dawson .30 .7
202 Mike Greenwell .20 .5
203 Carlos Quintana .20 .5
204 Jeff Russell .20 .5
205 Aaron Sele .20 .5
206 Mo Vaughn .30 .7
207 Frank Viola .30 .7
208 Rob Dibble .30 .7
209 Roberto Kelly .20 .5
210 Kevin Mitchell .20 .5
211 Hal Morris .20 .5
212 Joe Oliver .20 .5
213 Jose Rijo .20 .5
214 Bip Roberts .20 .5
215 Chris Sabo .20 .5
216 Reggie Sanders .30 .7
217 Dante Bichette .30 .7
218 Jerald Clark .20 .5
219 Alex Cole .20 .5
220 Andres Galarraga .30 .7
221 Joe Girardi .20 .5
222 Charlie Hayes .20 .5
223 Roberto Mejia RC .20 .5
224 Armando Reynoso .20 .5
225 Eric Young .20 .5
226 Kevin Appier .30 .7
227 George Brett 2.00 5.0
228 David Cone .30 .7
229 Phil Hiatt .20 .5
230 Felix Jose .20 .5
231 Wally Joyner .30 .7
232 Mike Macfarlane .20 .5
233 Brian McRae .20 .5
234 Jeff Montgomery .20 .5
235 Rob Deer .20 .5
236 Cecil Fielder .30 .7
237 Travis Fryman .30 .7
238 Mike Henneman .20 .5
239 Tony Phillips .20 .5
240 Mickey Tettleton .20 .5
241 Alan Trammell .30 .7
242 David Wells .30 .7
243 Lou Whitaker .30 .7
244 Rick Aguilera .20 .5
245 Scott Erickson .20 .5
246 Brian Harper .20 .5
247 Kent Hrbek .30 .7
248 Chuck Knoblauch .30 .7
249 Shane Mack .20 .5
250 David McCarty .20 .5
251 Pedro Munoz .20 .5
252 Dave Winfield .30 .7

53 Alex Fernandez .20 .50
54 Ozzie Guillen .30 .75
55 Bo Jackson .75 2.00
56 Lance Johnson .20 .50
57 Ron Karkovice .20 .50
58 Jack McDowell .20 .50
59 Tim Raines .30 .75
60 Frank Thomas .75 2.00
61 Robin Ventura .30 .75
62 Jim Abbott .50 1.25
63 Steve Farr .20 .50
64 Jimmy Key .30 .75
65 Don Mattingly 2.00 5.00
66 Paul O'Neill .50 1.25
67 Mike Stanley .20 .50
68 Danny Tartabull .20 .50
69 Bob Wickman .20 .50
70 Bernie Williams .50 1.25
71 Jason Bere FOIL .40 1.00
72 Roger Cedeno FOIL RC .60 1.50
73 Johnny Damon FOIL RC 3.00 8.00
74 Russ Davis FOIL RC .60 1.50
75 Carlos Delgado FOIL 1.50 4.00
76 Carl Everett FOIL .60 1.50
77 Cliff Floyd FOIL .30 .75
78 Alex Gonzalez FOIL .40 1.00
79 Derek Jeter FOIL RC ! 200.00 500.00
80 Chipper Jones FOIL 1.50 4.00
81 Javier Lopez FOIL .50 1.25
82 Chad Mottola FOIL RC .40 1.00
83 Marc Newfield FOIL .40 1.00
84 Eduardo Perez FOIL .40 1.00
85 Manny Ramirez FOIL 2.00 5.00
86 Todd Steverson FOIL RC .40 1.00
87 Michael Tucker FOIL .40 1.00
88 Allen Watson FOIL .40 1.00
89 Rondell White FOIL .60 1.50
90 Dmitri Young FOIL .60 1.50

1993 SP Platinum Power

ards from this 20-card standard-size were inserted ne every nine packs and feature power hitters from e American and National Leagues.

OMPLETE SET (20) 10.00 25.00
TATED ODDS 1:9
P1 Albert Belle .75 2.00
P2 Barry Bonds 5.00 12.00
P3 Joe Carter .50 1.25
P4 Will Clark 1.25 3.00
P5 Darren Daulton .75 2.00
P6 Cecil Fielder .75 2.00
P7 Ron Gant .75 2.00
P8 Juan Gonzalez .75 2.00
P9 Ken Griffey Jr. 4.00 10.00
P10 Dave Hollins .50 1.25
P11 David Justice .75 2.00
P12 Fred McGriff 1.25 3.00
P13 Mark McGwire 5.00 12.00
P14 Dean Palmer .75 2.00
P15 Mike Piazza 5.00 12.00
P16 Tim Salmon 1.25 3.00
P17 Ryne Sandberg 3.00 8.00
P18 Gary Sheffield .75 2.00
P19 Frank Thomas 2.00 5.00
P20 Matt Williams .75 2.00

1994 SP Previews

hese 15 cards were distributed regionally as inserts second series Upper Deck hobby packs. They were serted at a rate of one in 35. The manner of stribution was five cards per Central, East and West egion. The cards are nearly identical to the basic SP sue. Card fronts differ in that the region is at ottom right where the team name is located on the P cards.

OMPLETE SET (15) 75.00 150.00
OMPLETE CENTRAL (5) 25.00 60.00
OMPLETE EAST (5) 15.00 40.00
OMPLETE WEST (5) 25.00 60.00
TATED ODDS 1:35 REG'L SER.2 UD HOBBY
R1 Jeff Bagwell 2.00 5.00
R2 Michael Jordan 8.00 20.00
R3 Kirby Puckett 3.00 8.00
R4 Manny Ramirez 3.00 8.00
R5 Frank Thomas 3.00 8.00
R1 Roberto Alomar 2.00 5.00
R2 Cliff Floyd 1.25 3.00
R3 Javier Lopez 1.25 3.00
R4 Don Mattingly 8.00 20.00
R5 Cal Ripken 10.00 25.00
R1 Barry Bonds 8.00 20.00
R2 Juan Gonzalez 1.25 3.00

WR3 Ken Griffey Jr. 6.00 15.00
WR4 Mike Piazza 6.00 15.00
WR5 Tim Salmon 2.00 5.00

1994 SP

This 200-card standard-size set distributed in foil packs contains the game's top players and prospects. The first 20 cards in the set are Foil Prospects which are brighter and more metallic than the rest of the set. These cards therefore are highly condition sensitive. Cards 21-200 are in alphabetical order by team nickname. Rookie Cards include Brad Fullmer, Derrek Lee, Chan Ho Park and Alex Rodriguez.

COMPLETE SET (200) 50.00 100.00
COMMON CARD (21-200) .07 .20
COMMON FOIL (1-20) .20 .50
REGULAR CARDS HAVE GOLD HOLOGRAMS
FOIL CARDS CONDITION SENSITIVE
1 Mike Bell FOIL RC .20 .50
2 D.J. Boston FOIL RC .20 .50
3 Johnny Damon FOIL .75 2.00
4 Brad Fullmer FOIL RC .40 1.00
5 Joey Hamilton FOIL .20 .50
6 Todd Hollandsworth FOIL .20 .50
7 Brian L.Hunter FOIL .20 .50
8 LaTroy Hawkins FOIL RC .40 1.00
9 Brooks Kieschnick FOIL RC .20 .50
10 Derrek Lee FOIL RC 5.00 12.00
11 Trot Nixon FOIL RC 1.50 4.00
12 Alex Ochoa FOIL .20 .50
13 Chan Ho Park FOIL RC .75 2.00
14 Kirk Presley FOIL RC .20 .50
15 Alex Rodriguez FOIL RC 20.00 50.00
16 Jose Silva FOIL RC .20 .50
17 Terrell Wade FOIL RC .20 .50
18 Billy Wagner FOIL RC 1.50 4.00
19 Glenn Williams FOIL RC .20 .50
20 Preston Wilson FOIL .40 1.00
21 Brian Anderson RC .15 .40
22 Chad Curtis .07 .20
23 Chili Davis .15 .40
24 Bo Jackson .40 1.00
25 Mark Langston .07 .20
26 Tim Salmon .25 .60
27 Jeff Bagwell .25 .60
28 Craig Biggio .25 .60
29 Ken Caminiti .15 .40
30 Doug Drabek .07 .20
31 John Hudek RC .07 .20
32 Greg Swindell .07 .20
33 Brent Gates .07 .20
34 Rickey Henderson .40 1.00
35 Steve Karsay .07 .20
36 Mark McGwire 1.00 2.50
37 Ruben Sierra .15 .40
38 Terry Steinbach .07 .20
39 Roberto Alomar .25 .60
40 Joe Carter .15 .40
41 Carlos Delgado .25 .60
42 Alex Gonzalez .07 .20
43 Juan Guzman .07 .20
44 Paul Molitor .15 .40
45 John Olerud .15 .40
46 Devon White .15 .40
47 Steve Avery .07 .20
48 Jeff Blauser .07 .20
49 Tom Glavine .25 .60
50 David Justice .15 .40
51 Roberto Kelly .07 .20
52 Ryan Klesko .15 .40
53 Javier Lopez .15 .40
54 Greg Maddux .60 1.50
55 Fred McGriff .25 .60
56 Ricky Bones .07 .20
57 Cal Eldred .07 .20
58 Brian Harper .07 .20
59 Pat Listach .07 .20
60 B.J. Surhoff .15 .40
61 Greg Vaughn .07 .20
62 Bernard Gilkey .07 .20
63 Gregg Jefferies .07 .20
64 Ray Lankford .15 .40
65 Ozzie Smith .60 1.50
66 Bob Tewksbury .07 .20
67 Mark Whiten .07 .20
68 Todd Zeile .07 .20
69 Mark Grace .25 .60
70 Randy Myers .07 .20
71 Ryne Sandberg .60 1.50
72 Sammy Sosa .40 1.00
73 Steve Trachsel .07 .20
74 Rick Wilkins .07 .20
75 Brett Butler .15 .40
76 Delino DeShields .07 .20
77 Orel Hershiser .15 .40
78 Eric Karros .15 .40
79 Raul Mondesi .15 .40
80 Mike Piazza .75 2.00
81 Tim Wallach .07 .20
82 Moises Alou .15 .40
83 Cliff Floyd .15 .40
84 Marquis Grissom .15 .40
85 Pedro Martinez .40 1.00
86 Larry Walker .15 .40
87 John Wetteland .15 .40
88 Rondell White .15 .40
89 Rod Beck .07 .20
90 Barry Bonds 1.00 2.50
91 John Burkett .07 .20
92 Royce Clayton .07 .20
93 Billy Swift .07 .20
94 Robby Thompson .07 .20
95 Matt Williams .15 .40
96 Carlos Baerga .07 .20
97 Albert Belle .15 .40
98 Kenny Lofton .15 .40
99 Dennis Martinez .15 .40
100 Eddie Murray .40 1.00
101 Manny Ramirez .40 1.00
102 Eric Anthony .07 .20
103 Chris Bosio .07 .20
104 Jay Buhner .15 .40
105 Ken Griffey Jr. .75 2.00
106 Randy Johnson .40 1.00
107 Edgar Martinez .25 .60
108 Chuck Carr .07 .20
109 Jeff Conine .15 .40
110 Carl Everett .15 .40
111 Chris Hammond .07 .20
112 Bryan Harvey .07 .20
113 Charles Johnson .15 .40
114 Gary Sheffield .15 .40
115 Bobby Bonilla .15 .40
116 Dwight Gooden .15 .40
117 Todd Hundley .07 .20
118 Bobby Jones .07 .20
119 Jeff Kent .25 .60
120 Bret Saberhagen .15 .40
121 Jeffrey Hammonds .07 .20
122 Chris Hoiles .07 .20
123 Ben McDonald .07 .20
124 Mike Mussina .25 .60
125 Rafael Palmeiro .25 .60
126 Cal Ripken 1.25 3.00
127 Lee Smith .15 .40
128 Derek Bell .07 .20
129 Andy Benes .07 .20
130 Tony Gwynn .50 1.25
131 Trevor Hoffman .25 .60
132 Phil Plantier .07 .20
133 Bip Roberts .07 .20
134 Darren Daulton .15 .40
135 Lenny Dykstra .15 .40
136 Dave Hollins .07 .20
137 Danny Jackson .07 .20
138 John Kruk .15 .40
139 Kevin Stocker .07 .20
140 Jay Bell .15 .40
141 Carlos Garcia .07 .20
142 Jeff King .07 .20
143 Orlando Merced .07 .20
144 Andy Van Slyke .25 .60
145 Paul Wagner .07 .20
146 Jose Canseco .25 .60
147 Will Clark .25 .60
148 Juan Gonzalez .15 .40
149 Tom Henke .07 .20
150 Dean Palmer .15 .40
151 Ivan Rodriguez .25 .60
152 Roger Clemens .75 2.00
153 Scott Cooper .07 .20
154 Andre Dawson .15 .40
155 Mike Greenwell .07 .20
156 Aaron Sele .07 .20
157 Mo Vaughn .15 .40
158 Bret Boone .15 .40
159 Barry Larkin .25 .60
160 Kevin Mitchell .07 .20
161 Jose Rijo .07 .20
162 Deion Sanders .25 .60
163 Reggie Sanders .15 .40
164 Dante Bichette .15 .40
165 Ellis Burks .15 .40
166 Andres Galarraga .15 .40
167 Charlie Hayes .07 .20
168 David Nied .07 .20
169 Walt Weiss .07 .20
170 Kevin Appier .15 .40
171 David Cone .15 .40
172 Jeff Granger .07 .20
173 Felix Jose .07 .20
174 Wally Joyner .15 .40
175 Brian McRae .07 .20
176 Cecil Fielder .15 .40
177 Travis Fryman .15 .40
178 Mike Henneman .07 .20
179 Tony Phillips .07 .20
180 Mickey Tettleton .07 .20
181 Alan Trammell .15 .40
182 Rick Aguilera .07 .20
183 Rich Becker .07 .20
184 Scott Erickson .07 .20
185 Chuck Knoblauch .15 .40
186 Kirby Puckett .40 1.00
187 Dave Winfield .15 .40
188 Wilson Alvarez .07 .20
189 Jason Bere .07 .20
190 Alex Fernandez .07 .20
191 Julio Franco .15 .40
192 Jack McDowell .07 .20
193 Frank Thomas .40 1.00
194 Robin Ventura .15 .40
195 Jim Abbott .25 .60
196 Wade Boggs .25 .60
197 Jimmy Key .15 .40
198 Don Mattingly 1.00 2.50
199 Paul O'Neill .25 .60
200 Danny Tartabull .07 .20
P24 Ken Griffey Jr. Promo 1.00 2.50

1994 SP Die Cuts

COMPLETE SET (200) 75.00 150.00
*STARS: .75X TO 2X BASIC CARDS
*ROOKIES: .6X TO 1.5X BASIC CARDS
ONE DIE CUT PER PACK
DIE CUTS HAVE SILVER HOLOGRAMS
10 Derrek Lee FOIL 6.00 15.00
15 Alex Rodriguez FOIL 25.00 60.00

1994 SP Holoviews

Randomly inserted in SP foil packs at a rate of one in five, this 38-card set contains top stars and prospects.

STATED ODDS 1:5
1 Roberto Alomar 1.25 3.00
2 Kevin Appier .75 2.00
3 Jeff Bagwell 1.25 3.00
4 Jose Canseco 1.25 3.00
5 Roger Clemens 4.00 10.00
6 Carlos Delgado 1.25 3.00
7 Cecil Fielder .75 2.00
8 Cliff Floyd .75 2.00
9 Travis Fryman .75 2.00
10 Andres Galarraga .75 2.00
11 Juan Gonzalez .75 2.00
12 Ken Griffey Jr. 4.00 10.00
13 Tony Gwynn 2.50 6.00
14 Jeffrey Hammonds .60 1.50
15 Bo Jackson 2.00 5.00
16 Michael Jordan 6.00 15.00
17 David Justice .75 2.00
18 Steve Karsay .60 1.50
19 Jeff Kent 1.25 3.00
20 Brooks Kieschnick .60 1.50
21 Ryan Klesko .75 2.00
22 John Kruk .75 2.00
23 Barry Larkin 1.25 3.00
24 Pat Listach .60 1.50
25 Don Mattingly 5.00 12.00
26 Mark McGwire 5.00 12.00
27 Raul Mondesi .75 2.00
28 Trot Nixon 2.50 6.00
29 Mike Piazza 3.00 8.00
30 Kirby Puckett 2.00 5.00
31 Manny Ramirez 2.00 5.00
32 Cal Ripken 6.00 15.00
33 Alex Rodriguez 10.00 25.00
34 Tim Salmon 1.25 3.00
35 Gary Sheffield .75 2.00
36 Ozzie Smith 3.00 8.00
37 Sammy Sosa 2.00 5.00
38 Andy Van Slyke 1.25 3.00

1994 SP Holoviews Die Cuts

*DIE CUTS: 2.5X TO 6X BASIC HOLO
*DIE CUTS: 1.5X TO 4X BASIC HOLO RC YR
STATED ODDS 1:75
12 Ken Griffey Jr. 30.00 80.00
16 Michael Jordan 75.00 150.00
33 Alex Rodriguez 150.00 300.00

1995 SP

This set consists of 207 cards being sold in eight-card, hobby-only packs with a suggested retail price of $3.99. Subsets featured are Salute (1-4) and Premier Prospects (5-24). The only notable Rookie Card in this set is Hideo Nomo. Dealers who ordered a certain quantity of Upper Deck baseball cases received as a bonus, a certified autographed SP card of Ken Griffey Jr.

COMPLETE SET (207) 15.00 40.00
COMMON CARD (1-207) .07 .20
COMMON FOIL (5-24) .20 .50
GRIFFEY AU SENT TO DEALERS AS BONUS
1 Cal Ripken Salute 1.25 3.00
2 Nolan Ryan Salute 1.50 4.00
3 George Brett Salute 1.00 2.50
4 Mike Schmidt Salute .60 1.50
5 Dustin Hermanson FOIL .20 .50
6 Antonio Osuna FOIL .20 .50
7 Mark Grudzielanek FOIL RC .50 1.25
8 Ray Durham FOIL .30 .75
9 Ugueth Urbina FOIL .20 .50
10 Ruben Rivera FOIL .20 .50
11 Curtis Goodwin FOIL .20 .50
12 Jimmy Hurst FOIL .20 .50
13 Jose Malave FOIL .20 .50
14 Hideo Nomo FOIL RC 1.50 4.00
15 Juan Acevedo RC FOIL .20 .50
16 Tony Clark FOIL .20 .50
17 Jim Pittsley FOIL .20 .50
18 Freddy Adrian Garcia RC FOIL .20 .50
19 Carlos Perez RC FOIL .30 .75
20 Raul Casanova FOIL RC .20 .50
21 Quilvio Veras FOIL .20 .50
22 Edgardo Alfonzo FOIL .20 .50
23 Marty Cordova FOIL .20 .50
24 C.J. Nitkowski FOIL .20 .50
25 Wade Boggs CL .15 .40
26 Dave Winfield CL .07 .20
27 Eddie Murray CL .25 .60
28 David Justice .15 .40
29 Marquis Grissom .15 .40
30 Fred McGriff .25 .60
31 Greg Maddux .60 1.50
32 Tom Glavine .25 .60
33 Steve Avery .07 .20
34 Chipper Jones .40 1.00
35 Sammy Sosa .40 1.00
36 Jaime Navarro .07 .20
37 Randy Myers .07 .20
38 Mark Grace .25 .60
39 Todd Zeile .07 .20
40 Brian McRae .07 .20
41 Reggie Sanders .15 .40
42 Ron Gant .15 .40
43 Deion Sanders .25 .60
44 Bret Boone .15 .40
45 Barry Larkin .25 .60
46 Jose Rijo .07 .20
47 Jason Bates .07 .20
48 Andres Galarraga .15 .40
49 Bill Swift .07 .20
50 Larry Walker .15 .40
51 Vinny Castilla .15 .40
52 Dante Bichette .15 .40
53 Jeff Conine .15 .40
54 John Burkett .07 .20
55 Gary Sheffield .15 .40
56 Andre Dawson .15 .40
57 Terry Pendleton .15 .40
58 Charles Johnson .15 .40
59 Brian L.Hunter .07 .20
60 Jeff Bagwell .25 .60
61 Craig Biggio .25 .60
62 Phil Nevin .15 .40
63 Doug Drabek .07 .20
64 Derek Bell .07 .20
65 Raul Mondesi .15 .40
66 Eric Karros .15 .40
67 Roger Cedeno .07 .20
68 Delino DeShields .07 .20
69 Ramon Martinez .07 .20
70 Mike Piazza .60 1.50
71 Billy Ashley .07 .20
72 Jeff Fassero .07 .20
73 Shane Andrews .07 .20
74 Wil Cordero .07 .20
75 Tony Tarasco .07 .20
76 Rondell White .15 .40
77 Pedro Martinez .25 .60
78 Moises Alou .15 .40
79 Rico Brogna .07 .20
80 Bobby Bonilla .15 .40
81 Jeff Kent .15 .40
82 Brett Butler .15 .40
83 Bobby Jones .07 .20
84 Bill Pulsipher .07 .20
85 Bret Saberhagen .15 .40
86 Gregg Jefferies .07 .20
87 Lenny Dykstra .15 .40
88 Dave Hollins .07 .20
89 Charlie Hayes .07 .20
90 Darren Daulton .15 .40
91 Curt Schilling .15 .40
92 Heathcliff Slocumb .07 .20
93 Carlos Garcia .07 .20
94 Denny Neagle .15 .40
95 Jay Bell .15 .40
96 Orlando Merced .07 .20
97 Dave Clark .07 .20
98 Bernard Gilkey .07 .20
99 Scott Cooper .07 .20
100 Ozzie Smith .60 1.50
101 Tom Henke .07 .20
102 Ken Hill .07 .20
103 Brian Jordan .15 .40
104 Ray Lankford .15 .40
105 Tony Gwynn .50 1.25
106 Andy Benes .07 .20
107 Ken Caminiti .15 .40
108 Steve Finley .15 .40
109 Joey Hamilton .07 .20
110 Bip Roberts .07 .20
111 Eddie Williams .07 .20
112 Rod Beck .07 .20
113 Matt Williams .15 .40
114 Glenallen Hill .07 .20
115 Barry Bonds 1.00 2.50
116 Robby Thompson .07 .20
117 Mark Portugal .07 .20
118 Brady Anderson .15 .40
119 Mike Mussina .25 .60
120 Rafael Palmeiro .25 .60
121 Chris Hoiles .07 .20
122 Harold Baines .15 .40
123 Jeffrey Hammonds .07 .20
124 Tim Naehring .07 .20
125 Mo Vaughn .15 .40
126 Mike Macfarlane .07 .20
127 Roger Clemens .75 2.00
128 John Valentin .07 .20
129 Aaron Sele .07 .20
130 Jose Canseco .25 .60
131 J.T. Snow .15 .40
132 Mark Langston .07 .20
133 Chili Davis .15 .40
134 Chuck Finley .15 .40
135 Tim Salmon .25 .60
136 Tony Phillips .07 .20
137 Jason Bere .07 .20
138 Robin Ventura .15 .40
139 Tim Raines .15 .40
140 Frank Thomas .40 1.00
140A Frank Thomas ERR .40 1.00
141 Alex Fernandez .07 .20
142 Jim Abbott .25 .60
143 Wilson Alvarez .07 .20
144 Carlos Baerga .07 .20
145 Albert Belle .15 .40
146 Jim Thome .25 .60
147 Dennis Martinez .15 .40
148 Eddie Murray .40 1.00
149 Dave Winfield .15 .40
150 Kenny Lofton .15 .40
151 Manny Ramirez .25 .60
152 Chad Curtis .07 .20
153 Lou Whitaker .15 .40
154 Alan Trammell .15 .40
155 Cecil Fielder .15 .40
156 Kirk Gibson .15 .40
157 Michael Tucker .07 .20
158 Jon Nunnally .07 .20
159 Wally Joyner .15 .40
160 Kevin Appier .15 .40
161 Jeff Montgomery .07 .20
162 Greg Gagne .07 .20
163 Ricky Bones .07 .20
164 Cal Eldred .07 .20
165 Greg Vaughn .07 .20
166 Kevin Seitzer .07 .20
167 Jose Valentin .07 .20
168 Joe Oliver .07 .20
169 Rick Aguilera .07 .20
170 Kirby Puckett .40 1.00
171 Scott Stahoviak .07 .20
172 Kevin Tapani .07 .20
173 Chuck Knoblauch .15 .40
174 Rich Becker .07 .20
175 Don Mattingly 1.00 2.50
176 Jack McDowell .07 .20
177 Jimmy Key .15 .40
178 Paul O'Neill .25 .60
179 John Wetteland .15 .40
180 Wade Boggs .25 .60
181 Derek Jeter 1.00 2.50
182 Rickey Henderson .40 1.00
183 Terry Steinbach .07 .20
184 Ruben Sierra .15 .40
185 Mark McGwire 1.00 2.50
186 Todd Stottlemyre .07 .20
187 Dennis Eckersley .15 .40
188 Alex Rodriguez 1.00 2.50
189 Randy Johnson .40 1.00
190 Ken Griffey Jr. .75 2.00
191 Tino Martinez .25 .60
192 Jay Buhner .15 .40
193 Edgar Martinez .25 .60
194 Mickey Tettleton .07 .20
195 Juan Gonzalez .15 .40
196 Benji Gil .07 .20
197 Dean Palmer .15 .40
198 Ivan Rodriguez .25 .60
199 Kenny Rogers .15 .40
200 Will Clark .25 .60
201 Roberto Alomar .25 .60
202 David Cone .15 .40
203 Paul Molitor .15 .40
204 Shawn Green .15 .40
205 Joe Carter .15 .40
206 Alex Gonzalez .07 .20
207 Pat Hentgen .07 .20
P100 Ken Griffey Jr. Promo 1.00 2.50
AU100 Ken Griffey Jr. AU 30.00 60.00

1995 SP Silver

COMPLETE SET (207) 40.00 100.00
*STARS: 1X TO 2.5X BASIC CARDS
*ROOKIES: .75X TO 2X BASIC CARDS
ONE PER PACK

1995 SP Platinum Power

This 20-card set was randomly inserted in packs at a rate of one in five. This die-cut set is comprised of the top home run hitters in baseball.

COMPLETE SET (20) 8.00 20.00
STATED ODDS 1:5
PP1 Jeff Bagwell .30 .75
PP2 Barry Bonds 1.25 3.00
PP3 Ron Gant .20 .50
PP4 Fred McGriff .30 .75
PP5 Raul Mondesi .20 .50
PP6 Mike Piazza .75 2.00
PP7 Larry Walker .20 .50
PP8 Matt Williams .20 .50
PP9 Albert Belle .20 .50
PP10 Cecil Fielder .20 .50
PP11 Juan Gonzalez .20 .50
PP12 Ken Griffey Jr. 1.00 2.50
PP13 Mark McGwire 1.25 3.00
PP14 Eddie Murray .50 1.25
PP15 Manny Ramirez .30 .75
PP16 Cal Ripken 1.50 4.00
PP17 Tim Salmon .30 .75
PP18 Frank Thomas .50 1.25
PP19 Jim Thome .30 .75
PP20 Mo Vaughn .20 .50

1995 SP Special FX

This 48-card set was randomly inserted in packs at a rate of one in 75. The set is comprised of the top names in baseball. The cards are numbered on the back "X/48."

COMPLETE SET (48) 50.00 120.00
STATED ODDS 1:75
1 Jose Canseco 1.00 2.50
2 Roger Clemens 3.00 8.00
3 Mo Vaughn .75 2.00
4 Tim Salmon .75 2.00
5 Chuck Finley .75 2.00
6 Robin Ventura .75 2.00
7 Jason Bere .75 2.00
8 Carlos Baerga .75 2.00
9 Albert Belle .75 2.00
10 Kenny Lofton .75 2.00
11 Manny Ramirez 1.25 3.00
12 Jeff Montgomery .75 2.00
13 Kirby Puckett 2.00 5.00
14 Wade Boggs 1.25 3.00
15 Don Mattingly 4.00 10.00
16 Cal Ripken 6.00 15.00
17 Ruben Sierra .75 2.00
18 Ken Griffey Jr. 10.00 25.00
19 Randy Johnson 2.00 5.00
20 Alex Rodriguez 6.00 15.00
21 Will Clark .75 2.00
22 Juan Gonzalez 1.25 3.00
23 Roberto Alomar 1.25 3.00
24 Joe Carter .75 2.00
25 Alex Gonzalez .75 2.00
26 Paul Molitor 2.00 5.00
27 Ryan Klesko .75 2.00
28 Fred McGriff 1.25 3.00
29 Greg Maddux 6.00 15.00
30 Sammy Sosa 2.00 5.00
31 Bret Boone .75 2.00
32 Barry Larkin 1.25 3.00
33 Reggie Sanders .75 2.00
34 Dante Bichette .75 2.00
35 Andres Galarraga 1.25 3.00
36 Charles Johnson .75 2.00
37 Gary Sheffield .75 2.00
38 Jeff Bagwell 1.25 3.00
39 Craig Biggio 1.25 3.00
40 Eric Karros .75 2.00
41 Billy Ashley .75 2.00
42 Raul Mondesi .75 2.00
43 Mike Piazza 2.00 5.00
44 Rondell White .75 2.00
45 Bret Saberhagen .75 2.00
46 Tony Gwynn 2.00 5.00
47 Melvin Nieves .75 2.00
48 Matt Williams .75 2.00

1996 SP Previews FanFest

These eight standard-size cards were issued to promote the 1996 Upper Deck SP Issue. The fronts feature a color action photo as well as a small inset player shot. The 1996 All-Star game logo as well as the SP logo are on the bottom left corner. The backs have another photo as well as some biographical information.

COMPLETE SET (8)	15.00	40.00
1 Ken Griffey Jr.	4.00	10.00
2 Frank Thomas	1.50	4.00
3 Albert Belle	.60	1.50
4 Mo Vaughn	.60	1.50
5 Barry Bonds	2.50	6.00
6 Mike Piazza	4.00	10.00
7 Matt Williams	.75	2.00
8 Sammy Sosa	2.00	5.00

1996 SP

The 1996 SP set was issued in one series totalling 188 cards. The eight-card packs retailed for $4.19 each. Cards number 1-20 feature color action player photos with "Premier Prospects" printed in silver foil across the top and the player's name and team at the bottom in the border. The backs carry player information and statistics. Cards number 21-185 display unique player photos with an outer wood-grain border and inner thin platinum foil border as well as a small inset player shot. The only notable Rookie Card in this set is Darin Erstad.

COMPLETE SET (188)	12.00	30.00
SUBSET CARDS HALF VALUE OF BASE CARDS		
1 Rey Ordonez FOIL	.15	.40
2 George Arias FOIL	.15	.40
3 Osvaldo Fernandez FOIL	.15	.40
4 Darin Erstad FOIL RC	2.00	5.00
5 Paul Wilson FOIL	.15	.40
6 Richard Hidalgo FOIL	.15	.40
7 Justin Thompson FOIL	.15	.40
8 Jimmy Haynes FOIL	.15	.40
9 Edgar Renteria FOIL	.15	.40
10 Ruben Rivera FOIL	.15	.40
11 Chris Snopek FOIL	.15	.40
12 Billy Wagner FOIL	.15	.40
13 Mike Grace FOIL RC	.15	.40
14 Todd Greene FOIL	.15	.40
15 Karim Garcia FOIL	.15	.40
16 John Wasdin FOIL	.15	.40
17 Jason Kendall FOIL	.15	.40
18 Bob Abreu FOIL	.40	1.00
19 Jermaine Dye FOIL	.15	.40
20 Jason Schmidt FOIL	.25	.60
21 Javy Lopez	.15	.40
22 Ryan Klesko	.15	.40
23 Tom Glavine	.25	.60
24 John Smoltz	.25	.60
25 Greg Maddux	.60	1.50
26 Chipper Jones	.40	1.00
27 Fred McGriff	.25	.60
28 David Justice	.15	.40
29 Roberto Alomar	.25	.60
30 Cal Ripken	1.25	3.00
31 B.J. Surhoff	.15	.40
32 Bobby Bonilla	.15	.40
33 Mike Mussina	.25	.60
34 Randy Myers	.15	.40
35 Rafael Palmeiro	.25	.60
36 Brady Anderson	.15	.40
37 Tim Naehring	.15	.40
38 Jose Canseco	.25	.60
39 Roger Clemens	.75	2.00
40 Mo Vaughn	.15	.40
41 John Valentin	.15	.40
42 Kevin Mitchell	.15	.40
43 Chili Davis	.15	.40
44 Garret Anderson	.15	.40
45 Tim Salmon	.25	.60
46 Chuck Finley	.15	.40
47 Troy Percival	.15	.40
48 Jim Abbott	.25	.60
49 J.T. Snow	.15	.40
50 Jim Edmonds	.15	.40
51 Sammy Sosa	.40	1.00
52 Brian McRae	.15	.40
53 Ryne Sandberg	.60	1.50
54 Jaime Navarro	.15	.40
55 Mark Grace	.25	.60
56 Harold Baines	.15	.40
57 Robin Ventura	.15	.40
58 Tony Phillips	.15	.40
59 Alex Fernandez	.15	.40
60 Frank Thomas	.40	1.00
61 Ray Durham	.15	.40
62 Bret Boone	.15	.40
63 Reggie Sanders	.15	.40
64 Pete Schourek	.15	.40
65 Barry Larkin	.25	.60
66 John Smiley	.15	.40
67 Carlos Baerga	.15	.40
68 Jim Thome	.25	.60
69 Eddie Murray	.40	1.00
70 Albert Belle	.15	.40
71 Dennis Martinez	.15	.40
72 Jack McDowell	.15	.40
73 Kenny Lofton	.15	.40
74 Manny Ramirez	.25	.60
75 Dante Bichette	.15	.40
76 Vinny Castilla	.15	.40
77 Andres Galarraga	.15	.40
78 Walt Weiss	.15	.40
79 Ellis Burks	.15	.40
80 Larry Walker	.15	.40
81 Cecil Fielder	.15	.40
82 Melvin Nieves	.15	.40
83 Travis Fryman	.15	.40
84 Chad Curtis	.15	.40
85 Alan Trammell	.15	.40
86 Gary Sheffield	.15	.40
87 Charles Johnson	.15	.40
88 Andre Dawson	.15	.40
89 Jeff Conine	.15	.40
90 Greg Colbrunn	.15	.40
91 Derek Bell	.15	.40
92 Brian L.Hunter	.15	.40
93 Doug Drabek	.15	.40
94 Craig Biggio	.25	.60
95 Jeff Bagwell	.25	.60
96 Kevin Appier	.15	.40
97 Jeff Montgomery	.15	.40
98 Michael Tucker	.15	.40
99 Bip Roberts	.15	.40
100 Johnny Damon	.25	.60
101 Eric Karros	.15	.40
102 Raul Mondesi	.15	.40
103 Ramon Martinez	.15	.40
104 Ismael Valdes	.15	.40
105 Mike Piazza	.60	1.50
106 Hideo Nomo	.40	1.00
107 Chan Ho Park	.15	.40
108 Ben McDonald	.15	.40
109 Kevin Seitzer	.15	.40
110 Greg Vaughn	.15	.40
111 Jose Valentin	.15	.40
112 Rick Aguilera	.15	.40
113 Marty Cordova	.15	.40
114 Brad Radke	.15	.40
115 Kirby Puckett	.40	1.00
116 Chuck Knoblauch	.15	.40
117 Paul Molitor	.15	.40
118 Pedro Martinez	.25	.60
119 Mike Lansing	.15	.40
120 Rondell White	.15	.40
121 Moises Alou	.15	.40
122 Mark Grudzielanek	.15	.40
123 Jeff Fassero	.15	.40
124 Rico Brogna	.15	.40
125 Jason Isringhausen	.15	.40
126 Jeff Kent	.15	.40
127 Bernard Gilkey	.15	.40
128 Todd Hundley	.15	.40
129 David Cone	.15	.40
130 Andy Pettitte	.25	.60
131 Wade Boggs	.25	.60
132 Paul O'Neill	.25	.60
133 Ruben Sierra	.15	.40
134 John Wetteland	.15	.40
135 Derek Jeter	1.00	2.50
136 Geronimo Berroa	.15	.40
137 Terry Steinbach	.15	.40
138 Ariel Prieto	.15	.40
139 Scott Brosius	.15	.40
140 Mark McGwire	1.00	2.50
141 Lenny Dykstra	.15	.40
142 Todd Zeile	.15	.40
143 Benito Santiago	.15	.40
144 Mickey Morandini	.15	.40
145 Gregg Jefferies	.15	.40
146 Denny Neagle	.15	.40
147 Orlando Merced	.15	.40
148 Charlie Hayes	.15	.40
149 Carlos Garcia	.15	.40
150 Jay Bell	.15	.40
151 Ray Lankford	.15	.40
152 Alan Benes	.15	.40
Andy Benes		
153 Dennis Eckersley	.15	.40
154 Gary Gaetti	.15	.40
155 Ozzie Smith	.60	1.50
156 Ron Gant	.15	.40
157 Brian Jordan	.15	.40
158 Ken Caminiti	.15	.40
159 Rickey Henderson	.40	1.00
160 Tony Gwynn	.50	1.25
161 Wally Joyner	.15	.40
162 Andy Ashby	.15	.40
163 Steve Finley	.15	.40
164 Glenallen Hill	.15	.40
165 Matt Williams	.15	.40
166 Barry Bonds	1.00	2.50
167 William VanLandingham	.15	.40
168 Rod Beck	.15	.40
169 Randy Johnson	.40	1.00
170 Ken Griffey Jr.	.75	2.00
171 Alex Rodriguez	.75	2.00
172 Edgar Martinez	.25	.60
173 Jay Buhner	.15	.40
174 Russ Davis	.15	.40
175 Juan Gonzalez	.15	.40
176 Mickey Tettleton	.15	.40
177 Will Clark	.25	.60
178 Ken Hill	.15	.40
179 Dean Palmer	.15	.40
180 Ivan Rodriguez	.25	.60
181 Carlos Delgado	.15	.40
182 Alex Gonzalez	.15	.40
183 Shawn Green	.15	.40
184 Juan Guzman	.15	.40
185 Joe Carter	.15	.40
186 Hideo Nomo CL	.25	.60
187 Cal Ripken CL	.60	1.50
188 Ken Griffey Jr. CL	.50	1.25

1996 SP Baseball Heroes

This 10-card set was randomly inserted at the rate of one in 96 packs. It continues the insert set that was started in 1990 featuring ten of the top players in baseball. Please note these cards are condition sensitive and trade for premiums in Mint.

COMPLETE SET (10)	30.00	80.00
STATED ODDS 1:96		
CONDITION SENSITIVE SET		
82 Frank Thomas	4.00	10.00
83 Albert Belle	1.50	4.00
84 Barry Bonds	6.00	15.00
85 Chipper Jones	4.00	10.00
86 Hideo Nomo	4.00	10.00
87 Mike Piazza	4.00	10.00
88 Manny Ramirez	2.50	6.00
89 Greg Maddux	6.00	15.00
90 Ken Griffey Jr.	8.00	20.00
NNO Ken Griffey Jr. HDR	8.00	20.00

1996 SP Marquee Matchups

Randomly inserted at the rate of one in five packs, this 20-card set highlights two superstars' cards with a common matching stadium background photograph in a blue border.

COMPLETE SET (20)	15.00	40.00
STATED ODDS 1:5		
*DIE CUTS: 1.2X TO 3X BASIC MARQUEE		
DC STATED ODDS 1:61		
MM1 Ken Griffey Jr.	2.00	5.00
MM2 Hideo Nomo	1.00	2.50
MM3 Derek Jeter	2.50	6.00
MM4 Rey Ordonez	.40	1.00
MM5 Tim Salmon	.40	1.00
MM6 Mike Piazza	1.00	2.50
MM7 Mark McGwire	1.50	4.00
MM8 Barry Bonds	1.50	4.00
MM9 Cal Ripken	3.00	8.00
MM10 Greg Maddux	1.50	4.00
MM11 Albert Belle	.40	1.00
MM12 Barry Larkin	.60	1.50
MM13 Jeff Bagwell	.60	1.50
MM14 Juan Gonzalez	.40	1.00
MM15 Frank Thomas	1.00	2.50
MM16 Sammy Sosa	1.00	2.50
MM17 Mike Mussina	.60	1.50
MM18 Chipper Jones	1.00	2.50
MM19 Roger Clemens	1.25	3.00
MM20 Fred McGriff	.60	1.50

1996 SP Special FX

Randomly inserted at the rate of one in five packs, this 48-card set features a color action player cutout on a gold foil background with a holoview diamond shaped insert containing a black-and-white player portrait.

COMPLETE SET (48)	50.00	100.00
STATED ODDS 1:5		
*DIE CUTS: 1X TO 2.5X BASIC SPECIAL FX		
DIE CUTS STATED ODDS 1:75		
1 Greg Maddux	3.00	8.00
2 Eric Karros	.75	2.00
3 Mike Piazza	3.00	8.00
4 Raul Mondesi	.75	2.00
5 Hideo Nomo	2.00	5.00
6 Jim Edmonds	.75	2.00
7 Jason Isringhausen	.75	2.00
8 Jay Buhner	.75	2.00
9 Barry Larkin	1.25	3.00
10 Ken Griffey Jr.	4.00	10.00
11 Gary Sheffield	.75	2.00
12 Craig Biggio	1.25	3.00
13 Paul Wilson	.75	2.00
14 Rondell White	.75	2.00
15 Chipper Jones	2.00	5.00
16 Kirby Puckett	2.00	5.00
17 Ron Gant	.75	2.00
18 Wade Boggs	1.25	3.00
19 Fred McGriff	1.25	3.00
20 Cal Ripken	6.00	15.00
21 Jason Kendall	.75	2.00
22 Johnny Damon	1.25	3.00
23 Kenny Lofton	.75	2.00
24 Roberto Alomar	1.25	3.00
25 Barry Bonds	5.00	12.00
26 Dante Bichette	.75	2.00
27 Mark McGwire	5.00	12.00
28 Rafael Palmeiro	1.25	3.00
29 Juan Gonzalez	.75	2.00
30 Albert Belle	.75	2.00
31 Randy Johnson	2.00	5.00
32 Jose Canseco	1.25	3.00
33 Sammy Sosa	2.00	5.00
34 Eddie Murray	2.00	5.00
35 Frank Thomas	2.00	5.00
36 Tom Glavine	1.25	3.00
37 Matt Williams	.75	2.00
38 Roger Clemens	4.00	10.00
39 Paul Molitor	.75	2.00
40 Tony Gwynn	2.50	6.00
41 Mo Vaughn	.75	2.00
42 Tim Salmon	1.25	3.00
43 Manny Ramirez	1.25	3.00
44 Jeff Bagwell	1.25	3.00
45 Edgar Martinez	1.25	3.00
46 Rey Ordonez	.75	2.00
47 Osvaldo Fernandez	.75	2.00
48 Derek Jeter	5.00	12.00

1997 SP

The 1997 SP set was issued in one series totalling 183 cards and was distributed in eight-card packs with a suggested retail of $4.39. Although unconfirmed by the manufacturer, it is perceived in some circles that cards numbered between 160 and 180 are in slightly shorter supply. Notable Rookie Cards include Jose Cruz Jr. and Hideki Irabu.

COMPLETE SET (184)	15.00	40.00
1 Andruw Jones FOIL	.40	1.00
2 Kevin Orie FOIL	.20	.50
3 Nomar Garciaparra FOIL	1.00	2.50
4 Jose Guillen FOIL	.30	.75
5 Todd Walker FOIL	.20	.50
6 Derrick Gibson FOIL	.20	.50
7 Aaron Boone FOIL	.30	.75
8 Bartolo Colon FOIL	.30	.75
9 Derrek Lee FOIL	.40	1.00
10 Vladimir Guerrero FOIL	.60	1.50
11 Wilton Guerrero FOIL	.20	.50
12 Luis Castillo FOIL	.20	.50
13 Jason Dickson FOIL	.20	.50
14 Bubba Trammell FOIL RC	.30	.75
15 Jose Cruz Jr. FOIL RC	.30	.75
16 Eddie Murray	.40	1.00
17 Darin Erstad	.15	.40
18 Garret Anderson	.15	.40
19 Jim Edmonds	.15	.40
20 Tim Salmon	.25	.60
21 Chuck Finley	.15	.40
22 John Smoltz	.25	.60
23 Greg Maddux	.60	1.50
24 Kenny Lofton	.15	.40
25 Chipper Jones	.40	1.00
26 Ryan Klesko	.15	.40
27 Javy Lopez	.15	.40
28 Fred McGriff	.25	.60
29 Roberto Alomar	.25	.60
30 Rafael Palmeiro	.25	.60
31 Mike Mussina	.25	.60
32 Brady Anderson	.15	.40
33 Rocky Coppinger	.15	.40
34 Cal Ripken	1.25	3.00
35 Mo Vaughn	.15	.40
36 Steve Avery	.15	.40
37 Tom Gordon	.15	.40
38 Tim Naehring	.15	.40
39 Troy O'Leary	.15	.40
40 Sammy Sosa	.40	1.00
41 Brian McRae	.15	.40
42 Mel Rojas	.15	.40
43 Ryne Sandberg	.60	1.50
44 Mark Grace	.25	.60
45 Albert Belle	.15	.40
46 Robin Ventura	.15	.40
47 Roberto Hernandez	.15	.40
48 Ray Durham	.15	.40
49 Harold Baines	.15	.40
50 Frank Thomas	.40	1.00
51 Bret Boone	.15	.40
52 Reggie Sanders	.15	.40
53 Deion Sanders	.25	.60
54 Hal Morris	.15	.40
55 Barry Larkin	.25	.60
56 Jim Thome	.25	.60
57 Marquis Grissom	.15	.40
58 David Justice	.15	.40
59 Charles Nagy	.15	.40
60 Manny Ramirez	.25	.60
61 Matt Williams	.15	.40
62 Jack McDowell	.15	.40
63 Vinny Castilla	.15	.40
64 Dante Bichette	.15	.40
65 Andres Galarraga	.15	.40
66 Ellis Burks	.15	.40
67 Larry Walker	.15	.40
68 Eric Young	.15	.40
69 Brian L. Hunter	.15	.40
70 Travis Fryman	.15	.40
71 Tony Clark	.15	.40
72 Bobby Higginson	.15	.40
73 Melvin Nieves	.15	.40
74 Jeff Conine	.15	.40
75 Gary Sheffield	.15	.40
76 Moises Alou	.15	.40
77 Edgar Renteria	.15	.40
78 Alex Fernandez	.15	.40
79 Charles Johnson	.15	.40
80 Bobby Bonilla	.15	.40
81 Darryl Kile	.15	.40
82 Derek Bell	.15	.40
83 Shane Reynolds	.15	.40
84 Craig Biggio	.25	.60
85 Jeff Bagwell	.25	.60
86 Billy Wagner	.15	.40
87 Chili Davis	.15	.40
88 Kevin Appier	.15	.40
89 Jay Bell	.15	.40
90 Johnny Damon	.25	.60
91 Jeff King	.15	.40
92 Hideo Nomo	.40	1.00
93 Todd Hollandsworth	.15	.40
94 Eric Karros	.15	.40
95 Mike Piazza	.60	1.50
96 Ramon Martinez	.15	.40
97 Todd Worrell	.15	.40
98 Raul Mondesi	.15	.40
99 Dave Nilsson	.15	.40
100 John Jaha	.15	.40
101 Jose Valentin	.15	.40
102 Jeff Cirillo	.15	.40
103 Jeff D'Amico	.15	.40
104 Ben McDonald	.15	.40
105 Paul Molitor	.15	.40
106 Rich Becker	.15	.40
107 Frank Rodriguez	.15	.40
108 Marty Cordova	.15	.40
109 Terry Steinbach	.15	.40
110 Chuck Knoblauch	.15	.40
111 Mark Grudzielanek	.15	.40
112 Mike Lansing	.15	.40
113 Pedro Martinez	.25	.60
114 Henry Rodriguez	.15	.40
115 Rondell White	.15	.40
116 Rey Ordonez	.15	.40
117 Carlos Baerga	.15	.40
118 Lance Johnson	.15	.40
119 Bernard Gilkey	.15	.40
120 Todd Hundley	.15	.40
121 John Franco	.15	.40
122 Bernie Williams	.25	.60
123 David Cone	.15	.40
124 Cecil Fielder	.15	.40
125 Derek Jeter	1.00	2.50
126 Tino Martinez	.25	.60
127 Mariano Rivera	.40	1.00
128 Andy Pettitte	.25	.60
129 Wade Boggs	.25	.60
130 Mark McGwire	1.00	2.50
131 Jose Canseco	.25	.60
132 Geronimo Berroa	.15	.40
133 Jason Giambi	.15	.40
134 Ernie Young	.15	.40
135 Scott Rolen	.25	.60
136 Ricky Bottalico	.15	.40
137 Curt Schilling	.15	.40
138 Gregg Jefferies	.15	.40
139 Mickey Morandini	.15	.40
140 Jason Kendall	.15	.40
141 Kevin Elster	.15	.40
142 Al Martin	.15	.40
143 Joe Randa	.15	.40
144 Jason Schmidt	.15	.40
145 Ray Lankford	.15	.40
146 Brian Jordan	.15	.40
147 Andy Benes	.15	.40
148 Alan Benes	.15	.40
149 Gary Gaetti	.15	.40
150 Ron Gant	.15	.40
151 Dennis Eckersley	.15	.40
152 Rickey Henderson	.40	1.00
153 Joey Hamilton	.15	.40
154 Ken Caminiti	.15	.40
155 Tony Gwynn	.50	1.25
156 Steve Finley	.15	.40
157 Trevor Hoffman	.15	.40
158 Greg Vaughn	.15	.40
159 J.T. Snow	.15	.40
160 Barry Bonds	1.00	2.50
161 Glenallen Hill	.15	.40
162 Bill Van Landingham	.15	.40
163 Jeff Kent	.15	.40
164 Jay Buhner	.15	.40
165 Ken Griffey Jr.	.75	2.00
166 Alex Rodriguez	.60	1.50
167 Randy Johnson	.40	1.00
168 Edgar Martinez	.25	.60
169 Dan Wilson	.15	.40
170 Ivan Rodriguez	.25	.60
171 Roger Pavlik	.15	.40
172 Will Clark	.25	.60
173 Dean Palmer	.15	.40
174 Rusty Greer	.15	.40
175 Juan Gonzalez	.15	.40
176 John Wetteland	.15	.40
177 Joe Carter	.15	.40
178 Ed Sprague	.15	.40
179 Carlos Delgado	.15	.40
180 Roger Clemens	.75	2.00
181 Juan Guzman	.15	.40
182 Pat Hentgen	.15	.40
183 Ken Griffey Jr. CL	.50	1.25
184 Hideki Irabu RC	.15	.40

1997 SP Game Film

Randomly inserted in packs, this 10-card set features actual game film that highlights the accomplishments of some of the League's greatest players. Only 500 of each card in this crash numbered, limited edition set were produced.

COMPLETE SET (10)	125.00	250.00
RANDOM INSERTS IN PACKS		
STATED PRINT RUN 500 SERIAL #'d SETS		
GF1 Alex Rodriguez	12.00	30.00
GF2 Frank Thomas	10.00	25.00
GF3 Andruw Jones	4.00	10.00
GF4 Cal Ripken	30.00	80.00
GF5 Mike Piazza	10.00	25.00
GF6 Derek Jeter	25.00	60.00
GF7 Mark McGwire	15.00	40.00
GF8 Chipper Jones	10.00	25.00
GF9 Barry Bonds	15.00	40.00
GF10 Ken Griffey Jr.	20.00	50.00

1997 SP Griffey Heroes

This 10-card continuation insert set pays special tribute to one of the game's most talented players and features color photos of Ken Griffey Jr. Only 2,000 of each card in this crash numbered, limited edition set were produced.

COMPLETE SET (10)	20.00	50.00
COMMON CARD (91-100)	3.00	8.00

1997 SP Inside Info

Inserted one in every 30-pack box, this 25-card set features color player photos on original cards with an exclusive pull-out panel that details the accomplishments of the League's brightest stars. Please note these cards are condition sensitive and trade for premium values in Mint condition.

COMPLETE SET (25)	75.00	150.00
ONE PER SEALED BOX		
CONDITION SENSITIVE SET		
1 Ken Griffey Jr.	5.00	12.00
2 Mark McGwire	6.00	15.00
3 Kenny Lofton	1.00	2.50
4 Paul Molitor	1.00	2.50
5 Frank Thomas	2.50	6.00
6 Greg Maddux	4.00	10.00
7 Mo Vaughn	1.00	2.50
8 Cal Ripken	8.00	20.00
9 Jeff Bagwell	1.50	4.00
10 Alex Rodriguez	4.00	10.00
11 John Smoltz	1.50	4.00
12 Manny Ramirez	1.50	4.00
13 Sammy Sosa	2.50	6.00
14 Vladimir Guerrero	4.00	10.00
15 Albert Belle	1.00	2.50
16 Mike Piazza	4.00	10.00
17 Derek Jeter	6.00	15.00
18 Scott Rolen	1.50	4.00
19 Tony Gwynn	3.00	8.00
20 Barry Bonds	6.00	15.00
21 Ken Caminiti	1.00	2.50
22 Chipper Jones	2.50	6.00
23 Juan Gonzalez	1.00	2.50
24 Roger Clemens	5.00	12.00
25 Andruw Jones	2.50	6.00

1997 SP Marquee Matchups

Randomly inserted in packs at a rate of one in five, this 20-card set features color player images on die-cut cards that match-up the best pitchers and hitters from around the League.

COMPLETE SET (20)	20.00	50.00
STATED ODDS 1:5		
MM1 Ken Griffey Jr.	1.50	4.00
MM2 Andres Galarraga	.30	.75
MM3 Barry Bonds	2.00	5.00
MM4 Mark McGwire	2.00	5.00
MM5 Mike Piazza	1.25	3.00
MM6 Tim Salmon	.50	1.25
MM7 Tony Gwynn	1.00	2.50
MM8 Alex Rodriguez	1.25	3.0
MM9 Chipper Jones	.75	2.0
MM10 Derek Jeter	2.00	5.0
MM11 Manny Ramirez	.50	1.2
MM12 Jeff Bagwell	.50	1.2
MM13 Greg Maddux	1.25	3.0
MM14 Cal Ripken	2.50	6.0
MM15 Mo Vaughn	.30	.7
MM16 Gary Sheffield	.30	.7
MM17 Jim Thome	.50	1.2
MM18 Barry Larkin	.50	1.2
MM19 Frank Thomas	.75	2.0
MM20 Sammy Sosa	.75	2.0

1997 SP Special FX

Randomly inserted in packs at a rate of one in nine, this 48-card set features color player photos on Holoview cards with the Special F/X die-cut design. Cards numbers 1-47 are from 1997 with card number 49 featuring a design from 1996. There is no card number 48.

COMPLETE SET (48)	100.00	200.0
STATED ODDS 1:9		
1 Ken Griffey Jr.	4.00	10.0
2 Frank Thomas	2.00	5.0
3 Barry Bonds	5.00	12.0
4 Albert Belle	.75	2.0
5 Mike Piazza	3.00	8.0
6 Greg Maddux	3.00	8.0
7 Chipper Jones	2.00	5.0
8 Cal Ripken	6.00	15.0
9 Jeff Bagwell	1.25	3.0
10 Alex Rodriguez	3.00	8.0
11 Mark McGwire	5.00	12.0
12 Kenny Lofton	.75	2.0
13 Juan Gonzalez	.75	2.0
14 Mo Vaughn	.75	2.0
15 John Smoltz	1.25	3.0
16 Derek Jeter	5.00	12.0
17 Tony Gwynn	2.50	6.0
18 Ivan Rodriguez	1.25	3.0
19 Barry Larkin	1.25	3.0
20 Sammy Sosa	2.00	5.0
21 Mike Mussina	1.25	3.0
22 Gary Sheffield	.75	2.0
23 Brady Anderson	.75	2.0
24 Roger Clemens	4.00	10.0
25 Ken Caminiti	.75	2.0
26 Roberto Alomar	1.25	3.0
27 Hideo Nomo	2.00	5.0
28 Bernie Williams	1.25	3.0
29 Todd Hundley	.75	2.0
30 Manny Ramirez	1.25	3.0
31 Eric Karros	.75	2.0
32 Tim Salmon	1.25	3.0
33 Jay Buhner	.75	2.0
34 Andy Pettitte	1.25	3.0
35 Jim Thome	1.25	3.0
36 Ryne Sandberg	3.00	8.0
37 Matt Williams	.75	2.0
38 Ryan Klesko	.75	2.0
39 Jose Canseco	1.25	3.0
40 Paul Molitor	.75	2.0
41 Eddie Murray	2.00	5.0
42 Darin Erstad	.75	2.0
43 Todd Walker	1.00	2.5
44 Wade Boggs	1.25	3.0
45 Andruw Jones	2.00	5.0
46 Scott Rolen	1.25	3.0
47 Vladimir Guerrero	3.00	8.0
49 Alex Rodriguez '96	4.00	10.0

1997 SP SPx Force

Randomly inserted in packs, this 10-card die-cut s features head photos of four of the very best players on each card with an "X" in the background and players' and teams' names on one side. Only 500 o each card in this crash numbered, limited edition s were produced.

COMPLETE SET (10)	100.00	200.0
RANDOM INSERTS IN PACKS		
STATED PRINT RUN 500 SERIAL #'d SETS		
1 Griffey Buhn Gala Bich	12.50	30.0
2 McGwire Belle B.And Fielder	15.00.	40.0
3 F.Thom Mo Bagw Camin	6.00	15.0
4 Sosa Bonds Cans Sheff	6.00	15.0
5 Madd Clem Smoltz R.John	10.00	25.0
6 A.Rod Jeter Chipper Ordon	15.00	40.0
7 Piazza Nomo Mond T.Holl	10.00	25.0
8 J.Gonz M.Ram Alom I.Rod	4.00	10.0

9 Gwynn 8.00 20.00
Boggs
Murray
Molit
10 Vlad 10.00 25.00
Rolen
Andruw
T.Walk

1997 SP SPx Force Autographs

Randomly inserted in packs, this 10-card set is an autographed parallel version of the regular SPx Force set. Only 100 of each card in this crash numbered, limited edition set were produced. Mo Vaughn packed out as an exchange card.

STATED PRINT RUN 100 SERIAL #'d SETS
1 Ken Griffey Jr. 150.00 250.00
2 Albert Belle 15.00 40.00
3 Mo Vaughn 15.00 40.00
4 Gary Sheffield 20.00 50.00
5 Greg Maddux 75.00 150.00
6 Alex Rodriguez 100.00 175.00
7 Todd Hollandsworth 10.00 25.00
8 Roberto Alomar 20.00 50.00
9 Tony Gwynn 40.00 80.00
10 Andruw Jones 6.00 15.00

1997 SP Vintage Autographs

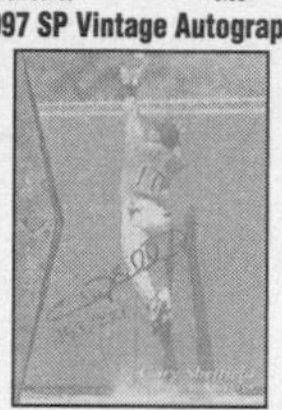

Randomly inserted in packs, this set features authenticated original 1993-1996 SP cards that have been autographed by the pictured player. The print runs are listed after year following the player's name in our checklist. Some of the very short printed autographs are listed but not priced. Each card came in the pack along with a standard size certificate of authenticity. These certificates are usually included when these autographed cards are traded. The 1997 Mo Vaughn card was available only as a mail-in exchange. Upper Deck seeded 250 '97 SP Vaughn cards into packs each carrying a large circular sticker on front. UD sent Mo 300 cards to sign, hoping that he'd sign at least 250 cards and actually received 293 cards back. The additional 43 cards were sent to UD's Quality Assurance area. An additional Mo Vaughn card, hailing from 1995, surfaced in early 2001. This set now stands as one of the most important issues of the 1990's in that it was the first to feature the popular "buy-back" concept widely used in the 2000's.

RANDOM INSERTS IN PACKS
PRINT RUNS B/WN 4-367 COPIES PER
NO PRICING ON QTY OF 25 OR LESS
1 Jeff Bagwell 93/7
2 Jeff Bagwell 95/173 30.00 60.00
3 Jeff Bagwell 96/292 12.00 30.00
4 Jeff Bagwell 96 MM/23
5 Jay Buhner 95/57 6.00 15.00
6 Jay Buhner 96/79 6.00 15.00
7 Jay Buhner 96 FX/27 6.00 15.00
8 Ken Griffey Jr. 93/16
9 Ken Griffey Jr. 93 PP/5
10 Ken Griffey Jr. 94/103 50.00 100.00
11 Ken Griffey Jr. 95/38 75.00 150.00
12 Ken Griffey Jr. 96/312 40.00 80.00
13 Tony Gwynn 93/17
14 Tony Gwynn 94/367 15.00 40.00
15 Tony Gwynn 94 HV/31 60.00 120.00
16 Tony Gwynn 95/64 30.00 60.00
17 Tony Gwynn 96/20
18 Todd Hollandsworth 94/167 6.00 15.00
19 Chipper Jones 93/34 50.00 100.00
20 Chipper Jones 95/60 40.00 80.00
21 Chipper Jones 96/102 30.00 60.00
22 Rey Ordonez 96/111 6.00 15.00
23 Rey Ordonez 96 MM/40 10.00 25.00
24 Alex Rodriguez 94/94 1000.00 1600.00
25 Alex Rodriguez 95/63 60.00 120.00
26 Alex Rodriguez 96/73 60.00 120.00
27 Gary Sheffield 94/130 15.00 40.00
28 Gary Sheffield 94 HVDC/4
29 Gary Sheffield 95/221 10.00 25.00
30 Gary Sheffield 96/58 30.00 60.00
31 Mo Vaughn 95/75 6.00 15.00
32 Mo Vaughn 97/293 6.00 15.00

1998 SP Authentic

The 1998 SP Authentic set was issued in one series totalling 198 cards. The five-card packs retailed for $4.99 each. The set contains the topical subset: Future Watch (1-30). Rookie Cards include Magglio Ordonez. A sample card featuring Ken Griffey Jr. was issued prior to the product's release and distributed along with dealer order forms. The card is identical to the basic issue Griffey Jr. card (number 123) except for the term "SAMPLE" in red print running diagonally against the card back.

COMPLETE SET (198) 15.00 40.00
1 Travis Lee FOIL .15 .40
2 Mike Caruso FOIL .15 .40
3 Kerry Wood FOIL .20 .50
4 Mark Kotsay FOIL .15 .40
5 Magglio Ordonez FOIL RC 5.00 12.00
6 Scott Elarton FOIL .15 .40
7 Carl Pavano FOIL .15 .40
8 A.J. Hinch FOIL .15 .40
9 Rolando Arrojo FOIL RC .15 .40
10 Ben Grieve FOIL .15 .40
11 Gabe Alvarez FOIL .15 .40
12 Mike Kinkade FOIL RC .15 .40
13 Bruce Chen FOIL .15 .40
14 Juan Encarnacion FOIL .15 .40
15 Todd Helton FOIL .25 .60
16 Aaron Boone FOIL .15 .40
17 Sean Casey FOIL .15 .40
18 Ramon Hernandez FOIL .15 .40
19 Daryle Ward FOIL .15 .40
20 Paul Konerko FOIL .15 .40
21 David Ortiz FOIL .50 1.25
22 Derrek Lee FOIL .25 .60
23 Brad Fullmer FOIL .15 .40
24 Javier Vazquez FOIL .15 .40
25 Miguel Tejada FOIL .40 1.00
26 Dave Dellucci FOIL RC .25 .60
27 Alex Gonzalez FOIL .15 .40
28 Matt Clement FOIL .15 .40
29 Masato Yoshii FOIL RC .15 .40
30 Russell Branyan FOIL .15 .40
31 Chuck Finley .15 .40
32 Jim Edmonds .15 .40
33 Darin Erstad .15 .40
34 Jason Dickson .15 .40
35 Tim Salmon .25 .60
36 Cecil Fielder .15 .40
37 Todd Greene .15 .40
38 Andy Benes .15 .40
39 Jay Bell .15 .40
40 Matt Williams .15 .40
41 Brian Anderson .15 .40
42 Karim Garcia .15 .40
43 Javy Lopez .15 .40
44 Tom Glavine .25 .60
45 Greg Maddux .60 1.50
46 Andruw Jones .25 .60
47 Chipper Jones .40 1.00
48 Ryan Klesko .15 .40
49 John Smoltz .25 .60
50 Andres Galarraga .15 .40
51 Rafael Palmeiro .25 .60
52 Mike Mussina .25 .60
53 Roberto Alomar .25 .60
54 Joe Carter .15 .40
55 Cal Ripken 1.25 3.00
56 Brady Anderson .15 .40
57 Mo Vaughn .15 .40
58 John Valentin .15 .40
59 Dennis Eckersley .15 .40
60 Nomar Garciaparra .60 1.50
61 Pedro Martinez .25 .60
62 Jeff Blauser .15 .40
63 Kevin Orie .15 .40
64 Henry Rodriguez .15 .40
65 Mark Grace .25 .60
66 Albert Belle .15 .40
67 Mike Cameron .15 .40
68 Robin Ventura .15 .40
69 Frank Thomas .40 1.00
70 Barry Larkin .25 .60
71 Brett Tomko .15 .40
72 Willie Greene .15 .40
73 Reggie Sanders .15 .40
74 Sandy Alomar Jr. .15 .40
75 Kenny Lofton .15 .40
76 Jaret Wright .15 .40
77 David Justice .15 .40
78 Omar Vizquel .25 .60
79 Manny Ramirez .25 .60
80 Jim Thome .25 .60
81 Travis Fryman .15 .40
82 Neifi Perez .15 .40
83 Mike Lansing .15 .40
84 Vinny Castilla .15 .40
85 Larry Walker .15 .40
86 Dante Bichette .15 .40
87 Darryl Kile .15 .40
88 Justin Thompson .15 .40
89 Damion Easley .15 .40
90 Tony Clark .15 .40
91 Bobby Higginson .15 .40
92 Brian Hunter .15 .40
93 Edgar Renteria .15 .40
94 Craig Counsell .15 .40
95 Mike Piazza .60 1.50
96 Livan Hernandez .15 .40
97 Todd Zeile .15 .40
98 Richard Hidalgo .15 .40
99 Moises Alou .15 .40
100 Jeff Bagwell .25 .60
101 Mike Hampton .15 .40
102 Craig Biggio .25 .60
103 Dean Palmer .15 .40
104 Tim Belcher .15 .40
105 Jeff King .15 .40
106 Jeff Conine .15 .40
107 Johnny Damon .25 .60
108 Hideo Nomo .40 1.00
109 Raul Mondesi .15 .40
110 Gary Sheffield .15 .40
111 Ramon Martinez .15 .40
112 Chan Ho Park .15 .40
113 Eric Young .15 .40
114 Charles Johnson .15 .40
115 Eric Karros .15 .40
116 Bobby Bonilla .15 .40
117 Jeromy Burnitz .15 .40
118 Cal Eldred .15 .40
119 Jeff D'Amico .15 .40
120 Marquis Grissom .15 .40
121 Dave Nilsson .15 .40
122 Brad Radke .15 .40
123 Marty Cordova .15 .40
124 Ron Coomer .15 .40
125 Paul Molitor .15 .40
126 Todd Walker .15 .40
127 Rondell White .15 .40
128 Mark Grudzielanek .15 .40
129 Carlos Perez .15 .40
130 Vladimir Guerrero .40 1.00
131 Dustin Hermanson .15 .40
132 Butch Huskey .15 .40
133 John Franco .15 .40
134 Rey Ordonez .15 .40
135 Todd Hundley .15 .40
136 Edgardo Alfonzo .15 .40
137 Bobby Jones .15 .40
138 John Olerud .15 .40
139 Chili Davis .15 .40
140 Tino Martinez .25 .60
141 Andy Pettitte .25 .60
142 Chuck Knoblauch .15 .40
143 Bernie Williams .25 .60
144 David Cone .15 .40
145 Derek Jeter 1.00 2.50
146 Paul O'Neill .25 .60
147 Rickey Henderson .40 1.00
148 Jason Giambi .15 .40
149 Kenny Rogers .15 .40
150 Scott Rolen .25 .60
151 Curt Schilling .15 .40
152 Ricky Bottalico .15 .40
153 Mike Lieberthal .15 .40
154 Francisco Cordova .15 .40
155 Jose Guillen .15 .40
156 Jason Schmidt .15 .40
157 Jason Kendall .15 .40
158 Kevin Young .15 .40
159 Delino DeShields .15 .40
160 Mark McGwire 1.00 2.50
161 Ray Lankford .15 .40
162 Brian Jordan .15 .40
163 Ron Gant .15 .40
164 Todd Stottlemyre .15 .40
165 Ken Caminiti .15 .40
166 Kevin Brown .25 .60
167 Trevor Hoffman .15 .40
168 Steve Finley .15 .40
169 Wally Joyner .15 .40
170 Tony Gwynn .50 1.25
171 Shawn Estes .15 .40
172 J.T. Snow .15 .40
173 Jeff Kent .15 .40
174 Robb Nen .15 .40
175 Barry Bonds 1.00 2.50
176 Randy Johnson .40 1.00
177 Edgar Martinez .25 .60
178 Jay Buhner .15 .40
179 Alex Rodriguez .60 1.50
180 Ken Griffey Jr. .75 2.00
181 Ken Cloude .15 .40
182 Wade Boggs .25 .60
183 Tony Saunders .15 .40
184 Wilson Alvarez .15 .40
185 Fred McGriff .25 .60
186 Roberto Hernandez .15 .40
187 Kevin Stocker .15 .40
188 Fernando Tatis .15 .40
189 Will Clark .25 .60
190 Juan Gonzalez .15 .40
191 Rusty Greer .15 .40
192 Ivan Rodriguez .25 .60
193 Jose Canseco .25 .60
194 Carlos Delgado .15 .40
195 Roger Clemens .75 2.00
196 Pat Hentgen .15 .40
197 Randy Myers .15 .40
198 Ken Griffey Jr. CL .50 1.25
S123 Ken Griffey Jr. Sample 1.00 2.50

1998 SP Authentic Chirography

Randomly inserted in packs at a rate of one in 25, this 31-card set is autographed by the league's top players. The Ken Griffey Jr. card was actually not available in packs. Instead, an exchange card was printed and seeded into packs. Collectors had until July 27th, 1999 to redeem these Griffey exchange cards. A selection of players were short-printed to 400 or 800 copies. These cards, however, are not serial numbered.

STATED ODDS 1:25
1000 OR MORE OF EACH UNLESS STATED
SP PRINT RUNS STATED BELOW
GRIFFEY EXCH.DEADLINE 07/27/99
AJ Andruw Jones 6.00 15.00
AR Alex Rodriguez SP/800 40.00 100.00
BG Ben Grieve 6.00 15.00
CJ Charles Johnson 6.00 15.00
CP Chipper Jones SP/800 30.00 80.00
DE Darin Erstad 6.00 15.00
GS Gary Sheffield 10.00 25.00
IR Ivan Rodriguez 8.00 20.00
JC Jose Cruz Jr. 6.00 15.00
JW Jaret Wright 6.00 15.00
KG Ken Griffey Jr. SP/400 100.00 200.00
KGEX Ken Griffey Jr. EXCH 6.00 15.00
LH Livan Hernandez 6.00 15.00
MK Mark Kotsay 6.00 15.00
MM Mike Mussina 20.00 50.00
MT Miguel Tejada 6.00 15.00
MV Mo Vaughn SP/800 6.00 15.00
NG Nomar Garciaparra SP/400 20.00 50.00
PK Paul Konerko 6.00 15.00
PM Paul Molitor SP/800 10.00 25.00
RA Roberto Alomar SP/800 15.00 40.00
RB Russell Branyan 6.00 15.00
RC Roger Clemens SP/400 30.00 60.00
RL Ray Lankford 6.00 15.00
SC Sean Casey 6.00 15.00
SR Scott Rolen 6.00 15.00
TC Tony Clark 6.00 15.00
TG Tony Gwynn SP/850 20.00 50.00
TH Todd Helton 10.00 25.00
TL Travis Lee 6.00 15.00
VG Vladimir Guerrero 12.00 30.00

1998 SP Authentic Griffey 300th HR Redemption

This 5" by 7" card is the redemption one received for mailing in the Ken Griffey Jr. 300 Home Run card available in the SP Authentic packs.

300 Ken Griffey Jr. 15.00 40.00

1998 SP Authentic Game Jersey 5 x 7

These attractive 5" by 7" memorabilia cards are the items one received when redeeming the SP Authentic Trade Cards (of which were randomly seeded into 1998 SP Authentic packs at a rate of 1:291). The 5 x 7 cards feature a larger swatch of the jersey on them as compared to a standard size Game Jersey card. The exchange deadline expired back on August 1st, 1999.

ONE PER JERSEY TRADE CARD VIA MAIL
PRINT RUNS B/WN 125-415 COPIES PER
EXCH.DEADLINE WAS 8/1/99
1 Ken Griffey Jr./125 40.00 80.00
2 Gary Sheffield/125 10.00 25.00
3 Greg Maddux/125 40.00 80.00
4 Alex Rodriguez/125 40.00 80.00
5 Tony Gwynn/415 20.00 50.00
6 Jay Buhner/125 10.00 25.00

1998 SP Authentic Sheer Dominance

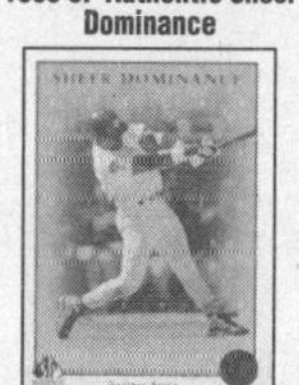

Randomly inserted in packs at a rate of one in three, this 42-card set has a mix of stars and young players and were issued in three different versions.

COMPLETE SET (42) 40.00 100.00
STATED ODDS 1:3
*GOLD: 1.25X TO 3X BASIC DOMINANCE
GOLD: RANDOM INSERTS IN PACKS
GOLD PRINT RUN 2000 SERIAL #'d SETS
*TITANIUM: 3X TO 8X BASIC DOMINANCE
TITANIUM: RANDOM INSERTS IN PACKS
TITANIUM PRINT RUN 100 SERIAL #'d SETS
SD1 Ken Griffey Jr. 2.00 5.00
SD2 Rickey Henderson 1.00 2.50
SD3 Jaret Wright .40 1.00
SD4 Craig Biggio .60 1.50
SD5 Travis Lee .40 1.00
SD6 Kenny Lofton .40 1.00
SD7 Raul Mondesi .40 1.00
SD8 Cal Ripken 3.00 8.00
SD9 Matt Williams .40 1.00
SD10 Mark McGwire 2.50 6.00
SD11 Alex Rodriguez 1.50 4.00
SD12 Fred McGriff .60 1.50
SD13 Scott Rolen .60 1.50
SD14 Paul Molitor .60 1.50
SD15 Nomar Garciaparra 1.50 4.00
SD16 Vladimir Guerrero 1.00 2.50
SD17 Andruw Jones .60 1.50
SD18 Manny Ramirez .60 1.50
SD19 Tony Gwynn 1.25 3.00
SD20 Barry Bonds 2.50 6.00
SD21 Ben Grieve .40 1.00
SD22 Ivan Rodriguez .60 1.50
SD23 Jose Cruz Jr. 1.00 2.50
SD24 Pedro Martinez .60 1.50
SD25 Chipper Jones 1.00 2.50
SD26 Albert Belle .40 1.00
SD27 Todd Helton .60 1.50
SD28 Paul Konerko .40 1.00
SD29 Sammy Sosa 1.00 2.50
SD30 Frank Thomas 1.00 2.50
SD31 Greg Maddux 1.50 4.00
SD32 Randy Johnson 1.00 2.50
SD33 Larry Walker .40 1.00
SD34 Roberto Alomar .60 1.50
SD35 Roger Clemens 2.00 5.00
SD36 Mo Vaughn .40 1.00
SD37 Jim Thome .60 1.50
SD38 Jeff Bagwell .60 1.50
SD39 Tino Martinez .60 1.50
SD40 Mike Piazza 1.50 4.00
SD41 Derek Jeter 2.50 6.00
SD42 Juan Gonzalez .40 1.00

1998 SP Authentic Trade Cards

Randomly seeded into packs at a rate of 1:291, these fifteen different trade cards could be redeemed for an assortion of UDA material. Specific quantities for each item are detailed below after each player name. The deadline to redeem these cards was August 1st, 1999. It is important to note that the redemption items came from UDA back stock and in many cases the card is far mor valuable than the redemption prize.

COMMON CARD (B1-B5) 6.00 15.00
COMMON CARD (J1-J6) 6.00 15.00
COMMON CARD (KG1-KG4) 6.00 15.00
STATED ODDS 1:291
PRINT RUNS LISTED BELOW
EXCHANGE DEADLINE WAS 8/1/99
GRIFFEY GLOVE/JERS.TOO SCARCE TO PRICE
B1 R.Alomar Ball/100 10.00 25.00
B2 A.Belle Ball/100 6.00 15.00
B3 B.Jordan Ball/50 6.00 15.00
B4 R.Mondesi Ball/100 6.00 15.00
B5 R.Ventura Ball/50 10.00 25.00
J1 J.Buhner Jsy Card/125 6.00 15.00
J2 K.Griffey Jr. Jsy Card/125 30.00 80.00
J3 T.Gwynn Jsy Card/415 10.00 25.00
J4 G.Maddux Jsy Card/125 25.00 60.00
J5 A.Rodriguez Jsy Card/125 20.00 50.00
J6 G.Sheffield Jsy Card/125 6.00 15.00
KG1 K.Griffey Jr.300 Card/1000 8.00 20.00
KG2 K.Griffey Jr.AU Glove/30
KG3 K.Griffey Jr.AU Jersey/30
KG4 K.Griffey Jr.Standee/200 12.50 30.00

1999 SP Authentic

The 1999 SP Authentic set was issued in one series totalling 135 cards and distributed in five-card packs with a suggested retail price of $4.99. The fronts feature color action player photos with player information printed on the backs. The set features the following limited edition subsets: Future Watch (91-120) serially numbered to 2700 and Season to Remember (121-135) numbered to 2700 also. 350 Ernie Banks A Piece of History 500 Club bat cards were randomly seeded into packs. Also, Banks signed and numbered twenty additional copies. Pricing for these bat cards can be referenced under 1999 Upper Deck A Piece of History 500 Club.

COMP.SET w/o SP's (90) 10.00 25.00
COMMON CARD (1-90) .15 .40
COMMON FW (91-120) 4.00 10.00
FW PRINT RUN 2700 SERIAL #'d SUBSETS
COMMON STR (121-135) 1.25 3.00
STR PRINT RUN 2700 SERIAL #'d SUBSETS
91-135 RANDOM IN PACKS
E.BANKS BAT LISTED W/UD APH 500 CLUB
1 Mo Vaughn .15 .40
2 Jim Edmonds .15 .40
3 Darin Erstad .15 .40
4 Travis Lee .15 .40
5 Matt Williams .15 .40
6 Randy Johnson .40 1.00
7 Chipper Jones .40 1.00
8 Greg Maddux .60 1.50
9 Andruw Jones .25 .60
10 Andres Galarraga .15 .40
11 Tom Glavine .25 .60
12 Cal Ripken 1.25 3.00
13 Brady Anderson .15 .40
14 Albert Belle .15 .40
15 Nomar Garciaparra .60 1.50
16 Donnie Sadler .15 .40
17 Pedro Martinez .25 .60
18 Sammy Sosa .40 1.00
19 Kerry Wood .15 .40
20 Mark Grace .25 .60
21 Mike Caruso .15 .40
22 Frank Thomas .40 1.00
23 Paul Konerko .15 .40
24 Sean Casey .15 .40
25 Barry Larkin .25 .60
26 Kenny Lofton .15 .40
27 Manny Ramirez .25 .60
28 Jim Thome .25 .60
29 Bartolo Colon .15 .40
30 Jaret Wright .15 .40
31 Larry Walker .15 .40
32 Todd Helton .25 .60
33 Tony Clark .15 .40
34 Dean Palmer .15 .40
35 Mark Kotsay .15 .40
36 Cliff Floyd .15 .40
37 Ken Caminiti .15 .40
38 Craig Biggio .25 .60
39 Jeff Bagwell .25 .60
40 Moises Alou .15 .40
41 Johnny Damon .25 .60
42 Larry Sutton .15 .40
43 Kevin Brown .25 .60
44 Gary Sheffield .15 .40
45 Raul Mondesi .15 .40
46 Jeromy Burnitz .15 .40
47 Jeff Cirillo .15 .40
48 Todd Walker .15 .40
49 David Ortiz .40 1.00
50 Brad Radke .15 .40
51 Vladimir Guerrero .40 1.00
52 Rondell White .15 .40
53 Brad Fullmer .15 .40
54 Mike Piazza .60 1.50
55 Robin Ventura .15 .40
56 John Olerud .15 .40
57 Derek Jeter 1.00 2.50
58 Tino Martinez .25 .60
59 Bernie Williams .25 .60
60 Roger Clemens .75 2.00
61 Ben Grieve .15 .40
62 Miguel Tejada .15 .40
63 A.J. Hinch .15 .40
64 Scott Rolen .25 .60
65 Curt Schilling .15 .40
66 Doug Glanville .15 .40
67 Aramis Ramirez .15 .40
68 Tony Womack .15 .40
69 Jason Kendall .15 .40
70 Tony Gwynn .50 1.25
71 Wally Joyner .15 .40
72 Greg Vaughn .15 .40
73 Barry Bonds 1.00 2.50
74 Ellis Burks .15 .40
75 Jeff Kent .15 .40
76 Ken Griffey Jr. .75 2.00
77 Alex Rodriguez .60 1.50
78 Edgar Martinez .25 .60
79 Mark McGwire 1.00 2.50
80 Eli Marrero .15 .40
81 Matt Morris .15 .40
82 Rolando Arrojo .15 .40
83 Quinton McCracken .15 .40
84 Jose Canseco .25 .60
85 Ivan Rodriguez .25 .60
86 Juan Gonzalez .15 .40
87 Royce Clayton .15 .40
88 Shawn Green .15 .40
89 Jose Cruz Jr. .15 .40
90 Carlos Delgado .15 .40
91 Troy Glaus FW 5.00 12.00
92 George Lombard FW 4.00 10.00
93 Ryan Minor FW 4.00 10.00
94 Calvin Pickering FW 4.00 10.00
95 Jin Ho Cho FW 4.00 10.00
96 Russ Branyan FW 4.00 10.00
97 Derrick Gibson FW 4.00 10.00
98 Gabe Kapler FW 4.00 10.00
99 Matt Anderson FW 4.00 10.00
100 Preston Wilson FW 4.00 10.00
101 Alex Gonzalez FW 4.00 10.00
102 Carlos Beltran FW 4.00 10.00
103 Dee Brown FW 4.00 10.00
104 Jeremy Giambi FW 4.00 10.00
105 Angel Pena FW 4.00 10.00
106 Geoff Jenkins FW 4.00 10.00
107 Corey Koskie FW 4.00 10.00
108 A.J. Pierzynski FW 4.00 10.00
109 Michael Barrett FW 4.00 10.00
110 Fernando Seguignol FW 4.00 10.00
111 Mike Kinkade FW 4.00 10.00
112 Ricky Ledee FW 4.00 10.00
113 Mike Lowell FW 4.00 10.00
114 Eric Chavez FW 4.00 10.00
115 Matt Clement FW 4.00 10.00
116 Shane Monahan FW 4.00 10.00
117 J.D. Drew FW 4.00 10.00
118 Bubba Trammell FW 4.00 10.00
119 Kevin Witt FW 4.00 10.00
120 Roy Halladay FW 10.00 25.00
121 Mark McGwire STR 5.00 12.00
122 M.McGwire 4.00 10.00
S.Sosa STR
123 Sammy Sosa STR 2.00 5.00
124 Ken Griffey Jr. STR 4.00 10.00
125 Cal Ripken STR 6.00 15.00
126 Juan Gonzalez STR 1.25 3.00
127 Kerry Wood STR 1.25 3.00
128 Trevor Hoffman STR 1.25 3.00
129 Barry Bonds STR 5.00 12.00
130 Alex Rodriguez STR 3.00 8.00
131 Ben Grieve STR 1.25 3.00
132 Tom Glavine STR 1.25 3.00
133 David Wells STR 1.25 3.00
134 Mike Piazza STR 3.00 8.00
135 Scott Brosius STR 1.25 3.00

1999 SP Authentic Chirography

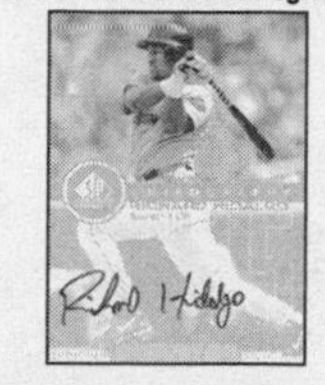

Randomly inserted in packs at the rate of one in 24, this 39-card set features color player photos with the pictured player's autograph at the bottom of the photo. Exchange cards for Ken Griffey Jr., Cal Ripken, Ruben Rivera and Scott Rolen were seeded into packs. The expiration date for the exchange cards was February 24th, 2000. Prices in our checklist refer to the actual autograph cards.

STATED ODDS 1:24
EXCH.DEADLINE 02/24/00
AG Alex Gonzalez 3.00 8.00
BC Bruce Chen 3.00 8.00
BF Brad Fullmer 3.00 8.00
BG Ben Grieve 3.00 8.00
CB Carlos Beltran 10.00 25.00
CJ Chipper Jones 30.00 80.00
CK Corey Koskie 4.00 10.00
CP Calvin Pickering 3.00 8.00
CR Cal Ripken 60.00 120.00
EC Eric Chavez 4.00 10.00
GK Gabe Kapler 4.00 10.00
GL George Lombard 3.00 8.00
GM Greg Maddux 50.00 120.00
GMJ Gary Matthews Jr. 3.00 8.00
GV Greg Vaughn 3.00 8.00
IR Ivan Rodriguez 15.00 40.00
JD J.D. Drew 4.00 10.00
JG Jeremy Giambi 3.00 8.00
JR Ken Griffey Jr. 60.00 150.00
JT Jim Thome 25.00 60.00
KW Kevin Witt 3.00 8.00
KW Kerry Wood 10.00 25.00
MA Matt Anderson 3.00 8.00
MK Mike Kinkade 3.00 8.00
ML Mike Lowell 5.00 12.00
NG Nomar Garciaparra 20.00 50.00
RB Russell Branyan 3.00 8.00
RH Richard Hidalgo 3.00 8.00
RL Ricky Ledee 3.00 8.00
RM Ryan Minor 3.00 8.00
RR Ruben Rivera 3.00 8.00
SM Shane Monahan 3.00 8.00
SR Scott Rolen 6.00 15.00
TG Tony Gwynn 10.00 25.00
TGL Troy Glaus 5.00 12.00
TH Todd Helton 8.00 20.00
TL Travis Lee 3.00 8.00
TW Todd Walker 4.00 10.00
VG Vladimir Guerrero 8.00 20.00
CRX Cal Ripken EXCH 4.00 10.00
JRX Ken Griffey Jr. EXCH 5.00 12.00
RRX Ruben Rivera EXCH .40 1.00
SRX Scott Rolen EXCH 1.00 2.50

1999 SP Authentic Chirography Gold

These scarce parallel versions of the Chirography cards were all serial numbered to the featured player's jersey number. The serial numbering was done by hand and is on the front of the card. In addition, gold ink was used on the card fronts (a flat grey front was used on the more common basic Chirography cards). While we only have pricing on some of the cards in this set, we are printing the checklist so collectors can know how many cards are available of each player. The same four players featured on exchange cards in the basic chirography (Griffey, Ripken, Rivera and Rolen) also had exchange cards in this set. The deadline for redeeming these cards was February 24th, 2000. Our listed price refers to the actual autograph cards.

RANDOM INSERTS IN PACKS
CARDS SERIAL #'d TO PLAYER'S JERSEY
NO PRICING ON QTY OF 25 OR LESS
EXCHANGE DEADLINE 02/24/00
AG Alex Gonzalez/22
BC Bruce Chen/48 10.00 25.00
BF Brad Fullmer/20
BG Ben Grieve/14
CB Carlos Beltran/36 40.00 100.00
CJ Chipper Jones/10
CK Corey Koskie/47 15.00 40.00
CP Calvin Pickering/6
CR Cal Ripken/8
EC Eric Chavez/30 15.00 40.00
GK Gabe Kapler/51 15.00 40.00
GL George Lombard/26 10.00 25.00
GM Greg Maddux/31 125.00 250.00
GMJ Gary Matthews Jr./68 10.00 25.00
GV Greg Vaughn/23

IR Ivan Rodriguez/7
JD J.D. Drew/8
JG Jeremy Giambi/15
JR Ken Griffey Jr./24
JT Jim Thome/25
KW Kevin Witt/6
KW Kerry Wood/34 30.00 60.00
MA Matt Anderson/14
MK Mike Kinkade/33 10.00 25.00
ML Mike Lowell/60 20.00 50.00
NG Nomar Garciaparra/5
RB Russ Branyan/66 10.00 25.00
RH Richard Hidalgo/15
RL Ricky Ledee/38 10.00 25.00
RM Ryan Minor/10
RR Ruben Rivera/28 10.00 25.00
SM Shane Monahan/12
SR Scott Rolen/17
TG Tony Gwynn/19
TGL Troy Glaus/14
TH Todd Helton/17
TL Travis Lee/16
TW Todd Walker/12
VG Vladimir Guerrero/27 60.00 120.00
CRX Cal Ripken EXCH
JRX Ken Griffey Jr. EXCH
RRX Ruben Rivera EXCH
SRX Scott Rolen EXCH

1999 SP Authentic Epic Figures

Randomly inserted in packs at the rate of one in seven, this 30-card set features action color photos of some of the game's most impressive players.
COMPLETE SET (30) 40.00 100.00
STATED ODDS 1:7
E1 Mo Vaughn .60 1.50
E2 Travis Lee .60 1.50
E3 Andres Galarraga .60 1.50
E4 Andruw Jones 1.00 2.50
E5 Chipper Jones 1.50 4.00
E6 Greg Maddux 2.50 6.00
E7 Cal Ripken 5.00 12.00
E8 Nomar Garciaparra 2.50 6.00
E9 Sammy Sosa 1.50 4.00
E10 Frank Thomas 1.50 4.00
E11 Kerry Wood .60 1.50
E12 Kenny Lofton .60 1.50
E13 Manny Ramirez 1.00 2.50
E14 Larry Walker .60 1.50
E15 Jeff Bagwell 1.00 2.50
E16 Paul Molitor 1.50 4.00
E17 Vladimir Guerrero 1.50 4.00
E18 Derek Jeter 4.00 10.00
E19 Tino Martinez 1.00 2.50
E20 Mike Piazza 2.50 6.00
E21 Ben Grieve .60 1.50
E22 Scott Rolen 1.00 2.50
E23 Mark McGwire 4.00 10.00
E24 Tony Gwynn 2.00 5.00
E25 Barry Bonds 4.00 10.00
E26 Ken Griffey Jr. 3.00 8.00
E27 Alex Rodriguez 2.50 6.00
E28 J.D. Drew .60 1.50
E29 Juan Gonzalez .60 1.50
E30 Kevin Brown 1.00 2.50

1999 SP Authentic Home Run Chronicles

Inserted one per pack, this 70-card set features action color photos of players who were the leading sluggers of the 1998 season.
COMPLETE SET (70) 25.00 60.00
*DIE CUTS: 5X TO 12X BASIC HR CHRON.
DIE CUTS RANDOM INSERTS IN PACKS
DIE CUT PRINT RUN 70 SERIAL #'d SETS
HR1 Mark McGwire 1.50 4.00
HR2 Sammy Sosa .40 1.00
HR3 Ken Griffey Jr. .75 2.00
HR4 Mark McGwire 1.00 2.50
HR5 Mark McGwire 1.00 2.50
HR6 Albert Belle .15 .40
HR7 Jose Canseco .25 .60
HR8 Juan Gonzalez .15 .40
HR9 Manny Ramirez .25 .60
HR10 Rafael Palmeiro .40 1.00
HR11 Mo Vaughn .15 .40
HR12 Carlos Delgado .15 .40
HR13 Nomar Garciaparra .60 1.50
HR14 Barry Bonds 1.00 2.50
HR15 Alex Rodriguez .60 1.50
HR16 Tony Clark .15 .40
HR17 Jim Thome .25 .60
HR18 Edgar Martinez .25 .60
HR19 Frank Thomas .40 1.00
HR20 Greg Vaughn .15 .40
HR21 Vinny Castilla .15 .40
HR22 Andres Galarraga .15 .40
HR23 Moises Alou .15 .40
HR24 Jeromy Burnitz .15 .40
HR25 Vladimir Guerrero .40 1.00
HR26 Jeff Bagwell .25 .60
HR27 Chipper Jones .40 1.00
HR28 Javier Lopez .15 .40
HR29 Mike Piazza .60 1.50
HR30 Andruw Jones .25 .60
HR31 Henry Rodriguez .15 .40
HR32 Jeff Kent .15 .40
HR33 Ray Lankford .15 .40
HR34 Scott Rolen .25 .60
HR35 Raul Mondesi .15 .40
HR36 Ken Caminiti .15 .40
HR37 J.D. Drew .15 .40
HR38 Troy Glaus .25 .60
HR39 Gabe Kapler .15 .40
HR40 Alex Rodriguez .60 1.50
HR41 Ken Griffey Jr. .75 2.00
HR42 Sammy Sosa .40 1.00
HR43 Mark McGwire 1.00 2.50
HR44 Sammy Sosa .40 1.00
HR45 Mark McGwire 1.00 2.50
HR46 Vinny Castilla .15 .40
HR47 Sammy Sosa .40 1.00
HR48 Mark McGwire 1.00 2.50
HR49 Sammy Sosa .40 1.00
HR50 Greg Vaughn .15 .40
HR51 Sammy Sosa .40 1.00
HR52 Mark McGwire 1.00 2.50
HR53 Sammy Sosa .40 1.00
HR54 Mark McGwire 1.00 2.50
HR55 Sammy Sosa .40 1.00
HR56 Ken Griffey Jr. .75 2.00
HR57 Sammy Sosa .40 1.00
HR58 Mark McGwire 1.00 2.50
HR59 Sammy Sosa .40 1.00
HR60 Mark McGwire 1.00 2.50
HR61 Mark McGwire 1.50 4.00
HR62 Mark McGwire 2.00 5.00
HR63 Mark McGwire 1.00 2.50
HR64 Mark McGwire 1.00 2.50
HR65 Mark McGwire 1.00 2.50
HR66 Sammy Sosa 2.00 5.00
HR67 Mark McGwire 1.00 2.50
HR68 Mark McGwire 1.00 2.50
HR69 Mark McGwire 1.00 2.50
HR70 Mark McGwire 4.00 10.00

1999 SP Authentic Redemption Cards

Randomly inserted in packs at the rate of one in 864, this 10-card set features hand-numbered cards that could be redeemed for various items autographed by the player named on the card. The expiration date for these cards was March 1st, 2000.
STATED ODDS 1:864
EXPIRATION DATE: 03/01/00
PRICES BELOW REFER TO TRADE CARDS
1 K.Griffey Jr. AU Jersey/25
2 K.Griffey Jr. AU Baseball/75
3 K.Griffey Jr. AU SI Cover/75
4 K.Griffey Jr. AU Mini Helmet/75
5 M.McGwire AU 62 Ticket/1
6 M.McGwire AU 70 Ticket/3
7 K.Griffey Jr. Standee/300 6.00 15.00
8 K.Griffey Jr. Glove Card/200 20.00 50.00
9 K.Griffey Jr. HR Cel Card/346 12.50 30.00
10 K.Griffey Jr. SI Cover/200 10.00 25.00

1999 SP Authentic Reflections

Randomly inserted in packs at the rate of one in 23, this 30-card set features color action photos of some of the game's best players and printed using Dot Matrix technology.
COMPLETE SET (30) 30.00 80.00
STATED ODDS 1:23
R1 Mo Vaughn .60 1.50
R2 Travis Lee .60 1.50
R3 Andres Galarraga 1.00 2.50
R4 Andruw Jones .60 1.50
R5 Chipper Jones 1.50 4.00
R6 Greg Maddux 2.00 5.00
R7 Cal Ripken 5.00 12.00
R8 Nomar Garciaparra 1.00 2.50
R9 Sammy Sosa 1.50 4.00
R10 Frank Thomas 1.50 4.00
R11 Kerry Wood .60 1.50
R12 Kenny Lofton .60 1.50
R13 Manny Ramirez 1.50 4.00
R14 Larry Walker 1.00 2.50
R15 Jeff Bagwell 1.00 2.50
R16 Paul Molitor 1.50 4.00
R17 Vladimir Guerrero 1.00 2.50
R18 Derek Jeter 4.00 10.00
R19 Tino Martinez .60 1.50
R20 Mike Piazza 1.50 4.00
R21 Ben Grieve .60 1.50
R22 Scott Rolen 1.00 2.50
R23 Mark McGwire 2.50 6.00
R24 Tony Gwynn 1.50 4.00
R25 Barry Bonds 2.50 6.00
R26 Ken Griffey Jr 3.00 8.00
R27 Alex Rodriguez 2.00 5.00
R28 J.D. Drew .60 1.50
R29 Juan Gonzalez .60 1.50
R30 Roger Clemens 2.00 5.00

2000 SP Authentic

The 2000 SP Authentic product was initially released in late July, 2000 as a 135-card set. Each pack contained five cards and carried a suggested retail price of $4.99. The basic set features 90 veteran players, a 15-card SP Superstars subset serial numbered to 2500, and a 30-card Future Watch subset also serial numbered to 2500. In late December, Upper Deck released their UD Rookie Update brand, which contained a selection of cards to append the 2000 SP Authentic, SPx and UD Pros and Prospects brands. For SP Authentic, sixty new cards were intended, but card number 165 was never created due to problems at the manufacturer. Cards 136-164 are devoted to an extension of the Future Watch prospect subset established in the basic set. Similar to the basic set's FW cards, these Update cards are serial numbered, but only 1,700 copies of each card were produced (as compared to the 2,500 print run for the "first series" cards). Cards 166-195 feature a selection of established veterans either initially not included in the basic set or traded to new teams. Notable Rookie Cards include Xavier Nady, Kazuhiro Sasaki and Barry Zito. Also, a selection of A Piece of History 3000 Club Tris Speaker and Paul Waner memorabilia cards were randomly seeded into packs. 350 bat cards and five hand-numbered, combination bat chip and autograph cut cards for each player were produced. Pricing for these memorabilia cards can be referenced under 2000 Upper Deck A Piece of History 3000 Club. Finally, a Ken Griffey Jr. sample card was distributed to dealers and hobby media in June, 2000 (several weeks prior to the basic product's national release). The card can be readily distinguished by the large "SAMPLE" text running diagonally across the back.
COMP.BASIC w/o SP's (90) 10.00 25.00
COMP.UPDATE w/o SP'S (30) 4.00 10.00
COMMON CARD (1-90) .15 .40
COMMON SUP (91-105) .40 1.00
91-105 PRINT RUN 2500 SERIAL #'d SETS
COMMON FW (106-135) .60 1.50
FW 106-135 PR.RUN 2500 SERIAL #'d SETS
COMMON FW (136-164) .75 2.00
FW 136-164 PRINT RUN 1700 #'d SETS
COMMON CARD (166-195) .25 .60
136-195 DISTRIBUTED IN ROOKIE UPD.PACKS
CARD NUMBER 165 DOES NOT EXIST
WANER/SPEAKER 3K LIST.W/UD 3000 CLUB
1 Mo Vaughn .15 .40
2 Troy Glaus .15 .40
3 Jason Giambi .15 .40
4 Tim Hudson .25 .60
5 Eric Chavez .15 .40
6 Shannon Stewart .15 .40
7 Raul Mondesi .15 .40
8 Carlos Delgado .15 .40
9 Jose Canseco .25 .60
10 Vinny Castilla .15 .40
11 Greg Vaughn .15 .40
12 Manny Ramirez .40 1.00
13 Roberto Alomar .25 .60
14 Jim Thome .25 .60
15 Richie Sexson .15 .40
16 Alex Rodriguez .50 1.25
17 Freddy Garcia .15 .40
18 John Olerud .15 .40
19 Albert Belle .15 .40
20 Cal Ripken 1.25 3.00
21 Mike Mussina .25 .60
22 Ivan Rodriguez .25 .60
23 Gabe Kapler .15 .40
24 Rafael Palmeiro .25 .60
25 Nomar Garciaparra .25 .60
26 Pedro Martinez .25 .60
27 Carl Everett .15 .40
28 Carlos Beltran .25 .60
29 Jermaine Dye .15 .40
30 Juan Gonzalez .15 .40
31 Dean Palmer .15 .40
32 Corey Koskie .15 .40
33 Jacque Jones .15 .40
34 Frank Thomas .40 1.00
35 Paul Konerko .15 .40
36 Magglio Ordonez .25 .60
37 Bernie Williams .25 .60
38 Derek Jeter 1.00 2.50
39 Roger Clemens .50 1.25
40 Mariano Rivera .50 1.25
41 Jeff Bagwell .25 .60
42 Craig Biggio .25 .60
43 Jose Lima .15 .40
44 Moises Alou .15 .40
45 Chipper Jones .40 1.00
46 Greg Maddux .50 1.25
47 Andruw Jones .15 .40
48 Andres Galarraga .25 .60
49 Jeromy Burnitz .15 .40
50 Geoff Jenkins .15 .40
51 Mark McGwire .60 1.50
52 Fernando Tatis .15 .40
53 J.D. Drew .15 .40
54 Sammy Sosa .40 1.00
55 Kerry Wood .15 .40
56 Mark Grace .25 .60
57 Matt Williams .15 .40
58 Randy Johnson .40 1.00
59 Erubiel Durazo .15 .40
60 Gary Sheffield .15 .40
61 Kevin Brown .15 .40
62 Shawn Green .15 .40
63 Vladimir Guerrero .25 .60
64 Michael Barrett .15 .40
65 Barry Bonds .60 1.50
66 Jeff Kent .15 .40
67 Russ Ortiz .15 .40
68 Preston Wilson .15 .40
69 Mike Lowell .15 .40
70 Mike Piazza .40 1.00
71 Mike Hampton .15 .40
72 Robin Ventura .15 .40
73 Edgardo Alfonzo .15 .40
74 Tony Gwynn .40 1.00
75 Ryan Klesko .15 .40
76 Trevor Hoffman .25 .60
77 Scott Rolen .25 .60
78 Bob Abreu .15 .40
79 Mike Lieberthal .15 .40
80 Curt Schilling .25 .60
81 Jason Kendall .15 .40
82 Brian Giles .15 .40
83 Kris Benson .15 .40
84 Ken Griffey Jr. .75 2.00
85 Sean Casey .15 .40
86 Pokey Reese .15 .40
87 Barry Larkin .25 .60
88 Larry Walker .25 .60
89 Todd Helton .25 .60
90 Jeff Cirillo .15 .40
91 Ken Griffey Jr. SUP 2.00 5.00
92 Mark McGwire SUP 1.50 4.00
93 Chipper Jones SUP 1.00 2.50
94 Derek Jeter SUP 2.50 6.00
95 Shawn Green SUP .40 1.00
96 Pedro Martinez SUP .60 1.50
97 Mike Piazza SUP 1.00 2.50
98 Alex Rodriguez SUP 1.25 3.00
99 Jeff Bagwell SUP .60 1.50
100 Cal Ripken SUP 3.00 8.00
101 Sammy Sosa SUP 1.00 2.50
102 Barry Bonds SUP 1.50 4.00
103 Jose Canseco SUP .60 1.50
104 Nomar Garciaparra SUP .60 1.50
105 Ivan Rodriguez SUP .60 1.50
106 Rick Ankiel FW 1.00 2.50
107 Pat Burrell FW .60 1.50
108 Vernon Wells FW .60 1.50
109 Nick Johnson FW .60 1.50
110 Kip Wells FW .60 1.50
111 Matt Riley FW .60 1.50
112 Alfonso Soriano FW 1.50 4.00
113 Josh Beckett FW 1.25 3.00
114 Danys Baez FW RC .60 1.50
115 Travis Dawkins FW .60 1.50
116 Eric Gagne FW .60 1.50
117 Mike Lamb FW RC .60 1.50
118 Eric Munson FW .60 1.50
119 Wilfredo Rodriguez FW RC .60 1.50
120 Kazuhiro Sasaki FW RC 1.50 4.00
121 Chad Hutchinson FW .60 1.50
122 Peter Bergeron FW .60 1.50
123 Wascar Serrano FW RC .60 1.50
124 Tony Armas Jr. FW .60 1.50
125 Ramon Ortiz FW .60 1.50
126 Adam Kennedy FW .60 1.50
127 Joe Crede FW .60 1.50
128 Roosevelt Brown FW .60 1.50
129 Mark Mulder FW .60 1.50
130 Brad Penny FW .60 1.50
131 Terrence Long FW .60 1.50
132 Ruben Mateo FW .60 1.50
133 Wily Mo Pena FW .60 1.50
134 Rafael Furcal FW 1.00 2.50
135 Mario Encarnacion FW .60 1.50
136 Barry Zito FW RC 6.00 15.00
137 Aaron McNeal FW RC .75 2.00
138 Timo Perez FW RC 1.25 3.00
139 Sun Woo Kim FW RC .75 2.00
140 Xavier Nady FW RC 2.00 5.00
141 Matt Wheatland FW RC .75 2.00
142 Brent Abernathy FW RC .75 2.00
143 Cory Vance FW RC .75 2.00
144 Scott Heard FW RC .75 2.00
145 Mike Meyers FW RC 1.25 3.00
146 Ben Diggins FW RC .75 2.00
147 Luis Matos FW RC .75 2.00
148 Ben Sheets FW RC 2.00 5.00
149 Kurt Ainsworth FW RC .75 2.00
150 Dave Krynzel FW RC .75 2.00
151 Alex Cabrera FW RC .75 2.00
152 Mike Tonis FW RC .75 2.00
153 Dane Sardinha FW RC .75 2.00
154 Keith Ginter FW RC .75 2.00
155 David Espinosa FW RC .75 2.00
156 Joe Torres FW RC .75 2.00
157 Daylan Holt FW RC .75 2.00
158 Koyie Hill FW RC .75 2.00
159 Brad Wilkerson FW RC 2.00 5.00
160 Juan Pierre FW RC 4.00 10.00
161 Matt Ginter FW RC .75 2.00
162 Dane Artman FW RC .75 2.00
163 Jon Rauch FW RC .75 2.00
164 Sean Burnett FW RC .75 2.00
166 Darin Erstad .25 .60
167 Ben Grieve .25 .60
168 David Wells .25 .60
169 Fred McGriff .40 1.00
170 Bob Wickman .25 .60
171 Al Martin .25 .60
172 Melvin Mora .40 1.00
173 Ricky Ledee .25 .60
174 Dante Bichette .25 .60
175 Mike Sweeney .25 .60
176 Bobby Higginson .25 .60
177 Matt Lawton .25 .60
178 Charles Johnson .25 .60
179 David Justice .25 .60
180 Richard Hidalgo .25 .60
181 B.J. Surhoff .25 .60
182 Richie Sexson .25 .60
183 Jim Edmonds .25 .60
184 Rondell White .25 .60
185 Curt Schilling .40 1.00
186 Tom Goodwin .25 .60
187 Jose Vidro .25 .60
188 Ellis Burks .25 .60
189 Henry Rodriguez .25 .60
190 Mike Bordick .25 .60
191 Eric Owens .25 .60
192 Travis Lee .25 .60
193 Kevin Young .25 .60
194 Aaron Boone .25 .60
195 Todd Hollandsworth .25 .60
SPA Ken Griffey Jr. Sample 1.00 2.50

2000 SP Authentic Limited

*LIMITED 1-90: 8X TO 20X BASIC
*LTD 91-105: 3X TO 8X BASIC
*LTD 106-135: 2X TO 5X BASIC
*LTD 106-135 RC: 1.5X TO 4X BASIC
STATED PRINT RUN 100 SERIAL #'d SETS

2000 SP Authentic Buybacks

Representatives at Upper Deck purchased back a selection of vintage SP brand trading cards from 1993-1999, featuring 29 different players. The "vintage" cards were all purchased in 2000 through hobby dealers. Each card was then hand-numbered in blue ink sharpie on front (please see listings for print runs), affixed with a serial numbered UDA hologram on back and packaged with a 2 1/2" by 3 1/2" UDA Certificate of Authenticity (of which had a hologram with a matching serial number of the signed card). The Certificate of Authenticity and the signed card were placed together in a soft plastic "penny" sleeve and then randomly seeded into 2000 SP Authentic packs at a rate of 1:95. Jeff Bagwell, Ken Griffey, Andruw Jones, Chipper Jones, Manny Ramirez and Alex Rodriguez did not manage to sign their cards in time for packout, thus exchange cards were created and seeded into packs for these players. The exchange cards did NOT specify the actual vintage card that the bearer would receive back in the mail. The deadline to redeem the exchange cards was March 30th, 2001. Pricing for cards with production of 25 or fewer cards is not provided due to scarcity.
STATED ODDS 1:95
PRINT RUNS B/WN 1-539 COPIES PER
NO PRICING ON QTY OF 25 OR LESS
1 Jeff Bagwell 93/58 12.50 30.00
2 Jeff Bagwell 94/46 12.50 30.00
3 Jeff Bagwell 95/60 12.50 30.00
4 Jeff Bagwell 96/74 12.50 30.00
5 Jeff Bagwell 97/53 12.50 30.00
6 Jeff Bagwell 98/38 12.50 30.00
7 Jeff Bagwell 99/539 10.00 25.00
9 Craig Biggio 93/59 15.00 40.00
10 Craig Biggio 94/69 15.00 40.00
11 Craig Biggio 95/171 10.00 25.00
12 Craig Biggio 96/71 15.00 40.00
13 Craig Biggio 97/46 15.00 40.00
14 Craig Biggio 98/40 15.00 40.00
15 Craig Biggio 99/125 10.00 25.00
22 Barry Bonds 99/520 30.00 60.00
23 Jose Canseco 93/29 20.00 50.00
29 Jose Canseco 99/502 15.00 40.00
31 Sean Casey 99/139 6.00 15.00
32 Roger Clemens 93/68 15.00 40.00
33 Roger Clemens 94/60 15.00 40.00
34 Roger Clemens 95/68 15.00 40.00
35 Roger Clemens 96/68 15.00 40.00
38 Roger Clemens 99/134 15.00 40.00
39 Jason Giambi 97/34 20.00 50.00
41 Tom Glavine 93/99 15.00 40.00
42 Tom Glavine 94/107 15.00 40.00
43 Tom Glavine 95/91 15.00 40.00
44 Tom Glavine 96/42 10.00 25.00
45 Tom Glavine 98/40 20.00 50.00
46 Tom Glavine 99/138 15.00 40.00
47 Shawn Green 96/55 15.00 40.00
48 Shawn Green 99/530 10.00 25.00
55 Ken Griffey Jr. 99/403 40.00 80.00
63 Tony Gwynn 99/129 25.00 60.00
64 Tony Gwynn 99/369 20.00 50.00
70 Derek Jeter 99/119 100.00 200.00
71 Randy Johnson 93/60 20.00 50.00
72 Randy Johnson 94/45 20.00 50.00
73 Randy Johnson 95/70 20.00 50.00
74 Randy Johnson 96/60 20.00 50.00
77 Randy Johnson 99/113 40.00 80.00
78 Andruw Jones 97/70 10.00 25.00
79 Andruw Jones 98/56 15.00 40.00
80 Andruw Jones 99/531 6.00 15.00
85 Chipper Jones 97/63 40.00 80.00
87 Chipper Jones 99/541 30.00 60.00
89 Kenny Lofton 94/100 8.00 20.00
90 Kenny Lofton 95/84 8.00 20.00
91 Kenny Lofton 96/34 20.00 50.00
92 Kenny Lofton 97/82 12.50 30.00
94 Kenny Lofton 99/99 12.50 30.00
95 Javy Lopez 93/106 6.00 15.00
96 Javy Lopez 94/160 6.00 15.00
97 Javy Lopez 96/99 6.00 15.00
98 Javy Lopez 97/61 10.00 25.00
99 Javy Lopez 98/26 12.50 30.00
106 Greg Maddux 99/504 40.00 80.00
107 Paul O'Neill 93/110 8.00 20.00
108 Paul O'Neill 94/97 12.00 30.00
109 Paul O'Neill 95/142 8.00 20.00
110 Paul O'Neill 96/70 8.00 20.00
116 Manny Ramirez 97/42 20.00 50.00
117 Manny Ramirez 98/36 20.00 50.00
118 Manny Ramirez 99/532 12.50 30.00
126 Cal Ripken 99/510 20.00 50.00
128 Alex Rodriguez 95/57 40.00 80.00
129 Alex Rodriguez 96/37 40.00 80.00
132 Alex Rodriguez 99/408 30.00 60.00
134 Ivan Rodriguez 93/29 30.00 60.00
139 Ivan Rodriguez 98/27 30.00 60.00
142 Scott Rolen 98/31 20.00 50.00
148 Frank Thomas 98/29 30.00 60.00
149 Frank Thomas 99/100 15.00 40.00
150 Greg Vaughn 93/79 4.00 10.00
151 Greg Vaughn 94/75 4.00 10.00
152 Greg Vaughn 95/155 4.00 10.00
153 Greg Vaughn 96/113 4.00 10.00
154 Greg Vaughn 97/29 8.00 20.00
155 Greg Vaughn 99/527 4.00 10.00
156 Mo Vaughn 93/119 6.00 15.00
157 Mo Vaughn 94/96 6.00 15.00
158 Mo Vaughn 95/121 6.00 15.00
159 Mo Vaughn 96/114 6.00 15.00
160 Mo Vaughn 97/61 10.00 25.00
161 Mo Vaughn 98/29 12.50 30.00
162 Mo Vaughn 99/537 4.00 10.00
163 Robin Ventura 93/59 10.00 25.00
164 Robin Ventura 94/49 10.00 25.00
165 Robin Ventura '95/125 6.00 15.00
166 Robin Ventura 96/55 10.00 25.00
167 Robin Ventura 97/44 10.00 25.00
168 Robin Ventura 98/28 12.50 30.00
169 Robin Ventura 99/370 6.00 15.00
170 Matt Williams 93/55 15.00 40.00
171 Matt Williams 94/50 15.00 40.00
172 Matt Williams 95/137 10.00 25.00
173 Matt Williams 96/77 10.00 25.00
174 Matt Williams 97/54 15.00 40.00
175 Matt Williams 98/29 20.00 50.00
176 Matt Williams 99/529 10.00 25.00
177 Preston Wilson '94/249 6.00 15.00
178 Preston Wilson '99/195 6.00 15.00
179 Authentication Card .20 .50

2000 SP Authentic Chirography

Randomly inserted into packs at one in 23, this 42-card insert features autographed cards of modern superstar players. Please note that there were also autographs of Sandy Koufax inserted into this set. There were a number of cards in this set that packed out as exchange cards, the exchange cards must be sent to Upper Deck by 03/30/01.
STATED ODDS 1:23
EXCHANGE DEADLINE 03/30/01
AJ Andruw Jones 6.00 15.00
AR Alex Rodriguez 30.00 60.00
AS Alfonso Soriano 4.00 10.00
BB Barry Bonds 50.00 120.00
BP Ben Petrick 4.00 10.00
CBE Carlos Beltran 10.00 25.00
CJ Chipper Jones 30.00 80.00
CR Cal Ripken 30.00 80.00
DJ Derek Jeter 125.00 300.00
EC Eric Chavez 6.00 15.00
ED Erubiel Durazo 4.00 10.00
EM Eric Munson 4.00 10.00
EY Ed Yarnall 4.00 10.00
IR Ivan Rodriguez 12.00 30.00
JB Jeff Bagwell 10.00 25.00
JC Jose Canseco 6.00 15.00
JD J.D. Drew 6.00 15.00
JG Jason Giambi 6.00 15.00
JK Josh Kalinowski 4.00 10.00
JL Jose Lima 4.00 10.00
JMA Joe Mays 4.00 10.00
JMO Jim Morris 8.00 20.00
JOB John Bale 4.00 10.00
KL Kenny Lofton 8.00 20.00
MQ Mark Quinn 4.00 10.00
MR Manny Ramirez 10.00 25.00
MRI Matt Riley 4.00 10.00
MV Mo Vaughn 6.00 15.00
NJ Nick Johnson 6.00 15.00
PB Pat Burrell 4.00 10.00
RA Rick Ankiel 6.00 15.00
RC Roger Clemens 30.00 60.00
RF Rafael Furcal 6.00 15.00
RP Robert Person 4.00 10.00
SC Sean Casey 4.00 10.00
SK Sandy Koufax 75.00 200.00
SR Scott Rolen 4.00 10.00
TG Tony Gwynn 20.00 50.00
TGL Troy Glaus 4.00 10.00
VG Vladimir Guerrero 10.00 25.00
VW Vernon Wells 4.00 10.00
WG Wilton Guerrero 4.00 10.00

2000 SP Authentic Chirography Gold

Randomly inserted into packs, this 42-card insert is a complete parallel of the SP Authentic Chirography set. All Gold cards have a G suffix on the card number (for example Rick Ankiel's card is number G-RA). For the handful of exchange cards that were seeded into packs, this was the key manner to differentiate them from basic Chirography cards. Please note exchange cards (with a redemption deadline of 03/30/01) were seeded into packs for Andruw Jones, Alex Rodriguez, Chipper Jones, Jeff Bagwell, Manny Ramirez, Pat Burrell, Rick Ankiel and Scott Rolen. In addition, about 50% of Jose Lima's cards went into packs as real autographs and the remainder packed out as exchange cards.
STATED PRINT RUNS LISTED BELOW
NO PRICING ON QTY OF 25 OR LESS
EXCHANGE DEADLINE 03/30/01
GAS Alfonso Soriano/53 8.00 20.00
GED Erubiel Durazo/44 6.00 15.00
GEY Ed Yarnall/41 6.00 15.00
GJC Jose Canseco/33 50.00 120.00
GJK Josh Kalinowski/62 6.00 15.00
GJL Jose Lima/42 6.00 15.00
GJMA Joe Mays/53 6.00 15.00
GJMO Jim Morris/63 30.00 80.00
GJOB John Bale/49 6.00 15.00
GMV Mo Vaughn/42 12.00 30.00
GNJ Nick Johnson/63 10.00 25.00
GPB Pat Burrell/33 15.00 40.00
GRA Rick Ankiel/66 10.00 25.00
GRP Robert Person/31 6.00 15.00
GVG Vladimir Guerrero/27 50.00 100.00

2000 SP Authentic Cornerstones

Randomly inserted into packs at one in 23, this seven-card insert features players that are the cornerstones of their teams. Card backs carry a "C" prefix.
COMPLETE SET (7) 8.00 20.00
STATED ODDS 1:23
C1 Ken Griffey Jr 2.00 5.00
C2 Cal Ripken 3.00 8.00
C3 Mike Piazza 1.00 2.50
C4 Derek Jeter 2.50 6.00
C5 Mark McGwire 1.50 4.00
C6 Nomar Garciaparra .60 1.50
C7 Sammy Sosa 1.00 2.50

2000 SP Authentic DiMaggio Memorabilia

Randomly inserted into packs, this three-card insert features game-used memorabilia cards of Joe DiMaggio. This set features a Game-Used Jersey card (numbered to 500), a Game-Used Jersey card Gold (numbered to 56), and a Game-Used Jersey/Cu Autograph card (numbered to 5).
STATED PRINT RUNS LISTED BELOW
1 J.DiMaggio Jsy/500 30.00 60.00
2 J.DiMaggio Jsy Gold/56 100.00 200.00

2000 SP Authentic Midsummer Classics

Randomly inserted into packs at one in 12, this 10-card insert features perennial All-Stars. Card backs carry a "MC" prefix.
COMPLETE SET (10) 8.00 20.00
STATED ODDS 1:12
MC1 Cal Ripken 3.00 8.00
MC2 Roger Clemens 1.25 3.00
MC3 Jeff Bagwell .60 1.50
MC4 Barry Bonds 1.50 4.00
MC5 Jose Canseco .60 1.50
MC6 Frank Thomas 1.00 2.50
MC7 Mike Piazza 1.00 2.50
MC8 Tony Gwynn 1.00 2.50
MC9 Juan Gonzalez .40 1.00
MC10 Greg Maddux 1.25 3.00

2000 SP Authentic Premier Performers

Randomly inserted into packs at one in 12, this 10-card insert features prime-time players that leave it all on the field and hold nothing back. Card backs carry a "PP" prefix.
COMPLETE SET (10) 10.00 25.00
STATED ODDS 1:12
PP1 Mark McGwire 1.50 4.00
PP2 Alex Rodriguez 1.25 3.00

PP3 Cal Ripken 3.00 8.00
PP4 Nomar Garciaparra .60 1.50
PP5 Ken Griffey Jr. 2.00 5.00
PP6 Chipper Jones 1.00 2.50
PP7 Derek Jeter 2.50 6.00
PP8 Ivan Rodriguez .60 1.50
PP9 Vladimir Guerrero .60 1.50
PP10 Sammy Sosa 1.00 2.50

2000 SP Authentic Supremacy

Randomly inserted into packs at one in 23, this seven-card insert features players that any team would like to have. Card backs carry a "S" prefix.

COMPLETE SET (7) 4.00 10.00
STATED ODDS 1:23
S1 Alex Rodriguez 1.25 3.00
S2 Shawn Green .40 1.00
S3 Pedro Martinez .60 1.50
S4 Chipper Jones 1.00 2.50
S5 Tony Gwynn 1.00 2.50
S6 Ivan Rodriguez .60 1.50
S7 Jeff Bagwell .60 1.50

2000 SP Authentic United Nations

Randomly inserted into packs at one in four, this 10-card insert features players that have come from other countries to play in the Major Leagues. Card backs carry a "UN" prefix.

COMPLETE SET (10) 5.00 12.00
STATED ODDS 1:4
UN1 Sammy Sosa 1.00 2.50
UN2 Ken Griffey Jr. 2.00 5.00
UN3 Orlando Hernandez .40 1.00
UN4 Andres Galarraga .60 1.50
UN5 Kazuhiro Sasaki 1.00 2.50
UN6 Larry Walker .60 1.50
UN7 Vinny Castilla .40 1.00
UN8 Andruw Jones .40 1.00
UN9 Ivan Rodriguez .60 1.50
UN10 Chan Ho Park .60 1.50

2001 SP Authentic

SP Authentic was initially released as a 180-card set in September, 2001. An additional 60-card Update set was distributed within Upper Deck Rookie Update packs in late December, 2001. Each basic sealed box contained 24 packs plus two three-card bonus packs (one entitled Stars of Japan and another entitled Mantle Pinstripe Exclusives). Each basic pack of SP Authentic contained five cards and carried a suggested retail price of $4.99. Upper Deck Rookie Update packs contained four cards and carried an SRP of $4.99. The basic set is broken into the following components: basic veterans (1-90), Future Watch (91-135) and Superstars (136-180). Each Future Watch and Superstar subset card from the first series is serial numbered of 1250 copies. Though odds were not released by the manufacturer, information supplied by dealers breaking several cases indicate on average one in every 18 basic packs contains one of these serial-numbered cards. The Update set is broken down as follows: basic veterans (181-210) and Future Watch (211-240). Each Update Future Watch is serial numbered to 1500 copies. Notable Rookie Cards in the basic set include Albert Pujols, Tsuyoshi Shinjo and Ichiro Suzuki. Notable Rookie Cards in the Update set include Mark Prior and Mark Teixeira.

COMP.BASIC w/o SP's (90) 10.00 25.00
COMP.UPDATE w/o SP's (30) 4.00 10.00
COMMON CARD (1-90) .15 .40
COMMON FW (91-135) 3.00 8.00
FW 91-135 RANDOM INSERTS IN PACKS
FW 91-135 PRINT RUN 1250 SERIAL #'d SETS
COMMON SS (136-180) 2.00 5.00
SS 136-180 RANDOM INSERTS IN PACKS
SS 136-180 PRINT RUN 1250 SERIAL #'d SETS
COMMON CARD (181-210) .25 .60
COMMON CARD (211-240) 2.50 6.00
211-240 RANDOM IN ROOKIE UPD.PACKS
211-240 PRINT RUN 1500 SERIAL #'d SETS
181-240 DISTRIBUTED IN ROOKIE UPD.PACKS
1 Troy Glaus .15 .40
2 Darin Erstad .15 .40
3 Jason Giambi .15 .40
4 Tim Hudson .15 .40
5 Eric Chavez .15 .40
6 Miguel Tejada .15 .40
7 Jose Ortiz .15 .40
8 Carlos Delgado .15 .40
9 Tony Batista .15 .40
10 Raul Mondesi .15 .40
11 Aubrey Huff .15 .40
12 Greg Vaughn .15 .40
13 Roberto Alomar .25 .60
14 Juan Gonzalez .15 .40
15 Jim Thome .25 .60
16 Omar Vizquel .25 .60
17 Edgar Martinez .25 .60
18 Freddy Garcia .15 .40
19 Cal Ripken 1.25 3.00
20 Ivan Rodriguez .25 .60
21 Rafael Palmeiro .25 .60
22 Alex Rodriguez .50 1.25
23 Manny Ramirez Sox .25 .60
24 Pedro Martinez .25 .60
25 Nomar Garciaparra .60 1.50
26 Mike Sweeney .15 .40
27 Jermaine Dye .15 .40
28 Bobby Higginson .15 .40
29 Dean Palmer .15 .40
30 Matt Lawton .15 .40
31 Eric Milton .15 .40
32 Frank Thomas .40 1.00
33 Magglio Ordonez .15 .40
34 David Wells .15 .40
35 Paul Konerko .15 .40
36 Derek Jeter 1.00 2.50
37 Bernie Williams .25 .60
38 Roger Clemens .75 2.00
39 Mike Mussina .25 .60
40 Jorge Posada .25 .60
41 Jeff Bagwell .25 .60
42 Richard Hidalgo .15 .40
43 Craig Biggio .25 .60
44 Greg Maddux .60 1.50
45 Chipper Jones .40 1.00
46 Andruw Jones .25 .60
47 Rafael Furcal .15 .40
48 Tom Glavine .25 .60
49 Jeromy Burnitz .15 .40
50 Jeffrey Hammonds .15 .40
51 Mark McGwire 1.00 2.50
52 Jim Edmonds .15 .40
53 Rick Ankiel .15 .40
54 J.D. Drew .15 .40
55 Sammy Sosa .40 1.00
56 Corey Patterson .15 .40
57 Kerry Wood .15 .40
58 Randy Johnson .40 1.00
59 Luis Gonzalez .15 .40
60 Curt Schilling .15 .40
61 Gary Sheffield .15 .40
62 Shawn Green .15 .40
63 Kevin Brown .15 .40
64 Vladimir Guerrero .40 1.00
65 Jose Vidro .15 .40
66 Barry Bonds 1.00 2.50
67 Jeff Kent .15 .40
68 Livan Hernandez .15 .40
69 Preston Wilson .15 .40
70 Charles Johnson .15 .40
71 Ryan Dempster .15 .40
72 Mike Piazza .60 1.50
73 Al Leiter .15 .40
74 Edgardo Alfonzo .15 .40
75 Robin Ventura .15 .40
76 Tony Gwynn .50 1.25
77 Phil Nevin .15 .40
78 Trevor Hoffman .15 .40
79 Scott Rolen .25 .60
80 Pat Burrell .15 .40
81 Bob Abreu .15 .40
82 Jason Kendall .15 .40
83 Brian Giles .15 .40
84 Kris Benson .15 .40
85 Ken Griffey Jr. .75 2.00
86 Barry Larkin .25 .60
87 Sean Casey .15 .40
88 Todd Helton .25 .60
89 Mike Hampton .15 .40
90 Larry Walker .15 .40
91 Ichiro Suzuki FW RC 300.00 600.00
92 Wilson Betemit FW RC 6.00 15.00
93 Adrian Hernandez FW RC 3.00 8.00
94 Juan Uribe FW RC 4.00 10.00
95 Travis Hafner FW RC 20.00 50.00
96 Morgan Ensberg FW RC 6.00 15.00
97 Sean Douglass FW RC 3.00 8.00
98 Juan Diaz FW RC 3.00 8.00
99 Erick Almonte FW RC 3.00 8.00
100 Ryan Freel FW RC 3.00 8.00
101 Elpidio Guzman FW RC 3.00 8.00
102 Christian Parker FW RC 3.00 8.00
103 Josh Fogg FW RC 3.00 8.00
104 Bert Snow FW RC 3.00 8.00
105 Horacio Ramirez FW RC 4.00 10.00
106 Ricardo Rodriguez FW RC 3.00 8.00
107 Tyler Walker FW RC 3.00 8.00
108 Jose Mieses FW RC 3.00 8.00
109 Billy Sylvester FW RC 3.00 8.00
110 Martin Vargas FW RC 3.00 8.00
111 Andres Torres FW RC 3.00 8.00
112 Greg Miller FW RC 3.00 8.00
113 Alexis Gomez FW RC 3.00 8.00
114 Grant Balfour FW RC 3.00 8.00
115 Henry Mateo FW RC 3.00 8.00
116 Esix Snead FW RC 3.00 8.00
117 Jackson Melian FW RC 3.00 8.00
118 Nate Teut FW RC 3.00 8.00
119 Tsuyoshi Shinjo FW RC 4.00 10.00
120 Carlos Valderrama FW RC 3.00 8.00
121 Johnny Estrada FW RC 4.00 10.00
122 Jason Michaels FW RC 3.00 8.00
123 William Ortega FW RC 3.00 8.00
124 Jason Smith FW RC 3.00 8.00
125 Brian Lawrence FW RC 3.00 8.00
126 Albert Pujols FW RC 125.00 250.00
127 Wilkin Ruan FW RC 3.00 8.00
128 Josh Towers FW RC 4.00 10.00
129 Kris Keller FW RC 3.00 8.00
130 Nick Maness FW RC 3.00 8.00
131 Jack Wilson FW RC 4.00 10.00
132 Brandon Duckworth FW RC 3.00 8.00
133 Mike Penney FW RC 3.00 8.00
134 Jay Gibbons FW RC 4.00 10.00
135 Cesar Crespo FW RC 3.00 8.00
136 Ken Griffey Jr. SS 5.00 12.00
137 Mark McGwire SS 6.00 15.00
138 Derek Jeter SS 6.00 15.00
139 Alex Rodriguez SS 3.00 8.00
140 Sammy Sosa SS 2.50 6.00
141 Carlos Delgado SS 2.00 5.00
142 Cal Ripken SS 8.00 20.00
143 Pedro Martinez SS 2.00 5.00
144 Frank Thomas SS 2.50 6.00
145 Juan Gonzalez SS 2.00 5.00
146 Troy Glaus SS 2.00 5.00
147 Jason Giambi SS 2.00 5.00
148 Ivan Rodriguez SS 2.00 5.00
149 Chipper Jones SS 2.50 6.00
150 Vladimir Guerrero SS 2.50 6.00
151 Mike Piazza SS 4.00 10.00
152 Jeff Bagwell SS 2.00 5.00
153 Randy Johnson SS 2.50 6.00
154 Todd Helton SS 2.00 5.00
155 Gary Sheffield SS 2.00 5.00
156 Tony Gwynn SS 3.00 8.00
157 Barry Bonds SS 6.00 15.00
158 Nomar Garciaparra SS 4.00 10.00
159 Bernie Williams SS 2.00 5.00
160 Greg Vaughn SS 2.00 5.00
161 David Wells SS 2.00 5.00
162 Roberto Alomar SS 2.00 5.00
163 Jermaine Dye SS 2.00 5.00
164 Rafael Palmeiro SS 2.00 5.00
165 Andruw Jones SS 2.00 5.00
166 Preston Wilson SS 2.00 5.00
167 Edgardo Alfonzo SS 2.00 5.00
168 Pat Burrell SS 2.00 5.00
169 Jim Edmonds SS 2.00 5.00
170 Mike Hampton SS 2.00 5.00
171 Jeff Kent SS 2.00 5.00
172 Kevin Brown SS 2.00 5.00
173 Manny Ramirez Sox SS 2.00 5.00
174 Magglio Ordonez SS 2.00 5.00
175 Roger Clemens SS 5.00 12.00
176 Jim Thome SS 2.00 5.00
177 Barry Zito SS 2.00 5.00
178 Brian Giles SS 2.00 5.00
179 Rick Ankiel SS 2.00 5.00
180 Corey Patterson SS 2.00 5.00
181 Garret Anderson .25 .60
182 Jermaine Dye .25 .60
183 Shannon Stewart .25 .60
184 Ben Grieve .25 .60
185 Ellis Burks .25 .60
186 John Olerud .25 .60
187 Tony Batista .25 .60
188 Ruben Sierra .25 .60
189 Carl Everett .25 .60
190 Neifi Perez .25 .60
191 Tony Clark .25 .60
192 Doug Mientkiewicz .25 .60
193 Carlos Lee .25 .60
194 Jorge Posada .40 1.00
195 Lance Berkman 2.00 5.00
196 Ken Caminiti .25 .60
197 Ben Sheets .40 1.00
198 Matt Morris .25 .60
199 Fred McGriff .40 1.00
200 Mark Grace .40 1.00
201 Paul LoDuca .25 .60
202 Tony Armas Jr. .25 .60
203 Andres Galarraga .25 .60
204 Cliff Floyd .25 .60
205 Matt Lawton .25 .60
206 Ryan Klesko .25 .60
207 Jimmy Rollins .25 .60
208 Aramis Ramirez .25 .60
209 Aaron Boone .25 .60
210 Jose Ortiz .25 .60
211 Mark Prior FW RC 6.00 15.00
212 Mark Teixeira FW RC 10.00 25.00
213 Bud Smith FW RC 2.50 6.00
214 Wilmy Caceres FW RC 2.50 6.00
215 Dave Williams FW RC 2.50 6.00
216 Delvin James FW RC 2.50 6.00
217 Endy Chavez FW RC 2.50 6.00
218 Doug Nickle FW RC 2.50 6.00
219 Bret Prinz FW RC 2.50 6.00
220 Troy Mattes FW RC 2.50 6.00
221 Duaner Sanchez FW RC 2.50 6.00
222 Dewon Brazelton FW RC 2.50 6.00
223 Brian Bowles FW RC 2.50 6.00
224 Donaldo Mendez FW RC 2.50 6.00
225 Jorge Julio FW RC 2.50 6.00
226 Matt White FW RC 2.50 6.00
227 Casey Fossum FW RC 2.50 6.00
228 Mike Rivera FW RC 2.50 6.00
229 Joe Kennedy FW RC 3.00 8.00
230 Kyle Lohse FW RC 5.00 12.00
231 Juan Cruz FW RC 2.50 6.00
232 Jeremy Affeldt FW RC 2.50 6.00
233 Brandon Lyon FW RC 2.50 6.00
234 Brian Roberts FW RC 8.00 20.00
235 Willie Harris FW RC 2.50 6.00
236 Pedro Santana FW RC 2.50 6.00
237 Rafael Soriano FW RC 2.50 6.00
238 Steve Green FW RC 2.50 6.00
239 Junior Spivey FW RC 3.00 8.00
240 Rob Mackowiak FW RC 3.00 8.00
NNO Ken Griffey Jr. Promo 1.00 2.50

2001 SP Authentic Limited

*STARS 1-90: 10X TO 25X BASIC 1-90
*FW 91-135: 1X TO 2.5X BASIC 91-135
*SS 136-180: 1.5X TO 4X BASIC 136-180
STATED PRINT RUN 50 SERIAL #'d SETS
91 Ichiro Suzuki FW 1000.00 1500.00
126 Albert Pujols FW 250.00 500.00

2001 SP Authentic BuyBacks

For the third time in the history of the brand (including 1997 and 2000), Upper Deck incorporated Buyback cards into SP Authentic packs. Representatives from UD purchased varying quantities of actual previously released SP Authentic cards ranging from 1993 to 2000. The cards were then signed by the featured ballplayer, hand-numbered in blue ink on front and affixed with a serial-numbered hologram sticker on back (note: it's believed all 2001 hologram sticker numbers begin with the letters "AAA"). In addition to the actual signed card, each Buyback was distributed with a 2 1/2" by 3 1/2" Authenticity Guarantee card. Each of these cards featured a hologram with a matching serial-number and a note of congratulations from Upper Deck's CEO Richard McWilliam. Our listings for these cards feature the year of the card followed by the quantity produced. Thus, "Edgardo Alfonzo 95/77" indicates a 1995 SP Authentic Edgardo Alfonzo card of which 77 copies were made. Please note that several Buyback cards are too scarce for us to provide accurate pricing. Please see our magazine or website for pricing information on these cards as it's made available. The following players were seeded into packs as exchange cards: Roger Clemens, Cal Ripken and Frank Thomas. Collectors did not know which card of these players they would receive until it was mailed to them. Exchange deadline was 8/30/04.

STATED ODDS 1:144
STATED PRINT RUNS LISTED BELOW
NO PRICING ON QTY OF 25 OR LESS
1 Edgardo Alfonzo 95/77 10.00 25.00
3 Edgardo Alfonzo 00/280 10.00 25.00
4 Barry Bonds 93/75 40.00 80.00
5 Barry Bonds 94/103 40.00 80.00
6 Barry Bonds 95/31 40.00 80.00
8 Barry Bonds 96/49 40.00 80.00
11 Barry Bonds 00/146 40.00 80.00
12 Roger Clemens 00/145 20.00 50.00
13 Roger Clemens 99/150 20.00 50.00
16 Carlos Delgado 94/272 6.00 15.00
17 Carlos Delgado 96/81 10.00 25.00
19 Carlos Delgado 98/29 20.00 50.00
20 Carlos Delgado 00/169 6.00 15.00
21 Jim Edmonds 96/72 15.00 40.00
22 Jim Edmonds 97/38 30.00 60.00
26 Jason Giambi 00/290 6.00 15.00
27 Troy Glaus 00/340 6.00 15.00
28 Shawn Green 00/340 10.00 25.00
29 Ken Griffey Jr. 93/34 125.00 300.00
30 Ken Griffey Jr. 94/182 40.00 100.00
31 Ken Griffey Jr. 95/116 40.00 100.00
33 Ken Griffey Jr. 96/53 60.00 150.00
36 Ken Griffey Jr. 00/333 40.00 100.00
37 Tony Gwynn 93/101 20.00 50.00
38 Tony Gwynn 94/88 20.00 50.00
39 Tony Gwynn 95/179 20.00 50.00
40 Tony Gwynn 96/82 20.00 50.00
43 Tony Gwynn 00/95 20.00 50.00
44 Todd Helton 00/194 10.00 25.00
45 Tim Hudson 00/291 10.00 25.00
46 Randy Johnson 93/97 30.00 60.00
47 Randy Johnson 94/146 30.00 60.00
48 Randy Johnson 95/121 30.00 60.00
50 Randy Johnson 96/78 50.00 100.00
53 Randy Johnson 00/213 30.00 60.00
56 Andruw Jones 00/336 30.00 60.00
58 Chipper Jones 95/118 30.00 80.00
59 Chipper Jones 96/72 40.00 100.00
62 Chipper Jones 00/303 30.00 80.00
64 Cal Ripken 94/99 40.00 100.00
65 Cal Ripken 95/37 75.00 150.00
70 Cal Ripken 00/266 60.00 120.00
72 Alex Rodriguez 95/117 50.00 100.00
74 Alex Rodriguez 96/72 50.00 100.00
77 Alex Rodriguez 00/332 20.00 50.00
78 Ivan Rodriguez 93/89 10.00 25.00
81 Ivan Rodriguez 96/64 10.00 25.00
84 Ivan Rodriguez 00/163 10.00 25.00
85 Gary Sheffield 93/82 8.00 20.00
87 Gary Sheffield 95/70 8.00 20.00
88 Gary Sheffield 96/67 8.00 20.00
89 Gary Sheffield 97/43 12.50 30.00
90 Gary Sheffield 98/27 15.00 40.00
91 Gary Sheffield 00/146 5.00 12.00
92 Sammy Sosa 93/73 50.00 100.00
94 Sammy Sosa 95/30 50.00 100.00
97 Fernando Tatis 00/267 4.00 10.00
98 Frank Thomas 93/79 30.00 60.00
99 Frank Thomas 94/165 30.00 60.00
101 Frank Thomas 97/34 50.00 100.00
103 Frank Thomas 00/302 20.00 50.00
105 Mo Vaughn 93/94 10.00 25.00
106 Mo Vaughn 94/102 10.00 25.00
107 Mo Vaughn 95/129 6.00 15.00
109 Mo Vaughn 96/81 10.00 25.00
110 Mo Vaughn 97/36 15.00 40.00
112 Mo Vaughn 00/309 6.00 15.00
113 Robin Ventura 00/340 6.00 15.00
114 Matt Williams 00/340 10.00 25.00

2001 SP Authentic Chirography

Signed Chirography inserts were brought back for the fourth straight year within SP Authentic. Over 40 players were featured in the 2001 issue, with announced odds of 1:72 packs. Each card features a horizontal design and a small black and white action photo of the player at the side to allow the maximum amount of room for the featured player's autograph (of which is typically found signed in blue ink). Quantities produced for each card varied dramatically and shortly after the product was released, representatives at Upper Deck publicly announced print runs on a selection of the toughest cards to obtain. Those quantities have been added to our checklist following the featured player's name.

STATED ODDS 1:72
SP PRINT RUNS LISTED BELOW
SP'S ARE NOT SERIAL NUMBERED
SP PRINT RUNS PROVIDED BY UPPER DECK
AB Albert Belle 6.00 15.00
AJ Andruw Jones 6.00 15.00
AP Albert Pujols 250.00 400.00
AR Alex Rodriguez SP/229 * 40.00 100.00
BS Ben Sheets 4.00 10.00
CB Carlos Beltran 6.00 15.00
CD Carlos Delgado 4.00 10.00
CF Cliff Floyd 6.00 15.00
CJ Chipper Jones SP/184 * 30.00 60.00
CR Cal Ripken SP/109 * 50.00 100.00
DD Darren Dreifort SP/206 * 4.00 10.00
DER Darin Erstad 4.00 10.00
DES David Espinosa 4.00 10.00
DJ David Justice 8.00 20.00
DS Dane Sardinha 4.00 10.00
DW David Wells 15.00 40.00
EA Edgardo Alfonzo 6.00 15.00
JC Jose Canseco 10.00 25.00
JD J.D. Drew 8.00 20.00
JE Jim Edmonds 8.00 20.00
JG Jason Giambi 6.00 15.00
KG Ken Griffey Jr. SP/126 * 50.00 100.00
LG Luis Gonzalez SP/271 * 10.00 25.00
MB Milton Bradley 6.00 15.00
MK Mark Kotsay SP/228 * 6.00 15.00
MS Mike Sweeney 6.00 15.00
MV Mo Vaughn SP/103 * 6.00 15.00
MW Matt Williams 10.00 25.00
PB Pat Burrell 6.00 15.00
RF Rafael Furcal SP/222 * 6.00 15.00
RH Rick Helling SP/211 * 4.00 10.00
RJ Randy Johnson SP/143 * 40.00 100.00
RW Rondell White 6.00 15.00
SG Shawn Green SP/82 * 6.00 15.00
SS Sammy Sosa SP/76 * 50.00 100.00
TH Tim Hudson 4.00 10.00
TL Travis Lee SP/226 * 4.00 10.00
TOG Tony Gwynn SP/76 * 20.00 50.00
TOH Todd Helton SP/152 * 10.00 25.00
TRG Troy Glaus 6.00 15.00

2001 SP Authentic Chirography Gold

These scarce autograph cards are a straight parallel of the more commonly available Chirography cards. The Gold cards, however, were all produced to quantities mirroring the featured player's uniform number. Furthermore, the cards are individually numbered on front in blue ink and the imagery and design accents are printed in a subdued gold color (rather than the black and white design used on the basic Chirography cards). Many of these cards are too scarce for us to provide accurate pricing on.

STATED PRINT RUNS LISTED BELOW
NO PRICING ON QTY OF 25 OR LESS
GAB Albert Belle/88 20.00 50.00
GDD Darren Dreifort/37 10.00 25.00
GDES David Espinosa/79 10.00 25.00
GDJ David Justice/28 25.00 60.00
GDS Dane Sardinha/50 10.00 25.00
GDW David Wells/33 10.00 25.00
GKG Ken Griffey Jr./30 75.00 150.00
GMS Mike Sweeney/29 20.00 50.00
GMV Mo Vaughn/42 20.00 50.00
GRH Rick Helling/32 10.00 25.00
GRJ Randy Johnson/51 50.00 120.00

2001 SP Authentic Chirography Update

Randomly inserted into Upper Deck Rookie Update packs, thse eight cards feature autographs from leading players in the game. Cal Ripken and Ichiro Suzuki did not return their cards in time for inclusion in these packs and these cards are available as exchange cards. Those cards could be redeemed until September 13th, 2004. These cards are serial numbered to 250.

STATED PRINT RUN 250 SERIAL #'d SETS
SPCR Cal Ripken 40.00 80.00
SPDM Doug Mientkiewicz 6.00 15.00
SPIS Ichiro Suzuki 400.00 800.00
SPJP Jorge Posada 40.00 80.00
SPKG Ken Griffey Jr. 40.00 80.00
SPLB Lance Berkman 6.00 15.00
SPMS Mike Sweeney 6.00 15.00
SPTG Tony Gwynn 10.00 25.00

2001 SP Authentic Chirography Update Silver

STATED PRINT RUN 100 SERIAL #'d SETS
SPCR Cal Ripken 75.00 150.00
SPDM Doug Mientkiewicz 10.00 25.00
SPJP Jorge Posada 50.00 100.00
SPKG Ken Griffey Jr. 50.00 100.00
SPLB Lance Berkman 15.00 40.00
SPMS Mike Sweeney 10.00 25.00
SPTG Tony Gwynn 15.00 40.00

2001 SP Authentic Cooperstown Calling Game Jersey

This 22-card set features a selection of players that were voted in (or were soon to be voted in) to the baseball Hall of Fame in Cooperstown, NY. Each card features a swatch of game-used jersey incorporated into an attractive horizontal design. Though specific odds per pack were not released for this set, Upper Deck did release cumulative odds of 1:24 packs for finding a game-used jersey card from either of the Cooperstown Calling, UD Exclusives or UD Exclusives Combos sets within the SP Authentic product.

OVERALL JERSEY ODDS 1:24
SP PRINT RUNS PROVIDED BY UD
CCAD Andre Dawson 3.00 8.00
CCRM Bill Mazeroski 10.00 25.00
CCCR Cal Ripken 8.00 20.00
CCDM Don Mattingly 10.00 25.00
CCDW Dave Winfield 3.00 8.00
CCEM Eddie Murray 3.00 8.00
CCGC Gary Carter 3.00 8.00
CCGG Goose Gossage 3.00 8.00
CCIS Ichiro Suzuki SP 600.00 1500.00
CCJB Jeff Bagwell 3.00 8.00
CCKP Kirby Puckett 5.00 12.00
CCKS Kazuhiro Sasaki 2.00 5.00
CCMP Mike Piazza SP 10.00 25.00
CCMR Manny Ramirez Sox SP 5.00 12.00
CCOS Ozzie Smith 6.00 15.00
CCPM Pedro Martinez SP 3.00 8.00
CCPM Paul Molitor 4.00 10.00
CCRC Roger Clemens 8.00 20.00
CCRM Roger Maris SP/243 * 12.00 30.00
CCRS Ryne Sandberg 10.00 25.00
CCSG Steve Garvey 2.00 5.00
CCTG Tony Gwynn 5.00 12.00
CCWB Wade Boggs 3.00 8.00

2001 SP Authentic Stars of Japan

This 30-card dual player set features a selection of Japanese stars active in Major League baseball at the time of issue. The cards were distributed in special Stars of Japan packs of which were available as a bonus pack within each sealed box of 2001 SP Authentic baseball. Each Stars of Japan pack contained three cards and one in every 12 packs contained a memorabilia card.

COMPLETE SET (30) 20.00 50.00
ONE 3-CARD PACK PER SPA HOBBY BOX
RS1 I.Suzuki T.Shinjo 3.00 8.00
RS2 S.Hasegawa H.Irabu .75 2.00
RS3 T.Ohka M.Suzuki .75 2.00
RS4 T.Shinjo H.Irabu .75 2.00
RS5 I.Suzuki H.Nomo 4.00 10.00
RS6 T.Shinjo M.Suzuki .75 2.00
RS7 T.Shinjo K.Sasaki .75 2.00
RS8 H.Nomo T.Ohka .75 2.00
RS9 I.Suzuki M.Suzuki 3.00 8.00
RS10 H.Nomo S.Hasegawa .75 2.00
RS11 H.Nomo M.Yoshii .75 2.00
RS12 H.Nomo H.Irabu .75 2.00
RS13 S.Hasegawa K.Sasaki .75 2.00
RS14 S.Hasegawa M.Suzuki .75 2.00
RS15 T.Shinjo H.Nomo .75 2.00
RS16 T.Shinjo T.Ohka .75 2.00
RS17 I.Suzuki K.Sasaki 4.00 10.00
RS18 M.Yoshii H.Irabu .75 2.00
RS19 I.Suzuki T.Ohka 3.00 8.00
RS20 H.Irabu K.Sasaki .75 2.00
RS21 T.Shinjo M.Yoshii .75 2.00
RS22 I.Suzuki S.Hasegawa 3.00 8.00
RS23 M.Suzuki K.Sasaki .75 2.00
RS24 I.Suzuki H.Irabu 3.00 8.00
RS25 T.Ohka K.Sasaki .75 2.00
RS26 T.Shinjo S.Hasegawa .75 2.00
RS27 M.Yoshii K.Sasaki .75 2.00
RS28 H.Nomo K.Sasaki .75 2.00
RS29 I.Suzuki M.Yoshii 3.00 8.00
RS30 H.Nomo M.Suzuki .75 2.00

2001 SP Authentic Stars of Japan Game Ball

This six-card set features a selection of Japanese stars actively playing in the Major Leagues at the time of issue. Each card features a patch of game-used baseball. The cards were distributed in special Stars of Japan packs. Each sealed box of 2001 SP Authentic contained one three-card Stars of Japan pack inside. Though individual Jersey card odds were not announced, the cumulative odds of finding a memorabilia card (ball, base, bat or jersey) from a Stars of Japan packs was 1:12.

OVERALL MEMORABILIA ODDS 1:12 SOJ
SP PRINT RUNS PROVIDED BY UD
NO PRICING ON QTY OF 40 OR LESS
GOLD RANDOM INSERTS IN PACKS
GOLD PRINT RUN 25 SERIAL #'d SETS
GOLD NO PRICING DUE TO SCARCITY
BBHI Hideki Irabu 4.00 10.00
BBIS Ichiro Suzuki 40.00 80.00
BBKS Kazuhiro Sasaki 6.00 15.00
BBMY Masato Yoshii 4.00 10.00
BBTS Tsuyoshi Shinjo SP/50 * 6.00 15.00

2001 SP Authentic Stars of Japan Game Ball-Base Combos

This 14-card dual player set features a selection of Japanese stars actively playing in the Major Leagues at the time of issue. Each card features a piece of a game-used baseball coupled with a piece of game-used base. The cards were distributed in special Stars of Japan packs. Each sealed box of 2001 SP Authentic contained one three-card Stars of Japan pack inside.Though individual Jersey card odds were not announced, the cumulative odds of finding a memorabilia card (ball, base, bat or jersey) from a Stars of Japan packs was 1:12.

OVERALL SOJ COMBO ODDS 1:576 BASIC
SP PRINT RUNS PROVIDED BY UD
NO PRICING ON QTY OF 40 OR LESS
GOLD RANDOM INSERTS IN PACKS
GOLD PRINT RUN 25 SERIAL #'d SETS
GOLD NO PRICING DUE TO SCARCITY
HNKS Nomo/Sasaki SP/50 * 40.00 80.00
HNSH Nomo/Hasegawa 10.00 25.00
ISMY Ichiro/Yoshii 40.00 80.00
ISSH Ichiro/Hasegawa SP/72 * 60.00 120.00
TOKS Ohka/Sasaki 4.00 10.00

2001 SP Authentic Stars of Japan Game Bat

This three-card set features a selection of Japanese stars actively playing in the Major Leagues at the time of issue. Each card features a piece of game-used bat. The cards were distributed in special Stars of Japan packs. Each sealed box of 2001 SP Authentic contained one three-card Stars of Japan pack inside.Though individual Jersey card odds were not announced, the cumulative odds of finding a memorabilia card (ball, base, bat or jersey) from a Stars of Japan packs was 1:12.

OVERALL MEMORABILIA ODDS 1:12 SOJ

SP PRINT RUNS PROVIDED BY UD
NO PRICING ON QTY OF 40 OR LESS
GOLD RANDOM INSERTS IN PACKS
GOLD PRINT RUN 25 SERIAL #'d SETS
GOLD NO PRICING DUE TO SCARCITY
BMY Masato Yoshii 4.00 10.00

2001 SP Authentic Stars of Japan Game Bat-Jersey Combos

This 4-card dual player set features a selection of Japanese stars actively playing in the Major Leagues at the time of issue. Each card features a combination of a game-used bat chip or game-used jersey swatch from the featured players. The cards were distributed in special Stars of Japan packs. Each sealed box of 2001 SP Authentic contained one 3-card Stars of Japan pack inside.Though individual Jersey card odds were not announced, the cumulative odds of finding a memorabilia card (ball, base, bat or jersey) from a Stars of Japan packs was 1:12.

OVERALL SOJ COMBO ODDS 1:576 BASIC
SASAKI-HASEGAWA IS DUAL JERSEY
HASEGAWA SHINJO IS DUAL BAT
GOLD RANDOM INSERTS IN PACKS
GOLD PRINT RUN 25 SERIAL #'d SETS
GOLD NO PRICING DUE TO SCARCITY
BBHS Hasegawa/Shinjo 10.00 25.00
JBNN Nomo/Nomo 30.00 60.00
JBSN Sasaki/Nomo 10.00 25.00
JJSH Sasaki/Hasegawa 6.00 15.00

2001 SP Authentic Stars of Japan Game Jersey

This six-card set features a selection of Japanese stars actively playing in the Major Leagues at the time of issue. Each card features a swatch of game-used jersey. The cards were distributed in special Stars of Japan packs. Each sealed box of 2001 SP Authentic contained one three-card Stars of Japan pack inside. Though individual Jersey card odds were not announced, the cumulative odds of finding a memorabilia card (ball, base, bat or jersey) from a Stars of Japan packs was 1:12. Ichiro Suzuki's jersey card was not available at time of packout and an exchange card was seeded into packs in it's place. The exchange card had a redemption deadline of August 30th, 2004. Though not serial-numbered, officials at Upper Deck announced that only 260 copies of Ichiro's jersey card were produced.

OVERALL MEMORABILIA ODDS 1:12 SOJ
SP PRINT RUNS PROVIDED BY UD
GOLD RANDOM INSERTS IN PACKS
GOLD PRINT RUN 25 SERIAL #'d SETS
NO GOLD PRICING DUE TO SCARCITY
JHN Hideo Nomo 6.00 15.00
JIS Ichiro Suzuki SP/260 * 20.00 50.00
JKS Kazuhiro Sasaki 4.00 10.00
JMY Masato Yoshii 4.00 10.00
JSH Shigetoshi Hasegawa 4.00 10.00
JTS Tsuyoshi Shinjo 6.00 15.00

2001 SP Authentic Sultan of Swatch Memorabilia

This 21-card set features a selection of significant achievements from legendary slugger Babe Ruth's storied career. Each card features a swatch of game-used uniform (most likely pants) and is hand-numbered in blue ink on front to the year or statisitical figure of the featured event (i.e. card SOS3 highlights Ruth's 94 career wins as a pitcher, thus only 94 hand-numbered copies of that card were produced). Quantities on each card vary from as many as 94 copies to as few as 14 copies. The cards were randomly inserted into packs at an unspecified ratio.

PRINT RUNS B/WN 14-94 COPIES PER
NO PRICING ON QTY OF 24 OR LESS
SOS2 B.Ruth 29.2 Inn/29 250.00 500.00
SOS3 B.Ruth 94 Wins/94 250.00 500.00
SOS4 B.Ruth 54 HRs/54 250.00 500.00
SOS5 B.Ruth 59 HRs/59 250.00 500.00
SOS6 B.Ruth 3 HRs WS/26 250.00 500.00
SOS7 B.Ruth 60 HRs/27 250.00 500.00
SOS8 B.Ruth Called Shot/32 250.00 500.00
SOS13 B.Ruth 40 HRs/26 250.00 500.00
SOS14 B.Ruth HR Title/27 250.00 500.00
SOS15 B.Ruth 50 HRs/28 250.00 500.00
SOS16 B.Ruth Leads Way/29 250.00 500.00
SOS17 B.Ruth 49 HRs/30 250.00 500.00
SOS18 B.Ruth Last Title/31 250.00 500.00
SOS19 B.Ruth 1st AS/33 250.00 500.00
SOS20 B.Ruth 1st HOF/36 250.00 500.00
SOS21 B.Ruth House/48 250.00 500.00

2001 SP Authentic UD Exclusives Game Jersey

This 6-card set features a selection of superstars signed exclusively to Upper Deck for the rights to produce game-used jersey cards. Each card features a swatch of game-used jersey incorporated into an attractive horizontal design. Though specific odds per pack were not released for this set, Upper Deck did release cumulative odds of 1:24 packs for finding a game-used jersey card from either of the Cooperstown Calling, UD Exclusives or UD Exclusives Combos sets within the SP Authentic product. Shortly after release, representatives at Upper Deck publicly released print run information on several short prints. These quantities have been added to the end of the card description within our checklist.

OVERALL JERSEY ODDS 1:24
SP PRINT RUNS PROVIDED BY UD
AR Alex Rodriguez 6.00 15.00
GS Gary Sheffield 4.00 10.00
JD Joe DiMaggio SP/243 * 30.00 60.00
KG Ken Griffey Jr. 6.00 15.00
MM Mickey Mantle SP/243 * 75.00 150.00
SS Sammy Sosa 6.00 15.00

2001 SP Authentic UD Exclusives Game Jersey Combos

This six-card set features a selection of superstars signed exclusively to Upper Deck for the rights to produce game-used jersey cards. Each card features a swatch of game-used jersey from each featured player incorporated into an attractive horizontal design. Though specific odds per pack were not released for this set, Upper Deck did release cumulative odds of 1:24 packs for finding a game-used jersey card from either of the Cooperstown Calling, UD Exclusives or UD Exclusives Combos sets within the SP Authentic product. Shortly after release, representatives at Upper Deck publicly released print run information on several short prints. These quantities have been added to the end of the card description within our checklist.

OVERALL JERSEY ODDS 1:24
SP PRINT RUNS PROVIDED BY UD
GD Griffey/DiMag SP/98 * 60.00 120.00
MD Mantle/DiMag SP/98 * 75.00 150.00
MG Mantle/Griffey Jr. SP/98 * 75.00 150.00
RS A.Rodriguez/O.Smith 10.00 25.00
SD Sosa/Dawson 10.00 25.00
SW Sheffield/Winfield 10.00 25.00

2002 SP Authentic

This 230 card set was released in two separate series. The basic SP Authentic product (containing cards 1-170) was issued in September, 2002. Update cards 171-230 were distributed within packs of 2002 Upper Deck Rookie Update in mid-December, 2002. SP Authentic packs were issued in five card packs with a $5 SRP. Boxes contained 24 packs and were packed five to a case. Cards numbered 1 through 90 featured veterans while cards number 91 through 135 were part of the Future Watch subset and were printed to a stated print run of 1999 serial numbered sets. Cards numbered 136 through 170 were signed by the player and most of the cards were printed to a stated print run of 999 serial numbered sets. Cards number 146, 152 and 157 were printed to a stated print run of 249 serial numbered sets. Update cards 201-230 continued the Future Watch subset (focusing on rookies and prospects) and each card was serial numbered to 1999. Though pack odds for these cards were never released, we estimate the cards were seeded at an approximate rate of 1:7 Rookie Update packs. In addition, an exchange card with a redemption deadline of August 8th, 2005, good for a signed Joe DiMaggio poster was randomly inserted into SP Authentic packs.

COMP.LOW w/o SP's (90) 6.00 15.00
COMP.UPDATE w/o SP's (30) 4.00 10.00
COMMON CARD (1-90) .15 .40
COMMON (91-135/201-230) 2.00 5.00
91-135/201-230 PRINT 1999 SERIAL #'d SETS
COMMON CARD (136-170) 4.00 10.00
136-170 PRINT RUN 999 SERIAL #'d SETS
146/152/157 PRINT 249 SERIAL #'d SETS
91-170/201-230 RANDOM IN PACKS
COMMON CARD (171-200) .25 .60
DIMAG POSTER EXCH RANDOM IN PACKS
DIMAGGIO EXCH.DEADLINE 08/08/05
1 Troy Glaus .15 .40
2 Darin Erstad .15 .40
3 Barry Zito .15 .40
4 Eric Chavez .15 .40
5 Tim Hudson .15 .40
6 Miguel Tejada .15 .40
7 Carlos Delgado .15 .40
8 Shannon Stewart .15 .40
9 Ben Grieve .15 .40
10 Jim Thome .25 .60
11 C.C. Sabathia .15 .40
12 Ichiro Suzuki .75 2.00
13 Freddy Garcia .15 .40
14 Edgar Martinez .25 .60
15 Bret Boone .15 .40
16 Jeff Conine .15 .40
17 Alex Rodriguez .50 1.50
18 Juan Gonzalez .15 .40
19 Ivan Rodriguez .25 .60
20 Rafael Palmeiro .25 .60
21 Hank Blalock .25 .60
22 Pedro Martinez .25 .60
23 Manny Ramirez .25 .60
24 Nomar Garciaparra .60 1.50
25 Carlos Beltran .15 .40
26 Mike Sweeney .15 .40
27 Randall Simon .15 .40
28 Dmitri Young .15 .40
29 Bobby Higginson .15 .40
30 Corey Koskie .15 .40
31 Eric Milton .15 .40
32 Torii Hunter .15 .40
33 Joe Mays .15 .40
34 Frank Thomas .40 1.00
35 Mark Buehrle .15 .40
36 Magglio Ordonez .15 .40
37 Kenny Lofton .15 .40
38 Roger Clemens .75 2.00
39 Derek Jeter 1.00 2.50
40 Jason Giambi .15 .40
41 Bernie Williams .25 .60
42 Alfonso Soriano .15 .40
43 Lance Berkman .15 .40
44 Roy Oswalt .15 .40
45 Jeff Bagwell .25 .60
46 Craig Biggio .25 .60
47 Chipper Jones .40 1.00
48 Greg Maddux .60 1.50
49 Gary Sheffield .15 .40
50 Andruw Jones .25 .60
51 Ben Sheets .15 .40
52 Richie Sexson .15 .40
53 Albert Pujols .75 2.00
54 Matt Morris .15 .40
55 J.D. Drew .15 .40
56 Sammy Sosa .40 1.00
57 Kerry Wood .15 .40
58 Corey Patterson .15 .40
59 Mark Prior .25 .60
60 Randy Johnson .40 1.00
61 Luis Gonzalez .15 .40
62 Curt Schilling .15 .40
63 Shawn Green .15 .40
64 Kevin Brown .15 .40
65 Hideo Nomo .40 1.00
66 Vladimir Guerrero .40 1.00
67 Jose Vidro .15 .40
68 Barry Bonds 1.00 2.50
69 Jeff Kent .15 .40
70 Rich Aurilia .15 .40
71 Preston Wilson .15 .40
72 Josh Beckett .15 .40
73 Mike Lowell .15 .40
74 Roberto Alomar .25 .60
75 Mo Vaughn .15 .40
76 Jeromy Burnitz .15 .40
77 Mike Piazza .60 1.50
78 Sean Burroughs .15 .40
79 Phil Nevin .15 .40
80 Bobby Abreu .15 .40
81 Pat Burrell .15 .40
82 Scott Rolen .25 .60
83 Jason Kendall .15 .40
84 Brian Giles .15 .40
85 Ken Griffey Jr. .75 2.00
86 Adam Dunn .15 .40
87 Sean Casey .15 .40
88 Todd Helton .25 .60
89 Larry Walker .15 .40
90 Mike Hampton .15 .40
91 Brandon Puffer FW RC 2.00 5.00
92 Tom Shearn FW RC 2.00 5.00
93 Chris Baker FW RC 2.00 5.00
94 Gustavo Chacin FW RC 3.00 8.00
95 Joe Orloski FW RC 2.00 5.00
96 Mike Smith FW RC 2.00 5.00
97 John Ennis FW RC 2.00 5.00
98 John Foster FW RC 2.00 5.00
99 Kevin Gryboski FW RC 2.00 5.00
100 Brian Mallette FW RC 2.00 5.00
101 Takahito Nomura FW RC 2.00 5.00
102 So Taguchi FW RC 3.00 8.00
103 Jeremy Lambert FW RC 2.00 5.00
104 Jason Simontacchi FW RC 2.00 5.00
105 Jorge Sosa FW RC 3.00 8.00
106 Brandon Backe FW RC 3.00 8.00
107 P.J. Bevis FW RC 2.00 5.00
108 Jeremy Ward FW RC 2.00 5.00
109 Doug Devore FW RC 2.00 5.00
110 Ron Chiavacci FW 2.00 5.00
111 Ron Calloway FW RC 2.00 5.00
112 Nelson Castro FW RC 2.00 5.00
113 Deivis Santos FW 2.00 5.00
114 Earl Snyder FW RC 2.00 5.00
115 Julio Mateo FW RC 2.00 5.00
116 J.J. Putz FW RC 2.00 5.00
117 Allan Simpson FW RC 2.00 5.00
118 Satoru Komiyama FW RC 2.00 5.00
119 Adam Walker FW RC 2.00 5.00
120 Oliver Perez FW RC 3.00 8.00
121 Cliff Bartosh FW RC 2.00 5.00
122 Todd Donovan FW RC 2.00 5.00
123 Elio Serrano FW RC 2.00 5.00
124 Pete Zamora FW RC 2.00 5.00
125 Mike Gonzalez FW RC 2.00 5.00
126 Travis Hughes FW RC 2.00 5.00
127 Jorge De La Rosa FW RC 2.00 5.00
128 Anastacio Martinez FW RC 2.00 5.00
129 Colin Young FW RC 2.00 5.00
130 Nate Field FW RC 2.00 5.00
131 Tim Kalita FW RC 2.00 5.00
132 Julius Matos FW RC 2.00 5.00
133 Terry Pearson FW RC 2.00 5.00
134 Kyle Kane FW RC 2.00 5.00
135 Mitch Wylie FW RC 2.00 5.00
136 Rodrigo Rosario AU RC 4.00 10.00
137 Franklyn German AU RC 4.00 10.00
138 Reed Johnson AU RC 8.00 20.00
139 Luis Martinez AU RC 4.00 10.00
140 Michael Crudale AU RC 4.00 10.00
141 Francis Beltran AU RC 4.00 10.00
142 Steve Kent AU RC 4.00 10.00
143 Felix Escalona AU RC 4.00 10.00
144 Jose Valverde AU RC 6.00 15.00
145 Victor Alvarez AU RC 4.00 10.00
146 Kazuhisa Ishii AU/249 RC 8.00 20.00
147 Jorge Nunez AU RC 4.00 10.00
148 Eric Good AU RC 4.00 10.00
149 Luis Ugueto AU RC 4.00 10.00
150 Matt Thornton AU RC 4.00 10.00
151 Wilson Valdez AU RC 4.00 10.00
152 Han Izquierdo AU/249 RC 15.00 40.00
153 Jaime Cerda AU RC 4.00 10.00
154 Mark Corey AU RC 4.00 10.00
155 Tyler Yates AU RC 4.00 10.00
156 Steve Bechler AU RC 4.00 10.00
157 Ben Howard AU/249 RC 15.00 40.00
158 Anderson Machado AU RC 4.00 10.00
159 Jorge Padilla AU RC 4.00 10.00
160 Eric Junge AU RC 4.00 10.00
161 Adrian Burnside AU RC 4.00 10.00
162 Josh Hancock AU RC 8.00 20.00
163 Chris Booker AU RC 4.00 10.00
164 Cam Esslinger AU RC 4.00 10.00
165 Rene Reyes AU RC 4.00 10.00
166 Aaron Cook AU RC 6.00 15.00
167 Juan Brito AU RC 4.00 10.00
168 Miguel Ascencio AU RC 4.00 10.00
169 Kevin Frederick AU RC 4.00 10.00
170 Edwin Almonte AU RC 4.00 10.00
171 Erubiel Durazo .25 .60
172 Junior Spivey .25 .60
173 Geronimo Gil .25 .60
174 Cliff Floyd .25 .60
175 Brandon Larson .25 .60
176 Aaron Boone .25 .60
177 Shawn Estes .25 .60
178 Austin Kearns .25 .60
179 Joe Borchard .25 .60
180 Russell Branyan .25 .60
181 Jay Payton .25 .60
182 Andres Torres .25 .60
183 Andy Van Hekken .25 .60
184 Alex Sanchez .25 .60
185 Endy Chavez .25 .60
186 Bartolo Colon .25 .60
187 Raul Mondesi .25 .60
188 Robin Ventura .25 .60
189 Mike Mussina .40 1.00
190 Jorge Posada .40 1.00
191 Ted Lilly .25 .60
192 Ray Durham .25 .60
193 Brett Myers .25 .60
194 Marlon Byrd .25 .60
195 Vicente Padilla .25 .60
196 Josh Fogg .25 .60
197 Kenny Lofton .25 .60
198 Scott Rolen .40 1.00
199 Jason Lane .25 .60
200 Josh Phelps .25 .60
201 Travis Driskill FW RC 2.00 5.00
202 Howie Clark FW RC 2.00 5.00
203 Mike Mahoney FW 2.00 5.00
204 Brian Tallet FW RC 2.00 5.00
205 Kirk Saarloos FW RC 2.00 5.00
206 Barry Wesson FW RC 2.00 5.00
207 Aaron Guiel FW RC 2.00 5.00
208 Shawn Sedlacek FW RC 2.00 5.00
209 Jose Diaz FW RC 2.00 5.00
210 Jorge Nunez FW 2.00 5.00
211 Danny Mota FW RC 2.00 5.00
212 David Ross FW RC 3.00 8.00
213 Jayson Durocher FW RC 2.00 5.00
214 Shane Nance FW RC 2.00 5.00
215 Wil Nieves FW RC 2.00 5.00
216 Freddy Sanchez FW RC 4.00 10.00
217 Alex Pelaez FW RC 2.00 5.00
218 Jamey Carroll FW RC 3.00 8.00
219 J.J. Trujillo FW RC 2.00 5.00
220 Kevin Pickford FW RC 2.00 5.00
221 Clay Condrey FW RC 2.00 5.00
222 Chris Snelling FW RC 2.50 6.00
223 Cliff Lee FW RC 4.00 10.00
224 Jeremy Hill FW RC 2.00 5.00
225 Jose Rodriguez FW RC 2.00 5.00
226 Lance Carter FW RC 2.00 5.00
227 Ken Huckaby FW RC 2.00 5.00
228 Scott Wiggins FW RC 2.00 5.00
229 Corey Thurman FW RC 2.00 5.00
230 Kevin Cash FW RC 2.00 5.00
RJD Joe DiMaggio AU Poster 125.00 200.00

2002 SP Authentic Limited

*LTD 1-90: 5X TO 12X BASIC
*LTD 91-135: .6X TO 1.5X BASIC
*LTD 136-170: .4X TO 1X BASIC
*LTD 146/152/157: .3X TO .8X BASIC
STATED PRINT RUN 125 SERIAL #'d SETS

2002 SP Authentic Limited Gold

*GOLD 1-90: 10X TO 25X BASIC
*GOLD 91-135: 1X TO 2.5X BASIC
*GOLD 136-170: .6X TO 1.5X BASIC
*GOLD 146/152/157: .5X TO 1.2X BASIC
STATED PRINT RUN 50 SERIAL #'d SETS
146 Kazuhisa Ishii FW AU 30.00 60.00

2002 SP Authentic Chirography

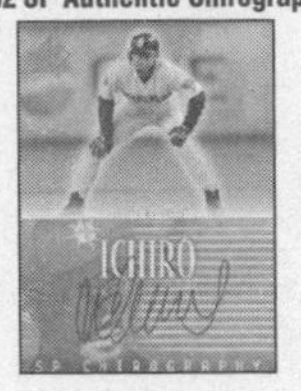

Bret Boone and Tony Gwynn are available only in the basic Chirography set. No Gold parallels were created for them. The following players packed out as redemption cards: Alex Rodriguez, Bret Boone, Sammy Sosa and Tony Gwynn. The deadline for exchange cards to be received by Upper Deck was September 10th, 2005.

STATED ODDS 1:72
STATED PRINT RUNS LISTED BELOW
EXCHANGE DEADLINE 9/10/05
AD Adam Dunn/348 10.00 25.00
AG Alex Graman/418 4.00 10.00
AR Alex Rodriguez/391 20.00 50.00
BB Barry Bonds/112 20.00 50.00
BBo Bret Boone/500 6.00 15.00
BZ Barry Zito/419 6.00 15.00
CF Cliff Floyd/313 6.00 15.00
CS C.C. Sabathia/442 10.00 25.00
DE Darin Erstad/80 6.00 15.00
DM Doug Mientkiewicz/478 6.00 15.00
FG Freddy Garcia/456 6.00 15.00
HB Hank Blalock/282 6.00 15.00
IS Ichiro Suzuki/78 300.00 500.00
JB John Buck/427 6.00 15.00
JG Jason Giambi/244 6.00 15.00
JL Jon Lieber/462 6.00 15.00
JM Joe Mays/469 4.00 10.00
KG Ken Griffey Jr./238 40.00 80.00
MBr Milton Bradley/470 6.00 15.00
MBu Mark Buehrle/438 12.50 30.00
MM Mark McGwire/50 150.00 300.00
MS Mike Sweeney/265 6.00 15.00
RS Richie Sexson/483 6.00 15.00
SB Sean Burroughs/275 4.00 10.00
SS Sammy Sosa/247 25.00 60.00
TG Tom Glavine/376 15.00 40.00
TGw Tony Gwynn/75 10.00 25.00

2002 SP Authentic Chirography Gold

Gold parallel cards were not created for Tony Gwynn and Bret Boone. Sammy Sosa and Alex Rodriguez packed out as exchange cards with a redemption deadline of September 10th, 2005.

SEE BECKETT.COM FOR PRINT RUNS
NO PRICING ON QTY OF 25 OR LESS
AD Adam Dunn/44 20.00 50.00
AG Alex Graman/76 6.00 15.00
BZ Barry Zito/75 10.00 25.00
CF Cliff Floyd/30 15.00 40.00
CS C.C. Sabathia/52 20.00 50.00
FG Freddy Garcia/34 15.00 40.00
IS Ichiro Suzuki/51 600.00 1200.00
JL Jon Lieber/32 15.00 40.00
KG Ken Griffey Jr./30 75.00 150.00
MBu Mark Buehrle/56 30.00 60.00
MS Mike Sweeney/29 15.00 40.00
TG Tom Glavine/47 15.00 40.00

2002 SP Authentic Game Jersey

Inserted into packs at stated odds of one in 24, these 38 cards feature some of the leading players along with a game-used memorabilia swatch. A few cards were issued in shorter supply and we have notated that in our checklist along with a stated print run when available.

STATED ODDS 1:24
SP INFO PROVIDED BY UPPER DECK
SP'S ARE NOT SERIAL-NUMBERED
JAJ Andruw Jones 6.00 15.00
JAP Andy Pettitte 6.00 15.00
JAR Alex Rodriguez 8.00 20.00
JBW Bernie Williams 6.00 15.00
JBZ Barry Zito 4.00 10.00
JCC C.C. Sabathia 4.00 10.00
JCD Carlos Delgado 4.00 10.00
JCJ Chipper Jones 6.00 15.00
JCS Curt Schilling 4.00 10.00
JDE Darin Erstad 4.00 10.00
JGM Greg Maddux 6.00 15.00
JGS Gary Sheffield 4.00 10.00
JIR Ivan Rodriguez 4.00 10.00
JIS Ichiro Suzuki SP 10.00 25.00
JJBA Jeff Bagwell 6.00 15.00
JJBU Jeromy Burnitz SP 6.00 15.00
JJE Jim Edmonds 4.00 10.00
JJGO Juan Gonzalez 4.00 10.00
JJGR Jason Giambi 4.00 10.00
JJK Jason Kendall 4.00 10.00
JJT Jim Thome 6.00 15.00
JKG Ken Griffey Jr. SP/95 * 8.00 20.00
JKI Kazuhisa Ishii 6.00 15.00
JMM Mark McGwire SP 75.00 150.00
JMO Magglio Ordonez 4.00 10.00
JMP Mike Piazza 6.00 15.00
JMR Manny Ramirez 6.00 15.00
JOV Omar Vizquel 6.00 15.00
JPW Preston Wilson 4.00 10.00
JRA Roberto Alomar 6.00 15.00
JRC Roger Clemens 8.00 20.00
JRJ Randy Johnson 6.00 15.00
JRV Robin Ventura 4.00 10.00
JSG Shawn Green 4.00 10.00
JSR Scott Rolen 6.00 15.00
JSS Sammy Sosa 6.00 15.00
JTH Todd Helton 6.00 15.00
JTS Tsuyoshi Shinjo 4.00 10.00

2002 SP Authentic Game Jersey Gold

Randomly inserted into packs, this is a parallel to the Game Jersey insert set. Each of these cards have a stated print run which matches the featured player's uniform number and we have notated that information in our checklist. If a card was issued to a stated print run of 25 or fewer, it is not priced due to market scarcity.

STATED PRINT RUNS LISTED BELOW
NO PRICING ON QTY OF 25 OR LESS
JAP Andy Pettitte/46 12.50 30.00
JBW Bernie Williams/51 12.50 30.00
JBZ Barry Zito/75 8.00 20.00
JCC C.C. Sabathia/52 8.00 20.00
JCS Curt Schilling/38 10.00 25.00
JGM Greg Maddux/31 40.00 80.00
JIS Ichiro Suzuki/51 60.00 120.00
JKG Ken Griffey Jr./30 15.00 40.00
JMO Magglio Ordonez/30 10.00 25.00
JMP Mike Piazza/31 40.00 80.00
JPW Preston Wilson/44 8.00 20.00
JRJ Randy Johnson/51 15.00 40.00

2002 SP Authentic Prospects Signatures

Inserted into packs at a stated rate of one in 36, these 12 cards feature signed cards of some leading baseball prospects.

STATED ODDS 1:36
PAG Alex Graman 3.00 8.00
PBH Bill Hall 4.00 10.00
PDM Dustan Mohr 3.00 8.00
PDW Danny Wright 3.00 8.00
PJC Jose Cueto 3.00 8.00
PJDE Jeff Deardorff 3.00 8.00
PJDI Jose Diaz 3.00 8.00
PKH Ken Huckaby 3.00 8.00
PMG Matt Guerrier 3.00 8.00
PMS Marcos Scutaro 6.00 15.00
PST Steve Torrealba 3.00 8.00
PXN Xavier Nady 3.00 8.00

2002 SP Authentic Signed Big Mac

Randomly inserted into packs, these 10 cards feature authentic autographs of retired superstar Mark McGwire. Each of these cards were signed to a different stated print run and we have notated that information in our checklist. If a card was signed to 25 or fewer copies, there is no pricing provided due to market scarcity.

RANDOM INSERTS IN PACKS
SEE BECKETT.COM FOR PRINT RUNS
NO PRICING ON QTY OF 25 OR LESS
MM6 Mark McGwire/70 75.00 200.00

2002 SP Authentic USA Future Watch

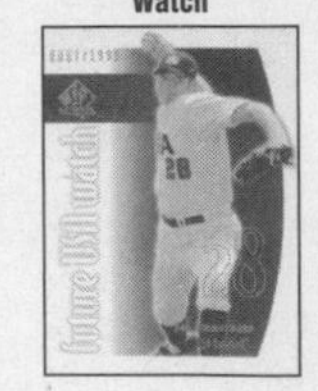

Randomly inserted into packs, these 22 cards feature players from the USA National Team. Each card was issued to a stated print run of 1999 serial numbered sets.

RANDOM INSERTS IN PACKS
STATED PRINT RUN 1999 SERIAL #'d SETS
USA1 Chad Cordero 4.00 10.00
USA2 Philip Humber 5.00 12.00
USA3 Grant Johnson 2.00 5.00
USA4 Wes Littleton 2.00 5.00
USA5 Kyle Sleeth 2.00 5.00
USA6 Huston Street 4.00 10.00
USA7 Brad Sullivan 2.00 5.00
USA8 Bob Zimmermann 2.00 5.00
USA9 Abe Alvarez 2.00 5.00
USA10 Kyle Bakker 2.00 5.00
USA11 Landon Powell 2.00 5.00
USA12 Clint Sammons 2.00 5.00
USA13 Michael Aubrey 3.00 8.00
USA14 Aaron Hill 4.00 10.00
USA15 Conor Jackson 6.00 15.00
USA16 Eric Patterson 3.00 8.00
USA17 Dustin Pedroia 10.00 25.00
USA18 Rickie Weeks 10.00 25.00
USA19 Shane Costa 2.00 5.00
USA20 Mark Jurich 2.00 5.00
USA21 Sam Fuld 6.00 15.00
USA22 Carlos Quentin 3.00 8.00

2002 SP Authentic Hawaii Sign of the Times Duke Snider

This card was distributed on February 27th, 2002 at Upper Deck's poolside reception during the Hawaii Trade Conference. Each attendee received either this signed Duke Snider card or a signed card of NFL legend John Riggins, both of which were hand-numbered to 500 copies in blue ink. Snider signed each card in blue ink sharpie across the front.

DS Duke Snider/500 12.50 30.00

2003 SP Authentic

This 239-card set was distributed in two separate series. The primary SP Authentic product was originally issued as a 189-card set released in May, 2003. These cards were issued in five card packs with an $5 SRP which were issued 24 packs to a box and 12 boxes to a case. Update cards 190-239 were issued randomly within packs of 2003 Upper Deck Finite and released in December, 2003. Cards numbered 1-90 featured commonly seeded veterans while cards 91-123 featured what was titled SP Rookie Archives (RA) and those cards were issued to a stated print run of 2500 serial numbered sets. Cards numbered 124 to 150 feature a subset called Back to 93 and those cards were issued to a stated print run of 1993 serial numbered sets. Cards numbered 151 through 189 feature Future Watch prospects (with 181 to 189 being autographed). Please note that cards numbered 151-180 were also issued to a stated print run of 2003 serial numbered sets and cards numbered 181-189 were issued to a stated print run of 500 serial numbered sets. The Jose Contreras signed card was issued either as a live card or an exchange card. The Contreras exchange card could be redeemed until May 21, 2006. Cards 190-239 (released at year's end) continued the Future Watch subset but each card was serial numbered to 699 copies.

91-123 PRINT RUN 2500 SERIAL #'d SETS
124-150 PRINT RUN 1993 SERIAL #'d SETS
151-180 PRINT RUN 2003 SERIAL #'d SETS
181-189 PRINT RUN 500 SERIAL #'d SETS
91-189 RANDOM INSERTS IN PACKS
190-239 RANDOM IN 03 UD FINITE PACKS
190-239 PRINT RUN 699 SERIAL #'d SETS
J.CONTRERAS IS PART LIVE/PART EXCH
J.CONTRERAS EXCH DEADLINE 05/21/06
1 Darin Erstad .15 .40
2 Garret Anderson .15 .40
3 Troy Glaus .15 .40
4 Eric Chavez .15 .40
5 Barry Zito .25 .60
6 Miguel Tejada .25 .60
7 Eric Hinske .15 .40
8 Carlos Delgado .15 .40
9 Josh Phelps .15 .40
10 Ben Grieve .15 .40
11 Carl Crawford .25 .60
12 Omar Vizquel .25 .60
13 Matt Lawton .15 .40

14 C.C. Sabathia	.25	.60
15 Ichiro Suzuki	.50	1.25
16 John Olerud	.15	.40
17 Freddy Garcia	.15	.40
18 Jay Gibbons	.15	.40
19 Tony Batista	.15	.40
20 Melvin Mora	.15	.40
21 Alex Rodriguez	.50	1.25
22 Rafael Palmeiro	.25	.60
23 Hank Blalock	.15	.40
24 Nomar Garciaparra	.25	.60
25 Pedro Martinez	.25	.60
26 Johnny Damon	.25	.60
27 Mike Sweeney	.15	.40
28 Carlos Febles	.15	.40
29 Carlos Beltran	.25	.60
30 Carlos Pena	.25	.60
31 Eric Munson	.15	.40
32 Bobby Higginson	.15	.40
33 Torii Hunter	.15	.40
34 Doug Mientkiewicz	.15	.40
35 Jacque Jones	.15	.40
36 Paul Konerko	.25	.60
37 Bartolo Colon	.15	.40
38 Magglio Ordonez	.25	.60
39 Derek Jeter	1.00	2.50
40 Bernie Williams	.25	.60
41 Jason Giambi	.15	.40
42 Alfonso Soriano	.25	.60
43 Roger Clemens	.50	1.25
44 Jeff Bagwell	.25	.60
45 Jeff Kent	.15	.40
46 Lance Berkman	.25	.60
47 Chipper Jones	.40	1.00
48 Andruw Jones	.15	.40
49 Gary Sheffield	.15	.40
50 Ben Sheets	.15	.40
51 Richie Sexson	.15	.40
52 Geoff Jenkins	.15	.40
53 Jim Edmonds	.25	.60
54 Albert Pujols	.50	1.25
55 Scott Rolen	.25	.60
56 Sammy Sosa	.40	1.00
57 Kerry Wood	.15	.40
58 Eric Karros	.15	.40
59 Luis Gonzalez	.15	.40
60 Randy Johnson	.40	1.00
61 Curt Schilling	.25	.60
62 Fred McGriff	.25	.60
63 Shawn Green	.15	.40
64 Paul Lo Duca	.15	.40
65 Vladimir Guerrero	.25	.60
66 Jose Vidro	.15	.40
67 Barry Bonds	.60	1.50
68 Rich Aurilia	.15	.40
69 Edgardo Alfonzo	.15	.40
70 Ivan Rodriguez	.25	.60
71 Mike Lowell	.15	.40
72 Derrek Lee	.15	.40
73 Tom Glavine	.25	.60
74 Mike Piazza	.40	1.00
75 Roberto Alomar	.25	.60
76 Ryan Klesko	.15	.40
77 Phil Nevin	.15	.40
78 Mark Kotsay	.15	.40
79 Jim Thome	.25	.60
80 Pat Burrell	.15	.40
81 Bobby Abreu	.15	.40
82 Jason Kendall	.15	.40
83 Brian Giles	.15	.40
84 Aramis Ramirez	.15	.40
85 Austin Kearns	.15	.40
86 Ken Griffey Jr.	.75	2.00
87 Adam Dunn	.25	.60
88 Larry Walker	.25	.60
89 Todd Helton	.25	.60
90 Preston Wilson	.15	.40
91 Derek Jeter RA	2.50	6.00
92 Johnny Damon RA	.60	1.50
93 Chipper Jones RA	1.00	2.50
94 Manny Ramirez RA	1.00	2.50
95 Trot Nixon RA	.40	1.00
96 Alex Rodriguez RA	1.25	3.00
97 Chan Ho Park RA	.60	1.50
98 Brad Fullmer RA	.40	1.00
99 Billy Wagner RA	.40	1.00
100 Hideo Nomo RA	1.00	2.50
101 Freddy Garcia RA	.40	1.00
102 Darin Erstad RA	.40	1.00
103 Jose Cruz Jr. RA	.40	1.00
104 Nomar Garciaparra RA	.60	1.50
105 Magglio Ordonez RA	.60	1.50
106 Kerry Wood RA	.40	1.00
107 Troy Glaus RA	.40	1.00
108 J.D. Drew RA	.40	1.00
109 Alfonso Soriano RA	.60	1.50
110 Danys Baez RA	.40	1.00
111 Kazuhiro Sasaki RA	.40	1.00
112 Barry Zito RA	.60	1.50
113 Brent Abernathy RA	.40	1.00
114 Ben Diggins RA	.40	1.00
115 Ben Sheets RA	.40	1.00
116 Brad Wilkerson RA	.40	1.00
117 Juan Pierre RA	.40	1.00
118 Jon Rauch RA	.40	1.00
119 Ichiro Suzuki RA	1.25	3.00
120 Albert Pujols RA	1.25	3.00
121 Mark Prior RA	.60	1.50
122 Mark Teixeira RA	.60	1.50
123 Kazuhisa Ishii RA	.40	1.00
124 Troy Glaus B93	.40	1.00
125 Randy Johnson B93	1.00	2.50
126 Curt Schilling B93	.60	1.50
127 Chipper Jones B93	1.00	2.50
128 Greg Maddux B93	1.25	3.00
129 Nomar Garciaparra B93	.60	1.50
130 Pedro Martinez B93	.60	1.50
131 Sammy Sosa B93	1.00	2.50
132 Mark Prior B93	.60	1.50
133 Ken Griffey Jr. B93	2.00	5.00
134 Adam Dunn B93	.60	1.50
135 Jeff Bagwell B93	.60	1.50
136 Vladimir Guerrero B93	.60	1.50
137 Mike Piazza B93	1.00	2.50
138 Tom Glavine B93	.60	1.50
139 Derek Jeter B93	2.50	6.00
140 Roger Clemens B93	1.25	3.00
141 Jason Giambi B93	.40	1.00
142 Alfonso Soriano B93	.60	1.50
143 Miguel Tejada B93	.60	1.50
144 Barry Zito B93	.60	1.50
145 Jim Thome B93	.60	1.50
146 Barry Bonds B93	1.50	4.00
147 Ichiro Suzuki B93	1.25	3.00
148 Albert Pujols B93	1.25	3.00
149 Alex Rodriguez B93	1.25	3.00
150 Carlos Delgado B93	.40	1.00
151 Rich Fischer FW RC	1.25	3.00
152 Brandon Webb FW RC	4.00	10.00
153 Rob Hammock FW RC	1.25	3.00
154 Matt Kata FW RC	1.25	3.00
155 Tim Olson FW RC	1.25	3.00
156 Oscar Villarreal FW RC	1.25	3.00
157 Michael Hessman FW RC	1.25	3.00
158 Daniel Cabrera FW RC	2.00	5.00
159 Jon Leicester FW RC	1.25	3.00
160 Todd Wellemeyer FW RC	1.25	3.00
161 Felix Sanchez FW RC	1.25	3.00
162 David Sanders FW RC	1.25	3.00
163 Josh Stewart FW RC	1.25	3.00
164 Arnie Munoz FW RC	1.25	3.00
165 Ryan Cameron FW RC	1.25	3.00
166 Clint Barmes FW RC	3.00	8.00
167 Josh Willingham FW RC	4.00	10.00
169 Willie Eyre FW RC	1.25	3.00
170 Brent Hoard FW RC	1.25	3.00
171 Terrmel Sledge FW RC	1.25	3.00
172 Phil Seibel FW RC	1.25	3.00
173 Craig Brazell FW RC	1.25	3.00
174 Jeff Duncan FW RC	1.25	3.00
176 Bernie Castro FW RC	1.25	3.00
177 Mike Nicolas FW RC	1.25	3.00
178 Rett Johnson FW RC	1.25	3.00
179 Bobby Madritsch FW RC	1.25	3.00
180 Chris Capuano FW RC	1.25	3.00
181 Hid Matsui FW AU RC	200.00	400.00
182 Jose Contreras FW AU RC	12.50	30.00
183 Lew Ford FW AU RC	10.00	25.00
184 Jeremy Griffiths FW AU RC	6.00	15.00
185 G.Quiroz FW AU RC	6.00	15.00
186 Alej Machado FW AU RC	6.00	15.00
187 Fran Cruceta FW AU RC	6.00	15.00
188 Prentice Redman FW AU RC	6.00	15.00
189 Shane Bazzell FW AU RC	6.00	15.00
190 Aaron Looper FW RC	1.25	3.00
191 Alex Prieto FW RC	1.25	3.00
192 Alfredo Gonzalez FW RC	1.25	3.00
193 Andrew Brown FW RC	1.25	3.00
194 Anthony Ferrari FW RC	1.25	3.00
195 Aquilino Lopez FW RC	1.25	3.00
196 Beau Kemp FW RC	1.25	3.00
197 Bo Hart FW RC	1.25	3.00
198 Chad Gaudin FW RC	1.25	3.00
199 Colin Porter FW RC	1.25	3.00
200 D.J. Carrasco FW RC	1.25	3.00
201 Dan Haren FW RC	6.00	15.00
202 Danny Garcia FW RC	1.25	3.00
203 Jon Switzer FW	1.25	3.00
204 Edwin Jackson FW RC	2.00	5.00
205 Fernando Cabrera FW RC	1.25	3.00
206 Garrett Atkins FW	1.25	3.00
207 Gerald Laird FW	1.25	3.00
208 Greg Jones FW RC	1.25	3.00
209 Ian Ferguson FW RC	1.25	3.00
210 Jason Roach FW RC	1.25	3.00
211 Jason Shiell FW RC	1.25	3.00
212 Jeremy Bonderman FW RC	5.00	12.00
213 Jeremy Wedel FW RC	1.25	3.00
214 Jhonny Peralta FW	1.25	3.00
215 Delmon Young FW RC	8.00	20.00
216 Jorge DePaula FW	1.25	3.00
217 Josh Hall FW RC	1.25	3.00
218 Julio Manon FW RC	1.25	3.00
219 Kevin Correia FW RC	1.25	3.00
220 Kevin Ohme FW RC	1.25	3.00
221 Kevin Tolar FW RC	1.25	3.00
222 Luis Ayala FW RC	1.25	3.00
223 Luis De Los Santos FW	1.25	3.00
224 Chad Cordero FW RC	1.25	3.00
225 Mark Malaska FW RC	1.25	3.00
226 Khalil Greene FW	2.00	5.00
227 Michael Nakamura FW RC	1.25	3.00
228 Michel Hernandez FW RC	1.25	3.00
229 Miguel Ojeda FW RC	1.25	3.00
230 Mike Neu FW RC	1.25	3.00
231 Nate Bland FW RC	1.25	3.00
232 Pete LaForest FW RC	1.25	3.00
233 Rickie Weeks FW RC	4.00	10.00
234 Rosman Garcia FW RC	1.25	3.00
235 Ryan Wagner FW RC	1.25	3.00
236 Lance Niekro FW	1.25	3.00
237 Tom Gregorio FW RC	1.25	3.00
238 Tommy Phelps FW	1.25	3.00
239 Wilfredo Ledezma FW RC	1.25	3.00

2003 SP Authentic Matsui Future Watch Autograph Parallel

RANDOM INSERTS IN PACKS
PRINT RUNS B/WN 10-75 COPIES PER
NO PRICING ON QTY OF 25 OR LESS

181A H.Matsui Bronze/75	175.00	300.00

2003 SP Authentic 500 HR Club

Randomly inserted into packs, this card featured members of the 500 homer club along with a game-used memorablia piece from each player. A gold parallel was also issued for this card and that card was issued to a stated print run of 25 serial numbered sets. The gold version is not priced due to market scarcity.

RANDOM INSERTS IN PACKS
GOLD PRINT RUN 25 SERIAL #'d CARDS
NO GOLD PRICING DUE TO SCARCITY

500 Sos/Ted/Mick/Mac/Bond	75.00	200.00

2003 SP Authentic Chirography

Randomly inserted into packs, these cards feature authentic autographs from the player pictured on the card. These cards marked the debut of Upper Deck using the "Band-Aid" approach to putting autographs on cards. What that means is that the player does not actually sign the card, instead the player signs a sticker which is then attached to the card. Please note that since these cards were issued to varying print runs, we have notated the stated print run next to the player's name in our checklist. Several players did not get their cards signed in time for inclusion in this product and those exchange cards could be redeemed until April 21, 2006. Please note that many cards in the various sets have notations but neither Mark Prior nor Corey Patterson used whatever notations they were supposed to throughout the course of this product.

PRINT RUNS B/WN 50-350 COPIES PER
NO BRONZE PRICING ON 25 OR LESS
SILVER PRINT B/WN 15-50 COPIES PER
NO SILVER PRICING ON 25 OR LESS
GOLD PRINT 10 SERIAL #'d SETS
NO GOLD PRICING DUE TO SCARCITY
EXCHANGE DEADLINE 05/21/06

AD Adam Dunn/170	6.00	15.00
BA Jeff Bagwell/175	30.00	60.00
CR Cal Ripken/250	30.00	80.00
FC Rafael Furcal/150	6.00	15.00
FG Freddy Garcia/345	6.00	15.00
FL Cliff Floyd/125	4.00	10.00
GA1 Garret Anderson/350	6.00	15.00
GI Jason Giambi/250	6.00	15.00
GJ Ken Griffey Jr./350	40.00	80.00
GL Brian Giles/225	6.00	15.00
IC Ichiro Suzuki/85	400.00	600.00
IS Ichiro Suzuki/75	400.00	600.00
JD Johnny Damon/245	6.00	15.00
JE2 Jim Edmonds/350	10.00	25.00
JM Joe Mays/245	4.00	10.00
JR Ken Griffey Jr./350	40.00	80.00
JT1 Jim Thome/250	15.00	40.00
KE Jason Kendall/145	6.00	15.00
LG1 Luis Gonzalez/195	6.00	15.00
MM Mark McGwire/50	175.00	300.00
RO Scott Rolen/345	6.00	15.00
RS Richie Sexson/245	6.00	15.00
SA Sammy Sosa/335	40.00	80.00
SO Sammy Sosa/335	20.00	50.00
SW Mike Sweeney/125	6.00	15.00
TO Torii Hunter/245	6.00	15.00
TS Tim Salmon/350	6.00	15.00

2003 SP Authentic Chirography Bronze

RANDOM INSERTS IN PACKS
PRINT RUNS B/WN 25-100 COPIES PER
NO PRICING ON QTY OF 25 OR LESS
EXCHANGE DEADLINE 05/21/06
A FEW CARDS FEATURE INSCRIPTIONS

AD Adam Dunn/50	15.00	40.00
BA Jeff Bagwell/50	40.00	100.00
CR Cal Ripken/75	40.00	100.00
FC Rafael Furcal/50	10.00	25.00
FG Freddy Garcia/100	10.00	25.00
FL Cliff Floyd/50	6.00	15.00
GI Jason Giambi/50	10.00	25.00
GJ Ken Griffey Jr./100	50.00	100.00
GL Brian Giles/50	10.00	25.00
IC Ichiro Suzuki ROY/50	1000.00	2000.00
IS Ichiro Suzuki MVP/50	1000.00	2000.00
JD Johnny Damon/100	10.00	25.00
JM Joe Mays/100	6.00	15.00
JR Ken Griffey Jr./100	50.00	100.00
KE Jason Kendall/50	10.00	25.00
RO Scott Rolen/100	25.00	60.00
RS Richie Sexson/100	10.00	25.00
SA Sammy Sosa/100	50.00	100.00
SO Sammy Sosa/100	30.00	60.00
SW Mike Sweeney/75	10.00	25.00
TO Torii Hunter/100	6.00	15.00

2003 SP Authentic Chirography Silver

RANDOM INSERTS IN PACKS
PRINT RUNS B/WN 15-50 COPIES PER
NO PRICING ON QTY OF 25 OR LESS
EXCHANGE DEADLINE 05/21/06
A FEW CARDS FEATURE INSCRIPTIONS

FG Freddy Garcia/50	15.00	40.00
JD Johnny Damon/50	15.00	40.00
JM Joe Mays/50	10.00	25.00
RO Scott Rolen/50	40.00	100.00
RS Richie Sexson/50	15.00	40.00
SA Sammy Sosa/50	50.00	100.00
SO Sammy Sosa/50	30.00	60.00
TO Torii Hunter/50	10.00	25.00

2003 SP Authentic Chirography Dodgers Stars

Randomly inserted in packs, these 11 cards feature retired Dodger stars and were issued to varying print runs. We have noted the stated print run in our checklist next to the player's name.

PRINT RUNS B/WN 170-345 COPIES PER
SILVER PRINT RUN 50 SERIAL #'d SETS
GOLD PRINT RUN 10 SERIAL #'d SETS
NO GOLD PRICING DUE TO SCARCITY

BB Bill Buckner/245	8.00	20.00
BI Bill Russell/245	6.00	15.00
CE Ron Cey/345	6.00	15.00
DL Davey Lopes/245	6.00	15.00
DN Don Newcombe/345	8.00	20.00
DS Duke Snider/345	10.00	25.00
JN Tommy John/170	6.00	15.00
MW Maury Wills/320	6.00	15.00
SG Steve Garvey/320	6.00	15.00
SU Don Sutton/245	6.00	15.00
SY Steve Yeager/345	6.00	15.00

2003 SP Authentic Chirography Dodgers Stars Bronze

*BRONZE: .6X TO 1.5X BASIC DODGER
RANDOM INSERTS IN PACKS
STATED PRINT RUN 100 SERIAL #'d SETS
T.JOHN PRINT RUN 75 SERIAL #'d CARDS
ALL HAVE DODGERS INSCRIPTION

2003 SP Authentic Chirography Dodgers Stars Silver

*SILVER: .75X TO 2X BASIC DODGER
RANDOM INSERTS IN PACKS
STATED PRINT RUN 50 SERIAL #'d SETS
MOST HAVE 81 WS CHAMPS INSCRIPTION

2003 SP Authentic Chirography Doubles

Randomly inserted into packs, these 15 cards feature signatures from two different players, who had a reason for commonality. These cards were issued to a stated print run of anywhere from 10 to 150 copies and we have placed that information next to the player's name in our checklist. Please note that cards with a stated print run of 25 or fewer are not priced due to market scarcity. In addition, a few cards were issued as exchange cards and those cards could be redeemed until May 21, 2006.

PRINT RUNS B/WN 10-150 COPIES PER
NO PRICING ON QTY OF 25 OR LESS
EXCHANGE DEADLINE 05/21/06

FB W.Ford/Y.Berra/75	75.00	200.00
FE C.Fisk/D.Evans/75	40.00	80.00
FM C.Fisk/B.Mazeroski/75	30.00	60.00
GG K.Griffey/J.Giambi/75	60.00	120.00
GR S.Garvey/R.Cey/75	30.00	60.00
JI K.Griffey/I.Suzuki/125	400.00	600.00
KR T.Kubek/B.Richardson/75	50.00	100.00
KT J.Koosman/T.Seaver/75	40.00	100.00
SJ S.Sosa/J.Giambi/75	30.00	60.00
WB M.Wilson/B.Buckner/150	25.00	60.00

2003 SP Authentic Chirography Flashback

Randomly inserted into packs, these cards feature an important moment from the player's career as well as authentic autograph. Most of these cards were issued to a stated print run of 350 copies but a few were Issued to differing amounts so we have noted the print run information next to the player's name in our checklist. In addition, some players did not return their autograph in time and those cards could be exchanged until May 21, 2006.

PRINT RUNS B/WN 55-350 COPIES PER
NO BRONZE PRICING ON QTY OF 25 OR LESS
SILVER PRINT B/WN 15-50 COPIES PER
NO SILVER PRICING ON QTY OF 25 OR LESS
GOLD PRINT RUN 10 SERIAL #'d SETS
NO GOLD PRICING DUE TO SCARCITY
EXCHANGE DEADLINE 05/21/06

BN Brian Giles/245	6.00	15.00
CF1 Cliff Floyd/350	6.00	15.00
GM Ken Griffey Jr./350	60.00	150.00
JA Jason Giambi/350	6.00	15.00
JE1 Jim Edmonds/350	10.00	25.00
LA Luis Gonzalez/200	8.00	20.00
MA Mark McGwire/55	150.00	300.00
SR Sammy Sosa/245	20.00	50.00

2003 SP Authentic Chirography Flashback Bronze

RANDOM INSERTS IN PACKS
PRINT RUNS B/WN 25-100 COPIES PER
NO PRICING ON QTY OF 25 OR LESS
EXCHANGE DEADLINE 05/21/06
MOST CARDS FEATURE INSCRIPTIONS

BN Brian Giles/50	10.00	25.00
GM Ken Griffey Jr./100	75.00	200.00
JA Jason Giambi/100	10.00	25.00
LA Luis Gonzalez/75	12.50	30.00
SR Sammy Sosa/100	20.00	50.00

2003 SP Authentic Chirography Flashback Silver

RANDOM INSERTS IN PACKS
PRINT RUNS B/WN 15-50 COPIES PER
NO PRICING ON QTY OF 25 OR LESS
EXCHANGE DEADLINE 05/21/06
MOST CARDS HAVE TEAM INSCRIPTION

JA0 Jason Giambi/50	12.50	30.00
SR Sammy Sosa/50	30.00	60.00

2003 SP Authentic Chirography Hall of Famers

Randomly inserted into packs, these 14 cards feature autographs of Hall of Famers. Since these cards were issued to varying print runs, we have identified the stated print run next to the player's name in our checklist.

PRINT RUNS B/WN 150-350 COPIES PER
SILVER PRINT B/WN 25-50 COPIES PER
NO SILVER PRICING ON QTY OF 25 OR LESS
GOLD PRINT RUN 10 SERIAL #'d SETS
NO GOLD PRICING DUE TO SCARCITY

BG Bob Gibson/245	12.50	30.00
CF Carlton Fisk/240	15.00	40.00
DS Duke Snider/250	10.00	25.00
DW2 Dave Winfield/350	10.00	25.00
GC1 Gary Carter/350	12.00	30.00
JB1 Johnny Bench/350	30.00	60.00
NR Nolan Ryan/170	50.00	120.00
OC Orlando Cepeda/245	10.00	25.00
RF Rollie Fingers/170	6.00	15.00
RR Robin Roberts/170	10.00	25.00
RY Robin Yount/350	20.00	50.00
TP Tony Perez/320	6.00	15.00
TS Tom Seaver/170	25.00	60.00
WF Whitey Ford/150	20.00	50.00

2003 SP Authentic Chirography Hall of Famers Bronze

RANDOM INSERTS IN PACKS
PRINT RUNS B/WN 50-100 COPIES PER
ALL HAVE HOF INSCRIPTION

BG Bob Gibson/100	20.00	50.00
CF Carlton Fisk/100	25.00	60.00
DS Duke Snider/100	15.00	40.00
NR Nolan Ryan/50	60.00	150.00
OC Orlando Cepeda/100	15.00	40.00
RF Rollie Fingers/50	10.00	25.00
RR Robin Roberts/50	15.00	40.00
TP Tony Perez/100	10.00	25.00
TS Tom Seaver/75	40.00	100.00
WF Whitey Ford/75	25.00	60.00

2003 SP Authentic Chirography Hall of Famers Silver

RANDOM INSERTS IN PACKS
PRINT RUNS B/WN 25-50 COPIES PER
NO PRICING ON QTY OF 25 OR LESS
ALL HAVE HOF YEAR INSCRIPTION

BG Bob Gibson/50	30.00	80.00
CF Carlton Fisk/50	30.00	80.00
DS Duke Snider/50	20.00	50.00
OC Orlando Cepeda/50	20.00	50.00
TP Tony Perez/50	12.50	30.00
TS Tom Seaver/50	50.00	120.00

2003 SP Authentic Chirography Triples

Randomly inserted in packs, these 12 cards feature autographs from three leading players. These cards were issued to stated print runs of anywhere from 10 to 75 copies and we are only providing pricing for cards with a stated print run of more than 10 copies. The following cards were available only as an exchange and those cards could be redeemed until May 21, 2006: Berra/Kubek/Richardson, Fisk/Carter/Gibson, Griffey Jr./Ichiro/Sosa, Griffey Jr./Sosa/Giambi, Giambi/Sosa/Griffey Jr., Ichiro/Sosa/Giambi, McGwire/Sosa/Griffey Jr., McGwire/Sosa/Ichiro and Seaver/Koosman/McGraw.

RANDOM INSERTS IN PACKS
PRINT RUN B/WN 10-75 COPIES PER CARD
NO PRICING ON QTY OF 10 OR LESS
EXCHANGE DEADLINE 05/21/06

BKR Berra/Kubek/Richardson	75.00	200.00
FCG Fisk/Carter/Gibson EXCH	40.00	100.00
GIS Griffey/Suzuki/Sosa EXCH	400.00	600.00
GLC Garvey/Lopes/Cey	50.00	100.00
GRC Garvey/Russell/Cey	50.00	100.00
GSG Griffey/Sosa/Giambi EXCH	150.00	250.00
GSJ Giambi/Sosa/Griffey	75.00	150.00
ISG Suzuki/Sosa/Giambi	250.00	500.00
SEA Salmon/Erstad/Anderson	30.00	60.00
SKM Seaver/Koosman/McGraw	60.00	150.00

2003 SP Authentic Chirography World Series Heroes

Randomly inserted into packs, these 17 cards feature players who were leading players in at least one World Series. Each of these cards were issued to varying print runs and we have identified the stated print run next to the player's name in our checklist. Andruw Jones did not return his cards in time for inclusion in this product so those exchange cards could be redeemed until May 21, 2006.

PRINT RUNS B/WN 145-350 COPIES PER
SILVER PRINT B/WN 25-50 COPIES PER
NO SILVER PRICING ON QTY OF 25 OR LESS
GOLD PRIN RUN 10 SERIAL #'d SETS
NO GOLD PRICING DUE TO SCARCITY
EXCHANGE DEADLINE 05/21/06

AJ1 Andruw Jones/350	8.00	20.00
BM Bill Mazeroski/245	8.00	20.00
CF Carlton Fisk/200	15.00	40.00
CR Cal Ripken/295	25.00	60.00
CS Curt Schilling/345	10.00	25.00
DE Darin Erstad/245	8.00	20.00
DJ David Justice/170	10.00	25.00
ER Edgar Renteria/220	8.00	20.00
GA Garret Anderson/245	8.00	20.00
GC Gary Carter/345	12.00	30.00
GO Luis Gonzalez/225	8.00	20.00
GS Ken Griffey Sr./295	8.00	20.00
JK Jerry Koosman/170	10.00	25.00
JP Jorge Posada/350	20.00	50.00
KG Kirk Gibson/145	10.00	25.00
TI Tim Salmon/245	10.00	25.00
TM Tug McGraw/170	20.00	50.00

2003 SP Authentic Chirography World Series Heroes Bronze

RANDOM INSERTS IN PACKS
PRINT RUNS B/WN 50-100 COPIES PER
EXCHANGE DEADLINE 05/21/06
ALL HAVE WS YEAR INSCRIPTION

BM Bill Mazeroski/100	12.00	30.00
CF Carlton Fisk/75	25.00	60.00
CS Curt Schilling/100	15.00	40.00
DE Darin Erstad/100	12.50	30.00
DJ David Justice/75	15.00	40.00
ER Edgar Renteria/75	12.50	30.00
GA Garret Anderson/100	12.50	30.00
GC Gary Carter/100	20.00	50.00
GO Luis Gonzalez/100	12.50	30.00
GS Ken Griffey Sr./100	12.50	30.00
JK Jerry Koosman/75	15.00	40.00
KG Kirk Gibson/50	15.00	40.00
TI Tim Salmon/100	15.00	40.00
TM Tug McGraw/100	30.00	80.00

2003 SP Authentic Chirography World Series Heroes Silver

RANDOM INSERTS IN PACKS
PRINT RUNS B/WN 25-50 COPIES PER
NO PRICING ON QTY OF 25 OR LESS
MOST FEATURE WS EVENT INSCRIPTIONS

BM Bill Mazeroski/50 15.00 40.00
CS Curt Schilling/50 20.00 50.00
DE Darin Erstad/50 15.00 40.00
DJ David Justice/50 20.00 50.00
GA Garret Anderson/50 20.00 50.00
GC Gary Carter/50 20.00 50.00
GO Luis Gonzalez/50 15.00 40.00
GS Ken Griffey Sr./50 15.00 40.00
JK Jerry Koosman/50 20.00 50.00
TI Tim Salmon/50 20.00 50.00
TM Tug McGraw Believe/50 50.00 100.00

2003 SP Authentic Chirography Yankees Stars

Randomly inserted into packs, these 14 cards feature not only Yankee stars of the past and present but also authentic autographs of the featured players. Since these cards were issued to varying print runs, we have identified the stated print run next to the player's name in our checklist.

RANDOM INSERTS IN PACKS
PRINT RUNS B/WN 210-350 COPIES PER
SILVER PRINT B/WN 25-75 COPIES PER
NO SILVER PRICING ON QTY OF 25 OR LESS
GOLD PRINT RUN 25 SERIAL #'d SETS
NO GOLD PRICING DUE TO SCARCITY

BR Bobby Richardson/320 10.00 25.00
DM Don Mattingly/295 20.00 50.00
DW1 Dave Winfield/350 12.00 30.00
HK Ralph Houk/245 6.00 15.00
JB Jim Bouton/345 6.00 15.00
JG Jason Giambi/275 6.00 15.00
KS Ken Griffey Sr./350 6.00 15.00
RC Roger Clemens/210 30.00 60.00
SL Sparky Lyle/345 6.00 15.00
ST Mel Stottlemyre/345 6.00 15.00
TH Tommy Henrich/345 8.00 20.00
TJ Tommy John/245 6.00 15.00
TK Tony Kubek/345 12.50 30.00
YB Yogi Berra/320 30.00 80.00

2003 SP Authentic Chirography Yankees Stars Bronze

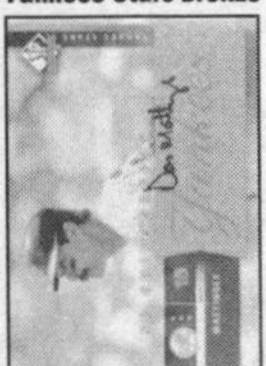

RANDOM INSERTS IN PACKS
PRINT RUNS B/WN 60-100 COPIES PER
MOST HAVE YANKEES INSCRIPTION

BR Bobby Richardson/100 15.00 40.00
DM Don Mattingly/100 30.00 80.00
HK Ralph Houk/100 10.00 25.00
JB Jim Bouton/100 10.00 25.00
JG Jason Giambi/60 10.00 25.00
KS Ken Griffey Sr./100 10.00 25.00
RC Roger Clemens/75 30.00 60.00
SL Sparky Lyle/100 10.00 25.00
ST Mel Stottlemyre/100 10.00 25.00
TH Tommy Henrich/100 12.50 30.00
TJ Tommy John/100 10.00 25.00
TK Tony Kubek/100 20.00 50.00
YB Yogi Berra/100 50.00 120.00

2003 SP Authentic Chirography Yankees Stars Silver

RANDOM INSERTS IN PACKS
PRINT RUNS B/WN 25-75 COPIES PER
NO PRICING ON QTY OF 25 OR LESS
MOST HAVE NEW YORK INSCRIPTION

BR Bobby Richardson/50 20.00 50.00
DM Don Mattingly/50 40.00 80.00
HK Ralph Houk/50 12.50 30.00
JB Jim Bouton/50 12.50 30.00
RC Roger Clemens/50 30.00 60.00
SL Sparky Lyle/50 12.50 30.00
ST Mel Stottlemyre/50 12.50 30.00
TH Tommy Henrich/50 15.00 40.00
TJ Tommy John/50 12.50 30.00
TK Tony Kubek/50 30.00 60.00
YB Yogi Berra/75 60.00 150.00

2003 SP Authentic Chirography Young Stars

Randomly inserted into packs, these 25 cards feature autographs of some of the leading young stars in baseball. These cards were issued to stated print runs of between 150 and 350 cards and we have notated that information in our checklist. Please note that Hee Seop Choi did not return his autographs in time for pack out and those exchange cards could be redeemed until May 21, 2006.

RANDOM INSERTS IN PACKS
PRINT RUNS B/WN 150-350 COPIES PER
BRONZE PRINT RUN 100 SERIAL #'d SETS
SILVER PRINT RUN 50 SERIAL #'d SETS
SILVER PRIOR PRINT RUN 25 #'d CARDS
NO SILVER PRIOR PRICING AVAILABLE
GOLD PRINT RUN 10 SERIAL #'d SETS
NO GOLD PRICING DUE TO SCARCITY
EXCHANGE DEADLINE 05/21/06

AP A.J. Pierzynski/245 6.00 15.00
BO Joe Borchard/245 4.00 10.00
BP1 Brandon Phillips/350 4.00 10.00
BZ Barry Zito/350 10.00 25.00
CP Corey Patterson/245 4.00 10.00
DH Drew Henson/245 4.00 10.00
DI1 Ben Diggins/350 4.00 10.00
EH Eric Hinske/245 4.00 10.00
FS Freddy Sanchez/350 6.00 15.00
HB Hank Blalock/245 6.00 15.00
JJ Jacque Jones/245 6.00 15.00
JJ1 Jimmy Journell/350 4.00 10.00
JL Jason Lane/245 6.00 15.00
JP Josh Phelps/245 4.00 10.00
JS Jayson Werth/350 4.00 10.00
MB Marlon Byrd/245 4.00 10.00
MI Doug Mientkiewicz/245 6.00 15.00
MP Mark Prior/150 10.00 25.00
MY Brett Myers/245 6.00 15.00
OH Orlando Hudson/245 4.00 10.00
OP Oliver Perez/245 6.00 15.00
PE Carlos Pena/245 4.00 10.00
SB Sean Burroughs/245 4.00 10.00
TX Mark Teixeira/245 4.00 10.00

2003 SP Authentic Chirography Young Stars Bronze

*BRONZE: .6X TO 1.5X BASIC YS
*BRONZE PRIOR: .75X TO 2X BASIC YS
RANDOM INSERTS IN PACKS
STATED PRINT RUN 100 SERIAL #'d SETS
PRIOR PRINT RUN 50 SERIAL #'d CARDS
MOST FEATURE CITY INSCRIPTION
EXCHANGE DEADLINE 05/21/06

2003 SP Authentic Chirography Young Stars Silver

*SILVER: .75X TO 2X BASIC YS
RANDOM INSERTS IN PACKS
STATED PRINT RUN 50 SERIAL #'d SETS
PRIOR PRINT RUN 25 SERIAL #'d CARDS
NO PRIOR PRICING DUE TO SCARCITY
EXCHANGE DEADLINE 05/21/06
MOST FEATURE TEAM INSCRIPTION

2003 SP Authentic Simply Splendid

COMMON CARD (TW1-TW30) 3.00 8.00
RANDOM INSERTS IN PACKS
STATED PRINT RUN 406 SERIAL #'d SETS

2003 SP Authentic Splendid Jerseys

RANDOM INSERTS IN PACKS
STATED PRINT RUN 406 SERIAL #'d SETS

SJTW Ted Williams 25.00 60.00

2003 SP Authentic Splendid Signatures

Randomly inserted in packs, these two cards feature autographs of current Red Sox star Nomar Garciaparra and retired Red Sox legend Ted Williams. Please note, that since these cards were issued after Williams passed on, that the Williams autographs are "cuts" while the Nomar autographs were signed for this product. Since the Williams card was issued to a stated print run of five serial numbered copies, no pricing is available for that card.

RANDOM INSERTS IN PACKS
STATED PRINT RUNS LISTED BELOW
NO T.WILLIAMS PRICING DUE TO SCARCITY

GA Nomar Garciaparra/406 10.00 25.00

2003 SP Authentic Splendid Swatches Pairs

Randomly inserted into packs, these nine cards feature a game-worn jersey swatch of retired Red Sox legend Ted Williams along with a game-used jersey swatch of another star. Each of the these cards were issued to a stated print run of 406 serial numbered sets. The two Williams/Nomar cards were not ready for pack-out and those were issued as a exchange cards with a redemption date of May 21, 2006.

RANDOM INSERTS IN PACKS
STATED PRINT RUN 406 SERIAL #'d SETS
EXCHANGE DEADLINE 05/21/06

IS T.Williams/I.Suzuki 20.00 50.00
JG T.Williams/J.Giambi 15.00 40.00
KG T.Williams/K.Griffey Jr. 20.00 50.00
MM T.Williams/M.McGwire 12.00 30.00
NM1 T.Williams/Nomar 10.00 25.00
NM2 T.Williams/Nomar 10.00 25.00
SS T.Williams/S.Sosa 10.00 25.00
TW T.Williams/M.Mantle 60.00 120.00

2003 SP Authentic Spotlight Godzilla

COMMON MATSUI (HM1-HM15) 3.00 8.00
STATED PRINT RUN 500 SERIAL #'d SETS
*RED: 1X TO 2.5X BASIC GODZILLA
RED PRINT RUN 55 SERIAL #'d SETS

2003 SP Authentic Superstar Flashback

RANDOM INSERTS IN PACKS
STATED PRINT RUN 2003 SERIAL #'d SETS

SF1 Tim Salmon .60 1.50
SF2 Darin Erstad .60 1.50
SF3 Troy Glaus .60 1.50
SF4 Randy Johnson 1.50 4.00
SF5 Curt Schilling 1.00 2.50
SF6 Steve Finley .60 1.50
SF7 Greg Maddux 2.00 5.00
SF8 Chipper Jones 1.50 4.00
SF9 Andruw Jones .60 1.50
SF10 Gary Sheffield .60 1.50
SF11 Manny Ramirez 1.50 4.00
SF12 Pedro Martinez 1.00 2.50
SF13 Nomar Garciaparra 1.00 2.50
SF14 Sammy Sosa 1.50 4.00
SF15 Frank Thomas 1.50 4.00
SF16 Kerry Wood .60 1.50
SF17 Paul Konerko 1.00 2.50
SF18 Corey Patterson .60 1.50
SF19 Mark Prior 1.00 2.50
SF20 Ken Griffey Jr. 3.00 8.00
SF21 Adam Dunn 1.00 2.50
SF22 Larry Walker 1.00 2.50
SF23 Preston Wilson .60 1.50
SF24 Todd Helton 1.00 2.50
SF25 Ivan Rodriguez 1.00 2.50
SF26 Josh Beckett .60 1.50
SF27 Jeff Bagwell 1.00 2.50
SF28 Jeff Kent .60 1.50
SF29 Lance Berkman 1.00 2.50
SF30 Carlos Beltran 1.00 2.50
SF31 Shawn Green .60 1.50
SF32 Richie Sexson .60 1.50
SF33 Vladimir Guerrero 1.00 2.50
SF34 Mike Piazza 1.50 4.00
SF35 Roberto Alomar 1.00 2.50
SF36 Roger Clemens 2.00 5.00
SF37 Derek Jeter 4.00 10.00
SF38 Jason Giambi .60 1.50
SF39 Bernie Williams 1.00 2.50
SF40 Nick Johnson .60 1.50
SF41 Alfonso Soriano 1.00 2.50
SF42 Miguel Tejada 1.00 2.50
SF43 Eric Chavez .60 1.50
SF44 Barry Zito 1.00 2.50
SF45 Jim Thome 1.00 2.50
SF46 Pat Burrell .60 1.50
SF47 Marlon Byrd .60 1.50
SF48 Jason Kendall .60 1.50
SF49 Aramis Ramirez .60 1.50
SF50 Brian Giles .60 1.50
SF51 Phil Nevin .60 1.50
SF52 Barry Bonds 2.50 6.00
SF53 Ichiro Suzuki 2.00 5.00
SF54 Scott Rolen 1.00 2.50
SF55 J.D. Drew .60 1.50
SF56 Albert Pujols 2.00 5.00
SF57 Mark Teixeira 1.00 2.50
SF58 Hank Blalock .60 1.50
SF59 Carlos Delgado .60 1.50
SF60 Roy Halladay 1.00 2.50

2004 SP Authentic

This 191 card set was released in June, 2004. The set was issued in five card packs with an $5 SRP which came 24 packs to a box and 12 boxes to a case. Cards numbered 1 through 90 featured veterans while cards numbered 91 through 132 and 178 through 191 feature rookies. With the exception of card 180, there were parallel versions issued of these cards and those cards all begin their serial numbering with 296. Card number 180 featuring Kazuo Matsui has a straight serial print run of card 1 through 999. Cards numbered 133 through 177 feature a mix of active and retired players with All-Star game memories and those cards were inserted at a stated rate of one in 24 with a stated print run of 999 serial numbered sets.

COMP.SET w/o SP's (90) 6.00 15.00
COMMON CARD (1-90) .15 .40
COMMON (91-132/178-191) 1.25 3.00
91-132/178-191 OVERALL FW ODDS 1:24
91-132/178-179/181-191 PRINT 704 #'d SETS
91-132/178-179/181-191 #'d FROM 296-999
CARD 180 PRINT RUN 999 #'d COPIES
CARD 180 #'d FROM 1-999
COMMON CARD (133-177) .40 1.00
133-177 STATED ODDS 1:24
133-177 PRINT RUN 999 SERIAL #'d SETS

1 Bret Boone .15 .40
2 Gary Sheffield .15 .40
3 Rafael Palmeiro .25 .60
4 Jorge Posada .25 .60
5 Derek Jeter 1.00 2.50
6 Garret Anderson .15 .40
7 Bartolo Colon .15 .40
8 Kevin Brown .15 .40
9 Shea Hillenbrand .15 .40
10 Ryan Klesko .15 .40
11 Bobby Abreu .15 .40
12 Scott Rolen .25 .60
13 Alfonso Soriano .25 .60
14 Jason Giambi .15 .40
15 Tom Glavine .25 .60
16 Hideo Nomo .40 1.00
17 Johan Santana .25 .60
18 Sammy Sosa .40 1.00
19 Rickie Weeks .15 .40
20 Barry Zito .15 .40
21 Kerry Wood .15 .40
22 Austin Kearns .15 .40
23 Shawn Green .15 .40
24 Miguel Cabrera .40 1.00
25 Richard Hidalgo .15 .40
26 Andruw Jones .15 .40
27 Randy Wolf .15 .40
28 David Ortiz .40 1.00
29 Roy Oswalt .25 .60
30 Vernon Wells .15 .40
31 Ben Sheets .15 .40
32 Mike Lowell .15 .40
33 Todd Helton .25 .60
34 Jacque Jones .15 .40
35 Mike Sweeney .15 .40
36 Hank Blalock .15 .40
37 Jason Schmidt .15 .40
38 Jeff Kent .15 .40
39 Josh Beckett .15 .40
40 Manny Ramirez .40 1.00
41 Torii Hunter .15 .40
42 Brian Giles .15 .40
43 Javier Vazquez .15 .40
44 Jim Edmonds .25 .60
45 Dmitri Young .15 .40
46 Preston Wilson .15 .40
47 Jeff Bagwell .25 .60
48 Pedro Martinez .25 .60
49 Eric Chavez .15 .40
50 Ken Griffey Jr. .75 2.00
51 Shannon Stewart .15 .40
52 Rafael Furcal .15 .40
53 Brandon Webb .15 .40
54 Juan Pierre .15 .40
55 Roger Clemens .50 1.25
56 Geoff Jenkins .15 .40
57 Lance Berkman .25 .60
58 Albert Pujols .50 1.25
59 Frank Thomas .40 1.00
60 Edgar Martinez .25 .60
61 Tim Hudson .25 .60
62 Eric Gagne .15 .40
63 Richie Sexson .15 .40
64 Corey Patterson .15 .40
65 Nomar Garciaparra .25 .60
66 Hideki Matsui .60 1.50
67 Mark Teixeira .25 .60
68 Troy Glaus .15 .40
69 Carlos Lee .15 .40
70 Mike Mussina .25 .60
71 Magglio Ordonez .25 .60
72 Roy Halladay .25 .60
73 Ichiro Suzuki .50 1.25
74 Randy Johnson .40 1.00
75 Luis Gonzalez .15 .40
76 Mark Prior .25 .60
77 Carlos Beltran .25 .60
78 Ivan Rodriguez .25 .60
79 Alex Rodriguez .50 1.25
80 Dontrelle Willis .15 .40
81 Mike Piazza .40 1.00
82 Curt Schilling .25 .60
83 Vladimir Guerrero .25 .60
84 Greg Maddux .50 1.25
85 Jim Thome .25 .60
86 Miguel Tejada .25 .60
87 Carlos Delgado .15 .40
88 Jose Reyes .25 .60
89 Matt Morris .15 .40
90 Mark Mulder .15 .40
91 Angel Chavez FW RC 1.25 3.00
92 Brandon Medders FW RC 1.25 3.00
93 Carlos Vasquez FW RC 1.25 3.00
94 Chris Aguila FW RC 1.25 3.00
95 Colby Miller FW RC 1.25 3.00
96 Dave Crouthers FW RC 1.25 3.00
97 Dennis Sarfate FW RC 1.25 3.00
98 Donnie Kelly FW RC 2.00 5.00
99 Merkin Valdez FW RC 1.25 3.00
100 Eddy Rodriguez FW RC 1.25 3.00
101 Edwin Moreno FW RC 1.25 3.00
102 Enemencio Pacheco FW RC 1.25 3.00
103 Roberto Novoa FW RC 1.25 3.00
104 Greg Dobbs FW RC 1.25 3.00
105 Hector Gimenez FW RC 1.25 3.00
106 Ian Snell FW RC 1.25 3.00
107 Jake Woods FW RC 1.25 3.00
108 Jamie Brown FW RC 1.25 3.00
109 Jason Frasor FW RC 1.25 3.00
110 Jerome Gamble FW RC 1.25 3.00
111 Jerry Gil FW RC 1.25 3.00
112 Jesse Harper FW RC 1.25 3.00
113 Jorge Vasquez FW RC 1.25 3.00
114 Jose Capellan FW RC 1.25 3.00
115 Josh Labandeira FW RC 1.25 3.00
116 Justin Hampson FW RC 1.25 3.00
117 Justin Huisman FW RC 1.25 3.00
118 Justin Leone FW RC 1.25 3.00
119 Lincoln Holdzkom FW RC 1.25 3.00
120 Lino Urdaneta FW RC 1.25 3.00
121 Mike Gosling FW RC 1.25 3.00
122 Mike Johnston FW RC 1.25 3.00
123 Mike Rouse FW RC 1.25 3.00
124 Scott Proctor FW RC 1.25 3.00
125 Roman Colon FW RC 1.25 3.00
126 Ronny Cedeno FW RC 1.25 3.00
127 Ryan Meaux FW RC 1.25 3.00
128 Scott Dohmann FW RC 1.25 3.00
129 Sean Henn FW RC 1.25 3.00
130 Tim Bausher FW RC 1.25 3.00
131 Tim Bittner FW RC 1.25 3.00
132 William Bergolla FW RC 1.25 3.00
133 Rick Ferrell ASM .40 1.00
134 Joe DiMaggio ASM 2.00 5.00
135 Bob Feller ASM .60 1.50
136 Ted Williams ASM 2.00 5.00
137 Stan Musial ASM 1.50 4.00
138 Larry Doby ASM .60 1.50
139 Red Schoendienst ASM .60 1.50
140 Enos Slaughter ASM .60 1.50
141 Stan Musial ASM 1.50 4.00
142 Mickey Mantle ASM 3.00 8.00
143 Ted Williams ASM 2.00 5.00
144 Mickey Mantle ASM 3.00 8.00
145 Stan Musial ASM 1.50 4.00
146 Tom Seaver ASM .60 1.50
147 Willie McCovey ASM .60 1.50
148 Bob Gibson ASM .60 1.50
149 Frank Robinson ASM .60 1.50
150 Joe Morgan ASM .60 1.50
151 Billy Williams ASM .60 1.50
152 Catfish Hunter ASM .60 1.50
153 Joe Morgan ASM .60 1.50
154 Joe Morgan ASM .60 1.50
155 Mike Schmidt ASM 1.50 4.00
156 Tommy Lasorda ASM .60 1.50
157 Robin Yount ASM 1.00 2.50
158 Nolan Ryan ASM 3.00 8.00
159 John Franco ASM .40 1.00
160 Nolan Ryan ASM 3.00 8.00
161 Ken Griffey Jr. ASM 2.00 5.00
162 Cal Ripken ASM 3.00 8.00
163 Ken Griffey Jr. ASM 2.00 5.00
164 Gary Sheffield ASM .40 1.00
165 Fred McGriff ASM .40 1.00
166 Hideo Nomo ASM 1.00 2.50
167 Mike Piazza ASM 1.00 2.50
168 Sandy Alomar Jr. ASM .40 1.00
169 Roberto Alomar ASM .60 1.50
170 Ted Williams ASM 2.00 5.00
171 Pedro Martinez ASM .60 1.50
172 Derek Jeter ASM 2.50 6.00
173 Cal Ripken ASM 3.00 8.00
174 Torii Hunter ASM .40 1.00
175 Alfonso Soriano ASM .60 1.50
176 Hank Blalock ASM .40 1.00
177 Ichiro Suzuki ASM 1.25 3.00
178 Orlando Rodriguez FW RC 1.25 3.00
179 Ramon Ramirez FW RC 1.25 3.00
180 Kazuo Matsui FW RC 2.00 5.00
181 Kevin Cave FW RC 1.25 3.00
182 John Gall FW RC 1.25 3.00
183 Freddy Guzman FW RC 1.25 3.00
184 Chris Oxspring FW RC 1.25 3.00
185 Rusty Tucker FW RC 1.25 3.00
186 Jorge Sequea FW RC 1.25 3.00
187 Carlos Hines FW RC 1.25 3.00
188 Michael Vento FW RC 1.25 3.00
189 Ryan Wing FW RC 1.25 3.00
190 Jeff Bennett FW RC 1.25 3.00
191 Luis A. Gonzalez FW RC 1.25 3.00

2004 SP Authentic 199/99

*199/99 1-90: 3X TO 8X BASIC
*199/99 91-132/178-191: 1X TO 2.5X BASIC
1-132/178-191 PRINT RUN SER. 99 #'d SETS
*199/99 133-177: .75X TO 2X BASIC
133-177 PRINT RUN 199 SERIAL #'d SETS
OVERALL PARALLEL ODDS 1:8

2004 SP Authentic 499/249

*499/249 1-90: 1.5X TO 4X BASIC
*499/249 133-177: .6X TO 1.5X BASIC
1-90/133-177 PRINT RUN 499 #'d SETS
*499/249 91-132/178-191: .75X TO 2X BASIC
91-132/178-191 PRINT RUN 249 #'d SETS
OVERALL PARALLEL ODDS 1:8

2004 SP Authentic Future Watch Autograph

STATED PRINT RUN 295 SERIAL #'d SETS
*AUTO 195: .5X TO 1.2X BASIC
AUTO 195 PRINT RUN 195 SERIAL #'d SETS
OVERALL FUTURE WATCH ODDS 1:24

91 Angel Chavez FW 4.00 10.00
92 Brandon Medders FW 4.00 10.00
93 Carlos Vasquez FW 6.00 15.00
94 Chris Aguila FW 4.00 10.00
95 Colby Miller FW 4.00 10.00
96 Dave Crouthers FW 4.00 10.00
97 Dennis Sarfate FW 4.00 10.00
98 Donnie Kelly FW 4.00 10.00
99 Merkin Valdez FW 4.00 10.00
100 Eddy Rodriguez FW 6.00 15.00
101 Edwin Moreno FW 4.00 10.00
102 Enemencio Pacheco FW 4.00 10.00
103 Roberto Novoa FW 4.00 10.00
104 Greg Dobbs FW 4.00 10.00
105 Hector Gimenez FW 4.00 10.00
106 Ian Snell FW 10.00 25.00
107 Jake Woods FW 4.00 10.00
108 Jamie Brown FW 4.00 10.00
109 Jason Frasor FW 4.00 10.00
110 Jerome Gamble FW 4.00 10.00
111 Jerry Gil FW 4.00 10.00
112 Jesse Harper FW 4.00 10.00
113 Jorge Vasquez FW 4.00 10.00
114 Jose Capellan FW 4.00 10.00
115 Josh Labandeira FW 4.00 10.00
116 Justin Hampson FW 4.00 10.00
117 Justin Huisman FW 4.00 10.00
118 Justin Leone FW 6.00 15.00
119 Lincoln Holdzkom FW 4.00 10.00
120 Lino Urdaneta FW 4.00 10.00
121 Mike Gosling FW 4.00 10.00
122 Mike Johnston FW 4.00 10.00
123 Mike Rouse FW 4.00 10.00
124 Scott Proctor FW 6.00 15.00
125 Roman Colon FW 4.00 10.00
126 Ronny Cedeno FW 6.00 15.00
127 Ryan Meaux FW 4.00 10.00
128 Scott Dohmann FW 4.00 10.00
129 Sean Henn FW 4.00 10.00
130 Tim Bausher FW 4.00 10.00
131 Tim Bittner FW 4.00 10.00
132 William Bergolla FW 4.00 10.00
178 Orlando Rodriguez FW 4.00 10.00
179 Ramon Ramirez FW 4.00 10.00
181 Kevin Cave FW 4.00 10.00
182 John Gall FW 6.00 15.00
183 Freddy Guzman FW 4.00 10.00
184 Chris Oxspring FW 4.00 10.00
185 Rusty Tucker FW 6.00 15.00
186 Jorge Sequea FW 4.00 10.00
187 Carlos Hines FW 4.00 10.00
188 Michael Vento FW 6.00 15.00
189 Ryan Wing FW 4.00 10.00
190 Jeff Bennett FW 4.00 10.00
191 Luis A. Gonzalez FW 6.00 15.00

2004 SP Authentic Buybacks

Jorge Posada did not return his cards in time for pack out and those cards could be redeemed until June 4, 2007.

OVERALL AUTO INSERT ODDS 1:12
PRINT RUNS B/WN 1-105 COPIES PER
NO PRICING ON QTY OF 14 OR LESS
EXCHANGE DEADLINE 06/04/07

AB1 Angel Berroa 04 VIN/70 4.00 10.00
AD1 Andre Dawson 04 SSC/50 6.00 15.00
AK1 Al Kaline 03 SP LC/20 30.00 80.00
AK2 Al Kaline 04 SSC/70 25.00 50.00
AL1 Al Leiter 04 FP/80 6.00 15.00
AL2 Al Leiter 04 UD/60 6.00 15.00
BA1 Bobby Abreu 03 CP/63 6.00 15.00
BA3 Bobby Abreu 03 SPx/63 6.00 15.00
BA4 Bobby Abreu 03 SS/64 6.00 15.00
BA5 Bobby Abreu 03 UDA/63 6.00 15.00
BA6 Bobby Abreu 04 DAS/53 6.00 15.00
BA7 Bobby Abreu 04 FP/53 6.00 15.00
BA8 Bobby Abreu 04 UD/65 6.00 15.00
BA9 Bobby Abreu 04 VIN/53 6.00 15.00
BB1 Bret Boone 03 CP/66 15.00 40.00
BB2 Bret Boone 03 PC/15 30.00 60.00
BB3 Bret Boone 03 SPx/29 20.00 50.00
BB4 Bret Boone 03 SS/44 15.00 40.00
BB5 Bret Boone 03 UDA/63 15.00 40.00
BB6 Bret Boone 04 DAS/57 15.00 40.00
BB7 Bret Boone 04 VIN/53 15.00 40.00
BD1 Bobby Doerr 03 SP LCB/50 6.00 15.00
BD2 Bobby Doerr 04 SSC/73 6.00 15.00
BG1 Bob Gibson 04 SSC/23 15.00 40.00
BH1 Bobby Hill 03 40M/40 4.00 10.00
BH2 Bobby Hill 03 UDA/17 8.00 20.00
BH3 Bobby Hill 04 FP/17 8.00 20.00
BH4 Bobby Hill 04 UD/17 8.00 20.00
BH5 Bobby Hill 04 VIN/34 6.00 15.00
BH1 Bo Hart 03 SPx/50 4.00 10.00
BH2 Bo Hart 04 VIN/45 4.00 10.00
BR1 B.Robinson 03 SP LC/50 10.00 25.00
BR2 B.Robinson 04 SSC/70 10.00 25.00
BS1 Ben Sheets 03 40M/25 10.00 25.00
BS2 Ben Sheets 03 CP/15 12.50 30.00
BS3 Ben Sheets 03 PC/15 12.50 30.00
BS4 Ben Sheets 03 SPx/15 12.50 30.00
BS5 Ben Sheets 04 DAS/15 12.50 30.00
BS7 Ben Sheets 04 UD/25 10.00 25.00
BS8 Ben Sheets 04 VIN/15 12.50 30.00
BW1 Brandon Webb 03 SPx/20 6.00 15.00
BW2 Brandon Webb 03 UD/65 4.00 10.00

Brandon Webb 04 DAS/50 4.00 10.00
Brandon Webb 04 FP/30 10.00 25.00
5 Brandon Webb 04 VIN/85 4.00 10.00
Barry Zito 03 40M/30 15.00 40.00
Barry Zito 03 CP/41 10.00 25.00
Barry Zito 03 HR/60 10.00 25.00
Barry Zito 03 PC/15 20.00 50.00
Barry Zito 03 SPx/46 10.00 25.00
Barry Zito 03 SS/63 10.00 25.00
Barry Zito 03 UDA/40 10.00 25.00
Barry Zito 04 FP/69 10.00 25.00
Barry Zito 04 UD/61 10.00 25.00
0 Barry Zito 04 VIN/50 10.00 25.00
Carlos Beltran 03 CP/15 12.50 30.00
Carlos Beltran 03 PC/15 12.50 30.00
Carlos Beltran 03 SS/15 12.50 30.00
Carlos Beltran 04 DAS/15 12.50 30.00
Carlos Beltran 04 VIN/15 12.50 30.00
C.Delgado 03 UDA/43 6.00 15.00
C.Fisk 03 SP LC/38 15.00 40.00
C.Fisk 03 SP LCB/55 15.00 40.00
1 Cliff Lee 04 FP/40 30.00 60.00
2 Cliff Lee 04 UD/50 30.00 60.00
Carlos Lee 04 FP/70 6.00 15.00
Carlos Lee 04 UD/70 6.00 15.00
Carlos Lee 04 VIN/70 6.00 15.00
01 Colin Porter 03 CP/60 4.00 10.00
03 Colin Porter 04 FP/70 4.00 10.00
C.Patterson 03 40M/20 6.00 15.00
C.Patterson 03 PC/20 6.00 15.00
3 C.Patterson 03 SPx/20 6.00 15.00
4 C.Patterson 03 SS/20 6.00 15.00
5 C.Patterson 04 FP/20 6.00 15.00
6 C.Patterson 04 UD/20 6.00 15.00
7 C.Patterson 04 VIN/20 6.00 15.00
Cal Ripken 04 SSC/45 75.00 150.00
1 C.Wang 04 FP/26 75.00 150.00
C.Yastrzemski 04 SSC/22 40.00 80.00
C.Zambrano 04 VIN/70 10.00 25.00
Derek Jeter 03 40M/30 90.00 180.00
Derek Jeter 03 HR/25 100.00 200.00
Derek Jeter 03 PC/25 100.00 200.00
Derek Jeter 03 SS/30 125.00 250.00
0 Derek Jeter 04 UD/25 100.00 200.00
1 Derek Jeter 04 VIN/25 100.00 200.00
1 Duke Snider 04 SSC/23 20.00 50.00
1 D.Willis 04 DAS/70 10.00 25.00
2 D.Willis 04 FP/80 10.00 25.00
3 D.Willis 04 UD SR/45 10.00 25.00
4 D.Willis 04 VIN/105 10.00 25.00
3 Delmon Young 04 VIN/35 15.00 40.00
1 Eric Chavez 03 40M/30 6.00 15.00
5 Eric Chavez 03 SS/25 6.00 15.00
1 Eric Gagne 03 40M/38 10.00 25.00
2 Eric Gagne 04 FP/26 15.00 40.00
3 Eric Gagne 04 UD/38 10.00 25.00
4 Eric Gagne 04 VIN/38 10.00 25.00
1 E.Martinez 04 DAS/70 15.00 40.00
1 G.Anderson 03 40M/30 10.00 25.00
4 G.Anderson 03 SS/20 10.00 25.00
5 G.Anderson 04 DAS/16 12.50 30.00
6 G.Anderson 04 VIN/16 12.50 30.00
1 Hank Blalock 03 40M/20 20.00 50.00
5 Hank Blalock 03 SS/15 12.50 30.00
1 H.Killebrew 03 SP LC/20 40.00 80.00
1 H.Ramirez 03 40M/25 6.00 15.00
3 Horacio Ramirez 04 UD/15 8.00 20.00
1 Josh Beckett 03 40M/21 15.00 40.00
3 Josh Beckett 03 HR/21 15.00 40.00
6 Josh Beckett 03 SS/21 15.00 40.00
1 Jim Edmonds 03 CP/25 15.00 40.00
2 Jim Edmonds 03 HR/15 20.00 50.00
3 Jim Edmonds 03 SPx/25 15.00 40.00
4 Jim Edmonds 03 SS/45 10.00 25.00
5 Jim Edmonds 03 UDA/25 15.00 40.00
6 Jim Edmonds 04 DAS/15 20.00 50.00
7 Jim Edmonds 04 FP/15 20.00 50.00
8 Jim Edmonds 04 UD/25 15.00 40.00
9 Jim Edmonds 04 VIN/15 20.00 50.00
E1 Jody Gerut 04 DAS/70 4.00 10.00
E2 Jody Gerut 04 VIN/70 4.00 10.00
1 Juan Gonzalez 03 40M/19 12.50 30.00
3 Juan Gonzalez 03 PC/19 12.50 30.00
5 Juan Gonzalez 03 SS/19 12.50 30.00
6 Juan Gonzalez 04 UD/19 12.50 30.00
7 Juan Gonzalez 04 VIN/20 10.00 25.00
1 Jacque Jones 03 40M/40 6.00 15.00
3 Jacque Jones 03 SPx/35 10.00 25.00
4 Jacque Jones 03 SS/35 10.00 25.00
1 Javy Lopez 03 40M/30 10.00 25.00
2 Javy Lopez 04 FP/18 12.50 30.00
3 Javy Lopez 04 UD/29 10.00 25.00
4 Javy Lopez 04 VIN/18 12.50 30.00
1 John Olerud 03 CP/50 10.00 25.00
2 John Olerud 03 SS/45 10.00 25.00
3 John Olerud 04 VIN/70 10.00 25.00
1 John Smoltz 04 FP/67 30.00 60.00
2 John Smoltz 04 UD/67 30.00 60.00
3 John Smoltz 04 VIN/70 30.00 60.00
1 Joe Torre 04 SSC/70 10.00 25.00
1 Javier Vazquez 04 DAS/70 6.00 15.00
2 Javier Vazquez 04 VIN/70 6.00 15.00
VS3 Jae Seo 04 UD/15 12.50 30.00
VS4 Jae Seo 04 VIN/15 12.50 30.00
1 Jer.Williams 04 UD/70 4.00 10.00
2 Jer.Williams 04 VIN/60 4.00 10.00
1 K.Grif 02 SUP Silv/45 50.00 100.00
3 K.Grif 02 SUP SK Blue/19 75.00 150.00
4 K.Grif 03 40M Blue/20 60.00 120.00
6 K.Grif 03 40M 92 AS/18 75.00 150.00
7 K.Grif 03 40M 97 AL/18 75.00 150.00
8 K.Grif 03 40MHR94 Blk/31 60.00 120.00
9 K.Grif 03 40MHR94 Blu/27 60.00 120.00
KG10 K.Grif 03 40MHR98 Sil/28 60.00 120.00
KG13 K.Grif 03 40M HR99 Sil/48 50.00 100.00
KG14 K.Grif 03 40M T40 Blu/35 60.00 120.00
KG15 K.Grif 03 40M T40 AL/29 50.00 120.00
KG16 K.Grif 03 GF Black/40 50.00 100.00
KG17 K.Grif 03 GF Blue/23 60.00 120.00
KG19 K.Grif 03 GF 92AS/19 75.00 150.00
KG20 K.Grif 03 HR 92AS/15 75.00 150.00
KG21 K.Grif 03 HR 97AL/37 60.00 120.00
KG23 K.Grif 03 MVP Blk/56 50.00 100.00
KG25 K.Grif 03 MVP GG/15 75.00 150.00
KG27 K.Grif 03 PC Black/27 60.00 120.00
KG30 K.Grif 03 PB Black/15 75.00 150.00
KG32 K.Grif 03 PB 56 HR/15 75.00 150.00
KG34 K.Grif 03 SPA 56 HR/15 75.00 150.00
KG35 K.Grif 03 SPA 92 AS/20 60.00 120.00
KG36 K.Grif 03 SPA B93/20 60.00 120.00
KG39 K.Grif 03 SPx 97 AL/26 60.00 120.00
KG40 K.Grif 03 SS 97 AL/32 50.00 120.00
KG42 K.Grif 03 VIC Blk/57 50.00 100.00
KG43 K.Grif 03 VIC 92 AS/18 75.00 150.00
KW1 Kerry Wood 03 40M/34 15.00 40.00
KW6 Kerry Wood 03 SS/34 15.00 40.00
LA1 L.Aparicio 03 SP LC/20 10.00 25.00
LG1 L.Gonzalez 03 40M HR/25 10.00 25.00
LG2 Luis Gonzalez 03 CP/20 10.00 25.00
LG3 Luis Gonzalez 03 HR/20 10.00 25.00
LG5 Luis Gonzalez 03 SS/40 6.00 15.00
LG9 Luis Gonzalez 04 VIN/20 10.00 25.00
MB1 Marlon Byrd 04 VIN/70 4.00 10.00
MC1 M.Cabrera 03 SPx/25 20.00 50.00
MC2 M.Cabrera 04 DAS/20 20.00 50.00
MC3 M.Cabrera 04 FP/20 20.00 50.00
MC4 M.Cabrera 04 VIN/20 20.00 50.00
ME1 M.Ensberg 04 FP/70 6.00 15.00
ME2 M.Ensberg 04 UD/70 6.00 15.00
ME3 M.Ensberg 04 VIN/70 6.00 15.00
MG1 Marcus Giles 04 VIN/70 6.00 15.00
MH1 Mike Hampton 03 UDA/60 4.00 10.00
MH2 Mike Hampton 04 FP/34 6.00 15.00
MH3 Mike Hampton 04 UD/47 4.00 10.00
MI1 Monte Irvin 03 SP LC/20 10.00 25.00
ML1 Mike Lowell 03 40M/19 8.00 20.00
ML2 Mike Lowell 04 DAS/19 8.00 20.00
ML3 Mike Lowell 04 FP/19 8.00 20.00
ML4 Mike Lowell 04 UD/19 8.00 20.00
ML5 Mike Lowell 04 VIN/19 8.00 20.00
MM2 Mike Mussina 03 HR/20 15.00 40.00
MM3 Mike Mussina 03 HR/25 15.00 40.00
MM5 Mike Mussina 03 SS/60 10.00 25.00
MM6 Mike Mussina 03 UDA/45 10.00 25.00
MM7 Mike Mussina 04 FP/58 10.00 25.00
MM8 Mike Mussina 04 UD/45 10.00 25.00
MM9 Mike Mussina 04 VIN/45 10.00 25.00
MP1 Mark Prior 03 40M/22 12.50 30.00
MP4 Mark Prior 03 HR/22 12.50 30.00
MP5 Mark Prior 03 PC/22 12.50 30.00
MP6 Mark Prior 03 SPx/22 12.50 30.00
MP7 Mark Prior 03 SS/22 12.50 30.00
MP10 Mark Prior 04 FP/22 12.50 30.00
MP11 Mark Prior 04 UD/22 12.50 30.00
MP12 Mark Prior 04 VIN/22 12.50 30.00
MS1 M.Schmidt 03 SP LC/20 20.00 50.00
MTE1 Miguel Tejada 03 CP/38 6.00 15.00
MTE2 Miguel Tejada 03 HR/36 10.00 25.00
MTE3 M.Tejada 03 SPx/30 15.00 40.00
MTE4 M.Tejada 03 UDA/58 10.00 25.00
MTE5 Miguel Tejada 04 DAS/37 10.00 25.00
MTE6 Miguel Tejada 04 VIN/70 6.00 15.00
MT1 M.Teix 03 40M RWB/45 10.00 25.00
MT4 Mark Teixeira 03 SPx/40 10.00 25.00
MT5 Mark Teixeira 03 SS/23 15.00 40.00
MT6 Mark Teixeira 03 SS/25 15.00 40.00
MT7 Mark Teixeira 03 UDA/21 15.00 40.00
MT10 Mark Teixeira 04 UD/23 15.00 40.00
MW1 Maury Wills 04 SSC/70 6.00 15.00
NR1 Nolan Ryan 03 UDA/20 60.00 120.00
OD1 Octavio Dotel 04 FP/70 4.00 10.00
OD2 Octavio Dotel 04 UD/70 4.00 10.00
OD3 Octavio Dotel 04 VIN/70 4.00 10.00
PB1 Pat Burrell 03 CP/50 6.00 15.00
PB2 Pat Burrell 03 HR/25 10.00 25.00
PB3 Pat Burrell 03 SS/50 6.00 15.00
PB4 Pat Burrell 03 UDA/50 6.00 15.00
PB5 Pat Burrell 04 VIN/68 6.00 15.00
PL1 P.LoDuca 03 40M RWB/60 6.00 15.00
PL2 Paul Lo Duca 04 VIN/60 6.00 15.00
PL3 P.Lo Duca 04 VIN BW/20 10.00 25.00
PR1 Phil Rizzuto 03 SP LC/21 15.00 40.00
RB3 Rocco Baldelli 03 SPx/15 12.50 30.00
RB7 R.Baldelli 04 PB Red/25 10.00 25.00
RB8 R.Baldelli 04 PB Blue/25 10.00 25.00
RHL1 Roy Halladay 03 40M/32 20.00 50.00
RHL5 Roy Halladay 04 UD/32 20.00 50.00
RHM1 R.Hammock 03 40M/35 6.00 15.00
RHM2 R.Hammock 03 PC/15 8.00 20.00
RHM4 R.Hammock 04 UD/30 6.00 15.00
RHR1 R.Hernandez 03 40M/55 4.00 10.00
RHR2 R.Hernandez 03 UDA/40 4.00 10.00
RI1 Raul Ibanez 04 FP/70 8.00 20.00
RI2 Raul Ibanez 04 UD/65 8.00 20.00
RI3 Raul Ibanez 04 VIN/70 8.00 20.00
RK1 Ralph Kiner 03 SP LC/20 15.00 40.00
RO1 Roy Oswalt 03 40M/44 6.00 15.00
RO2 Roy Oswalt 03 HR/55 6.00 15.00
RO3 Roy Oswalt 03 SS/20 10.00 25.00
RO4 Roy Oswalt 04 UD/52 6.00 15.00
RR1 R.Roberts 03 SP LC/15 12.50 30.00
RW1 Rickie Weeks 03 UD/30 15.00 40.00
RW2 Rickie Weeks 04 FP/15 12.50 30.00
RW3 Rickie Weeks 04 VIN/50 6.00 15.00
RY1 Robin Yount 03 SP LC/20 50.00 100.00
SG3 Shawn Green 03 SS/15 20.00 50.00
SG6 Shawn Green 04 FP/15 20.00 50.00
SG8 Shawn Green 04 VIN/15 20.00 50.00
SM1 S.Musial 03 SP LC/16 50.00 100.00
THO1 T.Hoffman 04 FP/67 10.00 25.00
THO2 T.Hoffman 04 UD/51 10.00 25.00
TH1 Travis Hafner 03 40M/32 6.00 15.00
TH4 Travis Hafner 03 SS/32 6.00 15.00
TS1 Tom Seaver 03 SP LC/15 30.00 80.00
VG1 Vlad Guerrero 03 CP/20 12.00 30.00
VG3 Vlad Guerrero 03 SPx/34 12.00 30.00
VG4 Vlad Guerrero 03 SS/27 12.00 30.00
VG5 Vlad Guerrero 03 UDA/54 10.00 25.00
VG6 Vlad Guerrero 04 DAS/27 12.00 30.00
VG7 Vlad Guerrero 04 FP/28 12.00 30.00
VG9 Vlad Guerrero 04 VIN/27 12.00 30.00
VW1 Vernon Wells 03 40M/15 12.50 30.00
WE1 Willie Eyre 03 40M/45 4.00 10.00
WE2 W.Eyre 03 40M RWB/45 4.00 10.00
YB1 Yogi Berra 03 SP LC/23 30.00 80.00

2004 SP Authentic Chirography

Jorge Posada and Ken Griffey Jr. did not return their cards in time for pack out and those cards could be redeemed until June 4, 2007. It is interesting to note that Griffey did return his buy-backed cards in time for inclusion in this product.

STATED PRINT RUN 75 SERIAL #'d SETS
BASIC CHIRO. HAVE RED BACKGROUNDS
*DT w/NOTE: .5X TO 1.2X BASIC
*DT w/o NOTE: .4X TO 1X BASIC
DUO TONE PRINT RUN 75 SERIAL #'d SETS
MOST DT FEATURE UNIFORM # NOTATION
*BRONZE: .4X TO 1X BASIC
BRONZE PRINT RUN 65 SERIAL #'d SETS
*BRONZE DT w/NOTE: .5X TO 1.5X BASIC
*BRONZE DT w/o NOTE: .4X TO 1X BASIC
BRONZE DUO TONE PRINT RUN 60 #'d SETS
MOST BRONZE DT FEATURE TEAM NAMES
*SILVER: .4X TO 1X BASIC
SILVER PRINT RUN 60 SERIAL #'d SETS
*SILVER DT w/NOTE: .6X TO 1.5X BASIC
*SILVER DT w/o NOTE: .5X TO 1.2X BASIC
SILVER DT PRINT RUN 30 SERIAL #'d SETS
MOST SILVER DT HAVE KEY ACHIEVEMENT
OVERALL AUTO INSERT ODDS 1:12
EXCHANGE DEADLINE 06/04/07
AK Austin Kearns 5.00 12.00
BA Bobby Abreu 8.00 20.00
BB Bret Boone 12.50 30.00
BH Bo Hart 5.00 12.00
BS Ben Sheets 8.00 20.00
BW Brandon Webb 6.00 15.00
BZ Barry Zito 8.00 20.00
CB Carlos Beltran 8.00 20.00
CL Cliff Lee 15.00 40.00
CP Colin Porter 5.00 12.00
CR Cal Ripken 40.00 80.00
CW Chien-Ming Wang 75.00 150.00
DE Dennis Eckersley 12.50 30.00
DJ Derek Jeter 100.00 200.00
DW Dontrelle Willis 12.50 30.00
DY Delmon Young 6.00 15.00
EC Eric Chavez 8.00 20.00
EG Eric Gagne 12.50 30.00
GA Garret Anderson 8.00 20.00
HA Robby Hammock 5.00 12.00
HB Hank Blalock 8.00 20.00
HE Runelvys Hernandez 5.00 12.00
HI Bobby Hill 5.00 12.00
HR Horacio Ramirez 5.00 12.00
HY Roy Halladay 12.50 30.00
JB Josh Beckett 8.00 20.00
JG Juan Gonzalez 10.00 25.00
JJ Jacque Jones 11 8.00 20.00
JL Javy Lopez 5.00 12.00
JR Jose Reyes 10.00 25.00
JS Jae Weong Seo 5.00 12.00
JV Javier Vazquez 5.00 12.00
JW Jerome Williams 5.00 12.00
KW Kerry Wood 6.00 15.00
MC Miguel Cabrera 20.00 50.00
ML Mike Lowell 8.00 20.00
MP Mark Prior 5.00 12.00
MT Mark Teixeira 12.50 30.00
PA Corey Patterson 5.00 12.00
PI Mike Piazza 25.00 60.00
PL Paul Lo Duca 8.00 20.00
RB Rocco Baldelli 8.00 20.00
RO Roy Oswalt 5.00 12.00
RW Rickie Weeks 8.00 20.00
TH Travis Hafner 5.00 12.00
VW Vernon Wells 8.00 20.00
WE Willie Eyre 5.00 12.00

2004 SP Authentic Chirography Gold

*GOLD p/r 40: .5X TO 1.2X BASIC
STATED PRINT RUN 40 SERIAL #'d SETS
EDGAR/LEITER/SMOLTZ 75 #'d COPIES PER
*GLD DT p/r 20 w/NOTE: .6X TO 1.5X p/r 40
*GLD DT p/r20 w/o NOTE: .5X TO 1.2X p/r 40
*GOLD DT p/r 75: .4X TO 1X GOLD p/r 75
GOLD DT PRINT RUN 20 SERIAL #'d SETS
MOST GOLD DT HAVE KEY ACHIEVEMENT
OVERALL AUTO INSERT ODDS 1:12
EXCHANGE DEADLINE 06/04/07
AL Al Leiter/75 10.00 25.00
AR Alex Rodriguez 100.00 175.00
EM Edgar Martinez/75 10.00 25.00
SM John Smoltz/75 20.00 50.00

2004 SP Authentic Chirography Dual

A few cards were not ready in time for pack out and those cards could be exchanged until June 4, 2007.

OVERALL AUTO INSERT ODDS 1:12
STATED PRINT RUN 50 SERIAL #'d SETS
EXCHANGE DEADLINE 06/04/07
BC B.Boone/E.Chavez 10.00 25.00
BL J.Beckett/M.Lowell 10.00 25.00
BP C.Beltran/C.Patterson 10.00 25.00
BT H.Blalock/M.Teixeira 6.00 15.00
EG D.Eckersley/E.Gagne 30.00 60.00
HW R.Halladay/V.Wells 30.00 60.00
JM J.Bench/M.Piazza 175.00 300.00
KG A.Kearns/K.Griffey Jr. 40.00 80.00
PB J.Posada/Y.Berra 50.00 100.00
RR A.Rodriguez/C.Ripken 250.00 500.00
SG I.Suzuki/K.Griffey Jr. 400.00 600.00
SM O.Smith/S.Musial 125.00 200.00
WC D.Willis/M.Cabrera 15.00 40.00
WJ C.Wang/D.Jeter 300.00 500.00
WR K.Wood/N.Ryan 175.00 300.00
WW B.Webb/D.Willis 30.00 60.00
ZC B.Zito/E.Chavez 30.00 60.00

2004 SP Authentic Chirography Hall of Famers

STATED PRINT RUN 40 SERIAL #'d SETS
*DUO TONE: .5X TO 1.2X BASIC
DUO TONE PRINT RUN 25 SERIAL #'d SETS
SOME DT FEATURE HOF NOTATION
OVERALL AUTO INSERT ODDS 1:12
AK Al Kaline 30.00 80.00
BD Bobby Doerr 10.00 25.00
BG Bob Gibson 15.00 40.00
BR B.Robinson UER B/W 15.00 40.00
CF Carlton Fisk 15.00 40.00
CY Carl Yastrzemski HOF 89 50.00 100.00
DE Dennis Eckersley 15.00 40.00
DS Duke Snider 15.00 40.00
HK Harmon Killebrew 20.00 50.00
JB Johnny Bench 30.00 60.00
KP Kirby Puckett 50.00 100.00
LA Luis Aparicio Hall of Famer 10.00 25.00
MI Monte Irvin 10.00 25.00
MS Mike Schmidt 30.00 80.00
NR Nolan Ryan 75.00 150.00
OS Ozzie Smith 50.00 100.00
PM Paul Molitor 10.00 25.00
PR Phil Rizzuto Hall of Famer 15.00 40.00
RK Ralph Kiner HOF 1975 10.00 25.00
RR Robin Roberts Hall of Famer 15.00 40.00
RY Robin Yount 50.00 100.00
SM Stan Musial 60.00 120.00
TP Tony Perez Hall of Famer 10.00 25.00
TS Tom Seaver 20.00 50.00
YB Yogi Berra 30.00 80.00

2004 SP Authentic Chirography Triple

A couple of cards were not totally ready at pack-out time and those cards could be exchanged until June 4, 2007.

OVERALL AUTO INSERT ODDS 1:12
STATED PRINT RUN 25 SERIAL #'d SETS
EXCHANGE DEADLINE 06/04/07
BWR Beck/Wood/Ryan 60.00 150.00
FBB Fisk/Bench/Berra 200.00 400.00
GSM Gibson/Ozzie/Musial 150.00 300.00
JVB Jeter/Vazquez/Berra 75.00 200.00
PRC Porter/Reyes/Cabrera 25.00 60.00
RBT A.Rod/Blalock/Teixeira 125.00 300.00
RRR A.Rod/Ripken/Rizz 75.00 200.00
SJB Ichiro/Jacque/Baldelli 250.00 500.00
WLE Wang/C.Lee/Eyre 60.00 150.00
WPB Webb/Prior/Beckett 60.00 150.00
YYM Yaz/Yount/Musial 200.00 400.00
ZHO Zito/Halladay/Oswalt 50.00 120.00

2004 SP Authentic USA Signatures 445

STATED PRINT RUN 445 SERIAL #'d SETS
*USA SIG 50: .6X TO 1.5X BASIC
USA SIG 50 PRINT RUN 50 #'d SETS
OVERALL AUTO INSERT ODDS 1:12
1 Ernie Young 4.00 10.00
2 Chris Burke 6.00 15.00
3 Jesse Crain 6.00 15.00
4 Justin Duchscherer 6.00 15.00
5 J.D. Durbin 4.00 10.00
6 Gerald Laird 6.00 15.00
7 John Grabow 4.00 10.00
8 Gabe Gross 6.00 15.00
9 J.J. Hardy 15.00 40.00
10 Jeremy Reed 6.00 15.00
11 Graham Koonce 4.00 10.00
12 Mike Lamb 4.00 10.00
13 Justin Leone 6.00 15.00
14 Ryan Madson 8.00 20.00
15 Joe Mauer 10.00 25.00
16 Todd Williams 4.00 10.00
17 Horacio Ramirez 4.00 10.00
18 Mike Rouse 4.00 10.00
19 Jason Stanford 4.00 10.00
20 John Van Benschoten 4.00 10.00
21 Grady Sizemore 12.50 30.00

2004 SP Authentic USA Signatures 50

OVERALL AUTO INSERT ODDS 1:12
STATED PRINT RUN 50 SERIAL #'d SETS*
9 J.J. Hardy 40.00 80.00

2005 SP Authentic

This set was released within two separate products . . SP Collection in October, 2005 (containing cards 1-100) and Upper Deck Update in February, 2006 (containing cards 101-186) . The SP Collection packs had five cards in each pack with an $6 SRP and those packs came 20 packs to a box and 16 boxes to a case. Upper Deck Update packs contained 5 cards and carried a $4.99 SRP. 24 packs were issued in each box. Of note, cards 105, 115, 118-119, 142, 154, 161, 180, 183 and 186 do not exist.

COMP.BASIC SET (100) 10.00 25.00
COMMON CARD (1-100) .15 .40
COMMON RETIRED 1-100 .15 .40
1-100 ISSUED IN 05 SP COLLECTION PACKS
COMMON AUTO (101-186) 4.00 10.00
101-186 ODDS APPX 1:8 '05 UD UPDATE
101-186 PRINT RUN 185 SERIAL #'d SETS
105, 115, 118-119, 142, 154 DO NOT EXIST
161, 180, 183, 186 DO NOT EXIST
1 A.J. Burnett .15 .40
2 Aaron Rowand .15 .40
3 Adam Dunn .25 .60
4 Adrian Beltre .40 1.00
5 Adrian Gonzalez .30 .75
6 Akinori Otsuka .15 .40
7 Albert Pujols .50 1.25
8 Andre Dawson .25 .60
9 Andruw Jones .15 .40
10 Aramis Ramirez .15 .40
11 Barry Larkin .25 .60
12 Ben Sheets .15 .40
13 Bo Jackson .40 1.00
14 Bobby Abreu .15 .40
15 Bobby Crosby .15 .40
16 Bronson Arroyo .15 .40
17 Cal Ripken 1.25 3.00
18 Carl Crawford .25 .60
19 Carlos Zambrano .25 .60
20 Casey Kotchman .15 .40
21 Cesar Izturis .15 .40
22 Chone Figgins .15 .40
23 Corey Patterson .15 .40
24 Craig Biggio .25 .60
25 Dale Murphy .40 1.00
26 Dallas McPherson .15 .40
27 Danny Haren .15 .40
28 Darryl Strawberry .15 .40
29 David Ortiz .40 1.00
30 David Wright .30 .75
31 Derek Jeter 1.00 2.50
32 Derrek Lee .15 .40
33 Don Mattingly .75 2.00
34 Dwight Gooden .15 .40
35 Edgar Renteria .15 .40
36 Eric Chavez .15 .40
37 Eric Gagne .15 .40
38 Gary Sheffield .15 .40
39 Gavin Floyd .15 .40
40 Pedro Martinez .25 .60
41 Greg Maddux .50 1.25
42 Hank Blalock .15 .40
43 Huston Street .15 .40
44 J.D. Drew .15 .40
45 Jake Peavy .15 .40
46 Jake Westbrook .15 .40
47 Jason Bay .15 .40
48 Austin Kearns .15 .40
49 Jeremy Reed .15 .40
50 Jim Rice .25 .60
51 Jimmy Rollins .25 .60
52 Joe Blanton .15 .40
53 Joe Mauer .30 .75
54 Johan Santana .25 .60
55 John Smoltz .40 1.00
56 Johnny Estrada .15 .40
57 Jose Reyes .25 .60
58 Ken Griffey Jr. .75 2.00
59 Kerry Wood .15 .40
60 Khalil Greene .15 .40
61 Marcus Giles .15 .40
62 Melvin Mora .15 .40
63 Mark Grace .25 .60
64 Mark Mulder .15 .40
65 Mark Prior .25 .60
66 Mark Teixeira .25 .60
67 Matt Clement .15 .40
68 Michael Young .15 .40
69 Miguel Cabrera .40 1.00
70 Miguel Tejada .25 .60
71 Mike Piazza .40 1.00
72 Mike Schmidt .75 2.00
73 Nolan Ryan 1.25 3.00
74 Oliver Perez .15 .40
75 Nick Johnson .15 .40
76 Paul Molitor .40 1.00
77 Rafael Palmeiro .25 .60
78 Randy Johnson .40 1.00
79 Reggie Jackson .25 .60
80 Rich Harden .15 .40
81 Rickie Weeks .15 .40
82 Robin Yount .40 1.00
83 Roger Clemens .50 1.25
84 Roy Oswalt .25 .60
85 Ryan Howard .30 .75
86 Ryne Sandberg .75 2.00
87 Scott Kazmir .40 1.00
88 Scott Rolen .25 .60
89 Sean Burroughs .15 .40
90 Sean Casey .15 .40
91 Shingo Takatsu .15 .40
92 Tim Hudson .25 .60
93 Tony Gwynn .50 1.25
94 Torii Hunter .15 .40
95 Travis Hafner .15 .40
96 Victor Martinez .25 .60
97 Vladimir Guerrero .25 .60
98 Wade Boggs .25 .60
99 Will Clark .25 .60
100 Yadier Molina .40 1.00
101 Adam Shabala AU RC 4.00 10.00
102 Ambiorix Burgos AU RC 4.00 10.00
103 Ambiorix Concepcion AU RC 4.00 10.00
104 Anibal Sanchez AU RC 6.00 15.00
106 Brandon McCarthy AU RC 8.00 20.00
107 Brian Burres AU RC 4.00 10.00
108 Carlos Ruiz AU RC 8.00 20.00
109 Casey Rogowski AU RC 4.00 10.00
110 Chad Orvella AU RC 4.00 10.00
111 Chris Resop AU RC 6.00 15.00
112 Chris Roberson AU RC 4.00 10.00
113 Chris Seddon AU RC 4.00 10.00
114 Colter Bean AU RC 6.00 15.00
116 Dave Gassner AU RC 4.00 10.00
117 Brian Anderson AU RC 6.00 15.00
120 Devon Lowery AU RC 4.00 10.00
121 Enrique Gonzalez AU RC 6.00 15.00
122 Eude Brito AU RC 4.00 10.00
123 Francisco Butto AU RC 4.00 10.00
124 Franquelis Osoria AU RC 4.00 10.00
125 Garrett Jones AU RC 10.00 25.00
126 Geovany Soto AU RC 4.00 10.00
127 Hayden Penn AU RC 6.00 15.00
128 Ismael Ramirez AU RC 4.00 10.00
129 Jared Gothreaux AU RC 4.00 10.00
130 Jason Hammel AU RC 4.00 10.00
131 Jeff Miller AU RC 4.00 10.00
132 Jeff Niemann AU RC 12.50 30.00
133 Joel Peralta AU RC 4.00 10.00
134 John Hattig AU RC 4.00 10.00
135 Jorge Campillo AU RC 4.00 10.00
136 Juan Morillo AU RC 4.00 10.00
137 Justin Verlander AU RC 75.00 200.00
138 Ryan Garko AU RC 4.00 10.00
139 Keiichi Yabu AU RC 6.00 15.00
140 Kendry Morales AU RC 10.00 25.00
141 Luis Hernandez AU RC 4.00 10.00
143 Luis O.Rodriguez AU RC 4.00 10.00
144 Luke Scott AU RC 10.00 25.00
145 Marcos Carvajal AU RC 4.00 10.00
146 Mark Woodyard AU RC 4.00 10.00
147 Matt A.Smith AU RC 4.00 10.00
148 Matthew Lindstrom AU RC 4.00 10.00
149 Miguel Negron AU RC 6.00 15.00
150 Mike Morse AU RC 10.00 25.00
151 Nate McLouth AU RC 6.00 15.00
152 Nelson Cruz AU RC 30.00 80.00
153 Nick Masset AU RC 4.00 10.00
155 Paulino Reynoso AU RC 4.00 10.00
156 Pedro Lopez AU RC 4.00 10.00
157 Pete Orr AU RC 4.00 10.00
158 Philip Humber AU RC 6.00 15.00
159 Prince Fielder AU RC 15.00 40.00
160 Randy Messenger AU RC 4.00 10.00
162 Raul Tablado AU RC 4.00 10.00
163 Ronny Paulino AU RC 6.00 15.00
164 Russ Rohlicek AU RC 4.00 10.00
165 Russell Martin AU RC 10.00 25.00
166 Scott Baker AU RC 6.00 15.00
167 Scott Munter AU RC 4.00 10.00
168 Sean Thompson AU RC 4.00 10.00
169 Sean Tracey AU RC 4.00 10.00
170 Shane Costa AU RC 4.00 10.00
171 Stephen Drew AU RC 12.50 30.00
172 Steve Schmoll AU RC 4.00 10.00
173 Tadahito Iguchi AU RC 15.00 40.00
174 Tony Giarratano AU RC 4.00 10.00
175 Tony Pena AU RC 4.00 10.00
176 Travis Bowyer AU RC 4.00 10.00
177 Ubaldo Jimenez AU RC 10.00 25.00
178 Wladimir Balentien AU RC 8.00 20.00
179 Yorman Bazardo AU RC 4.00 10.00
181 Ryan Zimmerman AU RC 40.00 100.00
182 Chris Denorfia AU RC 6.00 15.00
184 Jermaine Van Buren AU 4.00 10.00
185 Mark McLemore AU RC 4.00 10.00

2005 SP Authentic Jersey

STATED PRINT RUN 199 SERIAL #'d SETS
*GOLD: .5X TO 1.2X BASIC
GOLD PRINT RUN 99 SERIAL #'d SETS
ISSUED IN 05 SP COLLECTION PACKS
OVERALL GAME-USED ODDS 1:10
1 A.J. Burnett 2.00 5.00
2 Aaron Rowand 2.00 5.00
3 Adam Dunn 2.00 5.00
4 Adrian Beltre 2.00 5.00
5 Adrian Gonzalez 2.00 5.00
6 Akinori Otsuka 2.00 5.00
7 Albert Pujols 6.00 15.00
8 Andre Dawson 3.00 8.00
9 Andruw Jones 3.00 8.00
10 Aramis Ramirez 2.00 5.00
11 Barry Larkin 3.00 8.00
12 Ben Sheets 2.00 5.00
13 Bo Jackson 4.00 10.00
14 Bobby Abreu 2.00 5.00
15 Bobby Crosby 2.00 5.00
16 Bronson Arroyo 2.00 5.00
17 Cal Ripken Pants 8.00 20.00
18 Carl Crawford 2.00 5.00
19 Carlos Zambrano 2.00 5.00
20 Casey Kotchman 2.00 5.00
21 Cesar Izturis 2.00 5.00
22 Chone Figgins 2.00 5.00
23 Corey Patterson 2.00 5.00
24 Craig Biggio 3.00 8.00
25 Dale Murphy 4.00 10.00
26 Dallas McPherson 2.00 5.00
27 Danny Haren 2.00 5.00

28 Darryl Strawberry	3.00	8.00
29 David Ortiz	3.00	8.00
30 David Wright	4.00	10.00
31 Derek Jeter Pants	8.00	20.00
32 Derrek Lee	3.00	8.00
33 Don Mattingly	6.00	15.00
34 Dwight Gooden	3.00	8.00
35 Edgar Renteria	2.00	5.00
36 Eric Chavez	2.00	5.00
37 Eric Gagne	2.00	5.00
38 Gary Sheffield	2.00	5.00
39 Gavin Floyd	2.00	5.00
40 Pedro Martinez	3.00	8.00
41 Greg Maddux	4.00	10.00
42 Hank Blalock	2.00	5.00
43 Huston Street	3.00	8.00
44 J.D. Drew	2.00	5.00
45 Jake Peavy	2.00	5.00
46 Jake Westbrook	2.00	5.00
47 Jason Bay	2.00	5.00
48 Austin Kearns	2.00	5.00
49 Jeremy Reed	2.00	5.00
50 Jim Rice	3.00	8.00
51 Jimmy Rollins	2.00	5.00
52 Joe Blanton	2.00	5.00
53 Joe Mauer	4.00	10.00
54 Johan Santana	4.00	10.00
55 John Smoltz	3.00	8.00
56 Johnny Estrada	2.00	5.00
57 Jose Reyes	2.00	5.00
58 Ken Griffey Jr.	6.00	15.00
59 Kerry Wood	2.00	5.00
60 Khalil Greene	3.00	8.00
61 Marcus Giles	2.00	5.00
62 Melvin Mora	2.00	5.00
63 Mark Grace	4.00	10.00
64 Mark Mulder	2.00	5.00
65 Mark Prior	3.00	8.00
66 Mark Teixeria	3.00	8.00
67 Matt Clement	2.00	5.00
68 Michael Young	2.00	5.00
69 Miguel Cabrera	3.00	8.00
70 Miguel Tejada	2.00	5.00
71 Mike Piazza	4.00	10.00
72 Mike Schmidt	6.00	15.00
73 Nolan Ryan Pants	8.00	20.00
74 Oliver Perez	2.00	5.00
75 Nick Johnson	2.00	5.00
76 Paul Molitor	3.00	8.00
77 Rafael Palmeiro	4.00	10.00
78 Randy Johnson	4.00	10.00
79 Reggie Jackson	4.00	10.00
80 Rich Harden	2.00	5.00
81 Rickie Weeks	2.00	5.00
82 Robin Yount	4.00	10.00
83 Roger Clemens Pants	4.00	10.00
84 Roy Oswalt	2.00	5.00
85 Ryan Howard	10.00	25.00
86 Ryne Sandberg	6.00	15.00
87 Scott Kazmir	2.00	5.00
88 Scott Rolen	3.00	8.00
89 Sean Burroughs	2.00	5.00
90 Sean Casey	2.00	5.00
91 Shingo Takatsu	2.00	5.00
92 Tim Hudson	2.00	5.00
93 Tony Gwynn	4.00	10.00
94 Torii Hunter	2.00	5.00
95 Travis Hafner	2.00	5.00
96 Victor Martinez	2.00	5.00
97 Vladimir Guerrero	4.00	10.00
98 Wade Boggs	4.00	10.00
99 Will Clark	4.00	10.00
100 Yadier Molina	5.00	12.00

2005 SP Authentic Signature

PRINT RUNS B/WN 25-550 COPIES PER
GOLD PRINT RUN 10 SERIAL #'d SETS
NO GOLD PRICING DUE TO SCARCITY
ISSUED IN 05 SP COLLECTION PACKS
OVERALL AUTO ODDS 1:10

2 Aaron Rowand/550	10.00	25.00
3 Adam Dunn/25	10.00	25.00
4 Adrian Beltre/125	6.00	15.00
5 Adrian Gonzalez/550	6.00	15.00
6 Akinori Otsuka/475	6.00	15.00
7 Albert Pujols/25	150.00	250.00
8 Andre Dawson/125	6.00	15.00
9 Andruw Jones/25	20.00	50.00
10 Aramis Ramirez/475	6.00	15.00
11 Barry Larkin/125	20.00	50.00
12 Ben Sheets/350	6.00	15.00
13 Bo Jackson/25	40.00	80.00
15 Bobby Crosby/350	6.00	15.00
16 Bronson Arroyo/550	8.00	20.00
18 Carl Crawford/475	6.00	15.00
20 Casey Kotchman/550	6.00	15.00
21 Cesar Izturis/550	4.00	10.00
22 Chone Figgins/550	6.00	15.00
23 Corey Patterson/350	4.00	10.00
24 Craig Biggio/125	15.00	40.00
25 Dale Murphy/350	12.00	30.00
26 Dallas McPherson/550	4.00	10.00
27 Danny Haren/550	4.00	10.00
28 Darryl Strawberry/125	6.00	15.00
30 David Wright/350	12.50	30.00
31 Derek Jeter/150	125.00	300.00
32 Derrek Lee/350	10.00	25.00
33 Don Mattingly/25	40.00	80.00
34 Dwight Gooden/475	6.00	15.00
36 Eric Chavez/75	8.00	20.00
38 Gary Sheffield/25	15.00	40.00
89 Gavin Floyd/550	4.00	10.00
42 Hank Blalock/25	10.00	25.00
43 Huston Street/550	10.00	25.00
45 Jake Peavy/475	6.00	15.00
46 Jake Westbrook/550	4.00	10.00
47 Jason Bay/475	6.00	15.00
48 Austin Kearns/75	5.00	12.00
49 Jeremy Reed/550	4.00	10.00
50 Jim Rice/350	6.00	15.00
52 Joe Blanton/550	4.00	10.00
53 Joe Mauer/350	12.50	30.00
55 John Smoltz/25	20.00	50.00
57 Jose Reyes/475	6.00	15.00
59 Kerry Wood/25	10.00	25.00
60 Khalil Greene/350	10.00	25.00
62 Melvin Mora/475	6.00	15.00
63 Mark Grace/25	15.00	40.00
64 Mark Mulder/350	6.00	15.00
65 Mark Prior/25	10.00	25.00
66 Mark Teixeria/125	10.00	25.00
67 Matt Clement/350	6.00	15.00
68 Michael Young/475	6.00	15.00
69 Miguel Cabrera/125	12.50	30.00
70 Miguel Tejada/25	10.00	25.00
71 Mike Piazza/25	50.00	100.00
72 Mike Schmidt/25	40.00	80.00
73 Nolan Ryan/25	50.00	100.00
74 Oliver Perez/475	4.00	10.00
75 Nick Johnson/550	6.00	15.00
76 Paul Molitor/25	10.00	25.00
77 Rafael Palmeiro/25	15.00	40.00
78 Randy Johnson/25	50.00	100.00
79 Reggie Jackson/25	15.00	40.00
83 Roger Clemens/25	125.00	200.00
84 Roy Oswalt/125	6.00	15.00
85 Ryan Howard/550	10.00	25.00
86 Ryne Sandberg/25	40.00	80.00
87 Scott Kazmir/475	10.00	25.00
89 Sean Burroughs/475	4.00	10.00
91 Shingo Takatsu/550	6.00	15.00
92 Tim Hudson/25	10.00	25.00
93 Tony Gwynn/25	30.00	60.00
94 Torii Hunter/125	6.00	15.00
97 Vladimir Guerrero/25	15.00	40.00
98 Wade Boggs/25	15.00	40.00
99 Will Clark/25	20.00	50.00

2005 SP Authentic Honors

ISSUED IN 05 SP COLLECTION PACKS
OVERALL INSERT ODDS 1:10
STATED PRINT RUN 299 SERIAL #'d SETS

AB Adrian Beltre	1.50	4.00
AP Albert Pujols	2.00	5.00
AR Aramis Ramirez	.60	1.50
BC Bobby Crosby	.60	1.50
BJ Bo Jackson	1.50	4.00
BL Barry Larkin	1.00	2.50
BO Jeremy Bonderman	.60	1.50
BS Ben Sheets	.60	1.50
BU B.J. Upton	1.00	2.50
CA Miguel Cabrera	1.50	4.00
CC Carl Crawford	1.00	2.50
CP Corey Patterson	.60	1.50
CR Cal Ripken	5.00	12.00
CZ Carlos Zambrano	1.00	2.50
DG Dwight Gooden	.80	1.50
DJ Derek Jeter	4.00	10.00
DM Dale Murphy	1.50	4.00
DO David Ortiz	1.50	4.00
DW David Wright	1.25	3.00
GR Khalil Greene	.60	1.50
JB Jason Bay	.60	1.50
JM Joe Mauer	1.25	3.00
JP Jake Peavy	.60	1.50
JR Jimmy Rollins	1.00	2.50
JS Johan Santana	1.00	2.50
JW Jake Westbrook	.60	1.50
KG Ken Griffey Jr.	3.00	8.00
MC Dallas McPherson	.60	1.50
MG Marcus Giles	.60	1.50
MO Justin Morneau	1.00	2.50
MS Mike Schmidt	3.00	8.00
MT Mark Teixeria	1.00	2.50
MY Michael Young	.60	1.50
NR Nolan Ryan	5.00	12.00
OP Oliver Perez	.60	1.50
PM Paul Molitor	1.50	4.00
RC Roger Clemens	2.00	5.00
RE Jose Reyes	1.00	2.50
RH Rich Harden	.60	1.50
RS Ryne Sandberg	3.00	8.00
SK Scott Kazmir	1.50	4.00
SM John Smoltz	1.50	4.00
ST Shingo Takatsu	.60	1.50
TE Miguel Tejada	1.00	2.50
TG Tony Gwynn	2.00	5.00
TH Travis Hafner	.60	1.50
VM Victor Martinez	1.00	2.50
WB Wade Boggs	1.00	2.50
WC Will Clark	1.00	2.50
ZG Zack Greinke	1.50	4.00

2005 SP Authentic Honors Jersey

ISSUED IN 05 SP COLLECTION PACKS
OVERALL PREMIUM AU-GU ODDS 1:20
STATED PRINT RUN 130 SERIAL #'d SETS

AB Adrian Beltre	2.00	5.00
AP Albert Pujols	6.00	15.00
AR Aramis Ramirez	2.00	5.00
BC Bobby Crosby	2.00	5.00
BJ Bo Jackson	4.00	10.00
BL Barry Larkin	3.00	8.00
BO Jeremy Bonderman	2.00	5.00
BS Ben Sheets	2.00	5.00
BU B.J. Upton	2.00	5.00
CA Miguel Cabrera	3.00	8.00
CC Carl Crawford	2.00	5.00
CP Corey Patterson	2.00	5.00
CR Cal Ripken Pants	8.00	20.00
CZ Carlos Zambrano	2.00	5.00
DG Dwight Gooden	3.00	8.00
DJ Derek Jeter Pants	8.00	20.00
DM Dale Murphy	4.00	10.00
DO David Ortiz	3.00	8.00
DW David Wright	4.00	10.00
GR Khalil Greene	3.00	8.00
JB Jason Bay	2.00	5.00
JM Joe Mauer	4.00	10.00
JP Jake Peavy	2.00	5.00
JR Jimmy Rollins	2.00	5.00
JS Johan Santana	4.00	10.00
JW Jake Westbrook	2.00	5.00
KG Ken Griffey Jr.	6.00	15.00
MC Dallas McPherson	2.00	5.00
MG Marcus Giles	2.00	5.00
MO Justin Morneau	2.00	5.00
MS Mike Schmidt	6.00	15.00
MT Mark Teixeria	3.00	8.00
MY Michael Young	2.00	5.00
NR Nolan Ryan Pants	8.00	20.00
OP Oliver Perez	2.00	5.00
PM Paul Molitor	3.00	8.00
RC Roger Clemens Pants	4.00	10.00
RE Jose Reyes	2.00	5.00
RH Rich Harden	2.00	5.00
RS Ryne Sandberg	6.00	15.00
SK Scott Kazmir	2.00	5.00
SM John Smoltz	3.00	8.00
ST Shingo Takatsu	2.00	5.00
TE Miguel Tejada	2.00	5.00
TG Tony Gwynn	4.00	10.00
TH Travis Hafner	2.00	5.00
VM Victor Martinez	2.00	5.00
WB Wade Boggs	4.00	10.00
WC Will Clark	4.00	10.00
ZG Zack Greinke	2.00	5.00

2006 SP Authentic

This 300-card set was released in December, 2006. The set was issued in five-card packs, with an $4.99 SRP, which came 24 packs to a box and 12 boxes to a case. The first 100 cards of the set all feature veterans while cards 101-200 were inserted at a stated rate of one in eight and were issued to a stated print run of 899 serial numbered cards. The final 100-cards in this set all feature 2006 rookies and had between 125 and 899 serial numbered copies produced. These autograph cards were issued at a stated rate of one in 16. A few players did not return their signatures in time for pack out and those autographs could be redeemed until December 5, 2009.

COMP.SET w/o SP's (100)	6.00	15.00

101-200 STATED ODDS 1:8
101-200 PRINT RUN 899 #'d SETS
201-300 AU STATED ODDS 1:16
201-300 AU PRINTS B/WN 125-899 PER
EXCH: 214/235/242/247/249/253/277
EXCH: 279/280/291
EXCHANGE DEADLINE 12/05/09

1 Erik Bedard	.15	.40
2 Corey Patterson	.15	.40
3 Ramon Hernandez	.15	.40
4 Kris Benson	.15	.40
5 Miguel Batista	.15	.40
6 Orlando Hudson	.15	.40
7 Shawn Green	.15	.40
8 Jeff Francoeur	.40	1.00
9 Marcus Giles	.15	.40
10 Edgar Renteria	.15	.40
11 Tim Hudson	.25	.60
12 Tim Wakefield	.25	.60
13 Mark Loretta	.15	.40
14 Kevin Youkilis	.15	.40
15 Mike Lowell	.15	.40
16 Coco Crisp	.15	.40
17 Tadahito Iguchi	.15	.40
18 Scott Podsednik	.15	.40
19 Jermaine Dye	.15	.40
20 Jose Contreras	.15	.40
21 Carlos Zambrano	.25	.60
22 Aramis Ramirez	.15	.40
23 Jacque Jones	.15	.40
24 Austin Kearns	.15	.40
25 Felipe Lopez	.15	.40
26 Brandon Phillips	.15	.40
27 Aaron Harang	.15	.40
28 Cliff Lee	.25	.60
29 Jhonny Peralta	.15	.40
30 Jason Michaels	.15	.40
31 Clint Barmes	.15	.40
32 Brad Hawpe	.15	.40
33 Aaron Cook	.15	.40
34 Kenny Rogers	.15	.40
35 Carlos Guillen	.15	.40
36 Brian Moehler	.15	.40
37 Andy Pettitte	.25	.60
38 Wandy Rodriguez	.15	.40
39 Morgan Ensberg	.15	.40
40 Preston Wilson	.15	.40
41 Mark Grudzielanek	.15	.40
42 Angel Berroa	.15	.40
43 Jeremy Affeldt	.15	.40
44 Zack Greinke	.25	.60
45 Orlando Cabrera	.15	.40
46 Garret Anderson	.15	.40
47 Ervin Santana	.15	.40
48 Derek Lowe	.15	.40
49 Nomar Garciaparra	.25	.60
50 J.D. Drew	.15	.40
51 Rafael Furcal	.15	.40
52 Rickie Weeks	.15	.40
53 Geoff Jenkins	.15	.40
54 Bill Hall	.15	.40
55 Chris Capuano	.15	.40
56 Derrick Turnbow	.15	.40
57 Justin Morneau	.25	.60
58 Michael Cuddyer	.15	.40
59 Luis Castillo	.15	.40
60 Hideki Matsui	.40	1.00
61 Jason Giambi	.15	.40
62 Jorge Posada	.25	.60
63 Mariano Rivera	.50	1.25
64 Billy Wagner	.15	.40
65 Carlos Delgado	.15	.40
66 Jose Reyes	.25	.60
67 Nick Swisher	.25	.60
68 Bobby Crosby	.15	.40
69 Frank Thomas	.40	1.00
70 Ryan Howard	.30	.75
71 Pat Burrell	.15	.40
72 Jimmy Rollins	.25	.60
73 Craig Wilson	.15	.40
74 Freddy Sanchez	.15	.40
75 Sean Casey	.15	.40
76 Mike Piazza	.40	1.00
77 Dave Roberts	.25	.60
78 Chris Young	.15	.40
79 Noah Lowry	.15	.40
80 Armando Benitez	.15	.40
81 Pedro Feliz	.15	.40
82 Jose Lopez	.15	.40
83 Adrian Beltre	.40	1.00
84 Jamie Moyer	.15	.40
85 Jason Isringhausen	.15	.40
86 Jason Marquis	.15	.40
87 David Eckstein	.15	.40
88 Juan Encarnacion	.15	.40
89 Julio Lugo	.15	.40
90 Ty Wigginton	.15	.40
91 Jorge Cantu	.15	.40
92 Akinori Otsuka	.15	.40
93 Hank Blalock	.15	.40
94 Kevin Mench	.15	.40
95 Lyle Overbay	.15	.40
96 Shea Hillenbrand	.15	.40
97 B.J. Ryan	.15	.40
98 Tony Armas	.15	.40
99 Chad Cordero	.15	.40
100 Jose Guillen	.15	.40
101 Miguel Tejada	1.00	2.50
102 Brian Roberts	.60	1.50
103 Melvin Mora	.60	1.50
104 Brandon Webb	1.00	2.50
105 Chad Tracy	.60	1.50
106 Luis Gonzalez	.60	1.50
107 Andruw Jones	.60	1.50
108 Chipper Jones	1.50	4.00
109 John Smoltz	1.50	4.00
110 Curt Schilling	1.00	2.50
111 Josh Beckett	.60	1.50
112 David Ortiz	1.50	4.00
113 Manny Ramirez	1.50	4.00
114 Jason Varitek	1.50	4.00
115 Jim Thome	1.00	2.50
116 Paul Konerko	1.00	2.50
117 Javier Vazquez	.60	1.50
118 Mark Prior	1.00	2.50
119 Derrek Lee	.60	1.50
120 Greg Maddux	2.00	5.00
121 Ken Griffey Jr.	3.00	8.00
122 Adam Dunn	1.00	2.50
123 Bronson Arroyo	.60	1.50
124 Travis Hafner	.60	1.50
125 Victor Martinez	1.00	2.50
126 Grady Sizemore	1.00	2.50
127 C.C. Sabathia	1.00	2.50
128 Todd Helton	1.00	2.50
129 Matt Holliday	1.50	4.00
130 Garrett Atkins	.60	1.50
131 Jeff Francis	.60	1.50
132 Jeremy Bonderman	.60	1.50
133 Ivan Rodriguez	1.00	2.50
134 Chris Shelton	.60	1.50
135 Magglio Ordonez	1.00	2.50
136 Dontrelle Willis	.60	1.50
137 Miguel Cabrera	1.50	4.00
138 Roger Clemens	2.00	5.00
139 Roy Oswalt	1.00	2.50
140 Lance Berkman	1.00	2.50
141 Reggie Sanders	.60	1.50
142 Vladimir Guerrero	1.00	2.50
143 Bartolo Colon	.60	1.50
144 Chone Figgins	.60	1.50
145 Francisco Rodriguez	1.00	2.50
146 Brad Penny	.60	1.50
147 Jeff Kent	.60	1.50
148 Eric Gagne	.60	1.50
149 Carlos Lee	.60	1.50
150 Ben Sheets	.60	1.50
151 Johan Santana	1.00	2.50
152 Torii Hunter	.60	1.50
153 Joe Nathan	.60	1.50
154 Alex Rodriguez	2.00	5.00
155 Derek Jeter	4.00	10.00
156 Randy Johnson	1.50	4.00
157 Johnny Damon	1.00	2.50
158 Mike Mussina	1.00	2.50
159 Pedro Martinez	1.00	2.50
160 Tom Glavine	1.00	2.50
161 David Wright	1.25	3.00
162 Carlos Beltran	1.00	2.50
163 Rich Harden	.60	1.50
164 Barry Zito	1.00	2.50
165 Eric Chavez	.60	1.50
166 Huston Street	.60	1.50
167 Bobby Abreu	.60	1.50
168 Chase Utley	1.00	2.50
169 Brett Myers	.60	1.50
170 Jason Bay	.60	1.50
171 Zach Duke	.60	1.50
172 Jake Peavy	.60	1.50
173 Brian Giles	.60	1.50
174 Khalil Greene	.60	1.50
175 Trevor Hoffman	1.00	2.50
176 Jason Schmidt	.60	1.50
177 Randy Winn	.60	1.50
178 Omar Vizquel	1.00	2.50
179 Kenji Johjima	1.50	4.00
180 Ichiro Suzuki	2.00	5.00
181 Richie Sexson	.60	1.50
182 Felix Hernandez	1.00	2.50
183 Albert Pujols	2.00	5.00
184 Chris Carpenter	1.00	2.50
185 Jim Edmonds	1.00	2.50
186 Scott Rolen	1.00	2.50
187 Carl Crawford	1.00	2.50
188 Scott Kazmir	1.00	2.50
189 Jonny Gomes	.60	1.50
190 Mark Teixeira	1.00	2.50
191 Michael Young	.60	1.50
192 Kevin Millwood	.60	1.50
193 Vernon Wells	.60	1.50
194 Troy Glaus	.60	1.50
195 Roy Halladay	1.00	2.50
196 Alex Rios	.60	1.50
197 Nick Johnson	.60	1.50
198 Livan Hernandez	.60	1.50
199 Alfonso Soriano	1.00	2.50
200 Jose Vidro	.60	1.50
201 A.Rakers AU/399 (RC)	3.00	8.00
202 A.Pagan AU/399 (RC)	4.00	10.00
203 B.Hendrick AU/399 (RC)	3.00	8.00
204 B.Livingston AU/399 (RC)	3.00	8.00
205 D.Rasner AU/399 (RC)	3.00	8.00
206 B.Bannister AU/399 (RC)	4.00	10.00
207 B.Wilson AU/899 RC	10.00	25.00
208 B.Keppel AU/199 (RC)	6.00	15.00
209 C.Freeman AU/399 (RC)	3.00	8.00
210 C.Booker AU/899 (RC)	3.00	8.00
211 C.Britton AU/399 (RC)	4.00	10.00
212 C.Demaria AU/329 RC	4.00	10.00
213 C.Resop AU/899 (RC)	3.00	8.00
214 T.Gwynn Jr. AU/399 (RC)	4.00	10.00
215 E.Reed AU/399 (RC)	3.00	8.00
216 F.Castro AU/399 RC	8.00	20.00
217 F.Nieve AU/299 (RC)	4.00	10.00
218 F.Bynum AU/899 (RC)	3.00	8.00
219 G.Quiroz AU/399 (RC)	3.00	8.00
220 H.Kuo AU/899 (RC)	6.00	15.00
221 R.Theriot AU/399 RC	3.00	8.00
222 J.Taschner AU/899 (RC)	3.00	8.00
223 J.Bergmann AU/899 (RC)	3.00	8.00
224 J.Hammel AU/899 (RC)	5.00	12.00
225 J.Harris AU/399 RC	3.00	8.00
226 J.Accardo AU/399 RC	4.00	10.00
227 T.Taubenheim AU/399 RC	12.50	30.00
228 J.Zumaya AU/399 (RC)	6.00	15.00
229 J.Koronka AU/399 (RC)	3.00	8.00
230 E.Aybar AU/399 (RC)	3.00	8.00
231 J.Tata AU/399 RC	6.00	15.00
232 R.Martin AU/399 (RC)	5.00	12.00
233 J.Rupe AU/399 (RC)	3.00	8.00
234 K.Frandsen AU/399 (RC)	6.00	15.00
235 M.Prado AU/399 (RC)	6.00	15.00
236 M.Capps AU/399 (RC)	3.00	8.00
237 A.Montero AU/199 (RC)	4.00	10.00
238 M.Thompson AU/399 RC	3.00	8.00
239 N.McLouth AU/399 (RC)	4.00	10.00
240 P.Moylan AU/399 RC	3.00	8.00
241 R.Abercrom AU/399 (RC)	3.00	8.00
242 C.Quentin AU/399 (RC)	8.00	20.00
243 R.Flores AU/399 RC	3.00	8.00
244 R.Shealy AU/399 (RC)	8.00	20.00
245 M.Rouse AU/399 (RC)	3.00	8.00
246 S.Ramirez AU/399 (RC)	3.00	8.00
247 C.Hensley AU/899 (RC)	3.00	8.00
248 S.Schumaker AU/399 (RC)	6.00	15.00
249 E.Alfonzo AU/899 RC	3.00	8.00
250 S.Stemle AU/399 RC	3.00	8.00
251 T.Hamulack AU/399 (RC)	3.00	8.00
252 T.Pena Jr. AU/299 (RC)	4.00	10.00
253 E.Fruto AU/899 RC	3.00	8.00
254 W.Nieves AU/399 (RC)	4.00	10.00
255 J.Devine AU/399 RC	4.00	10.00
256 A.Wainwright AU/399 (RC)	12.50	30.00
257 A.Ethier AU/399 (RC)	6.00	15.00
258 B.Johnson AU/399 (RC)	3.00	8.00
259 B.Logan AU/399 RC	6.00	15.00
260 C.Denorfia AU/899 (RC)	4.00	10.00
261 A.Soler AU/299 RC	6.00	15.00
262 C.Ross AU/899 (RC)	6.00	15.00
263 D.Gassner AU/399 (RC)	3.00	8.00
264 F.Carmona AU/399 (RC)	10.00	25.00
265 J.Sowers AU/299 (RC)	10.00	25.00
266 J.Kubel AU/399 (RC)	4.00	10.00
267 J.VanBenSch AU/399 (RC)	3.00	8.00
268 J.Capellan AU/399 (RC)	3.00	8.00
269 J.Wilson AU/399 (RC)	3.00	8.00
270 K.Shoppach AU/399 (RC)	3.00	8.00
271 M.McBride AU/399 (RC)	4.00	10.00
272 M.Cain AU/399 (RC)	10.00	25.00
273 M.Jacobs AU/399 (RC)	6.00	15.00
274 P.Maholm AU/399 (RC)	4.00	10.00
275 C.Billingsley AU/399 (RC)	3.00	8.00
276 R.Lugo AU/399 (RC)	3.00	8.00
277 J.Lester AU/399 RC	15.00	40.00
278 S.Marshall AU/383 (RC)	6.00	15.00
279 Me.Cabrera AU/399 (RC)	15.00	40.00
280 Y.Petit AU/399 (RC)	3.00	8.00
281 A.Hernandez AU/299 (RC)	4.00	10.00
282 B.Anderson AU/699 (RC)	4.00	10.00
283 C.Hamels AU/299 (RC)	8.00	20.00
284 B.Bonser AU/299 (RC)	6.00	15.00
285 D.Uggla AU/199 (RC)	10.00	25.00
286 F.Liriano AU/299 (RC)	5.00	12.00
287 H.Ramirez AU/199 (RC)	12.50	30.00
288 I.Kinsler AU/299 (RC)	8.00	20.00
289 J.Hermida AU/299 (RC)	6.00	15.00
290 J.Papelbon AU/199 (RC)	20.00	50.00
291 J.Weaver AU/199 (RC)	12.50	30.00
292 J.Johnson AU/299 (RC)	6.00	15.00
293 J.Willingham AU/199 (RC)	6.00	15.00
294 J.Verlander AU/199 (RC)	20.00	50.00
295 S.Drew AU/299 (RC)	6.00	15.00
296 P.Fielder AU/125 (RC)	6.00	15.00
297 R.Zimmer AU/199 (RC)	10.00	25.00
298 T.Saito AU/283 RC	10.00	25.00
299 T.Buchholz AU/299 (RC)	4.00	10.00
300 Co.Jackson AU/299 (RC)	6.00	15.00

2006 SP Authentic Baseball Heroes

COMPLETE SET (70)	50.00	100.00

STATED ODDS 1:4

1 Albert Pujols	1.25	3.00
2 Andruw Jones	.40	1.00
3 Aramis Ramirez	.40	1.00
4 Brian Roberts	.40	1.00
5 Carl Crawford	.60	1.50
6 Carlos Lee	.40	1.00
7 Vladimir Guerrero	.60	1.50
8 Chris Carpenter	.60	1.50
9 Craig Biggio	.60	1.50
10 David Ortiz	1.00	2.50
11 David Wright	.75	2.00
12 Derrek Lee	.40	1.00
13 Dontrelle Willis	.40	1.00
14 Felix Hernandez	.60	1.50
15 Garrett Atkins	.40	1.00
16 Grady Sizemore	.60	1.50
17 Huston Street	.40	1.00
18 Jake Peavy	.40	1.00
19 Jason Bay	.40	1.00
20 Joe Mauer	.60	1.50
21 John Smoltz	1.00	2.50
22 Jonny Gomes	.40	1.00
23 Jorge Cantu	.40	1.00
24 Ken Griffey Jr.	2.00	5.00
25 Marcus Giles	.40	1.00
26 Mark Teixeira	.60	1.50
27 Matt Cain	2.50	6.00
28 Michael Young	.40	
29 Miguel Cabrera	1.00	
30 Johan Santana	.60	
31 Nick Swisher	.60	
32 Prince Fielder	2.00	
33 Joe Blanton	.40	
34 Roy Oswalt	.60	
35 Ryan Howard	.75	
36 Scott Kazmir	.60	
37 Tadahito Iguchi	.40	
38 Travis Hafner	.40	
39 Victor Martinez	.60	
40 Jose Reyes	.60	
41 C.Carpenter/A.Pujols	1.25	
42 A.Pujols/M.Cabrera	1.25	
43 K.Griffey Jr./A.Jones	2.00	
44 D.Lee/A.Ramirez	.40	
45 R.Howard/P.Fielder	2.00	
46 R.Oswalt/J.Peavy	.60	
47 C.Biggio/M.Ensberg	.60	
48 T.Hafner/D.Ortiz	1.00	
49 D.Jeter/D.Wright	2.50	
50 K.Griffey Jr./D.Jeter	2.50	
51 D.Jeter/M.Young	2.50	
52 S.Kazmir/D.Willis	.60	
53 G.Sizemore/J.Bay	.60	
54 M.Young/M.Teixeira	.60	
55 B.Roberts/T.Iguchi	.40	
56 Wang/Cain/Felix	2.50	
57 D.Lee/Pujols/Teixeira	1.25	
58 Griffey/Pujols/Cabrera	2.00	
59 Andruw/Smoltz/M.Giles	1.00	
60 Wood/D.Lee/Aramis	.40	
61 Aramis/Ensberg/Wright	.75	
62 Crawford/Cantu/Gomes	.60	
63 Smoltz/Carpenter/Peavy	1.00	
64 Hafner/V.Mart/Sizemore	.60	
65 Ortiz/Howard/Fielder	2.00	
66 Smoltz/Carp/Peavy/Willis	1.00	
67 Griffey/Jeter/Ortiz/Pujols	2.50	
68 Andruw/D.Lee/Ortiz/Teix	1.00	
69 Biggio/B.Rob/Giles/Iguchi	.60	
70 Wright/Teix/M.Cab/Bay	1.00	

2006 SP Authentic By the Let

STATED ODDS 1:24
PRINT RUNS B/WN 4-400 COPIES PER
EXCH: AJ, AR, CS, CZ, FH, FH2, GM, HO
EXCH: HU, JM, JR, JV, JW, KG, KG2, KG3
EXCH: KG4, KM, KW, MT, SM, TE
EXCHANGE DEADLINE 12/05/09

ABB A.J. Burnett B/50	6.00	15
ABE A.J. Burnett E/50	6.00	15
ABN A.J. Burnett N/50	6.00	15
ABR A.J. Burnett R/50	6.00	15
ABT A.J. Burnett T/100	6.00	15
ABU A.J. Burnett U/50	6.00	15.
ADD Adam Dunn D/50	10.00	25.
ADN Adam Dunn N/100	10.00	25.
ADU Adam Dunn U/50	10.00	25
AGG Tony Gwynn Jr. G/150	8.00	20
AGN Tony Gwynn Jr. N/300	8.00	20
AGW Tony Gwynn Jr. W/150	8.00	20.
AGY Tony Gwynn Jr. Y/150	8.00	20.
AJE Andruw Jones E/20	60.00	120.
AJJ Andruw Jones J/20	60.00	120
AJN Andruw Jones N/20	60.00	120
AJO Andruw Jones O/20	60.00	120
AJS Andruw Jones S/20	60.00	120
APJ Albert Pujols J/5	200.00	400.
APL Albert Pujols L/5	200.00	400.
APO Albert Pujols O/5	200.00	400.
APP Albert Pujols P/5	200.00	400.
APS Albert Pujols S/5	200.00	400.
APU Albert Pujols U/5	200.00	400.
AP2M Albert Pujols MVP M/10	200.00	400.
AP2P Albert Pujols MVP P/10	200.00	400.
AP2V Albert Pujols MVP V/10	200.00	400.
ARI Alex Rios I/100	20.00	40.
ARO Alex Rios O/100	20.00	40.
ARR Alex Rios R/100	20.00	40.
ARS Alex Rios S/100	20.00	40.
BAA Bronson Arroyo A/80	6.00	15.
BAO Bronson Arroyo O/160	6.00	15.
BAR Bronson Arroyo R/160	6.00	15.
BAY Bronson Arroyo Y/80	6.00	15.
BIB Chad Billingsley B/75	6.00	15.
BIE Chad Billingsley E/75	6.00	15.
BIG Chad Billingsley G/75	6.00	15.
BII Chad Billingsley I/150	6.00	15.
BIL Chad Billingsley L/225	6.00	15.
BIN Chad Billingsley N/75	6.00	15.
BIS Chad Billingsley S/75	6.00	15.
BIY Chad Billingsley Y/75	6.00	15.
BRB Brian Roberts B/14	40.00	80.
BRE Brian Roberts E/14	40.00	80.
BRO Brian Roberts O/14	40.00	80.
BRR Brian Roberts R/28	40.00	80.
BRS Brian Roberts S/14	40.00	80.
BRT Brian Roberts T/14	40.00	80.
BSE Ben Sheets E/250	6.00	15.
BSH Ben Sheets H/125	6.00	15.

S Ben Sheets S/250 6.00 15.00
T Ben Sheets T/125 6.00 15.00
N B.J. Upton N/20 25.00 50.00
O B.J. Upton O/20 25.00 50.00
P B.J. Upton P/20 25.00 50.00
T B.J. Upton T/20 25.00 50.00
U B.J. Upton U/20 25.00 50.00
B Craig Biggio B/55 30.00 60.00
G Craig Biggio G/110 30.00 60.00
I Craig Biggio I/110 30.00 60.00
O Craig Biggio O/55 30.00 60.00
A Chris Carpenter A/4 40.00 80.00
C Chris Carpenter C/4 40.00 80.00
E Chris Carpenter E/8 40.00 80.00
N Chris Carpenter N/4 40.00 80.00
P Chris Carpenter P/4 40.00 80.00
R Chris Carpenter R/8 40.00 80.00
T Chris Carpenter T/4 40.00 80.00
2C Chris Carpenter CY C/8 40.00 80.00
2G Chris Carpenter CY G/8 40.00 80.00
2N Chris Carpenter CY N/8 40.00 80.00
2O Chris Carpenter CY O/8 40.00 80.00
2U Chris Carpenter CY U/8 40.00 80.00
2Y Chris Carpenter CY Y/16 40.00 80.00
A Craig Hansen A/30 6.00 15.00
E Craig Hansen E/30 6.00 15.00
H Craig Hansen H/30 6.00 15.00
N Craig Hansen N/60 6.00 15.00
S Craig Hansen S/30 6.00 15.00
A Cole Hamels A/120 10.00 25.00
E Cole Hamels E/120 10.00 25.00
H Cole Hamels H/120 10.00 25.00
L Cole Hamels L/120 10.00 25.00
M Cole Hamels M/120 10.00 25.00
S Cole Hamels S/120 10.00 25.00
A C.C. Sabathia A/120 20.00 40.00
B C.C. Sabathia B/40 20.00 40.00
H C.C. Sabathia H/40 20.00 40.00
I C.C. Sabathia I/40 20.00 40.00
S C.C. Sabathia S/40 20.00 40.00
T C.C. Sabathia T/40 20.00 40.00
E Chase Utley E/25 30.00 60.00
L Chase Utley L/25 30.00 60.00
T Chase Utley T/25 30.00 60.00
U Chase Utley U/25 30.00 60.00
Y Chase Utley Y/25 30.00 60.00
A Carlos Zambrano A/34 50.00 100.00
B Carlos Zambrano B/17 50.00 100.00
M Carlos Zambrano M/17 50.00 100.00
N Carlos Zambrano N/17 50.00 100.00
O Carlos Zambrano O/17 50.00 100.00
R Carlos Zambrano R/17 50.00 100.00
Z Carlos Zambrano Z/17 50.00 100.00
HA Danny Haren A/180 8.00 20.00
HE Danny Haren E/180 8.00 20.00
HH Danny Haren H/180 8.00 20.00
HN Danny Haren N/180 8.00 20.00
HR Danny Haren R/180 8.00 20.00
JE Derek Jeter E/12 175.00 350.00
JJ Derek Jeter J/6 175.00 350.00
JR Derek Jeter R/6 175.00 350.00
JT Derek Jeter T/6 175.00 350.00
J2A Derek Jeter Captain A/10 175.00 350.00
J2C Derek Jeter Captain C/5 175.00 350.00
J2I Derek Jeter Captain I/5 175.00 350.00
J2N Derek Jeter Captain N/5 175.00 350.00
J2P Derek Jeter Captain P/5 175.00 350.00
J2T Derek Jeter Captain T/5 175.00 350.00
LE Derrek Lee E/400 6.00 15.00
LL Derrek Lee L/200 6.00 15.00
UA Dan Uggla A/100 10.00 25.00
UG Dan Uggla G/200 10.00 25.00
UL Dan Uggla L/100 10.00 25.00
UU Dan Uggla U/100 10.00 25.00
WI Dontrelle Willis I/300 6.00 15.00
WL Dontrelle Willis L/300 6.00 15.00
WS Dontrelle Willis S/150 6.00 15.00
WW Dontrelle Willis W/150 6.00 15.00
CA Eric Chavez A/75 20.00 40.00
CC Eric Chavez C/75 20.00 40.00
CE Eric Chavez E/75 20.00 40.00
CH Eric Chavez H/75 20.00 40.00
CV Eric Chavez V/75 20.00 40.00
CZ Eric Chavez Z/75 20.00 40.00
HA Felix Hernandez A/40 20.00 50.00
HD Felix Hernandez D/40 20.00 50.00
HE Felix Hernandez E/80 20.00 50.00
HH Felix Hernandez H/40 20.00 50.00
HN Felix Hernandez N/80 20.00 50.00
HR Felix Hernandez R/40 20.00 50.00
HZ Felix Hernandez Z/40 20.00 50.00
H2G Felix Hernandez King G/75 20.00 50.00
H2I Felix Hernandez King I/75 20.00 50.00
H2K Felix Hernandez King K/75 20.00 50.00
H2N Felix Hernandez King N/75 20.00 50.00
LA Francisco Liriano A/100 8.00 20.00
LI Francisco Liriano I/200 8.00 20.00
LL Francisco Liriano L/100 8.00 20.00
LN Francisco Liriano N/100 8.00 20.00
LO Francisco Liriano O/100 8.00 20.00
LR Francisco Liriano R/100 8.00 20.00
MA Greg Maddux A/25 75.00 150.00
MD Greg Maddux D/50 75.00 150.00
MM Greg Maddux M/25 75.00 150.00
MU Greg Maddux U/25 75.00 150.00
MX Greg Maddux X/25 75.00 150.00
BA Hank Blalock A/50 6.00 15.00
BB Hank Blalock B/50 6.00 15.00
BC Hank Blalock C/50 6.00 15.00
BK Hank Blalock K/50 6.00 15.00
BL Hank Blalock L/100 6.00 15.00
BO Hank Blalock O/50 6.00 15.00
KC Howie Kendrick C/75 6.00 15.00
HKD Howie Kendrick D/75 6.00 15.00
HKE Howie Kendrick E/75 6.00 15.00
HKI Howie Kendrick I/75 6.00 15.00
HKK Howie Kendrick K/150 6.00 15.00
HKN Howie Kendrick N/75 6.00 15.00
HKR Howie Kendrick R/75 6.00 15.00
HOA Trevor Hoffman A/8 10.00 25.00
HOF Trevor Hoffman F/16 10.00 25.00
HOH Trevor Hoffman H/8 10.00 25.00
HOM Trevor Hoffman M/8 10.00 25.00
HON Trevor Hoffman N/8 10.00 25.00
HOO Trevor Hoffman O/8 10.00 25.00
HRA Hanley Ramirez A/125 10.00 25.00
HRE Hanley Ramirez E/125 10.00 25.00
HRI Hanley Ramirez I/125 10.00 25.00
HRM Hanley Ramirez M/125 10.00 25.00
HRR Hanley Ramirez R/250 10.00 25.00
HRZ Hanley Ramirez Z/125 10.00 25.00
HSE Huston Street E/150 6.00 15.00
HSR Huston Street R/75 6.00 15.00
HSS Huston Street S/75 6.00 15.00
HST Huston Street T/150 6.00 15.00
HUD Tim Hudson D/50 20.00 40.00
HUH Tim Hudson H/50 20.00 40.00
HUN Tim Hudson N/50 20.00 40.00
HUO Tim Hudson O/50 20.00 40.00
HUS Tim Hudson S/50 20.00 40.00
HUU Tim Hudson U/50 20.00 40.00
IKE Ian Kinsler E/125 8.00 20.00
IKI Ian Kinsler I/125 8.00 20.00
IKK Ian Kinsler K/125 8.00 20.00
IKL Ian Kinsler L/125 8.00 20.00
IKN Ian Kinsler N/125 8.00 20.00
IKR Ian Kinsler R/125 8.00 20.00
IKS Ian Kinsler S/125 8.00 20.00
JBA Jason Bay A/110 6.00 15.00
JBB Jason Bay B/110 6.00 15.00
JBY Jason Bay Y/110 6.00 15.00
JB2O Jason Bay ROY O/50 6.00 15.00
JB2R Jason Bay ROY R/50 6.00 15.00
JB2Y Jason Bay ROY Y/50 6.00 15.00
JGE Jonny Gomes E/175 6.00 15.00
JGG Jonny Gomes G/175 6.00 15.00
JGM Jonny Gomes M/175 6.00 15.00
JGO Jonny Gomes O/175 6.00 15.00
JGS Jonny Gomes S/175 6.00 15.00
JHA Jeremy Hermida A/125 15.00 30.00
JHD Jeremy Hermida D/125 15.00 30.00
JHE Jeremy Hermida E/125 15.00 30.00
JHH Jeremy Hermida H/125 15.00 30.00
JHI Jeremy Hermida I/125 15.00 30.00
JHM Jeremy Hermida M/125 15.00 30.00
JHR Jeremy Hermida R/125 15.00 30.00
JMA Joe Mauer A/25 40.00 80.00
JME Joe Mauer E/25 40.00 80.00
JMM Joe Mauer M/25 40.00 80.00
JMR Joe Mauer R/25 40.00 80.00
JMU Joe Mauer U/25 40.00 80.00
JNA Joe Nathan A/200 6.00 15.00
JNH Joe Nathan H/100 6.00 15.00
JNN Joe Nathan N/200 6.00 15.00
JNT Joe Nathan T/100 6.00 15.00
JPA Jonathan Papelbon A/100 8.00 20.00
JPB Jonathan Papelbon B/100 8.00 20.00
JPE Jonathan Papelbon E/100 8.00 20.00
JPL Jonathan Papelbon L/100 8.00 20.00
JPN Jonathan Papelbon N/100 8.00 20.00
JPO Jonathan Papelbon O/100 8.00 20.00
JPP Jonathan Papelbon P/200 8.00 20.00
JRE Jose Reyes E/150 40.00 80.00
JRR Jose Reyes R/75 40.00 80.00
JRS Jose Reyes S/75 40.00 80.00
JRY Jose Reyes Y/75 40.00 80.00
JSE Jeremy Sowers E/50 25.00 50.00
JSO Jeremy Sowers O/50 25.00 50.00
JSR Jeremy Sowers R/50 25.00 50.00
JSS Jeremy Sowers S/100 25.00 50.00
JSW Jeremy Sowers W/50 25.00 50.00
JTE Jim Thome E/30 30.00 60.00
JTH Jim Thome H/30 30.00 60.00
JTM Jim Thome M/30 30.00 60.00
JTO Jim Thome O/30 30.00 60.00
JTT Jim Thome T/30 30.00 60.00
JVA Justin Verlander A/20 40.00 80.00
JVD Justin Verlander D/20 40.00 80.00
JVE Justin Verlander E/40 40.00 80.00
JVL Justin Verlander L/20 40.00 80.00
JVN Justin Verlander N/20 40.00 80.00
JVR Justin Verlander R/40 40.00 80.00
JVV Justin Verlander V/20 40.00 80.00
JWA Jered Weaver A/40 12.50 30.00
JWE Jered Weaver E/80 12.50 30.00
JWR Jered Weaver R/40 12.50 30.00
JWV Jered Weaver V/40 12.50 30.00
JWW Jered Weaver W/40 12.50 30.00
JZA Joel Zumaya A/250 6.00 15.00
JZM Joel Zumaya M/125 6.00 15.00
JZU Joel Zumaya U/125 6.00 15.00
JZY Joel Zumaya Y/125 6.00 15.00
JZZ Joel Zumaya Z/125 6.00 15.00
KGE Ken Griffey Jr. Reds E/25 75.00 150.00
KGF Ken Griffey Jr. Reds F/50 75.00 150.00
KGG Ken Griffey Jr. Reds G/25 75.00 150.00
KGI Ken Griffey Jr. Reds I/25 75.00 150.00
KGR Ken Griffey Jr. Reds R/25 75.00 150.00
KGY Ken Griffey Jr. Reds Y/25 75.00 150.00
KG2I Ken Griffey Jr. Junior I/25 75.00 150.00
KG2J Ken Griffey Jr. Junior J/25 75.00 150.00
KG2N Ken Griffey Jr. Junior N/25 75.00 150.00
KG2O Ken Griffey Jr. Junior O/25 75.00 150.00
KG2R Ken Griffey Jr. Junior R/25 75.00 150.00
KG2U Ken Griffey Jr. Junior U/25 75.00 150.00
KG3E Ken Griffey Jr. M's E/25 75.00 150.00
KG3F Ken Griffey Jr. M's F/50 75.00 150.00
KG3G Ken Griffey Jr. M's G/25 75.00 150.00
KG3I Ken Griffey Jr. M's I/25 75.00 150.00
KG3R Ken Griffey Jr. M's R/25 75.00 150.00
KG3Y Ken Griffey Jr. M's Y/25 75.00 150.00
KG4D Ken Griffey Jr. The Kid D/25 75.00 150.00
KG4E Ken Griffey Jr. The Kid E/25 75.00 150.00
KG4H Ken Griffey Jr. The Kid H/25 75.00 150.00
KG4I Ken Griffey Jr. The Kid I/25 75.00 150.00
KG4K Ken Griffey Jr. The Kid K/25 75.00 150.00
KG4T Ken Griffey Jr. The Kid T/25 75.00 150.00
KHE Khalil Greene E/225 6.00 15.00
KHG Khalil Greene G/75 6.00 15.00
KHN Khalil Greene N/75 6.00 15.00
KHR Khalil Greene R/75 6.00 15.00
KMA Kendry Morales A/20 10.00 25.00
KME Kendry Morales E/20 10.00 25.00
KML Kendry Morales L/20 10.00 25.00
KMM Kendry Morales M/20 10.00 25.00
KMO Kendry Morales O/20 10.00 25.00
KMR Kendry Morales R/20 10.00 25.00
KMS Kendry Morales S/20 10.00 25.00
KWD Kerry Wood D/10 40.00 80.00
KWO Kerry Wood O/20 40.00 80.00
KWW Kerry Wood W/10 40.00 80.00
LEE Carlos Lee E/50 20.00 40.00
LEL Carlos Lee L/25 20.00 40.00
MCA Miguel Cabrera A/70 40.00 80.00
MCB Miguel Cabrera B/35 40.00 80.00
MCC Miguel Cabrera C/35 40.00 80.00
MCE Miguel Cabrera E/35 40.00 80.00
MCR Miguel Cabrera R/70 40.00 80.00
MGE Marcus Giles E/136 6.00 15.00
MGG Marcus Giles G/136 6.00 15.00
MGI Marcus Giles I/136 6.00 15.00
MGL Marcus Giles L/136 6.00 15.00
MGS Marcus Giles S/136 6.00 15.00
MHA Matt Holliday A/37 15.00 40.00
MHD Matt Holliday D/37 15.00 40.00
MHH Matt Holliday H/37 15.00 40.00
MHI Matt Holliday I/37 15.00 40.00
MHL Matt Holliday L/74 15.00 40.00
MHO Matt Holliday O/37 15.00 40.00
MHY Matt Holliday Y/37 15.00 40.00
MMD Mark Mulder D/50 6.00 15.00
MME Mark Mulder E/50 6.00 15.00
MML Mark Mulder L/50 6.00 15.00
MMM Mark Mulder M/50 6.00 15.00
MMR Mark Mulder R/50 6.00 15.00
MMU Mark Mulder U/50 6.00 15.00
MOA Justin Morneau A/75 12.50 30.00
MOE Justin Morneau E/75 12.50 30.00
MOM Justin Morneau M/75 12.50 30.00
MON Justin Morneau N/75 12.50 30.00
MOO Justin Morneau O/75 12.50 30.00
MOR Justin Morneau R/75 12.50 30.00
MOU Justin Morneau U/75 12.50 30.00
MTA Mark Teixeira A/5 30.00 60.00
MTE Mark Teixeira E/10 30.00 60.00
MTI Mark Teixeira I/10 30.00 60.00
MTR Mark Teixeira R/5 30.00 60.00
MTT Mark Teixeira T/5 30.00 60.00
MTX Mark Teixeira X/5 30.00 60.00
MYG Michael Young G/50 12.50 30.00
MYN Michael Young N/50 12.50 30.00
MYO Michael Young O/50 12.50 30.00
MYU Michael Young U/50 12.50 30.00
MYY Michael Young Y/50 12.50 30.00
NSE Nick Swisher E/170 8.00 20.00
NSH Nick Swisher H/170 8.00 20.00
NSI Nick Swisher I/170 8.00 20.00
NSR Nick Swisher R/170 8.00 20.00
NSS Nick Swisher S/340 8.00 20.00
NSW Nick Swisher W/170 8.00 20.00
PEA Jake Peavy A/20 15.00 40.00
PEE Jake Peavy E/20 15.00 40.00
PEP Jake Peavy P/20 15.00 40.00
PEV Jake Peavy V/20 15.00 40.00
PEY Jake Peavy Y/20 15.00 40.00
RCC Roger Clemens C/15 30.00 60.00
RCE Roger Clemens E/30 30.00 60.00
RCL Roger Clemens L/15 30.00 60.00
RCM Roger Clemens M/15 30.00 60.00
RCN Roger Clemens N/15 30.00 60.00
RCS Roger Clemens S/15 30.00 60.00
RC2C Roger Clemens The Rocket C/15 30.00 60.00
RC2E Roger Clemens The Rocket E/30 30.00 60.00
RC2H Roger Clemens The Rocket H/15 30.00 60.00
RC2K Roger Clemens The Rocket K/15 30.00 60.00
RC2O Roger Clemens The Rocket O/15 30.00 60.00
RC2R Roger Clemens The Rocket R/15 30.00 60.00
RC2T Roger Clemens The Rocket T/30 30.00 60.00
ROA Roy Oswalt A/50 10.00 25.00
ROL Roy Oswalt L/50 10.00 25.00
ROO Roy Oswalt O/50 10.00 25.00
ROS Roy Oswalt S/50 10.00 25.00
ROT Roy Oswalt T/50 10.00 25.00
ROW Roy Oswalt W/50 10.00 25.00
RWE Rickie Weeks E/200 10.00 25.00
RWK Rickie Weeks K/100 10.00 25.00
RWS Rickie Weeks S/100 10.00 25.00
RWW Rickie Weeks W/100 10.00 25.00
RZA Ryan Zimmerman A/17 30.00 60.00
RZE Ryan Zimmerman E/17 30.00 60.00
RZI Ryan Zimmerman I/17 30.00 60.00
RZM Ryan Zimmerman M/51 30.00 60.00
RZN Ryan Zimmerman N/17 30.00 60.00
RZR Ryan Zimmerman R/17 30.00 60.00
RZZ Ryan Zimmerman Z/17 30.00 60.00
SKA Scott Kazmir A/6 50.00 100.00
SKI Scott Kazmir I/6 50.00 100.00
SKK Scott Kazmir K/6 50.00 100.00
SKM Scott Kazmir M/6 50.00 100.00
SKR Scott Kazmir R/6 50.00 100.00
SKZ Scott Kazmir Z/6 50.00 100.00
SML John Smoltz L/75 20.00 50.00
SMM John Smoltz M/75 20.00 50.00
SMO John Smoltz O/75 20.00 50.00
SMS John Smoltz S/75 20.00 50.00
SMT John Smoltz T/75 20.00 50.00
SMZ John Smoltz Z/75 20.00 50.00
TEA Miguel Tejada A/50 8.00 20.00
TED Miguel Tejada D/25 8.00 20.00
TEE Miguel Tejada E/25 8.00 20.00
TEJ Miguel Tejada J/25 8.00 20.00
TET Miguel Tejada T/25 8.00 20.00
THA Travis Hafner A/10 50.00 100.00
THE Travis Hafner E/10 50.00 100.00
THF Travis Hafner F/10 50.00 100.00
THH Travis Hafner H/10 50.00 100.00
THN Travis Hafner N/10 50.00 100.00
THR Travis Hafner R/10 50.00 100.00
TH2K Travis Hafner Pronk K/8 10.00 25.00
TH2N Travis Hafner Pronk N/8 10.00 25.00
TH2O Travis Hafner Pronk O/8 10.00 25.00
TH2P Travis Hafner Pronk P/8 10.00 25.00
TH2R Travis Hafner Pronk R/8 10.00 25.00
TIC Tadahito Iguchi C/20 20.00 50.00
TIG Tadahito Iguchi G/20 20.00 50.00
TIH Tadahito Iguchi H/20 20.00 50.00
TII Tadahito Iguchi I/40 20.00 50.00
TIU Tadahito Iguchi U/20 20.00 50.00
VGE Vladimir Guerrero E/50 20.00 50.00
VGG Vladimir Guerrero G/25 20.00 50.00
VGO Vladimir Guerrero O/25 20.00 50.00
VGR Vladimir Guerrero R/75 20.00 50.00
VGU Vladimir Guerrero U/25 20.00 50.00
VMA Victor Martinez A/75 6.00 15.00
VME Victor Martinez E/75 6.00 15.00
VMI Victor Martinez I/75 6.00 15.00
VMM Victor Martinez M/75 6.00 15.00
VMN Victor Martinez N/75 6.00 15.00
VMR Victor Martinez R/75 6.00 15.00
VMT Victor Martinez T/75 6.00 15.00
VMZ Victor Martinez Z/75 6.00 15.00
WIA Josh Willingham A/75 6.00 15.00
WIG Josh Willingham G/75 6.00 15.00
WIH Josh Willingham H/75 6.00 15.00
WII Josh Willingham I/150 6.00 15.00
WIL Josh Willingham L/150 6.00 15.00
WIM Josh Willingham M/75 6.00 15.00
WIN Josh Willingham N/75 6.00 15.00
WIW Josh Willingham W/75 6.00 15.00

2006 SP Authentic Chirography

STATED ODDS 1:96
PRINT RUNS B/WN 25-75 COPIES PER
NO PRICING ON QTY OF 25
EXCHANGE DEADLINE 12/05/09
AE Andre Ethier/75 12.50 30.00
AG Tony Gwynn Jr./75 6.00 15.00
AH Anderson Hernandez/75 4.00 10.00
AN Brian Anderson/75 4.00 10.00
AS Alfonso Soriano/75 12.50 30.00
AW Adam Wainwright/75 20.00 50.00
BA Brian Bannister/75 6.00 15.00
BB Brandon Backe/75 4.00 10.00
BC Bobby Crosby/75 6.00 15.00
BI Chad Billingsley/75 10.00 25.00
BL Boone Logan/75 4.00 10.00
BO Boof Bonser/75 4.00 10.00
BS Ben Sheets/75 10.00 25.00
CB Craig Biggio/75 15.00 40.00
CD Chris Denorfia/75 4.00 10.00
CF Choo Freeman/75 4.00 10.00
CG Carlos Guillen/75 10.00 25.00
CH Cole Hamels/75 10.00 25.00
CJ Conor Jackson/75 6.00 15.00
CK Casey Kotchman/75 4.00 10.00
CL Cliff Lee/75 15.00 40.00
CP Corey Patterson/75 6.00 15.00
CR Cody Ross/75 10.00 25.00
CS C.C. Sabathia/75 8.00 20.00
DB Denny Bautista/75 4.00 10.00
DD David DeJesus/75 6.00 15.00
DG David Gassner/75 4.00 10.00
DJ Derek Jeter/75 150.00 400.00
DU Dan Uggla/75 4.00 10.00
DW Dontrelle Willis/75 10.00 25.00
FC Fausto Carmona/75 4.00 10.00
FL Felipe Lopez/75 4.00 10.00
FT Frank Thomas/75 40.00 80.00
GA Garret Anderson/75 6.00 15.00
GR Ken Griffey Jr./75 60.00 120.00
HA Jeff Harris/75 4.00 10.00
HB Hank Blalock/75 6.00 15.00
HK Hong-Chih Kuo/75 50.00 100.00
HR Hanley Ramirez/75 6.00 15.00
IK Ian Kinsler/75 6.00 15.00
IR Ivan Rodriguez/75 20.00 50.00
JB Joe Blanton/75 6.00 15.00
JC Jose Capellan/75 4.00 10.00
JD Joey Devine/75 4.00 10.00
JE Johnny Estrada/75 4.00 10.00
JF Jeff Francis/75 10.00 25.00
JH Jeremy Hermida/75 6.00 15.00
JJ Josh Johnson/75 10.00 25.00
JK Jason Kubel/75 4.00 10.00
JL Jon Lester/75 15.00 40.00
JN Joe Nathan/75 6.00 15.00
JP Jonathan Papelbon/75 6.00 15.00
JR Josh Rupe/75 4.00 10.00
JS Jeremy Sowers/75 6.00 15.00
JW Josh Willingham/75 4.00 10.00
KF Keith Foulke/75 8.00 20.00
KG Khalil Greene/75 10.00 25.00
KM Kevin Mench/75 6.00 15.00
KS Kelly Shoppach/75 4.00 10.00
KY Kevin Youkilis/75 6.00 15.00
LI Francisco Liriano/75 6.00 15.00
LO Lyle Overbay/40 6.00 15.00
MC Matt Cain/75 40.00 80.00
MM Macay McBride/75 4.00 10.00
NS Nick Swisher/75 6.00 15.00
OP Oliver Perez/75 6.00 15.00
PM Paul Maholm/75 4.00 10.00
RE Eric Reed/75 4.00 10.00
RH Rich Harden/75 6.00 15.00
RZ Ryan Zimmerman/75 10.00 25.00
SC Sean Casey/75 10.00 25.00
SD Stephen Drew/75 6.00 15.00
SH Chris Shelton/75 20.00 50.00
SM Sean Marshall/75 12.50 30.00
SO Alay Soler/75 6.00 15.00
TB Taylor Buchholz/75 4.00 10.00
TH Travis Hafner/75 10.00 25.00
TP Tony Pena Jr./75 4.00 10.00
TS Takashi Saito/75 20.00 50.00
VA John Van Benschoten/75 4.00 10.00
VE Justin Verlander/75 50.00 100.00
VM Victor Martinez/75 10.00 25.00
WE Jered Weaver/75 4.00 10.00
WI Josh Wilson/75 4.00 10.00
WM Wily Mo Pena/75 6.00 15.00

2006 SP Authentic Sign of the Times

STATED ODDS 1:96
PRINT RUNS B/WN 25-75 COPIES PER
NO PRICING ON QTY OF 25
EXCHANGE DEADLINE 12/05/09
AB Adrian Beltre/75 10.00 25.00
AE Andre Ethier/75 12.50 30.00
AH Anderson Hernandez/75 4.00 10.00
AJ Andruw Jones/75 6.00 15.00
AN Brian Anderson/75 4.00 10.00
AR Aramis Ramirez/75 6.00 15.00
AS Alay Soler/75 6.00 15.00
AW Adam Wainwright/75 10.00 25.00
BA Bobby Abreu/75 30.00 60.00
BB Boof Bonser/75 4.00 10.00
BI Chad Billingsley/75 10.00 25.00
BJ Ben Johnson/75 4.00 10.00
BL Boone Logan/75 4.00 10.00
BR Brian Bannister/75 6.00 15.00
CA Matt Cain/75 10.00 25.00
CB Chris Booker/75 4.00 10.00
CC Carl Crawford/75 6.00 15.00
CD Chris Demaria/75 4.00 10.00
CH Cole Hamels/75 20.00 50.00
CR Cody Ross/75 10.00 25.00
CS Curt Schilling/75 20.00 50.00
CY Clay Hensley/75 4.00 10.00
DE Chris Denorfia/75 4.00 10.00
DG David Gassner/75 4.00 10.00
DJ Derek Jeter/75 100.00 175.00
DL Derrek Lee/75 6.00 15.00
DU Dan Uggla/75 12.50 30.00
EG Eric Gagne/75 10.00 25.00
ER Eric Reed/75 4.00 10.00
FC Fausto Carmona/75 10.00 25.00
FL Francisco Liriano/75 15.00 40.00
FR Ron Flores/75 4.00 10.00
GM Greg Maddux/75 60.00 120.00
HA Tim Hamulack/75 4.00 10.00
HE Jeremy Hermida/75 6.00 15.00
HR Hanley Ramirez/75 8.00 20.00
IK Ian Kinsler/75 6.00 15.00
JA Conor Jackson/75 6.00 15.00
JC Jose Capellan/75 4.00 10.00
JD J.D. Drew/75 6.00 15.00
JE Jered Weaver/75 20.00 50.00
JG Jose Guillen/75 4.00 10.00
JH Jason Hammel/75 4.00 10.00
JJ Josh Johnson/75 10.00 25.00
JK Jason Kendall/75 10.00 25.00
JM Joe Mauer/75 20.00 50.00
JP Jake Peavy/75 6.00 15.00
JS John Smoltz/75 10.00 25.00
JV John Van Benschoten/75 4.00 10.00
JW Josh Willingham/75 4.00 10.00
JY Jeremy Sowers/75 6.00 15.00
KG Ken Griffey Jr./75 60.00 120.00
KU Jason Kubel/75 4.00 10.00
MA Macay McBride/75 4.00 10.00
MC Miguel Cabrera/75 20.00 50.00
MI Mike Thompson/75 4.00 10.00
MJ Mike Jacobs/75 6.00 15.00
MK Mark Kotsay/75 6.00 15.00
MM Mark Mulder/75 6.00 15.00
MO Justin Morneau/75 6.00 15.00
MT Mark Teixeira/75 10.00 25.00
PA Jonathan Papelbon/75 10.00 25.00
PE Joel Peralta/75 4.00 10.00
PM Paul Maholm/75 4.00 10.00
RA Reggie Abercrombie/75 4.00 10.00
RF Rafael Furcal/75 6.00 15.00
RH Ramon Hernandez/75 10.00 25.00
RJ Randy Johnson/75 50.00 100.00
RM Russell Martin/75 4.00 10.00
RS Ryan Shealy/75 6.00 15.00
RW Rickie Weeks/75 10.00 25.00
RZ Ryan Zimmerman/75 20.00 50.00
SA Santiago Ramirez/75 4.00 10.00
SD Stephen Drew/75 20.00 50.00
SM Sean Marshall/75 10.00 25.00
SP Scott Podsednik/75 6.00 15.00
SS Skip Schumaker/75 4.00 10.00
ST Steve Stemle/75 4.00 10.00
TB Taylor Buchholz/75 4.00 10.00
TE Miguel Tejada/75 10.00 25.00
TH Tim Hudson/75 10.00 25.00
TP Tony Pena Jr./75 4.00 10.00
TS Takashi Saito/75 20.00 50.00
VE Justin Verlander/75 40.00 80.00
VG Vladimir Guerrero/75 15.00 40.00
VW Vernon Wells/75 6.00 15.00
WI Josh Wilson/75 4.00 10.00
YB Yuniesky Betancourt/75 6.00 15.00
ZG Zack Greinke/75 10.00 25.00

2006 SP Authentic WBC Future Watch

STATED ODDS 1:7
STATED PRINT RUN 999 SERIAL #'d SETS
1 Adrian Burnside 1.00 2.50
2 Gavin Fingleson 1.00 2.50
3 Bradley Harman 1.50 4.00
4 Brendan Kingman 1.00 2.50
5 Brett Roneberg 1.00 2.50
6 Paul Rutgers 1.00 2.50
7 Phil Stockman 1.00 2.50
8 Stubby Clapp 1.00 2.50
9 Steve Green 1.00 2.50
10 Pete LaForest 1.00 2.50
11 Adam Loewen 1.00 2.50
12 Ryan Radmanovich 1.00 2.50
13 Chenhao Li 1.00 2.50
14 Guangbiao Liu 1.00 2.50
15 Guogan Yang 1.00 2.50
16 Jingchao Wang 1.00 2.50
17 Lei Li 1.00 2.50
18 Lingfeng Sun 1.00 2.50
19 Nan Wang 1.00 2.50
20 Shuo Yang 1.00 2.50
21 Tao Bu 1.00 2.50
22 Wei Wang 1.00 2.50
23 Yi Feng 1.00 2.50
24 Chien-Ming Chiang 2.50 6.00
25 Yung-Chi Chen 1.50 4.00
26 Chia-Hsien Hseih 2.50 6.00
27 Chin-Lung Hu 1.00 2.50
28 En-Yu Lin 2.50 6.00
29 Wei-Lun Pan 2.50 6.00
30 Ariel Borrero 1.00 2.50
31 Yadel Marti 1.00 2.50
32 Yulieski Gourriel 3.00 8.00
33 Frederich Cepeda 1.00 2.50
34 Yadiel Pedroso 1.00 2.50
35 Pedro Luis Lazo 1.50 4.00
36 Elier Sanchez 1.00 2.50
37 Norberto Gonzalez 1.00 2.50
38 Carlos Tabares 1.00 2.50
39 Eduardo Paret 1.00 2.50
40 Osmany Urrutia 1.00 2.50
41 Alexei Ramirez 6.00 15.00
42 Yoandy Garlobo 1.00 2.50
43 Vicyohandry Odelin 1.00 2.50
44 Michel Enriquez 1.00 2.50
45 Ormari Romero 1.00 2.50
46 Ariel Pestano 1.00 2.50
47 Francisco Liriano 2.50 6.00
48 Dustin Delucchi 1.00 2.50
49 Tony Giarratano 1.00 2.50
50 Tom Gregorio 1.00 2.50
51 Mark Saccomanno 1.00 2.50
52 Takahiro Arai 1.50 4.00
53 Akinori Iwamura 3.00 8.00
54 Munenori Kawasaki 5.00 12.00
55 Nobuhiko Matsunaka 1.50 4.00
56 Daisuke Matsuzaka 3.00 8.00
57 Shinya Miyamoto 1.50 4.00
58 Tsuyoshi Nishioka 6.00 15.00
59 Tomoya Satozaki 1.50 4.00
60 Koji Uehara 3.00 8.00
61 Shunsuke Watanabe 1.00 2.50
62 Sadaharu Oh 6.00 15.00
63 Byung Kyu Lee 1.00 2.50
64 Ji Man Song 1.00 2.50
65 Jin Man Park 1.00 2.50
66 Jong Beom Lee 1.00 2.50
67 Jong Kook Kim 1.00 2.50
68 Min Han Son 1.00 2.50
69 Min Jae Kim 1.00 2.50
70 Seung Yeop Lee 1.50 4.00
71 Luis A. Garcia 1.00 2.50
72 Mario Valenzuela 1.00 2.50
73 Sharnol Adriana 1.00 2.50
74 Rob Cordemans 1.00 2.50
75 Michael Duursma 1.00 2.50
76 Percy Isenia 1.00 2.50
77 Sidney de Jong 1.00 2.50
78 Dirk Klooster 1.00 2.50
79 Raylince Legito 1.00 2.50
80 Shairon Martis 1.00 2.50
81 Harvey Monte 1.00 2.50
82 Hainley Statia 1.00 2.50
83 Roger Deago 1.00 2.50
84 Audes De Leon 1.00 2.50
85 Freddy Herrera 1.00 2.50
86 Yoni Lasso 1.00 2.50
87 Orlando Miller 1.00 2.50
88 Len Pecota 1.00 2.50
89 Federico Baez 1.00 2.50
90 Dicky Gonzalez 1.00 2.50
91 Josue Matos 1.00 2.50
92 Orlando Roman 1.00 2.50
93 Paul Bell 1.00 2.50
94 Kyle Botha 1.00 2.50
95 Jason Cook 1.00 2.50
96 Nicholas Dempsey 1.00 2.50
97 Victor Moreno 1.00 2.50
98 Ricardo Palma 1.00 2.50
99 Huston Street 1.00 2.50
100 Chase Utley 1.50 4.00

2007 SP Authentic

COMP.SET w/o RCs (100) 6.00 15.00
COMMON CARD (1-100) .15 .40
COMMON AU RC (101-158) 5.00 12.00
OVERALL BY THE LETTER AUTOS 1:12
AU RC PRINT RUN B/WN 20-120 COPIES PER
EXCHANGE DEADLINE 11/08/2008
1 Chipper Jones .40 1.00
2 Andruw Jones .15 .40
3 John Smoltz .40 1.00
4 Carlos Quentin .15 .40
5 Randy Johnson .40 1.00
6 Brandon Webb .25 .60
7 Alfonso Soriano .25 .60
8 Derrek Lee .15 .40
9 Aramis Ramirez .15 .40
10 Carlos Zambrano .15 .40
11 Ken Griffey Jr. .75 2.00
12 Adam Dunn .25 .60
13 Josh Hamilton .50 1.25
14 Todd Helton .25 .60
15 Jeff Francis .15 .40
16 Matt Holliday .40 1.00
17 Hanley Ramirez .25 .60
18 Dontrelle Willis .15 .40
19 Miguel Cabrera .40 1.00
20 Lance Berkman .25 .60
21 Roy Oswalt .25 .60
22 Carlos Lee .15 .40
23 Nomar Garciaparra .25 .60
24 Derek Lowe .15 .40
25 Juan Pierre .15 .40
26 Rafael Furcal .15 .40
27 Rickie Weeks .15 .40
28 Prince Fielder .25 .60
29 Ben Sheets .15 .40
30 David Wright .30 .75
31 Jose Reyes .25 .60
32 Tom Glavine .25 .60
33 Carlos Beltran .25 .60
34 Cole Hamels .30 .75
35 Jimmy Rollins .25 .60
36 Ryan Howard .30 .75
37 Jason Bay .25 .60
38 Freddy Sanchez .15 .40
39 Ian Snell .15 .40
40 Jake Peavy .15 .40
41 Greg Maddux .50 1.25
42 Trevor Hoffman .25 .60
43 Matt Cain .25 .60
44 Barry Zito .25 .60
45 Ray Durham .15 .40
46 Albert Pujols .50 1.25
47 Chris Carpenter .25 .60
48 Jim Edmonds .25 .60
49 Scott Rolen .25 .60
50 Ryan Zimmerman .25 .60
51 Felipe Lopez .15 .40
52 Austin Kearns .15 .40
53 Miguel Tejada .25 .60
54 Erik Bedard .15 .40
55 Daniel Cabrera .15 .40
56 David Ortiz .40 1.00
57 Curt Schilling .25 .60
58 Manny Ramirez .40 1.00

59 Jonathan Papelbon .40 1.00
60 Jim Thome .25 .60
61 Paul Konerko .25 .60
62 Bobby Jenks .15 .40
63 Grady Sizemore .25 .60
64 Victor Martinez .25 .60
65 Travis Hafner .15 .40
66 Ivan Rodriguez .25 .60
67 Justin Verlander .40 1.00
68 Joel Zumaya .15 .40
69 Jeremy Bonderman .15 .40
70 Gil Meche .15 .40
71 Mike Sweeney .15 .40
72 Mark Teahen .15 .40
73 Vladimir Guerrero .25 .60
74 Howie Kendrick .15 .40
75 Francisco Rodriguez .25 .60
76 Johan Santana .25 .60
77 Justin Morneau .25 .60
78 Joe Mauer .30 .75
79 Joe Nathan .15 .40
80a Alex Rodriguez .50 1.25
80b A.Rodriguez Angels 10.00 25.00
80c A.Rodriguez Cubs 12.00 30.00
80d A.Rodriguez Dodgers 12.00 30.00
80e A.Rodriguez Mets 12.00 30.00
80f A.Rodriguez Red Sox 12.00 30.00
81 Derek Jeter 1.00 2.50
82 Johnny Damon .25 .60
83 Chien-Ming Wang .25 .60
84 Rich Harden .15 .40
85 Mike Piazza .40 1.00
86 Dan Haren .15 .40
87 Ichiro Suzuki .50 1.25
88 Felix Hernandez .25 .60
89 Kenji Johjima .40 1.00
90 Adrian Beltre .40 1.00
91 Carl Crawford .25 .60
92 Scott Kazmir .25 .60
93 Delmon Young .25 .60
94 Michael Young .15 .40
95 Mark Teixeira .25 .60
96 Eric Gagne .15 .40
97 Hank Blalock .15 .40
98 Vernon Wells .15 .40
99 Roy Halladay .25 .60
100 Frank Thomas .40 1.00
101 Joaquin Arias AU/75 (RC) 5.00 12.00
102 Jeff Baker AU (RC) 5.00 12.00
103 M.Bourn AU/75 (RC) 6.00 15.00
104 Brian Burres AU/75 (RC) 6.00 15.00
105 Jared Burton AU/75 RC 6.00 15.00
106 Ryan Braun AU/50 (RC) 10.00 25.00
107a Y.Gallardo AU/75 (RC) 8.00 20.00
107b Yovani Gallardo AU/35 10.00 25.00
108a H.Gimenez AU/75 (RC) 6.00 15.00
108b Hector Gimenez AU/50 6.00 15.00
109 Alex Gordon AU/50 RC 10.00 25.00
110a J.Hamilton AU/50 (RC) 15.00 40.00
110b J.Hamilton AU/35 20.00 50.00
111a Justin Hampson AU/75 (RC) 5.00 12.00
111b Justin Hampson AU/50 5.00 12.00
112 Sean Henn AU/75 (RC) 10.00 25.00
113 P.Hughes AU (RC) 40.00 80.00
114 Kei Igawa AU/25 RC 8.00 20.00
115 A.Iwamura AU/20 RC 10.00 25.00
116a M.Reynolds AU/75 RC 5.00 12.00
116b Mark Reynolds AU/35 6.00 15.00
117a Homer Bailey AU/75 (RC) 4.00 10.00
117b Homer Bailey AU/50 (RC) 4.00 10.00
118a K.Kouzmanoff AU/75 (RC) 5.00 12.00
118b Kevin Kouzmanoff AU/40 5.00 12.00
119 Adam Lind AU/75 (RC) 6.00 15.00
120a Carlos Gomez AU/75 RC 8.00 20.00
120b Carlos Gomez AU/50 8.00 20.00
121a Glen Perkins AU/75 (RC) 5.00 12.00
121b Glen Perkins AU/50 5.00 12.00
122a R.Vanden Hurk AU/75 RC 5.00 12.00
122b Rick Vanden Hurk AU/35 5.00 12.00
123 Brad Salmon AU/75 RC 5.00 12.00
124a Zack Segovia AU/75 (RC) 5.00 12.00
124b Zack Segovia AU/50 5.00 12.00
125a Kurt Suzuki AU/75 (RC) 6.00 15.00
125b Kurt Suzuki AU/50 6.00 15.00
126a Chris Stewart AU/75 RC 5.00 12.00
126b Chris Stewart AU/50 5.00 12.00
127 Cesar Jimenez AU RC 5.00 12.00
128a Ryan Sweeney AU/50 (RC) 5.00 12.00
128b Ryan Sweeney AU/40 5.00 12.00
129a T.Tulowit AU/20 (RC) 15.00 40.00
129b T.Tulowit AU/10 15.00 40.00
130 Chase Wright AU/75 RC 6.00 15.00
131 Delmon Young AU/20 (RC) 5.00 12.00
132a Tony Abreu AU/75 RC 10.00 25.00
132b Tony Abreu AU/57 10.00 25.00
132c Tony Abreu AU/50 10.00 25.00
133 Brian Barden AU/75 RC 5.00 12.00
134a C.Thigpen AU/75 (RC) 4.00 10.00
134b Curtis Thigpen AU/40 4.00 10.00
135a Jon Coutlangus AU/75 (RC) 5.00 12.00
135b Jon Coutlangus AU/55 5.00 12.00
136a Kevin Cameron AU/75 RC 5.00 12.00
136b Kevin Cameron AU/50 5.00 12.00
137 Billy Butler AU/75 (RC) 6.00 15.00
138a A.Casilla AU/75 RC 5.00 12.00
138b Alexi Casilla AU/50 5.00 12.00
139 Kory Casto AU/75 (RC) 5.00 12.00
140 Matt Chico AU/75 (RC) 6.00 15.00
141 John Danks AU/75 RC 6.00 15.00
142 Andrew Miller AU/50 RC 8.00 20.00
143a B.Francisco AU/75 (RC) 6.00 15.00
143b Ben Francisco AU/40 6.00 15.00
144a Andy Gonzalez AU/75 RC 5.00 12.00
144b Andy Gonzalez AU/50 5.00 12.00
145 D.Hansack AU RC 6.00 15.00
146 Mike Rabelo AU/75 RC 6.00 15.00
147a Tim Lincecum AU/50 RC 20.00 50.00
147b Tim Lincecum AU/25 25.00 60.00
148a M.Lindstrom AU/75 (RC) 6.00 15.00
148b Matt Lindstrom AU/40 6.00 15.00
149a Jay Marshall AU/75 RC 5.00 12.00
149b Jay Marshall AU/50 5.00 12.00
150a D.Matsuzaka AU/20 RC 20.00 50.00
151a M.Montero AU/75 (RC) 5.00 12.00
151b Miguel Montero AU/60 5.00 12.00
152 Micah Owings AU/75 (RC) 6.00 15.00
153 Hunter Pence AU/75 (RC) 10.00 25.00
154a Brandon Wood AU/75 (RC) 6.00 15.00
155a Felix Pie AU/75 (RC) 6.00 15.00
155b Felix Pie AU/70 6.00 15.00
156 Danny Putnam AU/75 (RC) 6.00 15.00
157a Andy LaRoche AU/50 (RC) 5.00 12.00
157b Andy LaRoche AU/40 5.00 12.00
158a J.Saltalamac AU/75 (RC) 6.00 15.00
158b Jarrod Saltalamacchia AU/25 6.00 15.00
159 Doug Slaten AU/75 RC 6.00 15.00
160 Joe Smith AU/75 RC 8.00 20.00
161 Justin Upton AU/120 RC 10.00 25.00
162 J.Chamberlain AU/60 RC 8.00 20.00

2007 SP Authentic By the Letter Signatures

OVERALL BY THE LETTER AUTOS 1:12
PRINT RUNS B/WN 5-199 COPIES PER
NO PRICING ON SOME DUE TO SCARCITY
EXCHANGE DEADLINE 11/08/2008
1 Derek Jeter 150.00 300.00
2a Ken Griffey Jr./25 100.00 250.00
2b Ken Griffey Jr./20 100.00 250.00
4a Justin Verlander/25 25.00 60.00
4b Justin Verlander/15 30.00 80.00
5a Adrian Gonzalez/60 6.00 15.00
5b Adrian Gonzalez/50 6.00 15.00
8 Josh Beckett/15 10.00 25.00
9a Carlos Quentin/75 6.00 15.00
9b Carlos Quentin/50 6.00 15.00
10 Aramis Ramirez/25 6.00 15.00
11 Austin Kearns/50 6.00 15.00
12a B.J. Upton/25 8.00 20.00
12b B.J. Upton/15 8.00 20.00
13a Boof Bonser/75 6.00 15.00
13b Boof Bonser/50 6.00 15.00
14a Bronson Arroyo/75 6.00 15.00
14b Bronson Arroyo/10 10.00 25.00
15a Troy Tulowitzki 15.00 40.00
15b Troy Tulowitzki 15.00 40.00
16 Felix Pie/75 12.50 30.00
17 Alex Gordon/25 6.00 15.00
18a Chris Duffy/75 6.00 15.00
18b Chris Duffy 6.00 15.00
19a Chris Young/75 6.00 15.00
19b Chris Young/50 6.00 15.00
20a Cliff Lee/75 6.00 15.00
20b Cliff Lee/50 6.00 15.00
21a Cole Hamels/25 10.00 25.00
21b Cole Hamels/15 10.00 25.00
22 Adam Lind/75 8.00 20.00
23a Akinori Iwamura/25 6.00 15.00
23b Akinori Iwamura/15 6.00 15.00
24a Dan Uggla/25 8.00 20.00
24b Dan Uggla/21 8.00 20.00
25 Dan Haren/25 6.00 15.00
26 David Ortiz/10 40.00 80.00
27 Felix Hernandez/10 30.00 60.00
28a Tony Gwynn Jr. 6.00 15.00
28b Tony Gwynn Jr. 6.00 15.00
29a Josh Hamilton/75 10.00 30.00
29b Josh Hamilton/50 10.00 30.00
29c Josh Hamilton/10 15.00 40.00
30a Phil Hughes 6.00 15.00
30b Phil Hughes 8.00 20.00
31 Khalil Greene/25 12.50 30.00
32a Dontrelle Willis/25 6.00 15.00
32b Dontrelle Willis/20 6.00 15.00
33a Hanley Ramirez/50 10.00 25.00
33b Hanley Ramirez/25 12.00 30.00
34a Howie Kendrick/60 6.00 15.00
34b Howie Kendrick/50 6.00 15.00
35a Huston Street/50 6.00 15.00
35b Huston Street/25 8.00 20.00
37a Jason Bay/50 6.00 15.00
37b Jason Bay/25 10.00 25.00
40a Joe Mauer/25 50.00 100.00
40b Joe Mauer/15 50.00 100.00
41 Jonathan Papelbon/40 8.00 20.00
42a Tim Lincecum/50 15.00 40.00
42b Tim Lincecum/40 15.00 40.00
43a Matt Cain/75 8.00 20.00
43b Matt Cain/40 8.00 20.00
44 Victor Martinez/25 12.00 30.00
45 Chone Figgins/5 50.00 100.00
46 Ryan Zimmerman/25 12.00 30.00
47a Stephen Drew/25 6.00 15.00
47b Stephen Drew/10 6.00 15.00
48 Travis Hafner/25 6.00 15.00
49a Josh Willingham 6.00 15.00
49b Josh Willingham/50 6.00 15.00
50a Torii Hunter/25 8.00 20.00
51 Billy Butler/50 6.00 15.00
52a Justin Morneau/25 10.00 25.00
52b Justin Morneau/15 10.00 25.00
53a Andy LaRoche/75 6.00 15.00
53b Andy LaRoche/60 6.00 15.00
53c Andy LaRoche/50 6.00 15.00
54a Brandon Wood/75 6.00 15.00
54b Brandon Wood/50 6.00 15.00
55 Hunter Pence/75 12.00 30.00
56a Devern Hansack/199 6.00 15.00
56b Devern Hansack/75 6.00 15.00
56c Devern Hansack/50 10.00 25.00
58a Derrek Lee/25 8.00 50.00
58b Derrek Lee/10 8.00 20.00
59a Prince Fielder/25 8.00 20.00
59b Prince Fielder/10 10.00 25.00
60a Kevin Kouzmanoff/50 8.00 20.00

2007 SP Authentic Authentic Power

COMPLETE SET (50) 8.00 20.00
STATED ODDS 1:2
AP1 Adam Dunn .30 .75
AP2 Albert Pujols .60 1.50
AP3 Alex Rodriguez .60 1.50
AP4 Alfonso Soriano .30 .75
AP5 Andruw Jones .20 .50
AP6 Aramis Ramirez .20 .50
AP7 Bill Hall .20 .50
AP8 Carlos Beltran .30 .75
AP9 Carlos Delgado .20 .50
AP10 Carlos Lee .20 .50
AP11 Chase Utley .30 .75
AP12 Chipper Jones .50 1.25
AP13 Dan Uggla .20 .50
AP14 David Ortiz .50 1.25
AP15 David Wright .40 1.00
AP16 Derrek Lee .20 .50
AP17 Eric Chavez .20 .50
AP18 Frank Thomas .50 1.25
AP19 Garrett Atkins .20 .50
AP20 Gary Sheffield .20 .50
AP21 Hideki Matsui .50 1.25
AP22 J.D. Drew .20 .50
AP23 Jason Bay .30 .75
AP24 Jason Giambi .20 .50
AP25 Jeff Francoeur .50 1.25
AP26 Jermaine Dye .20 .50
AP27 Jim Thome .30 .75
AP28 Justin Morneau .30 .75
AP29 Ken Griffey Jr. 1.00 2.50
AP30 Lance Berkman .30 .75
AP31 Magglio Ordonez .30 .75
AP32 Manny Ramirez .50 1.25
AP33 Mark Teixeira .30 .75
AP34 Matt Holliday .50 1.25
AP35 Miguel Cabrera .50 1.25
AP36 Miguel Tejada .30 .75
AP37 Mike Piazza .50 1.25
AP38 Nick Swisher .30 .75
AP39 Pat Burrell .20 .50
AP40 Paul Konerko .30 .75
AP41 Prince Fielder .30 .75
AP42 Richie Sexson .20 .50
AP43 Ryan Howard .40 1.00
AP44 Sammy Sosa .50 1.25
AP45 Todd Helton .30 .75
AP46 Travis Hafner .20 .50
AP47 Troy Glaus .20 .50
AP48 Vernon Wells .20 .50
AP49 Victor Martinez .30 .75
AP50 Vladimir Guerrero .30 .75

2007 SP Authentic Authentic Speed

COMPLETE SET (50) 8.00 20.00
STATED ODDS 1:2
AS1 Alex Rios .20 .50
AS2 Alex Rodriguez .60 1.50
AS3 Alfonso Soriano .30 .75
AS4 B.J. Upton .20 .50
AS5 Bobby Abreu .20 .50
AS6 Brandon Phillips .20 .50
AS7 Brian Roberts .20 .50
AS8 Carl Crawford .30 .75
AS9 Carlos Beltran .30 .75
AS10 Chase Utley .30 .75
AS11 Chone Figgins .20 .50
AS12 Chris Burke .20 .50
AS13 Chris Duffy .20 .50
AS14 Coco Crisp .20 .50
AS15 Corey Patterson .20 .50
AS16 Dave Roberts .30 .75
AS17 David Wright .40 1.00
AS18 Derek Jeter 1.25 3.00
AS19 Edgar Renteria .20 .50
AS20 Eric Byrnes .20 .50
AS21 Felipe Lopez .20 .50
AS22 Gary Matthews .20 .50
AS23 Grady Sizemore .30 .75
AS24 Hanley Ramirez .30 .75
AS25 Ian Kinsler .30 .75
AS26 Ichiro Suzuki .60 1.50
AS27 Jacque Jones .20 .50
AS28 Jimmy Rollins .30 .75
AS29 Johnny Damon .30 .75
AS30 Jose Reyes .30 .75
AS31 Juan Pierre .20 .50
AS32 Julio Lugo .20 .50
AS33 Kenny Lofton .20 .50
AS34 Luis Castillo .20 .50
AS35 Marcus Giles .20 .50
AS36 Melky Cabrera .20 .50
AS37 Mike Cameron .20 .50
AS38 Orlando Cabrera .20 .50
AS39 Rafael Furcal .20 .50
AS40 Randy Winn .20 .50
AS41 Rickie Weeks .20 .50
AS42 Rocco Baldelli .20 .50
AS43 Ryan Freel .20 .50
AS44 Ryan Theriot .20 .50
AS45 Scott Podsednik .20 .50
AS46 Shane Victorino .20 .50
AS47 Tadahito Iguchi .20 .50
AS48 Torii Hunter .20 .50
AS49 Vernon Wells .20 .50
AS50 Willy Taveras .20 .50

2007 SP Authentic Chirography Dual

RANDOM INSERTS IN PACKS
PRINT RUNS B/WN 75-175 COPIES PER
EXCHANGE DEADLINE 11/05/2008
CG Chavez/Gordon/75 EXCH 8.00 20.00
CL Lincecum/Cain/175 40.00 80.00
HD Dunn/Hafner/75 8.00 20.00
HW Haren/Jer.Weaver/175 10.00 25.00
MI Matsuzaka/Iwamura/75 100.00 200.00
ML A.Miller/Lincecum/175 15.00 40.00
MZ Markakis/Zimmerman/75 10.00 25.00
RJ Ripken Jr./Jeter/75 EXCH 200.00 300.00
VH Hernandez/Verland/175 EXCH 50.00 100.00

2007 SP Authentic Sign of the Times Dual

RANDOM INSERTS IN PACKS
PRINT RUNS B/WN 75-175 COPIES PER
EXCHANGE DEADLINE 11/05/2008
BP Beckett/Papelbon/75 10.00 25.00
CJ Clemens/Jeter/75 150.00 400.00
CL Cain/Lincecum/175 75.00 150.00
CW Willis/Cabrera/75 20.00 50.00
FL Furcal/LaRoche/175 6.00 15.00
TK Teixeira/Kinsler/75 12.00 30.00
VM Verlander/Miller/75 12.00 30.00

2008 SP Authentic

This set was released on October 14, 2008. The base set consists of 191 cards. Cards 1-100 feature veterans, and cards 101-191 are rookies serial numbered of various quantities. Some rookie cards feature autographs, jerseys, or both.

COMP.SET w/o RCs (100) 8.00 20.00
COMMON CARD .15 .40
COMMON AU RC (101-191) 3.00 8.00
AU PRINT RUNS 149-999 PER
OVERALL AU ODDS 1:8 HOBBY
COMMON JSY AU RC (101-191) 4.00 10.00
JSY AU PRINT RUN 299-999 PER
OVERALL AU ODDS 1:8 HOBBY
EXCH DEADLINE 9/18/2010
1 Ken Griffey Jr. .75 2.00
2 Derek Jeter 1.00 2.50
3 Albert Pujols .50 1.25
4 Ichiro Suzuki .50 1.25
5 Daisuke Matsuzaka .25 .60
6 Vladimir Guerrero .25 .60
7 Magglio Ordonez .25 .60
8 Eric Chavez .15 .40
9 Randy Johnson .40 1.00
10 Ryan Braun .25 .60
11 Phil Hughes .15 .40
12 Joba Chamberlain .15 .40
13 B.J. Upton .25 .60
14 Frank Thomas .40 1.00
15 Greg Maddux .50 1.25
16 Delmon Young .25 .60
17 Carlos Beltran .25 .60
18 Derrek Lee .15 .40
19 Aramis Ramirez .15 .40
20 Miguel Tejada .25 .60
21 Manny Ramirez .40 1.00
22 Justin Upton .25 .60
23 Miguel Cabrera .40 1.00
24 Prince Fielder .25 .60
25 Adam Dunn .25 .60
26 Jose Reyes .25 .60
27 Chase Utley .25 .60
28 Jimmy Rollins .25 .60
29 Joe Blanton .15 .40
30 Mark Teixeira .25 .60
31 Brian McCann .25 .60
32 Russell Martin .15 .40
33 Ian Kinsler .25 .60
34 Travis Hafner .15 .40
35 Victor Martinez .25 .60
36 Grady Sizemore .25 .60
37 Alex Rodriguez .50 1.25
38 David Wright .25 .60
39 Ryan Howard .25 .60
40 Carlos Lee .15 .40
41 Lance Berkman .25 .60
42 Hunter Pence .25 .60
43 John Lackey .25 .60
44 C.C. Sabathia .25 .60
45 Michael Young .15 .40
46 Carl Crawford .25 .60
47 Carlos Pena .25 .60
48 Justin Verlander .40 1.00
49 Cole Hamels .30 .75
50 Carlos Zambrano .25 .60
51 Jake Peavy .15 .40
52 Khalil Greene .15 .40
53 Chris Young .15 .40
54 Vernon Wells .15 .40
55 Alex Rios .15 .40
56 Roy Halladay .25 .60
57 Roy Oswalt .25 .60
58 Ben Sheets .15 .40
59 J.J. Hardy .15 .40
60 Pedro Martinez .25 .60
61 Nick Swisher .25 .60
62 Curtis Granderson .25 .60
63 Johnny Damon .25 .60
64 Mariano Rivera .50 1.25
65 Josh Beckett .15 .40
66 Erik Bedard .15 .40
67 Johan Santana .25 .60
68 Joe Mauer .30 .75
69 Justin Morneau .25 .60
70 Torii Hunter .15 .40
71 Alex Gordon .25 .60
72 Jose Guillen .15 .40
73 Jim Thome .25 .60
74 Paul Konerko .25 .60
75 Josh Hamilton .25 .60
76 Hanley Ramirez .25 .60
77 Dontrelle Willis .15 .40
78 Dan Uggla .15 .40
79 Brandon Phillips .15 .40
80 Rick Ankiel .15 .40
81 Nick Markakis .30 .75
82 Ryan Zimmerman .25 .60
83 Brian Roberts .15 .40
84 Lastings Milledge .15 .40
85 Freddy Sanchez .15 .40
86 Barry Zito .25 .60
87 Matt Cain .25 .60
88 Andruw Jones .15 .40
89 Dan Haren .15 .40
90 Chien-Ming Wang .25 .60
91 Jonathan Papelbon .25 .60
92 Felix Hernandez .25 .60
93 David Ortiz .40 1.00
94 Jason Bay .25 .60
95 Matt Holliday .40 1.00
96 Troy Tulowitzki .40 1.00
97 Hideki Matsui .40 1.00
98 Jeff Francoeur .25 .60
99 Alfonso Soriano .25 .60
100 Curt Schilling .25 .60
101 Alex Romero Jsy AU/799 (RC) 4.00 10.00
102 Matt Tolbert Jsy AU/699 RC 5.00 12.00
103 Bobby Wilson AU/699 RC 6.00 15.00
104 B.Lillibridge AU/599 (RC) 5.00 12.00
105 Brian Barton AU/698 RC 6.00 15.00
106 B.Bass Jsy AU/799 (RC) 4.00 10.00
107 Brian Bixler AU/698 (RC) 3.00 8.00
108 Brian Bocock Jsy AU/599 RC 4.00 10.00
109 B.Badenhop AU/797 RC 3.00 8.00
110 C.Hu Jsy AU/999 (RC) 4.00 10.00
111 Chris Perez AU/699 RC 3.00 8.00
112 Buchholz Jsy AU/999 (RC) 5.00 12.00
114 Colt Morton Jsy AU/574 RC 4.00 10.00
115 Daric Barton Jsy AU/799 (RC) 4.00 10.00
116 Darren O'Day AU/798 RC 3.00 8.00
117 David Purcey AU/599 (RC) 3.00 8.00
118 D.Span Jsy AU/999 (RC) EXCH 8.00 20.00
119 E.Johnson AU/798 (RC) 3.00 8.00
120 E.Burriss AU/299 RC EXCH 4.00 10.00
121 E.Longoria Jsy AU/499 RC 15.00 40.00
122 Evan Meek Jsy AU/649 RC 5.00 12.00
123 Felipe Paulino Jsy AU/799 RC 4.00 10.00
125 German Duran AU/699 RC 3.00 8.00
126 Greg Reynolds AU/149 RC 3.00 8.00
127 Greg Smith Jsy AU/799 RC 5.00 12.00
128 Harvey Garcia Jsy AU/799 (RC) 4.00 10.00
129 Hernan Iribarren Jsy AU/799 (RC) 4.00 10.00
130 I.Kennedy Jsy AU/699 RC 6.00 15.00
131 J.R. Towles Jsy AU/499 RC 4.00 10.00
132 Jay Bruce Jsy AU/549 (RC) 4.00 10.00
133 Jayson Nix Jsy AU/299 (RC) EXCH 4.00 10.00
134 Jed Lowrie AU/499 (RC) 10.00 25.00
135 Jeff Clement AU/399 (RC) 4.00 10.00
136 Jonathan Herrera AU/699 RC 3.00 8.00
137 Joey Votto Jsy AU/999 (RC) 25.00 60.00
138 J.Cueto Jsy AU/999 RC 4.00 10.00
139 Jonathan Albaladejo Jsy AU/799 RC 4.00 10.00
140 J.Masterson AU/699 RC 6.00 15.00
141 J.Rugglano AU/149 RC 3.00 8.00
142 Kevin Hart Jsy AU/749 (RC) 4.00 10.00
143 K.Fukudome Jsy/799 RC 6.00 15.00
144 Luis Mendoza Jsy AU/299 (RC) 4.00 10.00
145 Luke Carlin AU/699 RC 6.00 15.00
146 L.Hochevar AU/798 RC 4.00 10.00
148 M.Hoffpauir AU/699 RC 8.00 20.00
149 Mike Parisi AU/699 RC 8.00 20.00
150 N.Adenhart AU/599 (RC) 10.00 25.00
151 Blackburn Jsy AU/799 RC 8.00 20.00
152 Nyjer Morgan Jsy AU/999 (RC) 4.00 10.00
153 Troncoso Jsy AU/399 RC 5.00 12.00
154 Randor Bierd Jsy AU/799 RC 4.00 10.00
155 R.Thompson AU/398 RC 5.00 12.00
156 Washington Jsy AU/799 (RC) 4.00 10.00
157 Ross Ohlendorf Jsy AU/999 RC 4.00 10.00
158 Steve Holm Jsy AU/999 RC 4.00 10.00
159 Wesley Wright Jsy AU/849 RC 4.00 10.00
160 Wladimir Balentien AU/599 (RC) 3.00 8.00
161 Alex Hinshaw AU/699 RC EXCH 5.00 12.00
162 Bobby Korecky AU/999 RC 3.00 8.00
163 Brad Harman AU/999 RC 5.00 12.00
164 Brandon Boggs AU/999 (RC) 3.00 8.00
165 Callix Crabbe AU/325 (RC) 3.00 8.00
166 Clay Timpner AU/649 (RC) 3.00 8.00
167 Clete Thomas AU/850 RC 3.00 8.00
168 Cory Wade AU/999 (RC) 3.00 8.00
169 Doug Mathis AU/999 RC 3.00 8.00
170 Eider Torres AU/999 (RC) 5.00 12.00
171 Gregorio Petit AU/999 RC 4.00 10.00
172 M.Aubrey AU/699 RC EXCH 4.00 10.00
173 Jesse Carlson AU/999 RC 8.00 20.00
174 Billy Buckner AU/999 (RC) 3.00 8.00
175 Josh Newman AU/699 RC 3.00 8.00
176 Matt Tupman AU/999 RC 5.00 12.00
177 Matt Joyce AU/999 RC 6.00 15.00
178 Paul Janish AU/999 (RC) 3.00 8.00
179 Robinzon Diaz AU/999 (RC) 3.00 8.00
180 Fernando Hernandez AU/999 RC 3.00 8.00
181 Brandon Jones AU/999 RC 3.00 8.00
182 Eddie Bonine AU/899 RC 3.00 8.00
183 Chris Smith AU/384 (RC) 6.00 15.00
184 J.Van Every AU/999 RC 4.00 10.00
185 Marino Salas AU/999 RC 4.00 10.00
186 Mike Aviles AU/899 RC 6.00 15.00
187 M.Boggs AU/699 (RC) EXCH 6.00 15.00
188 C.Carter AU/699 (RC) EXCH 5.00 12.00
189 Travis Denker AU/699 RC EXCH 3.00 8.00
190 Carlos Rosa AU/699 RC 5.00 12.00
191 E.Longoria AU/350 (RC) 6.00 15.00

2008 SP Authentic Gold

*GOLD 1-100: 5X TO 12X BASIC
*GLD AU RC: .75X TO 2X BASIC
*GLD JSY AU RC: .75X TO 2X BASIC
RANDOM INSERTS IN PACKS
PRINT RUN B/WN 10-50 SER.#'d SETS
NO VOTTO PRICING AVAILABLE
EXCH DEADLINE 9/18/2010
4 Ichiro Suzuki 20.00 50.00
121 Evan Longoria Jsy AU/50 40.00 100.00
191 Evan Longoria AU/50 75.00 150.00

2008 SP Authentic Authentic Achievements

STATED ODDS 1:2 HOBBY
AA1 Derek Jeter 2.00 5.00
AA2 Ken Griffey Jr. 1.50 4.00
AA3 Randy Johnson .75 2.00
AA4 Frank Thomas .75 2.00
AA5 Tom Glavine .50 1.25
AA6 Matt Holliday .75 2.00
AA7 Justin Verlander .75 2.00
AA8 Manny Ramirez .75 2.00
AA9 Scott Rolen .50 1.25
AA10 Brandon Webb .50 1.25
AA11 Erik Bedard .30 .75
AA12 Daisuke Matsuzaka .50 1.25
AA13 Johan Santana .50 1
AA14 Carlos Lee .30
AA15 Alfonso Soriano .50 1
AA16 Grady Sizemore .50 1
AA17 Jose Reyes .50 1
AA18 Chase Utley .50 1
AA19 Roy Oswalt .50 1
AA20 David Ortiz .75 2
AA21 Jake Peavy .30
AA22 Hanley Ramirez .50 1
AA23 Alex Rodriguez 1.00 2
AA24 Ryan Howard .50 1
AA25 David Wright .50 1
AA26 Trevor Hoffman .50 1
AA27 Prince Fielder .50 1
AA28 Ichiro Suzuki 1.00 2
AA29 Jimmy Rollins .50 1
AA30 Mariano Rivera 1.00 2
AA31 Pedro Martinez .50 1
AA32 Torii Hunter .30
AA33 Ivan Rodriguez .50 1
AA34 Jim Thome .50 1
AA35 Chipper Jones .75 2
AA36 John Smoltz .75 2
AA37 Jeff Kent .30
AA38 Albert Pujols 1.00 2
AA39 Lance Berkman .50 1
AA40 Justin Morneau .50 1.
AA41 Andruw Jones .30
AA42 Adam Dunn .50 1
AA43 Greg Maddux 1.00 2
AA44 Billy Wagner .30
AA45 Vladimir Guerrero .50 1.
AA46 C.C. Sabathia .50 1
AA47 Mark Teixeira .50 1.
AA48 Mark Buehrle .50 1
AA49 Miguel Cabrera .75 2
AA50 Josh Beckett .30

2008 SP Authentic By The Lett Autographs

OVERALL AU ODDS 1:8 HOBBY
ANNCD PRINT RUNS LISTED
SER.# ON CARDS ARE DIFFERENT
EXCH DEADLINE 9/18/2010
AD Adam Dunn/140 * 10.00 25.
AG Adrian Gonzalez/110 * 4.00 10.
BH Bill Hall/1570 * 8.00 20.
BP Brandon Phillips/1259 * 8.00 20.
BW Billy Wagner/125 * 20.00 50.
CB Chad Billingsley/1306 * 5.00 12.
CJ Chipper Jones/100 * 50.00 100.
CL Carlos Lee/160 * 10.00 25.
CW Chien-Ming Wang/80 * 40.00 80.
DA David Murphy/1837 * 10.00 25.
DJ Derek Jeter/240 * EXCH 125.00 250.
DM Daisuke Matsuzaka/125 * 30.00 60.
EE Edwin Encarnacion/1570 * 5.00 12.
FC Fausto Carmona/844 * 8.00 20.
GA Garrett Atkins/588 * 8.00 20.
GJ Geoff Jenkins/1200 * 5.00 12.
GS Grady Sizemore/240 * 12.00 30.
JB Joe Blanton/580 * 6.00 15.
JE Jeff Francoeur/275 * 12.00 30.
JF Jeff Francis/335 * 12.00 30.
JG Jeremy Guthrie/985 * 6.00 15.
JH Jeremy Hermida/505 * 5.00 12.
JL James Loney/1275 * EXCH 6.00 15.
JN Joe Nathan/365 * 5.00 12.
JO John Lackey/187 * 12.00 30.
JP Jonathan Papelbon/550 * 4.00 10.
JS Jon Lester/235 * 40.00 80.
KE Kevin Youkilis/365 * 15.00 40.
KG Ken Griffey Jr./275 * EXCH 100.00 175.
KJ Kelly Johnson/1399 * 5.00 12.
LB Lance Berkman/165 * 15.00 40.
ME Mark Ellis/995 * 5.00 12.
MG Matt Garza/235 * 8.00 20.
MK Matt Kemp/1369 * 12.00 30.
MM Melvin Mora/490 * EXCH 8.00 20.
NL Noah Lowry/1440 * 5.00 12.
NS Nick Swisher/1150 * 6.00 15.
PF Prince Fielder/245 * 6.00 15.
PH Phil Hughes/385 * 8.00 20.
PK Paul Konerko/175 * 15.00 40.
RH Rich Hill/220 * 6.00 15.
RM Russell Martin/265 * 8.00 20.
RO Roy Halladay/160 * 30.00 60.
SB Scott Baker/1248 * 6.00 15.
TG Tom Glavine/1082 * 5.00 12.
TT Troy Tulowitzki/252 * 10.00 25.

2008 SP Authentic Chirography Signatures Dual

OVERALL AU ODDS 1:8 HOBBY
PRINT RUNS B/WN 10-99 COPIES PER
NO PRICING ON MOST CARDS
EXCH DEADLINE 9/18/2010
GB T.Gorzelanny/C.Billingsley/96 12.50 30.0
HK P.Hughes/I.Kennedy/99 EXCH 10.00 25.0
MH D.Murphy/J.Hamilton/99 6.00 15.0
MK Nick Markakis 25.00 60.0
Matt Kemp/99
PE B.Phillips/E.Encarnacion/99 5.00 12.0

2008 SP Authentic Marquee Matchups

ATED ODDS 1:2 HOBBY
M1 D.Jeter/C.Schilling 2.00 5.00
M2 J.Beckett/D.Jeter 2.00 5.00
M3 A.Pujols/B.Lidge 1.00 2.50
M4 D.Matsuzaka/A.Rodriguez 1.00 2.50
M5 K.Griffey Jr./J.Smoltz 1.50 4.00
M6 J.Smoltz/D.Wright .75 2.00
M7 Jonathan Papelbon/Gary Sheffield .50 1.25
M8 R.Braun/R.Oswalt .50 1.25
M9 Mariano Rivera/David Ortiz 1.00 2.50
M10 C.Zambrano/A.Pujols 1.00 2.50
M11 Dontrelle Willis/Travis Hafner .30 .75
M12 Felix Hernandez/Victor Martinez .50 1.25
M13 Carlos Zambrano/Carlos Lee .50 1.25
M14 C.Wang/M.Ramirez .75 2.00
M15 Felix Hernandez/Justin Morneau .50 1.25
M16 I.Suzuki/F.Rodriguez 1.00 2.50
M17 Grady Sizemore/Erik Bedard .50 1.25
M18 V.Guerrero/J.Verlander .75 2.00
M19 D.Matsuzaka/I.Suzuki 1.00 2.50
M20 Alfonso Soriano/Chris Carpenter .50 1.25
M21 Hanley Ramirez/Pedro Martinez .50 1.25
M22 Chase Utley/Randy Johnson .75 2.00
M23 K.Griffey Jr./R.Oswalt 1.50 4.00
M24 R.Johnson/K.Griffey Jr. 1.50 4.00
M25 Jimmy Rollins/Johan Santana .50 1.25
M26 Matt Cain/Andruw Jones .50 1.25
M27 P.Martinez/R.Howard .50 1.25
M28 C.Hamels/D.Wright .60 1.50
M29 C.Jones/J.Santana .75 2.00
M30 Billy Wagner/Mark Teixeira .50 1.25
M31 C.C. Sabathia/Magglio Ordonez .50 1.25
M32 Jose Reyes/Tom Glavine .50 1.25
M33 D.Jeter/J.Papelbon 2.00 5.00
M34 J.Santana/A.Rodriguez 1.00 2.50
M35 Alfonso Soriano/Jake Peavy .50 1.25
M36 J.Santana/R.Howard .50 1.25
M37 Jake Peavy/Russell Martin .30 .75
M38 Carlos Zambrano/Prince Fielder .50 1.25
M39 Cole Hamels/Carlos Beltran .60 1.50
M40 J.Beckett/A.Rodriguez 1.00 2.50
M41 R.Halladay/D.Jeter 2.00 5.00
M42 H.Matsui/D.Matsuzaka .75 2.00
M43 C.C. Sabathia/Joe Mauer .60 1.50
M44 Francisco Rodriguez
Manny Ramirez .75 2.00
M45 J.Weaver/M.Cabrera .75 2.00
M46 D.Wright/J.Peavy .50 1.25
M47 G.Maddux/K.Griffey Jr. 1.50 4.00
M48 John Smoltz/Hanley Ramirez .75 2.00
M49 P.Martinez/A.Rodriguez 1.00 2.50
M50 Trevor Hoffman/Matt Holliday .75 2.00

2008 SP Authentic Rookie Exclusives

ANDOM INSERTS IN PACKS
H Alex Hinshaw 1.25 3.00
R Alex Romero 1.25 3.00
A Brian Barton 1.25 3.00
B Brandon Boggs 1.25 3.00
H Brad Harman 1.25 3.00
I Brian Bixler .75 2.00
K Bobby Korecky .75 2.00
O Brian Bocock .75 2.00
R Brian Bass .75 2.00
U Burke Badenhop 1.25 3.00
W Bobby Wilson .75 2.00
B Clay Buchholz 1.25 3.00
C Callix Crabbe .75 2.00
M Colt Morton 1.25 3.00
T Clay Timpner .75 2.00
U Johnny Cueto 2.00 5.00
W Cory Wade .75 2.00
B Daric Barton .75 2.00
M Doug Mathis .75 2.00
S Denard Span 1.25 3.00
B Emmanuel Burriss 1.25 3.00
J Elliot Johnson .75 2.00
M Evan Meek .75 2.00
T Eider Torres 1.25 3.00
H Fernando Hernandez .75 2.00
P Felipe Paulino 1.25 3.00
D German Duran 1.25 3.00
P Gregorio Petit 1.25 3.00
S Greg Smith .75 2.00
I Hernan Iribarren 1.25 3.00
K Ian Kennedy 2.00 5.00
A Jonathan Albaladejo 1.25 3.00
B Jay Bruce 2.50 6.00
C Jesse Carlson 1.25 3.00
H Jonathan Herrera 1.25 3.00
L Jed Lowrie .75 2.00
N Jayson Nix .75 2.00
T J.R. Towles 1.25 3.00
H Kevin Hart .75 2.00
C Luke Carlin .75 2.00
M Luis Mendoza .75 2.00
A Matt Tolbert 1.25 3.00
H Micah Hoffpauir 2.50 6.00
J Matt Joyce 2.00 5.00
MP Mike Parisi 1.25 3.00
MT Matt Tupman .75 2.00
NA Nick Adenhart .75 2.00
NB Nick Blackburn 1.25 3.00
NE Josh Newman 1.25 3.00
NM Nyjer Morgan .75 2.00
RA Alexei Ramirez 2.50 6.00
RB Randor Bierd .75 2.00
RD Robinzon Diaz .75 2.00
RI Rich Thompson 1.25 3.00
RO Ross Ohlendorf 1.25 3.00
RT Ramon Troncoso .75 2.00
RW Rico Washington .75 2.00
SH Steve Holm .75 2.00
TH Clete Thomas 1.25 3.00
WB Wladimir Balentien .75 2.00
WW Wesley Wright .75 2.00

2008 SP Authentic Sign of the Times Dual

OVERALL AU ODDS 1:8 HOBBY
PRINT RUNS B/WN 10-99 COPIES PER
MOST CARDS NOT PRICED
EXCH DEADLINE 9/18/2010
NW J.Nathan/B.Wagner/74 10.00 25.00
PW F.Pie/J.Willingham/99 6.00 15.00

2008 SP Authentic Sign of the Times Triple

OVERALL AU ODDS 1:8 HOBBY
PRINT RUNS B/WN 10-50 COPIES PER
NO PRICING ON QTY 14 OR LESS
EXCH DEADLINE 9/18/2010
HGK Jeremy Hermida
Carlos Gomez/Matt Kemp/50 10.00 25.00

2008 SP Authentic USA Junior National Team Jersey Autographs

OVERALL AU ODDS 1:8 HOBBY
STATED PRINT RUN 120 SER.#'d SETS
AA Andrew Aplin 10.00 25.00
AM Austin Maddox 5.00 12.00
CC Colton Cain 5.00 12.00
CG Cameron Garfield 12.50 30.00
CT Cecil Tanner 4.00 10.00
DN David Nick 4.00 10.00
DT Donovan Tate 10.00 25.00
FR Nick Franklin 5.00 12.00
HM Harold Martinez 10.00 25.00
JB Jake Barrett 6.00 15.00
MA Jeff Malm 6.00 15.00
ME Jonathan Meyer 8.00 20.00
MP Matthew Purke 8.00 20.00
MS Max Stassi 4.00 10.00
NF Nolan Fontana 5.00 12.00
TU Jacob Turner 6.00 15.00
WH Wes Hatton 10.00 25.00

2008 SP Authentic USA Junior National Team Patch Autographs

OVERALL AU ODDS 1:8 HOBBY
STATED PRINT RUN 50 SER.#'d SETS
AA Andrew Aplin 10.00 25.00
CC Colton Cain 10.00 25.00
DN David Nick 6.00 15.00
JB Jake Barrett 6.00 15.00
MS Max Stassi 10.00 25.00
NF Nolan Fontana 12.50 30.00
RW Ryan Weber 12.50 30.00
TU Jacob Turner 25.00 60.00
WH Wes Hatton 15.00 40.00

2008 SP Authentic USA National Team By the Letter Autographs

OVERALL AU ODDS 1:8 HOBBY
PRINT RUNS BW/N 50-181 PER
AG A.J. Griffin/105 4.00 10.00
AO Andrew Oliver/105 4.00 10.00
BS Blake Smith/105 4.00 10.00
CC Christian Colon/105 4.00 10.00
CH Chris Hernandez/180 4.00 10.00
DD Derek Dietrich/105 10.00 25.00
HM Hunter Morris/106 12.00 30.00
KD Kentrail Davis/103 12.00 30.00
KG Kyle Gibson/181 30.00 60.00
KR Kevin Rhoderick/172 4.00 10.00
KV Kendal Volz/105 4.00 10.00
MD Matt den Dekker/105 4.00 10.00
MG Micah Gibbs/180 4.00 10.00
ML Mike Leake/180 4.00 10.00
MM Mike Minor/105 4.00 10.00
RJ Ryan Jackson/104 4.00 10.00
SS Stephen Strasburg/105 25.00 60.00
TL Tyler Lyons/104 4.00 10.00

2009 SP Authentic

COMP.SET w/o AU's (200) 50.00 100.00
COMP.SET w/o SPs (100) 12.50 30.00
COMMON CARD (1-128) .15 .40
COMMON RC (129-170) 1.00 2.50
COMMON SP (171-200) .50 1.25
171-200 APPX.ODDS 1:8 HOBBY
COMMON SP (201-225) .60 1.50
201-225 RANDOMLY INSERTED
201-225 PRINT RUN 495 SER.#'d SETS
COMMON AUTO (226-250) 3.00 8.00
OVERALL AUTO ODDS 1:8 HOBBY
AUTO PRINT RUN B/WN 100-500 PER
1 Kosuke Fukudome .25 .60
2 Derek Jeter 1.00 2.50
3 Evan Longoria .25 .60
4 Yadier Molina .40 1.00
5 Albert Pujols .50 1.25
6 Ryan Howard .30 .75
7 Joe Mauer .30 .75
8 Ryan Braun .25 .60
9 Hunter Pence .25 .60
10 Gary Sheffield .15 .40
11 Ryan Zimmerman .25 .60
12 Alfonso Soriano .25 .60
13 Alex Rodriguez .50 1.25
14 Paul Konerko .25 .60
15 Dustin Pedroia .30 .75
16 Brian McCann .25 .60
17 Lance Berkman .25 .60
18 Daisuke Matsuzaka .25 .60
19 Josh Beckett .15 .40
20 Carlos Quentin .15 .40
21 Carlos Delgado .15 .40
22 Clayton Kershaw .75 2.00
23 Zack Greinke .25 .60
24 Ken Griffey Jr. .75 2.00
25 Mark Teixeira .25 .60
26 Chase Utley .25 .60
27 Vladimir Guerrero .25 .60
28 Prince Fielder .25 .60
29 Adrian Beltre .40 1.00
30 Magglio Ordonez .25 .60
31 Jon Lester .25 .60
32 Josh Hamilton .25 .60
33 Justin Morneau .25 .60
34 Felix Hernandez .25 .60
35 Cole Hamels .30 .75
36 Edinson Volquez .15 .40
37 Hideki Okajima .15 .40
38 Carlos Zambrano .25 .60
39 Aaron Harang .15 .40
40 Chien-Ming Wang .25 .60
41 Shin-Soo Choo .25 .60
42 Mariano Rivera .50 1.25
43 Josh Johnson .25 .60
44 Roy Oswalt .25 .60
45 Carlos Lee .15 .40
46 Ryan Dempster .15 .40
47 Ryan Ludwick .25 .60
48 Joakim Soria .15 .40
49 Jair Jurrjens .15 .40
50 John Danks .15 .40
51 Ichiro Suzuki .50 1.25
52 CC Sabathia .25 .60
53 Yovani Gallardo .15 .40
54 Ervin Santana .15 .40
55 Tim Lincecum .25 .60
56 Mark Buehrle .25 .60
57 Johan Santana .25 .60
58 Chad Billingsley .25 .60
59 Francisco Liriano .15 .40
60 Joey Votto .40 1.00
61 Matt Kemp .30 .75
62 Joba Chamberlain .15 .40
63 Hiroki Kuroda .15 .40
64 Brian Roberts .15 .40
65 Randy Johnson .40 1.00
66 Jay Bruce .25 .60
67 Curtis Granderson .30 .75
68 Hideki Matsui .40 1.00
69 Todd Helton .25 .60
70 Nick Markakis .30 .75
71 Andy Pettitte .25 .60
72 Ian Kinsler .25 .60
73 Brandon Inge .15 .40
74 Adrian Gonzalez .30 .75
75 Francisco Rodriguez .25 .60
76 Derek Lowe .15 .40
77 Carlos Beltran .25 .60
78 Matt Holliday .40 1.00
79 Jake Peavy .15 .40
80 Scott Kazmir .15 .40
81 David Ortiz .40 1.00
82 Dan Haren .15 .40
83 Hanley Ramirez .25 .60
84 Jim Thome .25 .60
85 Brad Hawpe .15 .40
86 Vernon Wells .15 .40
87 B.J. Upton .25 .60
88 James Shields .15 .40
89 Jason Giambi .15 .40
90 Adam Dunn .25 .60
91 Brandon Webb .25 .60
92 Roy Halladay .25 .60
93 Miguel Cabrera .40 1.00
94 Jose Reyes .25 .60
95 Chipper Jones .40 1.00
96 Grady Sizemore .25 .60
97 Jason Varitek .40 1.00
98 David Wright .30 .75
99 Manny Ramirez .40 1.00
100 Kevin Youkilis .15 .40
101 Bengie Molina .15 .40
102 Ivan Rodriguez .25 .60
103 Andruw Jones .15 .40
104 Jorge Cantu .15 .40
105 Corey Hart .15 .40
106 Adam Wainwright .25 .60
107 Raul Ibanez .25 .60
108 Jason Bay .25 .60
109 Chris Volstad .15 .40
110 Jermaine Dye .15 .40
111 Torii Hunter .15 .40
112 Brad Ziegler .15 .40
113 Carl Crawford .25 .60
114 Troy Tulowitzki .40 1.00
115 Aramis Ramirez .15 .40
116 Nomar Garciaparra .25 .60
117 Pedro Martinez .25 .60
118 Ryan Theriot .15 .40
119 Matt Cain .25 .60
120 Carlos Pena .25 .60
121 Nick Swisher .25 .60
122 Javier Vazquez .15 .40
123 John Lackey .25 .60
124 Jack Cust .15 .40
125 Justin Upton .25 .60
126 Michael Young .15 .40
127 Jeff Samardzija .25 .60
128 John Smoltz .40 1.00
129 Josh Reddick RC 1.50 4.00
130 Chris Tillman RC 1.50 4.00
131 Aaron Cunningham RC 1.00 2.50
132 Andrew McCutchen (RC) 5.00 12.00
133 Anthony Ortega RC 1.00 2.50
134 Anthony Swarzak (RC) 1.00 2.50
135 Antonio Bastardo RC 1.00 2.50
136 Brad Bergesen (RC) 1.00 2.50
137 Brett Cecil RC 1.00 2.50
138 Neftali Feliz RC 1.50 4.00
139 Chris Coghlan RC 2.50 6.00
140 Daniel Bard RC 1.00 2.50
141 Daniel Schlereth RC 1.00 2.50
142 Donald Veal RC 1.50 4.00
143 Brad Mills RC 1.00 2.50
144 David Huff RC 1.00 2.50
145 Elvis Andrus RC 2.50 6.00
146 Everth Cabrera RC 1.50 4.00
147 Mat Latos RC 3.00 8.00
148 Shairon Martis RC 1.50 4.00
149 Jess Todd RC 1.00 2.50
150 Jonathon Niese RC 1.50 4.00
151 Jose Mijares RC 2.50 6.00
152 Jhoulys Chacin RC 1.50 4.00
153 Kyle Blanks RC 1.50 4.00
154 Kris Medlen RC 2.50 6.00
155 Fu-Te Ni RC 1.50 4.00
156 Bud Norris RC 1.00 2.50
157 Julio Borbon RC 1.00 2.50
158 Mat Gamel RC 2.50 6.00
159 Matt LaPorta RC 1.50 4.00
160 Michael Bowden (RC) 1.00 2.50
161 Michael Saunders RC 2.50 6.00
162 Ricky Romero (RC) 1.50 4.00
163 Marc Rzepczynski RC 1.50 4.00
164 Ryan Perry RC 2.50 6.00
165 Sean O'Sullivan RC 1.00 2.50
166 Sean West (RC) 1.50 4.00
167 Trevor Cahill RC 2.50 6.00
168 Mike Carp (RC) 1.50 4.00
169 Vin Mazzaro RC 1.00 2.50
170 Wilkin Ramirez RC 1.00 2.50
171 Albert Pujols FG SP 1.50 4.00
172 Alfonso Soriano FG SP .75 2.00
173 Brandon Webb FG SP .75 2.00
174 Carlos Quentin FG SP .50 1.25
175 Carlos Zambrano FG SP .75 2.00
176 CC Sabathia FG SP .75 2.00
177 Chase Utley FG SP .75 2.00
178 Chipper Jones FG SP 1.25 3.00
179 Cole Hamels FG SP 1.00 2.50
180 Daisuke Matsuzaka FG SP .75 2.00
181 David Wright FG SP 1.00 2.50
182 Derek Jeter FG SP 3.00 8.00
183 Derek Lowe FG SP .50 1.25
184 Dustin Pedroia FG SP 1.00 2.50
185 Felix Hernandez FG SP .75 2.00
186 Grady Sizemore FG SP .75 2.00
187 Jason Giambi FG SP .50 1.25
188 Joba Chamberlain FG SP .50 1.25
189 Joe Mauer FG SP 1.00 2.50
190 Johan Santana FG SP .75 2.00
191 Jose Reyes FG SP .75 2.00
192 Josh Beckett FG SP .50 1.25
193 Josh Hamilton FG SP .75 2.00
194 Ken Griffey Jr. FG SP 2.50 6.00
195 Manny Ramirez FG SP 1.25 3.00
196 Prince Fielder FG SP .75 2.00
197 Randy Johnson FG SP 1.25 3.00
198 Ryan Braun FG SP .75 2.00
199 Ryan Howard FG SP 1.00 2.50
200 Tim Lincecum FG SP .75 2.00
201 A.J. Burnett FW FB .60 1.50
202 Adam Dunn FW FB 1.00 2.50
203 Alex Rodriguez FW FB 2.00 5.00
204 Alfonso Soriano FW FB 1.00 2.50
205 Andy Pettitte FW FB 1.00 2.50
206 Bobby Abreu FW FB .60 1.50
207 Carlos Beltran FW FB 1.00 2.50
208 Chipper Jones FW FB 1.50 4.00
209 Dan Haren FW FB .60 1.50
210 Derek Jeter FW FB 4.00 10.00
211 Derek Lowe FW FB .60 1.50
212 Gary Sheffield FW FB .60 1.50
213 Ivan Rodriguez FW FB 1.00 2.50
214 Jamie Moyer FW FB .60 1.50
215 Jason Giambi FW FB .60 1.50
216 Jim Thome FW FB 1.00 2.50
217 Johan Santana FW FB 1.00 2.50
218 John Smoltz FW FB 1.50 4.00
219 Johnny Damon FW FB 1.00 2.50
220 Josh Beckett FW FB .60 1.50
221 Ken Griffey Jr. FW FB 3.00 8.00
222 Manny Ramirez FW FB 1.50 4.00
223 Mark Teixeira FW FB 1.00 2.50
224 Randy Johnson FW FB 1.50 4.00
225 Tim Wakefield FW FB 1.00 2.50
226 Aaron Poreda AU/300 RC 3.00 8.00
227 B.Anderson AU/371 RC 5.00 12.00
228 M.LaPorta AU/225 5.00 12.00
229 C.Rasmus AU/300 (RC) 5.00 12.00
230 D.Price AU/222 RC 6.00 15.00
231 D.Holland AU/195 RC 5.00 12.00
232 D.Fowler AU/490 (RC) 5.00 12.00
233 F.Martinez AU/243 RC 8.00 20.00
234 G.Parra AU/299 RC 5.00 12.00
235 G.Beckham AU/136 RC 5.00 12.00
236 James McDonald AU/500 RC 8.00 20.00
237 James Parr AU/500 (RC) 3.00 8.00
238 J.Motte AU/415 (RC) 5.00 12.00
239 J.Schafer AU/475 (RC) 5.00 12.00
240 J.Zimmermann AU/417 RC 8.00 20.00
241 K Kawakami AU/425 RC 5.00 12.00
242 K.Uehara AU/200 RC 8.00 20.00
243 Luis Perdomo AU/275 RC 3.00 8.00
244 Tuiasosopo AU/500 (RC) 3.00 8.00
245 M.Wieters AU/200 RC 10.00 25.00
246 N.Reimold AU/135 (RC) 3.00 8.00
247 P.Sandoval AU/230 (RC) 6.00 15.00
248 R.Porcello AU/225 RC 10.00 25.00
249 T.Hanson AU/198 RC 8.00 20.00
250 T.Snider AU/100 RC 5.00 12.00

2009 SP Authentic Copper

*1-128 COPPER: 2X TO 5X BASIC
1-128 PRINT RUN 99 SER.#'d SETS
*129-170 COPPER: ..6X TO 1.5X BASIC
129-170 PRINT RUN 99 SER.#'d SETS
*171-200 COPPER: .6X TO 1.5X BASIC
171-200 PRINT RUN 99 SER.#'d SETS
*201-225 COPPER: 1.2X TO 3X BASIC
1-225 RANDOMLY INSERTED IN PACKS
201-225 PRINT RUN 29 SER.#'d SETS
OVERALL AUTO ODDS 1:8 HOBBY
AU PRINT RUNS B/WN 10-50 COPIES
NO PRICING ON QTY 25 OR LESS
226 Aaron Poreda AU/50 4.00 10.00
227 Brett Anderson AU/50 6.00 15.00
228 Matt LaPorta AU/50 6.00 15.00
229 Colby Rasmus AU/50 6.00 15.00
230 David Price AU/50 8.00 20.00
231 Derek Holland AU/35 6.00 15.00
232 Dexter Fowler AU/50 6.00 15.00
233 Fernando Martinez AU/50 10.00 25.00
234 Gerardo Parra AU/50 6.00 15.00
235 Gordon Beckham AU/40 6.00 15.00
236 James McDonald AU/50 10.00 25.00
237 James Parr AU/50 4.00 10.00
238 Jason Motte AU/50 6.00 15.00
239 Jordan Schafer AU/50 6.00 15.00
240 Jordan Zimmermann AU/50 10.00 25.00
241 Kenshin Kawakami AU/50 6.00 15.00
243 Luis Perdomo AU/50 4.00 10.00
244 Matt Tuiasosopo AU/50 4.00 10.00
247 Pablo Sandoval AU/50 8.00 20.00
240 Tommy Hanson AU/35 10.00 25.00

2009 SP Authentic Gold

*1-128 GOLD: 1.5X TO 4X BASIC
1-128 PRINT RUN 299 SER.#'d SETS
*129-170 GOLD: .6X TO 1.5X BASIC
129-170 PRINT RUN 299 SER.#'d SETS
*171-200 GOLD: .5X TO 1.2X BASIC
171-200 PRINT RUN 299 SER.#'d SETS
*201-225 GOLD: .5X TO 1.2X BASIC
1-225 RANDOMLY INSERTED IN PACKS
201-225 PRINT RUN 99 SER.#'d SETS
OVERALL AUTO ODDS 1:8 HOBBY
AU PRINT RUNS B/WN 25-125 COPIES
NO PRICING ON QTY 25 OR LESS
226 Aaron Poreda AU/124 3.00 8.00
227 Brett Anderson AU/125 5.00 12.00
228 Matt LaPorta AU/125 5.00 12.00
229 Colby Rasmus AU/100 5.00 12.00
230 David Price AU/125 6.00 15.00
231 Derek Holland AU/90 6.00 15.00
232 Dexter Fowler AU/125 5.00 12.00
233 Fernando Martinez AU/125 8.00 20.00
234 Gerardo Parra AU/125 5.00 12.00
235 Gordon Beckham AU/85 6.00 15.00
236 James McDonald AU/125 8.00 20.00
237 James Parr AU/125 3.00 8.00
230 Jason Motte AU/125 5.00 12.00
239 Jordan Schafer AU/125 5.00 12.00
240 Jordan Zimmermann AU/125 8.00 20.00
241 Kenshin Kawakami AU/125 5.00 12.00
243 Luis Perdomo AU/125 3.00 8.00
244 Matt Tuiasosopo AU/125 3.00 8.00
245 Matt Wieters AU/50 12.00 30.00
246 Nolan Reimold AU/65 4.00 10.00
247 Pablo Sandoval AU/75 8.00 20.00
248 Rick Porcello AU/75 12.00 30.00
249 Tommy Hanson AU/65 10.00 25.00
250 Travis Snider AU/50 6.00 15.00

2009 SP Authentic Silver

*1-128 SILVER: 2.5X TO 6X BASIC
1-128 PRINT RUN 59 SER.#'d SETS
*129-170 SILVER: .75X TO 2X BASIC
129-170 PRINT RUN 59 SER.#'d SETS
*171-200 SILVER: 2.5X TO 6X BASIC
1-200 RANDOMLY INSERTED IN PACKS
171-200 PRINT RUN 59 SER.#'d SETS
OVERALL AUTO ODDS 1:8 HOBBY
226-250 AU PR B/WN 4-25 SER.#'d SETS
NO 201-250 PRICING DUE TO SCARCITY

2009 SP Authentic By The Letter Rookie Signatures

OVERALL LETTER AU ODDS 1:12
SER.#'d B/WN 11-100 COPIES PER
TOTAL PRINT RUNS LISTED BELOW
EXCHANGE DEADLINE 9/18/2011
BA B.Anderson/599 * 6.00 15.00
CR Colby Rasmus/450 * 6.00 15.00
DF David Freese/450 * 12.00 30.00
DH Derek Holland/270 * 6.00 15.00
DP David Patton/600 * 6.00 15.00
DV Donald Veal/715 * 6.00 15.00
EA Elvis Andrus/660 * 10.00 25.00
EC Everth Cabrera/715 * 6.00 15.00
FO Dexter Fowler/715 * 6.00 15.00
GK George Kottaras/715 * 4.00 10.00
JM James McDonald/715 * 10.00 25.00
JS Jordan Schafer/510 * 6.00 15.00
JZ J.Zimmermann/297 * 10.00 25.00
KJ Kevin Jepsen/600 * 4.00 10.00
KK K.Kawakami/600 * 6.00 15.00
KU Koji Uehara/400 * 10.00 25.00
MO Jason Motte/600 * 6.00 15.00
MW Matt Wieters/165 * 12.00 30.00
PC Phil Coke/709 * 6.00 15.00
PD David Price/168 * 8.00 20.00
PE Ryan Perry/300 * 10.00 25.00
PR David Price/140 * 8.00 20.00
PS P.Sandoval/308 * 8.00 20.00
RP Rick Porcello/510 * 12.00 30.00
RR R.Romero/715 * 6.00 15.00
SM Shairon Martis/715 * 6.00 15.00
TC Trevor Cahill/510 * 10.00 25.00
TR Trevor Crowe/715 * 4.00 10.00
TS Travis Snider/540 * 6.00 15.00
UE Koji Uehara/190 * 10.00 25.00

2009 SP Authentic By The Letter Signatures

OVERALL LETTER AU ODDS 1:12
SER.#'d B/WN 2-60 COPIES PER
TOTAL PRINT RUNS LISTED BELOW
EXCHANGE DEADLINE 9/18/2011
AH Alex Hinshaw/473* 6.00 15.00
AR Alex Romero/400* 5.00 12.00
BJ B.Jones/360* 8.00 20.00
BM B.McCann/220* 12.00 30.00
BR Jay Bruce/350* 5.00 12.00
BU B.J. Upton/26* 8.00 20.00
CG C.Gonzalez/495* 6.00 15.00
CH C.Hu/120* 6.00 15.00
CJ Chipper Jones/24* 60.00 150.00
CK C.Kershaw/140* 100.00 250.00
CV Chris Volstad/300* 5.00 12.00
CW C.Wang/60* 40.00 80.00
DJ Derek Jeter/200* 150.00 250.00
DM D.Murphy/360* 5.00 12.00
DP David Purcey/341* 5.00 12.00
DU D.Pedroia/390* 20.00 50.00
EB Emmanuel Burriss/375* 5.00 12.00
EC Eric Chavez/54* 8.00 20.00
EL E.Longoria/60* 75.00 150.00
FH F.Hernandez/80* EXCH 20.00 50.00
GA Garrett Atkins/65* 8.00 20.00
GF Gavin Floyd/400* 6.00 15.00
GP Glen Perkins/385* 5.00 12.00
GS Geovany Soto/40* 20.00 50.00
HA Cole Hamels/100* 12.00 30.00
HP Hunter Pence/48* 8.00 20.00
HR H.Ramirez/52* 10.00 25.00
HU C.Hu/270* 10.00 25.00
JB Jay Bruce/494* 10.00 30.00
JC J.Chamberlain/150* 30.00 60.00
JJ J.Johnson/297* 6.00 15.00
JN Joe Nathan/324* 5.00 12.00
JT J.R. Towles/400* 5.00 12.00
KG K.Griffey Jr./144* 75.00 150.00
KM Kyle McClellan/390* 6.00 15.00
KS Kelly Shoppach/494* 5.00 12.00
KY K.Youkilis/260* 6.00 15.00
LE Jon Lester/270* 10.00 25.00
LJ Jed Lowrie/297* 10.00 25.00
MA Mike Aviles/500* 10.00 25.00
MC Matt Cain/400* 10.00 25.00
MD D.Murphy/385* 6.00 15.00
MG Matt Garza/450* 3.00 8.00
MN N.Markakis/315* 6.00 15.00
MO N.Morgan/385* 8.00 20.00
MR N.Markakis/360* 6.00 15.00
NA Joe Nathan/350* 5.00 12.00
NM N.McLouth/495* 3.00 8.00
PE D.Pedroia/408* 20.00 50.00
RB Ryan Braun/90* 40.00 80.00
RH R.Halladay/110* 40.00 80.00
RJ R.Johnson/21* 50.00 120.00
TT T.Tulowitzki/420* 12.00 30.00
UB B.J. Upton/210* 8.00 20.00
WA Cory Wade/400* 6.00 15.00

2009 SP Authentic Derek Jeter 1993 SP Buyback Autograph

RANDOMLY INSERTED IN PACKS
STATED PRINT RUN 93 SER.#'d SETS
279 Derek Jeter/93 2000.00 3000.00

2009 SP Authentic Pennant Run Heroes

STATED ODDS 1:20 HOBBY
PR1 Alfonso Soriano .60 1.50
PR2 B.J. Upton .60 1.50
PR3 Brad Lidge .40 1.00
PR4 Brandon Webb .60 1.50
PR5 Carlos Quentin .40 1.00
PR6 Chad Billingsley .60 1.50
PR7 Chase Utley .60 1.50
PR8 Chris B. Young .40 1.00
PR9 Clayton Kershaw 2.00 5.00
PR10 Cole Hamels .75 2.00
PR11 David Ortiz 1.00 2.50
PR12 David Price .75 2.00
PR13 Derek Jeter 2.50 6.00
PR14 Evan Longoria .60 1.50
PR15 John Lackey .60 1.50
PR16 Jonathan Papelbon .60 1.50
PR17 Kevin Youkilis .40 1.00
PR18 Lance Berkman .60 1.50
PR19 Magglio Ordonez .60 1.50
PR20 Mariano Rivera 1.25 3.00

2009 SP Authentic Platinum Power

STATED ODDS 1:10 HOBBY
PP1 A.J. Burnett .40 1.00
PP2 Adam Dunn .60 1.50
PP3 Adrian Gonzalez .75 2.00
PP4 Albert Pujols 1.25 3.00
PP5 Alex Rodriguez 1.25 3.00
PP6 Alfonso Soriano .60 1.50
PP7 Brandon Webb .60 1.50
PP8 Bronson Arroyo .40 1.00
PP9 Carlos Delgado .40 1.00
PP10 Carlos Lee .40 1.00
PP11 Carlos Pena .60 1.50
PP12 Carlos Quentin .40 1.00
PP13 CC Sabathia .60 1.50
PP14 Chad Billingsley .60 1.50
PP15 Chase Utley .60 1.50
PP16 Cole Hamels .75 2.00
PP17 Dan Haren .40 1.00
PP18 David Wright .75 2.00
PP19 Edinson Volquez .40 1.00
PP20 Evan Longoria .60 1.50
PP21 Felix Hernandez .60 1.50
PP22 Grady Sizemore .60 1.50
PP23 Ian Kinsler .60 1.50
PP24 Jack Cust .40 1.00
PP25 Jake Peavy .40 1.00
PP26 James Shields .40 1.00
PP27 Jason Bay .60 1.50
PP28 Jason Giambi .40 1.00
PP29 Javier Vazquez .40 1.00
PP30 Jermaine Dye .40 1.00
PP31 Jim Thome .60 1.50
PP32 Joey Votto 1.00 2.50
PP33 Johan Santana .60 1.50
PP34 Josh Beckett .40 1.00
PP35 Josh Hamilton .60 1.50
PP36 Josh Johnson .60 1.50
PP37 Justin Verlander 1.00 2.50
PP38 Lance Berkman .60 1.50
PP39 Manny Ramirez 1.00 2.50
PP40 Mark Teixeira .60 1.50
PP41 Matt Cain .60 1.50
PP42 Miguel Cabrera 1.00 2.50
PP43 Mike Jacobs .40 1.00
PP44 Nick Markakis .75 2.00
PP45 Prince Fielder .60 1.50
PP46 Randy Johnson 1.00 2.50
PP47 Ricky Nolasco .40 1.00
PP48 Roy Halladay .60 1.50
PP49 Roy Oswalt .60 1.50
PP50 Ryan Braun .60 1.50
PP51 Ryan Dempster .40 1.00
PP52 Ryan Howard .75 2.00
PP53 Ryan Ludwick .60 1.50
PP54 Scott Kazmir .40 1.00
PP55 Tim Lincecum .60 1.50
PP56 Ubaldo Jimenez .40 1.00
PP57 Vladimir Guerrero .60 1.50
PP58 Wandy Rodriguez .40 1.00
PP59 Yovani Gallardo .40 1.00
PP60 Zack Greinke .60 1.50

2009 SP Authentic Signatures

OVERALL AUTO ODDS 1:8 HOBBY
SP INFO PROVIDED BY UD
SAN Andy LaRoche SP 8.00 20.00
SAR Aaron Rowand SP 6.00 15.00
SAS Anibal Sanchez SP 3.00 8.00
SCB Chad Billingsley SP 5.00 12.00
SCH Chase Headley SP 4.00 10.00
SCW Cory Wade SP 5.00 12.00
SDB Daric Barton SP 5.00 12.00
SDE David Eckstein SP 8.00 20.00
SDJ Derek Jeter SP 150.00 250.00
SDL Derek Lowe SP 3.00 8.00
SDU Dan Uggla SP 4.00 10.00
SEB Emilio Bonifacio 3.00 8.00
SEJ Edwin Jackson SP 5.00 12.00
SFC Fausto Carmona SP 3.00 8.00
SFJ Jeff Francoeur SP 3.00 8.00
SFL Felipe Lopez SP 3.00 8.00
SGG Greg Golson SP 3.00 8.00
SGP Glen Perkins SP 3.00 8.00
SHE Jeremy Hermida SP 4.00 10.00
SHJ Josh Hamilton SP 12.50 30.00
SJD John Danks SP 4.00 10.00
SJH J.A. Happ 12.50 30.00
SJL John Lackey SP 20.00 50.00
SJM J.Masterson SP 8.00 20.00
SJS Joe Smith 3.00 8.00
SJS James Shields SP 5.00 12.00
SKG Ken Griffey Jr. SP 75.00 150.00
SKS Kurt Suzuki SP 4.00 10.00
SKY Kevin Youkilis SP 8.00 20.00
SLA Adam Lind SP 4.00 10.00
SMA D.Matsuzaka SP 40.00 80.00
SME Mark Ellis SP 3.00 8.00
SMG Matt Garza SP 4.00 10.00
SMU David Murphy SP 3.00 8.00
SNM Nick Markakis SP 15.00 40.00
SNS Nick Swisher SP 12.50 30.00
SRC Ryan Church SP 3.00 8.00
SRM Russell Martin SP 6.00 15.00
SRT Ryan Theriot 5.00 12.00
SSA Jarrod Saltalamacchia SP 3.00 8.00
SSM Sean Marshall 3.00 8.00
SSO Joakim Soria SP 3.00 8.00
STS Takashi Saito SP 20.00 50.00
SVM Victor Martinez SP 6.00 15.00

1996 SPx

This 1996 SPx set (produced by Upper Deck) was issued in one series totalling 60 cards. The one-card packs had a suggested retail price of $3.49. Printed on 32 pt. card stock with Holoview technology and a perimeter diecut design, the set features color player photos with a Holography background on the fronts and decorative foil stamping on the back. Two special cards are included in the set: a Ken Griffey Jr. Commemorative card was inserted one in every 75 packs and a Mike Piazza Tribute card inserted one in every 95 packs. An autographed version of each of these cards was inserted at the rate of one in 2,000.

COMPLETE SET (60) 12.50 30.00
GRIFFEY KG1 STATED ODDS 1:75
PIAZZA MP1 STATED ODDS 1:95
GRIFFEY AUTO STATED ODDS 1:2000
PIAZZA AUTO STATED ODDS 1:2000
1 Greg Maddux 1.25 3.00
2 Chipper Jones .75 2.00
3 Fred McGriff .50 1.25
4 Tom Glavine .50 1.25
5 Cal Ripken 2.50 6.00
6 Roberto Alomar .50 1.25
7 Rafael Palmeiro .50 1.25
8 Jose Canseco .50 1.25
9 Roger Clemens 1.50 4.00
10 Mo Vaughn .30 .75
11 Jim Edmonds .30 .75
12 Tim Salmon .50 1.25
13 Sammy Sosa .75 2.00
14 Ryne Sandberg 1.25 3.00
15 Mark Grace .50 1.25
16 Frank Thomas .75 2.00
17 Barry Larkin .50 1.25
18 Kenny Lofton .30 .75
19 Albert Belle .30 .75
20 Eddie Murray .75 2.00
21 Manny Ramirez .50 1.25
22 Dante Bichette .30 .75
23 Larry Walker .30 .75
24 Vinny Castilla .30 .75
25 Andres Galarraga .30 .75
26 Cecil Fielder .30 .75
27 Gary Sheffield .30 .75
28 Craig Biggio .50 1.25
29 Jeff Bagwell .50 1.25
30 Derek Bell .30 .75
31 Johnny Damon .50 1.25
32 Eric Karros .30 .75
33 Mike Piazza 1.25 3.00
34 Raul Mondesi .30 .75
35 Hideo Nomo .75 2.00
36 Kirby Puckett .75 2.00
37 Paul Molitor .30 .75
38 Marty Cordova .30 .75
39 Rondell White .30 .75
40 Jason Isringhausen .30 .75
41 Paul Wilson .30 .75
42 Rey Ordonez .30 .75
43 Derek Jeter 2.00 5.00
44 Wade Boggs .50 1.25
45 Mark McGwire 2.00 5.00
46 Jason Kendall .30 .75
47 Ron Gant .30 .75
48 Ozzie Smith 1.25 3.00
49 Tony Gwynn 1.00 2.50
50 Ken Caminiti .30 .75
51 Barry Bonds 2.00 5.00
52 Matt Williams .30 .75
53 Osvaldo Fernandez .30 .75
54 Jay Buhner .30 .75
55 Ken Griffey Jr. 1.50 4.00
56 Randy Johnson .75 2.00
57 Alex Rodriguez 1.50 4.00
58 Juan Gonzalez .30 .75
59 Joe Carter .30 .75
60 Carlos Delgado .30 .75
KG1 Ken Griffey Jr. Comm. 2.50 6.00
MP1 Mike Piazza Trib. 2.00 5.00
KGA1 Ken Griffey Jr. Auto. 60.00 120.00
MPA1 Mike Piazza Auto. 60.00 120.00
KG Ken Griffey Jr. Promo 1.25 3.00

1996 SPx Gold

*STARS: 1.25X TO 3X BASIC CARDS
STATED ODDS 1:7

1996 SPx Bound for Glory

Randomly inserted in packs at a rate of one in 24, this 10-card set features players with a chance to be long remembered.

COMPLETE SET (10) 30.00 80.00
STATED ODDS 1:24
1 Ken Griffey Jr. 4.00 10.00
2 Frank Thomas 2.00 5.00
3 Barry Bonds 5.00 12.00
4 Cal Ripken 6.00 15.00
5 Greg Maddux 3.00 8.00
6 Chipper Jones 2.00 5.00
7 Roberto Alomar 1.25 3.00
8 Manny Ramirez 1.25 3.00
9 Tony Gwynn 2.50 6.00
10 Mike Piazza 3.00 8.00

1997 SPx

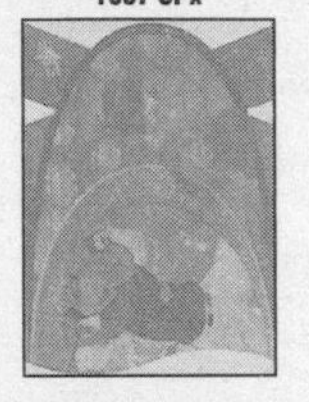

The 1997 SPx set (produced by Upper Deck) was issued in one series totalling 50 cards and was distributed in three-card hobby only packs with a suggested retail price of $5.99. The fronts feature color player images on a Holoview perimeter die cut design. The backs carry a player photo, player information, and career statistics. A sample card featuring Ken Griffey Jr. was distributed to dealers and hobby media several weeks prior to the products release.

COMPLETE SET (50) 20.00 50.00
1 Eddie Murray .60 1.50
2 Darin Erstad .25 .60
3 Tim Salmon .40 1.00
4 Andruw Jones .40 1.00
5 Chipper Jones .60 1.50
6 John Smoltz .40 1.00
7 Greg Maddux 1.00 2.50
8 Kenny Lofton .25 .60
9 Roberto Alomar .25 .60
10 Rafael Palmeiro .40 1.00
11 Brady Anderson .25 .60
12 Cal Ripken 2.00 5.00
13 Nomar Garciaparra 1.00 2.50
14 Mo Vaughn .25 .60
15 Ryne Sandberg 1.00 2.50
16 Sammy Sosa .60 1.50
17 Frank Thomas .60 1.50
18 Albert Belle .25 .60
19 Barry Larkin .40 1.00
20 Deion Sanders .40 1.00
21 Manny Ramirez .40 1.00
22 Jim Thome .40 1.00
23 Dante Bichette .25 .60
24 Andres Galarraga .25 .60
25 Larry Walker .25 .60
26 Gary Sheffield .25 .60
27 Jeff Bagwell .40 1.00
28 Raul Mondesi .25 .60
29 Hideo Nomo .60 1.50
30 Mike Piazza 1.00 2.50
31 Paul Molitor .25 .60
32 Todd Walker .25 .60
33 Vladimir Guerrero .60 1.50
34 Todd Hundley .25 .60
35 Andy Pettitte .40 1.00
36 Derek Jeter 1.50 4.00
37 Jose Canseco .40 1.00
38 Mark McGwire 1.50 4.00
39 Scott Rolen .40 1.00
40 Ron Gant .25 .60
41 Ken Caminiti .25 .60
42 Tony Gwynn .75 2.00
43 Barry Bonds 1.50 4.00
44 Jay Buhner .25 .60
45 Ken Griffey Jr. 1.25 3.00
46 Alex Rodriguez 1.00 2.50
47 Jose Cruz Jr. RC .40 1.00
48 Juan Gonzalez .25 .60
49 Ivan Rodriguez .40 1.00
50 Roger Clemens 1.25 3.00
S45 Ken Griffey Jr. Sample 1.00 2.50

1997 SPx Bronze

COMPLETE SET (50) 75.00 150.00
*STARS: 1X TO 2.5X BASIC CARDS
*ROOKIES: .6X TO 1.5X BASIC CARDS
RANDOM INSERTS IN PACKS

1997 SPx Gold

*STARS: 2.5X TO 6X BASIC CARDS
*ROOKIES: 1.5X TO 4X BASIC CARDS
STATED ODDS 1:17

1997 SPx Grand Finale

*STARS: 12.5X TO 30X BASIC CARDS
*ROOKIES: 5X TO 12X BASIC CARDS
RANDOM INSERTS IN PACKS
STATED PRINT RUN 50 SETS

1997 SPx Silver

*STARS: 1.5X TO 4X BASIC CARDS
*ROOKIES: 1X TO 2.5X BASIC CARDS
RANDOM INSERTS IN PACKS

1997 SPx Steel

COMPLETE SET (50) 40.00 100.00
*STARS: .6X TO 1.5X BASIC CARDS
*ROOKIES: .5X TO 1.2X BASIC CARDS
RANDOM INSERTS IN PACKS

1997 SPx Bound for Glory

Randomly inserted in packs, this 20-card set features color photos of promising great players on a Holoview die cut card design. Only 1,500 of each card was produced and are sequentially numbered.

COMPLETE SET (20) 40.00 100.00
RANDOM INSERTS IN PACKS
STATED PRINT RUN 1500 SERIAL #'d SETS
1 Andruw Jones 1.00 2.50
2 Chipper Jones 2.50 6.00
3 Greg Maddux 4.00 10.00
4 Kenny Lofton 1.00 2.50
5 Cal Ripken 8.00 20.00
6 Mo Vaughn 1.00 2.50
7 Frank Thomas 2.50 6.00
8 Albert Belle 1.00 2.50
9 Manny Ramirez 1.50 4.00
10 Gary Sheffield 1.00 2.50
11 Jeff Bagwell 1.50 4.00
12 Mike Piazza 2.50 6.00
13 Derek Jeter 6.00 15.00
14 Mark McGwire 4.00 10.00
15 Tony Gwynn 2.50 6.00
16 Ken Caminiti 1.00 2.50
17 Barry Bonds 4.00 10.00
18 Alex Rodriguez 3.00 8.00
19 Ken Griffey Jr. 5.00 12.00
20 Juan Gonzalez 1.00 2.50

1997 SPx Bound for Glory Supreme Signatures

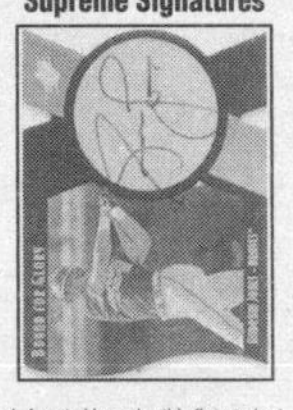

Randomly inserted in packs, this five-card set features unnumbered autographed Bound for Glory cards. Only 250 of each card was produced and signed and are sequentially numbered. The cards are checklisted below in alphabetical order.

RANDOM INSERTS IN PACKS
STATED PRINT RUN 250 SERIAL #'d SETS
1 Jeff Bagwell 40.00 80.00
2 Ken Griffey Jr. 75.00 150.00
3 Andruw Jones 10.00 25.00
4 Alex Rodriguez 50.00 120.00
5 Gary Sheffield 10.00 25.00

1997 SPx Cornerstones of the Game

Randomly inserted in packs, cards from this 10-card set display color photos of 20 top players. Two players are featured on each card using double Holoview technology. Only 500 of each card was produced and each is sequentially numbered on back.

COMPLETE SET (10) 50.00 100.00
RANDOM INSERTS IN PACKS
STATED PRINT RUN 500 SERIAL #'d SETS
1 K.Griffey Jr. 8.00 20.00
B.Bonds
2 F.Thomas 4.00 10.00
A.Belle
3 G.Maddux 6.00 15.00
C.Jones
4 T.Gwynn 4.00 10.00
P.Molitor
5 V.Guerrero 2.50 6.00
A.Jones
6 J.Bagwell 6.00 15.00
R.Sandberg
7 M.Piazza 4.00 10.00
I.Rodriguez
8 C.Ripken 12.00 30.00
E.Murray
9 M.McGwire 6.00 15.00
M.Vaughn
10 A.Rodriguez 10.00 25.00
D.Jeter

1998 SPx Finite Sample

A special Ken Griffey Jr. card serial numbered of 10,000 was issued as a promotional card and distributed within a silver foil wrapper along with a black and white information card to dealers with their first series order forms and at major industry events. The card is similar to Griffey's basic issue first series SPx Finite card (number 130) except for the lack of a card number on back, serial numbering to 10,000 coupled with the word "FINITE" running boldly across the back of the card in a diagonal manner.

1 Ken Griffey Jr. 2.50 6.00
2 Ken Griffey Jr. 2.50 6.00

1998 SPx Finite

The 1998 SPx Finite set contains a total of 180 cards, all serial numbered based upon specific subsets. The three-card packs retailed for $5.99 each and hit the market in June, 1998. The subsets and serial numbering are as follows: Youth Movement (1-30) - 5000 of each card, Power Explosion (31-50) - 4000 of each card, Basic Cards (51-140) - 9000 of each card, Star Focus (141-170) - 7000 of each card, Heroes of the Game (171-180) - 2000 of each card, Youth Movement (181-210) - 5000 of each card, Power Passion (211-240) - 7000 of each card, Basic Cards (241-330) - 9000 of each card, Tradewinds (331-350) - 4000 of each card and Cornerstones of the Game (351-360) -2000 of each card. Notable Rookie Cards include Kevin Millwood and Magglio Ordonez.

COMP.YM SER.1 (30) 8.00 20.00
COMMON YM (1-30) .30 .75
YM 1-30 PRINT RUN 5000 SERIAL #'d SETS
COMP.PE SER.1 (20) 8.00 20.00
COMMON PE (31-50) .30 .75
PE 31-50 PRINT RUN 4000 SERIAL #'d SETS
COMP.BASIC SER.1 (90) 20.00 50.00
COMMON CARD (51-140) .25 .60
BASIC 51-140 PR.RUN 9000 SERIAL #'d SETS
COMP.SF SER.1 (30) 12.00 30.00
COMMON SF (141-170) .25 .60
SF 141-170 PRINT RUN 7000 SERIAL #'d SETS
COMP.HG SER.1 (10) 10.00 25.00
COMMON HG (171-180) .40 1.00
HG 171-180 PRINT RUN 2000 #'d SETS
COMP.YM SER.2 (30) 8.00 20.00
COMMON YM (181-210) .30 .75
YM 181-210 PR.RUN 5000 SERIAL #'d SETS
COMP.PP SER.2 (30) 8.00 20.00
COMMON PP (211-240) .25 .60
PP 211-240 PRINT RUN 7000 SERIAL #'d SETS
COMP.BASIC SER.2 (90) 15.00 40.00
COMMON CARD (241-330) .25 .60
BASIC 241-330 PR.RUN 9000 SERIAL #'d SETS
COMP.TW SER.2 (20) 5.00 12.00
COMMON TW (331-350) .30 .75
TW 331-350 PR.RUN 4000 SERIAL #'d SETS
COMP.CG SER.2 (10) 8.00 20.00
COMMON CG (351-360) .40 1.00
CG 351-360 PRINT RUN 2000 #'d SETS
1 Nomar Garciaparra YM .50 1.25
2 Miguel Tejada YM .75 2.00
3 Mike Cameron YM .30 .75
4 Ken Cloude YM .30 .75
5 Jaret Wright YM .30 .75
6 Mark Kotsay YM .30 .75
7 Craig Counsell YM .30 .75
8 Jose Guillen YM .30 .75
9 Neifi Perez YM .30 .75
10 Jose Cruz Jr. YM .30 .75
11 Brett Tomko YM .30 .75
12 Matt Morris YM .30 .75
13 Justin Thompson YM .30 .75
14 Jeremi Gonzalez YM .30 .75
15 Scott Rolen YM .50 1.25
16 Vladimir Guerrero YM .50 1.25
17 Brad Fullmer YM .30 .75
18 Brian Giles YM .30 .75
19 Todd Dunwoody YM .30 .75
20 Ben Grieve YM .30 .75
21 Juan Encarnacion YM .30 .75
22 Aaron Boone YM .30 .75
23 Richie Sexson YM .30 .75
24 Richard Hidalgo YM .30 .75
25 Andruw Jones YM .30 .75
26 Todd Helton YM .50 1.25
27 Paul Konerko YM .30 .75
28 Dante Powell YM .30 .75
29 Eli Marrero YM .30 .75
30 Derek Jeter YM 2.00 5.00
31 Mike Piazza PE .75 2.00
32 Tony Clark PE .30 .75
33 Larry Walker PE .50 1.25
34 Jim Thome PE .50 1.25
35 Juan Gonzalez PE .30 .75
36 Jeff Bagwell PE .50 1.25
37 Jay Buhner PE .30 .75
38 Tim Salmon PE .30 .75
39 Albert Belle PE .30 .75
40 Mark McGwire PE 1.25 3.00
41 Sammy Sosa PE .75 2.00
42 Mo Vaughn PE .30 .75
43 Manny Ramirez PE .75 2.00
44 Tino Martinez PE .30 .75
45 Frank Thomas PE .75 2.00
46 Nomar Garciaparra PE .50 1.25
47 Alex Rodriguez PE 1.00 2.50
48 Chipper Jones PE .75 2.00
49 Barry Bonds PE 1.25 3.00
50 Ken Griffey Jr. PE 1.50 4.00
51 Jason Dickson .25 .60
52 Jim Edmonds .40 1.00
53 Darin Erstad .25 .60
54 Tim Salmon .25 .60
55 Chipper Jones .60 1.50
56 Ryan Klesko .25 .60
57 Tom Glavine .40 1.00
58 Denny Neagle .25 .60
59 John Smoltz .40 1.00
60 Javy Lopez .25 .60
61 Roberto Alomar .40 1.00
62 Rafael Palmeiro .40 1.00
63 Mike Mussina .40 1.00
64 Cal Ripken 2.00 5.00
65 Mo Vaughn .25 .60
66 Tim Naehring .25 .60
67 John Valentin .25 .60
68 Mark Grace .40 1.00
69 Kevin Orie .25 .60
70 Sammy Sosa .60 1.50
71 Albert Belle .25 .60
72 Frank Thomas .60 1.50
73 Robin Ventura .25 .60
74 David Justice .25 .60
75 Kenny Lofton .25 .60
76 Omar Vizquel .40 1.00
77 Manny Ramirez .60 1.50
78 Jim Thome .40 1.00
79 Dante Bichette .25 .60
80 Larry Walker .40 1.00
81 Vinny Castilla .25 .60
82 Ellis Burks .25 .60
83 Bobby Higginson .25 .60
84 Brian Hunter .25 .60
85 Tony Clark .25 .60
86 Mike Hampton .25 .60
87 Jeff Bagwell .40 1.00
88 Craig Biggio .40 1.00
89 Derek Bell .25 .60
90 Mike Piazza .60 1.50
91 Ramon Martinez .25 .60
92 Raul Mondesi .25 .60
93 Hideo Nomo .60 1.50
94 Eric Karros .25 .60
95 Paul Molitor .60 1.50
96 Marty Cordova .25 .60
97 Brad Radke .25 .60
98 Mark Grudzielanek .25 .60
99 Carlos Perez .25 .60
100 Rondell White .25 .60
101 Todd Hundley .25 .60
102 Edgardo Alfonzo .25 .60
103 John Franco .25 .60
104 John Olerud .25 .60
105 Tino Martinez .25 .60
106 David Cone .25 .60
107 Paul O'Neill .40 1.00
108 Andy Pettitte .40 1.00
109 Bernie Williams .40 1.00
110 Rickey Henderson .60 1.50
111 Jason Giambi .25 .60
112 Matt Stairs .25 .60
113 Gregg Jefferies .25 .60
114 Rico Brogna .25 .60
115 Curt Schilling .40 1.00
116 Jason Schmidt .25 .60
117 Jose Guillen .25 .60
118 Kevin Young .25 .60
119 Ray Lankford .25 .60
120 Mark McGwire 1.00 2.50
121 Delino DeShields .25 .60
122 Ken Caminiti .25 .60
123 Tony Gwynn .60 1.50
124 Trevor Hoffman .40 1.00
125 Barry Bonds 1.00 2.50
126 Jeff Kent .25 .60
127 Shawn Estes .25 .60
128 J.T. Snow .25 .60
129 Jay Buhner .25 .60
130 Ken Griffey Jr. 1.25 3.00
131 Dan Wilson .25 .60
132 Edgar Martinez .40 1.00
133 Alex Rodriguez .75 2.00
134 Rusty Greer .25 .60
135 Juan Gonzalez .25 .60
136 Fernando Tatis .25 .60
137 Ivan Rodriguez .40 1.00
138 Carlos Delgado .25 .60
139 Pat Hentgen .25 .60
140 Roger Clemens .75 2.00
141 Chipper Jones SF .60 1.50
142 Greg Maddux SF .75 2.00
143 Rafael Palmeiro SF .40 1.00
144 Mike Mussina SF .40 1.00
145 Cal Ripken SF 2.00 5.00
146 Nomar Garciaparra SF .40 1.00
147 Mo Vaughn SF .25 .60
148 Sammy Sosa SF .60 1.50
149 Albert Belle SF .25 .60
150 Frank Thomas SF .60 1.50
151 Jim Thome SF .40 1.00
152 Kenny Lofton SF .25 .60
153 Manny Ramirez SF .60 1.50
154 Larry Walker SF .40 1.00
155 Jeff Bagwell SF .40 1.00
156 Craig Biggio SF .40 1.00
157 Mike Piazza SF .60 1.50
158 Paul Molitor SF .60 1.50
159 Derek Jeter SF 1.50 4.00
160 Tino Martinez SF .25 .60
161 Curt Schilling SF .40 1.00
162 Mark McGwire SF 1.00 2.50
163 Tony Gwynn SF .60 1.50
164 Barry Bonds SF 1.00 2.50
165 Ken Griffey Jr. SF 1.25 3.00
166 Randy Johnson SF .60 1.50
167 Alex Rodriguez SF .75 2.00
168 Juan Gonzalez SF .25 .60
169 Ivan Rodriguez SF .40 1.00
170 Roger Clemens SF .75 2.00
171 Greg Maddux HG 1.25 3.00
172 Cal Ripken HG 3.00 8.00
173 Frank Thomas HG 1.00 2.50
174 Jeff Bagwell HG .60 1.50
175 Mike Piazza HG 1.00 2.50
176 Mark McGwire HG 1.50 4.00
177 Barry Bonds HG 1.50 4.00
178 Ken Griffey Jr. HG 2.00 5.00
179 Alex Rodriguez HG 1.25 3.00
180 Roger Clemens HG 1.25 3.00
181 Mike Caruso YM .30 .75
182 David Ortiz YM 1.00 2.50
183 Gabe Alvarez YM .30 .75
184 Gary Matthews Jr. YM RC .30 .75
185 Kerry Wood YM .30 .75
186 Carl Pavano YM .30 .75
187 Alex Gonzalez YM .30 .75
188 Masato Yoshii YM RC .30 .75
189 Larry Sutton YM .30 .75
190 Russell Branyan YM .30 .75
191 Bruce Chen YM .30 .75
192 Rolando Arrojo YM RC .30 .75
193 Ryan Christenson YM RC .30 .75
194 Cliff Politte YM .30 .75
195 A.J. Hinch YM .30 .75
196 Kevin Witt YM .30 .75
197 Daryle Ward YM .30 .75
198 Corey Koskie YM RC .30 .75
199 Mike Lowell YM RC 3.00 8.00
200 Travis Lee YM .30 .75
201 Kevin Millwood YM RC .75 2.00
202 Robert Smith YM .30 .75
203 Magglio Ordonez YM RC 1.25 3.00
204 Eric Milton YM .30 .75
205 Geoff Jenkins YM .30 .75
206 Rich Butler YM RC .30 .75
207 Mike Kinkade YM RC .30 .75
208 Braden Looper YM .30 .75
209 Matt Clement YM .30 .75
210 Derrek Lee YM .30 .75
211 Randy Johnson PP .60 1.50
212 John Smoltz PP .40 1.00
213 Roger Clemens PP .75 2.00
214 Curt Schilling PP .40 1.00
215 Pedro Martinez PP .40 1.00
216 Vinny Castilla PP .25 .60
217 Jose Cruz Jr. PP .25 .60
218 Jim Thome PP .40 1.00
219 Alex Rodriguez PP .75 2.00
220 Frank Thomas PP .60 1.50
221 Tim Salmon PP .25 .60
222 Larry Walker PP .40 1.00
223 Albert Belle PP .25 .60
224 Manny Ramirez PP .60 1.50
225 Mark McGwire PP 1.00 2.50
226 Mo Vaughn PP .25 .60
227 Andres Galarraga PP .40 1.00
228 Scott Rolen PP .40 1.00
229 Travis Lee PP .25 .60
230 Mike Piazza PP .60 1.50
231 Nomar Garciaparra PP .40 1.00
232 Andruw Jones PP .25 .60
233 Barry Bonds PP 1.00 2.50
234 Jeff Bagwell PP .40 1.00
235 Juan Gonzalez PP .25 .60
236 Tino Martinez PP .25 .60
237 Vladimir Guerrero PP .40 1.00
238 Rafael Palmeiro PP .40 1.00
239 Russell Branyan PP .25 .60
240 Ken Griffey Jr. PP 1.25 3.00
241 Cecil Fielder .25 .60
242 Chuck Finley .25 .60
243 Jay Bell .25 .60
244 Andy Benes .25 .60
245 Matt Williams .25 .60
246 Brian Anderson .25 .60
247 Dave Dellucci RC .40 1.00
248 Andres Galarraga .40 1.
249 Andruw Jones .25
250 Greg Maddux .75 2.
251 Brady Anderson .25
252 Joe Carter .25
253 Eric Davis .25
254 Pedro Martinez .40 1.
255 Nomar Garciaparra .40 1.
256 Dennis Eckersley .40 1.
257 Henry Rodriguez .25
258 Jeff Blauser .25
259 Jaime Navarro .25
260 Ray Durham .25
261 Chris Stynes .25
262 Willie Greene .25
263 Reggie Sanders .25
264 Bret Boone .25
265 Barry Larkin .40 1.
266 Travis Fryman .25
267 Charles Nagy .25
268 Sandy Alomar Jr. .25
269 Darryl Kile .25
270 Mike Lansing .25
271 Pedro Astacio .25
272 Damion Easley .25
273 Joe Randa .25
274 Luis Gonzalez .25
275 Mike Piazza .60 1.
276 Todd Zeile .25
277 Edgar Renteria .25
278 Livan Hernandez .25
279 Cliff Floyd .25
280 Moises Alou .25
281 Billy Wagner .25
282 Jeff King .25
283 Hal Morris .25
284 Johnny Damon .40 1.
285 Dean Palmer .25
286 Tim Belcher .25
287 Eric Young .25
288 Bobby Bonilla .25
289 Gary Sheffield .25
290 Chan Ho Park .40 1.0
291 Charles Johnson .25
292 Jeff Cirillo .25
293 Jeromy Burnitz .25
294 Jose Valentin .25
295 Marquis Grissom .25 .6
296 Todd Walker .25 .6
297 Terry Steinbach .25 .6
298 Rick Aguilera .25 .6
299 Vladimir Guerrero .40 1.0
300 Rey Ordonez .25
301 Butch Huskey .25
302 Bernard Gilkey .25 .6
303 Mariano Rivera .40 1.0
304 Chuck Knoblauch .25 .6
305 Derek Jeter 1.50 4.0
306 Ricky Bottalico .25 .6
307 Bob Abreu .25 .6
308 Scott Rolen .40 1.0
309 Al Martin .25 .6
310 Jason Kendall .25 .6
311 Brian Jordan .25 .6
312 Ron Gant .25 .6
313 Todd Stottlemyre .25 .6
314 Greg Vaughn .25 .6
315 Kevin Brown .25 .6
316 Wally Joyner .25 .6
317 Robb Nen .25 .6
318 Orel Hershiser .25 .6
319 Russ Davis .25 .6
320 Randy Johnson .60 1.5
321 Quinton McCracken .25 .6
322 Tony Saunders .25 .6
323 Wilson Alvarez .25 .6
324 Wade Boggs .40 1.0
325 Fred McGriff .40 1.0
326 Lee Stevens .25 .6
327 John Wetteland .25 .6
328 Jose Canseco .40 1.0
329 Randy Myers .25 .6
330 Jose Cruz Jr. .25 .6
331 Matt Williams TW .30 .75
332 Andres Galarraga TW .50 1.25
333 Walt Weiss TW .30 .75
334 Joe Carter TW .30 .75
335 Pedro Martinez TW .50 1.25
336 Henry Rodriguez TW .30 .75
337 Travis Fryman TW .30 .75
338 Darryl Kile TW .30 .75
339 Mike Lansing TW .30 .75
340 Mike Piazza TW .75 2.00
341 Moises Alou TW .30 .75
342 Charles Johnson TW .30 .75
343 Chuck Knoblauch TW .30 .75
344 Rickey Henderson TW .75 2.00
345 Kevin Brown TW .30 .75
346 Orel Hershiser TW .30 .75
347 Wade Boggs TW .50 1.25
348 Fred McGriff TW .50 1.25
349 Jose Canseco TW .50 1.25
350 Gary Sheffield TW .30 .75
351 Travis Lee CG .40 1.00
352 Nomar Garciaparra CG .60 1.50
353 Frank Thomas CG 1.00 2.50
354 Cal Ripken CG 3.00 8.00
355 Mark McGwire CG 1.50 4.00
356 Mike Piazza CG 1.00 2.50
357 Alex Rodriguez CG 1.25 3.00
358 Barry Bonds CG 1.50 4.00
359 Tony Gwynn CG 1.00 2.50
360 Ken Griffey Jr. CG 2.00 5.00

1998 SPx Finite Radiance

*YM RADIANCE: .5X TO 1.2X BASIC YM
YM 1-30 PRINT RUN 2500 SERIAL #'d SETS
*PE RADIANCE: .6X TO 1.5X BASIC PE
PE 31-50 PRINT RUN 1000 SERIAL #'d SETS
EXCH.CARDS MADE FOR #'s 39/40/41/46
EXCHANGE DEADLINE WAS 6/2/99
*BASIC RADIANCE: .5X TO 1.22X BASIC CARDS
BASIC 51-140 PR.RUN 4500 SERIAL #'d SETS
*SF RADIANCE: .5X TO 1.2X BASIC SF
SF 141-170 PRINT RUN 3500 SERIAL #'d SETS
*HG RADIANCE: 4X TO 10X BASIC HG
HG 171-180 PRINT RUN 100 SERIAL #'d SETS
*YM RADIANCE: .5X TO 1.2X BASIC YM
*YM RADIANCE RC's: .5X TO 1.2X BASIC YM
YM 181-210 PR.RUN 2500 SERIAL #'d SETS
*PP RADIANCE: .5X TO 1.2X BASIC PP
PP 211-240 PRINT RUN 3500 SERIAL #'d SETS
*BASIC RADIANCE: .5X TO 1.2X BASIC CARDS
BASIC 241-330 PR.RUN 4500 SERIAL #'d SETS
*TW RADIANCE: .6X TO 1.5X BASIC TW
TW 331-350 PR.RUN 1000 SERIAL #'d SETS
*CG RADIANCE: 4X TO 10X BASIC CG
CG 351-360 PRINT RUN 100 SERIAL #'d SETS
RANDOM INSERTS IN PACKS

1998 SPx Finite Spectrum

*YM SPECTRUM: 1X TO 2.5X BASIC YM
YM 1-30 PRINT RUN 1250 SERIAL #'d SETS
*PE SPECTRUM: 5X TO 12X BASIC PE
PE 31-50 PRINT RUN 50 SERIAL #'d SETS
*BASIC SPECTRUM: 1.25X TO 3X BASIC
BASIC 51-140 PR.RUN 2250 SERIAL #'d SETS
*SF SPECTRUM: 1.25X TO 3X BASIC SF
SF 141-170 PRINT RUN 1750 SERIAL #'d SETS
HG 171-180 PRINT RUN 1 SERIAL #'d SET
HG NOT PRICED DUE TO SCARCITY
*YM SPECTRUM: .75X TO 2X BASIC YM
*YM SPEC. RC's: .5X TO 1.2X BASIC YM
YM 181-210 PR.RUN 1250 SERIAL #'d SETS
*PP SPECTRUM: 1.25X TO 3X BASIC PP
PP 211-240 PRINT RUN 1750 SERIAL #'d SETS
*BASIC SPECTRUM: 1.25X TO 3X BASIC
BASIC 241-330 PR.RUN 2250 SERIAL #'d SETS
*TW SPECTRUM: 5X TO 12X BASIC TW
TW 331-350 PRINT RUN 50 SERIAL #'d SETS
CG 351-360 PRINT RUN 1 SERIAL #'d SET
CG NOT PRICED DUE TO SCARCITY
RANDOM INSERTS IN PACKS

1998 SPx Finite Home Run Hysteria

Randomly seeded exclusively into second series packs, these ten different inserts chronicle the epic home run race of the 1998 season. Each card is serial numbered to 62 on back.

RANDOM INSERTS IN SER.2 PACKS
STATED PRINT RUN 62 SERIAL #'d SETS
HR1 Ken Griffey Jr. 150.00 400.00
HR2 Mark McGwire 30.00 80.00
HR3 Sammy Sosa 20.00 50.00
HR4 Albert Belle 8.00 20.00
HR5 Alex Rodriguez 25.00 60.00
HR6 Greg Vaughn 8.00 20.00
HR7 Andres Galarraga 12.00 30.00
HR8 Vinny Castilla 8.00 20.00
HR9 Juan Gonzalez 8.00 20.00
HR10 Chipper Jones 20.00 50.00

1999 SPx

The 1999 SPx set (produced by Upper Deck) was issued in one series for a total of 120 cards and distributed in thee-card packs with a suggested retail price of $5.99. The set features color photos of 80 MLB verteran players (1-80) with 40 top rookies on subset cards (81-120) numbered to 1,999. J.D. Drew and Gabe Kapler autographed all 1,999 of their respective rookie cards. A Ken Griffey Jr. Sample card was distributed to dealers and hobby media several weeks prior to the product's release. This card is serial numbered "0000/0000" on front, has the word "SAMPLE" pasted across the back in red ink and is oddly numbered "24 East" on back (even though the basic cards have no regional references). Also, 350 Willie Mays A Piece of History 500 Home Run bat cards were randomly seeded into packs. Mays personally signed an additional 24 cards (matching his jersey number) - all of which were then serial numbered by hand and randomly seeded into packs. Pricing for these bat cards can be referenced under 1999 Upper Deck A Piece of History 500 Club.

COMP.SET w/o SP's (80) 10.00 25.00
COMMON MCGWIRE (1-10) .60 1.50
COMMON CARD (11-80) .20 .50
COMMON SP (81-120) 4.00 10.00
81-120 RANDOM INSERTS IN PACKS
81-120 PRINT RUN 1999 SERIAL #'d SETS
W.MAYS BAT LISTED W/UD APH 500 CLUB
1 Mark McGwire 61 1.25 3.00
2 Mark McGwire 62 1.25 3.00
3 Mark McGwire 63 .60 1.50
4 Mark McGwire 64 .60 1.50
5 Mark McGwire 65 .60 1.50
6 Mark McGwire 66 .60 1.50
7 Mark McGwire 67 .60 1.50
8 Mark McGwire 68 .60 1.50
9 Mark McGwire 69 .60 1.50
10 Mark McGwire 70 1.50 4.00
11 Mo Vaughn .20 .50
12 Darin Erstad .20 .50
13 Travis Lee .20 .50
14 Randy Johnson .50 1.25
15 Matt Williams .20 .50
16 Chipper Jones .50 1.25
17 Greg Maddux .75 2.00
18 Andruw Jones .30 .75
19 Andres Galarraga .20 .50
20 Cal Ripken 1.50 4.00
21 Albert Belle .20 .50
22 Mike Mussina .30 .75
23 Nomar Garciaparra .75 2.00
24 Pedro Martinez .30 .75
25 John Valentin .20 .50
26 Kerry Wood .20 .50
27 Sammy Sosa .50 1.25
28 Mark Grace .30 .75
29 Frank Thomas .50 1.25
30 Mike Caruso .20 .50
31 Barry Larkin .30 .75
32 Sean Casey .20 .50
33 Jim Thome .30 .75
34 Kenny Lofton .20 .50
35 Manny Ramirez .30 .75
36 Larry Walker .20 .50
37 Todd Helton .30 .75
38 Vinny Castilla .20 .50
39 Tony Clark .20 .50
40 Derrek Lee .30 .75
41 Mark Kotsay .20 .50
42 Jeff Bagwell .30 .75
43 Craig Biggio .30 .75
44 Moises Alou .20 .50
45 Larry Sutton .20 .50
46 Johnny Damon .30 .75
47 Gary Sheffield .20 .50
48 Raul Mondesi .20 .50
49 Jeromy Burnitz .20 .50
50 Todd Walker .20 .50
51 David Ortiz .50 1.25
52 Vladimir Guerrero .50 1.25
53 Rondell White .20 .50
54 Mike Piazza .75 2.00
55 Derek Jeter 1.25 3.00
56 Tino Martinez .30 .75
57 Roger Clemens 1.00 2.50
58 Ben Grieve .20 .50
59 A.J. Hinch .20 .50
60 Scott Rolen .30 .75
61 Doug Glanville .20 .50
62 Aramis Ramirez .20 .50
63 Jose Guillen .20 .50
64 Tony Gwynn .60 1.50
65 Greg Vaughn .20 .50
66 Ruben Rivera .20 .50
67 Barry Bonds 1.25 3.00
68 J.T. Snow .20 .50
69 Alex Rodriguez .75 2.00
70 Ken Griffey Jr. 1.00 2.50
71 Jay Buhner .20 .50
72 Mark McGwire 1.25 3.00
73 Fernando Tatis .20 .50
74 Quinton McCracken .20 .50
75 Wade Boggs .30 .75
76 Ivan Rodriguez .30 .75
77 Juan Gonzalez .20 .50
78 Rafael Palmeiro .30 .75
79 Jose Cruz Jr. .20 .50
80 Carlos Delgado .20 .50
81 Troy Glaus SP 6.00 15.00
82 Vladimir Nunez SP 4.00 10.00
83 George Lombard SP 4.00 10.00
84 Bruce Chen SP 4.00 10.00
85 Ryan Minor SP 4.00 10.00
86 Calvin Pickering SP 4.00 10.00
87 Jin Ho Cho SP 4.00 10.00
88 Russ Branyan SP 4.00 10.00
89 Derrick Gibson SP 4.00 10.00
90 Gabe Kapler SP AU 6.00 15.00
91 Matt Anderson SP 4.00 10.00
92 Robert Fick SP 4.00 10.00
93 Juan Encarnacion SP 4.00 10.00
94 Preston Wilson SP 4.00 10.00
95 Alex Gonzalez SP 4.00 10.00
96 Carlos Beltran SP 6.00 15.00
97 Jeremy Giambi SP 4.00 10.00
98 Dee Brown SP 4.00 10.00
99 Adrian Beltre SP 4.00 10.00
100 Alex Cora SP 4.00 10.00
101 Angel Pena SP 4.00 10.00
102 Geoff Jenkins SP 4.00 10.00
103 Ronnie Belliard SP 4.00 10.00
104 Corey Koskie SP 4.00 10.00
105 A.J. Pierzynski SP 4.00 10.00
106 Michael Barrett SP 4.00 10.00
107 Fernando Seguignol SP 4.00 10.00
108 Mike Kinkade SP 4.00 10.00
109 Mike Lowell SP 4.00 10.00
110 Ricky Ledee SP 4.00 10.00
111 Eric Chavez SP 4.00 10.00
112 Abraham Nunez SP 4.00 10.00
113 Matt Clement SP 4.00 10.00
114 Ben Davis SP 4.00 10.00
115 Mike Darr SP 4.00 10.00
116 Ramon E.Martinez SP RC 4.00 10.00
117 Carlos Guillen SP 4.00 10.00
118 Shane Monahan SP 4.00 10.00
119 J.D. Drew SP AU 4.00 10.00
120 Kevin Witt SP 4.00 10.00
24EAST Ken Griffey Jr. Sample 1.00 2.50

1999 SPx Finite Radiance

*RADIANCE 1-10: 5X TO 12X BASIC 1-10
*RADIANCE 11-80: 8X TO 20X BASIC 11 80
*RADIANCE 81-120: .75X TO 2X BASIC 81-120
THREE CARDS PER RADIANCE HOT PACK
STATED PRINT RUN 100 SERIAL #'D SETS
90 Gabe Kapler AU 10.00 25.00
119 J.D. Drew AU 10.00 25.00

1999 SPx Dominance

Randomly inserted into packs at the rate of one in 17, this 20-card set features color photos of some of the most dominant MLB superstars.

COMPLETE SET (20) 15.00 40.00
STATED ODDS 1:17
FB1 Chipper Jones 1.00 2.50
FB2 Greg Maddux 1.25 3.00
FB3 Cal Ripken 3.00 8.00
FB4 Nomar Garciaparra .60 1.50
FB5 Mo Vaughn .40 1.00
FB6 Sammy Sosa 1.00 2.50
FB7 Albert Belle .40 1.00
FB8 Frank Thomas 1.00 2.50
FB9 Jim Thome .60 1.50
FB10 Jeff Bagwell .60 1.50
FB11 Vladimir Guerrero .60 1.50
FB12 Mike Piazza 1.00 2.50
FB13 Derek Jeter 2.50 6.00
FB14 Tony Gwynn 1.00 2.50
FB15 Barry Bonds 1.50 4.00
FB16 Ken Griffey Jr. 2.00 5.00
FB17 Alex Rodriguez 1.25 3.00
FB18 Mark McGwire 1.50 4.00
FB19 J.D. Drew .40 1.00
FB20 Juan Gonzalez .40 1.00

1999 SPx Power Explosion

Randomly inserted in packs at the rate of one in three, this 30-card set features color action photos of some of the top power hitters of the game.

COMPLETE SET (30) 15.00 40.00
STATED ODDS 1:3
PE1 Troy Glaus .50 1.25
PE2 Mo Vaughn .30 .75
PE3 Travis Lee .30 .75
PE4 Chipper Jones .75 2.00
PE5 Andres Galarraga .30 .75
PE6 Brady Anderson .30 .75
PE7 Albert Belle .30 .75
PE8 Nomar Garciaparra 1.25 3.00
PE9 Sammy Sosa .75 2.00
PE10 Frank Thomas .75 2.00
PE11 Jim Thome .50 1.25
PE12 Manny Ramirez .50 1.25
PE13 Larry Walker .30 .75
PE14 Tony Clark .30 .75
PE15 Jeff Bagwell .50 1.25
PE16 Moises Alou .30 .75
PE17 Ken Caminiti .30 .75
PE18 Vladimir Guerrero .75 2.00
PE19 Mike Piazza 1.25 3.00
PE20 Tino Martinez .50 1.25
PE21 Ben Grieve .30 .75
PE22 Scott Rolen .50 1.25
PE23 Greg Vaughn .30 .75
PE24 Barry Bonds 2.00 5.00
PE25 Ken Griffey Jr. 1.50 4.00
PE26 Alex Rodriguez 1.25 3.00
PE27 Mark McGwire 2.00 5.00
PE28 J.D. Drew .30 .75
PE29 Juan Gonzalez .30 .75
PE30 Ivan Rodriguez .50 1.25

1999 SPx Premier Stars

Randomly inserted in packs at the rate of one in 17, this 30-card set features color action photos of some of the game's most powerful players captured on cards with a unique rainbow-foil design.

COMP. SET (PS1-PS30) 30.00 80.00
STATED ODDS 1:17
PS1 Mark McGwire 2.50 6.00
PS2 Sammy Sosa 1.50 4.00
PS3 Frank Thomas 1.50 4.00
PS4 J.D. Drew .60 1.50
PS5 Kerry Wood .60 1.50
PS6 Moises Alou .60 1.50
PS7 Kenny Lofton .60 1.50
PS8 Jeff Bagwell 1.00 2.50
PS9 Tony Clark .60 1.50
PS10 Roberto Alomar 1.00 2.50
PS11 Cal Ripken 5.00 12.00
PS12 Derek Jeter 4.00 10.00
PS13 Mike Piazza 1.50 4.00
PS14 Jose Cruz Jr. .60 1.50
PS15 Chipper Jones 1.50 4.00
PS16 Nomar Garciaparra 1.00 2.50
PS17 Greg Maddux 2.00 5.00
PS18 Scott Rolen 1.00 2.50
PS19 Vladimir Guerrero 1.00 2.50
PS20 Albert Belle .60 1.50
PS21 Ken Griffey Jr. 3.00 8.00
PS22 Alex Rodriguez 2.00 5.00
PS23 Ben Grieve .60 1.50
PS24 Juan Gonzalez .60 1.50
PS25 Barry Bonds 2.50 6.00
PS26 Roger Clemens 2.00 5.00
PS27 Tony Gwynn 1.50 4.00
PS28 Randy Johnson 1.50 4.00
PS29 Travis Lee .60 1.50
PS30 Mo Vaughn .60 1.50

1999 SPx Star Focus

Randomly inserted in packs at the rate of one in eight, this 30-card set features action color photos of some of the brightest stars in the game beside a black-and-white portrait of the player.

COMPLETE SET (30) 60.00 120.00
STATED ODDS 1:8
SF1 Chipper Jones 2.00 5.00
SF2 Greg Maddux 3.00 8.00
SF3 Cal Ripken 6.00 15.00
SF4 Nomar Garciaparra 3.00 8.00
SF5 Mo Vaughn .75 2.00
SF6 Sammy Sosa 2.00 5.00
SF7 Albert Belle .75 2.00
SF8 Frank Thomas 2.00 5.00
SF9 Jim Thome 1.25 3.00
SF10 Kenny Lofton .75 2.00
SF11 Manny Ramirez 1.25 3.00
SF12 Larry Walker .75 2.00
SF13 Jeff Bagwell 1.25 3.00
SF14 Craig Biggio 1.25 3.00
SF15 Randy Johnson 2.00 5.00
SF16 Vladimir Guerrero 2.00 5.00
SF17 Mike Piazza 3.00 8.00
SF18 Derek Jeter 5.00 12.00
SF19 Tino Martinez 1.25 3.00
SF20 Bernie Williams 2.00 5.00
SF21 Curt Schilling .75 2.00
SF22 Tony Gwynn 2.50 6.00
SF23 Barry Bonds 5.00 12.00
SF24 Ken Griffey Jr. 4.00 10.00
SF25 Alex Rodriguez 3.00 8.00
SF26 Mark McGwire 5.00 12.00
SF27 J.D. Drew .75 2.00
SF28 Juan Gonzalez .75 2.00
SF29 Ivan Rodriguez 1.25 3.00
SF30 Ben Grieve .75 2.00

1999 SPx Winning Materials

Randomly inserted into packs at the rate of one in 251, this eight-card set features color photos of top players with a piece of the player's game-worn jersey and game-used bat embedded in the card.

STATED ODDS 1:251
IR Ivan Rodriguez 6.00 15.00
JD J.D. Drew 6.00 15.00
JR Ken Griffey Jr. 25.00 60.00
TG Tony Gwynn 6.00 15.00
TH Todd Helton 6.00 15.00
TL Travis Lee 4.00 10.00
VC Vinny Castilla 6.00 15.00
VG Vladimir Guerrero 6.00 15.00

2000 SPx

The 2000 SPx (produced by Upper Deck) set was initially released in May, 2000 as a 120-card set. Each pack contained four cards and carried a suggested retail price of $5.99. The set featured 90-player cards, and a 30-card "Young Stars" subset. There are three tiers within the Young Stars subset. Tier one cards are serial numbered to 1000, Tier two cards are serial numbered to 1500 and autographed by the player and Tier three cards are serial numbered to 500 and autographed by the player. Redemption cards were issued for several of the autograph cards and they were to be postmarked by 1/24/01 and received by 2/3/01 to be valid for exchange. In late December, 2000, Upper Deck issued a new product called Rookie Update which contained a selection of new cards for SP Authentic, SPx and UD Pros and Prospects. Rookie Update packs contained four cards and the collector was guaranteed one card from each featured brand, plus a fourth card. For SPx, these "high series" cards were numbered 121-196. The Young Stars subset was extended with cards 121-151 and cards 182-196. Cards 121-135 and 182-196 featured a selection of prospects each serial numbered to 1600. Cards 136-151 featured a selection of prospect cards signed by the player and each serial numbered to 1500. Cards 152-181 contained a selection of veteran players that were either initially not included in the basic 120-card "first series" set or traded to new teams. Notable Rookie Cards include Xavier Nady, Kazuhiro Sasaki, Ben Sheets and Barry Zito. Also, a selection of A Piece of History 3000 Club Ty Cobb memorabilia cards were randomly seeded into packs. 350 bat cards, three hand-numbered autograph cut cards and one hand-numbered, combination bat chip and autograph cut card were produced. Pricing for these memorabilia cards can be referenced under 2000 Upper Deck A Piece of History 3000 Club.

COMP.BASIC w/o SP's (90) 10.00 25.00
COMP.UPDATE w/o SP's (30) 4.00 10.00
COMMON CARD (1-90) .20 .50
COMMON AU/1500 (91-120) 4.00 10.00
COMMON NO AU/1000 (91-120) .60 1.50
NO AU/1000 SEMIS 91-120 1.00 2.50
NO AU/1000 UNLISTED 91-120 1.50 4.00
91-120 RANDOM INSERTS IN PACKS
TIER 1 UNSIGNED 1000 SERIAL #'d SETS
TIER 2 SIGNED 1500 SERIAL #'d SETS
TIER 3 SIGNED 500 SERIAL #'d SETS
EXCHANGE DEADLINE 01/24/01
COMMON (121-135/182-196) .60 1.50
121-135/182-196 PRINT RUN 1600 #'d SETS
COMMON CARD (136-151) 4.00 10.00
136-151 PRINT RUN 1500 SERIAL #'d SETS
COMMON CARD (152-181) .30 .75
121-196 DISTRIBUTED IN ROOKIE UPD.PACKS
TY COBB 3K LISTED W/UD 3000 CLUB
1 Troy Glaus .20 .50
2 Mo Vaughn .20 .50
3 Ramon Ortiz .20 .50
4 Jeff Bagwell .30 .75
5 Moises Alou .20 .50
6 Craig Biggio .30 .75
7 Jose Lima .20 .50
8 Jason Giambi .20 .50
9 John Jaha .20 .50
10 Matt Stairs .20 .50
11 Chipper Jones .50 1.25
12 Greg Maddux .60 1.50
13 Andres Galarraga .30 .75
14 Andruw Jones .20 .50
15 Jeromy Burnitz .20 .50
16 Ron Belliard .20 .50
17 Carlos Delgado .20 .50
18 David Wells .20 .50
19 Tony Batista .20 .50
20 Shannon Stewart .20 .50
21 Sammy Sosa .50 1.25
22 Mark Grace .30 .75
23 Henry Rodriguez .20 .50
24 Mark McGwire .75 2.00
25 J.D. Drew .20 .50
26 Luis Gonzalez .20 .50
27 Randy Johnson .50 1.25
28 Matt Williams .20 .50
29 Steve Finley .20 .50
30 Shawn Green .20 .50
31 Kevin Brown .20 .50
32 Gary Sheffield .20 .50
33 Jose Canseco .30 .75
34 Greg Vaughn .20 .50
35 Vladimir Guerrero .30 .75
36 Michael Barrett .20 .50
37 Russ Ortiz .20 .50
38 Barry Bonds .75 2.00
39 Jeff Kent .20 .50
40 Richie Sexson .20 .50
41 Manny Ramirez .50 1.25
42 Jim Thome .30 .75
43 Roberto Alomar .30 .75
44 Edgar Martinez .30 .75
45 Alex Rodriguez .60 1.50
46 John Olerud .20 .50
47 Alex Gonzalez .20 .50
48 Cliff Floyd .20 .50
49 Mike Piazza .50 1.25
50 Al Leiter .20 .50
51 Robin Ventura .20 .50
52 Edgardo Alfonzo .20 .50
53 Albert Belle .20 .50
54 Cal Ripken 1.50 4.00
55 B.J. Surhoff .20 .50
56 Tony Gwynn .50 1.25
57 Trevor Hoffman .30 .75
58 Brian Giles .20 .50
59 Jason Kendall .20 .50
60 Kris Benson .20 .50
61 Bob Abreu .20 .50
62 Scott Rolen .30 .75
63 Curt Schilling .20 .50
64 Mike Lieberthal .20 .50
65 Sean Casey .20 .50
66 Dante Bichette .20 .50
67 Ken Griffey Jr. 1.00 2.50
68 Pokey Reese .20 .50
69 Mike Sweeney .20 .50
70 Carlos Febles .20 .50
71 Ivan Rodriguez .30 .75
72 Ruben Mateo .20 .50
73 Rafael Palmeiro .30 .75
74 Larry Walker .30 .75
75 Todd Helton .30 .75
76 Nomar Garciaparra .30 .75
77 Pedro Martinez .30 .75
78 Troy O'Leary .20 .50
79 Jacque Jones .20 .50
80 Corey Koskie .20 .50
81 Juan Gonzalez .20 .50
82 Dean Palmer .20 .50
83 Juan Encarnacion .20 .50
84 Frank Thomas .50 1.25
85 Magglio Ordonez .30 .75
86 Paul Konerko .20 .50
87 Bernie Williams .30 .75
88 Derek Jeter 1.25 3.00
89 Roger Clemens .60 1.50
90 Orlando Hernandez .20 .50
91 Vernon Wells AU/1500 6.00 15.00
92 Rick Ankiel AU/1500 6.00 15.00
93 Eric Chavez AU/1500 8.00 20.00
94 Alfonso Soriano AU/1500 8.00 20.00
95 Eric Gagne AU/1500 6.00 15.00
96 Rob Bell AU/1500 4.00 10.00
97 Matt Riley AU/1500 4.00 10.00
98 Josh Beckett AU/1500 8.00 20.00
99 Ben Petrick AU/1500 4.00 10.00
100 Rob Ramsay AU/1500 4.00 10.00
101 Scott Williamson AU/1500 4.00 10.00
102 Doug Davis AU/1500 6.00 15.00
103 Eric Munson AU/1500 4.00 10.00
104 Pat Burrell AU/500 8.00 20.00
105 Jim Morris AU/1500 15.00 40.00
106 Gabe Kapler AU/500 4.00 10.00
107 Lance Berkman/1000 1.00 2.50
108 Erubiel Durazo AU/1500 4.00 10.00
109 Tim Hudson AU/1500 6.00 15.00
110 Ben Davis AU/1500 4.00 10.00
111 Nick Johnson AU/1500 6.00 15.00
112 Octavio Dotel AU/1500 4.00 10.00
113 Jerry Hairston/1000 .60 1.50
114 Ruben Mateo/1000 .60 1.50
115 Chris Singleton/1000 .60 1.50
116 Bruce Chen AU/1500 4.00 10.00
117 Derrick Gibson/1000 .60 1.50
118 Carlos Beltran AU/500 12.00 30.00
119 Freddy Garcia AU/1500 6.00 15.00
120 Preston Wilson AU/1500 6.00 15.00
121 Brad Wilkerson/1600 RC 1.50 4.00
122 Roy Oswalt/1600 RC 10.00 25.00
123 Wascar Serrano/1600 RC .60 1.50
124 Sean Burnett/1600 RC .60 1.50
125 Alex Cabrera/1600 RC .60 1.50
126 Timo Perez/1600 RC 1.00 2.50
127 Juan Pierre/1600 RC 3.00 8.00
128 Daylan Holt/1600 RC .60 1.50
129 Tomokazu Ohka/1600 RC .60 1.50
130 Kazuhiro Sasaki/1600 RC 1.50 4.00
131 Kurt Ainsworth/1600 RC .60 1.50
132 Brent Abernathy/1600 RC .60 1.50
133 Danys Baez/1600 RC .60 1.50
134 Brad Cresse/1600 RC .60 1.50
135 Ryan Franklin/1600 RC .60 1.50
136 Mike Lamb AU/1500 RC 6.00 15.00
137 David Espinosa AU/1500 RC 4.00 10.00
138 Matt Wheatland AU/1500 RC 4.00 10.00
139 Xavier Nady AU/1500 RC 8.00 20.00
140 Scott Heard AU/1500 RC 4.00 10.00
141 P.Coco AU/1500 UER54 RC 4.00 10.00
142 Justin Miller AU/1500 RC 4.00 10.00
143 Dave Krynzel AU/1500 RC 4.00 10.00
144 Dane Sardinha AU/1500 RC 4.00 10.00
145 Ben Sheets AU/1500 RC 6.00 15.00
146 Leo Estrella AU/1500 RC 4.00 10.00
147 Ben Diggins AU/1500 RC 4.00 10.00
148 Barry Zito AU/1500 RC 6.00 15.00
149 Joe Torres AU/1500 RC 4.00 10.00
150 Mike Meyers AU/1500 RC 4.00 10.00
151 Kris Wilson AU/1500 RC 4.00 10.00
152 Darin Erstad .30 .75
153 Richard Hidalgo .30 .75
154 Eric Chavez .30 .75
155 B.J. Surhoff .30 .75
156 Richie Sexson .30 .75
157 Raul Mondesi .30 .75
158 Rondell White .30 .75
159 Jim Edmonds .30 .75
160 Curt Schilling .50 1.25
161 Tom Goodwin .30 .75
162 Fred McGriff .50 1.25
163 Jose Vidro .30 .75
164 Ellis Burks .30 .75
165 David Segui .30 .75
166 Aaron Sele .30 .75
167 Henry Rodriguez .30 .75
168 Mike Bordick .30 .75
169 Mike Mussina .50 1.25
170 Ryan Klesko .30 .75
171 Kevin Young .30 .75
172 Travis Lee .30 .75
173 Aaron Boone .30 .75
174 Jermaine Dye .30 .75
175 Ricky Ledee .30 .75
176 Jeffrey Hammonds .30 .75
177 Carl Everett .30 .75
178 Matt Lawton .30 .75
179 Bobby Higginson .30 .75
180 Charles Johnson .30 .75
181 David Justice .30 .75
182 Joey Nation/1600 RC .60 1.50
183 Rico Washington/1600 RC .60 1.50
184 Luis Matos/1600 RC .60 1.50
185 Chris Wakeland/1600 RC .60 1.50
186 Sun Woo Kim/1600 RC .60 1.50
187 Keith Ginter/1600 RC .60 1.50
188 Geraldo Guzman/1600 RC .60 1.50
189 Jay Spurgeon/1600 RC .60 1.50
190 Jace Brewer/1600 RC .60 1.50
191 Juan Guzman/1600 RC .60 1.50
192 Ross Gload/1600 RC .60 1.50
193 Paxton Crawford/1600 RC .60 1.50
194 Ryan Kohlmeier/1600 RC .60 1.50
195 Julio Zuleta/1600 RC .60 1.50
196 Matt Ginter/1600 RC .60 1.50

2000 SPx Radiance

*RADIANCE 1-90: 6X TO 15X BASIC
COMMON CARD (91-120) 3.00 8.00
SEMISTARS 91-120 5.00 12.00
UNLISTED STARS 91-120 8.00 20.00
STATED PRINT RUN 100 SERIAL #'d SETS
DUPE VERSIONS EXIST FOR 98/103/106
91 Vernon Wells 3.00 8.00
92 Rick Ankiel 5.00 12.00
93 Eric Chavez 3.00 8.00
94 Alfonso Soriano 8.00 20.00
95 Eric Gagne 3.00 8.00
96 Rob Bell 3.00 8.00
97 Matt Riley 3.00 8.00
98 Josh Beckett 6.00 15.00
98A John Bale * 3.00 8.00
98B Alex Escobar * 3.00 8.00
98C Joe Mays * 3.00 8.00
98D Calvin Pickering * 3.00 8.00
98E Dave Roberts * 5.00 12.00
98F Jared Sandberg * 3.00 8.00
98G Dernell Stenson * 3.00 8.00
98H Reggie Taylor * 3.00 8.00
98I Ed Yarnall * 3.00 8.00
99 Ben Petrick 3.00 8.00
100 Rob Ramsay 3.00 8.00
101 Scott Williamson 3.00 8.00
102 Doug Davis 3.00 8.00
103 Eric Munson 3.00 8.00
103A Tony Armas Jr. * 3.00 8.00
103B Travis Dawkins * 3.00 8.00
103C Mike Lamb * 3.00 8.00
103D Rico Washington * 3.00 8.00
104 Pat Burrell 3.00 8.00
105 Jim Morris 8.00 20.00
106 Gabe Kapler 3.00 8.00
106A Adam Piatt * 3.00 8.00
106B Mark Quinn * 3.00 8.00
107 Lance Berkman 5.00 12.00
108 Erubiel Durazo 3.00 8.00
109 Tim Hudson 5.00 12.00
110 Ben Davis 3.00 8.00
111 Nick Johnson 3.00 8.00
112 Octavio Dotel 3.00 8.00
113 Jerry Hairston 3.00 8.00

114 Ruben Mateo 3.00 8.00
115 Chris Singleton 3.00 8.00
116 Bruce Chen 3.00 8.00
117 Derrick Gibson 3.00 8.00
118 Carlos Beltran 5.00 12.00
119 Freddy Garcia 3.00 8.00
120 Preston Wilson 3.00 8.00

2000 SPx Foundations

Randomly inserted into packs at one 32, this 10-card insert features players that are the cornerstones teams build around. Card backs carry a "F" prefix.

COMPLETE SET (10) 10.00 25.00
STATED ODDS 1:32
F1 Ken Griffey Jr. 2.00 5.00
F2 Nomar Garciaparra .60 1.50
F3 Cal Ripken 3.00 8.00
F4 Chipper Jones 1.00 2.50
F5 Mike Piazza 1.00 2.50
F6 Derek Jeter 2.50 6.00
F7 Manny Ramirez 1.00 2.50
F8 Jeff Bagwell .60 1.50
F9 Tony Gwynn 1.00 2.50
F10 Larry Walker .60 1.50

2000 SPx Heart of the Order

Randomly inserted into packs at one in eight, this 20-card insert features players that can lift their teams to victory with one swing of the bat. Card backs carry a "H" prefix.

COMPLETE SET (20) 12.50 30.00
STATED ODDS 1:8
H1 Bernie Williams .60 1.50
H2 Mike Piazza 1.00 2.50
H3 Ivan Rodriguez .60 1.50
H4 Mark McGwire 1.50 4.00
H5 Manny Ramirez 1.00 2.50
H6 Ken Griffey Jr. 2.00 5.00
H7 Matt Williams .40 1.00
H8 Sammy Sosa 1.00 2.50
H9 Mo Vaughn .40 1.00
H10 Carlos Delgado .40 1.00
H11 Brian Giles .40 1.00
H12 Chipper Jones 1.00 2.50
H13 Sean Casey .40 1.00
H14 Tony Gwynn 1.00 2.50
H15 Barry Bonds 1.50 4.00
H16 Carlos Beltran .60 1.50
H17 Scott Rolen .60 1.50
H18 Juan Gonzalez .40 1.00
H19 Larry Walker .60 1.50
H20 Vladimir Guerrero .60 1.50

2000 SPx Highlight Heroes

Randomly inserted into packs at one in 16, this 10-card insert features players that have a flair for heroics. Card backs carry a "HH" prefix.

COMPLETE SET (10) 6.00 15.00
STATED ODDS 1:16
HH1 Pedro Martinez .60 1.50
HH2 Ivan Rodriguez .60 1.50
HH3 Carlos Beltran .60 1.50
HH4 Nomar Garciaparra .60 1.50
HH5 Ken Griffey Jr. 2.00 5.00
HH6 Randy Johnson 1.00 2.50
HH7 Chipper Jones 1.00 2.50
HH8 Scott Williamson .40 1.00
HH9 Larry Walker .60 1.50
HH10 Mark McGwire 1.50 4.00

2000 SPx Power Brokers

Randomly inserted into packs at one in eight, this 20-card insert features some of the greatest power hitters of all time. Card backs carry a "PB" prefix.

COMPLETE SET (20) 10.00 25.00
STATED ODDS 1:8
PB1 Rafael Palmeiro .60 1.50
PB2 Carlos Delgado .40 1.00
PB3 Ken Griffey Jr. 2.00 5.00
PB4 Matt Stairs .40 1.00
PB5 Mike Piazza 1.00 2.50
PB6 Vladimir Guerrero .60 1.50
PB7 Chipper Jones 1.00 2.50
PB8 Mark McGwire 1.50 4.00
PB9 Matt Williams .40 1.00
PB10 Juan Gonzalez .40 1.00
PB11 Shawn Green .40 1.00
PB12 Sammy Sosa 1.00 2.50
PB13 Brian Giles .40 1.00
PB14 Jeff Bagwell .60 1.50
PB15 Alex Rodriguez 1.25 3.00
PB16 Frank Thomas 1.00 2.50
PB17 Larry Walker .60 1.50
PB18 Albert Belle .40 1.00
PB19 Dean Palmer .40 1.00
PB20 Mo Vaughn .40 1.00

2000 SPx Signatures

Randomly inserted into packs at one in 179, this 15-card insert features autographed cards of some of the hottest players in major league baseball. The following players went out as stickered exchange cards: Jeff Bagwell (100 percent), Ken Griffey Jr. (100 percent), Tony Gwynn (25 percent), Vladimir Guerrero (50 percent), Manny Ramirez (100 percent) and Ivan Rodriguez (25 percent). The exchange deadline for the stickered cards was February 3rd, 2001. Card backs carry a "X" prefix followed by the players initials.

STATED ODDS 1:179
EXCHANGE DEADLINE 02/03/01
XBB Barry Bonds 50.00 120.00
XCJ Chipper Jones 30.00 60.00
XCR Cal Ripken 50.00 100.00
XDJ Derek Jeter 100.00 200.00
XIR Ivan Rodriguez 15.00 30.00
XJB Jeff Bagwell 15.00 40.00
XJC Jose Canseco 10.00 25.00
XKG Ken Griffey Jr. 60.00 150.00
XMR Manny Ramirez 12.00 25.00
XOH Orlando Hernandez 60.00 120.00
XRC Roger Clemens 25.00 60.00
XSC Sean Casey 6.00 15.00
XSR Scott Rolen 4.00 10.00
XTG Tony Gwynn 25.00 60.00
XVG Vladimir Guerrero 6.00 15.00

2000 SPx SPXcitement

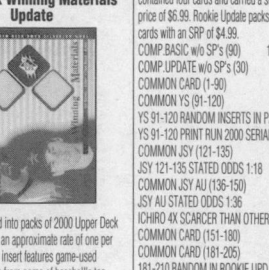

Randomly inserted into packs at one in four, this 20-card insert features some of the most exciting players in the major leagues. Card backs carry a "XC" prefix.

COMPLETE SET (20) 12.50 30.00
STATED ODDS 1:4
XC1 Nomar Garciaparra .60 1.50
XC2 Mark McGwire 1.50 4.00
XC3 Derek Jeter 2.50 6.00
XC4 Cal Ripken 3.00 8.00
XC5 Barry Bonds 1.50 4.00
XC6 Alex Rodriguez 1.25 3.00
XC7 Scott Rolen .60 1.50
XC8 Pedro Martinez .60 1.50
XC9 Sean Casey .40 1.00
XC10 Sammy Sosa 1.00 2.50
XC11 Randy Johnson 1.00 2.50
XC12 Ivan Rodriguez .60 1.50
XC13 Frank Thomas 1.00 2.50
XC14 Greg Maddux 1.25 3.00
XC15 Tony Gwynn 1.00 2.50
XC16 Ken Griffey Jr. 2.00 5.00
XC17 Carlos Beltran .60 1.50
XC18 Mike Piazza 1.00 2.50
XC19 Chipper Jones 1.00 2.50
XC20 Craig Biggio .60 1.50

2000 SPx Untouchable Talents

Randomly inserted into packs at one in 96, this 10-card insert features players that have skills that are unmatched. Card backs carry a "UT" prefix.

COMPLETE SET (10) 15.00 40.00
STATED ODDS 1:96
UT1 Mark McGwire 4.00 10.00
UT2 Ken Griffey Jr. 5.00 12.00
UT3 Shawn Green 1.00 2.50
UT4 Ivan Rodriguez 1.50 4.00
UT5 Sammy Sosa 2.50 6.00
UT6 Derek Jeter 6.00 15.00
UT7 Sean Casey 1.00 2.50
UT8 Chipper Jones 2.50 6.00
UT9 Pedro Martinez 1.50 4.00
UT10 Vladimir Guerrero 1.50 4.00

2000 SPx Winning Materials

Randomly inserted into first series packs, this 30-card insert features game-used memorabilia cards from some of the top names in baseball. The set includes Bat/Jersey cards, Cap/Jersey cards, Ball/Jersey cards, and autographed Bat/Jersey cards. Card backs carry the players initals. Please note that the Ken Griffey Jr. autographed Bat/Jersey cards, and the Manny Ramirez autographed Bat/Jersey cards were both redemptions with an exchang deadline of 12/31/2000.

BAT-JERSEY STATED ODDS 1:112
OTHER CARDS RANDOM INSERTS IN PACKS
SERIAL #'d PRINT RUNS FROM 50-250 PER
AU SERIAL #'d PRINT RUNS FROM 2-25 PER
NO PRICING ON QTY OF 25 OR LESS
EXCHANGE DEADLINE 12/31/00
AR1 A.Rodriguez Bat-Jsy 10.00 25.00
AR2 A.Rodriguez Cap-Jsy/100 10.00 25.00
AR3 A.Rodriguez Ball-Jsy/50 30.00 60.00
BB1 B.Bonds Bat-Jsy 5.00 12.00
BB2 B.Bonds Cap-Jsy/100 15.00 40.00
BW B.Williams Bat-Jsy 6.00 15.00
DJ1 D.Jeter Bat-Jsy 20.00 50.00
DJ2 D.Jeter Ball-Jsy/50 50.00 100.00
EC1 E.Chavez Bat-Jsy 4.00 10.00
EC2 E.Chavez Cap-Jsy/100 6.00 15.00
GM G.Maddux Bat-Jsy 10.00 25.00
IR I.Rodriguez Bat-Jsy 6.00 15.00
JB1 J.Bagwell Bat-Jsy 6.00 15.00
JB2 J.Bagwell Ball-Jsy/50 15.00 40.00
JC J.Canseco Bat-Jsy 6.00 15.00
JL1 J.Lopez Bat-Jsy 4.00 10.00
JL2 J.Lopez Cap-Jsy 6.00 15.00
KG1 K.Griffey Jr. Bat-Jsy 10.00 25.00
KG2 K.Griffey Jr. Ball-Jsy/50 30.00 60.00
MM1 McGwire Ball-Base/250 12.50 30.00
MM2 McGwire Ball-Base/250 12.50 30.00
MR1 M.Ramirez Bat-Jsy 6.00 15.00
MW M.Williams Bat-Jsy 4.00 10.00
PM P.Martinez Cap-Jsy/100 10.00 25.00
PO P.O'Neill Bat-Jsy 6.00 15.00
VG1 V.Guerrero Bat-Jsy 6.00 15.00
VG2 V.Guerrero Cap-Jsy/100 10.00 25.00
VG3 V.Guerrero Ball-Jsy/50 15.00 40.00
GL T.Glaus Bat-Jsy 4.00 10.00
TGW1 T.Gwynn Bat-Jsy 6.00 15.00
TGW2 T.Gwynn Ball-Jsy/50 20.00 50.00
TGW3 T.Gwynn Cap-Jsy/100 12.50 30.00

2000 SPx Winning Materials Update

Randomly inserted into packs of 2000 Upper Deck Rookie Update (at an approximate rate of one per box), this 28-card insert features game-used memorabilia cards from some of baseball's top athletes. The set also includes a few members of the 2000 USA Olympic Baseball team. Card backs carry the player's initials as numbering.

MKGD T.Dawkins M.Kinkade 1.25 3.00
BAAE B.Abernathy A.Everett 1.25 3.00
BWEY B.Wilkerson E.Young 3.00 8.00
CRTG C.Ripken T.Gwynn 10.00 25.00
DJAR D.Jeter A.Rodriguez 8.00 20.00
DJNG D.Jeter N.Garciaparra 8.00 20.00
FTMO F.Thomas M.Ordonez 3.00 8.00
GSR Griffey/Sosa/A-Rod 6.00 15.00
GWBS Ben Sheets 3.00 8.00
GWDM Doug Mientkiewicz 1.25 3.00
GWEY Ernie Young 1.25 3.00
GWJC John Cotton 1.25 3.00
GWMN Mike Neill 1.25 3.00
GWSB Sean Burroughs 1.25 3.00
IRRP I.Rodriguez R.Palmeiro 2.00 5.00
JGR Jeter/Nomar/A-Rod 8.00 20.00
JBCB J.Bagwell C.Biggio 2.00 5.00
JCBB J.Canseco B.Boonds 5.00 12.00
KGSS K.Griffey Jr. S.Sosa 6.00 15.00
MMKG M.McGwire K.Griffey Jr. 6.00 15.00
MMRA M.McGwire R.Ankiel 5.00 12.00
MMSS M.McGwire S.Sosa 5.00 12.00
MPRV M.Piazza R.Ventura 3.00 8.00
NGPM Nomar Pedro 2.00 5.00
RCPM R.Clemens P.Martinez 4.00 10.00
SBBS S.Burroughs B.Sheets 3.00 8.00

2000 SPx Winning Materials Update Numbered

Randomly inserted into 2001 Rookie Update packs, this 3-card insert features game-used memorabilia from three different major leaguers on the same card. These rare gems are individually serial numbered to 50. Card backs carry the players initials as numbering

STATED PRINT RUN 50 SERIAL #'d SETS
CBG Canseco/Bonds/Griffey 60.00 120.00
GSM Griffey/Sosa/McGwire 30.00 60.00
JGR Jeter/Nomar/A-Rod 50.00 100.00

2001 SPx

The 2001 SPx product was initially released in early May, 2001, and featured a 150-card base set. 60 additional update cards (151-210) were distributed within Upper Deck Rookie Update packs in late December, 2001. The base set is broken into tiers as follows: Base Veterans (1-90), Young Stars (91-120) serial numbered to 2000, Rookie Jerseys (121-135), and Jersey Autographs (136-150). The Rookie Update SPx cards were broken into tiers as follows: base veterans (151-180) and Young Stars (181-210) serial numbered to 1500. Cards 206-210, in addition to being serial-numbered of 1,500 copies per, also feature on-card autographs. Each basic pack contained four cards and carried a suggested retail price of $6.99. Rookie Update packs contained four cards with an SRP of $4.99.

COMP.BASIC w/o SP's (90) 10.00 25.00
COMP.UPDATE w/o SP's (30) 4.00 10.00
COMMON CARD (1-90) .20 .50
COMMON YS (91-120) 2.00 5.00
YS 91-120 RANDOM INSERTS IN PACKS
YS 91-120 PRINT RUN 2000 SERIAL #'d SETS
COMMON JSY (121-135) 3.00 8.00
JSY 121-135 STATED ODDS 1:18
COMMON JSY AU (136-150) 4.00 10.00
JSY AU STATED ODDS 1:36
ICHIRO 4X SCARCER THAN OTHER JSY AU'S
COMMON CARD (151-180) .30 .75
COMMON CARD (181-205) 2.00 5.00
181-210 RANDOM IN ROOKIE UPD.PACKS
181-210 PRINT RUN 1500 SERIAL #'d SETS
151-210 DISTRIBUTED IN ROOKIE UPD.PACKS
EXCHANGE DEADLINE 12/10/04
1 Darin Erstad .20 .50
2 Troy Glaus .20 .50
3 Mo Vaughn .20 .50
4 Johnny Damon .30 .75
5 Jason Giambi .20 .50
6 Tim Hudson .20 .50
7 Miguel Tejada .20 .50
8 Carlos Delgado .20 .50
9 Raul Mondesi .20 .50
10 Tony Batista .20 .50
11 Ben Grieve .20 .50
12 Greg Vaughn .20 .50
13 Juan Gonzalez .20 .50
14 Jim Thome .30 .75
15 Roberto Alomar .30 .75
16 John Olerud .20 .50
17 Edgar Martinez .30 .75
18 Albert Belle .20 .50
19 Cal Ripken 1.50 4.00
20 Ivan Rodriguez .30 .75
21 Rafael Palmeiro .30 .75
22 Alex Rodriguez .60 1.50
23 Nomar Garciaparra .75 2.00
24 Pedro Martinez .30 .75
25 Manny Ramirez Sox .30 .75
26 Jermaine Dye .20 .50
27 Mark Quinn .20 .50
28 Carlos Beltran .20 .50
29 Tony Clark .20 .50
30 Bobby Higginson .20 .50
31 Eric Milton .20 .50
32 Matt Lawton .20 .50
33 Frank Thomas .50 1.25
34 Magglio Ordonez .20 .50
35 Ray Durham .20 .50
36 David Wells .20 .50
37 Derek Jeter 1.25 3.00
38 Bernie Williams .30 .75
39 Roger Clemens 1.00 2.50
40 David Justice .20 .50
41 Jeff Bagwell .30 .75
42 Richard Hidalgo .20 .50
43 Moises Alou .20 .50
44 Chipper Jones .50 1.25
45 Andruw Jones .30 .75
46 Greg Maddux .75 2.00
47 Rafael Furcal .20 .50
48 Jeromy Burnitz .20 .50
49 Geoff Jenkins .20 .50
50 Mark McGwire 1.25 3.00
51 Jim Edmonds .20 .50
52 Rick Ankiel .20 .50
53 Edgar Renteria .20 .50
54 Sammy Sosa .50 1.25
55 Kerry Wood .20 .50
56 Rondell White .20 .50
57 Randy Johnson .50 1.25
58 Steve Finley .20 .50
59 Matt Williams .20 .50
60 Luis Gonzalez .20 .50
61 Kevin Brown .20 .50
62 Gary Sheffield .20 .50
63 Shawn Green .20 .50
64 Vladimir Guerrero .50 1.25
65 Jose Vidro .20 .50
66 Barry Bonds 1.25 3.00
67 Jeff Kent .20 .50
68 Livan Hernandez .20 .50
69 Preston Wilson .20 .50
70 Charles Johnson .20 .50
71 Cliff Floyd .20 .50
72 Mike Piazza .75 2.00
73 Edgardo Alfonzo .20 .50
74 Jay Payton .20 .50
75 Robin Ventura .20 .50
76 Tony Gwynn .60 1.50
77 Phil Nevin .20 .50
78 Ryan Klesko .20 .50
79 Scott Rolen .30 .75
80 Pat Burrell .20 .50
81 Bob Abreu .20 .50
82 Brian Giles .20 .50
83 Kris Benson .20 .50
84 Jason Kendall .20 .50
85 Ken Griffey Jr. 1.00 2.50
86 Barry Larkin .30 .75
87 Sean Casey .20 .50
88 Todd Helton .30 .75
89 Larry Walker .20 .50
90 Mike Hampton .20 .50
91 Billy Sylvester YS RC 2.00 5.00
92 Josh Towers YS RC 3.00 8.00
93 Zach Day YS RC 2.00 5.00
94 Martin Vargas YS RC 2.00 5.00
95 Adam Pettyjohn YS RC 2.00 5.00
96 Andres Torres YS RC 2.00 5.00
97 Kris Keller YS RC 2.00 5.00
98 Blaine Neal YS RC 2.00 5.00
99 Kyle Kessel YS RC 2.00 5.00
100 Greg Miller YS RC 2.00 5.00
101 Shawn Sonnier YS 2.00 5.00
102 Alexis Gomez YS RC 2.00 5.00
103 Grant Balfour YS RC 2.00 5.00
104 Henry Mateo YS RC 2.00 5.00
105 Wilken Ruan YS RC 2.00 5.00
106 Nick Maness YS RC 2.00 5.00
107 Jason Michaels YS RC 2.00 5.00
108 Esix Snead YS RC 2.00 5.00
109 William Ortega YS RC 2.00 5.00
110 David Elder YS RC 2.00 5.00
111 Jackson Melian YS RC 2.00 5.00
112 Nate Teut YS RC 2.00 5.00
113 Jason Smith YS RC 2.00 5.00
114 Mike Penney YS RC 2.00 5.00
115 Jose Mieses YS RC 2.00 5.00
116 Juan Pena YS 2.00 5.00
117 Brian Lawrence YS RC 2.00 5.00
118 Jeremy Owens YS RC 2.00 5.00
119 Carlos Valderrama YS RC 2.00 5.00
120 Rafael Soriano YS RC 2.00 5.00
121 Horacio Ramirez JSY RC 4.00 10.00
122 Ricardo Rodriguez JSY RC 3.00 8.00
123 Juan Diaz JSY RC 3.00 8.00
124 Donnie Bridges JSY 3.00 8.00
125 Tyler Walker JSY RC 3.00 8.00
126 Erick Almonte JSY RC 3.00 8.00
127 Jesus Colome JSY 3.00 8.00
128 Ryan Freel JSY RC 4.00 10.00
129 Elpidio Guzman JSY RC 3.00 8.00
130 Jack Cust JSY 3.00 8.00
131 Eric Hinske JSY RC 4.00 10.00
132 Josh Fogg JSY RC 3.00 8.00
133 Juan Uribe JSY RC 4.00 10.00
134 Bert Snow JSY RC 3.00 8.00
135 Pedro Feliz JSY 3.00 8.00
136 Wilson Betemit JSY AU RC 4.00 10.00
137 Sean Douglass JSY AU RC 4.00 10.00
138 Dernell Stenson JSY AU 4.00 10.00
139 Brandon Inge JSY AU 4.00 10.00
140 Mor.Ensberg JSY AU RC 4.00 10.00
141 Brian Cole JSY AU 6.00 15.00
142 A.Hernandez JSY AU RC 4.00 10.00
143 B.Duckworth JSY AU RC 4.00 10.00
144 Jack Wilson JSY AU RC 4.00 10.00
145 Travis Hafner JSY AU RC 4.00 10.00
146 Carlos Pena JSY AU 6.00 15.00
147 Corey Patterson JSY AU 4.00 10.00
148 Xavier Nady JSY AU 4.00 10.00
149 Jason Hart JSY AU 4.00 10.00
150 I.Suzuki JSY AU RC 1000.00 1500.00
151 Garret Anderson .30 .75
152 Jermaine Dye .30 .75
153 Shannon Stewart .30 .75
154 Toby Hall .30 .75
155 C.C. Sabathia .30 .75
156 Bret Boone .30 .75
157 Tony Batista .30 .75
158 Gabe Kapler .30 .75
159 Carl Everett .30 .75
160 Mike Sweeney .30 .75
161 Dean Palmer .30 .75
162 Doug Mientkiewicz .30 .75
163 Carlos Lee .30 .75
164 Mike Mussina .50 1.25
165 Lance Berkman .30 .75
166 Ken Caminiti .30 .75
167 Ben Sheets .50 1.25
168 Matt Morris .30 .75
169 Fred McGriff .50 1.25
170 Curt Schilling .30 .75
171 Paul LoDuca .30 .75
172 Javier Vazquez .30 .75
173 Rich Aurilia .30 .75
174 A.J. Burnett .30 .75
175 Al Leiter .30 .75
176 Mark Kotsay .30 .75
177 Jimmy Rollins .30 .75
178 Aramis Ramirez .30 .75
179 Aaron Boone .30 .75
180 Jeff Cirillo .30 .75
181 Johnny Estrada YS RC 3.00 8.00
182 Dave Williams YS RC 2.00 5.00
183 Donaldo Mendez YS RC 2.00 5.00
184 Junior Spivey YS RC 3.00 8.00
185 Jay Gibbons YS RC 3.00 8.00
186 Kyle Lohse YS RC 5.00 12.00
187 Willie Harris YS RC 2.00 5.00
188 Juan Cruz YS RC 2.00 5.00
189 Joe Kennedy YS RC 3.00 8.00
190 Duaner Sanchez YS RC 2.00 5.00
191 Jorge Julio YS RC 2.00 5.00
192 Cesar Crespo YS RC 2.00 5.00
193 Casey Fossum YS RC 2.00 5.00
194 Brian Roberts YS RC 6.00 15.00
195 Troy Mattes YS RC 2.00 5.00
196 Rob Mackowiak YS RC 3.00 8.00
197 Tsuyoshi Shinjo YS RC 3.00 8.00
198 Nick Punto YS RC 2.00 5.00
199 Wilmy Caceres YS RC 2.00 5.00
200 Jeremy Affeldt YS RC 2.00 5.00
201 Bret Prinz YS RC 2.00 5.00
202 Delvin James YS RC 2.00 5.00
203 Luis Pineda YS RC 2.00 5.00
204 Matt White YS RC 2.00 5.00
205 Brandon Knight YS RC 2.00 5.00
206 Albert Pujols YS AU RC 250.00 500.00
207 Mark Teixeira YS AU RC 12.50 30.00
208 Mark Prior YS AU RC 8.00 20.00
209 Dewon Brazelton YS AU RC 6.00 15.00
210 Bud Smith YS AU RC 6.00 15.00

2001 SPx Spectrum

*STARS 1-90: 12.5X TO 30X BASIC CARDS
*YS 91-120: 1X TO 2.5X BASIC CARDS
STATED PRINT RUN 50 SERIAL #'d SETS

2001 SPx Foundations

Randomly inserted into packs at one in eight, this 12-card insert features players that are the major foundation that keeps their respective ballclubs together. Card backs carry a "F" prefix.

COMPLETE SET (12) 20.00 50.00
STATED ODDS 1:8
F1 Mark McGwire 3.00 8.00
F2 Jeff Bagwell .75 2.00
F3 Alex Rodriguez 1.50 4.00
F4 Ken Griffey Jr. 2.50 6.00
F5 Andruw Jones .75 2.00
F6 Cal Ripken 4.00 10.00
F7 Barry Bonds 3.00 8.00
F8 Derek Jeter 3.00 8.00
F9 Frank Thomas 1.25 3.00
F10 Sammy Sosa 1.25 3.00
F11 Tony Gwynn 1.50 4.00
F12 Vladimir Guerrero 1.25 3.00

2001 SPx SPXcitement

Randomly inserted into packs at one in eight, this 12-card insert features players that are known for bringing excitement to the game. Card backs carry an "X" prefix.

COMPLETE SET (12) 20.00 50.00
STATED ODDS 1:8
X1 Alex Rodriguez 1.50 4.00
X2 Jason Giambi .75 2.00
X3 Ken Griffey Jr. 2.50 6.00
X4 Sammy Sosa 1.25 3.00
X5 Frank Thomas 1.25 3.00
X6 Todd Helton .75 2.00
X7 Mark McGwire 3.00 8.00
X8 Mike Piazza 2.00 5.00
X9 Derek Jeter 3.00 8.00
X10 Vladimir Guerrero 1.25 3.00
X11 Carlos Delgado .75 2.00
X12 Chipper Jones 1.25 3.00

2001 SPx Untouchable Talents

Randomly inserted into packs at one in 15, this six-card insert features players whose skills are unmatched. Card backs carry a "UT" prefix.

COMPLETE SET (6) 15.00 40.00
STATED ODDS 1:15
UT1 Ken Griffey Jr. 2.50 6.00
UT2 Mike Piazza 2.00 5.00
UT3 Mark McGwire 3.00 8.00
UT4 Alex Rodriguez 1.50 4.00
UT5 Sammy Sosa 2.00 5.00
UT6 Derek Jeter 3.00 8.00

2001 SPx Winning Materials Ball-Base

Randomly inserted into packs, this 13-card insert features actual swatches of both game-used baseball and base. Card backs carry a "B" prefix followed by the player's initials. Each card is individually serial numbered to 250.

STATED PRINT RUN 250 SERIAL #'d SETS
BAJ Andruw Jones 10.00 25.00
BAR Alex Rodriguez 10.00 25.00
BBB Barry Bonds 20.00 50.00
BCJ Chipper Jones 10.00 25.00
BDJ Derek Jeter 20.00 50.00
BFT Frank Thomas 10.00 25.00
BKG Ken Griffey Jr. 15.00 40.00
BMM Mark McGwire 12.00 30.00
BMP Mike Piazza 10.00 25.00
BNG Nomar Garciaparra 10.00 25.00
BPM Pedro Martinez 10.00 25.00
BSS Sammy Sosa 10.00 25.00
BVG Vladimir Guerrero 10.00 25.00

2001 SPx Winning Materials Base Duos

Randomly inserted into packs, this 10-card insert features actual swatches of game-used bases. Card backs carry a "B2" prefix followed by the player's initials. Each card is individually serial numbered to 50.

STATED PRINT RUN 50 SERIAL #'d SETS
B2GJ N.Garciaparra/D.Jeter 12.50 30.00
B2JG D.Jeter/J.Giambi 10.00 25.00
B2JP D.Jeter/M.Piazza 12.50 30.00
B2MG M.McGwire/K.Grif 10.00 25.00
B2MR M.McGwire/A.Rod 10.00 25.00
B2MS M.McGwire/S.Sosa 12.50 30.00
B2PB M.Piazza/B.Bonds 12.50 30.00
B2PM M.Piazza/M.McGwire 10.00 25.00
B2RJ A.Rodriguez/D.Jeter 10.00 25.00
B2TR F.Thomas/A.Rodriguez 10.00 25.00

2001 SPx Winning Materials Bat-Jersey

Randomly inserted into packs, this 21-card insert features actual swatches of both game-used bats and jerseys. Card backs carry the player's initials as numbering.

STATED ODDS 1:18
ASTERISKS PERCEIVED SHORTER SUPPLY
AJ1 Andruw Jones AS 2.50 6.00
AJ2 Andruw Jones 2.50 6.00
AR1 Alex Rodriguez AS 5.00 12.00
AR2 Alex Rodriguez AS 5.00 12.00
BB1 Barry Bonds AS 6.00 15.00
BB2 Barry Bonds 6.00 15.00
CD Carlos Delgado AS * 1.50 4.00
CJ1 Chipper Jones AS 4.00 10.00
CJ2 Chipper Jones 4.00 10.00
CR Cal Ripken 12.00 30.00
FT Frank Thomas 4.00 10.00
IR1 Ivan Rodriguez AS 2.50 6.00
IR2 Ivan Rodriguez 2.50 6.00
JD Joe DiMaggio 40.00 100.00
JE Jim Edmonds * 2.50 6.00
KG1 Ken Griffey Jr. AS 8.00 20.00
KG2 Ken Griffey Jr. 8.00 20.00
RA Rick Ankiel * 1.50 4.00
RJ1 Randy Johnson AS 4.00 10.00
RJ2 Randy Johnson 4.00 10.00
SS Sammy Sosa 2.50 6.00

2001 SPx Winning Materials Jersey Duos

Randomly inserted into packs, this 13-card insert features actual swatches of game-used jerseys. Card backs carry both player's initials as numbering. Each card is individually serial numbered to 50.

STATED PRINT RUN 50 SERIAL #'d SETS
AJCJ A.Jones/C.Jones 15.00 40.00
ARCR A.Rod/C.Ripken 50.00 100.00
BBSS B.Bonds/S.Sosa 30.00 60.00

JDW C.Jones/D.Wells 15.00 40.00
RAR I.Rod/A.Rod 40.00 80.00
GAR K.Griffey Jr./A.Rod AS 40.00 80.00
GBB K.Griffey/B.Bonds AS 50.00 100.00
GJD Griffey Jr./DiMaggio 40.00 80.00
GKG Griffey Jr./Griffey Jr. AS 40.00 80.00
GRJ Griffey Jr./Johnson AS 15.00 40.00
GSS K.Griffey Jr./S.Sosa 40.00 80.00
SCD S.Sosa/C.Delgado 15.00 40.00
SFT S.Sosa/F.Thomas 15.00 40.00

2001 SPx Winning Materials Update Duos

Inserted into 2001 Upper Deck Rookie Update packs at a rate of one in 15, these cards feature two players and a memorabilia piece from each of them.

STATED ODDS 1:15
GOLD RANDOM INSERTS IN PACKS
GOLD PRINT RUN 25 SERIAL #'d SETS
NO GOLD PRICING DUE TO SCARCITY
EACH CARD FEATURES DUAL JSY SWATCH

APJE A.Pujols/J.Edmonds 10.00 25.00
ASKS A.Sele/K.Sasaki 1.50 4.00
BBLG B.Bonds/L.Gonzalez 6.00 15.00
BWMR B.Williams/M.Rivera 4.00 10.00
BWRJ B.Williams/R.Jackson 3.00 8.00
CPBK C.Park/B.Kim 2.50 6.00
CPFV C.Park/F.Valenzuela 8.00 20.00
CREM C.Ripken/E.Murray 8.00 20.00
CRX2 C.Ripken/C.Ripken 8.00 20.00
CSRJ C.Schilling/R.Johnson 4.00 10.00
EMJM E.Milton/J.Mays 1.50 4.00
FTMO F.Thomas/M.Ordonez 4.00 10.00
GSSG G.Sheffield/S.Green 1.50 4.00
HNMY H.Nomo/M.Yoshii 4.00 10.00
IRAR I.Rodriguez/A.Rodriguez 5.00 12.00
JBCB J.Bagwell/C.Biggio 2.50 6.00
JBRY J.Burnitz/R.Yount 4.00 10.00
JGBB J.Giambi/B.Bonds 6.00 15.00
KGSC K.Griffey Jr./S.Casey 5.00 12.00
LWTH L.Walker/T.Helton 2.50 6.00
MPEA M.Piazza/E.Alfonzo 4.00 10.00
MRJG M.Ramirez Sox/J.Gonzalez 4.00 10.00
PMGM P.Martinez/G.Maddux 6.00 15.00
PMRJ P.Martinez/R.Johnson 4.00 10.00
SRBA S.Rolen/B.Abreu 2.50 6.00
SSEB S.Sosa/E.Banks 4.00 10.00
SSJG S.Sosa/J.Giambi 2.50 6.00
TGCR T.Gwynn/C.Ripken 10.00 25.00
TGDW T.Gwynn/D.Winfield 4.00 10.00
TGX2 T.Gwynn/T.Gwynn 4.00 10.00
TSHN T.Shinjo/H.Nomo 4.00 10.00

2001 SPx Winning Materials Update Trios

Inserted into 2001 Upper Deck Rookie Update Packs at a rate of one in 15, these 22 cards feature three players as well as a piece of game-worn jersey memorabilia from each one.

STATED ODDS 1:15
GOLD RANDOM INSERTS IN PACKS
GOLD PRINT RUN 25 SERIAL #'d SETS
NO GOLD PRICING DUE TO SCARCITY
ALL FEATURE THREE JSY SWATCHES

BGG Bonds/L.Gonz/Griffey 12.00 30.00
BTD Bagwell/Thomas/Delgado 6.00 15.00
CHN Clemens/Hudson/Nomo 10.00 25.00
DEA Drew/Edmonds/Abreu 4.00 10.00
DOP Delgado/M.Ordonez/Pujols 10.00 25.00
GWS L.Gonz/M.Will/Schilling 4.00 10.00
GZH Giambi/Zito/Hudson 4.00 10.00
HDG Helton/Delgado/Giambi 6.00 15.00
JAF C.Jones/A.Jones/Furcal 6.00 15.00
KBA Kent/Bonds/Aurilia 10.00 25.00
MGJ Maddux/Glavine/A.Jones 10.00 25.00
PPV Payton/Piazza/Ventura 8.00 20.00
PWO Pettitte/B.Williams/O'Neill 6.00 15.00
RPK I.Rod/Piazza/Kendall 8.00 20.00
RRK A.Rod/I.Rod/Kapler 8.00 20.00
SJC Schilling/R.John/Clemens 8.00 20.00
SKB Sheffield/Karros/K.Brown 4.00 10.00
SSM Sele/Ichiro/E.Martinez 12.50 30.00
SYN Sasaki/Yoshii/Nomo 6.00 15.00
TDK Thomas/Durham/Konerko 6.00 15.00
TGA Thome/J.Gonz/R.Alomar 4.00 10.00
VRF Vizquel/A.Rod/Furcal 8.00 20.00

2002 SPx

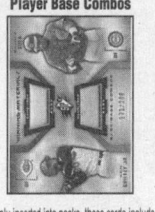

This 280-card set was issued in two separate brands. The SPx product itself was released in late April, 2002 and contained cards 1-250. These cards were issued in four card packs of which were distributed at a rate of 18 packs per box and 14 boxes per case. Cards numbered from 91 through 120 feature either a portrait or an action shot of a prospect. Both the portrait and the action shot were issued with separate stated print runs of 1800 serial numbered cards (for a total of 3,600 of each player in the subset). Cards 121-150 were not serial-numbered but instead feature autographs and were seeded into packs at a rate of 1:18. Cards numbered 151 through 190 were issued and featured jersey swatches of leading major league players. These cards had a stated print run of either 700 or 800 serial numbered cards. High series cards 191-250 were distributed in mid-December, 2002 within packs of 2002 Upper Deck Rookie Update. Cards 191-220 feature veterans on new teams and were commonly distributed in all packs. Cards 221-250 feature prospects and were signed by the player. In addition, the card were serial numbered to 825 copies. Though stated pack odds were not released by the manufacturer, we believe these signed cards were seeded at an approximate rate of 1:16 Upper Deck Rookie Update packs.

COMP.LOW w/o SP's (90) 10.00 25.00
COMP.UPDATE w/o SP's (30) 4.00 10.00
91-120 RANDOM INSERTS IN PACKS
91-120 ACTION 1800 SERIAL #'d SETS
91-120 PORTRAIT 1800 SERIAL #'d SETS
91-120 ACTION/PORTRAIT EQUAL VALUE
121-150 STATED ODDS 1:18
151-190 RANDOM INSERTS IN PACKS
151-190 PR.RUN 700-800 SER.#'d OF EACH
221-250 RANDOM IN ROOKIE UPD.PACKS
221-250 PRINT RUN 825 SERIAL #'d SETS
191-250 ISSUED IN ROOKIE UPDATE PACKS

1 Troy Glaus .20 .50
2 Darin Erstad .20 .50
3 David Justice .20 .50
4 Tim Hudson .20 .50
5 Miguel Tejada .20 .50
6 Barry Zito .20 .50
7 Carlos Delgado .20 .50
8 Shannon Stewart .20 .50
9 Greg Vaughn .20 .50
10 Toby Hall .20 .50
11 Jim Thome .30 .75
12 C.C. Sabathia .20 .50
13 Ichiro Suzuki 1.00 2.50
14 Edgar Martinez .30 .75
15 Freddy Garcia .20 .50
16 Mike Cameron .20 .50
17 Jeff Conine .20 .50
18 Tony Batista .20 .50
19 Alex Rodriguez .60 1.50
20 Rafael Palmeiro .30 .75
21 Ivan Rodriguez .30 .75
22 Carl Everett .20 .50
23 Pedro Martinez .30 .75
24 Manny Ramirez .30 .75
25 Nomar Garciaparra .75 2.00
26 Johnny Damon Sox .30 .75
27 Mike Sweeney .20 .50
28 Carlos Beltran .20 .50
29 Dmitri Young .20 .50
30 Joe Mays .20 .50
31 Doug Mientkiewicz .20 .50
32 Cristian Guzman .20 .50
33 Corey Koskie .20 .50
34 Frank Thomas .50 1.25
35 Magglio Ordonez .20 .50
36 Mark Buehrle .20 .50
37 Bernie Williams .30 .75
38 Roger Clemens 1.00 2.50
39 Derek Jeter 1.25 3.00
40 Jason Giambi .20 .50
41 Mike Mussina .30 .75
42 Lance Berkman .20 .50
43 Jeff Bagwell .30 .75
44 Roy Oswalt .20 .50
45 Greg Maddux .75 2.00
46 Chipper Jones .50 1.25
47 Andruw Jones .30 .75
48 Gary Sheffield .20 .50
49 Geoff Jenkins .20 .50
50 Richie Sexson .20 .50
51 Ben Sheets .20 .50
52 Albert Pujols 1.00 2.50
53 J.D. Drew .20 .50
54 Jim Edmonds .20 .50
55 Sammy Sosa .50 1.25
56 Moises Alou .20 .50
57 Kerry Wood .20 .50
58 Jon Lieber .20 .50
59 Fred McGriff .30 .75
60 Randy Johnson .50 1.25
61 Luis Gonzalez .20 .50
62 Curt Schilling .20 .50
63 Kevin Brown .20 .50
64 Hideo Nomo .50 1.25
65 Shawn Green .20 .50
66 Vladimir Guerrero .50 1.25
67 Jose Vidro .20 .50
68 Barry Bonds 1.25 3.00
69 Jeff Kent .20 .50
70 Rich Aurilia .20 .50
71 Cliff Floyd .20 .50
72 Josh Beckett .20 .50
73 Preston Wilson .20 .50
74 Mike Piazza .75 2.00
75 Mo Vaughn .20 .50
76 Jeromy Burnitz .20 .50
77 Roberto Alomar .30 .75
78 Phil Nevin .20 .50
79 Ryan Klesko .20 .50
80 Scott Rolen .30 .75
81 Bobby Abreu .20 .50
82 Jimmy Rollins .20 .50
83 Brian Giles .20 .50
84 Aramis Ramirez .20 .50
85 Ken Griffey Jr. 1.00 2.50
86 Sean Casey .20 .50
87 Barry Larkin .30 .75
88 Mike Hampton .20 .50
89 Larry Walker .20 .50
90 Todd Helton .30 .75
91A Ron Calloway YS RC 3.00 8.00
91P Ron Calloway YS RC 3.00 8.00
92A Joe Orloski YS RC 3.00 8.00
92P Joe Orloski YS RC 3.00 8.00
93A Anderson Machado YS RC 3.00 8.00
93P Anderson Machado YS RC 3.00 8.00
94A Eric Good YS RC 3.00 8.00
94P Eric Good YS RC 3.00 8.00
95A Reed Johnson YS RC 4.00 10.00
95P Reed Johnson YS RC 4.00 10.00
96A Brendan Donnelly YS RC 3.00 8.00
96P Brendan Donnelly YS RC 3.00 8.00
97A Chris Baker YS RC 3.00 8.00
97P Chris Baker YS RC 3.00 8.00
98A Wilson Valdez YS RC 3.00 8.00
98P Wilson Valdez YS RC 3.00 8.00
99A Scotty Layfield YS RC 3.00 8.00
99P Scotty Layfield YS RC 3.00 8.00
100A P.J. Bevis YS RC 3.00 8.00
100P P.J. Bevis YS RC 3.00 8.00
101A Edwin Almonte YS RC 3.00 8.00
101P Edwin Almonte YS RC 3.00 8.00
102A Francis Beltran YS RC 3.00 8.00
102P Francis Beltran YS RC 3.00 8.00
103A Val Pascucci YS 3.00 8.00
103P Val Pascucci YS 3.00 8.00
104A Nelson Castro YS RC 3.00 8.00
104P Nelson Castro YS RC 3.00 8.00
105A Michael Crudale YS RC 3.00 8.00
105P Michael Crudale YS RC 3.00 8.00
106A Colin Young YS RC 3.00 8.00
106P Colin Young YS RC 3.00 8.00
107A Todd Donovan YS RC 3.00 8.00
107P Todd Donovan YS RC 3.00 8.00
108A Felix Escalona YS RC 3.00 8.00
108P Felix Escalona YS RC 3.00 8.00
109A Brandon Backe YS RC 4.00 10.00
109P Brandon Backe YS RC 4.00 10.00
110A Corey Thurman YS RC 3.00 8.00
110P Corey Thurman YS RC 3.00 8.00
111A Kyle Kane YS RC 3.00 8.00
111P Kyle Kane YS RC 3.00 8.00
112A Allan Simpson YS RC 3.00 8.00
112P Allan Simpson YS RC 3.00 8.00
113A Jose Valverde YS RC 3.00 8.00
113P Jose Valverde YS RC 6.00 15.00
114A Chris Booker YS RC 3.00 8.00
114P Chris Booker YS RC 3.00 8.00
115A Brandon Puffer YS RC 3.00 8.00
115P Brandon Puffer YS RC 3.00 8.00
116A John Foster YS RC 3.00 8.00
116P John Foster YS RC 3.00 8.00
117A Cliff Bartosh YS RC 3.00 8.00
117P Cliff Bartosh YS RC 3.00 8.00
118A Gustavo Chacin YS RC 4.00 10.00
118P Gustavo Chacin YS RC 4.00 10.00
119A Steve Kent YS RC 3.00 8.00
119P Steve Kent YS RC 3.00 8.00
120A Nate Field YS RC 3.00 8.00
120P Nate Field YS RC 3.00 8.00
121 Victor Alvarez AU RC 4.00 10.00
122 Steve Bechler AU RC 4.00 10.00
123 Adrian Burnside AU RC 4.00 10.00
124 Marlon Byrd AU 6.00 15.00
125 Jaime Cerda AU RC 4.00 10.00
126 Brandon Claussen AU 6.00 15.00
127 Mark Corey AU RC 4.00 10.00
128 Doug Devore AU RC 4.00 10.00
129 Kazuhisa Ishii AU SP RC 4.00 10.00
130 John Ennis AU RC 4.00 10.00
131 Kevin Frederick AU RC 4.00 10.00
132 Josh Hancock AU RC 8.00 20.00
133 Ben Howard AU RC 4.00 10.00
134 Orlando Hudson AU 6.00 15.00
135 Hansel Izquierdo AU RC 4.00 10.00
136 Eric Junge AU RC 4.00 10.00
137 Austin Kearns AU 6.00 15.00
138 Victor Martinez AU 8.00 20.00
139 Luis Martinez AU RC 4.00 10.00
140 Danny Mota AU RC 4.00 10.00
141 Jorge Padilla AU RC 4.00 10.00
142 Andy Pratt AU RC 4.00 10.00
143 Rene Reyes AU RC 4.00 10.00
144 Rodrigo Rosario AU RC 4.00 10.00
145 Tom Shearn AU RC 4.00 10.00
146 So Taguchi AU SP RC 6.00 15.00
147 Dennis Tankersley AU 6.00 15.00
148 Matt Thornton AU RC 4.00 10.00
149 Jeremy Ward AU RC 4.00 10.00
150 Mitch Wylie AU RC 4.00 10.00
151 Pedro Martinez JSY/800 2.50 6.00
152 Cal Ripken JSY/800 12.00 30.00
153 Roger Clemens JSY/800 5.00 12.00
154 Bernie Williams JSY/800 2.50 6.00
155 Jason Giambi JSY/700 1.50 4.00
156 Robin Ventura JSY/800 1.50 4.00
157 Carlos Delgado JSY/800 1.50 4.00
158 Frank Thomas JSY/800 4.00 10.00
159 Magglio Ordonez JSY/800 2.50 6.00
160 Jim Thome JSY/800 2.50 6.00
161 Darin Erstad JSY/800 1.50 4.00
162 Tim Salmon JSY/800 1.50 4.00
163 Tim Hudson JSY/800 2.50 6.00
164 Barry Zito JSY/800 1.50 4.00
165 Ichiro Suzuki JSY/800 5.00 12.00
166 Edgar Martinez JSY/800 2.50 6.00
167 Alex Rodriguez JSY/800 5.00 12.00
168 Ivan Rodriguez JSY/800 2.50 6.00
169 Juan Gonzalez JSY/800 1.50 4.00
170 Greg Maddux JSY/800 6.00 15.00
171 Chipper Jones JSY/800 4.00 10.00
172 Andruw Jones JSY/800 1.50 4.00
173 Tom Glavine JSY/800 2.50 6.00
174 Mike Piazza JSY/800 4.00 10.00
175 Roberto Alomar JSY/800 2.50 6.00
176 Scott Rolen JSY/800 2.50 6.00
177 Sammy Sosa JSY/800 4.00 10.00
178 Moises Alou JSY/800 1.50 4.00
179 Ken Griffey Jr. JSY/700 8.00 20.00
180 Jeff Bagwell JSY/800 2.50 6.00
181 Jim Edmonds JSY/800 2.50 6.00
182 J.D. Drew JSY/800 1.50 4.00
183 Brian Giles JSY/800 1.50 4.00
184 Randy Johnson JSY/800 4.00 10.00
185 Curt Schilling JSY/800 2.50 6.00
186 Luis Gonzalez JSY/800 1.50 4.00
187 Todd Helton JSY/800 2.50 6.00
188 Shawn Green JSY/800 1.50 4.00
189 David Wells JSY/800 1.50 4.00
190 Jeff Kent JSY/800 1.50 4.00
191 Tom Glavine .50 1.25
192 Cliff Floyd .30 .75
193 Mark Prior .50 1.25
194 Corey Patterson .30 .75
195 Paul Konerko .30 .75
196 Adam Dunn .30 .75
197 Joe Borchard .30 .75
198 Carlos Pena .30 .75
199 Juan Encarnacion .30 .75
200 Luis Castillo .30 .75
201 Torii Hunter .30 .75
202 Hee Seop Choi .30 .75
203 Bartolo Colon .30 .75
204 Raul Mondesi .30 .75
205 Jeff Weaver .30 .75
206 Eric Munson .30 .75
207 Alfonso Soriano .30 .75
208 Ray Durham .30 .75
209 Eric Chavez .30 .75
210 Brett Myers .30 .75
211 Jeremy Giambi .30 .75
212 Vicente Padilla .30 .75
213 Felipe Lopez .30 .75
214 Sean Burroughs .30 .75
215 Kenny Lofton .30 .75
216 Scott Rolen .50 1.25
217 Carl Crawford .30 .75
218 Juan Gonzalez .30 .75
219 Orlando Hudson .30 .75
220 Eric Hinske .30 .75
221 Adam Walker AU RC 4.00 10.00
222 Aaron Cook AU RC 6.00 15.00
223 Cam Esslinger AU RC 4.00 10.00
224 Kirk Saarloos AU RC 4.00 10.00
225 Jose Diaz AU RC 4.00 10.00
226 David Ross AU RC 60.00 150.00
227 Jayson Durocher AU RC 4.00 10.00
228 Brian Mallette AU RC 4.00 10.00
229 Aaron Guiel AU RC 4.00 10.00
230 Jorge Nunez AU RC 4.00 10.00
231 Satoru Komiyama AU RC 6.00 15.00
232 Tyler Yates AU RC 4.00 10.00
233 Pete Zamora AU RC 4.00 10.00
234 Mike Gonzalez AU RC 4.00 10.00
235 Oliver Perez AU RC 4.00 10.00
236 Julius Matos AU RC 6.00 15.00
237 Andy Shibilo AU RC 4.00 10.00
238 Jason Simontacchi AU RC 4.00 10.00
239 Ron Chiavacci AU 4.00 10.00
240 Deivis Santos AU 4.00 10.00
241 Travis Driskill AU RC 4.00 10.00
242 Jorge De La Rosa AU RC 4.00 10.00
243 Anastacio Martinez AU RC 4.00 10.00
244 Earl Snyder AU RC 4.00 10.00
245 Freddy Sanchez AU RC 12.00 30.00
246 Miguel Asencio AU RC 4.00 10.00
247 Juan Brito AU RC 4.00 10.00
248 Franklyn German AU RC 4.00 10.00
249 Chris Snelling AU RC 6.00 15.00
250 Ken Huckaby AU RC 4.00 10.00

2002 SPx SuperStars Swatches Gold

*GOLD JSY: .6X TO 1.5X BASIC JSY
RANDOM INSERTS IN PACKS
STATED PRINT RUN 150 SERIAL #'d SETS

2002 SPx SuperStars Swatches Silver

*SILVER JSY: .4X TO 1X BASIC JSY
RANDOM INSERTS IN PACKS
STATED PRINT RUN 400 SERIAL #'d SETS

2002 SPx Winning Materials 2-Player Base Combos

Randomly inserted into packs, these cards include bases used by both players featured on the card. These cards were issued to a stated print run of 200 serial numbered sets.

RANDOM INSERTS IN PACKS
STATED PRINT RUN 200 SERIAL #'d SETS

BBG B.Bonds S.Green 10.00 25.00
BGR Troy Glaus Alex Rodriguez 8.00 20.00
BGS Ken Griffey Jr. Sammy Sosa 12.00 30.00
BIM Ichiro Suzuki Edgar Martinez 8.00 20.00
BPE Mike Piazza Jim Edmonds 6.00 15.00
BPI Albert Pujols Ichiro Suzuki 12.00 30.00
BRJ Alex Rodriguez Derek Jeter 10.00 25.00
BSG Sammy Sosa Luis Gonzalez 6.00 15.00
BSR Kazuhiro Sasaki Mariano Rivera 6.00 15.00
BWJ Bernie Williams Derek Jeter 12.00 30.00

2002 SPx Winning Materials 2-Player Jersey Combos

Inserted at stated odds of one in 18, these 29 cards feature not only the players but a jersey swatch from each player. A few players were issued in lesser quantities and we have notated that with an SP in our checklist. Other players were issued in larger quantities and we have notated that with an asterisk next to the player's name.

STATED ODDS 1:18
SP INFO PROVIDED BY UPPER DECK
DP PERCEIVED AS LARGER SUPPLY

WMAR A.Rodriguez I.Rodriguez 6.00 15.00
WMBA J.Burnitz/E.Alfonzo 2.00 5.00
WMBG J.Bagwell/J.Gonzalez 3.00 8.00
WMBR J.Bagwell/A.Rodriguez DP 6.00 15.00
WMDH J.Dye/T.Hudson 3.00 8.00
WMDS C.Delgado/S.Stewart 2.00 5.00
WMED J.Edmonds/J.Drew 3.00 8.00
WMGC K.Griffey Jr./S.Casey SP 10.00 25.00
WMGK S.Green/E.Karros 2.00 5.00
WMGR J.Gonzalez/I.Rodriguez 3.00 8.00
WMHW M.Hampton/L.Walker 3.00 8.00
WMJJ C.Jones/A.Jones 5.00 12.00
WMJS R.Johnson/C.Schilling 5.00 12.00
WMKG J.Kendall/B.Giles 2.00 5.00
WMLH A.Leiter/M.Hampton 2.00 5.00
WMMC E.Martinez/M.Cameron 3.00 8.00
WMMJ G.Maddux/C.Jones 8.00 20.00
WMNM H.Nomo/P.Martinez SP 5.00 12.00
WMPA M.Piazza/R.Alomar DP 5.00 12.00
WMRA S.Rolen/B.Abreu 3.00 8.00
WMRP I.Rodriguez/C.Park 3.00 8.00
WMSE A.Sele/D.Erstad 2.00 5.00
WMSH K.Sasaki/S.Hasegawa 2.00 5.00
WMSP S.Sosa/C.Patterson 5.00 12.00
WMTO F.Thomas/M.Ordonez 5.00 12.00
WMTS J.Thome/C.Sabathia DP 3.00 8.00
WMVR O.Vizquel/A.Rodriguez 6.00 15.00
WMWG B.Williams/J.Giambi DP 3.00 8.00
WMWP D.Wells/J.Posada DP 3.00 8.00

2002 SPx Winning Materials USA Jersey Combos

Randomly inserted into packs, these 23 cards feature two uniform swatches from players who played for the USA National team. These cards had a stated print run of 150 serial numbered sets.

RANDOM INSERTS IN PACKS
STATED PRINT RUN 150 SERIAL #'d SETS

USAAH B.Abernathy/O.Hudson 6.00 15.00
USAAW M.Anderson/J.Weaver 6.00 15.00
USABT S.Burroughs/M.Teixeira 10.00 25.00
USAGB J.Giambi/S.Burroughs 6.00 15.00
USAGT J.Giambi/M.Teixeira 10.00 25.00
USAHD O.Hudson/J.Deardorff 6.00 15.00
USAHP D.Hermanson/M.Prior 6.00 15.00
USAJC J.Jones/M.Cuddyer 6.00 15.00
USAKB A.Kearns/S.Burroughs 6.00 15.00
USAKC A.Kearns/M.Cuddyer 6.00 15.00
USAMG D.Mientk/J.Giambi 6.00 15.00
USAMO M.Morris/R.Oswalt 6.00 15.00
USAMP M.Morris/M.Prior 6.00 15.00
USAMW M.Morris/J.Weaver 6.00 15.00
USAPB M.Prior/D.Brazelton 6.00 15.00
USARE B.Roberts/A.Everett 6.00 15.00
USASD M.Kotsay/S.Burroughs 6.00 15.00
USATB B.Abernathy/D.Braz 6.00 15.00
USATP M.Teixeira/M.Prior 10.00 25.00
USAWB J.Weaver/D.Brazelton 6.00 15.00
USAWH J.Weaver/D.Hermanson 6.00 15.00
USAHOU R.Oswalt/A.Everett 6.00 15.00
USAMIN D.Mientk/M.Cuddyer 6.00 15.00

2003 SPx

This 199 card set was released in two series. The primary 178-card set was issued in August, 2003 followed up with 21 Update cards randomly seeded within a special rookie pack within sealed boxes of 2003 Upper Deck Finite baseball (of which was released in December, 2003). The primary SPx product was distributed in four card packs carrying an SRP of $7. Each sealed box contained 18 packs and each sealed case contained 14 boxes. Cards numbered 1 to 125 featured veterans with 25 short print cards inserted. Cards numbered 126 through 160 featured rookie cards which were issued to a stated print run of 999 serial numbered sets. Cards 161 and 162 featured New York Yankees rookies Hideki Matsui and Jose Contreras. The Matsui card was issued to a serial numbered print run of 864 copies while the Contreras was issued to a serial numbered print run of 800 copies. Both cards were signed while the Matsui also included a game-used jersey swatch. Cards numbered 163 through 178 featured both autographs and jersey swatches of the featured player and those cards were issued to a stated print run of 1224 cards. The Update cards 179-193 featured a selection of prospects and each card was serial numbered to 150 copies. For reasons unknown to us, the set then skipped to cards 381-387, of which featured additional prospects on cards enriched with both certified autographs and game jersey swatches. These "high number" cards were printed to a serial numbered quantity of 355 copies each.

COMP.LO SET w/o SP's (100) 10.00 25.00
COMP.LO SET w/ SP's (125) 20.00 50.00
COMMON CARD (1-125) .20 .50
COMMON SP (1-125) .60 1.50
SP: 4/9/13/20/22/26/35/53/60/64/70/72
SP: 79/82-84/91/94/101/105/108/111
SP: 114/116/125
COMMON CARD (126-160) 1.00 2.50
126-160 PRINT RUN 999 SERIAL #'d SETS
COMMON CARD (161-178) 6.00 15.00
CARD 161 PRINT RUN 864 SERIAL #'d COPIES
CARD 162 PRINT RUN 800 SERIAL #'d COPIES
163-178 PRINT RUN 1224 SERIAL #'d SETS
126-178 RANDOM INSERTS IN SPx PACKS
COMMON CARD (179-193) 2.50 6.00
179-193 RANDOM IN UD FINITE BONUS PACK
179-193 PRINT RUN 150 SERIAL #'d SETS
COMMON CARD (381-387) 6.00 15.00
381-387 RANDOM IN UD FINITE BONUS PACK
381-387 PRINT RUN 355 SERIAL #'d SETS

1 Darin Erstad .20 .50
2 Garret Anderson .20 .50
3 Tim Salmon .20 .50
4 Troy Glaus SP .60 1.50
5 Luis Gonzalez .20 .50
6 Randy Johnson .50 1.25
7 Curt Schilling .30 .75
8 Lyle Overbay .20 .50
9 Andruw Jones SP .60 1.50
10 Gary Sheffield .20 .50
11 Rafael Furcal .20 .50
12 Greg Maddux .60 1.50
13 Chipper Jones SP 1.50 4.00
14 Tony Batista .20 .50
15 Rodrigo Lopez .20 .50
16 Jay Gibbons .20 .50
17 Byung-Hyun Kim .20 .50
18 Johnny Damon .30 .75
19 Derek Lowe .20 .50
20 Nomar Garciaparra SP 1.00 2.50
21 Pedro Martinez .30 .75
22 Manny Ramirez SP 1.50 4.00
23 Mark Prior .30 .75
24 Kerry Wood .20 .50
25 Corey Patterson .20 .50
26 Sammy Sosa SP 1.50 4.00
27 Moises Alou .20 .50
28 Magglio Ordonez .30 .75
29 Frank Thomas .50 1.25
30 Paul Konerko .30 .75
31 Bartolo Colon .20 .50
32 Adam Dunn .30 .75
33 Austin Kearns .20 .50
34 Aaron Boone .20 .50
35 Ken Griffey Jr. SP 3.00 8.00
36 Omar Vizquel .30 .75
37 C.C. Sabathia .30 .75
38 Jason Davis .20 .50
39 Travis Hafner .20 .50
40 Brandon Phillips .20 .50
41 Larry Walker .30 .75
42 Preston Wilson .20 .50
43 Jay Payton .20 .50
44 Todd Helton .30 .75
45 Carlos Pena .30 .75
46 Eric Munson .20 .50
47 Ivan Rodriguez .30 .75
49 Alex Gonzalez .20 .50
50 Roy Oswalt .30 .75
51 Craig Biggio .30 .75
52 Jeff Bagwell .30 .75
53 Dontrelle Willis SP .60 1.50
54 Mike Sweeney .20 .50
55 Carlos Beltran .30 .75
56 Brent Mayne .20 .50
57 Hideo Nomo .50 1.25
58 Rickey Henderson .50 1.25
59 Adrian Beltre .50 1.25
60 Miguel Cabrera SP 8.00 20.00
61 Kazuhisa Ishii .20 .50
62 Ben Sheets .20 .50
63 Richie Sexson .20 .50
64 Torii Hunter SP .60 1.50
65 Jacque Jones .20 .50
66 Joe Mays .20 .50
67 Corey Koskie .20 .50
68 A.J. Pierzynski .20 .50
69 Jose Vidro .20 .50
70 Vladimir Guerrero SP 1.00 2.50
71 Tom Glavine .30 .75
72 Jose Reyes SP 1.50 4.00
73 Aaron Heilman .20 .50
74 Mike Piazza .50 1.25
75 Jorge Posada .30 .75
77 Robin Ventura .20 .50
78 Mariano Rivera .60 1.50
79 Roger Clemens SP 2.00 5.00
80 Jason Giambi .20 .50
81 Bernie Williams .30 .75
82 Alfonso Soriano SP 1.00 2.50
83 Derek Jeter SP 4.00 10.00
84 Miguel Tejada SP 1.00 2.50
85 Eric Chavez .20 .50
86 Tim Hudson .30 .75
87 Barry Zito .30 .75
88 Mark Mulder .20 .50
89 Erubiel Durazo .20 .50
90 Pat Burrell .20 .50
91 Jim Thome SP 1.00 2.50
92 Bobby Abreu .20 .50
93 Brian Giles .20 .50
94 Reggie Sanders SP .60 1.50
95 Kenny Lofton .20 .50
96 Ryan Klesko .20 .50
97 Sean Burroughs .20 .50
98 Edgardo Alfonzo .20 .50
99 Rich Aurilia .20 .50
100 Jose Cruz Jr. .20 .50
101 Barry Bonds SP 2.50 6.00
102 Mike Cameron .20 .50
103 Kazuhiro Sasaki .20 .50
104 Bret Boone .20 .50
105 Ichiro Suzuki SP 2.00 5.00
106 J.D. Drew .20 .50
107 Jim Edmonds .30 .75
108 Scott Rolen SP 1.00 2.50
109 Matt Morris .20 .50
110 Tino Martinez .20 .50
111 Albert Pujols SP 2.00 5.00
112 Damian Rolls .20 .50
113 Carl Crawford .20 .50
114 Rocco Baldelli SP .60 1.50
115 Hank Blalock .20 .50
116 Alex Rodriguez SP 2.00 5.00
117 Kevin Mench .20 .50
118 Rafael Palmeiro .30 .75
119 Mark Teixeira .30 .75
120 Shannon Stewart .20 .50

121 Vernon Wells	.20	.50
122 Josh Phelps	.20	.50
123 Eric Hinske	.20	.50
124 Orlando Hudson	.20	.50
125 Carlos Delgado SP	.60	1.50
126 Jason Roach ROO RC	1.00	2.50
127 Dan Haren ROO RC	5.00	12.00
128 Luis Ayala ROO RC	1.00	2.50
129 Bo Hart ROO RC	1.00	2.50
130 Wilfredo Ledezma ROO RC	1.00	2.50
131 Rick Roberts ROO RC	1.00	2.50
132 Miguel Ojeda ROO RC	1.00	2.50
133 Aquilino Lopez ROO RC	1.00	2.50
134 Roger Deago ROO RC	1.00	2.50
135 Arnie Munoz ROO RC	1.00	2.50
136 Brent Hoard ROO RC	1.00	2.50
137 Termel Sledge ROO RC	1.00	2.50
138 Ryan Cameron ROO RC	1.00	2.50
139 Prentice Redman ROO RC	1.00	2.50
140 Clint Barmes ROO RC	2.50	6.00
141 Jeremy Griffiths ROO RC	1.00	2.50
142 Jon Leicester ROO RC	1.00	2.50
143 Brandon Webb ROO RC	3.00	8.00
144 Todd Wellemeyer ROO RC	1.00	2.50
145 Felix Sanchez ROO RC	1.00	2.50
146 Anthony Ferrari ROO RC	1.00	2.50
147 Ian Ferguson ROO RC	1.00	2.50
148 Michael Nakamura ROO RC	1.00	2.50
149 Lew Ford ROO RC	1.00	2.50
150 Nate Bland ROO RC	1.00	2.50
151 David Matranga ROO RC	1.00	2.50
152 Edgar Gonzalez ROO RC	1.00	2.50
153 Carlos Mendez ROO RC	1.00	2.50
154 Jason Gilfillan ROO RC	1.00	2.50
155 Mike Neu ROO RC	1.00	2.50
156 Jason Shiell ROO RC	1.00	2.50
157 Jeff Duncan ROO RC	1.00	2.50
158 Oscar Villarreal ROO RC	1.00	2.50
159 Diegomar Markwell ROO RC	1.00	2.50
160 Joe Valentine ROO RC	1.00	2.50
161 Hideki Matsui AU JSY RC	100.00	200.00
162 Jose Contreras AU RC	20.00	40.00
163 Willie Eyre AU JSY RC	6.00	15.00
164 Matt Bruback AU JSY RC	6.00	15.00
165 Rett Johnson AU JSY RC	6.00	15.00
166 Jeremy Griffiths AU JSY	6.00	15.00
167 Fran Cruceta AU JSY RC	6.00	15.00
168 Fern Cabrera AU JSY RC	6.00	15.00
169 Jhonny Peralta AU JSY	6.00	15.00
170 Shane Bazzell AU JSY RC	6.00	15.00
171 Bob Madritsch AU JSY RC	10.00	25.00
172 Phil Seibel AU JSY RC	6.00	15.00
173 J.Willingham AU JSY RC	6.00	15.00
174 Rob Hammock AU JSY RC	6.00	15.00
175 A.Machado AU JSY RC	6.00	15.00
176 David Sanders AU JSY RC	6.00	15.00
177 Matt Kata AU JSY RC	6.00	15.00
178 Heath Bell AU JSY RC	6.00	15.00
179 Chad Gaudin ROO RC	2.50	6.00
180 Chris Capuano ROO RC	2.50	6.00
181 Danny Garcia ROO RC	2.50	6.00
182 Delmon Young ROO	15.00	40.00
183 Edwin Jackson ROO RC	4.00	10.00
184 Greg Jones ROO RC	2.50	6.00
185 Jeremy Bonderman ROO RC	10.00	25.00
186 Jorge DePaula ROO	2.50	6.00
187 Khalil Greene ROO	4.00	10.00
188 Chad Cordero ROO RC	2.50	6.00
189 Miguel Cabrera ROO	20.00	50.00
190 Rich Harden ROO	4.00	10.00
191 Rickie Weeks ROO	8.00	20.00
192 Rosman Garcia ROO RC	2.50	6.00
193 Tom Gregorio ROO RC	2.50	6.00
381 Andrew Brown AU JSY RC	6.00	15.00
382 Delm Young AU JSY RC	12.50	30.00
383 Colin Porter AU JSY RC	6.00	15.00
385 Rick. Weeks AU JSY RC	10.00	25.00
386 David Matranga AU JSY RC	6.00	15.00
387 Bo Hart AU JSY	6.00	15.00

2003 SPx Spectrum

*SPECTRUM 1-125 p/r 51-75: 5X TO 12X
*SPECTRUM 1-125 p/r 36-50: 6X TO 15X
*SPECTRUM 1-125 p/r 26-35: 8X TO 20X
*SPECTRUM 1-125 p/r 51-75: 1.25X TO 3X SP
*SPECTRUM 1-125 p/r 36-50: 1.5X TO 4X SP
*SPECTRUM 1-125 p/r 26-35: 2X TO 5X SP
1-125 PRINT RUNS B/WN 1-75 COPIES PER
*SPECTRUM 126-160: 2X TO 5X BASIC
126-160 PRINT RUN 125 SERIAL #'d SETS
161-178 PRINT RUN 25 SERIAL #'d SETS
161-178 NO PRICING DUE TO SCARCITY

2003 SPx Game Used Combos

Randomly inserted into packs, these 42 cards feature two players along with game-used memorabilia of each player. Since these cards were issued in varying quantities, we have notated the print run next to the card in our checklist. Please note that if a card was issued to a print run of 25 or fewer copies, no pricing is provided due to market scarcity.

PRINT RUNS B/WN 10-90 COPIES PER
NO PRICING ON QTY OF 25 OR LESS

BK J.Bagwell/J.Kent/90	15.00	40.00
BM B.Bonds/R.Maris/50	30.00	60.00
BT B.Bonds/T.Williams/50	125.00	250.00
CA C.Ripken/A.Rodriguez/50	125.00	200.00
CC J.Contreras/R.Clemens/50	20.00	50.00
CL C.Ripken/L.Gehrig/90	150.00	300.00
CM J.Contreras/P.Martinez/90	15.00	40.00
EG D.Erstad/T.Glaus/90	10.00	25.00
FC C.Fisk/G.Carter/90	15.00	40.00
GC G.Maddux/C.Jones/90	20.00	50.00
GD K.Griffey Jr./A.Dunn/90	30.00	60.00
GR K.Griffey Jr./S.Sosa/90	30.00	60.00
GS J.Giambi/A.Soriano/90	10.00	25.00
HJ H.Matsui/J.Giambi/50	50.00	100.00
IA I.Suzuki/A.Pujols/50	150.00	250.00
JJ C.Jones/A.Jones/90	15.00	40.00
MB M.Mantle/B.Bonds/50	50.00	120.00
MD M.Mantle/D.Jeter/50	150.00	250.00
MG P.Martinez/Nomar/90	30.00	60.00
MJ H.Matsui/D.Jeter/90	60.00	120.00
MS H.Matsui/I.Suzuki/50	250.00	400.00
MW M.Mantle/T.Williams/50	75.00	150.00
NI H.Nomo/K.Ishii/50	40.00	80.00
PM R.Palmeiro/F.McGriff/90	15.00	40.00
RC N.Ryan/R.Clemens/90	20.00	50.00
RG A.Rod/N.Garciaparra/90	30.00	60.00
RR C.Ripken/S.Rolen/90	25.00	60.00
RS N.Ryan/T.Seaver/90	75.00	150.00
RT A.Rodriguez/M.Tejada/90	20.00	50.00
SB S.Sosa/B.Bonds/90	30.00	60.00
SJ C.Schilling/R.Johnson/90	15.00	40.00
SN I.Suzuki/H.Nomo/90	125.00	200.00
SP S.Sosa/R.Palmeiro/90	15.00	40.00

2003 SPx Stars Autograph Jersey

Randomly inserted in packs, these cards feature both a game-used jersey swatch as well as an authentic signature. Since these cards were issued in varying print runs, we have notated the stated print run next to their name in our checklist.

PRINT RUNS B/WN 195-790 COPIES PER
SPECTRUM PRINT RUN 1 SERIAL #'d SET
NO SPECTRUM PRICING DUE TO SCARCITY

CJ0 Chipper Jones/195	40.00	80.00
CS Curt Schilling/490	12.00	30.00
JG Jason Giambi/315	15.00	40.00
KG Ken Griffey Jr./690	30.00	80.00
LB Lance Berkman/590	6.00	15.00
LG Luis Gonzalez/790	6.00	15.00
MP Mark Prior/490	8.00	20.00
NM Nomar Garciaparra/195	15.00	40.00
PB Pat Burrell/590	10.00	25.00
TG Troy Glaus/490	6.00	15.00
VG Vladimir Guerrero/390	10.00	25.00

2003 SPx Winning Materials 375

LOGO'S CONSECUTIVELY #'d FROM 41-375
NUMBERS CONSECUTIVELY #'d FROM 1-40
CARDS CUMULATIVELY SERIAL #'d TO 375
*WIN.MAT 250: .5X TO 1.2X WIN.MAT 375
NUMBERS CONSECUTIVELY #'d FROM 1-28
LOGOS CONSECUTIVELY #'d FROM 29-250
WM 250 CUMULATIVELY SERIAL #'d TO 250
LOGO/NUMBER PRINTS PROVIDED BY UD

AJ1A Andruw Jones Logo	1.50	4.00
AJ1B Andruw Jones Num	3.00	8.00
AP1A Albert Pujols Logo	5.00	12.00
AP1B Albert Pujols Num	10.00	25.00
AR1A Alex Rodriguez Logo	5.00	12.00
AR1B Alex Rodriguez Num	10.00	25.00
AS1A Alfonso Soriano Logo	2.50	6.00
AS1B Alfonso Soriano Num	5.00	12.00
BW1A Bernie Williams Logo	2.50	6.00
BW1B Bernie Williams Num	5.00	12.00
BZ1A Barry Zito Logo	2.50	6.00
BZ1B Barry Zito Num	5.00	12.00
CD1A Carlos Delgado Logo	1.50	4.00
CD1B Carlos Delgado Num	3.00	8.00
CJ1A Chipper Jones Logo	4.00	10.00
CJ1B Chipper Jones Num	8.00	20.00
CS1A Curt Schilling Logo	2.50	6.00
CS1B Curt Schilling Num	5.00	12.00
FT1A Frank Thomas Logo	4.00	10.00
FT1B Frank Thomas Num	8.00	20.00
GM1A Greg Maddux Logo	5.00	12.00
GM1B Greg Maddux Num	10.00	25.00
GS1A Gary Sheffield Logo	1.50	4.00
GS1B Gary Sheffield Num	3.00	8.00
HM1A Hideki Matsui Logo	8.00	20.00
HM1B Hideki Matsui Num	15.00	40.00
HN1A Hideo Nomo Logo	4.00	10.00
HN1B Hideo Nomo Num	8.00	20.00
IR1A Ivan Rodriguez Logo	2.50	6.00
IR1B Ivan Rodriguez Num	5.00	12.00
IS1A Ichiro Suzuki Logo	5.00	12.00
IS1B Ichiro Suzuki Num	10.00	25.00
JB1A Jeff Bagwell Logo	2.50	6.00
JB1B Jeff Bagwell Num	5.00	12.00
JG1A Jason Giambi Logo	1.50	4.00
JG1B Jason Giambi Num	3.00	8.00
JK1A Jeff Kent Logo	1.50	4.00
JK1B Jeff Kent Num	3.00	8.00
JT1A Jim Thome Logo	2.50	6.00
JT1B Jim Thome Num	5.00	12.00
KG1A Ken Griffey Jr. Logo	8.00	20.00
KG1B Ken Griffey Jr. Num	15.00	40.00
LB1A Lance Berkman Logo	2.50	6.00
LB1B Lance Berkman Num	5.00	12.00
LG1A Luis Gonzalez Logo	1.50	4.00
LG1B Luis Gonzalez Num	3.00	8.00
MA1A Mark Prior Logo	2.50	6.00
MA1B Mark Prior Num	5.00	12.00
MP1A Mike Piazza Logo	4.00	10.00
MP1B Mike Piazza Num	8.00	20.00
MR1A Manny Ramirez Logo	4.00	10.00
MR1B Manny Ramirez Num	8.00	20.00
MT1A Miguel Tejada Logo	2.50	6.00
MT1B Miguel Tejada Num	5.00	12.00
PB1A Pat Burrell Logo	1.50	4.00
PB1B Pat Burrell Num	3.00	8.00
PM1A Pedro Martinez Logo	2.50	6.00
PM1B Pedro Martinez Num	5.00	12.00
RA1A Roberto Alomar Logo	2.50	6.00
RA1B Roberto Alomar Num	5.00	12.00
RC1A Roger Clemens Logo	5.00	12.00
RC1B Roger Clemens Num	10.00	25.00
RF1A Rafael Furcal Logo	1.50	4.00
RF1B Rafael Furcal Num	3.00	8.00
RJ1A Randy Johnson Logo	4.00	10.00
RJ1B Randy Johnson Num	8.00	20.00
SG1A Shawn Green Logo	1.50	4.00
SG1B Shawn Green Num	3.00	8.00
SS1A Sammy Sosa Logo	4.00	10.00
SS1B Sammy Sosa Num	8.00	20.00
TG1A Tom Glavine Logo	2.50	6.00
TG1B Tom Glavine Num	5.00	12.00
TH1A Torii Hunter Logo	1.50	4.00
TH1B Torii Hunter Num	3.00	8.00
TO1A Todd Helton Logo	2.50	6.00
TO1B Todd Helton Num	5.00	12.00
TR1A Troy Glaus Logo	1.50	4.00
TR1B Troy Glaus Num	3.00	8.00
VG1A Vladimir Guerrero Logo	2.50	6.00
VG1B Vladimir Guerrero Num	5.00	12.00

2003 SPx Winning Materials 175

NUMBERS CONSECUTIVELY #'d FROM 1-20
LOGOS CONSECUTIVELY #'d FROM 21-175
CARDS CUMULATIVELY SERIAL #'d TO 175
*WM LOGO 50: .5X TO 1.2X WM LOGO 175
WM 50 NUMBERS CONSECUTIVELY #'d 1-10
WM 50 LOGOS CONSECUTIVELY #'d 11-50
WM 50 CUMULATIVELY SERIAL #'d TO 50
NO NUMBER PRICING DUE TO SCARCITY
LOGO/NUMBER PRINTS PROVIDED BY UD

AJ2A Andruw Jones Logo	2.00	5.00
AP2A Albert Pujols Logo	6.00	15.00
AR2A Alex Rodriguez Logo	6.00	15.00
AS2A Alfonso Soriano Logo	3.00	8.00
BW2A Bernie Williams Logo	3.00	8.00
BZ2A Barry Zito Logo	3.00	8.00
CD2A Carlos Delgado Logo	2.00	5.00
CJ2A Chipper Jones Logo	5.00	12.00
CS2A Curt Schilling Logo	3.00	8.00
FT2A Frank Thomas Logo	5.00	12.00
GM2A Greg Maddux Logo	6.00	15.00
GS2A Gary Sheffield Logo	2.00	5.00
HM2A Hideki Matsui Logo	10.00	25.00
HN2A Hideo Nomo Logo	5.00	12.00
IR2A Ivan Rodriguez Logo	3.00	8.00
IS2A Ichiro Suzuki Logo	6.00	15.00
JB2A Jeff Bagwell Logo	3.00	8.00
JG2A Jason Giambi Logo	2.00	5.00
JK2A Jeff Kent Logo	2.00	5.00
JT2A Jim Thome Logo	3.00	8.00
KG2A Ken Griffey Jr. Logo	10.00	25.00
LB2A Lance Berkman Logo	3.00	8.00
LG2A Luis Gonzalez Logo	2.00	5.00
MM2A M.Mantle Pants Logo	60.00	150.00
MP2RA Mark Prior Logo	3.00	8.00
MP2A Mike Piazza Logo	5.00	12.00
MR2A Manny Ramirez Logo	5.00	12.00
MT2A Miguel Tejada Logo	3.00	8.00
PB2A Pat Burrell Logo	2.00	5.00
PM2A Pedro Martinez Logo	3.00	8.00
RA2A Roberto Alomar Logo	3.00	8.00
RC2A Roger Clemens Logo	6.00	15.00
RF2A Rafael Furcal Logo	2.00	5.00
RJ2A Randy Johnson Logo	5.00	12.00
SG2A Shawn Green Logo	2.00	5.00
SS2A Sammy Sosa Logo	5.00	12.00
TGL2A Troy Glaus Logo	2.00	5.00
TG2A Tom Glavine Logo	3.00	8.00
THE2A Todd Helton Logo	3.00	8.00
TH2A Torii Hunter Logo	2.00	5.00
TW2A T.Williams Pants Logo	20.00	50.00
VG2A Vladimir Guerrero Logo	3.00	8.00

2003 SPx Young Stars Autograph Jersey

20 of the 23 cards within this set were randomly inserted in 2003 SPx packs (released in August, 2003). Serial #'d print runs for the 20 low series cards range between 964-1460 copies each. An additional three cards (all of which are much scarcer with serial #'d print runs of only 355 copies per), were randomly seeded in packs of 2003 Upper Deck Finite of which was released in December, 2003. These cards feature game-used jersey swatches and authentic autographs from each player. Since these cards were issued in varying quantities, we have noted the stated print run next to the player's name in our checklist. Rocco Baldelli did not return his autographs prior to packout thus an exchange card with a redemption deadline of August 15th, 2006 was placed into packs.

PRINT RUNS B/WN 355-1460 COPIES PER
SPECTRUM PRINT RUN 25 SERIAL #'d SETS
NO SPECTRUM PRICING DUE TO SCARCITY
EXCHANGE DEADLINE 08/15/06

AD Adam Dunn/1295	6.00	15.00
AK Austin Kearns/964	6.00	15.00
BM Brett Myers/1295	6.00	15.00
BP Brandon Phillips/1295	6.00	15.00
CG Chris George/1260	6.00	15.00
DW Dontrelle Willis/355	12.50	30.00
EH Eric Hinske/1295	6.00	15.00
HB Hank Blalock/1295	6.00	15.00
JA Jason Jennings/1295	6.00	15.00
JBA Josh Bard/1295	6.00	15.00
JJ Jacque Jones/1260	6.00	15.00
JP Josh Phelps/1295	6.00	15.00
KA Kurt Ainsworth/1460	6.00	15.00
KG Khalil Greene/355	20.00	50.00
KS Kirk Saarloos/1295	6.00	15.00
MD Michael Cuddyer/1156	6.00	15.00
MK Mike Kinkade/1295	6.00	15.00
MT Mark Teixeira/1295	10.00	25.00
NJ Nick Johnson/1295	6.00	15.00
RB Rocco Baldelli/1295	6.00	15.00
RH Rich Harden/355	6.00	15.00
RO Roy Oswalt/1295	6.00	15.00
SB Sean Burroughs/1295	6.00	15.00

2004 SPx

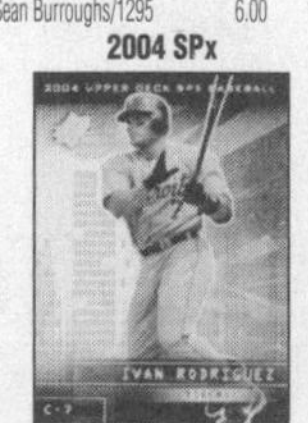

This 202-card set was released in December, 2004. The set was issued in four-card packs with an $7 SRP which came 18 packs to a box and 14 boxes to a case. The first 100 cards of this set feature active veterans while cards 101 through 110 feature retired greats. Cards 111 through 202 feature rookies either issued to different tiers or with both a jersey swatch and an autograph.

COMP.SET w/o SP's (100)	10.00	25.00
COMMON CARD (1-100)	.20	.50
COMMON CARD (101-110)	.60	1.50
101-110 STATED ODDS 1:18		
COMMON CARD (111-145)	.60	1.50
111-145 PRINT RUN 1599 SERIAL #'d SETS		
COMMON CARD (146-154)	1.50	4.00
146-154 PRINT RUN 499 SERIAL #'d SETS		
COMMON CARD (155-160)	1.50	4.00
155-160 PRINT RUN 299 SERIAL #'d SETS		
111-160 ODDS W/SPECTRUM 1:9		
COMMON CARD (161-202)	6.00	15.00
161-202 ODDS W/SPECTRUM 1:18		
161-202 PRINT RUN 799 SERIAL #'d SETS		
EXCHANGE DEADLINE 12/03/07		
MASTER PLATE ODDS 1:2500		
MASTER PLATE PRINT RUN 1 #'d SET		
NO PLATE PRICING DUE TO SCARCITY		
1 Alfonso Soriano	.30	.75
2 Todd Helton	.30	.75
3 Andruw Jones	.20	.50
4 Eric Gagne	.20	.50
5 Craig Wilson	.20	.50
6 Brian Giles	.20	.50
7 Miguel Tejada	.30	.75
8 Kevin Brown	.20	.50
9 Shawn Green	.20	.50
10 Ben Sheets	.20	.50
11 John Smoltz	.50	1.25
12 Tim Hudson	.30	.75
13 Jason Schmidt	.20	.50
14 Paul Konerko	.30	.75
15 Randy Johnson	.50	1.25
16 Roy Oswalt	.30	.75
17 Mike Lowell	.20	.50
18 Carlos Lee	.20	.50
19 Sean Burroughs	.20	.50
20 Edgar Renteria	.20	.50
21 Michael Young	.20	.50
22 Jose Vidro	.20	.50
23 Scott Rolen	.30	.75
24 Rafael Furcal	.20	.50
25 Tom Glavine	.30	.75
26 Scott Podsednik	.20	.50
27 Gary Sheffield	.20	.50
28 Eric Chavez	.20	.50
29 Mark Prior	.30	.75
30 Chipper Jones	.50	1.25
31 Frank Thomas	.50	1.25
32 Victor Martinez	.20	.50
33 Jake Peavy	.20	.50
34 Carlos Beltran	.30	.75
35 Roy Halladay	.30	.75
36 Mark Teixeira	.30	.75
37 Jacque Jones	.20	.50
38 Mike Sweeney	.20	.50
39 Troy Glaus	.20	.50
40 Pat Burrell	.20	.50
41 Ichiro Suzuki	.60	1.50
42 Vladimir Guerrero	.30	.75
43 Bobby Abreu	.20	.50
44 Jim Edmonds	.30	.75
45 Garret Anderson	.20	.50
46 J.D. Drew	.20	.50
47 C.C. Sabathia	.30	.75
48 Joe Mauer	.40	1.00
49 Phil Nevin	.20	.50
50 Hank Blalock	.20	.50
51 Carlos Zambrano	.30	.75
52 Mike Piazza	.50	1.25
53 Manny Ramirez	.50	1.25
54 Lance Berkman	.30	.75
55 Delmon Young	.30	.75
56 Nomar Garciaparra	.30	.75
57 Alex Rodriguez	.60	1.50
58 Rickie Weeks	.20	.50
59 Adrian Beltre	.50	1.25
60 Albert Pujols	.60	1.50
61 Richie Sexson	.20	.50
62 Magglio Ordonez	.30	.75
63 Derrek Lee	.20	.50
64 Sammy Sosa	.50	1.25
65 Jason Giambi	.20	.50
66 Curt Schilling	.30	.75
67 Jorge Posada	.30	.75
68 Rafael Palmeiro	.30	.75
69 Jeff Kent	.20	.50
70 Jose Reyes	.30	.75
71 David Ortiz	.50	1.25
72 Aubrey Huff	.20	.50
73 Jim Thome	.30	.75
74 Andy Pettitte	.30	.75
75 Barry Zito	.30	.75
76 Carlos Delgado	.20	.50
77 Hideki Matsui	.75	2.00
78 Sean Casey	.20	.50
79 Luis Gonzalez	.20	.50
80 Marcus Giles	.20	.50
81 Preston Wilson	.20	.50
82 Javy Lopez	.20	.50
83 Mark Mulder	.20	.50
84 Derek Jeter	1.25	3.00
85 Miguel Cabrera	.50	1.25
86 Vernon Wells	.20	.50
87 Roger Clemens	.60	1.50
88 Lyle Overbay	.20	.50
89 Bret Boone	.20	.50
90 Melvin Mora	.20	.50
91 Greg Maddux	.60	1.50
92 Kerry Wood	.20	.50
93 Ivan Rodriguez	.30	.75
94 Pedro Martinez	.30	.75
95 Jeff Bagwell	.30	.75
96 Torii Hunter	.20	.50
97 Ken Griffey Jr.	1.00	2.50
98 Mike Mussina	.30	.75
99 Oliver Perez	.20	.50
100 Josh Beckett	.20	.50
101 Bob Gibson LGD	1.00	2.50
102 Cal Ripken LGD	5.00	12.00
103 Ted Williams LGD	3.00	8.00
104 Nolan Ryan LGD	5.00	12.00
105 Mickey Mantle LGD	5.00	12.00
106 Ernie Banks LGD	1.50	4.00
107 Joe DiMaggio LGD	3.00	8.00
108 Stan Musial LGD	2.50	6.00
109 Tom Seaver LGD	1.00	2.50
110 Mike Schmidt LGD	2.50	6.00
111 Jerry Gil T1 RC	.60	1.50
112 Dioner Navarro T1 RC	1.00	2.50
113 Bartolome Fortunato T1 RC	.60	1.50
114 Carlos Hines T1 RC	.60	1.50
115 Franklyn Gracesqui T1 RC	.60	1.50
116 Aarom Baldiris T1 RC	.60	1.50
117 Casey Daigle T1 RC	.60	1.50
118 Joey Gathright T1 RC	.60	1.50
119 William Bergolla T1 RC	.60	1.50
120 Jeff Bennett T1 RC	.60	1.50
121 Lincoln Holdzkom T1 RC	.60	1.50
122 Jorge Vasquez T1 RC	.60	1.50
123 Donnie Kelly T1 RC	1.00	2.50
124 Yadier Molina T1 RC	8.00	20.00
125 Ryan Wing T1 RC	.60	1.50
126 Justin Germano T1 RC	.60	1.50
127 Freddy Guzman T1 RC	.60	1.50
128 Onil Joseph T1 RC	.60	1.50
129 Roman Colon T1 RC	.60	1.50
130 Roberto Novoa T1 RC	.60	1.50
131 Renyel Pinto T1 RC	.60	1.50
132 Evan Rust T1 RC	.60	1.50
133 Orlando Rodriguez T1 RC	.60	1.50
134 Edwardo Sierra T1 RC	.60	1.50
135 Mike Rose T1 RC	.60	1.50
136 Phil Stockman T1 RC	.60	1.50
137 Greg Dobbs T1 RC	.60	1.50
138 Brad Halsey T1 RC	.60	1.50
139 David Aardsma T1 RC	.60	1.50
140 Joe Hietpas T1 RC	.60	1.50
141 Josh Labandeira T1 RC	.60	1.50
142 Mariano Gomez T1 RC	.60	1.50
143 Jeff Bajenaru T1 RC	.60	1.50
144 Travis Blackley T1 RC	.60	1.50
145 Abe Alvarez T1 RC	.60	1.50
146 Ramon Ramirez T2 RC	1.50	4.00
147 Edwin Moreno T2 RC	1.50	4.00
148 Ronny Cedeno T2 RC	1.50	4.00
149 Hector Gimenez T2 RC	1.50	4.00
150 Carlos Vasquez T2 RC	1.50	4.00
151 Jesse Crain T2 RC	2.50	6.00
152 Logan Kensing T2 RC	1.50	4.00
153 Sean Henn T2 RC	1.50	4.00
154 Rusty Tucker T2 RC	1.50	4.00
155 Justin Lehr T3 RC	1.50	4.00
156 Ian Snell T3 RC	1.50	4.00
157 Merkin Valdez T3 RC	1.50	4.00
158 Scott Proctor T3 RC	1.50	4.00
159 Jose Capellan T3 RC	1.50	4.00
160 Kazuo Matsui T3 RC	2.50	6.00
161 Chris Oxspring AU JSY RC	6.00	15.00
162 Jimmy Serrano AU JSY RC	6.00	15.00
163 Jeff Keppinger AU JSY RC	8.00	20.00
164 B.Medders AU JSY RC	6.00	15.00
165 Brian Dallimore AU JSY RC	6.00	15.00
166 Chad Bentz AU JSY RC	6.00	15.00
167 Chris Aguila AU JSY RC	6.00	15.00
168 Chris Saenz AU JSY RC	6.00	15.00
169 Frank Francisco AU JSY RC	6.00	15.00
170 Colby Miller AU JSY RC	6.00	15.00
172 Charles Thomas AU JSY RC	6.00	15.00
173 Dennis Sarfate AU JSY RC	6.00	15.00
174 Lance Cormier AU JSY RC	6.00	15.00
175 Joe Horgan AU JSY RC	6.00	15.00
176 Fernando Nieve AU JSY RC	6.00	15.00
177 Jake Woods AU JSY RC	6.00	15.00
178 Matt Treanor AU JSY RC	6.00	15.00
179 Jerome Gamble AU JSY RC	6.00	15.00
180 John Gall AU JSY RC	10.00	25.00
181 Jorge Sequea AU JSY RC	6.00	15.00
182 Justin Hampson AU JSY RC	6.00	15.00
183 Justin Huisman AU JSY RC	6.00	15.00
184 Justin Knoedler AU JSY RC	6.00	15.00
185 Justin Leone AU JSY RC	10.00	25.00
186 Scott Atchison AU JSY RC	6.00	15.00
187 Jon Knott AU JSY RC	6.00	15.00
188 Kevin Cave AU JSY RC	6.00	15.00
189 Jason Frasor AU JSY RC	6.00	15.00
190 George Sherrill AU JSY RC	6.00	15.00
191 Mike Gosling AU JSY RC	6.00	15.00
192 Mike Johnston AU JSY RC	6.00	15.00
193 Mike Rouse AU JSY RC	6.00	15.00
194 Nick Regilio AU JSY RC	6.00	15.00
195 Ryan Meaux AU JSY RC	6.00	15.00
196 Scott Dohmann AU JSY RC	6.00	15.00
197 Shawn Camp AU JSY RC	6.00	15.00
198 Shawn Hill AU JSY RC	6.00	15.00
199 Shingo Takatsu AU JSY RC	6.00	15.00
200 Tim Bausher AU JSY RC	6.00	15.00
201 Tim Bittner AU JSY RC	6.00	15.00
202 Scott Kazmir AU JSY RC	6.00	15.00

2004 SPx Spectrum

*SPEC 1-100: 6X TO 15X BASIC
*SPEC 101-110: 2X TO 5X
1-110 STATED ODDS 1:252
111-160 W/BASIC OVERALL ODDS 1:9
161-202 W/BASIC OVERALL ODDS 1:18
STATED PRINT RUN 25 SERIAL #'d SETS
111-202 NO PRICING DUE TO SCARCITY
EXCHANGE DEADLINE 12/03/07

2004 SPx SuperScripts Rookies

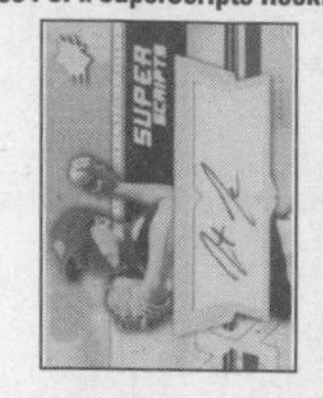

OVERALL SUPERSCRIPT ODDS 1:18
EXCHANGE DEADLINE 12/03/07

AS Alfredo Simon	4.00	10.00
CH Carlos Hines	4.00	10.00
CV Carlos Vasquez	6.00	15.00
DK Donnie Kelly	10.00	25.00
ES Edwardo Sierra	6.00	15.00
IO Ivan Ochoa	4.00	10.00
IS Ian Snell	8.00	20.00
JL Justin Lehr	4.00	10.00
LA Josh Labandeira	4.00	10.00
LH Lincoln Holdzkom	4.00	10.00
MG Mariano Gomez	4.00	10.00
MV Merkin Valdez	4.00	10.00
PS Phil Stockman	4.00	10.00
RR Ramon Ramirez	4.00	10.00
RU Evan Rust	4.00	10.00
SH Sean Henn	4.00	10.00
SP Scott Proctor	6.00	15.00
VE Michael Vento	6.00	15.00

2004 SPx SuperScripts Stars

OVERALL SUPERSCRIPT ODDS 1:18
SP INFO PROVIDED BY UPPER DECK

AP Albert Pujols SP	60.00	150.00
CR Cal Ripken SP	40.00	100.00
DJ Derek Jeter SP	75.00	200.00
EC Eric Chavez	6.00	15.00
JB Josh Beckett	8.00	20.00
KG Ken Griffey Jr.	30.00	80.00
MP Mark Prior	6.00	15.00
NG Nomar Garciaparra SP	12.00	30.00
NR Nolan Ryan SP	30.00	80.00
TE Miguel Tejada	6.00	15.00

2004 SPx SuperScripts Young Stars

OVERALL SUPERSCRIPT ODDS 1:18

BC Bobby Crosby	6.00	15.00
BW Brandon Webb	6.00	15.00
DW Dontrelle Willis	6.00	15.00
DY Delmon Young	6.00	15.00
EJ Edwin Jackson	6.00	15.00
JM Joe Mauer	12.00	30.00
JR Jose Reyes	6.00	15.00
MC Miguel Cabrera	20.00	50.00
MT Mark Teixeira	10.00	25.00
RH Rich Harden	6.00	15.00
RO Roy Oswalt	6.00	15.00
RW Rickie Weeks	6.00	15.00

2004 SPx Swatch Supremacy Signatures Stars

STATED PRINT RUN 275 SERIAL #'d SETS
*SPECTRUM: .75X TO 1.5X BASIC
SPECTRUM PRINT RUN 25 #'d SETS
OVERALL SWATCH SUP.ODDS 1:18

AP Albert Pujols	60.00	150.00
CR Cal Ripken	30.00	80.00
DJ Derek Jeter	100.00	200.00
DL Derrek Lee	10.00	25.00
EC Eric Chavez	6.00	15.00
GA Garret Anderson	10.00	25.00
KG Ken Griffey Jr.	40.00	100.00
MP Mark Prior	15.00	40.00
NG Nomar Garciaparra	15.00	40.00
NR Nolan Ryan	60.00	120.00

2004 SPx Swatch Supremacy Signatures Young Stars

STATED PRINT RUN 999 SERIAL #'d SETS
*SPECTRUM: .6X TO 1.5X BASIC
SPECTRUM PRINT RUN 25 #'d SETS
OVERALL SWATCH SUP.ODDS 1:18
AB Angel Berroa 4.00 10.00
AE Adam Eaton 4.00 10.00
BC Bobby Crosby 4.00 10.00
BS Ben Sheets 4.00 10.00
BW Brandon Webb 4.00 10.00
CC Chad Cordero 4.00 10.00
CK Casey Kotchman 4.00 10.00
CL Cliff Lee 4.00 10.00
CP Corey Patterson 4.00 10.00
DW Dontrelle Willis 4.00 10.00
GR Khalil Greene 4.00 10.00
HB Hank Blalock 4.00 10.00
HR Horacio Ramirez 4.00 10.00
JB Josh Beckett 4.00 10.00
JM Joe Mauer 12.00 30.00
JP Jake Peavy 4.00 10.00
JR Jose Reyes 6.00 15.00
JW Jerome Williams 4.00 10.00
LO Lyle Overbay 4.00 10.00
MC Miguel Cabrera 20.00 50.00
MG Marcus Giles 4.00 10.00
MT Mark Teixeira 6.00 15.00
MY Michael Young 6.00 15.00
RB Rocco Baldelli 4.00 10.00
RH Rich Harden 4.00 10.00
RO Roy Oswalt 4.00 10.00
RW Rickie Weeks 4.00 10.00
SB Sean Burroughs 4.00 10.00
SP Scott Podsednik 4.00 10.00

2004 SPx Winning Materials Dual Jersey

*SPECTRUM: .6X TO 1.5X BASIC
SPECTRUM PRINT RUN 25 #'d SETS
OVERALL WINNING MTL.ODDS 1:18
ALL HAVE GAME-WORN & DP SWATCHES
AP Albert Pujols 6.00 15.00
BE Josh Beckett 2.00 5.00
CD Carlos Delgado 2.00 5.00
CJ Chipper Jones 5.00 12.00
DJ Derek Jeter 12.00 30.00
EC Eric Chavez 2.00 5.00
GM Greg Maddux 6.00 15.00
GS Gary Sheffield 2.00 5.00
HB Hank Blalock 2.00 5.00
HM Hideki Matsui 8.00 20.00
IS Ichiro Suzuki 6.00 15.00
JB Jeff Bagwell 3.00 8.00
JG Jason Giambi 2.00 5.00
JP Jorge Posada 3.00 8.00
JR Jose Reyes 3.00 8.00
JT Jim Thome 3.00 8.00
KB Kevin Brown 2.00 5.00
MM Mike Mussina 3.00 8.00
MP Mark Prior 3.00 8.00
MR Manny Ramirez 5.00 12.00
PI Mike Piazza 5.00 12.00
RC Roger Clemens 6.00 15.00
RP Rafael Palmeiro 3.00 8.00
SG Shawn Green 2.00 5.00
SR Scott Rolen 3.00 8.00
SS Sammy Sosa 5.00 12.00
TE Miguel Tejada 3.00 8.00
TG Troy Glaus 2.00 5.00
VG Vladimir Guerrero 3.00 8.00

2005 SPx

These cards were issued as part of the SP Collection packs. For details on those packs, please see the write-up for SP Authentic.

COMP.BASIC SET (100) 10.00 25.00
COMMON CARD (1-100) .15 .40
COMMON RC (1-100) .25 .60
1-100 ISSUED IN 05 SP COLLECTION PACKS
COMMON AUTO (101-180) 4.00 10.00
101-180 ODDS APPX 1:8 '05 UD UPDATE
101-180 PRINT RUN 185 SERIAL #'d SETS
105, 117, 139, 149, 155, 172 DO NOT EXIST
175, 178, 180 DO NOT EXIST
1 Aaron Harang .15 .40
2 Aaron Rowand .15 .40
3 Aaron Miles .15 .40
4 Adrian Gonzalez .30 .75
5 Alex Rios .15 .40
6 Angel Berroa .15 .40
7 B.J. Upton .25 .60
8 Brandon Claussen .15 .40
9 Andy Marte .15 .40
10 Brandon Webb .25 .60
11 Bronson Arroyo .25 .60
12 Casey Kotchman .15 .40
13 Cesar Izturis .15 .40
14 Chad Cordero .15 .40
15 Chad Tracy .15 .40
16 Charles Thomas .15 .40
17 Chase Utley .25 .60
18 Chone Figgins .15 .40
19 Chris Burke .15 .40
20 Cliff Lee .25 .60
21 Clint Barmes .15 .40
22 Coco Crisp .15 .40
23 Bill Hall .15 .40
24 Dallas McPherson .15 .40
25 Brad Halsey .15 .40
26 Daniel Cabrera .15 .40
27 Danny Haren .15 .40
28 Dave Bush .15 .40
29 David DeJesus .15 .40
30 D.J. Houlton RC .25 .60
31 Derek Jeter 1.00 2.50
32 Dewon Brazelton .15 .40
33 Edwin Jackson .15 .40
34 Brad Hawpe .15 .40
35 Brandon Inge .15 .40
36 Brett Myers .15 .40
37 Garrett Atkins .15 .40
38 Gavin Floyd .15 .40
39 Grady Sizemore .25 .60
40 Guillermo Mota .15 .40
41 Carlos Guillen .15 .40
42 Gustavo Chacin .15 .40
43 Huston Street .15 .40
44 Chris Duffy .15 .40
45 J.D. Closser .15 .40
46 J.J. Hardy .15 .40
47 Jason Bartlett .15 .40
48 Jason DuBois .15 .40
49 Chris Shelton .15 .40
50 Jason Lane .15 .40
51 Jayson Werth .25 .60
52 Jeff Baker .15 .40
53 Jeff Francis .15 .40
54 Jeremy Bonderman .15 .40
55 Jeremy Reed .15 .40
56 Jerome Williams .15 .40
57 Jesse Crain .15 .40
58 Chris Young .25 .60
59 Jhonny Peralta .15 .40
60 Joe Blanton .15 .40
61 Joe Crede .15 .40
62 Joel Pineiro .15 .40
63 Joey Gathright .15 .40
64 John Buck .15 .40
65 Jonny Gomes .15 .40
66 Jorge Cantu .15 .40
67 Dan Johnson .15 .40
68 Jose Valverde .15 .40
69 Ervin Santana .15 .40
70 Justin Morneau .25 .60
71 Keiichi Yabu RC .25 .60
72 Ken Griffey Jr. .75 2.00
73 Jason Repko .15 .40
74 Kevin Youkilis .15 .40
75 Koyie Hill .15 .40
76 Laynce Nix .15 .40
77 Luke Scott RC .60 1.50
78 Juan Rivera .15 .40
79 Justin Duchscherer .15 .40
80 Mark Teahen .15 .40
81 Lance Niekro .15 .40
82 Michael Cuddyer .15 .40
83 Nick Swisher .25 .60
84 Noah Lowry .15 .40
85 Matt Holliday .40 1.00
86 Reed Johnson .15 .40
87 Rich Harden .15 .40
88 Robb Quinlan .15 .40
89 Nick Johnson .15 .40
90 Ryan Howard .30 .75
91 Nook Logan .15 .40
92 Steve Schmoll RC .25 .60
93 Tadahito Iguchi RC .40 1.00
94 Willy Taveras .15 .40
95 Wily Mo Pena .15 .40
96 Xavier Nady .15 .40
97 Yadier Molina .40 1.00
98 Yhency Brazoban .15 .40
99 Ryan Freel .15 .40
100 Zack Greinke .40 1.00
101 Adam Shabala AU RC 4.00 10.00
102 Ambiorix Burgos AU RC 4.00 10.00
103 Ambiorix Concepcion AU RC 4.00 10.00
104 Anibal Sanchez AU RC 6.00 15.00
106 Brandon McCarthy AU RC 6.00 15.00
107 Brian Burres AU RC 4.00 10.00
108 Carlos Ruiz AU RC 8.00 20.00
109 Casey Rogowski AU RC 4.00 10.00
110 Chad Orvella AU RC 4.00 10.00
111 Chris Resop AU RC 6.00 15.00
112 Chris Roberson AU RC 4.00 10.00
113 Chris Seddon AU RC 4.00 10.00
114 Colter Bean AU RC 6.00 15.00
115 Dave Gassner AU RC 4.00 10.00
116 Brian Anderson AU RC 6.00 15.00
118 Devon Lowery AU RC 4.00 10.00
119 Enrique Gonzalez AU RC 6.00 15.00
120 Eude Brito AU RC 4.00 10.00
121 Francisco Butto AU RC 4.00 10.00
122 Franquelis Osoria AU RC 4.00 10.00
123 Garrett Jones AU RC 10.00 25.00
124 Geovany Soto AU RC 10.00 25.00
125 Hayden Penn AU RC 6.00 15.00
126 Ismael Ramirez AU RC 4.00 10.00
127 Jared Gothreaux AU RC 4.00 10.00
128 Jason Hammel AU RC 10.00 25.00
129 Jeff Miller AU RC 4.00 10.00
130 Jeff Niemann AU RC 5.00 12.00
131 Joel Peralta AU RC 4.00 10.00
132 John Hattig AU RC 4.00 10.00
133 Jorge Campillo AU RC 4.00 10.00
134 Juan Morillo AU RC 4.00 10.00
135 Justin Verlander AU RC 75.00 200.00
136 Ryan Garko AU RC 4.00 10.00
137 Kendry Morales AU RC 10.00 25.00
138 Luis Hernandez AU RC 4.00 10.00
140 Luis O.Rodriguez AU RC 4.00 10.00
141 Mark Woodyard AU RC 4.00 10.00
142 Matt A.Smith AU RC 4.00 10.00
143 Matthew Lindstrom AU RC 4.00 10.00
144 Miguel Negron AU RC 6.00 15.00
145 Mike Morse AU RC 6.00 15.00
146 Nate McLouth AU RC 6.00 15.00
147 Nelson Cruz AU RC 20.00 50.00
148 Nick Masset AU RC 4.00 10.00
150 Paulino Reynoso AU RC 4.00 10.00
151 Pedro Lopez AU RC 4.00 10.00
152 Philip Humber AU RC 6.00 15.00
153 Prince Fielder AU RC 12.00 30.00
154 Randy Messenger AU RC 4.00 10.00
156 Raul Tablado AU RC 4.00 10.00
157 Ronny Paulino AU RC 6.00 15.00
158 Russ Rohlicek AU RC 4.00 10.00
159 Russell Martin AU RC 10.00 25.00
160 Scott Baker AU RC 6.00 15.00
161 Scott Munter AU RC 4.00 10.00
162 Sean Thompson AU RC 4.00 10.00
163 Sean Tracey AU RC 4.00 10.00
164 Shane Costa AU RC 4.00 10.00
165 Stephen Drew AU RC 12.50 30.00
166 Tony Giarratano AU RC 4.00 10.00
167 Tony Pena AU RC 4.00 10.00
168 Travis Bowyer AU RC 4.00 10.00
169 Ubaldo Jimenez AU RC 10.00 25.00
170 Wladimir Balentien AU RC 6.00 15.00
171 Yorman Bazardo AU RC 4.00 10.00
173 Ryan Zimmerman AU RC 20.00 50.00
174 Chris Denorfia AU RC 6.00 15.00
176 Jermaine Van Buren AU 4.00 10.00
177 Mark McLemore AU RC 4.00 10.00
179 Ryan Speier AU RC 4.00 10.00

2005 SPx Jersey

STATED PRINT RUN 199 SERIAL #'d SETS
*SPECTRUM: .5X TO 1.2X BASIC
SPECTRUM PRINT RUN 99 SERIAL #'d SETS
ISSUED IN 05 SP COLLECTION PACKS
OVERALL GAME-USED ODDS 1:10
1 Aaron Harang 2.00 5.00
2 Aaron Rowand 2.00 5.00
3 Aaron Miles 2.00 5.00
4 Adrian Gonzalez 2.00 5.00
5 Alex Rios 2.00 5.00
6 Angel Berroa 2.00 5.00
7 B.J. Upton 2.00 5.00
8 Brandon Claussen 2.00 5.00
9 Andy Marte 2.00 5.00
10 Brandon Webb 2.00 5.00
11 Bronson Arroyo 2.00 5.00
12 Casey Kotchman 2.00 5.00
13 Cesar Izturis 2.00 5.00
14 Chad Cordero 2.00 5.00
15 Chad Tracy 2.00 5.00
16 Charles Thomas 2.00 5.00
17 Chase Utley 3.00 8.00
18 Chone Figgins 2.00 5.00
19 Chris Burke 2.00 5.00
20 Cliff Lee 2.00 5.00
21 Clint Barmes 2.00 5.00
22 Coco Crisp 2.00 5.00
23 Bill Hall 2.00 5.00
24 Dallas McPherson 2.00 5.00
25 Brad Halsey 2.00 5.00
26 Daniel Cabrera 2.00 5.00
27 Danny Haren 2.00 5.00
28 Dave Bush 2.00 5.00
29 David DeJesus 2.00 5.00
30 D.J. Houlton 2.00 5.00
31 Derek Jeter Pants 8.00 20.00
32 Dewon Brazelton 2.00 5.00
33 Edwin Jackson 2.00 5.00
34 Brad Hawpe 2.00 5.00
35 Brandon Inge 2.00 5.00
36 Brett Myers 2.00 5.00
37 Garrett Atkins 2.00 5.00
38 Gavin Floyd 2.00 5.00
39 Grady Sizemore 3.00 8.00
40 Guillermo Mota 2.00 5.00
41 Carlos Guillen 2.00 5.00
42 Gustavo Chacin 2.00 5.00
43 Huston Street 3.00 8.00
44 Chris Duffy 2.00 5.00
45 J.D. Closser 2.00 5.00
46 J.J. Hardy 2.00 5.00
47 Jason Bartlett 2.00 5.00
48 Jason DuBois 2.00 5.00
49 Chris Shelton 4.00 10.00
50 Jason Lane 2.00 5.00
51 Jayson Werth 2.00 5.00
52 Jeff Baker 2.00 5.00
53 Jeff Francis 2.00 5.00
54 Jeremy Bonderman 2.00 5.00
55 Jeremy Reed 2.00 5.00
56 Jerome Williams 2.00 5.00
57 Jesse Crain 2.00 5.00
58 Chris Young 2.00 5.00
59 Jhonny Peralta 2.00 5.00
60 Joe Blanton 2.00 5.00
61 Joe Crede 2.00 5.00
62 Joel Pineiro 2.00 5.00
63 Joey Gathright 2.00 5.00
64 John Buck 2.00 5.00
65 Jonny Gomes 2.00 5.00
66 Jorge Cantu 2.00 5.00
67 Dan Johnson 2.00 5.00
68 Jose Valverde 2.00 5.00
69 Ervin Santana 2.00 5.00
70 Justin Morneau 2.00 5.00
71 Keiichi Yabu 2.00 5.00
72 Ken Griffey Jr. 6.00 15.00
73 Jason Repko 2.00 5.00
74 Kevin Youkilis 2.00 5.00
75 Koyie Hill 2.00 5.00
76 Laynce Nix 2.00 5.00
77 Luke Scott 4.00 10.00
78 Juan Rivera 2.00 5.00
79 Justin Duchscherer 2.00 5.00
80 Mark Teahen 2.00 5.00
81 Lance Niekro 2.00 5.00
82 Michael Cuddyer 2.00 5.00
83 Nick Swisher 2.00 5.00
84 Noah Lowry 2.00 5.00
85 Matt Holliday 2.50 6.00
86 Reed Johnson 2.00 5.00
87 Rich Harden 2.00 5.00
88 Robb Quinlan 2.00 5.00
89 Nick Johnson 2.00 5.00
90 Ryan Howard 10.00 25.00
91 Nook Logan 2.00 5.00
92 Steve Schmoll 2.00 5.00
93 Tadahito Iguchi 12.50 30.00
94 Willy Taveras 2.00 5.00
95 Wily Mo Pena 2.00 5.00
96 Xavier Nady 2.00 5.00
97 Yadier Molina 2.00 5.00
98 Yhency Brazoban 2.00 5.00
99 Ryan Freel 2.00 5.00
100 Zack Greinke 2.00 5.00

2005 SPx Signature

PRINT RUNS B/WN 50-350 COPIES PER
SPECTRUM PRINT RUN 10 SERIAL #'d SETS
NO SPECTRUM PRICING DUE TO SCARCITY
OVERALL AUTO ODDS 1:10
1 Aaron Harang/350 6.00 15.00
2 Aaron Rowand/150 10.00 25.00
4 Adrian Gonzalez/225 10.00 25.00
6 Angel Berroa/150 4.00 10.00
7 B.J. Upton/50 8.00 20.00
8 Brandon Claussen/350 4.00 10.00
9 Andy Marte/350 4.00 10.00
11 Bronson Arroyo/350 6.00 15.00
12 Casey Kotchman/225 6.00 15.00
13 Cesar Izturis/150 4.00 10.00
14 Chad Cordero/350 6.00 15.00
15 Chad Tracy/350 4.00 10.00
16 Charles Thomas/350 4.00 10.00
17 Chase Utley/50 10.00 25.00
18 Chone Figgins/150 6.00 15.00
19 Chris Burke/350 4.00 10.00
20 Cliff Lee/225 12.50 30.00
21 Clint Barmes/350 6.00 15.00
22 Coco Crisp/225 10.00 25.00
23 Bill Hall/350 4.00 10.00
24 Dallas McPherson/150 4.00 10.00
25 Brad Halsey/350 4.00 10.00
26 Daniel Cabrera/350 4.00 10.00
27 Danny Haren/225 4.00 10.00
28 Dave Bush/350 4.00 10.00
29 David DeJesus/225 4.00 10.00
30 D.J. Houlton/350 4.00 10.00
31 Derek Jeter/50 90.00 150.00
32 Dewon Brazelton/225 4.00 10.00
33 Edwin Jackson/150 4.00 10.00
34 Brad Hawpe/350 10.00 25.00
35 Brandon Inge/350 4.00 10.00
36 Brett Myers/150 6.00 15.00
37 Garrett Atkins/350 4.00 10.00
38 Gavin Floyd/150 4.00 10.00
39 Grady Sizemore/350 12.50 30.00
40 Guillermo Mota/225 4.00 10.00
41 Carlos Guillen/150 6.00 15.00
42 Gustavo Chacin/350 6.00 15.00
43 Huston Street/350 10.00 25.00
44 Chris Duffy/225 4.00 10.00
45 J.D. Closser/350 4.00 10.00
46 J.J. Hardy/350 20.00 50.00
47 Jason Bartlett/350 4.00 10.00
48 Jason DuBois/350 4.00 10.00
50 Jason Lane/350 4.00 10.00
51 Jayson Werth/350 4.00 10.00
52 Jeff Baker/350 4.00 10.00
53 Jeff Francis/150 4.00 10.00
54 Jeremy Bonderman/50 8.00 20.00
55 Jeremy Reed/150 6.00 15.00
56 Jerome Williams/50 8.00 20.00
57 Jesse Crain/350 4.00 10.00
59 Jhonny Peralta/350 6.00 15.00
60 Joe Blanton/350 4.00 10.00
61 Joe Crede/350 10.00 25.00
62 Joel Pineiro/150 6.00 15.00
63 Joey Gathright/350 4.00 10.00
64 John Buck/350 4.00 10.00
65 Jonny Gomes/350 6.00 15.00
66 Jorge Cantu/350 6.00 15.00
67 Dan Johnson/350 6.00 15.00
68 Jose Valverde/350 4.00 10.00
69 Ervin Santana/350 6.00 15.00
70 Justin Morneau/50 8.00 20.00
71 Keiichi Yabu/350 6.00 15.00
73 Jason Repko/350 10.00 25.00
74 Kevin Youkilis/225 8.00 20.00
75 Koyie Hill/350 4.00 10.00
76 Laynce Nix/150 4.00 10.00
77 Luke Scott/350 20.00 50.00
78 Juan Rivera/225 4.00 10.00
79 Justin Duchscherer/350 4.00 10.00
80 Mark Teahen/350 4.00 10.00
81 Lance Niekro/350 4.00 10.00
82 Michael Cuddyer/350 4.00 10.00
84 Noah Lowry/150 6.00 15.00
85 Matt Holliday/225 6.00 15.00
86 Reed Johnson/350 4.00 10.00
88 Robb Quinlan/350 4.00 10.00
89 Nick Johnson/150 6.00 15.00
90 Ryan Howard/225 10.00 25.00
91 Nook Logan/350 4.00 10.00
92 Steve Schmoll/350 4.00 10.00
93 Tadahito Iguchi/50 125.00 200.00
95 Wily Mo Pena/150 6.00 15.00
96 Xavier Nady/150 4.00 10.00
98 Yhency Brazoban/350 4.00 10.00
100 Zack Greinke/150 10.00 25.00

2005 SPx SPxtreme Stats

ISSUED IN 05 SP COLLECTION PACKS
OVERALL INSERT ODDS 1:10
STATED PRINT RUN 299 SERIAL #'d SETS
AB Adrian Beltre 1.50 4.00
AD Adam Dunn 1.00 2.50
AJ Andruw Jones .60 1.50
AP Albert Pujols 2.00 5.00
AR Aramis Ramirez .60 1.50
BA Bobby Abreu .60 1.50
BC Bobby Crosby .60 1.50
BS Ben Sheets .60 1.50
CB Craig Biggio 1.00 2.50
CC Carl Crawford 1.00 2.50
CP Corey Patterson .60 1.50
CZ Carlos Zambrano 1.00 2.50
DJ Derek Jeter 4.00 10.00
DL Derrek Lee .60 1.50
DO David Ortiz 1.50 4.00
DW David Wright 1.25 3.00
EC Eric Chavez .60 1.50
EG Eric Gagne .60 1.50
ER Edgar Renteria .60 1.50
GM Greg Maddux 2.00 5.00
GR Khalil Greene .60 1.50
GS Gary Sheffield .60 1.50
HB Hank Blalock .60 1.50
HU Torii Hunter .60 1.50
JD J.D. Drew .60 1.50
JM Joe Mauer 1.25 3.00
JP Jake Peavy .60 1.50
JR Jose Reyes 1.00 2.50
KG Ken Griffey Jr. 3.00 8.00
KW Kerry Wood .60 1.50
MC Miguel Cabrera 1.50 4.00
MM Mark Mulder .60 1.50
MO Melvin Mora .60 1.50
MP Mark Prior 1.00 2.50
MT Mark Teixeira 1.00 2.50
MY Michael Young .60 1.50
OP Oliver Perez .60 1.50
PI Mike Piazza 1.50 4.00
RC Roger Clemens 2.00 5.00
RJ Randy Johnson 1.50 4.00
RO Roy Oswalt 1.00 2.50
RP Rafael Palmeiro 1.00 2.50
SA Johan Santana 1.00 2.50
SC Sean Casey .60 1.50
SM John Smoltz 1.50 4.00
SR Scott Rolen 1.00 2.50
TE Miguel Tejada 1.00 2.50
TH Tim Hudson 1.00 2.50
VG Vladimir Guerrero 1.00 2.50
VM Victor Martinez 1.00 2.50

2005 SPx SPxtreme Stats Jersey

ISSUED IN 05 SP COLLECTION PACKS
OVERALL PREMIUM AU-GU ODDS 1:20
STATED PRINT RUN 130 SERIAL #'d SETS
AB Adrian Beltre 2.00 5.00
AD Adam Dunn 2.00 5.00
AJ Andruw Jones 3.00 8.00
AP Albert Pujols 6.00 15.00
AR Aramis Ramirez 2.00 5.00
BA Bobby Abreu 2.00 5.00
BC Bobby Crosby 2.00 5.00
BS Ben Sheets 2.00 5.00
CB Craig Biggio 3.00 8.00
CC Carl Crawford 2.00 5.00
CP Corey Patterson 2.00 5.00
CZ Carlos Zambrano 2.00 5.00
DJ Derek Jeter Pants 8.00 20.00
DL Derrek Lee 3.00 8.00
DO David Ortiz 3.00 8.00
DW David Wright 4.00 10.00
EC Eric Chavez 2.00 5.00
EG Eric Gagne 2.00 5.00
ER Edgar Renteria 2.00 5.00
GM Greg Maddux 4.00 10.00
GR Khalil Greene 3.00 8.00
GS Gary Sheffield 2.00 5.00
HB Hank Blalock 2.00 5.00
HU Torii Hunter 2.00 5.00
JD J.D. Drew 2.00 5.00
JM Joe Mauer 4.00 10.00
JP Jake Peavy 2.00 5.00
JR Jose Reyes 2.00 5.00
KG Ken Griffey Jr. 6.00 15.00
KW Kerry Wood 2.00 5.00
MC Miguel Cabrera 3.00 8.00
MM Mark Mulder 2.00 5.00
MO Melvin Mora 2.00 5.00
MP Mark Prior 3.00 8.00
MT Mark Teixeira 3.00 8.00
MY Michael Young 2.00 5.00
OP Oliver Perez 2.00 5.00
PI Mike Piazza 4.00 10.00
RC Roger Clemens Pants 4.00 10.00
RJ Randy Johnson 4.00 10.00
RO Roy Oswalt 2.00 5.00
RP Rafael Palmeiro 3.00 8.00
SA Johan Santana 4.00 10.00
SC Sean Casey 2.00 5.00
SM John Smoltz 3.00 8.00
SR Scott Rolen 3.00 8.00
TE Miguel Tejada 2.00 5.00
TH Tim Hudson 2.00 5.00
VG Vladimir Guerrero 4.00 10.00
VM Victor Martinez 2.00 5.00

2006 SPx

This 160-card set was released in September, 2006. The set was issued in four-card packs, which came 18 packs per box and 14 boxes per case. The first 100 cards feature veteran players which were sequenced in alphabetical order by team while the final 60 cards feature signed cards of 2006 rookies. Those cards were issued to stated print runs between 190 and 999 serial numbered copies and were inserted into packs at a stated rate of one in nine. A few players did not sign their cards in time for pack out and those autographs could be redeemed until September 7, 2008.

COMP.BASIC SET (100) 10.00 25.00
COMMON CARD (1-100) .15 .40
COMMON AU p/r 659-999 4.00 10.00
COMMON AU p/r 350-500 4.00 10.00
OVERALL 101-161 AU ODDS 1:9
101-161 AU EXCH DEADLINE 09/07/08
101-161 AU PRINT RUN B/WN 190-999 PER
101-161 PRINTING PLATE ODDS 1:224
101-161 PLATES PRINT RUN 1 SET PER CLR
101-161 PLATES FEATURE AUTOS
BLACK-CYAN-MAGENTA-YELLOW ISSUED
NO PLATE PRICING DUE TO SCARCITY
EXQUISITE EXCH ODDS 1:36
EXQUISITE EXCH DEADLINE 07/27/07
1 Luis Gonzalez .15 .40
2 Chad Tracy .15 .40
3 Brandon Webb .25 .60
4 Andruw Jones .15 .40
5 Chipper Jones .40 1.00
6 John Smoltz .40 1.00
7 Tim Hudson .25 .60
8 Miguel Tejada .25 .60
9 Brian Roberts .15 .40
10 Ramon Hernandez .15 .40
11 Curt Schilling .25 .60
12 David Ortiz .40 1.00
13 Manny Ramirez .40 1.00
14 Jason Varitek .40 1.00
15 Josh Beckett .15 .40
16 Greg Maddux .50 1.25
17 Derrek Lee .15 .40
18 Mark Prior .25 .60
19 Aramis Ramirez .15 .40
20 Jim Thome .25 .60
21 Paul Konerko .25 .60
22 Scott Podsednik .15 .40
23 Jose Contreras .15 .40
24 Ken Griffey Jr. .75 2.00
25 Adam Dunn .25 .60
26 Felipe Lopez .15 .40
27 Travis Hafner .15 .40
28 Victor Martinez .25 .60
29 Grady Sizemore .25 .60
30 Jhonny Peralta .15 .40
31 Todd Helton .25 .60
32 Garrett Atkins .15 .40
33 Clint Barmes .15 .40
34 Ivan Rodriguez .25 .60
35 Chris Shelton .15 .40
36 Jeremy Bonderman .15 .40
37 Miguel Cabrera .40 1.00
38 Dontrelle Willis .15 .40
39 Lance Berkman .25 .60
40 Morgan Ensberg .15 .40
41 Roy Oswalt .25 .60
42 Reggie Sanders .15 .40
43 Mike Sweeney .15 .40
44 Vladimir Guerrero .25 .60
45 Bartolo Colon .15 .40
46 Chone Figgins .15 .40
47 Nomar Garciaparra .25 .60
48 Jeff Kent .15 .40
49 J.D. Drew .15 .40
50 Carlos Lee .15 .40
51 Ben Sheets .15 .40
52 Rickie Weeks .15 .40
53 Johan Santana .25 .60
54 Torii Hunter .15 .40
55 Joe Mauer .25 .60
56 Pedro Martinez .25 .60
57 David Wright .30 .75
58 Carlos Beltran .25 .60
59 Carlos Delgado .15 .40
60 Jose Reyes .25 .60
61 Derek Jeter 1.00 2.50
62 Alex Rodriguez .50 1.25
63 Randy Johnson .40 1.00
64 Hideki Matsui .40 1.00
65 Gary Sheffield .15 .40
66 Rich Harden .15 .40
67 Eric Chavez .15 .40
68 Huston Street .15 .40
69 Bobby Crosby .15 .40
70 Bobby Abreu .15 .40
71 Ryan Howard .30 .75
72 Chase Utley .25 .60
73 Pat Burrell .15 .40
74 Jason Bay .15 .40
75 Sean Casey .15 .40
76 Mike Piazza .40 1.00
77 Jake Peavy .15 .40
78 Brian Giles .15 .40
79 Milton Bradley .15 .40
80 Omar Vizquel .25 .60
81 Jason Schmidt .15 .40
82 Ichiro Suzuki .50 1.25
83 Felix Hernandez .25 .60
84 Richie Sexson .15 .40
85 Albert Pujols .50 1.25
86 Chris Carpenter .25 .60
87 Scott Rolen .25 .60
88 Jim Edmonds .25 .60
89 Carl Crawford .25 .60
90 Jonny Gomes .15 .40
91 Scott Kazmir .25 .60
92 Mark Teixeira .25 .60
93 Michael Young .15 .40
94 Phil Nevin .15 .40
95 Vernon Wells .15 .40
96 Roy Halladay .25 .60
97 Troy Glaus .15 .40
98 Alfonso Soriano .25 .60
99 Nick Johnson .15 .40
100 Jose Vidro .15 .40
101 Conor Jackson AU/999 (RC) 6.00 15.00
102 J.Weaver AU/299 (RC) EXCH 8.00 20.00
103 Macay McBride AU/999 (RC) 4.00 10.00
104 Aaron Rakers AU/499 (RC) 4.00 10.00
105 J.Papelbon AU/499 (RC) 5.00 12.00
106 J.Bergmann AU/999 RC 4.00 10.00
107 S.Drew AU/350 (RC) 6.00 15.00
108 Chris Denorfia AU/999 (RC) 4.00 10.00
109 Kelly Shoppach AU/999 (RC) 4.00 10.00

110 Ryan Shealy AU/999 (RC) 4.00 10.00
111 Josh Wilson AU/999 (RC) 4.00 10.00
112 Brian Anderson AU/999 (RC) 4.00 10.00
113 J.Verlander AU/749 (RC) 25.00 60.00
114 J.Hermida AU/999 (RC) 6.00 15.00
115 M.Jacobs AU/999 (RC) 6.00 15.00
116 Josh Johnson AU/999 (RC) 8.00 20.00
117 Hanley Ramirez AU/659 (RC) 6.00 15.00
118 Chris Resop AU/999 (RC) 4.00 10.00
119 J.Willingham AU/999 (RC) 4.00 10.00
120 Cole Hamels AU/499 (RC) 10.00 25.00
121 Matt Cain AU/999 (RC) 10.00 25.00
122 Steve Stemle AU/999 RC 4.00 10.00
123 Tim Hamulack AU/999 (RC) 4.00 10.00
124 Choo Freeman AU/999 (RC) 4.00 10.00
125 H.Kuo AU/999 (RC) 8.00 20.00
126 Cody Ross AU/999 (RC) 4.00 10.00
127 Jose Capellan AU/999 (RC) 4.00 10.00
128 Prince Fielder AU/190 (RC) 15.00 40.00
129 David Gassner AU/999 (RC) 4.00 10.00
130 Jason Kubel AU/999 (RC) 4.00 10.00
131 F.Liriano AU/299 (RC) 6.00 15.00
132 A.Hernandez AU/999 (RC) 6.00 15.00
133 Joey Devine AU/499 RC 4.00 10.00
134 Chris Booker AU/999 (RC) 4.00 10.00
135 Matt Capps AU/999 (RC) 4.00 10.00
136 Paul Maholm AU/999 (RC) 4.00 10.00
137 N.McLouth AU/999 (RC) 6.00 15.00
138 J.Van Benschoten AU/999 (RC) 4.00 10.00
139 Jeff Harris AU/999 RC 4.00 10.00
140 Ben Johnson AU/999 (RC) 4.00 10.00
141 Wil Nieves AU/999 (RC) 4.00 10.00
142 G.Quiroz AU/999 (RC) 4.00 10.00
143 Josh Rupe AU/500 (RC) 4.00 10.00
144 Skip Schumaker AU/999 (RC) 4.00 10.00
145 Jack Taschner AU/999 (RC) 4.00 10.00
146 A.Wainwright AU/999 (RC) 6.00 15.00
147 Alay Soler AU/499 RC 4.00 10.00
148 Kendry Morales AU/999 (RC) 6.00 15.00
149 Ian Kinsler AU/999 (RC) 8.00 20.00
150 Jason Hammel AU/999 (RC) 4.00 10.00
151 C.Billingsley AU/499 (RC) 12.00 30.00
152 Boof Bonser AU/999 (RC) 6.00 15.00
153 Peter Moylan AU/999 RC 4.00 10.00
154 Chris Britton AU/999 RC 4.00 10.00
155 Takashi Saito AU/999 RC 6.00 15.00
156 Scott Dunn AU/999 (RC) 4.00 10.00
157 J.Zumaya AU/299 (RC) EXCH 4.00 10.00
158 Dan Uggla AU/999 (RC) 6.00 15.00
159 Taylor Buchholz AU/999 (RC) 4.00 10.00

2006 SPx Spectrum

*SPECTRUM 1-100: 2X TO 5X BASIC
STATED ODDS 1:3

2006 SPx Next In Line

STATED ODDS 1:9
AW Adam Wainwright 1.00 2.50
BA Brian Anderson .60 1.50
BB Brian Bannister .60 1.50
BJ Ben Johnson .60 1.50
CJ Conor Jackson 1.00 2.50
DU Dan Uggla 1.00 2.50
FH Felix Hernandez 1.00 2.50
FL Francisco Liriano 1.50 4.00
HR Hanley Ramirez 1.00 2.50
HS Huston Street .60 1.50
IK Ian Kinsler 2.00 5.00
JB Josh Barfield .60 1.50
JE Jered Weaver 2.00 5.00
JH Jeremy Hermida .60 1.50
JL James Loney 1.00 2.50
JP Jonathan Papelbon 3.00 8.00
JS Jeremy Sowers .60 1.50
JV Justin Verlander 5.00 12.00
JW Josh Willingham 1.00 2.50
LE Jon Lester 2.50 6.00
MC Matt Cain 4.00 10.00
MJ Mike Jacobs .60 1.50
AS Alay Soler .60 1.50
PF Prince Fielder 3.00 8.00
RC Ryan Church .60 1.50
RH Ryan Howard 1.25 3.00
RZ Ryan Zimmerman 2.00 5.00
SO Scott Olsen .60 1.50
TB Taylor Buchholz .60 1.50
TI Travis Ishikawa 1.00 2.50

2006 SPx SPxtra Info

STATED ODDS 1:9
AJ Andruw Jones .60 1.50
AP Albert Pujols 2.00 5.00
BA Bobby Abreu .60 1.50
BG Brian Giles .60 1.50
CC Carl Crawford 1.00 2.50
CL Carlos Lee .60 1.50
DJ Derek Jeter 4.00 10.00
DL Derrek Lee .60 1.50
DO David Ortiz 1.50 4.00
DW Dontrelle Willis .60 1.50
EC Eric Chavez .60 1.50
HE Todd Helton 1.00 2.50
IR Ivan Rodriguez 1.00 2.50
IS Ichiro Suzuki 2.00 5.00
JB Jason Bay .60 1.50
JK Jeff Kent .60 1.50
JS Johan Santana 1.00 2.50
JT Jim Thome 1.00 2.50
KG Ken Griffey Jr. 3.00 8.00
LG Luis Gonzalez .60 1.50
MT Miguel Tejada 1.00 2.50
NJ Nick Johnson .60 1.50
PM Pedro Martinez 1.00 2.50
RO Roy Oswalt 1.00 2.50
RS Reggie Sanders .60 1.50
SC Jason Schmidt .60 1.50
TE Mark Teixeira 1.00 2.50
TH Travis Hafner .60 1.50
VG Vladimir Guerrero 1.00 2.50
VW Vernon Wells .60 1.50

2006 SPx SPxciting Signature

RANDOM INSERTS IN PACKS
PRINT RUNS B/WN 10-30 COPIES PER
NO PRICING ON MOST DUE TO SCARCITY
JP Jonathan Papelbon/30 10.00 25.00
MC Matt Cain/30 40.00 80.00
PE Jake Peavy/30 6.00 15.00

2006 SPx SPxtreme Team

STATED ODDS 1:9
AD Adam Dunn 1.00 2.50
AJ Andruw Jones .60 1.50
AP Albert Pujols 2.00 5.00
AR Alex Rodriguez 2.00 5.00
AS Alfonso Soriano 1.00 2.50
BA Bobby Abreu .60 1.50
CC Chris Carpenter 1.00 2.50
CD Carlos Delgado .60 1.50
CL Carlos Lee .60 1.50
CR Carl Crawford 1.00 2.50
DJ Derek Jeter 4.00 10.00
DL Derrek Lee .60 1.50
DO David Ortiz 1.50 4.00
DW David Wright 1.25 3.00
GS Grady Sizemore 1.00 2.50
HA Travis Hafner .60 1.50
HM Hideki Matsui 1.50 4.00
HO Ryan Howard 1.25 3.00
IS Ichiro Suzuki 2.00 5.00
JB Jason Bay .60 1.50
JK Jeff Kent .60 1.50
JP Jake Peavy .60 1.50
JR Jose Reyes 1.00 2.50
JS Johan Santana 1.00 2.50
JT Jim Thome 1.00 2.50
KG Ken Griffey Jr. 3.00 8.00
LB Lance Berkman 1.00 2.50
MC Miguel Cabrera 1.50 4.00
MR Manny Ramirez 1.50 4.00
MT Mark Teixeira 1.00 2.50
MY Michael Young .60 1.50
PF Prince Fielder 3.00 8.00
PK Paul Konerko 1.00 2.50
PM Pedro Martinez 1.00 2.50
RH Rich Harden .60 1.50
TE Miguel Tejada 1.00 2.50
TH Todd Helton 1.00 2.50
VG Vladimir Guerrero 1.00 2.50
VM Victor Martinez 1.00 2.50
VW Vernon Wells .60 1.50

2006 SPx WBC All-World Team

STATED ODDS 1:9
1 Brett Willemburg .60 1.50
2 Bradley Harman 1.00 2.50
3 Adam Stern .60 1.50
4 Jason Bay .60 1.50
5 Adam Loewen .60 1.50
6 Wei Wang .60 1.50
7 Yi Feng .60 1.50
8 Yung Chi Chen 1.00 2.50
9 Chin-Lung Hu .60 1.50
10 Wei-Lun Pan 1.50 4.00
11 Yoandy Garlobo .60 1.50
12 Frederich Cepeda .60 1.50
13 Osmany Urrutia .60 1.50
14 Yulieski Gourriel 2.00 5.00
15 Yadel Marti .60 1.50
16 Pedro Luis Lazo 1.00 2.50
17 Adrian Beltre 1.50 4.00
18 David Ortiz 1.50 4.00
19 Albert Pujols 2.00 5.00
20 Bartolo Colon .60 1.50
21 Miguel Tejada 1.00 2.50
22 Mike Piazza 1.50 4.00
23 Jason Grilli .60 1.50
24 Nobuhiko Matsunaka 1.00 2.50
25 Tomoya Satozaki 1.00 2.50
26 Ichiro Suzuki 2.00 5.00
27 Hitoshi Tamura 1.00 2.50
28 Daisuke Matsuzaka 2.00 5.00
29 Koji Uehara 2.00 5.00
30 Jong Beom Lee .60 1.50
31 Seung Yeop Lee 1.00 2.50
32 Jae Seo .60 1.50
33 Min Han Son .60 1.50
34 Chan Ho Park 1.00 2.50
35 Jorge Cantu .60 1.50
36 Miguel Ojeda .60 1.50
37 Andruw Jones .60 1.50
38 Shairon Martis .60 1.50
39 Carlos Lee .60 1.50
40 Carlos Beltran 1.00 2.50
41 Javy Lopez .60 1.50
42 Javier Vazquez .60 1.50
43 Ken Griffey Jr. 3.00 8.00
44 Derek Jeter 4.00 10.00
45 Alex Rodriguez 2.00 5.00
46 Derrek Lee .60 1.50
47 Roger Clemens 2.00 5.00
48 Miguel Cabrera 1.50 4.00
49 Victor Martinez 1.00 2.50
50 Johan Santana 1.00 2.50

2006 SPx Winning Big Materials

STATED ODDS 1:252
PRINT RUNS B/WN 5-40 COPIES PER
NO PRICING ON QTY 26 OR LESS
PRICING IS FOR 2-3 CLR PATCHES
AB Adrian Beltre/40 50.00 100.00
AI Akinori Iwamura/30 200.00 300.00
AJ Andruw Jones/40 50.00 100.00
AP Ariel Pestano/30 50.00 100.00
AR Alex Rios/55 30.00 60.00
AS Alfonso Soriano/40 50.00 100.00
BA Bobby Abreu/40 50.00 100.00
BW Bernie Williams/40 75.00 120.00
CB Carlos Beltran/40 50.00 100.00
CD Carlos Delgado/40 30.00 60.00
CL Carlos Lee/40 30.00 60.00
CZ Carlos Zambrano/40 75.00 150.00
DL Derrek Lee/40 50.00 100.00
DO David Ortiz/30 30.00 60.00
EB Erik Bedard/40 30.00 60.00
EP Eduardo Paret/30 30.00 60.00
FC Frederich Cepeda/30 50.00 100.00
GY Guogan Yang/52 30.00 60.00
HC Hee Seop Choi/32 50.00 100.00
HT Hitoshi Tamura/30 200.00 300.00
IR Ivan Rodriguez/40 30.00 60.00
JB Jason Bay/40 50.00 100.00
JD Johnny Damon/40 50.00 100.00
JF Jeff Francis/40 30.00 60.00
JS Johan Santana/40 50.00 100.00
JV Jason Varitek/40 50.00 100.00
KU Koji Uehara/30 250.00 400.00
LO Javy Lopez/40 30.00 60.00
MA Moises Alou/53 30.00 60.00
MC Miguel Cabrera/40 50.00 100.00
ME Michel Enriquez/30 50.00 100.00
MF Maikel Folch/30 50.00 100.00
MK Munenori Kawasaki/30 250.00 400.00
MO Michihiro Ogasawara/30 300.00 400.00
MP Mike Piazza/40 60.00 150.00
MT Miguel Tejada/40 50.00 100.00
NM Nobuhiko Matsunaka/30 225.00 350.00
NS Naoyuki Shimizu/30 150.00 300.00
OU Osmany Urrutia/30 30.00 60.00
PE Wily Mo Pena/60 30.00 60.00
PL Pedro Luis Lazo/30 50.00 100.00
SW Shunsuke Watanabe/30 200.00 300.00
TN Tsuyoshi Nishioka/30 250.00 400.00
TW Tsuyoshi Wada/30 150.00 300.00
VM Victor Martinez/40 50.00 100.00
VO Vicyohandry Odelin/30 50.00 100.00
WL Wei-Chu Lin/45 200.00 400.00
WP Wei-Lun Pan/38 200.00 300.00
YG Yulieski Gourriel/30 50.00 100.00
YM Yunieski Maya/30 50.00 100.00

2006 SPx Winning Materials

STATED ODDS 1:18
AI Akinori Iwamura 8.00 20.00
AJ Andruw Jones 4.00 10.00
AP Ariel Pestano 3.00 8.00
AR Alex Rodriguez 6.00 15.00
AS Alfonso Soriano 3.00 8.00
BA Bobby Abreu 3.00 8.00
CB Carlos Beltran 3.00 8.00
CD Carlos Delgado 3.00 8.00
DL Derrek Lee 3.00 8.00
DO David Ortiz 4.00 10.00
EP Eduardo Paret 3.00 8.00
FC Frederich Cepeda 3.00 8.00
HC Hee Seop Choi 3.00 8.00
HT Hitoshi Tamura 8.00 20.00
IS Ichiro Suzuki 15.00 40.00
JB Jason Bay 3.00 8.00
JD Johnny Damon 3.00 8.00
JL Jong Beom Lee 3.00 8.00
JS Johan Santana 4.00 10.00
KG Ken Griffey Jr. 6.00 15.00
KU Koji Uehara 8.00 20.00
MC Miguel Cabrera 4.00 10.00
ME Michel Enriquez 3.00 8.00
MF Maikel Folch 3.00 8.00
MK Munenori Kawasaki 10.00 25.00
MO Michihiro Ogasawara 8.00 20.00
MP Mike Piazza 4.00 10.00
MS Min Han Son 4.00 10.00
MT Miguel Tejada 3.00 8.00
NM Nobuhiko Matsunaka 6.00 15.00
NS Naoyuki Shimizu 6.00 15.00
OU Osmany Urrutia 3.00 8.00
PL Pedro Luis Lazo 4.00 10.00
PU Albert Pujols 8.00 20.00
RC Roger Clemens 6.00 15.00
SW Shunsuke Watanabe 8.00 20.00
TN Tsuyoshi Nishioka 8.00 20.00
TW Tsuyoshi Wada 10.00 25.00
VM Victor Martinez 3.00 8.00
VO Vicyohandry Odelin 4.00 10.00
YG Yulieski Gourriel 3.00 8.00
YM Yunieski Maya 3.00 8.00

2007 SPx

This 150-card set was released in May, 2007. The set was issued in the hobby in three-card packs which came 10 packs per box and 10 boxes per case. Cards numbered 1-100 feature veterans while cards 101-150 (with the exception of Daisuke Matsuzaka (card #128) are signed rookie cards. The stated odds for the signed rookie cards were one in three packs. A few players did not return their signatures in time for pack out and those cards could be redeemed until May 10, 2010. The veteran cards were sequenced in alphabetical order by team.

COMMON CARD (1-100) .30 .75
COMMON AU RC (101-150) 3.00 8.00
OVERALL 101-150 AU RC ODDS 1:3
101-150 AU RC EXCH DEADLINE 05/10/2010
ASTERISK EQUALS PARTIAL EXCH
APPX.PRINTING PLATE ODDS 2 PER CASE
PLATES PRINT RUN 1 SET PER COLOR
BLACK-CYAN-MAGENTA-YELLOW ISSUED
NO PLATE PRICING DUE TO SCARCITY
1 Miguel Tejada .50 1.25
2 Brian Roberts .30 .75
3 Melvin Mora .30 .75
4 David Ortiz .75 2.00
5 Manny Ramirez .75 2.00
6 Jason Varitek .75 2.00
7 Curt Schilling .50 1.25
8 Jim Thome .50 1.25
9 Paul Konerko .50 1.25
10 Jermaine Dye .30 .75
11 Travis Hafner .30 .75
12 Victor Martinez .50 1.25
13 Grady Sizemore .50 1.25
14 C.C. Sabathia .50 1.25
15 Ivan Rodriguez .50 1.25
16 Magglio Ordonez .50 1.25
17 Carlos Guillen .30 .75
18 Justin Verlander .75 2.00
19 Shane Costa .30 .75
20 Emil Brown .30 .75
21 Mark Teahen .30 .75
22 Vladimir Guerrero .50 1.25
23 Jered Weaver .50 1.25
24 Juan Rivera .30 .75
25 Justin Morneau .50 1.25
26 Joe Mauer .60 1.50
27 Torii Hunter .30 .75
28 Johan Santana .50 1.25
29 Derek Jeter 2.00 5.00
30 Alex Rodriguez 1.00 2.50
31 Johnny Damon .50 1.25
32 Jason Giambi .30 .75
33 Bobby Crosby .30 .75
34 Nick Swisher .50 1.25
35 Eric Chavez .30 .75
36 Ichiro Suzuki 1.00 2.50
37 Raul Ibanez .50 1.25
38 Richie Sexson .30 .75
39 Carl Crawford .50 1.25
40 Rocco Baldelli .30 .75
41 Scott Kazmir .50 1.25
42 Michael Young .30 .75
43 Mark Teixeira .50 1.25
44 Ian Kinsler .50 1.25
45 Troy Glaus .30 .75
46 Vernon Wells .30 .75
47 Roy Halladay .50 1.25
48 Lyle Overbay .30 .75
49 Brandon Webb .50 1.25
50 Conor Jackson .30 .75
51 Stephen Drew .30 .75
52 Chipper Jones .75 2.00
53 Andruw Jones .30 .75
54 Adam LaRoche .30 .75
55 John Smoltz .75 2.00
56 Derrek Lee .30 .75
57 Aramis Ramirez .30 .75
58 Carlos Zambrano .50 1.25
59 Ken Griffey Jr. 1.50 4.00
60 Adam Dunn .50 1.25
61 Aaron Harang .30 .75
62 Todd Helton .50 1.25
63 Matt Holliday .75 2.00
64 Garrett Atkins .30 .75
65 Miguel Cabrera .75 2.00
66 Hanley Ramirez .50 1.25
67 Dontrelle Willis .30 .75
68 Lance Berkman .50 1.25
69 Roy Oswalt .50 1.25
70 Craig Biggio .50 1.25
71 J.D. Drew .30 .75
72 Nomar Garciaparra .50 1.25
73 Rafael Furcal .30 .75
74 Jeff Kent .30 .75
75 Prince Fielder .50 1.25
76 Bill Hall .30 .75
77 Rickie Weeks .30 .75
78 Jose Reyes .50 1.25
79 David Wright .60 1.50
80 Carlos Delgado .30 .75
81 Carlos Beltran .50 1.25
82 Ryan Howard .60 1.50
83 Chase Utley .50 1.25
84 Jimmy Rollins .50 1.25
85 Jason Bay .50 1.25
86 Freddy Sanchez .30 .75
87 Zach Duke .30 .75
88 Trevor Hoffman .50 1.25
89 Adrian Gonzalez .60 1.50
90 Chris Young .30 .75
91 Ray Durham .30 .75
92 Omar Vizquel .50 1.25
93 Jason Schmidt .30 .75
94 Albert Pujols 1.00 2.50
95 Scott Rolen .50 1.25
96 Jim Edmonds .50 1.25
97 Chris Carpenter .50 1.25
98 Alfonso Soriano .50 1.25
99 Ryan Zimmerman .50 1.25
100 Nick Johnson .30 .75
101 Delmon Young AU (RC) 8.00 20.00
102 A.Miller AU RC EXCH * 3.00 8.00
103 Troy Tulowitzki AU (RC) 4.00 10.00
104 Jeff Fiorentino AU (RC) 3.00 8.00
105 David Murphy AU (RC) 3.00 8.00
106 T.Lincecum AU RC 10.00 25.00
107 P.Hughes AU (RC) EXCH 6.00 15.00
108 K.Kouzmanoff AU (RC) EXCH 6.00 15.00
109 A.Lind AU (RC) EXCH * 3.00 8.00
110 M.Reynolds AU RC EXCH 8.00 20.00
111 Kevin Hooper AU (RC) 3.00 8.00
112 Mitch Maier AU RC 3.00 8.00
113 Homer Bailey AU (RC) 5.00 12.00
114 Dennis Sarfate AU (RC) 3.00 8.00
115 Drew Anderson AU RC 3.00 8.00
116 Miguel Montero AU (RC) 3.00 8.00
117 G.Perkins AU (RC) EXCH 3.00 8.00
119 Tim Gradoville AU RC 3.00 8.00
120 Ryan Braun AU (RC) 6.00 15.00
121 Chris Narveson AU (RC) 3.00 8.00
122 P.Misch AU (RC) EXCH * 3.00 8.00
123 Juan Salas AU (RC) 3.00 8.00
124 Beltran Perez AU (RC) 3.00 8.00
125 Joaquin Arias AU (RC) 3.00 8.00
126 Philip Humber AU (RC) 3.00 8.00
127 Kei Igawa AU RC 10.00 25.00
128 Daisuke Matsuzaka AU RC 20.00 50.00
129 Andy Cannizaro AU RC 6.00 15.00
130 Ubaldo Jimenez AU (RC) 5.00 12.00
131 Fred Lewis AU (RC) 6.00 15.00
132 Ryan Sweeney AU (RC) 3.00 8.00
133 Jeff Baker AU (RC) 3.00 8.00
134 Michael Bourn AU (RC) 3.00 8.00
135 Akinori Iwamura AU RC 6.00 15.00
136 Oswaldo Navarro AU RC 3.00 8.00
137 Hunter Pence AU (RC) 6.00 15.00
138 Jon Knott AU (RC) 3.00 8.00
139 J.Hampson AU (RC) EXCH 3.00 8.00
140 J.Salazar AU (RC) EXCH 3.00 8.00
141 Juan Morillo AU (RC) 3.00 8.00
142 Delwyn Young AU (RC) 3.00 8.00
143 Brian Burres AU (RC) 5.00 12.00
144 Chris Stewart AU RC 3.00 8.00
145 Eric Stults AU RC 3.00 8.00
146 Carlos Maldonado AU (RC) 3.00 8.00
147 Angel Sanchez AU RC 3.00 8.00
148 Cesar Jimenez AU RC 3.00 8.00
149 Shawn Riggans AU (RC) 3.00 8.00
150 John Nelson AU (RC) 3.00 8.00

2007 SPx Autofacts Preview

ONE PER HOBBY BOX TOPPER
EXCH DEADLINE 05/10/2010
AI Akinori Iwamura 15.00 40.00
AL Adam Lind 5.00 12.00
AS Angel Sanchez 3.00 8.00
BP Beltran Perez 3.00 8.00
BR Jeremy Brown 3.00 8.00
CM Carlos Maldonado 3.00 8.00
CN Chris Narveson 3.00 8.00
DS Dennis Sarfate 3.00 8.00
DW Dewayne Wise 5.00 12.00
DY Delmon Young 6.00 15.00
ES Eric Stults 3.00 8.00
FL Fred Lewis 5.00 12.00
GP Glen Perkins 3.00 8.00
JA Joaquin Arias 3.00 8.00
JB Jeff Baker 3.00 8.00
JH Justin Hampson 3.00 8.00
JK Jon Knott 3.00 8.00
JM Juan Morillo 3.00 8.00
JN John Nelson 3.00 8.00
JS Juan Salas 3.00 8.00
JW Jason Wood 3.00 8.00
KH Kevin Hooper 3.00 8.00
KI Kei Igawa 6.00 15.00
KK Kevin Kouzmanoff 5.00 12.00
MB Michael Bourn 5.00 12.00
MM Miguel Montero 3.00 8.00
PH Philip Humber 5.00 12.00
PM Patrick Misch 3.00 8.00
SA Jeff Salazar 3.00 8.00
SR Shawn Riggans 3.00 8.00
ST Chris Stewart 3.00 8.00
TT Troy Tulowitzki 10.00 25.00
YO Delwyn Young 3.00 8.00

2007 SPx Iron Man

COMMON CARD 1.50 4.00
APPX.ODDS 1:3
STATED PRINT RUN 699 SER.#'d SETS
APPX.PRINTING PLATE ODDS 2 PER CASE
PLATES PRINT RUN 1 SET PER COLOR
BLACK-CYAN-MAGENTA-YELLOW ISSUED
NO PLATE PRICING DUE TO SCARCITY

2007 SPx Iron Man Platinum

COMMON CARD 15.00 40.00
RANDOM INSERTS IN PACKS
STATED PRINT RUN 1 SER.#'d SET

2007 SPx Iron Man Memorabilia

COMMON CARD 10.00 25.00
APPX. SIX GAME-USED PER BOX
STATED PRINT RUN 25 SER.#'d SETS

2007 SPx Iron Man Signatures

COMMON CARD 150.00 300.00
RANDOM INSERTS IN PACKS
STATED PRINT RUN 1 SER.#'d SET

2007 SPx Winning Materials 199 Bronze

APPX. SIX GAME-USED PER BOX
STATED PRINT RUN 199 SER.#'d SETS
APPX.PRINTING PLATE ODDS 2 PER CASE
PLATES PRINT RUN 1 SET PER COLOR
BLACK-CYAN-MAGENTA-YELLOW ISSUED
NO PLATE PRICING DUE TO SCARCITY
AB A.J. Burnett/199 3.00 8.00
AD Adam Dunn/199 3.00 8.00
AE Andre Ethier/199 3.00 8.00
AJ Andruw Jones/199 3.00 8.00
AL Adam LaRoche/199 3.00 8.00
AP Albert Pujols/199 6.00 15.00
AR Aramis Ramirez/199 3.00 8.00
AS Anibal Sanchez/199 3.00 8.00
BA Bobby Abreu/199 4.00 10.00
BG Brian Giles/199 3.00 8.00
BL Joe Blanton/199 3.00 8.00
BM Brian McCann/199 3.00 8.00
BO Jeremy Bonderman/199 3.00 8.00
BR Brian Roberts/199 3.00 8.00
BS Ben Sheets/199 3.00 8.00
BU B.J. Upton/199 3.00 8.00
CA Miguel Cabrera/199 3.00 8.00
CB Craig Biggio/199 4.00 10.00
CC Chris Carpenter/199 3.00 8.00
CF Chone Figgins/199 3.00 8.00
CH Cole Hamels/199 4.00 10.00
CJ Chipper Jones/199 4.00 10.00
CL Roger Clemens/199 6.00 15.00
CN Robinson Cano/199 4.00 10.00
CR Carl Crawford/199 3.00 8.00
CU Chase Utley/199 4.00 10.00
CW Chien-Ming Wang/199 6.00 15.00
DJ Derek Jeter/199 8.00 20.00
DJ2 Derek Jeter/199 8.00 20.00
DL Derrek Lee/199 3.00 8.00
DO David Ortiz/199 4.00 10.00
DU Dan Uggla/199 3.00 8.00
DW Dontrelle Willis/199 3.00 8.00
EC Eric Chavez/199 3.00 8.00
FH Felix Hernandez/199 4.00 10.00
FL Francisco Liriano/199 3.00 8.00
FS Freddy Sanchez/199 3.00 8.00
FT Frank Thomas/199 4.00 10.00
GA Garrett Atkins/199 3.00 8.00
HA Travis Hafner/199 3.00 8.00
HE Todd Helton/199 4.00 10.00
HI Rich Hill/199 3.00 8.00
HK Howie Kendrick/199 3.00 8.00
HN Rich Harden/199 3.00 8.00
HR Hanley Ramirez/199 4.00 10.00
HS Huston Street/199 3.00 8.00
IK Ian Kinsler/199 3.00 8.00
IR Ivan Rodriguez/199 4.00 10.00
JB Jason Bay/199 3.00 8.00
JE Jim Edmonds/199 3.00 8.00
JF Jeff Francoeur/199 4.00 10.00
JJ Josh Johnson/199 3.00 8.00
JL Chad Billingsley/199 3.00 8.00
JM Joe Mauer/199 4.00 10.00
JN Joe Nathan/199 3.00 8.00
JP Jake Peavy/199 3.00 8.00
JR Jose Reyes/199 3.00 8.00
JS Jeremy Sowers/199 3.00 8.00
JT Jim Thome/199 3.00 8.00
JV Justin Verlander/199 4.00 10.00
JW Jered Weaver/199 3.00 8.00
JZ Joel Zumaya/199 3.00 8.00
KG Ken Griffey Jr./199 6.00 15.00

KG2 Ken Griffey Jr./199 6.00 15.00
KH Khalil Greene/199 4.00 10.00
KU Hong-Chih Kuo/199 8.00 20.00
LE Jon Lester/199 4.00 10.00
LG Luis Gonzalez/199 3.00 8.00
MC Matt Cain/199 3.00 8.00
ME Melky Cabrera/199 3.00 8.00
MH Matt Holliday/199 4.00 10.00
MO Justin Morneau/199 3.00 8.00
MT Mark Teixeira/199 3.00 8.00
NM Nick Markakis/199 4.00 10.00
NS Nick Swisher/199 3.00 8.00
PA Jonathan Papelbon/199 4.00 10.00
PF Prince Fielder/199 4.00 10.00
PL Paul LoDuca/199 3.00 8.00
RC Cal Ripken /199 6.00 15.00
RI Alex Rios/199 3.00 8.00
RJ Randy Johnson/199 3.00 8.00
RO Roy Oswalt/199 3.00 8.00
RW Rickie Weeks/199 3.00 8.00
RZ Ryan Zimmerman/199 3.00 8.00
SA Alfonso Soriano/199 3.00 8.00
SD Stephen Drew/199 3.00 8.00
SH James Shields/199 3.00 8.00
SK Scott Kazmir/199 3.00 8.00
SM John Smoltz/199 4.00 10.00
SO Scott Olsen/199 3.00 8.00
SR Scott Rolen/199 4.00 10.00
TE Miguel Tejada/199 3.00 8.00
TG Tom Glavine/199 4.00 10.00
TH Trevor Hoffman/199 3.00 8.00
TO Torii Hunter/199 3.00 8.00
VG Vladimir Guerrero/199 4.00 10.00
VM Victor Martinez/199 3.00 8.00
WE David Wells/199 3.00 8.00
WI Josh Willingham/199 3.00 8.00
YB Yuniesky Betancourt/199 3.00 8.00

2007 SPx Winning Materials 199 Gold

*199 GOLD: .4X TO 1X 199 BRONZE
APPX. SIX GAME-USED PER BOX
STATED PRINT RUN 199 SER.#'d SETS

2007 SPx Winning Materials 199 Silver

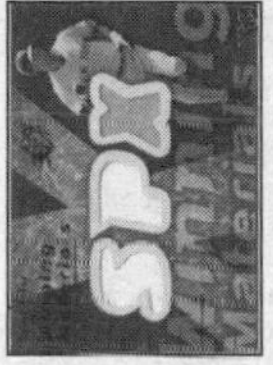

*199 SILVER: .4X TO 1X 199 BRONZE
APPX. SIX GAME-USED PER BOX
STATED PRINT RUN 199 SER.#'d SETS

2007 SPx Winning Materials 175 Blue

*175 BLUE: .4X TO 1X 199 BRONZE
APPX. SIX GAME-USED PER BOX
STATED PRINT RUN 175 SER.#'d SETS

2007 SPx Winning Materials 175 Green

*175 GREEN: .4X TO 1X 199 BRONZE
APPX. SIX GAME-USED PER BOX
STATED PRINT RUN 175 SER.#'d SETS

2007 SPx Winning Materials 99 Gold

*99 GOLD: .5X TO 1.2X 199 BRONZE
APPX. SIX GAME-USED PER BOX
STATED PRINT RUN 99 SER.#'d SETS

2007 SPx Winning Materials 99 Silver

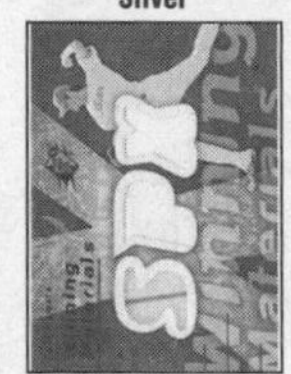

*99 SILVER: .5X TO 1.2X 199 BRONZE
APPX. SIX GAME-USED PER BOX
STATED PRINT RUN 99 SER.#'d SETS

2007 SPx Winning Materials Dual Gold

APPX. SIX GAME-USED PER BOX
STATED PRINT RUN 50 SER.#'d SETS
AB A.J. Burnett/50 5.00 12.00
AD Adam Dunn/50 5.00 12.00
AE Andre Ethier/50 5.00 12.00
AJ Andruw Jones/50 5.00 12.00
AL Adam LaRoche/50 5.00 12.00
AP Albert Pujols/50 10.00 25.00
AR Aramis Ramirez/50 5.00 12.00
AS Anibal Sanchez/50 5.00 12.00
BA Bobby Abreu/50 6.00 15.00
BG Brian Giles/50 5.00 12.00
BL Joe Blanton/50 5.00 12.00
BM Brian McCann/50 5.00 12.00
BO Jeremy Bonderman/50 5.00 12.00
BR Brian Roberts/50 5.00 12.00
BS Ben Sheets/50 5.00 12.00
BU B.J. Upton/50 5.00 12.00
CA Miguel Cabrera/50 5.00 12.00
CB Craig Biggio/50 6.00 15.00
CC Chris Carpenter/50 5.00 12.00
CF Chone Figgins/50 5.00 12.00
CH Cole Hamels/50 6.00 15.00
CJ Chipper Jones/50 6.00 15.00
CL Roger Clemens/50 10.00 25.00
CN Robinson Cano/50 6.00 15.00
CR Carl Crawford/50 5.00 12.00
CU Chase Utley/50 6.00 15.00
CW Chien-Ming Wang/50 10.00 25.00
DJ Derek Jeter/50 12.50 30.00
DJ2 Derek Jeter/50 12.50 30.00
DL Derrek Lee/50 5.00 12.00
DO David Ortiz/50 6.00 15.00
DU Dan Uggla/50 6.00 15.00
DW Dontrelle Willis/50 5.00 12.00
EC Eric Chavez/50 5.00 12.00
FH Felix Hernandez/50 6.00 15.00
FL Francisco Liriano/50 5.00 12.00
FS Freddy Sanchez/50 5.00 12.00
FT Frank Thomas/50 6.00 15.00
GA Garrett Atkins/50 5.00 12.00
HA Travis Hafner/50 5.00 12.00
HE Todd Helton/50 6.00 15.00
HI Rich Hill/50 5.00 12.00
HK Howie Kendrick/50 5.00 12.00
HN Rich Harden/50 5.00 12.00
HR Hanley Ramirez/50 6.00 15.00
HS Huston Street/50 5.00 12.00
IK Ian Kinsler/50 5.00 12.00
IR Ivan Rodriguez/50 6.00 15.00
JB Jason Bay/50 5.00 12.00
JE Jim Edmonds/50 5.00 12.00
JF Jeff Francoeur/50 6.00 15.00
JJ Josh Johnson/50 5.00 12.00
JL Chad Billingsley/50 5.00 12.00
JM Joe Mauer/50 6.00 15.00
JN Joe Nathan/50 5.00 12.00
JP Jake Peavy/50 5.00 12.00
JR Jose Reyes/50 5.00 12.00
JS Jeremy Sowers/50 5.00 12.00
JT Jim Thome/50 6.00 15.00
JV Justin Verlander/50 6.00 15.00
JW Jered Weaver/50 5.00 12.00
JZ Joel Zumaya/50 5.00 12.00
KG Ken Griffey Jr./50 10.00 25.00
KG2 Ken Griffey Jr./50 10.00 25.00
KH Khalil Greene/50 6.00 15.00
KU Hong-Chih Kuo/50 12.50 30.00
LE Jon Lester/50 6.00 15.00
LG Luis Gonzalez/50 5.00 12.00
MC Matt Cain/50 5.00 12.00
ME Melky Cabrera/50 5.00 12.00
MH Matt Holliday/50 6.00 15.00
MO Justin Morneau/50 5.00 12.00
MT Mark Teixeira/50 5.00 12.00
NM Nick Markakis/50 6.00 15.00
NS Nick Swisher/50 5.00 12.00
PA Jonathan Papelbon/50 6.00 15.00
PF Prince Fielder/50 6.00 15.00
PL Paul LoDuca/50 5.00 12.00
RC Cal Ripken /50 10.00 25.00
RI Alex Rios/50 5.00 12.00
RJ Randy Johnson/50 5.00 12.00
RO Roy Oswalt/50 5.00 12.00
RW Rickie Weeks/50 5.00 12.00
RZ Ryan Zimmerman/50 5.00 12.00
SA Alfonso Soriano/50 5.00 12.00
SD Stephen Drew/50 5.00 12.00
SH James Shields/50 5.00 12.00
SK Scott Kazmir/50 5.00 12.00
SM John Smoltz/50 5.00 12.00
SO Scott Olsen/50 5.00 12.00
SR Scott Rolen/50 5.00 12.00
TE Miguel Tejada/50 5.00 12.00
TG Tom Glavine/50 5.00 12.00
TH Trevor Hoffman/50 5.00 12.00
TO Torii Hunter/50 5.00 12.00
VG Vladimir Guerrero/50 6.00 15.00
VM Victor Martinez/50 5.00 12.00
WE David Wells/50 5.00 12.00
WI Josh Willingham/50 5.00 12.00
YB Yuniesky Betancourt/50 5.00 12.00

2007 SPx Winning Materials Dual Silver

*DUAL SILVER: .4X TO 1X DUAL GOLD
APPX. SIX GAME-USED PER BOX
STATED PRINT RUN 50 SER.#'d SETS

2007 SPx Winning Materials Patches Gold

APPX. SIX GAME-USED PER BOX
PRINT RUNS B/WN 3-99 COPIES PER
NO VERLANDER PRICING DUE TO SCARCITY
AB A.J. Burnett/99 4.00 10.00
AD Adam Dunn/99 4.00 10.00
AF Andre Ethier/99 5.00 12.00
AJ Andruw Jones/99 5.00 12.00
AL Adam LaRoche/99 4.00 10.00
AP Albert Pujols/99 15.00 40.00
AR Aramis Ramirez/99 4.00 10.00
AS Anibal Sanchez/54 4.00 10.00
BA Bobby Abreu/99 6.00 15.00
BG Brian Giles/99 4.00 10.00
BL Joe Blanton/99 4.00 10.00
BM Brian McCann/99 6.00 15.00
BO Jeremy Bonderman/99 6.00 15.00
BR Brian Roberts/99 4.00 10.00
BS Ben Sheets/99 4.00 10.00
BU B.J. Upton/99 10.00 25.00
CA Miguel Cabrera/99 5.00 12.00
CB Craig Biggio/99 6.00 15.00
CC Chris Carpenter/99 5.00 12.00
CF Chone Figgins/99 4.00 10.00
CH Cole Hamels/99 6.00 15.00
CJ Chipper Jones/99 6.00 15.00
CL Roger Clemens/99 15.00 40.00
CN Robinson Cano/99 6.00 15.00
CR Carl Crawford/99 5.00 12.00
CU Chase Utley/99 6.00 15.00
CW Chien-Ming Wang/99 15.00 40.00
DJ Derek Jeter/99 20.00 50.00
DJ2 Derek Jeter/99 20.00 50.00
DL Derrek Lee/99 4.00 10.00
DO David Ortiz/99 6.00 15.00
DU Dan Uggla/99 4.00 10.00
DW Dontrelle Willis/99 4.00 10.00
EC Eric Chavez/99 4.00 10.00
FH Felix Hernandez/99 5.00 12.00
FL Francisco Liriano/99 6.00 15.00
FS Freddy Sanchez/99 4.00 10.00
FT Frank Thomas/99 10.00 25.00
GA Garrett Atkins/99 4.00 10.00
HA Travis Hafner/99 4.00 10.00
HE Todd Helton/99 5.00 12.00
HI Rich Hill/99 4.00 10.00
HK Howie Kendrick/34 6.00 15.00
HN Rich Harden/99 4.00 10.00
HR Hanley Ramirez/99 5.00 12.00
HS Huston Street/99 4.00 10.00
IK Ian Kinsler/99 4.00 10.00
IR Ivan Rodriguez/99 5.00 12.00
JB Jason Bay/99 5.00 12.00
JE Jim Edmonds/99 5.00 12.00
JF Jeff Francoeur/99 10.00 25.00
JJ Josh Johnson/99 4.00 10.00
JL Chad Billingsley/99 4.00 10.00
JM Joe Mauer/99 6.00 15.00
JN Joe Nathan/99 4.00 10.00
JP Jake Peavy/99 4.00 10.00
JR Jose Reyes/99 6.00 15.00
JS Jeremy Sowers/99 4.00 10.00
JT Jim Thome/99 5.00 12.00
JW Jered Weaver/99 5.00 12.00
JZ Joel Zumaya/99 5.00 12.00
KG Ken Griffey Jr./99 12.50 30.00
KG2 Ken Griffey Jr./99 12.50 30.00
KH Khalil Greene/99 5.00 12.00
KU Hong-Chih Kuo/99 5.00 12.00
LE Jon Lester/99 5.00 12.00
LG Luis Gonzalez/99 4.00 10.00
MC Matt Cain/99 5.00 12.00
ME Melky Cabrera/99 4.00 10.00
MH Matt Holliday/99 5.00 12.00
MO Justin Morneau/99 4.00 10.00
MT Mark Teixeira/99 5.00 12.00
NM Nick Markakis/99 10.00 25.00
NS Nick Swisher/99 6.00 15.00
PA Jonathan Papelbon/99 6.00 15.00
PF Prince Fielder/99 6.00 15.00
PL Paul LoDuca/99 5.00 12.00
RC Cal Ripken /99 12.50 30.00
RI Alex Rios/99 4.00 10.00
RJ Randy Johnson/99 6.00 15.00
RO Roy Oswalt/99 5.00 12.00
RW Rickie Weeks/99 4.00 10.00
RZ Ryan Zimmerman/99 10.00 25.00
SA Alfonso Soriano/99 5.00 12.00
SD Stephen Drew/99 5.00 12.00
SH James Shields/99 4.00 10.00
SK Scott Kazmir/99 5.00 12.00
SM John Smoltz/99 10.00 25.00
SO Scott Olsen/99 4.00 10.00
SR Scott Rolen/99 4.00 10.00
TE Miguel Tejada/99 4.00 10.00
TG Tom Glavine/99 6.00 15.00
TH Trevor Hoffman/99 5.00 12.00
TO Torii Hunter/99 5.00 12.00
VG Vladimir Guerrero/99 10.00 25.00
VM Victor Martinez/99 4.00 10.00
WE David Wells/99 4.00 10.00
WI Josh Willingham/99 4.00 10.00
YB Yuniesky Betancourt/99 4.00 10.00

2007 SPx Winning Materials Patches Silver

*PATCH SILVER: .4X TO 1X PATCH GOLD
APPX. SIX GAME-USED PER BOX
PRINT RUN B/WN 3-99 COPIES PER
NO PRICING ON QTY 27 OR LESS
JV Justin Verlander/99 6.00 15.00
LE Jon Lester/37 6.00 15.00

2007 SPx Winning Materials Patches Bronze

*PATCH BRONZE: .5X TO 1.2X PATCH GOLD
APPX. SIX GAME-USED PER BOX
STATED PRINT RUN 50 SER.#'d SETS
AR Aramis Ramirez/50 4.00 10.00
LE Jon Lester/50 6.00 15.00
MH Matt Holliday/50 5.00 12.00

2007 SPx Winning Trios Bronze

*BRONZE: .5X TO 1.2X GOLD
APPX. SIX GAME-USED PER BOX
STATED PRINT RUN 30 SER.#'d SETS

2007 SPx Winning Trios Gold

APPX. SIX GAME-USED PER BOX
STATED PRINT RUN 75 SER.#'d SETS
WT1 Griffey Jr./Pujols/Jeter 20.00 50.00
WT2 Uggla/Hanley/Willingham 10.00 25.00
WT3 Willis/J.Johnson/Anibal 6.00 15.00
WT4 Berkman/Papi/Hafner 10.00 25.00
WT5 Peavy/Oswalt/Sheets 6.00 15.00
WT6 Verlander/Bonderman/Pudge 10.00 25.00
WT7 J.Reyes/Hanley/S.Drew 10.00 25.00
WT8 Mig.Cabrera/Zimmerman/B.Upton 10.00 25.00
WT9 Jer.Weaver/Verlander/Papelbon 10.00 25.00
WT10 Jeter/Big Unit/Abreu 10.00 25.00
WT11 Ensberg/Biggio/Berkman 6.00 15.00
WT12 Francoeur/LaRoche/ McCann 10.00 25.00
WT13 Mauer/McCann/V.Martinez 10.00 25.00
WT14 Crawford/Sizemore/J.Reyes 10.00 25.00
WT15 F.Garcia/Zambrano/Santana 6.00 15.00
WT16 Vlad/Abreu/Soriano 10.00 25.00
WT17 Morneau/Mauer/Santana 10.00 25.00
WT18 Delgado/J.Reyes/Beltran 6.00 15.00
WT19 Billingsley/Ethier/Kemp 10.00 25.00
WT20 Thome/Dye/Iguchi 10.00 25.00
WT21 Utley/Rowand/Rollins 10.00 25.00
WT22 Ordonez/Pudge/Granderson 15.00 40.00
WT23 Pujols/Carpenter/Rolen 15.00 40.00
WT24 Shields/B.Upton/Crawford 6.00 15.00
WT25 Kendrick/Jer.Weaver/Napoli 6.00 15.00
WT26 Uggla/Kendrick/Kinsler 6.00 15.00
WT27 Roberts/Mig.Tejada/Markakis 10.00 25.00
WT28 Jer.Weaver/Verlander/Pelfrey 10.00 25.00
WT29 Hamels/Hill/Liriano 10.00 25.00
WT30 Anibal/Lowe/Big Unit 6.00 15.00
WT31 Zimmerman/Prince/Uggla 10.00 25.00
WT32 Hoffman/Nathan/Street 6.00 15.00
WT33 Burnett/Rios/Wells 6.00 15.00
WT34 Weeks/Prince/Sheets 10.00 25.00
WT35 Betancourt/Beltre/F.Hernandez 10.00 25.00
WT36 Verlander/Zumaya/Bonderman 10.00 25.00
WT37 Wagner/J.Reyes/Lo Duca 6.00 15.00
WT38 Sowers/Sabathia/Martinez 6.00 15.00
WT39 S.Drew/Webb/C.Jackson 6.00 15.00
WT40 F.Hernandez
Jer.Weaver/Verlander 10.00 25.00
WT41 Griffey Jr./Big Hurt/Pudge 10.00 25.00
WT42 Jeter/Ripken Jr./J.Reyes 10.00 25.00

2007 SPx Winning Trios Silver

*SILVER: .4X TO 1X GOLD
APPX. SIX GAME-USED PER BOX
STATED PRINT RUN 50 SER.#'d SETS

2007 SPx Young Stars Signatures

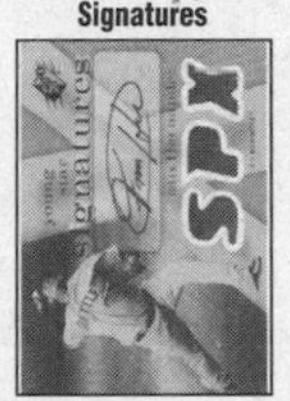

STATED ODDS 1:12
EXCH DEADLINE 05/10/2010
APPX.PRINTING PLATE ODDS 2 PER CASE
PLATES PRINT RUN 1 SET PER COLOR
BLACK-CYAN-MAGENTA-YELLOW ISSUED
NO PLATE PRICING DUE TO SCARCITY
AE Andre Ethier 3.00 8.00
AG Adrian Gonzalez 6.00 15.00
AM Andrew Miller 10.00 25.00
AS Anibal Sanchez 3.00 8.00
BU B.J. Upton 6.00 15.00
CA Matt Cain 8.00 20.00
CH Cole Hamels 6.00 15.00
CQ Carlos Quentin 3.00 8.00
DJ Derek Jeter EXCH 125.00 300.00
DU Dan Uggla 6.00 15.00
DY Delmon Young 6.00 15.00
FH Felix Hernandez 10.00 25.00
FL Francisco Liriano 4.00 10.00
HA Rich Harden 5.00 12.00
HI Rich Hill 6.00 15.00
HK Howie Kendrick 6.00 15.00
HR Hanley Ramirez 4.00 10.00
JB Jeremy Brown 3.00 8.00
JJ Josh Johnson 8.00 20.00
JL Jon Lester 6.00 15.00
JM Joe Mauer 12.00 30.00
JP Jonathan Papelbon 6.00 15.00
JR Jose Reyes 4.00 10.00
JS Jeremy Sowers 3.00 8.00
JV Justin Verlander 25.00 60.00
JW Jered Weaver 3.00 8.00
JZ Joel Zumaya 4.00 10.00
KG Ken Griffey Jr. 50.00 120.00
KU Hong-Chih Kuo 4.00 10.00
LO James Loney 3.00 8.00
MO Justin Morneau 6.00 15.00
NM Nick Markakis 10.00 25.00
PH Philip Humber 5.00 12.00
RW Rickie Weeks 5.00 12.00
RZ Ryan Zimmerman EXCH 3.00 8.00
SD Stephen Drew EXCH 4.00 10.00
ST Scott Thorman 5.00 12.00
TT Troy Tulowitzki 6.00 15.00
WI Josh Willingham 3.00 8.00

2008 SPx

OVERALL AU ODDS FOUR PER BOX
1 Brandon Webb .40 1.00
2 Chris B. Young .25 .60
3 Eric Byrnes .25 .60
4 Dan Haren .25 .60
5 Mark Teixeira .40 1.00
6 Chipper Jones .60 1.50
7 John Smoltz .60 1.50
8 Erik Bedard .25 .60
9 Nick Markakis .50 1.25
10 Brian Roberts .25 .60
11 David Ortiz .60 1.50
12 Curt Schilling .40 1.00
13 Manny Ramirez .60 1.50
14 Daisuke Matsuzaka .40 1.00
15 Josh Beckett .25 .60
16 Derrek Lee .25 .60
17 Alfonso Soriano .40 1.00
18 Carlos Zambrano .40 1.00
19 Aramis Ramirez .25 .60
20 Jermaine Dye .25 .60
21 Jim Thome .40 1.00
22 Nick Swisher .40 1.00
23 Ken Griffey Jr. 1.25 3.00
24 Adam Dunn .40 1.00
25 Brandon Phillips .25 .60
26 Grady Sizemore .40 1.00
27 Victor Martinez .40 1.00
28 C.C. Sabathia .40 1.00
29 Travis Hafner .25 .60
30 Matt Holliday .60 1.50
31 Todd Helton .40 1.00
32 Troy Tulowitzki .60 1.50
33 Magglio Ordonez .40 1.00
34 Gary Sheffield .25 .60
35 Justin Verlander .60 1.50
36 Curtis Granderson .40 1.00
37 Miguel Cabrera .60 1.50
38 Hanley Ramirez .40 1.00
39 Dan Uggla .25 .60
40 Miguel Tejada .40 1.00
41 Lance Berkman .40 1.00
42 Hunter Pence .40 1.00
43 Carlos Lee .25 .60
44 Alex Gordon .40 1.00
45 David DeJesus .25 .60
46 Vladimir Guerrero .40 1.00
47 Jered Weaver .40 1.00
48 Torii Hunter .25 .60
49 Andruw Jones .25 .60
50 Rafael Furcal .25 .60
51 Russell Martin .25 .60
52 Brad Penny .25 .60
53 Ryan Braun .40 1.00
54 Prince Fielder .40 1.00
55 J.J. Hardy .25 .60
56 Justin Morneau .40 1.00
57 Johan Santana .40 1.00
58 Joe Mauer .50 1.25
59 Delmon Young .40 1.00
60 Jose Reyes .40 1.00
61 David Wright .40 1.00
62 Carlos Beltran .40 1.00
63 Pedro Martinez .40 1.00
64 Chien-Ming Wang .40 1.00
65 Alex Rodriguez .75 2.00
66 Derek Jeter 1.50 4.00
67 Robinson Cano .40 1.00
68 Hideki Matsui .60 1.50
69 Joe Blanton .25 .60
70 Jack Cust .25 .60
71 Cole Hamels .50 1.25
72 Jimmy Rollins .40 1.00
73 Ryan Howard .40 1.00
74 Chase Utley .40 1.00
75 Jason Bay .40 1.00
76 Freddy Sanchez .25 .60
77 Jake Peavy .25 .60
78 Greg Maddux .75 2.00
79 Adrian Gonzalez .40 1.00
80 Barry Zito .40 1.00
81 Omar Vizquel .40 1.00
82 Tim Lincecum .40 1.00
83 Ichiro Suzuki .75 2.00
84 Felix Hernandez .40 1.00
85 Kenji Johjima .25 .60
86 Albert Pujols .75 2.00
87 Scott Rolen .40 1.00
88 Chris Carpenter .40 1.00
89 Rick Ankiel .25 .60
90 Scott Kazmir .40 1.00
91 Carl Crawford .40 1.00
92 B.J. Upton .40 1.00
93 Michael Young .25 .60
94 Josh Hamilton .40 1.00
95 Hank Blalock .25 .60
96 Roy Halladay .40 1.00
97 Vernon Wells .25 .60
98 Alex Rios .25 .60
99 Ryan Zimmerman .40 1.00
100 Dmitri Young .25 .60
101 Billy Murphy AU (RC) 3.00 8.00
102 Emilio Bonifacio AU RC 5.00 12.00
103 Brandon Jones AU RC 3.00 8.00
104 Clint Sammons AU (RC) 3.00 8.00
105 Clay Buchholz AU (RC) 8.00 20.00
106 Kevin Hart AU (RC) 3.00 8.00
107 Donny Lucy AU (RC) 3.00 8.00
108 Lance Broadway AU (RC) 3.00 8.00
109 Joey Votto AU (RC) 30.00 60.00
110 Ryan Hanigan AU RC 4.00 10.00
111 Joe Koshansky AU (RC) 3.00 8.00
112 Josh Newman AU RC 3.00 8.00
113 Seth Smith AU (RC) 3.00 8.00
114 Chris Seddon AU (RC) 3.00 8.00
115 Harvey Garcia AU (RC) 3.00 8.00
116 Felipe Paulino AU RC 3.00 8.00
117 J.R. Towles AU RC 4.00 10.00
118 Josh Anderson AU (RC) 3.00 8.00
119 Troy Patton AU (RC) 3.00 8.00
120 Billy Buckner AU (RC) 3.00 8.00
121 Luke Hochevar AU RC 3.00 8.00
122 Chin-Lung Hu AU (RC) 6.00 15.00
124 Jose Morales AU (RC) 6.00 15.00
126 Alberto Gonzalez AU RC 3.00 8.00
127 Bronson Sardinha AU (RC) 3.00 8.00
128 Ian Kennedy AU RC 6.00 15.00
129 Ross Ohlendorf AU RC 3.00 8.00
130 Daric Barton AU (RC) 6.00 15.00
131 Jerry Blevins AU RC 3.00 8.00
132 Dave Davidson AU RC 3.00 8.00
133 Nyjer Morgan AU (RC) 3.00 8.00
134 Steve Pearce AU RC 6.00 15.00
135 Colt Morton AU RC 3.00 8.00
136 Eugenio Velez AU RC 3.00 8.00
138 Rob Johnson AU (RC) 3.00 8.00
139 Wladimir Balentien AU (RC) 3.00 8.00
140 Justin Ruggiano AU RC 3.00 8.00
141 Bill White AU RC 3.00 8.00
142 Luis Mendoza AU (RC) 3.00 8.00
143 Jonathan Albaladejo AU RC 3.00 8.00
145 Ross Detwiler AU RC 6.00 15.00
146 J.Bruce AU (RC) UER 6.00 15.00
147 C.Gonzalez AU (RC) 20.00 50.00
148 E.Longoria AU RC 10.00 25.00
150 M.Scherzer AU RC 100.00 250.00
151 C.Kershaw AU RC 125.00 300.00
152 A.Ramirez AU RC 4.00 10.00

2008 SPx Silver

*SILVER AU: .4X TO 1X BASIC AU RC
RANDOM INSERT IN BOX TOPPER PACK
CARDS 146-150 DO NOT EXIST

2008 SPx Babe Ruth American Legend

COMMON RUTH 20.00 50.00
OVERALL ODDS ONE PER CASE
STATED PRINT RUN 1 SER.#'d SET

2008 SPx Ken Griffey Jr. American Hero

COMMON GRIFFEY 1.25 3.00
RANDOM INSERTS IN PACKS
STATED PRINT RUN 725 SER.#'d SETS

2008 SPx Ken Griffey Jr. American Hero Boxscore

COMMON GRIFFEY 12.00 30.00
OVERALL ODDS ONE PER CASE
STATED PRINT RUN 1 SER.#'d SET

2008 SPx Ken Griffey Jr. American Hero Memorabilia

COMMON GRIFFEY 12.50 30.00
OVERALL MEM ODDS SIX PER BOX
STATED PRINT RUN 25 SER.#'d SETS

2008 SPx Ken Griffey Jr. American Hero Signature

COMMON GRIFFEY 100.00 200.00
OVERALL AU ODDS FOUR PER BOX
STATED PRINT RUN 3 SER.#'d SETS

2008 SPx Superstar Signatures

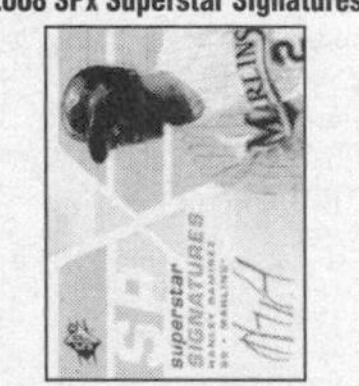

OVERALL AU ODDS FOUR PER BOX
EXCHANGE DEADLINE 4/28/2010
BW Brandon Webb 6.00 15.00
DJ Derek Jeter 100.00 175.00
DM Daisuke Matsuzaka 20.00 50.00
DU Dan Uggla 6.00 15.00
HR Hanley Ramirez 8.00 20.00
KG Ken Griffey Jr. 30.00 80.00
MH Matt Holliday 10.00 25.00
MT Mark Teixeira 10.00 25.00
PF Prince Fielder 4.00 10.00
SR Scott Rolen 5.00 12.00
TG Tom Glavine 10.00 25.00
TH Travis Hafner 5.00 12.00
VG Vladimir Guerrero 8.00 20.00
VM Victor Martinez 4.00 10.00

2008 SPx Winning Materials SPx 150

OVERALL GU ODDS SIX PER BOX
STATED PRINT RUN 150 SER.#'d SETS
AB A.J. Burnett 3.00 8.00
AE Andre Ethier 3.00 8.00
AG Adrian Gonzalez 3.00 8.00
AH Aaron Harang 3.00 8.00
AJ Andruw Jones 3.00 8.00
AK Austin Kearns 3.00 8.00
AL Adam LaRoche 3.00 8.00
AP Albert Pujols 5.00 12.00
AP Andy Pettitte 4.00 10.00
AR Aaron Rowand 3.00 8.00
AS Alfonso Soriano 3.00 8.00
BA Bobby Abreu 3.00 8.00
BC Bartolo Colon 3.00 8.00
BE Adrian Beltre 3.00 8.00
BG Brian Giles 3.00 8.00
BM Brian McCann 3.00 8.00
BS Ben Sheets 3.00 8.00
BU B.J. Upton 3.00 8.00
BW Billy Wagner 4.00 10.00
CA Chris Carpenter 3.00 8.00
CB Carlos Beltran 3.00 8.00
CC Chad Cordero 3.00 8.00
CD Carlos Delgado 3.00 8.00
CG Carlos Guillen 3.00 8.00
CH Chris Burke 3.00 8.00
CK Casey Kotchman 3.00 8.00
CL Carlos Lee 3.00 8.00
CS Curt Schilling 3.00 8.00
CU Chase Utley 5.00 12.00
CZ Carlos Zambrano 3.00 8.00
DH Dan Haren 3.00 8.00
DJ Derek Jeter 10.00 25.00
DL Derrek Lee 3.00 8.00
DO David Ortiz 3.00 8.00
DU Dan Uggla 3.00 8.00
DW Dontrelle Willis 3.00 8.00
DY Jermaine Dye 3.00 8.00
EC Eric Chavez 3.00 8.00
FH Felix Hernandez 3.00 8.00
FL Francisco Liriano 3.00 8.00
GA Garret Anderson 3.00 8.00
GA Garrett Atkins 3.00 8.00
GJ Geoff Jenkins 3.00 8.00
GM Greg Maddux 5.00 12.00
GO Alex Gordon 5.00 12.00
GR Curtis Granderson 3.00 8.00
GS Grady Sizemore 3.00 8.00
HA Cole Hamels 3.00 8.00
HB Hank Blalock 3.00 8.00
HE Todd Helton 3.00 8.00
HO Trevor Hoffman 3.00 8.00
HR Hanley Ramirez 3.00 8.00
HU Torii Hunter 3.00 8.00
IR Ivan Rodriguez 4.00 10.00
JA Conor Jackson 3.00 8.00
JB Josh Barfield 3.00 8.00
JD J.D. Drew 3.00 8.00
JE Jim Edmonds 4.00 10.00
JF Jeff Francoeur 4.00 10.00
JG Jason Giambi 3.00 8.00
JH Jhonny Peralta 3.00 8.00
JJ J.J. Hardy 3.00 8.00
JK Jeff Kent 3.00 8.00
JM Joe Mauer 3.00 8.00
JN Joe Nathan 3.00 8.00
JO Josh Beckett 4.00 10.00
JP Jake Peavy 3.00 8.00
JR Jose Reyes 3.00 8.00
JS Johan Santana 3.00 8.00
JT Jim Thome 3.00 8.00
JV Jason Varitek 4.00 10.00
KJ Kenji Johjima 3.00 8.00
KY Kevin Youkilis 4.00 10.00
LB Lance Berkman 3.00 8.00
LG Luis Gonzalez 3.00 8.00
MC Miguel Cabrera 3.00 8.00
MH Matt Holliday 3.00 8.00
MO Justin Morneau 3.00 8.00
MR Manny Ramirez 4.00 10.00
MT Mark Teixeira 3.00 8.00
MY Michael Young 3.00 8.00
OR Magglio Ordonez 3.00 8.00
PA Jonathan Papelbon 4.00 10.00
PF Prince Fielder 4.00 10.00
PM Pedro Martinez 3.00 8.00
PO Jorge Posada 3.00 8.00
RA Aramis Ramirez 3.00 8.00
RH Roy Halladay 3.00 8.00
RJ Randy Johnson 3.00 8.00
RO Roy Oswalt 3.00 8.00
SM John Smoltz 4.00 10.00
TE Miguel Tejada 3.00 8.00
TH Tim Hudson 3.00 8.00
TR Travis Hafner 3.00 8.00
VE Justin Verlander 3.00 8.00
VG Vladimir Guerrero 3.00 8.00
VW Vernon Wells 3.00 8.00

2008 SPx Winning Materials Baseball 99

*BB 99: .4X TO 1X WM SPX 150
OVERALL GU ODDS SIX PER BOX
STATED PRINT RUN 99 SER.#'d SETS
KG Ken Griffey Jr. 5.00 12.00
RF Rafael Furcal 3.00 8.00

2008 SPx Winning Materials Dual Jersey Number

*DUAL JN: .5X TO 1.2X WM SPX 150
OVERALL GU ODDS SIX PER BOX
PRINT RUNS B/WN 35-46 COPIES PER
CJ Chipper Jones/46 5.00 12.00

2008 SPx Winning Materials Dual Limited Patch SPx

*DUAL LTD PATCH: .6X TO 1.5X LTD PATCH SPX
OVERALL GU ODDS SIX PER BOX
PRINT RUNS B/WN 23-50 COPIES PER
NO PRICING ON QTY 25 OR LESS
KG Ken Griffey Jr. 15.00 40.00

2008 SPx Winning Materials Dual SPx

*DUAL SPX: .5X TO 1.2X WM SPX 150
OVERALL GU ODDS SIX PER BOX
STATED PRINT RUN 50 SER.#'d SETS

2008 SPx Winning Materials Jersey Number 125

*JN 125: .4X TO 1X WM SPX 150
OVERALL GU ODDS SIX PER BOX
STATED PRINT RUN 125 SER.#'d SETS
RF Rafael Furcal 3.00 8.00

2008 SPx Winning Materials Limited Patch SPx

OVERALL GU ODDS SIX PER BOX
PRINT RUNS B/WN 72-99 COPIES PER
AB A.J. Burnett 4.00 10.00
AE Andre Ethier 4.00 10.00
AG Adrian Gonzalez 4.00 10.00
AH Aaron Harang 4.00 10.00
AJ Andruw Jones 4.00 10.00
AK Austin Kearns 4.00 10.00
AL Adam LaRoche 4.00 10.00
AP Albert Pujols 10.00 25.00
AR Aaron Rowand 4.00 10.00
AS Alfonso Soriano 4.00 10.00
AT Garrett Atkins 4.00 10.00
BA Bobby Abreu 4.00 10.00
BC Bartolo Colon 4.00 10.00
BE Adrian Beltre 4.00 10.00
BG Brian Giles 4.00 10.00
BM Brian McCann/72 4.00 10.00
BS Ben Sheets/97 4.00 10.00
BU B.J. Upton 4.00 10.00
BW Billy Wagner 5.00 12.00
CA Chris Carpenter 4.00 10.00
CB Carlos Beltran 4.00 10.00
CC Chad Cordero 4.00 10.00
CD Carlos Delgado 4.00 10.00
CG Carlos Guillen 4.00 10.00
CH Chris Burke 4.00 10.00
CJ Chipper Jones 5.00 12.00
CK Casey Kotchman 4.00 10.00
CL Carlos Lee 4.00 10.00
CS Curt Schilling 4.00 10.00
CU Chase Utley 5.00 12.00
CZ Carlos Zambrano 4.00 10.00
DH Dan Haren 4.00 10.00
DJ Derek Jeter/76 15.00 40.00
DL Derrek Lee 4.00 10.00
DO David Ortiz 5.00 12.00
DU Dan Uggla 4.00 10.00
DW Dontrelle Willis 4.00 10.00
DY Jermaine Dye 4.00 10.00
EC Eric Chavez 4.00 10.00
FH Felix Hernandez 4.00 10.00
FL Francisco Liriano 4.00 10.00
GA Garret Anderson 4.00 10.00
GJ Geoff Jenkins 4.00 10.00
GM Greg Maddux 6.00 15.00
GO Alex Gordon 6.00 15.00
GR Curtis Granderson 4.00 10.00
GS Grady Sizemore 4.00 10.00
HA Cole Hamels 4.00 10.00
HB Hank Blalock 4.00 10.00
HE Todd Helton 4.00 10.00
HO Trevor Hoffman 4.00 10.00
HR Hanley Ramirez 4.00 10.00
HU Torii Hunter 4.00 10.00
IR Ivan Rodriguez 5.00 12.00
JA Conor Jackson/80 4.00 10.00
JB Josh Barfield 4.00 10.00
JD J.D. Drew 4.00 10.00
JE Jim Edmonds 5.00 12.00
JF Jeff Francoeur 5.00 12.00
JG Jason Giambi 4.00 10.00
JH Jhonny Peralta 4.00 10.00
JJ J.J. Hardy 4.00 10.00
JK Jeff Kent 4.00 10.00
JM Joe Mauer 4.00 10.00
JN Joe Nathan 4.00 10.00
JO Josh Beckett 5.00 12.00
JP Jake Peavy 4.00 10.00
JR Jose Reyes 4.00 10.00
JS Johan Santana 4.00 10.00
JT Jim Thome 4.00 10.00
JV Jason Varitek 5.00 12.00
KG Ken Griffey Jr. 6.00 15.00
KJ Kenji Johjima 4.00 10.00
KY Kevin Youkilis 5.00 12.00
LB Lance Berkman 4.00 10.00
LG Luis Gonzalez 4.00 10.00
MC Miguel Cabrera 4.00 10.00
MH Matt Holliday 4.00 10.00
MO Justin Morneau 4.00 10.00
MR Manny Ramirez 5.00 12.00
MT Mark Teixeira 4.00 10.00
MY Michael Young 4.00 10.00
OR Magglio Ordonez 4.00 10.00
PA Jonathan Papelbon 5.00 12.00
PE Andy Pettitte 4.00 10.00
PF Prince Fielder 5.00 12.00
PM Pedro Martinez 4.00 10.00
PO Jorge Posada 4.00 10.00
RA Aramis Ramirez 4.00 10.00
RF Rafael Furcal 4.00 10.00
RH Roy Halladay 4.00 10.00
RJ Randy Johnson 4.00 10.00
RO Roy Oswalt 4.00 10.00
SM John Smoltz 5.00 12.00
TE Miguel Tejada/83 4.00 10.00
TH Tim Hudson 4.00 10.00
TR Travis Hafner 4.00 10.00
VE Justin Verlander 4.00 10.00
VG Vladimir Guerrero 4.00 10.00
VW Vernon Wells 4.00 10.00

2008 SPx Winning Materials Limited Patch Team Initials

*LTD PATCH TI: .5X TO 1.2X LTD PATCH SPX
OVERALL GU ODDS SIX PER BOX
PRINT RUNS B/WN 40-50 COPIES PER

2008 SPx Winning Materials MLB 125

*MLB 125: .4X TO 1X WM SPX 150
OVERALL GU ODDS SIX PER BOX
STATED PRINT RUN 125 SER.#'d SETS
RF Rafael Furcal 3.00 8.00

2008 SPx Winning Materials Position 75

*POS 75: .4X TO 1X WM SPX 150
OVERALL GU ODDS SIX PER BOX
STATED PRINT RUN 75 SER.#'d SETS

2008 SPx Winning Materials SPx Die Cut 150

*SPX DC 150: .4X TO 1X SPX 150
OVERALL GU ODDS SIX PER BOX
STATED PRINT RUN 150 SER.#'d SETS

2008 SPx Winning Materials Team Initials 99

*TI 99: .4X TO 1X WM SPX 150
OVERALL GU ODDS SIX PER BOX
STATED PRINT RUN 99 SER.#'d SETS
KG Ken Griffey Jr. 5.00 12.00
RF Rafael Furcal 3.00 8.00

2008 SPx Winning Materials UD Logo

*LOGO 99: .4X TO 1X WM SPX 150
OVERALL GU ODDS SIX PER BOX
PRINT RUNS B/WN 26-99 COPIES PER
KG Ken Griffey Jr./26 8.00 20.00
RF Rafael Furcal 3.00 8.00

2008 SPx Winning Trios

OVERALL GU ODDS SIX PER BOX
STATED PRINT RUN 75 SER.#'d SETS
GOLD 25 PRINT RUN 25 SER.#'d SETS
NO GOLD 25 PRICING DUE TO SCARCITY
GOLD 15 PRINT RUN 15 SER.#'d SETS
NO GOLD 15 PRICING DUE TO SCARCITY
LTD.PATCH PRINT RUN 25 SER.#'d SETS
NO LTD.PATCH PRICING DUE TO SCARCITY
AGK Anderson/Vlad/Kotchman 4.00 10.00
BHJ Beltre/Hernandez/Johjima 4.00 10.00
BSS Beckett/Santana/Sabathia 4.00 10.00
CRP Carpenter/Rolen/Pujols 6.00 15.00
CRU Cabrera/Ramirez/Uggla 4.00 10.00
DBR Delgado/Beltran/Reyes 4.00 10.00
DOP Delgado/Papi/Pujols 8.00 20.00
GHL Gallardo/Hughes/Lincecum 6.00 15.00
GIB Gordon/Iwamura/Braun 20.00 50.00
GJP Griffey Jr./Jeter/Pujols 15.00 40.00
GMW Glavine/Pedro/Wagner 8.00 20.00
HAH Helton/Atkins/Holliday 5.00 12.00
HDF Hafner/Dunn/Fielder 5.00 12.00
HFB Hardy/Prince/Braun 8.00 20.00
HRR Hardy/Reyes/Ramirez 4.00 10.00
HSS Hafner/Sizemore/Sabathia 4.00 10.00
JBH Jones/Beltran/Hunter 4.00 10.00
JDY Jackson/Drew/Young 4.00 10.00
JRR Jones/Rolen/Ramirez 5.00 12.00
JST Chipper/Smoltz/Teixeira 6.00 15.00
KFE Kent/Furcal/Ethier 5.00 12.00
KUY Kazmir/Upton/Young 4.00 10.00
LBO Lee/Berkamn/Oswalt 4.00 10.00
LCL Lowry/Cain/Lincecum 6.00 15.00
LRZ Lee/Soriano/Zambrano 6.00 15.00
MGS Maddux/Glavine/Smoltz 15.00 40.00
MHP Maddux/Hoffman/Peavy 6.00 15.00
MPB VMart/Peralta/Barfield 4.00 10.00
MSM Morneau/Santana/Mauer 5.00 12.00
OGV Ordonez/Grander/Verland 10.00 25.00
PJP Pettitte/Jeter/Posada 10.00 25.00
RJC ARod/Jeter/Cano 30.00 60.00
RMM IRod/VMart/Mauer 5.00 12.00
SBP Schilling/Beckett/Papelbon 6.00 15.00
SOH Sheets/Oswalt/Harang 4.00 10.00
SRG Sheffield/IRod/Guillen 6.00 15.00
TDB Thome/Dye/Buehrle 5.00 12.00
UHR Utley/Hamels/Rowand 6.00 15.00
UKU Utley/Insler/Uggla 4.00 10.00
VOY Varitek/Papi/Youkilis 12.50 30.00
WHB Wells/Halladay/Burnett 5.00 12.00
ZPH Zambrano/Peavy/Harang 4.00 10.00

2008 SPx Young Star Signatures

OVERALL AU ODDS FOUR PER BOX
EXCHANGE DEADLINE 4/28/2010
AC Alexi Casilla 3.00 8.00
AE Andre Ethier 3.00 8.00
BB Brian Bannister 4.00 10.00
BM Brian McCann 4.00 10.00
BU Brian Burres 4.00 10.00
CD Chris Duncan 6.00 15.00
CH Cole Hamels 8.00 20.00
CY Chris B. Young 5.00 12.00
FC Fausto Carmona 4.00 10.00
FL Francisco Liriano 4.00 10.00
IK Ian Kinsler 3.00 8.00
JA Joaquin Arias 3.00 8.00
JD John Danks 3.00 8.00
JJ Josh Johnson 5.00 12.00
JL James Loney 6.00 15.00
JS Jarrod Saltalamacchia 3.00 8.00
JV Justin Verlander 10.00 25.00
JW Josh Willingham 3.00 8.00
JZ Joel Zumaya 3.00 8.00
KK Kevin Kouzmanoff 3.00 8.00
MA Nick Markakis 6.00 15.00
MC Matt Chico 3.00 8.00
MF Mike Fontenot 5.00 12.00
MO Micah Owings 4.00 10.00
MR Mark Reynolds 5.00 12.00
NM Nate McLouth 3.00 8.00
PH Phil Hughes 3.00 8.00
RB Ryan Braun 5.00 12.00
RG Ryan Garko 3.00 8.00
RM Russell Martin 6.00 15.00
SD Stephen Drew 4.00 10.00
SH James Shields 5.00 12.00
TB Travis Buck 4.00 10.00
TG Tom Gorzelanny 3.00 8.00
TT Troy Tulowitzki 4.00 10.00

2009 SPx

This set was released on March 24, 2009. The base set consists of 123 cards.

COMP.SET w/o AU's (100) 12.50 30.00
COMMON CARD (1-100) .20 .50
COMMON AU RC (101-123) 4.00 10.00
OVERALL AUTO ODDS 1:18
AU RC PRINT RUN 99 SER.#'d SETS
1 Ichiro Suzuki .60 1.50
2 Rick Ankiel .20 .50
3 Garrett Atkins .20 .50
4 Jason Bay .30 .75
5 Josh Beckett .20 .50
6 Erik Bedard .20 .50
7 Carlos Beltran .30 .75
8 Lance Berkman .30 .75
9 Ryan Braun .30 .75
10 Jay Bruce .30 .75
11 Miguel Cabrera .50 1.25
12 Matt Cain .30 .75
13 Joba Chamberlain .20 .50
14 Carl Crawford .30 .75
15 Jack Cust .20 .50
16 Joe DiMaggio 1.00 2.50
17 Ryan Doumit .20 .50
18 Justin Duchscherer .20 .50
19 Adam Dunn .30 .75
20 Prince Fielder .30 .75
21 Kosuke Fukudome .30 .75
22 Troy Glaus .20 .50
23 Tom Glavine .30 .75
24 Adrian Gonzalez .40 1.00
25 Alex Gordon .30 .75
26 Zack Greinke .30 .75
27 Ken Griffey Jr. 1.00 2.50
28 Vladimir Guerrero .30 .75
29 Travis Hafner .20 .50
30 Roy Halladay .30 .75
31 Cole Hamels .40 1.00
32 Josh Hamilton .30 .75
33 Rich Harden .20 .50
34 Dan Haren .20 .50
35 Felix Hernandez .30 .75
36 Trevor Hoffman .30 .75
37 Matt Holliday .50 1.25
38 Ryan Howard .40 1.00
39 Torii Hunter .20 .50
40 Derek Jeter 1.25 3.00
41 Randy Johnson .50 1.25
42 Chipper Jones .50 1.25
43 Scott Kazmir .20 .50
44 Matt Kemp .40 1.00
45 Clayton Kershaw 1.00 2.50
46 Ian Kinsler .30 .75
47 John Lackey .30 .75
48 Carlos Lee .20 .50
49 Derrek Lee .20 .50
50 Tim Lincecum .30 .75
51 Evan Longoria .30 .75
52 Nick Markakis .40 1.00
53 Russell Martin .20 .50
54 Victor Martinez .30 .75
55 Hideki Matsui .50 1.25
56 Daisuke Matsuzaka .30 .75
57 Joe Mauer .40 1.00
58 Brian McCann .30 .75
59 Nate McLouth .20 .50
60 Lastings Milledge .20 .50
61 Justin Morneau .30 .75
62 Magglio Ordonez .30 .75
63 David Ortiz .50 1.25
64 Roy Oswalt .30 .75
65 Jonathan Papelbon .30 .75
66 Jake Peavy .20 .50
67 Dustin Pedroia .40 1.00
68 Brandon Phillips .20 .50
69 Albert Pujols .60 1.50
70 Carlos Quentin .20 .50
71 Aramis Ramirez .20 .50
72 Hanley Ramirez .30 .75
73 Manny Ramirez .50 1.25
74 Jose Reyes .30 .75
75 Alex Rios .20 .50
76 Mariano Rivera .60 1.50
77 Brian Roberts .20 .50
78 Alex Rodriguez .60 1.50
79 Ivan Rodriguez .30 .75
80 Jimmy Rollins .30 .75
81 CC Sabathia .30 .75
82 Johan Santana .30 .75
83 Grady Sizemore .30 .75
84 John Smoltz .50 1.25
85 Alfonso Soriano .30 .75
86 Mark Teixeira .30 .75
87 Miguel Tejada .30 .75
88 Jim Thome .30 .75
89 Troy Tulowitzki .50 1.25
90 Dan Uggla .20 .50
91 B.J. Upton .30 .75
92 Chase Utley .30 .75
93 Edinson Volquez .20 .50
94 Chien-Ming Wang .30 .75
95 Brandon Webb .30 .75
96 Vernon Wells .20 .50
97 David Wright .40 1.00
98 Michael Young .20 .50
99 Carlos Zambrano .30 .75
100 Ryan Zimmerman .30 .75
101 David Price AU RC 20.00 50.00
102 A.Cunningham AU RC 12.50 30.00
103 A.Salome AU (RC) 10.00 25.00
104 C.Gillaspie AU RC 10.00 25.00
105 C.Lambert AU (RC) 8.00 20.00
106 D.Fowler AU (RC) 10.00 25.00
107 F.Cervelli AU RC EXCH 10.00 25.00
108 G.Golson AU (RC) 8.00 20.00
109 Josh Geer AU (RC) 4.00 10.00
110 J.Outman AU RC 4.00 10.00
111 James Parr AU (RC) 8.00 20.00
112 K.Ka'aihue AU (RC) 6.00 15.00
113 Luis Cruz AU RC 10.00 25.00
114 L.Marson AU (RC) 15.00 40.00
115 M.Antonelli AU RC 4.00 10.00
116 M.Bowden AU (RC) 4.00 10.00
117 Mat Gamel AU RC 15.00 40.00
118 Tuiasosopo AU (RC) 15.00 40.00
119 Phil Coke AU RC 12.50 30.00
120 J.McDonald AU RC 10.00 25.00
121 S.Martis AU RC EXCH 4.00 10.00
122 Travis Snider AU RC 8.00 20.00
123 Wade LeBlanc AU RC 4.00 10.00
124 Matt Wieters AU RC 15.00 40.00
125 Colby Rasmus AU (RC) 4.00 10.00
126 Josh Reddick AU RC 4.00 10.00
127 Mat Latos AU RC 4.00 10.00
128 A.McCutchen AU (RC) 50.00 120.00
129 Chris Tillman AU RC 6.00 15.00
130 Koji Uehara AU RC 20.00 50.00

2009 SPx Flashback Fabrics

OVERALL MEM ODDS 4 PER BOX
FFAG Adrian Gonzalez 3.00 8.00
FFAJ Andruw Jones 3.00 8.00
FFAP Andy Pettitte 3.00 8.00
FFBA Bobby Abreu 3.00 8.00
FFCC Coco Crisp 3.00 8.00
FFCD Carlos Delgado 3.00 8.00
FFCL Carlos Lee 3.00 8.00
FFCS Curt Schilling 3.00 8.00
FFDA Johnny Damon 3.00 8.00
FFFT Frank Thomas 4.00 10.00
FFGJ Geoff Jenkins 3.00 8.00
FFIR Ivan Rodriguez 4.00 10.00
FFJE Jim Edmonds 3.00 8.00
FFJV Jose Valverde 3.00 8.00
FFKM Kevin Millwood 3.00 8.00
FFLG Luis Gonzalez Pants 3.00 8.00
FFMA Moises Alou 3.00 8.00
FFMG Magglio Ordonez 3.00 8.00
FFMR Manny Ramirez 5.00 12.00
FFMT Mark Teixeira 4.00 10.00
FFOC Orlando Cabrera 3.00 8.00
FFPM Pedro Martinez 3.00 8.00
FFRJ Randy Johnson Pants 3.00 8.00
FFSR Scott Rolen 3.00 8.00
FFVG Vladimir Guerrero 3.00 8.00

2009 SPx Game Jersey

OVERALL MEM ODDS 4 PER BOX
GJBU B.J. Upton 3.00 8.00
GJCZ Carlos Zambrano 3.00 8.00
GJDJ Derek Jeter 10.00 25.00
GJDL Derrek Lee 3.00 8.00
GJDO David Ortiz 3.00 8.00
GJFL Francisco Liriano 3.00 8.00
GJGJ Geoff Jenkins 3.00 8.00
GJHR Hanley Ramirez 3.00 8.00
GJJD Jermaine Dye 3.00 8.00
GJJL John Lackey 3.00 8.00
GJJS John Smoltz 3.00 8.00
GJJT Jim Thome 3.00 8.00
GJJV Justin Verlander 3.00 8.00
GJKF Kosuke Fukudome 4.00 10.00
GJKW Kerry Wood 3.00 8.00
GJMR Manny Ramirez 3.00 8.00
GJMT Miguel Tejada 3.00 8.00
GJRH Roy Halladay 3.00 8.00
GJSA Johan Santana 3.00 8.00
GJTH Travis Hafner 3.00 8.00
GJTT Troy Tulowitzki 3.00 8.00

2009 SPx Game Jersey Autographs

OVERALL AUTO ODDS 1:18
GJAAE Andre Ethier 8.00 20.00
GJAAK Austin Kearns 4.00 10.00
GJAAL Adam LaRoche 4.00 10.00
GJAAM Andrew Miller 10.00 25.00
GJAAR Aaron Rowand 8.00 20.00
GJAAX Alex Romero 4.00 10.00
GJABA Brian Barton 4.00 10.00
GJABC Bobby Crosby 4.00 10.00
GJABE Josh Beckett 15.00 40.00
GJABG Brian Giles 4.00 10.00
GJABH Bill Hall 4.00 10.00
GJABM Brian McCann 5.00 12.00
GJABP Brandon Phillips 6.00 15.00
GJABR Brian Roberts 15.00 40.00
GJABW Brandon Webb 10.00 25.00
GJACB Chad Billingsley 8.00 20.00
GJACC Chris Carpenter 10.00 25.00
GJACD Chris Duncan 10.00 25.00
GJACF Chone Figgins 6.00 15.00
GJACH Cole Hamels 30.00 60.00
GJACJ Chipper Jones 50.00 100.00
GJACL Clay Buchholz 10.00 25.00
GJACR Coco Crisp 8.00 20.00
GJADL Derrek Lee 10.00 25.00
GJADS Denard Span 10.00 25.00
GJADU Dan Uggla 5.00 12.00
GJAEC Eric Chavez 4.00 10.00
GJAEM Evan Meek 4.00 10.00
GJAEV Edinson Volquez 6.00 15.00
GJAFC Fausto Carmona 4.00 10.00
GJAFH Felix Hernandez 12.50 30.00
GJAFL Francisco Liriano 5.00 12.00
GJAFP Felix Pie 4.00 10.00
GJAFT Frank Thomas 40.00 80.00
GJAGJ Geoff Jenkins 4.00 10.00
GJAHA Craig Hansen 4.00 10.00
GJAHC Hong-Chih Kuo 10.00 25.00
GJAHK Howie Kendrick 5.00 12.00
GJAHR Hanley Ramirez 8.00 20.00
GJAIK Ian Kinsler 10.00 25.00
GJAJB Jason Bay 10.00 25.00
GJAJC Johnny Cueto 6.00 15.00
GJAJH Jeremy Hermida 4.00 10.00
GJAJJ Josh Johnson 6.00 15.00
GJAJL John Lackey 5.00 12.00
GJAJN Joe Nathan 8.00 20.00
GJAJP Jonathan Papelbon 4.00 10.00
GJAJR J.R. Towles 4.00 10.00
GJAJV Joey Votto 15.00 40.00
GJAJZ Joel Zumaya 4.00 10.00
GJALA Andy LaRoche 4.00 10.00
GJALE Jon Lester 15.00 40.00
GJALS Luke Scott 4.00 10.00
GJAML Mark Loretta 4.00 10.00
GJAMO Justin Morneau 8.00 20.00
GJANS Nick Swisher 6.00 15.00
GJAPF Prince Fielder 12.50 30.00
GJAPH Phil Hughes 8.00 20.00
GJARA Aramis Ramirez 6.00 15.00
GJARH Ramon Hernandez 8.00 20.00
GJASD Stephen Drew 8.00 20.00
GJATH Travis Hafner 4.00 10.00
GJATT Troy Tulowitzki 8.00 20.00
GJAVE Justin Verlander 15.00 40.00
GJAVM Victor Martinez 5.00 12.00
GJAWI Josh Willingham 4.00 10.00
GJAZG Zack Greinke 12.50 30.00

2009 SPx Game Patc

OVERALL MEM ODDS 4 PER BOX
PRINT RUNS B/WN 50-99 COPIES PER
PRICING FOR 1-2 COLOR PATCHES
GJBU B.J. Upton 5.00 12.00
GJCZ Carlos Zambrano 6.00 15.00
GJDJ Derek Jeter/50 30.00 60.00
GJDL Derrek Lee 6.00 15.00
GJDO David Ortiz 5.00 12.00
GJFL Francisco Liriano 6.00 15.00
GJGJ Geoff Jenkins 5.00 12.00
GJHR Hanley Ramirez 6.00 15.00
GJJD Jermaine Dye 5.00 12.00
GJJL John Lackey 5.00 12.00
GJJS John Smoltz 8.00 20.00
GJJT Jim Thome 5.00 12.00
GJJV Justin Verlander 5.00 12.00
GJKF Kosuke Fukudome 8.00 20.00
GJKW Kerry Wood 5.00 12.00
GJMR Manny Ramirez 6.00 15.00
GJMT Miguel Tejada 5.00 12.00
GJRH Roy Halladay 6.00 15.00
GJSA Johan Santana 6.00 15.00
GJTH Travis Hafner 5.00 12.00
GJTT Troy Tulowitzki 5.00 12.00

2009 SPx Joe DiMaggio Career Highlights

COMMON DIMAGGIO (1-100) 3.00 8.00
STATED PRINT RUN 425 SER.#'d SETS
JD1 Joe DiMaggio 2.50 6.00
JD2 Joe DiMaggio 2.50 6.00
JD3 Joe DiMaggio 2.50 6.00
JD4 Joe DiMaggio 2.50 6.00
JD5 Joe DiMaggio 2.50 6.00
JD6 Joe DiMaggio 2.50 6.00
JD7 Joe DiMaggio 2.50 6.00
JD8 Joe DiMaggio 2.50 6.00
JD9 Joe DiMaggio 2.50 6.00
JD10 Joe DiMaggio 2.50 6.00
JD11 Joe DiMaggio 2.50 6.00
JD12 Joe DiMaggio 2.50 6.00
JD13 Joe DiMaggio 2.50 6.00
JD14 Joe DiMaggio 2.50 6.00
JD15 Joe DiMaggio 2.50 6.00
JD16 Joe DiMaggio 2.50 6.00
JD17 Joe DiMaggio 2.50 6.00
JD18 Joe DiMaggio 2.50 6.00
JD19 Joe DiMaggio 2.50 6.00
JD20 Joe DiMaggio 2.50 6.00
JD21 Joe DiMaggio 2.50 6.00
JD22 Joe DiMaggio 2.50 6.00
JD23 Joe DiMaggio 2.50 6.00
JD24 Joe DiMaggio 2.50 6.00
JD25 Joe DiMaggio 2.50 6.00
JD26 Joe DiMaggio 2.50 6.00
JD27 Joe DiMaggio 2.50 6.00
JD28 Joe DiMaggio 2.50 6.00
JD29 Joe DiMaggio 2.50 6.00
JD30 Joe DiMaggio 2.50 6.00
JD31 Joe DiMaggio 2.50 6.00
JD32 Joe DiMaggio 2.50 6.00
JD33 Joe DiMaggio 2.50 6.00
JD34 Joe DiMaggio 2.50 6.00
JD35 Joe DiMaggio 2.50 6.00
JD36 Joe DiMaggio 2.50 6.00
JD37 Joe DiMaggio 2.50 6.00
JD38 Joe DiMaggio 2.50 6.00
JD39 Joe DiMaggio 2.50 6.00
JD40 Joe DiMaggio 2.50 6.00
JD41 Joe DiMaggio 2.50 6.00
JD42 Joe DiMaggio 2.50 6.00
JD43 Joe DiMaggio 2.50 6.00
JD44 Joe DiMaggio 2.50 6.00
JD45 Joe DiMaggio 2.50 6.00
JD46 Joe DiMaggio 2.50 6.00
JD47 Joe DiMaggio 2.50 6.00
JD48 Joe DiMaggio 2.50 6.00
JD49 Joe DiMaggio 2.50 6.00
JD50 Joe DiMaggio 2.50 6.00
JD51 Joe DiMaggio 2.50 6.00
JD52 Joe DiMaggio 2.50 6.00
JD53 Joe DiMaggio 2.50 6.00
JD54 Joe DiMaggio 2.50 6.00
JD55 Joe DiMaggio 2.50 6.00
JD56 Joe DiMaggio 2.50 6.00
JD57 Joe DiMaggio 2.50 6.00
JD58 Joe DiMaggio 2.50 6.00
JD59 Joe DiMaggio 2.50 6.00
JD60 Joe DiMaggio 2.50 6.00
JD61 Joe DiMaggio 2.50 6.00
JD62 Joe DiMaggio 2.50 6.00
JD63 Joe DiMaggio 2.50 6.00
JD64 Joe DiMaggio 2.50 6.00
JD65 Joe DiMaggio 2.50 6.00
JD66 Joe DiMaggio 2.50 6.00
JD67 Joe DiMaggio 2.50 6.00
JD68 Joe DiMaggio 2.50 6.00
JD69 Joe DiMaggio 2.50 6.00
JD70 Joe DiMaggio 2.50 6.00
JD71 Joe DiMaggio 2.50 6.00
JD72 Joe DiMaggio 2.50 6.00
JD73 Joe DiMaggio 2.50 6.00
JD74 Joe DiMaggio 2.50 6.00
JD75 Joe DiMaggio 2.50 6.00
JD76 Joe DiMaggio 2.50 6.00
JD77 Joe DiMaggio 2.50 6.00
JD78 Joe DiMaggio 2.50 6.00
JD79 Joe DiMaggio 2.50 6.00
JD80 Joe DiMaggio 2.50 6.00
JD81 Joe DiMaggio 2.50 6.00
JD82 Joe DiMaggio 2.50 6.00
JD83 Joe DiMaggio 2.50 6.00
JD84 Joe DiMaggio 2.50 6.00
JD85 Joe DiMaggio 2.50 6.00
JD86 Joe DiMaggio 2.50 6.00
JD87 Joe DiMaggio 2.50 6.00
JD88 Joe DiMaggio 2.50 6.00
JD89 Joe DiMaggio 2.50 6.00
JD90 Joe DiMaggio 2.50 6.00
JD91 Joe DiMaggio 2.50 6.00
JD92 Joe DiMaggio 2.50 6.00
JD93 Joe DiMaggio 2.50 6.00
JD94 Joe DiMaggio 2.50 6.00
JD95 Joe DiMaggio 2.50 6.00
JD96 Joe DiMaggio 2.50 6.00
JD97 Joe DiMaggio 2.50 6.00
JD98 Joe DiMaggio 2.50 6.00
JD99 Joe DiMaggio 2.50 6.00
JD100 Joe DiMaggio 2.50 6.00

2009 SPx Mystery Rookie Redemption

RANDOM INSERTS IN PACKS
EXCHANGE DEADLINE 6/30/2011
NO EXCH Card 20.00 50.00

2009 SPx Winning Materials

OVERALL MEM ODDS 4 PER BOX
WMAS Alfonso Soriano 3.00 8.00
WMCJ Chipper Jones 4.00 10.00
WMCW Chien-Ming Wang 4.00 10.00
WMDJ Derek Jeter 6.00 15.00
WMDM Daisuke Matsuzaka 6.00 15.00
WMJB Josh Beckett 3.00 8.00
WMJM Justin Morneau 3.00 8.00
WMJP Jake Peavy 3.00 8.00
WMJR Jose Reyes 3.00 8.00
WMLB Lance Berkman 3.00 8.00
WMMC Miguel Cabrera 3.00 8.00
WMMH Matt Holliday 3.00 8.00
WMMR Mariano Rivera 6.00 15.00
WMMT Mark Teixeira 4.00 10.00
WMPF Prince Fielder 3.00 8.00
WMRA Manny Ramirez 3.00 8.00
WMRB Ryan Braun 4.00 10.00
WMRL Ryan Ludwick 4.00 10.00
WMSK Scott Kazmir 3.00 8.00
WMTL Tim Lincecum 5.00 12.00

2009 SPx Winning Materials Patch

OVERALL MEM ODDS 4 PER BOX
PRINT RUNS B/WN 59-99 COPIES PER
PRICING FOR 1-2 COLOR PATCHES
WMAS Alfonso Soriano 6.00 15.00
WMCJ Chipper Jones 10.00 25.00
WMCW Chien-Ming Wang 8.00 20.00
WMDJ Derek Jeter 20.00 50.00
WMJB Josh Beckett 6.00 15.00
WMJM Justin Morneau 5.00 12.00
WMJP Jake Peavy 5.00 12.00
WMJR Jose Reyes 10.00 25.00
WMLB Lance Berkman 5.00 12.00
WMMC Miguel Cabrera 5.00 12.00
WMMH Matt Holliday 5.00 12.00
WMMR Mariano Rivera 12.50 30.00
WMMT Mark Teixeira 5.00 12.00
WMPF Prince Fielder 5.00 12.00
WMRA Manny Ramirez 6.00 15.00
WMRB Ryan Braun/59 10.00 25.00
WMRL Ryan Ludwick 6.00 15.00
WMSK Scott Kazmir 5.00 12.00
WMTL Tim Lincecum 6.00 15.00

2009 SPx Winning Materials Dual

OVERALL MEM ODDS 4 PER BOX
BH A.Burnett/R.Halladay 3.00 8.00
GE K.Griffey/J.Edmonds 5.00 12.00
GR K.Greene/J.Reyes 4.00 10.00
GS R.Sexson/J.Giambi 3.00 8.00
HB J.Baker/M.Holliday 3.00 8.00
JD J.DiMaggio/D.Jeter 40.00 80.00
JY R.Johnson/C.Young 4.00 10.00
KT P.Konerko/J.Thome 3.00 8.00
LL A.LaRoche/A.LaRoche 3.00 8.00
ML Matsuzaka/Lincecum 5.00 12.00
PS J.Peavy/C.Sabathia 4.00 10.00
RB J.Bay/M.Ramirez 4.00 10.00
RO D.Ortiz/M.Ramirez 4.00 10.00
RP Papelbon/M.Rivera 4.00 10.00

2009 SPx Winning Materials Quad

OVERALL MEM ODDS 4 PER BOX
BDBM Braun/Duncan/Bald/Markakis 8.00 20.00
BUUB Ryan Braun/Dan Uggla
Chase Utley/Lance Berkman 4.00 10.00
DJCP DiMaggio/Jeter/Cano/Posada 30.00 60.00
DTGS Dye/Thome/Grif/Swisher 5.00 12.00
HFBS Hardy/Prince/Hall/Sheets 5.00 12.00
HHBN Matt Holliday/Todd Helton
Jeff Baker/Jayson Nix 4.00 10.00
HRBB Matt Holliday/Manny
Ramirez/Pat Burrell/Ryan Braun 4.00 10.00
HRNB Trevor Hoffman/Mariano Rivera/Joe
Nathan/Brad Lidge 4.00 10.00
HSLC Trevor Hoffman/Takashi Saito/Brad
Lidge/Chad Cordero 4.00 10.00
JTJF Chipper/Teix/Andruw/Furcal 6.00 15.00
KFSK Matt Kemp/Rafael Furcal
Takashi Saito/Hong-Chih Kuo 4.00 10.00
MMPV Brian McCann/Joe Mauer/Jorge
Posada/Jason Varitek 4.00 10.00
OEYV Papi/Ellsbury/Youkilis/Varitek 10.00 25.00
OGDF David Ortiz/Jason Giambi/Carlos
Delgado/Prince Fielder 4.00 10.00
OGTS David Ortiz/Jason Giambi
Jim Thome/Gary Sheffield 4.00 10.00
PCLZ Pujols/Carp/D.Lee/Zambrano 8.00 20.00
PLKL Peavy/Lince/Kazmir/Liriano 8.00 20.00
PMSL Papel/DiceK/Schilling/Lester 20.00 50.00
PRMV Posada/Pudge/Mauer/Varitek 5.00 12.00
RGBN Manny/Grif/Bay/Nady 5.00 12.00
RLZW Aramis/D.Lee/Zambrano/Wood 6.00 15.00
RRTD Reyes/Hanley/Tulo/S.Drew 6.00 15.00
RUJC Hanley/Uggla/Jeter/Cano 10.00 25.00
SZCO Ben Sheets/Carlos Zambrano
Chris Carpenter/Roy Oswalt 4.00 10.00
UPRI Utley/Phillips/Roberts/Iwamura 5.00 12.00
VGSZ Verland/Grand/Shef/Zumaya 6.00 15.00

2009 SPx Winning Materials Triple

OVERALL MEM ODDS 4 PER BOX
AKD Garrett Atkins 4.00 10.00
Kevin Kouzmanoff
Blake DeWitt
BCM Brian Barton 4.00 10.00
Chris Carpenter
Mark Mulder
CGV Cabrera/Grand/Verlander 8.00 20.00
DOF Jermaine Dye 4.00 10.00
Magglio Ordonez
Jeff Francoeur
FJH Prince Fielder 4.00 10.00
J.J. Hardy
Bill Hall
KCM Paul Konerko 4.00 10.00
Miguel Cabrera
Justin Morneau
KIB Scott Kazmir 4.00 10.00
Akinori Iwamura
Rocco Baldelli
KSB Jeff Kent 4.00 10.00
Freddy Sanchez
Josh Barfield
KSK Kuroda/Saito/Kuo 6.00 15.00
MBK Kevin Millwood 4.00 10.00
Hank Blalock
Ian Kinsler
MLY Mauer/Liriano/Delmon 6.00 15.00
NLB Joe Nathan 4.00 10.00
Francisco Liriano
Scott Baker
PCS Jonathan Papelbon 4.00 10.00
Chad Cordero
Joakim Soria
PJG Andy Pettitte 4.00 10.00
Randy Johnson
Tom Glavine
PKD Penny/Kent/DeWitt 5.00 12.00
RBE Manny/Bay/Ellsbury 6.00 15.00
RMD Manny/Pedro/Damon 8.00 20.00
SDM Schilling/Beckett/Matsuzaka 5.00 12.00
TCB Thomas/Crosby/Buck 10.00 25.00
TGB Teahen/Greinke/Butler 5.00 12.00
WNP Kerry Wood 4.00 10.00
Joe Nathan
Jonathan Papelbon

1991 Stadium Club

This 600-card standard size set marked Topps first premium quality set. The set was issued in two separate series of 300 cards each. Cards were distributed in plastic wrapped packs. Series II cards were also available at McDonald's restaurants in the Northeast at three cards per pack. The set created a stir in the hobby upon release with dazzling full-color borderless photos and slick, glossy card stock. The back of each card has the basic biographical information as well as making use of the Fastball BARS system and an inset photo of the player's Topps rookie card. Notable Rookie Cards include Jeff Bagwell.

COMPLETE SET (600) 12.00 30.00
COMPLETE SERIES 1 (300) 8.00 20.00
COMPLETE SERIES 2 (300) 8.00 20.00
1 Dave Stewart Tuxedo .20 .50
2 Wally Joyner .20 .50
3 Shawon Dunston .08 .25
4 Darren Daulton .20 .50
5 Will Clark .30 .75
6 Sammy Sosa .50 1.25
7 Dan Plesac .08 .25
8 Marquis Grissom .20 .50
9 Erik Hanson .08 .25
10 Geno Petralli .08 .25
11 Jose Rijo .08 .25
12 Carlos Quintana .08 .25
13 Junior Ortiz .08 .25
14 Bob Walk .08 .25
15 Mike Macfarlane .08 .25
16 Eric Yelding .08 .25
17 Bryn Smith .08 .25
18 Bip Roberts .08 .25
19 Mike Scioscia .08 .25
20 Mark Williamson .08 .25
21 Don Mattingly 1.25 3.00
22 John Franco .20 .50
23 Chet Lemon .08 .25
24 Tom Henke .08 .25
25 Jerry Browne .08 .25
26 Dave Justice .20 .50
27 Mark Langston .08 .25
28 Damon Berryhill .08 .25
29 Kevin Bass .08 .25
30 Scott Fletcher .08 .25
31 Moises Alou .20 .50
32 Dave Valle .08 .25
33 Jody Reed .08 .25
34 Dave West .08 .25
35 Kevin McReynolds .08 .25
36 Pat Combs .08 .25
37 Eric Davis .20 .50
38 Bret Saberhagen .20 .50
39 Stan Javier .08 .25
40 Chuck Cary .08 .25
41 Tony Phillips .08 .25
42 Lee Smith .20 .50
43 Tim Teufel .08 .25
44 Lance Dickson RC .15 .40
45 Greg Litton .08 .25
46 Ted Higuera .08 .25
47 Edgar Martinez .30 .75
48 Steve Avery .08 .25
49 Walt Weiss .08 .25
50 David Segui .08 .25
51 Andy Benes .08 .25
52 Karl Rhodes .08 .25
53 Neal Heaton .08 .25
54 Danny Gladden .08 .25
55 Luis Rivera .08 .25
56 Kevin Brown .20 .50
57 Frank Thomas .50 1.25
58 Terry Mulholland .08 .25
59 Dick Schofield .08 .25
60 Ron Darling .08 .25
61 Sandy Alomar Jr. .08 .25
62 Dave Stieb .08 .25
63 Alan Trammell .20 .50
64 Matt Nokes .08 .25
65 Lenny Harris .08 .25
66 Milt Thompson .08 .25
67 Storm Davis .08 .25
68 Joe Oliver .08 .25
69 Andres Galarraga .20 .50
70 Ozzie Guillen .20 .50
71 Ken Howell .08 .25
72 Garry Templeton .08 .25
73 Derrick May .08 .25
74 Xavier Hernandez .08 .25
75 Dave Parker .20 .50
76 Rick Aguilera .20 .50
77 Robby Thompson .08 .25
78 Pete Incaviglia .08 .25
79 Bob Welch .08 .25
80 Randy Milligan .08 .25
81 Chuck Finley .20 .50
82 Alvin Davis .08 .25
83 Tim Naehring .08 .25
84 Jay Bell .20 .50
85 Joe Magrane .08 .25
86 Howard Johnson .08 .25
87 Jack McDowell .08 .25
88 Kevin Seitzer .08 .25
89 Bruce Ruffin .08 .25
90 Fernando Valenzuela .20 .50
91 Terry Kennedy .08 .25
92 Barry Larkin .30 .75
93 Larry Walker .50 1.25
94 Luis Salazar .08 .25
95 Gary Sheffield .20 .50
96 Bobby Witt .08 .25
97 Lonnie Smith .08 .25
98 Bryan Harvey .08 .25
99 Mookie Wilson .20 .50
100 Dwight Gooden .20 .50
101 Lou Whitaker .20 .50
102 Ron Karkovice .08 .25
103 Jesse Barfield .08 .25
104 Jose DeJesus .08 .25
105 Benito Santiago .20 .50
106 Brian Holman .08 .25
107 Rafael Ramirez .08 .25
108 Ellis Burks .20 .50
109 Mike Bielecki .08 .25
110 Kirby Puckett .50 1.25
111 Terry Shumpert .08 .25
112 Chuck Crim .08 .25
113 Todd Benzinger .08 .25
114 Brian Barnes RC .15 .40
115 Carlos Baerga .08 .25
116 Kal Daniels .08 .25
117 Dave Johnson .08 .25
118 Andy Van Slyke .30 .75
119 John Burkett .08 .25
120 Rickey Henderson .50 1.25
121 Tim Jones .08 .25
122 Daryl Irvine RC .08 .25
123 Ruben Sierra .20 .50
124 Jim Abbott .30 .75
125 Daryl Boston .08 .25
126 Greg Maddux .75 2.00
127 Von Hayes .08 .25
128 Mike Fitzgerald .08 .25
129 Wayne Edwards .08 .25
130 Greg Briley .08 .25
131 Rob Dibble .20 .50
132 Gene Larkin .08 .25
133 David Wells .20 .50
134 Steve Balboni .08 .25
135 Greg Vaughn .08 .25
136 Mark Davis .08 .25
137 Dave Rhode .08 .25
138 Eric Show .08 .25
139 Bobby Bonilla .20 .50
140 Dana Kiecker .08 .25
141 Gary Pettis .08 .25
142 Dennis Boyd .08 .25
143 Mike Benjamin .08 .25
144 Luis Polonia .08 .25
145 Doug Jones .08 .25
146 Al Newman .08 .25
147 Alex Fernandez .08 .25
148 Bill Doran .08 .25
149 Kevin Elster .08 .25
150 Len Dykstra .20 .50
151 Mike Gallego .08 .25
152 Tim Belcher .08 .25
153 Jay Buhner .20 .50
154 Ozzie Smith UER .75 2.00
155 Jose Canseco .30 .75
156 Gregg Olson .08 .25
157 Charlie O'Brien .08 .25
158 Frank Tanana .08 .25
159 George Brett 1.25 3.00
160 Jeff Huson .08 .25
161 Kevin Tapani .08 .25
162 Jerome Walton .08 .25
163 Charlie Hayes .08 .25
164 Chris Bosio .08 .25
165 Chris Sabo .08 .25
166 Lance Parrish .20 .50
167 Don Robinson .08 .25
168 Manny Lee .08 .25
169 Dennis Rasmussen .08 .25
170 Wade Boggs .30 .75
171 Bob Geren .08 .25
172 Mackey Sasser .08 .25
173 Julio Franco .20 .50
174 Otis Nixon .08 .25
175 Bert Blyleven .20 .50
176 Craig Biggio .30 .75
177 Eddie Murray .50 1.25
178 Randy Tomlin RC .15 .40
179 Tino Martinez .50 1.25
180 Carlton Fisk .30 .75
181 Dwight Smith .08 .25
182 Scott Garrelts .08 .25
183 Jim Gantner .08 .25
184 Dickie Thon .08 .25
185 John Farrell .08 .25
186 Cecil Fielder .20 .50
187 Glenn Braggs .08 .25
188 Allan Anderson .08 .25
189 Kurt Stillwell .08 .25
190 Jose Oquendo .08 .25
191 Joe Orsulak .08 .25
192 Ricky Jordan .08 .25
193 Kelly Downs .08 .25
194 Delino DeShields .08 .25
195 Omar Vizquel .30 .75
196 Mark Carreon .08 .25
197 Mike Harkey .08 .25
198 Jack Howell .08 .25
199 Lance Johnson .08 .25
200 Nolan Ryan TUX 2.00 5.00
201 John Marzano .08 .25
202 Doug Drabek .08 .25
203 Mark Lemke .08 .25
204 Steve Sax .08 .25
205 Greg Harris .08 .25
206 B.J. Surhoff .20 .50
207 Todd Burns .08 .25
208 Jose Gonzalez .08 .25
209 Mike Scott .08 .25
210 Dave Magadan .08 .25
211 Dante Bichette .20 .50
212 Trevor Wilson .08 .25
213 Hector Villanueva .08 .25
214 Dan Pasqua .08 .25
215 Greg Colbrunn RC .25 .60
216 Mike Jeffcoat .08 .25
217 Harold Reynolds .20 .50
218 Paul O'Neill .30 .75
219 Mark Guthrie .08 .25
220 Barry Bonds 1.50 4.00
221 Jimmy Key .20 .50
222 Billy Ripken .08 .25
223 Tom Pagnozzi .08 .25
224 Bo Jackson .50 1.25
225 Sid Fernandez .08 .25
226 Mike Marshall .08 .25
227 John Kruk .20 .50
228 Mike Fetters .08 .25
229 Eric Anthony .08 .25
230 Ryne Sandberg .75 2.00
231 Carney Lansford .20 .50
232 Melido Perez .08 .25
233 Jose Lind .08 .25
234 Darryl Hamilton .08 .25
235 Tom Browning .08 .25
236 Spike Owen .08 .25
237 Juan Gonzalez .50 1.25
238 Felix Fermin .08 .25
239 Keith Miller .08 .25
240 Mark Gubicza .08 .25
241 Kent Anderson .08 .25
242 Alvaro Espinoza .08 .25
243 Dale Murphy .30 .75
244 Orel Hershiser .20 .50
245 Paul Molitor .20 .50
246 Eddie Whitson .08 .25
247 Joe Girardi .20 .50
248 Kent Hrbek .20 .50
249 Bill Sampen .08 .25
250 Kevin Mitchell .08 .25
251 Mariano Duncan .08 .25
252 Scott Bradley .08 .25
253 Mike Greenwell .08 .25
254 Tom Gordon .08 .25
255 Todd Zeile .08 .25
256 Bobby Thigpen .08 .25
257 Gregg Jefferies .08 .25
258 Kenny Rogers .20 .50
259 Shane Mack .08 .25
260 Zane Smith .08 .25
261 Mitch Williams .08 .25
262 Jim Deshaies .08 .25
263 Dave Winfield .20 .50
264 Ben McDonald .08 .25
265 Randy Ready .08 .25
266 Pat Borders .08 .25
267 Jose Uribe .08 .25
268 Derek Lilliquist .08 .25
269 Greg Brock .08 .25
270 Ken Griffey Jr. 1.25 3.00
271 Jeff Gray RC .08 .25
272 Danny Tartabull .08 .25
273 Dennis Martinez .20 .50
274 Robin Ventura .20 .50
275 Randy Myers .08 .25
276 Jack Daugherty .08 .25
277 Greg Gagne .08 .25
278 Jay Howell .08 .25
279 Mike LaValliere .08 .25
280 Rex Hudler .08 .25
281 Mike Simms RC .08 .25
282 Kevin Maas .08 .25
283 Jeff Ballard .08 .25
284 Dave Henderson .08 .25
285 Pete O'Brien .08 .25
286 Brook Jacoby .08 .25
287 Mike Henneman .08 .25
288 Greg Olson .08 .25
289 Greg Myers .08 .25
290 Mark Grace .30 .75
291 Shawn Abner .08 .25
292 Frank Viola .20 .50
293 Lee Stevens .08 .25
294 Jason Grimsley .08 .25
295 Matt Williams .20 .50
296 Ron Robinson .08 .25
297 Tom Brunansky .08 .25
298 Checklist 1-100 .08 .25
299 Checklist 101-200 .08 .25
300 Checklist 201-300 .08 .25
301 Darryl Strawberry .20 .50
302 Bud Black .08 .25
303 Harold Baines .20 .50
304 Roberto Alomar .30 .75
305 Norm Charlton .08 .25
306 Gary Thurman .08 .25
307 Mike Felder .08 .25
308 Tony Gwynn .60 1.50
309 Roger Clemens 1.50 4.00
310 Andre Dawson .20 .50
311 Scott Radinsky .08 .25
312 Bob Melvin .08 .25
313 Kirk McCaskill .08 .25
314 Pedro Guerrero .20 .50
315 Walt Terrell .08 .25
316 Sam Horn .08 .25
317 Wes Chamberlain UER RC .25 .60
318 Pedro Munoz RC .15 .40
319 Roberto Kelly .08 .25
320 Mark Portugal .08 .25
321 Tim McIntosh .08 .25
322 Jesse Orosco .08 .25
323 Gary Green .08 .25
324 Greg Harris .08 .25
325 Hubie Brooks .08 .25
326 Chris Nabholz .08 .25
327 Terry Pendleton .20 .50
328 Eric King .08 .25
329 Chili Davis .20 .50
330 Anthony Telford RC .08 .25
331 Kelly Gruber .08 .25
332 Dennis Eckersley .20 .50
333 Mel Hall .08 .25
334 Bob Kipper .08 .25
335 Willie McGee .20 .50
336 Steve Olin .08 .25
337 Steve Buechele .08 .25
338 Scott Leius .08 .25
339 Hal Morris .08 .25
340 Jose Offerman .08 .25
341 Kent Mercker .08 .25
342 Ken Griffey Sr. .20 .50
343 Pete Harnisch .08 .25
344 Kirk Gibson .20 .50
345 Dave Smith .08 .25
346 Dave Martinez .08 .25
347 Atlee Hammaker .08 .25
348 Brian Downing .08 .25
349 Todd Hundley .08 .25
350 Candy Maldonado .08 .25
351 Dwight Evans .30 .75
352 Steve Searcy .08 .25
353 Gary Gaetti .20 .50
354 Jeff Reardon .20 .50
355 Travis Fryman .20 .50
356 Dave Righetti .20 .50
357 Fred McGriff .30 .75
358 Don Slaught .08 .25
359 Gene Nelson .08 .25
360 Billy Spiers .08 .25
361 Lee Guetterman .08 .25
362 Darren Lewis .08 .25
363 Duane Ward .08 .25
364 Lloyd Moseby .08 .25
365 John Smoltz .30 .75
366 Felix Jose .08 .25
367 David Cone .20 .50
368 Wally Backman .08 .25
369 Jeff Montgomery .08 .25
370 Rich Garces RC .15 .40
371 Billy Hatcher .08 .25
372 Bill Swift .08 .25
373 Jim Eisenreich .08 .25
374 Rob Ducey .08 .25
375 Tim Crews .08 .25
376 Steve Finley .20 .50
377 Jeff Blauser .08 .25
378 Willie Wilson .08 .25
379 Gerald Perry .08 .25
380 Jose Mesa .08 .25
381 Pat Kelly RC .25 .60
382 Matt Merullo .08 .25
383 Ivan Calderon .08 .25
384 Scott Chiamparino .08 .25
385 Lloyd McClendon .08 .25
386 Dave Bergman .08 .25
387 Ed Sprague .08 .25
388 Jeff Bagwell RC 1.25 3.00
389 Brett Butler .20 .50
390 Larry Andersen .08 .25
391 Glenn Davis .08 .25
392 Alex Cole UER .08 .25
Front photo actually
Otis Nixon
393 Mike Heath .08 .25
394 Danny Darwin .08 .25
395 Steve Lake .08 .25
396 Tim Layana .08 .25
397 Terry Leach .08 .25
398 Bill Wegman .08 .25
399 Mark McGwire 1.50 4.00
400 Mike Boddicker .08 .25
401 Steve Howe .08 .25
402 Bernard Gilkey .08 .25
403 Thomas Howard .08 .25
404 Rafael Belliard .08 .25
405 Tom Candiotti .08 .25
406 Rene Gonzales .08 .25
407 Chuck McElroy .08 .25
408 Paul Sorrento .08 .25
409 Randy Johnson .60 1.50
410 Brady Anderson .20 .50
411 Dennis Cook .08 .25
412 Mickey Tettleton .08 .25
413 Mike Stanton .08 .25
414 Ken Oberkfell .08 .25
415 Rick Honeycutt .08 .25
416 Nelson Santovenia .08 .25
417 Bob Tewksbury .08 .25
418 Brent Mayne .08 .25
419 Steve Farr .08 .25
420 Phil Stephenson .08 .25
421 Jeff Russell .08 .25
422 Chris James .08 .25
423 Tim Leary .08 .25
424 Gary Carter .20 .50
425 Glenallen Hill .08 .25
426 Matt Young UER .08 .25
427 Sid Bream .08 .25
428 Greg Swindell .08 .25
429 Scott Aldred .08 .25
430 Cal Ripken 1.50 4.00
431 Bill Landrum .08 .25
432 Earnest Riles .08 .25
433 Danny Jackson .08 .25
434 Casey Candaele .08 .25
435 Ken Hill .08 .25
436 Jaime Navarro .08 .25
437 Lance Blankenship .08 .25
438 Randy Velarde .08 .25
439 Frank DiPino .08 .25
440 Carl Nichols .08 .25
441 Jeff M. Robinson .08 .25
442 Deion Sanders .30 .75
443 Vicente Palacios .08 .25
444 Devon White .20 .50
445 John Cerutti .08 .25
446 Tracy Jones .08 .25
447 Jack Morris .20 .50
448 Mitch Webster .08 .25
449 Bob Ojeda .08 .25
450 Oscar Azocar .08 .25
451 Luis Aquino .08 .25
452 Mark Whiten .08 .25
453 Stan Belinda .08 .25
454 Ron Gant .20 .50
455 Jose DeLeon .08 .25
456 Mark Salas UER .08 .25
Back has 85T photo,
but calls it 86T
457 Junior Felix .08 .25
458 Wally Whitehurst .08 .25
459 Phil Plantier RC .25 .60
460 Juan Berenguer .08 .25
461 Franklin Stubbs .08 .25
462 Joe Boever .08 .25
463 Tim Wallach .08 .25
464 Mike Moore .08 .25
465 Albert Belle .20 .50
466 Mike Witt .08 .25
467 Craig Worthington .08 .25
468 Jerald Clark .08 .25
469 Scott Terry .08 .25
470 Milt Cuyler .08 .25
471 John Smiley .08 .25
472 Charles Nagy .08 .25
473 Alan Mills .08 .25
474 John Russell .08 .25
475 Bruce Hurst .08 .25
476 Andujar Cedeno .08 .25
477 Dave Eiland .08 .25
478 Brian McRae RC .25 .60
479 Mike LaCoss .08 .25
480 Chris Gwynn .08 .25
481 Jamie Moyer .20 .50
482 John Olerud .20 .50
483 Efrain Valdez RC .08 .25
484 Sil Campusano .08 .25
485 Pascual Perez .08 .25
486 Gary Redus .08 .25
487 Andy Hawkins .08 .25
488 Cory Snyder .08 .25
489 Chris Hoiles .08 .25
490 Ron Hassey .08 .25
491 Gary Wayne .08 .25
492 Mark Lewis .08 .25
493 Scott Coolbaugh .08 .25
494 Gerald Young .08 .25
495 Juan Samuel .08 .25
496 Willie Fraser .08 .25
497 Jeff Treadway .08 .25
498 Vince Coleman .08 .25
499 Cris Carpenter .08 .25
500 Jack Clark .20 .50
501 Kevin Appier .20 .50
502 Rafael Palmeiro .30 .75
503 Hensley Meulens .08 .25
504 George Bell .08 .25
505 Tony Pena .08 .25
506 Roger McDowell .08 .25
507 Luis Sojo .08 .25
508 Mike Schooler .08 .25
509 Robin Yount .75 2.00
510 Jack Armstrong .08 .25
511 Rick Cerone .08 .25
512 Curt Wilkerson .08 .25
513 Joe Carter .20 .50
514 Tim Burke .08 .25
515 Tony Fernandez .08 .25
516 Ramon Martinez .08 .25
517 Tim Hulett .08 .25
518 Terry Steinbach .08 .25
519 Pete Smith .08 .25
520 Ken Caminiti .20 .50
521 Shawn Boskie .08 .25
522 Mike Pagliarulo .08 .25
523 Tim Raines .20 .50
524 Alfredo Griffin .08 .25
525 Henry Cotto .08 .25
526 Mike Stanley .08 .25
527 Charlie Leibrandt .08 .25
528 Jeff King .08 .25
529 Eric Plunk .08 .25
530 Tom Lampkin .08 .25
531 Steve Bedrosian .08 .25
532 Tom Herr .08 .25
533 Craig Lefferts .08 .25
534 Jeff Reed .08 .25
535 Mickey Morandini .08 .25
536 Greg Cadaret .08 .25
537 Ray Lankford .20 .50
538 John Candelaria .08 .25
539 Rob Deer .08 .25
540 Brad Arnsberg .08 .25
541 Mike Sharperson .08 .25
542 Jeff D. Robinson .08 .25
543 Mo Vaughn .20 .50
544 Jeff Parrett .08 .25
545 Willie Randolph .20 .50
546 Herm Winningham .08 .25
547 Jeff Innis .08 .25
548 Chuck Knoblauch .20 .50
549 Tommy Greene UER .08 .25
Born in North Carolina,
not South Carolina
550 Jeff Hamilton .08 .25
551 Barry Jones .08 .25
552 Ken Dayley .08 .25
553 Rick Dempsey .08 .25
554 Greg Smith .08 .25
555 Mike Devereaux .08 .25
556 Keith Comstock .08 .25
557 Paul Faries RC .08 .25
558 Tom Glavine .30 .75
559 Craig Grebeck .08 .25
560 Scott Erickson .08 .25
561 Joel Skinner .08 .25
562 Mike Morgan .08 .25
563 Dave Gallagher .08 .25
564 Todd Stottlemyre .08 .25
565 Rich Rodriguez RC .08 .25
566 Craig Wilson RC .08 .25
567 Jeff Brantley .08 .25
568 Scott Kamieniecki RC .25 .60
569 Steve Decker RC .15 .40
570 Juan Agosto .08 .25
571 Tommy Gregg .08 .25
572 Kevin Wickander .08 .25
573 Jamie Quirk UER .08 .25
Rookie card is 1976,
but card back is 1990
574 Jerry Don Gleaton .08 .25
575 Chris Hammond .08 .25
576 Luis Gonzalez RC .60 1.50
577 Russ Swan .08 .25
578 Jeff Conine RC .40 1.00
579 Charlie Hough .20 .50
580 Jeff Kunkel .08 .25
581 Darrel Akerfelds .08 .25
582 Jeff Manto .08 .25
583 Alejandro Pena .08 .25
584 Mark Davidson .08 .25
585 Bob MacDonald RC .15 .40
586 Paul Assenmacher .08 .25
587 Dan Wilson RC .25 .60
588 Tom Bolton .08 .25
589 Brian Harper .08 .25
590 John Habyan .08 .25
591 John Orton .08 .25
592 Mark Gardner .08 .25
593 Turner Ward RC .25 .60
594 Bob Patterson .08 .25
595 Ed Nunez .08 .25
596 Gary Scott UER RC .15 .40
597 Scott Bankhead .08 .25

598 Checklist 301-400	.08	.25
599 Checklist 401-500	.08	.25
600 Checklist 501-600	.08	.25

1991 Stadium Club Charter Member

This 50-card multi-sport standard-size set was sent to charter members in the Topps Stadium Club. The sports represented in the set are baseball (1-32), football (33-41), and hockey (42-50). The cards feature on the fronts full-bleed posed and action glossy color player photos. The player's name is shown in the light blue stripe that intersects the Stadium Club logo near the bottom of the picture. The words "Charter Member" are printed in gold foil lettering immediately below the stripe. The back design features a newspaper-like masthead (The Stadium Club Herald) complete with a headline announcing a major event in the player's season with copy below providing more information about the event. The cards are unnumbered and arranged below alphabetically within sports. Topps apparently made two printings of this set, which are most easily identifiable by the small asterisks on the bottom left of the card backs. The first printing cards have one asterisk, the second printing cards have two. The display box that contained the cards also included a Nolan Ryan bronze metallic card and a key chain. Very early members of the Stadium Club received a large size bronze metallic Nolan Ryan 1990 Topps card. It is valued below as well as the normal size Ryan metallic card. A third varation on the Ryan medallion has been found. This is another version of the 1991 Stadium Club charter member bronze medallion, except this one has a 24K logo on it. It is suspected that this might be a Home Shopping Newtork variety. No pricing is provided at this time for this piece due to lack of market information.

COMP.FACT SET (50)	6.00	15.00
1 Sandy Alomar	.10	.30
2 George Brett	.60	1.50
3 Barry Bonds	.40	1.00
4 Ellis Burks	.10	.30
5 Eric Davis	.10	.30
6 Delino DeShields	.07	.20
7 Doug Drabek	.07	.20
8 Cecil Fielder	.10	.30
9 Carlton Fisk	.20	.50
10 Ken Griffey Jr.	1.50	4.00
Ken Griffey Sr.		
11 Billy Hatcher	.07	.20
12 Andy Hawkins	.07	.20
13 Rickey Henderson	.20	.50
A.L. Recognizes		
Rickey As MVP		
14 Rickey Henderson	.20	.50
Rickey is A.L.'s		
Leading Thief		
15 Randy Johnson	.30	.75
16 Dave Justice	.30	.75
17 Mark Langston	.07	.20
Mike Witt		
18 Kevin Maas	.07	.20
19 Ramon Martinez	.10	.30
20 Willie McGee	.07	.20
21 Terry Mulholland	.07	.20
22 Jose Offerman	.07	.20
23 Melido Perez	.07	.20
24 Nolan Ryan	1.25	3.00
A No-Hitter For		
The Ages		
25 Nolan Ryan	1.25	3.00
Nolan Ryan Earns/300th Career Win		
26 Ryne Sandberg	.60	1.50
27 Dave Stewart	.10	.30
28 Dave Stieb	.07	.20
29 Bobby Thigpen	.07	.20
30 Fernando Valenzuela	.10	.30
31 Frank Viola	.07	.20
32 Bob Welch	.10	.30
NNO Nolan Ryan Bronze Medal.	6.00	15.00
NNO N.Ryan Bronze Medal. Lge.	80.00	200.00
NNO Nolan Ryan Bronze	.75	2.00
Medallion small/1991 Stadium C		

1991 Stadium Club Members Only

This 50-card multi-sport standard-size set was sent in three installments to members in the Topps Stadium Club. The first and second installments featured baseball players (card numbers 1-10 and 11-30), while the third spotlighted football (31-37) and hockey (38-50) players. The cards feature on the fronts full-bleed posed and action glossy color player photos. The player's name is shown in the light blue stripe that intersects the Stadium Club logo near the bottom of the picture. The words "Members Only" are printed in gold foil lettering immediately below the stripe. The back design features a newspaper-like masthead (The Stadium Club Herald) complete with a headline announcing a major event in the player's season with copy below providing more information about the event. The cards are unnumbered and arranged below alphabetically according to and within installments.

COMPLETE SET (50)	6.00	15.00
1 Wilson Alvarez	.07	.20
2 Andy Ashby	.07	.20
3 Tommy Greene	.07	.20
4 Rickey Henderson	.20	.50
Rickey Is Top		
Thief in History		
5 Denny Martinez	.07	.20
6 Paul Molitor	.30	.75
7 Nolan Ryan	1.25	3.00
Ryan Extends Record		
With 7th No-Hitte		
8 Robby Thompson	.07	.20
9 Dave Winfield	.30	.75
10 Orioles No-Hitter	.07	.20
Bob Milacki		
Mike Flanagan		
Mar		
11 Jeff Bagwell	1.25	3.00
12 Roger Clemens	.50	1.25
13 David Cone	.08	.25
14 Carlton Fisk	.20	.50
15 Julio Franco	.07	.20
16 Tom Glavine	.08	.25
17 Pete Harnisch	.07	.20
18 Rickey Henderson	.20	.50
Rickey Leads A.L. In		
Thefts For		
19 Howard Johnson	.07	.20
20 Chuck Knoblauch	.07	.20
21 Ray Lankford	.07	.20
22 Jack Morris	.08	.25
23 Terry Pendleton	.08	.25
NL's Leading Batsman		
24 Terry Pendleton	.08	.25
Close MVP Race		
Favors Terry		
25 Jeff Reardon	.07	.20
26 Cal Ripken	1.25	3.00
27 Nolan Ryan	1.25	3.00
Ryan's 22nd Straight		
Year With Over/		
28 Bret Saberhagen	.07	.20
29 Cecil Fielder	.15	.40
Jose Canseco		
30 Braves No Hitter	.07	.20
Kent Mercker		
Mark Wohlers		
Alej		

1992 Stadium Club Dome

The 1992 Stadium Club Dome set (issued by Topps) features 100 top draft picks, 56 1991 All-Star Game cards, 25 1991 Team U.S.A. cards, and 19 1991 Championship and World Series cards, all packaged in a factory set box inside a molded-plastic SkyDome display. Topps actually references this set as a 1991 set and the copyright lines on the card backs say 1991, but the set was released well into 1992. Rookie Cards in this set include Shawn Green and Manny Ramirez.

COMP.FACT.SET (200)	6.00	15.00
ORIGINALLY INTENDED AS A 1991 RELEASE		
1 Terry Adams RC	.20	.50
2 Tommy Adams RC	.08	.25
3 Rick Aguilera	.05	.15
4 Ron Allen RC	.08	.25
5 Roberto Alomar	.08	.25
6 Sandy Alomar Jr.	.02	.10
7 Greg Anthony RC	.08	.25
8 James Austin RC	.08	.25
9 Steve Avery	.02	.10
10 Harold Baines	.05	.15
11 Brian Barber RC	.08	.25
12 Jon Barnes RC	.08	.25
13 George Bell	.02	.10
14 Doug Bennett RC	.08	.25
15 Sean Bergman RC	.20	.50
16 Craig Biggio	.08	.25
17 Bill Bliss RC	.08	.25
18 Wade Boggs	.08	.25
19 Bobby Bonilla	.05	.15
20 Russell Brock RC	.08	.25
21 Tarrik Brock RC	.08	.25
22 Tom Browning	.02	.10
23 Brett Butler	.05	.15
24 Ivan Calderon	.02	.10
25 Joe Carter	.05	.15
26 Joe Caruso RC	.08	.25
27 Dan Cholowsky RC	.08	.25
28 Will Clark	.08	.25
29 Roger Clemens	.40	1.00
30 Shawn Curran RC	.08	.25
31 Chris Curtis RC	.08	.25
32 Chili Davis	.05	.15
33 Andre Dawson	.05	.15
34 Joe DeBerry RC	.08	.25
35 John Dettmer	.02	.10
36 Rob Dibble	.05	.15
37 John Donati RC	.08	.25
38 Dave Doorneweerd RC	.08	.25
39 Darren Dreifort	.02	.10
40 Mike Durant RC	.08	.25
41 Chris Durkin RC	.08	.25
42 Dennis Eckersley	.05	.15
43 Brian Edmondson RC	.08	.25
44 Vaughn Eshelman RC	.08	.25
45 Shawn Estes RC	.20	.50
46 Jorge Fabregas RC	.20	.50
47 Jon Farrell RC	.08	.25
48 Cecil Fielder	.05	.15
49 Carlton Fisk	.08	.25
50 Tim Flannelly RC	.08	.25
51 Cliff Floyd RC	.60	1.50
52 Julio Franco	.05	.15
53 Greg Gagne	.02	.10
54 Chris Gambs RC	.08	.25
55 Ron Gant	.05	.15
56 Brent Gates RC	.08	.25
57 Dwayne Gerald RC	.08	.25
58 Jason Giambi	.40	1.00
59 Benji Gil RC	.20	.50
60 Mark Gipner RC	.08	.25
61 Danny Gladden	.02	.10
62 Tom Glavine	.08	.25
63 Jimmy Gonzalez RC	.08	.25
64 Jeff Granger	.02	.10
65 Dan Grapenthien RC	.08	.25
66 Dennis Gray RC	.08	.25
67 Shawn Green RC	.75	2.00
68 Tyler Green RC	.08	.25
69 Todd Greene	.02	.10
70 Ken Griffey Jr.	.40	1.00
71 Kelly Gruber	.02	.10
72 Ozzie Guillen	.05	.15
73 Tony Gwynn	.25	.60
74 Shane Halter RC	.08	.25
75 Jeffrey Hammonds	.05	.15
76 Larry Hanlon RC	.08	.25
77 Pete Harnisch	.02	.10
78 Mike Harrison RC	.08	.25
79 Bryan Harvey	.02	.10
80 Scott Hatteberg RC	.20	.50
81 Rick Helling	.02	.10
82 Dave Henderson	.02	.10
83 Rickey Henderson	.20	.50
84 Tyrone Hill RC	.08	.25
85 Todd Hollandsworth RC	.20	.50
86 Brian Holliday RC	.08	.25
87 Terry Horn RC	.08	.25
88 Jeff Hostetler RC	.08	.25
89 Kent Hrbek	.05	.15
90 Mark Hubbard RC	.08	.25
91 Charles Johnson	.05	.15
92 Howard Johnson	.02	.10
93 Todd Johnson	.02	.10
94 Bobby Jones RC	.20	.50
95 Dan Jones RC	.08	.25
96 Felix Jose	.02	.10
97 David Justice	.02	.10
98 Jimmy Key	.05	.15
99 Marc Kroon RC	.08	.25
100 John Kruk	.05	.15
101 Mark Langston	.02	.10
102 Barry Larkin	.08	.25
103 Mike LaValliere	.02	.10
104 Scott Leius	.02	.10
105 Mark Lemke	.02	.10
106 Donnie Leshnock	.02	.10
107 Jimmy Lewis RC	.08	.25
108 Shane Livesy RC	.08	.25
109 Ryan Long RC	.08	.25
110 Trevor Mallory RC	.08	.25
111 Dennis Martinez	.05	.15
112 Justin Mashore RC	.08	.25
113 Jason McDonald	.02	.10
114 Jack McDowell	.02	.10
115 Tom McKinnon RC	.08	.25
116 Billy McMillon	.02	.10
117 Buck McNabb RC	.08	.25
118 Jim Mecir RC	.08	.25
119 Dan Melendez	.02	.10
120 Shawn Miller RC	.08	.25
121 Trever Miller RC	.08	.25
122 Paul Molitor	.05	.15
123 Vincent Moore RC	.08	.25
124 Mike Morgan	.02	.10
125 Jack Morris WS	.02	.10
126 Jack Morris AS	.02	.10
127 Sean Mulligan RC	.08	.25
128 Eddie Murray AS	.20	.50
129 Mike Neill RC	.20	.50
130 Phil Nevin	.40	1.00
131 Mark O'Brien RC	.08	.25
132 Alex Ochoa RC	.08	.25
133 Chad Ogea RC	.08	.25
134 Greg Olson	.02	.10
135 Paul O'Neill	.08	.25
136 Jared Osentowski RC	.08	.25
137 Mike Pagliarulo	.02	.10
138 Rafael Palmeiro	.08	.25
139 Rodney Pedraza RC	.08	.25
140 Tony Phillips P	.02	.10
141 Scott Pisciotta RC	.08	.25
142 Chris Pritchett RC	.08	.25
143 Jason Pruitt RC	.08	.25
144 Kirby Puckett WS UER	.20	.50
Championship series		
AB and BA is wrong		
145 Kirby Puckett AS	.20	.50
146 Manny Ramirez RC	2.50	6.00
147 Eddie Ramos RC	.08	.25
148 Mark Ratekin RC	.08	.25
149 Jeff Reardon	.05	.15
150 Sean Rees RC	.08	.25
151 Pokey Reese RC	.20	.50
152 Desmond Relaford RC	.08	.25
153 Eric Richardson RC	.08	.25
154 Cal Ripken	.60	1.50
155 Chris Roberts	.02	.10
156 Mike Robertson RC	.08	.25
157 Steve Rodriguez	.02	.10
158 Mike Rossiter RC	.08	.25
159 Scott Ruffcorn RC	.08	.25
160 Chris Sabo	.02	.10
161 Juan Samuel	.02	.10
162 Ryne Sandberg UER	.30	.75
163 Scott Sanderson	.02	.10
164 Benny Santiago	.05	.15
165 Gene Schall RC	.08	.25
166 Chad Schoenvogel RC	.08	.25
167 Chris Seelbach RC	.08	.25
168 Aaron Sele RC	.20	.50
169 Basil Shabazz RC	.08	.25
170 Al Shirley RC	.08	.25
171 Paul Shuey	.02	.10
172 Ruben Sierra	.02	.10
173 John Smiley	.02	.10
174 Lee Smith	.05	.15
175 Ozzie Smith	.30	.75
176 Tim Smith RC	.08	.25
177 Zane Smith	.02	.10
178 John Smoltz	.08	.25
179 Scott Stahoviak RC	.08	.25
180 Kennie Steenstra	.02	.10
181 Kevin Stocker RC	.08	.25
182 Chris Stynes RC	.20	.50
183 Danny Tartabull	.02	.10
184 Brien Taylor RC	.20	.50
185 Todd Taylor	.02	.10
186 Larry Thomas RC	.08	.25
187 Ozzie Timmons RC	.08	.25
See also 188		
188 David Tuttle UER	.02	.10
Mistakenly numbered		
as 187 on card		
189 Andy Van Slyke	.08	.25
190 Frank Viola	.05	.15
191 Michael Walkden RC	.08	.25
192 Jeff Ware	.02	.10
193 Allen Watson RC	.08	.25
194 Steve Whitaker RC	.08	.25
195 Jerry Willard	.02	.10
196 Craig Wilson	.02	.10
197 Chris Wimmer	.02	.10
198 Steve Wojciechowski RC	.08	.25
199 Joel Wolfe RC	.08	.25
200 Ivan Zweig	.02	.10

1992 Stadium Club

The 1992 Stadium Club baseball card set consists of 900 standard-size cards issued in three series of 300 cards each. Cards were issued in plastic wrapped packs. A card-like application form for membership in Topps Stadium Club was inserted in each pack. Card numbers 591-610 form a "Members Choice" subset.

COMPLETE SET (900)	20.00	50.00
COMPLETE SERIES 1 (300)	6.00	15.00
COMPLETE SERIES 2 (300)	6.00	15.00
COMPLETE SERIES 3 (300)	6.00	15.00
1 Cal Ripken UER	.60	1.50
2 Eric Yelding	.02	.10
3 Geno Petralli	.02	.10
4 Wally Backman	.02	.10
5 Milt Cuyler	.02	.10
6 Kevin Bass	.02	.10
7 Dante Bichette	.05	.15
8 Ray Lankford	.05	.15
9 Mel Hall	.02	.10
10 Joe Carter	.05	.15
11 Juan Samuel	.02	.10
12 Jeff Montgomery	.02	.10
13 Glenn Braggs	.02	.10
14 Henry Cotto	.02	.10
15 Deion Sanders	.08	.25
16 Dick Schofield	.02	.10
17 David Cone	.05	.15
18 Chili Davis	.05	.15
19 Tom Foley	.02	.10
20 Ozzie Guillen	.05	.15
21 Luis Salazar	.02	.10
22 Terry Steinbach	.02	.10
23 Chris James	.02	.10
24 Jeff King	.02	.10
25 Carlos Quintana	.02	.10
26 Mike Maddux	.02	.10
27 Tommy Greene	.02	.10
28 Jeff Russell	.02	.10
29 Steve Finley	.05	.15
30 Mike Flanagan	.02	.10
31 Darren Lewis	.02	.10
32 Mark Lee	.02	.10
33 Willie Fraser	.02	.10
34 Mike Henneman	.02	.10
35 Kevin Maas	.02	.10
36 Dave Hansen	.02	.10
37 Erik Hanson	.02	.10
38 Bill Doran	.02	.10
39 Mike Boddicker	.02	.10
40 Vince Coleman	.02	.10
41 Devon White	.05	.15
42 Mark Gardner	.02	.10
43 Scott Lewis	.02	.10
44 Juan Berenguer	.02	.10
45 Carney Lansford	.05	.15
46 Curt Wilkerson	.02	.10
47 Shane Mack	.02	.10
48 Bip Roberts	.02	.10
49 Greg A. Harris	.02	.10
50 Ryne Sandberg	.30	.75
51 Mark Whiten	.02	.10
52 Jack McDowell	.02	.10
53 Jimmy Jones	.02	.10
54 Steve Lake	.02	.10
55 Bud Black	.02	.10
56 Dave Valle	.02	.10
57 Kevin Reimer	.02	.10
58 Rich Gedman UER	.02	.10
Wrong BARS chart used		
59 Travis Fryman	.05	.15
60 Steve Avery	.02	.10
61 Francisco de la Rosa	.02	.10
62 Scott Hemond	.02	.10
63 Hal Morris	.02	.10
64 Hensley Meulens	.02	.10
65 Frank Castillo	.02	.10
66 Gene Larkin	.02	.10
67 Jose DeLeon	.02	.10
68 Al Osuna	.02	.10
69 Dave Cochrane	.02	.10
70 Robin Ventura	.05	.15
71 John Cerutti	.02	.10
72 Kevin Gross	.02	.10
73 Ivan Calderon	.02	.10
74 Mike Macfarlane	.02	.10
75 Stan Belinda	.02	.10
76 Shawn Hillegas	.02	.10
77 Pat Borders	.02	.10
78 Jim Vatcher	.02	.10
79 Bobby Rose	.02	.10
80 Roger Clemens	.40	1.00
81 Craig Worthington	.02	.10
82 Jeff Treadway	.02	.10
83 Jamie Quirk	.02	.10
84 Randy Bush	.02	.10
85 Anthony Young	.02	.10
86 Trevor Wilson	.02	.10
87 Jaime Navarro	.02	.10
88 Les Lancaster	.02	.10
89 Pat Kelly	.02	.10
90 Alvin Davis	.02	.10
91 Larry Andersen	.02	.10
92 Rob Deer	.02	.10
93 Mike Sharperson	.02	.10
94 Lance Parrish	.05	.15
95 Cecil Espy	.02	.10
96 Tim Spehr	.02	.10
97 Dave Stieb	.02	.10
98 Terry Mulholland	.02	.10
99 Dennis Boyd	.02	.10
100 Barry Larkin	.08	.25
101 Ryan Bowen	.02	.10
102 Felix Fermin	.02	.10
103 Luis Alicea	.02	.10
104 Tim Hulett	.02	.10
105 Rafael Belliard	.02	.10
106 Mike Gallego	.02	.10
107 Dave Righetti	.05	.15
108 Jeff Schaefer	.02	.10
109 Ricky Bones	.02	.10
110 Scott Erickson	.02	.10
111 Matt Nokes	.02	.10
112 Bob Scanlan	.02	.10
113 Tom Candiotti	.02	.10
114 Sean Berry	.02	.10
115 Kevin Morton	.02	.10
116 Scott Fletcher	.02	.10
117 B.J. Surhoff	.05	.15
118 Dave Magadan UER	.02	.10
Born Tampa, not Tamps		
119 Bill Gullickson	.02	.10
120 Marquis Grissom	.05	.15
121 Lenny Harris	.02	.10
122 Wally Joyner	.05	.15
123 Kevin Brown	.05	.15
124 Braulio Castillo	.02	.10
125 Eric King	.02	.10
126 Mark Portugal	.02	.10
127 Calvin Jones	.02	.10
128 Mike Heath	.02	.10
129 Todd Van Poppel	.02	.10
130 Benny Santiago	.05	.15
131 Gary Thurman	.02	.10
132 Joe Girardi	.02	.10
133 Dave Eiland	.02	.10
134 Orlando Merced	.02	.10
135 Joe Orsulak	.02	.10
136 John Burkett	.02	.10
137 Ken Dayley	.02	.10
138 Ken Hill	.02	.10
139 Walt Terrell	.02	.10
140 Mike Scioscia	.02	.10
141 Junior Felix	.02	.10
142 Ken Caminiti	.05	.15
143 Carlos Baerga	.02	.10
144 Tony Fossas	.02	.10
145 Craig Grebeck	.02	.10
146 Scott Bradley	.02	.10
147 Kent Mercker	.02	.10
148 Derrick May	.02	.10
149 Jerald Clark	.02	.10
150 George Brett	.50	1.25
151 Luis Quinones	.02	.10
152 Mike Pagliarulo	.02	.10
153 Jose Guzman	.02	.10
154 Charlie O'Brien	.02	.10
155 Darren Holmes	.02	.10
156 Joe Boever	.02	.10
157 Rich Monteleone	.02	.10
158 Reggie Harris	.02	.10
159 Roberto Alomar	.08	.25
160 Robby Thompson	.02	.10
161 Chris Hoiles	.02	.10
162 Tom Pagnozzi	.02	.10
163 Omar Vizquel	.08	.25
164 John Candelaria	.02	.10
165 Terry Shumpert	.02	.10
166 Andy Mota	.02	.10
167 Scott Bailes	.02	.10
168 Jeff Blauser	.02	.10
169 Steve Olin	.02	.10
170 Doug Drabek	.02	.10
171 Dave Bergman	.02	.10
172 Eddie Whitson	.02	.10
173 Gilberto Reyes	.02	.10
174 Mark Grace	.08	.25
175 Paul O'Neill	.08	.25
176 Greg Cadaret	.02	.10
177 Mark Williamson	.02	.10
178 Casey Candaele	.02	.10
179 Candy Maldonado	.02	.10
180 Lee Smith	.05	.15
181 Harold Reynolds	.05	.15
182 David Justice	.05	.15
183 Lenny Webster	.02	.10
184 Donn Pall	.02	.10
185 Gerald Alexander	.02	.10
186 Jack Clark	.05	.15
187 Stan Javier	.02	.10
188 Ricky Jordan	.02	.10
189 Franklin Stubbs	.02	.10
190 Dennis Eckersley	.05	.15
191 Danny Tartabull	.02	.10
192 Pete O'Brien	.02	.10
193 Mark Lewis	.02	.10
194 Mike Felder	.02	.10
195 Mickey Tettleton	.02	.10
196 Dwight Smith	.02	.10
197 Shawn Abner	.02	.10
198 Jim Leyritz UER	.02	.10
Career totals less		
than 1991 totals		
199 Mike Devereaux	.02	.10
200 Craig Biggio	.08	.25
201 Kevin Elster	.02	.10
202 Rance Mulliniks	.02	.10
203 Tony Fernandez	.02	.10
204 Allan Anderson	.02	.10
205 Herm Winningham	.02	.10
206 Tim Jones	.02	.10
207 Ramon Martinez	.02	.10
208 Teddy Higuera	.02	.10
209 John Kruk	.05	.15
210 Jim Abbott	.08	.25
211 Dean Palmer	.05	.15
212 Mark Davis	.02	.10
213 Jay Buhner	.05	.15
214 Jesse Barfield	.02	.10
215 Kevin Mitchell	.02	.10
216 Mike LaValliere	.02	.10
217 Mark Wohlers	.02	.10
218 Dave Henderson	.02	.10
219 Dave Smith	.02	.10
220 Albert Belle	.05	.15
221 Spike Owen	.02	.10
222 Jeff Gray	.02	.10
223 Paul Gibson	.02	.10
224 Bobby Thigpen	.02	.10
225 Mike Mussina	.20	.50
226 Darrin Jackson	.02	.10
227 Luis Gonzalez	.05	.15
228 Greg Briley	.02	.10
229 Brent Mayne	.02	.10
230 Paul Molitor	.05	.15
231 Al Leiter	.05	.15
232 Andy Van Slyke	.08	.25
233 Ron Tingley	.02	.10
234 Bernard Gilkey	.02	.10
235 Kent Hrbek	.05	.15
236 Eric Karros	.05	.15
237 Randy Velarde	.02	.10
238 Andy Allanson	.02	.10
239 Willie McGee	.05	.15
240 Juan Gonzalez	.08	.25
241 Karl Rhodes	.02	.10
242 Luis Mercedes	.02	.10
243 Bill Swift	.02	.10
244 Tommy Gregg	.02	.10
245 David Howard	.02	.10
246 Dave Hollins	.02	.10
247 Kip Gross	.02	.10
248 Walt Weiss	.02	.10
249 Mackey Sasser	.02	.10
250 Cecil Fielder	.05	.15
251 Jerry Browne	.02	.10
252 Doug Dascenzo	.02	.10
253 Darryl Hamilton	.02	.10
254 Dann Bilardello	.02	.10
255 Luis Rivera	.02	.10
256 Larry Walker	.08	.25
257 Ron Karkovice	.02	.10
258 Bob Tewksbury	.02	.10
259 Jimmy Key	.05	.15
260 Bernie Williams	.08	.25
261 Gary Wayne	.02	.10
262 Mike Simms UER	.02	.10
Reversed negative		
263 John Orton	.02	.10
264 Marvin Freeman	.02	.10
265 Mike Jeffcoat	.02	.10
266 Roger Mason	.02	.10
267 Edgar Martinez	.08	.25
268 Henry Rodriguez	.02	.10
269 Sam Horn	.02	.10
270 Brian McRae	.02	.10
271 Kirt Manwaring	.02	.10
272 Mike Bordick	.02	.10
273 Chris Sabo	.02	.10
274 Jim Olander	.02	.10
275 Greg W. Harris	.02	.10
276 Dan Gakeler	.02	.10
277 Bill Sampen	.02	.10
278 Joel Skinner	.02	.10
279 Curt Schilling	.08	.25
280 Dale Murphy	.08	.25
281 Lee Stevens	.02	.10
282 Lonnie Smith	.02	.10
283 Manuel Lee	.02	.10
284 Shawn Boskie	.02	.10
285 Kevin Seitzer	.02	.10
286 Stan Royer	.02	.10
287 John Dopson	.02	.10
288 Scott Bullett RC	.02	.10
289 Ken Patterson	.02	.10
290 Todd Hundley	.02	.10
291 Tim Leary	.02	.10
292 Brett Butler	.05	.15
293 Gregg Olson	.02	.10
294 Jeff Brantley	.02	.10
295 Brian Holman	.02	.10
296 Brian Harper	.02	.10
297 Brian Bohanon	.02	.10
298 Checklist 1-100	.02	.10
299 Checklist 101-200	.02	.10
300 Checklist 201-300	.02	.10
301 Frank Thomas	.20	.50
302 Lloyd McClendon	.02	.10
303 Brady Anderson	.05	.15
304 Julio Valera	.02	.10
305 Mike Aldrete	.02	.10
306 Joe Oliver	.02	.10
307 Todd Stottlemyre	.02	.10
308 Rey Sanchez RC	.05	.15
309 Gary Sheffield UER	.05	.15
310 Andujar Cedeno	.02	.10
311 Kenny Rogers	.05	.15
312 Bruce Hurst	.02	.10
313 Mike Schooler	.02	.10
314 Mike Benjamin	.02	.10
315 Chuck Finley	.05	.15
316 Mark Lemke	.02	.10
317 Scott Livingstone	.02	.10
318 Chris Nabholz	.02	.10
319 Mike Humphreys	.02	.10
320 Pedro Guerrero	.05	.15
321 Willie Banks	.02	.10
322 Tom Goodwin	.02	.10
323 Hector Wagner	.02	.10
324 Wally Ritchie	.02	.10
325 Mo Vaughn	.05	.15
326 Joe Klink	.02	.10
327 Cal Eldred	.02	.10
328 Daryl Boston	.02	.10
329 Mike Huff	.02	.10
330 Jeff Bagwell	.20	.50
331 Bob Milacki	.02	.10
332 Tom Prince	.02	.10
333 Pat Tabler	.02	.10
334 Ced Landrum	.02	.10
335 Reggie Jefferson	.02	.10
336 Mo Sanford	.02	.10
337 Kevin Ritz	.02	.10
338 Gerald Perry	.02	.10
339 Jeff Hamilton	.02	.10
340 Tim Wallach	.02	.10
341 Jeff Huson	.02	.10
342 Jose Melendez	.02	.10
343 Willie Wilson	.02	.10
344 Mike Stanton	.02	.10
345 Joel Johnston	.02	.10
346 Lee Guetterman	.02	.10
347 Francisco Oliveras	.02	.10
348 Dave Burba	.02	.10
349 Tim Crews	.02	.10
350 Scott Leius	.02	.10
351 Danny Cox	.02	.10
352 Wayne Housie	.02	.10
353 Chris Donnels	.02	.10
354 Chris George	.02	.10
355 Gerald Young	.02	.10
356 Roberto Hernandez	.02	.10
357 Neal Heaton	.02	.10
358 Todd Frohwirth	.02	.10
359 Jose Vizcaino	.02	.10
360 Jim Thome	.20	.50
361 Craig Wilson	.02	.10
362 Dave Haas	.02	.10
363 Billy Hatcher	.02	.10
364 John Barfield	.02	.10
365 Luis Aquino	.02	.10
366 Charlie Leibrandt	.02	.10
367 Howard Farmer	.02	.10
368 Bryn Smith	.02	.10
369 Mickey Morandini	.02	.10
370 Jose Canseco	.08	.25
See also 597		
371 Jose Uribe	.02	.10
372 Bob MacDonald	.02	.10
373 Luis Sojo	.02	.10
374 Craig Shipley	.02	.10
375 Scott Bankhead	.02	.10
376 Greg Gagne	.02	.10
377 Scott Cooper	.02	.10
378 Jose Offerman	.02	.10

379 Bill Spiers .02 .10
380 John Smiley .02 .10
381 Jeff Carter .02 .10
382 Heathcliff Slocumb .02 .10
383 Jeff Tackett .02 .10
384 John Kiely .02 .10
385 John Vander Wal .02 .10
386 Omar Olivares .02 .10
387 Ruben Sierra .05 .15
388 Tom Gordon .02 .10
389 Charles Nagy .02 .10
390 Dave Stewart .05 .15
391 Pete Harnisch .02 .10
392 Tim Burke .02 .10
393 Roberto Kelly .02 .10
394 Freddie Benavides .02 .10
395 Tom Glavine .08 .25
396 Wes Chamberlain .02 .10
397 Eric Gunderson .02 .10
398 Dave West .02 .10
399 Ellis Burks .05 .15
400 Ken Griffey Jr. .40 1.00
401 Thomas Howard .02 .10
402 Juan Guzman .02 .10
403 Mitch Webster .02 .10
404 Matt Merullo .02 .10
405 Steve Buechele .02 .10
406 Danny Jackson .02 .10
407 Felix Jose .02 .10
408 Doug Piatt .02 .10
409 Jim Eisenreich .02 .10
410 Bryan Harvey .02 .10
411 Jim Austin .02 .10
412 Jim Poole .02 .10
413 Glenallen Hill .02 .10
414 Gene Nelson .02 .10
415 Ivan Rodriguez .20 .50
416 Frank Tanana .02 .10
417 Steve Decker .02 .10
418 Jason Grimsley .02 .10
419 Tim Layana .02 .10
420 Don Mattingly .50 1.25
421 Jerome Walton .02 .10
422 Rob Ducey .02 .10
423 Andy Benes .02 .10
424 John Marzano .02 .10
425 Gene Harris .02 .10
426 Tim Raines .05 .15
427 Bret Barberie .02 .10
428 Harvey Pulliam .02 .10
429 Cris Carpenter .02 .10
430 Howard Johnson .02 .10
431 Orel Hershiser .05 .15
432 Brian Hunter .02 .10
433 Kevin Tapani .02 .10
434 Rick Reed .02 .10
435 Ron Witmeyer RC .02 .10
436 Gary Gaetti .05 .15
437 Alex Cole .02 .10
438 Chito Martinez .02 .10
439 Greg Litton .02 .10
440 Julio Franco .05 .15
441 Mike Munoz .02 .10
442 Erik Pappas .02 .10
443 Pat Combs .02 .10
444 Lance Johnson .02 .10
445 Ed Sprague .02 .10
446 Mike Greenwell .02 .10
447 Milt Thompson .02 .10
448 Mike Magnante RC .02 .10
449 Chris Haney .02 .10
450 Robin Yount .30 .75
451 Rafael Ramirez .02 .10
452 Gino Minutelli .02 .10
453 Tom Lampkin .02 .10
454 Tony Perezchica .02 .10
455 Dwight Gooden .05 .15
456 Mark Guthrie .02 .10
457 Jay Howell .02 .10
458 Gary DiSarcina .02 .10
459 John Smoltz .08 .25
460 Will Clark .08 .25
461 Dave Otto .02 .10
462 Rob Maurer RC .02 .10
463 Dwight Evans .08 .25
464 Tom Brunansky .02 .10
465 Shawn Hare RC .02 .10
466 Geronimo Pena .02 .10
467 Alex Fernandez .02 .10
468 Greg Myers .02 .10
469 Jeff Fassero .02 .10
470 Len Dykstra .05 .15
471 Jeff Johnson .02 .10
472 Russ Swan .02 .10
473 Archie Corbin .02 .10
474 Chuck McElroy .02 .10
475 Mark McGwire .50 1.25
476 Wally Whitehurst .02 .10
477 Tim McIntosh .02 .10
478 Sid Bream .02 .10
479 Jeff Juden .02 .10
480 Carlton Fisk .08 .25
481 Jeff Plympton .02 .10
482 Carlos Martinez .02 .10
483 Jim Gott .02 .10
484 Bob McClure .02 .10
485 Tim Teufel .02 .10
486 Vicente Palacios .02 .10
487 Jeff Reed .02 .10
488 Tony Phillips .02 .10
489 Mel Rojas .02 .10
490 Ben McDonald .02 .10
491 Andres Santana .02 .10
492 Chris Beasley .02 .10
493 Mike Timlin .02 .10
494 Brian Downing .02 .10
495 Kirk Gibson .05 .15
496 Scott Sanderson .02 .10
497 Nick Esasky .02 .10
498 Johnny Guzman RC .02 .10
499 Mitch Williams .02 .10
500 Kirby Puckett .20 .50
501 Mike Harkey .02 .10
502 Jim Gantner .02 .10
503 Bruce Egloff .02 .10
504 Josias Manzanillo RC .02 .10
505 Delino DeShields .02 .10
506 Rheal Cormier .02 .10
507 Jay Bell .05 .15
508 Rich Rowland RC .02 .10
509 Scott Servais .02 .10
510 Terry Pendleton .05 .15
511 Rich DeLucia .02 .10
512 Warren Newson .02 .10
513 Paul Faries .02 .10
514 Kal Daniels .02 .10
515 Jarvis Brown .02 .10
516 Rafael Palmeiro .08 .25
517 Kelly Downs .02 .10
518 Steve Chitren .02 .10
519 Moises Alou .05 .15
520 Wade Boggs .08 .25
521 Pete Schourek .02 .10
522 Scott Terry .02 .10
523 Kevin Appier .05 .15
524 Gary Redus .02 .10
525 George Bell .02 .10
526 Jeff Kaiser .02 .10
527 Alvaro Espinoza .02 .10
528 Luis Polonia .02 .10
529 Darren Daulton .05 .15
530 Norm Charlton .02 .10
531 John Olerud .05 .15
532 Dan Plesac .02 .10
533 Billy Ripken .02 .10
534 Rod Nichols .02 .10
535 Joey Cora .02 .10
536 Harold Baines .05 .15
537 Bob Ojeda .02 .10
538 Mark Leonard .02 .10
539 Danny Darwin .02 .10
540 Shawon Dunston .02 .10
541 Pedro Munoz .02 .10
542 Mark Gubicza .02 .10
543 Kevin Baez .02 .10
544 Todd Zeile .02 .10
545 Don Slaught .02 .10
546 Tony Eusebio .05 .15
547 Alonzo Powell .02 .10
548 Gary Pettis .02 .10
549 Brian Barnes .02 .10
550 Lou Whitaker .05 .15
551 Keith Mitchell .02 .10
552 Oscar Azocar .02 .10
553 Stu Cole RC .02 .10
554 Steve Wapnick .02 .10
555 Derek Bell .05 .15
556 Luis Lopez .02 .10
557 Anthony Telford .02 .10
558 Tim Mauser .02 .10
559 Glen Sutko .02 .10
560 Darryl Strawberry .05 .15
561 Tom Bolton .02 .10
562 Cliff Young .02 .10
563 Bruce Walton .02 .10
564 Chico Walker .02 .10
565 John Franco .05 .15
566 Paul McClellan .02 .10
567 Paul Abbott .02 .10
568 Gary Varsho .02 .10
569 Carlos Maldonado RC .02 .10
570 Kelly Gruber .02 .10
571 Jose Oquendo .02 .10
572 Steve Frey .02 .10
573 Tino Martinez .08 .25
574 Bill Haselman .02 .10
575 Eric Anthony .02 .10
576 John Habyan .02 .10
577 Jeff McNeely .02 .10
578 Chris Bosio .02 .10
579 Joe Grahe .02 .10
580 Fred McGriff .08 .25
581 Rick Honeycutt .02 .10
582 Matt Williams .05 .15
583 Cliff Brantley .02 .10
584 Rob Dibble .05 .15
585 Skeeter Barnes .02 .10
586 Greg Hibbard .02 .10
587 Randy Milligan .02 .10
588 Checklist 301-400 .02 .10
589 Checklist 401-500 .02 .10
590 Checklist 501-600 .02 .10
591 Frank Thomas MC .08 .25
592 David Justice MC .02 .10
593 Roger Clemens MC .20 .50
594 Steve Avery MC .02 .10
595 Cal Ripken MC .30 .75
596 Barry Larkin MC UER .05 .15
Ranked in AL,
should be NL
597 Jose Canseco MC UER .05 .15
Mistakenly numbered
370 on card back
598 Will Clark MC .05 .15
599 Cecil Fielder MC .05 .15
600 Ryne Sandberg MC .20 .50
601 Chuck Knoblauch MC .02 .10
602 Dwight Gooden MC .02 .10
603 Ken Griffey Jr. MC .25 .60
604 Barry Bonds MC .40 1.00
605 Nolan Ryan MC .30 .75
606 Jeff Bagwell MC .08 .25
607 Robin Yount MC .20 .50
608 Bobby Bonilla MC .02 .10
609 George Brett MC .25 .60
610 Howard Johnson MC .02 .10
611 Esteban Beltre .02 .10
612 Mike Christopher .02 .10
613 Troy Afenir .02 .10
614 Mariano Duncan .02 .10
615 Doug Henry RC .02 .10
616 Doug Jones .02 .10
617 Alvin Davis .02 .10
618 Craig Lefferts .02 .10
619 Kevin McReynolds .02 .10
620 Barry Bonds .60 1.50
621 Turner Ward .02 .10
622 Joe Magrane .02 .10
623 Mark Parent .02 .10
624 Tom Browning .02 .10
625 John Smiley .02 .10
626 Steve Wilson .02 .10
627 Mike Gallego .02 .10
628 Sammy Sosa .20 .50
629 Rico Rossy .02 .10
630 Royce Clayton .02 .10
631 Clay Parker .02 .10
632 Pete Smith .02 .10
633 Jeff McKnight .02 .10
634 Jack Daugherty .02 .10
635 Steve Sax .02 .10
636 Joe Hesketh .02 .10
637 Vince Horsman .02 .10
638 Eric King .02 .10
639 Joe Boever .02 .10
640 Jack Morris .05 .15
641 Arthur Rhodes .02 .10
642 Bob Melvin .02 .10
643 Rick Wilkins .02 .10
644 Scott Scudder .02 .10
645 Bip Roberts .02 .10
646 Julio Valera .02 .10
647 Kevin Campbell .02 .10
648 Steve Searcy .02 .10
649 Scott Kamieniecki .02 .10
650 Kurt Stillwell .02 .10
651 Bob Welch .02 .10
652 Andres Galarraga .05 .15
653 Mike Jackson .02 .10
654 Bo Jackson .20 .50
655 Sid Fernandez .02 .10
656 Mike Bielecki .02 .10
657 Jeff Reardon .05 .15
658 Wayne Rosenthal .02 .10
659 Eric Bullock .02 .10
660 Eric Davis .05 .15
661 Randy Tomlin .02 .10
662 Tom Edens .02 .10
663 Rob Murphy .02 .10
664 Leo Gomez .02 .10
665 Greg Maddux .30 .75
666 Greg Vaughn .02 .10
667 Wade Taylor .02 .10
668 Brad Arnsberg .02 .10
669 Mike Moore .02 .10
670 Mark Langston .02 .10
671 Barry Jones .02 .10
672 Bill Landrum .02 .10
673 Greg Swindell .02 .10
674 Wayne Edwards .02 .10
675 Greg Olson .02 .10
676 Bill Pulsipher RC .02 .10
677 Bobby Witt .02 .10
678 Mark Carreon .02 .10
679 Patrick Lennon .02 .10
680 Ozzie Smith .30 .75
681 John Briscoe .02 .10
682 Matt Young .02 .10
683 Jeff Conine .05 .15
684 Phil Stephenson .02 .10
685 Ron Darling .02 .10
686 Bryan Hickerson RC .02 .10
687 Dale Sveum .02 .10
688 Kirk McCaskill .02 .10
689 Rich Amaral .02 .10
690 Danny Tartabull .02 .10
691 Donald Harris .02 .10
692 Doug Davis .02 .10
693 John Farrell .02 .10
694 Paul Gibson .02 .10
695 Kenny Lofton .08 .25
696 Mike Fetters .02 .10
697 Rosario Rodriguez .02 .10
698 Chris Jones .02 .10
699 Jeff Manto .02 .10
700 Rick Sutcliffe .05 .15
701 Scott Bankhead .02 .10
702 Donnie Hill .02 .10
703 Todd Worrell .02 .10
704 Rene Gonzales .02 .10
705 Rick Cerone .02 .10
706 Tony Pena .02 .10
707 Paul Sorrento .02 .10
708 Gary Scott .02 .10
709 Junior Noboa .02 .10
710 Wally Joyner .05 .15
711 Charlie Hayes .02 .10
712 Rich Rodriguez .02 .10
713 Rudy Seanez .02 .10
714 Jim Bullinger .02 .10
715 Jeff M. Robinson .02 .10
716 Jeff Branson .02 .10
717 Andy Ashby .02 .10
718 Dave Burba .02 .10
719 Rich Gossage .05 .15
720 Randy Johnson .20 .50
721 David Wells .05 .15
722 Paul Kilgus .02 .10
723 Dave Martinez .02 .10
724 Denny Neagle .05 .15
725 Andy Stankiewicz .02 .10
726 Rick Aguilera .05 .15
727 Junior Ortiz .02 .10
728 Storm Davis .02 .10
729 Don Robinson .02 .10
730 Ron Gant .05 .15
731 Paul Assenmacher .02 .10
732 Mike Gardiner .02 .10
733 Milt Hill .02 .10
734 Jeremy Hernandez RC .02 .10
735 Ken Hill .02 .10
736 Xavier Hernandez .02 .10
737 Gregg Jefferies .02 .10
738 Dick Schofield .02 .10
739 Ron Robinson .02 .10
740 Sandy Alomar Jr. .02 .10
741 Mike Stanley .02 .10
742 Butch Henry RC .02 .10
743 Floyd Bannister .02 .10
744 Brian Drahman .02 .10
745 Dave Winfield .05 .15
746 Bob Walk .02 .10
747 Chris James .02 .10
748 Don Prybylinski RC .02 .10
749 Dennis Rasmussen .02 .10
750 Rickey Henderson .20 .50
751 Chris Hammond .02 .10
752 Bob Kipper .02 .10
753 Dave Rohde .02 .10
754 Hubie Brooks .02 .10
755 Bret Saberhagen .05 .15
756 Jeff D. Robinson .02 .10
757 Pat Listach RC .05 .15
758 Bill Wegman .02 .10
759 John Wetteland .05 .15
760 Phil Plantier .02 .10
761 Wilson Alvarez .02 .10
762 Scott Aldred .02 .10
763 Armando Reynoso RC .05 .15
764 Todd Benzinger .02 .10
765 Kevin Mitchell .02 .10
766 Gary Sheffield .05 .15
767 Allan Anderson .02 .10
768 Rusty Meacham .02 .10
769 Rick Parker .02 .10
770 Nolan Ryan .75 2.00
771 Jeff Ballard .02 .10
772 Cory Snyder .02 .10
773 Denis Boucher .02 .10
774 Jose Gonzalez .02 .10
775 Juan Guerrero .02 .10
776 Ed Nunez .02 .10
777 Scott Ruskin .02 .10
778 Terry Leach .02 .10
779 Carl Willis .02 .10
780 Bobby Bonilla .05 .15
781 Duane Ward .02 .10
782 Joe Slusarski .02 .10
783 David Segui .02 .10
784 Kirk Gibson .05 .15
785 Frank Viola .02 .10
786 Keith Miller .02 .10
787 Mike Morgan .02 .10
788 Kim Batiste .02 .10
789 Sergio Valdez .02 .10
790 Eddie Taubensee RC .05 .15
791 Jack Armstrong .02 .10
792 Scott Fletcher .02 .10
793 Steve Farr .02 .10
794 Dan Pasqua .02 .10
795 Eddie Murray .20 .50
796 John Morris .02 .10
797 Francisco Cabrera .02 .10
798 Mike Perez .02 .10
799 Ted Wood .02 .10
800 Jose Rijo .02 .10
801 Danny Gladden .02 .10
802 Archi Cianfrocco RC .02 .10
803 Monty Fariss .02 .10
804 Roger McDowell .02 .10
805 Randy Myers .02 .10
806 Kirk Dressendorfer .02 .10
807 Zane Smith .02 .10
808 Glenn Davis .02 .10
809 Torey Lovullo .02 .10
810 Andre Dawson .05 .15
811 Bill Pecota .02 .10
812 Ted Power .02 .10
813 Willie Blair .02 .10
814 Dave Fleming .02 .10
815 Chris Gwynn .02 .10
816 Jody Reed .02 .10
817 Mark Dewey .02 .10
818 Kyle Abbott .02 .10
819 Tom Henke .02 .10
820 Kevin Seitzer .02 .10
821 Al Newman .02 .10
822 Tim Sherrill .02 .10
823 Chuck Crim .02 .10
824 Darren Reed .02 .10
825 Tony Gwynn .25 .60
826 Steve Foster .02 .10
827 Steve Howe .02 .10
828 Brook Jacoby .02 .10
829 Rodney McCray .02 .10
830 Chuck Knoblauch .05 .15
831 John Wehner .02 .10
832 Scott Garrelts .02 .10
833 Alejandro Pena .02 .10
834 Jeff Parrett UER .02 .10
Kentucky
835 Juan Bell .02 .10
836 Lance Dickson .02 .10
837 Darryl Kile .05 .15
838 Efrain Valdez .02 .10
839 Bob Zupcic RC .02 .10
840 George Bell .02 .10
841 Dave Gallagher .02 .10
842 Tim Belcher .02 .10
843 Jeff Shaw .02 .10
844 Mike Fitzgerald .02 .10
845 Gary Carter .05 .15
846 John Russell .02 .10
847 Eric Hillman RC .02 .10
848 Mike Witt .02 .10
849 Curt Wilkerson .02 .10
850 Alan Trammell .05 .15
851 Rex Hudler .02 .10
852 Mike Walkden RC .02 .10
853 Kevin Ward .02 .10
854 Tim Naehring .02 .10
855 Bill Swift .02 .10
856 Damon Berryhill .02 .10
857 Mark Eichhorn .02 .10
858 Hector Villanueva .02 .10
859 Jose Lind .02 .10
860 Dennis Martinez .05 .15
861 Bill Krueger .02 .10
862 Mike Kingery .02 .10
863 Jeff Innis .02 .10
864 Derek Lilliquist .02 .10
865 Reggie Sanders .05 .15
866 Ramon Garcia .02 .10
867 Bruce Ruffin .02 .10
868 Dickie Thon .02 .10
869 Melido Perez .02 .10
870 Ruben Amaro .02 .10
871 Alan Mills .02 .10
872 Matt Sinatro .02 .10
873 Eddie Zosky .02 .10
874 Pete Incaviglia .02 .10
875 Tom Candiotti .02 .10
876 Bob Patterson .02 .10
877 Neal Heaton .02 .10
878 Terrel Hansen RC .02 .10
879 Dave Eiland .02 .10
880 Von Hayes .02 .10
881 Tim Scott .02 .10
882 Otis Nixon .02 .10
883 Herm Winningham .02 .10
884 Dion James .02 .10
885 Dave Wainhouse .02 .10
886 Frank DiPino .02 .10
887 Dennis Cook .02 .10
888 Jose Mesa .02 .10
889 Mark Leiter .02 .10
890 Willie Randolph .05 .15
891 Craig Colbert .02 .10
892 Dwayne Henry .02 .10
893 Jim Lindeman .02 .10
894 Charlie Hough .05 .15
895 Gil Heredia RC .05 .15
896 Scott Champarino .02 .10
897 Lance Blankenship .02 .10
898 Checklist 601-700 .02 .10
899 Checklist 701-800 .02 .10
900 Checklist 801-900 .02 .10

1992 Stadium Club First Draft Picks

This three-card standard-size set, featuring Major League Baseball's Number 1 draft pick for 1990, 1991, and 1992, was randomly inserted into 1992 Stadium Club Series III packs at an approximate rate of 1:72. One card also was mailed to each member of Topps Stadium Club.

RANDOM INSERTS IN SER.3 PACKS
ONE CARD SENT TO EACH ST.CLUB MEMBER
1 Chipper Jones 2.00 5.00
2 Brien Taylor .75 2.00
3 Phil Nevin .75 2.00

1992 Stadium Club Master Photos

In the first package of materials sent to 1992 Topps Stadium Club members, along with an 11-card boxed set, members received a randomly chosen "Master Photo" printed on (approximately) 5" by 7" white card stock to demonstrate how the photos are cropped to create a borderless design. Each master photo has the Topps Stadium Club logo and the words "Master Photo" above a gold foil picture frame enclosing the color player photo. The backs are blank. The cards are unnumbered and checklisted below alphabetically. Master photos were also available through a special promotion at Walmart as an insert one-per-box in specially marked wax boxes of regular Topps Stadium Club cards.

COMPLETE SET (15) 8.00 20.00
1 Wade Boggs .50 1.25
2 Barry Bonds .75 2.00
3 Jose Canseco .50 1.25
4 Will Clark .40 1.00
5 Cecil Fielder .20 .50
6 Dwight Gooden .20 .50
7 Ken Griffey Jr. 1.25 3.00
8 Rickey Henderson .60 1.50
9 Lance Johnson .08 .25
10 Cal Ripken 2.00 5.00
11 Nolan Ryan 2.00 5.00
12 Deion Sanders .40 1.00
13 Darryl Strawberry .20 .50
14 Danny Tartabull .08 .25
15 Frank Thomas .60 1.50

1992 Stadium Club East Coast National

These cards were selected from the regular Stadium Club series and were printed for the Gloria Rothstein's East Coast National Convention. The fronts feature borderless color player photos with the East Coast National Convention logo printed in gold foil in a top corner while the backs display a mini reprint of the player's rookie card and "BARS" (Baseball Analysis and Reporting System) statistics. The cards are checklisted below according to their numbers in the regular series.

COMPLETE SET (100) 100.00 200.00
601 Chuck Knoblauch MC 2.00 5.00
602 Doc Gooden MC .75 2.00
603 Ken Griffey Jr. MC 12.50 30.00
604 Barry Bonds MC 8.00 20.00
605 Nolan Ryan MC 20.00 50.00
606 Jeff Bagwell MC 6.00 15.00
607 Robin Yount MC 3.00 8.00
608 Bobby Bonilla MC .40 1.00
609 George Brett MC 10.00 25.00
610 Howard Johnson MC .40 1.00
611 Esteban Beltre .40 1.00
612 Mike Christopher .40 1.00
613 Troy Afenir .40 1.00
619 Kevin McReynolds .40 1.00
620 Barry Bonds 8.00 20.00
622 Joe Magrane .40 1.00
623 Mark Parent .40 1.00
626 Steve Wilson .40 1.00
629 Rico Rossy .40 1.00
631 Clay Parker .40 1.00
633 Jeff McKnight .40 1.00
637 Vince Horsman .40 1.00
638 Eric King .40 1.00
639 Joe Boever .40 1.00
641 Arthur Rhodes .40 1.00
647 Kevin Campbell .40 1.00
653 Mike Jackson .40 1.00
661 Randy Tomlin .40 1.00
665 Greg Maddux 12.50 30.00
668 Brad Arnsberg .40 1.00
671 Barry Jones .40 1.00
672 Bill Landrum .40 1.00
673 Greg Swindell .40 1.00
676 Bill Pulsipher .40 1.00
679 Patrick Lennon .40 1.00
681 John Briscoe .40 1.00
684 Phil Stephenson .40 1.00
685 Ron Darling .40 1.00
686 Bryan Hickerson .40 1.00
688 Kirk McCaskill .40 1.00
689 Rich Amaral .40 1.00
692 Doug Davis .40 1.00
693 John Farrell .40 1.00
700 Rick Sutcliffe .75 2.00
704 Rene Gonzalez .40 1.00
713 Rudy Seanez .40 1.00
714 Jim Bullinger .40 1.00
716 Jeff Branson .40 1.00
717 Andy Ashby .40 1.00
725 Andy Stankiewicz .40 1.00
733 Milt Hill .40 1.00
739 Ron Robinson .40 1.00
742 Butch Henry .40 1.00
747 Chris James .40 1.00
749 Dennis Rasmussen .40 1.00
753 Dave Rohde .40 1.00
757 Pat Listach .40 1.00
758 Bill Wegman .40 1.00
763 Armando Reynoso .40 1.00
765 Kevin Mitchell .40 1.00
766 Gary Sheffield 3.00 8.00
769 Rick Parker .40 1.00
771 Jeff Ballard .40 1.00
772 Cory Snyder .40 1.00
774 Jose Gonzalez .40 1.00
775 Juan Guerrero .40 1.00
776 Ed Nunez .40 1.00
778 Terry Leach .40 1.00
782 Joe Slusarski .40 1.00
784 Kirk Gibson .75 2.00
788 Kim Batiste .40 1.00
802 Archi Cianfrocco .40 1.00
806 Kirk Dressendorfer .40 1.00
807 Zane Smith .40 1.00
814 Dave Fleming .40 1.00
815 Chris Gwynn .40 1.00
817 Mark Dewey .40 1.00
819 Tom Henke .75 2.00
822 Tim Sherrill .40 1.00
826 Steve Foster .40 1.00
831 John Wehner .40 1.00
832 Scott Garrelts .40 1.00
840 George Bell .40 1.00
841 Dave Gallagher .40 1.00
846 John Russell .40 1.00
847 Eric Hillman .40 1.00
852 Mike Walkden .40 1.00
855 Bill Swift .40 1.00
864 Derek Lilliquist .40 1.00
876 Bob Patterson .40 1.00
878 Terrel Hansen .40 1.00
881 Tim Scott .40 1.00
886 Frank DiPino .40 1.00
891 Craig Colbert .40 1.00
892 Dwayne Henry .40 1.00
893 Jim Lindeman .40 1.00
895 Gil Heredia .40 1.00
898 Checklist .40 1.00
899 Checklist .40 1.00
900 Checklist .40 1.00

1992 Stadium Club Members Only

This 50-card standard-size set was sent to 1992 Stadium Club members in four installments. In addition to the Stadium Club cards, the first installment included one "Top Draft Picks of the '90s" card (as a bonus) and a randomly chosen "Master Photo" printed on 5" by 7" white card stock. The third and fourth installments included hockey and football players in addition to baseball players. The cards feature full-bleed glossy color player photos. The fronts of the regular cards have the words "Members Only" printed in gold foil at the bottom along with the player's name and the Stadium Club logo. The backs feature a stadium scene with the scoreboard displaying, in yellow neon, a career highlight. The cards are unnumbered and checklisted below alphabetically, with the two-player cards listed at the end.

COMPLETE SET (50) 12.00 30.00
1 Carlos Baerga .07 .20
2 Wade Boggs .20 .50
3 Barry Bonds .30 .75
4 Bret Boone .07 .20
5 Pat Borders .07 .20
6 George Brett .40 1.00
7 George Brett .40 1.00
8 Jim Bullinger .07 .20
9 Gary Carter .15 .40
10 Andujar Cedeno .07 .20
11 Roger Clemens .50 1.25
Matt Young
12 Dennis Eckersley .15 .40
13 Dennis Eckersley .15 .40
14 Dave Eiland .07 .20
15 Ken Griffey Jr. 1.50 4.00
16 Kevin Gross .07 .20
17 Bo Jackson .20 .50
18 Eric Karros .07 .20
19 Pat Listach .07 .20
20 Greg Maddux .75 2.00
21 Mickey Morandini .07 .20
22 Jack Morris .15 .40
23 Eddie Murray .20 .50
24 Eddie Murray .20 .50
25 Bip Roberts .07 .20
26 Nolan Ryan/27 Seasons 1.00 2.50
27 Nolan Ryan/1993 Seasons His Finale 1.00 2.50
28 Gary Sheffield .15 .40
Dwight Gooden
29 Gary Sheffield .15 .40
Fred McGriff
30 Lee Smith .15 .40
31 Ozzie Smith/(2,000th Hit) .50 1.25
32 Ozzie Smith/(7,000th Career Assist) .50 1.25
33 Ozzie Smith .50 1.25
34 Bobby Thigpen .07 .20
35 Dave Winfield .20 .50
36 Robin Yount .20 .50

1992 Stadium Club National Convention

These cards were selected from the regular Stadium Club series and were printed for the National Convention in Atlanta. The fronts feature borderless color player photos with the National Convention logo printed in gold foil in a top corner while the backs display a mini reprint of the player's rookie card and "BARS" (Baseball Analysis and Reporting System) statistics. The cards are checklisted below according to their numbers in the regular series.

COMPLETE SET (100) 75.00 150.00
616 Doug Jones .75 2.00
617 Alvin Davis .40 1.00
618 Craig Lefferts .40 1.00
621 Turner Ward .40 1.00
625 John Smiley .40 1.00
627 Mike Gallego .40 1.00
630 Royce Clayton .40 1.00
634 Jack Daugherty .40 1.00
635 Steve Sax .40 1.00
636 Joe Hesketh .40 1.00

643 Rick Wilkins .40 1.00
644 Scott Scudder .40 1.00
645 Bip Roberts .40 1.00
650 Kurt Stillwell .40 1.00
652 Andres Galarraga 2.00 5.00
657 Jeff Reardon .75 2.00
660 Eric Davis .75 2.00
662 Tom Edens .40 1.00
675 Greg Olson .40 1.00
678 Mark Carreon .40 1.00
680 Ozzie Smith 25.00 60.00
682 Matt Young .40 1.00
690 Danny Tartabull .40 1.00
691 Donald Harris .40 1.00
695 Kenny Lofton 3.00 8.00
697 Rosario Rodriguez .40 1.00
701 Scott Bankhead .40 1.00
705 Rick Cerone .40 1.00
706 Tony Pena .40 1.00
709 Junior Noboa .40 1.00
710 Wally Joyner .75 2.00
711 Charlie Hayes .40 1.00
712 Rich Rodriguez .40 1.00
721 David Wells 1.25 3.00
723 Dave Martinez .40 1.00
726 Rick Aguilera .75 2.00
727 Junior Ortiz .40 1.00
729 Don Robinson .40 1.00
730 Ron Gant .75 2.00
731 Paul Assenmacher .40 1.00
732 Mark Gardiner .40 1.00
735 Ken Hill .40 1.00
736 Xavier Hernandez .40 1.00
737 Gregg Jefferies .40 1.00
740 Sandy Alomar .40 1.00
741 Mike Stanley .40 1.00
744 Brian Drahman .40 1.00
746 Bob Walk .40 1.00
751 Chris Hammond .40 1.00
759 John Wetteland .75 2.00
760 Phil Plantier .40 1.00
761 Wilson Alvarez .75 2.00
773 Dennis Boucher .40 1.00
777 Scott Ruskin .40 1.00
779 Carl Willis .40 1.00
783 David Segui .40 1.00
786 Keith Miller .40 1.00
790 Eddie Taubensee .40 1.00
791 Jack Armstrong .40 1.00
792 Scott Fletcher .40 1.00
793 Steve Farr .40 1.00
794 Dan Pasqua .40 1.00
797 Francisco Cabrera .40 1.00
798 Mike Perez .40 1.00
801 Danny Gladden .40 1.00
803 Monty Fariss .40 1.00
804 Roger McDowell .40 1.00
805 Randy Myers .75 2.00
808 Glenn Davis .40 1.00
809 Torey Lovullo .40 1.00
816 Jody Reed .40 1.00
825 Tony Gwynn 10.00 25.00
827 Steve Howe .40 1.00
828 Brook Jacoby .40 1.00
829 Rodney McCray .40 1.00
830 Chuck Knoblauch 3.00 8.00
835 Juan Bell .40 1.00
836 Lance Dickson .40 1.00
837 Darryl Kile .40 1.00
842 Tim Belcher .40 1.00
843 Jeff Shaw .40 1.00
844 Mike Fitzgerald .40 1.00
845 Gary Carter 5.00 12.00
850 Alan Trammell 1.25 3.00
851 Rex Hudler .75 2.00
856 Damon Berryhill .40 1.00
857 Mark Eichhorn .40 1.00
858 Hector Villanueva .40 1.00
860 Denny Martinez .75 2.00
865 Reggie Sanders .75 2.00
869 Melido Perez .40 1.00
874 Pete Incaviglia .40 1.00
875 Tom Candiotti .40 1.00
877 Neal Heaton .40 1.00
879 Dave Eiland .40 1.00
882 Otis Nixon .40 1.00
883 Herm Winningham .40 1.00
884 Dion James .40 1.00
887 Dennis Cook .40 1.00
894 Charlie Hough .75 2.00

1993 Stadium Club Murphy

This 200-card boxed set features 1992 All-Star Game cards, 1992 Team USA cards, and 1992 Championship and World Series cards. Topps actually refers to this set as a 1992 issue, but the set was released in 1993. This set is housed in a replica of San Diego's Jack Murphy Stadium, site of the 1992 All-Star Game. Production was limited to 8,000 cases, with 16 boxes per case. The set includes 100 Draft Pick cards, 56 All-Star cards, 25 Team USA cards, and 19 cards commemorating the 1992 National and American League Championship Series and the World Series. Notable Rookie Cards in this set include Derek Jeter, Jason Kendall, Shannon Stewart and Preston Wilson. A second year Team USA Nomar Garciaparra is featured in this set as well.

COMP.FACT.SET (212) 75.00 150.00
COMPLETE SET (200) 60.00 120.00
COMMON CARD (1-200) .05 .15
COMMON RC .05 .15
STATED PRINT RUN 128,000 SETS
1 Dave Winfield WS .05 .15
2 Juan Guzman AS .05 .15
3 Tony Gwynn AS .40 1.00
4 Chris Roberts USA .05 .15
5 Benny Santiago .10 .30
6 Sherard Clinkscales RC .05 .15
7 Jon Nunnally RC .20 .50
8 Chuck Knoblauch .10 .30
9 Bob Wolcott RC .05 .15
10 Steve Rodriguez USA .05 .15
11 Mark Williams RC .05 .15
12 Danny Clyburn RC .05 .15
13 Darren Dreifort USA .05 .15
14 Andy Van Slyke .20 .50
15 Wade Boggs AS .20 .50
16 Scott Patton RC .05 .15
17 Gary Sheffield AS .10 .30
18 Ron Villone USA .05 .15
19 Roberto Alomar ALCS .20 .50
20 Marc Valdes USA .05 .15
21 Daron Kirkreit USA .05 .15
22 Jeff Granger USA .05 .15
23 Levon Largusa RC .05 .15
24 Jimmy Key .10 .30
25 Kevin Pearson RC .05 .15
26 Michael Moore RC .05 .15
27 Preston Wilson RC .60 1.50
28 Kirby Puckett AS .30 .75
29 Tim Crabtree RC .05 .15
30 Bip Roberts .05 .15
31 Kelly Gruber .05 .15
32 Tony Fernandez .05 .15
33 Jason Angel RC .05 .15
34 Calvin Murray USA .05 .15
35 Chad McConnell .05 .15
36 Jason Moler USA .05 .15
37 Mark Lemke .05 .15
38 Tom Knauss RC .05 .15
39 Larry Mitchell RC .05 .15
40 Doug Mirabelli RC .20 .50
41 Everett Stull RC .05 .15
42 Chris Wimmer USA .05 .15
43 Dan Serafini RC .05 .15
44 Ryne Sandberg AS .50 1.25
45 Steve.Lyons RC .05 .15
46 Ryan Freeburg RC .05 .15
47 Ruben Sierra .10 .30
48 David Mysel RC .05 .15
49 Joe Hamilton RC .05 .15
50 Steve Rodriguez .05 .15
51 Tim Wakefield .30 .75
52 Scott Gentile RC .05 .15
53 Doug Jones .05 .15
54 Willie Brown RC .05 .15
55 Chad Mottola RC .20 .50
56 Ken Griffey Jr. AS .60 1.50
57 Jon Lieber RC 1.00 2.50
58 Dennis Martinez .10 .30
59 Joe Petcka RC .05 .15
60 Benji Simonton RC .05 .15
61 Brett Backlund RC .05 .15
62 Damon Berryhill .05 .15
63 Juan Guzman ALCS .05 .15
64 Doug Hecker RC .05 .15
65 Jamie Arnold RC .05 .15
66 Bob Tewksbury .05 .15
67 Tim Leger RC .05 .15
68 Todd Etler RC .05 .15
69 Lloyd McClendon .05 .15
70 Kurt Ehmann RC .05 .15
71 Rick Magdaleno RC .05 .15
72 Tom Pagnozzi .05 .15
73 Jeffrey Hammonds USA .05 .15
74 Joe Carter AS .10 .30
75 Chris Holt RC .10 .30
76 Charles Johnson USA .10 .30
77 Bob Walk .05 .15
78 Fred McGriff AS .20 .50
79 Tom Evans RC .05 .15
80 Scott Klingenbeck RC .05 .15
81 Chad McConnell USA .05 .15
82 Chris Eddy RC .05 .15
83 Phil Nevin USA .10 .30
84 John Kruk .10 .30
85 Tony Sheffield RC .05 .15
86 John Smoltz .20 .50
87 Trevor Humphry RC .05 .15
88 Charles Nagy .05 .15
89 Sean Runyan RC .05 .15
90 Mike Gulan RC .05 .15
91 Darren Daulton .10 .30
92 Otis Nixon .05 .15
93 Nomar Garciaparra USA 2.00 5.00
94 Larry Walker AS .10 .30
95 Hut Smith RC .05 .15
96 Rick Helling USA .05 .15
97 Roger Clemens AS .60 1.50
98 Ron Gant .10 .30
99 Kenny Felder RC .05 .15
100 Steve Murphy RC .05 .15
101 Mike Smith RC .05 .15
102 Terry Pendleton .10 .30
103 Tim Davis USA .05 .15
104 Jeff Patzke RC .05 .15
105 Craig Wilson USA .05 .15
106 Tom Glavine AS .20 .50
107 Mark Langston .05 .15
108 Mark Thompson RC .05 .15
109 Eric Owens RC .05 .15
110 Keith Johnson RC .05 .15
111 Robin Ventura AS .10 .30
112 Ed Sprague .05 .15
113 Jeff Schmidt RC .05 .15
114 Don Wengert RC .05 .15
115 Craig Biggio .20 .50
116 Kenny Carlyle RC .05 .15
117 Derek Jeter RC 40.00 100.00
118 Manuel Lee .05 .15
119 Jeff Haas RC .05 .15
120 Roger Bailey RC .05 .15
121 Sean Lowe RC .05 .15
122 Rick Aguilera .05 .15
123 Sandy Alomar Jr. .05 .15
124 Derek Wallace RC .05 .15
125 B.J.Wallace USA .05 .15
126 Greg Maddux AS .50 1.25
127 Tim Moore RC .05 .15
128 Lee Smith .10 .30
129 Todd Steverson RC .05 .15
130 Chris Widger RC .20 .50
131 Paul Molitor AS .10 .30
132 Chris Smith RC .05 .15
133 Chris Gomez RC .20 .50
134 Jimmy Baron RC .05 .15
135 John Smoltz .20 .50
136 Pat Borders .05 .15
137 Donnie Leshnock .05 .15
138 Gus Gandarillas RC .05 .15
139 Will Clark .20 .50
140 Ryan Luzinski RC .05 .15
141 Cal Ripken AS 1.00 2.50
142 B.J.Wallace .05 .15
143 Trey Beamon RC .20 .50
144 Norm Charlton .05 .15
145 Mike Mussina AS .20 .50
146 Billy Owens RC .05 .15
147 Ozzie Smith AS .50 1.25
148 Jason Kendall RC .60 1.50
149 Mike Matthews RC .05 .15
150 David Spykstra RC .05 .15
151 Benji Grigsby RC .05 .15
152 Sean Smith RC .05 .15
153 Mark McGwire AS .75 2.00
154 David Cone .10 .30
155 Shon Walker RC .05 .15
156 Jason Giambi USA .40 1.00
157 Jack McDowell AS .05 .15
158 Paxton Briley RC .05 .15
159 Edgar Martinez .20 .50
160 Brian Sackinsky RC .05 .15
161 Barry Bonds AS .75 2.00
162 Roberto Kelly .05 .15
163 Jeff Alkire .05 .15
164 Mike Sharperson .05 .15
165 Jamie Taylor RC .05 .15
166 John Saffer UER RC .05 .15
167 Jerry Browne .05 .15
168 Travis Fryman AS .10 .30
169 Brady Anderson .10 .30
170 Chris Roberts .05 .15
171 Lloyd Peever RC .05 .15
172 Francisco Cabrera .05 .15
173 Ramiro Martinez RC .05 .15
174 Jeff Alkire USA .05 .15
175 Ivan Rodriguez AS .20 .50
176 Kevin Brown .10 .30
177 Chad Roper RC .05 .15
178 Rod Henderson RC .05 .15
179 Dennis Eckersley .10 .30
180 Shannon Stewart RC .60 1.50
181 DeShawn Warren RC .05 .15
182 Lonnie Smith .05 .15
183 Willie Adams USA .05 .15
184 Jeff Montgomery .05 .15
185 Damon Hollins RC .20 .50
186 Byron Mathews RC .05 .15
187 Harold Baines .10 .30
188 Rick Greene USA .05 .15
189 Carlos Baerga AS .05 .15
190 Brandon Cromer RC .05 .15
191 Roberto Alomar AS .20 .50
192 Rich Ireland RC .05 .15
193 Steve Montgomery RC .05 .15
194 Brant Brown RC .05 .15
195 Ritchie Moody RC .05 .15
196 Michael Tucker USA .05 .15
197 Jason Varitek USA 2.00 5.00
198 David Manning RC .05 .15
199 Marquis Riley RC .05 .15
200 Jason Giambi .40 1.00

1993 Stadium Club Murphy Master Photos

COMPLETE SET (12) 2.00 5.00
ONE MP SET PER MURPHY FACTORY SET
STATED PRINT RUN 128,000 SETS
UNNUMBERED LARGE CARDS
1 Sandy Alomar Jr. AS .05 .15
2 Tom Glavine AS .20 .50
3 Ken Griffey Jr. AS .60 1.50
4 Tony Gwynn AS .40 1.00
5 Chuck Knoblauch AS .10 .30
6 Chad Mottola .20 .50
7 Kirby Puckett AS .30 .75
8 Chris Roberts USA .05 .15
9 Ryne Sandberg AS .50 1.25
10 Gary Sheffield AS .10 .30
11 Larry Walker AS .10 .30
12 Preston Wilson .75 2.00

1993 Stadium Club

The 1993 Stadium Club baseball set consists of 750 standard-size cards issued in three series of 300, 300, and 150 cards respectively. Each series closes with a Members Choice subset (291-300, 591-600, and 746-750.

COMPLETE SET (750) 12.50 30.00
COMPLETE SERIES 1 (300) 5.00 12.00
COMPLETE SERIES 2 (300) 5.00 12.00
COMPLETE SERIES 3 (150) 4.00 10.00
1 Pat Borders .05 .15
2 Greg Maddux .50 1.25
3 Daryl Boston .05 .15
4 Bob Ayrault .05 .15
5 Tony Phillips IF .05 .15
6 Damion Easley .05 .15
7 Kip Gross .05 .15
8 Jim Thome .20 .50
9 Tim Belcher .05 .15
10 Gary Wayne .05 .15
11 Sam Militello .05 .15
12 Mike Magnante .05 .15
13 Tim Wakefield .30 .75
14 Tim Hulett .05 .15
15 Rheal Cormier .05 .15
16 Juan Guerrero .05 .15
17 Rich Gossage .10 .30
18 Tim Laker RC .05 .15
19 Darrin Jackson .05 .15
20 Jack Clark .10 .30
21 Roberto Hernandez .05 .15
22 Dean Palmer .10 .30
23 Harold Reynolds .10 .30
24 Dan Plesac .05 .15
25 Brent Mayne .05 .15
26 Pat Hentgen .05 .15
27 Luis Sojo .05 .15
28 Ron Gant .10 .30
29 Paul Gibson .05 .15
30 Bip Roberts .05 .15
31 Mickey Tettleton .05 .15
32 Randy Velarde .05 .15
33 Brian McRae .05 .15
34 Wes Chamberlain .05 .15
35 Wayne Kirby .05 .15
36 Rey Sanchez .05 .15
37 Jesse Orosco .05 .15
38 Mike Stanton .05 .15
39 Royce Clayton .05 .15
40 Cal Ripken UER 1.00 2.50
41 John Dopson .05 .15
42 Gene Larkin .05 .15
43 Tim Raines .10 .30
44 Randy Myers .05 .15
45 Clay Parker .05 .15
46 Mike Scioscia .05 .15
47 Pete Incaviglia .05 .15
48 Todd Van Poppel .05 .15
49 Ray Lankford .10 .30
50 Eddie Murray .30 .75
51 Barry Bonds COR .75 2.00
51A Barry Bonds ERR .75 2.00
52 Gary Thurman .05 .15
53 Bob Wickman .05 .15
54 Joey Cora .05 .15
55 Kenny Rogers .10 .30
56 Mike Devereaux .05 .15
57 Kevin Seitzer .05 .15
58 Rafael Belliard .05 .15
59 David Wells .10 .30
60 Mark Clark .05 .15
61 Carlos Baerga .05 .15
62 Scott Brosius .10 .30
63 Jeff Grotewold .05 .15
64 Rick Wrona .05 .15
65 Kurt Knudsen .05 .15
66 Lloyd McClendon .05 .15
67 Omar Vizquel .20 .50
68 Jose Vizcaino .05 .15
69 Rob Ducey .05 .15
70 Casey Candaele .05 .15
71 Ramon Martinez .05 .15
72 Todd Hundley .05 .15
73 John Marzano .05 .15
74 Derek Parks .05 .15
75 Jack McDowell .05 .15
76 Tim Scott .05 .15
77 Mike Mussina .20 .50
78 Delino DeShields .05 .15
79 Chris Bosio .05 .15
80 Mike Bordick .05 .15
81 Rod Beck .05 .15
82 Ted Power .05 .15
83 John Kruk .10 .30
84 Steve Shifflett .05 .15
85 Danny Tartabull .05 .15
86 Mike Greenwell .05 .15
87 Jose Melendez .05 .15
88 Craig Wilson .05 .15
89 Melvin Nieves .05 .15
90 Ed Sprague .05 .15
91 Willie McGee .10 .30
92 Joe Orsulak .05 .15
93 Jeff King .05 .15
94 Dan Pasqua .05 .15
95 Brian Harper .05 .15
96 Joe Oliver .05 .15
97 Shane Turner .05 .15
98 Lenny Harris .05 .15
99 Jeff Parrett .05 .15
100 Luis Polonia .05 .15
101 Kent Bottenfield .05 .15
102 Albert Belle .10 .30
103 Mike Maddux .05 .15
104 Randy Tomlin .05 .15
105 Andy Stankiewicz .05 .15
106 Rico Rossy .05 .15
107 Joe Hesketh .05 .15
108 Dennis Powell .05 .15
109 Derrick May .05 .15
110 Pete Harnisch .05 .15
111 Kent Mercker .05 .15
112 Scott Fletcher .05 .15
113 Rex Hudler .05 .15
114 Chico Walker .05 .15
115 Rafael Palmeiro .20 .50
116 Mark Leiter .05 .15
117 Pedro Munoz .05 .15
118 Jim Bullinger .05 .15
119 Ivan Calderon .05 .15
120 Mike Timlin .05 .15
121 Rene Gonzales .05 .15
122 Greg Vaughn .05 .15
123 Mike Flanagan .05 .15
124 Mike Hartley .05 .15
125 Jeff Montgomery .05 .15
126 Mike Gallego .05 .15
127 Don Slaught .05 .15
128 Charlie O'Brien .05 .15
129 Jose Offerman .05 .15
Can be found with home town missing on back
130 Mark Wohlers .05 .15
131 Eric Fox .05 .15
132 Doug Strange .05 .15
133 Jeff Frye .05 .15
134 Wade Boggs UER .20 .50
Redundantly lists lefty breakdown
135 Lou Whitaker .10 .30
136 Craig Grebeck .05 .15
137 Rich Rodriguez .05 .15
138 Jay Bell .10 .30
139 Felix Fermin .05 .15
140 Dennis Martinez .10 .30
141 Eric Anthony .05 .15
142 Roberto Alomar .20 .50
143 Darren Lewis .05 .15
144 Mike Blowers .05 .15
145 Scott Bankhead .05 .15
146 Jeff Reboulet .05 .15
147 Frank Viola .10 .30
148 Bill Pecota .05 .15
149 Carlos Hernandez .05 .15
150 Bobby Witt .05 .15
151 Sid Bream .05 .15
152 Todd Zeile .05 .15
153 Dennis Cook .05 .15
154 Brian Bohanon .05 .15
155 Pat Kelly .05 .15
156 Milt Cuyler .05 .15
157 Juan Bell .05 .15
158 Randy Milligan .05 .15
159 Mark Gardner .05 .15
160 Pat Tabler .05 .15
161 Jeff Reardon .10 .30
162 Ken Patterson .05 .15
163 Bobby Bonilla .10 .30
164 Tony Pena .05 .15
165 Greg Swindell .05 .15
166 Kirk McCaskill .05 .15
167 Doug Drabek .05 .15
168 Franklin Stubbs .05 .15
169 Ron Tingley .05 .15
170 Willie Banks .05 .15
171 Sergio Valdez .05 .15
172 Mark Lemke .05 .15
173 Robin Yount .50 1.25
174 Storm Davis .05 .15
175 Dan Walters .05 .15
176 Steve Farr .05 .15
177 Curt Wilkerson .05 .15
178 Luis Alicea .05 .15
179 Russ Swan .05 .15
180 Mitch Williams .05 .15
181 Wilson Alvarez .05 .15
182 Carl Willis .05 .15
183 Craig Biggio .20 .50
184 Sean Berry .05 .15
185 Trevor Wilson .05 .15
186 Jeff Tackett .05 .15
187 Ellis Burks .10 .30
188 Jeff Branson .05 .15
189 Matt Nokes .05 .15
190 John Smiley .05 .15
191 Danny Gladden .05 .15
192 Mike Boddicker .05 .15
193 Roger Pavlik .05 .15
194 Paul Sorrento .05 .15
195 Vince Coleman .05 .15
196 Gary DiSarcina .05 .15
197 Rafael Bournigal .05 .15
198 Mike Schooler .05 .15
199 Scott Ruskin .05 .15
200 Frank Thomas .30 .75
201 Kyle Abbott .05 .15
202 Mike Perez .05 .15
203 Andre Dawson .10 .30
204 Bill Swift .05 .15
205 Alejandro Pena .05 .15
206 Dave Winfield .10 .30
207 Andujar Cedeno .05 .15
208 Terry Steinbach .05 .15
209 Chris Hammond .05 .15
210 Todd Burns .05 .15
211 Hipolito Pichardo .05 .15
212 John Kiely .05 .15
213 Tim Teufel .05 .15
214 Lee Guetterman .05 .15
215 Geronimo Pena .05 .15
216 Brett Butler .10 .30
217 Bryan Hickerson .05 .15
218 Rick Trlicek .05 .15
219 Lee Stevens .05 .15
220 Roger Clemens .60 1.50
221 Carlton Fisk .20 .50
222 Chili Davis .10 .30
223 Walt Terrell .05 .15
224 Jim Eisenreich .05 .15
225 Ricky Bones .05 .15
226 Henry Rodriguez .05 .15
227 Ken Hill .05 .15
228 Rick Wilkins .05 .15
229 Ricky Jordan .05 .15
230 Bernard Gilkey .05 .15
231 Tim Fortugno .05 .15
232 Geno Petralli .05 .15
233 Jose Rijo .05 .15
234 Jim Leyritz .05 .15
235 Kevin Campbell .05 .15
236 Al Osuna .05 .15
237 Pete Smith .05 .15
238 Pete Schourek .05 .15
239 Moises Alou .10 .30
240 Donn Pall .05 .15
241 Denny Neagle .10 .30
242 Dan Peltier .05 .15
243 Scott Scudder .05 .15
244 Juan Guzman .05 .15
245 Dave Burba .05 .15
246 Rick Sutcliffe .10 .30
247 Tony Fossas .05 .15
248 Mike Munoz .05 .15
249 Tim Salmon .20 .50
250 Rob Murphy .05 .15
251 Roger McDowell .05 .15
252 Lance Parrish .10 .30
253 Cliff Brantley .05 .15
254 Scott Leius .05 .15
255 Carlos Martinez .05 .15
256 Vince Horsman .05 .15
257 Oscar Azocar .05 .15
258 Craig Shipley .05 .15
259 Ben McDonald .05 .15
260 Jeff Brantley .05 .15
261 Damon Berryhill .05 .15
262 Joe Grahe .05 .15
263 Dave Hansen .05 .15
264 Rich Amaral .05 .15
265 Tim Pugh RC .05 .15
266 Dion James .05 .15
267 Frank Tanana .05 .15
268 Stan Belinda .05 .15
269 Jeff Kent .30 .75
270 Bruce Ruffin .05 .15
271 Xavier Hernandez .05 .15
272 Darrin Fletcher .05 .15
273 Tino Martinez .20 .50
274 Benny Santiago .10 .30
275 Scott Radinsky .05 .15
276 Mariano Duncan .05 .15
277 Kenny Lofton .10 .30
278 Dwight Smith .05 .15
279 Joe Carter .10 .30
280 Tim Jones .05 .15
281 Jeff Huson .05 .15
282 Phil Plantier .05 .15
283 Kirby Puckett .30 .75
284 Johnny Guzman .05 .15
285 Mike Morgan .05 .15
286 Chris Sabo .05 .15
287 Matt Williams .10 .30
288 Checklist 1-100 .05 .15
289 Checklist 101-200 .05 .15
290 Checklist 201-300 .05 .15
291 Dennis Eckersley MC .10 .30
292 Eric Karros MC .05 .15
293 Pat Listach MC .05 .15
294 Andy Van Slyke MC .10 .30
295 Robin Ventura MC .05 .15
296 Tom Glavine MC .10 .30
297 Juan Gonzalez MC UER .05 .15
Misspelled Gonzales
298 Travis Fryman MC .05 .15
299 Larry Walker MC .10 .30
300 Gary Sheffield MC .05 .15
301 Chuck Finley .10 .30
302 Luis Gonzalez .10 .30
303 Darryl Hamilton .05 .15
304 Bien Figueroa .05 .15
305 Ron Darling .05 .15
306 Jonathan Hurst .05 .15
307 Mike Sharperson .05 .15
308 Mike Christopher .05 .15
309 Marvin Freeman .05 .15
310 Jay Buhner .10 .30
311 Butch Henry .05 .15
312 Greg W. Harris .05 .15
313 Darren Daulton .10 .30
314 Chuck Knoblauch .10 .30
315 Greg A. Harris .05 .15
316 John Franco .10 .30
317 John Wehner .05 .15
318 Donald Harris .05 .15
319 Benny Santiago .10 .30
320 Larry Walker .10 .30
321 Randy Knorr .05 .15
322 Ramon Martinez RC .05 .15
323 Mike Stanley .05 .15
324 Bill Wegman .05 .15
325 Tom Candiotti .05 .15
326 Glenn Davis .05 .15
327 Chuck Crim .05 .15
328 Scott Livingstone .05 .15
329 Eddie Taubensee .05 .15
330 George Bell .05 .15
331 Edgar Martinez .20 .50
332 Paul Assenmacher .05 .15
333 Steve Hosey .05 .15
334 Mo Vaughn .10 .30
335 Bret Saberhagen .10 .30
336 Mike Trombley .05 .15
337 Mark Lewis .05 .15
338 Terry Pendleton .10 .30
339 Dave Hollins .05 .15
340 Jeff Conine .10 .30
341 Bob Tewksbury .05 .15
342 Billy Ashley .05 .15
343 Zane Smith .05 .15
344 John Wetteland .10 .30
345 Chris Hoiles .05 .15
346 Frank Castillo .05 .15
347 Bruce Hurst .05 .15
348 Kevin McReynolds .05 .15
349 Dave Henderson .05 .15
350 Ryan Bowen .05 .15
351 Sid Fernandez .05 .15
352 Mark Whiten .05 .15
353 Nolan Ryan 1.25 3.00
354 Rick Aguilera .05 .15
355 Mark Langston .05 .15
356 Jack Morris .10 .30
357 Rob Deer .05 .15
358 Dave Fleming .05 .15
359 Lance Johnson .05 .15
360 Joe Millette .05 .15
361 Wil Cordero .05 .15
362 Chito Martinez .05 .15
363 Scott Servais .05 .15
364 Bernie Williams .20 .50
365 Pedro Martinez .60 1.50
366 Ryne Sandberg .50 1.25
367 Brad Ausmus .30 .75
368 Scott Cooper .05 .15
369 Rob Dibble .10 .30
370 Walt Weiss .05 .15
371 Mark Davis .05 .15
372 Orlando Merced .05 .15
373 Mike Jackson .05 .15
374 Kevin Appier .10 .30
375 Esteban Beltre .05 .15
376 Joe Slusarski .05 .15
377 William Suero .05 .15
378 Pete O'Brien .05 .15
379 Alan Embree .05 .15
380 Lenny Webster .05 .15
381 Eric Davis .10 .30
382 Duane Ward .05 .15
383 John Habyan .05 .15
384 Jeff Bagwell .20 .50
385 Ruben Amaro .05 .15
386 Julio Valera .05 .15
387 Robin Ventura .10 .30
388 Archi Cianfrocco .05 .15
389 Skeeter Barnes .05 .15
390 Tim Costo .05 .15
391 Luis Mercedes .05 .15
392 Jeremy Hernandez .05 .15
393 Shawon Dunston .05 .15
394 Andy Van Slyke .20 .50
395 Kevin Maas .05 .15
396 Kevin Brown .10 .30
397 J.T. Bruett .05 .15
398 Darryl Strawberry .10 .30
399 Tom Pagnozzi .05 .15
400 Sandy Alomar Jr. .05 .15
401 Keith Miller .05 .15
402 Rich DeLucia .05 .15
403 Shawn Abner .05 .15
404 Howard Johnson .05 .15
405 Mike Benjamin .05 .15
406 Roberto Mejia RC .05 .15
407 Mike Butcher .05 .15
408 Deion Sanders UER .20 .50
Braves on front and Yankees on back
409 Todd Stottlemyre .05 .15
410 Scott Kamieniecki .05 .15
411 Doug Jones .05 .15
412 John Burkett .05 .15
413 Lance Blankenship .05 .15
414 Jeff Parrett .05 .15
415 Barry Larkin .20 .50
416 Alan Trammell .10 .30
417 Mark Kiefer .05 .15
418 Gregg Olson .05 .15
419 Mark Grace .20 .50

420 Shane Mack .05 .15
421 Bob Walk .05 .15
422 Curt Schilling .10 .30
423 Erik Hanson .05 .15
424 George Brett .75 2.00
425 Reggie Jefferson .05 .15
426 Mark Portugal .05 .15
427 Ron Karkovice .05 .15
428 Matt Young .05 .15
429 Troy Neel .05 .15
430 Hector Fajardo .05 .15
431 Dave Righetti .10 .30
432 Pat Listach .05 .15
433 Jeff Innis .05 .15
434 Bob MacDonald .05 .15
435 Brian Jordan .10 .30
436 Jeff Blauser .05 .15
437 Mike Myers RC .05 .15
438 Frank Seminara .05 .15
439 Rusty Meacham .05 .15
440 Greg Briley .05 .15
441 Derek Lilliquist .05 .15
442 John Vander Wal .05 .15
443 Scott Erickson .05 .15
444 Bob Scanlan .05 .15
445 Todd Frohwirth .05 .15
446 Tom Goodwin .05 .15
447 William Pennyfeather .05 .15
448 Travis Fryman .10 .30
449 Mickey Morandini .05 .15
450 Greg Olson .05 .15
451 Trevor Hoffman .30 .75
452 Dave Magadan .05 .15
453 Shawn Jeter .05 .15
454 Andres Galarraga .10 .30
455 Ted Wood .05 .15
456 Freddie Benavides .05 .15
457 Junior Felix .05 .15
458 Alex Cole .05 .15
459 John Orton .05 .15
460 Eddie Zosky .05 .15
461 Dennis Eckersley .10 .30
462 Lee Smith .10 .30
463 John Smoltz .20 .50
464 Ken Caminiti .10 .30
465 Melido Perez .05 .15
466 Tom Marsh .05 .15
467 Jeff Nelson .05 .15
468 Jesse Levis .05 .15
469 Chris Nabholz .05 .15
470 Mike Macfarlane .05 .15
471 Reggie Sanders .10 .30
472 Chuck McElroy .05 .15
473 Kevin Gross .05 .15
474 Matt Whiteside RC .05 .15
475 Cal Eldred .05 .15
476 Dave Gallagher .05 .15
477 Len Dykstra .10 .30
478 Mark McGwire .75 2.00
479 David Segui .05 .15
480 Mike Henneman .05 .15
481 Bret Barberie .05 .15
482 Steve Sax .05 .15
483 Dave Valle .05 .15
484 Danny Darwin .05 .15
485 Devon White .10 .30
486 Eric Plunk .05 .15
487 Jim Gott .05 .15
488 Scooter Tucker .05 .15
489 Omar Olivares .05 .15
490 Greg Myers .05 .15
491 Brian Hunter .05 .15
492 Kevin Tapani .05 .15
493 Rich Monteleone .05 .15
494 Steve Buechele .05 .15
495 Bo Jackson .30 .75
496 Mike LaValliere .05 .15
497 Mark Leonard .05 .15
498 Daryl Boston .05 .15
499 Jose Canseco .20 .50
500 Brian Barnes .05 .15
501 Randy Johnson .30 .75
502 Tim McIntosh .05 .15
503 Cecil Fielder .10 .30
504 Derek Bell .05 .15
505 Kevin Koslofski .05 .15
506 Darren Holmes .05 .15
507 Brady Anderson .10 .30
508 John Valentin .05 .15
509 Jerry Browne .05 .15
510 Fred McGriff .20 .50
511 Pedro Astacio .05 .15
512 Gary Gaetti .10 .30
513 John Burke RC .05 .15
514 Dwight Gooden .10 .30
515 Thomas Howard .05 .15
516 Darrell Whitmore RC UER .05 .15
11 games played in 1992; should be 121
517 Ozzie Guillen .10 .30
518 Darryl Kile .10 .30
519 Rich Rowland .05 .15
520 Carlos Delgado .30 .75
521 Doug Henry .05 .15
522 Greg Colbrunn .05 .15
523 Tom Gordon .05 .15
524 Ivan Rodriguez .20 .50
525 Kent Hrbek .10 .30
526 Eric Young .05 .15
527 Rod Brewer .05 .15
528 Eric Karros .10 .30
529 Marquis Grissom .10 .30
530 Rico Brogna .05 .15
531 Sammy Sosa .30 .75
532 Bret Boone .10 .30
533 Luis Rivera .05 .15
534 Hal Morris .05 .15
535 Monty Fariss .05 .15
536 Leo Gomez .05 .15
537 Wally Joyner .10 .30
538 Tony Gwynn .40 1.00
539 Mike Williams .05 .15
540 Juan Gonzalez .10 .30
541 Ryan Klesko .10 .30
542 Ryan Thompson .05 .15
543 Chad Curtis .05 .15
544 Orel Hershiser .10 .30
545 Carlos Garcia .05 .15
546 Bob Welch .05 .15
547 Vinny Castilla .30 .75
548 Ozzie Smith .50 1.25
549 Luis Salazar .05 .15
550 Mark Guthrie .05 .15
551 Charles Nagy .05 .15
552 Alex Fernandez .05 .15
553 Mel Rojas .05 .15
554 Orestes Destrade .05 .15
555 Mark Gubicza .05 .15
556 Steve Finley .10 .30
557 Don Mattingly .75 2.00
558 Rickey Henderson .30 .75
559 Tommy Greene .05 .15
560 Arthur Rhodes .05 .15
561 Alfredo Griffin .05 .15
562 Will Clark .20 .50
563 Bob Zupcic .05 .15
564 Chuck Carr .05 .15
565 Henry Cotto .05 .15
566 Billy Spiers .05 .15
567 Jack Armstrong .05 .15
568 Kurt Stillwell .05 .15
569 David McCarty .05 .15
570 Joe Vitiello .05 .15
571 Gerald Williams .05 .15
572 Dale Murphy .20 .50
573 Scott Aldred .05 .15
574 Bill Gullickson .05 .15
575 Bobby Thigpen .05 .15
576 Glenallen Hill .05 .15
577 Dwayne Henry .05 .15
578 Calvin Jones .05 .15
579 Al Martin .05 .15
580 Ruben Sierra .10 .30
581 Andy Benes .05 .15
582 Anthony Young .05 .15
583 Shawn Boskie .05 .15
584 Scott Pose RC .05 .15
585 Mike Piazza 1.25 3.00
586 Donovan Osborne .05 .15
587 Jim Austin .05 .15
588 Checklist 301-400 .05 .15
589 Checklist 401-500 .05 .15
590 Checklist 501-600 .05 .15
591 Ken Griffey Jr. MC .40 1.00
592 Ivan Rodriguez MC .10 .30
593 Carlos Baerga MC .05 .15
594 Fred McGriff MC .10 .30
595 Mark McGwire MC .40 1.00
596 Roberto Alomar MC .10 .30
597 Kirby Puckett MC .20 .50
598 Marquis Grissom MC .05 .15
599 John Smoltz MC .10 .30
600 Ryne Sandberg MC .30 .75
601 Wade Boggs .20 .50
602 Jeff Reardon .10 .30
603 Billy Ripken .05 .15
604 Bryan Harvey .05 .15
605 Carlos Quintana .05 .15
606 Greg Hibbard .05 .15
607 Ellis Burks .10 .30
608 Greg Swindell .05 .15
609 Dave Winfield .10 .30
610 Charlie Hough .10 .30
611 Chili Davis .10 .30
612 Jody Reed .05 .15
613 Mark Williamson .05 .15
614 Phil Plantier .05 .15
615 Jim Abbott .20 .50
616 Dante Bichette .10 .30
617 Mark Eichhorn .05 .15
618 Gary Sheffield .10 .30
619 Richie Lewis RC .05 .15
620 Joe Girardi .05 .15
621 Jaime Navarro .05 .15
622 Willie Wilson .05 .15
623 Scott Fletcher .05 .15
624 Bud Black .05 .15
625 Tom Brunansky .05 .15
626 Steve Avery .05 .15
627 Paul Molitor .10 .30
628 Gregg Jefferies .05 .15
629 Dave Stewart .10 .30
630 Javier Lopez .20 .50
631 Greg Gagne .05 .15
632 Roberto Kelly .05 .15
633 Mike Fetters .05 .15
634 Ozzie Canseco .05 .15
635 Jeff Russell .05 .15
636 Pete Incaviglia .05 .15
637 Tom Henke .05 .15
638 Chipper Jones .30 .75
639 Jimmy Key .10 .30
640 Dave Martinez .05 .15
641 Dave Stieb .05 .15
642 Milt Thompson .05 .15
643 Alan Mills .05 .15
644 Tony Fernandez .05 .15
645 Randy Bush .05 .15
646 Joe Magrane .05 .15
647 Ivan Calderon .05 .15
648 Jose Guzman .05 .15
649 John Olerud .10 .30
650 Tom Glavine .20 .50
651 Julio Franco .10 .30
652 Armando Reynoso .05 .15
653 Felix Jose .05 .15
654 Ben Rivera .05 .15
655 Andre Dawson .10 .30
656 Mike Harkey .05 .15
657 Kevin Seitzer .05 .15
658 Lonnie Smith .05 .15
659 Norm Charlton .05 .15
660 David Justice .10 .30
661 Fernando Valenzuela .10 .30
662 Dan Wilson .10 .30
663 Mark Gardner .05 .15
664 Doug Dascenzo .05 .15
665 Greg Maddux .50 1.25
666 Harold Baines .10 .30
667 Randy Myers .05 .15
668 Harold Reynolds .10 .30
669 Candy Maldonado .05 .15
670 Al Leiter .10 .30
671 Jerald Clark .05 .15
672 Doug Drabek .05 .15
673 Kirk Gibson .10 .30
674 Steve Reed RC .05 .15
675 Mike Felder .05 .15
676 Ricky Gutierrez .05 .15
677 Spike Owen .05 .15
678 Otis Nixon .05 .15
679 Scott Sanderson .05 .15
680 Mark Carreon .05 .15
681 Troy Percival .20 .50
682 Kevin Stocker .05 .15
683 Jim Converse RC .05 .15
684 Barry Bonds .75 2.00
685 Greg Gohr .05 .15
686 Tim Wallach .05 .15
687 Matt Mieske .05 .15
688 Robby Thompson .05 .15
689 Brien Taylor .05 .15
690 Kirt Manwaring .05 .15
691 Mike Lansing RC .10 .30
692 Steve Decker .05 .15
693 Mike Moore .05 .15
694 Kevin Mitchell .05 .15
695 Phil Hiatt .05 .15
696 Tony Tarasco RC .05 .15
697 Benji Gil .05 .15
698 Jeff Juden .05 .15
699 Kevin Reimer .05 .15
700 Andy Ashby .05 .15
701 John Jaha .05 .15
702 Tim Bogar RC .05 .15
703 David Cone .10 .30
704 Willie Greene .05 .15
705 David Hulse RC .05 .15
706 Cris Carpenter .05 .15
707 Ken Griffey Jr. .60 1.50
708 Steve Bedrosian .05 .15
709 Dave Nilsson .05 .15
710 Paul Wagner .05 .15
711 B.J. Surhoff .10 .30
712 Rene Arocha RC .10 .30
713 Manuel Lee .05 .15
714 Brian Williams .05 .15
715 Sherman Obando RC .05 .15
716 Terry Mulholland .05 .15
717 Paul O'Neill .20 .50
718 David Nied .05 .15
719 J.T. Snow RC .20 .50
720 Nigel Wilson .05 .15
721 Mike Bielecki .05 .15
722 Kevin Young .10 .30
723 Charlie Leibrandt .05 .15
724 Frank Bolick .05 .15
725 Jon Shave RC .05 .15
726 Steve Cooke .05 .15
727 Domingo Martinez RC .05 .15
728 Todd Worrell .05 .15
729 Jose Lind .05 .15
730 Jim Tatum RC .05 .15
731 Mike Hampton .10 .30
732 Mike Draper .05 .15
733 Henry Mercedes .05 .15
734 John Johnstone RC .05 .15
735 Mitch Webster .05 .15
736 Russ Springer .05 .15
737 Rob Natal .05 .15
738 Steve Howe .05 .15
739 Darrell Sherman RC .05 .15
740 Pat Mahomes .05 .15
741 Alex Arias .05 .15
742 Damon Buford .05 .15
743 Charlie Hayes .05 .15
744 Guillermo Velasquez .05 .15
745 CL 601-750 UER .05 .15
650 Tom Glavine
746 Frank Thomas MC .20 .50
747 Barry Bonds MC .40 1.00
748 Roger Clemens MC .30 .75
749 Joe Carter MC .05 .15
750 Greg Maddux MC .30 .75

1993 Stadium Club First Day Issue

*STARS: 8X TO 20X BASIC CARDS
STATED ODDS 1:24 H/R, 1:15 JUMBO
BEWARE OF TRANSFERRED FDI LOGOS

1993 Stadium Club Members Only Parallel

COMPLETE FACT.SET (760) 75.00 150.00
COMMON CARD (1-750) .20 .50
*STARS: 2X TO 4X BASIC CARDS
*ROOKIES: 1.5X to 3X BASIC CARDS
MA1 Robin Yount 1.50 4.00
MA2 George Brett 3.00 8.00
MA3 David Nied .60 1.50
MA4 Nigel Wilson .60 1.50
MB1 W.Clark 3.00 8.00
M.McGwire
MB2 D.Gooden 1.50 4.00
D.Mattingly
MB3 R.Sandberg 2.00 5.00
F.Thomas
MB4 D.Strawberry 2.50 6.00
K.Griffey
MC1 David Nied .60 1.50
MC2 Charlie Hough .60 1.50

1993 Stadium Club Inserts

This 10-card set was randomly inserted in all series of Stadium Club packs, the first four in series 1, the second four in series 2 and the last two in series 3. The themes of the standard-size cards differ from series to series, but the basic design -- borderless color action shots on the fronts -- remains the same throughout. The series 1 and 3 cards are numbered on the back, the series 2 cards are unnumbered. No matter what series, all of these inserts were included one every 15 packs.

COMPLETE SET (10) 5.00 12.00
COMPLETE SERIES 1 (4) .75 2.00
COMPLETE SERIES 2 (4) 4.00 10.00
COMPLETE SERIES 3 (2) .20 .50
COMMON SER.1 CARD (A1-A4) .10 .30
COMMON SER.2 CARD (B1-B4) .10 .30
COMMON SER.3 CARD (C1-C2) .10 .30
A1-A4 SER.1 STATED ODDS 1:15
B1-B4 SER.2 STATED ODDS 1:15
C1-C2 SER.3 STATED ODDS 1:15
A1 Robin Yount 1.00 2.50
A2 George Brett 1.50 4.00
A3 David Nied .10 .30
A4 Nigel Wilson .10 .30
B1 M.McGwire 1.50 4.00
W.Clark
B2 D.Gooden 1.50 4.00
D.Mattingly
B3 F.Thomas .60 1.50
R.Sandberg
B4 K.Griffey Jr. 1.25 3.00
D.Strawberry
C1 David Nied .10 .30
C2 Charlie Hough .25 .60

1993 Stadium Club Master Photos

Each of the three Stadium Club series features Master Photos, uncropped versions of the regular Stadium Club cards. Each Master Photo is inlaid in a 5" by 7" white frame and bordered with a prismatic foil trim. The Master Photos were made available to the public in two ways. First, one in every 24 packs included a Master Photo winner card redeemable for a group of three Master Photos until Jan. 31, 1994. Second, each hobby box contained one Master Photo. The cards are unnumbered and checklisted below in alphabetical order within series I (1-12), II (13-24), and III (25-30). Two different versions of these master photos were issued, one with and one without the "Members Only" gold foil seal at the upper right corner. The "Members Only" Master Photos were only available with the direct-mail solicited 750-card Stadium Club Members Only set.

COMPLETE SET (30) 10.00 25.00
COMPLETE SERIES 1 (12) 2.50 6.00
COMPLETE SERIES 2 (12) 3.00 8.00
COMPLETE SERIES 3 (6) 4.00 10.00
STATED ODDS 1:24 HOB/RET, 1:15 JUM
THREE JUMBOS VIA MAIL PER WINNER CARD
ONE JUMBO PER HOBBY BOX
1 Carlos Baerga .08 .25
2 Delino DeShields .08 .25
3 Brian McRae .08 .25
4 Sam Militello .08 .25
5 Joe Oliver .08 .25
6 Kirby Puckett .50 1.25
7 Cal Ripken 1.50 4.00
8 Bip Roberts .08 .25
9 Mike Scioscia .08 .25
10 Rick Sutcliffe .20 .50
11 Danny Tartabull .08 .25
12 Tim Wakefield .50 1.25
13 George Brett 1.25 3.00
14 Jose Canseco .30 .75
15 Will Clark .30 .75
16 Travis Fryman .20 .50
17 Dwight Gooden .20 .50
18 Mark Grace .30 .75
19 Rickey Henderson .50 1.25
20 Mark McGwire 1.25 3.00
21 Nolan Ryan 2.00 5.00
22 Ruben Sierra .20 .50
23 Darryl Strawberry .20 .50
24 Larry Walker .20 .50
25 Barry Bonds 1.25 3.00
26 Ken Griffey Jr. 1.00 2.50
27 Greg Maddux .75 2.00
28 David Nied .08 .25
29 J.T.Snow .30 .75
30 Brien Taylor .08 .25

1993 Stadium Club Master Photos Members Only Parallel

*MEMBERS ONLY: .5X TO 1.2X BASIC

1993 Stadium Club Ultra-Pro

The ten cards in this set measure the standard size and were available singly as limited edition random inserts in the Topps Stadium Club Ultra-Pro Platinum collector pages refill packs (1-6) and individual semi-rigid card protector packs (7-10). In light of a marketing partnership with the Rembrandt Company, this ten-card set was produced by Stadium Club to mark the launch of a new accessory line of premium card storage accessory products. Reportedly no more than 150,000 sets were produced. Willie Mays is Barry Bonds' godfather.

COMPLETE SET (10) 8.00 20.00
1 Barry Bonds 1.00 2.50
Willie Mays
Bobby Bonds
2 Willie Mays 1.25 3.00
Leaning on bat
3 Bobby Bonds .40 1.00
Kneeling, leaning on bat
4 Barry Bonds .75 2.00
Bat extended
5 Barry Bonds .75 2.00
Bobby Bonds
6 Willie Mays 1.25 3.00
Squatting posture, glove in hand
7 Barry Bonds .75 2.00
Dressed in suit
8 Bobby Bonds .75 2.00
Willie Mays
9 Willie Mays 1.25 3.00
Kneeling, bat in right hand
10 Barry Bonds .75 2.00
Dressed in tuxedo

1993 Stadium Club Members Only

This 59-card standard-size set was mailed out to Stadium Club Members in four separate mailings. Each box contained several sports. The fronts have full-bleed color action player photos with the words "Members Only" printed in gold foil at the bottom along with the player's name and the Stadium Club logo. On a multi-colored background, the horizontal backs carry player information and a computer generated drawing of a baseball player. The cards are unnumbered and checklisted below alphabetically according to sport as follows: baseball (1-28), basketball (29-44), football (45-53), and hockey (54-59).

COMPLETE SET (59) 10.00 20.00
1 Jim Abbott .08 .25
2 Barry Bonds .30 .75
3 Chris Bosio .07 .20
4 George Brett .50 1.25
5 Jay Buhner .08 .25
6 Joe Carter .08 .25
Belts 3 for Fifth
Time in Career
7 Joe Carter .08 .25
Carter's Dramatics
Give Jays Series C
8 Carlton Fisk .15 .40
9 Travis Fryman .07 .20
10 Mark Grace .08 .25
11 Ken Griffey Jr. 1.50 4.00
12 Darryl Kile .07 .20
13 Darren Lewis .07 .20
14 Greg Maddux .75 2.00
15 Jack McDowell .07 .20
16 Paul Molitor .25 .60
17 Eddie Murray .25 .60
18 Mike Piazza 1.25 3.00
Home Run Record
for Rookie Catchers
19 Mike Piazza 1.25 3.00
NL Rookie Honors
20 Kirby Puckett .50 1.25
21 Jeff Reardon .08 .25
22 Tim Salmon .08 .25
23 Curt Schilling .25 .60
24 Lee Smith .08 .25
25 Dave Stewart .08 .25
26 Frank Thomas 1.00 2.50
27 Mark Whiten .07 .20
28 Dave Winfield .25 .60

1994 Stadium Club Pre-Production

COMPLETE SET (9) 2.50 6.00
6 Al Martin .20 .50
15 Junior Ortiz .20 .50
36 Tim Salmon .50 1.25
56 Jerry Spradlin .20 .50
122 Tom Pagnozzi .20 .50
123 Ron Gant .30 .75
125 Dennis Eckersley .60 1.50
135 Jose Lind .20 .50
238 Barry Bonds 1.00 2.50

1994 Stadium Club

The 720 standard-size cards comprising this set were issued two series of 270 and a third series of 180. There are a number of subsets including Home Run Club (258-268), Tale of Two Players (525/526), Division Leaders (527-532), Quick Starts (533-538), Career Contributors (541-543), Rookie Rocker (626-630), Rookie Rocket (631-634) and Fantastic Finishes (714-719). Rookie Cards include Jeff Cirillo and Chan Ho Park.

COMPLETE SET (720) 25.00 60.00
COMPLETE SERIES 1 (270) 8.00 20.00
COMPLETE SERIES 2 (270) 8.00 20.00
COMPLETE SERIES 3 (180) 6.00 15.00
SUBSET CARDS HALF VALUE OF BASE CARDS
1 Robin Yount .50 1.25
2 Rick Wilkins .05 .15
3 Steve Scarsone .05 .15
4 Gary Sheffield .10 .30
5 George Brett .75 2.00
6 Al Martin .05 .15
7 Joe Oliver .05 .15
8 Stan Belinda .05 .15
9 Denny Hocking .05 .15
10 Roberto Alomar .20 .50
11 Luis Polonia .05 .15
12 Scott Hemond .05 .15
13 Jody Reed .05 .15
14 Mel Rojas .05 .15
15 Junior Ortiz .05 .15
16 Harold Baines .10 .30
17 Brad Pennington .05 .15
18 Jay Bell .10 .30
19 Tom Henke .05 .15
20 Jeff Branson .05 .15
21 Roberto Mejia .05 .15
22 Pedro Munoz .05 .15
23 Matt Nokes .05 .15
24 Jack McDowell .05 .15
25 Cecil Fielder .10 .30
26 Tony Fossas .05 .15
27 Jim Eisenreich .05 .15
28 Anthony Young .05 .15
29 Chuck Carr .05 .15
30 Jeff Treadway .05 .15
31 Chris Nabholz .05 .15
32 Tom Candiotti .05 .15
33 Mike Maddux .05 .15
34 Nolan Ryan 1.25 3.00
35 Luis Gonzalez .10 .30
36 Tim Salmon .20 .50
37 Mark Whiten .05 .15
38 Roger McDowell .05 .15
39 Royce Clayton .05 .15
40 Troy Neel .05 .15
41 Mike Harkey .05 .15
42 Darrin Fletcher .05 .15
43 Wayne Kirby .05 .15
44 Rich Amaral .05 .15
45 Robb Nen UER .10 .30
46 Tim Teufel .05 .15
47 Steve Cooke .05 .15
48 Jeff McNeely .05 .15
49 Jeff Montgomery .05 .15
50 Skeeter Barnes .05 .15
51 Scott Stahoviak .05 .15
52 Pat Kelly .05 .15
53 Brady Anderson .10 .30
54 Mariano Duncan .05 .15
55 Brian Bohanon .05 .15
56 Jerry Spradlin .05 .15
57 Ron Karkovice .05 .15
58 Jeff Gardner .05 .15
59 Bobby Bonilla .10 .30
60 Tino Martinez .20 .50
61 Todd Benzinger .05 .15
62 Steve Trachsel .05 .15
63 Brian Jordan .10 .30
64 Steve Bedrosian .05 .15
65 Brent Gates .05 .15
66 Shawn Green .30 .75
67 Sean Berry .05 .15
68 Joe Klink .05 .15
69 Fernando Valenzuela .10 .30
70 Andy Tomberlin .05 .15
71 Tony Pena .05 .15
72 Eric Young .05 .15
73 Chris Gomez .05 .15
74 Paul O'Neill .20 .50
75 Ricky Gutierrez .05 .15
76 Brad Holman .05 .15
77 Lance Painter .05 .15
78 Mike Butcher .05 .15
79 Sid Bream .05 .15
80 Sammy Sosa .30 .75
81 Felix Fermin .05 .15
82 Todd Hundley .05 .15
83 Kevin Higgins .05 .15
84 Todd Pratt .05 .15
85 Ken Griffey Jr. .60 1.50
86 John O'Donoghue .05 .15
87 Rick Renteria .05 .15
88 John Burkett .05 .15
89 Jose Vizcaino .05 .15
90 Kevin Seitzer .05 .15
91 Bobby Witt .05 .15
92 Chris Turner .05 .15
93 Omar Vizquel .20 .50
94 David Justice .10 .30
95 David Segui .05 .15
96 Dave Hollins .05 .15
97 Doug Strange .05 .15
98 Jerald Clark .05 .15
99 Mike Moore .05 .15
100 Joey Cora .05 .15
101 Scott Kamieniecki .05 .15
102 Andy Benes .05 .15
103 Chris Bosio .05 .15
104 Rey Sanchez .05 .15
105 John Jaha .05 .15
106 Otis Nixon .05 .15
107 Rickey Henderson .30 .75
108 Jeff Bagwell .20 .50
109 Gregg Jefferies .05 .15
110 Alomar .10 .30
Molitor
Olerud
111 Gant .10 .30
Justice
McGriff
112 Gonzalez .20 .50
Palmeiro
Palmer
113 Greg Swindell .05 .15
114 Bill Haselman .05 .15
115 Phil Plantier .05 .15
116 Ivan Rodriguez .20 .50
117 Kevin Tapani .05 .15
118 Mike LaValliere .05 .15
119 Tim Costo .05 .15
120 Mickey Morandini .05 .15
121 Brett Butler .10 .30
122 Tom Pagnozzi .05 .15
123 Ron Gant .10 .30
124 Damion Easley .05 .15
125 Dennis Eckersley .10 .30
126 Matt Mieske .05 .15
127 Cliff Floyd .10 .30
128 Julian Tavarez RC .10 .30
129 Arthur Rhodes .05 .15
130 Dave West .05 .15
131 Tim Naehring .05 .15
132 Freddie Benavides .05 .15
133 Paul Assenmacher .05 .15
134 David McCarty .05 .15
135 Jose Lind .05 .15
136 Reggie Sanders .10 .30
137 Don Slaught .05 .15
138 Andujar Cedeno .05 .15
139 Rob Deer .05 .15
140 Mike Piazza .60 1.50
141 Moises Alou .10 .30
142 Tom Foley .05 .15
143 Benito Santiago .10 .30
144 Sandy Alomar Jr. .05 .15
145 Carlos Hernandez .05 .15
146 Luis Alicea .05 .15
147 Tom Lampkin .05 .15
148 Ryan Klesko .10 .30
149 Juan Guzman .05 .15
150 Scott Servais .05 .15
151 Tony Gwynn .40 1.00

152 Tim Wakefield .20 .50
153 David Nied .05 .15
154 Chris Haney .05 .15
155 Danny Bautista .05 .15
156 Randy Velarde .05 .15
157 Darrin Jackson .05 .15
158 J.R. Phillips .05 .15
159 Greg Gagne .05 .15
160 Luis Aquino .05 .15
161 John Vander Wal .05 .15
162 Randy Myers .05 .15
163 Ted Power .05 .15
164 Scott Brosius .10 .30
165 Len Dykstra .10 .30
166 Jacob Brumfield .05 .15
167 Bo Jackson .30 .75
168 Eddie Taubensee .05 .15
169 Carlos Baerga .05 .15
170 Tim Bogar .05 .15
171 Jose Canseco .20 .50
172 Greg Blosser UER/(Gregg on front) .05 .15
173 Chili Davis .10 .30
174 Randy Knorr .05 .15
175 Mike Perez .05 .15
176 Henry Rodriguez .05 .15
177 Brian Turang RC .05 .15
178 Roger Pavlik .05 .15
179 Aaron Sele .05 .15
180 F.McGriff .20 .50
G.Sheffield
181 J.T.Snow .20 .50
T.Salmon
182 Roberto Hernandez .05 .15
183 Jeff Reboulet .05 .15
184 John Doherty .05 .15
185 Danny Sheaffer .05 .15
186 Bip Roberts .05 .15
187 Dennis Martinez .10 .30
188 Darryl Hamilton .05 .15
189 Eduardo Perez .05 .15
190 Pete Harnisch .05 .15
191 Rich Gossage .10 .30
192 Mickey Tettleton .05 .15
193 Lenny Webster .05 .15
194 Lance Johnson .05 .15
195 Don Mattingly .75 2.00
196 Gregg Olson .05 .15
197 Mark Gubicza .05 .15
198 Scott Fletcher .05 .15
199 Jon Shave .05 .15
200 Tim Mauser .05 .15
201 Jeromy Burnitz .10 .30
202 Rob Dibble .10 .30
203 Will Clark .20 .50
204 Steve Buechele .05 .15
205 Brian Williams .05 .15
206 Carlos Garcia .05 .15
207 Mark Clark .05 .15
208 Rafael Palmeiro .20 .50
209 Eric Davis .10 .30
210 Pat Meares .05 .15
211 Chuck Finley .10 .30
212 Jason Bere .05 .15
213 Gary DiSarcina .05 .15
214 Tony Fernandez .05 .15
215 B.J. Surhoff .10 .30
216 Lee Guetterman .05 .15
217 Tim Wallach .05 .15
218 Kirt Manwaring .05 .15
219 Albert Belle .10 .30
220 Dwight Gooden .10 .30
221 Archi Cianfrocco .05 .15
222 Terry Mulholland .05 .15
223 Hipolito Pichardo .05 .15
224 Kent Hrbek .10 .30
225 Craig Grebeck .05 .15
226 Todd Jones .05 .15
227 Mike Bordick .05 .15
228 John Olerud .10 .30
229 Jeff Blauser .05 .15
230 Alex Arias .05 .15
231 Bernard Gilkey .05 .15
232 Denny Neagle .10 .30
233 Pedro Borbon .05 .15
234 Dick Schofield .05 .15
235 Matias Carrillo .05 .15
236 Juan Bell .05 .15
237 Mike Hampton .10 .30
238 Barry Bonds .75 2.00
239 Cris Carpenter .05 .15
240 Eric Karros .10 .30
241 Greg McMichael .05 .15
242 Pat Hentgen .05 .15
243 Tim Pugh .05 .15
244 Vinny Castilla .10 .30
245 Charlie Hough .10 .30
246 Bobby Munoz .05 .15
247 Kevin Baez .05 .15
248 Todd Frohwirth .05 .15
249 Charlie Hayes .05 .15
250 Mike Macfarlane .05 .15
251 Danny Darwin .05 .15
252 Ben Rivera .05 .15
253 Dave Henderson .05 .15
254 Steve Avery .05 .15
255 Tim Belcher .05 .15
256 Dan Plesac .05 .15
257 Jim Thome .20 .50
258 Albert Belle HR .10 .30
259 Barry Bonds HR .40 1.00
260 Ron Gant HR .05 .15
261 Juan Gonzalez HR .05 .15
262 Ken Griffey Jr. HR .40 1.00
263 David Justice HR .05 .15
264 Fred McGriff HR .10 .30
265 Rafael Palmeiro HR .10 .30
266 Mike Piazza HR .30 .75
267 Frank Thomas HR .20 .50
268 Matt Williams HR .05 .15
269 Checklist 1-135 .05 .15
270 Checklist 136-270 .05 .15
271 Mike Stanley .05 .15
272 Tony Tarasco .05 .15
273 Teddy Higuera .05 .15
274 Ryan Thompson .05 .15
275 Rick Aguilera .05 .15
276 Ramon Martinez .05 .15
277 Orlando Merced .05 .15
278 Guillermo Velasquez .05 .15
279 Mark Hutton .05 .15
280 Larry Walker .10 .30
281 Kevin Gross .05 .15
282 Jose Offerman .05 .15
283 Jim Leyritz .05 .15
284 Jamie Moyer .10 .30
285 Frank Thomas .30 .75
286 Derek Bell .05 .15
287 Derrick May .05 .15
288 Dave Winfield .10 .30
289 Curt Schilling .10 .30
290 Carlos Quintana .05 .15
291 Bob Natal .05 .15
292 David Cone .10 .30
293 Al Osuna .05 .15
294 Bob Hamelin .05 .15
295 Chad Curtis .05 .15
296 Danny Jackson .05 .15
297 Bob Welch .05 .15
298 Felix Jose .05 .15
299 Jay Buhner .10 .30
300 Joe Carter .10 .30
301 Kenny Lofton .10 .30
302 Kirk Rueter .05 .15
303 Kim Batiste .05 .15
304 Mike Morgan .05 .15
305 Pat Borders .05 .15
306 Rene Arocha .05 .15
307 Ruben Sierra .10 .30
308 Steve Finley .10 .30
309 Travis Fryman .10 .30
310 Zane Smith .05 .15
311 Willie Wilson .05 .15
312 Trevor Hoffman .20 .50
313 Terry Pendleton .10 .30
314 Salomon Torres .05 .15
315 Robin Ventura .10 .30
316 Randy Tomlin .05 .15
317 Dave Stewart .10 .30
318 Mike Benjamin .05 .15
319 Matt Turner .05 .15
320 Manny Ramirez .30 .75
321 Kevin Young .05 .15
322 Ken Caminiti .10 .30
323 Joe Girardi .05 .15
324 Jeff McKnight .05 .15
325 Gene Harris .05 .15
326 Devon White .10 .30
327 Darryl Kile .10 .30
328 Craig Paquette .05 .15
329 Cal Eldred .05 .15
330 Bill Swift .05 .15
331 Alan Trammell .10 .30
332 Armando Reynoso .05 .15
333 Brent Mayne .05 .15
334 Chris Donnels .05 .15
335 Darryl Strawberry .10 .30
336 Dean Palmer .10 .30
337 Frank Castillo .05 .15
338 Jeff King .05 .15
339 John Franco .10 .30
340 Kevin Appier .10 .30
341 Lance Blankenship .05 .15
342 Mark McLemore .05 .15
343 Pedro Astacio .05 .15
344 Rich Batchelor .05 .15
345 Ryan Bowen .05 .15
346 Terry Steinbach .05 .15
347 Troy O'Leary .05 .15
348 Willie Blair .05 .15
349 Wade Boggs .20 .50
350 Tim Raines .10 .30
351 Scott Livingstone .05 .15
352 Rod Correia .05 .15
353 Ray Lankford .10 .30
354 Pat Listach .05 .15
355 Milt Thompson .05 .15
356 Miguel Jimenez .05 .15
357 Marc Newfield .05 .15
358 Mark McGwire .75 2.00
359 Kirby Puckett .30 .75
360 Kent Mercker .05 .15
361 John Kruk .10 .30
362 Jeff Kent .20 .50
363 Hal Morris .05 .15
364 Edgar Martinez .20 .50
365 Dave Magadan .05 .15
366 Dante Bichette .10 .30
367 Chris Hammond .05 .15
368 Bret Saberhagen .10 .30
369 Billy Ripken .05 .15
370 Bill Gullickson .05 .15
371 Andre Dawson .10 .30
372 Roberto Kelly .05 .15
373 Cal Ripken 1.00 2.50
374 Craig Biggio .20 .50
375 Dan Pasqua .05 .15
376 Dave Nilsson .05 .15
377 Duane Ward .05 .15
378 Greg Vaughn .05 .15
379 Jeff Fassero .05 .15
380 Jerry DiPoto .05 .15
381 John Patterson .05 .15
382 Kevin Brown .10 .30
383 Kevin Roberson .05 .15
384 Joe Orsulak .05 .15
385 Hilly Hathaway .05 .15
386 Mike Greenwell .05 .15
387 Orestes Destrade .05 .15
388 Mike Gallego .05 .15
389 Ozzie Guillen .10 .30
390 Raul Mondesi .10 .30
391 Scott Lydy .05 .15
392 Tom Urbani .05 .15
393 Wil Cordero .05 .15
394 Tony Longmire .05 .15
395 Todd Zeile .05 .15
396 Scott Cooper .05 .15
397 Ryne Sandberg .50 1.25
398 Ricky Bones .05 .15
399 Phil Clark .05 .15
400 Orel Hershiser .10 .30
401 Mike Henneman .05 .15
402 Mark Lemke .05 .15
403 Mark Grace .20 .50
404 Ken Ryan .05 .15
405 John Smoltz .20 .50
406 Jeff Conine .10 .30
407 Greg Harris .05 .15
408 Doug Drabek .05 .15
409 Dave Fleming .05 .15
410 Danny Tartabull .05 .15
411 Chad Kreuter .05 .15
412 Brad Ausmus .20 .50
413 Ben McDonald .05 .15
414 Barry Larkin .20 .50
415 Bret Barberie .05 .15
416 Chuck Knoblauch .10 .30
417 Ozzie Smith .50 1.25
418 Ed Sprague .05 .15
419 Matt Williams .10 .30
420 Jeremy Hernandez .05 .15
421 Jose Bautista .05 .15
422 Kevin Mitchell .05 .15
423 Manuel Lee .05 .15
424 Mike Devereaux* .05 .15
425 Omar Olivares .05 .15
426 Rafael Belliard .05 .15
427 Richie Lewis .05 .15
428 Ron Darling .05 .15
429 Shane Mack .05 .15
430 Tim Hulett .05 .15
431 Wally Joyner .10 .30
432 Wes Chamberlain .05 .15
433 Tom Browning .05 .15
434 Scott Radinsky .05 .15
435 Rondell White .10 .30
436 Rod Beck .05 .15
437 Rheal Cormier .05 .15
438 Randy Johnson .30 .75
439 Pete Schourek .05 .15
440 Mo Vaughn .10 .30
441 Mike Timlin .05 .15
442 Mark Langston .05 .15
443 Lou Whitaker .10 .30
444 Kevin Stocker .05 .15
445 Ken Hill .05 .15
446 John Wetteland .10 .30
447 J.T. Snow .10 .30
448 Erik Pappas .05 .15
449 David Hulse .05 .15
450 Darren Daulton .10 .30
451 Chris Hoiles .05 .15
452 Bryan Harvey .05 .15
453 Darren Lewis .05 .15
454 Andres Galarraga .10 .30
455 Joe Hesketh .05 .15
456 Jose Valentin .05 .15
457 Dan Peltier .05 .15
458 Joe Boever .05 .15
459 Kevin Rogers .05 .15
460 Craig Shipley .05 .15
461 Alvaro Espinoza .05 .15
462 Wilson Alvarez .05 .15
463 Cory Snyder .05 .15
464 Candy Maldonado .05 .15
465 Blas Minor .05 .15
466 Rod Bolton .05 .15
467 Kenny Rogers .10 .30
468 Greg Myers .05 .15
469 Jimmy Key .10 .30
470 Tony Castillo .05 .15
471 Mike Stanton .05 .15
472 Deion Sanders .20 .50
473 Tito Navarro .05 .15
474 Mike Gardiner .05 .15
475 Steve Reed .05 .15
476 John Roper .05 .15
477 Mike Trombley .05 .15
478 Charles Nagy .05 .15
479 Larry Casian .05 .15
480 Eric Hillman .05 .15
481 Bill Wertz .05 .15
482 Jeff Schwarz .05 .15
483 John Valentin .05 .15
484 Carl Willis .05 .15
485 Gary Gaetti .10 .30
486 Bill Pecota .05 .15
487 John Smiley .05 .15
488 Mike Mussina .20 .50
489 Mike Ignasiak .05 .15
490 Billy Brewer .05 .15
491 Jack Voigt .05 .15
492 Mike Munoz .05 .15
493 Lee Tinsley .05 .15
494 Bob Wickman .05 .15
495 Roger Salkeld .05 .15
496 Thomas Howard .05 .15
497 Mark Davis .05 .15
498 Dave Clark .05 .15
499 Turk Wendell .05 .15
500 Rafael Bournigal .05 .15
501 Chip Hale .05 .15
502 Matt Whiteside .05 .15
503 Brian Koelling .05 .15
504 Jeff Reed .05 .15
505 Paul Wagner .05 .15
506 Torey Lovullo .05 .15
507 Curt Leskanic .05 .15
508 Derek Lilliquist .05 .15
509 Joe Magrane .05 .15
510 Mackey Sasser .05 .15
511 Lloyd McClendon .05 .15
512 Jayhawk Owens .05 .15
513 Woody Williams .05 .15
514 Gary Redus .05 .15
515 Tim Spehr .05 .15
516 Jim Abbott .20 .50
517 Lou Frazier .05 .15
518 Erik Plantenberg RC .05 .15
519 Tim Worrell .05 .15
520 Brian McRae .05 .15
521 Chan Ho Park RC .30 .75
522 Mark Wohlers .05 .15
523 Geronimo Pena .05 .15
524 Andy Ashby .05 .15
525 T.Raines .05 .15
A.Dawson TALE
526 Paul Molitor TALE .05 .15
527 Joe Carter DL .05 .15
528 Frank Thomas DL .20 .50
529 Ken Griffey Jr. DL .40 1.00
530 David Justice DL .05 .15
531 Gregg Jefferies DL .05 .15
532 Barry Bonds DL .40 1.00
533 John Kruk QS .05 .15
534 Roger Clemens QS .30 .75
535 Cecil Fielder QS .05 .15
536 Ruben Sierra QS .05 .15
537 Tony Gwynn QS .20 .50
538 Tom Glavine QS .10 .30
539 Checklist 271-405 UER
(number on back is 269) .05 .15
540 Checklist 406-540 UER
(numbered 270 on back) .05 .15
541 Ozzie Smith CC .30 .75
542 Eddie Murray ATL .20 .50
543 Lee Smith ATL .05 .15
544 Greg Maddux .50 1.25
545 Denis Boucher .05 .15
546 Mark Gardner .05 .15
547 Bo Jackson .30 .75
548 Eric Anthony .05 .15
549 Delino DeShields .05 .15
550 Turner Ward .05 .15
551 Scott Sanderson .05 .15
552 Hector Carrasco .05 .15
553 Tony Phillips .05 .15
554 Melido Perez .05 .15
555 Mike Felder .05 .15
556 Jack Morris .10 .30
557 Rafael Palmeiro .20 .50
558 Shane Reynolds .05 .15
559 Pete Incaviglia .05 .15
560 Greg Harris .05 .15
561 Matt Walbeck .05 .15
562 Todd Van Poppel .05 .15
563 Todd Stottlemyre .05 .15
564 Ricky Bones .05 .15
565 Mike Jackson .05 .15
566 Kevin McReynolds .05 .15
567 Melvin Nieves .05 .15
568 Juan Gonzalez .10 .30
569 Frank Viola .10 .30
570 Vince Coleman .05 .15
571 Brian Anderson RC .10 .30
572 Omar Vizquel .20 .50
573 Bernie Williams .20 .50
574 Tom Glavine .20 .50
575 Mitch Williams .05 .15
576 Shawon Dunston .05 .15
577 Mike Lansing .05 .15
578 Greg Pirkl .05 .15
579 Sid Fernandez .05 .15
580 Doug Jones .05 .15
581 Walt Weiss .05 .15
582 Tim Belcher .05 .15
583 Alex Fernandez .05 .15
584 Alex Cole .05 .15
585 Greg Cadaret .05 .15
586 Bob Tewksbury .05 .15
587 Dave Hansen .05 .15
588 Kurt Abbott RC .05 .15
589 Rick White RC .05 .15
590 Kevin Bass .05 .15
591 Geronimo Berroa .05 .15
592 Jaime Navarro .05 .15
593 Steve Farr .05 .15
594 Jack Armstrong .05 .15
595 Steve Howe .05 .15
596 Jose Rijo .05 .15
597 Otis Nixon .05 .15
598 Robby Thompson .05 .15
599 Kelly Stinnett RC .10 .30
600 Carlos Delgado .20 .50
601 Brian Johnson RC .05 .15
602 Gregg Olson .05 .15
603 Jim Edmonds .30 .75
604 Mike Blowers .05 .15
605 Lee Smith .10 .30
606 Pat Rapp .05 .15
607 Mike Magnante .05 .15
608 Karl Rhodes .05 .15
609 Jeff Juden .05 .15
610 Rusty Meacham .05 .15
611 Pedro Martinez .30 .75
612 Todd Worrell .05 .15
613 Stan Javier .05 .15
614 Mike Hampton .10 .30
615 Jose Guzman .05 .15
616 Xavier Hernandez .05 .15
617 David Wells .10 .30
618 John Habyan .05 .15
619 Chris Nabholz .05 .15
620 Bobby Jones .05 .15
621 Chris James .05 .15
622 Ellis Burks .10 .30
623 Erik Hanson .05 .15
624 Pat Meares .05 .15
625 Harold Reynolds .10 .30
626 Bob Hamelin RR .05 .15
627 Manny Ramirez RR .20 .50
628 Ryan Klesko RR .05 .15
629 Carlos Delgado RR .10 .30
630 Javier Lopez RR .10 .30
631 Steve Karsay RR .05 .15
632 Rick Helling RR .05 .15
633 Steve Trachsel RR .05 .15
634 Hector Carrasco RR .05 .15
635 Andy Stankiewicz .05 .15
636 Paul Sorrento .05 .15
637 Scott Erickson .05 .15
638 Chipper Jones .30 .75
639 Luis Polonia .05 .15
640 Howard Johnson .05 .15
641 John Dopson .05 .15
642 Jody Reed .05 .15
643 Lonnie Smith UER .05 .15
Card numbered 543
644 Mark Portugal .05 .15
645 Paul Molitor .10 .30
646 Paul Assenmacher .05 .15
647 Hubie Brooks .05 .15
648 Gary Wayne .05 .15
649 Sean Berry .05 .15
650 Roger Clemens .60 1.50
651 Brian R. Hunter .05 .15
652 Wally Whitehurst .05 .15
653 Allen Watson .05 .15
654 Rickey Henderson .30 .75
655 Sid Bream .05 .15
656 Dan Wilson .05 .15
657 Ricky Jordan .05 .15
658 Sterling Hitchcock .05 .15
659 Darrin Jackson .05 .15
660 Junior Felix .05 .15
661 Tom Brunansky .05 .15
662 Jose Vizcaino .05 .15
663 Mark Leiter .05 .15
664 Gil Heredia .05 .15
665 Fred McGriff .20 .50
666 Will Clark .20 .50
667 Al Leiter .10 .30
668 James Mouton .05 .15
669 Billy Bean .05 .15
670 Scott Leius .05 .15
671 Bret Boone .10 .30
672 Darren Holmes .05 .15
673 Dave Weathers .05 .15
674 Eddie Murray .30 .75
675 Felix Fermin .05 .15
676 Chris Sabo .05 .15
677 Billy Spiers .05 .15
678 Aaron Sele .05 .15
679 Juan Samuel .05 .15
680 Julio Franco .10 .30
681 Heathcliff Slocumb .05 .15
682 Dennis Martinez .10 .30
683 Jerry Browne .05 .15
684 Pedro A.Martinez RC .05 .15
685 Rex Hudler .05 .15
686 Willie McGee .10 .30
687 Andy Van Slyke .20 .50
688 Pat Mahomes .05 .15
689 Dave Henderson .05 .15
690 Tony Eusebio .05 .15
691 Rick Sutcliffe .10 .30
692 Willie Banks .05 .15
693 Alan Mills .05 .15
694 Jeff Treadway .05 .15
695 Alex Gonzalez .05 .15
696 David Segui .05 .15
697 Rick Helling .05 .15
698 Bip Roberts .05 .15
699 Jeff Cirillo RC .10 .30
700 Terry Mulholland .05 .15
701 Marvin Freeman .05 .15
702 Jason Bere .05 .15
703 Javier Lopez .10 .30
704 Greg Hibbard .05 .15
705 Tommy Greene .05 .15
706 Marquis Grissom .10 .30
707 Brian Harper .05 .15
708 Steve Karsay .05 .15
709 Jeff Brantley .05 .15
710 Jeff Russell .05 .15
711 Bryan Hickerson .05 .15
712 Jim Pittsley RC .05 .15
713 Bobby Ayala .05 .15
714 John Smoltz .20 .50
715 Jose Rijo .05 .15
716 Greg Maddux FAN .30 .75
717 Matt Williams FAN .05 .15
718 Frank Thomas FAN .20 .50
719 Ryne Sandberg FAN .30 .75
720 Checklist .05 .15

1994 Stadium Club First Day Issue

COMPLETE SET (720) 1500.00 2500.00
*STARS: 8X TO 20X BASIC CARDS
*ROOKIES: 6X TO 15X BASIC CARDS
STATED ODDS 1:24 H/R, 1:15 JUMBO
STATED PRINT RUN 2000 SETS
BEWARE OF TRANSFERRED FDI LOGOS

1994 Stadium Club Golden Rainbow

COMPLETE SET (720) 75.00 150.00
COMPLETE SERIES 1 (270) 25.00 60.00
COMPLETE SERIES 2 (270) 25.00 60.00
COMPLETE SERIES 3 (180) 15.00 40.00
*STARS: 1.25X TO 3X BASIC CARDS
*ROOKIES: 1X TO 2.5X BASIC CARDS
ONE PER PACK/TWO PER JUMBO

1994 Stadium Club Members Only Parallel

COMPLETE FACT.SET (770) 100.00 200.00
*1ST SERIES MEMBERS ONLY: 4X BASIC CARDS
2ND AND 3RD SERIES STARS: 6X BASIC CARDS
F1 Jeff Bagwell 1.50 4.00
F2 Albert Belle .60 1.50
F3 Barry Bonds 3.00 8.00
F4 Juan Gonzalez 1.25 3.00
F5 Ken Griffey Jr. 6.00 15.00
F6 Marquis Grissom .40 1.00
F7 David Justice 1.25 3.00
F8 Mike Piazza 3.00 8.00
F9 Tim Salmon 1.25 3.00
F10 Frank Thomas 2.50 6.00
DD1 Mike Piazza 3.00 8.00
DD2 Dave Winfield 1.25 3.00
DD3 John Kruk .60 1.50
DD4 Cal Ripken 6.00 15.00
DD5 Jack McDowell 2.50 6.00
DD6 Barry Bonds 3.00 8.00
DD7 Ken Griffey Jr. 6.00 15.00
DD8 Tim Salmon 1.25 3.00
DD9 Frank Thomas 2.00 5.00
DD10 Jeff Kent 1.25 3.00
DD11 Randy Johnson 1.50 4.00
DD12 Darren Daulton .60 1.50
ST1 Atlanta Braves D .30 .75
L
WS
ST2 Chicago Cubs .60 1.50
ST3 Cin.Reds .40 1.00
R.Sand
Lark D
ST4 Colorado Rockies .20 .50
ST5 Florida Marlins .20 .50
ST6 Houston Astros .30 .75
ST7 L.A.Dodgers 2.00 5.00
Piazza D
ST8 Montreal Expos .30 .75
ST9 New York Mets .20 .50
ST10 Philadelphia Phillies .20 .50
ST11 Pittsburgh Pirates .30 .75
ST12 St.Louis Cardinals .20 .50
ST13 San Diego Padres .20 .50
ST14 S.F.Giants .40 1.00
M.Williams
ST15 Baltimore Orioles 2.50 6.00
Ripken
ST16 Boston Red Sox D .20 .50
ST17 California Angels .60 1.50
ST18 Chicago White Sox .20 .50
ST19 Cle.Indians .40 1.00
Bel
Bae
Lof D
L
ST20 Detroit Tigers .30 .75
ST21 Kansas City Royals .20 .50
ST22 Milwaukee Brewers .20 .50
ST23 Minnesota Twins 1.25 3.00
Puckett
ST24 N.Y.Yankees 1.25 3.00
Mattingly
ST25 Oakland Athletics .20 .50
ST26 Seattle Mariners D .40 1.00
ST27 Tex.Rangers .60 1.50
Cans
Gonz
ST28 Toronto Blue Jays .20 .50

1994 Stadium Club Dugout Dir

Randomly inserted at a rate of one per six packs, these standard-size cards feature some of baseball's most popular and colorful players by sports cartoonists Daniel Guidera and Steve Benson. The cards resemble basic Stadium Club cards except for a Dugout Dirt logo at the bottom. Backs contain a cartoon. Cards 1-4 were found in first series packs with cards 5-8 and 9-12 were inserted in second series and third series packs respectively.

COMPLETE SET (12) 4.00 10.00
COMPLETE SERIES 1 (4) 2.00 5.00
COMPLETE SERIES 2 (4) 1.25 3.00
COMPLETE SERIES 3 (4) 1.25 3.00
STATED ODDS 1:6 H/R, 1:3 JUM
1 Mike Piazza .60 1.50
2 Dave Winfield .10 .30
3 John Kruk .10 .30
4 Cal Ripken 1.00 2.50
5 Jack McDowell .05 .15
6 Barry Bonds .75 2.00
7 Ken Griffey Jr. .60 1.50
8 Tim Salmon .20 .50
9 Frank Thomas .30 .75
10 Jeff Kent .20 .50
11 Randy Johnson .30 .75
12 Darren Daulton .10 .30

1994 Stadium Club Finest

This set contains 10 standard-size metallic cards of top players. They were randomly inserted one in six third series packs. Jumbo versions measuring approximately five inches by seven inches were issued for retail repacks.

COMPLETE SET (10) 10.00 25.00
SER.3 STATED ODDS 1:6
*JUMBOS: .6X TO 1.5X BASIC SC FINEST
JUMBOS DISTRIBUTED IN RETAIL PACKS
F1 Jeff Bagwell .60 1.50
F2 Albert Belle .40 1.00
F3 Barry Bonds 2.50 6.00
F4 Juan Gonzalez .40 1.00
F5 Ken Griffey Jr. 2.00 5.00
F6 Marquis Grissom .40 1.00
F7 David Justice .40 1.00
F8 Mike Piazza 2.00 5.00
F9 Tim Salmon .60 1.50
F10 Frank Thomas 1.00 2.50

1994 Stadium Club Super Teams

Randomly inserted at a rate of one per 24 first series packs only, this 28-card standard-size features one card for each of the 28 MLB teams. Collectors holding team cards could redeem them for special prizes if those teams won a division title, a league championship, or the World Series. But, since the strike affected the 1994 season, Topps postponed the promotion until the 1995 season. The expiration was pushed back to January 31, 1996.

COMPLETE SET (28) 20.00 50.00
SER.1 STAT.ODDS 1:24 HOB/RET, 1:15 JUMBO
CONTEST APPLIED TO 1995 SEASON
WINNERS LISTED UNDER 1995 STAD.CLUB
ST1 Atlanta DLWS 1.00 2.50
ST2 Chicago Cubs .40 1.00
ST3 Cincinnati .60 1.50
B.Larkin D
ST4 Colorado Rockies .40 1.00
ST5 Florida Marlins .40 1.00
ST6 Houston Astros .40 1.00
ST7 Los Angeles 2.00 5.00
M.Piazza D
ST8 Montreal Expos .40 1.00
ST9 New York Mets .40 1.00
ST10 Philadelphia Phillies .40 1.00
ST11 Pittsburgh Pirates .60 1.50
ST12 St.Louis Cardinals .40 1.00
ST13 San Diego Padres .40 1.00
ST14 San Francisco .40 1.00
M.Williams
ST15 Baltimore 3.00 8.00
C.Ripken
ST16 Boston .40 1.00
J.Valentin D
ST17 California Angels .40 1.00
ST18 Chicago White Sox .40 1.00
ST19 Cleveland .40 1.00
Belle
Lofton DL
ST20 Detroit Tigers .40 1.00
ST21 Kansas City Royals .40 1.00
ST22 Milwaukee Brewers .40 1.00

23 Minnesota 1.00 2.50
Puckett
24 New York 2.50 6.00
Mattingly
25 Oakland Athletics .40 1.00
26 Seattle .40 1.00
Buhner D
27 Texas .40 1.00
Gonzalez
28 Toronto Blue Jays .40 1.00

1994 Stadium Club Superstar Samplers

ary Sheffield 2.00 5.00
Roberto Alomar 1.25 3.00
Jack McDowell .40 1.00
Cecil Fielder .60 1.50
Tim Salmon .60 1.50
Bobby Bonilla .60 1.50
Ken Griffey Jr. 4.00 10.00
David Justice 1.25 3.00
8 Jeff Bagwell 2.00 5.00
9 Gregg Jefferies .40 1.00
7 Cliff Floyd 1.00 2.50
0 Mike Piazza 3.00 8.00
1 Tony Gwynn 3.00 8.00
5 Len Dykstra .40 1.00
9 Carlos Baerga .40 1.00
1 Jose Canseco 2.00 5.00
5 Don Mattingly 1.50 4.00
3 Will Clark 1.25 3.00
8 Rafael Palmeiro 1.50 4.00
9 Albert Belle .60 1.50
28 John Olerud .60 1.50
38 Barry Bonds 3.00 8.00
80 Larry Walker 1.50 4.00
85 Frank Thomas 2.00 5.00
00 Joe Carter .60 1.50
20 Manny Ramirez 2.00 5.00
59 Kirby Puckett 2.00 5.00
73 Cal Ripken 6.00 15.00
90 Raul Mondesi .60 1.50
97 Ryne Sandberg 2.50 6.00
03 Mark Grace 1.00 2.50
14 Barry Larkin 1.25 3.00
19 Matt Williams 1.00 2.50
38 Randy Johnson 2.50 6.00
440 Mo Vaughn .60 1.50
450 Darren Daulton .60 1.50
454 Andres Galarraga 1.25 3.00
544 Greg Maddux 4.00 10.00
568 Juan Gonzalez 1.25 3.00
574 Tom Glavine 1.50 4.00
645 Paul Molitor 1.50 4.00
650 Roger Clemens 3.00 8.00
665 Fred McGriff 1.00 2.50
687 Andy Van Slyke .40 1.00
706 Marquis Grissom .60 1.50

1994 Stadium Club Members Only 50

Issued to Stadium Club members, this 50-card standard-size set features 45 regular Stadium Club cards as well as five Stadium Club Finest cards.

COMPLETE SET (50) 8.00 20.00
1 Juan Gonzalez .30 .75
2 Tom Henke .02 .10
3 John Kruk .08 .25
4 Paul Molitor .30 .75
5 David Justice .08 .25
6 Rafael Palmeiro .25 .60
7 John Smoltz .25 .60
8 Matt Williams .15 .40
9 John Olerud .08 .25
10 Mark Grace .15 .40
11 Joe Carter .08 .25
12 Wilson Alvarez .08 .25
13 Len Dykstra .08 .25
14 Kevin Appier .08 .25
15 Andres Galarraga .25 .60
16 Mark Langston .02 .10
17 Ken Griffey Jr. 1.00 2.50
18 Albert Belle .08 .25
19 Gregg Jefferies .02 .10
20 Duane Ward .02 .10
21 Jack McDowell .02 .10
22 Randy Johnson .30 .75
23 Tom Glavine .25 .60
24 Barry Bonds .60 1.50
25 Chuck Carr .02 .10
26 Ron Gant .08 .25
27 Kenny Lofton .15 .40
28 Mike Piazza .60 1.50
29 Frank Thomas .40 1.00
30 Fred McGriff .15 .40
31 Bryan Harvey .02 .10
32 John Burkett .02 .10
33 Roberto Alomar .25 .60
34 Cecil Fielder .08 .25
35 Marquis Grissom .08 .25
36 Randy Myers .02 .10
37 Tony Phillips .02 .10
38 Rickey Henderson .30 .75
39 Luis Polonia .02 .10
40 Jose Rijo .02 .10
41 Jeff Montgomery .02 .10
42 Greg Maddux .75 2.00
43 Tony Gwynn .60 1.50
44 Rod Beck .02 .10
45 Carlos Baerga .08 .25
46 Wil Cordero FIN .20 .50
47 Tim Salmon FIN .75 2.00
48 Mike Lansing FIN .20 .50
49 J.T. Snow FIN .20 .50
50 Jeff Conine FIN .30 .75

1994 Stadium Club Team

This 360-card standard-size set features 30 players from 12 teams. The cards are checklisted alphabetically according to teams.

COMPLETE SET (360) 15.00 40.00
1 Barry Bonds .75 2.00
2 Royce Clayton .02 .10
3 Kirt Manwaring .02 .10
4 J.R. Phillips .02 .10
5 Robby Thompson .02 .10
6 Willie McGee .07 .20
7 Steve Hosey .02 .10
8 Dave Burba .02 .10
9 Steve Scarsone .02 .10
10 Salomon Torres .02 .10
11 Bryan Hickerson .02 .10
12 Mike Benjamin .02 .10
13 Mark Carreon .02 .10
14 Rich Monteleone .02 .10
15 Dave Martinez .02 .10
16 Bill Swift .02 .10
17 Jeff Reed .02 .10
18 John Patterson .02 .10
19 Darren Lewis .02 .10
20 Mark Portugal .02 .10
21 Trevor Wilson .02 .10
22 Matt Williams .15 .40
23 Kevin Rogers .02 .10
24 Luis Mercedes .02 .10
25 Mike Jackson .02 .10
26 Steve Frey .02 .10
27 Tony Menendez .02 .10
28 John Burkett .02 .10
29 Todd Benzinger .02 .10
30 Rod Beck .02 .10
31 Greg Maddux 1.00 2.50
32 Steve Avery .02 .10
33 Milt Hill .02 .10
34 Charlie O'Brien .02 .10
35 John Smoltz .07 .20
36 Jarvis Brown .02 .10
37 Dave Gallagher .02 .10
38 Ryan Klesko .15 .40
39 Kent Mercker .02 .10
40 Terry Pendleton .02 .10
41 Ron Gant .07 .20
42 Pedro Borbon Jr. .02 .10
43 Steve Bedrosian .02 .10
44 Ramon Caraballo .02 .10
45 Tyler Houston .02 .10
46 Mark Lemke .02 .10
47 Fred McGriff .15 .40
48 Jose Oliva .02 .10
49 David Justice .25 .60
50 Chipper Jones .75 2.00
51 Tony Tarasco .02 .10
52 Javier Lopez .15 .40
53 Mark Wohlers .02 .10
54 Deion Sanders .25 .60
55 Greg McMichael .02 .10
56 Tom Glavine .40 1.00
57 Bill Pecota .02 .10
58 Mike Stanton .02 .10
59 Rafael Belliard .02 .10
60 Jeff Blauser .02 .10
61 Bryan Harvey .02 .10
62 Bret Barberie .02 .10
63 Rick Renteria .02 .10
64 Chris Hammond .02 .10
65 Pat Rapp .02 .10
66 Nigel Wilson .02 .10
67 Gary Sheffield .40 1.00
68 Jerry Browne .02 .10
69 Charlie Hough .07 .20
70 Orestes Destrade .07 .20
71 Mario Diaz .02 .10
72 Ryan Bowen .02 .10
73 Carl Everett .07 .20
74 Richie Lewis .02 .10
75 Bob Natal .02 .10
76 Rich Rodriguez .02 .10
77 Darrell Whitmore .02 .10
78 Matt Turner .02 .10
79 Benito Santiago .07 .20
80 Robb Nen .07 .20
81 Dave Magadan .02 .10
82 Brian Drahman .02 .10
83 Mark Gardner .02 .10
84 Chuck Carr .02 .10
85 Alex Arias .02 .10
86 Kurt Abbott .02 .10
87 Joe Klink .02 .10
88 Jeff Mutis .02 .10
89 Dave Weathers .02 .10
90 Jeff Conine .07 .20
91 Andres Galarraga .25 .60
92 Vinny Castilla .07 .20
93 Roberto Mejia .02 .10
94 Darrell Sherman .02 .10
95 Mike Harkey .02 .10
96 Danny Sheaffer .02 .10
97 Pedro Castellano .02 .10
98 Walt Weiss .02 .10
99 Greg W. Harris .02 .10
100 Jayhawk Owens .02 .10
101 Bruce Ruffin .02 .10
102 Mike Munoz .02 .10
103 Armando Reynoso .02 .10
104 Eric Young .07 .20
105 Dante Bichette .07 .20
106 Marvin Freeman .02 .10
107 Joe Girardi .07 .20
108 Kent Bottenfield .02 .10
109 Howard Johnson .02 .10
110 Nelson Liriano .02 .10
111 David Nied .02 .10
112 Steve Reed .02 .10
113 Eric Wedge .07 .20
114 Charlie Hayes .02 .10
115 Ellis Burks .15 .40
116 Willie Blair .02 .10
117 Darren Holmes .02 .10
118 Curtis Leskanic .02 .10
119 Lance Painter .02 .10
120 Jim Tatum .02 .10
121 Frank Thomas .50 1.25
122 Jack McDowell .02 .10
123 Ron Karkovice .02 .10
124 Mike LaValliere .02 .10
125 Scott Radinsky .02 .10
126 Robin Ventura .15 .40
127 Scott Ruffcorn .02 .10
128 Steve Sax .02 .10
129 Roberto Hernandez .07 .20
130 Jose DeLeon .02 .10
131 Rod Bolton .02 .10
132 Wilson Alvarez .02 .10
133 Craig Grebeck .02 .10
134 Lance Johnson .02 .10
135 Kirk McCaskill .02 .10
136 Tim Raines .07 .20
137 Jeff Schwarz .02 .10
138 Warren Newson .02 .10
139 Norberto Martin .02 .10
140 Mike Huff .02 .10
141 Ozzie Guillen .15 .40
142 Alex Fernandez .02 .10
143 Joey Cora .02 .10
144 Jason Bere .02 .10
145 James Baldwin .07 .20
146 Esteban Beltre .02 .10
147 Julio Franco .07 .20
148 Matt Merullo .02 .10
149 Dan Pasqua .02 .10
150 Darrin Jackson .02 .10
151 Joe Carter .07 .20
152 Danny Cox .02 .10
153 Roberto Alomar .25 .60
154 Woody Williams .15 .40
155 Duane Ward .02 .10
156 Ed Sprague .02 .10
157 Domingo Martinez .02 .10
158 Pat Hentgen .07 .20
159 Shawn Green .40 1.00
160 Dick Schofield .02 .10
161 Paul Molitor .40 1.00
162 Darnell Coles .02 .10
163 Willie Canate .02 .10
164 Domingo Cedeno .02 .10
165 Pat Borders .02 .10
166 Greg Cadaret .02 .10
167 Tony Castillo .02 .10
168 Carlos Delgado .40 1.00
169 Scott Brow .02 .10
170 Juan Guzman .02 .10
171 Al Leiter .07 .20
172 John Olerud .15 .40
173 Todd Stottlemyre .02 .10
174 Devon White .07 .20
175 Paul Spoljaric .02 .10
176 Randy Knorr .02 .10
177 Huck Flener .02 .10
178 Rob Butler .02 .10
179 Dave Stewart .07 .20
180 Mike Timlin .02 .10
181 Don Mattingly .75 2.00
182 Mark Hutton .02 .10
183 Mike Gallego .02 .10
184 Jim Abbott .07 .20
185 Paul Gibson .02 .10
186 Scott Kamieniecki .02 .10
187 Sam Horn .02 .10
188 Melido Perez .02 .10
189 Randy Velarde .02 .10
190 Gerald Williams .02 .10
191 Dave Silvestri .02 .10
192 Jim Leyritz .02 .10
193 Steve Howe .02 .10
194 Russ Davis .02 .10
195 Paul Assenmacher .02 .10
196 Pat Kelly .02 .10
197 Mike Stanley .02 .10
198 Bernie Williams .30 .75
199 Paul O'Neill .25 .60
200 Donn Pall .02 .10
201 Xavier Hernandez .02 .10
202 Jim Austin .02 .10
203 Sterling Hitchcock .07 .20
204 Wade Boggs .40 1.00
205 Jimmy Key .07 .20
206 Matt Nokes .02 .10
207 Bobby Munoz .02 .10
208 Luis Polonia .02 .10
209 Danny Tartabull .07 .20
210 Bob Wickman .02 .10
211 Len Dykstra .07 .20
212 Kim Batiste .02 .10
213 Tony Longmire .02 .10
214 Terry Mulholland .02 .10
215 Pete Incaviglia .02 .10
216 Doug Jones .07 .20
217 Mariano Duncan .02 .10
218 Jeff Juden .02 .10
219 Milt Thompson .02 .10
220 Dave West .02 .10
221 Roger Mason .02 .10
222 Tommy Greene .02 .10
223 Larry Andersen .02 .10
224 Jim Eisenreich .02 .10
225 Dave Hollins .02 .10
226 John Kruk .07 .20
227 Todd Pratt .02 .10
228 Ricky Jordan .02 .10
229 Curt Schilling .60 1.50
230 Mike Williams .02 .10
231 Heathcliff Slocumb .02 .10
232 Ben Rivera .02 .10
233 Mike Lieberthal .07 .20
234 Mickey Morandini .02 .10
235 Danny Jackson .02 .10
236 Kevin Foster .02 .10
237 Darren Daulton .07 .20
238 Wes Chamberlain .02 .10
239 Tyler Green .02 .10
240 Kevin Stocker .02 .10
241 Juan Gonzalez .30 .75
242 Rick Honeycutt .02 .10
243 Bruce Hurst .02 .10
244 Steve Dreyer .02 .10
245 Brian Bohanon .02 .10
246 Benji Gil .02 .10
247 Jon Shave .02 .10
248 Manuel Lee .02 .10
249 Donald Harris .02 .10
250 Jose Canseco .30 .75
251 David Hulse .02 .10
252 Kenny Rogers .02 .10
253 Jeff Huson .02 .10
254 Dan Peltier .02 .10
255 Mike Scioscia .07 .20
256 Jack Armstrong .02 .10
257 Rob Ducey .02 .10
258 Will Clark .25 .60
259 Cris Carpenter .02 .10
260 Kevin Brown .15 .40
261 Jeff Frye .02 .10
262 Jay Howell .02 .10
263 Roger Pavlik .02 .10
264 Gary Redus .02 .10
265 Ivan Rodriguez .40 1.00
266 Matt Whiteside .02 .10
267 Doug Strange .02 .10
268 Billy Ripken .02 .10
269 Dean Palmer .07 .20
270 Tom Henke .02 .10
271 Cal Ripken 1.50 4.00
272 Mark McLemore .07 .20
273 Sid Fernandez .07 .20
274 Sherman Obando .02 .10
275 Paul Carey .02 .10
276 Mike Oquist .02 .10
277 Alan Mills .02 .10
278 Harold Baines .07 .20
279 Mike Mussina .40 1.00
280 Arthur Rhodes .02 .10
281 Kevin McGehee .02 .10
282 Mark Eichhorn .02 .10
283 Damon Buford .02 .10
284 Ben McDonald .02 .10
285 David Segui .02 .10
286 Brad Pennington .02 .10
287 Jamie Moyer .15 .40
288 Chris Hoiles .02 .10
289 Mike Cook .02 .10
290 Brady Anderson .07 .20
291 Chris Sabo .02 .10
292 Jack Voigt .02 .10
293 Jim Poole .02 .10
294 Jeff Tackett .02 .10
295 Rafael Palmeiro .30 .75
296 Alex Ochoa .02 .10
297 John O'Donoghue .02 .10
298 Tim Hulett .02 .10
299 Mike Devereaux .02 .10
300 Manny Alexander .02 .10
301 Ozzie Smith .40 1.00
302 Omar Olivares .02 .10
303 Rheal Cormier .02 .10
304 Donovan Osborne .02 .10
305 Mark Whiten .02 .10
306 Todd Zeile .07 .20
307 Geronimo Pena .02 .10
308 Brian Jordan .07 .20
309 Luis Alicea .02 .10
310 Ray Lankford .07 .20
311 Stan Royer .02 .10
312 Bob Tewksbury .02 .10
313 Jose Oquendo .02 .10
314 Steve Dixon .02 .10
315 Rene Arocha .02 .10
316 Bernard Gilkey .02 .10
317 Gregg Jefferies .02 .10
318 Rob Murphy .02 .10
319 Tom Pagnozzi .02 .10
320 Mike Perez .02 .10
321 Tom Urbani .02 .10
322 Allen Watson .02 .10
323 Erik Pappas .02 .10
324 Paul Kilgus .02 .10
325 John Habyan .02 .10
326 Rod Brewer .02 .10
327 Rich Batchelor .02 .10
328 Tripp Cromer .02 .10
329 Gerald Perry .02 .10
330 Les Lancaster .02 .10
331 Ryne Sandberg .75 2.00
332 Derrick May .02 .10
333 Steve Buechele .02 .10
334 Willie Banks .02 .10
335 Larry Luebbers .02 .10
336 Tommy Shields .02 .10
337 Eric Yelding .02 .10
338 Rey Sanchez .02 .10
339 Mark Grace .15 .40
340 Jose Bautista .02 .10
341 Frank Castillo .02 .10
342 Jose Guzman .02 .10
343 Rafael Novoa .02 .10
344 Karl Rhodes .02 .10
345 Steve Trachsel .02 .10
346 Rick Wilkins .02 .10
347 Sammy Sosa .60 1.50
348 Kevin Roberson .02 .10
349 Mark Parent .02 .10
350 Randy Myers .07 .20
351 Glenallen Hill .02 .10
352 Lance Dickson .02 .10
353 Shawn Boskie .02 .10
354 Shawon Dunston .07 .20
355 Dan Plesac .02 .10
356 Jose Vizcaino .02 .10
357 Willie Wilson .02 .10
358 Turk Wendell .02 .10
359 Mike Morgan .02 .10
360 Jim Bullinger .02 .10

1994 Stadium Club Team First Day Issue

*FIRST DAY: 5X to 12X BASIC CARDS
RANDOM INSERTS IN PACKS

1994 Stadium Club Team Finest

This 12-card standard-size set consists of one player from each of the 12 teams featured in the 1994 Stadium Club team series. The cards were randomly inserted in 12-card foil packs. Also one card was included in the 30-card team sets sold in blister packs. The cards are identical in design with the regular series, except for the metallic sheen characteristic of the Finest series.

COMPLETE SET (12) 12.50 30.00
1 Roberto Alomar .75 2.00
2 Barry Bonds 2.00 5.00
3 Len Dykstra .40 1.00
4 Andres Galarraga .75 2.00
5 Juan Gonzalez .75 2.00
6 David Justice .75 2.00
7 Don Mattingly 1.50 4.00
8 Cal Ripken 4.00 10.00
9 Ryne Sandberg 2.00 5.00
10 Gary Sheffield 1.00 2.50
11 Ozzie Smith 1.50 4.00
12 Frank Thomas .75 2.00

1994 Stadium Club Draft Picks

This 90-card standard-size set features players chosen in the June 1994 MLB draft and photographed in their major league uniforms. Each 24-pack box included four First Day Issue Draft Pick cards randomly packed, one in every six packs. Early cards of Nomar Garciaparra, Ben Grieve and Terrence Long are featured in this set.

COMPLETE SET (90) 4.00 10.00
1 Jacob Shumate XRC .08 .25
2 C.J. Nitkowski XRC .08 .25
3 Doug Million XRC .08 .25
4 Matt Smith XRC .08 .25
5 Kevin Lovinger XRC .08 .25
6 Alberto Castillo XRC .08 .25
7 Mike Russell XRC .08 .25
8 Dan Lock XRC .08 .25
9 Tom Szimanski XRC .08 .25
10 Aaron Boone XRC .20 .50
11 Jayson Peterson XRC .08 .25
12 Mark Johnson XRC .08 .25
13 Cade Gaspar XRC .08 .25
14 George Lombard XRC .08 .25
15 Russ Johnson .08 .25
16 Travis Miller XRC .08 .25
17 Jay Payton XRC .20 .50
18 Brian Buchanan XRC .08 .25
19 Jacob Cruz XRC .15 .40
20 Gary Rath XRC .08 .25
21 Ramon Castro XRC .08 .25
22 Tommy Davis XRC .08 .25
23 Tony Terry XRC .08 .25
24 Jerry Whittaker XRC .08 .25
25 Mike Darr XRC .08 .25
26 Doug Webb XRC .08 .25
27 Jason Camilli XRC .08 .25
28 Brad Rigby XRC .08 .25
29 Ryan Nye XRC .08 .25
30 Carl Dale XRC .08 .25
31 Andy Taulbee XRC .08 .25
32 Trey Moore XRC .08 .25
33 John Crowther XRC .08 .25
34 Joe Giuliano XRC .08 .25
35 Brian Rose XRC .08 .25
36 Paul Failla XRC .08 .25
37 Brian Meadows XRC .08 .25
38 Oscar Robles XRC .15 .40
39 Mike Metcalfe XRC .08 .25
40 Larry Barnes XRC .08 .25
41 Paul Ottavinia XRC .08 .25
42 Chris McBride XRC .08 .25
43 Ricky Stone XRC .08 .25
44 Billy Blythe XRC .08 .25
45 Eddie Priest XRC .08 .25
46 Scott Forster XRC .08 .25
47 Eric Pickett XRC .08 .25
48 Matt Beaumont .08 .25
49 Darrell Nicholas XRC .08 .25
50 Mike A. Hampton XRC .08 .25
51 Paul O'Malley XRC .08 .25
52 Steve Shoemaker XRC .08 .25
53 Jason Sikes XRC .08 .25
54 Bryan Farson XRC .08 .25
55 Yates Hall XRC .08 .25
56 Troy Brohawn XRC .08 .25
57 Dan Hower XRC .08 .25
58 Clay Caruthers XRC .08 .25
59 Pepe McNeal XRC .08 .25
60 Ray Ricken XRC .08 .25
61 Scott Shores XRC .08 .25
62 Eddie Brooks XRC .08 .25
63 Dave Kauflin XRC .08 .25
64 David Meyer XRC .08 .25
65 Geoff Blum XRC .20 .50
66 Roy Marsh XRC .08 .25
67 Ryan Beeney XRC .08 .25
68 Derek Dukart XRC .08 .25
69 Nomar Garciaparra 1.25 3.00
70 Jason Kelly XRC .08 .25
71 Jesse Ibarra XRC .08 .25
72 Bucky Buckles XRC .08 .25
73 Mark Little XRC .08 .25
74 Heath Murray XRC .08 .25
75 Greg Morris XRC .08 .25
76 Mike Halperlin XRC .08 .25
77 Wes Helms XRC .15 .40
78 Ray Brown XRC .08 .25
79 Kevin L.Brown XRC .15 .40
80 Paul Konerko XRC 2.00 5.00
81 Mike Thurman XRC .08 .25
82 Paul Wilson .08 .25
83 Terrence Long XRC .15 .40
84 Ben Grieve XRC .15 .40
85 Mark Farris XRC .08 .25
86 Bret Wagner .08 .25
87 Dustin Hermanson .08 .25
88 Kevin Witt XRC .15 .40
89 Corey Pointer XRC .08 .25
90 Tim Grieve XRC .08 .25

1994 Stadium Club Draft Picks First Day Issue

COMPLETE SET (90) 60.00 120.00
*FIRST DAY: 1.25X TO 3X BASIC CARDS
RANDOM INSERTS IN PACKS

1994 Stadium Club Draft Picks Members Only

*MEMBERS ONLY: 1.25X TO 3X BASIC CARD

1995 Stadium Club

The 1995 Stadium Club baseball card set was issued in three series of 270, 225 and 135 standard-size cards for a total of 630. The cards were distributed in 14-card packs at a suggested retail price of $2.50 and contained 24 packs per box. Notable Rookie Cards include Mark Grudzielanek, Bobby Higginson and Hideo Nomo.

COMPLETE SET (630) 12.50 30.00
COMPLETE SERIES 1 (270) 5.00 12.00
COMPLETE SERIES 2 (225) 4.00 10.00
COMPLETE SERIES 3 (135) 3.00 8.00
SUBSET CARDS HALF VALUE OF BASE CARDS
1 Cal Ripken 1.00 2.50
2 Bo Jackson .30 .75
3 Bryan Harvey .05 .15
4 Curt Schilling .10 .30
5 Bruce Ruffin .05 .15
6 Travis Fryman .10 .30
7 Jim Abbott .20 .50
8 David McCarty .05 .15
9 Gary Gaetti .10 .30
10 Roger Clemens .60 1.50
11 Carlos Garcia .05 .15
12 Lee Smith .10 .30
13 Bobby Ayala .05 .15
14 Charles Nagy .05 .15
15 Lou Frazier .05 .15
16 Rene Arocha .05 .15
17 Carlos Delgado .10 .30
18 Steve Finley .10 .30
19 Ryan Klesko .10 .30
20 Cal Eldred .05 .15
21 Rey Sanchez .05 .15
22 Ken Hill .05 .15
23 Benito Santiago .10 .30
24 Julian Tavarez .05 .15
25 Jose Vizcaino .05 .15
26 Andy Benes .05 .15
27 Mariano Duncan .05 .15
28 Checklist A .05 .15
29 Shawon Dunston .05 .15
30 Rafael Palmeiro .20 .50
31 Dean Palmer .10 .30
32 Andres Galarraga .10 .30
33 Joey Cora .05 .15
34 Mickey Tettleton .05 .15
35 Barry Larkin .20 .50
36 Carlos Baerga .05 .15
37 Orel Hershiser .10 .30
38 Jody Reed .05 .15
39 Paul Molitor .10 .30
40 Jim Edmonds .20 .50
41 Bob Tewksbury .05 .15
42 John Patterson .05 .15
43 Ray McDavid .05 .15
44 Zane Smith .05 .15
45 Bret Saberhagen SE .05 .15
46 Greg Maddux SE .30 .75
47 Frank Thomas SE .20 .50
48 Carlos Baerga SE .05 .15
49 Billy Spiers .05 .15
50 Stan Javier .05 .15
51 Rex Hudler .05 .15
52 Denny Hocking .05 .15
53 Todd Worrell .05 .15
54 Mark Clark .05 .15
55 Hipolito Pichardo .05 .15
56 Bob Wickman .05 .15
57 Raul Mondesi .10 .30
58 Steve Cooke .05 .15
59 Rod Beck .05 .15
60 Tim Davis .05 .15
61 Jeff Kent .10 .30
62 John Valentin .05 .15
63 Alex Arias .05 .15
64 Steve Reed .05 .15
65 Ozzie Smith .50 1.25
66 Terry Pendleton .10 .30
67 Kenny Rogers .10 .30
68 Vince Coleman .05 .15
69 Tom Pagnozzi .05 .15
70 Roberto Alomar .20 .50
71 Darrin Jackson .05 .15
72 Dennis Eckersley .10 .30
73 Jay Buhner .10 .30
74 Darren Lewis .05 .15
75 Dave Weathers .05 .15
76 Matt Walbeck .05 .15
77 Brad Ausmus .10 .30
78 Danny Bautista .05 .15
79 Bob Hamelin .05 .15
80 Steve Trachsel .05 .15
81 Ken Ryan .05 .15
82 Chris Turner .05 .15
83 David Segui .05 .15
84 Ben McDonald .05 .15
85 Wade Boggs .20 .50
86 John Vander Wal .05 .15
87 Sandy Alomar Jr. .05 .15
88 Ron Karkovice .05 .15

89 Doug Jones .05 .15
90 Gary Sheffield .10 .30
91 Ken Caminiti .10 .30
92 Chris Bosio .05 .15
93 Kevin Tapani .05 .15
94 Walt Weiss .05 .15
95 Erik Hanson .05 .15
96 Ruben Sierra .10 .30
97 Nomar Garciaparra .75 2.00
98 Terrence Long .05 .15
99 Jacob Shumate .05 .15
100 Paul Wilson .05 .15
101 Kevin Witt .05 .15
102 Paul Konerko .40 1.00
103 Ben Grieve .05 .15
104 Mark Johnson RC .15 .40
105 Cade Gaspar RC .05 .15
106 Mark Farris .05 .15
107 Dustin Hermanson .05 .15
108 Scott Elarton RC .15 .40
109 Doug Million .05 .15
110 Matt Smith .05 .15
111 Brian Buchanan RC .05 .15
112 Jayson Peterson RC .05 .15
113 Bret Wagner .05 .15
114 C.J. Nitkowski RC .15 .40
115 Ramon Castro RC .15 .40
116 Rafael Bournigal .05 .15
117 Jeff Fassero .05 .15
118 Bobby Bonilla .10 .30
119 Ricky Gutierrez .05 .15
120 Roger Pavlik .05 .15
121 Mike Greenwell .05 .15
122 Deion Sanders .20 .50
123 Charlie Hayes .05 .15
124 Paul O'Neill .20 .50
125 Jay Bell .10 .30
126 Royce Clayton .05 .15
127 Willie Banks .05 .15
128 Mark Wohlers .05 .15
129 Todd Jones .05 .15
130 Todd Stottlemyre .05 .15
131 Will Clark .20 .50
132 Wilson Alvarez .05 .15
133 Chili Davis .10 .30
134 Dave Burba .05 .15
135 Chris Hoiles .05 .15
136 Jeff Blauser .05 .15
137 Jeff Reboulet .05 .15
138 Bret Saberhagen .10 .30
139 Kirk Rueter .05 .15
140 Dave Nilsson .05 .15
141 Pat Borders .05 .15
142 Ron Darling .05 .15
143 Derek Bell .05 .15
144 Dave Hollins .05 .15
145 Juan Gonzalez .10 .30
146 Andre Dawson .10 .30
147 Jim Thome .20 .50
148 Larry Walker .10 .30
149 Mike Piazza .50 1.25
150 Mike Perez .05 .15
151 Steve Avery .05 .15
152 Dan Wilson .05 .15
153 Andy Van Slyke .20 .50
154 Junior Felix .05 .15
155 Jack McDowell .05 .15
156 Danny Tartabull .05 .15
157 Willie Blair .05 .15
158 Wm.VanLandingham .05 .15
159 Robb Nen .10 .30
160 Lee Tinsley .05 .15
161 Ismael Valdes .05 .15
162 Juan Guzman .05 .15
163 Scott Servais .05 .15
164 Cliff Floyd .10 .30
165 Allen Watson .05 .15
166 Eddie Taubensee .05 .15
167 Scott Hemond .05 .15
168 Jeff Tackett .05 .15
169 Chad Curtis .05 .15
170 Rico Brogna .05 .15
171 Luis Polonia .05 .15
172 Checklist B .05 .15
173 Lance Johnson .05 .15
174 Sammy Sosa .30 .75
175 Mike Macfarlane .05 .15
176 Darryl Hamilton .05 .15
177 Rick Aguilera .05 .15
178 Dave West .05 .15
179 Mike Gallego .05 .15
180 Marc Newfield .05 .15
181 Steve Buechele .05 .15
182 David Wells .10 .30
183 Tom Glavine .20 .50
184 Joe Girardi .05 .15
185 Craig Biggio .20 .50
186 Eddie Murray .30 .75
187 Kevin Gross .05 .15
188 Sid Fernandez .05 .15
189 John Franco .10 .30
190 Bernard Gilkey .05 .15
191 Matt Williams .10 .30
192 Darrin Fletcher .05 .15
193 Jeff Conine .10 .30
194 Ed Sprague .05 .15
195 Eduardo Perez .05 .15
196 Scott Livingstone .05 .15
197 Ivan Rodriguez .20 .50
198 Orlando Merced .05 .15
199 Ricky Bones .05 .15
200 Javier Lopez .10 .30
201 Miguel Jimenez .05 .15
202 Terry McGriff .05 .15
203 Mike Lieberthal .10 .30
204 David Cone .10 .30
205 Todd Hundley .05 .15
206 Ozzie Guillen .10 .30
207 Alex Cole .05 .15
208 Tony Phillips .05 .15
209 Jim Eisenreich .05 .15
210 Greg Vaughn BES .05 .15
211 Barry Larkin BES .10 .30
212 Don Mattingly BES .40 1.00
213 Mark Grace BES .10 .30
214 Jose Canseco BES .10 .30
215 Joe Carter BES .05 .15
216 David Cone BES .05 .15
217 Sandy Alomar Jr. BES .05 .15
218 Al Martin BES .05 .15
219 Roberto Kelly BES .05 .15
220 Paul Sorrento .05 .15
221 Tony Fernandez .05 .15
222 Stan Belinda .05 .15
223 Mike Stanley .05 .15
224 Doug Drabek .05 .15
225 Todd Van Poppel .05 .15
226 Matt Mieske .05 .15
227 Tino Martinez .20 .50
228 Andy Ashby .05 .15
229 Midre Cummings .05 .15
230 Jeff Frye .05 .15
231 Hal Morris .05 .15
232 Jose Lind .05 .15
233 Shawn Green .10 .30
234 Rafael Belliard .05 .15
235 Randy Myers .05 .15
236 Frank Thomas CE .20 .50
237 Darren Daulton CE .05 .15
238 Sammy Sosa CE .20 .50
239 Cal Ripken CE .50 1.25
240 Jeff Bagwell CE .10 .30
241 Ken Griffey Jr. .60 1.50
242 Brett Butler .10 .30
243 Derrick May .05 .15
244 Pat Listach .05 .15
245 Mike Bordick .05 .15
246 Mark Langston .05 .15
247 Randy Velarde .05 .15
248 Julio Franco .10 .30
249 Chuck Knoblauch .10 .30
250 Bill Gullickson .05 .15
251 Dave Henderson .05 .15
252 Bret Boone .10 .30
253 Al Martin .05 .15
254 Armando Benitez .05 .15
255 Wil Cordero .05 .15
256 Al Leiter .10 .30
257 Luis Gonzalez .10 .30
258 Charlie O'Brien .05 .15
259 Tim Wallach .05 .15
260 Scott Sanders .05 .15
261 Tom Henke .05 .15
262 Otis Nixon .05 .15
263 Darren Daulton .10 .30
264 Manny Ramirez .20 .50
265 Bret Barberie .05 .15
266 Mel Rojas .05 .15
267 John Burkett .05 .15
268 Brady Anderson .10 .30
269 John Roper .05 .15
270 Shane Reynolds .05 .15
271 Barry Bonds .75 2.00
272 Alex Fernandez .05 .15
273 Brian McRae .05 .15
274 Todd Zeile .05 .15
275 Greg Swindell .05 .15
276 Johnny Ruffin .05 .15
277 Troy Neel .05 .15
278 Eric Karros .10 .30
279 John Hudek .05 .15
280 Thomas Howard .05 .15
281 Joe Carter .10 .30
282 Mike Devereaux .05 .15
283 Butch Henry .05 .15
284 Reggie Jefferson .05 .15
285 Mark Lemke .05 .15
286 Jeff Montgomery .05 .15
287 Ryan Thompson .05 .15
288 Paul Shuey .05 .15
289 Mark McGwire .75 2.00
290 Bernie Williams .20 .50
291 Mickey Morandini .05 .15
292 Scott Leius .05 .15
293 David Hulse .05 .15
294 Greg Gagne .05 .15
295 Moises Alou .10 .30
296 Geronimo Berroa .05 .15
297 Eddie Zambrano .05 .15
298 Alan Trammell .10 .30
299 Don Slaught .05 .15
300 Jose Rijo .05 .15
301 Joe Ausanio .05 .15
302 Tim Raines .10 .30
303 Melido Perez .05 .15
304 Kent Mercker .05 .15
305 James Mouton .05 .15
306 Luis Lopez .05 .15
307 Mike Kingery .05 .15
308 Willie Greene .05 .15
309 Cecil Fielder .10 .30
310 Scott Kamieniecki .05 .15
311 Mike Greenwell BES .05 .15
312 Bobby Bonilla BES .05 .15
313 Andres Galarraga BES .05 .15
314 Cal Ripken BES .50 1.25
315 Matt Williams BES .05 .15
316 Tom Pagnozzi BES .05 .15
317 Len Dykstra BES .05 .15
318 Frank Thomas BES .20 .50
319 Kirby Puckett BES .30 .75
320 Mike Piazza BES .30 .75
321 Jason Jacome .05 .15
322 Brian Hunter .05 .15
323 Brent Gates .05 .15
324 Jim Converse .05 .15
325 Damion Easley .05 .15
326 Dante Bichette .10 .30
327 Kurt Abbott .05 .15
328 Scott Cooper .05 .15
329 Mike Henneman .05 .15
330 Orlando Miller .05 .15
331 John Kruk .10 .30
332 Jose Oliva .05 .15
333 Reggie Sanders .10 .30
334 Omar Vizquel .20 .50
335 Devon White .10 .30
336 Mike Morgan .05 .15
337 J.R. Phillips .05 .15
338 Gary DiSarcina .05 .15
339 Joey Hamilton .05 .15
340 Randy Johnson .30 .75
341 Jim Leyritz .05 .15
342 Bobby Jones .05 .15
343 Jaime Navarro .05 .15
344 Bip Roberts .05 .15
345 Steve Karsay .05 .15
346 Kevin Stocker .05 .15
347 Jose Canseco .20 .50
348 Bill Wegman .05 .15
349 Rondell White .10 .30
350 Mo Vaughn .10 .30
351 Joe Orsulak .05 .15
352 Pat Meares .05 .15
353 Albie Lopez .05 .15
354 Edgar Martinez .20 .50
355 Brian Jordan .10 .30
356 Tommy Greene .05 .15
357 Chuck Carr .05 .15
358 Pedro Astacio .05 .15
359 Russ Davis .05 .15
360 Chris Hammond .05 .15
361 Gregg Jefferies .05 .15
362 Shane Mack .05 .15
363 Fred McGriff .20 .50
364 Pat Rapp .05 .15
365 Bill Swift .05 .15
366 Checklist .05 .15
367 Robin Ventura .10 .30
368 Bobby Witt .05 .15
369 Karl Rhodes .05 .15
370 Eddie Williams .05 .15
371 John Jaha .05 .15
372 Steve Howe .05 .15
373 Leo Gomez .05 .15
374 Hector Fajardo .05 .15
375 Jeff Bagwell .20 .50
376 Mark Acre .05 .15
377 Wayne Kirby .05 .15
378 Mark Portugal .05 .15
379 Jesus Tavarez .05 .15
380 Jim Lindeman .05 .15
381 Don Mattingly .75 2.00
382 Trevor Hoffman .10 .30
383 Chris Gomez .05 .15
384 Garret Anderson .10 .30
385 Bobby Munoz .05 .15
386 Jon Lieber .05 .15
387 Rick Helling .05 .15
388 Marvin Freeman .05 .15
389 Juan Castillo .05 .15
390 Jeff Cirillo .05 .15
391 Sean Berry .05 .15
392 Hector Carrasco .05 .15
393 Mark Grace .20 .50
394 Pat Kelly .05 .15
395 Tim Naehring .05 .15
396 Greg Pirkl .05 .15
397 John Smoltz .20 .50
398 Robby Thompson .05 .15
399 Rick White .05 .15
400 Frank Thomas .30 .75
401 Jeff Conine CS .05 .15
402 Jose Valentin CS .05 .15
403 Carlos Baerga CS .05 .15
404 Rick Aguilera CS .05 .15
405 Wilson Alvarez CS .05 .15
406 Juan Gonzalez CS .05 .15
407 Barry Larkin CS .10 .30
408 Ken Hill CS .05 .15
409 Chuck Carr CS .05 .15
410 Tim Raines CS .05 .15
411 Bryan Eversgerd .05 .15
412 Phil Plantier .05 .15
413 Josias Manzanillo .05 .15
414 Roberto Kelly .05 .15
415 Rickey Henderson .30 .75
416 John Smiley .05 .15
417 Kevin Brown .10 .30
418 Jimmy Key .10 .30
419 Wally Joyner .10 .30
420 Roberto Hernandez .05 .15
421 Felix Fermin .05 .15
422 Checklist .05 .15
423 Greg Vaughn .05 .15
424 Ray Lankford .10 .30
425 Greg Maddux .50 1.25
426 Mike Mussina .20 .50
427 Geronimo Pena .05 .15
428 David Nied .05 .15
429 Scott Erickson .05 .15
430 Kevin Mitchell .05 .15
431 Mike Lansing .05 .15
432 Brian Anderson .05 .15
433 Jeff King .05 .15
434 Ramon Martinez .05 .15
435 Kevin Seitzer .05 .15
436 Salomon Torres .05 .15
437 Brian L.Hunter .05 .15
438 Melvin Nieves .05 .15
439 Mike Kelly .05 .15
440 Marquis Grissom .10 .30
441 Chuck Finley .10 .30
442 Len Dykstra .10 .30
443 Ellis Burks .10 .30
444 Harold Baines .10 .30
445 Kevin Appier .10 .30
446 David Justice .10 .30
447 Darryl Kile .10 .30
448 John Olerud .10 .30
449 Greg McMichael .05 .15
450 Kirby Puckett .30 .75
451 Jose Valentin .05 .15
452 Rick Wilkins .05 .15
453 Arthur Rhodes .05 .15
454 Pat Hentgen .05 .15
455 Tom Gordon .05 .15
456 Tom Candiotti .05 .15
457 Jason Bere .05 .15
458 Wes Chamberlain .05 .15
459 Greg Colbrunn .05 .15
460 John Doherty .05 .15
461 Kevin Foster .05 .15
462 Mark Whiten .05 .15
463 Terry Steinbach .05 .15
464 Aaron Sele .05 .15
465 Kirt Manwaring .05 .15
466 Darren Hall .05 .15
467 Delino DeShields .05 .15
468 Andujar Cedeno .05 .15
469 Billy Ashley .05 .15
470 Kenny Lofton .10 .30
471 Pedro Munoz .05 .15
472 John Wetteland .10 .30
473 Tim Salmon .20 .50
474 Denny Neagle .10 .30
475 Tony Gwynn .40 1.00
476 Vinny Castilla .10 .30
477 Steve Dreyer .05 .15
478 Jeff Shaw .05 .15
479 Chad Ogea .05 .15
480 Scott Ruffcorn .05 .15
481 Lou Whitaker .10 .30
482 J.T. Snow .10 .30
483 Rich Rowland .05 .15
484 Denny Martinez .10 .30
485 Pedro Martinez .20 .50
486 Rusty Greer .10 .30
487 Dave Fleming .05 .15
488 John Dettmer .05 .15
489 Albert Belle .10 .30
490 Ravelo Manzanillo .05 .15
491 Henry Rodriguez .05 .15
492 Andrew Lorraine .05 .15
493 Dwayne Hosey .05 .15
494 Mike Blowers .05 .15
495 Turner Ward .05 .15
496 Fred McGriff EC .10 .30
497 Sammy Sosa EC .20 .50
498 Barry Larkin EC .10 .30
499 Andres Galarraga EC .05 .15
500 Gary Sheffield EC .05 .15
501 Jeff Bagwell EC .10 .30
502 Mike Piazza EC .30 .75
503 Moises Alou EC .05 .15
504 Bobby Bonilla EC .05 .15
505 Darren Daulton EC .05 .15
506 Jeff King EC .05 .15
507 Ray Lankford EC .05 .15
508 Tony Gwynn EC .20 .50
509 Barry Bonds EC .40 1.00
510 Cal Ripken EC .50 1.25
511 Mo Vaughn EC .05 .15
512 Tim Salmon EC .10 .30
513 Frank Thomas EC .20 .50
514 Albert Belle EC .05 .15
515 Cecil Fielder EC .05 .15
516 Kevin Appier EC .05 .15
517 Greg Vaughn EC .05 .15
518 Kirby Puckett EC .20 .50
519 Paul O'Neill EC .10 .30
520 Ruben Sierra EC .05 .15
521 Ken Griffey Jr. EC .40 1.00
522 Will Clark EC .10 .30
523 Joe Carter EC .05 .15
524 Antonio Osuna .05 .15
525 Glenallen Hill .05 .15
526 Alex Gonzalez .05 .15
527 Dave Stewart .10 .30
528 Ron Gant .10 .30
529 Jason Bates .05 .15
530 Mike Macfarlane .05 .15
531 Esteban Loaiza .05 .15
532 Joe Randa .10 .30
533 Dave Winfield .10 .30
534 Danny Darwin .05 .15
535 Pete Harnisch .05 .15
536 Joey Cora .05 .15
537 Jaime Navarro .05 .15
538 Marty Cordova .05 .15
539 Andujar Cedeno .05 .15
540 Mickey Tettleton .05 .15
541 Andy Van Slyke .20 .50
542 Carlos Perez RC .15 .40
543 Chipper Jones .30 .75
544 Tony Fernandez .05 .15
545 Tom Henke .05 .15
546 Pat Borders .05 .15
547 Chad Curtis .05 .15
548 Ray Durham .10 .30
549 Joe Oliver .05 .15
550 Jose Mesa .05 .15
551 Steve Finley .10 .30
552 Otis Nixon .05 .15
553 Jacob Brumfield .05 .15
554 Bill Swift .05 .15
555 Quilvio Veras .05 .15
556 Hideo Nomo RC 1.00 2.50
557 Joe Vitiello .05 .15
558 Mike Perez .05 .15
559 Charlie Hayes .05 .15
560 Brad Radke RC .30 .75
561 Darren Bragg .05 .15
562 Orel Hershiser .10 .30
563 Edgardo Alfonzo .05 .15
564 Doug Jones .05 .15
565 Andy Pettitte .20 .50
566 Benito Santiago .10 .30
567 John Burkett .05 .15
568 Brad Clontz .05 .15
569 Jim Abbott .20 .50
570 Joe Rosselli .05 .15
571 Mark Grudzielanek RC .30 .75
572 Dustin Hermanson .05 .15
573 Benji Gil .05 .15
574 Mark Whiten .05 .15
575 Mike Ignasiak .05 .15
576 Kevin Ritz .05 .15
577 Paul Quantrill .05 .15
578 Andre Dawson .10 .30
579 Jerald Clark .05 .15
580 Frank Rodriguez .05 .15
581 Mark Kiefer .05 .15
582 Trevor Wilson .05 .15
583 Gary Wilson RC .05 .15
584 Andy Stankiewicz .05 .15
585 Felipe Lira .05 .15
586 Michael Mimbs RC .05 .15
587 Jon Nunnally .05 .15
588 Tomas Perez RC .05 .15
589 Chad Fonville .05 .15
590 Todd Hollandsworth .05 .15
591 Roberto Petagine .05 .15
592 Mariano Rivera .75 2.00
593 Mark McLemore .05 .15
594 Bobby Witt .05 .15
595 Jose Offerman .05 .15
596 Jason Christiansen RC .05 .15
597 Jeff Manto .05 .15
598 Jim Dougherty RC .05 .15
599 Juan Acevedo RC .05 .15
600 Troy O'Leary .05 .15
601 Ron Villone .05 .15
602 Tripp Cromer .05 .15
603 Steve Scarsone .05 .15
604 Lance Parrish .10 .30
605 Ozzie Timmons .05 .15
606 Ray Holbert .05 .15
607 Tony Phillips .05 .15
608 Phil Plantier .05 .15
609 Shane Andrews .05 .15
610 Heathcliff Slocumb .05 .15
611 Bob Higginson RC .30 .75
612 Bob Tewksbury .05 .15
613 Terry Pendleton .10 .30
614 Scott Cooper TA .05 .15
615 John Wetteland TA .05 .15
616 Ken Hill TA .05 .15
617 Marquis Grissom TA .05 .15
618 Larry Walker TA .05 .15
619 Derek Bell TA .05 .15
620 David Cone TA .05 .15
621 Ken Caminiti TA .05 .15
622 Jack McDowell TA .05 .15
623 Vaughn Eshelman TA .05 .15
624 Brian McRae TA .05 .15
625 Gregg Jefferies TA .05 .15
626 Kevin Brown TA .05 .15
627 Lee Smith TA .05 .15
628 Tony Tarasco TA .05 .15
629 Brett Butler TA .05 .15
630 Jose Canseco TA .10 .30

1995 Stadium Club First Day Issue

COMPLETE SET (270) 125.00 250.00
COMMON CARD (1-270) .75 2.00
*STARS: 5X TO 12X BASIC CARDS
*ROOKIES: 3X TO 8X BASIC CARDS
*DP STARS: 1.25X TO 3X BASIC CARDS
RANDOM INSERTS IN TOPPS SER.2 PACKS
TEN PER TOPPS FACTORY SET
DPs INSERTED IN TOPPS SER.1 & 2 PACKS
BEWARE OF TRANSFERRED FDI LOGOS

1995 Stadium Club Members Only Parallel

COMP.SET w/o VR (755) 125.00 250.00
*MEM.ONLY 1-630: 1.5X TO 4X BASIC CARDS
CB1 Chipper Jones 3.00 8.00
CB2 Dustin Hermanson .30 .75
CB3 Ray Durham .60 1.50
CB4 Phil Nevin .30 .75
CB5 Billy Ashley .08 .25
CB6 Shawn Green .75 2.00
CB7 Jason Bates .08 .25
CB8 Benji Gil .08 .25
CB9 Marty Cordova .08 .25
CB10 Quilvio Veras .30 .75
CB11 Mark Grudzielanek .30 .75
CB12 Ruben Rivera .08 .25
CB13 Bill Pulsipher .08 .25
CB14 Derek Jeter 6.00 15.00
CB15 LaTroy Hawkins .08 .25
CC1 Mike Piazza 3.00 8.00
CC2 Ruben Sierra .08 .25
CC3 Tony Gwynn 3.00 8.00
CC4 Frank Thomas 2.50 6.00
CC5 Fred McGriff .60 1.50
CC6 Rafael Palmeiro .75 2.00
CC7 Bobby Bonilla .08 .25
CC8 Chili Davis .30 .75
CC9 Hal Morris .08 .25
CC10 Jose Canseco 1.25 3.00
CC11 Jay Bell .30 .75
CC12 Kirby Puckett 2.50 6.00
CC13 Gary Sheffield .75 2.00
CC14 Bob Hamelin .08 .25
CC15 Jeff Bagwell 1.25 3.00
CC16 Albert Belle .30 .75
CC17 Sammy Sosa 3.00 8.00
CC18 Ken Griffey Jr. 6.00 15.00
CC19 Todd Zeile .30 .75
CC20 Mo Vaughn .30 .75
CC21 Moises Alou .30 .75
CC22 Paul O'Neill .30 .75
CC23 Andres Galarraga .75 2.00
CC24 Greg Vaughn .30 .75
CC25 Len Dykstra .30 .75
CC26 Joe Carter .30 .75
CC27 Barry Bonds 3.00 8.00
CC28 Cecil Fielder .30 .75
PZ1 Jeff Bagwell 1.25 3.00
PZ2 Albert Belle .30 .75
PZ3 Barry Bonds 3.00 8.00
PZ4 Joe Carter .30 .75
PZ5 Cecil Fielder .30 .75
PZ6 Andres Galarraga .75 2.00
PZ7 Ken Griffey Jr. 6.00 15.00
PZ8 Paul Molitor .75 2.00
PZ9 Fred McGriff .60 1.50
PZ10 Rafael Palmeiro .75 2.00
PZ11 Frank Thomas 2.50 6.00
PZ12 Matt Williams .60 1.50
RL1 Jeff Bagwell 1.25 3.00
RL2 Mark McGwire 5.00 12.00
RL3 Ozzie Smith 2.50 6.00
RL4 Paul Molitor .75 2.00
RL5 Darryl Strawberry .08 .25
RL6 Eddie Murray .75 2.00
RL7 Tony Gwynn 3.00 8.00
RL8 Jose Canseco 1.25 3.00
RL9 Howard Johnson .08 .25
RL10 Andre Dawson .60 1.50
RL11 Matt Williams .60 1.50
RL12 Tim Raines .30 .75
RL13 Fred McGriff .60 1.50
RL14 Ken Griffey Jr. 6.00 15.00
RL15 Gary Sheffield .75 2.00
RL16 Dennis Eckersley .30 .75
RL17 Kevin Mitchell .08 .25
RL18 Will Clark .75 2.00
RL19 Darren Daulton .30 .75
RL20 Paul O'Neill .75 2.00
RL21 Julio Franco .08 .25
RL22 Albert Belle .30 .75
RL23 Juan Gonzalez 1.25 3.00
RL24 Kirby Puckett 2.50 6.00
RL25 Joe Carter .30 .75
RL26 Frank Thomas 2.50 6.00
RL27 Cal Ripken 6.00 15.00
RL28 John Olerud .30 .75
RL29 Ruben Sierra .30 .75
RL30 Barry Bonds 3.00 8.00
RL31 Cecil Fielder .30 .75
RL32 Roger Clemens 3.00 8.00
RL33 Don Mattingly 3.00 8.00
RL34 Terry Pendleton .08 .25
RL35 Rickey Henderson 1.25 3.00
RL36 Dave Winfield 1.25 3.00
RL37 Edgar Martinez .60 1.50
RL38 Wade Boggs 1.25 3.00
RL39 Willie McGee .30 .75
RL40 Andres Galarraga .75 2.00
SS1 Roberto Alomar .75 2.00
SS2 Barry Bonds 3.00 8.00
SS3 Jay Buhner .30 .7
SS4 Chuck Carr .08 .2
SS5 Don Mattingly 3.00 8.0
SS6 Raul Mondesi .60 1.5
SS7 Tim Salmon .75 2.0
SS8 Deion Sanders .30 .7
SS9 Devon White .08 .2
SS10 Mark Whiten .08 .2
SS11 Ken Griffey Jr. 6.00 15.0
SS12 Marquis Grissom .08 .2
SS13 Paul O'Neill .30 .7
SS14 Kenny Lofton .08 .2
SS15 Larry Walker .75 2.0
SS16 Scott Cooper .08 .2
SS17 Barry Larkin .75 2.0
SS18 Matt Williams .60 1.5
SS19 John Wetteland .30 .7
SS20 Randy Johnson 1.25 3.0
VRE1 Barry Bonds 3.00 8.0
VRE2 Ken Griffey Jr. 6.00 15.0
VRE3 Jeff Bagwell 1.25 3.0
VRE4 Albert Belle .30 .75
VRE5 Frank Thomas 2.50 6.0
VRE6 Tony Gwynn 3.00 8.0
VRE7 Kenny Lofton .30 .75
VRE8 Deion Sanders .75 2.0
VRE9 Ken Hill .08 .25
VRE10 Jimmy Key .30 .75

1995 Stadium Club Super Team Division Winners

COMP.BRAVES SET (11) 3.00 8.00
COMP.DODGERS SET (11) 3.00 8.00
COMP.INDIANS SET (11) 2.50 6.00
COMP.MARINERS SET (11) 3.00 8.00
COMP.REDS SET (11) 1.25 3.00
COMP.RED SOX SET (11) 2.50 6.00
COMMON SUPER TEAM .40 1.00
ONE TEAM SET PER '94 SUPER TEAM WINNER
B1T Braves DW Super Team .40 1.00
B19 Ryan Klesko .25 .60
B128 Mark Wohlers .10 .30
B151 Steve Avery .10 .30
B183 Tom Glavine .40 1.00
B200 Javy Lopez .25 .60
B393 Fred McGriff .40 1.00
B397 John Smoltz .40 1.00
B425 Greg Maddux 1.00 2.50
B446 Dave Justice .25 .60
B543 Chipper Jones .60 1.50
D7T Dodgers DW Super Team .40 1.00
D57 Raul Mondesi .25 .60
D149 Mike Piazza 1.00 2.50
D161 Ismael Valdes .10 .30
D242 Brett Butler .25 .60
D259 Tim Wallach .10 .30
D278 Eric Karros .25 .60
D434 Ramon Martinez .10 .30
D456 Tom Candiotti .10 .30
D467 Delino Deshields .10 .30
D556 Hideo Nomo 2.00 5.00
I19T Indians DW Super Team .40 1.00
I36 Carlos Baerga .10 .30
I147 Jim Thome .40 1.00
I186 Eddie Murray .60 1.50
I264 Manny Ramirez .40 1.00
I334 Omar Vizquel .40 1.00
I470 Kenny Lofton .25 .60
I484 Dennis Martinez .25 .60
I489 Albert Belle .25 .60
I550 Jose Mesa .10 .30
I562 Orel Hershiser .25 .60
M26T Mariners DW Super Team .40 1.00
M73 Jay Buhner .25 .60
M92 Chris Bosio .10 .30
M152 Dan Wilson .10 .30
M227 Tino Martinez .40 1.00
M241 Ken Griffey Jr. 1.25 3.00
M340 Randy Johnson .60 1.50
M354 Edgar Martinez .40 1.00
M421 Felix Fermin .10 .30
M494 Mike Blowers .10 .30
M536 Joey Cora .10 .30
RE3T Reds DW Super Team
RE35 Barry Larkin .40 1.00
RE231 Hal Morris .10 .30
RE252 Bret Boone .25 .60
RE280 Thomas Howard .10 .30
RE300 Jose Rijo .10 .30
RE333 Reggie Sanders .25 .60
RE392 Hector Carrasco .10 .30
RE416 John Smiley .10 .30
RE528 Ron Gant .25 .60
RE566 Benito Santiago .25 .60
RS1T Red Sox DW Super Team .40 1.00
RS10 Roger Clemens 1.25 3.00
RS62 John Valentin .10 .30
RS121 Mike Greenwell .10 .30
RS160 Lee Tinsley .10 .30
RS347 Jose Canseco .40 1.00
RS350 Mo Vaughn .25 .60
RS395 Tim Naehring .10 .30

464 Aaron Sele .10 .30
530 Mike Macfarlane .10 .30
600 Troy O'Leary .10 .30

1995 Stadium Club Super Team Master Photos

MP.BRAVES SET (10) 4.00 10.00
MP.INDIANS SET (10) 3.00 8.00
E TEAM SET PER '94 SUPER TEAM WINNER
teve Avery .15 .40
om Glavine .50 1.25
hipper Jones .75 2.00
ave Justice .30 .75
yan Klesko .30 .75
avy Lopez .30 .75
reg Maddux 1.25 3.00
red McGriff .50 1.25
ohn Smoltz .50 1.25
Mark Wohlers .15 .40
Carlos Baerga .15 .40
Albert Belle .30 .75
Orel Hershiser .30 .75
Kenny Lofton .30 .75
Dennis Martinez .30 .75
Jose Mesa .15 .40
Eddie Murray .75 2.00
Manny Ramirez .50 1.25
Jim Thome .50 1.25
Omar Vizquel .50 1.25

1995 Stadium Club Super Team World Series

OMP.WS SET (585) 50.00 120.00
OMP.EC/TA SET (45) 6.00 15.00
STARS: .6X TO 1.5X BASIC CARDS
ROOKIES: .6X TO 1.5X BASIC CARDS
ONE SET VIA MAIL PER 1994 BRAVES SUP.TM
SER.3 EC AND TA SUBSETS SHIPPED LATER

1995 Stadium Club Virtual Reality

COMPLETE SET (270) 40.00 100.00
COMPLETE SERIES 1 (135) 20.00 50.00
COMPLETE SERIES 2 (135) 20.00 50.00
*STARS: .75X TO 2X BASIC CARDS
ONE PER PACK/TWO PER RACK PACK

1995 Stadium Club Virtual Reality Members Only

COMPLETE FACT.SET (270) 40.00 100.00
*MEMBERS ONLY: 2X BASIC CARDS

1995 Stadium Club Clear Cut

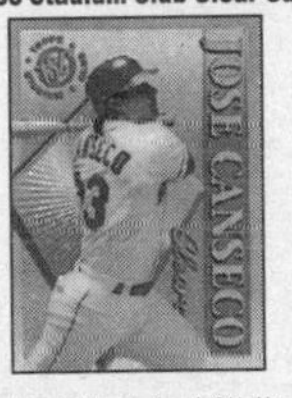

Randomly inserted at a rate of one in 24 hobby and retail packs, this 28-card set features a full color action photo of the player against a clear acetate background with the player's name printed vertically.

COMPLETE SET (28) 30.00 80.00
COMPLETE SERIES 1 (14) 15.00 40.00
COMPLETE SERIES 2 (14) 15.00 40.00
STATED ODDS 1:24 HOB/RET,1:10 RACK
CC1 Mike Piazza 4.00 10.00
CC2 Ruben Sierra 1.00 2.50
CC3 Tony Gwynn 3.00 8.00
CC4 Frank Thomas 2.50 6.00
CC5 Fred McGriff 1.50 4.00
CC6 Rafael Palmeiro 1.50 4.00
CC7 Bobby Bonilla 1.00 2.50
CC8 Chili Davis 1.00 2.50
CC9 Hal Morris .50 1.25
CC10 Jose Canseco 1.50 4.00
CC11 Jay Bell 1.00 2.50
CC12 Kirby Puckett 2.50 6.00
CC13 Gary Sheffield 1.00 2.50
CC14 Bob Hamelin .50 1.25
CC15 Jeff Bagwell 1.50 4.00
CC16 Albert Belle 1.00 2.50
CC17 Sammy Sosa 2.50 6.00
CC18 Ken Griffey Jr. 5.00 12.00
CC19 Todd Zeile .50 1.25
CC20 Mo Vaughn 1.00 2.50
CC21 Moises Alou 1.00 2.50
CC22 Paul O'Neill 1.50 4.00
CC23 Andres Galarraga 1.00 2.50
CC24 Greg Vaughn .50 1.25
CC25 Len Dykstra 1.00 2.50
CC26 Joe Carter 1.00 2.50
CC27 Barry Bonds 6.00 15.00
CC28 Cecil Fielder 1.00 2.50

1995 Stadium Club Crunch Time

This 20-card standard-size set features home run hitters and was randomly inserted in first series rack packs. The cards are numbered as "X" of 20 in the upper right corner.

COMPLETE SET (20) 20.00 50.00
ONE PER SER.1 RACK PACK
1 Jeff Bagwell .75 2.00
2 Kirby Puckett 1.25 3.00
3 Frank Thomas 1.25 3.00
4 Albert Belle .50 1.25
5 Julio Franco .50 1.25
6 Jose Canseco .75 2.00
7 Paul Molitor .50 1.25
8 Joe Carter .50 1.25
9 Ken Griffey Jr. 2.50 6.00
10 Larry Walker .50 1.25
11 Dante Bichette .50 1.25
12 Carlos Baerga .25 .60
13 Fred McGriff .75 2.00
14 Ruben Sierra .50 1.25
15 Will Clark .75 2.00
16 Moises Alou .50 1.25
17 Rafael Palmeiro .75 2.00
18 Travis Fryman .50 1.25
19 Barry Bonds 3.00 8.00
20 Cal Ripken 4.00 10.00

1995 Stadium Club Crystal Ball

This 15-card standard-size set was inserted into series three packs at a rate of one in 24. Fifteen leading 1995 rookies and prospects were featured in this set. The player is identified on the top and the cards are numbered with a "CB" prefix in the upper left corner.

COMPLETE SET (15) 30.00 80.00
SER.3 STATED ODDS 1:24
CB1 Chipper Jones 4.00 10.00
CB2 Dustin Hermanson .75 2.00
CB3 Ray Durham 1.50 4.00
CB4 Phil Nevin 1.50 4.00
CB5 Billy Ashley .75 2.00
CB6 Shawn Green 1.50 4.00
CB7 Jason Bates .75 2.00
CB8 Benji Gil .75 2.00
CB9 Marty Cordova .75 2.00
CB10 Quilvio Veras .75 2.00
CB11 Mark Grudzielanek 2.50 6.00
CB12 Ruben Rivera .75 2.00
CB13 Bill Pulsipher .75 2.00
CB14 Derek Jeter 8.00 20.00
CB15 LaTroy Hawkins .75 2.00

1995 Stadium Club Phone Cards

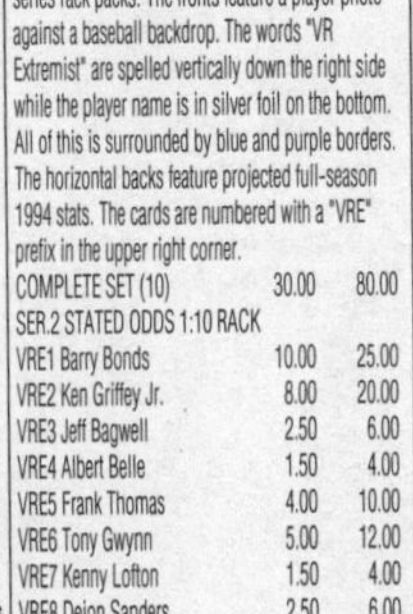

These phone cards were randomly inserted into packs. The prizes for these cards were as follows. The Gold Winner card was redeemable for the ring depicted on the front of the card. The silver winner card was redeemable for a set of all 39 phone cards. The regular winner card was redeemable for a Ring Leaders set. The fronts feature a photo of a specific ring while the backs have game information. If the card was not a winner for any of the prizes, it was still good for three minutes of time. The phone cards expired on January 1, 1996. If the PIN number is revealed the value is a percentage of an untouched card.

COMPLETE REGULAR SET (13) 8.00 20.00
COMMON REGULAR CARD 1.00 2.50
COMPLETE SILVER SET (13) 15.00 30.00
COMMON SILVER CARD 2.00 4.00
COMPLETE GOLD SET (13) 30.00 75.00
COMMON GOLD CARD 4.00 8.00
*PIN NUMBER REVEALED: .25X to .50X HI

1995 Stadium Club Power Zone

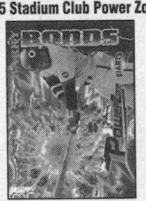

This 12-card standard-size set was inserted into series three packs at a rate of one in 24. The cards are numbered in the upper right corner with a "PZ" prefix.

COMPLETE SET (12) 20.00 50.00
SER.3 STATED ODDS 1:24
PZ1 Jeff Bagwell 1.50 4.00
PZ2 Albert Belle 1.00 2.50
PZ3 Barry Bonds 6.00 15.00
PZ4 Joe Carter 1.00 2.50
PZ5 Cecil Fielder 1.00 2.50
PZ6 Andres Galarraga 1.00 2.50
PZ7 Ken Griffey Jr. 5.00 12.00
PZ8 Paul Molitor 1.00 2.50
PZ9 Fred McGriff 1.50 4.00
PZ10 Rafael Palmeiro 1.50 4.00
PZ11 Frank Thomas 2.50 6.00
PZ12 Matt Williams 1.00 2.50

1995 Stadium Club Ring Leaders

Randomly inserted in packs, this set features players who have won various awards or titles. This set was also redeemable as a prize with winning regular phone cards. This set features Stadium Club's "Power Matrix Technology," which makes the cards shine and glow. The horizontal fronts feature a player photo, rings in both upper corners as well as other designs that make for a very busy front. The backs have information on how the player earned his rings, along with a player photo and some other pertinent information.

COMPLETE SET (40) 40.00 100.00
COMPLETE SERIES 1 (20) 20.00 50.00
COMPLETE SERIES 2 (20) 20.00 50.00
STATED ODDS 1:24 HOB/RET,1:10 RACK
ONE SET VIA MAIL PER PHONE WINNER
RL1 Jeff Bagwell 1.25 3.00
RL2 Mark McGwire 5.00 12.00
RL3 Ozzie Smith 3.00 8.00
RL4 Paul Molitor .75 2.00
RL5 Darryl Strawberry .75 2.00
RL6 Eddie Murray 2.00 5.00
RL7 Tony Gwynn 2.50 6.00
RL8 Jose Canseco 1.25 3.00
RL9 Howard Johnson .75 2.00
RL10 Andre Dawson .75 2.00
RL11 Matt Williams .75 2.00
RL12 Tim Raines .75 2.00
RL13 Fred McGriff 1.25 3.00
RL14 Ken Griffey Jr. 4.00 10.00
RL15 Gary Sheffield .75 2.00
RL16 Dennis Eckersley .75 2.00
RL17 Kevin Mitchell .75 2.00
RL18 Will Clark 1.25 3.00
RL19 Darren Daulton .75 2.00
RL20 Paul O'Neill 1.25 3.00
RL21 Julio Franco .75 2.00
RL22 Albert Belle .75 2.00
RL23 Juan Gonzalez .75 2.00
RL24 Kirby Puckett 2.00 5.00
RL25 Joe Carter .75 2.00
RL26 Frank Thomas 2.00 5.00
RL27 Cal Ripken 6.00 15.00
RL28 John Olerud .75 2.00
RL29 Ruben Sierra .75 2.00
RL30 Barry Bonds 5.00 12.00
RL31 Cecil Fielder .75 2.00
RL32 Roger Clemens 4.00 10.00
RL33 Don Mattingly 5.00 12.00
RL34 Terry Pendleton .75 2.00
RL35 Rickey Henderson 2.00 5.00
RL36 Dave Winfield .75 2.00
RL37 Edgar Martinez 1.25 3.00
RL38 Wade Boggs 1.25 3.00
RL39 Willie McGee .75 2.00
RL40 Andres Galarraga .75 2.00

1995 Stadium Club Super Skills

This 20-card set was randomly inserted into hobby packs. The cards are numbered in the upper left as "X" of 9.

COMPLETE SET (20) 30.00 80.00
COMPLETE SERIES 1 (9) 12.50 30.00
COMPLETE SERIES 2 (11) 15.00 40.00
STATED ODDS 1:24 HOBBY
SS1 Roberto Alomar 1.50 4.00
SS2 Barry Bonds 6.00 15.00
SS3 Jay Buhner 1.00 2.50
SS4 Chuck Carr .50 1.25
SS5 Don Mattingly 6.00 15.00
SS6 Raul Mondesi 1.00 2.50
SS7 Tim Salmon 1.50 4.00
SS8 Deion Sanders 1.50 4.00
SS9 Devon White 1.00 2.50
SS10 Mark Whiten .50 1.25
SS11 Ken Griffey Jr. 5.00 12.00
SS12 Marquis Grissom 1.00 2.50
SS13 Paul O'Neill 1.50 4.00
SS14 Kenny Lofton 1.00 2.50
SS15 Larry Walker 1.00 2.50
SS16 Scott Cooper .50 1.25
SS17 Barry Larkin 1.50 4.00
SS18 Matt Williams 1.00 2.50
SS19 John Wetteland 1.00 2.50
SS20 Randy Johnson 2.50 6.00

1995 Stadium Club Virtual Extremists

This 10-card set was inserted randomly into second series rack packs. The fronts feature a player photo against a baseball backdrop. The words "VR Extremist" are spelled vertically down the right side while the player name is in silver foil on the bottom. All of this is surrounded by blue and purple borders. The horizontal backs feature projected full-season 1994 stats. The cards are numbered with a "VRE" prefix in the upper right corner.

COMPLETE SET (10) 30.00 80.00
SER.2 STATED ODDS 1:10 RACK
VRE1 Barry Bonds 10.00 25.00
VRE2 Ken Griffey Jr. 8.00 20.00
VRE3 Jeff Bagwell 2.50 6.00
VRE4 Albert Belle 1.50 4.00
VRE5 Frank Thomas 4.00 10.00
VRE6 Tony Gwynn 5.00 12.00
VRE7 Kenny Lofton 1.50 4.00
VRE8 Deion Sanders 2.50 6.00
VRE9 Ken Hill .75 2.00
VRE10 Jimmy Key 1.50 4.00

1995 Stadium Club Members Only 50

Topps produced a 50-card boxed set for each of the four major sports. With their club membership, members received one set of their choice and had the option of purchasing additional sets for $10.00 each. Player section was based on 1994 leaders from both leagues in various statistical categories. The five Finest cards (46-50) represent Topps' selection of the top rookies of 1994. The color action photos on the fronts have brightly-colored backgrounds and carry the distinctive Topps Stadium Club Members Only gold foil seal. The backs present a second color photo and player profile.

COMP. FACT SET (50) 8.00 20.00
1 Moises Alou .08 .25
2 Jeff Bagwell .40 1.00
3 Albert Belle .08 .25
4 Andy Benes .02 .10
5 Dante Bichette .08 .25
6 Craig Biggio .20 .50
7 Wade Boggs .40 1.00
8 Barry Bonds .60 1.50
9 Brett Butler .08 .25
10 Jose Canseco .40 1.00
11 Joe Carter .08 .25
12 Vince Coleman .02 .10
13 Jeff Conine .02 .10
14 Cecil Fielder .08 .25
15 John Franco .08 .25
16 Julio Franco .08 .25
17 Travis Fryman .08 .25
18 Andres Galarraga .30 .75
19 Ken Griffey Jr. 1.25 3.00
20 Marquis Grissom .02 .10
21 Tony Gwynn .75 2.00
22 Ken Hill .02 .10
23 Randy Johnson .50 1.25
24 Lance Johnson .02 .10
25 Jimmy Key .08 .25
26 Chuck Knoblauch .20 .50
27 Ray Lankford .08 .25
28 Darren Lewis .02 .10
29 Kenny Lofton .20 .50
30 Greg Maddux 1.00 2.50
31 Fred McGriff .20 .50
32 Kevin Mitchell .02 .10
33 Paul Molitor .40 1.00
34 Hal Morris .02 .10
35 Paul O'Neill .08 .25
36 Rafael Palmeiro .30 .75
37 Tony Phillips .02 .10
38 Mike Piazza 1.00 2.50
39 Kirby Puckett .50 1.25
40 Cal Ripken 1.50 4.00
41 Deion Sanders .30 .75
42 Lee Smith .08 .25
43 Frank Thomas .50 1.25
44 Larry Walker .30 .75
45 Matt Williams .20 .50
46 Manny Ramirez .40 1.00
47 Joey Hamilton .02 .10
48 Raul Mondesi .20 .50
49 Bob Hamelin .02 .10
50 Ryan Klesko .08 .25

1995 Stadium Club Members Only Finest Bronze

COMPLETE SET (4) 20.00 50.00
1 Bob Hamelin 1.25 3.00
2 Greg Maddux 15.00 40.00
3 David Cone 2.00 5.00
4 Raul Mondesi 2.00 5.00

1996 Stadium Club

The 1996 Stadium Club set consists of 450 cards with cards 1-225 in first series packs and 226-450 in second series packs. The product was primarily distributed in first and second series foil-wrapped packs.There was also a factory set, which included the Mantle insert cards, packaged in mini-cereal box type cartons and made available through retail outlets. The set includes a Team TSC subset (181-270). These subset cards were slightly shortprinted in comparison to the other cards in the set. Though not confirmed by the manufacturer, it is believed that card number 22 (Roberto Hernandez) is a short-print.

COMPLETE SET (450) 25.00 60.00
COMP.CEREAL SET (454) 25.00 60.00
COMPLETE SERIES 1 (225) 12.50 30.00
COMPLETE SERIES 2 (225) 12.50 30.00
COMMON (1-180/271-450) .10 .30
COMMON TSC SP (181-270) .20 .50
SILVER FOIL: ONLY IN CEREAL SETS
1 Hideo Nomo .30 .75
2 Paul Molitor .10 .30
3 Garret Anderson .10 .30
4 Jose Mesa .10 .30
5 Vinny Castilla .10 .30
6 Mike Mussina .20 .50
7 Ray Durham .10 .30
8 Jack McDowell .10 .30
9 Juan Gonzalez .10 .30
10 Chipper Jones .30 .75
11 Deion Sanders .20 .50
12 Rondell White .10 .30
13 Tom Henke .10 .30
14 Derek Bell .10 .30
15 Randy Myers .10 .30
16 Randy Johnson .30 .75
17 Len Dykstra .10 .30
18 Bill Pulsipher .10 .30
19 Greg Colbrunn .10 .30
20 David Wells .10 .30
21 Chad Curtis .10 .30
22 Roberto Hernandez SP 2.00 5.00
23 Kirby Puckett .30 .75
24 Joe Vitiello .10 .30
25 Roger Clemens .60 1.50
26 Al Martin .10 .30
27 Chad Ogea .10 .30
28 David Segui .10 .30
29 Joey Hamilton .10 .30
30 Dan Wilson .10 .30
31 Chad Fonville .10 .30
32 Bernard Gilkey .10 .30
33 Kevin Seitzer .10 .30
34 Shawn Green .10 .30
35 Rick Aguilera .10 .30
36 Gary DiSarcina .10 .30
37 Jaime Navarro .10 .30
38 Doug Jones .10 .30
39 Brent Gates .10 .30
40 Dean Palmer .10 .30
41 Pat Rapp .10 .30
42 Tony Clark .10 .30
43 Bill Swift .10 .30
44 Randy Velarde .10 .30
45 Matt Williams .10 .30
46 John Mabry .10 .30
47 Mike Fetters .10 .30
48 Orlando Miller .10 .30
49 Tom Glavine .20 .50
50 Delino DeShields .10 .30
51 Scott Erickson .10 .30
52 Andy Van Slyke .20 .50
53 Jim Bullinger .10 .30
54 Lyle Mouton .10 .30
55 Bret Saberhagen .10 .30
56 Benito Santiago .10 .30
57 Dan Miceli .10 .30
58 Carl Everett .10 .30
59 Rod Beck .10 .30
60 Phil Nevin .10 .30
61 Jason Giambi .10 .30
62 Paul Menhart .10 .30
63 Eric Karros .10 .30
64 Allen Watson .10 .30
65 Jeff Cirillo .10 .30
66 Lee Smith .10 .30
67 Sean Berry .10 .30
68 Luis Sojo .10 .30
69 Jeff Montgomery .10 .30
70 Todd Hundley .10 .30
71 John Burkett .10 .30
72 Mark Gubicza .10 .30
73 Don Mattingly .75 2.00
74 Jeff Brantley .10 .30
75 Matt Walbeck .10 .30
76 Steve Parris .10 .30
77 Ken Caminiti .10 .30
78 Kirt Manwaring .10 .30
79 Greg Vaughn .10 .30
80 Pedro Martinez .20 .50
81 Benji Gil .10 .30
82 Heathcliff Slocumb .10 .30
83 Joe Girardi .10 .30
84 Sean Bergman .10 .30
85 Matt Karchner .10 .30
86 Butch Huskey .10 .30
87 Mike Morgan .10 .30
88 Todd Worrell .10 .30
89 Mike Bordick .10 .30
90 Bip Roberts .10 .30
91 Mike Hampton .10 .30
92 Troy O'Leary .10 .30
93 Wally Joyner .10 .30
94 Dave Stevens .10 .30
95 Cecil Fielder .10 .30
96 Wade Boggs .20 .50
97 Hal Morris .10 .30
98 Mickey Tettleton .10 .30
99 Jeff Kent .10 .30
100 Denny Martinez .10 .30
101 Luis Gonzalez .10 .30
102 John Jaha .10 .30
103 Javier Lopez .10 .30
104 Mark McGwire .75 2.00
105 Ken Griffey Jr. .60 1.50
106 Darren Daulton .10 .30
107 Bryan Rekar .10 .30
108 Mike Macfarlane .10 .30
109 Gary Gaetti .10 .30
110 Shane Reynolds .10 .30
111 Pat Meares .10 .30
112 Jason Schmidt .20 .50
113 Otis Nixon .10 .30
114 John Franco .10 .30
115 Marc Newfield .10 .30
116 Andy Benes .10 .30
117 Ozzie Guillen .10 .30
118 Brian Jordan .10 .30
119 Terry Pendleton .10 .30
120 Chuck Finley .10 .30
121 Scott Stahoviak .10 .30
122 Sid Fernandez .10 .30
123 Derek Jeter .75 2.00
124 John Smiley .10 .30
125 David Bell .10 .30
126 Brett Butler .10 .30
127 Doug Drabek .10 .30
128 J.T. Snow .10 .30
129 Joe Carter .10 .30
130 Dennis Eckersley .10 .30
131 Marty Cordova .10 .30
132 Greg Maddux .50 1.25
133 Tom Goodwin .10 .30
134 Andy Ashby .10 .30
135 Paul Sorrento .10 .30
136 Ricky Bones .10 .30
137 Shawon Dunston .10 .30
138 Moises Alou .10 .30
139 Mickey Morandini .10 .30
140 Ramon Martinez .10 .30
141 Royce Clayton .10 .30
142 Brad Ausmus .10 .30
143 Kenny Rogers .10 .30
144 Tim Naehring .10 .30
145 Chris Gomez .10 .30
146 Bobby Bonilla .10 .30
147 Wilson Alvarez .10 .30
148 Johnny Damon .20 .50
149 Pat Hentgen .10 .30
150 Andres Galarraga .10 .30
151 David Cone .10 .30
152 Lance Johnson .10 .30
153 Carlos Garcia .10 .30
154 Doug Johns .10 .30
155 Midre Cummings .10 .30
156 Steve Sparks .10 .30
157 Sandy Martinez .10 .30
158 Wm. Van Landingham .10 .30
159 David Justice .10 .30
160 Mark Grace .20 .50
161 Robb Nen .10 .30
162 Mike Greenwell .10 .30
163 Brad Radke .10 .30
164 Edgardo Alfonzo .10 .30
165 Mark Leiter .10 .30
166 Walt Weiss .10 .30
167 Mel Rojas .10 .30
168 Bret Boone .10 .30
169 Ricky Bottalico .10 .30
170 Bobby Higginson .10 .30
171 Trevor Hoffman .10 .30
172 Jay Bell .10 .30
173 Gabe White .10 .30
174 Curtis Goodwin .10 .30
175 Tyler Green .10 .30
176 Roberto Alomar .20 .50
177 Sterling Hitchcock .10 .30
178 Ryan Klesko .10 .30
179 Donne Wall .10 .30
180 Brian McRae .10 .30
181 Will Clark TSC SP .30 .75
182 Frank Thomas TSC SP .40 1.00
183 Jeff Bagwell TSC SP .20 .50
184 Mo Vaughn TSC SP .20 .50
185 Tino Martinez TSC SP .30 .75
186 Craig Biggio TSC SP .30 .75
187 Chuck Knoblauch TSC SP .20 .50
188 Carlos Baerga TSC SP .20 .50
189 Quilvio Veras TSC SP .20 .50
190 Luis Alicea TSC SP .20 .50
191 Jim Thome TSC SP .30 .75
192 Mike Blowers TSC SP .20 .50
193 Robin Ventura TSC SP .20 .50
194 Jeff King TSC SP .20 .50
195 Tony Phillips TSC SP .20 .50
196 John Valentin TSC SP .20 .50
197 Barry Larkin TSC SP .30 .75
198 Cal Ripken TSC SP 1.25 3.00
199 Omar Vizquel TSC SP .30 .75
200 Kurt Abbott TSC SP .20 .50
201 Albert Belle TSC SP .20 .50
202 Barry Bonds TSC SP 1.00 2.50
203 Ron Gant TSC SP .20 .50
204 Dante Bichette TSC SP .20 .50
205 Jeff Conine TSC SP .20 .50
206 Jim Edmonds TSC SP .20 .50
207 Stan Javier TSC SP .20 .50
208 Kenny Lofton TSC SP .20 .50
209 Ray Lankford TSC SP .20 .50
210 Bernie Williams TSC SP .30 .75
211 Jay Buhner TSC SP .20 .50
212 Paul O'Neill TSC SP .30 .75
213 Tim Salmon TSC SP .30 .75
214 Reggie Sanders TSC SP .20 .50
215 Manny Ramirez TSC SP .30 .75
216 Mike Piazza TSC SP .60 1.50
217 Mike Stanley TSC SP .20 .50
218 Tony Eusebio TSC SP .20 .50
219 Chris Hoiles TSC SP .20 .50
220 Ron Karkovice TSC SP .20 .50
221 Edgar Martinez TSC SP .30 .75
222 Chili Davis TSC SP .20 .50
223 Jose Canseco TSC SP .20 .50
224 Eddie Murray TSC SP .40 1.00
225 Geronimo Berroa TSC SP .20 .50
226 Chipper Jones TSC SP .40 1.00
227 Garret Anderson TSC SP .20 .50
228 Marty Cordova TSC SP .20 .50
229 Jon Nunnally TSC SP .20 .50
230 Brian L.Hunter TSC SP .20 .50
231 Shawn Green TSC SP .20 .50
232 Ray Durham TSC SP .20 .50
233 Alex Gonzalez TSC SP .20 .50
234 Bobby Higginson TSC SP .20 .50
235 Randy Johnson TSC SP .40 1.00
236 Al Leiter TSC SP .20 .50
237 Tom Glavine TSC SP .30 .75
238 Kenny Rogers TSC SP .20 .50
239 Mike Hampton TSC SP .20 .50
240 David Wells TSC SP .20 .50
241 Jim Abbott TSC SP .30 .75
242 Denny Neagle TSC SP .20 .50
243 Wilson Alvarez TSC SP .20 .50
244 John Smiley TSC SP .20 .50
245 Greg Maddux TSC SP .30 .75
246 Andy Ashby TSC SP .20 .50
247 Hideo Nomo TSC SP .40 1.00
248 Pat Rapp TSC SP .20 .50
249 Tim Wakefield TSC SP .20 .50
250 John Smoltz TSC SP .30 .75
251 Joey Hamilton TSC SP .20 .50
252 Frank Castillo TSC SP .20 .50
253 Denny Martinez TSC SP .20 .50
254 Jaime Navarro TSC SP .20 .50
255 Karim Garcia TSC SP .20 .50
256 Bob Abreu TSC SP .40 1.00
257 Butch Huskey TSC SP .20 .50
258 Ruben Rivera TSC SP .20 .50
259 Johnny Damon TSC SP .30 .75
260 Derek Jeter TSC SP 1.00 2.50
261 Dennis Eckersley TSC SP .20 .50
262 Jose Mesa TSC SP .20 .50
263 Tom Henke TSC SP .20 .50
264 Rick Aguilera TSC SP .20 .50
265 Randy Myers TSC SP .20 .50
266 John Franco TSC SP .20 .50
267 Jeff Brantley TSC SP .20 .50
268 John Wetteland TSC SP .20 .50
269 Mark Wohlers TSC SP .20 .50
270 Rod Beck TSC SP .20 .50
271 Barry Larkin .20 .50
272 Paul O'Neill .20 .50
273 Bobby Jones .10 .30
274 Will Clark .20 .50
275 Steve Avery .10 .30
276 Jim Edmonds .10 .30
277 John Olerud .10 .30
278 Carlos Perez .10 .30
279 Chris Hoiles .10 .30
280 Jeff Conine .10 .30
281 Jim Eisenreich .10 .30
282 Jason Jacome .10 .30
283 Ray Lankford .10 .30
284 John Wasdin .10 .30
285 Frank Thomas .30 .75
286 Jason Isringhausen .10 .30
287 Glenallen Hill .10 .30
288 Esteban Loaiza .10 .30
289 Bernie Williams .20 .50
290 Curtis Leskanic .10 .30
291 Scott Cooper .10 .30
292 Curt Schilling .10 .30
293 Eddie Murray .30 .75
294 Rick Krivda .10 .30
295 Domingo Cedeno .10 .30
296 Jeff Fassero .10 .30
297 Albert Belle .10 .30
298 Craig Biggio .20 .50
299 Fernando Vina .10 .30
300 Edgar Martinez .20 .50
301 Tony Gwynn .40 1.00
302 Felipe Lira .10 .30
303 Mo Vaughn .10 .30
304 Alex Fernandez .10 .30
305 Keith Lockhart .10 .30
306 Roger Pavlik .10 .30
307 Lee Tinsley .10 .30
308 Omar Vizquel .20 .50
309 Scott Servais .10 .30
310 Danny Tartabull .10 .30
311 Chili Davis .10 .30
312 Cal Eldred .10 .30
313 Roger Cedeno .10 .30
314 Chris Hammond .10 .30
315 Rusty Greer .10 .30
316 Brady Anderson .10 .30
317 Ron Villone .10 .30
318 Mark Carreon .10 .30
319 Larry Walker .10 .30
320 Pete Harnisch .10 .30
321 Robin Ventura .10 .30
322 Tim Belcher .10 .30
323 Tony Tarasco .10 .30
324 Juan Guzman .10 .30
325 Kenny Lofton .10 .30
326 Kevin Foster .10 .30

327 Wil Cordero .10 .30
328 Troy Percival .10 .30
329 Turk Wendell .10 .30
330 Thomas Howard .10 .30
331 Carlos Baerga .10 .30
332 B.J. Surhoff .10 .30
333 Jay Buhner .10 .30
334 Andujar Cedeno .10 .30
335 Jeff King .10 .30
336 Dante Bichette .10 .30
337 Alan Trammell .10 .30
338 Scott Leius .10 .30
339 Chris Snopek .10 .30
340 Roger Bailey .10 .30
341 Jacob Brumfield .10 .30
342 Jose Canseco .20 .50
343 Rafael Palmeiro .20 .50
344 Quilvio Veras .10 .30
345 Darrin Fletcher .10 .30
346 Carlos Delgado .10 .30
347 Tony Eusebio .10 .30
348 Ismael Valdes .10 .30
349 Terry Steinbach .10 .30
350 Orel Hershiser .10 .30
351 Kurt Abbott .10 .30
352 Jody Reed .10 .30
353 David Howard .10 .30
354 Ruben Sierra .10 .30
355 John Ericks .10 .30
356 Buck Showalter .10 .30
357 Jim Thome .20 .50
358 Geronimo Berroa .10 .30
359 Robby Thompson .10 .30
360 Jose Vizcaino .10 .30
361 Jeff Frye .10 .30
362 Kevin Appier .10 .30
363 Pat Kelly .10 .30
364 Ron Gant .10 .30
365 Luis Alicea .10 .30
366 Armando Benitez .10 .30
367 Rico Brogna .10 .30
368 Manny Ramirez .20 .50
369 Mike Lansing .10 .30
370 Sammy Sosa .30 .75
371 Don Wengert .10 .30
372 Dave Nilsson .10 .30
373 Sandy Alomar Jr. .10 .30
374 Joey Cora .10 .30
375 Larry Thomas .10 .30
376 John Valentin .10 .30
377 Kevin Ritz .10 .30
378 Steve Finley .10 .30
379 Frank Rodriguez .10 .30
380 Ivan Rodriguez .20 .50
381 Alex Ochoa .10 .30
382 Mark Lemke .10 .30
383 Scott Brosius .10 .30
384 James Mouton .10 .30
385 Mark Langston .10 .30
386 Ed Sprague .10 .30
387 Joe Oliver .10 .30
388 Steve Ontiveros .10 .30
389 Rey Sanchez .10 .30
390 Mike Henneman .10 .30
391 Jose Valentin .10 .30
392 Tom Candiotti .10 .30
393 Damon Buford .10 .30
394 Erik Hanson .10 .30
395 Mark Smith .10 .30
396 Pete Schourek .10 .30
397 John Flaherty .10 .30
398 Dave Martinez .10 .30
399 Tommy Greene .10 .30
400 Gary Sheffield .10 .30
401 Glenn Dishman .10 .30
402 Barry Bonds .75 2.00
403 Tom Pagnozzi .10 .30
404 Todd Stottlemyre .10 .30
405 Tim Salmon .20 .50
406 John Hudek .10 .30
407 Fred McGriff .20 .50
408 Orlando Merced .10 .30
409 Brian Barber .10 .30
410 Ryan Thompson .10 .30
411 Mariano Rivera .60 1.50
412 Eric Young .10 .30
413 Chris Bosio .10 .30
414 Chuck Knoblauch .10 .30
415 Jamie Moyer .10 .30
416 Chan Ho Park .10 .30
417 Mark Portugal .10 .30
418 Tim Raines .10 .30
419 Antonio Osuna .10 .30
420 Todd Zeile .10 .30
421 Steve Wojciechowski .10 .30
422 Marquis Grissom .10 .30
423 Norm Charlton .10 .30
424 Cal Ripken 1.00 2.50
425 Gregg Jefferies .10 .30
426 Mike Stanton .10 .30
427 Tony Fernandez .10 .30
428 Jose Rijo .10 .30
429 Jeff Bagwell .20 .50
430 Raul Mondesi .10 .30
431 Travis Fryman .10 .30
432 Ron Karkovice .10 .30
433 Alan Benes .10 .30
434 Tony Phillips .10 .30
435 Reggie Sanders .10 .30
436 Andy Pettitte .20 .50
437 Matt Lawton RC .10 .30
438 Jeff Blauser .10 .30
439 Michael Tucker .10 .30
440 Mark Loretta .10 .30
441 Charlie Hayes .10 .30
442 Mike Piazza .50 1.25
443 Shane Andrews .10 .30
444 Jeff Suppan .10 .30
445 Steve Rodriguez .10 .30
446 Mike Matheny .10 .30
447 Trenidad Hubbard .10 .30
448 Denny Hocking .10 .30
449 Mark Grudzielanek .10 .30
450 Joe Randa .10 .30
NNO Roger Clemens 2.00 5.00
Extreme Gold PROMO

1996 Stadium Club Members Only Parallel

COMP.SET W/INSERTS (555) 250.00 500.00
COMPLETE BASE SET (450) 100.00 200.00
COMMON CARD (1-450) .10 .25
COMMON MANTLE (MMA1-MMA19) 2.00 5.00
*MEMBERS ONLY: 6X BASIC CARDS
M1 Jeff Bagwell 1.50 4.00
M2 Barry Bonds 4.00 10.00
M3 Jose Canseco 1.50 4.00
M4 Roger Clemens 4.00 10.00
M5 Dennis Eckersley .60 1.50
M6 Greg Maddux 5.00 12.00
M7 Cal Ripken 8.00 20.00
M8 Frank Thomas 3.00 8.00
BB1 Sammy Sosa 4.00 10.00
BB2 Barry Bonds 4.00 10.00
BB3 Reggie Sanders .40 1.00
BB4 Craig Biggio .75 2.00
BB5 Raul Mondesi .75 2.00
BB6 Ron Gant .40 1.00
BB7 Ray Lankford .60 1.50
BB8 Glenallen Hill .40 1.00
BB9 Chad Curtis .40 1.00
BB10 John Valentin .60 1.50
MH1 Frank Thomas 3.00 8.00
MH2 Ken Griffey Jr. 8.00 20.00
MH3 Hideo Nomo 1.50 4.00
MH4 Ozzie Smith 1.50 4.00
MH5 Will Clark 1.25 3.00
MH6 Jack McDowell .40 1.00
MH7 Andres Galarraga 1.25 3.00
MH8 Roger Clemens 4.00 10.00
MH9 Deion Sanders .60 1.50
MH10 Mo Vaughn .60 1.50
MM1 H.Nomo 2.00 5.00
R.Johnson
MM2 M.Piazza 5.00 12.00
I.Rodriguez
MM3 F.McGriff 3.00 8.00
F.Thomas
MM4 C.Biggio .75 2.00
C.Baerga
MM5 V.Castilla 1.50 4.00
W.Boggs
MM6 B.Larkin 8.00 20.00
C.Ripken
MM7 B.Bonds 3.00 8.00
A.Belle
MM8 L.Dykstra .60 1.50
K.Lofton
MM9 T.Gwynn 4.00 10.00
K.Puckett
MM10 R.Gant .75 2.00
E.Martinez
PC1 Albert Belle .60 1.50
PC2 Barry Bonds 1.50 4.00
PC3 Ken Griffey Jr. 8.00 20.00
PC4 Tony Gwynn 4.00 10.00
PC5 Edgar Martinez .75 2.00
PC6 Rafael Palmeiro 1.25 3.00
PC7 Mike Piazza 4.00 10.00
PC8 Frank Thomas 3.00 8.00
PP1 Albert Belle .60 1.50
PP2 Mark McGwire 6.00 15.00
PP3 Jose Canseco 1.50 4.00
PP4 Mike Piazza 4.00 10.00
PP5 Ron Gant .60 1.50
PP6 Ken Griffey Jr. 8.00 20.00
PP7 Mo Vaughn .60 1.50
PP8 Cecil Fielder .60 1.50
PP9 Tim Salmon 1.25 3.00
PP10 Frank Thomas 3.00 8.00
PP11 Juan Gonzalez 1.50 4.00
PP12 Andres Galarraga 1.25 3.00
PP13 Fred McGriff .75 2.00
PP14 Jay Buhner .60 1.50
PP15 Dante Bichette .60 1.50
PS1 Randy Johnson 1.50 4.00
PS2 Hideo Nomo 2.00 5.00
PS3 Albert Belle .60 1.50
PS4 Dante Bichette .60 1.50
PS5 Jay Buhner .60 1.50
PS6 Frank Thomas 3.00 8.00
PS7 Mark McGwire 6.00 15.00
PS8 Rafael Palmeiro 1.25 3.00
PS9 Mo Vaughn .60 1.50
PS10 Sammy Sosa 4.00 10.00
PS11 Larry Walker 1.25 3.00
PS12 Gary Gaetti .60 1.50
PS13 Tim Salmon 1.25 3.00
PS14 Barry Bonds 4.00 10.00
PS15 Jim Edmonds 1.25 3.00
TSCA1 Cal Ripken 8.00 20.00
TSCA2 Albert Belle .60 1.50
TSCA3 Tom Glavine 1.25 3.00
TSCA4 Jeff Conine .40 1.00
TSCA5 Ken Griffey Jr. 8.00 20.00
TSCA6 Hideo Nomo 1.50 4.00
TSCA7 Greg Maddux 4.00 10.00
TSCA8 Chipper Jones 4.00 10.00
TSCA9 Randy Johnson 1.50 4.00
TSCA10 Jose Mesa .40 1.00

1996 Stadium Club Bash and Burn

Randomly inserted in packs at a rate of one in 24 (retail) and one in 48 (hobby), this ten card set features power/speed players.

COMPLETE SET (10) 15.00 40.00
SER.2 STATED ODDS 1:48 HOB, 1:24 RET
BB1 Sammy Sosa 4.00 10.00
BB2 Barry Bonds 10.00 25.00
BB3 Reggie Sanders 1.50 4.00
BB4 Craig Biggio 2.50 6.00
BB5 Raul Mondesi 1.50 4.00
BB6 Ron Gant 1.50 4.00
BB7 Ray Lankford 1.50 4.00
BB8 Glenallen Hill 1.50 4.00
BB9 Chad Curtis 1.50 4.00
BB10 John Valentin 1.50 4.00

1996 Stadium Club Extreme Players Bronze

One hundred and seventy nine different players were featured on Extreme Player game cards randomly issued in 1996 Stadium Club first and second series packs. Each player has three versions: Bronze, Silver and Gold. All of these cards parallel their corresponding regular issue card except for the Bronze foil "Extreme Players" logo on each card front and the "EP" suffix on the card number, thus creating a skip-numbered set. The Bronze cards listed below were seeded at a rate of 1:12 packs. At the conclusion of the 1996 regular season, an Extreme Player from each of ten positions was identified as a winner based on scores calculated from their actual playing statistics. The 10 winning players are noted with a "W" below. Prior to the December 31st, 1996 deadline, each of the ten winning Extreme Players Bronze cards was redeemable for a 10-card set of Extreme Winners Bronze. Unredeemed winners are now in much shorter supply than other cards in this set and carry premium values.

COMP.BRONZE SET (180) 125.00 250.00
COMP.BRONZE SER.1 (90) 50.00 120.00
COMP.BRONZE SER.2 (90) 50.00 120.00
*BRONZE: 2X TO 5X BASE CARD HI
BRONZE STATED ODDS 1:12
*SILVER SINGLES: .6X TO 1.5X BRONZE
*SILVER WIN: .6X TO 1.5X BRONZE WIN
SILVER STATED ODDS 1:24
*GOLD SINGLES: 1.25X TO 3X BRONZE
*GOLD WIN: 1.25X TO 3X BRONZE WIN
GOLD STATED ODDS 1:48
BRONZE WINNERS LISTED BELOW
SKIP-NUMBERED 179-CARD SET
77 Ken Caminiti W 1.50 4.00
88 Todd Worrell W .60 1.50
105 Ken Griffey Jr. W 6.00 15.00
132 Greg Maddux W 5.00 12.00
150 Andres Galarraga W 1.50 4.00
271 Barry Larkin W 1.50 4.00
400 Gary Sheffield W 2.00 5.00
402 Barry Bonds W 8.00 20.00
414 Chuck Knoblauch W 1.25 3.00
442 Mike Piazza W 5.00 12.00

1996 Stadium Club Extreme Winners Bronze

This 10-card skip-numbered set was only available to collectors who redeemed one of the ten winning Bronze Extreme Players cards before the December 31st, 1996 deadline. The cards parallel the Extreme Players cards inserted in Stadium Club packs except for their distinctive diffraction foil fronts.

COMPLETE SET (10) 10.00 25.00
ONE SET VIA MAIL PER BRONZE WINNER
*SILVER: 1.25X TO 3X BRONZE WINNER
ONE SILV.SET VIA MAIL PER SILV.WINNER
*GOLD: 5X TO 12X BRONZE WINNERS
ONE GOLD CARD VIA MAIL PER GOLD WNR.
EW1 Greg Maddux 1.50 4.00
EW2 Mike Piazza 1.50 4.00
EW3 Andres Galarraga .40 1.00
EW4 Chuck Knoblauch .40 1.00
EW5 Ken Caminiti .40 1.00
EW6 Barry Larkin .60 1.50
EW7 Barry Bonds 2.50 6.00
EW8 Ken Griffey Jr. 2.00 5.00
EW9 Gary Sheffield .40 1.00
EW10 Todd Worrell .40 1.00

1996 Stadium Club Mantle

Randomly inserted at a rate of one card in every 24 packs in series one, one in 12 packs in series two, this 19-card retrospective set chronicles Mantle's career with classic photography, celebrity quotes and highlights from each year. The cards are double foil-stamped. The series one cards feature black-and-white photos, series two color photos. Mantle's name is printed across a silver foil facade of Yankee Stadium on each card top. Cereal Box factory sets include these cards with gold foil. They are valued the same as the pack inserts.

COMPLETE SET (19) 30.00 60.00
COMPLETE SERIES 1 (9) 15.00 40.00
COMMON CARD (MM1-MM9) 2.00 5.00
COMMON CARD (MM10-MM19) 1.25 3.00
SER.1 STATED ODDS 1:24
SER.2 STATED ODDS 1:12

1996 Stadium Club Megaheroes

Randomly inserted at a rate of one in every 48 hobby and 24 retail packs, this 10-card set features super-heroic players matched with a comic book-style illustration depicting their nicknames.

COMPLETE SET (10) 15.00 40.00
SER.1 STATED ODDS 1:48 HOB, 1:24 RET
MH1 Frank Thomas 2.00 5.00
MH2 Ken Griffey Jr. 4.00 10.00
MH3 Hideo Nomo 2.00 5.00
MH4 Ozzie Smith 2.00 5.00
MH5 Will Clark 1.25 3.00
MH6 Jack McDowell .75 2.00
MH7 Andres Galarraga .75 2.00
MH8 Roger Clemens 4.00 10.00
MH9 Deion Sanders 1.25 3.00
MH10 Mo Vaughn .75 2.00

1996 Stadium Club Metalists

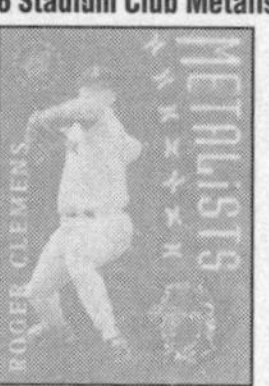

Randomly inserted in packs at a rate of one in 96 (retail) and one in 48 (hobby), this eight-card set features players with two or more MLB awards and is printed on laser-cut foil board.

COMPLETE SET (8) 15.00 40.00
SER.2 STATED ODDS 1:48 HOB, 1:96 RET
M1 Jeff Bagwell 1.00 2.50
M2 Barry Bonds 4.00 10.00
M3 Jose Canseco 1.00 2.50
M4 Roger Clemens 3.00 8.00
M5 Dennis Eckersley .60 1.50
M6 Greg Maddux 2.50 6.00
M7 Cal Ripken 5.00 12.00
M8 Frank Thomas 1.50 4.00

1996 Stadium Club Midsummer Matchups

Randomly inserted at a rate of one in every 48 hobby and 24 retail packs, this 10-card set salutes 1995 National League and American League All-Stars as they are matched back-to-back by position on these two-sided etched foil cards.

COMPLETE SET (10) 25.00 60.00
SER.1 STATED ODDS 1:48 HOB, 1:24 RET
M1 H.Nomo 2.00 5.00
R.Johnson
M2 M.Piazza 3.00 8.00
I.Rodriguez
M3 F.Thomas 2.00 5.00
F.McGriff
M4 C.Biggio 1.25 3.00
C.Baerga
M5 V.Castilla 1.25 3.00
W.Boggs
M6 C.Ripken 6.00 15.00
B.Larkin
M7 B.Bonds 5.00 12.00
A.Belle
M8 K.Lofton .75 2.00
L.Dykstra
M9 T.Gwynn 2.50 6.00
K.Puckett
M10 R.Gant 1.25 3.00
E.Martinez

1996 Stadium Club Power Packed

Randomly inserted in packs at a rate of one in 48, this 15-card set features the biggest, most powerful hitters in the League. Printed on Power Matrix, the cards carry diagrams showing where the players hit the ball over the fence and how far.

COMPLETE SET (15) 25.00 60.00
SER.2 STATED ODDS 1:48 RETAIL
PP1 Albert Belle 1.00 2.50
PP2 Mark McGwire 6.00 15.00
PP3 Jose Canseco 1.50 4.00
PP4 Mike Piazza 4.00 10.00
PP5 Ron Gant 1.00 2.50
PP6 Ken Griffey Jr. 5.00 12.00
PP7 Mo Vaughn 1.00 2.50
PP8 Cecil Fielder 1.00 2.50
PP9 Tim Salmon 1.50 4.00
PP10 Frank Thomas 2.50 6.00
PP11 Juan Gonzalez 1.00 2.50
PP12 Andres Galarraga 1.00 2.50
PP13 Fred McGriff 1.50 4.00
PP14 Jay Buhner 1.00 2.50
PP15 Dante Bichette 1.00 2.50

1996 Stadium Club Power Streak

Randomly inserted at a rate of one in every 24 hobby packs and 48 retail packs, this 15-card set spotlights baseball's most awesome power hitters and strikeout artists.

COMPLETE SET (15) 25.00 60.00
SER.1 STATED ODDS 1:24 HOB, 1:48 RET
PS1 Randy Johnson 2.50 6.00
PS2 Hideo Nomo 2.50 6.00
PS3 Albert Belle 1.00 2.50
PS4 Dante Bichette 1.00 2.50
PS5 Jay Buhner 1.00 2.50
PS6 Frank Thomas 2.50 6.00
PS7 Mark McGwire 6.00 15.00
PS8 Rafael Palmeiro 1.50 4.00
PS9 Mo Vaughn 1.00 2.50
PS10 Sammy Sosa 2.50 6.00
PS11 Larry Walker 1.00 2.50
PS12 Gary Gaetti 1.00 2.50
PS13 Tim Salmon 1.50 4.00
PS14 Barry Bonds 6.00 15.00
PS15 Jim Edmonds 1.00 2.50

1996 Stadium Club Prime Cuts

Randomly inserted at a rate of one in every 36 hobby and 72 retail packs, this eight card set highlights hitters with the purest swings. The cards are numbered on the back with a "PC" prefix.

COMPLETE SET (8) 20.00 50.00
SER.1 STATED ODDS 1:36 HOB, 1:72 RET
PC1 Albert Belle .75 2.00
PC2 Barry Bonds 5.00 12.00
PC3 Ken Griffey Jr. 4.00 10.00
PC4 Tony Gwynn 2.50 6.00
PC5 Edgar Martinez 1.25 3.00
PC6 Rafael Palmeiro 1.25 3.00
PC7 Mike Piazza 3.00 8.00
PC8 Frank Thomas 2.00 5.00

1996 Stadium Club TSC Awards

Randomly inserted in packs at a rate of one in 24 (retail) and one in 48 (hobby), this ten-card set features players whom TSC baseball experts voted to win various awards and is printed on diffraction foil.

COMPLETE SET (10) 15.00 40.00
SER.2 STATED ODDS 1:48 HOB, 1:24 RET
1 Cal Ripken 5.00 12.00
2 Albert Belle .60 1.50
3 Tom Glavine 1.00 2.50
4 Jeff Conine .60 1.50
5 Ken Griffey Jr. 3.00 8.00
6 Hideo Nomo 1.50 4.00
7 Greg Maddux 2.50 6.00
8 Chipper Jones 1.50 4.00
9 Randy Johnson 1.50 4.00
10 Jose Mesa .60 1.50

1996 Stadium Club Members Only 50

This 50-card set features color player photos of Topps' selection of 45 (numbers 1-45) of the top 1995 American and National League players. The set includes five Finest Cards (numbers 46-50) which represent Topps' selection of the top rookies from 1995. The backs carry information about the player.

COMP. FACT SET (50) 8.00 20.00
1 Carlos Baerga .02 .10
2 Derek Bell .02 .10
3 Albert Belle .08 .25
4 Dante Bichette .08 .25
5 Craig Biggio .15 .40
6 Wade Boggs .30 .75
7 Barry Bonds .50 1.25
8 Jay Buhner .08 .25
9 Vinny Castilla .08 .25
10 Jeff Conine .02 .10
11 Jim Edmonds .25 .60
12 Steve Finley .08 .25
13 Andres Galarraga .25 .60
14 Mark Grace .15 .40
15 Tony Gwynn .60 1.50
16 Lance Johnson .02 .10
17 Randy Johnson .30 .75
18 Eric Karros .08 .25
19 Chuck Knoblauch .15 .40
20 Barry Larkin .25 .60
21 Kenny Lofton .15 .40
22 Greg Maddux .75 2.00
23 Edgar Martinez .15 .40
24 Tino Martinez .08 .25
25 Mark McGwire .60 1.50
26 Brian McRae .02 .10
27 Jose Mesa .02 .10
28 Eddie Murray .30 .75
29 Mike Mussina .25 .60
30 Randy Myers .02 .10
31 Hideo Nomo .30 .75
32 Rafael Palmeiro .30 .75
33 Tony Phillips .02 .10
34 Mike Piazza .75 2.00
35 Kirby Puckett .40 1.00
36 Manny Ramirez .30 .75
37 Tim Salmon .15 .40
38 Reggie Sanders .02 .10
39 Sammy Sosa .50 1.25
40 Frank Thomas .30 .75
41 Jim Thome .30 .75
42 John Valentin .02 .10
43 Mo Vaughn .08 .25
44 Quilvio Veras .02 .10
45 Larry Walker .30 .75
46 Hideo Nomo FIN .60 1.50
47 Marty Cordova FIN .08 .25
48 Chipper Jones FIN 1.25 3.00
49 Garret Anderson FIN .40 1.00
50 Andy Pettitte FIN .25 .60

1997 Stadium Club Pre-Production

Each Topps wholesale account received one of these three Pre-Production sample cards along with their order forms for 1997 Stadium Club Series 1 baseball. The cards were designed to provide wholesale customers with a sneak preview of the upcoming Stadium Club release. The design parallels the regular issue cards excpt for the PP-prefixed numbering. In addition, the term "Pre-Production Sample" replaces the line of 1996 statistics on back.

COMPLETE SET (3) 2.00 5.00
PP1 Chipper Jones 1.25 3.00
PP2 Kenny Lofton .40 1.00
PP3 Gary Sheffield 1.00 2.50

1997 Stadium Club

Cards from this 390 card set were distributed in eight-card hobby and retail packs (SRP $3) and 13-card hobby collector packs (SRP $5). Card fronts feature color action player photos printed on 20 pt. card stock with Topps Super Color processing, Hi-gloss laminating, embossing and double foil stamping. The backs carry player information and statistics. In addition to the standard selection of major leaguers, the set contains a 15-card TSC 20 subset (181-195) featuring a selection of top young prospects. These subset cards were inserted one in every two eight-card first series packs and one per 13-card first series pack. First series cards were released in February, 1997. The 195-card Series tw set was issued in six-card retail packs with a suggested retail price of $2 and in nine-card hobby packs with a suggested retail price of $3. The secon series set features a 15-card Stadium Sluggers subset (376-390) with an insertion rate of one in every two hobby and three retail Series 2 packs. Second series cards were released in April, 1997. Please note that cards 361 and 374 do not exist. Du to an error at the manufacturer both Mike Sweeney and Tom Pagnozzi had their cards numbered as 274. In addition, Jermaine Dye and Brant Brown both had their cards numbered as 351. These numbering errors were never corrected and no premiums in value are associated.

COMPLETE SET (390) 30.00 60.00
COMPLETE SERIES 1 (195) 12.50 30.00
COMPLETE SERIES 2 (195) 12.50 30.00
COMMON (1-180/196-375) .10 .30
COM.SP (181-195/376-390) .30 .75
181-195 SER.1 ODDS 1:2 HOB/RET, 1:1 HTA
376-390 SER.2 ODDS 1:2 HOB, 1:3 RET
CARDS 361 AND 374 DON'T EXIST
SWEENEY AND PAGNOZZI NUMBERED 274
J.DYE AND B.BROWN NUMBERED 351
1 Chipper Jones .30 .75
2 Gary Sheffield .10 .30
3 Kenny Lofton .10 .30
4 Brian Jordan .10 .30
5 Mark McGwire .75 2.00
6 Charles Nagy .10 .30
7 Tim Salmon .20 .50
8 Cal Ripken 1.00 2.50
9 Jeff Conine .10 .30
10 Paul Molitor .10 .30
11 Mariano Rivera .30 .75
12 Pedro Martinez .20 .50
13 Jeff Bagwell .20 .50
14 Bobby Bonilla .10 .30
15 Barry Bonds .75 2.00
16 Ryan Klesko .10 .30
17 Barry Larkin .20 .50
18 Jim Thome .20 .50
19 Jay Buhner .10 .30
20 Juan Gonzalez .10 .30
21 Mike Mussina .20 .50
22 Kevin Appier .10 .30
23 Eric Karros .10 .30
24 Steve Finley .10 .30
25 Ed Sprague .10 .30
26 Bernard Gilkey .10 .30
27 Tony Phillips .10 .30
28 Henry Rodriguez .10 .30
29 John Smoltz .20 .50
30 Dante Bichette .10 .30
31 Mike Piazza .50 1.25
32 Paul O'Neill .20 .50
33 Billy Wagner .10 .30
34 Reggie Sanders .10 .30
35 John Jaha .10 .30
36 Eddie Murray .30 .75
37 Eric Young .10 .30
38 Roberto Hernandez .10 .30
39 Pat Hentgen .10 .30
40 Sammy Sosa .30 .75
41 Todd Hundley .10 .30
42 Mo Vaughn .10 .30
43 Robin Ventura .10 .30
44 Mark Grudzielanek .10 .30
45 Shane Reynolds .10 .30
46 Andy Pettitte .20 .50
47 Fred McGriff .20 .50
48 Rey Ordonez .10 .30
49 Will Clark .20 .50
50 Ken Griffey Jr. .60 1.50
51 Todd Worrell .10 .30
52 Rusty Greer .10 .30
53 Mark Grace .20 .50
54 Tom Glavine .20 .50
55 Derek Jeter .75 2.00
56 Rafael Palmeiro .20 .50
57 Bernie Williams .20 .50
58 Marty Cordova .10 .30
59 Andres Galarraga .10 .30
60 Ken Caminiti .10 .30
61 Garret Anderson .10 .30
62 Denny Martinez .10 .30
63 Mike Greenwell .10 .30
64 David Segui .10 .30
65 Julio Franco .10 .30
66 Rickey Henderson .30 .75
67 Ozzie Guillen .10 .30
68 Pete Harnisch .10 .30
69 Chan Ho Park .10 .30
70 Harold Baines .10 .30
71 Mark Clark .10 .30
72 Steve Avery .10 .30
73 Brian Hunter .10 .30
74 Pedro Astacio .10 .30
75 Jack McDowell .10 .30
76 Gregg Jefferies .10 .30
77 Jason Kendall .10 .30
78 Todd Walker .10 .30

79 B.J. Surhoff .10 .30
80 Moises Alou .10 .30
81 Fernando Vina .10 .30
82 Darryl Strawberry .10 .30
83 Jose Rosado .10 .30
84 Chris Gomez .10 .30
85 Chili Davis .10 .30
86 Alan Benes .10 .30
87 Todd Hollandsworth .10 .30
88 Jose Vizcaino .10 .30
89 Edgardo Alfonzo .10 .30
90 Ruben Rivera .10 .30
91 Donovan Osborne .10 .30
92 Doug Glanville .10 .30
93 Gary DiSarcina .10 .30
94 Brooks Kieschnick .10 .30
95 Bobby Jones .10 .30
96 Raul Casanova .10 .30
97 Jermaine Allensworth .10 .30
98 Kenny Rogers .10 .30
99 Mark McLemore .10 .30
100 Jeff Fassero .10 .30
101 Sandy Alomar Jr. .10 .30
102 Chuck Finley .10 .30
103 Eric Owens .10 .30
104 Billy McMillon .10 .30
105 Dwight Gooden .10 .30
106 Sterling Hitchcock .10 .30
107 Doug Drabek .10 .30
108 Paul Wilson .10 .30
109 Chris Snopek .10 .30
110 Al Leiter .10 .30
111 Bob Tewksbury .10 .30
112 Todd Greene .10 .30
113 Jose Valentin .10 .30
114 Delino DeShields .10 .30
115 Mike Bordick .10 .30
116 Pat Meares .10 .30
117 Mariano Duncan .10 .30
118 Steve Trachsel .10 .30
119 Luis Castillo .10 .30
120 Andy Benes .10 .30
121 Donne Wall .10 .30
122 Alex Gonzalez .10 .30
123 Dan Wilson .10 .30
124 Omar Vizquel .20 .50
125 Devon White .10 .30
126 Darryl Hamilton .10 .30
127 Orlando Merced .10 .30
128 Royce Clayton .10 .30
129 William VanLandingham .10 .30
130 Terry Steinbach .10 .30
131 Jeff Blauser .10 .30
132 Jeff Cirillo .10 .30
133 Roger Pavlik .10 .30
134 Danny Tartabull .10 .30
135 Jeff Montgomery .10 .30
136 Bobby Higginson .10 .30
137 Mike Grace .10 .30
138 Kevin Elster .10 .30
139 Brian Giles RC .60 1.50
140 Rod Beck .10 .30
141 Ismael Valdes .10 .30
142 Scott Brosius .10 .30
143 Mike Fetters .10 .30
144 Gary Gaetti .10 .30
145 Mike Lansing .10 .30
146 Glenallen Hill .10 .30
147 Shawn Green .10 .30
148 Mel Rojas .10 .30
149 Joey Cora .10 .30
150 John Smiley .10 .30
151 Marvin Benard .10 .30
152 Curt Schilling .10 .30
153 Dave Nilsson .10 .30
154 Edgar Renteria .10 .30
155 Joey Hamilton .10 .30
156 Carlos Garcia .10 .30
157 Nomar Garciaparra .50 1.25
158 Kevin Ritz .10 .30
159 Keith Lockhart .10 .30
160 Justin Thompson .10 .30
161 Terry Adams .10 .30
162 Jamey Wright .10 .30
163 Otis Nixon .10 .30
164 Michael Tucker .10 .30
165 Mike Stanley .10 .30
166 Ben McDonald .10 .30
167 John Mabry .10 .30
168 Troy O'Leary .10 .30
169 Mel Nieves .10 .30
170 Bret Boone .10 .30
171 Mike Timlin .10 .30
172 Scott Rolen .20 .50
173 Reggie Jefferson .10 .30
174 Neifi Perez .10 .30
175 Brian McRae .10 .30
176 Tom Goodwin .10 .30
177 Aaron Sele .10 .30
178 Benito Santiago .10 .30
179 Frank Rodriguez .10 .30
180 Eric Davis .10 .30
181 Andruw Jones 2000 SP .30 .75
182 Todd Walker 2000 SP .30 .75
183 Wes Helms 2000 SP .30 .75
184 N.Figueroa 2000 SP RC .30 .75
185 Vlad.Guerrero 2000 SP .50 1.25
186 Billy McMillon 2000 SP .30 .75
187 Todd Helton 2000 SP .50 1.25
188 N.Garciaparra 2000 SP 1.00 2.50
189 Katsuhiro Maeda 2000 SP .30 .75
190 Russell Branyan 2000 SP .30 .75
191 Glendon Rusch 2000 SP .30 .75
192 Bartolo Colon 2000 SP .30 .75
193 Scott Rolen 2000 SP .30 .75
194 Angel Echevarria 2000 SP .30 .75
195 Bob Abreu 2000 SP .30 .75
196 Greg Maddux .50 1.25
197 Joe Carter .10 .30
198 Alex Ochoa .10 .30
199 Ellis Burks .10 .30
200 Ivan Rodriguez .20 .50
201 Marquis Grissom .10 .30
202 Trevor Hoffman .10 .30
203 Matt Williams .10 .30
204 Carlos Delgado .10 .30
205 Ramon Martinez .10 .30
206 Chuck Knoblauch .10 .30
207 Juan Guzman .10 .30
208 Derek Bell .10 .30
209 Roger Clemens .60 1.50
210 Vladimir Guerrero .30 .75
211 Cecil Fielder .10 .30
212 Hideo Nomo .30 .75
213 Frank Thomas .30 .75
214 Greg Vaughn .10 .30
215 Javy Lopez .10 .30
216 Raul Mondesi .10 .30
217 Wade Boggs .20 .50
218 Carlos Baerga .10 .30
219 Tony Gwynn .40 1.00
220 Tino Martinez .20 .50
221 Vinny Castilla .10 .30
222 Lance Johnson .10 .30
223 David Justice .10 .30
224 Rondell White .10 .30
225 Dean Palmer .10 .30
226 Jim Edmonds .10 .30
227 Albert Belle .10 .30
228 Alex Fernandez .10 .30
229 Ryne Sandberg .50 1.25
230 Jose Mesa .10 .30
231 David Cone .10 .30
232 Troy Percival .10 .30
233 Edgar Martinez .20 .50
234 Jose Canseco .20 .50
235 Kevin Brown .10 .30
236 Ray Lankford .10 .30
237 Karim Garcia .10 .30
238 J.T. Snow .10 .30
239 Dennis Eckersley .10 .30
240 Roberto Alomar .20 .50
241 John Valentin .10 .30
242 Ron Gant .10 .30
243 Geronimo Berroa .10 .30
244 Manny Ramirez .20 .50
245 Travis Fryman .10 .30
246 Denny Neagle .10 .30
247 Randy Johnson .30 .75
248 Darin Erstad .10 .30
249 Mark Wohlers .10 .30
250 Ken Hill .10 .30
251 Larry Walker .10 .30
252 Craig Biggio .20 .50
253 Brady Anderson .10 .30
254 John Wetteland .10 .30
255 Andruw Jones .20 .50
256 Turk Wendell .10 .30
257 Jason Isringhausen .10 .30
258 Jaime Navarro .10 .30
259 Sean Berry .10 .30
260 Albie Lopez .10 .30
261 Jay Bell .10 .30
262 Bobby Witt .10 .30
263 Tony Clark .10 .30
264 Tim Wakefield .10 .30
265 Brad Radke .10 .30
266 Tim Belcher .10 .30
267 Nerio Rodriguez RC .10 .30
268 Roger Cedeno .10 .30
269 Tim Naehring .10 .30
270 Kevin Tapani .10 .30
271 Joe Randa .10 .30
272 Randy Myers .10 .30
273 Dave Burba .10 .30
274 Mike Sweeney .10 .30
275 Danny Graves .10 .30
276 Chad Mottola .10 .30
277 Ruben Sierra .10 .30
278 Norm Charlton .10 .30
279 Scott Servais .10 .30
280 Jacob Cruz .10 .30
281 Mike Macfarlane .10 .30
282 Rich Becker .10 .30
283 Shannon Stewart .10 .30
284 Gerald Williams .10 .30
285 Jody Reed .10 .30
286 Jeff D'Amico .10 .30
287 Walt Weiss .10 .30
288 Jim Leyritz .10 .30
289 Francisco Cordova .10 .30
290 F.P. Santangelo .10 .30
291 Scott Erickson .10 .30
292 Hal Morris .10 .30
293 Ray Durham .10 .30
294 Andy Ashby .10 .30
295 Darryl Kile .10 .30
296 Jose Paniagua .10 .30
297 Mickey Tettleton .10 .30
298 Joe Girardi .10 .30
299 Rocky Coppinger .10 .30
300 Bob Abreu .20 .50
301 John Olerud .10 .30
302 Paul Shuey .10 .30
303 Jeff Brantley .10 .30
304 Bob Wells .10 .30
305 Kevin Seitzer .10 .30
306 Shawon Dunston .10 .30
307 Jose Herrera .10 .30
308 Butch Huskey .10 .30
309 Jose Offerman .10 .30
310 Rick Aguilera .10 .30
311 Greg Gagne .10 .30
312 John Burkett .10 .30
313 Mark Thompson .10 .30
314 Alvaro Espinoza .10 .30
315 Todd Stottlemyre .10 .30
316 Al Martin .10 .30
317 James Baldwin .10 .30
318 Cal Eldred .10 .30
319 Sid Fernandez .10 .30
320 Mickey Morandini .10 .30
321 Robb Nen .10 .30
322 Mark Lemke .10 .30
323 Pete Schourek .10 .30
324 Marcus Jensen .10 .30
325 Rich Aurilia .10 .30
326 Jeff King .10 .30
327 Scott Stahoviak .10 .30
328 Ricky Otero .10 .30
329 Antonio Osuna .10 .30
330 Chris Hoiles .10 .30
331 Luis Gonzalez .10 .30
332 Wil Cordero .10 .30
333 Johnny Damon .20 .50
334 Mark Langston .10 .30
335 Orlando Miller .10 .30
336 Jason Giambi .10 .30
337 Damian Jackson .10 .30
338 David Wells .10 .30
339 Bip Roberts .10 .30
340 Matt Ruebel .10 .30
341 Tom Candiotti .10 .30
342 Wally Joyner .10 .30
343 Jimmy Key .10 .30
344 Tony Batista .10 .30
345 Paul Sorrento .10 .30
346 Ron Karkovice .10 .30
347 Wilson Alvarez .10 .30
348 John Flaherty .10 .30
349 Rey Sanchez .10 .30
350 John Vander Wal .10 .30
351 Jermaine Dye .10 .30
352 Mike Hampton .10 .30
353 Greg Colbrunn .10 .30
354 Heathcliff Slocumb .10 .30
355 Ricky Bottalico .10 .30
356 Marty Janzen .10 .30
357 Orel Hershiser .10 .30
358 Rex Hudler .10 .30
359 Amaury Telemaco .10 .30
360 Darrin Fletcher .10 .30
361 Brant Brown UER .10 .30
362 Russ Davis .10 .30
363 Allen Watson .10 .30
364 Mike Lieberthal .10 .30
365 Dave Stevens .10 .30
366 Jay Powell .10 .30
367 Tony Fossas .10 .30
368 Bob Wolcott .10 .30
369 Mark Loretta .10 .30
370 Shawn Estes .10 .30
371 Sandy Martinez .10 .30
372 Wendell Magee Jr. .10 .30
373 John Franco .10 .30
374 Tom Pagnozzi UER .10 .30
375 Willie Adams .10 .30
376 Chipper Jones SS SP .50 1.25
377 Mo Vaughn SS SP .30 .75
378 Frank Thomas SS SP .50 1.25
379 Albert Belle SS SP .30 .75
380 Andres Galarraga SS SP .30 .75
381 Gary Sheffield SS SP .30 .75
382 Jeff Bagwell SS SP .30 .75
383 Mike Piazza SS SP 1.00 2.50
384 Mark McGwire SS SP 1.50 4.00
385 Ken Griffey Jr. SS SP 1.25 3.00
386 Barry Bonds SS SP 1.50 4.00
387 Juan Gonzalez SS SP .30 .75
388 Brady Anderson SS SP .30 .75
389 Ken Caminiti SS SP .30 .75
390 Jay Buhner SS SP .30 .75

1997 Stadium Club Matrix

*STARS: 4X TO 10X BASIC CARDS
STATED ODDS 1:12 H/R, 1:18 ANCO, 1:6 HCP
CARDS 1-60 DISTRIBUTED IN SERIES 1
CARDS 196-255 DISTRIBUTED IN SERIES 2

1997 Stadium Club Members Only Parallel

COMP.FACT SET (497) 200.00 400.00
COMPLETE SERIES 1 (235) 100.00 200.00
COMPLETE SERIES 2 (242) 100.00 200.00
COMMON CARD .10 .25
*MEMBERS ONLY: 6X BASIC CARDS
I1 Eddie Murray 1.50 4.00
I2 Paul Molitor 1.50 4.00
I3 Todd Hundley .75 2.00
I4 Roger Clemens 4.00 10.00
I5 Barry Bonds 2.00 5.00
I6 Mark McGwire 10.00 25.00
I7 Brady Anderson .75 2.00
I8 Barry Larkin 1.50 4.00
I9 Ken Caminiti 1.25 3.00
I10 Hideo Nomo 1.50 4.00
I11 Bernie Williams 1.50 4.00
I12 Juan Gonzalez 1.50 4.00
I13 Andy Pettitte 1.25 3.00
I14 Albert Belle .75 2.00
I15 John Smoltz .75 2.00
I16 Brian Jordan .40 1.00
I17 Derek Jeter 10.00 25.00
I18 Ken Caminiti .75 2.00
I19 John Wetteland .75 2.00
I20 Brady Anderson .75 2.00
I21 Andruw Jones 2.00 5.00
I22 Jim Leyritz .40 1.00
M1 Derek Jeter 10.00 25.00
M2 Mark Grudzielanek .75 2.00
M3 Jacob Cruz .40 1.00
M4 Ray Durham 1.25 3.00
M5 Tony Clark .75 2.00
M6 Chipper Jones 5.00 12.00
M7 Luis Castillo .75 2.00
M8 Carlos Delgado 2.00 5.00
M9 Brant Brown .40 1.00
M10 Jason Kendall 1.25 3.00
M11 Alan Benes .40 1.00
M12 Rey Ordonez .40 1.00
M13 Justin Thompson .40 1.00
M14 Jermaine Allensworth .40 1.00
M15 Brian L. Hunter .40 1.00
M16 Marty Cordova .40 1.00
M17 Edgar Renteria .40 1.00
M18 Karim Garcia .40 1.00
M19 Todd Greene .40 1.00
M20 Paul Wilson .40 1.00
M21 Andruw Jones 2.00 5.00
M22 Todd Walker .40 1.00
M23 Alex Ochoa .40 1.00
M24 Bartolo Colon 1.50 4.00
M25 Wendell Magee Jr. .40 1.00
M26 Jose Rosado .40 1.00
M27 Katsuhiro Maeda .40 1.00
M28 Bob Abreu 1.50 4.00
M29 Brooks Kieschnick .40 1.00
M30 Derrick Gibson .40 1.00
M31 Mike Sweeney 2.00 5.00
M32 Jeff D'Amico .40 1.00
M33 Chad Mottola .40 1.00
M34 Chris Snopek .40 1.00
M35 Jaime Bluma .40 1.00
M36 Vladimir Guerrero 3.00 8.00
M37 Nomar Garciaparra 6.00 15.00
M38 Scott Rolen 1.50 4.00
M39 Dmitri Young .75 2.00
M40 Neifi Perez .75 2.00
FB1 Jeff Bagwell 2.00 5.00
FB2 Albert Belle .75 2.00
FB3 Barry Bonds 5.00 12.00
FB4 Andres Galarraga 1.50 4.00
FB5 Ken Griffey Jr. 10.00 25.00
FB6 Brady Anderson .75 2.00
FB7 Mark McGwire 8.00 20.00
FB8 Chipper Jones 5.00 12.00
FB9 Frank Thomas 3.00 8.00
FB10 Mike Piazza 6.00 15.00
FB11 Mo Vaughn .75 2.00
FB12 Juan Gonzalez 2.00 5.00
PG1 Brady Anderson .75 2.00
PG2 Albert Belle .75 2.00
PG3 Dante Bichette .75 2.00
PG4 Barry Bonds 5.00 12.00
PG5 Jay Buhner .75 2.00
PG6 Tony Gwynn 5.00 12.00
PG7 Chipper Jones 5.00 12.00
PG8 Mark McGwire 8.00 20.00
PG9 Gary Sheffield 1.50 4.00
PG10 Frank Thomas 4.00 10.00
PG11 Juan Gonzalez 2.00 5.00
PG12 Ken Caminiti .75 2.00
PG13 Kenny Lofton .75 2.00
PG14 Jeff Bagwell 2.00 5.00
PG15 Ken Griffey Jr. 10.00 25.00
PG16 Cal Ripken 10.00 25.00
PG17 Mo Vaughn .75 2.00
PG18 Mike Piazza 5.00 12.00
PG19 Derek Jeter 10.00 25.00
PG20 Andres Galarraga 1.50 4.00
PL1 Ivan Rodriguez 2.00 5.00
PL2 Ken Caminiti .75 2.00
PL3 Barry Bonds 5.00 12.00
PL4 Ken Griffey Jr. 10.00 25.00
PL5 Greg Maddux 6.00 15.00
PL6 Craig Biggio 1.25 3.00
PL7 Andres Galarraga 1.50 4.00
PL8 Kenny Lofton .75 2.00
PL9 Barry Larkin 1.50 4.00
PL10 Mark Grace 1.50 4.00
PL11 Rey Ordonez .40 1.00
PL12 Roberto Alomar 1.50 4.00
PL13 Derek Jeter 10.00 25.00

1997 Stadium Club Co-Signers

Randomly inserted in first series eight-card hobby packs at a rate of one in 168 and first series 13-card hobby collector packs at a rate of one in 96, cards (CO1-CO5) from this dual-sided, dual-player set feature color action player photos printed on 20pt. card stock with authentic signatures of two major league stand-outs per card. The last five cards (CO6-CO10) were randomly inserted in second series 10-card hobby packs with a rate of one in 168 and inserted with a rate of one in 96 Hobby Collector packs.

STATED ODDS 1:168 HOBBY, 1:96 HCP
CO1 D.Jeter/A.Pettitte 125.00 250.00
CO2 P.Wilson/T.Hundley 6.00 15.00
CO3 J.Dye/M.Wohlers 12.50 30.00
CO4 S.Rolen/G.Jefferies 8.00 20.00
CO5 J.Kendall/T.Holland 6.00 15.00
CO6 R.Ventura/A.Benes 10.00 25.00
CO7 R.Mondesi/E.Karros 6.00 15.00
CO8 N.Garciaparra/R.Ordon 20.00 50.00
CO9 R.White/M.Cordova 6.00 15.00
CO10 T.Gwynn/K.Garcia 12.50 30.00

1997 Stadium Club Firebrand Redemption

Randomly inserted exclusively into first series eight-card retail packs at a rate of one in 36, these redemption cards feature a selection of the leagues top sluggers. Due to circumstances beyond the manufacturers control, they were not able to insert the actual etched-wood cards into packs and had to resort to these redemption cards.

SER.1 STAT.ODDS 1:24 HOB/RET,1:36 ANCO
*WOOD: 5X TO 1.2X BASIC FIREBRAND
ONE WOOD CARD VIA MAIL PER EXCH.CARD
F1 Jeff Bagwell 1.50 4.00
F2 Albert Belle 1.00 2.50
F3 Barry Bonds 6.00 15.00
F4 Andres Galarraga 1.00 2.50
F5 Ken Griffey Jr. 5.00 12.00
F6 Brady Anderson 1.00 2.50
F7 Mark McGwire 6.00 15.00
F8 Chipper Jones 2.50 6.00
F9 Frank Thomas 2.50 6.00
F10 Mike Piazza 4.00 10.00
F11 Mo Vaughn 1.00 2.50
F12 Juan Gonzalez 1.00 2.50

1997 Stadium Club Instavision

The first ten cards of this 22-card set were randomly inserted in first series eight-card packs at a rate of one in 24 and first series 13-card packs at a rate of 1:12. The last 12 cards were inserted in series two packs at the rate of one in 24 and one in 12 in hobby collector packs. The set highlights some of the 1996 season's most exciting moments through exclusive holographic video action.

COMPLETE SET (22) 20.00 50.00
COMPLETE SERIES 1 (10) 10.00 25.00
COMPLETE SERIES 2 (12) 10.00 25.00
STATED ODDS 1:24 HOB/RET, 1:36 ANCO
I1 Eddie Murray 1.50 4.00
I2 Paul Molitor .60 1.50
I3 Todd Hundley .60 1.50
I4 Roger Clemens 3.00 8.00
I5 Barry Bonds 4.00 10.00
I6 Mark McGwire 4.00 10.00
I7 Brady Anderson .60 1.50
I8 Barry Larkin 1.00 2.50
I9 Ken Caminiti .60 1.50
I10 Hideo Nomo 1.50 4.00
I11 Bernie Williams 1.00 2.50
I12 Juan Gonzalez .60 1.50
I13 Andy Pettitte 1.00 2.50
I14 Albert Belle .60 1.50
I15 John Smoltz 1.00 2.50
I16 Brian Jordan .60 1.50
I17 Derek Jeter 4.00 10.00
I18 Ken Caminiti .60 1.50
I19 John Wetteland .60 1.50
I20 Brady Anderson .60 1.50
I21 Andruw Jones 1.00 2.50
I22 Jim Leyritz .60 1.50

1997 Stadium Club Millennium

Randomly inserted in first and second series eight-card packs at a rate of one in 24 and 13-card packs at a rate of 1:12, this 40-card set features color player photos of breakthrough stars of Major League Baseball reproduced using state-of-the-art advanced embossed holographic technology.

COMPLETE SET (40) 60.00 120.00
COMPLETE SERIES 1 (20) 20.00 50.00
COMPLETE SERIES 2 (20) 30.00 80.00
STATED ODDS 1:24H/R, 1:36ANCO, 1:12HCP
M1 Derek Jeter 8.00 20.00
M2 Mark Grudzielanek .60 1.50
M3 Jacob Cruz .60 1.50
M4 Ray Durham 1.00 2.50
M5 Tony Clark .60 1.50
M6 Chipper Jones 2.50 6.00
M7 Luis Castillo .60 1.50
M8 Carlos Delgado 1.00 2.50
M9 Brant Brown .60 1.50
M10 Jason Kendall 1.00 2.50
M11 Alan Benes .60 1.50
M12 Rey Ordonez .60 1.50
M13 Justin Thompson .60 1.50
M14 Jermaine Allensworth .60 1.50
M15 Brian Hunter .60 1.50
M16 Marty Cordova .60 1.50
M17 Edgar Renteria 1.00 2.50
M18 Karim Garcia .60 1.50
M19 Todd Greene .60 1.50
M20 Paul Wilson .60 1.50
M21 Andruw Jones 1.50 4.00
M22 Todd Walker .60 1.50
M23 Alex Ochoa .60 1.50
M24 Bartolo Colon 1.00 2.50
M25 Wendell Magee Jr. .60 1.50
M26 Jose Rosado .60 1.50
M27 Katsuhiro Maeda .60 1.50
M28 Bob Abreu .60 1.50
M29 Brooks Kieschnick .60 1.50
M30 Derrick Gibson .60 1.50
M31 Mike Sweeney 1.00 2.50
M32 Jeff D'Amico .60 1.50
M33 Chad Mottola .60 1.50
M34 Chris Snopek .60 1.50
M35 Jaime Bluma .60 1.50
M36 Vladimir Guerrero 2.50 6.00
M37 Nomar Garciaparra 5.00 12.00
M38 Scott Rolen 1.50 4.00
M39 Dmitri Young 1.00 2.50
M40 Neifi Perez .60 1.50

1997 Stadium Club Patent Leather

Randomly inserted in second series retail packs only at a rate of one in 36, this 13-card set features action player images standing in a baseball glove and with an inner die-cut glove background printed on leather card stock.

COMPLETE SET (13) 60.00 120.00
SER.2 STATED ODDS 1:36 RETAIL
PL1 Ivan Rodriguez 2.50 6.00
PL2 Ken Caminiti 1.50 4.00
PL3 Barry Bonds 10.00 25.00
PL4 Ken Griffey Jr. 8.00 20.00
PL5 Greg Maddux 6.00 15.00
PL6 Craig Biggio 2.50 6.00
PL7 Andres Galarraga 1.50 4.00
PL8 Kenny Lofton 1.50 4.00
PL9 Barry Larkin 2.50 6.00
PL10 Mark Grace 2.50 6.00
PL11 Rey Ordonez 1.50 4.00
PL12 Roberto Alomar 2.50 6.00
PL13 Derek Jeter 10.00 25.00

1997 Stadium Club Pure Gold

Randomly inserted in first and second series eight-card packs at a rate of one in 72 and 13-card packs at a rate of one in 36, this 20-card set features color action star player photos reproduced on 20 pt. embossed gold mirror foilboard.

COMPLETE SET (20) 100.00 200.00
COMPLETE SERIES 1 (10) 50.00 120.00
COMPLETE SERIES 2 (10) 100.00 200.00
STATED ODDS 1:72H/R, 1:108ANCO, 1:36HCP
PG1 Brady Anderson 1.25 3.00
PG2 Albert Belle 1.25 3.00
PG3 Dante Bichette 1.25 3.00
PG4 Barry Bonds 8.00 20.00
PG5 Jay Buhner 1.25 3.00
PG6 Tony Gwynn 4.00 10.00
PG7 Chipper Jones 3.00 8.00
PG8 Mark McGwire 8.00 20.00
PG9 Gary Sheffield 1.25 3.00
PG10 Frank Thomas 3.00 8.00
PG11 Juan Gonzalez 1.25 3.00
PG12 Ken Caminiti 1.25 3.00
PG13 Kenny Lofton 1.25 3.00
PG14 Jeff Bagwell 2.00 5.00
PG15 Ken Griffey Jr. 6.00 15.00
PG16 Cal Ripken 10.00 25.00
PG17 Mo Vaughn 1.25 3.00
PG18 Mike Piazza 5.00 12.00
PG19 Derek Jeter 8.00 20.00
PG20 Andres Galarraga 1.25 3.00

1998 Stadium Club

The 1998 Stadium Club set was issued in two separate 200-card series and distributed in six-card retail packs for $2, nine-card hobby packs for $3, and 15-card Home Team Advantage packs for $5. The card fronts feature action color player photos with player information displayed on the backs. The series one set included odd numbered cards only and series two included even numbered cards only. The set contains the topical subsets: Future Stars (odd-numbered 361-379), Draft Picks (odd-numbered 381-399) and Traded (even-numbered 356-400). Two separate Cal Ripken Sound Chip cards were distributed as chiptoppers in Home Team Advantage boxes. The second series features a 23-card Transaction subset (356-400). Second series cards were released in April, 1998. Rookie Cards include Jack Cust, Kevin Millwood and Magglio Ordonez.

COMPLETE SET (400) 30.00 80.00
COMPLETE SERIES 1 (200) 15.00 40.00
COMPLETE SERIES 2 (200) 15.00 40.00
ODD CARDS DISTRIBUTED IN SER.1 PACKS
EVEN CARDS DISTRIBUTED IN SER.2 PACKS
ONE RIPKEN SOUND CHIP PER HTA BOX
1 Chipper Jones .30 .75
2 Frank Thomas .30 .75
3 Vladimir Guerrero .30 .75
4 Ellis Burks .10 .30
5 John Franco .10 .30
6 Paul Molitor .10 .30
7 Rusty Greer .10 .30
8 Todd Hundley .10 .30
9 Brett Tomko .10 .30
10 Eric Karros .10 .30
11 Mike Cameron .10 .30
12 Jim Edmonds .10 .30
13 Bernie Williams .20 .50
14 Denny Neagle .10 .30
15 Jason Dickson .10 .30
16 Sammy Sosa .30 .75
17 Brian Jordan .10 .30
18 Jose Vidro .10 .30
19 Scott Spiezio .10 .30
20 Jay Buhner .10 .30
21 Jim Thome .20 .50
22 Sandy Alomar Jr. .10 .30
23 Livan Hernandez .10 .30
24 Roberto Alomar .20 .50
25 Chris Gomez .10 .30
26 John Wetteland .10 .30
27 Willie Greene .10 .30
28 Gregg Jefferies .10 .30
29 Johnny Damon .20 .50
30 Barry Larkin .20 .50
31 Chuck Knoblauch .10 .30
32 Mo Vaughn .10 .30
33 Tony Clark .10 .30
34 Marty Cordova .10 .30
35 Vinny Castilla .10 .30
36 Jeff King .10 .30
37 Reggie Jefferson .10 .30
38 Mariano Rivera .30 .75
39 Jermaine Allensworth .10 .30
40 Livan Hernandez .10 .30
41 Heathcliff Slocumb .10 .30
42 Jacob Cruz .10 .30
43 Barry Bonds .75 2.00
44 Dave Magadan .10 .30
45 Chan Ho Park .10 .30
46 Jeremi Gonzalez .10 .30
47 Jeff Cirillo .10 .30
48 Delino DeShields .10 .30
49 Craig Biggio .20 .50
50 Benito Santiago .10 .30
51 Mark Clark .10 .30
52 Fernando Vina .10 .30
53 F.P. Santangelo .10 .30
54 Pep Harris .10 .30
55 Edgar Renteria .10 .30
56 Jeff Bagwell .20 .50
57 Jimmy Key .10 .30
58 Bartolo Colon .10 .30
59 Curt Schilling .10 .30
60 Steve Finley .10 .30
61 Andy Ashby .10 .30
62 John Burkett .10 .30
63 Orel Hershiser .10 .30

64 Pokey Reese .10 .30
65 Scott Servais .10 .30
66 Todd Jones .10 .30
67 Javy Lopez .10 .30
68 Robin Ventura .10 .30
69 Miguel Tejada .30 .75
70 Raul Casanova .10 .30
71 Reggie Sanders .10 .30
72 Edgardo Alfonzo .10 .30
73 Dean Palmer .10 .30
74 Todd Stottlemyre .10 .30
75 David Wells .10 .30
76 Troy Percival .10 .30
77 Albert Belle .10 .30
78 Pat Hentgen .10 .30
79 Brian Hunter .10 .30
80 Richard Hidalgo .10 .30
81 Darren Oliver .10 .30
82 Mark Wohlers .10 .30
83 Cal Ripken 1.00 2.50
84 Hideo Nomo .30 .75
85 Derrek Lee .20 .50
86 Stan Javier .10 .30
87 Rey Ordonez .10 .30
88 Randy Johnson .30 .75
89 Jeff Kent .10 .30
90 Brian McRae .10 .30
91 Manny Ramirez .20 .50
92 Trevor Hoffman .10 .30
93 Doug Glanville .10 .30
94 Todd Walker .10 .30
95 Andy Benes .10 .30
96 Jason Schmidt .10 .30
97 Mike Matheny .10 .30
98 Tim Naehring .10 .30
99 Keith Lockhart .10 .30
100 Jose Rosado .10 .30
101 Roger Clemens .60 1.50
102 Pedro Astacio .10 .30
103 Mark Bellhorn .10 .30
104 Paul O'Neill .20 .50
105 Darin Erstad .10 .30
106 Mike Lieberthal .10 .30
107 Wilson Alvarez .10 .30
108 Mike Mussina .20 .50
109 George Williams .10 .30
110 Cliff Floyd .10 .30
111 Shawn Estes .10 .30
112 Mark Grudzielanek .10 .30
113 Tony Gwynn .40 1.00
114 Alan Benes .10 .30
115 Terry Steinbach .10 .30
116 Greg Maddux .50 1.25
117 Andy Pettitte .20 .50
118 Dave Nilsson .10 .30
119 Deivi Cruz .10 .30
120 Carlos Delgado .10 .30
121 Scott Hatteberg .10 .30
122 John Olerud .10 .30
123 Todd Dunwoody .10 .30
124 Garret Anderson .10 .30
125 Royce Clayton .10 .30
126 Dante Powell .10 .30
127 Tom Glavine .20 .50
128 Gary DiSarcina .10 .30
129 Terry Adams .10 .30
130 Raul Mondesi .10 .30
131 Dan Wilson .10 .30
132 Al Martin .10 .30
133 Mickey Morandini .10 .30
134 Rafael Palmeiro .20 .50
135 Juan Encarnacion .10 .30
136 Jim Pittsley .10 .30
137 Magglio Ordonez RC 1.25 3.00
138 Will Clark .20 .50
139 Todd Helton .20 .50
140 Kelvim Escobar .10 .30
141 Esteban Loaiza .10 .30
142 John Jaha .10 .30
143 Jeff Fassero .10 .30
144 Harold Baines .10 .30
145 Butch Huskey .10 .30
146 Pat Meares .10 .30
147 Brian Giles .10 .30
148 Ramiro Mendoza .10 .30
149 John Smoltz .20 .50
150 Felix Martinez .10 .30
151 Jose Valentin .10 .30
152 Brad Rigby .10 .30
153 Ed Sprague .10 .30
154 Mike Hampton .10 .30
155 Carlos Perez .10 .30
156 Ray Lankford .10 .30
157 Bobby Bonilla .10 .30
158 Bill Mueller .10 .30
159 Jeffrey Hammonds .10 .30
160 Charles Nagy .10 .30
161 Rich Loiselle RC .10 .30
162 Al Leiter .10 .30
163 Larry Walker .10 .30
164 Chris Hoiles .10 .30
165 Jeff Montgomery .10 .30
166 Francisco Cordova .10 .30
167 James Baldwin .10 .30
168 Mark McLemore .10 .30
169 Kevin Appier .10 .30
170 Jamey Wright .10 .30
171 Nomar Garciaparra .50 1.25
172 Matt Franco .10 .30
173 Armando Benitez .10 .30
174 Jeromy Burnitz .10 .30
175 Ismael Valdes .10 .30
176 Lance Johnson .10 .30
177 Paul Sorrento .10 .30
178 Rondell White .10 .30
179 Kevin Elster .10 .30
180 Jason Giambi .10 .30
181 Carlos Baerga .10 .30
182 Russ Davis .10 .30
183 Ryan McGuire .10 .30
184 Eric Young .10 .30
185 Ron Gant .10 .30
186 Manny Alexander .10 .30
187 Scott Karl .10 .30
188 Brady Anderson .10 .30
189 Randall Simon .10 .30
190 Tim Belcher .10 .30
191 Jaret Wright .10 .30
192 Dante Bichette .10 .30
193 John Valentin .10 .30
194 Darren Bragg .10 .30
195 Mike Sweeney .10 .30
196 Craig Counsell .10 .30
197 Jaime Navarro .10 .30
198 Todd Dunn .10 .30
199 Ken Griffey Jr. .60 1.50
200 Juan Gonzalez .10 .30
201 Billy Wagner .10 .30
202 Tino Martinez .20 .50
203 Mark McGwire .75 2.00
204 Jeff D'Amico .10 .30
205 Rico Brogna .10 .30
206 Todd Hollandsworth .10 .30
207 Chad Curtis .10 .30
208 Tom Goodwin .10 .30
209 Neifi Perez .10 .30
210 Derek Bell .10 .30
211 Quilvio Veras .10 .30
212 Greg Vaughn .10 .30
213 Kirk Rueter .10 .30
214 Arthur Rhodes .10 .30
215 Cal Eldred .10 .30
216 Bill Taylor .10 .30
217 Todd Greene .10 .30
218 Mario Valdez .10 .30
219 Ricky Bottalico .10 .30
220 Frank Rodriguez .10 .30
221 Rich Becker .10 .30
222 Roberto Duran RC .10 .30
223 Ivan Rodriguez .20 .50
224 Mike Jackson .10 .30
225 Deion Sanders .20 .50
226 Tony Womack .10 .30
227 Mark Kotsay .10 .30
228 Steve Trachsel .10 .30
229 Ryan Klesko .10 .30
230 Ken Cloude .10 .30
231 Luis Gonzalez .10 .30
232 Gary Gaetti .10 .30
233 Michael Tucker .10 .30
234 Shawn Green .10 .30
235 Ariel Prieto .10 .30
236 Kirt Manwaring .10 .30
237 Omar Vizquel .20 .50
238 Matt Beech .10 .30
239 Justin Thompson .10 .30
240 Bret Boone .10 .30
241 Derek Jeter .75 2.00
242 Ken Caminiti .10 .30
243 Jose Offerman .10 .30
244 Kevin Tapani .10 .30
245 Jason Kendall .10 .30
246 Jose Guillen .10 .30
247 Mike Bordick .10 .30
248 Dustin Hermanson .10 .30
249 Darrin Fletcher .10 .30
250 Dave Hollins .10 .30
251 Ramon Martinez .10 .30
252 Hideki Irabu .10 .30
253 Mark Grace .20 .50
254 Jason Isringhausen .10 .30
255 Jose Cruz Jr. .10 .30
256 Brian Johnson .10 .30
257 Brad Ausmus .10 .30
258 Andruw Jones .20 .50
259 Doug Jones .10 .30
260 Jeff Shaw .10 .30
261 Chuck Finley .10 .30
262 Gary Sheffield .10 .30
263 David Segui .10 .30
264 John Smiley .10 .30
265 Tim Salmon .20 .50
266 J.T. Snow .10 .30
267 Alex Fernandez .10 .30
268 Matt Stairs .10 .30
269 B.J. Surhoff .10 .30
270 Keith Foulke .10 .30
271 Edgar Martinez .20 .50
272 Shannon Stewart .10 .30
273 Eduardo Perez .10 .30
274 Wally Joyner .10 .30
275 Kevin Young .10 .30
276 Eli Marrero .10 .30
277 Brad Radke .10 .30
278 Jamie Moyer .10 .30
279 Joe Girardi .10 .30
280 Troy O'Leary .10 .30
281 Jeff Frye .10 .30
282 Jose Offerman .10 .30
283 Scott Erickson .10 .30
284 Sean Berry .10 .30
285 Shigetoshi Hasegawa .10 .30
286 Felix Heredia .10 .30
287 Willie McGee .10 .30
288 Alex Rodriguez .50 1.25
289 Ugueth Urbina .10 .30
290 Jon Lieber .10 .30
291 Fernando Tatis .10 .30
292 Chris Stynes .10 .30
293 Bernard Gilkey .10 .30
294 Joey Hamilton .10 .30
295 Matt Karchner .10 .30
296 Paul Wilson .10 .30
297 Damion Easley .10 .30
298 Kevin Millwood RC .40 1.00
299 Ellis Burks .10 .30
300 Jerry DiPoto .10 .30
301 Jermaine Dye .10 .30
302 Travis Lee .10 .30
303 Ron Coomer .10 .30
304 Matt Williams .10 .30
305 Bobby Higginson .10 .30
306 Jorge Fabregas .10 .30
307 Jon Nunnally .10 .30
308 Jay Bell .10 .30
309 Jason Schmidt .10 .30
310 Andy Benes .10 .30
311 Sterling Hitchcock .10 .30
312 Jeff Suppan .10 .30
313 Shane Reynolds .10 .30
314 Willie Blair .10 .30
315 Scott Rolen .20 .50
316 Wilson Alvarez .10 .30
317 David Justice .10 .30
318 Fred McGriff .20 .50
319 Bobby Jones .10 .30
320 Wade Boggs .20 .50
321 Tim Wakefield .10 .30
322 Tony Saunders .10 .30
323 David Cone .10 .30
324 Roberto Hernandez .10 .30
325 José Canseco .20 .50
326 Kevin Stocker .10 .30
327 Gerald Williams .10 .30
328 Quinton McCracken .10 .30
329 Mark Gardner .10 .30
330 Ben Grieve .10 .30
331 Kevin Brown .20 .50
332 Mike Lowell RC .60 1.50
333 Jed Hansen .10 .30
334 Abraham Nunez .10 .30
335 John Thomson .10 .30
336 Masato Yoshii RC .15 .40
337 Mike Piazza .50 1.25
338 Brad Fullmer .10 .30
339 Ray Durham .10 .30
340 Kerry Wood .15 .40
341 Kevin Polcovich .10 .30
342 Russ Johnson .10 .30
343 Darryl Hamilton .10 .30
344 David Ortiz .40 1.00
345 Kevin Orie .10 .30
346 Mike Caruso .10 .30
347 Juan Guzman .10 .30
348 Ruben Rivera .10 .30
349 Rick Aguilera .10 .30
350 Bobby Estalella .10 .30
351 Bobby Witt .10 .30
352 Paul Konerko .10 .30
353 Matt Morris .10 .30
354 Carl Pavano .10 .30
355 Todd Zeile .10 .30
356 Kevin Brown TR .20 .50
357 Alex Gonzalez .10 .30
358 Chuck Knoblauch TR .10 .30
359 Joey Cora .10 .30
360 Mike Lansing TR .10 .30
361 Adrian Beltre .10 .30
362 Dennis Eckersley TR .10 .30
363 A.J. Hinch .10 .30
364 Kenny Lofton TR .10 .30
365 Alex Gonzalez .10 .30
366 Henry Rodriguez TR .10 .30
367 Mike Stoner RC .10 .30
368 Darryl Kile TR .10 .30
369 Kevin McGlinchy .10 .30
370 Walt Weiss TR .10 .30
371 Kris Benson .10 .30
372 Cecil Fielder TR .10 .30
373 Dermal Brown .10 .30
374 Rod Beck TR .10 .30
375 Eric Milton .10 .30
376 Travis Fryman TR .10 .30
377 Preston Wilson .10 .30
378 Chili Davis TR .10 .30
379 Travis Lee .10 .30
380 Jim Leyritz TR .10 .30
381 Vernon Wells .10 .30
382 Joe Carter TR .10 .30
383 J.J. Davis .10 .30
384 Marquis Grissom TR .10 .30
385 Mike Cuddyer RC .40 1.00
386 Rickey Henderson TR .30 .75
387 Chris Enochs RC .10 .30
388 Andres Galarraga TR .10 .30
389 Jason Dellaero .10 .30
390 Robb Nen TR .10 .30
391 Mark Mangum .10 .30
392 Jeff Blauser TR .10 .30
393 Adam Kennedy .10 .30
394 Bob Abreu TR .10 .30
395 Jack Cust RC .75 2.00
396 Jose Vizcaino TR .10 .30
397 Jon Garland .10 .30
398 Pedro Martinez TR .20 .50
399 Aaron Akin .10 .30
400 Jeff Conine TR .10 .30
NNO Cal Ripken Sound Chip 1 6.00 15.00
NNO Cal Ripken Sound Chip 2 6.00 15.00

1998 Stadium Club First Day Issue

*STARS: 6X TO 15X BASIC CARDS
*ROOKIES: 6X TO 15X BASIC CARDS
SER.1 STATED ODDS 1:42 RETAIL PACKS
SER.2 STATED ODDS 1:47 RETAIL PACKS
STATED PRINT RUN 200 SERIAL #'d SETS

1998 Stadium Club One Of A Kind

*STARS: 8X TO 20X BASIC CARDS
*ROOKIES: 8X TO 20X BASIC CARDS
SER.1 STATED ODDS 1:21 HOB, 1:13 HTA
SER.2 STATED ODDS 1:24 HOB, 1:14 HTA
STATED PRINT RUN 150 SERIAL #'d SETS

1998 Stadium Club Co-Signers

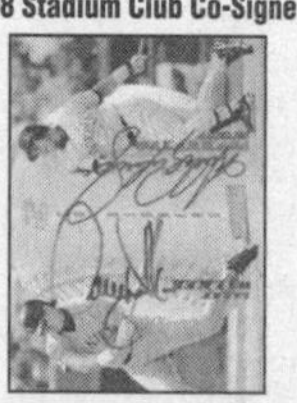

Randomly inserted exclusively in first and second series hobby and Home Team Advantage packs, this 36-card set features color photos of two top players on each card along with their autographs. These cards were released in three different levels of scarcity: A, B and C. Seeding rates are as follows: Series 1 Group A 1:4372 hobby and 1:2623 HTA, Series 1 Group B 1:1457 hobby and 1:874 HTA, Series 1 Group C 1:121 hobby and 1:73 HTA, Series 2 Group A 1:4702 hobby and 1:2821 HTA, Series 2 Group B 1:1567 hobby and 1:940 HTA and Series 2 Group C 1:131 hobby and 1:78 HTA. The scarce group A cards (rumored to be only 25 of each made) are the most difficult to obtain.

SER.1 A ODDS 1:4372 HOB, 1:2623 HTA
SER.2 A ODDS 1:4702 HOB, 1:2821 HTA
SER.1 B ODDS 1:1457 HOB, 1:874 HTA
SER.2 B ODDS 1:1567 HOB, 1:940 HTA
SER.1 C ODDS 1:121 HOB, 1:73 HTA
SER.2 C ODDS 1:131 HOB, 1: 78 HTA
CS1 N.Garciaparra/S.Rolen A 60.00 120.00
CS2 N.Garciaparra/D.Jeter B 175.00 300.00
CS3 N.Garciaparra/E.Karros C 20.00 50.00
CS4 S.Rolen/D.Jeter C 100.00 200.00
CS5 S.Rolen/E.Karros B 6.00 15.00
CS6 D.Jeter/E.Karros A 75.00 150.00
CS7 T.Lee/J.Cruz Jr. B 6.00 15.00
CS8 T.Lee/M.Kotsay C 6.00 15.00
CS9 T.Lee/P.Konerko A 40.00 80.00
CS10 J.Cruz Jr./M.Kotsay A 20.00 50.00
CS11 J.Cruz Jr./P.Konerko C 6.00 15.00
CS12 M.Kotsay/P.Konerko B 10.00 25.00
CS13 T.Gwynn/L.Walker A 150.00 300.00
CS14 T.Gwynn/M.Grudz. C 15.00 40.00
CS15 T.Gwynn/A.Galarraga B 60.00 120.00
CS16 L.Walker/M.Grudz. B 40.00 80.00
CS17 L.Walker/A.Galarraga C 15.00 40.00
CS18 A.Galarraga/M.Grudz. A 20.00 50.00
CS19 S.Alomar/R.Alomar A 15.00 40.00
CS20 S.Alomar/A.Pettitte C 15.00 40.00
CS21 S.Alomar/T.Martinez B 30.00 60.00
CS22 R.Alomar/A.Pettitte B 8.00 20.00
CS23 R.Alomar/T.Martinez C 20.00 50.00
CS24 A.Pettitte/T.Martinez A 60.00 120.00
CS25 T.Clark/T.Hundley A 20.00 50.00
CS26 T.Clark/T.Salmon B 20.00 50.00
CS27 T.Clark/R.Ventura C 6.00 15.00
CS28 T.Hundley/T.Salmon C 6.00 15.00
CS29 T.Hundley/R.Ventura B 15.00 40.00
CS30 T.Salmon/R.Ventura A 40.00 80.00
CS31 R.Clemens/R.Johnson B 100.00 200.00
CS32 R.Clemens/J.Wright A 75.00 150.00
CS33 R.Clemens/M.Morris C 20.00 50.00
CS34 R.Johnson/J.Wright C 30.00 80.00
CS35 R.Johnson/M.Morris A 20.00 50.00
CS36 J.Wright/M.Morris B 15.00 40.00

1998 Stadium Club In The Wings

Randomly inserted in first series hobby and retail packs at the rate of one in 36 and first series Home Team Advantage packs at a rate of one in 12, this 15-card set features color photos of some of the top young players in the league.

COMPLETE SET (15) 15.00 40.00
SER.1 STATED ODDS 1:36 H/R, 1:12 HTA
W1 Juan Encarnacion 1.50 4.00
W2 Brad Fullmer 1.50 4.00
W3 Ben Grieve 1.50 4.00
W4 Todd Helton 2.50 6.00
W5 Richard Hidalgo 1.50 4.00
W6 Russ Johnson 1.50 4.00
W7 Paul Konerko 1.50 4.00
W8 Mark Kotsay 1.50 4.00
W9 Derrek Lee 2.50 6.00
W10 Travis Lee 1.50 4.00
W11 Eli Marrero 1.50 4.00
W12 David Ortiz 5.00 12.00
W13 Randall Simon 1.50 4.00
W14 Shannon Stewart 1.50 4.00
W15 Fernando Tatis 1.50 4.00

1998 Stadium Club Never Compromise

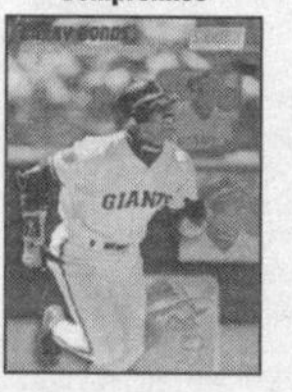

Randomly inserted in first series hobby and retail packs at the rate of one in 12 and first series HTA packs at the rate of one in four, this 20-card set features color photos of top players who never compromise in their game play.

COMPLETE SET (20) 30.00 80.00
SER.1 STATED ODDS 1:12 H/R, 1:4 HTA
NC1 Cal Ripken 4.00 10.00
NC2 Ivan Rodriguez .75 2.00
NC3 Ken Griffey Jr. 2.50 6.00
NC4 Frank Thomas 1.25 3.00
NC5 Tony Gwynn 1.50 4.00
NC6 Mike Piazza 2.00 5.00
NC7 Randy Johnson 1.25 3.00
NC8 Greg Maddux 2.00 5.00
NC9 Roger Clemens 2.50 6.00
NC10 Derek Jeter 3.00 8.00
NC11 Chipper Jones 1.25 3.00
NC12 Barry Bonds 3.00 8.00
NC13 Larry Walker .50 1.25
NC14 Jeff Bagwell .75 2.00
NC15 Barry Larkin .75 2.00
NC16 Ken Caminiti .50 1.25
NC17 Mark McGwire 3.00 8.00
NC18 Manny Ramirez .75 2.00
NC19 Tim Salmon .75 2.00
NC20 Paul Molitor .50 1.25

1998 Stadium Club Playing With Passion

Randomly seeded into second series hobby and retail packs at a rate of one in 12 and second series Home Team Advantage packs at a rate of one in four, cards from this 10-card set feature a selection of players who've got true fire in their hearts and the burning desire to win.

COMPLETE SET (10) 10.00 25.00
SER.2 STATED ODDS 1:12 H/R, 1:4 HTA
P1 Bernie Williams .60 1.50
P2 Jim Edmonds .40 1.00
P3 Chipper Jones 1.00 2.50
P4 Cal Ripken 3.00 8.00
P5 Craig Biggio .60 1.50
P6 Juan Gonzalez .40 1.00
P7 Alex Rodriguez 1.50 4.00
P8 Tino Martinez .60 1.50
P9 Mike Piazza 1.50 4.00
P10 Ken Griffey Jr. 2.00 5.00

1998 Stadium Club Royal Court

Randomly seeded into second series hobby and retail packs at a rate of one in 36 and second series Home Team Advantage packs at a rate of one in 12, cards from this 15-card set feature a selection of players that have proven their talent and dedication that they've got what it takes to achieve royalty. Players are broken into groups of ten Kings (veterans) and five Princes (rookies). Each card features a special Unilustre technology on front.

COMPLETE SET (15) 20.00 50.00
SER.2 STATED ODDS 1:36 H/R, 1:12 HTA
RC1 Ken Griffey Jr. 4.00 10.00
RC2 Frank Thomas 2.00 5.00
RC3 Mike Piazza 2.00 5.00
RC4 Chipper Jones 2.00 5.00
RC5 Mark McGwire 3.00 8.00
RC6 Cal Ripken 6.00 15.00
RC7 Jeff Bagwell 1.25 3.00
RC8 Barry Bonds 3.00 8.00
RC9 Juan Gonzalez .75 2.00
RC10 Alex Rodriguez 2.50 6.00
RC11 Travis Lee .75 2.00
RC12 Paul Konerko .75 2.00
RC13 Todd Helton 1.25 3.00
RC14 Ben Grieve .75 2.00
RC15 Mark Kotsay .75 2.00

1998 Stadium Club Triumvirate Luminous

Randomly inserted in first and second series retail packs at the rate of one in 48, the cards of this 54-card set feature color photos of three teammates that can be fused together to make one big card. These laser cut cards use Luminous technology.

STATED ODDS 1:48 RETAIL
*LUMINESCENT: 1.25X TO 3X LUMINOUS
LUMINESCENT STATED ODDS 1:192 RETAIL
*ILLUMINATOR: 2X TO 5X LUMINOUS
ILLUMINATOR STATED ODDS 1:384 RETAIL
T1A Chipper Jones 2.50 6.00
T1B Andruw Jones 1.50 4.00
T1C Kenny Lofton 1.00 2.50
T2A Derek Jeter 6.00 15.00
T2B Bernie Williams 1.50 4.00
T2C Tino Martinez 1.50 4.00
T3A Jay Buhner 1.00 2.50
T3B Edgar Martinez 1.50 4.00
T3C Ken Griffey Jr. 5.00 12.00
T4A Albert Belle 1.00 2.50
T4B Robin Ventura 1.00 2.50
T4C Frank Thomas 2.50 6.00
T5A Brady Anderson 1.00 2.50
T5B Cal Ripken 8.00 20.00
T5C Rafael Palmeiro 1.50 4.00
T6A Mike Piazza 4.00 10.00
T6B Raul Mondesi 1.00 2.50
T6C Eric Karros 1.00 2.50
T7A Vinny Castilla 1.00 2.50
T7B Andres Galarraga 1.00 2.50
T7C Larry Walker 1.00 2.50
T8A Jim Thome 1.50 4.00
T8B Manny Ramirez 1.50 4.00
T8C David Justice 1.00 2.50
T9A Mike Mussina 1.50 4.00
T9B Greg Maddux 4.00 10.00
T9C Randy Johnson 2.50 6.00
T10A Mike Piazza 4.00 10.00
T10B Sandy Alomar Jr. 1.00 2.50
T10C Ivan Rodriguez 1.50 4.00
T11A Mark McGwire 6.00 15.00
T11B Tino Martinez 1.50 4.00
T11C Frank Thomas 2.50 6.00
T12A Roberto Alomar 1.50 4.00
T12B Chuck Knoblauch 1.00 2.50
T12C Craig Biggio 1.50 4.00
T13A Cal Ripken 8.00 20.00
T13B Chipper Jones 2.50 6.00
T13C Ken Caminiti 1.00 2.50
T14A Derek Jeter 6.00 15.00
T14B Nomar Garciaparra 4.00 10.00
T14C Alex Rodriguez 4.00 10.00
T15A Barry Bonds 6.00 15.00
T15B David Justice 1.00 2.50
T15C Albert Belle 1.00 2.50
T16A Bernie Williams 1.50 4.00
T16B Ken Griffey Jr. 5.00 12.00
T16C Ray Lankford 1.00 2.50
T17A Tim Salmon 1.50 4.00
T17B Larry Walker 1.00 2.50
T17C Tony Gwynn 3.00 8.00
T18A Paul Molitor 1.00 2.50
T18B Edgar Martinez 1.50 4.00
T18C Juan Gonzalez 1.00 2.50

1999 Stadium Club

This 355-card set of 1999 Stadium Club cards was distributed in two separate series of 170 and 185 cards respectively. Six-card hobby and six-card retail packs each carried a suggested retail price of $2. 15-card Home Team Advantage packs (SRP of $5) were also distributed. All pack types contained a trifold/checklist info card. The card fronts feature color action player photos printed on 20 pt. card stock. The backs carry player information and career statistics. Draft Pick and Future Stars cards 141-160 and 336-355 were shortprinted at the following rates: 1:3 hobby/retail packs, one per HTA pack. Key Rookie Cards include Pat Burrell, Nick Johnson and Austin Kearns.

COMPLETE SET (355) 30.00 60.00
COMPLETE SERIES 1 (170) 12.50 30.00
COMP.SER.1 w/o SP's (150) 6.00 15.00
COMPLETE SERIES 2 (185) 12.50 30.00
COMP.SER.2 w/o SP's (165) 6.00 15.00
COMMON (1-140/161-170) .10 .30
COMMON CARD (171-335) .10 .30
COMM.SP (141-160/336-355) .75 2.00
SP ODDS 1:3 HOB/RET, 1 PER HTA
1 Alex Rodriguez .50 1.25
2 Chipper Jones .30 .75
3 Rusty Greer .10 .30
4 Jim Edmonds .10 .30
5 Ron Gant .10 .30
6 Kevin Polcovich .10 .30
7 Darryl Strawberry .10 .30
8 Bill Mueller .10 .30
9 Vinny Castilla .10 .30
10 Wade Boggs .20 .50
11 Jose Lima .10 .30
12 Darren Dreifort .10 .30
13 Jay Bell .10 .30
14 Ben Grieve .10 .30
15 Shawn Green .10 .30
16 Andres Galarraga .10 .30
17 Bartolo Colon .10 .30
18 Francisco Cordova .10 .30
19 Paul O'Neill .20 .50
20 Trevor Hoffman .10 .30
21 Darren Oliver .10 .30
22 John Franco .10 .30
23 Eli Marrero .10 .30
24 Roberto Hernandez .10 .30
25 Craig Biggio .20 .50
26 Brad Fullmer .10 .30
27 Scott Erickson .10 .30
28 Tom Gordon .10 .30
29 Brian Hunter .10 .30
30 Raul Mondesi .10 .30
31 Rick Reed .10 .30
32 Jose Canseco .20 .50
33 Robb Nen .10 .30
34 Turner Ward .10 .30
35 Orlando Hernandez .10 .30
36 Jeff Shaw .10 .30
37 Matt Lawton .10 .30
38 David Wells .10 .30
39 Bob Abreu .10 .30
40 Jeromy Burnitz .10 .30
41 Deivi Cruz .10 .30
42 Derek Bell .10 .30
43 Rico Brogna .10 .30
44 Dmitri Young .10 .30
45 Chuck Knoblauch .10 .30
46 Johnny Damon .20 .50
47 Brian Meadows .10 .30
48 Jeremi Gonzalez .10 .30
49 Gary DiSarcina .10 .30
50 Frank Thomas .30 .75
51 F.P. Santangelo .10 .30
52 Tom Candiotti .10 .30
53 Shane Reynolds .10 .30
54 Rod Beck .10 .30
55 Rey Ordonez .10 .30
56 Todd Helton .20 .50
57 Mickey Morandini .10 .30
58 Jorge Posada .20 .50
59 Mike Mussina .20 .50
60 Al Leiter .10 .30
61 David Segui .10 .30
62 Brian McRae .10 .30
63 Fred McGriff .20 .50
64 Brett Tomko .10 .30
65 Derek Jeter .75 2.00
66 Sammy Sosa .30 .75
67 Kenny Rogers .10 .30
68 Dave Nilsson .10 .30
69 Eric Young .10 .30
70 Mark McGwire .75 2.00
71 Kenny Lofton .10 .30
72 Tom Glavine .20 .50
73 Joey Hamilton .10 .30
74 John Valentin .10 .30

75 Mariano Rivera .30 .75
76 Ray Durham .10 .30
77 Tony Clark .10 .30
78 Livan Hernandez .10 .30
79 Rickey Henderson .30 .75
80 Vladimir Guerrero .30 .75
81 J.T. Snow .10 .30
82 Juan Guzman .10 .30
83 Darryl Hamilton .10 .30
84 Matt Anderson .10 .30
85 Travis Lee .10 .30
86 Joe Randa .10 .30
87 Dave Dellucci .10 .30
88 Moises Alou .10 .30
89 Alex Gonzalez .10 .30
90 Tony Womack .10 .30
91 Neifi Perez .10 .30
92 Travis Fryman .10 .30
93 Masato Yoshii .10 .30
94 Woody Williams .10 .30
95 Ray Lankford .10 .30
96 Roger Clemens .60 1.50
97 Dustin Hermanson .10 .30
98 Joe Carter .10 .30
99 Jason Schmidt .10 .30
100 Greg Maddux .50 1.25
101 Kevin Tapani .10 .30
102 Charles Johnson .10 .30
103 Derrek Lee .20 .50
104 Pete Harnisch .10 .30
105 Dante Bichette .10 .30
106 Scott Brosius .10 .30
107 Mike Caruso .10 .30
108 Eddie Taubensee .10 .30
109 Jeff Fassero .10 .30
110 Marquis Grissom .10 .30
111 Jose Hernandez .10 .30
112 Chan Ho Park .10 .30
113 Wally Joyner .10 .30
114 Bobby Estalella .10 .30
115 Pedro Martinez .20 .50
116 Shawn Estes .10 .30
117 Walt Weiss .10 .30
118 John Mabry .10 .30
119 Brian Johnson .10 .30
120 Jim Thome .20 .50
121 Bill Spiers .10 .30
122 John Olerud .10 .30
123 Jeff King .10 .30
124 Tim Belcher .10 .30
125 John Wetteland .10 .30
126 Tony Gwynn .40 1.00
127 Brady Anderson .10 .30
128 Randy Winn .10 .30
129 Andy Fox .10 .30
130 Eric Karros .10 .30
131 Kevin Millwood .10 .30
132 Andy Benes .10 .30
133 Andy Ashby .10 .30
134 Ron Coomer .10 .30
135 Juan Gonzalez .10 .30
136 Randy Johnson .30 .75
137 Aaron Sele .10 .30
138 Edgardo Alfonzo .10 .30
139 B.J. Surhoff .10 .30
140 Jose Vizcaino .10 .30
141 Chad Moeller SP RC .75 2.00
142 Mike Zywica SP RC .75 2.00
143 Angel Pena SP .75 2.00
144 Nick Johnson SP RC 1.00 2.50
145 C.Chiaramonte SP RC .75 2.00
146 Kit Pellow SP RC .75 2.00
147 Clayton Andrews SP RC .75 2.00
148 Jerry Hairston Jr. SP .75 2.00
149 Jason Tyner SP RC .75 2.00
150 Chip Ambres SP RC .75 2.00
151 Pat Burrell SP RC 1.50 4.00
152 Josh McKinley SP RC .75 2.00
153 Choo Freeman SP RC .75 2.00
154 Rick Elder SP RC .75 2.00
155 Eric Valent SP RC .75 2.00
156 Jeff Winchester SP RC .75 2.00
157 Mike Nannini SP RC .75 2.00
158 Mamon Tucker SP RC .75 2.00
159 Nate Bump SP RC .75 2.00
160 Andy Brown SP RC .75 2.00
161 Troy Glaus .20 .50
162 Adrian Beltre .10 .30
163 Mitch Meluskey .10 .30
164 Alex Gonzalez .10 .30
165 George Lombard .10 .30
166 Eric Chavez .10 .30
167 Ruben Mateo .10 .30
168 Calvin Pickering .10 .30
169 Gabe Kapler .10 .30
170 Bruce Chen .10 .30
171 Darin Erstad .10 .30
172 Sandy Alomar Jr. .10 .30
173 Miguel Cairo .10 .30
174 Jason Kendall .10 .30
175 Cal Ripken 1.00 2.50
176 Darryl Kile .10 .30
177 David Cone .10 .30
178 Mike Sweeney .10 .30
179 Royce Clayton .10 .30
180 Curt Schilling .10 .30
181 Barry Larkin .20 .50
182 Eric Milton .10 .30
183 Ellis Burks .10 .30
184 A.J. Hinch .10 .30
185 Garret Anderson .10 .30
186 Sean Bergman .10 .30
187 Shannon Stewart .10 .30
188 Bernard Gilkey .10 .30
189 Jeff Blauser .10 .30
190 Andruw Jones .20 .50
191 Omar Daal .10 .30
192 Jeff Kent .10 .30
193 Mark Kotsay .10 .30
194 Dave Burba .10 .30
195 Bobby Higginson .10 .30
196 Hideki Irabu .10 .30
197 Jamie Moyer .10 .30
198 Doug Glanville .10 .30
199 Quinton McCracken .10 .30
200 Ken Griffey Jr. .60 1.50
201 Mike Lieberthal .10 .30
202 Carl Everett .10 .30
203 Omar Vizquel .20 .50
204 Mike Lansing .10 .30
205 Manny Ramirez .20 .50
206 Ryan Klesko .10 .30
207 Jeff Montgomery .10 .30
208 Chad Curtis .10 .30
209 Rick Helling .10 .30
210 Justin Thompson .10 .30
211 Tom Goodwin .10 .30
212 Todd Dunwoody .10 .30
213 Kevin Young .10 .30
214 Tony Saunders .10 .30
215 Gary Sheffield .10 .30
216 Jaret Wright .10 .30
217 Quilvio Veras .10 .30
218 Marty Cordova .10 .30
219 Tino Martinez .20 .50
220 Scott Rolen .20 .50
221 Fernando Tatis .10 .30
222 Damion Easley .10 .30
223 Aramis Ramirez .10 .30
224 Brad Radke .10 .30
225 Nomar Garciaparra .50 1.25
226 Magglio Ordonez .10 .30
227 Andy Pettitte .20 .50
228 David Ortiz .30 .75
229 Todd Jones .10 .30
230 Larry Walker .10 .30
231 Tim Wakefield .10 .30
232 Jose Guillen .10 .30
233 Gregg Olson .10 .30
234 Ricky Gutierrez .10 .30
235 Todd Walker .10 .30
236 Abraham Nunez .10 .30
237 Sean Casey .10 .30
238 Greg Norton .10 .30
239 Bret Saberhagen .10 .30
240 Bernie Williams .20 .50
241 Tim Salmon .20 .50
242 Jason Giambi .10 .30
243 Fernando Vina .10 .30
244 Darrin Fletcher .10 .30
245 Mike Bordick .10 .30
246 Dennis Reyes .10 .30
247 Hideo Nomo .30 .75
248 Kevin Stocker .10 .30
249 Mike Hampton .10 .30
250 Kerry Wood .10 .30
251 Ismael Valdes .10 .30
252 Pat Hentgen .10 .30
253 Scott Spiezio .10 .30
254 Chuck Finley .10 .30
255 Troy Glaus .20 .50
256 Bobby Jones .10 .30
257 Wayne Gomes .10 .30
258 Rondell White .10 .30
259 Todd Zeile .10 .30
260 Matt Williams .10 .30
261 Henry Rodriguez .10 .30
262 Matt Stairs .10 .30
263 Jose Valentin .10 .30
264 David Justice .10 .30
265 Javy Lopez .10 .30
266 Matt Morris .10 .30
267 Steve Trachsel .10 .30
268 Edgar Martinez .20 .50
269 Al Martin .10 .30
270 Ivan Rodriguez .20 .50
271 Carlos Delgado .10 .30
272 Mark Grace .20 .50
273 Ugueth Urbina .10 .30
274 Jay Buhner .10 .30
275 Mike Piazza .50 1.25
276 Rick Aguilera .10 .30
277 Javier Valentin .10 .30
278 Brian Anderson .10 .30
279 Cliff Floyd .10 .30
280 Barry Bonds .75 2.00
281 Troy O'Leary .10 .30
282 Seth Greisinger .10 .30
283 Mark Grudzielanek .10 .30
284 Jose Cruz Jr. .10 .30
285 Jeff Bagwell .20 .50
286 John Smoltz .20 .50
287 Jeff Cirillo .10 .30
288 Richie Sexson .10 .30
289 Charles Nagy .10 .30
290 Pedro Martinez .20 .50
291 Juan Encarnacion .10 .30
292 Phil Nevin .10 .30
293 Terry Steinbach .10 .30
294 Miguel Tejada .20 .50
295 Dan Wilson .10 .30
296 Chris Peters .10 .30
297 Brian Moehler .10 .30
298 Jason Christiansen .10 .30
299 Kelly Stinnett .10 .30
300 Dwight Gooden .10 .30
301 Randy Velarde .10 .30
302 Kirt Manwaring .10 .30
303 Jeff Abbott .10 .30
304 Dave Hollins .10 .30
305 Kerry Ligtenberg .10 .30
306 Aaron Boone .10 .30
307 Carlos Hernandez .10 .30
308 Mike Difelice .10 .30
309 Brian Meadows .10 .30
310 Tim Bogar .10 .30
311 Greg Vaughn TR .10 .30
312 Brant Brown TR .10 .30
313 Steve Finley TR .10 .30
314 Bret Boone TR .10 .30
315 Albert Belle TR .10 .30
316 Robin Ventura TR .10 .30
317 Eric Davis TR .10 .30
318 Todd Hundley TR .10 .30
319 Roger Clemens TR .60 1.50
320 Kevin Brown TR .10 .30
321 Jose Offerman TR .10 .30
322 Brian Jordan TR .10 .30
323 Mike Cameron TR .10 .30
324 Bobby Bonilla TR .10 .30
325 Roberto Alomar TR .20 .50
326 Ken Caminiti TR .10 .30
327 Todd Stottlemyre TR .10 .30
328 Randy Johnson TR .30 .75
329 Luis Gonzalez TR .10 .30
330 Rafael Palmeiro TR .20 .50
331 Devon White TR .10 .30
332 Will Clark TR .20 .50
333 Dean Palmer TR .10 .30
334 Gregg Jefferies TR .10 .30
335 Mo Vaughn TR .10 .30
336 Brad Lidge SP RC 1.50 4.00
337 Chris George SP RC .75 2.00
338 Austin Kearns SP RC 1.50 4.00
339 Matt Belisle SP RC .75 2.00
340 Nate Cornejo SP RC .75 2.00
341 Matt Holliday SP RC 3.00 8.00
342 J.M. Gold SP RC .75 2.00
343 Matt Roney SP RC .75 2.00
344 Seth Etherton SP RC .75 2.00
345 Adam Everett SP RC .75 2.00
346 Marlon Anderson SP .75 2.00
347 Ron Belliard SP .75 2.00
348 Fernando Seguignol SP .75 2.00
349 Michael Barrett SP .75 2.00
350 Dernell Stenson SP .75 2.00
351 Ryan Anderson SP .75 2.00
352 Ramon Hernandez SP .75 2.00
353 Jeremy Giambi SP .75 2.00
354 Ricky Ledee SP .75 2.00
355 Carlos Lee SP .75 2.00

1999 Stadium Club First Day Issue

*STARS: 6X TO 15X BASIC CARDS
*SP 141-160/336-355: 2X TO 5X BASIC SP
SER.1 STATED ODDS 1:75 RETAIL
SER.2 STATED ODDS 1:60 RETAIL
SER.1 PRINT RUN 170 SERIAL #'d SETS
SER.2 PRINT RUN 200 SERIAL #'d SETS

1999 Stadium Club One of a Kind

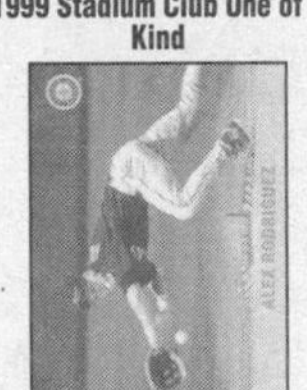

*STARS: 6X TO 15X BASIC CARDS
*SP'S 141-160/336-355: 2X TO 5X BASIC
SER.1 STATED ODDS 1:53 HOBBY, 1:21 HTA
SER.2 STATED ODDS 1:48 HOBBY, 1:19 HTA
STATED PRINT RUN 150 SERIAL #'d SETS

1999 Stadium Club Autographs

This 10-card set features color player photos with the pictured player's autograph and a gold-foil Topps Certified Autograph Issue stamp on the card front. They were inserted exclusively into retail packs as follows: series 1 1:1107, series 2 1:877.

SER.1 STATED ODDS 1:1107 RETAIL
SER.2 STATED ODDS 1:877 RETAIL
CARDS 1-5 IN SER.1, 6-10 IN SER.2
SCA1 Alex Rodriguez 40.00 80.00
SCA2 Chipper Jones 20.00 50.00
SCA3 Barry Bonds 100.00 175.00
SCA4 Tino Martinez 10.00 25.00
SCA5 Ben Grieve 6.00 15.00
SCA6 Juan Gonzalez 10.00 25.00
SCA7 Vladimir Guerrero 8.00 20.00
SCA8 Albert Belle 6.00 15.00
SCA9 Kerry Wood 10.00 25.00
SCA10 Todd Helton 10.00 25.00

1999 Stadium Club Chrome

Randomly inserted in packs at the rate of one in 24 hobby and retail packs and one in six HTA packs, this 40-card set features color player photos printed using chromium technology which gives the cards the shimmering metallic light of fresh steel.

COMPLETE SET (40) 60.00 120.00
COMPLETE SERIES 1 (20) 30.00 60.00
COMPLETE SERIES 2 (20) 25.00 60.00
STATED ODDS 1:24 HOB/RET, 1:6 HTA
*REFRACTORS: 1X TO 2.5X BASIC CHROME
REFRACTOR ODDS 1:96 HOB/RET, 1:24 HTA
SCC1 Nomar Garciaparra 2.50 6.00
SCC2 Kerry Wood .60 1.50
SCC3 Jeff Bagwell 1.00 2.50
SCC4 Ivan Rodriguez 1.00 2.50
SCC5 Albert Belle .60 1.50
SCC6 Gary Sheffield .60 1.50
SCC7 Andruw Jones 1.00 2.50
SCC8 Kevin Brown .60 1.50
SCC9 David Cone .60 1.50
SCC10 Darin Erstad .60 1.50
SCC11 Manny Ramirez 1.00 2.50
SCC12 Larry Walker .60 1.50
SCC13 Mike Piazza 2.50 6.00
SCC14 Cal Ripken 5.00 12.00
SCC15 Pedro Martinez 1.00 2.50
SCC16 Greg Vaughn .60 1.50
SCC17 Barry Bonds 4.00 10.00
SCC18 Mo Vaughn .60 1.50
SCC19 Bernie Williams 1.00 2.50
SCC20 Ken Griffey Jr. 3.00 8.00
SCC21 Alex Rodriguez 2.50 6.00
SCC22 Chipper Jones 1.50 4.00
SCC23 Ben Grieve .60 1.50
SCC24 Frank Thomas 1.50 4.00
SCC25 Derek Jeter 4.00 10.00
SCC26 Sammy Sosa 1.50 4.00
SCC27 Mark McGwire 4.00 10.00
SCC28 Vladimir Guerrero 1.50 4.00
SCC29 Greg Maddux 2.50 6.00
SCC30 Juan Gonzalez .60 1.50
SCC31 Troy Glaus 1.00 2.50
SCC32 Adrian Beltre .60 1.50
SCC33 Mitch Meluskey .60 1.50
SCC34 Alex Gonzalez .60 1.50
SCC35 George Lombard .60 1.50
SCC36 Eric Chavez .60 1.50
SCC37 Ruben Mateo .60 1.50
SCC38 Calvin Pickering .60 1.50
SCC39 Gabe Kapler .60 1.50
SCC40 Bruce Chen .60 1.50

1999 Stadium Club Co-Signers

Randomly inserted in hobby packs only, this 42-card set features color player photos with their autographs and Topps "Certified Autograph Issue" stamp. Cards 1-21 were seeded in first series packs and 22-42 in second series. The cards are divided into four groups. Group A was signed by all four players appearing on the cards. Groups B-D are dual player cards featuring two autographs. Series 1 hobby pack insertion rates are as follows: Group A 1:45,213, Group B 1:3617, Group C 1:1006, and Group D 1:102. Series 2 hobby pack insertion rates are as follows: Group A 1:43,369, Group B 1:8984, Group C 1:2975 and Group D 1:251. Series 2 HTA pack insertion rates are as follows: Group A 1:18,171, Group B 1:3533, Group C 1:1189 and Group D 1:100. Pricing is available for all cards where possible.

SER.1 A ODDS 1:45213 HOB, 1:18085 HTA
SER.2 A ODDS 1:43639 HOB, 1:18171 HTA
SER.1 B ODDS 1:9043 HOB, 1:3617 HTA
SER.2 B ODDS 1:8984 HOB, 1:3533 HTA
SER.1 C ODDS 1:3104 HOB, 1:1006 HTA
SER.2 C ODDS 1:2975 HOB, 1:1189 HTA
SER.1 D ODDS 1:254 HOB, 1:102 HTA
SER.2 D ODDS 1:251 HOB, 1:100 HTA
NO GROUP A PRICING DUE TO SCARCITY
NO SER.2 GROUP B PRICING AVAILABLE
CS1 B.Grieve/R.Sexson D 8.00 20.00
CS2 T.Helton/T.Glaus D 8.00 20.00
CS3 A.Rodriguez/S.Rolen D 30.00 60.00
CS4 D.Jeter/C.Jones D 300.00 400.00
CS5 C.Floyd/E.Marrero D 8.00 20.00
CS6 J.Buhner/K.Young D 8.00 20.00
CS7 B.Grieve/T.Glaus C 15.00 40.00
CS8 T.Helton/R.Sexson C 15.00 40.00
CS9 A.Rodriguez/C.Jones C 90.00 150.00
CS10 D.Jeter/S.Rolen C 125.00 250.00
CS11 C.Floyd/K.Young C 8.00 20.00
CS12 J.Buhner/E.Marrero B 8.00 20.00
CS13 B.Grieve/T.Helton B 30.00 60.00
CS14 R.Sexson/T.Glaus B 30.00 60.00
CS15 A.Rodriguez/D.Jeter B 250.00 500.00
CS16 C.Jones/S.Rolen B 60.00 120.00
CS17 C.Floyd/J.Buhner B 15.00 40.00
CS18 E.Marrero/K.Young B 8.00 20.00
CS19 Grieve/Helton/Sexson/Glaus A
CS20 A.Rod/Jeter/Jones/Rolen A
CS21 Floyd/Buhner/Marrero/Young A
CS22 E.Alfonzo/J.Guillen D 8.00 20.00
CS23 M.Lowell/R.Rincon D 8.00 20.00
CS24 J.Gonzalez/V.Castilla D 8.00 20.00
CS25 M.Alou/R.Clemens D 15.00 40.00
CS26 S.Spiezio/T.Womack D 6.00 15.00
CS27 F.Vina/Q.Veras D 6.00 15.00
CS28 E.Alfonzo/R.Rincon C 8.00 20.00
CS29 J.Guillen/M.Lowell C 8.00 20.00
CS30 J.Gonzalez/M.Alou C 8.00 20.00
CS31 R.Clemens/V.Castilla C 30.00 60.00
CS32 S.Spiezio/F.Vina C 6.00 15.00
CS33 T.Womack/Q.Veras B 8.00 20.00
CS34 E.Alfonzo/M.Lowell B 15.00 40.00
CS35 J.Guillen/R.Rincon B 15.00 40.00
CS36 J.Gonzalez/R.Clemens B 150.00 250.00
CS37 M.Alou/V.Castilla B 30.00 60.00
CS38 S.Spiezio/Q.Veras B 8.00 20.00
CS39 T.Womack/F.Vina B 8.00 20.00
CS40 Alfonzo/Guillen/Lowell/Rincon A
CS41 Gonzalez/Alou/Clemens/Castilla A
CS42 Spiezio/Womack/Vina/Veras A

1999 Stadium Club Never Compromise

Randomly inserted in packs at the rate of one in 12 hobby and retail packs and one in four HTA packs, this 10-card set features color action photos of top players.

COMPLETE SET (20) 20.00 50.00
COMPLETE SERIES 1 (10) 15.00 40.00
COMPLETE SERIES 2 (10) 8.00 20.00
STATED ODDS 1:12 HOB/RET, 1:4 HTA
NC1 Mark McGwire 2.00 5.00
NC2 Sammy Sosa .75 2.00
NC3 Ken Griffey Jr. 1.50 4.00
NC4 Greg Maddux 1.25 3.00
NC5 Barry Bonds 2.00 5.00
NC6 Alex Rodriguez 1.25 3.00
NC7 Darin Erstad .30 .75
NC8 Roger Clemens 1.50 4.00
NC9 Nomar Garciaparra 1.25 3.00
NC10 Derek Jeter 2.00 5.00
NC11 Cal Ripken 2.50 6.00
NC12 Mike Piazza 1.25 3.00
NC13 Kerry Wood .30 .75
NC14 Andres Galarraga .30 .75
NC15 Vinny Castilla .30 .75
NC16 Jeff Bagwell .50 1.25
NC17 Chipper Jones .75 2.00
NC18 Eric Chavez .30 .75
NC19 Orlando Hernandez .30 .75
NC20 Troy Glaus .50 1.25

1999 Stadium Club Triumvirate Luminous

Randomly inserted in hobby packs at the rate of one in 36 and in retail packs at the rate of one in 48, this 24-card set features color player photos printed on cards made to fit together to form eight different long cards.

COMPLETE SET (48) 150.00 300.00
COMPLETE SERIES 1 (24) 60.00 120.00
COMPLETE SERIES 2 (24) 75.00 150.00
STATED ODDS 1:36 H, 1:48 R, 1:18 HTA
*ILLUMINATOR: 2X TO 5X LUMINOUS
ILLUM.ODDS 1:288 H, 1:384 R, 1:144 HTA
*LUMINESCENT: 1X TO 2.5X LUMINOUS
L'SCENT.ODDS 1:144 H, 1:192 R, 1:72 HTA
T1A Greg Vaughn .75 2.00
T1B Ken Caminiti .75 2.00
T1C Tony Gwynn 2.50 6.00
T2A Andruw Jones 1.25 3.00
T2B Chipper Jones 2.00 5.00
T2C Andres Galarraga .75 2.00
T3A Jay Buhner .75 2.00
T3B Ken Griffey Jr. 4.00 10.00
T3C Alex Rodriguez 3.00 8.00
T4A Derek Jeter 5.00 12.00
T4B Tino Martinez 1.25 3.00
T4C Bernie Williams 1.25 3.00
T5A Brian Jordan .75 2.00
T5B Ray Lankford .75 2.00
T5C Mark McGwire 5.00 12.00
T6A Jeff Bagwell 1.25 3.00
T6B Craig Biggio 1.25 3.00
T6C Randy Johnson 2.00 5.00
T7A Nomar Garciaparra 3.00 8.00
T7B Pedro Martinez 1.25 3.00
T7C Mo Vaughn .75 2.00
T8A Sammy Sosa 2.00 5.00
T8B Mark Grace 1.25 3.00
T8C Kerry Wood .75 2.00
T9A Alex Rodriguez 3.00 8.00
T9B Nomar Garciaparra 3.00 8.00
T9C Derek Jeter 5.00 12.00
T10A Todd Helton 1.25 3.00
T10B Travis Lee .75 2.00
T10C Pat Burrell 1.25 3.00
T11A Greg Maddux 3.00 8.00
T11B Kerry Wood .75 2.00
T11C Tom Glavine 1.25 3.00
T12A Chipper Jones 2.00 5.00
T12B Vinny Castilla .75 2.00
T12C Scott Rolen 1.25 3.00
T13A Juan Gonzalez .75 2.00
T13B Ken Griffey Jr. 10.00 25.00
T13C Ben Grieve .75 2.00
T14A Sammy Sosa 2.00 5.00
T14B Vladimir Guerrero 2.00 5.00
T14C Barry Bonds 5.00 12.00
T15A Frank Thomas 2.00 5.00
T15B Jim Thome 1.25 3.00
T15C Tino Martinez 1.25 3.00
T16A Mark McGwire 5.00 12.00
T16B Andres Galarraga .75 2.00
T16C Jeff Bagwell 1.25 3.00

1999 Stadium Club Video Replay

Randomly inserted in Series two hobby and retail packs at the rate of one in 12 and HTA packs at the rate of one in four, this five-card set features live-action video images of top players on lenticular cards.

COMPLETE SET (5) 5.00 12.00
SER.2 STATED ODDS 1:12 HOB/RET, 1:4 HTA
VR1 Mark McGwire 1.50 4.00
VR2 Sammy Sosa .60 1.50
VR3 Ken Griffey Jr. 1.25 3.00
VR4 Kerry Wood .25 .60
VR5 Alex Rodriguez 1.00 2.50

2000 Stadium Club Pre-Production

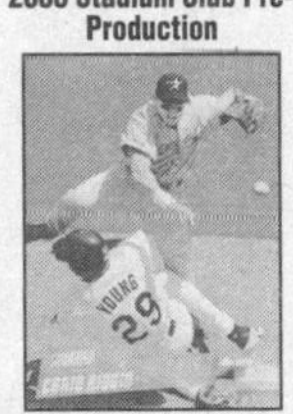

These three cards were issued by Topps to preview their 2000 Stadium Club set. The cards were distributed as a set within a sealed cello wrapper to dealers and hobby media several weeks before the product's release. The cards, while they are in the style of the 2000 set, are differentiated by having a "PP" prefix.

COMPLETE SET (3) 1.25 3.00
PP1 Ivan Rodriguez .60 1.50
PP2 Magglio Ordonez .60 1.50
PP3 Craig Biggio .60 1.50

2000 Stadium Club

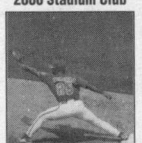

This 250-card single series set was released in February, 2000. Six-card hobby and retail packs carried an SRP of $2.00. There was also a HTC (Home Team Collector) fourteen card pack issued with a SRP of $5.00. The last 50 cards were printed in shorter supply the first 200 cards. These cards were inserted one in five packs and one per HTC pack. This was the first time the Stadium Club set was issued in a single series. Notable Rookie Cards at the time included Rick Asadoorian and Bobby Bradley.

COMPLETE SET (250) 50.00 120.00
COMP.SET w/o SP'S (200) 12.50 30.00
COMMON CARD (1-200) .12 .30
COMMON SP (201-250) .75 2.00
SP 201-250 ODDS 1:5 HOB/RET, 1:1 HTC
1 Nomar Garciaparra .20 .50
2 Brian Jordan .12 .30
3 Mark Grace .20 .50
4 Jeromy Burnitz .12 .30
5 Shane Reynolds .12 .30
6 Alex Gonzalez .12 .30
7 Jose Offerman .12 .30
8 Orlando Hernandez .12 .30
9 Mike Caruso .12 .30
10 Tony Clark .12 .30
11 Sean Casey .12 .30
12 Johnny Damon .20 .50
13 Dante Bichette .12 .30
14 Kevin Young .12 .30
15 Juan Gonzalez .12 .30
16 Chipper Jones .30 .75
17 Quilvio Veras .12 .30
18 Trevor Hoffman .20 .50
19 Roger Cedeno .12 .30
20 Ellis Burks .12 .30
21 Richie Sexson .12 .30
22 Gary Sheffield .12 .30
23 Delino DeShields .12 .30
24 Wade Boggs .20 .50
25 Ray Lankford .12 .30
26 Kevin Appier .12 .30
27 Roy Halladay .20 .50
28 Harold Baines .20 .50
29 Todd Zeile .12 .30
30 Barry Larkin .20 .50
31 Ron Coomer .12 .30
32 Jorge Posada .20 .50
33 Magglio Ordonez .20 .50
34 Brian Giles .12 .30
35 Jeff Kent .12 .30
36 Henry Rodriguez .12 .30
37 Fred McGriff .20 .50
38 Shawn Green .12 .30
39 Derek Bell .12 .30
40 Ben Grieve .12 .30
41 Dave Nilsson .12 .30
42 Mo Vaughn .12 .30
43 Rondell White .12 .30
44 Doug Glanville .12 .30
45 Paul O'Neill .20 .50
46 Carlos Lee .12 .30
47 Vinny Castilla .12 .30
48 Mike Sweeney .12 .30
49 Rico Brogna .12 .30
50 Alex Rodriguez .40 1.00
51 Luis Castillo .12 .30
52 Kevin Brown .12 .30
53 Jose Vidro .12 .30
54 John Smoltz .30 .75
55 Garret Anderson .12 .30
56 Matt Stairs .12 .30
57 Omar Vizquel .20 .50
58 Tom Goodwin .12 .30
59 Scott Brosius .12 .30
60 Robin Ventura .12 .30
61 B.J. Surhoff .12 .30
62 Andy Ashby .12 .30
63 Chris Widger .12 .30
64 Tim Hudson .20 .50
65 Javy Lopez .12 .30
66 Tim Salmon .12 .30
67 Warren Morris .12 .30
68 John Wetteland .12 .30
69 Gabe Kapler .12 .30
70 Bernie Williams .20 .50
71 Rickey Henderson .30 .75
72 Andruw Jones .12 .30
73 Eric Young .12 .30
74 Bob Abreu .12 .30
75 David Cone .12 .30
76 Rusty Greer .12 .30
77 Ron Belliard .12 .30
78 Troy Glaus .12 .30
79 Mike Hampton .12 .30
80 Miguel Tejada .20 .50
81 Jeff Cirillo .12 .30
82 Todd Hundley .12 .30
83 Roberto Alomar .20 .50
84 Charles Johnson .12 .30
85 Rafael Palmeiro .20 .50
86 Doug Mientkiewicz .12 .30
87 Mariano Rivera .40 1.00
88 Neifi Perez .12 .30
89 Jermaine Dye .12 .30
90 Ivan Rodriguez .20 .50
91 Jay Buhner .12 .30
92 Pokey Reese .12 .30
93 John Olerud .12 .30
94 Brady Anderson .12 .30
95 Manny Ramirez .30 .75
96 Keith Osik RC .12 .30
97 Mickey Morandini .12 .30
98 Matt Williams .12 .30
99 Eric Karros .12 .30
100 Ken Griffey Jr. .60 1.50
101 Bret Boone .12 .30
102 Ryan Klesko .12 .30
103 Craig Biggio .20 .50

104 John Jaha .12 .30
105 Vladimir Guerrero .20 .50
106 Devon White .12 .30
107 Tony Womack .12 .30
108 Marvin Benard .12 .30
109 Kenny Lofton .12 .30
110 Preston Wilson .12 .30
111 Al Leiter .12 .30
112 Reggie Sanders .12 .30
113 Scott Williamson .12 .30
114 Deivi Cruz .12 .30
115 Carlos Beltran .20 .50
116 Ray Durham .12 .30
117 Ricky Ledee .12 .30
118 Torii Hunter .12 .30
119 John Valentin .12 .30
120 Scott Rolen .20 .50
121 Jason Kendall .12 .30
122 Dave Martinez .12 .30
123 Jim Thome .20 .50
124 David Bell .12 .30
125 Jose Canseco .20 .50
126 Jose Lima .12 .30
127 Carl Everett .12 .30
128 Kevin Millwood .12 .30
129 Bill Spiers .12 .30
130 Omar Daal .12 .30
131 Miguel Cairo .12 .30
132 Mark Grudzielanek .12 .30
133 David Justice .12 .30
134 Russ Ortiz .12 .30
135 Mike Piazza .30 .75
136 Brian Meadows .12 .30
137 Tony Gwynn .30 .75
138 Cal Ripken 1.00 2.50
139 Kris Benson .12 .30
140 Larry Walker .20 .50
141 Cristian Guzman .12 .30
142 Tino Martinez .12 .30
143 Chris Singleton .12 .30
144 Lee Stevens .12 .30
145 Rey Ordonez .12 .30
146 Russ Davis .12 .30
147 J.T. Snow .12 .30
148 Luis Gonzalez .12 .30
149 Marquis Grissom .12 .30
150 Greg Maddux .40 1.00
151 Fernando Tatis .12 .30
152 Jason Giambi .12 .30
153 Carlos Delgado .12 .30
154 Joe McEwing .12 .30
155 Raul Mondesi .12 .30
156 Rich Aurilia .12 .30
157 Alex Fernandez .12 .30
158 Albert Belle .12 .30
159 Pat Meares .12 .30
160 Mike Lieberthal .12 .30
161 Mike Cameron .12 .30
162 Juan Encarnacion .12 .30
163 Chuck Knoblauch .12 .30
164 Pedro Martinez .20 .50
165 Randy Johnson .30 .75
166 Shannon Stewart .12 .30
167 Jeff Bagwell .20 .50
168 Edgar Renteria .12 .30
169 Barry Bonds .50 1.25
170 Steve Finley .12 .30
171 Brian Hunter .12 .30
172 Tom Glavine .20 .50
173 Mark Kotsay .12 .30
174 Tony Fernandez .12 .30
175 Sammy Sosa .30 .75
176 Geoff Jenkins .12 .30
177 Adrian Beltre .30 .75
178 Jay Bell .12 .30
179 Mike Bordick .12 .30
180 Ed Sprague .12 .30
181 Dave Roberts .20 .50
182 Greg Vaughn .12 .30
183 Brian Daubach .12 .30
184 Damion Easley .12 .30
185 Carlos Febles .12 .30
186 Kevin Tapani .12 .30
187 Frank Thomas .30 .75
188 Roger Clemens .40 1.00
189 Mike Benjamin .12 .30
190 Curt Schilling .20 .50
191 Edgardo Alfonzo .12 .30
192 Mike Mussina .20 .50
193 Todd Helton .20 .50
194 Todd Jones .12 .30
195 Dean Palmer .12 .30
196 John Flaherty .12 .30
197 Derek Jeter .75 2.00
198 Todd Walker .12 .30
199 Brad Ausmus .12 .30
200 Mark McGwire .50 1.25
201 Erubiel Durazo SP .75 2.00
202 Nick Johnson SP .75 2.00
203 Ruben Mateo SP .75 2.00
204 Lance Berkman SP 1.25 3.00
205 Pat Burrell SP .75 2.00
206 Pablo Ozuna SP .75 2.00
207 Roosevelt Brown SP .75 2.00
208 Alfonso Soriano SP 2.00 5.00
209 A.J. Burnett SP .75 2.00
210 Rafael Furcal SP 1.25 3.00
211 Scott Morgan SP .75 2.00
212 Adam Piatt SP .75 2.00
213 Dee Brown SP .75 2.00
214 Corey Patterson SP .75 2.00
215 Mickey Lopez SP .75 2.00
216 Rob Ryan SP .75 2.00
217 Sean Burroughs SP .75 2.00
218 Jack Cust SP .75 2.00
219 John Patterson SP .75 2.00
220 Kit Pellow SP .75 2.00
221 Chad Hermansen SP .75 2.00
222 Daryle Ward SP .75 2.00
223 Jayson Werth SP 1.25 3.00
224 Jason Standridge SP .75 2.00
225 Mark Mulder SP .75 2.00
226 Peter Bergeron SP .75 2.00
227 Willi Mo Pena SP .75 2.00
228 Aramis Ramirez SP .75 2.00
229 John Sneed SP RC .75 2.00
230 Wilton Veras SP .75 2.00
231 Josh Hamilton 2.50 6.00
232 Eric Munson SP .75 2.00
233 Bobby Bradley SP RC .75 2.00
234 Larry Bigbie SP RC .75 2.00
235 B.J. Garbe SP RC .75 2.00
236 Brett Myers SP RC 2.50 6.00
237 Jason Stumm SP RC .75 2.00
238 Corey Myers SP RC .75 2.00
239 Ryan Christianson SP RC .75 2.00
240 David Walling SP .75 2.00
241 Josh Girdley SP .75 2.00
242 Omar Ortiz SP .75 2.00
243 Jason Jennings SP .75 2.00
244 Kyle Snyder SP .75 2.00
245 Jay Gehrke SP .75 2.00
246 Mike Paradis SP .75 2.00
247 Chance Caple SP RC .75 2.00
248 Ben Christensen SP RC .75 2.00
249 Brad Baker SP RC .75 2.00
250 Rick Asadoorian SP RC .75 2.00

2000 Stadium Club First Day Issue

*1ST DAY: 10X TO 25X BASIC
*SP'S 201-250: 1.5X TO 4X BASIC
STATED ODDS 1:36 RETAIL
STATED PRINT RUN 150 SERIAL #'d SETS

2000 Stadium Club One of a Kind

*ONE KIND 1-250: 10X TO 25X BASIC
*ONE 201-250: 1.5X TO 4X BASIC
STATED ODDS 1:27 HOBBY, 1:11 HTC
STATED PRINT RUN 150 SERIAL #'d SETS

2000 Stadium Club Bats of Brilliance

Issued at a rate of one in 12 hobby packs, one in 15 retail packs and one in six HTC packs these 10 cards feature some of the best clutch hitters in the game.

COMPLETE SET (10) 8.00 20.00
STATED ODDS 1:12 HOB, 1:15 RET, 1:6 HTC
*DIE CUTS: 1.25X TO 3X BASIC BATS
DIE CUT ODDS 1:60 HOB, 1:75 RET, 1:30 HTC
BB1 Mark McGwire 1.50 4.00
BB2 Sammy Sosa .60 1.50
BB3 Jose Canseco .40 1.00
BB4 Jeff Bagwell .40 1.00
BB5 Ken Griffey Jr. 1.25 3.00
BB6 Nomar Garciaparra 1.00 2.50
BB7 Mike Piazza 1.00 2.50
BB8 Alex Rodriguez 1.00 2.50
BB9 Vladimir Guerrero .60 1.50
BB10 Chipper Jones .60 1.50

2000 Stadium Club Capture the Action

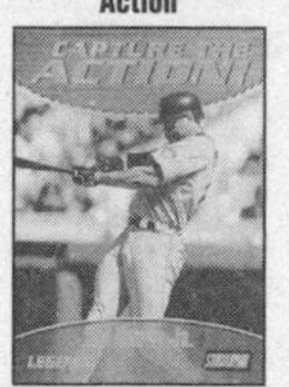

Inserted one in 12 hobby and retail packs and one in six HTC packs, these 20 cards feature players who continually hustle when on the field. This set is broken up into three groups: Rookies (CA1 through CA5); Stars (CA6 through CA14) and Legends (CA15 through CA20).

COMPLETE SET (20) 15.00 40.00
STATED ODDS 1:12 HOB/RET, 1:6 HTC
*GAME VIEW: 5X TO 12X BASIC CAPTURE
GAME VIEW ODDS 1:508 HOB, 1:203 HTC
GAME VIEW PRINT RUN 100 SERIAL #'d SETS
CA1 Josh Hamilton 1.25 3.00
CA2 Pat Burrell .40 1.00
CA3 Erubiel Durazo .40 1.00
CA4 Alfonso Soriano 1.00 2.50
CA5 A.J. Burnett .40 1.00
CA6 Alex Rodriguez 1.25 3.00
CA7 Sean Casey .40 1.00
CA8 Derek Jeter 2.50 6.00
CA9 Vladimir Guerrero .60 1.50
CA10 Nomar Garciaparra .60 1.50
CA11 Mike Piazza 1.00 2.50
CA12 Ken Griffey Jr. 2.00 5.00
CA13 Sammy Sosa 1.00 2.50
CA14 Juan Gonzalez .40 1.00
CA15 Mark McGwire 1.50 4.00
CA16 Ivan Rodriguez .60 1.50
CA17 Barry Bonds 1.50 4.00
CA18 Wade Boggs .60 1.50
CA19 Tony Gwynn 1.00 2.50
CA20 Cal Ripken 3.00 8.00

2000 Stadium Club Chrome Preview

Inserted at a rate of one in 24 for hobby and retail and one in 12 HTC packs, these 20 cards preview the "Chrome" set. These cards carry a "SCC" prefix.

COMPLETE SET (20) 20.00 50.00
STATED ODDS 1:24 HOB/RET, 1:12 HTC
*REFRACTOR: 1.25X TO 3X BASIC CHR.PREV.
REFRACTOR ODDS 1:120 HOB/RET, 1:60 HTC
SCC1 Nomar Garciaparra 1.00 2.50
SCC2 Juan Gonzalez .60 1.50
SCC3 Chipper Jones 1.50 4.00
SCC4 Alex Rodriguez 2.00 5.00
SCC5 Ivan Rodriguez 1.00 2.50
SCC6 Manny Ramirez 1.50 4.00
SCC7 Ken Griffey Jr. 3.00 8.00
SCC8 Vladimir Guerrero 1.00 2.50
SCC9 Mike Piazza 1.50 4.00
SCC10 Pedro Martinez 1.00 2.50
SCC11 Jeff Bagwell 1.00 2.50
SCC12 Barry Bonds 2.50 6.00
SCC13 Sammy Sosa 1.50 4.00
SCC14 Derek Jeter 4.00 10.00
SCC15 Mark McGwire 2.50 6.00
SCC16 Erubiel Durazo .60 1.50
SCC17 Nick Johnson .60 1.50
SCC18 Pat Burrell .60 1.50
SCC19 Alfonso Soriano 1.50 4.00
SCC20 Adam Piatt .60 1.50

2000 Stadium Club Co-Signers

Inserted in hobby packs only at different rates, these 15 cards feature a pair of players who have signed these cards. The odds are broken down like this: Group A was issued one every 10,184 hobby packs and one every 4060 HTC packs. Group B was issued one every 5092 hobby packs and one every 2032 HTC packs. Group C was issued one every 508 hobby packs and one every 203 HTC packs.

A ODDS 1:10,184 HOB, 1:4060 HTC
B ODDS 1:5,092 HOB, 1:2,030 HTC
C ODDS 1:508 HOB, 1:203 HTC
CO1 A.Rodriguez/D.Jeter A 300.00 600.00
CO2 D.Jeter/O.Vizquel B 150.00 300.00
CO3 A.Rodriguez/R.Ordonez B 90.00 150.00
CO4 D.Jeter/R.Ordonez B 100.00 175.00
CO5 O.Vizquel/A.Rodriguez B 90.00 150.00
CO6 R.Ordonez/O.Vizquel C 15.00 40.00
CO7 W.Boggs/R.Ventura C 15.00 40.00
CO8 R.Johnson/M.Mussina C 30.00 80.00
CO9 P.Burrell/M.Ordonez C 10.00 25.00
CO10 C.Hermansen/P.Burrell C 6.00 15.00
CO11 M.Ordonez/C.Herm C 10.00 25.00
CO12 J.Hamilton/C.Myers C 12.00 30.00
CO13 B.Garbe/J.Hamilton C 40.00 80.00
CO14 C.Myers/B.Garbe C 6.00 15.00
CO15 T.Martinez/F.McGriff C 20.00 50.00

2000 Stadium Club Lone Star Signatures

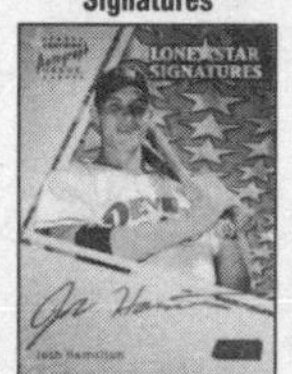

Issued at different rates throughout the various packaging, these 16 cards feature signed cards of various stars. The cards were inserted at these rates: Group 1 was inserted at a rate of one in 1981 retail packs, one in 1979 hobby packs and one in 792 HTC packs. Group 2 was inserted at a rate of one in 2421 retail packs, one in 2374 hobby packs and one in 946 HTC packs. Group 3 was issued at the same rate as Group 1 (1:1979 hobby, 1:1981 retail; 1:792 HTC packs). Group 4 were issued at a rate of one in 424 hobby packs, one in 423 retail packs and one in 169 HTC packs. These cards are authenticated with a "Topps Certified Autograph" stamp as well as a "Topps3M" sticker.

G1 ODDS 1:1,979 HOB, 1:1,981 RET, 1:792 HTC
G2 ODDS 1:2,374 HOB,1:2,421 RET,1:946 HTC
G3 ODDS 1:1,979 HOB, 1:1,981 RET, 1:792 HTC
G4 ODDS 1:424 HOB, 1:423 RET, 1:169 HTC
LS1 Derek Jeter G1 150.00 400.00
LS2 Alex Rodriguez G1 40.00 80.00
LS3 Wade Boggs G1 20.00 50.00
LS4 Robin Ventura G1 10.00 25.00
LS5 Randy Johnson G2 40.00 80.00
LS6 Mike Mussina G2 10.00 25.00
LS7 Tino Martinez G3 20.00 50.00
LS8 Fred McGriff G3 6.00 15.00
LS9 Omar Vizquel G4 12.50 30.00
LS10 Rey Ordonez G4 4.00 10.00
LS11 Pat Burrell G4 6.00 15.00
LS12 Chad Hermansen G4 4.00 10.00
LS13 Magglio Ordonez G4 6.00 15.00
LS14 Josh Hamilton 30.00 60.00
LS15 Corey Myers G4 4.00 10.00
LS16 B.J. Garbe G4 4.00 10.00

2000 Stadium Club Onyx Extreme

Inserted at a rate of one in 12 hobby, one in 15 retail and one in six HTC packs, these 10 cards feature 10 cards printed using black styrene technology with silver foil stamping.

COMPLETE SET (10) 8.00 20.00
STATED ODDS 1:12 HOB, 1:15 RET, 1:6 HTC
*DIE CUTS: 1.25X TO 3X BASIC ONYX
DIE CUT ODDS 1:60 HOB, 1:75 RET, 1:30 HTC
OE1 Ken Griffey Jr. 2.00 5.00
OE2 Derek Jeter 2.50 6.00
OE3 Vladimir Guerrero .60 1.50
OE4 Nomar Garciaparra .60 1.50
OE5 Barry Bonds 1.50 4.00
OE6 Alex Rodriguez 1.25 3.00
OE7 Sammy Sosa 1.00 2.50
OE8 Ivan Rodriguez .60 1.50
OE9 Larry Walker .60 1.50
OE10 Andruw Jones .40 1.00

2000 Stadium Club Scenes

Inserted as a box-topper in hobby and HTC boxes, these eight cards which measure 2 1/2" by 4 11/16" feature superstar players in a special "widevision" format.

COMPLETE SET (8) 10.00 25.00
ONE PER HOBBY/HTC BOX CHIP-TOPPER
SCS1 Mark McGwire 1.50 4.00
SCS2 Alex Rodriguez 1.25 3.00
SCS3 Cal Ripken 3.00 8.00
SCS4 Sammy Sosa 1.00 2.50
SCS5 Derek Jeter 2.50 6.00
SCS6 Ken Griffey Jr. 2.00 5.00
SCS7 Nomar Garciaparra .60 1.50
SCS8 Chipper Jones 1.00 2.50

2000 Stadium Club Souvenir

Inserted exclusively into hobby packs at a rate of one in 339 hobby packs and one in 136 HTC packs, these cards feature die-cut technology which incorporates an actual piece of a game-used uniform.

STATED ODDS 1:339 HOB, 1:136 HTC
S1 Wade Boggs 10.00 25.00
S2 Edgardo Alfonzo 4.00 10.00
S3 Robin Ventura 6.00 15.00

2000 Stadium Club 3 X 3 Luminous

Inserted at a rate of one in 18 hobby, one in 24 retail and one in nine HTC packs, these 30 cards can be fused together to form one very oversized card. The luminous variety is the most common of the three forms used (Luminous, Luminescent and Illuminator).

COMPLETE SET (30) 25.00 50.00
STATED ODDS 1:18 HOB, 1:24 RET, 1:9 HTC
*ILLUMINATOR: 1.5X TO 4X LUMINOUS
ILLUM ODDS 1:144 HOB, 1:192 RET, 1:72 HTC
*L'SCENT: .75X TO 2X LUMINOUS
L'SCENT ODDS 1:72 HOB, 1:96 RET, 1:36 HTC
1A Randy Johnson 1.50 4.00
1B Pedro Martinez 1.00 2.50
1C Greg Maddux 2.00 5.00
2A Mike Piazza 1.50 4.00
2B Ivan Rodriguez 1.00 2.50
2C Mike Lieberthal .60 1.50
3A Mark McGwire 2.50 6.00
3B Jeff Bagwell 1.00 2.50
3C Sean Casey .60 1.50
4A Craig Biggio 1.00 2.50
4B Roberto Alomar 1.00 2.50
4C Jay Bell .60 1.50
5A Chipper Jones 1.50 4.00
5B Matt Williams .60 1.50
5C Robin Ventura .60 1.50
6A Alex Rodriguez 2.00 5.00
6B Derek Jeter 4.00 10.00
6C Nomar Garciaparra 1.00 2.50
7A Barry Bonds 2.50 6.00
7B Luis Gonzalez .60 1.50
7C Dante Bichette .60 1.50
8A Ken Griffey Jr. 3.00 8.00
8B Bernie Williams 1.00 2.50
8C Andruw Jones .60 1.50
9A Manny Ramirez 1.50 4.00
9B Sammy Sosa 1.50 4.00
9C Juan Gonzalez .60 1.50
10A Jose Canseco 1.00 2.50
10B Frank Thomas 1.50 4.00
10C Rafael Palmeiro 1.00 2.50

2001 Stadium Club Pre-Production

This three-card set was distributed to dealers and hobby media in a sealed cello wrap bag several weeks prior to the release of 2001 Stadium Club. The cards can be distinguished from their basic issue counterparts by their "PP" prefixed numbering.

COMPLETE SET (3) 1.20 3.00
PP1 Andruw Jones .60 1.50
PP2 Jorge Posada .30 .75
PP3 Jeff Bagwell .60 1.50

2001 Stadium Club

The 2001 Stadium Club product was released in late December, 2000 and features a 200-card base set. The set is broken into tiers as follows: 175 Base Veterans and 25 Prospects (1:6). Each pack contained seven cards and carried a suggested retail price of $1.99.

COMPLETE SET (200) 50.00 120.00
COMP.SET w/o SP's (175) 10.00 25.00
SP STATED ODDS 1:6
SP's: 153/156-157/161-162/166-170/186-200
1 Nomar Garciaparra .20 .50
2 Chipper Jones .30 .75
3 Jeff Bagwell .20 .50
4 Chad Kreuter .12 .30
5 Randy Johnson .30 .75
6 Mike Hampton .12 .30
7 Barry Larkin .20 .50
8 Bernie Williams .20 .50
9 Chris Singleton .12 .30
10 Larry Walker .20 .50
11 Brad Ausmus .12 .30
12 Ron Coomer .12 .30
13 Edgardo Alfonzo .12 .30
14 Delino DeShields .12 .30
15 Tony Gwynn .30 .75
16 Andruw Jones .20 .50
17 Raul Mondesi .12 .30
18 Troy Glaus .12 .30
19 Ben Grieve .12 .30
20 Sammy Sosa .20 .50
21 Fernando Vina .12 .30
22 Jeromy Burnitz .12 .30
23 Jay Bell .12 .30
24 Pete Harnisch .12 .30
25 Barry Bonds .50 1.25
26 Eric Karros .12 .30
27 Alex Gonzalez .12 .30
28 Mike Lieberthal .12 .30
29 Juan Encarnacion .12 .30
30 Derek Jeter .75 2.00
31 Luis Sojo .12 .30
32 Eric Milton .12 .30
33 Aaron Boone .12 .30
34 Roberto Alomar .20 .50
35 John Olerud .12 .30
36 Orlando Cabrera .12 .30
37 Shawn Green .12 .30
38 Roger Cedeno .12 .30
39 Garret Anderson .12 .30
40 Jim Thome .20 .50
41 Gabe Kapler .12 .30
42 Mo Vaughn .12 .30
43 Sean Casey .12 .30
44 Preston Wilson .12 .30
45 Javy Lopez .12 .30
46 Ryan Klesko .12 .30
47 Ray Durham .12 .30
48 Dean Palmer .12 .30
49 Jorge Posada .20 .50
50 Alex Rodriguez .40 1.00
51 Tom Glavine .20 .50
52 Ray Lankford .12 .30
53 Jose Canseco .20 .50
54 Tim Salmon .20 .50
55 Cal Ripken 1.00 2.50
56 Bob Abreu .12 .30
57 Robin Ventura .12 .30
58 Damion Easley .12 .30
59 Paul O'Neill .20 .50
60 Ivan Rodriguez .20 .50
61 Carl Everett .12 .30
62 Doug Glanville .12 .30
63 Jeff Kent .12 .30
64 Jay Buhner .12 .30
65 Cliff Floyd .12 .30
66 Rick Ankiel .12 .30
67 Mark Grace .20 .50
68 Brian Jordan .12 .30
69 Craig Biggio .20 .50
70 Carlos Delgado .12 .30
71 Brad Radke .12 .30
72 Greg Maddux .50 1.25
73 Al Leiter .12 .30
74 Pokey Reese .12 .30
75 Todd Helton .20 .50
76 Mariano Rivera .30 .75
77 Shane Spencer .12 .30
78 Jason Kendall .12 .30
79 Chuck Knoblauch .12 .30
80 Scott Rolen .20 .50
81 Jose Offerman .12 .30
82 J.T. Snow .12 .30
83 Pat Meares .12 .30
84 Quilvio Veras .12 .30
85 Edgar Renteria .12 .30
86 Luis Matos .12 .30
87 Adrian Beltre .30 .75
88 Luis Gonzalez .12 .30
89 Rickey Henderson .30 .75
90 Brian Giles .12 .30
91 Carlos Febles .12 .30
92 Tino Martinez .20 .50
93 Magglio Ordonez .12 .30
94 Rafael Furcal .12 .30
95 Mike Mussina .20 .50
96 Gary Sheffield .12 .30
97 Kenny Lofton .12 .30
98 Fred McGriff .20 .50
99 Ken Caminiti .12 .30
100 Mark McGwire .50 1.25
101 Tom Goodwin .12 .30
102 Mark Grudzielanek .12 .30
103 Derek Bell .12 .30
104 Mike Lowell .12 .30
105 Jeff Cirillo .12 .30
106 Orlando Hernandez .12 .30
107 Jose Valentin .12 .30
108 Warren Morris .12 .30
109 Mike Williams .12 .30
110 Greg Zaun .12 .30
111 Jose Vidro .12 .30
112 Omar Vizquel .20 .50
113 Vinny Castilla .12 .30
114 Gregg Jefferies .12 .30
115 Kevin Brown .12 .30
116 Shannon Stewart .12 .30
117 Marquis Grissom .12 .30
118 Manny Ramirez .30 .75
119 Albert Belle .12 .30
120 Bret Boone .12 .30
121 Johnny Damon .20 .50
122 Juan Gonzalez .12 .30
123 David Justice .12 .30
124 Jeffrey Hammonds .12 .30
125 Ken Griffey Jr. .60 1.50
126 Mike Sweeney .12 .30
127 Tony Clark .12 .30
128 Todd Zeile .12 .30
129 Mark Johnson .12 .30
130 Matt Williams .12 .30
131 Geoff Jenkins .12 .30
132 Jason Giambi .12 .30
133 Steve Finley .12 .30
134 Derrek Lee .12 .30
135 Royce Clayton .12 .30
136 Joe Randa .12 .30
137 Rafael Palmeiro .20 .50
138 Kevin Young .12 .30
139 Mike Redmond .12 .30
140 Vladimir Guerrero .30 .75
141 Greg Vaughn .12 .30
142 Jermaine Dye .12 .30
143 Roger Clemens .50 1.25
144 Denny Hocking .12 .30
145 Frank Thomas .30 .75
146 Carlos Beltran .12 .30
147 Eric Young .12 .30
148 Pat Burrell .12 .30
149 Pedro Martinez .20 .50
150 Mike Piazza .30 .75
151 Adrian Gonzalez 1.25 3.00
152 Adam Johnson .20 .50
153 Luis Montanez SP RC 1.25 3.00
154 Mike Stodolka .20 .50
155 Phil Dumatrait .20 .50
156 Sean Burnett SP 1.25 3.00
157 Dominic Rich SP RC 1.25 3.00
158 Adam Wainwright .30 .75
159 Scott Thorman .20 .50
160 Scott Heard SP 1.25 3.00
161 Chad Petty SP RC 1.25 3.00
162 Matt Wheatland .20 .50
163 Bryan Digby .20 .50
164 Rocco Baldelli .20 .50
165 Grady Sizemore .75 2.00
166 Brian Sellier SP RC 1.25 3.00
167 Rick Brosseau SP RC 1.25 3.00
168 Shawn Fagan SP RC 1.25 3.00
169 Sean Smith SP 1.25 3.00
170 Chris Bass SP RC 1.25 3.00
171 Corey Patterson .20 .50
172 Sean Burroughs .20 .50
173 Ben Petrick .20 .50
174 Mike Glendenning .20 .50
175 Barry Zito .30 .75
176 Milton Bradley .20 .50
177 Bobby Bradley .20 .50
178 Jason Hart .20 .50
179 Ryan Anderson .20 .50
180 Ben Sheets .20 .50
181 Adam Everett .20 .50
182 Alfonso Soriano .30 .75
183 Josh Hamilton .30 .75
184 Eric Munson .20 .50
185 Chin-Feng Chen .20 .50
186 Tim Christman SP RC 1.25 3.00
187 J.R. House SP 1.25 3.00
188 Brandon Parker SP RC 1.25 3.00
189 Sean Fesh SP RC 1.25 3.00
190 Joel Pineiro SP 1.25 3.00
191 Oscar Ramirez SP RC 1.25 3.00
192 Alex Santos SP RC 1.25 3.00
193 Eddy Reyes SP RC 1.25 3.00
194 Mike Jacobs SP RC 3.00 8.00
195 Erick Almonte SP RC 1.25 3.00
196 Brandon Claussen SP RC 1.25 3.00
197 Kris Keller SP RC 1.25 3.00
198 Wilson Betemit SP RC 2.00 5.00
199 Andy Phillips SP RC 3.00 8.00
200 Adam Pettyjohn SP RC 1.25 3.00

2001 Stadium Club Beam Team

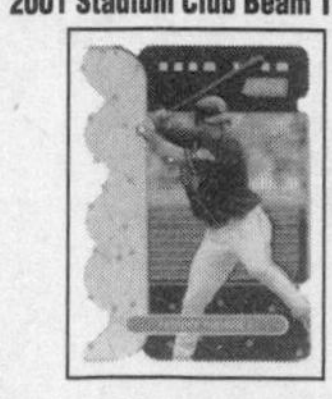

Randomly inserted into packs at one in 175 Hobby, and one in 68 HTA, this 30-card die-cut insert set features players who possess unparalleled style to accompany their world-class talent. Please note that these cards are individually serial numbered to 500, and that the card backs carry a "BT" prefix.

STATED ODDS 1:175 HOB, 1:68 HTA
STATED PRINT RUN 500 SERIAL #'d SETS
BT1 Sammy Sosa 5.00 12.00
BT2 Mark McGwire 12.50 30.00
BT3 Vladimir Guerrero 5.00 12.00
BT4 Chipper Jones 5.00 12.00
BT5 Manny Ramirez 3.00 8.00
BT6 Derek Jeter 15.00 40.00
BT7 Alex Rodriguez 6.00 15.00
BT8 Cal Ripken 15.00 40.00
BT9 Ken Griffey Jr. 10.00 25.00
BT10 Greg Maddux 8.00 20.00
BT11 Barry Bonds 12.50 30.00
BT12 Pedro Martinez 3.00 8.00
BT13 Nomar Garciaparra 8.00 20.00
BT14 Randy Johnson 5.00 12.00
BT15 Frank Thomas 5.00 12.00
BT16 Ivan Rodriguez 3.00 8.00
BT17 Jeff Bagwell 3.00 8.00
BT18 Mike Piazza 8.00 20.00
BT19 Todd Helton 3.00 8.00
BT20 Shawn Green 2.00 5.00
BT21 Juan Gonzalez 2.00 5.00
BT22 Larry Walker 2.00 5.00
BT23 Tony Gwynn 8.00 20.00
BT24 Pat Burrell 2.00 5.00
BT25 Rafael Furcal 2.00 5.00
BT26 Corey Patterson 2.00 5.00
BT27 Chin-Feng Chen 2.00 5.00
BT28 Sean Burroughs 2.00 5.00
BT29 Ryan Anderson 2.00 5.00
BT30 Josh Hamilton 4.00 10.00

2001 Stadium Club Capture the Action

Randomly inserted into packs at one in eight HOB/RET and one in two HTA, this 15-card insert features transformer technology that open up to enlarged action photos of ballplayers at the top of their game. Card backs carry a "CA" prefix.

COMPLETE SET (15) 8.00 20.00
STATED ODDS 1:8 HOB/RET, 1:2 HTA
*GAME VIEW: 10X TO 25X BASIC CAPTURE
GAME VIEW ODDS 1:577 HOBBY, 1:224 HTA
GAME VIEW PRINT RUN 100 SERIAL #'d SETS
CA1 Cal Ripken 1.50 4.00
CA2 Alex Rodriguez .60 1.50
CA3 Mike Piazza .75 2.00
CA4 Mark McGwire 1.25 3.00
CA5 Greg Maddux .75 2.00
CA6 Derek Jeter 1.25 3.00
CA7 Chipper Jones .50 1.25
CA8 Pedro Martinez .40 1.00
CA9 Ken Griffey Jr. 1.00 2.50
CA10 Nomar Garciaparra .75 2.00
CA11 Randy Johnson .50 1.25
CA12 Sammy Sosa .50 1.25
CA13 Vladimir Guerrero .50 1.25
CA14 Barry Bonds 1.25 3.00
CA15 Ivan Rodriguez .40 1.00

2001 Stadium Club Co-Signers

Randomly inserted into packs at one in 962 Hobby and one in 374 HTA packs, this nine-card insert features authenticated autographs of two players on the same card. Please note that the Chipper Jones/Troy Glaus and the Corey Patterson/Nick Johnson cards packed out as exchange cards, and must be redeemed by 11/30/01.

STATED ODDS 1:962 HOB, 1:374 HTA
CO1 N.Garciaparra D.Jeter 250.00 400.00
CO2 R.Alomar/E.Alfonzo 20.00 50.00
CO3 R.Ankiel/K.Millwood 15.00 40.00
CO4 C.Jones/T.Glaus 40.00 80.00
CO5 M.Ordonez/B.Abreu 15.00 40.00
CO6 A.Piatt/S.Burroughs 10.00 25.00
CO7 C.Patterson/N.Johnson 15.00 40.00
CO8 A.Gonzalez/R.Baldelli 20.00 50.00
CO9 A.Johnson/M.Stodolka 10.00 25.00

2001 Stadium Club Diamond Pearls

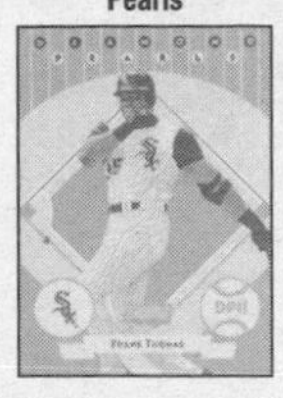

Randomly inserted into packs at one in eight HOB/RET packs, and one in 3 HTA packs; this 20-card insert features players that are the most sought after treasures in the game today. Card backs carry a "DP" prefix.

COMPLETE SET (20) 12.50 30.00
STATED ODDS 1:8 HOB/RET, 1:3 HTA
DP1 Ken Griffey Jr. 1.50 4.00
DP2 Alex Rodriguez 1.00 2.50
DP3 Derek Jeter 2.00 5.00
DP4 Chipper Jones .75 2.00
DP5 Nomar Garciaparra 1.25 3.00
DP6 Vladimir Guerrero .75 2.00
DP7 Jeff Bagwell .60 1.50
DP8 Cal Ripken 2.50 6.00
DP9 Sammy Sosa .75 2.00
DP10 Mark McGwire 2.00 5.00
DP11 Frank Thomas .75 2.00
DP12 Pedro Martinez .60 1.50
DP13 Manny Ramirez .60 1.50
DP14 Randy Johnson .75 2.00
DP15 Barry Bonds 2.00 5.00
DP16 Ivan Rodriguez .60 1.50
DP17 Greg Maddux 1.25 3.00
DP18 Mike Piazza 1.25 3.00
DP19 Todd Helton .60 1.50
DP20 Shawn Green .60 1.50

2001 Stadium Club King of the Hill Dirt Relic

Randomly inserted into packs at one in 20 HTA, this five-card insert features game-used dirt cards from the pitchers mound of today's top pitchers. The Topps Company announced that the ten exchange subjects from Stadium Club Play at the Plate, King of the Hill, and Souvenirs contain the wrong card back stating that they were autographed. None of these cards are actually autographed. Also note that these cards were inserted into packs with a white "waxpaper" covering to protect the cards. Card backs carry a "KH" prefix. Please note that Greg Maddux and Rick Ankiel both packed out as exchange cards and must be returned to Topps by 11/30/01.

STATED ODDS 1:20 HTA
KH1 Pedro Martinez 4.00 10.00
KH2 Randy Johnson 4.00 10.00
KH3 Greg Maddux ERR 4.00 10.00
KH4 Rick Ankiel ERR 3.00 8.00
KH5 Kevin Brown 3.00 8.00

2001 Stadium Club Lone Star Signatures

Randomly inserted into packs, this 18-card inserrt features authentic autographs from some of the Major Leagues most prolific players. Please note that this insert was broken into four tiers as follows: Group A (1:937 HOB/RET, 1:364 HTA), Group B (1:1010 HOB/RET, 1:392 HTA), Group C (1:1541 HOB/RET, 1:600 HTA), and Group D (1:354 HOB/RET, 1:138 HTA). The overall odds for pulling an autograph was one in 181 HOB/RET and one in 70 HTA.

GROUP A ODDS 1:937 H/R 1:364 HTA
GROUP B ODDS 1:1010 H/R 1:392 HTA
GROUP C ODDS 1:1541 H/R 1:600 HTA
GROUP D ODDS 1:354 H/R 1:138 HTA
OVERALL ODDS 1:181 H/R, 1:70 HTA
LS1 Nomar Garciaparra A 20.00 50.00
LS2 Derek Jeter A 100.00 250.00
LS3 Edgardo Alfonzo A 10.00 25.00
LS4 Roberto Alomar A 10.00 25.00
LS5 Magglio Ordonez A 10.00 25.00
LS6 Bobby Abreu A 6.00 15.00
LS7 Chipper Jones A 30.00 60.00
LS8 Troy Glaus A 15.00 40.00
LS9 Nick Johnson B 6.00 15.00
LS10 Adam Piatt B 6.00 15.00
LS11 Sean Burroughs B 4.00 10.00
LS12 Corey Patterson B 4.00 10.00
LS13 Rick Ankiel C 10.00 25.00
LS14 Kevin Millwood C 6.00 15.00
LS15 Adrian Gonzalez D 8.00 20.00
LS16 Adam Johnson D 4.00 10.00
LS17 Rocco Baldelli D 6.00 15.00
LS18 Mike Stodolka D 4.00 10.00

2001 Stadium Club Play at the Plate Dirt Relic

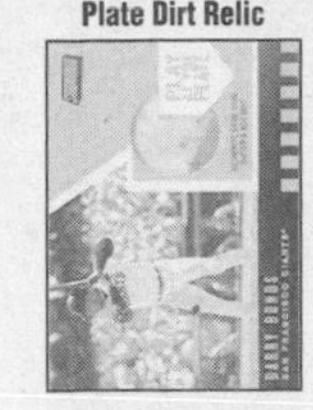

Randomly inserted into packs at one in 10 HTA, this nine-card insert features game-used dirt from the batter's box in which these top players played in. The Topps Company announced that the ten exchange subjects from Stadium Club Play at the Plate, King of the Hill, and Souvenirs contain the wrong card back stating that they were autographed. None of these cards are actually autographed. Please note that both Chipper Jones and Jeff Bagwell are number PP6. Also note that these cards were inserted into packs with a white "waxpaper" covering to protect the cards. The exchange deadline for these cards was 11/30/01.

STATED ODDS 1:10 HTA
CARD NUMBER PP9 DOES NOT EXIST
PP1 Mark McGwire ERR 15.00 40.00
PP2 Sammy Sosa ERR 2.50 6.00
PP3 Vladimir Guerrero 4.00 10.00
PP4 Ken Griffey Jr. ERR 8.00 20.00
PP5 Mike Piazza 4.00 10.00
PP6 Jeff Bagwell ERR 2.50 6.00
PP6 Chipper Jones ERR 4.00 10.00
PP7 Barry Bonds 6.00 15.00
PP8 Alex Rodriguez 5.00 12.00
PP10 N.Garciaparra ERR 2.50 6.00

2001 Stadium Club Prospect Performance

Randomly inserted into packs at one in 262 HOB/RET and one in 102 HTA, this 20-card insert features game-used jersey cards from some of the hottest young players in the Major Leagues. Card backs carry a "PRP" prefix.

STATED ODDS 1:262 HOB/RET, 1:102 HTA
PRP1 Chin-Feng Chen 40.00 80.00
PRP2 Bobby Bradley 3.00 8.00
PRP3 Tomokazu Ohka 4.00 10.00
PRP4 Kurt Ainsworth 3.00 8.00
PRP5 Craig Anderson 3.00 8.00
PRP6 Josh Hamilton 6.00 15.00
PRP7 Felipe Lopez 4.00 10.00
PRP8 Ryan Anderson 3.00 8.00
PRP9 Alex Escobar 3.00 8.00
PRP10 Ben Sheets 6.00 15.00
PRP11 Ntema Ndungidi 3.00 8.00
PRP12 Eric Munson 3.00 8.00
PRP13 Aaron Myette 3.00 8.00
PRP14 Jack Cust 3.00 8.00
PRP15 Julio Zuleta 3.00 8.00
PRP16 Corey Patterson 3.00 8.00
PRP17 Carlos Pena 3.00 8.00
PRP18 Marcus Giles 4.00 10.00
PRP19 Travis Wilson 3.00 8.00
PRP20 Barry Zito 6.00 15.00

2001 Stadium Club Souvenirs

Randomly inserted into HTA packs, this eight-card insert features game-used bat cards and game-used jersey cards of modern superstars. Card backs carry a "SCS" prefix. Please note that the Topps Company announced that the ten exchange subjects from Stadium Club Play at the Plate, King of the Hill, and Souvenirs contain the wrong card back stating that they were autographed. None of these cards are actually autographed. Also note that cards of Scolt Rolen, Matt Lawton, Jose Vidro, and Pat Burrell all packed out as exchange cards. These cards needed to have been returned to Topps by 11/30/01.

GROUP A BAT ODDS 1:849 H/R, 1:330 HTA
GROUP B BAT ODDS 1:2164 H/R, 1:847 HTA
JERSEY ODDS 1:216 H/R, 1:84 HTA
OVERALL ODDS 1:160 HOB, 1:62 HTA
SCS1 S.Rolen Bat A ERR 6.00 15.00
SCS2 Larry Walker Bat B 6.00 15.00
SCS3 Rafael Furcal Bat A 6.00 15.00
SCS4 Darin Erstad Bat A 6.00 15.00
SCS5 Mike Sweeney Jsy 4.00 10.00
SCS6 Matt Lawton Jsy ERR 4.00 10.00
SCS7 Jose Vidro Jsy ERR 4.00 10.00
SCS8 Pat Burrell Jsy ERR 4.00 10.00

2001 Stadium Club Super Teams

Randomly inserted into packs at 1:874 Hobby/Retail and 1:339 HTA, this 30-card insert featured exchange cards for special prizes. If your team won, you were entered into a drawing to win season tickets, signed 8 x 10 photos, or a Super Teams card set paralleling the basic Stadium Club cards. Card backs carry a 'ST" prefix. Please note the deadline to have exchanged these cards was December 1, 2001.

2002 Stadium Club

This 125 card set was issued in late 2001. The set was issued in either six card regular packs or 15 card HTA packs. Cards numbered 101-125 were short printed and are serial numbered to 2999.

COMP.SET w/o SP's (100) 12.50 30.00
COMMON CARD (1-100) .10 .30
COMMON CARD (101-125) 10.00 25.00
101-125 PRINT RUN 2999 SERIAL #'d SETS
101-115 ODDS 1:42 HOB, 1:50 RET, 1:7 HTA
116-125 ODDS 1:60 HOB, 1:74 RET, 1:11 HTA
BONDS AU BALL ODDS 1:147 HTA
BONDS AU BALL PRINT RUN 500
BONDS AU BALL EXCH.DEADLINE 11/30/03
1 Pedro Martinez .20 .50
2 Derek Jeter .75 2.00
3 Chipper Jones .30 .75
4 Roberto Alomar .20 .50
5 Albert Pujols 5.00 12.00
6 Bret Boone .10 .30
7 Alex Rodriguez .40 1.00
8 Jose Cruz Jr. .10 .30
9 Mike Hampton .10 .30
10 Vladimir Guerrero .30 .75
11 Jim Edmonds .10 .30
12 Luis Gonzalez .10 .30
13 Jeff Kent .10 .30
14 Mike Piazza .50 1.25
15 Ben Sheets .10 .30
16 Tsuyoshi Shinjo .10 .30
17 Pat Burrell - Rolen Photo .10 .30
18 Jermaine Dye .10 .30
19 Rafael Furcal .10 .30
20 Randy Johnson .30 .75
21 Carlos Delgado .10 .30
22 Roger Clemens .60 1.50
23 Eric Chavez .10 .30
24 Nomar Garciaparra .50 1.25
25 Ivan Rodriguez .20 .50
26 Juan Gonzalez .10 .30
27 Reggie Sanders .10 .30
28 Jeff Bagwell .20 .50
29 Kazuhiro Sasaki .10 .30
30 Larry Walker .10 .30
31 Ben Grieve .10 .30
32 David Justice .10 .30
33 David Wells .10 .30
34 Kevin Brown .10 .30
35 Miguel Tejada .10 .30
36 Jorge Posada .20 .50
37 Javy Lopez .10 .30
38 Cliff Floyd .10 .30
39 Carlos Lee .10 .30
40 Manny Ramirez .20 .50
41 Jim Thome .20 .50
42 Pokey Reese .10 .30
43 Scott Rolen .20 .50
44 Richie Sexson .10 .30
45 Dean Palmer .10 .30
46 Rafael Palmeiro .20 .50
47 Alfonso Soriano .10 .30
48 Craig Biggio .20 .50
49 Troy Glaus .10 .30
50 Andruw Jones .20 .50
51 Ichiro Suzuki .60 1.50
52 Kenny Lofton .10 .30
53 Hideo Nomo .30 .75
54 Magglio Ordonez .10 .30
55 Brad Penny .10 .30
56 Omar Vizquel .20 .50
57 Mike Sweeney .10 .30
58 Gary Sheffield .10 .30
59 Ken Griffey Jr. .60 1.50
60 Curt Schilling .10 .30
61 Bobby Higginson .10 .30
62 Terrence Long .10 .30
63 Moises Alou .10 .30
64 Sandy Alomar Jr. .10 .30
65 Cristian Guzman .10 .30
66 Sammy Sosa .30 .75
67 Jose Vidro .10 .30
68 Edgar Martinez .20 .50
69 Jason Giambi .10 .30
70 Mark McGwire .75 2.00
71 Barry Bonds .75 2.00
72 Greg Vaughn .10 .30
73 Phil Nevin .10 .30
74 Jason Kendall .10 .30
75 Greg Maddux .50 1.25
76 Jeromy Burnitz .10 .30
77 Mike Mussina .20 .50
78 Johnny Damon .20 .50
79 Shawn Green .10 .30
80 Jimmy Rollins .10 .30
81 Edgardo Alfonzo .10 .30
82 Barry Larkin .20 .50
83 Raul Mondesi .10 .30
84 Preston Wilson .10 .30
85 Mike Lieberthal .10 .30
86 J.D. Drew .10 .30
87 Ryan Klesko .10 .30
88 David Segui .10 .30
89 Derek Bell .10 .30
90 Bernie Williams .20 .50
91 Doug Mientkiewicz .10 .30
92 Rich Aurilia .10 .30
93 Ellis Burks .10 .30
94 Placido Polanco .10 .30
95 Darin Erstad .10 .30
96 Brian Giles .10 .30
97 Geoff Jenkins .10 .30
98 Kerry Wood .10 .30
99 Mariano Rivera .30 .75
100 Todd Helton .20 .50
101 Adam Dunn FS 10.00 25.00
102 Grant Balfour FS 10.00 25.00
103 Jae Seo FS 10.00 25.00
104 Hank Blalock FS 10.00 25.00
105 Chris George FS 10.00 25.00
106 Jack Cust FS 10.00 25.00
107 Juan Cruz FS 10.00 25.00
108 Adrian Gonzalez FS 10.00 25.00
109 Nick Johnson FS 10.00 25.00
110 Jeff DaVanon FS 10.00 25.00
111 Juan Diaz FS 10.00 25.00
112 Brandon Duckworth FS 10.00 25.00
113 Jason Lane FS 10.00 25.00
114 Seung Song FS 10.00 25.00
115 Morgan Ensberg FS 10.00 25.00
116 Marlyn Tisdale FY RC 10.00 25.00
117 Jason Botts FY RC 6.00 15.00
118 Henry Pichardo FY RC 10.00 25.00
119 John Rodriguez FY RC 10.00 25.00
120 Mike Peeples FY RC 10.00 25.00
121 Rob Bowen EFY RC 10.00 25.00
122 Jeremy Affeldt EFY 10.00 25.00
123 Jorge Buret EFY RC 10.00 25.00
124 Manny Ravelo EFY RC 10.00 25.00
125 Eudy Lajara EFY RC 10.00 25.00
NNO B.Bonds AU Ball 50.00 100.00

2002 Stadium Club All-Star Relics

Randomly inserted in packs, these 28 cards feature relics of players who participated in the All-Star game. Depending on which group the player belonged to there could be between 400 and 4800 of each card printed.

GROUP 1 ODDS 1:477 H, 1:548 R, 1:80 HTA
GROUP 1 PRINT RUN 400 SERIAL #'d SETS
GROUP 2 ODDS 1:795 H, 1:915 R, 1:133 HTA
GROUP 2 PRINT RUN 800 SERIAL #'d SETS
GROUP 3 ODDS 1:199 H, 1:247 R, 1:33 HTA
GROUP 3 PRINT RUN 1200 SERIAL #'d SETS
GROUP 4 ODDS 1:199 H, 1:247 R, 1:33 HTA
GROUP 4 PRINT RUN 2400 SERIAL #'d SETS
GROUP 5 ODDS 1:265 H, 1:305 R, 1:44 HTA
GROUP 5 PRINT RUN 3600 SERIAL #'d SETS
GROUP 6 ODDS 1:397 H, 1:457 R, 1:67 HTA
GROUP 6 PRINT RUN 4800 SERIAL #'d SETS
SCASAP Albert Pujols Bat G2 6.00 15.00
SCASBB Barry Bonds Uni G6 12.50 30.00
SCASBG Brian Giles Bat G2 4.00 10.00
SCASCF Cliff Floyd Bat G1 4.00 10.00
SCASCG C.Guzman Bat G1 4.00 10.00
SCASCJ Chipper Jones Jsy G3 6.00 15.00
SCASEM Edgar Martinez Jsy G3 6.00 15.00
SCASIR Ivan Rodriguez Uni G4 6.00 15.00
SCASJG Juan Gonzalez Bat G1 4.00 10.00
SCASJK Jeff Kent Bat G1 4.00 10.00
SCASJO John Olerud Jsy G3 4.00 10.00
SCASJP Jorge Posada Bat G1 6.00 15.00
SCASKS Kaz Sasaki Jsy G3 4.00 10.00
SCASLW Larry Walker Jsy G4 4.00 10.00
SCASMA Moises Alou Bat G1 4.00 10.00
SCASMC Mike Cameron Bat G1 4.00 10.00
SCASMO Magg Ordonez Bat G1 4.00 10.00
SCASMP Mike Piazza Uni G3 15.00 40.00
SCASMR M,Ramirez Uni G5 6.00 15.00
SCASMS Mike Sweeney Bat G1 4.00 10.00
SCASRA Roberto Alomar Uni G5 4.00 10.00
SCASRJ Randy Johnson Jsy G4 6.00 15.00
SCASRK Ryan Klesko Jsy G3 4.00 10.00
SCASSC Sean Casey Bat G1 4.00 10.00
SCASTG Tony Gwynn Jsy G4 8.00 20.00
SCASTH Todd Helton Jsy G3 6.00 15.00
SCASBRB Bret Boone Bat G3 4.00 10.00
SCASLG3 Luis Gonzalez Bat G2 4.00 10.00

2002 Stadium Club Chasing 500-500

Randomly inserted in packs, these three cards feature memorabilia from Barry Bonds as he chases becoming the first member of the 500 homer, 500 stolen base club.

DUAL ODDS 1:3209 HOBBY, 1:1290 HTA
JSY ODDS 1:1072 HOBBY, 1:427 HTA
MULTIPLE ODDS 1:3209 HOBBY, 1:1290 HTA
C55BB1 Barry Bonds Dual 10.00 25.00
C55BB2 Barry Bonds Jsy/600 8.00 20.00
C55BB3 Barry Bonds Mult/200 15.00 40.00

2002 Stadium Club Passport to the Majors

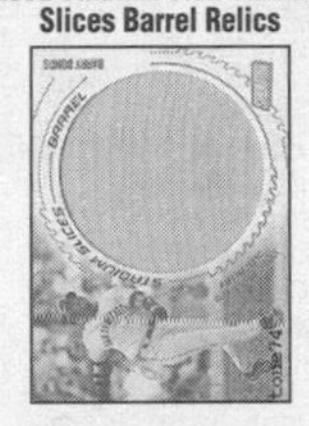

Randomly inserted in packs, these cards feature foreign players as well as a game-used relic. The jersey relics are serial numbered to 1200 while the bats are printed to differing amounts. The specific print information is notated in our checklist.

BAT ODDS 1:795 HOB, 1:915 RET, 1:133 HTA
JSY/UNI ODDS 1:84 HOB, 1:96 RET, 1:14 HTA
BAT PRINT RUNS LISTED BELOW
JSY/UNI PRINT RUN 1200 SERIAL #'d SETS
PTMAG Andres Galarraga Jsy/1200 4.00 10.00
PTMAJ Andruw Jones Jsy/1200 6.00 15.00
PTMAP Albert Pujols Bat/450 20.00 50.00
PTMAS Alf Soriano Bat/400 4.00 10.00
PTMBA Bob Abreu Bat/450 4.00 10.00
PTMBC Bartolo Colon Uni/1200 4.00 10.00
PTMCL Carlos Lee Jsy/1200 4.00 10.00
PTMCP Chan Ho Park Jsy/1200 4.00 10.00
PTMEA Edgardo Alfonzo Jsy/1200 4.00 10.00
PTMIR Ivan Rodriguez Uni/1200 6.00 15.00
PTMJG Juan Gonzalez Jsy/1200 4.00 10.00
PTMJL Javier Lopez Jsy/1200 4.00 10.00
PTMKS Kazuhiro Sasaki Jsy/1200 4.00 10.00
PTMLW Larry Walker Jsy/1200 4.00 10.00
PTMMO Magglio Ordonez Jsy/1200 4.00 10.00
PTMMR Manny Ramirez Jsy/1200 6.00 15.00
PTMMT Miguel Tejada Bat/375 4.00 10.00
PTMPM Pedro Martinez Jsy/1200 6.00 15.00
PTMRA Roberto Alomar Uni/1200 6.00 15.00
PTMRF Rafael Furcal Jsy/1200 4.00 10.00
PTMRM Raul Mondesi Jsy/1200 4.00 10.00
PTMRP Rafael Palmeiro Jsy/1200 6.00 15.00
PTMSH Shig Hasegawa Jsy/1200 4.00 10.00
PTMTS Tsuy Shinjo Bat/400 4.00 10.00
PTMWB Wilson Betemit Bat/325 4.00 10.00

2002 Stadium Club Reel Time

Inserted at a rate of one in eight hobby/retail packs and one in four HTA packs this 20 card set features players who constantly make the highlight reel.

COMPLETE SET (20) 15.00 40.00
STATED ODDS 1:8 H/R, 1:4 HTA
RT1 Luis Gonzalez .75 2.00
RT2 Derek Jeter 2.50 6.00
RT3 Ken Griffey Jr. 2.00 5.00
RT4 Alex Rodriguez 1.25 3.00
RT5 Barry Bonds 2.50 6.00
RT6 Ichiro Suzuki 2.00 5.00
RT7 Carlos Delgado .75 2.00
RT8 Manny Ramirez .75 2.00
RT9 Mike Piazza 1.50 4.00
RT10 Mark McGwire 2.50 6.00
RT11 Todd Helton .75 2.00
RT12 Vladimir Guerrero 1.00 2.50
RT13 Jim Thome .75 2.00
RT14 Rich Aurilia .75 2.00
RT15 Bret Boone .75 2.00
RT16 Roberto Alomar .75 2.00
RT17 Jason Giambi .75 2.00
RT18 Chipper Jones 1.00 2.50
RT19 Albert Pujols 2.00 5.00
RT20 Sammy Sosa 1.00 2.50

2002 Stadium Club Stadium Shots

Inserted at a rate of one in 12 hobby/retail packs and one in six HTA packs, these 10 cards feature 10 sluggers known for their long homers.

COMPLETE SET (10) 10.00 25.00
STATED ODDS 1:12 H/R, 1:6 HTA
SS1 Sammy Sosa 1.00 2.50
SS2 Manny Ramirez 1.00 2.50
SS3 Jason Giambi 1.00 2.50
SS4 Mike Piazza 1.50 4.00
SS5 Barry Bonds 2.50 6.00
SS6 Ken Griffey Jr. 2.00 5.00
SS7 Juan Gonzalez 1.00 2.50
SS8 Jeff Bagwell 1.00 2.50
SS9 Jim Thome 1.00 2.50
SS10 Mark McGwire 2.50 6.00

2002 Stadium Club Stadium Slices Barrel Relics

These five cards were inserted in packs and feature bat slices cut from the barrel of the bat. Each card is printed to a different amount and that information is notated in our checklist.

GROUP A ODDS 1:4289 HOBBY, 1:1700 HTA
GROUP B ODDS 1:6768 HOBBY, 1:2680 HTA
GROUP C ODDS 1:6465 HOBBY, 1:2581 HTA
GROUP D ODDS 1:6101 HOBBY, 1:2489 HTA
SCSSAP Albert Pujols B/95 15.00 40.00
SCSSBB Barry Bonds C/100 40.00 80.00
SCSSBW Bern Williams A/100 12.50 30.00
SCSSIR Ivan Rodriguez D/105 12.50 30.00
SCSSLG Luis Gonzalez A/75 12.50 30.00

2002 Stadium Club Stadium Slices Handle Relics

These five cards were inserted in packs and feature bat slices cut from the handle of the bat. Each card is printed to a different amount and that information is notated in our checklist.

GROUP A ODDS 1:3671 HOBBY, 1:1483 HTA
GROUP B ODDS 1:3580 HOBBY, 1:1422 HTA
GROUP C ODDS 1:3384 HOBBY, 1:1366 HTA
GROUP D ODDS 1:3209 HOBBY, 1:1290 HTA
GROUP E ODDS 1:3050 HOBBY, 1:1222 HTA
SCSSAP Albert Pujols C/190 10.00 25.00
SCSSBB Barry Bonds A/175 12.50 30.00
SCSSBW Bernie Williams E/210 8.00 20.00
SCSSIR Ivan Rodriguez B/180 8.00 20.00
SCSSLG Luis Gonzalez D/200 8.00 20.00

2002 Stadium Club Stadium Slices Trademark Relics

These five cards were inserted in packs and feature bat slices cut from the middle of the bat. Each card is printed to a different amount and that information is notated in our checklist.

GROUP A ODDS 1:6101 HOBBY, 1:2489 HTA
GROUP B ODDS 1:5853 HOBBY, 1:2323 HTA
GROUP C ODDS 1:4922 HOBBY, 1:1991 HTA
GROUP D ODDS 1:4559 HOBBY, 1:1834 HTA
GROUP E ODDS 1:3800 HOBBY, 1:1515 HTA
PRINT RUNS B/WN 105-170 COPIES PER
PRINT RUN INFO PROVIDED BY TOPPS
SCSSAP Albert Pujols C/130 12.00 30.00
SCSSBB Barry Bonds A/105 20.00 50.00
SCSSBW Bernie Williams B/110 10.00 25.00
SCSSIR Ivan Rodriguez E/170 10.00 25.00
SCSSLG Luis Gonzalez D/140 10.00 25.00

2002 Stadium Club World Champion Relics

Inserted at different odds depending on what type of relic, these 69 cards feature game-used relics from World Series ring holders. The Rickey Henderson card was short printed and we have notated this information in our checklist.

BAT ODDS 1:94 H, 1:108 R, 1:16 HTA
JERSEY ODDS 1:106 H, 1:122 R, 1:18 HTA
PANTS ODDS 1:795 H, 1:1022 R, 1:133 HTA
SPIKES 1:38,400 H, 1:51,696 R, 1:6335 HTA
WCAB Al Bumbry Bat 4.00 10.00
WCAL Al Leiter Jsy 6.00 15.00
WCAT Alan Trammell Bat 6.00 15.00
WCBB Bert Blyleven Jsy 6.00 15.00
WCBD Bucky Dent Bat 6.00 15.00
WCBM Bill Madlock Bat 6.00 15.00
WCBW Bernie Williams Bat 8.00 20.00
WCBRB Bob Boone Jsy 6.00 15.00
WCCC Chris Chambliss Bat 6.00 15.00
WCCJ Chipper Jones Bat 10.00 25.00
WCCK Chuck Knoblauch Bat 6.00 15.00
WCDB Don Baylor Bat 6.00 15.00
WCDC Dave Concepcion Bat 6.00 15.00
WCDJ David Justice Bat 6.00 15.00
WCDL Dave Lopes Bat 6.00 15.00
WCDP Dave Parker Bat 6.00 15.00
WCDW Dave Winfield Bat 6.00 15.00
WCED Eric Davis Bat 6.00 15.00
WCES Ed Sprague Jsy 4.00 10.00
WCEM1 Eddie Murray Bat 10.00 25.00
WCEM2 Eddie Murray Jsy 10.00 25.00
WCFM Fred McGriff Jsy 8.00 20.00
WCFV Fernando Valenzuela Bat 6.00 15.00
WCGB George Brett Bat 12.00 30.00
WCGF George Foster Bat 6.00 15.00
WCGH George Hendrick Bat 6.00 15.00
WCGL Greg Luzinski Bat 6.00 15.00
WCGM Greg Maddux Jsy 12.50 30.00
WCGC1 Gary Carter Bat 6.00 15.00
WCGC2 Gary Carter Jsy 6.00 15.00
WCHM Hal McRae Bat 6.00 15.00
WCJB Johnny Bench Bat 10.00 25.00
WCJC Joe Carter Jsy 6.00 15.00
WCJL Javy Lopez Bat 6.00 15.00
WCJO John Olerud Jsy 6.00 15.00
WCJP Jorge Posada Bat 8.00 20.00
WCJS John Smoltz Jsy 8.00 20.00
WCJV Jose Vizcaino Bat 4.00 10.00
WCJC1 Jose Canseco Yank Bat 8.00 20.00
WCJC2 Jose Canseco A's Bat 8.00 20.00
WCKG Ken Griffey Sr. Bat 8.00 20.00
WCKH Keith Hernandez Bat 6.00 15.00
WCKP Kirby Puckett Bat 15.00 40.00
WCKG1 Kirk Gibson Bat 6.00 15.00
WCKG2 Kirk Gibson Jsy 6.00 15.00
WCLW Lou Whitaker Bat 6.00 15.00
WCLVP Lou Piniella Bat 6.00 15.00
WCMA Moises Alou Bat 6.00 15.00
WCMS Mike Scioscia Bat 6.00 15.00
WCMW Mookie Wilson Bat 6.00 15.00
WCMJS Mike Schmidt Bat 10.00 25.00
WCOH Orel Hershiser Jsy 6.00 15.00
WCOS Ozzie Smith Bat 15.00 40.00
WCPG Phil Garner Bat 6.00 15.00
WCPM Paul Molitor Bat 6.00 15.00
WCPO Paul O'Neill Pants 8.00 20.00
WCRA Roberto Alomar Pants 8.00 20.00
WCRC Ron Cey Bat 6.00 15.00
WCRJ Reggie Jackson Bat 8.00 20.00
WCSB Scott Brosius Bat 6.00 15.00
WCTG Tom Glavine Jsy 8.00 20.00
WCTM Thurman Munson Bat 30.00 60.00
WCTP Tony Perez Bat 6.00 15.00
WCTLM Tino Martinez Bat 8.00 20.00
WCWB Wade Boggs Bat 8.00 20.00
WCWH Willie Hernandez Jsy 6.00 15.00
WCWR Willie Randolph Bat 6.00 15.00
WCWS Willie Stargell Bat 8.00 20.00

2003 Stadium Club

This 125 card set was released in November, 2002. This set marked the conclusion of the 13 year run of Stadium Club product being released as a baseball brand by Topps. This set was issued in either 10 card packs or 20 card HTA packs. The 10-card packs were issued 10 cards to a pack with 24 packs to a box and 12 boxes to a case with an SRP of $3 per pack. The 20-card HTA packs were issued 10 packs to a box and eight boxes to a case with an SRP of $10 per pack. Cards numbered from 101 through 113 featured future stars while cards numbered 114 through 125 feature players in their first year on a Stadium Club card. Cards numbered 101 through 125 were issued with different photos depending on whether or not they came from hobby or retail packs. These cards have two different varieties in all the parallel sets as well. Sets are considered complete at 125 cards - with one copy of either the hobby or retail versions of cards 101-125.

COMP.MASTER SET (150) 30.00 60.00
COMPLETE SET (125) 20.00 40.00
COMMON CARD (1-100) .12 .30
COMMON CARD (101-115) .20 .50
COMMON CARD (116-125) .40 1.00
1 Rafael Furcal .12 .30
2 Randy Winn .12 .30
3 Eric Chavez .12 .30
4 Fernando Vina .12 .30
5 Pat Burrell .12 .30
6 Derek Jeter .75 2.00
7 Ivan Rodriguez .20 .50
8 Eric Hinske .12 .30
9 Roberto Alomar .20 .50
10 Tony Batista .12 .30
11 Jacque Jones .12 .30
12 Alfonso Soriano .20 .50
13 Omar Vizquel .20 .50
14 Paul Konerko .20 .50
15 Shawn Green .12 .30
16 Garret Anderson .12 .30
17 Darin Erstad .12 .30
18 Johnny Damon .20 .50
19 Juan Gonzalez .12 .30
20 Luis Gonzalez .12 .30
21 Sean Burroughs .12 .30
22 Mark Prior .20 .50
23 Javier Vazquez .12 .30
24 Shannon Stewart .12 .30
25 Jay Gibbons .12 .30
26 A.J. Pierzynski .12 .30
27 Vladimir Guerrero .20 .50
28 Austin Kearns .12 .30
29 Shea Hillenbrand .12 .30
30 Magglio Ordonez .20 .50
31 Mike Cameron .12 .30
32 Tim Salmon .12 .30
33 Brian Jordan .12 .30
34 Moises Alou .12 .30
35 Rich Aurilia .12 .30
36 Nick Johnson .12 .30
37 Junior Spivey .12 .30
38 Curt Schilling .20 .50
39 Jose Vidro .12 .30
40 Orlando Cabrera .12 .30
41 Jeff Bagwell .20 .50
42 Mo Vaughn .12 .30
43 Luis Castillo .12 .30
44 Vicente Padilla .12 .30
45 Pedro Martinez .20 .50
46 John Olerud .12 .30
47 Tom Glavine .20 .50
48 Torii Hunter .12 .30
49 J.D. Drew .12 .30
50 Alex Rodriguez .40 1.00
51 Randy Johnson .30 .75
52 Richie Sexson .12 .30
53 Jimmy Rollins .20 .50
54 Cristian Guzman .12 .30
55 Tim Hudson .20 .50
56 Mark Buehrle .20 .50
57 Paul Lo Duca .12 .30
58 Aramis Ramirez .12 .30
59 Todd Helton .20 .50
60 Lance Berkman .20 .50
61 Josh Beckett .12 .30
62 Bret Boone .12 .30
63 Miguel Tejada .20 .50
64 Nomar Garciaparra .20 .50
65 Albert Pujols .40 1.00
66 Chipper Jones .30 .75
67 Scott Rolen .20 .50
68 Kerry Wood .12 .30
69 Jorge Posada .20 .50
70 Ichiro Suzuki .40 1.00
71 Jeff Kent .12 .30
72 David Eckstein .12 .30
73 Phil Nevin .12 .30
74 Brian Giles .12 .30
75 Barry Zito .20 .50
76 Andruw Jones .12 .30
77 Jim Thome .20 .50
78 Robert Fick .12 .30
79 Rafael Palmeiro .20 .50
80 Barry Bonds .50 1.25
81 Gary Sheffield .12 .30
82 Jim Edmonds .20 .50
83 Kazuhisa Ishii .12 .30
84 Jose Hernandez .12 .30
85 Jason Giambi .12 .30
86 Mark Mulder .12 .30
87 Roger Clemens .40 1.00
88 Troy Glaus .12 .30
89 Carlos Delgado .12 .30
90 Mike Sweeney .12 .30
91 Ken Griffey Jr. .60 1.50
92 Manny Ramirez .30 .75
93 Ryan Klesko .12 .30
94 Larry Walker .20 .50
95 Adam Dunn .20 .50
96 Raul Ibanez .20 .50
97 Preston Wilson .12 .30
98 Roy Oswalt .20 .50
99 Sammy Sosa .30 .75
100 Mike Piazza .30 .75
101H Jose Reyes FS .50 1.25
101R Jose Reyes FS .50 1.25
102H Ed Rogers FS .20 .50
102R Ed Rogers FS .20 .50
103H Hank Blalock FS .20 .50
103R Hank Blalock FS .20 .50
104H Mark Teixeira FS .30 .75
104R Mark Teixeira FS .30 .75
105H Orlando Hudson FS .20 .50
105R Orlando Hudson FS .20 .50
106H Drew Henson FS .20 .50
106R Drew Henson FS .20 .50
107H Joe Mauer FS .50 1.25
107R Joe Mauer FS .50 1.25
108H Carl Crawford FS .30 .75
108R Carl Crawford FS .30 .75
109H Marlon Byrd FS .20 .50
109R Marlon Byrd FS .20 .50
110H Jason Stokes FS .20 .50
110R Jason Stokes FS .20 .50
111H Miguel Cabrera FS 2.50 6.00
111R Miguel Cabrera FS 2.50 6.00
112H Wilson Betemit FS .20 .50
112R Wilson Betemit FS .20 .50
113H Jerome Williams FS .20 .50
113R Jerome Williams FS .20 .50
114H Walter Young FYP .20 .50
114R Walter Young FYP .20 .50
115H Juan Camacho FYP RC .40 1.00
115R Juan Camacho FYP RC .40 1.00
116H Chris Duncan FYP RC 1.25 3.00
116R Chris Duncan FYP RC 1.25 3.00
117H Franklin Gutierrez FYP RC 1.00 2.50
117R Franklin Gutierrez FYP RC 1.00 2.50
118H Adam LaRoche FYP .40 1.00
118R Adam LaRoche FYP .40 1.00
119H Manuel Ramirez FYP RC .40 1.00
119R Manuel Ramirez FYP RC .40 1.00
120H Il Kim FYP RC .40 1.00
120R Il Kim FYP RC .40 1.00
121H Wayne Lydon FYP RC .40 1.00
121R Wayne Lydon FYP RC .40 1.00
122H Daryl Clark FYP RC .40 1.00
122R Daryl Clark FYP RC .40 1.00
123H Sean Pierce FYP .40 1.00
123R Sean Pierce FYP .40 1.00
124H Andy Marte FYP RC .40 1.00
124R Andy Marte FYP RC .40 1.00
125H Matthew Peterson FYP RC .40 1.00
125R Matthew Peterson FYP RC .40 1.00

2003 Stadium Club Photographer's Proof

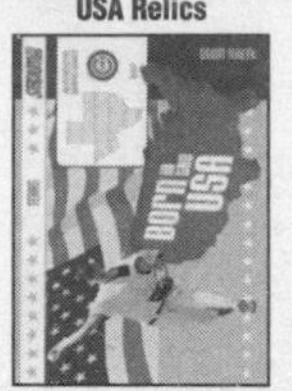

*PROOF 1-100: 4X TO 10X BASIC
*PROOF 101-115: 2.5X TO 6X BASIC
*PROOF 116-125: 1.25X TO 3X BASIC
1-100 ODDS 1:39 H, 1:23 HTA, 1:34 R
101-125 ODDS 1:61 H, 1:17 HTA, 1:92 R
STATED PRINT RUN 299 SERIAL #'d SETS

2003 Stadium Club Royal Gold

*GOLD 1-100: 1X TO 2.5X BASIC
*GOLD 101-115: 1X TO 2.5X BASIC
*GOLD 116-125: .75X TO 2X BASIC
STATED ODDS 1:1 HOB, 1:1 HTA
101-125 HOB/RET PHOTOS EQUAL VALUE

2003 Stadium Club Beam Team

Inserted into packs at a stated rate of one in 12 hobby, one in 12 retail and one in two HTA, these 20 cards feature some of the hottest talents in baseball.
STATED ODDS 1:12 HOB/RET, 1:2 HTA
BT1 Lance Berkman .60 1.50
BT2 Barry Bonds 1.50 4.00
BT3 Carlos Delgado .40 1.00
BT4 Adam Dunn .60 1.50
BT5 Nomar Garciaparra .60 1.50
BT6 Jason Giambi .40 1.00
BT7 Brian Giles .40 1.00
BT8 Shawn Green .40 1.00
BT9 Vladimir Guerrero .60 1.50
BT10 Todd Helton .60 1.50
BT11 Derek Jeter 2.50 6.00
BT12 Chipper Jones 1.00 2.50
BT13 Jeff Kent .40 1.00
BT14 Mike Piazza 1.00 2.50
BT15 Alex Rodriguez 1.25 3.00
BT16 Ivan Rodriguez .60 1.50
BT17 Sammy Sosa 1.00 2.50
BT18 Ichiro Suzuki 1.25 3.00
BT19 Miguel Tejada .60 1.50
BT20 Larry Walker .60 1.50

2003 Stadium Club Born in the USA Relics

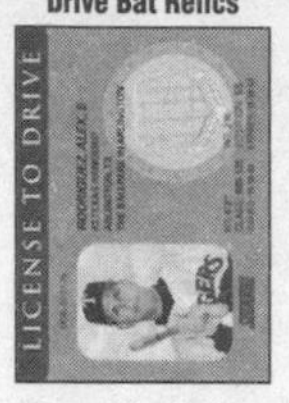

Inserted into packs at different odds depending on what type of game-used memorabilia piece was used, these 50 cards feature those memorabilia pieces cut into the shape of the player's home state.
BAT ODDS 1:76 H, 1:23 HTA, 1:89 R
JERSEY ODDS 1:52 H, 1:15 HTA, 1:61 R
UNIFORM ODDS 1:413 H, 1:126 HTA, 1:484 R
AB A.J. Burnett Jsy 4.00 10.00
AD Adam Dunn Bat 4.00 10.00
AR Alex Rodriguez Bat 10.00 25.00
BB Bret Boone Jsy 4.00 10.00
BF Brad Fullmer Bat 4.00 10.00
BL Barry Larkin Jsy 6.00 15.00
CB Craig Biggio Jsy 6.00 15.00
CF Cliff Floyd Bat 4.00 10.00
CJ Chipper Jones Jsy 6.00 15.00
CP Corey Patterson Bat 4.00 10.00
EC Eric Chavez Uni 4.00 10.00
EM Eric Milton Jsy 4.00 10.00
FT Frank Thomas Bat 6.00 15.00
GM Greg Maddux Jsy 6.00 15.00
GS Gary Sheffield Bat 4.00 10.00
JB Jeff Bagwell Jsy 6.00 15.00
JD Johnny Damon Bat 6.00 15.00
JDD J.D. Drew Bat 4.00 10.00
JE Jim Edmonds Jsy 4.00 10.00
JH Josh Hamilton 8.00 20.00
JNB Jeromy Burnitz Bat 4.00 10.00
JO John Olerud Jsy 4.00 10.00
JS John Smoltz Jsy 6.00 15.00
JT Jim Thome Jsy 6.00 15.00
KW Kerry Wood Bat 6.00 15.00
LG Luis Gonzalez Bat 4.00 10.00
MG Mark Grace Jsy 6.00 15.00
MP Mike Piazza Jsy 6.00 15.00
MV Mo Vaughn Bat 4.00 10.00
MW Matt Williams Bat 4.00 10.00
NG Nomar Garciaparra Bat 10.00 25.00
PB Pat Burrell Bat 4.00 10.00
PK Paul Konerko Bat 4.00 10.00
PW Preston Wilson Jsy 4.00 10.00
RA Rich Aurilia Jsy 4.00 10.00
RH Rickey Henderson Bat 6.00 15.00
RJ Randy Johnson Bat 6.00 15.00
RK Ryan Klesko Bat 4.00 10.00
RS Richie Sexson Bat 4.00 10.00
RV Robin Ventura Bat 4.00 10.00
SB Sean Burroughs Bat 4.00 10.00
SG Shawn Green Bat 4.00 10.00
SR Scott Rolen Bat 6.00 15.00
TC Tony Clark Bat 4.00 10.00
TH Todd Helton Bat 6.00 15.00
TJH Toby Hall Bat 4.00 10.00
TL Terrence Long Uni 4.00 10.00
TM Tino Martinez Bat 6.00 15.00
TRL Travis Lee Bat 4.00 10.00
WM Willie Mays Bat 12.50 30.00

2003 Stadium Club Clubhouse Exclusive

Inserted into packs at a different rate depending on how many memorabilia pieces are used, these four cards feature game-worn memorabilia pieces of Cardinals star Albert Pujols.
JSY ODDS 1:488 H, 1:178 HTA
BAT-JSY ODDS 1:2073 H, 1:758 HTA
BAT-JSY-SPK ODDS 1:2750 H, 1:1016 HTA
BAT-HAT-JSY-SPK ODDS 1:1016 HTA
CE1 Albert Pujols Jsy 8.00 20.00
CE2 Albert Pujols Bat-Jsy 15.00 40.00
CE3 Albert Pujols Bat-Jsy-Spike 50.00 100.00

2003 Stadium Club Co-Signers

Randomly inserted into packs, these two cards feature a pair of important baseball players who each signed cards for this set. This set features the first Masanori Murakami (the first Japanese player to play in the majors) certified signed cards. Murakami, to honor his heritage, signed an equivalent amount of cards in English and Japanese.
GROUP A STATED ODDS 1:339 HTA
GROUP B STATED ODDS 1:1016 HTA
MURAKAMI AU 50% ENGLISH/50% JAPAN
AM H.Aaron/W.Mays A 300.00 600.00
MI M.Murakami/K.Ishii B 175.00 300.00

2003 Stadium Club License to Drive Bat Relics

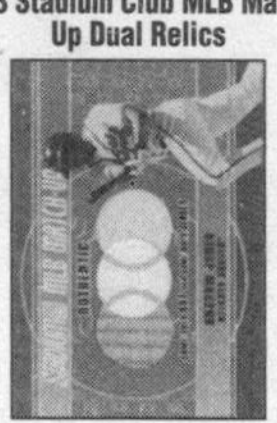

Inserted into packs at a stated rate of one in 98 hobby, one in 114 retail and one in 29 HTA, these 25 cards feature game-used bat relics of players who have driven in 100 runs in a season.
STATED ODDS 1:98 H, 1:29 HTA, 1:114 R
AB Adrian Beltre 4.00 10.00
AD Adam Dunn 4.00 10.00
AJ Andruw Jones 6.00 15.00
ANR Aramis Ramirez 4.00 10.00
AP Albert Pujols 8.00 20.00
AR Alex Rodriguez 10.00 25.00
BW Bernie Williams 6.00 15.00
CJ Chipper Jones 6.00 15.00
EC Eric Chavez 4.00 10.00
FT Frank Thomas 6.00 15.00
GS Gary Sheffield 4.00 10.00
IR Ivan Rodriguez 6.00 15.00
JG Juan Gonzalez 4.00 10.00
LB Lance Berkman 4.00 10.00
LG Luis Gonzalez 4.00 10.00
LW Larry Walker 4.00 10.00
MA Moises Alou 4.00 10.00
MP Mike Piazza 10.00 25.00
NG Nomar Garciaparra 10.00 25.00
RA Roberto Alomar 6.00 15.00
RP Rafael Palmeiro 6.00 15.00
SG Shawn Green 4.00 10.00
SR Scott Rolen 6.00 15.00
TH Todd Helton 6.00 15.00
TM Tino Martinez 6.00 15.00

2003 Stadium Club MLB Match-Up Dual Relics

Inserted into hobby packs at a stated rate of one in 485, one in 570 retail and HTA packs at one in 148, these five cards feature both a game-worn jersey swatch as well as a game-used bat relic of the featured players.
STATED ODDS 1:485 H, 1:148 HTA, 1:570 R
AJ Andruw Jones 2.50 6.00
AP Albert Pujols 8.00 20.00
BB Bret Boone 2.50 6.00
GM Greg Maddux 8.00 20.00
TH Todd Helton 4.00 10.00

2003 Stadium Club Shots

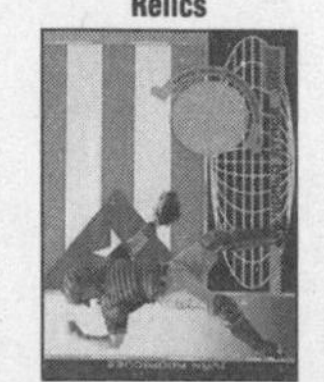

Inserted into hobby packs at a stated rate of one in 24, retail packs at one in 24 and HTA packs at a stated rate of one in four, these 10 cards feature players who are known for their long distance slugging.
STATED ODDS 1:24 HOB/RET, 1:4 HTA
SS1 Lance Berkman .60 1.50
SS2 Barry Bonds 1.50 4.00
SS3 Jason Giambi .40 1.00
SS4 Shawn Green .40 1.00
SS5 Miguel Tejada .60 1.50
SS6 Paul Konerko .60 1.50
SS7 Mike Piazza 1.00 2.50
SS8 Alex Rodriguez 1.25 3.00
SS9 Sammy Sosa 1.00 2.50
SS10 Gary Sheffield .40 1.00

2003 Stadium Club Stadium Slices Barrel Relics

Inserted into hobby packs at a stated rate of one in 550 and HTA packs at a stated rate of one in 204, these 10 cards feature game-used bat pieces taken from the barrel.
AJ Andruw Jones 15.00 40.00
AP Albert Pujols 20.00 50.00
AR Alex Rodriguez 30.00 60.00
CD Carlos Delgado 10.00 25.00
GS Gary Sheffield 10.00 25.00
MP Mike Piazza 30.00 60.00
NG Nomar Garciaparra 12.50 30.00
RA Roberto Alomar 10.00 25.00
RP Rafael Palmeiro 15.00 40.00
TH Todd Helton 15.00 40.00

2003 Stadium Club Stadium Slices Handle Relics

Inserted into hobby packs at a stated rate of one in 237 and HTA packs at a stated rate of one in 86, these 10 cards feature game-used bat pieces taken from the handle.
STATED ODDS 1:237 HOB, 1:86 HTA
AJ Andruw Jones 8.00 20.00
AP Albert Pujols 10.00 25.00
AR Alex Rodriguez 12.50 30.00
CD Carlos Delgado 5.00 12.00
GS Gary Sheffield 5.00 12.00
MP Mike Piazza 12.50 30.00
NG Nomar Garciaparra 15.00 40.00
RA Roberto Alomar 8.00 20.00
RP Rafael Palmeiro 8.00 20.00
TH Todd Helton 8.00 20.00

2003 Stadium Club Stadium Slices Trademark Relics

Inserted into hobby packs at a stated rate of one in 415 and HTA packs at a stated rate of one in 151, these 10 cards feature game-used bat pieces taken from the middle of the bat.
STATED ODDS 1:415 HOB, 1:151 HTA
AJ Andruw Jones 10.00 25.00
AP Albert Pujols 12.50 30.00
AR Alex Rodriguez 15.00 40.00
CD Carlos Delgado 6.00 15.00
GS Gary Sheffield 6.00 15.00
MP Mike Piazza 15.00 40.00
NG Nomar Garciaparra 20.00 50.00
RA Roberto Alomar 10.00 25.00
RP Rafael Palmeiro 10.00 25.00
TH Todd Helton 10.00 25.00

2003 Stadium Club World Stage Relics

Inserted into packs at a different rate depending on whether or not it is a bat or a jersey, these 10 cards feature game-used memorabilia pieces of players born outside the continental U.S.
BAT ODDS 1:809 H, 1:246 HTA, 1:950 R
JSY ODDS 1:118 H, 1:36 HTA, 1:138 R
AB Adrian Beltre Jsy 3.00 8.00
AP Albert Pujols Jsy 8.00 20.00
AS Alfonso Soriano Bat 4.00 10.00
BK Byung-Hyun Kim Jsy 4.00 10.00
HN Hideo Nomo Bat 10.00 25.00
IR Ivan Rodriguez Jsy 4.00 10.00
KI Kazuhisa Ishii Jsy 3.00 8.00
KS Kazuhiro Sasaki Jsy 3.00 8.00
MT Miguel Tejada Jsy 3.00 8.00
TS Tsuyoshi Shinjo Bat 4.00 10.00

2008 Stadium Club

This set was released on November 5, 2008.
COMMON CARD(1-100) .40 1.00
COMMON 999 (1-100) .75 2.00
COMMON RC (1-150) .40 1.00
COMMON RC 999 (1-150) .60 1.50
COMMON AU RC (151-185) 4.00 10.00
AU RC A ODDS 1:3
AU RC B ODDS 1:8
EXCHANGE DEADLINE 10/31/2010
PRINTING PLATE ODDS 1:85 HOBBY
PRINT.PLATE AUTO ODDS 1:198 HOBBY
PLATE PRINT RUN 1 SET PER COLOR
BLACK-CYAN-MAGENTA-YELLOW ISSUED
NO PLATE PRICING DUE TO SCARCITY
1 Chase Utley .60 1.50
2 Tim Lincecum .60 1.50
3 Ryan Zimmerman/999 1.00 2.50
4 Todd Helton .60 1.50
5 Russell Martin .40 1.00
6 Curtis Granderson/999 1.00 2.50
7 Torii Hunter .40 1.00
8 Mark Teixeira .60 1.50
9 Alfonso Soriano/999 1.00 2.50
10 C.C. Sabathia .60 1.50
11 David Ortiz 1.00 2.50
12 Miguel Tejada/999 1.00 2.50
13 Alex Rodriguez 1.25 3.00
14 Prince Fielder .60 1.50
15 Alex Gordon/999 1.00 2.50
16 Jake Peavy .40 1.00
17 B.J. Upton .60 1.50
18 Michael Young/999 1.00 2.50
19 Jason Bay .60 1.50
20 Jorge Posada .60 1.50
21 Jacoby Ellsbury/999 1.25 3.00
22 Nick Markakis .75 2.00
23 Tom Glavine .60 1.50
24 Justin Upton/999 1.00 2.50
25 Edinson Volquez .40 1.00
26 Miguel Cabrera 1.00 2.50
27 Carlos Lee/999 .60 1.50
28 Ryan Church .40 1.00
29 Delmon Young .60 1.50
30 Carlos Quentin/999 .60 1.50
31 Carl Crawford .60 1.50
32 Roy Halladay .60 1.50
33 Brandon Webb/999 1.00 2.50
34 Brian Roberts .40 1.00
35 Ken Griffey Jr. 2.00 5.00
36 Troy Tulowitzki/999 1.50 4.00
37 Hanley Ramirez .60 1.50
38 Hunter Pence .60 1.50
39 Johnny Damon/999 1.00 2.50
40 Eric Chavez .40 1.00
41 Adrian Gonzalez .60 1.50
42 Carlos Pena/999 1.00 2.50
43 Felix Hernandez .60 1.50
44 Magglio Ordonez .60 1.50
45 Josh Beckett/999 .60 1.50
46 Fausto Carmona .40 1.00
47 Chris Young .40 1.00
48 John Lackey/999 1.00 2.50
49 John Smoltz 1.00 2.50
50 David Wright .60 1.50
51 Ichiro Suzuki/999 2.00 5.00
52 Vernon Wells .40 1.00
53 Josh Hamilton .60 1.50
54 Albert Pujols/999 2.00 5.00
55 Dustin Pedroia .60 1.50
56 Garrett Atkins .40 1.00
57 Roy Oswalt/999 1.00 2.50
58 Jose Reyes .60 1.50
59 Derek Jeter 2.50 6.00
60 Scott Kazmir/999 1.00 2.50
61 Vladimir Guerrero .60 1.50
62 Joba Chamberlain .40 1.00
63 Kevin Youkilis/999 .60 1.50
64 Victor Martinez .60 1.50
65 Nick Swisher .60 1.50
66 Carlos Beltran/999 1.00 2.50
67 Joe Mauer .75 2.00
68 Gary Sheffield .40 1.00
69 Cole Hamels/999 1.25 3.00
70 Brian McCann .60 1.50
71 Grady Sizemore .60 1.50
72 Robinson Cano/999 1.00 2.50
73 Greg Maddux 1.25 3.00
74 Rich Harden .40 1.00
75 Ryan Howard/999 1.00 2.50
76 Johan Santana .60 1.50
77 Dan Uggla .40 1.00
78 Justin Verlander/999 1.50 4.00
79 Derrek Lee .40 1.00
80 Ryan Braun .60 1.50
81 Lance Berkman/999 1.00 2.50
82 Manny Ramirez 1.00 2.50
83 Chipper Jones 1.00 2.50
84 Daisuke Matsuzaka/999 1.00 2.50
85 Matt Holliday 1.00 2.50
86 Justin Morneau .60 1.50
87 Jimmy Rollins/999 1.00 2.50
88 Hideki Matsui 1.00 2.50
89 Pedro Martinez .60 1.50
90 Carlos Zambrano/999 1.00 2.50
91 Jackie Robinson 1.00 2.50
92 Mickey Mantle 3.00 8.00
93 Ty Cobb/999 2.50 6.00
94 J.DiMaggio Cut Out
95 Honus Wagner 1.00 2.50
96 Babe Ruth/999 4.00 10.00
97 Nolan Ryan 3.00 8.00
98 Roberto Clemente 2.50 6.00
99 Ted Williams/999 3.00 8.00
100 Tom Seaver .60 1.50
101a Luke Hochevar RC .60 1.50
101b Luke Hochevar VAR/999 1.00 2.50
102a Daric Barton/999 (RC) .60 1.50
102b Daric Barton VAR/999 (RC) .60 1.50
103a Nick Adenhart (RC) .40 1.00
103b Nick Adenhart VAR/999 .60 1.50
104a Gregor Blanco (RC) .40 1.00
104b Gregor Blanco VAR/999 .60 1.50
105a Chris Carter/999 (RC) 1.00 2.50
105b Chris Carter VAR/999 (RC) 1.00 2.50
106a Eric Hurley (RC) .40 1.00
106b Eric Hurley VAR/999 .60 1.50
107a Clayton Kershaw RC 6.00 15.00
107b Clayton Kershaw VAR/999 10.00 25.00
108a Evan Longoria/999 RC 2.50 6.00
108b Evan Longoria VAR/999 RC 2.50 6.00
109a Garrett Mock (RC) .40 1.00
109b Garrett Mock VAR/999 .60 1.50
110a David Purcey (RC) .40 1.00
110b David Purcey VAR/999 .60 1.50
111a Ryan Tucker/999 (RC) .60 1.50
111b Ryan Tucker VAR/999 (RC) .60 1.50
112a Joey Votto (RC) 1.50 4.00
112b Joey Votto VAR/999 2.50 6.00
113a Jeff Clement (RC) .60 1.50
113b Jeff Clement VAR/999 1.00 2.50
114a Michael Aubrey/999 RC 1.00 2.50
114b Michael Aubrey VAR RC/999 1.00 2.50
115a Brandon Boggs .60 1.50
115b Brandon Boggs VAR/999 1.00 2.50
116a Johnny Cueto RC 1.00 2.50
116b Johnny Cueto VAR/999 1.50 4.00
117a Hernan Iribarren/999 (RC) 1.00 2.50
117b Hernan Iribarren VAR/999 (RC) 1.00 2.50
118a Masahide Kobayashi RC .60 1.50
118b Masahide Kobayashi VAR/999 1.00 2.50
119a Jed Lowrie (RC) .40 1.00
119b Jed Lowrie VAR/999 .60 1.50
120a Greg Reynolds/999 RC 1.00 2.50
120b Greg Reynolds VAR/999 RC 1.00 2.50
121a Matt Tolbert RC .60 1.50
121b Matt Tolbert VAR/999 1.00 2.50
122a Jonathan Herrera RC .60 1.50
122b Jonathan Herrera VAR/999 1.00 2.50
123a J.R. Towles/999 RC 1.00 2.50
123b J.R. Towles VAR/999 RC 1.00 2.50
124a Armando Galarraga RC .60 1.50
124b Armando Galarraga VAR/999 1.00 2.50
125a Josh Banks (RC) .40 1.00
125b Josh Banks VAR/999 .60 1.50
126a Mitch Boggs/999 (RC) .60 1.50
126b Mitch Boggs VAR/999 (RC) .60 1.50
127a Blake DeWitt (RC) .60 1.50
127b Blake DeWitt VAR/999 1.00 2.50
128a Carlos Gonzalez (RC) 1.00 2.50
128b Carlos Gonzalez VAR/999 1.50 4.00
129a Elliot Johnson/999 (RC) .60 1.50
129b Elliot Johnson VAR/999 (RC) .60 1.50
130a Brian Barton RC .60 1.50
130b Brian Barton VAR/999 1.00 2.50
131a Sean Rodriguez (RC) .40 1.00
131b Sean Rodriguez VAR/999 .60 1.50
132a Kosuke Fukudome/999 RC 2.00 5.00
132b Kosuke Fukudome VAR/999 RC 2.00 5.00
133a Chin-Lung Hu (RC) .40 1.00
133b Chin-Lung Hu VAR/999 .60 1.50
134a Wladimir Balentien (RC) .40 1.00
134b Wladimir Balentien VAR/999 .60 1.50
135a Jeff Niemann/999 (RC) .60 1.50
135b Jeff Niemann VAR/999 (RC) .60 1.50
136a Jay Bruce (RC) 1.25 3.00
136b Jay Bruce VAR/999 2.00 5.00
137a Brandon Jones RC .60 1.50
137b Brandon Jones VAR/999 1.50 4.00
138a Justin Masterson/999 RC 1.50 4.00
138b Justin Masterson VAR/999 RC 1.50 4.00
139a Jayson Nix (RC) .40 1.00
139b Jayson Nix VAR/999 .60 1.50
140a Max Scherzer RC 5.00 12.00
140b Max Scherzer VAR/999 8.00 20.00
141a Mike Aviles/999 RC 1.00 2.50
141b Mike Aviles VAR/999 RC 1.00 2.50
142a Greg Smith RC .40 1.00
142b Greg Smith VAR/999 .60 1.50
143a Nick Blackburn RC .60 1.50
143b Nick Blackburn VAR/999 1.00 2.50
144a Justin Ruggiano/999 RC 1.00 2.50
144b Justin Ruggiano VAR/999 RC 1.00 2.50
145a Clay Buchholz .60 1.50
145b Clay Buchholz VAR/999 (RC) 1.00 2.50

46a German Duran RC .60 1.50
46b German Duran VAR/999 1.00 2.50
47a Radhames Liz/999 RC 1.00 2.50
47b Radhames Liz VAR/999 RC 1.00 2.50
48a Chris Perez RC .60 1.50
48b Chris Perez VAR/999 1.00 2.50
49a Hiroki Kuroda RC 1.00 2.50
49b Hiroki Kuroda VAR/999 1.50 4.00
50a Gregorio Petit RC .60 1.50
50b Gregorio Petit VAR/999 1.00 2.50
151 Emmanuel Burriss AU RC EXCH A 4.00 10.00
152 Elliot Johnson AU A 4.00 10.00
153 Jonathan Van Every AU RC A 4.00 10.00
154 Darren O'Day AU RC A 4.00 10.00
155 Matt Joyce AU RC A 6.00 15.00
156 Burke Badenhop AU RC A 4.00 10.00
157 Brent Lillibridge AU (RC) A 4.00 10.00
158 Johnny Cueto AU RC A 8.00 20.00
159 Jeff Niemann AU A 4.00 10.00
160 John Bowker AU (RC) A 4.00 10.00
161 Brandon Boggs AU A 4.00 10.00
162 Justin Masterson AU A 6.00 15.00
163 Masahide Kobayashi AU A 5.00 12.00
164 Nick Adenhart AU A 4.00 10.00
165 Chris Perez AU EXCH A 4.00 10.00
166 Gregor Blanco AU A 4.00 10.00
167 Travis Denker AU RC A 4.00 10.00
168 Jeff Clement AU EXCH A 4.00 10.00
169 Evan Longoria AU A 10.00 25.00
170 Greg Smith AU A 4.00 10.00
171 Jay Bruce AU (RC) B 6.00 15.00
172 Brian Barton AU B 6.00 15.00
173 Max Scherzer AU B 75.00 200.00
174 Blake DeWitt AU B 4.00 10.00
175 Jed Lowrie AU B 6.00 15.00
176 Clayton Kershaw AU B 75.00 200.00
177 Jonathan Albaladejo AU RC B 4.00 10.00
178 Josh Banks AU B 4.00 10.00
179 Brian Horwitz AU RC B 4.00 10.00
180 Micah Hoffpauir AU RC B 8.00 20.00
181 Robinzon Diaz AU (RC) B 4.00 10.00
182 Nick Evans AU RC B 6.00 15.00
183 J.Mather AU RC EXCH B 5.00 12.00
184 Danny Herrera AU RC B 4.00 10.00
185 Eugenio Velez AU RC B 4.00 10.00

2008 Stadium Club First Day Issue

*1ST DAY VET 1-100: .6X TO 1.5X BASIC
*1ST DAY RC 101-150: .6X TO 1.5X BASIC
APPX. ODDS TEN PER HOBBY BOX
STATED PRINT RUN 599 SER.#'d SETS

2008 Stadium Club First Day Issue Unnumbered

*1ST UNUM VET 1-100: .5X TO 1.2X BAS
*1ST UNUM RC 101-150: .5X TO 1.2X BAS
RANDOM INSERTS IN RETAIL BACKS

2008 Stadium Club Photographer's Proof Blue

*BLUE VET 1-100: 1X TO 2.5X BASIC
*BLUE 999 1-100: .6X TO 1.5X BASIC
*BLUE RC 101-150: 1X TO 2.5X BASIC
*BLUE 999 101-150: .6X TO 1.5X BASIC
NON-AU BLUE ODDS 1:5 HOBBY
*BLUE AU: .5X TO 1.2X BASIC
AU BLUE ODDS 1:29 HOBBY
BLUE PRINT RUN 99 SER.#'d SETS

2008 Stadium Club Photographer's Proof Gold

*GLD VET 1-100: 1.2X TO 3X BASIC
*GLD 999 1-100: .75X TO 2X BASIC
*GLD RC 101-150: 1.2X TO 3X BASIC
*GLD 999 101-150: .75X TO 2X BASIC
NON-AU GOLD ODDS 1:9 HOBBY
*GLD AU: .6X TO 1.5X BASIC
AU GOLD ODDS 1:62 HOBBY
GOLD PRINT RUN 50 SER.#'d SETS

2008 Stadium Club Beam Team Autographs

GROUP A ODDS 1:13 HOBBY
GROUP B ODDS 1:6 HOBBY
GROUP C ODDS 1:11 HOBBY
PRINTING PLATE ODDS 1:198 HOBBY
PLATE PRINT RUN 1 SET PER COLOR
BLACK-CYAN-MAGENTA-YELLOW ISSUED
NO PLATE PRICING DUE TO SCARCITY
EXCHANGE DEADLINE 10/31/2010
AG Adrian Gonzalez C 6.00 15.00
BH Brad Hawpe C 4.00 10.00
BP Brandon Phillips B 4.00 10.00
BT Brad Thompson C 8.00 20.00
CC Carl Crawford C 6.00 15.00
CCR Callix Crabbe C 4.00 10.00
CD Carlos Delgado C 6.00 15.00
CF Chone Figgins B 4.00 10.00
CM Carlos Marmol C 4.00 10.00
CMO Craig Monroe B 4.00 10.00
CP Carlos Pena C 6.00 15.00
CV Claudio Vargas C 4.00 10.00
CVI Carlos Villanueva B 4.00 10.00
CW C.J. Wilson B 4.00 10.00
DH Dan Haren C 6.00 15.00
DS Darryl Strawberry B 8.00 20.00
DY Delwyn Young A 4.00 10.00
ER Edwar Ramirez C 4.00 10.00
FL Francisco Liriano C 5.00 12.00
FP Felix Pie B 4.00 10.00
FS Freddy Sanchez C 4.00 10.00
GC Gary Carter C 10.00 25.00
GD German Duran B 4.00 10.00
GP Glen Perkins B 4.00 10.00
GS Gary Sheffield C 6.00 15.00
GSM Greg Smith C 4.00 10.00
JB Jason Bartlett C 4.00 10.00
JC Jack Cust C 5.00 12.00
JCR Jesse Crain A 4.00 10.00
JGA Joey Gathright C 4.00 10.00
JGU Jeremy Guthrie C 4.00 10.00
JH Josh Hamilton B 4.00 10.00
JJ Jair Jurrjens C 5.00 12.00
JL John Lackey B 5.00 12.00
JN Jayson Nix A 4.00 10.00
JP Jonathan Papelbon C 8.00 20.00
JPO Johnny Podres B 4.00 10.00
JR Jose Reyes C 8.00 20.00
JS Jeff Salazar B 4.00 10.00
KS Kevin Slowey B 5.00 12.00
LM Lastings Milledge B 4.00 10.00
ME Mark Ellis C 4.00 10.00
MK Mark Kotsay C 4.00 10.00
MN Mike Napoli C 4.00 10.00
MT Marcus Thames C 4.00 10.00
MTO Matt Tolbert A 4.00 10.00
NR Nate Robertson B 4.00 10.00
RC Robinson Cano B 6.00 15.00
RP Ronny Paulino B 4.00 10.00
TG Tom Gorzelanny C 4.00 10.00
TJ Todd Jones B 4.00 10.00
YP Yusmeiro Petit A 4.00 10.00

2008 Stadium Club Beam Team Autographs Black and White

*B AND W: .5X TO 1.2X BASIC
STATED ODDS 1:19 HOBBY
STATED PRINT RUN 99 SER.#'d SETS
EXCHANGE DEADLINE 10/31/2010

2008 Stadium Club Beam Team Autographs Gold

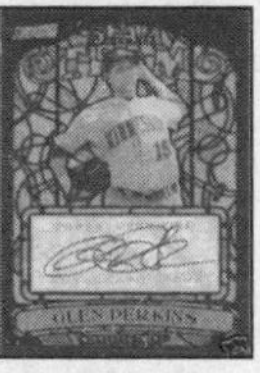

*GOLD: .5X TO 1.2X BASIC
STATED ODDS 1:40 HOBBY
STATED PRINT RUN 50 SER.#'d SETS
EXCHANGE DEADLINE 10/31/2010

2008 Stadium Club Ceremonial Cuts

STATED ODDS 1:34 HOBBY
STATED PRINT RUN 199 SER.#'d SETS
BR Babe Ruth 15.00 40.00
GB George Bush 10.00 25.00
JF Jimmie Foxx 8.00 20.00
JR Jackie Robinson 12.50 30.00
LG Lou Gehrig 15.00 40.00
MO Mel Ott 8.00 20.00
RH Rogers Hornsby 8.00 20.00
TC Ty Cobb 12.50 30.00
TW Ted Williams 12.50 30.00

2008 Stadium Club Ceremonial Cuts Photographer's Proof Blue

*BLUE: .5X TO 1.2X BASIC
STATED ODDS 1:28 HOBBY
STATED PRINT RUN 99 SER.#'d SETS

2008 Stadium Club Stadium Slices

STATED ODDS 1:23 HOBBY
PRINT RUNS B/WN 89-428 COPIES PER
AP Albert Pujols/428 10.00 25.00
AR Alex Rodriguez/89 30.00 60.00
DM Daisuke Matsuzaka/428 5.00 12.00
DO David Ortiz/428 4.00 10.00
GG Goose Gossage/89 15.00 40.00
HM Hideki Matsui/428 6.00 15.00
IS Ichiro Suzuki/428 10.00 25.00
JT Joe Torre/89 15.00 40.00
LP Lou Piniella/89 8.00 20.00
MM Mickey Mantle/89 15.00 40.00
MR Mariano Rivera/428 6.00 15.00
RJ Reggie Jackson/89 10.00 25.00
TM Thurman Munson/89 30.00 60.00
WF Whitey Ford/89 20.00 50.00
YB Yogi Berra/89 20.00 50.00

2008 Stadium Club Stadium Slices Photographer's Proof Blue

*BLUE: .5X TO 1.2X BASIC
STATED ODDS 1:28 HOBBY
PRINT RUNS B/WN 25-99 SER.#'d SETS
NO PRICING ON QTY 25 OR LESS

2008 Stadium Club Stadium Slices Photographer's Proof Gold

*GOLD: .5X TO 1.2X BASIC
STATED ODDS 1:55 HOBBY
PRINT RUNS B/WN 5-50 SER.#'d SETS
NO PRICING ON QTY 5 OR LESS

2008 Stadium Club Triumvirate Memorabilia Autographs

STATED ODDS 1:26 HOBBY
PRINT RUNS B/WN 49-99 SER.#'d SETS
EXCHANGE DEADLINE 10/31/2010
AD Adam Dunn 8.00 20.00
AP Albert Pujols 100.00 200.00
AR Aramis Ramirez 12.00 30.00
ARI Alex Rios 6.00 15.00
AS Alfonso Soriano 15.00 40.00
BU B.J. Upton 6.00 15.00
CC Carl Crawford 12.00 30.00
CL Carlos Lee 6.00 15.00
CW Chien-Ming Wang 30.00 60.00
DL Derrek Lee 12.00 30.00
DO David Ortiz 30.00 60.00
HR Hanley Ramirez 10.00 25.00
JF Jeff Francoeur 10.00 25.00
JM Justin Morneau 15.00 40.00
JP Jake Peavy 6.00 15.00
JPA Jonathan Papelbon 15.00 40.00
JU Justin Upton 8.00 20.00
MH Matt Holliday 12.00 30.00
MO Magglio Ordonez/49 6.00 15.00
MR Mariano Rivera 75.00 150.00
MT Miguel Tejada 10.00 25.00
RM Russ Martin 8.00 20.00
SK Scott Kazmir 8.00 20.00
TH Torii Hunter 12.00 30.00
TLH Todd Helton 10.00 25.00
TT Troy Tulowitzki 6.00 15.00
VG Vladimir Guerrero 12.00 30.00
VW Vernon Wells 10.00 25.00

2014 Stadium Club

COMPLETE SET (200) 25.00 60.00
1 Ken Griffey Jr. 1.00 2.50
2 Matt Holliday .50 1.25
3 Babe Ruth 1.25 3.00
4 Jon Singleton RC .40 1.00
5 Curtis Granderson .40 1.00
6 Shane Victorino .40 1.00
7 Adrian Gonzalez .40 1.00
8 Stephen Strasburg .50 1.25
9 Hisashi Iwakuma .40 1.00
10 Sergio Romo .30 .75
11 Max Scherzer .50 1.25
12 Gio Gonzalez .40 1.00
13 Stan Musial .75 2.00
14 Travis d'Arnaud RC .40 1.00
15 Mark Trumbo .30 .75
16 Nolan Arenado .60 1.50
17 Michael Cuddyer .30 .75
18 Derek Jeter 2.50 6.00
19 Jered Weaver .40 1.00
20 Ivan Rodriguez .40 1.00
21 Roy Halladay .40 1.00
22 Matt Adams .30 .75
23 John Smoltz .50 1.25
24 Anthony Rizzo .75 2.00
25 Edwin Encarnacion .50 1.25
26 Elvis Andrus .40 1.00
27 Lou Gehrig 1.00 2.50
28 Giancarlo Stanton .50 1.25
29 Jose Reyes .40 1.00
30 Andrew McCutchen .50 1.25
31 Todd Helton .40 1.00
32 Ernie Banks .50 1.25
33 Tony Cingrani .40 1.00
34 Jordan Zimmermann .40 1.00
35 Brian Dozier .40 1.00
36 Randy Johnson .50 1.25
37 Hunter Pence .40 1.00
38 Robinson Cano .40 1.00
39 Chase Utley .40 1.00
40 Justin Verlander .50 1.25
41 Shin-Soo Choo .40 1.00
42 Jackie Robinson .50 1.25
43 Pedro Martinez .40 1.00
44 Hank Aaron 1.00 2.50
45 Gregory Polanco RC .50 1.25
46 Rickey Henderson .50 1.25
47 Oscar Taveras RC .40 1.00
48 Jacoby Ellsbury .40 1.00
49 Michael Choice RC .30 .75
50 Mike Trout 2.50 6.00
51 Chris Davis .30 .75
52 Manny Machado .50 1.25
53 Willie Mays 1.00 2.50
54 Wil Myers .30 .75
55 Andrew Heaney RC .30 .75
56 Nick Castellanos RC 1.00 2.50
57 Jayson Werth .40 1.00
58 Zack Wheeler .40 1.00
59 Jonathan Schoop RC .30 .75
60 Albert Pujols .60 1.50
61 Alex Guerrero RC .40 1.00
62 Starling Marte .40 1.00
63 Billy Butler .30 .75
64 Tim Lincecum .40 1.00
65 Yu Darvish .50 1.25
66 Matt Cain .40 1.00
67 Ozzie Smith .60 1.50
68 Adrian Beltre .50 1.25
69 Freddie Freeman .60 1.50
70 Justin Upton .40 1.00
71 Ian Kinsler .40 1.00
72 Ty Cobb .75 2.00
73 Matt Carpenter .50 1.25
74 Josh Donaldson .40 1.00
75 Pablo Sandoval .40 1.00
76 Taijuan Walker RC .30 .75
77 Al Kaline .50 1.25
78 Josh Hamilton .40 1.00
79 Brandon Phillips .30 .75
80 Roger Clemens .60 1.50
81 Anibal Sanchez .30 .75
82 Evan Longoria .40 1.00
83 Brooks Robinson .40 1.00
84 Aroldis Chapman .50 1.25
85 Kolten Wong RC .40 1.00
86 David Wright .40 1.00
87 Joey Votto .50 1.25
88 Wilmer Flores RC .40 1.00
89 Yordano Ventura RC .40 1.00
90 Jose Altuve .40 1.00
91 Miguel Cabrera .50 1.25
92 CC Sabathia .40 1.00
93 Chris Owings RC .30 .75
94 George Springer RC 1.25 3.00
95 Mark McGwire 1.00 2.50
96 Johnny Cueto .40 1.00
97 Yasiel Puig .50 1.25
98 Victor Martinez .40 1.00
99 Trevor Rosenthal .40 1.00
100 Jose Abreu RC 2.50 6.00
101 Mike Napoli .30 .75
102 Adam Jones .40 1.00
103 Adam Eaton .30 .75
104 Nolan Ryan 1.50 4.00
105 Troy Tulowitzki .50 1.25
106 Eric Hosmer .40 1.00
107 Zack Greinke .40 1.00
108 Pedro Alvarez .30 .75
109 Jeff Bagwell .40 1.00
110 Xander Bogaerts RC 1.00 2.50
111 Duke Snider .40 1.00
112 Albert Belle .30 .75
113 Johnny Bench .50 1.25
114 Bob Feller .40 1.00
115 Jason Heyward .40 1.00
116 Andrelton Simmons .30 .75
117 Don Mattingly 1.00 2.50
118 Alex Gordon .40 1.00
119 Sonny Gray .40 1.00
120 Jose Bautista .40 1.00
121 Carlos Gonzalez .40 1.00
122 Craig Kimbrel .40 1.00
123 Andre Dawson .40 1.00
124 Billy Hamilton RC .40 1.00
125 Madison Bumgarner .40 1.00
126 Torii Hunter .30 .75
127 Roberto Clemente 1.25 3.00
128 Marcus Stroman RC .50 1.25
129 Hanley Ramirez .40 1.00
130 Starlin Castro .30 .75
131 Dustin Pedroia .50 1.25
132 Wilin Rosario .30 .75
133 Ted Williams 1.00 2.50
134 Carlos Beltran .40 1.00
135 Eddie Butler RC .30 .75
136 Jason Kipnis .40 1.00
137 Julio Teheran .40 1.00
138 Wade Boggs .40 1.00
139 Koji Uehara .30 .75
140 Mookie Betts RC 15.00 40.00
141 Evan Gattis .30 .75
142 Matt Harvey .40 1.00
143 Jean Segura .40 1.00
144 Yoenis Cespedes .50 1.25
145 Matt Kemp .40 1.00
146 Jay Bruce .40 1.00
147 Bo Jackson .50 1.25
148 Salvador Perez .40 1.00
149 Mike Piazza .50 1.25
150 Clayton Kershaw 1.00 2.50
151 Sandy Koufax 1.00 2.50
152 Nelson Cruz .50 1.25
153 Bryce Harper .75 2.00
154 Chris Sale .50 1.25
155 Michael Wacha .40 1.00
156 Prince Fielder .40 1.00
157 Jurickson Profar .40 1.00
158 Hyun-Jin Ryu .40 1.00
159 Mariano Rivera .60 1.50
160 Joe Mauer .40 1.00
161 Tony Gwynn .50 1.25
162 Jose Canseco .40 1.00
163 Masahiro Tanaka RC 1.00 2.50
164 Ryan Braun .40 1.00
165 Cole Hamels .40 1.00
166 Mat Latos .40 1.00
167 Domonic Brown .40 1.00
168 Adam Wainwright .40 1.00
169 Shelby Miller .40 1.00
170 Ryan Howard .40 1.00
171 Robin Yount .50 1.25
172 Arismendy Alcantara RC .30 .75
173 Mike Schmidt .75 2.00
174 Yadier Molina .50 1.25
175 Jose Fernandez .50 1.25
176 Jeff Samardzija .30 .75
177 Eddie Murray .40 1.00
178 Greg Maddux .60 1.50
179 Felix Hernandez .40 1.00
180 Ian Desmond .30 .75
181 C.J. Cron RC .30 .75
182 David Ortiz .50 1.25
183 Carlos Gomez .30 .75
184 Cliff Lee .40 1.00
185 Buster Posey .60 1.50
186 Carl Crawford .40 1.00
187 Christian Yelich .60 1.50
188 George Brett 1.00 2.50
189 David Price .40 1.00
190 Todd Frazier .40 1.00
191 Gerrit Cole .50 1.25
192 Brett Lawrie .40 1.00
193 R.A. Dickey .40 1.00
194 Tom Seaver .40 1.00
195 Chris Archer .30 .75
196 Ryan Zimmerman .40 1.00
197 Cal Ripken Jr. 1.50 4.00
198 Carlos Santana .40 1.00
199 Paul Goldschmidt .50 1.25
200 Joe DiMaggio 1.00 2.50

2014 Stadium Club Electric Foil

*ELECTRIC: 1.5X TO 4X BASIC
*ELECTRIC RC: 1.5X TO 4X BASIC
STATED ODDS 1:9 MINI BOX
1 Ken Griffey Jr. 6.00 15.00
18 Derek Jeter 20.00 50.00
29 Jose Reyes 5.00 12.00
67 Ozzie Smith 6.00 15.00
100 Jose Abreu 8.00 20.00
104 Nolan Ryan 10.00 25.00
117 Don Mattingly 8.00 20.00
127 Roberto Clemente 6.00 15.00
159 Mariano Rivera 8.00 20.00
161 Tony Gwynn 5.00 12.00
173 Mike Schmidt 6.00 15.00
188 George Brett 6.00 15.00
197 Cal Ripken Jr. 6.00 15.00

2014 Stadium Club Foilboard

*FOILBOARD: 4X TO 10X BASIC
*FOILBOARD RC: 4X TO 10X BASIC
STATED ODDS 1:11 MINI BOX
STATED PRINT RUN 25 SER.#'d SETS
1 Ken Griffey Jr. 20.00 50.00
18 Derek Jeter 50.00 120.00
29 Jose Reyes 8.00 20.00
37 Hunter Pence 6.00 15.00
67 Ozzie Smith 8.00 20.00
86 David Wright 10.00 25.00
90 Jose Altuve 12.00 30.00
95 Mark McGwire 15.00 40.00
97 Yasiel Puig 20.00 50.00
100 Jose Abreu 15.00 40.00
104 Nolan Ryan 25.00 60.00
117 Don Mattingly 15.00 40.00
127 Roberto Clemente 15.00 40.00
159 Mariano Rivera 15.00 40.00
161 Tony Gwynn 10.00 25.00
173 Mike Schmidt 10.00 25.00
178 Greg Maddux 10.00 25.00
188 George Brett 10.00 25.00
197 Cal Ripken Jr. 30.00 80.00

2014 Stadium Club Gold

*GOLD: 1.2X TO 3X BASIC
*GOLD RC: 1.2X TO 3X BASIC
STATED ODDS 1:3 MINI BOX
18 Derek Jeter 15.00 40.00
29 Jose Reyes 5.00 12.00
67 Ozzie Smith 5.00 12.00
100 Jose Abreu 6.00 15.00
104 Nolan Ryan 8.00 20.00
117 Don Mattingly 6.00 15.00
127 Roberto Clemente 5.00 12.00
159 Mariano Rivera 6.00 15.00
161 Tony Gwynn 4.00 10.00
173 Mike Schmidt 5.00 12.00
188 George Brett 5.00 12.00
197 Cal Ripken Jr. 5.00 12.00

2014 Stadium Club Rainbow

*RAINBOW: .6X TO 1.5X BASIC
*RAINBOW RC: .6X TO 1.5X BASIC
RANDOM INSERTS IN PACKS
18 Derek Jeter 10.00 25.00

2014 Stadium Club Autographs

OVERALL ONE AUTO PER MINI BOX
EXCHANGE DEADLINE 9/30/2017
SCAAA Arismendy Alcantara 2.50 6.00
SCAAE Adam Eaton 2.50 6.00
SCAAH Andrew Heaney 2.50 6.00
SCACA Chase Anderson 2.50 6.00
SCACBL Charlie Blackmon 8.00 20.00
SCACCR C.J. Cron 2.50 6.00
SCACF Cliff Floyd 2.50 6.00
SCACO Chris Owings 2.50 6.00
SCACY Christian Yelich 10.00 25.00
SCADA Dean Anna 2.50 6.00
SCADS Danny Salazar 4.00 10.00
SCAEG Evan Gattis 2.50 6.00
SCAEJ Erik Johnson 2.50 6.00
SCAGP Gregory Polanco 4.00 10.00
SCAGS George Springer 12.00 30.00
SCAJA Jose Abreu 15.00 40.00
SCAJJ James Jones 2.50 6.00
SCAJK Joe Kelly 2.50 6.00
SCAJL Junior Lake 2.50 6.00
SCAJM Jake Marisnick 2.50 6.00
SCAJSA Jarrod Saltalamacchia 2.50 6.00
SCAJSC Jonathan Schoop 5.00 12.00
SCAJSE Jean Segura 3.00 8.00
SCAJT Julio Teheran 3.00 8.00
SCAKU Koji Uehara 25.00 60.00
SCAKW Kolten Wong 3.00 8.00
SCALH Livan Hernandez 2.50 6.00
SCALS Luis Sardinas 2.50 6.00
SCAMA Matt Adams 2.50 6.00
SCAMBE Mookie Betts 100.00 250.00
SCAMCA Matt Carpenter 8.00 20.00
SCAMH Mario Hollands 3.00 8.00
SCAMST Marcus Stroman 5.00 12.00
SCAMW Maury Wills 4.00 10.00
SCAMZ Mike Zunino 2.50 6.00
SCAOT Oscar Taveras 3.00 8.00
SCAOV Omar Vizquel 15.00 40.00
SCARE Roenis Elias 2.50 6.00
SCARM Rafael Montero 2.50 6.00
SCASG Sonny Gray 6.00 15.00
SCASM Shelby Miller 10.00 25.00
SCASMA Starling Marte 5.00 12.00
SCASR Stefen Romero 2.50 6.00
SCATC Tony Cingrani 3.00 8.00
SCATW Taijuan Walker 2.50 6.00
SCAYS Yangervis Solarte 2.50 6.00
SCAZW Zack Wheeler 8.00 20.00

2014 Stadium Club Autographs Gold

*GOLD: .75X TO 2X BASIC
STATED ODDS 1:30 MINI BOX
STATED PRINT RUN 25 SER.#'d SETS
EXCHANGE DEADLINE 9/30/2017
SCAAB Albert Belle 20.00 50.00
SCAAD Andre Dawson 12.00 30.00
SCACR Cal Ripken Jr. 150.00 300.00
SCAFM Fred McGriff 40.00 100.00
SCAGM Greg Maddux 150.00 250.00
SCAJC Jose Canseco EXCH 25.00 60.00
SCAJG Juan Gonzalez 15.00 40.00
SCAJS John Smoltz 50.00 120.00
SCAJV Joey Votto 30.00 80.00
SCAKG Ken Griffey Jr. 150.00 250.00
SCAMN Mike Napoli 30.00 80.00
SCAMS Mike Schmidt 40.00 100.00
SCAMT Mike Trout 200.00 300.00
SCAPG Paul Goldschmidt 20.00 50.00
SCARP Rafael Palmeiro 20.00 50.00
SCATP Terry Pendleton 10.00 25.00
SCATT Troy Tulowitzki 30.00 80.00
SCAYP Yasiel Puig 125.00 250.00

2014 Stadium Club Autographs Rainbow

*RAINBOW: .6X TO 1.5X BASIC
STATED ODDS 1:18 MINI BOX
STATED PRINT RUN 50 SER.#'d SETS
EXCHANGE DEADLINE 9/30/2017
SCAAB Albert Belle 10.00 25.00
SCACK Clayton Kershaw 90.00 150.00
SCACSA Chris Sale 12.00 30.00
SCAJC Jose Canseco EXCH 20.00 50.00
SCAJG Juan Gonzalez 12.00 30.00
SCAMM Mike Minor 4.00 10.00
SCAMN Mike Napoli 25.00 60.00
SCAPG Paul Goldschmidt 15.00 40.00
SCATP Terry Pendleton 8.00 20.00

2014 Stadium Club Beam Team

STATED ODDS 1:3 MINI BOX
BT1 Miguel Cabrera 1.25 3.00
BT2 Max Scherzer 1.25 3.00
BT3 Clayton Kershaw 2.50 6.00
BT4 Wil Myers .75 2.00
BT5 Jose Fernandez 1.25 3.00
BT6 Troy Tulowitzki 1.25 3.00
BT7 Mike Trout 6.00 15.00
BT8 Joey Votto 1.25 3.00
BT9 Adam Jones 1.00 2.50
BT10 David Wright 1.00 2.50
BT11 Dustin Pedroia 1.25 3.00
BT12 Yadier Molina 1.25 3.00
BT13 Manny Machado 1.25 3.00
BT14 Evan Longoria 1.00 2.50
BT15 Yu Darvish 1.25 3.00
BT16 David Ortiz 1.25 3.00
BT17 Derek Jeter 4.00 10.00
BT18 Andrew McCutchen 1.25 3.00
BT19 Bryce Harper 2.00 5.00
BT20 Felix Hernandez 1.00 2.50
BT21 Robinson Cano 1.00 2.50
BT22 Jacoby Ellsbury 1.00 2.50
BT23 Adam Wainwright 1.00 2.50
BT24 Masahiro Tanaka 3.00 8.00
BT25 Dylan Bundy 1.00 2.50

2014 Stadium Club Beam Team Gold

*GOLD: 2.5X TO 6X BASIC
STATED ODDS 1:36 MINI BOX
BT17 Derek Jeter 50.00 120.00

2014 Stadium Club Field Access

RANDOM INSERTS IN PACKS
FA1 Mike Trout 6.00 15.00
FA2 Andrew McCutchen 1.25 3.00
FA3 Buster Posey 1.50 4.00
FA4 Bryce Harper 2.00 5.00
FA5 Willie Mays 2.50 6.00
FA6 Babe Ruth 3.00 8.00
FA7 David Wright 1.00 2.50
FA8 Hank Aaron 2.50 6.00
FA9 Roger Clemens 1.50 4.00
FA10 Stan Musial 2.00 5.00
FA11 Greg Maddux 1.50 4.00
FA12 Rickey Henderson 1.25 3.00
FA13 Randy Johnson 1.25 3.00
FA14 Miguel Cabrera 1.25 3.00
FA15 Yasiel Puig 1.25 3.00
FA16 Johnny Bench 1.25 3.00

FA17 Joe Mauer 1.00 2.50
FA18 Clayton Kershaw 2.50 6.00
FA19 Ken Griffey Jr. 2.50 6.00
FA20 Nolan Ryan 4.00 10.00
FA21 Justin Verlander 1.25 3.00
FA22 Derek Jeter 3.00 8.00
FA23 Jose Fernandez 1.25 3.00
FA24 Mark McGwire 2.50 6.00
FA25 Robinson Cano 1.00 2.50

2014 Stadium Club Field Access Electric Foil

*ELECTRIC FOIL: 1X TO 2.5X BASIC
STATED ODDS 1:88 MINI BOX
STATED PRINT RUN 25 SER.#'D SETS
FA1 Mike Trout 15.00 40.00
FA3 Buster Posey 12.00 30.00
FA13 Randy Johnson 10.00 25.00
FA18 Clayton Kershaw 12.00 30.00
FA19 Ken Griffey Jr. 25.00 60.00
FA20 Nolan Ryan 30.00 80.00
FA22 Derek Jeter 25.00 60.00

2014 Stadium Club Field Access Gold

*GOLD: .75X TO 2X BASIC
STATED ODDS 1:44 MINI BOX
STATED PRINT RUN 50 SER.#'D SETS

2014 Stadium Club Field Access Rainbow

*RAINBOW: .6X TO 1.5X BASIC
STATED ODDS 1:23 MINI BOX
STATED PRINT RUN 99 SER.#'D SETS
FA19 Ken Griffey Jr. 10.00 25.00
FA20 Nolan Ryan 10.00 25.00
FA22 Derek Jeter 10.00 25.00

2014 Stadium Club Future Stars Die Cut

STATED ODDS 1:3 MINI BOX
FS1 Jose Fernandez .75 2.00
FS2 Gerrit Cole .75 2.00
FS3 Michael Wacha .60 1.50
FS4 Wil Myers .50 1.25
FS5 Yasiel Puig .75 2.00
FS6 Xander Bogaerts 1.50 4.00
FS7 Billy Hamilton .60 1.50
FS8 Jose Abreu 4.00 10.00
FS9 Masahiro Tanaka 1.50 4.00
FS10 George Springer 2.00 5.00

2014 Stadium Club Future Stars Die Cut Gold

*GOLD: 2X TO 5X BASIC
STATED ODDS 1:218 MINI BOX
STATED PRINT RUN 25 SER.#'d SETS
FS7 Billy Hamilton 10.00 25.00

2014 Stadium Club Legends Die Cut

STATED ODDS 1:3 MINI BOX
LDC1 Stan Musial 1.50 4.00
LDC2 Greg Maddux 1.25 3.00
LDC3 Rickey Henderson 1.00 2.50
LDC4 Randy Johnson 1.00 2.50
LDC5 Johnny Bench 1.00 2.50
LDC6 George Brett 2.00 5.00
LDC7 Cal Ripken Jr. 3.00 8.00
LDC8 Ken Griffey Jr. 2.00 5.00
LDC9 Nolan Ryan 3.00 8.00
LDC10 Sandy Koufax 2.00 5.00

2014 Stadium Club Legends Die Cut Gold

*GOLD: 3X TO 8X BASIC
STATED ODDS 1:218 MINI BOX
STATED PRINT RUN 25 SER.#'d SETS
LDC4 Randy Johnson 12.00 30.00
LDC8 Ken Griffey Jr. 30.00 80.00

2014 Stadium Club Lone Star Signatures

STATED ODDS 1:219 MINI BOX
EXCHANGE DEADLINE 9/30/2017
LSSCK Clayton Kershaw EXCH 100.00 200.00
LSSHA Hank Aaron EXCH 100.00 200.00
LSSIR Ivan Rodriguez 20.00 50.00
LSSMM Mark McGwire 150.00 250.00
LSSMS Max Scherzer 40.00 100.00
LSSMW Michael Wacha EXCH 20.00 50.00
LSSNR Nolan Ryan EXCH 100.00 200.00
LSSRC Roger Clemens EXCH 50.00 120.00
LSSWM Willie Mays EXCH 125.00 250.00
LSSYD Yu Darvish EXCH 60.00 150.00

2014 Stadium Club Triumvirates Luminous

STATED ODDS 1:3 MINI BOX
T1A Hanley Ramirez 1.50 4.00
T1B Clayton Kershaw 4.00 10.00
T1C Yasiel Puig 2.00 5.00
T2A Albert Pujols 2.50 6.00
T2B Derek Jeter 5.00 12.00
T2C David Ortiz 2.00 5.00
T3A Adam Jones 1.50 4.00
T3B Mike Trout 10.00 25.00
T3C Giancarlo Stanton 2.00 5.00
T4A Stephen Strasburg 2.00 5.00
T4B Justin Verlander 2.00 5.00
T4C Adam Wainwright 1.50 4.00
T5A Troy Tulowitzki 2.00 5.00
T5B Miguel Cabrera 2.00 5.00
T5C Robinson Cano 1.50 4.00
T6A Andrew McCutchen 2.00 5.00
T6B Bryce Harper 3.00 8.00
T6C Carlos Gonzalez 1.50 4.00
T7A Yu Darvish 2.00 5.00
T7B Masahiro Tanaka 4.00 10.00
T7C Hyun-Jin Ryu 1.50 4.00
T8A Buster Posey 2.50 6.00
T8B Yadier Molina 2.00 5.00
T8C Joe Mauer 1.50 4.00
T9A Evan Longoria 1.50 4.00
T9B Manny Machado 2.00 5.00
T9C David Wright 1.50 4.00
T10A Xander Bogaerts 4.00 10.00
T10B Jose Abreu 6.00 15.00
T10C George Springer 5.00 12.00

2014 Stadium Club Triumvirates Illuminator

*ILLUMINATOR: 1X TO 2.5X BASIC
STATED ODDS 1:36 MINI BOX
T1B Clayton Kershaw 20.00 50.00
T2B Derek Jeter 50.00 120.00
T3B Mike Trout 40.00 100.00
T8A Buster Posey 12.00 30.00
T10B Jose Abreu 60.00 150.00

2014 Stadium Club Triumvirates Luminescent

*LUMINESCENT: .6X TO 1.5X BASIC
STATED ODDS 1:12 MINI BOX
T2B Derek Jeter 12.00 30.00

2015 Stadium Club

COMPLETE SET (300) 40.00 80.00
1 Fernando Valenzuela .25 .60
2 Sonny Gray .30 .75
3 David Cone .25 .60
4 Huston Street .25 .60
5 Anthony Ranaudo RC .50 1.25
6 J.J. Hardy .25 .60
7 Brandon Moss .25 .60
8 Mark Reynolds .25 .60
9 Rick Porcello .30 .75
10 Zach Britton .30 .75
11 Mark Buehrle .30 .75
12 Giancarlo Stanton .40 1.00
13 Ernie Banks .40 1.00
14 Mark Teixeira .30 .75
15 Adrian Beltre .40 1.00
16 Robinson Cano .30 .75
17 Jacoby Ellsbury .30 .75
18 Zack Wheeler .30 .75
19 Scott Kazmir .25 .60
20 Eric Chavez .25 .60
21 Patrick Corbin .30 .75
22 Ivan Rodriguez .30 .75
23 Ozzie Smith .50 1.25
24 Dale Murphy .40 1.00
25 Matt Holliday .40 1.00
26 Juan Lagares .25 .60
27 Carlos Santana .30 .75
28 Dallas Keuchel .30 .75
29 Trevor Rosenthal .30 .75
30 Dilson Herrera RC .60 1.50
31 Albert Belle .25 .60
32 Nolan Arenado .50 1.25
33 Cal Ripken Jr. 1.25 3.00
34 Mariano Rivera .50 1.25
35 Ryne Sandberg .75 2.00
36 Frank Robinson .30 .75
37 Carlos Ruiz .25 .60
38 Jonathan Lucroy .30 .75
39 Josh Donaldson .30 .75
40 Josh Hamilton .30 .75
41 Gregory Polanco .30 .75
42 Jordan Zimmermann .30 .75
43 Jose Bautista .30 .75
44 Todd Frazier .30 .75
45 Matt Shoemaker .30 .75
46 Yonder Alonso .25 .60
47 Michael Brantley .30 .75
48 Steven Moya .30 .75
49 Kurt Suzuki .25 .60
50 Ender Inciarte RC .50 1.25
51 Miguel Cabrera .40 1.00
52 Jake Marisnick .25 .60
53 Chipper Jones .40 1.00
54 Bip Roberts .25 .60
55 Lucas Duda .30 .75
56 Hunter Pence .30 .75
57 Marcus Stroman .30 .75
58 Jason Giambi .25 .60
59 Adrian Gonzalez .30 .75
60 James Shields .25 .60
61 Joe Mauer .30 .75
62 Paul Goldschmidt .40 1.00
63 Matt Adams .25 .60
64 Brett Gardner .30 .75
65 Jackie Robinson .40 1.00
66 Seth Smith .25 .60
67 Don Mattingly .75 2.00
68 Brooks Robinson .30 .75
69 Chris Sale .40 1.00
70 James McCann RC .75 2.00
71 Curtis Granderson .30 .75
72 Madison Bumgarner .30 .75
73 Starling Marte .30 .75
74 Adam Wainwright .30 .75
75 Lou Brock .30 .75
76 Bo Jackson .40 1.00
77 Marcell Ozuna .40 1.00
78 Juan Gonzalez .25 .60
79 Bartolo Colon .25 .60
80 Andrew Heaney .25 .60
81 Monte Irvin .30 .75
82 Deion Sanders .30 .75
83 Sean Doolittle .25 .60
84 Andrelton Simmons .25 .60
85 Joey Votto .40 1.00
86 Wily Peralta .25 .60
87 Christian Yelich .50 1.25
88 Chris Davis .25 .60
89 Joc Pederson RC 1.00 2.50
90 Justin Morneau .30 .75
91 Dusty Baker .25 .60
92 Jorge Soler RC .75 2.00
93 Andy Van Slyke .25 .60
94 Wei-Yin Chen .25 .60
95 Rob Dibble .25 .60
96 Jonathan Papelbon .30 .75
97 Evan Gattis .25 .60
98 Jim Rice .30 .75
99 Chase Utley .30 .75
100 Alex Cobb .25 .60
101 Mookie Betts .60 1.50
102 Cliff Lee .30 .75
103 Kennys Vargas .25 .60
104 Billy Hamilton .30 .75
105 Devin Mesoraco .25 .60
106 Shin-Soo Choo .30 .75
107 Ron Gant .25 .60
108 Buster Posey .50 1.25
109 David Price .30 .75
110 Terry Pendleton .25 .60
111 Whitey Ford .30 .75
112 Paul Konerko .30 .75
113 Buck Farmer RC .50 1.25
114 Gary Sheffield .25 .60
115 Jason Heyward .30 .75
116 Maikel Franco RC .60 1.50
117 Lenny Dykstra .25 .60
118 Yasiel Puig .40 1.00
119 Pedro Alvarez .25 .60
120 Victor Martinez .30 .75
121 Luis Aparicio .25 .60
122 Mike Minor .25 .60
123 Lenny Harris .25 .60
124 Cliff Floyd .25 .60
125 Jake Arrieta .30 .75
126 Rougned Odor .30 .75
127 Alfredo Simon .25 .60
128 Cory Spangenberg .25 .60
129 Adam Eaton .25 .60
130 John Olerud .25 .60
131 Phil Hughes .25 .60
132 Jered Weaver .25 .60
133 Kenley Jansen .30 .75
134 Mitch Moreland .25 .60
135 Mike Trout 2.00 5.00
136 Reggie Jackson .30 .75
137 Rondell White .25 .60
138 Ben Zobrist .30 .75
139 Andrew McCutchen .40 1.00
140 Jay Bruce .30 .75
141 Edwin Escobar .25 .60
142 Anthony Rendon .40 1.00
143 Mickey Tettleton .25 .60
144 Prince Fielder .30 .75
145 R.A. Dickey .30 .75
146 Mike Mussina .30 .75
147 Henderson Alvarez .25 .60
148 Kevin Gausman .25 .60
149 Orlando Cepeda .30 .75
150 Jacob deGrom .40 1.00
151 Andrew Cashner .25 .60
152 Jose Abreu .40 1.00
153 Mark McGwire .60 1.50
154 J.D. Martinez .40 1.00
155 Nick Swisher .30 .75
156 Chris Carter .25 .60
157 Orlando Hernandez .25 .60
158 Eric Hosmer .30 .75
159 Torii Hunter .25 .60
160 Elvis Andrus .30 .75
161 Ryan Braun .30 .75
162 Craig Kimbrel .30 .75
163 C.J. Wilson .25 .60
164 Carlton Fisk .30 .75
165 Willie Stargell .30 .75
166 Ian Kinsler .30 .75
167 Edwin Encarnacion .40 1.00
168 Carlos Baerga .25 .60
169 Brock Holt .25 .60
170 Albert Pujols .50 1.25
171 Jimmy Rollins .30 .75
172 Yoenis Cespedes .30 .75
173 Gary Brown RC .50 1.25
174 George Springer .30 .75
175 Drew Stubbs .25 .60
176 Matt Barnes RC .50 1.25
177 Guilder Rodriguez RC .50 1.25
178 Steve Pearce .40 1.00
179 Bud Norris .25 .60
180 Adam LaRoche .25 .60
181 Alcides Escobar .30 .75
182 Clayton Kershaw .75 2.00
183 Travis Ishikawa .25 .60
184 David Ortiz .40 1.00
185 Josh Harrison .30 .75
186 Lou Gehrig .75 2.00
187 Xander Bogaerts .40 1.00
188 Jhonny Peralta .25 .60
189 Jeurys Familia .30 .75
190 Stan Musial .60 1.50
191 Joe Panik .30 .75
192 Kolten Wong .30 .75
193 David Wright .30 .75
194 Carlos Gomez .25 .60
195 Yan Gomes .25 .60
196 Brandon Finnegan RC .50 1.25
197 Dalton Pompey RC .60 1.50
198 Cole Hamels .30 .75
199 Ryan Howard .30 .75
200 Mike Morse .25 .60
201 Rafael Montero .25 .60
202 Stephen Strasburg .40 1.00
203 Javier Baez RC 4.00 10.00
204 Raul Ibanez .30 .75
205 Jose Altuve .30 .75
206 Julio Teheran .30 .75
207 Doug Fister .25 .60
208 Masahiro Tanaka .30 .75
209 Mike Zunino .25 .60
210 George Brett .75 2.00
211 Justin Verlander .40 1.00
212 Rusney Castillo RC .60 1.50
213 Kyle Seager .25 .60
214 Brandon Crawford .30 .75
215 Adam Jones .30 .75
216 Bryce Harper .60 1.50
217 Yu Darvish .40 1.00
218 Nelson Cruz .40 1.00
219 C.J. Cron .25 .60
220 Jake Peavy .25 .60
221 Nick Castellanos .40 1.00
222 Tanner Roark .25 .60
223 Lorenzo Cain .25 .60
224 Kendall Graveman RC .50 1.25
225 Kristopher Negron RC .50 1.25
226 Dennis Eckersley .30 .75
227 Jon Singleton .30 .75
228 Chris Sabo .25 .60
229 Dayan Viciedo .25 .60
230 Billy Butler .25 .60
231 Joe Morgan .30 .75
232 Corey Dickerson .25 .60
233 Felix Hernandez .30 .75
234 Brandon Guyer .25 .60
235 Johnny Cueto .30 .75
236 Yusmeiro Petit .25 .60
237 Mike Moustakas .30 .75
238 Roberto Alomar .30 .75
239 Roger Clemens .50 1.25
240 Josh Beckett .25 .60
241 Garrett Richards .30 .75
242 Troy Tulowitzki .40 1.00
243 Salvador Perez .30 .75
244 Daniel Norris .25 .60
245 Edgar Martinez .30 .75
246 Adam Dunn .30 .75
247 Matt Williams .25 .60
248 Alex Gordon .30 .75
249 Daniel Murphy .30 .75
250 Manny Machado .40 1.00
251 Jayson Werth .30 .75
252 Tom Glavine .30 .75
253 Hisashi Iwakuma .30 .75
254 Evan Longoria .30 .75
255 Dellin Betances .30 .75
256 David Robertson .25 .60
257 Paul Molitor .40 1.00
258 Zack Greinke .30 .75
259 Greg Maddux .50 1.25
260 Ken Griffey Jr. .75 2.00
261 Jake Odorizzi .25 .60
262 Luis Gonzalez .25 .60
263 Anthony Rizzo .60 1.50
264 Alex Rodriguez .50 1.25
265 Tony Gwynn .40 1.00
266 Derek Jeter 1.00 2.50
267 Corey Kluber .30 .75
268 Matt Carpenter .40 1.00
269 Angel Pagan .25 .60
270 Kevin Kiermaier .30 .75
271 Russell Martin .25 .60
272 Alexander Guerrero (RC) .60 1.50
273 Mike Piazza .40 1.00
274 Tim Hudson .30 .75
275 Freddie Freeman .50 1.25
276 Jonathan Schoop .25 .60
277 Oswaldo Arcia .25 .60
278 Omar Vizquel .30 .75
279 Joe DiMaggio .75 2.00
280 Rymer Liriano RC .50 1.25
281 Yordano Ventura .30 .75
282 Fred McGriff .30 .75
283 Aaron Sanchez .60 1.50
284 Jose Fernandez .40 1.00
285 Hanley Ramirez .30 .75
286 Tyson Ross .25 .60
287 Pablo Sandoval .30 .75
288 David Peralta .25 .60
289 Danny Santana .25 .60
290 Dwight Gooden .25 .60
291 Arismendy Alcantara .25 .60
292 Fernando Rodney .25 .60
293 Trevor May RC .50 1.25
294 Wil Myers .25 .60
295 Michael Taylor .25 .60
296 Max Scherzer .40 1.00
297 Wade Davis .25 .60
298 Larry Doby .30 .75
299 Jake Lamb RC .75 2.00
300 Kris Bryant RC 10.00 25.00

2015 Stadium Club Black

*BLACK: 3X TO 8X BASIC
*BLACK RC: 1.5X TO 4X BASIC RC
STATED ODDS 1:8 HOBBY
ANNCD PRINT RUN 201 SETS

2015 Stadium Club Black and White

*B/W: 8X TO 20X BASIC
*B/W RC: 4X TO 10X BASIC RC
STATED ODDS 1:46 HOBBY
ANNCD PRINT RUN 17 SETS
89 Joc Pederson 60.00 150.00
266 Derek Jeter 60.00 150.00
300 Kris Bryant 100.00 250.00

2015 Stadium Club Foilboard

*FOIL: 6X TO 15X BASIC
*FOIL RC: 3X TO 8X BASIC RC
STATED ODDS 1:65 HOBBY
STATED PRINT RUN 25 SER.#'d SETS
89 Joc Pederson 50.00 120.00
266 Derek Jeter 50.00 120.00
300 Kris Bryant 75.00 200.00

2015 Stadium Club Gold

*GOLD: 1.5X TO 4X BASIC
*GOLD RC: .75X TO 2X BASIC RC
STATED ODDS 1:3 HOBBY

2015 Stadium Club Autographs

STATED ODDS 1:10 HOBBY
EXCHANGE DEADLINE 5/31/2018
SCAAA Arismendy Alcantara 3.00 8.00
SCAAB Archie Bradley 3.00 8.00
SCAAC Alex Cobb 3.00 8.00
SCAARZ Anthony Rizzo 15.00 40.00
SCAASZ Aaron Sanchez 4.00 10.00
SCABFN Brandon Finnegan 3.00 8.00
SCACB Carlos Baerga 8.00 20.00
SCACC C.J. Cron 3.00 8.00
SCACF Cliff Floyd 3.00 8.00
SCACKR Corey Kluber 5.00 12.00
SCACR Carlos Rodon 5.00 12.00
SCACS Chris Sale 5.00 12.00
SCACW Christian Walker 6.00 15.00
SCACY Christian Yelich 12.00 30.00
SCADB Dellin Betances 5.00 12.00
SCADC David Cone 10.00 25.00
SCADH Dilson Herrera 4.00 10.00
SCADN Daniel Norris 3.00 8.00
SCADP Dalton Pompey 5.00 12.00
SCAED Eric Davis 8.00 20.00
SCAEG Evan Gattis 3.00 8.00
SCAGR Garrett Richards 4.00 10.00
SCAGS George Springer 12.00 30.00
SCAJB Javier Baez 8.00 50.00
SCAJC Jarred Cosart 3.00 8.00
SCAJDM Jacob deGrom 20.00 50.00
SCAJF Jose Fernandez 20.00 50.00
SCAJH Jason Heyward 30.00 80.00
SCAJK Jung-Ho Kang 40.00 100.00
SCAJLS Juan Lagares 3.00 8.00
SCAJPA Joe Panik 4.00 10.00
SCAJPN Joc Pederson 12.00 30.00
SCAKB Kris Bryant 100.00 250.00
SCAKGA Kevin Gausman 3.00 8.00
SCAKGN Kendall Graveman 3.00 8.00
SCAKS Kyle Seager 3.00 8.00
SCAKV Kennys Vargas 3.00 8.00
SCALH Livan Hernandez 3.00 8.00
SCAMA Matt Adams 4.00 10.00
SCAMB Matt Barnes 3.00 8.00
SCAMCR Matt Carpenter 8.00 20.00
SCAMFO Maikel Franco 4.00 10.00
SCAMS Matt Shoemaker 4.00 10.00
SCAMST Marcus Stroman 4.00 10.00
SCAMTR Michael Taylor 3.00 8.00
SCAMW Matt Williams 3.00 8.00
SCANS Noah Syndergaard 20.00 50.00
SCAOV Omar Vizquel 8.00 20.00
SCARL Rymer Liriano 3.00 8.00
SCASG Sonny Gray 4.00 10.00
SCASM Starling Marte 4.00 10.00
SCATR Tyson Ross 3.00 8.00
SCATW Taijuan Walker 3.00 8.00
SCAWM Wil Myers 6.00 15.00
SCAYT Yasmany Tomas 20.00 50.00
SCAZW Zack Wheeler 8.00 20.00

2015 Stadium Club Autographs Black

*BLACK: .6X TO 1.5X BASIC
STATED ODDS 1:87 HOBBY
STATED PRINT RUN 50 SER.#'d SETS
EXCHANGE DEADLINE 5/31/2018
SCACKW Clayton Kershaw EXCH 60.00 150.00
SCAJDN Josh Donaldson 12.00 30.00
SCAJS Jorge Soler 10.00 25.00
SCAPG Paul Goldschmidt 25.00 60.00

2015 Stadium Club Autographs Gold

*GOLD: .75X TO 2X BASIC
STATED ODDS 1:142 HOBBY
STATED PRINT RUN 25 SER.#'d SETS
EXCHANGE DEADLINE 5/31/2018
SCABH Bryce Harper 250.00 350.00
SCABP Buster Posey 100.00 200.00
SCACKW Clayton Kershaw EXCH 75.00 200.00
SCADO David Ortiz 90.00 150.00
SCADW David Wright 50.00 120.00
SCAEL Evan Longoria 25.00 60.00
SCAFF Freddie Freeman 20.00 50.00
SCAFV Fernando Valenzuela 30.00 80.00
SCAJA Jose Abreu 40.00 100.00
SCAJDN Josh Donaldson 15.00 40.00
SCAJH Jason Heyward 50.00 120.00
SCAJS Jorge Soler 12.00 30.00
SCAJV Joey Votto 50.00 120.00
SCAMP Mike Piazza 90.00 150.00
SCAMR Mariano Rivera 100.00 250.00
SCAPG Paul Goldschmidt 30.00 80.00

2015 Stadium Club Contact Sheet

COMPLETE SET (25) 15.00 40.00
STATED ODDS 1:8 HOBBY
*WHITE/99: .6X TO 1.5X BASIC
*GOLD/50: 1.5X TO 4X BASIC
*ORANGE/25: 2.5X TO 6X BASIC
CS1 Mike Trout 5.00 12.00
CS2 Andrew McCutchen 1.00 2.50
CS3 Buster Posey 1.25 3.00
CS4 Giancarlo Stanton 1.00 2.50
CS5 Troy Tulowitzki 1.00 2.50
CS6 Josh Donaldson .75 2.00
CS7 Miguel Cabrera 1.00 2.50
CS8 Evan Longoria .75 2.00
CS9 Jose Bautista .75 2.00
CS10 Yasiel Puig 1.00 2.50
CS11 Robinson Cano .75 2.00
CS12 Manny Machado 1.00 2.50
CS13 Adrian Beltre 1.00 2.50
CS14 Paul Goldschmidt 1.00 2.50
CS15 Jason Heyward .75 2.00
CS16 Anthony Rendon 1.00 2.50
CS17 Dustin Pedroia 1.00 2.50
CS18 Anthony Rizzo 1.50 4.00
CS19 Alex Gordon .75 2.00
CS20 Carlos Gomez .60 1.50
CS21 Joey Votto 1.00 2.50
CS22 Bryce Harper 1.50 4.00
CS23 David Wright .75 2.00
CS24 Jose Abreu 1.00 2.50
CS25 Jacoby Ellsbury .75 2.00

2015 Stadium Club Crystal Ball

STATED ODDS 1:355 HOBBY
STATED PRINT RUN 70 SER.#'d SETS
*GOLD/30: .5X TO 1.2X BASIC
CB01 Mike Trout 80.00 200.00
CB02 Bryce Harper 25.00 60.00
CB03 Jorge Soler 15.00 40.00
CB04 Yordano Ventura 12.00 30.00
CB05 George Springer 12.00 30.00
CB06 Mookie Betts 25.00 60.00
CB07 Javier Baez 80.00 200.00
CB08 Taijuan Walker 10.00 25.00
CB09 Jacob deGrom 15.00 40.00
CB10 Daniel Norris 10.00 25.00

2015 Stadium Club Legends Die Cut

COMPLETE SET (10) 10.00 25.00
RANDOM INSERTS IN PACKS
*GOLD/25: 2.5X TO 6X BASIC
LDC01 Babe Ruth 2.50 6.00
LDC02 Ty Cobb 1.50 4.00
LDC03 Jackie Robinson 1.00 2.50
LDC04 Willie Mays 2.00 5.00
LDC05 Ted Williams 2.00 5.00
LDC06 Roberto Clemente 2.50 6.00
LDC07 Nolan Ryan 3.00 8.00
LDC08 Randy Johnson 1.00 2.50
LDC09 Roger Clemens 1.25 3.00
LDC10 Tony Gwynn 1.00 2.50

2015 Stadium Club Lone Star Signatures

STATED ODDS 1:2244 HOBBY
STATED PRINT RUN 25 SER.#'d SETS
EXCHANGE DEADLINE 5/31/2018
LSSAJ Adam Jones 20.00 50.00
LSSCH Cole Hamels 20.00 50.00
LSSGS Giancarlo Stanton EXCH 50.00 120.00
LSSJA Jose Abreu 25.00 60.00
LSSJD Josh Donaldson 20.00 50.00
LSSMR Mariano Rivera 100.00 250.00
LSSMT Mike Trout 200.00 400.00
LSSPG Paul Goldschmidt 40.00 100.00
LSSRC Robinson Cano 20.00 50.00
LSSRJ Randy Johnson 90.00 150.00
LSSTT Troy Tulowitzki 30.00 80.00

2015 Stadium Club Triumvirates Luminous

STATED ODDS 1:16 HOBBY
*LUMINESCENT: .6X TO 1.5X BASIC
*ILLUMINATOR: 1.5X TO 4X BASIC
T1A David Price 1.25 3.00
T1B Miguel Cabrera 1.50 4.00
T1C Victor Martinez 1.25 3.00
T2A Matt Harvey 1.25 3.00
T2B Jacob deGrom 1.50 4.00
T2C Zack Wheeler 1.25 3.00
T3A Adam Wainwright 1.25 3.00
T3B Jason Heyward 1.25 3.00
T3C Yadier Molina 1.50 4.00
T4A Jorge Soler 1.50 4.00
T4B Javier Baez 8.00 20.00
T4C Starlin Castro 1.00 2.50
T5A Jose Fernandez 1.50 4.00
T5B Giancarlo Stanton 1.50 4.00
T5C Christian Yelich 2.00 5.00
T6A Bryce Harper 2.50 6.00
T6B Stephen Strasburg 1.50 4.00
T6C Anthony Rendon 1.50 4.00
T7A Andrew McCutchen 1.50 4.00
T7B Starling Marte 1.25 3.00
T7C Gregory Polanco 1.25 3.00
T8A Eric Hosmer 1.25 3.00
T8B Salvador Perez 1.25 3.00
T8C Alex Gordon 1.25 3.00
T9A Josh Donaldson 1.25 3.00
T9B Evan Longoria 1.25 3.00
T9C Pablo Sandoval 1.25 3.00
T10A Yasiel Puig 1.50 4.00
T10B Jose Abreu 1.50 4.00
T10C Rusney Castillo 1.25 3.00

2015 Stadium Club True Colors

STATED ODDS 1:16 HOBBY
*REF: .6X TO 1.5X BASIC
*GOLD REF: .75X TO 2X BASIC
*ELEC.REF/25: 4X TO 10X BASIC
TCAAG Adrian Gonzalez .75 2.00
TCAAP Albert Pujols 1.25 3.00
TCABH Bryce Harper 1.50 4.00
TCABP Buster Posey 1.25 3.00
TCACK Clayton Kershaw 2.00 5.00
TCADO David Ortiz 1.00 2.50
TCAFV Fernando Valenzuela .60 1.50
TCAGS Giancarlo Stanton 1.00 2.50
TCAJA Jose Abreu 1.00 2.50
TCAJM Joe Mauer .75 2.00
TCAJP Joe Panik .75 2.00
TCALG Luis Gonzalez .60 1.50
TCAMB Madison Bumgarner .75 2.00
TCAMC Miguel Cabrera 1.00 2.50
TCAMM Mike Mussina .75 2.00
TCAMP Mike Piazza 1.00 2.50
TCAMR Mariano Rivera 1.25 3.00
TCAMT Mike Trout 5.00 12.00
TCAPG Paul Goldschmidt 1.00 2.50
TCARB Ryan Braun .75 2.00
TCARC Roger Clemens 1.25 3.00
TCATS Tom Seaver .75 2.00
TCAWM Willie Mays 2.00 5.00
TCAYD Yu Darvish 1.00 2.50
TCAYP Yasiel Puig 1.00 2.50

2016 Stadium Club

COMP.SET w/o SP's (300) 40.00 100.00
1 Gary Sanchez RC 1.50 4.00
2 Garrett Richards .30 .75
3 Matt Kemp .30 .75
4 Kevin Kiermaier .30 .75
5 Jay Bruce .30 .75
6 Brandon Phillips .25 .60
7 Edwin Encarnacion .40 1.00
8 Stephen Vogt .30 .75
9 Addison Russell .40 1.00
10 Jose Altuve .30 .75
11 Todd Frazier .30 .75
12 Jon Lester .30 .75
13 Sandy Koufax .75 2.00
14 Chris Davis .25 .60
15 Ozzie Smith .50 1.25
16 Greg Holland .25 .60
17 Raul Mondesi RC
18 Willie McCovey .30 .75
19 Marco Estrada .25 .60
20A Al Leiter .25 .60
20B Al Leiter SP 6.00 15.00
Holding head
21 Carson Smith .25 .60
22 Matt Reynolds .25 .60
23 Nolan Arenado .50 1.25
24 Michael Reed RC .50 1.25
25 Chris Archer .25 .60
26 Steven Matz .30 .75
27 Anthony Gose .25 .60
28 Dee Gordon .25 .60
29 Rob Refsnyder RC .60 1.50
30 Jose Bautista .30 .75
31 Brett Gardner .30 .75
32 Bob Feller .30 .75
33 Mitch Moreland .25 .60
34 Santiago Casilla .25 .60
35 Kendrys Morales .25 .60
36 Nomar Mazara RC .75 2.00
37 Yadier Molina .40 1.00
38 Frank Thomas .40 1.00
39 Michael Brantley .30 .75
40 Kyle Waldrop .30 .75
41 Reggie Jackson .30 .75
42 Francisco Lindor .75 2.00
43 Joc Pederson .30 .75
44 Mark Melancon .25 .60
45 Craig Biggio .30 .75
46 Greg Bird RC .60 1.50
47 Brandon Crawford .30 .75
48 Harold Baines .30 .75
49 Brett Anderson .25 .60
50 Whitey Ford .30 .75
51 Ken Griffey Jr. .75 2.00
52 Yangervis Solarte .25 .60
53 Chris Heston .25 .60
54 Matt Duffy .25 .60
55 Stephen Strasburg .40 1.00
56A Yordano Ventura .30 .75
56B Yordano Ventura SP 8.00 20.00
Sunglasses
57 Huston Street .25 .60
58 Eddie Murray .30 .75
59 Ken Giles .25 .60
60 Carl Yastrzemski .60 1.50
61 Miguel Almonte RC .50 1.25
62 Luke Jackson RC .50 1.25
63 Orlando Cepeda .30 .75
64 Lucas Duda .30 .75
65 Ender Inciarte .25 .60
66 Catfish Hunter .30 .75
67 Yu Darvish .40 1.00
68 Raisel Iglesias .30 .75
69A Clayton Kershaw .75 2.00
69B Kershaw SP Batting 20.00 50.00
70 Dennis Eckersley .30 .75
71 Luis Gonzalez .30 .75
72 Tom Murphy RC .50 1.25
73 Chris Tillman .25 .60
74 Maikel Franco .30 .75
75 Hank Aaron .75 2.00
76 Tyson Ross .25 .60
77 Tyler White RC .50 1.25
78A James Shields .25 .60
78B James Shields SP 6.00 15.00
Brown jersey

79 Marquis Grissom .25 .60
80A Nolan Ryan 1.25 3.00
80B Ryan SP HOF 30.00 80.00
81A Miguel Sano RC .75 2.00
81B Sano SP Dugout 10.00 25.00
82 Blake Swihart .30 .75
83 Tom Seaver .30 .75
84 Logan Forsythe .25 .60
85 J.J. Hardy .25 .60
86 Andrew Miller .30 .75
87 Lou Gehrig .75 2.00
88 Devin Mesoraco .25 .60
89 Erick Aybar .25 .60
90 Jason Kipnis .30 .75
91 Kenta Maeda RC 1.00 2.50
92 Max Scherzer .40 1.00
93 C.J. Wilson .25 .60
94 Adrian Beltre .40 1.00
95 Francisco Cervelli .25 .60
96 Adam Eaton .25 .60
97 Eric Hosmer .30 .75
98 Ian Kinsler .30 .75
99 Justin Turner .30 .75
100 Carlos Gonzalez .30 .75
101 Archie Bradley .25 .60
102 Ichiro Suzuki .50 1.25
103 Mark McGwire .60 1.50
104 Cole Hamels .30 .75
105 Bryce Harper .60 1.50
106 Sonny Gray .30 .75
107 Jake Arrieta .30 .75
108 Omar Vizquel .30 .75
109 Josh Reddick .25 .60
110 Salvador Perez .30 .75
111 Matt Carpenter .40 1.00
112 Curt Schilling .30 .75
113 Andrew McCutchen .40 1.00
114 David Ortiz .40 1.00
115 Paul Goldschmidt .40 1.00
116 J.T. Realmuto .40 1.00
117 Charlie Blackmon .40 1.00
118 Brian Dozier .30 .75
119 Mark Teixeira .30 .75
120A Mike Moustakas .30 .75
120B Mike Moustakas SP w/Dog 8.00 20.00
121A Masahiro Tanaka .30 .75
121B Masahiro Tanaka SP Batting 8.00 20.00
122A Greg Maddux .50 1.25
122B Maddux SP w/Chipper 15.00 40.00
123 Willie Stargell .30 .75
124 Felix Hernandez .30 .75
125A Corey Kluber .30 .75
125B Corey Kluber SP Batting 8.00 20.00
126 Roberto Clemente 1.00 2.50
127 Max Kepler RC .75 2.00
128 Dallas Keuchel .30 .75
129 Adam Jones .30 .75
130 Jason Heyward .30 .75
131 Gerrit Cole .40 1.00
132 Carlos Correa .40 1.00
133 David Price .30 .75
134 Adrian Gonzalez .30 .75
135 Phil Niekro .30 .75
136 Derek Norris .25 .60
137A Josh Harrison .25 .60
137B Josh Harrison SP Throwing 10.00 25.00
138 Shawn Tolleson .25 .60
139 Matt Harvey .30 .75
140 Gio Gonzalez .30 .75
141 Mookie Betts .60 1.50
142A Corey Seager RC 4.00 10.00
142B Seager SP Helmet 25.00 60.00
143 Jim Abbott .25 .60
144 Kole Calhoun .25 .60
145 Carl Edwards Jr. RC .60 1.50
146 Johnny Bench .40 1.00
147A Henry Owens RC .60 1.50
147B Henry Owens SP Green jersey 8.00 20.00
148 Danny Salazar .30 .75
149 Jeurys Familia .30 .75
150 Jorge De La Rosa .25 .60
151A Stephen Piscotty RC .75 2.00
151B Stephen Piscotty SP w/Bat 10.00 25.00
152 Albert Pujols .50 1.25
153 Yovani Gallardo .25 .60
154 Yoenis Cespedes .40 1.00
155 Marcus Semien .25 .60
156 Randal Grichuk .25 .60
157 Mike Leake .25 .60
158 Gary Carter .30 .75
159 Trevor Story RC 2.00 5.00
160 Miguel Cabrera .40 1.00
161 Alex Rodriguez .50 1.25
162 T.J. House .25 .60
163 Billy Hamilton .30 .75
164 DJ LeMahieu .40 1.00
165 Zach Lee RC .50 1.25
166 Freddy Galvis .25 .60
167 Micah Johnson .25 .60
168 Javier Baez .50 1.25
169 Kevin Pillar .25 .60
170 Colby Lewis .25 .60
171 Randy Johnson .40 1.00
172 Buster Posey .50 1.25
173 Nathan Eovaldi .30 .75
174 Victor Martinez .30 .75
175 Frankie Montas RC .60 1.50
176 Alex Colome .25 .60
177 Monte Irvin .30 .75
178 Brandon Drury RC .75 2.00
179 Lou Brock .30 .75
180 George Brett .75 2.00
181 Manny Banuelos .40 1.00
182 Ryan Braun .30 .75
183 Brad Ziegler .25 .60
184 Byron Buxton .30 .75
185 Jorge Soler .40 1.00
186 A.J. Ramos .25 .60
187 Johnny Cueto .30 .75
188 Colin Rea RC .50 1.25
189 Chris Sale .40 1.00
190 Erasmo Ramirez .25 .60
191 Frank Viola .25 .60
192 Delino DeShields .25 .60
193 Melvin Upton Jr. .30 .75
194 Willie Mays .75 2.00
195 Hisashi Iwakuma .30 .75
196 Adam Wainwright .30 .75
197 Zack Greinke .30 .75
198 Roberto Osuna .25 .60
199 Hector Rondon .25 .60
200A Jose Fernandez .40 1.00
200B Jose Fernandez SP Batting 6.00 15.00
201 Nelson Cruz .40 1.00
202 Daniel Murphy .30 .75
203A Alex Gordon .30 .75
203B Alex Gordon SP Sunglasses 8.00 20.00
204 Andre Ethier .30 .75
205 Christian Yelich .50 1.25
206 Josh Hamilton .30 .75
207 Anthony Rizzo .60 1.50
208 Edgar Martinez .30 .75
209A Julio Teheran .30 .75
209B Julio Teheran SP Batting 8.00 20.00
210 Luis Severino RC .60 1.50
211 Didi Gregorius .30 .75
212 Jonathan Lucroy .30 .75
213 Fernando Valenzuela .25 .60
214A Madison Bumgarner .30 .75
214B Bumgarner SP Batting 20.00 50.00
215 Jimmy Paredes .25 .60
216 Noah Syndergaard .30 .75
217 Carlos Santana .30 .75
218 Brandon Belt .30 .75
219 Kevin Plawecki .25 .60
220 Jung Ho Kang .25 .60
221 Jacob deGrom .40 1.00
222 Evan Longoria .30 .75
223 Nomar Garciaparra .30 .75
224 David Wright .30 .75
225 Trea Turner RC 1.50 4.00
226 Scott Kazmir .25 .60
227 Robin Yount .40 1.00
228 Jeremy Hellickson .25 .60
229 Babe Ruth 1.00 2.50
230 Jayson Werth .30 .75
231 Starlin Castro .25 .60
232 Sean Doolittle .25 .60
233 Robinson Cano .30 .75
234 Kyle Gibson .30 .75
235 Russell Martin .25 .60
236 Kris Bryant .50 1.25
237 Richie Shaffer RC .50 1.25
238 Jhonny Peralta .25 .60
239 Shelby Miller .30 .75
240 Brock Holt .25 .60
241 Rick Porcello .25 .60
242 Collin McHugh .25 .60
243 Hunter Pence .30 .75
244 Andres Galarraga .30 .75
245 Ketel Marte RC 1.00 2.50
246 Josh Donaldson .30 .75
247 Cameron Rupp .25 .60
248 Ted Williams .75 2.00
249 Yasmany Tomas .25 .60
250A Bartolo Colon .25 .60
250B Bartolo Colon SP Batting 6.00 15.00
251 Jon Gray .25 .60
252 Phil Hughes .25 .60
253 Paul Molitor .40 1.00
254 Dustin Pedroia .40 1.00
255 Wade Davis .25 .60
256 Rusney Castillo .25 .60
257 Joe Morgan .30 .75
258 Jose Peraza RC .60 1.50
259 Aroldis Chapman .40 1.00
260 Ryan Howard .30 .75
261 Johnny Damon .30 .75
262 Joey Votto .40 1.00
263 J.D. Martinez .40 1.00
264A A.J. Pollock .25 .60
264B A.J. Pollock SP Batting 6.00 15.00
265A Hector Olivera RC .60 1.50
265B Hector Olivera SP w/Bat 8.00 20.00
266 Edinson Volquez .25 .60
267 John Smoltz .40 1.00
268 Jordan Zimmermann .30 .75
269 Hector Santiago .25 .60
270 Prince Fielder .30 .75
271 Martin Prado .25 .60
272A Michael Conforto .30 .75
272B Conforto SP Gray jrsy 8.00 20.00
273 Brian Johnson RC .50 1.25
274 Giancarlo Stanton .40 1.00
275 David Peralta .25 .60
276 Francisco Liriano .25 .60
277A Kyle Schwarber RC 1.50 4.00
277B Schwarber SP Blue jrsy 20.00 50.00
278 Khris Davis .40 1.00
279 Joe Panik .30 .75
280A Mike Trout 2.00 5.00
280B Trout SP w/Bag 50.00 125.00
281 Peter O'Brien RC .50 1.25
282 Joe Mauer .30 .75
283 Rougned Odor .30 .75
284 Freddie Freeman .50 1.25
285 Trevor May .25 .60
286 Harmon Killebrew .40 1.00
287 Blake Snell RC .60 1.50
288 Jose Abreu .40 1.00
289 Anthony DeSclafani .25 .60
290 Manny Machado .40 1.00
291 George Springer .30 .75
292 Shin-Soo Choo .30 .75
293 Cal Ripken Jr. 1.25 3.00
294 Jackie Robinson .40 1.00
295A Aaron Nola RC 1.00 2.50
295B Aaron Nola SP Red jersey 12.00 30.00
296 Byung-Ho Park RC .60 1.50
297 Wade Boggs .30 .75
298 Curtis Granderson .30 .75
299 Kyle Seager .25 .60
300 Matt Wisler .25 .60

2016 Stadium Club Black

*BLACK: 2.5X TO 6X BASIC
*BLACK RC: 1.2X TO 3X BASIC RC

2016 Stadium Club Black and White

*B/W: 8X TO 20X BASIC
*B/W RC: 4X TO 10X BASIC RC

2016 Stadium Club Foilboard

*FOIL: 8X TO 20X BASIC
*FOIL RC: 4X TO 10X BASIC RC

2016 Stadium Club Gold

*GOLD: 1.5X TO 4X BASIC
*GOLD RC: .75X TO 2X BASIC RC

2016 Stadium Club Autographs

EXCHANGE DEADLINE 6/30/2018
SCAAC Alex Colome 3.00 8.00
SCAAGA Andres Galarraga 5.00 12.00
SCAAN Aaron Nola 6.00 15.00
SCAAP A.J. Pollock 3.00 8.00
SCAAR Addison Russell
SCABB Brandon Belt 4.00 10.00
SCABC Brandon Crawford 15.00 40.00
SCABD Brandon Drury 5.00 12.00
SCABHP Byung-Ho Park 4.00 10.00
SCABJ Brian Johnson 3.00 8.00
SCABP Buster Posey
SCACC Carlos Correa
SCACE Carl Edwards Jr. 4.00 10.00
SCACH Chris Heston 3.00 8.00
SCACK Clayton Kershaw
SCACRA Colin Rea 3.00 8.00
SCACRJ Cal Ripken Jr.
SCACSE Chris Sale
SCACSH Carson Smith 3.00 8.00
SCACSR Corey Seager
SCADK Dallas Keuchel
SCADL DJ LeMahieu 10.00 25.00
SCAFL Francisco Lindor 12.00 30.00
SCAFV Fernando Valenzuela
SCAGB Greg Bird 4.00 10.00
SCAGH Greg Holland 3.00 8.00
SCAGM Greg Maddux
SCAHB Harold Baines 5.00 12.00
SCAHOA Hector Olivera 4.00 10.00
SCAHOS Henry Owens 4.00 10.00
SCAI Ichiro Suzuki
SCAJA Jose Altuve
SCAJG Jon Gray
SCAJPK Joe Panik 10.00 25.00
SCAJPS Jimmy Paredes 3.00 8.00
SCAJR J.T. Realmuto 10.00 25.00
SCAKB Kris Bryant
SCAKC Kole Calhoun 5.00 12.00
SCAKG Ken Griffey Jr.
SCAKM Ketel Marte 6.00 15.00
SCAKMA Kenta Maeda 30.00 80.00
SCAKP Kevin Plawecki 3.00 8.00
SCAKS Kyle Schwarber 25.00 60.00
SCAKW Kyle Waldrop 4.00 10.00
SCALG Luis Gonzalez
SCALJ Luke Jackson 3.00 8.00
SCALS Luis Severino 6.00 15.00
SCAMA Miguel Almonte 3.00 8.00
SCAMC Michael Conforto
SCAMM Mark McGwire
SCAMR Michael Reed 3.00 8.00
SCAMS Miguel Sano 10.00 25.00
SCAMT Mike Trout
SCAMW Matt Wisler 3.00 8.00
SCANG Nomar Garciaparra
SCANM Nomar Mazara 30.00 80.00
SCANS Noah Syndergaard
SCAOV Omar Vizquel 4.00 10.00
SCAPM Paul Molitor
SCAPN Phil Niekro
SCAPO Peter O'Brien 3.00 8.00
SCARCA Robinson Cano
SCARM Raul Mondesi 4.00 10.00
SCARR Rob Refsnyder 4.00 10.00
SCARS Richie Shaffer 3.00 8.00
SCASK Sandy Koufax
SCASMR Shelby Miller
SCASMZ Steven Matz 6.00 15.00
SCASP Stephen Piscotty 5.00 12.00
SCATH T.J. House 3.00 8.00
SCATMA Trevor May 3.00 8.00
SCATMY Tom Murphy 3.00 8.00
SCATS Trevor Story EXCH 20.00 50.00
SCATTR Trea Turner 20.00 50.00
SCAWD Wade Davis 3.00 8.00
SCAZL Zach Lee 3.00 8.00

2016 Stadium Club Autographs Black

*BLACK: .5X TO 1.2X BASIC
STATED PRINT RUN 50 SER.#'d SETS
EXCHANGE DEADLINE 6/30/2018
SCAAR Addison Russell 20.00 50.00
SCABP Buster Posey 50.00 120.00
SCACC Carlos Correa
SCACK Clayton Kershaw
SCACRJ Cal Ripken Jr. 50.00 120.00
SCACSE Chris Sale 15.00 40.00
SCACSR Corey Seager 50.00 120.00
SCADK Dallas Keuchel 10.00 25.00
SCAFV Fernando Valenzuela 20.00 50.00
SCAGM Greg Maddux
SCAJA Jose Altuve 25.00 60.00
SCAJG Jon Gray 10.00 25.00
SCAKB Kris Bryant 75.00 200.00
SCALG Luis Gonzalez 6.00 15.00
SCAMC Michael Conforto 15.00 40.00
SCAMM Mark McGwire
SCAMT Mike Trout
SCANG Nomar Garciaparra
SCANS Noah Syndergaard 30.00 80.00
SCAPM Paul Molitor 15.00 40.00
SCAPN Phil Niekro 10.00 25.00
SCARCA Robinson Cano
SCASK Sandy Koufax
SCASMR Shelby Miller 5.00 12.00

2016 Stadium Club Autographs Gold

*GOLD: .75X TO 2X BASIC
STATED PRINT RUN 25 SER.#'d SETS
EXCHANGE DEADLINE 6/30/2018
SCAAR Addison Russell 25.00 60.00
SCABP Buster Posey 75.00 200.00
SCACC Carlos Correa 150.00 250.00
SCACK Clayton Kershaw 125.00 250.00
SCACRJ Cal Ripken Jr. 75.00 200.00
SCACSE Chris Sale 25.00 60.00
SCACSR Corey Seager 75.00 200.00
SCADK Dallas Keuchel 15.00 40.00
SCAFV Fernando Valenzuela 30.00 80.00
SCAGM Greg Maddux 60.00 150.00
SCAJA Jose Altuve 40.00 100.00
SCAJG Jon Gray 15.00 40.00
SCAKB Kris Bryant 125.00 300.00
SCALG Luis Gonzalez 10.00 25.00
SCAMC Michael Conforto 20.00 50.00
SCAMM Mark McGwire 75.00 200.00
SCAMT Mike Trout 200.00 400.00
SCANG Nomar Garciaparra 50.00 120.00
SCANS Noah Syndergaard 50.00 120.00
SCAPM Paul Molitor 25.00 60.00
SCAPN Phil Niekro 15.00 40.00
SCARCA Robinson Cano 25.00 60.00
SCASK Sandy Koufax 300.00 500.00
SCASMR Shelby Miller 8.00 20.00

2016 Stadium Club Beam Team

COMPLETE SET (25) 25.00 60.00
*GOLD/25: 1X TO 2.5X BASIC
BT01 Carlos Correa 2.00 5.00
BT02 Kris Bryant 2.50 6.00
BT03 Mike Trout 10.00 25.00
BT04 Yu Darvish 2.00 5.00
BT05 Omar Vizquel 1.50 4.00
BT06 Don Mattingly 4.00 10.00
BT07 Robinson Cano 1.50 4.00
BT08 Yoenis Cespedes 2.00 5.00
BT09 Hector Olivera 1.50 4.00
BT10 Aaron Nola 2.50 6.00
BT11 Nomar Garciaparra 1.50 4.00
BT12 Miguel Sano 2.00 5.00
BT13 Noah Syndergaard 1.50 4.00
BT14 Corey Seager 10.00 25.00
BT15 Matt Harvey 1.50 4.00
BT16 Yadier Molina 2.00 5.00
BT17 Madison Bumgarner 1.50 4.00
BT18 Buster Posey 2.50 6.00
BT19 Bryce Harper 3.00 8.00
BT20 David Wright 1.50 4.00
BT21 Clayton Kershaw 4.00 10.00
BT22 David Ortiz 2.00 5.00
BT23 Jose Abreu 2.00 5.00
BT24 Giancarlo Stanton 2.00 5.00
BT25 Andrew McCutchen 2.00 5.00

2016 Stadium Club Contact Sheet

COMPLETE SET (10) 4.00 10.00
*WHITE/99: .75X TO 2X BASIC
*GOLD/50: 1.2X TO 3X BASIC
*ORANGE/25: 5X TO 12X BASIC
CS1 Bryce Harper 1.00 2.50
CS2 Mike Trout 3.00 8.00
CS3 Josh Donaldson .50 1.25
CS4 Albert Pujols .75 2.00
CS5 Michael Conforto .50 1.25
CS6 Kris Bryant .75 2.00
CS7 Miguel Cabrera .60 1.50
CS8 Buster Posey .75 2.00
CS9 Carlos Correa .60 1.50
CS10 Nolan Arenado .75 2.00

2016 Stadium Club Instavision

*GOLD/25: .6X TO 1.5X BASIC
IV1 Mike Trout 30.00 80.00
IV2 Kris Bryant 8.00 20.00
IV3 Buster Posey 8.00 20.00
IV4 Clayton Kershaw 12.00 30.00
IV5 Bryce Harper 10.00 25.00
IV6 Matt Harvey 5.00 12.00
IV7 Andrew McCutchen 6.00 15.00
IV8 Josh Donaldson 5.00 12.00
IV9 Carlos Correa 6.00 15.00
IV10 Yadier Molina 6.00 15.00

2016 Stadium Club ISOmetrics

COMPLETE SET (25) 15.00 40.00
*GOLD/50: 1X TO 2.5X BASIC
I1 Josh Donaldson .75 2.00
I2 Mike Trout 5.00 12.00
I3 Kevin Kiermaier .75 2.00
I4 Dallas Keuchel .75 2.00
I5 Manny Machado 1.00 2.50
I6 Ian Kinsler .75 2.00
I7 Adrian Beltre 1.00 2.50
I8 Nelson Cruz 1.00 2.50
I9 Mookie Betts 1.50 4.00
I10 Miguel Cabrera 1.00 2.50
I11 Bryce Harper 1.50 4.00
I12 Zack Greinke .75 2.00
I13 Jake Arrieta .75 2.00
I14 Kris Bryant 1.25 3.00
I15 Clayton Kershaw 2.00 5.00
I16 Carlos Correa 1.00 2.50
I17 Paul Goldschmidt 1.00 2.50
I18 Joey Votto 1.00 2.50
I19 Max Scherzer 1.00 2.50
I20 Dee Gordon .60 1.50
I21 David Price .75 2.00
I22 Chris Sale 1.00 2.50
I23 A.J. Pollock .60 1.50
I24 Buster Posey 1.25 3.00
I25 Nolan Arenado 1.25 3.00

2016 Stadium Club Legends Die Cut

COMPLETE SET (10) 15.00 40.00
*GOLD/25: 4X TO 10X BASIC
LDC1 Robin Yount 1.00 2.50
LDC2 Robin Roberts .75 2.00
LDC3 Willie McCovey .75 2.00
LDC4 Johnny Bench 1.00 2.50
LDC5 Brooks Robinson .75 2.00
LDC6 Lou Gehrig 2.00 5.00
LDC7 Whitey Ford .75 2.00
LDC8 Tom Seaver .75 2.00
LDC9 Ozzie Smith 1.25 3.00
LDC10 Reggie Jackson .75 2.00

2016 Stadium Club Lone Star Signatures

EXCHANGE DEADLINE 6/30/2018
LSSBH Bryce Harper 75.00 200.00
LSSBP Buster Posey 25.00 60.00
LSSCC Carlos Correa 60.00 150.00
LSSCK Clayton Kershaw 60.00 150.00
LSSCR Cal Ripken Jr. 60.00 150.00
LSSCS Chris Sale 25.00 60.00
LSSDW David Wright
LSSKB Kris Bryant
LSSMP Mike Piazza 50.00 120.00
LSSOV Omar Vizquel
LSSPN Phil Niekro 20.00 50.00
LSSRC Robinson Cano 20.00 50.00
LSSYD Yu Darvish 30.00 80.00

2016 Stadium Club Triumvirates Luminous

*LUMINESCENT: .6X TO 1.5X BASIC
*ILLUMINATOR: 1.5X TO 4X BASIC
T1A Buster Posey 2.00 5.00
T1B Madison Bumgarner 1.25 3.00
T1C Hunter Pence 1.25 3.00
T2A Aroldis Chapman 1.50 4.00
T2B Andrew Miller 1.25 3.00
T2C Dellin Betances 1.25 3.00
T3A Lorenzo Cain 1.00 2.50
T3B Salvador Perez 1.25 3.00
T3C Kendrys Morales 1.00 2.50
T4A Jacob deGrom 1.50 4.00
T4B Noah Syndergaard 1.25 3.00
T4C Matt Harvey 1.25 3.00
T5A Kris Bryant 2.00 5.00
T5B Kyle Schwarber 3.00 8.00
T5C Addison Russell 1.50 4.00
T6A Miguel Sano 1.50 4.00
T6B Francisco Lindor 1.50 4.00
T6C Carlos Correa 1.50 4.00
T7A Mike Trout 8.00 20.00
T7B Josh Donaldson 1.25 3.00
T7C Bryce Harper 2.50 6.00
T8A Zack Greinke 1.25 3.00
T8B Jake Arrieta 1.25 3.00
T8C Dallas Keuchel 1.25 3.00
T9A Adrian Beltre 1.50 4.00
T9B Prince Fielder 1.25 3.00
T9C Mitch Moreland 1.00 2.50
T10A Michael Wacha 1.25 3.00
T10B Adam Wainwright 1.25 3.00
T10C Trevor Rosenthal 1.25 3.00

2017 Stadium Club

COMP.SET w/o SP's (300) 40.00 100.00
SP VAR ODDS 1:72 HOBBY
1 Albert Almora .25 .60
2 Mike Moustakas .25 .60
3 Noah Syndergaard .30 .75
4A Nelson Cruz .40 1.00
4B Nelson Cruz SP w/ bat 8.00 20.00
5 Aroldis Chapman .40 1.00
6 Adam Jones .30 .75
7 C.J. Cron .25 .60
8A Yu Darvish .40 1.00
8B Clayton Kershaw SP portrait w ball in hand 8.00 20.00
9 Greg Maddux .50 1.25
10 Danny Santana .25 .60
11 Harmon Killebrew .40 1.00
12 JaCoby Jones RC .50 1.25
13 Jake Thompson .25 .60
14A Ben Zobrist .30 .75
14B Zbrst SP WS trophy 10.00 25.00
15 Jorge Soler .40 1.00
16 Matt Harvey .30 .75
17 Didi Gregorius .30 .75
18 Fernando Rodney .25 .60
19 DJ LeMahieu .40 1.00
20A Dansby Swanson RC 1.00 2.50
20B Swnsn SP Glv on hat 12.00 30.00
21 Randy Johnson .40 1.00
22 Adam Duvall .40 1.00
23 Yasmany Tomas .25 .60
24 Zack Greinke .30 .75
25 Mark Melancon .25 .60
26 Eric Hosmer .30 .75
27 David Peralta .25 .60
28 Joe Mauer .30 .75
29 John Smoltz .40 1.00
30 Danny Duffy .25 .60
31A Salvador Perez .30 .75
31B Salvador Perez SP wearing catcher's gear 8.00 20.00
32A Brandon Phillips .25 .60
32B Brandon Phillips SP front of jersey visible 6.00 15.00
33 Yadier Molina .40 1.00
34 Greg Bird .30 .75
35 Nomar Mazara .25 .60
36 Willson Contreras .40 1.00
37A Jose Bautista .30 .75
37B Jose Bautista SP w cigar and goggles 8.00 20.00
38 Robert Gsellman .25 .60
39A Bryce Harper .60 1.50
39B Hrpr SP Hat over heart 12.00 30.00
40 Jose Peraza .30 .75
41A Kris Bryant .50 1.25
41B Bryant SP w/WWE belt 10.00 25.00
42A Justin Verlander .40 1.00
42B Justin Verlander SP in batting cage 8.00 20.00
43 Jharel Cotton RC .40 1.00
44 Jacoby Ellsbury .30 .75
45 Kyle Seager .25 .60
46 Trayce Thompson .30 .75
47 Ryan Braun .30 .75
48 Tanner Roark .25 .60
49 Masahiro Tanaka .30 .75
50 Todd Frazier .30 .75
51 Travis Jankowski .25 .60
52 Jason Varitek .40 1.00
53A Anthony Rizzo .60 1.50
53B Rizzo SP WS parade 12.00 30.00
54 Kevin Pillar .25 .60
55 Hank Aaron .75 2.00
56 Ian Kinsler .30 .75
57 Josh Bell RC 1.00 2.50
58 Christian Friedrich .25 .60
59 Josh Donaldson .30 .75
60 Clay Buchholz .25 .60
61 Rod Carew .30 .75
62 Mark Trumbo .25 .60
63A Jason Heyward .30 .75
63B Jason Heyward SP unbuttoned jersey 6.00 15.00
64 Aaron Judge RC 5.00 12.00
65 Zach Britton .30 .75
66 Teoscar Hernandez RC 1.25 3.00
67 Whitey Ford .30 .75
68 Braden Shipley .25 .60
69 Jay Bruce .30 .75
70 Ken Griffey Jr. .75 2.00
71 J.T. Realmuto .40 1.00
72 Johnny Damon .30 .75
73 Julio Teheran .30 .75
74 Andrew Miller .30 .75
75A Eduardo Nunez .25 .60
75B Eduardo Nunez SP sitting down 5.00 12.00
76 Hunter Pence .30 .75
77 Rick Porcello .30 .75
78 Denard Span .25 .60
79 Matt Olson .40 1.00
80 Henry Owens .25 .60
81 Carlos Rodon .30 .75
82 Mitch Moreland .25 .60
83 Matt Strahm .25 .60
84 Chad Pinder RC .40 1.00
85 Matt Duffy .25 .60
86 Ichiro .50 1.25
87 Tony Cingrani .30 .75
88 Rickey Henderson .40 1.00
89 Hunter Renfroe RC .50 1.25
90 Matt Wieters .40 1.00
91 Pat Neshek .25 .60
92 Alex Gordon .30 .75
93 Brad Miller .30 .75
94A Carlos Correa .40 1.00
94B Correa SP w/Altuve 8.00 20.00
95 Corey Dickerson .25 .60
96 Adam Conley .25 .60
97 Troy Tulowitzki .40 1.00
98 Stephen Piscotty .30 .75
99A Paul Goldschmidt .40 1.00
99B Gldschmdt SP Pntng bat 10.00 25.00
100 Brian Dozier .40 1.00
101 Lucas Giolito .30 .75
102 Billy Wagner .25 .60
103 Gabriel Ynoa .25 .60
104 Ryon Healy RC .50 1.25
105 Ty Blach .25 .60
106 Brandon Belt .30 .75
107 Alex Reyes RC .50 1.25
108 Jorge Alfaro RC .50 1.25
109 Mallex Smith .25 .60
110 Michael Conforto .30 .75
111 Yoan Moncada RC 1.25 3.00
112 Michael Lorenzen .25 .60
113 David Price .30 .75
114A Nolan Arenado .50 1.25
114B Nolan Arenado SP face visible 10.00 25.00
115 Logan Forsythe .25 .60
116A Jose Altuve .30 .75
116B Altuve SP Portrait 12.00 30.00
117A Wil Myers .25 .60
117B Wil Myers SP standing w bat in hands 8.00 20.00
118 Yandy Diaz RC .75 2.00
119 David Wright .30 .75
120A Jon Lester .30 .75
120B Jon Lester SP holding up World Series trophy 8.00 20.00
121 Tim Anderson .40 1.00
122 Adrian Gonzalez .30 .75
123A Kyle Hendricks .40 1.00
123B Kyle Hendricks SP no hat 8.00 20.00
124 Shawn O'Malley .25 .60
125 Randal Grichuk .25 .60
126 Brooks Robinson .30 .75
127 J.J. Hardy .25 .60
128 Luis Severino .30 .75
129 Jason Kipnis .30 .75
130A Jonathan Villar .25 .60
130B Jonathan Villar SP looking towards the sky 8.00 20.00
131A Manny Machado .40 1.00
131B Machado SP In dugout 12.00 30.00
132 Scooter Gennett .30 .75
133A Jeff Bagwell .30 .75
133B Jeff Bagwell SP signing autographs 6.00 15.00
134 Carlos Gonzalez .30 .75
135 Jameson Taillon .30 .75
136 Troy Mancini RC .75 2.00
137 Derek Jeter 1.00 2.50
138 Renato Nunez RC .75 2.00
139 Marcus Stroman .30 .75
140 Miguel Cabrera .40 1.00
141 Omar Vizquel .30 .75
142 Frank Thomas .40 1.00
143 Carlos Beltran .30 .75
144 Joey Votto .40 1.00
145 Aledmys Diaz .30 .75
146 Byron Buxton .30 .75
147 Kyle Zimmer RC .40 1.00
148 Carson Fulmer RC .40 1.00
149A Andrew Benintendi RC 1.50 4.00
149B Bnntndi SP w/C.Yng 15.00 40.00
150 Felix Hernandez .30 .75
151A Tim Raines .30 .75
151B Tim Raines SP hitting off of a tee 6.00 15.00
152 Gregory Polanco .30 .75
153 Roy Oswalt .30 .75
154 Lou Gehrig .75 2.00
155 Corey Seager .40 1.00
156 Lucas Duda .25 .60
157 Gerrit Cole .40 1.00
158A Francisco Lindor .40 1.00
158B Lindor SP No hat 8.00 20.00
159 Johnny Bench .40 1.00
160 Julio Urias .40 1.00
161 Tyler Glasnow RC .50 1.25
162 Andrew McCutchen .40 1.00
163 Don Mattingly .75 2.00
164 Kenta Maeda .30 .75
165A Addison Russell .40 1.00
165B Addison Russell SP World Series hat on 8.00 20.00
166 Javier Lopez .25 .60
167 Tommy Joseph .40 1.00
168 Sandy Koufax .75 2.00
169A Matt Carpenter .40 1.00
169B Matt Carpenter SP w/ bat 8.00 20.00
170 Ryne Sandberg .75 2.00
171 Manuel Margot RC .40 1.00
172 Brandon Crawford .30 .75
173 Steven Matz .30 .75
174A Aaron Nola .30 .75
174B Aaron Nola SP stretching 6.00 15.00
175 Mark McGwire .60 1.50
176A Dustin Pedroia .40 1.00
176B Dustin Pedroia SP red jersey 8.00 20.00
177 Robinson Cano .30 .75
178 Zach McAllister .25 .60
179 Brad Ziegler .25 .60
180 A.J. Reed .25 .60
181 Nolan Ryan 1.25 3.00
182 Kevin Kiermaier .30 .75
183A Jose Abreu .40 1.00
183B Jose Abreu SP portrait w/ bat 8.00 20.00
184 Cameron Maybin .25 .60
185 Gary Carter .30 .75
186 Kendrys Morales .25 .60
187 Dexter Fowler .30 .75
188 Reynaldo Lopez RC .40 1.00
189 Justin Upton .30 .75

190 Xander Bogaerts .40 1.00
191 Cole Hamels .30 .75
192 A.J. Pollock .25 .60
193 Jackie Robinson .40 1.00
194 Andres Galarraga .30 .75
195A Alex Bregman RC 1.50 4.00
195B Brgmn SP w/Correa 20.00 50.00
196 Victor Martinez .30 .75
197 Tyler Skaggs .25 .60
198 Ryan Schimpf .25 .60
199 Roman Quinn .25 .60
200 Dave Winfield .30 .75
201A Trea Turner .30 .75
201B Turner SP Blue jrsy 6.00 15.00
202 Alex Colome .25 .60
203A Hernan Perez .25 .60
203B Hernan Perez SP w
Scooter Gennett 5.00 12.00
204A Kyle Schwarber .40 1.00
204B Schwrbr SP WS hat 8.00 20.00
205 Warren Spahn .30 .75
206 Duke Snider .30 .75
207 Charlie Blackmon .40 1.00
208 J.A. Happ .30 .75
209 Hisashi Iwakuma .30 .75
210 Garrett Richards .30 .75
211 Zach Davies .25 .60
212 Christian Yelich .50 1.25
213 Jonathan Lucroy .30 .75
214 Max Scherzer .40 1.00
215 Willie Stargell .30 .75
216 Odubel Herrera .30 .75
217 Ender Inciarte .40 1.00
218 Ozzie Smith .50 1.25
219 Aaron Sanchez .30 .75
220A Jose Berrios .30 .75
220B Jose Berrios
SP standing in hallway 6.00 15.00
221 Cal Ripken Jr. 1.25 3.00
222 Miguel Sano .30 .75
223A Jake Arrieta .30 .75
223B Jake Arrieta SP w/ David Ross 6.00 15.00
224 Drew Pomeranz .30 .75
225 Yangervis Solarte .25 .60
226 Mookie Betts .60 1.50
227 Jose Canseco .30 .75
228 Gavin Cecchini RC .40 1.00
229 Jordan Zimmermann .30 .75
230A Clayton Kershaw .75 2.00
230B Krshw SP Ball in hand 15.00 40.00
231A Giancarlo Stanton .40 1.00
231B Giancarlo Stanton SP sitting 6.00 15.00
232 Joe Musgrove RC .40 1.00
233A Mike Trout 2.00 5.00
233B Trout SP Petting dog 40.00 100.00
234 Bo Jackson .40 1.00
235 Yulieski Gurriel RC .60 1.50
236 Bobby Abreu .25 .60
237 Ervin Santana .25 .60
238A Sonny Gray .30 .75
238B Gray SP w/Hahn 10.00 25.00
239 Chris Davis .25 .60
240 Andrelton Simmons .25 .60
241 Elvis Andrus .30 .75
242 Carl Yastrzemski .60 1.50
243 Jose De Leon RC .40 1.00
244 Raimel Tapia RC .50 1.25
245 Chris Sale .40 1.00
246A Javier Baez .50 1.25
246B Baez SP WS trophy 10.00 25.00
247A Gary Sanchez .40 1.00
247B Sanchez SP Towel 8.00 20.00
248 David Ortiz .40 1.00
249 Chipper Jones .40 1.00
250 Dee Gordon .25 .60
251 Tyler Naquin .25 .60
252 Luke Weaver RC .50 1.25
253A Evan Longoria .30 .75
253B Evan Longoria SP w/ David Ortiz 8.00 20.00
254 Maikel Franco .30 .75
255 Seth Lugo RC .40 1.00
256 Michael Fulmer .25 .60
257 Daniel Murphy .30 .75
258 Stephen Vogt .30 .75
259 Adrian Beltre .40 1.00
260 Ted Williams .75 2.00
261 Luis Perdomo .25 .60
262 Joc Pederson .30 .75
263 Freddie Freeman .50 1.25
264 Rougned Odor .30 .75
265 Matt Shoemaker .30 .75
266A Starling Marte .30 .75
266B Starling Marte SP Gregory Polanco 8.00 20.00
Andrew McCutchen
267 Hunter Dozier RC .40 1.00
268A Jacob deGrom .40 1.00
268B Jacob deGrom SP
spining iPad on finger 8.00 20.00
269A Albert Pujols .50 1.25
269B Pujols SP w/Cabrera 10.00 25.00
270 Steven Wright .25 .60
271 Joe Panik .30 .75
272 Jeremy Hazelbaker .30 .75
273 A.J. Ramos .25 .60
274 Ian Desmond .25 .60
275 Stephen Strasburg .40 1.00
276 Martin Prado .25 .60
277A Billy Hamilton .30 .75
277B Billy Hamilton SP
getting cooler dumped 8.00 20.00
278A Buster Posey .50 1.25
278B Posey SP Sitting 10.00 25.00
279 Trevor Story .40 1.00
280 Ken Giles .25 .60
281 Edwin Encarnacion .40 1.00
282 Max Kepler .30 .75
283 Willie McCovey .30 .75
284 Chase Anderson .25 .60
285A Orlando Arcia RC .60 1.50
285B Orlando Arcia SP sitting w/ bat 8.00 20.00
286 David Ross .25 .60
287 Derrek Lee .25 .60
288 Tyler Austin .40 1.00
289 Reggie Jackson .30 .75
290 Jon Gray .25 .60
291 Jimmy Nelson .25 .60
292 Alex Dickerson .25 .60
293 David Dahl RC .50 1.25
294 George Springer .30 .75
295 Jayson Werth .30 .75
296 Shelby Miller .30 .75
297 Curtis Granderson .30 .75
298 Dan Vogelbach .40 1.00
299 Corey Kluber .30 .75
300 Eddie Rosario .30 .75

2017 Stadium Club Black and White Orange Foil

*BW ORNG: 5X TO 12X BASIC
*BW ORNG RC: 3X TO 8X BASIC RC
STATED ODDS 1:48 HOBBY
64 Aaron Judge 60.00 150.00
70 Ken Griffey Jr. 25.00 60.00
137 Derek Jeter 40.00 100.00
181 Nolan Ryan 20.00 50.00
221 Cal Ripken Jr. 25.00 60.00
233 Mike Trout 25.00 60.00

2017 Stadium Club Black Foil

*BLK FOIL: 1.5X TO 4X BASIC
*BLK FOIL RC: 1X TO 2.5X BASIC RC
STATED ODDS 1:8 HOBBY
64 Aaron Judge 15.00 40.00

2017 Stadium Club Gold Foil

*GLD FOIL: 1X TO 2.5X BASIC
*GLD FOIL RC: .6X TO 1.5X BASIC RC
STATED ODDS 1:3 HOBBY
64 Aaron Judge 10.00 25.00

2017 Stadium Club Rainbow Foil

*RAINBOW: 8X TO 20X BASIC
*RAINBOW RC: 5X TO 12X BASIC RC
STATED ODDS 1:96 HOBBY
STATED PRINT RUN 25 SER.#'d SETS
41 Kris Bryant 40.00 100.00
64 Aaron Judge 100.00 250.00
86 Ichiro 30.00 80.00
116 Jose Altuve 20.00 50.00
137 Derek Jeter 60.00 150.00
163 Don Mattingly 25.00 60.00
168 Sandy Koufax 40.00 100.00
181 Nolan Ryan 40.00 100.00
221 Cal Ripken Jr. 40.00 100.00
233 Mike Trout 40.00 100.00

2017 Stadium Club Sepia

*SEPIA: 1.5X TO 4X BASIC
*SEPIA RC: 1X TO 2.5X BASIC RC
INSERTED IN RETAIL PACKS
64 Aaron Judge 15.00 40.00
137 Derek Jeter 12.00 30.00
163 Don Mattingly 12.00 30.00
181 Nolan Ryan 8.00 20.00
221 Cal Ripken Jr. 15.00 40.00

2017 Stadium Club Chrome

STATED ODDS 1:16 HOBBY
SCC1 Sandy Koufax 2.50 6.00
SCC2 Hank Aaron 2.50 6.00
SCC3 Mike Trout 6.00 15.00
SCC4 Ichiro 1.50 4.00
SCC5 Bryce Harper 2.00 5.00
SCC6 Ken Griffey Jr. 2.50 6.00
SCC7 Greg Maddux 1.50 4.00
SCC8 Randy Johnson 1.25 3.00
SCC9 Buster Posey 1.50 4.00
SCC10 Cal Ripken Jr. 4.00 10.00
SCC11 Bo Jackson 1.25 3.00
SCC12 Carl Yastrzemski 2.00 5.00
SCC13 Mark McGwire 2.00 5.00
SCC14 Nolan Ryan 4.00 10.00
SCC15 Reggie Jackson 1.00 2.50
SCC16 Rickey Henderson 1.25 3.00
SCC17 Kris Bryant 1.50 4.00
SCC18 Chipper Jones 1.25 3.00
SCC19 David Ortiz 1.25 3.00
SCC20 Ryne Sandberg 2.50 6.00
SCC21 Carlos Correa 1.25 3.00
SCC22 Clayton Kershaw 2.50 6.00
SCC23 Don Mattingly 2.50 6.00
SCC24 Frank Thomas 1.25 3.00
SCC25 Ryan Braun 1.00 2.50
SCC26 David Wright 1.00 2.50
SCC27 Corey Seager 1.25 3.00
SCC28 Bobby Abreu .75 2.00
SCC29 John Smoltz 1.25 3.00
SCC30 Ozzie Smith 1.50 4.00
SCC31 David Price 1.00 2.50
SCC32 Dustin Pedroia 1.25 3.00
SCC33 Manny Machado 1.25 3.00
SCC34 Yoan Moncada 2.50 6.00
SCC35 Freddie Freeman 1.50 4.00
SCC36 Chris Sale 1.25 3.00
SCC37 Jacob deGrom 1.25 3.00
SCC38 Kenta Maeda 1.00 2.50
SCC39 Anthony Rizzo 2.00 5.00
SCC40 Nolan Arenado 1.50 4.00
SCC41 Julio Urias 1.25 3.00
SCC42 Kyle Schwarber 1.25 3.00
SCC43 Noah Syndergaard 1.00 2.50
SCC44 Addison Russell 1.25 3.00
SCC45 Albert Almora .75 2.00
SCC46 Dexter Fowler 1.00 2.50
SCC47 Francisco Lindor 1.25 3.00
SCC48 Jose Altuve 1.00 2.50
SCC49 Matt Carpenter 1.25 3.00
SCC50 Dansby Swanson 2.00 5.00
SCC51 Yulieski Gurriel 1.25 3.00
SCC52 Sonny Gray 1.00 2.50
SCC53 Jameson Taillon 1.00 2.50
SCC54 Lucas Giolito 1.00 2.50
SCC55 Miguel Sano 1.00 2.50
SCC56 Joc Pederson 1.00 2.50
SCC57 Alex Bregman 3.00 8.00
SCC58 Hunter Dozier .75 2.00
SCC59 Andres Galarraga 1.00 2.50
SCC60 Kyle Seager .75 2.00
SCC61 Omar Vizquel 1.00 2.50
SCC62 George Springer 1.00 2.50
SCC63 Kendrys Morales .75 2.00
SCC64 Starling Marte 1.00 2.50
SCC65 Trevor Story 1.25 3.00
SCC66 David Dahl 1.00 2.50
SCC67 Alex Reyes 1.00 2.50
SCC68 Tyler Glasnow 1.00 2.50
SCC69 Roy Oswalt 1.00 2.50
SCC70 Steven Matz 1.00 2.50
SCC71 Trea Turner 1.00 2.50
SCC72 Willson Contreras 1.25 3.00
SCC73 Stephen Piscotty 1.00 2.50
SCC74 Greg Bird 1.00 2.50
SCC75 Randal Grichuk .75 2.00
SCC76 Aaron Judge 10.00 25.00
SCC77 Andrew Benintendi 2.50 6.00
SCC78 Luke Weaver 1.00 2.50
SCC79 Jose De Leon .75 2.00
SCC80 Aaron Nola 1.00 2.50
SCC81 Aledmys Diaz 1.00 2.50
SCC82 Gavin Cecchini .75 2.00
SCC83 Jharel Cotton .75 2.00
SCC84 Joe Musgrove .75 2.00
SCC85 Jose Canseco 1.00 2.50
SCC86 Tim Anderson 1.25 3.00
SCC87 Ryon Healy 1.00 2.50
SCC88 Michael Fulmer .75 2.00
SCC89 Jeff Bagwell 1.00 2.50
SCC90 Tim Raines 1.00 2.50

2017 Stadium Club Chrome Refractors

*REF: 1X TO 2.5X BASIC
STATED ODDS 1:64 HOBBY
SCC76 Aaron Judge 25.00 60.00

2017 Stadium Club Contact Sheet

COMPLETE SET (15) 8.00 20.00
STATED ODDS 1:8 HOBBY
*GOLD: .75X TO 2X BASIC
*BLACK/99: 1.2X TO 3X BASIC
*ORANGE/50: 2.5X TO 6X BASIC
CSAB Alex Bregman 1.50 4.00
CSAR Addison Russell .60 1.50
CSCC Carlos Correa .60 1.50
CSDL DJ LeMahieu .60 1.50
CSDM Daniel Murphy .50 1.25
CSGS Giancarlo Stanton .60 1.50
CSI Ichiro .75 2.00
CSJA Jose Altuve .50 1.25
CSJB Jose Bautista .50 1.25
CSJD Josh Donaldson .50 1.25
CSJV Joey Votto .60 1.50
CSMB Mookie Betts 1.00 2.50
CSMC Miguel Cabrera .60 1.50
CSMT Mike Trout 3.00 8.00
CSRC Robinson Cano .50 1.25

2017 Stadium Club Instavision

STATED ODDS 1:256 HOBBY
*GOLD/50: .6X TO 1.5X BASIC
*BLACK/25: .75X TO 2X BASIC
IAJ Aaron Judge 30.00 80.00
IBH Bryce Harper 6.00 15.00
ICK Clayton Kershaw 8.00 20.00
IDJ Derek Jeter 12.00 30.00
IFL Francisco Lindor 4.00 10.00
IHA Hank Aaron 8.00 20.00
IKB Kris Bryant 15.00 40.00
IMB Mookie Betts 6.00 15.00
IMF Michael Fulmer 6.00 15.00
IMT Mike Trout 15.00 40.00

2017 Stadium Club Lone Star Signatures

STATED ODDS 1:1593 HOBBY
PRINT RUNS B/WN 10-25 COPIES PER
NO PRICING ON QTY 15 OR LESS
EXCHANGE DEADLINE 5/31/2019
LSSAG Andres Galarraga/25
LSSAR Anthony Rizzo/25 25.00 60.00
LSSCS Corey Seager/25 50.00 120.00
LSSDO David Ortiz
LSSJC Jose Canseco/25 25.00 60.00
LSSKB Kris Bryant EXCH
LSSOV Omar Vizquel/25 25.00 60.00

2017 Stadium Club Power Zone

STATED ODDS 1:8 HOBBY
*GOLD: .75X TO 2X BASIC
*BLACK/99: 1.2X TO 3X BASIC
*ORANGE/50: 2.5X TO 6X BASIC
PZAB Adrian Beltre .60 1.50
PZAG Andres Galarraga .50 1.25
PZAP Albert Pujols .75 2.00
PZAR Anthony Rizzo 1.00 2.50
PZBH Bryce Harper 1.00 2.50
PZBJ Bo Jackson .60 1.50
PZCJ Chipper Jones .60 1.50
PZCS Corey Seager .60 1.50
PZDO David Ortiz .60 1.50
PZEE Edwin Encarnacion .60 1.50
PZFF Freddie Freeman .75 2.00
PZFT Frank Thomas .60 1.50
PZGS Giancarlo Stanton .60 1.50
PZJC Jose Canseco .50 1.25
PZJD Josh Donaldson .50 1.25
PZKB Kris Bryant .75 2.00
PZKG Ken Griffey Jr. 1.25 3.00
PZMC Miguel Cabrera .60 1.50
PZMM Manny Machado .60 1.50
PZMMC Mark McGwire 1.00 2.50
PZMT Mike Trout 3.00 8.00
PZNA Nolan Arenado .75 2.00
PZRB Ryan Braun .50 1.25
PZRC Robinson Cano .50 1.25
PZYC Yoenis Cespedes .60 1.50

2017 Stadium Club Scoreless Streak

COMPLETE SET (25) 10.00 25.00
STATED ODDS 1:8 HOBBY
*GOLD: .75X TO 2X BASIC
*BLACK/99: 1.2X TO 3X BASIC
*ORANGE/50: 2.5X TO 6X BASIC
SSAC Aroldis Chapman .60 1.50
SSAN Aaron Nola .50 1.25
SSAR Alex Reyes .50 1.25
SSCK Clayton Kershaw 1.25 3.00
SSCKR Corey Kluber .50 1.25
SSCM Carlos Martinez .50 1.25
SSCS Chris Sale .60 1.50
SSDP David Price .50 1.25
SSFH Felix Hernandez .50 1.25
SSJA Jake Arrieta .50 1.25
SSJC Johnny Cueto .50 1.25
SSJD Jacob deGrom .60 1.50
SSJL Jon Lester .50 1.25
SSJU Julio Urias .60 1.50
SSJV Justin Verlander .60 1.50
SSKM Kenta Maeda .50 1.25
SSMF Michael Fulmer .40 1.00
SSMS Max Scherzer .60 1.50
SSMSN Marcus Stroman .50 1.25
SSMT Masahiro Tanaka .50 1.25
SSNS Noah Syndergaard .50 1.25
SSSG Sonny Gray .50 1.25
SSSS Stephen Strasburg .60 1.50
SSYD Yu Darvish .60 1.50
SSZG Zack Greinke .50 1.25

2017 Stadium Club Autographs

STATED ODDS 1:10 HOBBY
EXCHANGE DEADLINE 5/31/2019
SCAAB Andrew Benintendi 25.00 60.00
SCAABN Alex Bregman 12.00 30.00
SCAAD Aledmys Diaz 4.00 10.00
SCAAGA Andres Galarraga 4.00 10.00
SCAAJE Aaron Judge 75.00 200.00
SCAAN Aaron Nola 5.00 12.00
SCAAR Alex Reyes 5.00 12.00
SCAARD A.J. Reed 3.00 8.00
SCABA Bobby Abreu 6.00 15.00
SCABH Bryce Harper
SCABP Buster Posey
SCABS Braden Shipley EXCH 3.00 8.00
SCABW Billy Wagner 5.00 12.00
SCACA Christian Arroyo EXCH 15.00 40.00
SCACC Carlos Correa
SCACF Carson Fulmer 3.00 8.00
SCACS Corey Seager
SCADJ Derek Jeter
SCADL Derrek Lee 3.00 8.00
SCADS Dansby Swanson
SCADV Dan Vogelbach 5.00 12.00
SCAFL Francisco Lindor 15.00 40.00
SCAGB Greg Bird 4.00 10.00
SCAGC Gavin Cecchini 3.00 8.00
SCAHA Hank Aaron
SCAHD Hunter Dozier 5.00 12.00
SCAHO Henry Owens 3.00 8.00
SCAI Ichiro
SCAJA Jose Altuve EXCH 25.00 60.00
SCAJAO Jorge Alfaro 4.00 10.00
SCAJBZ Javier Baez 12.00 30.00
SCAJC Jharel Cotton 3.00 8.00
SCAJCO Jose Canseco 6.00 15.00
SCAJDN Johnny Damon
SCAJH Jeremy Hazelbaker 4.00 10.00
SCAJM Joe Musgrove 3.00 8.00
SCAJTN Jake Thompson 3.00 8.00
SCAJU Julio Urias EXCH 6.00 15.00
SCAJV Jason Varitek
SCAKB Kris Bryant
SCAKS Kyle Schwarber EXCH
SCAKSR Kyle Seager 3.00 8.00
SCALW Luke Weaver 4.00 10.00
SCAMC Matt Carpenter 8.00 20.00
SCAMO Matt Olson EXCH 10.00 25.00
SCAMSM Matt Strahm 3.00 8.00
SCAMT Mike Trout
SCAOV Omar Vizquel 5.00 12.00
SCARGN Robert Gsellman 3.00 8.00
SCARHY Ryon Healy 4.00 10.00
SCARL Reynaldo Lopez 3.00 8.00
SCARO Roy Oswalt 12.00 30.00
SCARQ Roman Quinn 3.00 8.00
SCARSF Ryan Schimpf 3.00 8.00
SCART Raimel Tapia 4.00 10.00
SCASK Sandy Koufax
SCASL Seth Lugo 3.00 8.00
SCASW Steven Wright 3.00 8.00
SCATA Tyler Austin 5.00 12.00
SCATAN Tim Anderson 5.00 12.00
SCATB Ty Blach 3.00 8.00
SCATC Tim Cooney 3.00 8.00
SCATG Tyler Glasnow EXCH 4.00 10.00
SCATH Teoscar Hernandez 10.00 25.00
SCATM Trey Mancini 6.00 15.00
SCATN Tyler Naquin 3.00 8.00
SCAYG Yulieski Gurriel 10.00 25.00
SCAYMA Yoan Moncada

2017 Stadium Club Autographs Black Foil

*BLACK: .75X TO 2X BASIC
STATED ODDS 1:256 HOBBY
STATED PRINT RUN 25 SER.#'d SETS
EXCHANGE DEADLINE 5/31/2019
SCACS Corey Seager 40.00 100.00

2017 Stadium Club Autographs Gold Foil

*GOLD: .5X TO 1.2X BASIC
STATED ODDS 1:140 HOBBY
STATED PRINT RUN 50 SER.#'d SETS
EXCHANGE DEADLINE 5/31/2019
SCADS Dansby Swanson 40.00 100.00
SCAFL Francisco Lindor 25.00 60.00

2017 Stadium Club Autographs Mystery Redemption

EXCHANGE DEADLINE 5/31/2019
SCACB Cody Bellinger 75.00 200.00
SCAIH Ian Happ 75.00 200.00

2017 Stadium Club Beam Team

STATED ODDS 1:16 HOBBY
*GOLD: 1X TO 2.5X BASIC
*BLACK/99: 1.2X TO 3X BASIC
*ORANGE/50: 2.5X TO 6X BASIC
BTAB Andrew Benintendi 1.50 4.00
BTAR Anthony Rizzo 1.25 3.00
BTARL Addison Russell .75 2.00
BTBH Bryce Harper 1.25 3.00
BTBP Buster Posey 1.00 2.50
BTCC Carlos Correa .75 2.00
BTCK Clayton Kershaw 1.50 4.00
BTCS Corey Seager .75 2.00
BTDJ Derek Jeter 2.00 5.00
BTDP Dustin Pedroia .75 2.00
BTDS Dansby Swanson 1.25 3.00
BTFF Freddie Freeman 1.00 2.50
BTFL Francisco Lindor .75 2.00
BTGS Gary Sanchez .75 2.00
BTJA Jose Altuve .60 1.50
BTJD Jacob deGrom .75 2.00
BTJU Julio Urias .75 2.00
BTJV Justin Verlander .75 2.00
BTKB Kris Bryant 1.00 2.50
BTKS Kyle Schwarber .75 2.00
BTMM Manny Machado .75 2.00
BTMT Mike Trout 4.00 10.00
BTNA Nolan Arenado 1.00 2.50
BTNS Noah Syndergaard .60 1.50
BTRC Robinson Cano .60 1.50

2018 Stadium Club

COMPLETE SET (300) 25.00 60.00
1 Sandy Alcantara RC .20 .50
2 Miguel Cabrera .30 .75
3 Clint Frazier RC .60 1.50
4 Darryl Strawberry .20 .50
5 Johnny Cueto .25 .60
6 Carlos Gonzalez .25 .60
7 Alex Mejia RC .30 .75
8 Starlin Castro .20 .50
9 Zack Godley .20 .50
10 Matt Kemp .25 .60
11 Tzu-Wei Lin .25 .60
12 Andrew McCutchen .30 .75
13 Justin Bour .30 .75
14 Daniel Murphy .25 .60
15 Hanley Ramirez .25 .60
16 Carlos Rodon .25 .60
17 Zack Granite RC .25 .60
18 Christian Villanueva RC .30 .75
19 Garrett Richards .25 .60
20 Stephen Strasburg .30 .75
21 Robinson Cano .25 .60
22 Kevin Kiermaier .25 .60
23 Carlos Martinez .25 .60
24 Carlos Santana .25 .60
25 Marcell Ozuna .30 .75
26 Niko Goodrum RC .50 1.25
27 Michael Conforto .25 .60
28 Billy Hamilton .25 .60
29 Johnny Bench .30 .75
30 Javier Baez .40 1.00
31 Jose Quintana .20 .50
32 Carlos Correa .30 .75
33 Evan Longoria .25 .60
34 Manny Margot .20 .50
35 Marcus Stroman .25 .60
36 Gerrit Cole .30 .75
37 Victor Robles RC .75 2.00
38 Jake Arrieta .25 .60
39 Wil Myers .25 .60
40 Justin Smoak .20 .50
41 Corey Kluber .25 .60
42 Jacob deGrom .30 .75
43 Michael Fulmer .20 .50
44 Matt Olson .20 .50
45 J.P. Crawford RC .30 .75
46 Dallas Keuchel .25 .60
47 Matt Carpenter .30 .75
48 Mike Trout 1.50 4.00
49 Mike Moustakas .25 .60
50 Adam Jones .25 .60
51 Taijuan Walker .20 .50
52 Paul Goldschmidt .30 .75
53 Jake Lamb .25 .60
54 Masahiro Tanaka .25 .60
55 Lucas Giolito .25 .60
56 Jon Lester .25 .60
57 Luiz Gohara RC .30 .75
58 Francisco Lindor .30 .75
59 Yonder Alonso .20 .50
60 Aaron Altherr .20 .50
61 Anthony Rendon .30 .75
62 Tyler Glasnow .20 .50
63 Ian Kinsler .25 .60
64 Ender Inciarte .20 .50
65 Andrelton Simmons .20 .50
66 Jose Ramirez .25 .60
67 A.J. Minter RC .40 1.00
68 Ozzie Smith .40 1.00
69 Max Scherzer .30 .75
70 Noah Syndergaard .25 .60
71 Chris Sale .30 .75
72 Bo Jackson .30 .75
73 George Springer .25 .60
74 Ichiro .40 1.00
75 Ryne Sandberg .60 1.50
76 Eddie Rosario .30 .75
77 Paul Blackburn RC .30 .75
78 Yoenis Cespedes .30 .75
79 Mike Clevinger .25 .60
80 Andy Pettitte .25 .60
81 Will Clark .25 .60
82 Felix Jorge RC .30 .75
83 Joey Votto .30 .75
84 Nicky Delmonico RC .30 .75
85 Josh Reddick .20 .50
86 Dansby Swanson .30 .75
87 Nicholas Castellanos .30 .75
88 Andrew Stevenson RC .30 .75
89 Brandon Woodruff RC .40 1.00
90 Jose Canseco .25 .60
91 Dustin Fowler RC .30 .75
92 Kyle Farmer RC .30 .75
93 Nick Williams RC .40 1.00
94 Justin Upton .25 .60
95 Yasiel Puig .30 .75
96 J.D. Martinez .30 .75
97 Miguel Sano .25 .60
98 Jon Gray .20 .50
99 Jay Bruce .25 .60
100 Cam Gallagher RC .30 .75
101 Jack Flaherty RC .50 1.25
102 Richard Urena RC .30 .75
103 Tim Raines .25 .60
104 Hunter Renfroe .20 .50
105 Tomas Nido RC .30 .75
106 Austin Barnes .25 .60
107 Keon Broxton .20 .50
108 Erick Fedde RC .30 .75
109 Whit Merrifield .30 .75
110 Ozzie Albies RC 1.00 2.50
111 Cody Bellinger .60 1.50
112 Robbie Ray .20 .50
113 Tommy Pham .20 .50
114 Victor Caratini RC .40 1.00
115 Greg Allen RC .30 .75
116 Rougned Odor .20 .50
117 Rafael Devers RC 1.00 2.50
118 Xander Bogaerts .30 .75
119 Mitch Haniger .25 .60
120 Breyvic Valera RC .30 .75
121 Ryder Jones RC .30 .75
122 Chris Davis .20 .50
123 Craig Kimbrel .25 .60
124 Trevor Bauer .30 .75
125 Chipper Jones .30 .75
126 Max Kepler .25 .60
127 Yadier Molina .30 .75
128 Jose Berrios .25 .60
129 Manny Machado .30 .75
130 Eric Hosmer .25 .60
131 Matt Chapman .30 .75
132 Tyler Mahle RC .40 1.00
133 Nolan Ryan 1.00 2.50
134 Lucas Sims RC .30 .75
135 Chance Sisco RC .40 1.00
136 Christian Yelich .40 1.00
137 Josh Harrison .20 .50
138 Shohei Ohtani RC 2.00 5.00
139 Garrett Cooper RC .30 .75
140 Miguel Andujar RC 1.25 3.00
141 Jim Thome .25 .60
142 Chris Taylor .25 .60
143 Tim Locastro RC .30 .75
144 Luis Castillo .25 .60
145 Giancarlo Stanton .30 .75
146 Lance McCullers .20 .50
147 Ryan McMahon RC .40 1.00
148 Todd Frazier .25 .60
149 John Smoltz .30 .75
150 Justin Verlander .30 .75
151 Justin Turner .25 .60
152 Dwight Gooden .20 .50
153 Cameron Maybin .20 .50
154 Brandon Crawford .25 .60
155 Francisco Mejia RC .40 1.00
156 German Marquez .20 .50
157 Brett Gardner .25 .60
158 Dillon Maples RC .30 .75
159 Trey Mancini .25 .60
160 Cal Ripken Jr. 1.00 2.50
161 Rickey Henderson .30 .75
162 Brad Ziegler .20 .50
163 Ryan Zimmerman .25 .60
164 Barry Larkin .25 .60
165 Anthony Rizzo .50 1.25
166 Wade Boggs .25 .60
167 Dexter Fowler .25 .60
168 Chris Archer .20 .50
169 Trea Turner .25 .60
170 J.D. Davis RC .40 1.00
171 Don Mattingly .60 1.50
172 CC Sabathia .25 .60
173 Anthony Banda RC .30 .75
174 Kenley Jansen .25 .60
175 Mookie Betts .50 1.25
176 Dennis Eckersley .25 .60
177 Sean Newcomb .25 .60
178 Andrew Benintendi .30 .75
179 Bryce Harper .50 1.25
180 Ted Williams .60 1.50
181 Roberto Clemente .75 2.00
182 Aroldis Chapman .30 .75
183 Elvis Andrus .25 .60
184 Jeff Bagwell .25 .60
185 Jose Abreu .30 .75
186 Greg Bird .25 .60
187 Dustin Pedroia .30 .75
188 Bob Gibson .25 .60
189 Lewis Brinson .20 .50
190 Ian Happ .25 .60
191 Raisel Iglesias .25 .60
192 Buster Posey .40 1.00
193 Joc Pederson .25 .60
194 Joe Mauer .25 .60
195 Sonny Gray .25 .60
196 Pat Neshek .20 .50
197 Rhys Hoskins RC 1.25 3.00
198 Keury Mella RC .30 .75
199 Joey Gallo .25 .60
200 Jackie Robinson .30 .75
201 Kris Bryant .40 1.00
202 Yoan Moncada .30 .75
203 Zack Cozart .20 .50
204 Charlie Blackmon .30 .75
205 Austin Hays RC .50 1.25
206 Cole Hamels .25 .60
207 Nelson Cruz .30 .75
208 Greg Maddux .40 1.00
209 Dillon Peters RC .30 .75
210 Victor Arano RC .30 .75
211 Luis Severino .25 .60
212 Corey Seager .30 .75
213 Didi Gregorius .25 .60
214 Parker Bridwell RC .30 .75
215 Willson Contreras .30 .75
216 Anthony Santander RC .30 .75
217 Max Fried RC 1.25 3.00
218 Jimmie Sherfy RC .30 .75
219 Josh Donaldson .25 .60
220 Walker Buehler RC 1.50 4.00
221 Ryan Braun .25 .60
222 Domingo Santana .25 .60
223 Hank Aaron .60 1.50
224 Josh Hader .20 .50
225 Lorenzo Cain .20 .50
226 Starling Marte .25 .60
227 Andrew Miller .25 .60
228 Frank Thomas .30 .75
229 Paul DeJong .30 .75
230 Archie Bradley .20 .50
231 Julio Urias .30 .75
232 Freddie Freeman .40 1.00
233 Troy Scribner RC .30 .75
234 Adrian Beltre .25 .60
235 Orlando Arcia .20 .50
236 Albert Pujols .40 1.00
237 Kyle Seager .20 .50
238 Zach Davies .20 .50
239 Edwin Encarnacion .30 .75
240 David Price .25 .60
241 Aaron Judge .75 2.00
242 George Brett .60 1.50
243 Adam Duvall .30 .75
244 Yu Darvish .30 .75
245 Byron Buxton .25 .60
246 Alex Bregman .30 .75
247 Josh Bell .25 .60
248 Mariano Rivera .40 1.00
249 Nomar Mazara .20 .50
250 Mike Foltynewicz .20 .50
251 Dee Gordon .20 .50
252 Felix Hernandez .25 .60
253 Aaron Nola .25 .60
254 Jorge Alfaro .20 .50
255 Gregory Polanco .25 .60
256 Reggie Jackson .25 .60
257 Gary Sanchez .30 .75
258 Kenta Maeda .25 .60
259 Eric Thames .20 .50
260 Amed Rosario RC .40 1.00
261 Hunter Pence .25 .60
262 Randy Johnson .30 .75
263 Willie Calhoun RC .40 1.00
264 Alex Wood .20 .50
265 Travis Shaw .20 .50
266 Alex Verdugo RC .50 1.25
267 Avisail Garcia .25 .60
268 A.J. Pollock .25 .60
269 Zack Greinke .25 .60
270 Carlos Carrasco .20 .50
271 Jose Altuve .25 .60
272 Salvador Perez .25 .60
273 Kyle Schwarber .30 .75

74 Dominic Smith RC .30 .75
75 Derek Jeter .75 2.00
76 Clayton Kershaw .60 1.50
77 Yuli Gurriel .25 .60
78 Marwin Gonzalez .20 .50
79 Brian Anderson RC .40 1.00
80 Harrison Bader RC .50 1.25
81 Brian Dozier .25 .60
82 Mark McGwire .50 1.25
83 Jonathan Schoop .20 .50
84 Tyler Wade RC .40 1.00
85 Mike Piazza .30 .75
86 Addison Russell .25 .60
87 J.T. Realmuto .30 .75
88 Sandy Koufax .60 1.50
89 Jason Heyward .25 .60
90 Nolan Arenado .40 1.00
91 Edwin Diaz .25 .60
92 Jen-Ho Tseng RC .30 .75
93 Jackie Bradley Jr. .30 .75
94 Sean Manaea .20 .50
95 Mitch Garver RC .30 .75
96 Jackson Stephens RC .30 .75
97 Khris Davis .30 .75
98 Tim Beckham .25 .60
99 Trevor Story .30 .75
100 Hideki Matsui .30 .75

2018 Stadium Club Black and White Orange Foil

*BW ORNG: 5X TO 12X BASIC
*BW ORNG RC: 3X TO 8X BASIC RC
STATED ODDS 1:48 HOBBY

2018 Stadium Club Black Foil

*BLK FOIL: 1.5X TO 4X BASIC
*BLK FOIL RC: 1X TO 2.5X BASIC RC
STATED ODDS 1:8 HOBBY

2018 Stadium Club Rainbow Foil

*RAINBOW: 8X TO 20X BASIC
*RAINBOW RC: 5X TO 12X BASIC RC
STATED ODDS 1:145 HOBBY
STATED PRINT RUN 25 SER.#'d SETS

2018 Stadium Club Red Foil

*RED FOIL: 1X TO 2.5X BASIC
*RED FOIL RC: .6X TO 1.5X BASIC RC
STATED ODDS 1:3 HOBBY

2018 Stadium Club Sepia

*SEPIA: 2X TO 5X BASIC
*SEPIA RC: 1.2X TO 3X BASIC RC
INSERTED IN RETAIL PACKS

2018 Stadium Club Photo Variations

STATED ODDS 1:109 HOBBY
Frazier Jumping 10.00 25.00
2 Correa WS Celebrtn 8.00 20.00
7 Robles Bat 12.00 30.00
48 Trout Running 40.00 100.00
52 Gldschmdt Wht jsy 8.00 20.00
58 Lindor Diving 25.00 60.00
59 Scherzer Red jsy 15.00 40.00
70 Syndergaard Throwing 6.00 15.00
71 Sale Bullpen 20.00 50.00
72 Jackson Brkng Bat 25.00 60.00
81 Clark Jsy back 30.00 80.00
83 Votto Fielding 8.00 20.00
100 Ripken w Mascot 60.00 150.00
111 Bellinger Running 15.00 40.00
17 Devers Red jsy 15.00 40.00
125 Jones Bubble 8.00 20.00
129 Machado Towel 8.00 20.00
33 Ryan Wht jsu 25.00 60.00
138 Ohtani Pitching 40.00 100.00
145 Stanton Cage 8.00 20.00
150 Vrlndr Jsy back 8.00 20.00
165 Rizzo Fielding 15.00 40.00
169 Turner Bunting 10.00 25.00
171 Mtngly Gray jsy 12.00 30.00
175 Betts Flag 25.00 60.00
178 Benintendi Catching 8.00 20.00
179 Harper High-five 25.00 60.00
180 Williams Color 15.00 40.00
181 Clemente Elastic 15.00 40.00
192 Posey Sliding 10.00 25.00
197 Hoskins Sunglasses 20.00 50.00
200 Robinson Running 8.00 20.00
201 Bryant Batting 15.00 40.00
213 Gleyber Torres 100.00 250.00
223A Aaron Running 15.00 40.00
223B Ronald Acuna 100.00 250.00
228 Thomas Cage 8.00 20.00
241 Judge Bat 50.00 120.00
242 Brett Blue jsy 25.00 60.00
244 Darvish Pnstrp jsy 8.00 20.00
248 Rivera Ball 10.00 25.00
260 Rosario Batting 20.00 50.00
262 Johnson Batting 15.00 40.00
271 Altuve Batting 6.00 15.00
275 Jeter Jumping 30.00 80.00
276 Kershaw w Kids 15.00 40.00
282 McGwire Grn jsy 12.00 30.00
285 Piazza Gear 8.00 20.00
288 Koufax Color 40.00 100.00
290 Arenado Pstripe jsy 10.00 25.00

2018 Stadium Club Autographs

STATED ODDS 1:10 HOBBY
EXCHANGE DEADLINE 5/30/2020
*RED/50: .5X TO 1.2X BASIC
*BLACK/25: .6X TO 1.5X BASIC
SCAAA Aaron Altherr 4.00 10.00
SCAAB Anthony Banda 3.00 8.00
SCAABA Austin Barnes 4.00 10.00
SCAAH Austin Hays 6.00 15.00
SCAAME Alex Mejia 3.00 8.00
SCAAMI A.J. Minter 4.00 10.00
SCAAR Anthony Rizzo 20.00 50.00
SCAARO Amed Rosario 4.00 10.00
SCAAS Anthony Santander 3.00 8.00
SCAAST Andrew Stevenson 3.00 8.00
SCAAW Alex Wood 3.00 8.00
SCABH Bryce Harper
SCABJ Bo Jackson
SCABV Breyvic Valera 3.00 8.00
SCABW Brandon Woodruff 4.00 10.00
SCACG Cam Gallagher 3.00 8.00
SCACS Carlos Santana 6.00 15.00
SCACT Chris Taylor 4.00 10.00
SCACV Christian Villanueva 3.00 8.00
SCADF Dustin Fowler 3.00 8.00
SCADG Dwight Gooden 8.00 20.00
SCADJ Derek Jeter
SCADM Don Mattingly 60.00 150.00
SCADMA Dillon Maples 3.00 8.00
SCADSM Dominic Smith 3.00 8.00
SCADST Darryl Strawberry 10.00 25.00
SCAFL Francisco Lindor 15.00 40.00
SCAFM Francisco Mejia 6.00 15.00
SCAFT Frank Thomas 40.00 100.00
SCAGA Greg Allen 3.00 8.00
SCAGC Garrett Cooper 3.00 8.00
SCAGT Gleyber Torres 75.00 200.00
SCAHA Hank Aaron 100.00 250.00
SCAHB Harrison Bader 8.00 20.00
SCAIH Ian Happ 8.00 20.00
SCAI Ichiro
SCAJA Jose Altuve 40.00 100.00
SCAJBE Jose Berrios 4.00 10.00
SCAJBO Justin Bour 3.00 8.00
SCAJC Jose Canseco 10.00 25.00
SCAJD J.D. Davis 4.00 10.00
SCAJF Jack Flaherty 15.00 40.00
SCAJH Jose Ramirez 10.00 25.00
SCAJS Jimmie Sherfy 3.00 8.00
SCAJST Jackson Stephens 3.00 8.00
SCAJV Joey Votto 40.00 100.00
SCAKB Kris Bryant
SCAKBR Keon Broxton 5.00 12.00
SCAKD Khris Davis 6.00 15.00
SCAKF Kyle Farmer 3.00 8.00
SCAKM Keury Mella 3.00 8.00
SCAKS Kyle Schwarber 10.00 25.00
SCALC Luis Castillo 4.00 10.00
SCAMA Miguel Andujar 10.00 25.00
SCAMFR Max Fried 6.00 15.00
SCAMIG Miguel Gomez 3.00 8.00
SCAMM Manny Machado 25.00 60.00
SCAMMC Mark McGwire 30.00 80.00
SCAMO Matt Olson 3.00 8.00
SCAMT Mike Trout 250.00 400.00
SCAND Nicky Delmonico 3.00 8.00
SCANG Niko Goodrum 5.00 12.00
SCANR Nolan Ryan 75.00 200.00
SCANSY Noah Syndergaard 15.00 40.00
SCAOA Ozzie Albies 20.00 50.00
SCAPB Paul Blackburn 3.00 8.00
SCAPD Paul DeJong 5.00 12.00
SCAPE Phillip Evans 3.00 8.00
SCAPG Paul Goldschmidt 20.00 50.00
SCARA Ronald Acuna 150.00 400.00
SCARD Rafael Devers 30.00 80.00
SCARH Rhys Hoskins 15.00 40.00
SCARJ Ryder Jones 3.00 8.00
SCARR Raudy Read 3.00 8.00
SCARU Richard Urena 3.00 8.00
SCASA Sandy Alcantara 3.00 8.00
SCASG Sonny Gray 10.00 25.00
SCASN Sean Newcomb 4.00 10.00
SCASO Shohei Ohtani EXCH 200.00 400.00
SCATB Tim Beckham 4.00 10.00
SCATL Tzu-Wei Lin 4.00 10.00
SCATLO Tim Locastro 3.00 8.00
SCATMA Trey Mancini 4.00 10.00
SCATN Tomas Nido 3.00 8.00
SCATP Tommy Pham 3.00 8.00
SCATS Troy Scribner 3.00 8.00
SCATW Tyler Wade 4.00 10.00
SCAVA Victor Arano 3.00 8.00
SCAVC Victor Caratini 4.00 10.00
SCAVR Victor Robles 10.00 25.00
SCAWCO Willson Contreras 10.00 25.00
SCAWM Whit Merrifield 8.00 20.00
SCAYA Yonder Alonso 3.00 8.00

2018 Stadium Club Beam Team

STATED ODDS 1:16 HOBBY
BTAB Andrew Benintendi .75 2.00
BTAJ Aaron Judge 2.00 5.00
BTAR Anthony Rizzo 1.25 3.00
BTARO Amed Rosario .60 1.50
BTBH Bryce Harper 1.25 3.00
BTCB Cody Bellinger 1.50 4.00
BTCC Carlos Correa .75 2.00
BTCF Clint Frazier 1.00 2.50
BTCK Clayton Kershaw 1.50 4.00
BTCS Corey Seager .75 2.00
BTDJ Derek Jeter 2.00 5.00
BTFL Francisco Lindor .75 2.00
BTGS Gary Sanchez .75 2.00
BTGST Giancarlo Stanton .75 2.00
BTJA Jose Altuve .60 1.50
BTJV Joey Votto .75 2.00
BTKB Kris Bryant 1.00 2.50
BTMB Mookie Betts 1.25 3.00
BTMM Manny Machado .75 2.00
BTMT Mike Trout 4.00 10.00
BTNS Noah Syndergaard .60 1.50
BTPG Paul Goldschmidt .75 2.00
BTRD Rafael Devers 1.50 4.00
BTRH Rhys Hoskins 2.00 5.00
BTSO Shohei Ohtani 3.00 8.00

2018 Stadium Club Beam Team Black

*BLACK: 1.2X TO 3X BASIC
STATED ODDS 1:438 HOBBY
STATED PRINT RUN 99 SER.#'d SETS
BTSO Shohei Ohtani 30.00 80.00

2018 Stadium Club Beam Team Orange

*ORANGE: 3X TO 8X BASIC
STATED ODDS 1:868 HOBBY
STATED PRINT RUN 50 SER.#'d SETS
BTSO Shohei Ohtani 60.00 150.00

2018 Stadium Club Beam Team Red

*RED: 1X TO 2.5X BASIC
STATED ODDS 1:256 HOBBY
BTSO Shohei Ohtani 20.00 50.00

2018 Stadium Club Chrome

STATED ODDS 1:16 HOBBY
*REF: .6X TO 1.5X BASIC
*GOLD MINT: 2.5X TO 6X BASIC
SCC3 Clint Frazier 1.50 4.00
SCC4 Darryl Strawberry .75 2.00
SCC12 Andrew McCutchen 1.25 3.00
SCC21 Robinson Cano 1.00 2.50
SCC27 Michael Conforto 1.00 2.50
SCC29 Johnny Bench 1.25 3.00
SCC30 Javier Baez 1.50 4.00
SCC32 Carlos Correa 1.25 3.00
SCC37 Victor Robles 2.00 5.00
SCC45 J.P. Crawford .75 2.00
SCC48 Mike Trout 8.00 20.00
SCC54 Masahiro Tanaka 1.00 2.50
SCC58 Francisco Lindor 1.25 3.00
SCC68 Ozzie Smith 1.50 4.00
SCC69 Max Scherzer 1.25 3.00
SCC70 Noah Syndergaard 1.00 2.50
SCC71 Chris Sale 1.25 3.00
SCC72 Bo Jackson 1.25 3.00
SCC73 George Springer 1.00 2.50
SCC74 Ichiro 1.50 4.00
SCC75 Ryne Sandberg 2.50 6.00
SCC80 Andy Pettitte 1.00 2.50
SCC83 Joey Votto 1.25 3.00
SCC84 Nicky Delmonico .75 2.00
SCC90 Jose Canseco 1.00 2.50
SCC93 Nick Williams 1.00 2.50
SCC97 Miguel Sano 1.00 2.50
SCC100 Cal Ripken Jr. 4.00 10.00
SCC101 Jack Flaherty 1.25 3.00
SCC104 Hunter Renfroe .75 2.00
SCC110 Ozzie Albies 2.50 6.00
SCC111 Cody Bellinger 2.50 6.00
SCC117 Rafael Devers 2.50 6.00
SCC125 Chipper Jones 1.25 3.00
SCC128 Jose Berrios 1.00 2.50
SCC129 Manny Machado 1.25 3.00
SCC132 Tyler Mahle 1.00 2.50
SCC133 Nolan Ryan 4.00 10.00
SCC138 Shohei Ohtani 10.00 25.00
SCC141 Jim Thome 1.00 2.50
SCC145 Giancarlo Stanton 1.25 3.00
SCC149 John Smoltz 1.25 3.00
SCC152 Dwight Gooden .75 2.00
SCC155 Francisco Mejia 1.00 2.50
SCC159 Trey Mancini 1.00 2.50
SCC161 Rickey Henderson 1.25 3.00
SCC164 Barry Larkin 1.00 2.50
SCC165 Anthony Rizzo 2.00 5.00
SCC166 Wade Boggs 1.00 2.50
SCC169 Trea Turner 1.00 2.50
SCC171 Don Mattingly 2.50 6.00
SCC176 Dennis Eckersley 1.00 2.50
SCC178 Andrew Benintendi 1.25 3.00
SCC179 Bryce Harper 2.00 5.00
SCC190 Ian Happ 1.00 2.50
SCC192 Buster Posey 1.50 4.00
SCC195 Sonny Gray 1.00 2.50
SCC197 Rhys Hoskins 3.00 8.00
SCC201 Kris Bryant 1.50 4.00
SCC205 Austin Hays 1.25 3.00
SCC208 Greg Maddux 1.50 4.00
SCC211 Luis Severino 1.00 2.50
SCC212 Corey Seager 1.00 2.50
SCC215 Willson Contreras 1.25 3.00
SCC220 Walker Buehler 4.00 10.00
SCC223 Hank Aaron 2.50 6.00
SCC228 Frank Thomas 1.25 3.00
SCC232 Freddie Freeman 1.50 4.00
SCC241 Aaron Judge 3.00 8.00
SCC244 Yu Darvish 1.25 3.00
SCC245 Byron Buxton 1.00 2.50
SCC246 Alex Bregman 1.25 3.00
SCC248 Mariano Rivera 1.50 4.00
SCC256 Reggie Jackson 1.00 2.50
SCC257 Gary Sanchez 1.25 3.00
SCC260 Amed Rosario 1.00 2.50
SCC262 Randy Johnson 1.25 3.00
SCC263 Willie Calhoun 1.00 2.50
SCC266 Alex Verdugo 1.25 3.00
SCC271 Jose Altuve 1.00 2.50
SCC273 Kyle Schwarber 1.25 3.00
SCC274 Dominic Smith .75 2.00
SCC275 Derek Jeter 3.00 8.00
SCC276 Clayton Kershaw 2.50 6.00
SCC280 Harrison Bader 1.25 3.00
SCC282 Mark McGwire 2.00 5.00
SCC286 Addison Russell 1.00 2.50
SCC288 Sandy Koufax 2.50 6.00
SCC290 Nolan Arenado 1.50 4.00
SCC300 Hideki Matsui 1.25 3.00

2018 Stadium Club Instavision

STATED ODDS 1:321 HOBBY
*RED/50: .5X TO 1.2X BASIC
*BLACK/25: .75X TO 2X BASIC
IAJ Aaron Judge 12.00 30.00
IBH Bryce Harper 8.00 20.00
IBP Buster Posey 6.00 15.00
ICB Cody Bellinger 10.00 25.00
ICC Carlos Correa 5.00 12.00
IGS Giancarlo Stanton 5.00 12.00
IKB Kris Bryant 6.00 15.00
IMT Mike Trout 25.00 60.00
IRD Rafael Devers 10.00 25.00
ISO Shohei Ohtani 20.00 50.00

2018 Stadium Club Lone Star Signatures

STATED ODDS 1:2363 HOBBY
PRINT RUNS B/WN 5-25 COPIES PER
NO PRICING ON QTY 10 OR LESS
EXCHANGE DEADLINE 5/30/2020
LSSAJ Aaron Judge EXCH
LSSAR Amed Rosario/25 8.00 20.00
LSSBH Bryce Harper
LSSDJ Derek Jeter
LSSFL Francisco Lindor EXCH 60.00 150.00
LSSFT Frank Thomas
LSSKB Kris Bryant
LSSNS Noah Syndergaard/25 8.00 20.00
LSSRD Rafael Devers EXCH 25.00 60.00

2018 Stadium Club Never Compromise

STATED ODDS 1:8 HOBBY
*RED: .75X TO 2X BASIC
*BLACK/99: 1.5X TO 4X BASIC
*ORANGE/50: 3X TO 8X BASIC
NCAB Andrew Benintendi .50 1.25
NCAJ Aaron Judge 1.25 3.00
NCAR Anthony Rizzo .75 2.00
NCARO Amed Rosario .40 1.00
NCBH Bryce Harper .75 2.00
NCCB Cody Bellinger 1.00 2.50
NCCC Carlos Correa .50 1.25
NCCF Clint Frazier .60 1.50
NCCJ Chipper Jones .50 1.25
NCCR Cal Ripken Jr. 1.50 4.00
NCDJ Derek Jeter 1.25 3.00
NCFL Francisco Lindor .50 1.25
NCFT Frank Thomas .50 1.25
NCGS Giancarlo Stanton .50 1.25
NCJA Jose Altuve .40 1.00
NCJS John Smoltz .50 1.25
NCJV Joey Votto .50 1.25
NCKB Kris Bryant .60 1.50
NCMM Manny Machado .50 1.25
NCMMC Mark McGwire .75 2.00
NCMT Mike Trout 2.50 6.00
NCNS Noah Syndergaard .40 1.00
NCRD Rafael Devers 1.00 2.50
NCRH Rhys Hoskins 1.25 3.00
NCSO Shohei Ohtani 2.00 5.00

2018 Stadium Club Power Zone

STATED ODDS 1:8 HOBBY
*RED: .75X TO 2X BASIC
*BLACK/99: 1.5X TO 4X BASIC
*ORANGE/50: 3X TO 8X BASIC
PZAJ Aaron Judge 1.25 3.00
PZAM Andrew McCutchen .50 1.25
PZAR Anthony Rizzo .75 2.00
PZBH Bryce Harper .75 2.00
PZCB Cody Bellinger 1.00 2.50
PZCC Carlos Correa .50 1.25
PZGS Gary Sanchez .50 1.25
PZGSP George Springer .40 1.00
PZJD Josh Donaldson .40 1.00
PZJG Joey Gallo .40 1.00
PZJM J.D. Martinez .50 1.25
PZJU Justin Upton .40 1.00
PZJV Joey Votto .50 1.25
PZKB Kris Bryant .60 1.50
PZKD Khris Davis .50 1.25
PZKS Kyle Schwarber .50 1.25
PZMM Manny Machado .50 1.25
PZMO Marcell Ozuna .50 1.25
PZMT Mike Trout 2.50 6.00
PZNA Nolan Arenado .60 1.50
PZNC Nelson Cruz .50 1.25
PZPG Paul Goldschmidt .50 1.25
PZRD Rafael Devers 1.00 2.50
PZRH Rhys Hoskins 1.25 3.00
PZSO Shohei Ohtani 2.00 5.00

2018 Stadium Club Special Forces

STATED ODDS 1:8 HOBBY
*RED: .75X TO 2X BASIC
*BLACK/99: 1.5X TO 4X BASIC
*ORANGE/50: 3X TO 8X BASIC
SFAJ Aaron Judge 1.25 3.00
SFAR Anthony Rizzo .75 2.00
SFBH Bryce Harper .75 2.00
SFBP Buster Posey .60 1.50
SFCB Cody Bellinger 1.00 2.50
SFCC Carlos Correa .50 1.25
SFCK Clayton Kershaw 1.00 2.50
SFGS Giancarlo Stanton .50 1.25
SFJA Jose Altuve .40 1.00
SFJV Justin Verlander .50 1.25
SFJVO Joey Votto .50 1.25
SFKB Kris Bryant .60 1.50
SFMS Max Scherzer .50 1.25
SFMT Mike Trout 2.50 6.00
SFSO Shohei Ohtani 2.00 5.00

2019 Stadium Club

1 Mookie Betts .50 1.25
2 Kyle Schwarber .30 .75
3 Touki Toussaint RC .40 1.00
4 Josh Donaldson .25 .60
5 David Dahl .20 .50
6 Kyle Wright RC .50 1.25
7 David Fletcher RC 1.00 2.50
8 Max Scherzer .30 .75
9 David Price .25 .60
10 Javier Baez .40 1.00
11 Andrew Benintendi .30 .75
12 Brooks Robinson .25 .60
13 Ted Williams .60 1.50
14 Cedric Mullins RC .50 1.25
15 Zack Greinke .25 .60
16 Fred McGriff .25 .60
17 Jackie Bradley Jr. .30 .75
18 Willson Contreras .25 .60
19 Albert Almora Jr. .25 .60
20 Eugenio Suarez .25 .60
21 Charlie Blackmon .30 .75
22 Giancarlo Stanton .30 .75
23 Jose Peraza .25 .60
24 Frank Thomas .30 .75
25 Ernie Banks .30 .75
26 Cal Ripken Jr. 1.00 2.50
27 Freddie Freeman .40 1.00
28 Eddie Murray .25 .60
29 Christy Mathewson .30 .75
30 Carlos Correa .30 .75
31 Lance McCullers Jr. .20 .50
32 Trey Mancini .25 .60
33 Jake Lamb .25 .60
34 Trevor Bauer .30 .75
35 Francisco Lindor .30 .75
36 J.D. Martinez .30 .75
37 Carlos Carrasco .20 .50
38 Ryne Sandberg .60 1.50
39 Rafael Devers .40 1.00
40 Ender Inciarte .20 .50
41 A.J. Pollock .20 .50
42 Luis Castillo .25 .60
43 Carlos Santana .25 .60
44 Alex Bregman .30 .75
45 Albert Pujols .40 1.00
46 Michael Kopech RC .60 1.50
47 Scooter Gennett .25 .60
48 Tim Anderson .30 .75
49 Bryse Wilson RC .40 1.00
50 Mike Foltynewicz .30 .75
51 Robbie Ray .20 .50
52 DJ Stewart RC .40 1.00
53 Nolan Arenado .40 1.00
54 Hank Aaron .60 1.50
55 Cole Hamels .25 .60
56 Ronald Acuna Jr. 1.50 4.00
57 Carlos Rodon .25 .60
58 Joey Votto .30 .75
59 Tony Gwynn .30 .75
60 Mike Trout 1.50 4.00
61 Jim Palmer .25 .60
62 Barry Larkin .25 .60
63 Dustin Pedroia .30 .75
64 Jon Lester .25 .60
65 Yoan Moncada .30 .75
66 Shohei Ohtani .40 1.00
67 Justin Verlander .30 .75
68 Carl Yastrzemski .50 1.25
69 David Peralta .20 .50
70 Jackie Robinson .30 .75
71 Kris Bryant .40 1.00
72 Shane Bieber UER 8.00 20.00
73 Yasiel Puig .30 .75
74 Jake Bauers RC .50 1.25
75 Mark Trumbo .20 .50
76 Chris Sale .30 .75
77 Jose Abreu .30 .75
78 Chipper Jones .30 .75
79 Eloy Jimenez RC 1.25 3.00
80 Matt Kemp .25 .60
81 Jose Ramirez .25 .60
82 Dansby Swanson .30 .75
83 Justin Upton .25 .60
84 Andrelton Simmons .20 .50
85 Xander Bogaerts .30 .75
86 Johnny Bench .30 .75
87 Christian Yelich .40 1.00
88 Fernando Tatis Jr. RC 8.00 20.00
89 Kole Calhoun .20 .50
90 Eddie Mathews .30 .75
91 Yu Darvish .30 .75
92 Corey Kluber .25 .60
93 Matt Harvey .25 .60
94 Adam Jones .25 .60
95 Archie Bradley .20 .50
96 Ketel Marte .25 .60
97 Ozzie Albies .30 .75
98 Dale Murphy .30 .75
99 Wade Boggs .25 .60
100 Anthony Rizzo .50 1.25
101 Max Muncy .25 .60
102 Andrew McCutchen .30 .75
103 Enrique Hernandez .25 .60
104 Corbin Burnes RC .50 1.25
105 Nicholas Castellanos .30 .75
106 Kyle Tucker RC .60 1.50
107 Miguel Sano .25 .60
108 Willians Astudillo .20 .50
109 Khris Davis .30 .75
110 Jean Segura .30 .75
111 Gerrit Cole .30 .75
112 Michael Conforto .25 .60
113 Brandon Nimmo .25 .60
114 Justin Turner .25 .60
115 Roberto Clemente .75 2.00
116 Walker Buehler .40 1.00
117 Brian Anderson .20 .50
118 Trevor Richards RC .30 .75
119 Luis Severino .25 .60
120 Mike Piazza .30 .75
121 Jorge Alfaro .20 .50
122 Yuli Gurriel .25 .60
123 Miguel Andujar .30 .75
124 Orlando Arcia .20 .50
125 Michael Fulmer .20 .50
126 Billy Hamilton .25 .60
127 Jake Arrieta .25 .60
128 Jose Berrios .25 .60
129 Josh James RC .50 1.25
130 Jeff McNeil RC .75 2.00
131 Reggie Jackson .30 .75
132 Rickey Henderson .30 .75
133 Jacob deGrom .30 .75
134 Jeff Bagwell .25 .60
135 Eddie Rosario .25 .60
136 Ryan Braun .25 .60
137 Gary Sanchez .30 .75
138 Miguel Cabrera .30 .75
139 Darryl Strawberry .20 .50
140 Myles Straw RC .50 1.25
141 Derek Jeter .75 2.00
142 Adalberto Mondesi .25 .60
143 Kenley Jansen .25 .60
144 Josh Hader .20 .50
145 Mark McGwire .50 1.25
146 Cody Bellinger .60 1.50
147 Julio Urias .30 .75
148 Dallas Keuchel .25 .60
149 Alex Gordon .25 .60
150 Lewis Brinson .20 .50
151 Ramon Laureano RC .60 1.50
152 Aaron Nola .25 .60
153 Gleyber Torres .60 1.50
154 Didi Gregorius .25 .60
155 Rhys Hoskins .40 1.00
156 George Springer .25 .60
157 Don Mattingly .60 1.50
158 Joc Pederson .25 .60
159 Noah Syndergaard .25 .60
160 Jesus Aguilar .20 .50
161 Clayton Kershaw .60 1.50
162 Stephen Piscotty .20 .50
163 Matthew Boyd .20 .50
164 Matt Chapman .30 .75
165 Ryan O'Hearn RC .40 1.00
166 J.T. Realmuto .30 .75
167 Robinson Cano .25 .60
168 Christin Stewart RC .40 1.00
169 Nelson Cruz .30 .75
170 Jose Altuve .25 .60
171 Eric Thames .20 .50
172 Lorenzo Cain .20 .50
173 Mariano Rivera .40 1.00
174 Dennis Eckersley .25 .60
175 Corey Seager .30 .75
176 Matt Olson .20 .50
177 Whit Merrifield .30 .75
178 Bo Jackson .30 .75
179 Max Kepler .25 .60
180 Jonathan Schoop .20 .50
181 Masahiro Tanaka .20 .50
182 Robin Yount .30 .75
183 Amed Rosario .25 .60
184 Odubel Herrera .25 .60
185 Jose Canseco .25 .60
186 George Brett .60 1.50
187 Todd Frazier .25 .60
188 Brad Keller RC .30 .75
189 Starlin Castro .20 .50
190 Niko Goodrum .25 .60
191 Nick Martini RC .30 .75
192 Sandy Koufax .60 1.50
193 Byron Buxton .25 .60
194 Aaron Judge .75 2.00
195 Hyun-Jin Ryu .25 .60
196 Travis Shaw .20 .50
197 Hideki Matsui .30 .75
198 Salvador Perez .25 .60
199 Edwin Diaz .25 .60
200 Chris Taylor .40 1.00
201 Harmon Killebrew .25 .60
202 Wil Myers .20 .50
203 Johnny Mize .25 .60
204 Mel Ott .30 .75
205 Warren Spahn .25 .60
206 Roy Halladay .25 .60
207 Patrick Wisdom RC .30 .75
208 Carlton Fisk .25 .60
209 Felix Hernandez .25 .60
210 Franmil Reyes .20 .50
211 Jack Flaherty .30 .75
212 Starling Marte .25 .60
213 Blake Snell .25 .60
214 Victor Robles .40 1.00
215 Ty Cobb .50 1.25
216 Justus Sheffield RC .50 1.25
217 Trevor Story .30 .75
218 Marcus Stroman .25 .60
219 Ryan Zimmerman .25 .60
220 Stephen Strasburg .30 .75
221 Danny Jansen RC .30 .75
222 Johnny Cueto .25 .60
223 Edgar Martinez .25 .60
224 Mitch Haniger .25 .60
225 Juan Marichal .25 .60
226 Manny Machado .30 .75
227 Yadier Molina .30 .75
228 Mike Moustakas .25 .60
229 Josh Bell .25 .60
230 Reese McGuire RC .50 1.25
231 Pee Wee Reese .25 .60
232 Lourdes Gurriel Jr. .25 .60
233 Sammy Sosa .30 .75
234 Dereck Rodriguez .20 .50
235 Anthony Rendon .30 .75
236 Honus Wagner .30 .75
237 Justin Smoak .20 .50
238 Steven Duggar RC .40 1.00
239 Luis Urias RC .50 1.25
240 Joey Gallo .25 .60
241 Shin-Soo Choo .25 .60
242 Kevin Kramer RC .40 1.00
243 Ichiro .40 1.00
244 Buster Posey .40 1.00
245 Lou Gehrig .60 1.50
246 Juan Soto 1.00 2.50
247 Austin Meadows .25 .60
248 Willie Calhoun .20 .50
249 Jeff Samardzija .20 .50
250 Duke Snider .25 .60
251 Nolan Ryan 1.00 2.50
252 Dee Gordon .20 .50
253 Jameson Taillon .25 .60
254 Sean Reid-Foley RC .30 .75
255 Paul DeJong .30 .75
256 Roger Maris .30 .75
257 Ken Griffey Jr. .60 1.50
258 Roberto Alomar .25 .60
259 Babe Ruth .75 2.00
260 German Marquez .20 .50
261 Brian Dozier .25 .60
262 Bob Feller .25 .60
263 Brandon Crawford .25 .60
264 Felipe Vazquez .20 .50
265 Edwin Encarnacion .30 .75
266 Bob Gibson .25 .60
267 Kevin Newman RC .50 1.25
268 Vladimir Guerrero .25 .60
269 Francisco Mejia .25 .60
270 Craig Kimbrel .25 .60
271 Kyle Freeland .25 .60
272 Pete Alonso RC 2.50 6.00
273 Rogers Hornsby .25 .60
274 Yusei Kikuchi RC .50 1.25
275 Adrian Beltre .30 .75
276 Ozzie Smith .40 1.00
277 Carlos Martinez .25 .60
278 Al Kaline .30 .75
279 Rougned Odor .25 .60
280 Trea Turner .30 .75
281 David Ortiz .30 .75
282 Marcell Ozuna .30 .75
283 Eric Hosmer .25 .60
284 Matt Carpenter .30 .75
285 Paul Goldschmidt .30 .75
286 Todd Helton .25 .60
287 Kevin Kiermaier .25 .60
288 Rod Carew .25 .60
289 Ian Kinsler .25 .60
290 Stan Musial .50 1.25
291 Bryce Harper .50 1.25
292 Chris Archer .20 .50
293 Rowdy Tellez RC .50 1.25
294 Evan Longoria .25 .60
295 Tommy Pham .20 .50
296 Hunter Renfroe .20 .50
297 Nomar Mazara .20 .50
298 Harrison Bader .25 .60
299 Elvis Andrus .25 .60
300 Will Clark .25 .60
301 Vladimir Guerrero Jr. RC 5.00 12.00

2019 Stadium Club Black and White

*BW: 5X TO 12X BASIC
*BW RC: 3X TO 8X BASIC RC
STATED ODDS 1:48 HOBBY
79 Eloy Jimenez 15.00 40.00
272 Pete Alonso 30.00 80.00

2019 Stadium Club Black Foil

*BLK FOIL: 1.5X TO 4X BASIC
*BLK FOIL RC: 1X TO 2.5X BASIC RC
STATED ODDS 1:8 HOBBY
272 Pete Alonso 10.00 25.00

2019 Stadium Club Rainbow Foil

*RAINBOW: 8X TO 20X BASIC
*RAINBOW RC: 5X TO 12X BASIC RC
STATED ODDS 1:147 HOBBY
STATED PRINT RUN 25 SER.#'d SETS
79 Eloy Jimenez 20.00 50.00
272 Pete Alonso 50.00 120.00

2019 Stadium Club Red Foil

*RED FOIL: 1X TO 2.5X BASIC
*RED FOIL RC: .6X TO 1.5X BASIC RC
STATED ODDS 1:3 HOBBY
272 Pete Alonso 6.00 15.00

2019 Stadium Club Sepia

*SEPIA: 2X TO 5X BASIC
*SEPIA RC: 1.2X TO 3X BASIC RC
STATED ODDS 1:8 BLASTER
79 Eloy Jimenez 6.00 15.00
272 Pete Alonso 15.00 40.00

2019 Stadium Club Photo Variations

STATED ODDS 1:110 HOBBY
1 Mookie Betts 10.00 25.00
8 Max Scherzer 6.00 15.00
10 Javier Baez 8.00 20.00
11 Andrew Benintendi 6.00 15.00
24 Frank Thomas 6.00 15.00
26 Cal Ripken Jr. 20.00 50.00
27 Freddie Freeman 8.00 20.00
30 Carlos Correa 6.00 15.00
35 Francisco Lindor 6.00 15.00
38 Ryne Sandberg 12.00 30.00
44 Alex Bregman 6.00 15.00
54 Hank Aaron 12.00 30.00
56 Ronald Acuna Jr. 30.00 80.00
58 Joey Votto 6.00 15.00
60 Mike Trout 40.00 100.00
66 Shohei Ohtani 8.00 20.00
67 Justin Verlander 6.00 15.00
71 Kris Bryant 10.00 25.00
76 Chris Sale 6.00 15.00
78 Chipper Jones 6.00 15.00
79 Eloy Jimenez 15.00 40.00
87 Christian Yelich 8.00 20.00
88 Fernando Tatis Jr. 40.00 100.00
100 Anthony Rizzo 10.00 25.00
102 Andrew McCutchen 6.00 15.00
106 Kyle Tucker 8.00 20.00
123 Miguel Andujar 6.00 15.00
131 Reggie Jackson 5.00 12.00
132 Rickey Henderson 10.00 25.00
137 Gary Sanchez 6.00 15.00
141 Derek Jeter 15.00 40.00
145 Mark McGwire 10.00 25.00
155 Rhys Hoskins 8.00 20.00
157 Don Mattingly 12.00 30.00
161 Clayton Kershaw 12.00 30.00
170 Jose Altuve 5.00 12.00
173 Mariano Rivera 8.00 20.00
192 Sandy Koufax 12.00 30.00
194 Aaron Judge 15.00 40.00
197 Hideki Matsui 6.00 15.00
Holding key
206 Roy Halladay 5.00 12.00
227 Yadier Molina 6.00 15.00
243 Ichiro 8.00 20.00
244 Buster Posey 8.00 20.00
246 Juan Soto 20.00 50.00
257 Ken Griffey Jr. 12.00 30.00
272 Pete Alonso 30.00 80.00
274 Yusei Kikuchi 6.00 15.00
285 Paul Goldschmidt 6.00 15.00
291 Bryce Harper 10.00 25.00

2019 Stadium Club Autographs

STATED ODDS 1:10 HOBBY
EXCHANGE DEADLINE 5/31/2021
SCAAC Adam Cimber 6.00 15.00
SCAAD Austin Dean 3.00 8.00
SCAAG Adolis Garcia 3.00 8.00
SCABG Bob Gibson 25.00 60.00
SCABJ Bo Jackson EXCH
SCABK Brad Keller 3.00 8.00
SCABL Brandon Lowe 10.00 25.00
SCABN Brandon Nimmo 4.00 10.00
SCABS Blake Snell 6.00 15.00
SCABW Bryse Wilson 4.00 10.00
SCACA Chance Adams 3.00 8.00
SCACB Corbin Burnes 6.00 15.00
SCACD Corey Dickerson 3.00 8.00
SCACH Cesar Hernandez 3.00 8.00
SCACR Cal Ripken Jr. 50.00 120.00
SCACS Chris Shaw 5.00 12.00
SCADD Dean Deetz 3.00 8.00
SCADF David Fletcher 6.00 15.00
SCADH Dakota Hudson 4.00 10.00
SCADJ David Justice 10.00 25.00
SCADM Dale Murphy 40.00 100.00
SCADR Dereck Rodriguez 3.00 8.00
SCADS Darryl Strawberry 12.00 30.00
SCAEJ Eloy Jimenez 30.00 80.00
SCAEM Edgar Martinez 20.00 50.00
SCAFA Francisco Arcia 5.00 12.00
SCAFL Francisco Lindor 20.00 50.00
SCAFP Freddy Peralta 5.00 12.00
SCAI Ichiro
SCAJH Josh Hader 3.00 8.00
SCAJR Josh Rogers 3.00 8.00
SCAJS Juan Soto 40.00 100.00
SCAKA Kolby Allard 5.00 12.00
SCAKB Kris Bryant
SCAKK Kevin Kramer 4.00 10.00
SCAKN Kevin Newman 5.00 12.00
SCAKT Kyle Tucker 15.00 40.00
SCAKW Kyle Wright 5.00 12.00
SCALO Luis Ortiz 3.00 8.00
SCALV Luke Voit 25.00 60.00
SCAMC Matt Chapman 10.00 25.00
SCAMF Mike Foltynewicz 5.00 12.00
SCAMK Michael Kopech 6.00 15.00
SCAMM Miles Mikolas 5.00 12.00
SCAMS Myles Straw 5.00 12.00
SCAMT Mike Trout
SCANB Nick Burdi 3.00 8.00
SCANC Nicholas Ciuffo 3.00 8.00
SCANM Nick Martini 3.00 8.00
SCANR Nolan Ryan
SCANS Noah Syndergaard 4.00 10.00
SCAOA Ozzie Albies 10.00 25.00
SCAOH Odubel Herrera 4.00 10.00
SCAPA Peter Alonso 50.00 120.00
SCAPG Paul Goldschmidt 20.00 50.00
SCAPW Patrick Wisdom 3.00 8.00
SCARA Ronald Acuna Jr. 60.00 150.00
SCARB Ray Black 3.00 8.00
SCARH Rhys Hoskins 15.00 40.00
SCARL Ramon Laureano 5.00 12.00
SCARO Ryan O'Hearn 3.00 8.00
SCART Rowdy Tellez 5.00 12.00
SCASG Scooter Gennett 4.00 10.00
SCASR Sean Reid-Foley 3.00 8.00
SCAST Stephen Tarpley 4.00 10.00
SCATB Trevor Bauer 5.00 12.00
SCATR Trevor Richards 3.00 8.00
SCATS Tyler Skaggs 6.00 15.00
SCATT Touki Toussaint 4.00 10.00
SCATW Taylor Ward 3.00 8.00
SCAVG Vladimir Guerrero Jr. 75.00 200.00
SCAWA Willians Astudillo 10.00 25.00
SCAWC Will Clark 40.00 100.00
SCAYM Yadier Molina 30.00 80.00
SCACMU Cedric Mullins 5.00 12.00
SCACST Christin Stewart 4.00 10.00
SCADJA Danny Jansen 3.00 8.00
SCADMA Don Mattingly 50.00 120.00
SCADPO Daniel Poncedeleon 5.00 12.00
SCADSA Dennis Santana 3.00 8.00
SCADST DJ Stewart 4.00 10.00
SCAFTA Fernando Tatis Jr. 100.00 250.00
SCAFVA Framber Valdez 6.00 15.00
SCAJAL Jose Altuve 15.00 40.00
SCAJBA Jake Bauers 5.00 12.00
SCAJBE Jalen Beeks 3.00 8.00
SCAJBR Jose Briceno 3.00 8.00
SCAJCA Jake Cave 4.00 10.00
SCAJMA Juan Marichal 15.00 40.00
SCAJSH Justus Sheffield 5.00 12.00
SCAJSP Jeffrey Springs 3.00 8.00
SCAMMG Mark McGwire 40.00 25.00
SCAMMU Max Muncy 8.00 20.00
SCARBO Ryan Borucki 3.00 8.00
SCARMC Reese McGuire 5.00 12.00

2019 Stadium Club Autographs Black Foil

*BLACK FOIL: .6X TO 1.5X BASIC
STATED ODDS 1:274 HOBBY
STATED PRINT RUN 25 SER.#'d SETS
EXCHANGE DEADLINE 5/31/2021
SCAMK Michael Kopech 15.00 40.00
SCAOA Ozzie Albies 25.00 60.00
SCAPA Peter Alonso 100.00 250.00
SCAPG Paul Goldschmidt 40.00 100.00
SCAVG Vladimir Guerrero Jr. 150.00 400.00

2019 Stadium Club Autographs Red Foil

*RED FOIL: .5X TO 1.2X BASIC
STATED ODDS 1:152 HOBBY
STATED PRINT RUN 50 SER.#'d SETS
EXCHANGE DEADLINE 5/31/2021
SCAOA Ozzie Albies 20.00 50.00
SCAPA Peter Alonso 75.00 200.00
SCAVG Vladimir Guerrero Jr. 125.00 300.00

2019 Stadium Club Beam Team

STATED ODDS 1:16 HOBBY
*RED: 1X TO 2.5X BASIC
*BLACK/99: 1.2X TO 3X BASIC
*ORANGE/50: 3X TO 8X BASIC
BT1 Javier Baez 1.00 2.50
BT2 Derek Jeter 2.00 5.00
BT3 Mike Trout 4.00 10.00
BT4 Shohei Ohtani 1.00 2.50
BT5 Ichiro 1.00 2.50
BT6 Bryce Harper 1.25 3.00
BT7 Aaron Judge 2.00 5.00
BT8 Cal Ripken Jr. 2.50 6.00
BT9 Kris Bryant 1.00 2.50
BT10 Joey Votto .75 2.00
BT11 Manny Machado .75 2.00
BT12 Anthony Rizzo 1.25 3.00
BT13 Jose Altuve .60 1.50
BT14 Paul Goldschmidt .75 2.00
BT15 Francisco Lindor .75 2.00
BT16 Yadier Molina .75 2.00
BT17 Jacob deGrom .75 2.00
BT18 Ronald Acuna Jr. 4.00 10.00
BT19 Alex Bregman .75 2.00
BT20 Gleyber Torres 1.50 4.00
BT21 Chris Sale .75 2.00
BT22 Christian Yelich 1.00 2.50
BT23 Ken Griffey Jr. 1.50 4.00
BT24 Tony Gwynn .75 2.00
BT25 Juan Soto 2.50 6.00

2019 Stadium Club Chrome

STATED ODDS 1:16 HOBBY
SCC1 Sandy Koufax 4.00 10.00
SCC2 Derek Jeter 3.00 8.00
SCC3 Hank Aaron 2.50 6.00
SCC4 Mike Trout 6.00 15.00
SCC5 Shohei Ohtani 1.50 4.00
SCC6 Ichiro 1.50 4.00
SCC7 Mariano Rivera 1.50 4.00
SCC8 Bryce Harper 2.00 5.00
SCC9 Aaron Judge 3.00 8.00
SCC10 Buster Posey 1.50 4.00
SCC11 Clayton Kershaw 2.50 6.00
SCC12 Cal Ripken Jr. 4.00 10.00
SCC13 Johnny Bench 1.25 3.00
SCC14 Nolan Ryan 4.00 10.00
SCC15 Bo Jackson 1.25 3.00
SCC16 Masahiro Tanaka 1.00 2.50
SCC17 Hideki Matsui 1.25 3.00
SCC18 Reggie Jackson 1.00 2.50
SCC19 Rickey Henderson 1.25 3.00
SCC20 Mark McGwire 2.00 5.00
SCC21 Chipper Jones 1.25 3.00
SCC22 Kris Bryant 1.50 4.00
SCC23 Wade Boggs 1.00 2.50
SCC24 Ryne Sandberg 2.50 6.00
SCC25 Anthony Rizzo 2.00 5.00
SCC26 Frank Thomas 1.25 3.00
SCC27 Joey Votto 1.25 3.00
SCC28 Manny Machado 1.25 3.00
SCC29 Barry Larkin 1.00 2.50
SCC30 Jose Altuve 1.00 2.50
SCC31 Don Mattingly 2.50 6.00
SCC32 Jose Ramirez 1.00 2.50
SCC33 Gary Sanchez 1.25 3.00
SCC34 Ozzie Smith 1.50 4.00
SCC35 Andrew McCutchen 1.25 3.00
SCC36 Gleyber Torres 2.50 6.00
SCC37 Chris Sale 1.25 3.00
SCC38 George Springer 1.00 2.50
SCC39 Freddie Freeman 1.50 4.00
SCC40 Francisco Lindor 1.25 3.00
SCC41 Noah Syndergaard 1.00 2.50
SCC42 Miguel Andujar 1.25 3.00
SCC43 Yadier Molina 1.25 3.00
SCC44 Bob Gibson 1.00 2.50
SCC45 Andrew Benintendi 1.25 3.00
SCC46 Willson Contreras 1.00 2.50
SCC47 Luis Severino 1.00 2.50
SCC48 Jacob deGrom 1.25 3.00
SCC49 Kyle Schwarber 1.25 3.00
SCC50 Alex Bregman 1.25 3.00
SCC51 Darryl Strawberry .75 2.00
SCC52 Dennis Eckersley 1.00 2.50
SCC53 Ronald Acuna Jr. 6.00 15.00
SCC54 Rafael Devers 1.50 4.00
SCC55 Rhys Hoskins 1.50 4.00
SCC56 Juan Soto 4.00 10.00
SCC57 Charlie Blackmon 1.25 3.00
SCC58 Trevor Bauer 1.25 3.00
SCC59 Victor Robles 1.50 4.00
SCC60 Christian Yelich 1.50 4.00
SCC61 Ken Griffey Jr. 2.50 6.00
SCC62 Sammy Sosa 1.25 3.00
SCC63 Ozzie Albies 1.25 3.00
SCC64 Jose Canseco 1.00 2.50
SCC65 Blake Snell 1.00 2.50
SCC66 Khris Davis 1.25 3.00
SCC67 Roy Halladay 1.00 2.50
SCC68 Jack Flaherty 1.00 2.50
SCC69 Whit Merrifield 1.25 3.00
SCC70 Michael Kopech 1.50 4.00
SCC71 Justus Sheffield 1.25 3.00
SCC72 Eloy Jimenez 3.00 8.00
SCC73 Kyle Wright 1.25 3.00
SCC74 Kyle Tucker 1.50 4.00
SCC75 Touki Toussaint 1.00 2.50
SCC76 Pete Alonso 10.00 25.00
SCC77 Nolan Arenado 1.50 4.00
SCC78 Jeff McNeil 2.00 5.00
SCC79 Ryan O'Hearn .75 2.00
SCC80 Fernando Tatis Jr. 20.00 50.00
SCC81 Albert Pujols 1.50 4.00
SCC82 Giancarlo Stanton 1.25 3.00
SCC83 Mookie Betts 2.00 5.00
SCC84 Carlos Correa 1.25 3.00
SCC85 Max Scherzer 1.25 3.00
SCC86 J.D. Martinez 1.25 3.00
SCC87 Trea Turner 1.00 2.50
SCC88 Javier Baez 1.50 4.00
SCC89 Corey Seager 1.25 3.00
SCC90 Cody Bellinger 2.50 6.00

2019 Stadium Club Chrome Gold Mint

*GOLD MINT: 2.5X TO 6X BASIC
STATED ODDS 1:257 HOBBY
SCC2 Derek Jeter 40.00 100.00
SCC4 Mike Trout 50.00 120.00
SCC53 Ronald Acuna Jr. 40.00 100.00
SCC76 Pete Alonso 75.00 200.00

2019 Stadium Club Chrome Orange Refractors

*ORNG: 1.2X TO 3X BASIC
STATED ODDS 1:124 HOBBY
STATED PRINT RUN 99 SER.#'d SETS
SCC2 Derek Jeter 20.00 50.00
SCC4 Mike Trout 25.00 60.00
SCC53 Ronald Acuna Jr. 20.00 50.00
SCC76 Pete Alonso 40.00 100.00

2019 Stadium Club Chrome Refractors

*REF: .6X TO 1.5X BASIC
STATED ODDS 1:64 HOBBY
SCC4 Mike Trout 15.00 40.00
SCC53 Ronald Acuna Jr. 10.00 25.00
SCC76 Pete Alonso 20.00 50.00

2019 Stadium Club Emperors of the Zone

STATED ODDS 1:8 HOBBY
*RED: .75X TO 2X BASIC
*BLACK/99: 1.5X TO 4X BASIC
*ORANGE/50: 3X TO 8X BASIC
EZ1 Shohei Ohtani .60 1.50
EZ2 Pedro Martinez .40 1.00
EZ3 Clayton Kershaw 1.00 2.50
EZ4 Masahiro Tanaka .40 1.00
EZ5 Nolan Ryan 1.50 4.00
EZ6 Andy Pettitte .40 1.00
EZ7 Tom Glavine .40 1.00
EZ8 Zack Greinke .40 1.00
EZ9 John Smoltz .50 1.25
EZ10 Chris Sale .50 1.25
EZ11 Corey Kluber .40 1.00
EZ12 Trevor Bauer .50 1.25
EZ13 Noah Syndergaard .40 1.00
EZ14 Gerrit Cole .50 1.25
EZ15 Jacob deGrom .50 1.25
EZ16 Luis Severino .40 1.00
EZ17 Stephen Strasburg .50 1.25
EZ18 Dennis Eckersley .40 1.00
EZ19 Aaron Nola .40 1.00
EZ20 Blake Snell .40 1.00
EZ21 Walker Buehler .60 1.50
EZ22 Mariano Rivera .60 1.50
EZ23 Yusei Kikuchi .50 1.25
EZ24 Justin Verlander .50 1.25
EZ25 Max Scherzer .50 1.25

2019 Stadium Club Instavision

STATED ODDS 1:321 HOBBY
*RED/50: .5X TO 1.2X BASIC
*BLACK/25: .75X TO 2X BASIC
IV1 Cal Ripken Jr. 15.00 40.00
IV2 Javier Baez 6.00 15.00
IV3 Ken Griffey Jr. 10.00 25.00
IV4 Justin Verlander 5.00 12.00
IV5 Mark McGwire 8.00 20.00
IV6 Manny Machado 5.00 12.00
IV7 Bryce Harper 8.00 20.00
IV8 Mike Trout 25.00 60.00
IV9 Aaron Judge 12.00 30.00
IV10 Ichiro 6.00 15.00

2019 Stadium Club Lone Star Signatures

STATED ODDS 1:2138 HOBBY
PRINT RUNS B/WN 5-25 COPIES PER
NO PRICING ON QTY 15 OR LESS
EXCHANGE DEADLINE 5/31/2021
LSABG Bob Gibson/25 25.00
LSACS Chris Sale/25 10.00 25.00
LSADJ Derek Jeter
LSAEJ Eloy Jimenez/25 40.00 100.00
LSAFL Francisco Lindor/25
LSAJd Jacob deGrom/25 20.00 50.00
LSASO Shohei Ohtani
LSAVG Vladimir Guerrero Jr./25 125.00 300.00
LSAWC Will Clark/25 30.00 80.00
LSAYM Yadier Molina/25 30.00 80.00

2019 Stadium Club Oversized Box Toppers

INSERTED IN HOBBY BOXES
OBVI Ichiro 2.00 5.00
OBVAJ Aaron Judge 4.00 10.00
OBVAR Anthony Rizzo 2.50 6.00
OBVBG Bob Gibson 1.25 3.00
OBVBH Bryce Harper 2.50 6.00
OBVBJ Bo Jackson 1.50 4.00
OBVBP Buster Posey 2.00 5.00
OBVBR Babe Ruth 4.00 10.00
OBVCB Charlie Blackmon 1.50 4.00
OBVCF Carlton Fisk 1.25 3.00
OBVCJ Chipper Jones 1.50 4.00
OBVCK Clayton Kershaw 3.00 8.00
OBVCR Cal Ripken Jr. 5.00 12.00
OBVCS Chris Sale 1.50 4.00
OBVDJ Derek Jeter 4.00 10.00
OBVDM Don Mattingly 6.00 15.00
OBVDO David Ortiz 1.50 4.00
OBVFL Francisco Lindor 1.50 4.00
OBVHA Hank Aaron 3.00 8.00
OBVJA Jose Altuve 1.25 3.00
OBVJB Javier Baez 2.00 5.00
OBVJM Juan Marichal 1.25 3.00
OBVJR Jackie Robinson 1.50 4.00
OBVJS Juan Soto 5.00 12.00
OBVJV Joey Votto 1.50 4.00
OBVKB Kris Bryant 2.00 5.00
OBVKD Khris Davis 1.50 4.00
OBVKS Kyle Schwarber 1.50 4.00
OBVLG Lou Gehrig 3.00 8.00
OBVMB Mookie Betts 2.50 6.00
OBVMC Matt Carpenter 1.50 4.00
OBVMM Manny Machado 1.50 4.00
OBVMR Mariano Rivera 2.00 5.00
OBVMS Max Scherzer 1.50 4.00
OBVMT Mike Trout 8.00 20.00
OBVNA Nolan Arenado 2.00 5.00
OBVNR Nolan Ryan 5.00 12.00
OBVNS Noah Syndergaard 1.25 3.00
OBVOA Ozzie Albies 1.50 4.00
OBVRA Ronald Acuna Jr. 8.00 20.00
OBVRC Roberto Clemente 4.00 10.00
OBVRH Rhys Hoskins 2.00 5.00
OBVSK Sandy Koufax 5.00 12.00
OBVSO Shohei Ohtani 2.00 5.00
OBVTW Ted Williams 3.00 8.00
OBVYM Yadier Molina 1.50 4.00
OBVABE Andrew Benintendi 1.50 4.00
OBVABR Alex Bregman 1.50 4.00
OBVMMC Mark McGwire 2.50 6.00
OBVRHE Rickey Henderson 1.50 4.00

2019 Stadium Club Power Zone

STATED ODDS 1:8 HOBBY
*RED: .75X TO 2X BASIC
*BLACK/99: 1.5X TO 4X BASIC
*ORANGE/50: 3X TO 8X BASIC
PZ1 Shohei Ohtani .60 1.50
PZ2 Mike Trout 2.50 6.00
PZ3 Bryce Harper .75 2.00
PZ4 Aaron Judge 1.25 3.00
PZ5 Mark McGwire .75 2.00
PZ6 Cal Ripken Jr. 1.50 4.00
PZ7 Hideki Matsui .50 1.25
PZ8 Kris Bryant .60 1.50
PZ9 Chipper Jones .50 1.25
PZ10 Will Clark .40 1.00
PZ11 Francisco Lindor .50 1.25
PZ12 Miguel Andujar .50 1.25
PZ13 Todd Helton .40 1.00
PZ14 Alex Bregman .50 1.25
PZ15 Ronald Acuna Jr. 2.50 6.00
PZ16 Kyle Schwarber .50 1.25
PZ17 Rhys Hoskins .60 1.50
PZ18 Christian Yelich .60 1.50
PZ19 Khris Davis .50 1.25
PZ20 Gleyber Torres 1.00 2.50
PZ21 Mike Piazza .50 1.25
PZ22 Bo Jackson .50 1.25
PZ23 Matt Carpenter .50 1.25
PZ24 Vladimir Guerrero .40 1.00
PZ25 Ken Griffey Jr. 1.00 2.50

2019 Stadium Club Warp Speed

STATED ODDS 1:8 HOBBY
*RED: .75X TO 2X BASIC
*BLACK/99: 1.5X TO 4X BASIC
*ORANGE/50: 3X TO 8X BASIC
WS1 Ronald Acuna Jr. 2.50 6.00
WS2 Trea Turner .40 1.00
WS3 Francisco Lindor .50 1.25
WS4 Billy Hamilton .40 1.00
WS5 Harrison Bader .40 1.00
WS6 Adalberto Mondesi .40 1.00
WS7 Trevor Story .50 1.25
WS8 Victor Robles .60 1.50
WS9 Mike Trout 2.50 6.00
WS10 Whit Merrifield .50 1.25
WS11 Amed Rosario .40 1.00
WS12 Mookie Betts .75 2.00
WS13 Dee Gordon .30 .75
WS14 Javier Baez .60 1.50
WS15 Byron Buxton .40 1.00

2020 Stadium Club

1 Mike Trout 1.50 4.00
2 Nelson Cruz .30 .75
3 Babe Ruth .75 2.00
4 Justus Sheffield .30 .75
5 Bobby Bradley RC .40 1.00
6 Abraham Toro RC .40 1.00
7 Michel Baez RC .30 .75
8 Michael Conforto .25 .60
9 Jameson Taillon .25 .60
10 Chris Sale .30 .75
11 Matt Olson .20 .50
12 David Dahl .20 .50
13 Yadier Molina .30 .75
14 Anthony Rizzo .50 1.25
15 DJ LeMahieu .30 .75
16 Michael Chavis .25 .60
17 J.T. Realmuto .30 .75
18 Giancarlo Stanton .30 .75
19 Eddie Rosario .25 .60
20 Mitch Garver .20 .50
21 Xander Bogaerts .30 .75
22 Jose Ramirez .25 .60
23 Dylan Cease RC .60 1.50
24 Walker Buehler .40 1.00
25 Yasmani Grandal .20 .50
26 Sean Murphy RC .50 1.25
27 Mike Clevinger .25 .60
28 Max Muncy .25 .60
29 Lorenzo Cain .20 .50
30 Bryce Harper .50 1.25
31 John Means .20 .50
32 Yuli Gurriel .20 .50
33 Albert Pujols .40 1.00
34 Anthony Kay RC .30 .75
35 Lou Gehrig .60 1.50
36 Aristides Aquino RC .60 1.50
37 Mark Canha .20 .50
38 Eugenio Suarez .25 .60
39 Ryan Zimmerman .25 .60
40 Blake Snell .25 .60
41 Jonathan Villar .20 .50
42 Michael Brantley .25 .60
43 Byron Buxton .25 .60
44 Tommy Edman .30 .75
45 Justin Turner .25 .60
46 Joey Gallo .30 .75
47 Robel Garcia RC .30 .75
48 George Springer .25 .60
49 Josh VanMeter .20 .50
50 Mike Moustakas .25 .60
51 Adbert Alzolay RC .40 1.00
52 Mike Schmidt .50 1.25
53 Brusdar Graterol RC .50 1.25
54 David Wright .25 .60
55 Lucas Giolito .25 .60
56 Robinson Cano .25 .60
57 Shun Yamaguchi RC .40 1.00
58 Jason Varitek .30 .75
59 Sean Doolittle .20 .50
60 Josh Donaldson .25 .60
61 Dale Murphy .30 .75
62 Austin Meadows .25 .60
63 Yoan Moncada .30 .75
64 Yoshi Tsutsugo RC .40 1.00
65 Dario Agrazal RC .40 1.00
66 Aaron Hicks .25 .60
67 Ted Williams .60 1.50
68 Paul Goldschmidt .30 .75
69 Yordan Alvarez RC 1.50 4.00
70 Bob Feller .25 .60
71 Carl Yastrzemski .50 1.25
72 Zack Collins RC .40 1.00
73 Ketel Marte .25 .60
74 Brandon Woodruff .20 .50
75 Nolan Ryan 1.00 2.50
76 Mike Soroka .30 .75
77 Andrew McCutchen .30 .75
78 Sean Manaea .20 .50
79 Jose Abreu .30 .75
80 Mike Brosseau RC .60 1.50
81 Randal Grichuk .20 .50
82 Kirby Yates .20 .50
83 Max Kepler .25 .60
84 Adrian Morejon RC .30 .75
85 Kyle Hendricks .30 .75
86 Yu Chang RC .50 1.25
87 Clayton Kershaw .60 1.50
88 Starling Marte .25 .60
89 Adalberto Mondesi .30 .75
90 Tommy La Stella .20 .50
91 Max Scherzer .30 .75
92 Luke Voit .40 1.00
93 Kwang-Hyun Kim RC 1.00 2.50
94 Masahiro Tanaka .30 .75
95 Jesus Luzardo RC .60 1.50
96 Mark McGwire .50 1.25
97 Brendan Rodgers .30 .75
98 Sam Hilliard RC .50 1.25
99 Nomar Garciaparra .25 .60
100 Javier Baez .40 1.00
101 James Marvel RC .30 .75
102 Barry Larkin .25 .60
103 Hideki Matsui .30 .75
104 Juan Soto 1.00 2.50
105 Junior Fernandez RC .30 .75
106 Cal Ripken Jr. 1.00 2.50
107 Kris Bryant .40 1.00
108 Yusei Kikuchi .25 .60
109 Trey Mancini .30 .75
110 Ernie Banks .30 .75
111 Luis Severino .25 .60
112 Bo Bichette RC 5.00 12.00
113 Darryl Strawberry .20 .50
114 Robbie Ray .20 .50
115 Ramon Laureano .30 .75
116 Ronald Acuna Jr. 1.25 3.00
117 Miguel Cabrera .30 .75
118 Jacob deGrom .30 .75
119 Derek Dietrich .25 .60
120 Nolan Arenado .40 1.00
121 Nick Markakis .25 .60
122 Carter Kieboom .25 .60
123 Carlos Correa .30 .75
124 Keston Hiura .40 1.00
125 Sonny Gray .25 .60
126 Travis Demeritte RC .40 1.00
127 Miguel Sano .25 .60
128 Lourdes Gurriel Jr. .25 .60
129 Alex Young RC .30 .75
130 Cody Bellinger .60 1.50
131 Joey Votto .30 .75
132 Jeff McNeil .25 .60
133 Victor Robles .40 1.00
134 Didi Gregorius .25 .60
135 J.D. Martinez .30 .75
136 Zack Greinke .25 .60
137 Hyun-Jin Ryu .25 .60
138 Aaron Judge .75 2.00
139 Trevor Story .30 .75
140 Willie Mays .60 1.50
141 Danny Jansen .20 .50
142 Adam Wainwright .25 .60
143 Will Smith .40 1.00
144 Lewis Thorpe RC .30 .75
145 Shohei Ohtani .40 1.00
146 Jose Canseco .25 .60
147 Gleyber Torres .60 1.50
148 Honus Wagner .30 .75
149 Jose Urquidy RC .40 1.00
150 Rod Carew .25 .60
151 Nick Solak RC .50 1.25
152 Trent Grisham RC 1.25 3.00
153 Roberto Alomar .25 .60
154 Brian Anderson .20 .50
155 Joey Lucchesi .20 .50
156 Matt Thaiss RC .40 1.00
157 Marcell Ozuna .30 .75
158 Noah Syndergaard .25 .60
159 Roberto Clemente .75 2.00
160 Tony Gwynn .30 .75
161 Manny Machado .30 .75
162 Jaylin Davis RC .50 1.25
163 Nomar Mazara .20 .50
164 Pete Alonso .75 2.00
165 Stephen Strasburg .30 .75
166 Ozzie Smith .40 1.00
167 Trevor Bauer .30 .75
168 Ryne Sandberg .60 1.50
169 Chris Paddack .30 .75
170 Seth Brown RC .30 .75
171 Tim Lincecum .25 .60
172 Jeff Bagwell .25 .60
173 Freddie Freeman .40 1.00
174 Gio Urshela .30 .75
175 Justin Dunn RC .40 1.00
176 Dallas Keuchel .25 .60
177 Yasiel Puig .30 .75
178 Barry Zito .25 .60
179 Marcus Semien .20 .50
180 Josh Bell .25 .60
181 Josh Hader .20 .50
182 Aroldis Chapman .30 .75
183 Andres Munoz RC .40 1.00
184 Brandon Lowe .30 .75
185 Buster Posey .40 1.00
186 Austin Nola RC .50 1.25
187 Stan Musial .50 1.25
188 Fernando Tatis Jr. 1.25 3.00
189 Jorge Posada .25 .60
190 Dakota Hudson .25 .60
191 Francisco Lindor .30 .75
192 Hank Aaron .60 1.50
193 Jack Flaherty .25 .60
194 Matt Chapman .30 .75
195 Andrew Benintendi .30 .75
196 Marcus Stroman .25 .60
197 Mike Yastrzemski .50 1.25
198 Shed Long .25 .60
199 David Ortiz .30 .75
200 Will Clark .25 .60
201 Kerry Wood .20 .50
202 Patrick Corbin .25 .60
203 Chipper Jones .30 .75
204 Patrick Sandoval RC .50 1.25
205 Corey Kluber .25 .60
206 Salvador Perez .25 .60
207 Shane Bieber .30 .75
208 Domingo Leyba RC .40 1.00
209 Charlie Morton .30 .75
210 Eduardo Escobar .20 .50
211 Lance McCullers Jr. .20 .50
212 Jorge Soler .30 .75
213 Josh Rojas RC .30 .75
214 Ty Cobb .50 1.25
215 Gary Sanchez .30 .75
216 Rhys Hoskins .40 1.00
217 Logan Webb RC .40 1.00
218 Mookie Betts .60 1.50
219 Hunter Harvey RC .50 1.25
220 Paul DeJong .30 .75
221 Dan Vogelbach .20 .50
222 Elvis Andrus .25 .60
223 Matthew Boyd .20 .50
224 Edgar Martinez .25 .60
225 Nick Senzel .30 .75
226 Hunter Dozier .20 .50
227 Justin Verlander .30 .75
228 Khris Davis .30 .75
229 Tim Anderson .30 .75
230 Jordan Yamamoto RC .40 1.00
231 Al Kaline .30 .75
232 Jake Fraley RC .40 1.00
233 Nick Castellanos .30 .75
234 Rafael Devers .40 1.00
235 Carlos Santana .25 .60
236 Alex Bregman .30 .75
237 Brendan McKay RC .50 1.25
238 Amed Rosario .25 .60
239 Austin Hays .30 .75
240 A.J. Puk RC .60 1.50
241 Kyle Tucker .25 .60
242 George Brett .60 1.50
243 Aaron Nola .30 .75
244 Ichiro .40 1.00
245 Willi Castro RC .50 1.25
246 Trea Turner .25 .60
247 Gerrit Cole .50 1.25
248 Yu Darvish .30 .75
249 Kyle Lewis RC 5.00 12.00
250 Tyler Glasnow .20 .50
251 Luis Arraez .40 1.00
252 Brock Burke RC .30 .75
253 Nico Hoerner RC 1.25 3.00
254 Jose Berrios .25 .60
255 Dustin May RC 1.25 3.00
256 Bryan Reynolds .25 .60
257 Frank Thomas .30 .75
258 Isan Diaz RC .50 1.25
259 Joc Pederson .25 .60
260 Willie Calhoun .20 .50
261 Charlie Blackmon .30 .75
262 Zac Gallen RC .75 2.00
263 Corey Seager .30 .75
264 Cavan Biggio .40 1.00
265 Christian Walker .25 .60
266 Kolten Wong .25 .60
267 Mitch Keller .30 .75
268 Luis Castillo .25 .60
269 Aaron Civale RC .50 1.25
270 Ken Griffey Jr. .60 1.50
271 Logan Allen RC .30 .75
272 Don Mattingly .60 1.50
273 Austin Riley .50 1.25
274 Felix Hernandez .25 .60
275 Bubba Starling RC .60 1.50
276 Kyle Schwarber .30 .75
277 Johnny Bench .30 .75
278 Jose Altuve .25 .60
279 Mitch Haniger .25 .60
280 Dansby Swanson .30 .75
281 Josh Staumont RC .30 .75
282 Sheldon Neuse RC .40 1.00
283 Anthony Rendon .30 .75
284 James Karinchak RC .50 1.25
285 Shogo Akiyama .30 .75
286 Ozzie Albies .30 .75
287 Tommy Pham .20 .50
288 Vladimir Guerrero Jr. .60 1.50
289 Luis Robert RC 6.00 15.00
290 Sandy Koufax .60 1.50
291 Willson Contreras .30 .75
292 Christian Yelich .40 1.00
293 Randy Johnson .30 .75
294 T.J. Zeuch RC .30 .75
295 Jake Rogers RC .30 .75
296 Eduardo Rodriguez .20 .50
297 Mauricio Dubon RC .40 1.00
298 Gavin Lux RC 2.00 5.00
299 Randy Arozarena RC 2.50 6.00
300 Eloy Jimenez .60 1.50

2020 Stadium Club Black and White

BW: 5X TO 12X BASIC
BW RC: 3X TO 8X BASIC RC
STATED ODDS 1:48 HOBBY

2020 Stadium Club Black Foil

BLACK: 1.5X TO 4X BASIC
BLACK RC: 1X TO 2.5X BASIC RC
STATED ODDS 1:8 RETAIL

2020 Stadium Club Blue Foil

BLUE/50: 6X TO 15X BASIC
BLUE RC/50: 4X TO 10X BASIC RC
STATED ODDS 1:95 HOBBY
STATED PRINT RUN 50 SER.#'d SETS
9 Yordan Alvarez 20.00 50.00
04 Juan Soto 20.00 50.00
38 Aaron Judge 20.00 50.00
88 Fernando Tatis Jr. 25.00 60.00
92 Hank Aaron 25.00 60.00
44 Ichiro 12.00 30.00
70 Ken Griffey Jr. 40.00 100.00
90 Sandy Koufax 20.00 50.00

2020 Stadium Club Rainbow Foil

RAINBOW/25: 8X TO 20X BASIC
RAINBOW RC/25: 5X TO 1X BASIC RC
STATED ODDS 1:188 HOBBY
STATED PRINT RUN 25 SER.#'d SETS
Mike Trout 60.00 150.00
Babe Ruth 25.00 60.00
9 Yordan Alvarez 40.00 100.00
1 Carl Yastrzemski 15.00 40.00
04 Juan Soto 25.00 60.00
38 Aaron Judge 40.00 100.00
88 Fernando Tatis Jr. 40.00 100.00
92 Hank Aaron 30.00 80.00
44 Ichiro 15.00 40.00
70 Ken Griffey Jr. 50.00 120.00
90 Sandy Koufax 25.00 60.00

2020 Stadium Club Red Foil

RED: 1X TO 2.5X BASIC
RED RC: .6X TO 1.5X BASIC RC
STATED ODDS 1:3 HOBBY

2020 Stadium Club Sepia

SEPIA: 2X TO 5X BASIC
SEPIA RC: 1.2X TO 3X BASIC RC
STATED ODDS 1:8 RETAIL

2020 Stadium Club Autographs

STATED ODDS 1:9 HOBBY
EXCHANGE DEADLINE 7/31/22
S Mike Schmidt
AA Aristides Aquino 6.00 15.00
AJ Aaron Judge
AM Andres Munoz 4.00 10.00
AN Austin Nola 5.00 12.00
AT Abraham Toro 4.00 10.00
AY Alex Young 3.00 8.00
BB Bo Bichette EXCH 100.00 250.00
BG Brusdar Graterol 5.00 12.00
BH Bryce Harper
BL Brandon Lowe 8.00 20.00
BR Bryan Reynolds 4.00 10.00
BZ Barry Zito 8.00 20.00
CB Cavan Biggio 10.00 25.00
CJ Chipper Jones 60.00 150.00
CK Carter Kieboom 6.00 15.00
CY Christian Yelich
DL Domingo Leyba 4.00 10.00
DM Dustin May 20.00 50.00
DS Darryl Strawberry 25.00 60.00
DV Dan Vogelbach 3.00 8.00
DW David Wright 50.00 120.00
EJ Eloy Jimenez 15.00 40.00
EM Edgar Martinez 25.00 60.00
GL Gavin Lux EXCH 50.00 120.00
GT Gleyber Torres 30.00 80.00
GU Gio Urshela 12.00 30.00
JC Jose Canseco 15.00 40.00
JD Justin Dunn 4.00 10.00
JF Junior Fernandez 3.00 8.00
JK James Karinchak 8.00 20.00
JL Jesus Luzardo 10.00 25.00
JM James Marvel 3.00 8.00
JR Jake Rogers 3.00 8.00
JS Josh Staumont 3.00 8.00
JU Jose Urquidy 4.00 10.00
JV Josh VanMeter 3.00 8.00
JY Jordan Yamamoto 4.00 10.00
KB Kris Bryant
KL Kyle Lewis 40.00 100.00
KY Kirby Yates 12.00 30.00
LR Luis Robert 75.00 200.00
MB Mike Brosseau 6.00 15.00
MD Mauricio Dubon 4.00 10.00
MG Mitch Garver 8.00 20.00
MO Matt Olson 6.00 15.00
MT Matt Thaiss 4.00 10.00
MY Mike Yastrzemski 25.00 60.00
NH Nico Hoerner 12.00 30.00
NS Nick Solak 5.00 12.00
PA Pete Alonso 30.00 80.00
RA Randy Arozarena 50.00 120.00
RG Robel Garcia 3.00 8.00
RH Rhys Hoskins 15.00 40.00
SH Sam Hilliard 5.00 12.00
SL Shed Long 4.00 10.00
SM Sean Murphy 5.00 12.00
SN Sheldon Neuse 4.00 10.00
TA Tim Anderson 10.00 25.00
TD Travis Demeritte 4.00 10.00
TG Trent Grisham 10.00 25.00
TL Tim Lincecum 40.00 100.00
ATZ T.J. Zeuch 3.00 8.00
AVG Vladimir Guerrero Jr. 40.00 100.00
AVR Victor Robles 6.00 15.00
AWC Willi Castro 8.00 20.00
AWS Will Smith 8.00 20.00
AXB Xander Bogaerts 25.00 60.00
AYA Yordan Alvarez 30.00 80.00
AYG Yasmani Grandal 5.00 12.00
AZC Zack Collins 4.00 10.00
AZG Zac Gallen 6.00 15.00
AAKA Anthony Kay 3.00 8.00
AAME Austin Meadows 6.00 15.00
ABBR Bobby Bradley 4.00 10.00
ABBU Brock Burke 3.00 8.00
ADCE Dylan Cease 6.00 15.00
ADMA Don Mattingly 50.00 120.00
AJAL Jose Altuve 15.00 40.00
AJDA Jaylin Davis 5.00 12.00
AJdG Jacob deGrom 40.00 100.00
AJFR Jake Fraley 4.00 10.00
AJME John Means 3.00 8.00
AJMN Jeff McNeil 8.00 20.00
AJRO Josh Rojas 3.00 8.00
AJSO Jorge Soler 8.00 20.00
AJST Juan Soto 75.00 200.00
AJVA Jason Varitek 40.00 100.00
AKHE Kyle Hendricks 10.00 25.00
AKHI Keston Hiura 10.00 25.00
ALGI Lucas Giolito 10.00 25.00
AMBA Michel Baez 3.00 8.00
AMMC Mark McGwire 50.00 120.00
AMMU Max Muncy 6.00 15.00
AMSO Mike Soroka 10.00 25.00
AMTR Mike Trout 400.00 800.00
ARAJ Ronald Acuna Jr. 60.00 150.00
ARAL Roberto Alomar 40.00 100.00
ARLA Ramon Laureano 5.00 12.00
ATLS Tommy La Stella 3.00 8.00
AWCL Will Clark 30.00 80.00

2020 Stadium Club Autographs Black

*BLACK/25: .6X TO 1.5X BASIC
STATED ODDS 1:754 HOBBY
STATED PRINT RUN 25 SER.#'d SETS
EXCHANGE DEADLINE 7/31/22
AGL Gavin Lux EXCH 125.00 300.00
AKL Kyle Lewis 75.00 200.00

2020 Stadium Club Autographs Red

*RED/50: .5X TO 1.2X BASIC
STATED ODDS 1:388 HOBBY
STATED PRINT RUN 50 SER.#'d SETS
EXCHANGE DEADLINE 7/31/22
AGL Gavin Lux EXCH 100.00 250.00

2020 Stadium Club Bash and Burn

STATED ODDS 1:8 HOBBY
*RED: .6X TO 1.5X BASIC
BAB1 Ronald Acuna Jr. 2.50 6.00
BAB2 Mike Trout 3.00 8.00
BAB3 Shohei Ohtani .75 2.00
BAB4 Christian Yelich .75 2.00
BAB5 Vladimir Guerrero Jr. 1.25 3.00
BAB6 Juan Soto 2.00 5.00
BAB7 Fernando Tatis Jr. 2.50 6.00
BAB8 Bryce Harper 1.00 2.50
BAB9 Rickey Henderson .60 1.50
BAB10 Victor Robles .75 2.00
BAB11 Ken Griffey Jr. 1.25 3.00
BAB12 Gavin Lux 2.50 6.00
BAB13 Jose Altuve .50 1.25
BAB14 Bo Bichette 3.00 8.00
BAB15 Mookie Betts 1.25 3.00

2020 Stadium Club Bash and Burn Black

*BLACK/99: .8X TO 2X BASIC
STATED ODDS 1:952 HOBBY
STATED PRINT RUN 99 SER.#'d SETS
BAB11 Ken Griffey Jr. 8.00 20.00

2020 Stadium Club Bash and Burn Orange

*ORANGE/50: 1.5X TO 4X BASIC
STATED ODDS 1:1883 HOBBY
STATED PRINT RUN 50 SER.#'d SETS
BAB11 Ken Griffey Jr. 15.00 40.00

2020 Stadium Club Chrome Insert

STATED ODDS 1:6 HOBBY
1 Mike Trout 6.00 15.00
13 Yadier Molina 1.25 3.00
14 Anthony Rizzo 2.00 5.00
18 Giancarlo Stanton 1.25 3.00
21 Xander Bogaerts 1.25 3.00
23 Dylan Cease 1.50 4.00
24 Walker Buehler 1.50 4.00
26 Sean Murphy 1.25 3.00
30 Bryce Harper 2.00 5.00
33 Albert Pujols 1.50 4.00
34 Anthony Kay .75 2.00
36 Aristides Aquino 1.50 4.00
47 Robel Garcia .75 2.00
48 George Springer 1.00 2.50
51 Adbert Alzolay 1.00 2.50
54 David Wright 1.00 2.50
68 Paul Goldschmidt 1.25 3.00
69 Yordan Alvarez 4.00 10.00
72 Zack Collins 1.00 2.50
75 Nolan Ryan 4.00 10.00
77 Andrew McCutchen 1.25 3.00
87 Clayton Kershaw 2.50 6.00
91 Max Scherzer 1.25 3.00
94 Masahiro Tanaka 1.25 3.00
95 Jesus Luzardo 1.50 4.00
96 Mark McGwire 2.00 5.00
100 Javier Baez 1.50 4.00
102 Barry Larkin 1.00 2.50
103 Hideki Matsui 1.25 3.00
104 Juan Soto 5.00 12.00
106 Cal Ripken Jr. 4.00 10.00
107 Kris Bryant 1.50 4.00
112 Bo Bichette 12.00 30.00
113 Darryl Strawberry .75 2.00
116 Ronald Acuna Jr. 5.00 12.00
118 Jacob deGrom 1.25 3.00
120 Nolan Arenado 1.50 4.00
123 Carlos Correa 1.25 3.00
124 Keston Hiura 1.50 4.00
130 Cody Bellinger 2.50 6.00
131 Joey Votto 1.25 3.00
138 Aaron Judge 3.00 8.00
139 Trevor Story 1.25 3.00
145 Shohei Ohtani 1.50 4.00
147 Gleyber Torres 2.50 6.00
151 Nick Solak 1.25 3.00
158 Noah Syndergaard 1.00 2.50
160 Tony Gwynn 1.25 3.00
161 Manny Machado 1.25 3.00
162 Jaylin Davis 1.25 3.00
164 Pete Alonso 3.00 8.00
165 Stephen Strasburg 1.25 3.00
173 Freddie Freeman 1.50 4.00
180 Josh Bell 1.00 2.50
185 Buster Posey 1.50 4.00
188 Fernando Tatis Jr. 5.00 12.00
191 Francisco Lindor 1.25 3.00
192 Hank Aaron 2.50 6.00
193 Jack Flaherty 1.00 2.50
199 David Ortiz 1.25 3.00
200 Will Clark 1.00 2.50
203 Chipper Jones 1.25 3.00
216 Rhys Hoskins 1.50 4.00
218 Mookie Betts 2.50 6.00
227 Justin Verlander 1.25 3.00
233 Nick Castellanos 1.25 3.00
234 Rafael Devers 1.50 4.00
236 Alex Bregman 1.25 3.00
237 Brendan McKay 1.25 3.00
240 A.J. Puk 1.50 4.00
244 Ichiro 1.50 4.00
247 Gerrit Cole 2.00 5.00
249 Kyle Lewis 8.00 20.00
253 Nico Hoerner 3.00 8.00
255 Dustin May 3.00 8.00
257 Frank Thomas 1.25 3.00
262 Zac Gallen 2.00 5.00
270 Ken Griffey Jr. 2.50 6.00
272 Don Mattingly 2.50 6.00
278 Jose Altuve 1.00 2.50
283 Anthony Rendon 1.25 3.00
286 Ozzie Albies 1.25 3.00
288 Vladimir Guerrero Jr. 2.50 6.00
290 Sandy Koufax 2.50 6.00
291 Willson Contreras 1.25 3.00
292 Christian Yelich 1.50 4.00
293 Randy Johnson 1.25 3.00
295 Jake Rogers .75 2.00
296 Gavin Lux 5.00 12.00
300 Eloy Jimenez 2.50 6.00

2020 Stadium Club Chrome Insert Gold Mint

*GOLD MINT: 2X TO 5X BASIC
STATED ODDS 1:256 HOBBY
1 Mike Trout 60.00 150.00
69 Yordan Alvarez 50.00 120.00
104 Juan Soto 30.00 80.00
188 Fernando Tatis Jr. 50.00 120.00
249 Kyle Lewis 60.00 150.00
270 Ken Griffey Jr. 50.00 120.00
298 Gavin Lux 50.00 120.00

2020 Stadium Club Chrome Insert Orange Refractors

*ORANGE/99: 1.2X TO 3X BASIC
STATED ODDS 1:159 HOBBY
STATED PRINT RUN 99 SER.#'d SETS
1 Mike Trout 40.00 100.00
69 Yordan Alvarez 30.00 80.00
104 Juan Soto 20.00 50.00
188 Fernando Tatis Jr. 30.00 80.00
249 Kyle Lewis 40.00 100.00
270 Ken Griffey Jr. 30.00 80.00

2020 Stadium Club Chrome Insert Refractors

*REF.: .8X TO 2X BASIC
STATED ODDS 1:64 HOBBY
1 Mike Trout 25.00 60.00
249 Kyle Lewis 25.00 60.00
270 Ken Griffey Jr. 20.00 50.00

2020 Stadium Club Emperors of the Zone

STATED ODDS 1:16 HOBBY
*RED: .6X TO 1.5X BASIC
EOZ1 Mike Soroka .60 1.50
EOZ2 Chris Paddack .60 1.50
EOZ3 Lucas Giolito .50 1.25
EOZ4 Shohei Ohtani .75 2.00
EOZ5 Sonny Gray .50 1.25
EOZ6 Mike Clevinger .50 1.25
EOZ7 Shane Bieber .60 1.50
EOZ8 Gerrit Cole 1.00 2.50
EOZ9 Justin Verlander .60 1.50
EOZ10 Zack Greinke .50 1.25
EOZ11 Clayton Kershaw 1.25 3.00
EOZ12 Walker Buehler .75 2.00
EOZ13 Jacob deGrom .60 1.50
EOZ14 Jack Flaherty .50 1.25
EOZ15 Max Scherzer .60 1.50
EOZ16 Brendan McKay .60 1.50
EOZ17 Aaron Nola .60 1.50
EOZ18 Stephen Strasburg .60 1.50
EOZ19 Chris Sale .60 1.50
EOZ20 Noah Syndergaard .50 1.25
EOZ21 Luis Severino .50 1.25
EOZ22 Blake Snell .50 1.25
EOZ23 Tyler Glasnow .40 1.00
EOZ24 Jose Berrios .50 1.25
EOZ25 Patrick Corbin .50 1.25

2020 Stadium Club Emperors of the Zone Black

*BLACK/99: .8X TO 2X BASIC
STATED ODDS 1:571 HOBBY
EOZ11 Clayton Kershaw 5.00 12.00

2020 Stadium Club Emperors of the Zone Orange

*ORANGE/50: 1.5X TO 4X BASIC
STATED ODDS 1:1131 HOBBY
STATED PRINT RUN 50 SER.#'d SETS
EOZ11 Clayton Kershaw 10.00 25.00

2020 Stadium Club In the Wings

STATED ODDS 1:16 HOBBY
*RED: .6X TO 1.5X BASIC
ITW1 Ronald Acuna Jr. 2.50 6.00
ITW2 Vladimir Guerrero Jr. 1.25 3.00
ITW3 Juan Soto 2.00 5.00
ITW4 Fernando Tatis Jr. 2.50 6.00
ITW5 Victor Robles .75 2.00
ITW6 Bo Bichette 3.00 8.00
ITW7 Aristides Aquino .75 2.00
ITW8 Gavin Lux 2.50 6.00
ITW9 Gleyber Torres 1.25 3.00
ITW10 Kyle Tucker .50 1.25
ITW11 Ozzie Albies .60 1.50
ITW12 Yordan Alvarez 2.00 5.00
ITW13 Pete Alonso 1.50 4.00
ITW14 Keston Hiura .75 2.00
ITW15 Rafael Devers .75 2.00
ITW16 Shane Bieber .60 1.50
ITW17 Jack Flaherty .50 1.25
ITW18 Shohei Ohtani .75 2.00
ITW19 Walker Buehler .75 2.00
ITW20 Chris Paddack .60 1.50
ITW21 Mike Soroka .60 1.50
ITW22 Eloy Jimenez 1.25 3.00
ITW23 Cody Bellinger 1.25 3.00
ITW24 Jesus Luzardo .75 2.00
ITW25 Nico Hoerner 1.50 4.00

2020 Stadium Club In the Wings Black

*BLACK/99: .8X TO 2X BASIC
STATED ODDS 1:571 HOBBY
STATED PRINT RUN 99 SER.#'d SETS
ITW9 Gleyber Torres 6.00 15.00

2020 Stadium Club In the Wings Orange

*ORANGE/50: 1.5X TO 4X BASIC
STATED ODDS 1:1131 HOBBY
STATED PRINT RUN 50 SER.#'d SETS
ITW9 Gleyber Torres 12.00 30.00

2020 Stadium Club Instavision

STATED ODDS 1:256 HOBBY
IVC1 Ronald Acuna Jr. 6.00 15.00
IVC2 Vladimir Guerrero Jr. 5.00 12.00
IVC3 Fernando Tatis Jr. 10.00 25.00
IVC4 Peter Alonso 6.00 15.00
IVC5 Mike Trout 12.00 30.00
IVC6 Bryce Harper 6.00 15.00
IVC7 Luis Robert 15.00 40.00
IVC8 Gavin Lux 5.00 12.00
IVC9 Yordan Alvarez 5.00 12.00
IVC10 Bo Bichette 12.00 30.00

2020 Stadium Club Instavision Black

*BLACK/25: .8X TO 2X BASIC
STATED ODDS 1:5630 HOBBY
STATED PRINT RUN 25 SER.#'d SETS
IVC3 Fernando Tatis Jr. 40.00 100.00
IVC4 Peter Alonso 20.00 50.00
IVC5 Mike Trout 40.00 100.00
IVC7 Luis Robert 125.00 300.00
IVC10 Bo Bichette 30.00 80.00

2020 Stadium Club Instavision Red

*RED/50: .5X TO 1.2X BASIC
STATED ODDS 1:2828 HOBBY
STATED PRINT RUN 50 SER.#'d SETS
IVC3 Fernando Tatis Jr. 20.00 50.00
IVC4 Peter Alonso 12.00 30.00
IVC5 Mike Trout 25.00 60.00
IVC7 Luis Robert 75.00 200.00
IVC10 Bo Bichette 20.00 50.00

2020 Stadium Club Lone Star Signatures

STATED ODDS 1:4471 HOBBY
PRINT RUNS B/WN 10-25 COPIES PER
NO PRICING ON QTY 15 OR LESS
EXCHANGE DEADLINE 7/31/22
LSSBH Bryce Harper
LSSCY Christian Yelich/25 EXCH 50.00 120.00
LSSDJ Derek Jeter/25
LSSDW David Wright/25 60.00 150.00
LSSFT Frank Thomas/25 60.00 150.00
LSSGL Gavin Lux/25 EXCH 100.00 250.00
LSSJS Juan Soto/25 60.00 150.00
LSSPA Pete Alonso/25 60.00 150.00
LSSYA Yordan Alvarez/25 60.00 150.00
LSSBBI Bo Bichette/25 EXCH 60.00 150.00
LSSKGJ Ken Griffey Jr.
LSSRAJ Ronald Acuna Jr./25

2020 Stadium Club Oversized Box Toppers

STATED ODDS 1 PER HOBBY BOX
OBB Barry Bonds 2.50 6.00
OBS Mike Schmidt 2.50 6.00
OBAA Aristides Aquino 2.00 5.00
OBAJ Aaron Judge 10.00 25.00
OBBB Bo Bichette 8.00 20.00
OBBH Bryce Harper 2.50 6.00
OBBZ Barry Zito 1.25 3.00
OBCI Ichiro 5.00 12.00
OBCJ Chipper Jones 1.50 4.00
OBCR Cal Ripken Jr. 5.00 12.00
OBCY Christian Yelich 2.00 5.00
OBDM Dale Murphy 1.50 4.00
OBDS Darryl Strawberry 1.00 2.50
OBEM Edgar Martinez 1.25 3.00
OBFL Francisco Lindor 1.50 4.00
OBFT Fernando Tatis Jr. 6.00 15.00
OBGL Gavin Lux 6.00 15.00
OBGT Gleyber Torres 3.00 8.00
OBHA Hank Aaron 3.00 8.00
OBHM Hideki Matsui 1.50 4.00
OBJd Jacob deGrom 1.50 4.00
OBJL Jesus Luzardo 2.00 5.00
OBJS Juan Soto 5.00 12.00
OBJV Jason Varitek 1.50 4.00
OBKB Kris Bryant 2.00 5.00
OBKG Ken Griffey Jr. 10.00 25.00
OBKL Kyle Lewis 8.00 20.00
OBMM Mark McGwire 8.00 20.00
OBMS Max Scherzer 1.50 4.00
OBNA Nolan Arenado 2.00 5.00
OBNR Nolan Ryan 8.00 20.00
OBOA Ozzie Albies 1.50 4.00
OBPA Pete Alonso 4.00 10.00
OBPG Paul Goldschmidt 1.50 4.00
OBRA Roberto Alomar 1.25 3.00
OBRH Rhys Hoskins 2.00 5.00
OBRJ Randy Johnson 1.50 4.00
OBSB Shane Bieber 1.50 4.00
OBSO Shohei Ohtani 2.00 5.00
OBTL Tim Lincecum 1.25 3.00
OBVG Vladimir Guerrero Jr. 3.00 8.00
OBVR Victor Robles 2.00 5.00
OBWC Will Clark 1.25 3.00
OBXB Xander Bogaerts 1.50 4.00
OBYA Yordan Alvarez 5.00 12.00
OBDMA Dustin May 4.00 10.00
OBDMT Don Mattingly 3.00 8.00
OBFTH Frank Thomas 1.50 4.00
OBJCO Jose Canseco 1.25 3.00
OBRAJ Ronald Acuna Jr. 6.00 15.00

2020 Stadium Club Oversized Widevision

STATED ODDS 1 PER BLASTER BOX
30 Bryce Harper 8.00 20.00
68 Paul Goldschmidt 1.25 3.00
69 Yordan Alvarez 4.00 10.00
75 Nolan Ryan 8.00 20.00
96 Mark McGwire 2.00 5.00
100 Javier Baez 1.50 4.00
104 Juan Soto 10.00 25.00
107 Kris Bryant 1.50 4.00
116 Ronald Acuna Jr. 5.00 12.00
118 Jacob deGrom 5.00 12.00
120 Nolan Arenado 1.50 4.00
130 Cody Bellinger 2.50 6.00
138 Aaron Judge 3.00 8.00
147 Gleyber Torres 2.50 6.00
164 Pete Alonso 3.00 8.00
188 Fernando Tatis Jr. 12.00 30.00
192 Hank Aaron 2.50 6.00
218 Mookie Betts 2.50 6.00
227 Justin Verlander 1.25 3.00
244 Ichiro 1.50 4.00
249 Kyle Lewis 6.00 15.00
288 Vladimir Guerrero Jr. 2.50 6.00
290 Sandy Koufax 2.50 6.00
292 Christian Yelich 1.50 4.00
298 Gavin Lux 5.00 12.00

2020 Stadium Club Power Zone

STATED ODDS 1:16 HOBBY
*RED: .6X TO 1.5X BASIC
PZ1 Darryl Strawberry .40 1.00
PZ2 Pete Alonso 1.50 4.00
PZ3 Mike Trout 3.00 8.00
PZ4 Shohei Ohtani .75 2.00
PZ5 Christian Yelich .75 2.00
PZ6 Chipper Jones .60 1.50
PZ7 Ronald Acuna Jr. 2.50 6.00
PZ8 Vladimir Guerrero Jr. 1.25 3.00
PZ9 Juan Soto 2.00 5.00
PZ10 Fernando Tatis Jr. 2.50 6.00
PZ11 Mark McGwire 1.00 2.50
PZ12 Rhys Hoskins .75 2.00
PZ13 Bryce Harper 1.00 2.50
PZ14 Aaron Judge 1.50 4.00
PZ15 Jeff Bagwell .50 1.25
PZ16 Francisco Lindor .60 1.50
PZ17 Frank Thomas .60 1.50
PZ18 Eloy Jimenez 1.25 3.00
PZ19 Kris Bryant .75 2.00
PZ20 Anthony Rizzo 1.00 2.50
PZ21 David Wright .50 1.25
PZ22 Nolan Arenado .75 2.00
PZ23 Gleyber Torres 1.25 3.00
PZ24 Yordan Alvarez 2.00 5.00
PZ25 Ken Griffey Jr. 1.25 3.00

2020 Stadium Club Power Zone Black

*BLACK/99: .8X TO 2X BASIC
STATED ODDS 1:571 HOBBY
STATED PRINT RUN 99 SER.#'d SETS
PZ25 Ken Griffey Jr. 10.00 25.00

2020 Stadium Club Power Zone Orange

*ORANGE/50: 1.5X TO 4X BASIC
STATED ODDS 1:1131 HOBBY
STATED PRINT RUN 50 SER.#'d SETS
PZ14 Aaron Judge 15.00 40.00
PZ25 Ken Griffey Jr. 20.00 50.00

2020 Stadium Club Chrome

1 Mike Trout 4.00 10.00
2 Nelson Cruz .60 1.50
3 Babe Ruth 1.50 4.00
4 Justus Sheffield .60 1.50
5 Bobby Bradley RC .75 2.00
6 Abraham Toro RC .75 2.00
7 Michel Baez RC .60 1.50
8 Michael Conforto .50 1.25
9 Jameson Taillon .50 1.25
10 Chris Sale .60 1.50
11 Matt Olson .40 1.00
12 David Dahl .40 1.00
13 Yadier Molina .60 1.50
14 Anthony Rizzo 1.00 2.50
15 DJ LeMahieu .60 1.50
16 Michael Chavis .50 1.25
17 J.T. Realmuto .60 1.50
18 Giancarlo Stanton .60 1.50
19 Eddie Rosario .50 1.25
20 Mitch Garver .40 1.00
21 Xander Bogaerts .60 1.50
22 Jose Ramirez .50 1.25
23 Dylan Cease RC 1.25 3.00
24 Walker Buehler .75 2.00
25 Yasmani Grandal .40 1.00
26 Sean Murphy RC 1.00 2.50
27 Mike Clevinger .50 1.25
28 Max Muncy .50 1.25
29 Lorenzo Cain .40 1.00
30 Bryce Harper 1.00 2.50
31 John Means .40 1.00
32 Yuli Gurriel .50 1.25
33 Albert Pujols .75 2.00
34 Anthony Kay RC .60 1.50
35 Lou Gehrig 1.25 3.00
36 Aristides Aquino RC 1.25 3.00
37 Mark Canha .40 1.00
38 Eugenio Suarez .50 1.25
39 Ryan Zimmerman .50 1.25
40 Blake Snell .50 1.25
41 Jonathan Villar .40 1.00
42 Michael Brantley .50 1.25
43 Byron Buxton .50 1.25
44 Tommy Edman .60 1.50
45 Justin Turner .50 1.25
46 Joey Gallo .60 1.50
47 Robel Garcia RC .60 1.50
48 George Springer .50 1.25
49 Josh VanMeter .40 1.00
50 Mike Moustakas .50 1.25
51 Adbert Alzolay RC .75 2.00
52 Mike Schmidt 1.00 2.50
53 Brusdar Graterol RC 1.00 2.50
54 David Wright .50 1.25
55 Lucas Giolito .50 1.25
56 Robinson Cano .50 1.25
57 Shun Yamaguchi RC .75 2.00
58 Jason Varitek .60 1.50
59 Sean Doolittle .40 1.00
60 Josh Donaldson .50 1.25
61 Dale Murphy .60 1.50
62 Austin Meadows .50 1.25
63 Yoan Moncada .60 1.50
64 Yoshi Tsutsugo RC .75 2.00
65 Dario Agrazal RC .75 2.00
66 Aaron Hicks .50 1.25
67 Ted Williams 1.25 3.00
68 Paul Goldschmidt .60 1.50
69 Yordan Alvarez RC 3.00 8.00
70 Bob Feller .50 1.25
71 Carl Yastrzemski 1.00 2.50
72 Zack Collins RC .75 2.00
73 Ketel Marte .50 1.25
74 Brandon Woodruff .40 1.00
75 Nolan Ryan 2.00 5.00
76 Mike Soroka .60 1.50
77 Andrew McCutchen .60 1.50
78 Sean Manaea .40 1.00
79 Jose Abreu .60 1.50
80 Mike Brosseau RC 1.25 3.00
81 Randal Grichuk .40 1.00
82 Kirby Yates .40 1.00
83 Max Kepler .50 1.25
84 Adrian Morejon RC .60 1.50
85 Kyle Hendricks .60 1.50
86 Yu Chang RC 1.00 2.50
87 Clayton Kershaw 1.25 3.00
88 Starling Marte .50 1.25
89 Adalberto Mondesi .60 1.50
90 Tommy La Stella .40 1.00
91 Max Scherzer .60 1.50
92 Luke Voit .75 2.00
93 Kwang-Hyun Kim RC 2.00 5.00
94 Masahiro Tanaka .60 1.50
95 Jesus Luzardo RC 1.25 3.00
96 Mark McGwire 1.00 2.50
97 Brendan Rodgers .60 1.50
98 Sam Hilliard RC 1.00 2.50
99 Nomar Garciaparra .50 1.25
100 Javier Baez .75 2.00
101 James Marvel RC .60 1.50
102 Barry Larkin .50 1.25
103 Hideki Matsui .60 1.50
104 Juan Soto 3.00 7.00
105 Junior Fernandez RC .60 1.50
106 Cal Ripken Jr. 2.00 5.00
107 Kris Bryant .75 2.00
108 Yusei Kikuchi .50 1.25
109 Trey Mancini .60 1.50
110 Ernie Banks .60 1.50
111 Luis Severino .50 1.25
112 Bo Bichette RC 6.00 15.00
113 Darryl Strawberry .40 1.00
114 Robbie Ray .40 1.00
115 Ramon Laureano .60 1.50
116 Ronald Acuna Jr. 4.00 10.00
117 Miguel Cabrera .60 1.50
118 Jacob deGrom .60 1.50
119 Derek Dietrich .50 1.25
120 Nolan Arenado .75 2.00
121 Nick Markakis .50 1.25
122 Carter Kieboom .50 1.25
123 Carlos Correa .60 1.50
124 Keston Hiura .75 2.00
125 Sonny Gray .50 1.25
126 Travis Demeritte RC .75 2.00
127 Miguel Sano .50 1.25
128 Lourdes Gurriel Jr. .50 1.25
129 Alex Young RC .60 1.50
130 Cody Bellinger 1.25 3.00
131 Joey Votto .60 1.50
132 Jeff McNeil .50 1.25
133 Victor Robles .75 2.00
134 Didi Gregorius .50 1.25
135 J.D. Martinez .60 1.50
136 Zack Greinke .50 1.25
137 Hyun-Jin Ryu .50 1.25
138 Aaron Judge 1.50 4.00
139 Trevor Story .60 1.50
140 Willie Mays 1.25 3.00
141 Danny Jansen .40 1.00
142 Adam Wainwright .50 1.25
143 Will Smith .75 2.00
144 Lewis Thorpe RC .60 1.50
145 Shohei Ohtani .75 2.00
146 Jose Canseco .50 1.25
147 Gleyber Torres 1.25 3.00
148 Honus Wagner .60 1.50
149 Jose Urquidy RC .75 2.00
150 Rod Carew .50 1.25
151 Nick Solak RC 1.00 2.50
152 Trent Grisham RC 2.50 6.00
153 Roberto Alomar .50 1.25
154 Brian Anderson .40 1.00
155 Joey Lucchesi .40 1.00
156 Matt Thaiss RC .75 2.00
157 Marcell Ozuna .60 1.50
158 Noah Syndergaard .50 1.25
159 Roberto Clemente 1.50 4.00
160 Tony Gwynn .60 1.50
161 Manny Machado .60 1.50
162 Jaylin Davis RC 1.00 2.50
163 Nomar Mazara .40 1.00
164 Pete Alonso 1.50 4.00
165 Stephen Strasburg .60 1.50
166 Ozzie Smith .75 2.00
167 Trevor Bauer .60 1.50
168 Ryne Sandberg 1.25 3.00
169 Chris Paddack .60 1.50
170 Seth Brown RC .60 1.50
171 Tim Lincecum .50 1.25
172 Jeff Bagwell .50 1.25
173 Freddie Freeman .75 2.00
174 Gio Urshela .60 1.50
175 Justin Dunn RC .75 2.00
176 Dallas Keuchel .50 1.25
177 Yasiel Puig .60 1.50
178 Barry Zito .50 1.25
179 Marcus Semien .40 1.00
180 Josh Bell .50 1.25
181 Josh Hader .40 1.00
182 Aroldis Chapman .60 1.50
183 Andres Munoz RC .75 2.00
184 Brandon Lowe .60 1.50
185 Buster Posey .75 2.00
186 Austin Nola RC 1.00 2.50
187 Stan Musial 1.00 2.50
188 Fernando Tatis Jr. 2.50 6.00
189 Jorge Posada .50 1.25
190 Dakota Hudson .50 1.25
191 Francisco Lindor .60 1.50
192 Hank Aaron 1.25 3.00
193 Jack Flaherty .50 1.25
194 Matt Chapman .60 1.50
195 Andrew Benintendi .60 1.50
196 Marcus Stroman .50 1.25
197 Mike Yastrzemski 1.00 2.50
198 Shed Long RC .75 2.00
199 David Ortiz .60 1.50
200 Will Clark .50 1.25
201 Kerry Wood .40 1.00
202 Patrick Corbin .50 1.25
203 Chipper Jones .60 1.50
204 Patrick Sandoval RC 1.00 2.50
205 Corey Kluber .50 1.25
206 Salvador Perez .50 1.25
207 Shane Bieber .60 1.50
208 Domingo Leyba RC .75 2.00
209 Charlie Morton .60 1.50
210 Eduardo Escobar .40 1.00
211 Lance McCullers Jr. .40 1.00

212 Jorge Soler .60 1.50
213 Josh Rojas RC .60 1.50
214 Ty Cobb 1.00 2.50
215 Gary Sanchez .60 1.50
216 Rhys Hoskins .75 2.00
217 Logan Webb RC .75 2.00
218 Mookie Betts 1.25 3.00
219 Hunter Harvey RC 1.00 2.50
220 Paul DeJong .60 1.50
221 Dan Vogelbach .40 1.00
222 Elvis Andrus .50 1.25
223 Matthew Boyd .40 1.00
224 Edgar Martinez .50 1.25
225 Nick Senzel .60 1.50
226 Hunter Dozier .40 1.00
227 Justin Verlander .60 1.50
228 Khris Davis .60 1.50
229 Tim Anderson .60 1.50
230 Jordan Yamamoto RC .75 2.00
231 Al Kaline .60 1.50
232 Jake Fraley RC .75 2.00
233 Nick Castellanos .60 1.50
234 Rafael Devers .75 2.00
235 Carlos Santana .50 1.25
236 Alex Bregman .60 1.50
237 Brendan McKay RC 1.00 2.50
238 Amed Rosario .50 1.25
239 Austin Hays .60 1.50
240 A.J. Puk RC 1.25 3.00
241 Kyle Tucker .50 1.25
242 George Brett 1.25 3.00
243 Aaron Nola .60 1.50
244 Ichiro .75 2.00
245 Willi Castro RC 1.00 2.50
246 Trea Turner .50 1.25
247 Gerrit Cole 1.00 2.50
248 Yu Darvish .60 1.50
249 Kyle Lewis RC 5.00 12.00
250 Tyler Glasnow .40 1.00
251 Luis Arraez .75 2.00
252 Brock Burke RC .60 1.50
253 Nico Hoerner RC 2.50 6.00
254 Jose Berrios .50 1.25
255 Dustin May RC 2.50 6.00
256 Bryan Reynolds .50 1.25
257 Frank Thomas .60 1.50
258 Isan Diaz RC 1.00 2.50
259 Joc Pederson .50 1.25
260 Willie Calhoun .40 1.00
261 Charlie Blackmon .60 1.50
262 Zac Gallen RC 1.50 4.00
263 Corey Seager .60 1.50
264 Cavan Biggio .75 2.00
265 Christian Walker .50 1.25
266 Kolten Wong .50 1.25
267 Mitch Keller .60 1.50
268 Luis Castillo .50 1.25
269 Aaron Civale RC 1.00 2.50
270 Ken Griffey Jr. 2.00 5.00
271 Logan Allen RC .60 1.50
272 Don Mattingly 1.25 3.00
273 Austin Riley 1.00 2.50
274 Felix Hernandez .50 1.25
275 Bubba Starling RC 1.25 3.00
276 Kyle Schwarber .60 1.50
277 Johnny Bench .60 1.50
278 Jose Altuve .50 1.25
279 Mitch Haniger .50 1.25
280 Dansby Swanson .60 1.50
281 Josh Staumont RC .60 1.50
282 Sheldon Neuse RC .75 2.00
283 Anthony Rendon .60 1.50
284 James Karinchak RC 1.00 2.50
285 Shogo Akiyama RC 1.00 2.50
286 Ozzie Albies .60 1.50
287 Tommy Pham .40 1.00
288 Vladimir Guerrero Jr. 1.25 3.00
289 Luis Robert RC 12.00 30.00
290 Sandy Koufax 1.25 3.00
291 Willson Contreras .60 1.50
292 Christian Yelich .75 2.00
293 Randy Johnson .60 1.50
294 T.J. Zeuch RC .60 1.50
295 Jake Rogers RC .60 1.50
296 Eduardo Rodriguez .40 1.00
297 Mauricio Dubon RC .75 2.00
298 Gavin Lux RC 4.00 10.00
299 Randy Arozarena RC 5.00 12.00
300 Eloy Jimenez 1.25 3.00
301 David Price .50 1.25
302 Derek Jeter 1.50 4.00
303 Dylan Bundy .50 1.25
304 Renato Nunez .50 1.25
305 Hanser Alberto .40 1.00
306 Carlton Fisk .50 1.25
307 Wade Boggs .50 1.25
308 Roger Clemens .75 2.00
309 Cole Hamels .50 1.25
310 Jon Lester .50 1.25
311 Franmil Reyes .40 1.00
312 Carlos Carrasco .40 1.00
313 Ryan McMahon .40 1.00
314 Ryan Braun .50 1.25
315 Robin Yount .60 1.50
316 Brandon Nimmo .50 1.25
317 Gary Carter .50 1.25
318 Miguel Andujar .60 1.50
319 Eric Hosmer .50 1.25
320 Hunter Renfroe .40 1.00
321 Wil Myers .40 1.00
322 Jeff Samardzija .40 1.00
323 Evan Longoria .50 1.25
324 J.P. Crawford .40 1.00
325 Dee Gordon .40 1.00
326 Luis Urias .50 1.25
327 Francisco Mejia .50 1.25
328 Zach Wheeler .50 1.25
329 Danny Mendick RC .75 2.00
330 Rangel Ravelo RC .75 2.00
331 Tim Lopes RC .75 2.00
332 Dom Nunez RC .75 2.00
333 Tony Gonsolin RC 2.50 6.00
334 Tyler Alexander RC 1.00 2.50
335 Yonathan Daza RC .75 2.00
336 Randy Dobnak RC 1.25 3.00
337 Bryan Abreu RC .60 1.50
338 Clint Frazier .50 1.25
339 Frankie Montas .40 1.00
340 Eric Thames .40 1.00
341 Alex Verdugo .50 1.25
342 Max Fried .60 1.50
343 Ian Happ .50 1.25
344 Jason Heyward .50 1.25
345 Kenley Jansen .50 1.25
346 Jorge Polanco .50 1.25
347 Dinelson Lamet .40 1.00
348 Mike Minor .40 1.00
349 Edwin Encarnacion .60 1.50
350 Danny Santana .40 1.00
351 Kenta Maeda .50 1.25
352 Justin Upton .50 1.25
353 Jake Odorizzi .40 1.00
354 J.D. Davis .40 1.00
355 Chris Archer .40 1.00
356 Miles Mikolas .40 1.00
357 Starlin Castro .40 1.00
358 Michael Kopech .75 2.00
359 Willy Adames .40 1.00
360 Johnny Cueto .50 1.25
361 Kyle Seager .40 1.00
362 Kole Calhoun .40 1.00
363 Justin Smoak .40 1.00
364 Domingo Santana .50 1.25
365 Julio Teheran .50 1.25
366 Jesus Aguilar .40 1.00
367 Kevin Pillar .40 1.00
368 Howie Kendrick .40 1.00
369 Lewis Brinson .40 1.00
370 Yoenis Cespedes .60 1.50
371 Hunter Pence .50 1.25
372 Ryan O'Hearn .40 1.00
373 Alex Gordon .50 1.25
374 David Bednar RC .60 1.50
375 Jon Berti RC .60 1.50
376 Ryan McBroom RC .75 2.00
377 Chad Wallach RC .60 1.50
378 Scott Heineman RC .60 1.50
379 Edwin Rios RC 1.50 4.00
380 Brian O'Grady RC .60 1.50
381 Jack Mayfield RC .60 1.50
382 Lamonte Wade Jr. RC 1.00 2.50
383 Kyle Garlick RC 1.00 2.50
384 Seth Mejias-Brean RC .60 1.50
385 Garrett Stubbs RC .60 1.50
386 Kean Wong RC .75 2.00
387 Tyrone Taylor RC .60 1.50
388 Jose Rodriguez RC .60 1.50
389 Tom Eshelman RC .75 2.00
390 Robert Dugger RC .60 1.50
391 Emmanuel Clase RC .75 2.00
392 Jonathan Hernandez RC .60 1.50
393 Rogelio Armenteros RC .75 2.00
394 Danny Hultzen RC .75 2.00
395 Kevin Ginkel RC .60 1.50
396 Mariano Rivera .75 2.00
397 Vladimir Guerrero .50 1.25
398 Mike Piazza .60 1.50
399 Rickey Henderson .60 1.50
400 Jackie Robinson .60 1.50

2020 Stadium Club Chrome Gold Refractors

*GOLD REF.: 2X TO 5X BASIC
*GOLD REF.RC: 1.2X TO 3X BASIC RC
STATED ODDS 1:27 HOBBY
STATED PRINT RUN 50 SER.#'d SETS
1 Mike Trout 60.00 150.00
3 Babe Ruth 15.00 40.00
35 Lou Gehrig 15.00 40.00
67 Ted Williams 15.00 40.00
69 Yordan Alvarez 25.00 60.00
75 Nolan Ryan 15.00 40.00
104 Juan Soto 40.00 100.00
112 Bo Bichette 40.00 100.00
192 Hank Aaron 10.00 25.00
244 Ichiro 15.00 40.00
270 Ken Griffey Jr. 50.00 120.00
289 Luis Robert 75.00 200.00
290 Sandy Koufax 12.00 30.00
299 Randy Arozarena 50.00 120.00
302 Derek Jeter 40.00 100.00

2020 Stadium Club Chrome Orange Refractors

*ORNG REF.: 3X TO 8X BASIC
*ORNG REF.RC: 2X TO 5X BASIC RC
STATED ODDS 1:31 HOBBY
STATED PRINT RUN 25 SER.#'d SETS
1 Mike Trout 100.00 250.00
3 Babe Ruth 25.00 60.00
35 Lou Gehrig 25.00 60.00
67 Ted Williams 12.00 30.00
69 Yordan Alvarez 40.00 100.00
75 Nolan Ryan 25.00 60.00
104 Juan Soto 60.00 150.00
112 Bo Bichette 125.00 300.00
192 Hank Aaron 15.00 40.00
244 Ichiro 25.00 60.00
270 Ken Griffey Jr. 75.00 200.00
272 Don Mattingly 50.00 120.00
289 Luis Robert 125.00 300.00
290 Sandy Koufax 20.00 50.00
299 Randy Arozarena 75.00 200.00
302 Derek Jeter 60.00 150.00

2020 Stadium Club Chrome Refractors

*REF.: 1.2X TO 3X BASIC
*REF.RC: .8X TO 2X BASIC RC
STATED ODDS 1:2 HOBBY
1 Mike Trout 15.00 40.00
69 Yordan Alvarez 12.00 30.00
104 Juan Soto 12.00 30.00
112 Bo Bichette 20.00 50.00
270 Ken Griffey Jr. 8.00
289 Luis Robert 40.00 100.00
299 Randy Arozarena 15.00 40.00

2020 Stadium Club Chrome X-Fractors

*XFRAC.: 1.5X TO 5X BASIC
*XFRAC.RC: 1X TO 2.5X BASIC RC
STATED ODDS 4 PER BLASTER
1 Mike Trout 20.00 50.00
69 Yordan Alvarez 15.00 40.00
75 Nolan Ryan 10.00 25.00
104 Juan Soto 15.00 40.00
112 Bo Bichette 25.00 60.00
244 Ichiro 10.00 25.00
270 Ken Griffey Jr. 15.00 40.00
289 Luis Robert 50.00 120.00
299 Randy Arozarena 20.00 50.00
302 Derek Jeter 10.00 25.00

2020 Stadium Club Chrome Autographs

STATED ODDS 1:17 HOBBY
EXCHANGE DEADLINE 10/31/2022
CAAB Abraham Toro 4.00 10.00
CAAK Anthony Kay 3.00 8.00
CAAQ Aristides Aquino 15.00 40.00
CABH Bryce Harper 150.00 400.00
CABO Bo Bichette EXCH
CABS Blake Snell 8.00 20.00
CADC Dylan Cease 6.00 15.00
CADM Dustin May 15.00 40.00
CAEJ Eloy Jimenez
CAGL Gavin Lux
CAGT Gleyber Torres 40.00 100.00
CAJA Jake Rogers 3.00 8.00
CAJD Jaylin Davis 5.00 12.00
CAJF Jack Flaherty 20.00 50.00
CAJL Jesus Luzardo 10.00 25.00
CAJN Junior Fernandez 3.00 8.00
CAJS Juan Soto 150.00 400.00
CAJU Justin Dunn 4.00 10.00
CAJY Jordan Yamamoto 4.00 10.00
CAKH Keston Hiura 6.00 15.00
CAKL Kyle Lewis 50.00 120.00
CALW Logan Webb 4.00 10.00
CAMC Brendan McKay 8.00 20.00
CAMS Mike Soroka 12.00 30.00
CAMY Mike Yastrzemski 15.00 40.00
CANA Nolan Arenado
CANH Nico Hoerner 12.00 30.00
CANS Nick Solak 5.00 12.00
CAPA Pete Alonso
CAPG Paul Goldschmidt 25.00 60.00
CARA Ronald Acuna Jr. 100.00 250.00
CARG Robel Garcia 3.00 8.00
CASB Seth Brown 3.00 8.00
CASM Sean Murphy 6.00 15.00
CASO Shohei Ohtani 150.00 400.00
CAVG Vladimir Guerrero Jr. 40.00 100.00
CAYA Yordan Alvarez EXCH
CAZC Zack Collins 4.00 10.00
UAAM Andres Munoz 4.00 10.00
UAAR Austin Riley 15.00 40.00
UABA Bryan Abreu 3.00 8.00
UACB Cody Bellinger EXCH
UADJ Derek Jeter
UADL Domingo Leyba 4.00 10.00
UADN Dom Nunez 4.00 10.00
UAJF Jake Fraley 4.00 10.00
UAJR Josh Rojas 6.00 15.00
UAJS Josh Staumont 3.00 8.00
UAJU Jose Urquidy 4.00 10.00
UALR Luis Robert EXCH
UAMD Mauricio Dubon 4.00 10.00
UAMR Mike Brosseau 6.00 15.00
UAMT Matt Thaiss 4.00 10.00
UARA Randy Arozarena 60.00 150.00
UARD Randy Dobnak 10.00 25.00
UATA Tyler Alexander 5.00 12.00
UATD Travis Demeritte 4.00 10.00
UATE Tommy Edman 10.00 25.00
UATG Tony Gonsolin EXCH 12.00 30.00
UATL Tim Lopes 4.00 10.00
UAWC Willi Castro 15.00 40.00
UAYD Yonathan Daza 4.00 10.00

2020 Stadium Club Chrome Autographs Gold Refractors

*GOLD REF.: .5X TO 1.2X BASIC
STATED ODDS 1:171 HOBBY
STATED PRINT RUN 50 SER.#'d SETS
EXCHANGE DEADLINE 10/31/2022
CAMS Mike Soroka 20.00 50.00
UAWC Willi Castro 40.00 100.00

2020 Stadium Club Chrome Autographs Orange Refractors

*ORANGE REF.: .6X TO 1.5X BASIC
STATED ODDS 1:185 HOBBY
STATED PRINT RUN 25 SER.#'d SETS
EXCHANGE DEADLINE 10/31/2022
CAEJ Eloy Jimenez 40.00 100.00
CAJS Juan Soto 800.00 1500.00
CAMS Mike Soroka 25.00 601.00
UAWC Willi Castro 50.00 120.00

2020 Stadium Club Chrome Beam Team

STATED ODDS 1:4 HOBBY
BT1 Pete Alonso 3.00 8.00
BT2 Mike Trout 8.00 20.00
BT3 Shohei Ohtani 1.50 4.00
BT4 Christian Yelich 1.50 4.00
BT5 Ronald Acuna Jr. 5.00 12.00
BT6 Vladimir Guerrero Jr. 2.50 6.00
BT7 Juan Soto 4.00 10.00
BT8 Ken Griffey Jr. 4.00 10.00
BT9 Fernando Tatis Jr. 5.00 12.00
BT10 Bryce Harper 2.00 5.00
BT11 Aaron Judge 3.00 8.00
BT12 Luis Robert 8.00 20.00
BT13 Yordan Alvarez 4.00 10.00
BT14 Bo Bichette 6.00 15.00
BT15 Gavin Lux 5.00 12.00
BT16 Francisco Lindor 1.25 3.00
BT17 Clayton Kershaw 2.50 6.00
BT18 Walker Buehler 1.50 4.00
BT19 Max Scherzer 1.25 3.00
BT20 Kris Bryant 1.50 4.00
BT21 Cody Bellinger 2.50 6.00
BT22 Rafael Devers 1.50 4.00
BT23 Justin Verlander 1.25 3.00
BT24 Mookie Betts 2.50 6.00
BT25 Gleyber Torres 2.50 6.00

2020 Stadium Club Chrome Beam Team Gold Refractors

*GOLD REF.: 1.5X TO 4X BASIC
STATED ODDS 1:423 HOBBY
STATED PRINT RUN 50 SER.#'d SETS
BT2 Mike Trout 75.00 200.00
BT5 Ronald Acuna Jr. 40.00 100.00
BT7 Juan Soto 40.00 100.00
BT9 Fernando Tatis Jr. 40.00 100.00
BT10 Bryce Harper 12.00 30.00
BT12 Luis Robert 50.00 120.00
BT13 Yordan Alvarez 30.00 80.00
BT24 Mookie Betts 30.00 80.00

2020 Stadium Club Chrome Beam Team Orange Refractors

*ORANGE REF.: 2X TO 5X BASIC
STATED ODDS 1:482 HOBBY
STATED PRINT RUN 25 SER.#'d SETS
BT2 Mike Trout 100.00 250.00
BT5 Ronald Acuna Jr. 50.00 120.00
BT7 Juan Soto 50.00 120.00
BT9 Fernando Tatis Jr. 50.00 120.00
BT10 Bryce Harper 25.00 60.00
BT12 Luis Robert 100.00 250.00
BT13 Yordan Alvarez 40.00 100.00
BT24 Mookie Betts 40.00 100.00

2020 Stadium Club Chrome Emperors of the Zone

STATED ODDS 1:14 HOBBY
*GOLD REF.: 1.5X TO 4X BASIC
*ORANGE REF.: 2X TO 5X BASIC
EOZ1 Mike Soroka 1.25 3.00
EOZ2 Chris Paddack 1.25 3.00
EOZ3 Lucas Giolito 1.00 2.50
EOZ4 Shohei Ohtani 1.50 4.00
EOZ5 Sonny Gray 1.00 2.50
EOZ6 Mike Clevinger 1.00 2.50
EOZ7 Shane Bieber 1.25 3.00
EOZ8 Gerrit Cole 2.00 5.00
EOZ9 Justin Verlander 1.25 3.00
EOZ10 Zack Greinke 1.00 2.50
EOZ11 Clayton Kershaw 2.50 6.00
EOZ12 Walker Buehler 1.50 4.00
EOZ13 Jacob deGrom 1.25 3.00
EOZ14 Jack Flaherty 1.00 2.50
EOZ15 Max Scherzer 1.25 3.00
EOZ16 Brendan McKay 1.25 3.00
EOZ17 Aaron Nola 1.25 3.00
EOZ18 Stephen Strasburg 1.25 3.00
EOZ19 Chris Sale 1.25 3.00
EOZ20 Noah Syndergaard 1.00 2.50
EOZ21 Luis Severino 1.00 2.50
EOZ22 Blake Snell 1.00 2.50
EOZ23 Tyler Glasnow .75 2.00
EOZ24 Jose Berrios 1.00 2.50
EOZ25 Patrick Corbin 1.00 2.50

2020 Stadium Club Chrome Lone Star Signatures

STATED ODDS 1:2086 HOBBY
PRINT RUNS B/WN 10-25 COPIES PER
NO PRICING QTY 15 OR LESS
EXCHANGE DEADLINE 10/31/2022
LSSGL Gavin Lux 40.00 100.00
LSSHA Hank Aaron
LSSMT Mike Trout
LSSPA Pete Alonso 40.00 100.00
LSSFTJ Fernando Tatis Jr. 125.00 300.00
LSSRAJ Ronald Acuna Jr.
LSSVGJ Vladimir Guerrero Jr. 40.00 100.00

2020 Stadium Club Chrome Power Zone

STATED ODDS 1:14 HOBBY
PZ1 Darryl Strawberry .75 2.00
PZ2 Pete Alonso 3.00 8.00
PZ3 Mike Trout 6.00 15.00
PZ4 Shohei Ohtani 1.50 4.00
PZ5 Christian Yelich 1.50 4.00
PZ6 Chipper Jones 1.25 3.00
PZ7 Ronald Acuna Jr. 5.00 12.00
PZ8 Vladimir Guerrero Jr. 2.50 6.00
PZ9 Juan Soto 4.00 10.00
PZ10 Fernando Tatis Jr. 5.00 12.00
PZ11 Mark McGwire 2.00 5.00
PZ12 Rhys Hoskins 1.50 4.00
PZ13 Bryce Harper 2.00 5.00
PZ14 Aaron Judge 3.00 8.00
PZ15 Jeff Bagwell 1.00 2.50
PZ16 Francisco Lindor 1.25 3.00
PZ17 Frank Thomas 1.25 3.00
PZ18 Eloy Jimenez 2.50 6.00
PZ19 Kris Bryant 1.50 4.00
PZ20 Anthony Rizzo 2.00 5.00
PZ21 David Wright 1.00 2.50
PZ22 Nolan Arenado 1.50 4.00
PZ23 Gleyber Torres 2.50 6.00
PZ24 Yordan Alvarez 4.00 10.00
PZ25 Ken Griffey Jr. 2.50 6.00

2020 Stadium Club Chrome Power Zone Gold Refractors

*GOLD REF.: 1.5X TO 4X BASIC
STATED ODDS 1:423 HOBBY
STATED PRINT RUN 50 SER.#'d SETS
PZ3 Mike Trout 30.00 80.00
PZ9 Juan Soto 25.00 60.00

1911 T205 Gold Border

The cards in this 218-card set measure approximately 1 1/2" by 2 5/8". The T205 set (catalog designation), also known as the "Gold Border" set, was issued in 1911 in packages of the following cigarette brands: American Beauty, Broadleaf, Cycle, Drum, Hassan, Honest Long Cut, Piedmont, Polar Bear, Sovereign and Sweet Caporal. All the above were products of the American Tobacco Company, and the ads for the various brands appear below the biographical section on the back of each card. There are pose variations noted in the checklist (which is alphabetized and numbered for reference) and there are 12 minor league cards of a more ornate design which are somewhat scarce. The numbers below correspond to alphabetical order within category, i.e., major leaguers and minor leaguers are alphabetized separately. The gold borders of T205 cards chip easily and they are hard to find in "Mint" or even "Near Mint" condition, due to this there is a high premium on these high condition cards. Listed pricing for raw cards references "EX" condition.

COMPLETE SET (218) 15000.00 40000.00
COMMON MAJOR (1-186) 90.00 150.00
COM. MINOR (187-198) 150.00 300.00
1 Ed Abbaticchio 60.00 100.00
2 Merle (Doc) Adkins 125.00 200.00
3 Red Ames 60.00 100.00
4 Jimmy Archer 60.00 100.00
5 Jimmy Austin 60.00 100.00
6 Bill Bailey 60.00 100.00
7 Frank Baker 175.00 300.00
8 Neal Ball 60.00 100.00
9 Cy Barger Full B 60.00 100.00
10 Cy Barger Part B 250.00 400.00
11 Jack Barry 60.00 100.00
12 Emil Batch 125.00 200.00
13 Johnny Bates 60.00 100.00
14 Fred Beck 60.00 100.00
15 Beals Becker 60.00 100.00
16 George Bell 60.00 100.00
17 Chief Bender 175.00 300.00
18 Bill Bergen 60.00 100.00
19 Bob Bescher 60.00 100.00
20 Joe Birmingham 60.00 100.00
21 Russ Blackburne 60.00 100.00
22 Kitty Bransfield 60.00 100.00
23 R.Bresnahan Closed 175.00 300.00
24 R.Bresnahan Open 300.00 500.00
25 Al Bridwell 60.00 100.00
26 Mordecai Brown 175.00 300.00
27 Bobby Byrne 60.00 100.00
28 Hick Cady 150.00 250.00
29 Howie Camnitz 60.00 100.00
30 Bill Carrigan 60.00 100.00
31 Frank Chance 175.00 300.00
32A Hal Chase Both - Ends 125.00 200.00
32B Hal Chase Both - Extends 125.00 200.00
33 Hal Chase Left Ear 300.00 500.00
34 Eddie Cicotte 250.00 400.00
35 Fred Clarke 150.00 250.00
36 Ty Cobb 2500.00 4000.00
37 E.Collins Mouth Closed 175.00 300.00
38 E.Collins Mouth Open 350.00 600.00
39 Jimmy Collins 250.00 400.00
40 Frank Corridon 60.00 100.00
41A Otis Crandall (Otis) 150.00 250.00
41B Otis Crandall (Olis) 90.00 150.00
42 Lou Criger 60.00 100.00
43 Bill Dahlen 250.00 400.00
44 Jake Daubert 60.00 100.00
45 Jim Delahanty 60.00 100.00
46 Art Devlin 60.00 100.00
47 Josh Devore 60.00 100.00
48 Walt Dickson 60.00 100.00
49 Jiggs Donohue 250.00 400.00
50 Red Dooin 60.00 100.00
51 Mickey Doolan 60.00 100.00
52A Patsy Dougherty Red 150.00 250.00
52B Patsy Dougherty White 150.00 250.00
53 Tom Downey 60.00 100.00
54 Larry Doyle 60.00 100.00
55 Hugh Duffy 175.00 300.00
56 Jack Dunn 175.00 300.00
57 Jimmy Dygert 60.00 100.00
58 Dick Egan 60.00 100.00
59 Kid Elberfeld 60.00 100.00
60 Clyde Engle 60.00 100.00
61 Steve Evans 60.00 100.00
62 Johnny Evers 300.00 500.00
63 Bob Ewing 60.00 100.00
64 George Ferguson 60.00 100.00
65 Ray Fisher 175.00 300.00
66 Art Fletcher 60.00 100.00
67 John Flynn 60.00 100.00
68 Russ Ford Dark Cap 60.00 100.00
69 Russ Ford Light Cap 250.00 400.00
70 Bill Foxen 60.00 100.00
71 James Frick 150.00 250.00
72 Art Fromme 60.00 100.00
73 Earl Gardner 60.00 100.00
74 Harry Gaspar 60.00 100.00
75 George Gibson 60.00 100.00
76 Wilbur Good 60.00 100.00
77 P.Graham Cubs 250.00 400.00
78 P.Graham Rustlers 60.00 100.00
79 Eddie Grant 250.00 400.00
80A Dolly Gray w/o Stats 150.00 250.00
80B Dolly Gray w/Stats 600.00 1000.00
81 Clark Griffith 175.00 300.00
82 Bob Groom 60.00 100.00
83 Charles Hanford 150.00 250.00
84 Robert Harmon 60.00 100.00
Both ears
85 Robert Harmon 250.00 400.00
Left ear only
86 Topsy Hartsel 60.00 100.00
87 Arnold Hauser 60.00 100.00
88 Charlie Hemphill 60.00 100.00
89 Buck Herzog 60.00 100.00
90A D.Hoblitzell No Stats 7000.00 12000.00
90B D.Hoblitzell w/CIN 90.00 150.00
90C D.Hoblitzell (Hoblitzel) 350.00 600.00
90D D.Hoblitzell w/o CIN 350.00 600.00
91 Danny Hoffman 60.00 100.00
92 Miller Huggins 175.00 300.00
93 John Hummell 60.00 100.00
94 Fred Jacklitsch 60.00 100.00
95 Hughie Jennings MG 175.00 300.00
96 Walter Johnson 1000.00 1800.00
97 Davy Jones 60.00 100.00
98 Tom Jones 60.00 100.00
99 Addie Joss 900.00 1500.00
100 Ed Karger 250.00 400.00
101 Ed Killian 60.00 100.00
102 Red Kleinow 250.00 400.00
103 John Kling 60.00 100.00
104 John Knight 60.00 100.00
105 Ed Konetchy 60.00 100.00
106 Harry Krause 60.00 100.00
107 Rube Kroh 60.00 100.00
108 Frank Lang 60.00 100.00
109 Frank LaPorte 60.00 100.00
110A Arlie Latham (A.) 125.00 200.00
110B Arlie Latham (W.A.) 250.00 400.00
111 Tommy Leach 60.00 100.00
112 Wyatt Lee 90.00 150.00
113 Sam Leever 60.00 100.00
114A Lefty Leifield (A.) 150.00 250.00
114B Lefty Leifield (A.P.) 250.00 400.00
115 Ed Lennox 60.00 100.00
116 Paddy Livingston 60.00 100.00
117 Hans Lobert 60.00 100.00
118 Bris Lord 60.00 100.00
119 Harry Lord 60.00 100.00
120 John Lush 60.00 100.00
121 Nick Maddox 60.00 100.00
122 Sherry Magee 60.00 100.00
123 Rube Marquard 175.00 300.00
124 Christy Mathewson 1000.00 1800.00
125 Al Mattern 60.00 100.00
126 Lewis McAllister 90.00 150.00
127 George McBride 60.00 100.00
128 Amby McConnell 60.00 100.00
129 Pryor McElveen 60.00 100.00
130 John McGraw MG 175.00 300.00
131 Harry McIntire 60.00 100.00
132 Matty McIntyre 60.00 100.00
133 Larry McLean 60.00 100.00
134 Fred Merkle 60.00 100.00
135 George Merritt 150.00 250.00
136 Chief Meyers 60.00 100.00
137 Clyde Milan 60.00 100.00
138 Dots Miller 60.00 100.00
139 Mike Mitchell 60.00 100.00
140A Pat Moran Extra Stat 900.00 1500.00
140B Pat Moran 60.00 100.00
141 George Moriarity 60.00 100.00
142 George Mullin 60.00 100.00
143 Danny Murphy 60.00 100.00
144 Red Murray 60.00 100.00
145 John Nee 150.00 250.00
146 Tom Needham 60.00 100.00
147 Rebel Oakes 60.00 100.00
148 Rube Oldring 60.00 100.00
149 Charley O'Leary 60.00 100.00
150 Fred Olmstead 60.00 100.00
151 Orval Overall 60.00 100.00
152 Freddy Parent 60.00 100.00
153 Dode Paskert 60.00 100.00
154 Fred Payne 60.00 100.00
155 Barney Pelty 60.00 100.00
156 Jack Pfiester 60.00 100.00
157 James Phelan 150.00 250.00
158 Ed Phelps 60.00 100.00
159 Decon Phillippe 60.00 100.00
160 Jack Quinn 60.00 100.00
161 Bugs Raymond 250.00 400.00
162 Ed Reulbach 60.00 100.0
163 Lewis Richie 60.00 100.0
164 Jack Rowan 175.00 300.0
165 Nap Rucker 60.00 100.0
166 Doc Scanlan 250.00 400.0
167 Germany Schaefer 60.00 100.0
168 Admiral Schlei 60.00 100.0
169 Boss Schmidt 60.00 100.0
170 Wildfire Schulte 60.00 100.0
171 Jim Scott 60.00 100.0
172 Bayard Sharpe 60.00 100.0
173 David Shean 175.00 300.0
Chicago Cubs
174 David Shean 60.00 100.0
Boston Rustlers
175 Jimmy Sheckard 60.00 100.0
176 Hack Simmons 60.00 100.0
177 Tony Smith 60.00 100.0
178 Fred Snodgrass 60.00 100.0
179 Tris Speaker 500.00 800.0
180 Jake Stahl 60.00 100.0
181 Oscar Stanage 60.00 100.0
182 Harry Steinfeldt 60.00 100.0
183 George Stone 60.00 100.0
184 George Stovall 60.00 100.0
185 Gabby Street 60.00 100.0
186 George Suggs 250.00 400.0
187 Ed Summers 60.00 100.0
188 Jeff Sweeney 250.00 400.0
189 Lee Tannehill 60.00 100.0
190 Ira Thomas 60.00 100.0
191 Joe Tinker 175.00 300.0
192 John Titus 60.00 100.0
193 Terry Turner 250.00 400.0
194 Hippo Vaughn 300.00 500.0
195 Heinie Wagner 175.00 300.0
196 B.Wallace w/cap 150.00 250.0
197A B.Wallace w/o Cap 1 Line 1200.00 2000.0
197B B.Wallace w/o Cap 2 Lines 700.00 1200.0
198 Ed Walsh 500.00 800.0
199 Zach Wheat 175.00 300.0
200 Doc White 60.00 100.0
201 Kirby White 250.00 400.0
202A Irvin K. Wilhelm 350.00 600.0
202B Irvin K. Wilhelm Missing Letter 175.00 300.0
203 Ed Willett 60.00 100.0
204 Owen Wilson 60.00 100.0
205 H.Wiltse Both Ears 60.00 100.0
206 H.Wiltse Right Ear 250.00 400.0
207 Harry Wolter 60.00 100.0
208 Cy Young 1000.00 1800.0

1909-11 T206

The T206 set was and is the most popular of all the tobacco issues. The set was issued from 1909 to 1911 with sixteen different brands of cigarettes: American Beauty, Broadleaf, Cycle, Carolina Bright Drum, El Principe de Gales, Hindu, Lenox, Old Mill Piedmont, Polar Bear, Sovereign, Sweet Caporal, Tolstoi, and Uzit. There was also an extremely rare Cobb back version for the Ty Cobb Red Portrait tha it's believed was issued as a promotional card. Pricing for the Cobb back card is unavailable and it typically not considered part of the complete 524-card set. The minor league cards are supposedly slightly more difficult to obtain than the cards of the major leaguers, with the Southern League player cards being definitively more difficult. Minor Leagu players were obtained from the American Associati and the Eastern league. Southern League players were obtained from a variety of leagues including th following: South Atlantic League, Southern League Texas League, and Virginia League. Series 150 (notated as such on the card backs) was issued between February 1909 thru the end of May, 1909. Series 350 was issued from the end of May, 1909 thru April, 1910. The last series 350 to 460 was issued in late December 1910 through early 1911. The set price below does not include ultra-expensi Wagner, Plank, Magie error, or Doyle variation. The Wagner card is one of the most sought after cards i the hobby. This card was pulled from circulation almost immediately after being issued. Estimates of how many Wagners are in existence generally settle on around 50 to 60 copies. The backs vary in scarc as follows: Exceedingly Rare: Ty Cobb; Rare: Drum Uzit, Lenox, Broadleaf 460 and Hindu; Scarce: Broadleaf 350, Carolina brights, Hindu Red; Less Common: American Beauty, Cycle and Tolstoi; Readily Available: El Principe de Gales, Old Mill, Polar Bear and Sovereign and Common: Piedmont and Sweet Caporal. Listed prices refer to the Piedmont and Sweet caporal backs in raw "EX" condition. Of note, the O'Hara St. Louis and Demm St. Louis cards were only issued with Polar Bear backs and are are priced as such. Pricing is unavailable for the unbelieveably rare Joe Doyle Na variation (perhaps a dozen or fewer copies exist) in addition to the Bud Shappe and Fred nodgrass printing variaitons. Finally, unlike the other cards in this set, listed raw pricing for the famed Honus Wagner references "Good" condition insetad of "EX

COMPLETE SET (520) 30000.00 80000.0
COMMON MAJOR (1-389) 50.00 100.0
COMMON MINOR (390-475) 50.00 100.0
COM. SO. LEA. (476-523) 125.00 250.0
CARDS PRICED IN EXMT CONDITION
HONUS WAGNER PRICED IN GOOD CONDITION
1 Ed Abbaticchio Blue 85.00 135.0
2 Ed Abbaticchio Brown 85.00 135.0
3 Fred Abbott 60.00 100.0
4 Bill Abstein 60.00 100.0
5 Doc Adkins 125.00 200.0

6 Whitey Alperman 60.00 100.00
7 Red Ames Hands at 150.00 250.00
8 Red Ames Hands over 60.00 100.00
9 Red Ames 60.00 100.00
Portrait
10 John Anderson 60.00 100.00
11 Frank Arellanes 60.00 100.00
12 Herman Armbruster 60.00 100.00
13 Harry Arndt 70.00 120.00
14 Jake Atz 60.00 100.00
15 Home Run Baker 250.00 400.00
16 Neal Ball 60.00 100.00
Cleveland
17 Neal Ball 60.00 100.00
New York
18 Jap Barbeau 60.00 100.00
19 Cy Barger 60.00 100.00
20 Jack Barry 60.00 100.00
21 Shad Barry 60.00 100.00
22 Jack Bastian 175.00 300.00
23 Emil Batch 60.00 100.00
24 Johnny Bates 60.00 100.00
25 Harry Bay 175.00 300.00
26 Ginger Beaumont 60.00 100.00
27 Fred Beck 60.00 100.00
28 Beals Becker 60.00 100.00
29 Jake Beckley 175.00 300.00
30 George Bell Follow 60.00 100.00
31 George Bell Hands above 60.00 100.00
32 Chief Bender Pitching 250.00 400.00
33 Chief Bender 250.00 400.00
Pitching Trees in Back
34 Chief Bender 300.00 500.00
Portrait
35 Bill Bergen 60.00 100.00
Batting
36 Bill Bergen 60.00 100.00
Catching
37 Heinie Berger 60.00 100.00
38 Bill Bernhard 175.00 300.00
39 Bob Bescher Hands 60.00 100.00
40 Bob Bescher 60.00 100.00
Portrait
41 Joe Birmingham 90.00 150.00
42 Lena Blackburne 60.00 100.00
43 Jack Bliss 60.00 100.00
44 Frank Bowerman 60.00 100.00
45 Bill Bradley with Bat 60.00 100.00
46 Bill Bradley 60.00 100.00
Portrait
47 David Brain 60.00 100.00
48 Kitty Bransfield 60.00 100.00
49 Roy Brashear 60.00 100.00
50 Ted Breitenstein 175.00 300.00
51 Roger Bresnahan 175.00 300.00
Portrait
52 Roger Bresnahan 175.00 300.00
with Bat
53 Al Bridwell 60.00 100.00
No Cap
54 Al Bridwell 60.00 100.00
with Cap
55 George Brown Chicago 125.00 200.00
56 George Brown Washington 300.00 500.00
57 Mordecai Brown Chicago 200.00 350.00
58 Mordecai Brown Cubs 350.00 600.00
59 Mordecai Brown 300.00 500.00
Portrait
60 Al Burch 125.00 200.00
Batting
61 Al Burch 60.00 100.00
Fielding
62 Fred Burchell 60.00 100.00
63 Jimmy Burke 60.00 100.00
64 Bill Burns 60.00 100.00
65 Donie Bush 60.00 100.00
66 John Butler 60.00 100.00
67 Bobby Byrne 60.00 100.00
68 Howie Camnitz 60.00 100.00
Arm at Side
69 Howie Camnitz Folded 60.00 100.00
70 Howie Camnitz Hands 60.00 100.00
71 Billy Campbell 60.00 100.00
72 Scoops Carey 175.00 300.00
73 Charley Carr 60.00 100.00
74 Bill Carrigan 60.00 100.00
75 Doc Casey 60.00 100.00
76 Peter Cassidy 60.00 100.00
77 Frank Chance 250.00 400.00
Batting
78 F.Chance Portrait Red 300.00 500.00
79 F.Chance Portrait Yel 250.00 400.00
80 Bill Chappelle 60.00 100.00
81 Chappie Charles 60.00 100.00
82 Hal Chase Dark Cap 90.00 150.00
83 Hal Chase 150.00 250.00
Holding Trophy
84 Hal Chase 90.00 150.00
Portrait Blue
85 Hal Chase 250.00 400.00
Portrait Pink
86 Hal Chase White Cap 125.00 200.00
87 Jack Chesbro 250.00 400.00
88 Ed Cicotte 175.00 300.00
89 Bill Clancy (Clancey) 60.00 100.00
90 Fred Clarke 250.00 400.00
Holding Bat
91 Fred Clarke 250.00 400.00
Portrait
92 Josh Clark (Clarke) ML 60.00 100.00
93 J.J. (Nig) Clarke 60.00 100.00
94 Bill Clymer 60.00 100.00
95 Ty Cobb 1500.00 2500.00
Bat off Shoulder
96 Ty Cobb 1500.00 2500.00
Bat on Shoulder
97 Ty Cobb 3500.00 5000.00
Portrait Green
98 Ty Cobb 1200.00 2000.00
Portrait Red
99 Cad Coles 175.00 300.00
100 Eddie Collins 200.00 350.00
101 Jimmy Collins 175.00 300.00
102 Bunk Congalton ML 60.00 100.00
103 Wid Conroy 60.00 100.00
Fielding
104 Wid Conroy 60.00 100.00
with Bat
105 Harry Covaleski (Coveleski) 60.00 100.00
106 Doc Crandall 60.00 100.00
No Cap
107 Doc Crandall 60.00 100.00
with Cap
108 Bill Cranston 175.00 300.00
109 Gavvy Cravath 60.00 100.00
110 Sam Crawford 250.00 400.00
Throwing
111 Sam Crawford 250.00 400.00
with Bat
112 Birdie Cree 60.00 100.00
113 Lou Criger 60.00 100.00
114 Dode Criss UER 60.00 100.00
115 Monte Cross 60.00 100.00
116 Bill Dahlen 90.00 150.00
Boston
117 Bill Dahlen 300.00 500.00
Brooklyn
118 Paul Davidson 60.00 100.00
119 George Davis 175.00 300.00
120 Harry Davis 60.00 100.00
Davis on Front
121 Harry Davis 60.00 100.00
H.Davis on Front
122 Frank Delehanty 60.00 100.00
123 Jim Delehanty 60.00 100.00
124 Ray Demmitt 70.00 120.00
New York
125 Ray Demmitt 6000.00 10000.00
St. Louis
126 Rube Dessau 85.00 135.00
127 Art Devlin 60.00 100.00
128 Josh Devore 60.00 100.00
129 Bill Dineen 60.00 100.00
130 Mike Donlin 125.00 200.00
Fielding
131 Mike Donlin Sitting 60.00 100.00
132 Mike Donlin 60.00 100.00
with Bat
133 Jiggs Donahue (Donohue) 60.00 100.00
134 Wild Bill Donovan 60.00 100.00
Portrait
135 Wild Bill Donovan 60.00 100.00
Throwing
136 Red Dooin 60.00 100.00
137 Mickey Doolan 60.00 100.00
Batting
138 Mickey Doolan 60.00 100.00
Fielding
139 Mickey Doolin 60.00 100.00
Portrait (Doolan)
140 Gus Dorner ML 60.00 100.00
141 Gus Dorner
Card Spelled Dopner on Back
142 Patsy Dougherty 60.00 100.00
Arm in Air
143 Patsy Dougherty 60.00 100.00
Portrait
144 Tom Downey 60.00 100.00
Batting
145 Tom Downey 60.00 100.00
Fielding
146 Jerry Downs 60.00 100.00
147 Joe Doyle 350.00 600.00
148 Joe Doyle Nat'l
149 Larry Doyle Portrait 60.00 100.00
150 Larry Doyle 60.00 100.00
Throwing
151 Larry Doyle 60.00 100.00
with Bat
152 Jean Dubuc 60.00 100.00
153 Hugh Duffy 175.00 300.00
154 Jack Dunn Baltimore 60.00 100.00
155 Joe Dunn 60.00 100.00
Brooklyn
156 Bull Durham 60.00 100.00
157 Jimmy Dygert 60.00 100.00
158 Ted Easterly 60.00 100.00
159 Dick Egan 90.00 150.00
160 Kid Elberfeld 60.00 100.00
Fielding
161 Kid Elberfeld Port NY 60.00 100.00
162 Kid Elberfeld Port Wash 1800.00 3000.00
163 Roy Ellam 175.00 300.00
164 Clyde Engle 60.00 100.00
165 Steve Evans 60.00 100.00
166 J.Evers Portrait 350.00 600.00
167 J.Evers Chi Shirt 250.00 400.00
168 J.Evers Cubs Shirt 500.00 800.00
169 Bob Ewing 60.00 100.00
170 Cecil Ferguson 60.00 100.00
171 Hobe Ferris 60.00 100.00
172 Lou Fiene 60.00 100.00
Portrait
173 Lou Fiene 60.00 100.00
Throwing
174 Steamer Flanagan 60.00 100.00
175 Art Fletcher 60.00 100.00
176 Elmer Flick 175.00 300.00
177 Russ Ford 60.00 100.00
178 Ed Foster 175.00 300.00
179 Jerry Freeman 60.00 100.00
180 John Frill 60.00 100.00
181 Charlie Fritz 175.00 300.00
182 Art Fromme 60.00 100.00
183 Chick Gandil 175.00 300.00
184 Bob Ganley 60.00 100.00
185 John Ganzel 60.00 100.00
186 Harry Gasper (Gaspar) 60.00 100.00
187 Rube Geyer 60.00 100.00
188 George Gibson 60.00 100.00
189 Billy Gilbert 60.00 100.00
190 Wilbur Goode (Good) 60.00 100.00
191 Bill Graham 60.00 100.00
St. Louis
192 Peaches Graham 70.00 120.00
193 Dolly Gray 60.00 100.00
194 Ed Greminger 175.00 300.00
195 Clark Griffith 175.00 300.00
Batting
196 Clark Griffith 175.00 300.00
Portrait
197 Moose Grimshaw 60.00 100.00
198 Bob Groom 60.00 100.00
199 Tom Guiheen 175.00 300.00
200 Ed Hahn 60.00 100.00
201 Bob Hall 60.00 100.00
202 Bill Hallman 60.00 100.00
203 Jack Hannifan (Hannifin) 60.00 100.00
204 Bill Hart Little Rock 175.00 300.00
205 Jimmy Hart Montgomery 175.00 300.00
206 Topsy Hartsel 60.00 100.00
207 Jack Hayden 60.00 100.00
208 J.Ross Helm 175.00 300.00
209 Charlie Hemphill 60.00 100.00
210 Buck Herzog 60.00 100.00
Boston
211 Buck Herzog 60.00 100.00
New York
212 Gordon Hickman 175.00 300.00
213 Bill Hinchman 60.00 100.00
214 Harry Hinchman 60.00 100.00
215 Doc Hoblitzell 60.00 100.00
216 Danny Hoffman 60.00 100.00
St. Louis
217 Izzy Hoffman Providence 60.00 100.00
218 Solly Hofman 60.00 100.00
219 Buck Hooker 175.00 300.00
220 Del Howard 60.00 100.00
Chicago
221 Ernie Howard Savannah 175.00 300.00
222 Harry Howell 60.00 100.00
Hand at Waist
223 Harry Howell 60.00 100.00
Portrait
224 M.Huggins Mouth 175.00 300.00
225 M.Huggins Portrait 175.00 300.00
226 Rudy Hulswitt 60.00 100.00
227 John Hummel 60.00 100.00
228 George Hunter 60.00 100.00
229 Frank Isbell 60.00 100.00
230 Fred Jacklitsch 60.00 100.00
231 Jimmy Jackson 60.00 100.00
232 H.Jennings Both 175.00 300.00
233 H.Jennings One 175.00 300.00
234 H.Jennings Portrait 175.00 300.00
235 Walter Johnson Hands 700.00 1200.00
236 Walter Johnson Port 1000.00 1800.00
237 Davy Jones 60.00 100.00
Detroit
238 Fielder Jones 60.00 100.00
Hands at Hips
239 Fielder Jones 60.00 100.00
Portrait
240 Tom Jones 60.00 100.00
St. Louis
241 Dutch Jordan Atlanta 175.00 300.00
242 Tim Jordan Batting 60.00 100.00
243 Tim Jordan Portrait 60.00 100.00
244 Addie Joss 175.00 300.00
Pitching
245 Addie Joss 250.00 400.00
Portrait
246 Ed Karger 60.00 100.00
247 Willie Keeler 350.00 600.00
Portrait
248 Willie Keeler Batting 350.00 600.00
249 Joe Kelley 150.00 250.00
250 J.F. Kiernan 300.00 500.00
251 Ed Killian 60.00 100.00
Pitching
252 Ed Killian 60.00 100.00
Portrait
253 Frank King 175.00 300.00
254 Rube Kisinger (Kissinger) 60.00 100.00
255 Red Kleinow 300.00 500.00
Boston
256 Red Kleinow NY Catch 60.00 100.00
257 Red Kleinow NY Bat 60.00 100.00
258 Johnny Kling 60.00 100.00
259 Otto Knabe 60.00 100.00
260 Jack Knight 60.00 100.00
Portrait
261 Jack Knight 60.00 100.00
with Bat
262 Ed Konetchy Glove Lo 60.00 100.00
263 Ed Konetchy Glove Hi 60.00 100.00
264 Harry Krause 60.00 100.00
Pitching
265 Harry Krause 60.00 100.00
Portrait
266 Rube Kroh 60.00 100.00
267 Otto Kruger (Krueger) 60.00 100.00
268 James LaFitte 175.00 300.00
269 Nap Lajoie 500.00 800.00
Portrait
270 Nap Lajoie 400.00 700.00
Throwing
271 Nap Lajoie 400.00 700.00
with Bat
272 Joe Lake NY 60.00 100.00
273 Joe Lake Stl No Ball 60.00 100.00
274 Joe Lake Stl with Ball 60.00 100.00
275 Frank LaPorte 60.00 100.00
276 Arlie Latham 60.00 100.00
277 Bill Lattimore 60.00 100.00
278 Jimmy Lavender 60.00 100.00
279 Tommy Leach 60.00 100.00
Bending Over
280 Tommy Leach 60.00 100.00
Portrait
281 Lefty Leifield 60.00 100.00
Batting
282 Lefty Leifield 60.00 100.00
Pitching
283 Ed Lennox 60.00 100.00
284 Harry Lentz 250.00 400.00
(Sentz) SL
285 Glenn Liebhardt 60.00 100.00
286 Vive Lindaman 60.00 100.00
287 Perry Lipe 175.00 300.00
288 Paddy Livingstone 60.00 100.00
(Livingston)
289 Hans Lobert 60.00 100.00
290 Harry Lord 60.00 100.00
291 Harry Lumley 60.00 100.00
292 Carl Lundgren 500.00 800.00
Chicago
293 Carl Lundgren Kansas City 125.00 200.00
294 Nick Maddox 60.00 100.00
294 Sherry Magie Portrait ERR 15000.00 25000.00
295 Sherry Magee 60.00 100.00
with Bat
296 Sherry Magee 150.00 250.00
Portrait
298 Bill Malarkey 60.00 100.00
299 Bill Maloney 60.00 100.00
300 George Manion 175.00 300.00
301 Rube Manning 60.00 100.00
Batting
302 Rube Manning 60.00 100.00
Pitching
303 R.Marquard Follow 175.00 300.00
304 R.Marquard Hands 175.00 300.00
305 R.Marquard Portrait 200.00 350.00
306 Doc Marshall 60.00 100.00
307 C.Mathewson Drk Cap 700.00 1200.00
308 C.Mathewson Portrait 900.00 1500.00
309 C.Mathewson Wht Cap 900.00 1500.00
310 Al Mattern 60.00 100.00
311 John McAleese 60.00 100.00
312 George McBride 60.00 100.00
313 Pat McCauley 175.00 300.00
314 Moose McCormick 60.00 100.00
315 Pryor McElveen 60.00 100.00
316 Dennis McGann 60.00 100.00
317 Jim McGinley 60.00 100.00
318 Iron Man McGinnity 175.00 300.00
319 Stoney McGlynn 60.00 100.00
320 J.McGraw Finger 250.00 400.00
321 J.McGraw Glove-Hip 250.00 400.00
322 J.McGraw w/o Cap 250.00 400.00
323 J.McGraw w/Cap 250.00 400.00
324 Harry McIntyre 60.00 100.00
Brooklyn
325 Harry McIntyre 60.00 100.00
Brooklyn-Chicago
326 Matty McIntyre 60.00 100.00
Detroit
327 Larry McLean 60.00 100.00
328 George McQuillan 60.00 100.00
Ball in Hand
329 George McQuillan 60.00 100.00
with Bat
330 Fred Merkle Portrait 70.00 120.00
331 Fred Merkle Throwing 90.00 150.00
332 George Merritt 60.00 100.00
333 Chief Meyers 60.00 100.00
334 Chief Myers 70.00 120.00
Batting (Meyers)
335 Chief Myers 60.00 100.00
Fielding (Meyers)
336 Clyde Milan 60.00 100.00
337 Molly Miller Dallas 175.00 300.00
338 Dots Miller 60.00 100.00
Pittsburgh
339 Bill Milligan 60.00 100.00
340 Fred Mitchell Toronto 60.00 100.00
341 Mike Mitchell 60.00 100.00
Cincinnati
342 Dan Moeller 60.00 100.00
343 Carleton Molesworth 175.00 300.00
344 Herbie Moran Providence 60.00 100.00
345 Pat Moran 60.00 100.00
Chicago
346 George Moriarty 60.00 100.00
347 Mike Mowrey 60.00 100.00
348 Dom Mullaney 175.00 300.00
349 George Mullen 60.00 100.00
(Mullin)
350 George Mullin 60.00 100.00
with Bat
351 George Mullin Throwing 60.00 100.00
352 Danny Murphy 60.00 100.00
Batting
353 Danny Murphy 60.00 100.00
Throwing
354 Red Murray 60.00 100.00
Batting
355 Red Murray 60.00 100.00
Portrait
356 Billy Nattress 60.00 100.00
357 Tom Needham 60.00 100.00
358 Simon Nicholls 60.00 100.00
Hands on Knees
359 Simon Nichols 60.00 100.00
Batting (Nicholls)
360 Harry Niles 60.00 100.00
361 Rebel Oakes 60.00 100.00
362 Frank Oberlin 60.00 100.00
363 Peter O'Brien 60.00 100.00
364 Bill O'Hara NY 60.00 100.00
365 Bill O'Hara Stl 6000.00 10000.00
366 Rube Oldring 60.00 100.00
Batting
367 Rube Oldring 60.00 100.00
Fielding
368 Charley O'Leary 60.00 100.00
Hands on Knees
369 Charley O'Leary 60.00 100.00
Portrait
370 William O'Neil 150.00 250.00
371 Albert Orth 175.00 300.00
372 William Otey 175.00 300.00
373 Orval Overall 60.00 100.00
Hand at Face
374 Orval Overall 60.00 100.00
Hands at Waist
375 Orval Overall 60.00 100.00
Portrait
376 Frank Owen (Owens) 60.00 100.00
377 George Paige 175.00 300.00
378 Freddy Parent 60.00 100.00
379 Dode Paskert 60.00 100.00
380 Jim Pastorius 60.00 100.00
381 Harry Pattee 60.00 100.00
382 Fred Payne 60.00 100.00
383 Barney Pelty 60.00 100.00
Horizontal
384 Barney Pelty 60.00 100.00
Vertical
385 Hub Perdue 175.00 300.00
386 George Perring 60.00 100.00
387 Arch Persons 175.00 300.00
388 Jeff Pfeffer 60.00 100.00
389 Jeff Pfeffer ERR
Chicago
390 Jake Pfeister 60.00 100.00
Seated (Pfiester)
391 Jake Pfeister 60.00 100.00
Throwing (Pfiester)
392 Jimmy Phelan 60.00 100.00
393 Ed Phelps 60.00 100.00
394 Deacon Phillippe. 60.00 100.00
395 Ollie Pickering 60.00 100.00
396 Eddie Plank 45000.00 60000.00
397 Phil Poland 60.00 100.00
398 Jack Powell 60.00 100.00
399 Mike Powers 60.00 100.00
400 Billy Purtell 60.00 100.00
401 Ambrose Puttman (Puttmann) 85.00 135.00
402 Lee Quillen (Quillin) 60.00 100.00
403 Jack Quinn 60.00 100.00
404 Newt Randall 60.00 100.00
405 Bugs Raymond 60.00 100.00
406 Ed Reagan 175.00 300.00
407 Ed Reulbach Glove 60.00 100.00
408 Ed Reulbach 70.00 120.00
No Glove
409 Dutch Revelle 175.00 300.00
410 Bob Rhoades Hands 60.00 100.00
411 Bob Rhoades Right 60.00 100.00
412 Charlie Rhodes 60.00 100.00
413 Claude Ritchey 60.00 100.00
414 Lou Ritter 60.00 100.00
415 Ike Rockenfeld 175.00 300.00
416 Claude Rossman 60.00 100.00
417 Nap Rucker 60.00 100.00
Portrait
418 Nap Rucker 60.00 100.00
Throwing
419 Dick Rudolph 60.00 100.00
420 Ray Ryan 175.00 300.00
421 Germany Schaefer Det 60.00 100.00
422 Germany Schaefer Wash 60.00 100.00
423 George Schirm 85.00 135.00
424 Larry Schlafly 60.00 100.00
425 Admiral Schlei 60.00 100.00
Batting
426 Admiral Schlei 60.00 100.00
Catching
427 Admiral Schlei 60.00 100.00
Portrait
428 Boss Schmidt 60.00 100.00
Portrait
429 Boss Schmidt 60.00 100.00
Throwing
430 Ossee Schreck (Schreckengost) 70.00 120.00
431 Wildfire Schulte 60.00 100.00
Back View
432 Wildfire Schulte 175.00 300.00
Front View
433 Jim Scott 60.00 100.00
434 Charles Seitz 175.00 300.00
435 Cy Seymour 60.00 100.00
Batting
436 Cy Seymour 60.00 100.00
Portrait
437 Cy Seymour 60.00 100.00
Throwing
438 Spike Shannon 60.00 100.00
439 Bud Sharpe 60.00 100.00
440 Bud Shappe ERR
(Sharpe) ML
441 Frank Shaughnessy SL 175.00 300.00
442 Al Shaw 60.00 100.00
St. Louis
443 Hunky Shaw Providence 60.00 100.00
444 Jimmy Sheckard Glove 60.00 100.00
445 Jimmy Sheckard 60.00 100.00
No Glove
446 Bill Shipke 60.00 100.00
447 Jimmy Slagle 60.00 100.00
448 Carlos Smith Shreveport 175.00 300.00
449 Frank Smith Chi-Bos 350.00 600.00
450 Frank Smith Chi F.Smith 60.00 100.00
451 Frank Smith Chi Whit Cap 60.00 100.00
452 Heinie Smith Buffalo 60.00 100.00
453 Happy Smith 60.00 100.00
Brooklyn
454 Sid Smith Atlanta 175.00 300.00
455 F.Snodgrass Batting 60.00 100.00
456 F.nodgrass Batting ERR
457 F.Snodgrass Catching 60.00 100.00
458 Bob Spade 60.00 100.00
459 Tris Speaker 600.00 1000.00
460 Tubby Spencer 60.00 100.00
461 Jake Stahl Glove 85.00 135.00
462 Jake Stahl No Glove 60.00 100.00
463 Oscar Stanage 60.00 100.00
464 Dolly Stark 175.00 300.00
465 Charlie Starr 60.00 100.00
466 Harry Steinfeldt 60.00 100.00
with Bat
467 Harry Steinfeldt 60.00 100.00
Portrait
468 Jim Stephens 60.00 100.00
469 George Stone 60.00 100.00
470 George Stovall 60.00 100.00
Batting
471 George Stovall 60.00 100.00
Portrait
472 Sam Strang 60.00 100.00
473 Gabby Street 60.00 100.00
Catching
474 Gabby Street 60.00 100.00
Portrait
475 Billy Sullivan 60.00 100.00
476 Ed Summers 60.00 100.00
477 Bill Sweeney 60.00 100.00
Boston
478 Jeff Sweeney 60.00 100.00
New York
479 Jesse Tannehill 60.00 100.00
Washington
480 Lee Tannehill Chi L.Tannehill 60.00 100.00
481 Lee Tannehill Chi Tannehill 60.00 100.00
482 Dummy Taylor 60.00 100.00
483 Fred Tenney 60.00 100.00
484 Tony Thebo 175.00 300.00
485 Jake Thielman 90.00 150.00
486 Ira Thomas 60.00 100.00
487 Woodie Thornton 175.00 300.00
488 J.Tinker Bat off Shldr 250.00 400.00
489 J.Tinker Bat on Shldr 400.00 800.00
490 J.Tinker Hand-Knee 350.00 600.00
491 J.Tinker Portrait 350.00 600.00
492 John Titus 60.00 100.00
493 Terry Turner 60.00 100.00
494 Bob Unglaub 60.00 100.00
495 Juan Violat (Viola) 175.00 300.00
496 R.Waddell Portrait 250.00 400.00
497 R.Waddell Throwing 250.00 400.00
498 Heinie Wagner on Left 60.00 100.00
499 Heinie Wagner on Right 60.00 100.00
500 Honus Wagner 800000.001500000.00
501 Bobby Wallace 175.00 300.00
502 Ed Walsh 250.00 400.00
503 Jack Warhop 60.00 100.00
504 Jake Weimer 60.00 100.00
505 James Westlake 175.00 300.00
506 Zack Wheat 200.00 350.00
507 Doc White Pitching 60.00 100.00
508 Doc White Portrait 60.00 100.00
509 Foley White Houston 175.00 300.00
510 Jack White Buffalo 60.00 100.00
511 Kaiser Wilhelm Hands 60.00 100.00
512 Kaiser Wilhelm 60.00 100.00
with Bat
513 Ed Willett 60.00 100.00
with Bat
514 Ed Willetts 60.00 100.00
Throwing (Willett)
515 Jimmy Williams 60.00 100.00
516 Vic Willis Pitt 200.00 350.00
517 Vic Willis Stl Throw 175.00 300.00
518 Vic Willis Stl Bat 175.00 300.00
519 Owen Wilson 60.00 100.00
520 Hooks Wiltse 60.00 100.00
Pitching
521 Hooks Wiltse Portrait 60.00 100.00
522 Hooks Wiltse Sweater 60.00 100.00
523 Lucky Wright 60.00 100.00
524 Cy Young Bare Hand 700.00 1200.00
525 Cy Young w/Glove 700.00 1200.00
526 Cy Young 1000.00 1800.00
Portrait
527 Irv Young Minneapolis 70.00 120.00
528 Heinie Zimmerman: 60.00 100.00

2019 Timeless Treasures

RANDOM INSERTS IN PACKS
*GOLD/199: 1.2X TO 3X
*BLUE/99: 1.5X TO 4X
*RED/50: 2X TO 5X
*HOLO SLVR/25: 3X TO 8X
1 Pete Alonso RC 2.00 5.00
2 Eloy Jimenez .60 1.50
3 Fernando Tatis Jr. 2.00 5.00
4 Cole Tucker .25 .60
5 Kyle Tucker .30 .75
6 Yusei Kikuchi .25 .60
7 Chris Paddack .30 .75
8 Nathaniel Lowe .20 .50
9 Bryce Harper .40 1.00
10 Aaron Judge .60 1.50
11 Kris Bryant .30 .75
12 Shohei Ohtani .30 .75
13 Michael Chavis .25 .60
14 Carter Kieboom .25 .60
15 Didi Gregorius .20 .50
16 Justin Turner .20 .50
17 Austin Riley .75 2.00
18 Michael Conforto .20 .50
19 Vladimir Guerrero Jr. 2.50 6.00
20 Trey Mancini .20 .50

2020 Timeless Treasures

RANDOM INSERTS IN PACKS
1 Shogo Akiyama RC .40 1.00
2 Yordan Alvarez RC 1.25 3.00
3 Bo Bichette RC 3.00 8.00
4 Aristides Aquino RC .50 1.25
5 Gavin Lux RC 1.50 4.00
6 Yoshitomo Tsutsugo RC .30 .75
7 Brendan McKay RC .40 1.00
8 Luis Robert RC 4.00 10.00
9 A.J. Puk RC .50 1.25
10 Kyle Lewis RC 4.00 10.00
11 Logan Allen RC .25 .60
12 Zac Gallen RC .60 1.50
13 Isan Diaz RC .40 1.00
14 Bobby Bradley RC .30 .75
15 Adbert Alzolay RC .30 .75
16 Walker Buehler .30 .75
17 Trevor Story .25 .60
18 Freddie Freeman .30 .75
19 Starling Marte .20 .50
20 Jack Flaherty .20 .50

2020 Timeless Treasures Signatures

RANDOM INSERTS IN PACKS
PRINT RUNS B/WN 5-99 COPIES PER
NO PRICING QTY 15 OR LESS
EXCHANGE DEADLINE 3/18/2022
1 Shogo Akiyama/49 6.00 15.00
2 Yordan Alvarez/50 20.00 50.00
3 Bo Bichette/30 30.00 80.00
4 Aristides Aquino/60 8.00 20.00
6 Yoshitomo Tsutsugo/99 8.00 20.00
8 Luis Robert EXCH/99 75.00 200.00
9 A.J. Puk/99 6.00 15.00
10 Kyle Lewis/99 25.00 60.00
11 Logan Allen/96 3.00 8.00
12 Zac Gallen/49 10.00 25.00
13 Isan Diaz/59 5.00 12.00
14 Bobby Bradley/96 4.00 10.00
15 Adbert Alzolay/99 4.00 10.00

1951 Topps Blue Backs

The cards in this 52-card set measure approximately 2" by 2 5/8". The 1951 Topps series of blue-backed baseball cards could be used to play a baseball game by shuffling the cards and drawing them from a pile. These cards (packaged two adjoined in a penny pack) were marketed with a piece of caramel candy, which often melted or was squashed in such a way as to damage the card and wrapper (despite the fact that a paper shield was inserted between candy and card). Blue Backs are more difficult to obtain than the similarly styled Red Backs. The set is denoted on the cards as "Set B" and the Red Back set is correspondingly Set A. The only notable Rookie Card in the set is Billy Pierce.

COMPLETE SET (52) 800.00 1500.00
WRAPPER (1-CENT) 150.00 200.00
1 Eddie Yost 35.00 60.00
2 Hank Majeski 15.00 30.00
3 Richie Ashburn 125.00 200.00
4 Del Ennis 15.00 30.00
5 Johnny Pesky 15.00 30.00
6 Red Schoendienst 60.00 100.00
7 Gerry Staley RC 15.00 30.00
8 Dick Sisler 15.00 30.00
9 Johnny Sain 30.00 50.00
10 Joe Page 30.00 50.00
11 Johnny Groth 15.00 30.00
12 Sam Jethroe 20.00 40.00
13 Mickey Vernon 15.00 30.00
14 George Munger 15.00 30.00
15 Eddie Joost 15.00 30.00
16 Murry Dickson 15.00 30.00

17 Roy Smalley 15.00 30.00
18 Ned Garver 15.00 30.00
19 Phil Masi 15.00 30.00
20 Ralph Branca 30.00 50.00
21 Billy Johnson 15.00 30.00
22 Bob Kuzava 15.00 30.00
23 Dizzy Trout 20.00 40.00
24 Sherman Lollar 15.00 30.00
25 Sam Mele 15.00 30.00
26 Chico Carrasquel RC 20.00 40.00
27 Andy Pafko 15.00 30.00
28 Harry Brecheen 15.00 30.00
29 Granville Hamner 15.00 30.00
30 Enos Slaughter 60.00 100.00
31 Lou Brissie 15.00 30.00
32 Bob Elliott 20.00 40.00
33 Don Lenhardt RC 15.00 30.00
34 Earl Torgeson 15.00 30.00
35 Tommy Byrne RC 15.00 30.00
36 Cliff Fannin 15.00 30.00
37 Bobby Doerr 60.00 100.00
38 Irv Noren 15.00 30.00
39 Ed Lopat 30.00 50.00
40 Vic Wertz 15.00 30.00
41 Johnny Schmitz 15.00 30.00
42 Bruce Edwards 15.00 30.00
43 Willie Jones 15.00 30.00
44 Johnny Wyrostek 15.00 30.00
45 Billy Pierce RC 30.00 50.00
46 Gerry Priddy 15.00 30.00
47 Herman Wehmeier 15.00 30.00
48 Billy Cox 20.00 40.00
49 Hank Sauer 20.00 40.00
50 Johnny Mize 60.00 100.00
51 Eddie Waitkus 20.00 40.00
52 Sam Chapman 30.00 50.00

1951 Topps Red Backs

The cards in this 52-card set measure approximately 2" by 2 5/8". The 1951 Topps Red Back set is identical in style to the Blue Back set of the same year. The cards have rounded corners and were designed to be used as a baseball game. Zernial, number 36, is listed with either the White Sox or Athletics, and Holmes, number 52, with either the Braves or Hartford. The set is denoted on the cards as "Set A" and the Blue Back set is correspondingly Set B. The cards were packaged as two connected cards along with a piece of caramel in a penny pack. There were 120 penny packs in a box. The most notable Rookie Card in the set is Monte Irvin.

COMPLETE SET (54) 400.00 1000.00
WRAPPER (1-CENT) 4.00 5.00
1 Yogi Berra 100.00 250.00
2 Sid Gordon 5.00 10.00
3 Ferris Fain 6.00 12.00
4 Vern Stephens 6.00 12.00
5 Phil Rizzuto 35.00 60.00
6 Allie Reynolds 10.00 20.00
7 Howie Pollet 5.00 10.00
8 Early Wynn 12.50 25.00
9 Roy Sievers 7.50 15.00
10 Mel Parnell 6.00 15.00
11 Gene Hermanski 6.00 15.00
12 Jim Hegan 6.00 15.00
13 Dale Mitchell 6.00 15.00
14 Wayne Terwilliger 5.00 12.00
15 Ralph Kiner 12.50 25.00
16 Preacher Roe 7.50 15.00
17 Gus Bell RC 7.50 15.00
18 Jerry Coleman 7.50 15.00
19 Dick Kokos 5.00 10.00
20 Dom DiMaggio 10.00 20.00
21 Larry Jansen 6.00 12.00
22 Bob Feller 30.00 80.00
23 Ray Boone RC 7.50 15.00
24 Hank Bauer 10.00 20.00
25 Cliff Chambers 5.00 10.00
26 Luke Easter RC 7.50 15.00
27 Wally Westlake 6.00 12.00
28 Elmer Valo 5.00 10.00
29 Bob Kennedy RC 6.00 12.00
30 Warren Spahn 35.00 60.00
31 Gil Hodges 30.00 50.00
32 Henry Thompson 6.00 12.00
33 William Werle 5.00 10.00
34 Grady Hatton 5.00 10.00
35 Al Rosen 7.50 15.00
36A Gus Zernial Chic 20.00 40.00
36B Gus Zernial Phila 10.00 20.00
37 Wes Westrum RC 6.00 12.00
38 Duke Snider 35.00 60.00
39 Ted Kluszewski 12.50 25.00
40 Mike Garcia 7.50 15.00
41 Whitey Lockman 6.00 12.00
42 Ray Scarborough 5.00 10.00
43 Maurice McDermott 5.00 10.00
44 Sid Hudson 5.00 10.00
45 Andy Seminick 6.00 12.00
46 Billy Goodman 6.00 12.00
47 Tommy Glaviano RC 5.00 10.00
48 Eddie Stanky 6.00 12.00
49 Al Zarilla 5.00 10.00
50 Monte Irvin RC 20.00 40.00
51 Eddie Robinson 5.00 10.00
52A T.Holmes Boston 20.00 40.00
52B T.Holmes Hartford 12.50 25.00

1952 Topps

The cards in this 407-card set measure approximately 2 5/8" by 3 3/4". The 1952 Topps set is Topps' first truly major set. Card numbers 1 to 80 were issued with red or black backs, both of which are less plentiful than card numbers 81 to 250. In fact, the first series is considered the most difficult with respect to finding perfect condition cards. Card number 48 (Joe Page) and number 49 (Johnny Sain) can be found with each other's write-up on their back. However, many dealers today believe that all cards numbered 1-250 were produced in the same quantities. Card numbers 251 to 310 are somewhat scarce and numbers 311 to 407 are quite scarce. Cards 281-300 were single printed compared to the other cards in the next to last series. Cards 311-313 were double printed on the last high number printing sheet. The key card in the set is Mickey Mantle, number 311, which was Mickey's first of many Topps cards. A minor variation on cards from 311 through 313 is that they exist with the stitching on the number circle in the back pointing right or left. There seems to be no print run difference between the two versions. Card number 307, Frank Campos, can be found in a scarce version with with one red star and one black star next to the words "Topps Baseball" on the back. In the early 1980's, Topps issued a standard-size reprint set of the 52 Topps set. These cards were issued only as a factory set. Five people portrayed in the regular set: Billy Loes (number 20), Dom DiMaggio (number 22), Saul Rogovin (number 159), Solly Hemus (number 196) and Tommy Holmes (number 289) are not in the reprint set. Although rarely seen, salesman sample panels of three cards containing the fronts of regular cards with ad information on the back do exist.

COMP.MASTER SET (487) 100000.00 200000.00
COMPLETE SET (407) 75000.00 150000.00
COMMON CARD (1-80) 35.00 60.00
COMMON CARD (81-250) 20.00 40.00
COMMON CARD (251-310) 30.00 50.00
COMMON CARD (311-407) 150.00 250.00
WRAPPER (1-CENT) 200.00 250.00
WRAPPER (5-CENT) 75.00 100.00
1 Andy Pafko 3000.00 5000.00
1A Andy Pafko Black 1800.00 3000.00
2 Pete Runnels RC 150.00 250.00
2A Pete Runnels Black RC 150.00 250.00
3 Hank Thompson 40.00 70.00
3A Hank Thompson Black 40.00 70.00
4 Don Lenhardt 60.00 150.00
4A Don Lenhardt Black 50.00 120.00
5 c 50.00 120.00
5A Larry Jansen Black 50.00 120.00
6 Grady Hatton 35.00 60.00
6A Grady Hatton Black 35.00 60.00
7 Wayne Terwilliger 35.00 60.00
7A Wayne Terwilliger Black 35.00 60.00
8 Fred Marsh RC 40.00 100.00
8A Fred Marsh Black RC 40.00 100.00
9 Robert Hogue RC 35.00 60.00
9A Robert Hogue Black RC 35.00 60.00
10 Al Rosen 40.00 70.00
10A Al Rosen Black 40.00 70.00
11 Phil Rizzuto 250.00 400.00
11A Phil Rizzuto Black 200.00 350.00
12 Monty Basgall RC 35.00 60.00
12A Monty Basgall Black RC 35.00 60.00
13 Johnny Wyrostek 40.00 100.00
13A Johnny Wyrostek Black 40.00 100.00
14 Bob Elliott 40.00 70.00
14A Bob Elliott Black 40.00 70.00
15 Johnny Pesky 40.00 70.00
15A Johnny Pesky Black 40.00 70.00
16 Gene Hermanski 35.00 60.00
16A Gene Hermanski Black 35.00 60.00
17 Jim Hegan 40.00 70.00
17A Jim Hegan Black 40.00 70.00
18 Merrill Combs RC 35.00 60.00
18A Merrill Combs Black RC 35.00 60.00
19 Johnny Bucha RC 35.00 60.00
19A Johnny Bucha Black RC 35.00 60.00
20 Billy Loes SP RC 90.00 150.00
20A Billy Loes Black RC 90.00 150.00
21 Ferris Fain 40.00 70.00
21A Ferris Fain Black 40.00 70.00
22 Dom DiMaggio 75.00 125.00
22A Dom DiMaggio Black 60.00 100.00
23 Billy Goodman 40.00 70.00
23A Billy Goodman Black 40.00 70.00
24 Luke Easter 50.00 80.00
24A Luke Easter Black 50.00 80.00
25 Johnny Groth 35.00 60.00
25A Johnny Groth Black 35.00 60.00
26 Monte Irvin 75.00 200.00
26A Monte Irvin Black 75.00 200.00
27 Sam Jethroe 40.00 70.00
27A Sam Jethroe Black 40.00 70.00
28 Jerry Priddy 40.00 100.00
28A Jerry Priddy Black 40.00 100.00
29 Ted Kluszewski 75.00 125.00
29A Ted Kluszewski Black 75.00 125.00
30 Mel Parnell 40.00 70.00
30A Mel Parnell Black 40.00 70.00
31 Gus Zernial Baseballs 50.00 80.00
31A Gus Zernial Black 50.00 80.00
Posed with six baseballs
32 Eddie Robinson 35.00 60.00
32A Eddie Robinson Black 35.00 60.00
33 Warren Spahn 175.00 300.00
33A Warren Spahn Black 175.00 300.00
34 Elmer Valo 40.00 100.00
34A Elmer Valo Black 40.00 100.00
35 Hank Sauer 40.00 70.00
35A Hank Sauer Black 40.00 70.00
36 Gil Hodges 200.00 400.00
36A Gil Hodges Black 200.00 400.00
37 Duke Snider 150.00 400.00
37A Duke Snider Black 150.00 400.00
38 Wally Westlake 35.00 60.00
38A Wally Westlake Black 35.00 60.00
39 Dizzy Trout 40.00 70.00
39A Dizzy Trout Black 40.00 70.00
40 Irv Noren 40.00 70.00
40A Irv Noren Black 40.00 70.00
41 Bob Wellman RC 35.00 60.00
41A Bob Wellman Black RC 35.00 60.00
42 Lou Kretlow RC 35.00 60.00
42A Lou Kretlow Black RC 35.00 60.00
43 Ray Scarborough 35.00 60.00
43A Ray Scarborough Black 35.00 60.00
44 Con Dempsey RC 35.00 60.00
44A Con Dempsey Black RC 35.00 60.00
45 Eddie Joost 35.00 60.00
45A Eddie Joost Black 35.00 60.00
46 Gordon Goldsberry RC 35.00 60.00
46A Gordon Goldsberry Black RC 35.00 60.00
47 Willie Jones 40.00 70.00
47A Willie Jones Black 40.00 70.00
48A Joe Page ERR BLA 250.00 400.00
48B Joe Page COR BLA 75.00 125.00
48C Joe Page COR Red 75.00 125.00
49A John Sain ERR BLA 250.00 400.00
49B John Sain COR BLA 75.00 125.00
49C Joe Page COR Red 75.00 125.00
50 Marv Rickert RC 35.00 60.00
50A Marv Rickert Black RC 35.00 60.00
51 Jim Russell 35.00 60.00
51A Jim Russell Black 35.00 60.00
52 Don Mueller 40.00 70.00
52A Don Mueller Black 40.00 70.00
53 Chris Van Cuyk RC 30.00 80.00
53A Chris Van Cuyk Black RC 30.00 80.00
54 Leo Kiely RC 40.00 100.00
54A Leo Kiely Black RC 35.00 60.00
55 Ray Boone 50.00 80.00
55A Ray Boone Black 50.00 80.00
56 Tommy Glaviano 35.00 60.00
56A Tommy Glaviano Black 35.00 60.00
57 Ed Lopat 60.00 100.00
57A Ed Lopat Black 60.00 100.00
58 Bob Mahoney RC 35.00 60.00
58A Bob Mahoney Black RC 35.00 60.00
59 Robin Roberts 75.00 200.00
59A Robin Roberts Black 75.00 200.00
60 Sid Hudson 35.00 60.00
60A Sid Hudson Black 35.00 60.00
61 Tookie Gilbert 35.00 60.00
61A Tookie Gilbert Black 35.00 60.00
62 Chuck Stobbs RC 35.00 60.00
62A Chuck Stobbs Black RC 35.00 60.00
63 Howie Pollet 50.00 120.00
63A Howie Pollet Black 50.00 120.00
64 Roy Sievers 40.00 70.00
64A Roy Sievers Black 40.00 70.00
65 Enos Slaughter 75.00 200.00
65A Enos Slaughter Black 75.00 200.00
66 Preacher Roe 60.00 100.00
66A Preacher Roe Black 60.00 100.00
67 Allie Reynolds 75.00 125.00
67A Allie Reynolds Black 75.00 125.00
68 Cliff Chambers 35.00 60.00
68A Cliff Chambers Black 35.00 60.00
69 Virgil Stallcup 35.00 60.00
69A Virgil Stallcup Black 35.00 60.00
70 Al Zarilla 35.00 60.00
70A Al Zarilla Black 35.00 60.00
71 Tom Upton RC 35.00 60.00
71A Tom Upton Black RC 35.00 60.00
72 Karl Olson RC 35.00 60.00
72A Karl Olson Black RC 35.00 60.00
73 Bill Werle 35.00 60.00
73A Bill Werle Black 35.00 60.00
74 Andy Hansen RC 35.00 60.00
74A Andy Hansen Black RC 35.00 60.00
75 Wes Westrum 40.00 70.00
75A Wes Westrum Black 40.00 70.00
76 Eddie Stanky 50.00 120.00
76A Eddie Stanky Black 50.00 120.00
77 Bob Kennedy 40.00 70.00
77A Bob Kennedy Black 40.00 70.00
78 Ellis Kinder 40.00 100.00
78A Ellis Kinder Black 40.00 100.00
79 Gerry Staley 35.00 60.00
79A Gerry Staley Black 35.00 60.00
80 Herman Wehmeier 50.00 80.00
80A Herman Wehmeier Black 50.00 80.00
81 Vernon Law 50.00 80.00
82 Duane Pillette 20.00 40.00
83 Billy Johnson 20.00 40.00
84 Vern Stephens 30.00 50.00
85 Bob Kuzava 30.00 50.00
86 Ted Gray 20.00 40.00
87 Dale Coogan 20.00 50.00
88 Bob Feller 150.00 400.00
89 Johnny Lipon 20.00 50.00
90 Mickey Grasso 20.00 50.00
91 Red Schoendienst 60.00 150.00
92 Dale Mitchell 30.00 50.00
93 Al Sima RC 20.00 40.00
94 Sam Mele 20.00 40.00
95 Ken Holcombe 25.00 60.00
96 Willard Marshall 20.00 40.00
97 Earl Torgeson 25.00 60.00
98 Billy Pierce 30.00 50.00
99 Gene Woodling 35.00 60.00
100 Del Rice 30.00 80.00
101 Max Lanier 20.00 40.00
102 Bill Kennedy 20.00 40.00
103 Cliff Mapes 20.00 40.00
104 Don Kolloway 20.00 50.00
105 Johnny Pramesa 20.00 40.00
106 Mickey Vernon 20.00 50.00
107 Connie Ryan 20.00 40.00
108 Jim Konstanty 35.00 60.00
109 Ted Wilks 20.00 50.00
110 Dutch Leonard 20.00 40.00
111 Peanuts Lowrey 20.00 40.00
112 Hank Majeski 20.00 40.00
113 Dick Sisler 30.00 50.00
114 Willard Ramsdell 20.00 40.00
115 George Munger 20.00 50.00
116 Carl Scheib 20.00 40.00
117 Sherm Lollar 30.00 50.00
118 Ken Raffensberger 20.00 40.00
119 Mickey McDermott 20.00 40.00
120 Bob Chakales RC 25.00 60.00
121 Gus Niarhos 20.00 40.00
122 Jackie Jensen 50.00 80.00
123 Eddie Yost 30.00 50.00
124 Monte Kennedy 20.00 50.00
125 Bill Rigney 20.00 40.00
126 Fred Hutchinson 30.00 50.00
127 Paul Minner RC 20.00 40.00
128 Don Bollweg RC 20.00 40.00
129 Johnny Mize 75.00 200.00
130 Sheldon Jones 25.00 60.00
131 Morrie Martin RC 20.00 40.00
132 Clyde Kluttz RC 20.00 40.00
133 Al Widmar 20.00 40.00
134 Joe Tipton 20.00 40.00
135 Dixie Howell 20.00 40.00
136 Johnny Schmitz 20.00 40.00
137 Roy McMillan RC 30.00 50.00
138 Bill MacDonald 20.00 40.00
139 Ken Wood 20.00 40.00
140 Johnny Antonelli 35.00 60.00
141 Clint Hartung 20.00 40.00
142 Harry Perkowski RC 20.00 40.00
143 Les Moss 20.00 40.00
144 Ed Blake RC 20.00 40.00
145 Joe Haynes 20.00 40.00
146 Frank House RC 20.00 40.00
147 Bob Young RC 20.00 40.00
148 Johnny Klippstein 20.00 40.00
149 Dick Kryhoski 20.00 40.00
150 Ted Beard 20.00 40.00
151 Wally Post RC 30.00 50.00
152 Al Evans 20.00 40.00
153 Bob Rush 20.00 40.00
154 Joe Muir RC 20.00 40.00
155 Frank Overmire 20.00 40.00
156 Frank Hiller RC 20.00 40.00
157 Bob Usher 20.00 40.00
158 Eddie Waitkus 20.00 40.00
159 Saul Rogovin RC 20.00 40.00
160 Owen Friend 20.00 40.00
161 Bud Byerly RC 20.00 40.00
162 Del Crandall 30.00 50.00
163 Stan Rojek 20.00 40.00
164 Walt Dubiel 20.00 40.00
165 Eddie Kazak 20.00 40.00
166 Paul LaPalme RC 20.00 40.00
167 Bill Howerton 20.00 40.00
168 Charlie Silvera RC 35.00 60.00
169 Howie Judson 20.00 40.00
170 Gus Bell 30.00 50.00
171 Ed Erautt RC 20.00 40.00
172 Eddie Miksis 30.00 80.00
173 Roy Smalley 20.00 40.00
174 Clarence Marshall RC 20.00 40.00
175 Billy Martin RC 300.00 500.00
176 Hank Edwards 20.00 40.00
177 Bill Wight 20.00 40.00
178 Cass Michaels 20.00 40.00
179 Frank Smith RC 20.00 40.00
180 Charlie Maxwell RC 30.00 50.00
181 Bob Swift 20.00 40.00
182 Billy Hitchcock 20.00 40.00
183 Erv Dusak 20.00 40.00
184 Bob Ramazzotti 20.00 40.00
185 Bill Nicholson 30.00 50.00
186 Walt Masterson 20.00 40.00
187 Bob Miller 20.00 40.00
188 Clarence Podbielan RC 20.00 40.00
189 Pete Reiser 35.00 60.00
190 Don Johnson RC 20.00 40.00
191 Yogi Berra 500.00 800.00
192 Myron Ginsberg RC 30.00 80.00
193 Harry Simpson RC 30.00 50.00
194 Joe Hatten 20.00 40.00
195 Minnie Minoso RC 100.00 250.00
196 Solly Hemus RC 35.00 60.00
197 George Strickland RC 20.00 40.00
198 Phil Haugstad RC 20.00 40.00
199 George Zuverink RC 20.00 40.00
200 Ralph Houk RC 40.00 100.00
201 Alex Kellner 20.00 50.00
202 Joe Collins RC 40.00 100.00
203 Curt Simmons 35.00 60.00
204 Ron Northey 20.00 40.00
205 Clyde King 35.00 60.00
206 Joe Ostrowski RC 30.00 80.00
207 Mickey Harris 20.00 40.00
208 Marlin Stuart RC 20.00 40.00
209 Howie Fox 20.00 40.00
210 Dick Fowler 20.00 40.00
211 Ray Coleman 20.00 40.00
212 Ned Garver 20.00 40.00
213 Nippy Jones 20.00 40.00
214 Johnny Hopp 30.00 50.00
215 Hank Bauer 40.00 100.00
216 Richie Ashburn 100.00 250.00
217 Snuffy Stirnweiss 30.00 50.00
218 Clyde McCullough 20.00 40.00
219 Bobby Shantz 30.00 80.00
220 Joe Presko RC 20.00 50.00
221 Granny Hamner 20.00 40.00
222 Hoot Evers 20.00 40.00
223 Del Ennis 30.00 50.00
224 Bruce Edwards 20.00 40.00
225 Frank Baumholtz 20.00 40.00
226 Dave Philley 20.00 40.00
227 Joe Garagiola 40.00 100.00
228 Al Brazle 20.00 40.00
229 Gene Bearden UER 20.00 40.00
230 Matt Batts 20.00 40.00
231 Sam Zoldak 20.00 50.00
232 Billy Cox 30.00 50.00
233 Bob Friend RC 50.00 80.00
234 Steve Souchock RC 20.00 40.00
235 Walt Dropo 25.00 60.00
236 Ed Fitzgerald 20.00 40.00
237 Jerry Coleman 30.00 80.00
238 Art Houtteman 20.00 40.00
239 Rocky Bridges RC 30.00 50.00
240 Jack Phillips RC 20.00 50.00
241 Tommy Byrne 25.00 60.00
242 Tom Poholsky RC 20.00 40.00
243 Larry Doby 100.00 250.00
244 Vic Wertz 30.00 80.00
245 Sherry Robertson 20.00 40.00
246 George Kell 60.00 150.00
247 Randy Gumpert 20.00 40.00
248 Frank Shea 20.00 40.00
249 Bobby Adams 20.00 40.00
250 Carl Erskine 50.00 120.00
251 Chico Carrasquel 30.00 50.00
252 Vern Bickford 30.00 50.00
253 Johnny Berardino 30.00 80.00
254 Joe Dobson 30.00 50.00
255 Clyde Vollmer 30.00 50.00
256 Pete Suder 30.00 50.00
257 Bobby Avila 40.00 100.00
258 Steve Gromek 35.00 60.00
259 Bob Addis RC 30.00 50.00
260 Pete Castiglione 30.00 50.00
261 Willie Mays 3000.00 6000.00
262 Virgil Trucks 30.00 80.00
263 Harry Brecheen 35.00 60.00
264 Roy Hartsfield 30.00 50.00
265 Chuck Diering 30.00 50.00
266 Murry Dickson 30.00 50.00
267 Sid Gordon 35.00 60.00
268 Bob Lemon 100.00 250.00
269 Willard Nixon 30.00 50.00
270 Lou Brissie 30.00 50.00
271 Jim Delsing 30.00 80.00
272 Mike Garcia 50.00 80.00
273 Erv Palica 30.00 50.00
274 Ralph Branca 75.00 125.00
275 Pat Mullin 30.00 50.00
276 Jim Wilson RC 30.00 50.00
277 Early Wynn 100.00 250.00
278 Allie Clark 30.00 80.00
279 Eddie Stewart 30.00 50.00
280 Cloyd Boyer 50.00 80.00
281 Tommy Brown SP 50.00 80.00
282 Birdie Tebbetts SP 50.00 80.00
283 Phil Masi SP 35.00 60.00
284 Hank Arft SP 35.00 60.00
285 Cliff Fannin SP 40.00 100.00
286 Joe DeMaestri SP RC 35.00 60.00
287 Steve Bilko SP 30.00 80.00
288 Chet Nichols SP RC 50.00 80.00
289 Tommy Holmes SP 60.00 100.00
290 Joe Astroth SP 30.00 60.00
291 Gil Coan SP 35.00 60.00
292 Floyd Baker SP 35.00 60.00
293 Sibby Sisti SP 35.00 60.00
294 Walker Cooper SP 35.00 60.00
295 Phil Cavarretta SP 50.00 80.00
296 Red Rolfe MG SP 40.00 100.00
297 Andy Seminick SP 35.00 60.00
298 Bob Ross SP RC 35.00 60.00
299 Ray Murray SP RC 35.00 60.00
300 Barney McCosky SP 50.00 80.00
301 Bob Porterfield 30.00 50.00
302 Max Surkont RC 25.00 60.00
303 Harry Dorish 30.00 50.00
304 Sam Dente 30.00 50.00
305 Paul Richards MG 35.00 60.00
306 Lou Sleater RC 25.00 60.00
307 Frank Campos RC 30.00 50.00
Two red stars on back in copyright line
307A Frank Campos Star
307B Frank Campos RC
Partial top left border on front
308 Luis Aloma 30.00 50.00
309 Jim Busby 35.00 60.00
310 George Metkovich 60.00 100.00
311 Mickey Mantle DP 80000.00 120000.00
311B Mickey Mantle DP 80000.00 120000.00
312 Jackie Robinson 6000.00 12000.00
312B Jackie Robinson Stitch 6000.00 12000.00
313 Bobby Thomson DP 200.00 350.00
313B Bobby Thomson Stitch 200.00 350.00
314 Roy Campanella 1500.00 2500.00
315 Leo Durocher MG 350.00 600.00
316 Dave Williams RC 175.00 300.00
317 Conrado Marrero 175.00 300.00
318 Harold Gregg RC 175.00 300.00
319 Rube Walker RC 150.00 400.00
320 John Rutherford RC 175.00 300.00
321 Joe Black RC 350.00 500.00
322 Randy Jackson RC 175.00 300.00
323 Bubba Church 150.00 250.00
324 Warren Hacker 125.00 300.00
325 Bill Serena 175.00 300.00
326 George Shuba RC 350.00 500.00
327 Al Wilson RC 125.00 300.00
328 Bob Borkowski RC 175.00 300.00
329 Ike Delock RC 175.00 300.00
330 Turk Lown RC 175.00 300.00
331 Tom Morgan RC 175.00 300.00
332 Tony Bartirome RC 1500.00 2500.00
333 Pee Wee Reese 1000.00 2000.00
334 Wilmer Mizell RC 175.00 300.00
335 Ted Lepcio RC 150.00 250.00
336 Dave Koslo 150.00 250.00
337 Jim Hearn 175.00 300.00
338 Sal Yvars RC 175.00 300.00
339 Russ Meyer 175.00 300.00
340 Bob Hooper 175.00 300.00
341 Hal Jeffcoat 175.00 300.00
342 Clem Labine RC 350.00 500.00
343 Dick Gernert RC 150.00 250.00
344 Ewell Blackwell 175.00 300.00
345 Sammy White RC 150.00 250.00
346 George Spencer RC 150.00 250.00
347 Joe Adcock 250.00 400.00
348 Robert Kelly RC 150.00 250.00
349 Bob Cain 150.00 250.00
350 Cal Abrams 175.00 300.00
351 Alvin Dark 175.00 300.00
352 Karl Drews 175.00 300.00
353 Bobby Del Greco RC 175.00 300.00
354 Fred Hatfield RC 175.00 300.00
355 Bobby Morgan 175.00 300.00
356 Toby Atwell RC 175.00 300.00
357 Smoky Burgess 175.00 300.00
358 John Kucab RC 175.00 300.00
359 Dee Fondy RC 150.00 400.00
360 George Crowe RC 150.00 250.00
361 Bill Posedel CO 150.00 250.00
362 Ken Heintzelman 175.00 300.00
363 Dick Rozek RC 175.00 300.00
364 Clyde Sukeforth CO RC 175.00 300.00
365 Cookie Lavagetto CO 200.00 500.00
366 Dave Madison RC 150.00 250.00
367 Ben Thorpe RC 175.00 300.00
368 Ed Wright RC 175.00 300.00
369 Dick Groat RC 350.00 500.00
370 Billy Hoeft RC 250.00 600.00
371 Bobby Hofman 150.00 250.00
372 Gil McDougald RC 300.00 500.00
373 Jim Turner CO RC 250.00 400.00
374 Al Benton RC 150.00 250.00
375 John Merson RC 150.00 250.00
376 Faye Throneberry RC 150.00 250.00
377 Chuck Dressen MG 250.00 400.00
378 Leroy Fusselman RC 175.00 300.00
379 Joe Rossi RC 150.00 250.00
380 Clem Koshorek RC 150.00 250.00
381 Milton Stock CO RC 175.00 300.00
382 Sam Jones RC 200.00 350.00
383 Del Wilber RC 150.00 250.00
384 Frank Crosetti CO 300.00 500.00
385 Herman Franks CO RC 150.00 250.00
386 Ed Yuhas RC 175.00 300.00
387 Billy Meyer MG 150.00 250.00
388 Bob Chipman 150.00 250.00
389 Ben Wade RC 175.00 300.00
390 Rocky Nelson RC 175.00 300.00
391 Ben Chapman CO UER 150.00 250.00
392 Hoyt Wilhelm RC 800.00 1500.00
393 Ebba St.Claire RC 150.00 250.00
394 Billy Herman CO 350.00 600.00
395 Jake Pitler CO 175.00 300.00
396 Dick Williams RC 300.00 500.00
397 Forrest Main RC 150.00 250.00
398 Hal Rice 150.00 250.00
399 Jim Fridley RC 150.00 250.00
400 Bill Dickey CO 500.00 1200.00
401 Bob Schultz RC 175.00 300.00
402 Earl Harrist RC 175.00 300.00
403 Bill Miller RC 175.00 300.00
404 Dick Brodowski RC 175.00 300.00
405 Eddie Pellagrini 175.00 300.00
406 Joe Nuxhall RC 800.00 1500.00
407 Eddie Mathews RC 4000.00 8000.00

1953 Topps

The cards in this 274-card set measure 2 5/8" by 3 3/4". Card number 69, Dick Brodowksi, features the first known drawing of a player during a night game. Although the last card is numbered 280, there are only 274 cards in the set since numbers 253, 261, 267, 268, 271, and 275 were never issued. The 1953 Topps series contains line drawings of players in full color. The name and team panel at the card base is easily damaged, making it very difficult to complete a mint set. The high number series, 221 to 280, was produced in shorter supply late in the year and hence is more difficult to complete than the lower numbers. The key cards in the set are Mickey Mantle (82) and Willie Mays (244). The key Rookie Cards in this set are Roy Face, Jim Gilliam, and Johnny Podres, all from the last series. There are a number of double-printed cards (actually not double but 50 percent more of each of these numbers were printed compared to the other cards in the series) indicated by DP in the checklist below. There were five players (10 Smoky Burgess, 44 Ellis Kinder, 61 Early Wynn, 72 Fred Hutchinson, and 81 Joe Black) held out of the first run of 1-85 (but printed in with numbers 86-165), who are each marked by SP in the checklist below. In addition, there are five numbers which were printed with the more plentiful series 166-220; these cards (94, 107, 131, 145, and 156) are also indicated by DP in the checklist below. All these aforementioned cards from 86 through 165 and the fiye short prints come with the biographical information on the back in either white or black lettering. These seem to be printed in equal quantities and no price differential is given for either variety. The cards were issued in one-card penny packs or six-card nickel packs. The nickel packs were issued 24 to a box. There were some three-card advertising panels produced by Topps; the players include Johnny Mize/Clem Koshorek/Toby Atwell; Jim Hearn/Johnny Groth/Sherman Lollar and Mickey Mantle/Johnny Wyrostek/

COMPLETE SET (274) 10000.00 20000.00
COMMON CARD (1-165) 15.00 30.00
COMMON DP (1-165) 7.50 15.00
COMMON CARD (166-220) 12.50 25.00
COMMON CARD (221-280) 50.00 100.00
NOT ISSUED (253/261/267)
NOT ISSUED (268/271/275)
WRAP.(1-CENT, DATED) 150.00 200.00
WRAP.(1-CENT,NO DATE) 250.00 300.00
WRAP.(5-CENT, DATED) 300.00 400.00
WRAP.(5-CENT,NO DATE) 275.00 350.00
1 Jackie Robinson DP 600.00 1200.00
2 Luke Easter DP 10.00 20.00
3 George Crowe 25.00 40.00
4 Ben Wade 15.00 30.00
5 Joe Dobson 15.00 30.00
6 Sam Jones 25.00 40.00
7 Bob Borkowski DP 7.50 15.00
8 Clem Koshorek DP 7.50 15.00
9 Joe Collins 50.00 120.00
10 Smoky Burgess SP 50.00 80.00
11 Sal Yvars 15.00 30.00
12 Howie Judson DP 7.50 15.00
13 Conrado Marrero DP 12.00 30.00
14 Clem Labine DP 10.00 20.00
15 Bobo Newsom DP RC 10.00 20.00
16 Peanuts Lowrey DP 7.50 15.00
17 Billy Hitchcock 15.00 30.00
18 Ted Lepcio DP 7.50 15.00
19 Mel Parnell DP 10.00 20.00
20 Hank Thompson 25.00 40.00
21 Billy Johnson 15.00 30.00
22 Howie Fox 15.00 30.00
23 Toby Atwell DP 7.50 15.00
24 Ferris Fain 25.00 40.00
25 Ray Boone 25.00 40.00
26 Dale Mitchell DP 10.00 20.00
27 Roy Campanella DP 100.00 250.00
28 Eddie Pellagrini 15.00 30.00
29 Hal Jeffcoat 15.00 30.00
30 Willard Nixon 15.00 30.00
31 Ewell Blackwell 35.00 60.00
32 Clyde Vollmer 15.00 30.00
33 Bob Kennedy DP 12.00 30.00
34 George Shuba 25.00 40.00
35 Irv Noren DP 7.50 15.00
36 Johnny Groth DP 7.50 15.00
37 Eddie Mathews DP 75.00 200.00
38 Jim Hearn DP 7.50 15.00
39 Eddie Miksis 15.00 30.00
40 John Lipon 15.00 40.00
41 Enos Slaughter 50.00 120.00
42 Gus Zernial DP 10.00 20.00
43 Gil McDougald 35.00 60.00
44 Ellis Kinder SP 35.00 60.00
45 Grady Hatton DP 7.50 15.00
46 Johnny Klippstein DP 7.50 15.00
47 Bubba Church DP 7.50 15.00
48 Bob Del Greco DP 7.50 15.00
49 Faye Throneberry DP 7.50 15.00

0 Chuck Dressen MG DP 10.00 20.00
1 Frank Campos DP 7.50 15.00
2 Ted Gray DP 7.50 15.00
3 Sherm Lollar DP 10.00 20.00
4 Bob Feller DP 100.00 250.00
5 Maurice McDermott DP 7.50 15.00
6 Gerry Staley DP 7.50 15.00
7 Carl Scheib 15.00 30.00
8 George Metkovich 15.00 30.00
9 Karl Drews DP 7.50 15.00
0 Cloyd Boyer DP 7.50 15.00
1 Early Wynn SP 40.00 100.00
2 Monte Irvin DP 60.00 150.00
3 Gus Niarhos DP 7.50 15.00
4 Dave Philley 15.00 30.00
5 Earl Harrist 15.00 30.00
6 Minnie Minoso 35.00 60.00
7 Roy Sievers DP 10.00 20.00
8 Del Rice 15.00 30.00
9 Dick Brodowski 15.00 30.00
0 Ed Yuhas 15.00 30.00
1 Tony Bartirome 15.00 30.00
2 Fred Hutchinson SP 35.00 60.00
3 Eddie Robinson 15.00 30.00
4 Joe Rossi 15.00 30.00
5 Mike Garcia 25.00 40.00
6 Pee Wee Reese 125.00 300.00
7 Johnny Mize DP 50.00 120.00
8 Red Schoendienst 50.00 80.00
9 Johnny Wyrostek 15.00 30.00
0 Jim Hegan 25.00 40.00
1 Joe Black SP 50.00 80.00
2 Mickey Mantle 5000.00 10000.00
3 Howie Pollet 15.00 30.00
4 Bob Hooper DP 7.50 15.00
5 Bobby Morgan DP 7.50 15.00
6 Billy Martin 75.00 200.00
7 Ed Lopat 40.00 100.00
8 Willie Jones DP 7.50 15.00
9 Chuck Stobbs DP 7.50 15.00
0 Hank Edwards DP 7.50 15.00
1 Ebba St.Claire DP 15.00 40.00
2 Paul Minner DP 7.50 15.00
3 Hal Rice DP 7.50 15.00
4 Bill Kennedy DP 7.50 15.00
5 Willard Marshall DP 7.50 15.00
6 Virgil Trucks 25.00 40.00
7 Don Kolloway DP 12.00 30.00
8 Cal Abrams DP 7.50 15.00
9 Dave Madison 15.00 30.00
00 Bill Miller 15.00 30.00
01 Ted Wilks 15.00 30.00
02 Connie Ryan DP 7.50 15.00
03 Joe Astroth DP 7.50 15.00
04 Yogi Berra 250.00 500.00
05 Joe Nuxhall DP 10.00 20.00
06 Johnny Antonelli 25.00 40.00
07 Danny O'Connell DP 7.50 15.00
08 Bob Porterfield DP 12.00 30.00
09 Alvin Dark 35.00 60.00
10 Herman Wehmeier DP 7.50 15.00
11 Hank Sauer DP 15.00 40.00
12 Ned Garver DP 12.00 30.00
13 Jerry Priddy 15.00 30.00
14 Phil Rizzuto 100.00 250.00
15 George Spencer 15.00 30.00
16 Frank Smith DP 7.50 15.00
17 Sid Gordon DP 12.00 30.00
18 Gus Bell DP 10.00 20.00
19 Johnny Sain SP 40.00 100.00
20 Davey Williams 25.00 40.00
21 Walt Dropo 25.00 40.00
22 Elmer Valo 15.00 30.00
23 Tommy Byrne DP 12.00 30.00
24 Sibby Sisti DP 7.50 15.00
25 Dick Williams DP 10.00 20.00
26 Bill Connelly DP RC 7.50 15.00
27 Clint Courtney DP RC 7.50 15.00
28 Wilmer Mizell DP 10.00 20.00
Inconsistent design,
logo on front with
black birds
29 Keith Thomas RC 15.00 30.00
30 Turk Lown DP 15.00 40.00
31 Harry Byrd DP RC 7.50 15.00
32 Tom Morgan 15.00 30.00
33 Gil Coan 15.00 30.00
34 Rube Walker 25.00 40.00
35 Al Rosen DP 10.00 20.00
36 Ken Heintzelman DP 7.50 15.00
37 John Rutherford DP 7.50 15.00
38 George Kell 50.00 80.00
39 Sammy White 15.00 30.00
40 Tommy Glaviano 15.00 30.00
41 Allie Reynolds DP 40.00 100.00
42 Vic Wertz 25.00 40.00
43 Billy Pierce 20.00 50.00
44 Bob Schultz DP 7.50 15.00
45 Harry Dorish DP 7.50 15.00
46 Granny Hamner 15.00 30.00
47 Warren Spahn 100.00 250.00
48 Mickey Grasso 15.00 30.00
49 Dom DiMaggio DP 20.00 50.00
50 Harry Simpson DP 12.00 30.00
51 Hoyt Wilhelm 50.00 120.00
52 Bob Adams DP 7.50 15.00
53 Andy Seminick DP 7.50 15.00
54 Dick Groat 40.00 100.00
55 Dutch Leonard 15.00 30.00
56 Jim Rivera DP RC 10.00 25.00
57 Bob Addis DP 15.00 40.00
58 Johnny Logan RC 20.00 50.00
59 Wayne Terwilliger DP 7.50 15.00

160 Bob Young 15.00 30.00
161 Vern Bickford DP 7.50 15.00
162 Ted Kluszewski 40.00 100.00
163 Fred Hatfield DP 7.50 15.00
164 Frank Shea DP 7.50 15.00
165 Billy Hoeft 15.00 30.00
166 Billy Hunter RC 15.00 40.00
167 Art Schult RC 15.00 40.00
168 Willard Schmidt RC 12.50 25.00
169 Dizzy Trout 15.00 30.00
170 Bill Werle 12.50 25.00
171 Bill Glynn RC 12.00 30.00
172 Rip Repulski RC 12.50 25.00
173 Preston Ward 12.50 25.00
174 Billy Loes 15.00 30.00
175 Ron Kline RC 12.50 25.00
176 Don Hoak RC 25.00 40.00
177 Jim Dyck RC 12.00 30.00
178 Jim Waugh RC 12.50 25.00
179 Gene Hermanski 12.50 25.00
180 Virgil Stallcup 12.50 25.00
181 Al Zarilla 12.50 25.00
182 Bobby Hofman 12.50 25.00
183 Stu Miller RC 25.00 40.00
184 Hal Brown RC 12.50 25.00
185 Jim Pendleton RC 12.50 25.00
186 Charlie Bishop RC 15.00 40.00
187 Jim Fridley 12.50 25.00
188 Andy Carey RC 25.00 60.00
189 Ray Jablonski RC 12.50 25.00
190 Dixie Walker CO 15.00 30.00
191 Ralph Kiner 60.00 150.00
192 Wally Westlake 12.00 30.00
193 Mike Clark RC 12.50 25.00
194 Eddie Kazak 12.50 25.00
195 Ed McGhee RC 12.50 25.00
196 Bob Keegan RC 12.50 25.00
197 Del Crandall 25.00 40.00
198 Forrest Main 12.50 25.00
199 Marion Fricano RC 12.50 25.00
200 Gordon Goldsberry 12.50 25.00
201 Paul LaPalme 12.50 25.00
202 Carl Sawatski RC 12.50 25.00
203 Cliff Fannin 12.50 25.00
204 Dick Bokelman RC 12.50 25.00
205 Vern Benson RC 12.50 25.00
206 Ed Bailey RC 15.00 30.00
207 Whitey Ford 125.00 300.00
208 Jim Wilson 12.00 30.00
209 Jim Greengrass RC 12.50 25.00
210 Bob Cerv RC 25.00 40.00
211 J.W. Porter RC 12.50 25.00
212 Jack Dittmer RC 15.00 40.00
213 Ray Scarborough 20.00 50.00
214 Bill Bruton RC 25.00 40.00
215 Gene Conley RC 15.00 30.00
216 Jim Hughes RC 12.50 25.00
217 Murray Wall RC 12.50 25.00
218 Les Fusselman 12.50 25.00
219 Pete Runnels UER 15.00 30.00
Photo actually
Don Johnson
220 Satchel Paige UER 600.00 1200.00
221 Bob Milliken RC 50.00 100.00
222 Vic Janowicz DP RC 25.00 50.00
223 Johnny O'Brien DP RC 25.00 50.00
224 Lou Sleater DP 25.00 50.00
225 Bobby Shantz 75.00 125.00
226 Ed Erautt 50.00 100.00
227 Morrie Martin 50.00 100.00
228 Hal Newhouser 90.00 150.00
229 Rocky Krsnich RC 50.00 100.00
230 Johnny Lindell DP 25.00 50.00
231 Solly Hemus DP 25.00 50.00
232 Dick Kokos 50.00 100.00
233 Al Aber RC 50.00 100.00
234 Ray Murray DP 25.00 50.00
235 John Hetki DP RC 25.00 50.00
236 Harry Perkowski DP 25.00 50.00
237 Bud Podbielan DP 25.00 50.00
238 Cal Hogue DP RC 25.00 50.00
239 Jim Delsing 25.00 60.00
240 Fred Marsh 50.00 100.00
241 Al Sima DP 25.00 50.00
242 Charlie Silvera 75.00 125.00
243 Carlos Bernier DP RC 25.00 50.00
244 Willie Mays 2000.00 4000.00
245 Bill Norman CO 50.00 100.00
246 Roy Face RC DP RC 40.00 100.00
247 Mike Sandlock DP RC 25.00 50.00
248 Gene Stephens DP RC 25.00 50.00
249 Eddie O'Brien RC 50.00 100.00
250 Bob Wilson RC 50.00 100.00
251 Sid Hudson 75.00 200.00
252 Hank Foiles RC 50.00 100.00
254 Preacher Roe DP 50.00 120.00
255 Dixie Howell 50.00 100.00
256 Les Peden RC 50.00 100.00
257 Bob Boyd RC 50.00 100.00
258 Jim Gilliam RC 250.00 400.00
259 Roy McMillan DP 25.00 50.00
260 Sam Calderone RC 50.00 100.00
262 Bob Oldis RC 50.00 100.00
263 Johnny Podres RC 150.00 400.00
264 Gene Woodling DP 30.00 60.00
265 Jackie Jensen 75.00 125.00
266 Bob Cain 50.00 100.00
269 Duane Pillette 50.00 100.00
270 Vern Stephens 75.00 125.00
272 Bill Antonello RC 30.00 80.00
273 Harvey Haddix RC 100.00 250.00
274 John Riddle CO 50.00 100.00
276 Ken Raffensberger 50.00 100.00

277 Don Lund RC 50.00 100.00
278 Willie Miranda RC 50.00 100.00
279 Joe Coleman DP 25.00 50.00
280 Milt Bolling RC 200.00 400.00

1954 Topps

The cards in this 250-card set measure approximately 2 5/8" by 3 3/4". Each of the cards in the 1954 Topps set contains a large "head" shot of the player in color plus a smaller full-length photo in black and white set against a color background. The cards were issued in one-card penny packs or five-card nickel packs. Fifteen-card cello packs have also been seen. The penny packs came 120 to a box while the nickel packs came 24 to a box. The nickel boxes had a drawing of Ted Williams along with his name printed on the box to indicate that Williams was part of this product. This set contains the Rookie Cards of Hank Aaron, Ernie Banks, and Al Kaline and two separate cards of Ted Williams (number 1 and number 250). Conspicuous by his absence is Mickey Mantle who apparently was the exclusive property of Bowman during 1954 (and 1955). The first two issues of Sports Illustrated magazine contained "card" inserts on regular paper stock. The first issue showed actual cards in the set in color, while the second issue showed some created cards of New York Yankees players in black and white, including Mickey Mantle. There was also a Canadian printing of the first 50 cards. These cards can be easily discerned as they have "grey" backs rather than the white backs of the American printed cards. To celebrate this set as the first Topps set to feature Ted Williams, his visage is also featured on the five cent box. The Canadian cards came four cards to a pack and 36 packs to a box and cost five cents when issued.

COMPLETE SET (250) 6000.00 12000.00
COMMON (1-50/76-250) 7.50 15.00
COMMON CARD (51-75) 12.50 25.00
WRAP.(1-CENT, DATED) 150.00 200.00
WRAP.(1-CENT, UNDAT) 100.00 150.00
WRAP.(5-CENT, DATED) 250.00 300.00
WRAP.(5-CENT, UNDAT) 200.00 250.00
1 Ted Williams 400.00 800.00
2 Gus Zernial 12.50 25.00
3 Monte Irvin 30.00 80.00
4 Hank Sauer 12.50 25.00
5 Ed Lopat 12.50 25.00
6 Pete Runnels 12.50 25.00
7 Ted Kluszewski 15.00 40.00
8 Bob Young 7.50 15.00
9 Harvey Haddix 12.50 25.00
10 Jackie Robinson 250.00 600.00
11 Paul Leslie Smith RC 7.50 15.00
12 Del Crandall 12.50 25.00
13 Billy Martin 60.00 100.00
14 Preacher Roe UER 12.00 30.00
15 Al Rosen 12.50 25.00
16 Vic Janowicz 12.50 25.00
17 Phil Rizzuto 40.00 100.00
18 Walt Dropo 12.50 25.00
19 Johnny Lipon 7.50 15.00
20 Warren Spahn 75.00 125.00
21 Bobby Shantz 12.50 25.00
22 Jim Greengrass 7.50 15.00
23 Luke Easter 12.50 25.00
24 Granny Hamner 7.50 15.00
25 Harvey Kuenn RC 20.00 40.00
26 Ray Jablonski 7.50 15.00
27 Ferris Fain 12.50 25.00
28 Paul Minner 7.50 15.00
29 Jim Hegan 12.50 25.00
30 Eddie Mathews 50.00 120.00
31 Johnny Klippstein 7.50 15.00
32 Duke Snider 50.00 120.00
33 Johnny Schmitz 7.50 15.00
34 Jim Rivera 7.50 15.00
35 Junior Gilliam 25.00 50.00
36 Hoyt Wilhelm 25.00 60.00
37 Whitey Ford 60.00 150.00
38 Eddie Stanky MG 12.50 25.00
39 Sherm Lollar 12.50 25.00
40 Mel Parnell 12.50 25.00
41 Willie Jones 7.50 15.00
42 Don Mueller 12.50 25.00
43 Dick Groat 12.50 25.00
44 Ned Garver 7.50 15.00
45 Richie Ashburn 50.00 80.00
46 Ken Raffensberger 7.50 15.00
47 Ellis Kinder 7.50 15.00
48 Billy Hunter 12.50 25.00
49 Ray Murray 7.50 15.00
50 Yogi Berra 100.00 250.00
51 Johnny Lindell 12.50 25.00
52 Vic Power RC 15.00 30.00
53 Jack Dittmer 12.50 25.00
54 Vern Stephens 15.00 30.00
55 Phil Cavarretta MG 15.00 30.00
56 Willie Miranda 12.50 25.00
57 Luis Aloma 12.50 25.00
58 Bob Wilson 12.50 25.00

59 Gene Conley 15.00 30.00
60 Frank Baumholtz 12.50 25.00
61 Bob Cain 12.50 25.00
62 Eddie Robinson 12.50 25.00
63 Johnny Pesky 15.00 30.00
64 Hank Thompson 12.50 25.00
65 Bob Swift CO 12.50 25.00
66 Ted Lepcio 12.50 25.00
67 Jim Willis RC 12.50 25.00
68 Sam Calderone 12.50 25.00
69 Bud Podbielan 12.50 25.00
70 Larry Doby 75.00 200.00
71 Frank Smith 12.50 25.00
72 Preston Ward 12.50 25.00
73 Wayne Terwilliger 12.50 25.00
74 Bill Taylor RC 12.50 25.00
75 Fred Haney MG RC 12.50 25.00
76 Bob Scheffing CO 10.00 25.00
77 Ray Boone 12.50 25.00
78 Ted Kazanski RC 7.50 15.00
79 Andy Pafko 12.50 25.00
80 Jackie Jensen 12.50 25.00
81 Dave Hoskins RC 7.50 15.00
82 Milt Bolling 7.50 15.00
83 Joe Collins 12.00 30.00
84 Dick Cole RC 7.50 15.00
85 Bob Turley RC 20.00 40.00
86 Billy Herman CO 12.50 25.00
87 Roy Face 12.50 25.00
88 Matt Batts 7.50 15.00
89 Howie Pollet 7.50 15.00
90 Willie Mays 500.00 1000.00
91 Bob Oldis 7.50 15.00
92 Wally Westlake 7.50 15.00
93 Sid Hudson 7.50 15.00
94 Ernie Banks RC 1500.00 3000.00
95 Hal Rice 7.50 15.00
96 Charlie Silvera 12.50 25.00
97 Jerald Hal Lane RC 7.50 15.00
98 Joe Black 20.00 40.00
99 Bobby Hofman 7.50 15.00
100 Bob Keegan 7.50 15.00
101 Gene Woodling 12.50 25.00
102 Gil Hodges 40.00 100.00
103 Jim Lemon RC 7.50 15.00
104 Mike Sandlock 7.50 15.00
105 Andy Carey 12.50 25.00
106 Dick Kokos 12.00 30.00
107 Duane Pillette 7.50 15.00
108 Thornton Kipper RC 7.50 15.00
109 Bill Bruton 12.50 25.00
110 Harry Dorish 7.50 15.00
111 Jim Delsing 7.50 15.00
112 Bill Renna RC 7.50 15.00
113 Bob Boyd 7.50 15.00
114 Dean Stone RC 7.50 15.00
115 Rip Repulski 7.50 15.00
116 Steve Bilko 7.50 15.00
117 Solly Hemus 7.50 15.00
118 Carl Scheib 7.50 15.00
119 Johnny Antonelli 12.50 25.00
120 Roy McMillan 12.50 25.00
121 Clem Labine 12.00 30.00
122 Johnny Logan 12.50 25.00
123 Bobby Adams 7.50 15.00
124 Marion Fricano 7.50 15.00
125 Harry Perkowski 7.50 15.00
126 Ben Wade 7.50 15.00
127 Steve O'Neill MG 7.50 15.00
128 Hank Aaron RC 3000.00 8000.00
129 Forrest Jacobs RC 7.50 15.00
130 Hank Bauer 12.50 25.00
131 Reno Bertoia RC 12.50 25.00
132 Tommy Lasorda RC 150.00 400.00
133 Del Baker CO 7.50 15.00
134 Cal Hogue 7.50 15.00
135 Joe Presko 7.50 15.00
136 Connie Ryan 7.50 15.00
137 Wally Moon RC 20.00 40.00
138 Bob Borkowski 7.50 15.00
139 J.O'Brien/E.O'Brien 25.00 50.00
140 Tom Wright 7.50 15.00
141 Joey Jay RC 12.50 25.00
142 Tom Poholsky 7.50 15.00
143 Rollie Hemsley CO 7.50 15.00
144 Bill Werle 7.50 15.00
145 Elmer Valo 7.50 15.00
146 Don Johnson 7.50 15.00
147 Johnny Riddle CO 7.50 15.00
148 Bob Trice RC 7.50 15.00
149 Al Robertson 7.50 15.00
150 Dick Kryhoski 7.50 15.00
151 Alex Grammas RC 7.50 15.00
152 Michael Blyzka RC 7.50 15.00
153 Al Walker 12.50 25.00
154 Mike Fornieles RC 7.50 15.00
155 Bob Kennedy 12.50 25.00
156 Joe Coleman 12.50 25.00
157 Don Lenhardt 12.50 25.00
158 Peanuts Lowrey 7.50 15.00
159 Dave Philley 7.50 15.00
160 Ralph Kress CO 7.50 15.00
161 John Hetki 7.50 15.00
162 Herman Wehmeier 7.50 15.00
163 Frank House 7.50 15.00
164 Stu Miller 12.50 25.00
165 Jim Pendleton 7.50 15.00
166 Johnny Podres 20.00 50.00
167 Don Lund 7.50 15.00
168 Morrie Martin 12.50 25.00
169 Jim Hughes 20.00 40.00
170 Dusty Rhodes RC 12.50 25.00
171 Leo Kiely 10.00 25.00

172 Harold Brown RC 7.50 15.00
173 Jack Harshman RC 7.50 15.00
174 Tom Qualters RC 7.50 15.00
175 Frank Leja RC 12.50 25.00
176 Robert Keely CO 12.00 30.00
177 Bob Milliken 7.50 15.00
178 Bill Glynn UER 7.50 15.00
179 Gair Allie RC 7.50 15.00
180 Wes Westrum 12.50 25.00
181 Mel Roach RC 7.50 15.00
182 Chuck Harmon RC 7.50 15.00
183 Earle Combs CO 12.50 25.00
184 Ed Bailey 7.50 15.00
185 Chuck Stobbs 7.50 15.00
186 Karl Olson 7.50 15.00
187 Heinie Manush CO 12.50 25.00
188 Dave Jolly RC 7.50 15.00
189 Bob Ross 7.50 15.00
190 Ray Herbert RC 7.50 15.00
191 Dick Schofield RC 12.50 25.00
192 Ellis Deal CO 7.50 15.00
193 Johnny Hopp CO 12.50 25.00
194 Bill Sarni RC 7.50 15.00
195 Billy Consolo RC 7.50 15.00
196 Stan Jok RC 7.50 15.00
197 Lynwood Rowe CO 12.50 25.00
198 Carl Sawatski 7.50 15.00
199 Glenn Rocky Nelson 7.50 15.00
200 Larry Jansen 12.50 25.00
201 Al Kaline RC 750.00 1500.00
202 Bob Purkey RC 12.50 25.00
203 Harry Brecheen CO 12.50 25.00
204 Angel Scull RC 7.50 15.00
205 Johnny Sain 20.00 50.00
206 Ray Crone RC 7.50 15.00
207 Tom Oliver CO RC 7.50 15.00
208 Grady Hatton 7.50 15.00
209 Chuck Thompson RC 7.50 15.00
210 Bob Buhl RC 12.50 25.00
211 Don Hoak 12.50 25.00
212 Bob Micelotta RC 7.50 15.00
213 Johnny Fitzpatrick CO RC 7.50 15.00
214 Arnie Portocarrero RC 7.50 15.00
215 Ed McGhee 12.50 25.00
216 Al Sima 7.50 15.00
217 Paul Schreiber CO RC 7.50 15.00
218 Fred Marsh 7.50 15.00
219 Chuck Kress RC 7.50 15.00
220 Ruben Gomez RC 12.50 25.00
221 Dick Brodowski 7.50 15.00
222 Bill Wilson RC 7.50 15.00
223 Joe Haynes CO 12.00 30.00
224 Dick Weik RC 7.50 15.00
225 Don Liddle RC 7.50 15.00
226 Jehosie Heard RC 12.50 25.00
227 Buster Mills CO RC 7.50 15.00
228 Gene Hermanski 7.50 15.00
229 Bob Talbot RC 7.50 15.00
230 Bob Kuzava 12.50 25.00
231 Roy Smalley 7.50 15.00
232 Lou Limmer RC 7.50 15.00
233 Augie Galan CO 10.00 25.00
234 Jerry Lynch RC 7.50 15.00
235 Vern Law 12.50 25.00
236 Paul Penson RC 7.50 15.00
237 Mike Ryba CO RC 7.50 15.00
238 Al Aber 7.50 15.00
239 Bill Skowron RC 30.00 80.00
240 Sam Mele 12.50 25.00
241 Robert Miller RC 7.50 15.00
242 Curt Roberts RC 7.50 15.00
243 Ray Blades CO RC 7.50 15.00
244 Leroy Wheat RC 7.50 15.00
245 Roy Sievers 12.50 25.00
246 Howie Fox 7.50 15.00
247 Ed Mayo CO 7.50 15.00
248 Al Smith RC 12.50 25.00
249 Wilmer Mizell 12.50 25.00
250 Ted Williams 300.00 600.00

1955 Topps

The cards in this 206-card set measure approximately 2 5/8" by 3 3/4". Both the large "head" shot and the smaller full-length photos used on each card of the 1955 Topps set are in color. The card fronts were designed horizontally for the first time in Topps' history. The first card features Dusty Rhodes, hitting star and MVP in the New York Giants' 1954 World Series sweep over the Cleveland Indians. A "high" series, 161 to 210, is more difficult to find than cards 1 to 160. Numbers 175, 186, 203, and 209 were never issued. To fill in for the four cards not issued in the high number series, Topps double printed four players, those appearing on cards 170, 172, 184, and 188. Cards were issued in one-card penny packs or six-card nickel packs (which came 36 packs to a box) and 15-card cello packs (rarely seen). Although rarely seen, there exist salesman sample panels of three cards containing the fronts of regular cards with ad information for the 1955 Topps regular and the 1955 Topps Doubleheaders on the back. One panel depicts (from top to bottom) Danny Schell, Jake Thies, and Howie Pollet. Another Panel consists of Jackie Robinson, Bill Taylor and Curt Roberts. The key Rookie Cards in this set are Ken Boyer, Roberto Clemente, Harmon Killebrew, and Sandy Koufax. The Frank Sullivan card has a very noticable print dot which appears on some of the cards but not all of the cards. We are not listing that card as a variation at this point, but we will continue to monitor information about that card.

COMPLETE SET (206) 5000.00 10000.00
COMMON CARD (1-150) 6.00 12.00
COMMON CARD (151-160) 10.00 20.00
COMMON CARD (161-210) 15.00 30.00
NOT ISSUED (175/186/203/209)
WRAP.(1-CENT, DATED) 100.00 150.00
WRAP.(1-CENT, UNDAT) 40.00 50.00
WRAP.(5-CENT, DATED) 100.00 150.00
WRAP.(5-CENT, UNDAT) 75.00 100.00
1 Dusty Rhodes 25.00 60.00
2 Ted Williams 400.00 800.00
3 Art Fowler RC 7.50 15.00
4 Al Kaline 75.00 200.00
5 Jim Gilliam 30.00 80.00
6 Stan Hack MG RC 12.50 25.00
7 Jim Hegan 20.00 50.00
8 Harold Smith RC 6.00 12.00
9 Robert Miller 6.00 12.00
10 Bob Keegan 6.00 12.00
11 Ferris Fain 7.50 15.00
12 Vernon Jake Thies RC 6.00 12.00
13 Fred Marsh 6.00 12.00
14 Jim Finigan RC 6.00 12.00
15 Jim Pendleton 6.00 12.00
16 Roy Sievers 7.50 15.00
17 Bobby Hofman 6.00 12.00
18 Russ Kemmerer RC 6.00 12.00
19 Billy Herman CO 7.50 15.00
20 Andy Carey 7.50 15.00
21 Alex Grammas 6.00 12.00
22 Bill Skowron 15.00 40.00
23 Jack Parks RC 6.00 12.00
24 Hal Newhouser 30.00 80.00
25 Johnny Podres 20.00 50.00
26 Dick Groat 20.00 50.00
27 Billy Gardner RC 7.50 15.00
28 Ernie Banks 125.00 300.00
29 Herman Wehmeier 6.00 12.00
30 Vic Power 7.50 15.00
31 Warren Spahn 60.00 150.00
32 Warren McGhee 6.00 12.00
33 Tom Qualters 6.00 12.00
34 Wayne Terwilliger 10.00 25.00
35 Dave Jolly 6.00 12.00
36 Leo Kiely 6.00 12.00
37 Joe Cunningham RC 7.50 15.00
38 Bob Turley 12.00 30.00
39 Bill Glynn 6.00 12.00
40 Don Hoak 7.50 15.00
41 Chuck Stobbs 10.00 25.00
42 John Windy McCall RC 6.00 12.00
43 Harvey Haddix 7.50 15.00
44 Harold Valentine RC 6.00 12.00
45 Hank Sauer 7.50 15.00
46 Ted Kazanski 6.00 12.00
47 Hank Aaron 500.00 1000.00
48 Bob Kennedy 7.50 15.00
49 J.W. Porter 6.00 12.00
50 Jackie Robinson 300.00 600.00
51 Jim Hughes 7.50 15.00
52 Bill Tremel RC 6.00 12.00
53 Bill Taylor 6.00 12.00
54 Lou Limmer 6.00 12.00
55 Rip Repulski 6.00 12.00
56 Ray Jablonski 6.00 12.00
57 Billy O'Dell RC 6.00 12.00
58 Jim Rivera 10.00 25.00
59 Gair Allie 8.00 20.00
60 Dean Stone 8.00 20.00
61 Forrest Jacobs 6.00 12.00
62 Thornton Kipper 6.00 12.00
63 Joe Collins 12.00 30.00
64 Gus Triandos RC 12.00 30.00
65 Ray Boone 7.50 15.00
66 Ron Jackson RC 6.00 12.00
67 Wally Moon 7.50 15.00
68 Jim Davis RC 6.00 12.00
69 Ed Bailey 7.50 15.00
70 Al Rosen 12.00 30.00
71 Ruben Gomez 6.00 12.00
72 Karl Olson 6.00 15.00
73 Jack Shepard RC 6.00 12.00
74 Bob Borkowski 10.00 25.00
75 Sandy Amoros RC 12.00 30.00
76 Howie Pollet 6.00 12.00
77 Arnie Portocarrero 6.00 12.00
78 Gordon Jones RC 6.00 12.00
79 Clyde Danny Schell RC 6.00 12.00
80 Bob Grim RC 7.50 15.00
81 Gene Conley 7.50 15.00
82 Chuck Harmon 6.00 12.00
83 Tom Brewer RC 6.00 12.00
84 Camilo Pascual RC 7.50 15.00
85 Don Mossi RC 12.50 25.00
86 Bill Wilson 6.00 12.00
87 Frank House 6.00 12.00
88 Bob Skinner RC 7.50 15.00
89 Joe Frazier RC 7.50 15.00
90 Karl Spooner RC 7.50 15.00
91 Milt Bolling 6.00 12.00
92 Don Zimmer RC 40.00 100.00
93 Steve Bilko 6.00 12.00
94 Reno Bertoia 6.00 12.00
95 Preston Ward 6.00 12.00

96 Chuck Bishop 6.00 12.00
97 Carlos Paula RC 6.00 12.00
98 John Riddle CO 6.00 12.00
99 Frank Leja 6.00 12.00
100 Monte Irvin 40.00 100.00
101 Johnny Gray RC 6.00 12.00
102 Wally Westlake 10.00 25.00
103 Chuck White RC 6.00 12.00
104 Jack Harshman 8.00 20.00
105 Chuck Diering 6.00 12.00
106 Frank Sullivan RC 15.00 40.00
107 Curt Roberts 6.00 12.00
108 Rube Walker 7.50 15.00
109 Ed Lopat 12.00 30.00
110 Gus Zernial 8.00 20.00
111 Bob Milliken 7.50 15.00
112 Nelson King RC 6.00 12.00
113 Harry Brecheen CO 7.50 15.00
114 Louis Ortiz RC 6.00 12.00
115 Ellis Kinder 10.00 25.00
116 Tom Hurd RC 6.00 12.00
117 Mel Roach 10.00 25.00
118 Bob Purkey 12.00 30.00
119 Bob Lennon RC 6.00 12.00
120 Ted Kluszewski 20.00 50.00
121 Bill Renna 10.00 25.00
122 Carl Sawatski 6.00 12.00
123 Sandy Koufax RC 125.00 2500.00
124 Harmon Killebrew RC 250.00 500.00
125 Ken Boyer RC 40.00 100.00
126 Dick Hall RC 6.00 12.00
127 Dale Long RC 7.50 15.00
128 Ted Lepcio 6.00 12.00
129 Elvin Tappe 7.50 15.00
130 Mayo Smith MG RC 10.00 25.00
131 Grady Hatton 6.00 12.00
132 Bob Trice 6.00 12.00
133 Dave Hoskins 6.00 12.00
134 Joey Jay 7.50 15.00
135 Johnny O'Brien 7.50 15.00
136 Veston (Bunky) Stewart RC 6.00 12.00
137 Harry Elliott RC 6.00 12.00
138 Ray Herbert 6.00 12.00
139 Steve Kraly RC 6.00 12.00
140 Mel Parnell 7.50 15.00
141 Tom Wright 6.00 12.00
142 Jerry Lynch 10.00 25.00
143 John Schofield 7.50 15.00
144 Joe Amalfitano RC 6.00 12.00
145 Elmer Valo 6.00 12.00
146 Dick Donovan RC 6.00 12.00
147 Hugh Pepper RC 6.00 12.00
148 Hal Brown 6.00 12.00
149 Ray Crone 6.00 12.00
150 Mike Higgins MG 6.00 12.00
151 Ralph Kress CO 10.00 20.00
152 Harry Agganis RC 60.00 100.00
153 Bud Podbielan 12.50 25.00
154 Willie Miranda 15.00 40.00
155 Eddie Mathews 60.00 150.00
156 Joe Black 40.00 100.00
157 Robert Miller 12.00 30.00
158 Tommy Carroll RC 12.50 25.00
159 Johnny Schmitz 10.00 20.00
160 Ray Narleski RC 10.00 20.00
161 Chuck Tanner RC 20.00 40.00
162 Joe Coleman 15.00 30.00
163 Faye Throneberry 15.00 30.00
164 Roberto Clemente RC 2500.00 5000.00
165 Don Johnson 15.00 30.00
166 Hank Bauer 50.00 80.00
167 Tom Casagrande RC 15.00 30.00
168 Duane Pillette 15.00 30.00
169 Bob Oldis 20.00 40.00
170 Jim Pearce DP RC 7.50 15.00
171 Dick Brodowski 15.00 30.00
172 Frank Baumholtz DP 7.50 15.00
173 Bob Kline RC 15.00 30.00
174 Rudy Minarcin RC 15.00 30.00
176 Norm Zauchin RC 15.00 30.00
177 Al Robertson 15.00 40.00
178 Bobby Adams 15.00 30.00
179 Jim Bolger RC 25.00 60.00
180 Clem Labine 30.00 80.00
181 Roy McMillan 20.00 40.00
182 Humberto Robinson RC 15.00 30.00
183 Anthony Jacobs RC 15.00 30.00
184 Harry Perkowski DP 7.50 15.00
185 Don Ferrarese RC 15.00 30.00
187 Gil Hodges 60.00 150.00
188 Charlie Silvera DP 7.50 15.00
189 Phil Rizzuto 60.00 150.00
190 Gene Woodling 25.00 60.00
191 Eddie Stanky MG 20.00 40.00
192 Jim Delsing 20.00 40.00
193 Johnny Sain 30.00 60.00
194 Willie Mays 500.00 1000.00
195 Ed Roebuck RC 40.00 100.00
196 Gale Wade RC 15.00 30.00
197 Al Smith 30.00 60.00
198 Yogi Berra 250.00 500.00
199 Bert Hamric RC 20.00 40.00
200 Jackie Jensen 30.00 60.00
201 Sherman Lollar 20.00 40.00
202 Jim Owens RC 30.00 80.00
204 Frank Smith 15.00 30.00
205 Gene Freese RC 40.00 100.00
206 Pete Daley RC 15.00 30.00
207 Billy Consolo 30.00 80.00
208 Ray Moore RC 20.00 40.00
210 Duke Snider 250.00 500.00

1955 Topps Double Header

The cards in this 66-card set measure approximately 2 1/16" by 4 7/8". Borrowing a design from the T201 Mecca series, Topps issued a 132-player "Double Header" set in a separate wrapper in 1955. Each player is numbered in the biographical section on the reverse. When open, with perforated flap up, one player is revealed; when the flap is lowered, or closed, the player design on top incorporates a portion of the inside player artwork. When the cards are placed side by side, a continuous ballpark background is formed. Some cards have been found without perforations, and all players pictured appear in the low series of the 1955 regular issue. The cards were issued in one-card penny packs which came 120 packs to a box with a piece of bubble gum.

COMPLETE SET (66)	2500.00	4000.00
WRAPPER (5-CENT)	150.00	200.00
1 A. Rosen	30.00	50.00
C. Diering		
3 M.Irvin	35.00	60.00
R.Kemmerer		
5 Ted Kazanski and	25.00	40.00
6 Gordon Jones		
7 Bill Taylor and	25.00	40.00
8 Billy O'Dell		
9 J.W. Porter and	25.00	40.00
10 Thornton Kipper		
11 Curt Roberts and	25.00	40.00
12 Arnie Portocarrero		
13 Wally Westlake and	30.00	50.00
14 Frank House		
15 Rube Walker and	30.00	50.00
16 Lou Limmer		
17 Dean Stone and	25.00	40.00
18 Charlie White		
19 Karl Spooner and	30.00	50.00
20 Jim Hughes		
21 B.Skowron	35.00	60.00
F.Sullivan		
23 Jack Shepard and	25.00	40.00
24 Stan Hack MG		
25 J.Robinson	150.00	250.00
D.Hoak		
27 Dusty Rhodes and	30.00	50.00
28 Jim Davis		
29 Vic Power and	25.00	40.00
30 Ed Bailey		
31 H.Pollet	125.00	200.00
E.Banks		
33 Jim Pendleton and	25.00	40.00
34 Gene Conley		
35 Karl Olson and	25.00	40.00
36 Andy Carey		
37 W. Moon	30.00	50.00
J. Cunningham		
39 Freddie Marsh and/40 Vernon Thies	25.00	40.00
41 E.Lopat	35.00	60.00
H.Haddix		
43 Leo Kiely and	25.00	40.00
44 Chuck Stobbs		
45 A.Kaline	125.00	200.00
H.Valentine		
47 Forrest Jacobs and	25.00	40.00
48 Johnny Gray		
49 Ron Jackson and	25.00	40.00
50 Jim Finigan		
51 Ray Jablonski and	25.00	40.00
52 Bob Keegan		
53 B.Herman	50.00	80.00
S.Amoros		
55 Chuck Harmon and	25.00	40.00
56 Bob Skinner		
57 Dick Hall and	25.00	40.00
58 Bob Grim		
59 Billy Glynn and	30.00	50.00
60 Bob Miller		
61 Billy Gardner and	25.00	40.00
62 John Hetki		
63 B. Borkowski	25.00	40.00
B. Turley		
65 Joe Collins and	25.00	40.00
66 Jack Harshman		
67 Jim Hegan and	25.00	40.00
68 Jack Parks		
69 T.Williams	250.00	500.00
M.Smith		
71 Gair Allie and	25.00	40.00
72 Grady Hatton		
73 Jerry Lynch and	25.00	40.00
74 Harry Brecheen CO		
75 Tom Wright and	25.00	40.00
76 Vernon Stewart		
77 Dave Hoskins and	25.00	40.00
78 Warren McGhee		
79 Roy Sievers and	30.00	50.00
80 Art Fowler		
81 Danny Schell and	25.00	40.00
82 Gus Triandos		
83 Joe Frazier and	25.00	40.00
84 Don Mossi		
85 Elmer Valo and	25.00	40.00
86 Hector Brown		
87 Bob Kennedy and	30.00	50.00
88 Windy McCall		
89 Ruben Gomez and	25.00	40.00
90 Jim Rivera		
91 Louis Ortiz and	25.00	40.00
92 Milt Bolling		
93 Carl Sawatski and	25.00	40.00
94 El Tappe		
95 Dave Jolly and	25.00	40.00
96 Bobby Hofman		
97 P.Ward	35.00	60.00
D.Zimmer		
99 B. Renna	30.00	50.00
D. Groat		
101 Bill Wilson and	25.00	40.00
102 Bill Tremel		
103 H. Sauer	30.00	50.00
C. Pascual		
105 H.Aaron	300.00	500.00
R.Herbert		
107 Alex Grammas and	25.00	40.00
108 Tom Qualters		
109 H.Newhouser	35.00	60.00
C.Bishop		
111 H.Killebrew	125.00	200.00
J.Podres		
113 Ray Boone and	25.00	40.00
114 Bob Purkey		
115 Dale Long and	30.00	50.00
116 Ferris Fain		
117 Steve Bilko and	25.00	40.00
118 Bob Milliken		
119 Mel Parnell and	30.00	50.00
120 Tom Hurd		
121 T.Kluszewski	50.00	80.00
J.Owens		
123 Gus Zernial and	25.00	40.00
124 Bob Trice		
125 Rip Repulski and	25.00	40.00
126 Ted Lepcio		
127 W.Spahn	90.00	150.00
T.Brewer		
129 J.Gilliam	50.00	80.00
E.Kinder		
131 Herm Wehmeier and	25.00	40.00
132 Wayne Terwilliger		

1956 Topps

The cards in this 340-card set measure approximately 2 5/8" by 3 3/4". Following up with another horizontally oriented card in 1956, Topps improved the format by layering the color "head" shot onto an actual action sequence involving the player. Cards 1 to 180 come with either white or gray backs: in the 1 to 100 sequence gray backs are less common and in the 101 to 180 sequence white backs are less common. The team cards, used for the first time in a regular set by Topps, are found dated 1955, or undated, with the team name appearing on either side. The dated team cards in the first series were not printed on the gray stock. The two unnumbered checklist cards are highly prized (must be unmarked to qualify as excellent or mint). The complete set price below does not include the unnumbered checklist cards or any of the variations. The set was issued in one-card penny packs or six-card nickel packs. The six card nickel packs came 24 to a box with 24 boxes in a case while the once cent packs came 120 to a box. Both types of packs included a piece of bubble gum. Promotional three card strips were issued for this set. Among those strips were one featuring Johnny O'Brien/Harvey Haddix and Frank House. The key Rookie Cards in this set are Walt Alston, Luis Aparicio, and Roger Craig. There are ten double-printed cards in the first series as evidenced by the discovery of an uncut sheet of 110 cards (10 by 11); these DP's are listed below.

COMPLETE SET (340)	8000.00	15000.00
COMMON CARD (1-100)	5.00	10.00
COMMON CARD (101-180)	6.00	12.00
COMMON CARD (261-340)	6.00	12.00
COMMON CARD (181-260)	7.50	15.00
WRAP.(1-CENT)	200.00	250.00
WRAP.(1-CENT, REPEAT)	75.00	100.00
WRAPPER (5-CENT)	150.00	200.00
*1-100 GRAY BACK: .5X TO 1.2X		
*101-180 WHITE BACK: .5X TO 1.2X		
1 Will Harridge PRES	75.00	125.00
2 Warren Giles PRES DP	15.00	40.00
3 Elmer Valo	7.50	15.00
4 Carlos Paula	7.50	15.00
5 Ted Williams	300.00	500.00
6 Ray Boone	15.00	25.00
7 Ron Negray RC	5.00	10.00
8 Walter Alston MG RC	25.00	40.00
9 Ruben Gomez DP	5.00	10.00
10 Warren Spahn	40.00	100.00
11A Chicago Cubs TC Center	15.00	30.00
11B Chicago Cubs TC D'55	50.00	80.00
11C Chicago Cubs TC Left	15.00	30.00
12 Andy Carey	7.50	15.00
13 Roy Face	7.50	15.00
14 Ken Boyer DP	12.00	30.00
15 Ernie Banks DP	75.00	200.00
16 Hector Lopez RC	8.00	20.00
17 Gene Conley	7.50	15.00
18 Dick Donovan	5.00	10.00
19 Chuck Diering DP	5.00	10.00
20 Al Kaline	50.00	120.00
21 Joe Collins DP	7.50	15.00
22 Jim Finigan	5.00	10.00
23 Fred Marsh	5.00	10.00
24 Dick Groat	10.00	25.00
25 Ted Kluszewski	20.00	50.00
26 Grady Hatton	5.00	10.00
27 Nelson Burbrink DP RC	5.00	10.00
28 Bobby Hofman	5.00	10.00
29 Jack Harshman	5.00	10.00
30 Jackie Robinson DP	300.00	600.00
31 Hank Aaron UER DP	150.00	400.00
32 Frank House	5.00	10.00
33 Roberto Clemente	250.00	600.00
34 Tom Brewer DP	5.00	10.00
35 Al Rosen	12.00	30.00
36 Rudy Minarcin	7.50	15.00
37 Alex Grammas	10.00	25.00
38 Bob Kennedy	7.50	15.00
39 Don Mossi	7.50	15.00
40 Bob Turley	7.50	15.00
41 Hank Sauer	7.50	15.00
42 Sandy Amoros	20.00	50.00
43 Ray Moore	5.00	10.00
44 Windy McCall	5.00	10.00
45 Gus Zernial	7.50	15.00
46 Gene Freese DP	5.00	10.00
47 Art Fowler	5.00	10.00
48 Jim Hegan	12.00	30.00
49 Pedro Ramos RC	8.00	20.00
50 Dusty Rhodes DP	7.50	15.00
51 Ernie Oravetz RC	5.00	10.00
52 Bob Grim DP	7.50	15.00
53 Arnie Portocarrero	5.00	10.00
54 Bob Keegan	5.00	10.00
55 Wally Moon	7.50	15.00
56 Dale Long	7.50	15.00
57 Duke Maas RC	5.00	10.00
58 Ed Roebuck	15.00	25.00
59 Jose Santiago RC	5.00	10.00
60 Mayo Smith MG DP	5.00	10.00
61 Bill Skowron	20.00	50.00
62 Hal Smith	7.50	15.00
63 Roger Craig RC	25.00	40.00
64 Luis Arroyo RC	5.00	10.00
65 Johnny O'Brien	7.50	15.00
66 Bob Speake DP RC	5.00	10.00
67 Vic Power	7.50	15.00
68 Chuck Stobbs	5.00	10.00
69 Chuck Tanner	7.50	15.00
70 Jim Rivera	5.00	10.00
71 Frank Sullivan	5.00	10.00
72A Philadelphia Phillies TC Center	15.00	30.00
72B Philadelphia Phillies TC D'55	50.00	80.00
72C Philadelphia Phillies TC Left DP	15.00	30.00
73 Wayne Terwilliger	5.00	10.00
74 Jim King RC	5.00	10.00
75 Roy Sievers DP	7.50	15.00
76 Ray Crone	5.00	10.00
77 Harvey Haddix	10.00	25.00
78 Herman Wehmeier	5.00	10.00
79 Sandy Koufax	200.00	400.00
80 Gus Triandos DP	5.00	10.00
81 Wally Westlake	5.00	10.00
82 Bill Renna DP	5.00	10.00
83 Karl Spooner	7.50	15.00
84 Babe Birrer RC	5.00	10.00
85A Cleveland Indians TC Center	15.00	30.00
85B Cleveland Indians TC D'55	50.00	80.00
85C Cleveland Indians TC Left	15.00	30.00
86 Ray Jablonski DP	5.00	10.00
87 Dean Stone	5.00	10.00
88 Johnny Kucks RC	7.50	15.00
89 Norm Zauchin	5.00	10.00
90A Cincinnati Redlegs TC Center	15.00	30.00
90B Cincinnati Reds TC D'55	50.00	80.00
90C Cincinnati Reds TC Left	15.00	30.00
91 Gail Harris RC	5.00	10.00
92 Bob Red Wilson	5.00	10.00
93 George Susce	5.00	10.00
94 Ron Kline UER	5.00	10.00
Facimile auto is J.Robert Klein		
95A Milwaukee Braves TC Center	20.00	40.00
95B Milwaukee Braves TC D'55	50.00	80.00
95C Milwaukee Braves TC Left	20.00	40.00
96 Bill Tremel	5.00	10.00
97 Jerry Lynch	7.50	15.00
98 Camilo Pascual	7.50	15.00
99 Don Zimmer	15.00	40.00
100A Baltimore Orioles TC Center	20.00	40.00
100B Baltimore Orioles TC D'55	50.00	80.00
100C Baltimore Orioles TC Left	20.00	40.00
101 Roy Campanella	90.00	150.00
102 Jim Davis	6.00	12.00
103 Willie Miranda	6.00	12.00
104 Bob Lennon	6.00	12.00
105 Al Smith	6.00	12.00
106 Joe Astroth	6.00	12.00
107 Eddie Mathews	40.00	100.00
108 Laurin Pepper	6.00	12.00
109 Enos Slaughter	20.00	50.00
110 Yogi Berra	75.00	200.00
111 Boston Red Sox TC	20.00	40.00
112 Dee Fondy	6.00	12.00
113 Phil Rizzuto	50.00	120.00
114 Jim Owens	7.50	15.00
115 Jackie Jensen	7.50	15.00
116 Eddie O'Brien	6.00	12.00
117 Virgil Trucks	7.50	15.00
118 Nellie Fox	20.00	50.00
119 Larry Jackson RC	8.00	20.00
120 Richie Ashburn	35.00	60.00
121 Pittsburgh Pirates TC	20.00	40.00
122 Willard Nixon	6.00	12.00
123 Roy McMillan	7.50	15.00
124 Don Kaiser	6.00	12.00
125 Minnie Minoso	20.00	50.00
126 Jim Brady RC	6.00	12.00
127 Willie Jones	7.50	15.00
128 Eddie Yost	7.50	15.00
129 Jake Martin RC	6.00	12.00
130 Willie Mays	200.00	500.00
131 Bob Roselli RC	6.00	12.00
132 Bobby Avila	6.00	12.00
133 Ray Narleski	6.00	12.00
134 St. Louis Cardinals TC	20.00	40.00
135 Mickey Mantle	1250.00	2500.00
136 Johnny Logan	7.50	15.00
137 Al Silvera RC	6.00	12.00
138 Johnny Antonelli	7.50	15.00
139 Tommy Carroll	7.50	15.00
140 Herb Score RC	20.00	50.00
141 Joe Frazier	6.00	12.00
142 Gene Baker	6.00	12.00
143 Jim Piersall	7.50	15.00
144 Leroy Powell RC	6.00	12.00
145 Gil Hodges	30.00	80.00
146 Washington Nationals TC	20.00	40.00
147 Earl Torgeson	6.00	12.00
148 Alvin Dark	12.00	30.00
149 Dixie Howell	6.00	12.00
150 Duke Snider	50.00	120.00
151 Spook Jacobs	7.50	15.00
152 Billy Hoeft	7.50	15.00
153 Frank Thomas	10.00	25.00
154 Dave Pope	6.00	12.00
155 Harvey Kuenn	7.50	15.00
156 Wes Westrum	7.50	15.00
157 Dick Brodowski	6.00	12.00
158 Wally Post	7.50	15.00
159 Clint Courtney	6.00	12.00
160 Billy Pierce	7.50	15.00
161 Joe DeMaestri	6.00	12.00
162 Dave Gus Bell	7.50	15.00
163 Gene Woodling	7.50	15.00
164 Harmon Killebrew	60.00	150.00
165 Red Schoendienst	25.00	60.00
166 Brooklyn Dodgers TC	50.00	120.00
167 Harry Dorish	6.00	12.00
168 Sammy White	6.00	12.00
169 Bob Nelson RC	6.00	12.00
170 Bill Virdon	7.50	15.00
171 Jim Wilson	6.00	12.00
172 Frank Torre RC	7.50	15.00
173 Johnny Podres	20.00	50.00
174 Glen Gorbous RC	6.00	12.00
175 Del Crandall	7.50	15.00
176 Alex Kellner	6.00	12.00
177 Hank Bauer	15.00	40.00
178 Joe Black	7.50	15.00
179 Harry Chiti	6.00	12.00
180 Robin Roberts	30.00	50.00
181 Billy Martin	40.00	100.00
182 Paul Minner	8.00	20.00
183 Stan Lopata	10.00	20.00
184 Don Bessent RC	12.00	30.00
185 Bill Bruton	10.00	20.00
186 Ron Jackson	7.50	15.00
187 Early Wynn	25.00	60.00
188 Chicago White Sox TC	30.00	50.00
189 Ned Garver	7.50	15.00
190 Carl Furillo	15.00	40.00
191 Frank Lary	10.00	20.00
192 Smoky Burgess	10.00	20.00
193 Wilmer Mizell	10.00	20.00
194 Monte Irvin	40.00	100.00
195 George Kell	25.00	60.00
196 Tom Poholsky	7.50	15.00
197 Granny Hamner	7.50	15.00
198 Ed Fitzgerald	7.50	15.00
199 Hank Thompson	10.00	20.00
200 Bob Feller	60.00	150.00
201 Rip Repulski	7.50	15.00
202 Jim Hearn	7.50	15.00
203 Bill Tuttle	7.50	15.00
204 Art Swanson RC	7.50	15.00
205 Whitey Lockman	10.00	20.00
206 Erv Palica	7.50	15.00
207 Jim Small RC	7.50	15.00
208 Elston Howard	25.00	60.00
209 Max Surkont	7.50	15.00
210 Mike Garcia	10.00	20.00
211 Murry Dickson	7.50	15.00
212 Johnny Temple	7.50	15.00
213 Detroit Tigers	35.00	60.00
214 Bob Rush	7.50	15.00
215 Tommy Byrne	10.00	25.00
216 Jerry Schoonmaker RC	7.50	15.00
217 Billy Klaus	7.50	15.00
218 Joe Nuxhall UER	10.00	20.00
219 Lew Burdette	12.00	30.00
220 Del Ennis	10.00	20.00
221 Bob Friend	10.00	25.00
222 Dave Philley	7.50	15.00
223 Randy Jackson	7.50	15.00
224 Bud Podbielan	7.50	15.00
225 Gil McDougald	15.00	40.00
226 New York Giants	25.00	60.00
227 Russ Meyer	7.50	15.00
228 Mickey Vernon	10.00	20.00
229 Harry Brecheen CO	10.00	20.00
230 Chico Carrasquel	10.00	25.00
231 Bob Hale RC	7.50	15.00
232 Toby Atwell	7.50	15.00
233 Carl Erskine	20.00	50.00
234 Pete Runnels	12.00	30.00
235 Don Newcombe	30.00	80.00
236 Kansas City Athletics	20.00	40.00
237 Jose Valdivielso RC	7.50	15.00
238 Walt Dropo	10.00	20.00
239 Harry Simpson	7.50	15.00
240 Whitey Ford	60.00	150.00
241 Don Mueller UER	10.00	20.00
242 Hershell Freeman	7.50	15.00
243 Sherm Lollar	10.00	20.00
244 Bob Buhl	15.00	40.00
245 Billy Goodman	10.00	20.00
246 Tom Gorman	7.50	15.00
247 Bill Sarni	7.50	15.00
248 Bob Porterfield	7.50	15.00
249 Johnny Klippstein	7.50	15.00
250 Larry Doby	40.00	100.00
251 New York Yankees TC UER	75.00	200.00
252 Vern Law	10.00	20.00
253 Irv Noren	18.00	30.00
254 George Crowe	7.50	15.00
255 Bob Lemon	25.00	60.00
256 Tom Hurd	7.50	15.00
257 Bobby Thomson	18.00	30.00
258 Art Ditmar	7.50	15.00
259 Sam Jones	10.00	20.00
260 Pee Wee Reese	60.00	150.00
261 Bobby Shantz	7.50	15.00
262 Howie Pollet	6.00	12.00
263 Bob Miller	6.00	12.00
264 Ray Monzant RC	6.00	12.00
265 Sandy Consuegra	6.00	12.00
266 Don Ferrarese	6.00	12.00
267 Bob Nieman	6.00	12.00
268 Dale Mitchell	7.50	15.00
269 Jack Meyer RC	8.00	20.00
270 Billy Loes	12.00	30.00
271 Foster Castleman RC	6.00	12.00
272 Danny O'Connell	6.00	12.00
273 Walker Cooper	6.00	12.00
274 Frank Baumholtz	6.00	12.00
275 Jim Greengrass	6.00	12.00
276 George Zuverink	6.00	12.00
277 Daryl Spencer	6.00	12.00
278 Chet Nichols	6.00	12.00
279 Johnny Groth	6.00	12.00
280 Jim Gilliam	25.00	40.00
281 Art Houtteman	6.00	12.00
282 Warren Hacker	6.00	12.00
283 Hal Smith RC UER	10.00	25.00
Wrong Facsimile Autograph, belongs to Hal W. Smith		
284 Ike Delock	6.00	12.00
285 Eddie Miksis	6.00	12.00
286 Bill Wight	6.00	12.00
287 Bobby Adams	6.00	12.00
288 Bob Cerv	25.00	60.00
289 Hal Jeffcoat	6.00	12.00
290 Curt Simmons	10.00	25.00
291 Frank Kellert RC	6.00	12.00
292 Luis Aparicio RC	75.00	200.00
293 Stu Miller	15.00	25.00
294 Ernie Johnson	7.50	15.00
295 Clem Labine	12.00	30.00
296 Andy Seminick	6.00	12.00
297 Bob Skinner	7.50	15.00
298 Johnny Schmitz	6.00	12.00
299 Charlie Neal	25.00	40.00
300 Vic Wertz	7.50	15.00
301 Marv Grissom	6.00	12.00
302 Eddie Robinson	6.00	12.00
303 Jim Dyck	6.00	12.00
304 Frank Malzone	7.50	15.00
305 Brooks Lawrence	6.00	12.00
306 Curt Roberts	6.00	12.00
307 Hoyt Wilhelm	20.00	50.00
308 Chuck Harmon	6.00	12.00
309 Don Blasingame RC	10.00	25.00
310 Steve Gromek	6.00	12.00
311 Hal Naragon	6.00	12.00
312 Andy Pafko	7.50	15.00
313 Gene Stephens	6.00	12.00
314 Hobie Landrith	6.00	12.00
315 Milt Bolling	6.00	12.00
316 Jerry Coleman	10.00	25.00
317 Al Aber	6.00	12.00
318 Fred Hatfield	6.00	12.00
319 Jack Crimian RC	6.00	12.00
320 Joe Adcock	7.50	15.00
321 Jim Konstanty	7.50	15.00
322 Karl Olson	6.00	12.00
323 Willard Schmidt	6.00	12.00
324 Rocky Bridges	7.50	15.00
325 Don Liddle	6.00	12.00
326 Connie Johnson RC	6.00	12.00
327 Bob Wiesler RC	6.00	12.00
328 Preston Ward	6.00	12.00
329 Lou Berberet RC	6.00	12.00
330 Jim Busby	7.50	15.00
331 Dick Hall	6.00	12.00
332 Don Larsen	40.00	100.00
333 Rube Walker	10.00	25.00
334 Bob Miller	7.50	15.00
335 Don Hoak	8.00	20.00
336 Ellis Kinder	10.00	25.00
337 Bobby Morgan	6.00	12.00
338 Jim Delsing	6.00	12.00
339 Rance Pless RC	6.00	12.00
340 Mickey McDermott	35.00	60.00
CL1 Checklist 1/3	175.00	300.00
CL2 Checklist 2/4	175.00	300.00

1957 Topps

The cards in this 407-card set measure 2 1/2" by 3 1/2". In 1957, Topps returned to the vertical obverse, adopted what we now call the standard card size, and used a large, uncluttered color photo for the first time since 1952. Cards in the series 265 to 352 and the unnumbered checklist cards are scarcer than other cards in the set. However within this scarce series (265-352) there are 22 cards which were printed in double the quantity of the other cards in the series; these 22 double prints are indicated by DP in the checklist below. The first star combination cards, cards 400 and 407, are quite popular with collectors. They feature the big stars of the previous season's World Series teams, the Dodgers (Furillo, Hodges, Campanella, and Snider) and Yankees (Berra and Mantle). The complete set price below does not include the unnumbered checklist cards. Confirmed packaging includes one-cent penny packs and six-card nickel packs. Cello packs are definately known to exist and some collectors remember buying rack packs of 57's as well. The key Rookie Cards in this set are Jim Bunning, Rocky Colavito, Don Drysdale, Whitey Herzog, Tony Kubek, Bill Mazeroski, Bobby Richardson, Brooks Robinson, and Frank Robinson.

COMPLETE SET (407)	6000.00	12000.00
COMMON CARD (1-88)	5.00	10.00
COMMON CARD (89-176)	4.00	8.00
COMMON CARD (177-264)	4.00	8.00
COMMON CARD (265-352)	10.00	20.00
COMMON CARD (353-407)	4.00	8.00
COMMON DP (265-352)	6.00	12.00
WRAPPER (1-CENT)	250.00	300.00
WRAPPER (5-CENT)	150.00	200.00
1 Ted Williams	150.00	400.00
2 Yogi Berra	60.00	150.00
3 Dale Long	8.00	20.00
4 Johnny Logan	8.00	20.00
5 Sal Maglie	10.00	25.00
6 Hector Lopez	6.00	15.00
7 Luis Aparicio	15.00	40.00
8 Don Mossi	6.00	15.00
9 Johnny Temple	6.00	15.00
10 Willie Mays	150.00	400.00
11 George Zuverink	4.00	10.00
12 Dick Groat	8.00	20.00
13 Wally Burnette RC	4.00	10.00
14 Bob Nieman	10.00	25.00
15 Robin Roberts	20.00	50.00
16 Walt Moryn	4.00	10.00
17 Billy Gardner	4.00	10.00
18 Don Drysdale RC	125.00	300.00
19 Bob Wilson	4.00	10.00
20 Hank Aaron UER	150.00	400.00
21 Frank Sullivan	4.00	10.00
22 Jerry Snyder UER	4.00	10.00
23 Sherm Lollar	6.00	15.00
24 Bill Mazeroski RC	60.00	150.00
25 Whitey Ford	60.00	150.00
26 Bob Boyd	4.00	10.00
27 Ted Kazanski	4.00	10.00
28 Gene Conley	6.00	15.00
29 Whitey Herzog RC	12.00	30.00
30 Pee Wee Reese	40.00	100.00
31 Ron Northey	4.00	10.00
32 Hershell Freeman	4.00	10.00
33 Jim Small	4.00	10.00
34 Tom Sturdivant RC	6.00	15.00
35 Frank Robinson RC	300.00	600.00
36 Bob Grim	4.00	10.00
37 Frank Torre	6.00	15.00
38 Nellie Fox	25.00	60.00
39 Al Worthington RC	4.00	10.00
40 Early Wynn	10.00	25.00
41 Hal W. Smith	4.00	10.00
42 Dee Fondy	4.00	10.00
43 Connie Johnson	4.00	10.00
44 Joe DeMaestri	4.00	10.00
45 Carl Furillo	15.00	40.00
46 Robert J. Miller	4.00	10.00
47 Don Blasingame	4.00	10.00
48 Bill Bruton	6.00	15.00
49 Daryl Spencer	4.00	10.00
50 Herb Score	12.00	30.00
51 Clint Courtney	4.00	10.00
52 Lee Walls	4.00	10.00
53 Clem Labine	8.00	20.00
54 Elmer Valo	4.00	10.00
55 Ernie Banks	60.00	150.00
56 Dave Sisler RC	4.00	10.00
57 Jim Lemon	6.00	15.00
58 Ruben Gomez	4.00	10.00
59 Dick Williams	6.00	15.00
60 Billy Hoeft	6.00	15.00
61 Dusty Rhodes	6.00	15.00
62 Billy Martin	25.00	60.00
63 Ike Delock	4.00	10.00
64 Pete Runnels	6.00	15.00
65 Wally Moon	6.00	15.00
66 Brooks Lawrence	4.00	10.00
67 Chico Carrasquel	4.00	10.00
68 Ray Crone	4.00	10.00
69 Roy McMillan	6.00	15.00
70 Richie Ashburn	20.00	50.00
71 Murry Dickson	4.00	10.00
72 Bill Tuttle	4.00	10.00
73 George Crowe	4.00	10.00
74 Vito Valentinetti RC	4.00	10.00
75 Jimmy Piersall	6.00	15.00
76 Roberto Clemente	125.00	300.00
77 Paul Foytack RC	4.00	10.00
78 Vic Wertz	6.00	15.00
79 Lindy McDaniel RC	6.00	15.00
80 Gil Hodges	30.00	80.00
81 Herman Wehmeier	4.00	10.00
82 Elston Howard	12.00	30.00
83 Lou Skizas RC	4.00	10.00
84 Moe Drabowsky RC	6.00	15.00
85 Larry Doby	20.00	50.00
86 Bill Sarni	4.00	10.00
87 Tom Gorman	4.00	10.00
88 Harvey Kuenn	6.00	15.00
89 Roy Sievers	6.00	15.00
90 Warren Spahn	30.00	80.00
91 Mack Burk RC	3.00	8.00
92 Mickey Vernon	6.00	15.00
93 Hal Jeffcoat	3.00	8.00
94 Bobby Del Greco	3.00	8.00
95 Mickey Mantle	600.00	1200.00
96 Hank Aguirre RC	3.00	8.00
97 New York Yankees TC	30.00	80.00
98 Alvin Dark	6.00	15.00
99 Bob Keegan	3.00	8.00
100 W.Giles/W.Harridge	6.00	15.00
101 Chuck Stobbs	3.00	8.00
102 Ray Boone	6.00	15.00
103 Joe Nuxhall	6.00	15.00
104 Hank Foiles	3.00	8.00
105 Johnny Antonelli	6.00	15.00
106 Ray Moore	3.00	8.00
107 Jim Rivera	3.00	8.00
108 Tommy Byrne	6.00	15.00
109 Hank Thompson	3.00	8.00
110 Bill Virdon	6.00	15.00
111 Hal R. Smith	3.00	8.00
112 Tom Brewer	3.00	8.00
113 Wilmer Mizell	6.00	15.00
114 Milwaukee Braves TC	8.00	20.00
115 Jim Gilliam	20.00	50.00
116 Mike Fornieles	3.00	8.00
117 Joe Adcock	8.00	20.00
118 Bob Porterfield	3.00	8.00
119 Stan Lopata	3.00	8.00
120 Bob Lemon	12.00	30.00
121 Clete Boyer RC	12.00	30.00
122 Ken Boyer	10.00	25.00
123 Steve Ridzik	3.00	8.00
124 Dave Philley	3.00	8.00
125 Al Kaline	40.00	100.00
126 Bob Wiesler	3.00	8.00
127 Bob Buhl	6.00	15.00
128 Ed Bailey	6.00	15.00
129 Saul Rogovin	3.00	8.00
130 Don Newcombe	12.00	30.00
131 Milt Bolling	3.00	8.00
132 Art Ditmar	6.00	15.00
133 Del Crandall	6.00	15.00
134 Don Kaiser	3.00	8.00
135 Bill Skowron	15.00	40.00
136 Jim Hegan	6.00	15.00
137 Bob Rush	3.00	8.00
138 Minnie Minoso	10.00	25.00
139 Lou Kretlow	3.00	8.00
140 Frank Thomas	6.00	15.00
141 Al Aber	3.00	8.00
142 Charley Thompson	3.00	8.00
143 Andy Pafko	8.00	20.00
144 Ray Narleski	3.00	8.00
145 Al Smith	3.00	8.00
146 Don Ferrarese	3.00	8.00
147 Al Walker	3.00	8.00
148 Don Mueller	6.00	15.00
149 Bob Kennedy	6.00	15.00
150 Bob Friend	6.00	15.00
151 Willie Miranda	3.00	8.00
152 Jack Harshman	3.00	8.00
153 Karl Olson	3.00	8.00
154 Red Schoendienst	12.00	30.0
155 Jim Brosnan	6.00	15.0
156 Gus Triandos	6.00	15.0
157 Wally Post	6.00	15.0
158 Curt Simmons	6.00	15.0
159 Solly Drake RC	3.00	8.0
160 Billy Pierce	6.00	15.0
161 Pittsburgh Pirates TC	6.00	15.0
162 Jack Meyer	3.00	8.0
163 Sammy White	3.00	8.0
164 Tommy Carroll	3.00	8.0
165 Ted Kluszewski	60.00	150.0
166 Roy Face	6.00	15.0
167 Vic Power	6.00	15.0
168 Frank Lary	6.00	15.0
169 Herb Plews RC	3.00	8.0
170 Duke Snider	40.00	100.
171 Boston Red Sox TC	6.00	15.
172 Gene Woodling	6.00	15.
173 Roger Craig	6.00	15.
174 Willie Jones	3.00	8.
175 Don Larsen	15.00	40.
176A Gene Bakep ERR	150.00	400.
176B Gene Baker COR	6.00	15.
177 Eddie Yost	6.00	15.
178 Don Bessent	3.00	8.
179 Ernie Oravetz	3.00	8.

180 Gus Bell 6.00 15.00
181 Dick Donovan 3.00 8.00
182 Hobie Landrith 3.00 8.00
183 Chicago Cubs TC 6.00 15.00
184 Tito Francona RC 3.00 8.00
185 Johnny Kucks 6.00 15.00
186 Jim King 6.00 15.00
187 Virgil Trucks 6.00 15.00
188 Felix Mantilla RC 6.00 15.00
189 Willard Nixon 3.00 8.00
190 Randy Jackson 3.00 8.00
191 Joe Margoneri RC 3.00 8.00
192 Jerry Coleman 6.00 15.00
193 Del Rice 3.00 8.00
194 Hal Brown 3.00 8.00
195 Bobby Avila 3.00 8.00
196 Larry Jackson 6.00 15.00
197 Hank Sauer 6.00 15.00
198 Detroit Tigers TC 6.00 15.00
199 Vern Law 6.00 15.00
200 Gil McDougald 10.00 25.00
201 Sandy Amoros 6.00 15.00
202 Dick Gernert 3.00 8.00
203 Hoyt Wilhelm 15.00 40.00
204 Kansas City Athletics TC 6.00 15.00
205 Charlie Maxwell 6.00 15.00
206 Willard Schmidt 3.00 8.00
207 Gordon Billy Hunter 3.00 8.00
208 Lou Burdette 6.00 15.00
209 Bob Skinner 6.00 15.00
210 Roy Campanella 40.00 100.00
211 Camilo Pascual 6.00 15.00
212 Rocky Colavito RC 40.00 100.00
213 Les Moss 3.00 8.00
214 Philadelphia Phillies TC 6.00 15.00
215 Enos Slaughter 15.00 40.00
216 Marv Grissom 3.00 8.00
217 Gene Stephens 3.00 8.00
218 Ray Jablonski 3.00 8.00
219 Tom Acker RC 3.00 8.00
220 Jackie Jensen 8.00 20.00
221 Dixie Howell 3.00 8.00
222 Alex Grammas 3.00 8.00
223 Frank House 3.00 8.00
224 Marv Blaylock 3.00 8.00
225 Harry Simpson 3.00 8.00
226 Preston Ward 3.00 8.00
227 Gerry Staley 3.00 8.00
228 Smoky Burgess UER 6.00 15.00
229 George Susce 3.00 8.00
230 George Kell 12.00 30.00
231 Solly Hemus 3.00 8.00
232 Whitey Lockman 6.00 15.00
233 Art Fowler 3.00 8.00
234 Dick Cole 3.00 8.00
235 Tom Poholsky 3.00 8.00
236 Joe Ginsberg 3.00 8.00
237 Foster Castleman 3.00 8.00
238 Eddie Robinson 3.00 8.00
239 Tom Morgan 3.00 8.00
240 Hank Bauer 20.00 50.00
241 Joe Lonnett RC 3.00 8.00
242 Charlie Neal 6.00 15.00
243 St. Louis Cardinals TC 6.00 15.00
244 Billy Loes 6.00 15.00
245 Rip Repulski 3.00 8.00
246 Jose Valdivielso 3.00 8.00
247 Turk Lown 3.00 8.00
248 Jim Finigan 3.00 8.00
249 Dave Pope 3.00 8.00
250 Eddie Mathews 30.00 80.00
251 Baltimore Orioles TC 6.00 15.00
252 Carl Erskine 6.00 15.00
253 Gus Zernial 6.00 15.00
254 Ron Negray 3.00 8.00
255 Charlie Silvera 6.00 15.00
256 Ron Kline 3.00 8.00
257 Walt Dropo 3.00 8.00
258 Steve Gromek 3.00 8.00
259 Eddie O'Brien 3.00 8.00
260 Del Ennis 6.00 15.00
261 Bob Chakales 3.00 8.00
262 Bobby Thomson 6.00 15.00
263 George Strickland 3.00 8.00
264 Bob Turley 6.00 15.00
265 Harvey Haddix DP 5.00 12.00
266 Ken Kuhn DP RC 5.00 12.00
267 Danny Kravitz RC 8.00 20.00
268 Jack Collum 8.00 20.00
269 Bob Cerv 12.00 30.00
270 Washington Senators TC 25.00 60.00
271 Danny O'Connell DP 5.00 12.00
272 Bobby Shantz 15.00 40.00
273 Jim Davis 8.00 20.00
274 Don Hoak 6.00 15.00
275 Cleveland Indians TC UER 25.00 60.00
276 Jim Pyburn RC 8.00 20.00
277 Johnny Podres DP 25.00 60.00
278 Fred Hatfield DP 5.00 12.00
279 Bob Thurman RC 8.00 20.00
280 Alex Kellner 8.00 20.00
281 Gail Harris 8.00 20.00
282 Jack Dittmer DP 5.00 12.00
283 Wes Covington DP RC 5.00 12.00
284 Don Zimmer 15.00 40.00
285 Ned Garver 8.00 20.00
286 Bobby Richardson RC 50.00 120.00
287 Sam Jones 8.00 20.00
288 Ted Lepcio 8.00 20.00
289 Jim Bolger DP 5.00 12.00
290 Andy Carey DP 15.00 40.00
291 Windy McCall 8.00 20.00
292 Billy Klaus 8.00 20.00
293 Ted Abernathy RC 8.00 20.00
294 Rocky Bridges DP 5.00 12.00
295 Joe Collins DP 15.00 40.00
296 Johnny Klippstein 8.00 20.00
297 Jack Crimian 8.00 20.00
298 Irv Noren DP 5.00 12.00
299 Chuck Harmon 8.00 20.00
300 Mike Garcia 12.00 30.00
301 Sammy Esposito DP RC 8.00 20.00
302 Sandy Koufax DP 150.00 400.00
303 Billy Goodman 12.00 30.00
304 Joe Cunningham 12.00 30.00
305 Chico Fernandez 8.00 20.00
306 Darrell Johnson DP RC 5.00 12.00
307 Jack D. Phillips DP 5.00 12.00
308 Dick Hall 8.00 20.00
309 Jim Busby DP 5.00 12.00
310 Max Surkont DP 5.00 12.00
311 Al Pilarcik DP RC 5.00 12.00
312 Tony Kubek DP RC 40.00 100.00
313 Mel Parnell 6.00 15.00
314 Ed Bouchee DP RC 5.00 12.00
315 Lou Berberet DP 5.00 12.00
316 Billy O'Dell 8.00 20.00
317 New York Giants TC 30.00 80.00
318 Mickey McDermott 8.00 20.00
319 Gino Cimoli RC 8.00 20.00
320 Neil Chrisley RC 8.00 20.00
321 John Red Murff RC 8.00 20.00
322 Cincinnati Reds TC 30.00 80.00
323 Wes Westrum 12.00 30.00
324 Brooklyn Dodgers TC 40.00 100.00
325 Frank Bolling 8.00 20.00
326 Pedro Ramos 8.00 20.00
327 Jim Pendleton 8.00 20.00
328 Brooks Robinson RC 500.00 1000.00
329 Chicago White Sox TC 25.00 60.00
330 Jim Wilson 8.00 20.00
331 Ray Katt 8.00 20.00
332 Bob Bowman RC 8.00 20.00
333 Ernie Johnson 8.00 20.00
334 Jerry Schoonmaker 8.00 20.00
335 Granny Hamner 8.00 20.00
336 Haywood Sullivan RC 15.00 40.00
337 Rene Valdes RC 10.00 25.00
338 Jim Bunning RC 100.00 250.00
339 Bob Speake 8.00 20.00
340 Bill Wight 8.00 20.00
341 Don Gross RC 8.00 20.00
342 Gene Mauch 12.00 30.00
343 Taylor Phillips RC 6.00 15.00
344 Paul LaPalme 8.00 20.00
345 Paul Smith 8.00 20.00
346 Dick Littlefield 8.00 20.00
347 Hal Naragon 8.00 20.00
348 Jim Hearn 8.00 20.00
349 Nellie King 8.00 20.00
350 Eddie Miksis 8.00 20.00
351 Dave Hillman RC 8.00 20.00
352 Ellis Kinder 8.00 20.00
353 Cal Neeman RC 3.00 8.00
354 Rip Coleman RC 3.00 8.00
355 Frank Malzone 6.00 15.00
356 Faye Throneberry 3.00 8.00
357 Earl Torgeson 3.00 8.00
358 Jerry Lynch 6.00 15.00
359 Tom Cheney RC 3.00 8.00
360 Johnny Groth 3.00 8.00
361 Curt Barclay RC 3.00 8.00
362 Roman Mejias RC 6.00 15.00
363 Eddie Kasko RC 3.00 8.00
364 Cal McLish RC 6.00 15.00
365 Ozzie Virgil RC 3.00 8.00
366 Ken Lehman 3.00 8.00
367 Ed Fitzgerald 3.00 8.00
368 Bob Purkey 3.00 8.00
369 Milt Graff RC 3.00 8.00
370 Warren Hacker 3.00 8.00
371 Bob Lennon 3.00 8.00
372 Norm Zauchin 3.00 8.00
373 Pete Whisenant RC 3.00 8.00
374 Don Cardwell RC 3.00 8.00
375 Jim Landis RC 6.00 15.00
376 Don Elston RC 3.00 8.00
377 Andre Rodgers RC 3.00 8.00
378 Elmer Singleton 3.00 8.00
379 Don Lee RC 3.00 8.00
380 Walker Cooper 3.00 8.00
381 Dean Stone 3.00 8.00
382 Jim Brideweser 3.00 8.00
383 Juan Pizarro RC 3.00 8.00
384 Bobby G. Smith RC 3.00 8.00
385 Art Houtteman 3.00 8.00
386 Lyle Luttrell RC 3.00 8.00
387 Jack Sanford RC 6.00 15.00
388 Pete Daley 3.00 8.00
389 Dave Jolly 3.00 8.00
390 Reno Bertoia 3.00 8.00
391 Ralph Terry RC 6.00 15.00
392 Chuck Tanner 8.00 20.00
393 Raul Sanchez RC 3.00 8.00
394 Luis Arroyo 6.00 15.00
395 Bubba Phillips 3.00 8.00
396 Casey Wise RC 3.00 8.00
397 Roy Smalley 3.00 8.00
398 Al Cicotte RC 6.00 15.00
399 Billy Consolo 3.00 8.00
400 Fur/Hodges/Campy/Snider 60.00 150.00
401 Earl Battey RC 6.00 15.00
402 Jim Pisoni RC 3.00 8.00
403 Dick Hyde RC 3.00 8.00
404 Harry Anderson RC 3.00 8.00
405 Duke Maas 3.00 8.00
406 Bob Hale 3.00 8.00
407 Y.Berra/M.Mantle 250.00 500.00
CC1 Contest May 4 40.00 100.00
CC2 Contest May 25 40.00 100.00
CC3 Contest June 22 50.00 120.00
CC4 Contest July 19 50.00 120.00
NNO Checklist 1/2 Bazooka 100.00 250.00
NNO Checklist 1/2 Blony 100.00 250.00
NNO Checklist 2/3 Bazooka 150.00 400.00
NNO Checklist 2/3 Blony 150.00 400.00
NNO Checklist 3/4 Bazooka 400.00 800.00
NNO Checklist 3/4 Blony 300.00 600.00
NNO Checklist 4/5 Bazooka 500.00 1000.00
NNO Checklist 4/5 Blony 400.00 800.00
NNO Lucky Penny Charm 40.00 100.00

1958 Topps

This is a 494-card standard-size set. Card number 145, which was supposedly to be Ed Bouchee, was not issued. The 1958 Topps set contains the first Sport Magazine All-Star Selection series (475-495) and expanded use of combination cards. For the first time team cards carried series checklists on back (Milwaukee, Detroit, Baltimore, and Cincinnati are also found with players listed alphabetically). In the first series some cards were issued with yellow name (YN) or team (YT) lettering, as opposed to the common white lettering. They are explicitly noted below. Cards were issued in one-card penny packs or six-card nickel packs. In the last series, All-Star cards of Stan Musial and Mickey Mantle were triple printed; the cards they replaced (443, 446, 450, and 462) on the printing sheet were hence printed in shorter supply than other cards in the last series and are marked with an SP in the list below. The All-Star card of Musial marked his first appearance on a Topps card. Technically the New York Giants team card (19) is an error as the Giants had already moved to San Francisco. The key Rookie Cards in this set are Orlando Cepeda, Curt Flood, Roger Maris, and Vada Pinson. These cards were issued in varying formats, including one cent packs which were issued 120 to a box.

COMP. MASTER SET (534) 6000.00 12000.00
COMPLETE SET (494) 4000.00 8000.00
COMMON CARD (1-110) 6.00 12.00
COMMON CARD (111-495) 4.00 8.00
WRAPPER (1-CENT) 75.00 100.00
WRAPPER (5-CENT) 100.00 125.00
1 Ted Williams 200.00 400.00
2A Bob Lemon 12.00 30.00
2B Bob Lemon YT 25.00 60.00
3 Alex Kellner 5.00 12.00
4 Hank Foiles 5.00 12.00
5 Willie Mays 125.00 300.00
6 George Zuverink 5.00 12.00
7 Dale Long 6.00 15.00
8A Eddie Kasko 5.00 12.00
8B Eddie Kasko YN 15.00 40.00
9 Hank Bauer 20.00 50.00
10 Lou Burdette 8.00 20.00
11A Jim Rivera 5.00 12.00
11B Jim Rivera YT 15.00 40.00
12 George Crowe 5.00 12.00
13A Billy Hoeft 5.00 12.00
13B Billy Hoeft YN 15.00 40.00
14 Rip Repulski 5.00 12.00
15 Jim Lemon 6.00 15.00
16 Charlie Neal 6.00 15.00
17 Felix Mantilla 5.00 12.00
18 Frank Sullivan 5.00 12.00
19 San Francisco Giants TC 15.00 40.00
20A Gil McDougald 8.00 20.00
20B Gil McDougald YN 25.00 60.00
21 Curt Barclay 5.00 12.00
22 Hal Naragon 5.00 12.00
23A Bill Tuttle 5.00 12.00
23B Bill Tuttle YN 15.00 40.00
24A Hobie Landrith 5.00 12.00
24B Hobie Landrith YN 20.00 50.00
25 Don Drysdale 40.00 100.00
26 Ron Jackson 5.00 12.00
27 Bud Freeman 5.00 12.00
28 Jim Busby 5.00 12.00
29 Ted Lepcio 5.00 12.00
30A Hank Aaron 125.00 300.00
30B Hank Aaron YN 250.00 500.00
31 Tex Clevenger RC 5.00 12.00
32A J.W. Porter 5.00 12.00
32B J.W. Porter YN 15.00 40.00
33A Cal Neeman 5.00 12.00
33B Cal Neeman YT 15.00 40.00
34 Bob Thurman 5.00 12.00
35A Don Mossi 5.00 12.00
35B Don Mossi YT 15.00 40.00
36 Ted Kazanski 5.00 12.00
37 Mike McCormick UER RC 6.00 15.00
38 Dick Gernert 5.00 12.00
39 Bob Martyn RC 5.00 12.00
40 George Kell 10.00 25.00
41 Dave Hillman 5.00 12.00
42 John Roseboro RC 12.00 30.00
43 Sal Maglie 6.00 15.00
44 Washington Senators TC 8.00 20.00
45 Dick Groat 6.00 15.00
46A Lou Sleater 5.00 12.00
46B Lou Sleater YN 15.00 40.00
47 Roger Maris RC 300.00 600.00
48 Chuck Harmon 5.00 12.00
49 Smoky Burgess 6.00 15.00
50A Billy Pierce 6.00 15.00
50B Billy Pierce YT 15.00 40.00
51 Del Rice 5.00 12.00
52A Roberto Clemente 125.00 300.00
52B Roberto Clemente YT 250.00 500.00
53A Morrie Martin 5.00 12.00
53B Morrie Martin YN 15.00 40.00
54 Norm Siebern RC 8.00 20.00
55 Chico Carrasquel 5.00 12.00
56 Bill Fischer RC 5.00 12.00
57A Tim Thompson 5.00 12.00
57B Tim Thompson YN 15.00 40.00
58A Art Schult 5.00 12.00
58B Art Schult YT 15.00 40.00
59 Dave Sisler 5.00 12.00
60A Del Ennis 6.00 15.00
60B Del Ennis YN 15.00 40.00
61A Darrell Johnson 5.00 12.00
61B Darrell Johnson YN 15.00 40.00
62 Joe DeMaestri 5.00 12.00
63 Joe Nuxhall 6.00 15.00
64 Joe Lonnett 5.00 12.00
65A Von McDaniel RC 5.00 12.00
65B Von McDaniel YN 15.00 40.00
66 Lee Walls 5.00 12.00
67 Joe Ginsberg 5.00 12.00
68 Daryl Spencer 5.00 12.00
69 Wally Burnette 5.00 12.00
70A Al Kaline 40.00 100.00
70B Al Kaline YN 100.00 250.00
71 Los Angeles Dodgers TC 25.00 60.00
72 Bud Byerly UER 5.00 12.00
73 Pete Daley 5.00 12.00
74 Roy Face 6.00 15.00
75 Gus Bell 6.00 15.00
76A Dick Farrell RC 5.00 12.00
76B Dick Farrell YT 15.00 40.00
77A Don Zimmer 6.00 15.00
77B Don Zimmer YT 15.00 40.00
78A Ernie Johnson 6.00 15.00
78B Ernie Johnson YN 15.00 40.00
79A Dick Williams 6.00 15.00
79B Dick Williams YT 15.00 40.00
80 Dick Drott RC 5.00 12.00
81A Steve Boros RC 5.00 12.00
81B Steve Boros YT 15.00 40.00
82 Ron Kline 5.00 12.00
83 Bob Hazle RC 5.00 12.00
84 Billy O'Dell 5.00 12.00
85A Luis Aparicio 12.00 30.00
85B Luis Aparicio YT 30.00 80.00
86 Valmy Thomas RC 5.00 12.00
87 Johnny Kucks 5.00 12.00
88 Duke Snider 25.00 60.00
89 Billy Klaus 5.00 12.00
90 Robin Roberts 15.00 40.00
91 Chuck Tanner 6.00 15.00
92A Clint Courtney 5.00 12.00
92B Clint Courtney YN 15.00 40.00
93 Sandy Amoros 6.00 15.00
94 Bob Skinner 6.00 15.00
95 Frank Bolling 5.00 12.00
96 Joe Durham RC 5.00 12.00
97A Larry Jackson 5.00 12.00
97B Larry Jackson YN 15.00 40.00
98A Billy Hunter 5.00 12.00
98B Billy Hunter YN 15.00 40.00
99 Bobby Adams 5.00 12.00
100A Early Wynn 12.00 30.00
100B Early Wynn YT 30.00 80.00
101A Bobby Richardson 12.00 30.00
101B B.Richardson YN 25.00 60.00
102 George Strickland 5.00 12.00
103 Jerry Lynch 6.00 15.00
104 Jim Pendleton 5.00 12.00
105 Billy Gardner 5.00 12.00
106 Dick Schofield 6.00 15.00
107 Ossie Virgil 5.00 12.00
108A Jim Landis 5.00 12.00
108B Jim Landis YT 15.00 40.00
109 Herb Plews 5.00 12.00
110 Johnny Logan 6.00 15.00
111 Stu Miller 4.00 10.00
112 Gus Zernial 4.00 10.00
113 Jerry Walker RC 3.00 8.00
114 Irv Noren 4.00 10.00
115 Jim Bunning 12.00 30.00
116 Dave Philley 3.00 8.00
117 Frank Torre 4.00 10.00
118 Harvey Haddix 4.00 10.00
119 Harry Chiti 3.00 8.00
120 Johnny Podres 10.00 25.00
121 Eddie Miksis 3.00 8.00
122 Walt Moryn 3.00 8.00
123 Dick Tomanek RC 3.00 8.00
124 Bobby Usher 3.00 8.00
125 Alvin Dark 4.00 10.00
126 Stan Palys RC 3.00 8.00
127 Tom Sturdivant 8.00 20.00
128 Willie Kirkland RC 3.00 8.00
129 Jim Derrington RC 3.00 8.00
130 Jackie Jensen 4.00 10.00
131 Bob Henrich RC 3.00 8.00
132 Vern Law 4.00 10.00
133 Russ Nixon RC 3.00 8.00
134 Philadelphia Phillies TC 6.00 15.00
135 Mike MoeDrabowsky 4.00 10.00
136 Jim Finigan 3.00 8.00
137 Russ Kemmerer 3.00 8.00
138 Earl Torgeson 3.00 8.00
139 George Brunet RC 3.00 8.00
140 Wes Covington 4.00 10.00
141 Ken Lehman 3.00 8.00
142 Enos Slaughter 20.00 50.00
143 Billy Muffett RC 3.00 8.00
144 Bobby Morgan 3.00 8.00
146 Dick Gray RC 3.00 8.00
147 Don McMahon RC 3.00 8.00
148 Billy Consolo 3.00 8.00
149 Tom Acker 3.00 8.00
150 Mickey Mantle 500.00 1000.00
151 Buddy Pritchard RC 3.00 8.00
152 Johnny Antonelli 4.00 10.00
153 Les Moss 3.00 8.00
154 Harry Byrd 3.00 8.00
155 Hector Lopez 4.00 10.00
156 Dick Hyde 3.00 8.00
157 Dee Fondy 3.00 8.00
158 Cleveland Indians TC 6.00 15.00
159 Taylor Phillips 3.00 8.00
160 Don Hoak 4.00 10.00
161 Don Larsen 15.00 40.00
162 Gil Hodges 20.00 50.00
163 Jim Wilson 3.00 8.00
164 Bob Taylor RC 3.00 8.00
165 Bob Nieman 3.00 8.00
166 Danny O'Connell 3.00 8.00
167 Frank Baumann RC 3.00 8.00
168 Joe Cunningham 3.00 8.00
169 Ralph Terry 4.00 10.00
170 Vic Wertz 4.00 10.00
171 Harry Anderson 3.00 8.00
172 Don Gross 3.00 8.00
173 Eddie Yost 3.00 8.00
174 Kansas City Athletics TC 6.00 15.00
175 Marv Throneberry RC 6.00 15.00
176 Bob Buhl 4.00 10.00
177 Al Smith 3.00 8.00
178 Ted Kluszewski 10.00 25.00
179 Willie Miranda 3.00 8.00
180 Lindy McDaniel 4.00 10.00
181 Willie Jones 3.00 8.00
182 Joe Caffie RC 3.00 8.00
183 Dave Jolly 3.00 8.00
184 Elvin Tappe 3.00 8.00
185 Ray Boone 4.00 10.00
186 Jack Meyer 3.00 8.00
187 Sandy Koufax 100.00 250.00
188 Milt Bolling UER 3.00 8.00
189 George Susce 3.00 8.00
190 Red Schoendienst 10.00 25.00
191 Art Ceccarelli RC 3.00 8.00
192 Milt Graff 3.00 8.00
193 Jerry Lumpe RC 3.00 8.00
194 Roger Craig 4.00 10.00
195 Whitey Lockman 4.00 10.00
196 Mike Garcia 4.00 10.00
197 Haywood Sullivan 4.00 10.00
198 Bill Virdon 4.00 10.00
199 Don Blasingame 3.00 8.00
200 Bob Keegan 3.00 8.00
201 Jim Bolger 3.00 8.00
202 Woody Held RC 3.00 8.00
203 Al Walker 3.00 8.00
204 Leo Kiely 3.00 8.00
205 Johnny Temple 4.00 10.00
206 Bob Shaw RC 3.00 8.00
207 Solly Hemus 3.00 8.00
208 Cal McLish 3.00 8.00
209 Bob Anderson RC 3.00 8.00
210 Wally Moon 4.00 10.00
211 Pete Burnside RC 3.00 8.00
212 Bubba Phillips 3.00 8.00
213 Red Wilson 3.00 8.00
214 Willard Schmidt 3.00 8.00
215 Jim Gilliam 6.00 15.00
216 St. Louis Cardinals TC 6.00 15.00
217 Jack Harshman 3.00 8.00
218 Dick Rand RC 3.00 8.00
219 Camilo Pascual 4.00 10.00
220 Tom Brewer 3.00 8.00
221 Jerry Kindall RC 3.00 8.00
222 Bud Daley RC 3.00 8.00
223 Andy Pafko 4.00 10.00
224 Bob Grim 4.00 10.00
225 Billy Goodman 4.00 10.00
226 Bob Smith RC 3.00 8.00
227 Gene Stephens 3.00 8.00
228 Duke Maas 3.00 8.00
229 Frank Zupo RC 3.00 8.00
230 Richie Ashburn 15.00 40.00
231 Lloyd Merritt RC 3.00 8.00
232 Reno Bertoia 3.00 8.00
233 Mickey Vernon 4.00 10.00
234 Carl Sawatski 3.00 8.00
235 Tom Gorman 3.00 8.00
236 Ed Fitzgerald 3.00 8.00
237 Bill Wight 3.00 8.00
238 Bill Mazeroski 20.00 50.00
239 Chuck Stobbs 3.00 8.00
240 Bill Skowron 15.00 40.00
241 Dick Littlefield 3.00 8.00
242 Johnny Klippstein 3.00 8.00
243 Larry Raines RC 3.00 8.00
244 Don Demeter RC 3.00 8.00
245 Frank Lary 4.00 10.00
246 New York Yankees TC 30.00 80.00
247 Casey Wise 3.00 8.00
248 Herman Wehmeier 3.00 8.00
249 Ray Moore 3.00 8.00
250 Roy Sievers 4.00 10.00
251 Warren Hacker 3.00 8.00
252 Bob Trowbridge RC 3.00 8.00
253 Don Mueller 4.00 10.00
254 Alex Grammas 3.00 8.00
255 Bob Turley 4.00 10.00
256 Chicago White Sox TC 6.00 15.00
257 Hal Smith 3.00 8.00
258 Carl Erskine 6.00 15.00
259 Al Pilarcik 3.00 8.00
260 Frank Malzone 4.00 10.00
261 Turk Lown 3.00 8.00
262 Johnny Groth 3.00 8.00
263 Eddie Bressoud RC 4.00 10.00
264 Jack Sanford 4.00 10.00
265 Pete Runnels 4.00 10.00
266 Connie Johnson 3.00 8.00
267 Sherm Lollar 4.00 10.00
268 Granny Hamner 3.00 8.00
269 Paul Smith 3.00 8.00
270 Warren Spahn 30.00 80.00
271 Billy Martin 15.00 40.00
272 Ray Crone 3.00 8.00
273 Hal Smith 3.00 8.00
274 Rocky Bridges 3.00 8.00
275 Elston Howard 15.00 40.00
276 Bobby Avila 3.00 8.00
277 Virgil Trucks 4.00 10.00
278 Mack Burk 3.00 8.00
279 Bob Boyd 3.00 8.00
280 Jim Piersall 4.00 10.00
281 Sammy Taylor RC 3.00 8.00
282 Paul Foytack 3.00 8.00
283 Ray Shearer RC 3.00 8.00
284 Ray Katt 3.00 8.00
285 Frank Robinson 40.00 100.00
286 Gino Cimoli 3.00 8.00
287 Sam Jones 4.00 10.00
288 Harmon Killebrew 50.00 120.00
289 B.Shantz/L.Burdette 4.00 10.00
290 Dick Donovan 3.00 8.00
291 Don Landrum RC 3.00 8.00
292 Ned Garver 3.00 8.00
293 Gene Freese 3.00 8.00
294 Hal Jeffcoat 3.00 8.00
295 Minnie Minoso 10.00 25.00
296 Ryne Duren RC 15.00 40.00
297 Don Buddin RC 3.00 8.00
298 Jim Hearn 3.00 8.00
299 Harry Simpson 3.00 8.00
300 W.Harridge/W.Giles 6.00 15.00
301 Randy Jackson 3.00 8.00
302 Mike Baxes RC 3.00 8.00
303 Neil Chrisley 3.00 8.00
304 H.Kuenn/A.Kaline 10.00 25.00
305 Clem Labine 4.00 10.00
306 Whammy Douglas RC 3.00 8.00
307 Brooks Robinson 60.00 150.00
308 Paul Giel 4.00 10.00
309 Gail Harris 3.00 8.00
310 Ernie Banks 50.00 120.00
311 Bob Purkey 3.00 8.00
312 Boston Red Sox TC 6.00 15.00
313 Bob Rush 3.00 8.00
314 D.Snider/W.Alston 15.00 40.00
315 Bob Friend 4.00 10.00
316 Tito Francona 4.00 10.00
317 Albie Pearson RC 4.00 10.00
318 Frank House 3.00 8.00
319 Lou Skizas 3.00 8.00
320 Whitey Ford 40.00 100.00
321 T.Kluszewski/T.Williams 25.00 60.00
322 Harding Peterson RC 4.00 10.00
323 Elmer Valo 3.00 8.00
324 Hoyt Wilhelm 10.00 25.00
325 Joe Adcock 4.00 10.00
326 Bob Miller 3.00 8.00
327 Chicago Cubs TC 6.00 15.00
328 Ike Delock 3.00 8.00
329 Bob Cerv 4.00 10.00
330 Ed Bailey 4.00 10.00
331 Pedro Ramos 3.00 8.00
332 Jim King 3.00 8.00
333 Andy Carey 4.00 10.00
334 B.Friend/B.Pierce 4.00 10.00
335 Ruben Gomez 3.00 8.00
336 Bert Hamric 3.00 8.00
337 Hank Aguirre 3.00 8.00
338 Walt Dropo 4.00 10.00
339 Fred Hatfield 3.00 8.00
340 Don Newcombe 15.00 40.00
341 Pittsburgh Pirates TC 6.00 15.00
342 Jim Brosnan 4.00 10.00
343 Orlando Cepeda RC 75.00 200.00
344 Bob Porterfield 3.00 8.00
345 Jim Hegan 4.00 10.00
346 Steve Bilko 3.00 8.00
347 Don Rudolph RC 3.00 8.00
348 Chico Fernandez 3.00 8.00
349 Murry Dickson 3.00 8.00
350 Ken Boyer 10.00 25.00
351 Cran/Math/Aaron/Adcock 30.00 80.00
352 Herb Score 6.00 15.00
353 Stan Lopata 3.00 8.00
354 Art Ditmar 4.00 10.00
355 Bill Bruton 4.00 10.00
356 Bob Malkmus RC 3.00 8.00
357 Danny McDevitt RC 3.00 8.00
358 Gene Baker 3.00 8.00
359 Billy Loes 4.00 10.00
360 Roy McMillan 4.00 10.00
361 Mike Fornieles 3.00 8.00
362 Ray Jablonski 3.00 8.00
363 Don Elston 3.00 8.00
364 Earl Battey 3.00 8.00
365 Tom Morgan 3.00 8.00
366 Gene Green RC 3.00 8.00
367 Jack Urban RC 3.00 8.00
368 Rocky Colavito 25.00 60.00
369 Ralph Lumenti RC 3.00 8.00
370 Yogi Berra 50.00 120.00
371 Marty Keough RC 3.00 8.00
372 Don Cardwell 3.00 8.00
373 Joe Pignatano RC 3.00 8.00
374 Brooks Lawrence 3.00 8.00
375 Pee Wee Reese 30.00 80.00
376 Charley Rabe RC 3.00 8.00
377A Milwaukee Braves TC Alpha 6.00 15.00
377B Milwaukee Braves TC Num 40.00 100.00
378 Hank Sauer 4.00 10.00
379 Ray Herbert 3.00 8.00
380 Charlie Maxwell 4.00 10.00
381 Hal Brown 3.00 8.00
382 Al Cicotte 3.00 8.00
383 Lou Berberet 3.00 8.00
384 John Goryl RC 3.00 8.00
385 Wilmer Mizell 4.00 10.00
386 Bailey/Tebbets/F.Rob 6.00 15.00
387 Wally Post 4.00 10.00
388 Billy Moran RC 3.00 8.00
389 Bill Taylor 3.00 8.00
390 Del Crandall 4.00 10.00
391 Dave Melton RC 3.00 8.00
392 Bennie Daniels RC 3.00 8.00
393 Tony Kubek 12.00 30.00
394 Jim Grant RC 3.00 8.00
395 Willard Nixon 3.00 8.00
396 Dutch Dotterer RC 3.00 8.00
397A Detroit Tigers TC Alpha 6.00 15.00
397B Detroit Tigers TC Num 40.00 100.00
398 Gene Woodling 4.00 10.00
399 Marv Grissom 3.00 8.00
400 Nellie Fox 12.00 30.00
401 Don Bessent 3.00 8.00
402 Bobby Gene Smith 3.00 8.00
403 Steve Korcheck RC 3.00 8.00
404 Curt Simmons 4.00 10.00
405 Ken Aspromonte RC 3.00 8.00
406 Vic Power 4.00 10.00
407 Carlton Willey RC 4.00 10.00
408A Baltimore Orioles TC Alpha 6.00 15.00
408B Baltimore Orioles TC Num 40.00 100.00
409 Frank Thomas 4.00 10.00
410 Murray Wall 3.00 8.00
411 Tony Taylor RC 4.00 10.00
412 Gerry Staley 3.00 8.00
413 Jim Davenport RC 3.00 8.00
414 Sammy White 3.00 8.00
415 Bob Bowman 3.00 8.00
416 Foster Castleman 3.00 8.00
417 Carl Furillo 6.00 15.00
418 M.Mantle/H.Aaron 125.00 300.00
419 Bobby Shantz 4.00 10.00
420 Vada Pinson RC 20.00 50.00
421 Dixie Howell 3.00 8.00
422 Norm Zauchin 3.00 8.00
423 Phil Clark RC 3.00 8.00
424 Larry Doby UER 20.00 50.00
425 Sammy Esposito 3.00 8.00
426 Johnny O'Brien 4.00 10.00
427 Al Worthington 3.00 8.00
428A Cincinnati Reds TC Alpha 6.00 15.00
428B Cincinnati Reds TC Num 40.00 100.00
429 Gus Triandos 4.00 10.00
430 Bobby Thomson 4.00 10.00
431 Gene Conley 4.00 10.00
432 John Powers RC 3.00 8.00
433A Pancho Herrera COR RC 4.00 10.00
433B Pancho Herrer ERR 2500.00 5000.00
433C Pancho Herre ERR
433D Pancho Herr ERR
434 Harvey Kuenn 4.00 10.00
435 Ed Roebuck 4.00 10.00
436 W.Mays/D.Snider 25.00 60.00
437 Bob Speake 3.00 8.00
438 Whitey Herzog 4.00 10.00
439 Ray Narleski 3.00 8.00
440 Eddie Mathews 25.00 60.00
441 Jim Marshall RC 4.00 10.00
442 Phil Paine RC 3.00 8.00
443 Billy Harrell SP RC 8.00 20.00
444 Danny Kravitz 3.00 8.00
445 Bob Smith RC 3.00 8.00
446 Carroll Hardy SP RC 8.00 20.00
447 Ray Monzant 3.00 8.00
448 Charlie Lau RC 4.00 10.00
449 Gene Fodge RC 3.00 8.00
450 Preston Ward SP 8.00 20.00
451 Joe Taylor RC 3.00 8.00
452 Roman Mejias 3.00 8.00
453 Tom Qualters 3.00 8.00
454 Harry Hanebrink RC 3.00 8.00
455 Hal Griggs RC 3.00 8.00
456 Dick Brown RC 3.00 8.00
457 Milt Pappas RC 4.00 10.00
458 Julio Becquer RC 3.00 8.00
459 Ron Blackburn RC 3.00 8.00
460 Chuck Essegian RC 3.00 8.00
461 Ed Mayer RC 3.00 8.00
462 Gary Geiger SP RC 8.00 20.00
463 Vito Valentinetti 3.00 8.00
464 Curt Flood RC 20.00 50.00
465 Arnie Portocarrero 3.00 8.00
466 Pete Whisenant 3.00 8.00
467 Glen Hobbie RC 3.00 8.00
468 Bob Schmidt RC 3.00 8.00
469 Don Ferrarese 3.00 8.00
470 R.C. Stevens RC 3.00 8.00
471 Lenny Green RC 3.00 8.00
472 Joey Jay 4.00 10.00
473 Bill Renna 3.00 8.00
474 Roman Semproch RC 3.00 8.00
475 F.Haney/C.Stengel AS 15.00 40.00
476 Stan Musial AS TP 25.00 60.00
477 Bill Skowron AS 4.00 10.00

478 Johnny Temple AS UER 3.00 8.00
479 Nellie Fox AS 6.00 15.00
480 Eddie Mathews AS 15.00 40.00
481 Frank Malzone AS 3.00 8.00
482 Ernie Banks AS 25.00 60.00
483 Luis Aparicio AS 10.00 25.00
484 Frank Robinson AS 25.00 60.00
485 Ted Williams AS 50.00 120.00
486 Willie Mays AS 40.00 100.00
487 Mickey Mantle AS TP 75.00 200.00
488 Hank Aaron AS 30.00 80.00
489 Jackie Jensen AS 4.00 10.00
490 Ed Bailey AS 3.00 8.00
491 Sherm Lollar AS 3.00 8.00
492 Bob Friend AS 10.00 25.00
493 Bob Turley AS 4.00 10.00
494 Warren Spahn AS 10.00 25.00
495 Herb Score AS 6.00 15.00
NNO Contest Cards 15.00 40.00
NNO Felt Emblem Insert

1959 Topps

The cards in this 572-card set measure 2 1/2" by 3 1/2". The 1959 Topps set contains bust pictures of the players in a colored circle. Card numbers 551 to 572 are Sporting News All-Star Selections. High numbers 507 to 572 have the card number in a black background on the reverse rather than a green background as in the lower numbers. The high numbers are more difficult to obtain. Several cards in the 300s exist with or without an extra traded or option line on the back of the card. Cards 199 to 286 exist with either white or gray backs. There is no price differential for either colored back. Cards 461 to 470 contain "Highlights" while cards 116 to 146 give an alphabetically ordered listing of "Rookie Prospects." These Rookie Prospects (RP) were Topps' first organized inclusion of untested "Rookie" cards. Card 440 features Lew Burdette erroneously posing as a left-handed pitcher. Cards were issued in one-card penny packs or six-card nickel packs. There were some three-card advertising panels produced by Topps; the players included are from the first series. Panels which had Ted Kluszewski's card back on the back included Don McMahon/Red Wilson/Bob Boyd; Joe Pignatano/Sam Jones/Jack Urban also with Kluszewski's card on back. Strips with Nellie Fox on the back included Billy Hunter/Chuck Stobbs/Carl Sawatski; Vito Valentinetti/Ken Lehman/Ed Bouchee; Mel Roach/Brooks Lawrence/Warren Spahn. Other panels include Harvey Kuenn/Alex Grammas/ Bob Cerv; and Bob Cerv/Jim Bolger/Mickey Mantle. When separated, these advertising cards are distinguished by the non-standard card back, i.e., part of an advertisement for the 1959 Topps set instead of the typical statistics and biographical information about the player pictured. The key Rookie Cards in this set are Felipe Alou, Sparky Anderson (called George on the card), Norm Cash, Bob Gibson, and Bill White.

COMPLETE SET (572) 4000.00 8000.00
COMMON CARD (1-110) 3.00 6.00
COMMON CARD (111-506) 2.00 4.00
COMMON CARD (507-572) 7.50 15.00
WRAPPER (1-CENT) 100.00 125.00
WRAPPER (5-CENT) 75.00 100.00
1 Ford Frick COMM 40.00 100.00
2 Eddie Yost 4.00 8.00
3 Don McMahon 4.00 8.00
4 Albie Pearson 4.00 8.00
5 Dick Donovan 4.00 8.00
6 Alex Grammas 3.00 6.00
7 Al Pilarcik 3.00 6.00
8 Philadelphia Phillies CL 50.00 80.00
9 Paul Giel 4.00 8.00
10 Mickey Mantle 400.00 800.00
11 Billy Hunter 4.00 8.00
12 Vern Law 4.00 8.00
13 Dick Gernert 3.00 6.00
14 Pete Whisenant 3.00 6.00
15 Dick Drott 3.00 6.00
16 Joe Pignatano 3.00 6.00
17 Thomas/Murtaugh/Klusz 4.00 8.00
18 Jack Urban 3.00 6.00
19 Eddie Bressoud 3.00 6.00
20 Duke Snider 25.00 60.00
21 Connie Johnson 3.00 6.00
22 Al Smith 4.00 8.00
23 Murry Dickson 4.00 8.00
24 Red Wilson 3.00 6.00
25 Don Hoak 4.00 8.00
26 Chuck Stobbs 3.00 6.00
27 Andy Pafko 4.00 8.00
28 Al Worthington 3.00 6.00
29 Jim Bolger 3.00 6.00
30 Nellie Fox 15.00 30.00
31 Ken Lehman 3.00 6.00
32 Don Buddin 3.00 6.00
33 Ed Fitzgerald 3.00 6.00
34 Al Kaline/C.Maxwell 12.00 30.00
35 Ted Kluszewski 10.00 25.00
36 Hank Aguirre 3.00 6.00
37 Gene Green 3.00 6.00
38 Morrie Martin 3.00 6.00
39 Ed Bouchee 3.00 6.00
40A Warren Spahn ERR 50.00 80.00
40B Warren Spahn ERR 60.00 100.00
40C Warren Spahn COR 35.00 60.00
41 Bob Martyn 3.00 6.00
42 Murray Wall 3.00 6.00
43 Steve Bilko 3.00 6.00
44 Vito Valentinetti 3.00 6.00
45 Andy Carey 4.00 8.00
46 Bill R. Henry 3.00 6.00
47 Jim Finigan 3.00 6.00
48 Baltimore Orioles CL 12.50 25.00
49 Bill Hall RC 3.00 6.00
50 Willie Mays 60.00 150.00
51 Rip Coleman 3.00 6.00
52 Coot Veal RC 3.00 6.00
53 Stan Williams RC 4.00 8.00
54 Mel Roach 3.00 6.00
55 Tom Brewer 3.00 6.00
56 Carl Sawatski 3.00 6.00
57 Al Cicotte 3.00 6.00
58 Eddie Miksis 3.00 6.00
59 Irv Noren 4.00 8.00
60 Bob Turley 4.00 8.00
61 Dick Brown 3.00 6.00
62 Tony Taylor 4.00 8.00
63 Jim Hearn 3.00 6.00
64 Joe DeMaestri 3.00 6.00
65 Frank Torre 4.00 8.00
66 Joe Ginsberg 3.00 6.00
67 Brooks Lawrence 3.00 6.00
68 Dick Schofield 4.00 8.00
69 San Francisco Giants CL 12.50 25.00
70 Harvey Kuenn 4.00 8.00
71 Don Bessent 3.00 6.00
72 Bill Renna 3.00 6.00
73 Ron Jackson 4.00 8.00
74 Lemon/Lavagetto/Sievers 4.00 8.00
75 Sam Jones 4.00 8.00
76 Bobby Richardson 12.00 30.00
77 John Goryl 3.00 6.00
78 Pedro Ramos 3.00 6.00
79 Harry Chiti 3.00 6.00
80 Minnie Minoso 6.00 12.00
81 Hal Jeffcoat 3.00 6.00
82 Bob Boyd 3.00 6.00
83 Bob Smith 3.00 6.00
84 Reno Bertoia 3.00 6.00
85 Harry Anderson 3.00 6.00
86 Bob Keegan 4.00 8.00
87 Danny O'Connell 3.00 6.00
88 Herb Score 6.00 12.00
89 Billy Gardner 3.00 6.00
90 Bill Skowron 6.00 12.00
91 Herb Moford RC 3.00 6.00
92 Dave Philley 3.00 6.00
93 Julio Becquer 3.00 6.00
94 Chicago White Sox CL 20.00 40.00
95 Carl Willey 3.00 6.00
96 Lou Berberet 3.00 6.00
97 Jerry Lynch 4.00 8.00
98 Arnie Portocarrero 3.00 6.00
99 Ted Kazanski 3.00 6.00
100 Bob Cerv 4.00 8.00
101 Alex Kellner 3.00 6.00
102 Felipe Alou RC 15.00 30.00
103 Billy Goodman 4.00 8.00
104 Del Rice 4.00 8.00
105 Lee Walls 3.00 6.00
106 Hal Woodeshick RC 3.00 6.00
107 Norm Larker RC 4.00 8.00
108 Zack Monroe RC 4.00 8.00
109 Bob Schmidt 3.00 6.00
110 George Witt RC 4.00 8.00
111 Cincinnati Redlegs CL 7.50 15.00
112 Billy Consolo 2.00 4.00
113 Taylor Phillips 2.00 4.00
114 Earl Battey 4.00 8.00
115 Mickey Vernon 4.00 8.00
116 Bob Allison RS RC 6.00 12.00
117 John Blanchard RS RC 6.00 12.00
118 John Buzhardt RS RC 2.50 5.00
119 Johnny Callison RS RC 6.00 12.00
120 Chuck Coles RS RC 2.50 5.00
121 Bob Conley RS RC 2.50 5.00
122 Bennie Daniels RS 2.50 5.00
123 Don Dillard RS RC 2.50 5.00
124 Dan Dobbek RS RC 2.50 5.00
125 Ron Fairly RS RC 6.00 12.00
126 Eddie Haas RS RC 2.50 5.00
127 Kent Hadley RS RC 2.50 5.00
128 Bob Hartman RS RC 2.50 5.00
129 Frank Herrera RS 2.50 5.00
130 Lou Jackson RS RC 2.50 5.00
131 Deron Johnson RS RC 6.00 12.00
132 Don Lee RS 2.50 5.00
133 Bob Lillis RS RC 2.50 5.00
134 Jim McDaniel RS RC 2.50 5.00
135 Gene Oliver RS RC 2.50 5.00
136 Jim O'Toole RS RC 2.50 5.00
137 Dick Ricketts RS RC 2.50 5.00
138 John Romano RS RC 2.50 5.00
139 Ed Sadowski RS RC 2.50 5.00
140 Charlie Secrest RS RC 2.50 5.00
141 Joe Shipley RS RC 2.50 5.00
142 Dick Stigman RS RC 2.50 5.00
143 Willie Tasby RS RC 2.50 5.00
144 Jerry Walker RS 2.50 5.00
145 Dom Zanni RS RC 2.50 5.00
146 Jerry Zimmerman RS RC 2.50 5.00
147 Long/Banks/Moryn 15.00 30.00
148 Mike McCormick 4.00 8.00
149 Jim Bunning 12.00 30.00
150 Stan Musial 40.00 100.00
151 Bob Malkmus 2.00 4.00
152 Johnny Klippstein 2.00 4.00
153 Jim Marshall 2.00 4.00
154 Ray Herbert 2.00 4.00
155 Enos Slaughter 10.00 25.00
156 B.Pierce/R.Roberts 6.00 12.00
157 Felix Mantilla 2.00 4.00
158 Walt Dropo 2.00 4.00
159 Bob Shaw 4.00 8.00
160 Dick Groat 4.00 8.00
161 Frank Baumann 2.00 4.00
162 Bobby G. Smith 2.00 4.00
163 Sandy Koufax 100.00 250.00
164 Johnny Groth 2.00 4.00
165 Bill Bruton 2.00 4.00
166 Minoso/Colavito/Doby 15.00 30.00
167 Duke Maas 2.00 4.00
168 Carroll Hardy 2.00 4.00
169 Ted Abernathy 2.00 4.00
170 Gene Woodling 4.00 8.00
171 Willard Schmidt 2.00 4.00
172 Kansas City Athletics CL 7.50 15.00
173 Bill Monbouquette RC 4.00 8.00
174 Jim Pendleton 2.00 4.00
175 Dick Farrell 4.00 8.00
176 Preston Ward 2.00 4.00
177 John Briggs RC 2.00 4.00
178 Ruben Amaro RC 6.00 12.00
179 Don Rudolph 2.00 4.00
180 Yogi Berra 50.00 120.00
181 Bob Porterfield 2.00 4.00
182 Milt Graff 2.00 4.00
183 Stu Miller 4.00 8.00
184 Harvey Haddix 4.00 8.00
185 Jim Busby 2.00 4.00
186 Mudcat Grant 4.00 8.00
187 Bubba Phillips 4.00 8.00
188 Juan Pizarro 2.00 4.00
189 Neil Chrisley 2.00 4.00
190 Bill Virdon 4.00 8.00
191 Russ Kemmerer 2.00 4.00
192 Charlie Beamon RC 2.00 4.00
193 Sammy Taylor 2.00 4.00
194 Jim Brosnan 4.00 8.00
195 Rip Repulski 2.00 4.00
196 Billy Moran 2.00 4.00
197 Ray Semproch 2.00 4.00
198 Jim Davenport 4.00 8.00
199 Leo Kiely 2.00 4.00
200 W.Giles NL PRES 4.00 8.00
201 Tom Acker 2.00 4.00
202 Roger Maris 50.00 120.00
203 Ossie Virgil 2.00 4.00
204 Casey Wise 2.00 4.00
205 Don Larsen 4.00 8.00
206 Carl Furillo 6.00 12.00
207 George Strickland 2.00 4.00
208 Willie Jones 2.00 4.00
209 Lenny Green 2.00 4.00
210 Ed Bailey 2.00 4.00
211 Bob Blaylock RC 2.00 4.00
212 H.Aaron/E.Mathews 25.00 60.00
213 Jim Rivera 4.00 8.00
214 Marcelino Solis RC 2.00 4.00
215 Jim Lemon 4.00 8.00
216 Andre Rodgers 2.00 4.00
217 Carl Erskine 6.00 12.00
218 Roman Mejias 2.00 4.00
219 George Zuverink 2.00 4.00
220 Frank Malzone 4.00 8.00
221 Bob Bowman 2.00 4.00
222 Bobby Shantz 4.00 8.00
223 St. Louis Cardinals CL 7.50 15.00
224 Claude Osteen RC 4.00 8.00
225 Johnny Logan 4.00 8.00
226 Art Ceccarelli 2.00 4.00
227 Hal W. Smith 2.00 4.00
228 Don Gross 2.00 4.00
229 Vic Power 4.00 8.00
230 Bill Fischer 2.00 4.00
231 Ellis Burton RC 2.00 4.00
232 Eddie Kasko 2.00 4.00
233 Paul Foytack 2.00 4.00
234 Chuck Tanner 4.00 8.00
235 Valmy Thomas 2.00 4.00
236 Ted Bowsfield RC 2.00 4.00
237 McDougald/Turley/B.Rich 6.00 12.00
238 Gene Baker 2.00 4.00
239 Bob Trowbridge 2.00 4.00
240 Hank Bauer 6.00 15.00
241 Billy Muffett 2.00 4.00
242 Ron Samford RC 2.00 4.00
243 Marv Grissom 2.00 4.00
244 Dick Gray 2.00 4.00
245 Ned Garver 2.00 4.00
246 J.W. Porter 2.00 4.00
247 Don Ferrarese 2.00 4.00
248 Boston Red Sox CL 7.50 15.00
249 Bobby Adams 2.00 4.00
250 Billy O'Dell 2.00 4.00
251 Clete Boyer 6.00 12.00
252 Ray Boone 4.00 8.00
253 Seth Morehead RC 2.00 4.00
254 Zeke Bella RC 2.00 4.00
255 Del Ennis 4.00 8.00
256 Jerry Davie RC 2.00 4.00
257 Leon Wagner RC 4.00 8.00
258 Fred Kipp RC 2.00 4.00
259 Jim Pisoni 2.00 4.00
260 Early Wynn UER 10.00 25.00
261 Gene Stephens 2.00 4.00
262 Podres/Labine/Drysdale 6.00 12.00
263 Bud Daley 2.00 4.00
264 Chico Carrasquel 2.00 4.00
265 Ron Kline 2.00 4.00
266 Woody Held 2.00 4.00
267 John Romonosky RC 2.00 4.00
268 Tito Francona 4.00 8.00
269 Jack Meyer 2.00 4.00
270 Gil Hodges 15.00 30.00
271 Orlando Pena RC 2.00 4.00
272 Jerry Lumpe 2.00 4.00
273 Joey Jay 4.00 8.00
274 Jerry Kindall 4.00 8.00
275 Jack Sanford 4.00 8.00
276 Pete Daley 2.00 4.00
277 Turk Lown 4.00 8.00
278 Chuck Essegian 2.00 4.00
279 Ernie Johnson 2.00 4.00
280 Frank Bolling 2.00 4.00
281 Walt Craddock RC 2.00 4.00
282 R.C. Stevens 2.00 4.00
283 Russ Heman RC 2.00 4.00
284 Steve Korcheck 2.00 4.00
285 Joe Cunningham 2.00 4.00
286 Dean Stone 2.00 4.00
287 Don Zimmer 6.00 12.00
288 Dutch Dotterer 2.00 4.00
289 Johnny Kucks 4.00 8.00
290 Wes Covington 2.00 4.00
291 P.Ramos/C.Pascual 2.00 4.00
292 Dick Williams 4.00 8.00
293 Ray Moore 2.00 4.00
294 Hank Foiles 2.00 4.00
295 Billy Martin 12.00 30.00
296 Ernie Broglio RC 2.00 4.00
297 Jackie Brandt RC 2.00 4.00
298 Tex Clevenger 2.00 4.00
299 Billy Klaus 2.00 4.00
300 Richie Ashburn 15.00 40.00
301 Earl Averill Jr. RC 2.00 4.00
302 Don Mossi 4.00 8.00
303 Marty Keough 2.00 4.00
304 Chicago Cubs CL 7.50 15.00
305 Curt Raydon RC 2.00 4.00
306 Jim Gilliam 4.00 8.00
307 Curt Barclay 2.00 4.00
308 Norm Siebern 2.00 4.00
309 Sal Maglie 4.00 8.00
310 Luis Aparicio 12.00 30.00
311 Norm Zauchin 2.00 4.00
312 Don Newcombe 4.00 8.00
313 Frank House 2.00 4.00
314 Don Cardwell 2.00 4.00
315 Joe Adcock 4.00 8.00
316A Ralph Lumenti UER 2.00 4.00
316B Ralph Lumenti UER 50.00 80.00
317 R.Ashburn/W.Mays 20.00 50.00
318 Rocky Bridges 2.00 4.00
319 Dave Hillman 2.00 4.00
320 Bob Skinner 4.00 8.00
321A Bob Giallombardo RC 4.00 8.00
321B Bob Giallombardo ERR 50.00 80.00
322A Harry Hanebrink TR 4.00 8.00
322B H.Hanebrink ERR 50.00 80.00
323 Frank Sullivan 2.00 4.00
324 Don Demeter 2.00 4.00
325 Ken Boyer 6.00 12.00
326 Marv Throneberry 4.00 8.00
327 Gary Bell RC 2.00 4.00
328 Lou Skizas 2.00 4.00
329 Detroit Tigers CL 7.50 15.00
330 Gus Triandos 4.00 8.00
331 Steve Boros 2.00 4.00
332 Ray Monzant 2.00 4.00
333 Harry Simpson 2.00 4.00
334 Glen Hobbie 2.00 4.00
335 Johnny Temple 4.00 8.00
336A Billy Loes TR 4.00 8.00
336B Billy Loes ERR 50.00 80.00
337 George Crowe 2.00 4.00
338 Sparky Anderson RC 25.00 60.00
339 Roy Face 4.00 8.00
340 Roy Sievers 4.00 8.00
341 Tom Qualters 2.00 4.00
342 Ray Jablonski 2.00 4.00
343 Billy Hoeft 2.00 4.00
344 Russ Nixon 2.00 4.00
345 Gil McDougald 6.00 15.00
346 D.Sisler/T.Brewer 2.00 4.00
347 Bob Buhl 2.00 4.00
348 Ted Lepcio 2.00 4.00
349 Hoyt Wilhelm 8.00 20.00
350 Ernie Banks 40.00 100.00
351 Earl Torgeson 2.00 4.00
352 Robin Roberts 12.00 30.00
353 Curt Flood 4.00 8.00
354 Pete Burnside 2.00 4.00
355 Jimmy Piersall 4.00 8.00
356 Bob Mabe RC 2.00 4.00
357 Dick Stuart RC 4.00 8.00
358 Ralph Terry 2.00 4.00
359 Bill White RC 10.00 20.00
360 Al Kaline 25.00 60.00
361 Willard Nixon 2.00 4.00
362A Dolan Nichols RC 2.00 4.00
362B Dolan Nichols ERR 50.00 80.00
363 Bobby Avila 2.00 4.00
364 Danny McDevitt 2.00 4.00
365 Gus Bell 4.00 8.00
366 Humberto Robinson 2.00 4.00
367 Cal Neeman 2.00 4.00
368 Don Mueller 4.00 8.00
369 Dick Tomanek 2.00 4.00
370 Pete Runnels 4.00 8.00
371 Dick Brodowski 2.00 4.00
372 Jim Hegan 4.00 8.00
373 Herb Plews 2.00 4.00
374 Art Ditmar 4.00 8.00
375 Bob Nieman 2.00 4.00
376 Hal Naragon 2.00 4.00
377 John Antonelli 4.00 8.00
378 Gail Harris 2.00 4.00
379 Bob Miller 2.00 4.00
380 Hank Aaron 75.00 200.00
381 Mike Baxes 2.00 4.00
382 Curt Simmons 4.00 8.00
383 D.Larsen/C.Stengel 6.00 12.00
384 Dave Sisler 2.00 4.00
385 Sherm Lollar 4.00 8.00
386 Jim Delsing 2.00 4.00
387 Don Drysdale 15.00 40.00
388 Bob Will RC 2.00 4.00
389 Joe Nuxhall 4.00 8.00
390 Orlando Cepeda 12.00 30.00
391 Milt Pappas 4.00 8.00
392 Whitey Herzog 4.00 8.00
393 Frank Lary 4.00 8.00
394 Randy Jackson 2.00 4.00
395 Elston Howard 10.00 25.00
396 Bob Rush 2.00 4.00
397 Washington Senators CL 7.50 15.00
398 Wally Post 4.00 8.00
399 Larry Jackson 2.00 4.00
400 Jackie Jensen 4.00 8.00
401 Ron Blackburn 2.00 4.00
402 Hector Lopez 4.00 8.00
403 Clem Labine 4.00 8.00
404 Hank Sauer 4.00 8.00
405 Roy McMillan 4.00 8.00
406 Solly Drake 2.00 4.00
407 Moe Drabowsky 4.00 8.00
408 N.Fox/L.Aparicio 20.00 40.00
409 Gus Zernial 4.00 8.00
410 Billy Pierce 4.00 8.00
411 Whitey Lockman 4.00 8.00
412 Stan Lopata 2.00 4.00
413 Camilo Pascual UER 4.00 8.00
414 Dale Long 4.00 8.00
415 Bill Mazeroski 10.00 25.00
416 Haywood Sullivan 4.00 8.00
417 Virgil Trucks 4.00 8.00
418 Gino Cimoli 2.00 4.00
419 Milwaukee Braves CL 7.50 15.00
420 Rocky Colavito 15.00 30.00
421 Herman Wehmeier 2.00 4.00
422 Hobie Landrith 2.00 4.00
423 Bob Grim 4.00 8.00
424 Ken Aspromonte 2.00 4.00
425 Del Crandall 4.00 8.00
426 Gerry Staley 4.00 8.00
427 Charlie Neal 4.00 8.00
428 Kline/Friend/Law/Face 2.00 4.00
429 Bobby Thomson 4.00 8.00
430 Whitey Ford 25.00 60.00
431 Whammy Douglas 2.00 4.00
432 Smoky Burgess 4.00 8.00
433 Billy Harrell 2.00 4.00
434 Hal Griggs 2.00 4.00
435 Frank Robinson 40.00 100.00
436 Granny Hamner 2.00 4.00
437 Ike Delock 2.00 4.00
438 Sammy Esposito 2.00 4.00
439 Brooks Robinson 40.00 100.00
440 Lew Burdette UER 4.00 8.00
441 John Roseboro 4.00 8.00
442 Ray Narleski 2.00 4.00
443 Daryl Spencer 2.00 4.00
444 Ron Hansen RC 4.00 8.00
445 Cal McLish 2.00 4.00
446 Rocky Nelson 2.00 4.00
447 Bob Anderson 2.00 4.00
448 Vada Pinson UER 10.00 25.00
449 Tom Gorman 2.00 4.00
450 Eddie Mathews 25.00 60.00
451 Jimmy Constable RC 2.00 4.00
452 Chico Fernandez 2.00 4.00
453 Les Moss 2.00 4.00
454 Phil Clark 2.00 4.00
455 Larry Doby 10.00 25.00
456 Jerry Casale RC 2.00 4.00
457 Los Angeles Dodgers CL 15.00 30.00
458 Gordon Jones 2.00 4.00
459 Bill Tuttle 2.00 4.00
460 Bob Friend 4.00 8.00
461 Mickey Mantle BT 40.00 100.00
462 Rocky Colavito BT 6.00 12.00
463 Al Kaline BT 15.00 30.00
464 Willie Mays BT 25.00 60.00
465 Roy Sievers BT 4.00 8.00
466 Billy Pierce BT 4.00 8.00
467 Hank Aaron BT 20.00 50.00
468 Duke Snider BT 10.00 20.00
469 Ernie Banks BT 12.00 30.00
470 Stan Musial BT 15.00 30.00
471 Tom Sturdivant 2.00 4.00
472 Gene Freese 2.00 4.00
473 Mike Fornieles 2.00 4.00
474 Moe Thacker RC 2.00 4.00
475 Jack Harshman 2.00 4.00
476 Cleveland Indians CL 7.50 15.00
477 Barry Latman RC 2.00 4.00
478 Roberto Clemente UER 125.00 300.00
479 Lindy McDaniel 4.00 8.00
480 Red Schoendienst 10.00 25.00
481 Charlie Maxwell 4.00 8.00
482 Russ Meyer 2.00 4.00
483 Clint Courtney 2.00 4.00
484 Willie Kirkland 2.00 4.00
485 Ryne Duren 4.00 8.00
486 Sammy White 2.00 4.00
487 Hal Brown 2.00 4.00
488 Walt Moryn 2.00 4.00
489 John Powers 2.00 4.00
490 Frank Thomas 4.00 8.00
491 Don Blasingame 2.00 4.00
492 Gene Conley 4.00 8.00
493 Jim Landis 4.00 8.00
494 Don Pavletich RC 2.00 4.00
495 Johnny Podres 8.00 20.00
496 Wayne Terwilliger UER 2.00 4.00
497 Hal R. Smith 2.00 4.00
498 Dick Hyde 2.00 4.00
499 Johnny O'Brien 4.00 8.00
500 Vic Wertz 4.00 8.00
501 Bob Tiefenauer RC 2.00 4.00
502 Alvin Dark 4.00 8.00
503 Jim Owens 2.00 4.00
504 Ossie Alvarez RC 2.00 4.00
505 Tony Kubek 10.00 25.00
506 Bob Purkey 2.00 4.00
507 Bob Hale 7.50 15.00
508 Art Fowler 7.50 15.00
509 Norm Cash RC 30.00 80.00
510 New York Yankees CL 50.00 120.00
511 George Susce 7.50 15.00
512 George Altman RC 7.50 15.00
513 Tommy Carroll 7.50 15.00
514 Bob Gibson RC 600.00 1200.00
515 Harmon Killebrew 40.00 100.00
516 Mike Garcia 10.00 20.00
517 Joe Koppe RC 7.50 15.00
518 Mike Cueller UER RC 15.00 40.00
Sic, Cuellar
519 Runnels/Gernert/Malzone 10.00 20.00
520 Don Elston 7.50 15.00
521 Gary Geiger 7.50 15.00
522 Gene Snyder RC 7.50 15.00
523 Harry Bright RC 7.50 15.00
524 Larry Osborne RC 7.50 15.00
525 Jim Coates RC 10.00 20.00
526 Bob Speake 7.50 15.00
527 Solly Hemus 7.50 15.00
528 Pittsburgh Pirates CL 50.00 80.00
529 George Bamberger RC 10.00 20.00
530 Wally Moon 10.00 20.00
531 Ray Webster RC 7.50 15.00
532 Mark Freeman RC 7.50 15.00
533 Darrell Johnson 10.00 20.00
534 Faye Throneberry 7.50 15.00
535 Ruben Gomez 7.50 15.00
536 Danny Kravitz 7.50 15.00
537 Rudolph Arias RC 7.50 15.00
538 Chick King 7.50 15.00
539 Gary Blaylock RC 7.50 15.00
540 Willie Miranda 7.50 15.00
541 Bob Thurman 7.50 15.00
542 Jim Perry RC 12.00 30.00
543 Skinner/Virdon/Clemente 25.00 60.00
544 Lee Tate RC 7.50 15.00
545 Tom Morgan 7.50 15.00
546 Al Schroll 7.50 15.00
547 Jim Baxes RC 7.50 15.00
548 Elmer Singleton 7.50 15.00
549 Howie Nunn RC 7.50 15.00
550 R.Campanella Courage 40.00 100.00
551 Fred Haney AS MG 7.50 15.00
552 Casey Stengel AS MG 18.00 30.00
553 Orlando Cepeda AS 18.00 30.00
554 Bill Skowron AS 10.00 20.00
555 Bill Mazeroski AS 15.00 40.00
556 Nellie Fox AS 20.00 40.00
557 Ken Boyer AS 18.00 30.00
558 Frank Malzone AS 7.50 15.00
559 Ernie Banks AS 25.00 60.00
560 Luis Aparicio AS 25.00 40.00
561 Hank Aaron AS 40.00 100.00
562 Al Kaline AS 20.00 50.00
563 Willie Mays AS 40.00 100.00
564 Mickey Mantle AS 125.00 300.00
565 Wes Covington AS 10.00 20.00
566 Roy Sievers AS 7.50 15.00
567 Del Crandall AS 7.50 15.00
568 Gus Triandos AS 7.50 15.00
569 Bob Friend AS 7.50 15.00
570 Bob Turley AS 7.50 15.00
571 Warren Spahn AS 30.00 50.00
572 Billy Pierce AS 25.00 40.00

1960 Topps

The cards in this 572-card set measure 2 1/2" by 3 1/2". The 1960 Topps set is the first Topps standard size issue to use a horizontally oriented front. World Series cards appeared for the first time (385 to 391), and there is a Rookie Prospect (RP) series (117-148), the most famous of which is Carl Yastrzemski, and a Sport Magazine All-Star Selection (AS) series (553-572). There are 16 manager cards listed alphabetically from 212 through 227. The 1959 Topps All-Rookie team is featured on cards 316-325. This was the first time the Topps All-Rookie team was ever selected and the only time that all of the cards were placed together in a subset. The coaching staff of each team was also afforded their own card in a 16-card subset (455-470). There is no price differential for either color back. The high series (507-572) were printed on a more limited basis than the rest of the set. The team cards have series checklists on the reverse. Cards were issued in one-card penny packs, six-card nickel packs (which came 24 to a box), 10 cent cello packs (which came 36 packs to a box) and 36-card rack packs which cost 29 cents . Three card ad-sheets have been seen. One such sheet features Wayne Terwilliger, Kent Hadley and Faye Throneberry on the front with Gene Woodling and an Ad on the back. Another sheet featured Hank Foiles/Hobie Landrith and Hal Smith on the front. The key Rookie Cards in this set are Jim Kaat, Willie McCovey and Carl Yastrzemski. Recently, a Kent Hadley was discovered with a Kansas City A's logo on the front, while this card was rumoured to exist for years, this is the first known spotting of the card. According the published reports at the time, seven copies of the Hadley card, along with the Gino Cimoli and the Faye Throneberry cards were produced. Each series of this set had different card backs. Cards numbered 1-110 had cream colored white back, cards numbered 111-198 had grey backs, cards number 119-286 had cream colored white backs, cards numbered 287-

COMPLETE SET (572) 2500.00 6000.00
COMMON CARD (1-440) 1.50 4.00
COMMON CARD (441-506) 3.00 8.00
COMMON CARD (507-572) 6.00 15.00
WRAPPER (1-CENT) 500.00 1000.00
WRAP. (1-CENT REPEAT) 250.00 500.00
WRAPPER (5-CENT) 15.00 40.00
1 Early Wynn 20.00 50.00
2 Roman Mejias 1.50 4.00
3 Joe Adcock 2.50 6.00
4 Bob Purkey 1.50 4.00
5 Wally Moon 2.50 6.00
6 Lou Berberet 1.50 4.00
7 W.Mays/B.Rigney 12.00 30.00
8 Bud Daley 1.50 4.00
9 Faye Throneberry 1.50 4.00
9A Faye Throneberry
10 Ernie Banks 40.00 100.00
11 Norm Siebern 1.50 4.00
12 Milt Pappas 2.50 6.00
13 Wally Post 2.50 6.00
14 Jim Grant 2.50 6.00
15 Pete Runnels 2.50 6.00
16 Ernie Broglio 2.50 6.00
17 Johnny Callison 2.50 6.00
18 Los Angeles Dodgers CL 20.00 50.00
19 Felix Mantilla 1.50 4.00
20 Roy Face 2.50 6.00
21 Dutch Dotterer 1.50 4.00
22 Rocky Bridges 1.50 4.00
23 Eddie Fisher RC 1.50 4.00
24 Dick Gray 1.50 4.00
25 Roy Sievers 2.50 6.00
26 Wayne Terwilliger 1.50 4.00
27 Dick Drott 1.50 4.00
28 Brooks Robinson 25.00 60.00
29 Clem Labine 2.50 6.00
30 Tito Francona 1.50 4.00
31 Sammy Esposito 1.50 4.00
32 J.O'Toole/V.Pinson 1.50 4.00
33 Tom Morgan 1.50 4.00
34 Sparky Anderson 6.00 15.00
35 Whitey Ford 30.00 80.00
36 Russ Nixon 1.50 4.00
37 Bill Bruton 1.50 4.00
38 Jerry Casale 1.50 4.00
39 Earl Averill Jr. 1.50 4.00
40 Joe Cunningham 1.50 4.00
41 Barry Latman 1.50 4.00
42 Hobie Landrith 1.50 4.00
43 Washington Senators CL 4.00 10.00
44 Bobby Locke RC 1.50 4.00
45 Roy McMillan 2.50 6.00
46 Jack Fisher RC 1.50 4.00
47 Don Zimmer 2.50 6.00
48 Hal W. Smith 1.50 4.00
49 Curt Raydon 1.50 4.00
50 Al Kaline 25.00 60.00
51 Jim Coates 2.50 6.00
52 Dave Philley 1.50 4.00
53 Jackie Brandt 1.50 4.00
54 Mike Fornieles 1.50 4.00
55 Bill Mazeroski 15.00 40.00
56 Steve Korcheck 1.50 4.00
57 T.Lown/G.Staley 1.50 4.00
58 Gino Cimoli 1.50 4.00
58A Gino Cimoli Cards
59 Juan Pizarro 1.50 4.00
60 Gus Triandos 2.50 6.00
61 Eddie Kasko 1.50 4.00
62 Roger Craig 2.50 6.00
63 George Strickland 1.50 4.00
64 Jack Meyer 1.50 4.00
65 Elston Howard 2.50 6.00
66 Bob Trowbridge 1.50 4.00
67 Jose Pagan RC 1.50 4.00
68 Dave Hillman 1.50 4.00
69 Billy Goodman 2.50 6.00
70 Lew Burdette UER 2.50 6.00
71 Marty Keough 1.50 4.00
72 Detroit Tigers CL 10.00 25.00

73 Bob Gibson 40.00 100.00
74 Walt Moryn 1.50 4.00
75 Vic Power 2.50 6.00
76 Bill Fischer 1.50 4.00
77 Hank Foiles 1.50 4.00
78 Bob Grim 1.50 4.00
79 Walt Dropo 1.50 4.00
80 Johnny Antonelli 2.50 6.00
81 Russ Snyder RC 1.50 4.00
82 Ruben Gomez 1.50 4.00
83 Tony Kubek 8.00 20.00
84 Hal R. Smith 1.50 4.00
85 Frank Lary 2.50 6.00
86 Dick Gernert 1.50 4.00
87 John Romonosky 1.50 4.00
88 John Roseboro 2.50 6.00
89 Hal Brown 1.50 4.00
90 Bobby Avila 1.50 4.00
91 Bennie Daniels 1.50 4.00
92 Whitey Herzog 2.50 6.00
93 Art Schult 1.50 4.00
94 Leo Kiely 1.50 4.00
95 Frank Thomas 2.50 6.00
96 Ralph Terry 2.50 6.00
97 Ted Lepcio 1.50 4.00
98 Gordon Jones 1.50 4.00
99 Lenny Green 1.50 4.00
100 Nellie Fox 15.00 40.00
101 Bob Miller RC 1.50 4.00
102 Kent Hadley 1.50 4.00
102A Kent Hadley A's
103 Dick Farrell 2.50 6.00
104 Dick Schofield 2.50 6.00
105 Larry Sherry RC 2.50 6.00
106 Billy Gardner 1.50 4.00
107 Carlton Willey 1.50 4.00
108 Pete Daley 1.50 4.00
109 Clete Boyer 6.00 15.00
110 Cal McLish 1.50 4.00
111 Vic Wertz 2.50 6.00
112 Jack Harshman 1.50 4.00
113 Bob Skinner 1.50 4.00
114 Ken Aspromonte 1.50 4.00
115 R.Face/H.Wilhelm 2.50 6.00
116 Jim Rivera 1.50 4.00
117 Tom Borland RS 1.50 4.00
118 Bob Bruce RS RC 1.50 4.00
119 Chico Cardenas RS RC 2.50 6.00
120 Duke Carmel RS RC 1.50 4.00
121 Camilo Carreon RS RC 1.50 4.00
122 Don Dillard RS 1.50 4.00
123 Dan Dobbek RS 1.50 4.00
124 Jim Donohue RS RC 1.50 4.00
125 Dick Ellsworth RS RC 2.50 6.00
126 Chuck Estrada RS RC 1.50 4.00
127 Ron Hansen RS 2.50 6.00
128 Bill Harris RS RC 1.50 4.00
129 Bob Hartman RS 1.50 4.00
130 Frank Herrera RS 1.50 4.00
131 Ed Hobaugh RS RC 1.50 4.00
132 Frank Howard RS RC 12.00 30.00
133 Julian Javier RS RC 2.50 6.00
134 Deron Johnson RS 2.50 6.00
135 Ken Johnson RS RC 1.50 4.00
136 Jim Kaat RS RC 30.00 80.00
137 Lou Klimchock RS RC 1.50 4.00
138 Art Mahaffey RS RC 2.50 6.00
139 Carl Mathias RS RC 1.50 4.00
140 Julio Navarro RS RC 1.50 4.00
141 Jim Proctor RS RC 1.50 4.00
142 Bill Short RS RC 1.50 4.00
143 Al Spangler RS RC 1.50 4.00
144 Al Stieglitz RS RC 1.50 4.00
145 Jim Umbricht RS RC 1.50 4.00
146 Ted Wieand RS RC 1.50 4.00
147 Bob Will RS 1.50 4.00
148 C.Yastrzemski RS RC 150.00 400.00
149 Bob Nieman 1.50 4.00
150 Billy Pierce 2.50 6.00
151 San Francisco Giants CL 4.00 10.00
152 Gail Harris 1.50 4.00
153 Bobby Thomson 6.00 15.00
154 Jim Davenport 2.50 6.00
155 Charlie Neal 2.50 6.00
156 Art Ceccarelli 1.50 4.00
157 Rocky Nelson 2.50 6.00
158 Wes Covington 2.50 6.00
159 Jim Piersall 2.50 6.00
160 M.Mantle/K.Boyer 40.00 100.00
161 Ray Narleski 1.50 4.00
162 Sammy Taylor 1.50 4.00
163 Hector Lopez 2.50 6.00
164 Cincinnati Reds CL 4.00 10.00
165 Jack Sanford 2.50 6.00
166 Chuck Essegian 1.50 4.00
167 Valmy Thomas 1.50 4.00
168 Alex Grammas 1.50 4.00
169 Jake Striker RC 1.50 4.00
170 Del Crandall 2.50 6.00
171 Johnny Groth 1.50 4.00
172 Willie Kirkland 1.50 4.00
173 Billy Martin 10.00 25.00
174 Cleveland Indians CL 4.00 10.00
175 Pedro Ramos 1.50 4.00
176 Vada Pinson 2.50 6.00
177 Johnny Kucks 1.50 4.00
178 Woody Held 1.50 4.00
179 Rip Coleman 1.50 4.00
180 Harry Simpson 1.50 4.00
181 Billy Loes 2.50 6.00
182 Glen Hobbie 1.50 4.00
183 Eli Grba RC 1.50 4.00
184 Gary Geiger 1.50 4.00
185 Jim Owens 1.50 4.00
186 Dave Sisler 1.50 4.00
187 Jay Hook RC 1.50 4.00
188 Dick Williams 2.50 6.00
189 Don McMahon 1.50 4.00
190 Gene Woodling 2.50 6.00
191 Johnny Klippstein 1.50 4.00
192 Danny O'Connell 1.50 4.00
193 Dick Hyde 1.50 4.00
194 Bobby Gene Smith 1.50 4.00
195 Lindy McDaniel 2.50 6.00
196 Andy Carey 2.50 6.00
197 Ron Kline 1.50 4.00
198 Jerry Lynch 2.50 6.00
199 Dick Donovan 2.50 6.00
200 Willie Mays 75.00 200.00
201 Larry Osborne 1.50 4.00
202 Fred Kipp 1.50 4.00
203 Sammy White 1.50 4.00
204 Ryne Duren 2.50 6.00
205 Johnny Logan 2.50 6.00
206 Claude Osteen 2.50 6.00
207 Bob Boyd 1.50 4.00
208 Chicago White Sox CL 4.00 10.00
209 Ron Blackburn 1.50 4.00
210 Harmon Killebrew 25.00 60.00
211 Taylor Phillips 1.50 4.00
212 Walter Alston MG 4.00 10.00
213 Chuck Dressen MG 2.50 6.00
214 Jimmy Dykes MG 2.50 6.00
215 Bob Elliott MG 2.50 6.00
216 Joe Gordon MG 2.50 6.00
217 Charlie Grimm MG 2.50 6.00
218 Solly Hemus MG 1.50 4.00
219 Fred Hutchinson MG 2.50 6.00
220 Billy Jurges MG 1.50 4.00
221 Cookie Lavagetto MG 1.50 4.00
222 Al Lopez MG 4.00 10.00
223 Danny Murtaugh MG 2.50 6.00
224 Paul Richards MG 2.50 6.00
225 Bill Rigney MG 1.50 4.00
226 Eddie Sawyer MG 1.50 4.00
227 Casey Stengel MG 12.00 30.00
228 Ernie Johnson 2.50 6.00
229 Joe M. Morgan RC 1.50 4.00
230 Burdette/Spahn/Buhl 4.00 10.00
231 Hal Naragon 1.50 4.00
232 Jim Busby 1.50 4.00
233 Don Elston 1.50 4.00
234 Don Demeter 1.50 4.00
235 Gus Bell 2.50 6.00
236 Dick Ricketts 1.50 4.00
237 Elmer Valo 1.50 4.00
238 Danny Kravitz 1.50 4.00
239 Joe Shipley 1.50 4.00
240 Luis Aparicio 12.00 30.00
241 Albie Pearson 2.50 6.00
242 St. Louis Cardinals CL 4.00 10.00
243 Bubba Phillips 1.50 4.00
244 Hal Griggs 1.50 4.00
245 Eddie Yost 2.50 6.00
246 Lee Maye RC 2.50 6.00
247 Gil McDougald 4.00 10.00
248 Del Rice 1.50 4.00
249 Earl Wilson RC 2.50 6.00
250 Stan Musial 50.00 120.00
251 Bob Malkmus 1.50 4.00
252 Ray Herbert 1.50 4.00
253 Eddie Bressoud 1.50 4.00
254 Arnie Portocarrero 1.50 4.00
255 Jim Gilliam 6.00 15.00
256 Dick Brown 1.50 4.00
257 Gordy Coleman RC 1.50 4.00
258 Dick Groat 2.50 6.00
259 George Altman 1.50 4.00
260 R.Colavito/T.Francona 6.00 15.00
261 Pete Burnside 1.50 4.00
262 Hank Bauer 2.50 6.00
263 Darrell Johnson 1.50 4.00
264 Robin Roberts 10.00 25.00
265 Rip Repulski 1.50 4.00
266 Joey Jay 2.50 6.00
267 Jim Marshall 1.50 4.00
268 Al Worthington 1.50 4.00
269 Gene Green 1.50 4.00
270 Bob Turley 2.50 6.00
271 Julio Becquer 1.50 4.00
272 Fred Green RC 2.50 6.00
273 Neil Chrisley 1.50 4.00
274 Tom Acker 1.50 4.00
275 Curt Flood 8.00 20.00
276 Ken McBride RC 1.50 4.00
277 Harry Bright 1.50 4.00
278 Stan Williams 2.50 6.00
279 Chuck Tanner 2.50 6.00
280 Frank Sullivan 1.50 4.00
281 Ray Boone 2.50 6.00
282 Joe Nuxhall 2.50 6.00
283 Johnny Blanchard 2.50 6.00
284 Don Gross 1.50 4.00
285 Harry Anderson 1.50 4.00
286 Ray Semproch 1.50 4.00
287 Felipe Alou 2.50 6.00
288 Bob Mabe 1.50 4.00
289 Willie Jones 1.50 4.00
290 Jerry Lumpe 1.50 4.00
291 Bob Keegan 1.50 4.00
292 J.Pignatano/J.Roseboro 2.50 6.00
293 Gene Conley 2.50 6.00
294 Tony Taylor 2.50 6.00
295 Gil Hodges 12.00 30.00
296 Nelson Chittum RC 1.50 4.00
297 Reno Bertoia 1.50 4.00
298 George Witt 1.50 4.00
299 Earl Torgeson 1.50 4.00
300 Hank Aaron 100.00 250.00
301 Jerry Davie 1.50 4.00
302 Philadelphia Phillies CL 4.00 10.00
303 Billy O'Dell 1.50 4.00
304 Joe Ginsberg 1.50 4.00
305 Richie Ashburn 12.00 30.00
306 Frank Baumann 1.50 4.00
307 Gene Oliver 1.50 4.00
308 Dick Hall 1.50 4.00
309 Bob Hale 1.50 4.00
310 Frank Malzone 2.50 6.00
311 Raul Sanchez 1.50 4.00
312 Charley Lau 2.50 6.00
313 Turk Lown 1.50 4.00
314 Chico Fernandez 1.50 4.00
315 Bobby Shantz 4.00 10.00
316 W.McCovey ASR RC 100.00 250.00
317 Pumpsie Green ASR RC 2.50 6.00
318 Jim Baxes ASR 2.50 6.00
319 Joe Koppe ASR 2.50 6.00
320 Bob Allison ASR 2.50 6.00
321 Ron Fairly ASR 2.50 6.00
322 Willie Tasby ASR 2.50 6.00
323 John Romano ASR 2.50 6.00
324 Jim Perry ASR 2.50 6.00
325 Jim O'Toole ASR 2.50 6.00
326 Roberto Clemente 100.00 250.00
327 Ray Sadecki RC 1.50 4.00
328 Earl Battey 1.50 4.00
329 Zack Monroe 1.50 4.00
330 Harvey Kuenn 2.50 6.00
331 Henry Mason RC 1.50 4.00
332 New York Yankees CL 20.00 50.00
333 Danny McDevitt 1.50 4.00
334 Ted Abernathy 1.50 4.00
335 Red Schoendienst 10.00 25.00
336 Ike Delock 1.50 4.00
337 Cal Neeman 1.50 4.00
338 Ray Monzant 1.50 4.00
339 Harry Chiti 1.50 4.00
340 Harvey Haddix 2.50 6.00
341 Carroll Hardy 1.50 4.00
342 Casey Wise 1.50 4.00
343 Sandy Koufax 60.00 150.00
344 Clint Courtney 1.50 4.00
345 Don Newcombe 2.50 6.00
346 J.C. Martin UER RC 2.50 6.00
347 Ed Bouchee 1.50 4.00
348 Barry Shetrone RC 1.50 4.00
349 Moe Drabowsky 2.50 6.00
350 Mickey Mantle 500.00 1000.00
351 Don Nottebart RC 1.50 4.00
352 Bell/F.Robinson/Lynch 4.00 10.00
353 Don Larsen 10.00 25.00
354 Bob Lillis 1.50 4.00
355 Bill White 2.50 6.00
356 Joe Amalfitano 1.50 4.00
357 Al Schroll 1.50 4.00
358 Joe DeMaestri 1.50 4.00
359 Buddy Gilbert RC 1.50 4.00
360 Herb Score 2.50 6.00
361 Bob Oldis 2.50 6.00
362 Russ Kemmerer 1.50 4.00
363 Gene Stephens 1.50 4.00
364 Paul Foytack 1.50 4.00
365 Minnie Minoso 10.00 25.00
366 Dallas Green RC 4.00 10.00
367 Bill Tuttle 1.50 4.00
368 Daryl Spencer 1.50 4.00
369 Billy Hoeft 1.50 4.00
370 Bill Skowron 4.00 10.00
371 Bud Byerly 1.50 4.00
372 Frank House 1.50 4.00
373 Don Hoak 2.50 6.00
374 Bob Buhl 2.50 6.00
375 Dale Long 4.00 10.00
376 John Briggs 1.50 4.00
377 Roger Maris 50.00 100.00
378 Stu Miller 2.50 6.00
379 Red Wilson 1.50 4.00
380 Bob Shaw 1.50 4.00
381 Milwaukee Braves CL 4.00 10.00
382 Ted Bowsfield 1.50 4.00
383 Leon Wagner 1.50 4.00
384 Don Cardwell 1.50 4.00
385 Charlie Neal WS1 3.00 8.00
386 Charlie Neal WS2 3.00 8.00
387 Carl Furillo WS3 3.00 8.00
388 Gil Hodges WS4 5.00 12.00
389 L.Aparicio WS5 w/M.Wills 4.00 10.00
390 Scrambling After Ball WS6 3.00 8.00
391 Champs Celebrate WS 3.00 8.00
392 Tex Clevenger 1.50 4.00
393 Smoky Burgess 2.50 6.00
394 Norm Larker 2.50 6.00
395 Hoyt Wilhelm 8.00 20.00
396 Steve Bilko 1.50 4.00
397 Don Blasingame 1.50 4.00
398 Mike Cuellar 2.50 6.00
399 Pappas/Fisher/Walker 2.50 6.00
400 Rocky Colavito 8.00 20.00
401 Bob Duliba RC 1.50 4.00
402 Dick Stuart 6.00 15.00
403 Ed Sadowski 1.50 4.00
404 Bob Rush 1.50 4.00
405 Bobby Richardson 10.00 25.00
406 Billy Klaus 1.50 4.00
407 Gary Peters UER RC 2.50 6.00
408 Carl Furillo 4.00 10.00
409 Ron Samford 1.50 4.00
410 Sam Jones 2.50 6.00
411 Ed Bailey 1.50 4.00
412 Bob Anderson 1.50 4.00
413 Kansas City Athletics CL 4.00 10.00
414 Don Williams RC 1.50 4.00
415 Bob Cerv 1.50 4.00
416 Humberto Robinson 1.50 4.00
417 Chuck Cottier RC 1.50 4.00
418 Don Mossi 2.50 6.00
419 George Crowe 1.50 4.00
420 Eddie Mathews 20.00 50.00
421 Duke Maas 1.50 4.00
422 John Powers 1.50 4.00
423 Ed Fitzgerald 1.50 4.00
424 Pete Whisenant 1.50 4.00
425 Johnny Podres 2.50 6.00
426 Ron Jackson 1.50 4.00
427 Al Grunwald RC 1.50 4.00
428 Al Smith 1.50 4.00
429 Nellie Fox/H.Kuenn 4.00 10.00
430 Art Ditmar 1.50 4.00
431 Andre Rodgers 1.50 4.00
432 Chuck Stobbs 1.50 4.00
433 Irv Noren 1.50 4.00
434 Brooks Lawrence 2.50 6.00
435 Gene Freese 1.50 4.00
436 Marv Throneberry 2.50 6.00
437 Bob Friend 2.50 6.00
438 Jim Coker RC 1.50 4.00
439 Tom Brewer 1.50 4.00
440 Jim Lemon 2.50 6.00
441 Gary Bell 4.00 10.00
442 Joe Pignatano 3.00 8.00
443 Charlie Maxwell 3.00 8.00
444 Jerry Kindall 3.00 8.00
445 Warren Spahn 30.00 80.00
446 Ellis Burton 3.00 8.00
447 Ray Moore 3.00 8.00
448 Jim Gentile RC 8.00 20.00
449 Jim Brosnan 3.00 8.00
450 Orlando Cepeda 30.00 80.00
451 Curt Simmons 3.00 8.00
452 Ray Webster 3.00 8.00
453 Vern Law 10.00 25.00
454 Hal Woodeshick 3.00 8.00
455 Baltimore Coaches 3.00 8.00
456 Red Sox Coaches 4.00 10.00
457 Cubs Coaches 3.00 8.00
458 White Sox Coaches 3.00 8.00
459 Reds Coaches 3.00 8.00
460 Indians Coaches 6.00 15.00
461 Tigers Coaches 4.00 10.00
462 Athletics Coaches 3.00 8.00
463 Dodgers Coaches 3.00 8.00
464 Braves Coaches 3.00 8.00
465 Yankees Coaches 10.00 25.00
466 Phillies Coaches 3.00 8.00
467 Pirates Coaches 3.00 8.00
468 Cardinals Coaches 3.00 8.00
469 Giants Coaches 3.00 8.00
470 Senators Coaches 3.00 8.00
471 Ned Garver 3.00 8.00
472 Alvin Dark 3.00 8.00
473 Al Cicotte 3.00 8.00
474 Haywood Sullivan 3.00 8.00
475 Don Drysdale 25.00 60.00
476 Lou Johnson RC 3.00 8.00
477 Don Ferrarese 3.00 8.00
478 Frank Torre 3.00 8.00
479 Georges Maranda RC 3.00 8.00
480 Yogi Berra 50.00 120.00
481 Wes Stock RC 3.00 8.00
482 Frank Bolling 3.00 8.00
483 Camilo Pascual 3.00 8.00
484 Pittsburgh Pirates CL 15.00 40.00
485 Ken Boyer 6.00 15.00
486 Bobby Del Greco 3.00 8.00
487 Tom Sturdivant 3.00 8.00
488 Norm Cash 10.00 25.00
489 Steve Ridzik 3.00 8.00
490 Frank Robinson 25.00 60.00
491 Mel Roach 3.00 8.00
492 Larry Jackson 3.00 8.00
493 Duke Snider 25.00 60.00
494 Baltimore Orioles CL 10.00 25.00
495 Sherm Lollar 3.00 8.00
496 Bill Virdon 4.00 10.00
497 John Tsitouris 3.00 8.00
498 Al Pilarcik 3.00 8.00
499 Johnny James RC 4.00 10.00
500 Johnny Temple 3.00 8.00
501 Bob Schmidt 3.00 8.00
502 Jim Bunning 20.00 50.00
503 Don Lee 3.00 8.00
504 Seth Morehead 3.00 8.00
505 Ted Kluszewski 10.00 25.00
506 Lee Walls 3.00 8.00
507 Dick Stigman 6.00 15.00
508 Billy Consolo 6.00 15.00
509 Tommy Davis RC 20.00 50.00
510 Gerry Staley 6.00 15.00
511 Ken Walters RC 6.00 15.00
512 Joe Gibbon RC 6.00 15.00
513 Chicago Cubs CL 12.50 30.00
514 Steve Barber RC 6.00 15.00
515 Stan Lopata 6.00 15.00
516 Marty Kutyna RC 6.00 15.00
517 Charlie James RC 10.00 25.00
518 Tony Gonzalez RC 6.00 15.00
519 Ed Roebuck 6.00 15.00
520 Don Buddin 6.00 15.00
521 Mike Lee RC 6.00 15.00
522 Ken Hunt RC 12.50 30.00
523 Clay Dalrymple RC 6.00 15.00
524 Bill Henry 6.00 15.00
525 Marv Breeding RC 6.00 15.00
526 Paul Giel 10.00 25.00
527 Jose Valdivielso 10.00 25.00
528 Ben Johnson RC 6.00 15.00
529 Norm Sherry RC 8.00 20.00
530 Mike McCormick 6.00 15.00
531 Sandy Amoros 10.00 25.00
532 Mike Garcia 8.00 20.00
533 Lu Clinton RC 6.00 15.00
534 Ken MacKenzie RC 6.00 15.00
535 Whitey Lockman 6.00 15.00
536 Wynn Hawkins RC 6.00 15.00
537 Boston Red Sox CL 12.50 30.00
538 Frank Barnes RC 6.00 15.00
539 Gene Baker 6.00 15.00
540 Jerry Walker 6.00 15.00
541 Tony Curry RC 6.00 15.00
542 Ken Hamlin RC 6.00 15.00
543 Elio Chacon RC 6.00 15.00
544 Bill Monbouquette 8.00 20.00
545 Carl Sawatski 6.00 15.00
546 Hank Aguirre 6.00 15.00
547 Bob Aspromonte RC 8.00 20.00
548 Don Mincher RC 6.00 15.00
549 John Buzhardt 6.00 15.00
550 Jim Landis 6.00 15.00
551 Ed Rakow RC 6.00 15.00
552 Walt Bond RC 6.00 15.00
553 Bill Skowron AS 8.00 20.00
554 Willie McCovey AS 30.00 80.00
555 Nellie Fox AS 10.00 25.00
556 Charlie Neal AS 6.00 15.00
557 Frank Malzone AS 6.00 15.00
558 Eddie Mathews AS 15.00 40.00
559 Luis Aparicio AS 12.50 30.00
560 Ernie Banks AS 30.00 80.00
561 Al Kaline AS 20.00 50.00
562 Joe Cunningham AS 6.00 15.00
563 Mickey Mantle AS 125.00 300.00
564 Willie Mays AS 50.00 120.00
565 Roger Maris AS 50.00 100.00
566 Hank Aaron AS 40.00 100.00
567 Sherm Lollar AS 6.00 15.00
568 Del Crandall AS 6.00 15.00
569 Camilo Pascual AS 6.00 15.00
570 Don Drysdale AS 25.00 60.00
571 Billy Pierce AS 6.00 15.00
572 Johnny Antonelli AS 12.50 30.00
NNO Iron-On Team Transfer

1961 Topps

The cards in this 587-card set measure 2 1/2" by 3 1/2". In 1961, Topps returned to the vertical obverse format. Introduced for the first time were "League Leaders" (41-50) and separate, numbered checklist cards. Two number 463s exist: the Braves team card carrying that number was meant to be number 426. There are three versions of the second series checklist card number 98; the variations are distinguished by the color of the "CHECKLIST" headline on the front of the card, the color of the printing of the card number on the bottom of the reverse, and the presence of the copyright notice running vertically on the card back. There are two groups of managers (131-139/219-226) as well as separate subsets of World Series cards (306-313), Baseball Thrills (401-410), MVP's of the 1950's (AL 471-478/NL 479-486) and Sporting News All-Stars (566-589). The usual last series scarcity (523-589) exists. Some collectors believe that 61 high numbers are the toughest of all the Topps hi series numbers. The set actually totals 587 cards since numbers 587 and 588 were never issued. These card advertising promos have been seen: Dan Dobbek/Russ Nixon/60 NL Pitching Leaders on the front along with an ad and Roger Maris on the back.Other strips feature Jack Kralick/Dick Stigman/Joe Christopher; Ed Roebuck/Bob Schmidt/Zoilo Versalles; Lindy (McDaniel) Shows Larry (Jackson)/John Blanchard/Johnny Kucks. Cards were issued in one-card penny packs, five-card nickel packs, 10 cent cello packs (which came 36 to a box) and 36-card rack packs which cost 29 cents. The one card packs came 120 to a box. The key Rookie Cards in this set are Juan Marichal, Ron Santo and Billy Williams.

COMPLETE SET (587) 2500.00 6000.00
COMMON CARD (1-370) 1.25 3.00
COMMON CARD (371-446) 1.50 4.00
COMMON CARD (447-522) 3.00 8.00
COMMON CARD (523-589) 12.50 30.00
NOT ISSUED (587/588)
WRAPPER (1-CENT) 100.00 200.00
WRAP.(1-CENT, REPEAT) 50.00 100.00
WRAPPER (5-CENT) 15.00 40.00
1 Dick Groat 12.00 30.00
2 Roger Maris 60.00 150.00
3 John Buzhardt 1.25 3.00
4 Lenny Green 1.25 3.00
5 John Romano 1.25 3.00
6 Ed Roebuck 1.25 3.00
7 Chicago White Sox TC 3.00 8.00
8 Dick Williams UER 2.50 6.00
Blurb states career high in RBI, however his career high in RBI was in 1959
9 Bob Purkey 1.25 3.00
10 Brooks Robinson 15.00 40.00
11 Curt Simmons 2.50 6.00
12 Moe Thacker 1.25 3.00
13 Chuck Cottier 1.25 3.00
14 Don Mossi 2.50 6.00
15 Willie Kirkland 1.25 3.00
16 Billy Muffett 1.25 3.00
17 Checklist 1 4.00 10.00
18 Jim Grant 2.50 6.00
19 Clete Boyer 3.00 8.00
20 Robin Roberts 8.00 20.00
21 Zoilo Versalles UER RC 3.00 8.00
22 Clem Labine 2.50 6.00
23 Don Demeter 1.25 3.00
24 Ken Johnson 2.50 6.00
25 Pinson/Bell/F.Robinson 3.00 8.00
26 Wes Stock 1.25 3.00
27 Jerry Kindall 1.25 3.00
28 Hector Lopez 2.50 6.00
29 Don Nottebart 1.25 3.00
30 Nellie Fox 10.00 25.00
31 Bob Schmidt 1.25 3.00
32 Ray Sadecki 1.25 3.00
33 Gary Geiger 1.25 3.00
34 Wynn Hawkins 1.25 3.00
35 Ron Santo RC 40.00 100.00
36 Jack Kralick RC 1.25 3.00
37 Charley Maxwell 2.50 6.00
38 Bob Lillis 1.25 3.00
39 Leo Posada RC 1.25 3.00
40 Bob Turley 2.50 6.00
41 Groat/Mays/Clemente LL 10.00 25.00
42 Runnels/Minoso/Skow LL 3.00 8.00
43 Banks/Aaron/Mathews LL 10.00 25.00
44 Mante/Maris/Colavito LL 25.00 60.00
45 McCormick/Drysdale LL 3.00 8.00
46 Baumann/Bunning/Dit LL 3.00 8.00
47 Broglio/Spahn/Burdette LL 3.00 8.00
48 Estrada/Perry/Daley LL 3.00 8.00
49 Drysdale/Koufax LL 8.00 20.00
50 Bunning/Ramos/Wynn LL 3.00 8.00
51 Detroit Tigers TC 3.00 8.00
52 George Crowe 1.25 3.00
53 Russ Nixon 1.25 3.00
54 Earl Francis RC 1.25 3.00
55 Jim Davenport 2.50 6.00
56 Russ Kemmerer 1.25 3.00
57 Marv Throneberry 2.50 6.00
58 Joe Schaffernoth RC 1.25 3.00
59 Jim Woods 1.25 3.00
60 Woody Held 1.25 3.00
61 Ron Piche RC 1.25 3.00
62 Al Pilarcik 1.25 3.00
63 Jim Kaat 3.00 8.00
64 Alex Grammas 1.25 3.00
65 Ted Kluszewski 3.00 8.00
66 Bill Henry 1.25 3.00
67 Ossie Virgil 1.25 3.00
68 Deron Johnson 2.50 6.00
69 Earl Wilson 2.50 6.00
70 Bill Virdon 2.50 6.00
71 Jerry Adair 1.25 3.00
72 Stu Miller 2.50 6.00
73 Al Spangler 1.25 3.00
74 Joe Pignatano 1.25 3.00
75 L.McDaniel/L.Jackson 2.50 6.00
76 Harry Anderson 1.25 3.00
77 Dick Stigman 1.25 3.00
78 Lee Walls 2.50 6.00
79 Joe Ginsberg 1.25 3.00
80 Harmon Killebrew 12.00 30.00
81 Tracy Stallard RC 1.25 3.00
82 Joe Christopher RC 1.25 3.00
83 Bob Bruce 1.25 3.00
84 Lee Maye 1.25 3.00
85 Jerry Walker 1.25 3.00
86 Los Angeles Dodgers TC 3.00 8.00
87 Joe Amalfitano 1.25 3.00
88 Richie Ashburn 6.00 15.00
89 Billy Martin 10.00 25.00
90 Gerry Staley 1.25 3.00
91 Walt Moryn 1.25 3.00
92 Hal Naragon 1.25 3.00
93 Tony Gonzalez 1.25 3.00
94 Johnny Kucks 1.25 3.00
95 Norm Cash 3.00 8.00
96 Billy O'Dell 1.25 3.00
97 Jerry Lynch 2.50 6.00
98A Checklist 2 Red 4.00 10.00
98B Checklist 2 Yellow B/W 4.00 10.00
98C Checklist 2 Yellow W/B 4.00 10.00
99 Don Buddin UER 1.25 3.00
100 Harvey Haddix 2.50 6.00
101 Bubba Phillips 1.25 3.00
102 Gene Stephens 1.25 3.00
103 Ruben Amaro 1.25 3.00
104 John Blanchard 3.00 8.00
105 Carl Willey 1.25 3.00
106 Whitey Herzog 1.25 3.00
107 Seth Morehead 1.25 3.00
108 Dan Dobbek 1.25 3.00
109 Johnny Podres 3.00 8.00
110 Vada Pinson 3.00 8.00
111 Jack Meyer 1.25 3.00
112 Chico Fernandez 1.25 3.00
113 Mike Fornieles 1.25 3.00
114 Hobie Landrith 1.25 3.00
115 Johnny Antonelli 2.50 6.00
116 Joe DeMaestri 1.25 3.00
117 Dale Long 2.50 6.00
118 Chris Cannizzaro RC 1.25 3.00
119 Siebern/Bauer/Lumpe 2.50 6.00
120 Eddie Mathews 12.50 30.00
121 Eli Grba 2.50 6.00
122 Chicago Cubs TC 3.00 8.00
123 Billy Gardner 1.25 3.00
124 J.C. Martin 1.25 3.00
125 Steve Barber 1.25 3.00
126 Dick Stuart 2.50 6.00
127 Ron Kline 1.25 3.00
128 Rip Repulski 1.25 3.00
129 Ed Hobaugh 1.25 3.00
130 Norm Larker 1.25 3.00
131 Paul Richards MG 2.50 6.00
132 Al Lopez MG 3.00 8.00
133 Ralph Houk MG 2.50 6.00
134 Mickey Vernon MG 2.50 6.00
135 Fred Hutchinson MG 2.50 6.00
136 Walter Alston MG 3.00 8.00
137 Chuck Dressen MG 2.50 6.00
138 Danny Murtaugh MG 2.50 6.00
139 Solly Hemus MG 2.50 6.00
140 Gus Triandos 2.50 6.00
141 Billy Williams RC 40.00 100.00
142 Luis Arroyo 2.50 6.00
143 Russ Snyder 1.25 3.00
144 Jim Coker 1.25 3.00
145 Bob Buhl 2.50 6.00
146 Marty Keough 1.25 3.00
147 Ed Rakow 1.25 3.00
148 Julian Javier 2.50 6.00
149 Bob Oldis 1.25 3.00
150 Willie Mays 40.00 100.00
151 Jim Donohue 1.25 3.00
152 Earl Torgeson 1.25 3.00
153 Don Lee 1.25 3.00
154 Bobby Del Greco 1.25 3.00
155 Johnny Temple 2.50 6.00
156 Ken Hunt 2.50 6.00
157 Cal McLish 1.25 3.00
158 Pete Daley 1.25 3.00
159 Baltimore Orioles TC 3.00 8.00
160 Whitey Ford UER 20.00 50.00
161 Sherman Jones UER RC 1.25 3.00
162 Jay Hook 1.25 3.00
163 Ed Sadowski 1.25 3.00
164 Felix Mantilla 1.25 3.00
165 Gino Cimoli 1.25 3.00
166 Danny Kravitz 1.25 3.00
167 San Francisco Giants TC 3.00 8.00
168 Tommy Davis 3.00 8.00
169 Don Elston 1.25 3.00
170 Al Smith 1.25 3.00
171 Paul Foytack 1.25 3.00
172 Don Dillard 1.25 3.00
173 Malzone/Wertz/Jensen 2.50 6.00
174 Ray Semproch 1.25 3.00
175 Gene Freese 1.25 3.00
176 Ken Aspromonte 1.25 3.00
177 Don Larsen 2.50 6.00
178 Bob Nieman 1.25 3.00
179 Joe Koppe 1.25 3.00
180 Bobby Richardson 8.00 20.00
181 Fred Green 1.25 3.00
182 Dave Nicholson RC 1.25 3.00
183 Andre Rodgers 1.25 3.00
184 Steve Bilko 2.50 6.00
185 Herb Score 2.50 6.00
186 Elmer Valo 2.50 6.00
187 Billy Klaus 1.25 3.00
188 Jim Marshall 1.25 3.00
189A Checklist 3 Copyright 263 4.00 10.00
189B Checklist 3 Copyright 264 4.00 10.00
190 Stan Williams 2.50 6.00
191 Mike de la Hoz RC 1.25 3.00
192 Dick Brown 1.25 3.00
193 Gene Conley 2.50 6.00
194 Gordy Coleman 2.50 6.00
195 Jerry Casale 1.25 3.00
196 Ed Bouchee 1.25 3.00
197 Dick Hall 1.25 3.00
198 Carl Sawatski 1.25 3.00
199 Bob Boyd 1.25 3.00
200 Warren Spahn 15.00 40.00
201 Pete Whisenant 1.25 3.00
202 Al Neiger RC 1.25 3.00
203 Eddie Bressoud 1.25 3.00
204 Bob Skinner 2.50 6.00
205 Billy Pierce 2.50 6.00
206 Gene Green 1.25 3.00
207 S.Koufax/J.Podres 15.00 40.00
208 Larry Osborne 1.25 3.00
209 Ken McBride 1.25 3.00
210 Pete Runnels 2.50 6.00
211 Bob Gibson 25.00 60.00
212 Haywood Sullivan 2.50 6.00
213 Bill Stafford RC 1.25 3.00
214 Danny Murphy RC 2.50 6.00
215 Gus Bell 2.50 6.00
216 Ted Bowsfield 1.25 3.00
217 Mel Roach 1.25 3.00
218 Hal Brown 1.25 3.00
219 Gene Mauch MG 2.50 6.00
220 Alvin Dark MG 2.50 6.00
221 Mike Higgins MG 1.25 3.00
222 Jimmy Dykes MG 2.50 6.00
223 Bob Scheffing MG 1.25 3.00
224 Joe Gordon MG 2.50 6.00
225 Bill Rigney MG 2.50 6.00
226 Cookie Lavagetto MG 2.50 6.00
227 Juan Pizarro 1.25 3.00
228 New York Yankees TC 20.00 50.00

229 Rudy Hernandez RC 1.25 3.00
230 Don Hoak 2.50 6.00
231 Dick Drott 1.25 3.00
232 Bill White 2.50 6.00
233 Joey Jay 2.50 6.00
234 Ted Lepcio 1.25 3.00
235 Camilo Pascual 2.50 6.00
236 Don Gile RC 1.25 3.00
237 Billy Loes 2.50 6.00
238 Jim Gilliam 2.50 6.00
239 Dave Sisler 1.25 3.00
240 Ron Hansen 1.25 3.00
241 Al Cicotte 1.25 3.00
242 Hal Smith 1.25 3.00
243 Frank Lary 2.50 6.00
244 Chico Cardenas 2.50 6.00
245 Joe Adcock 2.50 6.00
246 Bob Davis RC 1.25 3.00
247 Billy Goodman 2.50 6.00
248 Ed Keegan RC 1.25 3.00
249 Cincinnati Reds TC 3.00 8.00
250 V.Law/R.Face 2.50 6.00
251 Bill Bruton 1.25 3.00
252 Bill Short 1.25 3.00
253 Sammy Taylor 1.25 3.00
254 Ted Sadowski RC 2.50 6.00
255 Vic Power 2.50 6.00
256 Billy Hoeft 1.25 3.00
257 Carroll Hardy 1.25 3.00
258 Jack Sanford 2.50 6.00
259 John Schaive RC 1.25 3.00
260 Don Drysdale 15.00 40.00
261 Charlie Lau 2.50 6.00
262 Tony Curry 1.25 3.00
263 Ken Hamlin 1.25 3.00
264 Glen Hobbie 1.25 3.00
265 Tony Kubek 5.00 12.00
266 Lindy McDaniel 2.50 6.00
267 Norm Siebern 1.25 3.00
268 Ike Delock 1.25 3.00
269 Harry Chiti 1.25 3.00
270 Bob Friend 2.50 6.00
271 Jim Landis 1.25 3.00
272 Tom Morgan 1.25 3.00
273A Checklist 4 Copyright 336 6.00 15.00
273B Checklist 4 Copyright 339 4.00 10.00
274 Gary Bell 1.25 3.00
275 Gene Woodling 2.50 6.00
276 Ray Rippelmeyer RC 1.25 3.00
277 Hank Foiles 1.25 3.00
278 Don McMahon 1.25 3.00
279 Jose Pagan 1.25 3.00
280 Frank Howard 3.00 8.00
281 Frank Sullivan 1.25 3.00
282 Faye Throneberry 1.25 3.00
283 Bob Anderson 1.25 3.00
284 Dick Gernert 1.25 3.00
285 Sherm Lollar 2.50 6.00
286 George Witt 1.25 3.00
287 Carl Yastrzemski 60.00 150.00
288 Albie Pearson 2.50 6.00
289 Ray Moore 1.25 3.00
290 Stan Musial 40.00 100.00
291 Tex Clevenger 1.25 3.00
292 Jim Baumer RC 1.25 3.00
293 Tom Sturdivant 1.25 3.00
294 Don Blasingame 1.25 3.00
295 Milt Pappas 2.50 6.00
296 Wes Covington 2.50 6.00
297 Kansas City Athletics TC 3.00 8.00
298 Jim Golden RC 1.25 3.00
299 Clay Dalrymple 1.25 3.00
300 Mickey Mantle 300.00 600.00
301 Chet Nichols 1.25 3.00
302 Al Heist RC 1.25 3.00
303 Gary Peters 2.50 6.00
304 Rocky Nelson 1.25 3.00
305 Mike McCormick 2.50 6.00
306 Bill Virdon WS1 4.00 10.00
307 Mickey Mantle WS2 40.00 100.00
308 Bobby Richardson WS3 5.00 12.00
309 Gino Cimoli WS4 4.00 10.00
310 Roy Face WS5 4.00 10.00
311 Whitey Ford WS6 6.00 15.00
312 Bill Mazeroski WS7 20.00 50.00
313 Pirates Celebrate WS 6.00 15.00
314 Bob Miller 1.25 3.00
315 Earl Battey 2.50 6.00
316 Bobby Gene Smith 1.25 3.00
317 Jim Brewer RC 1.25 3.00
318 Danny O'Connell 1.25 3.00
319 Valmy Thomas 1.25 3.00
320 Lou Burdette 2.50 6.00
321 Marv Breeding 1.25 3.00
322 Bill Kunkel RC 2.50 6.00
323 Sammy Esposito 1.25 3.00
324 Hank Aguirre 1.25 3.00
325 Wally Moon 2.50 6.00
326 Dave Hillman 1.25 3.00
327 Matty Alou RC 8.00 20.00
328 Jim O'Toole 2.50 6.00
329 Julio Becquer 1.25 3.00
330 Rocky Colavito 8.00 20.00
331 Ned Garver 1.25 3.00
332 Dutch Dotterer UER 1.25 3.00
333 Fritz Brickell RC 1.25 3.00
334 Walt Bond 1.25 3.00
335 Frank Bolling 1.25 3.00
336 Don Mincher 2.50 6.00
337 Wynn/Lopez/Score 3.00 8.00
338 Don Landrum 1.25 3.00
339 Gene Baker 1.25 3.00
340 Vic Wertz 2.50 6.00
341 Jim Owens 1.25 3.00
342 Clint Courtney 1.25 3.00
343 Earl Robinson RC 1.25 3.00
344 Sandy Koufax 50.00 100.00
345 Jimmy Piersall 3.00 8.00
346 Howie Nunn 1.25 3.00
347 St. Louis Cardinals TC 3.00 8.00
348 Steve Boros 1.25 3.00
349 Danny McDevitt 1.25 3.00
350 Ernie Banks 20.00 50.00
351 Jim King 1.25 3.00
352 Bob Shaw 1.25 3.00
353 Howie Bedell RC 1.25 3.00
354 Billy Harrell 2.50 6.00
355 Bob Allison 3.00 8.00
356 Ryne Duren 1.25 3.00
357 Daryl Spencer 1.25 3.00
358 Earl Averill Jr. 2.50 6.00
359 Dallas Green 1.25 3.00
360 Frank Robinson 20.00 50.00
361A Checklist 5 No Ad on Back 6.00 15.00
361B Checklist 5 Ad on Back 6.00 15.00
362 Frank Funk RC 1.25 3.00
363 John Roseboro 2.50 6.00
364 Moe Drabowsky 2.50 6.00
365 Jerry Lumpe 1.25 3.00
366 Eddie Fisher 1.25 3.00
367 Jim Rivera 1.25 3.00
368 Bennie Daniels 1.25 3.00
369 Dave Philley 1.25 3.00
370 Roy Face 2.50 6.00
371 Bill Skowron SP 12.00 30.00
372 Bob Hendley RC 1.50 4.00
373 Boston Red Sox TC 3.00 8.00
374 Paul Giel 1.50 4.00
375 Ken Boyer 5.00 12.00
376 Mike Roarke RC 2.50 6.00
377 Ruben Gomez 1.50 4.00
378 Wally Post 2.50 6.00
379 Bobby Shantz 1.50 4.00
380 Minnie Minoso 3.00 8.00
381 Dave Wickersham RC 1.50 4.00
382 Frank Thomas 2.50 6.00
383 McCormick/Sanford/O'Dell 2.50 6.00
384 Chuck Essegian 1.50 4.00
385 Jim Perry 2.50 6.00
386 Joe Hicks 1.50 4.00
387 Duke Maas 1.50 4.00
388 Roberto Clemente 50.00 120.00
389 Ralph Terry 2.50 6.00
390 Del Crandall 3.00 8.00
391 Winston Brown RC 1.50 4.00
392 Reno Bertoia 1.50 4.00
393 D.Cardwell/G.Hobbie 1.50 4.00
394 Ken Walters 1.50 4.00
395 Chuck Estrada 2.50 6.00
396 Bob Aspromonte 1.50 4.00
397 Hal Woodeshick 1.50 4.00
398 Hank Bauer 2.50 6.00
399 Cliff Cook RC 1.50 4.00
400 Vernon Law 40.00 100.00
401 Babe Ruth 60th HR 25.00 60.00
402 Don Larsen Perfect SP 10.00 25.00
403 26 Inning Tie/Oeschger/Cadore 3.00 8.00
404 Rogers Hornsby .424 5.00 12.00
405 Lou Gehrig Streak 20.00 50.00
406 Mickey Mantle 565 HR 40.00 100.00
407 Jack Chesbro Wins 41 3.00 8.00
408 Christy Mathewson K's SP 8.00 20.00
409 Walter Johnson Shutout 8.00 20.00
410 Harvey Haddix 12 Perfect 3.00 8.00
411 Tony Taylor 2.50 6.00
412 Larry Sherry 2.50 6.00
413 Eddie Yost 2.50 6.00
414 Dick Donovan 2.50 6.00
415 Hank Aaron 75.00 200.00
416 Dick Howser RC 3.00 8.00
417 Juan Marichal SP RC 100.00 250.00
418 Ed Bailey 2.50 6.00
419 Tom Borland 1.50 4.00
420 Ernie Broglio 2.50 6.00
421 Ty Cline SP RC 8.00 20.00
422 Bud Daley 1.50 4.00
423 Charlie Neal SP 8.00 20.00
424 Turk Lown 1.50 4.00
425 Yogi Berra 40.00 100.00
426 Milwaukee Braves TC UER 5.00 12.00
427 Dick Ellsworth 2.50 6.00
428 Ray Barker SP RC 8.00 20.00
429 Al Kaline 15.00 40.00
430 Bill Mazeroski SP 10.00 25.00
431 Chuck Stobbs 1.50 4.00
432 Coot Veal 2.50 6.00
433 Art Mahaffey 1.50 4.00
434 Tom Brewer 1.50 4.00
435 Orlando Cepeda UER 12.00 30.00
436 Jim Maloney SP RC 8.00 20.00
437A Checklist 6 440 Louis 6.00 15.00
437B Checklist 6 440 Luis 6.00 15.00
438 Curt Flood 3.00 8.00
439 Phil Regan RC 2.50 6.00
440 Luis Aparicio 8.00 20.00
441 Dick Bertell RC 1.50 4.00
442 Gordon Jones 1.50 4.00
443 Duke Snider 12.00 30.00
444 Joe Nuxhall 2.50 6.00
445 Frank Malzone 2.50 6.00
446 Bob Taylor 1.50 4.00
447 Harry Bright 3.00 8.00
448 Del Rice 6.00 15.00
449 Bob Bolin RC 3.00 8.00
450 Jim Lemon 3.00 8.00
451 Spencer/White/Broglio 3.00 8.00
452 Bob Allen RC 3.00 8.00
453 Dick Schofield 3.00 8.00
454 Pumpsie Green 3.00 8.00
455 Early Wynn 6.00 15.00
456 Hal Bevan 3.00 8.00
457 Johnny James 3.00 8.00
458 Willie Tasby 3.00 8.00
459 Terry Fox RC 4.00 10.00
460 Gil Hodges 10.00 25.00
461 Smoky Burgess 6.00 15.00
462 Lou Klimchock 3.00 8.00
463 Jack Fisher See 426 3.00 8.00
464 Lee Thomas RC 4.00 10.00
465 Roy McMillan 6.00 15.00
466 Ron Moeller RC 3.00 8.00
467 Cleveland Indians TC 5.00 12.00
468 John Callison 4.00 10.00
469 Ralph Lumenti 3.00 8.00
470 Roy Sievers 4.00 10.00
471 Phil Rizzuto MVP 12.00 30.00
472 Yogi Berra MVP 25.00 60.00
473 Bob Shantz MVP 3.00 8.00
474 Al Rosen MVP 4.00 10.00
475 Mickey Mantle MVP 100.00 250.00
476 Jackie Jensen MVP 4.00 10.00
477 Nellie Fox MVP 6.00 15.00
478 Roger Maris MVP 25.00 60.00
479 Jim Konstanty MVP 3.00 8.00
480 Roy Campanella MVP 15.00 40.00
481 Hank Sauer MVP 3.00 8.00
482 Willie Mays MVP 25.00 60.00
483 Don Newcombe MVP 5.00 12.00
484 Hank Aaron MVP 25.00 60.00
485 Ernie Banks MVP 20.00 50.00
486 Dick Groat MVP 4.00 10.00
487 Gene Oliver 3.00 8.00
488 Joe McClain RC 4.00 10.00
489 Walt Dropo 3.00 8.00
490 Jim Bunning 10.00 25.00
491 Philadelphia Phillies TC 5.00 12.00
492 R.Fairly White 4.00 10.00
492B R.Fairly Green 8.00 20.00
493 Don Zimmer UER 5.00 12.00
494 Tom Cheney 4.00 10.00
495 Elston Howard 10.00 25.00
496 Ken MacKenzie 3.00 8.00
497 Willie Jones 3.00 8.00
498 Ray Herbert 3.00 8.00
499 Chuck Schilling RC 3.00 8.00
500 Harvey Kuenn 6.00 15.00
501 John DeMerit RC 3.00 8.00
502 Choo Choo Coleman RC 4.00 10.00
503 Tito Francona 3.00 8.00
504 Billy Consolo 3.00 8.00
505 Red Schoendienst 8.00 20.00
506 Willie Davis RC 8.00 20.00
507 Pete Burnside 3.00 8.00
508 Rocky Bridges 3.00 8.00
509 Camilo Carreon 3.00 8.00
510 Art Ditmar 3.00 8.00
511 Joe M. Morgan 3.00 8.00
512 Bob Will 3.00 8.00
513 Jim Brosnan 3.00 8.00
514 Jake Wood RC 3.00 8.00
515 Jackie Brandt 3.00 8.00
516A Checklist 7 6.00 15.00
(C on front partially covers Braves cap)
516B Checklist 7 6.00 15.00
(C on front fully above Braves cap)
517 Willie McCovey 25.00 60.00
518 Andy Carey 3.00 8.00
519 Jim Pagliaroni RC 3.00 8.00
520 Joe Cunningham 3.00 8.00
521 N.Sherry/L.Sherry 3.00 8.00
522 Dick Farrell UER 6.00 15.00
523 Joe Gibbon 15.00 40.00
524 Johnny Logan 12.00 30.00
525 Ron Perranoski RC 30.00 60.00
526 R.C. Stevens 12.50 30.00
527 Gene Leek RC 12.50 30.00
528 Pedro Ramos 12.50 30.00
529 Bob Roselli 12.50 30.00
530 Bob Malkmus 12.50 30.00
531 Jim Coates 20.00 50.00
532 Bob Hale 12.50 30.00
533 Jack Curtis RC 12.50 30.00
534 Eddie Kasko 15.00 40.00
535 Larry Jackson 12.50 30.00
536 Bill Tuttle 12.50 30.00
537 Bobby Locke 12.50 30.00
538 Chuck Hiller RC 12.50 30.00
539 Johnny Klippstein 12.50 30.00
540 Jackie Jensen 15.00 40.00
541 Roland Sheldon RC 20.00 50.00
542 Minnesota Twins TC 30.00 60.00
543 Roger Craig 15.00 40.00
544 George Thomas RC 20.00 50.00
545 Hoyt Wilhelm 30.00 60.00
546 Marty Kutyna 12.50 30.00
547 Leon Wagner 12.50 30.00
548 Ted Wills 12.50 30.00
549 Hal R. Smith 12.50 30.00
550 Frank Baumann 12.50 30.00
551 George Altman 15.00 40.00
552 Jim Archer RC 12.50 30.00
553 Bill Fischer 12.50 30.00
554 Pittsburgh Pirates TC 40.00 80.00
555 Sam Jones 12.50 30.00
556 Ken R. Hunt RC 12.50 30.00
557 Jose Valdivielso 12.50 30.00
558 Don Ferrarese 12.50 30.00
559 Jim Gentile 30.00 80.00
560 Barry Latman 15.00 40.00
561 Charley James 12.50 30.00
562 Bill Monbouquette 12.50 30.00
563 Bob Cerv 30.00 80.00
564 Don Cardwell 12.50 30.00
565 Felipe Alou 20.00 50.00
566 Paul Richards AS MG 12.50 30.00
567 Danny Murtaugh AS MG 12.50 30.00
568 Bill Skowron AS 12.00 30.00
569 Frank Herrera AS 15.00 40.00
570 Nellie Fox AS 30.00 60.00
571 Bill Mazeroski AS 30.00 60.00
572 Brooks Robinson AS 25.00 60.00
573 Ken Boyer AS 15.00 40.00
574 Luis Aparicio AS 30.00 60.00
575 Ernie Banks AS 40.00 80.00
576 Roger Maris AS 50.00 120.00
577 Hank Aaron AS 50.00 120.00
578 Mickey Mantle AS 150.00 400.00
579 Willie Mays AS 50.00 120.00
580 Al Kaline AS 20.00 50.00
581 Frank Robinson AS 25.00 60.00
582 Earl Battey AS 12.50 30.00
583 Del Crandall AS 12.50 30.00
584 Jim Perry AS 12.50 30.00
585 Bob Friend AS 12.50 30.00
586 Whitey Ford AS 25.00 60.00
589 Warren Spahn AS 30.00 80.00

1961 Topps Magic Rub-Offs

There are 36 "Magic Rub-Offs" in this set of inserts also marketed in packages of 1961 Topps baseball cards. Each rub off measures 2 1/16" by 3 1/16". Of this number, 18 are team designs (numbered 1-18 below), while the remaining 18 depict players (numbered 19-36 below). The latter, one from each team, were apparently selected for their unusual nicknames.

COMPLETE SET (36) 150.00 300.00
COMMON RUB-OFF (1-18) .75 2.00
COMMON PLAYER (19-36) 2.00 5.00
1 Detroit Tigers 2.00 5.00
2 New York Yankees 2.50 6.00
3 Minnesota Twins 1.25 3.00
4 Washington Senators 1.25 3.00
5 Boston Red Sox 2.00 5.00
6 Los Angeles Angels 1.25 3.00
7 Kansas City A's 1.25 3.00
8 Baltimore Orioles 1.25 3.00
9 Chicago White Sox 1.25 3.00
10 Cleveland Indians 1.25 3.00
11 Pittsburgh Pirates 1.25 3.00
12 San Francisco Giants 1.25 3.00
13 Los Angeles Dodgers 2.50 6.00
14 Philadelphia Phillies 1.25 3.00
15 Cincinnati Redlegs 1.25 3.00
16 St. Louis Cardinals 1.25 3.00
17 Chicago Cubs 1.25 3.00
18 Milwaukee Braves 1.25 3.00
19 John Romano 4.00 10.00
20 Ray Moore 4.00 10.00
21 Ernie Banks 20.00 50.00
22 Charlie Maxwell 4.00 10.00
23 Yogi Berra 20.00 50.00
24 Henry Dutch Dotterer 4.00 10.00
25 Jim Brosnan 4.00 10.00
26 Billy Martin 8.00 20.00
27 Jackie Brandt 4.00 10.00
28 Duke Mass/(sic, Maas) 5.00 12.00
29 Pete Runnels 5.00 12.00
30 Joe Gordon MG 5.00 12.00
31 Sam Jones 4.00 10.00
32 Walt Moryn 4.00 10.00
33 Harvey Haddix 5.00 12.00
34 Frank Howard 6.00 15.00
35 Turk Lown 4.00 10.00
36 Frank Herrera 4.00 10.00

1961 Topps Stamps

There are 207 different baseball players depicted in this stamp series, which was issued as an insert in packages of the regular Topps cards of 1961. The set is actually comprised of 208 stamps: 104 players are pictured on brown stamps and 104 players appear on green stamps, with Kaline found in both colors. The stamps were issued in attached pairs and an album was sold separately (10 cents) at retail outlets. Each stamp measures 1 3/8" by 1 3/16". Stamps are unnumbered but are presented here in alphabetical order by team, Chicago Cubs (1-12), Cincinnati Reds (13-24), Los Angeles Dodgers (25-36), Milwaukee Braves (37-48), Philadelphia Phillies (49-60), Pittsburgh Pirates (61-72), San Francisco Giants (73-84), St. Louis Cardinals (85-96), Baltimore Orioles AL (97-107), Boston Red Sox (108-119), Chicago White Sox (120-131), Cleveland Indians (132-143), Detroit Tigers (144-155), Kansas City A's (156-168), Los Angeles Angels (169-175), Minnesota Twins (176-187), New York Yankees (188-200) and Washington Senators (201-207).

COMPLETE SET (207) 300.00 600.00
1 George Altman .75 2.00
2 Bob Anderson .75 2.00
brown
3 Richie Ashburn 2.00 5.00
4 Ernie Banks 3.00 8.00
5 Ed Bouchee .75 2.00
6 Jim Brewer .75 2.00
7 Dick Ellsworth .75 2.00
8 Don Elston .75 2.00
9 Ron Santo 2.00 5.00
10 Sammy Taylor .75 2.00
11 Bob Will .75 2.00
12 Billy Williams 2.00 5.00
13 Ed Bailey .75 2.00
14 Gus Bell .75 2.00
15 Jim Brosnan .75 2.00
brown
16 Chico Cardenas .75 2.00
17 Gene Freese .75 2.00
18 Eddie Kasko .75 2.00
19 Jerry Lynch .75 2.00
20 Billy Martin 2.00 5.00
21 Jim O'Toole .75 2.00
22 Vada Pinson 1.25 3.00
23 Wally Post .75 2.00
brown
24 Frank Robinson 3.00 8.00
25 Tommy Davis 1.25 3.00
26 Don Drysdale 2.00 5.00
27 Frank Howard 1.25 3.00
Brown
28 Norm Larker .75 2.00
29 Wally Moon .75 2.00
brown
30 Charlie Neal .75 2.00
31 Johnny Podres 1.25 3.00
32 Ed Roebuck .75 2.00
33 Johnny Roseboro .75 2.00
34 Larry Sherry .75 2.00
35 Duke Snider 3.00 8.00
36 Stan Williams .75 2.00
37 Hank Aaron 10.00 25.00
38 Joe Adcock .75 2.00
39 Bill Bruton .75 2.00
40 Bob Buhl .75 2.00
41 Wes Covington .75 2.00
brown
42 Del Crandall .75 2.00
43 Joey Jay .75 2.00
44 Felix Mantilla .75 2.00
45 Eddie Mathews 3.00 8.00
46 Roy McMillan .75 2.00
47 Warren Spahn 3.00 8.00
48 Carlton Willey .75 2.00
brown
49 John Buzhardt .75 2.00
50 Johnny Callison .75 2.00
51 Tony Curry .75 2.00
52 Clay Dalrymple .75 2.00
brown
53 Bobby Del Greco .75 2.00
brown
54 Dick Farrell .75 2.00
brown
55 Tony Gonzalez .75 2.00
56 Pancho Herrera .75 2.00
57 Art Mahaffey .75 2.00
58 Robin Roberts 1.25 3.00
59 Tony Taylor .75 2.00
60 Lee Walls .75 2.00
61 Smoky Burgess .75 2.00
62 Roy Face (brown) .75 2.00
63 Bob Friend .75 2.00
64 Dick Groat 1.25 3.00
65 Don Hoak .75 2.00
66 Vern Law .75 2.00
67 Bill Mazeroski 1.25 3.00
68 Rocky Nelson .75 2.00
69 Bob Skinner .75 2.00
70 Hal Smith .75 2.00
71 Dick Stuart .75 2.00
72 Bill Virdon .75 2.00
73 Don Blasingame .75 2.00
74 Eddie Bressoud .75 2.00
brown
75 Orlando Cepeda 1.25 3.00
76 Jim Davenport .75 2.00
77 Harvey Kuenn 1.25 3.00
Brown
78 Hobie Landrith .75 2.00
79 Juan Marichal 2.00 5.00
80 Willie Mays 10.00 25.00
81 Mike McCormick .75 2.00
82 Willie McCovey 3.00 8.00
83 Billy O'Dell .75 2.00
84 Jack Sanford .75 2.00
85 Ken Boyer 1.25 3.00
86 Curt Flood 1.25 3.00
87 Alex Grammas .75 2.00
brown
88 Larry Jackson .75 2.00
89 Julian Javier .75 2.00
90 Ron Kline .75 2.00
brown
91 Lindy McDaniel .75 2.00
92 Stan Musial 6.00 15.00
93 Curt Simmons .75 2.00
brown
94 Hal Smith .75 2.00
95 Daryl Spencer .75 2.00
96 Bill White .75 2.00
brown
97 Steve Barber .75 2.00
98 Jackie Brandt .75 2.00
brown
99 Marv Breeding .75 2.00
100 Chuck Estrada .75 2.00
101 Jim Gentile .75 2.00
102 Ron Hansen .75 2.00
103 Milt Pappas .75 2.00
104 Brooks Robinson 3.00 8.00
105 Gene Stephens .75 2.00
106 Gus Triandos .75 2.00
107 Hoyt Wilhelm 1.25 3.00
108 Tom Brewer .75 2.00
109 Gene Conley .75 2.00
brown
110 Ike Delock .75 2.00
brown
111 Gary Geiger .75 2.00
112 Jackie Jensen 1.25 3.00
113 Frank Malzone .75 2.00
114 Bill Monbouquette .75 2.00
115 Russ Nixon .75 2.00
116 Pete Runnels .75 2.00
117 Willie Tasby .75 2.00
118 Vic Wertz .75 2.00
brown
119 Carl Yastrzemski 6.00 15.00
120 Luis Aparicio 1.25 3.00
121 Russ Kemmerer .75 2.00
brown
122 Jim Landis .75 2.00
123 Sherman Lollar .75 2.00
124 J.C. Martin .75 2.00
125 Minnie Minoso 1.25 3.00
126 Billy Pierce .75 2.00
127 Bob Shaw .75 2.00
128 Roy Sievers .75 2.00
129 Al Smith .75 2.00
130 Gerry Staley .75 2.00
brown
131 Early Wynn 1.25 3.00
132 Johnny Antonelli .75 2.00
brown
133 Ken Aspromonte .75 2.00
134 Tito Francona .75 2.00
135 Jim Grant .75 2.00
136 Woody Held .75 2.00
137 Barry Latman .75 2.00
138 Jim Perry .75 2.00
139 Jimmy Piersall 1.25 3.00
140 Bubba Phillips .75 2.00
141 Vic Power .75 2.00
142 John Romano .75 2.00
143 Johnny Temple .75 2.00
144 Hank Aguirre .75 2.00
brown
145 Frank Bolling .75 2.00
146 Steve Boros .75 2.00
brown
147 Jim Bunning 1.25 3.00
148 Norm Cash 1.25 3.00
149 Harry Chiti .75 2.00
150 Chico Fernandez .75 2.00
151 Dick Gernert .75 2.00
152A Al Kaline (green) 3.00 8.00
152B Al Kaline (brown) 3.00 8.00
153 Frank Lary .75 2.00
154 Charlie Maxwell .75 2.00
155 Dave Sisler .75 2.00
156 Hank Bauer .75 2.00
157 Bob Boyd (brown) .75 2.00
158 Andy Carey .75 2.00
159 Bud Daley .75 2.00
160 Dick Hall .75 2.00
161 J.C. Hartman .75 2.00
162 Ray Herbert .75 2.00
163 Whitey Herzog 1.25 3.00
164 Jerry Lumpe .75 2.00
brown
165 Norm Siebern .75 2.00
166 Marv Throneberry .75 2.00
167 Bill Tuttle .75 2.00
168 Dick Williams .75 2.00
169 Jerry Casale .75 2.00
brown
170 Bob Cerv .75 2.00
171 Ned Garver .75 2.00
172 Ken Hunt .75 2.00
173 Ted Kluszewski 2.00 5.00
174 Ed Sadowski .75 2.00
brown
175 Eddie Yost .75 2.00
176 Bob Allison .75 2.00
177 Earl Battey .75 2.00
brown
178 Reno Bertoia .75 2.00
179 Billy Gardner .75 2.00
180 Jim Kaat 1.25 3.00
181 Harmon Killebrew 3.00 8.00
182 Jim Lemon .75 2.00
183 Camilo Pascual .75 2.00
184 Pedro Ramos .75 2.00
185 Chuck Stobbs .75 2.00
186 Zoilo Versalles .75 2.00
187 Pete Whisenant .75 2.00
188 Luis Arroyo .75 2.00
brown
189 Yogi Berra 5.00 12.00
190 John Blanchard .75 2.00
191 Clete Boyer .75 2.00
192 Art Ditmar .75 2.00
193 Whitey Ford 5.00 12.00
194 Elston Howard 2.00 5.00
195 Tony Kubek 2.00 5.00
196 Mickey Mantle 50.00 100.00
197 Roger Maris 10.00 25.00
198 Bobby Shantz .75 2.00
199 Bill Stafford .75 2.00
200 Bob Turley .75 2.00
201 Bud Daley .75 2.00
brown
202 Dick Donovan .75 2.00
203 Bobby Klaus .75 2.00
204 Johnny Klippstein .75 2.00
205 Dale Long .75 2.00
206 Ray Semproch .75 2.00
207 Gene Woodling .75 2.00
XX Stamp Album 8.00 20.00

1962 Topps

The cards in this 598-card set measure 2 1/2" by 3 1/2". The 1962 Topps set contains a mini-series spotlighting Babe Ruth (135-144). Other subsets in the set include League Leaders (51-60), World Series cards (232-237), In Action cards (311-319), NL All Stars (390-399), AL All Stars (466-475), and Rookie Prospects (591-598). The All-Star selections were again provided by Sport Magazine, as in 1958 and 1960. The second series had two distinct printings which are distinguishable by numerous color and pose variations. Those cards with a distinctive "green tint" are valued at a slight premuim as they are basically the result of a flawed printing process occurring early in the second series run. Card number 139 exists as A: Babe Ruth Special card, B: Hal Reniff with arms over head, or C: Hal Reniff in the same pose as card number 159. In addition, two poses exist for these cards: 129, 132, 134, 147, 174, 176, and 190. The high number series, 523 to 598, is somewhat more difficult to obtain than other cards in the set. Within the last series (523-598) there are 43 cards which were printed in lesser quantities; these are marked SP in the checklist below. In particular, the Rookie Parade subset (591-598) of this last series is even more difficult. This was the first year Topps produced multi-player Rookie Cards. The set price listed does not include the pose variations (see checklist below for individual values). A three card ad sheet has been seen. The players on the front include AL HR leaders, Barney Schultz and Carl Sawatski, while the back features an ad and a Roger Maris card. Cards were issued in one-card penny packs as well as five-card nickel packs. The five card packs came 24 to a box. The key Rookie Cards in this set are Lou Brock, Tim McCarver, Gaylord Perry, and Bob Uecker.

COMP. MASTER SET (689) 5000.00 10000.00
COMPLETE SET (598) 4000.00 8000.00
COMMON CARD (1-370) 2.00 5.00
COMMON CARD (371-446) 2.50 6.00
COMMON CARD (447-522) 5.00 12.00
COMMON CARD (523-598) 8.00 20.00
WRAPPER (1-CENT) 50.00 100.00
WRAPPER (5-CENT) 12.50 30.00
1 Roger Maris 100.00 250.00
2 Jim Brosnan 2.00 5.00
3 Pete Runnels 2.00 5.00
4 John DeMerit 3.00 8.00
5 Sandy Koufax UER 50.00 120.00
6 Marv Breeding 2.00 5.00
7 Frank Thomas 4.00 10.00
8 Ray Herbert 2.00 5.00
9 Jim Davenport 3.00 8.00
10 Roberto Clemente 75.00 200.00
11 Tom Morgan 2.00 5.00
12 Harry Craft MG 3.00 8.00
13 Dick Howser 3.00 8.00
14 Bill White 3.00 8.00
15 Dick Donovan 2.00 5.00
16 Darrell Johnson 2.00 5.00
17 Johnny Callison 3.00 8.00
18 M.Mantle/W.Mays 60.00 150.00
19 Ray Washburn RC 2.00 5.00
20 Rocky Colavito 6.00 15.00
21 Jim Kaat 3.00 8.00
22A Checklist 1 ERR 5.00 12.00
22B Checklist 1 COR 5.00 12.00
23 Norm Larker 2.00 5.00
24 Detroit Tigers TC 4.00 10.00
25 Ernie Banks 30.00 80.00
26 Chris Cannizzaro 3.00 8.00
27 Chuck Cottier 2.00 5.00
28 Minnie Minoso 4.00 10.00
29 Casey Stengel MG 10.00 25.00
30 Eddie Mathews 20.00 50.00
31 Tom Tresh RC 12.00 30.00
32 John Roseboro 3.00 8.00
33 Don Larsen 3.00 8.00

Card	Low	High
34 Johnny Temple	3.00	8.00
35 Don Schwall RC	4.00	10.00
36 Don Leppert RC	2.00	5.00
37 Latman/Stigman/Perry	2.00	5.00
38 Gene Stephens	2.00	5.00
39 Joe Koppe	2.00	5.00
40 Orlando Cepeda	10.00	25.00
41 Cliff Cook	2.00	5.00
42 Jim King	2.00	5.00
43 Los Angeles Dodgers TC	4.00	10.00
44 Don Taussig RC	2.00	5.00
45 Brooks Robinson	20.00	50.00
46 Jack Baldschun RC	2.00	5.00
47 Bob Will	2.00	5.00
48 Ralph Terry	3.00	8.00
49 Hal Jones RC	2.00	5.00
50 Stan Musial	30.00	80.00
51 Cash/Kaline/Howard LL	3.00	8.00
52 Clemente/Pins/Boyer LL	10.00	25.00
53 Maris/Mantle/Kill LL	30.00	80.00
54 Cepeda/Mays/F.Rob LL	8.00	20.00
55 Donovan/Staff/Mossi LL	3.00	8.00
56 Spahn/O'Toole/Simm LL	3.00	8.00
57 Ford/Lary/Bunning LL	3.00	8.00
58 Spahn/Jay/O'Toole LL	3.00	8.00
59 Pascual/Ford/Bunning LL	3.00	8.00
60 Koufax/Will/Drysdale LL	8.00	20.00
61 St. Louis Cardinals TC	4.00	10.00
62 Steve Boros	2.00	5.00
63 Tony Cloninger RC	3.00	8.00
64 Russ Snyder	2.00	5.00
65 Bobby Richardson	4.00	10.00
66 Cuno Barragan RC	2.00	5.00
67 Harvey Haddix	3.00	8.00
68 Ken Hunt	2.00	5.00
69 Phil Ortega RC	2.00	5.00
70 Harmon Killebrew	15.00	40.00
71 Dick LeMay RC	2.00	5.00
72 Boros/Scheffing/Wood	2.00	5.00
73 Nellie Fox	8.00	20.00
74 Bob Lillis	3.00	8.00
75 Milt Pappas	3.00	8.00
76 Howie Bedell	2.00	5.00
77 Tony Taylor	3.00	8.00
78 Gene Green	2.00	5.00
79 Ed Hobaugh	2.00	5.00
80 Vada Pinson	3.00	8.00
81 Jim Pagliaroni	2.00	5.00
82 Deron Johnson	3.00	8.00
83 Larry Jackson	2.00	5.00
84 Lenny Green	2.00	5.00
85 Gil Hodges	10.00	25.00
86 Donn Clendenon RC	3.00	8.00
87 Mike Roarke	2.00	5.00
88 Ralph Houk MG	3.00	8.00
89 Barney Schultz RC	2.00	5.00
90 Jimmy Piersall	3.00	8.00
91 J.C. Martin	2.00	5.00
92 Sam Jones	2.00	5.00
93 John Blanchard	3.00	8.00
94 Jay Hook	3.00	8.00
95 Don Hoak	3.00	8.00
96 Eli Grba	2.00	5.00
97 Tito Francona	2.00	5.00
98 Checklist 2	5.00	12.00
99 Boog Powell RC	15.00	40.00
100 Warren Spahn	15.00	40.00
101 Carroll Hardy	2.00	5.00
102 Al Schroll	2.00	5.00
103 Don Blasingame	2.00	5.00
104 Ted Savage RC	2.00	5.00
105 Don Mossi	3.00	8.00
106 Carl Sawatski	2.00	5.00
107 Mike McCormick	3.00	8.00
108 Willie Davis	3.00	8.00
109 Bob Shaw	2.00	5.00
110 Bill Skowron	3.00	8.00
110A Bill Skowron Green Tint	3.00	8.00
111 Dallas Green	3.00	8.00
111A Dallas Green Green Tint	3.00	8.00
112 Hank Foiles	2.00	5.00
112A Hank Foiles Green Tint	2.00	5.00
113 Chicago White Sox TC	4.00	10.00
113A Chicago White Sox TC Green Tint	4.00	10.00
114 Howie Koplitz RC	2.00	5.00
114A Howie Koplitz Green Tint	2.00	5.00
115 Bob Skinner	3.00	8.00
115A Bob Skinner Green Tint	3.00	8.00
116 Herb Score	3.00	8.00
116A Herb Score Green Tint	3.00	8.00
117 Gary Geiger	3.00	8.00
117A Gary Geiger Green Tint	3.00	8.00
118 Julian Javier	3.00	8.00
118A Julian Javier Green Tint	3.00	8.00
119 Danny Murphy	2.00	5.00
119A Danny Murphy Green Tint	2.00	5.00
120 Bob Purkey	2.00	5.00
120A Bob Purkey Green Tint	2.00	5.00
121 Billy Hitchcock	2.00	5.00
121A Billy Hitchcock Green Tint	2.00	5.00
122 Norm Bass RC	2.00	5.00
122A Norm Bass Green Tint	2.00	5.00
123 Mike de la Hoz	2.00	5.00
123A Mike de la Hoz Green Tint	2.00	5.00
124 Bill Pleis RC	2.00	5.00
124A Bill Pleis Green Tint	2.00	5.00
125 Gene Woodling	3.00	8.00
125A Gene Woodling Green Tint	3.00	8.00
126 Al Cicotte	2.00	5.00
126A Al Cicotte Green Tint	2.00	5.00
127 Siebern/Bauer/Lumpe	2.00	5.00
127A Siebern/Bauer/Lumpe Green Tint	2.00	5.00
128 Art Fowler	2.00	5.00
128A Art Fowler Green Tint	2.00	5.00
129A Lee Walls Facing Right	2.00	5.00
129B Lee Walls Face Lft Grn	12.50	30.00
130 Frank Bolling	2.00	5.00
130A Frank Bolling Green Tint	2.00	5.00
131 Pete Richert RC	2.00	5.00
131A Pete Richert Green Tint	2.00	5.00
132A Los Angeles Angels TC w/o inset	4.00	10.00
132B Los Angeles Angels TC w/inset	12.50	30.00
133 Felipe Alou	3.00	8.00
133A Felipe Alou Green Tint	3.00	8.00
134A Billy Hoeft Blue Sky	2.00	5.00
134B Billy Hoeft Green Sky	12.50	30.00
135 Babe as a Boy	8.00	20.00
135A Babe as a Boy Green	8.00	20.00
136 Babe Joins Yanks	8.00	20.00
136A Babe Joins Yanks Green	8.00	20.00
137 Babe with Mgr. Huggins	10.00	25.00
137A Babe with Mgr. Huggins Green	10.00	25.00
138 The Famous Slugger	8.00	20.00
138A The Famous Slugger Green	8.00	20.00
139A1 Babe Hits 60 (Pole)	12.50	30.00
139A2 Babe Hits 60 (No Pole)	12.50	30.00
139B Hal Reniff Portrait	6.00	15.00
139C Hal Reniff Pitching	30.00	60.00
140 Gehrig and Ruth	20.00	50.00
140A Gehrig and Ruth Green	20.00	50.00
141 Twilight Years	12.00	30.00
141A Twilight Years Green	12.00	30.00
142 Coaching the Dodgers	8.00	20.00
142A Coaching the Dodgers Green	8.00	20.00
143 Greatest Sports Hero	8.00	20.00
143A Greatest Sports Hero Green	8.00	20.00
144 Farewell Speech	8.00	20.00
144A Farewell Speech Green	8.00	20.00
145 Barry Latman	2.00	5.00
145A Barry Latman Green Tint	2.00	5.00
146 Don Demeter	2.00	5.00
146A Don Demeter Green Tint	2.00	5.00
147A Bill Kunkel Portrait	2.00	5.00
147B Bill Kunkel Pitching	12.50	30.00
148 Wally Post	2.00	5.00
148A Wally Post Green Tint	2.00	5.00
149 Bob Duliba	2.00	5.00
149A Bob Duliba Green Tint	2.00	5.00
150 Al Kaline	20.00	50.00
150A Al Kaline Green Tint	20.00	50.00
151 Johnny Klippstein	2.00	5.00
151A Johnny Klippstein Green Tint	2.00	5.00
152 Mickey Vernon MG	3.00	8.00
152A Mickey Vernon MG Green Tint	3.00	8.00
153 Pumpsie Green	2.50	6.00
153A Pumpsie Green Green Tint	2.50	6.00
154 Lee Thomas	2.50	6.00
154A Lee Thomas Green Tint	2.50	6.00
155 Stu Miller	2.50	6.00
155A Stu Miller Green Tint	2.50	6.00
156 Merritt Ranew RC	2.00	5.00
156A Merritt Ranew Green Tint	2.00	5.00
157 Wes Covington	3.00	8.00
157A Wes Covington Green Tint	3.00	8.00
158 Milwaukee Braves TC	4.00	10.00
158A Milwaukee Braves TC Green Tint	6.00	15.00
159 Hal Reniff RC	3.00	8.00
160 Dick Stuart	3.00	8.00
160A Dick Stuart Green Tint	3.00	8.00
161 Frank Baumann	2.00	5.00
161A Frank Baumann Green Tint	2.00	5.00
162 Sammy Drake RC	2.00	5.00
162A Sammy Drake Green Tint	2.00	5.00
163 B.Gardner/C.Boyer	3.00	8.00
163A B.Gardner/C.Boyer Green Tint	3.00	8.00
164 Hal Naragon	2.00	5.00
164A Hal Naragon Green Tint	2.00	5.00
165 Jackie Brandt	2.00	5.00
165A Jackie Brandt Green Tint	2.00	5.00
166 Don Lee	2.00	5.00
166A Don Lee Green Tint	2.00	5.00
167 Tim McCarver RC	15.00	40.00
167A Tim McCarver Green Tint	12.50	30.00
168 Leo Posada	2.00	5.00
168A Leo Posada Green Tint	2.00	5.00
169 Bob Cerv	4.00	10.00
169A Bob Cerv Green Tint	4.00	10.00
170 Ron Santo	12.00	30.00
170A Ron Santo Green Tint	12.00	30.00
171 Dave Sisler	2.00	5.00
171A Dave Sisler Green Tint	2.00	5.00
172 Fred Hutchinson MG	3.00	8.00
172A Fred Hutchinson MG Green Tint	3.00	8.00
173 Chico Fernandez	2.00	5.00
173A Chico Fernandez Green Tint	2.00	5.00
174A Carl Willey w/o Cap	2.00	5.00
174B Carl Willey w/Cap	12.50	30.00
175 Frank Howard	4.00	10.00
175A Frank Howard Green Tint	4.00	10.00
176A Eddie Yost Portrait	2.00	5.00
176B Eddie Yost Batting	12.50	30.00
177 Bobby Shantz	3.00	8.00
177A Bobby Shantz Green Tint	3.00	8.00
178 Camilo Carreon	2.00	5.00
178A Camilo Carreon Green Tint	2.00	5.00
179 Tom Sturdivant	2.00	5.00
179A Tom Sturdivant Green Tint	2.00	5.00
180 Bob Allison	4.00	10.00
180A Bob Allison Green Tint	4.00	10.00
181 Paul Brown RC	2.00	5.00
181A Paul Brown Green Tint	2.00	5.00
182 Bob Nieman	2.00	5.00
182A Bob Nieman Green Tint	2.00	5.00
183 Roger Craig	3.00	8.00
183A Roger Craig Green Tint	3.00	8.00
184 Haywood Sullivan	3.00	8.00
184A Haywood Sullivan Green Tint	3.00	8.00
185 Roland Sheldon	4.00	10.00
185A Roland Sheldon Green Tint	4.00	10.00
186 Mack Jones RC	2.00	5.00
186A Mack Jones Green Tint	2.00	5.00
187 Gene Conley	2.00	5.00
187A Gene Conley Green Tint	2.00	5.00
188 Chuck Hiller	2.00	5.00
188A Chuck Hiller Green Tint	2.00	5.00
189 Dick Hall	2.00	5.00
189A Dick Hall Green Tint	2.00	5.00
190A Wally Moon Portrait	3.00	8.00
190B Wally Moon Batting	12.50	30.00
191 Jim Brewer	2.00	5.00
191A Jim Brewer Green Tint	2.00	5.00
192A Checklist 3 w/o Comma	5.00	12.00
192B Checklist 3 w/Comma	6.00	15.00
193 Eddie Kasko	2.00	5.00
193A Eddie Kasko Green Tint	2.00	5.00
194 Dean Chance RC	3.00	8.00
194A Dean Chance Green Tint	3.00	8.00
195 Joe Cunningham	2.00	5.00
195A Joe Cunningham Green Tint	2.00	5.00
196 Terry Fox	2.00	5.00
196A Terry Fox Green Tint	2.00	5.00
197 Daryl Spencer	2.00	5.00
198 Johnny Keane MG	2.00	5.00
199 Gaylord Perry RC	50.00	120.00
200 Mickey Mantle	400.00	800.00
201 Ike Delock	2.00	5.00
202 Carl Warwick RC	2.00	5.00
203 Jack Fisher	2.00	5.00
204 Johnny Weekly RC	2.00	5.00
205 Gene Freese	2.00	5.00
206 Washington Senators TC	4.00	10.00
207 Pete Burnside	2.00	5.00
208 Billy Martin	8.00	20.00
209 Jim Frogosi RC	6.00	15.00
210 Roy Face	3.00	8.00
211 F.Bolling/R.McMillan	2.00	5.00
212 Jim Owens	2.00	5.00
213 Richie Ashburn	8.00	20.00
214 Dom Zanni	2.00	5.00
215 Woody Held	2.00	5.00
216 Ron Kline	2.00	5.00
217 Walter Alston MG	4.00	10.00
218 Joe Torre RC	40.00	100.00
219 Al Downing RC	3.00	8.00
220 Roy Sievers	3.00	8.00
221 Bill Short	2.00	5.00
222 Jerry Zimmerman	2.00	5.00
223 Alex Grammas	2.00	5.00
224 Don Rudolph	2.00	5.00
225 Frank Malzone	3.00	8.00
226 San Francisco Giants TC	4.00	10.00
227 Bob Tiefenauer	2.00	5.00
228 Dale Long	4.00	10.00
229 Jesus McFarlane RC	2.00	5.00
230 Camilo Pascual	3.00	8.00
231 Ernie Bowman RC	2.00	5.00
232 Ellie Howard WS1	4.00	10.00
233 Joey Jay WS2	4.00	10.00
234 Roger Maris WS3	15.00	40.00
235 Whitey Ford WS4	6.00	15.00
236 Yanks Crush Reds WS5	4.00	10.00
237 Yanks Celebrate WS	4.00	10.00
238 Norm Sherry	2.00	5.00
239 Cecil Butler RC	2.00	5.00
240 George Altman	2.00	5.00
241 Johnny Kucks	2.00	5.00
242 Mel McGaha MG RC	2.00	5.00
243 Robin Roberts	6.00	15.00
244 Don Gile	2.00	5.00
245 Ron Hanson	2.00	5.00
246 Art Ditmar	2.00	5.00
247 Joe Pignatano	2.00	5.00
248 Bob Aspromonte	3.00	8.00
249 Ed Keegan	2.00	5.00
250 Norm Cash	4.00	10.00
251 New York Yankees TC	20.00	50.00
252 Earl Francis	2.00	5.00
253 Harry Chiti CO	2.00	5.00
254 Gordon Windhorn RC	2.00	5.00
255 Juan Pizarro	2.00	5.00
256 Elio Chacon	3.00	8.00
257 Jack Spring RC	2.00	5.00
258 Marty Keough	2.00	5.00
259 Lou Klimchock	2.00	5.00
260 Billy Pierce	3.00	8.00
261 George Alusik RC	2.00	5.00
262 Bob Schmidt	2.00	5.00
263 Purkey/Turner/Jay	2.00	5.00
264 Dick Ellsworth	3.00	8.00
265 Joe Adcock	3.00	8.00
266 John Anderson RC	2.00	5.00
267 Dan Dobbek	2.00	5.00
268 Ken McBride	2.00	5.00
269 Bob Oldis	2.00	5.00
270 Dick Groat	3.00	8.00
271 Ray Rippelmeyer	2.00	5.00
272 Earl Robinson	2.00	5.00
273 Gary Bell	2.00	5.00
274 Sammy Taylor	2.00	5.00
275 Norm Siebern	2.00	5.00
276 Hal Kolstad RC	2.00	5.00
277 Checklist 4	6.00	15.00
278 Ken Johnson	3.00	8.00
279 Hobie Landrith UER	3.00	8.00
280 Johnny Podres	3.00	8.00
281 Jake Gibbs RC	4.00	10.00
282 Dave Hillman	2.00	5.00
283 Charlie Smith RC	2.00	5.00
284 Ruben Amaro	2.00	5.00
285 Curt Simmons	3.00	8.00
286 Al Lopez MG	4.00	10.00
287 George Witt	2.00	5.00
288 Billy Williams	20.00	50.00
289 Mike Krsnich RC	2.00	5.00
290 Jim Gentile	3.00	8.00
291 Hal Stowe RC	2.00	5.00
292 Jerry Kindall	2.00	5.00
293 Bob Miller	3.00	8.00
294 Philadelphia Phillies TC	4.00	10.00
295 Vern Law	3.00	8.00
296 Ken Hamlin	2.00	5.00
297 Ron Perranoski	3.00	8.00
298 Bill Tuttle	2.00	5.00
299 Don Wert RC	2.00	5.00
300 Willie Mays	100.00	250.00
301 Galen Cisco RC	2.00	5.00
302 Johnny Edwards RC	2.00	5.00
303 Frank Torre	3.00	8.00
304 Dick Farrell	3.00	8.00
305 Jerry Lumpe	2.00	5.00
306 L.McDaniel/L.Jackson	2.00	5.00
307 Jim Grant	3.00	8.00
308 Neil Chrisley	3.00	8.00
309 Moe Morhardt RC	2.00	5.00
310 Whitey Ford	20.00	50.00
311 Tony Kubek IA	3.00	8.00
312 Warren Spahn IA	6.00	15.00
313 Roger Maris IA	40.00	80.00
314 Rocky Colavito IA	3.00	8.00
315 Whitey Ford IA	6.00	15.00
316 Harmon Killebrew IA	6.00	15.00
317 Stan Musial IA	8.00	20.00
318 Mickey Mantle IA	40.00	100.00
319 Mike McCormick IA	2.00	5.00
320 Hank Aaron	60.00	150.00
321 Lee Stange RC	2.00	5.00
322 Alvin Dark MG	3.00	8.00
323 Don Landrum	2.00	5.00
324 Joe McClain	2.00	5.00
325 Luis Aparicio	10.00	25.00
326 Tom Parsons RC	2.00	5.00
327 Ozzie Virgil	2.00	5.00
328 Ken Walters	2.00	5.00
329 Bob Bolin	2.00	5.00
330 John Romano	2.00	5.00
331 Moe Drabowsky	3.00	8.00
332 Don Buddin	2.00	5.00
333 Frank Cipriani RC	2.00	5.00
334 Boston Red Sox TC	4.00	10.00
335 Bill Bruton	2.00	5.00
336 Billy Muffett	2.00	5.00
337 Jim Marshall	3.00	8.00
338 Billy Gardner	2.00	5.00
339 Jose Valdivielso	2.00	5.00
340 Don Drysdale	15.00	40.00
341 Mike Hershberger RC	2.00	5.00
342 Ed Rakow	2.00	5.00
343 Albie Pearson	3.00	8.00
344 Ed Bauta RC	2.00	5.00
345 Chuck Schilling	2.00	5.00
346 Jack Kralick	2.00	5.00
347 Chuck Hinton RC	2.00	5.00
348 Larry Burright RC	2.00	5.00
349 Paul Foytack	2.00	5.00
350 Frank Robinson	30.00	80.00
351 J.Torre/D.Crandall	3.00	8.00
352 Frank Sullivan	2.00	5.00
353 Bill Mazeroski	6.00	15.00
354 Roman Mejias	3.00	8.00
355 Steve Barber	2.00	5.00
356 Tom Haller RC	2.00	5.00
357 Jerry Walker	2.00	5.00
358 Tommy Davis	3.00	8.00
359 Bobby Locke	2.00	5.00
360 Yogi Berra	40.00	80.00
361 Bob Hendley	2.00	5.00
362 Ty Cline	2.00	5.00
363 Bob Roselli	2.00	5.00
364 Ken Hunt	2.00	5.00
365 Charlie Neal	3.00	8.00
366 Phil Regan	3.00	8.00
367 Checklist 5	6.00	15.00
368 Bob Tillman RC	2.00	5.00
369 Ted Bowsfield	2.00	5.00
370 Ken Boyer	4.00	10.00
371 Earl Battey	2.50	6.00
372 Jack Curtis	2.50	6.00
373 Al Heist	2.50	6.00
374 Gene Mauch MG	4.00	10.00
375 Ron Fairly	4.00	10.00
376 Bud Daley	3.00	8.00
377 John Orsino RC	2.50	6.00
378 Bennie Daniels	2.50	6.00
379 Chuck Essegian	2.50	6.00
380 Lou Burdette	4.00	10.00
381 Chico Cardenas	4.00	10.00
382 Dick Williams	3.00	8.00
383 Ray Sadecki	2.50	6.00
384 Kansas City Athletics TC	4.00	10.00
385 Early Wynn	6.00	15.00
386 Don Mincher	3.00	8.00
387 Lou Brock RC	150.00	400.00
388 Ryne Duren	3.00	8.00
389 Smoky Burgess	4.00	10.00
390 Orlando Cepeda AS	4.00	10.00
391 Bill Mazeroski AS	4.00	10.00
392 Ken Boyer AS UER	3.00	8.00
393 Roy McMillan AS	2.50	6.00
394 Hank Aaron AS	25.00	60.00
395 Willie Mays AS	20.00	50.00
396 Frank Robinson AS	10.00	25.00
397 John Roseboro AS	2.50	6.00
398 Don Drysdale AS	6.00	15.00
399 Warren Spahn AS	8.00	20.00
400 Elston Howard	4.00	10.00
401 O.Cepeda/R.Maris	15.00	40.00
402 Gino Cimoli	2.50	6.00
403 Chet Nichols	2.50	6.00
404 Tim Harkness RC	3.00	8.00
405 Jim Perry	3.00	8.00
406 Bob Taylor	2.50	6.00
407 Hank Aguirre	2.50	6.00
408 Gus Bell	3.00	8.00
409 Pittsburgh Pirates TC	4.00	10.00
410 Al Smith	2.50	6.00
411 Danny O'Connell	2.50	6.00
412 Charlie James	2.50	6.00
413 Matty Alou	4.00	10.00
414 Joe Gaines RC	2.50	6.00
415 Bill Virdon	4.00	10.00
416 Bob Scheffing MG	2.50	6.00
417 Joe Azcue RC	2.50	6.00
418 Andy Carey	2.50	6.00
419 Bob Bruce	3.00	8.00
420 Gus Triandos	3.00	8.00
421 Ken MacKenzie	3.00	8.00
422 Steve Bilko	2.50	6.00
423 R.Face/H.Wilhelm	4.00	10.00
424 Al McBean RC	2.50	6.00
425 Carl Yastrzemski	40.00	100.00
426 Bob Farley RC	2.50	6.00
427 Jake Wood	2.50	6.00
428 Joe Hicks	2.50	6.00
429 Billy O'Dell	2.50	6.00
430 Tony Kubek	6.00	15.00
431 Bob Buck Rodgers RC	3.00	8.00
432 Jim Pendleton	2.50	6.00
433 Jim Archer	2.50	6.00
434 Clay Dalrymple	2.50	6.00
435 Larry Sherry	3.00	8.00
436 Felix Mantilla	3.00	8.00
437 Ray Moore	2.50	6.00
438 Dick Brown	2.50	6.00
439 Jerry Buchek RC	2.50	6.00
440 Joey Jay	2.50	6.00
441 Checklist 6	6.00	15.00
442 Wes Stock	2.50	6.00
443 Del Crandall	3.00	8.00
444 Ted Wills	2.50	6.00
445 Vic Power	3.00	8.00
446 Don Elston	2.50	6.00
447 Willie Kirkland	5.00	12.00
448 Joe Gibbon	5.00	12.00
449 Jerry Adair	5.00	12.00
450 Jim O'Toole	6.00	15.00
451 Jose Tartabull RC	6.00	15.00
452 Earl Averill Jr.	5.00	12.00
453 Cal McLish	5.00	12.00
454 Floyd Robinson RC	5.00	12.00
455 Luis Arroyo	6.00	15.00
456 Joe Amalfitano	6.00	15.00
457 Lou Clinton	5.00	12.00
458A Bob Buhl Emblem	6.00	15.00
458B Bob Buhl No Emblem	20.00	50.00
459 Ed Bailey	5.00	12.00
460 Jim Bunning	8.00	20.00
461 Ken Hubbs RC	10.00	25.00
462A Willie Tasby Emblem	5.00	12.00
462B Willie Tasby No Emblem	20.00	50.00
463 Hank Bauer MG	6.00	15.00
464 Al Jackson RC	6.00	15.00
465 Cincinnati Reds TC	8.00	20.00
466 Norm Cash AS	6.00	15.00
467 Chuck Schilling AS	5.00	12.00
468 Brooks Robinson AS	12.00	30.00
469 Luis Aparicio AS	6.00	15.00
470 Al Kaline AS	20.00	50.00
471 Mickey Mantle AS	100.00	250.00
472 Rocky Colavito AS	6.00	15.00
473 Elston Howard AS	6.00	15.00
474 Frank Lary AS	5.00	12.00
475 Whitey Ford AS	8.00	20.00
476 Baltimore Orioles TC	8.00	20.00
477 Andre Rodgers	5.00	12.00
478 Don Zimmer	8.00	20.00
479 Joel Horlen RC	5.00	12.00
480 Harvey Kuenn	6.00	15.00
481 Vic Wertz	6.00	15.00
482 Sam Mele MG	5.00	12.00
483 Don McMahon	5.00	12.00
484 Dick Schofield	5.00	12.00
485 Pedro Ramos	5.00	12.00
486 Jim Gilliam	6.00	15.00
487 Jerry Lynch	5.00	12.00
488 Hal Brown	5.00	12.00
489 Julio Gotay RC	5.00	12.00
490 Clete Boyer UER	6.00	15.00
491 Leon Wagner	5.00	12.00
492 Hal W. Smith	6.00	15.00
493 Danny McDevitt	5.00	12.00
494 Sammy White	5.00	12.00
495 Don Cardwell	5.00	12.00
496 Wayne Causey RC	5.00	12.00
497 Ed Bouchee	6.00	15.00
498 Jim Donohue	5.00	12.00
499 Zoilo Versalles	6.00	15.00
500 Duke Snider	20.00	50.00
501 Claude Osteen	6.00	15.00
502 Hector Lopez	6.00	15.00
503 Danny Murtaugh MG	6.00	15.00
504 Eddie Bressoud	5.00	12.00
505 Juan Marichal	15.00	40.00
506 Charlie Maxwell	6.00	15.00
507 Ernie Broglio	6.00	15.00
508 Gordy Coleman	6.00	15.00
509 Dave Giusti RC	6.00	15.00
510 Jim Lemon	5.00	12.00
511 Bubba Phillips	5.00	12.00
512 Mike Fornieles	5.00	12.00
513 Whitey Herzog	6.00	15.00
514 Sherm Lollar	6.00	15.00
515 Stan Williams	6.00	15.00
516A Checklist 7 White	6.00	15.00
516B Checklist 7 Yellow	6.00	15.00
517 Dave Wickersham	5.00	12.00
518 Lee Maye	5.00	12.00
519 Bob Johnson RC	5.00	12.00
520 Bob Friend	6.00	15.00
521 Jacke Davis UER RC	5.00	12.00
522 Lindy McDaniel	6.00	15.00
523 Russ Nixon SP	12.50	30.00
524 Howie Nunn SP	12.50	30.00
525 George Thomas	8.00	20.00
526 Hal Woodeshick SP	12.50	30.00
527 Dick McAuliffe RC	12.50	30.00
528 Turk Lown	8.00	20.00
529 John Schaive SP	12.50	30.00
530 Bob Gibson SP	60.00	150.00
531 Bobby G. Smith	8.00	20.00
532 Dick Stigman	8.00	20.00
533 Charley Lau SP	12.50	30.00
534 Tony Gonzalez SP	12.50	30.00
535 Ed Roebuck	8.00	20.00
536 Dick Gernert	8.00	20.00
537 Cleveland Indians TC	20.00	50.00
538 Jack Sanford	8.00	20.00
539 Billy Moran	8.00	20.00
540 Jim Landis	12.50	30.00
541 Don Nottebart SP	12.50	30.00
542 Dave Philley	8.00	20.00
543 Bob Allen SP	12.50	30.00
544 Willie McCovey SP	60.00	150.00
545 Hoyt Wilhelm SP	20.00	50.00
546 Moe Thacker SP	12.50	30.00
547 Don Ferrarese	8.00	20.00
548 Bobby Del Greco	8.00	20.00
549 Bill Rigney MG SP	12.50	30.00
550 Art Mahaffey SP	12.50	30.00
551 Harry Bright	8.00	20.00
552 Chicago Cubs TC	20.00	50.00
553 Jim Coates	12.50	30.00
554 Bubba Morton SP RC	12.50	30.00
555 John Buzhardt SP	12.50	30.00
556 Al Spangler	8.00	20.00
557 Bob Anderson SP	12.50	30.00
558 John Goryl	8.00	20.00
559 Mike Higgins MG	8.00	20.00
560 Chuck Estrada SP	12.50	30.00
561 Gene Oliver SP	12.50	30.00
562 Bill Henry	8.00	20.00
563 Ken Aspromonte	8.00	20.00
564 Bob Grim	8.00	20.00
565 Jose Pagan	8.00	20.00
566 Marty Kutyna SP	12.50	30.00
567 Tracy Stallard SP	12.50	30.00
568 Jim Golden	8.00	20.00
569 Ed Sadowski SP	12.50	30.00
570 Bill Stafford SP	12.50	30.00
571 Billy Klaus SP	12.50	30.00
572 Bob G. Miller SP	12.50	30.00
573 Johnny Logan	8.00	20.00
574 Dean Stone	8.00	20.00
575 Red Schoendienst SP	20.00	50.00
576 Russ Kemmerer SP	12.50	30.00
577 Dave Nicholson SP	12.50	30.00
578 Jim Duffalo RC	8.00	20.00
579 Jim Schaffer SP RC	12.50	30.00
580 Bill Monbouquette	8.00	20.00
581 Mel Roach	8.00	20.00
582 Ron Piche	8.00	20.00
583 Larry Osborne	8.00	20.00
584 Minnesota Twins TC SP	30.00	60.00
585 Glen Hobbie SP	12.50	30.00
586 Sammy Esposito SP	12.50	30.00
587 Frank Funk SP	12.50	30.00
588 Birdie Tebbetts MG	8.00	20.00
589 Bob Turley	12.50	30.00
590 Curt Flood	12.50	30.00
591 Sam McDowell SP RC	40.00	80.00
592 Jim Bouton SP RC	30.00	80.00
593 Rookie Pitchers SP	20.00	50.00
594 Bob Uecker SP RC	100.00	250.00
595 Rookie Infielders SP	20.00	50.00
596 Joe Pepitone SP RC	50.00	120.00
597 Rookie Infield SP	20.00	50.00
598 Rookie Outfielders SP	40.00	80.00

1962 Topps Bucks

There are 96 "Baseball Bucks" in this unusual set released in its own one-cent package in 1962. Each "buck" measures 1 3/4" by 4 1/8". Each depicts a player with accompanying biography and facsimile autograph to the left. To the right is found a drawing of the player's home stadium. His team and position are listed under the ribbon design containing his name. The team affiliation and league are also indicated within circles on the reverse.

Card	Low	High
COMPLETE SET (96)	600.00	1200.00
WRAPPER (1-CENT)	20.00	50.00
1 Hank Aaron	30.00	60.00
2 Joe Adcock	2.50	6.00
3 George Altman	2.00	5.00
4 Jim Archer	2.00	5.00
5 Richie Ashburn	10.00	25.00
6 Ernie Banks	15.00	40.00
7 Earl Battey	2.00	5.00
8 Gus Bell	2.00	5.00
9 Yogi Berra	15.00	40.00
10 Ken Boyer	3.00	8.00
11 Jackie Brandt	2.00	5.00
12 Jim Bunning	10.00	25.00
13 Lew Burdette	2.50	6.00
14 Don Cardwell	2.00	5.00
15 Norm Cash	3.00	8.00
16 Orlando Cepeda	8.00	20.00
17 Roberto Clemente	100.00	200.00
18 Rocky Colavito	6.00	15.00
19 Chuck Cottier	2.00	5.00
20 Roger Craig	2.50	6.00
21 Bennie Daniels	2.00	5.00
22 Don Demeter	2.00	5.00
23 Don Drysdale	12.50	30.00
24 Chuck Estrada	2.00	5.00
25 Dick Farrell	2.00	5.00
26 Whitey Ford	15.00	40.00
27 Nellie Fox	10.00	25.00
28 Tito Francona	2.00	5.00
29 Bob Friend	2.00	5.00
30 Jim Gentile	2.50	6.00
31 Dick Gernert	2.00	5.00
32 Lenny Green	2.00	5.00
33 Dick Groat	2.50	6.00
34 Woodie Held	2.00	5.00
35 Don Hoak	2.00	5.00
36 Gil Hodges	10.00	25.00
37 Elston Howard	6.00	15.00
38 Frank Howard	3.00	8.00
39 Dick Howser	2.50	6.00
40 Ken Hunt	2.00	5.00
41 Larry Jackson	2.00	5.00
42 Joey Jay	2.00	5.00
43 Al Kaline	15.00	40.00
44 Harmon Killebrew	10.00	25.00
45 Sandy Koufax	40.00	80.00
46 Harvey Kuenn	2.50	6.00
47 Jim Landis	2.00	5.00
48 Norm Larker	2.00	5.00
49 Frank Lary	2.00	5.00
50 Jerry Lumpe	2.00	5.00
51 Art Mahaffey	2.00	5.00
52 Frank Malzone	2.00	5.00
53 Felix Mantilla	2.00	5.00
54 Mickey Mantle	100.00	200.00
55 Roger Maris	20.00	50.00
56 Eddie Mathews	10.00	25.00
57 Willie Mays	30.00	60.00
58 Ken McBride	2.00	5.00
59 Mike McCormick	2.00	5.00
60 Stu Miller	2.00	5.00
61 Minnie Minoso	3.00	8.00
62 Wally Moon	2.50	6.00
63 Stan Musial	30.00	60.00
64 Danny O'Connell	2.00	5.00
65 Jim O'Toole	2.00	5.00
66 Camilo Pascual	2.00	5.00
67 Jim Perry	2.50	6.00
68 Jimmy Piersall	2.50	6.00
69 Vada Pinson	3.00	8.00
70 Juan Pizarro	2.00	5.00
71 Johnny Podres	2.50	6.00
72 Vic Power	2.00	5.00
73 Bob Purkey	2.00	5.00
74 Pedro Ramos	2.00	5.00
75 Brooks Robinson	15.00	40.00
76 Floyd Robinson	2.00	5.00
77 Frank Robinson	15.00	40.00
78 John Romano	2.00	5.00
79 Pete Runnels	2.00	5.00
80 Don Schwall	2.00	5.00
81 Bobby Shantz	2.00	5.00
82 Norm Siebern	2.00	5.00
83 Roy Sievers	2.00	5.00
84 Hal Smith	2.00	5.00
85 Warren Spahn	10.00	25.00
86 Dick Stuart	2.50	6.00
87 Tony Taylor	2.00	5.00
88 Lee Thomas	2.50	6.00
89 Gus Triandos	2.00	5.00
90 Leon Wagner	2.00	5.00
91 Jerry Walker	2.00	5.00
92 Bill White	3.00	8.00
93 Billy Williams	10.00	25.00
94 Gene Woodling	2.50	6.00
95 Early Wynn	10.00	25.00
96 Carl Yastrzemski	15.00	40.00

1962 Topps Stamps

The 201 baseball player stamps inserted into the Topps regular issue of 1962 are color photos set upon red or yellow backgrounds (100 players for each color). They came in two-stamp panels with a small additional strip which contained advertising for an album. Roy Sievers appears with Kansas City or Philadelphia; the set price includes both versions. Each stamp measures 1 3/8" by 1 7/8". Stamps are unnumbered but are presented here in alphabetical order by team, Baltimore Orioles AL (1-10), Boston Red Sox (11-20), Chicago White Sox (21-30), Cleveland Indians (31-40), Detroit Tigers (41-50), Kansas City A's (51-61), Los Angeles Angels (62-71), Minnesota Twins (72-81), New York Yankees (82-91), Washington Senators (92-101), Chicago Cubs NL (102-111), Cincinnati Reds (112-121), Houston Colt .45's (122-131), Los Angeles Dodgers (132-141), Milwaukee Braves (142-151), New York Mets (152-161), Philadelphia Phillies (162-171), Pittsburgh Pirates (172-181), St. Louis Cardinals (182-191) and San Francisco Giants (192-201). For some time there has been the rumored existence of a

Roy Sievers stamp wearing an A's cap but it has yet to be confirmed.
COMPLETE SET (201) 200.00 400.00
1 Baltimore Emblem .40 1.00
2 Jerry Adair .40 1.00
3 Jackie Brandt .40 1.00
4 Chuck Estrada .40 1.00
5 Jim Gentile .60 1.50
6 Ron Hansen .40 1.00
7 Milt Pappas .60 1.50
8 Brooks Robinson 3.00 8.00
9 Gus Triandos .60 1.50
10 Hoyt Wilhelm 1.00 2.50
11 Boston Emblem .40 1.00
12 Mike Fornieles .40 1.00
13 Gary Geiger .40 1.00
14 Frank Malzone .60 1.50
15 Bill Monbouquette .40 1.00
16 Russ Nixon .40 1.00
17 Pete Runnels .60 1.50
18 Chuck Schilling .40 1.00
19 Don Schwall .40 1.00
20 Carl Yastrzemski 5.00 12.00
21 Chicago Emblem .40 1.00
22 Luis Aparicio 1.00 2.50
23 Camilo Carreon .40 1.00
24 Nellie Fox 1.50 4.00
25 Ray Herbert .40 1.00
26 Jim Landis .40 1.00
27 J.C. Martin .40 1.00
28 Juan Pizzaro .40 1.00
29 Floyd Robinson .40 1.00
30 Early Wynn 1.00 2.50
31 Cleveland Emblem .40 1.00
32 Ty Cline .40 1.00
33 Dick Donovan .40 1.00
34 Tito Francona .40 1.00
35 Woody Held .40 1.00
36 Barry Latman .40 1.00
37 Jim Perry .60 1.50
38 Bubba Phillips .40 1.00
39 Vic Power .40 1.00
40 Johnny Romano .40 1.00
41 Detroit Emblem .40 1.00
42 Steve Boros .40 1.00
43 Bill Bruton .40 1.00
44 Jim Bunning 1.00 2.50
45 Norm Cash 1.00 2.50
46 Rocky Colavito 1.00 2.50
47 Al Kaline 3.00 8.00
48 Frank Lary .60 1.50
49 Don Mossi .60 1.50
50 Jake Wood .40 1.00
51 Kansas City Emblem .40 1.00
52 Jim Archer .40 1.00
53 Dick Howser 1.00 2.50
54 Jerry Lumpe .40 1.00
55 Leo Posada .40 1.00
56 Bob Shaw .40 1.00
57 Norm Siebern .40 1.00
59 Gene Stephens .40 1.00
60 Haywood Sullivan .40 1.00
61 Jerry Walker .40 1.00
62 Los Angeles Emblem .40 1.00
63 Steve Bilko .40 1.00
64 Ted Bowsfield .40 1.00
65 Ken Hunt .40 1.00
66 Ken McBride .40 1.00
67 Albie Pearson .40 1.00
68 Bob Rodgers .60 1.50
69 George Thomas .40 1.00
70 Lee Thomas .60 1.50
71 Leon Wagner .40 1.00
72 Minnesota Emblem .40 1.00
73 Bob Allison .60 1.50
74 Earl Battey .40 1.00
75 Lenny Green .40 1.00
76 Harmon Killebrew 2.50 6.00
77 Jack Kralick .40 1.00
78 Camilo Pascual .60 1.50
79 Pedro Ramos .40 1.00
80 Bill Tuttle .40 1.00
81 Zoilo Versailles .60 1.50
82 New York Emblem .60 1.50
83 Yogi Berra 5.00 12.00
84 Clete Boyer 1.00 2.50
85 Whitey Ford 4.00 10.00
86 Elston Howard 1.50 4.00
87 Tony Kubek 1.00 2.50
88 Mickey Mantle 30.00 60.00
89 Roger Maris 8.00 20.00
90 Bobby Richardson 1.00 2.50
91 Bill Skowron 1.00 2.50
92 Washington Emblem .40 1.00
93 Chuck Cottier .40 1.00
94 Pete Daley .40 1.00
95 Bennie Daniels .40 1.00
96 Chuck Hinton .40 1.00
97 Bob Johnson .40 1.00
98 Joe McClain .40 1.00
99 Danny O'Connell .40 1.00
100 Jimmy Piersall 1.00 2.50
101 Gene Woodling .60 1.50
102 Chicago Emblem .40 1.00
103 George Altman .40 1.00
104 Ernie Banks 3.00 8.00
105 Dick Bertell .40 1.00
106 Don Cardwell .40 1.00
107 Dick Ellsworth .40 1.00
108 Glen Hobbie .40 1.00
109 Ron Santo 1.00 2.50
110 Barney Schultz .40 1.00
111 Billy Williams 1.00 2.50
112 Cincinnati Emblem .40 1.00
113 Gordon Coleman .40 1.00
114 Johnny Edwards .40 1.00
115 Gene Freese .40 1.00
116 Joey Jay .40 1.00
117 Eddie Kasko .40 1.00
118 Jim O'Toole .40 1.00
119 Vada Pinson 1.00 2.50
120 Bob Purkey .40 1.00
121 Frank Robinson 3.00 8.00
122 Houston Emblem .40 1.00
123 Joe Amalfitano .40 1.00
124 Bob Aspromonte .40 1.00
125 Dick Farrell .40 1.00
126 Al Heist .40 1.00
127 Sam Jones .40 1.00
128 Bobby Shantz .60 1.50
129 Hal W. Smith .40 1.00
130 Al Spangler .40 1.00
131 Bob Tiefenauer .40 1.00
132 Los Angeles Emblem .40 1.00
133 Don Drysdale 2.50 6.00
134 Ron Fairly .60 1.50
135 Frank Howard 1.00 2.50
136 Sandy Koufax 6.00 15.00
137 Wally Moon .60 1.50
138 Johnny Podres 1.00 2.50
139 John Roseboro .40 1.00
140 Duke Snider 4.00 10.00
141 Daryl Spencer .40 1.00
142 Milwaukee Emblem .40 1.00
143 Hank Aaron 6.00 15.00
144 Joe Adcock .60 1.50
145 Frank Bolling .40 1.00
146 Lou Burdette 1.00 2.50
147 Del Crandall .40 1.00
148 Eddie Mathews 2.50 6.00
149 Roy McMillan .40 1.00
150 Warren Spahn 3.00 8.00
151 Joe Torre 2.00 5.00
152 New York Emblem .60 1.50
153 Gus Bell .60 1.50
154 Roger Craig 1.00 2.50
155 Gil Hodges 2.50 6.00
156 Jay Hook .60 1.50
157 Hobie Landrith .60 1.50
158 Felix Mantilla .60 1.50
159 Bob L. Miller .60 1.50
160 Lee Walls .60 1.50
161 Don Zimmer 1.00 2.50
162 Philadelphia Emblem .40 1.00
163 Ruben Amaro .40 1.00
164 Jack Baldschun .40 1.00
165 Johnny Callison UER .60 1.50
Name spelled Callizon
166 Clay Dalrymple .40 1.00
167 Don Demeter .40 1.00
168 Tony Gonzalez .40 1.00
169 Roy Sievers 1.00 2.50
Phils, see also 58
170 Tony Taylor .60 1.50
171 Art Mahaffey .40 1.00
172 Pittsburgh Emblem .40 1.00
173 Smoky Burgess .60 1.50
174 Roberto Clemente 15.00 40.00
175 Roy Face 1.00 2.50
176 Bob Friend .60 1.50
177 Dick Groat 1.00 2.50
178 Don Hoak .40 1.00
179 Bill Mazeroski 1.50 4.00
180 Dick Stuart .60 1.50
181 Bill Virdon 1.00 2.50
182 St. Louis Emblem .40 1.00
183 Ken Boyer 1.00 2.50
184 Larry Jackson .40 1.00
185 Julian Javier .40 1.00
186 Tim McCarver 1.50 4.00
187 Lindy McDaniel .40 1.00
188 Minnie Minoso 1.00 2.50
189 Stan Musial 6.00 15.00
190 Ray Sadecki .40 1.00
191 Bill White 1.00 2.50
192 San Francisco Emblem .40 1.00
193 Felipe Alou 1.00 2.50
194 Ed Bailey .40 1.00
195 Orlando Cepeda 1.00 2.50
196 Jim Davenport 1.00 2.50
197 Harvey Kuenn 1.00 2.50
198 Juan Marichal 1.50 4.00
199 Willie Mays 8.00 20.00
200 Mike McCormick .60 1.50
201 Stu Miller .40 1.00
NNO Stamp Album 8.00 20.00

1963 Topps

The cards in this 576-card set measure 2 1/2" by 3 1/2". The sharp color photographs of the 1963 set are a vivid contrast to the drab pictures of 1962. In addition to the "League Leaders" series (1-10) and World Series cards (142-148), the seventh and last series of cards (523-576) contains seven rookie cards (each depicting four players). Cards were issued, among other ways, in one-card penny packs and five-card nickel packs. There were some three-card advertising panels produced by Topps; the players included are from the first series; one panel shows Hoyt Wilhelm, Don Lock, and Bob Duliba on the front with a Stan Musial ad/endorsement on one of the backs. Key Rookie Cards in this set are Bill Freehan, Tony Oliva, Pete Rose, Willie Stargell and Rusty Staub.

COMPLETE SET (576) 3000.00 8000.00
COMMON CARD (1-196) 1.50 4.00
COMMON CARD (197-283) 2.00 5.00
COMMON CARD (284-370) 2.00 5.00
COMMON CARD (371-446) 2.00 5.00
COMMON CARD (447-522) 10.00 25.00
COMMON CARD (523-576) 6.00 15.00
WRAPPER (1-CENT) 15.00 40.00
WRAPPER (5-CENT) 12.50 30.00
1 F.Rob/Musial/Aaron LL 10.00 25.00
2 Runnels/Mantle/Rob LL 20.00 50.00
3 Mays/Aaron/Rob/Cep/Banks LL 20.00 50.00
4 Kill/Cash/Colav/Maris LL 10.00 25.00
5 Koufax/Gibson/Drysdale LL 10.00 25.00
6 Aguirre/Roberts/Ford LL 4.00 10.00
7 Drysdale/Sanf/Purk LL 4.00 10.00
8 Terry/Donovan/Bunning LL 3.00 8.00
9 Drysdale/Koufax/Gibson LL 12.50 30.00
10 Pascual/Bunning/Kaat LL 3.00 8.00
11 Lee Walls 1.50 4.00
12 Steve Barber 1.50 4.00
13 Philadelphia Phillies TC 3.00 8.00
14 Pedro Ramos 1.50 4.00
15 Ken Hubbs UER NPO 4.00 10.00
16 Al Smith 1.50 4.00
17 Ryne Duren 3.00 8.00
18 Burg/Stu/Clemente/Skin 20.00 50.00
19 Pete Burnside 1.50 4.00
20 Tony Kubek 6.00 15.00
21 Marty Keough 1.50 4.00
22 Curt Simmons 3.00 8.00
23 Ed Lopat MG 3.00 8.00
24 Bob Bruce 1.50 4.00
25 Al Kaline 25.00 60.00
26 Ray Moore 1.50 4.00
27 Choo Choo Coleman 3.00 8.00
28 Mike Fornieles 1.50 4.00
29A Rookie Stars 1962 4.00 10.00
29B Rookie Stars 1963 1.50 4.00
30 Harvey Kuenn 3.00 8.00
31 Cal Koonce RC 1.50 4.00
32 Tony Gonzalez 1.50 4.00
33 Bo Belinsky 3.00 8.00
34 Dick Schofield 1.50 4.00
35 John Buzhardt 1.50 4.00
36 Jerry Kindall 1.50 4.00
37 Jerry Lynch 1.50 4.00
38 Bud Daley 3.00 8.00
39 Los Angeles Angels TC 3.00 8.00
40 Vic Power 3.00 8.00
41 Charley Lau 3.00 8.00
42 Stan Williams 3.00 8.00
43 C.Stengel/G.Woodling 3.00 8.00
44 Terry Fox 1.50 4.00
45 Bob Aspromonte 1.50 4.00
46 Tommie Aaron RC 3.00 8.00
47 Don Lock RC 1.50 4.00
48 Birdie Tebbetts MG 3.00 8.00
49 Dal Maxvill RC 3.00 8.00
50 Billy Pierce 3.00 8.00
51 George Alusik 1.50 4.00
52 Chuck Schilling 1.50 4.00
53 Joe Moeller RC 3.00 8.00
54A Dave DeBusschere 62 6.00 15.00
54B Dave DeBusschere 63 RC 3.00 8.00
55 Bill Virdon 3.00 8.00
56 Dennis Bennett RC 1.50 4.00
57 Billy Moran 1.50 4.00
58 Bob Will 1.50 4.00
59 Craig Anderson 1.50 4.00
60 Elston Howard 3.00 8.00
61 Ernie Bowman 1.50 4.00
62 Bob Hendley 1.50 4.00
63 Cincinnati Reds TC 3.00 8.00
64 Dick McAuliffe 3.00 8.00
65 Jackie Brandt 1.50 4.00
66 Mike Joyce RC 1.50 4.00
67 Ed Charles 1.50 4.00
68 G.Hodges/D.Snider 10.00 25.00
69 Bud Zipfel RC 1.50 4.00
70 Jim O'Toole 3.00 8.00
71 Bobby Wine RC 3.00 8.00
72 Johnny Romano 1.50 4.00
73 Bobby Bragan MG RC 3.00 8.00
74 Denny Lemaster RC 1.50 4.00
75 Bob Allison 3.00 8.00
76 Earl Wilson 3.00 8.00
77 Al Spangler 1.50 4.00
78 Marv Throneberry 3.00 8.00
79 Checklist 1 5.00 12.00
80 Jim Gilliam 3.00 8.00
81 Jim Schaffer 1.50 4.00
82 Ed Rakow 1.50 4.00
83 Charley James 1.50 4.00
84 Ron Kline 1.50 4.00
85 Tom Haller 3.00 8.00
86 Charley Maxwell 3.00 8.00
87 Bob Veale 3.00 8.00
88 Ron Hansen 1.50 4.00
89 Dick Stigman 1.50 4.00
90 Gordy Coleman 3.00 8.00
91 Dallas Green 3.00 8.00
92 Hector Lopez 3.00 8.00
93 Galen Cisco 1.50 4.00
94 Bob Schmidt 1.50 4.00
95 Larry Jackson 1.50 4.00
96 Lou Clinton 1.50 4.00
97 Bob Duliba 1.50 4.00
98 George Thomas 1.50 4.00
99 Jim Umbricht 1.50 4.00
100 Joe Cunningham 1.50 4.00
101 Joe Gibbon 1.50 4.00
102A Checklist 2 Red 5.00 12.00
Yellow
102B Checklist 2 White 5.00 12.00
Red
103 Chuck Essegian 1.50 4.00
104 Lew Krausse RC 1.50 4.00
105 Ron Fairly 3.00 8.00
106 Bobby Bolin 1.50 4.00
107 Jim Hickman 3.00 8.00
108 Hoyt Wilhelm 4.00 10.00
109 Lee Maye 1.50 4.00
110 Rich Rollins 3.00 8.00
111 Al Jackson 1.50 4.00
112 Dick Brown 1.50 4.00
113 Don Landrum UER 1.50 4.00
114 Dan Osinski RC 1.50 4.00
115 Carl Yastrzemski 30.00 80.00
116 Jim Brosnan 3.00 8.00
117 Jacke Davis 1.50 4.00
118 Sherm Lollar 1.50 4.00
119 Bob Lillis 1.50 4.00
120 Roger Maris 40.00 100.00
121 Jim Hannan RC 1.50 4.00
122 Julio Gotay 1.50 4.00
123 Frank Howard 3.00 8.00
124 Dick Howser 3.00 8.00
125 Robin Roberts 8.00 20.00
126 Bob Uecker 25.00 60.00
127 Bill Tuttle 1.50 4.00
128 Matty Alou 3.00 8.00
129 Gary Bell 1.50 4.00
130 Dick Groat 3.00 8.00
131 Washington Senators TC 3.00 8.00
132 Jack Hamilton 1.50 4.00
133 Gene Freese 1.50 4.00
134 Bob Scheffing MG 1.50 4.00
135 Richie Ashburn 10.00 25.00
136 Ike Delock 1.50 4.00
137 Mack Jones 1.50 4.00
138 W.Mays/S.Musial 25.00 60.00
139 Earl Averill Jr. 1.50 4.00
140 Frank Lary 3.00 8.00
141 Manny Mota RC 3.00 8.00
142 Whitey Ford WS1 8.00 20.00
143 Jack Sanford WS2 3.00 8.00
144 Roger Maris WS3 10.00 25.00
145 Chuck Hiller WS4 3.00 8.00
146 Tom Tresh WS5 3.00 8.00
147 Billy Pierce WS6 3.00 8.00
148 Ralph Terry WS7 3.00 8.00
149 Marv Breeding 1.50 4.00
150 Johnny Podres 3.00 8.00
151 Pittsburgh Pirates TC 3.00 8.00
152 Ron Nischwitz 1.50 4.00
153 Hal Smith 1.50 4.00
154 Walter Alston MG 3.00 8.00
155 Bill Stafford 1.50 4.00
156 Roy McMillan 3.00 8.00
157 Diego Segui RC 3.00 8.00
158 Tommy Harper RC 3.00 8.00
159 Jim Pagliaroni 1.50 4.00
160 Juan Pizarro 1.50 4.00
161 Frank Torre 3.00 8.00
162 Minnesota Twins TC 3.00 8.00
163 Don Larsen 3.00 8.00
164 Bubba Morton 1.50 4.00
165 Jim Kaat 3.00 8.00
166 Johnny Keane MG 1.50 4.00
167 Jim Fregosi 3.00 8.00
168 Russ Nixon 1.50 4.00
169 Gaylord Perry 10.00 25.00
170 Joe Adcock 3.00 8.00
171 Steve Hamilton RC 1.50 4.00
172 Gene Oliver 1.50 4.00
173 Tresh/Mantle/Richardson 50.00 120.00
174 Larry Burright 1.50 4.00
175 Bob Buhl 3.00 8.00
176 Jim King 1.50 4.00
177 Bubba Phillips 1.50 4.00
178 Johnny Edwards 1.50 4.00
179 Ron Piche 1.50 4.00
180 Bill Skowron 3.00 8.00
181 Sammy Esposito 3.00 8.00
182 Albie Pearson 3.00 8.00
183 Joe Pepitone 3.00 8.00
184 Vern Law 3.00 8.00
185 Chuck Hiller 1.50 4.00
186 Jerry Zimmerman 1.50 4.00
187 Willie Kirkland 1.50 4.00
188 Eddie Bressoud 1.50 4.00
189 Dave Giusti 3.00 8.00
190 Minnie Minoso 3.00 8.00
191 Checklist 3 5.00 12.00
192 Clay Dalrymple 1.50 4.00
193 Andre Rodgers 1.50 4.00
194 Joe Nuxhall 3.00 8.00
195 Manny Jimenez 1.50 4.00
196 Doug Camilli 1.50 4.00
197 Roger Craig 3.00 8.00
198 Lenny Green 2.00 5.00
199 Joe Amalfitano 2.00 5.00
200 Mickey Mantle 300.00 600.00
201 Cecil Butler 2.00 5.00
202 Boston Red Sox TC 3.00 8.00
203 Chico Cardenas 3.00 8.00
204 Don Nottebart 2.00 5.00
205 Luis Aparicio 6.00 15.00
206 Ray Washburn 2.00 5.00
207 Ken Hunt 2.00 5.00
208 Rookie Stars 2.00 5.00
209 Hobie Landrith 2.00 5.00
210 Sandy Koufax 75.00 200.00
211 Fred Whitfield RC 2.00 5.00
212 Glen Hobbie 2.00 5.00
213 Billy Hitchcock MG 2.00 5.00
214 Orlando Pena 2.00 5.00
215 Bob Skinner 3.00 8.00
216 Gene Conley 3.00 8.00
217 Joe Christopher 2.00 5.00
218 Lary/Mossi/Bunning 3.00 8.00
219 Chuck Cottier 2.00 5.00
220 Camilo Pascual 3.00 8.00
221 Cookie Rojas RC 3.00 8.00
222 Chicago Cubs TC 3.00 8.00
223 Eddie Fisher 2.00 5.00
224 Mike Roarke 2.00 5.00
225 Joey Jay 2.00 5.00
226 Julian Javier 3.00 8.00
227 Jim Grant 3.00 8.00
228 Tony Oliva RC 30.00 80.00
229 Willie Davis 3.00 8.00
230 Pete Runnels 3.00 8.00
231 Eli Grba UER 2.00 5.00
232 Frank Malzone 3.00 8.00
233 Casey Stengel MG 8.00 20.00
234 Dave Nicholson 2.00 5.00
235 Billy O'Dell 2.00 5.00
236 Bill Bryan RC 2.00 5.00
237 Jim Coates 3.00 8.00
238 Lou Johnson 2.00 5.00
239 Harvey Haddix 3.00 8.00
240 Rocky Colavito 6.00 15.00
241 Billy Smith RC 2.00 5.00
242 E.Banks/H.Aaron 30.00 80.00
243 Don Leppert 2.00 5.00
244 John Tsitouris 2.00 5.00
245 Gil Hodges 8.00 20.00
246 Lee Stange 2.00 5.00
247 New York Yankees TC 25.00 60.00
248 Tito Francona 2.00 5.00
249 Leo Burke RC 2.00 5.00
250 Stan Musial 40.00 100.00
251 Jack Lamabe 2.00 5.00
252 Ron Santo 12.00 30.00
253 Rookie Stars 2.00 5.00
254 Mike Hershberger 2.00 5.00
255 Bob Shaw 2.00 5.00
256 Jerry Lumpe 2.00 5.00
257 Hank Aguirre 2.00 5.00
258 Alvin Dark MG 3.00 8.00
259 Johnny Logan 3.00 8.00
260 Jim Gentile 3.00 8.00
261 Bob Miller 2.00 5.00
262 Ellis Burton 2.00 5.00
263 Dave Stenhouse 2.00 5.00
264 Phil Linz 2.00 5.00
265 Vada Pinson 3.00 8.00
266 Bob Allen 2.00 5.00
267 Carl Sawatski 2.00 5.00
268 Don Demeter 2.00 5.00
269 Don Mincher 2.00 5.00
270 Felipe Alou 3.00 8.00
271 Dean Stone 2.00 5.00
272 Danny Murphy 2.00 5.00
273 Sammy Taylor 2.00 5.00
274 Checklist 4 5.00 12.00
275 Eddie Mathews 20.00 50.00
276 Barry Shetrone 2.00 5.00
277 Dick Farrell 2.00 5.00
278 Chico Fernandez 2.00 5.00
279 Wally Moon 3.00 8.00
280 Bob Buck Rodgers 2.00 5.00
281 Tom Sturdivant 2.00 5.00
282 Bobby Del Greco 2.00 5.00
283 Roy Sievers 3.00 8.00
284 Dave Sisler 2.00 5.00
285 Dick Stuart 3.00 8.00
286 Stu Miller 3.00 8.00
287 Dick Bertell 2.00 5.00
288 Chicago White Sox TC 4.00 10.00
289 Hal Brown 2.00 5.00
290 Bill White 3.00 8.00
291 Don Rudolph 2.00 5.00
292 Pumpsie Green 3.00 8.00
293 Bill Pleis 2.00 5.00
294 Bill Rigney MG 2.00 5.00
295 Ed Roebuck 2.00 5.00
296 Doc Edwards 2.00 5.00
297 Jim Golden 2.00 5.00
298 Don Dillard 2.00 5.00
299 Rookie Stars 3.00 8.00
300 Willie Mays 75.00 200.00
301 Bill Fischer 2.00 5.00
302 Whitey Herzog 3.00 8.00
303 Earl Francis 2.00 5.00
304 Harry Bright 2.00 5.00
305 Don Hoak 2.00 5.00
306 E.Battey/E.Howard 4.00 10.00
307 Chet Nichols 2.00 5.00
308 Camilo Carreon 2.00 5.00
309 Jim Brewer 2.00 5.00
310 Tommy Davis 3.00 8.00
311 Joe McClain 2.00 5.00
312 Houston Colts TC 10.00 25.00
313 Ernie Broglio 2.00 5.00
314 John Goryl 2.00 5.00
315 Ralph Terry 3.00 8.00
316 Norm Sherry 3.00 8.00
317 Sam McDowell 3.00 8.00
318 Gene Mauch MG 3.00 8.00
319 Joe Gaines 2.00 5.00
320 Warren Spahn 30.00 80.00
321 Gino Cimoli 2.00 5.00
322 Bob Turley 3.00 8.00
323 Bill Mazeroski 20.00 50.00
324 Vic Davalillo RC 3.00 8.00
325 Jack Sanford 2.00 5.00
326 Hank Foiles 2.00 5.00
327 Paul Foytack 2.00 5.00
328 Dick Williams 3.00 8.00
329 Lindy McDaniel 3.00 8.00
330 Chuck Hinton 2.00 5.00
331 Stafford/Pierce 3.00 8.00
332 Joel Horlen 3.00 8.00
333 Carl Warwick 2.00 5.00
334 Wynn Hawkins 2.00 5.00
335 Leon Wagner 2.00 5.00
336 Ed Bauta 2.00 5.00
337 Los Angeles Dodgers TC 10.00 25.00
338 Russ Kemmerer 2.00 5.00
339 Ted Bowsfield 2.00 5.00
340 Yogi Berra P 50.00 100.00
CO
341 Jack Baldschun 2.00 5.00
342 Gene Woodling 3.00 8.00
343 Johnny Pesky MG 3.00 8.00
344 Don Schwall 2.00 5.00
345 Brooks Robinson 20.00 50.00
346 Billy Hoeft 2.00 5.00
347 Joe Torre 8.00 20.00
348 Vic Wertz 3.00 8.00
349 Zoilo Versalles 3.00 8.00
350 Bob Purkey 2.00 5.00
351 Al Luplow 2.00 5.00
352 Ken Johnson 2.00 5.00
353 Billy Williams 25.00 60.00
354 Dom Zanni 2.00 5.00
355 Dean Chance 3.00 8.00
356 John Schaive 2.00 5.00
357 George Altman 2.00 5.00
358 Milt Pappas 3.00 8.00
359 Haywood Sullivan 3.00 8.00
360 Don Drysdale 20.00 50.00
361 Clete Boyer 4.00 10.00
362 Checklist 5 5.00 12.00
363 Dick Radatz 3.00 8.00
364 Howie Goss 2.00 5.00
365 Jim Bunning 8.00 20.00
366 Tony Taylor 3.00 8.00
367 Tony Cloninger 2.00 5.00
368 Ed Bailey 2.00 5.00
369 Jim Lemon 2.00 5.00
370 Dick Donovan 2.00 5.00
371 Rod Kanehl 3.00 8.00
372 Don Lee 2.00 5.00
373 Jim Campbell RC 2.00 5.00
374 Claude Osteen 3.00 8.00
375 Ken Boyer 6.00 15.00
376 John Wyatt RC 2.00 5.00
377 Baltimore Orioles TC 4.00 10.00
378 Bill Henry 2.00 5.00
379 Bob Anderson 2.00 5.00
380 Ernie Banks UER 50.00 100.00
381 Frank Baumann 2.00 5.00
382 Ralph Houk MG 4.00 10.00
383 Pete Richert 2.00 5.00
384 Bob Tillman 2.00 5.00
385 Art Mahaffey 2.00 5.00
386 Rookie Stars 2.00 5.00
387 Al McBean 2.00 5.00
388 Jim Davenport 3.00 8.00
389 Frank Sullivan 2.00 5.00
390 Hank Aaron 75.00 200.00
391 Bill Dailey RC 2.00 5.00
392 Romano/Francona 2.00 5.00
393 Ken MacKenzie 3.00 8.00
394 Tim McCarver 6.00 15.00
395 Don McMahon 2.00 5.00
396 Joe Koppe 2.00 5.00
397 Kansas City Athletics TC 4.00 10.00
398 Boog Powell 15.00 40.00
399 Dick Ellsworth 2.00 5.00
400 Frank Robinson 30.00 80.00
401 Jim Bouton 15.00 40.00
402 Mickey Vernon MG 3.00 8.00
403 Ron Perranoski 3.00 8.00
404 Bob Oldis 2.00 5.00
405 Floyd Robinson 2.00 5.00
406 Howie Koplitz 2.00 5.00
407 Rookie Stars 3.00 8.00
408 Billy Gardner 2.00 5.00
409 Roy Face 3.00 8.00
410 Earl Battey 2.00 5.00
411 Jim Constable 2.00 5.00
412 Podres/Drysdale/Koufax 30.00 80.00
413 Jerry Walker 2.00 5.00
414 Ty Cline 2.00 5.00
415 Bob Gibson 40.00 100.00
416 Alex Grammas 2.00 5.00
417 San Francisco Giants TC 4.00 10.00
418 John Orsino 2.00 5.00
419 Tracy Stallard 2.00 5.00
420 Bobby Richardson 6.00 15.00
421 Tom Morgan 2.00 5.00
422 Fred Hutchinson MG 3.00 8.00
423 Ed Hobaugh 2.00 5.00
424 Charlie Smith 2.00 5.00
425 Smoky Burgess 3.00 8.00
426 Barry Latman 2.00 5.00
427 Bernie Allen 2.00 5.00
428 Carl Boles RC 2.00 5.00
429 Lou Burdette 3.00 8.00
430 Norm Siebern 2.00 5.00
431A Checklist 6 White 5.00 12.00
Red
431B Checklist 6 Black 12.50 30.00
Orange
432 Roman Mejias 2.00 5.00
433 Denis Menke 2.00 5.00
434 John Callison 3.00 8.00
435 Woody Held 3.00 8.00
436 Tim Harkness 3.00 8.00
437 Bill Bruton 2.00 5.00
438 Wes Stock 2.00 5.00
439 Don Zimmer 3.00 8.00
440 Juan Marichal 20.00 50.00
441 Lee Thomas 3.00 8.00
442 J.C. Hartman RC 2.00 5.00
443 Jimmy Piersall 3.00 8.00
444 Jim Maloney 3.00 8.00
445 Norm Cash 4.00 10.00
446 Whitey Ford 20.00 50.00
447 Felix Mantilla 10.00 25.00
448 Jack Kralick 10.00 25.00
449 Jose Tartabull 10.00 25.00
450 Bob Friend 12.50 30.00
451 Cleveland Indians TC 15.00 40.00
452 Barney Schultz 10.00 25.00
453 Jake Wood 10.00 25.00
454A Art Fowler White 10.00 25.00
454B Art Fowler Orange 12.50 30.00
455 Ruben Amaro 10.00 25.00
456 Jim Coker 10.00 25.00
457 Tex Clevenger 10.00 25.00
458 Al Lopez MG 12.50 30.00
459 Dick LeMay 10.00 25.00
460 Del Crandall 12.50 30.00
461 Norm Bass 10.00 25.00
462 Wally Post 10.00 25.00
463 Joe Schaffernoth 10.00 25.00
464 Ken Aspromonte 10.00 25.00
465 Chuck Estrada 10.00 25.00
466 Bill Freehan SP RC 20.00 50.00
467 Phil Ortega 10.00 25.00
468 Carroll Hardy 12.50 30.00
469 Jay Hook 12.50 30.00
470 Tom Tresh SP 30.00 60.00
471 Ken Retzer 10.00 25.00
472 Lou Brock 60.00 150.00
473 New York Mets TC 50.00 100.00
474 Jack Fisher 10.00 25.00
475 Gus Triandos 12.50 30.00
476 Frank Funk 10.00 25.00
477 Donn Clendenon 12.50 30.00
478 Paul Brown 10.00 25.00
479 Ed Brinkman RC 10.00 25.00
480 Bill Monbouquette 10.00 25.00
481 Bob Taylor 10.00 25.00
482 Felix Torres 10.00 25.00
483 Jim Owens UER 10.00 25.00
484 Dale Long SP 12.50 30.00
485 Jim Landis 10.00 25.00
486 Ray Sadecki 10.00 25.00
487 John Roseboro 12.50 30.00
488 Jerry Adair 10.00 25.00
489 Paul Toth RC 10.00 25.00
490 Willie McCovey 40.00 100.00
491 Harry Craft MG 10.00 25.00
492 Dave Wickersham 10.00 25.00
493 Walt Bond 10.00 25.00
494 Phil Regan 10.00 25.00
495 Frank Thomas SP 12.50 30.00
496 Rookie Stars 12.50 30.00
497 Bennie Daniels 10.00 25.00
498 Eddie Kasko 10.00 25.00
499 J.C. Martin 10.00 25.00
500 Harmon Killebrew SP 40.00 100.00
501 Joe Azcue 10.00 25.00
502 Daryl Spencer 10.00 25.00
503 Milwaukee Braves TC 15.00 40.00
504 Bob Johnson 10.00 25.00
505 Curt Flood 15.00 40.00
506 Gene Green 10.00 25.00
507 Roland Sheldon 12.50 30.00
508 Ted Savage 10.00 25.00
509A Checklist 7 Centered 12.50 30.00
509B Checklist 7 Right 12.50 30.00
510 Ken McBride 10.00 25.00
511 Charlie Neal 12.50 30.00
512 Cal McLish 10.00 25.00
513 Gary Geiger 10.00 25.00
514 Larry Osborne 10.00 25.00
515 Don Elston 10.00 25.00
516 Purnell Goldy RC 10.00 25.00
517 Hal Woodeshick 10.00 25.00
518 Don Blasingame 10.00 25.00
519 Claude Raymond RC 10.00 25.00
520 Orlando Cepeda 15.00 40.00
521 Dan Pfister 10.00 25.00
522 Rookie Stars 12.50 30.00
523 Bill Kunkel 6.00 15.00
524 St. Louis Cardinals TC 12.50 30.00
525 Nellie Fox 15.00 40.00
526 Dick Hall 6.00 15.00
527 Ed Sadowski 6.00 15.00
528 Carl Willey 6.00 15.00
529 Wes Covington 6.00 15.00
530 Don Mossi 8.00 20.00
531 Sam Mele MG 6.00 15.00
532 Steve Boros 6.00 15.00
533 Bobby Shantz 8.00 20.00
534 Ken Walters 6.00 15.00
535 Jim Perry 8.00 20.00
536 Norm Larker 6.00 15.00

'ete Rose RC 800.00 1500.00
ieorge Brunet 6.00 15.00
Vayne Causey 6.00 15.00
Roberto Clemente 125.00 300.00
Ron Moeller 6.00 15.00
.ou Klimchock 6.00 15.00
Russ Snyder 6.00 15.00
Rusty Staub RC 30.00 80.00
Jose Pagan 6.00 15.00
Hal Reniff 8.00 20.00
Gus Bell 6.00 15.00
Tom Satriano RC 6.00 15.00
Rookie Stars 6.00 15.00
Duke Snider 20.00 50.00
Billy Klaus 6.00 15.00
Detroit Tigers TC 10.00 25.00
Willie Stargell RC 150.00 400.00
Hank Fischer RC 6.00 15.00
John Blanchard 8.00 20.00
Al Worthington 6.00 15.00
Cuno Barragan 6.00 15.00
Ron Hunt RC 8.00 20.00
Danny Murtaugh MG 6.00 15.00
Ray Herbert 6.00 15.00
Mike De La Hoz 6.00 15.00
Dave McNally RC 15.00 40.00
Mike McCormick 6.00 15.00
George Banks RC 6.00 15.00
Larry Sherry 6.00 15.00
Cliff Cook 6.00 15.00
Jim Duffalo 6.00 15.00
Bob Sadowski 6.00 15.00
Luis Arroyo 8.00 20.00
Frank Bolling 6.00 15.00
Johnny Klippstein 6.00 15.00
Jack Spring 6.00 15.00
Coot Veal 6.00 15.00
Hal Kolstad 6.00 15.00
Don Cardwell 6.00 15.00
Johnny Temple 12.50 30.00

1963 Topps Peel-Offs

k-on inserts were found in several series of the 3 Topps cards. Each sticker measures 1 1/4" by 2 ". They are found either with blank backs or with ructions on the reverse. Stick-ons with the ruction backs are a little tougher to find. The er photo is in color inside an oval with name, n and postion below. Since these inserts were numbered, they are ordered below alphabetically.

MPLETE SET (46) 300.00 600.00
ank Aaron 15.00 40.00
uis Aparicio 5.00 12.00
ichie Ashburn 6.00 15.00
ob Aspromonte 1.50 4.00
rnie Banks 8.00 20.00
en Boyer 2.50 6.00
im Bunning 60.00 120.00
ohnny Callison 1.50 4.00
Roberto Clemente 30.00 60.00
Orlando Cepeda 5.00 12.00
Rocky Colavito 4.00 10.00
Tommy Davis 2.00 5.00
Dick Donovan 1.50 4.00
Don Drysdale 6.00 15.00
Dick Farrell 1.50 4.00
Jim Gentile 2.00 5.00
Ray Herbert 1.50 4.00
Chuck Hinton 1.50 4.00
Ken Hubbs 2.50 6.00
Al Jackson 1.50 4.00
Al Kaline 8.00 20.00
Harmon Killebrew 5.00 12.00
Sandy Koufax 12.50 30.00
Jerry Lumpe 1.50 4.00
Art Mahaffey 1.50 4.00
Mickey Mantle 50.00 100.00
Willie Mays 20.00 50.00
Bill Mazeroski 4.00 10.00
Bill Monbouquette 1.50 4.00
Stan Musial 12.50 30.00
Camilo Pascual 1.50 4.00
Bob Purkey 1.50 4.00
Bobby Richardson 2.50 6.00
Brooks Robinson 8.00 20.00
5 Floyd Robinson 1.50 4.00
5 Frank Robinson 8.00 20.00
7 Bob Rodgers 1.50 4.00
3 Johnny Romano 1.50 4.00
9 Jack Sanford 1.50 4.00
) Norm Siebern 1.50 4.00
1 Warren Spahn 5.00 12.00
2 Dave Stenhouse 1.50 4.00
3 Ralph Terry 1.50 4.00
4 Lee Thomas 2.00 5.00
5 Bill White 2.00 5.00
6 Carl Yastrzemski 10.00 25.00

1964 Topps

The cards in this 587-card set measure 2 1/2" by 3 1/2". Players in the 1964 Topps baseball series were easy to sort by team due to the giant block lettering found at the top of each card. The name and position of the player are found underneath the picture, and the card is numbered in a ball design on the orange-colored back. The usual last series scarcity holds for this set (523 to 587). Subsets within this set include League Leaders (1-12) and World Series cards (136-140). Among other vehicles, cards were issued in one-card penny packs as well as five-card nickel packs. There were some three-card advertising panels produced by Topps; the players included are from the first series; Panels with Mickey Mantle card backs include Walt Alston/Bill Henry/Vada Pinson; Carl Willey/White Sox Rookies/Bob Friend; and Jimmie Hall/Ernie Broglio/A.L. ERA Leaders on the front with a Mickey Mantle card back on one of the backs. The key Rookie Cards in this set are Richie Allen, Tony Conigliaro, Tommy John, Tony LaRussa, Phil Niekro and Lou Piniella.

COMPLETE SET (587) 2500.00 5000.00
COMMON CARD (1-196) 1.25 3.00
COMMON CARD (197-370) 1.50 4.00
COMMON CARD (371-522) 3.00 8.00
COMMON CARD (523-587) 6.00 15.00
WRAPPER (1-CENT) 50.00 100.00
WRAP.(1-CENT, REPEAT) 60.00 120.00
WRAPPER (5-CENT) 12.50 30.00
WRAPPER (5-CENT, COIN) 15.00 40.00
1 Koufax/Ells/Friend LL 12.50 30.00
2 Peters/Pizarro/Pascual LL 3.00 8.00
3 Koufax/Marichal/Spahn LL 8.00 20.00
4 Ford/Pascual/Bouton LL 3.00 8.00
5 Koufax/Malon/Drysdale LL 6.00 15.00
6 Pascual/Bunning/Stigman LL 3.00 8.00
7 Clemente/Groat/Aaron LL 12.00 30.00
8 Yaz/Kaline/Rollins LL 10.00 25.00
9 Aaron/McCov/Mays/Cep LL 20.00 50.00
10 Killebrew/Stuart/Allison LL 3.00 8.00
11 Aaron/Boyer/White LL 10.00 25.00
12 Stuart/Kaline/Killebrew LL 3.00 8.00
13 Hoyt Wilhelm 8.00 20.00
14 D.Nen RC/N.Willhite RC 1.25 3.00
15 Zoilo Versalles 2.50 6.00
16 John Boozer 1.25 3.00
17 Willie Kirkland 1.25 3.00
18 Billy O'Dell 1.25 3.00
19 Don Wert 1.25 3.00
20 Bob Friend 2.50 6.00
21 Yogi Berra MG 25.00 60.00
22 Jerry Adair 1.25 3.00
23 Chris Zachary RC 1.25 3.00
24 Carl Sawatski 1.25 3.00
25 Bill Monbouquette 1.25 3.00
26 Gino Cimoli 1.25 3.00
27 New York Mets TC 3.00 8.00
28 Claude Osteen 2.50 6.00
29 Lou Brock 30.00 80.00
30 Ron Perranoski 2.50 6.00
31 Dave Nicholson 1.25 3.00
32 Dean Chance 2.50 6.00
33 S.Ellis/M.Queen 2.50 6.00
34 Jim Perry 2.50 6.00
35 Eddie Mathews 20.00 30.00
36 Hal Reniff 1.25 3.00
37 Smoky Burgess 2.50 6.00
38 Jim Wynn RC 12.00 30.00
39 Hank Aguirre 1.25 3.00
40 Dick Groat 2.50 6.00
41 W.McCovey/L.Wagner 3.00 8.00
42 Moe Drabowsky 2.50 6.00
43 Roy Sievers 2.50 6.00
44 Duke Carmel 1.25 3.00
45 Milt Pappas 2.50 6.00
46 Ed Brinkman 1.25 3.00
47 J.Alou RC/R.Herbel 2.50 6.00
48 Bob Perry RC 1.25 3.00
49 Bill Henry 1.25 3.00
50 Mickey Mantle 250.00 600.00
51 Pete Richert 1.25 3.00
52 Chuck Hinton 1.25 3.00
53 Denis Menke 1.25 3.00
54 Sam Mele MG 1.25 3.00
55 Ernie Banks 40.00 100.00
56 Hal Brown 1.25 3.00
57 Tim Harkness 2.50 6.00
58 Don Demeter 2.50 6.00
59 Ernie Broglio 1.25 3.00
60 Frank Malzone 2.50 6.00
61 B.Rodgers/E.Sadowski 2.50 6.00
62 Ted Savage 1.25 3.00
63 John Orsino 1.25 3.00
64 Ted Abernathy 1.25 3.00
65 Felipe Alou 2.50 6.00
66 Eddie Fisher 1.25 3.00
67 Detroit Tigers TC 2.50 6.00
68 Willie Davis 2.50 6.00
69 Clete Boyer 2.50 6.00
70 Joe Torre 3.00 8.00
71 Jack Spring 1.25 3.00
72 Chico Cardenas 2.50 6.00
73 Jimmie Hall RC 3.00 8.00
74 B.Priddy RC/T.Butters 1.25 3.00
75 Wayne Causey 1.25 3.00
76 Checklist 1 4.00 10.00
77 Jerry Walker 1.25 3.00
78 Merritt Ranew 1.25 3.00
79 Bob Heffner RC 1.25 3.00
80 Vada Pinson 3.00 8.00
81 N.Fox/H.Killebrew 5.00 12.00
82 Jim Davenport 2.50 6.00
83 Gus Triandos 2.50 6.00
84 Carl Willey 1.25 3.00
85 Pete Ward 1.25 3.00
86 Al Downing 2.50 6.00
87 St. Louis Cardinals TC 2.50 6.00
88 John Roseboro 2.50 6.00
89 Boog Powell 2.50 6.00
90 Earl Battey 1.25 3.00
91 Bob Bailey 2.50 6.00
92 Steve Ridzik 1.25 3.00
93 Gary Geiger 1.25 3.00
94 J.Britton RC/L.Maxie RC 1.25 3.00
95 George Altman 1.25 3.00
96 Bob Buhl 2.50 6.00
97 Jim Fregosi 2.50 6.00
98 Bill Bruton 1.25 3.00
99 Al Stanek RC 1.25 3.00
100 Elston Howard 2.50 6.00
101 Walt Alston MG 3.00 8.00
102 Checklist 2 4.00 10.00
103 Curt Flood 2.50 6.00
104 Art Mahaffey 2.50 6.00
105 Woody Held 1.25 3.00
106 Joe Nuxhall 2.50 6.00
107 B.Howard RC/F.Kruetzer RC 1.25 3.00
108 John Wyatt 1.25 3.00
109 Rusty Staub 2.50 6.00
110 Albie Pearson 2.50 6.00
111 Don Elston 1.25 3.00
112 Bob Tillman 1.25 3.00
113 Grover Powell RC 2.50 6.00
114 Don Lock 1.25 3.00
115 Frank Bolling 1.25 3.00
116 J.Ward RC/T.Oliva 10.00 25.00
117 Earl Francis 1.25 3.00
118 John Blanchard 2.50 6.00
119 Gary Kolb RC 1.25 3.00
120 Don Drysdale 15.00 40.00
121 Pete Runnels 2.50 6.00
122 Don McMahon 1.25 3.00
123 Jose Pagan 1.25 3.00
124 Orlando Pena 1.25 3.00
125 Pete Rose UER 200.00 500.00
126 Russ Snyder 1.25 3.00
127 A.Gatewood RC/D.Simpson 1.25 3.00
128 Mickey Lolich RC 15.00 40.00
129 Amado Samuel 1.25 3.00
130 Gary Peters 2.50 6.00
131 Steve Boros 1.25 3.00
132 Milwaukee Braves TC 2.50 6.00
133 Jim Grant 2.50 6.00
134 Don Zimmer 2.50 6.00
135 Johnny Callison 2.50 6.00
136 Sandy Koufax WS1 8.00 20.00
137 Willie Davis WS2 3.00 8.00
138 Ron Fairly WS3 3.00 8.00
139 Frank Howard WS4 3.00 8.00
140 Dodgers Celebrate WS 3.00 8.00
141 Danny Murtaugh MG 2.50 6.00
142 John Bateman 1.25 3.00
143 Bubba Phillips 1.25 3.00
144 Al Worthington 1.25 3.00
145 Norm Siebern 1.25 3.00
146 T.John RC/B.Chance RC 15.00 40.00
147 Ray Sadecki 1.25 3.00
148 J.C. Martin 1.25 3.00
149 Paul Foytack 1.25 3.00
150 Willie Mays 60.00 150.00
151 Kansas City Athletics TC 2.50 6.00
152 Denny Lemaster 1.25 3.00
153 Dick Williams 2.50 6.00
154 Dick Tracewski RC 2.50 6.00
155 Duke Snider 12.50 30.00
156 Bill Dailey 1.25 3.00
157 Gene Mauch MG 2.50 6.00
158 Ken Johnson 1.25 3.00
159 Charlie Dees RC 1.25 3.00
160 Ken Boyer 2.50 6.00
161 Dave McNally 2.50 6.00
162 D.Sisler/V.Pinson 2.50 6.00
163 Donn Clendenon 2.50 6.00
164 Bud Daley 1.25 3.00
165 Jerry Lumpe 1.25 3.00
166 Marty Keough 1.25 3.00
167 M.Brumley RC/L.Piniella RC 12.50 30.00
168 Al Weis 1.25 3.00
169 Del Crandall 2.50 6.00
170 Dick Radatz 2.50 6.00
171 Ty Cline 1.25 3.00
172 Cleveland Indians TC 2.50 6.00
173 Ryne Duren 2.50 6.00
174 Doc Edwards 1.25 3.00
175 Billy Williams 10.00 25.00
176 Tracy Stallard 1.25 3.00
177 Harmon Killebrew 12.00 30.00
178 Hank Bauer MG 2.50 6.00
179 Carl Warwick 1.25 3.00
180 Tommy Davis 2.50 6.00
181 Dave Wickersham 1.25 3.00
182 C.Yastrzemski/C.Schilling 6.00 15.00
183 Ron Taylor 1.25 3.00
184 Al Luplow 1.25 3.00
185 Jim O'Toole 2.50 6.00
186 Roman Mejias 1.25 3.00
187 Ed Roebuck 1.25 3.00
188 Checklist 3 4.00 10.00
189 Bob Hendley 1.25 3.00
190 Bobby Richardson 3.00 8.00
191 Clay Dalrymple 2.50 6.00
192 J.Boccabella RC/B.Cowan RC 1.25 3.00
193 Jerry Lynch 1.25 3.00
194 John Goryl 1.25 3.00
195 Floyd Robinson 1.25 3.00
196 Jim Gentile 1.25 3.00
197 Frank Lary 2.50 6.00
198 Len Gabrielson 1.50 4.00
199 Joe Azcue 1.50 4.00
200 Sandy Koufax 40.00 100.00
201 S.Bowens RC/W.Bunker RC 2.50 6.00
202 Galen Cisco 2.50 6.00
203 John Kennedy RC 2.50 6.00
204 Matty Alou 2.50 6.00
205 Nellie Fox 5.00 12.00
206 Steve Hamilton 2.50 6.00
207 Fred Hutchinson MG 2.50 6.00
208 Wes Covington 2.50 6.00
209 Bob Allen 1.50 4.00
210 Carl Yastrzemski 20.00 50.00
211 Jim Coker 1.50 4.00
212 Pete Lovrich 1.50 4.00
213 Los Angeles Angels TC 2.50 6.00
214 Ken McMullen 2.50 6.00
215 Ray Herbert 1.50 4.00
216 Mike de la Hoz 1.50 4.00
217 Jim King 1.50 4.00
218 Hank Fischer 1.50 4.00
219 A.Downing/J.Bouton 2.50 6.00
220 Dick Ellsworth 2.50 6.00
221 Bob Saverine 1.50 4.00
222 Billy Pierce 2.50 6.00
223 George Banks 1.50 4.00
224 Tommie Sisk 1.50 4.00
225 Roger Maris 30.00 80.00
226 J.Grote RC/L.Yellen RC 2.50 6.00
227 Barry Latman 1.50 4.00
228 Felix Mantilla 1.50 4.00
229 Charley Lau 2.50 6.00
230 Brooks Robinson 15.00 40.00
231 Dick Calmus RC 1.50 4.00
232 Al Lopez MG 3.00 8.00
233 Hal Smith 1.50 4.00
234 Gary Bell 1.50 4.00
235 Ron Hunt 1.50 4.00
236 Bill Faul 1.50 4.00
237 Chicago Cubs TC 2.50 6.00
238 Roy McMillan 2.50 6.00
239 Herm Starrette RC 1.50 4.00
240 Bill White 2.50 6.00
241 Jim Owens 1.50 4.00
242 Harvey Kuenn 2.50 6.00
243 R.Allen RC/J.Hernstein 12.50 30.00
244 Tony LaRussa RC 12.50 30.00
245 Dick Stigman 1.50 4.00
246 Manny Mota 2.50 6.00
247 Dave DeBusschere 2.50 6.00
248 Johnny Pesky MG 2.50 6.00
249 Doug Camilli 1.50 4.00
250 Al Kaline 15.00 40.00
251 Choo Choo Coleman 2.50 6.00
252 Ken Aspromonte 1.50 4.00
253 Wally Post 2.50 6.00
254 Don Hoak 2.50 6.00
255 Lee Thomas 2.50 6.00
256 Johnny Weekly 1.50 4.00
257 San Francisco Giants TC 2.50 6.00
258 Garry Roggenburk 1.50 4.00
259 Harry Bright 1.50 4.00
260 Frank Robinson 25.00 60.00
261 Jim Hannan 1.50 4.00
262 M.Shannon RC/H.Fanok 3.00 8.00
263 Chuck Estrada 1.50 4.00
264 Jim Landis 1.50 4.00
265 Jim Bunning 5.00 12.00
266 Gene Freese 1.50 4.00
267 Wilbur Wood RC 2.50 6.00
268 D.Murtaugh/B.Virdon 2.50 6.00
269 Ellis Burton 1.50 4.00
270 Rich Rollins 2.50 6.00
271 Bob Sadowski RC 1.50 4.00
272 Jake Wood 1.50 4.00
273 Mel Nelson 1.50 4.00
274 Checklist 4 4.00 10.00
275 John Tsitouris 1.50 4.00
276 Jose Tartabull 2.50 6.00
277 Ken Retzer 1.50 4.00
278 Bobby Shantz 2.50 6.00
279 Joe Koppe 1.50 4.00
280 Juan Marichal 12.00 30.00
281 J.Gibbs/T.Metcalf RC 1.50 4.00
282 Bob Bruce 1.50 4.00
283 Tom McCraw RC 1.50 4.00
284 Dick Schofield 1.50 4.00
285 Robin Roberts 6.00 15.00
286 Don Landrum 1.50 4.00
287 T.Conig.RC/B.Spans.RC 20.00 50.00
288 Al Moran 1.50 4.00
289 Frank Funk 1.50 4.00
290 Bob Allison 2.50 6.00
291 Phil Ortega 1.50 4.00
292 Mike Roarke 1.50 4.00
293 Philadelphia Phillies TC 2.50 6.00
294 Ken L. Hunt 1.50 4.00
295 Roger Craig 2.50 6.00
296 Ed Kirkpatrick 1.50 4.00
297 Ken MacKenzie 1.50 4.00
298 Harry Craft MG 1.50 4.00
299 Bill Stafford 1.50 4.00
300 Hank Aaron 60.00 150.00
301 Larry Brown RC 1.50 4.00
302 Dan Pfister 1.50 4.00
303 Jim Campbell 1.50 4.00
304 Bob Johnson 1.50 4.00
305 Jack Lamabe 1.50 4.00
306 Willie Mays/O.Cepeda 15.00 40.00
307 Joe Gibbon 1.50 4.00
308 Gene Stephens 1.50 4.00
309 Paul Toth 1.50 4.00
310 Jim Gilliam 2.50 6.00
311 Tom W. Brown RC 2.50 6.00
312 F.Fisher RC/F.Gladding RC 1.50 4.00
313 Chuck Hiller 1.50 4.00
314 Jerry Buchek 1.50 4.00
315 Bo Belinsky 2.50 6.00
316 Gene Oliver 1.50 4.00
317 Al Smith 1.50 4.00
318 Minnesota Twins TC 2.50 6.00
319 Paul Brown 1.50 4.00
320 Rocky Colavito 5.00 12.00
321 Bob Lillis 1.50 4.00
322 George Brunet 1.50 4.00
323 John Buzhardt 1.50 4.00
324 Casey Stengel MG 6.00 15.00
325 Hector Lopez 2.50 6.00
326 Ron Brand RC 1.50 4.00
327 Don Blasingame 1.50 4.00
328 Bob Shaw 1.50 4.00
329 Russ Nixon 1.50 4.00
330 Tommy Harper 2.50 6.00
331 Maris/Cash/Mantle/Kaline 60.00 150.00
332 Ray Washburn 1.50 4.00
333 Billy Moran 1.50 4.00
334 Lew Krausse 1.50 4.00
335 Don Mossi 2.50 6.00
336 Andre Rodgers 1.50 4.00
337 A.Ferrara RC/J.Torborg RC 2.50 6.00
338 Jack Kralick 1.50 4.00
339 Walt Bond 1.50 4.00
340 Joe Cunningham 1.50 4.00
341 Jim Roland 1.50 4.00
342 Willie Stargell 20.00 50.00
343 Washington Senators TC 2.50 6.00
344 Phil Linz 2.50 6.00
345 Frank Thomas 3.00 8.00
346 Joey Jay 1.50 4.00
347 Bobby Wine 2.50 6.00
348 Ed Lopat MG 2.50 6.00
349 Art Fowler 1.50 4.00
350 Willie McCovey 12.00 30.00
351 Dan Schneider 1.50 4.00
352 Eddie Bressoud 1.50 4.00
353 Wally Moon 2.50 6.00
354 Dave Giusti 1.50 4.00
355 Vic Power 2.50 6.00
356 B.McCool RC/C.Ruiz 2.50 6.00
357 Charley James 1.50 4.00
358 Ron Kline 1.50 4.00
359 Jim Schaffer 1.50 4.00
360 Joe Pepitone 5.00 12.00
361 Jay Hook 1.50 4.00
362 Checklist 5 4.00 10.00
363 Dick McAuliffe 2.50 6.00
364 Joe Gaines 1.50 4.00
365 Cal McLish 2.50 6.00
366 Nelson Mathews 1.50 4.00
367 Fred Whitfield 1.50 4.00
368 F.Ackley RC/D.Buford RC 2.50 6.00
369 Jerry Zimmerman 1.50 4.00
370 Hal Woodeshick 1.50 4.00
371 Frank Howard 3.00 8.00
372 Howie Koplitz 3.00 8.00
373 Pittsburgh Pirates TC 5.00 12.00
374 Bobby Bolin 3.00 8.00
375 Ron Santo 4.00 10.00
376 Dave Morehead 3.00 8.00
377 Bob Skinner 3.00 8.00
378 W.Woodward RC/J.Smith 4.00 10.00
379 Tony Gonzalez 3.00 8.00
380 Whitey Ford 15.00 40.00
381 Bob Taylor 3.00 8.00
382 Wes Stock 3.00 8.00
383 Bill Rigney MG 3.00 8.00
384 Ron Hansen 3.00 8.00
385 Curt Simmons 4.00 10.00
386 Lenny Green 3.00 8.00
387 Terry Fox 3.00 8.00
388 J.O'Donoghue RC/G.Williams 4.00 10.00
389 Jim Umbricht 4.00 10.00
390 Orlando Cepeda 10.00 25.00
391 Sam McDowell 4.00 10.00
392 Jim Pagliaroni 3.00 8.00
393 C.Stengel/E.Kranepool 6.00 15.00
394 Bob Miller 3.00 8.00
395 Tom Tresh 4.00 10.00
396 Dennis Bennett 3.00 8.00
397 Chuck Cottier 3.00 8.00
398 B.Haas/D.Smith 4.00 10.00
399 Jackie Brandt 3.00 8.00
400 Warren Spahn 15.00 40.00
401 Charlie Maxwell 3.00 8.00
402 Tom Sturdivant 3.00 8.00
403 Cincinnati Reds TC 5.00 12.00
404 Tony Martinez 3.00 8.00
405 Ken McBride 3.00 8.00
406 Al Spangler 3.00 8.00
407 Bill Freehan 4.00 10.00
408 J.Stewart RC/F.Burdette RC 3.00 8.00
409 Bill Fischer 3.00 8.00
410 Dick Stuart 4.00 10.00
411 Lee Walls 3.00 8.00
412 Ray Culp 4.00 10.00
413 Johnny Keane MG 3.00 8.00
414 Jack Sanford 3.00 8.00
415 Tony Kubek 10.00 25.00
416 Lee Maye 3.00 8.00
417 Don Cardwell 3.00 8.00
418 D.Knowles RC/B.Narum RC 4.00 10.00
419 Ken Harrelson RC 6.00 15.00
420 Jim Maloney 4.00 10.00
421 Camilo Carreon 3.00 8.00
422 Jack Fisher 3.00 8.00
423 H.Aaron/W.Mays 40.00 100.00
424 Dick Bertell 3.00 8.00
425 Norm Cash 4.00 10.00
426 Bob Rodgers 3.00 8.00
427 Don Rudolph 3.00 8.00
428 A.Skeen RC/P.Smith RC 3.00 8.00
429 Tim McCarver 4.00 10.00
430 Juan Pizarro 3.00 8.00
431 George Alusik 3.00 8.00
432 Ruben Amaro 4.00 10.00
433 New York Yankees TC 15.00 40.00
434 Don Nottebart 3.00 8.00
435 Vic Davalillo 3.00 8.00
436 Charlie Neal 4.00 10.00
437 Ed Bailey 3.00 8.00
438 Checklist 6 6.00 15.00
439 Harvey Haddix 4.00 10.00
440 Roberto Clemente UER 75.00 200.00
441 Bob Duliba 3.00 8.00
442 Pumpsie Green 4.00 10.00
443 Chuck Dressen MG 4.00 10.00
444 Larry Jackson 3.00 8.00
445 Bill Skowron 4.00 10.00
446 Julian Javier 6.00 15.00
447 Ted Bowsfield 3.00 8.00
448 Cookie Rojas 4.00 10.00
449 Deron Johnson 4.00 10.00
450 Steve Barber 3.00 8.00
451 Joe Amalfitano 3.00 8.00
452 G.Garrido RC/J.Hart RC 4.00 10.00
453 Frank Baumann 3.00 8.00
454 Tommie Aaron 4.00 10.00
455 Bernie Allen 3.00 8.00
456 W.Parker RC/J.Werhas RC 4.00 10.00
457 Jesse Gonder 3.00 8.00
458 Ralph Terry 4.00 10.00
459 P.Charton RC/D.Jones RC 3.00 8.00
460 Bob Gibson 25.00 60.00
461 George Thomas 3.00 8.00
462 Birdie Tebbetts MG 3.00 8.00
463 Don Leppert 3.00 8.00
464 Dallas Green 6.00 15.00
465 Mike Hershberger 3.00 8.00
466 D.Green RC/A.Monteagudo RC 4.00 10.00
467 Bob Aspromonte 3.00 8.00
468 Gaylord Perry 15.00 40.00
469 F.Norman RC/S.Slaughter RC 4.00 10.00
470 Jim Bouton 5.00 12.00
471 Gates Brown RC 4.00 10.00
472 Vern Law 4.00 10.00
473 Baltimore Orioles TC 5.00 12.00
474 Larry Sherry 4.00 10.00
475 Ed Charles 3.00 8.00
476 R.Carty RC/D.Kelley RC 6.00 15.00
477 Mike Joyce 3.00 8.00
478 Dick Howser 4.00 10.00
479 D.Bakenhaster RC/J.Lewis RC 3.00 8.00
480 Bob Purkey 3.00 8.00
481 Chuck Schilling 3.00 8.00
482 J.Briggs RC/D.Cater RC 4.00 10.00
483 Fred Valentine RC 3.00 8.00
484 Bill Pleis 3.00 8.00
485 Tom Haller 3.00 8.00
486 Bob Kennedy MG 3.00 8.00
487 Mike McCormick 4.00 10.00
488 P.Mikkelsen RC/B.Meyer RC 6.00 15.00
489 Julio Navarro 3.00 8.00
490 Ron Fairly 4.00 10.00
491 Ed Rakow 3.00 8.00
492 J.Beauchamp RC/M.White RC 3.00 8.00
493 Don Lee 3.00 8.00
494 Al Jackson 3.00 8.00
495 Bill Virdon 4.00 10.00
496 Chicago White Sox TC 5.00 12.00
497 Jeoff Long RC 3.00 8.00
498 Dave Stenhouse 3.00 8.00
499 C.Slamon RC/G.Seyfried RC 3.00 8.00
500 Camilo Pascual 4.00 10.00
501 Bob Veale 4.00 10.00
502 B.Knoop RC/B.Lee RC 3.00 8.00
503 Earl Wilson 3.00 8.00
504 Claude Raymond 3.00 8.00
505 Stan Williams 3.00 8.00
506 Bobby Bragan MG 3.00 8.00
507 Johnny Edwards 3.00 8.00
508 Diego Segui 3.00 8.00
509 G.Alley RC/O.McFarlane RC 4.00 10.00
510 Lindy McDaniel 4.00 10.00
511 Lou Jackson 4.00 10.00
512 W.Horton RC/J.Sparma RC 6.00 15.00
513 Don Larsen 4.00 10.00
514 Jim Hickman 4.00 10.00
515 Johnny Romano 3.00 8.00
516 J.Arrigo RC/D.Siebler RC 3.00 8.00
517A Checklist 7 ERR 10.00 25.00
517B Checklist 7 COR 6.00 15.00
518 Carl Bouldin 3.00 8.00
519 Charlie Smith 3.00 8.00
520 Jack Baldschun 4.00 10.00
521 Tom Satriano 3.00 8.00
522 Bob Tiefenauer 3.00 8.00
523 Lou Burdette UER 8.00 20.00
524 J.Dickson RC/B.Klaus RC 6.00 15.00
525 Al McBean 6.00 15.00
526 Lou Clinton 6.00 15.00
527 Larry Bearnarth 6.00 15.00
528 D.Duncan RC/T.Reynolds RC 8.00 20.00
529 Alvin Dark MG 8.00 20.00
530 Leon Wagner 6.00 15.00
531 Los Angeles Dodgers TC 10.00 25.00
532 B.Bloomfield RC/J.Nossek RC 6.00 15.00
533 Johnny Klippstein 6.00 15.00
534 Gus Bell 6.00 15.00
535 Phil Regan 6.00 15.00
536 L.Elliot/J.Stephenson RC 6.00 15.00
537 Dan Osinski 6.00 15.00
538 Minnie Minoso 8.00 20.00
539 Roy Face 8.00 20.00
540 Luis Aparicio 15.00 40.00
541 P.Roof/P.Niekro RC 50.00 120.00
542 Don Mincher 6.00 15.00
543 Bob Uecker 20.00 50.00
544 S.Hertz RC/J.Hoerner RC 6.00 15.00
545 Max Alvis 6.00 15.00
546 Joe Christopher 6.00 15.00
547 Gil Hodges MG 6.00 15.00
548 W.Schurr RC/P.Speckenbach RC 8.00 20.00
549 Joe Moeller 6.00 15.00
550 Ken Hubbs MEM 15.00 40.00
551 Billy Hoeft 6.00 15.00
552 T.Kelley RC/S.Siebert RC 6.00 15.00
553 Jim Brewer 6.00 15.00
554 Hank Foiles 6.00 15.00
555 Lee Stange 6.00 15.00
556 S.Dillon RC/R.Locke RC 6.00 15.00
557 Leo Burke 6.00 15.00
558 Don Schwall 6.00 15.00
559 Dick Phillips 6.00 15.00
560 Dick Farrell 6.00 15.00
561 D.Bennett RC/R.Wise RC 8.00 20.00
562 Pedro Ramos 6.00 15.00
563 Dal Maxvill 8.00 20.00
564 J.McCabe RC/J.McNertney RC 8.00 20.00
565 Stu Miller 6.00 15.00
566 Ed Kranepool 8.00 20.00
567 Jim Kaat 8.00 20.00
568 P.Gagliano RC/C.Peterson RC 6.00 15.00
569 Fred Newman 6.00 15.00
570 Bill Mazeroski 20.00 50.00
571 Gene Conley 6.00 15.00
572 D.Gray RC/D.Egan 6.00 15.00
573 Jim Duffalo 6.00 15.00
574 Manny Jimenez 6.00 15.00
575 Tony Cloninger 6.00 15.00
576 J.Hinsley RC/B.Wakefield RC 6.00 15.00
577 Gordy Coleman 6.00 15.00
578 Glen Hobbie 6.00 15.00
579 Boston Red Sox TC 10.00 25.00
580 Johnny Podres 8.00 20.00
581 P.Gonzalez/A.Moore RC 8.00 20.00
582 Rod Kanehl 8.00 20.00
583 Tito Francona 6.00 15.00
584 Joel Horlen 6.00 15.00
585 Tony Taylor 8.00 20.00
586 Jimmy Piersall 8.00 20.00
587 Bennie Daniels 8.00 20.00

1964 Topps Coins

This set of 164 unnumbered coins issued in 1964 is sometimes divided into two sets -- the regular series (1-120) and the all-star series (121-164). Each metal coin is approximately 1 1/2" in diameter. The regular series features gold and silver coins with a full color photo of the player, including the background of the photo. The player's name, team and position are delineated on the coin front. The back includes the line "Collect the entire set of 120 all-stars". The all-star series (denoted AS in the checklist below) contains a full color cutout photo of the player on a solid background. The fronts feature the line "1964 All-stars" along with the name only of the player. The backs contain the line "Collect all 44 special stars". Mantle, Causey and Hinton appear in two variations each. The complete set price below includes all variations. Some dealers believe the following coins are short printed: Callison, Tresh, Rollins, Santo, Pappas, Freehan, Hendley, Staub, Bateman and O'Dell.

COMPLETE SET (167) 500.00 1000.00
1 Don Zimmer 2.50 6.00
2 Jim Wynn 2.00 5.00
3 Johnny Orsino 1.50 4.00
4 Jim Bouton 2.00 5.00
5 Dick Groat 2.00 5.00
6 Leon Wagner 1.50 4.00
7 Frank Malzone 1.50 4.00
8 Steve Barber 1.50 4.00
9 Johnny Romano 1.50 4.00
10 Tom Tresh 2.50 6.00
11 Felipe Alou 2.00 5.00
12 Dick Stuart 2.00 5.00
13 Claude Osteen 1.50 4.00
14 Juan Pizarro 1.50 4.00
15 Donn Clendenon 1.50 4.00
16 Jimmie Hall 1.50 4.00
17 Al Jackson 1.50 4.00
18 Brooks Robinson 10.00 25.00
19 Bob Allison 2.00 5.00
20 Ed Roebuck 1.50 4.00
21 Pete Ward 1.50 4.00
22 Willie McCovey 4.00 10.00
23 Elston Howard 4.00 10.00
24 Diego Segui 1.50 4.00

25 Ken Boyer 2.50 6.00
26 Carl Yastrzemski 10.00 25.00
27 Bill Mazeroski 4.00 10.00
28 Jerry Lumpe 1.50 4.00
29 Woody Held 1.50 4.00
30 Dick Radatz 1.50 4.00
31 Luis Aparicio 2.50 6.00
32 Dave Nicholson 1.50 4.00
33 Eddie Mathews 10.00 25.00
34 Don Drysdale 8.00 20.00
35 Ray Culp 1.50 4.00
36 Juan Marichal 4.00 10.00
37 Frank Robinson 10.00 25.00
38 Chuck Hinton 1.50 4.00
39 Floyd Robinson 1.50 4.00
40 Tommy Harper 2.00 5.00
41 Ron Hansen 1.50 4.00
42 Ernie Banks 10.00 25.00
43 Jesse Gonder 1.50 4.00
44 Billy Williams 2.50 6.00
45 Vada Pinson 2.00 5.00
46 Rocky Colavito 5.00 12.00
47 Bill Monbouquette 1.50 4.00
48 Max Alvis 1.50 4.00
49 Norm Siebern 1.50 4.00
50 Johnny Callison 2.00 5.00
51 Rich Rollins 1.50 4.00
52 Ken McBride 1.50 4.00
53 Don Lock 1.50 4.00
54 Ron Fairly 2.00 5.00
55 Roberto Clemente 40.00 80.00
56 Dick Ellsworth 1.50 4.00
57 Tommy Davis 2.00 5.00
58 Tony Gonzalez 1.50 4.00
59 Bob Gibson 8.00 20.00
60 Jim Maloney 2.00 5.00
61 Frank Howard 2.00 5.00
62 Jim Pagliaroni 1.50 4.00
63 Orlando Cepeda 2.50 6.00
64 Ron Perranoski 1.50 4.00
65 Curt Flood 2.50 6.00
66 Alvin McBean 1.50 4.00
67 Dean Chance 1.50 4.00
68 Ron Santo 2.50 6.00
69 Jack Baldschun 1.50 4.00
70 Milt Pappas 2.00 5.00
71 Gary Peters 1.50 4.00
72 Bobby Richardson 2.50 6.00
73 Lee Thomas 1.50 4.00
74 Hank Aguirre 1.50 4.00
75 Carlton Willey 1.50 4.00
76 Camilo Pascual 2.00 5.00
77 Bob Friend 2.00 5.00
78 Bill White 2.00 5.00
79 Norm Cash 2.50 6.00
80 Willie Mays 30.00 60.00
81 Leon Carmel 1.50 4.00
82 Pete Rose 40.00 80.00
83 Hank Aaron 15.00 40.00
84 Bob Aspromonte 1.50 4.00
85 Jim O'Toole 1.50 4.00
86 Vic Davalillo 2.00 5.00
87 Bill Freehan 2.00 5.00
88 Warren Spahn 4.00 10.00
89 Ken Hunt 1.50 4.00
90 Denis Menke 1.50 4.00
91 Dick Farrell 1.50 4.00
92 Jim Hickman 2.00 5.00
93 Jim Bunning 2.50 6.00
94 Bob Hendley 1.50 4.00
95 Ernie Broglio 1.50 4.00
96 Rusty Staub 2.00 5.00
97 Lou Brock 4.00 10.00
98 Jim Fregosi 2.00 5.00
99 Jim Grant 1.50 4.00
100 Al Kaline 8.00 20.00
101 Earl Battey 2.00 5.00
102 Wayne Causey 1.50 4.00
103 Chuck Schilling 1.50 4.00
104 Boog Powell 2.50 6.00
105 Dave Wickersham 1.50 4.00
106 Sandy Koufax 10.00 25.00
107 John Bateman 2.00 5.00
108 Ed Brinkman 1.50 4.00
109 Al Downing 1.50 4.00
110 Joe Azcue 1.50 4.00
111 Albie Pearson 1.50 4.00
112 Harmon Killebrew 8.00 20.00
113 Tony Taylor 2.00 5.00
114 Larry Jackson 1.50 4.00
115 Billy O'Dell 2.00 5.00
116 Don Demeter 2.00 5.00
117 Ed Charles 1.50 4.00
118 Joe Torre 4.00 10.00
119 Don Nottebart 1.50 4.00
120 Mickey Mantle 50.00 100.00
121 Joe Pepitone AS 2.00 5.00
122 Dick Stuart AS 2.00 5.00
123 Bobby Richardson AS 2.50 6.00
124 Jerry Lumpe AS 1.50 4.00
125 Brooks Robinson AS 8.00 20.00
126 Frank Malzone AS 1.50 4.00
127 Luis Aparicio AS 2.50 6.00
128 Jim Fregosi AS 2.00 5.00
129 Al Kaline AS 6.00 15.00
130 Leon Wagner AS 1.50 4.00
131A Mickey Mantle AS Bat R 20.00 50.00
131B Mickey Mantle AS Bat L 20.00 50.00
132 Albie Pearson AS 1.50 4.00
133 Harmon Killebrew AS 6.00 15.00
134 Carl Yastrzemski AS 10.00 25.00
135 Elston Howard AS 2.50 6.00
136 Earl Battey AS 1.50 4.00
137 Camilo Pascual AS 1.50 4.00
138 Jim Bouton AS 2.00 5.00
139 Whitey Ford AS 8.00 20.00
140 Gary Peters AS 1.50 4.00
141 Bill White AS 2.00 5.00
142 Orlando Cepeda AS 2.50 6.00
143 Bill Mazeroski AS 4.00 10.00
144 Tony Taylor AS 1.50 4.00
145 Ken Boyer AS 2.50 6.00
146 Ron Santo AS 2.50 6.00
147 Dick Groat AS 2.00 5.00
148 Roy McMillan AS 1.50 4.00
149 Hank Aaron AS 10.00 25.00
150 Roberto Clemente AS 12.50 30.00
151 Willie Mays AS 12.50 30.00
152 Vada Pinson AS 2.00 5.00
153 Tommy Davis AS 2.00 5.00
154 Frank Robinson AS 8.00 20.00
155 Joe Torre AS 4.00 10.00
156 Tim McCarver AS 2.00 5.00
157 Juan Marichal AS 4.00 10.00
158 Jim Maloney AS 2.00 5.00
159 Sandy Koufax AS 10.00 25.00
160 Warren Spahn AS 4.00 10.00
161A Wayne Causey AS NL 6.00 15.00
161B Wayne Causey AS American League 2.00 5.00
162A Chuck Hinton AS NL 8.00 20.00
162B Chuck Hinton AS American League 2.00 5.00
163 Bob Aspromonte AS 1.50 4.00
164 Ron Hunt AS 1.50 4.00

1964 Topps Giants

The cards in this 60-card set measure approximately 3 1/8" by 5 1/4". The 1964 Topps Giants are postcard size cards containing color player photographs. They are numbered on the backs, which also contain biographical information presented in a newspaper format. These "giant size" cards were distributed in both cellophane and waxed gum packs apart from the Topps regular issue of 1964. The gum packs contain three cards. The Cards 3, 28, 42, 45, 47, 51 and 60 are more difficult to find and are indicated by SP in the checklist below.

COMPLETE SET (60) 250.00 600.00
COMMON CARD (1-60) .60 1.50
COMMON SP'S 4.00 10.00
WRAPPER (5-CENT) 15.00 40.00
1 Gary Peters .75 2.00
2 Ken Johnson .60 1.50
3 Sandy Koufax SP 50.00 120.00
4 Bob Bailey .60 1.50
5 Milt Pappas .75 2.00
6 Ron Hunt .60 1.50
7 Whitey Ford 8.00 20.00
8 Roy McMillan .60 1.50
9 Rocky Colavito 2.00 5.00
10 Jim Bunning 1.25 3.00
11 Roberto Clemente 25.00 60.00
12 Al Kaline 8.00 20.00
13 Nellie Fox 5.00 12.00
14 Tony Gonzalez .60 1.50
15 Jim Gentile .75 2.00
16 Dean Chance .75 2.00
17 Dick Ellsworth .75 2.00
18 Jim Fregosi .75 2.00
19 Dick Groat .75 2.00
20 Chuck Hinton .60 1.50
21 Elston Howard .75 2.00
22 Dick Farrell .60 1.50
23 Albie Pearson .60 1.50
24 Frank Howard .75 2.00
25 Mickey Mantle 60.00 150.00
26 Joe Torre 2.00 5.00
27 Eddie Brinkman .60 1.50
28 Bob Friend SP 8.00 20.00
29 Frank Robinson 10.00 25.00
30 Bill Freehan .75 2.00
31 Warren Spahn 6.00 15.00
32 Camilo Pascual .75 2.00
33 Pete Ward .60 1.50
34 Jim Maloney .75 2.00
35 Dave Wickersham .60 1.50
36 Johnny Callison .75 2.00
37 Juan Marichal 1.25 3.00
38 Harmon Killebrew 6.00 15.00
39 Luis Aparicio 1.25 3.00
40 Dick Radatz .60 1.50
41 Bob Gibson 12.00 30.00
42 Dick Stuart SP 5.00 12.00
43 Tommy Davis .75 2.00
44 Tony Oliva 1.25 3.00
45 Wayne Causey SP 6.00 15.00
46 Max Alvis .60 1.50
47 Galen Cisco SP 10.00 25.00
48 Carl Yastrzemski 8.00 20.00
49 Hank Aaron 25.00 60.00
50 Brooks Robinson 8.00 20.00
51 Willie Mays SP 40.00 100.00
52 Billy Williams 1.25 3.00
53 Juan Pizarro .60 1.50
54 Leon Wagner .60 1.50
55 Orlando Cepeda 1.25 3.00
56 Vada Pinson .75 2.00
57 Ken Boyer 1.25 3.00
58 Ron Santo 1.25 3.00
59 John Romano .60 1.50
60 Bill Skowron SP 12.00 30.00

1964 Topps Stand-Ups

In 1964 Topps produced a die-cut "Stand-Up" card design for the first time since their Connie Mack and Current All Stars of 1951. These cards were issued in both one cent and five cent packs. The cards have full-length, color player photos set against a green and yellow background. Of the 77 cards in the set, 22 were single printed and these are marked in the checklist below with an SP. These unnumbered cards are standard-size (2 1/2" by 3 1/2"), blank backed, and have been numbered here for reference in alphabetical order of players. Interestingly there were four different wrapper designs used for this set. All the design variations are valued at the same price.

COMPLETE SET (77) 2500.00 4000.00
COMMON CARD (1-77) 4.00 10.00
COMMON CARD SP 15.00 40.00
WRAPPER (1-CENT) 75.00 150.00
WRAPPER (5-CENT) 175.00 350.00
1 Hank Aaron 75.00 200.00
2 Hank Aguirre 5.00 12.00
3 George Altman 8.00 20.00
4 Max Alvis 5.00 12.00
5 Bob Aspromonte 5.00 12.00
6 Jack Baldschun SP 20.00 50.00
7 Ernie Banks 50.00 100.00
8 Steve Barber 5.00 12.00
9 Earl Battey 5.00 12.00
10 Ken Boyer 10.00 25.00
11 Ernie Broglio 5.00 12.00
12 John Callison 8.00 20.00
13 Norm Cash SP 40.00 80.00
14 Wayne Causey 5.00 12.00
15 Orlando Cepeda 10.00 25.00
16 Ed Charles 8.00 20.00
17 Roberto Clemente 125.00 250.00
18 Donn Clendenon SP 20.00 50.00
19 Rocky Colavito 15.00 40.00
20 Ray Culp SP 30.00 60.00
21 Tommy Davis 8.00 20.00
22 Don Drysdale SP 75.00 150.00
23 Dick Ellsworth 5.00 12.00
24 Dick Farrell 5.00 12.00
25 Jim Fregosi 8.00 20.00
26 Bob Friend 5.00 12.00
27 Jim Gentile 8.00 20.00
28 Jesse Gonder SP 20.00 50.00
29 Tony Gonzalez SP 20.00 50.00
30 Dick Groat 10.00 25.00
31 Woody Held 5.00 12.00
32 Chuck Hinton 5.00 12.00
33 Elston Howard 10.00 25.00
34 Frank Howard SP 40.00 80.00
35 Ron Hunt 8.00 20.00
36 Al Jackson 5.00 12.00
37 Ken Johnson 5.00 12.00
38 Al Kaline 50.00 100.00
39 Harmon Killebrew 50.00 100.00
40 Sandy Koufax 100.00 200.00
41 Don Lock SP 20.00 50.00
42 Jerry Lumpe SP 20.00 50.00
43 Jim Maloney 8.00 20.00
44 Frank Malzone 5.00 12.00
45 Mickey Mantle 300.00 600.00
46 Juan Marichal SP 60.00 120.00
47 Eddie Mathews SP 75.00 150.00
48 Willie Mays 100.00 250.00
49 Bill Mazeroski 15.00 40.00
50 Ken McBride 5.00 12.00
51 Willie McCovey SP 60.00 120.00
52 Claude Osteen 8.00 20.00
53 Jim O'Toole 5.00 12.00
54 Camilo Pascual 8.00 20.00
55 Albie Pearson SP 30.00 60.00
56 Gary Peters 5.00 12.00
57 Vada Pinson 8.00 20.00
58 Juan Pizarro 5.00 12.00
59 Boog Powell 10.00 25.00
60 Bobby Richardson 10.00 25.00
61 Brooks Robinson 50.00 100.00
62 Floyd Robinson 5.00 12.00
63 Frank Robinson 50.00 100.00
64 Ed Roebuck SP 20.00 50.00
65 Rich Rollins 5.00 12.00
66 John Romano 5.00 12.00
67 Ron Santo SP 40.00 80.00
68 Norm Siebern 5.00 12.00
69 Warren Spahn SP 75.00 150.00
70 Dick Stuart SP 30.00 60.00
71 Lee Thomas 5.00 12.00
72 Joe Torre 10.00 25.00
73 Pete Ward 5.00 12.00
74 Bill White SP 30.00 60.00
75 Billy Williams SP 60.00 120.00
76 Hal Woodeshick SP 20.00 50.00
77 Carl Yastrzemski SP 250.00 500.00

1964 Topps Tattoos Inserts

These tattoos measure 1 9/16" by 3 1/2" and are printed in color on very thin paper. One side gives instructions for applying the tattoo. The picture side gives either the team logo and name (on tattoos numbered 1-20 below) or the player's face, name and team (21-75 below). The tattoos are unnumbered and are presented below in alphabetical order within type for convenience. This set was issued in one cent packs which came 120 to a box. The boxes had photos of Whitey Ford on them.

COMPLETE SET (75) 600.00 1200.00
COMMON TATOO (1-20) 1.50 4.00
COMMON TATOO (21-75) 3.00 8.00
8 Detroit Tigers 2.00 5.00
11 Los Angeles Dodgers 5.00 12.00
14 New York Mets 2.00 5.00
15 New York Yankees 5.00 12.00
21 Hank Aaron 60.00 120.00
22 Max Alvis 3.00 8.00
23 Hank Aguirre 3.00 8.00
24 Ernie Banks 30.00 60.00
25 Steve Barber 3.00 8.00
26 Ken Boyer 5.00 12.00
27 John Callison 3.00 8.00
28 Norm Cash 4.00 10.00
29 Wayne Causey 3.00 8.00
30 Orlando Cepeda 8.00 20.00
31 Rocky Colavito 8.00 20.00
32 Ray Culp 3.00 8.00
33 Vic Davalillo 3.00 8.00
34 Moe Drabowsky 3.00 8.00
35 Dick Ellsworth 3.00 8.00
36 Curt Flood 5.00 12.00
37 Bill Freehan 4.00 10.00
38 Jim Fregosi 4.00 10.00
39 Bob Friend 3.00 8.00
40 Dick Groat 5.00 12.00
41 Woody Held 3.00 8.00
42 Frank Howard 5.00 12.00
43 Al Jackson 3.00 8.00
44 Larry Jackson 3.00 8.00
45 Ken Johnson 3.00 8.00
46 Al Kaline 30.00 60.00
47 Harmon Killebrew 15.00 40.00
48 Sandy Koufax 60.00 120.00
49 Don Lock 3.00 8.00
50 Frank Malzone 4.00 10.00
51 Mickey Mantle 150.00 300.00
52 Eddie Mathews 20.00 50.00
53 Willie Mays 60.00 120.00
54 Bill Mazeroski 6.00 15.00
55 Ken McBride 3.00 8.00
56 Bill Monbouquette 3.00 8.00
57 Dave Nicholson 3.00 8.00
58 Claude Osteen 3.00 8.00
59 Milt Pappas 4.00 10.00
60 Camilo Pascual 3.00 8.00
61 Albie Pearson 3.00 8.00
62 Ron Perranoski 3.00 8.00
63 Gary Peters 3.00 8.00
64 Boog Powell 5.00 12.00
65 Frank Robinson 20.00 50.00
66 Johnny Romano 3.00 8.00
67 Norm Siebern 3.00 8.00
68 Warren Spahn 20.00 50.00
69 Dick Stuart 4.00 10.00
70 Lee Thomas 3.00 8.00
71 Joe Torre 6.00 15.00
72 Pete Ward 3.00 8.00
73 Carlton Willey 3.00 8.00
74 Billy Williams 15.00 40.00
75 Carl Yastrzemski 30.00 60.00

1965 Topps

The cards in this 598-card set measure 2 1/2" by 3 1/2". The cards comprising the 1965 Topps set have team names located within a distinctive pennant design below the picture. The cards have blue borders on the reverse and were issued by series. Within this last series (523-598) there are 44 cards that were printed in lesser quantities than the other cards in that series; these shorter-printed cards are marked by SP in the checklist below. Featured subsets within this set include League Leaders (1-12) and World Series cards (132-139). This was the last year Topps issued one-card penny packs. Card were also issued in five-card nickel packs. The key Rookie Cards in this set are Steve Carlton, Jim "Catfish" Hunter, Joe Morgan, Mansori Murakami and Tony Perez.

COMPLETE SET (598) 2500.00 5000.00
COMMON CARD (1-196) .75 2.00
COMMON CARD (197-283) 1.00 2.50
COMMON CARD (284-370) 1.50 4.00
COMMON CARD (371-598) 3.00 8.00
WRAPPER (1-CENT) 60.00 120.00
WRAPPER (5-CENT) 50.00 100.00
1 Oliva/Howard/Brooks LL 8.00 20.00
2 Clemente/Aaron/Carty LL 20.00 50.00
3 Killebrew/Mantle/Powell LL 25.00 60.00
4 Mays/B.Will/Cepeda LL 10.00 25.00
5 Brooks/Kill/Mantle LL 25.00 60.00
6 Boyer/Mays Santo LL 8.00 20.00
7 D.Chance/J.Horlen LL 2.00 5.00
8 S.Koufax/D.Ellsworth LL 8.00 20.00
9 Chance/Peters/Wick LL 2.00 5.00
10 Jackson/Sad/Marichal LL 2.00 5.00
11 Downing/Chance/Pascual LL 2.00 5.00
12 Veale/Drysdale/Gibson LL 4.00 10.00
13 Pedro Ramos 1.50 4.00
14 Len Gabrielson .75 2.00
15 Robin Roberts 8.00 20.00
16 Joe Morgan RC DP 75.00 200.00
17 Johnny Romano .75 2.00
18 Bill McCool .75 2.00
19 Gates Brown 1.50 4.00
20 Jim Bunning 4.00 10.00
21 Don Blasingame .75 2.00
22 Charlie Smith .75 2.00
23 Bob Tiefenauer .75 2.00
24 Minnesota Twins TC 2.50 6.00
25 Al McBean .75 2.00
26 Bobby Knoop .75 2.00
27 Dick Bertell .75 2.00
28 Barney Schultz .75 2.00
29 Felix Mantilla .75 2.00
30 Jim Bouton 2.50 6.00
31 Mike White .75 2.00
32 Herman Franks MG .75 2.00
33 Jackie Brandt .75 2.00
34 Cal Koonce .75 2.00
35 Ed Charles .75 2.00
36 Bobby Wine .75 2.00
37 Fred Gladding .75 2.00
38 Jim King .75 2.00
39 Gerry Arrigo .75 2.00
40 Frank Howard 2.50 6.00
41 B.Howard/M.Staehle RC .75 2.00
42 Earl Wilson 1.50 4.00
43 Mike Shannon 1.50 4.00
44 Wade Blasingame RC .75 2.00
45 Roy McMillan 1.50 4.00
46 Bob Lee .75 2.00
47 Tommy Harper 1.50 4.00
48 Claude Raymond 1.50 4.00
49 C.Blefary RC/J.Miller 1.50 4.00
50 Juan Marichal 10.00 25.00
51 Bill Bryan .75 2.00
52 Ed Roebuck .75 2.00
53 Dick McAuliffe 1.50 4.00
54 Joe Gibbon .75 2.00
55 Tony Conigliaro 6.00 15.00
56 Ron Kline .75 2.00
57 St. Louis Cardinals TC 2.50 6.00
58 Fred Talbot RC .75 2.00
59 Nate Oliver .75 2.00
60 Jim O'Toole 1.50 4.00
61 Chris Cannizzaro .75 2.00
62 Jim Kaat UER DP 6.00 15.00
63 Ty Cline .75 2.00
64 Lou Burdette 1.50 4.00
65 Tony Kubek 4.00 10.00
66 Bill Rigney MG .75 2.00
67 Harvey Haddix 1.50 4.00
68 Del Crandall 1.50 4.00
69 Bill Virdon 1.50 4.00
70 Bill Skowron 2.50 6.00
71 John O'Donoghue .75 2.00
72 Tony Gonzalez .75 2.00
73 Dennis Ribant RC .75 2.00
74 R.Petrocelli RC/J.Steph RC 4.00 10.00
75 Deron Johnson 1.50 4.00
76 Sam McDowell 2.50 6.00
77 Doug Camilli .75 2.00
78 Dal Maxvill .75 2.00
79A Checklist 1 Cannizzaro 4.00 10.00
79B Checklist 1 C.Cannizzaro 4.00 10.00
80 Turk Farrell .75 2.00
81 Don Buford 1.50 4.00
82 S.Alomar RC/J.Braun RC 2.50 6.00
83 George Thomas .75 2.00
84 Ron Herbel .75 2.00
85 Willie Smith RC .75 2.00
86 Buster Narum .75 2.00
87 Nelson Mathews .75 2.00
88 Jack Lamabe .75 2.00
89 Mike Hershberger .75 2.00
90 Rich Rollins 1.50 4.00
91 Chicago Cubs TC 2.50 6.00
92 Dick Howser 1.50 4.00
93 Jack Fisher .75 2.00
94 Charlie Lau 1.50 4.00
95 Bill Mazeroski DP 10.00 25.00
96 Sonny Siebert 1.50 4.00
97 Pedro Gonzalez .75 2.00
98 Bob Miller .75 2.00
99 Gil Hodges MG 2.50 6.00
100 Ken Boyer 4.00 10.00
101 Fred Newman .75 2.00
102 Steve Boros .75 2.00
103 Harvey Kuenn 1.50 4.00
104 Checklist 2 4.00 10.00
105 Chico Salmon .75 2.00
106 Gene Oliver .75 2.00
107 P.Corrales RC/C.Shockley RC 1.50 4.00
108 Don Mincher .75 2.00
109 Walt Bond .75 2.00
110 Ron Santo 2.50 6.00
111 Lee Thomas 1.50 4.00
112 Derrell Griffith RC .75 2.00
113 Steve Barber .75 2.00
114 Jim Hickman 1.50 4.00
115 Bobby Richardson 4.00 10.00
116 D.Dowling RC/B.Tolan RC 1.50 4.00
117 Wes Stock .75 2.00
118 Hal Lanier RC 1.50 4.00
119 John Kennedy .75 2.00
120 Frank Robinson 30.00 80.00
121 Gene Alley 1.50 4.00
122 Bill Pleis .75 2.00
123 Frank Thomas 1.50 4.00
124 Tom Satriano .75 2.00
125 Juan Pizarro .75 2.00
126 Los Angeles Dodgers TC 2.50 6.00
127 Frank Lary .75 2.00
128 Vic Davalillo .75 2.00
129 Bennie Daniels .75 2.00
130 Al Kaline 20.00 50.00
131 Johnny Keane MG .75 2.00
132 Cards Take Opener WS1 4.00 10.00
133 Mel Stottlemyre WS2 2.50 6.00
134 Mickey Mantle WS3 30.00 80.00
135 Ken Boyer WS4 4.00 10.00
136 Tim McCarver WS5 2.50 6.00
137 Jim Bouton WS6 2.50 6.00
138 Bob Gibson WS7 5.00 12.00
139 Cards Celebrate WS 2.50 6.00
140 Dean Chance 1.50 4.00
141 Charlie James .75 2.00
142 Bill Monbouquette .75 2.00
143 J.Gelnar RC/J.May RC .75 2.00
144 Ed Kranepool 1.50 4.00
145 Luis Tiant RC 12.00 30.00
146 Ron Hansen .75 2.00
147 Dennis Bennett .75 2.00
148 Willie Kirkland .75 2.00
149 Wayne Schurr .75 2.00
150 Brooks Robinson 20.00 50.00
151 Kansas City Athletics TC 2.50 6.00
152 Phil Ortega .75 2.00
153 Norm Cash 10.00 25.00
154 Bob Humphreys RC .75 2.00
155 Roger Maris 40.00 100.00
156 Bob Sadowski .75 2.00
157 Zoilo Versalles 1.50 4.00
158 Dick Sisler .75 2.00
159 Jim Duffalo .75 2.00
160 Roberto Clemente UER 60.00 150.00
161 Frank Baumann .75 2.00
162 Russ Nixon .75 2.00
163 Johnny Briggs .75 2.00
164 Al Spangler .75 2.00
165 Dick Ellsworth .75 2.00
166 G.Culver RC/T.Agee RC 1.50 4.00
167 Bill Wakefield .75 2.00
168 Dick Green .75 2.00
169 Dave Vineyard RC .75 2.00
170 Hank Aaron 75.00 200.00
171 Jim Roland .75 2.00
172 Jimmy Piersall 2.50 6.00
173 Detroit Tigers TC 2.50 6.00
174 Joey Jay .75 2.00
175 Bob Aspromonte .75 2.00
176 Willie McCovey 15.00 40.00
177 Pete Mikkelsen .75 2.00
178 Dalton Jones .75 2.00
179 Hal Woodeshick .75 2.00
180 Bob Allison 1.50 4.00
181 D.Loun RC/J.McCabe .75 2.00
182 Mike de la Hoz .75 2.00
183 Dave Nicholson .75 2.00
184 John Boozer .75 2.00
185 Max Alvis .75 2.00
186 Billy Cowan .75 2.00
187 Casey Stengel MG 10.00 25.00
188 Sam Bowens .75 2.00
189 Checklist 3 4.00 10.00
190 Bill White 2.50 6.00
191 Phil Regan 1.50 4.00
192 Jim Coker .75 2.00
193 Gaylord Perry 8.00 20.00
194 B.Kelso RC/R.Reichardt RC .75 2.00
195 Bob Veale 1.50 4.00
196 Ron Fairly 1.50 4.00
197 Diego Segui 1.00 2.50
198 Smoky Burgess 1.50 4.00
199 Bob Heffner 1.00 2.50
200 Joe Torre 2.50 6.00
201 S.Valdespino RC/C.Tovar RC 1.50 4.00
202 Leo Burke 1.00 2.50
203 Dallas Green 1.50 4.00
204 Russ Snyder 1.00 2.50
205 Warren Spahn 10.00 25.00
206 Willie Horton 1.50 4.00
207 Pete Rose 75.00 200.00
208 Tommy John 2.50 6.00
209 Pittsburgh Pirates TC 2.50 6.00
210 Jim Fregosi 1.50 4.00
211 Steve Ridzik 1.00 2.50
212 Ron Brand 1.00 2.50
213 Jim Davenport 1.00 2.50
214 Bobby Purkey 1.00 2.50
215 Pete Ward 1.00 2.50
216 Al Worthington 1.00 2.50
217 Walter Alston MG 2.50 6.00
218 Dick Schofield 1.00 2.50
219 Bob Meyer 1.00 2.50
220 Billy Williams 25.00 60.00
221 John Tsitouris 1.00 2.50
222 Bob Tillman 1.00 2.50
223 Dan Osinski 1.00 2.50
224 Bob Chance 1.00 2.50
225 Bo Belinsky 1.50 4.00
226 E.Jimenez RC/J.Gibbs 2.50 6.00
227 Bobby Klaus 1.00 2.50
228 Jack Sanford 1.00 2.50
229 Lou Clinton 1.00 2.50
230 Ray Sadecki 1.00 2.50
231 Jerry Adair 1.00 2.50
232 Steve Blass RC 1.50 4.00
233 Don Zimmer 1.50 4.00
234 Chicago White Sox TC 2.50 6.00
235 Chuck Hinton 1.00 2.50
236 Denny McLain RC 25.00 60.00
237 Bernie Allen 1.00 2.50
238 Joe Moeller 1.00 2.50
239 Doc Edwards 1.00 2.50
240 Bob Bruce 1.00 2.50
241 Mack Jones 1.00 2.50
242 George Brunet 1.00 2.50
243 T.Davidson RC/T.Helms RC 1.50
244 Lindy McDaniel 1.50
245 Joe Pepitone 2.50
246 Tom Butters 1.50
247 Wally Moon 1.50
248 Gus Triandos 1.50
249 Dave McNally 1.50
250 Willie Mays 75.00 20
251 Billy Herman MG 1.50
252 Pete Richert 1.00
253 Danny Cater 1.00
254 Roland Sheldon 1.00
255 Camilo Pascual 1.50
256 Tito Francona 1.00
257 Jim Wynn 1.50
258 Larry Bearnarth 1.00
259 J.Northrup RC/R.Oyler RC 2.50
260 Don Drysdale 20.00 5
261 Duke Carmel 1.00
262 Bud Daley 1.00 2
263 Marty Keough 1.00 2
264 Bob Buhl 1.50 4
265 Jim Pagliaroni 1.00 2
266 Bert Campaneris RC 10.00 2
267 Washington Senators TC 2.50
268 Ken McBride 1.00 2
269 Frank Bolling 1.00 2
270 Milt Pappas 1.50 4
271 Don Wert 1.50 4
272 Chuck Schilling 1.00 2
273 Checklist 4 4.00 10
274 Lum Harris MG RC 1.00 2
275 Dick Groat 2.50 6
276 Hoyt Wilhelm 10.00 25
277 Johnny Lewis 1.00 2
278 Ken Retzer 1.00 2
279 Dick Tracewski 1.00 2
280 Dick Stuart 1.50 4
281 Bill Stafford 1.00 2
282 D.Est RC/M.Murakami RC 20.00 50
283 Fred Whitfield 1.00 2
284 Nick Willhite 1.50 4
285 Ron Hunt 1.50 4
286 J.Dickson/A.Monteagudo 1.50 4
287 Gary Kolb 1.50 4
288 Jack Hamilton 1.50 4
289 Gordy Coleman 2.50 6
290 Wally Bunker 2.50 6
291 Jerry Lynch 1.50 4
292 Larry Yellen 1.50 4
293 Los Angeles Angels TC 2.50 6
294 Tim McCarver 4.00 10
295 Dick Radatz 2.50 6
296 Tony Taylor 2.50 6
297 Dave DeBusschere 4.00 10
298 Jim Stewart 1.50 4
299 Jerry Zimmerman 1.50 4
300 Sandy Koufax 75.00 200
301 Birdie Tebbetts MG 2.50 6
302 Al Stanek 1.50 4.
303 John Orsino 1.50 4
304 Dave Stenhouse 1.50 4
305 Rico Carty 2.50 6
306 Bubba Phillips 1.50 4.
307 Barry Latman 1.50 4.
308 C.Jones RC/T.Parsons 2.50 6.
309 Steve Hamilton 2.50 6.
310 Johnny Callison 2.50 6.
311 Orlando Pena 1.50 4.
312 Joe Nuxhall 1.50 4.
313 Jim Schaffer 1.50 4.
314 Sterling Slaughter 1.50 4.
315 Frank Malzone 2.50 6.
316 Cincinnati Reds TC 2.50 6.
317 Don McMahon 1.50 4.
318 Matty Alou 2.50 6.
319 Ken McMullen 1.50 4.
320 Bob Gibson 25.00 60.
321 Rusty Staub 4.00 10.
322 Rick Wise 2.50 6.
323 Hank Bauer MG 2.50 6.
324 Bobby Locke 1.50 4.
325 Donn Clendenon 2.50 6.
326 Dwight Siebler 1.50 4.0
327 Denis Menke 1.50 4.0
328 Eddie Fisher 1.50 4.0
329 Hawk Taylor 1.50 4.
330 Whitey Ford 20.00 50.
331 A.Ferrara/J.Purdin RC 2.50 6.
332 Ted Abernathy 1.50 4.0
333 Tom Reynolds 1.50 4.0
334 Vic Roznovsky RC 1.50 4.0
335 Mickey Lolich 8.00 20.0
336 Woody Held 1.50 4.0
337 Mike Cuellar 2.50 6.0
338 Philadelphia Phillies TC 2.50 6.0
339 Ryne Duren 2.50 6.0
340 Tony Oliva 20.00 50.0
341 Bob Bolin 1.50 4.0
342 Bob Rodgers 2.50 6.0
343 Mike McCormick 2.50 6.0
344 Wes Parker 2.50 6.0
345 Floyd Robinson 1.50 4.0
346 Bobby Bragan MG 1.50 4.0
347 Roy Face 2.50 6.0
348 George Banks 1.50 4.0
349 Larry Miller RC 1.50 4.0
350 Mickey Mantle 400.00 800.0
351 Jim Perry 2.50 6.0
352 Alex Johnson RC 2.50 6.0

Jerry Lumpe	1.50	4.00
B.Ott RC/J.Warner RC	1.50	4.00
Vada Pinson	4.00	10.00
Bill Spanswick	1.50	4.00
Carl Warwick	1.50	4.00
Albie Pearson	2.50	6.00
Ken Johnson	1.50	4.00
Orlando Cepeda	6.00	15.00
Checklist 5	5.00	12.00
Don Schwall	1.50	4.00
Bob Johnson	1.50	4.00
Galen Cisco	1.50	4.00
Jim Gentile	2.50	6.00
Dan Schneider	1.50	4.00
Leon Wagner	1.50	4.00
K.Berry RC/J.Gibson RC	2.50	6.00
Phil Linz	2.50	6.00
Herman Thomas Davis	2.50	6.00
Frank Kreutzer	3.00	8.00
2 Clay Dalrymple	3.00	8.00
3 Curt Simmons	3.00	8.00
4 J.Cardenal RC/D.Simpson	3.00	8.00
5 Dave Wickersham	3.00	8.00
Jim Landis	3.00	8.00
Willie Stargell	25.00	60.00
3 Chuck Estrada	3.00	8.00
9 San Francisco Giants TC	3.00	8.00
Rocky Colavito	10.00	25.00
Al Jackson	3.00	8.00
2 J.C. Martin	3.00	8.00
3 Felipe Alou	6.00	15.00
4 Johnny Klippstein	3.00	8.00
5 Carl Yastrzemski	30.00	80.00
6 P.Jaeckel RC/F.Norman	3.00	8.00
7 Johnny Podres	6.00	15.00
8 John Blanchard	6.00	15.00
9 Don Larsen	6.00	15.00
0 Bill Freehan	6.00	15.00
1 Mel McGaha MG	3.00	8.00
2 Bob Friend	6.00	15.00
3 Ed Kirkpatrick	3.00	8.00
4 Jim Hannan	3.00	8.00
5 Jim Ray Hart	3.00	8.00
6 Frank Bertaina RC	3.00	8.00
7 Jerry Buchek	3.00	8.00
8 D.Neville RC/A.Shamsky RC	6.00	15.00
9 Ray Herbert	3.00	8.00
0 Harmon Killebrew	30.00	80.00
1 Carl Willey	3.00	8.00
2 Joe Amalfitano	3.00	8.00
03 Boston Red Sox TC	3.00	8.00
04 Stan Williams	3.00	8.00
05 John Roseboro	8.00	20.00
06 Ralph Terry	6.00	15.00
07 Lee Maye	3.00	8.00
08 Larry Sherry	3.00	8.00
09 J.Beauchamp RC/L.Dierker RC	6.00	15.00
10 Luis Aparicio	10.00	25.00
11 Roger Craig	6.00	15.00
12 Bob Bailey	3.00	8.00
13 Hal Reniff	3.00	8.00
14 Al Lopez MG	6.00	15.00
15 Curt Flood	8.00	20.00
16 Jim Brewer	3.00	8.00
17 Ed Brinkman	3.00	8.00
18 Johnny Edwards	3.00	8.00
19 Ruben Amaro	3.00	8.00
420 Larry Jackson	3.00	8.00
421 G.Dotter RC/J.Ward	3.00	8.00
422 Aubrey Gatewood	3.00	8.00
423 Jesse Gonder	3.00	8.00
424 Gary Bell	3.00	8.00
425 Wayne Causey	3.00	8.00
426 Milwaukee Braves TC	3.00	8.00
427 Bob Saverine	3.00	8.00
428 Bob Shaw	3.00	8.00
429 Don Demeter	3.00	8.00
430 Gary Peters	3.00	8.00
431 N.Briles RC/W.Spiezio RC	6.00	15.00
432 Jim Grant	6.00	15.00
433 John Bateman	3.00	8.00
434 Dave Morehead	3.00	8.00
435 Willie Davis	6.00	15.00
436 Don Elston	3.00	8.00
437 Chico Cardenas	6.00	15.00
438 Harry Walker MG	3.00	8.00
439 Moe Drabowsky	6.00	15.00
440 Tom Tresh	6.00	15.00
441 Denny Lemaster	3.00	8.00
442 Vic Power	3.00	8.00
443 Checklist 6	5.00	12.00
444 Bob Hendley	3.00	8.00
445 Don Lock	3.00	8.00
446 Art Mahaffey	3.00	8.00
447 Julian Javier	6.00	15.00
448 Lee Stange	3.00	8.00
449 J.Hinsley/G.Kroll RC	6.00	15.00
450 Elston Howard	6.00	15.00
451 Jim Owens	3.00	8.00
452 Gary Geiger	3.00	8.00
453 W.Crawford RC/J.Werhas	6.00	15.00
454 Ed Rakow	3.00	8.00
455 Norm Siebern	3.00	8.00
456 Bill Henry	3.00	8.00
457 Bob Kennedy MG	6.00	15.00
458 John Buzhardt	3.00	8.00
459 Frank Kostro	3.00	8.00
460 Richie Allen	15.00	40.00
461 C.Carroll RC/P.Niekro	25.00	60.00
462 Lew Krausse UER	3.00	8.00
463 Manny Mota	6.00	15.00
464 Ron Piche	3.00	8.00
465 Tom Haller	6.00	15.00
466 P.Craig RC/D.Nen	3.00	8.00
467 Ray Washburn	3.00	8.00
468 Larry Brown	3.00	8.00
469 Don Nottebart	3.00	8.00
470 Yogi Berra P/CO	25.00	60.00
471 Billy Hoeft	3.00	8.00
472 Don Pavletich	3.00	8.00
473 P.Blair RC/D.Johnson RC	6.00	15.00
474 Cookie Rojas	6.00	15.00
475 Clete Boyer	6.00	15.00
476 Billy O'Dell	3.00	8.00
477 Steve Carlton RC	100.00	250.00
478 Wilbur Wood	6.00	15.00
479 Ken Harrelson	6.00	15.00
480 Joel Horlen	3.00	8.00
481 Cleveland Indians TC	4.00	10.00
482 Bob Priddy	3.00	8.00
483 George Smith RC	3.00	8.00
484 Ron Perranoski	8.00	20.00
485 Nellie Fox P	6.00	15.00
CO		
486 T.Egan/P.Rogan RC	3.00	8.00
487 Woody Woodward	6.00	15.00
488 Ted Wills	3.00	8.00
489 Gene Mauch MG	6.00	15.00
490 Earl Battey	3.00	8.00
491 Tracy Stallard	3.00	8.00
492 Gene Freese	3.00	8.00
493 B.Roman RC/B.Brubaker RC	3.00	8.00
494 Jay Ritchie RC	3.00	8.00
495 Joe Christopher	3.00	8.00
496 Joe Cunningham	3.00	8.00
497 K.Henderson RC/J.Hiatt RC	6.00	15.00
498 Gene Stephens	3.00	8.00
499 Stu Miller	6.00	15.00
500 Eddie Mathews	20.00	50.00
501 R.Gagliano RC/J.Rittwage RC	3.00	8.00
502 Don Cardwell	3.00	8.00
503 Phil Gagliano	3.00	8.00
504 Jerry Grote	6.00	15.00
505 Ray Culp	3.00	8.00
506 Sam Mele MG	3.00	8.00
507 Sammy Ellis	3.00	8.00
508 Checklist 7	5.00	12.00
509 B.Guindon RC/G.Vezendy RC	3.00	8.00
510 Ernie Banks	30.00	80.00
511 Ron Locke	3.00	8.00
512 Cap Peterson	3.00	8.00
513 New York Yankees TC	15.00	40.00
514 Joe Azcue	3.00	8.00
515 Vern Law	6.00	15.00
516 Al Weis	3.00	8.00
517 P.Schaal RC/J.Warner	6.00	15.00
518 Ken Rowe	3.00	8.00
519 Bob Uecker UER	20.00	50.00
520 Tony Cloninger	3.00	8.00
521 D.Bennett/M.Steevens RC	3.00	8.00
522 Hank Aguirre	3.00	8.00
523 Mike Brumley SP	5.00	12.00
524 Dave Giusti SP	5.00	12.00
525 Eddie Bressoud	3.00	8.00
526 J.Odom/J.Hunter SP RC	50.00	120.00
527 Jeff Torborg SP	5.00	12.00
528 George Altman	3.00	8.00
529 Jerry Fosnow SP RC	5.00	12.00
530 Jim Maloney	6.00	15.00
531 Chuck Hiller	3.00	8.00
532 Hector Lopez	6.00	15.00
533 R.Swob/T.McGraw SP RC	15.00	40.00
534 John Herrnstein	3.00	8.00
535 Jack Kralick SP	5.00	12.00
536 Andre Rodgers SP	5.00	12.00
537 Lopez/Roof/May RC	3.00	8.00
538 Chuck Dressen MG SP	5.00	12.00
539 Herm Starrette	3.00	8.00
540 Lou Brock SP	40.00	100.00
541 G.Bollo RC/B.Locker RC	3.00	8.00
542 Lou Klimchock	3.00	8.00
543 Ed Connolly SP RC	5.00	12.00
544 Howie Reed RC	3.00	8.00
545 Jesus Alou SP	10.00	25.00
546 Davis/Hed/Bark/Weav RC	3.00	8.00
547 Jake Wood SP	5.00	12.00
548 Dick Stigman	3.00	8.00
549 R.Pena RC/G.Beckert RC	8.00	20.00
550 Mel Stottlemyre SP RC	20.00	50.00
551 New York Mets TC SP	12.50	30.00
552 Julio Gotay	3.00	8.00
553 Coombs/Ratliff/McClure RC	3.00	8.00
554 Chico Ruiz SP	5.00	12.00
555 Jack Baldschun SP	5.00	12.00
556 R.Schoendienst SP	10.00	25.00
557 Jose Santiago RC	3.00	8.00
558 Tommie Sisk	3.00	8.00
559 Ed Bailey SP	5.00	12.00
560 Boog Powell SP	8.00	20.00
561 Dab/Kek/Valle/Lefebvre RC	6.00	15.00
562 Billy Moran	3.00	8.00
563 Julio Navarro	3.00	8.00
564 Mel Nelson	3.00	8.00
565 Ernie Broglio SP	5.00	12.00
566 Blanco/Moschitto/Lopez RC	5.00	12.00
567 Tommie Aaron	3.00	8.00
568 Ron Taylor SP	5.00	12.00
569 Gino Cimoli SP	5.00	12.00
570 Claude Osteen SP	6.00	15.00
571 Ossie Virgil SP	5.00	12.00
572 Baltimore Orioles TC SP	10.00	25.00
573 Jim Lonborg SP RC	10.00	25.00
574 Roy Sievers	6.00	15.00
575 Jose Pagan	3.00	8.00
576 Terry Fox SP	5.00	12.00
577 Knowles/Busch/Schein RC	5.00	12.00
578 Camilo Carreon SP	5.00	12.00
579 Dick Smith SP	5.00	12.00
580 Jimmie Hall SP	5.00	12.00
581 Tony Perez SP RC	50.00	120.00
582 Bob Schmidt SP	5.00	12.00
583 Wes Covington SP	5.00	12.00
584 Harry Bright	6.00	15.00
585 Hank Fischer	3.00	8.00
586 Tom McCraw SP UER	5.00	12.00
Name is spelled McGraw on the back		
587 Joe Sparma	3.00	8.00
588 Lenny Green	3.00	8.00
589 F.Linzy RC/B.Schroder RC	5.00	12.00
590 John Wyatt	3.00	8.00
591 Bob Skinner SP	5.00	12.00
592 Frank Bork SP RC	5.00	12.00
593 J.Sullivan RC/J.Moore RC SP	5.00	12.00
594 Joe Gaines	3.00	8.00
595 Don Lee	3.00	8.00
596 Don Landrum SP	5.00	12.00
597 Nossek/Sevcik/Reese RC	3.00	8.00
598 Al Downing SP	10.00	25.00

1965 Topps Embossed

The cards in this 72-card set measure approximately 2 1/8" by 3 1/2". The 1965 Topps Embossed set contains gold foil cameo player portraits. Each league had 36 representatives set on blue backgrounds for the AL and red backgrounds for the NL. The Topps embossed set was distributed as inserts in packages of the regular 1965 baseball series.

COMPLETE SET (72)	150.00	300.00
1 Carl Yastrzemski	4.00	10.00
2 Ron Fairly	.75	2.00
3 Max Alvis	.75	2.00
4 Jim Ray Hart	.75	2.00
5 Bill Skowron	1.25	3.00
6 Ed Kranepool	.75	2.00
7 Tim McCarver	1.25	3.00
8 Sandy Koufax	8.00	20.00
9 Donn Clendenon	.75	2.00
10 John Romano	.75	2.00
11 Mickey Mantle	40.00	100.00
12 Joe Torre	2.00	5.00
13 Al Kaline	4.00	10.00
14 Al McBean	.75	2.00
15 Don Drysdale	2.00	5.00
16 Brooks Robinson	4.00	10.00
17 Jim Bunning	1.25	3.00
18 Gary Peters	.75	2.00
19 Roberto Clemente	25.00	60.00
20 Milt Pappas	.75	2.00
21 Wayne Causey	.75	2.00
22 Frank Robinson	2.00	5.00
23 Bill Mazeroski	2.00	5.00
24 Diego Segui	.75	2.00
25 Jim Bouton	1.25	3.00
26 Eddie Mathews	2.50	6.00
27 Willie Mays	10.00	25.00
28 Ron Santo	1.25	3.00
29 Boog Powell	1.25	3.00
30 Ken McBride	.75	2.00
31 Leon Wagner	.75	2.00
32 Johnny Callison	.75	2.00
33 Zoilo Versalles	.75	2.00
34 Jack Baldschun	.75	2.00
35 Ron Hunt	.75	2.00
36 Richie Allen	2.00	5.00
37 Frank Malzone	.75	2.00
38 Bob Allison	.75	2.00
39 Jim Fregosi	1.25	3.00
40 Billy Williams	1.25	3.00
41 Bill Freehan	1.25	3.00
42 Vada Pinson	1.25	3.00
43 Bill White	1.25	3.00
44 Roy McMillan	.75	2.00
45 Orlando Cepeda	1.25	3.00
46 Rocky Colavito	2.00	5.00
47 Ken Boyer	1.25	3.00
48 Dick Radatz	.75	2.00
49 Tommy Davis	1.25	3.00
50 Walt Bond	.75	2.00
51 John Orsino	.75	2.00
52 Joe Christopher	.75	2.00
53 Al Spangler	.75	2.00
54 Jim King	.75	2.00
55 Mickey Lolich	1.25	3.00
56 Harmon Killebrew	2.50	6.00
57 Bob Shaw	.75	2.00
58 Ernie Banks	4.00	10.00
59 Hank Aaron	15.00	40.00
60 Chuck Hinton	.75	2.00
61 Bob Aspromonte	.75	2.00
62 Lee Maye	.75	2.00
63 Joe Cunningham	.75	2.00
64 Pete Ward	.75	2.00
65 Bobby Richardson	1.25	3.00
66 Dean Chance	.75	2.00
67 Dick Ellsworth	.75	2.00
68 Jim Maloney	.75	2.00
69 Bob Gibson	2.00	5.00
70 Earl Battey	.75	2.00
71 Tony Kubek	1.25	3.00
72 Jack Kralick	.75	2.00

1965 Topps Transfers Inserts

The 1965 Topps transfers (2" by 3") were issued in series of 24 each as inserts in three of the regular 1965 Topps cards series. Thirty-six of the transfers feature blue bands at the top and bottom while 36 feature red bands at the top and bottom. The team name and position are listed in the top band while the player's name is listed in the bottom band. Transfers 1-36 have blue panels whereas 37-72 have red panels. These unnumbered transfers are ordered below alphabetically by player's name within each color group. Transfers of Bob Veale and Carl Yastrzemski are supposedly tougher to find than the others in the set; they are marked below by SP.

COMPLETE SET (72)	200.00	400.00
1 Bob Allison	1.00	2.50
2 Max Alvis	1.00	2.50
3 Luis Aparicio	2.50	6.00
4 Walt Bond	1.00	2.50
5 Jim Bouton	1.50	4.00
6 Jim Bunning	2.50	6.00
7 Rico Carty	1.50	4.00
8 Wayne Causey	1.00	2.50
9 Orlando Cepeda	2.50	6.00
10 Dean Chance	1.00	2.50
11 Tony Conigliaro	1.50	4.00
12 Bill Freehan	1.50	4.00
13 Jim Fregosi	1.50	4.00
14 Bob Gibson	4.00	10.00
15 Dick Green	1.50	4.00
16 Tom Haller	1.00	2.50
17 Larry Jackson	1.00	2.50
18 Bobby Knoop	1.00	2.50
19 Jim Maloney	1.50	4.00
20 Juan Marichal	2.50	6.00
21 Lee Maye	1.00	2.50
22 Jim O'Toole	1.00	2.50
23 Camilo Pascual	1.00	2.50
24 Vada Pinson	1.50	4.00
25 Juan Pizarro	1.00	2.50
26 Bobby Richardson	2.50	6.00
27 Bob Rodgers	1.00	2.50
28 John Roseboro	1.00	2.50
29 Dick Stuart	1.50	4.00
30 Luis Tiant	1.50	4.00
31 Joe Torre	2.50	6.00
32 Bob Veale SP	5.00	12.00
33 Leon Wagner	1.00	2.50
34 Dave Wickersham	1.00	2.50
35 Billy Williams	2.50	6.00
36 Carl Yastrzemski SP	20.00	50.00
37 Hank Aaron	15.00	40.00
38 Richie Allen	4.00	10.00
39 Bob Aspromonte	1.00	2.50
40 Ken Boyer	2.50	6.00
41 Johnny Callison	1.50	4.00
42 Dean Chance	1.00	2.50
43 Joe Christopher	1.00	2.50
44 Roberto Clemente	30.00	60.00
45 Rocky Colavito	4.00	10.00
46 Tommy Davis	1.50	4.00
47 Don Drysdale	4.00	10.00
48 Chuck Hinton	1.00	2.50
49 Elston Howard	2.50	6.00
50 Ron Hunt	1.00	2.50
51 Al Kaline	8.00	20.00
52 Harmon Killebrew	5.00	12.00
53 Jim King	1.00	2.50
54 Ron Kline	1.00	2.50
55 Sandy Koufax	15.00	40.00
56 Ed Kranepool	1.00	2.50
57 Mickey Mantle	60.00	120.00
58 Willie Mays	15.00	40.00
59 Bill Mazeroski	4.00	10.00
60 Tony Oliva	2.50	6.00
61 Milt Pappas	1.00	2.50
62 Gary Peters	1.00	2.50
63 Boog Powell	2.50	6.00
64 Dick Radatz	1.00	2.50
65 Brooks Robinson	8.00	20.00
66 Frank Robinson	4.00	10.00
67 Ron Santo	2.50	6.00
68 Diego Segui	1.00	2.50
69 Bill Skowron	1.50	4.00
70 Al Spangler	1.00	2.50
71 Pete Ward	1.00	2.50
72 Bill White	1.50	4.00

1966 Topps

The cards in this 598-card set measure 2 1/2" by 3 1/2". There are the same number of cards as in the 1965 set. Once again, the seventh series cards (523 to 598) are considered more difficult to obtain than the cards of any other series in the set. Within this last series there are 43 cards that were printed in lesser quantities than the other cards in that series; these shorter-printed cards are marked by SP in the checklist below. Among other ways, cards were issued in five-card nickel wax packs, 12-card dime cello packs which came 36 packs to a box and 12 boxes to a case. These cards were also issued in 36-card rack packs which cost 29 cents. These rack packs were issued 48 to a case. The only featured subset within this set is League Leaders (215-226). Noteworthy Rookie Cards in the set include Jim Palmer (126), Ferguson Jenkins (254), and Don Sutton (288). Jim Palmer is described in the bio (on his card back) as a left-hander.

COMPLETE SET (598)	2500.00	5000.00
COMMON CARD (1-109)	.60	1.50
COMMON CARD (110-283)	.75	2.00
COMMON CARD (284-370)	1.25	3.00
COMMON CARD (371-446)	2.00	5.00
COMMON CARD (447-522)	4.00	10.00
COMMON CARD (523-598)	6.00	15.00
COMMON SP (523-598)	12.50	30.00
WRAPPER (5-CENT)	10.00	25.00
1 Willie Mays	100.00	250.00
2 Ted Abernathy	.60	1.50
3 Sam Mele MG	.60	1.50
4 Ray Culp	.60	1.50
5 Jim Fregosi	.75	2.00
6 Chuck Schilling	.60	1.50
7 Tracy Stallard	.60	1.50
8 Floyd Robinson	.60	1.50
9 Clete Boyer	.75	2.00
10 Tony Cloninger	.60	1.50
11 B.Alyea RC/P.Craig	.60	1.50
12 John Tsitouris	.60	1.50
13 Lou Johnson	.75	2.00
14 Norm Siebern	.60	1.50
15 Vern Law	.75	2.00
16 Larry Brown	.60	1.50
17 John Stephenson	.60	1.50
18 Roland Sheldon	.60	1.50
19 San Francisco Giants TC	2.00	5.00
20 Willie Horton	.75	2.00
21 Don Nottebart	.60	1.50
22 Joe Nossek	.60	1.50
23 Jack Sanford	.60	1.50
24 Don Kessinger RC	1.50	4.00
25 Pete Ward	.60	1.50
26 Ray Sadecki	.60	1.50
27 D.Knowles/A.Etchebarren RC	.60	1.50
28 Phil Niekro	8.00	20.00
29 Mike Brumley	.60	1.50
30 Pete Rose UER DP	40.00	100.00
31 Jack Cullen	.75	2.00
32 Adolfo Phillips RC	.60	1.50
33 Jim Pagliaroni	.60	1.50
34 Checklist 1	3.00	8.00
35 Ron Swoboda	1.50	4.00
36 Jim Hunter UER DP	8.00	20.00
37 Billy Herman MG	.75	2.00
38 Ron Nischwitz	.60	1.50
39 Ken Henderson	.60	1.50
40 Jim Grant	.60	1.50
41 Don LeJohn RC	.60	1.50
42 Aubrey Gatewood	.60	1.50
43A D.Landrum Dark Button	.75	2.00
43B D.Landrum Airbrush Button	8.00	20.00
43C D.Landrum No Button	.75	2.00
44 B.Davis/T.Kelley	.60	1.50
45 Jim Gentile	.75	2.00
46 Howie Koplitz	.60	1.50
47 J.C. Martin	.60	1.50
48 Paul Blair	.75	2.00
49 Woody Woodward	.75	2.00
50 Mickey Mantle DP	200.00	500.00
51 Gordon Richardson RC	.60	1.50
52 W.Covington/J.Callison	1.50	4.00
53 Bob Duliba	.60	1.50
54 Jose Pagan	.60	1.50
55 Ken Harrelson	.75	2.00
56 Sandy Valdespino	.60	1.50
57 Jim Lefebvre	.75	2.00
58 Dave Wickersham	.60	1.50
59 Cincinnati Reds TC	2.00	5.00
60 Curt Flood	1.50	4.00
61 Bob Bolin	.60	1.50
62A Merritt Ranew Sold Line	.75	2.00
62B Merritt Ranew NTR	12.50	30.00
63 Jim Stewart	.60	1.50
64 Bob Bruce	.60	1.50
65 Leon Wagner	.60	1.50
66 Al Weis	.60	1.50
67 C.Jones/D.Selma RC	1.50	4.00
68 Hal Reniff	.60	1.50
69 Ken Hamlin	.60	1.50
70 Carl Yastrzemski	25.00	60.00
71 Frank Carpin RC	.60	1.50
72 Tony Perez	20.00	50.00
73 Jerry Zimmerman	.60	1.50
74 Don Mossi	.75	2.00
75 Tommy Davis	.75	2.00
76 Red Schoendienst MG	1.50	4.00
77 John Orsino	.60	1.50
78 Frank Linzy	.60	1.50
79 Joe Pepitone	1.50	4.00
80 Richie Allen	2.50	6.00
81 Ray Oyler	.60	1.50
82 Bob Hendley	.60	1.50
83 Albie Pearson	.75	2.00
84 J.Beauchamp/D.Kelley	.60	1.50
85 Eddie Fisher	.60	1.50
86 John Bateman	.60	1.50
87 Dan Napoleon	.60	1.50
88 Fred Whitfield	.60	1.50
89 Ted Davidson	.60	1.50
90 Luis Aparicio	3.00	8.00
91A Bob Uecker TR	4.00	10.00
91B Bob Uecker NTR	15.00	40.00
92 New York Yankees TC	6.00	15.00
93 Jim Lonborg DP	.75	2.00
94 Matty Alou	.75	2.00
95 Pete Richert	.60	1.50
96 Felipe Alou	1.50	4.00
97 Jim Merritt RC	.60	1.50
98 Don Demeter	.60	1.50
99 W.Stargell/D.Clendenon	2.50	6.00
100 Sandy Koufax	50.00	100.00
101A Checklist 2 Spahn ERR	6.00	15.00
101B Cheklist 2 Henry COR	4.00	10.00
102 Ed Kirkpatrick	.60	1.50
103A Dick Groat TR	.75	2.00
103B Dick Groat NTR	15.00	40.00
104A Alex Johnson TR	.75	2.00
104B Alex Johnson NTR	12.50	30.00
105 Milt Pappas	.75	2.00
106 Rusty Staub	1.50	4.00
107 L.Stahl RC/R.Tompkins RC	.60	1.50
108 Bobby Klaus	.60	1.50
109 Ralph Terry	.75	2.00
110 Ernie Banks	40.00	100.00
111 Gary Peters	.75	2.00
112 Manny Mota	1.50	4.00
113 Hank Aguirre	.75	2.00
114 Jim Gosger	.75	2.00
115 Bill Henry	.75	2.00
116 Walter Alston MG	2.50	6.00
117 Jake Gibbs	.75	2.00
118 Mike McCormick	.75	2.00
119 Art Shamsky	.75	2.00
120 Harmon Killebrew	12.00	30.00
121 Ray Herbert	.75	2.00
122 Joe Gaines	.75	2.00
123 F.Bork/J.May	.75	2.00
124 Tug McGraw	1.50	4.00
125 Lou Brock	25.00	60.00
126 Jim Palmer UER RC	50.00	120.00
127 Ken Berry	.75	2.00
128 Jim Landis	.75	2.00
129 Jack Kralick	.75	2.00
130 Joe Torre	2.50	6.00
131 California Angels TC	2.00	5.00
132 Orlando Cepeda	3.00	8.00
133 Don McMahon	.75	2.00
134 Wes Parker	1.50	4.00
135 Dave Morehead	.75	2.00
136 Woody Held	.75	2.00
137 Pat Corrales	.75	2.00
138 Roger Repoz RC	.75	2.00
139 B.Browne RC/D.Young RC	.75	2.00
140 Jim Maloney	1.50	4.00
141 Tom McCraw	.75	2.00
142 Don Dennis RC	.75	2.00
143 Jose Tartabull	1.50	4.00
144 Don Schwall	.75	2.00
145 Bill Freehan	1.50	4.00
146 George Altman	.75	2.00
147 Lum Harris MG	.75	2.00
148 Bob Johnson	.75	2.00
149 Dick Nen	.75	2.00
150 Rocky Colavito	3.00	8.00
151 Gary Wagner RC	.75	2.00
152 Frank Malzone	1.50	4.00
153 Rico Carty	1.50	4.00
154 Chuck Hiller	.75	2.00
155 Marcelino Lopez	.75	2.00
156 D.Schofield/H.Lanier	.75	2.00
157 Rene Lachemann	.75	2.00
158 Jim Brewer	.75	2.00
159 Chico Ruiz	.75	2.00
160 Whitey Ford	20.00	50.00
161 Jerry Lumpe	.75	2.00
162 Lee Maye	.75	2.00
163 Tito Francona	.75	2.00
164 T.Agee/M.Staehle	1.50	4.00
165 Don Lock	.75	2.00
166 Chris Krug RC	.75	2.00
167 Boog Powell	2.50	6.00
168 Dan Osinski	.75	2.00
169 Duke Sims RC	.75	2.00
170 Cookie Rojas	1.50	4.00
171 Nick Willhite	.75	2.00
172 New York Mets TC	2.00	5.00
173 Al Spangler	.75	2.00
174 Ron Taylor	.75	2.00
175 Bert Campaneris	1.50	4.00
176 Jim Davenport	.75	2.00
177 Hector Lopez	.75	2.00
178 Bob Tillman	.75	2.00
179 D.Aust RC/B.Tolan	1.50	4.00
180 Vada Pinson	1.50	4.00
181 Al Worthington	.75	2.00
182 Jerry Lynch	.75	2.00
183A Checklist 3 Large Print	3.00	8.00
183B Checklist 3 Small Print	3.00	8.00
184 Denis Menke	.75	2.00
185 Bob Buhl	1.50	4.00
186 Ruben Amaro	.75	2.00
187 Chuck Dressen MG	1.50	4.00
188 Al Luplow	.75	2.00
189 John Roseboro	1.50	4.00
190 Jimmie Hall	.75	2.00
191 Darrell Sutherland RC	.75	2.00
192 Vic Power	1.50	4.00
193 Dave McNally	1.50	4.00
194 Washington Senators TC	2.00	5.00
195 Joe Morgan	30.00	80.00
196 Don Pavletich	.75	2.00
197 Sonny Siebert	.75	2.00
198 Mickey Stanley RC	2.50	6.00
199 Skowron/Romano/Robinson	1.50	4.00
200 Eddie Mathews	6.00	15.00
201 Jim Dickson	.75	2.00
202 Clay Dalrymple	.75	2.00
203 Jose Santiago	.75	2.00
204 Chicago Cubs TC	2.00	5.00
205 Tom Tresh	1.50	4.00
206 Al Jackson	.75	2.00
207 Frank Quilici RC	.75	2.00
208 Bob Miller	.75	2.00
209 F.Fisher/J.Hiller RC	1.50	4.00
210 Bill Mazeroski	10.00	25.00
211 Frank Kreutzer	.75	2.00
212 Ed Kranepool	1.50	4.00
213 Fred Newman	.75	2.00
214 Tommy Harper	1.50	4.00
215 Clemente/Aaron/Mays LL	30.00	80.00
216 Oliva/Yaz/Davalillo LL	2.00	5.00
217 Mays/McCovey/B.Will LL	10.00	25.00
218 Conigliaro/Cash/Horton LL	2.00	5.00
219 Johnson/F.Rob/Mays LL	10.00	25.00
220 Colavito/Horton/Oliva LL	2.00	5.00
221 Koufax/Marichal/Law LL	5.00	12.00
222 McDowell/Fisher/Siebert LL	2.00	5.00
223 Koufax/Clon/Drysdale LL	8.00	20.00
224 Grant/Stottlemyre/Kaat LL	2.00	5.00
225 Koufax/Veale/Gibson LL	12.00	30.00
226 McDowell/Lolich/McLain LL	2.00	5.00
227 Russ Nixon	.75	2.00
228 Larry Dierker	1.50	4.00
229 Hank Bauer MG	1.50	4.00
230 Johnny Callison	1.50	4.00
231 Floyd Weaver	.75	2.00
232 Glenn Beckert	1.50	4.00
233 Dom Zanni	.75	2.00
234 R.Beck RC/R.White RC	3.00	8.00
235 Don Cardwell	.75	2.00
236 Mike Hershberger	.75	2.00
237 Billy O'Dell	.75	2.00
238 Los Angeles Dodgers TC	2.00	5.00
239 Orlando Pena	.75	2.00
240 Earl Battey	.75	2.00
241 Dennis Ribant	.75	2.00
242 Jesus Alou	.75	2.00
243 Nelson Briles	1.50	4.00
244 C.Harrison RC//S.Jackson	.75	2.00
245 John Buzhardt	.75	2.00
246 Ed Bailey	.75	2.00
247 Carl Warwick	.75	2.00
248 Pete Mikkelsen	.75	2.00
249 Bill Rigney MG	.75	2.00
250 Sammy Ellis	.75	2.00
251 Ed Brinkman	.75	2.00
252 Denny Lemaster	.75	2.00
253 Don Wert	.75	2.00
254 Fergie Jenkins RC	50.00	120.00
255 Willie Stargell	15.00	40.00
256 Lew Krausse	.75	2.00
257 Jeff Torborg	1.50	4.00
258 Dave Giusti	.75	2.00
259 Boston Red Sox TC	2.00	5.00
260 Bob Shaw	.75	2.00
261 Ron Hansen	.75	2.00
262 Jack Hamilton	.75	2.00
263 Tom Egan	.75	2.00
264 A.Kosco RC/T.Uhlaender RC	.75	2.00
265 Stu Miller	1.50	4.00
266 Pedro Gonzalez UER	.75	2.00
267 Joe Sparma	.75	2.00
268 John Blanchard	.75	2.00
269 Don Heffner MG	.75	2.00
270 Claude Osteen	1.50	4.00
271 Hal Lanier	.75	2.00
272 Jack Baldschun	.75	2.00
273 B.Aspromonte/R.Staub	1.50	4.00
274 Buster Narum	.75	2.00
275 Tim McCarver	1.50	4.00
276 Jim Bouton	1.50	4.00
277 George Thomas	.75	2.00
278 Cal Koonce	.75	2.00
279A Checklist 4 Black Cap	3.00	8.00
279B Checklist 4 Red Cap	3.00	8.00
280 Bobby Knoop	.75	2.00
281 Bruce Howard	.75	2.00
282 Johnny Lewis	.75	2.00
283 Jim Perry	1.50	4.00
284 Bobby Wine	1.25	3.00
285 Luis Tiant	2.00	5.00
286 Gary Geiger	1.25	3.00
287 Jack Aker RC	1.25	3.00
288 D.Sutton RC/B.Singer RC	40.00	100.00
289 Larry Sherry	1.25	3.00
290 Ron Santo	2.00	5.00
291 Moe Drabowsky	2.00	5.00
292 Jim Coker	1.25	3.00
293 Mike Shannon	2.00	5.00
294 Steve Ridzik	1.25	3.00
295 Jim Ray Hart	2.00	5.00
296 Johnny Keane MG	2.00	5.00
297 Jim Owens	1.25	3.00
298 Rico Petrocelli	2.00	5.00
299 Lew Burdette	2.00	5.00
300 Bob Clemente	75.00	200.00
301 Greg Bollo	1.25	3.00
302 Ernie Bowman	1.25	3.00
303 Cleveland Indians TC	2.00	5.00
304 John Herrnstein	1.25	3.00

Card	Low	High
305 Camilo Pascual	2.00	5.00
306 Ty Cline	1.25	3.00
307 Clay Carroll	2.00	5.00
308 Tom Haller	2.00	5.00
309 Diego Segui	1.25	3.00
310 Frank Robinson	15.00	40.00
311 T.Helms/D.Simpson	2.00	5.00
312 Bob Saverine	1.25	3.00
313 Chris Zachary	1.25	3.00
314 Hector Valle	1.25	3.00
315 Norm Cash	2.00	5.00
316 Jack Fisher	1.25	3.00
317 Dalton Jones	1.25	3.00
318 Harry Walker MG	1.25	3.00
319 Gene Freese	1.25	3.00
320 Bob Gibson	20.00	50.00
321 Rick Reichardt	1.25	3.00
322 Bill Faul	1.25	3.00
323 Ray Barker	1.25	3.00
324 John Boozer UER	1.25	3.00
1965 Record is incorrect		
325 Vic Davalillo	1.25	3.00
326 Atlanta Braves TC	2.00	5.00
327 Bernie Allen	1.25	3.00
328 Jerry Grote	2.00	5.00
329 Pete Charton	1.25	3.00
330 Ron Fairly	2.00	5.00
331 Ron Herbel	1.25	3.00
332 Bill Bryan	1.25	3.00
333 J.Coleman RC/J.French RC	1.25	3.00
334 Marty Keough	1.25	3.00
335 Juan Pizarro	1.25	3.00
336 Gene Alley	2.00	5.00
337 Fred Gladding	1.25	3.00
338 Dal Maxvill	1.25	3.00
339 Del Crandall	2.00	5.00
340 Dean Chance	2.00	5.00
341 Wes Westrum MG	2.00	5.00
342 Bob Humphreys	1.25	3.00
343 Joe Christopher	1.25	3.00
344 Steve Blass	2.00	5.00
345 Bob Allison	2.00	5.00
346 Mike de la Hoz	1.25	3.00
347 Phil Regan	2.00	5.00
348 Baltimore Orioles TC	3.00	8.00
349 Cap Peterson	1.25	3.00
350 Mel Stottlemyre	3.00	8.00
351 Fred Valentine	1.25	3.00
352 Bob Aspromonte	1.25	3.00
353 Al McBean	1.25	3.00
354 Smoky Burgess	2.00	5.00
355 Wade Blasingame	1.25	3.00
356 O.Johnson RC/K.Sanders RC	1.25	3.00
357 Gerry Arrigo	1.25	3.00
358 Charlie Smith	1.25	3.00
359 Johnny Briggs	1.25	3.00
360 Ron Hunt	1.25	3.00
361 Tom Satriano	1.25	3.00
362 Gates Brown	2.00	5.00
363 Checklist 5	4.00	10.00
364 Nate Oliver	1.25	3.00
365 Roger Maris UER	40.00	100.00
366 Wayne Causey	1.25	3.00
367 Mel Nelson	1.25	3.00
368 Charlie Lau	2.00	5.00
369 Jim King	1.25	3.00
370 Chico Cardenas	1.25	3.00
371 Lee Stange	2.00	5.00
372 Harvey Kuenn	3.00	8.00
373 J.Hiatt/D.Estelle	3.00	8.00
374 Bob Locker	2.00	5.00
375 Donn Clendenon	3.00	8.00
376 Paul Schaal	2.00	5.00
377 Turk Farrell	2.00	5.00
378 Dick Tracewski	2.00	5.00
379 St. Louis Cardinals TC	4.00	10.00
380 Tony Conigliaro	4.00	10.00
381 Hank Fischer	2.00	5.00
382 Phil Roof	2.00	5.00
383 Jackie Brandt	2.00	5.00
384 Al Downing	3.00	8.00
385 Ken Boyer	4.00	10.00
386 Gil Hodges MG	3.00	8.00
387 Howie Reed	2.00	5.00
388 Don Mincher	2.00	5.00
389 Jim O'Toole	3.00	8.00
390 Brooks Robinson	20.00	50.00
391 Chuck Hinton	2.00	5.00
392 B.Hands RC/R.Hundley RC	3.00	8.00
393 George Brunet	2.00	5.00
394 Ron Brand	2.00	5.00
395 Len Gabrielson	2.00	5.00
396 Jerry Stephenson	2.00	5.00
397 Bill White	3.00	8.00
398 Danny Cater	2.00	5.00
399 Ray Washburn	2.00	5.00
400 Zoilo Versalles	3.00	8.00
401 Ken McMullen	2.00	5.00
402 Jim Hickman	2.00	5.00
403 Fred Talbot	2.00	5.00
404 Pittsburgh Pirates TC	4.00	10.00
405 Elston Howard	3.00	8.00
406 Joey Jay	2.00	5.00
407 John Kennedy	2.00	5.00
408 Lee Thomas	3.00	8.00
409 Billy Hoeft	2.00	5.00
410 Al Kaline	15.00	40.00
411 Gene Mauch MG	2.00	5.00
412 Sam Bowens	2.00	5.00
413 Johnny Romano	2.00	5.00
414 Dan Coombs	2.00	5.00
415 Max Alvis	2.00	5.00
416 Phil Ortega	2.00	5.00
417 J.McGlothlin RC/E.Sukla RC	2.00	5.00
418 Phil Gagliano	2.00	5.00
419 Mike Ryan	2.00	5.00
420 Juan Marichal	12.00	30.00
421 Roy McMillan	3.00	8.00
422 Ed Charles	2.00	5.00
423 Ernie Broglio	2.00	5.00
424 L.May RC/D.Osteen RC	4.00	10.00
425 Bob Veale	3.00	8.00
426 Chicago White Sox TC	4.00	10.00
427 John Miller	2.00	5.00
428 Sandy Alomar	2.00	5.00
429 Bill Monbouquette	2.00	5.00
430 Don Drysdale	12.00	30.00
431 Walt Bond	2.00	5.00
432 Bob Heffner	2.00	5.00
433 Alvin Dark MG	3.00	8.00
434 Willie Kirkland	2.00	5.00
435 Jim Bunning	6.00	15.00
436 Julian Javier	3.00	8.00
437 Al Stanek	2.00	5.00
438 Willie Smith	2.00	5.00
439 Pedro Ramos	2.00	5.00
440 Deron Johnson	3.00	8.00
441 Tommie Sisk	2.00	5.00
442 E.Barnowski RC/E.Watt RC	2.00	5.00
443 Bill Wakefield	2.00	5.00
444 Checklist 6	4.00	10.00
445 Jim Kaat	4.00	10.00
446 Mack Jones	2.00	5.00
447 D.Ellsw UER Hubbs	6.00	15.00
448 Eddie Stanky MG	4.00	10.00
449 Joe Moeller	4.00	10.00
450 Tony Oliva	6.00	15.00
451 Barry Latman	4.00	10.00
452 Joe Azcue	4.00	10.00
453 Ron Kline	4.00	10.00
454 Jerry Buchek	4.00	10.00
455 Mickey Lolich	6.00	15.00
456 D.Brandon RC/J.Foy RC	4.00	10.00
457 Joe Gibbon	4.00	10.00
458 Manny Jiminez	4.00	10.00
459 Bill McCool	4.00	10.00
460 Curt Blefary	4.00	10.00
461 Roy Face	6.00	15.00
462 Bob Rodgers	4.00	10.00
463 Philadelphia Phillies TC	6.00	15.00
464 Larry Bearnarth	4.00	10.00
465 Don Buford	4.00	10.00
466 Ken Johnson	4.00	10.00
467 Vic Roznovsky	4.00	10.00
468 Johnny Podres	6.00	15.00
469 B.Murcer RC/D.Womack RC	15.00	40.00
470 Sam McDowell	6.00	15.00
471 Bob Skinner	4.00	10.00
472 Terry Fox	4.00	10.00
473 Rich Rollins	4.00	10.00
474 Dick Schofield	4.00	10.00
475 Dick Radatz	4.00	10.00
476 Bobby Bragan MG	4.00	10.00
477 Steve Barber	4.00	10.00
478 Tony Gonzalez	4.00	10.00
479 Jim Hannan	4.00	10.00
480 Dick Stuart	4.00	10.00
481 Bob Lee	4.00	10.00
482 J.Boccabella/D.Dowling	4.00	10.00
483 Joe Nuxhall	4.00	10.00
484 Wes Covington	4.00	10.00
485 Bob Bailey	4.00	10.00
486 Tommy John	6.00	15.00
487 Al Ferrara	4.00	10.00
488 George Banks	4.00	10.00
489 Curt Simmons	4.00	10.00
490 Bobby Richardson	10.00	25.00
491 Dennis Bennett	4.00	10.00
492 Kansas City Athletics TC	6.00	15.00
493 Johnny Klippstein	4.00	10.00
494 Gordy Coleman	4.00	10.00
495 Dick McAuliffe	6.00	15.00
496 Lindy McDaniel	4.00	10.00
497 Chris Cannizzaro	4.00	10.00
498 L.Walker RC/W.Fryman RC	4.00	10.00
499 Wally Bunker	4.00	10.00
500 Hank Aaron	60.00	150.00
501 John O'Donoghue	4.00	10.00
502 Lenny Green UER	4.00	10.00
503 Steve Hamilton	6.00	15.00
504 Grady Hatton MG	4.00	10.00
505 Jose Cardenal	4.00	10.00
506 Bo Belinsky	6.00	15.00
507 Johnny Edwards	4.00	10.00
508 Steve Hargan RC	6.00	15.00
509 Jake Wood	4.00	10.00
510 Hoyt Wilhelm	10.00	25.00
511 B.Barton RC/T.Fuentes RC	4.00	10.00
512 Dick Stigman	4.00	10.00
513 Camilo Carreon	4.00	10.00
514 Hal Woodeshick	4.00	10.00
515 Frank Howard	6.00	15.00
516 Eddie Bressoud	4.00	10.00
517A Checklist 7 White Sox	6.00	15.00
517B Checklist 7 W.Sox	6.00	15.00
518 H.Hippauf RC/A.Umbach RC	4.00	10.00
519 Bob Friend	6.00	15.00
520 Jim Wynn	6.00	15.00
521 John Wyatt	4.00	10.00
522 Phil Linz	4.00	10.00
523 Bob Sadowski	4.00	10.00
524 O.Brown RC/D.Mason RC SP	20.00	50.00
525 Gary Bell SP	12.50	30.00
526 Minnesota Twins TC SP	50.00	100.00
527 Julio Navarro	6.00	15.00
528 Jesse Gonder SP	12.50	30.00
529 Elia/Higgins/Voss RC	6.00	15.00
530 Robin Roberts	20.00	50.00
531 Joe Cunningham	6.00	15.00
532 A.Monteagudo SP	12.50	30.00
533 Jerry Adair SP	12.50	30.00
534 D.Eilers RC/R.Gardner RC	6.00	15.00
535 Willie Davis SP	15.00	40.00
536 Dick Egan	6.00	15.00
537 Herman Franks MG	6.00	15.00
538 Bob Allen SP	12.50	30.00
539 B.Heath RC/C.Sembera RC	10.00	25.00
540 Denny McLain SP	40.00	100.00
541 Gene Oliver SP	12.50	30.00
542 George Smith	6.00	15.00
543 Roger Craig SP	12.50	30.00
544 Hoerner/Kernek/Williams RC SP	12.50	30.00
545 Dick Green SP	12.50	30.00
546 Dwight Siebler	10.00	25.00
547 Horace Clarke SP RC	60.00	150.00
548 Gary Kroll SP	12.50	30.00
549 A.Closter RC/C.Cox RC	6.00	15.00
550 Willie McCovey SP	50.00	100.00
551 Bob Purkey SP	12.50	30.00
552 B.Tebbetts MG SP	12.50	30.00
553 P.Garrett RC/J.Warner	6.00	15.00
554 Jim Northrup SP	12.50	30.00
555 Ron Perranoski SP	12.50	30.00
556 Mel Queen SP	12.50	30.00
557 Felix Mantilla SP	12.50	30.00
558 Grilli/Magrini/Scott RC	8.00	20.00
559 Roberto Pena SP	12.50	30.00
560 Joel Horlen	6.00	15.00
561 Choo Choo Coleman SP	50.00	120.00
562 Russ Snyder	10.00	25.00
563 P.Cimino RC/C.Tovar RC	6.00	15.00
564 Bob Chance SP	12.50	30.00
565 Jimmy Piersall SP	15.00	40.00
566 Mike Cuellar SP	12.50	30.00
567 Dick Howser SP	15.00	40.00
568 P.Lindblad RC/R.Stone RC	6.00	15.00
569 Orlando McFarlane SP	12.50	30.00
570 Art Mahaffey SP	12.50	30.00
571 Dave Roberts SP	12.50	30.00
572 Bob Priddy	6.00	15.00
573 Derrell Griffith	6.00	15.00
574 B.Hepler RC/B.Murphy RC	6.00	15.00
575 Earl Wilson	6.00	15.00
576 Dave Nicholson SP	12.50	30.00
577 Jack Lamabe SP	12.50	30.00
578 Chi Chi Olivo SP RC	12.50	30.00
579 Bertaina/Brabender/Johnson RC	8.00	20.00
580 Billy Williams SP	30.00	60.00
581 Tony Martinez	6.00	15.00
582 Garry Roggenburk	6.00	15.00
583 Tigers TC SP UER	60.00	120.00
584 F.Fernandez RC/F.Peterson RC	6.00	15.00
585 Tony Taylor	10.00	25.00
586 Claude Raymond SP	12.50	30.00
587 Dick Bertell	6.00	15.00
588 C.Dobson RC/K.Suarez RC	6.00	15.00
589 Lou Klimchock SP	12.50	30.00
590 Bill Skowron SP	15.00	40.00
591 B.Shirley RC/G.Jackson RC SP	125.00	300.00
592 Andre Rodgers	6.00	15.00
593 Doug Camilli SP	12.50	30.00
594 Chico Salmon	6.00	15.00
595 Larry Jackson	6.00	15.00
596 N.Colbert RC/G.Sims RC SP	12.50	30.00
597 John Sullivan	6.00	15.00
598 Gaylord Perry SP	60.00	150.00

1966 Topps Rub-Offs

There are 120 "rub-offs" in the Topps insert set of 1966, of which 100 depict players and the remaining 20 show team pennants. Each rub off measures 2 1/16" by 3". The color player photos are vertical while the team pennants are horizontal; both types of transfer have a large black printer's mark. These rub-offs were originally printed in rolls of 20 and are frequently still found this way. These rub-offs were issued one per wax pack and three per rack pack. Since these rub-offs are unnumbered, they are ordered below alphabetically within type, players (1-100) and team pennants (101-120).

Card	Low	High
COMPLETE SET (120)	200.00	400.00
COMMON RUB-OFF (1-120)	.60	1.50
COMMON PEN. (101-120)	.40	1.00
1 Hank Aaron	10.00	25.00
2 Jerry Adair	.60	1.50
3 Richie Allen	.75	2.00
4 Jesus Alou	.75	2.00
5 Max Alvis	.60	1.50
6 Bob Aspromonte	.60	1.50
7 Ernie Banks	4.00	10.00
8 Earl Battey	.60	1.50
9 Curt Blefary	.60	1.50
10 Ken Boyer	1.25	3.00
11 Bob Bruce	.60	1.50
12 Jim Bunning	1.25	3.00
13 Johnny Callison	.75	2.00
14 Bert Campaneris	.75	2.00
15 Jose Cardenal	.60	1.50
16 Dean Chance	.75	2.00
17 Ed Charles	.60	1.50
18 Roberto Clemente	30.00	60.00
19 Tony Cloninger	.60	1.50
20 Rocky Colavito	2.00	5.00
21 Tony Conigliaro	.75	2.00
22 Vic Davalillo	.60	1.50
23 Willie Davis	.75	2.00
24 Don Drysdale	2.00	5.00
25 Sammy Ellis	.60	1.50
26 Dick Ellsworth	.60	1.50
27 Ron Fairly	.75	2.00
28 Dick Farrell	.60	1.50
29 Eddie Fisher	.60	1.50
30 Jack Fisher	.60	1.50
31 Curt Flood	.75	2.00
32 Whitey Ford	2.00	5.00
33 Bill Freehan	.75	2.00
34 Jim Fregosi	.75	2.00
35 Bob Gibson	2.00	5.00
36 Jim Grant	.60	1.50
37 Jimmie Hall	.60	1.50
38 Ken Harrelson	.75	2.00
39 Jim Ray Hart	.60	1.50
40 Joel Horlen	.60	1.50
41 Willie Horton	.75	2.00
42 Frank Howard	.75	2.00
43 Deron Johnson	.60	1.50
44 Al Kaline	4.00	10.00
45 Harmon Killebrew	3.00	8.00
46 Bobby Knoop	.60	1.50
47 Sandy Koufax	8.00	20.00
48 Ed Kranepool	.60	1.50
49 Gary Kroll	.60	1.50
50 Don Landrum	.60	1.50
51 Vern Law	.75	2.00
52 Johnny Lewis	.60	1.50
53 Don Lock	.60	1.50
54 Mickey Lolich	.75	2.00
55 Jim Maloney	.75	2.00
56 Felix Mantilla	.60	1.50
57 Mickey Mantle	30.00	60.00
58 Juan Marichal	2.00	5.00
59 Eddie Mathews	3.00	8.00
60 Willie Mays	10.00	25.00
61 Bill Mazeroski	2.00	5.00
62 Dick McAuliffe	.60	1.50
63 Tim McCarver	.75	2.00
64 Willie McCovey	2.00	5.00
65 Sam McDowell	.75	2.00
66 Ken McMullen	.60	1.50
67 Denis Menke	.60	1.50
68 Bill Monbouquette	.60	1.50
69 Joe Morgan	2.00	5.00
70 Fred Newman	.60	1.50
71 John O'Donoghue	.60	1.50
72 Tony Oliva	1.25	3.00
73 Johnny Orsino	.60	1.50
74 Phil Ortega	.60	1.50
75 Milt Pappas	.75	2.00
76 Dick Radatz	.75	2.00
77 Bobby Richardson	1.25	3.00
78 Pete Richert	.60	1.50
79 Brooks Robinson	4.00	10.00
80 Floyd Robinson	.60	1.50
81 Frank Robinson	2.00	5.00
82 Cookie Rojas	.60	1.50
83 Pete Rose	12.50	30.00
84 John Roseboro	.75	2.00
85 Ron Santo	1.25	3.00
86 Bill Skowron	.75	2.00
87 Willie Stargell	2.00	5.00
88 Mel Stottlemyre	.75	2.00
89 Dick Stuart	.60	1.50
90 Ron Swoboda	.75	2.00
91 Fred Talbot	.60	1.50
92 Ralph Terry	.75	2.00
93 Joe Torre	2.00	5.00
94 Tom Tresh	1.25	3.00
95 Bob Veale	.60	1.50
96 Pete Ward	.60	1.50
97 Bill White	.75	2.00
98 Billy Williams	1.25	3.00
99 Jim Wynn	.75	2.00
100 Carl Yastrzemski	5.00	12.00
101 Baltimore Orioles	1.00	2.50
102 Boston Red Sox	1.00	2.50
103 California Angels	.40	1.00
104 Chicago Cubs	.40	1.00
105 Chicago White Sox	.40	1.00
106 Cincinnati Reds	.40	1.00
107 Cleveland Indians	.40	1.00
108 Detroit Tigers	1.00	2.50
109 Houston Astros	.40	1.00
110 Kansas City Athletics	.40	1.00
111 Los Angeles Dodgers	1.00	2.50
112 Atlanta Braves	.40	1.00
113 Minnesota Twins	.40	1.00
114 New York Mets	1.00	2.50
115 New York Yankees	1.50	4.00
116 Philadelphia Phillies	.40	1.00
117 Pittsburgh Pirates	.40	1.00
118 San Francisco Giants	.40	1.00
119 St. Louis Cardinals	.40	1.00
120 Washington Senators	1.00	2.50

1967 Topps

The cards in this 609-card set measure 2 1/2" by 3 1/2". The 1967 Topps series is considered by some collectors to be one of the company's finest accomplishments in baseball card production. Excellent color photographs are combined with easy-to-read backs. Cards 458 to 533 are slightly harder to find than numbers 1 to 457, and the inevitable high series (534 to 609) exists. Each checklist card features a small circular picture of a popular player included in that series. Printing discrepancies resulted in some high series cards being in shorter supply. The checklist below identifies (by DP) 22 double-printed high numbers; of the 76 cards in the last series, 54 cards were short printed and the other 22 cards are much more plentiful. Featured subsets within this set include World Series cards (151-155) and League Leaders (233-244). A limited number of "proof" Roger Maris cards were produced. These cards are blank backed and Maris is listed as a New York Yankee on it. Some Bob Bolin cards: (number 252) have a white smear in between his names. Another tough variation that has been recently discovered involves card number 58 Paul Schaal. The tough version has a green bat above his name. The key Rookie Cards in the set are high number cards of Rod Carew and Tom Seaver. Confirmed methods of selling these cards include five-card nickel wax packs. Although rarely seen, there exists a salesman's sample panel of three cards that pictures Earl Battey, Manny Mota, and Gene Brabender with ad information on the back about the "new" Topps cards.

Card	Low	High
COMPLETE SET (609)	2500.00	6000.00
COMMON CARD (1-109)	.60	1.50
COMMON CARD (110-283)	.75	2.00
COMMON CARD (284-370)	1.00	2.50
COMMON CARD (371-457)	1.50	4.00
COMMON CARD (458-533)	2.50	6.00
COMMON CARD (534-609)	6.00	15.00
COMMON DP (534-609)	3.00	8.00
WRAPPER (5-CENT)	10.00	25.00
1 Robinson/Bauer/Robinson DP	15.00	40.00
2 Jack Hamilton	.60	1.50
3 Duke Sims	.60	1.50
4 Hal Lanier	.60	1.50
5 Whitey Ford UER	20.00	50.00
6 Dick Simpson	.60	1.50
7 Don McMahon	.60	1.50
8 Chuck Harrison	.60	1.50
9 Ron Hansen	.60	1.50
10 Matty Alou	1.50	4.00
11 Barry Moore RC	.60	1.50
12 J.Campanis RC/B.Singer	1.50	4.00
13 Joe Sparma	.60	1.50
14 Phil Linz	1.50	4.00
15 Earl Battey	.60	1.50
16 Bill Hands	.60	1.50
17 Jim Gosger	.60	1.50
18 Gene Oliver	.60	1.50
19 Jim McGlothlin	.60	1.50
20 Orlando Cepeda	12.00	30.00
21 Dave Bristol MG RC	.60	1.50
22 Gene Brabender	.60	1.50
23 Larry Elliot	.60	1.50
24 Bob Allen	.60	1.50
25 Elston Howard	1.50	4.00
26A Bob Priddy NTR	12.50	30.00
26B Bob Priddy TR	1.50	4.00
27 Bob Saverine	.60	1.50
28 Barry Latman	.60	1.50
29 Tom McCraw	.60	1.50
30 Al Kaline DP	12.00	30.00
31 Jim Brewer	.60	1.50
32 Bob Bailey	1.50	4.00
33 S.Bando RC/R.Schwartz RC	2.50	6.00
34 Pete Cimino	.60	1.50
35 Rico Carty	1.50	4.00
36 Bob Tillman	.60	1.50
37 Rick Wise	1.50	4.00
38 Bob Johnson	.60	1.50
39 Curt Simmons	1.50	4.00
40 Rick Reichardt	.60	1.50
41 Joe Hoerner	.60	1.50
42 New York Mets TC	4.00	10.00
43 Chico Salmon	.60	1.50
44 Joe Nuxhall	1.50	4.00
45 Roger Maris	25.00	60.00
45A R.Maris Yanks/Blank Back	900.00	1500.00
46 Lindy McDaniel	1.50	4.00
47 Ken McMullen	.60	1.50
48 Bill Freehan	1.50	4.00
49 Roy Face	1.50	4.00
50 Tony Oliva	2.50	6.00
51 D.Adlesh RC/W.Bales RC	.60	1.50
52 Dennis Higgins	.60	1.50
53 Clay Dalrymple	.60	1.50
54 Dick Green	.60	1.50
55 Don Drysdale	15.00	40.00
56 Jose Tartabull	1.50	4.00
57 Pat Jarvis RC	1.50	4.00
58A Paul Schaal	8.00	20.00
Green Bat		
58B P.Schaal Normal Bat	.60	1.50
59 Ralph Terry	1.50	4.00
60 Luis Aparicio	8.00	20.00
61 Gordy Coleman	.60	1.50
62 Frank Robinson CL1	3.00	8.00
63 L.Brock/C.Flood	3.00	8.00
64 Fred Valentine	.60	1.50
65 Tom Haller	1.50	4.00
66 Manny Mota	1.50	4.00
67 Ken Berry	.60	1.50
68 Bob Buhl	1.50	4.00
69 Vic Davalillo	.60	1.50
70 Ron Santo	12.00	30.00
71 Camilo Pascual	1.50	4.00
72 G.Korince ERR RC/T.Matchick RC	.60	1.50
73 Rusty Staub	2.50	6.00
74 Wes Stock	.60	1.50
75 George Scott	1.50	4.00
76 Jim Barbieri RC	.60	1.50
77 Dooley Womack	1.50	4.00
78 Pat Corrales	.60	1.50
79 Bubba Morton	.60	1.50
80 Jim Maloney	1.50	4.00
81 Eddie Stanky MG	1.50	4.00
82 Steve Barber	.60	1.50
83 Ollie Brown	.60	1.50
84 Tommie Sisk	.60	1.50
85 Johnny Callison	1.50	4.00
86A Mike McCormick NTR	12.50	30.00
86B Mike McCormick TR	1.50	4.00
87 George Altman	.60	1.50
88 Mickey Lolich	1.50	4.00
89 Felix Millan RC	1.50	4.00
90 Jim Nash RC	.60	1.50
91 Johnny Lewis	.60	1.50
92 Ray Washburn	.60	1.50
93 S.Bahnsen RC/B.Murcer	1.50	4.00
94 Ron Fairly	1.50	4.00
95 Sonny Siebert	.60	1.50
96 Art Shamsky	.60	1.50
97 Mike Cuellar	1.50	4.00
98 Rich Rollins	.60	1.50
99 Lee Stange	.60	1.50
100 Frank Robinson DP	15.00	40.00
101 Ken Johnson	.60	1.50
102 Philadelphia Phillies TC	1.50	4.00
103A Mickey Mantle CL2 DP D.Mc	12.00	30.00
103B Mickey Mantle CL2 DP D Mc		
104 Minnie Rojas RC	.60	1.50
105 Ken Boyer	2.50	6.00
106 Randy Hundley	1.50	4.00
107 Joel Horlen	.60	1.50
108 Alex Johnson	1.50	4.00
109 R.Colavito/L.Wagner	2.50	6.00
110 Jack Aker	1.50	4.00
111 John Kennedy	.75	2.00
112 Dave Wickersham	.75	2.00
113 Dave Nicholson	.75	2.00
114 Jack Baldschun	.75	2.00
115 Paul Casanova RC	.75	2.00
116 Herman Franks MG	.75	2.00
117 Darrell Brandon	.75	2.00
118 Bernie Allen	.75	2.00
119 Wade Blasingame	.75	2.00
120 Floyd Robinson	.75	2.00
121 Eddie Bressoud	.75	2.00
122 George Brunet	.75	2.00
123 J.Price RC/L.Walker	1.50	4.00
124 Jim Stewart	.75	2.00
125 Moe Drabowsky	1.50	4.00
126 Tony Taylor	.75	2.00
127 John O'Donoghue	.75	2.00
128A Ed Spiezio	.75	2.00
128B Ed Spiezio		
Partial last name on front		
129 Phil Roof	.75	2.00
130 Phil Regan	1.50	4.00
131 New York Yankees TC	8.00	20.00
132 Ozzie Virgil	.75	2.00
133 Ron Kline	.75	2.00
134 Gates Brown	2.50	6.00
135 Deron Johnson	1.50	4.00
136 Carroll Sembera	.75	2.00
137 Rookie Stars	.75	2.00
Ron Clark RC		
Jim Ollum RC		
138 Dick Kelley	.75	2.00
139 Dalton Jones	1.50	4.00
140 Willie Stargell	12.00	30.00
141 John Miller	.75	2.00
142 Jackie Brandt	.75	2.00
143 P.Ward/D.Buford	.75	2.00
144 Bill Hepler	.75	2.00
145 Larry Brown	.75	2.00
146 Steve Carlton	25.00	60.00
147 Tom Egan	.75	2.00
148 Adolfo Phillips	.75	2.00
149 Joe Moeller	.75	2.00
150 Mickey Mantle	150.00	400.00
151 Moe Drabowsky WS1	2.00	5.00
152 Jim Palmer WS2	3.00	8.00
153 Paul Blair WS3	2.00	[illegible]
154 Robinson/McNally WS4	2.00	[illegible]
155 Orioles Celebrate WS	2.00	[illegible]
156 Ron Herbel	.75	[illegible]
157 Danny Cater	.75	[illegible]
158 Jimmie Coker	.75	[illegible]
159 Bruce Howard	.75	[illegible]
160 Willie Davis	1.50	[illegible]
161 Dick Williams MG	1.50	[illegible]
162 Billy O'Dell	.75	[illegible]
163 Vic Roznovsky	.75	[illegible]
164 Dwight Siebler UER	.75	[illegible]
165 Cleon Jones	1.50	[illegible]
166 Eddie Mathews	10.00	25[illegible]
167 J.Coleman RC/T.Cullen RC	.75	[illegible]
168 Ray Culp	.75	[illegible]
169 Horace Clarke	1.50	[illegible]
170 Dick McAuliffe	1.50	4[illegible]
171 Cal Koonce	.75	[illegible]
172 Bill Heath	.75	2[illegible]
173 St. Louis Cardinals TC	1.50	4[illegible]
174 Dick Radatz	1.50	4[illegible]
175 Bobby Knoop	.75	2[illegible]
176 Sammy Ellis	.75	2[illegible]
177 Tito Fuentes	.60	1[illegible]
178 John Buzhardt	.75	2[illegible]
179 C.Vaughan RC/C.Epshaw RC	1.50	4[illegible]
180 Curt Blefary	.75	2[illegible]
181 Terry Fox	.75	2[illegible]
182 Ed Charles	.75	2[illegible]
183 Jim Pagliaroni	.75	2[illegible]
184 George Thomas	.75	2[illegible]
185 Ken Holtzman RC	1.50	4[illegible]
186 E.Kranepool/R.Swoboda	1.50	4[illegible]
187 Pedro Ramos	.75	2[illegible]
188 Ken Harrelson	1.50	4[illegible]
189 Chuck Hinton	.75	2[illegible]
190 Turk Farrell	.75	2[illegible]
191A W.Mays CL3 214 Tom	4.00	10[illegible]
191B W.Mays CL3 214 Dick	5.00	12[illegible]
192 Fred Gladding	.75	2[illegible]
193 Jose Cardenal	1.50	4.[illegible]
194 Bob Allison	1.50	4.[illegible]
195 Al Jackson	.75	2.[illegible]
196 Johnny Romano	.75	2.[illegible]
197 Ron Perranoski	1.50	4.[illegible]
198 Chuck Hiller	.75	2[illegible]
199 Billy Hitchcock MG	.75	2.[illegible]
200 Willie Mays UER	50.00	120.[illegible]
201 Hal Reniff	1.50	4.[illegible]
202 Johnny Edwards	.75	2.[illegible]
203 Al McBean	.75	2.[illegible]
204 M.Epstein RC/T.Phoebus RC	2.50	6.[illegible]
205 Dick Groat	1.50	4.[illegible]
206 Dennis Bennett	.75	2.[illegible]
207 John Orsino	.75	2.[illegible]
208 Jack Lamabe	.75	2.[illegible]
209 Joe Nossek	.75	2.[illegible]
210 Bob Gibson	15.00	40.[illegible]
211 Minnesota Twins TC	1.50	4.[illegible]
212 Chris Zachary	.75	2.[illegible]
213 Jay Johnstone RC	1.50	4.[illegible]
214 Tom Kelley	.75	2.[illegible]
215 Ernie Banks	30.00	80.0[illegible]
216 A.Kaline/N.Cash	8.00	20.[illegible]
217 Rob Gardner	.75	2.[illegible]
218 Wes Parker	1.50	4.[illegible]
219 Clay Carroll	1.50	4.[illegible]
220 Jim Ray Hart	1.50	4.[illegible]
221 Woody Fryman	1.50	4.[illegible]
222 D.Osteen/L.May	1.50	4.0[illegible]
223 Mike Ryan	1.50	4.0[illegible]
224 Walt Bond	.75	2.0[illegible]
225 Mel Stottlemyre	2.50	6.0[illegible]
226 Julian Javier	1.50	4.0[illegible]
227 Paul Lindblad	.75	2.0[illegible]
228 Gil Hodges MG	2.50	6.0[illegible]
229 Larry Jackson	.75	2.0[illegible]
230 Boog Powell	2.50	6.0[illegible]
231 John Bateman	.75	2.0[illegible]
232 Don Buford	.75	2.0[illegible]
233 Peters/Horlen/Hargan LL	1.50	4.0[illegible]
234 Koufax/Cuellar/Marichal LL	10.00	25.0[illegible]
235 Kaat/McLain/Wilson LL	2.50	6.0[illegible]
236 Koufax/Mari/Gibs/Perry LL	10.00	25.0[illegible]
237 McDowell/Kaat/Wilson LL	2.50	6.0[illegible]
238 Koufax/Bunning/Veale LL	8.00	20.0[illegible]
239 F.Rob/Oliva/Kaline LL	4.00	10.0[illegible]
240 Alou/Alou/Carty LL	2.50	6.0[illegible]
241 F.Rob/Killebrew/Powell LL	4.00	10.0[illegible]
242 Aaron/Clemente/Allen LL	20.00	50.0[illegible]
243 F.Rob/Killebrew/Powell LL	4.00	10.0[illegible]
244 Aaron/Allen/Mays LL	12.00	30.0[illegible]
245 Curt Flood	2.50	6.0[illegible]
246 Jim Perry	1.50	4.0[illegible]
247 Jerry Lumpe	.75	2.0[illegible]
248 Gene Mauch MG	1.50	4.0[illegible]
249 Nick Willhite	.75	2.0[illegible]
250 Hank Aaron UER	40.00	100.0[illegible]
251 Woody Held	.75	2.0[illegible]
252 Bob Bolin	.75	2.0[illegible]
253 B.Davis/G.Gil RC	.75	2.0[illegible]
254 Milt Pappas	1.50	4.0[illegible]
255 Frank Howard	1.50	4.0[illegible]
256 Bob Hendley	.75	2.0[illegible]
257 Charlie Smith	.75	2.0[illegible]
258 Lee Maye	.75	2.0[illegible]
259 Don Dennis	.75	2.0[illegible]
260 Jim Lefebvre	1.50	4.0[illegible]

Card	Low	High
261 John Wyatt	.75	2.00
262 Kansas City Athletics TC	1.50	4.00
263 Hank Aguirre	.75	2.00
264 Ron Swoboda	1.50	4.00
265 Lou Burdette	1.50	4.00
266 W.Stargell/D.Clendenon	1.50	4.00
267 Don Schwall	.75	2.00
268 Johnny Briggs	.75	2.00
269 Don Nottebart	.75	2.00
270 Zoilo Versalles	.75	2.00
271 Eddie Watt	.75	2.00
272 B.Connors RC/D.Dowling	1.50	4.00
273 Dick Lines RC	.75	2.00
274 Bob Aspromonte	.75	2.00
275 Fred Whitfield	.75	2.00
276 Bruce Brubaker	.75	2.00
277 Steve Whitaker RC	2.50	6.00
278 Jim Kaat CL4	3.00	8.00
279 Frank Linzy	.75	2.00
280 Tony Conigliaro	3.00	8.00
281 Bob Rodgers	.75	2.00
282 John Odom	.75	2.00
283 Gene Alley	1.50	4.00
284 Johnny Podres	1.50	4.00
285 Lou Brock	15.00	40.00
286 Wayne Causey	1.00	2.50
287 G.Goosen RC/B.Shirley	1.00	2.50
288 Denny Lemaster	1.00	2.50
289 Tom Tresh	2.00	5.00
290 Bill White	2.00	5.00
291 Jim Hannan	1.00	2.50
292 Don Pavletich	1.00	2.50
293 Ed Kirkpatrick	1.00	2.50
294 Walter Alston MG	3.00	8.00
295 Sam McDowell	2.00	5.00
296 Glenn Beckert	2.00	5.00
297 Dave Morehead	2.00	5.00
298 Ron Davis RC	1.00	2.50
299 Norm Siebern	1.00	2.50
300 Jim Kaat	2.00	5.00
301 Jesse Gonder	1.00	2.50
302 Baltimore Orioles TC	3.00	8.00
303 Gil Blanco	1.00	2.50
304 Phil Gagliano	1.00	2.50
305 Earl Wilson	2.00	5.00
306 Bud Harrelson RC	2.00	5.00
307 Jim Beauchamp	1.00	2.50
308 Al Downing	2.00	5.00
309 J.Callison/R.Allen	2.00	5.00
310 Gary Peters	1.00	2.50
311 Ed Brinkman	1.00	2.50
312 Don Mincher	1.00	2.50
313 Bob Lee	1.00	2.50
314 M.Andrews RC/R.Smith RC	3.00	8.00
315 Billy Williams	12.00	30.00
316 Jack Kralick	1.00	2.50
317 Cesar Tovar	1.00	2.50
318 Dave Giusti	1.00	2.50
319 Paul Blair	2.00	5.00
320 Gaylord Perry	6.00	15.00
321 Mayo Smith MG	1.00	2.50
322 Jose Pagan	1.00	2.50
323 Mike Hershberger	1.00	2.50
324 Hal Woodeshick	1.00	2.50
325 Chico Cardenas	2.00	5.00
326 Bob Uecker	10.00	25.00
327 California Angels TC	3.00	8.00
328 Clete Boyer UER	2.00	5.00
329 Charlie Lau	2.00	5.00
330 Claude Osteen	2.00	5.00
331 Joe Foy	2.00	5.00
332 Jesus Alou	1.00	2.50
333 Fergie Jenkins	10.00	25.00
334 H.Killebrew/B.Allison	4.00	10.00
335 Bob Veale	2.00	5.00
336 Joe Azcue	1.00	2.50
337 Joe Morgan	12.00	30.00
338 Bob Locker	1.00	2.50
339 Chico Ruiz	1.00	2.50
340 Joe Pepitone	3.00	8.00
341 D.Dietz RC/B.Sorrell	1.00	2.50
342 Hank Fischer	1.00	2.50
343 Tom Satriano	1.00	2.50
344 Ossie Chavarria RC	1.00	2.50
345 Stu Miller	2.00	5.00
346 Jim Hickman	1.00	2.50
347 Grady Hatton MG	1.00	2.50
348 Tug McGraw	2.00	5.00
349 Bob Chance	1.00	2.50
350 Joe Torre	10.00	25.00
351 Vern Law	2.00	5.00
352 Ray Oyler	1.00	2.50
353 Bill McCool	1.00	2.50
354 Chicago Cubs TC	3.00	8.00
355 Carl Yastrzemski	25.00	60.00
356 Larry Jaster RC	1.00	2.50
357 Bill Skowron	2.00	5.00
358 Ruben Amaro	1.00	2.50
359 Dick Ellsworth	1.00	2.50
360 Leon Wagner	1.00	2.50
361 Roberto Clemente CL5	8.00	20.00
362 Darold Knowles	1.00	2.50
363 Davey Johnson	2.00	5.00
364 Claude Raymond	1.00	2.50
365 John Roseboro	2.00	5.00
366 Andy Kosco	1.00	2.50
367 B.Kelso/D.Wallace RC	1.00	2.50
368 Jack Hiatt	1.00	2.50
369 Jim Hunter	10.00	25.00
370 Tommy Davis	2.00	5.00
371 Jim Lonborg	3.00	8.00
372 Mike de la Hoz	1.50	4.00
373 D.Josephson RC/F.Klages RC DP	1.50	4.00
374A Mel Queen ERR	8.00	20.00
374B Mel Queen COR DP	1.50	4.00
375 Jake Gibbs	3.00	8.00
376 Don Lock DP	1.50	4.00
377 Luis Tiant	3.00	8.00
378 Detroit Tigers TC UER	3.00	8.00
379 Jerry May DP	1.50	4.00
380 Dean Chance DP	1.50	4.00
381 Dick Schofield DP	1.50	4.00
382 Dave McNally	3.00	8.00
383 Ken Henderson DP	1.50	4.00
384 J.Cosman RC/D.Hughes RC	1.50	4.00
385 Jim Fregosi	3.00	8.00
386 Dick Selma DP	1.50	4.00
387 Cap Peterson DP	1.50	4.00
388 Arnold Earley DP	1.50	4.00
389 Alvin Dark MG DP	3.00	8.00
390 Jim Wynn DP	3.00	8.00
391 Wilbur Wood DP	3.00	8.00
392 Tommy Harper DP	3.00	8.00
393 Jim Bouton DP	3.00	8.00
394 Jake Wood DP	1.50	4.00
395 Chris Short RC	3.00	8.00
396 D.Menke/T.Cloninger	1.50	4.00
397 Willie Smith DP	1.50	4.00
398 Jeff Torborg	3.00	8.00
399 Al Worthington DP	1.50	4.00
400 Bob Clemente DP	60.00	120.00
401 Jim Coates	1.50	4.00
402A G.Jackson/B.Wilson Stat Line	8.00	20.00
402B G.Jackson/B.Wilson RC DP	3.00	8.00
403 Dick Nen	1.50	4.00
404 Nelson Briles	3.00	8.00
405 Russ Snyder	1.50	4.00
406 Lee Elia DP	1.50	4.00
407 Cincinnati Reds TC	3.00	8.00
408 Jim Northrup DP	3.00	8.00
409 Ray Sadecki	1.50	4.00
410 Lou Johnson DP	1.50	4.00
411 Dick Howser DP	1.50	4.00
412 N.Miller RC/D.Rader RC	3.00	8.00
413 Jerry Grote	1.50	4.00
414 Casey Cox	1.50	4.00
415 Sonny Jackson	1.50	4.00
416 Roger Repoz	1.50	4.00
417A Bob Bruce ERR	12.50	30.00
417B Bob Bruce COR DP	1.50	4.00
418 Sam Mele MG	1.50	4.00
419 Don Kessinger DP	3.00	8.00
420 Denny McLain	5.00	12.00
421 Dal Maxvill DP	1.50	4.00
422 Hoyt Wilhelm	6.00	15.00
423 W.Mays/W.McCovey DP	25.00	60.00
424 Pedro Gonzalez	1.50	4.00
425 Pete Mikkelsen	1.50	4.00
426 Lou Clinton	1.50	4.00
427A Ruben Gomez ERR	8.00	20.00
427B Ruben Gomez COR DP	1.50	4.00
428 T.Hutton RC/G.Michael RC DP	3.00	8.00
429 Garry Roggenburk DP	1.50	4.00
430 Pete Rose	50.00	120.00
431 Ted Uhlaender	1.50	4.00
432 Jimmie Hall DP	1.50	4.00
433 Al Luplow DP	1.50	4.00
434 Eddie Fisher DP	1.50	4.00
435 Mack Jones DP	1.50	4.00
436 Pete Ward	1.50	4.00
437 Washington Senators TC	3.00	8.00
438 Chuck Dobson	1.50	4.00
439 Byron Browne	1.50	4.00
440 Steve Hargan	1.50	4.00
441 Jim Davenport	1.50	4.00
442 B.Robinson RC/J.Verbanic RC DP	3.00	8.00
443 Tito Francona DP	1.50	4.00
444 George Smith	1.50	4.00
445 Don Sutton	10.00	25.00
446 Russ Nixon DP	1.50	4.00
447A Bo Belinsky ERR DP	1.50	4.00
447B Bo Belinsky COR	3.00	8.00
448 Harry Walker MG DP	1.50	4.00
449 Orlando Pena	1.50	4.00
450 Richie Allen	3.00	8.00
451 Fred Newman DP	1.50	4.00
452 Ed Kranepool	3.00	8.00
453 Aurelio Monteagudo DP	1.50	4.00
454A J.Marichal CL6 No Ear DP	5.00	12.00
454B Juan Marichal CL6 w/Ear DP	5.00	12.00
455 Tommie Agee	3.00	8.00
456 Phil Niekro UER	6.00	15.00
457 Andy Etchebarren DP	3.00	8.00
458 Lee Thomas	2.50	6.00
459 D.Bosman RC/P.Craig	2.50	6.00
460 Harmon Killebrew	15.00	40.00
461 Bob Miller	5.00	12.00
462 Bob Barton	2.50	6.00
463 S.McDowell/S.Siebert	5.00	12.00
464 Dan Coombs	2.50	6.00
465 Willie Horton	5.00	12.00
466 Bobby Wine	8.00	20.00
467 Jim O'Toole	2.50	6.00
468 Ralph Houk MG	2.50	6.00
469 Len Gabrielson	2.50	6.00
470 Bob Shaw	2.50	6.00
471 Rene Lachemann	2.50	6.00
472 J.Gelnar/G.Spriggs RC	2.50	6.00
473 Jose Santiago	2.50	6.00
474 Bob Tolan	4.00	10.00
475 Jim Palmer	20.00	50.00
476 Tony Perez SP	30.00	60.00
477 Atlanta Braves TC	6.00	15.00
478 Bob Humphreys	2.50	6.00
479 Gary Bell	2.50	6.00
480 Willie McCovey	15.00	40.00
481 Leo Durocher MG	8.00	20.00
482 Bill Monbouquette	2.50	6.00
483 Jim Landis	2.50	6.00
484 Jerry Adair	2.50	6.00
485 Tim McCarver	10.00	25.00
486 R.Reese RC/B.Whitby RC	2.50	6.00
487 Tommie Reynolds	2.50	6.00
488 Gerry Arrigo	2.50	6.00
489 Doug Clemens RC	2.50	6.00
490 Tony Cloninger	2.50	6.00
491 Sam Bowens	2.50	6.00
492 Pittsburgh Pirates TC	6.00	15.00
493 Phil Ortega	2.50	6.00
494 Bill Rigney MG	2.50	6.00
495 Fritz Peterson	2.50	6.00
496 Orlando McFarlane	2.50	6.00
497 Ron Campbell RC	2.50	6.00
498 Larry Dierker	5.00	12.00
499 G.Culver/J.Vidal RC	2.50	6.00
500 Juan Marichal	15.00	40.00
501 Jerry Zimmerman	2.50	6.00
502 Derrell Griffith	2.50	6.00
503 Los Angeles Dodgers TC	8.00	20.00
504 Orlando Martinez RC	2.50	6.00
505 Tommy Helms	5.00	12.00
506 Smoky Burgess	2.50	6.00
507 E.Barnowski/L.Haney RC	2.50	6.00
508 Dick Hall	2.50	6.00
509 Jim King	2.50	6.00
510 Bill Mazeroski	8.00	20.00
511 Don Wert	2.50	6.00
512 Red Schoendienst MG	10.00	25.00
513 Marcelino Lopez	2.50	6.00
514 John Werhas	2.50	6.00
515 Bert Campaneris	5.00	12.00
516 San Francisco Giants TC	6.00	15.00
517 Fred Talbot	5.00	12.00
518 Denis Menke	2.50	6.00
519 Ted Davidson	2.50	6.00
520 Max Alvis	2.50	6.00
521 B.Powell/C.Blefary	5.00	12.00
522 John Stephenson	2.50	6.00
523 Jim Merritt	2.50	6.00
524 Felix Mantilla	2.50	6.00
525 Ron Hunt	2.50	6.00
526 P.Dobson RC/G.Korince RC	2.50	6.00
527 Dennis Ribant	2.50	6.00
528 Rico Petrocelli	8.00	20.00
529 Gary Wagner	2.50	6.00
530 Felipe Alou	5.00	12.00
531 B.Robinson CL7 DP	6.00	15.00
532 Jim Hicks RC	2.50	6.00
533 Jack Fisher	2.50	6.00
534 Hank Bauer MG DP	3.00	8.00
535 Donn Clendenon	10.00	25.00
536 J.Niekro RC/P.Popovich RC	40.00	100.00
537 Chuck Estrada DP	3.00	8.00
538 J.C. Martin	6.00	15.00
539 Dick Egan DP	3.00	8.00
540 Norm Cash	25.00	60.00
541 Joe Gibbon	6.00	15.00
542 R.Monday RC/T.Pierce RC DP	10.00	25.00
543 Dan Schneider	6.00	15.00
544 Cleveland Indians TC	12.50	30.00
545 Jim Grant	10.00	25.00
546 Woody Woodward	10.00	25.00
547 R.Gibson RC/B.Rohr RC DP	3.00	8.00
548 Tony Gonzalez DP	3.00	8.00
549 Jack Sanford	6.00	15.00
550 Vada Pinson DP	4.00	10.00
551 Doug Camilli DP	3.00	8.00
552 Ted Savage	15.00	40.00
553 M.Hegan RC/T.Tillotson	15.00	40.00
554 Andre Rodgers DP	3.00	8.00
555 Don Cardwell	12.00	30.00
556 Al Weis DP	3.00	8.00
557 Al Ferrara	10.00	25.00
558 M.Belanger RC/B.Dillman RC	40.00	100.00
559 Dick Tracewski DP	3.00	8.00
560 Jim Bunning	40.00	100.00
561 Sandy Alomar	15.00	40.00
562 Steve Blass DP	3.00	8.00
563 Joe Adcock	15.00	40.00
564 A.Harris RC/A.Pointer RC DP	3.00	8.00
565 Lew Krausse	10.00	25.00
566 Gary Geiger DP	5.00	12.00
567 Steve Hamilton	15.00	40.00
568 John Sullivan	15.00	40.00
569 Rod Carew RC DP	250.00	600.00
570 Maury Wills	40.00	80.00
571 Larry Sherry	10.00	25.00
572 Don Demeter	10.00	25.00
573 Chicago White Sox TC	12.50	30.00
574 Jerry Buchek	10.00	25.00
575 Dave Boswell RC	6.00	15.00
576 R.Hernandez RC/N.Gigon RC	15.00	40.00
577 Bill Short	6.00	15.00
578 John Boccabella	6.00	15.00
579 Bill Henry	6.00	15.00
580 Rocky Colavito	75.00	150.00
581 Tom Seaver RC	600.00	1500.00
582 Jim Owens DP	3.00	8.00
583 Ray Barker	15.00	40.00
584 Jimmy Piersall	15.00	40.00
585 Wally Bunker	10.00	25.00
586 Manny Jimenez	6.00	15.00
587 D.Shaw RC/G.Sutherland RC	15.00	40.00
588 Johnny Klippstein DP	3.00	8.00
589 Dave Ricketts DP	3.00	8.00
590 Pete Richert	6.00	15.00
591 Ty Cline	10.00	25.00
592 J.Shellenback RC/R.Willis RC	10.00	25.00
593 Wes Westrum MG	20.00	50.00
594 Dan Osinski	15.00	40.00
595 Cookie Rojas	10.00	25.00
596 Galen Cisco DP	3.00	8.00
597 Ted Abernathy	6.00	15.00
598 W.Williams RC/E.Stroud RC	10.00	25.00
599 Bob Duliba DP	3.00	8.00
600 Brooks Robinson	200.00	400.00
601 Bill Bryan DP	3.00	8.00
602 Juan Pizarro	15.00	40.00
603 T.Talton RC/R.Webster RC	10.00	25.00
604 Boston Red Sox TC	60.00	120.00
605 Mike Shannon	20.00	50.00
606 Ron Taylor	10.00	25.00
607 Mickey Stanley	20.00	50.00
608 R.Nye RC/J.Upham RC DP	3.00	8.00
609 Tommy John	50.00	120.00

1967 Topps Posters Inserts

The wrappers of the 1967 Topps cards have this 32-card set advertised as follows: "Extra -- All Star Pin-Up Inside." Printed on (5" by 7") paper in full color, these "All-Star" inserts have fold lines which are generally not very noticeable when stored carefully. They are numbered, blank-backed, and carry a facsimile autograph.

Card	Low	High
COMPLETE SET (32)	50.00	100.00
1 Boog Powell	1.00	2.50
2 Bert Campaneris	.75	2.00
3 Brooks Robinson	1.50	4.00
4 Tommie Agee	.50	1.25
5 Carl Yastrzemski	2.00	5.00
6 Mickey Mantle	12.00	30.00
7 Frank Howard	.75	2.00
8 Sam McDowell	.75	2.00
9 Orlando Cepeda	1.25	3.00
10 Chico Cardenas	.50	1.25
11 Roberto Clemente	4.00	10.00
12 Willie Mays	3.00	8.00
13 Cleon Jones	.50	1.25
14 Johnny Callison	.75	2.00
15 Hank Aaron	2.50	6.00
16 Don Drysdale	1.25	3.00
17 Bobby Knoop	.50	1.25
18 Tony Oliva	1.00	2.50
19 Frank Robinson	1.25	3.00
20 Denny McLain	1.00	2.50
21 Al Kaline	1.50	4.00
22 Joe Pepitone	.75	2.00
23 Harmon Killebrew	1.50	4.00
24 Leon Wagner	.50	1.25
25 Joe Morgan	1.25	3.00
26 Ron Santo	1.00	2.50
27 Joe Torre	1.00	2.50
28 Juan Marichal	1.00	2.50
29 Matty Alou	.50	1.25
30 Felipe Alou	.75	2.00
31 Ron Hunt	.50	1.25
32 Willie McCovey	1.25	3.00

1968 Topps

The cards in this 598-card set measure 2 1/2" by 3 1/2". The 1968 Topps set includes Sporting News All-Star Selections as card numbers 361 to 380. Other subsets in the set include League Leaders (1-12) and World Series cards (151-158). The front of each checklist card features a picture of a popular player inside a circle. Higher numbers 458 to 598 are slightly more difficult to obtain. The first series looks different from the other series, as it has a lighter, wider mesh background on the card front. The later series all had a much darker, finer mesh pattern. Among other fashions, cards were issued in five-card nickel packs. Those five cent packs were issued 24 packs to a box. Thirty-six card rack packs with an SRP of 29 cents were also issued. The key Rookie Cards in the set are Johnny Bench and Nolan Ryan. Lastly, some cards were also issued along with the "Win-A-Card" board game from Milton Bradley that included cards from the 1965 Topps Hot Rods and 1967 Topps football card sets. This version of these cards is somewhat difficult to distinguish, but are often found with a slight touch of the 1967 football set white border on the front top or bottom edge as well as a brighter yellow card back instead of the darker yellow or gold color. The known cards from this product include card numbers 16, 20, 34, 45, 108, and 149.

Card	Low	High
COMPLETE SET (598)	1500.00	4000.00
COMMON CARD (1-457)	.75	2.00
COMMON CARD (458-598)	1.50	4.00
WRAPPER (5-CENT)	10.00	25.00
1 Clemente/Gonz/Alou LL	10.00	25.00
2 Yaz/F.Rob/Kaline LL	6.00	15.00
3 Cep/Clemente/Aaron LL	15.00	40.00
4 Yaz/Killebrew/F.Rob LL	6.00	15.00
5 Aaron/Santo/McCovey LL	8.00	20.00
6 Yaz/Killebrew/Howard LL	3.00	8.00
7 Niekro/Bunning/Short LL	1.50	4.00
8 Horlen/Peters/Siebert LL	1.50	4.00
9 McCor/Jenkins/Bunning LL	1.50	4.00
10A Lonb/Wils/Chance LL ERR	1.50	4.00
10B Lonb/Wils/Chance LL COR	1.50	4.00
11 Bunning/jenkins/Perry LL	2.50	6.00
12 Lonborg/McDow/Chance LL	1.50	4.00
13 Chuck Hartenstein RC	.75	2.00
14 Jerry McNertney	.75	2.00
15 Ron Hunt	.75	2.00
16 L.Piniella/R.Scheinblum	2.50	6.00
17 Dick Hall	.75	2.00
18 Mike Hershberger	.75	2.00
19 Juan Pizarro	.75	2.00
20 Brooks Robinson	12.00	30.00
21 Ron Davis	.75	2.00
22 Pat Dobson	1.50	4.00
23 Chico Cardenas	1.50	4.00
24 Bobby Locke	.75	2.00
25 Julian Javier	1.50	4.00
26 Darrell Brandon	.75	2.00
27 Gil Hodges MG	8.00	20.00
28 Ted Uhlaender	.75	2.00
29 Joe Verbanic	.75	2.00
30 Joe Torre	2.50	6.00
31 Ed Stroud	.75	2.00
32 Joe Gibbon	.75	2.00
33 Pete Ward	.75	2.00
34 Al Ferrara	.75	2.00
35 Steve Hargan	.75	2.00
36 B.Moose RC/B.Robertson RC	1.50	4.00
37 Billy Williams	10.00	25.00
38 Tony Pierce	.75	2.00
39 Cookie Rojas	.75	2.00
40 Denny McLain	10.00	25.00
41 Julio Gotay	.75	2.00
42 Larry Haney	.75	2.00
43 Gary Bell	.75	2.00
44 Frank Kostro	.75	2.00
45 Tom Seaver	40.00	100.00
46 Dave Ricketts	.75	2.00
47 Ralph Houk MG	1.50	4.00
48 Ted Davidson	.75	2.00
49A E.Brinkman White	.75	2.00
49B E.Brinkman Yellow Tm	20.00	50.00
50 Willie Mays	40.00	100.00
51 Bob Locker	.75	2.00
52 Hawk Taylor	.75	2.00
53 Gene Alley	1.50	4.00
54 Stan Williams	.75	2.00
55 Felipe Alou	1.50	4.00
56 D.Leonhard RC/D.May RC	.75	2.00
57 Dan Schneider	.75	2.00
58 Eddie Mathews	6.00	15.00
59 Don Lock	.75	2.00
60 Ken Holtzman	1.50	4.00
61 Reggie Smith	1.50	4.00
62 Chuck Dobson	.75	2.00
63 Dick Kenworthy RC	.75	2.00
64 Jim Merritt	.75	2.00
65 John Roseboro	1.50	4.00
66A Casey Cox White	.75	2.00
66B C.Cox Yellow Tm	50.00	100.00
67 Checklist 1/Kaat	2.50	6.00
68 Ron Willis	.75	2.00
69 Tom Tresh	1.50	4.00
70 Bob Veale	1.50	4.00
71 Vern Fuller RC	.75	2.00
72 Tommy John	2.50	6.00
73 Jim Ray Hart	1.50	4.00
74 Milt Pappas	1.50	4.00
75 Don Mincher	.75	2.00
76 J.Britton/R.Reed RC	1.50	4.00
77 Don Wilson RC	1.50	4.00
78 Jim Northrup	2.50	6.00
79 Ted Kubiak RC	.75	2.00
80 Rod Carew	20.00	50.00
81 Larry Jackson	.75	2.00
82 Sam Bowens	.75	2.00
83 John Stephenson	.75	2.00
84 Bob Tolan	.75	2.00
85 Gaylord Perry	6.00	15.00
86 Willie Stargell	15.00	40.00
87 Dick Williams MG	1.50	4.00
88 Phil Regan	1.50	4.00
89 Jake Gibbs	1.50	4.00
90 Vada Pinson	1.50	4.00
91 Jim Ollom	.75	2.00
92 Ed Kranepool	1.50	4.00
93 Tony Cloninger	.75	2.00
94 Lee Maye	.75	2.00
95 Bob Aspromonte	.75	2.00
96 F.Coggins RC/D.Nold	.75	2.00
97 Tom Phoebus	.75	2.00
98 Gary Sutherland	.75	2.00
99 Rocky Colavito	3.00	8.00
100 Bob Gibson	20.00	50.00
101 Glenn Beckert	1.50	4.00
102 Jose Cardenal	1.50	4.00
103 Don Sutton	3.00	8.00
104 Dick Dietz	.75	2.00
105 Al Downing	1.50	4.00
106 Dalton Jones	.75	2.00
107A Checklist 2/Marichal Wide	2.50	6.00
107B Checklist 2/J.Marichal Fine	2.50	6.00
108 Don Pavletich	.75	2.00
109 Bert Campaneris	1.50	4.00
110 Hank Aaron	40.00	100.00
111 Rich Reese	.75	2.00
112 Woody Fryman	.75	2.00
113 T.Matchick/D.Patterson RC	1.50	4.00
114 Ron Swoboda	1.50	4.00
115 Sam McDowell	1.50	4.00
116 Ken McMullen	.75	2.00
117 Larry Jaster	.75	2.00
118 Mark Belanger	1.50	4.00
119 Ted Savage	.75	2.00
120 Mel Stottlemyre	1.50	4.00
121 Jimmie Hall	.75	2.00
122 Gene Mauch MG	1.50	4.00
123 Jose Santiago	.75	2.00
124 Nate Oliver	.75	2.00
125 Joel Horlen	.75	2.00
126 Bobby Etheridge RC	.75	2.00
127 Paul Lindblad	.75	2.00
128 T.Dukes RC/A.Harris	.75	2.00
129 Mickey Stanley	2.50	6.00
130 Tony Perez	10.00	25.00
131 Frank Bertaina	.75	2.00
132 Bud Harrelson	1.50	4.00
133 Fred Whitfield	.75	2.00
134 Pat Jarvis	.75	2.00
135 Paul Blair	1.50	4.00
136 Randy Hundley	1.50	4.00
137 Minnesota Twins TC	1.50	4.00
138 Ruben Amaro	.75	2.00
139 Chris Short	.75	2.00
140 Tony Conigliaro	3.00	8.00
141 Dal Maxvill	.75	2.00
142 B.Bradford RC/B.Voss	.75	2.00
143 Pete Cimino	.75	2.00
144 Joe Morgan	8.00	20.00
145 Don Drysdale	12.00	30.00
146 Sal Bando	1.50	4.00
147 Frank Linzy	.75	2.00
148 Dave Bristol MG	.75	2.00
149 Bob Saverine	.75	2.00
150 Roberto Clemente	40.00	100.00
151 Lou Brock WS1	4.00	10.00
152 Carl Yastrzemski WS2	4.00	10.00
153 Nelson Briles WS3	2.00	5.00
154 Bob Gibson WS4	4.00	10.00
155 Jim Lonborg WS5	2.00	5.00
156 Rico Petrocelli WS6	2.00	5.00
157 St. Louis Wins It WS7	2.00	5.00
158 Cardinals Celebrate WS	2.00	5.00
159 Don Kessinger	1.50	4.00
160 Earl Wilson	1.50	4.00
161 Norm Miller	.75	2.00
162 H.Gilson RC/M.Torrez RC	1.50	4.00
163 Gene Brabender	.75	2.00
164 Ramon Webster	.75	2.00
165 Tony Oliva	2.50	6.00
166 Claude Raymond	.75	2.00
167 Elston Howard	2.50	6.00
168 Los Angeles Dodgers TC	1.50	4.00
169 Bob Bolin	.75	2.00
170 Jim Fregosi	1.50	4.00
171 Don Nottebart	.75	2.00
172 Walt Williams	.75	2.00
173 John Boozer	.75	2.00
174 Bob Tillman	.75	2.00
175 Maury Wills	2.50	6.00
176 Bob Allen	.75	2.00
177 N.Ryan RC/J.Koosman RC	500.00	1200.00
178 Don Wert	1.50	4.00
179 Bill Stoneman RC	.75	2.00
180 Curt Flood	2.50	6.00
181 Jerry Zimmerman	.75	2.00
182 Dave Giusti	.75	2.00
183 Bob Kennedy MG	1.50	4.00
184 Lou Johnson	.75	2.00
185 Tom Haller	.75	2.00
186 Eddie Watt	.75	2.00
187 Sonny Jackson	.75	2.00
188 Cap Peterson	.75	2.00
189 Bill Landis RC	.75	2.00
190 Bill White	1.50	4.00
191 Dan Frisella RC	.75	2.00
192A Checklist 3/Yaz Ball	3.00	8.00
192B Checklist 3/Yaz Game	3.00	8.00
193 Jack Hamilton	.75	2.00
194 Don Buford	.75	2.00
195 Joe Pepitone	1.50	4.00
196 Gary Nolan RC	1.50	4.00
197 Larry Brown	.75	2.00
198 Roy Face	1.50	4.00
199 R.Rodriguez RC/D.Osteen	.75	2.00
200 Orlando Cepeda	10.00	25.00
201 Mike Marshall RC	1.50	4.00
202 Adolfo Phillips	.75	2.00
203 Dick Kelley	.75	2.00
204 Andy Etchebarren	.75	2.00
205 Juan Marichal	3.00	8.00
206 Cal Ermer MG RC	.75	2.00
207 Carroll Sembera	.75	2.00
208 Willie Davis	1.50	4.00
209 Tim Cullen	.75	2.00
210 Gary Peters	.75	2.00
211 J.C. Martin	.75	2.00
212 Dave Morehead	.75	2.00
213 Chico Ruiz	.75	2.00
214 S.Bahnsen/F.Fernandez	1.50	4.00
215 Jim Bunning	3.00	8.00
216 Bubba Morton	.75	2.00
217 Dick Farrell	.75	2.00
218 Ken Suarez	.75	2.00
219 Rob Gardner	.75	2.00
220 Harmon Killebrew	12.00	30.00
221 Atlanta Braves TC	1.50	4.00
222 Jim Hardin RC	.75	2.00
223 Ollie Brown	.75	2.00
224 Jack Aker	.75	2.00
225 Richie Allen	2.50	6.00
226 Jimmie Price	.75	2.00
227 Joe Hoerner	.75	2.00
228 J.Billingham RC/J.Fairey RC	1.50	4.00
229 Fred Klages	.75	2.00
230 Pete Rose	30.00	80.00
231 Dave Baldwin RC	.75	2.00
232 Denis Menke	.75	2.00
233 George Scott	1.50	4.00
234 Bill Monbouquette	.75	2.00
235 Ron Santo	3.00	8.00
236 Tug McGraw	2.50	6.00
237 Alvin Dark MG	1.50	4.00
238 Tom Satriano	.75	2.00
239 Bill Henry	.75	2.00
240 Al Kaline	15.00	40.00
241 Felix Millan	.75	2.00
242 Moe Drabowsky	1.50	4.00
243 Rich Rollins	.75	2.00
244 John Donaldson RC	.75	2.00
245 Tony Gonzalez	.75	2.00
246 Fritz Peterson	1.50	4.00
247 Johnny Bench RC	125.00	300.00
248 Fred Valentine	.75	2.00
249 Bill Singer	.75	2.00
250 Carl Yastrzemski	15.00	40.00
251 Manny Sanguillen RC	2.50	6.00
252 California Angels TC	1.50	4.00
253 Dick Hughes	.75	2.00
254 Cleon Jones	1.50	4.00
255 Dean Chance	1.50	4.00
256 Norm Cash	8.00	20.00
257 Phil Niekro	8.00	20.00
258 J.Arcia RC/B.Schlesinger	.75	2.00
259 Ken Boyer	2.50	6.00
260 Jim Wynn	1.50	4.00
261 Dave Duncan	1.50	4.00
262 Rick Wise	1.50	4.00
263 Horace Clarke	1.50	4.00
284 Ted Abernathy	.75	2.00
265 Tommy Davis	1.50	4.00
266 Paul Popovich	.75	2.00
267 Herman Franks MG	.75	2.00
268 Bob Humphreys	.75	2.00
269 Bob Tiefenauer	.75	2.00
270 Matty Alou	1.50	4.00
271 Bobby Knoop	.75	2.00
272 Ray Culp	.75	2.00
273 Dave Johnson	1.50	4.00
274 Mike Cuellar	1.50	4.00
275 Tim McCarver	2.50	6.00
276 Jim Roland	.75	2.00
277 Jerry Buchek	.75	2.00
278 Checklist 4/Cepeda	2.50	6.00
279 Bill Hands	.75	2.00
280 Mickey Mantle	200.00	500.00
281 Jim Campanis	.75	2.00
282 Rick Monday	1.50	4.00
283 Mel Queen	.75	2.00
284 Johnny Briggs	.75	2.00
285 Dick McAuliffe	2.50	6.00
286 Cecil Upshaw	.75	2.00
287 M.Abarbanel RC/C.Carlos RC	.75	2.00
288 Dave Wickersham	.75	2.00
289 Woody Held	.75	2.00
290 Willie McCovey	15.00	40.00
291 Dick Lines	.75	2.00
292 Art Shamsky	.75	2.00
293 Bruce Howard	.75	2.00
294 Red Schoendienst MG	6.00	15.00
295 Sonny Siebert	.75	2.00
296 Byron Browne	.75	2.00
297 Russ Gibson	.75	2.00
298 Jim Brewer	.75	2.00
299 Gene Michael	1.50	4.00
300 Rusty Staub	1.50	4.00
301 G.Mitterwald RC/R.Renick RC	.75	2.00
302 Gerry Arrigo	.75	2.00
303 Dick Green	1.50	4.00
304 Sandy Valdespino	.75	2.00
305 Minnie Rojas	.75	2.00
306 Mike Ryan	.75	2.00
307 John Hiller	1.50	4.00
308 Pittsburgh Pirates TC	1.50	4.00
309 Ken Henderson	.75	2.00
310 Luis Aparicio	6.00	15.00
311 Jack Lamabe	.75	2.00
312 Curt Blefary	.75	2.00
313 Al Weis	.75	2.00
314 B.Rohr/G.Spriggs	.75	2.00
315 Zoilo Versalles	.75	2.00
316 Steve Barber	.75	2.00
317 Ron Brand	.75	2.00
318 Chico Salmon	.75	2.00

319 George Culver .75 2.00
320 Frank Howard 1.50 4.00
321 Leo Durocher MG 2.50 6.00
322 Dave Boswell .75 2.00
323 Deron Johnson 1.50 4.00
324 Jim Nash .75 2.00
325 Manny Mota 1.50 4.00
326 Dennis Ribant .75 2.00
327 Tony Taylor 1.50 4.00
328 C.Vinson RC/J.Weaver RC .75 2.00
329 Duane Josephson .75 2.00
330 Roger Maris 20.00 50.00
331 Dan Osinski .75 2.00
332 Doug Rader 1.50 4.00
333 Ron Herbel .75 2.00
334 Baltimore Orioles TC 1.50 4.00
335 Bob Allison 1.50 4.00
336 John Purdin .75 2.00
337 Bill Robinson 1.50 4.00
338 Bob Johnson .75 2.00
339 Rich Nye .75 2.00
340 Max Alvis .75 2.00
341 Jim Lemon MG .75 2.00
342 Ken Johnson .75 2.00
343 Jim Gosger .75 2.00
344 Donn Clendenon 1.50 4.00
345 Bob Hendley .75 2.00
346 Jerry Adair .75 2.00
347 George Brunet .75 2.00
348 L.Colton RC/D.Thoenen RC .75 2.00
349 Ed Spiezio 1.50 4.00
350 Hoyt Wilhelm 5.00 12.00
351 Bob Barton .75 2.00
352 Jackie Hernandez RC .75 2.00
353 Mack Jones .75 2.00
354 Pete Richert .75 2.00
355 Ernie Banks 25.00 60.00
356A Checklist 5/Holtzman Center 2.50 6.00
356B Checklist 5/Holtzman Right 2.50 6.00
357 Len Gabrielson .75 2.00
358 Mike Epstein .75 2.00
359 Joe Moeller .75 2.00
360 Willie Horton 2.50 6.00
361 Harmon Killebrew AS 8.00 20.00
362 Orlando Cepeda AS 2.50 6.00
363 Rod Carew AS 3.00 8.00
364 Joe Morgan AS 3.00 8.00
365 Brooks Robinson AS 3.00 8.00
366 Ron Santo AS 2.50 6.00
367 Jim Fregosi AS 1.50 4.00
368 Gene Alley AS 1.50 4.00
369 Carl Yastrzemski AS 10.00 25.00
370 Hank Aaron AS 20.00 50.00
371 Tony Oliva AS 2.50 6.00
372 Lou Brock AS 6.00 15.00
373 Frank Robinson AS 3.00 8.00
374 Roberto Clemente AS 20.00 50.00
375 Bill Freehan AS 1.50 4.00
376 Tim McCarver AS 1.50 4.00
377 Joel Horlen AS 1.50 4.00
378 Bob Gibson AS 3.00 8.00
379 Gary Peters AS 1.50 4.00
380 Ken Holtzman AS 1.50 4.00
381 Boog Powell 1.50 4.00
382 Ramon Hernandez .75 2.00
383 Steve Whitaker .75 2.00
384 B.Henry/H.McRae RC 2.50 6.00
385 Jim Hunter 8.00 20.00
386 Greg Goossen .75 2.00
387 Joe Foy .75 2.00
388 Ray Washburn .75 2.00
389 Jay Johnstone 1.50 4.00
390 Bill Mazeroski 6.00 15.00
391 Bob Priddy .75 2.00
392 Grady Hatton MG .75 2.00
393 Jim Perry 1.50 4.00
394 Tommie Aaron 2.50 6.00
395 Camilo Pascual 1.50 4.00
396 Bobby Wine .75 2.00
397 Vic Davalillo .75 2.00
398 Jim Grant .75 2.00
399 Ray Oyler 1.50 4.00
400A Mike McCormick YT 1.50 4.00
400B M.McCormick White Tm 400.00 800.00
401 Mets Team 1.50 4.00
402 Mike Hegan 1.50 4.00
403 John Buzhardt .75 2.00
404 Floyd Robinson .75 2.00
405 Tommy Helms 1.50 4.00
406 Dick Ellsworth .75 2.00
407 Gary Kolb .75 2.00
408 Steve Carlton 20.00 50.00
409 F.Peters RC/R.Stone .75 2.00
410 Ferguson Jenkins 4.00 10.00
411 Ron Hansen .75 2.00
412 Clay Carroll 1.50 4.00
413 Tom McCraw .75 2.00
414 Mickey Lolich 3.00 8.00
415 Johnny Callison 1.50 4.00
416 Bill Rigney MG .75 2.00
417 Willie Crawford .75 2.00
418 Eddie Fisher .75 2.00
419 Jack Hiatt .75 2.00
420 Cesar Tovar .75 2.00
421 Ron Taylor .75 2.00
422 Rene Lachemann .75 2.00
423 Fred Gladding .75 2.00
424 Chicago White Sox TC 1.50 4.00
425 Jim Maloney 1.50 4.00
426 Hank Allen .75 2.00
427 Dick Calmus .75 2.00
428 Vic Roznovsky .75 2.00
429 Tommie Sisk .75 2.00
430 Rico Petrocelli 1.50 4.00
431 Dooley Womack .75 2.00
432 B.Davis/J.Vidal .75 2.00
433 Bob Rodgers .75 2.00
434 Ricardo Joseph RC .75 2.00
435 Ron Perranoski 1.50 4.00
436 Hal Lanier .75 2.00
437 Don Cardwell .75 2.00
438 Lee Thomas 1.50 4.00
439 Lum Harris MG .75 2.00
440 Claude Osteen 1.50 4.00
441 Alex Johnson 1.50 4.00
442 Dick Bosman .75 2.00
443 Joe Azcue .75 2.00
444 Jack Fisher .75 2.00
445 Mike Shannon 1.50 4.00
446 Ron Kline .75 2.00
447 G.Korince/F.Lasher RC 1.50 4.00
448 Gary Wagner .75 2.00
449 Gene Oliver .75 2.00
450 Jim Kaat 2.50 6.00
451 Al Spangler .75 2.00
452 Jesus Alou .75 2.00
453 Sammy Ellis .75 2.00
454A Checklist 6/F.Rob Complete 3.00 8.00
454B Checklist 6/F.Rob Partial 3.00 8.00
455 Rico Carty 1.50 4.00
456 John O'Donoghue .75 2.00
457 Jim Lefebvre 1.50 4.00
458 Lew Krausse 2.50 6.00
459 Dick Simpson 1.50 4.00
460 Jim Lonborg 2.50 6.00
461 Chuck Hiller 1.50 4.00
462 Barry Moore 1.50 4.00
463 Jim Schaffer 1.50 4.00
464 Don McMahon 1.50 4.00
465 Tommie Agee 4.00 10.00
466 Bill Dillman 1.50 4.00
467 Dick Howser 4.00 10.00
468 Larry Sherry 1.50 4.00
469 Ty Cline 1.50 4.00
470 Bill Freehan 4.00 10.00
471 Orlando Pena 1.50 4.00
472 Walter Alston MG 2.50 6.00
473 Al Worthington 1.50 4.00
474 Paul Schaal 1.50 4.00
475 Joe Niekro 2.50 6.00
476 Woody Woodward 1.50 4.00
477 Philadelphia Phillies TC 3.00 8.00
478 Dave McNally 2.50 6.00
479 Phil Gagliano 2.50 6.00
480 Oliva/Chico/Clemente 25.00 60.00
481 John Wyatt 1.50 4.00
482 Jose Pagan 1.50 4.00
483 Darold Knowles 1.50 4.00
484 Phil Roof 1.50 4.00
485 Ken Berry 2.50 6.00
486 Cal Koonce 1.50 4.00
487 Lee May 4.00 10.00
488 Dick Tracewski 2.50 6.00
489 Wally Bunker 1.50 4.00
490 Kill/Mays/Mantle 75.00 200.00
491 Denny Lemaster 1.50 4.00
492 Jeff Torborg 2.50 6.00
493 Jim McGlothlin 1.50 4.00
494 Ray Sadecki 1.50 4.00
495 Leon Wagner 1.50 4.00
496 Steve Hamilton 2.50 6.00
497 St. Louis Cardinals TC 3.00 8.00
498 Bill Bryan 2.50 6.00
499 Steve Blass 2.50 6.00
500 Frank Robinson 12.50 30.00
501 John Odom 2.50 6.00
502 Mike Andrews 1.50 4.00
503 Al Jackson 2.50 6.00
504 Russ Snyder 1.50 4.00
505 Joe Sparma 4.00 10.00
506 Clarence Jones RC 1.50 4.00
507 Wade Blasingame 1.50 4.00
508 Duke Sims 1.50 4.00
509 Dennis Higgins 1.50 4.00
510 Ron Fairly 4.00 10.00
511 Bill Kelso 1.50 4.00
512 Grant Jackson 1.50 4.00
513 Hank Bauer MG 2.50 6.00
514 Al McBean 1.50 4.00
515 Russ Nixon 1.50 4.00
516 Pete Mikkelsen 1.50 4.00
517 Diego Segui 2.50 6.00
518A Checklist 7/Boyer ERR 5.00 12.00
518B Checklist 7/Boyer COR 5.00 12.00
519 Jerry Stephenson 1.50 4.00
520 Lou Brock 15.00 40.00
521 Don Shaw 1.50 4.00
522 Wayne Causey 1.50 4.00
523 John Tsitouris 1.50 4.00
524 Andy Kosco 2.50 6.00
525 Jim Davenport 1.50 4.00
526 Bill Denehy 1.50 4.00
527 Tito Francona 1.50 4.00
528 Detroit Tigers TC 30.00 60.00
529 Bruce Von Hoff RC 1.50 4.00
530 B.Robinson/F.Robinson 15.00 40.00
531 Chuck Hinton 1.50 4.00
532 Luis Tiant 5.00 12.00
533 Wes Parker 2.50 6.00
534 Bob Miller 2.50 6.00
535 Danny Cater 2.50 6.00
536 Bill Short 1.50 4.00
537 Norm Siebern 2.50 6.00
538 Manny Jimenez 2.50 6.00
539 J.Ray RC/M.Ferraro RC 1.50 4.00
540 Nelson Briles 2.50 6.00
541 Sandy Alomar 2.50 6.00
542 John Boccabella 1.50 4.00
543 Bob Lee 1.50 4.00
544 Mayo Smith MG 5.00 12.00
545 Lindy McDaniel 2.50 6.00
546 Roy White 2.50 6.00
547 Dan Coombs 1.50 4.00
548 Bernie Allen 1.50 4.00
549 C.Motton RC/R.Nelson RC 1.50 4.00
550 Clete Boyer 2.50 6.00
551 Darrell Sutherland 1.50 4.00
552 Ed Kirkpatrick 1.50 4.00
553 Hank Aguirre 1.50 4.00
554 Oakland Athletics TC 4.00 10.00
555 Jose Tartabull 2.50 6.00
556 Dick Selma 1.50 4.00
557 Frank Quilici 2.50 6.00
558 Johnny Edwards 1.50 4.00
559 C.Taylor RC/L.Walker 1.50 4.00
560 Paul Casanova 1.50 4.00
561 Lee Elia 1.50 4.00
562 Jim Bouton 8.00 20.00
563 Ed Charles 1.50 4.00
564 Eddie Stanky MG 2.50 6.00
565 Larry Dierker 2.50 6.00
566 Ken Harrelson 2.50 6.00
567 Clay Dalrymple 1.50 4.00
568 Willie Smith 1.50 4.00
569 I.Murrell RC/L.Rohr RC 1.50 4.00
570 Rick Reichardt 1.50 4.00
571 Tony LaRussa 5.00 12.00
572 Don Bosch RC 1.50 4.00
573 Joe Coleman 1.50 4.00
574 Cincinnati Reds TC 4.00 10.00
575 Jim Palmer 20.00 50.00
576 Dave Adlesh 1.50 4.00
577 Fred Talbot 1.50 4.00
578 Orlando Martinez 1.50 4.00
579 L.Hisle RC/M.Lum RC 4.00 10.00
580 Bob Bailey 1.50 4.00
581 Garry Roggenburk 1.50 4.00
582 Jerry Grote 4.00 10.00
583 Gates Brown 4.00 10.00
584 Larry Shepard MG RC 1.50 4.00
585 Wilbur Wood 2.50 6.00
586 Jim Pagliaroni 2.50 6.00
587 Roger Repoz 1.50 4.00
588 Dick Schofield 1.50 4.00
589 R.Clark/M.Ogier RC 1.50 4.00
590 Tommy Harper 2.50 6.00
591 Dick Nen 1.50 4.00
592 John Bateman 1.50 4.00
593 Lee Stange 1.50 4.00
594 Phil Linz 2.50 6.00
595 Phil Ortega 1.50 4.00
596 Charlie Smith 1.50 4.00
597 Bill McCool 1.50 4.00
598 Jerry May 2.50 6.00

1968 Topps Game

The cards in this 33-card set measure approximately 2 1/4" by 3 1/4". This "Game" card set of players, issued as inserts with the regular third series 1968 Topps baseball cards, was patterned directly after the Red Back and Blue Back sets of 1951. Each card has a color player photo set upon a white background, with a facsimile autograph underneath the picture. The cards have blue backs, and were also sold in boxed sets, which had an original cost of 15 cents on a limited basis.

COMPLETE SET (33) 125.00 300.00
COMP.FACT SET (33) 125.00 300.00
1 Matty Alou 1.00 2.50
2 Mickey Mantle 50.00 120.00
3 Carl Yastrzemski 10.00 25.00
4 Hank Aaron 15.00 40.00
5 Harmon Killebrew 8.00 20.00
6 Roberto Clemente 20.00 50.00
7 Frank Robinson 8.00 20.00
8 Willie Mays 15.00 40.00
9 Brooks Robinson 8.00 20.00
10 Tommy Davis .75 2.00
11 Bill Freehan 1.00 2.50
12 Claude Osteen .75 2.00
13 Gary Peters .75 2.00
14 Jim Lonborg .75 2.00
15 Steve Hargan .75 2.00
16 Dean Chance .75 2.00
17 Mike McCormick .75 2.00
18 Tim McCarver 1.00 2.50
19 Ron Santo 1.25 3.00
20 Tony Gonzalez .75 2.00
21 Frank Howard 1.00 2.50
22 George Scott .75 2.00
23 Richie Allen 1.25 3.00
24 Jim Wynn 1.00 2.50
25 Gene Alley .75 2.00
26 Rick Monday .75 2.00
27 Al Kaline 6.00 15.00
28 Rusty Staub 1.00 2.50
29 Rod Carew 6.00 15.00
30 Pete Rose 15.00 40.00
31 Joe Torre 1.25 3.00
32 Orlando Cepeda 1.25 3.00
33 Jim Fregosi 1.00 2.50

1969 Topps

The cards in this 664-card set measure 2 1/2" by 3 1/2". The 1969 Topps set includes Sporting News All-Star Selections as card numbers 416 to 435. Other popular subsets within this set include League Leaders (1-12) and World Series cards (162-169). The fifth series contains several variations; the more difficult variety consists of cards with the player's first name, last name, and/or position in white letters instead of lettering in some other color. These are designated in the checklist below by WL (white letters). Each checklist card features a different popular player's picture inside a circle on the front of the checklist card. Two different team identifications of Clay Dalrymple and Donn Clendenon exist, as indicated in the checklist. The key Rookie Cards in this set are Rollie Fingers, Reggie Jackson, and Graig Nettles. This was the last year that Topps issued multi-player special star cards, ending a 13-year tradition, which they had begun in 1957. There were cropping differences in checklist cards 57, 214, and 412, due to their each being printed with two different series. The differences are difficult to explain and have not been greatly sought by collectors; hence they are not listed explicitly in the list below. The All-Star cards 426-435, when turned over and placed together, form a puzzle back of Pete Rose. This would turn out to be the final year that Topps issued cards in five-card nickel wax packs. Cards were also issued in thirty-six card rack packs which were sold for 29 cents.

COMP. MASTER SET (695) 2500.00 5000.00
COMPLETE SET (664) 1500.00 3000.00
COMMON (1-218/328-512) .60 1.50
COMMON CARD (219-327) 1.00 2.50
COMMON CARD (513-588) .75 2.00
COMMON CARD (589-664) 1.25 3.00
WRAPPER (5-CENT) 8.00 20.00
1 Yaz/Cater/Oliva LL 10.00 25.00
2 Rose/Alou/Alou LL 3.00 8.00
3 Harrelson/Howard/North LL 1.50 4.00
4 McCovey/Santo/B.Will LL 2.50 6.00
5 Howard/Horton/Harrelson LL 1.50 4.00
6 McCovey/Allen/Banks LL 2.50 6.00
7 Tiant/McDow/McNally LL 1.50 4.00
8 Gibson/Bolin/Veale LL 2.50 6.00
9 McLain/McNal/Tiant/Stott LL 1.50 4.00
10 Marichal/Gibson/Jenkins LL 3.00 8.00
11 McDowell/McLain/Tiant LL 1.50 4.00
12 Gibson/Jenkins/Singer LL 1.50 4.00
13 Mickey Stanley 1.00 2.50
14 Al McBean .60 1.50
15 Boog Powell 1.50 4.00
16 C.Gutierrez RC/R.Robertson RC .60 1.50
17 Mike Marshall 1.00 2.50
18 Dick Schofield .60 1.50
19 Ken Suarez .60 1.50
20 Ernie Banks 20.00 50.00
21 Jose Santiago .60 1.50
22 Jesus Alou 1.00 2.50
23 Lew Krausse .60 1.50
24 Walt Alston MG 1.50 4.00
25 Roy White 1.00 2.50
26 Clay Carroll 1.00 2.50
27 Bernie Allen .60 1.50
28 Mike Ryan .60 1.50
29 Dave Morehead .60 1.50
30 Bob Allison 1.00 2.50
31 G.Gentry RC/A.Otis RC 1.00 2.50
32 Sammy Ellis .60 1.50
33 Wayne Causey .60 1.50
34 Gary Peters .60 1.50
35 Joe Morgan 12.00 30.00
36 Luke Walker .60 1.50
37 Curt Motton .60 1.50
38 Zoilo Versalles 1.00 2.50
39 Dick Hughes .60 1.50
40 Mayo Smith MG .60 1.50
41 Bob Barton .60 1.50
42 Tommy Harper 1.00 2.50
43 Joe Niekro 1.00 2.50
44 Danny Cater .60 1.50
45 Maury Wills 1.00 2.50
46 Fritz Peterson 1.00 2.50
47A P.Popovich Thick Airbrush 1.00 2.50
47B P.Popovich Light Airbrush 1.00 2.50
47C P.Popovich C on Helmet 10.00 25.00
48 Brant Alyea .60 1.50
49A S.Jones/E.Rodriguez ERR 10.00 25.00
49B S.Jones RC/E.Rodriguez RC .60 1.50
50 Roberto Clemente UER 40.00 100.00
51 Woody Fryman 1.00 2.50
52 Mike Andrews .60 1.50
53 Sonny Jackson .60 1.50
54 Cisco Carlos .60 1.50
55 Jerry Grote 1.00 2.50
56 Rich Reese .60 1.50
57 Checklist 1/McLain 2.50 6.00
58 Fred Gladding .60 1.50
59 Jay Johnstone 1.00 2.50
60 Nelson Briles 1.00 2.50
61 Jimmie Hall .60 1.50
62 Chico Salmon .60 1.50
63 Jim Hickman 1.00 2.50
64 Bill Monbouquette .60 1.50
65 Willie Davis 1.00 2.50
66 M.Adamson RC/M.Rettenmund RC .60 1.50
67 Bill Stoneman 1.00 2.50
68 Dave Duncan 1.00 2.50
69 Steve Hamilton 1.00 2.50
70 Tommy Helms 1.00 2.50
71 Steve Whitaker 1.00 2.50
72 Ron Taylor .60 1.50
73 Johnny Briggs .60 1.50
74 Preston Gomez MG .60 1.50
75 Luis Aparicio 2.50 6.00
76 Norm Miller .60 1.50
77A R.Perranoski No LA 1.00 2.50
77B R.Perranoski LA Cap 10.00 25.00
78 Tom Satriano .60 1.50
79 Milt Pappas 1.00 2.50
80 Norm Cash 1.00 2.50
81 Mel Queen .60 1.50
82 R.Hebner RC/A.Oliver RC 3.00 8.00
83 Mike Ferraro 1.00 2.50
84 Bob Humphreys .60 1.50
85 Lou Brock 15.00 40.00
86 Pete Richert .60 1.50
87 Horace Clarke 1.00 2.50
88 Rich Nye .60 1.50
89 Russ Gibson .60 1.50
90 Jerry Koosman 1.00 2.50
91 Alvin Dark MG 1.00 2.50
92 Jack Billingham 1.00 2.50
93 Joe Foy 1.00 2.50
94 Hank Aguirre .60 1.50
95 Johnny Bench 60.00 150.00
96 Denny Lemaster .60 1.50
97 Buddy Bradford .60 1.50
98 Dave Giusti .60 1.50
99A D.Morris RC/G.Nettles RC 6.00 15.00
99B D.Morris/G.Nettles ERR 6.00 15.00
100 Hank Aaron 50.00 120.00
101 Daryl Patterson .60 1.50
102 Jim Davenport .60 1.50
103 Roger Repoz .60 1.50
104 Steve Blass .60 1.50
105 Rick Monday 1.00 2.50
106 Jim Hannan .60 1.50
107A Checklist 2/Gibson ERR 2.50 6.00
107B Checklist 2/Gibson COR 3.00 8.00
108 Tony Taylor 1.00 2.50
109 Jim Lonborg 1.00 2.50
110 Mike Shannon 1.00 2.50
111 John Morris RC .60 1.50
112 J.C. Martin 1.00 2.50
113 Dave May .60 1.50
114 A.Closter/J.Cumberland RC 1.00 2.50
115 Bill Hands .60 1.50
116 Chuck Harrison .60 1.50
117 Jim Fairey 1.00 2.50
118 Stan Williams .60 1.50
119 Doug Rader 1.00 2.50
120 Pete Rose 25.00 60.00
121 Joe Grzenda RC .60 1.50
122 Ron Fairly 1.00 2.50
123 Wilbur Wood 1.00 2.50
124 Hank Bauer MG 1.00 2.50
125 Ray Sadecki .60 1.50
126 Dick Tracewski .60 1.50
127 Kevin Collins 1.00 2.50
128 Tommie Aaron 1.00 2.50
129 Bill McCool .60 1.50
130 Carl Yastrzemski 20.00 50.00
131 Chris Cannizzaro .60 1.50
132 Dave Baldwin .60 1.50
133 Johnny Callison 1.00 2.50
134 Jim Weaver .60 1.50
135 Tommy Davis 1.00 2.50
136 S.Huntz RC/M.Torrez .60 1.50
137 Wally Bunker .60 1.50
138 John Bateman .60 1.50
139 Andy Kosco .60 1.50
140 Jim Lefebvre 1.00 2.50
141 Bill Dillman .60 1.50
142 Woody Woodward .60 1.50
143 Joe Nossek .60 1.50
144 Bob Hendley .60 1.50
145 Max Alvis .60 1.50
146 Jim Perry 1.00 2.50
147 Leo Durocher MG 1.50 4.00
148 Lee Stange .60 1.50
149 Ollie Brown 1.00 2.50
150 Denny McLain 1.50 4.00
151A C.Dalrymple Portrait .60 1.50
151B C.Dalrymple Catch 6.00 15.00
152 Tommie Sisk .60 1.50
153 Ed Brinkman .60 1.50
154 Jim Britton .60 1.50
155 Pete Ward .60 1.50
156 H.Gilson/L.McFadden RC .60 1.50
157 Bob Rodgers 1.00 2.50
158 Joe Gibbon .60 1.50
159 Jerry Adair .60 1.50
160 Vada Pinson 1.00 2.50
161 John Purdin .60 1.50
162 Bob Gibson WS1 3.00 8.00
163 Willie Horton WS2 2.50 6.00
164 T.McCarver w/Maris WS3 5.00 12.00
165 Lou Brock WS4 3.00 8.00
166 Al Kaline WS5 3.00 8.00
167 Jim Northrup WS6 2.50 6.00
168 M.Lolich/B.Gibson WS7 3.00 8.00
169 Tigers Celebrate WS 2.50 6.00
170 Frank Howard 1.00 2.50
171 Glenn Beckert 1.00 2.50
172 Jerry Stephenson .60 1.50
173 B.Christian RC/G.Nyman RC .60 1.50
174 Grant Jackson .60 1.50
175 Jim Bunning 2.50 6.00
176 Joe Azcue .60 1.50
177 Ron Reed .60 1.50
178 Ray Oyler 1.00 2.50
179 Don Pavletich .60 1.50
180 Willie Horton 1.00 2.50
181 Mel Nelson .60 1.50
182 Bill Rigney MG .60 1.50
183 Don Shaw 1.00 2.50
184 Roberto Pena .60 1.50
185 Tom Phoebus .60 1.50
186 Johnny Edwards .60 1.50
187 Leon Wagner .60 1.50
188 Rick Wise 1.00 2.50
189 J.Lahoud RC/J.Thibodeau RC .60 1.50
190 Willie Mays 60.00 150.00
191 Lindy McDaniel 1.00 2.50
192 Jose Pagan .60 1.50
193 Don Cardwell 1.00 2.50
194 Ted Uhlaender .60 1.50
195 John Odom .60 1.50
196 Lum Harris MG .60 1.50
197 Dick Selma .60 1.50
198 Willie Smith .60 1.50
199 Jim French .60 1.50
200 Bob Gibson 25.00 60.00
201 Russ Snyder .60 1.50
202 Don Wilson 1.00 2.50
203 Dave Johnson 1.00 2.50
204 Jack Hiatt .60 1.50
205 Rick Reichardt .60 1.50
206 L.Hisle/B.Lersch RC 1.00 2.50
207 Roy Face 1.00 2.50
208A D.Clendenon Houston 1.00 2.50
208B D.Clendenon Expos 6.00 15.00
209 Larry Haney UER .60 1.50
210 Felix Millan .60 1.50
211 Galen Cisco .60 1.50
212 Tom Tresh 1.00 2.50
213 Gerry Arrigo .60 1.50
214 Checklist 3 2.50 6.00
215 Rico Petrocelli 1.00 2.50
216 Don Sutton 2.50 6.00
217 John Donaldson .60 1.50
218 John Roseboro 1.00 2.50
219 Freddie Patek RC 1.50 4.00
220 Sam McDowell 1.50 4.00
221 Art Shamsky 1.50 4.00
222 Duane Josephson 1.00 2.50
223 Tom Dukes 1.50 4.00
224 B.Harrelson RC/S.Kealey RC 1.00 2.50
225 Don Kessinger 1.00 2.50
226 Bruce Howard 1.00 2.50
227 Frank Johnson RC 1.00 2.50
228 Dave Leonhard 1.00 2.50
229 Don Lock 1.00 2.50
230 Rusty Staub UER 1.50 4.00
231 Pat Dobson 1.50 4.00
232 Dave Ricketts 1.00 2.50
233 Steve Barber 1.50 4.00
234 Dave Bristol MG 1.00 2.50
235 Jim Hunter 4.00 10.00
236 Manny Mota 1.50 4.00
237 Bobby Cox RC 25.00 60.00
238 Ken Johnson 1.00 2.50
239 Bob Taylor 1.50 4.00
240 Ken Harrelson 1.50 4.00
241 Jim Brewer 1.00 2.50
242 Frank Kostro 1.00 2.50
243 Ron Kline 1.00 2.50
244 R.Fosse RC/G.Woodson RC 1.50 4.00
245 Ed Charles 1.50 4.00
246 Joe Coleman 1.00 2.50
247 Gene Oliver 1.00 2.50
248 Bob Priddy 1.00 2.50
249 Ed Spiezio 1.50 4.00
250 Frank Robinson 20.00 50.00
251 Ron Herbel 1.00 2.50
252 Chuck Cottier 1.00 2.50
253 Jerry Johnson RC 1.00 2.50
254 Joe Schultz MG RC 1.50 4.00
255 Steve Carlton 15.00 40.00
256 Gates Brown 1.50 4.00
257 Jim Ray 1.00 2.50
258 Jackie Hernandez 1.50 4.00
259 Bill Short 1.00 2.50
260 Reggie Jackson RC 150.00 400.00
261 Bob Johnson 1.00 2.50
262 Mike Kekich 1.50 4.00
263 Jerry May 1.00 2.50
264 Bill Landis 1.00 2.50
265 Chico Cardenas 1.50 4.00
266 T.Hutton/A.Foster RC 1.50 4.00
267 Vicente Romo RC 1.00 2.50
268 Al Spangler 1.50 4.00
269 Al Weis 1.50 4.00
270 Mickey Lolich 1.50 4.00
271 Larry Stahl 1.50 4.00
272 Ed Stroud 1.00 2.50
273 Ron Willis 1.00 2.50
274 Clyde King MG 1.00 2.50
275 Vic Davalillo 1.00 2.50
276 Gary Wagner 1.00 2.50
277 Elrod Hendricks RC 1.00 2.50
278 Gary Geiger UER 1.00
279 Roger Nelson 1.50
280 Alex Johnson 1.50
281 Ted Kubiak 1.00
282 Pat Jarvis 1.00
283 Sandy Alomar 1.50
284 J.Robertson RC/M.Wegener RC 1.50
285 Don Mincher 1.50
286 Dock Ellis RC 1.50
287 Jose Tartabull 1.50
288 Ken Holtzman 1.50
289 Bart Shirley 1.00
290 Jim Kaat 1.50
291 Vern Fuller 1.00
292 Al Downing 1.50
293 Dick Dietz 1.00
294 Jim Lemon MG 1.00
295 Tony Perez 12.00
296 Andy Messersmith RC 1.50
297 Deron Johnson 1.00
298 Dave Nicholson 1.00
299 Mark Belanger 1.50
300 Felipe Alou 1.50
301 Darrell Brandon 1.50
302 Jim Pagliaroni 1.00
303 Cal Koonce 1.50
304 B.Davis/C.Gaston RC 2.50
305 Dick McAuliffe 1.50
306 Jim Grant 1.50
307 Gary Kolb 1.50
308 Wade Blasingame 1.00
309 Walt Williams 1.00
310 Tom Haller 1.00
311 Sparky Lyle RC 4.00
312 Lee Elia 1.00
313 Bill Robinson 1.00
314 Checklist 4/Drysdale 2.50
315 Eddie Fisher 1.00
316 Hal Lanier 1.00
317 Bruce Look RC 1.00
318 Jack Fisher 1.00
319 Ken McMullen UER 1.00
320 Dal Maxvill 1.00
321 Jim McAndrew RC 1.00
322 Jose Vidal 1.50
323 Larry Miller 1.50
324 L.Cain RC/D.Campbell RC 1.50
325 Jose Cardenal 1.50
326 Gary Sutherland 1.50
327 Willie Crawford 1.00
328 Joel Horlen .60
329 Rick Joseph .60
330 Tony Conigliaro 1.50
331 G.Garrido/T.House RC .60
332 Fred Talbot .60
333 Ivan Murrell .60
334 Phil Roof .60
335 Bill Mazeroski 2.50
336 Jim Roland .60
337 Marty Martinez RC .60
338 Del Unser RC .60
339 S.Mingori RC/J.Pena RC .60
340 Dave McNally 1.00
341 Dave Adlesh .60
342 Bubba Morton .60
343 Dan Frisella .60
344 Tom Matchick .60
345 Frank Linzy .60
346 Wayne Comer RC .60
347 Randy Hundley 1.00
348 Steve Hargan .60
349 Dick Williams MG 1.00
350 Richie Allen 1.50
351 Carroll Sembera .60
352 Paul Schaal .60
353 Jeff Torborg .60
354 Nate Oliver .60
355 Phil Niekro 8.00
356 Frank Quilici .60
357 Carl Taylor .60
358 G.Lauzerique RC/R.Rodriguez .60
359 Dick Kelley .60
360 Jim Wynn 1.00
361 Gary Holman RC .60
362 Jim Maloney 1.00
363 Russ Nixon .60
364 Tommie Agee 1.00
365 Jim Fregosi 1.00
366 Bo Belinsky .60
367 Lou Johnson 1.00
368 Vic Roznovsky .60
369 Bob Skinner MG .60
370 Juan Marichal 3.00
371 Sal Bando 1.00
372 Adolfo Phillips .60
373 Fred Lasher .60
374 Bob Tillman .60
375 Harmon Killebrew 20.00
376 M.Fiore RC/J.Rooker RC .60
377 Gary Bell 1.00
378 Jose Herrera RC .60
379 Ken Boyer 1.00
380 Stan Bahnsen 1.00
381 Ed Kranepool 1.00
382 Pat Corrales 1.00
383 Casey Cox .60
384 Larry Shepard MG .60
385 Orlando Cepeda 2.50
386 Jim McGlothlin .60
387 Bobby Klaus .60
388 Tom McCraw .60
389 Dan Coombs .60
390 Bill Freehan 1.00

1 Ray Culp .60 1.50
2 Bob Burda RC .60 1.50
3 Gene Brabender 1.00 2.50
4 L.Piniella/M.Staehle 2.50 6.00
5 Chris Short .60 1.50
6 Jim Campanis .60 1.50
7 Chuck Dobson .60 1.50
8 Tito Francona .60 1.50
9 Bob Bailey 1.00 2.50
0 Don Drysdale 10.00 25.00
1 Jake Gibbs 1.00 2.50
2 Ken Boswell RC 1.00 2.50
3 Bob Miller .60 1.50
4 V.LaRose RC/G.Ross RC 1.00 2.50
5 Lee May 1.00 2.50
6 Phil Ortega .60 1.50
7 Tom Egan .60 1.50
8 Nate Colbert .60 1.50
9 Bob Moose .60 1.50
0 Al Kaline 10.00 25.00
1 Larry Dierker 1.00 2.50
2 Checklist 5/Mantle DP 12.00 30.00
3 Roland Sheldon 1.00 2.50
4 Duke Sims .60 1.50
5 Ray Washburn .60 1.50
6 Willie McCovey AS 3.00 8.00
7 Ken Harrelson AS 1.25 3.00
8 Tommy Helms AS 1.25 3.00
19 Rod Carew AS 4.00 10.00
20 Ron Santo AS 1.50 4.00
21 Brooks Robinson AS 3.00 8.00
22 Don Kessinger AS 1.25 3.00
23 Bert Campaneris AS 1.50 4.00
24 Pete Rose AS 10.00 25.00
25 Carl Yastrzemski AS 10.00 25.00
26 Curt Flood AS 1.50 4.00
27 Tony Oliva AS 1.50 4.00
28 Lou Brock AS 2.50 6.00
29 Willie Horton AS 1.25 3.00
30 Johnny Bench AS 20.00 50.00
31 Bill Freehan AS 1.50 4.00
32 Bob Gibson AS 6.00 15.00
33 Denny McLain AS 1.25 3.00
34 Jerry Koosman AS 1.25 3.00
35 Sam McDowell AS 1.00 2.50
36 Gene Alley 1.00 2.50
437 Luis Alcaraz RC .60 1.50
438 Gary Waslewski RC .60 1.50
439 E.Herrmann RC/D.Lazar RC .60 1.50
440A Willie McCovey 6.00 15.00
440B Willie McCovey WL 50.00 100.00
441A Dennis Higgins .60 1.50
441B Dennis Higgins WL 10.00 25.00
442 Ty Cline .60 1.50
443 Don Wert .60 1.50
444A Joe Moeller .60 1.50
444B Joe Moeller WL 10.00 25.00
445 Bobby Knoop .60 1.50
446 Claude Raymond .60 1.50
447A Ralph Houk MG 1.00 2.50
447B Ralph Houk MG WL 10.00 25.00
448 Bob Tolan 1.00 2.50
449 Paul Lindblad .60 1.50
450 Billy Williams 12.00 30.00
451A Rich Rollins 1.00 2.50
451B Rich Rollins WL 10.00 25.00
452A Al Ferrara .60 1.50
452B Al Ferrara WL 10.00 25.00
453 Mike Cuellar 1.00 2.50
454A L.Colton/D.Money RC 1.00 2.50
454B L.Colton/D.Money WL 10.00 25.00
455 Sonny Siebert .60 1.50
456 Bud Harrelson 1.00 2.50
457 Dalton Jones .60 1.50
458 Curt Blefary .60 1.50
459 Dave Boswell .60 1.50
460 Joe Torre 1.50 4.00
461A Mike Epstein .60 1.50
461B Mike Epstein WL 10.00 25.00
462 R.Schoendienst MG 1.00 2.50
463 Dennis Ribant .60 1.50
464A Dave Marshall RC .60 1.50
464B Dave Marshall WL 10.00 25.00
465 Tommy John 1.50 4.00
466 John Boccabella 1.00 2.50
467 Tommie Reynolds .60 1.50
468A B.Dal Canton RC/B.Robertson .60 1.50
468B B.Dal Canton/B.Robertson WL 10.00 25.00
469 Chico Ruiz .60 1.50
470A Mel Stottlemyre 1.00 2.50
470B Mel Stottlemyre WL 12.50 30.00
471A Ted Savage .60 1.50
471B Ted Savage WL 10.00 25.00
472 Jim Price .60 1.50
473A Jose Arcia .60 1.50
473B Jose Arcia WL 10.00 25.00
474 Tom Murphy RC .60 1.50
475 Tim McCarver 1.50 4.00
476A K.Brett RC/G.Moses 1.00 2.50
476B K.Brett/G.Moses WL 12.50 30.00
477 Jeff James RC .60 1.50
478 Don Buford .60 1.50
479 Richie Scheinblum .60 1.50
480 Tom Seaver 25.00 60.00
481 Bill Melton RC 1.00 2.50
482A Jim Gosger .60 1.50
482B Jim Gosger WL 10.00 25.00
483 Ted Abernathy .60 1.50
484 Joe Gordon MG 1.00 2.50
485A Gaylord Perry 4.00 10.00
485B Gaylord Perry WL 40.00 80.00
486A Paul Casanova .60 1.50
486B Paul Casanova WL 10.00 25.00
487 Denis Menke .60 1.50
488 Joe Sparma .60 1.50
489 Clete Boyer 1.00 2.50
490 Matty Alou 1.00 2.50
491A J.Crider RC/G.Mitterwald .60 1.50
491B J.Crider/G.Mitterwald WL 10.00 25.00
492 Tony Cloninger .60 1.50
493A Wes Parker 1.00 2.50
493B Wes Parker WL 10.00 25.00
494 Ken Berry .60 1.50
495 Bert Campaneris 1.00 2.50
496 Larry Jaster .60 1.50
497 Julian Javier 1.00 2.50
498 Juan Pizarro 1.00 2.50
499 D.Bryant RC/S.Shea RC .60 1.50
500A Mickey Mantle UER 150.00 400.00
500B Mickey Mantle UER WL 1000.00 2000.00
501A Tony Gonzalez 1.00 2.50
501B Tony Gonzalez WL 10.00 25.00
502 Minnie Rojas .60 1.50
503 Larry Brown .60 1.50
504 Checklist 6/B.Robinson 3.00 8.00
505A Bobby Bolin .60 1.50
505B Bobby Bolin WL 10.00 25.00
506 Paul Blair 1.00 2.50
507 Cookie Rojas 1.00 2.50
508 Moe Drabowsky 1.00 2.50
509 Manny Sanguillen 1.00 2.50
510 Rod Carew 15.00 40.00
511A Diego Segui 1.00 2.50
511B Diego Segui WL 10.00 25.00
512 Cleon Jones 1.00 2.50
513 Camilo Pascual 1.25 3.00
514 Mike Lum .75 2.00
515 Dick Green .75 2.00
516 Earl Weaver MG RC 8.00 20.00
517 Mike McCormick 1.25 3.00
518 Fred Whitfield .75 2.00
519 J.Kenney RC/L.Boehmer RC .75 2.00
520 Bob Veale 1.25 3.00
521 George Thomas .75 2.00
522 Joe Hoerner .75 2.00
523 Bob Chance .75 2.00
524 J.Laboy RC/F.Wicker RC 1.25 3.00
525 Earl Wilson 1.25 3.00
526 Hector Torres RC .75 2.00
527 Al Lopez MG 2.00 5.00
528 Claude Osteen 1.25 3.00
529 Ed Kirkpatrick 1.25 3.00
530 Cesar Tovar .75 2.00
531 Dick Farrell .75 2.00
532 Phoeb/Hard/McNally/Cuellar 1.25 3.00
533 Nolan Ryan 125.00 300.00
534 Jerry McNertney 1.25 3.00
535 Phil Regan 1.25 3.00
536 D.Breeden RC/D.Roberts RC .75 2.00
537 Mike Paul RC .75 2.00
538 Charlie Smith .75 2.00
539 T.Williams/M.Epstein 5.00 12.00
540 Curt Flood 1.25 3.00
541 Joe Verbanic .75 2.00
542 Bob Aspromonte .75 2.00
543 Fred Newman .75 2.00
544 M.Kilkenny RC/R.Woods RC .75 2.00
545 Willie Stargell 12.00 30.00
546 Jim Nash .75 2.00
547 Billy Martin MG 2.00 5.00
548 Bob Locker .75 2.00
549 Ron Brand .75 2.00
550 Brooks Robinson 12.50 30.00
551 Wayne Granger RC .75 2.00
552 T.Sizemore RC/B.Sudakis RC 1.25 3.00
553 Ron Davis .75 2.00
554 Frank Bertaina .75 2.00
555 Jim Ray Hart 1.25 3.00
556 Bando/Campaneris/Cater 1.25 3.00
557 Frank Fernandez .75 2.00
558 Tom Burgmeier RC 1.25 3.00
559 J.Hague RC/J.Hicks .75 2.00
560 Luis Tiant 1.25 3.00
561 Ron Clark .75 2.00
562 Bob Watson RC 3.00 8.00
563 Marty Pattin RC 1.25 3.00
564 Gil Hodges MG 4.00 10.00
565 Hoyt Wilhelm 3.00 8.00
566 Ron Hansen .75 2.00
567 E.Jimenez/J.Shellenback .75 2.00
568 Cecil Upshaw .75 2.00
569 Billy Harris .60 1.50
570 Ron Santo 3.00 8.00
571 Cap Peterson .75 2.00
572 W.McCovey/J.Marichal 6.00 15.00
573 Jim Palmer 12.00 30.00
574 George Scott 1.25 3.00
575 Bill Singer 1.25 3.00
576 R.Stone/B.Wilson .75 2.00
577 Mike Hegan 1.25 3.00
578 Don Bosch .75 2.00
579 Dave Nelson RC .75 2.00
580 Jim Northrup 1.25 3.00
581 Gary Nolan 1.25 3.00
582A Checklist 7/Oliva White 2.50 6.00
582B Checklist 7/Oliva Red 3.00 8.00
583 Clyde Wright RC .75 2.00
584 Don Mason .75 2.00
585 Ron Swoboda 1.25 3.00
586 Tim Cullen .75 2.00
587 Joe Rudi RC 3.00 8.00
588 Bill White 1.25 3.00
589 Joe Pepitone 2.00 5.00
590 Rico Carty 2.00 5.00
591 Mike Hedlund 1.25 3.00
592 R.Robles RC/A.Santorini RC 2.00 5.00
593 Don Nottebart 1.25 3.00
594 Dooley Womack 1.25 3.00
595 Lee Maye 1.25 3.00
596 Chuck Hartenstein 1.25 3.00
597 Rollie Fingers RC 40.00 100.00
598 Ruben Amaro 1.25 3.00
599 John Boozer 1.25 3.00
600 Tony Oliva 3.00 8.00
601 Tug McGraw 3.00 8.00
602 Distaso/Young/Qualls RC 2.00 5.00
603 Joe Keough RC 1.25 3.00
604 Bobby Etheridge 1.25 3.00
605 Dick Ellsworth 1.25 3.00
606 Gene Mauch MG 2.00 5.00
607 Dick Bosman 1.25 3.00
608 Dick Simpson 1.25 3.00
609 Phil Gagliano 1.25 3.00
610 Jim Hardin 1.25 3.00
611 Didier/Hriniak/Niebauer RC 2.00 5.00
612 Jack Aker 2.00 5.00
613 Jim Beauchamp 1.25 3.00
614 T.Griffin RC/S.Guinn RC 1.25 3.00
615 Len Gabrielson 1.25 3.00
616 Don McMahon 1.25 3.00
617 Jesse Gonder 1.25 3.00
618 Ramon Webster 1.25 3.00
619 Butler/Kelly/Rios RC 2.00 5.00
620 Dean Chance 2.00 5.00
621 Bill Voss 1.25 3.00
622 Dan Osinski 1.25 3.00
623 Hank Allen 1.25 3.00
624 Chaney/Dyer/Harmon RC 2.00 5.00
625 Mack Jones UER 2.00 5.00
626 Gene Michael 2.00 5.00
627 George Stone RC 1.25 3.00
628 Conigliaro/O'Brien/Wenz RC 2.00 5.00
629 Jack Hamilton 1.25 3.00
630 Bobby Bonds RC 15.00 40.00
631 John Kennedy 2.00 5.00
632 Jon Warden RC 1.25 3.00
633 Harry Walker MG 1.25 3.00
634 Andy Etchebarren 1.25 3.00
635 George Culver 1.25 3.00
636 Woody Held 1.25 3.00
637 DaVanon/Reberger/Kirby RC 2.00 5.00
638 Ed Sprague RC 1.25 3.00
639 Barry Moore 1.25 3.00
640 Ferguson Jenkins 8.00 20.00
641 Darwin/Miller/Dean RC 2.00 5.00
642 John Hiller 1.25 3.00
643 Billy Cowan 1.25 3.00
644 Chuck Hinton 1.25 3.00
645 George Brunet 1.25 3.00
646 D.McGinn RC/C.Morton RC 2.00 5.00
647 Dave Wickersham 1.25 3.00
648 Bobby Wine 2.00 5.00
649 Al Jackson 1.25 3.00
650 Ted Williams MG 8.00 20.00
651 Gus Gil 2.00 5.00
652 Eddie Watt 1.25 3.00
653 Aurelio Rodriguez UER RC 2.00 5.00
654 May/Secrist/Morales RC 2.00 5.00
655 Mike Hershberger 1.25 3.00
656 Dan Schneider 1.25 3.00
657 Bobby Murcer 3.00 8.00
658 Hall/Burbach/Miles RC 1.25 3.00
659 Johnny Podres 2.00 5.00
660 Reggie Smith 2.00 5.00
661 Jim Merritt 1.25 3.00
662 Drago/Spriggs/Oliver RC 2.00 5.00
663 Dick Radatz 2.00 5.00
664 Ron Hunt 2.00 5.00

1969 Topps Decals

The 1969 Topps Decal Inserts are a set of 48 unnumbered decals issued as inserts in packages of 1969 Topps regular issue cards. Each decal is approximately 1" by 1 1/2" although including the plain backing the measurement is 1 3/4" by 2 1/8". The decals appear to be miniature versions of the Topps regular issue of that year. The copyright notice on the side indicates that these decals were produced in the United Kingdom. Most of the players on the decals are stars.

COMPLETE SET (48) 250.00 500.00
1 Hank Aaron 20.00 50.00
2 Richie Allen 3.00 8.00
3 Felipe Alou 2.00 5.00
4 Matty Alou 2.00 5.00
5 Luis Aparicio 3.00 8.00
6 Roberto Clemente 30.00 60.00
7 Donn Clendenon 1.50 4.00
8 Tommy Davis 2.00 5.00
9 Don Drysdale 4.00 10.00
10 Joe Foy 1.50 4.00
11 Jim Fregosi 2.00 5.00
12 Bob Gibson 4.00 10.00
13 Tony Gonzalez 1.50 4.00
14 Tom Haller 1.50 4.00
15 Ken Harrelson 2.00 5.00
16 Tommy Helms 1.50 4.00
17 Willie Horton 2.00 5.00
18 Frank Howard 2.00 5.00
19 Reggie Jackson 20.00 50.00
20 Ferguson Jenkins 3.00 8.00
21 Harmon Killebrew 6.00 15.00
22 Jerry Koosman 2.00 5.00
23 Mickey Mantle 50.00 100.00
24 Willie Mays 10.00 25.00
25 Tim McCarver 2.00 5.00
26 Willie McCovey 4.00 10.00
27 Sam McDowell 2.00 5.00
28 Denny McLain 2.00 5.00
29 Dave McNally 2.00 5.00
30 Don Mincher 1.50 4.00
31 Rick Monday 2.00 5.00
32 Tony Oliva 3.00 8.00
33 Camilo Pascual 1.50 4.00
34 Rick Reichardt 1.50 4.00
35 Frank Robinson 4.00 10.00
36 Pete Rose 20.00 50.00
37 Ron Santo 3.00 8.00
38 Tom Seaver 12.50 30.00
39 Dick Selma 1.50 4.00
40 Chris Short 1.50 4.00
41 Rusty Staub 3.00 8.00
42 Mel Stottlemyre 2.00 5.00
43 Luis Tiant 2.00 5.00
44 Pete Ward 1.50 4.00
45 Hoyt Wilhelm 3.00 8.00
46 Maury Wills 3.00 8.00
47 Jim Wynn 2.00 5.00
48 Carl Yastrzemski 8.00 20.00

1969 Topps Deckle Edge

The cards in this 33-card set measure approximately 2 1/4" by 3 1/4". This unusual black and white insert set derives its name from the serrated border, or edge, of the cards. The cards were included as inserts in the regularly issued Topps baseball third series of 1969. Card number 11 is found with either Hoyt Wilhelm or Jim Wynn, and number 22 with either Rusty Staub or Joe Foy. The set price below does include all variations. The set numbering is arranged in team order by league except for cards 11 and 22.

COMPLETE SET (35) 50.00 100.00
1 Brooks Robinson 2.50 6.00
2 Boog Powell 1.25 3.00
3 Ken Harrelson .60 1.50
4 Carl Yastrzemski 3.00 8.00
5 Jim Fregosi .75 2.00
6 Luis Aparicio 1.25 3.00
7 Luis Tiant .75 2.00
8 Denny McLain 1.25 3.00
9 Willie Horton .75 2.00
10 Bill Freehan .75 2.00
11A Hoyt Wilhelm 3.00 8.00
11B Jim Wynn 6.00 15.00
12 Rod Carew 1.50 4.00
13 Mel Stottlemyre .75 2.00
14 Rick Monday .60 1.50
15 Tommy Davis .75 2.00
16 Frank Howard .75 2.00
17 Felipe Alou .75 2.00
18 Don Kessinger .60 1.50
19 Ron Santo 1.25 3.00
20 Tommy Helms .60 1.50
21 Pete Rose 5.00 12.00
22A Rusty Staub .75 2.00
22B Joe Foy 10.00 25.00
23 Tom Haller .60 1.50
24 Maury Wills 1.25 3.00
25 Jerry Koosman .75 2.00
26 Richie Allen 1.50 4.00
27 Roberto Clemente 8.00 20.00
28 Curt Flood 1.25 3.00
29 Bob Gibson 1.50 4.00
30 Al Ferrara .60 1.50
31 Willie McCovey 1.50 4.00
32 Juan Marichal 1.25 3.00
33 Willie Mays 5.00 12.00

1970 Topps

The cards in this 720-card set measure 2 1/2" by 3 1/2". The Topps set for 1970 has color photos surrounded by white frame lines and gray borders. The backs have a blue biographical section and a yellow record section. All-Star selections are featured on cards 450 to 469. Other topical subsets within this set include League Leaders (61-72), Playoffs cards (195-202), and World Series cards (305-310). There are graduations of scarcity, terminating in the high series (634-720), which are outlined in the value summary. Cards were issued in ten-card dime packs as well as thirty-three card cello packs which sold for a quarter and were encased in a small Topps box, and in 54-card rack packs which sold for 39 cents. The key Rookie Card in this set is Thurman Munson.

COMPLETE SET (720) 1250.00 2500.00
COMMON CARD (1-132) .30 .75
COMMON CARD (133-372) .40 1.00
COMMON CARD (373-459) .60 1.50
COMMON CARD (460-546) .75 2.00
COMMON CARD (547-633) 1.50 4.00
COMMON CARD (634-720) 4.00 10.00
WRAPPER (10-CENT) 8.00 20.00
1 New York Mets TC 12.50 30.00
2 Diego Segui .40 1.00
3 Darrel Chaney .30 .75
4 Tom Egan .30 .75
5 Wes Parker .40 1.00
6 Grant Jackson .30 .75
7 G.Boyd RC/R.Nagelson RC .30 .75
8 Jose Martinez RC .30 .75
9 Checklist 1 5.00 12.00
10 Carl Yastrzemski 8.00 20.00
11 Nate Colbert .30 .75
12 John Hiller .30 .75
13 Jack Hiatt .30 .75
14 Hank Allen .30 .75
15 Larry Dierker .30 .75
16 Charlie Metro MG RC .30 .75
17 Hoyt Wilhelm 1.50 4.00
18 Carlos May .40 1.00
19 John Boccabella .30 .75
20 Dave McNally .40 1.00
21 V.Blue RC/G.Tenace RC 1.50 4.00
22 Ray Washburn .30 .75
23 Bill Robinson .40 1.00
24 Dick Selma .30 .75
25 Cesar Tovar .30 .75
26 Tug McGraw .75 2.00
27 Chuck Hinton .30 .75
28 Billy Wilson .30 .75
29 Sandy Alomar .40 1.00
30 Matty Alou .40 1.00
31 Marty Pattin .40 1.00
32 Harry Walker MG .30 .75
33 Don Wert .30 .75
34 Willie Crawford .30 .75
35 Joel Horlen .30 .75
36 D.Breeden/B.Carbo RC .40 1.00
37 Dick Drago .30 .75
38 Mack Jones .30 .75
39 Mike Nagy RC .30 .75
40 Rich Allen .75 2.00
41 George Lauzerique .30 .75
42 Tito Fuentes .30 .75
43 Jack Aker .30 .75
44 Roberto Pena .30 .75
45 Dave Johnson .40 1.00
46 Ken Rudolph RC .30 .75
47 Bob Miller .30 .75
48 Gil Garrido .30 .75
49 Tim Cullen .30 .75
50 Tommie Agee .40 1.00
51 Bob Christian .30 .75
52 Bruce Dal Canton .30 .75
53 John Kennedy .30 .75
54 Jeff Torborg .40 1.00
55 John Odom .30 .75
56 J.Lis RC/S.Reid RC .30 .75
57 Pat Kelly .30 .75
58 Dave Marshall .30 .75
59 Dick Ellsworth .30 .75
60 Jim Wynn .40 1.00
61 Rose/Clemente/Jones LL 5.00 12.00
62 Carew/Smith/Oliva LL .75 2.00
63 McCovey/Santo/Perez LL .75 2.00
64 Kill/Powell/Jackson LL 1.50 4.00
65 McCovey/Aaron/May LL 5.00 12.00
66 Kill/Howard/Jackson LL 1.50 4.00
67 Marichal/Carlton/Gibson LL 1.50 4.00
68 Bosman/Palmer/Cuellar LL .40 1.00
69 Seav/Niek/Jenk/Mari LL 1.50 4.00
70 McLain/Cuellar/Boswell LL .40 1.00
71 Jenkins/Gibson/Singer LL .75 2.00
72 McDowell/Lolich/Mess LL .40 1.00
73 Wayne Granger .30 .75
74 G.Washburn RC/W.Wolf .30 .75
75 Jim Kaat .40 1.00
76 Carl Taylor UER .30 .75
Collecting is spelled incorrectly in the cartoon
77 Frank Linzy .30 .75
78 Joe Lahoud .30 .75
79 Clay Kirby .30 .75
80 Don Kessinger .40 1.00
81 Dave May .30 .75
82 Frank Fernandez .30 .75
83 Don Cardwell .30 .75
84 Paul Casanova .30 .75
85 Max Alvis .30 .75
86 Lum Harris MG .30 .75
87 Steve Renko RC .30 .75
88 M.Fuentes RC/D.Baney RC .40 1.00
89 Juan Rios .30 .75
90 Tim McCarver .40 1.00
91 Rich Morales .30 .75
92 George Culver .30 .75
93 Rick Renick .30 .75
94 Freddie Patek .40 1.00
95 Earl Wilson .40 1.00
96 L.Lee RC/J.Reuss RC .40 1.00
97 Joe Moeller .30 .75
98 Gates Brown .40 1.00
99 Bobby Pfeil RC .30 .75
100 Mel Stottlemyre .40 1.00
101 Bobby Floyd .30 .75
102 Joe Rudi .40 1.00
103 Frank Reberger .30 .75
104 Gerry Moses .30 .75
105 Tony Gonzalez .30 .75
106 Darold Knowles .30 .75
107 Bobby Etheridge .30 .75
108 Tom Burgmeier .30 .75
109 G.Jestadt RC/C.Morton .30 .75
110 Bob Moose .30 .75
111 Mike Hegan .40 1.00
112 Dave Nelson .30 .75
113 Jim Ray .30 .75
114 Gene Michael .40 1.00
115 Alex Johnson .40 1.00
116 Sparky Lyle .40 1.00
117 Don Young .30 .75
118 George Mitterwald .30 .75
119 Chuck Taylor RC .30 .75
120 Sal Bando .40 1.00
121 F.Beene RC/T.Crowley RC .30 .75
122 George Stone .30 .75
123 Don Gutteridge MG RC .30 .75
124 Larry Jaster .30 .75
125 Deron Johnson .30 .75
126 Marty Martinez .30 .75
127 Joe Coleman .30 .75
128A Checklist 2 R Perranoski 2.50 6.00
128B Checklist 2 R. Perranoski 2.50 6.00
129 Jimmie Price .30 .75
130 Ollie Brown .30 .75
131 R.Lamb RC/B.Stinson RC .30 .75
132 Jim McGlothlin .30 .75
133 Clay Carroll .40 1.00
134 Danny Walton RC .40 1.00
135 Dick Dietz .40 1.00
136 Steve Hargan .40 1.00
137 Art Shamsky .40 1.00
138 Joe Foy .40 1.00
139 Rich Nye .40 1.00
140 Reggie Jackson 20.00 50.00
141 D.Cash RC/J.Jeter RC .60 1.50
142 Fritz Peterson .40 1.00
143 Phil Gagliano .40 1.00
144 Ray Culp .40 1.00
145 Rico Carty .60 1.50
146 Danny Murphy .40 1.00
147 Angel Hermoso RC .40 1.00
148 Earl Weaver MG 1.25 3.00
149 Billy Champion RC .40 1.00
150 Harmon Killebrew 3.00 8.00
151 Dave Roberts .40 1.00
152 Ike Brown RC .40 1.00
153 Gary Gentry .40 1.00
154 J.Miles/J.Dukes RC .40 1.00
155 Denis Menke .40 1.00
156 Eddie Fisher .40 1.00
157 Manny Mota .60 1.50
158 Jerry McNertney .60 1.50
159 Tommy Helms .60 1.50
160 Phil Niekro 2.00 5.00
161 Richie Scheinblum .40 1.00
162 Jerry Johnson .40 1.00
163 Syd O'Brien .40 1.00
164 Ty Cline .40 1.00
165 Ed Kirkpatrick .40 1.00
166 Al Oliver 1.25 3.00
167 Bill Burbach .40 1.00
168 Dave Watkins RC .40 1.00
169 Tom Hall .40 1.00
170 Billy Williams 2.00 5.00
171 Jim Nash .40 1.00
172 G.Hill RC/R.Garr RC .60 1.50
173 Jim Hicks .40 1.00
174 Ted Sizemore .60 1.50
175 Dick Bosman .40 1.00
176 Jim Ray Hart .60 1.50
177 Jim Northrup .60 1.50
178 Denny Lemaster .40 1.00
179 Ivan Murrell .40 1.00
180 Tommy John .60 1.50
181 Sparky Anderson MG 2.00 5.00
182 Dick Hall .40 1.00
183 Jerry Grote .60 1.50
184 Ray Fosse .40 1.00
185 Don Mincher .60 1.50
186 Rick Joseph .40 1.00
187 Mike Hedlund .40 1.00
188 Manny Sanguillen .60 1.50
189 Thurman Munson RC 50.00 120.00
190 Joe Torre 1.25 3.00
191 Vicente Romo .40 1.00
192 Jim Qualls .40 1.00
193 Mike Wegener .40 1.00
194 Chuck Manuel RC 1.00 2.50
195 Tom Seaver NLCS1 10.00 25.00
196 Ken Boswell NLCS2 .75 2.00
197 Nolan Ryan NLCS3 12.50 30.00
198 Mets Celebrate/w/Ryan 6.00 15.00
199 Mike Cuellar ALCS1 .75 2.00
200 Boog Powell ALCS2 1.25 3.00
201 B.Powell/A.Etch ALCS3 .75 2.00
202 Orioles Celebrate ALCS .75 2.00
203 Rudy May .40 1.00
204 Len Gabrielson .40 1.00
205 Bert Campaneris .60 1.50
206 Clete Boyer .60 1.50
207 N.McRae RC/B.Reed RC .40 1.00
208 Fred Gladding .40 1.00
209 Ken Suarez .40 1.00
210 Juan Marichal 2.00 5.00
211 Ted Williams MG UER 10.00 25.00
212 Al Santorini .40 1.00
213 Andy Etchebarren .40 1.00
214 Ken Boswell .40 1.00
215 Reggie Smith .60 1.50
216 Chuck Hartenstein .40 1.00
217 Ron Hansen .40 1.00
218 Ron Stone .40 1.00
219 Jerry Kenney .40 1.00
220 Steve Carlton 8.00 20.00
221 Ron Brand .40 1.00
222 Jim Rooker .40 1.00
223 Nate Oliver .40 1.00
224 Steve Barber .60 1.50
225 Lee May .60 1.50
226 Ron Perranoski .40 1.00
227 J.Mayberry RC/B.Watkins RC .60 1.50
228 Aurelio Rodriguez .40 1.00
229 Rich Robertson .40 1.00
230 Brooks Robinson 8.00 20.00
231 Luis Tiant .60 1.50
232 Bob Didier .40 1.00
233 Lew Krausse .40 1.00
234 Tommy Dean .40 1.00
235 Mike Epstein .40 1.00
236 Bob Veale .40 1.00
237 Russ Gibson .40 1.00
238 Jose Laboy .40 1.00
239 Ken Berry .40 1.00
240 Ferguson Jenkins 2.00 5.00
241 A.Fitzmorris RC/S.Northey RC .40 1.00
242 Walter Alston MG 1.25 3.00
243 Joe Sparma .40 1.00
244A Checklist 3 Red Bat 2.50 6.00
244B Checklist 3 Brown Bat 2.50 6.00
245 Leo Cardenas .40 1.00
246 Jim McAndrew .40 1.00
247 Lou Klimchock .40 1.00
248 Jesus Alou .40 1.00
249 Bob Locker .40 1.00
250 Willie McCovey UER 4.00 10.00
251 Dick Schofield .40 1.00
252 Lowell Palmer RC .40 1.00
253 Ron Woods .40 1.00
254 Camilo Pascual .40 1.00
255 Jim Spencer RC .40 1.00
256 Vic Davalillo .40 1.00
257 Dennis Higgins .40 1.00
258 Paul Popovich .40 1.00
259 Tommie Reynolds .40 1.00
260 Claude Osteen .40 1.00
261 Curt Motton .40 1.00
262 J.Morales RC/J.Williams RC .40 1.00
263 Duane Josephson .40 1.00
264 Rich Hebner .40 1.00
265 Randy Hundley .40 1.00
266 Wally Bunker .40 1.00
267 H.Hill RC/P.Ratliff .40 1.00
268 Claude Raymond .40 1.00
269 Cesar Gutierrez .40 1.00
270 Chris Short .40 1.00
271 Greg Goossen .60 1.50
272 Hector Torres .40 1.00
273 Ralph Houk MG .60 1.50
274 Gerry Arrigo .40 1.00
275 Duke Sims .40 1.00
276 Ron Hunt .40 1.00
277 Paul Doyle RC .40 1.00
278 Tommie Aaron .40 1.00
279 Bill Lee RC .60 1.50
280 Donn Clendenon .60 1.50
281 Casey Cox .40 1.00
282 Steve Huntz .40 1.00
283 Angel Bravo RC .40 1.00
284 Jack Baldschun .40 1.00
285 Paul Blair .60 1.50
286 J.Jenkins RC/B.Buckner RC 8.00 20.00
287 Fred Talbot .40 1.00
288 Larry Hisle .60 1.50
289 Gene Brabender .40 1.00
290 Rod Carew 10.00 25.00
291 Leo Durocher MG 1.25 3.00
292 Eddie Leon RC .40 1.00
293 Bob Bailey .60 1.50
294 Jose Azcue .40 1.00
295 Cecil Upshaw .40 1.00
296 Woody Woodward .40 1.00
297 Curt Blefary .40 1.00
298 Ken Henderson .40 1.00
299 Buddy Bradford .40 1.00
300 Tom Seaver 12.00 30.00
301 Chico Salmon .40 1.00
302 Jeff James .40 1.00
303 Brant Alyea .40 1.00
304 Bill Russell RC 2.00 5.00
305 Don Buford WS1 1.50 4.00
306 Donn Clendenon WS2 1.50 4.00
307 Tommie Agee WS3 1.50 4.00
308 J.C. Martin WS4 1.50 4.00
309 Jerry Koosman WS5 1.50 4.00
310 Mets Celebrate WS 2.00 5.00
311 Dick Green .40 1.00
312 Mike Torrez .40 1.00
313 Mayo Smith MG .40 1.00
314 Bill McCool .40 1.00
315 Luis Aparicio 4.00 10.00
316 Skip Guinn .40 1.00
317 B.Conigliaro/L.Alvarado RC .60 1.50
318 Willie Smith .40 1.00
319 Clay Dalrymple .40 1.00
320 Jim Maloney .60 1.50
321 Lou Piniella .60 1.50
322 Luke Walker .40 1.00
323 Wayne Comer .40 1.00
324 Tony Taylor .60 1.50
325 Dave Boswell .40 1.00
326 Bill Voss .40 1.00
327 Hal King RC .40 1.00
328 George Brunet .40 1.00
329 Chris Cannizzaro .40 1.00
330 Lou Brock 10.00 25.00
331 Chuck Dobson .40 1.00
332 Bobby Wine .40 1.00
333 Bobby Murcer .60 1.50

334 Phil Regan .40 1.00
335 Bill Freehan .60 1.50
336 Del Unser .40 1.00
337 Mike McCormick .60 1.50
338 Paul Schaal .40 1.00
339 Johnny Edwards .40 1.00
340 Tony Conigliaro 1.25 3.00
341 Bill Sudakis .40 1.00
342 Wilbur Wood .60 1.50
343A Checklist 4 Red Bat 2.50 6.00
343B Checklist 4 Brown Bat 2.50 6.00
344 Marcelino Lopez .40 1.00
345 Al Ferrara .40 1.00
346 Red Schoendienst MG .60 1.50
347 Russ Snyder .40 1.00
348 M.Jorgensen RC/J.Hudson RC .60 1.50
349 Steve Hamilton .40 1.00
350 Roberto Clemente 30.00 80.00
351 Tom Murphy .40 1.00
352 Bob Barton .40 1.00
353 Stan Williams .40 1.00
354 Amos Otis .60 1.50
355 Doug Rader .40 1.00
356 Fred Lasher .40 1.00
357 Bob Burda .40 1.00
358 Pedro Borbon RC .60 1.50
359 Phil Roof .40 1.00
360 Curt Flood .60 1.50
361 Ray Jarvis .40 1.00
362 Joe Hague .40 1.00
363 Tom Shopay RC .40 1.00
364 Dan McGinn .40 1.00
365 Zoilo Versalles .40 1.00
366 Barry Moore .40 1.00
367 Mike Lum .40 1.00
368 Ed Herrmann .40 1.00
369 Alan Foster .40 1.00
370 Tommy Harper .60 1.50
371 Rod Gaspar RC .40 1.00
372 Dave Giusti .40 1.00
373 Roy White .75 2.00
374 Tommie Sisk .60 1.50
375 Johnny Callison .75 2.00
376 Lefty Phillips MG RC .60 1.50
377 Bill Butler .60 1.50
378 Jim Davenport .60 1.50
379 Tom Tischinski RC .60 1.50
380 Tony Perez 2.50 6.00
381 B.Brooks RC/M.Olivo RC .60 1.50
382 Jack DiLauro RC .60 1.50
383 Mickey Stanley .75 2.00
384 Gary Neibauer .60 1.50
385 George Scott .75 2.00
386 Bill Dillman .60 1.50
387 Baltimore Orioles TC 1.25 3.00
388 Byron Browne .60 1.50
389 Jim Shellenback .60 1.50
390 Willie Davis .75 2.00
391 Larry Brown .60 1.50
392 Walt Hriniak .75 2.00
393 John Gelnar .60 1.50
394 Gil Hodges MG 1.50 4.00
395 Walt Williams .60 1.50
396 Steve Blass .75 2.00
397 Roger Repoz .60 1.50
398 Bill Stoneman .60 1.50
399 New York Yankees TC 1.25 3.00
400 Denny McLain 1.50 4.00
401 J.Harrell RC/B.Williams RC .60 1.50
402 Ellie Rodriguez .60 1.50
403 Jim Bunning 5.00 12.00
404 Rich Reese .60 1.50
405 Bill Hands .60 1.50
406 Mike Andrews .60 1.50
407 Bob Watson .75 2.00
408 Paul Lindblad .60 1.50
409 Bob Tolan .60 1.50
410 Boog Powell 1.50 4.00
411 Los Angeles Dodgers TC 1.25 3.00
412 Larry Burchart .60 1.50
413 Sonny Jackson .60 1.50
414 Paul Edmondson RC .60 1.50
415 Julian Javier .75 2.00
416 Joe Verbanic .60 1.50
417 John Bateman .60 1.50
418 John Donaldson .60 1.50
419 Ron Taylor .60 1.50
420 Ken McMullen .75 2.00
421 Pat Dobson .75 2.00
422 Kansas City Royals TC 1.25 3.00
423 Jerry May .60 1.50
424 Mike Kilkenny .60 1.50
425 Bobby Bonds 2.50 6.00
426 Bill Rigney MG .60 1.50
427 Fred Norman .60 1.50
428 Don Buford .60 1.50
429 R.Bobb RC/J.Cosman .60 1.50
430 Andy Messersmith .75 2.00
431 Ron Swoboda .75 2.00
432A Checklist 5 Yellow Ltr 2.50 6.00
432B Checklist 5 White Ltr 2.50 6.00
433 Ron Bryant RC .75 2.00
434 Felipe Alou .75 2.00
435 Nelson Briles .75 2.00
436 Philadelphia Phillies TC 1.25 3.00
437 Danny Cater .60 1.50
438 Pat Jarvis .60 1.50
439 Lee Maye .60 1.50
440 Bill Mazeroski 2.50 6.00
441 John O'Donoghue .60 1.50
442 Gene Mauch MG .75 2.00
443 Al Jackson .60 1.50
444 B.Farmer RC/J.Matias RC .60 1.50
445 Vada Pinson .75 2.00
446 Billy Grabarkewitz RC .60 1.50
447 Lee Stange .60 1.50
448 Houston Astros TC 1.25 3.00
449 Jim Palmer 10.00 25.00
450 Willie McCovey AS 8.00 20.00
451 Boog Powell AS 1.50 4.00
452 Felix Millan AS .75 2.00
453 Rod Carew AS 2.50 6.00
454 Ron Santo AS 1.50 4.00
455 Brooks Robinson AS 2.50 6.00
456 Don Kessinger AS .75 2.00
457 Rico Petrocelli AS 1.50 4.00
458 Pete Rose AS 12.00 30.00
459 Reggie Jackson AS 8.00 20.00
460 Matty Alou AS 1.25 3.00
461 Carl Yastrzemski AS 8.00 20.00
462 Hank Aaron AS 20.00 50.00
463 Frank Robinson AS 10.00 25.00
464 Johnny Bench AS 15.00 40.00
465 Bill Freehan AS 1.25 3.00
466 Juan Marichal AS 2.00 5.00
467 Denny McLain AS 1.25 3.00
468 Jerry Koosman AS 1.25 3.00
469 Sam McDowell AS 1.25 3.00
470 Willie Stargell 8.00 20.00
471 Chris Zachary .75 2.00
472 Atlanta Braves TC 1.50 4.00
473 Don Bryant .75 2.00
474 Dick Kelley .75 2.00
475 Dick McAuliffe 1.25 3.00
476 Don Shaw .75 2.00
477 A.Severinsen RC/R.Freed RC .75 2.00
478 Bobby Heise RC .75 2.00
479 Dick Woodson RC .75 2.00
480 Glenn Beckert 1.25 3.00
481 Jose Tartabull .75 2.00
482 Tom Hilgendorf RC .75 2.00
483 Gail Hopkins RC .75 2.00
484 Gary Nolan 1.25 3.00
485 Jay Johnstone 1.25 3.00
486 Terry Harmon .75 2.00
487 Cisco Carlos .75 2.00
488 J.C. Martin .75 2.00
489 Eddie Kasko MG .75 2.00
490 Bill Singer 1.25 3.00
491 Graig Nettles 2.00 5.00
492 K.Lampard RC/S.Spinks RC .75 2.00
493 Lindy McDaniel 1.25 3.00
494 Larry Stahl .75 2.00
495 Dave Morehead .75 2.00
496 Steve Whitaker .75 2.00
497 Eddie Watt .75 2.00
498 Al Weis .75 2.00
499 Skip Lockwood 1.25 3.00
500 Hank Aaron 25.00 60.00
501 Chicago White Sox TC 1.50 4.00
502 Rollie Fingers 10.00 25.00
503 Dal Maxvill .75 2.00
504 Don Pavletich .75 2.00
505 Ken Holtzman 1.25 3.00
506 Ed Stroud .75 2.00
507 Pat Corrales .75 2.00
508 Joe Niekro 1.25 3.00
509 Montreal Expos TC 1.50 4.00
510 Tony Oliva 2.00 5.00
511 Joe Hoerner .75 2.00
512 Billy Harris .75 2.00
513 Preston Gomez MG .75 2.00
514 Steve Hovley RC .75 2.00
515 Don Wilson 1.25 3.00
516 J.Ellis RC/J.Lyttle RC .75 2.00
517 Joe Gibbon .75 2.00
518 Bill Melton .75 2.00
519 Don McMahon .75 2.00
520 Willie Horton 1.25 3.00
521 Cal Koonce .75 2.00
522 California Angels TC 1.50 4.00
523 Jose Pena .75 2.00
524 Alvin Dark MG 1.25 3.00
525 Jerry Adair .75 2.00
526 Ron Herbel .75 2.00
527 Don Bosch .75 2.00
528 Elrod Hendricks .75 2.00
529 Bob Aspromonte .75 2.00
530 Bob Gibson 10.00 25.00
531 Ron Clark .75 2.00
532 Danny Murtaugh MG 1.25 3.00
533 Buzz Stephen RC .75 2.00
534 Minnesota Twins TC 1.50 4.00
535 Andy Kosco .75 2.00
536 Mike Kekich .75 2.00
537 Joe Morgan 10.00 25.00
538 Bob Humphreys .75 2.00
539 D.Doyle RC/L.Bowa RC 3.00 8.00
540 Gary Peters .75 2.00
541 Bill Heath .75 2.00
542A Checklist 6 Brown Bat 2.50 6.00
542B Checklist 6 Gray Bat 2.50 6.00
543 Clyde Wright .75 2.00
544 Cincinnati Reds TC 1.50 4.00
545 Ken Harrelson 1.25 3.00
546 Ron Reed .75 2.00
547 Rick Monday 2.50 6.00
548 Howie Reed 1.50 4.00
549 St. Louis Cardinals TC 2.50 6.00
550 Frank Howard 2.50 6.00
551 Dock Ellis 2.50 6.00
552 O'Riley/Paepke/Rico RC 1.50 4.00
553 Jim Lefebvre 2.50 6.00
554 Tom Timmermann RC 1.50 4.00
555 Orlando Cepeda 5.00 12.00
556 Dave Bristol MG 2.50 6.00
557 Ed Kranepool 2.50 6.00
558 Vern Fuller 1.50 4.00
559 Tommy Davis 2.50 6.00
560 Gaylord Perry 5.00 12.00
561 Tom McCraw 1.50 4.00
562 Ted Abernathy 1.50 4.00
563 Boston Red Sox TC 2.50 6.00
564 Johnny Briggs 1.50 4.00
565 Jim Hunter 8.00 20.00
566 Gene Alley 2.50 6.00
567 Bob Oliver 1.50 4.00
568 Stan Bahnsen 2.50 6.00
569 Cookie Rojas 2.50 6.00
570 Jim Fregosi 2.50 6.00
571 Jim Brewer 1.50 4.00
572 Frank Quilici 1.50 4.00
573 Corkins/Robles/Slocum RC 1.50 4.00
574 Bobby Bolin 2.50 6.00
575 Cleon Jones 2.50 6.00
576 Milt Pappas 2.50 6.00
577 Bernie Allen 1.50 4.00
578 Tom Griffin 1.50 4.00
579 Detroit Tigers TC 2.50 6.00
580 Pete Rose 30.00 60.00
581 Tom Satriano 1.50 4.00
582 Mike Paul 1.50 4.00
583 Hal Lanier 1.50 4.00
584 Al Downing 2.50 6.00
585 Rusty Staub 3.00 8.00
586 Rickey Clark RC 1.50 4.00
587 Jose Arcia 1.50 4.00
588A Checklist 7 Adolfo 3.00 8.00
588B Checklist 7 Adolpho 2.50 6.00
589 Joe Keough 1.50 4.00
590 Mike Cuellar 2.50 6.00
591 Mike Ryan UER 1.50 4.00
592 Daryl Patterson 1.50 4.00
593 Chicago Cubs TC 3.00 8.00
594 Jake Gibbs 1.50 4.00
595 Maury Wills 5.00 12.00
596 Mike Hershberger 2.50 6.00
597 Sonny Siebert 1.50 4.00
598 Joe Pepitone 2.50 6.00
599 Stelmaszek/Martin/Such RC 1.50 4.00
600 Willie Mays 40.00 100.00
601 Pete Richert 1.50 4.00
602 Ted Savage 1.50 4.00
603 Ray Oyler 1.50 4.00
604 Clarence Gaston 2.50 6.00
605 Rick Wise 2.50 6.00
606 Chico Ruiz 1.50 4.00
607 Gary Waslewski 1.50 4.00
608 Pittsburgh Pirates TC 2.50 6.00
609 Buck Martinez RC 2.50 6.00
610 Jerry Koosman 3.00 8.00
611 Norm Cash 2.50 6.00
612 Jim Hickman 2.50 6.00
613 Dave Baldwin 2.50 6.00
614 Mike Shannon 2.50 6.00
615 Mark Belanger 2.50 6.00
616 Jim Merritt 1.50 4.00
617 Jim French 1.50 4.00
618 Billy Wynne RC 1.50 4.00
619 Norm Miller 1.50 4.00
620 Jim Perry 2.50 6.00
621 McQueen/Evans/Kester RC 5.00 12.00
622 Don Sutton 5.00 12.00
623 Horace Clarke 2.50 6.00
624 Clyde King MG 1.50 4.00
625 Dean Chance 1.50 4.00
626 Dave Ricketts 1.50 4.00
627 Gary Wagner 1.50 4.00
628 Wayne Garrett RC 1.50 4.00
629 Merv Rettenmund 1.50 4.00
630 Ernie Banks 25.00 60.00
631 Oakland Athletics TC 2.50 6.00
632 Gary Sutherland 1.50 4.00
633 Roger Nelson 1.50 4.00
634 Bud Harrelson 6.00 15.00
635 Bob Allison 6.00 15.00
636 Jim Stewart 4.00 10.00
637 Cleveland Indians TC 5.00 12.00
638 Frank Bertaina 4.00 10.00
639 Dave Campbell 6.00 15.00
640 Al Kaline 25.00 60.00
641 Al McBean 4.00 10.00
642 Garrett/Lund/Tatum RC 4.00 10.00
643 Jose Pagan 4.00 10.00
644 Gerry Nyman 4.00 10.00
645 Don Money 6.00 15.00
646 Jim Britton 4.00 10.00
647 Tom Matchick 4.00 10.00
648 Larry Haney 4.00 10.00
649 Jimmie Hall 4.00 10.00
650 Sam McDowell 6.00 15.00
651 Jim Gosger 4.00 10.00
652 Rich Rollins 6.00 15.00
653 Moe Drabowsky 4.00 10.00
654 Gamble/Day/Mangual RC 8.00 20.00
655 John Roseboro 6.00 15.00
656 Jim Hardin 4.00 10.00
657 San Diego Padres TC 6.00 15.00
658 Ken Tatum RC 4.00 10.00
659 Pete Ward 4.00 10.00
660 Johnny Bench 60.00 150.00
661 Jerry Robertson 4.00 10.00
662 Frank Lucchesi MG RC 4.00 10.00
663 Tito Francona 4.00 10.00
664 Bob Robertson 4.00 10.00
665 Jim Lonborg 6.00 15.00
666 Adolpho Phillips 4.00 10.00
667 Bob Meyer 6.00 15.00
668 Bob Tillman 4.00 10.00
669 Johnson/Lazar/Scott RC 4.00 10.00
670 Ron Santo 10.00 25.00
671 Jim Campanis 4.00 10.00
672 Leon McFadden 4.00 10.00
673 Ted Uhlaender 4.00 10.00
674 Dave Leonhard 4.00 10.00
675 Jose Cardenal 6.00 15.00
676 Washington Senators TC 5.00 12.00
677 Woodie Fryman 4.00 10.00
678 Dave Duncan 6.00 15.00
679 Ray Sadecki 4.00 10.00
680 Rico Petrocelli 6.00 15.00
681 Bob Garibaldi RC 4.00 10.00
682 Dalton Jones 4.00 10.00
683 Geishart/McRae/Simpson RC 6.00 15.00
684 Jack Fisher 4.00 10.00
685 Tom Haller 4.00 10.00
686 Jackie Hernandez 4.00 10.00
687 Bob Priddy 4.00 10.00
688 Ted Kubiak 6.00 15.00
689 Frank Tepedino RC 6.00 15.00
690 Ron Fairly 6.00 15.00
691 Joe Grzenda 4.00 10.00
692 Duffy Dyer 4.00 10.00
693 Bob Johnson 4.00 10.00
694 Gary Ross 4.00 10.00
695 Bobby Knoop 4.00 10.00
696 San Francisco Giants TC 5.00 12.00
697 Jim Hannan 4.00 10.00
698 Tom Tresh 6.00 15.00
699 Hank Aguirre 4.00 10.00
700 Frank Robinson 25.00 60.00
701 Jack Billingham 4.00 10.00
702 Johnson/Klimkowski/Zepp RC 4.00 10.00
703 Lou Marone RC 4.00 10.00
704 Frank Baker RC 4.00 10.00
705 Tony Cloninger UER 4.00 10.00
706 John McNamara MG RC 4.00 10.00
707 Kevin Collins 4.00 10.00
708 Jose Santiago 4.00 10.00
709 Mike Fiore 4.00 10.00
710 Felix Millan 4.00 10.00
711 Ed Brinkman 4.00 10.00
712 Nolan Ryan 100.00 250.00
713 Seattle Pilots TC 10.00 25.00
714 Al Spangler 4.00 10.00
715 Mickey Lolich 6.00 15.00
716 Campisi/Cleveland/Guzman RC 6.00 15.00
717 Tom Phoebus 4.00 10.00
718 Ed Spiezio 4.00 10.00
719 Jim Roland 4.00 10.00
720 Rick Reichardt 6.00 15.00

1970 Topps Booklets

Inserted into packages of the 1970 Topps (and O-Pee-Chee) regular issue of cards, there are 24 miniature biographies of ballplayers in the set. Each numbered paper booklet, which features one player per team, contains six pages of comic book style story and a checklist of the booklet is available on the back page. These little booklets measure approximately 2 1/2" by 3 7/16".

COMPLETE SET (24) 15.00 40.00
COMMON CARD (1-16) .40 1.00
COMMON CARD (17-24) .40 1.00
1 Mike Cuellar .40 1.00
2 Rico Petrocelli .40 1.00
3 Jay Johnstone .40 1.00
4 Walt Williams .40 1.00
5 Vada Pinson .40 1.00
6 Bill Freehan .40 1.00
7 Wally Bunker .40 1.00
8 Tony Oliva .60 1.50
9 Bobby Murcer .40 1.00
10 Reggie Jackson 2.50 6.00
11 Tommy Harper .40 1.00
12 Mike Epstein .40 1.00
13 Orlando Cepeda .60 1.50
14 Ernie Banks 1.50 4.00
15 Pete Rose 2.50 6.00
16 Denis Menke .40 1.00
17 Bill Singer .40 1.00
18 Rusty Staub .60 1.50
19 Cleon Jones .40 1.00
20 Deron Johnson .40 1.00
21 Bob Moose .40 1.00
22 Bob Gibson 1.00 2.50
23 Al Ferrara .40 1.00
24 Willie Mays 3.00 8.00

1970 Topps Posters Inserts

In 1970 Topps raised its price per package of cards to ten cents, and a series of 24 color posters was included as a bonus to the collector. Each thin-paper poster is numbered and features a large portrait and a smaller black and white action pose. It was folded five times to fit in the packaging. Each poster measures 8 11/16" by 9 5/8".

COMPLETE SET (24) 30.00 60.00
1 Joe Horlen .60 1.50
2 Phil Niekro .75 2.00
3 Willie Davis .60 1.50
4 Lou Brock 2.00 5.00
5 Ron Santo 1.25 3.00
6 Ken Harrelson .60 1.50
7 Willie McCovey 2.00 5.00
8 Rick Wise .60 1.50
9 Andy Messersmith .60 1.50
10 Ron Fairly .60 1.50
11 Johnny Bench 4.00 10.00
12 Frank Robinson 2.00 5.00
13 Tommie Agee .60 1.50
14 Roy White .60 1.50
15 Larry Dierker .60 1.50
16 Rod Carew 2.00 5.00
17 Don Mincher .60 1.50
18 Ollie Brown .60 1.50
19 Ed Kirkpatrick .60 1.50
20 Reggie Smith .75 2.00
21 Roberto Clemente 8.00 20.00
22 Frank Howard .75 2.00
23 Bert Campaneris .75 2.00
24 Denny McLain .75 2.00

1970 Topps Scratchoffs

The 1970 Topps Scratch-off inserts are heavy cardboard, folded inserts issued with the regular card series of those years. Unfolded, they form a game board upon which a baseball game is played by means of rubbing off black ink from the playing squares to reveal moves. Inserts with white centers were issued in 1970 and inserts with red centers in 1971. Unfolded, these inserts measure 3 3/8" by 5". Obviously, a card which has been scratched off can be considered to be in no better than vg condition.

COMPLETE SET (24) 20.00 50.00
COMMON CARD (1-24) .40 1.00
1 Hank Aaron 3.00 8.00
2 Rich Allen .60 1.50
3 Luis Aparicio 1.00 2.50
4 Sal Bando .60 1.50
5 Glenn Beckert .40 1.00
6 Dick Bosman .40 1.00
7 Nate Colbert .40 1.00
8 Mike Hegan .40 1.00
9 Mack Jones .40 1.00
10 Al Kaline 2.00 5.00
11 Harmon Killebrew 2.00 5.00
12 Juan Marichal 1.00 2.50
13 Tim McCarver .60 1.50
14 Sam McDowell .60 1.50
15 Claude Osteen .40 1.00
16 Tony Perez 1.00 2.50
17 Lou Piniella .60 1.50
18 Boog Powell 1.00 2.50
19 Tom Seaver 2.00 5.00
20 Jim Spencer .40 1.00
21 Willie Stargell 1.50 4.00
22 Mel Stottlemyre .60 1.50
23 Jim Wynn .60 1.50
24 Carl Yastrzemski 2.50 6.00

1971 Topps

The cards in this 752-card set measure 2 1/2" by 3 1/2". The 1971 Topps set is a challenge to complete in strict mint condition because the black obverse border is easily scratched and damaged. An unusual feature of this set is that the player is also pictured in black and white on the back of the card. Featured subsets within this set include League Leaders (61-72), Playoffs cards (195-202), and World Series cards (327-332). Cards 524-643 and the last series (644-752) are somewhat scarce. The last series was printed in two sheets of 132. On the printing sheets 44 cards were printed in 50 percent greater quantity than the other 66 cards. These 66 (slightly) shorter-printed numbers are identified in the checklist below by SP. The key Rookie Cards in this set are the multi-player Rookie Card of Dusty Baker and Don Baylor and the individual cards of Bert Blyleven, Dave Concepcion, Steve Garvey, and Ted Simmons. The Jim Northrup and Jim Nash cards have been seen with our without printing "blotches" on the card. There is still debate on whether those two cards are just printing issues or legitimate variations. Among the ways these cards were issued was in 54-card rack packs which retailed for 39 cents.

COMPLETE SET (752) 1500.00 3000.00
COMMON CARD (1-393) .60 1.50
COMMON CARD (394-523) 1.00 2.50
COMMON CARD (524-643) 1.50 4.00
COMMON CARD (644-752) 3.00 8.00
COMMON SP (644-752) 5.00 12.00
WRAPPER (10-CENT) 6.00 15.00
1 Baltimore Orioles TC 8.00 20.00
2 Dock Ellis .75 2.00
3 Dick McAuliffe .75 2.00
4 Vic Davalillo .75 2.00
5 Thurman Munson 60.00 120.00
6 Ed Spiezio .60 1.50
7 Jim Holt RC .60 1.50
8 Mike McQueen 1.50
9 George Scott .75 2.00
10 Claude Osteen .60 1.50
11 Elliott Maddox RC .60 1.50
12 Johnny Callison .75 2.00
13 C.Brinkman RC/D.Moloney RC .60 1.50
14 Dave Concepcion RC 15.00 40.00
15 Andy Messersmith .75 2.00
16 Ken Singleton RC 1.50 4.00
17 Billy Sorrell .60 1.50
18 Norm Miller .60 1.50
19 Skip Pitlock RC .60 1.50
20 Reggie Jackson 30.00 80.00
21 Dan McGinn .60 1.50
22 Phil Roof .60 1.50
23 Oscar Gamble .60 1.50
24 Rich Hand RC .60 1.50
25 Clarence Gaston .75 2.00
26 Bert Blyleven RC 30.00 80.00
27 F.Cambria RC/G.Clines RC .60 1.50
28 Ron Klimkowski .60 1.50
29 Don Buford .60 1.50
30 Phil Niekro 8.00 20.00
31 Eddie Kasko MG .60 1.50
32 Jerry DaVanon .60 1.50
33 Del Unser .60 1.50
34 Sandy Vance RC .60 1.50
35 Lou Piniella .75 2.00
36 Dean Chance .75 2.00
37 Rich McKinney RC .60 1.50
38 Jim Colborn RC .60 1.50
39 L.LaGrow RC/G.Lamont RC .75 2.00
40 Lee May .75 2.00
41 Rick Austin RC .60 1.50
42 Boots Day .60 1.50
43 Steve Kealey .60 1.50
44 Johnny Edwards .60 1.50
45 Jim Hunter 6.00 15.00
46 Dave Campbell .75 2.00
47 Johnny Jeter .60 1.50
48 Dave Baldwin .60 1.50
49 Don Money .60 1.50
50 Willie McCovey 10.00 25.00
51 Steve Kline RC .60 1.50
52 O.Brown RC/E.Williams RC .60 1.50
53 Paul Blair .75 2.00
54 Checklist 1 4.00 10.00
55 Steve Carlton 12.00 30.00
56 Duane Josephson .60 1.50
57 Von Joshua RC .60 1.50
58 Bill Lee .75 2.00
59 Gene Mauch MG .75 2.00
60 Dick Bosman .60 1.50
61 Johnson/Yaz/Oliva LL 1.50 4.00
62 Carty/Torre/Sang LL .75 2.00
63 Howard/Conig/Powell LL 1.50 4.00
64 Bench/Perez/B.Will LL 2.50 6.00
65 Howard/Killebrew/Yaz LL 1.50 4.00
66 Bench/B.Will/Perez LL 2.50 6.00
67 Segui/Palmer/Wright LL 1.50 4.00
68 Seaver/Simp/Walk LL 1.50 4.00
69 Cuellar/McNally/Perry LL .75 2.00
70 Gibson/Perry/Jenkins LL 2.50 6.00
71 McDowell/Lolich/John LL .75 2.00
72 Seaver/Gibson/Jenkins LL 2.50 6.00
73 George Brunet .60 1.50
74 P.Hamm RC/J.Nettles RC .60 1.50
75 Gary Nolan .60 1.50
76 Ted Savage .60 1.50
77 Mike Compton RC .60 1.50
78 Jim Spencer .60 1.50
79 Wade Blasingame .60 1.50
80 Bill Melton .60 1.50
81 Felix Millan .60 1.50
82 Casey Cox .60 1.50
83 T.Foli RC/R.Bobb .75 2.00
84 Marcel Lachemann RC .60 1.50
85 Billy Grabarkewitz .60 1.50
86 Mike Kilkenny .60 1.50
87 Jack Heidemann RC .60 1.50
88 Hal King .60 1.50
89 Ken Brett .60 1.50
90 Joe Pepitone .75 2.00
91 Bob Lemon MG .75 2.00
92 Fred Wenz .60 1.50
93 N.McRae/D.Riddleberger .60 1.50
94 Don Hahn RC .60 1.50
95 Luis Tiant .75 2.00
96 Joe Hague .60 1.50
97 Floyd Wicker .60 1.50
98 Joe Decker RC .60 1.50
99 Mark Belanger .75 2.00
100 Pete Rose 25.00 60.00
101 Les Cain .60 1.50
102 K.Forsch RC/L.Howard RC .75 2.00
103 Rich Severson RC .60 1.50
104 Dan Frisella .60 1.50
105 Tony Conigliaro .75 2.00
106 Tom Dukes .60 1.50
107 Roy Foster RC .60 1.50
108 John Cumberland .60 1.50
109 Steve Hovley .60 1.50
110 Bill Mazeroski 10.00 25.00
111 L.Colson RC/B.Mitchell RC .60 1.50
112 Manny Mota .75 2.00
113 Jerry Crider .60 1.50
114 Billy Conigliaro .60 1.50
115 Donn Clendenon .75 2.00
116 Ken Sanders .60 1.50
117 Ted Simmons RC 60.00 150.00
118 Cookie Rojas .75 2.00
119 Frank Lucchesi MG .60 1.50
120 Willie Horton .75 2.00
121 J.Dunegan/R.Skidmore RC .60 1.50
122 Eddie Watt .60 1.50
123A Checklist 2 Right 4.00 10.00
123B Checklist 2 Centered 4.00 10.00
124 Don Gullett RC .75 2.00
125 Ray Fosse .60 1.50
126 Danny Coombs .60 1.50
127 Danny Thompson RC .75 2.00
128 Frank Johnson .60 1.50
129 Aurelio Monteagudo .60 1.50
130 Denis Menke .60 1.50
131 Curt Blefary .60 1.50
132 Jose Laboy .60 1.50
133 Mickey Lolich .75 2.00
134 Jose Arcia .60 1.50
135 Rick Monday .75 2.00
136 Duffy Dyer .60 1.50
137 Marcelino Lopez .60 1.50
138 J.Lis/W.Montanez RC .75 2.00
139 Paul Casanova .60 1.50
140 Gaylord Perry 2.50 6.00
141 Frank Quilici .60 1.50
142 Mack Jones .60 1.50
143 Steve Blass .75 2.00
144 Jackie Hernandez .60 1.50
145 Bill Singer .75 2.00
146 Ralph Houk MG .75 2.00
147 Bob Priddy .60 1.50
148 John Mayberry .75 2.00
149 Mike Hershberger .60 1.50
150 Sam McDowell .75 2.00
151 Tommy Davis .75 2.00
152 L.Allen RC/W.Llenas RC .60 1.50
153 Gary Ross .60 1.50
154 Cesar Gutierrez .60 1.50
155 Ken Henderson .60 1.50
156 Bart Johnson .60 1.50
157 Bob Bailey .75 2.00
158 Jerry Reuss .75 2.00
159 Jarvis Tatum .60 1.50
160 Tom Seaver 15.00 40.00
161 Coin Checklist 4.00 10.00
162 Jack Billingham .60 1.50
163 Buck Martinez .75 2.00
164 F.Duffy RC/M.Wilcox RC .75 2.00
165 Cesar Tovar .60 1.50
166 Joe Hoerner .60 1.50
167 Tom Grieve RC .75 2.00
168 Bruce Dal Canton .60 1.50
169 Ed Herrmann .60 1.50
170 Mike Cuellar .75 2.00
171 Bobby Wine .60 1.50
172 Duke Sims .60 1.50
173 Gil Garrido .60 1.50
174 Dave LaRoche RC .60 1.50
175 Jim Hickman .60 1.50
176 B.Montgomery RC/D.Griffin RC .75 2.00
177 Hal McRae .75 2.00
178 Dave Duncan .75 2.00
179 Mike Corkins .60 1.50
180 Al Kaline UER 20.00 50.00
181 Hal Lanier .60 1.50
182 Al Downing .75 2.00
183 Gil Hodges MG 1.50 4.00
184 Stan Bahnsen .60 1.50
185 Julian Javier .60 1.50
186 Bob Spence RC .60 1.50
187 Ted Abernathy .60 1.50
188 B.Valentine RC/M.Strahler RC 6.00 15.00
189 George Mitterwald .60 1.50
190 Bob Tolan .60 1.50
191 Mike Andrews .60 1.50
192 Billy Wilson .60 1.50
193 Bob Grich RC 1.50 4.00
194 Mike Lum .60 1.50
195 Boog Powell ALCS .75 2.00
196 Dave McNally ALCS .75 2.00
197 Jim Palmer ALCS 1.50 4.00
198 Orioles Celebrate ALCS .75 2.00
199 Ty Cline NLCS .75 2.00
200 Bobby Tolan NLCS .75 2.00
201 Ty Cline NLCS .75 2.00
202 Reds Celebrate NLCS .75 2.00
203 Larry Gura RC .75 2.00
204 B.Smith RC/G.Kopacz RC .60 1.50
205 Gerry Moses .60 1.50
206 Checklist 3 4.00 10.00
207 Alan Foster .60 1.50
208 Billy Martin MG 1.50 4.00
209 Steve Renko .60 1.50
210 Rod Carew 12.00 30.00
211 Phil Hennigan RC .60 1.50
212 Rich Hebner .75 2.00
213 Frank Baker RC .60 1.50
214 Al Ferrara .60 1.50
215 Diego Segui .60 1.50
216 R.Cleveland/L.Melendez RC .60 1.50
217 Ed Stroud .60 1.50
218 Tony Cloninger .60 1.50
219 Elrod Hendricks .60 1.50
220 Ron Santo 1.50 4.00
221 Dave Morehead .60 1.50
222 Bob Watson .75 2.00
223 Cecil Upshaw .60 1.50
224 Alan Gallagher RC .60 1.50
225 Gary Peters .60 1.50
226 Bill Russell .75 2.00
227 Floyd Weaver .60 1.50
228 Wayne Garrett .60 1.50
229 Jim Hannan .60 1.50
230 Willie Stargell 20.00 50.00
231 V.Colbert RC/J.Lowenstein RC .75 2.00
232 John Strohmayer RC .60 1.50
233 Larry Bowa .75 2.00
234 Jim Lyttle .60 1.50
235 Nate Colbert .60 1.50
236 Bob Humphreys .60 1.50
237 Cesar Cedeno RC .75 2.00

Chuck Dobson	.60	1.50
Red Schoendienst MG	.75	2.00
Clyde Wright	.60	1.50
Dave Nelson	.60	1.50
Jim Ray	.60	1.50
Carlos May	.60	1.50
Bob Tillman	.60	1.50
Jim Kaat	.75	2.00
Tony Taylor	.60	1.50
J.Cram RC/P.Splittorff RC	.75	2.00
Hoyt Wilhelm	2.50	6.00
Chico Salmon	.60	1.50
Johnny Bench	25.00	60.00
Frank Reberger	.60	1.50
Eddie Leon	.60	1.50
Bill Sudakis	.60	1.50
Cal Koonce	.60	1.50
Bob Robertson	.75	2.00
Tony Gonzalez	.60	1.50
Nelson Briles	.75	2.00
3 Dick Green	.60	1.50
9 Dave Marshall	.60	1.50
) Tommy Harper	.75	2.00
Darold Knowles	.60	1.50
2 J.Williams/D.Robinson RC	.60	1.50
3 John Ellis	.60	1.50
4 Joe Morgan	15.00	40.00
5 Jim Northrup	.75	2.00
6 Bill Stoneman	.60	1.50
7 Rich Morales	.60	1.50
8 Philadelphia Phillies TC	1.50	4.00
9 Gail Hopkins	.60	1.50
) Rico Carty	.75	2.00
1 Bill Zepp	.60	1.50
2 Tommy Helms	.75	2.00
3 Pete Richert	.60	1.50
4 Ron Slocum	.60	1.50
5 Vada Pinson	.75	2.00
6 M.Davison RC/G.Foster RC	15.00	40.00
7 Cary Waslewski	.60	1.50
8 Jerry Grote	.75	2.00
79 Lefty Phillips MG	.60	1.50
0 Ferguson Jenkins	2.50	6.00
1 Danny Walton	.60	1.50
2 Jose Pagan	.60	1.50
3 Dick Such	.60	1.50
34 Jim Gosger	.60	1.50
35 Sal Bando	.75	2.00
36 Jerry McNertney	.60	1.50
37 Mike Fiore	.60	1.50
38 Joe Moeller	.60	1.50
39 Chicago White Sox TC	1.50	4.00
90 Tony Oliva	1.50	4.00
91 George Culver	.60	1.50
92 Jay Johnstone	.75	2.00
93 Pat Corrales	.75	2.00
94 Steve Dunning RC	.60	1.50
95 Bobby Bonds	1.50	4.00
96 Tom Timmermann	.60	1.50
97 Johnny Briggs	.60	1.50
98 Jim Nelson RC	.60	1.50
99 Ed Kirkpatrick	.60	1.50
00 Brooks Robinson	20.00	50.00
01 Earl Wilson	.60	1.50
02 Phil Gagliano	.60	1.50
03 Lindy McDaniel	.75	2.00
04 Ron Brand	.60	1.50
05 Reggie Smith	.75	2.00
06 Jim Nash	.60	1.50
07 Don Wert	.60	1.50
08 St. Louis Cardinals TC	1.50	4.00
09 Dick Ellsworth	.60	1.50
10 Tommie Agee	.75	2.00
11 Lee Stange	.60	1.50
312 Harry Walker MG	.60	1.50
313 Tom Hall	.60	1.50
314 Jeff Torborg	.75	2.00
315 Ron Fairly	.75	2.00
316 Fred Scherman RC	.60	1.50
317 J.Driscoll RC/A.Mangual	.60	1.50
318 Rudy May	.60	1.50
319 Ty Cline	.60	1.50
320 Dave McNally	.75	2.00
321 Tom Matchick	.60	1.50
322 Jim Beauchamp	.60	1.50
323 Billy Champion	.60	1.50
324 Graig Nettles	.75	2.00
325 Juan Marichal	10.00	25.00
326 Richie Scheinblum	.60	1.50
327 Boog Powell WS	.75	2.00
328 Don Buford WS	.75	2.00
329 Frank Robinson WS	1.50	4.00
330 Reds Stay Alive WS	.75	2.00
331 Brooks Robinson WS	2.50	6.00
332 Orioles Celebrate WS	.75	2.00
333 Clay Kirby	.60	1.50
334 Roberto Pena	.60	1.50
335 Jerry Koosman	.75	2.00
336 Detroit Tigers TC	1.50	4.00
337 Jesus Alou	.60	1.50
338 Gene Tenace	.75	2.00
339 Wayne Simpson	.60	1.50
340 Rico Petrocelli	.75	2.00
341 Steve Garvey RC	30.00	80.00
342 Frank Tepedino	.75	2.00
343 E.Acosta RC/M.May RC	.75	2.00
344 Ellie Rodriguez	.60	1.50
345 Joel Horlen	.60	1.50
346 Lum Harris MG	.60	1.50
347 Ted Uhlaender	.60	1.50
348 Fred Norman	.60	1.50
349 Rich Reese	.60	1.50
350 Billy Williams	2.50	6.00
351 Jim Shellenback	.60	1.50
352 Denny Doyle	.60	1.50
353 Carl Taylor	.60	1.50
354 Don McMahon	.60	1.50
355 Bud Harrelson	1.50	4.00
Nolan Ryan in photo		
356 Bob Locker	.60	1.50
357 Cincinnati Reds TC	1.50	4.00
358 Danny Cater	.60	1.50
359 Ron Reed	.60	1.50
360 Jim Fregosi	.75	2.00
361 Don Sutton	8.00	20.00
362 M.Adamson/R.Freed	.60	1.50
363 Mike Nagy	.60	1.50
364 Tommy Dean	.60	1.50
365 Bob Johnson	.60	1.50
366 Ron Stone	.60	1.50
367 Dalton Jones	.60	1.50
368 Bob Veale	.75	2.00
369 Checklist 4	4.00	10.00
370 Joe Torre	1.50	4.00
371 Jack Hiatt	.60	1.50
372 Lew Krausse	.60	1.50
373 Tom McCraw	.60	1.50
374 Clete Boyer	.75	2.00
375 Steve Hargan	.60	1.50
376 C.Mashore RC/E.McAnally RC	.60	1.50
377 Greg Garrett	.60	1.50
378 Tito Fuentes	.60	1.50
379 Wayne Granger	.60	1.50
380 Ted Williams MG	10.00	25.00
381 Fred Gladding	.60	1.50
382 Jake Gibbs	.60	1.50
383 Rod Gaspar	.60	1.50
384 Rollie Fingers	20.00	50.00
385 Maury Wills	1.50	4.00
386 Boston Red Sox TC	.75	2.00
387 Ron Herbel	.60	1.50
388 Al Oliver	1.50	4.00
389 Ed Brinkman	.60	1.50
390 Glenn Beckert	.75	2.00
391 S.Brye RC/C.Nash RC	.75	2.00
392 Grant Jackson	.60	1.50
393 Merv Rettenmund	.75	2.00
394 Clay Carroll	1.00	2.50
395 Roy White	1.50	4.00
396 Dick Schofield	1.00	2.50
397 Alvin Dark MG	1.50	4.00
398 Howie Reed	1.00	2.50
399 Jim French	1.00	2.50
400 Hank Aaron	40.00	100.00
401 Tom Murphy	1.00	2.50
402 Los Angeles Dodgers TC	2.50	6.00
403 Joe Coleman	1.00	2.50
404 B.Harris RC/R.Metzger RC	1.00	2.50
405 Leo Cardenas	1.00	2.50
406 Ray Sadecki	1.00	2.50
407 Joe Rudi	1.50	4.00
408 Rafael Robles	1.00	2.50
409 Don Pavletich	1.00	2.50
410 Ken Holtzman	1.50	4.00
411 George Spriggs	1.00	2.50
412 Jerry Johnson	1.00	2.50
413 Pat Kelly	1.00	2.50
414 Woodie Fryman	1.00	2.50
415 Mike Hegan	1.00	2.50
416 Gene Alley	1.00	2.50
417 Dick Hall	1.00	2.50
418 Adolfo Phillips	1.00	2.50
419 Ron Hansen	1.00	2.50
420 Jim Merritt	1.00	2.50
421 John Stephenson	1.00	2.50
422 Frank Bertaina	1.00	2.50
423 D.Saunders/T.Marting RC	1.00	2.50
424 Roberto Rodriquez	1.00	2.50
425 Doug Rader	1.50	4.00
426 Chris Cannizzaro	1.00	2.50
427 Bernie Allen	1.00	2.50
428 Jim McAndrew	1.00	2.50
429 Chuck Hinton	1.00	2.50
430 Wes Parker	1.50	4.00
431 Tom Burgmeier	1.00	2.50
432 Bob Didier	1.00	2.50
433 Skip Lockwood	1.00	2.50
434 Gary Sutherland	1.00	2.50
435 Jose Cardenal	1.50	4.00
436 Wilbur Wood	1.50	4.00
437 Danny Murtaugh MG	1.50	4.00
438 Mike McCormick	1.50	4.00
439 G.Luzinski RC/S.Reid	8.00	20.00
440 Bert Campaneris	1.50	4.00
441 Milt Pappas	1.50	4.00
442 California Angels TC	1.50	4.00
443 Rich Robertson	1.00	2.50
444 Jimmie Price	1.00	2.50
445 Art Shamsky	1.00	2.50
446 Bobby Bolin	1.00	2.50
447 Cesar Geronimo RC	1.50	4.00
448 Dave Roberts	1.00	2.50
449 Brant Alyea	1.00	2.50
450 Bob Gibson	20.00	50.00
451 Joe Keough	1.00	2.50
452 John Boccabella	1.00	2.50
453 Terry Crowley	1.00	2.50
454 Mike Paul	1.00	2.50
455 Don Kessinger	1.50	4.00
456 Bob Meyer	1.00	2.50
457 Willie Smith	1.00	2.50
458 R.Lolich RC/D.Lemonds RC	1.00	2.50
459 Jim Lefebvre	1.00	2.50
460 Fritz Peterson	1.00	2.50
461 Jim Ray Hart	1.00	2.50
462 Washington Senators TC	2.50	6.00
463 Tom Kelley	1.00	2.50
464 Aurelio Rodriguez	1.00	2.50
465 Tim McCarver	2.50	6.00
466 Ken Berry	1.00	2.50
467 Al Santorini	1.00	2.50
468 Frank Fernandez	1.00	2.50
469 Bob Aspromonte	1.00	2.50
470 Bob Oliver	1.00	2.50
471 Tom Griffin	1.00	2.50
472 Ken Rudolph	1.00	2.50
473 Gary Wagner	1.00	2.50
474 Jim Fairey	1.00	2.50
475 Ron Perranoski	1.00	2.50
476 Dal Maxvill	1.00	2.50
477 Earl Weaver MG	2.50	6.00
478 Bernie Carbo	1.00	2.50
479 Dennis Higgins	1.00	2.50
480 Manny Sanguillen	1.50	4.00
481 Daryl Patterson	1.00	2.50
482 San Diego Padres TC	2.50	6.00
483 Gene Michael	1.00	2.50
484 Don Wilson	1.00	2.50
485 Ken McMullen	1.00	2.50
486 Steve Huntz	1.00	2.50
487 Paul Schaal	1.00	2.50
488 Jerry Stephenson	1.00	2.50
489 Luis Alvarado	1.00	2.50
490 Deron Johnson	1.00	2.50
491 Jim Hardin	1.00	2.50
492 Ken Boswell	1.00	2.50
493 Dave May	1.00	2.50
494 R.Garr/R.Kester	1.50	4.00
495 Felipe Alou	1.50	4.00
496 Woody Woodward	1.00	2.50
497 Horacio Pina RC	1.00	2.50
498 John Kennedy	1.00	2.50
499 Checklist 5	4.00	10.00
500 Jim Perry	1.50	4.00
501 Andy Etchebarren	1.00	2.50
502 Chicago Cubs TC	2.50	6.00
503 Gates Brown	1.50	4.00
504 Ken Wright RC	1.00	2.50
505 Ollie Brown	1.00	2.50
506 Bobby Knoop	1.00	2.50
507 George Stone	1.00	2.50
508 Roger Repoz	1.00	2.50
509 Jim Grant	1.00	2.50
510 Ken Harrelson	1.50	4.00
511 Chris Short w/Rose	1.50	4.00
512 D.Mills RC/M.Garman RC	1.00	2.50
513 Nolan Ryan	60.00	150.00
514 Ron Woods	1.00	2.50
515 Carl Morton	1.00	2.50
516 Ted Kubiak	1.00	2.50
517 Charlie Fox MG RC	1.00	2.50
518 Joe Grzenda	1.00	2.50
519 Willie Crawford	1.00	2.50
520 Tommy John	2.50	6.00
521 Leron Lee	1.00	2.50
522 Minnesota Twins TC	2.50	6.00
523 John Odom	1.00	2.50
524 Mickey Stanley	2.50	6.00
525 Ernie Banks	50.00	120.00
526 Ray Jarvis	1.50	4.00
527 Cloon Jones	2.50	6.00
528 Wally Bunker	1.50	4.00
529 Hernandez/Bucker/Perez RC	2.50	6.00
530 Carl Yastrzemski	20.00	50.00
531 Mike Torrez	1.50	4.00
532 Bill Rigney MG	1.50	4.00
533 Mike Ryan	1.50	4.00
534 Luke Walker	1.50	4.00
535 Curt Flood	2.50	6.00
536 Claude Raymond	1.50	4.00
537 Tom Egan	1.50	4.00
538 Angel Bravo	1.50	4.00
539 Larry Brown	1.50	4.00
540 Larry Dierker	2.50	6.00
541 Bob Burda	1.50	4.00
542 Bob Miller	1.50	4.00
543 New York Yankees TC	4.00	10.00
544 Vida Blue	2.50	6.00
545 Dick Dietz	1.50	4.00
546 John Matias	1.50	4.00
547 Pat Dobson	2.50	6.00
548 Don Mason	1.50	4.00
549 Jim Brewer	2.50	6.00
550 Harmon Killebrew	20.00	50.00
551 Frank Linzy	1.50	4.00
552 Buddy Bradford	1.50	4.00
553 Kevin Collins	1.50	4.00
554 Lowell Palmer	1.50	4.00
555 Walt Williams	1.50	4.00
556 Jim McGlothlin	1.50	4.00
557 Tom Satriano	1.50	4.00
558 Hector Torres	1.50	4.00
559 Cox/Gogolewsk/Jones RC	1.50	4.00
560 Rusty Staub	2.50	6.00
561 Syd O'Brien	1.50	4.00
562 Dave Giusti	1.50	4.00
563 San Francisco Giants TC	3.00	8.00
564 Al Fitzmorris	1.50	4.00
565 Jim Wynn	2.50	6.00
566 Tim Cullen	1.50	4.00
567 Walt Alston MG	6.00	15.00
568 Sal Campisi	1.50	4.00
569 Ivan Murrell	1.50	4.00
570 Jim Palmer	10.00	25.00
571 Ted Sizemore	1.50	4.00
572 Jerry Kenney	1.50	4.00
573 Ed Kranepool	2.50	6.00
574 Jim Bunning	3.00	8.00
575 Bill Freehan	2.50	6.00
576 Garrett/Davis/Jestadt RC	1.50	4.00
577 Jim Lonborg	2.50	6.00
578 Ron Hunt	1.50	4.00
579 Marty Pattin	1.50	4.00
580 Tony Perez	20.00	50.00
581 Roger Nelson	1.50	4.00
582 Dave Cash	2.50	6.00
583 Ron Cook RC	1.50	4.00
584 Cleveland Indians TC	3.00	8.00
585 Willie Davis	2.50	6.00
586 Dick Woodson	1.50	4.00
587 Sonny Jackson	1.50	4.00
588 Tom Bradley RC	1.50	4.00
589 Bob Barton	1.50	4.00
590 Alex Johnson	2.50	6.00
591 Jackie Brown RC	1.50	4.00
592 Randy Hundley	2.50	6.00
593 Jack Aker	1.50	4.00
594 Chlupsa/Stinson/Hrabosky RC	2.50	6.00
595 Dave Johnson	2.50	6.00
596 Mike Jorgensen	1.50	4.00
597 Ken Suarez	1.50	4.00
598 Rick Wise	2.50	6.00
599 Norm Cash	2.50	6.00
600 Willie Mays	50.00	120.00
601 Ken Tatum	1.50	4.00
602 Marty Martinez	1.50	4.00
603 Pittsburgh Pirates TC	3.00	8.00
604 John Gelnar	1.50	4.00
605 Orlando Cepeda	6.00	15.00
606 Chuck Taylor	1.50	4.00
607 Paul Ratliff	1.50	4.00
608 Mike Wegener	1.50	4.00
609 Leo Durocher MG	3.00	8.00
610 Amos Otis	2.50	6.00
611 Tom Phoebus	1.50	4.00
612 Camilli/Ford/Mingori RC	1.50	4.00
613 Pedro Borbon	1.50	4.00
614 Billy Cowan	1.50	4.00
615 Mel Stottlemyre	2.50	6.00
616 Larry Hisle	2.50	6.00
617 Clay Dalrymple	1.50	4.00
618 Tug McGraw	2.50	6.00
619A Checklist 6 ERR w/o Copy	4.00	10.00
619B Checklist 6 COR w/Copy	2.50	6.00
620 Frank Howard	2.50	6.00
621 Ron Bryant	1.50	4.00
622 Joe Lahoud	1.50	4.00
623 Pat Jarvis	1.50	4.00
624 Oakland Athletics TC	3.00	8.00
625 Lou Brock	20.00	50.00
626 Freddie Patek	2.50	6.00
627 Steve Hamilton	1.50	4.00
628 John Bateman	1.50	4.00
629 John Hiller	2.50	6.00
630 Roberto Clemente	75.00	200.00
631 Eddie Fisher	1.50	4.00
632 Darrel Chaney	1.50	4.00
633 Brooks/Koegel/Northey RC	1.50	4.00
634 Phil Regan	1.50	4.00
635 Bobby Murcer	2.50	6.00
636 Denny Lemaster	1.50	4.00
637 Dave Bristol MG	1.50	4.00
638 Stan Williams	1.50	4.00
639 Tom Haller	1.50	4.00
640 Frank Robinson	15.00	40.00
641 New York Mets TC	6.00	15.00
642 Jim Roland	1.50	4.00
643 Rick Reichardt	1.50	4.00
644 Jim Stewart SP	5.00	12.00
645 Jim Maloney SP	6.00	15.00
646 Bobby Floyd SP	5.00	12.00
647 Juan Pizarro	3.00	8.00
648 Folkers/Martinez/Matlack SP RC	10.00	25.00
649 Sparky Lyle SP	15.00	40.00
650 Rich Allen SP	20.00	50.00
651 Jerry Robertson SP	5.00	12.00
652 Atlanta Braves TC	5.00	12.00
653 Russ Snyder SP	5.00	12.00
654 Don Shaw SP	5.00	12.00
655 Mike Epstein SP	5.00	12.00
656 Gerry Nyman SP	5.00	12.00
657 Jose Azcue	3.00	8.00
658 Paul Lindblad SP	5.00	12.00
659 Byron Browne SP	5.00	12.00
660 Ray Culp	3.00	8.00
661 Chuck Tanner MG SP	6.00	15.00
662 Mike Hedlund SP	5.00	12.00
663 Marv Staehle	3.00	8.00
664 Reynolds/Reynolds/Reynolds SP RC	5.00	12.00
665 Ron Swoboda SP	6.00	15.00
666 Gene Brabender SP	5.00	12.00
667 Pete Ward	3.00	8.00
668 Gary Neibauer	3.00	8.00
669 Ike Brown SP	5.00	12.00
670 Bill Hands	3.00	8.00
671 Bill Voss SP	5.00	12.00
672 Ed Crosby SP RC	5.00	12.00
673 Gerry Janeski SP RC	5.00	12.00
674 Montreal Expos TC	5.00	12.00
675 Dave Boswell	3.00	8.00
676 Tommie Reynolds	3.00	8.00
677 Jack DiLauro SP	5.00	12.00
678 George Thomas	3.00	8.00
679 Don O'Riley	3.00	8.00
680 Don Mincher SP	5.00	12.00
681 Bill Butler	3.00	8.00
682 Terry Harmon	3.00	8.00
683 Bill Burbach SP	5.00	12.00
684 Curt Motton	3.00	8.00
685 Moe Drabowsky	3.00	8.00
686 Chico Ruiz SP	5.00	12.00
687 Ron Taylor SP	5.00	12.00
688 S.Anderson MG SP	12.00	30.00
689 Frank Baker	3.00	8.00
690 Bob Moose	3.00	8.00
691 Bobby Heise	3.00	8.00
692 Haydel/Moret/Twitchell SP RC	5.00	12.00
693 Jose Pena SP	5.00	12.00
694 Rick Renick SP	5.00	12.00
695 Joe Niekro	5.00	12.00
696 Jerry Morales	3.00	8.00
697 Rickey Clark SP	5.00	12.00
698 Milwaukee Brewers TC SP	8.00	20.00
699 Jim Britton	3.00	8.00
700 Boog Powell SP	20.00	50.00
701 Bob Garibaldi	3.00	8.00
702 Milt Ramirez RC	3.00	8.00
703 Mike Kekich	3.00	8.00
704 J.C. Martin SP	5.00	12.00
705 Dick Selma SP	5.00	12.00
706 Joe Foy SP	5.00	12.00
707 Fred Lasher	3.00	8.00
708 Russ Nagelson SP	5.00	12.00
709 Baker/Baylor/Pac SP RC	50.00	120.00
710 Sonny Siebert	3.00	8.00
711 Larry Stahl SP	5.00	12.00
712 Jose Martinez	3.00	8.00
713 Mike Marshall SP	6.00	15.00
714 Dick Williams MG SP	6.00	15.00
715 Horace Clarke SP	6.00	15.00
716 Dave Leonhard	3.00	8.00
717 Tommie Aaron SP	5.00	12.00
718 Billy Wynne	3.00	8.00
719 Jerry May SP	5.00	12.00
720 Matty Alou	5.00	12.00
721 John Morris	3.00	8.00
722 Houston Astros TC SP	8.00	20.00
723 Vicente Romo SP	5.00	12.00
724 Tom Tischinski SP	5.00	12.00
725 Gary Gentry SP	5.00	12.00
726 Paul Popovich	3.00	8.00
727 Ray Lamb SP	5.00	12.00
728 Redmond/Lampard/Williams RC	3.00	8.00
729 Dick Billings RC	3.00	8.00
730 Jim Rooker	3.00	8.00
731 Jim Qualls SP	5.00	12.00
732 Bob Reed	3.00	8.00
733 Lee Maye SP	5.00	12.00
734 Rob Gardner SP	5.00	12.00
735 Mike Shannon SP	8.00	20.00
736 Mel Queen SP	5.00	12.00
737 Preston Gomez MG SP	5.00	12.00
738 Russ Gibson SP	5.00	12.00
739 Barry Lersch SP	5.00	12.00
740 Luis Aparicio SP	10.00	25.00
741 Skip Guinn	3.00	8.00
742 Kansas City Royals TC	5.00	12.00
743 John O'Donoghue SP	5.00	12.00
744 Chuck Manuel SP	5.00	12.00
745 Sandy Alomar SP	5.00	12.00
746 Andy Kosco	3.00	8.00
747 Severinsen/Spinks/Moore RC	3.00	8.00
748 John Purdin SP	5.00	12.00
749 Ken Szotkiewicz RC	3.00	8.00
750 Denny McLain SP	10.00	25.00
751 Al Weis SP	8.00	20.00
752 Dick Drago	5.00	12.00

1971 Topps Coins

This full-color set of 153 coins, which were inserted into packs, contains the photo of the player surrounded by a colored band, which contains the player's name, his team, his position and several stars. The backs contain the coin number, short biographical data and the line "Collect the entire set of 153 coins." The set was evidently produced in three groups of 51 as coins 1-51 have brass backs, coins 52-102 have chrome backs and coins 103-153 have blue backs. In fact it has been verified that the coins were printed in three sheets of 51 coins comprised of three rows of 17 coins. Each coin measures approximately 1 1/2" in diameter.

COMPLETE SET (153)	200.00	400.00
1 Clarence Gaston	1.00	2.50
2 Dave Johnson	1.00	2.50
3 Jim Bunning	2.00	5.00
4 Jim Spencer	.75	2.00
5 Felix Millan	.75	2.00
6 Gerry Moses	.75	2.00
7 Ferguson Jenkins	2.00	5.00
8 Felipe Alou	1.00	2.50
9 Jim McGlothlin	.75	2.00
10 Dick McAuliffe	.75	2.00
11 Joe Torre	2.00	5.00
12 Jim Perry	1.00	2.50
13 Bobby Bonds	1.25	3.00
14 Danny Cater	.75	2.00
15 Bill Mazeroski	2.00	5.00
16 Luis Aparicio	2.00	5.00
17 Doug Rader	.75	2.00
18 Vada Pinson	1.25	3.00
19 John Bateman	.75	2.00
20 Lew Krausse	.75	2.00
21 Billy Grabarkewitz	1.00	2.50
22 Frank Howard	1.25	3.00
23 Jerry Koosman	1.25	3.00
24 Rod Carew	2.00	5.00
25 Al Ferrara	.75	2.00
26 Dave McNally	1.00	2.50
27 Jim Hickman	.75	2.00
28 Sandy Alomar	1.00	2.50
29 Lee May	1.00	2.50
30 Rico Petrocelli	1.00	2.50
31 Don Money	.75	2.00
32 Jim Rooker	.75	2.00
33 Dick Dietz	.75	2.00
34 Roy White	1.00	2.50
35 Carl Morton	.75	2.00
36 Walt Williams	.75	2.00
37 Phil Niekro	2.00	5.00
38 Bill Freehan	1.00	2.50
39 Julian Javier	.75	2.00
40 Rick Monday	1.00	2.50
41 Don Wilson	.75	2.00
42 Ray Fosse	1.00	2.50
43 Art Shamsky	.75	2.00
44 Ted Savage	.75	2.00
45 Claude Osteen	.75	2.00
46 Ed Brinkman	.75	2.00
47 Matty Alou	1.00	2.50
48 Bob Oliver	.75	2.00
49 Danny Coombs	.75	2.00
50 Frank Robinson	2.00	5.00
51 Randy Hundley	.75	2.00
52 Cesar Tovar	1.00	2.50
53 Wayne Simpson	.75	2.00
54 Bobby Murcer	1.25	3.00
55 Carl Taylor	.75	2.00
56 Tommy John	1.00	2.50
57 Willie McCovey	2.00	5.00
58 Carl Yastrzemski	5.00	12.00
59 Bob Bailey	.75	2.00
60 Clyde Wright	.75	2.00
61 Orlando Cepeda	2.00	5.00
62 Al Kaline	4.00	10.00
63 Bob Gibson	2.00	5.00
64 Bert Campaneris	.75	2.00
65 Ted Sizemore	.75	2.00
66 Duke Sims	.75	2.00
67 Bud Harrelson	1.25	3.00
68 Gerald McNertney	.75	2.00
69 Jim Wynn	1.00	2.50
70 Dick Bosman	1.00	2.50
71 Roberto Clemente	12.50	30.00
72 Rich Reese	.75	2.00
73 Gaylord Perry	2.00	5.00
74 Boog Powell	1.00	2.50
75 Billy Williams	2.00	5.00
76 Bill Melton	.75	2.00
77 Nate Colbert	.75	2.00
78 Reggie Smith	1.00	2.50
79 Deron Johnson	.75	2.00
80 Jim Hunter	2.00	5.00
81 Bobby Tolan	1.00	2.50
82 Jim Northrup	.75	2.00
83 Ron Fairly	1.00	2.50
84 Alex Johnson	.75	2.00
85 Pat Jarvis	.75	2.00
86 Sam McDowell	1.00	2.50
87 Lou Brock	2.00	5.00
88 Danny Walton	.75	2.00
89 Denis Menke	.75	2.00
90 Jim Palmer	2.00	5.00
91 Tommy Agee	1.00	2.50
92 Duane Josephson	.75	2.00
93 Willie Davis	1.00	2.50
94 Mel Stottlemyre	1.00	2.50
95 Ron Santo	1.00	2.50
96 Amos Otis	1.00	2.50
97 Ken Henderson	.75	2.00
98 George Scott	1.00	2.50
99 Dock Ellis	1.00	2.50
100 Harmon Killebrew	4.00	10.00
101 Pete Rose	8.00	20.00
102 Rick Reichardt	.75	2.00
103 Cleon Jones	.75	2.00
104 Ron Perranoski	.75	2.00
105 Tony Perez	2.00	5.00
106 Mickey Lolich	1.00	2.50
107 Tim McCarver	1.00	2.50
108 Reggie Jackson	6.00	15.00
109 Chris Cannizzaro	.75	2.00
110 Steve Hargan	.75	2.00
111 Rusty Staub	1.00	2.50
112 Andy Messersmith	1.00	2.50
113 Rico Carty	1.00	2.50
114 Brooks Robinson	4.00	10.00
115 Steve Carlton	2.00	5.00
116 Mike Hegan	.75	2.00
117 Joe Morgan	2.00	5.00
118 Thurman Munson	5.00	12.00
119 Don Kessinger	.75	2.00
120 Joel Horlen	.75	2.00
121 Wes Parker	1.00	2.50
122 Sonny Siebert	.75	2.00
123 Willie Stargell	2.00	5.00
124 Ellie Rodgiuez	.75	2.00
125 Juan Marichal	2.00	5.00
126 Mike Epstein	.75	2.00
127 Tom Seaver	5.00	12.00
128 Tony Oliva	1.00	2.50
129 Jim Merritt	.75	2.00
130 Willie Horton	1.00	2.50
131 Rick Wise	.75	2.00
132 Sal Bando	1.00	2.50
133 Ollie Brown	.75	2.00
134 Ken Harrelson	1.00	2.50
135 Mack Jones	.75	2.00
136 Jim Fregosi	1.00	2.50
137 Hank Aaron	8.00	20.00
138 Fritz Peterson	.75	2.00
139 Joe Hague	.75	2.00
140 Tommy Harper	.75	2.00
141 Larry Dierker	.75	2.00
142 Tony Conigliaro	1.00	2.50
143 Glenn Beckert	.75	2.00
144 Carlos May	.75	2.00
145 Don Sutton	2.00	5.00
146 Paul Casanova	.75	2.00
147 Bob Moose	.75	2.00
148 Chico Cardenas	.75	2.00
149 Johnny Bench	6.00	15.00
150 Mike Cuellar	1.00	2.50
151 Donn Clendenon	.75	2.00
152 Lou Piniella	1.00	2.50
153 Willie Mays	10.00	25.00

1971 Topps Scratchoffs

These pack inserts featured the same players are the 1970 Topps Scratchoffs. However, the only difference is that the center of the game is red rather than black.

COMPLETE SET (24)	15.00	40.00
1 Hank Aaron	3.00	8.00
2 Rich Allen	.60	1.50
3 Luis Aparicio	1.50	4.00
4 Sal Bando	.40	1.00
5 Glenn Beckert	.40	1.00
6 Dick Bosman	.40	1.00
7 Nate Colbert	.40	1.00
8 Mike Hegan	.40	1.00
9 Mack Jones	.40	1.00
10 Al Kaline	2.00	5.00
11 Harmon Killebrew	2.00	5.00
12 Juan Marichal	1.50	4.00
13 Tim McCarver	.75	2.00
14 Sam McDowell	.50	1.25
15 Claude Osteen	.40	1.00
16 Tony Perez	1.25	3.00
17 Lou Piniella	.60	1.50
18 Boog Powell	.60	1.50
19 Tom Seaver	2.50	6.00
20 Jim Spencer	.40	1.00
21 Willie Stargell	2.00	5.00
22 Mel Stottlemyre	.50	1.25
23 Jim Wynn	.50	1.25
24 Carl Yastrzemski	2.00	5.00

1971 Topps Greatest Moments

The cards in this 55-card set measure 2 1/2" by 4 3/4". The 1971 Topps Greatest Moments set contains numbered cards depicting specific career highlights of current players. The obverses are black bordered and contain a small cameo picture of the left side; a deckle-bordered black and white action photo dominates the rest of the card. The backs are designed in newspaper style. Sometimes found in uncut sheets, this test set was retailed in gum packs on a very limited basis. Double prints (DP) are listed in our checklist; there were 22 double prints and 33 single prints.

COMPLETE SET (55)	750.00	1500.00
COMMON CARD (1-55)	8.00	20.00
COMMON DP	3.00	8.00
1 Thurman Munson DP	15.00	40.00
2 Hoyt Wilhelm	10.00	25.00
3 Rico Carty	8.00	20.00
4 Carl Morton DP	3.00	8.00
5 Sal Bando DP	4.00	10.00
6 Bert Campaneris DP	4.00	10.00
7 Jim Kaat	10.00	25.00
8 Harmon Killebrew	40.00	80.00
9 Brooks Robinson	40.00	80.00
10 Jim Perry	8.00	20.00
11 Tony Oliva	12.50	30.00
12 Vada Pinson	10.00	25.00
13 Johnny Bench	60.00	120.00
14 Tony Perez	12.50	30.00
15 Pete Rose DP	40.00	80.00
16 Jim Fregosi DP	4.00	10.00
17 Alex Johnson DP	3.00	8.00
18 Clyde Wright DP	3.00	8.00
19 Al Kaline DP	15.00	40.00
20 Denny McLain	12.50	30.00
21 Jim Northrup	8.00	20.00
22 Bill Freehan	8.00	20.00
23 Mickey Lolich	10.00	25.00
24 Bob Gibson DP	12.50	30.00
25 Tim McCarver DP	3.00	8.00
26 Orlando Cepeda DP	8.00	20.00
27 Lou Brock DP	12.50	30.00
28 Nate Colbert DP	3.00	8.00
29 Maury Wills	12.50	30.00
30 Wes Parker	8.00	20.00
31 Jim Wynn	10.00	25.00
32 Larry Dierker	10.00	25.00
33 Bill Melton	8.00	20.00
34 Joe Morgan	12.50	30.00
35 Rusty Staub	10.00	25.00
36 Ernie Banks DP	15.00	40.00
37 Billy Williams	12.50	30.00
38 Lou Piniella	10.00	25.00
39 Rico Petrocelli DP	4.00	10.00
40 Carl Yastrzemski DP	20.00	50.00
41 Willie Mays DP	50.00	100.00
42 Tommy Harper	8.00	20.00
43 Jim Bunning DP	4.00	10.00
44 Fritz Peterson	10.00	25.00
45 Roy White	10.00	25.00
46 Bobby Murcer	12.50	30.00
47 Reggie Jackson	100.00	200.00
48 Frank Howard	10.00	25.00
49 Dick Bosman	8.00	20.00
50 Sam McDowell DP	4.00	10.00
51 Luis Aparicio DP	4.00	10.00
52 Willie McCovey DP	12.50	30.00
53 Joe Pepitone	10.00	25.00
54 Jerry Grote	10.00	25.00
55 Bud Harrelson	8.00	20.00

1972 Topps

The cards in this 787-card set measure 2 1/2" by 3 1/2". The 1972 Topps set contained the most cards ever for a Topps set to that point in time. Features appearing for the first time were "Boyhood Photos" (341-348/491-498), Awards and Trophy cards (621-626), "In Action" (distributed throughout the set), and "Traded Cards" (751-757). Other subsets included League Leaders (85-96), Playoffs cards (221-222), and World Series cards (223-230). The curved lines of the color picture are a departure from the rectangular designs of other years. There is a series of intermediate scarcity (526-656) and the usual high numbers (657-787). The backs of cards 692, 694, 696, 700, 706 and 710 form a picture back of Tom Seaver. The backs of cards 698, 702, 704, 708, 712, 714 form a picture back of Tony Oliva. As in previous years, cards were issued in a variety of ways including ten-card wax packs which cost a dime, 28-card cello packs which cost a quarter and 54-card rack packs which cost 39 cents. The 10 cents wax packs were issued 24 packs to a box while the cello packs were also issued 24 packs to a box. Rookie Cards in this set include Ron Cey and Carlton Fisk.

COMPLETE SET (787) 1250.00 3000.00
COMMON CARD (1-132) .25 .60
COMMON CARD (133-263) .40 1.00
COMMON CARD (264-394) .50 1.25
COMMON CARD (395-525) .60 1.50
COMMON CARD (526-656) 1.50 4.00
COMMON CARD (657-787) 5.00 12.00
WRAPPER (10-CENT) 6.00 15.00
1 Pittsburgh Pirates TC 3.00 8.00
2 Ray Culp .25 .60
3 Bob Tolan .25 .60
4 Checklist 1-132 2.50 6.00
5 John Bateman .25 .60
6 Fred Scherman .25 .60
7 Enzo Hernandez .25 .60
8 Ron Swoboda .50 1.25
9 Stan Williams .25 .60
10 Amos Otis .50 1.25
11 Bobby Valentine .50 1.25
12 Jose Cardenal .25 .60
13 Joe Grzenda .25 .60
14 Koegel/Anderson/Twitchell RC .25 .60
15 Walt Williams .25 .60
16 Mike Jorgensen .25 .60
17 Dave Duncan .50 1.25
18A Juan Pizarro Yellow .25 .60
18B Juan Pizarro Green 2.00 5.00
19 Billy Cowan .25 .60
20 Don Wilson .25 .60
21 Atlanta Braves TC .60 1.50
22 Rob Gardner .25 .60
23 Ted Kubiak .25 .60
24 Ted Ford .25 .60
25 Bill Singer .25 .60
26 Andy Etchebarren .25 .60
27 Bob Johnson .25 .60
28 Gebhard/Brye Haydel RC .25 .60
29A Bill Bonham Yellow RC .25 .60
29B Bill Bonham Green 2.00 5.00
30 Rico Petrocelli .50 1.25
31 Cleon Jones .50 1.25
32 Cleon Jones IA .25 .60
33 Billy Martin MG 1.50 4.00
34 Billy Martin IA 1.00 2.50
35 Jerry Johnson .25 .60
36 Jerry Johnson IA .25 .60
37 Carl Yastrzemski 10.00 25.00
38 Carl Yastrzemski IA 6.00 15.00
39 Bob Barton .25 .60
40 Bob Barton IA .25 .60
41 Tommy Davis .50 1.25
42 Tommy Davis IA .25 .60
43 Rick Wise .50 1.25
44 Rick Wise IA .25 .60
45A Glenn Beckert Yellow .50 1.25
45B Glenn Beckert Green 2.00 5.00
46 Glenn Beckert IA .25 .60
47 John Ellis .25 .60
48 John Ellis IA .25 .60
49 Willie Mays 20.00 50.00
50 Willie Mays IA 10.00 25.00
51 Harmon Killebrew 3.00 8.00
52 Harmon Killebrew IA 1.50 4.00
53 Bud Harrelson .50 1.25
54 Bud Harrelson IA .25 .60
55 Clyde Wright .25 .60
56 Rich Chiles RC .25 .60
57 Bob Oliver .25 .60
58 Ernie McAnally .25 .60
59 Fred Stanley RC .25 .60
60 Manny Sanguillen .50 1.25
61 Hooten/Hisle/Stephenson RC .50 1.25
62 Angel Mangual .25 .60
63 Duke Sims .25 .60
64 Pete Broberg RC .25 .60
65 Cesar Cedeno .50 1.25
66 Ray Corbin RC .25 .60
67 Red Schoendienst MG 1.00 2.50
68 Jim York RC .25 .60
69 Roger Freed .25 .60
70 Mike Cuellar .50 1.25
71 California Angels TC .60 1.50
72 Bruce Kison RC .25 .60
73 Steve Huntz .25 .60
74 Cecil Upshaw .25 .60
75 Bert Campaneris .50 1.25
76 Don Carrithers RC .25 .60
77 Ron Theobald RC .25 .60
78 Steve Arlin RC .25 .60
79 C.Fisk RC/C.Cooper RC 25.00 60.00
80 Tony Perez 1.50 4.00
81 Mike Hedlund .25 .60
82 Ron Woods .25 .60
83 Dalton Jones .25 .60
84 Vince Colbert .25 .60
85 Torre/Garr/Beckert LL 1.00 2.50
86 Oliva/Murcer/Rett LL 1.00 2.50
87 Torre/Stargell/Aaron LL 5.00 12.00
88 Kill/F.Rob/Smith LL 1.50 4.00
89 Stargell/Aaron/May LL 4.00 10.00
90 Melton/Cash/Jackson LL 1.00 2.50
91 Seaver/Roberts/Wilson LL 1.00 2.50
92 Blue/Wood/Palmer LL 1.00 2.50
93 Jenkins/Carlton/Seaver LL 1.50 4.00
94 Lolich/Blue/Wood LL 1.00 2.50
95 Seaver/Jenkins/Stone LL 1.50 4.00
96 Lolich/Blue/Coleman LL 1.00 2.50
97 Tom Kelley .25 .60
98 Chuck Tanner MG .50 1.25
99 Ross Grimsley RC .25 .60
100 Frank Robinson 3.00 8.00
101 Grief/Richard/Busse RC 1.00 2.50
102 Lloyd Allen .25 .60
103 Checklist 133-263 2.50 6.00
104 Toby Harrah RC .50 1.25
105 Gary Gentry .25 .60
106 Milwaukee Brewers TC .60 1.50
107 Jose Cruz RC .50 1.25
108 Gary Waslewski .25 .60
109 Jerry May .25 .60
110 Ron Hunt .25 .60
111 Jim Grant .25 .60
112 Greg Luzinski .50 1.25
113 Rogelio Moret .25 .60
114 Bill Buckner .50 1.25
115 Jim Fregosi .50 1.25
116 Ed Farmer RC .25 .60
117A Cleo James Yellow RC .25 .60
117B Cleo James Green 2.00 5.00
118 Skip Lockwood .25 .60
119 Marty Perez .25 .60
120 Bill Freehan .50 1.25
121 Ed Sprague .25 .60
122 Larry Biittner RC .25 .60
123 Ed Acosta .25 .60
124 Closter/Torres/Hambright RC .25 .60
125 Dave Cash .50 1.25
126 Bart Johnson .25 .60
127 Duffy Dyer .25 .60
128 Eddie Watt .25 .60
129 Charlie Fox MG .25 .60
130 Bob Gibson 8.00 20.00
131 Jim Nettles .25 .60
132 Joe Morgan 2.50 6.00
133 Joe Keough .40 1.00
134 Carl Morton .40 1.00
135 Vada Pinson .75 2.00
136 Darrel Chaney .40 1.00
137 Dick Williams MG .75 2.00
138 Mike Kekich .40 1.00
139 Tim McCarver .75 2.00
140 Pat Dobson .75 2.00
141 Capra/Stanton/Matlack RC .75 2.00
142 Chris Chambliss RC 1.50 4.00
143 Garry Jestadt .40 1.00
144 Marty Pattin .40 1.00
145 Don Kessinger .75 2.00
146 Steve Kealey .40 1.00
147 Dave Kingman RC 6.00 15.00
148 Dick Billings .40 1.00
149 Gary Neibauer .40 1.00
150 Norm Cash .75 2.00
151 Jim Brewer .40 1.00
152 Gene Clines .40 1.00
153 Rick Auerbach RC .40 1.00
154 Ted Simmons 1.50 4.00
155 Larry Dierker .40 1.00
156 Minnesota Twins TC .75 2.00
157 Don Gullett .40 1.00
158 Jerry Kenney .40 1.00
159 John Boccabella .40 1.00
160 Andy Messersmith .75 2.00
161 Brock Davis .40 1.00
162 Bell/Porter/Reynolds RC .75 2.00
163 Tug McGraw 1.50 4.00
164 Tug McGraw IA .75 2.00
165 Chris Speier RC .75 2.00
166 Chris Speier IA .40 1.00
167 Deron Johnson .40 1.00
168 Deron Johnson IA .40 1.00
169 Vida Blue 1.50 4.00
170 Vida Blue IA .75 2.00
171 Darrell Evans 1.50 4.00
172 Darrell Evans IA .75 2.00
173 Clay Kirby .40 1.00
174 Clay Kirby IA .40 1.00
175 Tom Haller .40 1.00
176 Tom Haller IA .40 1.00
177 Paul Schaal .40 1.00
178 Paul Schaal IA .40 1.00
179 Dock Ellis .40 1.00
180 Dock Ellis IA .40 1.00
181 Ed Kranepool .75 2.00
182 Ed Kranepool IA .40 1.00
183 Bill Melton .40 1.00
184 Bill Melton IA .40 1.00
185 Ron Bryant .40 1.00
186 Ron Bryant IA .40 1.00
187 Gates Brown .40 1.00
188 Frank Lucchesi MG .40 1.00
189 Gene Tenace .75 2.00
190 Dave Giusti .40 1.00
191 Jeff Burroughs RC 1.50 4.00
192 Chicago Cubs TC .75 2.00
193 Kurt Bevacqua RC .40 1.00
194 Fred Norman .40 1.00
195 Orlando Cepeda 6.00 15.00
196 Mel Queen .40 1.00
197 Johnny Briggs .40 1.00
198 Hough/O'Brien/Strahler RC 4.00 10.00
199 Mike Fiore .40 1.00
200 Lou Brock 8.00 20.00
201 Phil Roof .40 1.00
202 Scipio Spinks .40 1.00
203 Ron Blomberg RC .40 1.00
204 Tommy Helms .40 1.00
205 Dick Drago .40 1.00
206 Dal Maxvill .40 1.00
207 Tom Egan .40 1.00
208 Milt Pappas .75 2.00
209 Joe Rudi .75 2.00
210 Denny McLain .75 2.00
211 Gary Sutherland .40 1.00
212 Grant Jackson .40 1.00
213 Parker/Kusnyer/Silverio RC .40 1.00
214 Mike McQueen .40 1.00
215 Alex Johnson .75 2.00
216 Joe Niekro .75 2.00
217 Roger Metzger .40 1.00
218 Eddie Kasko MG .40 1.00
219 Rennie Stennett RC .75 2.00
220 Jim Perry .75 2.00
221 NL Playoffs Bucs .75 2.00
222 AL Playoffs B.Robinson 1.50 4.00
223 Dave McNally WS .75 2.00
224 D.Johnson/M.Belanger WS .75 2.00
225 Manny Sanguillen WS .75 2.00
226 Roberto Clemente WS 3.00 8.00
227 Nellie Briles WS .75 2.00
228 F.Robinson/M.Sanguillen WS .75 2.00
229 Steve Blass WS .75 2.00
230 Pirates Celebrate WS .75 2.00
231 Casey Cox .40 1.00
232 Arnold/Barr/Rader RC .40 1.00
233 Jay Johnstone .75 2.00
234 Ron Taylor .40 1.00
235 Merv Rettenmund .40 1.00
236 Jim McGlothlin .40 1.00
237 New York Yankees TC .75 2.00
238 Leron Lee .40 1.00
239 Tom Timmermann .40 1.00
240 Rich Allen .75 2.00
241 Rollie Fingers 5.00 12.00
242 Don Mincher .40 1.00
243 Frank Linzy .40 1.00
244 Steve Braun RC .40 1.00
245 Tommie Agee .75 2.00
246 Tom Burgmeier .40 1.00
247 Milt May .40 1.00
248 Tom Bradley .40 1.00
249 Harry Walker MG .40 1.00
250 Boog Powell .75 2.00
251 Checklist 264-394 2.50 6.00
252 Ken Reynolds .40 1.00
253 Sandy Alomar .75 2.00
254 Boots Day .40 1.00
255 Jim Lonborg .75 2.00
256 George Foster .75 2.00
257 Foor/Hosley/Jata RC .40 1.00
258 Randy Hundley .40 1.00
259 Sparky Lyle .75 2.00
260 Ralph Garr .75 2.00
261 Steve Mingori .40 1.00
262 San Diego Padres TC .75 2.00
263 Felipe Alou .75 2.00
264 Tommy John .75 2.00
265 Wes Parker .75 2.00
266 Bobby Bolin .50 1.25
267 Dave Concepcion 1.50 4.00
268 D.Anderson RC/C.Floethe RC .50 1.25
269 Don Hahn .50 1.25
270 Jim Palmer 6.00 15.00
271 Ken Rudolph .50 1.25
272 Mickey Rivers RC .75 2.00
273 Bobby Floyd .50 1.25
274 Al Severinsen .50 1.25
275 Cesar Tovar .50 1.25
276 Gene Mauch MG .75 2.00
277 Elliott Maddox .50 1.25
278 Dennis Higgins .50 1.25
279 Larry Brown .50 1.25
280 Willie McCovey 2.50 6.00
281 Bill Parsons RC .50 1.25
282 Houston Astros TC .75 2.00
283 Darrell Brandon .50 1.25
284 Ike Brown .50 1.25
285 Gaylord Perry 2.50 6.00
286 Gene Alley .50 1.25
287 Jim Hardin .50 1.25
288 Johnny Jeter .50 1.25
289 Syd O'Brien .50 1.25
290 Sonny Siebert .50 1.25
291 Hal McRae .75 2.00
292 Hal McRae IA .50 1.25
293 Dan Frisella .50 1.25
294 Dan Frisella IA .50 1.25
295 Dick Dietz .50 1.25
296 Dick Dietz IA .50 1.25
297 Claude Osteen .75 2.00
298 Claude Osteen IA .50 1.25
299 Hank Aaron 25.00 60.00
300 Hank Aaron IA 8.00 20.00
301 George Mitterwald .50 1.25
302 George Mitterwald IA .50 1.25
303 Joe Pepitone .75 2.00
304 Joe Pepitone IA .50 1.25
305 Ken Boswell .50 1.25
306 Ken Boswell IA .50 1.25
307 Steve Renko .50 1.25
308 Steve Renko IA .50 1.25
309 Roberto Clemente 30.00 80.00
310 Roberto Clemente IA 12.00 30.00
311 Clay Carroll .50 1.25
312 Clay Carroll IA .50 1.25
313 Luis Aparicio 2.50 6.00
314 Luis Aparicio IA .75 2.00
315 Paul Splittorff .50 1.25
316 Bibby/Roque/Guzman RC .75 2.00
317 Rich Hand .50 1.25
318 Sonny Jackson .50 1.25
319 Aurelio Rodriguez .50 1.25
320 Steve Blass .75 2.00
321 Joe Lahoud .50 1.25
322 Jose Pena .50 1.25
323 Earl Weaver MG 1.50 4.00
324 Mike Ryan .50 1.25
325 Mel Stottlemyre .75 2.00
326 Pat Kelly .50 1.25
327 Steve Stone RC .75 2.00
328 Boston Red Sox TC .75 2.00
329 Roy Foster .50 1.25
330 Jim Hunter 2.50 6.00
331 Stan Swanson RC .50 1.25
332 Buck Martinez .50 1.25
333 Steve Barber .50 1.25
334 Fahey/Mason Ragland RC .50 1.25
335 Bill Hands .50 1.25
336 Marty Martinez .50 1.25
337 Mike Kilkenny .50 1.25
338 Bob Grich .75 2.00
339 Ron Cook .50 1.25
340 Roy White .75 2.00
341 Joe Torre KP .50 1.25
342 Wilbur Wood KP .50 1.25
343 Willie Stargell KP .50 1.25
344 Dave McNally KP .50 1.25
345 Rick Wise KP .50 1.25
346 Jim Fregosi KP .50 1.25
347 Tom Seaver KP 1.50 4.00
348 Sal Bando KP .50 1.25
349 Al Fitzmorris .50 1.25
350 Frank Howard .75 2.00
351 House/Kester/Britton .75 2.00
352 Dave LaRoche .50 1.25
353 Art Shamsky .50 1.25
354 Tom Murphy .50 1.25
355 Bob Watson .75 2.00
356 Gerry Moses .50 1.25
357 Woody Fryman .50 1.25
358 Sparky Anderson MG 1.50 4.00
359 Don Pavletich .50 1.25
360 Dave Roberts .50 1.25
361 Mike Andrews .50 1.25
362 New York Mets TC .75 2.00
363 Ron Klimkowski .50 1.25
364 Johnny Callison .75 2.00
365 Dick Bosman .75 2.00
366 Jimmy Rosario RC .50 1.25
367 Ron Perranoski .50 1.25
368 Danny Thompson .50 1.25
369 Jim Lefebvre .75 2.00
370 Don Buford .50 1.25
371 Denny Lemaster .50 1.25
372 L.Clemons RC/M.Montgomery RC .50 1.25
373 John Mayberry .75 2.00
374 Jack Heidemann .50 1.25
375 Reggie Cleveland .50 1.25
376 Andy Kosco .50 1.25
377 Terry Harmon .50 1.25
378 Checklist 395-525 2.50 6.00
379 Ken Berry .50 1.25
380 Earl Williams .50 1.25
381 Chicago White Sox TC .75 2.00
382 Joe Gibbon .50 1.25
383 Brant Alyea .50 1.25
384 Dave Campbell .75 2.00
385 Mickey Stanley .75 2.00
386 Jim Colborn .50 1.25
387 Horace Clarke .75 2.00
388 Charlie Williams RC .50 -1.25
389 Bill Rigney MG .50 1.25
390 Willie Davis .75 2.00
391 Ken Sanders .50 1.25
392 F.Cambria/R.Zisk RC .75 2.00
393 Curt Motton .50 1.25
394 Ken Forsch .75 2.00
395 Matty Alou .75 2.00
396 Paul Lindblad .60 1.50
397 Philadelphia Phillies TC .75 2.00
398 Larry Hisle .75 2.00
399 Milt Wilcox .75 2.00
400 Tony Oliva 1.50 4.00
401 Jim Nash .60 1.50
402 Bobby Heise .60 1.50
403 John Cumberland .60 1.50
404 Jeff Torborg .75 2.00
405 Ron Fairly .75 2.00
406 George Hendrick RC .75 2.00
407 Chuck Taylor .60 1.50
408 Jim Northrup .75 2.00
409 Frank Baker .60 1.50
410 Ferguson Jenkins 2.50 6.00
411 Bob Montgomery .60 1.50
412 Dick Kelley .60 1.50
413 D.Eddy RC/D.Lemonds .60 1.50
414 Bob Miller .60 1.50
415 Cookie Rojas .75 2.00
416 Johnny Edwards .60 1.50
417 Tom Hall .60 1.50
418 Tom Shopay .60 1.50
419 Jim Spencer .60 1.50
420 Steve Carlton 8.00 20.00
421 Ellie Rodriguez .60 1.50
422 Ray Lamb .60 1.50
423 Oscar Gamble .75 2.00
424 Bill Gogolewski .60 1.50
425 Ken Singleton .75 2.00
426 Ken Singleton IA .60 1.50
427 Tito Fuentes .60 1.50
428 Tito Fuentes IA .60 1.50
429 Bob Robertson .60 1.50
430 Bob Robertson IA .60 1.50
431 Clarence Gaston .75 2.00
432 Clarence Gaston IA .75 2.00
433 Johnny Bench 15.00 40.00
434 Johnny Bench IA 8.00 20.00
435 Reggie Jackson 12.00 30.00
436 Reggie Jackson IA 6.00 15.00
437 Maury Wills .75 2.00
438 Maury Wills IA .75 2.00
439 Billy Williams 2.50 6.00
440 Billy Williams IA 1.50 4.00
441 Thurman Munson 12.00 30.00
442 Thurman Munson IA 3.00 8.00
443 Ken Henderson .60 1.50
444 Ken Henderson IA .60 1.50
445 Tom Seaver 20.00 50.00
446 Tom Seaver IA 5.00 12.00
447 Willie Stargell 3.00 8.00
448 Willie Stargell IA 1.50 4.00
449 Bob Lemon MG .75 2.00
450 Mickey Lolich .75 2.00
451 Tony LaRussa 1.50 4.00
452 Ed Herrmann .60 1.50
453 Barry Lersch .75 2.00
454 Oakland Athletics TC .75 2.00
455 Tommy Harper .75 2.00
456 Mark Belanger .75 2.00
457 Fast/Thomas/Ivie RC .60 1.50
458 Aurelio Monteagudo .60 1.50
459 Rick Renick .60 1.50
460 Al Downing .60 1.50
461 Tim Cullen .60 1.50
462 Rickey Clark .60 1.50
463 Bernie Carbo .60 1.50
464 Jim Roland .60 1.50
465 Gil Hodges MG 1.50 4.00
466 Norm Miller .60 1.50
467 Steve Kline .60 1.50
468 Richie Scheinblum .60 1.50
469 Ron Herbel .60 1.50
470 Ray Fosse .60 1.50
471 Luke Walker .60 1.50
472 Phil Gagliano .60 1.50
473 Dan McGinn .60 1.50
474 Baylor/Harrison/Oates RC 6.00 15.00
475 Gary Nolan .75 2.00
476 Lee Richard RC .60 1.50
477 Tom Phoebus .60 1.50
478 Checklist 526-656 2.50 6.00
479 Don Shaw .60 1.50
480 Lee May .60 1.50
481 Billy Conigliaro .75 2.00
482 Joe Hoerner .60 1.50
483 Ken Suarez .60 1.50
484 Lum Harris MG .60 1.50
485 Phil Regan .75 2.00
486 John Lowenstein .60 1.50
487 Detroit Tigers TC .75 2.00
488 Mike Nagy .60 1.50
489 T.Humphrey RC/K.Lampard .60 1.50
490 Dave McNally .75 2.00
491 Lou Piniella KP .75 2.00
492 Mel Stottlemyre KP .75 2.00
493 Bob Bailey KP .75 2.00
494 Willie Horton KP .75 2.00
495 Bill Melton KP .75 2.00
496 Bud Harrelson KP .75 2.00
497 Jim Perry KP .75 2.00
498 Brooks Robinson KP 1.50 4.00
499 Vicente Romo .60 1.50
500 Joe Torre 1.50 4.00
501 Pete Hamm .60 1.50
502 Jackie Hernandez .60 1.50
503 Gary Peters .60 1.50
504 Ed Spiezio .60 1.50
505 Mike Marshall .75 2.00
506 Ley/Moyer/Tidrow RC .60 1.50
507 Fred Gladding .60 1.50
508 Elrod Hendricks .60 1.50
509 Don McMahon .60 1.50
510 Ted Williams MG 8.00 20.00
511 Tony Taylor .75 2.00
512 Paul Popovich .60 1.50
513 Lindy McDaniel .75 2.00
514 Ted Sizemore .60 1.50
515 Bert Blyleven 1.50 4.00
516 Oscar Brown .60 1.50
517 Ken Brett .60 1.50
518 Wayne Garrett .60 1.50
519 Ted Abernathy .60 1.50
520 Larry Bowa .75 2.00
521 Alan Foster .60 1.50
522 Los Angeles Dodgers TC .75 2.00
523 Chuck Dobson .60 1.50
524 E.Armbrister RC/M.Behney RC .60 1.50
525 Carlos May .75 2.00
526 Bob Bailey 2.50 6.00
527 Dave Leonhard 1.50 4.00
528 Ron Stone 1.50 4.00
529 Dave Nelson 2.50 6.00
530 Don Sutton 5.00 12.00
531 Freddie Patek 2.50 6.00
532 Fred Kendall RC 1.50 4.00
533 Ralph Houk MG 2.50 6.00
534 Jim Hickman 2.50 6.00
535 Ed Brinkman 1.50 4.00
536 Doug Rader 2.50 6.00
537 Bob Locker 1.50 4.00
538 Charlie Sands RC 1.50 4.00
539 Terry Forster RC 2.50 6.00
540 Felix Millan 1.50 4.00
541 Roger Repoz 1.50 4.00
542 Jack Billingham 1.50 4.00
543 Duane Josephson 1.50 4.00
544 Ted Martinez 1.50 4.00
545 Wayne Granger 1.50 4.00
546 Joe Hague 1.50 4.00
547 Cleveland Indians TC 3.00 8.00
548 Frank Reberger 1.50 4.00
549 Dave May 1.50 4.00
550 Brooks Robinson 8.00 20.00
551 Ollie Brown 1.50 4.00
552 Ollie Brown IA 1.50 4.00
553 Wilbur Wood 2.50 6.00
554 Wilbur Wood IA 1.50 4.00
555 Ron Santo 3.00 8.00
556 Ron Santo IA 2.50 6.00
557 John Odom 1.50 4.00
558 John Odom IA 1.50 4.00
559 Pete Rose 25.00 60.00
560 Pete Rose IA 10.00 25.00
561 Leo Cardenas 1.50 4.00
562 Leo Cardenas IA 1.50 4.00
563 Ray Sadecki 1.50 4.00
564 Ray Sadecki IA 1.50 4.00
565 Reggie Smith 2.50 6.00
566 Reggie Smith IA 1.50 4.00
567 Juan Marichal 6.00 15.00
568 Juan Marichal IA 2.50 6.00
569 Ed Kirkpatrick 1.50 4.00
570 Ed Kirkpatrick IA 1.50 4.00
571 Nate Colbert 1.50 4.00
572 Nate Colbert IA 1.50 4.00
573 Fritz Peterson 1.50 4.00
574 Fritz Peterson IA 1.50 4.00
575 Al Oliver 3.00 8.00
576 Leo Durocher MG 2.50 6.00
577 Mike Paul 2.50 6.00
578 Billy Grabarkewitz 1.50 4.00
579 Doyle Alexander RC 2.50 6.00
580 Lou Piniella 2.50 6.00
581 Wade Blasingame 1.50 4.00
582 Montreal Expos TC 3.00 8.00
583 Darold Knowles 1.50 4.00
584 Jerry McNertney 1.50 4.00
585 George Scott 2.50 6.00
586 Denis Menke 1.50 4.00
587 Billy Wilson 1.50 4.00
588 Jim Holt 1.50 4.00
589 Hal Lanier 1.50 4.00
590 Graig Nettles 3.00 8.00
591 Paul Casanova 1.50 4.00
592 Lew Krausse 1.50 4.00
593 Rich Morales 1.50 4.00
594 Jim Beauchamp 1.50 4.00
595 Nolan Ryan 40.00 100.00
596 Manny Mota 2.50 6.00
597 Jim Magnuson RC 1.50 4.00
598 Hal King 2.50 6.00
599 Billy Champion 1.50 4.00
600 Al Kaline 12.00 30.00
601 George Stone 1.50 4.00
602 Dave Bristol MG 1.50 4.00
603 Jim Ray 1.50 4.00
604A Checklist 657-787 Right Copy 5.00 12.00
604B Checklist 657-787 Left Copy 5.00 12.00
605 Nelson Briles 2.50 6.00
606 Luis Melendez 1.50 4.00
607 Frank Duffy 1.50 4.00
608 Mike Corkins 1.50 4.00
609 Tom Grieve 2.50 6.00
610 Bill Stoneman 2.50 6.00
611 Rich Reese 1.50 4.00
612 Joe Decker 1.50 4.00
613 Mike Ferraro 1.50 4.00
614 Ted Uhlaender 1.50 4.00
615 Steve Hargan 1.50 4.00
616 Joe Ferguson RC 2.50 6.00
617 Kansas City Royals TC 3.00 8.00
618 Rich Robertson 1.50 4.00
619 Rich McKinney 1.50 4.00
620 Phil Niekro 8.00 20.00
621 Commish Award 3.00 8.00
622 MVP Award 3.00 8.00
623 Cy Young Award 3.00 8.00
624 Minor Lg POY Award 3.00 8.00
625 Rookie of the Year 3.00 8.00
626 Babe Ruth Award 3.00 8.00
627 Moe Drabowsky 1.50 4.00
628 Terry Crowley 1.50 4.00
629 Paul Doyle 1.50 4.00
630 Rich Hebner 2.50
631 John Strohmayer 1.50
632 Mike Hegan 1.50
633 Jack Hiatt 1.50
634 Dick Woodson 1.50
635 Don Money 2.50
636 Bill Lee 2.50
637 Preston Gomez MG 1.50
638 Ken Wright 1.50
639 J.C. Martin 1.50
640 Joe Coleman 1.50
641 Mike Lum 1.50
642 Dennis Riddleberger RC 1.50
643 Russ Gibson 1.50
644 Bernie Allen 1.50
645 Jim Maloney 2.50
646 Chico Salmon 1.50
647 Bob Moose 1.50
648 Jim Lyttle 1.50
649 Pete Richert 1.50
650 Sal Bando 2.50
651 Cincinnati Reds TC 3.00
652 Marcelino Lopez 1.50
653 Jim Fairey 1.50
654 Horacio Pina 2.50
655 Jerry Grote 1.50
656 Rudy May 1.50
657 Bobby Wine 5.00 12
658 Steve Dunning 5.00 12
659 Bob Aspromonte 5.00 12
660 Paul Blair 6.00 15
661 Bill Virdon MG 5.00 12
662 Stan Bahnsen 5.00 12
663 Fran Healy RC 6.00 15
664 Bobby Knoop 5.00 12
665 Chris Short 5.00 12
666 Hector Torres 5.00 12
667 Ray Newman RC 5.00 12
668 Texas Rangers TC 12.50 30
669 Willie Crawford 5.00 12
670 Ken Holtzman 6.00 15
671 Donn Clendenon 6.00 15
672 Archie Reynolds 5.00 12
673 Dave Marshall 5.00 12.
674 John Kennedy 5.00 12.
675 Pat Jarvis 5.00 12.
676 Danny Cater 5.00 12.
677 Ivan Murrell 5.00 12.
678 Steve Luebber RC 5.00 12.
679 B.Fenwick RC/B.Stinson 5.00 12.
680 Dave Johnson 6.00 15.
681 Bobby Pfeil 5.00 12.
682 Mike McCormick 6.00 15.
683 Steve Hovley 5.00 12.
684 Hal Breeden RC 5.00 12.
685 Joel Horlen 5.00 12.
686 Steve Garvey 20.00 50.
687 Del Unser 5.00 12.
688 St. Louis Cardinals TC 8.00 20.
689 Eddie Fisher 5.00 12.
690 Willie Montanez 6.00 15.
691 Curt Blefary 5.00 12.
692 Curt Blefary IA 5.00 12.
693 Alan Gallagher 5.00 12.0
694 Alan Gallagher IA 5.00 12.0
695 Rod Carew 25.00 60.0
696 Rod Carew IA 12.00 30.0
697 Jerry Koosman 6.00 15.0
698 Jerry Koosman IA 6.00 15.0
699 Bobby Murcer 6.00 15.0
700 Bobby Murcer IA 6.00 15.0
701 Jose Pagan 5.00 12.0
702 Jose Pagan IA 5.00 12.0
703 Doug Griffin 5.00 12.0
704 Doug Griffin IA 5.00 12.0
705 Pat Corrales 6.00 15.0
706 Pat Corrales IA 5.00 12.0
707 Tim Foli 5.00 12.0
708 Tim Foli IA 5.00 12.0
709 Jim Kaat 6.00 15.0
710 Jim Kaat IA 6.00 15.0
711 Bobby Bonds 8.00 20.0
712 Bobby Bonds IA 6.00 15.0
713 Gene Michael 8.00 20.0
714 Gene Michael IA 6.00 15.0
715 Mike Epstein 5.00 12.0
716 Jesus Alou 5.00 12.0
717 Bruce Dal Canton 5.00 12.0
718 Del Rice MG 5.00 12.0
719 Cesar Geronimo 5.00 12.0
720 Sam McDowell 6.00 15.0
721 Eddie Leon 5.00 12.0
722 Bill Sudakis 5.00 12.0
723 Al Santorini 5.00 12.0
724 Curtis/Hinton/Scott RC 5.00 12.00
725 Dick McAuliffe 6.00 15.00
726 Dick Selma 5.00 12.00
727 Jose Laboy 5.00 12.00
728 Gail Hopkins 5.00 12.00
729 Bob Veale 6.00 15.00
730 Rick Monday 6.00 15.00
731 Baltimore Orioles TC 8.00 20.00
732 George Culver 5.00 12.00
733 Jim Ray Hart 6.00 15.00
734 Bob Burda 5.00 12.00
735 Diego Segui 5.00 12.00
736 Bill Russell 6.00 15.00
737 Len Randle RC 6.00 15.00
738 Jim Merritt 5.00 12.00
739 Don Mason 5.00 12.00
740 Rico Carty 6.00 15.00
741 Hutton/Milner/Miller RC 6.00 15.00
742 Jim Rooker 5.00 12.00

Card	Low	High
743 Cesar Gutierrez	5.00	12.00
744 Jim Slaton RC	5.00	12.00
745 Julian Javier	6.00	15.00
746 Lowell Palmer	5.00	12.00
747 Jim Stewart	5.00	12.00
748 Phil Hennigan	5.00	12.00
749 Walter Alston MG	8.00	20.00
750 Willie Horton	6.00	15.00
751 Steve Carlton TR	15.00	40.00
752 Joe Morgan TR	12.00	30.00
753 Denny McLain TR	8.00	20.00
754 Frank Robinson TR	10.00	25.00
755 Jim Fregosi TR	6.00	15.00
756 Rick Wise TR	6.00	15.00
757 Jose Cardenal TR	6.00	15.00
758 Gil Garrido	5.00	12.00
759 Chris Cannizzaro	5.00	12.00
760 Bill Mazeroski	10.00	25.00
761 Oglivie/Cey/Williams RC	20.00	50.00
762 Wayne Simpson	5.00	12.00
763 Ron Hansen	5.00	12.00
764 Dusty Baker	8.00	20.00
765 Ken McMullen	5.00	12.00
766 Steve Hamilton	5.00	12.00
767 Tom McCraw	6.00	15.00
768 Denny Doyle	5.00	12.00
769 Jack Aker	5.00	12.00
770 Jim Wynn	6.00	15.00
771 San Francisco Giants TC	8.00	20.00
772 Ken Tatum	5.00	12.00
773 Ron Brand	5.00	12.00
774 Luis Alvarado	5.00	12.00
775 Jerry Reuss	6.00	15.00
776 Bill Voss	5.00	12.00
777 Hoyt Wilhelm	10.00	25.00
778 Albury/Dempsey/Strickland RC	8.00	20.00
779 Tony Cloninger	5.00	12.00
780 Dick Green	5.00	12.00
781 Jim McAndrew	5.00	12.00
782 Larry Stahl	5.00	12.00
783 Les Cain	5.00	12.00
784 Ken Aspromonte	5.00	12.00
785 Vic Davalillo	5.00	12.00
786 Chuck Brinkman	5.00	12.00
787 Ron Reed	6.00	15.00

1973 Topps

The cards in this 660-card set measure 2 1/2" by 3 1/2". The 1973 Topps set marked the last year in which Topps marketed baseball cards in consecutive series. The last series (529-660) is more difficult to obtain. In some parts of the country, however, all five series were distributed together. Beginning in 1974, all Topps cards were printed at the same time, thus eliminating the "high number" factor. The set features team leader cards with small individual pictures of the coaching staff members and a larger picture of the manager. The "background" variations below with respect to these leader cards are subtle and are best understood after a side-by-side comparison of the two varieties. An "All-Time Leaders" series (471 478) appeared for the first time in this set. Kid Pictures appeared again for the second year in a row (341-346). Other topical subsets within the set included League Leaders (61-68), Playoffs cards (201-202), World Series cards (203-210), and Rookie Prospects (601-616). For the fourth and final time, cards were issued in ten-card dime packs which were issued 24 packs to a box, in addition, these cards were also released in 54-card rack packs which cost 39 cents upon release. The key Rookie Cards in this set are all in the Rookie Prospect series: Bob Boone, Dwight Evans, and Mike Schmidt.

Card	Low	High
COMPLETE SET (660)	600.00	1500.00
COMMON CARD (1-264)	.20	.50
COMMON CARD (265-396)	.30	.75
COMMON CARD (397-528)	.50	1.25
COMMON CARD (529-660)	1.25	3.00
WRAPPER (10-CENT, BAT)	6.00	15.00
WRAPPER (10-CENT)	6.00	15.00
1 Ruth/Aaron/Mays HR	25.00	60.00
2 Rich Hebner	.60	1.50
3 Jim Lonborg	.60	1.50
4 John Milner	.20	.50
5 Ed Brinkman	.20	.50
6 Mac Scarce RC	.20	.50
7 Texas Rangers TC	.75	2.00
8 Tom Hall	.20	.50
9 Johnny Oates	.60	1.50
10 Don Sutton	1.50	4.00
11 Chris Chambliss UER	.60	1.50
12A Don Zimmer MG w/o Ear	1.25	3.00
12B Don Zimmer MG w/Ear	.30	.75
13 George Hendrick	.60	1.50
14 Sonny Siebert	.20	.50
15 Ralph Garr	.60	1.50
16 Steve Braun	.20	.50
17 Fred Gladding	.20	.50
18 Leroy Stanton	.20	.50
19 Tim Foli	.20	.50
20 Stan Bahnsen	.20	.50
21 Randy Hundley	.60	1.50
22 Ted Abernathy	.20	.50
23 Dave Kingman	.60	1.50
24 Al Santorini	.20	.50
25 Roy White	.60	1.50
26 Pittsburgh Pirates TC	.75	2.00
27 Bill Gogolewski	.20	.50
28 Hal McRae	.60	1.50
29 Tony Taylor	.60	1.50
30 Tug McGraw	.60	1.50
31 Buddy Bell RC	1.00	2.50
32 Fred Norman	.20	.50
33 Jim Breazeale RC	.20	.50
34 Pat Dobson	.20	.50
35 Willie Davis	.60	1.50
36 Steve Barber	.20	.50
37 Bill Robinson	.60	1.50
38 Mike Epstein	.20	.50
39 Dave Roberts	.20	.50
40 Reggie Smith	.60	1.50
41 Tom Walker RC	.20	.50
42 Mike Andrews	.20	.50
43 Randy Moffitt RC	.20	.50
44 Rick Monday	.60	1.50
45 Ellie Rodriguez UER	.20	.50
46 Lindy McDaniel	.60	1.50
47 Luis Melendez	.20	.50
48 Paul Splittorff	.20	.50
49A Frank Quilici MG Solid	1.25	3.00
49B Frank Quilici MG Natural	.30	.75
50 Roberto Clemente	30.00	80.00
51 Chuck Seelbach RC	.20	.50
52 Denis Menke	.20	.50
53 Steve Dunning	.20	.50
54 Checklist 1-132	1.25	3.00
55 Jon Matlack	.60	1.50
56 Merv Rettenmund	.20	.50
57 Derrel Thomas	.20	.50
58 Mike Paul	.20	.50
59 Steve Yeager RC	.60	1.50
60 Ken Holtzman	.60	1.50
61 B.Williams/R.Carew LL	1.00	2.50
62 J.Bench/D.Allen LL	1.00	2.50
63 J.Bench/D.Allen LL	1.00	2.50
64 L.Brock/Campaneris LL	.60	1.50
65 S.Carlton/L.Tiant LL	.60	1.50
66 Carlton/Perry/Wood LL	.60	1.50
67 S.Carlton/N.Ryan LL	5.00	12.00
68 C.Carroll/S.Lyle LL	.60	1.50
69 Phil Gagliano	.20	.50
70 Milt Pappas	.60	1.50
71 Johnny Briggs	.20	.50
72 Ron Reed	.20	.50
73 Ed Herrmann	.20	.50
74 Billy Champion	.20	.50
75 Vada Pinson	.60	1.50
76 Doug Rader	.20	.50
77 Mike Torrez	.60	1.50
78 Richie Scheinblum	.20	.50
79 Jim Willoughby RC	.20	.50
80 Tony Oliva UER	1.00	2.50
81A W.Lockman MG w/Banks Solid	.60	1.50
81B W.Lockman MG w/Banks Natural	.60	1.50
82 Fritz Peterson	.20	.50
83 Leron Lee	.20	.50
84 Rollie Fingers	1.50	4.00
85 Ted Simmons	.60	1.50
86 Tom McCraw	.20	.50
87 Ken Boswell	.20	.50
88 Mickey Stanley	.60	1.50
89 Jack Billingham	.20	.50
90 Brooks Robinson	8.00	20.00
91 Los Angeles Dodgers TC	.75	2.00
92 Jerry Bell	.20	.50
93 Jesus Alou	.20	.50
94 Dick Billings	.20	.50
95 Steve Blass	.60	1.50
96 Doug Griffin	.20	.50
97 Willie Montanez	.60	1.50
98 Dick Woodson	.20	.50
99 Carl Taylor	.20	.50
100 Hank Aaron	20.00	50.00
101 Ken Henderson	.20	.50
102 Rudy May	.20	.50
103 Celerino Sanchez RC	.20	.50
104 Reggie Cleveland	.20	.50
105 Carlos May	.20	.50
106 Terry Humphrey	.20	.50
107 Phil Hennigan	.20	.50
108 Bill Russell	.60	1.50
109 Doyle Alexander	.60	1.50
110 Bob Watson	.60	1.50
111 Dave Nelson	.20	.50
112 Gary Ross	.20	.50
113 Jerry Grote	.60	1.50
114 Lynn McGlothen RC	.20	.50
115 Ron Santo	.60	1.50
116A Ralph Houk MG Solid	1.25	3.00
116B Ralph Houk MG Natural	.30	.75
117 Ramon Hernandez	.20	.50
118 John Mayberry	.60	1.50
119 Larry Bowa	.60	1.50
120 Joe Coleman	.20	.50
121 Dave Rader	.20	.50
122 Jim Strickland	.20	.50
123 Sandy Alomar	.60	1.50
124 Jim Hardin	.20	.50
125 Ron Fairly	.60	1.50
126 Jim Brewer	.20	.50
127 Milwaukee Brewers TC	.75	2.00
128 Ted Sizemore	.20	.50
129 Terry Forster	.60	1.50
130 Pete Rose	15.00	40.00
131A Eddie Kasko MG w/oEar	1.25	3.00
131B Eddie Kasko MG w/Ear	.60	1.50
132 Matty Alou	.60	1.50
133 Dave Roberts RC	.20	.50
134 Milt Wilcox	.20	.50
135 Lee May UER	.60	1.50
136A Earl Weaver MG Orange	.60	1.50
136B Earl Weaver MG Pale	1.25	3.00
137 Jim Beauchamp	.20	.50
138 Horacio Pina	.20	.50
139 Carmen Fanzone RC	.20	.50
140 Lou Piniella	1.00	2.50
141 Bruce Kison	.20	.50
142 Thurman Munson	10.00	25.00
143 John Curtis	.20	.50
144 Marty Perez	.20	.50
145 Bobby Bonds	1.00	2.50
146 Woodie Fryman	.20	.50
147 Mike Anderson	.20	.50
148 Dave Goltz	.20	.50
149 Ron Hunt	.20	.50
150 Wilbur Wood	.60	1.50
151 Wes Parker	.60	1.50
152 Dave May	.20	.50
153 Al Hrabosky	.60	1.50
154 Jeff Torborg	.60	1.50
155 Sal Bando	.60	1.50
156 Cesar Geronimo	.20	.50
157 Denny Riddleberger	.20	.50
158 Houston Astros TC	.75	2.00
159 Clarence Gaston	.60	1.50
160 Jim Palmer	2.50	6.00
161 Ted Martinez	.20	.50
162 Pete Broberg	.20	.50
163 Vic Davalillo	.20	.50
164 Monty Montgomery	.20	.50
165 Luis Aparicio	1.50	4.00
166 Terry Harmon	.20	.50
167 Steve Stone	.60	1.50
168 Jim Northrup	.60	1.50
169 Ron Schueler RC	.60	1.50
170 Harmon Killebrew	6.00	15.00
171 Bernie Carbo	.20	.50
172 Steve Kline	.20	.50
173 Hal Breeden	.20	.50
174 Goose Gossage RC	15.00	40.00
175 Frank Robinson	8.00	20.00
176 Chuck Taylor	.20	.50
177 Bill Plummer RC	.20	.50
178 Don Rose RC	.20	.50
179A Dick Williams w/Ear	1.50	4.00
179B Dick Williams w/o Ear	.60	1.50
180 Ferguson Jenkins	1.50	4.00
181 Jack Brohamer RC	.20	.50
182 Mike Caldwell RC	.60	1.50
183 Don Buford	.20	.50
184 Jerry Koosman	.60	1.50
185 Jim Wynn	.60	1.50
186 Bill Fahey	.20	.50
187 Luke Walker	.20	.50
188 Cookie Rojas	.60	1.50
189 Greg Luzinski	1.00	2.50
190 Bob Gibson	10.00	25.00
191 Detroit Tigers TC	1.00	2.50
192 Pat Jarvis	.20	.50
193 Carlton Fisk	12.00	30.00
194 Jorge Orta RC	.20	.50
195 Clay Carroll	.20	.50
196 Ken McMullen	.20	.50
197 Ed Goodson RC	.20	.50
198 Horace Clarke	.20	.50
199 Bert Blyleven	1.00	2.50
200 Billy Williams	1.50	4.00
201 George Hendrick ALCS	.60	1.50
202 George Foster NLCS	.60	1.50
203 Gene Tenace WS	.60	1.50
204 A's Two Straight WS	.60	1.50
205 Tony Perez WS	1.00	2.50
206 Gene Tenace WS	.60	1.50
207 Blue Moon Odom WS	.60	1.50
208 Johnny Bench WS	2.00	5.00
209 Bert Campaneris WS	.60	1.50
210 A's Win WS	.20	.50
211 Balor Moore	.20	.50
212 Joe Lahoud	.20	.50
213 Steve Garvey	6.00	15.00
214 Dave Hamilton RC	.20	.50
215 Dusty Baker	1.00	2.50
216 Toby Harrah	.60	1.50
217 Don Wilson	.20	.50
218 Aurelio Rodriguez	.20	.50
219 St. Louis Cardinals TC	1.00	2.50
220 Nolan Ryan	15.00	40.00
221 Fred Kendall	.20	.50
222 Rob Gardner	.20	.50
223 Bud Harrelson	.60	1.50
224 Bill Lee	.60	1.50
225 Al Oliver	.60	1.50
226 Ray Fosse	.20	.50
227 Wayne Twitchell	.20	.50
228 Bobby Darwin	.20	.50
229 Roric Harrison	.20	.50
230 Joe Morgan	8.00	20.00
231 Bill Parsons	.20	.50
232 Ken Singleton	.60	1.50
233 Ed Kirkpatrick	.20	.50
234 Bill North RC	.20	.50
235 Jim Hunter	1.50	4.00
236 Tito Fuentes	.20	.50
237A Eddie Mathews MG w/Ear	.60	1.50
237B Eddie Mathews MG w/o Ear	1.25	3.00
238 Tony Muser RC	.20	.50
239 Pete Richert	.20	.50
240 Bobby Murcer	.60	1.50
241 Dwain Anderson	.20	.50
242 George Culver	.20	.50
243 California Angels TC	1.00	2.50
244 Ed Acosta	.20	.50
245 Carl Yastrzemski	10.00	25.00
246 Ken Sanders	.20	.50
247 Del Unser	.20	.50
248 Jerry Johnson	.20	.50
249 Larry Biittner	.20	.50
250 Manny Sanguillen	.60	1.50
251 Roger Nelson	.20	.50
252A Charlie Fox MG Orange	1.50	4.00
252B Charlie Fox MG Pale	.60	1.50
253 Mark Belanger	.60	1.50
254 Bill Stoneman	.20	.50
255 Reggie Jackson	12.00	30.00
256 Chris Zachary	.20	.50
257A Yogi Berra MG Orange	1.25	3.00
257B Yogi Berra MG Pale	2.00	5.00
258 Tommy John	.60	1.50
259 Jim Holt	.20	.50
260 Gary Nolan	.60	1.50
261 Pat Kelly	.20	.50
262 Jack Aker	.20	.50
263 George Scott	.60	1.50
264 Checklist 133-264	1.25	3.00
265 Gene Michael	.60	1.50
266 Mike Lum	.30	.75
267 Lloyd Allen	.30	.75
268 Jerry Morales	.30	.75
269 Tim McCarver	.60	1.50
270 Luis Tiant	.60	1.50
271 Tom Hutton	.30	.75
272 Ed Farmer	.30	.75
273 Chris Speier	.30	.75
274 Darold Knowles	.30	.75
275 Tony Perez	1.50	4.00
276 Joe Lovitto RC	.30	.75
277 Bob Miller	.30	.75
278 Baltimore Orioles TC	.60	1.50
279 Mike Strahler	.30	.75
280 Al Kaline	8.00	20.00
281 Mike Jorgensen	.30	.75
282 Steve Hovley	.30	.75
283 Ray Sadecki	.30	.75
284 Glenn Borgmann RC	.30	.75
285 Don Kessinger	.60	1.50
286 Frank Linzy	.30	.75
287 Eddie Leon	.30	.75
288 Gary Gentry	.30	.75
289 Bob Oliver	.30	.75
290 Cesar Cedeno	.60	1.50
291 Rogelio Moret	.30	.75
292 Jose Cruz	.60	1.50
293 Bernie Allen	.30	.75
294 Steve Arlin	.30	.75
295 Bert Campaneris	.60	1.50
296 Sparky Anderson MG	1.00	2.50
297 Walt Williams	.30	.75
298 Ron Bryant	.30	.75
299 Ted Ford	.30	.75
300 Steve Carlton	6.00	15.00
301 Billy Grabarkewitz	.30	.75
302 Terry Crowley	.30	.75
303 Nelson Briles	.30	.75
304 Duke Sims	.30	.75
305 Willie Mays	40.00	100.00
306 Tom Burgmeier	.30	.75
307 Boots Day	.30	.75
308 Skip Lockwood	.30	.75
309 Paul Popovich	.30	.75
310 Dick Allen	.60	1.50
311 Joe Decker	.30	.75
312 Oscar Brown	.30	.75
313 Jim Ray	.30	.75
314 Ron Swoboda	.60	1.50
315 John Odom	.30	.75
316 San Diego Padres TC	.60	1.50
317 Danny Cater	.30	.75
318 Jim McGlothlin	.30	.75
319 Jim Spencer	.30	.75
320 Lou Brock	3.00	8.00
321 Rich Hinton	.30	.75
322 Garry Maddox RC	.60	1.50
323 Billy Martin MG	.60	1.50
324 Al Downing	.30	.75
325 Boog Powell	.60	1.50
326 Darrell Brandon	.30	.75
327 John Lowenstein	.30	.75
328 Bill Bonham	.30	.75
329 Ed Kranepool	.60	1.50
330 Rod Carew	3.00	8.00
331 Carl Morton	.30	.75
332 John Felske RC	.30	.75
333 Gene Clines	.30	.75
334 Freddie Patek	.30	.75
335 Bob Tolan	.30	.75
336 Tom Bradley	.30	.75
337 Dave Duncan	.60	1.50
338 Checklist 265-396	1.25	3.00
339 Dick Tidrow	.30	.75
340 Nate Colbert	.30	.75
341 Jim Palmer KP	1.00	2.50
342 Sam McDowell KP	.30	.75
343 Bobby Murcer KP	.30	.75
344 Jim Hunter KP	1.00	2.50
345 Chris Speier KP	.30	.75
346 Gaylord Perry KP	.60	1.50
347 Kansas City Royals TC	.60	1.50
348 Rennie Stennett	.30	.75
349 Dick McAuliffe	.30	.75
350 Tom Seaver	12.00	30.00
351 Jimmy Stewart	.30	.75
352 Don Stanhouse RC	.30	.75
353 Steve Brye	.30	.75
354 Billy Parker	.30	.75
355 Mike Marshall	.60	1.50
356 Chuck Tanner MG	1.50	4.00
357 Ross Grimsley	.30	.75
358 Jim Nettles	.30	.75
359 Cecil Upshaw	.30	.75
360 Joe Rudi UER	.60	1.50
361 Fran Healy	.30	.75
362 Eddie Watt	.30	.75
363 Jackie Hernandez	.30	.75
364 Rick Wise	.30	.75
365 Rico Petrocelli	.60	1.50
366 Brock Davis	.30	.75
367 Burt Hooton	.60	1.50
368 Bill Buckner	.60	1.50
369 Lerrin LaGrow	.30	.75
370 Willie Stargell	2.00	5.00
371 Mike Kekich	.30	.75
372 Oscar Gamble	.30	.75
373 Clyde Wright	.30	.75
374 Darrell Evans	.60	1.50
375 Larry Dierker	.60	1.50
376 Frank Duffy	.30	.75
377 Gene Mauch MG	1.50	4.00
378 Len Randle	.30	.75
379 Cy Acosta RC	.30	.75
380 Johnny Bench	10.00	25.00
381 Vicente Romo	.30	.75
382 Mike Hegan	.30	.75
383 Diego Segui	.30	.75
384 Don Baylor	1.50	4.00
385 Jim Perry	.60	1.50
386 Don Money	.30	.75
387 Jim Barr	.30	.75
388 Ben Oglivie	.60	1.50
389 New York Mets TC	1.50	4.00
390 Mickey Lolich	.60	1.50
391 Lee Lacy RC	.60	1.50
392 Dick Drago	.30	.75
393 Jose Cardenal	.30	.75
394 Sparky Lyle	.60	1.50
395 Roger Metzger	.30	.75
396 Grant Jackson	.30	.75
397 Dave Cash	.50	1.25
398 Rich Hand	.50	1.25
399 George Foster	.75	2.00
400 Gaylord Perry	2.00	5.00
401 Clyde Mashore	.50	1.25
402 Jack Hiatt	.50	1.25
403 Sonny Jackson	.50	1.25
404 Chuck Brinkman	.50	1.25
405 Cesar Tovar	.50	1.25
406 Paul Lindblad	.50	1.25
407 Felix Millan	.50	1.25
408 Jim Colborn	.50	1.25
409 Ivan Murrell	.50	1.25
410 Willie McCovey	2.50	6.00
411 Ray Corbin	.50	1.25
412 Manny Mota	.75	2.00
413 Tom Timmermann	.50	1.25
414 Ken Rudolph	.50	1.25
415 Marty Pattin	.50	1.25
416 Paul Schaal	.50	1.25
417 Scipio Spinks	.50	1.25
418 Bob Grich	.75	2.00
419 Casey Cox	.50	1.25
420 Tommie Agee	.50	1.25
421A B.Winkles MG RC Orange	.60	1.50
421B Bobby Winkles MG Pale	1.25	3.00
422 Bob Robertson	.50	1.25
423 Johnny Jeter	.50	1.25
424 Denny Doyle	.50	1.25
425 Alex Johnson	.50	1.25
426 Dave LaRoche	.50	1.25
427 Rick Auerbach	.50	1.25
428 Wayne Simpson	.50	1.25
429 Jim Fairey	.50	1.25
430 Vida Blue	.75	2.00
431 Gerry Moses	.50	1.25
432 Dan Frisella	.50	1.25
433 Willie Horton	.75	2.00
434 San Francisco Giants TC	1.25	3.00
435 Rico Carty	.75	2.00
436 Jim McAndrew	.50	1.25
437 John Kennedy	.50	1.25
438 Enzo Hernandez	.50	1.25
439 Eddie Fisher	.50	1.25
440 Glenn Beckert	.50	1.25
441 Gail Hopkins	.50	1.25
442 Dick Dietz	.50	1.25
443 Danny Thompson	.50	1.25
444 Ken Brett	.50	1.25
445 Ken Berry	.50	1.25
446 Jerry Reuss	.75	2.00
447 Joe Hague	.50	1.25
448 John Hiller	.50	1.25
449A K.Aspro MG w/Spahn Point	1.50	4.00
449B K.Aspro MG w/Spahn Round	1.50	4.00
450 Joe Torre	1.25	3.00
451 John Vukovich RC	.50	1.25
452 Paul Casanova	.50	1.25
453 Checklist 397-528	1.25	3.00
454 Tom Haller	.50	1.25
455 Bill Melton	.50	1.25
456 Dick Green	.50	1.25
457 John Strohmayer	.50	1.25
458 Jim Mason	.50	1.25
459 Jimmy Howarth RC	.50	1.25
460 Bill Freehan	.75	2.00
461 Mike Corkins	.50	1.25
462 Ron Blomberg	.50	1.25
463 Ken Tatum	.50	1.25
464 Chicago Cubs TC	1.25	3.00
465 Dave Giusti	.50	1.25
466 Jose Arcia	.50	1.25
467 Mike Ryan	.50	1.25
468 Tom Griffin	.50	1.25
469 Dan Monzon RC	.50	1.25
470 Mike Cuellar	.75	2.00
471 Ty Cobb LDR	4.00	10.00
472 Lou Gehrig LDR	6.00	15.00
473 Hank Aaron LDR	8.00	20.00
474 Babe Ruth LDR	8.00	20.00
475 Ty Cobb LDR	6.00	15.00
476 Walter Johnson LDR	1.25	3.00
477 Cy Young LDR	1.25	3.00
478 Walter Johnson LDR	1.25	3.00
479 Hal Lanier	.50	1.25
480 Juan Marichal	2.00	5.00
481 Chicago White Sox TC	1.25	3.00
482 Rick Reuschel RC	1.25	3.00
483 Dal Maxvill	.50	1.25
484 Ernie McAnally	.50	1.25
485 Norm Cash	.75	2.00
486A D.Ozark MG RC Orange	.60	1.50
486B Danny Ozark MG Pale	1.25	3.00
487 Bruce Dal Canton	.50	1.25
488 Dave Campbell	.75	2.00
489 Jeff Burroughs	.75	2.00
490 Claude Osteen	.75	2.00
491 Bob Montgomery	.50	1.25
492 Pedro Borbon	.50	1.25
493 Duffy Dyer	.50	1.25
494 Rich Morales	.50	1.25
495 Tommy Helms	.50	1.25
496 Ray Lamb	.50	1.25
497A R.Schoen MG Orange	.75	2.00
497B R.Schoen MG Pale	1.25	3.00
498 Graig Nettles	1.25	3.00
499 Bob Moose	.50	1.25
500 Oakland Athletics TC	1.25	3.00
501 Larry Gura	.50	1.25
502 Bobby Valentine	1.25	3.00
503 Phil Niekro	2.00	5.00
504 Earl Williams	.50	1.25
505 Bob Bailey	.50	1.25
506 Bart Johnson	.50	1.25
507 Darrel Chaney	.50	1.25
508 Gates Brown	.50	1.25
509 Jim Nash	.50	1.25
510 Amos Otis	.75	2.00
511 Sam McDowell	.75	2.00
512 Dalton Jones	.50	1.25
513 Dave Marshall	.50	1.25
514 Jerry Kenney	.50	1.25
515 Andy Messersmith	.75	2.00
516 Danny Walton	.50	1.25
517A Bill Virdon MG w/o Ear	.60	1.50
517B Bill Virdon MG w/Ear	1.25	3.00
518 Bob Veale	.50	1.25
519 Johnny Edwards	.50	1.25
520 Mel Stottlemyre	.75	2.00
521 Atlanta Braves TC	1.25	3.00
522 Leo Cardenas	.50	1.25
523 Wayne Granger	.50	1.25
524 Gene Tenace	.75	2.00
525 Jim Fregosi	.75	2.00
526 Ollie Brown	.50	1.25
527 Dan McGinn	.50	1.25
528 Paul Blair	.50	1.25
529 Milt May	1.25	3.00
530 Jim Kaat	2.00	5.00
531 Ron Woods	1.25	3.00
532 Steve Mingori	1.25	3.00
533 Larry Stahl	1.25	3.00
534 Dave Lemonds	1.25	3.00
535 Johnny Callison	2.00	5.00
536 Philadelphia Phillies TC	2.50	6.00
537 Bill Slayback RC	1.25	3.00
538 Jim Ray Hart	2.00	5.00
539 Tom Murphy	1.25	3.00
540 Cleon Jones	2.00	5.00
541 Bob Bolin	1.25	3.00
542 Pat Corrales	2.00	5.00
543 Alan Foster	1.25	3.00
544 Von Joshua	1.25	3.00
545 Orlando Cepeda	3.00	8.00
546 Jim York	1.25	3.00
547 Bobby Heise	1.25	3.00
548 Don Durham RC	1.25	3.00
549 Whitey Herzog MG	2.00	5.00
550 Dave Johnson	2.00	5.00
551 Mike Kilkenny	1.25	3.00
552 J.C. Martin	1.25	3.00
553 Mickey Scott	1.25	3.00
554 Dave Concepcion	2.00	5.00
555 Bill Hands	1.25	3.00
556 New York Yankees TC	3.00	8.00
557 Bernie Williams	1.25	3.00
558 Jerry May	1.25	3.00
559 Barry Lersch	1.25	3.00
560 Frank Howard	2.00	5.00
561 Jim Geddes RC	1.25	3.00
562 Wayne Garrett	1.25	3.00
563 Larry Haney	1.25	3.00
564 Mike Thompson RC	1.25	3.00
565 Jim Hickman	1.25	3.00
566 Lew Krausse	1.25	3.00
567 Bob Fenwick	1.25	3.00
568 Ray Newman	1.25	3.00
569 Walt Alston MG	3.00	8.00
570 Bill Singer	2.00	5.00
571 Rusty Torres	1.25	3.00
572 Gary Sutherland	1.25	3.00
573 Fred Beene	1.25	3.00
574 Bob Didier	1.25	3.00
575 Dock Ellis	1.25	3.00
576 Montreal Expos TC	2.50	6.00
577 Eric Soderholm RC	1.25	3.00
578 Ken Wright	1.25	3.00
579 Tom Grieve	2.00	5.00
580 Joe Pepitone	2.00	5.00
581 Steve Kealey	1.25	3.00
582 Darrell Porter	2.00	5.00
583 Bill Greif	1.25	3.00
584 Chris Arnold	1.25	3.00
585 Joe Niekro	2.00	5.00
586 Bill Sudakis	1.25	3.00
587 Rich McKinney	1.25	3.00
588 Checklist 529-660	8.00	20.00
589 Ken Forsch	1.25	3.00
590 Deron Johnson	1.25	3.00
591 Mike Hedlund	1.25	3.00
592 John Boccabella	1.25	3.00
593 Jack McKeon MG RC	1.50	4.00
594 Vic Harris RC	1.25	3.00
595 Don Gullett	2.00	5.00
596 Boston Red Sox TC	2.50	6.00
597 Mickey Rivers	2.00	5.00
598 Phil Roof	1.25	3.00
599 Ed Crosby	1.25	3.00
600 Dave McNally	2.00	5.00
601 Robles/Pena/Stelmaszek RC	2.00	5.00
602 Behney/Garcia/Rau RC	2.00	5.00
603 Hughes/McNulty/Reitz RC	2.00	5.00
604 Jefferson/O'Toole/Stampe RC	2.00	5.00
605 Cabell/Bourque/Marquez RC	2.00	5.00
606 Matthews/Pac/Roque RC	2.00	5.00
607 Frias/Busse/Guerrero RC	2.00	5.00
608 Busby/Colpaert/Medich RC	2.00	5.00
609 Blanks/Garcia/Lopes RC	2.00	5.00
610 Freeman/Hough/Webb RC	2.00	5.00
611 Coggins/Wohlford/Zisk RC	2.00	5.00
612 Lawson/Reynolds/Strom RC	2.00	5.00
613 Boone/Jutze/Ivie RC	6.00	15.00
614 Bumbry/Evans/Spikes RC	30.00	80.00
615 Mike Schmidt RC	125.00	300.00
616 Angelini/Blateric/Garman RC	2.00	5.00
617 Rich Chiles	1.25	3.00
618 Andy Etchebarren	1.25	3.00
619 Billy Wilson	1.25	3.00
620 Tommy Harper	2.00	5.00
621 Joe Ferguson	2.00	5.00
622 Larry Hisle	2.00	5.00
623 Steve Renko	1.25	3.00
624 Leo Durocher MG	2.00	5.00
625 Angel Mangual	1.25	3.00
626 Bob Barton	1.25	3.00
627 Luis Alvarado	1.25	3.00
628 Jim Slaton	1.25	3.00
629 Cleveland Indians TC	2.50	6.00
630 Denny McLain	3.00	8.00
631 Tom Matchick	1.25	3.00
632 Dick Selma	1.25	3.00
633 Ike Brown	1.25	3.00
634 Alan Closter	1.25	3.00
635 Gene Alley	2.00	5.00
636 Rickey Clark	1.25	3.00
637 Norm Miller	1.25	3.00
638 Ken Reynolds	1.25	3.00
639 Willie Crawford	1.25	3.00
640 Dick Bosman	1.25	3.00
641 Cincinnati Reds TC	2.50	6.00
642 Jose Laboy	1.25	3.00
643 Al Fitzmorris	1.25	3.00
644 Jack Heidemann	1.25	3.00
645 Bob Locker	1.25	3.00
646 Del Crandall MG	1.50	4.00
647 George Stone	1.25	3.00
648 Tom Egan	1.25	3.00
649 Rich Folkers	1.25	3.00
650 Felipe Alou	2.00	5.00
651 Don Carrithers	1.25	3.00
652 Ted Kubiak	1.25	3.00
653 Joe Hoerner	1.25	3.00
654 Minnesota Twins TC	2.50	6.00
655 Clay Kirby	1.25	3.00
656 John Ellis	1.25	3.00
657 Bob Johnson	1.25	3.00
658 Elliott Maddox	1.25	3.00
659 Jose Pagan	1.25	3.00
660 Fred Scherman	2.00	5.00

1973 Topps Blue Team Checklists

This 24-card standard-size set is rather difficult to find. These blue-bordered team checklist cards are very similar in design to the mass produced red trim team checklist cards issued by Topps the next year. Reportedly these were inserts only found in the test packs that included all series. In addition, a collector could mail in 25 cents and receive a full uncut sheet of these cards. This offer was somewhat limited in terms of collectors mailing in for them.

Card	Low	High
COMPLETE SET (24)	75.00	150.00
COMMON TEAM (1-24)	3.00	8.00
16 New York Mets	4.00	10.00
17 New York Yankees	4.00	10.00

1974 Topps

The cards in this 660-card set measure 2 1/2" by 3 1/2". This year marked the first time Topps issued all the cards of its baseball set at the same time rather than in series. Among other methods, cards were issued in eight-card fifteen-cent wax packs and 42 card rack packs. The ten cent packs were issued 36 to a box. For the first time, factory sets were issued through the JC Penny's catalog. Sales were probably disappointing for it would be several years before factory sets were issued again. Some interesting variations were created by the rumored move of the San Diego Padres to Washington. Fifteen cards (13 players, the team card, and the rookie card (599) of the Padres were printed either as "San Diego" (SD) or "Washington." The latter are the scarcer variety and are denoted in the checklist below by WAS. Each team's manager and his coaches again have a combined card with small pictures of each coach below the larger photo of the team's manager. The first six cards in the set (1-6) feature Hank Aaron and his illustrious career. Other topical subsets included in the set are League Leaders (201-208), All-Star selections (331-339), Playoffs cards (470-471), World Series cards (472-479), and Rookie Prospects (596-608). The card backs for the All-Stars (331-339) have no statistics, but form a picture puzzle of Bobby Bonds, the 1973 All-Star Game MVP. The key Rookie Cards in this set are Ken Griffey Sr., Dave Parker and Dave Winfield.

COMPLETE SET (660) 300.00 800.00
COMP.FACT.SET (660) 500.00 1200.00
WRAPPERS (10-CENTS) 4.00 10.00
1 Hank Aaron 715 15.00 40.00
2 Hank Aaron 54-57 5.00 12.00
3 Hank Aaron 58-61 5.00 12.00
4 Hank Aaron 62-65 5.00 12.00
5 Hank Aaron 66-69 5.00 12.00
6 Hank Aaron 70-73 5.00 12.00
7 Jim Hunter 1.50 4.00
8 George Theodore RC .20 .50
9 Mickey Lolich .40 1.00
10 Johnny Bench 8.00 20.00
11 Jim Bibby .20 .50
12 Dave May .20 .50
13 Tom Hilgendorf .20 .50
14 Paul Popovich .20 .50
15 Joe Torre .75 2.00
16 Baltimore Orioles TC .40 1.00
17 Doug Bird RC .20 .50
18 Gary Thomasson RC .20 .50
19 Gerry Moses .20 .50
20 Nolan Ryan 12.00 30.00
21 Bob Gallagher RC .20 .50
22 Cy Acosta .20 .50
23 Craig Robinson RC .20 .50
24 John Hiller .40 1.00
25 Ken Singleton .40 1.00
26 Bill Campbell RC .20 .50
27 George Scott .40 1.00
28 Manny Sanguillen .40 1.00
29 Phil Niekro 1.25 3.00
30 Bobby Bonds .75 2.00
31 Preston Gomez MG .40 1.00
32A Johnny Grubb SD RC .40 1.00
32B Johnny Grubb WASH 1.50 4.00
33 Don Newhauser RC .20 .50
34 Andy Kosco .20 .50
35 Gaylord Perry 1.25 3.00
36 St. Louis Cardinals TC .40 1.00
37 Dave Sells RC .20 .50
38 Don Kessinger .40 1.00
39 Ken Suarez .20 .50
40 Jim Palmer 6.00 15.00
41 Bobby Floyd .20 .50
42 Claude Osteen .40 1.00
43 Jim Wynn .40 1.00
44 Mel Stottlemyre .40 1.00
45 Dave Johnson .40 1.00
46 Pat Kelly .20 .50
47 Dick Ruthven RC .20 .50
48 Dick Sharon RC .20 .50
49 Steve Renko .20 .50
50 Rod Carew 3.00 8.00
51 Bobby Heise .20 .50
52 Al Oliver .40 1.00
53A Fred Kendall SD .40 1.00
53B Fred Kendall WASH 1.50 4.00
54 Elias Sosa RC .20 .50
55 Frank Robinson 5.00 12.00
56 New York Mets TC .40 1.00
57 Darold Knowles .20 .50
58 Charlie Spikes .20 .50
59 Ross Grimsley .20 .50
60 Lou Brock 2.50 6.00
61 Luis Aparicio 1.25 3.00
62 Bob Locker .20 .50
63 Bill Sudakis .20 .50
64 Doug Rau .20 .50
65 Amos Otis .40 1.00
66 Sparky Lyle .40 1.00
67 Tommy Helms .20 .50
68 Grant Jackson .20 .50
69 Del Unser .20 .50
70 Dick Allen .75 2.00
71 Dan Frisella .20 .50
72 Aurelio Rodriguez .20 .50
73 Mike Marshall .75 2.00
74 Minnesota Twins TC .40 1.00
75 Jim Colborn .20 .50
76 Mickey Rivers .40 1.00
77A Rich Troedson SD RC .40 1.00
77B Rich Troedson WASH 1.50 4.00
78 Charlie Fox MG .40 1.00
79 Gene Tenace .40 1.00
80 Tom Seaver 10.00 25.00
81 Frank Duffy .20 .50
82 Dave Giusti .20 .50
83 Orlando Cepeda 1.25 3.00
84 Rick Wise .20 .50
85 Joe Morgan 3.00 8.00
86 Joe Ferguson .40 1.00
87 Fergie Jenkins 1.25 3.00
88 Freddie Patek .40 1.00
89 Jackie Brown .20 .50
90 Bobby Murcer .40 1.00
91 Ken Forsch .20 .50
92 Paul Blair .40 1.00
93 Rod Gilbreath RC .20 .50
94 Detroit Tigers TC .40 1.00
95 Steve Carlton 3.00 8.00
96 Jerry Hairston RC .20 .50
97 Bob Bailey .20 .50
98 Bert Blyleven .75 2.00
99 Del Crandall MG .40 1.00
100 Willie Stargell 2.50 6.00
101 Bobby Valentine .40 1.00
102A Bill Greif SD .40 1.00
102B Bill Greif WASH 1.50 4.00
103 Sal Bando .40 1.00
104 Ron Bryant .20 .50
105 Carlton Fisk 5.00 12.00
106 Harry Parker RC .20 .50
107 Alex Johnson .20 .50
108 Al Hrabosky .40 1.00
109 Bob Grich .40 1.00
110 Billy Williams 1.25 3.00
111 Clay Carroll .20 .50
112 Dave Lopes .75 2.00
113 Dick Drago .20 .50
114 California Angels TC .40 1.00
115 Willie Horton .40 1.00
116 Jerry Reuss .40 1.00
117 Ron Blomberg .20 .50
118 Bill Lee .40 1.00
119 Danny Ozark MG .40 1.00
120 Wilbur Wood .20 .50
121 Larry Lintz RC .20 .50
122 Jim Holt .20 .50
123 Nelson Briles .40 1.00
124 Bobby Coluccio RC .20 .50
125A Nate Colbert SD .40 1.00
125B Nate Colbert WASH 1.50 4.00
126 Checklist 1-132 1.25 3.00
127 Tom Paciorek .40 1.00
128 John Ellis .20 .50
129 Chris Speier .20 .50
130 Reggie Jackson 8.00 20.00
131 Bob Boone .75 2.00
132 Felix Millan .20 .50
133 David Clyde RC .40 1.00
134 Denis Menke .20 .50
135 Roy White .40 1.00
136 Rick Reuschel .40 1.00
137 Al Bumbry .40 1.00
138 Eddie Brinkman .20 .50
139 Aurelio Monteagudo .20 .50
140 Darrell Evans .75 2.00
141 Pat Bourque .20 .50
142 Pedro Garcia .20 .50
143 Dick Woodson .20 .50
144 Walter Alston MG 1.25 3.00
145 Dock Ellis .20 .50
146 Ron Fairly .40 1.00
147 Bart Johnson .20 .50
148A Dave Hilton SD .40 1.00
148B Dave Hilton WASH 1.50 4.00
149 Mac Scarce .20 .50
150 John Mayberry .40 1.00
151 Diego Segui .20 .50
152 Oscar Gamble .40 1.00
153 Jon Matlack .40 1.00
154 Houston Astros TC .40 1.00
155 Bert Campaneris .40 1.00
156 Randy Moffitt .20 .50
157 Vic Harris .20 .50
158 Jack Billingham .20 .50
159 Jim Ray Hart .20 .50
160 Brooks Robinson 6.00 15.00
161 Ray Burris UER RC .40 1.00
162 Bill Freehan .40 1.00
163 Ken Berry .20 .50
164 Tom House .20 .50
165 Willie Davis .40 1.00
166 Jack McKeon MG .40 1.00
167 Luis Tiant .75 2.00
168 Danny Thompson .20 .50
169 Steve Rogers RC .75 2.00
170 Bill Melton .20 .50
171 Eduardo Rodriguez RC .20 .50
172 Gene Clines .20 .50
173A Randy Jones SD RC .75 2.00
173B Randy Jones WASH 2.00 5.00
174 Bill Robinson .40 1.00
175 Reggie Cleveland .20 .50
176 John Lowenstein .20 .50
177 Dave Roberts .20 .50
178 Garry Maddox .40 1.00
179 Yogi Berra MG 2.00 5.00
180 Ken Holtzman .20 .50
181 Cesar Geronimo .20 .50
182 Lindy McDaniel .40 1.00
183 Johnny Oates .40 1.00
184 Texas Rangers TC .40 1.00
185 Jose Cardenal .20 .50
186 Fred Scherman .20 .50
187 Don Baylor .75 2.00
188 Rudy Meoli RC .20 .50
189 Jim Brewer .20 .50
190 Tony Oliva .75 2.00
191 Al Fitzmorris .20 .50
192 Mario Guerrero .20 .50
193 Tom Walker .20 .50
194 Darrell Porter .40 1.00
195 Carlos May .20 .50
196 Jim Fregosi .40 1.00
197A Vicente Romo SD .40 1.00
197B Vicente Romo WASH 1.50 4.00
198 Dave Cash .20 .50
199 Mike Kekich .20 .50
200 Cesar Cedeno .40 1.00
201 R.Carew/P.Rose LL 2.50 6.00
202 R.Jackson/W.Stargell LL 2.00 5.00
203 R.Jackson/W.Stargell LL 2.00 5.00
204 T.Harper/L.Brock LL .75 2.00
205 W.Wood/R.Bryant LL .20 .50
206 J.Palmer/T.Seaver LL 2.00 5.00
207 N.Ryan/T.Seaver LL 5.00 12.00
208 J.Hiller/M.Marshall LL .40 1.00
209 Ted Sizemore .20 .50
210 Bill Singer .20 .50
211 Chicago Cubs TC .40 1.00
212 Rollie Fingers 1.25 3.00
213 Dave Rader .20 .50
214 Billy Grabarkewitz .20 .50
215 Al Kaline UER 6.00 15.00
216 Ray Sadecki .20 .50
217 Tim Foli .20 .50
218 Johnny Briggs .20 .50
219 Doug Griffin .20 .50
220 Don Sutton 1.25 3.00
221 Chuck Tanner MG .40 1.00
222 Ramon Hernandez .20 .50
223 Jeff Burroughs .75 2.00
224 Roger Metzger .20 .50
225 Paul Splittorff .20 .50
226A San Diego Padres TC SD .75 2.00
226B San Diego Padres TC WASH 3.00 8.00
227 Mike Lum .20 .50
228 Ted Kubiak .20 .50
229 Fritz Peterson .20 .50
230 Tony Perez 1.50 4.00
231 Dick Tidrow .20 .50
232 Steve Brye .20 .50
233 Jim Barr .20 .50
234 John Milner .20 .50
235 Dave McNally .40 1.00
236 Red Schoendienst MG 1.25 3.00
237 Ken Brett .20 .50
238 F.Healy w/Munson .20 .50
239 Bill Russell .40 1.00
240 Joe Coleman .20 .50
241A Glenn Beckert SD .40 1.00
241B Glenn Beckert WASH 1.50 4.00
242 Bill Gogolewski .20 .50
243 Bob Oliver .20 .50
244 Carl Morton .20 .50
245 Cleon Jones .20 .50
246 Oakland Athletics TC .75 2.00
247 Rick Miller .20 .50
248 Tom Hall .20 .50
249 George Mitterwald .20 .50
250A Willie McCovey SD 3.00 8.00
250B Willie McCovey WASH 10.00 25.00
251 Graig Nettles .75 2.00
252 Dave Parker RC 15.00 40.00
253 John Boccabella .20 .50
254 Stan Bahnsen .20 .50
255 Larry Bowa .40 1.00
256 Tom Griffin .20 .50
257 Buddy Bell .75 2.00
258 Jerry Morales .20 .50
259 Bob Reynolds .20 .50
260 Ted Simmons .75 2.00
261 Jerry Bell .20 .50
262 Ed Kirkpatrick .20 .50
263 Checklist 133-264 1.25 3.00
264 Joe Rudi .40 1.00
265 Tug McGraw .75 2.00
266 Jim Northrup .40 1.00
267 Andy Messersmith .40 1.00
268 Tom Grieve .40 1.00
269 Bob Johnson .20 .50
270 Ron Santo .75 2.00
271 Bill Hands .20 .50
272 Paul Casanova .20 .50
273 Checklist 265-396 1.25 3.00
274 Fred Beene .20 .50
275 Ron Hunt .20 .50
276 Bobby Winkles MG .40 1.00
277 Gary Nolan .40 1.00
278 Cookie Rojas .40 1.00
279 Jim Crawford RC .20 .50
280 Carl Yastrzemski 10.00 25.00
281 San Francisco Giants TC .40 1.00
282 Doyle Alexander .40 1.00
283 Mike Schmidt 15.00 40.00
284 Dave Duncan .40 1.00
285 Reggie Smith .40 1.00
286 Tony Muser .20 .50
287 Clay Kirby .20 .50
288 Gorman Thomas RC .75 2.00
289 Rick Auerbach .20 .50
290 Vida Blue .40 1.00
291 Don Hahn .20 .50
292 Chuck Seelbach .20 .50
293 Milt May .20 .50
294 Steve Foucault RC .20 .50
295 Rick Monday .40 1.00
296 Ray Corbin .20 .50
297 Hal Breeden .20 .50
298 Roric Harrison .20 .50
299 Gene Michael .20 .50
300 Pete Rose 12.00 30.00
301 Bob Montgomery .20 .50
302 Rudy May .20 .50
303 George Hendrick .40 1.00
304 Don Wilson .20 .50
305 Tito Fuentes .20 .50
306 Earl Weaver MG 1.25 3.00
307 Luis Melendez .20 .50
308 Bruce Dal Canton .20 .50
309A Dave Roberts SD .40 1.00
309B Dave Roberts WASH 2.50 6.00
310 Terry Forster .40 1.00
311 Jerry Grote .40 1.00
312 Deron Johnson .20 .50
313 Barry Lersch .20 .50
314 Milwaukee Brewers TC .40 1.00
315 Ron Cey .75 2.00
316 Jim Perry .40 1.00
317 Richie Zisk .40 1.00
318 Jim Merritt .20 .50
319 Randy Hundley .20 .50
320 Dusty Baker .75 2.00
321 Steve Braun .20 .50
322 Ernie McAnally .20 .50
323 Richie Scheinblum .20 .50
324 Steve Kline .20 .50
325 Tommy Harper .40 1.00
326 Sparky Anderson MG 1.25 3.00
327 Tom Timmermann .20 .50
328 Skip Jutze .20 .50
329 Mark Belanger .40 1.00
330 Juan Marichal 2.00 5.00
331 C.Fisk/J.Bench AS 2.00 5.00
332 D.Allen/H.Aaron AS 3.00 8.00
333 R.Carew/J.Morgan AS 1.50 4.00
334 B.Robinson/R.Santo AS .75 2.00
335 B.Campaneris/C.Speier AS .40 1.00
336 B.Murcer/P.Rose AS 2.00 5.00
337 A.Otis/C.Cedeno AS .40 1.00
338 R.Jackson/B.Williams AS 2.00 5.00
339 J.Hunter/R.Wise AS 1.25 3.00
340 Thurman Munson 5.00 12.00
341 Dan Driessen RC .40 1.00
342 Jim Lonborg .40 1.00
343 Kansas City Royals TC .40 1.00
344 Mike Caldwell .20 .50
345 Bill North .20 .50
346 Ron Reed .20 .50
347 Sandy Alomar .40 1.00
348 Pete Richert .20 .50
349 John Vukovich .20 .50
350 Bob Gibson 6.00 15.00
351 Dwight Evans 1.25 3.00
352 Bill Stoneman .20 .50
353 Rich Coggins .20 .50
354 Whitey Lockman MG .40 1.00
355 Dave Nelson .20 .50
356 Jerry Koosman .40 1.00
357 Buddy Bradford .20 .50
358 Dal Maxvill .20 .50
359 Brent Strom .20 .50
360 Greg Luzinski .75 2.00
361 Don Carrithers .20 .50
362 Hal King .20 .50
363 New York Yankees TC .75 2.00
364A Cito Gaston SD .75 2.00
364B Cito Gaston WASH 3.00 8.00
365 Steve Busby .40 1.00
366 Larry Hisle .40 1.00
367 Norm Cash .75 2.00
368 Manny Mota .40 1.00
369 Paul Lindblad .20 .50
370 Bob Watson .40 1.00
371 Jim Slaton .20 .50
372 Ken Reitz .20 .50
373 John Curtis .20 .50
374 Marty Perez .20 .50
375 Earl Williams .20 .50
376 Jorge Orta .20 .50
377 Ron Woods .20 .50
378 Burt Hooton .40 1.00
379 Billy Martin MG .75 2.00
380 Bud Harrelson .40 1.00
381 Charlie Sands .20 .50
382 Bob Moose .20 .50
383 Philadelphia Phillies TC .40 1.00
384 Chris Chambliss .40 1.00
385 Don Gullett .40 1.00
386 Gary Matthews .75 2.00
387A Rich Morales SD .40 1.00
387B Rich Morales WASH 2.50 6.00
388 Phil Roof .20 .50
389 Gates Brown .20 .50
390 Lou Piniella .75 2.00
391 Billy Champion .20 .50
392 Dick Green .20 .50
393 Orlando Pena .20 .50
394 Ken Henderson .20 .50
395 Doug Rader .20 .50
396 Tommy Davis .40 1.00
397 George Stone .20 .50
398 Duke Sims .20 .50
399 Mike Paul .20 .50
400 Harmon Killebrew 6.00 15.00
401 Elliott Maddox .20 .50
402 Jim Rooker .20 .50
403 Darrell Johnson MG .40 1.00
404 Jim Howarth .20 .50
405 Ellie Rodriguez .20 .50
406 Steve Arlin .20 .50
407 Jim Wohlford .20 .50
408 Charlie Hough .40 1.00
409 Ike Brown .20 .50
410 Pedro Borbon .20 .50
411 Frank Baker .20 .50
412 Chuck Taylor .20 .50
413 Don Money .40 1.00
414 Checklist 397-528 1.25 3.00
415 Gary Gentry .20 .50
416 Chicago White Sox TC .40 1.00
417 Rich Folkers .20 .50
418 Walt Williams .20 .50
419 Wayne Twitchell .20 .50
420 Ray Fosse .20 .50
421 Dan Fife RC .20 .50
422 Gonzalo Marquez .20 .50
423 Fred Stanley .20 .50
424 Jim Beauchamp .20 .50
425 Pete Broberg .20 .50
426 Rennie Stennett .20 .50
427 Bobby Bolin .20 .50
428 Gary Sutherland .20 .50
429 Dick Lange RC .20 .50
430 Matty Alou .40 1.00
431 Gene Garber RC .40 1.00
432 Chris Arnold .20 .50
433 Lerrin LaGrow .20 .50
434 Ken McMullen .20 .50
435 Dave Concepcion .75 2.00
436 Don Hood RC .20 .50
437 Jim Lyttle .20 .50
438 Ed Herrmann .20 .50
439 Norm Miller .20 .50
440 Jim Kaat .75 2.00
441 Tom Ragland .20 .50
442 Alan Foster .20 .50
443 Tom Hutton .20 .50
444 Vic Davalillo .20 .50
445 George Medich .20 .50
446 Len Randle .20 .50
447 Frank Quilici MG .40 1.00
448 Ron Hodges RC .20 .50
449 Tom McCraw .20 .50
450 Rich Hebner .40 1.00
451 Tommy John .75 2.00
452 Gene Hiser .20 .50
453 Balor Moore .20 .50
454 Kurt Bevacqua .20 .50
455 Tom Bradley .20 .50
456 Dave Winfield RC 20.00 50.00
457 Chuck Goggin RC .20 .50
458 Jim Ray .20 .50
459 Cincinnati Reds TC .75 2.00
460 Boog Powell .75 2.00
461 John Odom .20 .50
462 Luis Alvarado .20 .50
463 Pat Dobson .20 .50
464 Jose Cruz .75 2.00
465 Dick Bosman .20 .50
466 Dick Billings .20 .50
467 Winston Llenas .20 .50
468 Pepe Frias .20 .50
469 Joe Decker .20 .50
470 Reggie Jackson ALCS 2.00 5.00
471 Jon Matlack NLCS .40 1.00
472 Darold Knowles WS1 .40 1.00
473 Willie Mays WS 6.00 15.00
474 Bert Campaneris WS3 .40 1.00
475 Rusty Staub WS4 .40 1.00
476 Cleon Jones WS5 .40 1.00
477 Reggie Jackson WS 2.00 5.00
478 Bert Campaneris WS7 .40 1.00
479 A's Celebrate WS .40 1.00
480 Willie Crawford .20 .50
481 Jerry Terrell RC .20 .50
482 Bob Didier .20 .50
483 Atlanta Braves TC .40 1.00
484 Carmen Fanzone .20 .50
485 Felipe Alou .75 2.00
486 Steve Stone .40 1.00
487 Ted Martinez .20 .50
488 Andy Etchebarren .20 .50
489 Danny Murtaugh MG .40 1.00
490 Vada Pinson .75 2.00
491 Roger Nelson .20 .50
492 Mike Rogodzinski RC .20 .50
493 Joe Hoerner .20 .50
494 Ed Goodson .20 .50
495 Dick McAuliffe .40 1.00
496 Tom Murphy .20 .50
497 Bobby Mitchell .20 .50
498 Pat Corrales .20 .50
499 Rusty Torres .20 .50
500 Lee May .40 1.00
501 Eddie Leon .20 .50
502 Dave LaRoche .20 .50
503 Eric Soderholm .20 .50
504 Joe Niekro .40 1.00
505 Bill Buckner .40 1.00
506 Ed Farmer .20 .50
507 Larry Stahl .20 .50
508 Montreal Expos TC .40 1.00
509 Jesse Jefferson .20 .50
510 Wayne Garrett .20 .50
511 Toby Harrah .40 1.00
512 Joe Lahoud .20 .50
513 Jim Campanis .20 .50
514 Paul Schaal .20 .50
515 Willie Montanez .20 .50
516 Horacio Pina .20 .50
517 Mike Hegan .20 .50
518 Derrel Thomas .20 .50
519 Bill Sharp RC .20 .50
520 Tim McCarver .75 2.00
521 Ken Aspromonte MG .40 1.00
522 J.R. Richard .75 2.00
523 Cecil Cooper .75 2.00
524 Bill Plummer .20 .50
525 Clyde Wright .20 .50
526 Frank Tepedino .40 1.00
527 Bobby Darwin .20 .50
528 Bill Bonham .20 .50
529 Horace Clarke .40 1.00
530 Mickey Stanley .40 1.00
531 Gene Mauch MG .40 1.00
532 Skip Lockwood .20 .50
533 Mike Phillips RC .20 .50
534 Eddie Watt .20 .50
535 Bob Tolan .20 .50
536 Duffy Dyer .20 .50
537 Steve Mingori .20 .50
538 Cesar Tovar .20 .50
539 Lloyd Allen .20 .50
540 Bob Robertson .20 .50
541 Cleveland Indians TC .40 1.00
542 Goose Gossage .75 2.00
543 Danny Cater .20 .50
544 Ron Schueler .20 .50
545 Billy Conigliaro .40 1.00
546 Mike Corkins .20 .50
547 Glenn Borgmann .20 .50
548 Sonny Siebert .20 .50
549 Mike Jorgensen .20 .50
550 Sam McDowell .40 1.00
551 Von Joshua .20 .50
552 Denny Doyle .20 .50
553 Jim Willoughby .20 .50
554 Tim Johnson RC .20 .50
555 Woodie Fryman .20 .50
556 Dave Campbell .40 1.00
557 Jim McGlothlin .20 .50
558 Bill Fahey .20 .50
559 Darrel Chaney .20 .50
560 Mike Cuellar .40 1.00
561 Ed Kranepool .40 1.00
562 Jack Aker .20 .50
563 Hal McRae .40 1.00
564 Mike Ryan .20 .50
565 Milt Wilcox .20 .50
566 Jackie Hernandez .20 .50
567 Boston Red Sox TC .40 1.00
568 Mike Torrez .40 1.00
569 Rick Dempsey .40 1.00
570 Ralph Garr .40 1.00
571 Rich Hand .20 .50
572 Enzo Hernandez .20 .50
573 Mike Adams RC .20 .50
574 Bill Parsons .20 .50
575 Steve Garvey 1.25 3.00
576 Scipio Spinks .20 .50
577 Mike Sadek RC .20 .50
578 Ralph Houk MG .40 1.00
579 Cecil Upshaw .20 .50
580 Jim Spencer .20 .50
581 Fred Norman .20 .50
582 Bucky Dent RC 2.00 5.00
583 Marty Pattin .20 .50
584 Ken Rudolph .20 .50
585 Merv Rettenmund .20 .50
586 Jack Brohamer .20 .50
587 Larry Christenson RC .20 .50
588 Hal Lanier .20 .50
589 Boots Day .20 .50
590 Roger Moret .20 .50
591 Sonny Jackson .20 .50
592 Ed Bane RC .20 .50
593 Steve Yeager .40 1.00
594 Leroy Stanton .20 .50
595 Steve Blass .40 1.00
596 Gar/Hold/Lit/Pole RC .20 .50
597 Chalk/Gam/Mac/Trillo RC .40 1.00
598 Ken Griffey RC 8.00 20.00
599A Dior/Freis/Ric/Shan WASH .75 2.00
599B Dior/Freis/Ric/Shan Lg 6.00 15.00
599C Dior/Freis/Ric/Shan Sm
600 Cash/Cox/Madlock/Sand RC 2.00 5.00
601 Arm/Bladt/Downing/McBride RC 1.25 3.00
602 Abb/Henn/Swan/Voss RC .40 1.00
603 Foote/Lund/Moore/Robles RC .20 .50
604 Hugh/Knox/Thornton/White RC 2.00 5.00
605 Alb/Frail/Kob/Tanana RC 1.50 4.00
606 Fuller/Howard/Smith/Velez RC .40 1.00
607 Fost/Hein/Ros/Taveras RC .40 1.00
608A Apod/Ban/D'Acq/Wall ERR .75 2.00
608B Apod/Ban/D'Acq/Wall RC .40 1.00
609 Rico Petrocelli .40 1.00
610 Dave Kingman .75 2.00
611 Rich Stelmaszek .20 .50
612 Luke Walker .20 .50
613 Dan Monzon .20 .50
614 Adrian Devine RC .40 1.00
615 Johnny Jeter UER .20 .50
616 Larry Gura .20 .50
617 Ted Ford .20 .5
618 Jim Mason .20 .5
619 Mike Anderson .20 .5
620 Al Downing .20 .5
621 Bernie Carbo .20 .5
622 Phil Gagliano .20 .5
623 Celerino Sanchez .20 .5
624 Bob Miller .20 .5
625 Ollie Brown .20 .5
626 Pittsburgh Pirates TC .40 1.0
627 Carl Taylor .20 .5
628 Ivan Murrell .20 .5
629 Rusty Staub .75 2.0
630 Tommie Agee .40 1.0
631 Steve Barber .20 .50
632 George Culver .20 .50
633 Dave Hamilton .20 .50
634 Eddie Mathews MG 1.25 3.0
635 Johnny Edwards .20 .50
636 Dave Goltz .20 .50
637 Checklist 529-660 1.25 3.0
638 Ken Sanders .20 .50
639 Joe Lovitto .20 .50
640 Milt Pappas .40 1.0
641 Chuck Brinkman .20 .50
642 Terry Harmon .20 .50
643 Los Angeles Dodgers TC .40 1.0
644 Wayne Granger .20 .50
645 Ken Boswell .20 .50
646 George Foster .75 2.0
647 Juan Beniquez RC .20 .50
648 Terry Crowley .20 .50
649 Fernando Gonzalez RC .20 .50
650 Mike Epstein .20 .50
651 Leron Lee .20 .50
652 Gail Hopkins .20 .50
653 Bob Stinson .20 .50
654A Jesus Alou NPOF 1.50 4.00
654B Jesus Alou COR .40 1.00
655 Mike Tyson RC .20 .50
656 Adrian Garrett .20 .50
657 Jim Shellenback .20 .50
658 Lee Lacy .20 .50
659 Joe Lis .20 .50
660 Larry Dierker .75 2.00

1974 Topps Traded

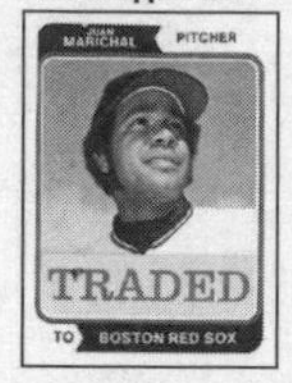

The cards in this 44-card set measure 2 1/2" by 3 1/2". The 1974 Topps Traded set contains 43 player cards and one unnumbered checklist card. The fronts have the word "traded" in block letters and the backs are designed in newspaper style. Card numbers are the same as in the regular set except they are followed by a "T." No known scarcities exist for this set. The cards were inserted in all packs toward the end of the production run. They were produced in large enough quantity that they are no scarcer than the regular Topps cards.

COMPLETE SET (44) 8.00 20.00
23T Craig Robinson .20 .50
42T Claude Osteen .30 .75
43T Jim Wynn .30 .75
51T Bobby Heise .20 .50
59T Ross Grimsley .20 .50
62T Bob Locker .20 .50
63T Bill Sudakis .20 .50
73T Mike Marshall .30 .75
123T Nelson Briles .30 .75
139T Aurelio Monteagudo .20 .50
151T Diego Segui .20 .50
165T Willie Davis .30 .75
175T Reggie Cleveland .20 .50
182T Lindy McDaniel .30 .75
186T Fred Scherman .20 .50
249T George Mitterwald .20 .50
262T Ed Kirkpatrick .20 .50
269T Bob Johnson .20 .50
270T Ron Santo .40 1.00
313T Barry Lersch .20 .50
319T Randy Hundley .30 .75
330T Juan Marichal .75 2.00
348T Pete Richert .20 .50
373T John Curtis .20 .50
390T Lou Piniella .40 1.00
428T Gary Sutherland .20 .50
454T Kurt Bevacqua .20 .50
458T Jim Ray .20 .50
485T Felipe Alou .40 1.00
486T Steve Stone .30 .75
496T Tom Murphy .20 .50
516T Horacio Pina .20 .50
534T Eddie Watt .20 .50
538T Cesar Tovar .20 .50
544T Ron Schueler .20 .50
579T Cecil Upshaw .20 .50
585T Merv Rettenmund .20 .50
612T Luke Walker .20 .50
616T Larry Gura .30 .75
618T Jim Mason .20 .50
630T Tommie Agee .30 .75

8T Terry Crowley .20 .50
9T Fernando Gonzalez .20 .50
0 Traded Checklist .60 1.50

1974 Topps Team Checklists

he cards in this 24-card set measure 2 1/2" by 3 /2". The 1974 series of checklists was issued in acks with the regular cards for that year. The cards re unnumbered (arbitrarily numbered below lphabetically by team name) and have bright red orders. The year and team name appear in a green anel decorated by a crossed bats design, below hich is a white area containing facsimile autographs f various players. The mustard-yellow and gray-olored backs list team members alphabetically, long with their card number, uniform number and osition. Uncut sheets of these cards were also vailable through a wrapper mail-in offer. The uncut heet value in NR/Mt or better condition is pproximately $150.

COMPLETE SET (24) 8.00 20.00
COMMON TEAM (1-24) .40 1.00

1975 Topps

The 1975 Topps set consists of 660 standard size cards. The design was radically different in appearance from sets of the preceding years. The most prominent change was the use of a two-color frame surrounding the picture area rather than a single, subdued color. A facsimile autograph appears on the picture, and the backs are printed in red and green on gray. Cards were released in ten-card wax packs, 18-card cello packs with a 25 cent SRP and were packaged 24 to a box and 15 boxes to a case, as well as in 42-card rack packs which cost 49 cents upon release. The cello packs were issued 24 to a box. Cards 189-212 depict the MVP's of both leagues from 1951 through 1974. The first seven cards (1-7) feature players (listed in alphabetical order) breaking records or achieving milestones during the previous season. Cards 306-313 picture league leaders in various statistical categories. Cards 459-466 depict the results of post-season action. Team cards feature a checklist back for players on that team and show a small inset photo of the manager on the front. The following players' regular issue cards are explicitly denoted as All-Stars, 1, 50, 80, 140, 170, 180, 260, 320, 350, 390, 400, 420, 440, 470, 530, 570, and 600. This set is quite popular with collectors, at least in part due to the fact that the Rookie Cards of George Brett, Gary Carter, Keith Hernandez, Fred Lynn, Jim Rice and Robin Yount are all in the set.

COMPLETE SET (660) 400.00 1000.00
WRAPPER (15-CENT) 3.00 8.00
1 Hank Aaron HL 12.00 30.00
2 Lou Brock HL 1.25 3.00
3 Bob Gibson HL 1.25 3.00
4 Al Kaline HL 6.00 15.00
5 Nolan Ryan HL 6.00 15.00
6 Mike Marshall HL .40 1.00
7 Ryan / Busby / Bosman HL 3.00 8.00
8 Rogelio Moret .20 .50
9 Frank Tepedino .40 1.00
10 Willie Davis .40 1.00
11 Bill Melton .20 .50
12 David Clyde .20 .50
13 Gene Locklear RC .40 1.00
14 Milt Wilcox .20 .50
15 Jose Cardenal .40 1.00
16 Frank Tanana .75 2.00
17 Dave Concepcion .75 2.00
18 Detroit Tigers CL/Houk .75 2.00
19 Jerry Koosman .40 1.00
20 Thurman Munson 10.00 25.00
21 Rollie Fingers 1.25 3.00
22 Dave Cash .20 .50
23 Bill Russell .40 1.00
24 Al Fitzmorris .20 .50
25 Lee May .40 1.00
26 Dave McNally .40 1.00
27 Ken Reitz .20 .50
28 Tom Murphy .20 .50
29 Dave Parker 1.25 3.00
30 Bert Blyleven .75 2.00
31 Dave Rader .20 .50
32 Reggie Cleveland .20 .50
33 Dusty Baker .75 2.00
34 Steve Renko .20 .50
35 Ron Santo .40 1.00
36 Joe Lovitto .20 .50
37 Dave Freisleben .20 .50
38 Buddy Bell .75 2.00
39 Andre Thornton .40 1.00
40 Bill Singer .20 .50
41 Cesar Geronimo .40 1.00
42 Joe Coleman .20 .50
43 Cleon Jones .40 1.00
44 Pat Dobson .20 .50
45 Joe Rudi .40 1.00
46 Philadelphia Phillies CL/Ozark .75 2.00
47 Tommy John .75 2.00
48 Freddie Patek .40 1.00
49 Larry Dierker .40 1.00
50 Brooks Robinson 3.00 8.00
51 Bob Forsch RC .40 1.00
52 Darrell Porter .40 1.00
53 Dave Giusti .20 .50
54 Eric Soderholm .20 .50
55 Bobby Bonds .75 2.00
56 Rick Wise .40 1.00
57 Dave Johnson .40 1.00
58 Chuck Taylor .20 .50
59 Ken Henderson .20 .50
60 Fergie Jenkins 1.25 3.00
61 Dave Winfield 6.00 15.00
62 Fritz Peterson .20 .50
63 Steve Swisher RC .20 .50
64 Dave Chalk .20 .50
65 Don Gullett .40 1.00
66 Willie Horton .40 1.00
67 Tug McGraw .40 1.00
68 Ron Blomberg .20 .50
69 John Odom .20 .50
70 Mike Schmidt 6.00 15.00
71 Charlie Hough .40 1.00
72 Kansas City Royals CL/McKeon .75 2.00
73 J.R. Richard .40 1.00
74 Mark Belanger .40 1.00
75 Ted Simmons .75 2.00
76 Ed Sprague .20 .50
77 Richie Zisk .40 1.00
78 Ray Corbin .20 .50
79 Gary Matthews .40 1.00
80 Carlton Fisk 6.00 15.00
81 Ron Reed .20 .50
82 Pat Kelly .20 .50
83 Jim Merritt .20 .50
84 Enzo Hernandez .20 .50
85 Bill Bonham .20 .50
86 Joe Lis .20 .50
87 George Foster .75 2.00
88 Tom Egan .20 .50
89 Jim Ray .20 .50
90 Rusty Staub .75 2.00
91 Dick Green .20 .50
92 Cecil Upshaw .20 .50
93 Davey Lopes .75 2.00
94 Jim Lonborg .40 1.00
95 John Mayberry .40 1.00
96 Mike Cosgrove RC .20 .50
97 Earl Williams .20 .50
98 Rich Folkers .20 .50
99 Mike Hegan .20 .50
100 Willie Stargell 1.50 4.00
101 Montreal Expos CL/Mauch .75 2.00
102 Joe Decker .20 .50
103 Rick Miller .20 .50
104 Bill Madlock .75 2.00
105 Buzz Capra .20 .50
106 Mike Hargrove UER RC 1.25 3.00
107 Jim Barr .20 .50
108 Tom Hall .20 .50
109 George Hendrick .40 1.00
110 Wilbur Wood .20 .50
111 Wayne Garrett .20 .50
112 Larry Hardy RC .20 .50
113 Elliott Maddox .20 .50
114 Dick Lange .20 .50
115 Joe Ferguson .20 .50
116 Lerrin LaGrow .20 .50
117 Baltimore Orioles CL/Weaver 1.25 3.00
118 Mike Anderson .20 .50
119 Tommy Helms .20 .50
120 Steve Busby UER .40 1.00
121 Bill North .20 .50
122 Al Hrabosky .40 1.00
123 Johnny Briggs .20 .50
124 Jerry Reuss .40 1.00
125 Ken Singleton .40 1.00
126 Checklist 1-132 1.25 3.00
127 Glenn Borgmann .20 .50
128 Bill Lee .40 1.00
129 Rick Monday .40 1.00
130 Phil Niekro 1.25 3.00
131 Toby Harrah .40 1.00
132 Randy Moffitt .20 .50
133 Dan Driessen .40 1.00
134 Ron Hodges .20 .50
135 Charlie Spikes .20 .50
136 Jim Mason .20 .50
137 Terry Forster .40 1.00
138 Del Unser .20 .50
139 Horacio Pina .20 .50
140 Steve Garvey 1.25 3.00
141 Mickey Stanley .40 1.00
142 Bob Reynolds .20 .50
143 Cliff Johnson RC .40 1.00
144 Jim Wohlford .20 .50
145 Ken Holtzman .40 1.00
146 San Diego Padres CL/McNamara .75 2.00
147 Pedro Garcia .20 .50
148 Jim Rooker .20 .50
149 Tim Foli .20 .50
150 Bob Gibson 2.50 6.00
151 Steve Brye .20 .50
152 Mario Guerrero .20 .50
153 Rick Reuschel .40 1.00
154 Mike Lum .20 .50
155 Jim Bibby .20 .50
156 Dave Kingman .75 2.00
157 Pedro Borbon .40 1.00
158 Jerry Grote .20 .50
159 Steve Arlin .20 .50
160 Graig Nettles .75 2.00
161 Stan Bahnsen .20 .50
162 Willie Montanez .20 .50
163 Jim Brewer .20 .50
164 Mickey Rivers .40 1.00
165 Doug Rader .40 1.00
166 Woodie Fryman .20 .50
167 Rich Coggins .20 .50
168 Bill Greif .20 .50
169 Cookie Rojas .20 .50
170 Bert Campaneris .40 1.00
171 Ed Kirkpatrick .20 .50
172 Boston Red Sox CL/Johnson 1.25 3.00
173 Steve Rogers .40 1.00
174 Bake McBride .40 1.00
175 Don Money .40 1.00
176 Burt Hooton .40 1.00
177 Vic Correll RC .20 .50
178 Cesar Tovar .20 .50
179 Tom Bradley .20 .50
180 Joe Morgan 8.00 20.00
181 Fred Beene .20 .50
182 Don Hahn .20 .50
183 Mel Stottlemyre .40 1.00
184 Jorge Orta .20 .50
185 Steve Carlton 3.00 8.00
186 Willie Crawford .20 .50
187 Denny Doyle .20 .50
188 Tom Griffin .20 .50
189 Y.Berra/Campanella MVP 1.50 4.00
190 B.Shantz/H.Sauer MVP .75 2.00
191 Al Rosen/Campanella MVP .75 2.00
192 Y.Berra/W.Mays MVP 1.50 4.00
193 Y.Berra/Campanella MVP 1.25 3.00
194 M.Mantle/D.Newcombe MVP 4.00 10.00
195 M.Mantle/H.Aaron MVP 6.00 15.00
196 J.Jensen/E.Banks MVP 1.25 3.00
197 N.Fox/E.Banks MVP .75 2.00
198 R.Maris/D.Groat MVP .75 2.00
199 R.Maris/F.Robinson MVP 1.25 3.00
200 M.Mantle/M.Wills MVP 4.00 10.00
201 E.Howard/S.Koufax MVP .75 2.00
202 B.Robinson/K.Boyer MVP .40 1.00
203 Z.Versalles/W.Mays MVP .75 2.00
204 F.Robinson/B.Clemente MVP 2.50 6.00
205 C.Yastrzemski/O.Cepeda MVP .75 2.00
206 D.McLain/B.Gibson MVP .75 2.00
207 H.Killebrew/W.McCovey MVP .40 1.00
208 B.Powell/J.Bench MVP .75 2.00
209 V.Blue/J.Torre MVP .75 2.00
210 R.Allen/J.Bench MVP .75 2.00
211 R.Jackson/P.Rose MVP 2.00 5.00
212 J.Burroughs/S.Garvey MVP .75 2.00
213 Oscar Gamble .40 1.00
214 Harry Parker .20 .50
215 Bobby Valentine .40 1.00
216 San Francisco Giants CL/Westrum .75 2.00
217 Lou Piniella .75 2.00
218 Jerry Johnson .20 .50
219 Ed Herrmann .20 .50
220 Don Sutton 1.25 3.00
221 Aurelio Rodriguez .20 .50
222 Dan Spillner RC .20 .50
223 Robin Yount RC 30.00 80.00
224 Ramon Hernandez .20 .50
225 Bob Grich .40 1.00
226 Bill Campbell .20 .50
227 Bob Watson .40 1.00
228 George Brett RC 60.00 150.00
229 Barry Foote .20 .50
230 Jim Hunter 1.50 4.00
231 Mike Tyson .20 .50
232 Diego Segui .20 .50
233 Billy Grabarkewitz .20 .50
234 Tom Grieve .40 1.00
235 Jack Billingham .40 1.00
236 California Angels CL/Williams .75 2.00
237 Carl Morton .40 1.00
238 Dave Duncan .40 1.00
239 George Stone .20 .50
240 Garry Maddox .40 1.00
241 Dick Tidrow .20 .50
242 Jay Johnstone .40 1.00
243 Jim Kaat .75 2.00
244 Bill Buckner .40 1.00
245 Mickey Lolich .75 2.00
246 St. Louis Cardinals CL/Schoen .75 2.00
247 Enos Cabell .20 .50
248 Randy Jones .75 2.00
249 Danny Thompson .20 .50
250 Ken Brett .20 .50
251 Fran Healy .20 .50
252 Fred Scherman .20 .50
253 Jesus Alou .20 .50
254 Mike Torrez .40 1.00
255 Dwight Evans .75 2.00
256 Billy Champion .20 .50
257 Checklist: 133-264 1.25 3.00
258 Dave LaRoche .20 .50
259 Len Randle .20 .50
260 Johnny Bench 10.00 25.00
261 Andy Hassler RC .20 .50
262 Rowland Office RC .20 .50
263 Jim Perry .40 1.00
264 John Milner .20 .50
265 Ron Bryant .20 .50
266 Sandy Alomar .40 1.00
267 Dick Ruthven .20 .50
268 Hal McRae .40 1.00
269 Doug Rau .20 .50
270 Ron Fairly .40 1.00
271 Gerry Moses .20 .50
272 Lynn McGlothen .20 .50
273 Steve Braun .20 .50
274 Vicente Romo .20 .50
275 Paul Blair .40 1.00
276 Chicago White Sox CL/Tanner .75 2.00
277 Frank Taveras .20 .50
278 Paul Lindblad .20 .50
279 Milt May .20 .50
280 Carl Yastrzemski 5.00 12.00
281 Jim Slaton .20 .50
282 Jerry Morales .20 .50
283 Steve Foucault .20 .50
284 Ken Griffey Sr. 1.50 4.00
285 Ellie Rodriguez .20 .50
286 Mike Jorgensen .20 .50
287 Roric Harrison .20 .50
288 Bruce Ellingsen RC .20 .50
289 Ken Rudolph .20 .50
290 Jon Matlack .20 .50
291 Bill Sudakis .20 .50
292 Ron Schueler .20 .50
293 Dick Sharon .20 .50
294 Geoff Zahn RC .20 .50
295 Vada Pinson .75 2.00
296 Alan Foster .20 .50
297 Craig Kusick RC .20 .50
298 Johnny Grubb .20 .50
299 Bucky Dent .75 2.00
300 Reggie Jackson 5.00 12.00
301 Dave Roberts .20 .50
302 Rick Burleson RC .40 1.00
303 Grant Jackson .20 .50
304 Pittsburgh Pirates CL/Murtaugh .75 2.00
305 Jim Colborn .20 .50
306 R.Carew/R.Garr LL .75 2.00
307 D.Allen/M.Schmidt LL 1.50 4.00
308 J.Burroughs/J.Bench LL .75 2.00
309 B.North/L.Brock LL .75 2.00
310 Hunter/Jenk/Mess/Niek LL .75 2.00
311 J.Hunter/B.Capra LL .75 2.00
312 N.Ryan/S.Carlton LL 5.00 12.00
313 T.Forster/M.Marshall LL .40 1.00
314 Buck Martinez .20 .50
315 Don Kessinger .40 1.00
316 Jackie Brown .20 .50
317 Joe Lahoud .20 .50
318 Ernie McAnally .20 .50
319 Johnny Oates .40 1.00
320 Pete Rose 12.00 30.00
321 Rudy May .20 .50
322 Ed Goodson .20 .50
323 Fred Holdsworth .20 .50
324 Ed Kranepool .40 1.00
325 Tony Oliva .75 2.00
326 Wayne Twitchell .20 .50
327 Jerry Hairston .20 .50
328 Sonny Siebert .20 .50
329 Ted Kubiak .20 .50
330 Mike Marshall .40 1.00
331 Cleveland Indians CL/Robinson .75 2.00
332 Fred Kendall .20 .50
333 Dick Drago .20 .50
334 Greg Gross RC .20 .50
335 Jim Palmer 2.50 6.00
336 Rennie Stennett .20 .50
337 Kevin Kobel .20 .50
338 Rich Stelmaszek .20 .50
339 Jim Fregosi .40 1.00
340 Paul Splittorff .20 .50
341 Hal Breeden .20 .50
342 Leroy Stanton .20 .50
343 Danny Frisella .20 .50
344 Ben Oglivie .40 1.00
345 Clay Carroll .40 1.00
346 Bobby Darwin .20 .50
347 Mike Caldwell .40 1.00
348 Tony Muser .40 1.00
349 Ray Sadecki .20 .50
350 Bobby Murcer .40 1.00
351 Bob Boone .75 2.00
352 Darold Knowles .20 .50
353 Luis Melendez .20 .50
354 Dick Bosman .20 .50
355 Chris Cannizzaro .20 .50
356 Rico Petrocelli .40 1.00
357 Ken Forsch UER .20 .50
358 Al Bumbry .40 1.00
359 Paul Popovich .20 .50
360 George Scott .40 1.00
361 Los Angeles Dodgers CL/Alston .75 2.00
362 Steve Hargan .20 .50
363 Carmen Fanzone .20 .50
364 Doug Bird .20 .50
365 Bob Bailey .20 .50
366 Ken Sanders .20 .50
367 Craig Robinson .20 .50
368 Vic Albury .20 .50
369 Merv Rettenmund .20 .50
370 Tom Seaver 10.00 25.00
371 Gates Brown .20 .50
372 John D'Acquisto .20 .50
373 Bill Sharp .20 .50
374 Eddie Watt .20 .50
375 Roy White .40 1.00
376 Steve Yeager .40 1.00
377 Tom Hilgendorf .20 .50
378 Derrel Thomas .20 .50
379 Bernie Carbo .20 .50
380 Sal Bando .40 1.00
381 John Curtis .20 .50
382 Don Baylor .75 2.00
383 Jim York .40 1.00
384 Milwaukee Brewers CL/Crandall .75 2.00
385 Dock Ellis .20 .50
386 Checklist: 265-396 UER 1.25 3.00
387 Jim Spencer .20 .50
388 Steve Stone .40 1.00
389 Tony Solaita RC .20 .50
390 Ron Cey .75 2.00
391 Don DeMola RC .20 .50
392 Bruce Bochte RC .40 1.00
393 Gary Gentry .20 .50
394 Larvell Blanks .20 .50
395 Bud Harrelson .40 1.00
396 Fred Norman .40 1.00
397 Bill Freehan .40 1.00
398 Elias Sosa .20 .50
399 Terry Harmon .20 .50
400 Dick Allen .75 2.00
401 Mike Wallace .20 .50
402 Bob Tolan .20 .50
403 Tom Buskey RC .20 .50
404 Ted Sizemore .20 .50
405 John Montague RC .20 .50
406 Bob Gallagher .20 .50
407 Herb Washington RC .75 2.00
408 Clyde Wright UER .20 .50
409 Bob Robertson .20 .50
410 Mike Cuellar UER .40 1.00
411 George Mitterwald .20 .50
412 Bill Hands .20 .50
413 Marty Pattin .20 .50
414 Manny Mota .40 1.00
415 John Hiller .40 1.00
416 Larry Lintz .20 .50
417 Skip Lockwood .20 .50
418 Leo Foster .20 .50
419 Dave Goltz .20 .50
420 Larry Bowa .75 2.00
421 New York Mets CL/Berra 1.25 3.00
422 Brian Downing .40 1.00
423 Clay Kirby .20 .50
424 John Lowenstein .20 .50
425 Tito Fuentes .20 .50
426 George Medich .20 .50
427 Clarence Gaston .40 1.00
428 Dave Hamilton .20 .50
429 Jim Dwyer RC .20 .50
430 Luis Tiant .75 2.00
431 Rod Gilbreath .20 .50
432 Ken Berry .20 .50
433 Larry Demery RC .20 .50
434 Bob Locker .20 .50
435 Dave Nelson .20 .50
436 Ken Frailing .20 .50
437 Al Cowens RC .40 1.00
438 Don Carrithers .20 .50
439 Ed Brinkman .20 .50
440 Andy Messersmith .40 1.00
441 Bobby Heise .20 .50
442 Maximino Leon RC .20 .50
443 Minnesota Twins CL/Quilici .75 2.00
444 Gene Garber .40 1.00
445 Felix Millan .20 .50
446 Bart Johnson .20 .50
447 Terry Crowley .20 .50
448 Frank Duffy .20 .50
449 Charlie Williams .20 .50
450 Willie McCovey 2.50 6.00
451 Rick Dempsey .40 1.00
452 Angel Mangual .20 .50
453 Claude Osteen .40 1.00
454 Doug Griffin .20 .50
455 Don Wilson .20 .50
456 Bob Coluccio .20 .50
457 Mario Mendoza RC .20 .50
458 Ross Grimsley .20 .50
459 1974 AL Championships .40 1.00
460 1974 NL Championships .75 2.00
461 Reggie Jackson WS1 2.00 5.00
462 W.Alston/J.Ferguson WS2 .40 1.00
463 Rollie Fingers WS3 .75 2.00
464 A's Batter WS4 .40 1.00
465 Joe Rudi WS5 .40 1.00
466 A's Do it Again WS .75 2.00
467 Ed Halicki RC .20 .50
468 Bobby Mitchell .20 .50
469 Tom Dettore RC .20 .50
470 Jeff Burroughs .40 1.00
471 Bob Stinson .20 .50
472 Bruce Dal Canton .20 .50
473 Ken McMullen .20 .50
474 Luke Walker .20 .50
475 Darrell Evans .40 1.00
476 Ed Figueroa RC .20 .50
477 Tom Hutton .20 .50
478 Tom Burgmeier .20 .50
479 Ken Boswell .20 .50
480 Carlos May .20 .50
481 Will McEnaney RC .40 1.00
482 Tom McCraw .20 .50
483 Steve Ontiveros .20 .50
484 Glenn Beckert .40 1.00
485 Sparky Lyle .40 1.00
486 Ray Fosse .20 .50
487 Houston Astros CL/Gomez .75 2.00
488 Bill Travers RC .20 .50
489 Cecil Cooper .75 2.00
490 Reggie Smith .40 1.00
491 Doyle Alexander .40 1.00
492 Rich Hebner .40 1.00
493 Don Stanhouse .20 .50
494 Pete LaCock RC .20 .50
495 Nelson Briles .40 1.00
496 Pepe Frias .20 .50
497 Jim Nettles .20 .50
498 Al Downing .20 .50
499 Marty Perez .20 .50
500 Nolan Ryan 20.00 50.00
501 Bill Robinson .40 1.00
502 Pat Bourque .20 .50
503 Fred Stanley .20 .50
504 Buddy Bradford .20 .50
505 Chris Speier .20 .50
506 Leron Lee .20 .50
507 Tom Carroll RC .20 .50
508 Bob Hansen RC .20 .50
509 Dave Hilton .20 .50
510 Vida Blue .40 1.00
511 Texas Rangers CL/Martin .75 2.00
512 Larry Milbourne RC .20 .50
513 Dick Pole .20 .50
514 Jose Cruz .75 2.00
515 Manny Sanguillen .40 1.00
516 Don Hood .20 .50
517 Checklist: 397-528 1.25 3.00
518 Leo Cardenas .20 .50
519 Jim Todd RC .20 .50
520 Amos Otis .40 1.00
521 Dennis Blair RC .20 .50
522 Gary Sutherland .20 .50
523 Tom Paciorek .40 1.00
524 John Doherty RC .20 .50
525 Tom House .20 .50
526 Larry Hisle .40 1.00
527 Mac Scarce .20 .50
528 Eddie Leon .20 .50
529 Gary Thomasson .20 .50
530 Gaylord Perry 1.25 3.00
531 Cincinnati Reds CL/Anderson 2.00 5.00
532 Gorman Thomas .40 1.00
533 Rudy Meoli .20 .50
534 Alex Johnson .20 .50
535 Gene Tenace .40 1.00
536 Bob Moose .20 .50
537 Tommy Harper .40 1.00
538 Duffy Dyer .20 .50
539 Jesse Jefferson .20 .50
540 Lou Brock 2.50 6.00
541 Roger Metzger .20 .50
542 Pete Broberg .20 .50
543 Larry Biittner .20 .50
544 Steve Mingori .20 .50
545 Billy Williams 1.25 3.00
546 John Knox .20 .50
547 Von Joshua .20 .50
548 Charlie Sands .20 .50
549 Bill Butler .20 .50
550 Ralph Garr .40 1.00
551 Larry Christenson .20 .50
552 Jack Brohamer .20 .50
553 John Boccabella .20 .50
554 Goose Gossage .75 2.00
555 Al Oliver .40 1.00
556 Tim Johnson .20 .50
557 Larry Gura .20 .50
558 Dave Roberts .20 .50
559 Bob Montgomery .20 .50
560 Tony Perez 1.50 4.00
561 Oakland Athletics CL/Dark .75 2.00
562 Gary Nolan .40 1.00
563 Wilbur Howard .20 .50
564 Tommy Davis .40 1.00
565 Joe Torre .75 2.00
566 Ray Burris .20 .50
567 Jim Sundberg RC .75 2.00
568 Dale Murray RC .20 .50
569 Frank White .40 1.00
570 Jim Wynn .40 1.00
571 Dave Lemanczyk RC .20 .50
572 Roger Nelson .20 .50
573 Orlando Pena .20 .50
574 Tony Taylor .20 .50
575 Gene Clines .20 .50
576 Phil Roof .20 .50
577 John Morris .20 .50
578 Dave Tomlin RC .20 .50
579 Skip Pitlock .20 .50
580 Frank Robinson 2.50 6.00
581 Darrel Chaney .20 .50
582 Eduardo Rodriguez .20 .50
583 Andy Etchebarren .20 .50
584 Mike Garman .20 .50
585 Chris Chambliss .40 1.00
586 Tim McCarver .75 2.00
587 Chris Ward RC .20 .50
588 Rick Auerbach .20 .50
589 Atlanta Braves CL/King .75 2.00
590 Cesar Cedeno .40 1.00
591 Glenn Abbott .20 .50
592 Balor Moore .20 .50
593 Gene Lamont .20 .50
594 Jim Fuller .20 .50
595 Joe Niekro .40 1.00
596 Ollie Brown .20 .50
597 Winston Llenas .20 .50
598 Bruce Kison .20 .50
599 Nate Colbert .20 .50
600 Rod Carew 3.00 8.00
601 Juan Beniquez .20 .50
602 John Vukovich .20 .50
603 Lew Krausse .20 .50
604 Oscar Zamora RC .20 .50
605 John Ellis .20 .50
606 Bruce Miller RC .20 .50
607 Jim Holt .20 .50
608 Gene Michael .20 .50
609 Elrod Hendricks .20 .50
610 Ron Hunt .20 .50
611 New York Yankees CL/Virdon .75 2.00
612 Terry Hughes .20 .50
613 Bill Parsons .20 .50
614 Kuc/Mill/Ruhle/Sieb RC .40 1.00
615 Darcy/Leonard/Und/Webb RC .75 2.00
616 Jim Rice RC 15.00 40.00
617 Cubb/DeCinces/Sand/Trillo RC .75 2.00
618 East/John/McGregor/Rhoden RC .40 1.00
619 Ayala/Nyman/Smith Turner RC .40 1.00
620 Gary Carter RC 15.00 40.00
621 Denny/Eastwick/Kern/Vein RC .75 2.00
622 Fred Lynn RC 6.00 15.00
623 K.Hern RC/P.Garner RC 4.00 10.00
624 Kon/Lavelle/Otten/Sol RC .40 1.00
625 Boog Powell .75 2.00
626 Larry Haney UER .20 .50
627 Tom Walker .20 .50
628 Ron LeFlore RC .40 1.00
629 Joe Hoerner .20 .50
630 Greg Luzinski .75 2.00
631 Lee Lacy .20 .50
632 Morris Nettles RC .20 .50
633 Paul Casanova .20 .50
634 Cy Acosta .20 .50
635 Chuck Dobson .20 .50
636 Charlie Moore .20 .50
637 Ted Martinez .20 .50
638 Chicago Cubs CL/Marshall .75 2.00
639 Steve Kline .20 .50
640 Harmon Killebrew 2.50 6.00
641 Jim Northrup .40 1.00
642 Mike Phillips .20 .50
643 Brent Strom .20 .50
644 Bill Fahey .20 .50
645 Danny Cater .20 .50
646 Checklist: 529-660 1.25 3.00
647 Claudell Washington RC .75 2.00
648 Dave Pagan RC .20 .50
649 Jack Heidemann .20 .50
650 Dave May .20 .50
651 John Morlan RC .20 .50
652 Lindy McDaniel .40 1.00
653 Lee Richard UER .20 .50
654 Jerry Terrell .20 .50
655 Rico Carty .40 1.00
656 Bill Plummer .20 .50
657 Bob Oliver .20 .50
658 Vic Harris .20 .50
659 Bob Apodaca .20 .50
660 Hank Aaron 20.00 50.00

1975 Topps Mini

COMPLETE SET (660) 300.00 600.00
*MINI VETS: .75X TO 1.5X BASIC CARDS
*MINI ROOKIES: .5X TO 1X BASIC RC

1976 Topps

The 1976 Topps set of 660 standard-size cards is known for its sharp color photographs and interesting presentation of subjects. Cards were issued in ten-card wax packs which cost 15 cents upon release, 42-card rack packs as well as cello packs and other options. Team cards feature a checklist back for players on that team and show a small inset photo of the manager on the front. A "Father and Son" series (66-70) spotlights five Major Leaguers whose fathers also made the "Big Show." Other subseries include "All Time All Stars" (341-350), "Record Breakers" from the previous season (1-6), League Leaders (191-205), Post-season cards (461-462), and Rookie Prospects (589-599). The following players' regular issue cards are explicitly denoted as All-Stars, 10, 48, 60, 140, 150, 165, 169, 240, 300, 370, 380, 395, 400, 420, 475, 500, 580, and 650. The key Rookie Cards in this set are Dennis Eckersley, Ron Guidry, and Willie Randolph. We've heard recent reports that this set was also issued in seven-card wax packs which cost a dime. Confirmation of that information would be appreciated.

COMPLETE SET (660) 300.00 600.00
1 Hank Aaron RB 10.00 25.00
2 Bobby Bonds RB .60 1.50
3 Mickey Lolich RB .30 .75
4 Dave Lopes RB .30 .75
5 Tom Seaver RB 2.00 5.00
6 Rennie Stennett RB .30 .75
7 Jim Umbarger RC .15 .40
8 Tito Fuentes .15 .40
9 Paul Lindblad .15 .40
10 Lou Brock 2.00 5.00
11 Jim Hughes .15 .40
12 Richie Zisk .30 .75

13 John Wockenfuss RC .15 .40
14 Gene Garber .30 .75
15 George Scott .30 .75
16 Bob Apodaca .15 .40
17 New York Yankees CL/Martin .60 1.50
18 Dale Murray .15 .40
19 George Brett 15.00 40.00
20 Bob Watson .30 .75
21 Dave LaRoche .15 .40
22 Bill Russell .30 .75
23 Brian Downing .15 .40
24 Cesar Geronimo .30 .75
25 Mike Torrez .30 .75
26 Andre Thornton .30 .75
27 Ed Figueroa .15 .40
28 Dusty Baker .60 1.50
29 Rick Burleson .30 .75
30 John Montefusco RC .30 .75
31 Len Randle .15 .40
32 Danny Frisella .15 .40
33 Bill North .15 .40
34 Mike Garman .15 .40
35 Tony Oliva .60 1.50
36 Frank Taveras .15 .40
37 John Hiller .30 .75
38 Garry Maddox .30 .75
39 Pete Broberg .15 .40
40 Dave Kingman .60 1.50
41 Tippy Martinez RC .30 .75
42 Barry Foote .15 .40
43 Paul Splittorff .15 .40
44 Doug Rader .30 .75
45 Boog Powell .60 1.50
46 Los Angeles Dodgers CL/Alston .60 1.50
47 Jesse Jefferson .15 .40
48 Dave Concepcion .60 1.50
49 Dave Duncan .30 .75
50 Fred Lynn 2.00 5.00
51 Ray Burris .15 .40
52 Dave Chalk .15 .40
53 Mike Beard RC .15 .40
54 Dave Rader .15 .40
55 Gaylord Perry 1.00 2.50
56 Bob Tolan .15 .40
57 Phil Garner .30 .75
58 Ron Reed .15 .40
59 Larry Hisle .30 .75
60 Jerry Reuss .30 .75
61 Ron LeFlore .30 .75
62 Johnny Oates .30 .75
63 Bobby Darwin .15 .40
64 Jerry Koosman .30 .75
65 Chris Chambliss .30 .75
66 Gus/Buddy Bell FS .30 .75
67 Bob/Ray Boone FS .30 .75
68 Joe/Joe Jr. Coleman FS .15 .40
69 Jim/Mike Hegan FS .15 .40
70 Roy/Roy Jr. Smalley FS .15 .40
71 Steve Rogers .30 .75
72 Hal McRae .30 .75
73 Baltimore Orioles CL/Weaver .60 1.50
74 Oscar Gamble .30 .75
75 Larry Dierker .30 .75
76 Willie Crawford .15 .40
77 Pedro Borbon .30 .75
78 Cecil Cooper .30 .75
79 Jerry Morales .15 .40
80 Jim Kaat .60 1.50
81 Darrell Evans .30 .75
82 Von Joshua .15 .40
83 Jim Spencer .15 .40
84 Brent Strom .15 .40
85 Mickey Rivers .30 .75
86 Mike Tyson .15 .40
87 Tom Burgmeier .15 .40
88 Duffy Dyer .15 .40
89 Vern Ruhle .15 .40
90 Sal Bando .30 .75
91 Tom Hutton .15 .40
92 Eduardo Rodriguez .15 .40
93 Mike Phillips .15 .40
94 Jim Dwyer .15 .40
95 Brooks Robinson 6.00 15.00
96 Doug Bird .15 .40
97 Wilbur Howard .15 .40
98 Dennis Eckersley RC 20.00 50.00
99 Lee Lacy .15 .40
100 Jim Hunter 1.25 3.00
101 Pete LaCock .15 .40
102 Jim Willoughby .15 .40
103 Biff Pocoroba RC .15 .40
104 Cincinnati Reds CL/Anderson 1.00 2.50
105 Gary Lavelle .15 .40
106 Tom Grieve .30 .75
107 Dave Roberts .15 .40
108 Don Kirkwood RC .15 .40
109 Larry Lintz .15 .40
110 Carlos May .15 .40
111 Danny Thompson .15 .40
112 Kent Tekulve RC .60 1.50
113 Gary Sutherland .15 .40
114 Jay Johnstone .30 .75
115 Ken Holtzman .30 .75
116 Charlie Moore .15 .40
117 Mike Jorgensen .15 .40
118 Boston Red Sox CL/Johnson .60 1.50
119 Checklist 1-132 .60 1.50
120 Rusty Staub .30 .75
121 Tony Solaita .15 .40
122 Mike Cosgrove .15 .40
123 Walt Williams .15 .40
124 Doug Rau .15 .40
125 Don Baylor .60 1.50
126 Tom Dettore .15 .40
127 Larvell Blanks .15 .40
128 Ken Griffey Sr. 1.00 2.50
129 Andy Etchebarren .15 .40
130 Luis Tiant .60 1.50
131 Bill Stein RC .15 .40
132 Don Hood .15 .40
133 Gary Matthews .30 .75
134 Mike Ivie .15 .40
135 Bake McBride .30 .75
136 Dave Goltz .15 .40
137 Bill Robinson .30 .75
138 Lerrin LaGrow .15 .40
139 Gorman Thomas .30 .75
140 Vida Blue .30 .75
141 Larry Parrish RC .60 1.50
142 Dick Drago .15 .40
143 Jerry Grote .15 .40
144 Al Fitzmorris .15 .40
145 Larry Bowa .30 .75
146 George Medich .15 .40
147 Houston Astros CL/Virdon .60 1.50
148 Stan Thomas RC .15 .40
149 Tommy Davis .30 .75
150 Steve Garvey 1.00 2.50
151 Bill Bonham .15 .40
152 Leroy Stanton .15 .40
153 Buzz Capra .15 .40
154 Bucky Dent .30 .75
155 Jack Billingham .30 .75
156 Rico Carty .30 .75
157 Mike Caldwell .15 .40
158 Ken Reitz .15 .40
159 Jerry Terrell .15 .40
160 Dave Winfield 6.00 15.00
161 Bruce Kison .15 .40
162 Jack Pierce RC .15 .40
163 Jim Slaton .15 .40
164 Pepe Mangual .15 .40
165 Gene Tenace .30 .75
166 Skip Lockwood .15 .40
167 Freddie Patek .30 .75
168 Tom Hilgendorf .15 .40
169 Graig Nettles .60 1.50
170 Rick Wise .15 .40
171 Greg Gross .15 .40
172 Texas Rangers CL/Lucchesi .60 1.50
173 Steve Swisher .15 .40
174 Charlie Hough .30 .75
175 Ken Singleton .30 .75
176 Dick Lange .15 .40
177 Marty Perez .15 .40
178 Tom Buskey .15 .40
179 George Foster .60 1.50
180 Goose Gossage .60 1.50
181 Willie Montanez .15 .40
182 Harry Rasmussen .15 .40
183 Steve Braun .15 .40
184 Bill Greif .15 .40
185 Dave Parker .60 1.50
186 Tom Walker .15 .40
187 Pedro Garcia .15 .40
188 Fred Scherman .15 .40
189 Claudell Washington .30 .75
190 Jon Matlack .15 .40
191 Madlock/Simm/Mang LL .30 .75
192 Carew/Lynn/Munson LL 1.00 2.50
193 Schmidt/King/Luz LL 1.25 3.00
194 Reggie/Scott/Mayb LL 1.25 3.00
195 Luz/Bench/Perez LL .60 1.50
196 Scott/Mayb/Lynn LL .15 .40
197 Lopes/Morgan/Brock LL .60 1.50
198 Rivers/Wash/Otis LL .15 .40
199 Seaver/Jones/Mess LL 1.00 2.50
200 Hunter/Palmer/Blue LL .60 1.50
201 Jones/Mess/Seaver LL .60 1.50
202 Palmer/Hunter/Eck LL 1.25 3.00
203 Seaver/Mont/Mess LL 1.00 2.50
204 Tanana/Blyleven/Perry LL .30 .75
205 A.Hrabosky/G.Gossage LL .30 .75
206 Manny Trillo .15 .40
207 Andy Hassler .15 .40
208 Mike Lum .15 .40
209 Alan Ashby RC .15 .40
210 Lee May .30 .75
211 Clay Carroll .15 .40
212 Pat Kelly .15 .40
213 Dave Heaverlo RC .15 .40
214 Eric Soderholm .15 .40
215 Reggie Smith .30 .75
216 Montreal Expos CL/Kuehl .60 1.50
217 Dave Freisleben .15 .40
218 John Knox .15 .40
219 Tom Murphy .15 .40
220 Manny Sanguillen .30 .75
221 Jim Todd .15 .40
222 Wayne Garrett .15 .40
223 Ollie Brown .15 .40
224 Jim York .15 .40
225 Roy White .30 .75
226 Jim Sundberg .30 .75
227 Oscar Zamora .15 .40
228 John Hale RC .15 .40
229 Jerry Remy RC .15 .40
230 Carl Yastrzemski 8.00 20.00
231 Tom House .15 .40
232 Frank Duffy .15 .40
233 Grant Jackson .15 .40
234 Mike Sadek .15 .40
235 Bert Blyleven .60 1.50
236 Kansas City Royals CL/Herzog .60 1.50
237 Dave Hamilton .15 .40
238 Larry Biittner .15 .40
239 John Curtis .15 .40
240 Pete Rose 15.00 40.00
241 Hector Torres .15 .40
242 Dan Meyer .15 .40
243 Jim Rooker .15 .40
244 Bill Sharp .15 .40
245 Felix Millan .15 .40
246 Cesar Tovar .15 .40
247 Terry Harmon .15 .40
248 Dick Tidrow .15 .40
249 Cliff Johnson .30 .75
250 Fergie Jenkins 1.00 2.50
251 Rick Monday .30 .75
252 Tim Nordbrook RC .15 .40
253 Bill Buckner .30 .75
254 Rudy Meoli .15 .40
255 Fritz Peterson .15 .40
256 Rowland Office .15 .40
257 Ross Grimsley .15 .40
258 Nyls Nyman .15 .40
259 Darrel Chaney .15 .40
260 Steve Busby .15 .40
261 Gary Thomasson .15 .40
262 Checklist 133-264 .60 1.50
263 Lyman Bostock RC .60 1.50
264 Steve Renko .15 .40
265 Willie Davis .30 .75
266 Alan Foster .15 .40
267 Aurelio Rodriguez .15 .40
268 Del Unser .15 .40
269 Rick Austin .15 .40
270 Willie Stargell 1.25 3.00
271 Jim Lonborg .30 .75
272 Rick Dempsey .30 .75
273 Joe Niekro .30 .75
274 Tommy Harper .30 .75
275 Rick Manning RC .30 .75
276 Mickey Scott .15 .40
277 Chicago Cubs CL/Marshall .60 1.50
278 Bernie Carbo .15 .40
279 Roy Howell RC .15 .40
280 Burt Hooton .30 .75
281 Dave May .15 .40
282 Dan Osborn RC .15 .40
283 Merv Rettenmund .15 .40
284 Steve Ontiveros .15 .40
285 Mike Cuellar .30 .75
286 Jim Wohlford .15 .40
287 Pete Mackanin .15 .40
288 Bill Campbell .15 .40
289 Enzo Hernandez .15 .40
290 Ted Simmons .30 .75
291 Ken Sanders .15 .40
292 Leon Roberts .15 .40
293 Bill Castro RC .15 .40
294 Ed Kirkpatrick .15 .40
295 Dave Cash .15 .40
296 Pat Dobson .15 .40
297 Roger Metzger .15 .40
298 Dick Bosman .15 .40
299 Champ Summers RC .15 .40
300 Johnny Bench 10.00 25.00
301 Jackie Brown .15 .40
302 Rick Miller .15 .40
303 Steve Foucault .15 .40
304 California Angels CL/Williams .60 1.50
305 Andy Messersmith .30 .75
306 Rod Gilbreath .15 .40
307 Al Bumbry .30 .75
308 Jim Barr .15 .40
309 Bill Melton .15 .40
310 Randy Jones .30 .75
311 Cookie Rojas .30 .75
312 Don Carrithers .15 .40
313 Dan Ford RC .15 .40
314 Ed Kranepool .15 .40
315 Al Hrabosky .30 .75
316 Robin Yount 8.00 20.00
317 John Candelaria RC .60 1.50
318 Bob Boone .60 1.50
319 Larry Gura .15 .40
320 Willie Horton .30 .75
321 Jose Cruz .60 1.50
322 Glenn Abbott .15 .40
323 Rob Sperring RC .15 .40
324 Jim Bibby .15 .40
325 Tony Perez 1.25 3.00
326 Dick Pole .15 .40
327 Dave Moates RC .15 .40
328 Carl Morton .15 .40
329 Joe Ferguson .15 .40
330 Nolan Ryan 12.00 30.00
331 San Diego Padres CL/McNamara .60 1.50
332 Charlie Williams .15 .40
333 Bob Coluccio .15 .40
334 Dennis Leonard .30 .75
335 Bob Grich .30 .75
336 Vic Albury .15 .40
337 Bud Harrelson .30 .75
338 Bob Bailey .15 .40
339 John Denny .30 .75
340 Jim Rice 10.00 25.00
341 Lou Gehrig ATG 5.00 12.00
342 Rogers Hornsby ATG 1.25 3.00
343 Pie Traynor ATG .60 1.50
344 Honus Wagner ATG 2.00 5.00
345 Babe Ruth ATG 8.00 20.00
346 Ty Cobb ATG 5.00 12.00
347 Ted Williams ATG 5.00 12.00
348 Mickey Cochrane ATG .60 1.50
349 Walter Johnson ATG 2.00 5.00
350 Lefty Grove ATG .60 1.50
351 Randy Hundley .30 .75
352 Dave Giusti .15 .40
353 Sixto Lezcano RC .30 .75
354 Ron Blomberg .15 .40
355 Steve Carlton 4.00 10.00
356 Ted Martinez .15 .40
357 Ken Forsch .15 .40
358 Buddy Bell .30 .75
359 Rick Reuschel .30 .75
360 Jeff Burroughs .30 .75
361 Detroit Tigers CL/Houk .60 1.50
362 Will McEnaney .30 .75
363 Dave Collins RC .30 .75
364 Elias Sosa .15 .40
365 Carlton Fisk 2.50 6.00
366 Bobby Valentine .30 .75
367 Bruce Miller .15 .40
368 Wilbur Wood .15 .40
369 Frank White .30 .75
370 Ron Cey .30 .75
371 Elrod Hendricks .15 .40
372 Rick Baldwin RC .15 .40
373 Johnny Briggs .15 .40
374 Dan Warthen RC .15 .40
375 Ron Fairly .30 .75
376 Rich Hebner .30 .75
377 Mike Hegan .15 .40
378 Steve Stone .30 .75
379 Ken Boswell .15 .40
380 Bobby Bonds .60 1.50
381 Denny Doyle .15 .40
382 Matt Alexander RC .15 .40
383 John Ellis .15 .40
384 Philadelphia Phillies CL/Ozark .60 1.50
385 Mickey Lolich .30 .75
386 Ed Goodson .15 .40
387 Mike Miley RC .15 .40
388 Stan Perzanowski RC .15 .40
389 Glenn Adams RC .15 .40
390 Don Gullett .30 .75
391 Jerry Hairston .15 .40
392 Checklist 265-396 .60 1.50
393 Paul Mitchell RC .15 .40
394 Fran Healy .15 .40
395 Jim Wynn .30 .75
396 Bill Lee .15 .40
397 Tim Foli .15 .40
398 Dave Tomlin .15 .40
399 Luis Melendez .15 .40
400 Rod Carew 2.50 6.00
401 Ken Brett .15 .40
402 Don Money .30 .75
403 Geoff Zahn .15 .40
404 Enos Cabell .15 .40
405 Rollie Fingers 1.00 2.50
406 Ed Herrmann .15 .40
407 Tom Underwood .15 .40
408 Charlie Spikes .15 .40
409 Dave Lemanczyk .15 .40
410 Ralph Garr .30 .75
411 Bill Singer .15 .40
412 Toby Harrah .30 .75
413 Pete Varney RC .15 .40
414 Wayne Garland .15 .40
415 Vada Pinson .60 1.50
416 Tommy John .60 1.50
417 Gene Clines .15 .40
418 Jose Morales RC .15 .40
419 Reggie Cleveland .15 .40
420 Joe Morgan 6.00 15.00
421 Oakland Athletics CL .60 1.50
422 Johnny Grubb .15 .40
423 Ed Halicki .15 .40
424 Phil Roof .15 .40
425 Rennie Stennett .15 .40
426 Bob Forsch .15 .40
427 Kurt Bevacqua .15 .40
428 Jim Crawford .15 .40
429 Fred Stanley .15 .40
430 Jose Cardenal .30 .75
431 Dick Ruthven .15 .40
432 Tom Veryzer .15 .40
433 Rick Waits RC .15 .40
434 Morris Nettles .15 .40
435 Phil Niekro 1.00 2.50
436 Bill Fahey .15 .40
437 Terry Forster .15 .40
438 Doug DeCinces .30 .75
439 Rick Rhoden .30 .75
440 John Mayberry .30 .75
441 Gary Carter 3.00 8.00
442 Hank Webb .15 .40
443 San Francisco Giants CL .60 1.50
444 Gary Nolan .30 .75
445 Rico Petrocelli .30 .75
446 Larry Haney .15 .40
447 Gene Locklear .30 .75
448 Tom Johnson .15 .40
449 Bob Robertson .15 .40
450 Jim Palmer 2.00 5.00
451 Buddy Bradford .15 .40
452 Tom Hausman RC .15 .40
453 Lou Piniella .60 1.50
454 Tom Griffin .15 .40
455 Dick Allen .60 1.50
456 Joe Coleman .15 .40
457 Ed Crosby .15 .40
458 Earl Williams .15 .40
459 Jim Brewer .15 .40
460 Cesar Cedeno .30 .75
461 NL/AL Champs .30 .75
462 1975 WS/Reds Champs .30 .75
463 Steve Hargan .15 .40
464 Ken Henderson .15 .40
465 Mike Marshall .30 .75
466 Bob Stinson .15 .40
467 Woodie Fryman .15 .40
468 Jesus Alou .15 .40
469 Rawly Eastwick .30 .75
470 Bobby Murcer .30 .75
471 Jim Burton .15 .40
472 Bob Davis RC .15 .40
473 Paul Blair .30 .75
474 Ray Corbin .15 .40
475 Joe Rudi .30 .75
476 Bob Moose .15 .40
477 Cleveland Indians CL/Robinson .60 1.50
478 Lynn McGlothen .15 .40
479 Bobby Mitchell .15 .40
480 Mike Schmidt 8.00 20.00
481 Rudy May .15 .40
482 Tim Hosley .15 .40
483 Mickey Stanley .15 .40
484 Eric Raich RC .15 .40
485 Mike Hargrove .30 .75
486 Bruce Dal Canton .15 .40
487 Leron Lee .15 .40
488 Claude Osteen .30 .75
489 Skip Jutze .15 .40
490 Frank Tanana .30 .75
491 Terry Crowley .15 .40
492 Marty Pattin .15 .40
493 Derrel Thomas .15 .40
494 Craig Swan .30 .75
495 Nate Colbert .15 .40
496 Juan Beniquez .15 .40
497 Joe McIntosh RC .15 .40
498 Glenn Borgmann .15 .40
499 Mario Guerrero .15 .40
500 Reggie Jackson 6.00 15.00
501 Billy Champion .15 .40
502 Tim McCarver .60 1.50
503 Elliott Maddox .15 .40
504 Pittsburgh Pirates CL/Murtaugh .60 1.50
505 Mark Belanger .30 .75
506 George Mitterwald .15 .40
507 Ray Bare RC .15 .40
508 Duane Kuiper RC .15 .40
509 Bill Hands .15 .40
510 Amos Otis .30 .75
511 Jamie Easterley .15 .40
512 Ellie Rodriguez .15 .40
513 Bart Johnson .15 .40
514 Dan Driessen .30 .75
515 Steve Yeager .30 .75
516 Wayne Granger .15 .40
517 John Milner .15 .40
518 Doug Flynn RC .15 .40
519 Steve Brye .15 .40
520 Willie McCovey 5.00 12.00
521 Jim Colborn .15 .40
522 Ted Sizemore .15 .40
523 Bob Montgomery .15 .40
524 Pete Falcone RC .15 .40
525 Billy Williams 1.00 2.50
526 Checklist 397-528 .60 1.50
527 Mike Anderson .15 .40
528 Dock Ellis .15 .40
529 Deron Johnson .15 .40
530 Don Sutton 1.00 2.50
531 New York Mets CL/Frazier .60 1.50
532 Milt May .15 .40
533 Lee Richard .15 .40
534 Stan Bahnsen .15 .40
535 Dave Nelson .15 .40
536 Mike Thompson .15 .40
537 Tony Muser .15 .40
538 Pat Darcy .15 .40
539 John Balaz RC .15 .40
540 Bill Freehan .30 .75
541 Steve Mingori .15 .40
542 Keith Hernandez .30 .75
543 Wayne Twitchell .15 .40
544 Pepe Frias .15 .40
545 Sparky Lyle .30 .75
546 Dave Rosello .15 .40
547 Roric Harrison .15 .40
548 Manny Mota .30 .75
549 Randy Tate RC .15 .40
550 Hank Aaron 15.00 40.00
551 Jerry DaVanon .15 .40
552 Terry Humphrey .15 .40
553 Randy Moffitt .15 .40
554 Ray Fosse .15 .40
555 Dyar Miller .15 .40
556 Minnesota Twins CL/Mauch .60 1.50
557 Dan Spillner .15 .40
558 Clarence Gaston .30 .75
559 Clyde Wright .15 .40
560 Jorge Orta .15 .40
561 Tom Carroll .15 .40
562 Adrian Garrett .15 .40
563 Larry Demery .15 .40
564 Kurt Bevacqua GUM .60 1.50
565 Tug McGraw .30 .75
566 Ken McMullen .15 .40
567 George Stone .15 .40
568 Rob Andrews RC .15 .40
569 Nelson Briles .30 .75
570 George Hendrick .30 .75
571 Don DeMola .15 .40
572 Rich Coggins .15 .40
573 Bill Travers .15 .40
574 Don Kessinger .30 .75
575 Dwight Evans .60 1.50
576 Maximino Leon .15 .40
577 Marc Hill .15 .40
578 Ted Kubiak .15 .40
579 Clay Kirby .15 .40
580 Bert Campaneris .30 .75
581 St. Louis Cardinals CL Schoendienst .60 1.50
582 Mike Kekich .15 .40
583 Tommy Helms .15 .40
584 Stan Wall RC .15 .40
585 Joe Torre .60 1.50
586 Ron Schueler .15 .40
587 Leo Cardenas .15 .40
588 Kevin Kobel .15 .40
589 Alc/Flanagan/Pac/Torr RC .60 1.50
590 Cruz/Lemon/Valen/Whit RC .30 .75
591 Grilli/Mitch/Sosa/Throop RC .30 .75
592 Randolph/McK/Roy/Sta RC 2.00 5.00
593 Andr/Crosby/Litell/Metzger RC .30 .75
594 Mer/Ott/Still/White RC .30 .75
595 DeFil/Lerch/Monge/Barr RC .30 .75
596 Rey/John/LeMas/Manuel RC .30 .75
597 Aase/Kucek/LaCorte/Pazik RC .30 .75
598 Cruz/Quirk/Turner/Wallis RC .30 .75
599 Dres/Guidry/McCl/Zach RC 5.00 12.00
600 Tom Seaver 6.00 15.00
601 Ken Rudolph .15 .40
602 Doug Konieczny .15 .40
603 Jim Holt .15 .40
604 Joe Lovitto .15 .40
605 Al Downing .15 .40
606 Milwaukee Brewers CL/Grammas .60 1.50
607 Rich Hinton .15 .40
608 Vic Correll .15 .40
609 Fred Norman .15 .40
610 Greg Luzinski .60 1.50
611 Rich Folkers .15 .40
612 Joe Lahoud .15 .40
613 Tim Johnson .15 .40
614 Fernando Arroyo RC .15 .40
615 Mike Cubbage .15 .40
616 Buck Martinez .15 .40
617 Darold Knowles .15 .40
618 Jack Brohamer .15 .40
619 Bill Butler .15 .40
620 Al Oliver .30 .75
621 Tom Hall .15 .40
622 Rick Auerbach .15 .40
623 Bob Allietta RC .15 .40
624 Tony Taylor .15 .40
625 J.R. Richard .30 .75
626 Bob Sheldon .15 .40
627 Bill Plummer .15 .40
628 John D'Acquisto .15 .40
629 Sandy Alomar .30 .75
630 Chris Speier .15 .40
631 Atlanta Braves CL/Bristol .60 1.50
632 Rogelio Moret .15 .40
633 John Stearns RC .30 .75
634 Larry Christenson .15 .40
635 Jim Fregosi .30 .75
636 Joe Decker .15 .40
637 Bruce Bochte .15 .40
638 Doyle Alexander .30 .75
639 Fred Kendall .15 .40
640 Bill Madlock .60 1.50
641 Tom Paciorek .30 .75
642 Dennis Blair .15 .40
643 Checklist 529-660 .60 1.50
644 Tom Bradley .15 .40
645 Darrell Porter .30 .75
646 John Lowenstein .15 .40
647 Ramon Hernandez .15 .40
648 Al Cowens .30 .75
649 Dave Roberts .15 .40
650 Thurman Munson 6.00 15.00
651 John Odom .15 .40
652 Ed Armbrister .15 .40
653 Mike Norris RC .30 .75
654 Doug Griffin .15 .40
655 Mike Vail RC .15 .40
656 Chicago White Sox CL/Tanner .60 1.50
657 Roy Smalley RC .30 .75
658 Jerry Johnson .15 .40
659 Ben Oglivie .30 .75
660 Davey Lopes .60 1.50

1976 Topps Traded

The cards in this 44-card set measure 2 1/2" by 3 1/2". The 1976 Topps Traded set contains 43 players and one unnumbered checklist card. The individuals pictured were traded after the Topps regular set was printed. A "Sports Extra" heading design is found on each picture and is also used to introduce the biographical section of the reverse. Each card is numbered according to the player's regular 1976 card with the addition of "T" to indicate his new status. As in 1974, the cards were inserted in all packs toward the end of the production run. According to published reports at the time, they were not released until April, 1976. Because they were produced in large quantities, they are no scarcer than the basic cards. Reports at the time indicated that a dealer could make approximately 35 sets from a vending case. The vending cases included both regular and traded cards.

COMPLETE SET (44) 12.50 30.00
27T Ed Figueroa .15 .40
28T Dusty Baker .60 1.50
44T Doug Rader .30 .75
58T Ron Reed .15 .40
74T Oscar Gamble .60 1.50
80T Jim Kaat .60 1.50
83T Jim Spencer .15 .40
85T Mickey Rivers .30 .75
99T Lee Lacy .15 .40
120T Rusty Staub .30 .75
127T Larvell Blanks .15 .40
146T George Medich .15 .40
158T Ken Reitz .15 .40
208T Mike Lum .15 .40
211T Clay Carroll .15 .40
231T Tom House .15 .40
250T Fergie Jenkins 1.25 3.00
259T Darrel Chaney .15 .40
292T Leon Roberts .15 .40
296T Pat Dobson .15 .40
309T Bill Melton .15 .40
338T Bob Bailey .15 .40
380T Bobby Bonds .60 1.50
383T John Ellis .15 .40
385T Mickey Lolich .30 .75
401T Ken Brett .15 .40
410T Ralph Garr .15 .40
411T Bill Singer .15 .40
428T Jim Crawford .15 .40
434T Morris Nettles .15 .40
464T Ken Henderson .15 .40
497T Joe McIntosh .15 .40
524T Pete Falcone .15 .40
527T Mike Anderson .15 .40
528T Dock Ellis .15 .40
532T Milt May .15 .40
554T Ray Fosse .15 .40
579T Clay Kirby .15 .40
583T Tommy Helms .15 .40
592T Willie Randolph 2.00 5.00
618T Jack Brohamer .15 .40
632T Rogelio Moret .15 .40
649T Dave Roberts .15 .40
NNO Traded Checklist .75 2.00

1977 Topps

In 1977 for the fifth consecutive year, Topps produced a 660-card standard-size baseball set. Among other fashions, this set was released in 10-card wax packs as well as thirty-nine card rack packs. The player's name, team affiliation, and his position are compactly arranged over the picture area and a facsimile autograph appears on the photo. Team cards feature a checklist of that team's players in the set and a small picture of the manager on the front of the card. Appearing for the first time are the series "Brothers" (631-634) and "Turn Back the Clock" (433-437). Other subseries in the set are League Leaders (1-8), Record Breakers (231-234), Playoffs cards (276-277), World Series cards (411-413), and Rookie Prospects (472-479/487-494). The following players' regular issue cards are explicitly denoted as All-Stars, 30, 70, 100, 120, 170, 210, 240, 265, 301, 347, 400, 420, 450, 500, 521, 550, 560, and 580. The key Rookie Cards in the set are Jack Clark, Andre Dawson, Mark "The Bird" Fidrych, Dennis Martinez and Dale Murphy. Cards numbered 23 or lower, that feature Yankees and do not follow the numbering checklisted below, are not necessarily error cards. Those cards were issued in the NY area and distributed by Burger King. There was an aluminum version of the Dale Murphy rookie card number 476 produced (legally) in the early '80s; proceeds from the sales originally priced at 10.00) of this "card" went to the Huntington's Disease Foundation.

COMPLETE SET (660) 200.00 500.00
1 G.Brett/B.Madlock LL 3.00 8.00
2 G.Nettles/M.Schmidt LL 1.00 2.50
3 L.May/G.Foster LL .60 1.50
4 B.North/D.Lopes LL .30 .75
5 J.Palmer/R.Jones LL .60 1.50
6 N.Ryan/T.Seaver LL 4.00 10.00
7 M.Fidrych/J.Denny LL .30 .75
8 B.Campbell/R.Eastwick LL .30 .75
9 Doug Rader .12 .30
10 Reggie Jackson 6.00 15.00
11 Rob Dressler .12 .30
12 Larry Haney .12 .30
13 Luis Gomez RC .12 .30
14 Tommy Smith .12 .30
15 Don Gullett .30 .75
16 Bob Jones RC .12 .30
17 Steve Stone .30 .75
18 Cleveland Indians CL/Robinson .60 1.50
19 John D'Acquisto .12 .30
20 Graig Nettles .60 1.50
21 Ken Forsch .12 .30
22 Bill Freehan .30 .75
23 Dan Driessen .12 .30

arl Morton .12 .30
wight Evans .60 1.50
ay Sadecki .12 .30
ill Buckner .30 .75
Voodie Fryman .12 .30
ucky Dent .30 .75
reg Luzinski .60 1.50
m Todd .12 .30
hecklist 1-132 .60 1.50
Vayne Garland .12 .30
alifornia Angels CL/Sherry .60 1.50
ennie Stennett .12 .30
ohn Ellis .12 .30
teve Hargan .12 .30
raig Kusick .12 .30
om Griffin .12 .30
obby Murcer .30 .75
im Kern .12 .30
ose Cruz .30 .75
ay Bare .12 .30
ud Harrelson .30 .75
awly Eastwick .12 .30
uck Martinez .12 .30
ynn McGlothen .12 .30
om Paciorek .30 .75
rant Jackson .12 .30
on Cey .30 .75
Milwaukee Brewers CL/Grammas .60 1.50
Ellis Valentine .12 .30
Paul Mitchell .12 .30
Sandy Alomar .30 .75
Jeff Burroughs .30 .75
Rudy May .12 .30
Marc Hill .12 .30
Chet Lemon .30 .75
Larry Christenson .12 .30
Jim Rice 1.50 4.00
Manny Sanguillen .30 .75
Eric Raich .12 .30
Tito Fuentes .12 .30
Larry Biittner .12 .30
Skip Lockwood .12 .30
Roy Smalley .30 .75
Joaquin Andujar RC .30 .75
Bruce Bochte .12 .30
Jim Crawford .12 .30
Johnny Bench 6.00 15.00
Dock Ellis .12 .30
Mike Anderson .12 .30
Charlie Williams .12 .30
Oakland Athletics CL/McKeon .60 1.50
Dennis Leonard .30 .75
Tim Foli .12 .30
Dyar Miller .12 .30
Bob Davis .12 .30
Don Money .30 .75
Andy Messersmith .30 .75
Juan Beniquez .12 .30
Jim Rooker .12 .30
Kevin Bell RC .12 .30
Ollie Brown .12 .30
Duane Kuiper .12 .30
6 Pat Zachry .12 .30
7 Glenn Borgmann .12 .30
8 Stan Wall .12 .30
9 Butch Hobson RC .30 .75
Cesar Cedeno .30 .75
1 John Verhoeven RC .12 .30
2 Dave Rosello .12 .30
3 Tom Poquette .12 .30
4 Craig Swan .12 .30
5 Keith Hernandez .30 .75
6 Lou Piniella .30 .75
7 Dave Heaverlo .12 .30
8 Milt May .12 .30
9 Tom Hausman .12 .30
00 Joe Morgan 1.50 4.00
01 Dick Bosman .12 .30
02 Jose Morales .12 .30
03 Mike Bacsik RC .12 .30
04 Omar Moreno RC .30 .75
05 Steve Yeager .30 .75
06 Mike Flanagan .30 .75
07 Bill Melton .12 .30
08 Alan Foster .12 .30
09 Jorge Orta .12 .30
10 Steve Carlton 4.00 10.00
11 Rico Petrocelli .30 .75
12 Bill Greif .12 .30
113 Toronto Blue Jays CL/Hartsfield .60 1.50
114 Bruce Dal Canton .12 .30
115 Rick Manning .12 .30
116 Joe Niekro .30 .75
117 Frank White .30 .75
118 Rick Jones RC .12 .30
119 John Stearns .12 .30
120 Rod Carew 4.00 10.00
121 Gary Nolan .12 .30
122 Ben Oglivie .30 .75
123 Fred Stanley .12 .30
124 George Mitterwald .12 .30
125 Bill Travers .12 .30
126 Rod Gilbreath .12 .30
127 Ron Fairly .30 .75
128 Tommy John .60 1.50
129 Mike Sadek .12 .30
130 Al Oliver .30 .75
131 Orlando Ramirez RC .12 .30
132 Chip Lang RC .12 .30
133 Ralph Garr .30 .75
134 San Diego Padres CL/McNamara .60 1.50
135 Mark Belanger .30 .75
136 Jerry Mumphrey RC .30 .75
137 Jeff Terpko RC .12 .30
138 Bob Stinson .12 .30
139 Fred Norman .12 .30
140 Mike Schmidt 5.00 12.00
141 Mark Littell .12 .30
142 Steve Dillard RC .12 .30
143 Ed Herrmann .12 .30
144 Bruce Sutter RC 10.00 25.00
145 Tom Veryzer .12 .30
146 Dusty Baker .60 1.50
147 Jackie Brown .12 .30
148 Fran Healy .12 .30
149 Mike Cubbage .12 .30
150 Tom Seaver 3.00 8.00
151 Johnny LeMaster .12 .30
152 Gaylord Perry 1.00 2.50
153 Ron Jackson RC .12 .30
154 Dave Giusti .12 .30
155 Joe Rudi .30 .75
156 Pete Mackanin .12 .30
157 Ken Brett .12 .30
158 Ted Kubiak .12 .30
159 Bernie Carbo .12 .30
160 Will McEnaney .12 .30
161 Garry Templeton RC .60 1.50
162 Mike Cuellar .30 .75
163 Dave Hilton .12 .30
164 Tug McGraw .30 .75
165 Jim Wynn .30 .75
166 Bill Campbell .12 .30
167 Rich Hebner .30 .75
168 Charlie Spikes .12 .30
169 Darold Knowles .12 .30
170 Thurman Munson 12.00 30.00
171 Ken Sanders .12 .30
172 John Milner .12 .30
173 Chuck Scrivener RC .12 .30
174 Nelson Briles .30 .75
175 Butch Wynegar RC .30 .75
176 Bob Robertson .12 .30
177 Bart Johnson .12 .30
178 Bombo Rivera RC .12 .30
179 Paul Hartzell RC .12 .30
180 Dave Lopes .30 .75
181 Ken McMullen .12 .30
182 Dan Spillner .12 .30
183 St.Louis Cardinals CL/V.Rapp .60 1.50
184 Bo McLaughlin RC .12 .30
185 Sixto Lezcano .12 .30
186 Doug Flynn .12 .30
187 Dick Pole .12 .30
188 Bob Tolan .12 .30
189 Rick Dempsey .30 .75
190 Ray Burris .12 .30
191 Doug Griffin .12 .30
192 Clarence Gaston .30 .75
193 Larry Gura .12 .30
194 Gary Matthews .30 .75
195 Ed Figueroa .12 .30
196 Len Randle .12 .30
197 Ed Ott .12 .30
198 Wilbur Wood .12 .30
199 Pepe Frias .12 .30
200 Frank Tanana .30 .75
201 Ed Kranepool .12 .30
202 Tom Johnson .12 .30
203 Ed Armbrister .12 .30
204 Jeff Newman RC .12 .30
205 Pete Falcone .12 .30
206 Boog Powell .60 1.50
207 Glenn Abbott .12 .30
208 Checklist 133-264 .60 1.50
209 Rob Andrews .12 .30
210 Fred Lynn .75 2.00
211 San Francisco Giants CL/Altobelli .60 1.50
212 Jim Mason .12 .30
213 Maximino Leon .12 .30
214 Darrell Porter .30 .75
215 Butch Metzger .12 .30
216 Doug DeCinces .30 .75
217 Tom Underwood .12 .30
218 John Wathan RC .30 .75
219 Joe Coleman .12 .30
220 Chris Chambliss .30 .75
221 Bob Bailey .12 .30
222 Francisco Barrios RC .12 .30
223 Earl Williams .12 .30
224 Rusty Torres .12 .30
225 Bob Apodaca .12 .30
226 Leroy Stanton .30 .75
227 Joe Sambito RC .12 .30
228 Minnesota Twins CL/Mauch .60 1.50
229 Don Kessinger .30 .75
230 Vida Blue .30 .75
231 George Brett RB 3.00 8.00
232 Minnie Minoso RB .30 .75
233 Jose Morales RB .12 .30
234 Nolan Ryan RB 5.00 12.00
235 Cecil Cooper .30 .75
236 Tom Buskey .12 .30
237 Gene Clines .12 .30
238 Tippy Martinez .12 .30
239 Bill Plummer .12 .30
240 Ron LeFlore .30 .75
241 Dave Tomlin .12 .30
242 Ken Henderson .12 .30
243 Ron Reed .12 .30
244 John Mayberry .30 .75
245 Rick Rhoden .30 .75
246 Mike Vail .12 .30
247 Chris Knapp RC .12 .30
248 Wilbur Howard .12 .30
249 Pete Redfern RC .12 .30
250 Bill Madlock .30 .75
251 Tony Muser .12 .30
252 Dale Murray .12 .30
253 John Hale .12 .30
254 Doyle Alexander .12 .30
255 George Scott .30 .75
256 Joe Hoerner .12 .30
257 Mike Miley .12 .30
258 Luis Tiant .30 .75
259 New York Mets CL/Frazier .60 1.50
260 J.R. Richard .30 .75
261 Phil Garner .30 .75
262 Al Cowens .30 .75
263 Mike Marshall .30 .75
264 Tom Hutton .12 .30
265 Mark Fidrych RC 1.25 3.00
266 Derrel Thomas .12 .30
267 Ray Fosse .12 .30
268 Rick Sawyer RC .12 .30
269 Joe Lis .12 .30
270 Dave Parker .60 1.50
271 Terry Forster .12 .30
272 Lee Lacy .12 .30
273 Eric Soderholm .12 .30
274 Don Stanhouse .12 .30
275 Mike Hargrove .30 .75
276 Chris Chambliss ALCS .60 1.50
277 Pete Rose NLCS 2.00 5.00
278 Danny Frisella .12 .30
279 Joe Wallis .12 .30
280 Jim Hunter 1.00 2.50
281 Roy Staiger .12 .30
282 Sid Monge .12 .30
283 Jerry DaVanon .12 .30
284 Mike Norris .12 .30
285 Brooks Robinson 5.00 12.00
286 Johnny Grubb .12 .30
287 Cincinnati Reds CL/Anderson .60 1.50
288 Bob Montgomery .12 .30
289 Gene Garber .30 .75
290 Amos Otis .30 .75
291 Jason Thompson RC .30 .75
292 Rogelio Moret .12 .30
293 Jack Brohamer .12 .30
294 George Medich .12 .30
295 Gary Carter 1.50 4.00
296 Don Hood .12 .30
297 Ken Reitz .12 .30
298 Charlie Hough .30 .75
299 Otto Velez .30 .75
300 Jerry Koosman .30 .75
301 Toby Harrah .30 .75
302 Mike Garman .12 .30
303 Gene Tenace .30 .75
304 Jim Hughes .12 .30
305 Mickey Rivers .30 .75
306 Rick Waits .12 .30
307 Gary Sutherland .12 .30
308 Gene Pentz RC .12 .30
309 Boston Red Sox CL/Zimmer .60 1.50
310 Larry Bowa .30 .75
311 Vern Ruhle .12 .30
312 Rob Belloir RC .12 .30
313 Paul Blair .30 .75
314 Steve Mingori .12 .30
315 Dave Chalk .12 .30
316 Steve Rogers .12 .30
317 Kurt Bevacqua .12 .30
318 Duffy Dyer .12 .30
319 Goose Gossage .60 1.50
320 Ken Griffey Sr. .60 1.50
321 Dave Goltz .12 .30
322 Bill Russell .30 .75
323 Larry Lintz .12 .30
324 John Curtis .12 .30
325 Mike Ivie .12 .30
326 Jesse Jefferson .12 .30
327 Houston Astros CL/Virdon .60 1.50
328 Tommy Boggs RC .12 .30
329 Ron Hodges .12 .30
330 George Hendrick .30 .75
331 Jim Colborn .12 .30
332 Elliott Maddox .12 .30
333 Paul Reuschel RC .12 .30
334 Bill Stein .12 .30
335 Bill Robinson .30 .75
336 Denny Doyle .12 .30
337 Ron Schueler .12 .30
338 Dave Duncan .30 .75
339 Adrian Devine .12 .30
340 Hal McRae .30 .75
341 Joe Kerrigan RC .12 .30
342 Jerry Remy .12 .30
343 Ed Halicki .12 .30
344 Brian Downing .30 .75
345 Reggie Smith .30 .75
346 Bill Singer .12 .30
347 George Foster .60 1.50
348 Brent Strom .12 .30
349 Jim Holt .12 .30
350 Larry Dierker .30 .75
351 Jim Sundberg .30 .75
352 Mike Phillips .12 .30
353 Stan Thomas .12 .30
354 Pittsburgh Pirates CL/Tanner .60 1.50
355 Lou Brock 1.50 4.00
356 Checklist 265-396 .60 1.50
357 Tim McCarver .60 1.50
358 Tom House .12 .30
359 Willie Randolph .60 1.50
360 Rick Monday .30 .75
361 Eduardo Rodriguez .12 .30
362 Tommy Davis .30 .75
363 Dave Roberts .12 .30
364 Vic Correll .12 .30
365 Mike Torrez .30 .75
366 Ted Sizemore .12 .30
367 Dave Hamilton .12 .30
368 Mike Jorgensen .12 .30
369 Terry Humphrey .12 .30
370 John Montefusco .12 .30
371 Kansas City Royals CL/Herzog .60 1.50
372 Rich Folkers .12 .30
373 Bert Campaneris .30 .75
374 Kent Tekulve .30 .75
375 Larry Hisle .30 .75
376 Nino Espinosa RC .12 .30
377 Dave McKay .12 .30
378 Jim Umbarger .12 .30
379 Larry Cox RC .12 .30
380 Lee May .30 .75
381 Bob Forsch .12 .30
382 Charlie Moore .12 .30
383 Stan Bahnsen .12 .30
384 Darrel Chaney .12 .30
385 Dave LaRoche .12 .30
386 Manny Mota .30 .75
387 New York Yankees CL/Martin 1.00 2.50
388 Terry Harmon .12 .30
389 Ken Kravec RC .12 .30
390 Dave Winfield 6.00 15.00
391 Dan Warthen .12 .30
392 Phil Roof .12 .30
393 John Lowenstein .12 .30
394 Bill Laxton RC .12 .30
395 Manny Trillo .12 .30
396 Tom Murphy .12 .30
397 Larry Herndon RC .30 .75
398 Tom Burgmeier .12 .30
399 Bruce Boisclair RC .12 .30
400 Steve Garvey 1.00 2.50
401 Mickey Scott .12 .30
402 Tommy Helms .12 .30
403 Tom Grieve .30 .75
404 Eric Rasmussen RC .12 .30
405 Claudell Washington .30 .75
406 Tim Johnson .12 .30
407 Dave Freisleben .12 .30
408 Cesar Tovar .12 .30
409 Pete Broberg .12 .30
410 Willie Montanez .12 .30
411 J.Morgan/J.Bench WS 1.00 2.50
412 Johnny Bench WS 1.00 2.50
413 Cincy Wins WS .30 .75
414 Tommy Harper .30 .75
415 Jay Johnstone .30 .75
416 Chuck Hartenstein .12 .30
417 Wayne Garrett .12 .30
418 Chicago White Sox CL/Lemon .60 1.50
419 Steve Swisher .12 .30
420 Rusty Staub .60 1.50
421 Doug Rau .12 .30
422 Freddie Patek .30 .75
423 Gary Lavelle .12 .30
424 Steve Brye .12 .30
425 Joe Torre .60 1.50
426 Dick Drago .12 .30
427 Dave Rader .12 .30
428 Texas Rangers CL/Lucchesi .60 1.50
429 Ken Boswell .12 .30
430 Fergie Jenkins 1.00 2.50
431 Dave Collins UER .30 .75
432 Buzz Capra .12 .30
433 Nate Colbert TBC .12 .30
434 Carl Yastrzemski TBC .60 1.50
435 Maury Wills TBC .30 .75
436 Bob Keegan TBC .12 .30
437 Ralph Kiner TBC .60 1.50
438 Marty Perez .12 .30
439 Gorman Thomas .30 .75
440 Jon Matlack .12 .30
441 Larvell Blanks .12 .30
442 Atlanta Braves CL/Bristol .60 1.50
443 Lamar Johnson .12 .30
444 Wayne Twitchell .12 .30
445 Ken Singleton .30 .75
446 Bill Bonham .12 .30
447 Jerry Turner .12 .30
448 Ellie Rodriguez .12 .30
449 Al Fitzmorris .12 .30
450 Pete Rose 5.00 12.00
451 Checklist 397-528 .60 1.50
452 Mike Caldwell .12 .30
453 Pedro Garcia .12 .30
454 Andy Etchebarren .12 .30
455 Rick Wise .12 .30
456 Leon Roberts .12 .30
457 Steve Luebber .12 .30
458 Leo Foster .12 .30
459 Steve Foucault .12 .30
460 Willie Stargell 1.00 2.50
461 Dick Tidrow .12 .30
462 Don Baylor .60 1.50
463 Jamie Quirk .12 .30
464 Randy Moffitt .12 .30
465 Rico Carty .30 .75
466 Fred Holdsworth .12 .30
467 Philadelphia Phillies CL/Ozark .60 1.50
468 Ramon Hernandez .12 .30
469 Pat Kelly .12 .30
470 Ted Simmons .30 .75
471 Del Unser .12 .30
472 Aase/McCl/Patt/Wehr RC .12 .30
473 Andre Dawson RC 20.00 50.00
474 Bailor/Gar/Reyn/Tav RC .30 .75
475 Batt/Camp/McGr/Sarm RC .30 .75
476 Dale Murphy RC 15.00 40.00
477 Ault/Dauer/Gonz/Mank RC .30 .75
478 Gid/Hoot/John/Lemong RC .30 .75
479 Assel/Gross/Mej/Woods RC .30 .75
480 Carl Yastrzemski 3.00 8.00
481 Roger Metzger .12 .30
482 Tony Solaita .12 .30
483 Richie Zisk .12 .30
484 Burt Hooton .30 .75
485 Roy White .30 .75
486 Ed Bane .12 .30
487 And/Glynn/Hend/Terl RC .30 .75
488 J.Clark/L.Mazzilli RC 1.25 3.00
489 Barker/Ler/Mint/Overy RC .30 .75
490 Almon/Klutts/McM/Wag RC .30 .75
491 Dennis Martinez RC 1.25 3.00
492 Armas/Kemp/Lop/Woods RC .30 .75
493 Krukow/Ott/Wheel/Will RC .30 .75
494 J.Gantner/B.Wills RC .60 1.50
495 Al Hrabosky .30 .75
496 Gary Thomasson .12 .30
497 Clay Carroll .12 .30
498 Sal Bando .30 .75
499 Pablo Torrealba .12 .30
500 Dave Kingman .60 1.50
501 Jim Bibby .12 .30
502 Randy Hundley .12 .30
503 Bill Lee .12 .30
504 Los Angeles Dodgers CL/Lasorda .60 1.50
505 Oscar Gamble .30 .75
506 Steve Grilli .12 .30
507 Mike Hegan .12 .30
508 Dave Pagan .12 .30
509 Cookie Rojas .30 .75
510 John Candelaria .12 .30
511 Bill Fahey .12 .30
512 Jack Billingham .12 .30
513 Jerry Terrell .12 .30
514 Cliff Johnson .12 .30
515 Chris Speier .12 .30
516 Bake McBride .30 .75
517 Pete Vuckovich RC .30 .75
518 Chicago Cubs CL/Franks .60 1.50
519 Don Kirkwood .12 .30
520 Garry Maddox .12 .30
521 Bob Grich .30 .75
522 Enzo Hernandez .12 .30
523 Rollie Fingers 1.00 2.50
524 Rowland Office .12 .30
525 Dennis Eckersley 4.00 10.00
526 Larry Parrish .30 .75
527 Dan Meyer .30 .75
528 Bill Castro .12 .30
529 Jim Essian RC .12 .30
530 Rick Reuschel .30 .75
531 Lyman Bostock .30 .75
532 Jim Willoughby .12 .30
533 Mickey Stanley .12 .30
534 Paul Splittorff .12 .30
535 Cesar Geronimo .12 .30
536 Vic Albury .12 .30
537 Dave Roberts .12 .30
538 Frank Taveras .12 .30
539 Mike Wallace .12 .30
540 Bob Watson .30 .75
541 John Denny .30 .75
542 Frank Duffy .12 .30
543 Ron Blomberg .12 .30
544 Gary Ross .10 .30
545 Bob Boone .30 .75
546 Baltimore Orioles CL/Weaver .60 1.50
547 Willie McCovey 1.50 4.00
548 Joel Youngblood RC .12 .30
549 Jerry Royster .12 .30
550 Randy Jones .12 .30
551 Bill North .12 .30
552 Pepe Mangual .12 .30
553 Jack Heidemann .12 .30
554 Bruce Kimm RC .12 .30
555 Dan Ford .12 .30
556 Doug Bird .12 .30
557 Jerry White .12 .30
558 Elias Sosa .12 .30
559 Alan Bannister RC .12 .30
560 Dave Concepcion .60 1.50
561 Pete LaCock .12 .30
562 Checklist 529-660 .60 1.50
563 Bruce Kison .12 .30
564 Alan Ashby .12 .30
565 Mickey Lolich .30 .75
566 Rick Miller .12 .30
567 Enos Cabell .12 .30
568 Carlos May .12 .30
569 Jim Lonborg .30 .75
570 Bobby Bonds .60 1.50
571 Darrell Evans .30 .75
572 Ross Grimsley .12 .30
573 Joe Ferguson .12 .30
574 Aurelio Rodriguez .12 .30
575 Dick Ruthven .12 .30
576 Fred Kendall .12 .30
577 Jerry Augustine RC .12 .30
578 Bob Randall RC .12 .30
579 Don Carrithers .12 .30
580 George Brett 8.00 20.00
581 Pedro Borbon .12 .30
582 Ed Kirkpatrick .12 .30
583 Paul Lindblad .12 .30
584 Ed Goodson .12 .30
585 Rick Burleson .30 .75
586 Steve Renko .12 .30
587 Rick Baldwin .12 .30
588 Dave Moates .12 .30
589 Mike Cosgrove .12 .30
590 Buddy Bell .30 .75
591 Chris Arnold .12 .30
592 Dan Briggs RC .12 .30
593 Dennis Blair .12 .30
594 Biff Pocoroba .12 .30
595 John Hiller .12 .30
596 Jerry Martin RC .12 .30
597 Seattle Mariners CL/Johnson .60 1.50
598 Sparky Lyle .30 .75
599 Mike Tyson .12 .30
600 Jim Palmer 1.50 4.00
601 Mike Lum .12 .30
602 Andy Hassler .12 .30
603 Willie Davis .30 .75
604 Jim Slaton .12 .30
605 Felix Millan .12 .30
606 Steve Braun .12 .30
607 Larry Demery .12 .30
608 Roy Howell .12 .30
609 Jim Barr .12 .30
610 Jose Cardenal .30 .75
611 Dave Lemanczyk .12 .30
612 Barry Foote .12 .30
613 Reggie Cleveland .12 .30
614 Greg Gross .12 .30
615 Phil Niekro 1.00 2.50
616 Tommy Sandt RC .12 .30
617 Bobby Darwin .12 .30
618 Pat Dobson .12 .30
619 Johnny Oates .30 .75
620 Don Sutton 1.00 2.50
621 Detroit Tigers CL/Houk .60 1.50
622 Jim Wohlford .12 .30
623 Jack Kucek .12 .30
624 Hector Cruz .12 .30
625 Ken Holtzman .30 .75
626 Al Bumbry .30 .75
627 Bob Myrick RC .12 .30
628 Mario Guerrero .12 .30
629 Bobby Valentine .30 .75
630 Bert Blyleven .60 1.50
631 Brett Brothers 2.50 6.00
632 Forsch Brothers .30 .75
633 May Brothers .30 .75
634 Reuschel Brothers UER .30 .75
635 Robin Yount 3.00 8.00
636 Santo Alcala .12 .30
637 Alex Johnson .12 .30
638 Jim Kaat .60 1.50
639 Jerry Morales .12 .30
640 Carlton Fisk 2.00 5.00
641 Dan Larson RC .12 .30
642 Willie Crawford .12 .30
643 Mike Pazik .12 .30
644 Matt Alexander .12 .30
645 Jerry Reuss .30 .75
646 Andres Mora RC .12 .30
647 Montreal Expos CL/Williams .60 1.50
648 Jim Spencer .12 .30
649 Dave Cash .12 .30
650 Nolan Ryan 12.00 30.00
651 Von Joshua .12 .30
652 Tom Walker .12 .30
653 Diego Segui .30 .75
654 Ron Pruitt RC .12 .30
655 Tony Perez 1.00 2.50
656 Ron Guidry .60 1.50
657 Mick Kelleher RC .12 .30
658 Marty Pattin .12 .30
659 Merv Rettenmund .12 .30
660 Willie Horton .60 1.50

1978 Topps

The cards in this 726-card set measure 2 1/2" by 3 1/2". As in previous years, this set was issued in many different ways: some of them include 14-card wax packs, 30-card supermarket packs which came 48 to a case and had an SRP of 20 cents and 39-card rack packs. The 1978 Topps set experienced an increase in number of cards from the previous five regular issue sets of 660. Card numbers 1 through 7 feature Record Breakers (RB) of the 1977 season. Other subsets within this set include League Leaders (201-208), Post-season cards (411-413), and Rookie Prospects (701-711). The key Rookie Cards in this set are the multi-player Rookie Card of Paul Molitor and Alan Trammell, Jack Morris, Eddie Murray, Lance Parrish, and Lou Whitaker. Many of the Molitor/Trammell cards are found with black printing smudges. The manager cards in the set feature a "then and now" format on the card front showing the manager as he looked during his playing days. While no scarcities exist, 66 of the cards are more abundant in supply, as they were "double printed." These 66 double-printed cards are noted in the checklist by DP. Team cards again feature a checklist of that team's players in the set on the back. Cards numbered 23 or lower, that feature Astros, Rangers, Tigers, or Yankees and do not follow the numbering checklisted below, are not necessarily error cards. They are undoubtedly Burger King cards, separate sets with their own pricing and mass distribution. The Bump Wills card has been seen with either no black mark or a major black mark on the front of the card. We will continue to investigate this card and see whether or not it should be considered a variation.

COMPLETE SET (726) 150.00 400.00
COMMON CARD (1-726) .10 .25
COMMON CARD DP .08 .20
1 Lou Brock RB 1.25 3.00
2 Sparky Lyle RB .25 .60
3 Willie McCovey RB 1.00 2.50
4 Brooks Robinson RB .50 1.25
5 Pete Rose RB 3.00 8.00
6 Nolan Ryan RB 6.00 15.00
7 Reggie Jackson RB 1.50 4.00
8 Mike Sadek .10 .25
9 Doug DeCinces .25 .60
10 Phil Niekro 1.00 2.50
11 Rick Manning .10 .25
12 Don Aase .10 .25
13 Art Howe RC .25 .60
14 Lerrin LaGrow .10 .25
15 Tony Perez DP .50 1.25
16 Roy White .25 .60
17 Mike Krukow .10 .25
18 Bob Grich .25 .60
19 Darrell Porter .25 .60
20 Pete Rose DP 5.00 12.00
21 Steve Kemp .10 .25
22 Charlie Hough .25 .60
23 Bump Wills .10 .25
24 Don Money DP .08 .20
25 Jon Matlack .10 .25
26 Rich Hebner .25 .60
27 Geoff Zahn .10 .25
28 Ed Ott .10 .25
29 Bob Lacey RC .10 .25
30 George Hendrick .25 .60
31 Glenn Abbott .10 .25
32 Garry Templeton .25 .60
33 Dave Lemanczyk .10 .25
34 Willie McCovey 1.25 3.00
35 Sparky Lyle .25 .60
36 Eddie Murray RC 15.00 40.00
37 Rick Waits .10 .25
38 Willie Montanez .10 .25
39 Floyd Bannister RC .10 .25
40 Carl Yastrzemski 4.00 10.00
41 Burt Hooton .25 .60
42 Jorge Orta .10 .25
43 Bill Atkinson RC .10 .25
44 Toby Harrah .25 .60
45 Mark Fidrych 1.00 2.50
46 Al Cowens .25 .60
47 Jack Billingham .10 .25
48 Don Baylor .50 1.25
49 Ed Kranepool .25 .60
50 Rick Reuschel .25 .60
51 Charlie Moore DP .08 .20
52 Jim Lonborg .25 .60
53 Phil Garner DP .10 .25
54 Tom Johnson .10 .25
55 Mitchell Page RC .10 .25
56 Randy Jones .10 .25
57 Dan Meyer .10 .25
58 Bob Forsch .10 .25
59 Otto Velez .10 .25
60 Thurman Munson 1.50 4.00
61 Larvell Blanks .10 .25
62 Jim Barr .10 .25
63 Don Zimmer MG .25 .60
64 Gene Pentz .10 .25
65 Ken Singleton .25 .60
66 Chicago White Sox CL .50 1.25
67 Claudell Washington .25 .60
68 Steve Foucault DP .08 .20
69 Mike Vail .10 .25
70 Goose Gossage .50 1.25
71 Terry Humphrey .10 .25
72 Andre Dawson 1.50 4.00
73 Andy Hassler .10 .25
74 Checklist 1-121 .50 1.25
75 Dick Ruthven .10 .25
76 Steve Ontiveros .10 .25
77 Ed Kirkpatrick .10 .25
78 Pablo Torrealba .10 .25
79 Darrell Johnson MG DP .08 .20
80 Ken Griffey Sr. .50 1.25
81 Pete Redfern .10 .25
82 San Francisco Giants CL .50 1.25
83 Bob Montgomery .10 .25
84 Kent Tekulve .25 .60
85 Ron Fairly .30 .75
86 Dave Tomlin .10 .25
87 John Lowenstein .10 .25
88 Mike Phillips .10 .25
89 Ken Clay RC .10 .25
90 Larry Bowa .50 1.25
91 Oscar Zamora .10 .25
92 Adrian Devine .10 .25
93 Bobby Cox DP .08 .20
94 Chuck Scrivener .10 .25
95 Jamie Quirk .10 .25
96 Baltimore Orioles CL .50 1.25
97 Stan Bahnsen .10 .25
98 Jim Essian .25 .60
99 Willie Hernandez RC .50 1.25
100 George Brett 8.00 20.00
101 Sid Monge .10 .25
102 Matt Alexander .10 .25
103 Tom Murphy .10 .25
104 Lee Lacy .10 .25

105 Reggie Cleveland .10 .25
106 Bill Plummer .10 .25
107 Ed Halicki .10 .25
108 Von Joshua .10 .25
109 Joe Torre MG .25 .60
110 Richie Zisk .10 .25
111 Mike Tyson .10 .25
112 Houston Astros CL .50 1.25
113 Don Carrithers .10 .25
114 Paul Blair .25 .60
115 Gary Nolan .10 .25
116 Tucker Ashford RC .10 .25
117 John Montague .10 .25
118 Terry Harmon .10 .25
119 Dennis Martinez 1.00 2.50
120 Gary Carter 1.00 2.50
121 Alvis Woods .10 .25
122 Dennis Eckersley 1.25 3.00
123 Manny Trillo .10 .25
124 Dave Rozema RC .10 .25
125 George Scott .25 .60
126 Paul Moskau RC .10 .25
127 Chet Lemon .25 .60
128 Bill Russell .25 .60
129 Jim Colborn .10 .25
130 Jeff Burroughs .25 .60
131 Bert Blyleven .50 1.25
132 Enos Cabell .10 .25
133 Jerry Augustine .10 .25
134 Steve Henderson RC .10 .25
135 Ron Guidry DP .50 1.25
136 Ted Sizemore .10 .25
137 Craig Kusick .10 .25
138 Larry Demery .10 .25
139 Wayne Gross .10 .25
140 Rollie Fingers 1.00 2.50
141 Ruppert Jones .10 .25
142 John Montefusco .10 .25
143 Keith Hernandez .25 .60
144 Jesse Jefferson .10 .25
145 Rick Monday .25 .60
146 Doyle Alexander .25 .60
147 Lee Mazzilli .10 .25
148 Andre Thornton .25 .60
149 Dale Murray .10 .25
150 Bobby Bonds .50 1.25
151 Milt Wilcox .10 .25
152 Ivan DeJesus RC .10 .25
153 Steve Stone .25 .60
154 Cecil Cooper DP .10 .25
155 Butch Hobson .10 .25
156 Andy Messersmith .25 .60
157 Pete LaCock DP .08 .20
158 Joaquin Andujar .25 .60
159 Lou Piniella .25 .60
160 Jim Palmer 1.25 3.00
161 Bob Boone .50 1.25
162 Paul Thormodsgard RC .10 .25
163 Bill North .10 .25
164 Bob Owchinko RC .10 .25
165 Rennie Stennett .10 .25
166 Carlos Lopez .10 .25
167 Tim Foli .10 .25
168 Reggie Smith .25 .60
169 Jerry Johnson .10 .25
170 Lou Brock 1.25 3.00
171 Pat Zachry .10 .25
172 Mike Hargrove .25 .60
173 Robin Yount UER 4.00 10.00
174 Wayne Garland .10 .25
175 Jerry Morales .10 .25
176 Milt May .10 .25
177 Gene Garber DP .10 .25
178 Dave Chalk .10 .25
179 Dick Tidrow .10 .25
180 Dave Concepcion .50 1.25
181 Ken Forsch .10 .25
182 Jim Spencer .10 .25
183 Doug Bird .10 .25
184 Checklist 122-242 .50 1.25
185 Ellis Valentine .10 .25
186 Bob Stanley DP RC .08 .20
187 Jerry Royster DP .08 .20
188 Al Bumbry .25 .60
189 Tom Lasorda MG DP 1.00 2.50
190 John Candelaria .25 .60
191 Rodney Scott RC .10 .25
192 San Diego Padres CL .50 1.25
193 Rich Chiles .10 .25
194 Derrel Thomas .10 .25
195 Larry Dierker .25 .60
196 Bob Bailor .10 .25
197 Nino Espinosa .10 .25
198 Ron Pruitt .10 .25
199 Craig Reynolds .10 .25
200 Reggie Jackson 3.00 8.00
201 D.Parker/R.Carew LL .50 1.25
202 G.Foster/J.Rice LL DP .25 .60
203 G.Foster/L.Hisle LL .25 .60
204 F.Taveras/F.Patek LL DP .10 .25
205 Carlton/Gol/Leon/Palm LL 1.00 2.50
206 P.Niekro/N.Ryan LL DP 2.50 6.00
207 J.Cand/F.Tanana LL DP .25 .60
208 R.Fingers/B.Campbell LL .50 1.25
209 Dock Ellis .10 .25
210 Jose Cardenal .10 .25
211 Earl Weaver MG DP .50 1.25
212 Mike Caldwell .10 .25
213 Alan Bannister .10 .25
214 California Angels CL .50 1.25
215 Darrell Evans .25 .60
216 Mike Paxton RC .10 .25
217 Rod Gilbreath .10 .25
218 Marty Pattin .10 .25
219 Mike Cubbage .10 .25
220 Pedro Borbon .10 .25
221 Chris Speier .10 .25
222 Jerry Martin .10 .25
223 Bruce Kison .10 .25
224 Jerry Tabb RC .10 .25
225 Don Gullett DP .10 .25
226 Joe Ferguson .10 .25
227 Al Fitzmorris .10 .25
228 Manny Mota DP .10 .25
229 Leo Foster .10 .25
230 Al Hrabosky .25 .60
231 Wayne Nordhagen RC .10 .25
232 Mickey Stanley .10 .25
233 Dick Pole .10 .25
234 Herman Franks MG .10 .25
235 Tim McCarver .25 .60
236 Terry Whitfield .10 .25
237 Rich Dauer .10 .25
238 Juan Beniquez .10 .25
239 Dyar Miller .10 .25
240 Gene Tenace .25 .60
241 Pete Vuckovich .25 .60
242 Barry Bonnell DP RC .08 .20
243 Bob McClure .10 .25
244 Montreal Expos CL DP .25 .60
245 Rick Burleson .25 .60
246 Dan Driessen .10 .25
247 Larry Christenson .10 .25
248 Frank White DP .25 .60
249 Dave Goltz DP .08 .20
250 Graig Nettles DP .25 .60
251 Don Kirkwood .10 .25
252 Steve Swisher DP .08 .20
253 Jim Kern .10 .25
254 Dave Collins .25 .60
255 Jerry Reuss .25 .60
256 Joe Altobelli MG RC .10 .25
257 Hector Cruz .10 .25
258 John Hiller .10 .25
259 Los Angeles Dodgers CL .50 1.25
260 Bert Campaneris .25 .60
261 Tim Hosley .10 .25
262 Rudy May .10 .25
263 Danny Walton .10 .25
264 Jamie Easterly .10 .25
265 Sal Bando DP .25 .60
266 Bob Shirley RC .10 .25
267 Doug Ault .10 .25
268 Gil Flores RC .10 .25
269 Wayne Twitchell .10 .25
270 Carlton Fisk 1.50 4.00
271 Randy Lerch DP .08 .20
272 Royle Stillman .10 .25
273 Fred Norman .10 .25
274 Freddie Patek .25 .60
275 Dan Ford .10 .25
276 Bill Bonham DP .08 .20
277 Bruce Boisclair .10 .25
278 Enrique Romo RC .10 .25
279 Bill Virdon MG .10 .25
280 Buddy Bell .25 .60
281 Eric Rasmussen DP .08 .20
282 New York Yankees CL 1.00 2.50
283 Omar Moreno .10 .25
284 Randy Moffitt .10 .25
285 Steve Yeager DP .25 .60
286 Ben Oglivie .25 .60
287 Kiko Garcia .10 .25
288 Dave Hamilton .10 .25
289 Checklist 243-363 .50 1.25
290 Willie Horton .25 .60
291 Gary Ross .10 .25
292 Gene Richards .10 .25
293 Mike Willis .10 .25
294 Larry Parrish .25 .60
295 Bill Lee .10 .25
296 Biff Pocoroba .10 .25
297 Warren Brusstar DP RC .08 .20
298 Tony Armas .25 .60
299 Whitey Herzog MG .25 .60
300 Joe Morgan 1.25 3.00
301 Buddy Schultz RC .10 .25
302 Chicago Cubs CL .50 1.25
303 Sam Hinds RC .10 .25
304 John Milner .10 .25
305 Rico Carty .25 .60
306 Joe Niekro .25 .60
307 Glenn Borgmann .10 .25
308 Jim Rooker .10 .25
309 Cliff Johnson .10 .25
310 Don Sutton 1.00 2.50
311 Jose Baez DP RC .08 .20
312 Greg Minton .10 .25
313 Andy Etchebarren .10 .25
314 Paul Lindblad .10 .25
315 Mark Belanger .25 .60
316 Henry Cruz DP .08 .20
317 Dave Johnson .10 .25
318 Tom Griffin .10 .25
319 Alan Ashby .10 .25
320 Fred Lynn .60 1.50
321 Santo Alcala .10 .25
322 Tom Paciorek .25 .60
323 Jim Fregosi DP .10 .25
324 Vern Rapp MG RC .10 .25
325 Bruce Sutter 1.25 3.00
326 Mike Lum DP .08 .20
327 Rick Langford DP RC .08 .20
328 Milwaukee Brewers CL .50 1.25
329 John Verhoeven .10 .25
330 Bob Watson .25 .60
331 Mark Littell .10 .25
332 Duane Kuiper .10 .25
333 Jim Todd .10 .25
334 John Stearns .10 .25
335 Bucky Dent .25 .60
336 Steve Busby .10 .25
337 Tom Grieve .25 .60
338 Dave Heaverlo .10 .25
339 Mario Guerrero .10 .25
340 Bake McBride .25 .60
341 Mike Flanagan .25 .60
342 Aurelio Rodriguez .10 .25
343 John Wathan DP .08 .20
344 Sam Ewing RC .10 .25
345 Luis Tiant .25 .60
346 Larry Biittner .10 .25
347 Terry Forster .10 .25
348 Del Unser .10 .25
349 Rick Camp DP .08 .20
350 Steve Garvey 1.00 2.50
351 Jeff Torborg .25 .60
352 Tony Scott RC .10 .25
353 Doug Bair RC .10 .25
354 Cesar Geronimo .10 .25
355 Bill Travers .10 .25
356 New York Mets CL .50 1.25
357 Tom Poquette .10 .25
358 Mark Lemongello .10 .25
359 Marc Hill .10 .25
360 Mike Schmidt 4.00 10.00
361 Chris Knapp .10 .25
362 Dave May .10 .25
363 Bob Randall .10 .25
364 Jerry Turner .10 .25
365 Ed Figueroa .10 .25
366 Larry Milbourne DP .08 .20
367 Rick Dempsey .25 .60
368 Balor Moore .10 .25
369 Tim Nordbrook .10 .25
370 Rusty Staub .50 1.25
371 Ray Burris .10 .25
372 Brian Asselstine .10 .25
373 Jim Willoughby .10 .25
374A Jose Morales .10 .25
Red stitching
374B Jose Morales
Black overprint stitching
375 Tommy John .50 1.25
376 Jim Wohlford .10 .25
377 Manny Sarmiento .10 .25
378 Bobby Winkles MG .10 .25
379 Skip Lockwood .10 .25
380 Ted Simmons .25 .60
381 Philadelphia Phillies CL .50 1.25
382 Joe Lahoud .10 .25
383 Mario Mendoza .10 .25
384 Jack Clark .50 1.25
385 Tito Fuentes .10 .25
386 Bob Gorinski RC .10 .25
387 Ken Holtzman .25 .60
388 Bill Fahey DP .08 .20
389 Julio Gonzalez RC .10 .25
390 Oscar Gamble .25 .60
391 Larry Haney .10 .25
392 Billy Almon .10 .25
393 Tippy Martinez .25 .60
394 Roy Howell DP .08 .20
395 Jim Hughes .10 .25
396 Bob Stinson DP .08 .20
397 Greg Gross .10 .25
398 Don Hood .10 .25
399 Pete Mackanin .10 .25
400 Nolan Ryan 10.00 25.00
401 Sparky Anderson MG .25 .60
402 Dave Campbell .10 .25
403 Bud Harrelson .25 .60
404 Detroit Tigers CL .50 1.25
405 Rawly Eastwick .10 .25
406 Mike Jorgensen .10 .25
407 Odell Jones RC .10 .25
408 Joe Zdeb RC .10 .25
409 Ron Schueler .10 .25
410 Bill Madlock .25 .60
411 Mickey Rivers ALCS .25 .60
412 Davey Lopes NLCS .25 .60
413 Reggie Jackson WS 1.50 4.00
414 Darold Knowles DP .08 .20
415 Ray Fosse .10 .25
416 Jack Brohamer .10 .25
417 Mike Garman DP .08 .20
418 Tony Muser .10 .25
419 Jerry Garvin RC .10 .25
420 Greg Luzinski .50 1.25
421 Junior Moore RC .10 .25
422 Steve Braun .10 .25
423 Dave Rosello .10 .25
424 Boston Red Sox CL .50 1.25
425 Steve Rogers DP .10 .25
426 Fred Kendall .10 .25
427 Mario Soto RC .25 .60
428 Joel Youngblood .10 .25
429 Mike Barlow RC .10 .25
430 Al Oliver .25 .60
431 Butch Metzger .10 .25
432 Terry Bulling RC .10 .25
433 Fernando Gonzalez .10 .25
434 Mike Norris .10 .25
435 Checklist 364-484 .50 1.25
436 Vic Harris DP .08 .20
437 Bo McLaughlin .10 .25
438 John Ellis .10 .25
439 Ken Kravec .10 .25
440 Dave Lopes .25 .60
441 Larry Gura .10 .25
442 Elliott Maddox .10 .25
443 Darrel Chaney .10 .25
444 Roy Hartsfield MG .10 .25
445 Mike Ivie .10 .25
446 Tug McGraw .25 .60
447 Leroy Stanton .10 .25
448 Bill Castro .10 .25
449 Tim Blackwell DP RC .08 .20
450 Tom Seaver 3.00 8.00
451 Minnesota Twins CL .50 1.25
452 Jerry Mumphrey .10 .25
453 Doug Flynn .10 .25
454 Dave LaRoche .10 .25
455 Bill Robinson .25 .60
456 Vern Ruhle .10 .25
457 Bob Bailey .10 .25
458 Jeff Newman .10 .25
459 Charlie Spikes .10 .25
460 Jim Hunter 1.00 2.50
461 Rob Andrews DP .08 .20
462 Rogelio Moret .10 .25
463 Kevin Bell .10 .25
464 Jerry Grote .10 .25
465 Hal McRae .25 .60
466 Dennis Blair .10 .25
467 Alvin Dark MG .25 .60
468 Warren Cromartie RC .25 .60
469 Rick Cerone .25 .60
470 J.R. Richard .25 .60
471 Roy Smalley .25 .60
472 Ron Reed .10 .25
473 Bill Buckner .25 .60
474 Jim Slaton .10 .25
475 Gary Matthews .25 .60
476 Bill Stein .10 .25
477 Doug Capilla RC .10 .25
478 Jerry Remy .10 .25
479 St. Louis Cardinals CL .50 1.25
480 Ron LeFlore .25 .60
481 Jackson Todd RC .10 .25
482 Rick Miller .10 .25
483 Ken Macha RC .10 .25
484 Jim Norris RC .10 .25
485 Chris Chambliss .25 .60
486 John Curtis .10 .25
487 Jim Tyrone .10 .25
488 Dan Spillner .10 .25
489 Rudy Meoli .10 .25
490 Amos Otis .25 .60
491 Scott McGregor .25 .60
492 Jim Sundberg .25 .60
493 Steve Renko .10 .25
494 Chuck Tanner MG .25 .60
495 Dave Cash .10 .25
496 Jim Clancy DP RC .08 .20
497 Glenn Adams .10 .25
498 Joe Sambito .10 .25
499 Seattle Mariners CL .50 1.25
500 George Foster .50 1.25
501 Dave Roberts .10 .25
502 Pat Rockett RC .10 .25
503 Ike Hampton RC .10 .25
504 Roger Freed .10 .25
505 Felix Millan .10 .25
506 Ron Blomberg .10 .25
507 Willie Crawford .10 .25
508 Johnny Oates .25 .60
509 Brent Strom .10 .25
510 Willie Stargell 1.00 2.50
511 Frank Duffy .10 .25
512 Larry Herndon .10 .25
513 Barry Foote .10 .25
514 Rob Sperring .10 .25
515 Tim Corcoran RC .10 .25
516 Gary Beare RC .10 .25
517 Andres Mora .10 .25
518 Tommy Boggs DP .08 .20
519 Brian Downing .25 .60
520 Larry Hisle .10 .25
521 Steve Staggs RC .10 .25
522 Dick Williams MG .25 .60
523 Donnie Moore RC .10 .25
524 Bernie Carbo .10 .25
525 Jerry Terrell .10 .25
526 Cincinnati Reds CL .50 1.25
527 Vic Correll .10 .25
528 Rob Picciolo RC .10 .25
529 Paul Hartzell .10 .25
530 Dave Winfield 1.50 4.00
531 Tom Underwood .10 .25
532 Skip Jutze .10 .25
533 Sandy Alomar .25 .60
534 Wilbur Howard .10 .25
535 Checklist 485-605 .50 1.25
536 Roric Harrison .10 .25
537 Bruce Bochte .10 .25
538 Johnny LeMaster .10 .25
539 Vic Davalillo DP .08 .20
540 Steve Carlton 1.50 4.00
541 Larry Cox .10 .25
542 Tim Johnson .10 .25
543 Larry Harlow DP RC .08 .20
544 Len Randle DP .08 .20
545 Bill Campbell .10 .25
546 Ted Martinez .10 .25
547 John Scott .10 .25
548 Billy Hunter MG DP .08 .20
549 Joe Kerrigan .10 .25
550 John Mayberry .25 .60
551 Atlanta Braves CL .50 1.25
552 Francisco Barrios .10 .25
553 Terry Puhl RC .25 .60
554 Joe Coleman .10 .25
555 Butch Wynegar .10 .25
556 Ed Armbrister .10 .25
557 Tony Solaita .10 .25
558 Paul Mitchell .10 .25
559 Phil Mankowski .10 .25
560 Dave Parker .50 1.25
561 Charlie Williams .10 .25
562 Glenn Burke RC .10 .25
563 Dave Rader .10 .25
564 Mick Kelleher .10 .25
565 Jerry Koosman .25 .60
566 Merv Rettenmund .10 .25
567 Dick Drago .10 .25
568 Tom Hutton .10 .25
569 Lary Sorensen RC .10 .25
570 Dave Kingman .50 1.25
571 Buck Martinez .10 .25
572 Rick Wise .10 .25
573 Luis Gomez .10 .25
574 Bob Lemon MG .50 1.25
575 Pat Dobson .10 .25
576 Sam Mejias .10 .25
577 Oakland Athletics CL .50 1.25
578 Buzz Capra .10 .25
579 Rance Mulliniks RC .10 .25
580 Rod Carew 1.50 4.00
581 Lynn McGlothen .10 .25
582 Fran Healy .10 .25
583 George Medich .10 .25
584 John Hale .10 .25
585 Woodie Fryman DP .08 .20
586 Ed Goodson .10 .25
587 John Urrea RC .10 .25
588 Jim Mason .10 .25
589 Bob Knepper RC .10 .25
590 Bobby Murcer .25 .60
591 George Zeber RC .10 .25
592 Bob Apodaca .10 .25
593 Dave Skaggs RC .10 .25
594 Dave Freisleben .10 .25
595 Sixto Lezcano .10 .25
596 Gary Wheelock .10 .25
597 Steve Dillard .10 .25
598 Eddie Solomon .10 .25
599 Gary Woods .10 .25
600 Frank Tanana .25 .60
601 Gene Mauch MG .25 .60
602 Eric Soderholm .10 .25
603 Will McEnaney .10 .25
604 Earl Williams .10 .25
605 Rick Rhoden .25 .60
606 Pittsburgh Pirates CL .50 1.25
607 Fernando Arroyo .10 .25
608 Johnny Grubb .10 .25
609 John Denny .10 .25
610 Garry Maddox .25 .60
611 Pat Scanlon RC .10 .25
612 Ken Henderson .10 .25
613 Marty Perez .10 .25
614 Joe Wallis .10 .25
615 Clay Carroll .10 .25
616 Pat Kelly .10 .25
617 Joe Nolan RC .10 .25
618 Tommy Helms .10 .25
619 Thad Bosley DP RC .08 .20
620 Willie Randolph .50 1.25
621 Craig Swan DP .08 .20
622 Champ Summers .10 .25
623 Eduardo Rodriguez .10 .25
624 Gary Alexander DP .08 .20
625 Jose Cruz .25 .60
626 Toronto Blue Jays CL DP .50 1.25
627 David Johnson .10 .25
628 Ralph Garr .25 .60
629 Don Stanhouse .10 .25
630 Ron Cey .50 1.25
631 Danny Ozark MG .10 .25
632 Rowland Office .10 .25
633 Tom Veryzer .10 .25
634 Len Barker .10 .25
635 Joe Rudi .25 .60
636 Jim Bibby .10 .25
637 Duffy Dyer .10 .25
638 Paul Splittorff .10 .25
639 Gene Clines .10 .25
640 Lee May DP .10 .25
641 Doug Rau .10 .25
642 Denny Doyle .10 .25
643 Tom House .10 .25
644 Jim Dwyer .10 .25
645 Mike Torrez .25 .60
646 Rick Auerbach DP .08 .20
647 Steve Dunning .10 .25
648 Gary Thomasson .10 .25
649 Moose Haas RC .10 .25
650 Cesar Cedeno .25 .60
651 Doug Rader .10 .25
652 Checklist 606-726 .50 1.25
653 Ron Hodges DP .08 .20
654 Pepe Frias .10 .25
655 Lyman Bostock .25 .60
656 Dave Garcia MG RC .10 .25
657 Bombo Rivera .10 .25
658 Manny Sanguillen .25 .60
659 Texas Rangers CL .50 1.25
660 Jason Thompson .25 .60
661 Grant Jackson .10 .25
662 Paul Dade RC .10 .25
663 Paul Reuschel .10 .25
664 Fred Stanley .10 .25
665 Dennis Leonard .25 .60
666 Billy Smith RC .10 .25
667 Jeff Byrd RC .10 .25
668 Dusty Baker .50 1.25
669 Pete Falcone .10 .25
670 Jim Rice 1.00 2.50
671 Gary Lavelle .10 .25
672 Don Kessinger .25 .60
673 Steve Brye .10 .25
674 Ray Knight RC 1.00 2.50
675 Jay Johnstone .25 .60
676 Bob Myrick .10 .25
677 Ed Herrmann .10 .25
678 Tom Burgmeier .10 .25
679 Wayne Garrett .10 .25
680 Vida Blue .25 .60
681 Rob Belloir .10 .25
682 Ken Brett .10 .25
683 Mike Champion .10 .25
684 Ralph Houk MG .25 .60
685 Frank Taveras .10 .25
686 Gaylord Perry 1.00 2.50
687 Julio Cruz RC .10 .25
688 George Mitterwald .10 .25
689 Cleveland Indians CL .50 1.25
690 Mickey Rivers .25 .60
691 Ross Grimsley .10 .25
692 Ken Reitz .10 .25
693 Lamar Johnson .10 .25
694 Elias Sosa .10 .25
695 Dwight Evans .50 1.25
696 Steve Mingori .10 .25
697 Roger Metzger .10 .25
698 Juan Bernhardt .10 .25
699 Jackie Brown .10 .25
700 Johnny Bench 6.00 15.00
701 Hume/Land/McC/Tay RC .25 .60
702 Nah/Pas/Sweet/Wer RC .25 .60
703 Jack Morris DP RC 6.00 15.00
704 Lou Whitaker RC 10.00 25.00
705 Berg/Milone/Hurdle/Nor RC .50 1.25
706 Cage/Cox/Put/Rev RC .25 .60
707 P.Molitor RC/A.Trammell RC 20.00 50.00
708 D.Murphy/L.Parrish RC 1.50 4.00
709 Burke/Keough/Rau/Schat RC .25 .60
710 Alston/Bos/Easler/Smith RC .50 1.25
711 Camp/Lamp/Mit/Tho DP RC .10 .25
712 Bobby Valentine .25 .60
713 Bob Davis .10 .25
714 Mike Anderson .10 .25
715 Jim Kaat .50 1.25
716 Clarence Gaston .25 .60
717 Nelson Briles .10 .25
718 Ron Jackson .10 .25
719 Randy Elliott RC .10 .25
720 Fergie Jenkins 1.00 2.50
721 Billy Martin MG .50 1.25
722 Pete Broberg .10 .25
723 John Wockenfuss .10 .25
724 Kansas City Royals CL .50 1.25
725 Kurt Bevacqua .10 .25
726 Wilbur Wood .50 1.25

1978 Topps Team Checklist Sheet

As part of a mail-away offer, Topps offered all 26 team checklist cards on an uncut sheet. These cards enabled the collector to have an easy reference for which card(s) he/she needed to finish their sets. When cut from the sheet, all cards measure the standard size.

1 Team Checklist Sheet 40.00 80.00

1978 Topps Zest

This set of five standard-size cards is very similar to the 1978 Topps regular issue. Although the cards were produced by Topps, they were used in a promotion for Zest Soap. The sponsor of the set, Zest Soap, is not mentioned anywhere on the cards. The card numbers are different and the backs are written in English and Spanish. By the choice of players in this small set, Zest appears to have been targeting the Hispanic community. Each player's card number in the regular 1978 Topps set is also given. A different photo was used for Montanez, showing his head and shoulders as a New York Met rather than as an Atlanta Brave in a batting stance as shown on Willie's Topps regular card.

COMPLETE SET (5) 2.50 6.00
1 Joaquin Andujar/78T-158 .60 1.50
2 Bert Campaneris/78T-260 .75 2.00
3 Ed Figueroa/78T-365 .40 1.00
4 Willie Montanez/78T-38 (different pose)(New Yo .60 1.50
5 Manny Mota/78T-228 .60 1.50

1979 Topps

The cards in this 726-card set measure 2 1/2" by 3 1/2". Topps continued with the same number of cards as in 1978. As in previous years, this set was released in many different formats, among them ar 12-card wax packs and 39-card rack packs which cost 59 cents upon release. Those rack packs came 24 packs to a box and three boxes to a case. Vario series spotlight League Leaders (1-8), "Season and Career Record Holders" (411-418), "Record Breakers" (201-206), and one "Prospects" card for each team (701-726). Team cards feature a checkli on back of that team's players in the set and a smal picture of the manager on the front of the card. The are 66 cards that were double printed and these are noted in the checklist by the abbreviation DP. Bum Wills (369) was initially depicted in a Ranger unifo but with a Blue Jays affiliation; later printings correctly labeled him with Texas. The set price includes either Wills card. The key Rookie Cards in this set are Pedro Guerrero, Carney Lansford, Ozzie Smith, Bob Welch and Willie Wilson. Cards numbered 23 or lower, which feature Phillies or Yankees and do not follow the numbering checklist below, are not necessarily error cards. They are undoubtedly Burger King cards, separate sets for each team with their own pricing and mass distribution.

COMPLETE SET (726) 150.00 400.0
COMMON CARD (1-726) .10 .25
COMMON CARD DP .08 .20
1 R.Carew/D.Parker LL 1.00 2.50
2 J.Rice/G.Foster LL .60 1.50
3 J.Rice/G.Foster LL .60 1.50
4 R.LeFlore/O.Moreno LL .30 .75
5 R.Guidry/G.Perry LL .30 .75
6 N.Ryan/J.Richard LL 2.00 5.00
7 R.Guidry/C.Swan LL .30 .75
8 R.Gossage/R.Fingers LL .60 1.50
9 Dave Campbell .10 .25
10 Lee May .30 .75
11 Marc Hill .10 .25
12 Dick Drago .10 .25
13 Paul Dade .10 .25
14 Rafael Landestoy RC .10 .25
15 Ross Grimsley .10 .25
16 Fred Stanley .10 .25
17 Donnie Moore .10 .25
18 Tony Solaita .10 .25
19 Larry Gura DP .08 .20
20 Joe Morgan DP 1.00 2.50
21 Kevin Kobel .10 .25
22 Mike Jorgensen .10 .25
23 Terry Forster .10 .25
24 Paul Molitor 6.00 15.00
25 Steve Carlton 1.25 3.00
26 Jamie Quirk .10 .25
27 Dave Goltz .10 .25
28 Steve Brye .10 .25
29 Rick Langford .10 .25
30 Dave Winfield 1.50 4.00
31 Tom House DP .08 .20
32 Jerry Mumphrey .10 .25
33 Dave Rozema .10 .25
34 Rob Andrews .10 .25
35 Ed Figueroa .10 .25
36 Alan Ashby .10 .25
37 Joe Kerrigan DP .08 .20
38 Bernie Carbo .10 .25
39 Dale Murphy 1.25 3.00
40 Dennis Eckersley 1.00 2.50
41 Minnesota Twins CL/Mauch .60 1.50
42 Ron Blomberg .10 .25
43 Wayne Twitchell .10 .25
44 Kurt Bevacqua .10 .25
45 Al Hrabosky .30 .75
46 Ron Hodges .10 .25
47 Fred Norman .10 .25
48 Merv Rettenmund .10 .25
49 Vern Ruhle .10 .25
50 Steve Garvey DP .60 1.50
51 Ray Fosse DP .08 .20
52 Randy Lerch .10 .25
53 Mick Kelleher .10 .25
54 Dell Alston DP .08 .20
55 Willie Stargell 1.00 2.50
56 John Hale .10 .25
57 Eric Rasmussen .10 .25
58 Bob Randall DP .08 .20
59 John Denny DP .08 .20
60 Mickey Rivers .30 .75
61 Bo Diaz .10 .25
62 Randy Moffitt .10 .25
63 Jack Brohamer .10 .25
64 Tom Underwood .10 .25
65 Mark Belanger .30 .75
66 Detroit Tigers CL/Moss .60 1.50
67 Jim Mason DP .08 .20
68 Joe Niekro DP .08 .20
69 Elliott Maddox .10 .25
70 John Candelaria .30 .75

Brian Downing .30 .75
Steve Mingori .10 .25
Ken Henderson .10 .25
Shane Rawley RC .10 .25
Steve Yeager .30 .75
Warren Cromartie .30 .75
Dan Briggs DP .08 .20
Elias Sosa .10 .25
Ted Cox .10 .25
Jason Thompson .30 .75
Roger Erickson RC .10 .25
2 New York Mets CL/Torre .60 1.50
Fred Kendall .10 .25
Greg Minton .10 .25
5 Gary Matthews .30 .75
6 Rodney Scott .10 .25
7 Pete Falcone .10 .25
8 Bob Molinaro RC .10 .25
9 Dick Tidrow .10 .25
0 Bob Boone .60 1.50
1 Terry Crowley .10 .25
2 Jim Bibby .10 .25
3 Phil Mankowski .10 .25
4 Len Barker .10 .25
5 Robin Yount 2.00 5.00
6 Cleveland Indians CL/Torborg .60 1.50
7 Sam Mejias .10 .25
8 Ray Burris .10 .25
9 John Wathan .30 .75
00 Tom Seaver DP 1.50 4.00
01 Roy Howell .10 .25
02 Mike Anderson .10 .25
03 Jim Todd .10 .25
04 Johnny Oates DP .10 .25
05 Rick Camp DP .08 .20
06 Frank Duffy .10 .25
07 Jesus Alou DP .08 .20
08 Eduardo Rodriguez .10 .25
109 Joel Youngblood .10 .25
110 Vida Blue .30 .75
111 Roger Freed .10 .25
112 Philadelphia Phillies CL/Ozark .60 1.50
113 Pete Redfern .10 .25
114 Cliff Johnson .10 .25
115 Nolan Ryan 8.00 20.00
116 Ozzie Smith RC 25.00 60.00
117 Grant Jackson .10 .25
118 Bud Harrelson .30 .75
119 Don Stanhouse .10 .25
120 Jim Sundberg .30 .75
121 Checklist 1-121 DP .30 .75
122 Mike Paxton .10 .25
123 Lou Whitaker 1.00 2.50
124 Dan Schatzeder .10 .25
125 Rick Burleson .10 .25
126 Doug Bair .10 .25
127 Thad Bosley .10 .25
128 Ted Martinez .10 .25
129 Marty Pattin DP .08 .20
130 Bob Watson DP .10 .25
131 Jim Clancy .10 .25
132 Rowland Office .10 .25
133 Bill Castro .10 .25
134 Alan Bannister .10 .25
135 Bobby Murcer .30 .75
136 Jim Kaat .30 .75
137 Larry Wolfe DP RC .08 .20
138 Mark Lee RC .10 .25
139 Luis Pujols RC .10 .25
140 Don Gullett .30 .75
141 Tom Paciorek .30 .75
142 Charlie Williams .10 .25
143 Tony Scott .10 .25
144 Sandy Alomar .10 .25
145 Rick Rhoden .10 .25
146 Duane Kuiper .10 .25
147 Dave Hamilton .10 .25
148 Bruce Boisclair .10 .25
149 Manny Sarmiento .10 .25
150 Wayne Cage .10 .25
151 John Hiller .10 .25
152 Rick Cerone .10 .25
153 Dennis Lamp .10 .25
154 Jim Gantner DP .10 .25
155 Dwight Evans .60 1.50
156 Buddy Solomon .10 .25
157 U.L. Washington UER .10 .25
158 Joe Sambito .10 .25
159 Roy White .30 .75
160 Mike Flanagan .60 1.50
161 Barry Foote .10 .25
162 Tom Johnson .10 .25
163 Glenn Burke .10 .25
164 Mickey Lolich .30 .75
165 Frank Taveras .10 .25
166 Leon Roberts .10 .25
167 Roger Metzger DP .08 .20
168 Dave Freisleben .10 .25
169 Bill Nahorodny .10 .25
170 Don Sutton 1.00 2.50
171 Gene Clines .10 .25
172 Mike Bruhert RC .10 .25
173 John Lowenstein .10 .25
174 Rick Auerbach .10 .25
175 George Hendrick .60 1.50
176 Aurelio Rodriguez .10 .25
177 Ron Reed .10 .25
178 Alvis Woods .10 .25
179 Jim Beattie DP RC .08 .20
180 Larry Hisle .10 .25
181 Mike Garman .10 .25
182 Tim Johnson .10 .25
183 Paul Splittorff .10 .25
184 Darrel Chaney .10 .25
185 Mike Torrez .30 .75
186 Eric Soderholm .10 .25
187 Mark Lemongello .10 .25
188 Pat Kelly .10 .25
189 Ed Whitson RC .10 .25
190 Ron Cey .30 .75
191 Mike Norris .10 .25
192 St. Louis Cardinals CL/Boyer .60 1.50
193 Glenn Adams .10 .25
194 Randy Jones .10 .25
195 Bill Madlock .30 .75
196 Steve Kemp DP .10 .25
197 Bob Apodaca .10 .25
198 Johnny Grubb .10 .25
199 Larry Milbourne .10 .25
200 Johnny Bench DP 2.00 5.00
201 Mike Edwards RB .10 .25
202 Ron Guidry RB .30 .75
203 J.R. Richard RB .10 .25
204 Pete Rose RB 2.00 5.00
205 John Stearns RB .10 .25
206 Sammy Stewart RB .10 .25
207 Dave Lemanczyk .10 .25
208 Clarence Gaston .10 .25
209 Reggie Cleveland .10 .25
210 Larry Bowa .30 .75
211 Dennis Martinez 1.00 2.50
212 Carney Lansford RC .60 1.50
213 Bill Travers .10 .25
214 Boston Red Sox CL/Zimmer .60 1.50
215 Willie McCovey 1.00 2.50
216 Wilbur Wood .10 .25
217 Steve Dillard .10 .25
218 Dennis Leonard .30 .75
219 Roy Smalley .30 .75
220 Cesar Geronimo .10 .25
221 Jesse Jefferson .10 .25
222 Bob Beall RC .10 .25
223 Kent Tekulve .30 .75
224 Dave Revering .10 .25
225 Goose Gossage .60 1.50
226 Ron Pruitt .10 .25
227 Steve Stone .30 .75
228 Vic Davalillo .10 .25
229 Doug Flynn .10 .25
230 Bob Forsch .10 .25
231 John Wockenfuss .10 .25
232 Jimmy Sexton RC .10 .25
233 Paul Mitchell .10 .25
234 Toby Harrah .30 .75
235 Steve Rogers .10 .25
236 Jim Dwyer .10 .25
237 Billy Smith .10 .25
238 Balor Moore .10 .25
239 Willie Horton .30 .75
240 Rick Reuschel .30 .75
241 Checklist 122-242 DP .30 .75
242 Pablo Torrealba .10 .25
243 Buck Martinez DP .10 .25
244 Pittsburgh Pirates CL/Tanner .60 1.50
245 Jeff Burroughs .30 .75
246 Darrell Jackson RC .10 .25
247 Tucker Ashford DP .08 .20
248 Pete LaCock .10 .25
249 Paul Thormodsgard .10 .25
250 Willie Randolph .30 .75
251 Jack Morris 1.00 2.50
252 Bob Stinson .10 .25
253 Rick Wise .10 .25
254 Luis Gomez .10 .25
255 Tommy John .60 1.50
256 Mike Sadek .10 .25
257 Adrian Devine .10 .25
258 Mike Phillips .10 .25
259 Cincinnati Reds CL/Anderson .60 1.50
260 Richie Zisk .10 .25
261 Mario Guerrero .10 .25
262 Nelson Briles .10 .25
263 Oscar Gamble .30 .75
264 Don Robinson RC .10 .25
265 Don Money .10 .25
266 Jim Willoughby .10 .25
267 Joe Rudi .30 .75
268 Julio Gonzalez .10 .25
269 Woodie Fryman .10 .25
270 Butch Hobson .30 .75
271 Rawly Eastwick .10 .25
272 Tim Corcoran .10 .25
273 Jerry Terrell .10 .25
274 Willie Norwood .10 .25
275 Junior Moore .10 .25
276 Jim Colborn .10 .25
277 Tom Grieve .30 .75
278 Andy Messersmith .30 .75
279 Jerry Grote DP .08 .20
280 Andre Thornton .30 .75
281 Vic Correll DP .08 .20
282 Toronto Blue Jays CL/Hartsfield .30 .75
283 Ken Kravec .10 .25
284 Johnnie LeMaster .10 .25
285 Bobby Bonds .60 1.50
286 Duffy Dyer UER .10 .25
287 Andres Mora .10 .25
288 Milt Wilcox .10 .25
289 Jose Cruz .60 1.50
290 Dave Lopes .30 .75
291 Tom Griffin .10 .25
292 Don Reynolds RC .10 .25
293 Jerry Garvin .10 .25
294 Pepe Frias .10 .25
295 Mitchell Page .10 .25
296 Preston Hanna RC .10 .25
297 Ted Sizemore .10 .25
298 Rich Gale RC .10 .25
299 Steve Ontiveros .10 .25
300 Rod Carew 1.25 3.00
301 Tom Hume .10 .25
302 Atlanta Braves CL/Cox .60 1.50
303 Lary Sorensen DP .08 .20
304 Steve Swisher .10 .25
305 Willie Montanez .10 .25
306 Floyd Bannister .10 .25
307 Larvell Blanks .10 .25
308 Bert Blyleven .60 1.50
309 Ralph Garr .30 .75
310 Thurman Munson 1.25 3.00
311 Gary Lavelle .10 .25
312 Bob Robertson .10 .25
313 Dyar Miller .10 .25
314 Larry Harlow .10 .25
315 Jon Matlack .10 .25
316 Milt May .10 .25
317 Jose Cardenal .30 .75
318 Bob Welch RC 1.00 2.50
319 Wayne Garrett .10 .25
320 Carl Yastrzemski 2.00 5.00
321 Gaylord Perry 1.00 2.50
322 Danny Goodwin RC .10 .25
323 Lynn McGlothen .10 .25
324 Mike Tyson .10 .25
325 Cecil Cooper .30 .75
326 Pedro Borbon .10 .25
327 Art Howe DP .10 .25
328 Oakland Athletics CL/McKeon .60 1.50
329 Joe Coleman .10 .25
330 George Brett 5.00 12.00
331 Mickey Mahler .10 .25
332 Gary Alexander .10 .25
333 Chet Lemon .30 .75
334 Craig Swan .10 .25
335 Chris Chambliss .30 .75
336 Bobby Thompson RC .10 .25
337 John Montague .10 .25
338 Vic Harris .10 .25
339 Ron Jackson .10 .25
340 Jim Palmer 1.00 2.50
341 Willie Upshaw RC .30 .75
342 Dave Roberts .10 .25
343 Ed Glynn .10 .25
344 Jerry Royster .10 .25
345 Tug McGraw .30 .75
346 Bill Buckner .30 .75
347 Doug Rau .10 .25
348 Andre Dawson 1.25 3.00
349 Jim Wright RC .10 .25
350 Garry Templeton .30 .75
351 Wayne Nordhagen DP .08 .20
352 Steve Renko .10 .25
353 Checklist 243-363 .60 1.50
354 Bill Bonham .10 .25
355 Lee Mazzilli .10 .25
356 San Francisco Giants CL/Altobelli .60 1.50
357 Jerry Augustine .10 .25
358 Alan Trammell 1.25 3.00
359 Dan Spillner DP .08 .20
360 Amos Otis .30 .75
361 Tom Dixon RC .10 .25
362 Mike Cubbage .10 .25
363 Craig Skok RC .10 .25
364 Gene Richards .10 .25
365 Sparky Lyle .30 .75
366 Juan Bernhardt .10 .25
367 Dave Skaggs .10 .25
368 Don Aase .10 .25
369A Bump Wills ERR 1.25 3.00
369B Bump Wills COR .75 2.00
370 Dave Kingman .60 1.50
371 Jeff Holly RC .10 .25
372 Lamar Johnson .10 .25
373 Lance Rautzhan .10 .25
374 Ed Herrmann .10 .25
375 Bill Campbell .10 .25
376 Gorman Thomas .30 .75
377 Paul Moskau .10 .25
378 Rob Picciolo DP .08 .20
379 Dale Murray .10 .25
380 John Mayberry .30 .75
381 Houston Astros CL/Virdon .60 1.50
382 Jerry Martin .10 .25
383 Phil Garner .30 .75
384 Tommy Boggs .10 .25
385 Dan Ford .10 .25
386 Francisco Barrios .10 .25
387 Gary Thomasson .10 .25
388 Jack Billingham .10 .25
389 Joe Zdeb .10 .25
390 Rollie Fingers 1.00 2.50
391 Al Oliver .30 .75
392 Doug Ault .10 .25
393 Scott McGregor .30 .75
394 Randy Stein RC .10 .25
395 Dave Cash .10 .25
396 Bill Plummer .10 .25
397 Sergio Ferrer RC .10 .25
398 Ivan DeJesus .10 .25
399 David Clyde .10 .25
400 Jim Rice .75 2.00
401 Ray Knight .30 .75
402 Paul Hartzell .10 .25
403 Tim Foli .10 .25
404 Chicago White Sox CL/Kessinger .60 1.50
405 Butch Wynegar DP .08 .20
406 Joe Wallis DP .08 .20
407 Pete Vuckovich .30 .75
408 Charlie Moore DP .08 .20
409 Willie Wilson RC .60 1.50
410 Darrell Evans .60 1.50
411 G.Sisler/T.Cobb ATL 1.00 2.50
412 H.Wilson/H.Aaron ATL 1.00 2.50
413 R.Maris/H.Aaron ATL 1.50 4.00
414 R.Hornsby/T.Cobb ATL 1.00 2.50
415 L.Brock/L.Brock ATL .60 1.50
416 J.Chesbro/C.Young ATL .30 .75
417 N.Ryan/W.Johnson ATL DP 2.00 5.00
418 D.Leonard/W.Johnson ATL DP .10 .25
419 Dick Ruthven .10 .25
420 Ken Griffey Sr. .30 .75
421 Doug DeCinces .30 .75
422 Ruppert Jones .10 .25
423 Bob Montgomery .10 .25
424 California Angels CL/Fregosi .60 1.50
425 Rick Manning .10 .25
426 Chris Speier .10 .25
427 Andy Replogle RC .10 .25
428 Bobby Valentine .30 .75
429 John Urrea DP .08 .20
430 Dave Parker .30 .75
431 Glenn Borgmann .10 .25
432 Dave Heaverlo .10 .25
433 Larry Biittner .10 .25
434 Ken Clay .10 .25
435 Gene Tenace .30 .75
436 Hector Cruz .10 .25
437 Rick Williams RC .10 .25
438 Horace Speed RC .10 .25
439 Frank White .30 .75
440 Rusty Staub .60 1.50
441 Lee Lacy .10 .25
442 Doyle Alexander .10 .25
443 Bruce Bochte .10 .25
444 Aurelio Lopez RC .10 .25
445 Steve Henderson .10 .25
446 Jim Lonborg .30 .75
447 Manny Sanguillen .30 .75
448 Moose Haas .10 .25
449 Bombo Rivera .10 .25
450 Dave Concepcion .60 1.50
451 Kansas City Royals CL/Herzog .60 1.50
452 Jerry Morales .10 .25
453 Chris Knapp .10 .25
454 Len Randle .10 .25
455 Bill Lee DP .08 .20
456 Chuck Baker RC .10 .25
457 Bruce Sutter 1.00 2.50
458 Jim Essian .10 .25
459 Sid Monge .10 .25
460 Graig Nettles .60 1.50
461 Jim Barr DP .08 .20
462 Otto Velez .10 .25
463 Steve Comer RC .10 .25
464 Joe Nolan .10 .25
465 Reggie Smith .30 .75
466 Mark Littell .10 .25
467 Don Kessinger DP .10 .25
468 Stan Bahnsen DP .08 .20
469 Lance Parrish .60 1.50
470 Garry Maddox DP .10 .25
471 Joaquin Andujar .30 .75
472 Craig Kusick .10 .25
473 Dave Roberts .10 .25
474 Dick Davis RC .10 .25
475 Dan Driessen .10 .25
476 Tom Poquette .10 .25
477 Bob Grich .30 .75
478 Juan Beniquez .10 .25
479 San Diego Padres CL/Craig .60 1.50
480 Fred Lynn .40 1.00
481 Skip Lockwood .10 .25
482 Craig Reynolds .10 .25
483 Checklist 364-484 DP .30 .75
484 Rick Waits .10 .25
485 Bucky Dent .30 .75
486 Bob Knepper .10 .25
487 Miguel Dilone .10 .25
488 Bob Owchinko .10 .25
489 Larry Cox UER .10 .25
490 Al Cowens .30 .75
491 Tippy Martinez .10 .25
492 Bob Bailor .10 .25
493 Larry Christenson .10 .25
494 Jerry White .10 .25
495 Tony Perez 1.00 2.50
496 Barry Bonnell DP .08 .20
497 Glenn Abbott .10 .25
498 Rich Chiles .10 .25
499 Texas Rangers CL/Corrales .60 1.50
500 Ron Guidry .30 .75
501 Junior Kennedy RC .10 .25
502 Steve Braun .10 .25
503 Terry Humphrey .10 .25
504 Larry McWilliams RC .10 .25
505 Ed Kranepool .10 .25
506 John D'Acquisto .10 .25
507 Tony Armas .30 .75
508 Charlie Hough .30 .75
509 Mario Mendoza UER .10 .25
510 Ted Simmons .60 1.50
511 Paul Reuschel DP .08 .20
512 Jack Clark .30 .75
513 Dave Johnson .30 .75
514 Mike Proly RC .10 .25
515 Enos Cabell .10 .25
516 Champ Summers DP .10 .25
517 Al Bumbry .30 .75
518 Jim Umbarger .10 .25
519 Ben Oglivie .30 .75
520 Gary Carter .75 2.00
521 Sam Ewing .10 .25
522 Ken Holtzman .30 .75
523 John Milner .10 .25
524 Tom Burgmeier .10 .25
525 Freddie Patek .10 .25
526 Los Angeles Dodgers CL/Lasorda .60 1.50
527 Lerrin LaGrow .10 .25
528 Wayne Gross DP .08 .20
529 Brian Asselstine .10 .25
530 Frank Tanana .30 .75
531 Fernando Gonzalez .10 .25
532 Buddy Schultz .10 .25
533 Leroy Stanton .10 .25
534 Ken Forsch .10 .25
535 Ellis Valentine .10 .25
536 Jerry Reuss .30 .75
537 Tom Veryzer .10 .25
538 Mike Ivie DP .08 .20
539 John Ellis .10 .25
540 Greg Luzinski .30 .75
541 Jim Slaton .10 .25
542 Rick Bosetti .10 .25
543 Kiko Garcia .10 .25
544 Fergie Jenkins 1.00 2.50
545 John Stearns .10 .25
546 Bill Russell .30 .75
547 Clint Hurdle .10 .25
548 Enrique Romo .10 .25
549 Bob Bailey .10 .25
550 Sal Bando .30 .75
551 Chicago Cubs CL/Franks .60 1.50
552 Jose Morales .10 .25
553 Denny Walling .10 .25
554 Matt Keough .10 .25
555 Biff Pocoroba .10 .25
556 Mike Lum .10 .25
557 Ken Brett .10 .25
558 Jay Johnstone .30 .75
559 Greg Pryor RC .10 .25
560 John Montefusco .10 .25
561 Ed Ott .10 .25
562 Dusty Baker .60 1.50
563 Roy Thomas .10 .25
564 Jerry Turner .10 .25
565 Rico Carty .30 .75
566 Nino Espinosa .10 .25
567 Richie Hebner .30 .75
568 Carlos Lopez .10 .25
569 Bob Sykes .10 .25
570 Cesar Cedeno .30 .75
571 Darrell Porter .30 .75
572 Rod Gilbreath .10 .25
573 Jim Kern .10 .25
574 Claudell Washington .30 .75
575 Luis Tiant .30 .75
576 Mike Parrott RC .10 .25
577 Milwaukee Brewers CL/Bamberger .60 1.50
578 Pete Broberg .10 .25
579 Greg Gross .10 .25
580 Ron Fairly .30 .75
581 Darold Knowles .10 .25
582 Paul Blair .30 .75
583 Julio Cruz .10 .25
584 Jim Rooker .10 .25
585 Hal McRae .60 1.50
586 Bob Horner RC .60 1.50
587 Ken Reitz .10 .25
588 Tom Murphy .10 .25
589 Terry Whitfield .10 .25
590 J.R. Richard .30 .75
591 Mike Hargrove .30 .75
592 Mike Krukow .10 .25
593 Rick Dempsey .30 .75
594 Bob Shirley .10 .25
595 Phil Niekro 1.00 2.50
596 Jim Wohlford .10 .25
597 Bob Stanley .10 .25
598 Mark Wagner .10 .25
599 Jim Spencer .10 .25
600 George Foster .30 .75
601 Dave LaRoche .10 .25
602 Checklist 485-605 .60 1.50
603 Rudy May .10 .25
604 Jeff Newman .10 .25
605 Rick Monday DP .10 .25
606 Montreal Expos CL/Williams .60 1.50
607 Omar Moreno .10 .25
608 Dave McKay .10 .25
609 Silvio Martinez RC .10 .25
610 Mike Schmidt 4.00 10.00
611 Jim Norris .10 .25
612 Rick Honeycutt RC .30 .75
613 Mike Edwards RC .10 .25
614 Willie Hernandez .30 .75
615 Ken Singleton .30 .75
616 Billy Almon .10 .25
617 Terry Puhl .10 .25
618 Jerry Remy .10 .25
619 Ken Landreaux RC .30 .75
620 Bert Campaneris .30 .75
621 Pat Zachry .10 .25
622 Dave Collins .30 .75
623 Bob McClure .10 .25
624 Larry Herndon .10 .25
625 Mark Fidrych 1.00 2.50
626 New York Yankees CL/Lemon .60 1.50
627 Gary Serum RC .10 .25
628 Del Unser .10 .25
629 Gene Garber .10 .25
630 Bake McBride .30 .75
631 Jorge Orta .10 .25
632 Don Kirkwood .10 .25
633 Rob Wilfong DP RC .08 .20
634 Paul Lindblad .10 .25
635 Don Baylor .60 1.50
636 Wayne Garland .10 .25
637 Bill Robinson .30 .75
638 Al Fitzmorris .10 .25
639 Manny Trillo .10 .25
640 Eddie Murray 4.00 10.00
641 Bobby Castillo RC .10 .25
642 Wilbur Howard DP .08 .20
643 Tom Hausman .10 .25
644 Manny Mota .30 .75
645 George Scott DP .10 .25
646 Rick Sweet .10 .25
647 Bob Lacey .10 .25
648 Lou Piniella .30 .75
649 John Curtis .10 .25
650 Pete Rose 6.00 15.00
651 Mike Caldwell .10 .25
652 Stan Papi RC .10 .25
653 Warren Brusstar DP .08 .20
654 Rick Miller .10 .25
655 Jerry Koosman .30 .75
656 Hosken Powell RC .10 .25
657 George Medich .10 .25
658 Taylor Duncan RC .10 .25
659 Seattle Mariners CL/Johnson .60 1.50
660 Ron LeFlore DP .10 .25
661 Bruce Kison .10 .25
662 Kevin Bell .10 .25
663 Mike Vail .10 .25
664 Doug Bird .10 .25
665 Lou Brock 1.00 2.50
666 Rich Dauer .10 .25
667 Don Hood .10 .25
668 Bill North .10 .25
669 Checklist 606-726 .60 1.50
670 Jim Hunter DP .60 1.50
671 Joe Ferguson DP .08 .20
672 Ed Halicki .10 .25
673 Tom Hutton .10 .25
674 Dave Tomlin .10 .25
675 Tim McCarver .60 1.50
676 Johnny Sutton RC .10 .25
677 Larry Parrish .30 .75
678 Geoff Zahn .10 .25
679 Derrel Thomas .10 .25
680 Carlton Fisk 1.25 3.00
681 John Henry Johnson RC .10 .25
682 Dave Chalk .10 .25
683 Dan Meyer DP .08 .20
684 Jamie Easterly DP .08 .20
685 Sixto Lezcano .10 .25
686 Ron Schueler DP .08 .20
687 Rennie Stennett .10 .25
688 Mike Willis .10 .25
689 Baltimore Orioles CL/Weaver .60 1.50
690 Buddy Bell DP .10 .25
691 Dock Ellis DP .08 .20
692 Mickey Stanley .10 .25
693 Dave Rader .10 .25
694 Burt Hooton .30 .75
695 Keith Hernandez .30 .75
696 Andy Hassler .10 .25
697 Dave Bergman .10 .25
698 Bill Stein .10 .25
699 Hal Dues RC .10 .25
700 Reggie Jackson DP 4.00 10.00
701 Corey/Flinn/Stewart RC .30 .75
702 Finch/Hancock/Ripley RC .30 .75
703 Anderson/Frost/Slater RC .30 .75
704 Baumgarten/Colbern/Squires RC .30 .75
705 Griffin/Norrid/Oliver RC .60 1.50
706 Stegman/Tobik/Young RC .30 .75
707 Bass/Gaudet/McGilberry RC .60 1.50
708 Bass/Romero/Yost RC .60 1.50
709 Perlozzo/Sofield/Stanfield RC .30 .75
710 Doyle/Heath/Rajsich RC .30 .75
711 Murphy/Robinson/Wirth RC .60 1.50
712 Anderson/Biercevicz McLaughlin RC .30 .75
713 Darwin/Putnam/Sample RC .60 1.50
714 Cruz/Kelly/Whitt RC .30 .75
715 Benedict/Hubbard/Whisenton RC .60 1.50
716 Geisel/Pagel/Thompson RC .30 .75
717 LaCoss/Oester/Spilman RC .30 .75
718 Bochy/Fischlin/Pisker RC 2.00 5.00
719 Guerrero/Law/Simpson RC .60 1.50
720 Fry/Pirtle/Sanderson RC .60 1.50
721 Berenguer/Bernard/Norman RC .30 .75
722 Morrison/Smith/Wright RC .60 1.50
723 Berra/Cotes/Wiltbank RC .30 .75
724 Bruno/Frazier/Kennedy RC .60 1.50
725 Beswick/Mura/Perkins RC .30 .75
726 Johnston/Strain/Tamargo RC .30 .75

1980 Topps

The cards in this 726-card set measure the standard size. In 1980 Topps released another set of the same size and number of cards as the previous two years. Distribution for these cards included 15-card wax packs as well as 42-card rack packs. The 15-card wax packs had an 25 cent SRP and came 36 packs to a box and 20 boxes to a case. A special experiment in 1980 was the issuance of a 28-card cello pack with a 59 cent SRP which had a three-pack of gum at the bottom so no cards would be damaged. As with those sets, Topps again produced 66 double-printed cards in the set; they are noted by DP in the checklist below. The player's name appears over the picture and his position and team are found in pennant design. Every card carries a facsimile autograph. Team cards feature a team checklist of players in the set on the back and the manager's name on the front. Cards 1-6 show Highlights (HL) of the 1979 season, cards 201-207 are League Leaders, and cards 661-686 feature American and National League rookie "Future Stars," one card for each team showing three young prospects. The key Rookie Card in this set is Rickey Henderson; other Rookie Cards included in this set are Dan Quisenberry, Dave Stieb and Rick Sutcliffe.

COMPLETE SET (726) 60.00 120.00
COMMON CARD (1-726) .10 .25
COMMON DP .08 .25
1 L.Brock/C.Yastrzemski HL 1.00 2.50
2 Willie McCovey HL .30 .75
3 Manny Mota HL .10 .25
4 Pete Rose HL 1.25 3.00
5 Garry Templeton HL .10 .25
6 Del Unser HL .10 .25
7 Mike Lum .10 .25
8 Craig Swan .10 .25
9 Steve Braun .10 .25
10 Dennis Martinez .30 .75
11 Jimmy Sexton .10 .25
12 John Curtis DP .10 .25
13 Ron Pruitt .10 .25
14 Dave Cash .30 .75
15 Bill Campbell .10 .25
16 Jerry Narron RC .10 .25
17 Bruce Sutter .60 1.50
18 Ron Jackson .10 .25
19 Balor Moore .10 .25
20 Dan Ford .10 .25
21 Manny Sarmiento .10 .25
22 Pat Putnam .10 .25
23 Derrel Thomas .10 .25
24 Jim Slaton .10 .25
25 Lee Mazzilli .30 .75
26 Marty Pattin .10 .25
27 Del Unser .10 .25
28 Bruce Kison .10 .25
29 Mark Wagner .10 .25
30 Vida Blue .30 .75
31 Jay Johnstone .10 .25
32 Julio Cruz DP .10 .25
33 Tony Scott .10 .25
34 Jeff Newman DP .10 .25
35 Luis Tiant .30 .75
36 Rusty Torres .10 .25
37 Kiko Garcia .10 .25
38 Dan Spillner DP .10 .25
39 Rowland Office .10 .25
40 Carlton Fisk 1.00 2.50
41 Texas Rangers CL/Corrales .30 .75
42 David Palmer RC .10 .25
43 Bombo Rivera .10 .25
44 Bill Fahey .10 .25
45 Frank White .30 .75
46 Rico Carty .30 .75
47 Bill Bonham DP .10 .25
48 Rick Miller .10 .25
49 Mario Guerrero .10 .25
50 J.R. Richard .30 .75
51 Joe Ferguson DP .10 .25
52 Warren Brusstar .10 .25
53 Ben Oglivie .30 .75
54 Dennis Lamp .10 .25
55 Bill Madlock .30 .75
56 Bobby Valentine .30 .75
57 Pete Vuckovich .30 .75
58 Doug Flynn .10 .25
59 Eddy Putman RC .10 .25
60 Bucky Dent .30 .75
61 Gary Serum .10 .25
62 Mike Ivie .10 .25
63 Bob Stanley .10 .25
64 Joe Nolan .10 .25
65 Al Bumbry .30 .75
66 Kansas City Royals CL/Frey .30 .75
67 Doyle Alexander .10 .25
68 Larry Harlow .10 .25
69 Rick Williams .10 .25
70 Gary Carter .60 1.50
71 John Milner DP .10 .25
72 Fred Howard DP RC .10 .25
73 Dave Collins .10 .25
74 Sid Monge .10 .25
75 Bill Russell .30 .75
76 John Stearns .10 .25
77 Dave Stieb RC .60 1.50
78 Ruppert Jones .10 .25
79 Bob Owchinko .10 .25
80 Ron LeFlore .30 .75
81 Ted Sizemore .10 .25
82 Houston Astros CL/Virdon .30 .75
83 Steve Trout RC .10 .25
84 Gary Lavelle .10 .25
85 Ted Simmons .30 .75
86 Dave Hamilton .10 .25
87 Pepe Frias .10 .25
88 Ken Landreaux .10 .25
89 Don Hood .10 .25
90 Manny Trillo .10 .25
91 Rick Dempsey .30 .75
92 Rick Rhoden .10 .25

93 Dave Roberts DP .10 .25
94 Neil Allen RC .10 .25
95 Cecil Cooper .30 .75
96 Oakland Athletics CL/Marshall .30 .75
97 Bill Lee .30 .75
98 Jerry Terrell .10 .25
99 Victor Cruz .10 .25
100 Johnny Bench 1.25 3.00
101 Aurelio Lopez .10 .25
102 Rich Dauer .10 .25
103 Bill Caudill RC .10 .25
104 Manny Mota .30 .75
105 Frank Tanana .30 .75
106 Jeff Leonard RC .60 1.50
107 Francisco Barrios .10 .25
108 Bob Horner .30 .75
109 Bill Travers .10 .25
110 Fred Lynn DP .20 .50
111 Bob Knepper .10 .25
112 Chicago White Sox CL/LaRussa .30 .75
113 Geoff Zahn .10 .25
114 Juan Beniquez .10 .25
115 Sparky Lyle .30 .75
116 Larry Cox .10 .25
117 Dock Ellis .30 .75
118 Phil Garner .30 .75
119 Sammy Stewart .10 .25
120 Greg Luzinski .30 .75
121 Checklist 1-121 .30 .75
122 Dave Rosello DP .10 .25
123 Lynn Jones RC .10 .25
124 Dave Lemanczyk .10 .25
125 Tony Perez .30 .75
126 Dave Tomlin .10 .25
127 Gary Thomasson .10 .25
128 Tom Burgmeier .10 .25
129 Craig Reynolds .10 .25
130 Amos Otis .30 .75
131 Paul Mitchell .10 .25
132 Biff Pocoroba .10 .25
133 Jerry Turner .10 .25
134 Matt Keough .10 .25
135 Bill Buckner .30 .75
136 Dick Ruthven .10 .25
137 John Castino RC .10 .25
138 Ross Baumgarten .10 .25
139 Dane Iorg RC .10 .25
140 Rich Gossage .30 .75
141 Gary Alexander .10 .25
142 Phil Huffman RC .10 .25
143 Bruce Bochte DP .10 .25
144 Steve Comer .10 .25
145 Darrell Evans .30 .75
146 Bob Welch .30 .75
147 Terry Puhl .10 .25
148 Manny Sanguillen .30 .75
149 Tom Hume .10 .25
150 Jason Thompson .10 .25
151 Tom Hausman DP .10 .25
152 John Fulgham RC .10 .25
153 Tim Blackwell .10 .25
154 Lary Sorensen .10 .25
155 Jerry Remy .10 .25
156 Tony Brizzolara RC .10 .25
157 Willie Wilson DP .20 .50
158 Rob Picciolo DP .10 .25
159 Ken Clay .10 .25
160 Eddie Murray 2.00 5.00
161 Larry Christenson .10 .25
162 Bob Randall .10 .25
163 Steve Swisher .10 .25
164 Greg Pryor .10 .25
165 Omar Moreno .10 .25
166 Glenn Abbott .10 .25
167 Jack Clark .30 .75
168 Rick Waits .10 .25
169 Luis Gomez .10 .25
170 Burt Hooton .30 .75
171 Fernando Gonzalez .10 .25
172 Ron Hodges .10 .25
173 John Henry Johnson .10 .25
174 Ray Knight .30 .75
175 Rick Reuschel .30 .75
176 Champ Summers .10 .25
177 Dave Heaverlo .10 .25
178 Tim McCarver .30 .75
179 Ron Davis RC .10 .25
180 Warren Cromartie .10 .25
181 Moose Haas .10 .25
182 Ken Reitz .10 .25
183 Jim Anderson DP .10 .25
184 Steve Renko DP .10 .25
185 Hal McRae .30 .75
186 Junior Moore .10 .25
187 Alan Ashby .10 .25
188 Terry Crowley .10 .25
189 Kevin Kobel .10 .25
190 Buddy Bell .30 .75
191 Ted Martinez .10 .25
192 Atlanta Braves CL/Cox .30 .75
193 Dave Goltz .10 .25
194 Mike Easler .10 .25
195 John Montefusco .10 .25
196 Lance Parrish .30 .75
197 Byron McLaughlin .10 .25
198 Dell Alston DP .10 .25
199 Mike LaCoss .10 .25
200 Jim Rice .30 .75
201 K.Hernandez/F.Lynn LL .30 .75
202 D.Kingman/G.Thomas LL .60 1.50
203 D.Winfield/D.Baylor LL .60 1.50
204 O.Moreno/W.Wilson LL .30 .75
205 Niekro/Niekro/Flan LL .30 .75
206 J.Richard/N.Ryan LL 2.00 5.00
207 J.Richard/R.Guidry LL .30 .75
208 Wayne Cage .10 .25
209 Von Joshua .10 .25
210 Steve Carlton .60 1.50
211 Dave Skaggs DP .10 .25
212 Dave Roberts .10 .25
213 Mike Jorgensen DP .10 .25
214 California Angels CL/Fregosi .30 .75
215 Sixto Lezcano .10 .25
216 Phil Mankowski .10 .25
217 Ed Halicki .10 .25
218 Jose Morales .10 .25
219 Steve Mingori .10 .25
220 Dave Concepcion .30 .75
221 Joe Cannon RC .10 .25
222 Ron Hassey RC .10 .25
223 Bob Sykes .10 .25
224 Willie Montanez .10 .25
225 Lou Piniella .30 .75
226 Bill Stein .10 .25
227 Len Barker .30 .75
228 Johnny Oates .30 .75
229 Jim Bibby .10 .25
230 Dave Winfield .60 1.50
231 Steve McCatty .10 .25
232 Alan Trammell .60 1.50
233 LaRue Washington RC .10 .25
234 Vern Ruhle .10 .25
235 Andre Dawson .60 1.50
236 Marc Hill .10 .25
237 Scott McGregor .30 .75
238 Rob Wilfong .10 .25
239 Don Aase .10 .25
240 Dave Kingman .30 .75
241 Checklist 122-242 .30 .75
242 Lamar Johnson .10 .25
243 Jerry Augustine .10 .25
244 St. Louis Cardinals CL/Boyer .30 .75
245 Phil Niekro .30 .75
246 Tim Foli DP .10 .25
247 Frank Riccelli .10 .25
248 Jamie Quirk .10 .25
249 Jim Clancy .10 .25
250 Jim Kaat .30 .75
251 Kip Young .10 .25
252 Ted Cox .10 .25
253 John Montague .10 .25
254 Paul Dade DP .10 .25
255 Dusty Baker DP .20 .50
256 Roger Erickson .10 .25
257 Larry Herndon .10 .25
258 Paul Moskau .10 .25
259 New York Mets CL/Torre .60 1.50
260 Al Oliver .30 .75
261 Dave Chalk .10 .25
262 Benny Ayala .10 .25
263 Dave LaRoche DP .10 .25
264 Bill Robinson .10 .25
265 Robin Yount 1.25 3.00
266 Bernie Carbo .10 .25
267 Dan Schatzeder .10 .25
268 Rafael Landestoy .10 .25
269 Dave Tobik .10 .25
270 Mike Schmidt DP 1.25 3.00
271 Dick Drago DP .10 .25
272 Ralph Garr .30 .75
273 Eduardo Rodriguez .10 .25
274 Dale Murphy 1.00 2.50
275 Jerry Koosman .30 .75
276 Tom Veryzer .10 .25
277 Rick Bosetti .10 .25
278 Jim Spencer .10 .25
279 Rob Andrews .10 .25
280 Gaylord Perry .30 .75
281 Paul Blair .30 .75
282 Seattle Mariners CL/Johnson .30 .75
283 John Ellis .10 .25
284 Larry Murray DP RC .10 .25
285 Don Baylor .30 .75
286 Darold Knowles DP .10 .25
287 John Lowenstein .10 .25
288 Dave Rozema .10 .25
289 Bruce Bochy .10 .25
290 Steve Garvey .60 1.50
291 Randy Scarberry RC .10 .25
292 Dale Berra .10 .25
293 Elias Sosa .10 .25
294 Charlie Spikes .10 .25
295 Larry Gura .10 .25
296 Dave Rader .10 .25
297 Tim Johnson .10 .25
298 Ken Holtzman .30 .75
299 Steve Henderson .10 .25
300 Ron Guidry .30 .75
301 Mike Edwards .10 .25
302 Los Angeles Dodgers CL/Lasorda .60 1.50
303 Bill Castro .10 .25
304 Butch Wynegar .10 .25
305 Randy Jones .30 .75
306 Denny Walling .10 .25
307 Rick Honeycutt .10 .25
308 Mike Hargrove .30 .75
309 Larry McWilliams .10 .25
310 Dave Parker .30 .75
311 Roger Metzger .10 .25
312 Mike Barlow .10 .25
313 Johnny Grubb .10 .25
314 Tim Stoddard RC .10 .25
315 Steve Kemp .30 .75
316 Bob Lacey .10 .25
317 Mike Anderson DP .10 .25
318 Jerry Reuss .30 .75
319 Chris Speier .10 .25
320 Dennis Eckersley .60 1.50
321 Keith Hernandez .30 .75
322 Claudell Washington .10 .25
323 Mick Kelleher .10 .25
324 Tom Underwood .10 .25
325 Dan Driessen .10 .25
326 Bo McLaughlin .10 .25
327 Ray Fosse DP .20 .50
328 Minnesota Twins CL/Mauch .30 .75
329 Bert Roberge RC .10 .25
330 Al Cowens .30 .75
331 Richie Hebner .10 .25
332 Enrique Romo .10 .25
333 Jim Norris DP .10 .25
334 Jim Beattie .10 .25
335 Willie McCovey .60 1.50
336 George Medich .10 .25
337 Carney Lansford .30 .75
338 John Wockenfuss .10 .25
339 John D'Acquisto .10 .25
340 Ken Singleton .30 .75
341 Jim Essian .30 .75
342 Odell Jones .10 .25
343 Mike Vail .10 .25
344 Randy Lerch .10 .25
345 Larry Parrish .30 .75
346 Buddy Solomon .10 .25
347 Harry Chappas RC .10 .25
348 Checklist 243-363 .30 .75
349 Jack Brohamer .10 .25
350 George Hendrick .30 .75
351 Bob Davis .10 .25
352 Dan Briggs .10 .25
353 Andy Hassler .10 .25
354 Rick Auerbach .10 .25
355 Gary Matthews .30 .75
356 San Diego Padres CL/Coleman .30 .75
357 Bob McClure .10 .25
358 Lou Whitaker .30 .75
359 Randy Moffitt .10 .25
360 Darrell Porter DP .20 .50
361 Wayne Garland .10 .25
362 Danny Goodwin .10 .25
363 Wayne Gross .10 .25
364 Ray Burris .10 .25
365 Bobby Murcer .30 .75
366 Rob Dressler .10 .25
367 Billy Smith .10 .25
368 Willie Aikens RC .10 .25
369 Jim Kern .10 .25
370 Cesar Cedeno .30 .75
371 Jack Morris .30 .75
372 Joel Youngblood .10 .25
373 Dan Petry DP RC .30 .75
374 Jim Gantner .30 .75
375 Ross Grimsley .10 .25
376 Gary Allenson RC .10 .25
377 Junior Kennedy .10 .25
378 Jerry Mumphrey .10 .25
379 Kevin Bell .10 .25
380 Garry Maddox .30 .75
381 Chicago Cubs CL/Gomez .30 .75
382 Dave Freisleben .10 .25
383 Ed Ott .10 .25
384 Joey McLaughlin RC .10 .25
385 Enos Cabell .10 .25
386 Darrell Jackson .10 .25
387A F.Stanley Yellow .75 2.00
387B F.Stanley Red Name .10 .25
388 Mike Paxton .10 .25
389 Pete LaCock .10 .25
390 Fergie Jenkins .30 .75
391 Tony Armas DP .20 .50
392 Milt Wilcox .10 .25
393 Ozzie Smith 4.00 10.00
394 Reggie Cleveland .10 .25
395 Ellis Valentine .10 .25
396 Dan Meyer .10 .25
397 Roy Thomas DP .10 .25
398 Barry Foote .10 .25
399 Mike Proly DP .10 .25
400 George Foster .30 .75
401 Pete Falcone .10 .25
402 Merv Rettenmund .10 .25
403 Pete Redfern DP .10 .25
404 Baltimore Orioles CL/Weaver .30 .75
405 Dwight Evans .60 1.50
406 Paul Molitor 1.50 4.00
407 Tony Solaita .10 .25
408 Bill North .10 .25
409 Paul Splittorff .10 .25
410 Bobby Bonds .30 .75
411 Frank LaCorte .10 .25
412 Thad Bosley .10 .25
413 Allen Ripley .10 .25
414 George Scott .30 .75
415 Bill Atkinson .10 .25
416 Tom Brookens RC .10 .25
417 Craig Chamberlain DP RC .10 .25
418 Roger Freed DP .10 .25
419 Vic Correll .10 .25
420 Butch Hobson .10 .25
421 Doug Bird .10 .25
422 Larry Milbourne .10 .25
423 Dave Frost .10 .25
424 New York Yankees CL/Howser .30 .75
425 Mark Belanger .30 .75
426 Grant Jackson .10 .25
427 Tom Hutton DP .10 .25
428 Pat Zachry .10 .25
429 Duane Kuiper .10 .25
430 Larry Hisle DP .10 .25
431 Mike Krukow .10 .25
432 Willie Norwood .10 .25
433 Rich Gale .10 .25
434 Johnnie LeMaster .10 .25
435 Don Gullett .30 .75
436 Billy Almon .10 .25
437 Joe Niekro .30 .75
438 Dave Revering .10 .25
439 Mike Phillips .10 .25
440 Don Sutton .30 .75
441 Eric Soderholm .10 .25
442 Jorge Orta .10 .25
443 Mike Parrott .10 .25
444 Alvis Woods .10 .25
445 Mark Fidrych .30 .75
446 Duffy Dyer .10 .25
447 Nino Espinosa .10 .25
448 Jim Wohlford .10 .25
449 Doug Bair .10 .25
450 George Brett 3.00 8.00
451 Cleveland Indians CL/Garcia .30 .75
452 Steve Dillard .10 .25
453 Mike Bacsik .10 .25
454 Tom Donohue RC .10 .25
455 Mike Torrez .30 .75
456 Frank Taveras .10 .25
457 Bert Blyleven .30 .75
458 Billy Sample .10 .25
459 Mickey Lolich DP .20 .50
460 Willie Randolph .30 .75
461 Dwayne Murphy .10 .25
462 Mike Sadek DP .10 .25
463 Jerry Royster .10 .25
464 John Denny .30 .75
465 Rick Monday .30 .75
466 Mike Squires .10 .25
467 Jesse Jefferson .10 .25
468 Aurelio Rodriguez .10 .25
469 Randy Niemann DP RC .10 .25
470 Bob Boone .30 .75
471 Hosken Powell DP .10 .25
472 Willie Hernandez .30 .75
473 Bump Wills .10 .25
474 Steve Busby .10 .25
475 Cesar Geronimo .30 .75
476 Bob Shirley .10 .25
477 Buck Martinez .10 .25
478 Gil Flores .10 .25
479 Montreal Expos CL/Williams .30 .75
480 Bob Watson .30 .75
481 Tom Paciorek .30 .75
482 Rickey Henderson RC 25.00 60.00
483 Bo Diaz .10 .25
484 Checklist 364-484 .30 .75
485 Mickey Rivers .30 .75
486 Mike Tyson DP .10 .25
487 Wayne Nordhagen .10 .25
488 Roy Howell .10 .25
489 Preston Hanna DP .10 .25
490 Lee May .30 .75
491 Steve Mura DP .10 .25
492 Todd Cruz RC .10 .25
493 Jerry Martin .10 .25
494 Craig Minetto RC .10 .25
495 Bake McBride .30 .75
496 Silvio Martinez .10 .25
497 Jim Mason .10 .25
498 Danny Darwin .10 .25
499 San Francisco Giants CL/Bristol .30 .75
500 Tom Seaver 1.25 3.00
501 Rennie Stennett .10 .25
502 Rich Wortham DP RC .10 .25
503 Mike Cubbage .10 .25
504 Gene Garber .10 .25
505 Bert Campaneris .30 .75
506 Tom Buskey .10 .25
507 Leon Roberts .10 .25
508 U.L. Washington .10 .25
509 Ed Glynn .10 .25
510 Ron Cey .30 .75
511 Eric Wilkins RC .10 .25
512 Jose Cardenal .10 .25
513 Tom Dixon DP .10 .25
514 Steve Ontiveros .10 .25
515 Mike Caldwell UER .10 .25
516 Hector Cruz .10 .25
517 Don Stanhouse .10 .25
518 Nelson Norman RC .10 .25
519 Steve Nicosia RC .10 .25
520 Steve Rogers .30 .75
521 Ken Brett .10 .25
522 Jim Morrison .10 .25
523 Ken Henderson .10 .25
524 Jim Wright DP .10 .25
525 Clint Hurdle .10 .25
526 Philadelphia Phillies CL/Green .30 .75
527 Doug Rau DP .10 .25
528 Adrian Devine .10 .25
529 Jim Barr .10 .25
530 Jim Sundberg DP .20 .50
531 Eric Rasmussen .10 .25
532 Willie Horton .30 .75
533 Checklist 485-605 .30 .75
534 Andre Thornton .30 .75
535 Bob Forsch .10 .25
536 Lee Lacy .10 .25
537 Alex Trevino RC .10 .25
538 Joe Strain .10 .25
539 Rudy May .10 .25
540 Pete Rose 3.00 8.00
541 Miguel Dilone .10 .25
542 Joe Coleman .10 .25
543 Pat Kelly .10 .25
544 Rick Sutcliffe RC .60 1.50
545 Jeff Burroughs .30 .75
546 Rick Langford .10 .25
547 John Wathan .10 .25
548 Dave Rajsich .10 .25
549 Larry Wolfe .10 .25
550 Ken Griffey Sr. .30 .75
551 Pittsburgh Pirates CL/Tanner .30 .75
552 Bill Nahorodny .10 .25
553 Dick Davis .10 .25
554 Art Howe .30 .75
555 Ed Figueroa .10 .25
556 Joe Rudi .30 .75
557 Mark Lee .10 .25
558 Alfredo Griffin .10 .25
559 Dale Murray .10 .25
560 Dave Lopes .30 .75
561 Eddie Whitson .10 .25
562 Joe Wallis .10 .25
563 Will McEnaney .10 .25
564 Rick Manning .10 .25
565 Dennis Leonard .10 .25
566 Bud Harrelson .30 .75
567 Skip Lockwood .10 .25
568 Gary Roenicke RC .10 .25
569 Terry Kennedy .10 .25
570 Roy Smalley .30 .75
571 Joe Sambito .10 .25
572 Jerry Morales DP .10 .25
573 Kent Tekulve .30 .75
574 Scot Thompson .10 .25
575 Ken Kravec .10 .25
576 Jim Dwyer .10 .25
577 Toronto Blue Jays CL/Mattick .30 .75
578 Scott Sanderson .10 .25
579 Charlie Moore .10 .25
580 Nolan Ryan 8.00 20.00
581 Bob Bailor .10 .25
582 Brian Doyle .10 .25
583 Bob Stinson .10 .25
584 Kurt Bevacqua .10 .25
585 Al Hrabosky .30 .75
586 Mitchell Page .10 .25
587 Garry Templeton .30 .75
588 Greg Minton .10 .25
589 Chet Lemon .30 .75
590 Jim Palmer .60 1.50
591 Rick Cerone .10 .25
592 Jon Matlack .30 .75
593 Jesus Alou .10 .25
594 Dick Tidrow .10 .25
595 Don Money .10 .25
596 Rick Matula RC .10 .25
597 Tom Poquette .10 .25
598 Fred Kendall DP .10 .25
599 Mike Norris .10 .25
600 Reggie Jackson 1.25 3.00
601 Buddy Schultz .10 .25
602 Brian Downing .30 .75
603 Jack Billingham DP .10 .25
604 Glenn Adams .10 .25
605 Terry Forster .30 .75
606 Cincinnati Reds CL/McNamara .30 .75
607 Woodie Fryman .10 .25
608 Alan Bannister .10 .25
609 Ron Reed .10 .25
610 Willie Stargell .60 1.50
611 Jerry Garvin DP .10 .25
612 Cliff Johnson .10 .25
613 Randy Stein .10 .25
614 John Hiller .10 .25
615 Doug DeCinces .30 .75
616 Gene Richards .10 .25
617 Joaquin Andujar .30 .75
618 Bob Montgomery DP .10 .25
619 Sergio Ferrer .10 .25
620 Richie Zisk .30 .75
621 Bob Grich .30 .75
622 Mario Soto .30 .75
623 Gorman Thomas .30 .75
624 Lerrin LaGrow .10 .25
625 Chris Chambliss .30 .75
626 Detroit Tigers CL/Anderson .30 .75
627 Pedro Borbon .10 .25
628 Doug Capilla .10 .25
629 Jim Todd .10 .25
630 Larry Bowa .30 .75
631 Mark Littell .10 .25
632 Barry Bonnell .10 .25
633 Bob Apodaca .10 .25
634 Glenn Borgmann DP .10 .25
635 John Candelaria .30 .75
636 Toby Harrah .30 .75
637 Joe Simpson .10 .25
638 Mark Clear RC .10 .25
639 Larry Biittner .10 .25
640 Mike Flanagan .30 .75
641 Ed Kranepool .30 .75
642 Ken Forsch DP .10 .25
643 John Mayberry .30 .75
644 Charlie Hough .30 .75
645 Rick Burleson .30 .75
646 Checklist 606-726 .30 .75
647 Milt May .10 .25
648 Roy White .30 .75
649 Tom Griffin .10 .25
650 Joe Morgan .60 1.50
651 Rollie Fingers .30 .75
652 Mario Mendoza .10 .25
653 Stan Bahnsen .10 .25
654 Bruce Boisclair DP .10 .25
655 Tug McGraw .30 .75
656 Larvell Blanks .10 .25
657 Dave Edwards RC .10 .25
658 Chris Knapp .10 .25
659 Milwaukee Brewers CL/Bamberger .30 .75
660 Rusty Staub .30 .75
661 Mark Corey .10 .25
Dave Ford RC
Wayne Krenchicki RC
662 Finch/O'Berry/Rainey RC .10 .25
663 Botting/Clark/Thon RC .30 .75
664 Colbern/Hoffman/Robinson RC .10 .25
665 Andersen/Cuellar/Wihtol RC .10 .25
666 Chris/Greene/Robbins RC .10 .25
667 Mart/Pasch/Quisenberry RC .30 .75
668 Boitano/Mueller/Sakata RC .10 .25
669 Graham/Sofield/Ward RC .30 .75
670 Brown/Gulden/Jones RC .10 .25
671 Bryant/Kingman/Morgan RC .30 .75
672 Beamon/Craig/Vasquez RC .10 .25
673 Allard/Gleaton/Mahlberg RC .10 .25
674 Edge/Kelly/Wilborn RC .10 .25
675 Benedict/Bradford/Miller RC .10 .25
676 Geisel/Macko/Pagel RC .10 .25
677 DeFreites/Pastore/Spilman RC .10 .25
678 Baldwin/Knicely/Ladd RC .10 .25
679 Beckwith/Hatcher/Patterson RC .30 .75
680 Bernazard/Miller/Tamargo RC .10 .25
681 Norman/Orosco/Scott RC .60 1.50
682 Aviles/Noles/Saucier RC .10 .25
683 Boyland/Lois/Saferight RC .10 .25
684 Frazier/Herr/O'Brien RC .30 .75
685 Flannery/Greer/Wilhelm RC .10 .25
686 Johnston/Littlejohn/Nastu RC .10 .25
687 Mike Heath DP .10 .25
688 Steve Stone .30 .75
689 Boston Red Sox CL/Zimmer .30 .75
690 Tommy John .30 .75
691 Ivan DeJesus .10 .25
692 Rawly Eastwick DP .20 .50
693 Craig Kusick .10 .25
694 Jim Rooker .10 .25
695 Reggie Smith .30 .75
696 Julio Gonzalez .10 .25
697 David Clyde .10 .25
698 Oscar Gamble .30 .75
699 Floyd Bannister .10 .25
700 Rod Carew DP .30 .75
701 Ken Oberkfell RC .10 .25
702 Ed Farmer .10 .25
703 Otto Velez .10 .25
704 Gene Tenace .30 .75
705 Freddie Patek .30 .75
706 Tippy Martinez .10 .25
707 Elliott Maddox .10 .25
708 Bob Tolan .10 .25
709 Pat Underwood RC .10 .25
710 Graig Nettles .30 .75
711 Bob Galasso RC .10 .25
712 Rodney Scott .10 .25
713 Terry Whitfield .10 .25
714 Fred Norman .10 .25
715 Sal Bando .30 .75
716 Lynn McGlothen .10 .25
717 Mickey Klutts DP .10 .25
718 Greg Gross .10 .25
719 Don Robinson .30 .75
720 Carl Yastrzemski DP .75 2.00
721 Paul Hartzell .10 .25
722 Jose Cruz .30 .75
723 Shane Rawley .10 .25
724 Jerry White .10 .25
725 Rick Wise .10 .25
726 Steve Yeager .30 .75

1981 Topps

The cards in this 726-card set measure the standard size. This set was issued primarily in 15-card wax packs and 50-card rack packs. League Leaders (1-8), Record Breakers (201-208), and Post-season cards (401-404) are the topical subsets. The team cards are all grouped together (661-686) and feature team checklist backs and a very small photo of the team's manager in the upper right corner of the obverse. The obverses carry the player's position and team in a baseball cap design, and the company name is printed in a small baseball. The backs are red and gray. The 66 double-printed cards are noted in the checklist by DP. Notable Rookie Cards in the set include Harold Baines, Kirk Gibson, Tim Raines, Jeff Reardon, and Fernando Valenzuela. During 1981, a promotion existed where collectors could order complete set in sheet form from Topps for $24.

COMPLETE SET (726) 25.00 60.00
COMMON CARD (1-726) .05 .15
COMMON CARD DP .05 .15
1 G.Brett/B.Buckner LL 1.25 3.00
2 Reggie/Ogliv/Schmidt LL .60 1.50
3 C.Cooper/M.Schmidt LL .60 1.50
4 R.Henderson/LeFlore LL 1.25 3.00
5 S.Stone/S.Carlton LL .15 .40
6 Len Barker/S.Carlton LL .15 .40
7 R.May/D.Sutton LL .15 .40
8 Quis/Fingers/Hume LL .15 .40
9 Pete LaCock DP .05 .1
10 Mike Flanagan .05 .1
11 Jim Wohlford DP .05 .1
12 Mark Clear .05 .1
13 Joe Charboneau RC .60 1.50
14 John Tudor RC .60 1.50
15 Larry Parrish .05 .15
16 Ron Davis .05 .15
17 Cliff Johnson .05 .15
18 Glenn Adams .05 .15
19 Jim Clancy .05 .15
20 Jeff Burroughs .15 .40
21 Ron Oester .05 .15
22 Danny Darwin .05 .15
23 Alex Trevino .05 .15
24 Don Stanhouse .05 .15
25 Sixto Lezcano .05 .15
26 U.L. Washington .05 .15
27 Champ Summers DP .05 .15
28 Enrique Romo .05 .15
29 Gene Tenace .15 .40
30 Jack Clark .15 .40
31 Checklist 1-121 DP .08 .25
32 Ken Oberkfell .05 .15
33 Rick Honeycutt .05 .15
34 Aurelio Rodriguez .05 .15
35 Mitchell Page .05 .15
36 Ed Farmer .05 .15
37 Gary Roenicke .05 .15
38 Win Remmerswaal RC .05 .15
39 Tom Veryzer .05 .15
40 Tug McGraw .15 .40
41 Babcock/Butcher/Gleaton RC .08 .25
42 Jerry White DP .05 .15
43 Jose Morales .05 .15
44 Larry McWilliams .05 .15
45 Enos Cabell .05 .15
46 Rick Bosetti .05 .15
47 Ken Brett .05 .15
48 Dave Skaggs .05 .15
49 Bob Shirley .05 .15
50 Dave Lopes .15 .40
51 Bill Robinson DP .05 .15
52 Hector Cruz .05 .15
53 Kevin Saucier .05 .15
54 Ivan DeJesus .05 .15
55 Mike Norris .05 .15
56 Buck Martinez .05 .15
57 Dave Roberts .05 .15
58 Joel Youngblood .05 .15
59 Dan Petry .05 .15
60 Willie Randolph .15 .40
61 Butch Wynegar .05 .15
62 Joe Pettini RC .05 .15
63 Steve Renko DP .05 .15
64 Brian Asselstine .05 .15
65 Scott McGregor .05 .15
66 Castillo/Ireland/M.Jones RC .08 .25
67 Ken Kravec .05 .15
68 Matt Alexander DP .05 .15
69 Ed Halicki .05 .15
70 Al Oliver DP .08 .25
71 Hal Dues .05 .15
72 Barry Evans DP RC .05 .15
73 Doug Bair .05 .15
74 Mike Hargrove .05 .15
75 Reggie Smith .15 .40
76 Mario Mendoza .05 .15
77 Mike Barlow .05 .15
78 Steve Dillard .05 .15
79 Bruce Robbins .05 .15
80 Rusty Staub .15 .40
81 Dave Stapleton RC .05 .15
82 Heep/Knicely/Sprowl RC .08 .25
83 Mike Proly .05 .15
84 Johnnie LeMaster .05 .15
85 Mike Caldwell .05 .15
86 Wayne Gross .05 .15
87 Rick Camp .05 .15
88 Joe Lefebvre RC .05 .15
89 Darrell Jackson .05 .15
90 Bake McBride .15 .40
91 Tim Stoddard DP .05 .15
92 Mike Easler .05 .15
93 Ed Glynn DP .05 .15
94 Harry Spilman DP .05 .15
95 Jim Sundberg .15 .40
96 Beard/Camacho/Dempsey RC .08 .25
97 Chris Speier .05 .15
98 Clint Hurdle .05 .15
99 Eric Wilkins .05 .15
100 Rod Carew .30 .75
101 Benny Ayala .05 .15
102 Dave Tobik .05 .15
103 Jerry Martin .05 .15
104 Terry Forster .15 .40
105 Jose Cruz .15 .40
106 Don Money .05 .15
107 Rich Wortham .05 .15
108 Bruce Benedict .05 .15
109 Mike Scott .15 .40
110 Carl Yastrzemski 1.00 2.50
111 Greg Minton .05 .15
112 Kuntz/Mullins/Sutherland RC .08 .25
113 Mike Phillips .05 .15
114 Tom Underwood .05 .15
115 Roy Smalley .15 .40
116 Joe Simpson .05 .15
117 Pete Falcone .05 .15
118 Kurt Bevacqua .05 .15
119 Tippy Martinez .05 .15
120 Larry Bowa .15 .40
121 Larry Harlow .05 .15

John Denny .05 .15
Al Cowens .05 .15
Jerry Garvin .05 .15
Andre Dawson .30 .75
Charlie Leibrandt RC .30 .75
Rudy Law .05 .15
Gary Allenson DP .05 .15
Art Howe .05 .15
Larry Gura .05 .15
Keith Moreland RC .05 .15
Tommy Boggs .05 .15
Jeff Cox RC .05 .15
Steve Mura .05 .15
Gorman Thomas .15 .40
Doug Capilla .05 .15
Hosken Powell .05 .15
Rich Dotson DP RC .05 .15
Oscar Gamble .05 .15
Bob Forsch .05 .15
Miguel Dilone .05 .15
Jackson Todd .05 .15
Dan Meyer .05 .15
4 Allen Ripley .05 .15
5 Mickey Rivers .05 .15
6 Bobby Castillo .05 .15
7 Dale Berra .05 .15
8 Randy Niemann .05 .15
9 Joe Nolan .05 .15
0 Mark Fidrych .15 .40
1 Claudell Washington .05 .15
2 John Urrea .05 .15
3 Tom Poquette .05 .15
4 Rick Langford .05 .15
5 Chris Chambliss .15 .40
6 Bob McClure .05 .15
7 John Wathan .05 .15
8 Fergie Jenkins .15 .40
9 Brian Doyle .05 .15
0 Garry Maddox .05 .15
1 Dan Graham .05 .15
52 Doug Corbett RC .05 .15
53 Bill Almon .05 .15
54 LaMarr Hoyt RC .30 .75
55 Tony Scott .05 .15
56 Floyd Bannister .05 .15
57 Terry Whitfield .05 .15
58 Don Robinson DP .05 .15
59 John Mayberry .05 .15
70 Ross Grimsley .05 .15
71 Gene Richards .05 .15
72 Gary Woods .05 .15
73 Bump Wills .05 .15
74 Doug Rau .05 .15
75 Dave Collins .05 .15
76 Mike Krukow .05 .15
77 Rick Peters RC .05 .15
78 Jim Essian DP .05 .15
79 Rudy May .05 .15
80 Pete Rose 2.00 5.00
81 Elias Sosa .05 .15
82 Bob Grich .15 .40
83 Dick Davis DP .05 .15
84 Jim Dwyer .05 .15
85 Dennis Leonard .05 .15
186 Wayne Nordhagen .05 .15
187 Mike Parrott .05 .15
188 Doug DeCinces .05 .15
189 Craig Swan .05 .15
190 Cesar Cedeno .15 .40
191 Rick Sutcliffe .15 .40
192 Harper/Miller/Ramirez RC .08 .25
193 Pete Vuckovich .05 .15
194 Rod Scurry RC .05 .15
195 Rich Murray RC .05 .15
196 Duffy Dyer .05 .15
197 Jim Kern .05 .15
198 Jerry Dybzinski RC .05 .15
199 Chuck Rainey .05 .15
200 George Foster .15 .40
201 Johnny Bench RB .30 .75
202 Steve Carlton RB .15 .40
203 Bill Gullickson RB .05 .15
204 R.LeFlore/R.Scott RB .15 .40
205 Pete Rose RB .60 1.50
206 Mike Schmidt RB .60 1.50
207 Ozzie Smith RB .75 2.00
208 Willie Wilson RB .05 .15
209 Dickie Thon DP .05 .15
210 Jim Palmer .30 .75
211 Derrel Thomas .05 .15
212 Steve Nicosia .05 .15
213 Al Holland RC .05 .15
214 Botting/Dorsey/J.Harris RC .08 .25
215 Larry Hisle .05 .15
216 John Henry Johnson .05 .15
217 Rich Hebner .05 .15
218 Paul Splittorff .05 .15
219 Ken Landreaux .05 .15
220 Tom Seaver .60 1.50
221 Bob Davis .05 .15
222 Jorge Orta .05 .15
223 Roy Lee Jackson RC .05 .15
224 Pat Zachry .05 .15
225 Ruppert Jones .05 .15
226 Manny Sanguillen DP .08 .25
227 Fred Martinez RC .05 .15
228 Tom Paciorek .05 .15
229 Rollie Fingers .15 .40
230 George Hendrick .15 .40
231 Joe Beckwith .05 .15
232 Mickey Klutts .05 .15
233 Skip Lockwood .05 .15
234 Lou Whitaker .30 .75
235 Scott Sanderson .05 .15
236 Mike Ivie .05 .15
237 Charlie Moore .05 .15
238 Willie Hernandez .05 .15
239 Rick Miller DP .05 .15
240 Nolan Ryan 3.00 8.00
241 Checklist 122-242 DP .08 .25
242 Chet Lemon .15 .40
243 Sal Butera RC .05 .15
244 Landrum/Olmsted/Rincon RC .08 .25
245 Ed Figueroa .05 .15
246 Ed Ott DP .05 .15
247 Glenn Hubbard DP .05 .15
248 Joey McLaughlin .05 .15
249 Larry Cox .05 .15
250 Ron Guidry .15 .40
251 Tom Brookens .05 .15
252 Victor Cruz .05 .15
253 Dave Bergman .05 .15
254 Ozzie Smith 2.00 5.00
255 Mark Littell .05 .15
256 Bombo Rivera .05 .15
257 Rennie Stennett .05 .15
258 Joe Price RC .05 .15
259 M.Wilson/H.Brooks RC 2.00 5.00
260 Ron Cey .15 .40
261 Rickey Henderson 4.00 10.00
262 Sammy Stewart .05 .15
263 Brian Downing .15 .40
264 Jim Norris .05 .15
265 John Candelaria .15 .40
266 Tom Herr .05 .15
267 Stan Bahnsen .05 .15
268 Jerry Royster .05 .15
269 Ken Forsch .05 .15
270 Greg Luzinski .15 .40
271 Bill Castro .05 .15
272 Bruce Kimm .05 .15
273 Stan Papi .05 .15
274 Craig Chamberlain .05 .15
275 Dwight Evans .30 .75
276 Dan Spillner .05 .15
277 Alfredo Griffin .05 .15
278 Rick Sofield .05 .15
279 Bob Knepper .05 .15
280 Ken Griffey .15 .40
281 Fred Stanley .05 .15
282 Anderson/Biercevicz/Craig RC .08 .25
283 Billy Sample .05 .15
284 Brian Kingman .05 .15
285 Jerry Turner .05 .15
286 Dave Frost .05 .15
287 Lenn Sakata .05 .15
288 Bob Clark .05 .15
289 Mickey Hatcher .05 .15
290 Bob Boone DP .08 .25
291 Aurelio Lopez .05 .15
292 Mike Squires .05 .15
293 Charlie Lea RC .05 .15
294 Mike Tyson DP .05 .15
295 Hal McRae .15 .40
296 Bill Nahorodny DP .05 .15
297 Bob Bailor .05 .15
298 Buddy Solomon .05 .15
299 Elliott Maddox .05 .15
300 Paul Molitor .60 1.50
301 Matt Keough .05 .15
302 F.Valenzuela/M.Scioscia RC 3.00 8.00
303 Johnny Oates .15 .40
304 John Castino .05 .15
305 Ken Clay .05 .15
306 Juan Beniquez DP .05 .15
307 Gene Garber .05 .15
308 Rick Manning .05 .15
309 Luis Salazar RC .30 .75
310 Vida Blue DP .08 .25
311 Freddie Patek .05 .15
312 Rick Rhoden .05 .15
313 Luis Pujols .05 .15
314 Rich Dauer .05 .15
315 Kirk Gibson RC 3.00 8.00
316 Craig Minetto .05 .15
317 Lonnie Smith .15 .40
318 Steve Yeager .15 .40
319 Rowland Office .05 .15
320 Tom Burgmeier .05 .15
321 Leon Durham RC .30 .75
322 Neil Allen .05 .15
323 Jim Morrison DP .05 .15
324 Mike Willis .05 .15
325 Ray Knight .15 .40
326 Biff Pocoroba .05 .15
327 Moose Haas .05 .15
328 Engle/Johnston/G.Ward .08 .25
329 Joaquin Andujar .15 .40
330 Frank White .15 .40
331 Dennis Lamp .05 .15
332 Lee Lacy DP .05 .15
333 Sid Monge .05 .15
334 Dane Iorg .05 .15
335 Rick Cerone .05 .15
336 Eddie Whitson .05 .15
337 Lynn Jones .05 .15
338 Checklist 243-363 .15 .40
339 John Ellis .05 .15
340 Bruce Kison .05 .15
341 Dwayne Murphy .05 .15
342 Eric Rasmussen DP .05 .15
343 Frank Taveras .05 .15
344 Byron McLaughlin .05 .15
345 Warren Cromartie .05 .15
346 Larry Christenson DP .05 .15
347 Harold Baines RC 1.25 3.00
348 Bob Sykes .05 .15
349 Glenn Hoffman RC .05 .15
350 J.R. Richard .15 .40
351 Otto Velez .05 .15
352 Dick Tidrow DP .05 .15
353 Terry Kennedy .05 .15
354 Mario Soto .15 .40
355 Bob Horner .15 .40
356 Stablein/Stimac/Tellmann RC .08 .25
357 Jim Slaton .05 .15
358 Mark Wagner .05 .15
359 Tom Hausman .05 .15
360 Willie Wilson .15 .40
361 Joe Strain .05 .15
362 Bo Diaz .05 .15
363 Geoff Zahn .05 .15
364 Mike Davis RC .08 .25
365 Graig Nettles DP .08 .25
366 Mike Ramsey RC .08 .25
367 Dennis Martinez .15 .40
368 Leon Roberts .05 .15
369 Frank Tanana .15 .40
370 Dave Winfield .30 .75
371 Charlie Hough .15 .40
372 Jay Johnstone .05 .15
373 Pat Underwood .05 .15
374 Tommy Hutton .05 .15
375 Dave Concepcion .15 .40
376 Ron Reed .05 .15
377 Jerry Morales .05 .15
378 Dave Rader .05 .15
379 Larry Sorensen .05 .15
380 Willie Stargell .30 .75
381 Lezcano/Macko/Martz RC .08 .25
382 Paul Mirabella RC .05 .15
383 Eric Soderholm DP .05 .15
384 Mike Sadek .05 .15
385 Joe Sambito .05 .15
386 Dave Edwards .05 .15
387 Phil Niekro .15 .40
388 Andre Thornton .15 .40
389 Marty Pattin .05 .15
390 Cesar Geronimo .05 .15
391 Dave Lemanczyk DP .05 .15
392 Lance Parrish .15 .40
393 Broderick Perkins .05 .15
394 Woodie Fryman .05 .15
395 Scot Thompson .05 .15
396 Bill Campbell .05 .15
397 Julio Cruz .05 .15
398 Ross Baumgarten .05 .15
399 Boddicker/Corey/Rayford RC .30 .75
400 Reggie Jackson .60 1.50
401 George Brett ALCS 1.00 2.50
402 NL Champs .30 .75
403 Larry Bowa WS .30 .75
404 Tug McGraw WS .30 .75
405 Nino Espinosa .05 .15
406 Dickie Noles .05 .15
407 Ernie Whitt .05 .15
408 Fernando Arroyo .05 .15
409 Larry Herndon .05 .15
410 Bert Campaneris .15 .40
411 Terry Puhl .05 .15
412 Britt Burns RC .05 .15
413 Tony Bernazard .05 .15
414 John Pacella DP RC .05 .15
415 Ben Oglivie .15 .40
416 Gary Alexander .05 .15
417 Dan Schatzeder .05 .15
418 Bobby Brown .05 .15
419 Tom Hume .05 .15
420 Keith Hernandez .15 .40
421 Bob Stanley .05 .15
422 Dan Ford .05 .15
423 Shane Rawley .05 .15
424 Lollar/Robinson/Werth RC .08 .25
425 Al Bumbry .05 .15
426 Warren Brusstar .05 .15
427 John D'Acquisto .05 .15
428 John Stearns .05 .15
429 Mick Kelleher .05 .15
430 Jim Bibby .05 .15
431 Dave Roberts .05 .15
432 Len Barker .15 .40
433 Rance Mulliniks .05 .15
434 Roger Erickson .05 .15
435 Jim Spencer .05 .15
436 Gary Lucas RC .05 .15
437 Mike Heath DP .05 .15
438 John Montefusco .05 .15
439 Denny Walling .05 .15
440 Jerry Reuss .05 .15
441 Ken Reitz .05 .15
442 Ron Pruitt .05 .15
443 Jim Beattie DP .05 .15
444 Garth Iorg .05 .15
445 Ellis Valentine .05 .15
446 Checklist 364-484 .15 .40
447 Junior Kennedy DP .05 .15
448 Tim Corcoran .05 .15
449 Paul Mitchell .05 .15
450 Dave Kingman DP .08 .25
451 Bando/Brennan/Wihtol RC .08 .25
452 Renie Martin .05 .15
453 Rob Wilfong DP .05 .15
454 Andy Hassler .05 .15
455 Rick Burleson .05 .15
456 Jeff Reardon RC .60 1.50
457 Mike Lum .05 .15
458 Randy Jones .05 .15
459 Greg Gross .05 .15
460 Rich Gossage .15 .40
461 Dave McKay .05 .15
462 Jack Brohamer .05 .15
463 Milt May .05 .15
464 Adrian Devine .05 .15
465 Bill Russell .15 .40
466 Bob Molinaro .05 .15
467 Dave Stieb .15 .40
468 John Wockenfuss .05 .15
469 Jeff Leonard .15 .40
470 Manny Trillo .05 .15
471 Mike Vail .05 .15
472 Dyar Miller DP .05 .15
473 Jose Cardenal .05 .15
474 Mike LaCoss .05 .15
475 Buddy Bell .15 .40
476 Jerry Koosman .15 .40
477 Luis Gomez .05 .15
478 Juan Eichelberger RC .05 .15
479 Tim Raines RC 1.50 4.00
480 Carlton Fisk .30 .75
481 Bob Lacey DP .05 .15
482 Jim Gantner .05 .15
483 Mike Griffin RC .08 .25
484 Max Venable DP RC .05 .15
485 Garry Templeton .15 .40
486 Marc Hill .05 .15
487 Dewey Robinson .05 .15
488 Damaso Garcia RC .05 .15
489 John Littlefield RC .05 .15
490 Eddie Murray 1.00 2.50
491 Gordy Pladson RC .05 .15
492 Barry Foote .05 .15
493 Dan Quisenberry .05 .15
494 Bob Walk RC .30 .75
495 Dusty Baker .15 .40
496 Paul Dade .05 .15
497 Fred Norman .05 .15
498 Pat Putnam .05 .15
499 Frank Pastore .05 .15
500 Jim Rice .15 .40
501 Tim Foli DP .05 .15
502 Bourjos/Hargesheimer/Rowland RC .08 .25
503 Steve McCatty .05 .15
504 Dale Murphy .30 .75
505 Jason Thompson .05 .15
506 Phil Huffman .05 .15
507 Jamie Quirk .05 .15
508 Rob Dressler .05 .15
509 Pete Mackanin .05 .15
510 Lee Mazzilli .15 .40
511 Wayne Garland .05 .15
512 Gary Thomasson .05 .15
513 Frank LaCorte .05 .15
514 George Riley RC .05 .15
515 Robin Yount 1.00 2.50
516 Doug Bird .05 .15
517 Richie Zisk .05 .15
518 Grant Jackson .05 .15
519 John Tamargo DP .05 .15
520 Steve Stone .05 .15
521 Sam Mejias .05 .15
522 Mike Colbern .05 .15
523 John Fulgham .05 .15
524 Willie Aikens .05 .15
525 Mike Torrez .05 .15
526 Bystrom/Loviglio/Wright RC .08 .25
527 Danny Goodwin .05 .15
528 Gary Matthews .15 .40
529 Dave LaRoche .05 .15
530 Steve Garvey .30 .75
531 John Curtis .05 .15
532 Bill Stein .05 .15
533 Jesus Figueroa RC .05 .15
534 Dave Smith RC .30 .75
535 Omar Moreno .05 .15
536 Bob Owchinko DP .05 .15
537 Ron Hodges .05 .15
538 Tom Griffin .05 .15
539 Rodney Scott .05 .15
540 Mike Schmidt DP .75 2.00
541 Steve Swisher .05 .15
542 Larry Bradford DP .05 .15
543 Terry Crowley .05 .15
544 Rich Gale .05 .15
545 Johnny Grubb .05 .15
546 Paul Moskau .05 .15
547 Mario Guerrero .05 .15
548 Dave Goltz .05 .15
549 Jerry Remy .05 .15
550 Tommy John .15 .40
551 Law/Pena/Perez RC .30 .75
552 Steve Trout .05 .15
553 Tim Blackwell .05 .15
554 Bert Blyleven .15 .40
555 Cecil Cooper .15 .40
556 Jerry Mumphrey .05 .15
557 Chris Knapp .05 .15
558 Barry Bonnell .05 .15
559 Willie Montanez .05 .15
560 Joe Morgan .30 .75
561 Dennis Littlejohn .05 .15
562 Checklist 485-605 .15 .40
563 Jim Kaat .15 .40
564 Ron Hassey DP .05 .15
565 Burt Hooton .05 .15
566 Del Unser .05 .15
567 Mark Bomback RC .05 .15
568 Dave Revering .05 .15
569 Al Williams DP RC .05 .15
570 Ken Singleton .15 .40
571 Todd Cruz .05 .15
572 Jack Morris .30 .75
573 Phil Garner .15 .40
574 Bill Caudill .05 .15
575 Tony Perez .30 .75
576 Reggie Cleveland .05 .15
577 Leal/Milner/Schrom RC .08 .25
578 Bill Gullickson RC .30 .75
579 Tim Flannery .05 .15
580 Don Baylor .15 .40
581 Roy Howell .05 .15
582 Gaylord Perry .15 .40
583 Larry Milbourne .05 .15
584 Randy Lerch .05 .15
585 Amos Otis .15 .40
586 Silvio Martinez .05 .15
587 Jeff Newman .05 .15
588 Gary Lavelle .05 .15
589 Lamar Johnson .05 .15
590 Bruce Sutter .30 .75
591 John Lowenstein .05 .15
592 Steve Comer .05 .15
593 Steve Kemp .05 .15
594 Preston Hanna DP .05 .15
595 Butch Hobson .05 .15
596 Jerry Augustine .05 .15
597 Rafael Landestoy .05 .15
598 George Vukovich DP RC .05 .15
599 Dennis Kinney RC .05 .15
600 Johnny Bench .60 1.50
601 Don Aase .05 .15
602 Bobby Murcer .15 .40
603 John Verhoeven .05 .15
604 Rob Picciolo .05 .15
605 Don Sutton .15 .40
606 Bereny/Combe/Householder DP RC .08 .25
607 David Palmer .05 .15
608 Greg Pryor .05 .15
609 Lynn McGlothen .05 .15
610 Darrell Porter .05 .15
611 Rick Matula DP .05 .15
612 Duane Kuiper .05 .15
613 Jim Anderson .05 .15
614 Dave Rozema .05 .15
615 Rick Dempsey .05 .15
616 Rick Wise .05 .15
617 Craig Reynolds .05 .15
618 John Milner .05 .15
619 Steve Henderson .05 .15
620 Dennis Eckersley .30 .75
621 Tom Donohue .05 .15
622 Randy Moffitt .05 .15
623 Sal Bando .15 .40
624 Bob Welch .15 .40
625 Bill Buckner .15 .40
626 Steffen/Ujdur/Weaver RC .08 .25
627 Luis Tiant .15 .40
628 Vic Correll .05 .15
629 Tony Armas .15 .40
630 Steve Carlton .30 .75
631 Ron Jackson .05 .15
632 Alan Bannister .05 .15
633 Bill Lee .15 .40
634 Doug Flynn .05 .15
635 Bobby Bonds .15 .40
636 Al Hrabosky .15 .40
637 Jerry Narron .05 .15
638 Checklist 606-726 .15 .40
639 Carney Lansford .15 .40
640 Dave Parker .15 .40
641 Mark Belanger .05 .15
642 Vern Ruhle .05 .15
643 Lloyd Moseby RC .30 .75
644 Ramon Aviles DP .05 .15
645 Rick Reuschel .15 .40
646 Marvis Foley RC .05 .15
647 Dick Drago .05 .15
648 Darrell Evans .15 .40
649 Manny Sarmiento .05 .15
650 Bucky Dent .15 .40
651 Pedro Guerrero .15 .40
652 John Montague .05 .15
653 Bill Fahey .05 .15
654 Ray Burris .05 .15
655 Dan Driessen .05 .15
656 Jon Matlack .05 .15
657 Mike Cubbage DP .05 .15
658 Milt Wilcox .05 .15
659 Flinn/Romero/Yost .30 .75
660 Gary Carter .30 .75
661 Orioles Team CL .15 .40
Earl Weaver MG
662 Red Sox Team CL .15 .40
Ralph Houk MG
663 Angels Team CL .15 .40
Jim Fregosi MG
664 White Sox Team .15 .40
Mgr.
Tony LaRussa/(Checklist back
665 Indians Team CL .15 .40
Dave Garcia MG
666 Tigers Team .15 .40
Mgr.
Sparky Anderson/(Checklist back
667 Royals Team CL .15 .40
Jim Frey MG
668 Brewers Team CL .15 .40
Bob Rodgers MG
669 Twins Team CL. .15 .40
John Goryl MG
670 Yankees Team CL .15 .40
Gene Michael MG
671 A's Team CL .30 .75
Billy Martin MG
672 Mariners Team CL .15 .40
Maury Wills MG
673 Rangers Team CL .15 .40
Don Zimmer MG
674 Blue Jays Team .15 .40
Mgr.
Bobby Mattick/(Checklist bac
675 Braves Team CL .15 .40
Bobby Cox MG
676 Cubs Team CL .15 .40
Joe Amalfitano MG
677 Reds Team CL .15 .40
John McNamara MG
678 Astros Team CL .15 .40
Bill Virdon MG
679 Dodgers Team CL .30 .75
Tom Lasorda MG
680 Expos Team CL .15 .40
Dick Williams MG
681 Mets Team CL .30 .75
Joe Torre MG
682 Phillies Team CL .15 .40
Dallas Green MG
683 Pirates Team CL .15 .40
Chuck Tanner MG
684 Cardinals Team .15 .40
Mgr.
Whitey Herzog/(Checklist bac
685 Padres Team CL .15 .40
Frank Howard MG
686 Giants Team CL .15 .40
Dave Bristol MG
687 Jeff Jones RC .05 .15
688 Kiko Garcia .05 .15
689 Bruce Hurst RC .30 .75
690 Bob Watson .05 .15
691 Dick Ruthven .05 .15
692 Lenny Randle .05 .15
693 Steve Howe RC .08 .25
694 Bud Harrelson DP .08 .25
695 Kent Tekulve .05 .15
696 Alan Ashby .05 .15
697 Rick Waits .05 .15
698 Mike Jorgensen .05 .15
699 Glenn Abbott .05 .15
700 George Brett 1.50 4.00
701 Joe Rudi .15 .40
702 George Medich .05 .15
703 Alvis Woods .05 .15
704 Bill Travers DP .05 .15
705 Ted Simmons .15 .40
706 Dave Ford .05 .15
707 Dave Cash .05 .15
708 Doyle Alexander .05 .15
709 Alan Trammell DP .20 .50
710 Ron LeFlore DP .08 .25
711 Joe Ferguson .05 .15
712 Bill Bonham .05 .15
713 Bill North .05 .15
714 Pete Redfern .05 .15
715 Bill Madlock .15 .40
716 Glenn Borgmann .05 .15
717 Jim Barr DP .05 .15
718 Larry Biittner .05 .15
719 Sparky Lyle .15 .40
720 Fred Lynn .15 .40
721 Toby Harrah .15 .40
722 Joe Niekro .05 .15
723 Bruce Bochte .05 .15
724 Lou Piniella .15 .40
725 Steve Rogers .15 .40
726 Rick Monday .15 .40

1981 Topps Traded

For the first time since 1976, Topps issued a 132-card factory boxed "traded" set in 1981, issued exclusively through hobby dealers. This set was sequentially numbered, alphabetically, from 727 to 858 and carries the same design as the regular issue 1981 Topps set. There are no key Rookie Cards in this set although Hubie Brooks, Tim Raines, Jeff Reardon, and Fernando Valenzuela are depicted in their rookie year for cards. The key extended Rookie Card in the set is Danny Ainge. According to reports at the time, dealers were required to order a minimum of two cases, which cost them $4.50 per set.

COMP.FACT.SET (132) 12.50 30.00
727 Danny Ainge XRC 2.00 5.00
728 Doyle Alexander .08 .25
729 Gary Alexander .08 .25
730 Bill Almon .08 .25
731 Joaquin Andujar .40 1.00
732 Bob Bailor .08 .25
733 Juan Beniquez .08 .25
734 Dave Bergman .08 .25
735 Tony Bernazard .08 .25
736 Larry Biittner .08 .25
737 Doug Bird .08 .25
738 Bert Blyleven .40 1.00
739 Mark Bomback .08 .25
740 Bobby Bonds .40 1.00
741 Rick Bosetti .08 .25
742 Hubie Brooks .75 2.00
743 Rick Burleson .08 .25
744 Ray Burris .08 .25
745 Jeff Burroughs .40 1.00
746 Enos Cabell .08 .25
747 Ken Clay .08 .25
748 Mark Clear .08 .25
749 Larry Cox .08 .25
750 Hector Cruz .08 .25
751 Victor Cruz .08 .25
752 Mike Cubbage .08 .25
753 Dick Davis .08 .25
754 Brian Doyle .08 .25
755 Dick Drago .08 .25
756 Leon Durham .40 1.00
757 Jim Dwyer .08 .25
758 Dave Edwards .08 .25
759 Jim Essian .08 .25
760 Bill Fahey .08 .25
761 Rollie Fingers .40 1.00
762 Carlton Fisk .75 2.00
763 Barry Foote .08 .25
764 Ken Forsch .08 .25
765 Kiko Garcia .08 .25
766 Cesar Geronimo .08 .25
767 Gary Gray XRC .08 .25
768 Mickey Hatcher .08 .25
769 Steve Henderson .08 .25
770 Marc Hill .08 .25
771 Butch Hobson .08 .25
772 Rick Honeycutt .08 .25
773 Roy Howell .08 .25
774 Mike Ivie .08 .25
775 Roy Lee Jackson .08 .25
776 Cliff Johnson .08 .25
777 Randy Jones .40 1.00
778 Ruppert Jones .08 .25
779 Mick Kelleher .08 .25
780 Terry Kennedy .08 .25
781 Dave Kingman .40 1.00
782 Bob Knepper .08 .25
783 Ken Kravec .08 .25
784 Bob Lacey .08 .25
785 Dennis Lamp .08 .25
786 Rafael Landestoy .08 .25
787 Ken Landreaux .08 .25
788 Carney Lansford .40 1.00
789 Dave LaRoche .08 .25
790 Joe Lefebvre .08 .25
791 Ron LeFlore .40 1.00
792 Randy Lerch .08 .25
793 Sixto Lezcano .08 .25
794 John Littlefield .08 .25
795 Mike Lum .08 .25
796 Greg Luzinski .40 1.00
797 Fred Lynn .40 1.00
798 Jerry Martin .08 .25
799 Buck Martinez .08 .25
800 Gary Matthews .40 1.00
801 Mario Mendoza .08 .25
802 Larry Milbourne .08 .25
803 Rick Miller .08 .25
804 John Montefusco .08 .25
805 Jerry Morales .08 .25
806 Jose Morales .08 .25
807 Joe Morgan .75 2.00
808 Jerry Mumphrey .08 .25
809 Gene Nelson XRC .08 .25
810 Ed Ott .08 .25
811 Bob Owchinko .08 .25
812 Gaylord Perry .40 1.00
813 Mike Phillips .08 .25
814 Darrell Porter .08 .25
815 Mike Proly .08 .25
816 Tim Raines 2.00 5.00
817 Lenny Randle .08 .25
818 Doug Rau .08 .25
819 Jeff Reardon .75 2.00
820 Ken Reitz .08 .25
821 Steve Renko .08 .25
822 Rick Reuschel .40 1.00
823 Dave Revering .08 .25
824 Dave Roberts .08 .25
825 Leon Roberts .08 .25
826 Joe Rudi .40 1.00
827 Kevin Saucier .08 .25
828 Tony Scott .08 .25
829 Bob Shirley .08 .25
830 Ted Simmons .40 1.00
831 Lary Sorensen .08 .25
832 Jim Spencer .08 .25
833 Harry Spilman .08 .25
834 Fred Stanley .08 .25
835 Rusty Staub .40 1.00
836 Bill Stein .08 .25
837 Joe Strain .08 .25
838 Bruce Sutter .75 2.00
839 Don Sutton .40 1.00
840 Steve Swisher .08 .25
841 Frank Tanana .40 1.00
842 Gene Tenace .40 1.00
843 Jason Thompson .08 .25
844 Dickie Thon .08 .25
845 Bill Travers .08 .25
846 Tom Underwood .08 .25
847 John Urrea .08 .25
848 Mike Vail .08 .25
849 Ellis Valentine .08 .25
850 Fernando Valenzuela 5.00 12.00
851 Pete Vuckovich .08 .25
852 Mark Wagner .08 .25
853 Bob Walk .40 1.00
854 Claudell Washington .08 .25
855 Dave Winfield .75 2.00

856 Geoff Zahn .08 .25
857 Richie Zisk .08 .25
858 Checklist 727-858 .08 .25

1982 Topps

The cards in this 792-card set measure the standard size. Cards were primarily distributed in 15-card wax packs and 51-card rack packs. The 1982 baseball series was the first of the largest sets Topps issued at one printing. The 66-card increase from the previous year's total eliminated the "double print" practice, that had occurred in every regular issue since 1978. Cards 1-6 depict Highlights of the strike-shortened 1981 season, cards 161-168 picture League Leaders, and there are subsets of AL (547-557) and NL (337-347) All-Stars (AS). The abbreviation "IA" in the checklist is given for the 40 "In Action" cards introduced in this set. The team cards are actually Team Leader (TL) cards picturing the batting average and ERA leader for that team with a checklist back. All 26 of these cards were available from Topps on a perforated sheet through an offer on wax pack wrappers. Notable Rookie Cards include Brett Butler, Chili Davis, Cal Ripken Jr., Lee Smith, and Dave Stewart. Be careful when purchasing blank-back Cal Ripken Jr. Rookie Cards. Those cards are extremely likely to be counterfeit.

COMPLETE SET (792) 30.00 80.00
1 Steve Carlton HL .10 .30
2 Ron Davis HL .05 .15
3 Tim Raines HL .10 .30
4 Pete Rose HL .25 .60
5 Nolan Ryan HL 1.25 3.00
6 Fernando Valenzuela HL .25 .60
7 Scott Sanderson .05 .15
8 Rich Dauer .05 .15
9 Ron Guidry .10 .30
10 Ron Guidry IA .05 .15
11 Gary Alexander .05 .15
12 Moose Haas .05 .15
13 Lamar Johnson .05 .15
14 Steve Howe .05 .15
15 Ellis Valentine .05 .15
16 Steve Comer .05 .15
17 Darrell Evans .10 .30
18 Fernando Arroyo .05 .15
19 Ernie Whitt .05 .15
20 Garry Maddox .05 .15
21 Cal Ripken RC 10.00 25.00
22 Jim Beattie .05 .15
23 Willie Hernandez .05 .15
24 Dave Frost .05 .15
25 Jerry Remy .05 .15
26 Jorge Orta .05 .15
27 Tom Herr .05 .15
28 John Urrea .05 .15
29 Dwayne Murphy .05 .15
30 Tom Seaver .50 1.25
31 Tom Seaver IA .10 .30
32 Gene Garber .05 .15
33 Jerry Morales .05 .15
34 Joe Sambito .05 .15
35 Willie Aikens .05 .15
36 Al Oliver .25 .60
Doc Medich TL
37 Dan Graham .05 .15
38 Charlie Lea .05 .15
39 Lou Whitaker .10 .30
40 Dave Parker .10 .30
41 Dave Parker IA .05 .15
42 Rick Sofield .05 .15
43 Mike Cubbage .05 .15
44 Britt Burns .05 .15
45 Rick Cerone .05 .15
46 Jerry Augustine .05 .15
47 Jeff Leonard .05 .15
48 Bobby Castillo .05 .15
49 Alvis Woods .05 .15
50 Buddy Bell .10 .30
51 Howell/Lezcano/Waller RC .30 .75
52 Larry Andersen .05 .15
53 Greg Gross .05 .15
54 Ron Hassey .05 .15
55 Rick Burleson .05 .15
56 Mark Littell .05 .15
57 Craig Reynolds .05 .15
58 John D'Acquisto .05 .15
59 Rich Gedman .30 .75
60 Tony Armas .10 .30
61 Tommy Boggs .05 .15
62 Mike Tyson .05 .15
63 Mario Soto .10 .30
64 Lynn Jones .05 .15
65 Terry Kennedy .05 .15
66 A.Howe/N.Ryan TL .75 2.00
67 Rich Gale .05 .15
68 Roy Howell .05 .15
69 Al Williams .05 .15
70 Tim Raines .25 .60
71 Roy Lee Jackson .05 .15
72 Rick Auerbach .05 .15
73 Buddy Solomon .05 .15
74 Bob Clark .05 .15
75 Tommy John .10 .30
76 Greg Pryor .05 .15
77 Miguel Dilone .05 .15
78 George Medich .05 .15
79 Bob Bailor .05 .15
80 Jim Palmer .10 .30
81 Jim Palmer IA .05 .15
82 Bob Welch .10 .30
83 Balboni/McGaf/Rob RC .30 .75
84 Rennie Stennett .05 .15
85 Lynn McGlothen .05 .15
86 Dane Iorg .05 .15
87 Matt Keough .05 .15
88 Biff Pocoroba .05 .15
89 Steve Henderson .05 .15
90 Nolan Ryan 2.50 6.00
91 Carney Lansford .10 .30
92 Brad Havens .05 .15
93 Larry Hisle .05 .15
94 Andy Hassler .05 .15
95 Ozzie Smith 1.00 2.50
96 George Brett .50 1.25
Larry Gura TL
97 Paul Moskau .05 .15
98 Terry Bulling .05 .15
99 Barry Bonnell .05 .15
100 Mike Schmidt 1.25 3.00
101 Mike Schmidt IA .50 1.25
102 Dan Briggs .05 .15
103 Bob Lacey .05 .15
104 Rance Mulliniks .05 .15
105 Kirk Gibson .50 1.25
106 Enrique Romo .05 .15
107 Wayne Krenchicki .05 .15
108 Bob Sykes .05 .15
109 Dave Revering .05 .15
110 Carlton Fisk .25 .60
111 Carlton Fisk IA .10 .30
112 Billy Sample .05 .15
113 Steve McCatty .05 .15
114 Ken Landreaux .05 .15
115 Gaylord Perry .10 .30
116 Jim Wohlford .05 .15
117 Rawly Eastwick .10 .30
118 Francona/Mills/Smith RC 2.00 5.00
119 Joe Pittman .05 .15
120 Gary Lucas .05 .15
121 Ed Lynch .05 .15
122 Jamie Easterly UER .05 .15
Photo actually
Reggie Cleveland
123 Danny Goodwin .05 .15
124 Reid Nichols .05 .15
125 Danny Ainge .10 .30
126 Claudell Washington .25 .60
Rick Mahler TL
127 Lonnie Smith .05 .15
128 Frank Pastore .05 .15
129 Checklist 1-132 .10 .30
130 Julio Cruz .05 .15
131 Stan Bahnsen .05 .15
132 Lee May .05 .15
133 Pat Underwood .05 .15
134 Dan Ford .05 .15
135 Andy Rincon .05 .15
136 Lenn Sakata .05 .15
137 George Cappuzzello .05 .15
138 Tony Pena .10 .30
139 Jeff Jones .05 .15
140 Ron LeFlore .10 .30
141 Bando/Brennan/Hayes RC .30 .75
142 Dave LaRoche .05 .15
143 Mookie Wilson .10 .30
144 Fred Breining .05 .15
145 Bob Horner .10 .30
146 Mike Griffin .05 .15
147 Denny Walling .05 .15
148 Mickey Klutts .05 .15
149 Pat Putnam .05 .15
150 Ted Simmons .10 .30
151 Dave Edwards .05 .15
152 Ramon Aviles .05 .15
153 Roger Erickson .05 .15
154 Dennis Werth .05 .15
155 Otto Velez .05 .15
156 Rickey Henderson .50 1.25
Steve McCatty TL
157 Steve Crawford .05 .15
158 Brian Downing .10 .30
159 Larry Biittner .05 .15
160 Luis Tiant .10 .30
161 Bill Madlock/Carney Lansford LL .10 .30
162 Mike Schmidt .50 1.25
Tony Armas
Dwight Evans
Bobby Grich
Eddie Murray LL
163 Mike Schmidt .50 1.25
Eddie Murray LL
164 Tim Raines .50 1.25
Rickey Henderson LL
165 Seav/Martinez/Morris LL .10 .30
166 Strikeout Leaders
Fernando Valenzuela/Len Barker .10 .30
167 N.Ryan/S.McCatty LL .75 2.00
168 Bruce Sutter .10 .30
Rollie Fingers LL
169 Charlie Leibrandt .05 .15
170 Jim Bibby .05 .15
171 Brenly/Davis/Tufts RC .60 1.50
172 Bill Gullickson .05 .15
173 Jamie Quirk .05 .15
174 Dave Ford .05 .15
175 Jerry Mumphrey .05 .15
176 Dewey Robinson .05 .15
177 John Ellis .05 .15
178 Dyar Miller .05 .15
179 Steve Garvey .10 .30
180 Steve Garvey IA .05 .15
181 Silvio Martinez .05 .15
182 Larry Herndon .05 .15
183 Mike Proly .05 .15
184 Mick Kelleher .05 .15
185 Phil Niekro .10 .30
186 Keith Hernandez .10 .30
Bob Forsch TL
187 Jeff Newman .05 .15
188 Randy Martz .05 .15
189 Glenn Hoffman .05 .15
190 J.R. Richard .10 .30
191 Tim Wallach RC .60 1.50
192 Broderick Perkins .05 .15
193 Darrell Jackson .05 .15
194 Mike Vail .05 .15
195 Paul Molitor .10 .30
196 Willie Upshaw .30 .75
197 Shane Rawley .05 .15
198 Chris Speier .05 .15
199 Don Aase .05 .15
200 George Brett 1.25 3.00
201 George Brett IA .60 1.50
202 Rick Manning .05 .15
203 Barfield/Miln/Wells RC .60 1.50
204 Gary Roenicke .05 .15
205 Neil Allen .05 .15
206 Tony Bernazard .05 .15
207 Rod Scurry .05 .15
208 Bobby Murcer .10 .30
209 Gary Lavelle .05 .15
210 Keith Hernandez .10 .30
211 Dan Petry .05 .15
212 Mario Mendoza .05 .15
213 Dave Stewart RC 1.00 2.50
214 Brian Asselstine .05 .15
215 Mike Krukow .05 .15
216 Chet Lemon .25 .60
Dennis Lamp TL
217 Bo McLaughlin .05 .15
218 Dave Roberts .05 .15
219 John Curtis .05 .15
220 Manny Trillo .05 .15
221 Jim Slaton .05 .15
222 Butch Wynegar .05 .15
223 Lloyd Moseby .05 .15
224 Bruce Bochte .05 .15
225 Mike Torrez .05 .15
226 Checklist 133-264 .25 .60
227 Ray Burris .05 .15
228 Sam Mejias .05 .15
229 Geoff Zahn .05 .15
230 Willie Wilson .10 .30
231 Davis/Dernier/Virgil RC .30 .75
232 Terry Crowley .05 .15
233 Duane Kuiper .05 .15
234 Ron Hodges .05 .15
235 Mike Easler .05 .15
236 John Martin RC .08 .25
237 Rusty Kuntz .05 .15
238 Kevin Saucier .05 .15
239 Jon Matlack .05 .15
240 Bucky Dent .10 .30
241 Bucky Dent IA .05 .15
242 Milt May .05 .15
243 Bob Owchinko .05 .15
244 Rufino Linares .05 .15
245 Ken Reitz .05 .15
246 Hubie Brooks .25 .60
Mike Scott TL
247 Pedro Guerrero .10 .30
248 Frank LaCorte .05 .15
249 Tim Flannery .05 .15
250 Tug McGraw .10 .30
251 Fred Lynn .10 .30
252 Fred Lynn IA .05 .15
253 Chuck Baker .05 .15
254 Jorge Bell RC .60 1.50
George Bell
255 Tony Perez .25 .60
256 Tony Perez IA .10 .30
257 Larry Harlow .05 .15
258 Bo Diaz .05 .15
259 Rodney Scott .10 .30
260 Bruce Sutter .25 .60
261 Bailey/Castillo/Rucker RC .05 .15
262 Doug Bair .05 .15
263 Victor Cruz .05 .15
264 Dan Quisenberry .05 .15
265 Al Bumbry .05 .15
266 Rick Leach .05 .15
267 Kurt Bevacqua .05 .15
268 Rickey Keeton .05 .15
269 Jim Essian .05 .15
270 Rusty Staub .10 .30
271 Larry Bradford .05 .15
272 Bump Wills .05 .15
273 Doug Bird .05 .15
274 Bob Ojeda RC .30 .75
275 Bob Watson .05 .15
276 Rod Carew .25 .60
Ken Forsch TL
277 Terry Puhl .05 .15
278 John Littlefield .05 .15
279 Bill Russell .10 .30
280 Ben Oglivie .10 .30
281 John Verhoeven .05 .15
282 Ken Macha .05 .15
283 Brian Allard .05 .15
284 Bobby Grich .10 .30
285 Sparky Lyle .10 .30
286 Bill Fahey .05 .15
287 Alan Bannister .05 .15
288 Garry Templeton .10 .30
289 Bob Stanley .05 .15
290 Ken Singleton .10 .30
291 Law/Long/Ray RC .10 .30
292 David Palmer .05 .15
293 Rob Picciolo .05 .15
294 Mike LaCoss .05 .15
295 Jason Thompson .05 .15
296 Bob Walk .05 .15
297 Clint Hurdle .05 .15
298 Danny Darwin .05 .15
299 Steve Trout .05 .15
300 Reggie Jackson .25 .60
301 Reggie Jackson IA .10 .30
302 Doug Flynn .05 .15
303 Bill Caudill .05 .15
304 Johnnie LeMaster .05 .15
305 Don Sutton .10 .30
306 Don Sutton IA .05 .15
307 Randy Bass .30 .75
308 Charlie Moore .05 .15
309 Pete Redfern .05 .15
310 Mike Hargrove .05 .15
311 Dusty Baker .10 .30
Burt Hooton TL
312 Lenny Randle .05 .15
313 John Harris .05 .15
314 Buck Martinez .05 .15
315 Burt Hooton .05 .15
316 Steve Braun .05 .15
317 Dick Ruthven .05 .15
318 Mike Heath .05 .15
319 Dave Rozema .05 .15
320 Chris Chambliss .10 .30
321 Chris Chambliss IA .05 .15
322 Garry Hancock .05 .15
323 Bill Lee .10 .30
324 Steve Dillard .05 .15
325 Jose Cruz .10 .30
326 Pete Falcone .05 .15
327 Joe Nolan .05 .15
328 Ed Farmer .05 .15
329 U.L. Washington .05 .15
330 Rick Wise .05 .15
331 Benny Ayala .05 .15
332 Don Robinson .05 .15
333 DiPino/Edwards/Porter RC .05 .15
334 Aurelio Rodriguez .05 .15
335 Jim Sundberg .10 .30
336 Tom Paciorek .25 .60
Glenn Abbott TL
337 Pete Rose AS .25 .60
338 Dave Lopes AS .05 .15
339 Mike Schmidt AS .50 1.25
340 Dave Concepcion AS .05 .15
341 Andre Dawson AS .05 .15
342A George Foster AS w/Auto .10 .30
342B George Foster AS w/o Auto .50 1.25
343 Dave Parker AS .05 .15
344 Gary Carter AS .05 .15
345 Fernando Valenzuela AS .25 .60
346 Tom Seaver AS ERR .10 .30
'ted'
346B Tom Seaver AS COR .10 .30
347 Bruce Sutter AS .05 .15
348 Derrel Thomas .05 .15
349 George Frazier .05 .15
350 Thad Bosley .05 .15
351 Brown/Comb/House RC .05 .15
352 Dick Davis .05 .15
353 Jack O'Connor .05 .15
354 Roberto Ramos .05 .15
355 Dwight Evans .25 .60
356 Denny Lewallyn .05 .15
357 Butch Hobson .05 .15
358 Mike Parrott .05 .15
359 Jim Dwyer .05 .15
360 Len Barker .05 .15
361 Rafael Landestoy .05 .15
362 Jim Wright UER .05 .15
Wrong Jim Wright
pictured
363 Bob Molinaro .05 .15
364 Doyle Alexander .05 .15
365 Bill Madlock .10 .30
366 Luis Salazar .25 .60
Juan Eichelberger TL
367 Jim Kaat .10 .30
368 Alex Trevino .05 .15
369 Champ Summers .05 .15
370 Mike Norris .05 .15
371 Jerry Don Gleaton .05 .15
372 Luis Gomez .05 .15
373 Gene Nelson .05 .15
374 Tim Blackwell .05 .15
375 Dusty Baker .10 .30
376 Chris Welsh .05 .15
377 Kiko Garcia .05 .15
378 Mike Caldwell .05 .15
379 Rob Wilfong .05 .15
380 Dave Stieb .10 .30
381 Bruce Hurst .05 .15
Dave Schmidt RC
Julio Valdez RC
382 Joe Simpson .05 .15
383A Pascual Perez ERR 15.00 40.00
383B Pascual Perez COR .10 .30
384 Keith Moreland .05 .15
385 Ken Forsch .05 .15
386 Jerry White .05 .15
387 Tom Veryzer .05 .15
388 Joe Rudi .10 .30
389 George Vukovich .05 .15
390 Eddie Murray .50 1.25
391 Dave Tobik .05 .15
392 Rick Bosetti .05 .15
393 Al Hrabosky .05 .15
394 Checklist 265-396 .25 .60
395 Omar Moreno .05 .15
396 John Castino .25 .60
Fernando Arroyo TL
397 Ken Brett .05 .15
398 Mike Squires .05 .15
399 Pat Zachry .05 .15
400 Johnny Bench .50 1.25
401 Johnny Bench IA .25 .60
402 Bill Stein .05 .15
403 Jim Tracy .10 .30
404 Dickie Thon .05 .15
405 Rick Reuschel .10 .30
406 Al Holland .05 .15
407 Danny Boone .05 .15
408 Ed Romero .05 .15
409 Don Cooper .05 .15
410 Ron Cey .10 .30
411 Ron Cey IA .05 .15
412 Luis Leal .05 .15
413 Dan Meyer .05 .15
414 Elias Sosa .05 .15
415 Don Baylor .10 .30
416 Marty Bystrom .05 .15
417 Pat Kelly .05 .15
418 Butcher/John/Schmidt RC .05 .15
419 Steve Stone .05 .15
420 George Hendrick .10 .30
421 Mark Clear .05 .15
422 Cliff Johnson .05 .15
423 Stan Papi .05 .15
424 Bruce Benedict .05 .15
425 John Candelaria .05 .15
426 Eddie Murray .25 .60
Sammy Stewart
427 Ron Oester .05 .15
428 LaMarr Hoyt .05 .15
429 John Wathan .05 .15
430 Vida Blue .10 .30
431 Vida Blue IA .05 .15
432 Mike Scott .10 .30
433 Alan Ashby .05 .15
434 Joe Lefebvre .05 .15
435 Robin Yount .75 2.00
436 Joe Strain .05 .15
437 Juan Berenguer .05 .15
438 Pete Mackanin .05 .15
439 Dave Righetti RC 1.00 2.50
440 Jeff Burroughs .05 .15
441 Heep/Smith/Sprowl RC .05 .15
442 Bruce Kison .05 .15
443 Mark Wagner .05 .15
444 Terry Forster .10 .30
445 Larry Parrish .05 .15
446 Wayne Garland .05 .15
447 Darrell Porter .05 .15
448 Darrell Porter IA .05 .15
449 Luis Aguayo .05 .15
450 Jack Morris .10 .30
451 Ed Miller .05 .15
452 Lee Smith RC 1.25 3.00
453 Art Howe .05 .15
454 Rick Langford .05 .15
455 Tom Burgmeier .05 .15
456 Bill Buckner .10 .30
Randy Martz TL
457 Tim Stoddard .05 .15
458 Willie Montanez .05 .15
459 Bruce Berenyi .05 .15
460 Jack Clark .10 .30
461 Rich Dotson .05 .15
462 Dave Chalk .05 .15
463 Jim Kern .05 .15
464 Juan Bonilla RC .08 .25
465 Lee Mazzilli .05 .15
466 Randy Lerch .05 .15
467 Mickey Hatcher .05 .15
468 Floyd Bannister .05 .15
469 Ed Ott .05 .15
470 John Mayberry .05 .15
471 Hammaker/Jones/Motley RC .05 .15
472 Oscar Gamble .05 .15
473 Mike Stanton .05 .15
474 Ken Oberkfell .05 .15
475 Alan Trammell .10 .30
476 Brian Kingman .05 .15
477 Steve Yeager .10 .30
478 Ray Searage .05 .15
479 Rowland Office .05 .15
480 Steve Carlton .25 .60
481 Steve Carlton IA .10 .30
482 Glenn Hubbard .05 .15
483 Gary Woods .05 .15
484 Ivan DeJesus .05 .15
485 Kent Tekulve .05 .15
486 Jerry Mumphrey .10 .30
Tommy John TL
487 Bob McClure .05 .15
488 Ron Jackson .05 .15
489 Rick Dempsey .05 .15
490 Dennis Eckersley .25 .60
491 Checklist 397-528 .25 .60
492 Joe Price .05 .15
493 Chet Lemon .10 .30
494 Hubie Brooks .05 .15
495 Dennis Leonard .05 .15
496 Johnny Grubb .05 .15
497 Jim Anderson .05 .15
498 Dave Bergman .05 .15
499 Paul Mirabella .05 .15
500 Rod Carew .25 .60
501 Rod Carew IA .10 .30
502 Steve Bedrosian RC UER .60 1.50
Photo actually Larry Owen
Brett Butler RC
Larry Owen
503 Julio Gonzalez .05 .15
504 Rick Peters .05 .15
505 Graig Nettles .10 .30
506 Graig Nettles IA .05 .15
507 Terry Harper .05 .15
508 Jody Davis RC .05 .15
509 Harry Spilman .05 .15
510 Fernando Valenzuela .50 1.25
511 Ruppert Jones .05 .15
512 Jerry Dybzinski .05 .15
513 Rick Rhoden .05 .15
514 Joe Ferguson .05 .15
515 Larry Bowa .10 .30
516 Larry Bowa IA .05 .15
517 Mark Brouhard .05 .15
518 Garth Iorg .05 .15
519 Glenn Adams .05 .15
520 Mike Flanagan .05 .15
521 Bill Almon .05 .15
522 Chuck Rainey .05 .15
523 Gary Gray .05 .15
524 Tom Hausman .05 .15
525 Ray Knight .10 .30
526 Warren Cromartie .25 .60
Bill Gullickson TL
527 John Henry Johnson .05 .15
528 Matt Alexander .05 .15
529 Allen Ripley .05 .15
530 Dickie Noles .05 .15
531 Bordi/Budaska/Moore RC .05 .15
532 Toby Harrah .10 .30
533 Joaquin Andujar .10 .30
534 Dave McKay .05 .15
535 Lance Parrish .10 .30
536 Rafael Ramirez .05 .15
537 Doug Capilla .05 .15
538 Lou Piniella .10 .30
539 Vern Ruhle .05 .15
540 Andre Dawson .10 .30
541 Barry Evans .05 .15
542 Ned Yost .05 .15
543 Bill Robinson .05 .15
544 Larry Christenson .05 .15
545 Reggie Smith .10 .30
546 Reggie Smith IA .05 .15
547 Rod Carew AS .10 .30
548 Willie Randolph AS .05 .15
549 George Brett AS .60 1.50
550 Bucky Dent AS .05 .15
551 Reggie Jackson AS .10 .30
552 Ken Singleton AS .05 .15
553 Dave Winfield AS .05 .15
554 Carlton Fisk AS .10 .30
555 Scott McGregor AS .05 .15
556 Jack Morris AS .05 .15
557 Rich Gossage AS .10 .30
558 John Tudor .10 .30
559 Mike Hargrove .10 .30
Bert Blyleven TL
560 Doug Corbett .05 .15
561 Brum/DeLeon/Roof RC .05 .15
562 Mike O'Berry .05 .15
563 Ross Baumgarten .05 .15
564 Doug DeCinces .05 .15
565 Jackson Todd .05 .15
566 Mike Jorgensen .05 .15
567 Bob Babcock .05 .15
568 Joe Pettini .05 .15
569 Willie Randolph .10 .30
570 Willie Randolph IA .05 .15
571 Glenn Abbott .05 .15
572 Juan Beniquez .05 .15
573 Rick Waits .05 .15
574 Mike Ramsey .05 .15
575 Al Cowens .05 .15
576 Milt May .25 .60
Vida Blue TL
577 Rick Monday .10 .30
578 Shooty Babitt .05 .15
579 Rick Mahler .05 .15
580 Bobby Bonds .10 .30
581 Ron Reed .05 .15
582 Luis Pujols .05 .15
583 Tippy Martinez .05 .15
584 Hosken Powell .05 .15
585 Rollie Fingers .10 .30
586 Rollie Fingers IA .05 .15
587 Tim Lollar .05 .15
588 Dale Berra .05 .15
589 Dave Stapleton .05 .15
590 Al Oliver .10 .30
591 Al Oliver IA .05 .15
592 Craig Swan .05 .15
593 Billy Smith .05 .15
594 Renie Martin .05 .15
595 Dave Collins .05 .15
596 Damaso Garcia .05 .15
597 Wayne Nordhagen .05 .15
598 Bob Galasso .05 .15
599 Lovig/Patt/Suth RC .05 .15
600 Dave Winfield .10
601 Sid Monge .05
602 Freddie Patek .05
603 Rich Hebner .05
604 Orlando Sanchez .05
605 Steve Rogers .10
606 John Mayberry .10
Dave Stieb TL
607 Leon Durham .05
608 Jerry Royster .05
609 Rick Sutcliffe .10
610 Rickey Henderson 1.50 4.
611 Joe Niekro .05
612 Gary Ward .05
613 Jim Gantner .05
614 Juan Eichelberger .05
615 Bob Boone .10
616 Bob Boone IA .05
617 Scott McGregor .05
618 Tim Foli .05
619 Bill Campbell .05
620 Ken Griffey .10
621 Ken Griffey IA .05
622 Dennis Lamp .05
623 Gardenhire/Leach/Leary RC .30 .7
624 Fergie Jenkins .10 .3
625 Hal McRae .10 .3
626 Randy Jones .05 .1
627 Enos Cabell .05 .1
628 Bill Travers .05 .1
629 John Wockenfuss .05 .1
630 Joe Charboneau .10 .3
631 Gene Tenace .10 .3
632 Bryan Clark RC .08 .2
633 Mitchell Page .05 .1
634 Checklist 529-660 .25 .6
635 Ron Davis .05 .15
636 Pete Rose .50 1.25
Steve Carlton TL
637 Rick Camp .05 .15
638 John Milner .05 .15
639 Ken Kravec .05 .15
640 Cesar Cedeno .10 .30
641 Steve Mura .05 .15
642 Mike Scioscia .10 .30
643 Pete Vuckovich .05 .15
644 John Castino .05 .15
645 Frank White .10 .30
646 Frank White IA .05 .15
647 Warren Brusstar .05 .15
648 Jose Morales .05 .15
649 Ken Clay .05 .15
650 Carl Yastrzemski .75 2.00
651 Carl Yastrzemski IA .50 1.25
652 Steve Nicosia .05 .15
653 Brunansky/Sanch/Scon RC .60 1.50
654 Jim Morrison .05 .15
655 Joel Youngblood .05 .15
656 Eddie Whitson .05 .15
657 Tom Poquette .05 .15
658 Tito Landrum .05 .15
659 Fred Martinez .05 .15
660 Dave Concepcion .10 .30
661 Dave Concepcion IA .05 .15
662 Luis Salazar .05 .15
663 Hector Cruz .05 .15
664 Dan Spillner .05 .15
665 Jim Clancy .05 .15
666 Steve Kemp .25 .60
Dan Petry TL
667 Jeff Reardon .10 .30
668 Dale Murphy .25 .60
669 Larry Milbourne .05 .15
670 Steve Kemp .05 .15
671 Mike Davis .05 .15
672 Bob Knepper .05 .15
673 Keith Drumwright .05 .15
674 Dave Goltz .05 .15
675 Cecil Cooper .10 .30
676 Sal Butera .05 .15
677 Alfredo Griffin .05 .15
678 Tom Paciorek .05 .15
679 Sammy Stewart .05 .15
680 Gary Matthews .10 .30
681 Marshall/Roen/Sax RC .60 1.50
682 Jesse Jefferson .05 .15
683 Phil Garner .10 .30
684 Harold Baines .10 .30
685 Bert Blyleven .10 .30
686 Gary Allenson .05 .15
687 Greg Minton .05 .15
688 Leon Roberts .05 .15
689 Lary Sorensen .05 .15
690 Dave Kingman .10 .30
691 Dan Schatzeder .05 .15
692 Wayne Gross .05 .15
693 Cesar Geronimo .05 .15
694 Dave Wehrmeister .05 .15
695 Warren Cromartie .05 .15
696 Bill Madlock .25 .60
Eddie Solomon TL
697 John Montefusco .05 .15
698 Tony Scott .05 .15
699 Dick Tidrow .05 .15
700 George Foster .10 .30
701 George Foster IA .05 .15
702 Steve Renko .05 .15
703 Cecil Cooper .25 .60
Pete Vuckovich TL
704 Mickey Rivers .05 .15
705 Mickey Rivers IA .05 .15
706 Barry Foote .05 .15
707 Mark Bomback .05 .15

Gene Richards .05 .15
Don Money .05 .15
Jerry Reuss .05 .15
Edler/Henderson/Walton RC .30 .75
Dennis Martinez .10 .30
Del Unser .05 .15
Jerry Koosman .10 .30
Willie Stargell .25 .60
Willie Stargell IA .10 .30
Rick Miller .05 .15
Charlie Hough .10 .30
Jerry Narron .05 .15
0 Greg Luzinski .10 .30
1 Greg Luzinski IA .05 .15
2 Jerry Martin .05 .15
3 Junior Kennedy .05 .15
4 Dave Rosello .05 .15
5 Amos Otis .10 .30
6 Amos Otis IA .05 .15
7 Sixto Lezcano .05 .15
8 Aurelio Lopez .05 .15
9 Jim Spencer .05 .15
0 Gary Carter .10 .30
1 Armstrong/Gwosdz/Kuhaulua RC .05 .15
2 Mike Lum .05 .15
3 Larry McWilliams .05 .15
4 Mike Ivie .05 .15
5 Rudy May .05 .15
36 Jerry Turner .05 .15
37 Reggie Cleveland .05 .15
38 Dave Engle .05 .15
39 Joey McLaughlin .05 .15
40 Dave Lopes .10 .30
41 Dave Lopes IA .05 .15
42 Dick Drago .05 .15
43 John Stearns .05 .15
44 Mike Witt .30 .75
45 Bake McBride .10 .30
46 Andre Thornton .05 .15
47 John Lowenstein .05 .15
48 Marc Hill .05 .15
49 Bob Shirley .05 .15
50 Jim Rice .10 .30
51 Rick Honeycutt .05 .15
52 Lee Lacy .05 .15
53 Tom Brookens .05 .15
54 Joe Morgan .10 .30
55 Joe Morgan IA .05 .15
56 Ken Griffey .10 .30
Tom Seaver TL
757 Tom Underwood .05 .15
758 Claudell Washington .05 .15
759 Paul Splittorff .05 .15
760 Bill Buckner .10 .30
761 Dave Smith .05 .15
762 Mike Phillips .05 .15
763 Tom Hume .05 .15
764 Steve Swisher .05 .15
765 Gorman Thomas .10 .30
766 Faedo/Hrbek/Laudner RC .60 1.50
767 Roy Smalley .05 .15
768 Jerry Garvin .05 .15
769 Richie Zisk .05 .15
770 Rich Gossage .10 .30
771 Rich Gossage IA .05 .15
772 Bert Campaneris .10 .30
773 John Denny .05 .15
774 Jay Johnstone .05 .15
775 Bob Forsch .05 .15
776 Mark Belanger .05 .15
777 Tom Griffin .05 .15
778 Kevin Hickey RC .08 .25
779 Grant Jackson .05 .15
780 Pete Rose 1.50 4.00
781 Pete Rose IA .50 1.25
782 Frank Taveras .05 .15
783 Greg Harris RC .08 .25
784 Milt Wilcox .05 .15
785 Dan Driessen .05 .15
786 Carney Lansford .25 .60
Mike Torrez TL
787 Fred Stanley .05 .15
788 Woodie Fryman .05 .15
789 Checklist 661-792 .25 .60
790 Larry Gura .05 .15
791 Bobby Brown .05 .15
792 Frank Tanana .10 .30

1982 Topps Blackless

During the 1982 Topps production, a whole sheet of cards were issued without the black ink. This caused the cards to have no facsimile autographs on the card front along with other processes missing. This affected mainly the A, B and C sheets.

COMPLETE SET (396) 1500.00 2500.00
8 Rich Dauer 2.00 5.00
9 Ron Guidry 3.00 8.00
10 Ron Guidry IA 2.50 6.00
11 Gary Alexander 2.00 5.00
12 Moose Haas 2.00 5.00
13 Lamar Johnson 2.00 5.00
14 Steve Howe 2.00 5.00
17 Darrell Evans 2.50 6.00
18 Fernando Arroyo 2.00 5.00
20 Garry Maddox 2.00 5.00
24 Dave Frost 2.00 5.00
26 Jorge Orta 2.00 5.00
28 John Urrea 2.00 5.00
31 Tom Seaver IA 7.50 15.00
35 Willie Aikens 2.00 5.00
37 Dan Graham 2.00 5.00
38 Charlie Lea 2.00 5.00
39 Lou Whitaker 3.00 8.00
40 Dave Parker 3.00 8.00
42 Rick Sofield 2.00 5.00
48 Bobby Castillo 2.00 5.00
49 Alvis Woods 2.00 5.00
50 Buddy Bell 2.50 6.00
52 Larry Andersen 2.00 5.00
54 Ron Hassey 2.00 5.00
55 Rick Burleson 2.00 5.00
60 Tony Armas 2.00 5.00
64 Lynn Jones 2.00 5.00
65 Terry Kennedy 2.00 5.00
67 Rich Gale 2.00 5.00
68 Roy Howell 2.00 5.00
70 Tim Raines 4.00 10.00
71 Roy Lee Jackson 2.00 5.00
72 Rick Auerbach 2.00 5.00
73 Buddy Solomon 2.00 5.00
74 Bob Clark 2.00 5.00
77 Miguel Dilone 2.00 5.00
78 Doc Medich 2.00 5.00
80 Jim Palmer 10.00 20.00
81 Jim Palmer IA 7.50 15.00
84 Rennie Stennett 2.00 5.00
87 Matt Keough 2.00 5.00
88 Biff Pocoroba 2.00 5.00
89 Steve Henderson 2.00 5.00
90 Nolan Ryan 25.00 50.00
91 Carney Lansford 2.50 6.00
92 Brad Havens 2.00 5.00
94 Andy Hassler 2.00 5.00
95 Ozzie Smith 12.50 30.00
98 Terry Bulling 2.00 5.00
99 Barry Bonnell 2.00 5.00
100 Mike Schmidt 20.00 40.00
101 Mike Schmidt IA 10.00 20.00
105 Kirk Gibson 4.00 10.00
107 Wayne Krenchicki 2.00 5.00
109 Dave Revering 2.00 5.00
110 Carlton Fisk 7.50 15.00
111 Carlton Fisk IA 4.00 10.00
112 Billy Sample 2.00 5.00
113 Steve McCatty 2.00 5.00
114 Ken Landreaux 2.00 5.00
115 Gaylord Perry 7.50 15.00
116 Jim Wohlford 2.00 5.00
117 Rawly Eastwick 2.00 5.00
119 Joe Pittman 2.00 5.00
120 Gary Lucas 2.00 5.00
122 Jamie Easterly 2.00 5.00
123 Danny Goodwin 2.00 5.00
125 Danny Ainge 4.00 10.00
127 Lonnie Smith 2.00 5.00
128 Frank Pastore 2.00 5.00
130 Julio Cruz 2.00 5.00
131 Stan Bahnsen 2.00 5.00
132 Lee May 2.50 6.00
134 Dan Ford 2.00 5.00
135 Andy Rincon 2.00 5.00
136 Lenn Sakata 2.00 5.00
137 George Cappuzzello 2.00 5.00
138 Tony Pena 2.50 6.00
140 Ron LeFlore 2.00 5.00
143 Mookie Wilson 2.50 6.00
147 Denny Walling 2.00 5.00
150 Ted Simmons 2.50 6.00
155 Otto Velez 2.00 5.00
157 Steve Crawford 2.00 5.00
158 Brian Downing 2.50 6.00
159 Larry Biittner 2.00 5.00
160 Luis Tiant 3.00 8.00
170 Jim Bibby 2.00 5.00
172 Bill Gullickson 2.00 5.00
173 Jamie Quirk 2.00 5.00
174 Dave Ford 2.00 5.00
175 Jerry Mumphrey 2.00 5.00
177 John Ellis 2.00 5.00
178 Dyar Miller 2.00 5.00
179 Steve Garvey 4.00 10.00
181 Silvio Martinez 2.00 5.00
183 Mike Proly 2.00 5.00
185 Phil Niekro 7.50 15.00
189 Glenn Hoffman 2.00 5.00
190 J.R. Richard 2.50 6.00
192 Broderick Perkins 2.00 5.00
198 Chris Speier 2.00 5.00
200 George Brett 20.00 40.00
201 George Brett IA 12.50 25.00
204 Gary Roenicke 2.00 5.00
209 Gary Lavelle 2.00 5.00
210 Keith Hernandez 3.00 8.00
211 Dan Petry 2.00 5.00
212 Mario Mendoza 2.00 5.00
215 Mike Krukow 2.00 5.00
220 Manny Trillo 2.00 5.00
221 Jim Slaton 2.00 5.00
222 Butch Wynegar 2.00 5.00
223 Lloyd Moseby 2.00 5.00
224 Bruce Bochte 2.00 5.00
225 Mike Torrez 2.00 5.00
228 Sam Mejias 2.00 5.00
230 Willie Wilson 2.50 6.00
232 Terry Crowley 2.00 5.00
233 Duane Kuiper 2.00 5.00
234 Ron Hodges 2.00 5.00
235 Mike Easler 2.00 5.00
237 Rusty Kuntz 2.00 5.00
238 Kevin Saucier 2.00 5.00
239 Jon Matlack 2.00 5.00
240 Bucky Dent 2.50 6.00
241 Bucky Dent IA 2.50 6.00
245 Ken Reitz 2.00 5.00
247 Pedro Guerrero 2.50 6.00
251 Fred Lynn 2.50 6.00
255 Tony Perez 7.50 15.00
256 Tony Perez IA 4.00 10.00
257 Larry Harlow 2.00 5.00
258 Bo Diaz 2.00 5.00
259 Rodney Scott 2.00 5.00
260 Bruce Sutter 6.00 15.00
262 Doug Bair 2.00 5.00
264 Dan Quisenberry 2.00 5.00
265 Al Bumbry 2.00 5.00
267 Kurt Bevacqua 2.00 5.00
270 Rusty Staub 2.50 6.00
272 Bump Wills 2.00 5.00
275 Bob Watson 2.50 6.00
278 John Littlefield 2.00 5.00
280 Ben Oglivie 2.00 5.00
281 John Verhoeven 2.00 5.00
282 Ken Macha 2.00 5.00
283 Brian Allard 2.00 5.00
285 Sparky Lyle 2.50 6.00
287 Alan Bannister 2.00 5.00
288 Garry Templeton 2.50 6.00
289 Bob Stanley 2.00 5.00
290 Ken Singleton 2.50 6.00
297 Clint Hurdle 2.50 6.00
299 Steve Trout 2.00 5.00
300 Reggie Jackson 12.50 30.00
302 Doug Flynn 2.00 5.00
305 Don Sutton 7.50 15.00
307 Randy Bass 2.00 5.00
308 Charlie Moore 2.00 5.00
310 Mike Hargrove 2.50 6.00
312 Lenny Randle 2.00 5.00
315 Burt Hooton 2.00 5.00
317 Dick Ruthven 2.00 5.00
323 Bill Lee 2.00 5.00
324 Steve Dillard 2.00 5.00
325 Jose Cruz 2.50 6.00
328 Ed Farmer 2.00 5.00
329 U.L. Washington 2.00 5.00
330 Rick Wise 2.00 5.00
332 Don Robinson 2.00 5.00
334 Aurelio Rodriguez 2.00 5.00
335 Jim Sundberg 2.00 5.00
339 Mike Schmidt AS 7.50 15.00
340 Dave Concepcion AS 2.50 6.00
342 George Foster AS 2.00 5.00
343 Dave Parker AS 2.00 5.00
344 Gary Carter AS 7.50 15.00
345 Fernando Valenzuela AS 2.50 6.00
349 George Frazier 2.00 5.00
352 Dick Davis 2.00 5.00
354 Roberto Ramos 2.00 5.00
355 Dwight Evans 4.00 10.00
357 Butch Hobson 2.00 5.00
359 Jim Dwyer 2.00 5.00
360 Len Barker 2.00 5.00
363 Bob Molinaro 2.00 5.00
365 Bill Madlock 3.00 8.00
370 Mike Norris 2.00 5.00
380 Dave Stieb 2.00 5.00
382 Joe Simpson 2.00 5.00
385 Ken Forsch 2.00 5.00
387 Tom Veryzer 2.00 5.00
388 Joe Rudi 2.00 5.00
390 Eddie Murray 10.00 20.00
397 Ken Brett 2.00 5.00
398 Mike Squires 2.00 5.00
399 Pat Zachry 2.00 5.00
400 Johnny Bench 12.50 25.00
406 Al Holland 2.00 5.00
409 Don Cooper 2.00 5.00
412 Luis Leal 2.00 5.00
413 Dan Meyer 2.00 5.00
415 Don Baylor 3.00 8.00
417 Pat Kelly 2.00 5.00
419 Steve Stone 2.50 6.00
420 George Hendrick 2.00 5.00
421 Mark Clear 2.00 5.00
422 Cliff Johnson 2.00 5.00
423 Stan Papi 2.00 5.00
424 Bruce Benedict 2.00 5.00
425 John Candelaria 2.00 5.00
430 Vida Blue 2.50 6.00
440 Jeff Burroughs 2.00 5.00
442 Bruce Kison 2.00 5.00
443 Mark Wagner 2.00 5.00
445 Larry Parrish 2.00 5.00
446 Wayne Garland 2.00 5.00
448 Darrell Porter IA 2.00 5.00
450 Jack Morris 4.00 10.00
451 Ed Miller 2.00 5.00
459 Bruce Berenyi 2.00 5.00
460 Jack Clark 3.00 8.00
461 Rich Dotson 2.00 5.00
462 Dave Chalk 2.00 5.00
463 Jim Kern 2.00 5.00
464 Juan Bonilla 2.00 5.00
465 Lee Mazzilli 2.00 5.00
467 Mickey Hatcher 2.00 5.00
468 Floyd Bannister 2.00 5.00
472 Oscar Gamble 2.00 5.00
475 Alan Trammell 3.00 8.00
477 Steve Yeager 2.00 5.00
480 Steve Carlton 12.50 25.00
481 Steve Carlton IA 10.00 20.00
484 Ivan DeJesus 2.00 5.00
490 Dennis Eckersley 7.50 15.00
492 Joe Price 2.00 5.00
493 Chet Lemon 2.00 5.00
494 Hubie Brooks 2.00 5.00
495 Dennis Leonard 2.00 5.00
496 Johnny Grubb 2.00 5.00
498 Dave Bergman 2.00 5.00
499 Paul Mirabella 2.00 5.00
500 Rod Carew 12.50 25.00
501 Rod Carew IA 10.00 20.00
503 Julio Gonzalez 2.00 5.00
507 Terry Harper 2.00 5.00
510 Fernando Valenzuela 4.00 10.00
511 Ruppert Jones 2.00 5.00
512 Jerry Dybzinski 2.00 5.00
515 Larry Bowa 2.50 6.00
518 Garth Iorg 2.00 5.00
519 Glenn Adams 2.00 5.00
520 Mike Flanagan 2.00 5.00
521 Bill Almon 2.00 5.00
523 Gary Gray 2.00 5.00
524 Tom Hausman 2.00 5.00
532 Toby Harrah 2.00 5.00
534 Dave McKay 2.00 5.00
536 Rafael Ramirez 2.00 5.00
540 Andre Dawson 4.00 10.00
541 Barry Evans 2.00 5.00
542 Ned Yost 2.50 6.00
543 Bill Robinson 2.00 5.00
547 Rod Carew AS 7.50 15.00
548 Willie Randolph AS 3.00 8.00
549 George Brett AS 12.50 25.00
550 Bucky Dent AS 2.00 5.00
551 Reggie Jackson AS 10.00 20.00
552 Ken Singleton AS 2.00 5.00
553 Dave Winfield AS 7.50 15.00
554 Carlton Fisk AS 7.50 15.00
555 Scott McGregor AS 2.00 5.00
556 Jack Morris AS 2.50 6.00
557 Rich Gossage AS 2.50 6.00
560 Doug Corbett 2.00 5.00
563 Ross Baumgarten 2.00 5.00
564 Doug DeCinces 2.50 6.00
565 Jackson Todd 2.00 5.00
567 Bob Babcock 2.00 5.00
568 Joe Pettini 2.00 5.00
569 Willie Randolph 3.00 8.00
573 Rick Waits 2.00 5.00
574 Mike Ramsey 2.00 5.00
575 Al Cowens 2.00 5.00
579 Rick Mahler 2.00 5.00
580 Bobby Bonds 2.50 6.00
581 Ron Reed 2.00 5.00
582 Luis Pujols 2.00 5.00
585 Rollie Fingers 7.50 15.00
588 Dale Berra 2.00 5.00
590 Al Oliver 2.50 6.00
594 Renie Martin 2.00 5.00
600 Dave Winfield 10.00 20.00
601 Sid Monge 2.00 5.00
602 Freddie Patek 2.00 5.00
603 Richie Hebner 2.00 5.00
608 Jerry Royster 2.00 5.00
610 Rickey Henderson 30.00 60.00
611 Joe Niekro 2.50 6.00
612 Gary Ward 2.00 5.00
613 Jim Gantner 2.00 5.00
615 Bob Boone 2.50 6.00
616 Bob Boone IA 2.50 6.00
622 Dennis Lamp 2.00 5.00
624 Fergie Jenkins 7.50 15.00
625 Hal McRae 2.50 6.00
626 Randy Jones 2.00 5.00
627 Enos Cabell 2.00 5.00
629 Johnny Wockenfuss 2.00 5.00
630 Joe Charboneau 2.50 6.00
632 Bryan Clark 2.00 5.00
635 Ron Davis 2.00 5.00
637 Rick Camp 2.00 5.00
640 Cesar Cedeno 2.50 6.00
645 Frank White 2.50 6.00
646 Frank White IA 2.00 5.00
648 Jose Morales 2.00 5.00
649 Ken Clay 2.00 5.00
654 Jim Morrison 2.00 5.00
655 Joel Youngblood 2.00 5.00
656 Eddie Whitson 2.00 5.00
661 Dave Concepcion IA 2.00 5.00
663 Hector Cruz 2.00 5.00
664 Dan Spillner 2.00 5.00
665 Jim Clancy 2.00 5.00
668 Dale Murphy 4.00 10.00
669 Larry Milbourne 2.00 5.00
670 Steve Kemp 2.00 5.00
672 Bob Knepper 2.00 5.00
675 Cecil Cooper 2.50 6.00
677 Alfredo Griffin 2.00 5.00
678 Tom Paciorek 2.00 5.00
684 Harold Baines 3.00 8.00
685 Bert Blyleven 4.00 10.00
686 Gary Allenson 2.00 5.00
690 Dave Kingman 2.50 6.00
691 Dan Schatzeder 2.00 5.00
694 Dave Wehrmeister 2.00 5.00
695 Warren Cromartie 2.00 5.00
700 George Foster 2.50 6.00
702 Steve Renko 2.00 5.00
704 Mickey Rivers 2.50 6.00
705 Mickey Rivers IA 2.00 5.00
706 Barry Foote 2.00 5.00
707 Mark Bomback 2.00 5.00
708 Gene Richards 2.00 5.00
710 Jerry Reuss 2.50 6.00
713 Del Unser 2.00 5.00
715 Willie Stargell 7.50 15.00
716 Willie Stargell IA 7.50 15.00
718 Charlie Hough 2.50 6.00
720 Greg Luzinski 2.50 6.00
721 Greg Luzinski IA 2.50 6.00
722 Jerry Martin 2.00 5.00
724 Dave Rosello 2.00 5.00
725 Amos Otis 2.00 5.00
730 Gary Carter 10.00 20.00
735 Rudy May 2.00 5.00
737 Reggie Cleveland 2.00 5.00
738 Dave Engle 2.00 5.00
739 Joey McLaughlin 2.00 5.00
740 Davey Lopes 2.50 6.00
741 Davey Lopes IA 2.50 6.00
742 Dick Drago 2.00 5.00
743 John Stearns 2.00 5.00
745 Bake McBride 2.00 5.00
747 John Lowenstein 2.00 5.00
748 Marc Hill 2.00 5.00
751 Rick Honeycutt 2.00 5.00
753 Tom Brookens 2.00 5.00
754 Joe Morgan 7.50 15.00
757 Tom Underwood 2.00 5.00
760 Bill Buckner 2.50 6.00
761 Dave Smith 2.00 5.00
764 Steve Swisher 2.00 5.00
765 Gorman Thomas 2.00 5.00
767 Roy Smalley 2.00 5.00
768 Jerry Garvin 2.00 5.00
769 Richie Zisk 2.00 5.00
771 Rich Gossage IA 2.50 6.00
775 Bob Forsch 2.00 5.00
776 Mark Belanger 2.00 5.00
777 Tom Griffin 2.00 5.00
778 Kevin Hickey 2.00 5.00
780 Pete Rose 20.00 40.00
781 Pete Rose IA 12.50 30.00
782 Frank Taveras 2.00 5.00
784 Milt Wilcox 2.00 5.00
788 Woodie Fryman 2.00 5.00
790 Larry Gura 2.00 5.00
792 Frank Tanana 2.00 5.00

1982 Topps Traded

The cards in this 132-card set measure the standard size. These sets were shipped to hobby dealers in 100-ct cases. The 1982 Topps Traded or extended series is distinguished by a "T" printed after the number (located on the reverse). This was the first time Topps began a tradition of newly numbering (and alphabetizing) their traded series from 1T to 132T. All 131 player photos used in the set are completely new. Of this total, 112 individuals are seen in the uniform of their new team, 11 youngsters have been elevated to single card status from multi-player "Future Stars" cards, and eight more are entirely new to the 1982 Topps lineup. The backs are almost completely red in color with black print. There are no key Rookie Cards in this set. Although the Cal Ripken card is this set's most valuable card, it is not his Rookie Card since he had already been included in the 1982 regular set, albeit on a multi-player card.

COMP.FACT.SET (132) 75.00 150.00
1T Doyle Alexander .20 .50
2T Jesse Barfield 1.25 3.00
3T Ross Baumgarten .20 .50
4T Steve Bedrosian .60 1.50
5T Mark Belanger .20 .50
6T Kurt Bevacqua .20 .50
7T Tim Blackwell .20 .50
8T Vida Blue .40 1.00
9T Bob Boone .40 1.00
10T Larry Bowa .40 1.00
11T Dan Briggs .20 .50
12T Bobby Brown .20 .50
13T Tom Brunansky 1.25 3.00
14T Jeff Burroughs .20 .50
15T Enos Cabell .20 .50
16T Bill Campbell .20 .50
17T Bobby Castillo .20 .50
18T Bill Caudill .20 .50
19T Cesar Cedeno .40 1.00
20T Dave Collins .20 .50
21T Doug Corbett .20 .50
22T Al Cowens .20 .50
23T Chili Davis 1.25 3.00
24T Dick Davis .20 .50
25T Ron Davis .20 .50
26T Doug DeCinces .20 .50
27T Ivan DeJesus .20 .50
28T Bob Dernier .20 .50
29T Bo Diaz .20 .50
30T Roger Erickson .20 .50
31T Jim Essian .20 .50
32T Ed Farmer .20 .50
33T Doug Flynn .20 .50
34T Tim Foli .20 .50
35T Dan Ford .20 .50
36T George Foster .40 1.00
37T Dave Frost .20 .50
38T Rich Gale .20 .50
39T Ron Gardenhire .60 1.50
40T Ken Griffey .40 1.00
41T Greg Harris .20 .50
42T Von Hayes .60 1.50
43T Larry Herndon .20 .50
44T Kent Hrbek 1.25 3.00
45T Mike Ivie .20 .50
46T Grant Jackson .20 .50
47T Reggie Jackson .75 2.00
48T Ron Jackson .20 .50
49T Fergie Jenkins .40 1.00
50T Lamar Johnson .20 .50
51T Randy Johnson XRC .20 .50
52T Jay Johnstone .20 .50
53T Mick Kelleher .20 .50
54T Steve Kemp .20 .50
55T Junior Kennedy .20 .50
56T Jim Kern .20 .50
57T Ray Knight .40 1.00
58T Wayne Krenchicki .20 .50
59T Mike Krukow .20 .50
60T Duane Kuiper .20 .50
61T Mike LaCoss .20 .50
62T Chet Lemon .40 1.00
63T Sixto Lezcano .20 .50
64T Dave Lopes .40 1.00
65T Jerry Martin .20 .50
66T Renie Martin .20 .50
67T John Mayberry .20 .50
68T Lee Mazzilli .40 1.00
69T Bake McBride .40 1.00
70T Dan Meyer .20 .50
71T Larry Milbourne .20 .50
72T Eddie Milner .20 .50
73T Sid Monge .20 .50
74T John Montefusco .20 .50
75T Jose Morales .20 .50
76T Keith Moreland .20 .50
77T Jim Morrison .20 .50
78T Rance Mulliniks .20 .50
79T Steve Mura .20 .50
80T Gene Nelson .20 .50
81T Joe Nolan .20 .50
82T Dickie Noles .20 .50
83T Al Oliver .40 1.00
84T Jorge Orta .20 .50
85T Tom Paciorek .20 .50
86T Larry Parrish .20 .50
87T Jack Perconte .20 .50
88T Gaylord Perry .40 1.00
89T Rob Picciolo .20 .50
90T Joe Pittman .20 .50
91T Hosken Powell .20 .50
92T Mike Proly .20 .50
93T Greg Pryor .20 .50
94T Charlie Puleo .20 .50
95T Shane Rawley .20 .50
96T Johnny Ray .60 1.50
97T Dave Revering .20 .50
98T Cal Ripken 60.00 150.00
99T Allen Ripley .20 .50
100T Bill Robinson .20 .50
101T Aurelio Rodriguez .20 .50
102T Joe Rudi .40 1.00
103T Steve Sax 1.25 3.00
104T Dan Schatzeder .20 .50
105T Bob Shirley .20 .50
106T Eric Show XRC .60 1.50
107T Roy Smalley .20 .50
108T Lonnie Smith .20 .50
109T Ozzie Smith 6.00 15.00
110T Reggie Smith .40 1.00
111T Lary Sorensen .20 .50
112T Elias Sosa .20 .50
113T Mike Stanton .20 .50
114T Steve Stroughter .20 .50
115T Champ Summers .20 .50
116T Rick Sutcliffe .40 1.00
117T Frank Tanana .40 1.00
118T Frank Taveras .20 .50
119T Garry Templeton .40 1.00
120T Alex Trevino .20 .50
121T Jerry Turner .20 .50
122T Ed VandeBerg .20 .50
123T Tom Veryzer .20 .50
124T Ron Washington XRC .40 1.00
125T Bob Watson .20 .50
126T Dennis Werth .20 .50
127T Eddie Whitson .20 .50
128T Rob Wilfong .20 .50
129T Bump Wills .20 .50
130T Gary Woods .20 .50
131T Butch Wynegar .20 .50
132T Checklist: 1-132 .20 .50

1983 Topps

The cards in this 792-card set measure the standard size. Cards were primarily issued in 15-card wax packs and 51-card rack packs. The wax packs had 15 cards in each pack with an 30 cent SRP and were packed 36 packs to a box and 20 boxes to a case. Each player card front features a large action shot with a small cameo portrait at bottom right. There are special series for AL and NL All Stars (386-407), League Leaders (701-708), and Record Breakers (1-6). In addition, there are 34 "Super Veteran" (SV) cards and six numbered checklist cards. The Super Veteran cards are oriented horizontally and show two pictures of the featured player, a recent picture and a picture showing the player as a rookie. The team cards are actually Team Leader (TL) cards picturing the batting and pitching leader for that team with a checklist back. Notable Rookie Cards include Wade Boggs, Tony Gwynn and Ryne Sandberg. In each wax pack a game card was included which included prizes all the way up to a trip and tickets to the World Series. Card prizes possible from these cards included the 1983 Topps League Leaders sheet as well as with enough run accumulation, ordering of a part of the 1983 Topps Mail-Away glossy set. The factory sets were available in JC Penney's Christmas Catalog for $15.99.

COMPLETE SET (792) 30.00 80.00
1 Tony Armas RB .10 .30
2 Rickey Henderson RB .50 1.25
3 Greg Minton RB .05 .15
4 Lance Parrish RB .05 .15
5 Manny Trillo RB .05 .15
6 John Wathan RB .05 .15
7 Gene Richards .05 .15
8 Steve Balboni .05 .15
9 Joey McLaughlin .05 .15
10 Gorman Thomas .10 .30
11 Billy Gardner MG .05 .15
12 Paul Mirabella .05 .15
13 Larry Herndon .05 .15
14 Frank LaCorte .05 .15
15 Ron Cey .10 .30
16 George Vukovich .05 .15
17 Kent Tekulve .05 .15
18 Kent Tekulve SV .05 .15
19 Oscar Gamble .05 .15
20 Carlton Fisk .25 .60
21 Orioles TL .25 .60
Murray
Palmer
22 Randy Martz .05 .15
23 Mike Heath .05 .15
24 Steve Mura .05 .15
25 Hal McRae .10 .30
26 Jerry Royster .05 .15
27 Doug Corbett .05 .15
28 Bruce Bochte .05 .15
29 Randy Jones .05 .15
30 Jim Rice .10 .30
31 Bill Gullickson .05 .15
32 Dave Dergman .05 .15
33 Jack O'Connor .05 .15
34 Paul Householder .05 .15
35 Rollie Fingers .10 .30
36 Rollie Fingers SV .05 .15
37 Darrell Johnson MG .05 .15
38 Tim Flannery .05 .15
39 Terry Puhl .05 .15
40 Fernando Valenzuela .10 .30
41 Jerry Turner .05 .15
42 Dale Murray .05 .15
43 Bob Dernier .05 .15
44 Don Robinson .05 .15
45 John Mayberry .05 .15
46 Richard Dotson .05 .15
47 Dave McKay .05 .15
48 Lary Sorensen .05 .15
49 Willie McGee RC 1.00 2.50
50 Bob Horner UER .10 .30
51 Cubs TL .05 .15
F.Jenkins
52 Onix Concepcion .05 .15
53 Mike Witt .05 .15
54 Jim Maler .05 .15
55 Mookie Wilson .10 .30
56 Chuck Rainey .05 .15
57 Tim Blackwell .05 .15
58 Al Holland .05 .15
59 Benny Ayala .05 .15
60 Johnny Bench .50 1.25
61 Johnny Bench SV .25 .60
62 Bob McClure .05 .15
63 Rick Monday .10 .30
64 Bill Stein .05 .15
65 Jack Morris .10 .30
66 Bob Lillis MG .05 .15
67 Sal Butera .05 .15
68 Eric Show RC .30 .75
69 Lee Lacy .05 .15
70 Steve Carlton .25 .60

1983 Topps

Card	Low	High
71 Steve Carlton SV	.10	.30
72 Tom Paciorek	.05	.15
73 Allen Ripley	.05	.15
74 Julio Gonzalez	.05	.15
75 Amos Otis	.10	.30
76 Rick Mahler	.05	.15
77 Hosken Powell	.05	.15
78 Bill Caudill	.05	.15
79 Mick Kelleher	.05	.15
80 George Foster	.10	.30
81 J.Mumphrey D.Righetti TL	.10	.30
82 Bruce Hurst	.05	.15
83 Ryne Sandberg RC	10.00	25.00
84 Milt May	.05	.15
85 Ken Singleton	.10	.30
86 Tom Hume	.05	.15
87 Joe Rudi	.10	.30
88 Jim Gantner	.05	.15
89 Leon Roberts	.05	.15
90 Jerry Reuss	.05	.15
91 Larry Milbourne	.05	.15
92 Mike LaCoss	.05	.15
93 John Castino	.05	.15
94 Dave Edwards	.05	.15
95 Alan Trammell	.10	.30
96 Dick Howser MG	.05	.15
97 Ross Baumgarten	.05	.15
98 Vance Law	.05	.15
99 Dickie Noles	.05	.15
100 Pete Rose	1.50	4.00
101 Pete Rose SV	.50	1.25
102 Dave Beard	.05	.15
103 Darrell Porter	.05	.15
104 Bob Walk	.05	.15
105 Don Baylor	.10	.30
106 Gene Nelson	.05	.15
107 Mike Jorgensen	.05	.15
108 Glenn Hoffman	.05	.15
109 Luis Leal	.05	.15
110 Ken Griffey	.10	.30
111 Montreal Expos TL BA: Al Oliver ERA: Steve Roger	.10	.30
112 Bob Shirley	.05	.15
113 Ron Roenicke	.05	.15
114 Jim Slaton	.05	.15
115 Chili Davis	.10	.30
116 Dave Schmidt	.05	.15
117 Alan Knicely	.05	.15
118 Chris Welsh	.05	.15
119 Tom Brookens	.05	.15
120 Len Barker	.05	.15
121 Mickey Hatcher	.05	.15
122 Jimmy Smith	.05	.15
123 George Frazier	.05	.15
124 Marc Hill	.05	.15
125 Leon Durham	.05	.15
126 Joe Torre MG	.10	.30
127 Preston Hanna	.05	.15
128 Mike Ramsey	.05	.15
129 Checklist: 1-132	.10	.30
130 Dave Stieb	.10	.30
131 Ed Ott	.05	.15
132 Todd Cruz	.05	.15
133 Jim Barr	.05	.15
134 Hubie Brooks	.05	.15
135 Dwight Evans	.25	.60
136 Willie Aikens	.05	.15
137 Woodie Fryman	.05	.15
138 Rick Dempsey	.05	.15
139 Bruce Berenyi	.05	.15
140 Willie Randolph	.10	.30
141 Indians TL BA: Toby Harrah ERA: Rick Sutcliffe/	.10	.30
142 Mike Caldwell	.05	.15
143 Joe Pettini	.05	.15
144 Mark Wagner	.05	.15
145 Don Sutton	.10	.30
146 Don Sutton SV	.05	.15
147 Rick Leach	.05	.15
148 Dave Roberts	.05	.15
149 Johnny Ray	.05	.15
150 Bruce Sutter	.25	.60
151 Bruce Sutter SV	.10	.30
152 Jay Johnstone	.05	.15
153 Jerry Koosman	.10	.30
154 Johnnie LeMaster	.05	.15
155 Dan Quisenberry	.05	.15
156 Billy Martin MG	.25	.60
157 Steve Bedrosian	.05	.15
158 Rob Wilfong	.05	.15
159 Mike Stanton	.05	.15
160 Dave Kingman	.10	.30
161 Dave Kingman SV	.05	.15
162 Mark Clear	.05	.15
163 Cal Ripken	4.00	10.00
164 David Palmer	.05	.15
165 Dan Driessen	.05	.15
166 John Pacella	.05	.15
167 Mark Brouhard	.05	.15
168 Juan Eichelberger	.05	.15
169 Doug Flynn	.05	.15
170 Steve Howe	.05	.15
171 Giants TL Joe Morgan	.10	.30
172 Vern Ruhle	.05	.15
173 Jim Morrison	.05	.15
174 Jerry Ujdur	.05	.15
175 Bo Diaz	.05	.15
176 Dave Righetti	.10	.30
177 Harold Baines	.10	.30
178 Luis Tiant	.10	.30
179 Luis Tiant SV	.05	.15
180 Rickey Henderson	1.00	2.50
181 Terry Felton	.05	.15
182 Mike Fischlin	.05	.15
183 Ed VandeBerg	.05	.15
184 Bob Clark	.05	.15
185 Tim Lollar	.05	.15
186 Whitey Herzog MG	.10	.30
187 Terry Leach	.05	.15
188 Rick Miller	.05	.15
189 Dan Schatzeder	.05	.15
190 Cecil Cooper	.10	.30
191 Joe Price	.05	.15
192 Floyd Rayford	.05	.15
193 Harry Spilman	.05	.15
194 Cesar Geronimo	.05	.15
195 Bob Stoddard	.05	.15
196 Bill Fahey	.05	.15
197 Jim Eisenreich RC	.30	.75
198 Kiko Garcia	.05	.15
199 Marty Bystrom	.05	.15
200 Rod Carew	.25	.60
201 Rod Carew SV	.10	.30
202 Blue Jays TL BA: Damaso Garcia ERA: Dave Stieb/	.10	.30
203 Mike Morgan	.05	.15
204 Junior Kennedy	.05	.15
205 Dave Parker	.10	.30
206 Ken Oberkfell	.05	.15
207 Rick Camp	.05	.15
208 Dan Meyer	.05	.15
209 Mike Moore RC	.30	.75
210 Jack Clark	.10	.30
211 John Denny	.05	.15
212 John Stearns	.05	.15
213 Tom Burgmeier	.05	.15
214 Jerry White	.05	.15
215 Mario Soto	.10	.30
216 Tony LaRussa MG	.10	.30
217 Tim Stoddard	.05	.15
218 Roy Howell	.05	.15
219 Mike Armstrong	.05	.15
220 Dusty Baker	.10	.30
221 Joe Niekro	.05	.15
222 Damaso Garcia	.05	.15
223 John Montefusco	.05	.15
224 Mickey Rivers	.05	.15
225 Enos Cabell	.05	.15
226 Enrique Romo	.05	.15
227 Chris Bando	.05	.15
228 Joaquin Andujar	.10	.30
229 Phillies TL S.Carlton	.05	.15
230 Fergie Jenkins	.10	.30
231 Fergie Jenkins SV	.05	.15
232 Tom Brunansky	.10	.30
233 Wayne Gross	.05	.15
234 Larry Andersen	.05	.15
235 Claudell Washington	.05	.15
236 Steve Renko	.05	.15
237 Dan Norman	.05	.15
238 Bud Black RC	.30	.75
239 Dave Stapleton	.05	.15
240 Rich Gossage	.10	.30
241 Rich Gossage SV	.05	.15
242 Joe Nolan	.05	.15
243 Duane Walker RC	.05	.15
244 Dwight Bernard	.05	.15
245 Steve Sax	.10	.30
246 George Bamberger MG	.05	.15
247 Dave Smith	.05	.15
248 Bake McBride	.10	.30
249 Checklist: 133-264	.10	.30
250 Bill Buckner	.10	.30
251 Alan Wiggins	.05	.15
252 Luis Aguayo	.05	.15
253 Larry McWilliams	.05	.15
254 Rick Cerone	.05	.15
255 Gene Garber	.05	.15
256 Gene Garber SV	.05	.15
257 Jesse Barfield	.10	.30
258 Manny Castillo	.05	.15
259 Jeff Jones	.05	.15
260 Steve Kemp	.05	.15
261 Tigers TL BA: Larry Herndon ERA: Dan Petry/(Che	.10	.30
262 Ron Jackson	.05	.15
263 Renie Martin	.05	.15
264 Jamie Quirk	.05	.15
265 Joel Youngblood	.05	.15
266 Paul Boris	.05	.15
267 Terry Francona	.10	.30
268 Storm Davis RC	.30	.75
269 Ron Oester	.05	.15
270 Dennis Eckersley	.25	.60
271 Ed Romero	.05	.15
272 Frank Tanana	.10	.30
273 Mark Belanger	.05	.15
274 Terry Kennedy	.05	.15
275 Ray Knight	.10	.30
276 Gene Mauch MG	.05	.15
277 Rance Mulliniks	.05	.15
278 Kevin Hickey	.05	.15
279 Greg Gross	.05	.15
280 Bert Blyleven	.10	.30
281 Andre Robertson	.05	.15
282 R.Smith w Sandberg	.50	1.25
283 Reggie Smith SV	.05	.15
284 Jeff Lahti	.05	.15
285 Lance Parrish	.10	.30
286 Rick Langford	.05	.15
287 Bobby Brown	.05	.15
288 Joe Cowley	.05	.15
289 Jerry Dybzinski	.05	.15
290 Jeff Reardon	.10	.30
291 Bill Madlock John Candelaria TL	.10	.30
292 Craig Swan	.05	.15
293 Glenn Gulliver	.05	.15
294 Dave Engle	.05	.15
295 Jerry Remy	.05	.15
296 Greg Harris	.05	.15
297 Ned Yost	.05	.15
298 Floyd Chiffer	.05	.15
299 George Wright RC	.30	.75
300 Mike Schmidt	1.25	3.00
301 Mike Schmidt SV	.50	1.25
302 Ernie Whitt	.05	.15
303 Miguel Dilone	.05	.15
304 Dave Rucker	.05	.15
305 Larry Bowa	.10	.30
306 Tom Lasorda MG	.25	.60
307 Lou Piniella	.10	.30
308 Jesus Vega	.05	.15
309 Jeff Leonard	.05	.15
310 Greg Luzinski	.10	.30
311 Glenn Brummer	.05	.15
312 Brian Kingman	.05	.15
313 Gary Gray	.05	.15
314 Ken Dayley	.05	.15
315 Rick Burleson	.05	.15
316 Paul Splittorff	.05	.15
317 Gary Rajsich	.05	.15
318 John Tudor	.10	.30
319 Lenn Sakata	.05	.15
320 Steve Rogers	.10	.30
321 Brewers TL Robin Yount	.50	1.25
322 Dave Van Gorder	.05	.15
323 Luis DeLeon	.05	.15
324 Mike Marshall	.05	.15
325 Von Hayes	.05	.15
326 Garth Iorg	.05	.15
327 Bobby Castillo	.05	.15
328 Craig Reynolds	.05	.15
329 Randy Niemann	.05	.15
330 Buddy Bell	.10	.30
331 Mike Krukow	.05	.15
332 Glenn Wilson	.30	.75
333 Dave LaRoche	.05	.15
334 Dave LaRoche SV	.05	.15
335 Steve Henderson	.05	.15
336 Rene Lachemann MG	.05	.15
337 Tito Landrum	.05	.15
338 Bob Owchinko	.05	.15
339 Terry Harper	.05	.15
340 Larry Gura	.05	.15
341 Doug DeCinces	.05	.15
342 Atlee Hammaker	.05	.15
343 Bob Bailor	.05	.15
344 Roger LaFrancois	.05	.15
345 Jim Clancy	.05	.15
346 Joe Pittman	.05	.15
347 Sammy Stewart	.05	.15
348 Alan Bannister	.05	.15
349 Checklist: 265-396	.10	.30
350 Robin Yount	.75	2.00
351 Reds TL BA: Cesar Cedeno ERA: Mario Soto/(Check	.10	.30
352 Mike Scioscia	.10	.30
353 Steve Comer	.05	.15
354 Randy Johnson RC	.05	.15
355 Jim Bibby	.05	.15
356 Gary Woods	.05	.15
357 Len Matuszek	.05	.15
358 Jerry Garvin	.05	.15
359 Dave Collins	.05	.15
360 Nolan Ryan	2.50	6.00
361 Nolan Ryan SV	1.25	3.00
362 Bill Almon	.05	.15
363 John Stuper	.05	.15
364 Brett Butler	.10	.30
365 Dave Lopes	.10	.30
366 Dick Williams MG	.05	.15
367 Bud Anderson	.05	.15
368 Richie Zisk	.05	.15
369 Jesse Orosco	.05	.15
370 Gary Carter	.10	.30
371 Mike Richardt	.05	.15
372 Terry Crowley	.05	.15
373 Kevin Saucier	.05	.15
374 Wayne Krenchicki	.05	.15
375 Pete Vuckovich	.05	.15
376 Ken Landreaux	.05	.15
377 Lee May	.05	.15
378 Lee May SV	.05	.15
379 Guy Sularz	.05	.15
380 Ron Davis	.05	.15
381 Red Sox TL BA: Jim Rice ERA: Bob Stanley/(Check	.10	.30
382 Bob Knepper	.05	.15
383 Ozzie Virgil	.05	.15
384 Dave Dravecky RC	.60	1.50
385 Mike Easler	.05	.15
386 Rod Carew AS	.10	.30
387 Bob Grich AS	.05	.15
388 George Brett AS	.60	1.50
389 Robin Yount AS	.50	1.25
390 Reggie Jackson AS	.10	.30
391 Rickey Henderson AS	.50	1.25
392 Fred Lynn AS	.05	.15
393 Carlton Fisk AS	.10	.30
394 Pete Vuckovich AS	.05	.15
395 Larry Gura AS	.05	.15
396 Dan Quisenberry AS	.05	.15
397 Pete Rose AS	.25	.60
398 Manny Trillo AS	.05	.15
399 Mike Schmidt AS	.50	1.25
400 Dave Concepcion AS	.05	.15
401 Dale Murphy AS	.10	.30
402 Andre Dawson AS	.05	.15
403 Tim Raines AS	.05	.15
404 Gary Carter AS	.05	.15
405 Steve Rogers AS	.05	.15
406 Steve Carlton AS	.10	.30
407 Bruce Sutter AS	.10	.30
408 Rudy May	.05	.15
409 Marvis Foley	.05	.15
410 Phil Niekro	.10	.30
411 Phil Niekro SV	.05	.15
412 Rangers TL BA: Buddy Bell ERA: Charlie Hough/(C	.10	.30
413 Matt Keough	.05	.15
414 Julio Cruz	.05	.15
415 Bob Forsch	.05	.15
416 Joe Ferguson	.05	.15
417 Tom Hausman	.05	.15
418 Greg Pryor	.05	.15
419 Steve Crawford	.05	.15
420 Al Oliver	.10	.30
421 Al Oliver SV	.05	.15
422 George Cappuzzello	.05	.15
423 Tom Lawless	.05	.15
424 Jerry Augustine	.05	.15
425 Pedro Guerrero	.10	.30
426 Earl Weaver MG	.10	.30
427 Roy Lee Jackson	.05	.15
428 Champ Summers	.05	.15
429 Eddie Whitson	.05	.15
430 Kirk Gibson	.10	.30
431 Gary Gaetti RC	.60	1.50
432 Porfirio Altamirano	.05	.15
433 Dale Berra	.05	.15
434 Dennis Lamp	.05	.15
435 Tony Armas	.10	.30
436 Bill Campbell	.05	.15
437 Rick Sweet	.05	.15
438 Dave LaPoint	.05	.15
439 Rafael Ramirez	.05	.15
440 Ron Guidry	.10	.30
441 Astros TL BA: Ray Knight ERA: Joe Niekro/(Check	.10	.30
442 Brian Downing	.10	.30
443 Don Hood	.05	.15
444 Wally Backman	.05	.15
445 Mike Flanagan	.05	.15
446 Reid Nichols	.05	.15
447 Bryn Smith	.05	.15
448 Darrell Evans	.10	.30
449 Eddie Milner	.05	.15
450 Ted Simmons	.10	.30
451 Ted Simmons SV	.05	.15
452 Lloyd Moseby	.05	.15
453 Lamar Johnson	.05	.15
454 Bob Welch	.10	.30
455 Sixto Lezcano	.05	.15
456 Lee Elia MG	.05	.15
457 Milt Wilcox	.05	.15
458 Ron Washington RC	.10	.25
459 Ed Farmer	.05	.15
460 Roy Smalley	.05	.15
461 Steve Trout	.05	.15
462 Steve Nicosia	.05	.15
463 Gaylord Perry	.10	.30
464 Gaylord Perry SV	.05	.15
465 Lonnie Smith	.05	.15
466 Tom Underwood	.05	.15
467 Rufino Linares	.05	.15
468 Dave Goltz	.05	.15
469 Ron Gardenhire	.05	.15
470 Greg Minton	.05	.15
471 Kansas City Royals TL BA: Willie Wilson ERA: Vid	.10	.30
472 Gary Allenson	.05	.15
473 John Lowenstein	.05	.15
474 Ray Burris	.05	.15
475 Cesar Cedeno	.10	.30
476 Rob Picciolo	.05	.15
477 Tom Niedenfuer	.05	.15
478 Phil Garner	.10	.30
479 Charlie Hough	.10	.30
480 Toby Harrah	.10	.30
481 Scot Thompson	.05	.15
482 Tony Gwynn RC	10.00	25.00
483 Lynn Jones	.05	.15
484 Dick Ruthven	.05	.15
485 Omar Moreno	.05	.15
486 Clyde King MG	.05	.15
487 Jerry Hairston	.05	.15
488 Alfredo Griffin	.05	.15
489 Tom Herr	.05	.15
490 Jim Palmer	.10	.30
491 Jim Palmer SV	.05	.15
492 Paul Serna	.05	.15
493 Steve McCatty	.05	.15
494 Bob Brenly	.05	.15
495 Warren Cromartie	.05	.15
496 Tom Veryzer	.05	.15
497 Rick Sutcliffe	.10	.30
498 Wade Boggs RC	6.00	15.00
499 Jeff Little	.05	.15
500 Reggie Jackson	.25	.60
501 Reggie Jackson SV	.10	.30
502 Braves TL Murphy Niekro	.25	.60
503 Moose Haas	.05	.15
504 Don Werner	.05	.15
505 Garry Templeton	.10	.30
506 Jim Gott RC	.30	.75
507 Tony Scott	.05	.15
508 Tom Filer	.05	.15
509 Lou Whitaker	.10	.30
510 Tug McGraw	.10	.30
511 Tug McGraw SV	.05	.15
512 Doyle Alexander	.05	.15
513 Fred Stanley	.05	.15
514 Rudy Law	.05	.15
515 Gene Tenace	.10	.30
516 Bill Virdon MG	.05	.15
517 Gary Ward	.05	.15
518 Bill Laskey	.05	.15
519 Terry Bulling	.05	.15
520 Fred Lynn	.10	.30
521 Bruce Benedict	.05	.15
522 Pat Zachry	.05	.15
523 Carney Lansford	.10	.30
524 Tom Brennan	.05	.15
525 Frank White	.10	.30
526 Checklist: 397-528	.10	.30
527 Larry Biittner	.05	.15
528 Jamie Easterly	.05	.15
529 Tim Laudner	.05	.15
530 Eddie Murray	.50	1.25
531 A's TL Rickey Henderson	.50	1.25
532 Dave Stewart	.10	.30
533 Luis Salazar	.05	.15
534 John Butcher	.05	.15
535 Manny Trillo	.05	.15
536 John Wockenfuss	.05	.15
537 Rod Scurry	.05	.15
538 Danny Heep	.05	.15
539 Roger Erickson	.05	.15
540 Ozzie Smith	.75	2.00
541 Britt Burns	.05	.15
542 Jody Davis	.05	.15
543 Alan Fowlkes	.05	.15
544 Larry Whisenton	.05	.15
545 Floyd Bannister	.05	.15
546 Dave Garcia MG	.05	.15
547 Geoff Zahn	.05	.15
548 Brian Giles	.05	.15
549 Charlie Puleo	.05	.15
550 Carl Yastrzemski	.75	2.00
551 Carl Yastrzemski SV	.50	1.25
552 Tim Wallach	.10	.30
553 Dennis Martinez	.10	.30
554 Mike Vail	.05	.15
555 Steve Yeager	.10	.30
556 Willie Upshaw	.05	.15
557 Rick Honeycutt	.05	.15
558 Dickie Thon	.05	.15
559 Pete Redfern	.05	.15
560 Ron LeFlore	.10	.30
561 Cardinals TL BA: Lonnie Smith ERA: Joaquin Anduj	.10	.30
562 Dave Rozema	.05	.15
563 Juan Bonilla	.05	.15
564 Sid Monge	.05	.15
565 Bucky Dent	.10	.30
566 Manny Sarmiento	.05	.15
567 Joe Simpson	.05	.15
568 Willie Hernandez	.05	.15
569 Jack Perconte	.05	.15
570 Vida Blue	.10	.30
571 Mickey Klutts	.05	.15
572 Bob Watson	.05	.15
573 Andy Hassler	.05	.15
574 Glenn Adams	.05	.15
575 Neil Allen	.05	.15
576 Frank Robinson MG	.25	.60
577 Luis Aponte	.05	.15
578 David Green RC	.30	.75
579 Rich Dauer	.05	.15
580 Tom Seaver	.50	1.25
581 Tom Seaver SV	.10	.30
582 Marshall Edwards	.05	.15
583 Terry Forster	.10	.30
584 Dave Hostetler RC	.05	.15
585 Jose Cruz	.10	.30
586 Frank Viola RC	1.00	2.50
587 Ivan DeJesus	.05	.15
588 Pat Underwood	.05	.15
589 Alvis Woods	.05	.15
590 Tony Pena	.05	.15
591 White Sox TL BA: Greg Luzinski ERA: LaMarr Hoyt#	.10	.30
592 Shane Rawley	.05	.15
593 Broderick Perkins	.05	.15
594 Eric Rasmussen	.05	.15
595 Tim Raines	.10	.30
596 Randy Johnson	.05	.15
597 Mike Proly	.05	.15
598 Dwayne Murphy	.05	.15
599 Don Aase	.05	.15
600 George Brett	1.25	3.00
601 Ed Lynch	.05	.15
602 Rich Gedman	.05	.15
603 Joe Morgan	.10	.30
604 Joe Morgan SV	.05	.15
605 Gary Roenicke	.05	.15
606 Bobby Cox MG	.10	.30
607 Charlie Leibrandt	.05	.15
608 Don Money	.05	.15
609 Danny Darwin	.05	.15
610 Steve Garvey	.10	.30
611 Bert Roberge	.05	.15
612 Steve Swisher	.05	.15
613 Mike Ivie	.05	.15
614 Ed Glynn	.05	.15
615 Garry Maddox	.05	.15
616 Bill Nahorodny	.05	.15
617 Butch Wynegar	.05	.15
618 LaMarr Hoyt	.05	.15
619 Keith Moreland	.05	.15
620 Mike Norris	.05	.15
621 New York Mets TL BA: Mookie Wilson ERA: Craig Sw	.10	.30
622 Dave Edler	.05	.15
623 Luis Sanchez	.05	.15
624 Glenn Hubbard	.05	.15
625 Ken Forsch	.05	.15
626 Jerry Martin	.05	.15
627 Doug Bair	.05	.15
628 Julio Valdez	.05	.15
629 Charlie Lea	.05	.15
630 Paul Molitor	.10	.30
631 Tippy Martinez	.05	.15
632 Alex Trevino	.05	.15
633 Vicente Romo	.05	.15
634 Max Venable	.05	.15
635 Graig Nettles	.10	.30
636 Graig Nettles SV	.05	.15
637 Pat Corrales MG	.05	.15
638 Dan Petry	.05	.15
639 Art Howe	.05	.15
640 Andre Thornton	.05	.15
641 Billy Sample	.05	.15
642 Checklist: 529-660	.10	.30
643 Bump Wills	.05	.15
644 Joe Lefebvre	.05	.15
645 Bill Madlock	.10	.30
646 Jim Essian	.05	.15
647 Bobby Mitchell	.05	.15
648 Jeff Burroughs	.05	.15
649 Tommy Boggs	.05	.15
650 George Hendrick	.10	.30
651 Angels TL Rod Carew	.10	.30
652 Butch Hobson	.05	.15
653 Ellis Valentine	.05	.15
654 Bob Ojeda	.05	.15
655 Al Bumbry	.05	.15
656 Dave Frost	.05	.15
657 Mike Gates	.05	.15
658 Frank Pastore	.05	.15
659 Charlie Moore	.05	.15
660 Mike Hargrove	.05	.15
661 Bill Russell	.10	.30
662 Joe Sambito	.05	.15
663 Tom O'Malley	.05	.15
664 Bob Molinaro	.05	.15
665 Jim Sundberg	.10	.30
666 Sparky Anderson MG	.10	.30
667 Dick Davis	.05	.15
668 Larry Christenson	.05	.15
669 Mike Squires	.05	.15
670 Jerry Mumphrey	.05	.15
671 Lenny Faedo	.05	.15
672 Jim Kaat	.10	.30
673 Jim Kaat SV	.05	.15
674 Kurt Bevacqua	.05	.15
675 Jim Beattie	.05	.15
676 Biff Pocoroba	.05	.15
677 Dave Revering	.05	.15
678 Juan Beniquez	.05	.15
679 Mike Scott	.10	.30
680 Andre Dawson	.10	.30
681 Dodgers Leaders BA: Pedro Guerrero ERA: Fernando	.10	.30
682 Bob Stanley	.05	.15
683 Dan Ford	.05	.15
684 Rafael Landestoy	.05	.15
685 Lee Mazzilli	.10	.30
686 Randy Lerch	.05	.15
687 U.L. Washington	.05	.15
688 Jim Wohlford	.05	.15
689 Ron Hassey	.05	.15
690 Kent Hrbek	.10	.30
691 Dave Tobik	.05	.15
692 Denny Walling	.05	.15
693 Sparky Lyle	.10	.30
694 Sparky Lyle SV	.05	.15
695 Ruppert Jones	.05	.15
696 Chuck Tanner MG	.05	.15
697 Barry Foote	.05	.15
698 Tony Bernazard	.05	.15
699 Lee Smith	.25	.60
700 Keith Hernandez	.10	.30
701 Willie Wilson Al Oliver LL	.10	.3
702 Reggie Thomas Kingman LL	.10	.3
703 RBI Leaders AL: Hal McRae NL: Dale Murphy NL: A	.25	.6
704 R.Henderson T.Raines LL	.50	1.2
705 L.Hoyt S.Carlton LL	.10	.3
706 F.Bannister Carlton LL	.10	.3
707 Rick Sutcliffe Steve Rogers LL	.10	.3
708 Leading Firemen AL: Dan Quisenberry NL: Bruce Su	.10	.3
709 Jimmy Sexton	.05	.15
710 Willie Wilson	.10	.30
711 Mariners TL BA: Bruce Bochte ERA: Jim Beattie/(	.10	.30
712 Bruce Kison	.05	.15
713 Ron Hodges	.05	.15
714 Wayne Nordhagen	.05	.15
715 Tony Perez	.25	.60
716 Tony Perez SV	.10	.30
717 Scott Sanderson	.05	.15
718 Jim Dwyer	.05	.15
719 Rich Gale	.05	.15
720 Dave Concepcion	.10	.30
721 John Martin	.05	.15
722 Jorge Orta	.05	.15
723 Randy Moffitt	.05	.15
724 Johnny Grubb	.05	.15
725 Dan Spillner	.05	.15
726 Harvey Kuenn MG	.05	.15
727 Chet Lemon	.10	.30
728 Ron Reed	.05	.15
729 Jerry Morales	.05	.15
730 Jason Thompson	.05	.15
731 Al Williams	.05	.15
732 Dave Henderson	.05	.15
733 Buck Martinez	.05	.15
734 Steve Braun	.05	.15
735 Tommy John	.10	.30
736 Tommy John SV	.05	.15
737 Mitchell Page	.05	.15
738 Tim Foli	.05	.15
739 Rick Ownbey	.05	.15
740 Rusty Staub	.10	.30
741 Rusty Staub SV	.05	.15
742 Padres TL BA: Terry Kennedy ERA: Tim Lollar/(Ch	.10	.30
743 Mike Torrez	.05	.15
744 Brad Mills	.05	.15
745 Scott McGregor	.05	.15
746 John Wathan	.05	.15
747 Fred Breining	.05	.15
748 Derrel Thomas	.05	.15
749 Jon Matlack	.05	.15
750 Ben Oglivie	.10	.30
751 Brad Havens	.05	.15
752 Luis Pujols	.05	.15
753 Elias Sosa	.05	.15
754 Bill Robinson	.05	.15
755 John Candelaria	.05	.15
756 Russ Nixon MG	.05	.15
757 Rick Manning	.05	.15
758 Aurelio Rodriguez	.05	.15
759 Doug Bird	.05	.15
760 Dale Murphy	.25	.60
761 Gary Lucas	.05	.15
762 Cliff Johnson	.05	.15
763 Al Cowens	.05	.15
764 Pete Falcone	.05	.15
765 Bob Boone	.10	.30
766 Barry Bonnell	.05	.15
767 Duane Kuiper	.05	.15
768 Chris Speier	.05	.15
769 Checklist: 661-792	.10	.30
770 Dave Winfield	.10	.30
771 Twins TL BA: Kent Hrbek ERA: Bobby Castillo/(Ch	.10	.30
772 Jim Kern	.05	.15
773 Larry Hisle	.05	.15
774 Alan Ashby	.05	.15
775 Burt Hooton	.05	.15
776 Larry Parrish	.05	.15
777 John Curtis	.05	.15
778 Rich Hebner	.05	.15
779 Rick Waits	.05	.15
780 Gary Matthews	.10	.30
781 Rick Rhoden	.05	.15
782 Bobby Murcer	.10	.30
783 Bobby Murcer SV	.05	.15
784 Jeff Newman	.05	.15
785 Dennis Leonard	.05	.15
786 Ralph Houk MG	.05	.15
787 Dick Tidrow	.05	.15
788 Dane Iorg	.05	.15
789 Bryan Clark	.05	.15
790 Bob Grich	.10	.30
791 Gary Lavelle	.05	.15
792 Chris Chambliss	.10	.30
XX Game Insert Card	.02	.10

1983 Topps Glossy Send-Ins

e cards in this 40-card set measure the standard . The 1983 Topps "Collector's Edition" or "All- r Set" (popularly known as "Glossies") consists of or ballplayer picture cards with shiny, glazed faces. The player's name appears in small print side the frame line at bottom left. The backs ntain no biography or record and list only the set es, the player's name, team, position, and the card mber.

Card	Low	High
MPLETE SET (40)	6.00	15.00
Carl Yastrzemski	.40	1.25
Mookie Wilson	.07	.20
Andre Thornton	.02	.10
Keith Hernandez	.07	.20
Robin Yount	.40	1.25
Terry Kennedy	.02	.10
Dave Winfield	.40	1.25
Mike Schmidt	.60	1.50
Buddy Bell	.07	.20
Fernando Valenzuela	.10	.30
Rich Gossage	.07	.20
2 Bob Horner	.02	.10
3 Toby Harrah	.02	.10
4 Pete Rose	.60	1.50
5 Cecil Cooper	.07	.20
6 Dale Murphy	.20	.50
7 Carlton Fisk	.40	1.25
8 Ray Knight	.02	.10
9 Jim Palmer	.30	1.00
0 Gary Carter	.12	1.00
1 Richie Zisk	.02	.10
2 Dusty Baker	.07	.20
23 Willie Wilson	.02	.10
24 Bill Buckner	.07	.20
25 Dave Stieb	.02	.10
26 Bill Madlock	.02	.10
27 Lance Parrish	.07	.20
28 Nolan Ryan	2.00	5.00
29 Rod Carew	.40	1.00
30 Al Oliver	.07	.20
31 George Brett	1.00	2.50
32 Jack Clark	.02	.10
33 Rickey Henderson	.75	2.00
34 Dave Concepcion	.07	.20
35 Kent Hrbek	.07	.20
36 Steve Carlton	.30	1.00
37 Eddie Murray	.50	1.25
38 Ruppert Jones	.02	.10
39 Reggie Jackson	.40	1.25
40 Bruce Sutter	.30	.75

1983 Topps Traded

For the third year in a row, Topps issued a 132-card standard-size Traded (or extended) set featuring some of the year's top rookies and players who had changed teams during the year. The cards were available through hobby dealers only in factory set form and were printed in Ireland by the Topps affiliate in that country. The set is numbered alphabetically by player. The Darryl Strawberry card number 108 can be found with either one or two asterisks (in the lower left corner of the reverse). There is no difference in value for either version. The key (extended) Rookie Cards in this set include Julio Franco, Tony Phillips and Darryl Strawberry.

Card	Low	High
COMP.FACT.SET (132)	15.00	40.00
1T Neil Allen	.08	.25
2T Bill Almon	.08	.25
3T Joe Altobelli MG	.08	.25
4T Tony Armas	.40	1.00
5T Doug Bair	.08	.25
6T Steve Baker	.08	.25
7T Floyd Bannister	.08	.25
8T Don Baylor	.40	1.00
9T Tony Bernazard	.08	.25
10T Larry Biittner	.08	.25
11T Dann Bilardello	.08	.25
12T Doug Bird	.08	.25
13T Steve Boros MG	.08	.25
14T Greg Brock	.08	.25
15T Mike C. Brown	.08	.25
16T Tom Burgmeier	.08	.25
17T Randy Bush	.08	.25
18T Bert Campaneris	.40	1.00
19T Ron Cey	.40	1.00
20T Chris Codiroli	.08	.25
21T Dave Collins	.08	.25
22T Terry Crowley	.08	.25
23T Julio Cruz	.08	.25
24T Mike Davis	.08	.25
25T Frank DiPino	.08	.25
26T Bill Doran XRC	.40	1.00
27T Jerry Dybzinski	.08	.25
28T Jamie Easterly	.08	.25
29T Juan Eichelberger	.08	.25
30T Jim Essian	.08	.25
31T Pete Falcone	.08	.25
32T Mike Ferraro MG	.08	.25
33T Terry Forster	.40	1.00
34T Julio Franco XRC	3.00	8.00
35T Rich Gale	.08	.25
36T Kiko Garcia	.08	.25
37T Steve Garvey	.40	1.00
38T Johnny Grubb	.08	.25
39T Mel Hall XRC	.40	1.00
40T Von Hayes	.08	.25
41T Danny Heep	.08	.25
42T Steve Henderson	.08	.25
43T Keith Hernandez	.40	1.00
44T Leo Hernandez	.08	.25
45T Willie Hernandez	.08	.25
46T Al Holland	.08	.25
47T Frank Howard MG	.40	1.00
48T Bobby Johnson	.08	.25
49T Cliff Johnson	.08	.25
50T Odell Jones	.08	.25
51T Mike Jorgensen	.08	.25
52T Bob Kearney	.08	.25
53T Steve Kemp	.08	.25
54T Matt Keough	.08	.25
55T Ron Kittle XRC	.75	2.00
56T Mickey Klutts	.08	.25
57T Alan Knicely	.08	.25
58T Mike Krukow	.08	.25
59T Rafael Landestoy	.08	.25
60T Carney Lansford	.40	1.00
61T Joe Lefebvre	.08	.25
62T Bryan Little	.08	.25
63T Aurelio Lopez	.08	.25
64T Mike Madden	.08	.25
65T Rick Manning	.08	.25
66T Billy Martin MG	.75	2.00
67T Lee Mazzilli	.40	1.00
68T Andy McGaffigan	.08	.25
69T Craig McMurtry	.08	.25
70T John McNamara MG	.08	.25
71T Orlando Mercado	.08	.25
72T Larry Milbourne	.08	.25
73T Randy Moffitt	.08	.25
74T Sid Monge	.08	.25
75T Jose Morales	.08	.25
76T Omar Moreno	.08	.25
77T Joe Morgan	.40	1.00
78T Mike Morgan	.08	.25
79T Dale Murray	.08	.25
80T Jeff Newman	.08	.25
81T Pete O'Brien XRC	.40	1.00
82T Jorge Orta	.08	.25
83T Alejandro Pena XRC	.75	2.00
84T Pascual Perez	.08	.25
85T Tony Perez	.75	2.00
86T Broderick Perkins	.08	.25
87T Tony Phillips XRC	.75	2.00
88T Charlie Puleo	.08	.25
89T Pat Putnam	.08	.25
90T Jamie Quirk	.08	.25
91T Doug Rader MG	.08	.25
92T Chuck Rainey	.08	.25
93T Bobby Ramos	.08	.25
94T Gary Redus XRC	.40	1.00
95T Steve Renko	.08	.25
96T Leon Roberts	.08	.25
97T Aurelio Rodriguez	.08	.25
98T Dick Ruthven	.08	.25
99T Daryl Sconiers	.08	.25
100T Mike Scott	.40	1.00
101T Tom Seaver	.75	2.00
102T John Shelby	.08	.25
103T Bob Shirley	.08	.25
104T Joe Simpson	.08	.25
105T Doug Sisk	.08	.25
106T Mike Smithson	.08	.25
107T Elias Sosa	.08	.25
108T Darryl Strawberry XRC	20.00	50.00
109T Tom Tellmann	.08	.25
110T Gene Tenace	.40	1.00
111T Gorman Thomas	.40	1.00
112T Dick Tidrow	.08	.25
113T Dave Tobik	.08	.25
114T Wayne Tolleson	.08	.25
115T Mike Torrez	.08	.25
116T Manny Trillo	.08	.25
117T Steve Trout	.08	.25
118T Lee Tunnell	.08	.25
119T Mike Vail	.08	.25
120T Ellis Valentine	.08	.25
121T Tom Veryzer	.08	.25
122T George Vukovich	.08	.25
123T Rick Waits	.08	.25
124T Greg Walker	.40	1.00
125T Chris Welsh	.08	.25
126T Len Whitehouse	.08	.25
127T Eddie Whitson	.08	.25
128T Jim Wohlford	.08	.25
129T Matt Young XRC	.40	1.00
130T Joel Youngblood	.08	.25
131T Pat Zachry	.08	.25
132T Checklist 1T-132T	.08	.25

1984 Topps

The cards in this 792-card set measure the standard size. Cards were primarily distributed in 15-card wax packs and 54-card rack packs. For the second year in a row, Topps utilized a dual picture on the front of the card. A portrait is shown in a square insert and an action shot is featured in the main photo. Card numbers 1-6 feature 1983 Highlights (HL), cards 131-138 depict League Leaders, card numbers 386-407 feature All-Stars, and card numbers 701-718 feature active Major League career leaders in various statistical categories. Each team leader (TL) card features the team's leading hitter and pitcher pictured on the front with a team checklist back. There are six numerical checklist cards in the set. The player cards feature team logos in the upper right corner of the reverse. The key Rookie Cards in this set are Don Mattingly and Darryl Strawberry. Topps tested a special send-in offer in Michigan and a few other states whereby collectors could obtain direct from Topps ten cards of their choice. Needless to say most people ordered the key (most valuable) players necessitating the printing of a special sheet to keep up with the demand. The special sheet had five cards of Darryl Strawberry, three cards of Don Mattingly, etc. The test was apparently a failure in Topps' eyes as they have never tried it again.

Card	Low	High
COMPLETE SET (792)	20.00	50.00
1 Steve Carlton HL	.08	.25
2 Rickey Henderson HL	.25	.60
3 Dan Quisenberry HL	.05	.15
Sets save record		
4 N.Ryan	.40	1.00
Carlton		
Perry HL		
5 Dave Righetti&	.08	.25
Bob Forsch&		
and Mike Warren HL/(		
6 J.Bench	.15	.40
G.Perry		
C.Yaz HL		
7 Gary Lucas	.05	.15
8 Don Mattingly RC	10.00	25.00
9 Jim Gott	.05	.15
10 Robin Yount	.40	1.00
11 Minnesota Twins TL	.08	.25
Kent Hrbek		
Ken Schrom/(Check		
12 Billy Sample	.05	.15
13 Scott Holman	.05	.15
14 Tom Brookens	.08	.25
15 Burt Hooton	.05	.15
16 Omar Moreno	.05	.15
17 John Denny	.05	.15
18 Dale Berra	.05	.15
19 Ray Fontenot	.05	.15
20 Greg Luzinski	.08	.25
21 Joe Altobelli MG	.05	.15
22 Bryan Clark	.05	.15
23 Keith Moreland	.05	.15
24 John Martin	.05	.15
25 Glenn Hubbard	.05	.15
26 Bud Black	.05	.15
27 Daryl Sconiers	.05	.15
28 Frank Viola	.15	.40
29 Danny Heep	.05	.15
30 Wade Boggs	.60	1.50
31 Andy McGaffigan	.05	.15
32 Bobby Ramos	.05	.15
33 Tom Burgmeier	.05	.15
34 Eddie Milner	.05	.15
35 Don Sutton	.08	.25
36 Denny Walling	.05	.15
37 Texas Rangers TL	.08	.25
Buddy Bell		
Rick Honeycutt/(Che		
38 Luis DeLeon	.05	.15
39 Garth Iorg	.05	.15
40 Dusty Baker	.08	.25
41 Tony Bernazard	.05	.15
42 Johnny Grubb	.05	.15
43 Ron Reed	.05	.15
44 Jim Morrison	.05	.15
45 Jerry Mumphrey	.05	.15
46 Ray Smith	.05	.15
47 Rudy Law	.05	.15
48 Julio Franco	.08	.25
49 John Stuper	.05	.15
50 Chris Chambliss	.08	.25
51 Jim Frey MG	.05	.15
52 Paul Splittorff	.05	.15
53 Juan Beniquez	.05	.15
54 Jesse Orosco	.05	.15
55 Dave Concepcion	.08	.25
56 Gary Allenson	.05	.15
57 Dan Schatzeder	.05	.15
58 Max Venable	.05	.15
59 Sammy Stewart	.05	.15
60 Paul Molitor	.08	.25
61 Chris Codiroli	.05	.15
62 Dave Hostetler	.05	.15
63 Ed VandeBerg	.05	.15
64 Mike Scioscia	.08	.25
65 Kirk Gibson	.25	.60
66 Astros TL	.40	1.00
Nolan Ryan		
67 Gary Ward	.05	.15
68 Luis Salazar	.05	.15
69 Rod Scurry	.05	.15
70 Gary Matthews	.08	.25
71 Leo Hernandez	.05	.15
72 Mike Squires	.05	.15
73 Jody Davis	.05	.15
74 Jerry Martin	.05	.15
75 Bob Forsch	.05	.15
76 Alfredo Griffin	.05	.15
77 Brett Butler	.08	.25
78 Mike Torrez	.05	.15
79 Rob Wilfong	.05	.15
80 Steve Rogers	.08	.25
81 Billy Martin MG	.15	.40
82 Doug Bird	.05	.15
83 Richie Zisk	.05	.15
84 Lenny Faedo	.05	.15
85 Atlee Hammaker	.05	.15
86 John Shelby	.05	.15
87 Frank Pastore	.05	.15
88 Rob Picciolo	.05	.15
89 Mike Smithson	.05	.15
90 Pedro Guerrero	.08	.25
91 Dan Spillner	.05	.15
92 Lloyd Moseby	.05	.15
93 Bob Knepper	.05	.15
94 Mario Ramirez	.05	.15
95 Aurelio Lopez	.08	.25
96 Kansas City Royals TL	.08	.25
Hal McRae		
Larry Gura/(Che		
97 LaMarr Hoyt	.05	.15
98 Steve Nicosia	.05	.15
99 Craig Lefferts RC	.05	.15
100 Reggie Jackson	.15	.40
101 Porfirio Altamirano	.05	.15
102 Ken Oberkfell	.05	.15
103 Dwayne Murphy	.05	.15
104 Ken Dayley	.05	.15
105 Tony Armas	.08	.25
106 Tim Stoddard	.05	.15
107 Ned Yost	.05	.15
108 Randy Moffitt	.05	.15
109 Brad Wellman	.05	.15
110 Ron Guidry	.08	.25
111 Bill Virdon MG	.05	.15
112 Tom Niedenfuer	.05	.15
113 Kelly Paris	.05	.15
114 Checklist 1-132	.08	.25
115 Andre Thornton	.05	.15
116 George Bjorkman	.05	.15
117 Tom Veryzer	.05	.15
118 Charlie Hough	.08	.25
119 John Wockenfuss	.05	.15
120 Keith Hernandez	.08	.25
121 Pat Sheridan	.05	.15
122 Cecilio Guante	.05	.15
123 Butch Wynegar	.05	.15
124 Damaso Garcia	.05	.15
125 Britt Burns	.05	.15
126 Braves TL	.15	.40
Dale Murphy		
127 Mike Madden	.05	.15
128 Rick Manning	.05	.15
129 Bill Laskey	.05	.15
130 Ozzie Smith	.40	1.00
131 W.Boggs	.25	.60
B.Madlock LL		
132 Mike Schmidt	.25	.60
J.Rice LL		
133 D.Murphy	.15	.40
Coop		
Rice LL		
134 T.Raines	.25	.60
R.Henderson LL		
135 John Denny	.25	.60
LaMarr Hoyt LL		
136 S.Carlton	.08	.25
J.Morris LL		
137 A.Hammaker	.08	.25
R.Honeycutt LL		
138 Al Holland	.08	.25
Dan Quisenberry LL		
139 Bert Campaneris	.08	.25
140 Storm Davis	.05	.15
141 Pat Corrales MG	.05	.15
142 Rich Gale	.05	.15
143 Jose Morales	.05	.15
144 Brian Harper RC	.15	.40
145 Gary Lavelle	.05	.15
146 Ed Romero	.05	.15
147 Dan Petry	.08	.25
148 Joe Lefebvre	.05	.15
149 Jon Matlack	.05	.15
150 Dale Murphy	.15	.40
151 Steve Trout	.05	.15
152 Glenn Brummer	.05	.15
153 Dick Tidrow	.05	.15
154 Dave Henderson	.08	.25
155 Frank White	.08	.25
156 A's TL	.25	.60
Rickey Henderson		
157 Gary Gaetti	.15	.40
158 John Curtis	.05	.15
159 Darryl Cias	.05	.15
160 Mario Soto	.08	.25
161 Junior Ortiz	.05	.15
162 Bob Ojeda	.05	.15
163 Lorenzo Gray	.05	.15
164 Scott Sanderson	.05	.15
165 Ken Singleton	.08	.25
166 Jamie Nelson	.05	.15
167 Marshall Edwards	.05	.15
168 Juan Bonilla	.05	.15
169 Larry Parrish	.05	.15
170 Jerry Reuss	.05	.15
171 Frank Robinson MG	.15	.40
172 Frank DiPino	.05	.15
173 Marvell Wynne	.15	.40
174 Juan Berenguer	.05	.15
175 Graig Nettles	.08	.25
176 Lee Smith	.08	.25
177 Jerry Hairston	.05	.15
178 Bill Krueger RC	.05	.15
179 Buck Martinez	.05	.15
180 Manny Trillo	.05	.15
181 Roy Thomas	.05	.15
182 Darryl Strawberry RC	1.25	3.00
183 Al Williams	.05	.15
184 Mike O'Berry	.05	.15
185 Sixto Lezcano	.05	.15
186 Cardinal TL	.08	.25
Lonnie Smith		
John Stuper/(Checklist		
187 Luis Aponte	.05	.15
188 Bryan Little	.05	.15
189 Tim Conroy	.05	.15
190 Ben Oglivie	.08	.25
191 Mike Boddicker	.05	.15
192 Nick Esasky	.05	.15
193 Darrell Brown	.05	.15
194 Domingo Ramos	.05	.15
195 Jack Morris	.08	.25
196 Don Slaught	.08	.25
197 Garry Hancock	.05	.15
198 Bill Doran RC*	.15	.40
199 Willie Hernandez	.05	.15
200 Andre Dawson	.08	.25
201 Bruce Kison	.05	.15
202 Bobby Cox MG	.08	.25
203 Matt Keough	.05	.15
204 Bobby Meacham	.05	.15
205 Greg Minton	.05	.15
206 Andy Van Slyke RC	.60	1.50
207 Donnie Moore	.05	.15
208 Jose Oquendo RC	.15	.40
209 Manny Sarmiento	.05	.15
210 Joe Morgan	.08	.25
211 Rick Sweet	.05	.15
212 Broderick Perkins	.05	.15
213 Bruce Hurst	.05	.15
214 Paul Householder	.05	.15
215 Tippy Martinez	.05	.15
216 White Sox TL	.08	.25
C.Fisk		
217 Alan Ashby	.05	.15
218 Rick Waits	.05	.15
219 Joe Simpson	.05	.15
220 Fernando Valenzuela	.08	.25
221 Cliff Johnson	.05	.15
222 Rick Honeycutt	.05	.15
223 Wayne Krenchicki	.05	.15
224 Sid Monge	.05	.15
225 Lee Mazzilli	.08	.25
226 Juan Eichelberger	.05	.15
227 Steve Braun	.05	.15
228 John Rabb	.05	.15
229 Paul Owens MG	.05	.15
230 Rickey Henderson	.40	1.00
231 Gary Woods	.05	.15
232 Tim Wallach	.05	.15
233 Checklist 133-264	.08	.25
234 Rafael Ramirez	.05	.15
235 Matt Young RC	.15	.40
236 Ellis Valentine	.05	.15
237 John Castino	.05	.15
238 Reid Nichols	.05	.15
239 Jay Howell	.05	.15
240 Eddie Murray	.25	.60
241 Bill Almon	.05	.15
242 Alex Trevino	.05	.15
243 Pete Ladd	.05	.15
244 Candy Maldonado	.05	.15
245 Rick Sutcliffe	.08	.25
246 Mets TL	.08	.25
Tom Seaver		
247 Onix Concepcion	.05	.15
248 Bill Dawley	.05	.15
249 Jay Johnstone	.05	.15
250 Bill Madlock	.08	.25
251 Tony Gwynn	1.00	2.50
252 Larry Christenson	.05	.15
253 Jim Wohlford	.05	.15
254 Shane Rawley	.05	.15
255 Bruce Benedict	.05	.15
256 Dave Geisel	.05	.15
257 Julio Cruz	.05	.15
258 Luis Sanchez	.05	.15
259 Sparky Anderson MG	.08	.25
260 Scott McGregor	.05	.15
261 Bobby Brown	.05	.15
262 Tom Candiotti RC	.30	.75
263 Jack Fimple	.05	.15
264 Doug Frobel RC	.05	.15
265 Donnie Hill	.05	.15
266 Steve Lubratich	.05	.15
267 Carmelo Martinez	.05	.15
268 Jack O'Connor	.05	.15
269 Aurelio Rodriguez	.05	.15
270 Jeff Russell RC	.15	.40
271 Moose Haas	.05	.15
272 Rick Dempsey	.05	.15
273 Charlie Puleo	.05	.15
274 Rick Monday	.08	.25
275 Len Matuszek	.05	.15
276 Angels TL	.08	.25
Rod Carew		
277 Eddie Whitson	.05	.15
278 George Bell	.08	.25
279 Ivan DeJesus	.05	.15
280 Floyd Bannister	.05	.15
281 Larry Milbourne	.05	.15
282 Jim Barr	.05	.15
283 Larry Biittner	.05	.15
284 Howard Bailey	.05	.15
285 Darrell Porter	.05	.15
286 Lary Sorensen	.05	.15
287 Warren Cromartie	.05	.15
288 Jim Beattie	.05	.15
289 Randy Johnson	.05	.15
290 Dave Dravecky	.05	.15
291 Chuck Tanner MG	.05	.15
292 Tony Scott	.05	.15
293 Ed Lynch	.05	.15
294 U.L. Washington	.05	.15
295 Mike Flanagan	.05	.15
296 Jeff Newman	.05	.15
297 Bruce Berenyi	.05	.15
298 Jim Gantner	.05	.15
299 John Butcher	.05	.15
300 Pete Rose	.75	2.00
301 Frank LaCorte	.05	.15
302 Barry Bonnell	.05	.15
303 Marty Castillo	.05	.15
304 Warren Brusstar	.05	.15
305 Roy Smalley	.05	.15
306 Dodgers TL	.08	.25
Pedro Guerrero		
Bob Welch/(Checklist		
307 Bobby Mitchell	.05	.15
308 Ron Hassey	.05	.15
309 Tony Phillips RC	.30	.75
310 Willie McGee	.08	.25
311 Jerry Koosman	.08	.25
312 Jorge Orta	.05	.15
313 Mike Jorgensen	.05	.15
314 Orlando Mercado	.05	.15
315 Bob Grich	.08	.25
316 Mark Bradley	.05	.15
317 Greg Pryor	.05	.15
318 Bill Gullickson	.05	.15
319 Al Bumbry	.05	.15
320 Bob Stanley	.05	.15
321 Harvey Kuenn MG	.05	.15
322 Ken Schrom	.05	.15
323 Alan Knicely	.05	.15
324 Alejandro Pena RC*	.30	.75
325 Darrell Evans	.08	.25
326 Bob Kearney	.05	.15
327 Ruppert Jones	.05	.15
328 Vern Ruhle	.05	.15
329 Pat Tabler	.05	.15
330 John Candelaria	.05	.15
331 Bucky Dent	.08	.25
332 Kevin Gross RC	.15	.40
333 Larry Herndon	.08	.25
334 Chuck Rainey	.05	.15
335 Don Baylor	.08	.25
336 Seattle Mariners TL	.08	.25
Pat Putnam		
Matt Young/(Chec		
337 Kevin Hagen	.05	.15
338 Mike Warren	.05	.15
339 Roy Lee Jackson	.05	.15
340 Hal McRae	.08	.25
341 Dave Tobik	.05	.15
342 Tim Foli	.05	.15
343 Mark Davis	.05	.15
344 Rick Miller	.05	.15
345 Kent Hrbek	.08	.25
346 Kurt Bevacqua	.05	.15
347 Allan Ramirez	.05	.15
348 Toby Harrah	.08	.25
349 Bob L. Gibson RC	.05	.15
350 George Foster	.08	.25
351 Russ Nixon MG	.05	.15
352 Dave Stewart	.08	.25
353 Jim Anderson	.05	.15
354 Jeff Burroughs	.05	.15
355 Jason Thompson	.05	.15
356 Glenn Abbott	.05	.15
357 Ron Cey	.08	.25
358 Bob Dernier	.05	.15
359 Jim Acker	.05	.15
360 Willie Randolph	.08	.25
361 Dave Smith	.05	.15
362 David Green	.05	.15
363 Tim Laudner	.05	.15
364 Scott Fletcher	.05	.15
365 Steve Bedrosian	.05	.15
366 Padres TL	.08	.25
Terry Kennedy		
Dave Dravecky/(Checklis		
367 Jamie Easterly	.05	.15
368 Hubie Brooks	.05	.15
369 Steve McCatty	.05	.15
370 Tim Raines	.08	.25
371 Dave Gumpert	.05	.15
372 Gary Roenicke	.05	.15
373 Bill Scherrer	.05	.15
374 Don Money	.05	.15
375 Dennis Leonard	.05	.15
376 Dave Anderson RC	.05	.15
377 Danny Darwin	.05	.15
378 Bob Brenly	.05	.15
379 Checklist 265-396	.08	.25
380 Steve Garvey	.08	.25
381 Ralph Houk MG	.05	.15
382 Chris Nyman	.05	.15
383 Terry Puhl	.05	.15
384 Lee Tunnell	.05	.15
385 Tony Perez	.15	.40
386 George Hendrick AS	.05	.15
387 Johnny Ray AS	.05	.15
388 Mike Schmidt AS	.25	.60
389 Ozzie Smith AS	.25	.60
390 Tim Raines AS	.05	.15
391 Dale Murphy AS	.08	.25
392 Andre Dawson AS	.05	.15
393 Gary Carter AS	.05	.15
394 Steve Rogers AS	.05	.15
395 Steve Carlton AS	.08	.25
396 Jesse Orosco AS	.05	.15
397 Eddie Murray AS	.15	.40
398 Lou Whitaker AS	.05	.15
399 George Brett AS	.25	.60
400 Cal Ripken AS	.75	2.00
401 Jim Rice AS	.05	.15
402 Dave Winfield AS	.05	.15
403 Lloyd Moseby AS	.05	.15
404 Ted Simmons AS	.05	.15
405 LaMarr Hoyt AS	.05	.15
406 Ron Guidry AS	.05	.15
407 Dan Quisenberry AS	.05	.15
408 Lou Piniella	.08	.25
409 Juan Agosto	.05	.15
410 Claudell Washington	.05	.15
411 Houston Jimenez	.05	.15
412 Doug Rader MG	.05	.15
413 Spike Owen RC	.15	.40
414 Mitchell Page	.05	.15
415 Tommy John	.08	.25
416 Dane Iorg	.05	.15
417 Mike Armstrong	.05	.15
418 Ron Hodges	.05	.15
419 John Henry Johnson	.05	.15
420 Cecil Cooper	.08	.25
421 Charlie Lea	.05	.15
422 Jose Cruz	.08	.25
423 Mike Morgan	.05	.15
424 Dann Bilardello	.05	.15
425 Steve Howe	.05	.15
426 Orioles TL	.60	1.50
Cal Ripken		
427 Rick Leach	.05	.15
428 Fred Breining	.05	.15
429 Randy Bush	.05	.15
430 Rusty Staub	.08	.25
431 Chris Bando	.05	.15
432 Charles Hudson	.05	.15
433 Rich Hebner	.05	.15
434 Harold Baines	.08	.25
435 Neil Allen	.05	.15
436 Rick Peters	.05	.15
437 Mike Proly	.05	.15
438 Biff Pocoroba	.05	.15
439 Bob Stoddard	.05	.15
440 Steve Kemp	.05	.15
441 Bob Lillis MG	.05	.15
442 Byron McLaughlin	.05	.15
443 Benny Ayala	.05	.15
444 Steve Renko	.05	.15
445 Jerry Remy	.05	.15
446 Luis Pujols	.05	.15
447 Tom Brunansky	.05	.15
448 Ben Hayes	.05	.15
449 Joe Pettini	.05	.15
450 Gary Carter	.08	.25
451 Bob Jones	.05	.15
452 Chuck Porter	.05	.15
453 Willie Upshaw	.05	.15
454 Joe Beckwith	.05	.15
455 Terry Kennedy	.05	.15
456 Cubs TL	.05	.15
F.Jenkins		
457 Dave Rozema	.05	.15
458 Kiko Garcia	.05	.15
459 Kevin Hickey	.05	.15
460 Dave Winfield	.08	.25
461 Jim Maler	.05	.15
462 Lee Lacy	.05	.15
463 Dave Engle	.05	.15
464 Jeff A. Jones	.05	.15
465 Mookie Wilson	.08	.25
466 Gene Garber	.05	.15
467 Mike Ramsey	.05	.15
468 Geoff Zahn	.05	.15
469 Tom O'Malley	.05	.15
470 Nolan Ryan	1.25	3.00
471 Dick Howser MG	.05	.15
472 Mike G. Brown RC	.05	.15
473 Jim Dwyer	.05	.15
474 Greg Bargar	.05	.15
475 Gary Redus RC*	.15	.40
476 Tom Tellmann	.05	.15
477 Rafael Landestoy	.05	.15
478 Alan Bannister	.05	.15
479 Frank Tanana	.08	.25
480 Ron Kittle	.05	.15
481 Mark Thurmond	.05	.15
482 Enos Cabell	.05	.15
483 Fergie Jenkins	.08	.25
484 Ozzie Virgil	.05	.15
485 Rick Rhoden	.05	.15
486 D.Baylor	.08	.25
R.Guidry TL		

Card	Low	High
487 Ricky Adams	.05	.15
488 Jesse Barfield	.08	.25
489 Dave Von Ohlen	.05	.15
490 Cal Ripken	1.50	4.00
491 Bobby Castillo	.05	.15
492 Tucker Ashford	.05	.15
493 Mike Norris	.05	.15
494 Chili Davis	.08	.25
495 Rollie Fingers	.08	.25
496 Terry Francona	.08	.25
497 Bud Anderson	.05	.15
498 Rich Gedman	.05	.15
499 Mike Witt	.05	.15
500 George Brett	.60	1.50
501 Steve Henderson	.05	.15
502 Joe Torre MG	.08	.25
503 Elias Sosa	.05	.15
504 Mickey Rivers	.05	.15
505 Pete Vuckovich	.05	.15
506 Ernie Whitt	.05	.15
507 Mike LaCoss	.05	.15
508 Mel Hall	.08	.25
509 Brad Havens	.05	.15
510 Alan Trammell	.08	.25
511 Marty Bystrom	.05	.15
512 Oscar Gamble	.05	.15
513 Dave Beard	.05	.15
514 Floyd Rayford	.05	.15
515 Gorman Thomas	.08	.25
516 Montreal Expos TL	.08	.25
Al Oliver		
Charlie Lea/(Checkl		
517 John Moses	.05	.15
518 Greg Walker	.15	.40
519 Ron Davis	.05	.15
520 Bob Boone	.08	.25
521 Pete Falcone	.05	.15
522 Dave Bergman	.05	.15
523 Glenn Hoffman	.05	.15
524 Carlos Diaz	.05	.15
525 Willie Wilson	.08	.25
526 Ron Oester	.05	.15
527 Checklist 397-528	.08	.25
528 Mark Brouhard	.05	.15
529 Keith Atherton	.05	.15
530 Dan Ford	.05	.15
531 Steve Boros MG	.05	.15
532 Eric Show	.05	.15
533 Ken Landreaux	.05	.15
534 Pete O'Brien RC*	.15	.40
535 Bo Diaz	.05	.15
536 Doug Bair	.05	.15
537 Johnny Ray	.05	.15
538 Kevin Bass	.05	.15
539 George Frazier	.05	.15
540 George Hendrick	.08	.25
541 Dennis Lamp	.05	.15
542 Duane Kuiper	.05	.15
543 Craig McMurtry	.05	.15
544 Cesar Geronimo	.05	.15
545 Bill Buckner	.08	.25
546 Indians TL	.08	.25
Mike Hargrove		
Lary Sorensen/(Checkli		
547 Mike Moore	.05	.15
548 Ron Jackson	.05	.15
549 Walt Terrell	.05	.15
550 Jim Rice	.08	.25
551 Scott Ullger	.05	.15
552 Ray Burris	.05	.15
553 Joe Nolan	.05	.15
554 Ted Power	.05	.15
555 Greg Brock	.05	.15
556 Joey McLaughlin	.05	.15
557 Wayne Tolleson	.05	.15
558 Mike Davis	.05	.15
559 Mike Scott	.08	.25
560 Carlton Fisk	.15	.40
561 Whitey Herzog MG	.08	.25
562 Manny Castillo	.05	.15
563 Glenn Wilson	.08	.25
564 Al Holland	.05	.15
565 Leon Durham	.05	.15
566 Jim Bibby	.05	.15
567 Mike Heath	.05	.15
568 Pete Filson	.05	.15
569 Bake McBride	.08	.25
570 Dan Quisenberry	.05	.15
571 Bruce Bochy	.05	.15
572 Jerry Royster	.05	.15
573 Dave Kingman	.08	.25
574 Brian Downing	.08	.25
575 Jim Clancy	.05	.15
576 Giants TL	.08	.25
Jeff Leonard		
Atlee Hammaker/(Checklis		
577 Mark Clear	.05	.15
578 Lenn Sakata	.05	.15
579 Bob James	.05	.15
580 Lonnie Smith	.05	.15
581 Jose DeLeon RC	.15	.40
582 Bob McClure	.05	.15
583 Derrel Thomas	.05	.15
584 Dave Schmidt	.05	.15
585 Dan Driessen	.05	.15
586 Joe Niekro	.05	.15
587 Von Hayes	.05	.15
588 Milt Wilcox	.05	.15
589 Mike Easler	.05	.15
590 Dave Stieb	.08	.25
591 Tony LaRussa MG	.08	.25
592 Andre Robertson	.05	.15
593 Jeff Lahti	.05	.15
594 Gene Richards	.05	.15
595 Jeff Reardon	.08	.25
596 Ryne Sandberg	1.00	2.50
597 Rick Camp	.05	.15
598 Rusty Kuntz	.05	.15
599 Doug Sisk	.05	.15
600 Rod Carew	.15	.40
601 John Tudor	.08	.25
602 John Wathan	.05	.15
603 Renie Martin	.05	.15
604 John Lowenstein	.05	.15
605 Mike Caldwell	.05	.15
606 Blue Jays TL	.08	.25
Lloyd Moseby		
Dave Stieb/(Checklist		
607 Tom Hume	.05	.15
608 Bobby Johnson	.05	.15
609 Dan Meyer	.05	.15
610 Steve Sax	.05	.15
611 Chet Lemon	.08	.25
612 Harry Spilman	.05	.15
613 Greg Gross	.05	.15
614 Len Barker	.05	.15
615 Garry Templeton	.08	.25
616 Don Robinson	.05	.15
617 Rick Cerone	.05	.15
618 Dickie Noles	.05	.15
619 Jerry Dybzinski	.05	.15
620 Al Oliver	.08	.25
621 Frank Howard MG	.08	.25
622 Al Cowens	.05	.15
623 Ron Washington	.05	.15
624 Terry Harper	.05	.15
625 Larry Gura	.05	.15
626 Bob Clark	.05	.15
627 Dave LaPoint	.05	.15
628 Ed Jurak	.05	.15
629 Rick Langford	.05	.15
630 Ted Simmons	.08	.25
631 Dennis Martinez	.08	.25
632 Tom Foley	.05	.15
633 Mike Krukow	.05	.15
634 Mike Marshall	.05	.15
635 Dave Righetti	.08	.25
636 Pat Putnam	.05	.15
637 Phillies TL	.08	.25
Gary Matthews		
John Denny/(Checklist		
638 George Vukovich	.05	.15
639 Rick Lysander	.05	.15
640 Lance Parrish	.15	.40
641 Mike Richardt	.05	.15
642 Tom Underwood	.05	.15
643 Mike C. Brown	.05	.15
644 Tim Lollar	.05	.15
645 Tony Pena	.05	.15
646 Checklist 529-660	.08	.25
647 Ron Roenicke	.05	.15
648 Len Whitehouse	.05	.15
649 Tom Herr	.05	.15
650 Phil Niekro	.08	.25
651 John McNamara MG	.05	.15
652 Rudy May	.05	.15
653 Dave Stapleton	.05	.15
654 Bob Bailor	.05	.15
655 Amos Otis	.08	.25
656 Bryn Smith	.05	.15
657 Thad Bosley	.05	.15
658 Jerry Augustine	.05	.15
659 Duane Walker	.05	.15
660 Ray Knight	.08	.25
661 Steve Yeager	.08	.25
662 Tom Brennan	.05	.15
663 Johnnie LeMaster	.05	.15
664 Dave Stegman	.05	.15
665 Buddy Bell	.08	.25
666 Tigers TL	.08	.25
Morris		
Whitak		
667 Vance Law	.05	.15
668 Larry McWilliams	.05	.15
669 Dave Lopes	.08	.25
670 Rich Gossage	.08	.25
671 Jamie Quirk	.05	.15
672 Ricky Nelson	.05	.15
673 Mike Walters	.05	.15
674 Tim Flannery	.05	.15
675 Pascual Perez	.05	.15
676 Brian Giles	.05	.15
677 Doyle Alexander	.05	.15
678 Chris Speier	.05	.15
679 Art Howe	.05	.15
680 Fred Lynn	.08	.25
681 Tom Lasorda MG	.15	.40
682 Dan Morogiello	.05	.15
683 Marty Barrett RC	.15	.40
684 Bob Shirley	.05	.15
685 Willie Aikens	.05	.15
686 Joe Price	.05	.15
687 Roy Howell	.05	.15
688 George Wright	.05	.15
689 Mike Fischlin	.05	.15
690 Jack Clark	.08	.25
691 Steve Lake	.05	.15
692 Dickie Thon	.05	.15
693 Alan Wiggins	.05	.15
694 Mike Stanton	.05	.15
695 Lou Whitaker	.08	.25
696 Pirates TL	.08	.25
Bill Madlock		
Rick Rhoden/(Checklist		
697 Dale Murray	.05	.15
698 Marc Hill	.05	.15
699 Dave Rucker	.05	.15
700 Mike Schmidt	.60	1.50
701 Madlock	.25	.60
Rose		
Parker LL		
702 Rose	.25	.60
Staub		
Perez LL		
703 Schmidt	.25	.60
Perez		
Kingm LL		
704 Tony Perez	.08	.25
Rusty Staub		
Al Oliver LL		
705 Morgan	.15	.40
Cedeno		
Bowa LL		
706 S.Carlton	.08	.25
Jenk		
Seaver LL		
707 N.Ryan	.60	1.50
Seaver		
Carlton LL		
708 Seaver	.08	.25
Carlton		
Rog LL		
709 NL Active Save	.08	.25
Bruce Sutter		
Tug McGraw		
Gene Gar		
710 Carew	.15	.40
Brett		
Cooper LL		
711 Carew	.08	.25
Camp		
Reggie LL		
712 Reggie	.08	.25
Nettles		
Luz LL		
713 Reggie	.08	.25
Simmons		
Nett LL		
714 AL Active Steals	.08	.25
Bert Campaneris		
Dave Lopes		
Oma		
715 Palmer	.08	.25
Sutton		
John LL		
716 AL Active Strikeout	.15	.40
Don Sutton		
Bert Blyleven		
Je		
717 Jim Palmer	.08	.25
Fingers LL		
718 Fingers	.08	.25
Goose		
Quis LL		
719 Andy Hassler	.05	.15
720 Dwight Evans	.15	.40
721 Del Crandall MG	.05	.15
722 Bob Welch	.08	.25
723 Rich Dauer	.05	.15
724 Eric Rasmussen	.05	.15
725 Cesar Cedeno	.08	.25
726 Brewers TL	.08	.25
Ted Simmons		
Moose Haas/(Checklist on		
727 Joel Youngblood	.05	.15
728 Tug McGraw	.08	.25
729 Gene Tenace	.08	.25
730 Bruce Sutter	.15	.40
731 Lynn Jones	.05	.15
732 Terry Crowley	.05	.15
733 Dave Collins	.05	.15
734 Odell Jones	.05	.15
735 Rick Burleson	.05	.15
736 Dick Ruthven	.05	.15
737 Jim Essian	.05	.15
738 Bill Schroeder	.05	.15
739 Bob Watson	.05	.15
740 Tom Seaver	.25	.60
741 Wayne Gross	.05	.15
742 Dick Williams MG	.05	.15
743 Don Hood	.05	.15
744 Jamie Allen	.05	.15
745 Dennis Eckersley	.15	.40
746 Mickey Hatcher	.05	.15
747 Pat Zachry	.05	.15
748 Jeff Leonard	.05	.15
749 Doug Flynn	.05	.15
750 Jim Palmer	.08	.25
751 Charlie Moore	.05	.15
752 Phil Garner	.08	.25
753 Doug Gwosdz	.05	.15
754 Kent Tekulve	.05	.15
755 Garry Maddox	.05	.15
756 Reds TL	.08	.25
Ron Oester		
Mario Soto/(Checklist on bac		
757 Larry Bowa	.08	.25
758 Bill Stein	.05	.15
759 Richard Dotson	.05	.15
760 Bob Horner	.08	.25
761 John Montefusco	.05	.15
762 Rance Mulliniks	.05	.15
763 Craig Swan	.05	.15
764 Mike Hargrove	.05	.15
765 Ken Forsch	.05	.15
766 Mike Vail	.05	.15
767 Carney Lansford	.08	.25
768 Champ Summers	.05	.15
769 Bill Caudill	.05	.15
770 Ken Griffey	.08	.25
771 Billy Gardner MG	.05	.15
772 Jim Slaton	.05	.15
773 Todd Cruz	.05	.15
774 Tom Gorman	.05	.15
775 Dave Parker	.08	.25
776 Craig Reynolds	.05	.15
777 Tom Paciorek	.05	.15
778 Andy Hawkins	.05	.15
779 Jim Sundberg	.08	.25
780 Steve Carlton	.15	.40
781 Checklist 661-792	.08	.25
782 Steve Balboni	.05	.15
783 Luis Leal	.05	.15
784 Leon Roberts	.05	.15
785 Joaquin Andujar	.08	.25
786 Red Sox TL	.15	.40
Boggs		
Ojeda		
787 Bill Campbell	.05	.15
788 Milt May	.05	.15
789 Bert Blyleven	.08	.25
790 Doug DeCinces	.05	.15
791 Terry Forster	.08	.25
792 Bill Russell	.08	.25

1984 Topps Tiffany

COMP.FACT.SET (792)	200.00	400.00

*STARS: 3X TO 8X BASIC CARDS
*ROOKIES: 2.5X TO 6X BASIC CARDS
DISTRIBUTED ONLY IN FACTORY SET FORM
FACTORY SET PRICE IS FOR SEALED SETS

1984 Topps Glossy All-Stars

The cards in this 22-card set measure the standard size. Unlike the 1983 Topps Glossy set which was not distributed with its regular baseball cards, the 1984 Topps Glossy set was distributed as inserts in Topps Rak-Paks. The set features the nine American and National League All-Stars who started in the 1983 All Star game in Chicago. The managers and team captains (Yastrzemski and Bench) complete the set. The cards are numbered on the back and are ordered by position within league (AL: 1-11 and NL: 12-22).

Card	Low	High
COMPLETE SET (22)	2.00	5.00
1 Harvey Kuenn MG	.01	.05
2 Rod Carew	.20	.50
3 Manny Trillo	.01	.05
4 George Brett	.40	1.00
5 Robin Yount	.20	.50
6 Jim Rice	.02	.10
7 Fred Lynn	.02	.10
8 Dave Winfield	.20	.50
9 Ted Simmons	.02	.10
10 Dave Stieb	.01	.05
11 Carl Yastrzemski CAPT	.20	.50
12 Whitey Herzog MG	.01	.05
13 Al Oliver	.02	.10
14 Steve Sax	.02	.10
15 Mike Schmidt	.30	.75
16 Ozzie Smith	.40	1.00
17 Tim Raines	.05	.15
18 Andre Dawson	.08	.25
19 Dale Murphy	.08	.25
20 Gary Carter	.15	.40
21 Mario Soto	.01	.05
22 Johnny Bench CAPT	.20	.50

1984 Topps Glossy Send-Ins

The cards in this 40-card set measure the standard size. Similar to last year's glossy set, this set was issued as a bonus prize to Topps All-Star Baseball Game cards found in wax packs. Twenty-five bonus runs from the game cards were necessary to obtain a five card subset of the series. There were eight different subsets of five cards. The cards are numbered and the set contains 20 stars from each league.

Card	Low	High
COMPLETE SET (40)	5.00	12.00
1 Pete Rose	.50	1.25
2 Lance Parrish	.07	.20
3 Steve Rogers	.02	.10
4 Eddie Murray	.40	1.00
5 Johnny Ray	.02	.10
6 Rickey Henderson	.75	2.00
7 Atlee Hammaker	.02	.10
8 Wade Boggs	.60	1.50
9 Gary Carter	.50	1.25
10 Jack Morris	.07	.20
11 Darrell Evans	.07	.20
12 George Brett	1.00	2.50
13 Bob Horner	.02	.10
14 Ron Guidry	.07	.20
15 Nolan Ryan	2.00	5.00
16 Dave Winfield	.40	1.00
17 Ozzie Smith	.75	2.00
18 Ted Simmons	.07	.20
19 Bill Madlock	.02	.10
20 Tony Armas	.02	.10
21 Al Oliver	.07	.20
22 Jim Rice	.07	.20
23 George Hendrick	.02	.10
24 Dave Stieb	.02	.10
25 Pedro Guerrero	.02	.10
26 Rod Carew	.40	1.00
27 Steve Carlton	.40	1.00
28 Dave Righetti	.07	.20
29 Darryl Strawberry	.20	.50
30 Lou Whitaker	.07	.20
31 Dale Murphy	.10	.30
32 LaMarr Hoyt	.02	.10
33 Jesse Orosco	.07	.20
34 Cecil Cooper	.07	.20
35 Andre Dawson	.20	.50
36 Robin Yount	.50	1.25
37 Tim Raines	.10	.30
38 Dan Quisenberry	.02	.10
39 Mike Schmidt	.75	2.00
40 Carlton Fisk	.60	1.50

1984 Topps Traded

In what was now standard procedure, Topps issued its standard-size Traded (or extended) set for the fourth year in a row. Several of 1984's top rookies not contained in the regular set are pictured in the Traded set. Extended Rookie Cards in this set include Dwight Gooden, Jimmy Key, Mark Langston, Jose Rijo, and Bret Saberhagen. Again this year, the Topps affiliate in Ireland printed the cards, and the cards were available through hobby channels only in factory set form. The set numbering is in alphabetical order by player's name. The 132-card sets were shipped to dealers in 100-ct set cases. A few cards have been seen with a "grey" logo for Topps, these cards draw a significant multiplier of the regular Topps Traded cards, but are not yet known in sufficient quantity to price in our checklist.

Card	Low	High
COMP.FACT.SET (132)	12.50	30.00
1T Willie Aikens	.15	.40
2T Luis Aponte	.15	.40
3T Mike Armstrong	.15	.40
4T Bob Bailor	.15	.40
5T Dusty Baker	.25	.60
6T Steve Balboni	.15	.40
7T Alan Bannister	.15	.40
8T Dave Beard	.15	.40
9T Joe Beckwith	.15	.40
10T Bruce Berenyi	.15	.40
11T Dave Bergman	.15	.40
12T Tony Bernazard	.15	.40
13T Yogi Berra MG	.60	1.50
14T Barry Bonnell	.15	.40
15T Phil Bradley	.40	1.00
16T Fred Breining	.15	.40
17T Bill Buckner	.25	.60
18T Ray Burris	.15	.40
19T John Butcher	.15	.40
20T Brett Butler	.25	.60
21T Enos Cabell	.15	.40
22T Bill Campbell	.15	.40
23T Bill Caudill	.15	.40
24T Bob Clark	.15	.40
25T Bryan Clark	.15	.40
26T Jaime Cocanower	.15	.40
27T Ron Darling XRC*	.75	2.00
28T Alvin Davis XRC	.40	1.00
29T Ken Dayley	.15	.40
30T Jeff Dedmon	.15	.40
31T Bob Dernier	.15	.40
32T Carlos Diaz	.15	.40
33T Mike Easler	.15	.40
34T Dennis Eckersley	.40	1.00
35T Jim Essian	.15	.40
36T Darrell Evans	.25	.60
37T Mike Fitzgerald	.15	.40
38T Tim Foli	.15	.40
39T George Frazier	.15	.40
40T Rich Gale	.15	.40
41T Barbaro Garbey	.15	.40
42T Dwight Gooden XRC	10.00	25.00
43T Rich Gossage	.25	.60
44T Wayne Gross	.15	.40
45T Mark Gubicza XRC	.40	1.00
46T Jackie Gutierrez	.15	.40
47T Mel Hall	.25	.60
48T Toby Harrah	.25	.60
49T Ron Hassey	.15	.40
50T Rich Hebner	.15	.40
51T Willie Hernandez	.15	.40
52T Ricky Horton	.15	.40
53T Art Howe	.15	.40
54T Dane Iorg	.15	.40
55T Brook Jacoby	.40	1.00
56T Mike Jeffcoat XRC	.20	.50
57T Dave Johnson MG	.15	.40
58T Lynn Jones	.15	.40
59T Ruppert Jones	.15	.40
60T Mike Jorgensen	.15	.40
61T Bob Kearney	.15	.40
62T Jimmy Key XRC	.75	2.00
63T Dave Kingman	.25	.60
64T Jerry Koosman	.25	.60
65T Wayne Krenchicki	.15	.40
66T Rusty Kuntz	.15	.40
67T Rene Lachemann MG	.15	.40
68T Frank LaCorte	.15	.40
69T Dennis Lamp	.15	.40
70T Mark Langston XRC	.75	2.00
71T Rick Leach	.15	.40
72T Craig Lefferts	.20	.50
73T Gary Lucas	.15	.40
74T Jerry Martin	.15	.40
75T Carmelo Martinez	.15	.40
76T Mike Mason XRC	.20	.50
77T Gary Matthews	.25	.60
78T Andy McGaffigan	.15	.40
79T Larry Milbourne	.15	.40
80T Sid Monge	.15	.40
81T Jackie Moore MG	.15	.40
82T Joe Morgan	.25	.60
83T Graig Nettles	.25	.60
84T Phil Niekro	.25	.60
85T Ken Oberkfell	.15	.40
86T Mike O'Berry	.15	.40
87T Al Oliver	.25	.60
88T Jorge Orta	.15	.40
89T Amos Otis	.25	.60
90T Dave Parker	.25	.60
91T Tony Perez	.40	1.00
92T Gerald Perry	.40	1.00
93T Gary Pettis	.15	.40
94T Rob Picciolo	.15	.40
95T Vern Rapp MG	.15	.40
96T Floyd Rayford	.15	.40
97T Randy Ready XRC	.40	1.00
98T Ron Reed	.15	.40
99T Gene Richards	.15	.40
100T Jose Rijo XRC	.75	2.00
101T Jeff D. Robinson	.15	.40
102T Ron Romanick	.15	.40
103T Pete Rose	2.00	5.00
104T Bret Saberhagen XRC	1.50	4.00
105T Juan Samuel XRC*	.75	2.00
106T Scott Sanderson	.15	.40
107T Dick Schofield XRC*	.40	1.00
108T Tom Seaver	.60	1.50
109T Jim Slaton	.15	.40
110T Mike Smithson	.15	.40
111T Lary Sorensen	.15	.40
112T Tim Stoddard	.15	.40
113T Champ Summers	.15	.40
114T Jim Sundberg	.25	.60
115T Rick Sutcliffe	.25	.60
116T Craig Swan	.15	.40
117T Tim Teufel XRC*	.40	1.00
118T Derrel Thomas	.15	.40
119T Gorman Thomas	.25	.60
120T Alex Trevino	.15	.40
121T Manny Trillo	.15	.40
122T John Tudor	.25	.60
123T Tom Underwood	.15	.40
124T Mike Vail	.15	.40
125T Tom Waddell	.15	.40
126T Gary Ward	.15	.40
127T Curt Wilkerson	.15	.40
128T Frank Williams	.15	.40
129T Glenn Wilson	.25	.60
130T John Wockenfuss	.15	.40
131T Ned Yost	.15	.40
132T Checklist 1T-132T	.15	.40

1984 Topps Traded Tiffany

COMP.FACT.SET (132)	30.00	80.00

*STARS: .6X TO 1.5X BASIC CARDS
*ROOKIES: 1X TO 2.5X BASIC CARDS
DISTRIBUTED ONLY IN FACTORY SET FORM
FACTORY SET PRICE IS FOR SEALED SETS

1985 Topps

The 1985 Topps set contains 792 standard-size full-color cards. Cards were primarily distributed in 15-card wax packs, 51-card rack packs and factory (usually available through retail catalogs) sets. The wax packs were issued with an 35 cent SRP and were packaged 36 packs to a box and 20 boxes to a case. Manager cards feature the team checklist on the reverse. Full color card fronts feature both the Top[illegible] and team logos along with the team name, player[illegible] name, and his position. The first ten cards (1-10) [illegible] Record Breakers, cards 131-143 are Father and Sons, and cards 701 to 722 portray All-Star selections. Cards 271-282 represent "First Draft Picks" still active in professional baseball and car[illegible] 389-404 feature selected members of the 1984 U.[illegible] Olympic Baseball Team. Rookie Cards include Ro[illegible] Clemens, Eric Davis, Shawon Dunston, Dwight Gooden, Orel Hershiser, Jimmy Key, Mark Langst[illegible] Mark McGwire, Terry Pendleton, Kirby Puckett and Bret Saberhagen.

Card	Low	High
COMPLETE SET (792)	20.00	[illegible]
COMP.FACT.SET (792)	90.00	[illegible]
1 Carlton Fisk RB	.08	[illegible]
2 Steve Garvey RB	.05	[illegible]
3 Dwight Gooden RB	.25	[illegible]
4 Cliff Johnson RB	.05	[illegible]
5 Joe Morgan RB	.05	[illegible]
6 Pete Rose RB	.15	[illegible]
7 Nolan Ryan RB	.60	[illegible]
8 Juan Samuel RB	.05	[illegible]
9 Bruce Sutter RB	.05	[illegible]
10 Don Sutton RB	.05	[illegible]
11 Ralph Houk MG	.05	[illegible]
12 Dave Lopes	.08	[illegible]
13 Tim Lollar	.05	[illegible]
14 Chris Bando	.05	[illegible]
15 Jerry Koosman	.08	[illegible]
16 Bobby Meacham	.05	[illegible]
17 Mike Scott	.08	[illegible]
18 Mickey Hatcher	.05	[illegible]
19 George Frazier	.05	[illegible]
20 Chet Lemon	.08	[illegible]
21 Lee Tunnell	.05	.15
22 Duane Kuiper	.05	.15
23 Bret Saberhagen RC	.40	1.00
24 Jesse Barfield	.08	.25
25 Steve Bedrosian	.05	.15
26 Roy Smalley	.05	.15
27 Bruce Berenyi	.05	.15
28 Dann Bilardello	.05	.15
29 Odell Jones	.05	.15
30 Cal Ripken	1.00	2.50
31 Terry Whitfield	.05	.15
32 Chuck Porter	.05	.15
33 Tito Landrum	.05	.15
34 Ed Nunez	.05	.15
35 Graig Nettles	.08	.25
36 Fred Breining	.05	.15
37 Reid Nichols	.05	.15
38 Jackie Moore MG	.05	.15
39 John Wockenfuss	.05	.15
40 Phil Niekro	.08	.25
41 Mike Fischlin	.05	.15
42 Luis Sanchez	.05	.15
43 Andre David	.05	.15
44 Dickie Thon	.05	.15
45 Greg Minton	.05	.15
46 Gary Woods	.05	.15
47 Dave Rozema	.05	.15
48 Tony Fernandez	.08	.25
49 Butch Davis	.05	.15
50 John Candelaria	.05	.15
51 Bob Watson	.05	.15
52 Jerry Dybzinski	.05	.15
53 Tom Gorman	.05	.15
54 Cesar Cedeno	.08	.25
55 Frank Tanana	.08	.25
56 Jim Dwyer	.05	.15
57 Pat Zachry	.05	.15
58 Orlando Mercado	.05	.15
59 Rick Waits	.05	.15
60 George Hendrick	.08	.25
61 Curt Kaufman	.05	.15
62 Mike Ramsey	.05	.15
63 Steve McCatty	.05	.15
64 Mark Bailey	.05	.15
65 Bill Buckner	.08	.25
66 Dick Williams MG	.05	.15
67 Rafael Santana	.05	.15
68 Von Hayes	.05	.15
69 Jim Winn	.05	.15
70 Don Baylor	.08	.25
71 Tim Laudner	.05	.15
72 Rick Sutcliffe	.08	.25
73 Rusty Kuntz	.05	.15
74 Mike Krukow	.05	.15
75 Willie Upshaw	.05	.15
76 Alan Bannister	.05	.15
77 Joe Beckwith	.05	.15
78 Scott Fletcher	.05	.15
79 Rick Mahler	.05	.15
80 Keith Hernandez	.08	.25
81 Lenn Sakata	.05	.15
82 Joe Price	.05	.15
83 Charlie Moore	.05	.15
84 Spike Owen	.05	.15
85 Mike Marshall	.05	.15
86 Don Aase	.05	.15
87 David Green	.05	.15
88 Bryn Smith	.05	.15
89 Jackie Gutierrez	.05	.15
90 Rich Gossage	.08	.25
91 Jeff Burroughs	.05	.15
92 Paul Owens MG	.05	.15
93 Don Schulze	.05	.15
94 Toby Harrah	.08	.25
95 Jose Cruz	.08	.25
96 Johnny Ray	.05	.15
97 Pete Filson	.05	.15
98 Steve Lake	.05	.15

Card	Low	High
99 Milt Wilcox	.05	.15
100 George Brett	.60	1.50
101 Jim Acker	.05	.15
102 Tommy Dunbar	.05	.15
103 Randy Lerch	.05	.15
104 Mike Fitzgerald	.05	.15
105 Ron Kittle	.05	.15
106 Pascual Perez	.05	.15
107 Tom Foley	.05	.15
108 Darnell Coles	.05	.15
109 Gary Roenicke	.05	.15
110 Alejandro Pena	.05	.15
111 Doug DeCinces	.05	.15
112 Tom Tellmann	.05	.15
113 Tom Herr	.05	.15
114 Bob James	.05	.15
115 Rickey Henderson	.30	.75
116 Dennis Boyd	.05	.15
117 Greg Gross	.05	.15
118 Eric Show	.05	.15
119 Pat Corrales MG	.05	.15
120 Steve Kemp	.05	.15
121 Checklist: 1-132	.05	.15
122 Tom Brunansky	.05	.15
123 Dave Smith	.05	.15
124 Rich Hebner	.05	.15
125 Kent Tekulve	.05	.15
126 Ruppert Jones	.05	.15
127 Mark Gubicza RC*	.15	.40
128 Ernie Whitt	.05	.15
129 Gene Garber	.05	.15
130 Al Oliver	.08	.25
131 Buddy	.08	.25
Gus Bell FS		
132 Yogi	.25	.60
Dale Berra FS		
133 Bob	.05	.15
Ray Boone FS		
134 Terry	.08	.25
Tito Francona FS		
135 Terry	.05	.15
Bob Kennedy FS		
136 Jeff	.05	.15
Bill Kunkel FS		
137 Vance	.08	.25
Vern Law FS		
138 Dick	.05	.15
Dick Schofield FS		
139 Joel	.05	.15
Bob Skinner FS		
140 Roy	.05	.15
Roy Smalley FS		
141 Mike	.05	.15
Dave Stenhouse FS		
142 Steve	.05	.15
Dizzy Trout FS		
143 Ozzie	.05	.15
Ossie Virgil FS		
144 Ron Gardenhire	.05	.15
145 Alvin Davis RC*	.15	.40
146 Gary Redus	.05	.15
147 Bill Swaggerty	.05	.15
148 Steve Yeager	.08	.25
149 Dickie Noles	.05	.15
150 Jim Rice	.08	.25
151 Moose Haas	.05	.15
152 Steve Braun	.05	.15
153 Frank LaCorte	.05	.15
154 Angel Salazar	.05	.15
155 Yogi Berra MG/TC	.25	.60
156 Craig Reynolds	.05	.15
157 Tug McGraw	.08	.25
158 Pat Tabler	.05	.15
159 Carlos Diaz	.05	.15
160 Lance Parrish	.08	.25
161 Ken Schrom	.05	.15
162 Benny Distefano	.05	.15
163 Dennis Eckersley	.15	.40
164 Jorge Orta	.05	.15
165 Dusty Baker	.08	.25
166 Keith Atherton	.05	.15
167 Rufino Linares	.05	.15
168 Garth Iorg	.05	.15
169 Dan Spillner	.05	.15
170 George Foster	.08	.25
171 Bill Stein	.05	.15
172 Jack Perconte	.05	.15
173 Mike Young	.05	.15
174 Rick Honeycutt	.05	.15
175 Dave Parker	.08	.25
176 Bill Schroeder	.05	.15
177 Dave Von Ohlen	.05	.15
178 Miguel Dilone	.05	.15
179 Tommy John	.08	.25
180 Dave Winfield	.08	.25
181 Roger Clemens RC	6.00	15.00
182 Tim Flannery	.05	.15
183 Larry McWilliams	.05	.15
184 Carmen Castillo	.05	.15
185 Al Holland	.05	.15
186 Bob Lillis MG	.05	.15
187 Mike Walters	.05	.15
188 Greg Pryor	.05	.15
189 Warren Brusstar	.05	.15
190 Rusty Staub	.08	.25
191 Steve Nicosia	.05	.15
192 Howard Johnson	.08	.25
193 Jimmy Key RC	.30	.75
194 Dave Stegman	.05	.15
195 Glenn Hubbard	.05	.15
196 Pete O'Brien	.05	.15
197 Mike Warren	.05	.15
198 Eddie Milner	.05	.15
199 Dennis Martinez	.08	.25
200 Reggie Jackson	.15	.40
201 Burt Hooton	.05	.15
202 Gorman Thomas	.08	.25
203 Bob McClure	.05	.15
204 Art Howe	.05	.15
205 Steve Rogers	.08	.25
206 Phil Garner	.08	.25
207 Mark Clear	.05	.15
208 Champ Summers	.05	.15
209 Bill Campbell	.05	.15
210 Gary Matthews	.08	.25
211 Clay Christiansen	.05	.15
212 George Vukovich	.05	.15
213 Billy Gardner MG	.05	.15
214 John Tudor	.08	.25
215 Bob Brenly	.05	.15
216 Jerry Don Gleaton	.05	.15
217 Leon Roberts	.05	.15
218 Doyle Alexander	.05	.15
219 Gerald Perry	.05	.15
220 Fred Lynn	.08	.25
221 Ron Reed	.05	.15
222 Hubie Brooks	.05	.15
223 Tom Hume	.05	.15
224 Al Cowens	.05	.15
225 Mike Boddicker	.05	.15
226 Juan Beniquez	.05	.15
227 Danny Darwin	.05	.15
228 Dion James	.05	.15
229 Dave LaPoint	.05	.15
230 Gary Carter	.08	.25
231 Dwayne Murphy	.05	.15
232 Dave Beard	.05	.15
233 Ed Jurak	.05	.15
234 Jerry Narron	.05	.15
235 Garry Maddox	.05	.15
236 Mark Thurmond	.05	.15
237 Julio Franco	.08	.25
238 Jose Rijo RC	.30	.75
239 Tim Teufel	.05	.15
240 Dave Stieb	.08	.25
241 Jim Frey MG	.05	.15
242 Greg Harris	.05	.15
243 Barbaro Garbey	.05	.15
244 Mike Jones	.05	.15
245 Chili Davis	.08	.25
246 Mike Norris	.05	.15
247 Wayne Tolleson	.05	.15
248 Terry Forster	.08	.25
249 Harold Baines	.08	.25
250 Jesse Orosco	.05	.15
251 Brad Gulden	.05	.15
252 Dan Ford	.05	.15
253 Sid Bream RC	.15	.40
254 Pete Vuckovich	.05	.15
255 Lonnie Smith	.05	.15
256 Mike Stanton	.05	.15
257 Bryan Little	.05	.15
258 Mike C. Brown	.05	.15
259 Gary Allenson	.05	.15
260 Dave Righetti	.08	.25
261 Checklist: 133-264	.05	.15
262 Greg Booker	.05	.15
263 Mel Hall	.05	.15
264 Joe Sambito	.05	.15
265 Juan Samuel	.05	.15
266 Frank Viola	.08	.25
267 Henry Cotto RC	.05	.15
268 Chuck Tanner MG	.05	.15
269 Doug Baker	.05	.15
270 Dan Quisenberry	.08	.25
271 Tim Foli FDP	.05	.15
272 Jeff Burroughs FDP	.05	.15
273 Bill Almon FDP	.05	.15
274 Floyd Bannister FDP	.05	.15
275 Harold Baines FDP	.05	.15
276 Bob Horner FDP	.05	.15
277 Al Chambers FDP	.05	.15
278 Darryl Strawberry FDP	.15	.40
279 Mike Moore FDP	.05	.15
280 Shawon Dunston FDP RC	.30	.75
281 Tim Belcher FDP RC	.15	.40
282 Shawn Abner FDP RC	.05	.15
283 Fran Mullins	.05	.15
284 Marty Bystrom	.05	.15
285 Dan Driessen	.05	.15
286 Rudy Law	.05	.15
287 Walt Terrell	.05	.15
288 Jeff Kunkel	.05	.15
289 Tom Underwood	.05	.15
290 Cecil Cooper	.08	.25
291 Bob Welch	.08	.25
292 Brad Komminsk	.05	.15
293 Curt Young	.05	.15
294 Tom Nieto	.05	.15
295 Joe Niekro	.05	.15
296 Ricky Nelson	.05	.15
297 Gary Lucas	.05	.15
298 Marty Barrett	.05	.15
299 Andy Hawkins	.05	.15
300 Rod Carew	.15	.40
301 John Montefusco	.05	.15
302 Tim Corcoran	.05	.15
303 Mike Jeffcoat	.05	.15
304 Gary Gaetti	.08	.25
305 Dale Berra	.05	.15
306 Rick Reuschel	.08	.25
307 Sparky Anderson MG	.08	.25
308 John Wathan	.05	.15
309 Mike Witt	.05	.15
310 Manny Trillo	.05	.15
311 Jim Gott	.05	.15
312 Marc Hill	.05	.15
313 Dave Schmidt	.05	.15
314 Ron Oester	.05	.15
315 Doug Sisk	.05	.15
316 John Lowenstein	.05	.15
317 Jack Lazorko	.05	.15
318 Ted Simmons	.08	.25
319 Jeff Jones	.05	.15
320 Dale Murphy	.15	.40
321 Ricky Horton	.05	.15
322 Dave Stapleton	.05	.15
323 Andy McGaffigan	.05	.15
324 Bruce Bochy	.05	.15
325 John Denny	.05	.15
326 Kevin Bass	.05	.15
327 Brook Jacoby	.05	.15
328 Bob Shirley	.05	.15
329 Ron Washington	.05	.15
330 Leon Durham	.05	.15
331 Bill Laskey	.05	.15
332 Brian Harper	.05	.15
333 Willie Hernandez	.05	.15
334 Dick Howser MG	.05	.15
335 Bruce Benedict	.05	.15
336 Rance Mulliniks	.05	.15
337 Billy Sample	.05	.15
338 Britt Burns	.05	.15
339 Danny Heep	.05	.15
340 Robin Yount	.40	1.00
341 Floyd Rayford	.05	.15
342 Ted Power	.05	.15
343 Bill Russell	.08	.25
344 Dave Henderson	.05	.15
345 Charlie Lea	.05	.15
346 Terry Pendleton RC	.30	.75
347 Rick Langford	.05	.15
348 Bob Boone	.08	.25
349 Domingo Ramos	.05	.15
350 Wade Boggs	.25	.60
351 Juan Agosto	.05	.15
352 Joe Morgan	.08	.25
353 Julio Solano	.05	.15
354 Andre Robertson	.05	.15
355 Bert Blyleven	.08	.25
356 Dave Meier	.05	.15
357 Rich Bordi	.05	.15
358 Tony Pena	.05	.15
359 Pat Sheridan	.05	.15
360 Steve Carlton	.08	.25
361 Alfredo Griffin	.05	.15
362 Craig McMurtry	.05	.15
363 Ron Hodges	.05	.15
364 Richard Dotson	.05	.15
365 Danny Ozark MG	.05	.15
366 Todd Cruz	.05	.15
367 Keefe Cato	.05	.15
368 Dave Bergman	.05	.15
369 R.J. Reynolds	.05	.15
370 Bruce Sutter	.08	.25
371 Mickey Rivers	.05	.15
372 Roy Howell	.05	.15
373 Mike Moore	.05	.15
374 Brian Downing	.08	.25
375 Jeff Reardon	.08	.25
376 Jeff Newman	.05	.15
377 Checklist: 265-396	.05	.15
378 Alan Wiggins	.05	.15
379 Charles Hudson	.05	.15
380 Ken Griffey	.08	.25
381 Roy Smith	.05	.15
382 Denny Walling	.05	.15
383 Rick Lysander	.05	.15
384 Jody Davis	.05	.15
385 Jose DeLeon	.05	.15
386 Dan Gladden RC	.15	.40
387 Buddy Biancalana	.05	.15
388 Bert Roberge	.05	.15
389 Rod Dedeaux OLY CO RC	.08	.25
390 Sid Akins OLY RC	.05	.15
391 Flavio Alfaro OLY RC	.05	.15
392 Don August OLY RC	.05	.15
393 Scott Bankhead OLY RC	.05	.15
394 Bob Caffrey OLY RC	.05	.15
395 Mike Dunne OLY RC	.05	.15
396 Gary Green OLY RC	.05	.15
397 John Hoover OLY RC	.05	.15
398 Shane Mack OLY RC	.15	.40
399 John Marzano OLY RC	.05	.15
400 Oddibe McDowell OLY RC	.15	.40
401 Mark McGwire OLY RC	10.00	25.00
402 Pat Pacillo OLY RC	.05	.15
403 Cory Snyder OLY RC	.30	.75
404 Bill Swift OLY RC	.15	.40
405 Tom Veryzer	.05	.15
406 Len Whitehouse	.05	.15
407 Bobby Ramos	.05	.15
408 Sid Monge	.05	.15
409 Brad Wellman	.05	.15
410 Bob Horner	.08	.25
411 Bobby Cox MG	.08	.25
412 Bud Black	.05	.15
413 Vance Law	.05	.15
414 Gary Ward	.05	.15
415 Ron Darling UER	.08	.25
416 Wayne Gross	.05	.15
417 John Franco RC	.30	.75
418 Ken Landreaux	.05	.15
419 Mike Caldwell	.05	.15
420 Andre Dawson	.08	.25
421 Dave Rucker	.05	.15
422 Carney Lansford	.08	.25
423 Barry Bonnell	.05	.15
424 Al Nipper	.05	.15
425 Mike Hargrove	.05	.15
426 Vern Ruhle	.05	.15
427 Mario Ramirez	.05	.15
428 Larry Andersen	.05	.15
429 Rick Cerone	.05	.15
430 Ron Davis	.05	.15
431 U.L. Washington	.05	.15
432 Thad Bosley	.05	.15
433 Jim Morrison	.05	.15
434 Gene Richards	.05	.15
435 Dan Petry	.05	.15
436 Willie Aikens	.05	.15
437 Al Jones	.05	.15
438 Joe Torre MG	.08	.25
439 Junior Ortiz	.05	.15
440 Fernando Valenzuela	.08	.25
441 Duane Walker	.05	.15
442 Ken Forsch	.05	.15
443 George Wright	.05	.15
444 Tony Phillips	.05	.15
445 Tippy Martinez	.05	.15
446 Jim Sundberg	.08	.25
447 Jeff Lahti	.05	.15
448 Derrel Thomas	.05	.15
449 Phil Bradley	.15	.40
450 Steve Garvey	.08	.25
451 Bruce Hurst	.05	.15
452 John Castino	.05	.15
453 Tom Waddell	.05	.15
454 Glenn Wilson	.05	.15
455 Bob Knepper	.05	.15
456 Tim Foli	.05	.15
457 Cecilio Guante	.05	.15
458 Randy Johnson	.05	.15
459 Charlie Leibrandt	.05	.15
460 Ryne Sandberg	.50	1.25
461 Marty Castillo	.05	.15
462 Gary Lavelle	.05	.15
463 Dave Collins	.05	.15
464 Mike Mason RC	.05	.15
465 Bob Grich	.08	.25
466 Tony LaRussa MG	.08	.25
467 Ed Lynch	.05	.15
468 Wayne Krenchicki	.05	.15
469 Sammy Stewart	.05	.15
470 Steve Sax	.05	.15
471 Pete Ladd	.05	.15
472 Jim Essian	.05	.15
473 Tim Wallach	.05	.15
474 Kurt Kepshire	.05	.15
475 Andre Thornton	.05	.15
476 Jeff Stone RC	.05	.15
477 Bob Ojeda	.05	.15
478 Kurt Bevacqua	.05	.15
479 Mike Madden	.05	.15
480 Lou Whitaker	.08	.25
481 Dale Murray	.05	.15
482 Harry Spilman	.05	.15
483 Mike Smithson	.05	.15
484 Larry Bowa	.08	.25
485 Matt Young	.05	.15
486 Steve Balboni	.05	.15
487 Frank Williams	.05	.15
488 Joel Skinner	.05	.15
489 Bryan Clark	.05	.15
490 Jason Thompson	.05	.15
491 Rick Camp	.05	.15
492 Dave Johnson MG	.05	.15
493 Orel Hershiser RC	.75	2.00
494 Rich Dauer	.05	.15
495 Mario Soto	.08	.25
496 Donnie Scott	.05	.15
497 Gary Pettis UER	.05	.15
498 Ed Romero	.05	.15
499 Danny Cox	.05	.15
500 Mike Schmidt	.60	1.50
501 Dan Schatzeder	.05	.15
502 Rick Miller	.05	.15
503 Tim Conroy	.05	.15
504 Jerry Willard	.05	.15
505 Jim Beattie	.05	.15
506 Franklin Stubbs	.05	.15
507 Ray Fontenot	.05	.15
508 John Shelby	.05	.15
509 Milt May	.05	.15
510 Kent Hrbek	.08	.25
511 Lee Smith	.08	.25
512 Tom Brookens	.05	.15
513 Lynn Jones	.05	.15
514 Jeff Cornell	.05	.15
515 Dave Concepcion	.08	.25
516 Roy Lee Jackson	.05	.15
517 Jerry Martin	.05	.15
518 Chris Chambliss	.08	.25
519 Doug Rader MG	.05	.15
520 LaMarr Hoyt	.05	.15
521 Rick Dempsey	.05	.15
522 Paul Molitor	.08	.25
523 Candy Maldonado	.05	.15
524 Rob Wilfong	.05	.15
525 Darrell Porter	.05	.15
526 David Palmer	.05	.15
527 Checklist: 397-528	.05	.15
528 Bill Krueger	.05	.15
529 Rich Gedman	.05	.15
530 Dave Dravecky	.05	.15
531 Joe Lefebvre	.05	.15
532 Frank DiPino	.05	.15
533 Tony Bernazard	.05	.15
534 Brian Dayett	.05	.15
535 Pat Putnam	.05	.15
536 Kirby Puckett RC	6.00	15.00
537 Don Robinson	.05	.15
538 Keith Moreland	.05	.15
539 Aurelio Lopez	.05	.15
540 Claudell Washington	.05	.15
541 Mark Davis	.05	.15
542 Don Slaught	.05	.15
543 Mike Squires	.05	.15
544 Bruce Kison	.05	.15
545 Lloyd Moseby	.05	.15
546 Brent Gaff	.05	.15
547 Pete Rose MG/TC	.15	.40
548 Larry Parrish	.05	.15
549 Mike Scioscia	.08	.25
550 Scott McGregor	.05	.15
551 Andy Van Slyke	.15	.40
552 Chris Codiroli	.05	.15
553 Bob Clark	.05	.15
554 Doug Flynn	.05	.15
555 Bob Stanley	.05	.15
556 Sixto Lezcano	.05	.15
557 Len Barker	.05	.15
558 Carmelo Martinez	.05	.15
559 Jay Howell	.05	.15
560 Bill Madlock	.08	.25
561 Darryl Motley	.05	.15
562 Houston Jimenez	.05	.15
563 Dick Ruthven	.05	.15
564 Alan Ashby	.05	.15
565 Kirk Gibson	.08	.25
566 Ed VandeBerg	.05	.15
567 Joel Youngblood	.05	.15
568 Cliff Johnson	.05	.15
569 Ken Oberkfell	.05	.15
570 Darryl Strawberry	.25	.60
571 Charlie Hough	.08	.25
572 Tom Paciorek	.05	.15
573 Jay Tibbs	.05	.15
574 Joe Altobelli MG	.05	.15
575 Pedro Guerrero	.08	.25
576 Jaime Cocanower	.05	.15
577 Chris Speier	.05	.15
578 Terry Francona	.08	.25
579 Ron Romanick	.05	.15
580 Dwight Evans	.15	.40
581 Mark Wagner	.05	.15
582 Ken Phelps	.05	.15
583 Bobby Brown	.05	.15
584 Kevin Gross	.05	.15
585 Butch Wynegar	.05	.15
586 Bill Scherrer	.05	.15
587 Doug Frobel	.05	.15
588 Bobby Castillo	.05	.15
589 Bob Dernier	.05	.15
590 Ray Knight	.08	.25
591 Larry Herndon	.05	.15
592 Jeff D. Robinson	.05	.15
593 Rick Leach	.05	.15
594 Curt Wilkerson	.05	.15
595 Larry Gura	.05	.15
596 Jerry Hairston	.05	.15
597 Brad Lesley	.05	.15
598 Jose Oquendo	.05	.15
599 Storm Davis	.05	.15
600 Pete Rose	.60	1.50
601 Tom Lasorda MG	.15	.40
602 Jeff Dedmon	.05	.15
603 Rick Manning	.05	.15
604 Daryl Sconiers	.05	.15
605 Ozzie Smith	.40	1.00
606 Rich Gale	.05	.15
607 Bill Almon	.05	.15
608 Craig Lefferts	.05	.15
609 Broderick Perkins	.05	.15
610 Jack Morris	.08	.25
611 Ozzie Virgil	.05	.15
612 Mike Armstrong	.05	.15
613 Terry Puhl	.05	.15
614 Al Williams	.05	.15
615 Marvell Wynne	.05	.15
616 Scott Sanderson	.05	.15
617 Willie Wilson	.08	.25
618 Pete Falcone	.05	.15
619 Jeff Leonard	.05	.15
620 Dwight Gooden RC	.75	2.00
621 Marvis Foley	.05	.15
622 Luis Leal	.05	.15
623 Greg Walker	.05	.15
624 Benny Ayala	.05	.15
625 Mark Langston RC	.30	.75
626 German Rivera	.05	.15
627 Eric Davis RC	.75	2.00
628 Rene Lachemann MG	.05	.15
629 Dick Schofield	.05	.15
630 Tim Raines	.08	.25
631 Bob Forsch	.05	.15
632 Bruce Bochte	.05	.15
633 Glenn Hoffman	.05	.15
634 Bill Dawley	.05	.15
635 Terry Kennedy	.05	.15
636 Shane Rawley	.05	.15
637 Brett Butler	.08	.25
638 Mike Pagliarulo	.05	.15
639 Ed Hodge	.05	.15
640 Steve Henderson	.05	.15
641 Rod Scurry	.05	.15
642 Dave Owen	.05	.15
643 Johnny Grubb	.05	.15
644 Mark Huismann	.05	.15
645 Damaso Garcia	.05	.15
646 Scot Thompson	.05	.15
647 Rafael Ramirez	.05	.15
648 Bob Jones	.05	.15
649 Sid Fernandez	.08	.25
650 Greg Luzinski	.08	.25
651 Jeff Russell	.05	.15
652 Joe Nolan	.05	.15
653 Mark Brouhard	.05	.15
654 Dave Anderson	.05	.15
655 Joaquin Andujar	.08	.25
656 Chuck Cottier MG	.05	.15
657 Jim Slaton	.05	.15
658 Mike Stenhouse	.05	.15
659 Checklist: 529-660	.05	.15
660 Tony Gwynn	.50	1.25
661 Steve Crawford	.05	.15
662 Mike Heath	.05	.15
663 Luis Aguayo	.05	.15
664 Steve Farr RC	.15	.40
665 Don Mattingly	1.00	2.50
666 Mike LaCoss	.05	.15
667 Dave Engle	.05	.15
668 Steve Trout	.05	.15
669 Lee Lacy	.05	.15
670 Tom Seaver	.15	.40
671 Dane Iorg	.05	.15
672 Juan Berenguer	.05	.15
673 Buck Martinez	.05	.15
674 Atlee Hammaker	.05	.15
675 Tony Perez	.15	.40
676 Albert Hall	.05	.15
677 Wally Backman	.05	.15
678 Joey McLaughlin	.05	.15
679 Bob Kearney	.05	.15
680 Jerry Reuss	.05	.15
681 Ben Oglivie	.08	.25
682 Doug Corbett	.05	.15
683 Whitey Herzog MG	.08	.25
684 Bill Doran	.05	.15
685 Bill Caudill	.05	.15
686 Mike Easler	.05	.15
687 Bill Gullickson	.05	.15
688 Len Matuszek	.05	.15
689 Luis DeLeon	.05	.15
690 Alan Trammell	.08	.25
691 Dennis Rasmussen	.05	.15
692 Randy Bush	.05	.15
693 Tim Stoddard	.05	.15
694 Joe Carter	.25	.60
695 Rick Rhoden	.05	.15
696 John Rabb	.05	.15
697 Onix Concepcion	.05	.15
698 George Bell	.08	.25
699 Donnie Moore	.05	.15
700 Eddie Murray	.25	.60
701 Eddie Murray AS	.15	.40
702 Damaso Garcia AS	.05	.15
703 George Brett AS	.25	.60
704 Cal Ripken AS	.60	1.50
705 Dave Winfield AS	.05	.15
706 Rickey Henderson AS	.15	.40
707 Tony Armas AS	.05	.15
708 Lance Parrish AS	.05	.15
709 Mike Boddicker AS	.05	.15
710 Frank Viola AS	.05	.15
711 Dan Quisenberry AS	.05	.15
712 Keith Hernandez AS	.05	.15
713 Ryne Sandberg AS	.25	.60
714 Mike Schmidt AS	.25	.60
715 Ozzie Smith AS	.25	.60
716 Dale Murphy AS	.08	.25
717 Tony Gwynn AS	.40	1.00
718 Jeff Leonard AS	.05	.15
719 Gary Carter AS	.05	.15
720 Rick Sutcliffe AS	.05	.15
721 Bob Knepper AS	.05	.15
722 Bruce Sutter AS	.05	.15
723 Dave Stewart	.08	.25
724 Oscar Gamble	.05	.15
725 Floyd Bannister	.05	.15
726 Al Bumbry	.05	.15
727 Frank Pastore	.05	.15
728 Bob Bailor	.05	.15
729 Don Sutton	.08	.25
730 Dave Kingman	.08	.25
731 Neil Allen	.05	.15
732 John McNamara MG	.05	.15
733 Tony Scott	.05	.15
734 John Henry Johnson	.05	.15
735 Garry Templeton	.08	.25
736 Jerry Mumphrey	.05	.15
737 Bo Diaz	.05	.15
738 Omar Moreno	.05	.15
739 Ernie Camacho	.05	.15
740 Jack Clark	.08	.25
741 John Butcher	.05	.15
742 Ron Hassey	.05	.15
743 Frank White	.08	.25
744 Doug Bair	.05	.15
745 Buddy Bell	.08	.25
746 Jim Clancy	.05	.15
747 Alex Trevino	.05	.15
748 Lee Mazzilli	.08	.25
749 Julio Cruz	.05	.15
750 Rollie Fingers	.08	.25
751 Kelvin Chapman	.05	.15
752 Bob Owchinko	.05	.15
753 Greg Brock	.05	.15
754 Larry Milbourne	.05	.15
755 Ken Singleton	.08	.25
756 Rob Picciolo	.05	.15
757 Willie McGee	.08	.25
758 Ray Burris	.05	.15
759 Jim Fanning MG	.05	.15
760 Nolan Ryan	1.25	3.00
761 Jerry Remy	.05	.15
762 Eddie Whitson	.05	.15
763 Kiko Garcia	.05	.15
764 Jamie Easterly	.05	.15
765 Willie Randolph	.08	.25
766 Paul Mirabella	.05	.15
767 Darrell Brown	.05	.15
768 Ron Cey	.08	.25
769 Joe Cowley	.05	.15
770 Carlton Fisk	.15	.40
771 Geoff Zahn	.05	.15
772 Johnnie LeMaster	.05	.15
773 Hal McRae	.08	.25
774 Dennis Lamp	.05	.15
775 Mookie Wilson	.08	.25
776 Jerry Royster	.05	.15
777 Ned Yost	.05	.15
778 Mike Davis	.05	.15
779 Nick Esasky	.05	.15
780 Mike Flanagan	.05	.15
781 Jim Gantner	.05	.15
782 Tom Niedenfuer	.05	.15
783 Mike Jorgensen	.05	.15
784 Checklist: 661-792	.05	.15
785 Tony Armas	.08	.25
786 Enos Cabell	.05	.15
787 Jim Wohlford	.05	.15
788 Steve Comer	.05	.15
789 Luis Salazar	.05	.15
790 Ron Guidry	.08	.25
791 Ivan DeJesus	.05	.15
792 Darrell Evans	.08	.25

1985 Topps Tiffany

COMP.FACT.SET (792)	300.00	500.00

*STARS: 3X TO 8X BASIC CARDS
*ROOKIES: 2.5X TO 6X BASIC CARDS
DISTRIBUTED ONLY IN FACTORY SET FORM
FACTORY SET PRICE IS FOR SEALED SETS

1985 Topps Glossy All-Stars

The cards in this 22-card set the standard size. Similar in design, both front and back, to last year's Glossy set, this edition features the managers, starting nine players and honorary captains of the National and American League teams in the 1984 All-Star game. The set is numbered on the reverse with players essentially ordered by position within league, NL: 1-11 and AL: 12-22.

Card	Low	High
COMPLETE SET (22)	2.00	5.00
1 Paul Owens MG	.01	.05
2 Steve Garvey	.05	.15
3 Ryne Sandberg	.40	1.00
4 Mike Schmidt	.30	.75
5 Ozzie Smith	.40	1.00
6 Tony Gwynn	.50	1.25
7 Dale Murphy	.07	.20
8 Darryl Strawberry	.02	.10
9 Gary Carter	.20	.50
10 Charlie Lea	.01	.05
11 Willie McCovey CAPT	.02	.10
12 Joe Altobelli MG	.01	.05
13 Rod Carew	.20	.50
14 Lou Whitaker	.02	.10
15 George Brett	.40	1.00
16 Cal Ripken	.75	2.00
17 Dave Winfield	.20	.50
18 Chet Lemon	.01	.05
19 Reggie Jackson	.20	.50
20 Lance Parrish	.01	.05
21 Dave Stieb	.01	.05
22 Hank Greenberg CAPT	.02	.10

1985 Topps Glossy Send-Ins

The cards in this 40-card set measure the standard size. Similar to last year's glossy set, this set was issued as a bonus prize to Topps All-Star Baseball Game cards found in wax packs. The set could be obtained by sending in the "Bonus Runs" from the "Winning Pitch" game insert cards. For 25 runs and 75 cents, a collector could send in for one of the eight different five card series plus automatically be entered in the Grand Prize Sweepstakes for a chance at a free trip to the All-Star game. The cards are numbered and contain 20 stars from each league.

Card	Low	High
COMPLETE SET (40)	4.00	10.00
1 Dale Murphy	.10	.30
2 Jesse Orosco	.07	.20
3 Bob Brenly	.02	.10
4 Mike Boddicker	.02	.10
5 Dave Kingman	.07	.20
6 Jim Rice	.07	.20
7 Frank Viola	.07	.20
8 Alvin Davis	.02	.10
9 Rick Sutcliffe	.02	.10
10 Pete Rose	.50	1.25

11 Leon Durham .02 .10
12 Joaquin Andujar .02 .10
13 Keith Hernandez .07 .20
14 Dave Winfield .30 .75
15 Reggie Jackson .30 .75
16 Alan Trammell .10 .30
17 Bert Blyleven .07 .20
18 Tony Armas .02 .10
19 Rich Gossage .07 .20
20 Jose Cruz .07 .20
21 Ryne Sandberg .75 2.00
22 Bruce Sutter .30 .75
23 Mike Schmidt .50 1.25
24 Cal Ripken 2.00 5.00
25 Dan Petry .02 .10
26 Jack Morris .07 .20
27 Don Mattingly 1.00 2.50
28 Eddie Murray .40 1.00
29 Tony Gwynn 1.00 2.50
30 Charlie Lea .02 .10
31 Juan Samuel .02 .10
32 Phil Niekro .30 .75
33 Alejandro Pena .02 .10
34 Harold Baines .07 .20
35 Dan Quisenberry .02 .10
36 Gary Carter .30 .75
37 Mario Soto .02 .10
38 Dwight Gooden .20 .50
39 Tom Brunansky .02 .10
40 Dave Stieb .02 .10

1985 Topps Traded

In its now standard procedure, Topps issued its standard-size Traded (or extended) set for the fifth year in a row. In addition to the typical factory set hobby distribution, Topps tested the limited issuance of these Traded cards in wax packs. Card design is identical to the regular-issue 1985 Topps set except for whiter card stock and T-suffixed numbering on back. The set numbering is in alphabetical order by player's name. The key extended Rookie Cards in this set include Vince Coleman, Ozzie Guillen, and Mickey Tettleton.

COMP.FACT.SET (132) 3.00 8.00
1T Don Aase .05 .15
2T Bill Almon .05 .15
3T Benny Ayala .05 .15
4T Dusty Baker .15 .40
5T George Bamberger MG .05 .15
6T Dale Berra .05 .15
7T Rich Bordi .05 .15
8T Daryl Boston XRC* .08 .25
9T Hubie Brooks .05 .15
10T Chris Brown XRC .08 .25
11T Tom Browning XRC* .20 .50
12T Al Bumbry .05 .15
13T Ray Burris .05 .15
14T Jeff Burroughs .05 .15
15T Bill Campbell .05 .15
16T Don Carman .05 .15
17T Gary Carter .15 .40
18T Bobby Castillo .05 .15
19T Bill Caudill .05 .15
20T Rick Cerone .05 .15
21T Bryan Clark .05 .15
22T Jack Clark .15 .40
23T Pat Clements .05 .15
24T Vince Coleman XRC .40 1.00
25T Dave Collins .05 .15
26T Danny Darwin .05 .15
27T Jim Davenport MG .05 .15
28T Jerry Davis .05 .15
29T Brian Dayett .05 .15
30T Ivan DeJesus .05 .15
31T Ken Dixon .05 .15
32T Mariano Duncan XRC .20 .50
33T John Felske MG .05 .15
34T Mike Fitzgerald .05 .15
35T Ray Fontenot .05 .15
36T Greg Gagne XRC* .20 .50
37T Oscar Gamble .05 .15
38T Scott Garrelts .05 .15
39T Bob L. Gibson .05 .15
40T Jim Gott .05 .15
41T David Green .05 .15
42T Alfredo Griffin .05 .15
43T Ozzie Guillen XRC 2.00 5.00
44T Eddie Haas MG .05 .15
45T Terry Harper .05 .15
46T Toby Harrah .15 .40
47T Greg Harris .15 .40
48T Ron Hassey .05 .15
49T Rickey Henderson 1.00 2.50
50T Steve Henderson .05 .15
51T George Hendrick .15 .40
52T Joe Hesketh .05 .15
53T Teddy Higuera XRC .20 .50
54T Donnie Hill .05 .15
55T Al Holland .05 .15
56T Burt Hooton .05 .15
57T Jay Howell .05 .15
58T Ken Howell .05 .15
59T LaMarr Hoyt .05 .15
60T Tim Hulett XRC* .08 .25
61T Bob James .05 .15
62T Steve Jeltz XRC .08 .25
63T Cliff Johnson .05 .15
64T Howard Johnson .15 .40
65T Ruppert Jones .05 .15
66T Steve Kemp .05 .15
67T Bruce Kison .05 .15
68T Alan Knicely .05 .15
69T Mike LaCoss .05 .15
70T Lee Lacy .05 .15
71T Dave LaPoint .05 .15
72T Gary Lavelle .05 .15
73T Vance Law .05 .15
74T Johnnie LeMaster .05 .15
75T Sixto Lezcano .05 .15
76T Tim Lollar .05 .15
77T Fred Lynn .15 .40
78T Billy Martin MG .30 .75
79T Ron Mathis .05 .15
80T Len Matuszek .05 .15
81T Gene Mauch MG .05 .15
82T Oddibe McDowell .20 .50
83T Roger McDowell XRC .20 .50
84T John McNamara MG .05 .15
85T Donnie Moore .05 .15
86T Gene Nelson .05 .15
87T Steve Nicosia .05 .15
88T Al Oliver .15 .40
89T Joe Orsulak XRC .20 .50
90T Rob Picciolo .05 .15
91T Chris Pittaro .05 .15
92T Jim Presley .20 .50
93T Rick Reuschel .15 .40
94T Bert Roberge .05 .15
95T Bob Rodgers MG .05 .15
96T Jerry Royster .05 .15
97T Dave Rozema .05 .15
98T Dave Rucker .05 .15
99T Vern Ruhle .05 .15
100T Paul Runge XRC .08 .25
101T Mark Salas .05 .15
102T Luis Salazar .05 .15
103T Joe Sambito .05 .15
104T Rick Schu .05 .15
105T Donnie Scott .05 .15
106T Larry Sheets XRC .08 .25
107T Don Slaught .05 .15
108T Roy Smalley .05 .15
109T Lonnie Smith .05 .15
110T Nate Snell UER/(Headings on back .05 .15
for a batter)
111T Chris Speier .05 .15
112T Mike Stenhouse .05 .15
113T Tim Stoddard .05 .15
114T Jim Sundberg .05 .15
115T Bruce Sutter .15 .40
116T Don Sutton .15 .40
117T Kent Tekulve .05 .15
118T Tom Tellmann .05 .15
119T Walt Terrell .05 .15
120T Mickey Tettleton XRC .20 .50
121T Derrel Thomas .05 .15
122T Rich Thompson .05 .15
123T Alex Trevino .05 .15
124T John Tudor .15 .40
125T Jose Uribe .05 .15
126T Bobby Valentine MG .15 .40
127T Dave Von Ohlen .05 .15
128T U.L. Washington .05 .15
129T Earl Weaver MG .15 .40
130T Eddie Whitson .05 .15
131T Herm Winningham .05 .15
132T Checklist 1-132 .05 .15

1985 Topps Traded Tiffany

COMP.FACT.SET (132) 20.00 50.00
*STARS: 1.5X TO 4X BASIC CARDS
*ROOKIES: 1.5X TO 4X BASIC CARDS
DISTRIBUTED ONLY IN FACTORY SET FORM
FACTORY SET PRICE IS FOR SEALED SETS

1986 Topps

This set consists of 792 standard-size cards. Cards were primarily distributed in 15-card wax packs, 48-card rack packs and factors sets. This was also the first year Topps offered a factory set to hobby dealers. Standard card fronts feature a black and white split border framing a color photo with team name on top and player name on bottom. Subsets include Pete Rose tribute (1-7), Record Breakers (201-207), Turn Back the Clock (401-405), All-Stars (701-722) and Team Leaders (seeded throughout the set). Manager cards feature the team checklist on the reverse. There are two uncorrected errors involving misnumbered cards; see card numbers 51, 57, 141, and 171 in the checklist below. The key Rookie Cards in this set are Darren Daulton, Len Dykstra, Cecil Fielder, and Mickey Tettleton.

COMPLETE SET (792) 10.00 25.00
COMP.X-MAS.SET (792) 60.00 120.00
1 Pete Rose .75 2.00
2 Rose Special: '63-'66 .08 .25
3 Rose Special: '67-'70 .08 .25
4 Rose Special: '71-'74 .08 .25
5 Rose Special: '75-'78 .08 .25
6 Rose Special: '79-'82 .08 .25
7 Rose Special: '83-'85 .08 .25
8 Dwayne Murphy .02 .10
9 Roy Smith .02 .10
10 Tony Gwynn .25 .60
11 Bob Ojeda .02 .10
12 Jose Uribe .02 .10
13 Bob Kearney .02 .10
14 Julio Cruz .02 .10
15 Eddie Whitson .02 .10
16 Rick Schu .02 .10
17 Mike Stenhouse .02 .10
18 Brent Gaff .02 .10
19 Rich Hebner .02 .10
20 Lou Whitaker .05 .15
21 George Bamberger MG .02 .10
22 Duane Walker .02 .10
23 Manuel Lee RC* .02 .10
24 Len Barker .02 .10
25 Willie Wilson .05 .15
26 Frank DiPino .02 .10
27 Ray Knight .05 .15
28 Eric Davis .15 .40
29 Tony Phillips .02 .10
30 Eddie Murray .15 .40
31 Jamie Easterly .02 .10
32 Steve Yeager .05 .15
33 Jeff Lahti .02 .10
34 Ken Phelps .02 .10
35 Jeff Reardon .05 .15
36 Tigers Leaders .05 .15
Lance Parrish
37 Mark Thurmond .02 .10
38 Glenn Hoffman .02 .10
39 Dave Rucker .02 .10
40 Ken Griffey .05 .15
41 Brad Wellman .02 .10
42 Geoff Zahn .02 .10
43 Dave Engle .02 .10
44 Lance McCullers .02 .10
45 Damaso Garcia .02 .10
46 Billy Hatcher .02 .10
47 Juan Berenguer .02 .10
48 Bill Almon .02 .10
49 Rick Manning .02 .10
50 Dan Quisenberry .02 .10
51 Bobby Wine MG ERR
(Checklist back)/(Number of ca .02 .10
52 Chris Welsh .02 .10
53 Len Dykstra RC .30 .75
54 John Franco .05 .15
55 Fred Lynn .05 .15
56 Tom Niedenfuer .02 .10
57 Bill Doran/(See also 51) .02 .10
58 Bill Krueger .02 .10
59 Andre Thornton .02 .10
60 Dwight Evans .08 .25
61 Karl Best .02 .10
62 Bob Boone .05 .15
63 Ron Roenicke .02 .10
64 Floyd Bannister .02 .10
65 Dan Driessen .02 .10
66 Cardinals Leaders .02 .10
Bob Forsch
67 Carmelo Martinez .02 .10
68 Ed Lynch .02 .10
69 Luis Aguayo .02 .10
70 Dave Winfield .05 .15
71 Ken Schrom .02 .10
72 Shawon Dunston .05 .15
73 Randy O'Neal .02 .10
74 Rance Mulliniks .02 .10
75 Jose DeLeon .02 .10
76 Dion James .02 .10
77 Charlie Leibrandt .02 .10
78 Bruce Benedict .02 .10
79 Dave Schmidt .02 .10
80 Darryl Strawberry .08 .25
81 Gene Mauch MG .02 .10
82 Tippy Martinez .02 .10
83 Phil Garner .05 .15
84 Curt Young .02 .10
85 Tony Perez w .05 .15
E.Davis
86 Tom Waddell .02 .10
87 Candy Maldonado .02 .10
88 Tom Nieto .02 .10
89 Randy St.Claire .02 .10
90 Garry Templeton .05 .15
91 Steve Crawford .02 .10
92 Al Cowens .02 .10
93 Scot Thompson .02 .10
94 Rich Bordi .02 .10
95 Ozzie Virgil .02 .10
96 Blue Jays Leaders .02 .10
Jim Clancy
97 Gary Gaetti .05 .15
98 Dick Ruthven .02 .10
99 Buddy Biancalana .02 .10
100 Nolan Ryan .75 2.00
101 Dave Bergman .02 .10
102 Joe Orsulak RC* .08 .25
103 Luis Salazar .02 .10
104 Sid Fernandez .02 .10
105 Gary Ward .02 .10
106 Ray Burris .02 .10
107 Rafael Ramirez .02 .10
108 Ted Power .02 .10
109 Len Matuszek .02 .10
110 Scott McGregor .02 .10
111 Roger Craig MG .05 .15
112 Bill Campbell .02 .10
113 U.L. Washington .02 .10
114 Mike C. Brown .02 .10
115 Jay Howell .02 .10
116 Brook Jacoby .02 .10
117 Bruce Kison .02 .10
118 Jerry Royster .02 .10
119 Barry Bonnell .02 .10
120 Steve Carlton .05 .15
121 Nelson Simmons .02 .10
122 Pete Filson .02 .10
123 Greg Walker .02 .10
124 Luis Sanchez .02 .10
125 Dave Lopes .05 .15
126 Mets Leaders .02 .10
Mookie Wilson
127 Jack Howell .02 .10
128 John Wathan .02 .10
129 Jeff Dedmon .02 .10
130 Alan Trammell .05 .15
131 Checklist: 1-132 .05 .15
132 Razor Shines .02 .10
133 Andy McGaffigan .02 .10
134 Carney Lansford .05 .15
135 Joe Niekro .02 .10
136 Mike Hargrove .02 .10
137 Charlie Moore .02 .10
138 Mark Davis .02 .10
139 Daryl Boston .02 .10
140 John Candelaria .02 .10
141 Chuck Cottier MG .02 .10
See also 171
142 Bob Jones .02 .10
143 Dave Van Gorder .02 .10
144 Doug Sisk .02 .10
145 Pedro Guerrero .05 .15
146 Jack Perconte .02 .10
147 Larry Sheets .02 .10
148 Mike Heath .02 .10
149 Brett Butler .05 .15
150 Joaquin Andujar .05 .15
151 Dave Stapleton .02 .10
152 Mike Morgan .02 .10
153 Ricky Adams .02 .10
154 Bert Roberge .02 .10
155 Bob Grich .05 .15
156 White Sox Leaders .02 .10
Richard Dotson
157 Ron Hassey .02 .10
158 Derrel Thomas .02 .10
159 Orel Hershiser UER .15 .40
160 Chet Lemon .05 .15
161 Lee Tunnell .02 .10
162 Greg Gagne .05 .15
163 Pete Ladd .02 .10
164 Steve Balboni .02 .10
165 Mike Davis .02 .10
166 Dickie Thon .02 .10
167 Zane Smith .02 .10
168 Jeff Burroughs .02 .10
169 George Wright .02 .10
170 Gary Carter .05 .15
171 Bob Rodgers MG ERR
(Checklist back)/(Number of c .02 .10
172 Jerry Reed .02 .10
173 Wayne Gross .02 .10
174 Brian Snyder .02 .10
175 Steve Sax .02 .10
176 Jay Tibbs .02 .10
177 Joel Youngblood .02 .10
178 Ivan DeJesus .02 .10
179 Stu Cliburn .02 .10
180 Don Mattingly .50 1.25
181 Al Nipper .02 .10
182 Bobby Brown .02 .10
183 Larry Andersen .02 .10
184 Tim Laudner .02 .10
185 Rollie Fingers .05 .15
186 Astros Leaders .02 .10
Jose Cruz
187 Scott Fletcher .02 .10
188 Bob Dernier .02 .10
189 Mike Mason .02 .10
190 George Hendrick .05 .15
191 Wally Backman .02 .10
192 Milt Wilcox .02 .10
193 Daryl Sconiers .02 .10
194 Craig McMurtry .02 .10
195 Dave Concepcion .05 .15
196 Doyle Alexander .02 .10
197 Enos Cabell .02 .10
198 Ken Dixon .02 .10
199 Dick Howser MG .02 .10
200 Mike Schmidt .40 1.00
201 Vince Coleman RB .05 .15
Most stolen bases&
season& rook
202 Dwight Gooden RB .08 .25
203 Keith Hernandez RB .02 .10
204 Phil Niekro RB .05 .15
Oldest shutout pitcher
205 Tony Perez RB .05 .15
Oldest grand slammer
206 Pete Rose RB .15 .40
207 Fernando Valenzuela RB .02 .10
Most cons. innings&
start
208 Ramon Romero .02 .10
209 Randy Ready .02 .10
210 Calvin Schiraldi .02 .10
211 Ed Wojna .02 .10
212 Chris Speier .02 .10
213 Bob Shirley .02 .10
214 Randy Bush .02 .10
215 Frank White .05 .15
216 A's Leaders .02 .10
Dwayne Murphy
217 Bill Scherrer .02 .10
218 Randy Hunt .02 .10
219 Dennis Lamp .02 .10
220 Bob Horner .05 .15
221 Dave Henderson .02 .10
222 Craig Gerber .02 .10
223 Atlee Hammaker .02 .10
224 Cesar Cedeno .05 .15
225 Ron Darling .05 .15
226 Lee Lacy .02 .10
227 Al Jones .02 .10
228 Tom Lawless .02 .10
229 Bill Gullickson .02 .10
230 Terry Kennedy .02 .10
231 Jim Frey MG .02 .10
232 Rick Rhoden .02 .10
233 Steve Lyons .02 .10
234 Doug Corbett .02 .10
235 Butch Wynegar .02 .10
236 Frank Eufemia .02 .10
237 Ted Simmons .05 .15
238 Larry Parrish .02 .10
239 Joel Skinner .02 .10
240 Tommy John .05 .15
241 Tony Fernandez .02 .10
242 Rich Thompson .02 .10
243 Johnny Grubb .02 .10
244 Craig Lefferts .02 .10
245 Jim Sundberg .05 .15
246 Steve Carlton TL .02 .10
247 Terry Harper .02 .10
248 Spike Owen .02 .10
249 Rob Deer .02 .10
250 Dwight Gooden .15 .40
251 Rich Dauer .02 .10
252 Bobby Castillo .02 .10
253 Dann Bilardello .02 .10
254 Ozzie Guillen RC .60 1.50
255 Tony Armas .05 .15
256 Kurt Kepshire .02 .10
257 Doug DeCinces .02 .10
258 Tim Burke .02 .10
259 Dan Pasqua .02 .10
260 Tony Pena .02 .10
261 Bobby Valentine MG .05 .15
262 Mario Ramirez .02 .10
263 Checklist: 133-264 .05 .15
264 Darren Daulton RC .20 .50
265 Ron Davis .02 .10
266 Keith Moreland .02 .10
267 Paul Molitor .02 .10
268 Mike Scott .05 .15
269 Dane Iorg .02 .10
270 Jack Morris .05 .15
271 Dave Collins .02 .10
272 Tim Tolman .02 .10
273 Jerry Willard .02 .10
274 Ron Gardenhire .02 .10
275 Charlie Hough .05 .15
276 Yankees Leaders .05 .15
Willie Randolph
277 Jaime Cocanower .02 .10
278 Sixto Lezcano .02 .10
279 Al Pardo .02 .10
280 Tim Raines .05 .15
281 Steve Mura .02 .10
282 Jerry Mumphrey .02 .10
283 Mike Fischlin .02 .10
284 Brian Dayett .02 .10
285 Buddy Bell .05 .15
286 Luis DeLeon .02 .10
287 John Christensen .02 .10
288 Don Aase .02 .10
289 Johnnie LeMaster .02 .10
290 Carlton Fisk .08 .25
291 Tom Lasorda MG .08 .25
292 Chuck Porter .02 .10
293 Chris Chambliss .05 .15
294 Danny Cox .02 .10
295 Kirk Gibson .05 .15
296 Geno Petralli .02 .10
297 Tim Lollar .02 .10
298 Craig Reynolds .02 .10
299 Bryn Smith .02 .10
300 George Brett .40 1.00
301 Dennis Rasmussen .02 .10
302 Greg Gross .02 .10
303 Curt Wardle .02 .10
304 Mike Gallego RC .02 .10
305 Phil Bradley .02 .10
306 Padres Leaders .02 .10
Terry Kennedy
307 Dave Sax .02 .10
308 Ray Fontenot .02 .10
309 John Shelby .02 .10
310 Greg Minton .02 .10
311 Dick Schofield .02 .10
312 Tom Filer .02 .10
313 Joe DeSa .02 .10
314 Frank Pastore .02 .10
315 Mookie Wilson .05 .15
316 Sammy Khalifa .02 .10
317 Ed Romero .02 .10
318 Terry Whitfield .02 .10
319 Rick Camp .02 .10
320 Jim Rice .05 .15
321 Earl Weaver MG .05 .15
322 Bob Forsch .02 .10
323 Jerry Davis .02 .10
324 Dan Schatzeder .02 .10
325 Juan Beniquez .02 .10
326 Kent Tekulve .02 .10
327 Mike Pagliarulo .02 .10
328 Pete O'Brien .02 .10
329 Kirby Puckett .40 1.00
330 Rick Sutcliffe .05 .15
331 Alan Ashby .02 .10
332 Darryl Motley .02 .10
333 Tom Henke .05 .15
334 Ken Oberkfell .02 .10
335 Don Sutton .05 .15
336 Indians Leaders .05 .15
Andre Thornton
337 Darnell Coles .02 .10
338 Jorge Bell .05 .15
339 Bruce Berenyi .02 .10
340 Cal Ripken .60 1.50
341 Frank Williams .02 .10
342 Gary Redus .02 .10
343 Carlos Diaz .02 .10
344 Jim Wohlford .02 .10
345 Donnie Moore .02 .10
346 Bryan Little .02 .10
347 Teddy Higuera RC* .08 .25
348 Cliff Johnson .02 .10
349 Mark Clear .02 .10
350 Jack Clark .05 .15
351 Chuck Tanner MG .02 .10
352 Harry Spilman .02 .10
353 Keith Atherton .02 .10
354 Tony Bernazard .02 .10
355 Lee Smith .05 .15
356 Mickey Hatcher .02 .10
357 Ed VandeBerg .02 .10
358 Rick Dempsey .02 .10
359 Mike LaCoss .02 .10
360 Lloyd Moseby .02 .10
361 Shane Rawley .02 .10
362 Tom Paciorek .02 .10
363 Terry Forster .05 .15
364 Reid Nichols .02 .10
365 Mike Flanagan .02 .10
366 Reds Leaders .05 .15
Dave Concepcion
367 Aurelio Lopez .02 .10
368 Greg Brock .02 .10
369 Al Holland .02 .10
370 Vince Coleman RC .20 .50
371 Bill Stein .02 .10
372 Ben Oglivie .05 .15
373 Urbano Lugo .02 .10
374 Terry Francona .05 .15
375 Rich Gedman .02 .10
376 Bill Dawley .02 .10
377 Joe Carter .05 .15
378 Bruce Bochte .02 .10
379 Bobby Meacham .02 .10
380 LaMarr Hoyt .02 .10
381 Ray Miller MG .02 .10
382 Ivan Calderon RC* .08 .25
383 Chris Brown RC .02 .10
384 Steve Trout .02 .10
385 Cecil Cooper .05 .15
386 Cecil Fielder RC .40 1.00
387 Steve Kemp .02 .10
388 Dickie Noles .02 .10
389 Glenn Davis .02 .10
390 Tom Seaver .08 .25
391 Julio Franco .05 .15
392 John Russell .02 .10
393 Chris Pittaro .02 .10
394 Checklist: 265-396 .05 .15
395 Scott Garrelts .02 .10
396 Red Sox Leaders .08 .25
Dwight Evans
397 Steve Buechele RC .08 .25
398 Earnie Riles .02 .10
399 Bill Swift .02 .10
400 Rod Carew .08 .25
401 Fernando Valenzuela TBC '81 .02 .10
402 Tom Seaver TBC .05 .15
403 Willie Mays TBC .15 .40
404 Frank Robinson TBC .05 .15
405 Roger Maris TBC .15 .40
406 Scott Sanderson .02 .10
407 Sal Butera .02 .10
408 Dave Smith .02 .10
409 Paul Runge RC .02 .10
410 Dave Kingman .05 .15
411 Sparky Anderson MG .05 .15
412 Jim Clancy .02 .10
413 Tim Flannery .02 .10
414 Tom Gorman .02 .10
415 Hal McRae .05 .15
416 Dennis Martinez .05 .15
417 R.J. Reynolds .02 .10
418 Alan Knicely .02 .10
419 Frank Wills .02 .10
420 Von Hayes .02 .10
421 David Palmer .02 .10
422 Mike Jorgensen .02 .10
423 Dan Spillner .02 .10
424 Rick Miller .02 .10
425 Larry McWilliams .02 .10
426 Brewers Leaders .02 .10
Charlie Moore
427 Joe Cowley .02 .10
428 Max Venable .02 .10
429 Greg Booker .02 .10
430 Kent Hrbek .05 .15
431 George Frazier .02 .10
432 Mark Bailey .02 .10
433 Chris Codiroli .02 .10
434 Curt Wilkerson .02 .10
435 Bill Caudill .02 .10
436 Doug Flynn .02 .10
437 Rick Mahler .02 .10
438 Clint Hurdle .02 .10
439 Rick Honeycutt .02 .10
440 Alvin Davis .02 .10
441 Whitey Herzog MG .08 .25
442 Ron Robinson .02 .10
443 Bill Buckner .05 .15
444 Alex Trevino .02 .10
445 Bert Blyleven .05 .15
446 Lenn Sakata .02 .10
447 Jerry Don Gleaton .02 .10
448 Herm Winningham .02 .10
449 Rod Scurry .02 .10
450 Graig Nettles .05 .15
451 Mark Brown .02 .10
452 Bob Clark .02 .10
453 Steve Jeltz .02 .10
454 Burt Hooton .02 .10
455 Willie Randolph .05 .15
456 Braves Leaders .08 .25
Dale Murphy
457 Mickey Tettleton RC .08 .25
458 Kevin Bass .02 .10
459 Luis Leal .02 .10
460 Leon Durham .02 .10
461 Walt Terrell .02 .10
462 Domingo Ramos .02 .10
463 Jim Gott .02 .10
464 Ruppert Jones .02 .10
465 Jesse Orosco .02 .10
466 Tom Foley .02 .10
467 Bob James .02 .10
468 Mike Scioscia .05 .15
469 Storm Davis .02 .10
470 Bill Madlock .05 .15
471 Bobby Cox MG .05 .15
472 Joe Hesketh .02 .10
473 Mark Brouhard .02 .10
474 John Tudor .05 .15
475 Juan Samuel .02 .10
476 Ron Mathis .02 .10
477 Mike Easler .02 .10
478 Andy Hawkins .02 .10
479 Bob Melvin .02 .10
480 Oddibe McDowell .02 .10
481 Scott Bradley .02 .10
482 Rick Lysander .02 .10
483 George Vukovich .02 .10
484 Donnie Hill .02 .10
485 Gary Matthews .05 .15
486 Angels Leaders .02 .10
Bobby Grich
487 Bret Saberhagen .05 .15
488 Lou Thornton .02 .10
489 Jim Winn .02 .10
490 Jeff Leonard .02 .10
491 Pascual Perez .02 .10
492 Kelvin Chapman .02 .10
493 Gene Nelson .02 .10
494 Gary Roenicke .02 .10
495 Mark Langston .05 .15
496 Jay Johnstone .02 .10
497 John Stuper .02 .10
498 Tito Landrum .02 .10
499 Bob L. Gibson .02 .10
500 Rickey Henderson .15 .40
501 Dave Johnson MG .02 .10
502 Glen Cook .02 .10
503 Mike Fitzgerald .02 .10
504 Denny Walling .02 .10
505 Jerry Koosman .05 .15
506 Bill Russell .05 .15
507 Steve Ontiveros RC .02 .10
508 Alan Wiggins .02 .10
509 Ernie Camacho .02 .10
510 Wade Boggs .08 .25
511 Ed Nunez .02 .10
512 Thad Bosley .02 .10
513 Ron Washington .02 .10
514 Mike Jones .02 .10
515 Darrell Evans .05 .15
516 Giants Leaders .02 .10
Greg Minton
517 Milt Thompson RC .08 .25
518 Buck Martinez .02 .10
519 Danny Darwin .02 .10
520 Keith Hernandez .05 .15
521 Nate Snell .02 .10
522 Bob Bailor .02 .10
523 Joe Price .02 .10
524 Darrell Miller .02 .10
525 Marvell Wynne .02 .10
526 Charlie Lea .02 .10
527 Checklist: 397-528 .05 .15
528 Terry Pendleton .05 .15
529 Marc Sullivan .02 .10
530 Rich Gossage .05 .15
531 Tony LaRussa MG .05 .15
532 Don Carman .02 .10
533 Billy Sample .02 .10
534 Jeff Calhoun .02 .10
535 Toby Harrah .05 .15
536 Jose Rijo .05 .15
537 Mark Salas .02 .10
538 Dennis Eckersley .08 .25
539 Glenn Hubbard .02 .10
540 Dan Petry .02 .10

541 Jorge Orta .02 .10
542 Don Schulze .02 .10
543 Jerry Narron .02 .10
544 Eddie Milner .02 .10
545 Jimmy Key .05 .15
546 Mariners Leaders .02 .10
Dave Henderson
547 Roger McDowell RC* .08 .25
548 Mike Young .02 .10
549 Bob Welch .05 .15
550 Tom Herr .02 .10
551 Dave LaPoint .02 .10
552 Marc Hill .02 .10
553 Jim Morrison .02 .10
554 Paul Householder .02 .10
555 Hubie Brooks .02 .10
556 John Denny .02 .10
557 Gerald Perry .02 .10
558 Tim Stoddard .02 .10
559 Tommy Dunbar .02 .10
560 Dave Righetti .05 .15
561 Bob Lillis MG .02 .10
562 Joe Beckwith .02 .10
563 Alejandro Sanchez .02 .10
564 Warren Brusstar .02 .10
565 Tom Brunansky .02 .10
566 Alfredo Griffin .02 .10
567 Jeff Barkley .02 .10
568 Donnie Scott .02 .10
569 Jim Acker .02 .10
570 Rusty Staub .05 .15
571 Mike Jeffcoat .02 .10
572 Paul Zuvella .02 .10
573 Tom Hume .02 .10
574 Ron Kittle .02 .10
575 Mike Boddicker .02 .10
576 Andre Dawson TL .02 .10
577 Jerry Reuss .02 .10
578 Lee Mazzilli .05 .15
579 Jim Slaton .02 .10
580 Willie McGee .05 .15
581 Bruce Hurst .02 .10
582 Jim Gantner .02 .10
583 Al Bumbry .02 .10
584 Brian Fisher RC .02 .10
585 Garry Maddox .02 .10
586 Greg Harris .02 .10
587 Rafael Santana .02 .10
588 Steve Lake .02 .10
589 Sid Bream .02 .10
590 Bob Knepper .02 .10
591 Jackie Moore MG .02 .10
592 Frank Tanana .05 .15
593 Jesse Barfield .05 .15
594 Chris Bando .02 .10
595 Dave Parker .05 .15
596 Onix Concepcion .02 .10
597 Sammy Stewart .02 .10
598 Jim Presley .02 .10
599 Rick Aguilera RC .08 .25
600 Dale Murphy .08 .25
601 Gary Lucas .02 .10
602 Mariano Duncan RC .08 .25
603 Bill Laskey .02 .10
604 Gary Pettis .02 .10
605 Dennis Boyd .02 .10
606 Royals Leaders .05 .15
Hal McRae
607 Ken Dayley .02 .10
608 Bruce Bochy .02 .10
609 Barbaro Garbey .02 .10
610 Ron Guidry .05 .15
611 Gary Woods .02 .10
612 Richard Dotson .02 .10
613 Roy Smalley .02 .10
614 Rick Waits .02 .10
615 Johnny Ray .02 .10
616 Glenn Brummer .02 .10
617 Lonnie Smith .02 .10
618 Jim Pankovits .02 .10
619 Danny Heep .02 .10
620 Bruce Sutter .05 .15
621 John Felske MG .02 .10
622 Gary Lavelle .02 .10
623 Floyd Rayford .02 .10
624 Steve McCatty .02 .10
625 Bob Brenly .02 .10
626 Roy Thomas .02 .10
627 Ron Oester .02 .10
628 Kirk McCaskill RC .08 .25
629 Mitch Webster .02 .10
630 Fernando Valenzuela .05 .15
631 Steve Braun .02 .10
632 Dave Von Ohlen .02 .10
633 Jackie Gutierrez .02 .10
634 Roy Lee Jackson .02 .10
635 Jason Thompson .02 .10
636 Lee Smith TL .02 .10
637 Rudy Law .02 .10
638 John Butcher .02 .10
639 Bo Diaz .02 .10
640 Jose Cruz .05 .15
641 Wayne Tolleson .02 .10
642 Ray Searage .02 .10
643 Tom Brookens .02 .10
644 Mark Gubicza .02 .10
645 Dusty Baker .05 .15
646 Mike Moore .02 .10
647 Mel Hall .02 .10
648 Steve Bedrosian .02 .10
649 Ronn Reynolds .02 .10
650 Dave Stieb .05 .15
651 Billy Martin MG .08 .25
TC
652 Tom Browning .02 .10
653 Jim Dwyer .02 .10
654 Ken Howell .02 .10
655 Manny Trillo .02 .10
656 Brian Harper .02 .10
657 Juan Agosto .02 .10
658 Rob Wilfong .02 .10
659 Checklist: 529-660 .05 .15
660 Steve Garvey .05 .15
661 Roger Clemens 1.50 4.00
662 Bill Schroeder .02 .10
663 Neil Allen .02 .10
664 Tim Corcoran .02 .10
665 Alejandro Pena .02 .10
666 Rangers Leaders .05 .15
Charlie Hough
667 Tim Teufel .02 .10
668 Cecilio Guante .02 .10
669 Ron Cey .05 .15
670 Willie Hernandez .02 .10
671 Lynn Jones .02 .10
672 Rob Picciolo .02 .10
673 Ernie Whitt .02 .10
674 Pat Tabler .02 .10
675 Claudell Washington .02 .10
676 Matt Young .02 .10
677 Nick Esasky .02 .10
678 Dan Gladden .02 .10
679 Britt Burns .02 .10
680 George Foster .05 .15
681 Dick Williams MG .02 .10
682 Junior Ortiz .02 .10
683 Andy Van Slyke .08 .25
684 Bob McClure .02 .10
685 Tim Wallach .02 .10
686 Jeff Stone .02 .10
687 Mike Trujillo .02 .10
688 Larry Herndon .05 .15
689 Dave Stewart .05 .15
690 Ryne Sandberg .30 .75
691 Mike Madden .02 .10
692 Dale Berra .02 .10
693 Tom Tellmann .02 .10
694 Garth Iorg .02 .10
695 Mike Smithson .02 .10
696 Dodgers Leaders .05 .15
Bill Russell
697 Bud Black .02 .10
698 Brad Komminsk .02 .10
699 Pat Corrales MG .02 .10
700 Reggie Jackson .08 .25
701 Keith Hernandez AS .02 .10
702 Tom Herr AS .02 .10
703 Tim Wallach AS .02 .10
704 Ozzie Smith AS .15 .40
705 Dale Murphy AS .05 .15
706 Pedro Guerrero AS .02 .10
707 Willie McGee AS .02 .10
708 Gary Carter AS .02 .10
709 Dwight Gooden AS .08 .25
710 John Tudor AS .02 .10
711 Jeff Reardon AS .02 .10
712 Don Mattingly AS .25 .60
713 Damaso Garcia AS .02 .10
714 George Brett AS .15 .40
715 Cal Ripken AS .15 .40
716 Rickey Henderson AS .08 .25
717 Dave Winfield AS .02 .10
718 George Bell AS .02 .10
719 Carlton Fisk AS .05 .15
720 Bret Saberhagen AS .02 .10
721 Ron Guidry AS .02 .10
722 Dan Quisenberry AS .02 .10
723 Marty Bystrom .02 .10
724 Tim Hulett .02 .10
725 Mario Soto .05 .15
726 Orioles Leaders .05 .15
Rick Dempsey
727 David Green .02 .10
728 Mike Marshall .02 .10
729 Jim Beattie .02 .10
730 Ozzie Smith .25 .60
731 Don Robinson .02 .10
732 Floyd Youmans .02 .10
733 Ron Romanick .02 .10
734 Marty Barrett .02 .10
735 Dave Dravecky .02 .10
736 Glenn Wilson .02 .10
737 Pete Vuckovich .02 .10
738 Andre Robertson .02 .10
739 Dave Rozema .02 .10
740 Lance Parrish .05 .15
741 Pete Rose MG .15 .40
TC
742 Frank Viola .05 .15
743 Pat Sheridan .02 .10
744 Lary Sorensen .02 .10
745 Willie Upshaw .02 .10
746 Denny Gonzalez .02 .10
747 Rick Cerone .02 .10
748 Steve Henderson .02 .10
749 Ed Jurak .02 .10
750 Gorman Thomas .05 .15
751 Howard Johnson .05 .15
752 Mike Krukow .02 .10
753 Dan Ford .02 .10
754 Pat Clements .02 .10
755 Harold Baines .05 .15
756 Pirates Leaders .02 .10
Rick Rhoden
757 Darrell Porter .02 .10
758 Dave Anderson .02 .10
759 Moose Haas .02 .10
760 Andre Dawson .05 .15
761 Don Slaught .02 .10
762 Eric Show .02 .10
763 Terry Puhl .02 .10
764 Kevin Gross .02 .10
765 Don Baylor .05 .15
766 Rick Langford .02 .10
767 Jody Davis .02 .10
768 Vern Ruhle .02 .10
769 Harold Reynolds RC .30 .75
770 Vida Blue .05 .15
771 John McNamara MG .02 .10
772 Brian Downing .05 .15
773 Greg Pryor .02 .10
774 Terry Leach .02 .10
775 Al Oliver .05 .15
776 Gene Garber .02 .10
777 Wayne Krenchicki .02 .10
778 Jerry Hairston .02 .10
779 Rick Reuschel .05 .15
780 Robin Yount .25 .60
781 Joe Nolan .02 .10
782 Ken Landreaux .02 .10
783 Ricky Horton .02 .10
784 Alan Bannister .02 .10
785 Bob Stanley .02 .10
786 Twins Leaders .02 .10
Mickey Hatcher
787 Vance Law .02 .10
788 Marty Castillo .02 .10
789 Kurt Bevacqua .02 .10
790 Phil Niekro .05 .15
791 Checklist: 661-792 .05 .15
792 Charles Hudson .02 .10

1986 Topps Tiffany

COMP.FACT.SET (792) 100.00 200.00
*STARS: 5X TO 12X BASIC CARDS
*ROOKIES: 5X TO 12X BASIC CARDS
DISTRIBUTED ONLY IN FACTORY SET FORM
FACTORY SET PRICE IS FOR SEALED SETS

1986 Topps Glossy All-Stars

This 22-card standard-size set was distributed as an insert, one card per rak pack. The players featured are the starting lineups of the 1985 All-Star Game played in Minnesota. The cards are very colorful and have a high gloss finish.

COMPLETE SET (22) 2.00 5.00
1 Sparky Anderson MG .01 .05
2 Eddie Murray .20 .50
3 Lou Whitaker .02 .10
4 George Brett .40 1.00
5 Cal Ripken .75 2.00
6 Jim Rice .02 .10
7 Rickey Henderson .20 .50
8 Dave Winfield .20 .50
9 Carlton Fisk .15 .40
10 Jack Morris .02 .10
11 AL Team Photo .01 .05
12 Dick Williams MG .01 .05
13 Steve Garvey .02 .10
14 Tom Herr .01 .05
15 Graig Nettles .02 .10
16 Ozzie Smith .40 1.00
17 Tony Gwynn .40 1.00
18 Dale Murphy .07 .20
19 Darryl Strawberry .02 .10
20 Terry Pendleton .01 .05
21 LaMarr Hoyt .01 .05
22 NL Team Photo .01 .05

1986 Topps Glossy Send-Ins

This 60-card glossy standard-size set was produced by Topps and distributed ten cards at a time based on the offer found on the wax packs. Each series of ten cards was available by sending in 1.00 plus six "special offer" cards inserted one per wax pack. The card backs are printed in red and blue on white card stock. The card fronts feature a white border and a green frame surrounding a full-color photo of the player.

COMPLETE SET (60) 5.00 12.00
1 Oddibe McDowell .02 .10
2 Reggie Jackson .30 .75
3 Fernando Valenzuela .07 .20
4 Jack Clark .02 .10
5 Rickey Henderson .40 1.25
6 Steve Balboni .02 .10
7 Keith Hernandez .07 .20
8 Lance Parrish .07 .20
9 Willie McGee .07 .20
10 Chris Brown .02 .10
11 Darryl Strawberry .07 .20
12 Ron Guidry .07 .20
13 Dave Parker .07 .20
14 Cal Ripken 1.50 4.00
15 Tim Raines .07 .20
16 Rod Carew .30 .75
17 Mike Schmidt .40 1.00
18 George Brett .75 2.00
19 Joe Hesketh .02 .10
20 Dan Pasqua .02 .10
21 Vince Coleman .07 .20
22 Tom Seaver .30 .75
23 Gary Carter .30 .75
24 Orel Hershiser .07 .20
25 Pedro Guerrero .02 .10
26 Wade Boggs .30 .75
27 Bret Saberhagen .07 .20
28 Carlton Fisk .30 .75
29 Kirk Gibson .07 .20
30 Brian Fisher .02 .10
31 Don Mattingly .75 2.00
32 Tom Herr .02 .10
33 Eddie Murray .30 .75
34 Ryne Sandberg .60 1.50
35 Dan Quisenberry .02 .10
36 Jim Rice .07 .20
37 Dale Murphy .10 .30
38 Steve Garvey .07 .20
39 Roger McDowell .02 .10
40 Earnie Riles .02 .10
41 Dwight Gooden .07 .20
42 Dave Winfield .30 .75
43 Dave Stieb .02 .10
44 Bob Horner .02 .10
45 Nolan Ryan 1.50 4.00
46 Ozzie Smith .75 2.00
47 George Bell .02 .10
48 Gorman Thomas .02 .10
49 Tom Browning .02 .10
50 Larry Sheets .02 .10
51 Pete Rose .40 1.00
52 Brett Butler .07 .20
53 John Tudor .02 .10
54 Phil Bradley .02 .10
55 Jeff Reardon .07 .20
56 Rich Gossage .07 .20
57 Tony Gwynn .75 2.00
58 Ozzie Guillen .20 .50
59 Glenn Davis .02 .10
60 Darrell Evans .02 .10

1986 Topps Wax Box Cards

Topps printed cards (each measuring the standard 2 1/2" by 3 1/2") on the bottoms of their wax pack boxes for their regular issue cards; there are four different boxes, each with four cards. These sixteen cards ("numbered" A through P) are listed below; they are not considered an integral part of the regular set but are considered a separate set. The order of the set is alphabetical by player's name. These wax box cards are styled almost exactly like the 1986 Topps regular issue cards. Complete boxes would be worth an additional 25 percent premium over the prices below. The card lettering is sequenced in alphabetical order.

COMPLETE SET (16) 3.00 8.00
A George Bell .07 .20
B Wade Boggs .40 1.00
C George Brett .75 2.00
D Vince Coleman .15 .40
E Carlton Fisk .40 1.00
F Dwight Gooden .15 .40
G Pedro Guerrero .15 .40
H Ron Guidry .15 .40
I Reggie Jackson .40 1.00
J Don Mattingly .75 2.00
K Oddibe McDowell .07 .20
L Willie McGee .15 .40
M Dale Murphy .30 .75
N Pete Rose .50 1.25
O Bret Saberhagen .15 .40
P Fernando Valenzuela .15 .40

1986 Topps Traded

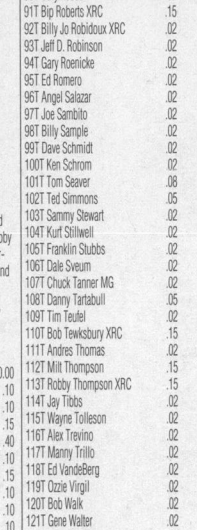

This 132-card standard-size Traded set was distributed in factory set form, which were packed 100 to a case, in a red and white box through hobby dealers. The cards are identical in style to regular-issue 1986 Topps cards except for whiter stock and t-suffixed numbering. The key extended Rookie Cards in this set are Barry Bonds, Bobby Bonilla, Jose Canseco, Will Clark, Andres Galarraga, Bo Jackson, Wally Joyner, John Kruk, and Kevin Mitchell.

COMP.FACT.SET (132) 12.50 30.00
1T Andy Allanson XRC .02 .10
2T Neil Allen .02 .10
3T Joaquin Andujar .05 .15
4T Paul Assenmacher .15 .40
5T Scott Bailes .02 .10
6T Don Baylor .05 .15
7T Steve Bedrosian .02 .10
8T Juan Beniquez .02 .10
9T Juan Berenguer .02 .10
10T Mike Bielecki .02 .10
11T Barry Bonds XRC 8.00 20.00
12T Bobby Bonilla XRC .30 .75
13T Juan Bonilla .02 .10
14T Rich Bordi .02 .10
15T Steve Boros MG .02 .10
16T Rick Burleson .02 .10
17T Bill Campbell .02 .10
18T Tom Candiotti .02 .10
19T John Cangelosi .02 .10
20T Jose Canseco XRC 2.50 6.00
21T Carmen Castillo .02 .10
22T Rick Cerone .02 .10
23T John Cerutti .02 .10
24T Will Clark XRC 5.00 12.00
25T Mark Clear .02 .10
26T Darnell Coles .02 .10
27T Dave Collins .02 .10
28T Tim Conroy .02 .10
29T Joe Cowley .02 .10
30T Joel Davis .02 .10
31T Rob Deer .02 .10
32T John Denny .02 .10
33T Mike Easler .02 .10
34T Mark Eichhorn .02 .10
35T Steve Farr .02 .10
36T Scott Fletcher .02 .10
37T Terry Forster .05 .15
38T Terry Francona .05 .15
39T Jim Fregosi MG .02 .10
40T Andres Galarraga XRC .40 1.00
41T Ken Griffey .05 .15
42T Bill Gullickson .02 .10
43T Jose Guzman XRC .02 .10
44T Moose Haas .02 .10
45T Billy Hatcher .02 .10
46T Mike Heath .02 .10
47T Tom Hume .02 .10
48T Pete Incaviglia XRC .15 .40
49T Dane Iorg .02 .10
50T Bo Jackson XRC 6.00 15.00
51T Wally Joyner XRC .30 .75
52T Charlie Kerfeld .02 .10
53T Eric King .02 .10
54T Bob Kipper .02 .10
55T Wayne Krenchicki .02 .10
56T John Kruk XRC .40 1.00
57T Mike LaCoss .02 .10
58T Pete Ladd .02 .10
59T Mike Laga .02 .10
60T Hal Lanier MG .02 .10
61T Dave LaPoint .02 .10
62T Rudy Law .02 .10
63T Rick Leach .02 .10
64T Tim Leary .02 .10
65T Dennis Leonard .02 .10
66T Jim Leyland MG XRC .20 .50
67T Steve Lyons .02 .10
68T Mickey Mahler .02 .10
69T Candy Maldonado .02 .10
70T Roger Mason XRC .02 .10
71T Bob McClure .02 .10
72T Andy McGaffigan .02 .10
73T Gene Michael MG .02 .10
74T Kevin Mitchell XRC .30 .75
75T Omar Moreno .02 .10
76T Jerry Mumphrey .02 .10
77T Phil Niekro .05 .15
78T Randy Niemann .02 .10
79T Juan Nieves .02 .10
80T Otis Nixon XRC .30 .75
81T Bob Ojeda .02 .10
82T Jose Oquendo .02 .10
83T Tom Paciorek .02 .10
84T David Palmer .02 .10
85T Frank Pastore .02 .10
86T Lou Piniella MG .05 .15
87T Dan Plesac .15 .40
88T Darrell Porter .02 .10
89T Rey Quinones .02 .10
90T Gary Redus .02 .10
91T Bip Roberts XRC .15 .40
92T Billy Jo Robidoux XRC .02 .10
93T Jeff D. Robinson .02 .10
94T Gary Roenicke .02 .10
95T Ed Romero .02 .10
96T Angel Salazar .02 .10
97T Joe Sambito .02 .10
98T Billy Sample .02 .10
99T Dave Schmidt .02 .10
100T Ken Schrom .02 .10
101T Tom Seaver .08 .25
102T Ted Simmons .05 .15
103T Sammy Stewart .02 .10
104T Kurt Stillwell .02 .10
105T Franklin Stubbs .02 .10
106T Dale Sveum .02 .10
107T Chuck Tanner MG .02 .10
108T Danny Tartabull .05 .15
109T Tim Teufel .02 .10
110T Bob Tewksbury XRC .15 .40
111T Andres Thomas .02 .10
112T Milt Thompson .15 .40
113T Robby Thompson XRC .15 .40
114T Jay Tibbs .02 .10
115T Wayne Tolleson .02 .10
116T Alex Trevino .02 .10
117T Manny Trillo .02 .10
118T Ed VandeBerg .02 .10
119T Ozzie Virgil .02 .10
120T Bob Walk .02 .10
121T Gene Walter .02 .10
122T Claudell Washington .02 .10
123T Bill Wegman XRC .02 .10
124T Dick Williams MG .02 .10
125T Mitch Williams XRC .15 .40
126T Bobby Witt XRC .15 .40
127T Todd Worrell XRC .15 .40
128T George Wright .02 .10
129T Ricky Wright .02 .10
130T Steve Yeager .05 .15
131T Paul Zuvella .02 .10
132T Checklist 1T-132T .02 .10

1986 Topps Traded Tiffany

COMP.FACT.SET (132) 200.00 400.00
*STARS: 5X TO 12X BASIC CARDS
*ROOKIES: 4X TO 10X BASIC CARDS
DISTRIBUTED ONLY IN FACTORY SET FORM
FACTORY SET PRICE IS FOR SEALED SETS
OPENED SETS SELL FOR 50-60% OF SEALED

1987 Topps

This set consists of 792 standard-size cards. Cards were primarily issued in 17-card wax packs, 50-card rack packs and factory sets. Card fronts feature wood grain borders encasing a color photo (reminiscent of Topps' classic 1962 baseball set). Subsets include Record Breakers (1-7), Turn Back the Clock (311-315), All-Star selections (595-616) and Team Leaders (scattered throughout the set). The manager cards contain a team checklist on back. The key Rookie Cards in this set are Barry Bonds, Bobby Bonilla, Will Clark, Bo Jackson, Wally Joyner, John Kruk, Barry Larkin, Rafael Palmeiro, Ruben Sierra, and Devon White.

COMPLETE SET (792) 10.00 25.00
COMP.FACT.SET (792) 15.00 40.00
COMP.HOBBY SET (792) 15.00 40.00
COMP.X-MAS.SET (792) 15.00 40.00
1 Roger Clemens RB .40 1.00
2 Jim Deshaies RB .01 .05
Most cons. K's&
start of game
3 Dwight Evans RB .05 .15
Earliest home run&
season
4 Davey Lopes RB .01 .05
Most steals& season&/40-year-old
5 Dave Righetti RB .01 .05
Most saves& season
6 Ruben Sierra RB .08 .25
7 Todd Worrell RB .01 .05
Most saves&
season& rookie
8 Terry Pendleton .02 .10
9 Jay Tibbs .01 .05
10 Cecil Cooper .02 .10
11 Indians Team/(Mound conference) .01 .05
12 Jeff Sellers .01 .05
13 Nick Esasky .01 .05
14 Dave Stewart .02 .10
15 Claudell Washington .01 .05
16 Pat Clements .01 .05
17 Pete O'Brien .01 .05
18 Dick Howser MG .01 .05
19 Matt Young .01 .05
20 Gary Carter .02 .10
21 Mark Davis .01 .05
22 Doug DeCinces .01 .05
23 Lee Smith .02 .10
24 Tony Walker .01 .05
25 Bert Blyleven .02 .10
26 Greg Brock .01 .05
27 Joe Cowley .01 .05
28 Rick Dempsey .01 .05
29 Jimmy Key .02 .10
30 Tim Raines .02 .10
31 Braves Team/(Glenn Hubbard and .01 .05
Rafael Ramirez)
32 Tim Leary .01 .05
33 Andy Van Slyke .05 .15
34 Jose Rijo .02 .10
35 Sid Bream .01 .05
36 Eric King .01 .05
37 Marvell Wynne .01 .05
38 Dennis Leonard .01 .05
39 Marty Barrett .01 .05
40 Dave Righetti .02 .10
41 Bo Diaz .01 .05
42 Gary Redus .01 .05
43 Gene Michael MG .01 .05
44 Greg Harris .01 .05
45 Jim Presley .01 .05
46 Dan Gladden .01 .05
47 Dennis Powell .01 .05
48 Wally Backman .01 .05
49 Terry Harper .01 .05
50 Dave Smith .01 .05
51 Mel Hall .01 .05
52 Keith Atherton .01 .05
53 Ruppert Jones .01 .05
54 Bill Dawley .01 .05
55 Tim Wallach .01 .05
56 Brewers Team/(Mound conference) .02 .10
57 Scott Nielsen .01 .05
58 Thad Bosley .01 .05
59 Ken Dayley .01 .05
60 Tony Pena .01 .05
61 Bobby Thigpen RC .08 .25
62 Bobby Meacham .01 .05
63 Fred Toliver .01 .05
64 Harry Spilman .01 .05
65 Tom Browning .01 .05
66 Marc Sullivan .01 .05
67 Bill Swift .01 .05
68 Tony LaRussa MG .02 .10
69 Lonnie Smith .01 .05
70 Charlie Hough .02 .10
71 Mike Aldrete .01 .05
72 Walt Terrell .01 .05
73 Dave Anderson .01 .05
74 Dan Pasqua .01 .05
75 Ron Darling .02 .10
76 Rafael Ramirez .01 .05
77 Bryan Oelkers .01 .05
78 Tom Foley .01 .05
79 Juan Nieves .01 .05
80 Wally Joyner RC .15 .40
81 Padres Team/(Andy Hawkins and .01 .05
Terry Kennedy)
82 Rob Murphy .01 .05
83 Mike Davis .01 .05
84 Steve Lake .01 .05
85 Kevin Bass .01 .05
86 Nate Snell .01 .05
87 Mark Salas .01 .05
88 Ed Wojna .01 .05
89 Ozzie Guillen .05 .15
90 Dave Stieb .02 .10
91 Harold Reynolds .02 .10
92A Urbano Lugo .05 .15
ERR (no trademark)
92B Urbano Lugo COR .01 .05
93 Jim Leyland MG .08 .25
TC RC *
94 Calvin Schiraldi .01 .05
95 Oddibe McDowell .01 .05
96 Frank Williams .01 .05
97 Glenn Wilson .01 .05
98 Bill Scherrer .01 .05
99 Darryl Motley/(Now with Braves .01 .05
on card front)
100 Steve Garvey .02 .10
101 Carl Willis RC .02 .10
102 Paul Zuvella .01 .05
103 Rick Aguilera .01 .05
104 Billy Sample .01 .05
105 Floyd Youmans .01 .05
106 Blue Jays Team/(George Bell and .01 .05
Jesse Barfield)
107 John Butcher .01 .05
108 Jim Gantner UER/(Brewers logo .01 .05
reversed)
109 R.J. Reynolds .01 .05
110 John Tudor .02 .10
111 Alfredo Griffin .01 .05
112 Alan Ashby .01 .05
113 Neil Allen .01 .05
114 Billy Beane .02 .10
115 Donnie Moore .01 .05
116 Bill Russell .02 .10
117 Jim Beattie .01 .05
118 Bobby Valentine MG .02 .10
119 Ron Robinson .01 .05
120 Eddie Murray .08 .25
121 Kevin Romine RC .01 .05
122 Jim Clancy .01 .05
123 John Kruk RC .20 .50
124 Ray Fontenot .01 .05
125 Bob Brenly .01 .05
126 Mike Loynd RC .02 .10
127 Vance Law .01 .05
128 Checklist 1-132 .01 .05
129 Rick Cerone .01 .05
130 Dwight Gooden .05 .15

131 Pirates Team/(Sid Bream and Tony Pena) .01 .05
132 Paul Assenmacher .08 .25
133 Jose Oquendo .01 .05
134 Rich Yett .01 .05
135 Mike Easler .01 .05
136 Ron Romanick .01 .05
137 Jerry Willard .01 .05
138 Roy Lee Jackson .01 .05
139 Devon White RC .15 .40
140 Bret Saberhagen .02 .10
141 Herm Winningham .01 .05
142 Rick Sutcliffe .02 .10
143 Steve Boros MG .01 .05
144 Mike Scioscia .02 .10
145 Charlie Kerfeld .01 .05
146 Tracy Jones .01 .05
147 Randy Niemann .01 .05
148 Dave Collins .01 .05
149 Ray Searage .01 .05
150 Wade Boggs .05 .15
151 Mike LaCoss .01 .05
152 Toby Harrah .02 .10
153 Duane Ward RC * .08 .25
154 Tom O'Malley .01 .05
155 Eddie Whitson .01 .05
156 Mariners Team/(Mound conference) .01 .05
157 Danny Darwin .01 .05
158 Tim Teufel .01 .05
159 Ed Olwine .01 .05
160 Julio Franco .02 .10
161 Steve Ontiveros .01 .05
162 Mike LaValliere RC * .08 .25
163 Kevin Gross .01 .05
164 Sammy Khalifa .01 .05
165 Jeff Reardon .02 .10
166 Bob Boone .02 .10
167 Jim Deshaies RC * .02 .10
168 Lou Piniella MG .02 .10
169 Ron Washington .01 .05
170 Bo Jackson RC 1.25 3.00
171 Chuck Cary .01 .05
172 Ron Oester .01 .05
173 Alex Trevino .01 .05
174 Henry Cotto .01 .05
175 Bob Stanley .01 .05
176 Steve Buechele .01 .05
177 Keith Moreland .01 .05
178 Cecil Fielder .02 .10
179 Bill Wegman .01 .05
180 Chris Brown .01 .05
181 Cardinals Team (Mound conference) .01 .05
182 Lee Lacy .01 .05
183 Andy Hawkins .01 .05
184 Bobby Bonilla RC .15 .40
185 Roger McDowell .01 .05
186 Bruce Benedict .01 .05
187 Mark Huismann .01 .05
188 Tony Phillips .01 .05
189 Joe Hesketh .01 .05
190 Jim Sundberg .02 .10
191 Charles Hudson .01 .05
192 Cory Snyder .01 .05
193 Roger Craig MG .02 .10
194 Kirk McCaskill .01 .05
195 Mike Pagliarulo .01 .05
196 Randy O'Neal UER (Wrong ML career W-L totals) .01 .05
197 Mark Bailey .01 .05
198 Lee Mazzilli .02 .10
199 Mariano Duncan .01 .05
200 Pete Rose .25 .60
201 John Cangelosi .01 .05
202 Ricky Wright .01 .05
203 Mike Kingery RC .02 .10
204 Sammy Stewart .01 .05
205 Graig Nettles .02 .10
206 Twins Team/(Frank Viola and Tim Laudner) .01 .05
207 George Frazier .01 .05
208 John Shelby .01 .05
209 Rick Schu .01 .05
210 Lloyd Moseby .01 .05
211 John Morris .01 .05
212 Mike Fitzgerald .01 .05
213 Randy Myers RC .15 .40
214 Omar Moreno .01 .05
215 Mark Langston .01 .05
216 B.J. Surhoff RC .15 .40
217 Chris Codiroli .01 .05
218 Sparky Anderson MG .02 .10
219 Cecilio Guante .01 .05
220 Joe Carter .02 .10
221 Vern Ruhle .01 .05
222 Denny Walling .01 .05
223 Charlie Leibrandt .01 .05
224 Wayne Tolleson .01 .05
225 Mike Smithson .01 .05
226 Max Venable .01 .05
227 Jamie Moyer RC .20 .50
228 Curt Wilkerson .01 .05
229 Mike Birkbeck .02 .10
230 Don Baylor .02 .10
231 Giants Team/(Bob Brenly and Jim Gott) .01 .05
232 Reggie Williams .01 .05
233 Russ Morman .01 .05
234 Pat Sheridan .01 .05
235 Alvin Davis .01 .05
236 Tommy John .02 .10
237 Jim Morrison .01 .05
238 Bill Krueger .01 .05
239 Juan Espino .01 .05
240 Steve Balboni .01 .05
241 Danny Heep .01 .05
242 Rick Mahler .01 .05
243 Whitey Herzog MG .02 .10
244 Dickie Noles .01 .05
245 Willie Upshaw .01 .05
246 Jim Dwyer .01 .05
247 Jeff Reed .01 .05
248 Gene Walter .01 .05
249 Jim Pankovits .01 .05
250 Teddy Higuera .01 .05
251 Rob Wilfong .01 .05
252 Dennis Martinez .02 .10
253 Eddie Milner .01 .05
254 Bob Tewksbury RC * .08 .25
255 Juan Samuel .01 .05
256 Royals TL George Brett .05 .15
257 Bob Forsch .01 .05
258 Steve Yeager .02 .10
259 Mike Greenwell RC .08 .25
260 Vida Blue .02 .10
261 Ruben Sierra RC .20 .50
262 Jim Winn .01 .05
263 Stan Javier .01 .05
264 Checklist 133-264 .01 .05
265 Darrell Evans .02 .10
266 Jeff Hamilton .01 .05
267 Howard Johnson .02 .10
268 Pat Corrales MG .01 .05
269 Cliff Speck .01 .05
270 Jody Davis .01 .05
271 Mike G. Brown .01 .05
272 Andres Galarraga .02 .10
273 Gene Nelson .01 .05
274 Jeff Hearron UER/(Duplicate 1986 stat line on ba .01 .05
275 LaMarr Hoyt .01 .05
276 Jackie Gutierrez .01 .05
277 Juan Agosto .01 .05
278 Gary Pettis .01 .05
279 Dan Plesac .01 .05
280 Jeff Leonard .01 .05
281 Reds TL Rose .08 .25
282 Jeff Calhoun .01 .05
283 Doug Drabek RC .15 .40
284 John Moses .01 .05
285 Dennis Boyd .01 .05
286 Mike Woodard .01 .05
287 Dave Von Ohlen .01 .05
288 Tito Landrum .01 .05
289 Bob Kipper .01 .05
290 Leon Durham .01 .05
291 Mitch Williams RC * .08 .25
292 Franklin Stubbs .01 .05
293 Bob Rodgers MG/(Checklist back & inconsistent des .01 .05
294 Steve Jeltz .01 .05
295 Len Dykstra .02 .10
296 Andres Thomas .01 .05
297 Don Schulze .01 .05
298 Larry Herndon .01 .05
299 Joel Davis .01 .05
300 Reggie Jackson .05 .15
301 Luis Aquino UER/(No trademark never corrected) .01 .05
302 Bill Schroeder .01 .05
303 Juan Berenguer .01 .05
304 Phil Garner .02 .10
305 John Franco .02 .10
306 Red Sox TL Seaver .02 .10
307 Lee Guetterman .01 .05
308 Don Slaught .01 .05
309 Mike Young .01 .05
310 Frank Viola .02 .10
311 Rickey Henderson TBC .05 .15
312 Reggie Jackson TBC .02 .10
313 Roberto Clemente TBC .08 .25
314 Carl Yastrzemski TBC .08 .25
315 Maury Wills TBC '62 .02 .10
316 Brian Fisher .01 .05
317 Clint Hurdle .01 .05
318 Jim Fregosi MG .01 .05
319 Greg Swindell RC .08 .25
320 Barry Bonds RC 4.00 10.00
321 Mike Laga .01 .05
322 Chris Bando .01 .05
323 Al Newman RC .01 .05
324 David Palmer .01 .05
325 Garry Templeton .02 .10
326 Mark Gubicza .01 .05
327 Dale Sveum .01 .05
328 Bob Welch .02 .10
329 Ron Roenicke .01 .05
330 Mike Scott .02 .10
331 Mets TL Carter Straw .02 .10
332 Joe Price .01 .05
333 Ken Phelps .01 .05
334 Ed Correa .01 .05
335 Candy Maldonado .01 .05
336 Allan Anderson RC .01 .05
337 Darrell Miller .01 .05
338 Tim Conroy .01 .05
339 Donnie Hill .01 .05
340 Roger Clemens .60 1.50
341 Mike C. Brown .01 .05
342 Bob James .01 .05
343 Hal Lanier MG .01 .05
344A Joe Niekro/(Copyright inside righthand border) .01 .05
344B Joe Niekro/(Copyright outside righthand border) .01 .05
345 Andre Dawson .02 .10
346 Shawon Dunston .01 .05
347 Mickey Brantley .01 .05
348 Carmelo Martinez .01 .05
349 Storm Davis .01 .05
350 Keith Hernandez .02 .10
351 Gene Garber .01 .05
352 Mike Felder .01 .05
353 Ernie Camacho .01 .05
354 Jamie Quirk .01 .05
355 Don Carman .01 .05
356 White Sox Team (Mound conference) .01 .05
357 Steve Fireovid .01 .05
358 Sal Butera .01 .05
359 Doug Corbett .01 .05
360 Pedro Guerrero .02 .10
361 Mark Thurmond .01 .05
362 Luis Quinones .01 .05
363 Jose Guzman .01 .05
364 Randy Bush .01 .05
365 Rick Rhoden .01 .05
366 Mark McGwire 1.50 4.00
367 Jeff Lahti .01 .05
368 John McNamara MG .01 .05
369 Brian Dayett .01 .05
370 Fred Lynn .02 .10
371 Mark Eichhorn .01 .05
372 Jerry Mumphrey .01 .05
373 Jeff Dedmon .01 .05
374 Glenn Hoffman .01 .05
375 Ron Guidry .02 .10
376 Scott Bradley .01 .05
377 John Henry Johnson .01 .05
378 Rafael Santana .01 .05
379 John Russell .01 .05
380 Rich Gossage .02 .10
381 Expos Team/(Mound conference) .01 .05
382 Rudy Law .01 .05
383 Ron Davis .01 .05
384 Johnny Grubb .01 .05
385 Orel Hershiser .05 .15
386 Dickie Thon .01 .05
387 T.R. Bryden .01 .05
388 Geno Petralli .01 .05
389 Jeff D. Robinson .01 .05
390 Gary Matthews .02 .10
391 Jay Howell .01 .05
392 Checklist 265-396 .01 .05
393 Pete Rose MG TC .05 .15
394 Mike Bielecki .01 .05
395 Damaso Garcia .01 .05
396 Tim Lollar .01 .05
397 Greg Walker .01 .05
398 Brad Havens .01 .05
399 Curt Ford .01 .05
400 George Brett .25 .60
401 Billy Joe Robidoux .01 .05
402 Mike Trujillo .01 .05
403 Jerry Royster .01 .05
404 Doug Sisk .01 .05
405 Brook Jacoby .01 .05
406 Yankees TL Hend Matt .20 .50
407 Jim Acker .01 .05
408 John Mizerock .01 .05
409 Milt Thompson .01 .05
410 Fernando Valenzuela .02 .10
411 Darnell Coles .01 .05
412 Eric Davis .05 .15
413 Moose Haas .01 .05
414 Joe Orsulak .01 .05
415 Bobby Witt RC .08 .25
416 Tom Nieto .01 .05
417 Pat Perry .01 .05
418 Dick Williams MG .01 .05
419 Mark Portugal RC * .08 .25
420 Will Clark RC .40 1.00
421 Jose DeLeon .01 .05
422 Jack Howell .01 .05
423 Jaime Cocanower .01 .05
424 Chris Speier .01 .05
425 Tom Seaver .05 .15
426 Floyd Rayford .01 .05
427 Edwin Nunez .01 .05
428 Bruce Bochy .01 .05
429 Tim Pyznarski .01 .05
430 Mike Schmidt .20 .50
431 Dodgers Team/(Mound conference) .01 .05
432 Jim Slaton .01 .05
433 Ed Hearn RC .01 .05
434 Mike Fischlin .01 .05
435 Bruce Sutter .02 .10
436 Andy Allanson RC .01 .05
437 Ted Power .01 .05
438 Kelly Downs RC .02 .10
439 Karl Best .01 .05
440 Willie McGee .02 .10
441 Dave Leiper .01 .05
442 Mitch Webster .01 .05
443 John Felske MG .01 .05
444 Jeff Russell .01 .05
445 Dave Lopes .02 .10
446 Chuck Finley RC .15 .40
447 Bill Almon .01 .05
448 Chris Bosio RC .08 .25
449 Pat Dodson .02 .10
450 Kirby Puckett .20 .50
451 Joe Sambito .01 .05
452 Dave Henderson .01 .05
453 Scott Terry RC .02 .10
454 Luis Salazar .01 .05
455 Mike Boddicker .01 .05
456 A's Team/(Mound conference) .01 .05
457 Len Matuszek .01 .05
458 Kelly Gruber .01 .05
459 Dennis Eckersley .05 .15
460 Darryl Strawberry .02 .10
461 Craig McMurtry .01 .05
462 Scott Fletcher .01 .05
463 Tom Candiotti .01 .05
464 Butch Wynegar .01 .05
465 Todd Worrell .01 .05
466 Kal Daniels .01 .05
467 Randy St.Claire .01 .05
468 George Bamberger MG .01 .05
469 Mike Diaz .01 .05
470 Dave Dravecky .01 .05
471 Ronn Reynolds .01 .05
472 Bill Doran .01 .05
473 Steve Farr .01 .05
474 Jerry Narron .01 .05
475 Scott Garrelts .01 .05
476 Danny Tartabull .01 .05
477 Ken Howell .01 .05
478 Tim Laudner .01 .05
479 Bob Sebra .01 .05
480 Jim Rice .02 .10
481 Phillies Team/(Glenn Wilson & Juan Samuel & and V .01 .05
482 Daryl Boston .01 .05
483 Dwight Lowry .01 .05
484 Jim Traber .01 .05
485 Tony Fernandez .01 .05
486 Otis Nixon .01 .05
487 Dave Gumpert .01 .05
488 Ray Knight .02 .10
489 Bill Gullickson .01 .05
490 Dale Murphy .05 .15
491 Ron Karkovice RC .08 .25
492 Mike Heath .01 .05
493 Tom Lasorda MG .05 .15
494 Barry Jones .01 .05
495 Gorman Thomas .02 .10
496 Bruce Bochte .01 .05
497 Dale Mohorcic .01 .05
498 Bob Kearney .01 .05
499 Bruce Ruffin RC .02 .10
500 Don Mattingly .25 .60
501 Craig Lefferts .01 .05
502 Dick Schofield .01 .05
503 Larry Andersen .01 .05
504 Mickey Hatcher .01 .05
505 Bryn Smith .01 .05
506 Orioles Team/(Mound conference) .01 .05
507 Dave L. Stapleton .01 .05
508 Scott Bankhead .01 .05
509 Enos Cabell .01 .05
510 Tom Henke .01 .05
511 Steve Lyons .01 .05
512 Dave Magadan RC .08 .25
513 Carmen Castillo .01 .05
514 Orlando Mercado .01 .05
515 Willie Hernandez .01 .05
516 Ted Simmons .02 .10
517 Mario Soto .02 .10
518 Gene Mauch MG .01 .05
519 Curt Young .01 .05
520 Jack Clark .02 .10
521 Rick Reuschel .02 .10
522 Checklist 397-528 .01 .05
523 Earnie Riles .01 .05
524 Bob Shirley .01 .05
525 Phil Bradley .01 .05
526 Roger Mason .01 .05
527 Jim Wohlford .01 .05
528 Ken Dixon .01 .05
529 Alvaro Espinoza RC .01 .05
530 Tony Gwynn .10 .30
531 Astros TL Y.Berra .02 .10
532 Jeff Stone .01 .05
533 Angel Salazar .01 .05
534 Scott Sanderson .01 .05
535 Tony Armas .02 .10
536 Terry Mulholland RC .08 .25
537 Rance Mulliniks .01 .05
538 Tom Niedenfuer .01 .05
539 Reid Nichols .01 .05
540 Terry Kennedy .01 .05
541 Rafael Belliard RC .08 .25
542 Ricky Horton .01 .05
543 Dave Johnson MG .01 .05
544 Zane Smith .01 .05
545 Buddy Bell .02 .10
546 Mike Morgan .01 .05
547 Rob Deer .01 .05
548 Bill Mooneyham .01 .05
549 Bob Melvin .01 .05
550 Pete Incaviglia RC * .08 .25
551 Frank Wills .01 .05
552 Larry Sheets .01 .05
553 Mike Maddux RC .01 .05
554 Buddy Biancalana .01 .05
555 Dennis Rasmussen .01 .05
556 Angels Team (Rene Lachemann CO & Mike Witt & and/ .01 .05
557 John Cerutti .01 .05
558 Greg Gagne .01 .05
559 Lance McCullers .01 .05
560 Glenn Davis .01 .05
561 Rey Quinones .01 .05
562 Bryan Clutterbuck .01 .05
563 John Stefero .01 .05
564 Larry McWilliams .01 .05
565 Dusty Baker .02 .10
566 Tim Hulett .01 .05
567 Greg Mathews .01 .05
568 Earl Weaver MG .02 .10
569 Wade Rowdon .01 .05
570 Sid Fernandez .01 .05
571 Ozzie Virgil .01 .05
572 Pete Ladd .01 .05
573 Hal McRae .02 .10
574 Manny Lee .01 .05
575 Pat Tabler .01 .05
576 Frank Pastore .01 .05
577 Dann Bilardello .01 .05
578 Billy Hatcher .01 .05
579 Rick Burleson .01 .05
580 Mike Krukow .01 .05
581 Cubs Team/(Ron Cey and Steve Trout) .01 .05
582 Bruce Berenyi .01 .05
583 Junior Ortiz .01 .05
584 Ron Kittle .01 .05
585 Scott Bailes .01 .05
586 Ben Oglivie .02 .10
587 Eric Plunk .01 .05
588 Wallace Johnson .01 .05
589 Steve Crawford .01 .05
590 Vince Coleman .01 .05
591 Spike Owen .01 .05
592 Chris Welsh .01 .05
593 Chuck Tanner MG .01 .05
594 Rick Anderson .01 .05
595 Keith Hernandez AS .01 .05
596 Steve Sax AS .01 .05
597 Mike Schmidt AS .08 .25
598 Ozzie Smith AS .08 .25
599 Tony Gwynn AS .05 .15
600 Dave Parker AS .01 .05
601 Darryl Strawberry AS .01 .05
602 Gary Carter AS .01 .05
603A Dwight Gooden AS NoTM .02 .10
603B Dwight Gooden AS TM .02 .10
604 Fernando Valenzuela AS .01 .05
605 Todd Worrell AS .01 .05
606 Don Mattingly AS .10 .30
606A Don Mattingly AS NoTM .40 1.00
607 Tony Bernazard AS .01 .05
608 Wade Boggs AS .02 .10
609 Cal Ripken AS .08 .25
610 Jim Rice AS .01 .05
611 Kirby Puckett AS .08 .25
612 George Bell AS .01 .05
613 Lance Parrish AS UER (Pitcher heading on back) .01 .05
614 Roger Clemens AS .40 1.00
615 Teddy Higuera AS .01 .05
616 Dave Righetti AS .01 .05
617 Al Nipper .01 .05
618 Tom Kelly MG .01 .05
619 Jerry Reed .01 .05
620 Jose Canseco .40 1.00
621 Danny Cox .01 .05
622 Glenn Braggs RC .02 .10
623 Kurt Stillwell .01 .05
624 Tim Burke .01 .05
625 Mookie Wilson .02 .10
626 Joel Skinner .01 .05
627 Ken Oberkfell .01 .05
628 Bob Walk .01 .05
629 Larry Parrish .01 .05
630 John Candelaria .01 .05
631 Tigers Team/(Mound conference) .01 .05
632 Rob Woodward .01 .05
633 Jose Uribe .01 .05
634 Rafael Palmeiro RC .60 1.50
635 Ken Schrom .01 .05
636 Darren Daulton .02 .10
637 Bip Roberts RC .08 .25
638 Rich Bordi .01 .05
639 Gerald Perry .01 .05
640 Mark Clear .01 .05
641 Domingo Ramos .01 .05
642 Al Pulido .01 .05
643 Ron Shepherd .01 .05
644 John Denny .01 .05
645 Dwight Evans .05 .15
646 Mike Mason .01 .05
647 Tom Lawless .01 .05
648 Barry Larkin RC 1.00 2.50
649 Mickey Tettleton .01 .05
650 Hubie Brooks .01 .05
651 Benny Distefano .01 .05
652 Terry Forster .02 .10
653 Kevin Mitchell RC * .15 .40
654 Checklist 529-660 .01 .05
655 Jesse Barfield .02 .10
656 Rangers Team/(Bobby Valentine MG and Ricky Wrigh .01 .05
657 Tom Waddell .01 .05
658 Robby Thompson RC * .08 .25
659 Aurelio Lopez .01 .05
660 Bob Horner .02 .10
661 Lou Whitaker .02 .10
662 Frank DiPino .01 .05
663 Cliff Johnson .01 .05
664 Mike Marshall .01 .05
665 Rod Scurry .01 .05
666 Von Hayes .01 .05
667 Ron Hassey .01 .05
668 Juan Bonilla .01 .05
669 Bud Black .01 .05
670 Jose Cruz .02 .10
671A Ray Soff ERR/(No D* before copyright line) .01 .05
671B Ray Soff COR/(D* before copyright line) .01 .05
672 Chili Davis .02 .10
673 Don Sutton .02 .10
674 Bill Campbell .01 .05
675 Ed Romero .01 .05
676 Charlie Moore .01 .05
677 Bob Grich .02 .10
678 Carney Lansford .02 .10
679 Kent Hrbek .02 .10
680 Ryne Sandberg .15 .40
681 George Bell .01 .05
682 Jerry Reuss .01 .05
683 Gary Roenicke .01 .05
684 Kent Tekulve .01 .05
685 Jerry Hairston .01 .05
686 Doyle Alexander .01 .05
687 Alan Trammell .02 .10
688 Juan Beniquez .01 .05
689 Darrell Porter .01 .05
690 Dane Iorg .01 .05
691 Dave Parker .02 .10
692 Frank White .02 .10
693 Terry Puhl .01 .05
694 Phil Niekro .02 .10
695 Chico Walker .01 .05
696 Gary Lucas .01 .05
697 Ed Lynch .01 .05
698 Ernie Whitt .01 .05
699 Ken Landreaux .01 .05
700 Dave Bergman .01 .05
701 Willie Randolph .02 .10
702 Greg Gross .01 .05
703 Dave Schmidt .01 .05
704 Jesse Orosco .01 .05
705 Bruce Hurst .01 .05
706 Rick Manning .01 .05
707 Bob McClure .01 .05
708 Scott McGregor .01 .05
709 Dave Kingman .02 .10
710 Gary Gaetti .02 .10
711 Ken Griffey .02 .10
712 Don Robinson .01 .05
713 Tom Brookens .01 .05
714 Dan Quisenberry .01 .05
715 Bob Dernier .01 .05
716 Rick Leach .01 .05
717 Ed VandeBerg .01 .05
718 Steve Carlton .02 .10
719 Tom Hume .01 .05
720 Richard Dotson .01 .05
721 Tom Herr .01 .05
722 Bob Knepper .01 .05
723 Brett Butler .02 .10
724 Greg Minton .01 .05
725 George Hendrick .02 .10
726 Frank Tanana .02 .10
727 Mike Moore .01 .05
728 Tippy Martinez .01 .05
729 Tom Paciorek .02 .10
730 Eric Show .01 .05
731 Dave Concepcion .02 .10
732 Manny Trillo .01 .05
733 Bill Caudill .01 .05
734 Bill Madlock .02 .10
735 Rickey Henderson .08 .25
736 Steve Bedrosian .01 .05
737 Floyd Bannister .01 .05
738 Jorge Orta .01 .05
739 Chet Lemon .02 .10
740 Rich Gedman .01 .05
741 Paul Molitor .02 .10
742 Andy McGaffigan .01 .05
743 Dwayne Murphy .01 .05
744 Roy Smalley .01 .05
745 Glenn Hubbard .01 .05
746 Bob Ojeda .01 .05
747 Johnny Ray .01 .05
748 Mike Flanagan .01 .05
749 Ozzie Smith .15 .40
750 Steve Trout .01 .05
751 Garth Iorg .01 .05
752 Dan Petry .01 .05
753 Rick Honeycutt .01 .05
754 Dave LaPoint .01 .05
755 Luis Aguayo .01 .05
756 Carlton Fisk .05 .15
757 Nolan Ryan .40 1.00
758 Tony Bernazard .01 .05
759 Joel Youngblood .01 .05
760 Mike Witt .01 .05
761 Greg Pryor .01 .05
762 Gary Ward .01 .05
763 Tim Flannery .01 .05
764 Bill Buckner .02 .10
765 Kirk Gibson .02 .10
766 Don Aase .01 .05
767 Ron Cey .02 .10
768 Dennis Lamp .01 .05
769 Steve Sax .01 .05
770 Dave Winfield .02 .10
771 Shane Rawley .01 .05
772 Harold Baines .02 .10
773 Robin Yount .15 .40
774 Wayne Krenchicki .01 .05
775 Joaquin Andujar .02 .10
776 Tom Brunansky .01 .05
777 Chris Chambliss .02 .10
778 Jack Morris .02 .10
779 Craig Reynolds .01 .05
780 Andre Thornton .01 .05
781 Atlee Hammaker .01 .05
782 Brian Downing .02 .10
783 Willie Wilson .02 .10
784 Cal Ripken .30 .75
785 Terry Francona .02 .10
786 Jimy Williams MG .01 .05
787 Alejandro Pena .01 .05
788 Tim Stoddard .01 .05
789 Dan Schatzeder .01 .05
790 Julio Cruz .01 .05
791 Lance Parrish UER/(No trademark & never corrected) .02 .10
792 Checklist 661-792 .01 .05

1987 Topps Tiffany

COMP.FACT.SET (792) 40.00 80.00
*STARS: 2.5X TO 6X BASIC CARDS
*ROOKIES: 2.5X TO 6X BASIC CARDS
DISTRIBUTED ONLY IN FACTORY SET FORM
FACTORY SET PRICE IS FOR SEALED SETS

1987 Topps Glossy All-Stars

This set of 22 glossy cards was inserted one per rack pack. Players selected for the set are the starting players (plus manager and two pitchers) in the 1986 All-Star Game in Houston. Cards measure the standard size and the backs feature red and blue printing on a white card stock.

COMPLETE SET (22) 2.00 5.00
1 Whitey Herzog MG .02 .10
2 Keith Hernandez .02 .10
3 Ryne Sandberg .40 1.00
4 Mike Schmidt .20 .50
5 Ozzie Smith .40 1.00
6 Tony Gwynn .40 1.00
7 Dale Murphy .07 .20
8 Darryl Strawberry .02 .10
9 Gary Carter .20 .50
10 Dwight Gooden .05 .15
11 Fernando Valenzuela .02 .10
12 Dick Howser MG .01 .05
13 Wally Joyner .02 .10
14 Lou Whitaker .02 .10
15 Wade Boggs .20 .50
16 Cal Ripken .75 2.00
17 Dave Winfield .20 .50
18 Rickey Henderson .25 .60
19 Kirby Puckett .30 .75
20 Lance Parrish .02 .10
21 Roger Clemens .40 1.00
22 Teddy Higuera .01 .05

1987 Topps Glossy Send-Ins

Topps issued this set through a mail-in offer explained and advertised on the wax packs. This 60-card set features glossy fronts with each card measuring the standard size. The offer provided your choice of any one of the six 10-card subsets (1-10, 11-20, etc.) for 1.00 plus six of the Special Offer ("Spring Fever Baseball") insert cards, which were found one per wax pack. The last two players (numerically) in each ten-card subset are actually "Hot Prospects." This set is highlighted by an early Barry Bonds card.

COMPLETE SET (60) 10.00 25.00
DISTRIBUTED VIA MAIL EXCH.PROGRAM
1 Don Mattingly .75 2.00
2 Tony Gwynn .40 1.00
3 Gary Gaetti .10 .30
4 Glenn Davis .07 .20
5 Roger Clemens 1.25 3.00
6 Dale Murphy .20 .50
7 Lou Whitaker .10 .30
8 Roger McDowell .07 .20

9 Cory Snyder .07 .20
10 Todd Worrell .10 .30
11 Gary Carter .10 .30
12 Eddie Murray .30 .75
13 Bob Knepper .07 .20
14 Harold Baines .10 .30
15 Jeff Reardon .10 .30
16 Joe Carter .10 .30
17 Dave Parker .10 .30
18 Wade Boggs .20 .50
19 Danny Tartabull .07 .20
20 Jim Deshaies .07 .20
21 Rickey Henderson .30 .75
22 Rob Deer .07 .20
23 Ozzie Smith .50 1.25
24 Dave Righetti .10 .30
25 Kent Hrbek .10 .30
26 Keith Hernandez .10 .30
27 Don Baylor .10 .30
28 Mike Schmidt .60 1.50
29 Pete Incaviglia .10 .30
30 Barry Bonds 4.00 10.00
31 George Brett .75 2.00
32 Darryl Strawberry .10 .30
33 Mike Witt .07 .20
34 Kevin Bass .07 .20
35 Jesse Barfield .07 .20
36 Bob Ojeda .07 .20
37 Cal Ripken 1.00 2.50
38 Vince Coleman .07 .20
39 Wally Joyner .20 .50
40 Robby Thompson .10 .30
41 Pete Rose .75 2.00
42 Jim Rice .10 .30
43 Tony Bernazard .07 .20
44 Eric Davis .20 .50
45 George Bell .07 .20
46 Hubie Brooks .07 .20
47 Jack Morris .10 .30
48 Tim Raines .10 .30
49 Mark Eichhorn .07 .20
50 Kevin Mitchell .10 .30
51 Dwight Gooden .20 .50
52 Doug DeCinces .07 .20
53 Fernando Valenzuela .10 .30
54 Reggie Jackson .20 .50
55 Johnny Ray .07 .20
56 Mike Pagliarulo .07 .20
57 Kirby Puckett .40 1.00
58 Lance Parrish .10 .30
59 Jose Canseco .60 1.50
60 Greg Mathews .07 .20

1987 Topps Rookies

Inserted in each supermarket jumbo pack is a card from this series of 22 of 1986's best rookies as determined by Topps. Jumbo packs consisted of 100 (regular issue 1987 Topps baseball) cards with a stick of gum plus the insert "Rookie" card. The card fronts are in full color and measure the standard size. The card backs are printed in red and blue on white card stock and are numbered at the bottom essentially by alphabetical order.

COMPLETE SET (22) 5.00 12.00
ONE PER RETAIL JUMBO PACK
1 Andy Allanson .08 .25
2 John Cangelosi .08 .25
3 Jose Canseco .75 2.00
4 Will Clark 1.00 2.50
5 Mark Eichhorn .08 .25
6 Pete Incaviglia .20 .50
7 Wally Joyner .30 .75
8 Eric King .08 .25
9 Dave Magadan .20 .50
10 John Morris .08 .25
11 Juan Nieves .08 .25
12 Rafael Palmeiro 2.00 5.00
13 Billy Joe Robidoux .08 .25
14 Bruce Ruffin .08 .25
15 Ruben Sierra .40 1.00
16 Cory Snyder .08 .25
17 Kurt Stillwell .08 .25
18 Dale Sveum .08 .25
19 Danny Tartabull .08 .25
20 Andres Thomas .08 .25
21 Robby Thompson .08 .25
22 Todd Worrell .20 .50

1987 Topps Wax Box Cards

This set of eight cards is really four different sets of two smaller (approximately 2 1/8" by 3") cards which were printed on the side of the wax pack box; these eight cards are lettered A through H and are very similar in design to the Topps regular issue cards. The order of the set is alphabetical by player's name. Complete boxes would be worth an additional 25 percent premium over the prices below. The card backs are done in a newspaper headline style describing something about that player that happened the previous season. The card backs feature blue and yellow ink on gray card stock.

COMPLETE SET (8) 1.25 3.00
A Don Baylor .08 .25
B Steve Carlton .30 .75
C Ron Cey .08 .25
D Cecil Cooper .02 .10
E Rickey Henderson .30 .75
F Jim Rice .08 .25
G Don Sutton .30 .75
H Dave Winfield .30 .75

1987 Topps Traded

This 132-card standard-size Traded set was distributed exclusively in factory set form in a special green and white box through hobby dealers. The card fronts are identical in style to the Topps regular issue except for whiter stock and t-suffixed numbering on back. The cards are ordered alphabetically by player's last name. The key extended Rookie Cards in this set are Ellis Burks, David Cone, Greg Maddux, Fred McGriff and Matt Williams.

COMP.FACT.SET (132) 5.00 12.00
1T Bill Almon .01 .05
2T Scott Bankhead .01 .05
3T Eric Bell .02 .10
4T Juan Beniquez .01 .05
5T Juan Berenguer .01 .05
6T Greg Booker .01 .05
7T Thad Bosley .01 .05
8T Larry Bowa MG .02 .10
9T Greg Brock .01 .05
10T Bob Brower .01 .05
11T Jerry Browne .02 .10
12T Ralph Bryant .01 .05
13T DeWayne Buice .01 .05
14T Ellis Burks XRC .20 .50
15T Ivan Calderon .01 .05
16T Jeff Calhoun .01 .05
17T Casey Candaele .01 .05
18T John Cangelosi .01 .05
19T Steve Carlton .02 .10
20T Juan Castillo .02 .10
21T Rick Cerone .01 .05
22T Ron Cey .02 .10
23T John Christensen .01 .05
24T David Cone XRC .30 .75
25T Chuck Crim .01 .05
26T Storm Davis .01 .05
27T Andre Dawson .02 .10
28T Rick Dempsey .01 .05
29T Doug Drabek .20 .50
30T Mike Dunne .01 .05
31T Dennis Eckersley .05 .15
32T Lee Elia MG .01 .05
33T Brian Fisher .01 .05
34T Terry Francona .02 .10
35T Willie Fraser .02 .10
36T Billy Gardner MG .01 .05
37T Ken Gerhart .01 .05
38T Dan Gladden .01 .05
39T Jim Gott .01 .05
40T Cecilio Guante .01 .05
41T Albert Hall .01 .05
42T Terry Harper .01 .05
43T Mickey Hatcher .01 .05
44T Brad Havens .01 .05
45T Neal Heaton .01 .05
46T Mike Henneman XRC .08 .25
47T Donnie Hill .01 .05
48T Guy Hoffman .01 .05
49T Brian Holton .01 .05
50T Charles Hudson .01 .05
51T Danny Jackson .01 .05
52T Reggie Jackson .05 .15
53T Chris James XRC .02 .10
54T Dion James .01 .05
55T Stan Jefferson .01 .05
56T Joe Johnson .01 .05
57T Terry Kennedy .01 .05
58T Mike Kingery .02 .10
59T Ray Knight .02 .10
60T Gene Larkin XRC .08 .25
61T Mike LaValliere .08 .25
62T Jack Lazorko .01 .05
63T Terry Leach .01 .05
64T Tim Leary .01 .05
65T Jim Lindeman .02 .10
66T Steve Lombardozzi .01 .05
67T Bill Long .01 .05
68T Barry Lyons .01 .05
69T Shane Mack .01 .05
70T Greg Maddux XRC 5.00 12.00
71T Bill Madlock .02 .10
72T Joe Magrane XRC .02 .10
73T Dave Martinez XRC .08 .25
74T Fred McGriff .25 .60
75T Mark McLemore .02 .10
76T Kevin McReynolds .01 .05
77T Dave Meads .01 .05
78T Eddie Milner .01 .05
79T Greg Minton .01 .05
80T John Mitchell XRC .02 .10
81T Kevin Mitchell .05 .15
82T Charlie Moore .01 .05
83T Jeff Musselman .01 .05
84T Gene Nelson .01 .05
85T Graig Nettles .02 .10
86T Al Newman .01 .05
87T Reid Nichols .01 .05
88T Tom Niedenfuer .01 .05
89T Joe Niekro .01 .05
90T Tom Nieto .01 .05
91T Matt Nokes XRC .08 .25
92T Dickie Noles .01 .05
93T Pat Pacillo .01 .05
94T Lance Parrish .02 .10
95T Tony Pena .01 .05
96T Luis Polonia XRC .08 .25
97T Randy Ready .01 .05
98T Jeff Reardon .02 .10
99T Gary Redus .01 .05
100T Jeff Reed .01 .05
101T Rick Rhoden .01 .05
102T Cal Ripken Sr. MG .01 .05
103T Wally Ritchie .01 .05
104T Jeff M. Robinson .01 .05
105T Gary Roenicke .01 .05
106T Jerry Royster .01 .05
107T Mark Salas .01 .05
108T Luis Salazar .01 .05
109T Benito Santiago .02 .10
110T Dave Schmidt .01 .05
111T Kevin Seitzer XRC .08 .25
112T John Shelby .01 .05
113T Steve Shields .01 .05
114T John Smiley XRC .08 .25
115T Chris Speier .01 .05
116T Mike Stanley XRC .08 .25
117T Terry Steinbach XRC .20 .50
118T Les Straker .01 .05
119T Jim Sundberg .02 .10
120T Danny Tartabull .01 .05
121T Tom Trebelhorn MG .01 .05
122T Dave Valle XRC .02 .10
123T Ed VandeBerg .01 .05
124T Andy Van Slyke .05 .15
125T Gary Ward .01 .05
126T Alan Wiggins .01 .05
127T Bill Wilkinson .01 .05
128T Frank Williams .01 .05
129T Matt Williams XRC .40 1.00
130T Jim Winn .01 .05
131T Matt Young .01 .05
132T Checklist 1T-132T .01 .05

1987 Topps Traded Tiffany

COMP.FACT.SET (132) 15.00 40.00
*STARS: 1.5X TO 4X BASIC CARDS
*ROOKIES: 2X TO 5X BASIC CARDS
DISTRIBUTED ONLY IN FACTORY SET FORM
FACTORY SET PRICE IS FOR SEALED SETS

1988 Topps

This set consists of 792 standard-size cards. The cards were primarily issued in 15-card wax packs, 42-card rack packs and factory sets. Card fronts feature white borders encasing a color photo with team name running across the top and player name diagonally across the bottom. Subsets include Record Breakers (1-7), All-Stars (386-407), Turn Back the Clock (661-665), and Team Leaders (scattered throughout the set). The manager cards contain a team checklist on back. The key Rookie Cards in this set are Ellis Burks, Ken Caminiti, Tom Glavine, and Matt Williams.

COMPLETE SET (792) 8.00 20.00
COMP.FACT.SET (792) 8.00 20.00
COMP.X-MAS.SET (792) 15.00 40.00
1 Vince Coleman RB .01 .05
2 Don Mattingly RB .10 .30
3 Mark McGwire RB .30 .75
3A Mark McGwire RB .30 .75
4 Eddie Murray RB .05 .15
Switch Home Runs,
Two Straight Games
No caption on front
4A Eddie Murray RB .20 .50
5 Phil Niekro .02 .10
Joe Niekro RB
6 Nolan Ryan RB .15 .40
7 Benito Santiago RB .01 .05
8 Kevin Elster .01 .05
9 Andy Hawkins .01 .05
10 Ryne Sandberg .15 .40
11 Mike Young .01 .05
12 Bill Schroeder .01 .05
13 Andres Thomas .01 .05
14 Sparky Anderson MG .02 .10
15 Chili Davis .02 .10
16 Kirk McCaskill .01 .05
17 Ron Oester .01 .05
18A Al Leiter ERR .20 .50
18B A.Leiter RC COR .20 .50
19 Mark Davidson .01 .05
20 Kevin Gross .01 .05
21 Wade Boggs .02 .10
Spike Owen TL
22 Greg Swindell .01 .05
23 Ken Landreaux .01 .05
24 Jim Deshaies .01 .05
25 Andres Galarraga .02 .10
26 Mitch Williams .01 .05
27 R.J. Reynolds .01 .05
28 Jose Nunez .01 .05
29 Angel Salazar .01 .05
30 Sid Fernandez .01 .05
31 Bruce Bochy .01 .05
32 Mike Morgan .01 .05
33 Rob Deer .01 .05
34 Ricky Horton .01 .05
35 Harold Baines .02 .10
36 Jamie Moyer .02 .10
37 Ed Romero .01 .05
38 Jeff Calhoun .01 .05
39 Gerald Perry .01 .05
40 Orel Hershiser .02 .10
41 Bob Melvin .01 .05
42 Bill Landrum .01 .05
43 Dick Schofield .01 .05
44 Lou Piniella MG .02 .10
45 Kent Hrbek .02 .10
46 Darnell Coles .01 .05
47 Joaquin Andujar .02 .10
48 Alan Ashby .01 .05
49 Dave Clark .01 .05
50 Hubie Brooks .01 .05
51 E.Murray/C.Ripken TL .15 .40
52 Don Robinson .01 .05
53 Curt Wilkerson .01 .05
54 Jim Clancy .01 .05
55 Phil Bradley .01 .05
56 Ed Hearn .01 .05
57 Tim Crews RC .08 .25
58 Dave Magadan .01 .05
59 Danny Cox .01 .05
60 Rickey Henderson .07 .20
61 Mark Knudson .01 .05
62 Jeff Hamilton .01 .05
63 Jimmy Jones .01 .05
64 Ken Caminiti RC .75 2.00
65 Leon Durham .01 .05
66 Shane Rawley .01 .05
67 Ken Oberkfell .01 .05
68 Dave Dravecky .01 .05
69 Mike Hart .01 .05
70 Roger Clemens .40 1.00
71 Gary Pettis .01 .05
72 Dennis Eckersley .05 .15
73 Randy Bush .01 .05
74 Tom Lasorda MG .05 .15
75 Joe Carter .02 .10
76 Dennis Martinez .02 .10
77 Tom O'Malley .01 .05
78 Dan Petry .01 .05
79 Ernie Whitt .01 .05
80 Mark Langston .01 .05
81 Ron Robinson .01 .05
John Franco TL
82 Darrel Akerfelds RC .01 .05
83 Jose Oquendo .01 .05
84 Cecilio Guante .01 .05
85 Howard Johnson .02 .10
86 Ron Karkovice .01 .05
87 Mike Mason .01 .05
88 Earnie Riles .01 .05
89 Gary Thurman RC .01 .05
90 Dale Murphy .05 .15
91 Joey Cora RC .08 .25
92 Len Matuszek .01 .05
93 Bob Sebra .01 .05
94 Chuck Jackson .01 .05
95 Lance Parrish .02 .10
96 Todd Benzinger RC .08 .25
97 Scott Garrelts .01 .05
98 Rene Gonzales RC .02 .10
99 Chuck Finley .02 .10
100 Jack Clark .02 .10
101 Allan Anderson .01 .05
102 Barry Larkin .05 .15
103 Curt Young .01 .05
104 Dick Williams MG .01 .05
105 Jesse Orosco .01 .05
106 Jim Walewander .01 .05
107 Scott Bailes .01 .05
108 Steve Lyons .01 .05
109 Joel Skinner .01 .05
110 Teddy Higuera .01 .05
111 Hubie Brooks .01 .05
Vance Law TL
112 Les Lancaster .01 .05
113 Kelly Gruber .01 .05
114 Jeff Russell .01 .05
115 Johnny Ray .01 .05
116 Jerry Don Gleaton .01 .05
117 James Steels .01 .05
118 Bob Welch .02 .10
119 Robbie Wine .01 .05
120 Kirby Puckett .07 .20
121 Checklist 1-132 .01 .05
122 Tony Bernazard .01 .05
123 Tom Candiotti .01 .05
124 Ray Knight .02 .10
125 Bruce Hurst .01 .05
126 Steve Jeltz .01 .05
127 Jim Gott .01 .05
128 Johnny Grubb .01 .05
129 Greg Minton .01 .05
130 Buddy Bell .02 .10
131 Don Schulze .01 .05
132 Donnie Hill .01 .05
133 Greg Mathews .01 .05
134 Chuck Tanner MG .01 .05
135 Dennis Rasmussen .01 .05
136 Brian Dayett .01 .05
137 Chris Bosio .01 .05
138 Mitch Webster .01 .05
139 Jerry Browne .01 .05
140 Jesse Barfield .02 .10
141 George Brett .07 .20
Bret Saberhagen TL
142 Andy Van Slyke .05 .15
143 Mickey Tettleton .01 .05
144 Don Gordon .01 .05
145 Bill Madlock .02 .10
146 Donell Nixon .02 .10
147 Bill Buckner .02 .10
148 Carmelo Martinez .01 .05
149 Ken Howell .01 .05
150 Eric Davis .02 .10
151 Bob Knepper .01 .05
152 Jody Reed RC .08 .25
153 John Habyan .01 .05
154 Jeff Stone .01 .05
155 Bruce Sutter .02 .10
156 Gary Matthews .02 .10
157 Atlee Hammaker .01 .05
158 Tim Hulett .01 .05
159 Brad Arnsberg .01 .05
160 Willie McGee .02 .10
161 Bryn Smith .01 .05
162 Mark McLemore .01 .05
163 Dale Mohorcic .01 .05
164 Dave Johnson MG .01 .05
165 Robin Yount .10 .30
166 Rick Rodriquez .01 .05
167 Rance Mulliniks .01 .05
168 Barry Jones .01 .05
169 Ross Jones .01 .05
170 Rich Gossage .02 .10
171 Shawon Dunston .01 .05
Manny Trillo TL
172 Lloyd McClendon RC .08 .25
173 Eric Plunk .01 .05
174 Phil Garner .02 .10
175 Kevin Bass .01 .05
176 Jeff Reed .01 .05
177 Frank Tanana .02 .10
178 Dwayne Henry .01 .05
179 Charlie Puleo .01 .05
180 Terry Kennedy .01 .05
181 David Cone .02 .10
182 Ken Phelps .01 .05
183 Tom Lawless .01 .05
184 Ivan Calderon .01 .05
185 Rick Rhoden .01 .05
186 Rafael Palmeiro .15 .40
187 Steve Kiefer .01 .05
188 John Russell .01 .05
189 Wes Gardner .01 .05
190 Candy Maldonado .01 .05
191 John Cerutti .01 .05
192 Devon White .02 .10
193 Brian Fisher .01 .05
194 Tom Kelly MG .01 .05
195 Dan Quisenberry .01 .05
196 Dave Engle .01 .05
197 Lance McCullers .01 .05
198 Franklin Stubbs .01 .05
199 Dave Meads .01 .05
200 Wade Boggs .05 .15
201 Bobby Valentine MG .01 .05
Pete O'Brien
Pete Incaviglia
Steve Buechele TL
202 Glenn Hoffman .01 .05
203 Fred Toliver .01 .05
204 Paul O'Neill .05 .15
205 Nelson Liriano RC .01 .05
206 Domingo Ramos .01 .05
207 John Mitchell RC .02 .10
208 Steve Lake .01 .05
209 Richard Dotson .01 .05
210 Willie Randolph .02 .10
211 Frank DiPino .01 .05
212 Greg Brock .01 .05
213 Albert Hall .01 .05
214 Dave Schmidt .01 .05
215 Von Hayes .01 .05
216 Jerry Reuss .01 .05
217 Harry Spilman .01 .05
218 Dan Schatzeder .01 .05
219 Mike Stanley .01 .05
220 Tom Henke .01 .05
221 Rafael Belliard .01 .05
222 Steve Farr .01 .05
223 Stan Jefferson .01 .05
224 Tom Trebelhorn MG .01 .05
225 Mike Scioscia .02 .10
226 Dave Lopes .02 .10
227 Ed Correa .01 .05
228 Wallace Johnson .01 .05
229 Jeff Musselman .01 .05
230 Pat Tabler .01 .05
231 B.Bonds/B.Bonilla .40 1.00
232 Bob James .01 .05
233 Rafael Santana .01 .05
234 Ken Dayley .01 .05
235 Gary Ward .01 .05
236 Ted Power .01 .05
237 Mike Heath .01 .05
238 Luis Polonia RC .08 .25
239 Roy Smalley .01 .05
240 Lee Smith .02 .10
241 Damaso Garcia .01 .05
242 Tom Niedenfuer .01 .05
243 Mark Ryal .01 .05
244 Jeff D. Robinson .01 .05
245 Rich Gedman .01 .05
246 Mike Campbell RC .01 .05
247 Thad Bosley .01 .05
248 Storm Davis .01 .05
249 Mike Marshall .01 .05
250 Nolan Ryan .40 1.00
251 Tom Foley .01 .05
252 Bob Brower .01 .05
253 Checklist 133-264 .01 .05
254 Lee Elia MG .01 .05
255 Mookie Wilson .02 .10
256 Ken Schrom .01 .05
257 Jerry Royster .01 .05
258 Ed Nunez .01 .05
259 Ron Kittle .01 .05
260 Vince Coleman .01 .05
261 Giants TL .01 .05
Five players
262 Drew Hall .01 .05
263 Glenn Braggs .01 .05
264 Les Straker .01 .05
265 Bo Diaz .01 .05
266 Paul Assenmacher .01 .05
267 Billy Bean RC .02 .10
268 Bruce Ruffin .01 .05
269 Ellis Burks RC .15 .40
270 Mike Witt .01 .05
271 Ken Gerhart .01 .05
272 Steve Ontiveros .01 .05
273 Garth Iorg .01 .05
274 Junior Ortiz .01 .05
275 Kevin Seitzer .01 .05
276 Luis Salazar .01 .05
277 Alejandro Pena .01 .05
278 Jose Cruz .02 .10
279 Randy St.Claire .01 .05
280 Pete Incaviglia .01 .05
281 Jerry Hairston .01 .05
282 Pat Perry .01 .05
283 Phil Lombardi .01 .05
284 Larry Bowa MG .02 .10
285 Jim Presley .01 .05
286 Chuck Crim .01 .05
287 Manny Trillo .01 .05
288 Pat Pacillo .01 .05
289 Dave Bergman .01 .05
290 Tony Fernandez .01 .05
291 Billy Hatcher .01 .05
Kevin Bass TL
292 Carney Lansford .02 .10
293 Doug Jones RC .08 .25
294 Al Pedrique .01 .05
295 Bert Blyleven .02 .10
296 Floyd Rayford .01 .05
297 Zane Smith .01 .05
298 Milt Thompson .01 .05
299 Steve Crawford .01 .05
300 Don Mattingly .25 .60
301 Bud Black .01 .05
302 Jose Uribe .01 .05
303 Eric Show .01 .05
304 George Hendrick .02 .10
305 Steve Sax .01 .05
306 Billy Hatcher .01 .05
307 Mike Trujillo .01 .05
308 Lee Mazzilli .02 .10
309 Bill Long .01 .05
310 Tom Herr .01 .05
311 Scott Sanderson .01 .05
312 Joey Meyer .01 .05
313 Bob McClure .01 .05
314 Jimy Williams MG .01 .05
315 Dave Parker .02 .10
316 Jose Rijo .02 .10
317 Tom Nieto .01 .05
318 Mel Hall .01 .05
319 Mike Loynd .01 .05
320 Alan Trammell .02 .10
321 Harold Baines .02 .10
Carlton Fisk TL
322 Vicente Palacios RC .01 .05
323 Rick Leach .01 .05
324 Danny Jackson .01 .05
325 Glenn Hubbard .01 .05
326 Al Nipper .01 .05
327 Larry Sheets .01 .05
328 Greg Cadaret .01 .05
329 Chris Speier .01 .05
330 Eddie Whitson .01 .05
331 Brian Downing .02 .10
332 Jerry Reed .01 .05
333 Wally Backman .01 .05
334 Dave LaPoint .01 .05
335 Claudell Washington .01 .05
336 Ed Lynch .01 .05
337 Jim Gantner .01 .05
338 Brian Holton UER .01 .05
1987 ERA .389,
should be 3.89
339 Kurt Stillwell .01 .05
340 Jack Morris .02 .10
341 Carmen Castillo .01 .05
342 Larry Andersen .01 .05
343 Greg Gagne .01 .05
344 Tony LaRussa MG .02 .10
345 Scott Fletcher .01 .05
346 Vance Law .01 .05
347 Joe Johnson .01 .05
348 Jim Eisenreich .01 .05
349 Bob Walk .01 .05
350 Will Clark .07 .20
351 Red Schoendienst CO .02 .10
Tony Pena TL
352 Bill Ripken RC .01 .05
353 Ed Olwine .01 .05
354 Marc Sullivan .01 .05
355 Roger McDowell .01 .05
356 Luis Aguayo .01 .05
357 Floyd Bannister .01 .05
358 Rey Quinones .01 .05
359 Tim Stoddard .01 .05
360 Tony Gwynn .10 .30
361 Greg Maddux .40 1.00
362 Juan Castillo .01 .05
363 Willie Fraser .01 .05
364 Nick Esasky .01 .05
365 Floyd Youmans .01 .05
366 Chet Lemon .02 .10
367 Tim Leary .01 .05
368 Gerald Young .01 .05
369 Greg Harris .01 .05
370 Jose Canseco .20 .50
371 Joe Hesketh .01 .05
372 Matt Williams RC .30 .75
373 Checklist 265-396 .01 .05
374 Doc Edwards MG .01 .05
375 Tom Brunansky .01 .05
376 Bill Wilkinson .01 .05
377 Sam Horn RC .02 .10
378 Todd Frohwirth .01 .05
379 Rafael Ramirez .01 .05
380 Joe Magrane RC .01 .05
381 Wally Joyner .02 .10
Jack Howell TL
382 Keith A. Miller RC .08 .25
383 Eric Bell .01 .05
384 Neil Allen .01 .05
385 Carlton Fisk .05 .15
386 Don Mattingly AS .10 .30
387 Willie Randolph AS .01 .05
388 Wade Boggs AS .02 .10
389 Alan Trammell AS .01 .05
390 George Bell AS .01 .05
391 Kirby Puckett AS .05 .15
392 Dave Winfield AS .01 .05
393 Matt Nokes AS .01 .05
394 Roger Clemens AS .20 .50
395 Jimmy Key AS .01 .05
396 Tom Henke AS .01 .05
397 Jack Clark AS .01 .05
398 Juan Samuel AS .01 .05
399 Tim Wallach AS .01 .05
400 Ozzie Smith AS .07 .20
401 Andre Dawson AS .01 .05
402 Tony Gwynn AS .05 .15
403 Tim Raines AS .01 .05
404 Benny Santiago AS .01 .05
405 Dwight Gooden AS .01 .05
406 Shane Rawley AS .01 .05
407 Steve Bedrosian AS .01 .05
408 Dion James .01 .05
409 Joel McKeon .01 .05
410 Tony Pena .01 .05
411 Wayne Tolleson .01 .05
412 Randy Myers .02 .10
413 John Christensen .01 .05
414 John McNamara MG .01 .05
415 Don Carman .01 .05
416 Keith Moreland .01 .05
417 Mark Ciardi .01 .05
418 Joel Youngblood .01 .05
419 Scott McGregor .01 .05
420 Wally Joyner .02 .10
421 Ed VandeBerg .01 .05
422 Dave Concepcion .02 .10
423 John Smiley RC .08 .25
424 Dwayne Murphy .01 .05
425 Jeff Reardon .02 .10
426 Randy Ready .01 .05
427 Paul Kilgus .01 .05
428 John Shelby .01 .05
429 Alan Trammell .02 .10
Kirk Gibson TL
430 Glenn Davis .01 .05
431 Casey Candaele .01 .05
432 Mike Moore .01 .05
433 Bill Pecota RC .01 .05
434 Rick Aguilera .01 .05
435 Mike Pagliarulo .01 .05
436 Mike Bielecki .01 .05
437 Fred Manrique .01 .05
438 Rob Ducey RC .01 .05
439 Dave Martinez .01 .05
440 Steve Bedrosian .01 .05
441 Rick Manning .01 .05
442 Tom Bolton .01 .05
443 Ken Griffey .02 .10
444 Cal Ripken Sr. MG UER .01 .05
two copyrights
445 Mike Krukow .01 .05
446 Doug DeCinces .01 .05
Now with Cardinals

on card front
447 Jeff Montgomery RC .08 .25
448 Mike Davis .01 .05
449 Jeff M. Robinson .01 .05
450 Barry Bonds .75 2.00
451 Keith Atherton .01 .05
452 Willie Wilson .02 .10
453 Dennis Powell .01 .05
454 Marvell Wynne .01 .05
455 Shawn Hillegas RC .01 .05
456 Dave Anderson .01 .05
457 Terry Leach .01 .05
458 Ron Hassey .01 .05
459 Dave Winfield .01 .05
Willie Randolph TL
460 Ozzie Smith .10 .30
461 Danny Darwin .01 .05
462 Don Slaught .01 .05
463 Fred McGriff .07 .20
464 Jay Tibbs .01 .05
465 Paul Molitor .02 .10
466 Jerry Mumphrey .01 .05
467 Don Aase .01 .05
468 Darren Daulton .02 .10
469 Jeff Dedmon .01 .05
470 Dwight Evans .05 .15
471 Donnie Moore .01 .05
472 Robby Thompson .01 .05
473 Joe Niekro .01 .05
474 Tom Brookens .01 .05
475 Pete Rose MG .20 .50
476 Dave Stewart .02 .10
477 Jamie Quirk .01 .05
478 Sid Bream .01 .05
479 Brett Butler .02 .10
480 Dwight Gooden .02 .10
481 Mariano Duncan .01 .05
482 Mark Davis .01 .05
483 Rod Booker .01 .05
484 Pat Clements .01 .05
485 Harold Reynolds .02 .10
486 Pat Keedy .01 .05
487 Jim Pankovits .01 .05
488 Andy McGaffigan .01 .05
489 Pedro Guerrero .01 .05
Fernando Valenzuela TL
490 Larry Parrish .01 .05
491 B.J. Surhoff .02 .10
492 Doyle Alexander .01 .05
493 Mike Greenwell .01 .05
494 Wally Ritchie .01 .05
495 Eddie Murray .07 .20
496 Guy Hoffman .01 .05
497 Kevin Mitchell .02 .10
498 Bob Boone .02 .10
499 Eric King .01 .05
500 Andre Dawson .02 .10
501 Tim Birtsas .01 .05
502 Dan Gladden .01 .05
503 Junior Noboa .01 .05
504 Bob Rodgers MG .01 .05
505 Willie Upshaw .01 .05
506 John Cangelosi .01 .05
507 Mark Gubicza .01 .05
508 Tim Teufel .01 .05
509 Bill Dawley .01 .05
510 Dave Winfield .02 .10
511 Joel Davis .01 .05
512 Alex Trevino .01 .05
513 Tim Flannery .01 .05
514 Pat Sheridan .01 .05
515 Juan Nieves .01 .05
516 Jim Sundberg .02 .10
517 Ron Robinson .01 .05
518 Greg Gross .01 .05
519 Harold Reynolds .01 .05
Phil Bradley TL
520 Dave Smith .01 .05
521 Jim Dwyer .01 .05
522 Bob Patterson .01 .05
523 Gary Roenicke .01 .05
524 Gary Lucas .01 .05
525 Marty Barrett .01 .05
526 Juan Berenguer .01 .05
527 Steve Henderson .01 .05
528A Checklist 397-528 .05 .15
ERR 455 S. Carlton
528B Checklist 397-528 .02 .10
COR 455 S. Hillegas
529 Tim Burke .01 .05
530 Gary Carter .02 .10
531 Rich Yett .01 .05
532 Mike Kingery .01 .05
533 John Farrell RC .02 .10
534 John Wathan MG .01 .05
535 Ron Guidry .02 .10
536 John Morris .01 .05
537 Steve Buechele .01 .05
538 Bill Wegman .01 .05
539 Mike LaValliere .01 .05
540 Bret Saberhagen .02 .10
541 Juan Beniquez .01 .05
542 Paul Noce .01 .05
543 Kent Tekulve .01 .05
544 Jim Traber .01 .05
545 Don Baylor .02 .10
546 John Candelaria .01 .05
547 Felix Fermin .01 .05
548 Shane Mack .01 .05
549 Albert Hall .02 .10
Dale Murphy
Ken Griffey
Dion James TL
550 Pedro Guerrero .02 .10
551 Terry Steinbach .02 .10
552 Mark Thurmond .01 .05
553 Tracy Jones .01 .05
554 Mike Smithson .01 .05
555 Brook Jacoby .01 .05
556 Stan Clarke .01 .05
557 Craig Reynolds .01 .05
558 Bob Ojeda .01 .05
559 Ken Williams RC .01 .05
560 Tim Wallach .01 .05
561 Rick Cerone .01 .05
562 Jim Lindeman .01 .05
563 Jose Guzman .01 .05
564 Frank Lucchesi MG .01 .05
565 Lloyd Moseby .01 .05
566 Charlie O'Brien RC .01 .05
567 Mike Diaz .01 .05
568 Chris Brown .01 .05
569 Charlie Leibrandt .01 .05
570 Jeffrey Leonard .01 .05
571 Mark Williamson .01 .05
572 Chris James .01 .05
573 Bob Stanley .01 .05
574 Graig Nettles .02 .10
575 Don Sutton .02 .10
576 Tommy Hinzo .01 .05
577 Tom Browning .01 .05
578 Gary Gaetti .02 .10
579 Gary Carter .01 .05
Kevin McReynolds TL
580 Mark McGwire .60 1.50
581 Tito Landrum .01 .05
582 Mike Henneman RC .08 .25
583 Dave Valle .01 .05
584 Steve Trout .01 .05
585 Ozzie Guillen .02 .10
586 Bob Forsch .01 .05
587 Terry Puhl .01 .05
588 Jeff Parrett .01 .05
589 Geno Petralli .01 .05
590 George Bell .02 .10
591 Doug Drabek .01 .05
592 Dale Sveum .01 .05
593 Bob Tewksbury .01 .05
594 Bobby Valentine MG .02 .10
595 Frank White .02 .10
596 John Kruk .02 .10
597 Gene Garber .01 .05
598 Lee Lacy .01 .05
599 Calvin Schiraldi .01 .05
600 Mike Schmidt .20 .50
601 Jack Lazorko .01 .05
602 Mike Aldrete .01 .05
603 Rob Murphy .01 .05
604 Chris Bando .01 .05
605 Kirk Gibson .07 .20
606 Moose Haas .01 .05
607 Mickey Hatcher .01 .05
608 Charlie Kerfeld .01 .05
609 Gary Gaetti .02 .10
Kent Hrbek TL
610 Keith Hernandez .02 .10
611 Tommy John .02 .10
612 Curt Ford .01 .05
613 Bobby Thigpen .01 .05
614 Herm Winningham .01 .05
615 Jody Davis .01 .05
616 Jay Aldrich .01 .05
617 Oddibe McDowell .01 .05
618 Cecil Fielder .02 .10
619 Mike Dunne .01 .05
Inconsistent design,
black name on front
620 Cory Snyder .01 .05
621 Gene Nelson .01 .05
622 Kal Daniels .01 .05
623 Mike Flanagan .01 .05
624 Jim Leyland MG .01 .05
625 Frank Viola .02 .10
626 Glenn Wilson .01 .05
627 Joe Boever .01 .05
628 Dave Henderson .01 .05
629 Kelly Downs .01 .05
630 Darrell Evans .02 .10
631 Jack Howell .01 .05
632 Steve Shields .01 .05
633 Barry Lyons .01 .05
634 Jose DeLeon .01 .05
635 Terry Pendleton .02 .10
636 Charles Hudson .01 .05
637 Jay Bell RC .15 .40
638 Steve Balboni .01 .05
639 Glenn Braggs .01 .05
Tony Muser CO TL
640 Gary Templeton .02 .10
Inconsistent design,
green border
641 Rick Honeycutt .01 .05
642 Bob Dernier .01 .05
643 Rocky Childress .01 .05
644 Terry McGriff .01 .05
645 Matt Nokes RC .08 .25
646 Checklist 529-660 .01 .05
647 Pascual Perez .01 .05
648 Al Newman .01 .05
649 DeWayne Buice .01 .05
650 Cal Ripken .30 .75
651 Mike Jackson RC .08 .25
652 Bruce Benedict .01 .05
653 Jeff Sellers .01 .05
654 Roger Craig MG .02 .10
655 Len Dykstra .02 .10
656 Lee Guetterman .01 .05
657 Gary Redus .01 .05
658 Tim Conroy .01 .05
Inconsistent design,
name in white
659 Bobby Meacham .01 .05
660 Rick Reuschel .02 .10
661 Nolan Ryan TBC '83 .20 .50
662 Jim Rice TBC .01 .05
663 Ron Blomberg TBC .01 .05
664 Bob Gibson TBC '68 .08 .25
665 Stan Musial TBC '63 .07 .20
666 Mario Soto .02 .10
667 Luis Quinones .01 .05
668 Walt Terrell .01 .05
669 Lance Parrish .01 .05
Mike Ryan CO TL
670 Dan Plesac .01 .05
671 Tim Laudner .01 .05
672 John Davis RC .01 .05
673 Tony Phillips .01 .05
674 Mike Fitzgerald .01 .05
675 Jim Rice .02 .10
676 Ken Dixon .01 .05
677 Eddie Milner .01 .05
678 Jim Acker .01 .05
679 Darrell Miller .01 .05
680 Charlie Hough .02 .10
681 Bobby Bonilla .02 .10
682 Jimmy Key .02 .10
683 Julio Franco .02 .10
684 Hal Lanier MG .01 .05
685 Ron Darling .02 .10
686 Terry Francona .02 .10
687 Mickey Brantley .01 .05
688 Jim Winn .01 .05
689 Tom Pagnozzi RC .02 .10
690 Jay Howell .01 .05
691 Dan Pasqua .01 .05
692 Mike Birkbeck .01 .05
693 Benito Santiago .02 .10
694 Eric Nolte .01 .05
695 Shawon Dunston .01 .05
696 Duane Ward .01 .05
697 Steve Lombardozzi .01 .05
698 Brad Havens .01 .05
699 Benito Santiago .02 .10
Tony Gwynn TL
700 George Brett .20 .50
701 Sammy Stewart .01 .05
702 Mike Gallego .01 .05
703 Bob Brenly .01 .05
704 Dennis Boyd .01 .05
705 Juan Samuel .01 .05
706 Rick Mahler .01 .05
707 Fred Lynn .02 .10
708 Gus Polidor .01 .05
709 George Frazier .01 .05
710 Darryl Strawberry .02 .10
711 Bill Gullickson .01 .05
712 John Moses .01 .05
713 Willie Hernandez .01 .05
714 Jim Fregosi MG .01 .05
715 Todd Worrell .01 .05
716 Lenn Sakata .01 .05
717 Jay Baller .01 .05
718 Mike Felder .01 .05
719 Denny Walling .01 .05
720 Tim Raines .02 .10
721 Pete O'Brien .01 .05
722 Manny Lee .01 .05
723 Bob Kipper .01 .05
724 Danny Tartabull .01 .05
725 Mike Boddicker .01 .05
726 Alfredo Griffin .01 .05
727 Greg Booker .01 .05
728 Andy Allanson .01 .05
729 George Bell .02 .10
Fred McGriff TL
730 John Franco .02 .10
731 Rick Schu .01 .05
732 David Palmer .01 .05
733 Spike Owen .01 .05
734 Craig Lefferts .01 .05
735 Kevin McReynolds .01 .05
736 Matt Young .01 .05
737 Butch Wynegar .01 .05
738 Scott Bankhead .01 .05
739 Daryl Boston .01 .05
740 Rick Sutcliffe .02 .10
741 Mike Easler .01 .05
742 Mark Clear .01 .05
743 Larry Herndon .01 .05
744 Whitey Herzog MG .02 .10
745 Bill Doran .01 .05
746 Gene Larkin RC .08 .25
747 Bobby Witt .01 .05
748 Reid Nichols .01 .05
749 Mark Eichhorn .01 .05
750 Bo Jackson .07 .20
751 Jim Morrison .01 .05
752 Mark Grant .01 .05
753 Danny Heep .01 .05
754 Mike LaCoss .01 .05
755 Ozzie Virgil .01 .05
756 Mike Maddux .01 .05
757 John Marzano .01 .05
758 Eddie Williams RC .02 .10
759 McGwire/Canseco TL UER .40 1.00
760 Mike Scott .02 .10
761 Tony Armas .02 .10
762 Scott Bradley .01 .05
763 Doug Sisk .01 .05
764 Greg Walker .01 .05
765 Neal Heaton .01 .05
766 Henry Cotto .01 .05
767 Jose Lind RC .08 .25
768 Dickie Noles .01 .05
Now with Tigers
on card front
769 Cecil Cooper .02 .10
770 Lou Whitaker .02 .10
771 Ruben Sierra .02 .10
772 Sal Butera .01 .05
773 Frank Williams .01 .05
774 Gene Mauch MG .01 .05
775 Dave Stieb .02 .10
776 Checklist 661-792 .01 .05
777 Lonnie Smith .01 .05
778A Keith Comstock ERR .75 2.00
778B Keith Comstock COR .01 .05
Blue Padres
779 Tom Glavine RC 1.25 3.00
780 Fernando Valenzuela .02 .10
781 Keith Hughes RC .01 .05
782 Jeff Ballard RC .01 .05
783 Ron Roenicke .01 .05
784 Joe Sambito .01 .05
785 Alvin Davis .01 .05
786 Joe Price .01 .05
Inconsistent design,
orange team name
787 Bill Almon .01 .05
788 Ray Searage .01 .05
789 Joe Carter .01 .05
Cory Snyder TL
790 Dave Righetti .02 .10
791 Ted Simmons .02 .10
792 John Tudor .02 .10

1988 Topps Tiffany

COMP.FACT.SET (792) 30.00 80.00
*STARS: 4X TO 10X BASIC CARDS
*ROOKIES: 3X TO 8X BASIC CARDS
DISTRIBUTED ONLY IN FACTORY SET FORM
FACTORY SET PRICE IS FOR SEALED SETS

1988 Topps Glossy All-Stars

This set of 22 glossy cards was inserted one per rack pack. Players selected for the set are the starting players (plus manager and honorary captain) in the 1987 All-Star Game in Oakland. Cards measure the standard size and the backs feature red and blue printing on a white card stock.

COMPLETE SET (22) 1.50 4.00
1 John McNamara MG .01 .05
2 Don Mattingly .40 1.00
3 Willie Randolph .02 .10
4 Wade Boggs .20 .50
5 Cal Ripken .75 2.00
6 George Bell .01 .05
7 Rickey Henderson .30 .75
8 Dave Winfield .15 .40
9 Terry Kennedy .01 .05
10 Bret Saberhagen .02 .10
11 Jim Hunter CAPT .08 .25
12 Dave Johnson MG .02 .10
13 Jack Clark .02 .10
14 Ryne Sandberg .40 1.00
15 Mike Schmidt .20 .50
16 Ozzie Smith .40 1.00
17 Eric Davis .02 .10
18 Andre Dawson .07 .20
19 Darryl Strawberry .02 .10
20 Gary Carter .15 .40
21 Mike Scott .01 .05
22 Billy Williams CAPT .08 .25

1988 Topps Glossy Send-Ins

Topps issued this set through a mail-in offer explained and advertised on the wax packs. This 60-card set features glossy fronts with each card measuring the standard size. The offer provided your choice of any one of the six 10-card subsets (1-10, 11-20, etc.) for 1.25 plus six of the Special Offer ("Spring Fever Baseball") insert cards, which were found one per wax pack. One complete set was obtainable by sending 7.50 plus 18 special offer cards. The last two players (numerically) in each ten-card subset are actually "Hot Prospects."

COMPLETE SET (60) 4.00 10.00
1 Andre Dawson .15 .40
2 Jesse Barfield .02 .10
3 Mike Schmidt .40 1.00
4 Ruben Sierra .07 .20
5 Mike Scott .02 .10
6 Cal Ripken 1.50 4.00
7 Gary Carter .30 .75
8 Kent Hrbek .07 .20
9 Kevin Seitzer .02 .10
10 Mike Henneman .07 .20
11 Don Mattingly .75 2.00
12 Tim Raines .07 .20
13 Roger Clemens .75 2.00
14 Ryne Sandberg .60 1.50
15 Tony Fernandez .07 .20
16 Eric Davis .07 .20
17 Jack Morris .07 .20
18 Tim Wallach .02 .10
19 Mike Dunne .02 .10
20 Mike Greenwell .02 .10
21 Dwight Evans .07 .20
22 Darryl Strawberry .07 .20
23 Cory Snyder .02 .10
24 Pedro Guerrero .02 .10
25 Rickey Henderson .40 1.25
26 Dale Murphy .15 .40
27 Kirby Puckett .40 1.00
28 Steve Bedrosian .02 .10
29 Devon White .07 .20
30 Benito Santiago .07 .20
31 George Bell .02 .10
32 Keith Hernandez .07 .20
33 Dave Stewart .07 .20
34 Dave Parker .07 .20
35 Tom Henke .02 .10
36 Willie McGee .07 .20
37 Alan Trammell .10 .30
38 Tony Gwynn .75 2.00
39 Mark McGwire .75 2.00
40 Joe Magrane .02 .10
41 Jack Clark .07 .20
42 Willie Randolph .07 .20
43 Juan Samuel .02 .10
44 Joe Carter .10 .30
45 Shane Rawley .02 .10
46 Dave Winfield .20 .50
47 Ozzie Smith .75 2.00
48 Wally Joyner .07 .20
49 B.J. Surhoff .07 .20
50 Ellis Burks .30 .75
51 Wade Boggs .30 .75
52 Howard Johnson .02 .10
53 George Brett .75 2.00
54 Dwight Gooden .07 .20
55 Jose Canseco .40 1.00
56 Lee Smith .07 .20
57 Paul Molitor .30 .75
58 Andres Galarraga .15 .40
59 Matt Nokes .02 .10
60 Casey Candaele .02 .10

1988 Topps Rookies

Inserted in each supermarket jumbo pack is a card from this series of 22 of 1987's best rookies as determined by Topps. Jumbo packs consisted of 100 (regular issue 1988 Topps baseball) cards with a stick of gum plus the insert "Rookie" card. The card fronts are in full color and measure the standard size. The card backs are printed in red and blue on white card stock and are numbered at the bottom.

COMPLETE SET (22) 10.00 25.00
ONE PER RETAIL JUMBO PACK
1 Bill Ripken .08 .25
2 Ellis Burks .40 1.00
3 Mike Greenwell .08 .25
4 DeWayne Buice .08 .25
5 Devon White .20 .50
6 Fred Manrique .08 .25
7 Mike Henneman .20 .50
8 Matt Nokes .08 .25
9 Kevin Seitzer .20 .50
10 B.J. Surhoff .20 .50
11 Casey Candaele .08 .25
12 Randy Myers .30 .75
13 Mark McGwire 6.00 15.00
14 Luis Polonia .08 .25
15 Terry Steinbach .20 .50
16 Mike Dunne .08 .25
17 Al Pedrique .08 .25
18 Benito Santiago .08 .25
19 Kelly Downs .08 .25
20 Joe Magrane .08 .25
21 Jerry Browne .08 .25
22 Jeff Musselman .08 .25

1988 Topps Wax Box Cards

The cards in this 16-card set measure the standard size. Cards have essentially the same design as the 1988 Topps regular issue set. The cards were printed on the bottoms of the regular issue wax pack boxes. These 16 cards, "lettered" A through P, are considered a separate set in their own right and are not typically included in a complete set of the regular issue 1988 Topps cards. The value of the panels uncut is slightly greater, perhaps by 25 percent greater, than the value of the individual cards cut up carefully. The card lettering is sequenced alphabetically by player's name.

COMPLETE SET (16) 2.00 5.00
A Don Baylor .07 .20
B Steve Bedrosian .02 .10
C Juan Beniquez .02 .10
D Bob Boone .07 .20
E Darrell Evans .07 .20
F Tony Gwynn .50 1.25
G John Kruk .07 .20
H Marvell Wynne .02 .10
I Joe Carter .15 .40
J Eric Davis .07 .20
K Howard Johnson .02 .10
L Darryl Strawberry .07 .20
M Rickey Henderson .40 1.00
N Nolan Ryan 1.00 2.50
O Mike Schmidt .30 .75
P Kent Tekulve .02 .10

1988 Topps Traded

This standard-size 132-card Traded set was distributed exclusively in factory set form in blue and white taped boxes through hobby dealers. The cards are identical in style to the Topps regular issue except for whiter stock and t-suffixed numbering on back. Cards are ordered alphabetically by player's last name. This set generated additional interest upon release due to the inclusion of members of the 1988 U.S. Olympic baseball team. These Olympians are indicated in the checklist below by OLY. The key extended Rookie Cards in this set are Jim Abbott, Roberto Alomar, Brady Anderson, Andy Benes, Jay Buhner, Ron Gant, Mark Grace, Tino Martinez, Charles Nagy, Robin Ventura and Walt Weiss.

COMP.FACT.SET (132) 3.00 8.00
1T Jim Abbott OLY XRC .75 2.00
2T Juan Agosto .02 .10
3T Luis Alicea XRC .20 .50
4T Roberto Alomar XRC .75 2.00
5T Brady Anderson XRC .30 .75
6T Jack Armstrong XRC .20 .50
7T Don August .02 .10
8T Floyd Bannister .02 .10
9T Bret Barberie OLY XRC .08 .25
10T Jose Bautista XRC .08 .25
11T Don Baylor .07 .20
12T Tim Belcher .02 .10
13T Buddy Bell .07 .20
14T Andy Benes OLY XRC .30 .75
15T Damon Berryhill XRC* .20 .50
16T Bud Black .02 .10
17T Pat Borders XRC .20 .50
18T Phil Bradley .02 .10
19T Jeff Branson XRC OLY .20 .50
20T Tom Brunansky .02 .10
21T Jay Buhner XRC .40 1.00
22T Brett Butler .07 .20
23T Jim Campanis OLY XRC .02 .10
24T Sil Campusano .02 .10
25T John Candelaria .02 .10
26T Jose Cecena .02 .10
27T Rick Cerone .02 .10
28T Jack Clark .07 .20
29T Kevin Coffman .02 .10
30T Pat Combs OLY XRC .08 .25
31T Henry Cotto .02 .10
32T Chili Davis .07 .20
33T Mike Davis .02 .10
34T Jose DeLeon .02 .10
35T Richard Dotson .02 .10
36T Cecil Espy XRC .02 .10
37T Tom Filer .02 .10
38T Mike Fiore OLY .02 .10
39T Ron Gant XRC .30 .75
40T Kirk Gibson .20 .50
41T Rich Gossage .07 .20
42T Mark Grace XRC .75 2.00
43T Alfredo Griffin .02 .10
44T Ty Griffin OLY .02 .10
45T Bryan Harvey XRC .20 .50
46T Ron Hassey .02 .10
47T Ray Hayward .02 .10
48T Dave Henderson .02 .10
49T Tom Herr .02 .10
50T Bob Horner .07 .20
51T Ricky Horton .02 .10
52T Jay Howell .02 .10
53T Glenn Hubbard .02 .10
54T Jeff Innis .02 .10
55T Danny Jackson .02 .10
56T Darrin Jackson XRC .08 .25
57T Roberto Kelly XRC .20 .50
58T Ron Kittle .02 .10
59T Ray Knight .07 .20
60T Vance Law .02 .10
61T Jeffrey Leonard .02 .10
62T Mike Macfarlane XRC .20 .50
63T Scotti Madison .02 .10
64T Kirt Manwaring .02 .10
65T Mark Marquess OLY CO .02 .10
66T Tino Martinez OLY XRC 1.25 3.00
67T Billy Masse OLY XRC .08 .25
68T Jack McDowell XRC .30 .75
69T Jack McKeon MG .07 .20
70T Larry McWilliams .02 .10
71T Mickey Morandini OLY XRC .20 .50
72T Keith Moreland .02 .10
73T Mike Morgan .02 .10
74T Charles Nagy OLY XRC .20 .50
75T Al Nipper .02 .10
76T Russ Nixon MG .02 .10
77T Jesse Orosco .02 .10
78T Joe Orsulak .02 .10
79T Dave Palmer .02 .10
80T Mark Parent XRC .02 .10
81T Dave Parker .07 .20
82T Dan Pasqua .02 .10
83T Melido Perez XRC .20 .50
84T Steve Peters .02 .10
85T Dan Petry .02 .10
86T Gary Pettis .02 .10
87T Jeff Pico .02 .10
88T Jim Poole OLY XRC .08 .25
89T Ted Power .02 .10
90T Rafael Ramirez .02 .10
91T Dennis Rasmussen .02 .10
92T Jose Rijo .07 .20
93T Ernie Riles .02 .10
94T Luis Rivera .02 .10
95T Doug Robbins OLY XRC .08 .25
96T Frank Robinson MG .10 .30
97T Cookie Rojas MG .02 .10
98T Chris Sabo XRC .30 .75
99T Mark Salas .02 .10
100T Luis Salazar .02 .10
101T Rafael Santana .02 .10
102T Nelson Santovenia .02 .10
103T Mackey Sasser XRC .20 .50
104T Calvin Schiraldi .02 .10
105T Mike Schooler .02 .10
106T Scott Servais OLY XRC .20 .50
107T Dave Silvestri OLY XRC .08 .25
108T Don Slaught .02 .10
109T Joe Slusarski OLY XRC .08 .25
110T Lee Smith .07 .20
111T Pete Smith XRC .08 .25
112T Jim Snyder MG .02 .10
113T Ed Sprague OLY XRC .20 .50
114T Pete Stanicek RC .02 .10
115T Kurt Stillwell .02 .10
116T Todd Stottlemyre XRC .20 .50
117T Bill Swift .02 .10
118T Pat Tabler .02 .10
119T Scott Terry .02 .10
120T Mickey Tettleton .02 .10
121T Dickie Thon .02 .10
122T Jeff Treadway XRC .20 .50
123T Willie Upshaw .02 .10
124T Robin Ventura OLY XRC .60 1.50
125T Ron Washington .02 .10
126T Walt Weiss XRC .30 .75
127T Bob Welch .07 .20
128T David Wells XRC .60 1.50
129T Glenn Wilson .02 .10
130T Ted Wood OLY XRC .08 .25
131T Don Zimmer MG .07 .20
132T Checklist 1T-132T .02 .10

1988 Topps Traded Tiffany

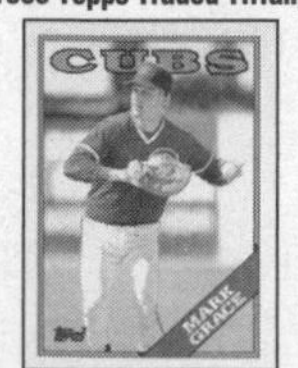

COMP.FACT.SET (132) 15.00 40.00
*STARS: 1.5X TO 4X BASIC CARDS
*ROOKIES: 2.5X TO 6X BASIC CARDS
DISTRIBUTED ONLY IN FACTORY SET FORM
FACTORY SET PRICE IS FOR SEALED SETS
66T Tino Martinez OLY 4.00 10.00

1989 Topps

This set consists of 792 standard-size cards. Cards were primarily issued in 15-card wax packs, 42-card rack packs and factory sets. Subsets in the set include Record Breakers (1-7), Turn Back the Clock (661-665), All-Star selections (386-407) and First Draft Picks, Future Stars and Team Leaders (all scattered throughout the set). The manager cards contain a team checklist on back. The key Rookie Cards in this set are Jim Abbott, Sandy Alomar Jr., Brady Anderson, Steve Avery, Andy Benes, Dante Bichette, Craig Biggio, Randy Johnson, Ramon Martinez, Gary Sheffield, John Smoltz, and Robin Ventura.

COMPLETE SET (792) 8.00 20.00
COMP.FACT.SET (792) 10.00 25.00
COMP.X-MAS.SET (792) 10.00 25.00
FS SUBSET VARIATIONS EXIST
FS PHOTOS ARE PLACED HIGHER/LOWER

1 George Bell RB .01 .05
Slams 3 HR on
Opening Day
2 Wade Boggs RB .02 .10
3 Gary Carter RB .01 .05
Sets Record for
Career Putouts
4 Andre Dawson RB .01 .05
Logs Double Figures
in HR and SB
5 Orel Hershiser RB .01 .05
Pitches 59
Scoreless Innings
6 Doug Jones RB UER .01 .05
Earns His 15th
Straight Save

Photo actually Chris Codiroli
7 Kevin McReynolds RB .01 .05
Steals 21 Without
Being Caught
8 Dave Eiland .01 .05
9 Tim Teufel .01 .05
10 Andre Dawson .02 .10
11 Bruce Sutter .02 .10
12 Dale Sveum .01 .05
13 Doug Sisk .01 .05
14 Tom Kelly MG .01 .05
15 Robby Thompson .01 .05
16 Ron Robinson .01 .05
17 Brian Downing .02 .10
18 Rick Rhoden .01 .05
19 Greg Gagne .01 .05
20 Steve Bedrosian .01 .05
21 Greg Walker TL .01 .05
22 Tim Crews .01 .05
23 Mike Fitzgerald .01 .05
24 Larry Andersen .01 .05
25 Frank White .02 .10
26 Dale Mohorcic .01 .05
27A Orestes Destrade .02 .10
F* next to copyright RC
27B Orestes Destrade .02 .10
E*F* next to
copyright VAR
28 Mike Moore .01 .05
29 Kelly Gruber .01 .05
30 Dwight Gooden .02 .10
31 Terry Francona .02 .10
32 Dennis Rasmussen .01 .05
33 B.J. Surhoff .01 .05
34 Ken Williams .01 .05
35 John Tudor UER .02 .10
With Red Sox in '84,should be Pirates
36 Mitch Webster .01 .05
37 Bob Stanley .01 .05
38 Paul Runge .01 .05
39 Mike Maddux .01 .05
40 Steve Sax .01 .05
41 Terry Mulholland .01 .05
42 Jim Eppard .01 .05
43 Guillermo Hernandez .01 .05
44 Jim Snyder MG .01 .05
45 Kal Daniels .01 .05
46 Mark Portugal .01 .05
47 Carney Lansford .02 .10
48 Tim Burke .01 .05
49 Craig Biggio RC 1.25 3.00
50 George Bell .02 .10
51 Mark McLemore TL .01 .05
52 Bob Brenly .01 .05
53 Ruben Sierra .02 .10
54 Steve Trout .01 .05
55 Julio Franco .02 .10
56 Pat Tabler .01 .05
57 Alejandro Pena .01 .05
58 Lee Mazzilli .02 .10
59 Mark Davis .01 .05
60 Tom Brunansky .01 .05
61 Neil Allen .01 .05
62 Alfredo Griffin .01 .05
63 Mark Clear .01 .05
64 Alex Trevino .01 .05
65 Rick Reuschel .02 .10
66 Manny Trillo .01 .05
67 Dave Palmer .01 .05
68 Darrell Miller .01 .05
69 Jeff Ballard .01 .05
70 Mark McGwire .40 1.00
71 Mike Boddicker .01 .05
72 John Moses .01 .05
73 Pascual Perez .01 .05
74 Nick Leyva MG .01 .05
75 Tom Henke .01 .05
76 Terry Blocker .01 .05
77 Doyle Alexander .01 .05
78 Jim Sundberg .02 .10
79 Scott Bankhead .01 .05
80 Cory Snyder .01 .05
81 Tim Raines TL .01 .05
82 Dave Leiper .01 .05
83 Jeff Blauser .01 .05
84 Bill Bene FDP .01 .05
85 Kevin McReynolds .01 .05
86 Al Nipper .01 .05
87 Larry Owen .01 .05
88 Darryl Hamilton RC .08 .25
89 Dave LaPoint .01 .05
90 Vince Coleman UER .01 .05
Wrong birth year
91 Floyd Youmans .01 .05
92 Jeff Kunkel .01 .05
93 Ken Howell .01 .05
94 Chris Speier .01 .05
95 Gerald Young .01 .05
96 Rick Cerone .01 .05
97 Greg Mathews .01 .05
98 Larry Sheets .01 .05
99 Sherman Corbett RC .01 .05
100 Mike Schmidt .20 .50
101 Les Straker .01 .05
102 Mike Gallego .01 .05
103 Tim Birtsas .01 .05
104 Dallas Green MG .01 .05
105 Ron Darling .02 .10
106 Willie Upshaw .01 .05
107 Jose DeLeon .01 .05
108 Fred Manrique .01 .05
109 Hipolito Pena .01 .05
110 Paul Molitor .02 .10
111 Eric Davis TL .01 .05
112 Jim Presley .01 .05
113 Lloyd Moseby .01 .05
114 Bob Kipper .01 .05
115 Jody Davis .01 .05
116 Jeff Montgomery .01 .05
117 Dave Anderson .01 .05
118 Checklist 1-132 .01 .05
119 Terry Puhl .01 .05
120 Frank Viola .02 .10
121 Garry Templeton .02 .10
122 Lance Johnson .01 .05
123 Spike Owen .01 .05
124 Jim Traber .01 .05
125 Mike Krukow .01 .05
126 Sid Bream .01 .05
127 Walt Terrell .01 .05
128 Milt Thompson .01 .05
129 Terry Clark .01 .05
130 Gerald Perry .01 .05
131 Dave Otto .01 .05
132 Curt Ford .01 .05
133 Bill Long .01 .05
134 Don Zimmer MG .02 .10
135 Jose Rijo .02 .10
136 Joey Meyer .01 .05
137 Geno Petralli .01 .05
138 Wallace Johnson .01 .05
139 Mike Flanagan .01 .05
140 Shawon Dunston .01 .05
141 Brook Jacoby TL .01 .05
142 Mike Diaz .01 .05
143 Mike Campbell .01 .05
144 Jay Bell .02 .10
145 Dave Stewart .02 .10
146 Gary Pettis .01 .05
147 DeWayne Buice .01 .05
148 Bill Pecota .01 .05
149 Doug Dascenzo .01 .05
150 Fernando Valenzuela .02 .10
151 Terry McGriff .01 .05
152 Mark Thurmond .01 .05
153 Jim Pankovits .01 .05
154 Don Carman .01 .05
155 Marty Barrett .01 .05
156 Dave Gallagher .01 .05
157 Tom Glavine .08 .25
158 Mike Aldrete .01 .05
159 Pat Clements .01 .05
160 Jeffrey Leonard .01 .05
161 Gregg Olson RC FDP UER .08 .25
Born Scribner, NE,
should be Omaha, NE
162 John Davis .01 .05
163 Bob Forsch .01 .05
164 Hal Lanier MG .01 .05
165 Mike Dunne .01 .05
166 Doug Jennings RC .01 .05
167 Steve Searcy FS .01 .05
168 Willie Wilson .02 .10
169 Mike Jackson .01 .05
170 Tony Fernandez .01 .05
171 Andres Thomas TL .01 .05
172 Frank Williams .01 .05
173 Mel Hall .01 .05
174 Todd Burns .01 .05
175 John Shelby .01 .05
176 Jeff Parrett .01 .05
177 Monty Fariss FDP .01 .05
178 Mark Grant .01 .05
179 Ozzie Virgil .01 .05
180 Mike Scott .02 .10
181 Craig Worthington .01 .05
182 Bob McClure .01 .05
183 Oddibe McDowell .01 .05
184 John Costello RC .01 .05
185 Claudell Washington .01 .05
186 Pat Perry .01 .05
187 Darren Daulton .02 .10
188 Dennis Lamp .01 .05
189 Kevin Mitchell .02 .10
190 Mike Witt .01 .05
191 Sil Campusano .01 .05
192 Paul Mirabella .01 .05
193 Sparky Anderson MG .02 .10
UER 553 Salazar
194 Greg W. Harris RC .02 .10
195 Ozzie Guillen .02 .10
196 Denny Walling .01 .05
197 Neal Heaton .01 .05
198 Danny Heep .01 .05
199 Mike Schooler RC .02 .10
200 George Brett .25 .60
201 Kelly Gruber TL .01 .05
202 Brad Moore .01 .05
203 Rob Ducey .01 .05
204 Brad Havens .01 .05
205 Dwight Evans .05 .15
206 Roberto Alomar .08 .25
207 Terry Leach .01 .05
208 Tom Pagnozzi .01 .05
209 Jeff Bittiger .01 .05
210 Dale Murphy .05 .15
211 Mike Pagliarulo .01 .05
212 Scott Sanderson .01 .05
213 Rene Gonzales .01 .05
214 Charlie O'Brien .01 .05
215 Kevin Gross .01 .05
216 Jack Howell .01 .05
217 Joe Price .01 .05
218 Mike LaValliere .01 .05
219 Jim Clancy .01 .05
220 Gary Gaetti .02 .10
221 Cecil Espy .01 .05
222 Mark Lewis FDP RC .08 .25
223 Jay Buhner .02 .10
224 Tony LaRussa MG .02 .10
225 Ramon Martinez RC .08 .25
226 Bill Doran .01 .05
227 John Farrell .01 .05
228 Nelson Santovenia .01 .05
229 Jimmy Key .02 .10
230 Ozzie Smith .15 .40
231 Roberto Alomar TL .08 .25
Gary Carter at plate
232 Ricky Horton .01 .05
233 Gregg Jefferies FS .01 .05
234 Tom Browning .01 .05
235 John Kruk .02 .10
236 Charles Hudson .01 .05
237 Glenn Hubbard .01 .05
238 Eric King .01 .05
239 Tim Laudner .01 .05
240 Greg Maddux .20 .50
241 Brett Butler .02 .10
242 Ed VandeBerg .01 .05
243 Bob Boone .02 .10
244 Jim Acker .01 .05
245 Jim Rice .02 .10
246 Rey Quinones .01 .05
247 Shawn Hillegas .01 .05
248 Tony Phillips .01 .05
249 Tim Leary .01 .05
250 Cal Ripken .30 .75
251 John Dopson .01 .05
252 Billy Hatcher .01 .05
253 Jose Alvarez RC .01 .05
254 Tom Lasorda MG .05 .15
255 Ron Guidry .02 .10
256 Benny Santiago .02 .10
257 Rick Aguilera .01 .05
258 Checklist 133-264 .01 .05
259 Larry McWilliams .01 .05
260 Dave Winfield .02 .10
261 Tom Brunansky .01 .05
Luis Alicea TL
262 Jeff Pico .01 .05
263 Mike Felder .01 .05
264 Rob Dibble RC .15 .40
265 Kent Hrbek .02 .10
266 Luis Aquino .01 .05
267 Jeff M. Robinson .01 .05
268 Keith Miller RC .08 .25
269 Tom Bolton .01 .05
270 Wally Joyner .02 .10
271 Jay Tibbs .01 .05
272 Ron Hassey .01 .05
273 Jose Lind .01 .05
274 Mark Eichhorn .01 .05
275 Danny Tartabull UER .01 .05
Born San Juan, PR
should be Miami, FL
276 Paul Kilgus .01 .05
277 Mike Davis .01 .05
278 Andy McGaffigan .01 .05
279 Scott Bradley .01 .05
280 Bob Knepper .01 .05
281 Gary Redus .01 .05
282 Cris Carpenter RC .02 .10
283 Andy Allanson .01 .05
284 Jim Leyland MG .02 .10
285 John Candelaria .01 .05
286 Darrin Jackson .02 .10
287 Juan Nieves .01 .05
288 Pat Sheridan .01 .05
289 Ernie Whitt .01 .05
290 John Franco .02 .10
291 Darryl Strawberry .01 .05
Keith Hernandez
Kevin McReynolds TL
292 Jim Corsi .01 .05
293 Glenn Wilson .01 .05
294 Juan Berenguer .01 .05
295 Scott Fletcher .01 .05
296 Ron Gant .02 .10
297 Oswald Peraza RC .01 .05
298 Chris James .01 .05
299 Steve Ellsworth .01 .05
300 Darryl Strawberry .02 .10
301 Charlie Leibrandt .01 .05
302 Gary Ward .01 .05
303 Felix Fermin .01 .05
304 Joel Youngblood .01 .05
305 Dave Smith .01 .05
306 Tracy Woodson .01 .05
307 Lance McCullers .01 .05
308 Ron Karkovice .01 .05
309 Mario Diaz .01 .05
310 Rafael Palmeiro .08 .25
311 Chris Bosio .01 .05
312 Tom Lawless .01 .05
313 Dennis Martinez .02 .10
314 Bobby Valentine MG .02 .10
315 Greg Swindell .01 .05
316 Walt Weiss .01 .05
317 Jack Armstrong RC .08 .25
318 Gene Larkin .01 .05
319 Greg Booker .01 .05
320 Lou Whitaker .02 .10
321 Jody Reed TL .01 .05
322 John Smiley .01 .05
323 Gary Thurman .01 .05
324 Bob Milacki .01 .05
325 Jesse Barfield .01 .05
326 Dennis Boyd .01 .05
327 Mark Lemke RC .15 .40
328 Rick Honeycutt .01 .05
329 Bob Melvin .01 .05
330 Eric Davis .02 .10
331 Curt Wilkerson .01 .05
332 Tony Armas .02 .10
333 Bob Ojeda .01 .05
334 Steve Lyons .01 .05
335 Dave Righetti .02 .10
336 Steve Balboni .01 .05
337 Calvin Schiraldi .01 .05
338 Jim Adduci .01 .05
339 Scott Bailes .01 .05
340 Kirk Gibson .02 .10
341 Jim Deshaies .01 .05
342 Tom Brookens .01 .05
343 Gary Sheffield FS RC .60 1.50
344 Tom Trebelhorn MG .01 .05
345 Charlie Hough .02 .10
346 Rex Hudler .01 .05
347 John Cerutti .01 .05
348 Ed Hearn .01 .05
349 Ron Jones .02 .10
350 Andy Van Slyke .05 .15
351 Bob Melvin .01 .05
Bill Fahey CO TL
352 Rick Schu .01 .05
353 Marvell Wynne .01 .05
354 Larry Parrish .01 .05
355 Mark Langston .01 .05
356 Kevin Elster .01 .05
357 Jerry Reuss .01 .05
358 Ricky Jordan RC .08 .25
359 Tommy John .02 .10
360 Ryne Sandberg .15 .40
361 Kelly Downs .01 .05
362 Jack Lazorko .01 .05
363 Rich Yett .01 .05
364 Rob Deer .01 .05
365 Mike Henneman .01 .05
366 Herm Winningham .01 .05
367 Johnny Paredes .01 .05
368 Brian Holton .01 .05
369 Ken Caminiti .05 .15
370 Dennis Eckersley .05 .15
371 Manny Lee .01 .05
372 Craig Lefferts .01 .05
373 Tracy Jones .01 .05
374 John Wathan MG .01 .05
375 Terry Pendleton .02 .10
376 Steve Lombardozzi .01 .05
377 Mike Smithson .01 .05
378 Checklist 265-396 .01 .05
379 Tim Flannery .01 .05
380 Rickey Henderson .08 .25
381 Larry Sheets TL .01 .05
382 John Smoltz RC .60 1.50
383 Howard Johnson .02 .10
384 Mark Salas .01 .05
385 Von Hayes .01 .05
386 Andres Galarraga AS .01 .05
387 Ryne Sandberg AS .08 .25
388 Bobby Bonilla AS .01 .05
389 Ozzie Smith AS .08 .25
390 Darryl Strawberry AS .01 .05
391 Andre Dawson AS .01 .05
392 Andy Van Slyke AS .02 .10
393 Gary Carter AS .01 .05
394 Orel Hershiser AS .02 .10
395 Danny Jackson AS .01 .05
396 Kirk Gibson AS .02 .10
397 Don Mattingly AS .10 .30
398 Julio Franco AS .01 .05
399 Wade Boggs AS .02 .10
400 Alan Trammell AS .01 .05
401 Jose Canseco AS .05 .15
402 Mike Greenwell AS .01 .05
403 Kirby Puckett AS .05 .15
404 Bob Boone AS .01 .05
405 Roger Clemens AS .20 .50
406 Frank Viola AS .01 .05
407 Dave Winfield AS .01 .05
408 Greg Walker .01 .05
409 Ken Dayley .01 .05
410 Jack Clark .02 .10
411 Mitch Williams .01 .05
412 Barry Lyons .01 .05
413 Mike Kingery .01 .05
414 Jim Fregosi MG .01 .05
415 Rich Gossage .02 .10
416 Fred Lynn .02 .10
417 Mike LaCoss .01 .05
418 Bob Dernier .01 .05
419 Tom Filer .01 .05
420 Joe Carter .02 .10
421 Kirk McCaskill .01 .05
422 Bo Diaz .01 .05
423 Brian Fisher .01 .05
424 Luis Polonia UER .01 .05
Wrong birthdate
425 Jay Howell .01 .05
426 Dan Gladden .01 .05
427 Eric Show .01 .05
428 Craig Reynolds .01 .05
429 Greg Gagne TL .01 .05
430 Mark Gubicza .01 .05
431 Luis Rivera .01 .05
432 Chad Kreuter RC .08 .25
433 Albert Hall .01 .05
434 Ken Patterson .01 .05
435 Len Dykstra .02 .10
436 Bobby Meacham .01 .05
437 Andy Benes FDP RC .15 .40
438 Greg Gross .01 .05
439 Frank DiPino .01 .05
440 Bobby Bonilla .02 .10
441 Jerry Reed .01 .05
442 Jose Oquendo .01 .05
443 Rod Nichols .01 .05
444 Moose Stubing MG .01 .05
445 Matt Nokes .01 .05
446 Rob Murphy .01 .05
447 Donell Nixon .01 .05
448 Eric Plunk .01 .05
449 Carmelo Martinez .01 .05
450 Roger Clemens .40 1.00
451 Mark Davidson .01 .05
452 Israel Sanchez .01 .05
453 Tom Prince .01 .05
454 Paul Assenmacher .01 .05
455 Johnny Ray .01 .05
456 Tim Belcher .01 .05
457 Mackey Sasser .01 .05
458 Donn Pall .01 .05
459 Dave Valle TL .01 .05
460 Dave Stieb .02 .10
461 Buddy Bell .02 .10
462 Jose Guzman .01 .05
463 Steve Lake .01 .05
464 Bryn Smith .01 .05
465 Mark Grace .08 .25
466 Chuck Crim .01 .05
467 Jim Walewander .01 .05
468 Henry Cotto .01 .05
469 Jose Bautista RC .01 .05
470 Lance Parrish .02 .10
471 Steve Curry .01 .05
472 Brian Harper .01 .05
473 Don Robinson .01 .05
474 Bob Rodgers MG .01 .05
475 Dave Parker .02 .10
476 Jon Perlman .01 .05
477 Dick Schofield .01 .05
478 Doug Drabek .01 .05
479 Mike Macfarlane RC .08 .25
480 Keith Hernandez .02 .10
481 Chris Brown .01 .05
482 Steve Peters .01 .05
483 Mickey Hatcher .01 .05
484 Steve Shields .01 .05
485 Hubie Brooks .01 .05
486 Jack McDowell .02 .10
487 Scott Lusader .01 .05
488 Kevin Coffman .01 .05
Now with Cubs
489 Mike Schmidt TL .05 .15
490 Chris Sabo RC .15 .40
491 Mike Birkbeck .01 .05
492 Alan Ashby .01 .05
493 Todd Benzinger .01 .05
494 Shane Rawley .01 .05
495 Candy Maldonado .01 .05
496 Dwayne Henry .01 .05
497 Pete Stanicek .01 .05
498 Dave Valle .01 .05
499 Don Heinkel .01 .05
500 Jose Canseco .08 .25
501 Vance Law .01 .05
502 Duane Ward .01 .05
503 Al Newman .01 .05
504 Bob Walk .01 .05
505 Pete Rose MG .20 .50
506 Kirt Manwaring .01 .05
507 Steve Farr .01 .05
508 Wally Backman .01 .05
509 Bud Black .01 .05
510 Bob Horner .02 .10
511 Richard Dotson .01 .05
512 Donnie Hill .01 .05
513 Jesse Orosco .01 .05
514 Chet Lemon .02 .10
515 Barry Larkin .05 .15
516 Eddie Whitson .01 .05
517 Greg Brock .01 .05
518 Bruce Ruffin .01 .05
519 Willie Randolph TL .01 .05
520 Rick Sutcliffe .02 .10
521 Mickey Tettleton .01 .05
522 Randy Kramer .01 .05
523 Andres Thomas .01 .05
524 Checklist 397-528 .01 .05
525 Chili Davis .02 .10
526 Wes Gardner .01 .05
527 Dave Henderson .01 .05
528 Luis Medina .01 .05
Lower left front
has white triangle
529 Tom Foley .01 .05
530 Nolan Ryan .40 1.00
531 Dave Hengel .01 .05
532 Jerry Browne .01 .05
533 Andy Hawkins .01 .05
534 Doc Edwards MG .01 .05
535 Todd Worrell UER .01 .05
4 wins in '88,
should be 5
536 Joel Skinner .01 .05
537 Pete Smith .01 .05
538 Juan Castillo .01 .05
539 Barry Jones .01 .05
540 Bo Jackson .08 .25
541 Cecil Fielder .02 .10
542 Todd Frohwirth .01 .05
543 Damon Berryhill .01 .05
544 Jeff Sellers .01 .05
545 Mookie Wilson .02 .10
546 Mark Williamson .01 .05
547 Mark McLemore .01 .05
548 Bobby Witt .01 .05
549 Jamie Moyer TL .01 .05
550 Orel Hershiser .02 .10
551 Randy Ready .01 .05
552 Greg Cadaret .01 .05
553 Luis Salazar .01 .05
554 Nick Esasky .01 .05
555 Bert Blyleven .02 .10
556 Bruce Fields .01 .05
557 Keith A. Miller .01 .05
558 Dan Pasqua .01 .05
559 Juan Agosto .01 .05
560 Tim Raines .02 .10
561 Luis Aguayo .01 .05
562 Danny Cox .01 .05
563 Bill Schroeder .01 .05
564 Russ Nixon MG .01 .05
565 Jeff Russell .01 .05
566 Al Pedrique .01 .05
567 David Wells UER .02 .10
Complete Pitching
Recor
568 Mickey Brantley .01 .05
569 German Jimenez .01 .05
570 Tony Gwynn UER .10 .30
571 Billy Ripken .01 .05
572 Atlee Hammaker .01 .05
573 Jim Abbott FDP RC .40 1.00
574 Dave Clark .01 .05
575 Juan Samuel .01 .05
576 Greg Minton .01 .05
577 Randy Bush .01 .05
578 John Morris .01 .05
579 Glenn Davis TL .01 .05
580 Harold Reynolds .02 .10
581 Gene Nelson .01 .05
582 Mike Marshall .01 .05
583 Paul Gibson .01 .05
584 Randy Velarde UER .01 .05
Signed 1935,
should be 1985
585 Harold Baines .02 .10
586 Joe Boever .01 .05
587 Mike Stanley .01 .05
588 Luis Alicea RC .08 .25
589 Dave Meads .01 .05
590 Andres Galarraga .02 .10
591 Jeff Musselman .01 .05
592 John Cangelosi .01 .05
593 Drew Hall .01 .05
594 Jimy Williams MG .01 .05
595 Teddy Higuera .01 .05
596 Kurt Stillwell .01 .05
597 Terry Taylor RC .02 .10
598 Ken Gerhart .01 .05
599 Tom Candiotti .01 .05
600 Wade Boggs .05 .15
601 Dave Dravecky .01 .05
602 Devon White .02 .10
603 Frank Tanana .01 .05
604 Paul O'Neill .05 .15
605A Bob Welch ERR 4.00 10.00
605B Bob Welch COR .02 .10
606 Rick Dempsey .01 .05
607 Willie Ansley FDP RC .02 .10
608 Phil Bradley .01 .05
609 Frank Tanana .01 .05
Alan Trammell
Mike Heath TL
610 Randy Myers .02 .10
611 Don Slaught .01 .05
612 Dan Quisenberry .01 .05
613 Gary Varsho .01 .05
614 Joe Hesketh .01 .05
615 Robin Yount .15 .40
616 Steve Rosenberg .01 .05
617 Mark Parent RC .01 .05
618 Rance Mulliniks .01 .05
619 Checklist 529-660 .01 .05
620 Barry Bonds .60 1.50
621 Rick Mahler .01 .05
622 Stan Javier .01 .05
623 Fred Toliver .01 .05
624 Jack McKeon MG .02 .10
625 Eddie Murray .08 .25
626 Jeff Reed .01 .05
627 Greg A. Harris .01 .05
628 Matt Williams .08 .25
629 Pete O'Brien .01 .05
630 Mike Greenwell .01 .05
631 Dave Bergman .01 .05
632 Bryan Harvey RC .08 .25
633 Daryl Boston .01 .05
634 Marvin Freeman .01 .05
635 Willie Randolph .02 .10
636 Bill Wilkinson .01 .05
637 Carmen Castillo .01 .05
638 Floyd Bannister .01 .05
639 Walt Weiss TL .01 .05
640 Willie McGee .02 .10
641 Curt Young .01 .05
642 Angel Salazar .01 .05
643 Louie Meadows RC .01 .05
644 Lloyd McClendon .01 .05
645 Jack Morris .02 .10
646 Kevin Bass .01 .05
647 Randy Johnson RC .75 2.00
648 Sandy Alomar FS RC .15 .40
649 Stu Cliburn .01 .05
650 Kirby Puckett .08 .25
651 Tom Niedenfuer .01 .05
652 Rich Gedman .01 .05
653 Tommy Barrett .01 .05
654 Whitey Herzog MG .02 .10
655 Dave Magadan .01 .05
656 Ivan Calderon .01 .05
657 Joe Magrane .01 .05
658 R.J. Reynolds .01 .05
659 Al Leiter .08 .25
660 Will Clark .05 .15
661 Dwight Gooden TBC 84 .01 .05
662 Lou Brock TBC79 .02 .10
663 Hank Aaron TBC74 .08 .25
664 Gil Hodges TBC 69 .02 .10
665B Tony Oliva TBC 64 .02 .10
COR fabricated
card
666 Randy St.Claire .01 .05
667 Dwayne Murphy .01 .05
668 Mike Bielecki .01 .05
669 Orel Hershiser .02 .10
Mike Scioscia TL
670 Kevin Seitzer .01 .05
671 Jim Gantner .01 .05
672 Allan Anderson .01 .05
673 Don Baylor .02 .10
674 Otis Nixon .01 .05
675 Bruce Hurst .01 .05
676 Ernie Riles .01 .05
677 Dave Schmidt .01 .05
678 Dion James .01 .05
679 Willie Fraser .01 .05
680 Gary Carter .02 .10
681 Jeff D. Robinson .01 .05
682 Rick Leach .01 .05
683 Jose Cecena .01 .05
684 Dave Johnson MG .01 .05
685 Jeff Treadway .01 .05
686 Scott Terry .01 .05
687 Alvin Davis .01 .05
688 Zane Smith .01 .05
689A Stan Jefferson 4.00 10.00
689B Stan Jefferson .01 .05
Violet triangle on
front bottom left
690 Doug Jones .01 .05
691 Roberto Kelly UER .01 .05
982
692 Steve Ontiveros .01 .05
693 Pat Borders RC .08 .25
694 Les Lancaster .01 .05
695 Carlton Fisk .05 .15
696 Don August .01 .05
697A Franklin Stubbs ERR 4.00 10.00
697B Franklin Stubbs .01 .05
Team name on front
in gray
698 Keith Atherton .01 .05
699 Al Pedrique TL .01 .05
Tony Gwynn sliding
700 Don Mattingly .25 .60
701 Storm Davis .01 .05
702 Jamie Quirk .01 .05
703 Scott Garrelts .01 .05
704 Carlos Quintana RC .02 .10
705 Terry Kennedy .01 .05
706 Pete Incaviglia .01 .05

707 Steve Jeltz .01 .05
708 Chuck Finley .02 .10
709 Tom Herr .01 .05
710 David Cone .02 .10
711 Candy Sierra .01 .05
712 Bill Swift .01 .05
713 Ty Griffin FDP .01 .05
714 Joe Morgan MG .02 .10
715 Tony Pena .01 .05
716 Wayne Tolleson .01 .05
717 Jamie Moyer .02 .10
718 Glenn Braggs .01 .05
719 Danny Darwin .01 .05
720 Tim Wallach .01 .05
721 Ron Tingley .01 .05
722 Todd Stottlemyre .01 .05
723 Rafael Belliard .01 .05
724 Jerry Don Gleaton .01 .05
725 Terry Steinbach .02 .10
726 Dickie Thon .01 .05
727 Joe Orsulak .01 .05
728 Charlie Puleo .01 .05
729 Steve Buechele TL .01 .05
Inconsistent design, team name on front surrounded by black, should be white
730 Danny Jackson .01 .05
731 Mike Young .01 .05
732 Steve Buechele .01 .05
733 Randy Bockus .01 .05
734 Jody Reed .01 .05
735 Roger McDowell .01 .05
736 Jeff Hamilton .01 .05
737 Norm Charlton RC .08 .25
738 Darnell Coles .01 .05
739 Brook Jacoby .01 .05
740 Dan Plesac .01 .05
741 Ken Phelps .01 .05
742 Mike Harkey FS RC .02 .10
743 Mike Heath .01 .05
744 Roger Craig MG .02 .10
745 Fred McGriff .05 .15
746 German Gonzalez UER .01 .05
Wrong birthdate
747 Wil Tejada .01 .05
748 Jimmy Jones .01 .05
749 Rafael Ramirez .01 .05
750 Bret Saberhagen .02 .10
751 Ken Oberkfell .01 .05
752 Jim Gott .01 .05
753 Jose Uribe .01 .05
754 Bob Brower .01 .05
755 Mike Scioscia .02 .10
756 Scott Medvin .01 .05
757 Brady Anderson RC .15 .40
758 Gene Walter .01 .05
759 Rob Deer TL .01 .05
760 Lee Smith .02 .10
761 Dante Bichette RC .15 .40
762 Bobby Thigpen .01 .05
763 Dave Martinez .01 .05
764 Robin Ventura FDP RC .30 .75
765 Glenn Davis .01 .05
766 Cecilio Guante .01 .05
767 Mike Capel .01 .05
768 Bill Wegman .01 .05
769 Junior Ortiz .01 .05
770 Alan Trammell .02 .10
771 Ron Kittle .01 .05
772 Ron Oester .01 .05
773 Keith Moreland .01 .05
774 Frank Robinson MG .05 .15
775 Jeff Reardon .02 .10
776 Nelson Liriano .01 .05
777 Ted Power .01 .05
778 Bruce Benedict .01 .05
779 Craig McMurtry .01 .05
780 Pedro Guerrero .02 .10
781 Greg Briley .02 .10
782 Checklist 661-792 .01 .05
783 Trevor Wilson RC .02 .10
784 Steve Avery FDP RC .08 .25
785 Ellis Burks .02 .10
786 Melido Perez .01 .05
787 Dave West RC .02 .10
788 Mike Morgan .01 .05
789 Bo Jackson TL .08 .25
790 Sid Fernandez .01 .05
791 Jim Lindeman .01 .05
792 Rafael Santana .01 .05

1989 Topps Tiffany

COMP.FACT.SET (792) 60.00 150.00
*STARS: 5X TO 12X BASIC CARDS
*ROOKIES: 5X TO 12X BASIC CARDS
DISTRIBUTED ONLY IN FACTORY SET FORM
FACTORY SET PRICE IS FOR SEALED SETS

1989 Topps Batting Leaders

The 1989 Topps Batting Leaders set contains 22 standard-size glossy cards. The fronts are bright red. The set depicts the 22 veterans with the highest lifetime batting averages. The cards were distributed one per Topps blister pack. These blister packs were sold exclusively through K-Mart stores. The cards in the set were numbered by K-Mart essentially in order of highest active career batting average entering the 1989 season.

COMPLETE SET (22) 30.00 60.00
1 Wade Boggs 3.00 8.00
2 Tony Gwynn 6.00 15.00
3 Don Mattingly 6.00 15.00
4 Kirby Puckett 5.00 12.00
5 George Brett 6.00 15.00
6 Pedro Guerrero .20 .50
7 Tim Raines .40 1.00
8 Keith Hernandez .40 1.00
9 Jim Rice .40 1.00
10 Paul Molitor 2.50 6.00
11 Eddie Murray 2.50 6.00
12 Willie McGee .40 1.00
13 Dave Parker .40 1.00
14 Julio Franco .40 1.00
15 Rickey Henderson 4.00 10.00
16 Kent Hrbek .40 1.00
17 Willie Wilson .20 .50
18 Johnny Ray .20 .50
19 Pat Tabler .20 .50
20 Carney Lansford .20 .50
21 Robin Yount 2.50 6.00
22 Alan Trammell .60 1.50

1989 Topps Glossy All-Stars

These glossy cards were inserted with Topps rack packs and honor the starting line-ups, managers, and honorary captains of the 1988 National and American League All-Star teams. The standard size cards are very similar in design to what Topps has used since 1984. The backs are printed in red and blue on white card stock.

COMPLETE SET (22) 1.25 3.00
1 Tom Kelly MG .01 .05
2 Mark McGwire .30 .75
3 Paul Molitor .15 .40
4 Wade Boggs .10 .30
5 Cal Ripken .60 1.50
6 Jose Canseco .08 .25
7 Rickey Henderson .25 .60
8 Dave Winfield .15 .40
9 Terry Steinbach .01 .05
10 Frank Viola .01 .05
11 Bobby Doerr CAPT .08 .25
12 Whitey Herzog MG .01 .05
13 Will Clark .07 .20
14 Ryne Sandberg .20 .50
15 Bobby Bonilla .02 .10
16 Ozzie Smith .20 .50
17 Vince Coleman .01 .05
18 Andre Dawson .07 .20
19 Darryl Strawberry .02 .10
20 Gary Carter .15 .40
21 Dwight Gooden .02 .10
22 Willie Stargell CAPT .08 .25

1989 Topps Glossy Send-Ins

The 1989 Topps Glossy Send-In set contains 60 standard-size cards. The fronts have color photos with white borders; the backs are light blue. The cards were distributed through the mail by Topps in six groups of ten cards. The last two cards out of each group of ten are young players or prospects.

COMPLETE SET (60) 8.00 20.00
1 Kirby Puckett .40 1.00
2 Eric Davis .07 .20
3 Joe Carter .07 .20
4 Andy Van Slyke .02 .10
5 Wade Boggs .25 .60
6 David Cone .07 .20
7 Kent Hrbek .07 .20
8 Darryl Strawberry .07 .20
9 Jay Buhner .07 .20
10 Ron Gant .07 .20
11 Will Clark .15 .40
12 Jose Canseco .30 .75
13 Juan Samuel .02 .10
14 George Brett .60 1.50
15 Benito Santiago .07 .20
16 Dennis Eckersley .25 .60
17 Gary Carter .25 .60
18 Frank Viola .02 .10
19 Roberto Alomar .60 1.50
20 Paul Gibson .02 .10
21 Dave Winfield .25 .60
22 Howard Johnson .02 .10
23 Roger Clemens .60 1.50
24 Bobby Bonilla .07 .20
25 Alan Trammell .10 .30
26 Kevin McReynolds .02 .10
27 George Bell .02 .10
28 Bruce Hurst .02 .10
29 Mark Grace .30 .75
30 Tim Belcher .02 .10
31 Mike Greenwell .02 .10
32 Glenn Davis .02 .10
33 Gary Gaetti .07 .20
34 Ryne Sandberg .60 1.50
35 Rickey Henderson .30 1.00
36 Dwight Evans .07 .20
37 Dwight Gooden .07 .20
38 Robin Yount .25 .60
39 Damon Berryhill .02 .10
40 Chris Sabo .02 .10
41 Mark McGwire .60 1.50
42 Ozzie Smith .60 1.50
43 Paul Molitor .25 .60
44 Andres Galarraga .15 .40
45 Dave Stewart .07 .20
46 Tom Browning .02 .10
47 Cal Ripken 1.25 3.00
48 Orel Hershiser .07 .20
49 Dave Gallagher .02 .10
50 Walt Weiss .02 .10
51 Don Mattingly .60 1.50
52 Tony Fernandez .02 .10
53 Tim Raines .07 .20
54 Jeff Reardon .07 .20
55 Kirk Gibson .07 .20
56 Jack Clark .02 .10
57 Danny Jackson .02 .10
58 Tony Gwynn .60 1.50
59 Cecil Espy .02 .10
60 Jody Reed .02 .10

1989 Topps Rookies

Inserted in each supermarket jumbo pack is a card from this series of 22 of 1988's best rookies as determined by Topps. Jumbo packs consisted of 100 (regular issue 1989 Topps baseball) cards with a stick of gum plus the insert "Rookie" card. The card fronts are in full color and measure the standard size. The card backs are printed in red and blue on white card stock and are numbered at the bottom. The order of the set is alphabetical by player's name.

COMPLETE SET (22) 5.00 12.00
1 Roberto Alomar 1.00 2.50
2 Brady Anderson .30 .75
3 Tim Belcher .08 .25
4 Damon Berryhill .08 .25
5 Jay Buhner .40 1.00
6 Kevin Elster .08 .25
7 Cecil Espy .08 .25
8 Dave Gallagher .08 .25
9 Ron Gant .40 1.00
10 Paul Gibson .08 .25
11 Mark Grace .75 2.00
12 Darrin Jackson .08 .25
13 Gregg Jefferies .20 .50
14 Ricky Jordan .08 .25
15 Al Leiter .40 1.00
16 Melido Perez .08 .25
17 Chris Sabo .08 .25
18 Nelson Santovenia .08 .25
19 Mackey Sasser .08 .25
20 Gary Sheffield 1.25 3.00
21 Walt Weiss .08 .25
22 David Wells .75 2.00

1989 Topps Wax Box Cards

The cards in this 16-card set measure the standard size. Cards have essentially the same design as the 1989 Topps regular issue set. The cards were printed on the bottoms of the regular issue wax pack boxes. These 16 cards, "lettered" A through P, are considered a separate set in their own right and are not typically included in a complete set of the regular issue 1989 Topps cards. The order of the set is alphabetical by player's name. The value of the panels uncut is slightly greater, perhaps by 25 percent greater, than the value of the individual cards cut up carefully. The sixteen cards in this set honor players (and one manager) who reached career milestones during the 1988 season.

COMPLETE SET (16) 3.00 8.00
A George Brett .40 1.00
B Bill Buckner .07 .20
C Darrell Evans .07 .20
D Rich Gossage .07 .20
E Greg Gross .02 .10
F Rickey Henderson .30 .75
G Keith Hernandez .07 .20
H Tom Lasorda MG .15 .40
I Jim Rice .07 .20
J Cal Ripken .75 2.00
K Nolan Ryan .75 2.00
L Mike Schmidt .30 .75
M Bruce Sutter .20 .50
N Don Sutton .20 .50
O Kent Tekulve .02 .10
P Dave Winfield .30 .75

1989 Topps Traded

The 1989 Topps Traded set contains 132 standard-size cards. The cards were distributed exclusively in factory set form in red and white taped boxes through hobby dealers. The cards are identical to the 1989 Topps regular issue cards except for whiter stock and t-suffixed numbering on back. Rookie Cards in this set include Ken Griffey Jr., Kenny Rogers, Deion Sanders and Omar Vizquel.

COMP.FACT.SET (132) 4.00 10.00
1T Don Aase .01 .05
2T Jim Abbott .20 .50
3T Kent Anderson .01 .05
4T Keith Atherton .01 .05
5T Wally Backman .01 .05
6T Steve Balboni .01 .05
7T Jesse Barfield .02 .10
8T Steve Bedrosian .01 .05
9T Todd Benzinger .01 .05
10T Geronimo Berroa .01 .05
11T Bert Blyleven .02 .10
12T Bob Boone .02 .10
13T Phil Bradley .01 .05
14T Jeff Brantley RC .08 .25
15T Kevin Brown .08 .25
16T Jerry Browne .01 .05
17T Chuck Cary .01 .05
18T Carmen Castillo .01 .05
19T Jim Clancy .01 .05
20T Jack Clark .02 .10
21T Bryan Clutterbuck .01 .05
22T Jody Davis .01 .05
23T Mike Devereaux .01 .05
24T Frank DiPino .01 .05
25T Benny Distefano .01 .05
26T John Dopson .01 .05
27T Len Dykstra .02 .10
28T Jim Eisenreich .01 .05
29T Nick Esasky .01 .05
30T Alvaro Espinoza .01 .05
31T Darrell Evans UER .02 .10
32T Junior Felix RC .02 .10
33T Felix Fermin .01 .05
34T Julio Franco .02 .10
35T Terry Francona .02 .10
36T Cito Gaston MG .01 .05
37T Bob Geren UER RC .01 .05
38T Tom Gordon RC .20 .50
39T Tommy Gregg .01 .05
40T Ken Griffey Sr. .02 .10
41T Ken Griffey Jr. RC 8.00 20.00
42T Kevin Gross .01 .05
43T Lee Guetterman .01 .05
44T Mel Hall .01 .05
45T Erik Hanson RC .08 .25
46T Gene Harris RC .02 .10
47T Andy Hawkins .01 .05
48T Rickey Henderson .08 .25
49T Tom Herr .01 .05
50T Ken Hill RC .08 .25
51T Brian Holman RC .02 .10
52T Brian Holton .01 .05
53T Art Howe MG .01 .05
54T Ken Howell .01 .05
55T Bruce Hurst .01 .05
56T Chris James .01 .05
57T Randy Johnson .60 1.50
58T Jimmy Jones .01 .05
59T Terry Kennedy .01 .05
60T Paul Kilgus .01 .05
61T Eric King .01 .05
62T Ron Kittle .01 .05
63T John Kruk .02 .10
64T Randy Kutcher .01 .05
65T Steve Lake .01 .05
66T Mark Langston .01 .05
67T Dave LaPoint .01 .05
68T Rick Leach .01 .05
69T Terry Leach .01 .05
70T Jim Lefebvre MG .01 .05
71T Al Leiter .08 .25
72T Jeffrey Leonard .01 .05
73T Derek Lilliquist RC .02 .10
74T Rick Mahler .01 .05
75T Tom McCarthy .01 .05
76T Lloyd McClendon .01 .05
77T Lance McCullers .01 .05
78T Oddibe McDowell .01 .05
79T Roger McDowell .01 .05
80T Larry McWilliams .01 .05
81T Randy Milligan .01 .05
82T Mike Moore .01 .05
83T Keith Moreland .01 .05
84T Mike Morgan .01 .05
85T Jamie Moyer .02 .10
86T Rob Murphy .01 .05
87T Eddie Murray .08 .25
88T Pete O'Brien .01 .05
89T Gregg Olson .08 .25
90T Steve Ontiveros .01 .05
91T Jesse Orosco .01 .05
92T Spike Owen .01 .05
93T Rafael Palmeiro .08 .25
94T Clay Parker .01 .05
95T Jeff Parrett .01 .05
96T Lance Parrish .02 .10
97T Dennis Powell .01 .05
98T Rey Quinones .01 .05
99T Doug Rader MG .01 .05
100T Willie Randolph .02 .10
101T Shane Rawley .01 .05
102T Randy Ready .01 .05
103T Bip Roberts .01 .05
104T Kenny Rogers RC .75 2.00
105T Ed Romero .01 .05
106T Nolan Ryan .60 1.50
107T Luis Salazar .01 .05
108T Juan Samuel .01 .05
109T Alex Sanchez RC .01 .05
110T Deion Sanders RC .60 1.50
111T Steve Sax .01 .05
112T Rick Schu .01 .05
113T Dwight Smith RC .08 .25
114T Lonnie Smith .01 .05
115T Billy Spiers RC .08 .25
116T Kent Tekulve .01 .05
117T Walt Terrell .01 .05
118T Milt Thompson .01 .05
119T Dickie Thon .01 .05
120T Jeff Torborg MG .01 .05
121T Jeff Treadway .01 .05
122T Omar Vizquel RC .40 1.00
123T Jerome Walton RC .08 .25
124T Gary Ward .01 .05
125T Claudell Washington .01 .05
126T Curt Wilkerson .01 .05
127T Eddie Williams .01 .05
128T Frank Williams .01 .05
129T Ken Williams .01 .05
130T Mitch Williams .01 .05
131T Steve Wilson RC .02 .10
132T Checklist 1T-132T .01 .05

1989 Topps Traded Tiffany

COMP.FACT.SET (132) 60.00 120.00
*STARS: 4X TO 10X BASIC CARDS
*ROOKIES: 4X TO 10X BASIC CARDS
DISTRIBUTED ONLY IN FACTORY SET FORM
FACTORY SET PRICE IS FOR SEALED SETS

1990 Topps

The 1990 Topps set contains 792 standard-size cards. Cards were issued primarily in wax packs, rack packs and hobby and retail Christmas factory sets. Card fronts feature various colored borders with the player's name at the bottom and team name at top. Subsets include All-Stars (385-407), Turn Back the Clock (661-665) and Draft Picks (scattered throughout the set). The key Rookie Cards in this set are Juan Gonzalez, Marquis Grissom, Sammy Sosa, Frank Thomas, Larry Walker and Bernie Williams. The Frank Thomas card (#414A) was printed without his name on the front, as well as portions of the black borders being omitted, creating a scarce variation. Several additional cards in the set were subsequently discovered missing portions of the black borders or missing some of the black printing in the backgrounds of the photos that occurred in the same printing that created the Thomas error. These cards are rarely seen and the Thomas card, for a newer issue, has experienced unprecedented growth as far as value. Be careful when purchasing the Frank Thomas NNOF version as counterfeits have been produced. A very few cards of President George Bush made their ways into packs. While these cards were supposed to have never been issued, a few collectors did receive these cards when opening packs.

COMPLETE SET (792) 8.00 20.00
COMP.FACT.SET (792) 10.00 25.00
COMP.X-MAS.SET (792) 15.00 40.00
BEWARE COUNTERFEIT THOMAS NNOF
1 Nolan Ryan .40 1.00
2 Nolan Ryan Mets .20 .50
3 Nolan Ryan Angels .20 .50
4 Nolan Ryan Astros .20 .50
5 N.Ryan Rangers UER .20 .50
Says Texas Stadium rather than Arlington Stadium
6 Vince Coleman RB .01 .05
7 Rickey Henderson RB .05 .15
8 Cal Ripken RB .08 .25
9 Eric Plunk .01 .05
10 Barry Larkin .05 .15
11 Paul Gibson .01 .05
12 Joe Girardi .05 .15
13 Mark Williamson .01 .05
14 Mike Fetters RC .08 .25
15 Teddy Higuera .01 .05
16 Kent Anderson .01 .05
17 Kelly Downs .01 .05
18 Carlos Quintana .01 .05
19 Al Newman .01 .05
20 Mark Gubicza .01 .05
21 Jeff Torborg MG .01 .05
22 Bruce Ruffin .01 .05
23 Randy Velarde .01 .05
24 Joe Hesketh .01 .05
25 Willie Randolph .02 .10
26 Don Slaught .01 .05
27 Rick Leach .01 .05
28 Duane Ward .01 .05
29 John Cangelosi .01 .05
30 David Cone .02 .10
31 Henry Cotto .01 .05
32 John Farrell .01 .05
33 Greg Walker .01 .05
34 Tony Fossas RC .01 .05
35 Benito Santiago .02 .10
36 John Costello .01 .05
37 Domingo Ramos .01 .05
38 Wes Gardner .01 .05
39 Curt Ford .01 .05
40 Jay Howell .01 .05
41 Matt Williams .02 .10
42 Jeff M. Robinson .01 .05
43 Dante Bichette .02 .10
44 Roger Salkeld FDP RC .02 .10
45 Dave Parker UER .02 .10
46 Rob Dibble .02 .10
47 Brian Harper .01 .05
48 Zane Smith .01 .05
49 Tom Lawless .01 .05
50 Glenn Davis .01 .05
51 Doug Rader MG .01 .05
52 Jack Daugherty RC .01 .05
53 Mike LaCoss .01 .05
54 Joel Skinner .01 .05
55 Darrell Evans UER .02 .10
HR total should be 414, not 424
56 Franklin Stubbs .01 .05
57 Greg Vaughn .01 .05
58 Keith Miller .01 .05
59 Ted Power .01 .05
60 George Brett .25 .60
61 Deion Sanders .08 .25
62 Ramon Martinez .01 .05
63 Mike Pagliarulo .01 .05
64 Danny Darwin .01 .05
65 Devon White .02 .10
66 Greg Litton .01 .05
67 Scott Sanderson .01 .05
68 Dave Henderson .01 .05
69 Todd Frohwirth .01 .05
70 Mike Greenwell .01 .05
71 Allan Anderson .01 .05
72 Jeff Huson RC .02 .10
73 Bob Milacki .01 .05
74 Jeff Jackson FDP RC .02 .10
75 Doug Jones .01 .05
76 Dave Valle .01 .05
77 Dave Bergman .01 .05
78 Mike Flanagan .01 .05
79 Ron Kittle .01 .05
80 Jeff Russell .01 .05
81 Bob Rodgers MG .01 .05
82 Scott Terry .01 .05
83 Hensley Meulens .01 .05
84 Ray Searage .01 .05
85 Juan Samuel .01 .05
86 Paul Kilgus .01 .05
87 Rick Luecken RC .01 .05
88 Glenn Braggs .01 .05
89 Clint Zavaras RC .01 .05
90 Jack Clark .02 .10
91 Steve Frey RC .01 .05
92 Mike Stanley .01 .05
93 Shawn Hillegas .01 .05
94 Herm Winningham .01 .05
95 Todd Worrell .01 .05
96 Jody Reed .01 .05
97 Curt Schilling .40 1.00
98 Jose Gonzalez .01 .05
99 Rich Monteleone .01 .05
100 Will Clark .05 .15
101 Shane Rawley .01 .05
102 Stan Javier .01 .05
103 Marvin Freeman .01 .05
104 Bob Knepper .01 .05
105 Randy Myers .02 .10
106 Charlie O'Brien .01 .05
107 Fred Lynn .01 .05
108 Rod Nichols .01 .05
109 Roberto Kelly .01 .05
110 Tommy Helms MG .01 .05
111 Ed Whited RC .01 .05
112 Glenn Wilson .01 .05
113 Manny Lee .01 .05
114 Mike Bielecki .01 .05
115 Tony Pena .01 .05
116 Floyd Bannister .01 .05
117 Mike Sharperson .01 .05
118 Erik Hanson .01 .05
119 Billy Hatcher .01 .05
120 John Franco .02 .10
121 Robin Ventura .08 .25
122 Shawn Abner .01 .05
123 Rich Gedman .01 .05
124 Dave Dravecky .02 .10
125 Kent Hrbek .02 .10
126 Randy Kramer .01 .05
127 Mike Devereaux .01 .05
128 Checklist 1 .01 .05
129 Ron Jones .01 .05
130 Bert Blyleven .02 .10
131 Matt Nokes .01 .05
132 Lance Blankenship .01 .05
133 Ricky Horton .01 .05
134 Earl Cunningham FDP RC .02 .10
135 Dave Magadan .01 .05
136 Kevin Brown .02 .10
137 Marty Pevey RC .01 .05
138 Al Leiter .08 .25
139 Greg Brock .01 .05
140 Andre Dawson .02 .10
141B John Hart MG RC .01 .05
142 Jeff Wetherby RC .01 .05
143 Rafael Belliard .01 .05
144 Bud Black .01 .05
145 Terry Steinbach .01 .05
146 Rob Richie RC .01 .05
147 Chuck Finley .02 .10
148 Edgar Martinez .05 .15
149 Steve Farr .01 .05
150 Kirk Gibson .02 .10
151 Rick Mahler .01 .05
152 Lonnie Smith .01 .05
153 Randy Milligan .01 .05
154 Mike Maddux .01 .05
155 Ellis Burks .05 .15
156 Ken Patterson .01 .05
157 Craig Biggio .08 .25
158 Craig Lefferts .01 .05
159 Mike Felder .01 .05
160 Dave Righetti .01 .05
161 Harold Reynolds .02 .10
162 Todd Zeile .02 .10
163 Phil Bradley .01 .05
164 Jeff Juden FDP RC .02 .10
165 Walt Weiss .01 .05
166 Bobby Witt .01 .05
167 Kevin Appier .02 .10
168 Jose Lind .01 .05
169 Richard Dotson .01 .05
170 George Bell .01 .05
171 Russ Nixon MG .01 .05
172 Tom Lampkin .01 .05
173 Tim Belcher .01 .05
174 Jeff Kunkel .01 .05
175 Mike Moore .01 .05
176 Luis Quinones .01 .05
177 Mike Henneman .01 .05
178 Chris James .01 .05
179 Brian Holton .01 .05
180 Tim Raines .02 .10
181 Juan Agosto .01 .05
182 Mookie Wilson .02 .10
183 Steve Lake .01 .05
184 Danny Cox .01 .05
185 Ruben Sierra .02 .10
186 Dave LaPoint .01 .05
187 Rick Wrona .01 .05
188 Mike Smithson .01 .05
189 Dick Schofield .01 .05
190 Rick Reuschel .01 .05
191 Pat Borders .01 .05
192 Don August .01 .05
193 Andy Benes .02 .10
194 Glenallen Hill .01 .05
195 Tim Burke .01 .05
196 Gerald Young .01 .05
197 Doug Drabek .01 .05
198 Mike Marshall .01 .05
199 Sergio Valdez RC .01 .05
200 Don Mattingly .25 .60
201 Cito Gaston MG .01 .05
202 Mike Macfarlane .01 .05
203 Mike Roesler RC .01 .05
204 Bob Dernier .01 .05
205 Mark Davis .01 .05
206 Nick Esasky .01 .05
207 Bob Ojeda .01 .05
208 Brook Jacoby .01 .05
209 Greg Mathews .01 .05
210 Ryne Sandberg .15 .40
211 John Cerutti .01 .05
212 Joe Orsulak .01 .05
213 Scott Bankhead .01 .05
214 Terry Francona .02 .10
215 Kirk McCaskill .01 .05
216 Ricky Jordan .01 .05
217 Don Robinson .01 .05
218 Wally Backman .01 .05
219 Donn Pall .01 .05
220 Barry Bonds .40 1.00
221 Gary Mielke RC .01 .05
222 Kurt Stillwell UER .01 .05
Graduate misspelled as gradute
223 Tommy Gregg .01 .05
224 Delino DeShields RC .08 .25
225 Jim Deshaies .01 .05
226 Mickey Hatcher .01 .05
227B Kevin Tapani RC .08 .25
228 Dave Martinez .01 .05
229 David Wells .02 .10

230 Keith Hernandez .02 .10
231 Jack McKeon MG .01 .05
232 Darnell Coles .01 .05
233 Ken Hill .02 .10
234 Mariano Duncan .01 .05
235 Jeff Reardon .02 .10
236 Hal Morris .01 .05
237 Kevin Ritz RC .01 .05
238 Felix Jose .01 .05
239 Eric Show .01 .05
240 Mark Grace .05 .15
241 Mike Krukow .01 .05
242 Fred Manrique .01 .05
243 Barry Jones .01 .05
244 Bill Schroeder .01 .05
245 Roger Clemens .40 1.00
246 Jim Eisenreich .01 .05
247 Jerry Reed .01 .05
248 Dave Anderson .01 .05
249 Mike Texas Smith RC .01 .05
250 Jose Canseco .05 .15
251 Jeff Blauser .01 .05
252 Otis Nixon .01 .05
253 Mark Portugal .01 .05
254 Francisco Cabrera .01 .05
255 Bobby Thigpen .01 .05
256 Marvell Wynne .01 .05
257 Jose DeLeon .01 .05
258 Barry Lyons .01 .05
259 Lance McCullers .01 .05
260 Eric Davis .02 .10
261 Whitey Herzog MG .02 .10
262 Checklist 2 .01 .05
263 Mel Stottlemyre Jr. .01 .05
264 Bryan Clutterbuck .01 .05
265 Pete O'Brien .01 .05
266 German Gonzalez .01 .05
267 Mark Davidson .01 .05
268 Rob Murphy .01 .05
269 Dickie Thon .01 .05
270 Dave Stewart .02 .10
271 Chet Lemon .01 .05
272 Bryan Harvey .01 .05
273 Bobby Bonilla .02 .10
274 Mauro Gozzo RC .01 .05
275 Mickey Tettleton .01 .05
276 Gary Thurman .01 .05
277 Lenny Harris .01 .05
278 Pascual Perez .01 .05
279 Steve Buechele .01 .05
280 Lou Whitaker .02 .10
281 Kevin Bass .01 .05
282 Derek Lilliquist .01 .05
283 Joey Belle .08 .25
284 Mark Gardner RC .02 .10
285 Willie McGee .02 .10
286 Lee Guetterman .01 .05
287 Vance Law .01 .05
288 Greg Briley .01 .05
289 Norm Charlton .01 .05
290 Robin Yount .15 .40
291 Dave Johnson MG .02 .10
292 Jim Gott .01 .05
293 Mike Gallego .01 .05
294 Craig McMurtry .01 .05
295 Fred McGriff .08 .25
296 Jeff Ballard .01 .05
297 Tommy Herr .01 .05
298 Dan Gladden .01 .05
299 Adam Peterson .01 .05
300 Bo Jackson .08 .25
301 Don Aase .01 .05
302B Marcus Lawton RC .01 .05
303 Rick Cerone .01 .05
304 Marty Clary .01 .05
305 Eddie Murray .08 .25
306 Tom Niedenfuer .01 .05
307 Bip Roberts .01 .05
308 Jose Guzman .01 .05
309 Eric Yelding RC .01 .05
310 Steve Bedrosian .01 .05
311 Dwight Smith .01 .05
312 Dan Quisenberry .01 .05
313 Gus Polidor .01 .05
314 Donald Harris FDP RC .01 .05
315 Bruce Hurst .01 .05
316 Carney Lansford .02 .10
317 Mark Guthrie RC .01 .05
318 Wallace Johnson .01 .05
319 Dion James .01 .05
320 Dave Stieb .02 .10
321 Joe Morgan MG .01 .05
322 Junior Ortiz .01 .05
323 Willie Wilson .01 .05
324 Pete Harnisch .01 .05
325 Robby Thompson .01 .05
326 Tom McCarthy .01 .05
327 Ken Williams .01 .05
328 Curt Young .01 .05
329 Oddibe McDowell .01 .05
330 Ron Darling .01 .05
331 Juan Gonzalez RC .40 1.00
332 Paul O'Neill .05 .15
333 Bill Wegman .01 .05
334 Johnny Ray .01 .05
335 Andy Hawkins .01 .05
336 Ken Griffey Jr. .40 1.00
337 Lloyd McClendon .01 .05
338 Dennis Lamp .01 .05
339 Dave Clark .01 .05
340 Fernando Valenzuela .02 .10
341 Tom Foley .01 .05
342 Alex Trevino .01 .05
343 Frank Tanana .01 .05
344 George Canale RC .01 .05
345 Harold Baines .02 .10
346 Jim Presley .01 .05
347 Junior Felix .01 .05
348 Gary Wayne .01 .05
349 Steve Finley .02 .10
350 Bret Saberhagen .02 .10
351 Roger Craig MG .01 .05
352 Bryn Smith .01 .05
353 Sandy Alomar Jr. .02 .10
Not listed as Jr.
on card front
354 Stan Belinda RC .02 .10
355 Marty Barrett .01 .05
356 Randy Ready .01 .05
357 Dave West .01 .05
358 Andres Thomas .01 .05
359 Jimmy Jones .01 .05
360 Paul Molitor .02 .10
361 Randy McCament RC .01 .05
362 Damon Berryhill .01 .05
363 Dan Petry .01 .05
364 Rolando Roomes .01 .05
365 Ozzie Guillen .02 .10
366 Mike Heath .01 .05
367 Mike Morgan .01 .05
368 Bill Doran .01 .05
369 Todd Burns .01 .05
370 Tim Wallach .01 .05
371 Jimmy Key .02 .10
372 Terry Kennedy .01 .05
373 Alvin Davis .01 .05
374 Steve Cummings RC .01 .05
375 Dwight Evans .05 .15
376 Checklist 3 UER .01 .05
Higuera misalphabet-
ized in Brewer list
377 Mickey Weston RC .01 .05
378 Luis Salazar .01 .05
379 Steve Rosenberg .01 .05
380 Dave Winfield .02 .10
381 Frank Robinson MG .05 .15
382 Jeff Musselman .01 .05
383B John Morris .01 .05
384 Pat Combs .01 .05
385B Fred McGriff AS .02 .10
386B Julio Franco AS .01 .05
387 Wade Boggs AS .02 .10
388 Cal Ripken AS .15 .40
389 Robin Yount AS .08 .25
390 Ruben Sierra AS .01 .05
391 Kirby Puckett AS .05 .15
392B Carlton Fisk AS .02 .10
393 Bret Saberhagen AS .01 .05
394 Jeff Ballard AS .01 .05
395B Jeff Russell AS .01 .05
396 Bart Giamatti MEM .08 .25
397 Will Clark AS .02 .10
398 Ryne Sandberg AS .08 .25
399 Howard Johnson AS .01 .05
400 Ozzie Smith AS .08 .25
401 Kevin Mitchell AS .01 .05
402 Eric Davis AS .01 .05
403 Tony Gwynn AS .05 .15
404B Craig Biggio AS .08 .25
405 Mike Scott AS .01 .05
406B Joe Magrane AS .01 .05
407 Mark Davis AS .01 .05
408 Trevor Wilson .01 .05
409 Tom Brunansky .01 .05
410 Joe Boever .01 .05
411 Ken Phelps .01 .05
412 Jamie Moyer .02 .10
413 Brian DuBois RC .01 .05
414A F.Thomas ERR NNOF 600.00 800.00
414B Frank Thomas RC 1.25 3.00
415 Shawon Dunston .01 .05
416 Dave Wayne Johnson RC .01 .05
417 Jim Gantner .01 .05
418 Tom Browning .01 .05
419 Beau Allred RC .01 .05
420 Carlton Fisk .05 .15
421 Greg Minton .01 .05
422 Pat Sheridan .01 .05
423 Fred Toliver .01 .05
424 Jerry Reuss .01 .05
425 Bill Landrum .01 .05
426 Jeff Hamilton UER .01 .05
427 Carmen Castillo .01 .05
428 Steve Davis RC .01 .05
429 Tom Kelly MG .01 .05
430 Pete Incaviglia .01 .05
431 Randy Johnson .20 .50
432 Damaso Garcia .01 .05
433 Steve Olin RC .08 .25
434 Mark Carreon .01 .05
435 Kevin Seitzer .01 .05
436 Mel Hall .01 .05
437 Les Lancaster .01 .05
438 Greg Myers .01 .05
439 Jeff Parrett .01 .05
440 Alan Trammell .02 .10
441 Bob Kipper .01 .05
442 Jerry Browne .01 .05
443 Cris Carpenter .01 .05
444 Kyle Abbott FDP RC .01 .05
445 Danny Jackson .01 .05
446 Dan Pasqua .01 .05
447 Atlee Hammaker .01 .05
448 Greg Gagne .01 .05
449 Dennis Rasmussen .01 .05
450 Rickey Henderson .08 .25
451 Mark Lemke .01 .05
452 Luis DeLosSantos .01 .05
453 Jody Davis .01 .05
454 Jeff King .01 .05
455 Jeffrey Leonard .01 .05
456 Chris Gwynn .01 .05
457 Gregg Jefferies .02 .10
458 Bob McClure .01 .05
459 Jim Lefebvre MG .01 .05
460 Mike Scott .01 .05
461 Carlos Martinez .01 .05
462 Denny Walling .01 .05
463 Drew Hall .01 .05
464 Jerome Walton .01 .05
465 Kevin Gross .01 .05
466 Rance Mulliniks .01 .05
467 Juan Nieves .01 .05
468 Bill Ripken .01 .05
469 John Kruk .02 .10
470 Frank Viola .01 .05
471 Mike Brumley .01 .05
472 Jose Uribe .01 .05
473 Joe Price .01 .05
474 Rich Thompson .01 .05
475 Bob Welch .01 .05
476 Brad Komminsk .01 .05
477 Willie Fraser .01 .05
478 Mike LaValliere .01 .05
479 Frank White .02 .10
480 Sid Fernandez .01 .05
481 Garry Templeton .01 .05
482 Steve Carter .01 .05
483 Alejandro Pena .01 .05
484 Mike Fitzgerald .01 .05
485 John Candelaria .01 .05
486 Jeff Treadway .01 .05
487 Steve Searcy .01 .05
488 Ken Oberkfell .01 .05
489 Nick Leyva MG .01 .05
490 Dan Plesac .01 .05
491 Dave Cochrane RC .01 .05
492 Ron Oester .01 .05
493 Jason Grimsley RC .02 .10
494 Terry Puhl .01 .05
495 Lee Smith .02 .10
496 Cecil Espy UER .01 .05
'88 stats have 3
SB's, should be 33
497 Dave Schmidt .01 .05
498 Rick Schu .01 .05
499 Bill Long .01 .05
500 Kevin Mitchell .01 .05
501 Matt Young .01 .05
502 Mitch Webster .01 .05
503 Randy St.Claire .01 .05
504 Tom O'Malley .01 .05
505 Kelly Gruber .01 .05
506 Tom Glavine .05 .15
507 Gary Redus .01 .05
508 Terry Leach .01 .05
509 Tom Pagnozzi .01 .05
510 Dwight Gooden .02 .10
511 Clay Parker .01 .05
512 Gary Pettis .01 .05
513 Mark Eichhorn .01 .05
514 Andy Allanson .01 .05
515 Len Dykstra .02 .10
516 Tim Leary .01 .05
517 Roberto Alomar .05 .15
518 Bill Krueger .01 .05
519 Bucky Dent MG .01 .05
520 Mitch Williams .01 .05
521 Craig Worthington .01 .05
522 Mike Dunne .01 .05
523 Jay Bell .02 .10
524 Daryl Boston .01 .05
525 Wally Joyner .02 .10
526 Checklist 4 .01 .05
527 Ron Hassey .01 .05
528 Kevin Wickander UER .01 .05
Monthly scoreboard
strikeout total was 2.2,
that was his innings
pitched total
529 Greg A. Harris .01 .05
530 Mark Langston .01 .05
531 Ken Caminiti .02 .10
532 Cecilio Guante .01 .05
533 Tim Jones .01 .05
534 Louie Meadows .01 .05
535 John Smoltz .08 .25
536 Bob Geren .01 .05
537 Mark Grant .01 .05
538 Bill Spiers UER .01 .05
Photo actually
George Canale
539 Neal Heaton .01 .05
540 Danny Tartabull .01 .05
541 Pat Perry .01 .05
542 Darren Daulton .02 .10
543 Nelson Liriano .01 .05
544 Dennis Boyd .01 .05
545 Kevin McReynolds .01 .05
546 Kevin Hickey .01 .05
547 Jack Howell .01 .05
548 Pat Clements .01 .05
549 Don Zimmer MG .01 .05
550 Julio Franco .02 .10
551 Tim Crews .01 .05
552 Mike Miss. Smith RC .01 .05
553 Scott Scudder UER .01 .05
Cedar Rap1ds
554 Jay Buhner .02 .10
555 Jack Morris .02 .10
556 Gene Larkin .01 .05
557 Jeff Innis RC .01 .05
558 Rafael Ramirez .01 .05
559 Andy McGaffigan .01 .05
560 Steve Sax .01 .05
561 Ken Dayley .01 .05
562 Chad Kreuter .01 .05
563 Alex Sanchez .01 .05
564 Tyler Houston FDP RC .08 .25
565 Scott Fletcher .01 .05
566 Mark Knudson .01 .05
567 Ron Gant .02 .10
568 John Smiley .01 .05
569 Ivan Calderon .01 .05
570 Cal Ripken .30 .75
571 Brett Butler .02 .10
572 Greg W. Harris .01 .05
573 Danny Heep .01 .05
574 Bill Swift .01 .05
575 Lance Parrish .01 .05
576 Mike Dyer RC .01 .05
577 Charlie Hayes .01 .05
578 Joe Magrane .01 .05
579 Art Howe MG .01 .05
580 Joe Carter .02 .10
581 Ken Griffey Sr. .02 .10
582 Rick Honeycutt .01 .05
583 Bruce Benedict .01 .05
584 Phil Stephenson .01 .05
585 Kal Daniels .01 .05
586 Edwin Nunez .01 .05
587 Lance Johnson .01 .05
588 Rick Rhoden .01 .05
589 Mike Aldrete .01 .05
590 Ozzie Smith .15 .40
591 Todd Stottlemyre .02 .10
592 R.J. Reynolds .01 .05
593 Scott Bradley .01 .05
594 Luis Sojo RC .01 .05
595 Greg Swindell .01 .05
596 Jose DeJesus .01 .05
597 Chris Bosio .01 .05
598 Brady Anderson .02 .10
599 Frank Williams .01 .05
600 Darryl Strawberry .02 .10
601 Luis Rivera .01 .05
602 Scott Garrelts .01 .05
603 Tony Armas .01 .05
604 Ron Robinson .01 .05
605 Mike Scioscia .01 .05
606 Storm Davis .01 .05
607 Steve Jeltz .01 .05
608 Eric Anthony RC .02 .10
609 Sparky Anderson MG .02 .10
610 Pedro Guerrero .01 .05
611 Walt Terrell .01 .05
612 Dave Gallagher .01 .05
613 Jeff Pico .01 .05
614 Nelson Santovenia .01 .05
615 Rob Deer .01 .05
616 Brian Holman .01 .05
617 Geronimo Berroa .01 .05
618 Ed Whitson .01 .05
619 Rob Ducey .01 .05
620 Tony Castillo .01 .05
621 Melido Perez .01 .05
622 Sid Bream .01 .05
623 Jim Corsi .01 .05
624B Darrin Jackson .01 .05
625 Roger McDowell .01 .05
626 Bob Melvin .01 .05
627 Jose Rijo .01 .05
628 Candy Maldonado .01 .05
629 Eric Hetzel .01 .05
630 Gary Gaetti .02 .10
631 John Wetteland .08 .25
632 Scott Lusader .01 .05
633 Dennis Cook .01 .05
634 Luis Polonia .01 .05
635 Brian Downing .01 .05
636 Jesse Orosco .01 .05
637 Craig Reynolds .01 .05
638 Jeff Montgomery .02 .10
639 Tony LaRussa MG .02 .10
640 Rick Sutcliffe .02 .10
641 Doug Strange RC .01 .05
642 Jack Armstrong .01 .05
643 Alfredo Griffin .01 .05
644 Paul Assenmacher .01 .05
645 Jose Oquendo .01 .05
646 Checklist 5 .01 .05
647 Rex Hudler .01 .05
648 Jim Clancy .01 .05
649 Dan Murphy RC .02 .10
650 Mike Witt .01 .05
651 Rafael Santana .01 .05
652 Mike Boddicker .01 .05
653 John Moses .01 .05
654 Paul Coleman FDP RC .02 .10
655 Gregg Olson .02 .10
656 Mackey Sasser .01 .05
657 Terry Mulholland .01 .05
658 Donell Nixon .01 .05
659 Greg Cadaret .01 .05
660 Vince Coleman .01 .05
661 Dick Howser TBC'85 .01 .05
UER Seaver's 300th
on 7/11/85, should
be 8/4/85
662 Mike Schmidt TBC'80 .08 .25
663 Fred Lynn TBC'75 .01 .05
664 Johnny Bench TBC'70 .05 .15
665 Sandy Koufax TBC'65 .20 .50
666 Brian Fisher .01 .05
667 Curt Wilkerson .01 .05
668 Joe Oliver .01 .05
669 Tom Lasorda MG .08 .25
670 Dennis Eckersley .02 .10
671 Bob Boone .02 .10
672 Roy Smith .01 .05
673 Joey Meyer .01 .05
674 Spike Owen .01 .05
675 Jim Abbott .05 .15
676 Randy Kutcher .01 .05
677 Jay Tibbs .01 .05
678 Kirt Manwaring UER .01 .05
'88 Phoenix stats
repeated
679 Gary Ward .01 .05
680 Howard Johnson .01 .05
681 Mike Schooler .01 .05
682 Dann Bilardello .01 .05
683 Kenny Rogers .02 .10
684 Julio Machado RC .01 .05
685 Tony Fernandez .01 .05
686 Carmelo Martinez .01 .05
687 Tim Birtsas .01 .05
688 Milt Thompson .01 .05
689 Rich Yett .01 .05
690 Mark McGwire .25 .60
691 Chuck Cary .01 .05
692 Sammy Sosa RC .75 2.00
693 Calvin Schiraldi .01 .05
694 Mike Stanton RC .08 .25
695 Tom Henke .01 .05
696 B.J. Surhoff .02 .10
697 Mike Davis .01 .05
698 Omar Vizquel .08 .25
699 Jim Leyland MG .01 .05
700 Kirby Puckett .08 .25
701 Bernie Williams RC .60 1.50
702 Tony Phillips .01 .05
703 Jeff Brantley .01 .05
704 Chip Hale RC .01 .05
705 Claudell Washington .01 .05
706 Geno Petralli .01 .05
707 Luis Aquino .01 .05
708 Larry Sheets .01 .05
709 Juan Berenguer .01 .05
710 Von Hayes .01 .05
711 Rick Aguilera .02 .10
712 Todd Benzinger .01 .05
713 Tim Drummond RC .01 .05
714 Marquis Grissom RC .15 .40
715 Greg Maddux .15 .40
716 Steve Balboni .01 .05
717 Ron Karkovice .01 .05
718 Gary Sheffield .08 .25
719 Wally Whitehurst .01 .05
720 Andres Galarraga .02 .10
721 Lee Mazzilli .01 .05
722 Felix Fermin .01 .05
723 Jeff D. Robinson .01 .05
724 Juan Bell .01 .05
725 Terry Pendleton .02 .10
726 Gene Nelson .01 .05
727 Pat Tabler .01 .05
728B Jim Acker .01 .05
729 Bobby Valentine MG .01 .05
730 Tony Gwynn .10 .30
731 Don Carman .01 .05
732 Ernest Riles .01 .05
733 John Dopson .01 .05
734 Kevin Elster .01 .05
735 Charlie Hough .02 .10
736 Rick Dempsey .01 .05
737 Chris Sabo .01 .05
738 Gene Harris .01 .05
739 Dale Sveum .01 .05
740 Jesse Barfield .01 .05
741 Steve Wilson .01 .05
742 Ernie Whitt .01 .05
743 Tom Candiotti .01 .05
744 Kelly Mann RC .01 .05
745 Hubie Brooks .01 .05
746 Dave Smith .01 .05
747 Randy Bush .01 .05
748 Doyle Alexander .01 .05
749 Mark Parent UER .01 .05
'87 BA .80,
should be .080
750 Dale Murphy .05 .15
751 Steve Lyons .01 .05
752 Tom Gordon .02 .10
753 Chris Speier .01 .05
754 Bob Walk .01 .05
755 Rafael Palmeiro .05 .15
756 Ken Howell .01 .05
757 Larry Walker RC .40 1.00
758 Mark Thurmond .01 .05
759 Tom Trebelhorn MG .01 .05
760 Wade Boggs .05 .15
761 Mike Jackson .01 .05
762 Doug Dascenzo .01 .05
763 Dennis Martinez .02 .10
764 Tim Teufel .01 .05
765 Chili Davis .02 .10
766 Brian Meyer .01 .05
767 Tracy Jones .01 .05
768 Chuck Crim .01 .05
769 Greg Hibbard RC .02 .10
770 Cory Snyder .01 .05
771 Pete Smith .01 .05
772 Jeff Reed .01 .05
773 Dave Leiper .01 .05
774 Ben McDonald RC .08 .25
775 Andy Van Slyke .05 .15
776 Charlie Leibrandt .01 .05
777 Tim Laudner .01 .05
778 Mike Jeffcoat .01 .05
779 Lloyd Moseby .01 .05
780 Orel Hershiser .02 .10
781 Mario Diaz .01 .05
782 Jose Alvarez .01 .05
783 Checklist 6 .01 .05
784 Scott Bailes .01 .05
785 Jim Rice .02 .10
786 Eric King .01 .05
787 Rene Gonzales .01 .05
788 Frank DiPino .01 .05
789 John Wathan MG .01 .05
790 Gary Carter .02 .10
791 Alvaro Espinoza .01 .05
792 Gerald Perry .01 .05
USA1 George Bush PRES
USA1 George Bush PRES
GLOSSY

1990 Topps Tiffany

COMP.FACT.SET (792) 100.00 200.00
*STARS: 6X TO 15X BASIC CARDS
*ROOKIES: 4X TO 10X BASIC CARDS
DISTRIBUTED ONLY IN FACTORY SET FORM
STATED PRINT RUN 15,000 SETS
FACTORY SET PRICE IS FOR SEALED SETS
414 Frank Thomas FDP 25.00 60.00

1990 Topps Batting Leaders

The 1990 Topps Batting Leaders set contains 22 standard-size cards. The front borders are emerald green, and the backs are white, blue and evergreen. This set, like the 1989 set of the same name, depicts the 22 major leaguers with the highest lifetime batting averages (minimum 765 games). The card numbers correspond to the player's rank in terms of career batting average. Many of the photos are the same as those from the 1989 set. The cards were distributed one per special 100-card Topps blister pack available only at K-Mart stores and were produced by Topps. The K-Mart logo does not appear anywhere on the cards themselves, although there is a Topps logo on the front and back of each card.

COMPLETE SET (22) 12.50 30.00
1 Wade Boggs 4.00 10.00
2 Tony Gwynn 8.00 20.00
3 Kirby Puckett 6.00 15.00
4 Don Mattingly 8.00 20.00
5 George Brett 8.00 20.00
6 Pedro Guerrero .40 1.00
7 Tim Raines .40 1.00
8 Paul Molitor 3.00 8.00
9 Jim Rice .40 1.00
10 Keith Hernandez .40 1.00
11 Julio Franco .40 1.00
12 Carney Lansford .40 1.00
13 Dave Parker .40 1.00
14 Willie McGee .40 1.00
15 Robin Yount 3.00 8.00
16 Tony Fernandez .40 1.00
17 Eddie Murray 3.00 8.00
18 Johnny Ray .40 1.00
19 Lonnie Smith .40 1.00
20 Phil Bradley .40 1.00
21 Rickey Henderson 5.00 12.00
22 Kent Hrbek .40 1.00

1990 Topps Glossy All-Stars

The 1990 Topps Glossy All-Star set contains 22 standard-size glossy cards. The front and back borders are white, and other design elements are red, blue and yellow. This set is almost identical to previous year sets of the same name. One card was included in each 1990 Topps rack pack. The players selected for the set were the starters, managers, and honorary captains in the previous year's All-Star Game.

COMPLETE SET (22) 1.25 3.00
1 Tom Lasorda MG .07 .20
2 Will Clark .07 .20
3 Ryne Sandberg .20 .50
4 Howard Johnson .01 .05
5 Ozzie Smith .25 .60
6 Kevin Mitchell .01 .05
7 Eric Davis .02 .10
8 Tony Gwynn .30 .75
9 Benito Santiago .02 .10
10 Rick Reuschel .01 .05
11 Don Drysdale CAPT .08 .25
12 Tony LaRussa MG .01 .05
13 Mark McGwire .30 .75
14 Julio Franco .02 .10
15 Wade Boggs .15 .40
16 Cal Ripken .60 1.50
17 Bo Jackson .08 .25
18 Kirby Puckett .15 .40
19 Ruben Sierra .02 .10
20 Terry Steinbach .01 .05
21 Dave Stewart .02 .10
22 Carl Yastrzemski CAPT .10 .30

1990 Topps Glossy Send-Ins

The 1990 Topps Glossy 60 set was issued as a mailaway by Topps for the eighth straight year. This standard-size, 60-card set features two young players among every ten players as Topps again broke down these cards into six series of ten cards each.

COMPLETE SET (60) 5.00 12.00
1 Ryne Sandberg .60 1.50
2 Nolan Ryan 2.00 5.00
3 Glenn Davis .02 .10
4 Dave Stewart .07 .20
5 Barry Larkin .15 .40
6 Carney Lansford .07 .20
7 Darryl Strawberry .07 .20
8 Steve Sax .02 .10
9 Carlos Martinez .02 .10
10 Gary Sheffield .30 .75
11 Don Mattingly 1.00 2.50
12 Mark Grace .40 1.00
13 Bret Saberhagen .07 .20
14 Mike Scott .02 .10
15 Robin Yount .20 .50
16 Ozzie Smith .60 1.50
17 Jeff Ballard .02 .10
18 Rick Reuschel .02 .10
19 Greg Briley .02 .10
20 Ken Griffey Jr. 1.25 3.00
21 Kevin Mitchell .02 .10
22 Wade Boggs .30 .75
23 Dwight Gooden .07 .20
24 George Bell .02 .10
25 Eric Davis .07 .20
26 Ruben Sierra .07 .20
27 Roberto Alomar .30 .75
28 Gary Gaetti .07 .20
29 Gregg Olson .02 .10
30 Tom Gordon .10 .30
31 Jose Canseco .30 .75
32 Pedro Guerrero .02 .10
33 Joe Carter .07 .20
34 Mike Scioscia .07 .20
35 Julio Franco .07 .20
36 Joe Magrane .02 .10
37 Rickey Henderson .40 1.00
38 Tim Raines .07 .20
39 Jerome Walton .02 .10
40 Bob Geren .02 .10
41 Andre Dawson .15 .40
42 Mark McGwire 1.00 2.50
43 Howard Johnson .02 .10
44 Bo Jackson .20 .50
45 Shawon Dunston .02 .10
46 Carlton Fisk .20 .50
47 Mitch Williams .02 .10
48 Kirby Puckett .40 1.00
49 Craig Worthington .02 .10
50 Jim Abbott .20 .50
51 Cal Ripken 2.00 5.00
52 Will Clark .15 .40
53 Dennis Eckersley .20 .50
54 Craig Biggio .10 .30
55 Fred McGriff .15 .40
56 Tony Gwynn .75 2.00
57 Mickey Tettleton .07 .20
58 Mark Davis .02 .10
59 Omar Vizquel .15 .40
60 Gregg Jefferies .02 .10

1990 Topps Rookies

The 1990 Topps Rookies set contains 33 standard-size glossy cards. The front and back borders are white, and other design elements are red, blue and yellow. This set is almost identical to previous year sets of the same name except that it contains 33 cards rather than only 22. One card was included in each 1990 Topps jumbo pack. The cards are numbered in alphabetical order.

COMPLETE SET (33)	10.00	25.00
ONE PER RETAIL JUMBO PACK		
1 Jim Abbott	.30	.75
2 Albert Belle	.40	1.00
3 Andy Benes	.20	.50
4 Greg Briley	.08	.25
5 Kevin Brown	.20	.50
6 Mark Carreon	.08	.25
7 Mike Devereaux	.08	.25
8 Junior Felix	.08	.25
9 Bob Geren	.08	.25
10 Tom Gordon	.20	.50
11 Ken Griffey Jr.	2.50	6.00
12 Pete Harnisch	.08	.25
13 Greg W. Harris	.08	.25
14 Greg Hibbard	.08	.25
15 Ken Hill	.08	.25
16 Gregg Jefferies	.08	.25
17 Jeff King	.08	.25
18 Derek Lilliquist	.08	.25
19 Carlos Martinez	.08	.25
20 Ramon Martinez	.08	.25
21 Bob Milacki	.08	.25
22 Gregg Olson	.08	.25
23 Donn Pall	.08	.25
24 Kenny Rogers	.20	.50
25 Gary Sheffield	.40	1.00
26 Dwight Smith	.08	.25
27 Billy Spiers	.08	.25
28 Omar Vizquel	.40	1.00
29 Jerome Walton	.08	.25
30 Dave West	.08	.25
31 John Wetteland	.20	.50
32 Steve Wilson	.08	.25
33 Craig Worthington	.08	.25

1990 Topps Wax Box Cards

The 1990 Topps wax box cards comprise four different box bottoms with four cards each, for a total of 16 standard-size cards. The front borders are green. The vertically oriented backs are yellowish green. These cards depict various career milestones achieved during the 1989 season. The card numbers are actually the letters A through P. The card ordering is alphabetical by player's name.

COMPLETE SET (16)	3.00	8.00
A Wade Boggs	.20	.50
B George Brett	.40	1.00
C Andre Dawson	.15	.40
D Darrell Evans	.07	.20
E Dwight Gooden	.07	.20
F Rickey Henderson	.30	.75
G Tom Lasorda MG	.10	.30
H Fred Lynn	.02	.10
I Mark McGwire	.50	1.25
J Dave Parker	.07	.20
K Jeff Reardon	.07	.20
L Rick Reuschel	.02	.10
M Jim Rice	.07	.20
N Cal Ripken	1.00	2.50
O Nolan Ryan	1.00	2.50
P Ryne Sandberg	.20	.50

1990 Topps Traded

The 1990 Topps Traded Set was the tenth consecutive year Topps issued a 132-card standard-size set at the end of the year. For the first time, Topps not only issued the set in factory set form but also distributed (on a significant basis) the set via seven-card wax packs. Unlike the factory set cards (which feature the whiter paper stock typical of the previous years Traded sets), the wax pack cards feature gray paper stock. Gray and white stock cards are equally valued. This set was arranged alphabetically by player and includes a mix of traded players and rookies for whom Topps did not include a card in the regular set. The key Rookie Cards in this set are Travis Fryman, Todd Hundley and Dave Justice.

COMPLETE SET (132)	1.25	3.00
COMP.FACT.SET (132)	1.25	3.00
1T Darrel Akerfelds	.01	.05
2T Sandy Alomar Jr.	.02	.10
3T Brad Arnsberg	.01	.05
4T Steve Avery	.01	.05
5T Wally Backman	.01	.05
6T Carlos Baerga RC	.08	.25
7T Kevin Bass	.01	.05
8T Willie Blair RC	.02	.10
9T Mike Blowers RC	.08	.25
10T Shawn Boskie RC	.02	.10
11T Daryl Boston	.01	.05
12T Dennis Boyd	.01	.05
13T Glenn Braggs	.01	.05
14T Hubie Brooks	.01	.05
15T Tom Brunansky	.01	.05
16T John Burkett	.01	.05
17T Casey Candaele	.01	.05
18T John Candelaria	.01	.05
19T Gary Carter	.02	.10
20T Joe Carter	.02	.10
21T Rick Cerone	.01	.05
22T Scott Coolbaugh RC	.01	.05
23T Bobby Cox MG	.02	.10
24T Mark Davis	.01	.05
25T Storm Davis	.01	.05
26T Edgar Diaz RC	.01	.05
27T Wayne Edwards RC	.01	.05
28T Mark Eichhorn	.01	.05
29T Scott Erickson RC	.08	.25
30T Nick Esasky	.01	.05
31T Cecil Fielder	.02	.10
32T John Franco	.02	.10
33T Travis Fryman RC	.15	.40
34T Bill Gullickson	.01	.05
35T Darryl Hamilton	.01	.05
36T Mike Harkey	.01	.05
37T Bud Harrelson MG	.01	.05
38T Billy Hatcher	.01	.05
39T Keith Hernandez	.02	.10
40T Joe Hesketh	.01	.05
41T Dave Hollins RC	.08	.25
42T Sam Horn	.01	.05
43T Steve Howard RC	.01	.05
44T Todd Hundley RC	.08	.25
45T Jeff Huson	.01	.05
46T Chris James	.01	.05
47T Stan Javier	.01	.05
48T David Justice RC	.20	.50
49T Jeff Kaiser	.01	.05
50T Dana Kiecker RC	.01	.05
51T Joe Klink RC	.01	.05
52T Brent Knackert RC	.02	.10
53T Brad Komminsk	.01	.05
54T Mark Langston	.01	.05
55T Tim Layana RC	.01	.05
56T Rick Leach	.01	.05
57T Terry Leach	.01	.05
58T Tim Leary	.01	.05
59T Craig Lefferts	.01	.05
60T Charlie Leibrandt	.01	.05
61T Jim Leyritz RC	.08	.25
62T Fred Lynn	.01	.05
63T Kevin Maas RC	.08	.25
64T Shane Mack	.01	.05
65T Candy Maldonado	.01	.05
66T Fred Manrique	.01	.05
67T Mike Marshall	.01	.05
68T Carmelo Martinez	.01	.05
69T John Marzano	.01	.05
70T Ben McDonald	.01	.05
71T Jack McDowell	.01	.05
72T John McNamara MG	.01	.05
73T Orlando Mercado	.01	.05
74T Stump Merrill MG RC	.01	.05
75T Alan Mills RC	.02	.10
76T Hal Morris	.01	.05
77T Lloyd Moseby	.01	.05
78T Randy Myers	.02	.10
79T Tim Naehring RC	.02	.10
80T Junior Noboa	.01	.05
81T Matt Nokes	.01	.05
82T Pete O'Brien	.01	.05
83T John Olerud RC	.20	.50
84T Greg Olson (C) RC	.02	.10
85T Junior Ortiz	.01	.05
86T Dave Parker	.02	.10
87T Rick Parker RC	.01	.05
88T Bob Patterson	.01	.05
89T Alejandro Pena	.01	.05
90T Tony Pena	.01	.05
91T Pascual Perez	.01	.05
92T Gerald Perry	.01	.05
93T Dan Petry	.01	.05
94T Gary Pettis	.01	.05
95T Tony Phillips	.01	.05
96T Lou Piniella MG	.02	.10
97T Luis Polonia	.01	.05
98T Jim Presley	.01	.05
99T Scott Radinsky RC	.02	.10
100T Willie Randolph	.02	.10
101T Jeff Reardon	.02	.10
102T Greg Riddoch MG RC	.01	.05
103T Jeff Robinson	.01	.05
104T Ron Robinson	.01	.05
105T Kevin Romine	.01	.05
106T Scott Ruskin RC	.01	.05
107T John Russell	.01	.05
108T Bill Sampen RC	.01	.05
109T Juan Samuel	.01	.05
110T Scott Sanderson	.01	.05
111T Jack Savage	.01	.05
112T Dave Schmidt	.01	.05
113T Red Schoendienst MG	.08	.25
114T Terry Shumpert RC	.01	.05
115T Matt Sinatro	.01	.05
116T Don Slaught	.01	.05
117T Bryn Smith	.01	.05
118T Lee Smith	.02	.10
119T Paul Sorrento RC	.08	.25
120T Franklin Stubbs UER	.01	.05
('84 says '99 and has		
the sa		
121T Russ Swan RC	.02	.10
122T Bob Tewksbury	.01	.05
123T Wayne Tolleson	.01	.05
124T John Tudor	.01	.05
125T Randy Veres	.01	.05
126T Hector Villanueva RC	.02	.10
127T Mitch Webster	.01	.05
128T Ernie Whitt	.01	.05
129T Frank Wills	.01	.05
130T Dave Winfield	.02	.10
131T Matt Young	.01	.05
132T Checklist 1T-132T	.01	.05

1990 Topps Traded Tiffany

COMP.FACT.SET (132)	15.00	40.00
*STARS: 6X TO 15X BASIC CARDS		
*ROOKIES: 6X TO 15X BASIC CARDS		
DISTRIBUTED ONLY IN FACTORY SET FORM		
STATED PRINT RUN 15,000 SETS		
FACTORY SET PRICE IS FOR SEALED SETS		

1991 Topps

This set marks Topps tenth consecutive year of issuing a 792-card standard-size set. Cards were primarily issued in wax packs, rack packs and factory sets. The fronts feature a full color player photo with a white border. Topps also commemorated their fortieth anniversary by including a "Topps 40" logo on the front and back of each card. Virtually all of the cards have been discovered without the 40th logo on the back. Subsets include Record Breakers (2-8) and All-Stars (386-407). In addition, First Draft Picks and Future Stars subset cards are scattered throughout the set. The key Rookie Cards include Chipper Jones and Brian McRae. As a special promotion Topps inserted (randomly) into their wax packs one of every previous card they ever issued.

COMPLETE SET (792)	8.00	20.00
COMP.FACT.SET (792)	10.00	25.00
SUBSET CARDS HALF VALUE OF BASE CARDS		
1 Nolan Ryan	.60	1.50
2 George Brett RB	.10	.30
3 Carlton Fisk RB	.02	.10
4 Kevin Maas RB	.01	.05
5 Cal Ripken RB	.15	.40
6 Nolan Ryan RB	.20	.50
7 Ryne Sandberg RB	.08	.25
8 Bobby Thigpen RB	.01	.05
9 Darrin Fletcher	.01	.05
10 Gregg Olson	.01	.05
11 Roberto Kelly	.01	.05
12 Paul Assenmacher	.01	.05
13 Mariano Duncan	.01	.05
14 Dennis Lamp	.01	.05
15 Von Hayes	.01	.05
16 Mike Heath	.01	.05
17 Jeff Brantley	.01	.05
18 Nelson Liriano	.01	.05
19 Jeff D. Robinson	.01	.05
20 Pedro Guerrero	.02	.10
21 Joe Morgan MG	.01	.05
22 Storm Davis	.01	.05
23 Jim Gantner	.01	.05
24 Dave Martinez	.01	.05
25 Tim Belcher	.01	.05
26 Luis Sojo UER	.01	.05
Born in Barquisimento,		
not Caracas		
27 Bobby Witt	.01	.05
28 Alvaro Espinoza	.01	.05
29 Bob Walk	.01	.05
30 Gregg Jefferies	.01	.05
31 Colby Ward RC	.01	.05
32 Mike Simms RC	.01	.05
33 Barry Jones	.01	.05
34 Atlee Hammaker	.01	.05
35 Greg Maddux	.15	.40
36 Donnie Hill	.01	.05
37 Tom Bolton	.01	.05
38 Scott Bradley	.01	.05
39 Jim Neidlinger RC	.01	.05
40 Kevin Mitchell	.01	.05
41 Ken Dayley	.01	.05
42 Chris Hoiles	.01	.05
43 Roger McDowell	.01	.05
44 Mike Felder	.01	.05
45 Chris Sabo	.01	.05
46 Tim Drummond	.01	.05
47 Brook Jacoby	.01	.05
48 Dennis Boyd	.01	.05
49A Pat Borders ERR	.08	.25
40 steals at		
Kinston in '86		
49B Pat Borders COR	.01	.05
0 steals at		
Kinston in '86		
50 Bob Welch	.01	.05
51 Art Howe MG	.01	.05
52 Francisco Oliveras	.01	.05
53 Mike Sharperson UER	.01	.05
Born in 1961, not 1960		
54 Gary Mielke	.01	.05
55 Jeffrey Leonard	.01	.05
56 Jeff Parrett	.01	.05
57 Jack Howell	.01	.05
58 Mel Stottlemyre Jr.	.01	.05
59 Eric Yelding	.01	.05
60 Frank Viola	.02	.10
61 Stan Javier	.01	.05
62 Lee Guetterman	.01	.05
63 Milt Thompson	.01	.05
64 Tom Herr	.01	.05
65 Bruce Hurst	.01	.05
66 Terry Kennedy	.01	.05
67 Rick Honeycutt	.01	.05
68 Gary Sheffield	.02	.10
69 Steve Wilson	.01	.05
70 Ellis Burks	.02	.10
71 Jim Acker	.01	.05
72 Junior Ortiz	.01	.05
73 Craig Worthington	.01	.05
74 Shane Andrews RC	.08	.25
75 Jack Morris	.02	.10
76 Jerry Browne	.01	.05
77 Drew Hall	.01	.05
78 Geno Petralli	.01	.05
79 Frank Thomas	.08	.25
80A Fernando Valenzuela	.15	.40
ERR 104 earned runs		
in '90 tied for		
league lead		
80B Fernando Valenzuela	.02	.10
COR 104 earned runs		
in '90 led league, 20		
CG's in 1986 now		
italicized		
81 Cito Gaston MG	.01	.05
82 Tom Glavine	.05	.15
83 Daryl Boston	.01	.05
84 Bob McClure	.01	.05
85 Jesse Barfield	.01	.05
86 Les Lancaster	.01	.05
87 Tracy Jones	.01	.05
88 Bob Tewksbury	.01	.05
89 Darren Daulton	.02	.10
90 Danny Tartabull	.01	.05
91 Greg Colbrunn RC	.08	.25
92 Danny Jackson	.01	.05
93 Ivan Calderon	.01	.05
94 John Dopson	.01	.05
95 Paul Molitor	.02	.10
96 Trevor Wilson	.01	.05
97A Brady Anderson ERR	.15	.40
September, 2 RBI and		
3 hits, should be 3		
RBI and 14 hits		
97B Brady Anderson COR	.02	.10
98 Sergio Valdez	.01	.05
99 Chris Gwynn	.01	.05
100 Don Mattingly COR	.25	.60
100A Don Mattingly ERR	.75	2.00
101 Rob Ducey	.01	.05
102 Gene Larkin	.01	.05
103 Tim Costo RC	.01	.05
104 Don Robinson	.01	.05
105 Kevin McReynolds	.01	.05
106 Ed Nunez	.01	.05
107 Luis Polonia	.01	.05
108 Matt Young	.01	.05
109 Greg Riddoch MG	.01	.05
110 Tom Henke	.01	.05
111 Andres Thomas	.01	.05
112 Frank DiPino	.01	.05
113 Carl Everett RC	.20	.50
114 Lance Dickson RC	.02	.10
115 Hubie Brooks	.01	.05
116 Mark Davis	.01	.05
117 Dion James	.01	.05
118 Tom Edens RC	.01	.05
119 Carl Nichols	.01	.05
120 Joe Carter	.02	.10
121 Eric King	.01	.05
122 Paul O'Neill	.05	.15
123 Greg A. Harris	.01	.05
124 Randy Bush	.01	.05
125 Steve Bedrosian	.01	.05
126 Bernard Gilkey	.01	.05
127 Joe Price	.01	.05
128 Travis Fryman	.02	.10
Front has SS		
back has SS-3B		
129 Mark Eichhorn	.01	.05
130 Ozzie Smith	.15	.40
131A Checklist 1 ERR	.08	.25
727 Phil Bradley		
131B Checklist 1 COR	.01	.05
717 Phil Bradley		
132 Jamie Quirk	.01	.05
133 Greg Briley	.01	.05
134 Kevin Elster	.01	.05
135 Jerome Walton	.01	.05
136 Dave Schmidt	.01	.05
137 Randy Ready	.01	.05
138 Jamie Moyer	.02	.10
139 Jeff Treadway	.01	.05
140 Fred McGriff	.05	.15
141 Nick Leyva MG	.01	.05
142 Curt Wilkerson	.01	.05
143 John Smiley	.01	.05
144 Dave Henderson	.01	.05
145 Lou Whitaker	.02	.10
146 Dan Plesac	.01	.05
147 Carlos Baerga	.01	.05
148 Rey Palacios	.01	.05
149 Al Osuna UER RC	.02	.10
150 Cal Ripken	.30	.75
151 Tom Browning	.01	.05
152 Mickey Hatcher	.01	.05
153 Bryan Harvey	.01	.05
154 Jay Buhner	.02	.10
155A Dwight Evans ERR	.20	.50
Led league with		
162 games in '82		
155B Dwight Evans COR	.05	.15
Tied for lead with		
162 games in '82		
156 Carlos Martinez	.01	.05
157 John Smoltz	.05	.15
158 Jose Uribe	.01	.05
159 Joe Boever	.01	.05
160 Vince Coleman UER	.01	.05
Wrong birth year,		
born 9/22/60		
161 Tim Leary	.01	.05
162 Ozzie Canseco	.01	.05
163 Dave Johnson	.01	.05
164 Edgar Diaz	.01	.05
165 Sandy Alomar Jr.	.01	.05
166 Harold Baines	.02	.10
167A Randy Tomlin ERR	.08	.25
Harriburg		
167B Randy Tomlin COR RC	.02	.10
168 John Olerud	.02	.10
169 Luis Aquino	.01	.05
170 Carlton Fisk	.05	.15
171 Tony LaRussa MG	.02	.10
172 Pete Incaviglia	.01	.05
173 Jason Grimsley	.01	.05
174 Ken Caminiti	.02	.10
175 Jack Armstrong	.01	.05
176 John Orton	.01	.05
177 Reggie Harris	.01	.05
178 Dave Valle	.01	.05
179 Pete Harnisch	.01	.05
180 Tony Gwynn	.10	.30
181 Duane Ward	.01	.05
182 Junior Noboa	.01	.05
183 Clay Parker	.01	.05
184 Gary Green	.01	.05
185 Joe Magrane	.01	.05
186 Rod Booker	.01	.05
187 Greg Cadaret	.01	.05
188 Damon Berryhill	.01	.05
189 Daryl Irvine RC	.01	.05
190 Matt Williams	.02	.10
191 Willie Blair	.01	.05
192 Rob Deer	.01	.05
193 Felix Fermin	.01	.05
194 Xavier Hernandez	.01	.05
195 Wally Joyner	.02	.10
196 Jim Vatcher RC	.01	.05
197 Chris Nabholz	.01	.05
198 R.J. Reynolds	.01	.05
199 Mike Hartley	.01	.05
200 Darryl Strawberry	.02	.10
201 Tom Kelly MG	.01	.05
202 Jim Leyritz	.01	.05
203 Gene Harris	.01	.05
204 Herm Winningham	.01	.05
205 Mike Perez RC	.01	.05
206 Carlos Quintana	.01	.05
207 Gary Wayne	.01	.05
208 Willie Wilson	.01	.05
209 Ken Howell	.01	.05
210 Lance Parrish	.02	.10
211 Brian Barnes RC	.01	.05
212 Steve Finley	.02	.10
213 Frank Wills	.01	.05
214 Joe Girardi	.01	.05
215 Dave Smith	.01	.05
216 Greg Gagne	.01	.05
217 Chris Bosio	.01	.05
218 Rick Parker	.01	.05
219 Jack McDowell	.01	.05
220 Tim Wallach	.01	.05
221 Don Slaught	.01	.05
222 Brian McRae RC	.08	.25
223 Allan Anderson	.01	.05
224 Juan Gonzalez	.08	.25
225 Randy Johnson	.10	.30
226 Alfredo Griffin	.01	.05
227 Steve Avery UER	.01	.05
Pitched 13 games for		
Durham in 1989, not 2		
228 Rex Hudler	.01	.05
229 Rance Mulliniks	.01	.05
230 Sid Fernandez	.01	.05
231 Doug Rader MG	.01	.05
232 Jose DeJesus	.01	.05
233 Al Leiter	.02	.10
234 Scott Erickson	.01	.05
235 Dave Parker	.02	.10
236A Frank Tanana ERR	.08	.25
Tied for lead with		
269 K's in '75		
236B Frank Tanana COR	.01	.05
Led league with		
269 K's in '75		
237 Rick Cerone	.01	.05
238 Mike Dunne	.01	.05
239 Darren Lewis	.01	.05
240 Mike Scott	.01	.05
241 Dave Clark UER	.01	.05
Career totals 19 HR		
and 5 3B, should		
be 22 and 3		
242 Mike LaCoss	.01	.05
243 Lance Johnson	.01	.05
244 Mike Jeffcoat	.01	.05
245 Kal Daniels	.01	.05
246 Kevin Wickander	.01	.05
247 Jody Reed	.01	.05
248 Tom Gordon	.01	.05
249 Bob Melvin	.01	.05
250 Dennis Eckersley	.02	.10
251 Mark Lemke	.01	.05
252 Mel Rojas	.01	.05
253 Garry Templeton	.01	.05
254 Shawn Boskie	.01	.05
255 Brian Downing	.01	.05
256 Greg Hibbard	.01	.05
257 Tom O'Malley	.01	.05
258 Chris Hammond	.01	.05
259 Hensley Meulens	.01	.05
260 Harold Reynolds	.02	.10
261 Bud Harrelson MG	.01	.05
262 Tim Jones	.01	.05
263 Checklist 2	.01	.05
264 Dave Hollins	.01	.05
265 Mark Gubicza	.01	.05
266 Carmelo Castillo	.01	.05
267 Mark Knudson	.01	.05
268 Tom Brookens	.01	.05
269 Joe Hesketh	.01	.05
270 Mark McGwire COR	.30	.75
270A Mark McGwire ERR	.75	2.00
271 Omar Olivares RC	.02	.10
272 Jeff King	.01	.05
273 Johnny Ray	.01	.05
274 Ken Williams	.01	.05
275 Alan Trammell	.02	.10
276 Bill Swift	.01	.05
277 Scott Coolbaugh	.01	.05
278 Alex Fernandez UER	.01	.05
No '90 White Sox stats		
279A Jose Gonzalez ERR	.08	.25
Photo actually		
Billy Bean		
279B Jose Gonzalez COR	.01	.05
280 Bret Saberhagen	.02	.10
281 Larry Sheets	.01	.05
282 Don Carman	.01	.05
283 Marquis Grissom	.02	.10
284 Billy Spiers	.01	.05
285 Jim Abbott	.05	.15
286 Ken Oberkfell	.01	.05
287 Mark Grant	.01	.05
288 Derrick May	.01	.05
289 Tim Birtsas	.01	.05
290 Steve Sax	.01	.05
291 John Wathan MG	.01	.05
292 Bud Black	.01	.05
293 Jay Bell	.02	.10
294 Mike Moore	.01	.05
295 Rafael Palmeiro	.05	.15
296 Mark Williamson	.01	.05
297 Manny Lee	.01	.05
298 Omar Vizquel	.05	.15
299 Scott Radinsky	.01	.05
300 Kirby Puckett	.08	.25
301 Steve Farr	.01	.05
302 Tim Teufel	.01	.05
303 Mike Boddicker	.01	.05
304 Kevin Reimer	.01	.05
305 Mike Scioscia	.01	.05
306A Lonnie Smith ERR	.15	.40
136 games in '90		
306B Lonnie Smith COR	.01	.05
135 games in '90		
307 Andy Benes	.01	.05
308 Tom Pagnozzi	.01	.05
309 Norm Charlton	.01	.05
310 Gary Carter	.02	.10
311 Jeff Pico	.01	.05
312 Charlie Hayes	.01	.05
313 Ron Robinson	.01	.05
314 Gary Pettis	.01	.05
315 Roberto Alomar	.05	.15
316 Gene Nelson	.01	.05
317 Mike Fitzgerald	.01	.05
318 Randy Kutcher	.02	.10
319 Jeff McKnight	.01	.05
320 Tony Fernandez	.01	.05
321 Bob Rodgers MG	.01	.05
322 Terry Shumpert	.01	.05
323 Cory Snyder	.01	.05
324A Ron Kittle ERR	.15	.40
Set another		
standard ...		
324B Ron Kittle COR	.01	.05
Tied another		
standard ...		
325 Brett Butler	.02	.10
326 Ken Patterson	.01	.05
327 Ron Hassey	.01	.05
328 Walt Terrell	.01	.05
329 Dave Justice UER	.02	.10
Drafted third round		
on card, should say		
fourth pick		
330 Dwight Gooden	.02	.10
331 Eric Anthony	.01	.05
332 Kenny Rogers	.02	.10
333 Chipper Jones RC	5.00	12.00
334 Todd Benzinger	.01	.05
335 Mitch Williams	.01	.05
336 Matt Nokes	.01	.05
337A Keith Comstock ERR	.08	.25
Cubs logo on front		
337B Keith Comstock COR	.01	.05
Mariners logo on front		
338 Luis Rivera	.01	.05
339 Larry Walker	.08	.25
340 Ramon Martinez	.01	.05
341 John Moses	.01	.05
342 Mickey Morandini	.01	.05
343 Jose Oquendo	.01	.05
344 Jeff Russell	.01	.05
345 Len Dykstra	.02	.10
346 Jesse Orosco	.01	.05
347 Greg Vaughn	.01	.05
348 Todd Stottlemyre	.01	.05
349 Dave Gallagher	.01	.05
350 Glenn Davis	.01	.05
351 Joe Torre MG	.02	.10
352 Frank White	.02	.10
353 Tony Castillo	.01	.05
354 Sid Bream	.01	.05
355 Chili Davis	.02	.10
356 Mike Marshall	.01	.05
357 Jack Savage	.01	.05
358 Mark Parent	.01	.05
359 Chuck Cary	.01	.05
360 Tim Raines	.02	.10
361 Scott Garrelts	.01	.05
362 Hector Villenueva	.01	.05
363 Rick Mahler	.01	.05
364 Dan Pasqua	.01	.05
365 Mike Schooler	.01	.05
366A Checklist 3 ERR	.08	.25
19 Carl Nichols		
366B Checklist 3 COR	.01	.05
119 Carl Nichols		
367 Dave Walsh RC	.01	.05
368 Felix Jose	.01	.05
369 Steve Searcy	.01	.05
370 Kelly Gruber	.01	.05
371 Jeff Montgomery	.01	.05
372 Spike Owen	.01	.05
373 Darrin Jackson	.01	.05
374 Larry Casian RC	.01	.05
375 Tony Pena	.01	.05
376 Mike Harkey	.01	.05
377 Rene Gonzales	.01	.05
378A Wilson Alvarez ERR	.08	.25
'89 Port Charlotte		
and '90 Birmingham		
stat lines omitted		
378B Wilson Alvarez COR	.01	.05
Text still says 143		
K's in 1988,		
whereas stats say 134		
379 Randy Velarde	.01	.05
380 Willie McGee	.02	.10
381 Jim Leyland MG	.01	.05
382 Mackey Sasser	.01	.05
383 Pete Smith	.01	.05
384 Gerald Perry	.01	.05
385 Mickey Tettleton	.01	.05
386 Cecil Fielder AS	.01	.05
387 Julio Franco AS	.01	.05
388 Kelly Gruber AS	.01	.05
389 Alan Trammell AS	.02	.10
390 Jose Canseco AS	.02	.10
391 Rickey Henderson AS	.05	.15
392 Ken Griffey Jr. AS	.20	.50
393 Carlton Fisk AS	.02	.10
394 Bob Welch AS	.01	.05
395 Chuck Finley AS	.01	.05
396 Bobby Thigpen AS	.01	.05
397 Eddie Murray AS	.05	.15
398 Ryne Sandberg AS	.08	.25
399 Matt Williams AS	.01	.05
400 Barry Larkin AS	.02	.10
401 Barry Bonds AS	.20	.50
402 Darryl Strawberry AS	.01	.05
403 Bobby Bonilla AS	.01	.05
404 Mike Scioscia AS	.01	.05
405 Doug Drabek AS	.01	.05
406 Frank Viola AS	.01	.05
407 John Franco AS	.01	.05
408 Earnest Riles	.01	.05
409 Mike Stanley	.01	.05
410 Dave Righetti	.02	.10
411 Lance Blankenship	.01	.05

412 Dave Bergman .01 .05
413 Terry Mulholland .01 .05
414 Sammy Sosa .08 .25
415 Rick Sutcliffe .02 .10
416 Randy Milligan .01 .05
417 Bill Krueger .01 .05
418 Nick Esasky .01 .05
419 Jeff Reed .01 .05
420 Bobby Thigpen .01 .05
421 Alex Cole .01 .05
422 Rick Reuschel .01 .05
423 Rafael Ramirez UER .01 .05
Born 1959, not 1958
424 Calvin Schiraldi .01 .05
425 Andy Van Slyke .05 .15
426 Joe Grahe RC .02 .10
427 Rick Dempsey .01 .05
428 John Barfield .01 .05
429 Stump Merrill MG .01 .05
430 Gary Gaetti .02 .10
431 Paul Gibson .01 .05
432 Delino DeShields .02 .10
433 Pat Tabler .01 .05
434 Julio Machado .01 .05
435 Kevin Maas .01 .05
436 Scott Bankhead .01 .05
437 Doug Dascenzo .01 .05
438 Vicente Palacios .01 .05
439 Dickie Thon .01 .05
440 George Bell .01 .05
441 Zane Smith .01 .05
442 Charlie O'Brien .01 .05
443 Jeff Innis .01 .05
444 Glenn Braggs .01 .05
445 Greg Swindell .01 .05
446 Craig Grebeck .01 .05
447 John Burkett .01 .05
448 Craig Lefferts .01 .05
449 Juan Berenguer .01 .05
450 Wade Boggs .05 .15
451 Neal Heaton .01 .05
452 Bill Schroeder .01 .05
453 Lenny Harris .01 .05
454A Kevin Appier ERR .15 .40
'90 Omaha stat
line omitted
454B Kevin Appier COR .02 .10
455 Walt Weiss .01 .05
456 Charlie Leibrandt .01 .05
457 Todd Hundley .01 .05
458 Brian Holman .01 .05
459 Tom Trebelhorn MG UER .01 .05
Pitching and batting
columns switched
460 Dave Stieb .01 .05
461 Robin Ventura .02 .10
462 Steve Frey .01 .05
463 Dwight Smith .01 .05
464 Steve Buechele .01 .05
465 Ken Griffey Sr. .02 .10
466 Charles Nagy .01 .05
467 Dennis Cook .01 .05
468 Tim Hulett .01 .05
469 Chet Lemon .01 .05
470 Howard Johnson .01 .05
471 Mike Lieberthal RC .15 .40
472 Kirt Manwaring .01 .05
473 Curt Young .01 .05
474 Phil Plantier RC .02 .10
475 Ted Higuera .01 .05
476 Glenn Wilson .01 .05
477 Mike Fetters .01 .05
478 Kurt Stillwell .01 .05
479 Bob Patterson UER .01 .05
Has a decimal point
between 7 and 9
480 Dave Magadan .01 .05
481 Eddie Whitson .01 .05
482 Tino Martinez .08 .25
483 Mike Aldrete .01 .05
484 Dave LaPoint .01 .05
485 Terry Pendleton .02 .10
486 Tommy Greene .01 .05
487 Rafael Belliard .01 .05
488 Jeff Manto .01 .05
489 Bobby Valentine MG .01 .05
490 Kirk Gibson .02 .10
491 Kurt Miller RC .01 .05
492 Ernie Whitt .01 .05
493 Jose Rijo .01 .05
494 Chris James .01 .05
495 Charlie Hough .02 .10
496 Marty Barrett .01 .05
497 Ben McDonald .01 .05
498 Mark Salas .01 .05
499 Melido Perez .01 .05
500 Will Clark .05 .15
501 Mike Bielecki .01 .05
502 Carney Lansford .02 .10
503 Roy Smith .01 .05
504 Julio Valera .01 .05
505 Chuck Finley .02 .10
506 Darnell Coles .01 .05
507 Steve Jeltz .01 .05
508 Mike York RC .01 .05
509 Glenallen Hill .01 .05
510 John Franco .02 .10
511 Steve Balboni .01 .05
512 Jose Mesa .01 .05
513 Jerald Clark .01 .05
514 Mike Stanton .01 .05
515 Alvin Davis .01 .05
516 Karl Rhodes .01 .05
517 Joe Oliver .01 .05
518 Cris Carpenter .01 .05
519 Sparky Anderson MG .02 .10
520 Mark Grace .05 .15
521 Joe Orsulak .01 .05
522 Stan Belinda .01 .05
523 Rodney McCray RC .01 .05
524 Darrel Akerfelds .01 .05
525 Willie Randolph .02 .10
526A Moises Alou ERR .15 .40
37 runs in 2 games
for '90 Pirates
526B Moises Alou COR .02 .10
0 runs in 2 games
for '90 Pirates
527A Checklist 4 ERR .08 .25
105 Keith Miller
719 Kevin McReynolds
527B Checklist 4 COR .01 .05
105 Kevin McReynolds
719 Keith Miller
528 Dennis Martinez .02 .10
529 Marc Newfield RC .02 .10
530 Roger Clemens .30 .75
531 Dave Rohde .01 .05
532 Kirk McCaskill .01 .05
533 Oddibe McDowell .01 .05
534 Mike Jackson .01 .05
535 Ruben Sierra UER .02 .10
Back reads 100 Runs
amd 100 RBI's
536 Mike Witt .01 .05
537 Jose Lind .01 .05
538 Bip Roberts .01 .05
539 Scott Terry .01 .05
540 George Brett .25 .60
541 Domingo Ramos .01 .05
542 Rob Murphy .01 .05
543 Junior Felix .01 .05
544 Alejandro Pena .01 .05
545 Dale Murphy .05 .15
546 Jeff Ballard .01 .05
547 Mike Pagliarulo .01 .05
548 Jaime Navarro .01 .05
549 John McNamara MG .01 .05
550 Eric Davis .02 .10
551 Bob Kipper .01 .05
552 Jeff Hamilton .01 .05
553 Joe Klink .01 .05
554 Brian Harper .01 .05
555 Turner Ward RC .02 .10
556 Gary Ward .01 .05
557 Wally Whitehurst .01 .05
558 Otis Nixon .01 .05
559 Adam Peterson .01 .05
560 Greg Smith .01 .05
561 Tim McIntosh .01 .05
562 Jeff Kunkel .01 .05
563 Brent Knackert .01 .05
564 Dante Bichette .02 .10
565 Craig Biggio .05 .15
566 Craig Wilson RC .01 .05
567 Dwayne Henry .01 .05
568 Ron Karkovice .01 .05
569 Curt Schilling .08 .25
570 Barry Bonds .40 1.00
571 Pat Combs .01 .05
572 Dave Anderson .01 .05
573 Rich Rodriguez UER RC .01 .05
574 John Marzano .01 .05
575 Robin Yount .15 .40
576 Jeff Kaiser .01 .05
577 Bill Doran .01 .05
578 Dave West .01 .05
579 Roger Craig MG .01 .05
580 Dave Stewart .02 .10
581 Luis Quinones .01 .05
582 Marty Clary .01 .05
583 Tony Phillips .01 .05
584 Kevin Brown .02 .10
585 Pete O'Brien .01 .05
586 Fred Lynn .01 .05
587 Jose Offerman UER .01 .05
Text says he signed
7/24/86, but bio
says 1988
588A Mark Whiten .01 .05
588B M.Whiten FTC UER 60.00 150.00
589 Scott Ruskin .01 .05
590 Eddie Murray .08 .25
591 Ken Hill .01 .05
592 B.J. Surhoff .02 .10
593A Mike Walker ERR .08 .25
'90 Canton-Akron
stat line omitted
593B Mike Walker COR .01 .05
594 Rich Garces RC .02 .10
595 Bill Landrum .01 .05
596 Ronnie Walden RC .02 .10
597 Jerry Don Gleaton .01 .05
598 Sam Horn .01 .05
599A Greg Myers ERR .08 .25
'90 Syracuse
stat line omitted
599B Greg Myers COR .01 .05
600 Bo Jackson .08 .25
601 Bob Ojeda .01 .05
602 Casey Candaele .01 .05
603A Wes Chamberlain ERR .15 .40
603B Wes Chamberlain COR RC .02 .10
604 Billy Hatcher .01 .05
605 Jeff Reardon .02 .10
606 Jim Gott .01 .05
607 Edgar Martinez .05 .15
608 Todd Burns .01 .05
609 Jeff Torborg MG .01 .05
610 Andres Galarraga .02 .10
611 Dave Eiland .01 .05
612 Steve Lyons .01 .05
613 Eric Show .01 .05
614 Luis Salazar .01 .05
615 Bert Blyleven .02 .10
616 Todd Zeile .01 .05
617 Bill Wegman .01 .05
618 Sil Campusano .01 .05
619 David Wells .02 .10
620 Ozzie Guillen .02 .10
621 Ted Power .01 .05
622 Jack Daugherty .01 .05
623 Jeff Blauser .01 .05
624 Tom Candiotti .01 .05
625 Terry Steinbach .01 .05
626 Gerald Young .01 .05
627 Tim Layana .01 .05
628 Greg Litton .01 .05
629 Wes Gardner .01 .05
630 Dave Winfield .02 .10
631 Mike Morgan .01 .05
632 Lloyd Moseby .01 .05
633 Kevin Tapani .01 .05
634 Henry Cotto .01 .05
635 Andy Hawkins .01 .05
636 Geronimo Pena .01 .05
637 Bruce Ruffin .01 .05
638 Mike Macfarlane .01 .05
639 Frank Robinson MG .05 .15
640 Andre Dawson .02 .10
641 Mike Henneman .01 .05
642 Hal Morris .01 .05
643 Jim Presley .01 .05
644 Chuck Crim .01 .05
645 Juan Samuel .01 .05
646 Andujar Cedeno .01 .05
647 Mark Portugal .01 .05
648 Lee Stevens .01 .05
649 Bill Sampen .01 .05
650 Jack Clark .02 .10
651 Alan Mills .01 .05
652 Kevin Romine .01 .05
653 Anthony Telford RC .01 .05
654 Paul Sorrento .01 .05
655 Erik Hanson .01 .05
656A Checklist 5 ERR .08 .25
348 Vicente Palacios
381 Jose Lind
537 Mike LaValliere
665 Jim Leyland
656B Checklist 5 ERR .08 .25
433 Vicente Palacios
Palacios should be 438
537 Jose Lind
665 Mike LaValliere
381 Jim Leyland
656C Checklist 5 COR .01 .05
438 Vicente Palacios
537 Jose Lind
665 Mike LaValliere
381 Jim Leyland
657 Mike Kingery .01 .05
658 Scott Aldred .01 .05
659 Oscar Azocar .01 .05
660 Lee Smith .02 .10
661 Steve Lake .01 .05
662 Ron Dibble .02 .10
663 Greg Brock .01 .05
664 John Farrell .01 .05
665 Mike LaValliere .01 .05
666 Danny Darwin .01 .05
667 Kent Anderson .01 .05
668 Bill Long .01 .05
669 Lou Piniella MG .02 .10
670 Rickey Henderson .08 .25
671 Andy McGaffigan .01 .05
672 Shane Mack .01 .05
673 Greg Olson UER .01 .05
6 RBI in '88 at Tidewater
and 2 RBI in '87,
should be 48 and 15
674A Kevin Gross ERR .08 .25
89 BB with Phillies
in '88 tied for
league lead
674B Kevin Gross COR .01 .05
89 BB with Phillies
in '88 led league
675 Tom Brunansky .01 .05
676 Scott Chiamparino .01 .05
677 Billy Ripken .01 .05
678 Mark Davidson .01 .05
679 Bill Bathe .01 .05
680 David Cone .02 .10
681 Jeff Schaefer .01 .05
682 Ray Lankford .02 .10
683 Derek Lilliquist .01 .05
684 Milt Cuyler .01 .05
685 Doug Drabek .01 .05
686 Mike Gallego .01 .05
687A John Cerutti ERR .08 .25
4.46 ERA in '90
687B John Cerutti COR .01 .05
4.76 ERA in '90
688 Rosario Rodriguez RC .01 .05
689 John Kruk .02 .10
690 Orel Hershiser .02 .10
691 Mike Blowers .01 .05
692A Efrain Valdez ERR .08 .25
692B Efrain Valdez COR RC .01 .05
693 Francisco Cabrera .01 .05
694 Randy Veres .01 .05
695 Kevin Seitzer .01 .05
696 Steve Olin .01 .05
697 Shawn Abner .01 .05
698 Mark Guthrie .01 .05
699 Jim Lefebvre MG .01 .05
700 Jose Canseco .05 .15
701 Pascual Perez .01 .05
702 Tim Naehring .01 .05
703 Juan Agosto .01 .05
704 Devon White .02 .10
705 Robby Thompson .01 .05
706A Brad Arnsberg ERR .08 .25
68.2 IP in '90
706B Brad Arnsberg COR .01 .05
62.2 IP in '90
707 Jim Eisenreich .01 .05
708 John Mitchell .01 .05
709 Matt Sinatro .01 .05
710 Kent Hrbek .02 .10
711 Jose DeLeon .01 .05
712 Ricky Jordan .01 .05
713 Scott Scudder .01 .05
714 Marvell Wynne .01 .05
715 Tim Burke .01 .05
716 Bob Geren .01 .05
717 Phil Bradley .01 .05
718 Steve Crawford .01 .05
719 Keith Miller .01 .05
720 Cecil Fielder .02 .10
721 Mark Lee RC .01 .05
722 Wally Backman .01 .05
723 Candy Maldonado .01 .05
724 David Segui .01 .05
725 Ron Gant .02 .10
726 Phil Stephenson .01 .05
727 Mookie Wilson .02 .10
728 Scott Sanderson .01 .05
729 Don Zimmer MG .01 .05
730 Barry Larkin .05 .15
731 Jeff Gray RC .01 .05
732 Franklin Stubbs .01 .05
733 Kelly Downs .01 .05
734 John Russell .01 .05
735 Ron Darling .01 .05
736 Dick Schofield .01 .05
737 Tim Crews .01 .05
738 Mel Hall .01 .05
739 Russ Swan .01 .05
740 Ryne Sandberg .15 .40
741 Jimmy Key .02 .10
742 Tommy Gregg .01 .05
743 Bryn Smith .01 .05
744 Nelson Santovenia .01 .05
745 Doug Jones .01 .05
746 John Shelby .01 .05
747 Tony Fossas .01 .05
748 Al Newman .01 .05
749 Greg W. Harris .01 .05
750 Bobby Bonilla .02 .10
751 Wayne Edwards .01 .05
752 Kevin Bass .01 .05
753 Paul Marak UER RC .01 .05
754 Bill Pecota .01 .05
755 Mark Langston .01 .05
756 Jeff Huson .01 .05
757 Mark Gardner .01 .05
758 Mike Devereaux .01 .05
759 Bobby Cox MG .01 .05
760 Benny Santiago .02 .10
761 Larry Andersen .01 .05
762 Mitch Webster .01 .05
763 Dana Kiecker .01 .05
764 Mark Carreon .01 .05
765 Shawon Dunston .01 .05
766 Jeff Robinson .01 .05
767 Dan Wilson RC .08 .25
768 Don Pall .01 .05
769 Tim Sherrill .01 .05
770 Jay Howell .01 .05
771 Gary Redus UER .01 .05
Born in Tanner,
should say Athens
772 Kent Mercker UER .01 .05
Born in Indianapolis,
should say Dublin, Ohio
773 Tom Foley .01 .05
774 Dennis Rasmussen .01 .05
775 Julio Franco .02 .10
776 Brent Mayne .01 .05
777 John Candelaria .01 .05
778 Dan Gladden .01 .05
779 Carmelo Martinez .01 .05
780A Randy Myers ERR .15 .40
15 career losses
780B Randy Myers COR .01 .05
19 career losses
781 Darryl Hamilton .01 .05
782 Jim Deshaies .01 .05
783 Joel Skinner .01 .05
784 Willie Fraser .01 .05
785 Scott Fletcher .01 .05
786 Eric Plunk .01 .05
787 Checklist 6 .01 .05
788 Bob Milacki .01 .05
789 Tom Lasorda MG .08 .25
790 Ken Griffey Jr. .40 1.00
791 Mike Benjamin .01 .05
792 Mike Greenwell .01 .05

1991 Topps Desert Shield

COMMON CARD (1-792) 2.50 6.00
DIST.TO ARMED FORCES IN SAUDI ARABIA
333 Chipper Jones 300.00 800.00

1991 Topps Micro

This 792 card set parallels the regular Topps issue. The cards are significantly smaller (slightly larger than a postage stamp) than the regular Topps cards and are valued at a percentage of the regular 1991 Topps cards.

COMPLETE FACT.SET (792) 8.00 20.00
*STARS: .4X to 1X BASIC CARDS

1991 Topps Tiffany

COMP.FACT.SET (792) 100.00 200.00
*STARS: 12.5X TO 30X BASIC CARDS
*ROOKIES: 6X TO 15X BASIC CARDS
DISTRIBUTED ONLY IN FACTORY SET FORM
FACTORY SET PRICE IS FOR SEALED SETS

1991 Topps Rookies

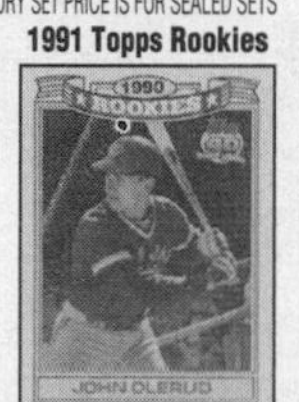

This set contains 33 standard-size cards and were distributed at a rate of one per retail jumbo pack. The front and back borders are white and other design elements are red, blue, and yellow. This set is identical to the previous year's set. Topps also commemorated its 40th anniversary by including a "Topps 40" logo on the front. The cards are unnumbered and checklisted below in alphabetical order.

COMPLETE SET (33) 8.00 20.00
1 Sandy Alomar .20 .50
2 Kevin Appier .20 .50
3 Steve Avery .08 .25
4 Carlos Baerga .20 .50
5 John Burkett .08 .25
6 Alex Cole .08 .25
7 Pat Combs .08 .25
8 Delino DeShields .20 .50
9 Travis Fryman .20 .50
10 Marquis Grissom .40 1.00
11 Mike Harkey .08 .25
12 Glenallen Hill .08 .25
13 Jeff Huson .08 .25
14 Felix Jose .08 .25
15 Dave Justice .60 1.50
16 Jim Leyritz .08 .25
17 Kevin Maas .08 .25
18 Ben McDonald .08 .25
19 Kent Mercker .08 .25
20 Hal Morris .08 .25
21 Chris Nabholz .08 .25
22 Tim Naehring .08 .25
23 Jose Offerman .08 .25
24 John Olerud .75 2.00
25 Scott Radinsky .08 .25
26 Scott Ruskin .08 .25
27 Kevin Tapani .08 .25
28 Frank Thomas 3.00 8.00
29 Randy Tomlin .08 .25
30 Greg Vaughn .20 .50
31 Robin Ventura .40 1.00
32 Larry Walker .60 1.50
33 Todd Zeile .20 .50

1991 Topps Wax Box Cards

Topps again in 1991 issued cards on the bottom of their wax pack boxes. There are four different boxes, each with four cards and a checklist on the side. These standard-size cards have yellow borders rather than the white borders of the regular issue cards, and they have different photos of the players. The backs are printed in pink and blue on gray cardboard stock and feature outstanding achievements of the players. The cards are numbered by letter on the back. The cards have the typical Topps 1991 design on the front of the card. The set was ordered in alphabetical order and lettered A-P.

COMPLETE SET (16) 2.50 6.00
A Bert Blyleven .07 .20
B George Brett .40 1.00
C Brett Butler .02 .10
D Andre Dawson .20 .50
E Dwight Evans .07 .20
F Carlton Fisk .25 .60
G Alfredo Griffin .02 .10
H Rickey Henderson .25 .60
I Willie McGee .07 .20
J Dale Murphy .20 .50
K Eddie Murray .25 .60
L Dave Parker .07 .20
M Jeff Reardon .07 .20
N Nolan Ryan 1.00 2.50
O Juan Samuel .02 .10
P Robin Yount .25 .60

1991 Topps Traded

The 1991 Topps Traded set contains 132 standard-size cards. The cards were issued primarily in factory set form through hobby dealers but were also made available on a limited basis in wax packs. The cards in the wax packs (gray backs) and collated factory sets (white backs) are from different card stock. Both versions are valued equally. The card design is identical to the regular issue 1991 Topps cards except for the whiter stock (for factory set cards) and T-suffixed numbering. The set is numbered in alphabetical order. The set includes a Team U.S.A. subset, featuring 25 of America's top collegiate players. The key Rookie Cards in this set are Jeff Bagwell, Jason Giambi, Luis Gonzalez, Charles Johnson and Ivan Rodriguez.

COMPLETE SET (132) 4.00 10.00
COMP.FACT.SET (132) 4.00 10.00
1T Juan Agosto .01 .05
2T Roberto Alomar .05 .15
3T Wally Backman .01 .05
4T Jeff Bagwell RC .60 1.50
5T Skeeter Barnes .01 .05
6T Steve Bedrosian .01 .05
7T Derek Bell .02 .10
8T George Bell .01 .05
9T Rafael Belliard .01 .05
10T Dante Bichette .02 .10
11T Bud Black .01 .05
12T Mike Boddicker .01 .05
13T Sid Bream .01 .05
14T Hubie Brooks .01 .05
15T Brett Butler .02 .10
16T Ivan Calderon .01 .05
17T John Candelaria .01 .05
18T Tom Candiotti .01 .05
19T Gary Carter .02 .10
20T Joe Carter .02 .10
21T Rick Cerone .01 .05
22T Jack Clark .02 .10
23T Vince Coleman .01 .05
24T Scott Coolbaugh .01 .05
25T Danny Cox .01 .05
26T Danny Darwin .01 .05
27T Chili Davis .02 .10
28T Glenn Davis .01 .05
29T Steve Decker RC .01 .05
30T Rob Deer .01 .05
31T Rich DeLucia RC .01 .05
32T John Dettmer USA RC .08 .25
33T Brian Downing .01 .05
34T Darren Dreifort USA RC .08 .25
35T Kirk Dressendorfer RC .01 .05
36T Jim Essian MG .01 .05
37T Dwight Evans .05 .15
38T Steve Farr .01 .05
39T Jeff Fassero RC .08 .25
40T Junior Felix .01 .05
41T Tony Fernandez .01 .05
42T Steve Finley .02 .10
43T Jim Fregosi MG .01 .05
44T Gary Gaetti .02 .10
45T Jason Giambi USA RC 3.00 8.00
46T Kirk Gibson .02 .10
47T Leo Gomez .02 .10
48T Luis Gonzalez RC .20 .50
49T Jeff Granger USA RC .08 .25
50T Todd Greene USA RC .20 .50
51T Jeffrey Hammonds USA RC .20 .50
52T Mike Hargrove MG .01 .05
53T Pete Harnisch .01 .05
54T Rick Helling USA RC .20 .50
55T Glenallen Hill .01 .05
56T Charlie Hough .02 .10
57T Pete Incaviglia .01 .05
58T Bo Jackson .08 .25
59T Danny Jackson .01 .05
60T Reggie Jefferson .01 .05
61T Charles Johnson USA RC .30 .75
62T Jeff Johnson RC .01 .05
63T Todd Johnson USA RC .08 .25
64T Barry Jones .01 .05
65T Chris Jones RC .02 .10
66T Scott Kamieniecki RC .02 .10
67T Pat Kelly RC .02 .10
68T Darryl Kile .02 .10
69T Chuck Knoblauch .02 .10
70T Bill Krueger .01 .05
71T Scott Leius .01 .05
72T Donnie Leshnock USA RC .08 .25
73T Mark Lewis .01 .05
74T Candy Maldonado .01 .05
75T Jason McDonald USA RC .08 .25
76T Willie McGee .02 .10
77T Fred McGriff .05 .15
78T Billy McMillon USA RC .08 .25
79T Hal McRae MG .02 .10
80T Dan Melendez USA RC .08 .25
81T Orlando Merced RC .02 .10
82T Jack Morris .02 .10
83T Phil Nevin USA RC .30 .75
84T Otis Nixon .01 .05
85T Johnny Oates MG .01 .05
86T Bob Ojeda .01 .05
87T Mike Pagliarulo .01 .05
88T Dean Palmer .02 .10
89T Dave Parker .02 .10
90T Terry Pendleton .02 .10
91T Tony Phillips (P) USA RC .08 .25
92T Doug Piatt RC .01 .05
93T Ron Polk USA CO .08 .25
94T Tim Raines .02 .10
95T Willie Randolph .02 .10
96T Dave Righetti .02 .10
97T Ernie Riles .01 .05
98T Chris Roberts USA RC .08 .25
99T Jeff D. Robinson .01 .05
100T Jeff M. Robinson .01 .05
101T Ivan Rodriguez RC 1.25 3.00
102T Steve Rodriguez USA RC .08 .25
103T Tom Runnells MG .01 .05
104T Scott Sanderson .01 .05
105T Bob Scanlan RC .01 .05
106T Pete Schourek RC .02 .10
107T Gary Scott RC .01 .05
108T Paul Shuey USA RC .20 .50
109T Doug Simons RC .01 .05
110T Dave Smith .01 .05
111T Cory Snyder .01 .05
112T Luis Sojo .01 .05
113T Kennie Steenstra USA RC .08 .25
114T Darryl Strawberry .02 .10
115T Franklin Stubbs .01 .05
116T Todd Taylor USA RC .08 .25
117T Wade Taylor RC .01 .05
118T Garry Templeton .01 .05
119T Mickey Tettleton .01 .05
120T Tim Teufel .01 .05
121T Mike Timlin RC .08 .25
122T David Tuttle USA RC .08 .25
123T Mo Vaughn .02 .10
124T Jeff Ware USA RC .08 .25
125T Devon White .02 .10
126T Mark Whiten .01 .05
127T Mitch Williams .01 .05
128T Craig Wilson USA RC .08 .25
129T Willie Wilson .01 .05
130T Chris Wimmer USA RC .08 .25
131T Ivan Zweig USA RC .08 .25
132T Checklist 1T-132T .01 .05

1991 Topps Traded Tiffany

COMP.FACT.SET (132) 75.00 150.00
*STARS: 12.5X TO 30X BASIC CARDS
*ROOKIES: 10X TO 25X BASIC CARDS
*USA ROOKIES: 6X TO 15X BASIC CARDS
DISTRIBUTED ONLY IN FACTORY SET FORM
FACTORY SET PRICE IS FOR SEALED SETS

1992 Topps

The 1992 Topps set contains 792 standard-size cards. Cards were distributed in plastic wrap packs, jumbo packs, rack packs and factory sets. The fronts have either posed or action color player photos on a white card face. Different color stripes frame the pictures, and the player's name and team name appear in two short color stripes respectively at the bottom. Special subsets included are Record Breakers (2-5), Prospects (58, 126, 179, 473, 551, 591, 618, 656, 676), and All-Stars (386-407). The key Rookie Cards in this set are Shawn Green and Manny Ramirez.

COMPLETE SET (792) 12.00 30.00
COMP.FACT.SET (802) 12.00 30.00
COMP.HOLIDAY SET (811) 15.00 40.00
1 Nolan Ryan .40 1.00
2 Rickey Henderson RB .05 .15
Most career SB's
Some cards have print
marks that show 1.991
on the front
3 Jeff Reardon RB .01 .05
4 Nolan Ryan RB .20 .50
5 Dave Winfield RB .01 .05
6 Brien Taylor RC .08 .25
7 Jim Olander .01 .05
8 Bryan Hickerson RC .02 .10
9 Jon Farrell RC .02 .10
10 Wade Boggs .05 .15
11 Jack McDowell .01 .05

12 Luis Gonzalez .02 .10
13 Mike Scioscia .01 .05
14 Wes Chamberlain .01 .05
15 Dennis Martinez .02 .10
16 Jeff Montgomery .01 .05
17 Randy Milligan .01 .05
18 Greg Cadaret .01 .05
19 Jamie Quirk .01 .05
20 Bip Roberts .01 .05
21 Buck Rodgers MG .01 .05
22 Bill Wegman .01 .05
23 Chuck Knoblauch .02 .10
24 Randy Myers .01 .05
25 Ron Gant .02 .10
26 Mike Bielecki .01 .05
27 Juan Gonzalez .05 .15
28 Mike Schooler .01 .05
29 Mickey Tettleton .01 .05
30 John Kruk .02 .10
31 Bryn Smith .01 .05
32 Chris Nabholz .01 .05
33 Carlos Baerga .01 .05
34 Jeff Juden .01 .05
35 Dave Righetti .02 .10
36 Scott Ruffcorn RC .02 .10
37 Luis Polonia .01 .05
38 Tom Candiotti .01 .05
39 Greg Olson .01 .05
40 Cal Ripken .75 2.00
41 Craig Lefferts .01 .05
42 Mike Macfarlane .01 .05
43 Jose Lind .01 .05
44 Rick Aguilera .02 .10
45 Gary Carter .02 .10
46 Steve Farr .01 .05
47 Rex Hudler .01 .05
48 Scott Scudder .01 .05
49 Damon Berryhill .01 .05
50 Ken Griffey Jr. .20 .50
51 Tom Runnells MG .01 .05
52 Juan Bell .01 .05
53 Tommy Gregg .01 .05
54 David Wells .02 .10
55 Rafael Palmeiro .05 .15
56 Charlie O'Brien .01 .05
57 Donn Pall .01 .05
58 Brad Ausmus RC .60 1.50
59 Mo Vaughn .02 .10
60 Tony Fernandez .01 .05
61 Paul O'Neill .05 .15
62 Gene Nelson .01 .05
63 Randy Ready .01 .05
64 Bob Kipper .01 .05
65 Willie McGee .02 .10
66 Scott Stahoviak RC .02 .10
67 Luis Salazar .01 .05
68 Marvin Freeman .01 .05
69 Kenny Lofton .05 .15
70 Gary Gaetti .02 .10
71 Erik Hanson .01 .05
72 Eddie Zosky .01 .05
73 Brian Barnes .01 .05
74 Scott Leius .01 .05
75 Bret Saberhagen .02 .10
76 Mike Gallego .01 .05
77 Jack Armstrong .01 .05
78 Ivan Rodriguez .08 .25
79 Jesse Orosco .01 .05
80 David Justice .02 .10
81 Ced Landrum .01 .05
82 Doug Simons .01 .05
83 Tommy Greene .01 .05
84 Leo Gomez .01 .05
85 Jose DeLeon .01 .05
86 Steve Finley .02 .10
87 Bob MacDonald .01 .05
88 Darrin Jackson .01 .05
89 Neal Heaton .01 .05
90 Robin Yount .15 .40
91 Jeff Reed .01 .05
92 Lenny Harris .01 .05
93 Reggie Jefferson .01 .05
94 Sammy Sosa .08 .25
95 Scott Bailes .01 .05
96 Tom McKinnon RC .02 .10
97 Luis Rivera .01 .05
98 Mike Harkey .01 .05
99 Jeff Treadway .01 .05
100 Jose Canseco .05 .15
101 Omar Vizquel .05 .15
102 Scott Kamieniecki .01 .05
103 Ricky Jordan .01 .05
104 Jeff Ballard .01 .05
105 Felix Jose .01 .05
106 Mike Boddicker .01 .05
107 Dan Pasqua .01 .05
108 Mike Timlin .01 .05
109 Roger Craig MG .01 .05
110 Ryne Sandberg .15 .40
111 Mark Carreon .01 .05
112 Oscar Azocar .01 .05
113 Mike Greenwell .01 .05
114 Mark Portugal .01 .05
115 Terry Pendleton .02 .10
116 Willie Randolph .02 .10
117 Scott Terry .01 .05
118 Chili Davis .02 .10
119 Mark Gardner .01 .05
120 Alan Trammell .02 .10
121 Derek Bell .02 .10
122 Gary Varsho .01 .05
123 Bob Ojeda .01 .05
124 Shawn Livsey RC .02 .10
125 Chris Hoiles .01 .05
126 Klesko/Jaha/Brogna/Staton .08 .25
127 Carlos Quintana .01 .05
128 Kurt Stillwell .01 .05
129 Melido Perez .01 .05
130 Alvin Davis .01 .05
131 Checklist 1-132 .01 .05
132 Eric Show .01 .05
133 Rance Mulliniks .01 .05
134 Darryl Kile .02 .10
135 Von Hayes .01 .05
136 Bill Doran .01 .05
137 Jeff D. Robinson .01 .05
138 Monty Fariss .01 .05
139 Jeff Innis .01 .05
140 Mark Grace UER .05 .15
Home Calie., should
be Calif.
141 Jim Leyland MG UER .02 .10
No closed parenthesis
after East in 1991
142 Todd Van Poppel .01 .05
143 Paul Gibson .01 .05
144 Bill Swift .01 .05
145 Danny Tartabull .01 .05
146 Al Newman .01 .05
147 Cris Carpenter .01 .05
148 Anthony Young .01 .05
149 Brian Bohanon .01 .05
150 Roger Clemens UER .20 .50
151 Jeff Hamilton .01 .05
152 Charlie Leibrandt .01 .05
153 Ron Karkovice .01 .05
154 Hensley Meulens .01 .05
155 Scott Bankhead .01 .05
156 Manny Ramirez RC 2.00 5.00
157 Keith Miller .01 .05
158 Todd Frohwirth .01 .05
159 Darrin Fletcher .01 .05
160 Bobby Bonilla .02 .10
161 Casey Candaele .01 .05
162 Paul Faries .01 .05
163 Dana Kiecker .01 .05
164 Shane Mack .01 .05
165 Mark Langston .01 .05
166 Geronimo Pena .01 .05
167 Andy Allanson .01 .05
168 Dwight Smith .01 .05
169 Chuck Crim .01 .05
170 Alex Cole .01 .05
171 Bill Plummer MG .01 .05
172 Juan Berenguer .01 .05
173 Brian Downing .01 .05
174 Steve Frey .01 .05
175 Orel Hershiser .02 .10
176 Ramon Garcia .01 .05
177 Dan Gladden .01 .05
178 Jim Acker .01 .05
179 DeJard/Bern/Moreno/Stank .01 .05
180 Kevin Mitchell .01 .05
181 Hector Villanueva .01 .05
182 Jeff Reardon .02 .10
183 Brent Mayne .01 .05
184 Jimmy Jones .01 .05
185 Benito Santiago .02 .10
186 Cliff Floyd RC .30 .75
187 Ernie Riles .01 .05
188 Jose Guzman .01 .05
189 Junior Felix .01 .05
190 Glenn Davis .01 .05
191 Charlie Hough .02 .10
192 Dave Fleming .01 .05
193 Omar Olivares .01 .05
194 Eric Karros .02 .10
195 David Cone .02 .10
196 Frank Castillo .01 .05
197 Glenn Braggs .01 .05
198 Scott Aldred .01 .05
199 Jeff Blauser .01 .05
200 Len Dykstra .02 .10
201 Buck Showalter MG RC .08 .25
202 Rick Honeycutt .01 .05
203 Greg Myers .01 .05
204 Trevor Wilson .01 .05
205 Jay Howell .01 .05
206 Luis Sojo .01 .05
207 Jack Clark .02 .10
208 Julio Machado .01 .05
209 Lloyd McClendon .01 .05
210 Ozzie Guillen .02 .10
211 Jeremy Hernandez RC .02 .10
212 Randy Velarde .01 .05
213 Les Lancaster .01 .05
214 Andy Mota .01 .05
215 Rich Gossage .02 .10
216 Brent Gates RC .02 .10
217 Brian Harper .01 .05
218 Mike Flanagan .01 .05
219 Jerry Browne .01 .05
220 Jose Rijo .01 .05
221 Skeeter Barnes .01 .05
222 Jaime Navarro .01 .05
223 Mel Hall .01 .05
224 Bret Barberie .01 .05
225 Roberto Alomar .05 .15
226 Pete Smith .01 .05
227 Daryl Boston .01 .05
228 Eddie Whitson .01 .05
229 Shawn Boskie .01 .05
230 Dick Schofield .01 .05
231 Brian Drahman .01 .05
232 John Smiley .01 .05
233 Mitch Webster .01 .05
234 Terry Steinbach .01 .05
235 Jack Morris .02 .10
236 Bill Pecota .01 .05
237 Jose Hernandez RC .08 .25
238 Greg Litton .01 .05
239 Brian Holman .01 .05
240 Andres Galarraga .02 .10
241 Gerald Young .01 .05
242 Mike Mussina .08 .25
243 Alvaro Espinoza .01 .05
244 Darren Daulton .02 .10
245 John Smoltz .05 .15
246 Jason Pruitt RC .02 .10
247 Chuck Finley .02 .10
248 Jim Gantner .01 .05
249 Tony Fossas .01 .05
250 Ken Griffey Sr. .02 .10
251 Kevin Elster .01 .05
252 Dennis Rasmussen .01 .05
253 Terry Kennedy .01 .05
254 Ryan Bowen .01 .05
255 Robin Ventura .02 .10
256 Mike Aldrete .01 .05
257 Jeff Russell .01 .05
258 Jim Lindeman .01 .05
259 Ron Darling .01 .05
260 Devon White .02 .10
261 Tom Lasorda MG .02 .10
262 Terry Lee .01 .05
263 Bob Patterson .01 .05
264 Checklist 133-264 .01 .05
265 Teddy Higuera .01 .05
266 Roberto Kelly .01 .05
267 Steve Bedrosian .01 .05
268 Brady Anderson .02 .10
269 Ruben Amaro .01 .05
270 Tony Gwynn .10 .30
271 Tracy Jones .01 .05
272 Jerry Don Gleaton .01 .05
273 Craig Grebeck .01 .05
274 Bob Scanlan .01 .05
275 Todd Zeile .01 .05
276 Shawn Green RC .40 1.00
277 Scott Chiamparino .01 .05
278 Darryl Hamilton .01 .05
279 Jim Clancy .01 .05
280 Carlos Martinez .01 .05
281 Kevin Appier .02 .10
282 John Wehner .01 .05
283 Reggie Sanders .02 .10
284 Gene Larkin .01 .05
285 Bob Welch .01 .05
286 Gilberto Reyes .01 .05
287 Pete Schourek .01 .05
288 Andujar Cedeno .01 .05
289 Mike Morgan .01 .05
290 Bo Jackson .08 .25
291 Phil Garner MG .02 .10
292 Ray Lankford .02 .10
293 Mike Henneman .01 .05
294 Dave Valle .01 .05
295 Alonzo Powell .01 .05
296 Tom Brunansky .01 .05
297 Kevin Brown .02 .10
298 Kelly Gruber .01 .05
299 Charles Nagy .01 .05
300 Don Mattingly .25 .60
301 Kirk McCaskill .01 .05
302 Joey Cora .01 .05
303 Dan Plesac .01 .05
304 Joe Oliver .01 .05
305 Tom Glavine .05 .15
306 Al Shirley RC .02 .10
307 Bruce Ruffin .01 .05
308 Craig Shipley .01 .05
309 Dave Martinez .01 .05
310 Jose Mesa .01 .05
311 Henry Cotto .01 .05
312 Mike LaValliere .01 .05
313 Kevin Tapani .01 .05
314 Jeff Huson .01 .05
315 Juan Samuel .01 .05
316 Curt Schilling .05 .15
317 Mike Bordick .01 .05
318 Steve Howe .01 .05
319 Tony Phillips .01 .05
320 George Bell .01 .05
321 Lou Piniella MG .02 .10
322 Tim Burke .01 .05
323 Milt Thompson .01 .05
324 Danny Darwin .01 .05
325 Joe Orsulak .01 .05
326 Eric King .01 .05
327 Jay Buhner .02 .10
328 Joel Johnston .01 .05
329 Franklin Stubbs .01 .05
330 Will Clark .05 .15
331 Steve Lake .01 .05
332 Chris Jones .01 .05
333 Pat Tabler .01 .05
334 Kevin Gross .01 .05
335 Dave Henderson .01 .05
336 Greg Anthony RC .02 .10
337 Alejandro Pena .01 .05
338 Shawn Abner .01 .05
339 Tom Browning .01 .05
340 Otis Nixon .01 .05
341 Bob Geren .01 .05
342 Tim Spehr .01 .05
343 John Vander Wal .01 .05
344 Jack Daugherty .01 .05
345 Zane Smith .01 .05
346 Rheal Cormier .01 .05
347 Kent Hrbek .02 .10
348 Rick Wilkins .01 .05
349 Steve Lyons .01 .05
350 Gregg Olson .01 .05
351 Greg Riddoch MG .01 .05
352 Ed Nunez .01 .05
353 Braulio Castillo .01 .05
354 Dave Bergman .01 .05
355 Warren Newson .01 .05
356 Luis Quinones .01 .05
357 Mike Witt .01 .05
358 Ted Wood .01 .05
359 Mike Moore .01 .05
360 Lance Parrish .02 .10
361 Barry Jones .01 .05
362 Javier Ortiz .01 .05
363 John Candelaria .01 .05
364 Glenallen Hill .01 .05
365 Duane Ward .01 .05
366 Checklist 265-396 .01 .05
367 Rafael Belliard .01 .05
368 Bill Krueger .01 .05
369 Steve Whitaker RC .02 .10
370 Shawon Dunston .01 .05
371 Dante Bichette .02 .10
372 Kip Gross .01 .05
373 Don Robinson .01 .05
374 Bernie Williams .05 .15
375 Bert Blyleven .02 .10
376 Chris Donnels .01 .05
377 Bob Zupcic RC .02 .10
378 Joel Skinner .01 .05
379 Steve Chitren .01 .05
380 Barry Bonds .40 1.00
381 Sparky Anderson MG .02 .10
382 Sid Fernandez .01 .05
383 Dave Hollins .01 .05
384 Mark Lee .01 .05
385 Tim Wallach .01 .05
386 Will Clark AS .02 .10
387 Ryne Sandberg AS .08 .25
388 Howard Johnson AS .01 .05
389 Barry Larkin AS .02 .10
390 Barry Bonds AS .20 .50
391 Ron Gant AS .01 .05
392 Bobby Bonilla AS .01 .05
393 Craig Biggio AS .02 .10
394 Dennis Martinez AS .01 .05
395 Tom Glavine AS .02 .10
396 Lee Smith AS .01 .05
397 Cecil Fielder AS .01 .05
398 Julio Franco AS .01 .05
399 Wade Boggs AS .02 .10
400 Cal Ripken AS .15 .40
401 Jose Canseco AS .05 .15
402 Joe Carter AS .01 .05
403 Ruben Sierra AS .01 .05
404 Matt Nokes AS .01 .05
405 Roger Clemens AS .08 .25
406 Jim Abbott AS .02 .10
407 Bryan Harvey AS .01 .05
408 Bob Milacki .01 .05
409 Geno Petralli .01 .05
410 Dave Stewart .02 .10
411 Mike Jackson .01 .05
412 Luis Aquino .01 .05
413 Tim Teufel .01 .05
414 Jeff Ware .01 .05
415 Jim Deshaies .01 .05
416 Ellis Burks .02 .10
417 Allan Anderson .01 .05
418 Alfredo Griffin .01 .05
419 Wally Whitehurst .01 .05
420 Sandy Alomar Jr. .01 .05
421 Juan Agosto .01 .05
422 Sam Horn .01 .05
423 Jeff Fassero .01 .05
424 Paul McClellan .01 .05
425 Cecil Fielder .02 .10
426 Tim Raines .02 .10
427 Eddie Taubensee RC .08 .25
428 Dennis Boyd .01 .05
429 Tony LaRussa MG .02 .10
430 Steve Sax .01 .05
431 Tom Gordon .01 .05
432 Billy Hatcher .01 .05
433 Cal Eldred .01 .05
434 Wally Backman .01 .05
435 Mark Eichhorn .01 .05
436 Mookie Wilson .02 .10
437 Scott Servais .01 .05
438 Mike Maddux .01 .05
439 Chico Walker .01 .05
440 Doug Drabek .01 .05
441 Rob Deer .01 .05
442 Dave West .01 .05
443 Spike Owen .01 .05
444 Tyrone Hill RC .02 .10
445 Matt Williams .02 .10
446 Mark Lewis .01 .05
447 David Segui .01 .05
448 Tom Pagnozzi .01 .05
449 Jeff Johnson .01 .05
450 Mark McGwire .25 .60
451 Tom Henke .01 .05
452 Wilson Alvarez .01 .05
453 Gary Redus .01 .05
454 Darren Holmes .01 .05
455 Pete O'Brien .01 .05
456 Pat Combs .01 .05
457 Hubie Brooks .01 .05
458 Frank Tanana .01 .05
459 Tom Kelly MG .01 .05
460 Andre Dawson .02 .10
461 Doug Jones .01 .05
462 Rich Rodriguez .01 .05
463 Mike Simms .01 .05
464 Mike Jeffcoat .01 .05
465 Barry Larkin .05 .15
466 Stan Belinda .01 .05
467 Lonnie Smith .01 .05
468 Greg Harris .01 .05
469 Jim Eisenreich .01 .05
470 Pedro Guerrero .02 .10
471 Jose DeJesus .01 .05
472 Rich Rowland RC .02 .10
473 Bolick/Paquette/Red/Russo .01 .05
474 Mike Rossiter RC .02 .10
475 Robby Thompson .01 .05
476 Randy Bush .01 .05
477 Greg Hibbard .01 .05
478 Dale Sveum .01 .05
479 Chito Martinez .01 .05
480 Scott Sanderson .01 .05
481 Tino Martinez .05 .15
482 Jimmy Key .02 .10
483 Terry Shumpert .01 .05
484 Mike Hartley .01 .05
485 Chris Sabo .01 .05
486 Bob Walk .01 .05
487 John Cerutti .01 .05
488 Scott Cooper .01 .05
489 Bobby Cox MG .02 .10
490 Julio Franco .02 .10
491 Jeff Brantley .01 .05
492 Mike Devereaux .01 .05
493 Jose Offerman .01 .05
494 Gary Thurman .01 .05
495 Carney Lansford .02 .10
496 Joe Grahe .01 .05
497 Andy Ashby .01 .05
498 Gerald Perry .01 .05
499 Dave Otto .01 .05
500 Vince Coleman .01 .05
501 Rob Mallicoat .01 .05
502 Greg Briley .01 .05
503 Pascual Perez .01 .05
504 Aaron Sele RC .08 .25
505 Bobby Thigpen .01 .05
506 Todd Benzinger .01 .05
507 Candy Maldonado .01 .05
508 Bill Gullickson .01 .05
509 Doug Dascenzo .01 .05
510 Frank Viola .02 .10
511 Kenny Rogers .02 .10
512 Mike Heath .01 .05
513 Kevin Bass .01 .05
514 Kim Batiste .01 .05
515 Delino DeShields .01 .05
516 Ed Sprague .01 .05
517 Jim Gott .01 .05
518 Jose Melendez .01 .05
519 Hal McRae MG .02 .10
520 Jeff Bagwell .08 .25
521 Joe Hesketh .01 .05
522 Milt Cuyler .01 .05
523 Shawn Hillegas .01 .05
524 Don Slaught .01 .05
525 Randy Johnson .08 .25
526 Doug Piatt .01 .05
527 Checklist 397-528 .01 .05
528 Steve Foster .01 .05
529 Joe Girardi .01 .05
530 Jim Abbott .05 .15
531 Larry Walker .05 .15
532 Mike Huff .01 .05
533 Mackey Sasser .01 .05
534 Benji Gil RC .08 .25
535 Dave Stieb .01 .05
536 Willie Wilson .01 .05
537 Mark Leiter .01 .05
538 Jose Uribe .01 .05
539 Thomas Howard .01 .05
540 Ben McDonald .01 .05
541 Jose Tolentino .01 .05
542 Keith Mitchell .01 .05
543 Jerome Walton .01 .05
544 Cliff Brantley .01 .05
545 Andy Van Slyke .05 .15
546 Paul Sorrento .01 .05
547 Herm Winningham .01 .05
548 Mark Guthrie .01 .05
549 Joe Torre MG .02 .10
550 Darryl Strawberry .02 .10
551 Chipper Jones .08 .25
552 Dave Gallagher .01 .05
553 Edgar Martinez .05 .15
554 Donald Harris .01 .05
555 Frank Thomas .08 .25
556 Storm Davis .01 .05
557 Dickie Thon .01 .05
558 Scott Garrelts .01 .05
559 Steve Olin .01 .05
560 Rickey Henderson .08 .25
561 Jose Vizcaino .01 .05
562 Wade Taylor .01 .05
563 Pat Borders .01 .05
564 Jimmy Gonzalez RC .02 .10
565 Lee Smith .02 .10
566 Bill Sampen .01 .05
567 Dean Palmer .02 .10
568 Bryan Harvey .01 .05
569 Tony Pena .01 .05
570 Lou Whitaker .02 .10
571 Randy Tomlin .01 .05
572 Greg Vaughn .01 .05
573 Kelly Downs .01 .05
574 Steve Avery UER .01 .05
Should be 13 games
for Durham in 1989
575 Kirby Puckett .08 .25
576 Heathcliff Slocumb .01 .05
577 Kevin Seitzer .01 .05
578 Lee Guetterman .01 .05
579 Johnny Oates MG .01 .05
580 Greg Maddux .15 .40
581 Stan Javier .01 .05
582 Vicente Palacios .01 .05
583 Mel Rojas .01 .05
584 Wayne Rosenthal RC .02 .10
585 Lenny Webster .01 .05
586 Rod Nichols .01 .05
587 Mickey Morandini .01 .05
588 Russ Swan .01 .05
589 Mariano Duncan .01 .05
590 Howard Johnson .01 .05
591 Burnitz/Brum/Coc/Dozier .02 .10
592 Denny Neagle .02 .10
593 Steve Decker .01 .05
594 Brian Barber RC .02 .10
595 Bruce Hurst .01 .05
596 Kent Mercker .01 .05
597 Mike Magnante RC .02 .10
598 Jody Reed .01 .05
599 Steve Searcy .01 .05
600 Paul Molitor .02 .10
601 Dave Smith .01 .05
602 Mike Fetters .01 .05
603 Luis Mercedes .01 .05
604 Chris Gwynn .01 .05
605 Scott Erickson .01 .05
606 Brook Jacoby .01 .05
607 Todd Stottlemyre .01 .05
608 Scott Bradley .01 .05
609 Mike Hargrove MG .02 .10
610 Eric Davis .02 .10
611 Brian Hunter .01 .05
612 Pat Kelly .01 .05
613 Pedro Munoz .01 .05
614 Al Osuna .01 .05
615 Matt Merullo .01 .05
616 Larry Andersen .01 .05
617 Junior Ortiz .01 .05
618 Hern/Hosey/McNeely/Pelt .01 .05
619 Danny Jackson .01 .05
620 George Brett .25 .60
621 Dan Gakeler .01 .05
622 Steve Buechele .01 .05
623 Bob Tewksbury .01 .05
624 Shawn Estes RC .08 .25
625 Kevin McReynolds .01 .05
626 Chris Haney .01 .05
627 Mike Sharperson .01 .05
628 Mark Williamson .01 .05
629 Wally Joyner .02 .10
630 Carlton Fisk .05 .15
631 Armando Reynoso RC .08 .25
632 Felix Fermin .01 .05
633 Mitch Williams .01 .05
634 Manuel Lee .01 .05
635 Harold Baines .02 .10
636 Greg Harris .01 .05
637 Orlando Merced .01 .05
638 Chris Bosio .01 .05
639 Wayne Housie .01 .05
640 Xavier Hernandez .01 .05
641 David Howard .01 .05
642 Tim Crews .01 .05
643 Rick Cerone .01 .05
644 Terry Leach .01 .05
645 Deion Sanders .05 .15
646 Craig Wilson .01 .05
647 Marquis Grissom .02 .10
648 Scott Fletcher .01 .05
649 Norm Charlton .01 .05
650 Jesse Barfield .01 .05
651 Joe Slusarski .01 .05
652 Bobby Rose .01 .05
653 Dennis Lamp .01 .05
654 Allen Watson RC .02 .10
655 Brett Butler .02 .10
656 Pem/H.Rod/Tinsley/G.Will .02 .10
657 Dave Johnson .01 .05
658 Checklist 529-660 .01 .05
659 Brian McRae .01 .05
660 Fred McGriff .05 .15
661 Bill Landrum .01 .05
662 Juan Guzman .01 .05
663 Greg Gagne .01 .05
664 Ken Hill .01 .05
665 Dave Haas .01 .05
666 Tom Foley .01 .05
667 Roberto Hernandez .01 .05
668 Dwayne Henry .01 .05
669 Jim Fregosi MG .01 .05
670 Harold Reynolds .02 .10
671 Mark Whiten .01 .05
672 Eric Plunk .01 .05
673 Todd Hundley .01 .05
674 Mo Sanford .01 .05
675 Bobby Witt .01 .05
676 Mil/Mahomes/Wendell/Salk .08 .25
677 John Marzano .01 .05
678 Joe Klink .01 .05
679 Pete Incaviglia .01 .05
680 Dale Murphy .05 .15
681 Rene Gonzales .01 .05
682 Andy Benes .01 .05
683 Jim Poole .01 .05
684 Trever Miller RC .02 .10
685 Scott Livingstone .01 .05
686 Rich DeLucia .01 .05
687 Harvey Pulliam .01 .05
688 Tim Belcher .01 .05
689 Mark Lemke .01 .05
690 John Franco .02 .10
691 Walt Weiss .01 .05
692 Scott Ruskin .01 .05
693 Jeff King .01 .05
694 Mike Gardiner .01 .05
695 Gary Sheffield .02 .10
696 Joe Boever .01 .05
697 Mike Felder .01 .05
698 John Habyan .01 .05
699 Cito Gaston MG .01 .05
700 Ruben Sierra .02 .10
701 Scott Radinsky .01 .05
702 Lee Stevens .01 .05
703 Mark Wohlers .01 .05
704 Curt Young .01 .05
705 Dwight Evans .05 .15
706 Rob Murphy .01 .05
707 Gregg Jefferies .01 .05
708 Tom Bolton .01 .05
709 Chris James .01 .05
710 Kevin Maas .01 .05
711 Ricky Bones .01 .05
712 Curt Wilkerson .01 .05
713 Roger McDowell .01 .05
714 Pokey Reese RC .08 .25
715 Craig Biggio .05 .15
716 Kirk Dressendorfer .01 .05
717 Ken Dayley .01 .05
718 B.J. Surhoff .02 .10
719 Terry Mulholland .01 .05
720 Kirk Gibson .02 .10
721 Mike Pagliarulo .01 .05
722 Walt Terrell .01 .05
723 Jose Oquendo .01 .05
724 Kevin Morton .01 .05
725 Dwight Gooden .02 .10
726 Kirt Manwaring .01 .05
727 Chuck McElroy .01 .05
728 Dave Burba .01 .05
729 Art Howe MG .01 .05
730 Ramon Martinez .01 .05
731 Donnie Hill .01 .05
732 Nelson Santovenia .01 .05
733 Bob Melvin .01 .05
734 Scott Hatteberg RC .08 .25
735 Greg Swindell .01 .05
736 Lance Johnson .01 .05
737 Kevin Reimer .01 .05
738 Dennis Eckersley .02 .10
739 Rob Ducey .01 .05
740 Ken Caminiti .02 .10
741 Mark Gubicza .01 .05
742 Bill Spiers .01 .05
743 Darren Lewis .01 .05
744 Chris Hammond .01 .05
745 Dave Magadan .01 .05
746 Bernard Gilkey .01 .05
747 Willie Banks .01 .05
748 Matt Nokes .01 .05
749 Jerald Clark .01 .05
750 Travis Fryman .02 .10
751 Steve Wilson .01 .05
752 Billy Ripken .01 .05
753 Paul Assenmacher .01 .05
754 Charlie Hayes .01 .05
755 Alex Fernandez .01 .05
756 Gary Pettis .01 .05
757 Rob Dibble .02 .10
758 Tim Naehring .01 .05
759 Jeff Torborg MG .01 .05
760 Ozzie Smith .15 .40
761 Mike Fitzgerald .01 .05
762 John Burkett .01 .05
763 Kyle Abbott .01 .05
764 Tyler Green RC .02 .10
765 Pete Harnisch .01 .05
766 Mark Davis .01 .05
767 Kal Daniels .01 .05
768 Jim Thome .08 .25
769 Jack Howell .01 .05
770 Sid Bream .01 .05
771 Arthur Rhodes .01 .05
772 Garry Templeton UER .01 .05
Stat heading in for pitchers
773 Hal Morris .01 .05
774 Bud Black .01 .05
775 Ivan Calderon .01 .05
776 Doug Henry RC .02 .10
777 John Olerud .02 .10
778 Tim Leary .01 .05
779 Jay Bell .02 .10
780 Eddie Murray .08 .25
781 Paul Abbott .01 .05
782 Phil Plantier .01 .05
783 Joe Magrane .01 .05
784 Ken Patterson .01 .05
785 Albert Belle .02 .10
786 Royce Clayton .01 .05
787 Checklist 661-792 .01 .05
788 Mike Stanton .01 .05
789 Bobby Valentine MG .01 .05
790 Joe Carter .02 .10
791 Danny Cox .01 .05
792 Dave Winfield .02 .10

1992 Topps Gold

COMPLETE SET (792) 30.00 80.00
COMP.FACT.SET (793) 30.00 80.00
*STARS: 6X TO 15X BASIC CARDS
*ROOKIES: 4X TO 10X BASIC CARDS
RANDOM INSERTS IN PACKS
TEN PER BASIC FACTORY SET
131 Terry Mathews .30 .75
264 Rod Beck .30 .75
366 Tony Perezchica .30 .75
527 Terry McDaniel .30 .75
658 John Ramos .30 .75
787 Brian Williams .30 .75
793 Brien Taylor AU/12000 5.00 12.00

1992 Topps Gold Winners

COMPLETE SET (792) 15.00 40.00
*STARS: 1.25X TO 3X BASIC CARDS
*ROOKIES: 1.25X TO 3X BASIC CARDS
REDEEMED WITH WINNING GAME CARDS
131 Terry Mathews .05 .15
264 Rod Beck .05 .15
366 Tony Perezchica .05 .15
527 Terry McDaniel .05 .15
658 John Ramos .05 .15
787 Brian Williams .05 .15

1992 Topps Micro

This 804 card parallel set was issued in factory set form only. The set is an exact replica of the regular issue 1992 Topps set (not including the Traded set).The cards, however, measure considerably smaller (1" by 1 3/8") than the regular cards. The set also includes 12 special gold foil parallel mini cards which are listed below. Please refer to the multipliers provided for values on the other singles.

COMPLETE FACT.SET (802) 12.50 30.00
COMMON GOLD INSERT .04 .10
*STARS: .4X TO 1X BASIC CARDS
G1 Nolan Ryan RB 1.00 2.50
G2 Rickey Henderson RB .20 .50
G10 Wade Boggs Gold .20 .50
G50 Ken Griffey Jr. 1.25 3.00
G100 Jose Canseco .20 .50
G270 Tony Gwynn .50 1.25
G300 Don Mattingly .50 1.25
G380 Barry Bonds .20 .50
G397 Cecil Fielder AS .02 .10
G403 Ruben Sierra AS .02 .10
G460 Andre Dawson .15 .40
G725 Dwight Gooden .07 .20

1992 Topps Traded

The 1992 Topps Traded set comprises 132 standard-size cards. The set was distributed exclusively in factory set form through hobby dealers. As in past editions, the set focuses on promising rookies, new managers, and players who changed teams. The set also includes a Team U.S.A. subset, featuring 25 of America's top college players and the Team U.S.A. coach. Card design is identical to the regular issue 1992 Topps cards except for the T-suffixed numbering. The cards are arranged in alphabetical order by player's last name. The key Rookie Cards in this set are Nomar Garciaparra, Brian Jordan and Jason Varitek.

COMP.FACT.SET (132) 10.00 25.00
1T Willie Adams USA RC .08 .25
2T Jeff Alkire USA RC .08 .25
3T Felipe Alou MG .07 .20
4T Moises Alou .07 .20
5T Ruben Amaro .02 .10
6T Jack Armstrong .02 .10
7T Scott Bankhead .02 .10
8T Tim Belcher .02 .10
9T George Bell .02 .10
10T Freddie Benavides .02 .10
11T Todd Benzinger .02 .10
12T Joe Boever .02 .10
13T Ricky Bones .02 .10
14T Bobby Bonilla .07 .20
15T Hubie Brooks .02 .10
16T Jerry Browne .02 .10
17T Jim Bullinger .02 .10
18T Dave Burba .02 .10
19T Kevin Campbell .02 .10
20T Tom Candiotti .02 .10
21T Mark Carreon .02 .10
22T Gary Carter .07 .20
23T Archi Cianfrocco RC .02 .10
24T Phil Clark .02 .10
25T Chad Curtis RC .15 .40
26T Eric Davis .07 .20
27T Tim Davis USA RC .08 .25
28T Gary DiSarcina .02 .10
29T Darren Dreifort USA .02 .10
30T Mariano Duncan .02 .10
31T Mike Fitzgerald .02 .10
32T John Flaherty RC .02 .10
33T Darrin Fletcher .02 .10
34T Scott Fletcher .02 .10
35T Ron Fraser USA CO RC .08 .25
36T Andres Galarraga .07 .20
37T Dave Gallagher .02 .10
38T Mike Gallego .02 .10
39T Nomar Garciaparra USA RC 5.00 12.00
40T Jason Giambi USA .40 1.00
41T Danny Gladden .02 .10
42T Rene Gonzales .02 .10
43T Jeff Granger USA .02 .10
44T Rick Greene USA RC .08 .25
45T Jeffrey Hammonds USA .07 .20
46T Charlie Hayes .02 .10
47T Von Hayes .02 .10
48T Rick Helling USA .02 .10
49T Butch Henry RC .02 .10
50T Carlos Hernandez .02 .10
51T Ken Hill .02 .10
52T Butch Hobson .02 .10
53T Vince Horsman .02 .10
54T Pete Incaviglia .02 .10
55T Gregg Jefferies .02 .10
56T Charles Johnson USA .07 .20
57T Doug Jones .02 .10
58T Brian Jordan RC .30 .75
59T Wally Joyner .07 .20
60T Daron Kirkreit USA RC .08 .25
61T Bill Krueger .02 .10
62T Gene Lamont MG .02 .10
63T Jim Lefebvre MG .02 .10
64T Danny Leon .02 .10
65T Pat Listach RC .15 .40
66T Kenny Lofton .10 .30
67T Dave Martinez .02 .10
68T Derrick May .02 .10
69T Kirk McCaskill .02 .10
70T Chad McConnell USA RC .08 .25
71T Kevin McReynolds .02 .10
72T Rusty Meacham .02 .10
73T Keith Miller .02 .10
74T Kevin Mitchell .02 .10
75T Jason Moler USA RC .08 .25
76T Mike Morgan .02 .10
77T Jack Morris .07 .20
78T Calvin Murray USA RC .30 .75
79T Eddie Murray .20 .50
80T Randy Myers .02 .10
81T Denny Neagle .07 .20
82T Phil Nevin USA .02 .10
83T Dave Nilsson .02 .10
84T Junior Ortiz .02 .10
85T Donovan Osborne .02 .10
86T Bill Pecota .02 .10
87T Melido Perez .02 .10
88T Mike Perez .02 .10
89T Hipolito Pichardo RC .02 .10
90T Willie Randolph .07 .20
91T Darren Reed .02 .10
92T Bip Roberts .02 .10
93T Chris Roberts USA .02 .10
94T Steve Rodriguez USA .02 .10
95T Bruce Ruffin .02 .10
96T Scott Ruskin .02 .10
97T Bret Saberhagen .07 .20
98T Rey Sanchez RC .15 .40
99T Steve Sax .02 .10
100T Curt Schilling .10 .30
101T Dick Schofield .02 .10
102T Gary Scott .02 .10
103T Kevin Seitzer .02 .10
104T Frank Seminara RC .02 .10
105T Gary Sheffield .07 .20
106T John Smiley .02 .10
107T Cory Snyder .02 .10
108T Paul Sorrento .02 .10
109T Sammy Sosa Cubs .60 1.50
110T Matt Stairs RC .20 .50
111T Andy Stankiewicz .02 .10
112T Kurt Stillwell .02 .10
113T Rick Sutcliffe .07 .20
114T Bill Swift .02 .10
115T Jeff Tackett .02 .10
116T Danny Tartabull .02 .10
117T Eddie Taubensee .07 .20
118T Dickie Thon .02 .10
119T Michael Tucker USA RC .30 .75
120T Scooter Tucker .02 .10
121T Marc Valdes USA RC .08 .25
122T Julio Valera .02 .10
123T Jason Varitek USA RC 5.00 12.00
124T Ron Villone USA RC .08 .25
125T Frank Viola .07 .20
126T B.J.Wallace USA RC .08 .25
127T Dan Walters .02 .10
128T Craig Wilson USA .02 .10
129T Chris Wimmer USA .02 .10
130T Dave Winfield .07 .20
131T Herm Winningham .02 .10
132T Checklist 1T-132T .02 .10

1992 Topps Traded Gold

COMP.FACT.SET (132) 15.00 40.00
*GOLD STARS: 1.5X TO 4X BASIC CARDS
*GOLD RC's: .75X TO 2X BASIC CARDS
GOLD SOLD ONLY IN FACTORY SET FORM

1993 Topps

The 1993 Topps baseball set consists of two series, respectively, of 396 and 429 standard-size cards. A Topps Gold card was inserted in every 15-card pack. In addition, hobby and retail factory sets were produced. The fronts feature color action player photos with white borders. The player's name appears in a stripe at the bottom of the picture, and this stripe and two short diagonal stripes at the bottom corners of the picture are team color-coded. The backs are colorful and carry a color head shot, biography, complete statistical information, with a career highlight if space permitted. Cards 401-411 comprise an All-Star subset. Rookie Cards in this set include Jim Edmonds, Derek Jeter and Jason Kendall.

COMPLETE SET (825) 20.00 50.00
COMP.HOBBY.SET (847) 20.00 50.00
COMP.RETAIL.SET (838) 20.00 50.00
COMPLETE SERIES 1 (396) 10.00 25.00
COMPLETE SERIES 2 (429) 10.00 25.00
1 Robin Yount .30 .75
2 Barry Bonds .60 1.50
3 Ryne Sandberg .30 .75
4 Roger Clemens .40 1.00
5 Tony Gwynn .25 .60
6 Jeff Tackett .02 .10
7 Pete Incaviglia .02 .10
8 Mark Wohlers .02 .10
9 Kent Hrbek .07 .20
10 Will Clark .10 .30
11 Eric Karros .07 .20
12 Lee Smith .07 .20
13 Esteban Beltre .02 .10
14 Greg Briley .02 .10
15 Marquis Grissom .07 .20
16 Dan Plesac .02 .10
17 Dave Hollins .02 .10
18 Terry Steinbach .02 .10
19 Ed Nunez .02 .10
20 Tim Salmon .10 .30
21 Luis Salazar .02 .10
22 Jim Eisenreich .02 .10
23 Todd Stottlemyre .02 .10
24 Tim Naehring .02 .10
25 John Franco .07 .20
26 Skeeter Barnes .02 .10
27 Carlos Garcia .02 .10
28 Joe Orsulak .02 .10
29 Dwayne Henry .02 .10
30 Fred McGriff .10 .30
31 Derek Lilliquist .02 .10
32 Don Mattingly .50 1.25
33 B.J. Wallace .02 .10
34 Juan Gonzalez .07 .20
35 John Smoltz .10 .30
36 Scott Servais .02 .10
37 Lenny Webster .02 .10
38 Chris James .02 .10
39 Roger McDowell .02 .10
40 Ozzie Smith .30 .75
41 Alex Fernandez .02 .10
42 Spike Owen .02 .10
43 Ruben Amaro .02 .10
44 Kevin Seitzer .02 .10
45 Dave Fleming .02 .10
46 Eric Fox .02 .10
47 Bob Scanlan .02 .10
48 Bert Blyleven .07 .20
49 Brian McRae .02 .10
50 Roberto Alomar .10 .30
51 Mo Vaughn .07 .20
52 Bobby Bonilla .07 .20
53 Frank Tanana .02 .10
54 Mike LaValliere .02 .10
55 Mark McLemore .02 .10
56 Chad Mottola RC .02 .10
57 Norm Charlton .02 .10
58 Jose Melendez .02 .10
59 Carlos Martinez .02 .10
60 Roberto Kelly .02 .10
61 Gene Larkin .02 .10
62 Rafael Belliard .02 .10
63 Al Osuna .02 .10
64 Scott Chiamparino .02 .10
65 Brett Butler .07 .20
66 John Burkett .02 .10
67 Felix Jose .02 .10
68 Omar Vizquel .10 .30
69 John Vander Wal .02 .10
70 Roberto Hernandez .02 .10
71 Ricky Bones .02 .10
72 Jeff Grotewold .02 .10
73 Mike Moore .02 .10
74 Steve Buechele .02 .10
75 Juan Guzman .02 .10
76 Kevin Appier .07 .20
77 Junior Felix .02 .10
78 Greg W. Harris .02 .10
79 Dick Schofield .02 .10
80 Cecil Fielder .07 .20
81 Lloyd McClendon .02 .10
82 David Segui .02 .10
83 Reggie Sanders .07 .20
84 Kurt Stillwell .02 .10
85 Sandy Alomar Jr. .02 .10
86 John Habyan .02 .10
87 Kevin Reimer .02 .10
88 Mike Stanton .02 .10
89 Eric Anthony .02 .10
90 Scott Erickson .02 .10
91 Craig Colbert .02 .10
92 Tom Pagnozzi .02 .10
93 Pedro Astacio .02 .10
94 Lance Johnson .02 .10
95 Larry Walker .07 .20
96 Russ Swan .02 .10
97 Scott Fletcher .02 .10
98 Derek Jeter RC 10.00 25.00
99 Mike Williams .02 .10
100 Mark McGwire .50 1.25
101 Jim Bullinger .02 .10
102 Brian Hunter .02 .10
103 Jody Reed .02 .10
104 Mike Butcher .02 .10
105 Gregg Jefferies .02 .10
106 Howard Johnson .02 .10
107 John Kiely .02 .10
108 Jose Lind .02 .10
109 Sam Horn .02 .10
110 Barry Larkin .10 .30
111 Bruce Hurst .02 .10
112 Brian Barnes .02 .10
113 Thomas Howard .02 .10
114 Mel Hall .02 .10
115 Robby Thompson .02 .10
116 Mark Lemke .02 .10
117 Eddie Taubensee .02 .10
118 David Hulse RC .02 .10
119 Pedro Munoz .02 .10
120 Ramon Martinez .02 .10
121 Todd Worrell .02 .10
122 Joey Cora .02 .10
123 Moises Alou .07 .20
124 Franklin Stubbs .02 .10
125 Pete O'Brien .02 .10
126 Bob Ayrault .02 .10
127 Carney Lansford .07 .20
128 Kal Daniels .02 .10
129 Joe Grahe .02 .10
130 Jeff Montgomery .02 .10
131 Dave Winfield .07 .20
132 Preston Wilson RC .30 .75
133 Steve Wilson .02 .10
134 Lee Guetterman .02 .10
135 Mickey Tettleton .02 .10
136 Jeff King .02 .10
137 Alan Mills .02 .10
138 Joe Oliver .02 .10
139 Gary Gaetti .07 .20
140 Gary Sheffield .07 .20
141 Dennis Cook .02 .10
142 Charlie Hayes .02 .10
143 Jeff Huson .02 .10
144 Kent Mercker .02 .10
145 Eric Young .02 .10
146 Scott Leius .02 .10
147 Bryan Hickerson .02 .10
148 Steve Finley .07 .20
149 Rheal Cormier .02 .10
150 Frank Thomas UER .20 .50
Categories leading
league are italicized
but not printed in red
151 Archi Cianfrocco .02 .10
152 Rich DeLucia .02 .10
153 Greg Vaughn .02 .10
154 Wes Chamberlain .02 .10
155 Dennis Eckersley .07 .20
156 Sammy Sosa .20 .50
157 Gary DiSarcina .02 .10
158 Kevin Koslofski .02 .10
159 Doug Linton .02 .10
160 Lou Whitaker .07 .20
161 Chad McConnell .02 .10
162 Joe Hesketh .02 .10
163 Tim Wakefield .20 .50
164 Leo Gomez .02 .10
165 Jose Rijo .02 .10
166 Tim Scott .02 .10
167 Steve Olin UER .02 .10
Born 10/4/65
should say 10/10/65
168 Kevin Maas .02 .10
169 Kenny Rogers .07 .20
170 David Justice .07 .20
171 Doug Jones .02 .10
172 Jeff Reboulet .02 .10
173 Andres Galarraga .07 .20
174 Randy Velarde .02 .10
175 Kirk McCaskill .02 .10
176 Darren Lewis .02 .10
177 Lenny Harris .02 .10
178 Jeff Fassero .02 .10
179 Ken Griffey Jr. .40 1.00
180 Darren Daulton .07 .20
181 John Jaha .02 .10
182 Ron Darling .02 .10
183 Greg Maddux .30 .75
184 Damion Easley .02 .10
185 Jack Morris .07 .20
186 Mike Magnante .02 .10
187 John Dopson .02 .10
188 Sid Fernandez .02 .10
189 Tony Phillips .02 .10
190 Doug Drabek .02 .10
191 Sean Lowe RC .02 .10
192 Bob Milacki .02 .10
193 Steve Foster .02 .10
194 Jerald Clark .02 .10
195 Pete Harnisch .02 .10
196 Pat Kelly .02 .10
197 Jeff Frye .02 .10
198 Alejandro Pena .02 .10
199 Junior Ortiz .02 .10
200 Kirby Puckett .20 .50
201 Jose Uribe .02 .10
202 Mike Scioscia .02 .10
203 Bernard Gilkey .02 .10
204 Dan Pasqua .02 .10
205 Gary Carter .07 .20
206 Henry Cotto .02 .10
207 Paul Molitor .07 .20
208 Mike Hartley .02 .10
209 Jeff Parrett .02 .10
210 Mark Langston .02 .10
211 Doug Dascenzo .02 .10
212 Rick Reed .02 .10
213 Candy Maldonado .02 .10
214 Danny Darwin .02 .10
215 Pat Howell .02 .10
216 Mark Leiter .02 .10
217 Kevin Mitchell .02 .10
218 Ben McDonald .02 .10
219 Bip Roberts .02 .10
220 Benny Santiago .07 .20
221 Carlos Baerga .02 .10
222 Bernie Williams .10 .30
223 Roger Pavlik .02 .10
224 Sid Bream .02 .10
225 Matt Williams .07 .20
226 Willie Banks .02 .10
227 Jeff Bagwell .10 .30
228 Tom Goodwin .02 .10
229 Mike Perez .02 .10
230 Carlton Fisk .10 .30
231 John Wetteland .07 .20
232 Tino Martinez .10 .30
233 Rick Greene .02 .10
234 Tim McIntosh .02 .10
235 Mitch Williams .02 .10
236 Kevin Campbell .02 .10
237 Jose Vizcaino .02 .10
238 Chris Donnels .02 .10
239 Mike Boddicker .02 .10
240 John Olerud .07 .20
241 Mike Gardiner .02 .10
242 Charlie O'Brien .02 .10
243 Rob Deer .02 .10
244 Denny Neagle .07 .20
245 Chris Sabo .02 .10
246 Gregg Olson .02 .10
247 Frank Seminara UER .02 .10
Acquired 12/3/98
248 Scott Scudder .02 .10
249 Tim Burke .02 .10
250 Chuck Knoblauch .07 .20
251 Mike Bielecki .02 .10
252 Xavier Hernandez .02 .10
253 Jose Guzman .02 .10
254 Cory Snyder .02 .10
255 Orel Hershiser .07 .20
256 Wil Cordero .02 .10
257 Luis Alicea .02 .10
258 Mike Schooler .02 .10
259 Craig Grebeck .02 .10
260 Duane Ward .02 .10
261 Bill Wegman .02 .10
262 Mickey Morandini .02 .10
263 Vince Horsman .02 .10
264 Paul Sorrento .02 .10
265 Andre Dawson .07 .20
266 Rene Gonzales .02 .10
267 Keith Miller .02 .10
268 Derek Bell .02 .10
269 Todd Steverson RC .02 .10
270 Frank Viola .07 .20
271 Wally Whitehurst .02 .10
272 Kurt Knudsen .02 .10
273 Dan Walters .02 .10
274 Rick Sutcliffe .07 .20
275 Andy Van Slyke .10 .30
276 Paul O'Neill .10 .30
277 Mark Whiten .02 .10
278 Chris Nabholz .02 .10
279 Todd Burns .02 .10
280 Tom Glavine .10 .30
281 Butch Henry .02 .10
282 Shane Mack .02 .10
283 Mike Jackson .02 .10
284 Henry Rodriguez .02 .10
285 Bob Tewksbury .02 .10
286 Ron Karkovice .02 .10
287 Mike Gallego .02 .10
288 Dave Cochrane .02 .10
289 Jesse Orosco .02 .10
290 Dave Stewart .07 .20
291 Tommy Greene .02 .10
292 Rey Sanchez .02 .10
293 Rob Ducey .02 .10
294 Brent Mayne .02 .10
295 Dave Stieb .02 .10
296 Luis Rivera .02 .10
297 Jeff Innis .02 .10
298 Scott Livingstone .02 .10
299 Bob Patterson .02 .10
300 Cal Ripken .60 1.50
301 Cesar Hernandez .02 .10
302 Randy Myers .02 .10
303 Brook Jacoby .02 .10
304 Melido Perez .02 .10
305 Rafael Palmeiro .10 .30
306 Damon Berryhill .02 .10
307 Dan Serafini RC .02 .10
308 Darryl Kile .07 .20
309 J.T. Bruett .02 .10
310 Dave Righetti .07 .20
311 Jay Howell .02 .10
312 Geronimo Pena .02 .10
313 Greg Hibbard .02 .10
314 Mark Gardner .02 .10
315 Edgar Martinez .10 .30
316 Dave Nilsson .02 .10
317 Kyle Abbott .02 .10
318 Willie Wilson .02 .10
319 Paul Assenmacher .02 .10
320 Tim Fortugno .02 .10
321 Rusty Meacham .02 .10
322 Pat Borders .02 .10
323 Mike Greenwell .02 .10
324 Willie Randolph .07 .20
325 Bill Gullickson .02 .10
326 Gary Varsho .02 .10
327 Tim Hulett .02 .10
328 Scott Ruskin .02 .10
329 Mike Maddux .02 .10
330 Danny Tartabull .02 .10
331 Kenny Lofton .07 .20
332 Geno Petralli .02 .10
333 Otis Nixon .02 .10
334 Jason Kendall RC .40 1.00
335 Mark Portugal .02 .10
336 Mike Pagliarulo .02 .10
337 Kirt Manwaring .02 .10
338 Bob Ojeda .02 .10
339 Mark Clark .02 .10
340 John Kruk .07 .20
341 Mel Rojas .02 .10
342 Erik Hanson .02 .10
343 Doug Henry .02 .10
344 Jack McDowell .02 .10
345 Harold Baines .07 .20
346 Chuck McElroy .02 .10
347 Luis Sojo .02 .10
348 Andy Stankiewicz .02 .10
349 Hipolito Pichardo .02 .10
350 Joe Carter .07 .20
351 Ellis Burks .07 .20
352 Pete Schourek .02 .10
353 Buddy Groom .02 .10
354 Jay Bell .07 .20
355 Brady Anderson .07 .20
356 Freddie Benavides .02 .10
357 Phil Stephenson .02 .10
358 Kevin Wickander .02 .10
359 Mike Stanley .02 .10
360 Ivan Rodriguez .10 .30
361 Scott Bankhead .02 .10
362 Luis Gonzalez .07 .20
363 John Smiley .02 .10
364 Trevor Wilson .02 .10
365 Tom Candiotti .02 .10
366 Craig Wilson .02 .10
367 Steve Sax .02 .10
368 Delino DeShields .02 .10
369 Jaime Navarro .02 .10
370 Dave Valle .02 .10
371 Mariano Duncan .02 .10
372 Rod Nichols .02 .10
373 Mike Morgan .02 .10
374 Julio Valera .02 .10
375 Wally Joyner .07 .20
376 Tom Henke .02 .10
377 Herm Winningham .02 .10
378 Orlando Merced .02 .10
379 Mike Munoz .02 .10
380 Todd Hundley .02 .10
381 Mike Flanagan .02 .10
382 Tim Belcher .02 .10
383 Jerry Browne .02 .10
384 Mike Benjamin .02 .10
385 Jim Leyritz .02 .10
386 Ray Lankford .07 .20
387 Devon White .07 .20
388 Jeremy Hernandez .02 .10
389 Brian Harper .02 .10
390 Wade Boggs .10 .30
391 Derrick May .02 .10
392 Travis Fryman .07 .20
393 Ron Gant .07 .20
394 Checklist 1-132 .02 .10
395 CL 133-264 UER .02 .10
Eckerlsey
396 Checklist 265-396 .02 .10
397 George Brett .50 1.25
398 Bobby Witt .02 .10
399 Daryl Boston .02 .10
400 Bo Jackson .20 .50
401 Fred McGriff .10 .30
Frank Thomas AS
402 Ryne Sandberg .20 .50
Carlos Baerga AS
403 Gary Sheffield .07 .20
Edgar Martinez AS
404 Barry Larkin .07 .20
Travis Fryman AS
405 Andy Van Slyke .25 .60
Ken Griffey Jr. AS
406 Larry Walker .10 .30
Kirby Puckett AS
407 Barry Bonds .30 .75
Joe Carter AS
408 Darren Daulton .07 .20
Brian Harper AS
409 Greg Maddux .20 .50
Roger Clemens AS
410 Tom Glavine .07 .20
Dave Fleming AS
411 Lee Smith .07 .20
Dennis Eckersley AS
412 Jamie McAndrew .02 .10
413 Pete Smith .02 .10
414 Juan Guerrero .02 .10
415 Todd Frohwirth .02 .10
416 Randy Tomlin .02 .10
417 B.J. Surhoff .07 .20
418 Jim Gott .02 .10
419 Mark Thompson RC .02 .10
420 Kevin Tapani .02 .10
421 Curt Schilling .07 .20
422 J.T. Snow RC .20 .50
423 Ryan Klesko .07 .20
424 John Valentin .02 .10
425 Joe Girardi .02 .10
426 Nigel Wilson .02 .10
427 Bob MacDonald .02 .10
428 Todd Zeile .02 .10
429 Milt Cuyler .02 .10
430 Eddie Murray .20 .50
431 Rich Amaral .02 .10
432 Pete Young .02 .10
433 Tom Schmidt RC .02 .10
434 Jack Armstrong .02 .10
435 Willie McGee .07 .20
436 Greg W. Harris .02 .10
437 Chris Hammond .02 .10
438 Ritchie Moody RC .02 .10
439 Bryan Harvey .02 .10
440 Ruben Sierra .07 .20
441 Don Lemon .02 .10
Todd Pridy RC
442 Kevin McReynolds .02 .10
443 Terry Leach .02 .10
444 David Nied .02 .10
445 Dale Murphy .10 .30
446 Luis Mercedes .02 .10
447 Keith Shepherd RC .02 .10
448 Ken Caminiti .07 .20
449 Jim Austin .02 .10
450 Darryl Strawberry .07 .20
451 Quinton McCracken RC .08 .25
452 Bob Wickman .02 .10
453 Victor Cole .02 .10
454 John Johnstone RC .02 .10
455 Chili Davis .07 .20
456 Scott Taylor .02 .10
457 Tracy Woodson .02 .10
458 David Wells .07 .20
459 Derek Wallace RC .02 .10
460 Randy Johnson .20 .50
461 Steve Reed RC .02 .10
462 Felix Fermin .02 .10
463 Scott Aldred .02 .10
464 Greg Colbrunn .02 .10
465 Tony Fernandez .02 .10
466 Mike Felder .02 .10
467 Lee Stevens .02 .10
468 Matt Whiteside RC .02 .10
469 Dave Hansen .02 .10
470 Rob Dibble .07 .20
471 Dave Gallagher .02 .10
472 Chris Gwynn .02 .10
473 Dave Henderson .02 .10
474 Ozzie Guillen .07 .20
475 Jeff Reardon .07 .20
476 Will Scalzitti RC .02 .10
477 Jimmy Jones .02 .10
478 Greg Cadaret .02 .10
479 Todd Pratt RC .02 .10
480 Pat Listach .02 .10
481 Ryan Luzinski RC .02 .10
482 Darren Reed .02 .10
483 Brian Griffiths RC .02 .10
484 John Wehner .02 .10
485 Glenn Davis .02 .10
486 Eric Wedge RC .07 .20
487 Jesse Hollins .02 .10
488 Manuel Lee .02 .10
489 Scott Fredrickson RC .02 .10
490 Omar Olivares .02 .10
491 Shawn Hare .02 .10
492 Tom Lampkin .02 .10
493 Jeff Nelson .02 .10
494 L.Lucca RC/E.Perez .02 .10
495 Ken Hill .02 .10
496 Reggie Jefferson .02 .10
497 Willie Brown RC .02 .10
498 Bud Black .02 .10
499 Chuck Crim .02 .10
500 Jose Canseco .10 .30
501 Johnny Oates MG .07 .20
Bobby Cox MG
502 Butch Hobson MG .02 .10
Jim Lefebvre MG
503 Buck Rodgers MG .07 .20
Tony Perez MG
504 Gene Lamont MG .07 .20
Don Baylor MG
505 Mike Hargrove MG .07 .20
Rene Lachemann MG
506 Sparky Anderson MG .07 .20
Art Howe MG
507 Hal McRae MG .07 .20

Tom Lasorda MG
508 Phil Garner MG .07 .20
Felipe Alou MG
509 Tom Kelly MG .02 .10
Jeff Torborg MG
510 Buck Showalter MG .07 .20
Jim Fregosi MG
511 Tony LaRussa MG .07 .20
Jim Leyland MG
512 Lou Piniella MG .07 .20
Joe Torre MG
513 Kevin Kennedy MG .02 .10
Jim Riggleman MG
514 Cito Gaston MG .07 .20
Dusty Baker MG
515 Greg Swindell .02 .10
516 Alex Arias .02 .10
517 Bill Pecota .02 .10
518 Benji Grigsby RC .02 .10
519 David Howard .02 .10
520 Charlie Hough .07 .20
521 Kevin Flora .02 .10
522 Shane Reynolds .02 .10
523 Doug Bochtler RC .02 .10
524 Chris Hoiles .02 .10
525 Scott Sanderson .02 .10
526 Mike Sharperson .02 .10
527 Mike Fetters .02 .10
528 Paul Quantrill .02 .10
529 Chipper Jones .20 .50
530 Sterling Hitchcock RC .08 .25
531 Joe Millette .02 .10
532 Tom Brunansky .02 .10
533 Frank Castillo .02 .10
534 Randy Knorr .02 .10
535 Jose Oquendo .02 .10
536 Dave Haas .02 .10
537 Jason Hutchins RC .02 .10
538 Jimmy Baron RC .02 .10
539 Kerry Woodson .02 .10
540 Ivan Calderon .02 .10
541 Denis Boucher .02 .10
542 Royce Clayton .02 .10
543 Reggie Williams .02 .10
544 Steve Decker .02 .10
545 Dean Palmer .07 .20
546 Hal Morris .02 .10
547 Ryan Thompson .02 .10
548 Lance Blankenship .02 .10
549 Hensley Meulens .02 .10
550 Scott Radinsky .02 .10
551 Eric Young .02 .10
552 Jeff Blauser .02 .10
553 Andujar Cedeno .02 .10
554 Arthur Rhodes .02 .10
555 Terry Mulholland .02 .10
556 Darryl Hamilton .02 .10
557 Pedro Martinez .40 1.00
558 Ryan Whitman RC .02 .10
559 Jamie Arnold RC .02 .10
560 Zane Smith .02 .10
561 Matt Nokes .02 .10
562 Bob Zupcic .02 .10
563 Shawn Boskie .02 .10
564 Mike Timlin .02 .10
565 Jerald Clark .02 .10
566 Rod Brewer .02 .10
567 Mark Carreon .02 .10
568 Andy Benes .02 .10
569 Shawn Barton RC .02 .10
570 Tim Wallach .02 .10
571 Dave Mlicki .02 .10
572 Trevor Hoffman .20 .50
573 John Patterson .02 .10
574 De Shawn Warren RC .02 .10
575 Monty Fariss .02 .10
576 Cliff Floyd .07 .20
577 Tim Costo .02 .10
578 Dave Magadan .02 .10
579 Jason Bates RC .02 .10
580 Walt Weiss .02 .10
581 Chris Haney .02 .10
582 Shawn Abner .02 .10
583 Marvin Freeman .02 .10
584 Casey Candaele .02 .10
585 Ricky Jordan .02 .10
586 Jeff Tabaka RC .02 .10
587 Manny Alexander .02 .10
588 Mike Trombley .02 .10
589 Carlos Hernandez .02 .10
590 Cal Eldred .02 .10
591 Alex Cole .02 .10
592 Phil Plantier .02 .10
593 Brett Merriman RC .02 .10
594 Jerry Nielsen .02 .10
595 Shawon Dunston .02 .10
596 Jimmy Key .07 .20
597 Gerald Perry .02 .10
598 Rico Brogna .02 .10
599 Clemente Nunez .02 .10
600 Bret Saberhagen .07 .20
601 Craig Shipley .02 .10
602 Henry Mercedes .02 .10
603 Jim Thome .10 .30
604 Rod Beck .02 .10
605 Chuck Finley .07 .20
606 Jayhawk Owens RC .02 .10
607 Dan Smith .02 .10
608 Bill Doran .02 .10
609 Lance Parrish .07 .20
610 Dennis Martinez .07 .20
611 Tom Gordon .02 .10
612 Byron Mathews RC .02 .10
613 Joel Adamson RC .02 .10
614 Brian Williams .02 .10
615 Steve Avery .02 .10
616 Midre Cummings RC .02 .10
617 Craig Lefferts .02 .10
618 Tony Pena .02 .10
619 Billy Spiers .02 .10
620 Todd Benzinger .02 .10
621 Greg Boyd RC .02 .10
622 Ben Rivera .02 .10
623 Al Martin .02 .10
624 Sam Militello UER .02 .10
Profile says drafted
in 1988, bio says
drafted in 1990
625 Rick Aguilera .02 .10
626 Dan Gladden .02 .10
627 Andres Berumen RC .02 .10
628 Kelly Gruber .02 .10
629 Cris Carpenter .02 .10
630 Mark Grace .10 .30
631 Jeff Brantley .02 .10
632 Chris Widger RC .08 .25
633 Three Russians .02 .10
634 Mo Sanford .02 .10
635 Albert Belle .07 .20
636 Tim Teufel .02 .10
637 Greg Myers .02 .10
638 Brian Bohanon .02 .10
639 Mike Bordick .02 .10
640 Dwight Gooden .07 .20
641 P.Leahy/G.Baugh RC .02 .10
642 Milt Hill .02 .10
643 Luis Aquino .02 .10
644 Dante Bichette .07 .20
645 Bobby Thigpen .02 .10
646 Rich Scheid RC .02 .10
647 Brian Sackinsky RC .02 .10
648 Ryan Hawblitzel .02 .10
649 Tom Marsh .02 .10
650 Terry Pendleton .07 .20
651 Rafael Bournigal .02 .10
652 Dave West .02 .10
653 Steve Hosey .02 .10
654 Gerald Williams .02 .10
655 Scott Cooper .02 .10
656 Gary Scott .02 .10
657 Mike Harkey .02 .10
658 J.Burnitz/S.Walker RC .07 .20
659 Ed Sprague .02 .10
660 Alan Trammell .07 .20
661 Garvin Alston RC .02 .10
662 Donovan Osborne .02 .10
663 Jeff Gardner .02 .10
664 Calvin Jones .02 .10
665 Darrin Fletcher .02 .10
666 Glenallen Hill .02 .10
667 Jim Rosenbohm RC .02 .10
668 Scott Lewis .02 .10
669 Kip Yaughn RC .02 .10
670 Julio Franco .07 .20
671 Dave Martinez .02 .10
672 Kevin Bass .02 .10
673 Todd Van Poppel .02 .10
674 Mark Gubicza .02 .10
675 Tim Raines .07 .20
676 Rudy Seanez .02 .10
677 Charlie Leibrandt .02 .10
678 Randy Milligan .02 .10
679 Kim Batiste .02 .10
680 Craig Biggio .10 .30
681 Darren Holmes .02 .10
682 John Candelaria .02 .10
683 Eddie Christian RC .02 .10
684 Pat Mahomes .02 .10
685 Bob Walk .02 .10
686 Russ Springer .02 .10
687 Tony Sheffield RC .02 .10
688 Dwight Smith .02 .10
689 Eddie Zosky .02 .10
690 Bien Figueroa .02 .10
691 Jim Tatum RC .02 .10
692 Chad Kreuter .02 .10
693 Rich Rodriguez .02 .10
694 Shane Turner .02 .10
695 Kent Bottenfield .02 .10
696 Jose Mesa .02 .10
697 Darrell Whitmore RC .02 .10
698 Ted Wood .02 .10
699 Chad Curtis .02 .10
700 Nolan Ryan .75 2.00
701 M.Piazza/C.Delgado 1.50 4.00
702 Tim Pugh RC .02 .10
703 Jeff Kent .20 .50
704 J.Goodrich/D.Figueroa RC .02 .10
705 Bob Welch .02 .10
706 Sherard Clinkscales RC .02 .10
707 Donn Pall .02 .10
708 Greg Olson .02 .10
709 Jeff Juden .02 .10
710 Mike Mussina .10 .30
711 Scott Chiamparino .02 .10
712 Stan Javier .02 .10
713 John Doherty .02 .10
714 Kevin Gross .02 .10
715 Greg Gagne .02 .10
716 Steve Cooke .02 .10
717 Steve Farr .02 .10
718 Jay Buhner .07 .20
719 Butch Henry .02 .10
720 David Cone .07 .20
721 Rick Wilkins .02 .10
722 Chuck Carr .02 .10
723 Kenny Felder RC .02 .10
724 Guillermo Velasquez .02 .10
725 Billy Hatcher .02 .10
726 Mike Veneziale RC .02 .10
727 Jonathan Hurst .02 .10
728 Steve Frey .02 .10
729 Mark Leonard .02 .10
730 Charles Nagy .02 .10
731 Donald Harris .02 .10
732 Travis Buckley RC .02 .10
733 Tom Browning .02 .10
734 Anthony Young .02 .10
735 Steve Shifflett .02 .10
736 Jeff Russell .02 .10
737 Wilson Alvarez .02 .10
738 Lance Painter RC .02 .10
739 Dave Weathers .02 .10
740 Len Dykstra .07 .20
741 Mike Devereaux .02 .10
742 R.Arocha RC/A.Embree .08 .25
743 Dave Landaker RC .02 .10
744 Chris George .02 .10
745 Eric Davis .07 .20
746 Lamar Rogers RC .02 .10
747 Carl Willis .02 .10
748 Stan Belinda .02 .10
749 Scott Kamieniecki .02 .10
750 Rickey Henderson .20 .50
751 Eric Hillman .02 .10
752 Pat Hentgen .02 .10
753 Jim Corsi .02 .10
754 Brian Jordan .07 .20
755 Bill Swift .02 .10
756 Mike Henneman .02 .10
757 Harold Reynolds .07 .20
758 Sean Berry .02 .10
759 Charlie Hayes .02 .10
760 Luis Polonia .02 .10
761 Darrin Jackson .02 .10
762 Mark Lewis .02 .10
763 Rob Maurer .02 .10
764 Willie Greene .02 .10
765 Vince Coleman .02 .10
766 Todd Revenig .02 .10
767 Rich Ireland RC .02 .10
768 Mike Macfarlane .02 .10
769 Francisco Cabrera .02 .10
770 Robin Ventura .07 .20
771 Kevin Ritz .02 .10
772 Chito Martinez .02 .10
773 Cliff Brantley .02 .10
774 Curt Leskanic RC .08 .25
775 Chris Bosio .02 .10
776 Jose Offerman .02 .10
777 Mark Guthrie .02 .10
778 Don Slaught .02 .10
779 Rich Monteleone .02 .10
780 Jim Abbott .10 .30
781 Jack Clark .07 .20
782 R.Mendoza/D.Roman RC .02 .10
783 Heathcliff Slocumb .02 .10
784 Jeff Branson .02 .10
785 Kevin Brown .07 .20
786 K.Ryan/Gandarillas RC .02 .10
787 Mike Matthews RC .02 .10
788 Mackey Sasser .02 .10
789 Jeff Conine UER .07 .20
No inclusion of 1990
RBI stats in career total
790 George Bell .02 .10
791 Pat Rapp .02 .10
792 Joe Boever .02 .10
793 Jim Poole .02 .10
794 Andy Ashby .02 .10
795 Deion Sanders .10 .30
796 Scott Brosius .07 .20
797 Brad Pennington .02 .10
798 Greg Blosser .02 .10
799 Jim Edmonds RC .75 2.00
800 Shawn Jeter .02 .10
801 Jesse Levis .02 .10
802 Phil Clark UER .02 .10
Word a is missing in
sentence beginning
with In 1992 ...
803 Ed Pierce RC .02 .10
804 Jose Valentin RC .08 .25
805 Terry Jorgensen .02 .10
806 Mark Hutton .02 .10
807 Troy Neel .02 .10
808 Bret Boone .07 .20
809 Cris Colon .02 .10
810 Domingo Martinez RC .02 .10
811 Javier Lopez .10 .30
812 Matt Walbeck RC .02 .10
813 Dan Wilson .07 .20
814 Scooter Tucker .02 .10
815 Billy Ashley .02 .10
816 Tim Laker RC .02 .10
817 Bobby Jones .07 .20
818 Brad Brink .02 .10
819 William Pennyfeather .02 .10
820 Stan Royer .02 .10
821 Doug Brocail .02 .10
822 Kevin Rogers .02 .10
823 Checklist 397-540 .02 .10
824 Checklist 541-691 .02 .10
825 Checklist 692-825 .02 .10

1993 Topps Gold

*STARS: 1X TO 2.5X BASIC CARDS
*ROOKIES: 1.25X TO 3X BASIC CARDS
GOLD CARDS 1 PER WAX PACK
GOLD CARDS 3 PER RACK PACK
GOLD CARDS 5 PER JUMBO PACK
GOLD CARDS 10 PER FACTORY SET
98 Derek Jeter 40.00 100.00
394 Bernardo Brito .08 .25
395 Jim McNamara .08 .25
396 Rich Sauveur .08 .25
823 Keith Brown .08 .25
824 Russ McGinnis .08 .25
825 Mike Walker UER .08 .25

1993 Topps Inaugural Marlins

COMP.FACT.SET (825) 75.00 150.00
*STARS: 2.5X TO 6X BASIC CARDS
*ROOKIES: 2.5X TO 6X BASIC CARDS
DISTRIBUTED IN FACTORY SET FORM ONLY
NO MORE THAN 10,000 SETS PRODUCED

1993 Topps Inaugural Rockies

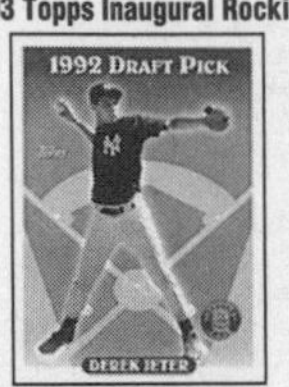

COMP.FACT.SET (825) 75.00 150.00
*STARS: 2.5X TO 6X BASIC CARDS
*ROOKIES: 2.5X TO 6X BASIC CARDS
NO MORE THAN 10,000 SETS PRODUCED

1993 Topps Micro

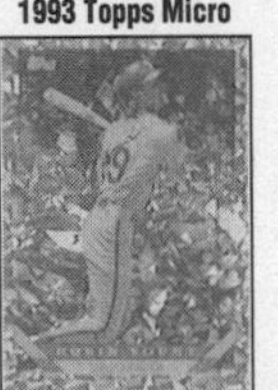

COMPLETE SET (825) 15.00 40.00
COMMON PRISM INSERT .04 .10
*MICRO: .25X TO .6X BASIC CARDS
98 Derek Jeter 15.00 40.00
P1 Robin Yount .20 .50
P20 Tim Salmon .15 .40
P32 Don Mattingly .50 1.25
P50 Roberto Alomar .15 .40
P150 Frank Thomas .40 1.00
P155 Dennis Eckersley .07 .20
P179 Ken Griffey Jr. 1.25 3.00
P200 Kirby Puckett .40 1.00
P397 George Brett .40 1.00
P426 Nigel Wilson .02 .10
P444 David Nied .02 .10
P700 Nolan Ryan 1.00 2.50

1993 Topps Black Gold

Topps Black Gold cards 1-22 were randomly inserted in series I packs while card numbers 23-44 were featured in series II packs. They were also inserted three per factory set. In the packs, the cards were inserted one every 72 hobby or retail packs; one every 12 jumbo packs and one every 24 rack packs. Hobbyists could obtain the set by collecting individual random insert cards or receive 11, 22, or 44 Black Gold cards by mail when they sent in special "You've Just Won" cards, which were randomly inserted in packs. Series I packs featured three different "You've Just Won" cards, entitling the holder to receive Group A (cards 1-11), Group B (cards 12-22), or Groups A and B (Cards 1-22). In a similar fashion, four "You've Just Won" cards were inserted in series II packs and entitled the holder to receive Group C (23-33), Group D (34-44), Groups C and D (23-44), or Groups A-D (1-44). By returning the "You've Just Won" card with $1.50 for postage and handling, the collector received not only the Black Gold cards won but also a special "You've Just Won" card and a congratulatory letter informing the collector that his/her name has been entered into a drawing for one of 500 uncut sheets of all 44 Topps Black Gold cards in a leatherette frame. These standard-size cards feature different color player photos than either the 1993 Topps regular issue or the Topps Gold issue. The player pictures are cut out and superimposed on a black gloss background. Inside white borders, gold refractory foil edges the top and bottom of the card face. On a black-and-gray pinstripe pattern inside white borders, the horizontal backs have a second cut out player photo and a player profile on a blue panel. The player's name appears in gold foil lettering on a blue-and-gray geometric shape. The first 22 cards are National Leaguers while the second 22 cards are American Leaguers. Winner cards C and D were both originally produced erroneously and later corrected; the error versions show the players from Winner A and B on the respective fronts of Winner cards C and D. There is no value difference in the variations at this time. The winner cards were redeemable until January 31, 1994.

COMPLETE SET (44) 6.00 15.00
COMP.SERIES 1 (22) 2.50 6.00
COMP.SERIES 2 (22) 4.00 10.00
STATED ODDS 1:72 H/R, 1:12 J, 1:24 RACK
STATED ODDS 1:35 34CT JUM, 1:37 18CT JUM
THREE PER FACTORY SET
1 Barry Bonds 1.00 2.50
2 Will Clark .20 .50
3 Darren Daulton .10 .30
4 Andre Dawson .10 .30
5 Delino DeShields .05 .15
6 Tom Glavine .20 .50
7 Marquis Grissom .10 .30
8 Tony Gwynn .40 1.00
9 Eric Karros .10 .30
10 Ray Lankford .10 .30
11 Barry Larkin .20 .50
12 Greg Maddux .50 1.25
13 Fred McGriff .20 .50
14 Joe Oliver .05 .15
15 Terry Pendleton .10 .30
16 Bip Roberts .05 .15
17 Ryne Sandberg .50 1.25
18 Gary Sheffield .10 .30
19 Lee Smith .10 .30
20 Ozzie Smith .50 1.25
21 Andy Van Slyke .20 .50
22 Larry Walker .10 .30
23 Roberto Alomar .20 .50
24 Brady Anderson .10 .30
25 Carlos Baerga .05 .15
26 Joe Carter .10 .30
27 Roger Clemens .60 1.50
28 Mike Devereaux .05 .15
29 Dennis Eckersley .10 .30
30 Cecil Fielder .10 .30
31 Travis Fryman .10 .30
32 Juan Gonzalez .10 .30
33 Ken Griffey Jr. .60 1.50
34 Brian Harper .05 .15
35 Pat Listach .05 .15
36 Kenny Lofton .10 .30
37 Edgar Martinez .20 .50
38 Jack McDowell .05 .15
39 Mark McGwire .75 2.00
40 Kirby Puckett .30 .75
41 Mickey Tettleton .05 .15
42 Frank Thomas .30 .75
43 Robin Ventura .10 .30
44 Dave Winfield .10 .30
A1 Winner A 1-11 EXCH 2.50 6.00
A2 Winner A 1-11 Prize .60 1.50
B1 Winner B 12-22 EXCH 2.50 6.00
B2 Winner B 12-22 Prize .60 1.50
C1 Winner C 23-33 EXCH 2.50 6.00
UER Cards 1-11 Pictured
C2 Winner C 23-33 Prize .60 1.50
D1 Winner D 34-44 EXCH 2.50 6.00
UER Cards 12-22 Pictured
D2 Winner D 34-44 Prize .60 1.50
AB1 Winner AB 1-22 EXCH 3.00 8.00
AB2 Winner AB 1-22 Prize .75 2.00
CD1 Winner CD 23-44 EXCH 3.00 8.00
CD2 Winner CD 23-44 Prize .75 2.00
ABCD1 Winner ABCD 1-44 EXCH 8.00 20.00
ABCD2 Winner ABCD 1-44 Prize 2.00 5.00

1993 Topps Traded

This 132-card standard-size set focuses on promising rookies, new managers, free agents, and players who changed teams. The set also includes 22 members of Team USA. The set has the same design on the front as the regular 1993 Topps issue. The backs are also the same design and carry a head shot, biography, stats, and career highlights. Rookie Cards in this set include Todd Helton.

COMP.FACT.SET (132) 10.00 25.00
1T Barry Bonds .60 1.50
2T Rich Renteria .02 .10
3T Aaron Sele .02 .10
4T Carlton Loewer USA RC .08 .25
5T Erik Pappas .02 .10
6T Greg McMichael RC .08 .25
7T Freddie Benavides .02 .10
8T Kirk Gibson .07 .20
9T Tony Fernandez .02 .10
10T Jay Gainer RC .08 .25
11T Orestes Destrade .02 .10
12T A.J. Hinch USA RC .20 .50
13T Bobby Munoz .02 .10
14T Tom Henke .02 .10
15T Rob Butler .02 .10
16T Gary Wayne .02 .10
17T David McCarty .02 .10
18T Walt Weiss .02 .10
19T Todd Helton USA RC 2.50 6.00
20T Mark Whiten .02 .10
21T Ricky Gutierrez .02 .10
22T Dustin Hermanson USA RC .40 1.00
23T Sherman Obando RC .08 .25
24T Mike Piazza 1.25 3.00
25T Jeff Russell .02 .10
26T Jason Bere .02 .10
27T Jack Voigt RC .08 .25
28T Chris Bosio .02 .10
29T Phil Hiatt .02 .10
30T Matt Beaumont USA RC .08 .25
31T Andres Galarraga .07 .20
32T Greg Swindell .02 .10
33T Vinny Castilla .20 .50
34T Pat Clougherty RC USA .08 .25
35T Greg Briley .02 .10
36T Dallas Green MG .02 .10
Davey Johnson MG
37T Tyler Green .02 .10
38T Craig Paquette .02 .10
39T Danny Sheaffer RC .08 .25
40T Jim Converse RC .08 .25
41T Terry Harvey USA RC .08 .25
42T Phil Plantier .02 .10
43T Doug Saunders RC .08 .25
44T Benny Santiago .07 .20
45T Dante Powell USA RC .08 .25
46T Jeff Parrett .02 .10
47T Wade Boggs .10 .30
48T Paul Molitor .07 .20
49T Turk Wendell .02 .10
50T David Wells .07 .20
51T Gary Sheffield .07 .20
52T Kevin Young .07 .20
53T Nelson Liriano .02 .10
54T Greg Maddux .30 .75
55T Derek Bell .02 .10
56T Matt Turner RC .08 .25
57T Charlie Nelson USA RC .08 .25
58T Mike Hampton .07 .20
59T Troy O'Leary RC .20 .50
60T Benji Gil .02 .10
61T Mitch Lyden RC .08 .25
62T J.T.Snow .10 .30
63T Damon Buford .02 .10
64T Gene Harris .02 .10
65T Randy Myers .02 .10
66T Felix Jose .02 .10
67T Todd Dunn USA RC .08 .25
68T Jimmy Key .07 .20
69T Pedro Castellano .02 .10
70T Mark Merila USA RC .08 .25
71T Rich Rodriguez .02 .10
72T Matt Mieske .02 .10
73T Pete Incaviglia .02 .10
74T Carl Everett .07 .20
75T Jim Abbott .10 .30
76T Luis Aquino .02 .10
77T Rene Arocha .07 .20
78T Jon Shave .02 .10
79T Todd Walker USA RC .40 1.00
80T Jack Armstrong .02 .10
81T Jeff Richardson .02 .10
82T Blas Minor .02 .10
83T Dave Winfield .07 .20
84T Paul O'Neill .10 .30
85T Steve Reich USA RC .08 .25
86T Chris Hammond .02 .10
87T Hilly Hathaway RC .08 .25
88T Fred McGriff .10 .30
89T Dave Telgheder RC .08 .25
90T Richie Lewis RC .08 .25
91T Brent Gates .02 .10
92T Andre Dawson .07 .20
93T Andy Barkett USA RC .08 .25
94T Doug Drabek .02 .10
95T Joe Klink .02 .10
96T Willie Blair .02 .10
97T Danny Graves USA RC .20 .50
98T Pat Meares RC .20 .50
99T Mike Lansing RC .20 .50
100T Marcos Armas RC .08 .25
101T Darren Grass USA RC .08 .25
102T Chris Jones .02 .10
103T Ken Ryan RC .08 .25
104T Ellis Burks .07 .20
105T Roberto Kelly .02 .10
106T Dave Magadan .02 .10
107T Paul Wilson USA RC .20 .50
108T Rob Natal .02 .10
109T Paul Wagner .02 .10
110T Jeromy Burnitz .07 .20
111T Monty Fariss .02 .10
112T Kevin Mitchell .02 .10
113T Scott Pose RC .08 .25
114T Dave Stewart .07 .20
115T Russ Johnson USA RC .08 .25
116T Armando Reynoso .02 .10
117T Geronimo Berroa .02 .10
118T Woody Williams RC .40 1.00
119T Tim Bogar RC .08 .25
120T Bob Scafa USA RC .08 .25
121T Henry Cotto .02 .10
122T Gregg Jefferies .02 .10
123T Norm Charlton .02 .10
124T Bret Wagner USA RC .08 .25
125T David Cone .07 .20
126T Daryl Boston .02 .10
127T Tim Wallach .02 .10
128T Mike Martin USA RC .08 .25
129T John Cummings RC .08 .25
130T Ryan Bowen .02 .10
131T John Powell USA RC .08 .25
132T Checklist 1-132 .02 .10

1994 Topps

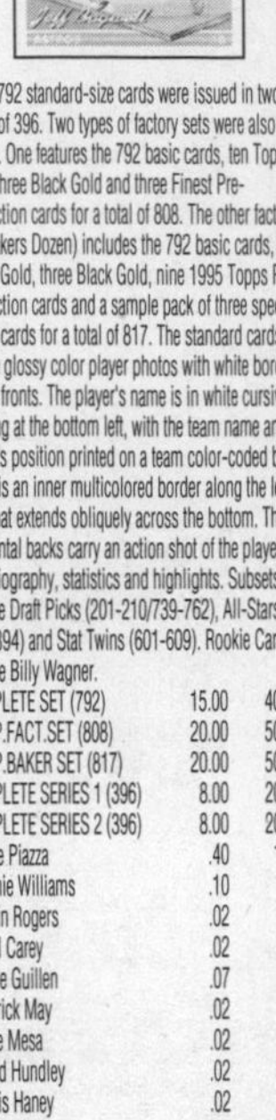

These 792 standard-size cards were issued in two series of 396. Two types of factory sets were also issued. One features the 792 basic cards, ten Topps Gold, three Black Gold and three Finest Pre-Production cards for a total of 808. The other factory set (Bakers Dozen) includes the 792 basic cards, ten Topps Gold, three Black Gold, nine 1995 Topps Pre-Production cards and a sample pack of three special Topps cards for a total of 817. The standard cards feature glossy color player photos with white borders on the fronts. The player's name is in white cursive lettering at the bottom left, with the team name and player's position printed on a team color-coded bar. There is an inner multicolored border along the left side that extends obliquely across the bottom. The horizontal backs carry an action shot of the player with biography, statistics and highlights. Subsets include Draft Picks (201-210/739-762), All-Stars (384-394) and Stat Twins (601-609). Rookie Cards include Billy Wagner.

COMPLETE SET (792) 15.00 40.00
COMP.FACT.SET (808) 20.00 50.00
COMP.BAKER SET (817) 20.00 50.00
COMPLETE SERIES 1 (396) 8.00 20.00
COMPLETE SERIES 2 (396) 8.00 20.00
1 Mike Piazza .40 1.00
2 Bernie Williams .10 .30
3 Kevin Rogers .02 .10
4 Paul Carey .02 .10
5 Ozzie Guillen .07 .20
6 Derrick May .02 .10
7 Jose Mesa .02 .10
8 Todd Hundley .02 .10
9 Chris Haney .02 .10
10 John Olerud .07 .20
11 Andujar Cedeno .02 .10
12 John Smiley .02 .10
13 Phil Plantier .02 .10
14 Willie Banks .02 .10
15 Jay Bell .07 .20
16 Doug Henry .02 .10
17 Lance Blankenship .02 .10
18 Greg W. Harris .02 .10
19 Scott Livingstone .02 .10
20 Bryan Harvey .02 .10
21 Wil Cordero .02 .10
22 Roger Pavlik .02 .10
23 Mark Lemke .02 .10
24 Jeff Nelson .02 .10
25 Todd Zeile .02 .10
26 Billy Hatcher .02 .10
27 Joe Magrane .02 .10
28 Tony Longmire .02 .10
29 Omar Daal .02 .10
30 Kirt Manwaring .02 .10
31 Melido Perez .02 .10
32 Tim Hulett .02 .10
33 Jeff Schwarz .02 .10
34 Nolan Ryan .75 2.00
35 Jose Guzman .02 .10
36 Felix Fermin .02 .10
37 Jeff Innis .02 .10
38 Brett Mayne .02 .10
39 Huck Flener RC .02 .10
40 Jeff Bagwell .10 .30
41 Kevin Wickander .02 .10
42 Ricky Gutierrez .02 .10
43 Pat Mahomes .02 .10
44 Jeff King .02 .10
45 Cal Eldred .02 .10
46 Craig Paquette .02 .10
47 Richie Lewis .02 .10
48 Tony Phillips .02 .10
49 Armando Reynoso .02 .10
50 Moises Alou .07 .20
51 Manuel Lee .02 .10
52 Otis Nixon .02 .10
53 Billy Ashley .02 .10
54 Mark Whiten .02 .10
55 Jeff Russell .02 .10
56 Chad Curtis .02 .10
57 Kevin Stocker .02 .10
58 Mike Jackson .02 .10
59 Matt Nokes .02 .10
60 Chris Bosio .02 .10
61 Damon Buford .02 .10
62 Tim Belcher .02 .10
63 Glenallen Hill .02 .10
64 Bill Wertz .02 .10
65 Eddie Murray .20 .50
66 Tom Gordon .02 .10
67 Alex Gonzalez .02 .10
68 Eddie Taubensee .02 .10
69 Jacob Brumfield .02 .10
70 Andy Benes .02 .10
71 Rich Becker .02 .10
72 Steve Cooke .02 .10
73 Billy Spiers .02 .10
74 Scott Brosius .07 .20
75 Alan Trammell .07 .20

Card	Low	High
76 Luis Aquino	.02	.10
77 Jerald Clark	.02	.10
78 Mel Rojas	.02	.10
79 Craig McClure RC	.02	.10
80 Jose Canseco	.10	.30
81 Greg McMichael	.02	.10
82 Brian Turang RC	.02	.10
83 Tom Urbani	.02	.10
84 Garret Anderson	.20	.50
85 Tony Pena	.02	.10
86 Ricky Jordan	.02	.10
87 Jim Gott	.02	.10
88 Pat Kelly	.02	.10
89 Bud Black	.02	.10
90 Robin Ventura	.07	.20
91 Rick Sutcliffe	.07	.20
92 Jose Bautista	.02	.10
93 Bob Ojeda	.02	.10
94 Phil Hiatt	.02	.10
95 Tim Pugh	.02	.10
96 Randy Knorr	.02	.10
97 Todd Jones	.02	.10
98 Ryan Thompson	.02	.10
99 Tim Mauser	.02	.10
100 Kirby Puckett	.20	.50
101 Mark Dewey	.02	.10
102 B.J. Surhoff	.07	.20
103 Sterling Hitchcock	.02	.10
104 Alex Arias	.02	.10
105 David Wells	.07	.20
106 Daryl Boston	.02	.10
107 Mike Stanton	.02	.10
108 Gary Redus	.02	.10
109 Delino DeShields	.02	.10
110 Lee Smith	.07	.20
111 Greg Litton	.02	.10
112 Frankie Rodriguez	.02	.10
113 Russ Springer	.02	.10
114 Mitch Williams	.02	.10
115 Eric Karros	.07	.20
116 Jeff Brantley	.02	.10
117 Jack Voigt	.02	.10
118 Jason Bere	.02	.10
119 Kevin Roberson	.02	.10
120 Jimmy Key	.07	.20
121 Reggie Jefferson	.02	.10
122 Jeromy Burnitz	.07	.20
123 Billy Brewer	.02	.10
124 Willie Canate	.02	.10
125 Greg Swindell	.02	.10
126 Hal Morris	.02	.10
127 Brad Ausmus	.10	.30
128 George Tsamis	.02	.10
129 Denny Neagle	.07	.20
130 Pat Listach	.02	.10
131 Steve Karsay	.02	.10
132 Bret Barberie	.02	.10
133 Mark Leiter	.02	.10
134 Greg Colbrunn	.02	.10
135 David Nied	.02	.10
136 Dean Palmer	.07	.20
137 Steve Avery	.02	.10
138 Bill Haselman	.02	.10
139 Tripp Cromer	.02	.10
140 Frank Viola	.07	.20
141 Rene Gonzales	.02	.10
142 Curt Schilling	.07	.20
143 Tim Wallach	.02	.10
144 Bobby Munoz	.02	.10
145 Brady Anderson	.07	.20
146 Rod Beck	.02	.10
147 Mike LaValliere	.02	.10
148 Greg Hibbard	.02	.10
149 Kenny Lofton	.07	.20
150 Dwight Gooden	.07	.20
151 Greg Gagne	.02	.10
152 Ray McDavid	.02	.10
153 Chris Donnels	.02	.10
154 Dan Wilson	.02	.10
155 Todd Stottlemyre	.02	.10
156 David McCarty	.02	.10
157 Paul Wagner	.02	.10
158 Derek Jeter UER	1.25	3.00
159 Mike Fetters	.02	.10
160 Scott Lydy	.02	.10
161 Darrell Whitmore	.02	.10
162 Bob MacDonald	.02	.10
163 Vinny Castilla	.07	.20
164 Denis Boucher	.02	.10
165 Ivan Rodriguez	.10	.30
166 Ron Gant	.07	.20
167 Tim Davis	.02	.10
168 Steve Dixon	.02	.10
169 Scott Fletcher	.02	.10
170 Terry Mulholland	.02	.10
171 Greg Myers	.02	.10
172 Brett Butler	.07	.20
173 Bob Wickman	.02	.10
174 Dave Martinez	.02	.10
175 Fernando Valenzuela	.07	.20
176 Craig Grebeck	.02	.10
177 Shawn Boskie	.02	.10
178 Albie Lopez	.02	.10
179 Butch Huskey	.02	.10
180 George Brett	.50	1.25
181 Juan Guzman	.02	.10
182 Eric Anthony	.02	.10
183 Rob Dibble	.07	.20
184 Craig Shipley	.02	.10
185 Kevin Tapani	.02	.10
186 Marcus Moore	.02	.10
187 Graeme Lloyd	.02	.10
188 Mike Bordick	.02	.10
189 Chris Hammond	.02	.10
190 Cecil Fielder	.07	.20
191 Curt Leskanic	.02	.10
192 Lou Frazier	.02	.10
193 Steve Dreyer RC	.02	.10
194 Javier Lopez	.07	.20
195 Edgar Martinez	.10	.30
196 Allen Watson	.02	.10
197 John Flaherty	.02	.10
198 Kurt Stillwell	.02	.10
199 Danny Jackson	.02	.10
200 Cal Ripken	.60	1.50
201 Mike Bell RC	.02	.10
202 Alan Benes RC	.08	.25
203 Matt Farner RC	.02	.10
204 Jeff Granger	.02	.10
205 Brooks Kieschnick RC	.02	.10
206 Jeremy Lee RC	.02	.10
207 Charles Peterson RC	.02	.10
208 Andy Rice RC	.02	.10
209 Billy Wagner RC	.60	1.50
210 Kelly Wunsch RC	.08	.25
211 Tom Candiotti	.02	.10
212 Domingo Jean	.02	.10
213 John Burkett	.02	.10
214 George Bell	.02	.10
215 Dan Plesac	.02	.10
216 Manny Ramirez	.20	.50
217 Mike Maddux	.02	.10
218 Kevin McReynolds	.02	.10
219 Pat Borders	.02	.10
220 Doug Drabek	.02	.10
221 Larry Luebbers RC	.02	.10
222 Trevor Hoffman	.10	.30
223 Pat Meares	.02	.10
224 Danny Miceli	.02	.10
225 Greg Vaughn	.02	.10
226 Scott Hemond	.02	.10
227 Pat Rapp	.02	.10
228 Kirk Gibson	.07	.20
229 Lance Painter	.02	.10
230 Larry Walker	.07	.20
231 Benji Gil	.02	.10
232 Mark Wohlers	.02	.10
233 Rich Amaral	.02	.10
234 Eric Pappas	.02	.10
235 Scott Cooper	.02	.10
236 Mike Butcher	.02	.10
237 Pride RC	.20	.50
Green		
Sweeney RC		
238 Kim Batiste	.02	.10
239 Paul Assenmacher	.02	.10
240 Will Clark	.10	.30
241 Jose Offerman	.02	.10
242 Todd Frohwirth	.02	.10
243 Tim Raines	.07	.20
244 Rick Wilkins	.02	.10
245 Bret Saberhagen	.07	.20
246 Thomas Howard	.02	.10
247 Stan Belinda	.02	.10
248 Rickey Henderson	.20	.50
249 Brian Williams	.02	.10
250 Barry Larkin	.10	.30
251 Jose Valentin	.02	.10
252 Lenny Webster	.02	.10
253 Blas Minor	.02	.10
254 Tim Teufel	.02	.10
255 Bobby Witt	.02	.10
256 Walt Weiss	.02	.10
257 Chad Kreuter	.02	.10
258 Roberto Mejia	.02	.10
259 Cliff Floyd	.07	.20
260 Julio Franco	.07	.20
261 Rafael Belliard	.02	.10
262 Marc Newfield	.02	.10
263 Gerald Perry	.02	.10
264 Ken Ryan	.02	.10
265 Chili Davis	.07	.20
266 Dave West	.02	.10
267 Royce Clayton	.02	.10
268 Pedro Martinez	.20	.50
269 Mark Hutton	.02	.10
270 Frank Thomas	.20	.50
271 Brad Pennington	.02	.10
272 Mike Harkey	.02	.10
273 Sandy Alomar Jr.	.02	.10
274 Dave Gallagher	.02	.10
275 Wally Joyner	.07	.20
276 Ricky Trlicek	.02	.10
277 Al Osuna	.02	.10
278 Pokey Reese	.02	.10
279 Kevin Higgins	.02	.10
280 Rick Aguilera	.02	.10
281 Orlando Merced	.02	.10
282 Mike Mohler	.02	.10
283 John Jaha	.02	.10
284 Robb Nen	.07	.20
285 Travis Fryman	.07	.20
286 Mark Thompson	.02	.10
287 Mike Lansing	.02	.10
288 Craig Lefferts	.02	.10
289 Damon Berryhill	.02	.10
290 Randy Johnson	.20	.50
291 Jeff Reed	.02	.10
292 Danny Darwin	.02	.10
293 J.T.Snow	.07	.20
294 Tyler Green	.02	.10
295 Chris Hoiles	.02	.10
296 Roger McDowell	.02	.10
297 Spike Owen	.02	.10
298 Salomon Torres	.02	.10
299 Wilson Alvarez	.02	.10
300 Ryne Sandberg	.30	.75
301 Derek Lilliquist	.02	.10
302 Howard Johnson	.02	.10
303 Greg Cadaret	.02	.10
304 Pat Hentgen	.02	.10
305 Craig Biggio	.10	.30
306 Scott Service	.02	.10
307 Melvin Nieves	.02	.10
308 Mike Trombley	.02	.10
309 Carlos Garcia	.02	.10
310 Robin Yount	.30	.75
311 Marcos Armas	.02	.10
312 Rich Rodriguez	.02	.10
313 Justin Thompson	.02	.10
314 Danny Sheaffer	.02	.10
315 Ken Hill	.02	.10
316 Terrell Wade RC	.02	.10
317 Cris Carpenter	.02	.10
318 Jeff Blauser	.02	.10
319 Ted Power	.02	.10
320 Ozzie Smith	.30	.75
321 John Dopson	.02	.10
322 Chris Turner	.02	.10
323 Pete Incaviglia	.02	.10
324 Alan Mills	.02	.10
325 Jody Reed	.02	.10
326 Rich Monteleone	.02	.10
327 Mark Carreon	.02	.10
328 Donn Pall	.02	.10
329 Matt Walbeck	.02	.10
330 Charley Nagy	.02	.10
331 Jeff McKnight	.02	.10
332 Jose Lind	.02	.10
333 Mike Timlin	.02	.10
334 Doug Jones	.02	.10
335 Kevin Mitchell	.02	.10
336 Luis Lopez	.02	.10
337 Shane Mack	.02	.10
338 Randy Tomlin	.02	.10
339 Matt Mieske	.02	.10
340 Mark McGwire	.50	1.25
341 Nigel Wilson	.02	.10
342 Danny Gladden	.02	.10
343 Mo Sanford	.02	.10
344 Sean Berry	.02	.10
345 Kevin Brown	.07	.20
346 Greg Olson	.02	.10
347 Dave Magadan	.02	.10
348 Rene Arocha	.02	.10
349 Carlos Quintana	.02	.10
350 Jim Abbott	.10	.30
351 Gary DiSarcina	.02	.10
352 Ben Rivera	.02	.10
353 Carlos Hernandez	.02	.10
354 Darren Lewis	.02	.10
355 Harold Reynolds	.07	.20
356 Scott Ruffcorn	.02	.10
357 Mark Gubicza	.02	.10
358 Paul Sorrento	.02	.10
359 Anthony Young	.02	.10
360 Mark Grace	.10	.30
361 Rob Butler	.02	.10
362 Kevin Bass	.02	.10
363 Eric Helfand	.02	.10
364 Derek Bell	.02	.10
365 Scott Erickson	.02	.10
366 Al Martin	.02	.10
367 Ricky Bones	.02	.10
368 Jeff Branson	.02	.10
369 J.Giambi	.20	.50
D.Bell RC		
370 Benito Santiago	.07	.20
371 John Doherty	.02	.10
372 Joe Girardi	.02	.10
373 Tim Scott	.02	.10
374 Marvin Freeman	.02	.10
375 Deion Sanders	.10	.30
376 Roger Salkeld	.02	.10
377 Bernard Gilkey	.02	.10
378 Tony Fossas	.02	.10
379 Mark McLemore UER	.02	.10
380 Darren Daulton	.07	.20
381 Chuck Finley	.07	.20
382 Mitch Webster	.02	.10
383 Gerald Williams	.02	.10
384 F.Thomas	.10	.30
F.McGriff AS		
385 R.Alomar	.07	.20
R.Thompson AS		
386 W.Boggs	.07	.20
M.Williams AS		
387 C.Ripken	.20	.50
J.Blauser AS		
388 K.Griffey	.25	.60
L.Dykstra AS		
389 J.Gonzalez	.07	.20
D.Justice AS		
390 A.Belle	.30	.75
B.Bonds AS		
391 M.Stanley	.20	.50
M.Piazza AS		
392 J.McDowell	.10	.30
G.Maddux AS		
393 J.Key	.07	.20
T.Glavine AS		
394 J.Montgomery	.02	.10
R.Myers AS		
395 Checklist 1-198	.02	.10
396 Checklist 199-396	.02	.10
397 Tim Salmon	.10	.30
398 Todd Benzinger	.02	.10
399 Frank Castillo	.02	.10
400 Ken Griffey Jr.	.40	1.00
401 John Kruk	.07	.20
402 Dave Telgheder	.02	.10
403 Gary Gaetti	.07	.20
404 Jim Edmonds	.20	.50
405 Don Slaught	.02	.10
406 Jose Oquendo	.02	.10
407 Bruce Ruffin	.02	.10
408 Phil Clark	.02	.10
409 Joe Klink	.02	.10
410 Lou Whitaker	.07	.20
411 Kevin Seitzer	.02	.10
412 Darrin Fletcher	.02	.10
413 Kenny Rogers	.07	.20
414 Bill Pecota	.02	.10
415 Dave Fleming	.02	.10
416 Luis Alicea	.02	.10
417 Paul Quantrill	.02	.10
418 Damion Easley	.02	.10
419 Wes Chamberlain	.02	.10
420 Harold Baines	.07	.20
421 Scott Radinsky	.02	.10
422 Rey Sanchez	.02	.10
423 Junior Ortiz	.02	.10
424 Jeff Kent	.10	.30
425 Brian McRae	.02	.10
426 Ed Sprague	.02	.10
427 Tom Edens	.02	.10
428 Willie Greene	.02	.10
429 Bryan Hickerson	.02	.10
430 Dave Winfield	.07	.20
431 Pedro Astacio	.02	.10
432 Mike Gallego	.02	.10
433 Dave Burba	.02	.10
434 Bob Walk	.02	.10
435 Darryl Hamilton	.02	.10
436 Vince Horsman	.02	.10
437 Bob Natal	.02	.10
438 Mike Henneman	.02	.10
439 Willie Blair	.02	.10
440 Dennis Martinez	.07	.20
441 Dan Peltier	.02	.10
442 Tony Tarasco	.02	.10
443 John Cummings	.02	.10
444 Geronimo Pena	.02	.10
445 Aaron Sele	.02	.10
446 Stan Javier	.02	.10
447 Mike Williams	.02	.10
448 D.J. Boston RC	.02	.10
449 Jim Poole	.02	.10
450 Carlos Baerga	.02	.10
451 Bob Scanlan	.02	.10
452 Lance Johnson	.02	.10
453 Eric Hillman	.02	.10
454 Keith Miller	.02	.10
455 Dave Stewart	.07	.20
456 Pete Harnisch	.02	.10
457 Roberto Kelly	.02	.10
458 Tim Worrell	.02	.10
459 Pedro Munoz	.02	.10
460 Orel Hershiser	.07	.20
461 Randy Velarde	.02	.10
462 Trevor Wilson	.02	.10
463 Jerry Goff	.02	.10
464 Bill Wegman	.02	.10
465 Dennis Eckersley	.07	.20
466 Jeff Conine	.07	.20
467 Joe Boever	.02	.10
468 Dante Bichette	.07	.20
469 Jeff Shaw	.02	.10
470 Rafael Palmeiro	.10	.30
471 Phil Leftwich RC	.02	.10
472 Jay Buhner	.07	.20
473 Bob Tewksbury	.02	.10
474 Tim Naehring	.02	.10
475 Tom Glavine	.10	.30
476 Dave Hollins	.02	.10
477 Arthur Rhodes	.02	.10
478 Joey Cora	.02	.10
479 Mike Morgan	.02	.10
480 Albert Belle	.07	.20
481 John Franco	.07	.20
482 Hipolito Pichardo	.02	.10
483 Duane Ward	.02	.10
484 Luis Gonzalez	.07	.20
485 Joe Oliver	.02	.10
486 Wally Whitehurst	.02	.10
487 Mike Benjamin	.02	.10
488 Eric Davis	.07	.20
489 Scott Kamieniecki	.02	.10
490 Kent Hrbek	.07	.20
491 John Hope RC	.02	.10
492 Jesse Orosco	.02	.10
493 Troy Neel	.02	.10
494 Ryan Bowen	.02	.10
495 Mickey Tettleton	.02	.10
496 Chris Jones	.02	.10
497 John Wetteland	.07	.20
498 David Hulse	.02	.10
499 Greg Maddux	.30	.75
500 Bo Jackson	.20	.50
501 Donovan Osborne	.02	.10
502 Mike Greenwell	.02	.10
503 Steve Frey	.02	.10
504 Jim Eisenreich	.02	.10
505 Robby Thompson	.02	.10
506 Leo Gomez	.02	.10
507 Dave Staton	.02	.10
508 Wayne Kirby	.02	.10
509 Tim Bogar	.02	.10
510 David Cone	.07	.20
511 Devon White	.07	.20
512 Xavier Hernandez	.02	.10
513 Tim Costo	.02	.10
514 Gene Harris	.02	.10
515 Jack McDowell	.02	.10
516 Kevin Gross	.02	.10
517 Scott Leius	.02	.10
518 Lloyd McClendon	.02	.10
519 Alex Diaz RC	.02	.10
520 Wade Boggs	.10	.30
521 Bob Welch	.02	.10
522 Henry Cotto	.02	.10
523 Mike Moore	.02	.10
524 Tim Laker	.02	.10
525 Andres Galarraga	.07	.20
526 Jamie Moyer	.07	.20
527 J.Hardtke RC	.02	.10
C.Sexton RC		
528 Sid Bream	.02	.10
529 Erik Hanson	.02	.10
530 Ray Lankford	.07	.20
531 Rob Deer	.02	.10
532 Rod Correia	.02	.10
533 Roger Mason	.02	.10
534 Mike Devereaux	.02	.10
535 Jeff Montgomery	.02	.10
536 Dwight Smith	.02	.10
537 Jeremy Hernandez	.02	.10
538 Ellis Burks	.07	.20
539 Bobby Jones	.02	.10
540 Paul Molitor	.07	.20
541 Jeff Juden	.02	.10
542 Chris Sabo	.02	.10
543 Larry Casian	.02	.10
544 Jeff Gardner	.02	.10
545 Ramon Martinez	.02	.10
546 Paul O'Neill	.10	.30
547 Steve Hosey	.02	.10
548 Dave Nilsson	.02	.10
549 Ron Darling	.02	.10
550 Matt Williams	.07	.20
551 Jack Armstrong	.02	.10
552 Bill Krueger	.02	.10
553 Freddie Benavides	.02	.10
554 Jeff Fassero	.02	.10
555 Chuck Knoblauch	.07	.20
556 Guillermo Velasquez	.02	.10
557 Joel Johnston	.02	.10
558 Tom Lampkin	.02	.10
559 Todd Van Poppel	.02	.10
560 Gary Sheffield	.07	.20
561 Skeeter Barnes	.02	.10
562 Darren Holmes	.02	.10
563 John Vander Wal	.02	.10
564 Mike Ignasiak	.02	.10
565 Fred McGriff	.10	.30
566 Luis Polonia	.02	.10
567 Mike Perez	.02	.10
568 John Valentin	.02	.10
569 Mike Felder	.02	.10
570 Tommy Greene	.02	.10
571 David Segui	.02	.10
572 Roberto Hernandez	.02	.10
573 Steve Wilson	.02	.10
574 Willie McGee	.07	.20
575 Randy Myers	.02	.10
576 Darrin Jackson	.02	.10
577 Eric Plunk	.02	.10
578 Mike Macfarlane	.02	.10
579 Doug Brocail	.02	.10
580 Steve Finley	.07	.20
581 John Roper	.02	.10
582 Danny Cox	.02	.10
583 Chip Hale	.02	.10
584 Scott Bullett	.02	.10
585 Kevin Reimer	.02	.10
586 Brent Gates	.02	.10
587 Matt Turner	.02	.10
588 Rich Rowland	.02	.10
589 Kent Bottenfield	.02	.10
590 Marquis Grissom	.07	.20
591 Doug Strange	.02	.10
592 Jay Howell	.02	.10
593 Omar Vizquel	.10	.30
594 Rheal Cormier	.02	.10
595 Andre Dawson	.07	.20
596 Hilly Hathaway	.02	.10
597 Todd Pratt	.02	.10
598 Mike Mussina	.10	.30
599 Alex Fernandez	.02	.10
600 Don Mattingly	.50	1.25
601 Frank Thomas MOG	.10	.30
602 Ryne Sandberg MOG	.20	.50
603 Wade Boggs MOG	.07	.20
604 Cal Ripken MOG	.30	.75
605 Barry Bonds MOG	.30	.75
606 Ken Griffey Jr. MOG	.25	.60
607 Kirby Puckett MOG	.10	.30
608 Darren Daulton MOG	.02	.10
609 Paul Molitor MOG	.02	.10
610 Terry Steinbach	.02	.10
611 Todd Worrell	.02	.10
612 Jim Thome	.10	.30
613 Chuck McElroy	.02	.10
614 John Habyan	.02	.10
615 Sid Fernandez	.02	.10
616 Jermaine Allensworth RC	.02	.10
617 Steve Bedrosian	.02	.10
618 Rob Ducey	.02	.10
619 Tom Browning	.02	.10
620 Tony Gwynn	.25	.60
621 Carl Willis	.02	.10
622 Kevin Young	.02	.10
623 Rafael Novoa	.02	.10
624 Jerry Browne	.02	.10
625 Charlie Hough	.07	.20
626 Chris Gomez	.02	.10
627 Steve Reed	.02	.10
628 Kirk Rueter	.02	.10
629 Matt Whiteside	.02	.10
630 David Justice	.07	.20
631 Brad Holman	.02	.10
632 Brian Jordan	.07	.20
633 Scott Bankhead	.02	.10
634 Torey Lovullo	.02	.10
635 Len Dykstra	.07	.20
636 Ben McDonald	.02	.10
637 Steve Howe	.02	.10
638 Jose Vizcaino	.02	.10
639 Bill Swift	.02	.10
640 Darryl Strawberry	.07	.20
641 Steve Farr	.02	.10
642 Tom Kramer	.02	.10
643 Joe Orsulak	.02	.10
644 Tom Henke	.02	.10
645 Joe Carter	.07	.20
646 Ken Caminiti	.07	.20
647 Reggie Sanders	.07	.20
648 Andy Ashby	.02	.10
649 Derek Parks	.02	.10
650 Andy Van Slyke	.10	.30
651 Juan Bell	.02	.10
652 Roger Smithberg	.02	.10
653 Chuck Carr	.02	.10
654 Bill Gullickson	.02	.10
655 Charlie Hayes	.02	.10
656 Chris Nabholz	.02	.10
657 Karl Rhodes	.02	.10
658 Pete Smith	.02	.10
659 Bret Boone	.07	.20
660 Gregg Jefferies	.02	.10
661 Bob Zupcic	.02	.10
662 Steve Sax	.02	.10
663 Mariano Duncan	.02	.10
664 Jeff Tackett	.02	.10
665 Mark Langston	.02	.10
666 Steve Buechele	.02	.10
667 Candy Maldonado	.02	.10
668 Woody Williams	.07	.20
669 Tim Wakefield	.10	.30
670 Danny Tartabull	.02	.10
671 Charlie O'Brien	.02	.10
672 Felix Jose	.02	.10
673 Bobby Ayala	.02	.10
674 Scott Servais	.02	.10
675 Roberto Alomar	.10	.30
676 Pedro A.Martinez RC	.02	.10
677 Eddie Guardado	.07	.20
678 Mark Lewis	.02	.10
679 Jaime Navarro	.02	.10
680 Ruben Sierra	.07	.20
681 Rick Renteria	.02	.10
682 Storm Davis	.02	.10
683 Cory Snyder	.02	.10
684 Ron Karkovice	.02	.10
685 Juan Gonzalez	.07	.20
686 Carlos Delgado	.10	.30
687 John Smoltz	.10	.30
688 Brian Dorsett	.02	.10
689 Omar Olivares	.02	.10
690 Mo Vaughn	.07	.20
691 Joe Grahe	.02	.10
692 Mickey Morandini	.02	.10
693 Tino Martinez	.10	.30
694 Brian Barnes	.02	.10
695 Mike Stanley	.02	.10
696 Mark Clark	.02	.10
697 Dave Hansen	.02	.10
698 Willie Wilson	.02	.10
699 Pete Schourek	.02	.10
700 Barry Bonds	.60	1.50
701 Kevin Appier	.07	.20
702 Tony Fernandez	.02	.10
703 Darryl Kile	.07	.20
704 Archi Cianfrocco	.02	.10
705 Jose Rijo	.02	.10
706 Brian Harper	.02	.10
707 Zane Smith	.02	.10
708 Dave Henderson	.02	.10
709 Angel Miranda UER	.02	.10
710 Orestes Destrade	.02	.10
711 Greg Gohr	.02	.10
712 Eric Young	.02	.10
713 Bullinger	.02	.10
Will		
Wat		
Welch		
714 Tim Spehr	.02	.10
715 Hank Aaron 715 HR	.20	.50
716 Nate Minchey	.02	.10
717 Mike Blowers	.02	.10
718 Kent Mercker	.02	.10
719 Tom Pagnozzi	.02	.10
720 Roger Clemens	.40	1.00
721 Eduardo Perez	.02	.10
722 Milt Thompson	.02	.10
723 Gregg Olson	.02	.10
724 Kirk McCaskill	.02	.10
725 Sammy Sosa	.20	.50
726 Alvaro Espinoza	.02	.10
727 Henry Rodriguez	.02	.10
728 Jim Leyritz	.02	.10
729 Steve Scarsone	.02	.10
730 Bobby Bonilla	.07	.20
731 Chris Gwynn	.02	.10
732 Al Leiter	.07	.20
733 Bip Roberts	.02	.10
734 Mark Portugal	.02	.10
735 Terry Pendleton	.07	.20
736 Dave Valle	.02	.10
737 Paul Kilgus	.02	.10
738 Greg A. Harris	.02	.10
739 Jon Ratliff RC	.02	.10
740 Kirk Presley RC	.02	.10
741 Josue Estrada RC	.02	.10
742 Wayne Gomes RC	.02	.10
743 Pat Watkins RC	.02	.10
744 Jamey Wright RC	.08	.25
745 Jay Powell RC	.02	.10
746 Ryan McGuire RC	.02	.10
747 Marc Barcelo RC	.02	.10
748 Sloan Smith RC	.02	.10
749 John Wasdin RC	.02	.10
750 Marc Valdes	.02	.10
751 Dan Ehler RC	.02	.10
752 Andre King RC	.02	.10
753 Greg Keagle RC	.02	.10
754 Jason Myers RC	.02	.10
755 Dax Winslett RC	.02	.10
756 Casey Whitten RC	.02	.10
757 Tony Fuduric RC	.02	.10
758 Greg Norton RC	.08	.25
759 Jeff D'Amico RC	.02	.10
760 Ryan Hancock RC	.02	.10
761 David Cooper RC	.02	.10
762 Kevin Orie RC	.02	.10
763 J.O'Donoghue	.02	.10
M.Oquist		
764 C.Bailey RC	.02	.10
S.Hatteberg		
765 M.Holzemer	.02	.10
P.Swingle RC		
766 J.Baldwin	.02	.10
R.Bolton		
767 J.Tavarez RC	.08	.25
J.DiPoto		
768 D.Bautista	.02	.10
S.Bergman		
769 B.Hamelin	.02	.10
J.Vitiello		
770 M.Kiefer	.02	.10
T.O'Leary		
771 D.Hocking	.02	.10
O.Munoz RC		
772 Russ Davis	.02	.10
B.Taylor		
773 K.Abbott	.08	.25
M.Jimenez		
774 K.King RC	.02	.10
Plantenberg RC		
775 J.Shave	.02	.10
D.Wilson		
776 D.Cedeno	.02	.10
P.Spoljaric		
777 C.Jones	.20	.50
R.Klesko		
778 S.Trachsel	.02	.10
T.Wendell		
779 J.Spradlin RC	.02	.10
J.Ruffin		
780 J.Bates	.02	.10
J.Burke		
781 C.Everett	.07	.20
D.Weathers		
782 J.Mouton	.02	.10
G.Mota		
783 R.Mondesi	.07	.20
B.Van Ryn		
784 R.White	.07	.20
G.White		
785 B.Pulsipher	.07	.20
B.Fordyce		
786 K.Foster RC	.02	.10
G.Schall		
787 Rich Aude RC	.02	.10
M.Cummings		
788 B.Barber	.02	.10
R.Batchelor		
789 B.Johnson RC	.02	.10
S.Sanders		
790 J.Phillips	.02	.10
R.Faneyte		
791 Checklist 3	.02	.10
792 Checklist 4	.02	.10

1994 Topps Gold

*STARS: 1.5X TO 4X BASIC CARDS
*ROOKIES: 1.25X TO 3X BASIC CARDS
ONE PER PACK OR MINIPACK
TWO PER FOURTH PACK OR MINI JUMBO

Card	Low	High
395 Bill Brennan	.15	.40
396 Jeff Bronkey	.15	.40
791 Mike Cook	.15	.40
792 Dan Pasqua	.15	.40

1994 Topps Spanish

*STARS: 3X to 6X BASIC CARDS
L1 Felipe Alou .30 .75
L2 Ruben Amaro .08 .25
L3 Luis Aparicio .40 1.00
L4 Rod Carew .40 1.00
L5 Chico Carrasquel .20 .50
L6 Orlando Cepeda .40 1.00
L7 Juan Marichal .40 1.00
L8 Minnie Minoso .30 .75
L9 Cookie Rojas .08 .25
L10 Luis Tiant .20 .50

1994 Topps Black Gold

Randomly inserted one in every 72 packs, this 44-card standard-size set was issued in two series of 22. Cards were also issued three per 1994 Topps factory set. Collectors had a chance, through redemption cards to receive all or part of the set. There are seven Winner redemption cards for a total 51 cards associated with this set. The set is considered complete with the 44 player cards. Card fronts feature color player action photos. The player's name at bottom and the team name at top are screened in gold foil. The backs contain a player photo and statistical rankings. The winner cards were redeemable until January 31, 1995

COMPLETE SET (44) 10.00 25.00
COMPLETE SERIES 1 (22) 6.00 15.00
COMPLETE SERIES 2 (22) 4.00 10.00
STAT.ODDS 1:72H/R,1:18J,1:24RAC,1:36CEL
THREE PER FACTORY SET
1 Roberto Alomar .25 .60
2 Carlos Baerga .07 .20
3 Albert Belle .15 .40
4 Joe Carter .15 .40
5 Cecil Fielder .15 .40
6 Travis Fryman .15 .40
7 Juan Gonzalez .15 .40
8 Ken Griffey Jr. .75 2.00
9 Chris Hoiles .07 .20
10 Randy Johnson .40 1.00
11 Kenny Lofton .15 .40
12 Jack McDowell .07 .20
13 Paul Molitor .15 .40
14 Jeff Montgomery .07 .20
15 John Olerud .15 .40
16 Rafael Palmeiro .25 .60
17 Kirby Puckett .40 1.00
18 Cal Ripken 1.25 3.00
19 Tim Salmon .25 .60
20 Mike Stanley .07 .20
21 Frank Thomas .40 1.00
22 Robin Ventura .15 .40
23 Jeff Bagwell .25 .60
24 Jay Bell .15 .40
25 Craig Biggio .25 .60
26 Jeff Blauser .07 .20
27 Barry Bonds 1.25 3.00
28 Darren Daulton .15 .40
29 Len Dykstra .15 .40
30 Andres Galarraga .15 .40
31 Ron Gant .15 .40
32 Tom Glavine .25 .60
33 Mark Grace .25 .60
34 Marquis Grissom .15 .40
35 Gregg Jefferies .07 .20
36 David Justice .15 .40
37 John Kruk .15 .40
38 Greg Maddux .60 1.50
39 Fred McGriff .25 .60
40 Randy Myers .07 .20
41 Mike Piazza .75 2.00
42 Sammy Sosa .40 1.00
43 Robby Thompson .07 .20
44 Matt Williams .15 .40
A Winner A 1-11 Expired .07 .20
B Winner B 12-22 .07 .20
C Winner C 23-33 .07 .20
D Winner D 34-44 .07 .20
AB Winner AB 1-22 10.00 25.00
CD Winner CD 23-44 10.00 25.00
ABCD Win.ABCD 1-44 75.00 150.00

1994 Topps Traded

This set consists of 132 standard-size cards featuring traded players in their new uniforms, rookies and draft choices. Factory sets consisted of 140 cards including a set of eight Topps Finest cards. Card fronts feature a player photo with the player's name, team and position at the bottom. The horizontal backs have a player photo to the left with complete career statistics and highlights. Rookie Cards include Rusty Greer, Ben Grieve, Paul Konerko Terrence Long and Chan Ho Park.

COMP.FACT.SET (140) 15.00 40.00
1T Paul Wilson .02 .10
2T Bill Taylor RC .40 1.00
3T Dan Wilson .02 .10
4T Mark Smith .02 .10
5T Toby Borland RC .08 .25
6T Dave Clark .02 .10
7T Dennis Martinez .07 .20
8T Dave Gallagher .02 .10
9T Josias Manzanillo .02 .10
10T Brian Anderson RC .40 1.00
11T Damon Berryhill .02 .10
12T Alex Cole .02 .10
13T Jacob Shumate RC .08 .25
14T Oddibe McDowell .02 .10
15T Willie Banks .02 .10
16T Jerry Browne .02 .10
17T Donnie Elliott .02 .10
18T Ellis Burks .07 .20
19T Chuck McElroy .02 .10
20T Luis Polonia .02 .10
21T Brian Harper .02 .10
22T Mark Portugal .02 .10
23T Dave Henderson .02 .10
24T Mark Acre RC .08 .25
25T Julio Franco .07 .20
26T Darren Hall RC .08 .25
27T Eric Anthony .02 .10
28T Sid Fernandez .02 .10
29T Rusty Greer RC .60 1.50
30T Riccardo Ingram RC .08 .25
31T Gabe White .02 .10
32T Tim Belcher .02 .10
33T Terrence Long RC .40 1.00
34T Mark Dalesandro RC .08 .25
35T Mike Kelly .02 .10
36T Jack Morris .07 .20
37T Jeff Brantley .02 .10
38T Larry Barnes RC .08 .25
39T Brian R. Hunter .02 .10
40T Otis Nixon .02 .10
41T Bret Wagner .02 .10
42T P.Martinez .20 .50
D.Deshields TR
43T Heathcliff Slocumb .02 .10
44T Ben Grieve RC .40 1.00
45T John Hudek RC .08 .25
46T Shawon Dunston .02 .10
47T Greg Colbrunn .02 .10
48T Joey Hamilton .02 .10
49T Marvin Freeman .02 .10
50T Terry Mulholland .02 .10
51T Keith Mitchell .02 .10
52T Dwight Smith .02 .10
53T Shawn Boskie .02 .10
54T Kevin Witt RC .40 1.00
55T Ron Gant .07 .20
56T Jason Schmidt RC 4.00 10.00
57T Jody Reed .02 .10
58T Rick Helling .02 .10
59T John Powell .02 .10
60T Eddie Murray .20 .50
61T Joe Hall RC .08 .25
62T Jorge Fabregas .02 .10
63T Mike Mordecai RC .08 .25
64T Ed Vosberg .02 .10
65T Rickey Henderson .20 .50
66T Tim Grieve RC .08 .25
67T Jon Lieber .07 .20
68T Chris Howard .02 .10
69T Matt Walbeck .02 .10
70T Chan Ho Park RC .60 1.50
71T Bryan Eversgerd RC .08 .25
72T John Dettmer .02 .10
73T Erik Hanson .02 .10
74T Mike Thurman RC .08 .25
75T Bobby Ayala .02 .10
76T Rafael Palmeiro .10 .30
77T Bret Boone .07 .20
78T Paul Shuey .02 .10
79T Kevin Foster RC .08 .25
80T Dave Magadan .02 .10
81T Bip Roberts .02 .10
82T Howard Johnson .02 .10
83T Xavier Hernandez .02 .10
84T Ross Powell RC .08 .25
85T Doug Million RC .08 .25
86T Geronimo Berroa .02 .10
87T Mark Farris RC .08 .25
88T Butch Henry .02 .10
89T Junior Felix .02 .10
90T Bo Jackson .20 .50
91T Hector Carrasco .02 .10
92T Charlie O'Brien .02 .10
93T Omar Vizquel .10 .30
94T David Segui .02 .10
95T Dustin Hermanson .02 .10
96T Gar Finnvold RC .08 .25
97T Dave Stevens .02 .10
98T Corey Pointer RC .08 .25
99T Felix Fermin .02 .10
100T Lee Smith .07 .20
101T Reid Ryan RC .40 1.00
102T Bobby Munoz .02 .10
103T D.Sanders .10 .30
R.Kelly TR
104T Turner Ward .02 .10
105T W.VanLandingham RC .08 .25
106T Vince Coleman .02 .10
107T Stan Javier .02 .10
108T Darrin Jackson .02 .10
109T C.J.Nitkowski RC .08 .25
110T Anthony Young .02 .10
111T Kurt Miller .02 .10
112T Paul Konerko RC 6.00 15.00
113T Walt Weiss .02 .10
114T Daryl Boston .02 .10
115T Will Clark .10 .30
116T Matt Smith RC .08 .25
117T Mark Leiter .02 .10
118T Gregg Olson .02 .10
119T Tony Pena .02 .10
120T Jose Vizcaino .02 .10
121T Rick White RC .08 .25
122T Rich Rowland .02 .10
123T Jeff Reboulet .02 .10
124T Greg Hibbard .02 .10
125T Chris Sabo .02 .10
126T Doug Jones .02 .10
127T Tony Fernandez .02 .10
128T Carlos Reyes RC .08 .25
129T Kevin L.Brown RC .40 1.00
130T Ryne Sandberg HL .50 1.25
131T Ryne Sandberg HL .50 1.25
132T Checklist 1-132 .02 .10

1994 Topps Traded Finest Inserts

Each Topps Traded factory set contained a complete eight card set of Finest Inserts. These cards are numbered separately and designed differently from the base cards. Each Finest Insert features a action shot of a player set against purple chrome background. The set highlights the top performers midway through the 1994 season, detailing their performances through July. The cards are numbered on back "X of 8".

COMPLETE SET (8) 2.00 5.00
ONE SET PER TRADED FACTORY SET
1 Greg Maddux .30 .75
2 Mike Piazza .40 1.00
3 Matt Williams .07 .20
4 Raul Mondesi .07 .20
5 Ken Griffey Jr. .40 1.00
6 Kenny Lofton .07 .20
7 Frank Thomas .20 .50
8 Manny Ramirez .20 .50

1995 Topps

These 660 standard-size cards feature color action player photos with white borders on the fronts. This set was released in two series. The first series contained 396 cards while the second series had 264 cards. Cards were distributed in 11-card packs (SRP $1.29), jumbo packs and factory sets. One "Own The Game" instant winner card has been inserted in every 120 packs. Rookie cards in this set include Rey Ordonez. Due to the 1994 baseball strike, it was publicly announced that production for this set was the lowest print run since 1966.

COMPLETE SET (660) 25.00 60.00
COMP.HOBBY SET (677) 30.00 80.00
COMP.RETAIL SET (677) 30.00 80.00
COMPLETE SERIES 1 (396) 15.00 40.00
COMPLETE SERIES 2 (264) 15.00 40.00
1 Frank Thomas .30 .75
2 Mickey Morandini .05 .15
3 Babe Ruth 100th B-Day .75 2.00
4 Scott Cooper .05 .15
5 David Cone .10 .30
6 Jacob Shumate .05 .15
7 Trevor Hoffman .10 .30
8 Shane Mack .05 .15
9 Delino DeShields .05 .15
10 Matt Williams .10 .30
11 Sammy Sosa .30 .75
12 Gary DiSarcina .05 .15
13 Kenny Rogers .10 .30
14 Jose Vizcaino .05 .15
15 Lou Whitaker .10 .30
16 Ron Darling .05 .15
17 Dave Nilsson .05 .15
18 Chris Hammond .05 .15
19 Sid Bream .05 .15
20 Denny Martinez .10 .30
21 Orlando Merced .05 .15
22 John Wetteland .10 .30
23 Mike Devereaux .05 .15
24 Rene Arocha .05 .15
25 Jay Buhner .10 .30
26 Darren Holmes .05 .15
27 Hal Morris .05 .15
28 Brian Buchanan RC .05 .15
29 Keith Miller .05 .15
30 Paul Molitor .10 .30
31 Dave West .05 .15
32 Tony Tarasco .05 .15
33 Scott Sanders .05 .15
34 Eddie Zambrano .05 .15
35 Ricky Bones .05 .15
36 John Valentin .05 .15
37 Kevin Tapani .05 .15
38 Tim Wallach .05 .15
39 Darren Lewis .05 .15
40 Travis Fryman .10 .30
41 Mark Leiter .05 .15
42 Jose Bautista .05 .15
43 Pete Smith .05 .15
44 Bret Barberie .05 .15
45 Dennis Eckersley .10 .30
46 Ken Hill .05 .15
47 Chad Ogea .05 .15
48 Pete Harnisch .05 .15
49 James Baldwin .05 .15
50 Mike Mussina .20 .50
51 Al Martin .05 .15
52 Mark Thompson .05 .15
53 Matt Smith .05 .15
54 Joey Hamilton .05 .15
55 Edgar Martinez .20 .50
56 John Smiley .05 .15
57 Rey Sanchez .05 .15
58 Mike Timlin .05 .15
59 Ricky Bottalico .05 .15
60 Jim Abbott .20 .50
61 Mike Kelly .05 .15
62 Brian Jordan .10 .30
63 Ken Ryan .05 .15
64 Matt Mieske .05 .15
65 Rick Aguilera .05 .15
66 Ismael Valdes .05 .15
67 Royce Clayton .05 .15
68 Junior Felix .05 .15
69 Harold Reynolds .10 .30
70 Juan Gonzalez .10 .30
71 Kelly Stinnett .05 .15
72 Carlos Reyes .05 .15
73 Dave Weathers .05 .15
74 Mel Rojas .05 .15
75 Doug Drabek .05 .15
76 Charles Nagy .05 .15
77 Tim Raines .10 .30
78 Midre Cummings .05 .15
79 Ray Brown RC .05 .15
80 Rafael Palmeiro .20 .50
81 Charlie Hayes .05 .15
82 Ray Lankford .10 .30
83 Tim Davis .05 .15
84 C.J. Nitkowski .05 .15
85 Andy Ashby .05 .15
86 Gerald Williams .05 .15
87 Terry Shumpert .05 .15
88 Heathcliff Slocumb .05 .15
89 Domingo Cedeno .05 .15
90 Mark Grace .20 .50
91 Brad Woodall RC .05 .15
92 Gar Finnvold .05 .15
93 Jaime Navarro .05 .15
94 Carlos Hernandez .05 .15
95 Mark Langston .05 .15
96 Chuck Carr .05 .15
97 Mike Gardiner .05 .15
98 Dave McCarty .05 .15
99 Cris Carpenter .05 .15
100 Barry Bonds .75 2.00
101 David Segui .05 .15
102 Scott Brosius .10 .30
103 Mariano Duncan .05 .15
104 Kenny Lofton .10 .30
105 Ken Caminiti .10 .30
106 Darrin Jackson .05 .15
107 Jim Poole .05 .15
108 Wil Cordero .05 .15
109 Danny Miceli .05 .15
110 Walt Weiss .05 .15
111 Tom Pagnozzi .05 .15
112 Terrence Long .05 .15
113 Bret Boone .10 .30
114 Daryl Boston .05 .15
115 Wally Joyner .10 .30
116 Rob Butler .05 .15
117 Rafael Belliard .05 .15
118 Luis Lopez .05 .15
119 Tony Fossas .05 .15
120 Len Dykstra .10 .30
121 Mike Morgan .05 .15
122 Denny Hocking .05 .15
123 Kevin Gross .05 .15
124 Todd Benzinger .05 .15
125 John Doherty .05 .15
126 Eduardo Perez .05 .15
127 Dan Smith .05 .15
128 Joe Orsulak .05 .15
129 Brent Gates .05 .15
130 Jeff Conine .10 .30
131 Doug Henry .05 .15
132 Paul Sorrento .05 .15
133 Mike Hampton .10 .30
134 Tim Spehr .05 .15
135 Julio Franco .10 .30
136 Mike Dyer .05 .15
137 Chris Sabo .05 .15
138 Rheal Cormier .05 .15
139 Paul Konerko .40 1.00
140 Dante Bichette .10 .30
141 Chuck McElroy .05 .15
142 Mike Stanley .05 .15
143 Bob Hamelin .05 .15
144 Tommy Greene .05 .15
145 John Smoltz .20 .50
146 Ed Sprague .05 .15
147 Ray McDavid .05 .15
148 Otis Nixon .05 .15
149 Turk Wendell .05 .15
150 Chris James .05 .15
151 Derek Parks .05 .15
152 Jose Offerman .05 .15
153 Tony Clark .10 .30
154 Chad Curtis .05 .15
155 Mark Portugal .05 .15
156 Bill Pulsipher .05 .15
157 Troy Neel .05 .15
158 Dave Winfield .10 .30
159 Bill Wegman .05 .15
160 Benito Santiago .10 .30
161 Jose Mesa .05 .15
162 Luis Gonzalez .10 .30
163 Alex Fernandez .05 .15
164 Freddie Benavides .05 .15
165 Ben McDonald .05 .15
166 Blas Minor .05 .15
167 Bret Wagner .05 .15
168 Mac Suzuki .05 .15
169 Roberto Mejia .05 .15
170 Wade Boggs .20 .50
171 Pokey Reese .05 .15
172 Hipolito Pichardo .05 .15
173 Kim Batiste .05 .15
174 Darren Hall .05 .15
175 Tom Glavine .20 .50
176 Phil Plantier .05 .15
177 Chris Howard .05 .15
178 Karl Rhodes .05 .15
179 LaTroy Hawkins .05 .15
180 Raul Mondesi .10 .30
181 Jeff Reed .05 .15
182 Milt Cuyler .05 .15
183 Jim Edmonds .20 .50
184 Hector Fajardo .05 .15
185 Jeff Kent .10 .30
186 Wilson Alvarez .05 .15
187 Geronimo Berroa .05 .15
188 Billy Spiers .05 .15
189 Derek Lilliquist .05 .15
190 Craig Biggio .20 .50
191 Roberto Hernandez .05 .15
192 Bob Natal .05 .15
193 Bobby Ayala .05 .15
194 Travis Miller RC .05 .15
195 Bob Tewksbury .05 .15
196 Rondell White .10 .30
197 Steve Cooke .05 .15
198 Jeff Branson .05 .15
199 Derek Jeter .75 2.00
200 Tim Salmon .20 .50
201 Steve Frey .05 .15
202 Kent Mercker .05 .15
203 Randy Johnson .30 .75
204 Todd Worrell .05 .15
205 Mo Vaughn .10 .30
206 Howard Johnson .05 .15
207 John Wasdin .05 .15
208 Eddie Williams .05 .15
209 Tim Belcher .05 .15
210 Jeff Montgomery .05 .15
211 Kirt Manwaring .05 .15
212 Ben Grieve .05 .15
213 Pat Hentgen .05 .15
214 Shawon Dunston .05 .15
215 Mike Greenwell .05 .15
216 Alex Diaz .05 .15
217 Pat Mahomes .05 .15
218 Dave Hansen .05 .15
219 Kevin Rogers .05 .15
220 Cecil Fielder .10 .30
221 Andrew Lorraine .05 .15
222 Jack Armstrong .05 .15
223 Todd Hundley .05 .15
224 Mark Acre .05 .15
225 Darrell Whitmore .05 .15
226 Randy Milligan .05 .15
227 Wayne Kirby .05 .15
228 Darryl Kile .10 .30
229 Bob Zupcic .05 .15
230 Jay Bell .10 .30
231 Dustin Hermanson .05 .15
232 Harold Baines .10 .30
233 Alan Benes .05 .15
234 Felix Fermin .05 .15
235 Ellis Burks .10 .30
236 Jeff Brantley .05 .15
237 Karim Garcia RC .05 .15
238 Matt Nokes .05 .15
239 Ben Rivera .05 .15
240 Joe Carter .10 .30
241 Jeff Granger .05 .15
242 Terry Pendleton .10 .30
243 Melvin Nieves .05 .15
244 Frankie Rodriguez .05 .15
245 Darryl Hamilton .05 .15
246 Brooks Kieschnick .05 .15
247 Todd Hollandsworth .05 .15
248 Joe Rosselli .05 .15
249 Bill Gullickson .05 .15
250 Chuck Knoblauch .10 .30
251 Kurt Miller .05 .15
252 Bobby Jones .05 .15
253 Lance Blankenship .05 .15
254 Matt Whiteside .05 .15
255 Darrin Fletcher .05 .15
256 Eric Plunk .05 .15
257 Shane Reynolds .05 .15
258 Norberto Martin .05 .15
259 Mike Thurman .05 .15
260 Andy Van Slyke .20 .50
261 Dwight Smith .05 .15
262 Allen Watson .05 .15
263 Dan Wilson .05 .15
264 Brent Mayne .05 .15
265 Bip Roberts .05 .15
266 Sterling Hitchcock .05 .15
267 Alex Gonzalez .05 .15
268 Greg Harris .05 .15
269 Ricky Jordan .05 .15
270 Johnny Ruffin .05 .15
271 Mike Stanton .05 .15
272 Rich Rowland .05 .15
273 Steve Trachsel .05 .15
274 Pedro Munoz .05 .15
275 Ramon Martinez .05 .15
276 Dave Henderson .05 .15
277 Chris Gomez .05 .15
278 Joe Grahe .05 .15
279 Rusty Greer .10 .30
280 John Franco .10 .30
281 Mike Bordick .05 .15
282 Jeff D'Amico .05 .15
283 Dave Magadan .05 .15
284 Tony Pena .05 .15
285 Greg Swindell .05 .15
286 Doug Million .05 .15
287 Gabe White .05 .15
288 Trey Beamon .05 .15
289 Arthur Rhodes .05 .15
290 Juan Guzman .05 .15
291 Jose Oquendo .05 .15
292 Willie Blair .05 .15
293 Eddie Taubensee .05 .15
294 Steve Howe .05 .15
295 Greg Maddux .50 1.25
296 Mike Macfarlane .05 .15
297 Curt Schilling .10 .30
298 Phil Clark .05 .15
299 Woody Williams .05 .15
300 Jose Canseco .20 .50
301 Aaron Sele .05 .15
302 Carl Willis .05 .15
303 Steve Buechele .05 .15
304 Dave Burba .05 .15
305 Orel Hershiser .10 .30
306 Damion Easley .05 .15
307 Mike Henneman .05 .15
308 Josias Manzanillo .05 .15
309 Kevin Seitzer .05 .15
310 Ruben Sierra .10 .30
311 Bryan Harvey .05 .15
312 Jim Thome .20 .50
313 Ramon Castro RC .15 .40
314 Lance Johnson .05 .15
315 Marquis Grissom .10 .30
316 Eddie Priest RC .05 .15
317 Paul Wagner .05 .15
318 Jamie Moyer .10 .30
319 Todd Zeile .05 .15
320 Chris Bosio .05 .15
321 Steve Reed .05 .15
322 Erik Hanson .05 .15
323 Luis Polonia .05 .15
324 Ryan Klesko .10 .30
325 Kevin Appier .10 .30
326 Jim Eisenreich .05 .15
327 Randy Knorr .05 .15
328 Craig Shipley .05 .15
329 Tim Naehring .05 .15
330 Randy Myers .05 .15
331 Alex Cole .05 .15
332 Jim Gott .05 .15
333 Mike Jackson .05 .15
334 John Flaherty .05 .15
335 Chili Davis .10 .30
336 Benji Gil .05 .15
337 Jason Jacome .05 .15
338 Stan Javier .05 .15
339 Mike Fetters .05 .15
340 Rich Renteria .05 .15
341 Kevin Witt .05 .15
342 Scott Servais .05 .15
343 Craig Grebeck .05 .15
344 Kirk Rueter .05 .15
345 Don Slaught .05 .15
346 Armando Benitez .05 .15
347 Ozzie Smith .50 1.25
348 Mike Blowers .05 .15
349 Armando Reynoso .05 .15
350 Barry Larkin .20 .50
351 Mike Williams .05 .15
352 Scott Kamieniecki .05 .15
353 Gary Gaetti .10 .30
354 Todd Stottlemyre .05 .15
355 Fred McGriff .20 .50
356 Tim Mauser .05 .15
357 Chris Gwynn .05 .15
358 Frank Castillo .05 .15
359 Jeff Reboulet .05 .15
360 Roger Clemens .60 1.50
361 Mark Carreon .05 .15
362 Chad Kreuter .05 .15
363 Mark Farris .05 .15
364 Bob Welch .05 .15
365 Dean Palmer .10 .30
366 Jeromy Burnitz .10 .30
367 B.J. Surhoff .10 .30
368 Mike Butcher .05 .15
369 B.Buckles RC .05 .15
B.Clontz
370 Eddie Murray .30 .75
371 Orlando Miller .05 .15
372 Ron Karkovice .05 .15
373 Richie Lewis .05 .15
374 Lenny Webster .05 .15
375 Jeff Tackett .05 .15
376 Tom Urbani .05 .15
377 Tino Martinez .20 .50
378 Mark Dewey .05 .15
379 Charles O'Brien .05 .15
380 Terry Mulholland .05 .15
381 Thomas Howard .05 .15
382 Chris Haney .05 .15
383 Billy Hatcher .05 .15
384 F.Thomas .20 .50
J.Bagwell AS
385 B.Boone .10 .30
C.Baerga AS
386 M.Williams .10 .30
W.Boggs AS
387 C.Ripken .30 .75
W.Cordero AS
388 K.Griffey Jr. .50 1.25
B.Bonds AS
389 T.Gwynn .10 .30
A.Belle AS
390 D.Bichette .20 .50
K.Puckett AS
391 M.Piazza .30 .75
M.Stanley AS
392 G.Maddux .30 .75
D.Cone AS
393 D.Jackson .05 .15
J.Key AS
394 J.Franco .05 .15
L.Smith AS
395 Checklist 1-198 .05 .15
396 Checklist 199-396 .05 .15
397 Ken Griffey Jr. .60 1.50
398 Rick Heiserman RC .05 .15
399 Don Mattingly .75 2.00
400 Henry Rodriguez .05 .15
401 Lenny Harris .05 .15
402 Ryan Thompson .05 .15
403 Darren Oliver .05 .15
404 Omar Vizquel .20 .50
405 Jeff Bagwell .20 .50
406 Doug Webb RC .05 .15
407 Todd Van Poppel .05 .15
408 Leo Gomez .05 .15
409 Mark Whiten .05 .15
410 Pedro A.Martinez .05 .15
411 Reggie Sanders .10 .30
412 Kevin Foster .05 .15
413 Danny Tartabull .05 .15
414 Jeff Blauser .05 .15
415 Mike Magnante .05 .15
416 Tom Candiotti .05 .15
417 Rod Beck .05 .15
418 Jody Reed .05 .15
419 Vince Coleman .05 .15
420 Danny Jackson .05 .15
421 Ryan Nye RC .05 .15
422 Larry Walker .10 .30
423 Russ Johnson DP .05 .15
424 Pat Borders .05 .15
425 Lee Smith .10 .30
426 Paul O'Neill .20 .50
427 Devon White .10 .30
428 Jim Bullinger .05 .15
429 Rob Welch RC .05 .15
430 Steve Avery .05 .15
431 Tony Gwynn .40 1.00
432 Pat Meares .05 .15
433 Bill Swift .05 .15
434 David Wells .10 .30
435 John Briscoe .05 .15
436 Roger Pavlik .05 .15
437 Jayson Peterson RC .05 .15
438 Roberto Alomar .20 .50
439 Billy Brewer .05 .15
440 Gary Sheffield .10 .30
441 Lou Frazier .05 .15
442 Terry Steinbach .05 .15
443 Jay Payton RC .30 .75
444 Jason Bere .05 .15
445 Denny Neagle .10 .30
446 Andres Galarraga .10 .30
447 Hector Carrasco .05 .15

448 Bill Risley .05 .15
449 Andy Benes .05 .15
450 Jim Leyritz .05 .15
451 Jose Oliva .05 .15
452 Greg Vaughn .05 .15
453 Rich Monteleone .05 .15
454 Tony Eusebio .05 .15
455 Chuck Finley .10 .30
456 Kevin Brown .10 .30
457 Joe Boever .05 .15
458 Bobby Munoz .05 .15
459 Bret Saberhagen .10 .30
460 Kurt Abbott .05 .15
461 Bobby Witt .05 .15
462 Cliff Floyd .10 .30
463 Mark Clark .05 .15
464 Andujar Cedeno .05 .15
465 Marvin Freeman .05 .15
466 Mike Piazza .50 1.25
467 Willie Greene .05 .15
468 Pat Kelly .05 .15
469 Carlos Delgado .10 .30
470 Willie Banks .05 .15
471 Matt Walbeck .05 .15
472 Mark McGwire .75 2.00
473 McKay Christensen RC .05 .15
474 Alan Trammell .10 .30
475 Tom Gordon .05 .15
476 Greg Colbrunn .05 .15
477 Darren Daulton .10 .30
478 Albie Lopez .05 .15
479 Robin Ventura .10 .30
480 Eddie Perez RC .15 .40
481 Bryan Eversgerd .05 .15
482 Dave Fleming .05 .15
483 Scott Livingstone .05 .15
484 Pete Schourek .05 .15
485 Bernie Williams .20 .50
486 Mark Lemke .05 .15
487 Eric Karros .10 .30
488 Scott Ruffcorn .05 .15
489 Billy Ashley .05 .15
490 Rico Brogna .05 .15
491 John Burkett .05 .15
492 Cade Gaspar RC .05 .15
493 Jorge Fabregas .05 .15
494 Greg Gagne .05 .15
495 Doug Jones .05 .15
496 Troy O'Leary .05 .15
497 Pat Rapp .05 .15
498 Butch Henry .05 .15
499 John Olerud .10 .30
500 John Hudek .05 .15
501 Jeff King .05 .15
502 Bobby Bonilla .10 .30
503 Albert Belle .10 .30
504 Rick Wilkins .05 .15
505 John Jaha .05 .15
506 Nigel Wilson .05 .15
507 Sid Fernandez .05 .15
508 Deion Sanders .20 .50
509 Gil Heredia .05 .15
510 Scott Elarton RC .15 .40
511 Melido Perez .05 .15
512 Greg McMichael .05 .15
513 Rusty Meacham .05 .15
514 Shawn Green .10 .30
515 Carlos Garcia .05 .15
516 Dave Stevens .05 .15
517 Eric Young .05 .15
518 Omar Daal .05 .15
519 Kirk Gibson .10 .30
520 Spike Owen .05 .15
521 Jacob Cruz RC .10 .30
522 Sandy Alomar Jr. .05 .15
523 Steve Bedrosian .05 .15
524 Ricky Gutierrez .05 .15
525 Dave Veres .05 .15
526 Gregg Jefferies .05 .15
527 Jose Valentin .05 .15
528 Robb Nen .10 .30
529 Jose Rijo .05 .15
530 Sean Berry .05 .15
531 Mike Gallego .05 .15
532 Roberto Kelly .05 .15
533 Kevin Stocker .05 .15
534 Kirby Puckett .30 .75
535 Chipper Jones .30 .75
536 Russ Davis .05 .15
537 Jon Lieber .05 .15
538 Trey Moore RC .05 .15
539 Joe Girardi .05 .15
540 Miguel Cairo RC .05 .15
541 Tony Phillips .05 .15
542 Brian Anderson .05 .15
543 Ivan Rodriguez .20 .50
544 Jeff Cirillo .05 .15
545 Joey Cora .05 .15
546 Chris Hoiles .05 .15
547 Bernard Gilkey .05 .15
548 Mike Lansing .05 .15
549 Jimmy Key .10 .30
550 Mark Wohlers .05 .15
551 Chris Clemons RC .05 .15
552 Vinny Castilla .10 .30
553 Mark Guthrie .05 .15
554 Mike Lieberthal .10 .30
555 Tommy Davis RC .05 .15
556 Robby Thompson .05 .15
557 Danny Bautista .05 .15
558 Will Clark .20 .50
559 Rickey Henderson .30 .75
560 Todd Jones .05 .15
561 Jack McDowell .05 .15
562 Carlos Rodriguez .05 .15
563 Mark Eichhorn .05 .15
564 Jeff Nelson .05 .15
565 Eric Anthony .05 .15
566 Randy Velarde .05 .15
567 Javier Lopez .10 .30
568 Kevin Mitchell .05 .15
569 Steve Karsay .05 .15
570 Brian Meadows RC .05 .15
571 Rey Ordonez RC .30 .75
572 John Kruk .10 .30
573 Scott Leius .05 .15
574 John Patterson .05 .15
575 Kevin Brown .10 .30
576 Mike Moore .05 .15
577 Manny Ramirez .20 .50
578 Jose Lind .05 .15
579 Derrick May .05 .15
580 Cal Eldred .05 .15
581 A.Boone RC .30 .75
D.Bell
582 J.T. Snow .10 .30
583 Luis Sojo .05 .15
584 Moises Alou .10 .30
585 Dave Clark .05 .15
586 Dave Hollins .05 .15
587 Nomar Garciaparra .75 2.00
588 Cal Ripken 1.00 2.50
589 Pedro Astacio .05 .15
590 J.R. Phillips .05 .15
591 Jeff Frye .05 .15
592 Bo Jackson .30 .75
593 Steve Ontiveros .05 .15
594 David Nied .05 .15
595 Brad Ausmus .10 .30
596 Carlos Baerga .05 .15
597 James Mouton .05 .15
598 Ozzie Guillen .10 .30
599 Johnny Damon .30 .75
600 Yorkis Perez .05 .15
601 Rich Rodriguez .05 .15
602 Mark McLemore .05 .15
603 Jeff Fassero .05 .15
604 John Roper .05 .15
605 Mark Johnson RC .15 .40
606 Wes Chamberlain .05 .15
607 Felix Jose .05 .15
608 Tony Longmire .05 .15
609 Duane Ward .05 .15
610 Brett Butler .10 .30
611 William VanLandingham .05 .15
612 Mickey Tettleton .05 .15
613 Brady Anderson .10 .30
614 Reggie Jefferson .05 .15
615 Mike Kingery .05 .15
616 Derek Bell .05 .15
617 Scott Erickson .05 .15
618 Bob Wickman .05 .15
619 Phil Leftwich .05 .15
620 David Justice .10 .30
621 Paul Wilson .05 .15
622 Pedro Martinez .20 .50
623 Terry Mathews .05 .15
624 Brian McRae .05 .15
625 Bruce Ruffin .05 .15
626 Steve Finley .10 .30
627 Ron Gant .10 .30
628 Rafael Bournigal .05 .15
629 Darryl Strawberry .10 .30
630 Luis Alicea .05 .15
631 Mark Smith .05 .15
632 C.Bailey .05 .15
S.Hatteberg
633 Todd Greene .10 .30
634 Rod Bolton .05 .15
635 Herbert Perry .05 .15
636 Sean Bergman .05 .15
637 J.Randa .10 .30
J.Vitiello
638 Jose Mercedes .05 .15
639 Marty Cordova .05 .15
640 R.Rivera .10 .30
A.Pettitte
641 W.Adams .05 .15
S.Spiezio
642 Eddy Diaz RC .05 .15
643 Jon Shave .05 .15
644 Paul Spoljaric .05 .15
645 Damon Hollins .05 .15
646 Doug Glanville .05 .15
647 Tim Belk .05 .15
648 Rod Pedraza .05 .15
649 Marc Valdes .05 .15
650 Rick Huisman .05 .15
651 Ron Coomer RC .05 .15
652 Carlos Perez RC .15 .40
653 Jason Isringhausen .10 .30
654 Kevin Jordan .05 .15
655 Esteban Loaiza .05 .15
656 John Frascatore .05 .15
657 Bryce Florie .05 .15
658 Keith Williams .05 .15
659 Checklist .05 .15
660 Checklist .05 .15

1995 Topps Cyberstats

COMPLETE SET (396) 12.00 30.00
COMPLETE SERIES 1 (198) 5.00 12.00
COMPLETE SERIES 2 (198) 8.00 20.00
*STARS: 1X TO 2.5X BASIC CARDS
ONE PER PACK/THREE PER JUMBO

1995 Topps Cyber Season in Review

COMPLETE SET (7) 4.00 10.00
1 Barry Bonds 1.50 4.00
2 Jose Canseco .75 2.00
3 Juan Gonzalez .60 1.50
4 Fred McGriff .40 1.00
5 Carlos Baerga .20 .50
6 Ryan Klesko .40 1.00
7 Kenny Lofton .30 .75

1995 Topps Finest Inserts

This 15-card standard-size set was inserted one every 36 Topps series two packs. This set featured the top 15 players in total bases from the 1994 season. The fronts feature a player photo, with his team identification and name on the bottom of the card. The horizontal backs feature another player photo along with a breakdown of how many of each type of hit each player got on the way to their season total. The set is sequenced in order of how they finished in the majors for the 1994 season.

COMPLETE SET (15) 25.00 60.00
SER.2 ODDS 1:36 HOB/RET, 1:20 JUM
1 Jeff Bagwell 1.25 3.00
2 Albert Belle .75 2.00
3 Ken Griffey Jr. 4.00 10.00
4 Frank Thomas 2.00 5.00
5 Matt Williams .75 2.00
6 Dante Bichette .75 2.00
7 Barry Bonds 5.00 12.00
8 Moises Alou .75 2.00
9 Andres Galarraga .75 2.00
10 Kenny Lofton .75 2.00
11 Rafael Palmeiro 1.25 3.00
12 Tony Gwynn 2.50 6.00
13 Kirby Puckett 2.00 5.00
14 Jose Canseco 1.25 3.00
15 Jeff Conine .75 2.00

1995 Topps League Leaders

Randomly inserted in jumbo packs at a rate of one in three and retail packs at a rate of one in six, this 50-card standard-size set showcases those that were among league leaders in various categories. Card fronts feature a player photo with a black background. The player's name appears in gold foil at the bottom and the category with which he led the league or was among the leaders is in yellow letters up the right side. The backs contain various graphs and where the player placed among the leaders.

COMPLETE SET (50) 20.00 50.00
COMPLETE SERIES 1 (25) 8.00 20.00
COMPLETE SERIES 2 (25) 12.50 30.00
STATED ODDS 1:6 RETAIL, 1:3 JUMBO
LL1 Albert Belle .25 .60
LL2 Kevin Mitchell .10 .30
LL3 Wade Boggs .40 1.00
LL4 Tony Gwynn .75 2.00
LL5 Moises Alou .25 .60
LL6 Andres Galarraga .25 .60
LL7 Matt Williams .25 .60
LL8 Barry Bonds 1.50 4.00
LL9 Frank Thomas .60 1.50
LL10 Jose Canseco .40 1.00
LL11 Jeff Bagwell .40 1.00
LL12 Kirby Puckett .60 1.50
LL13 Julio Franco .25 .60
LL14 Albert Belle .25 .60
LL15 Fred McGriff .40 1.00
LL16 Kenny Lofton .25 .60
LL17 Otis Nixon .10 .30
LL18 Brady Anderson .25 .60
LL19 Deion Sanders .40 1.00
LL20 Chuck Carr .10 .30
LL21 Pat Hentgen .10 .30
LL22 Andy Benes .10 .30
LL23 Roger Clemens 1.25 3.00
LL24 Greg Maddux 1.00 2.50
LL25 Pedro Martinez .10 .30
LL26 Paul O'Neill .40 1.00
LL27 Jeff Bagwell .40 1.00
LL28 Frank Thomas .60 1.50
LL29 Hal Morris .10 .30
LL30 Kenny Lofton .25 .60
LL31 Ken Griffey Jr. 1.25 3.00
LL32 Jeff Bagwell .40 1.00
LL33 Albert Belle .25 .60
LL34 Fred McGriff .40 1.00
LL35 Cecil Fielder .25 .60
LL36 Matt Williams .25 .60
LL37 Joe Carter .25 .60
LL38 Dante Bichette .25 .60
LL39 Frank Thomas .60 1.50
LL40 Mike Piazza 1.00 2.50
LL41 Craig Biggio .40 1.00
LL42 Vince Coleman .10 .30
LL43 Marquis Grissom .25 .60
LL44 Chuck Knoblauch .25 .60
LL45 Darren Lewis .10 .30
LL46 Randy Johnson .60 1.50
LL47 Jose Rijo .10 .30
LL48 Chuck Finley .25 .60
LL49 Bret Saberhagen .25 .60
LL50 Kevin Appier .25 .60

1995 Topps Opening Day

This 10-card standard-size set was inserted into all retail factory sets. The borderless fronts feature the player's photo set against a prismatic star background and the player's name on the bottom. In the lower right, the player's opening day highlight is mentioned and there is an "Opening Day" verbiage and logo in the upper right. The horizontal back has a player photo, description of the player's opening day as well as a line score for the player.

COMPLETE SET (10) 10.00 25.00
1 Kevin Appier .20 .50
2 Dante Bichette .40 1.00
3 Ken Griffey Jr. 8.00 20.00
4 Todd Hundley .40 1.00
5 John Jaha .20 .50
6 Fred McGriff .60 1.50
7 Raul Mondesi .40 1.00
8 Manny Ramirez 2.50 6.00
9 Danny Tartabull .20 .50
10 Devon White .40 1.00

1995 Topps Traded

This set contains 165 standard-size cards and was sold in 11-card packs for $1.29. The set features rookies, draft picks and players who had been traded. The fronts contain a photo with a white border. The backs have a player picture in a scoreboard and his statistics and information. Subsets featured are: At the Break (1T-10T) and All-Stars (156T-164T). Rookie Cards in this set include Michael Barrett, Carlos Beltran, Ben Davis, Hideo Nomo and Richie Sexson.

COMPLETE SET (165) 15.00 40.00
1T Frank Thomas AB .25 .60
2T Ken Griffey Jr. AB .50 1.25
3T Barry Bonds AB .50 1.25
4T Albert Belle AB .15 .40
5T Cal Ripken AB .60 1.50
6T Mike Piazza AB .40 1.00
7T Tony Gwynn AB .25 .60
8T Jeff Bagwell AB .15 .40
9T Mo Vaughn AB .07 .20
10T Matt Williams AB .07 .20
11T Ray Durham .15 .40
12T J.LeBron RC UER Beltran 1.50 4.00
13T Shawn Green .15 .40
14T Kevin Gross .07 .20
15T Jon Nunnally .07 .20
16T Brian Maxcy RC .08 .25
17T Mark Kiefer .07 .20
18T C.Beltran RC UER LeBron 4.00 10.00
19T Michael Mimbs RC .08 .25
20T Larry Walker .15 .40
21T Chad Curtis .07 .20
22T Jeff Barry .07 .20
23T Joe Oliver .07 .20
24T Tomas Perez RC .08 .25
25T Michael Barrett RC .40 1.00
26T Brian McRae .07 .20
27T Derek Bell .07 .20
28T Ray Durham .15 .40
29T Todd Williams .07 .20
30T Ryan Jaroncyk RC .07 .20
31T Todd Steverson .07 .20
32T Mike Devereaux .07 .20
33T Rheal Cormier .07 .20
34T Benny Santiago .15 .40
35T Bob Higginson RC .40 1.00
36T Jack McDowell .07 .20
37T Mike MacFarlane .07 .20
38T Tony McKnight RC .08 .25
39T Brian L.Hunter .07 .20
40T Hideo Nomo RC 1.50 4.00
41T Brett Butler .15 .40
42T Donovan Osborne .07 .20
43T Scott Karl .07 .20
44T Tony Phillips .07 .20
45T Marty Cordova .07 .20
46T Dave Mlicki .07 .20
47T Bronson Arroyo RC 2.50 6.00
48T John Burkett .07 .20
49T J.D.Smart RC .08 .25
50T Mickey Tettleton .07 .20
51T Todd Stottlemyre .07 .20
52T Mike Perez .07 .20
53T Terry Mulholland .07 .20
54T Edgardo Alfonzo .07 .20
55T Zane Smith .07 .20
56T Jacob Brumfield .07 .20
57T Andujar Cedeno .07 .20
58T Jose Parra .07 .20
59T Manny Alexander .07 .20
60T Tony Tarasco .07 .20
61T Orel Hershiser .15 .40
62T Tim Scott .07 .20
63T Felix Rodriguez RC .08 .25
64T Ken Hill .07 .20
65T Marquis Grissom .15 .40
66T Lee Smith .15 .40
67T Jason Bates .07 .20
68T Felipe Lira .07 .20
69T Alex Hernandez RC .08 .25
70T Tony Fernandez .07 .20
71T Scott Radinsky .07 .20
72T Jose Canseco .25 .60
73T Mark Grudzielanek RC .40 1.00
74T Ben Davis RC .08 .25
75T Jim Abbott .25 .60
76T Roger Bailey .07 .20
77T Gregg Jefferies .07 .20
78T Erik Hanson .07 .20
79T Brad Radke RC .40 1.00
80T Jaime Navarro .07 .20
81T John Wetteland .15 .40
82T Chad Fonville RC .08 .25
83T John Mabry .07 .20
84T Glenallen Hill .07 .20
85T Ken Caminiti .15 .40
86T Tom Goodwin .07 .20
87T Darren Bragg .07 .20
88T Robbie Bell RC .08 .25
89T Jeff Russell .07 .20
90T Dave Gallagher .07 .20
91T Steve Finley .15 .40
92T Vaughn Eshelman .07 .20
93T Kevin Jarvis .07 .20
94T Mark Gubicza .07 .20
95T Tim Wakefield .15 .40
96T Bob Tewksbury .07 .20
97T Sid Roberson RC .08 .25
98T Tom Henke .07 .20
99T Michael Tucker .07 .20
100T Jason Bates .07 .20
101T Otis Nixon .07 .20
102T Mark Whiten .07 .20
103T Dilson Torres RC .08 .25
104T Melvin Bunch RC .08 .25
105T Terry Pendleton .15 .40
106T Corey Jenkins RC .08 .25
107T Glenn Dishman RC .08 .25
108T Reggie Taylor RC .08 .25
109T Curtis Goodwin .07 .20
110T David Cone .15 .40
111T Antonio Osuna .07 .20
112T Paul Shuey .07 .20
113T Doug Jones .07 .20
114T Mark McLemore .07 .20
115T Kevin Ritz .07 .20
116T John Kruk .15 .40
117T Trevor Wilson .07 .20
118T Jerald Clark .07 .20
119T Julian Tavarez .07 .20
120T Tim Pugh .07 .20
121T Todd Zeile .07 .20
122T R.Sexson 1.50 4.00
B.Schneider RC
123T Bobby Witt .07 .20
124T Hideo Nomo ROY .60 1.50
125T Joey Cora .07 .20
126T Jim Scharrer RC .08 .25
127T Paul Quantrill .07 .20
128T Chipper Jones ROY .25 .60
129T Kenny James RC .08 .25
130T Mariano Rivera 4.00 10.00
131T Tyler Green .07 .20
132T Brad Clontz .07 .20
133T Jon Nunnally .07 .20
134T Dave Magadan .07 .20
135T Al Leiter .15 .40
136T Bret Barberie .07 .20
137T Bill Swift .07 .20
138T Scott Cooper .07 .20
139T Roberto Kelly .07 .20
140T Charlie Hayes .07 .20
141T Pete Harnisch .07 .20
142T Rich Amaral .07 .20
143T Rudy Seanez .07 .20
144T Pat Listach .07 .20
145T Quilvio Veras .07 .20
146T Jose Olmeda RC .08 .25
147T Roberto Petagine .07 .20
148T Kevin Brown .15 .40
149T Phil Plantier .07 .20
150T Carlos Perez .15 .40
151T Pat Borders .07 .20
152T Tyler Green .07 .20
153T Stan Belinda .07 .20
154T Dave Stewart .15 .40
155T Andre Dawson .15 .40
156T F.Thomas .25 .60
F.McGriff AS
157T C.Baerga .15 .40
C.Biggio AS
158T W.Boggs .15 .40
M.Williams AS
159T C.Ripken .40 1.00
O.Smith AS
160T K.Griffey .50 1.25
T.Gwynn AS
161T A.Belle .50 1.25
B.Bonds AS
162T K.Puckett .25 .60
L.Dykstra AS
163T I.Rodriguez .40 1.00
M.Piazza AS
164T H.Nomo .60 1.50
R.Johnson AS
165T Checklist .07 .20

1995 Topps Traded Proofs

NNO Shawn Green 4.00 10.00

1995 Topps Traded Power Boosters

This 10-card standard-size set was inserted in packs at a rate of one in 36. The set is comprised of parallel cards for the first 10 cards of the regular Topps Traded set which was the "At the Break" subset. The cards are done on extra-thick stock. The fronts have an action photo on a "Power Boosted" background, which is similar to diffraction technology, with the words "at the break" on the left side. The backs have a head shot and player information including his mid-season statistics for 1995 and previous years.

COMPLETE SET (10) 30.00 80.00
STATED ODDS 1:36
1 Frank Thomas 4.00 10.00
2 Ken Griffey Jr. 8.00 20.00
3 Barry Bonds 8.00 20.00
4 Albert Belle 2.50 6.00
5 Cal Ripken 10.00 25.00
6 Mike Piazza 6.00 15.00
7 Tony Gwynn 4.00 10.00
8 Jeff Bagwell 2.50 6.00
9 Mo Vaughn 1.25 3.00
10 Matt Williams 1.25 3.00

1996 Topps

This set consists of 440 standard-size cards. These cards were issued in 12-card foil packs with a suggested retail price of $1.29. The fronts feature full-color photos surrounded by a white background. Information on the backs includes a player photo, season and career stats and text. First series subsets include Star Power (1-6, 8-12), Draft Picks (13-26), AAA Stars (101-104), and Future Stars (210-219). A special Mickey Mantle card was issued as card number 7 (his uniform number) and became the last card to be issued as card number 7 in the Topps brand set. Rookie Cards in this set include Sean Casey, Geoff Jenkins and Daryle Ward.

COMPLETE SET (440) 15.00 40.00
COMP.HOBBY SET (449) 15.00 40.00
COMP.CEREAL SET (444) 20.00 50.00
COMPLETE SERIES 1 (220) 8.00 20.00
COMPLETE SERIES 2 (220) 8.00 20.00
COMMON CARD (1-440) .07 .20
COMMON RC .08 .25
SUBSET CARDS HALF VALUE OF BASE CARDS
ONE LAST DAY MANTLE PER HOBBY SET
1 Tony Gwynn STP .10 .30
2 Mike Piazza STP .20 .50
3 Greg Maddux STP .20 .50
4 Jeff Bagwell STP .07 .20
5 Larry Walker STP .07 .20
6 Barry Larkin STP .07 .20
7 Mickey Mantle 1.50 4.00
8 Tom Glavine STP .07 .20
9 Craig Biggio STP .07 .20
10 Barry Bonds STP .30 .75
11 Heathcliff Slocumb STP .07 .20
12 Matt Williams STP .07 .20
13 Todd Helton .40 1.00
14 Mark Redman .08 .25
15 Michael Barrett .08 .25
16 Ben Davis .08 .25
17 Juan LeBron .08 .25
18 Tony McKnight .08 .25
19 Ryan Jaroncyk .08 .25
20 Corey Jenkins .08 .25
21 Jim Scharrer .08 .25
22 Mark Bellhorn RC .40 1.00
23 Jarrod Washburn RC .30 .75
24 Geoff Jenkins RC .30 .75
25 Sean Casey RC 1.50 4.00
26 Brett Tomko RC .15 .40
27 Tony Fernandez .07 .20
28 Rich Becker .07 .20
29 Andujar Cedeno .07 .20
30 Paul Molitor .07 .20
31 Brent Gates .07 .20
32 Glenallen Hill .07 .20
33 Mike Macfarlane .07 .20
34 Manny Alexander .07 .20
35 Todd Zeile .07 .20
36 Joe Girardi .07 .20
37 Tony Tarasco .07 .20
38 Tim Belcher .07 .20
39 Tom Goodwin .07 .20
40 Orel Hershiser .07 .20
41 Tripp Cromer .07 .20
42 Sean Bergman .07 .20
43 Troy Percival .07 .20
44 Kevin Stocker .07 .20
45 Albert Belle .07 .20
46 Tony Eusebio .07 .20
47 Sid Roberson .07 .20
48 Todd Hollandsworth .07 .20
49 Mark Wohlers .07 .20
50 Kirby Puckett .20 .50
51 Darren Holmes .07 .20
52 Ron Karkovice .07 .20
53 Al Martin .07 .20
54 Pat Rapp .07 .20
55 Mark Grace .10 .30
56 Greg Gagne .07 .20
57 Stan Javier .07 .20
58 Scott Sanders .07 .20
59 J.T. Snow .07 .20
60 David Justice .07 .20
61 Royce Clayton .07 .20
62 Kevin Foster .07 .20
63 Tim Naehring .07 .20
64 Orlando Miller .07 .20
65 Mike Mussina .10 .30
66 Jim Eisenreich .07 .20
67 Felix Fermin .07 .20
68 Bernie Williams .10 .30
69 Robb Nen .07 .20
70 Ron Gant .07 .20
71 Felipe Lira .07 .20
72 Jacob Brumfield .07 .20
73 John Mabry .07 .20
74 Mark Carreon .07 .20
75 Carlos Baerga .07 .20
76 Jim Dougherty .07 .20
77 Ryan Thompson .07 .20
78 Scott Leius .07 .20
79 Roger Pavlik .07 .20
80 Gary Sheffield .07 .20
81 Julian Tavarez .07 .20
82 Andy Ashby .07 .20
83 Mark Lemke .07 .20
84 Omar Vizquel .10 .30
85 Darren Daulton .07 .20
86 Mike Lansing .07 .20
87 Rusty Greer .07 .20
88 Dave Stevens .07 .20
89 Jose Offerman .07 .20
90 Tom Henke .07 .20
91 Troy O'Leary .07 .20
92 Michael Tucker .07 .20
93 Marvin Freeman .07 .20
94 Alex Diaz .07 .20
95 John Wetteland .07 .20
96 Cal Ripken 2131 .75 2.00
97 Mike Mimbs .07 .20
98 Bobby Higginson .07 .20
99 Edgardo Alfonzo .07 .20
100 Frank Thomas .20 .50
101 Bob Abreu .20 .50
102 B.Givens .08 .25
T.J.Mathews
103 C.Pritchett .08 .25
T.Hubbard
104 E.Owens .08 .25
B.Huskey
105 Doug Drabek .07 .20
106 Tomas Perez .07 .20
107 Mark Leiter .07 .20
108 Joe Oliver .07 .20
109 Tony Castillo .07 .20
110 Checklist (1-110) .07 .20
111 Kevin Seitzer .07 .20
112 Pete Schourek .07 .20
113 Sean Berry .07 .20
114 Todd Stottlemyre .07 .20
115 Joe Carter .07 .20
116 Jeff King .07 .20
117 Dan Wilson .07 .20
118 Kurt Abbott .07 .20
119 Lyle Mouton .07 .20
120 Jose Rijo .07 .20
121 Curtis Goodwin .07 .20
122 Jose Valentin .07 .20
123 Ellis Burks .07 .20
124 David Cone .07 .20
125 Eddie Murray .20 .50
126 Brian Jordan .07 .20
127 Darrin Fletcher .07 .20
128 Curt Schilling .07 .20
129 Ozzie Guillen .07 .20
130 Kenny Rogers .07 .20
131 Tom Pagnozzi .07 .20
132 Garret Anderson .07 .20
133 Bobby Jones .07 .20
134 Chris Gomez .07 .20
135 Mike Stanley .07 .20
136 Hideo Nomo .20 .50
137 Jon Nunnally .07 .20

138 Tim Wakefield .07 .20
139 Steve Finley .07 .20
140 Ivan Rodriguez .10 .30
141 Quilvio Veras .07 .20
142 Mike Fetters .07 .20
143 Mike Greenwell .07 .20
144 Bill Pulsipher .07 .20
145 Mark McGwire .50 1.25
146 Frank Castillo .07 .20
147 Greg Vaughn .07 .20
148 Pat Hentgen .07 .20
149 Walt Weiss .07 .20
150 Randy Johnson .20 .50
151 David Segui .07 .20
152 Benji Gil .07 .20
153 Tom Candiotti .07 .20
154 Geronimo Berroa .07 .20
155 John Franco .07 .20
156 Jay Bell .07 .20
157 Mark Gubicza .07 .20
158 Hal Morris .07 .20
159 Wilson Alvarez .07 .20
160 Derek Bell .07 .20
161 Ricky Bottalico .07 .20
162 Bret Boone .07 .20
163 Brad Radke .07 .20
164 John Valentin .07 .20
165 Steve Avery .07 .20
166 Mark McLemore .07 .20
167 Danny Jackson .07 .20
168 Tino Martinez .10 .30
169 Shane Reynolds .07 .20
170 Terry Pendleton .07 .20
171 Jim Edmonds .07 .20
172 Esteban Loaiza .07 .20
173 Ray Durham .07 .20
174 Carlos Perez .07 .20
175 Raul Mondesi .07 .20
176 Steve Ontiveros .07 .20
177 Chipper Jones .20 .50
178 Otis Nixon .07 .20
179 John Burkett .07 .20
180 Gregg Jefferies .07 .20
181 Denny Martinez .07 .20
182 Ken Caminiti .07 .20
183 Doug Jones .07 .20
184 Brian McRae .07 .20
185 Don Mattingly .50 1.25
186 Mel Rojas .07 .20
187 Marty Cordova .07 .20
188 Vinny Castilla .07 .20
189 John Smoltz .10 .30
190 Travis Fryman .07 .20
191 Chris Hoiles .07 .20
192 Chuck Finley .07 .20
193 Ryan Klesko .07 .20
194 Alex Fernandez .07 .20
195 Dante Bichette .07 .20
196 Eric Karros .07 .20
197 Roger Clemens .40 1.00
198 Randy Myers .07 .20
199 Tony Phillips .07 .20
200 Cal Ripken .60 1.50
201 Rod Beck .07 .20
202 Chad Curtis .07 .20
203 Jack McDowell .07 .20
204 Gary Gaetti .07 .20
205 Ken Griffey Jr. .40 1.00
206 Ramon Martinez .07 .20
207 Jeff Kent .07 .20
208 Brad Ausmus .07 .20
209 Devon White .07 .20
210 Jason Giambi .07 .20
211 Nomar Garciaparra .30 .75
212 Billy Wagner .07 .20
213 Todd Greene .07 .20
214 Paul Wilson .07 .20
215 Johnny Damon .10 .30
216 Alan Benes .07 .20
217 Karim Garcia .07 .20
218 Dustin Hermanson .07 .20
219 Derek Jeter .50 1.25
220 Checklist (111-220) .07 .20
221 Kirby Puckett STP .10 .30
222 Cal Ripken STP .30 .75
223 Albert Belle STP .07 .20
224 Randy Johnson STP .10 .30
225 Wade Boggs STP .07 .20
226 Carlos Baerga STP .07 .20
227 Ivan Rodriguez STP .07 .20
228 Mike Mussina STP .07 .20
229 Frank Thomas STP .10 .30
230 Ken Griffey Jr. STP .25 .60
231 Jose Mesa STP .07 .20
232 Matt Morris RC .60 1.50
233 Craig Wilson RC .30 .75
234 Alvie Shepherd RC .08 .25
235 Randy Winn RC .30 .75
236 David Yocum RC .08 .25
237 Jason Brester RC .08 .25
238 Shane Monahan RC .08 .25
239 Brian McNichol RC .08 .25
240 Reggie Taylor .08 .25
241 Garrett Long .08 .25
242 Jonathan Johnson .08 .25
243 Jeff Liefer RC .08 .25
244 Brian Powell .08 .25
245 Brian Buchanan RC .08 .25
246 Mike Piazza .30 .75
247 Edgar Martinez .10 .30
248 Chuck Knoblauch .07 .20
249 Andres Galarraga .07 .20
250 Tony Gwynn .25 .60
251 Lee Smith .07 .20
252 Sammy Sosa .20 .50
253 Jim Thome .10 .30
254 Frank Rodriguez .07 .20
255 Charlie Hayes .07 .20
256 Bernard Gilkey .07 .20
257 John Smiley .07 .20
258 Brady Anderson .07 .20
259 Rico Brogna .07 .20
260 Kirt Manwaring .07 .20
261 Len Dykstra .07 .20
262 Tom Glavine .10 .30
263 Vince Coleman .07 .20
264 John Olerud .07 .20
265 Orlando Merced .07 .20
266 Kent Mercker .07 .20
267 Terry Steinbach .07 .20
268 Brian L. Hunter .07 .20
269 Jeff Fassero .07 .20
270 Jay Buhner .07 .20
271 Jeff Brantley .07 .20
272 Tim Raines .07 .20
273 Jimmy Key .07 .20
274 Mo Vaughn .07 .20
275 Andre Dawson .07 .20
276 Jose Mesa .07 .20
277 Brett Butler .07 .20
278 Luis Gonzalez .07 .20
279 Steve Sparks .07 .20
280 Chili Davis .07 .20
281 Carl Everett .07 .20
282 Jeff Cirillo .07 .20
283 Thomas Howard .07 .20
284 Paul O'Neill .10 .30
285 Pat Meares .07 .20
286 Mickey Tettleton .07 .20
287 Rey Sanchez .07 .20
288 Bip Roberts .07 .20
289 Roberto Alomar .10 .30
290 Ruben Sierra .07 .20
291 John Flaherty .07 .20
292 Bret Saberhagen .07 .20
293 Barry Larkin .10 .30
294 Sandy Alomar Jr. .07 .20
295 Ed Sprague .07 .20
296 Gary DiSarcina .07 .20
297 Marquis Grissom .07 .20
298 John Frascatore .07 .20
299 Will Clark .10 .30
300 Barry Bonds .60 1.50
301 Ozzie Smith .30 .75
302 Dave Nilsson .07 .20
303 Pedro Martinez .10 .30
304 Joey Cora .07 .20
305 Rick Aguilera .07 .20
306 Craig Biggio .10 .30
307 Jose Vizcaino .07 .20
308 Jeff Montgomery .07 .20
309 Moises Alou .07 .20
310 Robin Ventura .07 .20
311 David Wells .07 .20
312 Delino DeShields .07 .20
313 Trevor Hoffman .07 .20
314 Andy Benes .07 .20
315 Deion Sanders .10 .30
316 Jim Bullinger .07 .20
317 John Jaha .07 .20
318 Greg Maddux .30 .75
319 Tim Salmon .10 .30
320 Ben McDonald .07 .20
321 Sandy Martinez .07 .20
322 Dan Miceli .07 .20
323 Wade Boggs .10 .30
324 Ismael Valdes .07 .20
325 Juan Gonzalez .07 .20
326 Charles Nagy .07 .20
327 Ray Lankford .07 .20
328 Mark Portugal .07 .20
329 Bobby Bonilla .07 .20
330 Reggie Sanders .07 .20
331 Jamie Brewington RC .08 .25
332 Aaron Sele .07 .20
333 Pete Harnisch .07 .20
334 Cliff Floyd .07 .20
335 Cal Eldred .07 .20
336 Jason Bates .07 .20
337 Tony Clark .07 .20
338 Jose Herrera .07 .20
339 Alex Ochoa .07 .20
340 Mark Loretta .07 .20
341 Donne Wall .07 .20
342 Jason Kendall .07 .20
343 Shannon Stewart .07 .20
344 Brooks Kieschnick .07 .20
345 Chris Snopek .07 .20
346 Ruben Rivera .07 .20
347 Jeff Suppan .07 .20
348 Phil Nevin .07 .20
349 John Wasdin .07 .20
350 Jay Payton .07 .20
351 Tim Crabtree .07 .20
352 Rick Krivda .07 .20
353 Bob Wolcott .07 .20
354 Jimmy Haynes .07 .20
355 Herb Perry .07 .20
356 Ryne Sandberg .30 .75
357 Harold Baines .07 .20
358 Chad Ogea .07 .20
359 Lee Tinsley .07 .20
360 Matt Williams .07 .20
361 Randy Velarde .07 .20
362 Jose Canseco .10 .30
363 Larry Walker .07 .20
364 Kevin Appier .07 .20
365 Darryl Hamilton .07 .20
366 Jose Lima .07 .20
367 Javy Lopez .07 .20
368 Dennis Eckersley .07 .20
369 Jason Isringhausen .07 .20
370 Mickey Morandini .07 .20
371 Scott Cooper .07 .20
372 Jim Abbott .10 .30
373 Paul Sorrento .07 .20
374 Chris Hammond .07 .20
375 Lance Johnson .07 .20
376 Kevin Brown .07 .20
377 Luis Alicea .07 .20
378 Andy Pettitte .10 .30
379 Dean Palmer .07 .20
380 Jeff Bagwell .10 .30
381 Jaime Navarro .07 .20
382 Rondell White .07 .20
383 Erik Hanson .07 .20
384 Pedro Munoz .07 .20
385 Heathcliff Slocumb .07 .20
386 Wally Joyner .07 .20
387 Bob Tewksbury .07 .20
388 David Bell .07 .20
389 Fred McGriff .10 .30
390 Mike Henneman .07 .20
391 Robby Thompson .07 .20
392 Norm Charlton .07 .20
393 Cecil Fielder .07 .20
394 Benito Santiago .07 .20
395 Rafael Palmeiro .10 .30
396 Ricky Bones .07 .20
397 Rickey Henderson .20 .50
398 C.J. Nitkowski .07 .20
399 Shawon Dunston .07 .20
400 Manny Ramirez .10 .30
401 Bill Swift .07 .20
402 Chad Fonville .07 .20
403 Joey Hamilton .07 .20
404 Alex Gonzalez .07 .20
405 Roberto Hernandez .07 .20
406 Jeff Blauser .07 .20
407 LaTroy Hawkins .07 .20
408 Greg Colbrunn .07 .20
409 Todd Hundley .07 .20
410 Glenn Dishman .07 .20
411 Joe Vitiello .07 .20
412 Todd Worrell .07 .20
413 Wil Cordero .07 .20
414 Ken Hill .07 .20
415 Carlos Garcia .07 .20
416 Bryan Rekar .07 .20
417 Shawn Green .07 .20
418 Tyler Green .07 .20
419 Mike Blowers .07 .20
420 Kenny Lofton .07 .20
421 Denny Neagle .07 .20
422 Jeff Conine .07 .20
423 Mark Langston .07 .20
424 Ron Wright RC .30 .75
D.Lee
425 D.Ward RC .40 1.00
R.Sexson
426 Adam Riggs RC .08 .25
427 N.Perez .08 .25
E.Wilson
428 Bartolo Colon .20 .50
429 Marty Janzen RC .08 .25
430 Rich Hunter RC .08 .25
431 Dave Coggin RC .08 .25
432 R.Ibanez RC .60 1.50
P.Konerko
433 Marc Kroon .07 .20
434 S.Rolen .20 .50
S.Spiezio
435 V.Guerrero 1.00 2.50
A.Jones
436 Shane Spencer RC .15 .40
437 A.French .08 .25
D.Stovall RC
438 Michael Coleman RC .08 .25
Jacob Cruz
Richard Hidalgo
Charles Peterson
439 Jermaine Dye .07 .20
440 Checklist .07 .20
F7 Mickey Mantle Last Day 2.00 5.00
NNO Derek Jeter Tri-Card 20.00 50.00
NNO Mickey Mantle 1.25 3.00
Tribute Card, promotes the Mantle F

1996 Topps Classic Confrontations

These cards were inserted at a rate of one in every five-card Series one retail pack sold at Walmart. The first ten cards showcase hitters, while the last five cards feature pitchers. Inside white borders, the fronts show player cutouts on a brownish rock background featuring a shadow image of the player. The player's name is gold foil stamped across the bottom. The horizontal backs of the hitters' cards are aqua and present headshots and statistics. The backs of the pitchers cards are purple and present the same information.

COMPLETE SET (15) 2.50 6.00
ONE PER SPECIAL SER.1 RETAIL PACK
CC1 Ken Griffey Jr. .30 .75
CC2 Cal Ripken .50 1.25
CC3 Edgar Martinez .08 .25
CC4 Kirby Puckett .15 .40
CC5 Frank Thomas .15 .40
CC6 Barry Bonds .50 1.25
CC7 Reggie Sanders .05 .15
CC8 Andres Galarraga .05 .15
CC9 Tony Gwynn .20 .50
CC10 Mike Piazza .25 .60
CC11 Randy Johnson .15 .40
CC12 Mike Mussina .08 .25
CC13 Roger Clemens .30 .75
CC14 Tom Glavine .08 .25
CC15 Greg Maddux .25 .60

1996 Topps Mantle

Randomly inserted in Series one packs at a rate of one in nine hobby packs, one in six retail packs and one in two jumbo packs; these cards are reprints of the original Mickey Mantle cards issued from 1951 through 1969. The fronts look the same except for a commemorative stamp, while the backs clearly state that they are "Mickey Mantle Commemorative" cards and have a 1996 copyright date. These cards honor Yankee great Mickey Mantle, who passed away in August 1995 after a gallant battle against cancer. Based on evidence from an uncut sheet auctioned off at the 1996 Kit Young Hawaii Trade Show, some collectors/dealers believe that cards 15 through 19 were slightly shorter printed in relation to the other 14 cards.

COMPLETE SET (19) 20.00 50.00
COMMON MANTLE 2.50 6.00
SER.1 ODDS 1:9 HOB, 1:6 RET, 1:2 JUM
FOUR PER CEREAL FACT.SET
CARDS 15-19 SHORTPRINTED BY 20%
ONE CASE PER SER.2 HOB/JUM/VEND CASE
FINEST SER.2 ODDS 1:18 RET, 1:12 ANCO
REF.SER.2 ODDS 1:96 HOB, 1:144 RET
RDMP.SER.2 ODDS 1:72 ANCO, 1:108 RET

1996 Topps Mantle Finest

COMPLETE SET (19) 30.00 60.00
COMMON MANTLE (1-14) 3.00 8.00
COMMON MANTLE SP (15-19) 4.00 10.00
SER.2 STATED ODDS 1:18 RET, 1:12 ANCO
CARDS 15-19 SHORTPRINTED BY 20%
1 Mickey Mantle 1951 Bowman 6.00 15.00
2 Mickey Mantle 1952 Topps 6.00 15.00
3 Mickey Mantle 1953 Topps 3.00 8.00

1996 Topps Masters of the Game

Cards from this 20-card standard-size set were randomly inserted into first-series hobby packs at a rate of one in 18. In addition, every factory set contained two Masters of the Game cards. The cards are numbered with a "MG" prefix in the lower left corner.

COMPLETE SET (20) 12.50 30.00
SER.1 STATED ODDS 1:18 HOBBY
TWO PER HOBBY FACTORY SET
1 Dennis Eckersley .40 1.00
2 Denny Martinez .40 1.00
3 Eddie Murray 1.00 2.50
4 Paul Molitor .40 1.00
5 Ozzie Smith 1.50 4.00
6 Rickey Henderson 1.00 2.50
7 Tim Raines .40 1.00
8 Lee Smith .40 1.00
9 Cal Ripken 3.00 8.00
10 Chili Davis .40 1.00
11 Wade Boggs .60 1.50
12 Tony Gwynn 1.25 3.00
13 Don Mattingly 2.50 6.00
14 Bret Saberhagen .40 1.00
15 Kirby Puckett 1.00 2.50
16 Joe Carter .40 1.00
17 Roger Clemens 2.00 5.00
18 Barry Bonds 3.00 8.00
19 Greg Maddux 1.50 4.00
20 Frank Thomas 1.00 2.50

1996 Topps Mystery Finest

Randomly inserted in first-series packs at a rate of one in 36 hobby and retail packs and one in eight jumbo packs, this 26-card standard-size set features a bit of a mystery. The fronts have opaque coating that must be removed before the player can be identified. After the opaque coating is removed, the fronts feature a player photo surrounded by silver borders. The backs feature a choice of players along with a corresponding mystery finest trivia fact. Some of these cards were also issued with refractor fronts.

COMPLETE SET (26) 60.00 120.00
SER.1 STATED ODDS 1:36 HOB/RET, 1:8 JUM
*REF: 1.25X TO 3X BASIC MYSTERY FINEST
REF.SER.1 ODDS 1:216 HOB/RET, 1:36 JUM
M1 Hideo Nomo 2.00 5.00
M2 Greg Maddux 3.00 8.00
M3 Randy Johnson 2.00 5.00
M4 Chipper Jones 2.00 5.00
M5 Marty Cordova .75 2.00
M6 Garret Anderson .75 2.00
M7 Cal Ripken 6.00 15.00
M8 Kirby Puckett 2.00 5.00
M9 Tony Gwynn 2.50 6.00
M10 Manny Ramirez 1.25 3.00
M11 Jim Edmonds .75 2.00
M12 Mike Piazza 3.00 8.00
M13 Barry Bonds 6.00 15.00
M14 Raul Mondesi .75 2.00
M15 Sammy Sosa 2.00 5.00
M16 Ken Griffey Jr. 4.00 10.00
M17 Albert Belle .75 2.00
M18 Dante Bichette .75 2.00
M19 Mo Vaughn .75 2.00
M20 Jeff Bagwell 1.25 3.00
M21 Frank Thomas 2.00 5.00
M22 Hideo Nomo 2.00 5.00
M23 Cal Ripken 6.00 15.00
M24 Mike Piazza 3.00 8.00
M25 Ken Griffey Jr. 4.00 10.00
M26 Frank Thomas 2.00 5.00

1996 Topps Power Boosters

Randomly inserted into packs, these cards are a metallic version of 25 of the first 26 cards from the basic Topps set. Card numbers 1-6 and 8-12 were issued at a rate of one every 36 first series retail packs, while numbers 13-26 were issued in hobby packs at a rate of one in 36. Inserted in place of two basic cards, they are printed on 28 point stock and the fronts have prismatic foil printing. Card number 7, which is Mickey Mantle in the regular set, was not issued in a Power Booster form. A first year card of Sean Casey highlights this set.

COMPLETE SET (25) 75.00 150.00
COMP.STAR POW.SET (11) 25.00 50.00
COMMON STAR POW. (1-6/8-12) .75 2.00
STR.PWR.SER.1 ODDS 1:36 RETAIL
COMP.DRAFT PICKS SET (14) 1.25 3.00
COMMON DRAFT PICK (13-26) .75 2.00
DP SER.1 STATED ODDS 1:36 HOBBY
CARD #7 DOES NOT EXIST
1 Tony Gwynn 2.50 6.00
2 Mike Piazza 3.00 8.00
3 Greg Maddux 3.00 8.00
4 Jeff Bagwell 1.25 3.00
5 Larry Walker .75 2.00
6 Barry Larkin 1.25 3.00
8 Tom Glavine 1.25 3.00
9 Craig Biggio 1.25 3.00
10 Barry Bonds 6.00 15.00
11 Heathcliff Slocumb .75 2.00
12 Matt Williams .75 2.00
13 Todd Helton 3.00 8.00
14 Mark Redman .75 2.00
15 Michael Barrett .75 2.00
16 Ben Davis .75 2.00
17 Juan LeBron .75 2.00
18 Tony McKnight .75 2.00
19 Ryan Jaroncyk .75 2.00
20 Corey Jenkins .75 2.00
21 Jim Scharrer .75 2.00
22 Mark Bellhorn 4.00 10.00
23 Jarrod Washburn 3.00 8.00
24 Geoff Jenkins 3.00 8.00
25 Sean Casey 6.00 15.00
26 Brett Tomko 2.00 5.00

1996 Topps Profiles

Randomly inserted into Series one and two packs at a rate of one in 12 hobby and retail packs, one in six jumbo packs and one in eight ANCO packs;, this 20-card standard-size set features 10 players from each league. One card from the first series and two from the second series were also included in all Topps factory sets. Topps spokesmen Kirby Puckett (AL) and Tony Gwynn (NL) give opinions on players within their league. The fronts feature a player photo set against a silver-foil background. The player's name is on the bottom. A photo of either Gwynn or Puckett as well as the words "Profiles by ..." is on the right. The backs feature a player photo, some career data as well as Gwynn's or Puckett's opinion about the featured player. The cards are numbered with either an "AL or NL" prefix on the back depending on the player's league. The cards are sequenced in alphabetical order within league.

COMPLETE SET (40) 15.00 40.00
COMPLETE SERIES 1 (20) 12.50 30.00
COMPLETE SERIES 2 (20) 4.00 10.00
STAT.ODDS 1:12 HOB/RET,1:6 JUM,1:8 ANCO
1 SER.1 AND 2 SER.2 PER HOB.FACT.SET
AL1 Roberto Alomar .30 .75
AL2 Carlos Baerga .20 .50
AL3 Albert Belle .20 .50
AL4 Cecil Fielder .20 .50
AL5 Ken Griffey Jr. 1.00 2.50
AL6 Randy Johnson .50 1.25
AL7 Paul O'Neill .30 .75
AL8 Cal Ripken 1.50 4.00
AL9 Frank Thomas .50 1.25
AL10 Mo Vaughn .20 .50
AL11 Jay Buhner .20 .50
AL12 Marty Cordova .20 .50
AL13 Jim Edmonds .20 .50
AL14 Juan Gonzalez .20 .50
AL15 Kenny Lofton .20 .50
AL16 Edgar Martinez .30 .75
AL17 Don Mattingly 1.25 3.00
AL18 Mark McGwire 1.25 3.00
AL19 Rafael Palmeiro .30 .75
AL20 Tim Salmon .30 .75
NL1 Jeff Bagwell .30 .75
NL2 Derek Bell .20 .50
NL3 Barry Bonds 1.50 4.00
NL4 Greg Maddux .75 2.00
NL5 Fred McGriff .30 .75
NL6 Raul Mondesi .20 .50
NL7 Mike Piazza .75 2.00
NL8 Reggie Sanders .20 .50
NL9 Sammy Sosa .50 1.25
NL10 Larry Walker .20 .50
NL11 Dante Bichette .20 .50
NL12 Andres Galarraga .20 .50
NL13 Ron Gant .20 .50
NL14 Tom Glavine .30 .75
NL15 Chipper Jones .50 1.25
NL16 David Justice .20 .50
NL17 Barry Larkin .30 .75
NL18 Hideo Nomo .50 1.25
NL19 Gary Sheffield .20 .50
NL20 Matt Williams .20 .50

1996 Topps Road Warriors

This 20-card set was inserted only into Series two WalMart packs at a rate of one per pack and featured leading hitters of the majors. The set is sequenced in alphabetical order.

COMPLETE SET (20) 5.00 12.00
ONE PER SPECIAL SER.2 RETAIL PACK
RW1 Derek Bell .15 .40
RW2 Albert Belle .15 .40
RW3 Craig Biggio .25 .60
RW4 Barry Bonds 1.25 3.00
RW5 Jay Buhner .15 .40
RW6 Jim Edmonds .15 .40
RW7 Gary Gaetti .15 .40
RW8 Ron Gant .15 .40
RW9 Edgar Martinez .25 .60
RW10 Tino Martinez .25 .60
RW11 Mark McGwire 1.00 2.50
RW12 Mike Piazza .60 1.50
RW13 Manny Ramirez .25 .60
RW14 Tim Salmon .25 .60
RW15 Reggie Sanders .15 .40
RW16 Frank Thomas .40 1.00
RW17 John Valentin .15 .40
RW18 Mo Vaughn .15 .40
RW19 Robin Ventura .15 .40
RW20 Matt Williams .15 .40

1996 Topps Wrecking Crew

Randomly inserted in Series two hobby packs at a rate of one in 18, this 15-card set honors some of the hottest home run producers in the League. One card from this set was also inserted into Topps Hobby Factory sets. The cards feature color action player photos with foil stamping.

COMPLETE SET (15) 25.00 60.00
SER.2 STATED ODDS 1:18 HOBBY
ONE PER HOBBY FACTORY SET
WC1 Jeff Bagwell 1.25 3.00
WC2 Albert Belle .75 2.00
WC3 Barry Bonds 6.00 15.00
WC4 Jose Canseco 1.25 3.00
WC5 Joe Carter .75 2.00
WC6 Cecil Fielder .75 2.00
WC7 Ron Gant .75 2.00
WC8 Juan Gonzalez .75 2.00
WC9 Ken Griffey Jr 4.00 10.00
WC10 Fred McGriff 1.25 3.00
WC11 Mark McGwire 5.00 12.00
WC12 Mike Piazza 3.00 8.00
WC13 Frank Thomas 2.00 5.00
WC14 Mo Vaughn .75 2.00
WC15 Matt Williams .75 2.00

1997 Topps

This 495-card set was primarily distributed in first and second series 11-card packs with a suggested retail price of $1.29. In addition, eight-card retail packs, 40-card jumbo packs and 504-card factory sets (containing the complete 495-card set plus a random selection of eight insert cards and one hermetically sealed Willie Mays or Mickey Mantle Reprint insert) were made available. The card fronts feature a color action player photo with a gloss coating and a spot matte finish on the outside border with gold foil stamping. The backs carry another player photo, player information and statistics. The set includes the following subsets: Season Highlights (100-104, 462-466), Prospects (200-207, 487-494), the first ever expansion team cards of the Arizona Diamondbacks (249-251,468-469 and the Tampa Bay Devil Rays (252-253, 470-472) and Draft Picks (269-274, 477-483). Card 42 is a special Jackie Robinson tribute card commemorating the 50th anniversary of his contribution to baseball history and numbered for his Dodgers uniform number. Card number 7 does not exist because it was retired in honor of Mickey Mantle. Card number 84 does not exist because Mike Fetters' card was incorrectly numbered 61. Card number 277 does not exist because Chipper Jones' card was incorrectly numbered 276. Rookie Cards include Kris Benson and Eric Chavez. The Derek Jeter autograph card found at the end of our checklist was seeded one every 576 second series packs.

COMPLETE SET (495) 30.00 80.00
COMPLETE SERIES 1 (276) 15.00 40.00
COMPLETE SERIES 2 (220) 20.00 40.00
SUBSET CARDS HALF VALUE OF BASE CARDS
CARDS 7, 84 AND 277 DON'T EXIST
ELSTER AND FETTERS NUMBERED 61
CL 276 AND C.JONES NUMBERED 276
1 Barry Bonds .60 1.50
2 Tom Pagnozzi .07 .20
3 Terrell Wade .07 .20
4 Jose Valentin .07 .20
5 Mark Clark .07 .20
6 Brady Anderson .07 .20
8 Wade Boggs .10 .30
9 Scott Stahoviak .07 .20
10 Andres Galarraga .07 .20
11 Steve Avery .07 .20
12 Rusty Greer .07 .20
13 Derek Jeter .50 1.25
14 Ricky Bottalico .07 .20
15 Andy Ashby .07 .20
16 Paul Shuey .07 .20
17 F.P. Santangelo .07 .20
18 Royce Clayton .07 .20
19 Mike Mohler .07 .20
20 Mike Piazza .30 .75
21 Jaime Navarro .07 .20
22 Billy Wagner .07 .20
23 Mike Timlin .07 .20
24 Garret Anderson .07 .20
25 Ben McDonald .07 .20
26 Mel Rojas .07 .20
27 John Burkett .07 .20
28 Jeff King .07 .20
29 Reggie Jefferson .07 .20
30 Kevin Appier .07 .20
31 Felipe Lira .07 .20
32 Kevin Tapani .07 .20
33 Mark Portugal .07 .20
34 Carlos Garcia .07 .20
35 Joey Cora .07 .20
36 David Segui .07 .20
37 Mark Grace .10 .30
38 Erik Hanson .07 .20
39 Jeff D'Amico .07 .20
40 Jay Buhner .07 .20
41 B.J. Surhoff .07 .20
42 Jackie Robinson TRIB .20 .50
43 Roger Pavlik .07 .20
44 Hal Morris .07 .20
45 Mariano Duncan .07 .20
46 Harold Baines .07 .20

47 Jorge Fabregas	.07	.20
48 Jose Herrera	.07	.20
49 Jeff Cirillo	.07	.20
50 Tom Glavine	.10	.30
51 Pedro Astacio	.07	.20
52 Mark Gardner	.07	.20
53 Arthur Rhodes	.07	.20
54 Troy O'Leary	.07	.20
55 Bip Roberts	.07	.20
56 Mike Lieberthal	.07	.20
57 Shane Andrews	.07	.20
58 Scott Karl	.07	.20
59 Gary DiSarcina	.07	.20
60 Andy Pettitte	.10	.30
61 Kevin Elster	.07	.20
61B Mike Fetters UER	.07	.20
62 Mark McGwire	.50	1.25
63 Dan Wilson	.07	.20
64 Mickey Morandini	.07	.20
65 Chuck Knoblauch	.07	.20
66 Tim Wakefield	.07	.20
67 Raul Mondesi	.07	.20
68 Todd Jones	.07	.20
69 Albert Belle	.07	.20
70 Trevor Hoffman	.07	.20
71 Eric Young	.07	.20
72 Robert Perez	.07	.20
73 Butch Huskey	.07	.20
74 Brian McRae	.07	.20
75 Jim Edmonds	.07	.20
76 Mike Henneman	.07	.20
77 Frank Rodriguez	.07	.20
78 Danny Tartabull	.07	.20
79 Robb Nen	.07	.20
80 Reggie Sanders	.07	.20
81 Ron Karkovice	.07	.20
82 Benito Santiago	.07	.20
83 Mike Lansing	.07	.20
85 Craig Biggio	.10	.30
86 Mike Bordick	.07	.20
87 Ray Lankford	.07	.20
88 Charles Nagy	.07	.20
89 Paul Wilson	.07	.20
90 John Wetteland	.07	.20
91 Tom Candiotti	.07	.20
92 Carlos Delgado	.07	.20
93 Derek Bell	.07	.20
94 Mark Lemke	.07	.20
95 Edgar Martinez	.10	.30
96 Rickey Henderson	.20	.50
97 Greg Myers	.07	.20
98 Jim Leyritz	.07	.20
99 Mark Johnson	.07	.20
100 Dwight Gooden HL	.07	.20
101 Al Leiter HL	.07	.20
102 John Mabry HL	.07	.20
103 Alex Ochoa HL	.07	.20
104 Mike Piazza HL	.20	.50
105 Jim Thome	.10	.30
106 Ricky Otero	.07	.20
107 Jamey Wright	.07	.20
108 Frank Thomas	.20	.50
109 Jody Reed	.07	.20
110 Orel Hershiser	.07	.20
111 Terry Steinbach	.07	.20
112 Mark Loretta	.07	.20
113 Turk Wendell	.07	.20
114 Marvin Benard	.07	.20
115 Kevin Brown	.07	.20
116 Robert Person	.07	.20
117 Joey Hamilton	.07	.20
118 Francisco Cordova	.07	.20
119 John Smiley	.07	.20
120 Travis Fryman	.07	.20
121 Jimmy Key	.07	.20
122 Tom Goodwin	.07	.20
123 Mike Greenwell	.07	.20
124 Juan Gonzalez	.07	.20
125 Pete Harnisch	.07	.20
126 Roger Cedeno	.07	.20
127 Ron Gant	.07	.20
128 Mark Langston	.07	.20
129 Tim Crabtree	.07	.20
130 Greg Maddux	.30	.75
131 William VanLandingham	.07	.20
132 Wally Joyner	.07	.20
133 Randy Myers	.07	.20
134 John Valentin	.07	.20
135 Bret Boone	.07	.20
136 Bruce Ruffin	.07	.20
137 Chris Snopek	.07	.20
138 Paul Molitor	.07	.20
139 Mark McLemore	.07	.20
140 Rafael Palmeiro	.10	.30
141 Herb Perry	.07	.20
142 Luis Gonzalez	.07	.20
143 Doug Drabek	.07	.20
144 Ken Ryan	.07	.20
145 Todd Hundley	.07	.20
146 Ellis Burks	.07	.20
147 Ozzie Guillen	.07	.20
148 Rich Becker	.07	.20
149 Sterling Hitchcock	.07	.20
150 Bernie Williams	.10	.30
151 Mike Stanley	.07	.20
152 Roberto Alomar	.10	.30
153 Jose Mesa	.07	.20
154 Steve Trachsel	.07	.20
155 Alex Gonzalez	.07	.20
156 Troy Percival	.07	.20
157 John Smoltz	.10	.30
158 Pedro Martinez	.10	.30
159 Jeff Conine	.07	.20
160 Bernard Gilkey	.07	.20
161 Jim Eisenreich	.07	.20
162 Mickey Tettleton	.07	.20
163 Justin Thompson	.07	.20
164 Jose Offerman	.07	.20
165 Tony Phillips	.07	.20
166 Ismael Valdes	.07	.20
167 Ryne Sandberg	.30	.75
168 Matt Mieske	.07	.20
169 Geronimo Berroa	.07	.20
170 Otis Nixon	.07	.20
171 John Mabry	.07	.20
172 Shawon Dunston	.07	.20
173 Omar Vizquel	.10	.30
174 Chris Hoiles	.07	.20
175 Dwight Gooden	.07	.20
176 Wilson Alvarez	.07	.20
177 Todd Hollandsworth	.07	.20
178 Roger Salkeld	.07	.20
179 Rey Sanchez	.07	.20
180 Rey Ordonez	.07	.20
181 Denny Martinez	.07	.20
182 Ramon Martinez	.07	.20
183 Dave Nilsson	.07	.20
184 Marquis Grissom	.07	.20
185 Randy Velarde	.07	.20
186 Ron Coomer	.07	.20
187 Tino Martinez	.10	.30
188 Jeff Brantley	.07	.20
189 Steve Finley	.07	.20
190 Andy Benes	.07	.20
191 Terry Adams	.07	.20
192 Mike Blowers	.07	.20
193 Russ Davis	.07	.20
194 Darryl Hamilton	.07	.20
195 Jason Kendall	.07	.20
196 Johnny Damon	.10	.30
197 Dave Martinez	.07	.20
198 Mike Macfarlane	.07	.20
199 Norm Charlton	.07	.20
200 Damian Moss	.08	.25
201 Jenkins	.07	.20
Ibanez		
Cameron		
202 Sean Casey	.10	.30
203 J.Hansen	.07	.20
H.Bush		
F.Crespo		
204 K.Orie	.07	.20
G.Alvarez		
A.Boone		
205 B.Davis	.07	.20
K.Brown		
B.Estalella		
206 Bubba Trammell RC	.15	.40
207 Jarrod Washburn	.07	.20
208 Brian Hunter	.07	.20
209 Jason Giambi	.07	.20
210 Henry Rodriguez	.07	.20
211 Edgar Renteria	.07	.20
212 Edgardo Alfonzo	.07	.20
213 Fernando Vina	.07	.20
214 Shawn Green	.07	.20
215 Ray Durham	.07	.20
216 Joe Randa	.07	.20
217 Armando Reynoso	.07	.20
218 Eric Davis	.07	.20
219 Bob Tewksbury	.07	.20
220 Jacob Cruz	.07	.20
221 Glenallen Hill	.07	.20
222 Gary Gaetti	.07	.20
223 Donne Wall	.07	.20
224 Brad Clontz	.07	.20
225 Marty Janzen	.07	.20
226 Todd Worrell	.07	.20
227 John Franco	.07	.20
228 David Wells	.07	.20
229 Gregg Jefferies	.07	.20
230 Tim Naehring	.07	.20
231 Thomas Howard	.07	.20
232 Roberto Hernandez	.07	.20
233 Kevin Ritz	.07	.20
234 Julian Tavarez	.07	.20
235 Ken Hill	.07	.20
236 Greg Gagne	.07	.20
237 Bobby Chouinard	.07	.20
238 Joe Carter	.07	.20
239 Jermaine Dye	.07	.20
240 Antonio Osuna	.07	.20
241 Julio Franco	.07	.20
242 Mike Grace	.07	.20
243 Aaron Sele	.07	.20
244 David Justice	.07	.20
245 Sandy Alomar Jr.	.07	.20
246 Jose Canseco	.10	.30
247 Paul O'Neill	.10	.30
248 Sean Berry	.07	.20
249 N.Bierbrodt	.08	.25
K.Sweeney RC		
250 Vladimir Nunez RC	.08	.25
251 R.Hartman	.08	.25
D.Hayman RC		
252 A.Sanchez	.15	.40
M.Quatraro RC		
253 Ronni Seberino RC	.08	.25
254 Rex Hudler	.07	.20
255 Orlando Miller	.07	.20
256 Mariano Rivera	.20	.50
257 Brad Radke	.07	.20
258 Bobby Higginson	.07	.20
259 Jay Bell	.07	.20
260 Mark Grudzielanek	.07	.20
261 Lance Johnson	.07	.20
262 Ken Caminiti	.07	.20
263 J.T. Snow	.07	.20
264 Gary Sheffield	.07	.20
265 Darrin Fletcher	.07	.20
266 Eric Owens	.07	.20
267 Luis Castillo	.07	.20
268 Scott Rolen	.10	.30
269 T.Noel	.08	.25
J.Oliver RC		
270 Robert Stratton RC	.15	.40
271 Gil Meche RC	.40	1.00
272 E.Milton RC	.15	.40
D.Brown RC		
273 Chris Reitsma RC	.15	.40
274 J.Marquis	.30	.75
A.J.Zapp RC		
275 Checklist	.07	.20
276 Checklist	.07	.20
277 Chipper Jones UER276	.20	.50
278 Orlando Merced	.07	.20
279 Ariel Prieto	.07	.20
280 Al Leiter	.07	.20
281 Pat Meares	.07	.20
282 Darryl Strawberry	.07	.20
283 Jamie Moyer	.07	.20
284 Scott Servais	.07	.20
285 Delino DeShields	.07	.20
286 Danny Graves	.07	.20
287 Gerald Williams	.07	.20
288 Todd Greene	.07	.20
289 Rico Brogna	.07	.20
290 Derrick Gibson	.07	.20
291 Joe Girardi	.07	.20
292 Darren Lewis	.07	.20
293 Nomar Garciaparra	.30	.75
294 Greg Colbrunn	.07	.20
295 Jeff Bagwell	.10	.30
296 Brent Gates	.07	.20
297 Jose Vizcaino	.07	.20
298 Alex Ochoa	.07	.20
299 Sid Fernandez	.07	.20
300 Ken Griffey Jr.	.40	1.00
301 Chris Gomez	.07	.20
302 Wendell Magee	.07	.20
303 Darren Oliver	.07	.20
304 Mel Nieves	.07	.20
305 Sammy Sosa	.20	.50
306 George Arias	.07	.20
307 Jack McDowell	.07	.20
308 Stan Javier	.07	.20
309 Kimera Bartee	.07	.20
310 James Baldwin	.07	.20
311 Rocky Coppinger	.07	.20
312 Keith Lockhart	.07	.20
313 C.J. Nitkowski	.07	.20
314 Allen Watson	.07	.20
315 Darryl Kile	.07	.20
316 Amaury Telemaco	.07	.20
317 Jason Isringhausen	.07	.20
318 Manny Ramirez	.10	.30
319 Terry Pendleton	.07	.20
320 Tim Salmon	.10	.30
321 Eric Karros	.07	.20
322 Mark Whiten	.07	.20
323 Rick Krivda	.07	.20
324 Brett Butler	.07	.20
325 Randy Johnson	.20	.50
326 Eddie Taubensee	.07	.20
327 Mark Leiter	.07	.20
328 Kevin Gross	.07	.20
329 Ernie Young	.07	.20
330 Pat Hentgen	.07	.20
331 Rondell White	.07	.20
332 Bobby Witt	.07	.20
333 Eddie Murray	.20	.50
334 Tim Raines	.07	.20
335 Jeff Fassero	.07	.20
336 Chuck Finley	.07	.20
337 Willie Adams	.07	.20
338 Chan Ho Park	.07	.20
339 Jay Powell	.07	.20
340 Ivan Rodriguez	.10	.30
341 Jermaine Allensworth	.07	.20
342 Jay Payton	.07	.20
343 T.J. Mathews	.07	.20
344 Tony Batista	.07	.20
345 Ed Sprague	.07	.20
346 Jeff Kent	.07	.20
347 Scott Erickson	.07	.20
348 Jeff Suppan	.07	.20
349 Pete Schourek	.07	.20
350 Kenny Lofton	.07	.20
351 Alan Benes	.07	.20
352 Fred McGriff	.10	.30
353 Charlie O'Brien	.07	.20
354 Darren Bragg	.07	.20
355 Alex Fernandez	.07	.20
356 Al Martin	.07	.20
357 Bob Wells	.07	.20
358 Chad Mottola	.07	.20
359 Devon White	.07	.20
360 David Cone	.07	.20
361 Bobby Jones	.07	.20
362 Scott Sanders	.07	.20
363 Karim Garcia	.07	.20
364 Kirt Manwaring	.07	.20
365 Chili Davis	.07	.20
366 Mike Hampton	.07	.20
367 Chad Ogea	.07	.20
368 Curt Schilling	.07	.20
369 Phil Nevin	.07	.20
370 Roger Clemens	.40	1.00
371 Willie Greene	.07	.20
372 Kenny Rogers	.07	.20
373 Jose Rijo	.07	.20
374 Bobby Bonilla	.07	.20
375 Mike Mussina	.10	.30
376 Curtis Pride	.07	.20
377 Todd Walker	.07	.20
378 Jason Bere	.07	.20
379 Heathcliff Slocumb	.07	.20
380 Dante Bichette	.07	.20
381 Carlos Baerga	.07	.20
382 Livan Hernandez	.07	.20
383 Jason Schmidt	.07	.20
384 Kevin Stocker	.07	.20
385 Matt Williams	.07	.20
386 Bartolo Colon	.07	.20
387 Will Clark	.10	.30
388 Dennis Eckersley	.07	.20
389 Brooks Kieschnick	.07	.20
390 Ryan Klesko	.07	.20
391 Mark Carreon	.07	.20
392 Tim Worrell	.07	.20
393 Dean Palmer	.07	.20
394 Wil Cordero	.07	.20
395 Javy Lopez	.07	.20
396 Rich Aurilia	.07	.20
397 Greg Vaughn	.07	.20
398 Vinny Castilla	.07	.20
399 Jeff Montgomery	.07	.20
400 Cal Ripken	.60	1.50
401 Walt Weiss	.07	.20
402 Brad Ausmus	.07	.20
403 Ruben Rivera	.07	.20
404 Mark Wohlers	.07	.20
405 Rick Aguilera	.07	.20
406 Tony Clark	.07	.20
407 Lyle Mouton	.07	.20
408 Bill Pulsipher	.07	.20
409 Jose Rosado	.07	.20
410 Tony Gwynn	.25	.60
411 Cecil Fielder	.07	.20
412 John Flaherty	.07	.20
413 Lenny Dykstra	.07	.20
414 Ugueth Urbina	.07	.20
415 Brian Jordan	.07	.20
416 Bob Abreu	.10	.30
417 Craig Paquette	.07	.20
418 Sandy Martinez	.07	.20
419 Jeff Blauser	.07	.20
420 Barry Larkin	.10	.30
421 Kevin Seitzer	.07	.20
422 Tim Belcher	.07	.20
423 Paul Sorrento	.07	.20
424 Cal Eldred	.07	.20
425 Robin Ventura	.07	.20
426 John Olerud	.07	.20
427 Bob Wolcott	.07	.20
428 Matt Lawton	.07	.20
429 Rod Beck	.07	.20
430 Shane Reynolds	.07	.20
431 Mike James	.07	.20
432 Steve Wojciechowski	.07	.20
433 Vladimir Guerrero	.20	.50
434 Dustin Hermanson	.07	.20
435 Marty Cordova	.07	.20
436 Marc Newfield	.07	.20
437 Todd Stottlemyre	.07	.20
438 Jeffrey Hammonds	.07	.20
439 Dave Stevens	.07	.20
440 Hideo Nomo	.20	.50
441 Mark Thompson	.07	.20
442 Mark Lewis	.07	.20
443 Quinton McCracken	.07	.20
444 Cliff Floyd	.07	.20
445 Denny Neagle	.07	.20
446 John Jaha	.07	.20
447 Mike Sweeney	.07	.20
448 John Wasdin	.07	.20
449 Chad Curtis	.07	.20
450 Mo Vaughn	.07	.20
451 Donovan Osborne	.07	.20
452 Ruben Sierra	.07	.20
453 Michael Tucker	.07	.20
454 Kurt Abbott	.07	.20
455 Andruw Jones UER	.10	.30
456 Shannon Stewart	.07	.20
457 Scott Brosius	.07	.20
458 Juan Guzman	.07	.20
459 Ron Villone	.07	.20
460 Moises Alou	.07	.20
461 Larry Walker	.07	.20
462 Eddie Murray SH	.10	.30
463 Paul Molitor SH	.07	.20
464 Hideo Nomo SH	.07	.20
465 Barry Bonds SH	.30	.75
466 Todd Hundley SH	.07	.20
467 Rheal Cormier	.07	.20
468 J.Sandoval	.08	.25
J.Conti RC		
469 R.Barajas	.60	1.50
J.Rexrode RC		
470 Jared Sandberg RC	.08	.25
471 P.Wilder	.08	.25
C.Gunner RC		
472 M.DeCelle	.08	.25
M.McCain RC		
473 Todd Zeile	.07	.20
474 Neifi Perez	.07	.20
475 Jeromy Burnitz	.07	.20
476 Trey Beamon	.07	.20
477 J.Patterson	.30	.75
B.Looper RC		
478 Jake Westbrook RC	.20	.50
479 E.Chavez	.75	2.00
A.Eaton RC		
480 P.Tucci	.08	.25
J.Lawrence RC		
481 K.Benson	.20	.50
B.Koch RC		
482 J.Nicholson	.08	.25
A.Prater RC		
483 M.Kotsay	.30	.75
M.Johnson RC		
484 Armando Benitez	.07	.20
485 Mike Matheny	.07	.20
486 Jeff Reed	.07	.20
487 M.Bellhorn	.07	.20
R.Johnson		
E.Wilson		
488 R.Hidalgo	.07	.20
B.Grieve		
489 Konerko	.10	.30
D.Lee		
Wright		
490 Bill Mueller RC	.50	1.25
491 J.Abbott	.07	.20
S.Monahan		
E.Velazquez		
492 Jimmy Anderson RC	.08	.25
493 Carl Pavano	.07	.20
494 Nelson Figueroa RC	.08	.25
495 Checklist (277-400)	.07	.20
496 Checklist (401-496)	.07	.20
NNO Derek Jeter AU	125.00	250.00

1997 Topps All-Stars

Randomly inserted in Series one hobby and retail packs at a rate of one in 18 and one in every six jumbo packs, this 22-card set printed on rainbow foilboard features the top 11 players from each league and from each position as voted by the Topps Sports Department. The fronts carry a photo of a "first team" all-star player while the backs carry a different photo of that player alongside the "second team" and "third team" selections. Only the "first team" players are checklisted listed below.

COMPLETE SET (22)	10.00	25.00
SER.1 STATED ODDS 1:18 HOB/RET, 1:6 JUM		
AS1 Ivan Rodriguez	.40	1.00
AS2 Todd Hundley	.25	.60
AS3 Frank Thomas	.60	1.50
AS4 Andres Galarraga	.25	.60
AS5 Chuck Knoblauch	.25	.60
AS6 Eric Young	.25	.60
AS7 Jim Thome	.40	1.00
AS8 Chipper Jones	.60	1.50
AS9 Cal Ripken	2.00	5.00
AS10 Barry Larkin	.40	1.00
AS11 Albert Belle	.25	.60
AS12 Barry Bonds	2.00	5.00
AS13 Ken Griffey Jr.	1.25	3.00
AS14 Ellis Burks	.25	.60
AS15 Juan Gonzalez	.25	.60
AS16 Gary Sheffield	.25	.60
AS17 Andy Pettitte	.40	1.00
AS18 Tom Glavine	.40	1.00
AS19 Pat Hentgen	.25	.60
AS20 John Smoltz	.40	1.00
AS21 Roberto Hernandez	.25	.60
AS22 Mark Wohlers	.25	.60

1997 Topps Awesome Impact

Randomly inserted in second series 11-card retail packs at a rate of 1:18, cards from this 20-card set feature a selection of top young stars and prospects. Each card front features a color player action shot cut out against a silver prismatic background.

COMPLETE SET (20)	40.00	100.00
SER.2 STATED ODDS 1:18 RETAIL		
AI1 Jaime Bluma	1.25	3.00
AI2 Tony Clark	1.25	3.00
AI3 Jermaine Dye	1.25	3.00
AI4 Nomar Garciaparra	5.00	12.00
AI5 Vladimir Guerrero	3.00	8.00
AI6 Todd Hollandsworth	1.25	3.00
AI7 Derek Jeter	8.00	20.00
AI8 Andruw Jones	2.00	5.00
AI9 Chipper Jones	3.00	8.00
AI10 Jason Kendall	1.25	3.00
AI11 Brooks Kieschnick	1.25	3.00
AI12 Alex Ochoa	1.25	3.00
AI13 Rey Ordonez	1.25	3.00
AI14 Neifi Perez	1.25	3.00
AI15 Edgar Renteria	1.25	3.00
AI16 Mariano Rivera	3.00	8.00
AI17 Ruben Rivera	1.25	3.00
AI18 Scott Rolen	2.00	5.00
AI19 Billy Wagner	1.25	3.00
AI20 Todd Walker	1.25	3.00

1997 Topps Hobby Masters

Randomly inserted in first and second series hobby packs at a rate of one in 36, cards from this 10-card set honor twenty players picked by hobby dealers from across the country as their all-time favorites. Cards 1-10 were issued in first series packs and 11-20 in second series. Printed on 28-point diffraction foilboard, one card replaces two regular cards when inserted in packs. The fronts feature borderless color player photos on a background of the player's profile. The backs carry player information.

COMPLETE SET (20)	30.00	80.00
COMPLETE SERIES 1 (10)	15.00	40.00
COMPLETE SERIES 2 (10)	15.00	40.00
STATED ODDS 1:36 HOBBY		
HM1 Ken Griffey Jr.	3.00	8.00
HM2 Cal Ripken	5.00	12.00
HM3 Greg Maddux	2.50	6.00
HM4 Albert Belle	.60	1.50
HM5 Tony Gwynn	2.00	5.00
HM6 Jeff Bagwell	1.00	2.50
HM7 Randy Johnson	1.50	4.00
HM8 Raul Mondesi	.60	1.50
HM9 Juan Gonzalez	.60	1.50
HM10 Kenny Lofton	.60	1.50
HM11 Frank Thomas	1.50	4.00
HM12 Mike Piazza	2.50	6.00
HM13 Chipper Jones	1.50	4.00
HM14 Brady Anderson	.60	1.50
HM15 Ken Caminiti	.60	1.50
HM16 Barry Bonds	5.00	12.00
HM17 Mo Vaughn	.60	1.50
HM18 Derek Jeter	4.00	10.00
HM19 Sammy Sosa	1.50	4.00
HM20 Andres Galarraga	.60	1.50

1997 Topps Inter-League Finest

Randomly inserted in Series one hobby and retail packs at a rate of one in 36 and jumbo packs at a rate of one in 10; this 14-card set features top individual match-ups from inter-league rivalries. One player from each major league team is represented on each side of this double-sided set with a color photo and is covered with the patented Finest clear protector.

COMPLETE SET (14)	25.00	60.00
SER.1 ODDS 1:36 HOB/RET,1:10 JUM		
*REF.: 1X TO 2.5X BASIC INTER-LG		
REF.SER.1 ODDS 1:216 HOB/RET, 1:56 JUM		
ILM1 M.McGwire	4.00	10.00
B.Bonds		
ILM2 M.Piazza	2.50	6.00
T.Salmon		
ILM3 K.Griffey Jr.	3.00	8.00
D.Bichette		
ILM4 J.Gonzalez	2.00	5.00
T.Gwynn		
ILM5 S.Sosa	1.50	4.00
F.Thomas		
ILM6 A.Belle	.60	1.50
B.Larkin		
ILM7 J.Damon	.60	1.50
B.Jordan		
ILM8 P.Molitor	.60	1.50
J.King		
ILM9 J.Bagwell	1.00	2.50
J.Jaha		
ILM10 B.Williams	1.00	2.50
T.Hundley		
ILM11 J.Carter	.60	1.50
H.Rodriguez		
ILM12 C.Ripken	5.00	12.00
G.Jefferies		
ILM13 C.Jones	1.50	4.00
M.Vaughn		
ILM14 T.Fryman	.60	1.50
G.Sheffield		

1997 Topps Mantle

Randomly inserted at the rate of one in 12 Series one hobby/retail packs and one every three jumbo packs, this 16-card set features authentic reprints of Topps Mickey Mantle cards that were not reprinted last year. Each card is stamped with the commemorative gold foil logo.

COMPLETE SET (16)	40.00	100.00
COMMON MANTLE (21 36)	3.00	8.00
SER.1 ODDS 1:12 HOB/RET,1:3 JUM		
COMMON FINEST (21-36)	3.00	8.00
FINEST SER.2 1:24 HOB/RET, 1:6 JUM		
COMMON REF. (21-36)	12.50	30.00
REF.SER.2 1:216 HOB/RET,1:60 JUM		

1997 Topps Mays

Randomly inserted at the rate of one in eight first series hobby/retail packs and one every two jumbo packs; cards from this 27-card set feature reprints of both the Topps and Bowman vintage Mays cards . Each card front is highlighted by a special commemorative gold foil stamp. Randomly inserted in first series hobby packs only (at the rate of one in 2,400) are personally signed cards. A special 4 1/4" by 5 3/4" jumbo reprint of the 1952 Topps Willie Mays card was made available exclusively in special series one Wal-Mart boxes. Each box (shaped much like a cereal box) contained ten eight-card retail packs and the aforementioned jumbo card and retailed for $10.

COMPLETE SET (27)	30.00	60.00
COMMON MAYS (3-27)	1.50	4.00
SER.1 ODDS 1:8 HOB/RET, 1:2 JUM		
COMMON FINEST (1-27)	1.50	4.00
*'51-'52 FINEST: .4X TO 1X LISTED CARDS		
FINEST SER.2 1:20 HOB/RET,1:4 JUM		
COMMON REF. (1-27)	4.00	10.00
*'51-'52 REF: 1X TO 2.5X BASIC MAYS		
REF.SER.2 1:180 HOB/RET,1:48 JUM		
1 1951 Bowman	3.00	8.00
2 1952 Topps	2.50	6.00
J261 Willie Mays 1952 Jumbo	3.00	8.00

1997 Topps Mays Autographs

Acording to Topps, Mays signed about 65 each of the following cards: 51B, 52T, 53T, 55B, 55T, 57T, 58T, 60T, 60T AS, 61T, 61T AS, 63T, 64T, 65T, 66T, 69T, 70T, 72T, 73T. The cards all have a "Certified Topps Autograph" stamp on them.

COMMON CARD (1953-1958)	100.00	200.00
COMMON CARD (1960-1973)	78.00	150.00
SER.1 ODDS 1:2400 H/R, 1:625 JUM		
MAYS SIGNED APPX. 65 OF EACH CARD		
NO AU'S: 54B-56T-59T-62T-67T-68T-71T		
1 Willie Mays 1951 Bowman	100.00	200.00
2 Willie Mays 1952 Topps	100.00	200.00

1997 Topps Season's Best

This 25-card set was randomly inserted into Topps Series two packs at a rate of one every six hobby/retail packs and one per jumbo pack; this set features five top players from each of the following five statistical categories: Leading Looters (top base stealers), Bleacher Reachers (top home run hitters), Hill Toppers (most wins), Number Crunchers (most RBI's), Kings of Swings (top slugging percentages). The fronts display color player photos printed on prismatic illusion foilboard. The backs carry another player photo and statistics.

COMPLETE SET (25)	10.00	25.00
SER.2 STATED ODDS 1:6 HOB/RET, 1:1 JUM		
SB1 Tony Gwynn	1.00	2.50
SB2 Frank Thomas	.75	2.00
SB3 Ellis Burks	.30	.75
SB4 Paul Molitor	.30	.75
SB5 Chuck Knoblauch	.30	.75
SB6 Mark McGwire	2.00	5.00
SB7 Brady Anderson	.30	.75
SB8 Ken Griffey Jr.	1.50	4.00
SB9 Albert Belle	.30	.75
SB10 Andres Galarraga	.30	.75
SB11 Andres Galarraga	.30	.75
SB12 Albert Belle	.30	.75
SB13 Juan Gonzalez	.30	.75
SB14 Mo Vaughn	.30	.75
SB15 Rafael Palmeiro	.50	1.25
SB16 John Smoltz	.50	1.25
SB17 Andy Pettitte	.50	1.25
SB18 Pat Hentgen	.30	.75
SB19 Mike Mussina	.50	1.25
SB20 Andy Benes	.30	.75
SB21 Kenny Lofton	.30	.75
SB22 Tom Goodwin	.30	.75
SB23 Otis Nixon	.30	.75
SB24 Eric Young	.30	.75
SB25 Lance Johnson	.30	.75

1997 Topps Sweet Strokes

This 15-card retail only set was randomly inserted in series one retail packs at a rate of one in 12. Printed on Rainbow foilboard, the set features color photos of some of Baseball's top hitters.

COMPLETE SET (15)	15.00	40.00
SER.1 STATED ODDS 1:12 RETAIL		
SS1 Roberto Alomar	.60	1.50
SS2 Jeff Bagwell	.60	1.50
SS3 Albert Belle	.40	1.00
SS4 Barry Bonds	3.00	8.00
SS5 Mark Grace	.60	1.50
SS6 Ken Griffey Jr.	2.00	5.00
SS7 Tony Gwynn	1.25	3.00
SS8 Chipper Jones	1.00	2.50
SS9 Edgar Martinez	.60	1.50
SS10 Mark McGwire	2.50	6.00
SS11 Rafael Palmeiro	.60	1.50
SS12 Mike Piazza	1.50	4.00

SS13 Gary Sheffield .40 1.00
SS14 Frank Thomas 1.00 2.50
SS15 Mo Vaughn .40 1.00

1997 Topps Team Timber

Randomly inserted into all second series hobby/retail packs at a rate of 1:36 and second series Hobby Collector (jumbo) packs at a rate of 1:8, cards from this 16-card set highlight a selection of baseball's top sluggers. Each card features a simulated wood-grain stock, but the fronts are UV-coated, making the cards bow noticeably.

COMPLETE SET (16) 15.00 40.00
SER.2 STATED ODDS 1:36 HOB/RET, 1:8 JUM
TT1 Ken Griffey Jr. 2.00 5.00
TT2 Ken Caminiti .40 1.00
TT3 Bernie Williams .60 1.50
TT4 Jeff Bagwell .60 1.50
TT5 Frank Thomas 1.00 2.50
TT6 Andres Galarraga .40 1.00
TT7 Barry Bonds 3.00 8.00
TT8 Rafael Palmeiro .60 1.50
TT9 Brady Anderson .40 1.00
TT10 Juan Gonzalez .40 1.00
TT11 Mo Vaughn .40 1.00
TT12 Mark McGwire 2.50 6.00
TT13 Gary Sheffield .40 1.00
TT14 Albert Belle .40 1.00
TT15 Chipper Jones 1.00 2.50
TT16 Mike Piazza 1.50 4.00

1998 Topps

This 503-card set was distributed in two separate series: 282 cards in first series and 221 cards in second series. 11-card packs carried a suggested retail price of $1.29. Cards were also distributed in Home Team Advantage jumbo packs and hobby, retail and Christmas factory sets. Card fronts feature color action player photos printed on 16 pt. stock with player information and career statistics on the back. Card number 7 was permanently retired in 1996 to honor Mickey Mantle. Series one contains the following subsets: Draft Picks (245-249), Prospects (250-259), Season Highlights (265-269), Interleague (270-274) Checklists (275-276) and World Series (277-283). Series two contains Season Highlights (474-478), Interleague (479-483), Prospects (484-495/498-501) and Checklists (502-503). Rookie Cards of note include Ryan Anderson, Michael Cuddyer, Jack Cust and Troy Glaus. This set also features Topps long-awaited first regular-issue Alex Rodriguez card (504). The superstar shortstop was left out of all Topps sets for the first four years of his career due to a problem between Topps and Rodriguez's agent Scott Boras. Finally, as part of an agreement with the Baseball Hall of Fame, Topps produced commemorative admission tickets featuring Roberto Clemente memorabilia from the Hall in the form of a Topps card. These were the standard admission tickets for the shrine, and were also included one per case in 1998 Topps series two baseball.

COMPLETE SET (503) 25.00 60.00
COMP.HOBBY SET (511) 30.00 80.00
COMP.RETAIL SET (511) 30.00 80.00
COMPLETE SERIES 1 (282) 12.50 30.00
COMPLETE SERIES 2 (221) 12.50 30.00
CARD NUMBER 7 DOES NOT EXIST
1 Tony Gwynn .25 .60
2 Larry Walker .07 .20
3 Billy Wagner .07 .20
4 Denny Neagle .07 .20
5 Vladimir Guerrero .20 .50
6 Kevin Brown .10 .30
8 Mariano Rivera .20 .50
9 Tony Clark .07 .20
10 Deion Sanders .10 .30
11 Francisco Cordova .07 .20
12 Matt Williams .07 .20
13 Carlos Baerga .07 .20
14 Mo Vaughn .07 .20
15 Bobby Witt .07 .20
16 Matt Stairs .07 .20
17 Chan Ho Park .07 .20
18 Mike Bordick .07 .20
19 Michael Tucker .07 .20
20 Frank Thomas .20 .50
21 Roberto Clemente .40 1.00
22 Dmitri Young .07 .20
23 Steve Trachsel .07 .20
24 Jeff Kent .07 .20
25 Scott Rolen .10 .30
26 John Thomson .07 .20
27 Joe Vitiello .07 .20
28 Eddie Guardado .07 .20
29 Charlie Hayes .07 .20
30 Juan Gonzalez .07 .20
31 Garret Anderson .07 .20
32 John Jaha .07 .20
33 Omar Vizquel .10 .30
34 Brian Hunter .07 .20
35 Jeff Bagwell .10 .30
36 Mark Lemke .07 .20
37 Doug Glanville .07 .20
38 Dan Wilson .07 .20
39 Steve Cooke .07 .20
40 Chili Davis .07 .20
41 Mike Cameron .07 .20
42 F.P. Santangelo .07 .20
43 Brad Ausmus .07 .20
44 Gary DiSarcina .07 .20
45 Pat Hentgen .07 .20
46 Wilton Guerrero .07 .20
47 Devon White .07 .20
48 Danny Patterson .07 .20
49 Pat Meares .07 .20
50 Rafael Palmeiro .10 .30
51 Mark Gardner .07 .20
52 Jeff Blauser .07 .20
53 Dave Hollins .07 .20
54 Carlos Garcia .07 .20
55 Ben McDonald .07 .20
56 John Mabry .07 .20
57 Trevor Hoffman .07 .20
58 Tony Fernandez .07 .20
59 Rich Loiselle RC .07 .20
60 Mark Leiter .07 .20
61 Pat Kelly .07 .20
62 John Flaherty .07 .20
63 Roger Bailey .07 .20
64 Tom Gordon .07 .20
65 Ryan Klesko .07 .20
66 Darryl Hamilton .07 .20
67 Jim Eisenreich .07 .20
68 Butch Huskey .07 .20
69 Mark Grudzielanek .07 .20
70 Marquis Grissom .07 .20
71 Mark McLemore .07 .20
72 Gary Gaetti .07 .20
73 Greg Gagne .07 .20
74 Lyle Mouton .07 .20
75 Jim Edmonds .07 .20
76 Shawn Green .07 .20
77 Greg Vaughn .07 .20
78 Terry Adams .07 .20
79 Kevin Polcovich .07 .20
80 Troy O'Leary .07 .20
81 Jeff Shaw .07 .20
82 Rich Becker .07 .20
83 David Wells .07 .20
84 Steve Karsay .07 .20
85 Charles Nagy .07 .20
86 B.J. Surhoff .07 .20
87 Jamey Wright .07 .20
88 James Baldwin .07 .20
89 Edgardo Alfonzo .07 .20
90 Jay Buhner .07 .20
91 Brady Anderson .07 .20
92 Scott Servais .07 .20
93 Edgar Renteria .07 .20
94 Mike Lieberthal .07 .20
95 Rick Aguilera .07 .20
96 Walt Weiss .07 .20
97 Deivi Cruz .07 .20
98 Kurt Abbott .07 .20
99 Henry Rodriguez .07 .20
100 Mike Piazza .30 .75
101 Bill Taylor .07 .20
102 Todd Zeile .07 .20
103 Rey Ordonez .07 .20
104 Willie Greene .07 .20
105 Tony Womack .07 .20
106 Mike Sweeney .07 .20
107 Jeffrey Hammonds .07 .20
108 Kevin Orie .07 .20
109 Alex Gonzalez .07 .20
110 Jose Canseco .10 .30
111 Paul Sorrento .07 .20
112 Joey Hamilton .07 .20
113 Brad Radke .07 .20
114 Steve Avery .07 .20
115 Esteban Loaiza .07 .20
116 Stan Javier .07 .20
117 Chris Gomez .07 .20
118 Royce Clayton .07 .20
119 Orlando Merced .07 .20
120 Kevin Appier .07 .20
121 Mel Nieves .07 .20
122 Joe Girardi .07 .20
123 Rico Brogna .07 .20
124 Kent Mercker .07 .20
125 Manny Ramirez .10 .30
126 Jeromy Burnitz .07 .20
127 Kevin Foster .07 .20
128 Matt Morris .07 .20
129 Jason Dickson .07 .20
130 Tom Glavine .10 .30
131 Wally Joyner .07 .20
132 Rick Reed .07 .20
133 Todd Jones .07 .20
134 Dave Martinez .07 .20
135 Sandy Alomar Jr. .07 .20
136 Mike Lansing .07 .20
137 Sean Berry .07 .20
138 Doug Jones .07 .20
139 Todd Stottlemyre .07 .20
140 Jay Bell .07 .20
141 Jaime Navarro .07 .20
142 Chris Hoiles .07 .20
143 Joey Cora .07 .20
144 Scott Spiezio .07 .20
145 Joe Carter .07 .20
146 Jose Guillen .07 .20
147 Damion Easley .07 .20
148 Lee Stevens .07 .20
149 Alex Fernandez .07 .20
150 Randy Johnson .20 .50
151 J.T. Snow .07 .20
152 Chuck Finley .07 .20
153 Bernard Gilkey .07 .20
154 David Segui .07 .20
155 Dante Bichette .07 .20
156 Kevin Stocker .07 .20
157 Carl Everett .07 .20
158 Jose Valentin .07 .20
159 Pokey Reese .07 .20
160 Derek Jeter .50 1.25
161 Roger Pavlik .07 .20
162 Mark Wohlers .07 .20
163 Ricky Bottalico .07 .20
164 Ozzie Guillen .07 .20
165 Mike Mussina .10 .30
166 Gary Sheffield .07 .20
167 Hideo Nomo .20 .50
168 Mark Grace .10 .30
169 Aaron Sele .07 .20
170 Darryl Kile .07 .20
171 Shawn Estes .07 .20
172 Vinny Castilla .07 .20
173 Ron Coomer .07 .20
174 Jose Rosado .07 .20
175 Kenny Lofton .07 .20
176 Jason Giambi .07 .20
177 Hal Morris .07 .20
178 Darren Bragg .07 .20
179 Orel Hershiser .07 .20
180 Ray Lankford .07 .20
181 Hideki Irabu .07 .20
182 Kevin Young .07 .20
183 Javy Lopez .07 .20
184 Jeff Montgomery .07 .20
185 Mike Holtz .07 .20
186 George Williams .07 .20
187 Cal Eldred .07 .20
188 Tom Candiotti .07 .20
189 Glenallen Hill .07 .20
190 Brian Giles .07 .20
191 Dave Mlicki .07 .20
192 Garrett Stephenson .07 .20
193 Jeff Frye .07 .20
194 Joe Oliver .07 .20
195 Bob Hamelin .07 .20
196 Luis Sojo .07 .20
197 LaTroy Hawkins .07 .20
198 Kevin Elster .07 .20
199 Jeff Reed .07 .20
200 Dennis Eckersley .07 .20
201 Bill Mueller .07 .20
202 Russ Davis .07 .20
203 Armando Benitez .07 .20
204 Quilvio Veras .07 .20
205 Tim Naehring .07 .20
206 Quinton McCracken .07 .20
207 Raul Casanova .07 .20
208 Matt Lawton .07 .20
209 Luis Alicea .07 .20
210 Luis Gonzalez .07 .20
211 Allen Watson .07 .20
212 Gerald Williams .07 .20
213 David Bell .07 .20
214 Todd Hollandsworth .07 .20
215 Wade Boggs .10 .30
216 Jose Mesa .07 .20
217 Jamie Moyer .07 .20
218 Darren Daulton .07 .20
219 Mickey Morandini .07 .20
220 Rusty Greer .07 .20
221 Jim Bullinger .07 .20
222 Jose Offerman .07 .20
223 Matt Karchner .07 .20
224 Woody Williams .07 .20
225 Mark Loretta .07 .20
226 Mike Hampton .07 .20
227 Willie Adams .07 .20
228 Scott Hatteberg .07 .20
229 Rich Amaral .07 .20
230 Terry Steinbach .07 .20
231 Glendon Rusch .07 .20
232 Bret Boone .07 .20
233 Robert Person .07 .20
234 Jose Hernandez .07 .20
235 Doug Drabek .07 .20
236 Jason McDonald .07 .20
237 Chris Widger .07 .20
238 Tom Martin .07 .20
239 Dave Burba .07 .20
240 Pete Rose Jr. .07 .20
241 Bobby Ayala .07 .20
242 Tim Wakefield .07 .20
243 Dennis Springer .07 .20
244 Tim Belcher .07 .20
245 J.Garland .10 .30
G.Goetz
246 L.Berkman .10 .30
G.Davis
247 V.Wells .10 .30
A.Akin
248 A.Kennedy .07 .20
J.Romano
249 J.Dellaero .07 .20
T.Cameron
250 J.Sandberg .07 .20
A.Sanchez
251 P.Ortega .07 .20
J.Manias
252 Mike Stoner RC .07 .20
253 J.Patterson .07 .20
L.Rodriguez
254 R.Minor RC .10 .30
A.Beltre
255 B.Grieve .07 .20
D.Brown
256 Wood .10 .30
Pavano
Meche
257 D.Ortiz 1.00 2.50
Sexson
Ward
258 J.Encarn .07 .20
Winn
Vessel
259 Bens .07 .20
T.Smith RC
C.Dunc RC
260 Warren Morris RC .07 .20
261 R.Hernandez .07 .20
B.Davis
E.Marrero
262 E.Chavez .10 .30
R.Branyan
263 Ryan Jackson RC .07 .20
264 B.Fuentes RC .60 1.50
Clement
Halladay
265 Randy Johnson SH .10 .30
266 Kevin Brown SH .07 .20
267 R.Rincon .07 .20
F.Cordova SH
268 Nomar Garciaparra SH .20 .50
269 Tino Martinez SH .07 .20
270 Chuck Knoblauch IL .07 .20
271 Pedro Martinez IL .10 .30
272 Denny Neagle IL .07 .20
273 Juan Gonzalez IL .07 .20
274 Andres Galarraga IL .07 .20
275 Checklist (1-195) .07 .20
276 Checklist (196-283 .07 .20
inserts)
277 Moises Alou WS .07 .20
278 Sandy Alomar Jr. WS .07 .20
279 Gary Sheffield WS .07 .20
280 Matt Williams WS .07 .20
281 Livan Hernandez WS .07 .20
282 Chad Ogea WS .07 .20
283 Marlins Champs .07 .20
284 Tino Martinez .10 .30
285 Roberto Alomar .10 .30
286 Jeff King .07 .20
287 Brian Jordan .07 .20
288 Darin Erstad .07 .20
289 Ken Caminiti .07 .20
290 Jim Thome .10 .30
291 Paul Molitor .07 .20
292 Ivan Rodriguez .10 .30
293 Bernie Williams .10 .30
294 Todd Hundley .07 .20
295 Andres Galarraga .07 .20
296 Greg Maddux .30 .75
297 Edgar Martinez .10 .30
298 Ron Gant .07 .20
299 Derek Bell .07 .20
300 Roger Clemens .40 1.00
301 Rondell White .07 .20
302 Barry Larkin .10 .30
303 Robin Ventura .07 .20
304 Jason Kendall .07 .20
305 Chipper Jones .20 .50
306 John Franco .07 .20
307 Sammy Sosa .20 .50
308 Troy Percival .07 .20
309 Chuck Knoblauch .07 .20
310 Ellis Burks .07 .20
311 Al Martin .07 .20
312 Tim Salmon .10 .30
313 Moises Alou .07 .20
314 Lance Johnson .07 .20
315 Justin Thompson .07 .20
316 Will Clark .10 .30
317 Barry Bonds .60 1.50
318 Craig Biggio .10 .30
319 John Smoltz .10 .30
320 Cal Ripken .60 1.50
321 Ken Griffey Jr. .40 1.00
322 Paul O'Neill .10 .30
323 Todd Helton .10 .30
324 John Olerud .07 .20
325 Mark McGwire .50 1.25
326 Jose Cruz Jr. .07 .20
327 Jeff Cirillo .07 .20
328 Dean Palmer .07 .20
329 John Wetteland .07 .20
330 Steve Finley .07 .20
331 Albert Belle .07 .20
332 Curt Schilling .07 .20
333 Raul Mondesi .07 .20
334 Andruw Jones .10 .30
335 Nomar Garciaparra .30 .75
336 David Justice .07 .20
337 Andy Pettitte .10 .30
338 Pedro Martinez .10 .30
339 Travis Miller .07 .20
340 Chris Stynes .07 .20
341 Gregg Jefferies .07 .20
342 Jeff Fassero .07 .20
343 Craig Counsell .07 .20
344 Wilson Alvarez .07 .20
345 Bip Roberts .07 .20
346 Kelvim Escobar .07 .20
347 Mark Bellhorn .07 .20
348 Cory Lidle RC .60 1.50
349 Fred McGriff .10 .30
350 Chuck Carr .07 .20
351 Bob Abreu .07 .20
352 Juan Guzman .07 .20
353 Fernando Vina .07 .20
354 Andy Benes .07 .20
355 Dave Nilsson .07 .20
356 Bobby Bonilla .07 .20
357 Ismael Valdes .07 .20
358 Carlos Perez .07 .20
359 Kirk Rueter .07 .20
360 Bartolo Colon .07 .20
361 Mel Rojas .07 .20
362 Johnny Damon .10 .30
363 Geronimo Berroa .07 .20
364 Reggie Sanders .07 .20
365 Jermaine Allensworth .07 .20
366 Orlando Cabrera .07 .20
367 Jorge Fabregas .07 .20
368 Scott Stahoviak .07 .20
369 Ken Cloude .07 .20
370 Donovan Osborne .07 .20
371 Roger Cedeno .07 .20
372 Neifi Perez .07 .20
373 Chris Holt .07 .20
374 Cecil Fielder .07 .20
375 Marty Cordova .07 .20
376 Tom Goodwin .07 .20
377 Jeff Suppan .07 .20
378 Jeff Brantley .07 .20
379 Mark Langston .07 .20
380 Shane Reynolds .07 .20
381 Mike Fetters .07 .20
382 Todd Greene .07 .20
383 Ray Durham .07 .20
384 Carlos Delgado .07 .20
385 Jeff D'Amico .07 .20
386 Brian McRae .07 .20
387 Alan Benes .07 .20
388 Heathcliff Slocumb .07 .20
389 Eric Young .07 .20
390 Travis Fryman .07 .20
391 David Cone .07 .20
392 Otis Nixon .07 .20
393 Jeremi Gonzalez .07 .20
394 Jeff Juden .07 .20
395 Jose Vizcaino .07 .20
396 Ugueth Urbina .07 .20
397 Ramon Martinez .07 .20
398 Robb Nen .07 .20
399 Harold Baines .07 .20
400 Delino DeShields .07 .20
401 John Burkett .07 .20
402 Sterling Hitchcock .07 .20
403 Mark Clark .07 .20
404 Terrell Wade .07 .20
405 Scott Brosius .07 .20
406 Chad Curtis .07 .20
407 Brian Johnson .07 .20
408 Roberto Kelly .07 .20
409 Dave Dellucci RC .15 .40
410 Michael Tucker .07 .20
411 Mark Kotsay .07 .20
412 Mark Lewis .07 .20
413 Ryan McGuire .07 .20
414 Shawon Dunston .07 .20
415 Brad Rigby .07 .20
416 Scott Erickson .07 .20
417 Bobby Jones .07 .20
418 Darren Oliver .07 .20
419 John Smiley .07 .20
420 T.J. Mathews .07 .20
421 Dustin Hermanson .07 .20
422 Mike Timlin .07 .20
423 Willie Blair .07 .20
424 Manny Alexander .07 .20
425 Bob Tewksbury .07 .20
426 Pete Schourek .07 .20
427 Reggie Jefferson .07 .20
428 Ed Sprague .07 .20
429 Jeff Conine .07 .20
430 Roberto Hernandez .07 .20
431 Tom Pagnozzi .07 .20
432 Jaret Wright .07 .20
433 Livan Hernandez .07 .20
434 Andy Ashby .07 .20
435 Todd Dunn .07 .20
436 Bobby Higginson .07 .20
437 Rod Beck .07 .20
438 Jim Leyritz .07 .20
439 Matt Williams .07 .20
440 Brett Tomko .07 .20
441 Joe Randa .07 .20
442 Chris Carpenter .07 .20
443 Dennis Reyes .07 .20
444 Al Leiter .07 .20
445 Jason Schmidt .07 .20
446 Ken Hill .07 .20
447 Shannon Stewart .07 .20
448 Enrique Wilson .07 .20
449 Fernando Tatis .07 .20
450 Jimmy Key .07 .20
451 Darrin Fletcher .07 .20
452 John Valentin .07 .20
453 Kevin Tapani .07 .20
454 Eric Karros .07 .20
455 Jay Bell .07 .20
456 Walt Weiss .07 .20
457 Devon White .07 .20
458 Carl Pavano .07 .20
459 Mike Lansing .07 .20
460 John Flaherty .07 .20
461 Richard Hidalgo .07 .20
462 Quinton McCracken .07 .20
463 Karim Garcia .07 .20
464 Miguel Cairo .07 .20
465 Edwin Diaz .07 .20
466 Bobby Smith .07 .20
467 Yamil Benitez .07 .20
468 Rich Butler .07 .20
469 Ben Ford RC .07 .20
470 Bubba Trammell .07 .20
471 Brent Brede .07 .20
472 Brooks Kieschnick .07 .20
473 Carlos Castillo .07 .20
474 Brad Radke SH .07 .20
475 Roger Clemens SH .20 .50
476 Curt Schilling SH .07 .20
477 John Olerud SH .07 .20
478 Mark McGwire SH .25 .60
479 M.Piazza .25 .60
K.Griffey Jr. IL
480 J.Bagwell .10 .30
F.Thomas IL
481 C.Jones .10 .30
N.Garciaparra IL
482 L.Walker .07 .20
J.Gonzalez IL
483 G.Sheffield .07 .20
T.Martinez IL
484 D.Gib .07 .20
M.Colem
Hutchins
485 B.Rose .07 .20
Looper
Polite
486 E.Milton .07 .20
Marquis
C.Lee
487 Robert Fick RC .10 .30
488 A.Ramirez .10 .30
A.Gonz
Casey
489 D.Bridges .07 .20
T.Drew RC
490 D.McDonald .07 .20
N.Ndungidi RC
491 Ryan Anderson RC .07 .20
492 Troy Glaus RC .50 1.25
493 J.Werth .07 .20
D.Reichert RC
494 Michael Cuddyer RC .30 .75
495 Jack Cust RC .20 .50
496 Brian Anderson .07 .20
497 Tony Saunders .07 .20
498 J.Sandoval .07 .20
V.Nunez
499 B.Penny .10 .30
N.Bierbrodt
500 D.Carr .07 .20
L.Cruz RC
501 C.Bowers .07 .20
M.McCain
502 Checklist .07 .20
503 Checklist .07 .20
504 Alex Rodriguez .75 2.00

1998 Topps Minted in Cooperstown

*STARS: 5X TO 12X BASIC CARDS
*ROOKIES: 6X TO 15X BASIC CARDS
STATED ODDS: 1:8
CARD NUMBER 7 DOES NOT EXIST

1998 Topps Inaugural Devil Rays

COMP.FACT.SET (503) 40.00 100.00
*STARS: 1.5X TO 4X BASIC CARDS
*ROOKIES: 2.5X TO 6X BASIC CARDS
DISTRIBUTED ONLY IN FACT.SET FORM

1998 Topps Inaugural Diamondbacks

COMP.FACT.SET (503) 60.00 120.00
*STARS: 1.5X TO 4X BASIC CARDS
*ROOKIES: 2.5X TO 6X BASIC CARDS
DISTRIBUTED ONLY IN FACT.SET FORM

1998 Topps Baby Boomers

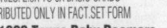

Randomly inserted in retail packs only at the rate of one in 36, this 15-card set features color photos of young players who have already made their mark in the game dispite less than three years in the majors.

COMPLETE SET (15) 5.00 12.00
SER.1 STATED ODDS 1:36 RETAIL
BB1 Derek Jeter 2.50 6.00
BB2 Scott Rolen .60 1.50
BB3 Nomar Garciaparra .60 1.50
BB4 Jose Cruz Jr. .40 1.00
BB5 Darin Erstad .40 1.00
BB6 Todd Helton .60 1.50
BB7 Tony Clark .40 1.00
BB8 Jose Guillen .40 1.00
BB9 Andruw Jones .40 1.00
BB10 Vladimir Guerrero .60 1.50
BB11 Mark Kotsay .40 1.00
BB12 Todd Greene .40 1.00
BB13 Andy Pettitte .60 1.50
BB14 Justin Thompson .40 1.00
BB15 Alan Benes .40 1.00

1998 Topps Clemente

Randomly inserted in first and second series packs at the rate of one in 18, cards from this 19-card set honor the memory of Roberto Clemente on the 25th anniversary of his untimely death with conventional reprints of his Topps cards. All odd numbered cards were seeded in first series packs. All even numbered cards were seeded in second series packs.

COMPLETE SET (19) 30.00 60.00
COMPLETE SERIES 1 (10) 12.50 30.00
COMPLETE SERIES 2 (9) 12.50 30.00
COMMON CARD (2-19) 1.50 4.00
STATED ODDS 1:18
ODD NUMBERS IN 1ST SERIES PACKS
EVEN NUMBERS IN 2ND SERIES PACKS
1 Roberto Clemente 1955 3.00 8.00

1998 Topps Clemente Memorabilia Madness

As a major promotion for 1998 Topps series one, Topps created 46 different Roberto Clemente exchange cards for a total of 854 prizes. All 46 prizes (including the quantity available of each prize) is detailed explicitly in the listings below. The quantity is noted immediately after the prize. All 854 exchange cards looked identical to each other on front and almost identical to each other on back. Card fronts feature a blue, purple and white dot matrix head shot of Clemente surrounded by burgundy borders. Card backs featured extensive guidelines and rules for the exchange program. The only difference for each card were the few sentences on back detailing which specific prize each of the 46 different cards could be exchanged for. Lucky collectors that got their hands on these scarce exchange cards had until August 31st, 1998 to redeem their prizes. Odds for pulling one of these cards was approximately 1:3,708 hobby packs and approximately 1:1,020 hobby collector packs. Prices for almost all of these exchange cards have been excluded due to scarcity and lack of market information.

COMMON CARD (1-46) 100.00 200.00
SER.1 ODDS 1:3708 HOBBY, 1:1020 HTA
SER.1 WILD CARD ODDS 1:72
NNO Wild Card .40 1.00

1998 Topps Clemente Sealed

*SEALED: .4X TO 1X BASIC CLEMENTE
ONE PER HOBBY FACTORY SET

1998 Topps Clemente Tins

COMMON TIN (1-4) 2.00 5.00

1998 Topps Clemente Tribute

Randomly inserted in packs at the rate of one in 12, this five-card set honors the memory of Roberto Clemente on the 25th anniversay of his untimely death and features color photos printed on mirror foilboard on newly designed cards.

COMPLETE SET (5) 3.00 8.00
COMMON CARD (RC1-RC5) .75 2.00
SER.1 STATED ODDS 1:12

1998 Topps Clout Nine

Randomly inserted in Topps Series two packs at the rate of one in 72, this nine-card set features color photos of the top players statiscally at each of the nine playing positions.

COMPLETE SET (9) 10.00 25.00
SER.2 STATED ODDS 1:72
C1 Edgar Martinez 1.25 3.00
C2 Mike Piazza 2.00 5.00
C3 Frank Thomas 2.00 5.00
C4 Craig Biggio 1.25 3.00
C5 Vinny Castilla .75 2.00
C6 Jeff Blauser .75 2.00
C7 Barry Bonds 3.00 8.00
C8 Ken Griffey Jr. 4.00 10.00
C9 Larry Walker 1.25 3.00

1998 Topps Etch-A-Sketch

Randomly inserted in Topps Series one packs at the rate of one in 36, this nine-card set features drawings by artist George Vlosich III of some of baseball's hottest superstars using an Etch A Sketch as a canvas.

COMPLETE SET (9) 12.50 30.00
SER.1 STATED ODDS 1:36
ES1 Albert Belle .50 1.25
ES2 Barry Bonds 4.00 10.00
ES3 Ken Griffey Jr. 2.50 6.00
ES4 Greg Maddux 2.00 5.00
ES5 Hideo Nomo 1.25 3.00
ES6 Mike Piazza 2.00 5.00
ES7 Cal Ripken 4.00 10.00
ES8 Frank Thomas 1.25 3.00
ES9 Mo Vaughn .50 1.25

1998 Topps Flashback

Randomly inserted in Topps Series one packs at the rate of one in 72, these two-sided cards of top players feature photographs of how they looked "then" as rookies on one side and how they look "now" as stars on the other.

COMPLETE SET (10) 12.00 30.00
SER.1 STATED ODDS 1:72
FB1 Barry Bonds 2.50 6.00
FB2 Ken Griffey Jr. 3.00 8.00
FB3 Paul Molitor 1.50 4.00
FB4 Randy Johnson 1.50 4.00
FB5 Cal Ripken 5.00 12.00
FB6 Tony Gwynn 1.50 4.00
FB7 Kenny Lofton .60 1.50
FB8 Gary Sheffield .60 1.50
FB9 Deion Sanders 1.00 2.50
FB10 Brady Anderson .60 1.50

1998 Topps Focal Points

Randomly inserted in Topps Series two hobby packs only at the rate of one in 36, this 15-card set features color photos of current superstars with a special focus on the skills that have put them at the top.

COMPLETE SET (15) 30.00 80.00
SER.2 STATED ODDS 1:36 HOBBY
FP1 Juan Gonzalez .75 2.00
FP2 Nomar Garciaparra 3.00 8.00
FP3 Jose Cruz Jr. .75 2.00
FP4 Cal Ripken 6.00 15.00
FP5 Ken Griffey Jr. 4.00 10.00
FP6 Ivan Rodriguez 1.25 3.00
FP7 Larry Walker .75 2.00
FP8 Barry Bonds 6.00 15.00
FP9 Roger Clemens 4.00 10.00
FP10 Frank Thomas 2.00 5.00
FP11 Chuck Knoblauch .75 2.00
FP12 Mike Piazza 3.00 8.00
FP13 Greg Maddux 3.00 8.00
FP14 Vladimir Guerrero 2.00 5.00
FP15 Andruw Jones 1.25 3.00

1998 Topps HallBound

Randomly inserted in Topps Series one hobby packs only at the rate of one in 36, this 15-card set features color photos of top stars who are bound for the Hall of Fame printed on foil mirrorboard cards.

COMPLETE SET (15) 20.00 50.00
SER.1 STATED ODDS 1:36 HOBBY
HB1 Paul Molitor .75 2.00
HB2 Tony Gwynn 2.50 6.00
HB3 Wade Boggs 1.25 3.00
HB4 Roger Clemens 4.00 10.00
HB5 Dennis Eckersley .75 2.00
HB6 Cal Ripken 6.00 15.00
HB7 Greg Maddux 3.00 8.00
HB8 Rickey Henderson 1.25 3.00
HB9 Ken Griffey Jr. 4.00 10.00
HB10 Frank Thomas 2.00 5.00
HB11 Mark McGwire 5.00 12.00
HB12 Barry Bonds 6.00 15.00
HB13 Mike Piazza 3.00 8.00
HB14 Juan Gonzalez .75 2.00
HB15 Randy Johnson 2.00 5.00

1998 Topps Milestones

Randomly inserted in Topps Series two retail packs only at the rate of one in 36, this ten-card set features color photos of players with the ability to set new records in the sport.

COMPLETE SET (10) 20.00 50.00
SER.2 STATED ODDS 1:36 RETAIL
MS1 Barry Bonds 5.00 12.00
MS2 Roger Clemens 3.00 8.00
MS3 Dennis Eckersley .60 1.50
MS4 Juan Gonzalez .60 1.50
MS5 Ken Griffey Jr. 3.00 8.00
MS6 Tony Gwynn 2.00 5.00
MS7 Greg Maddux 2.50 6.00
MS8 Mark McGwire 4.00 10.00
MS9 Cal Ripken 5.00 12.00
MS10 Frank Thomas 1.50 4.00

1998 Topps Mystery Finest

Randomly inserted in first series packs at the rate of one in 36, this 20-card set features color action player photos which showcase five of the 1997 season's most intriguing inter-league matchups.

COMPLETE SET (20) 30.00 80.00
SER.1 STATED ODDS 1:36
*REFRACTOR: 1X TO 2.5X BASIC MYS.FIN.
REFRACTOR SER.1 STATED ODDS: 1:144
ILM1 Chipper Jones 2.00 5.00
ILM2 Cal Ripken 6.00 15.00
ILM3 Greg Maddux 3.00 8.00
ILM4 Rafael Palmeiro 1.25 3.00
ILM5 Todd Hundley .75 2.00
ILM6 Derek Jeter 5.00 12.00
ILM7 John Olerud .75 2.00
ILM8 Tino Martinez 1.25 3.00
ILM9 Larry Walker .75 2.00
ILM10 Ken Griffey Jr. 4.00 10.00
ILM11 Andres Galarraga .75 2.00
ILM12 Randy Johnson 2.00 5.00
ILM13 Mike Piazza 3.00 8.00
ILM14 Jim Edmonds .75 2.00
ILM15 Eric Karros .75 2.00
ILM16 Tim Salmon 1.25 3.00
ILM17 Sammy Sosa 2.00 5.00
ILM18 Frank Thomas 2.00 5.00
ILM19 Mark Grace 1.25 3.00
ILM20 Albert Belle .75 2.00

1998 Topps Mystery Finest Bordered

Randomly inserted in Topps Series two packs at the rate of one in 36, this 20-card set features bordered color player photos of current hot players.

COMPLETE SET (20) 30.00 60.00
SER.2 STATED ODDS 1:36
*BORDERED REF: .75X TO 2X BORDERED
BORDERED REF.SER.2 ODDS 1:108
*BORDERLESS: .6X TO 1.5X BORDERED
BORDERLESS SER.2 ODDS 1:72
*BORDERLESS REF: 1.25X TO 3X BORDERED
BORDERLESS REF.SER.2 ODDS 1:288
M1 Nomar Garciaparra 3.00 8.00
M2 Chipper Jones 2.00 5.00
M3 Scott Rolen 1.25 3.00
M4 Albert Belle .75 2.00
M5 Mo Vaughn .75 2.00
M6 Jose Cruz Jr. .75 2.00
M7 Mark McGwire 5.00 12.00
M8 Derek Jeter 5.00 12.00
M9 Tony Gwynn 2.50 6.00
M10 Frank Thomas 2.00 5.00
M11 Tino Martinez 1.25 3.00
M12 Greg Maddux 3.00 8.00
M13 Juan Gonzalez .75 2.00
M14 Larry Walker .75 2.00
M15 Mike Piazza 3.00 8.00
M16 Cal Ripken 6.00 15.00
M17 Jeff Bagwell 1.25 3.00
M18 Andruw Jones 1.25 3.00
M19 Barry Bonds 6.00 15.00
M20 Ken Griffey Jr. 4.00 10.00

1998 Topps Rookie Class

Randomly inserted in Topps Series two packs at the rate of one in 12, this 10-card set features color photos of top young stars with less than one year's playing time in the Majors. The backs carry player information.

COMPLETE SET (10) 2.50 6.00
SER.2 STATED ODDS 1:12
R1 Travis Lee .30 .75
R2 Richard Hidalgo .30 .75
R3 Todd Helton .50 1.25
R4 Paul Konerko .30 .75
R5 Mark Kotsay .30 .75
R6 Derrek Lee .30 .75
R7 Eli Marrero .30 .75
R8 Fernando Tatis .30 .75
R9 Juan Encarnacion .30 .75
R10 Ben Grieve .30 .75

1999 Topps

The 1999 Topps set consisted of 462 standard-size cards. Each 11 card pack carried a suggested retail price of $1.29 per pack. Cards were also distributed in 40-card Home Team advantage jumbo packs, hobby, retail and Christmas factory sets. The Mark McGwire number 220 card was issued in 70 different varieties to honor his record setting season. The Sammy Sosa number 461 card was issued in 66 different varieties to honor his 1998 season. Basic sets are considered complete with any one of the 70 McGwire and 66 Sosa variations. A.J. Burnett, Pat Burrell, and Alex Escobar are the most notable Rookie Cards in the set. Card number 7 was not issued as Topps continues to honor the memory of Mickey Mantle. The Christmas factory set contains one Nolan Ryan finest reprint card as an added bonus, while the hobby and retail factory sets just contained the regular sets in a factory box.

COMPLETE SET (462) 25.00 60.00
COMP.HOBBY SET (462) 25.00 60.00
COMP.X-MAS SET (463) 25.00 60.00
COMPLETE SERIES 1 (241) 12.50 30.00
COMPLETE SERIES 2 (221) 12.50 30.00
COMP.MAC HR SET (70) 100.00 200.00
CARD 220 AVAIL.IN 70 VARIATIONS
COMP.SOSA HR SET (66) 60.00 120.00
CARD 461 AVAILABLE IN 66 VARIATIONS
CARD NUMBER 7 DOES NOT EXIST
SER.1 SET INCLUDES 1 CARD 220 VARIATION
SER.2 SET INCLUDES 1 CARD 461 VARIATION
1 Roger Clemens .40 1.00
2 Andres Galarraga .07 .20
3 Scott Brosius .07 .20
4 John Flaherty .07 .20
5 Jim Leyritz .07 .20
6 Ray Durham .07 .20
8 Jose Vizcaino .07 .20
9 Will Clark .10 .30
10 David Wells .07 .20
11 Jose Guillen .07 .20
12 Scott Hatteberg .07 .20
13 Edgardo Alfonzo .07 .20
14 Mike Bordick .07 .20
15 Manny Ramirez .10 .30
16 Greg Maddux .30 .75
17 David Segui .07 .20
18 Darryl Strawberry .07 .20
19 Brad Radke .07 .20
20 Kerry Wood .07 .20
21 Matt Anderson .07 .20
22 Derrek Lee .10 .30
23 Mickey Morandini .07 .20
24 Paul Konerko .07 .20
25 Travis Lee .07 .20
26 Ken Hill .07 .20
27 Kenny Rogers .07 .20
28 Paul Sorrento .07 .20
29 Quilvio Veras .07 .20
30 Todd Walker .07 .20
31 Ryan Jackson .07 .20
32 John Olerud .07 .20
33 Doug Glanville .07 .20
34 Nolan Ryan .75 2.00
35 Ray Lankford .07 .20
36 Mark Loretta .07 .20
37 Jason Dickson .07 .20
38 Sean Bergman .07 .20
39 Quinton McCracken .07 .20
40 Bartolo Colon .07 .20
41 Brady Anderson .07 .20
42 Chris Stynes .07 .20
43 Jorge Posada .10 .30
44 Justin Thompson .07 .20
45 Johnny Damon .10 .30
46 Armando Benitez .07 .20
47 Brant Brown .07 .20
48 Charlie Hayes .07 .20
49 Darren Dreifort .07 .20
50 Juan Gonzalez .07 .20
51 Chuck Knoblauch .07 .20
52 Todd Helton .10 .30
53 Rick Reed .07 .20
54 Chris Gomez .07 .20
55 Gary Sheffield .07 .20
56 Rod Beck .07 .20
57 Rey Sanchez .07 .20
58 Garret Anderson .07 .20
59 Jimmy Haynes .07 .20
60 Steve Woodard .07 .20
61 Rondell White .07 .20
62 Vladimir Guerrero .20 .50
63 Eric Karros .07 .20
64 Russ Davis .07 .20
65 Mo Vaughn .07 .20
66 Sammy Sosa .20 .50
67 Troy Percival .07 .20
68 Kenny Lofton .07 .20
69 Bill Taylor .07 .20
70 Mark McGwire .50 1.25
71 Roger Cedeno .07 .20
72 Javy Lopez .07 .20
73 Damion Easley .07 .20
74 Andy Pettitte .10 .30
75 Tony Gwynn .25 .60
76 Ricardo Rincon .07 .20
77 F.P. Santangelo .07 .20
78 Jay Bell .07 .20
79 Scott Servais .07 .20
80 Jose Canseco .10 .30
81 Roberto Hernandez .07 .20
82 Todd Dunwoody .07 .20
83 John Wetteland .07 .20
84 Mike Caruso .07 .20
85 Derek Jeter .50 1.25
86 Aaron Sele .07 .20
87 Jose Lima .07 .20
88 Ryan Christenson .07 .20
89 Jeff Cirillo .07 .20
90 Jose Hernandez .07 .20
91 Mark Kotsay .07 .20
92 Darren Bragg .07 .20
93 Albert Belle .07 .20
94 Matt Lawton .07 .20
95 Pedro Martinez .10 .30
96 Greg Vaughn .07 .20
97 Neifi Perez .07 .20
98 Gerald Williams .07 .20
99 Derek Bell .07 .20
100 Ken Griffey Jr. .40 1.00
101 David Cone .07 .20
102 Brian Johnson .07 .20
103 Dean Palmer .07 .20
104 Javier Valentin .07 .20
105 Trevor Hoffman .07 .20
106 Butch Huskey .07 .20
107 Dave Martinez .07 .20
108 Billy Wagner .07 .20
109 Shawn Green .07 .20
110 Ben Grieve .07 .20
111 Tom Goodwin .07 .20
112 Jaret Wright .07 .20
113 Aramis Ramirez .07 .20
114 Dmitri Young .07 .20
115 Hideki Irabu .07 .20
116 Roberto Kelly .07 .20
117 Jeff Fassero .07 .20
118 Mark Clark .07 .20
119 Jason McDonald .07 .20
120 Matt Williams .07 .20
121 Dave Burba .07 .20
122 Bret Saberhagen .07 .20
123 Deivi Cruz .07 .20
124 Chad Curtis .07 .20
125 Scott Rolen .10 .30
126 Lee Stevens .07 .20
127 J.T. Snow .07 .20
128 Rusty Greer .07 .20
129 Brian Meadows .07 .20
130 Jim Edmonds .07 .20
131 Ron Gant .07 .20
132 A.J. Hinch .07 .20
133 Shannon Stewart .07 .20
134 Brad Fullmer .07 .20
135 Cal Eldred .07 .20
136 Matt Walbeck .07 .20
137 Carl Everett .07 .20
138 Walt Weiss .07 .20
139 Fred McGriff .10 .30
140 Darin Erstad .07 .20
141 Dave Nilsson .07 .20
142 Eric Young .07 .20
143 Dan Wilson .07 .20
144 Jeff Reed .07 .20
145 Brett Tomko .07 .20
146 Terry Steinbach .07 .20
147 Seth Greisinger .07 .20
148 Pat Meares .07 .20
149 Livan Hernandez .07 .20
150 Jeff Bagwell .10 .30
151 Bob Wickman .07 .20
152 Omar Vizquel .10 .30
153 Eric Davis .07 .20
154 Larry Sutton .07 .20
155 Magglio Ordonez .07 .20
156 Eric Milton .07 .20
157 Darren Lewis .07 .20
158 Rick Aguilera .07 .20
159 Mike Lieberthal .07 .20
160 Robb Nen .07 .20
161 Brian Giles .07 .20
162 Jeff Brantley .07 .20
163 Gary DiSarcina .07 .20
164 John Valentin .07 .20
165 David Dellucci .07 .20
166 Chan Ho Park .07 .20
167 Masato Yoshii .07 .20
168 Jason Schmidt .07 .20
169 LaTroy Hawkins .07 .20
170 Bret Boone .07 .20
171 Jerry DiPoto .07 .20
172 Mariano Rivera .20 .50
173 Mike Cameron .07 .20
174 Scott Erickson .07 .20
175 Charles Johnson .07 .20
176 Bobby Jones .07 .20
177 Francisco Cordova .07 .20
178 Todd Jones .07 .20
179 Jeff Montgomery .07 .20
180 Mike Mussina .10 .30
181 Bob Abreu .07 .20
182 Ismael Valdes .07 .20
183 Andy Fox .07 .20
184 Woody Williams .07 .20
185 Denny Neagle .07 .20
186 Jose Valentin .07 .20
187 Darrin Fletcher .07 .20
188 Gabe Alvarez .07 .20
189 Eddie Taubensee .07 .20
190 Edgar Martinez .10 .30
191 Jason Kendall .07 .20
192 Darryl Kile .07 .20
193 Jeff King .07 .20
194 Rey Ordonez .07 .20
195 Andruw Jones .10 .30
196 Tony Fernandez .07 .20
197 Jamey Wright .07 .20
198 B.J. Surhoff .07 .20
199 Vinny Castilla .07 .20
200 David Wells HL .07 .20
201 Mark McGwire HL .25 .60
202 Sammy Sosa HL .10 .30
203 Roger Clemens HL .20 .50
204 Kerry Wood HL .07 .20
205 L.Berkman .15 .40
G.Kapler
206 Alex Escobar RC .15 .40
207 Peter Bergeron RC .08 .25
208 M.Barrett .08 .25
B.Davis
R.Fick
209 P.Cline .08 .25
R.Hernandez
J.Werth
210 R.Anderson .08 .25
Chen
Enochs
211 B.Penny .08 .25
Dotel
Lincoln
212 Chuck Abbott RC .08 .25
213 C.Jones .08 .25
J.Urban RC
214 T.Torcato .08 .25
A.McDowell RC
215 J.Tyner .08 .25
J.McKinley RC
216 M.Burch .08 .25
S.Etherton RC
217 R.Elder .08 .25
M.Tucker RC
218 J.M.Gold .08 .25
R.Mills RC
219 A.Brown .08 .25
C.Freeman RC
220A Mark McGwire HR 1 8.00 20.00
220B Mark McGwire HR 2 3.00 8.00
220C Mark McGwire HR 3 3.00 8.00
220D Mark McGwire HR 4 3.00 8.00
220E Mark McGwire HR 5 3.00 8.00
220F Mark McGwire HR 6 3.00 8.00
220G Mark McGwire HR 7 3.00 8.00
220H Mark McGwire HR 8 3.00 8.00
220I Mark McGwire HR 9 3.00 8.00
220J Mark McGwire HR 10 3.00 8.00
220K Mark McGwire HR 11 3.00 8.00
220L Mark McGwire HR 12 3.00 8.00
220M Mark McGwire HR 13 3.00 8.00
220N Mark McGwire HR 14 3.00 8.00
220O Mark McGwire HR 15 3.00 8.00
220P Mark McGwire HR 16 3.00 8.00
220Q Mark McGwire HR 17 3.00 8.00
220R Mark McGwire HR 18 3.00 8.00
220S Mark McGwire HR 19 3.00 8.00
220T Mark McGwire HR 20 3.00 8.00
220U Mark McGwire HR 21 3.00 8.00
220V Mark McGwire HR 22 3.00 8.00
220W Mark McGwire HR 23 3.00 8.00
220X Mark McGwire HR 24 3.00 8.00
220Y Mark McGwire HR 25 3.00 8.00
220Z Mark McGwire HR 26 3.00 8.00
220AA Mark McGwire HR 27 3.00 8.00
220AB Mark McGwire HR 28 3.00 8.00
220AC Mark McGwire HR 29 3.00 8.00
220AD Mark McGwire HR 30 3.00 8.00
220AE Mark McGwire HR 31 3.00 8.00
220AF Mark McGwire HR 32 3.00 8.00
220AG Mark McGwire HR 33 3.00 8.00
220AH Mark McGwire HR 34 3.00 8.00
220AI Mark McGwire HR 35 3.00 8.00
220AJ Mark McGwire HR 36 3.00 8.00
220AK Mark McGwire HR 37 3.00 8.00
220AL Mark McGwire HR 38 3.00 8.00
220AM Mark McGwire HR 39 3.00 8.00
220AN Mark McGwire HR 40 3.00 8.00
220AO Mark McGwire HR 41 3.00 8.00
220AP Mark McGwire HR 42 3.00 8.00
220AQ Mark McGwire HR 43 3.00 8.00
220AR Mark McGwire HR 44 3.00 8.00
220AS Mark McGwire HR 45 3.00 8.00
220AT Mark McGwire HR 46 3.00 8.00
220AU Mark McGwire HR 47 3.00 8.00
220AV Mark McGwire HR 48 3.00 8.00
220AW Mark McGwire HR 49 3.00 8.00
220AX Mark McGwire HR 50 3.00 8.00
220AY Mark McGwire HR 51 3.00 8.00
220AZ Mark McGwire HR 52 3.00 8.00
220BB Mark McGwire HR 53 3.00 8.00
220CC Mark McGwire HR 54 3.00 8.00
220DD Mark McGwire HR 55 3.00 8.00
220EE Mark McGwire HR 56 3.00 8.00
220FF Mark McGwire HR 57 3.00 8.00
220GG Mark McGwire HR 58 3.00 8.00
220HH Mark McGwire HR 59 3.00 8.00
220II Mark McGwire HR 60 3.00 8.00
220JJ Mark McGwire HR 61 6.00 15.00
220KK Mark McGwire HR 62 8.00 20.00
220LL Mark McGwire HR 63 3.00 8.00
220MM Mark McGwire HR 64 3.00 8.00
220NN Mark McGwire HR 65 3.00 8.00
220OO Mark McGwire HR 66 3.00 8.00
220PP Mark McGwire HR 67 3.00 8.00
220QQ Mark McGwire HR 68 3.00 8.00
220RR Mark McGwire HR 69 3.00 8.00
220SS Mark McGwire HR 70 10.00 25.00
221 Larry Walker LL .07 .20
222 Bernie Williams LL .07 .20
223 Mark McGwire LL .25 .60
224 Ken Griffey Jr. LL .25 .60
225 Sammy Sosa LL .10 .30
226 Juan Gonzalez LL .07 .20
227 Dante Bichette LL .07 .20
228 Alex Rodriguez LL .20 .50
229 Sammy Sosa LL .10 .30
230 Derek Jeter LL .25 .60
231 Greg Maddux LL .20 .50
232 Roger Clemens LL .20 .50
233 Ricky Ledee WS .07 .20
234 Chuck Knoblauch WS .07 .20
235 Bernie Williams WS .07 .20
236 Tino Martinez WS .07 .20
237 Orlando Hernandez WS .07 .20
238 Scott Brosius WS .07 .20
239 Andy Pettitte WS .07 .20
240 Mariano Rivera WS .10 .30
241 Checklist 1 .07 .20
242 Checklist 2 .07 .20
243 Tom Glavine .10 .30
244 Andy Benes .07 .20
245 Sandy Alomar Jr. .07 .20
246 Wilton Guerrero .07 .20
247 Alex Gonzalez .07 .20
248 Roberto Alomar .10 .30
249 Ruben Rivera .07 .20
250 Eric Chavez .07 .20
251 Ellis Burks .07 .20
252 Richie Sexson .07 .20
253 Steve Finley .07 .20
254 Dwight Gooden .07 .20
255 Dustin Hermanson .07 .20
256 Kirk Rueter .07 .20
257 Steve Trachsel .07 .20
258 Gregg Jefferies .07 .20
259 Matt Stairs .07 .20
260 Shane Reynolds .07 .20
261 Gregg Olson .07 .20
262 Kevin Tapani .07 .20
263 Matt Morris .07 .20
264 Carl Pavano .07 .20
265 Nomar Garciaparra .30 .75
266 Kevin Young .07 .20
267 Rick Helling .07 .20
268 Matt Franco .07 .20
269 Brian McRae .07 .20
270 Cal Ripken .60 1.50
271 Jeff Abbott .07 .20
272 Tony Batista .07 .20
273 Bill Simas .07 .20
274 Brian Hunter .07 .20
275 John Franco .07 .20
276 Devon White .07 .20
277 Rickey Henderson .20 .50
278 Chuck Finley .07 .20
279 Mike Blowers .07 .20
280 Mark Grace .10 .30
281 Randy Winn .07 .20
282 Bobby Bonilla .07 .20
283 David Justice .07 .20
284 Shane Monahan .07 .20
285 Kevin Brown .10 .30
286 Todd Zeile .07 .20
287 Al Martin .07 .20
288 Troy O'Leary .07 .20
289 Darryl Hamilton .07 .20
290 Tino Martinez .10 .30
291 David Ortiz .20 .50
292 Tony Clark .07 .20
293 Ryan Minor .07 .20
294 Mark Leiter .07 .20
295 Wally Joyner .07 .20
296 Cliff Floyd .07 .20
297 Shawn Estes .07 .20
298 Pat Hentgen .07 .20
299 Scott Elarton .07 .20
300 Alex Rodriguez .30 .75
301 Ozzie Guillen .07 .20
302 Hideo Nomo .20 .50
303 Ryan McGuire .07 .20
304 Brad Ausmus .07 .20
305 Alex Gonzalez .07 .20
306 Brian Jordan .07 .20
307 John Jaha .07 .20
308 Mark Grudzielanek .07 .20
309 Juan Guzman .07 .20
310 Tony Womack .07 .20
311 Dennis Reyes .07 .20
312 Marty Cordova .07 .20
313 Ramiro Mendoza .07 .20
314 Robin Ventura .07 .20
315 Rafael Palmeiro .10 .30
316 Ramon Martinez .07 .20
317 Pedro Astacio .07 .20
318 Dave Hollins .07 .20
319 Tom Candiotti .07 .20
320 Al Leiter .07 .20
321 Rico Brogna .07 .20
322 Reggie Jefferson .07 .20
323 Bernard Gilkey .07 .20
324 Jason Giambi .07 .20
325 Craig Biggio .10 .30
326 Troy Glaus .10 .30
327 Delino DeShields .07 .20
328 Fernando Vina .07 .20
329 John Smoltz .10 .30
330 Jeff Kent .07 .20
331 Roy Halladay .20 .50
332 Andy Ashby .07 .20
333 Tim Wakefield .07 .20
334 Roger Clemens .40 1.00
335 Bernie Williams .10 .30
336 Desi Relaford .07 .20
337 John Burkett .07 .20
338 Mike Hampton .07 .20
339 Royce Clayton .07 .20
340 Mike Piazza .30 .75
341 Jeremi Gonzalez .07 .20

342 Mike Lansing .07 .20
343 Jamie Moyer .07 .20
344 Ron Coomer .07 .20
345 Barry Larkin .10 .30
346 Fernando Tatis .07 .20
347 Chili Davis .07 .20
348 Bobby Higginson .07 .20
349 Hal Morris .07 .20
350 Larry Walker .07 .20
351 Carlos Guillen .07 .20
352 Miguel Tejada .07 .20
353 Travis Fryman .07 .20
354 Jarrod Washburn .07 .20
355 Chipper Jones .20 .50
356 Todd Stottlemyre .07 .20
357 Henry Rodriguez .07 .20
358 Eli Marrero .07 .20
359 Alan Benes .07 .20
360 Tim Salmon .10 .30
361 Luis Gonzalez .07 .20
362 Scott Spiezio .07 .20
363 Chris Carpenter .07 .20
364 Bobby Howry .07 .20
365 Raul Mondesi .07 .20
366 Ugueth Urbina .07 .20
367 Tom Evans .07 .20
368 Kerry Ligtenberg RC .08 .25
369 Adrian Beltre .07 .20
370 Ryan Klesko .07 .20
371 Wilson Alvarez .07 .20
372 John Thomson .07 .20
373 Tony Saunders .07 .20
374 Dave Mlicki .07 .20
375 Ken Caminiti .07 .20
376 Jay Buhner .07 .20
377 Bill Mueller .07 .20
378 Jeff Blauser .07 .20
379 Edgar Renteria .07 .20
380 Jim Thome .10 .30
381 Joey Hamilton .07 .20
382 Calvin Pickering .07 .20
383 Marquis Grissom .07 .20
384 Omar Daal .07 .20
385 Curt Schilling .07 .20
386 Jose Cruz Jr. .07 .20
387 Chris Widger .07 .20
388 Pete Harnisch .07 .20
389 Charles Nagy .07 .20
390 Tom Gordon .07 .20
391 Bobby Smith .07 .20
392 Derrick Gibson .07 .20
393 Jeff Conine .07 .20
394 Carlos Perez .07 .20
395 Barry Bonds .60 1.50
396 Mark McLemore .07 .20
397 Juan Encarnacion .07 .20
398 Wade Boggs .10 .30
399 Ivan Rodriguez .10 .30
400 Moises Alou .07 .20
401 Jeromy Burnitz .07 .20
402 Sean Casey .07 .20
403 Jose Offerman .07 .20
404 Joe Fontenot .07 .20
405 Kevin Millwood .07 .20
406 Lance Johnson .07 .20
407 Richard Hidalgo .07 .20
408 Mike Jackson .07 .20
409 Brian Anderson .07 .20
410 Jeff Shaw .07 .20
411 Preston Wilson .07 .20
412 Todd Hundley .07 .20
413 Jim Parque .07 .20
414 Justin Baughman .07 .20
415 Dante Bichette .07 .20
416 Paul O'Neill .10 .30
417 Miguel Cairo .07 .20
418 Randy Johnson .20 .50
419 Jesus Sanchez .07 .20
420 Carlos Delgado .07 .20
421 Ricky Ledee .07 .20
422 Orlando Hernandez .07 .20
423 Frank Thomas .20 .50
424 Pokey Reese .07 .20
425 C.Lee .15 .40
M.Lowell
426 M.Cuddyer .08 .25
DeRosa
Hairston
427 M.Anderson .15 .40
Belliard
Cabrera
428 M.Bowie .08 .25
P.Norton RC
Wolf
429 J.Cressend RC .15 .40
Rocker
430 R.Mateo .08 .25
M.Zywica RC
431 J.LaRue .08 .25
LeCroy
Meluskey
432 Gabe Kapler .15 .40
433 A.Kennedy .08 .25
M.Lopez RC
434 Jose Fernandez RC .08 .25
C.Truby
435 Doug Mientkiewicz RC .20 .50
436 R.Brown RC .08 .25
V.Wells
437 A.J. Burnett RC .30 .75
438 M.Belisle .08 .25
M.Roney RC
439 A.Kearns .60 1.50
C.George RC
440 N.Cornejo .08 .25
N.Bump RC
441 B.Lidge .60 1.50
M.Nannini RC
442 M.Holliday 1.50 4.00
J.Winchester RC
443 A.Everett .20 .50
C.Ambres RC
444 P.Burrell .60 1.50
E.Valent RC
445 Roger Clemens SK .20 .50
446 Kerry Wood SK .07 .20
447 Curt Schilling SK .07 .20
448 Randy Johnson SK .10 .30
449 Pedro Martinez SK .10 .30
450 Bagwell .20 .50
Galar
McGwire AT
451 Olerud .07 .20
Thome
Martinez AT
452 ARod .25 .60
Nomar
Jeter AT
453 Castilla .10 .30
Jones
Rolen AT
454 Sosa .25 .60
Griffey
Gonzalez AT
455 Bonds .30 .75
Ramirez
Walker AT
456 Thomas .20 .50
Salmon
Justice AT
457 Lee .07 .20
Helton
Grieve AT
458 Guerrero .07 .20
Vaughn
B.Will AT
459 Piazza .20 .50
IRod
Kendall AT
460 Clemens .20 .50
Wood
Maddux AT
461A Sammy Sosa HR 1 3.00 8.00
461B Sammy Sosa HR 2 1.25 3.00
461C Sammy Sosa HR 3 1.25 3.00
461D Sammy Sosa HR 4 1.25 3.00
461E Sammy Sosa HR 5 1.25 3.00
461F Sammy Sosa HR 6 1.25 3.00
461G Sammy Sosa HR 7 1.25 3.00
461H Sammy Sosa HR 8 1.25 3.00
461I Sammy Sosa HR 9 1.25 3.00
461J Sammy Sosa HR 10 1.25 3.00
461K Sammy Sosa HR 11 1.25 3.00
461L Sammy Sosa HR 12 1.25 3.00
461M Sammy Sosa HR 13 1.25 3.00
461N Sammy Sosa HR 14 1.25 3.00
461O Sammy Sosa HR 15 1.25 3.00
461P Sammy Sosa HR 16 1.25 3.00
461Q Sammy Sosa HR 17 1.25 3.00
461R Sammy Sosa HR 18 1.25 3.00
461S Sammy Sosa HR 19 1.25 3.00
461T Sammy Sosa HR 20 1.25 3.00
461U Sammy Sosa HR 21 1.25 3.00
461V Sammy Sosa HR 22 1.25 3.00
461W Sammy Sosa HR 23 1.25 3.00
461X Sammy Sosa HR 24 1.25 3.00
461Y Sammy Sosa HR 25 1.25 3.00
461Z Sammy Sosa HR 26 1.25 3.00
461AA Sammy Sosa HR 27 1.25 3.00
461AB Sammy Sosa HR 28 1.25 3.00
461AC Sammy Sosa HR 29 1.25 3.00
461AD Sammy Sosa HR 30 1.25 3.00
461AE Sammy Sosa HR 31 1.25 3.00
461AF Sammy Sosa HR 32 1.25 3.00
461AG Sammy Sosa HR 33 1.25 3.00
461AH Sammy Sosa HR 34 1.25 3.00
461AI Sammy Sosa HR 35 1.25 3.00
461AJ Sammy Sosa HR 36 1.25 3.00
461AK Sammy Sosa HR 37 1.25 3.00
461AL Sammy Sosa HR 38 1.25 3.00
461AM Sammy Sosa HR 39 1.25 3.00
461AN Sammy Sosa HR 40 1.25 3.00
461AO Sammy Sosa HR 41 1.25 3.00
461AP Sammy Sosa HR 42 1.25 3.00
461AR Sammy Sosa HR 43 1.25 3.00
461AS Sammy Sosa HR 44 1.25 3.00
461AT Sammy Sosa HR 45 1.25 3.00
461AU Sammy Sosa HR 46 1.25 3.00
461AV Sammy Sosa HR 47 1.25 3.00
461AW Sammy Sosa HR 48 1.25 3.00
461AX Sammy Sosa HR 49 1.25 3.00
461AY Sammy Sosa HR 50 1.25 3.00
461AZ Sammy Sosa HR 51 1.25 3.00
461BB Sammy Sosa HR 52 1.25 3.00
461CC Sammy Sosa HR 53 1.25 3.00
461DD Sammy Sosa HR 54 1.25 3.00
461EE Sammy Sosa HR 55 1.25 3.00
461FF Sammy Sosa HR 56 1.25 3.00
461GG Sammy Sosa HR 57 1.25 3.00
461HH Sammy Sosa HR 58 1.25 3.00
461II Sammy Sosa HR 59 1.25 3.00
461JJ Sammy Sosa HR 60 1.25 3.00
461KK Sammy Sosa HR 61 3.00 8.00
461LL Sammy Sosa HR 62 4.00 10.00
461MM Sammy Sosa HR 63 1.50 4.00
461NN Sammy Sosa HR 64 1.50 4.00
461OO Sammy Sosa HR 65 1.50 4.00
461PP Sammy Sosa HR 66 10.00 25.00
462 Checklist .07 .20
463 Checklist .07 .20

1999 Topps MVP Promotion

*STARS: 30X TO 80X BASIC CARDS
*ROOKIES: 12X TO 30X BASIC CARDS
SER.1 ODDS 1:515 HOB, 1:142 HTA
SER.2 ODDS 1:504 HOB, 1:139 HTA, 1:504 RET
STATED PRINT RUN 100 SETS
MVP PARALLELS ARE UNNUMBERED
EXCHANGE DEADLINE: 12/31/99
PRIZE CARDS MAILED OUT ON 2/15/00
35 Ray Lankford W 6.00 15.00
52 Todd Helton W 10.00 25.00
70 Mark McGwire W 40.00 100.00
96 Greg Vaughn W 6.00 15.00
101 David Cone W 6.00 15.00
125 Scott Rolen W 10.00 25.00
127 J.T. Snow W 6.00 15.00
139 Fred McGriff W 10.00 25.00
159 Mike Lieberthal W 6.00 15.00
198 B.J. Surhoff W 6.00 15.00
248 Roberto Alomar W 10.00 25.00
265 Nomar Garciaparra W 25.00 60.00
290 Tino Martinez W 10.00 25.00
292 Tony Clark W 6.00 15.00
300 Alex Rodriguez W 25.00 60.00
315 Rafael Palmeiro W 10.00 25.00
340 Mike Piazza W 25.00 60.00
346 Fernando Tatis W 6.00 15.00
350 Larry Walker W 6.00 15.00
352 Miguel Tejada W 6.00 15.00
355 Chipper Jones W 15.00 40.00
360 Tim Salmon W 10.00 25.00
365 Raul Mondesi W 6.00 15.00
416 Paul O'Neill W 10.00 25.00
418 Randy Johnson W 15.00 40.00

1999 Topps MVP Promotion Exchange

This 25-card set was available only to those lucky collectors who obtained one of the twenty-five winning player cards from the 1999 Topps MVP Promotion parallel set. Each week, throughout the 1999 season, Topps named a new Player of the Week, and that player's Topps MVP Promotion parallel card was made redeemable for this 25-card set. The deadline to exchange the winning cards was December 31st, 1999. The exchange cards shipped out in mid-February, 2000.

COMP.FACT.SET (25) 20.00 50.00
ONE SET VIA MAIL PER '99 MVP WINNER
MVP1 Raul Mondesi .60 1.50
MVP2 Tim Salmon 1.00 2.50
MVP3 Fernando Tatis .60 1.50
MVP4 Larry Walker .60 1.50
MVP5 Fred McGriff 1.00 2.50
MVP6 Nomar Garciaparra 2.50 6.00
MVP7 Rafael Palmeiro 1.00 2.50
MVP8 Randy Johnson 1.50 4.00
MVP9 Mike Lieberthal .60 1.50
MVP10 B.J. Surhoff .60 1.50
MVP11 Todd Helton 1.00 2.50
MVP12 Tino Martinez 1.00 2.50
MVP13 Scott Rolen 1.00 2.50
MVP14 Mike Piazza 2.50 6.00
MVP15 David Cone .60 1.50
MVP16 Tony Clark .60 1.50
MVP17 Roberto Alomar 1.00 2.50
MVP18 Miguel Tejada .60 1.50
MVP19 Alex Rodriguez 2.50 6.00
MVP20 J.T. Snow .60 1.50
MVP21 Ray Lankford .60 1.50
MVP22 Greg Vaughn .60 1.50
MVP23 Paul O'Neill 1.00 2.50
MVP24 Chipper Jones 1.50 4.00
MVP25 Mark McGwire 4.00 10.00

1999 Topps Oversize

COMPLETE SERIES 1 (8) 6.00 15.00
COMPLETE SERIES 2 (8) 6.00 15.00
ONE PER HTA OR HOBBY BOX

1999 Topps All-Matrix

This 30-card insert set consists of three thematic subsets (Club 40 are numbers 1-13, '99 Rookie Rush are number's 14-23 and Club K are numbers 24-30). All 30-cards feature silver foil dot-matrix technology. Cards were seeded exclusively into series 2 packs as follows: 1:18 hobby, 1:18 retail and 1:5 Home Team Advantage.

COMPLETE SET (30) 12.00 30.00
SER.2 ODDS 1:18 HOB/RET, 1:5 HTA
AM1 Mark McGwire 2.00 5.00
AM2 Sammy Sosa 1.25 3.00
AM3 Ken Griffey Jr. 2.50 6.00
AM4 Greg Vaughn .50 1.25
AM5 Albert Belle .50 1.25
AM6 Vinny Castilla .50 1.25
AM7 Jose Canseco .75 2.00
AM8 Juan Gonzalez .50 1.25
AM9 Manny Ramirez 1.25 3.00
AM10 Andres Galarraga .75 2.00
AM11 Rafael Palmeiro .75 2.00
AM12 Alex Rodriguez 1.50 4.00
AM13 Mo Vaughn .50 1.25
AM14 Eric Chavez .50 1.25
AM15 Gabe Kapler .50 1.25
AM16 Calvin Pickering .50 1.25
AM17 Ruben Mateo .50 1.25
AM18 Roy Halladay .75 2.00
AM19 Jeremy Giambi .50 1.25
AM20 Alex Gonzalez .50 1.25
AM21 Ron Belliard .50 1.25
AM22 Marlon Anderson .50 1.25
AM23 Carlos Lee .50 1.25
AM24 Kerry Wood .50 1.25
AM25 Roger Clemens 1.50 4.00
AM26 Curt Schilling .50 1.25
AM27 Kevin Brown .50 1.25
AM28 Randy Johnson 1.25 3.00
AM29 Pedro Martinez .75 2.00
AM30 Orlando Hernandez .50 1.25

1999 Topps All-Topps Mystery Finest

Randomly inserted in Topps Series two packs at the rate of one in 36, this 33-card set features 11 three-player positional parallels of the All-Topps subset printed using Finest technology. All three players are printed on the back, but the collector has to peel off the opaque protector to reveal who is on the front.

COMPLETE SET (33) 20.00 50.00
SER.2 ODDS 1:36 HOB/RET, 1:8 HTA
*REFRACTORS: 1X TO 2.5X BASIC ATMF
SER.2 REF.ODDS 1:144 HOB/RET, 1:32 HTA
M1 Jeff Bagwell .60 1.50
M2 Andres Galarraga .60 1.50
M3 Mark McGwire 1.50 4.00
M4 John Olerud .40 1.00
M5 Jim Thome .60 1.50
M6 Tino Martinez .40 1.00
M7 Alex Rodriguez 1.25 3.00
M8 Nomar Garciaparra .60 1.50
M9 Derek Jeter 2.50 6.00
M10 Vinny Castilla .40 1.00
M11 Chipper Jones 1.00 2.50
M12 Scott Rolen .60 1.50
M13 Sammy Sosa 1.00 2.50
M14 Ken Griffey Jr. 2.00 5.00
M15 Juan Gonzalez .40 1.00
M16 Barry Bonds 1.50 4.00
M17 Manny Ramirez 1.00 2.50
M18 Larry Walker .60 1.50
M19 Frank Thomas 1.00 2.50
M20 Tim Salmon .40 1.00
M21 Dave Justice .40 1.00
M22 Travis Lee .40 1.00
M23 Todd Helton .60 1.50
M24 Ben Grieve .40 1.00
M25 Vladimir Guerrero .60 1.50
M26 Greg Vaughn .40 1.00
M27 Bernie Williams .60 1.50
M28 Mike Piazza 1.00 2.50
M29 Ivan Rodriguez .60 1.50
M30 Jason Kendall .40 1.00
M31 Roger Clemens 1.25 3.00
M32 Kerry Wood .40 1.00
M33 Greg Maddux 1.25 3.00

1999 Topps Autographs

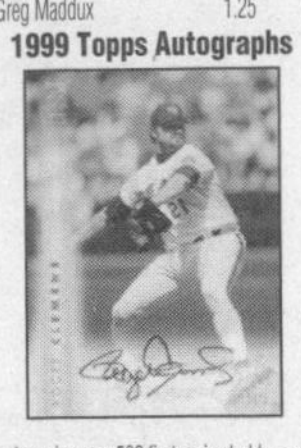

Inserted one in every 532 first series hobby packs, one in every 146 first series Home Team Advantage packs,d one in every 501 second series hobby packs and one in every 138 second series HTA packs, these cards feature an assortment of young and old players affixing their signature to these cards. Cards A1-A8 were distributed exclusively in first series packs and cards A9-A16 were distributed exclusively in second series packs. The fronts feature a player photo with the authentic autograph on the bottom.

SER.1 ODDS 1:532 HOB, 1:146 HTA
SER.2 ODDS 1:501 HOB, 1:138 HTA
A1 Roger Clemens 25.00 60.00
A2 Chipper Jones 25.00 60.00
A3 Scott Rolen 8.00 20.00
A4 Alex Rodriguez 20.00 50.00
A5 Andres Galarraga 8.00 20.00
A6 Rondell White 6.00 15.00
A7 Ben Grieve 4.00 10.00
A8 Troy Glaus 6.00 15.00
A9 Moises Alou 6.00 15.00
A10 Barry Bonds 75.00 200.00
A11 Vladimir Guerrero 12.00 30.00
A12 Andruw Jones 8.00 20.00
A13 Darin Erstad 6.00 15.00
A14 Shawn Green 8.00 20.00
A15 Eric Chavez 4.00 10.00
A16 Pat Burrell 4.00 10.00

1999 Topps Hall of Fame Collection

This 10 card set features Hall of Famers with photos of the plaques and a silhouetted photo. These cards were inserted one every 12 hobby packs and one every three HTA packs.

COMPLETE SET (10) 8.00 20.00
SER.1 ODDS 1:12 HOB/RET, 1:3 HTA
HOF1 Mike Schmidt 1.50 4.00
HOF2 Brooks Robinson .75 2.00
HOF3 Stan Musial 1.25 3.00
HOF4 Willie McCovey .75 2.00
HOF5 Eddie Mathews .75 2.00
HOF6 Reggie Jackson .75 2.00
HOF7 Ernie Banks .75 2.00
HOF8 Whitey Ford .75 2.00
HOF9 Bob Feller .75 2.00
HOF10 Yogi Berra .75 2.00

1999 Topps Lords of the Diamond

This die-cut insert set was inserted one every 18 hobby packs and one every five HTA packs. The words "Lords of the Diamond" are printed on the top while the players name is at the bottom. The middle of the card has the players photo.

COMPLETE SET (15) 10.00 25.00
SER.1 ODDS 1:18 HOB/RET, 1:5 HTA
LD1 Ken Griffey Jr. 2.00 5.00
LD2 Chipper Jones 1.00 2.50
LD3 Sammy Sosa 1.00 2.50
LD4 Frank Thomas 1.00 2.50
LD5 Mark McGwire 1.50 4.00
LD6 Jeff Bagwell .60 1.50
LD7 Alex Rodriguez 1.25 3.00
LD8 Juan Gonzalez .40 1.00
LD9 Barry Bonds 1.50 4.00
LD10 Nomar Garciaparra .60 1.50
LD11 Darin Erstad .40 1.00
LD12 Tony Gwynn 1.00 2.50
LD13 Andres Galarraga .60 1.50
LD14 Mike Piazza 1.00 2.50
LD15 Greg Maddux 1.25 3.00

1999 Topps New Breed

Fifteen of the young stars of the game are featured in this insert set. The cards were seeded into the 99 Topps packs at a rate of one every 18 hobby packs and one every five HTA packs.

COMPLETE SET (15) 10.00 25.00
SER.1 ODDS 1:18 HOB/RET, 1:5 HTA
NB1 Darin Erstad .30 .75
NB2 Brad Fullmer .30 .75
NB3 Kerry Wood .30 .75
NB4 Nomar Garciaparra 1.25 3.00
NB5 Travis Lee .30 .75
NB6 Scott Rolen .50 1.25
NB7 Todd Helton .50 1.25
NB8 Vladimir Guerrero .75 2.00
NB9 Derek Jeter 2.00 5.00
NB10 Alex Rodriguez 1.25 3.00
NB11 Ben Grieve .30 .75
NB12 Andruw Jones .50 1.25
NB13 Paul Konerko .30 .75
NB14 Aramis Ramirez .30 .75
NB15 Adrian Beltre .30 .75

1999 Topps Picture Perfect

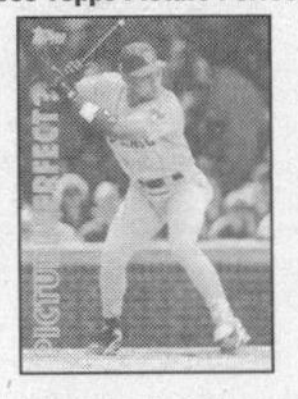

This 10 card insert set was inserted one every eight hobby packs and one every two HTA packs. These cards all contain a minor, very difficult to determine mistake and part of the charm is to figure out what the error is in the card.

COMPLETE SET (10) 6.00 15.00
SER.1 ODDS 1:8 HOB/RET, 1:2 HTA
P1 Ken Griffey Jr. .75 2.00
P2 Kerry Wood .15 .40
P3 Pedro Martinez .25 .60
P4 Mark McGwire 1.00 2.50
P5 Greg Maddux .60 1.50
P6 Sammy Sosa .40 1.00
P7 Greg Vaughn .15 .40
P8 Juan Gonzalez .15 .40
P9 Jeff Bagwell .25 .60
P10 Derek Jeter 1.00 2.50

1999 Topps Power Brokers

This 20 card set features leading baseball players. They were inserted at a seeded rate of one every 36 hobby/retail packs and one every eight HTA packs.

COMPLETE SET (20) 60.00 120.00
SER.1 ODDS 1:36 HOB/RET, 1:8 HTA
*REFRACTORS: 1X TO 2.5X BASIC BROKERS
SER.1 REF.ODDS 1:144 HOB/RET, 1:32 HTA
PB1 Mark McGwire 5.00 12.00
PB2 Andres Galarraga .75 2.00
PB3 Ken Griffey Jr. 4.00 10.00
PB4 Sammy Sosa 2.00 5.00
PB5 Juan Gonzalez .75 2.00
PB6 Alex Rodriguez 3.00 8.00
PB7 Frank Thomas 2.00 5.00
PB8 Jeff Bagwell 1.25 3.00
PB9 Vinny Castilla .75 2.00
PB10 Mike Piazza 3.00 8.00
PB11 Greg Vaughn .75 2.00
PB12 Barry Bonds 6.00 15.00
PB13 Mo Vaughn .75 2.00
PB14 Jim Thome 1.25 3.00
PB15 Larry Walker .75 2.00
PB16 Chipper Jones 2.00 5.00
PB17 Nomar Garciaparra 3.00 8.00
PB18 Manny Ramirez 1.25 3.00
PB19 Roger Clemens 4.00 10.00
PB20 Kerry Wood .75 2.00

1999 Topps Record Numbers

Randomly inserted in Series two hobby and retail packs at the rate of one in eight and HTA packs at a rate of one in two, this 10-card set features action color photos of record-setting players with silver foil highlights.

COMPLETE SET (10) 6.00 15.00
SER.2 ODDS 1:8 HOB/RET, 1:2 HTA
RN1 Mark McGwire 1.00 2.50
RN2 Mike Piazza .60 1.50
RN3 Curt Schilling .15 .40
RN4 Ken Griffey Jr. .75 2.00
RN5 Sammy Sosa .40 1.00
RN6 Nomar Garciaparra .60 1.50
RN7 Kerry Wood .15 .40
RN8 Roger Clemens .75 2.00
RN9 Cal Ripken 1.25 3.00
RN10 Mark McGwire 1.00 2.50

1999 Topps Record Numbers Gold

Randomly seeded in series two packs, these scarce gold-foiled cards parallel the more common "silver-foiled" Record Numbers inserts. The print run for each card was based upon the statistic specified on the card. Erroneous stated odds for these Gold cards were unfortunately printed on all series two wrappers According to sources at Topps the correct pack odds are as follows: RN1 1:151,320 hob, 1:38,016 HTA, 1:138,567 ret, RN2 1:28,317 hob, 1:7,797 HTA, 1:28,340 ret, RN3 1:32,134 hob, 1:8,848 HTA, 1:32,160 ret, RN4 1:29,288 hob, 1:8,064 HTA, 1:29,312 ret, RN5 1:907,920 hob, 1:133,056 HTA, 1:1,524,420 ret, RN6 1:605,280 hob, 1:88,704 HTA, 1:1,016,280 ret, RN7 1:907,920 hob, 1:133,056 HTA, 1:1,524,420 ret, RN8 1:907,920 hob, 1:133,056 HTA, 1:1,524,420 ret, RN9 1:3891 hob, 1:1069 HTA, 1:3888 ret, RN10 1:63,312 hob, 1:17,741 HTA, 1:63,510 ret. No pricing is available for cards with print runs of 30 or less.

RANDOM INSERTS IN ALL SER.2 PACKS
PRINT RUNS B/WN 20-2632 COPIES PER
NO PRICING ON QTY OF 30 OR LESS
RN1 Mark McGwire/70 50.00 100.00
RN2 Mike Piazza/362 6.00 15.00
RN3 Curt Schilling/319 3.00 8.00
RN4 Ken Griffey Jr./350 10.00 25.00
RN5 Sammy Sosa/20
RN6 Nomar Garciaparra/30
RN7 Kerry Wood/20
RN8 Roger Clemens/20
RN9 Cal Ripken/2632 6.00 15.00
RN10 Mark McGwire/162 15.00 40.00

1999 Topps Ryan

These cards reflect the Nolan Ryan Reprints of earlier Topps cards featuring the pitcher known for "Texas Heat". These cards are replicas of Ryan's cards and have a commemorative sticker placed on them as well. The cards were seeded one every 18 hobby/retail packs and one every five HTA packs. Odd-numbered cards (i.e. 1, 3, 5 etc.) were distributed in first series packs and even numbered cards were distributed in second series packs.

COMPLETE SET (27) 30.00 80.00
COMPLETE SERIES 1 (14) 15.00 40.00
COMPLETE SERIES 2 (13) 15.00 40.00
COMMON CARD (1-27) 2.00 5.00
STATED ODDS 1:18 HOB/RET, 1:5 HTA
ODD NUMBERS DISTRIBUTED IN SER.1
EVEN NUMBERS DISTRIBUTED IN SER.2
1 Nolan Ryan 1968 4.00 10.00

1999 Topps Ryan Autographs

Nolan Ryan signed a selection of all 27 cards for this reprint set. The autographed cards were issued one every 4,250 series one hobby packs, one in every 5,007 series two hobby packs and one every 1,176 series one HTA packs.

COMMON CARD (1-13) 125.00 200.00
COMMON CARD (14-27) 100.00 200.00
SER.1 ODDS 1:4260 HOB, 1:1172 HTA
SER.2 ODDS 1:5007 HOB
1 Nolan Ryan 1968 300.00 500.00

1999 Topps Traded

This set contains 121 cards and was distributed as factory boxed sets only. The fronts feature color action player photo. The backs carry player information. Rookie Cards include Sean Burroughs, Josh Hamilton, Corey Patterson and Alfonso Soriano.

COMP.FACT.SET (122) 15.00 40.00
COMPLETE SET (121) 12.50 30.00
DISTRIBUTED ONLY IN FACTORY SET FORM
FACT.SET PRICE IS FOR SEALED SET W/AUTO
T1 Seth Etherton .07 .20
T2 Mark Harriger RC .08 .25
T3 Matt Wise RC .08 .25
T4 Carlos Eduardo Hernandez RC .15 .40
T5 Julio Lugo RC .30 .75
T6 Mike Nannini .07 .20
T7 Justin Bowles RC .08 .25
T8 Mark Mulder RC .60 1.50
T9 Roberto Vaz RC .08 .25
T10 Felipe Lopez RC .60 1.50
T11 Matt Belisle .20 .50
T12 Micah Bowie .07 .20
T13 Ruben Quevedo RC .08 .25
T14 Jose Garcia RC .08 .25
T15 David Kelton RC .08 .25
T16 Phil Norton .07 .20
T17 Corey Patterson RC .40 1.00
T18 Ron Walker RC .08 .25
T19 Paul Hoover RC .08 .25
T20 Ryan Rupe RC .08 .25
T21 J.D. Closser RC .15 .40
T22 Rob Ryan RC .08 .25
T23 Steve Colyer RC .08 .25
T24 Bubba Crosby RC .25 .60
T25 Luke Prokopec RC .08 .25
T26 Matt Blank RC .08 .25
T27 Josh McKinley .07 .20
T28 Nate Bump .07 .20
T29 Giuseppe Chiaramonte RC .08 .25
T30 Arturo McDowell .07 .20
T31 Tony Torcato .07 .20
T32 Dave Roberts RC .25 .60
T33 C.C. Sabathia RC 4.00 10.00
T34 Sean Spencer RC .08 .25
T35 Chip Ambres .07 .20
T36 A.J. Burnett .40 1.00
T37 Mo Bruce RC .08 .25
T38 Jason Tyner .07 .20
T39 Mamon Tucker .07 .20
T40 Sean Burroughs RC .25 .60
T41 Kevin Eberwein RC .08 .25
T42 Junior Herndon RC .08 .25
T43 Bryan Wolff RC .08 .25
T44 Pat Burrell .50 1.25
T45 Eric Valent .07 .20
T46 Carlos Pena RC .20 .50
T47 Mike Zywica .07 .20
T48 Adam Everett .10 .30
T49 Juan Pena RC .15 .40
T50 Adam Dunn RC 1.50 4.00
T51 Austin Kearns .50 1.25
T52 Jacobo Sequea RC .08 .25
T53 Choo Freeman .07 .20
T54 Jeff Winchester .07 .20
T55 Matt Burch .07 .20
T56 Chris George .07 .20
T57 Scott Mullen RC .08 .25
T58 Kit Pellow .07 .20
T59 Mark Quinn RC .08 .25
T60 Nate Cornejo .08 .25
T61 Ryan Mills .07 .20
T62 Kevin Beirne RC .08 .25
T63 Kip Wells RC .15 .40
T64 Juan Rivera RC .40 1.00
T65 Alfonso Soriano RC 2.00 5.00
T66 Josh Hamilton RC 3.00 8.00
T67 Josh Girdley RC .08 .25
T68 Kyle Snyder RC .08 .25
T69 Mike Paradis RC .08 .25
T70 Jason Jennings RC .25 .60
T71 David Walling RC .08 .25
T72 Omar Ortiz RC .08 .25
T73 Jay Gehrke RC .15 .40
T74 Casey Burns RC .15 .40
T75 Carl Crawford RC 1.50 4.00
T76 Reggie Sanders .07 .20
T77 Will Clark .10 .30
T78 David Wells .07 .20
T79 Paul Konerko .07 .20
T80 Armando Benitez .07 .20
T81 Brant Brown .07 .20
T82 Mo Vaughn .07 .20
T83 Jose Canseco .10 .30
T84 Albert Belle .07 .20
T85 Dean Palmer .07 .20
T86 Greg Vaughn .07 .20
T87 Mark Clark .07 .20
T88 Pat Meares .07 .20
T89 Eric Davis .07 .20
T90 Brian Giles .07 .20
T91 Jeff Brantley .07 .20
T92 Bret Boone .07 .20
T93 Ron Gant .07 .20
T94 Mike Cameron .07 .20
T95 Charles Johnson .07 .20
T96 Denny Neagle .07 .20
T97 Brian Hunter .07 .20
T98 Jose Hernandez .07 .20
T99 Rick Aguilera .07 .20
T100 Tony Batista .07 .20
T101 Roger Cedeno .07 .20
T102 Creighton Gubanich RC .08 .25
T103 Tim Belcher .07 .20
T104 Bruce Aven .07 .20
T105 Brian Daubach RC .15 .40
T106 Ed Sprague .07 .20
T107 Michael Tucker .07 .20
T108 Homer Bush .07 .20
T109 Armando Reynoso .07 .20
T110 Brook Fordyce .07 .20
T111 Matt Mantei .07 .20
T112 Dave Mlicki .07 .20
T113 Kenny Rogers .07 .20
T114 Livan Hernandez .07 .20
T115 Butch Huskey .07 .20
T116 David Segui .07 .20
T117 Darryl Hamilton .07 .20
T118 Terry Mulholland .07 .20
T119 Randy Velarde .07 .20
T120 Bill Taylor .07 .20
T121 Kevin Appier .07 .20

1999 Topps Traded Autographs

Inserted one per factory box set, this 75-card set features autographed parallel version of the first 75 cards of the basic 1999 Topps Traded set. The card fronts have a light faded image on the base to accentuate the signature.

COMPLETE SET (75) 400.00 800.00
ONE AUTO PER FACTORY SET
T1 Seth Etherton 2.00 5.00
T2 Mark Harriger 3.00 8.00
T3 Matt Wise 3.00 8.00
T4 Carlos Eduardo Hernandez 3.00 8.00
T5 Julio Lugo 3.00 8.00
T6 Mike Nannini 2.00 5.00
T7 Justin Bowles 3.00 8.00
T8 Mark Mulder 4.00 10.00
T9 Roberto Vaz 2.00 5.00
T10 Felipe Lopez 3.00 8.00
T11 Matt Belisle 2.00 5.00
T12 Micah Bowie 2.00 5.00
T13 Ruben Quevedo 2.00 5.00
T14 Jose Garcia 3.00 8.00
T15 David Kelton 3.00 8.00
T16 Phil Norton 3.00 8.00
T17 Corey Patterson 3.00 8.00
T18 Ron Walker 2.00 5.00
T19 Paul Hoover 3.00 8.00
T20 Ryan Rupe 2.00 5.00
T21 J.D. Closser 3.00 8.00
T22 Rob Ryan 2.00 5.00
T23 Steve Colyer 2.00 5.00
T24 Bubba Crosby 3.00 8.00
T25 Luke Prokopec 2.00 5.00
T26 Matt Blank 3.00 8.00
T27 Josh McKinley 2.00 5.00
T28 Nate Bump 3.00 8.00
T29 Giuseppe Chiaramonte 2.00 5.00
T30 Arturo McDowell 2.00 5.00
T31 Tony Torcato 2.00 5.00
T32 Dave Roberts 4.00 10.00
T33 C.C. Sabathia 30.00 80.00
T34 Sean Spencer 2.00 5.00
T35 Chip Ambres 2.00 5.00
T36 A.J. Burnett 6.00 15.00
T37 Mo Bruce 2.00 5.00
T38 Jason Tyner 2.00 5.00
T39 Mamon Tucker 2.00 5.00
T40 Sean Burroughs 6.00 15.00
T41 Kevin Eberwein 2.00 5.00
T42 Junior Herndon 2.00 5.00
T43 Bryan Wolff 3.00 8.00
T44 Pat Burrell 6.00 15.00
T45 Eric Valent 3.00 8.00
T46 Carlos Pena 10.00 25.00
T47 Mike Zywica 3.00 8.00
T48 Adam Everett 6.00 15.00
T49 Juan Pena 3.00 8.00
T50 Adam Dunn 10.00 25.00
T51 Austin Kearns 4.00 10.00
T52 Jacobo Sequea 2.00 5.00
T53 Choo Freeman 3.00 8.00
T54 Jeff Winchester 2.00 5.00
T55 Matt Burch 3.00 8.00
T56 Chris George 2.00 5.00
T57 Scott Mullen 2.00 5.00
T58 Kit Pellow 2.00 5.00
T59 Mark Quinn 2.00 5.00
T60 Nate Cornejo 2.00 5.00
T61 Ryan Mills 2.00 5.00
T62 Kevin Beirne 3.00 8.00
T63 Kip Wells 3.00 8.00
T64 Juan Rivera 4.00 10.00
T65 Alfonso Soriano 15.00 40.00
T66 Josh Hamilton 20.00 50.00
T67 Josh Girdley 2.00 5.00
T68 Kyle Snyder 2.00 5.00
T69 Mike Paradis 2.00 5.00
T70 Jason Jennings 6.00 15.00
T71 David Walling 2.00 5.00
T72 Omar Ortiz 3.00 8.00
T73 Jay Gehrke 3.00 8.00
T74 Casey Burns 3.00 8.00
T75 Carl Crawford 4.00 10.00

2000 Topps

This 478 card set was issued in two separate series. The first series (containing cards 1-239) was released in December, 1999. The second series (containing cards 240-479) was released in April, 2000. The cards were issued in various formats including an eleven card hobby or retail pack with an SRP of $1.29 and a 40 card HomeTeam Advantage jumbo pack. Cards 1-200 and 240-440 are individual player cards with subsets as follows: Prospects (201-208/441-448), Draft Picks (209-220/449-455), Season Highlights (217-221/456-460), Post Season Highlights (222-228), 20th Century's Best (229-235/468-474), Magic Moments (236-240/475-479) and League Leaders (461-467). After the success Topps had with the multiple versions of Mark McGwire 220 and Sammy Sosa 461 in 1999, they made five versions each of the Magic Moments cards this year. Each Magic Moment variation featured different gold foil text on front commemorating a specific achievement in the featured player's career. Please note, that basic hand-collected sets are considered complete with the inclusion of any one of each of these Magic Moment cards. A reprint of the 1985 Mark McGwire Rookie Card was inserted one every 36 hobby and retail first series packs and one every eight HTA first series packs. Card number 7 was not issued as Topps continues to honor the memory of Mickey Mantle who wore that number during his career. Players with notable Rookie Cards in this set include Ben Sheets and Barry Zito.

COMPLETE SET (478) 20.00 50.00
COMP.HOBBY SET (478) 15.00 40.00
COMPLETE SERIES 1 (239) 10.00 25.00
COMPLETE SERIES 2 (240) 10.00 25.00
COMMON CARD (1-6/8-479) .07 .20
COMMON RC .15 .40
MCGWIRE MM SET (5) 3.00 8.00
MCGWIRE MM (236A-236E) 1.00 2.50
AARON MM SET (5) 3.00 8.00
AARON MM (237A-237E) 1.00 2.50
RIPKEN MM SET (5) 6.00 15.00
RIPKEN MM (238A-238E) 2.00 5.00
BOGGS MM SET (5) .75 2.00
BOGGS MM (239A-239E) .30 .75
GWYNN MM SET (5) 1.50 4.00
GWYNN MM (240A-240E) .50 1.25
GRIFFEY MM SET (5) 2.50 6.00
GRIFFEY MM (475A-475E) .75 2.00
BONDS MM SET (5) 3.00 8.00
BONDS MM (476A-476E) 1.00 2.50
SOSA MM SET (5) 1.50 4.00
SOSA MM (477A-477E) .50 1.25
JETER MM SET (5) 4.00 10.00
JETER MM (478A-478E) 1.25 3.00
A.ROD MM SET (5) 2.50 6.00
A.ROD MM (479A-479E) .75 2.00
CARD NUMBER 7 DOES NOT EXIST
SER.1 HAS ONLY 1 VERSION OF 236-240
SER.2 HAS ONLY 1 VERSION OF 475-479
MCGWIRE '85 ODDS 1:36 HOB/RET, 1:8 HTA
1 Mark McGwire .30 .75
2 Tony Gwynn .20 .50
3 Wade Boggs .12 .30
4 Cal Ripken .60 1.50
5 Matt Williams .07 .20
6 Jay Buhner .07 .20
8 Jeff Conine .07 .20
9 Todd Greene .07 .20
10 Mike Lieberthal .07 .20
11 Steve Avery .07 .20
12 Bret Saberhagen .07 .20
13 Magglio Ordonez .12 .30
14 Brad Radke .07 .20
15 Derek Jeter .50 1.25
16 Javy Lopez .07 .20
17 Russ Davis .07 .20
18 Armando Benitez .07 .20
19 B.J. Surhoff .07 .20
20 Darryl Kile .07 .20
21 Mark Lewis .07 .20
22 Mike Williams .07 .20
23 Mark McLemore .07 .20
24 Sterling Hitchcock .07 .20
25 Darin Erstad .07 .20
26 Ricky Gutierrez .07 .20
27 John Jaha .07 .20
28 Homer Bush .07 .20
29 Darrin Fletcher .07 .20
30 Mark Grace .12 .30
31 Fred McGriff .12 .30
32 Omar Daal .07 .20
33 Eric Karros .07 .20
34 Orlando Cabrera .07 .20
35 J.T. Snow .07 .20
36 Luis Castillo .07 .20
37 Rey Ordonez .07 .20
38 Bob Abreu .07 .20
39 Warren Morris .07 .20
40 Juan Gonzalez .07 .20
41 Mike Lansing .07 .20
42 Chili Davis .07 .20
43 Dean Palmer .07 .20
44 Hank Aaron .40 1.00
45 Jeff Bagwell .12 .30
46 Jose Valentin .07 .20
47 Shannon Stewart .07 .20
48 Kent Bottenfield .07 .20
49 Jeff Shaw .07 .20
50 Sammy Sosa .20 .50
51 Randy Johnson .20 .50
52 Benny Agbayani .07 .20
53 Dante Bichette .07 .20
54 Pete Harnisch .07 .20
55 Frank Thomas .20 .50
56 Jorge Posada .12 .30
57 Todd Walker .07 .20
58 Juan Encarnacion .07 .20
59 Mike Sweeney .07 .20
60 Pedro Martinez .12 .30
61 Lee Stevens .07 .20
62 Brian Giles .07 .20
63 Chad Ogea .07 .20
64 Ivan Rodriguez .12 .30
65 Roger Cedeno .07 .20
66 David Justice .07 .20
67 Steve Trachsel .07 .20
68 Eli Marrero .07 .20
69 Dave Nilsson .07 .20
70 Ken Caminiti .07 .20
71 Tim Raines .12 .30
72 Brian Jordan .07 .20
73 Jeff Blauser .07 .20
74 Bernard Gilkey .07 .20
75 John Flaherty .07 .20
76 Brent Mayne .07 .20
77 Jose Vidro .07 .20
78 David Bell .07 .20
79 Bruce Aven .07 .20
80 John Olerud .07 .20
81 Pokey Reese .07 .20
82 Woody Williams .07 .20
83 Ed Sprague .07 .20
84 Joe Girardi .12 .30
85 Barry Larkin .12 .30
86 Mike Caruso .07 .20
87 Bobby Higginson .07 .20
88 Roberto Kelly .07 .20
89 Edgar Martinez .12 .30
90 Mark Kotsay .07 .20
91 Paul Sorrento .07 .20
92 Eric Young .07 .20
93 Carlos Delgado .07 .20
94 Troy Glaus .07 .20
95 Ben Grieve .07 .20
96 Jose Lima .07 .20
97 Garret Anderson .07 .20
98 Luis Gonzalez .07 .20
99 Carl Pavano .07 .20
100 Alex Rodriguez .25 .60
101 Preston Wilson .07 .20
102 Ron Gant .07 .20
103 Brady Anderson .07 .20
104 Rickey Henderson .20 .50
105 Gary Sheffield .07 .20
106 Mickey Morandini .07 .20
107 Jim Edmonds .07 .20
108 Kris Benson .07 .20
109 Adrian Beltre .07 .20
110 Alex Fernandez .07 .20
111 Dan Wilson .07 .20
112 Mark Clark .07 .20
113 Greg Vaughn .07 .20
114 Neifi Perez .07 .20
115 Paul O'Neill .12 .30
116 Jermaine Dye .07 .20
117 Todd Jones .07 .20
118 Terry Steinbach .07 .20
119 Greg Norton .07 .20
120 Curt Schilling .12 .30
121 Todd Zeile .07 .20
122 Edgardo Alfonzo .07 .20
123 Ryan McGuire .07 .20
124 Rich Aurilia .07 .20
125 John Smoltz .20 .50
126 Bob Wickman .07 .20
127 Richard Hidalgo .07 .20
128 Chuck Finley .07 .20
129 Billy Wagner .07 .20
130 Todd Hundley .07 .20
131 Dwight Gooden .07 .20
132 Russ Ortiz .07 .20
133 Mike Lowell .07 .20
134 Reggie Sanders .07 .20
135 John Valentin .07 .20
136 Brad Ausmus .07 .20
137 Chad Kreuter .07 .20
138 David Cone .07 .20
139 Brook Fordyce .07 .20
140 Roberto Alomar .12 .30
141 Charles Nagy .07 .20
142 Brian Hunter .07 .20
143 Mike Mussina .12 .30
144 Robin Ventura .07 .20
145 Kevin Brown .07 .20
146 Pat Hentgen .07 .20
147 Ryan Klesko .07 .20
148 Derek Bell .07 .20
149 Andy Sheets .07 .20
150 Larry Walker .12 .30
151 Scott Williamson .07 .20
152 Jose Offerman .07 .20
153 Doug Mientkiewicz .07 .20
154 John Snyder RC .15 .40
155 Sandy Alomar Jr. .07 .20
156 Joe Nathan .07 .20
157 Lance Johnson .07 .20
158 Odalis Perez .07 .20
159 Hideo Nomo .20 .50
160 Steve Finley .07 .20
161 Dave Martinez .07 .20
162 Matt Walbeck .07 .20
163 Bill Spiers .07 .20
164 Fernando Tatis .07 .20
165 Kenny Lofton .07 .20
166 Paul Byrd .07 .20
167 Aaron Sele .07 .20
168 Eddie Taubensee .07 .20
169 Reggie Jefferson .07 .20
170 Roger Clemens .25 .60
171 Francisco Cordova .07 .20
172 Mike Bordick .07 .20
173 Wally Joyner .07 .20
174 Marvin Benard .07 .20
175 Jason Kendall .07 .20
176 Mike Stanley .07 .20
177 Chad Allen .07 .20
178 Carlos Beltran .12 .30
179 Deivi Cruz .07 .20
180 Chipper Jones .20 .50
181 Vladimir Guerrero .12 .30
182 Dave Burba .07 .20
183 Tom Goodwin .07 .20
184 Brian Daubach .07 .20
185 Jay Bell .07 .20
186 Roy Halladay .12 .30
187 Miguel Tejada .12 .30
188 Armando Rios .07 .20
189 Fernando Vina .07 .20
190 Eric Davis .07 .20
191 Henry Rodriguez .07 .20
192 Joe McEwing .07 .20
193 Jeff Kent .07 .20
194 Mike Jackson .07 .20
195 Mike Morgan .07 .20
196 Jeff Montgomery .07 .20
197 Jeff Zimmerman .07 .20
198 Tony Fernandez .07 .20
199 Jason Giambi .07 .20
200 Jose Canseco .12 .30
201 Alex Gonzalez .07 .20
202 J.Cust .07 .20
M.Colangelo
D.Brown
203 A.Soriano .20 .50
F.Lopez
P.Ozuna
204 Durazo .07 .20
Burrell
Johnson
205 J.Sneed RC .15 .40
K.Wells
M.Blank
206 J.Kalinowski .15 .40
M.Tejera
C.Mears
207 L.Berkman .12 .30
C.Patterson
R.Brown
208 K.Pellow .07 .20
K.Barker
R.Branyan
209 B.Garbe .15 .40
L.Bigbie
210 B.Bradley .15 .40
E.Munson
211 J.Girdley .07 .20
K.Snyder
212 C.Caple .15 .40
J.Jennings
213 B.Myers .50 1.25
R.Christianson
214 J.Stumm .15 .40
R.Purvis RC
215 D.Walling .07 .20
M.Paradis
216 O.Ortiz .07 .20
J.Gehrke
217 David Cone HL .07 .20
218 Jose Jimenez HL .07 .20
219 Chris Singleton HL .07 .20
220 Fernando Tatis HL .07 .20
221 Todd Helton HL .12 .30
222 Kevin Millwood DIV .07 .20
223 Todd Pratt DIV .07 .20
224 Orlando Hernandez DIV .07 .20
225 Pedro Martinez DIV .12 .30
226 Tom Glavine LCS .12 .30
227 Bernie Williams LCS .12 .30
228 Mariano Rivera WS .25 .60
229 Tony Gwynn 20CB .20 .50
230 Wade Boggs 20CB .12 .30
231 Lance Johnson CB .07 .20
232 Mark McGwire 20CB .30 .75
233 Rickey Henderson 20CB .20 .50
234 Rickey Henderson 20CB .20 .50
235 Roger Clemens 20CB .25 .60
236A M.McGwire MM 1st HR .75 2.00
236B M.McGwire MM 1987 ROY .75 2.00
236C M.McGwire MM 62nd HR .75 2.00
236D M.McGwire MM 70th HR .75 2.00
236E M.McGwire MM 500th HR .75 2.00
237A H.Aaron MM 1st Career HR 1.00 2.50
237B H.Aaron MM 1957 MVP 1.00 2.50
237C H.Aaron MM 3000th Hit 1.00 2.50
237D H.Aaron MM 715th HR 1.00 2.50
237E H.Aaron MM 755th HR 1.00 2.50
238A C.Ripken MM 1982 ROY 1.50 4.00
238B C.Ripken MM 1991 MVP 1.50 4.00
238C C.Ripken MM 2131 Game 1.50 4.00
238D C.Ripken MM Streak Ends 1.50 4.00
238E C.Ripken MM 400th HR 1.50 4.00
239A W.Boggs MM 1983 Batting .30 .75
239B W.Boggs MM 1988 Batting .30 .75
239C W.Boggs MM 2000th Hit .30 .75
239D W.Boggs MM 1996 Champs .30 .75
239E W.Boggs MM 3000th Hit .30 .75
240A T.Gwynn MM 1984 Batting .50 1.25
240B T.Gwynn MM 1984 NLCS .50 1.25
240C T.Gwynn MM 1995 Batting .50 1.25
240D T.Gwynn MM 1998 NLCS .50 1.25
240E T.Gwynn MM 3000th Hit .50 1.25
241 Tom Glavine .12 .30
242 David Wells .07 .20
243 Kevin Appier .07 .20
244 Troy Percival .07 .20
245 Ray Lankford .07 .20
246 Marquis Grissom .07 .20
247 Randy Winn .07 .20
248 Miguel Batista .07 .20
249 Darren Dreifort .07 .20
250 Barry Bonds .30 .75
251 Harold Baines .12 .30
252 Cliff Floyd .07 .20
253 Freddy Garcia .07 .20
254 Kenny Rogers .07 .20
255 Ben Davis .07 .20
256 Charles Johnson .07 .20
257 Bubba Trammell .07 .20
258 Desi Relaford .07 .20
259 Al Martin .07 .20
260 Andy Pettitte .12 .30
261 Carlos Lee .07 .20
262 Matt Lawton .07 .20
263 Andy Fox .07 .20
264 Chan Ho Park .12 .30
265 Billy Koch .07 .20
266 Dave Roberts .12 .30
267 Carl Everett .07 .20
268 Orel Hershiser .07 .20
269 Trot Nixon .07 .20
270 Rusty Greer .07 .20
271 Will Clark .12 .30
272 Quilvio Veras .07 .20
273 Rico Brogna .07 .20
274 Devon White .07 .20
275 Tim Hudson .12 .30
276 Mike Hampton .07 .20
277 Miguel Cairo .07 .20
278 Darren Oliver .07 .20
279 Jeff Cirillo .07 .20
280 Al Leiter .07 .20
281 Shane Andrews .07 .20
282 Carlos Febles .07 .20
283 Pedro Astacio .07 .20
284 Juan Guzman .07 .20
285 Orlando Hernandez .07 .20
286 Paul Konerko .07 .20
287 Tony Clark .07 .20
288 Aaron Boone .07 .20
289 Ismael Valdes .07 .20
290 Moises Alou .07 .20
291 Kevin Tapani .07 .20
292 John Franco .07 .20
293 Todd Zeile .07 .20
294 Jason Schmidt .07 .20
295 Johnny Damon .12 .30
296 Scott Brosius .07 .20
297 Travis Fryman .07 .20
298 Jose Vizcaino .07 .20
299 Eric Chavez .07 .20
300 Mike Piazza .20 .50
301 Matt Clement .07 .20
302 Cristian Guzman .07 .20
303 C.J. Nitkowski .07 .20
304 Michael Tucker .07 .20
305 Brett Tomko .07 .20
306 Mike Lansing .07 .20
307 Eric Owens .07 .20
308 Livan Hernandez .07 .20
309 Rondell White .07 .20
310 Todd Stottlemyre .07 .20
311 Chris Carpenter .12 .30
312 Ken Hill .07 .20
313 Mark Loretta .07 .20
314 John Rocker .07 .20
315 Richie Sexson .07 .20
316 Ruben Mateo .07 .20
317 Joe Randa .07 .20
318 Mike Sirotka .07 .20
319 Jose Rosado .07 .20
320 Matt Mantei .07 .20
321 Kevin Millwood .07 .20
322 Gary Disarcina .07 .20
323 Dustin Hermanson .07 .20
324 Mike Stanton .07 .20
325 Kirk Rueter .07 .20
326 Damian Miller RC .15 .40
327 Doug Glanville .07 .20
328 Scott Rolen .12 .30
329 Ray Durham .07 .20
330 Butch Huskey .07 .20
331 Mariano Rivera .25 .60
332 Darren Lewis .07 .20
333 Mike Timlin .07 .20
334 Mark Grudzielanek .07 .20
335 Mike Cameron .07 .20
336 Kelvim Escobar .07 .20
337 Bret Boone .07 .20
338 Mo Vaughn .07 .20
339 Craig Biggio .12 .30
340 Michael Barrett .07 .20
341 Marlon Anderson .07 .20
342 Bobby Jones .07 .20
343 John Halama .07 .20
344 Todd Ritchie .07 .20
345 Chuck Knoblauch .07 .20
346 Rick Reed .07 .20
347 Kelly Stinnett .07 .20
348 Tim Salmon .07 .20
349 A.J. Hinch .07 .20
350 Jose Cruz Jr. .07 .20
351 Roberto Hernandez .07 .20
352 Edgar Renteria .07 .20
353 Jose Hernandez .07 .20
354 Brad Fullmer .07 .20
355 Trevor Hoffman .12 .30
356 Troy O'Leary .07 .20
357 Justin Thompson .07 .20
358 Kevin Young .07 .20
359 Hideki Irabu .07 .20
360 Jim Thome .12 .30
361 Steve Karsay .07 .20
362 Octavio Dotel .07 .20
363 Omar Vizquel .12 .30
364 Raul Mondesi .07 .20
365 Shane Reynolds .07 .20
366 Bartolo Colon .07 .20
367 Chris Widger .07 .20
368 Gabe Kapler .07 .20
369 Bill Simas .07 .20
370 Tino Martinez .07 .20
371 John Thomson .07 .20
372 Delino Deshields .07 .20
373 Carlos Perez .07 .20
374 Eddie Perez .07 .20
375 Jeromy Burnitz .07 .20
376 Jimmy Haynes .07 .20
377 Travis Lee .07 .20
378 Darryl Hamilton .07 .20
379 Jamie Moyer .07 .20
380 Alex Gonzalez .07 .20
381 John Wetteland .07 .20
382 Vinny Castilla .07 .20
383 Jeff Suppan .07 .20
384 Jim Leyritz .07 .20
385 Robb Nen .07 .20
386 Wilson Alvarez .07 .20
387 Andres Galarraga .12 .30
388 Mike Remlinger .07 .20
389 Geoff Jenkins .07 .20
390 Matt Stairs .07 .20
391 Bill Mueller .07 .20
392 Mike Lowell .07 .20
393 Andy Ashby .07 .20
394 Ruben Rivera .07 .20
395 Todd Helton .12 .30
396 Bernie Williams .12 .30
397 Royce Clayton .07 .20
398 Manny Ramirez .20 .50
399 Kerry Wood .07 .20
400 Ken Griffey Jr. .40 1.00
401 Enrique Wilson .07 .20
402 Joey Hamilton .07 .20
403 Shawn Estes .07 .20
404 Ugueth Urbina .07 .20
405 Albert Belle .07 .20
406 Rick Helling .07 .20
407 Steve Parris .07 .20
408 Eric Milton .07 .20
409 Dave Mlicki .07 .20
410 Shawn Green .07 .20
411 Jaret Wright .07 .20
412 Tony Womack .07 .20
413 Vernon Wells .07 .20
414 Ron Belliard .07 .20
415 Ellis Burks .07 .20
416 Scott Erickson .07 .20

417 Rafael Palmeiro .12 .30
418 Damion Easley .07 .20
419 Jamey Wright .07 .20
420 Corey Koskie .07 .20
421 Bobby Howry .07 .20
422 Ricky Ledee .07 .20
423 Dmitri Young .07 .20
424 Sidney Ponson .07 .20
425 Greg Maddux .25 .60
426 Jose Guillen .07 .20
427 Jon Lieber .07 .20
428 Andy Benes .07 .20
429 Randy Velarde .07 .20
430 Sean Casey .07 .20
431 Torii Hunter .07 .20
432 Ryan Rupe .07 .20
433 David Segui .07 .20
434 Todd Pratt .07 .20
435 Nomar Garciaparra .12 .30
436 Denny Neagle .07 .20
437 Ron Coomer .07 .20
438 Chris Singleton .07 .20
439 Tony Batista .07 .20
440 Andruw Jones .07 .20
441 A.Huff .07 .20
S.Burroughs
A.Piatt
442 Furcal .12 .30
Dawkins
Dellaero
443 M.Lamb RC .15 .40
J.Crede
W.Veras
444 J.Zuleta .15 .40
J.Toca
D.Stenson
445 G.Maddux Jr. .15 .40
G.Matthews Jr.
T.Raines Jr.
446 M.Mulder .12 .30
C.Sabathia
M.Riley
447 S.Downs .15 .40
C.George
M.Belisle
448 D.Mirabelli .12 .30
B.Petrick
J.Werth
449 J.Hamilton .50 1.25
C.Meyers
450 B.Christensen .15 .40
R.Stahl
451 B.Zito 1.25 3.00
B.Sheets RC
452 K.Ainsworth .15 .40
T.Howington
453 R.Asadoorian .15 .40
V.Faison
454 K.Reed .15 .40
J.Heaverlo
455 M.MacDougal .25 .60
B.Baker
456 Mark McGwire SH .30 .75
457 Cal Ripken SH .60 1.50
458 Wade Boggs SH .12 .30
459 Tony Gwynn SH .20 .50
460 Jesse Orosco SH .07 .20
461 L.Walker .12 .30
N.Garciaparra LL
462 K.Griffey Jr. .40 1.00
M.McGwire LL
463 M.Ramirez .30 .75
M.McGwire LL
464 P.Martinez .20 .50
R.Johnson LL
465 P.Martinez .20 .50
R.Johnson LL
466 D.Jeter .50 1.25
L.Gonzalez LL
467 L.Walker .20 .50
M.Ramirez LL
468 Tony Gwynn 20CB .20 .50
469 Mark McGwire 20CB .30 .75
470 Frank Thomas 20CB .20 .50
471 Harold Baines 20CB .12 .30
472 Roger Clemens 20CB .25 .60
473 John Franco 20CB .07 .20
474 John Franco 20CB .07 .20
475A K.Griffey Jr. MM 350th HR 1.00 2.50
475B K.Griffey Jr. MM 1997 MVP 1.00 2.50
475C K.Griffey Jr. MM HR Dad 1.00 2.50
475D K.Griffey Jr. MM 1992 AS MVP 1.00 2.50
475E K.Griffey Jr. MM 50 HR 1997 1.00 2.50
476A B.Bonds MM 400HR/400SB .75 2.00
476B B.Bonds MM 40HR/40SB .75 2.00
476C B.Bonds MM 1993 MVP .75 2.00
476D B.Bonds MM 1990 MVP .75 2.00
476E B.Bonds MM 1992 MVP .75 2.00
477A S.Sosa MM 20 HR June .50 1.25
477B S.Sosa MM 66 HR 1998 .50 1.25
477C S.Sosa MM 60 HR 1999 .50 1.25
477D S.Sosa MM 1998 MVP .50 1.25
477E S.Sosa MM HR's 61/62 .50 1.25
478A D.Jeter MM 1996 ROY 1.25 3.00
478B D.Jeter MM Wins 1999 WS 1.25 3.00
478C D.Jeter MM Wins 1998 WS 1.25 3.00
478D D.Jeter MM Wins 1996 WS 1.25 3.00
478E D.Jeter MM 17 GM Hit Streak 1.25 3.00
479A A.Rodriguez MM 40HR/40SB .60 1.50
479B A.Rodriguez MM 100th HR .60 1.50
479C A.Rodriguez MM 1996 POY .60 1.50
479D A.Rodriguez MM Wins 1 Million .60 1.50
479E A.Rodriguez MM
1996 Batting Leader .60 1.50
NNO M.McGwire 85 Reprint 1.00 2.50

2000 Topps 20th Century Best Sequential

Inserted into first series hobby packs at an overall rate of one in 869 and one in 239 HTA packs, and into series two hobby packs at one in 362 and one in 100 HTA packs, these cards parallel the Century's Best subset within the base 2000 Topps set (cards 229-235/468-474). These insert cards, unlike the regular cards, feature "CB" prefixed numbering on back and have dramatic sparkling foil-coated fronts. Each card is sequentially numbered to the featured players highlighted career statistic.

SER.1 STATED ODDS 1:869 HOBBY, 1:239 HTA
SER.2 STATED ODDS 1:362 HOBBY, 1:100 HTA
PRINT RUNS B/WN 117-3316 COPIES PER
CB1 T.Gwynn AVG/339 10.00 25.00
CB2 W.Boggs 2B/578 6.00 15.00
CB3 L.Johnson 3B/117 6.00 15.00
CB4 M.McGwire HR/522 15.00 40.00
CB5 R.Henderson SB/1334 6.00 15.00
CB6 R.Henderson RUN/2103 6.00 15.00
CB7 R.Clemens WIN/247 12.00 30.00
CB8 Tony Gwynn HIT/3067 6.00 15.00
CB9 Mark McGwire SLG/587 15.00 40.00
CB10 Frank Thomas OBP/440 10.00 25.00
CB11 Harold Baines RBI/1583 4.00 10.00
CB12 Roger Clemens K's/3316 8.00 20.00
CB13 John Franco ERA/264 4.00 10.00
CB14 John Franco SV/416 4.00 10.00

2000 Topps Home Team Advantage

COMP.FACT.SET (479) 40.00 80.00
*HTA: .75X TO 2X BASIC CARDS
DISTRIBUTED ONLY IN HTA FACTORY SETS

2000 Topps MVP Promotion

SER.1 ODDS 1:510 HOB/RET, 1:140 HTA
SER.2 ODDS 1:378 HOB/RET, 1:104 HTA
STATED PRINT RUN 100 SETS
EXCHANGE DEADLINE 12/31/00
CARD NUMBERS 7 AND 44 DO NOT EXIST
MVP PARALLELS ARE UNNUMBERED
1 Mark McGwire 20.00 50.00
2 Tony Gwynn 12.00 30.00
3 Wade Boggs 8.00 20.00
4 Cal Ripken 40.00 100.00
5 Matt Williams 5.00 12.00
6 Jay Buhner 5.00 12.00
8 Jeff Conine 5.00 12.00
9 Todd Greene 5.00 12.00
10 Mike Lieberthal 5.00 12.00
11 Steve Avery 5.00 12.00
12 Bret Saberhagen 5.00 12.00
13 Magglio Ordonez W 8.00 20.00
14 Brad Radke 5.00 12.00
15 Derek Jeter W 30.00 80.00
16 Javy Lopez 5.00 12.00
17 Russ Davis 5.00 12.00
18 Armando Benitez 5.00 12.00
19 B.J. Surhoff 5.00 12.00
20 Darryl Kile 5.00 12.00
21 Mark Lewis 5.00 12.00
22 Mike Williams 5.00 12.00
23 Mark McLemore 5.00 12.00
24 Sterling Hitchcock 5.00 12.00
25 Darin Erstad 5.00 12.00
26 Ricky Gutierrez 5.00 12.00
27 John Jaha 5.00 12.00
28 Homer Bush 5.00 12.00
29 Darrin Fletcher 5.00 12.00
30 Mark Grace 8.00 20.00
31 Fred McGriff 8.00 20.00
32 Omar Daal 5.00 12.00
33 Eric Karros 5.00 12.00
34 Orlando Cabrera 5.00 12.00
35 J.T. Snow 5.00 12.00
36 Luis Castillo 5.00 12.00
37 Rey Ordonez 5.00 12.00
38 Bob Abreu 5.00 12.00
39 Warren Morris 5.00 12.00
40 Juan Gonzalez 5.00 12.00
41 Mike Lansing 5.00 12.00
42 Chili Davis 5.00 12.00
43 Dean Palmer 5.00 12.00
45 Jeff Bagwell W 8.00 20.00
46 Jose Valentin 5.00 12.00
47 Shannon Stewart 5.00 12.00
48 Kent Bottenfield 5.00 12.00
49 Jeff Shaw 5.00 12.00
50 Sammy Sosa W 12.00 30.00
51 Randy Johnson 12.00 30.00
52 Benny Agbayani 5.00 12.00
53 Dante Bichette W 5.00 12.00
54 Pete Harnisch 5.00 12.00
55 Frank Thomas W 12.00 30.00
56 Jorge Posada 8.00 20.00
57 Todd Walker 5.00 12.00
58 Juan Encarnacion 5.00 12.00
59 Mike Sweeney 5.00 12.00
60 Pedro Martinez W 8.00 20.00
61 Lee Stevens 5.00 12.00
62 Brian Giles 5.00 12.00
63 Chad Ogea 5.00 12.00
64 Ivan Rodriguez 8.00 20.00
65 Roger Cedeno 5.00 12.00
66 David Justice 5.00 12.00
67 Steve Trachsel 5.00 12.00
68 Eli Marrero 5.00 12.00
69 Dave Nilsson 5.00 12.00
70 Ken Caminiti 5.00 12.00
71 Tim Raines 8.00 20.00
72 Brian Jordan W 5.00 12.00
73 Jeff Blauser 5.00 12.00
74 Bernard Gilkey 5.00 12.00
75 John Flaherty 5.00 12.00
76 Brent Mayne 5.00 12.00
77 Jose Vidro 5.00 12.00
78 David Bell 5.00 12.00
79 Bruce Aven 5.00 12.00
80 John Olerud 5.00 12.00
81 Juan Guzman 5.00 12.00
82 Woody Williams 5.00 12.00
83 Ed Sprague 5.00 12.00
84 Joe Girardi 8.00 20.00
85 Barry Larkin 8.00 20.00
86 Mike Caruso 5.00 12.00
87 Bobby Higginson W 5.00 12.00
88 Roberto Kelly 5.00 12.00
89 Edgar Martinez 8.00 20.00
90 Mark Kotsay W 5.00 12.00
91 Paul Sorrento 5.00 12.00
92 Eric Young 5.00 12.00
93 Carlos Delgado W 5.00 12.00
94 Troy Glaus 5.00 12.00
95 Ben Grieve 5.00 12.00
96 Jose Lima 5.00 12.00
97 Garret Anderson 5.00 12.00
98 Luis Gonzalez 5.00 12.00
99 Carl Pavano 5.00 12.00
100 Alex Rodriguez 15.00 40.00
101 Preston Wilson 5.00 12.00
102 Ron Gant 5.00 12.00
103 Brady Anderson 5.00 12.00
104 Rickey Henderson 12.00 30.00
105 Gary Sheffield 5.00 12.00
106 Mickey Morandini 5.00 12.00
107 Jim Edmonds W 5.00 12.00
108 Kris Benson 5.00 12.00
109 Adrian Beltre W 12.00 30.00
110 Alex Fernandez 5.00 12.00
111 Dan Wilson 5.00 12.00
112 Mark Clark 5.00 12.00
113 Greg Vaughn 5.00 12.00
114 Neifi Perez 5.00 12.00
115 Paul O'Neill 8.00 20.00
116 Jermaine Dye W 5.00 12.00
117 Todd Jones 5.00 12.00
118 Terry Steinbach 5.00 12.00
119 Greg Norton 5.00 12.00
120 Curt Schilling 8.00 20.00
121 Todd Zeile 5.00 12.00
122 Edgardo Alfonzo 5.00 12.00
123 Ryan McGuire 5.00 12.00
124 Rich Aurilia 5.00 12.00
125 John Smoltz 12.00 30.00
126 Bob Wickman 5.00 12.00
127 Billy Wagner 5.00 12.00
128 Chuck Finley 5.00 12.00
129 Billy Wagner 5.00 12.00
130 Todd Hundley 5.00 12.00
131 Dwight Gooden 5.00 12.00
132 Russ Ortiz 5.00 12.00
133 Mike Lowell 5.00 12.00
134 Reggie Sanders 5.00 12.00
135 John Valentin 5.00 12.00
136 Brad Ausmus 5.00 12.00
137 Chad Kreuter 5.00 12.00
138 David Cone 5.00 12.00
139 Brook Fordyce 5.00 12.00
140 Roberto Alomar 8.00 20.00
141 Charles Nagy 5.00 12.00
142 Brian Hunter 5.00 12.00
143 Mike Mussina 8.00 20.00
144 Robin Ventura 5.00 12.00
145 Kevin Brown 5.00 12.00
146 Pat Hentgen 5.00 12.00
147 Ryan Klesko 5.00 12.00
148 Derek Bell W 5.00 12.00
149 Andy Sheets 5.00 12.00
150 Larry Walker 8.00 20.00
151 Scott Williamson 5.00 12.00
152 Jose Offerman 5.00 12.00
153 Doug Mientkiewicz 5.00 12.00
154 John Snyder 5.00 12.00
155 Sandy Alomar Jr. 5.00 12.00
156 Joe Nathan 5.00 12.00
157 Lance Johnson 5.00 12.00
158 Odalis Perez 5.00 12.00
159 Hideo Nomo 12.00 30.00
160 Steve Finley 5.00 12.00
161 Dave Martinez 5.00 12.00
162 Matt Walbeck 5.00 12.00
163 Bill Spiers 12.00 30.00
164 Fernando Tatis 5.00 12.00
165 Kenny Lofton W 5.00 12.00
166 Paul Byrd 5.00 12.00
167 Aaron Sele 5.00 12.00
168 Eddie Taubensee 12.00 30.00
169 Reggie Jefferson 5.00 12.00
170 Roger Clemens 15.00 40.00
171 Francisco Cordova 5.00 12.00
172 Mike Bordick 5.00 12.00
173 Wally Joyner 5.00 12.00
174 Marvin Benard 5.00 12.00
175 Jason Kendall 5.00 12.00
176 Mike Stanley 5.00 12.00
177 Chad Allen 5.00 12.00
178 Carlos Beltran 8.00 20.00
179 Deivi Cruz 5.00 12.00
180 Chipper Jones W 12.00 30.00
181 Vladimir Guerrero 8.00 20.00
182 Dave Burba 5.00 12.00
183 Tom Goodwin 5.00 12.00
184 Brian Daubach 5.00 12.00
185 Jay Bell 5.00 12.00
186 Roy Halladay 8.00 20.00
187 Miguel Tejada 8.00 20.00
188 Armando Rios 5.00 12.00
189 Fernando Vina 5.00 12.00
190 Eric Davis 5.00 12.00
191 Henry Rodriguez 5.00 12.00
192 Joe McEwing 5.00 12.00
193 Jeff Kent 5.00 12.00
194 Mike Jackson 5.00 12.00
195 Mike Morgan 5.00 12.00
196 Jeff Montgomery 5.00 12.00
197 Jeff Zimmerman 5.00 12.00
198 Tony Fernandez 5.00 12.00
199 Jason Giambi W 5.00 12.00
200 Jose Canseco 8.00 20.00
201 Alex Gonzalez 5.00 12.00
241 Tom Glavine 8.00 20.00
242 David Wells 5.00 12.00
243 Kevin Appier 5.00 12.00
244 Troy Percival 5.00 12.00
245 Ray Lankford 5.00 12.00
246 Marquis Grissom 5.00 12.00
247 Randy Winn 5.00 12.00
248 Miguel Batista 5.00 12.00
249 Darren Dreifort 5.00 12.00
250 Barry Bonds W 20.00 50.00
251 Harold Baines 8.00 20.00
252 Cliff Floyd 5.00 12.00
253 Freddy Garcia 5.00 12.00
254 Kenny Rogers 5.00 12.00
255 Ben Davis 5.00 12.00
256 Charles Johnson 5.00 12.00
257 Bubba Trammell 5.00 12.00
258 Desi Relaford 5.00 12.00
259 Al Martin 5.00 12.00
260 Andy Pettitte 8.00 20.00
261 Carlos Lee 5.00 12.00
262 Matt Lawton 5.00 12.00
263 Andy Fox 5.00 12.00
264 Chan Ho Park 8.00 20.00
265 Billy Koch 5.00 12.00
266 Dave Roberts 8.00 20.00
267 Carl Everett 5.00 12.00
268 Orel Hershiser 5.00 12.00
269 Trot Nixon 5.00 12.00
270 Rusty Greer 5.00 12.00
271 Will Clark W 8.00 20.00
272 Quilvio Veras 5.00 12.00
273 Rico Brogna 5.00 12.00
274 Devon White 5.00 12.00
275 Tim Hudson 8.00 20.00
276 Mike Hampton 5.00 12.00
277 Miguel Cairo 5.00 12.00
278 Darren Oliver 5.00 12.00
279 Jeff Cirillo 5.00 12.00
280 Al Leiter 5.00 12.00
281 Shane Andrews 5.00 12.00
282 Carlos Febles 5.00 12.00
283 Pedro Astacio 5.00 12.00
284 Juan Guzman 5.00 12.00
285 Orlando Hernandez 5.00 12.00
286 Paul Konerko 5.00 12.00
287 Tony Clark 5.00 12.00
288 Aaron Boone 5.00 12.00
289 Ismael Valdes 5.00 12.00
290 Moises Alou 5.00 12.00
291 Kevin Tapani 5.00 12.00
292 John Franco 5.00 12.00
293 Todd Zeile 5.00 12.00
294 Jason Schmidt 5.00 12.00
295 Johnny Damon 8.00 20.00
296 Scott Brosius 5.00 12.00
297 Travis Fryman 5.00 12.00
298 Jose Vizcaino 5.00 12.00
299 Eric Chavez 5.00 12.00
300 Mike Piazza 12.00 30.00
301 Matt Clement 5.00 12.00
302 Cristian Guzman 5.00 12.00
303 C.J. Nitkowski 5.00 12.00
304 Michael Tucker 5.00 12.00
305 Brett Tomko 5.00 12.00
306 Mike Lansing 5.00 12.00
307 Eric Owens 5.00 12.00
308 Livan Hernandez 5.00 12.00
309 Rondell White 5.00 12.00
310 Todd Stottlemyre 5.00 12.00
311 Chris Carpenter 8.00 20.00
312 Ken Hill 5.00 12.00
313 Mark Loretta 5.00 12.00
314 John Rocker 5.00 12.00
315 Richie Sexson 5.00 12.00
316 Ruben Mateo 5.00 12.00
317 Joe Randa 5.00 12.00
318 Mike Sirotka 5.00 12.00
319 Jose Rosado 5.00 12.00
320 Matt Mantei 5.00 12.00
321 Kevin Millwood 5.00 12.00
322 Gary Disarcina 5.00 12.00
323 Dustin Hermanson 5.00 12.00
324 Mike Stanton 5.00 12.00
325 Kirk Rueter 5.00 12.00
326 Damian Miller 5.00 12.00
327 Doug Glanville 5.00 12.00
328 Scott Rolen 8.00 20.00
329 Ray Durham 5.00 12.00
330 Butch Huskey 5.00 12.00
331 Mariano Rivera 15.00 40.00
332 Darren Lewis 5.00 12.00
333 Mike Timlin 5.00 12.00
334 Mark Grudzielanek 5.00 12.00
335 Mike Cameron 5.00 12.00
336 Kelvim Escobar 5.00 12.00
337 Bret Boone 5.00 12.00
338 Mo Vaughn 5.00 12.00
339 Craig Biggio 8.00 20.00
340 Michael Barrett 5.00 12.00
341 Marlon Anderson 5.00 12.00
342 Bobby Jones 5.00 12.00
343 John Halama 5.00 12.00
344 Todd Ritchie 5.00 12.00
345 Chuck Knoblauch 5.00 12.00
346 Rick Reed 5.00 12.00
347 Kelly Stinnett 5.00 12.00
348 Tim Salmon 5.00 12.00
349 A.J. Hinch 5.00 12.00
350 Jose Cruz Jr. W 5.00 12.00
351 Roberto Hernandez 5.00 12.00
352 Edgar Renteria 5.00 12.00
353 Jose Hernandez 5.00 12.00
354 Brad Fullmer 5.00 12.00
355 Trevor Hoffman 8.00 20.00
356 Troy O'Leary 5.00 12.00
357 Justin Thompson 5.00 12.00
358 Kevin Young 5.00 12.00
359 Hideki Irabu 5.00 12.00
360 Jim Thome 8.00 20.00
361 Steve Karsay 5.00 12.00
362 Octavio Dotel 5.00 12.00
363 Omar Vizquel 8.00 20.00
364 Raul Mondesi 5.00 12.00
365 Shane Reynolds 5.00 12.00
366 Bartolo Colon 5.00 12.00
367 Chris Widger 5.00 12.00
368 Gabe Kapler 5.00 12.00
369 Bill Simas 5.00 12.00
370 Tino Martinez 5.00 12.00
371 John Thomson 5.00 12.00
372 Delino Deshields 5.00 12.00
373 Carlos Perez 5.00 12.00
374 Eddie Perez 5.00 12.00
375 Jeromy Burnitz 5.00 12.00
376 Jimmy Haynes 5.00 12.00
377 Travis Lee 5.00 12.00
378 Darryl Hamilton 5.00 12.00
379 Jamie Moyer 5.00 12.00
380 Alex Gonzalez 5.00 12.00
381 John Wetteland 5.00 12.00
382 Vinny Castilla 5.00 12.00
383 Jeff Suppan 5.00 12.00
384 Jim Leyritz 5.00 12.00
385 Robb Nen 5.00 12.00
386 Wilson Alvarez 5.00 12.00
387 Andres Galarraga 8.00 20.00
388 Mike Remlinger 5.00 12.00
389 Geoff Jenkins 5.00 12.00
390 Matt Stairs 5.00 12.00
391 Bill Mueller 5.00 12.00
392 Mike Lowell 5.00 12.00
393 Andy Ashby 5.00 12.00
394 Ruben Rivera 5.00 12.00
395 Todd Helton W 8.00 20.00
396 Bernie Williams 8.00 20.00
397 Royce Clayton 5.00 12.00
398 Manny Ramirez W 12.00 30.00
399 Kerry Wood 5.00 12.00
400 Ken Griffey Jr. 25.00 60.00
401 Enrique Wilson 5.00 12.00
402 Joey Hamilton 5.00 12.00
403 Shawn Estes W 5.00 12.00
404 Ugueth Urbina 5.00 12.00
405 Albert Belle 5.00 12.00
406 Rick Helling 5.00 12.00
407 Steve Parris 5.00 12.00
408 Eric Milton 5.00 12.00
409 Dave Mlicki 5.00 12.00
410 Shawn Green 5.00 12.00
411 Jaret Wright 5.00 12.00
412 Tony Womack 5.00 12.00
413 Vernon Wells 5.00 12.00
414 Ron Belliard 5.00 12.00
415 Ellis Burks 5.00 12.00
416 Scott Erickson 5.00 12.00
417 Rafael Palmeiro 8.00 20.00
418 Damion Easley 5.00 12.00
419 Jamey Wright 5.00 12.00
420 Corey Koskie 5.00 12.00
421 Bobby Howry 5.00 12.00
422 Ricky Ledee 5.00 12.00
423 Dmitri Young 5.00 12.00
424 Sidney Ponson 5.00 12.00
425 Greg Maddux 15.00 40.00
426 Jose Guillen 5.00 12.00
427 Jon Lieber W 5.00 12.00
428 Andy Benes 5.00 12.00
429 Randy Velarde 5.00 12.00
430 Sean Casey 5.00 12.00
431 Torii Hunter 5.00 12.00
432 Ryan Rupe 5.00 12.00
433 David Segui 5.00 12.00
434 Todd Pratt 5.00 12.00
435 Nomar Garciaparra 8.00 20.00
436 Denny Neagle 5.00 12.00
437 Ron Coomer 5.00 12.00
438 Chris Singleton 5.00 12.00
439 Tony Batista 5.00 12.00
440 Andruw Jones 5.00 12.00

2000 Topps MVP Promotion Exchange

This 25-card set was available only to those lucky collectors who obtained one of the twenty-five winning player cards from the 2000 Topps MVP Promotion parallel set. Each week, throughout the 2000 season, Topps named a new Player of the Week, and that player's Topps MVP Promotion parallel card was made redeemable for this 25-card set. The deadline to exchange the winning cards was 12/31/00.

COMPLETE SET (25) 15.00 40.00
ONE SET VIA MAIL PER '00 MVP WINNER
MVP1 Pedro Martinez 1.00 2.50
MVP2 Jim Edmonds .60 1.50
MVP3 Derek Bell .60 1.50
MVP4 Jermaine Dye .60 1.50
MVP5 Jose Cruz Jr. .60 1.50
MVP6 Todd Helton 1.00 2.50
MVP7 Brian Jordan .60 1.50
MVP8 Shawn Estes .60 1.50
MVP9 Dante Bichette .60 1.50
MVP10 Carlos Delgado .60 1.50
MVP11 Bobby Higginson .60 1.50
MVP12 Mark Kotsay .60 1.50
MVP13 Magglio Ordonez 1.00 2.50
MVP14 Jon Lieber .60 1.50
MVP15 Frank Thomas 1.50 4.00
MVP16 Manny Ramirez 1.50 4.00
MVP17 Sammy Sosa 1.50 4.00
MVP18 Will Clark 1.00 2.50
MVP19 Jeff Bagwell 1.00 2.50
MVP20 Derek Jeter 4.00 10.00
MVP21 Adrian Beltre 1.50 4.00
MVP22 Kenny Lofton .60 1.50
MVP23 Barry Bonds 2.50 6.00
MVP24 Jason Giambi .60 1.50
MVP25 Chipper Jones 1.50 4.00

2000 Topps Oversize

COMPLETE SERIES 1 (8) 4.00 10.00
COMPLETE SERIES 2 (8) 4.00 10.00
ONE PER HOBBY AND HTA BOX
A1 Mark McGwire .75 2.00
A2 Hank Aaron 1.00 2.50
A3 Derek Jeter 1.25 3.00
A4 Sammy Sosa .50 1.25
A5 Alex Rodriguez .60 1.50
A6 Chipper Jones .50 1.25
A7 Cal Ripken 1.50 4.00
A8 Pedro Martinez .30 .75
B1 Barry Bonds .75 2.00
B2 Orlando Hernandez .20 .50
B3 Mike Piazza .50 1.25
B4 Manny Ramirez .50 1.25
B5 Ken Griffey Jr. 1.00 2.50
B6 Rafael Palmeiro .30 .75
B7 Greg Maddux .60 1.50
B8 Nomar Garciaparra .30 .75

2000 Topps 21st Century

Inserted one every 18 first series hobby and retail packs and one every five first series HTA packs, these 10 cards feature players who are among those expected to be among the best players in the first part of the 21st century.

COMPLETE SET (10) 4.00 10.00
SER.1 STATED ODDS 1:18 HOB/RET, 1:5 HTA
C1 Ben Grieve .15 .40
C2 Alex Gonzalez .15 .40
C3 Derek Jeter 1.00 2.50
C4 Sean Casey .15 .40
C5 Nomar Garciaparra .25 .60
C6 Alex Rodriguez .50 1.25
C7 Scott Rolen .25 .60
C8 Andruw Jones .15 .40
C9 Vladimir Guerrero .25 .60
C10 Todd Helton .25 .60

2000 Topps Aaron

For their year 2000 product, Topps chose to reprint cards of All-Time Home Run King, Hank Aaron. The cards were inserted one every 18 hobby and retail pack and one every five HTA packs in both first and second series. The even year cards were released in the first series and the odd year cards were issued in the second series. Each card can be easily detected from the original cards issued from the 1950-70s by the large gold foil logo on front and the glossy card stock.

COMPLETE SET (23) 30.00 60.00
COMPLETE SERIES 1 (12) 12.50 30.00
COMPLETE SERIES 2 (11) 12.50 30.00
STATED ODDS 1:18 HOB/RET, 1:5 HTA
EVEN YEAR CARDS DISTRIBUTED IN SER.1
ODD YEAR CARDS DISTRIBUTED IN SER.2
1 Hank Aaron 1954 2.00 5.00

2000 Topps Aaron Autographs

Due to the fact that Topps could not obtain actual signed Hank Aaron cards prior to pack out for first series in December, 2000 - Topps inserted into first series packs at a rate of one in 4361 hobby and retail and 1 in 1199 first series HTA packs exchange cards of which were redeemable (prior to the May 31st, 2000 deadline) for a signed Hank Aaron Reprint card. The 12 exchange cards distributed in series one were redeemable exclusively for specific even year Reprint cards. The 11 odd year Autographs were obtained by Topps well in time for the second series release in April, 2000 and thus those actual autographed cards were seeded directly into the series two packs.

COMMON CARD (2-23) 200.00 400.00
SER.1 ODDS 1:4361 HOB/RET, 1:1199 HTA
SER.2 ODDS 1:3672 HOB/RET, 1:1007 HTA
EVEN YEAR CARDS DISTRIBUTED IN SER.1
ODD YEAR CARDS DISTRIBUTED IN SER.2
SER.1 EXCHANGE DEADLINE: 05/31/00
1 Hank Aaron 1954 300.00 500.00

2000 Topps Aaron Chrome

COMPLETE SET (23) 40.00 80.00
COMPLETE SERIES 1 (11) 15.00 40.00
COMPLETE SERIES 2 (12) 15.00 40.00
COMMON CARD (1-23) 2.00 5.00
STATED ODDS 1:72 HOB/RET, 1:16 HTA
*CHROME REF: 1X TO 2.5X CHROME
CH.REF.ODDS 1:288 HOB/RET, 1:76 HTA
ODD YEAR CARDS DISTRIBUTED IN SER.1
EVEN YEAR CARDS DISTRIBUTED IN SER.2
1 Hank Aaron 1954 3.00 8.00

2000 Topps All-Star Rookie Team

Randomly inserted into packs at one in 36 HOB/RET packs and one in eight HTA packs, this 10-card insert set features players that had break-through seasons their first year. Card backs carry a "RT" prefix.

COMPLETE SET (10) 6.00 15.00
SER.2 STATED ODDS 1:36 HOB/RET, 1:8 HTA
RT1 Mark McGwire 1.25 3.00
RT2 Chuck Knoblauch .30 .75
RT3 Chipper Jones .75 2.00
RT4 Cal Ripken 2.50 6.00
RT5 Manny Ramirez .75 2.00
RT6 Jose Canseco .50 1.25
RT7 Ken Griffey Jr. 1.50 4.00
RT8 Mike Piazza .75 2.00
RT9 Dwight Gooden .30 .75
RT10 Billy Wagner .30 .75

2000 Topps All-Topps

Inserted one every 12 first series hobby and retail packs and one every three first series HTA packs, this set features 10 star National Leaguers, 10 star American Leaguers, and a comparision to Hall of Famers at their respective position. Each card is printed on silver foil-board with select metalization. The National League players were issued in series one, while the American League players were issued in series two.

COMPLETE SET (20) 6.00 15.00
COMPLETE N.L.TEAM (10) 3.00 8.00
COMPLETE A.L.TEAM (10) 3.00 8.00
N.L. CARDS DISTRIBUTED IN SERIES 1
A.L. CARDS DISTRIBUTED IN SERIES 2
STATED ODDS 1:12 HOB/RET, 1:3 HTA
AT1 Greg Maddux .50 1.25
AT2 Mike Piazza .40 1.00
AT3 Mark McGwire .60 1.50
AT4 Craig Biggio .25 .60
AT5 Chipper Jones .40 1.00
AT6 Barry Larkin .25 .60
AT7 Barry Bonds .60 1.50
AT8 Andruw Jones .15 .40
AT9 Sammy Sosa .40 1.00
AT10 Larry Walker .25 .60
AT11 Pedro Martinez .25 .60
AT12 Ivan Rodriguez .25 .60
AT13 Rafael Palmeiro .25 .60
AT14 Roberto Alomar .25 .60
AT15 Cal Ripken 1.25 3.00
AT16 Derek Jeter 1.00 2.50
AT17 Albert Belle .15 .40
AT18 Ken Griffey Jr. .75 2.00
AT19 Manny Ramirez .40 1.00
AT20 Jose Canseco .25 .60

2000 Topps Autographs

Inserted at various level of difficulty, these players signed autographs for the 2000 Topps product. Group A players were inserted one every 7589 first series hobby and retail packs and one every 2087 first series HTA packs. Group A players were issued at a rate of one every 5840 second series hobby and retail packs, and one every 1607 HTA packs. Group B players were inserted one every 4553 first series hobby and retail packs and one every 1252 first series HTA packs. Group B players were inserted at a rate of one every 2337 second series hobby and retail packs, and one every 643 HTA packs. Group C players were inserted one every 1518 first series hobby and retail packs and one every 417 first series HTA packs. Group C players were inserted one every 1169 second series hobby and retail packs, and one in every 321 HTA packs. Group D players were inserted one every 911 first series hobby and retails packs and one every 250 first series HTA packs. Group D players were inserted one in every 701 second series hobby and retail packs, and one in every 193 HTA packs. Group E autographs were issued one every 1138 first series hobby and retail packs and one every 313 first series HTA packs. Group E players were inserted one in every 1754 second series hobby and retail packs, and one in every 482 HTA packs. Originally intended to be a straight numerical run of TA1-TA15 for series one,

ds TA 4 (Sean Casey) and TA 15 (Carlos Beltran) re dropped and replaced with TA 20 (Vladimir errero) and TA 27 (Mike Sweeney).
R.1 GROUP A 1:7589 H/R, 1:2087 HTA
R.2 GROUP A 1:5840 H/R, 1:1607 HTA
R.1 GROUP B 1:4553 H/R, 1:1252 HTA
R.2 GROUP B 1:2337 H/R, 1:643 HTA
R.1 GROUP C 1:1518 H/R, 1:417 HTA
R.2 GROUP C 1:1169 H/R, 1:321 HTA
R.1 GROUP D 1:911 H/R, 1:250 HTA
R.2 GROUP D 1:701 H/R, 1:193 HTA
R.1 GROUP E 1:1138 H/R, 1:313 HTA
R.2 GROUP E 1:1754 H/R, 1:482 HTA
1 Alex Rodriguez A 50.00 100.00
2 Tony Gwynn A 30.00 80.00
3 Vinny Castilla B 10.00 25.00
4 Sean Casey B 10.00 25.00
5 Shawn Green C 15.00 40.00
6 Rey Ordonez C 6.00 15.00
7 Matt Lawton C 6.00 15.00
8 Tony Womack C 6.00 15.00
9 Gabe Kapler D 10.00 25.00
10 Pat Burrell D 10.00 25.00
11 Preston Wilson D 10.00 25.00
12 Troy Glaus D 6.00 15.00
13 Carlos Beltran D 10.00 25.00
14 Josh Girdley E 6.00 15.00
15 B.J. Garbe E 6.00 15.00
16 Derek Jeter A 100.00 250.00
17 Cal Ripken A 60.00 150.00
18 Ivan Rodriguez B 15.00 40.00
19 Rafael Palmeiro B 30.00 60.00
20 Vladimir Guerrero B 6.00 15.00
21 Raul Mondesi C 6.00 15.00
22 Scott Rolen C 6.00 15.00
23 Billy Wagner C 6.00 15.00
24 Fernando Tatis C 6.00 15.00
25 Ruben Mateo D 6.00 15.00
26 Carlos Febles D 6.00 15.00
27 Mike Sweeney D 10.00 25.00
28 Alex Gonzalez D 6.00 15.00
29 Miguel Tejada D 6.00 15.00
30 Josh Hamilton 10.00 40.00

2000 Topps Combos

ndomly inserted into packs at one in 18 hobby and ail packs, and one in every five HTA packs, this -card insert set showcases player groupings ified by a common theme, such as Home Run ngs, and features artist renderings of each player miniscent of Topps' classic 1959 set. Card backs rry a "TC" prefix.

OMPLETE SET (10) 12.50 30.00
ER.2 STATED ODDS 1:18 HOB/RET, 1:5 HTA
C1 Tribe-unal 1.00 2.50
C2 Ratter Raffler's 1.25 3.00
C3 Torre's Terrors 2.50 6.00
C4 All-Star Backstops 1.00 2.50
C5 Three of a Kind 2.50 6.00
C6 Home Run Kings 1.50 4.00
C7 Strikeout Kings 1.00 2.50
C8 Executive Producers 2.00 5.00
C9 MVP's 1.00 2.50
C10 3000 Hit Brigade 3.00 8.00

2000 Topps Hands of Gold

serted on every 18 first series hobby and retail acks and one every five first series HTA packs, this ven card set features players who have won at least e Gold Gloves. Each card is foil-stamped, die-cut d specially embossed.

OMPLETE SET (7) 5.00 12.00
ER.1 STATED ODDS 1:18 HOB/RET, 1:5 HTA
G1 Barry Bonds 1.50 4.00
G2 Ivan Rodriguez .60 1.50
G3 Ken Griffey Jr. 2.00 5.00
G4 Roberto Alomar .60 1.50
G5 Tony Gwynn 1.00 2.50
G6 Omar Vizquel .60 1.50
G7 Greg Maddux 1.25 3.00

2000 Topps Own the Game

ndomly inserted into series two hobby and retail cks at a rate one in every 12, and one in every ee series two HTA packs, this 30-card insert set atures the top statistical leaders in major league seball. Card backs carry an "OTG" prefix.

OMPLETE SET (30) 20.00 50.00
ER.2 STATED ODDS 1:12 HOB/RET, 1:3 HTA
TG1 Derek Jeter 2.50 6.00
TG2 B.J. Surhoff .40 1.00
TG3 Luis Gonzalez .40 1.00
TG4 Manny Ramirez 1.00 2.50
TG5 Rafael Palmeiro .60 1.50
TG6 Mark McGwire 1.50 4.00
TG7 Mark McGwire 1.50 4.00
TG8 Sammy Sosa 1.00 2.50
TG9 Ken Griffey Jr. 2.00 5.00
TG10 Larry Walker .60 1.50
TG11 Nomar Garciaparra .60 1.50
TG12 Derek Jeter 2.50 6.00
TG13 Larry Walker .60 1.50
TG14 Mark McGwire 1.50 4.00
TG15 Manny Ramirez 1.00 2.50
TG16 Pedro Martinez .60 1.50
TG17 Randy Johnson 1.00 2.50
TG18 Kevin Millwood .40 1.00
TG19 Randy Johnson 1.00 2.50
TG20 Pedro Martinez .60 1.50
TG21 Kevin Brown .40 1.00
TG22 Chipper Jones 1.00 2.50
TG23 Ivan Rodriguez .60 1.50
OTG24 Mariano Rivera 1.25 3.00
OTG25 Scott Williamson .40 1.00
OTG26 Carlos Beltran .60 1.50
OTG27 Randy Johnson 1.00 2.50
OTG28 Pedro Martinez .60 1.50
OTG29 Sammy Sosa 1.00 2.50
OTG30 Manny Ramirez 1.00 2.50

2000 Topps Perennial All-Stars

This set is inserted into first series hobby and retail packs at a rate of one in 18 and first series HTA packs at a rate of one every five packs. These 10 cards feature players who consistently achieve All-Star recognition.

COMPLETE SET (10) 6.00 15.00
SER.1 STATED ODDS 1:18 HOB/RET, 1:5 HTA
PA1 Ken Griffey Jr. 1.00 2.50
PA2 Derek Jeter 1.25 3.00
PA3 Sammy Sosa .50 1.25
PA4 Cal Ripken 1.50 4.00
PA5 Mike Piazza .50 1.25
PA6 Nomar Garciaparra .30 .75
PA7 Jeff Bagwell .30 .75
PA8 Barry Bonds .75 2.00
PA9 Alex Rodriguez .60 1.50
PA10 Mark McGwire .75 2.00

2000 Topps Power Players

Inserted into hobby and retail first series packs at a rate of one in eight and first series HTA packs at a rate one every other pack, this set features 20 of the best sluggers in baseball.

COMPLETE SET (20) 5.00 12.00
SER.1 STATED ODDS 1:8 HOB/RET, 1:2 HTA
P1 Juan Gonzalez .15 .40
P2 Ken Griffey Jr. .75 2.00
P3 Mark McGwire .60 1.50
P4 Nomar Garciaparra .25 .60
P5 Barry Bonds .60 1.50
P6 Mo Vaughn .15 .40
P7 Larry Walker .25 .60
P8 Alex Rodriguez .50 1.25
P9 Jose Canseco .25 .60
P10 Jeff Bagwell .25 .60
P11 Manny Ramirez .40 1.00
P12 Albert Belle .15 .40
P13 Frank Thomas .40 1.00
P14 Mike Piazza .40 1.00
P15 Chipper Jones .40 1.00
P16 Sammy Sosa .40 1.00
P17 Vladimir Guerrero .25 .60
P18 Scott Rolen .25 .60
P19 Raul Mondesi .15 .40
P20 Derek Jeter 1.00 2.50

2000 Topps Stadium Autograph Relics

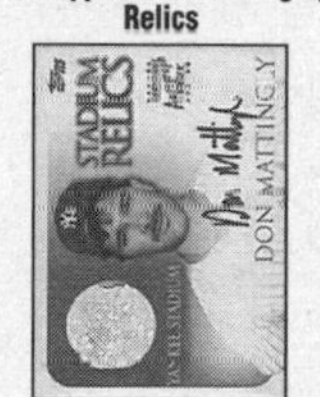

Exclusively inserted into first series HTA jumbo packs at a rate of one in 165 first series packs, and one in every 135 second series HTA packs, these cards feature a piece of a major league stadium (mostly infield bases) as well as a photo and an autograph of the featured superstar who played there. Among the venerable ballparks included in this set are Wrigley Field, Fenway Park and Yankee Stadium.

SER.1 STATED ODDS 1:165 HTA
SER.2 STATED ODDS 1:135 HTA
SR1 Don Mattingly 60.00 150.00
SR2 Carl Yastrzemski 50.00 120.00
SR3 Ernie Banks 50.00 120.00
SR4 Johnny Bench 60.00 150.00
SR5 Willie Mays 150.00 400.00
SR6 Mike Schmidt 40.00 80.00
SR7 Lou Brock 30.00 80.00
SR8 Al Kaline 30.00 80.00
SR9 Paul Molitor 25.00 60.00
SR10 Eddie Mathews 25.00 60.00

2000 Topps Limited

COMP.FACT.SET (619) 40.00 80.00
COMPLETE SET (478) 30.00 60.00
*STARS: 1.5X TO 4X BASIC CARDS
*YNG.STARS: 1.5X TO 4X BASIC CARDS
*ROOKIES: 1.5X TO 4X BASIC CARDS
*MAGIC MOMENTS: .75X TO 2X BASIC MM
MCGWIRE MM (236A-236E) 4.00 10.00
AARON MM (237A-237E) 3.00 8.00
RIPKEN MM (238A-238E) 5.00 12.00
BOGGS MM (239A-239E) 1.00 2.50
GWYNN MM (240A-240E) 2.50 6.00
GRIFFEY MM (475A-475E) 2.50 6.00
BONDS MM (476A-476E) 4.00 10.00
SOSA MM (477A-477E) 2.50 6.00
JETER MM (478A-478E) 5.00 12.00
A.ROD MM (479A-479E) 3.00 8.00
STATED PRINT RUN 4000 FACTORY SETS
MM PRINT RUN 800 OF EACH CARD
CARD NUMBER 7 DOES NOT EXIST

2000 Topps Limited 21st Century

COMPLETE SET (10) 6.00 15.00
*LIMITED: 1X TO 2.5X TOPPS 21ST CENT.
ONE SET PER FACTORY SET

2000 Topps Limited Aaron

COMPLETE SET (23) 30.00 60.00
*LIMITED: .3X TO .8X TOPPS AARON
ONE SET PER FACTORY SET
1 Hank Aaron 1954 3.00 8.00

2000 Topps Limited All-Star Rookie Team

COMPLETE SET (10) 10.00 25.00
*LIMITED: .5X TO 1.2X TOPPS AS ROOK.
ONE SET PER FACTORY SET

2000 Topps Limited All-Topps

COMPLETE SET (20) 15.00 40.00
*LIMITED: 1X TO 2.5X TOPPS ALL-TOPPS
ONE SET PER FACTORY SET

2000 Topps Limited Combos

COMPLETE SET (10) 12.50 30.00
*LIMITED: .5X TO 1.2X TOPPS COMBOS
ONE SET PER FACTORY SET

2000 Topps Limited Hands of Gold

COMPLETE SET (7) 6.00 15.00
*LIMITED: .5X TO 1.2X TOPPS HANDS
ONE SET PER FACTORY SET

2000 Topps Limited Own the Game

COMPLETE SET (30) 25.00 60.00
*LIMITED: .5X TO 1.2X TOPPS OTG
ONE SET PER FACTORY SET

2000 Topps Limited Perennial All-Stars

COMPLETE SET (10) 12.50 30.00
*LIMITED: 1X TO 2.5X TOPPS PER.AS
ONE SET PER FACTORY SET

2000 Topps Limited Power Players

COMPLETE SET (20) 12.50 30.00
*LIMITED: 1X TO 2.5X TOPPS POWER
ONE SET PER FACTORY SET

2000 Topps Traded

The 2000 Topps Traded sets were released in October, 2000 and featured a 135-card base set, and one additional autograph card. The set carried a suggested retail price of $29.99. Please note that each card in the base set carried a "T" prefix before the card number. Topps announced that due to the unavailability of certain players previously scheduled to sign autographs, Topps will include a small quantity of autographed cards from the 2000 Topps Baseball Rookies/Traded set into its 2000 Bowman Baseball Draft Picks and Prospects set. Notable Rookie Cards include Cristian Guerrero and J.R. House.

COMP.FACT.SET (136) 50.00 100.00
COMPLETE SET (135) 40.00 80.00
COMMON CARD (T1-T135) .12 .30
COMMON RC .12 .30
FACT.SET PRICE IS FOR SEALED SETS
T1 Mike MacDougal .20 .50
T2 Andy Tracy RC .12 .30
T3 Brandon Phillips RC .50 1.25
T4 Brandon Inge RC .75 2.00
T5 Robbie Morrison RC .12 .30
T6 Josh Pressley RC .12 .30
T7 Todd Moser RC .12 .30
T8 Rob Purvis .12 .30
T9 Chance Caple .12 .30
T10 Ben Sheets .30 .75
T11 Russ Jacobson RC .12 .30
T12 Brian Cole RC .12 .30
T13 Brad Baker .12 .30
T14 Alex Cintron RC .12 .30
T15 Lyle Overbay RC .20 .50
T16 Mike Edwards RC .12 .30
T17 Sean McGowan RC .12 .30
T18 Jose Molina .12 .30
T19 Marcos Castillo RC .12 .30
T20 Josue Espada RC .12 .30
T21 Alex Gordon RC .12 .30
T22 Rob Pugmire RC .12 .30
T23 Jason Stumm .12 .30
T24 Ty Howington .12 .30
T25 Brett Myers .40 1.00
T26 Maicer Izturis RC .20 .50
T27 John McDonald .12 .30
T28 Wilfredo Rodriguez RC .12 .30
T29 Carlos Zambrano RC .75 2.00
T30 Alejandro Diaz RC .12 .30
T31 Geraldo Guzman RC .12 .30
T32 J.R. House RC .12 .30
T33 Elvin Nina RC .12 .30
T34 Juan Pierre RC .60 1.50
T35 Ben Johnson RC .12 .30
T36 Jeff Bailey RC .12 .30
T37 Miguel Olivo RC .20 .50
T38 Francisco Rodriguez RC .75 2.00
T39 Tony Pena Jr. RC .12 .30
T40 Miguel Cabrera RC 30.00 80.00
T41 Asdrubal Oropeza RC .12 .30
T42 Junior Zamora RC .12 .30
T43 Jovanny Cedeno RC .12 .30
T44 John Sneed .12 .30
T45 Josh Kalinowski .12 .30
T46 Mike Young RC 1.25 3.00
T47 Rico Washington RC .12 .30
T48 Chad Durbin RC .12 .30
T49 Junior Brignac RC .12 .30
T50 Carlos Hernandez RC .12 .30
T51 Cesar Izturis RC .12 .30
T52 Oscar Salazar RC .12 .30
T53 Pat Strange RC .12 .30
T54 Rick Asadoorian .12 .30
T55 Keith Reed .12 .30
T56 Leo Estrella RC .12 .30
T57 Wascar Serrano RC .12 .30
T58 Richard Gomez RC .12 .30
T59 Ramon Santiago RC .12 .30
T60 Jovanny Sosa RC .12 .30
T61 Aaron Rowand RC .60 1.50
T62 Junior Guerrero RC .12 .30
T63 Luis Terrero RC .12 .30
T64 Brian Sanches RC .12 .30
T65 Scott Sobkowiak RC .12 .30
T66 Gary Majewski RC .12 .30
T67 Barry Zito 1.00 2.50
T68 Ryan Christianson .12 .30
T69 Cristian Guerrero RC .12 .30
T70 Tomas De La Rosa RC .12 .30
T71 Andrew Beinbrink RC .12 .30
T72 Ryan Knox RC .12 .30
T73 Alex Graman RC .12 .30
T74 Juan Guzman RC .12 .30
T75 Ruben Salazar RC .12 .30
T76 Luis Matos RC .12 .30
T77 Tony Mota RC .12 .30
T78 Doug Davis .12 .30
T79 Ben Christensen .12 .30
T80 Mike Lamb .12 .30
T81 Adrian Gonzalez RC 3.00 8.00
T82 Mike Stodolka RC .12 .30
T83 Adam Johnson RC .12 .30
T84 Matt Wheatland RC .12 .30
T85 Corey Smith RC .12 .30
T86 Rocco Baldelli RC .30 .75
T87 Keith Bucktrot RC .12 .30
T88 Adam Wainwright RC 1.25 3.00
T89 Scott Thorman RC .20 .50
T90 Tripper Johnson RC .12 .30
T91 Jim Edmonds Cards .12 .30
T92 Masato Yoshii .12 .30
T93 Adam Kennedy .12 .30
T94 Darryl Kile .12 .30
T95 Mark McLemore .12 .30
T96 Ricky Gutierrez .12 .30
T97 Juan Gonzalez .12 .30
T98 Melvin Mora .12 .30
T99 Dante Bichette .12 .30
T100 Lee Stevens .12 .30
T101 Roger Cedeno .12 .30
T102 John Olerud .12 .30
T103 Eric Young .12 .30
T104 Mickey Morandini .12 .30
T105 Travis Lee .12 .30
T106 Greg Vaughn .12 .30
T107 Todd Zeile .12 .30
T108 Chuck Finley .12 .30
T109 Ismael Valdes .12 .30
T110 Reggie Sanders .12 .30
T111 Pat Hentgen .12 .30
T112 Ryan Klesko .12 .30
T113 Derek Bell .12 .30
T114 Hideo Nomo .30 .75
T115 Aaron Sele .12 .30
T116 Fernando Vina .12 .30
T117 Wally Joyner .12 .30
T118 Brian Hunter .12 .30
T119 Joe Girardi .20 .50
T120 Omar Daal .12 .30
T121 Brook Fordyce .12 .30
T122 Jose Valentin .20 .50
T123 Curt Schilling .20 .50
T124 B.J. Surhoff .12 .30
T125 Henry Rodriguez .12 .30
T126 Mike Bordick .12 .30
T127 David Justice .12 .30
T128 Charles Johnson .12 .30
T129 Will Clark .20 .50
T130 Dwight Gooden .12 .30
T131 David Segui .12 .30
T132 Denny Neagle .12 .30
T133 Jose Canseco .20 .50
T134 Bruce Chen .12 .30
T135 Jason Bere .12 .30

2000 Topps Traded Autographs

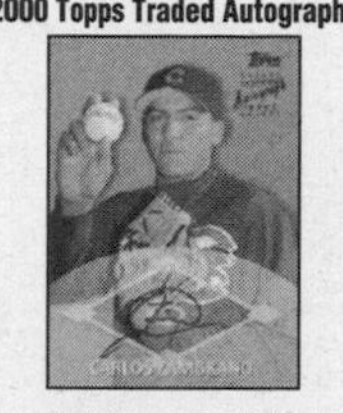

Randomly inserted into 2000 Topps Traded sets at a rate of one per sealed factory set, this 80-card set features autographed cards of some of the Major League's most talented prospects. Card backs carry a "TTA" prefix.

ONE PER FACTORY SET
TTA1 Mike MacDougal 3.00 8.00
TTA2 Andy Tracy 2.00 5.00
TTA3 Brandon Phillips 15.00 40.00
TTA4 Brandon Inge 12.50 30.00
TTA5 Robbie Morrison 2.00 5.00
TTA6 Josh Pressley 2.00 5.00
TTA7 Todd Moser 2.00 5.00
TTA8 Rob Purvis 3.00 8.00
TTA9 Chance Caple 2.00 5.00
TTA10 Ben Sheets 6.00 15.00
TTA11 Russ Jacobson 2.00 5.00
TTA12 Brian Cole 6.00 15.00
TTA13 Brad Baker 2.00 5.00
TTA14 Alex Cintron 3.00 8.00
TTA15 Lyle Overbay 10.00 25.00
TTA16 Mike Edwards 2.00 5.00
TTA17 Sean McGowan 2.00 5.00
TTA18 Jose Molina 5.00 12.00
TTA19 Marcos Castillo 2.00 5.00
TTA20 Josue Espada 2.00 5.00
TTA21 Alex Gordon 2.00 5.00
TTA22 Rob Pugmire 2.00 5.00
TTA23 Jason Stumm 2.00 5.00
TTA24 Ty Howington 2.00 5.00
TTA25 Brett Myers 10.00 25.00
TTA26 Maicer Izturis 6.00 15.00
TTA27 John McDonald 2.00 5.00
TTA28 Wilfredo Rodriguez 2.00 5.00
TTA29 Carlos Zambrano 5.00 12.00
TTA30 Alejandro Diaz 2.00 5.00
TTA31 Geraldo Guzman 2.00 5.00
TTA32 J.R. House 2.00 5.00
TTA33 Elvin Nina 2.00 5.00
TTA34 Juan Pierre 4.00 10.00
TTA35 Ben Johnson 10.00 25.00
TTA36 Jeff Bailey 2.00 5.00
TTA37 Miguel Olivo 5.00 12.00
TTA38 Francisco Rodriguez 15.00 40.00
TTA39 Tony Pena Jr. 2.00 5.00
TTA40 Miguel Cabrera 600.00 1000.00
TTA41 Asdrubal Oropeza 2.00 5.00
TTA42 Junior Zamora 2.00 5.00
TTA43 Jovanny Cedeno 2.00 5.00
TTA44 John Sneed 2.00 5.00
TTA45 Josh Kalinowski 3.00 8.00
TTA46 Mike Young 15.00 40.00
TTA47 Rico Washington 2.00 5.00
TTA48 Chad Durbin 2.00 5.00
TTA49 Junior Brignac 2.00 5.00
TTA50 Carlos Hernandez 3.00 8.00
TTA51 Cesar Izturis 6.00 15.00
TTA52 Oscar Salazar 2.00 5.00
TTA53 Pat Strange 2.00 5.00
TTA54 Rick Asadoorian 3.00 8.00
TTA55 Keith Reed 2.00 5.00
TTA56 Leo Estrella 2.00 5.00
TTA57 Wascar Serrano 2.00 5.00
TTA58 Richard Gomez 2.00 5.00
TTA59 Ramon Santiago 2.00 5.00
TTA60 Jovanny Sosa 2.00 5.00
TTA61 Aaron Rowand 8.00 20.00
TTA62 Junior Guerrero 2.00 5.00
TTA63 Luis Terrero 3.00 8.00
TTA64 Brian Sanches 2.00 5.00
TTA65 Scott Sobkowiak 2.00 5.00
TTA66 Gary Majewski 3.00 8.00
TTA67 Barry Zito 8.00 20.00
TTA68 Ryan Christianson 2.00 5.00
TTA69 Cristian Guerrero 2.00 5.00
TTA70 Tomas De La Rosa 2.00 5.00
TTA71 Andrew Beinbrink 3.00 8.00
TTA72 Ryan Knox 2.00 5.00
TTA73 Alex Graman 2.00 5.00
TTA74 Juan Guzman 2.00 5.00
TTA75 Ruben Salazar 2.00 5.00
TTA76 Luis Matos 2.00 5.00
TTA77 Tony Mota 2.00 5.00
TTA78 Doug Davis 6.00 15.00
TTA79 Ben Christensen 2.00 5.00
TTA80 Mike Lamb 6.00 15.00

2001 Topps

The 2001 Topps set featured 790 cards and was issued over two series. The set looks to bring back some of the heritage that Topps established in the past by bringing back Manager cards, dual-player prospect cards, and the 2000 season highlight cards. Notable Rookie Cards include Hee Seop Choi. Please note that some cards have been discovered with nothing printed on front but blank white except for the players name and 50th Topps anniversary logo printed in Gold. Factory sets include five special cards inserted specifically in those sets. Card number 7 was not issued as Topps continued to honor the memory of Mickey Mantle.

COMPLETE SET (790) 40.00 80.00
COMP.FACT.BLUE SET (795) 50.00 100.00
COMPLETE SERIES 1 (405) 20.00 40.00
COMPLETE SERIES 2 (385) 20.00 40.00
COMMON CARD (1-6/8-791) .07 .20
COMMON (352-376/727-751) .08 .25
CARD NO.7 DOES NOT EXIST
HISTORY SER.1 ODDS 1:911 H/R, 1:202 HTA
HISTORY SER.2 ODDS 1:686 H/R, 1:152 HTA
BO/DEION BAT SER.2 ODDS 1:30167 H/R
BO/DEION BAT SER.2 ODDS 1:6753 HTA
MANTLE VINTAGE SER.1 ODDS 1:27370 H/R
MANTLE VINTAGE SER.1 ODDS 1:6112 HTA
MANTLE VINTAGE SER.2 ODDS 1:21377 H/R
MANTLE VINTAGE SER.2 ODDS 1:4772 HTA
THOMSON/BRANCA SER.1 ODDS 1:7299 H/R
THOMSON/BRANCA SER.1 ODDS 1:1625 HTA
VINTAGE STARS SER.1 ODDS 1:4363 H/R
VINTAGE STARS SER.1 ODDS 1:970 HTA
VINTAGE STARS SER.2 ODDS 1:3656 H/R
VINTAGE STARS SER.2 ODDS 1:812 HTA
1 Cal Ripken .60 1.50
2 Chipper Jones .20 .50
3 Roger Cedeno .07 .20
4 Garret Anderson .07 .20
5 Robin Ventura .07 .20
6 Daryle Ward .07 .20
8 Craig Paquette .07 .20
9 Phil Nevin .07 .20
10 Jermaine Dye .07 .20
11 Chris Singleton .07 .20
12 Mike Stanton .07 .20
13 Brian Hunter .07 .20
14 Mike Redmond .07 .20
15 Jim Thome .10 .30
16 Brian Jordan .07 .20
17 Joe Girardi .07 .20
18 Steve Woodard .07 .20
19 Dustin Hermanson .07 .20
20 Shawn Green .07 .20
21 Todd Stottlemyre .07 .20
22 Dan Wilson .07 .20
23 Todd Pratt .07 .20
24 Derek Lowe .07 .20
25 Juan Gonzalez .07 .20
26 Clay Bellinger .07 .20
27 Jeff Fassero .07 .20
28 Pat Meares .07 .20
29 Eddie Taubensee .07 .20
30 Paul O'Neill .10 .30
31 Jeffrey Hammonds .07 .20
32 Pokey Reese .07 .20
33 Mike Mussina .10 .30
34 Rico Brogna .07 .20
35 Jay Buhner .07 .20
36 Steve Cox .07 .20
37 Quilvio Veras .07 .20
38 Marquis Grissom .07 .20
39 Shigetoshi Hasegawa .07 .20
40 Shane Reynolds .07 .20
41 Adam Piatt .07 .20
42 Luis Polonia .07 .20
43 Brook Fordyce .07 .20
44 Preston Wilson .07 .20
45 Ellis Burks .07 .20
46 Armando Rios .07 .20
47 Chuck Finley .07 .20
48 Dan Plesac .07 .20
49 Shannon Stewart .07 .20
50 Mark McGwire .50 1.25
51 Mark Loretta .07 .20
52 Gerald Williams .07 .20
53 Eric Young .07 .20
54 Peter Bergeron .07 .20
55 Dave Hansen .07 .20
56 Arthur Rhodes .07 .20
57 Bobby Jones .07 .20
58 Matt Clement .07 .20
59 Mike Benjamin .07 .20
60 Pedro Martinez .10 .30
61 Jose Canseco .10 .30
62 Matt Anderson .07 .20
63 Torii Hunter .07 .20
64 Carlos Lee .07 .20
65 David Cone .07 .20
66 Rey Sanchez .07 .20
67 Eric Chavez .07 .20
68 Rick Helling .07 .20
69 Manny Alexander .07 .20
70 John Franco .07 .20
71 Mike Bordick .07 .20
72 Andres Galarraga .07 .20
73 Jose Cruz Jr. .07 .20
74 Mike Matheny .07 .20
75 Randy Johnson .20 .50
76 Richie Sexson .07 .20
77 Vladimir Nunez .07 .20
78 Harold Baines .07 .20
79 Aaron Boone .07 .20
80 Darin Erstad .07 .20
81 Alex Gonzalez .07 .20
82 Gil Heredia .07 .20
83 Shane Andrews .07 .20
84 Todd Hundley .07 .20
85 Bill Mueller .07 .20
86 Mark McLemore .07 .20
87 Scott Spiezio .07 .20
88 Kevin McGlinchy .07 .20
89 Bubba Trammell .07 .20
90 Manny Ramirez .10 .30
91 Mike Lamb .07 .20
92 Scott Karl .07 .20
93 Brian Buchanan .07 .20
94 Chris Turner .07 .20
95 Mike Sweeney .07 .20
96 John Wetteland .07 .20
97 Rob Bell .07 .20
98 Pat Rapp .07 .20
99 John Burkett .07 .20
100 Derek Jeter .50 1.25
101 J.D. Drew .07 .20
102 Jose Offerman .07 .20
103 Rick Reed .07 .20
104 Will Clark .10 .30
105 Rickey Henderson .20 .50
106 Dave Berg .07 .20
107 Kirk Rueter .07 .20
108 Lee Stevens .07 .20
109 Jay Bell .07 .20
110 Fred McGriff .10 .30
111 Julio Zuleta .07 .20
112 Brian Anderson .07 .20
113 Orlando Cabrera .07 .20
114 Alex Fernandez .07 .20
115 Derek Bell .07 .20
116 Eric Owens .07 .20
117 Brian Bohanon .07 .20
118 Dennys Reyes .07 .20
119 Mike Stanley .07 .20
120 Jorge Posada .10 .30
121 Rich Becker .07 .20
122 Paul Konerko .07 .20
123 Mike Remlinger .07 .20
124 Travis Lee .07 .20
125 Ken Caminiti .07 .20
126 Kevin Barker .07 .20
127 Paul Quantrill .07 .20
128 Ozzie Guillen .07 .20
129 Kevin Tapani .07 .20
130 Mark Johnson .07 .20
131 Randy Wolf .07 .20
132 Michael Tucker .07 .20
133 Darren Lewis .07 .20
134 Joe Randa .07 .20
135 Jeff Cirillo .07 .20
136 David Ortiz .20 .50
137 Herb Perry .07 .20
138 Jeff Nelson .07 .20
139 Chris Stynes .07 .20
140 Johnny Damon .10 .30
141 Jeff Reboulet .07 .20
142 Jason Schmidt .07 .20
143 Charles Johnson .07 .20
144 Pat Burrell .07 .20
145 Gary Sheffield .07 .20
146 Tom Glavine .10 .30
147 Jason Isringhausen .07 .20
148 Chris Carpenter .07 .20
149 Jeff Suppan .07 .20
150 Ivan Rodriguez .10 .30
151 Luis Sojo .07 .20
152 Ron Villone .07 .20
153 Mike Sirotka .07 .20
154 Chuck Knoblauch .07 .20
155 Jason Kendall .07 .20
156 Dennis Cook .07 .20
157 Bobby Estalella .07 .20
158 Jose Guillen .07 .20
159 Thomas Howard .07 .20
160 Carlos Delgado .07 .20
161 Benji Gil .07 .20
162 Tim Bogar .07 .20
163 Kevin Elster .07 .20
164 Einar Diaz .07 .20
165 Andy Benes .07 .20
166 Adrian Beltre .07 .20
167 David Bell .07 .20
168 Turk Wendell .07 .20
169 Pete Harnisch .07 .20
170 Roger Clemens .40 1.00
171 Scott Williamson .07 .20
172 Kevin Jordan .07 .20
173 Brad Penny .07 .20
174 John Flaherty .07 .20
175 Troy Glaus .07 .20
176 Kevin Appier .07 .20
177 Walt Weiss .07 .20
178 Tyler Houston .07 .20
179 Michael Barrett .07 .20
180 Mike Hampton .07 .20
181 Francisco Cordova .07 .20
182 Mike Jackson .07 .20
183 David Segui .07 .20
184 Carlos Febles .07 .20
185 Roy Halladay .07 .20
186 Seth Etherton .07 .20
187 Charlie Hayes .07 .20
188 Fernando Tatis .07 .20
189 Steve Trachsel .07 .20
190 Livan Hernandez .07 .20
191 Joe Oliver .07 .20
192 Stan Javier .07 .20
193 B.J. Surhoff .07 .20
194 Rob Ducey .07 .20
195 Barry Larkin .10 .30

196 Danny Patterson .07 .20
197 Bobby Howry .07 .20
198 Dmitri Young .07 .20
199 Brian Hunter .07 .20
200 Alex Rodriguez .25 .60
201 Hideo Nomo .20 .50
202 Luis Alicea .07 .20
203 Warren Morris .07 .20
204 Antonio Alfonseca .07 .20
205 Edgardo Alfonzo .07 .20
206 Mark Grudzielanek .07 .20
207 Fernando Vina .07 .20
208 Willie Greene .07 .20
209 Homer Bush .07 .20
210 Jason Giambi .07 .20
211 Mike Morgan .07 .20
212 Steve Karsay .07 .20
213 Matt Lawton .07 .20
214 Wendell Magee Jr. .07 .20
215 Rusty Greer .07 .20
216 Keith Lockhart .07 .20
217 Billy Koch .07 .20
218 Todd Hollandsworth .07 .20
219 Raul Ibanez .07 .20
220 Tony Gwynn .25 .60
221 Carl Everett .07 .20
222 Hector Carrasco .07 .20
223 Jose Valentin .07 .20
224 Deivi Cruz .07 .20
225 Bret Boone .07 .20
226 Kurt Abbott .07 .20
227 Melvin Mora .07 .20
228 Danny Graves .07 .20
229 Jose Jimenez .07 .20
230 James Baldwin .07 .20
231 C.J. Nitkowski .07 .20
232 Jeff Zimmerman .07 .20
233 Mike Lowell .07 .20
234 Hideki Irabu .07 .20
235 Greg Vaughn .07 .20
236 Omar Daal .07 .20
237 Darren Dreifort .07 .20
238 Gil Meche .07 .20
239 Damian Jackson .07 .20
240 Frank Thomas .20 .50
241 Travis Miller .07 .20
242 Jeff Frye .07 .20
243 Dave Magadan .07 .20
244 Luis Castillo .07 .20
245 Bartolo Colon .07 .20
246 Steve Kline .07 .20
247 Shawon Dunston .07 .20
248 Rick Aguilera .07 .20
249 Omar Olivares .07 .20
250 Craig Biggio .10 .30
251 Scott Schoeneweis .07 .20
252 Dave Veres .07 .20
253 Ramon Martinez .07 .20
254 Jose Vidro .07 .20
255 Todd Helton .10 .30
256 Greg Norton .07 .20
257 Jacque Jones .07 .20
258 Jason Grimsley .07 .20
259 Dan Reichert .07 .20
260 Robb Nen .07 .20
261 Mark Clark .07 .20
262 Scott Hatteberg .07 .20
263 Doug Brocail .07 .20
264 Mark Johnson .07 .20
265 Eric Davis .07 .20
266 Terry Shumpert .07 .20
267 Kevin Millar .07 .20
268 Ismael Valdes .07 .20
269 Richard Hidalgo .07 .20
270 Randy Velarde .07 .20
271 Bengie Molina .07 .20
272 Tony Womack .07 .20
273 Enrique Wilson .07 .20
274 Jeff Brantley .07 .20
275 Rick Ankiel .07 .20
276 Terry Mulholland .07 .20
277 Ron Belliard .07 .20
278 Terrence Long .07 .20
279 Alberto Castillo .07 .20
280 Royce Clayton .07 .20
281 Joe McEwing .07 .20
282 Jason McDonald .07 .20
283 Ricky Bottalico .07 .20
284 Keith Foulke .07 .20
285 Brad Radke .07 .20
286 Gabe Kapler .07 .20
287 Pedro Astacio .07 .20
288 Armando Reynoso .07 .20
289 Darryl Kile .07 .20
290 Reggie Sanders .07 .20
291 Esteban Yan .07 .20
292 Joe Nathan .07 .20
293 Jay Payton .07 .20
294 Francisco Cordero .07 .20
295 Gregg Jefferies .07 .20
296 LaTroy Hawkins .07 .20
297 Jeff Tam RC .15 .40
298 Jacob Cruz .07 .20
299 Chris Holt .07 .20
300 Vladimir Guerrero .20 .50
301 Marvin Benard .07 .20
302 Alex Ramirez .07 .20
303 Mike Williams .07 .20
304 Sean Bergman .07 .20
305 Juan Encarnacion .07 .20
306 Russ Davis .07 .20
307 Hanley Frias .07 .20
308 Ramon Hernandez .07 .20
309 Matt Walbeck .07 .20
310 Bill Spiers .07 .20
311 Bob Wickman .07 .20
312 Sandy Alomar Jr. .07 .20
313 Eddie Guardado .07 .20
314 Shane Halter .07 .20
315 Geoff Jenkins .07 .20
316 Brian Meadows .07 .20
317 Damian Miller .07 .20
318 Darrin Fletcher .07 .20
319 Rafael Furcal .07 .20
320 Mark Grace .10 .30
321 Mark Mulder .07 .20
322 Joe Torre MG .10 .30
323 Bobby Cox MG .07 .20
324 Mike Scioscia MG .07 .20
325 Mike Hargrove MG .07 .20
326 Jimy Williams MG .07 .20
327 Jerry Manuel MG .07 .20
328 Buck Showalter MG .07 .20
329 Charlie Manuel MG .07 .20
330 Don Baylor MG .07 .20
331 Phil Garner MG .07 .20
332 Jack McKeon MG .07 .20
333 Tony Muser MG .07 .20
334 Buddy Bell MG .07 .20
335 Tom Kelly MG .07 .20
336 John Boles MG .07 .20
337 Art Howe MG .07 .20
338 Larry Dierker MG .07 .20
339 Lou Piniella MG .07 .20
340 Davey Johnson MG .07 .20
341 Larry Rothschild MG .07 .20
342 Davey Lopes MG .07 .20
343 Johnny Oates MG .07 .20
344 Felipe Alou MG .07 .20
345 Jim Fregosi MG .07 .20
346 Bobby Valentine MG .07 .20
347 Terry Francona MG .07 .20
348 Gene Lamont MG .07 .20
349 Tony LaRussa MG .07 .20
350 Bruce Bochy MG .07 .20
351 Dusty Baker MG .07 .20
352 A.Gonzalez .60 1.50
A.Johnson
353 M.Wheatland .08 .25
B.Digby
354 T.Johnson .08 .25
S.Thorman
355 P.Dumatrait .20 .50
A.Wainwright
356 David Parrish RC .08 .25
357 M.Folsom RC .15 .40
R.Baldelli
358 Dominic Rich RC .08 .25
359 M.Stodolka .08 .25
S.Burnett
360 D.Thompson .08 .25
C.Smith
361 D.Borrell RC .08 .25
J.Bourgeois RC
362 Josh Hamilton .20 .50
363 B.Zito .20 .50
C.Sabathia
364 Ben Sheets .20 .50
365 Howington .08 .25
Kalinowski
Girdley
366 Hee Seop Choi RC .20 .50
367 Bradley .15 .40
Ainsworth
Tsao
368 Glendenning .08 .25
Kelly
Silvestre
369 J.R. House .08 .25
370 Rafael Soriano RC .15 .40
371 T.Hafner RC 1.50 4.00
B.Jacobsen
372 Conti .08 .25
Wakeland
Cole
373 Seabol .30 .75
Huff
Crede
374 Everett .08 .25
Ortiz
Ginter
375 Hernandez .08 .25
Guzman
Eaton
376 Kielty .15 .40
Bradley
J.Rivera
377 Mark McGwire GM .25 .60
378 Don Larsen GM .07 .20
379 Bobby Thomson GM .07 .20
380 Bill Mazeroski GM .07 .20
381 Reggie Jackson GM .10 .30
382 Kirk Gibson GM .07 .20
383 Roger Maris GM .10 .30
384 Cal Ripken GM .30 .75
385 Hank Aaron GM .20 .50
386 Joe Carter GM .07 .20
387 Cal Ripken SH .60 1.50
388 Randy Johnson SH .10 .30
389 Ken Griffey Jr. SH .40 1.00
390 Troy Glaus SH .07 .20
391 Kazuhiro Sasaki SH .07 .20
392 S.Sosa .10 .30
T.Glaus LL
393 T.Helton .07 .20
E.Martinez LL
394 T.Helton .20 .50
N.Garciaparra LL
395 B.Bonds .30 .75
J.Giambi LL
396 T.Helton .07 .20
M.Ramirez LL
397 T.Helton .07 .20
D.Erstad LL
398 K.Brown .10 .30
P.Martinez LL
399 R.Johnson .10 .30
P.Martinez LL
400 Will Clark HL .10 .30
401 New York Mets HL .20 .50
402 New York Yankees HL .30 .75
403 Seattle Mariners HL .07 .20
404 Mike Hampton HL .07 .20
405 New York Yankees HL .40 1.00
406 New York Yankees Champs .75 2.00
407 Jeff Bagwell .10 .30
408 Brant Brown .07 .20
409 Brad Fullmer .07 .20
410 Dean Palmer .07 .20
411 Greg Zaun .07 .20
412 Jose Vizcaino .07 .20
413 Jeff Abbott .07 .20
414 Travis Fryman .07 .20
415 Mike Cameron .07 .20
416 Matt Mantei .07 .20
417 Alan Benes .07 .20
418 Mickey Morandini .07 .20
419 Troy Percival .07 .20
420 Eddie Perez .07 .20
421 Vernon Wells .07 .20
422 Ricky Gutierrez .07 .20
423 Carlos Hernandez .07 .20
424 Chan Ho Park .07 .20
425 Armando Benitez .07 .20
426 Sidney Ponson .07 .20
427 Adrian Brown .07 .20
428 Ruben Mateo .07 .20
429 Alex Ochoa .07 .20
430 Jose Rosado .07 .20
431 Masato Yoshii .07 .20
432 Corey Koskie .07 .20
433 Andy Pettitte .10 .30
434 Brian Daubach .07 .20
435 Sterling Hitchcock .07 .20
436 Timo Perez .07 .20
437 Shawn Estes .07 .20
438 Tony Armas Jr. .07 .20
439 Danny Bautista .07 .20
440 Randy Winn .07 .20
441 Wilson Alvarez .07 .20
442 Rondell White .07 .20
443 Jeromy Burnitz .07 .20
444 Kelvim Escobar .07 .20
445 Paul Bako .07 .20
446 Javier Vazquez .07 .20
447 Eric Gagne .07 .20
448 Kenny Lofton .07 .20
449 Mark Kotsay .07 .20
450 Jamie Moyer .07 .20
451 Delino DeShields .07 .20
452 Rey Ordonez .07 .20
453 Russ Ortiz .07 .20
454 Dave Burba .07 .20
455 Eric Karros .07 .20
456 Felix Martinez .07 .20
457 Tony Batista .07 .20
458 Bobby Higginson .07 .20
459 Jeff D'Amico .07 .20
460 Shane Spencer .07 .20
461 Brent Mayne .07 .20
462 Glendon Rusch .07 .20
463 Chris Gomez .07 .20
464 Jeff Shaw .07 .20
465 Damon Buford .07 .20
466 Mike DiFelice .07 .20
467 Jimmy Haynes .07 .20
468 Billy Wagner .07 .20
469 A.J. Hinch .07 .20
470 Gary DiSarcina .07 .20
471 Tom Lampkin .07 .20
472 Adam Eaton .07 .20
473 Brian Giles .07 .20
474 John Thomson .07 .20
475 Cal Eldred .07 .20
476 Ramiro Mendoza .07 .20
477 Scott Sullivan .07 .20
478 Scott Rolen .10 .30
479 Todd Ritchie .07 .20
480 Pablo Ozuna .07 .20
481 Carl Pavano .07 .20
482 Matt Morris .07 .20
483 Matt Stairs .07 .20
484 Tim Belcher .07 .20
485 Lance Berkman .07 .20
486 Brian Meadows .07 .20
487 Bob Abreu .07 .20
488 John VanderWal .07 .20
489 Donnie Sadler .07 .20
490 Damion Easley .07 .20
491 David Justice .07 .20
492 Ray Durham .07 .20
493 Todd Zeile .07 .20
494 Desi Relaford .07 .20
495 Cliff Floyd .07 .20
496 Scott Downs .07 .20
497 Barry Bonds .50 1.25
498 Jeff D'Amico .07 .20
499 Octavio Dotel .07 .20
500 Kent Mercker .07 .20
501 Craig Grebeck .07 .20
502 Roberto Hernandez .07 .20
503 Matt Williams .07 .20
504 Bruce Aven .07 .20
505 Brett Tomko .07 .20
506 Kris Benson .07 .20
507 Neifi Perez .07 .20
508 Alfonso Soriano .10 .30
509 Keith Osik .07 .20
510 Matt Franco .07 .20
511 Steve Finley .07 .20
512 Olmedo Saenz .07 .20
513 Esteban Loaiza .07 .20
514 Adam Kennedy .07 .20
515 Scott Elarton .07 .20
516 Moises Alou .07 .20
517 Bryan Rekar .07 .20
518 Darryl Hamilton .07 .20
519 Osvaldo Fernandez .07 .20
520 Kip Wells .07 .20
521 Bernie Williams .10 .30
522 Mike Darr .07 .20
523 Marlon Anderson .07 .20
524 Derrek Lee .10 .30
525 Ugueth Urbina .07 .20
526 Vinny Castilla .07 .20
527 David Wells .07 .20
528 Jason Marquis .07 .20
529 Orlando Palmeiro .07 .20
530 Carlos Perez .07 .20
531 J.T. Snow .07 .20
532 Al Leiter .07 .20
533 Jimmy Anderson .07 .20
534 Brett Laxton .07 .20
535 Butch Huskey .07 .20
536 Orlando Hernandez .07 .20
537 Magglio Ordonez .07 .20
538 Willie Blair .07 .20
539 Kevin Sefcik .07 .20
540 Chad Curtis .07 .20
541 John Halama .07 .20
542 Andy Fox .07 .20
543 Juan Guzman .07 .20
544 Frank Menechino RC .07 .20
545 Raul Mondesi .07 .20
546 Tim Salmon .10 .30
547 Ryan Rupe .07 .20
548 Jeff Reed .07 .20
549 Mike Mordecai .07 .20
550 Jeff Kent .07 .20
551 Wiki Gonzalez .07 .20
552 Kenny Rogers .07 .20
553 Kevin Young .07 .20
554 Brian Johnson .07 .20
555 Tom Goodwin .07 .20
556 Tony Clark .07 .20
557 Mac Suzuki .07 .20
558 Brian Moehler .07 .20
559 Jim Parque .07 .20
560 Mariano Rivera .20 .50
561 Trot Nixon .07 .20
562 Mike Mussina .10 .30
563 Nelson Figueroa .07 .20
564 Alex Gonzalez .07 .20
565 Benny Agbayani .07 .20
566 Ed Sprague .07 .20
567 Scott Erickson .07 .20
568 Abraham Nunez .07 .20
569 Jerry DiPoto .07 .20
570 Sean Casey .07 .20
571 Wilton Veras .07 .20
572 Joe Mays .07 .20
573 Bill Simas .07 .20
574 Doug Glanville .07 .20
575 Scott Sauerbeck .07 .20
576 Ben Davis .07 .20
577 Jesus Sanchez .07 .20
578 Ricardo Rincon .07 .20
579 John Olerud .07 .20
580 Curt Schilling .07 .20
581 Alex Cora .07 .20
582 Pat Hentgen .07 .20
583 Javy Lopez .07 .20
584 Ben Grieve .07 .20
585 Frank Castillo .07 .20
586 Kevin Stocker .07 .20
587 Mark Sweeney .07 .20
588 Ray Lankford .07 .20
589 Turner Ward .07 .20
590 Felipe Crespo .07 .20
591 Omar Vizquel .10 .30
592 Mike Lieberthal .07 .20
593 Ken Griffey Jr. .40 1.00
594 Troy O'Leary .07 .20
595 Dave Mlicki .07 .20
596 Manny Ramirez Sox .10 .30
597 Mike Lansing .07 .20
598 Rich Aurilia .07 .20
599 Russell Branyan .07 .20
600 Russ Johnson .07 .20
601 Greg Colbrunn .07 .20
602 Andruw Jones .10 .30
603 Henry Blanco .07 .20
604 Jarrod Washburn .07 .20
605 Tony Eusebio .07 .20
606 Aaron Sele .07 .20
607 Charles Nagy .07 .20
608 Ryan Klesko .07 .20
609 Dante Bichette .07 .20
610 Bill Haselman .07 .20
611 Jerry Spradlin .07 .20
612 Alex Rodriguez .25 .60
613 Jose Silva .07 .20
614 Darren Oliver .07 .20
615 Pat Mahomes .07 .20
616 Roberto Alomar .10 .30
617 Edgar Renteria .07 .20
618 Jon Lieber .07 .20
619 John Rocker .07 .20
620 Miguel Tejada .07 .20
621 Mo Vaughn .07 .20
622 Jose Lima .07 .20
623 Kerry Wood .07 .20
624 Mike Timlin .07 .20
625 Wil Cordero .07 .20
626 Albert Belle .07 .20
627 Bobby Jones .07 .20
628 Doug Mirabelli .07 .20
629 Jason Tyner .07 .20
630 Andy Ashby .07 .20
631 Jose Hernandez .07 .20
632 Devon White .07 .20
633 Ruben Rivera .07 .20
634 Steve Parris .07 .20
635 David McCarty .07 .20
636 Jose Canseco .10 .30
637 Todd Walker .07 .20
638 Stan Spencer .07 .20
639 Wayne Gomes .07 .20
640 Freddy Garcia .07 .20
641 Jeremy Giambi .07 .20
642 Luis Lopez .07 .20
643 John Smoltz .10 .30
644 Kelly Stinnett .07 .20
645 Kevin Brown .07 .20
646 Wilton Guerrero .07 .20
647 Al Martin .07 .20
648 Woody Williams .07 .20
649 Brian Rose .07 .20
650 Rafael Palmeiro .10 .30
651 Pete Schourek .07 .20
652 Kevin Jarvis .07 .20
653 Mark Redman .07 .20
654 Ricky Ledee .07 .20
655 Larry Walker .07 .20
656 Paul Byrd .07 .20
657 Jason Bere .07 .20
658 Rick White .07 .20
659 Calvin Murray .07 .20
660 Greg Maddux .30 .75
661 Ron Gant .07 .20
662 Eli Marrero .07 .20
663 Graeme Lloyd .07 .20
664 Trevor Hoffman .07 .20
665 Nomar Garciaparra .30 .75
666 Glenallen Hill .07 .20
667 Matt LeCroy .07 .20
668 Justin Thompson .07 .20
669 Brady Anderson .07 .20
670 Miguel Batista .07 .20
671 Erubiel Durazo .07 .20
672 Kevin Millwood .07 .20
673 Mitch Meluskey .07 .20
674 Luis Gonzalez .07 .20
675 Edgar Martinez .10 .30
676 Robert Person .07 .20
677 Benito Santiago .07 .20
678 Todd Jones .07 .20
679 Tino Martinez .10 .30
680 Carlos Beltran .07 .20
681 Gabe White .07 .20
682 Bret Saberhagen .07 .20
683 Jeff Conine .07 .20
684 Jaret Wright .07 .20
685 Bernard Gilkey .07 .20
686 Garrett Stephenson .07 .20
687 Jamey Wright .07 .20
688 Sammy Sosa .20 .50
689 John Jaha .07 .20
690 Ramon Martinez .07 .20
691 Robert Fick .07 .20
692 Eric Milton .07 .20
693 Denny Neagle .07 .20
694 Ron Coomer .07 .20
695 John Valentin .07 .20
696 Placido Polanco .07 .20
697 Tim Hudson .07 .20
698 Marty Cordova .07 .20
699 Chad Kreuter .07 .20
700 Frank Catalanotto .07 .20
701 Tim Wakefield .07 .20
702 Jim Edmonds .07 .20
703 Michael Tucker .07 .20
704 Cristian Guzman .07 .20
705 Joey Hamilton .07 .20
706 Mike Piazza .30 .75
707 Dave Martinez .07 .20
708 Mike Hampton .07 .20
709 Bobby Bonilla .07 .20
710 Juan Pierre .07 .20
711 John Parrish .07 .20
712 Kory DeHaan .07 .20
713 Brian Tollberg .07 .20
714 Chris Truby .07 .20
715 Emil Brown .07 .20
716 Ryan Dempster .07 .20
717 Rich Garces .07 .20
718 Mike Myers .07 .20
719 Luis Ordaz .07 .20
720 Kazuhiro Sasaki .07 .20
721 Mark Quinn .07 .20
722 Ramon Ortiz .07 .20
723 Kerry Ligtenberg .07 .20
724 Rolando Arrojo .07 .20
725 Tsuyoshi Shinjo RC .20 .50
726 Ichiro Suzuki RC 12.00 30.00

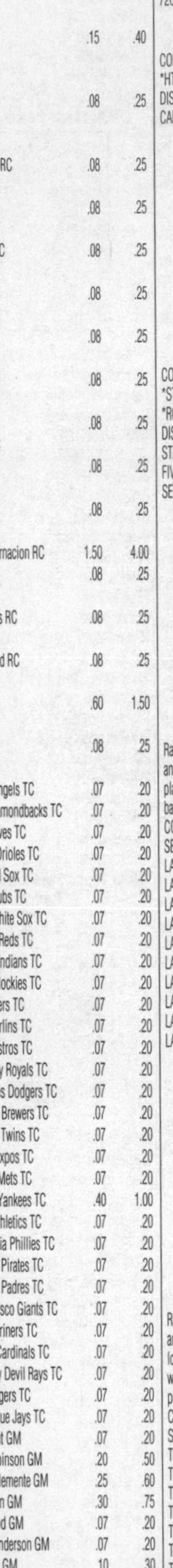

727 Oswalt .30 .75
Strange
Rauch
728 Jake Peavy RC UER .75 2.00
729 S.Smyth RC .08 .25
Bynum
Haynes
730 Cuddyer .08 .25
Lawrence
Freeman
731 C.Pena .08 .25
Barnes
Wise
732 Dawkins/Almonte/Lopez .08 .25
733 Escobar .08 .25
Valent
Wilkerson
734 Hall .08 .25
Barajas
Goldbach
735 Romano .15 .40
Giles
Ozuna
736 D.Brown .08 .25
Cust
V.Wells
737 L.Montanez RC .08 .25
D.Espinosa
738 J.Wayne RC .08 .25
A.Pluta RC
739 J.Axelson RC .08 .25
C.Cali RC
740 S.Boyd RC .08 .25
C.Morris RC
741 T.Arko RC .08 .25
D.Moylan RC
742 L.Cotto RC .08 .25
L.Escobar
743 B.Mims RC .08 .25
B.Williams RC
744 C.Russ RC .08 .25
B.Edwards
745 J.Torres .08 .25
B.Diggins
746 Edwin Encarnacion RC 1.50 4.00
747 B.Bass RC .08 .25
O.Ayala RC
748 M.Matthews RC .08 .25
J.Kaanoi
749 S.McFarland RC .08 .25
A.Sterrett RC
750 D.Krynzel .60 1.50
G.Sizemore
751 K.Bucktrot .08 .25
D.Sardinha
752 Anaheim Angels TC .07 .20
753 Arizona Diamondbacks TC .07 .20
754 Atlanta Braves TC .07 .20
755 Baltimore Orioles TC .07 .20
756 Boston Red Sox TC .07 .20
757 Chicago Cubs TC .07 .20
758 Chicago White Sox TC .07 .20
759 Cincinnati Reds TC .07 .20
760 Cleveland Indians TC .07 .20
761 Colorado Rockies TC .07 .20
762 Detroit Tigers TC .07 .20
763 Florida Marlins TC .07 .20
764 Houston Astros TC .07 .20
765 Kansas City Royals TC .07 .20
766 Los Angeles Dodgers TC .07 .20
767 Milwaukee Brewers TC .07 .20
768 Minnesota Twins TC .07 .20
769 Montreal Expos TC .07 .20
770 New York Mets TC .07 .20
771 New York Yankees TC .40 1.00
772 Oakland Athletics TC .07 .20
773 Philadelphia Phillies TC .07 .20
774 Pittsburgh Pirates TC .07 .20
775 San Diego Padres TC .07 .20
776 San Francisco Giants TC .07 .20
777 Seattle Mariners TC .07 .20
778 St. Louis Cardinals TC .07 .20
779 Tampa Bay Devil Rays TC .07 .20
780 Texas Rangers TC .07 .20
781 Toronto Blue Jays TC .07 .20
782 Bucky Dent GM .07 .20
783 Jackie Robinson GM .20 .50
784 Roberto Clemente GM .25 .60
785 Nolan Ryan GM .30 .75
786 Kerry Wood GM .07 .20
787 Rickey Henderson GM .07 .20
788 Lou Brock GM .10 .30
789 David Wells GM .07 .20
790 Andruw Jones GM .07 .20
791 Carlton Fisk GM .07 .20
TK B.Jackson/D.Sanders Bat 30.00 60.00
NNO B.Thomson/R.Branca AU 30.00 60.00

2001 Topps Employee

*STARS: 6X TO 15X BASIC CARDS
CARD NO.7 DOES NOT EXIST
726 Ichiro Suzuki 40.00 80.00

2001 Topps Gold

COMPLETE SET (790) 60.00 120.
*STARS: 10X TO 25X BASIC CARDS
*PROSPECTS 352-376/725/751: 4X TO 10X
*ROOKIES 352-376/725-751: 4X TO 10X
SER.1 STATED ODDS 1:17 H/R, 1:4 HTA
SER.2 STATED ODDS 1:14 H/R, 1:3 HTA
STATED PRINT RUN 2001 SERIAL #'d SETS
CARD NO.7 DOES NOT EXIST
726 Ichiro Suzuki 200.00 500.

2001 Topps Home Team Advantage

COMP.HTA.GOLD SET (790) 60.00 120.
*HTA: .75X TO 2X BASIC CARDS
DISTRIBUTED IN FACT.SET FORM ONLY
CARD NO.7 DOES NOT EXIST

2001 Topps Limited

COMP.FACT.SET (790) 60.00 150.
*STARS: 1.5X TO 4X BASIC CARDS
*ROOKIES: 1.5X TO 4X BASIC CARDS
DISTRIBUTED ONLY IN FACTORY SET FORM
STATED PRINT RUN 3805 SETS
FIVE ARCH.RSV.FUTURE REPRINTS PER SET
SEE TOPPS ARCH.RSV.FOR INSERT PRICING

2001 Topps A Look Ahead

Randomly inserted into packs at 1:25 Hobby/Retail and 1:5 HTA, this 10-card insert takes a look a players that are on their way to Cooperstown. Card backs carry a "LA" prefix.
COMPLETE SET (10) 12.50 30.
SER.1 STATED ODDS 1:25 H/R, 1:5 HTA
LA1 Vladimir Guerrero 1.00 2.
LA2 Derek Jeter 2.50 6.
LA3 Todd Helton .60 1.
LA4 Alex Rodriguez 1.25 3.
LA5 Ken Griffey Jr. 2.00 5.
LA6 Nomar Garciaparra 1.50 4.
LA7 Chipper Jones 1.00 2.
LA8 Ivan Rodriguez .60 1.
LA9 Pedro Martinez .60 1.
LA10 Rick Ankiel .40 1.

2001 Topps A Tradition Continues

Randomly inserted into packs at 1:17 Hobby/Retail and 1:5 HTA, this 30-card insert features players th look to carry the tradition of Major League Baseball well into the 21st century. Card backs carry a "TRC" prefix.
COMPLETE SET (30) 50.00 100.
SER.1 STATED ODDS 1:17 H/R, 1:5 HTA
TRC1 Chipper Jones 1.25 3.
TRC2 Cal Ripken 4.00 10.
TRC3 Mike Piazza 2.00 5.
TRC4 Ken Griffey Jr. 2.50 6.
TRC5 Randy Johnson 1.25 3.
TRC6 Derek Jeter 3.00 8.
TRC7 Scott Rolen .75 2.
TRC8 Nomar Garciaparra 2.00 5.
TRC9 Roberto Alomar .75 2.
TRC10 Greg Maddux 2.00 5.
TRC11 Ivan Rodriguez .75 2.
TRC12 Jeff Bagwell .75 2.
TRC13 Alex Rodriguez 1.50 4.
TRC14 Pedro Martinez .75 2.
TRC15 Sammy Sosa 1.25 3.
TRC16 Jim Edmonds .50 1.
TRC17 Mo Vaughn .50 1.

C18 Barry Bonds	3.00	8.00
C19 Larry Walker	.50	1.25
C20 Mark McGwire	3.00	8.00
C21 Vladimir Guerrero	1.25	3.00
C22 Andruw Jones	.75	2.00
C23 Todd Helton	.75	2.00
C24 Kevin Brown	.50	1.25
C25 Tony Gwynn	1.50	4.00
C26 Manny Ramirez	.75	2.00
C27 Roger Clemens	2.50	6.00
C28 Frank Thomas	1.25	3.00
C29 Shawn Green	.50	1.25
C30 Jim Thome	.75	2.00

001 Topps Base Hit Autograph Relics

erted in series two packs at a rate of one in 1,462 obby or retail packs and one in 325 HTA packs, se 28 cards features managers along with a game-ed base piece and an autograph.

R.2 STATED ODDS 1:1462 H/R, 1:325 HTA		
1 Mike Scioscia	40.00	80.00
2 Larry Dierker	20.00	50.00
3 Art Howe	40.00	80.00
4 Jim Fregosi	20.00	50.00
5 Bobby Cox	50.00	100.00
6 Davey Lopes	20.00	50.00
7 Tony LaRussa	40.00	80.00
8 Don Baylor	40.00	100.00
9 Larry Rothschild	20.00	50.00
10 Buck Showalter	20.00	50.00
11 Davey Johnson	20.00	50.00
12 Felipe Alou	40.00	80.00
13 Charlie Manuel	30.00	60.00
14 Lou Piniella	40.00	80.00
15 John Boles	20.00	50.00
16 Bobby Valentine	40.00	80.00
17 Mike Hargrove	40.00	80.00
18 Bruce Bochy	20.00	50.00
19 Terry Francona	60.00	120.00
20 Gene Lamont	20.00	50.00
21 Johnny Oates	50.00	100.00
22 Jimy Williams	20.00	50.00
23 Jack McKeon	40.00	80.00
24 Buddy Bell	40.00	80.00
25 Tony Muser	20.00	50.00
26 Phil Garner	40.00	80.00
27 Tom Kelly	20.00	50.00
28 Jerry Manuel	20.00	50.00

2001 Topps Before There Was Topps

sued in series two packs at a rate of one in 25 bby/retail packs and one in five HTA packs; these cards feature superstars who concluded their reer before Topps started their dominance of the rd market.

OMPLETE SET (10)	15.00	40.00
R.2 STATED ODDS 1:25 H/R, 1:5 HTA		
1 Lou Gehrig	2.50	6.00
2 Babe Ruth	4.00	10.00
3 Cy Young	1.25	3.00
4 Walter Johnson	1.25	3.00
5 Ty Cobb	2.00	5.00
6 Rogers Hornsby	1.25	3.00
7 Honus Wagner	1.25	3.00
8 Christy Mathewson	1.25	3.00
9 Grover Alexander	1.25	3.00
10 Joe DiMaggio	2.50	6.00

2001 Topps Combos

andomly inserted into packs at a rate of 1:12 obby/Retail and 1:4 HTA, this 20-card insert set airs up players that have put up similar statistics roughout their carrers. Card backs carry a "TC" efix. Instead of having photographs, these cards ature drawings of the featured players.

OMPLETE SET (20)	12.50	30.00
OMPLETE SERIES 1 (10)	6.00	15.00
OMPLETE SERIES 2 (10)	6.00	15.00
R.1 AND SER.2 ODDS 1:12 H/R, 1:4 HTA		
C1 Decades of Excellence	2.00	5.00
C2 Power Corner	.60	1.50
C3 Glove Birds	1.50	4.00
C4 Mound Marksmen	.60	1.50
C5 Tools of Success	.60	1.50
C6 Shortstop Supremacy	.75	2.00
C7 Big Red Machine	.75	2.00
C8 Latin Heat	.60	1.50
C9 Home Run Royalty	1.00	2.50
C10 New York State of Mind	.60	1.50
C11 Dodger Blue	1.25	3.00
C12 60 Home Run Club	1.50	4.00
C13 Heroes of Fenway	1.25	3.00
C14 Mound Masters	1.00	2.50
C15 Sweetness	1.25	3.00
C16 Ironmen	2.00	5.00
TC17 Southpaw Greatness	2.00	5.00
TC18 Best There is Was	.75	2.00
TC19 All in the Family	1.50	4.00
TC20 Barrier Breakers	.60	1.50

2001 Topps Golden Anniversary

Randomly inserted into packs at 1:10 Hobby/Retail and 1:1 HTA, this 50-card insert celibrates Topp's 50th Anniversary by taking a look at some of the all-time greats. Card backs carry a "GA" prefix.

COMPLETE SET (50)	40.00	80.00
SER.1 STATED ODDS 1:10 H/R, 1:1 HTA		
GA1 Hank Aaron	2.00	5.00
GA2 Ernie Banks	1.00	2.50
GA3 Mike Schmidt	2.00	5.00
GA4 Willie Mays	2.00	5.00
GA5 Johnny Bench	1.00	2.50
GA6 Tom Seaver	.60	1.50
GA7 Frank Robinson	.60	1.50
GA8 Sandy Koufax	3.00	8.00
GA9 Bob Gibson	.60	1.50
GA10 Ted Williams	2.00	5.00
GA11 Cal Ripken	3.00	8.00
GA12 Tony Gwynn	1.25	3.00
GA13 Mark McGwire	2.50	6.00
GA14 Ken Griffey Jr.	2.00	5.00
GA15 Greg Maddux	1.50	4.00
GA16 Roger Clemens	2.00	5.00
GA17 Barry Bonds	2.50	6.00
GA18 Rickey Henderson	1.00	2.50
GA19 Mike Piazza	1.50	4.00
GA20 Jose Canseco	.60	1.50
GA21 Derek Jeter	2.50	6.00
GA22 Nomar Garciaparra	1.50	4.00
GA23 Alex Rodriguez	1.25	3.00
GA24 Sammy Sosa	1.00	2.50
GA25 Ivan Rodriguez	.60	1.50
GA26 Vladimir Guerrero	1.00	2.50
GA27 Chipper Jones	1.00	2.50
GA28 Jeff Bagwell	.60	1.50
GA29 Pedro Martinez	.60	1.50
GA30 Randy Johnson	1.00	2.50
GA31 Pat Burrell	.40	1.00
GA32 Josh Hamilton	.75	2.00
GA33 Ryan Anderson	.40	1.00
GA34 Corey Patterson	.40	1.00
GA35 Eric Munson	.40	1.00
GA36 Sean Burroughs	.40	1.00
GA37 C.C. Sabathia	.40	1.00
GA38 Chin-Feng Chen	.40	1.00
GA39 Barry Zito	.60	1.50
GA40 Adrian Gonzalez	2.50	6.00
GA41 Mark McGwire	2.50	6.00
GA42 Nomar Garciaparra	1.50	4.00
GA43 Todd Helton	.60	1.50
GA44 Matt Williams	.40	1.00
GA45 Troy Glaus	.40	1.00
GA46 Geoff Jenkins	.40	1.00
GA47 Frank Thomas	1.00	2.50
GA48 Mo Vaughn	.40	1.00
GA49 Barry Larkin	.60	1.50
GA50 J.D. Drew	.40	1.00

2001 Topps Golden Anniversary Autographs

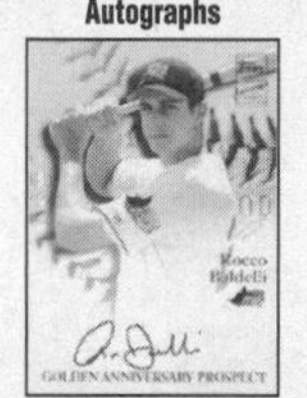

Randomly inserted into packs, this 98-card insert features authentic autographs of both modern day and former greats. Card backs carry a "GAA" prefix followed by the players initials. Please note that the Andy Pafko, Lou Brock, Rafael Furcal and Todd Zeile cards all packed out in series one packs as exchange cards with a redemption deadline of November 30th, 2001. In addition, Carlos Silva, Eddy Furniss, Phil Merrell and Carlos Silva packed out as exchange cards in series two packs with a redemption deadline of April 30th, 2003.

SER.1 GROUP A 1:22866 H/R, 1:5056 HTA		
SER.1 GROUP B 1:3054 H/R, 1:678 HTA		
SER.2 GROUP B 1:11781 H/R, 1:2612 HTA		
SER.1 GROUP C 1:1431 H/R, 1:318 HTA		
SER.2 GROUP C 1:4236 H/R, 1:942 HTA		
SER.1 GROUP D 1:18339H/R,1:4,095HTA		
SER.2 GROUP D 1:981 H/R, 1:218 HTA		
SER.1 GROUP E 1:13737 H/R,1:3,056HTA		
SER.2 GROUP E 1:14157 H/R, 1:3139 HTA		
SER.1 GROUP F 1:11015 H/R, 1:2438 HTA		
SER.2 GROUP F 1:3532 H/R, 1:785 HTA		
SER.1 GROUP G 1:625 H/R, 1:139 HTA		
SER.2 GROUP G 1:3532 H/R, 1:785 HTA		
SER.2 GROUP H 1:2,037 H/R, 1:452 HTA		
SER.2 GROUP I 1:481 H/R, 1:107 HTA		
SER.1 OVERALL 1:346 H/R, 1:77 HTA		
SER.2 OVERALL 1:216 H/R, 1:48 HTA		
SER.1 EXCH.DEADLINE 11/30/01		
SER.2 EXCH.DEADLINE 04/30/03		
SER.2 GROUP A 1:10583 H/R, 1:2355 HTA		
GAAAG Adrian Gonzalez G1-I2	4.00	10.00
GAAAH Aaron Herr I2	5.00	12.00
GAAAJ Adam Johnson G1-I2	4.00	10.00
GAAAO Augie Ojeda B2	10.00	25.00
GAAAP Andy Pafko C1	8.00	20.00
GAABB Barry Bonds B2	125.00	300.00
GAABE Brian Esposito I2	4.00	10.00
GAABG Bob Gibson C2	20.00	50.00
GAABK Bobby Kielty I2	6.00	15.00
GAABO Ben Oglivie D2	4.00	10.00
GAABR Brooks Robinson B1	30.00	80.00
GAABT Brian Tollberg I2	4.00	10.00
GAACC Chris Clapinski I2	6.00	15.00
GAACD Chad Durbin I2	6.00	15.00
GAACE Carl Erskine D2	4.00	10.00
GAACJ Chipper Jones B1	60.00	120.00
GAACL Colby Lewis I2	6.00	15.00
GAACR Chris Richard I2	6.00	15.00
GAACS Carlos Silva I2	12.00	30.00
GAACY Carl Yastrzemski C2	40.00	100.00
GAADA Dick Allen C1	10.00	25.00
GAADA Denny Abreu I2	4.00	10.00
GAADG Dick Groat D2	6.00	15.00
GAADT Derek Thompson I2	6.00	15.00
GAAEB Ernie Banks B1	100.00	250.00
GAAEB Eric Byrnes I2	10.00	25.00
GAAEF Eddy Furniss I2	4.00	10.00
GAAEM Eric Munson G2	4.00	10.00
GAAER Erasmo Ramirez I2	4.00	10.00
GAAGB George Bell D2	5.00	12.00
GAAGG Geraldo Guzman I2	4.00	10.00
GAAGM Gary Matthews D2	6.00	15.00
GAAGS Grady Sizemore I2	4.00	10.00
GAAGT Garry Templeton C1	4.00	10.00
GAAHA Hank Aaron B1	200.00	400.00
GAAJB Johnny Bench C2	50.00	100.00
GAAJC Jorge Cantu I2	6.00	15.00
GAAJL John Lackey I2	8.00	20.00
GAAJM Jason Marquis G1	4.00	10.00
GAAJR Joe Rudi C1	6.00	15.00
GAAJR Juan Rincon I2	6.00	15.00
GAAJS Juan Salas I2	4.00	10.00
GAAJV Jose Vidro F1	4.00	10.00
GAAJW Justin Wayne H2	4.00	10.00
GAAKG Kevin Gregg B2	8.00	20.00
GAAKH Ken Holtzman D2	6.00	15.00
GAAKT Kent Tekulve D2	8.00	20.00
GAALB Lou Brock B1	6.00	15.00
GAALM Luis Montanez H2	4.00	10.00
GAALR Luis Rivas I2	4.00	10.00
GAAMB Milton Bradley G2	6.00	15.00
GAAMC Mike Cuellar C1	8.00	20.00
GAAMG Mike Glendenning I2	4.00	10.00
GAAML Matt Lawton F2	5.00	12.00
GAAML Mike Lamb G1	4.00	10.00
GAAMM Mike Mussina	12.00	30.00
GAAMO Magglio Ordonez B1	12.00	30.00
GAAMS Mike Schmidt B1	60.00	120.00
GAAMS Mike Sweeney F2	4.00	10.00
GAAMS Mike Stodolka I2	4.00	10.00
GAAMW Matt Wheatland G1	4.00	10.00
GAAMW Michael Wenner I2	4.00	10.00
GAANG Nick Green I2	4.00	10.00
GAANJ Neil Jenkins I2	8.00	20.00
GAANR Nolan Ryan A2	175.00	350.00
GAAPB Pat Burrell G1	6.00	15.00
GAAPM Phil Merrell I2	4.00	10.00
GAARA Rick Ankiel D1	6.00	15.00
GAARB Rocco Baldelli G1-I2	4.00	10.00
GAARC Rod Carew B1	12.00	30.00
GAARF Rafael Furcal G1	6.00	15.00
GAARJ Reggie Jackson A2	125.00	200.00
GAARS Ron Swoboda C1	6.00	15.00
GAASH Scott Heard G1	4.00	10.00
GAASK Sandy Koufax A1	400.00	800.00
GAASM Stan Musial A2	175.00	300.00
GAASR Scott Rolen F2	5.00	12.00
GAAST Scott Thorman I2	4.00	10.00
GAATA Tony Alvarez I2	8.00	20.00
GAATH Todd Helton B2	4.00	10.00
GAATJ Tripper Johnson I2	4.00	10.00
GAATS Tom Seaver A2	75.00	200.00
GAAVL Vernon Law C1	6.00	15.00
GAAWD Willie Davis D2	10.00	25.00
GAAWF Whitey Ford C2	40.00	80.00
GAAWH Willie Hernandez C1	4.00	10.00
GAAWM Willie Mays A1	350.00	450.00
GAAWW Wilbur Wood D2	6.00	15.00
GAAYB Yogi Berra B1	50.00	120.00
GAAYH Yamid Haad I2	6.00	15.00
GAAYT Yorvit Torrealba I2	10.00	25.00
GAACCS Corey Smith I2	4.00	10.00
GAAGHB George Brett A2	125.00	250.00
GAAJDD J.D. Drew E2	5.00	12.00
GAAMAB Mike Bynum I2	4.00	10.00
GAAMFL Mike Lockwood I2	4.00	10.00
GAAMJS Mike Stodolka G1	4.00	10.00
GAAMJW Matt Wheatland I2	6.00	15.00
GAATDLR Tomas De la Rosa I2	6.00	15.00

2001 Topps Hit Parade Bat Relics

Issued in retail packs at odds of one in 2,607 these six cards feature players who have achieved major career milestones along with a piece of memorabilia.

SER.2 STATED ODDS 1:2607 RETAIL		
HP1 Reggie Jackson	12.50	30.00
HP2 Dave Winfield	12.50	30.00
HP3 Eddie Murray	12.50	30.00
HP4 Rickey Henderson	12.50	30.00
HP5 Robin Yount	12.50	30.00
HP6 Carl Yastrzemski	12.50	30.00

2001 Topps King of Kings Relics

Randomly inserted into packs at 1:2056 Hobby/Retail and 1:457 HTA, this four-card insert features game-used memorabilia from Nolan Ryan, Rickey Henderson, and Hank Aaron. Please note that a special fourth card containing game-used memorabilia of all three were inserted into HTA packs at 1:8903. Card backs carry a "KKG" prefix.

SER.1 STATED ODDS 1:2056 H/R, 1:457 HTA		
SER.2 GROUP A 1:7205 H/R, 1:1,605 HTA		
SER.2 GROUP B 1:2391 H/R, 1:531 HTA		
SER.1 KKGE ODDS 1:8903 HTA		
SER.2 KKLE2 ODDS 1:7615 HTA		
KKR1 Hank Aaron Jsy	10.00	25.00
KKR2 Nolan Ryan Jsy	15.00	40.00
KKR3 Rickey Henderson Jsy	10.00	25.00
KKR4 Mark McGwire Jsy B	10.00	25.00
KKR5 Bob Gibson Jsy A	10.00	25.00
KKR6 Nolan Ryan Jsy B	10.00	25.00
KKGE Aaron/Ryan/Henderson	175.00	300.00
KKLE2 McGwire/Gib/Ryan	300.00	500.00

2001 Topps Noteworthy

Inserted in hobby/retail packs at a rate of one in eight and HTA packs at a rate of one per pack; this 50-card set feature a mix of active and retired players who achieved significant feats during their career.

COMPLETE SET (50)	20.00	50.00
SER.2 STATED ODDS 1:8 H/R, 1:1 HTA		
TN1 Mark McGwire	1.50	4.00
TN2 Derek Jeter	1.50	4.00
TN3 Sammy Sosa	.60	1.50
TN4 Todd Helton	.40	1.00
TN5 Alex Rodriguez	.75	2.00
TN6 Chipper Jones	.60	1.50
TN7 Barry Bonds	1.50	4.00
TN8 Ken Griffey Jr.	1.25	3.00
TN9 Nomar Garciaparra	1.00	2.50
TN10 Frank Thomas	.60	1.50
TN11 Randy Johnson	.60	1.50
TN12 Cal Ripken	2.00	5.00
TN13 Mike Piazza	1.00	2.50
TN14 Ivan Rodriguez	.40	1.00
TN15 Jeff Bagwell	.40	1.00
TN16 Vladimir Guerrero	.60	1.50
TN17 Greg Maddux	1.00	2.50
TN18 Tony Gwynn	.75	2.00
TN19 Larry Walker	.40	1.00
TN20 Juan Gonzalez	.40	1.00
TN21 Scott Rolen	.40	1.00
TN22 Jason Giambi	.40	1.00
TN23 Jeff Kent	.40	1.00
TN24 Pat Burrell	.40	1.00
TN25 Pedro Martinez	.40	1.00
TN26 Willie Mays	1.50	4.00
TN27 Whitey Ford	.40	1.00
TN28 Jackie Robinson	.60	1.50
TN29 Ted Williams	1.50	4.00
TN30 Babe Ruth	3.00	8.00
TN31 Warren Spahn	.40	1.00
TN32 Nolan Ryan	2.50	6.00
TN33 Yogi Berra	.60	1.50
TN34 Mike Schmidt	1.50	4.00
TN35 Steve Carlton	.40	1.00
TN36 Brooks Robinson	.40	1.00
TN37 Bob Gibson	.40	1.00
TN38 Reggie Jackson	.40	1.00
TN39 Johnny Bench	.60	1.50
TN40 Ernie Banks	.60	1.50
TN41 Eddie Mathews	.60	1.50
TN42 Don Mattingly	1.50	4.00
TN43 Duke Snider	.40	1.00
TN44 Hank Aaron	1.50	4.00
TN45 Roberto Clemente	2.00	5.00
TN46 Harmon Killebrew	.60	1.50
TN47 Frank Robinson	.40	1.00
TN48 Stan Musial	1.25	3.00
TN49 Lou Brock	.40	1.00
TN50 Joe Morgan	.40	1.00

2001 Topps Originals Relics

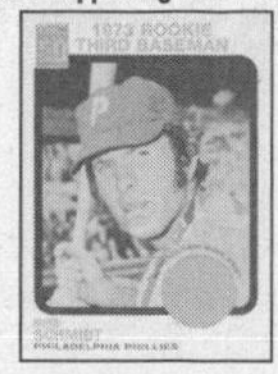

Randomly inserted into packs at different rates depening which series these cards were inserted in, this ten-card insert set features game-used jersey cards of players like Roberto Clemente and Carl Yastrzemski. Please note that the Willie Mays card is actually a game-used jacket.

SER.1 STATED ODDS 1:1172 H/R, 1:260 HTA		
SER.2 STATED ODDS 1:1023 H/R, 1:227 HTA		
1 Roberto Clemente 55 Jsy	50.00	120.00
2 Carl Yastrzemski 60 Jsy	15.00	40.00
3 Mike Schmidt 73 Jsy	10.00	25.00
4 Wade Boggs 83 Jsy	6.00	15.00
5 Chipper Jones 91 Jsy	10.00	25.00
6 Willie Mays 52 Jkt	15.00	40.00
7 Lou Brock 62 Jsy	10.00	25.00
8 Dave Parker 74 Jsy	6.00	15.00
9 Barry Bonds 86 Jsy	6.00	15.00
10 Alex Rodriguez 98 Jsy	10.00	25.00

2001 Topps Team Topps Legends Autographs

These signed cards were inserted into various 2001-2003 Topps products. As these cards were inserted into different products and some were exchange cards. Most players in this set were featured on reprinted versions of their classic Topps "rookie" and "final" cards. The checklist was originally comprised of cards TT1-TT50 (with each player having an R and F suffix (i.e. Willie Mays is featured on TT1F with his 1973 card and TT1R with his 1952 card). In late 2002 and throughout 2003, additional players were added to the set with checklist numbering outside of the TT1-TT50 schematic. The numbering for these late additions was based on player's initials (i.e. Lou Brock's card is TT-LB) and only reprints of their rookie-year cards were produced.

BOW.BEST GROUP A ODDS 1:404		
BOW.BEST GROUP B ODDS 1:67		
BOW.HERITAGE GROUP 1 ODDS 1:1570		
BOW.HERITAGE GROUP 2 ODDS 1:1556		
BOW.HERITAGE GROUP 3 ODDS 1:1937		
BOW.HERITAGE GROUP 4 ODDS 1:1453		
BOW.HERITAGE GROUP 5 ODDS 1:1899		
TOPPS TRD.GROUP A ODDS 1:1567		
TOPPS TRD.GROUP B ODDS 1:1881		
TOPPS TRD.GROUP C ODDS 1:626		
TOPPS TRD.GROUP D ODDS 1:TBD		
TOPPS TRD.OVERALL ODDS 1:361		
TOPPS AMERICAN PIE ODDS 1:211		
TOPPS GALLERY ODDS 1:286		
AP SUFFIX ON AMERICAN PIE DISTRIBUTION		
TOPPS AMER.PIE EXCH.DEADLINE 11/01/03		
TOPPS GALLERY EXCH.DEADLINE 06/30/03		
02 TOPPS EXCH.DEADLINE 12/01/03		
TT1F Willie Mays 73	125.00	250.00
TT1R Willie Mays 52	125.00	200.00
TT3F Stan Musial 63	40.00	80.00
TT3R Stan Musial 58 AS	40.00	80.00
TT6F Whitey Ford 67	20.00	50.00
TT6R Whitey Ford 53	15.00	40.00
TT7R Nolan Ryan 68	75.00	200.00
TT8F Carl Yastrzemski 83	40.00	80.00
TT8R Carl Yastrzemski 60	25.00	60.00
TT9R Brooks Robinson 57	25.00	60.00
TT10F Frank Robinson 75	12.00	30.00
TT10R Frank Robinson 57	20.00	50.00
TT11R Tom Seaver 67	30.00	80.00
TT11F Tom Seaver 87	30.00	80.00
TT12R Duke Snider 52	8.00	20.00
TT13F Warren Spahn 65	12.50	30.00
TT13R Warren Spahn 52	15.00	40.00
TT14F Johnny Bench 83	30.00	60.00
TT14R Johnny Bench 68	40.00	80.00
TT15R Reggie Jackson 69	40.00	80.00
TT16R Al Kaline 54	25.00	50.00
TT18F Bob Gibson 75	15.00	40.00
TT18R Bob Gibson 59	12.00	30.00
TT19R Mike Schmidt 73	25.00	60.00
TT20R Harmon Killebrew 55	40.00	80.00
TT21R Bob Feller 52	10.00	25.00
TT23F Gil McDougald 60	6.00	15.00
TT23R Gil McDougald 52	6.00	15.00
TT25F Luis Tiant 83	6.00	15.00
TT25R Luis Tiant 65	6.00	15.00
TT27F Andy Pafko 59	8.00	20.00
TT27R Andy Pafko 52	8.00	20.00
TT28F Herb Score 62	6.00	15.00
TT28R Herb Score 56	6.00	15.00
TT29F Bill Skowron 67	8.00	20.00
TT29R Bill Skowron 54	6.00	15.00
TT31F Clete Boyer 71	6.00	15.00
TT31R Clete Boyer 57	8.00	20.00
TT33F Vida Blue 87	6.00	15.00
TT33R Vida Blue 70	6.00	15.00
TT34R Don Larsen 56	8.00	20.00
TT35F Joe Pepitone 73	8.00	20.00
TT35R Joe Pepitone 62	6.00	15.00
TT36F Enos Slaughter 59	10.00	25.00
TT36R Enos Slaughter 52	15.00	40.00
TT37F Tug McGraw 85	12.50	30.00
TT37R Tug McGraw 65	12.50	30.00
TT38R Fergie Jenkins 66	8.00	20.00
TT40R Gaylord Perry 62	10.00	25.00
TT43F Bobby Thomson 60	8.00	20.00
TT43R Bobby Thomson 52	10.00	25.00
TT46F Robin Roberts 66	10.00	25.00
TT46R Robin Roberts 52	6.00	15.00
TT47F Frank Howard 73	6.00	15.00
TT47R Frank Howard 60	10.00	25.00
TT48F Bobby Richardson 66	6.00	15.00
TT48R Bobby Richardson 57	6.00	15.00
TT49R Tony Kubek 57	40.00	80.00
TT50F Mickey Lolich 80	6.00	15.00
TT50R Mickey Lolich 64	6.00	15.00
TT51RF Ralph Branca 52	6.00	15.00
TTGC Gary Carter 75	25.00	60.00
TTGG Rich Gossage 73	6.00	15.00
TTGN Graig Nettles 69	6.00	15.00
TTJB Jim Bunning 65	10.00	25.00
TTJM Joe Morgan 65	15.00	40.00
TTJP Jim Palmer 66	10.00	25.00
TTJS Johnny Sain 52	6.00	15.00
TTLA Luis Aparicio 56	10.00	25.00
TTLB Lou Brock 62	15.00	40.00
TTPB Paul Blair 65	6.00	15.00
TTRY Robin Yount 75	40.00	80.00
TTVL Vern Law 52	6.00	15.00

2001 Topps Through the Years Reprints

Randomly inserted into packs at 1:8 Hobby/Retail and 1:1 HTA, this 50-card set takes a look at some of the best players to every make it onto a Topps trading card.

COMPLETE SET (50)	20.00	50.00
SER.1 STATED ODDS 1:8 H/R, 1:1 HTA		
1 Yogi Berra '57	1.25	3.00
2 Roy Campanella '56	1.25	3.00
3 Willie Mays '53	2.00	5.00
4 Andy Pafko '52	1.25	3.00
5 Jackie Robinson '52	1.25	3.00
6 Stan Musial '59	1.50	4.00
7 Duke Snider '56	1.25	3.00
8 Warren Spahn '56	1.25	3.00
9 Ted Williams '54	3.00	8.00
10 Eddie Mathews '55	1.25	3.00
11 Willie McCovey '60	1.25	3.00
12 Frank Robinson '69	1.25	3.00
13 Ernie Banks '66	1.25	3.00
14 Hank Aaron '65	2.00	5.00
15 Sandy Koufax '61	2.50	6.00
16 Bob Gibson '68	1.25	3.00
17 Harmon Killebrew '67	1.25	3.00
18 Whitey Ford '64	1.25	3.00
19 Roberto Clemente '63	3.00	8.00
20 Juan Marichal '62	1.25	3.00
21 Johnny Bench '70	1.25	3.00
22 Willie Stargell '73	1.25	3.00
23 Joe Morgan '74	1.25	3.00
24 Carl Yastrzemski '71	1.50	4.00
25 Reggie Jackson '76	1.25	3.00
26 Tom Seaver '78	1.25	3.00
27 Steve Carlton '77	1.25	3.00
28 Jim Palmer '79	1.25	3.00
29 Rod Carew '72	1.25	3.00
30 George Brett '75	3.00	8.00
31 Roger Clemens '85	2.50	6.00
32 Don Mattingly '84	3.00	8.00
33 Ryne Sandberg '89	2.00	5.00
34 Mike Schmidt '81	2.00	5.00
35 Cal Ripken '82	4.00	10.00
36 Tony Gwynn '83	1.50	4.00
37 Ozzie Smith '87	2.00	5.00
38 Wade Boggs '88	1.25	3.00
39 Nolan Ryan '80	2.50	6.00
40 Robin Yount '86	1.25	3.00
41 Mark McGwire '99	2.50	6.00
42 Ken Griffey Jr. '92	2.00	5.00
43 Sammy Sosa '90	1.25	3.00
44 Alex Rodriguez '98	1.25	3.00
45 Barry Bonds '94	2.50	6.00
46 Mike Piazza '95	1.50	4.00
47 Chipper Jones '91	1.25	3.00
48 Greg Maddux '97	1.50	4.00
49 Nomar Garciaparra '97	1.50	4.00
50 Derek Jeter '93	3.00	8.00

2001 Topps What Could Have Been

Inserted at a rate of one in 25 hobby/retail packs or one in five HTA packs, these 10 cards feature stars of the Negro leagues who never got to play in the majors while they were at their peak.

COMPLETE SET (10)	10.00	25.00
SER.2 STATED ODDS 1:25 H/R, 1:5 HTA		
WCB1 Josh Gibson	2.00	5.00
WCB2 Satchel Paige	1.25	3.00
WCB3 Buck Leonard	.75	2.00
WCB4 James Bell	1.25	3.00
WCB5 Rube Foster	1.25	3.00
WCB6 Martin DiHigo	.75	2.00
WCB7 William Johnson	.75	2.00
WCB8 Mule Suttles	.75	2.00
WCB9 Ray Dandridge	.75	2.00
WCB10 John Lloyd	.75	2.00

2001 Topps Traded

The 2001 Topps Traded product was released in October 2001, and features a 265-card base set. The 2001 Topps Traded and the 2001 Topps Chrome Traded were combined and sold together. Each pack contained eight 2001 Topps Traded and two 2001 Topps Chrome Traded cards for a total of ten cards in each pack. The 265-card set is broken down as follows: 99 cards highlighting player deals made during the 2000 off-season and 2001 season; 60 future stars who have never appeared alone on a Topps card; 55 rookies who make their premiere on a Topps card; six managers (T145-T150) who've either switched teams or were newly hired for the 2001 season and 45 traded repints (T100 through T144) of rookie cards featured in past Topps Traded sets. The packs carried a 3.00 per pack SRP and came 24 packs to a box.

COMPLETE SET (265)	60.00	150.00
COMMON CARD (1-99/145-265)	.15	.40
COMMON REPRINT (100-144)	.40	1.00
REPRINTS ARE NOT SP'S!		
T1 Sandy Alomar Jr.	.15	.40
T2 Kevin Appier	.20	.50
T3 Brad Ausmus	.20	.50
T4 Derek Bell	.15	.40
T5 Bret Boone	.20	.50
T6 Rico Brogna	.15	.40
T7 Ellis Burks	.20	.50
T8 Ken Caminiti	.20	.50
T9 Roger Cedeno	.15	.40
T10 Royce Clayton	.15	.40
T11 Enrique Wilson	.15	.40
T12 Rheal Cormier	.15	.40
T13 Eric Davis	.20	.50
T14 Shawon Dunston	.15	.40
T15 Andres Galarraga	.20	.50
T16 Tom Gordon	.15	.40
T17 Mark Grace	.30	.75
T18 Jeffrey Hammonds	.15	.40
T19 Dustin Hermanson	.15	.40
T20 Quinton McCracken	.15	.40
T21 Todd Hundley	.15	.40
T22 Charles Johnson	.20	.50
T23 Marquis Grissom	.20	.50
T24 Jose Mesa	.15	.40
T25 Brian Boehringer	.15	.40
T26 John Rocker	.20	.50
T27 Jeff Frye	.15	.40
T28 Reggie Sanders	.20	.50
T29 David Segui	.15	.40
T30 Mike Sirotka	.15	.40
T31 Fernando Tatis	.15	.40
T32 Steve Trachsel	.15	.40
T33 Ismael Valdes	.15	.40
T34 Randy Velarde	.15	.40
T35 Ryan Kohlmeier	.15	.40
T36 Mike Bordick	.20	.50
T37 Kent Bottenfield	.15	.40
T38 Pat Rapp	.15	.40
T39 Jeff Nelson	.15	.40
T40 Ricky Bottalico	.15	.40
T41 Luke Prokopec	.15	.40
T42 Hideo Nomo	.50	1.25
T43 Bill Mueller	.20	.50
T44 Roberto Kelly	.15	.40
T45 Chris Holt	.15	.40
T46 Mike Jackson	.15	.40
T47 Devon White	.20	.50
T48 Gerald Williams	.15	.40
T49 Eddie Taubensee	.15	.40
T50 Brian Hunter	.15	.40
T51 Nelson Cruz	.15	.40
T52 Jeff Fassero	.15	.40
T53 Bubba Trammell	.15	.40
T54 Bo Porter	.15	.40
T55 Greg Norton	.15	.40
T56 Benito Santiago	.20	.50
T57 Ruben Rivera	.15	.40
T58 Dee Brown	.15	.40
T59 Jose Canseco	.30	.75
T60 Chris Michalak	.15	.40
T61 Tim Worrell	.15	.40

T62 Matt Clement .20 .50
T63 Bill Pulsipher .15 .40
T64 Troy Brohawn RC .15 .40
T65 Mark Kotsay .20 .50
T66 Jimmy Rollins .20 .50
T67 Shea Hillenbrand .20 .50
T68 Ted Lilly .15 .40
T69 Jermaine Dye .20 .50
T70 Jerry Hairston Jr. .15 .40
T71 John Mabry .15 .40
T72 Kurt Abbott .15 .40
T73 Eric Owens .15 .40
T74 Jeff Brantley .15 .40
T75 Roy Oswalt .50 1.25
T76 Doug Mientkiewicz .20 .50
T77 Rickey Henderson .50 1.25
T78 Jason Grimsley .15 .40
T79 Christian Parker RC .15 .40
T80 Donne Wall .15 .40
T81 Alex Arias .15 .40
T82 Willis Roberts .15 .40
T83 Ryan Minor .15 .40
T84 Jason LaRue .15 .40
T85 Ruben Sierra .20 .50
T86 Johnny Damon .30 .75
T87 Juan Gonzalez .20 .50
T88 C.C. Sabathia .20 .50
T89 Tony Batista .15 .40
T90 Jay Witasick .15 .40
T91 Brent Abernathy .15 .40
T92 Paul LoDuca .20 .50
T93 Wes Helms .15 .40
T94 Mark Wohlers .15 .40
T95 Rob Bell .15 .40
T96 Tim Redding .15 .40
T97 Bud Smith RC .15 .40
T98 Adam Dunn .30 .75
T99 I.Suzuki 8.00 20.00
A.Pujols ROY
T100 Carlton Fisk 81 .50 1.25
T101 Tim Raines 81 .40 1.00
T102 Juan Marichal 74 .40 1.00
T103 Dave Winfield 81 .40 1.00
T104 Reggie Jackson 82 .50 1.25
T105 Cal Ripken 82 2.50 6.00
T106 Ozzie Smith 82 1.25 3.00
T107 Tom Seaver 83 .50 1.25
T108 Lou Piniella 74 .40 1.00
T109 Dwight Gooden 84 .40 1.00
T110 Bret Saberhagen 84 .40 1.00
T111 Gary Carter 85 .40 1.00
T112 Jack Clark 85 .40 1.00
T113 Rickey Henderson 85 .75 2.00
T114 Barry Bonds 86 2.00 5.00
T115 Bobby Bonilla 86 .40 1.00
T116 Jose Canseco 86 .50 1.25
T117 Will Clark 86 .50 1.25
T118 Andres Galarraga 86 .40 1.00
T119 Bo Jackson 86 .75 2.00
T120 Wally Joyner 86 .40 1.00
T121 Ellis Burks 87 .40 1.00
T122 David Cone 87 .40 1.00
T123 Greg Maddux 87 1.25 3.00
T124 Willie Randolph 76 .40 1.00
T125 Dennis Eckersley 87 .40 1.00
T126 Matt Williams 87 .40 1.00
T127 Joe Morgan 81 .40 1.00
T128 Fred McGriff 87 .50 1.25
T129 Roberto Alomar 88 .50 1.25
T130 Lee Smith 88 .40 1.00
T131 David Wells 88 .40 1.00
T132 Ken Griffey Jr. 89 1.50 4.00
T133 Deion Sanders 89 .50 1.25
T134 Nolan Ryan 89 1.50 4.00
T135 David Justice 90 .40 1.00
T136 Joe Carter 91 .40 1.00
T137 Jack Morris 92 .40 1.00
T138 Mike Piazza 93 1.25 3.00
T139 Barry Bonds 93 2.00 5.00
T140 Terrence Long 94 .40 1.00
T141 Ben Grieve 94 .40 1.00
T142 Richie Sexson 95 .40 1.00
T143 Sean Burroughs 99 .40 1.00
T144 Alfonso Soriano 99 .50 1.25
T145 Bob Boone MG .20 .50
T146 Larry Bowa MG .20 .50
T147 Bob Brenly MG .15 .40
T148 Buck Martinez MG .15 .40
T149 Lloyd McClendon MG .15 .40
T150 Jim Tracy MG .15 .40
T151 Jared Abruzzo RC .15 .40
T152 Kurt Ainsworth .15 .40
T153 Willie Bloomquist .20 .50
T154 Ben Broussard .15 .40
T155 Bobby Bradley .15 .40
T156 Mike Bynum .15 .40
T157 A.J. Hinch .15 .40
T158 Ryan Christianson .15 .40
T159 Carlos Silva .15 .40
T160 Joe Crede .50 1.25
T161 Jack Cust .15 .40
T162 Ben Diggins .15 .40
T163 Phil Dumatrait .15 .40
T164 Alex Escobar .15 .40
T165 Miguel Olivo .15 .40
T166 Chris George .15 .40
T167 Marcus Giles .20 .50
T168 Keith Ginter .15 .40
T169 Josh Girdley .15 .40
T170 Tony Alvarez .15 .40
T171 Scott Seabol .15 .40
T172 Josh Hamilton .30 .75
T173 Jason Hart .15 .40
T174 Israel Alcantara .15 .40
T175 Jake Peavy .40 1.00
T176 Stubby Clapp RC .15 .40
T177 D'Angelo Jimenez .15 .40
T178 Nick Johnson .20 .50
T179 Ben Johnson .20 .50
T180 Larry Bigbie .15 .40
T181 Allen Levrault .15 .40
T182 Felipe Lopez .20 .50
T183 Sean Burnett .15 .40
T184 Nick Neugebauer .15 .40
T185 Austin Kearns .20 .50
T186 Corey Patterson .15 .40
T187 Carlos Pena .15 .40
T188 Ricardo Rodriguez RC .15 .40
T189 Juan Rivera .15 .40
T190 Grant Roberts .15 .40
T191 Adam Pettyjohn RC .15 .40
T192 Jared Sandberg .15 .40
T193 Xavier Nady .15 .40
T194 Dane Sardinha .15 .40
T195 Shawn Sonnier .15 .40
T196 Rafael Soriano .15 .40
T197 Brian Specht RC .15 .40
T198 Aaron Myette .15 .40
T199 Juan Uribe RC .20 .50
T200 Jayson Werth .15 .40
T201 Brad Wilkerson .15 .40
T202 Horacio Estrada .15 .40
T203 Joel Pineiro .20 .50
T204 Matt LeCroy .15 .40
T205 Michael Coleman .15 .40
T206 Ben Sheets .30 .75
T207 Eric Byrnes .15 .40
T208 Sean Burroughs .15 .40
T209 Ken Harvey .15 .40
T210 Travis Hafner 1.50 4.00
T211 Erick Almonte .15 .40
T212 Jason Belcher RC .15 .40
T213 Wilson Betemit RC .60 1.50
T214 Hank Blalock RC 1.00 2.50
T215 Danny Borrell .15 .40
T216 John Buck RC .20 .50
T217 Freddie Bynum RC .15 .40
T218 Noel Devarez RC .15 .40
T219 Juan Diaz RC .15 .40
T220 Felix Diaz RC .15 .40
T221 Josh Fogg RC .15 .40
T222 Matt Ford RC .15 .40
T223 Scott Heard .15 .40
T224 Ben Hendrickson RC .15 .40
T225 Cody Ross RC .60 1.50
T226 Adrian Hernandez RC .15 .40
T227 Alfredo Amezaga RC .15 .40
T228 Bob Keppel RC .15 .40
T229 Ryan Madson RC .30 .75
T230 Octavio Martinez RC .15 .40
T231 Hee Seop Choi .20 .50
T232 Thomas Mitchell .15 .40
T233 Luis Montanez .15 .40
T234 Andy Morales RC .15 .40
T235 Justin Morneau RC 3.00 8.00
T236 Toe Nash RC .15 .40
T237 Valentino Pascucci RC .15 .40
T238 Roy Smith RC .15 .40
T239 Antonio Perez RC .20 .50
T240 Chad Petty RC .15 .40
T241 Steve Smyth .15 .40
T242 Jose Reyes RC 3.00 8.00
T243 Eric Reynolds RC .15 .40
T244 Dominic Rich .15 .40
T245 Jason Richardson RC .15 .40
T246 Ed Rogers RC .15 .40
T247 Albert Pujols RC 20.00 50.00
T248 Esix Snead RC .15 .40
T249 Luis Torres RC .15 .40
T250 Matt White RC .15 .40
T251 Blake Williams .15 .40
T252 Chris Russ .15 .40
T253 Joe Kennedy RC .20 .50
T254 Jeff Randazzo RC .15 .40
T255 Beau Hale RC .15 .40
T256 Brad Hennessey RC .50 1.25
T257 Jake Gautreau RC .15 .40
T258 Jeff Mathis RC .20 .50
T259 Aaron Heilman RC .20 .50
T260 Bronson Sardinha RC .15 .40
T261 Irvin Guzman RC 1.50 4.00
T262 Gabe Gross RC .20 .50
T263 J.D. Martin RC .15 .40
T264 Chris Smith RC .15 .40
T265 Kenny Baugh RC .15 .40

2001 Topps Traded Gold

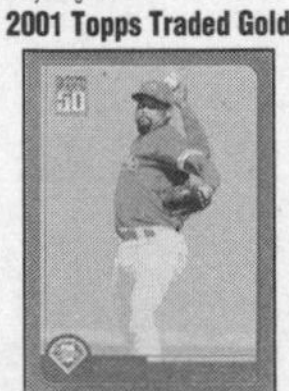

*STARS: 4X TO 10X BASIC CARDS
*REPRINTS: 1.5X TO 4X BASIC
*ROOKIES: 1X TO 2.5X BASIC
STATED ODDS 1:3
STATED PRINT RUN 2001 SERIAL #'d SETS
T247 Albert Pujols 150.00 400.00

2001 Topps Traded Autographs

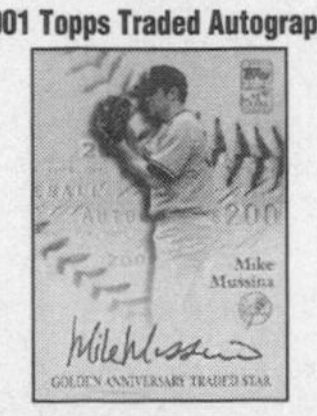

Inserted at a rate of one in 626, these cards share the same design as the 2001 Topps Golden Anniversary Autographs. The only difference is the front bottom of the card reads "Golden Anniversary Traded Star". The cards carry a 'TTA' prefix.
STATED ODDS 1:626
TTAJD Johnny Damon 10.00 25.00
TTAMM Mike Mussina 8.00 20.00

2001 Topps Traded Dual Jersey Relics

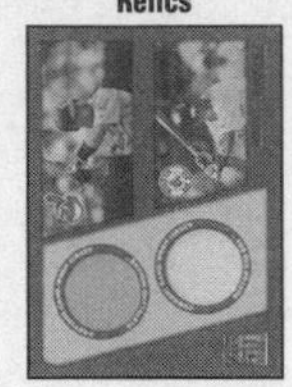

Inserted at a rate of one in 376, these cards highlight a player who has switched teams and feature a swatch of game-used jersey from both his former and current teams. The cards carry a 'TRR' prefix. Ben Grieve packed out as an exchange card.
STATED ODDS 1:376
TTRBG Ben Grieve 6.00 15.00
TTRDH Dustin Hermanson 6.00 15.00
TTRFT Fernando Tatis 6.00 15.00
TTRMR Manny Ramirez 8.00 20.00

2001 Topps Traded Farewell Dual Bat Relic

Inserted at a rate of one in 4693, this card features bat pieces from both Cal Ripken and Tony Gwynn and is a farewell tribute to both players. The card carries a 'FR' prefix.
STATED ODDS 1:4693
FRRG C.Ripken/T.Gwynn 25.00 60.00

2001 Topps Traded Hall of Fame Bat Relic

Inserted at a rate of one in 2796, this card features bat pieces from both Kirby Puckett and Dave Winfield and commemorates their entrance in Cooperstown. The card carries a 'HFR' prefix.
STATED ODDS 1:2796
HFRPW K.Puckett/D.Winfield 10.00 25.00

2001 Topps Traded Relics

Inserted at a rate of one in 29, this 33-card set features game used bats or jersey swatches for players who have switched teams this season. All jersey swatches represent each player's new team. The cards carry a 'TTR' prefix. An exchange card for a Matt Stairs Jersey card was packed out.
STATED ODDS 1:29
AG Andres Galarraga Bat 4.00 10.00
BB1 Bobby Bonilla Bat 4.00 10.00
BB2 Bret Boone Jsy 4.00 10.00
BM Bill Mueller Jsy 6.00 15.00
CJ Charles Johnson Jsy 4.00 10.00
DB Derek Bell Bat 4.00 10.00
DN Denny Neagle Jsy 4.00 10.00
DW David Wells Jsy 4.00 10.00
ED Eric Davis Bat 4.00 10.00
EW Enrique Wilson Bat 4.00 10.00
FM Fred McGriff Bat 6.00 15.00
GW Gerald Williams Bat 4.00 10.00
HR Hideo Nomo Jsy 10.00 25.00
JC Jose Canseco Bat 6.00 15.00
JD Jermaine Dye Bat SP 4.00 10.00
JD1 Johnny Damon Bat 6.00 15.00
JD2 Johnny Damon Jsy 6.00 15.00
JG Juan Gonzalez Bat 4.00 10.00
JH Jeffrey Hammonds Jsy 4.00 10.00
KC Ken Caminiti Bat 4.00 10.00
KS Kelly Stinnett Bat SP 4.00 10.00
MG1 Mark Grace Bat 6.00 15.00
MG2 Marquis Grissom Bat 4.00 10.00
MH Mike Hampton Jsy 4.00 10.00
MS Matt Stairs Jsy 4.00 10.00
NP Neifi Perez Bat 4.00 10.00
RB Rico Brogna Jsy 4.00 10.00
RG Ron Gant Bat 4.00 10.00
ROC Roger Cedeno Jsy 4.00 10.00
RS Ruben Sierra Bat 4.00 10.00
RSC Royce Clayton Bat 4.00 10.00
SA Sandy Alomar Jr. Bat 4.00 10.00
TH Todd Hundley Jsy 4.00 10.00
TR Tim Raines Jsy 4.00 10.00

2001 Topps Traded Rookie Relics

Inserted at a rate of one in 91, this 18-card set features bat pieces or jersey swatches for rookies. The cards carry a 'TRR' prefix. An exchange card for the Ed Rogers Bat card was seeded into packs.
STATED ODDS 1:91
TRRAB Angel Berroa Jsy 4.00 10.00
TRRAP Albert Pujols Bat SP 50.00 100.00
TRRBO Bill Ortega Jsy 3.00 8.00
TRRER Ed Rogers Bat SP 4.00 10.00
TRRHC Humberto Cota Jsy 3.00 8.00
TRRJL Jason Lane Jsy 3.00 8.00
TRRJS Jae Seo Jsy 3.00 8.00
TRRJS Jamal Strong Jsy 3.00 8.00
TRRJV Jose Valverde Jsy 3.00 8.00
TRRJY Jason Young Jsy 3.00 8.00
TRRNC Nate Cornejo Jsy 3.00 8.00
TRRNN Nick Neugebauer Jsy 3.00 8.00
TRRPF Pedro Feliz Jsy SP 3.00 8.00
TRRRS Richard Stahl Jsy 3.00 8.00
TRRSB Sean Burroughs Jsy 3.00 8.00
TRRTS Tsuyoshi Shinjo Bat SP 4.00 10.00
TRRWB Wilson Betemit Bat 4.00 10.00
TRRWR Wilkin Ruan Jsy 3.00 8.00

2001 Topps Traded Who Would Have Thought

Inserted at a rate of one in eight, this 20-card set portrays players who fans thought would never be traded. The cards carry a 'WWHT' prefix.
COMPLETE SET (20) 12.00 30.00
STATED ODDS 1:8
WWHT1 Nolan Ryan 2.50 6.00
WWHT2 Ozzie Smith 1.50 4.00
WWHT3 Tom Seaver .60 1.50
WWHT4 Steve Carlton .60 1.50
WWHT5 Reggie Jackson .60 1.50
WWHT6 Frank Robinson .60 1.50
WWHT7 Keith Hernandez .60 1.50
WWHT8 Andre Dawson .60 1.50
WWHT9 Lou Brock .60 1.50
WWHT10 Dennis Eckersley .60 1.50
WWHT11 Dave Winfield .60 1.50
WWHT12 Rod Carew .60 1.50
WWHT13 Willie Randolph .60 1.50
WWHT14 Dwight Gooden .60 1.50
WWHT15 Carlton Fisk .60 1.50
WWHT16 Dale Murphy .60 1.50
WWHT17 Paul Molitor .60 1.50
WWHT18 Gary Carter .60 1.50
WWHT19 Wade Boggs .60 1.50
WWHT20 Willie Mays 2.00 5.00

2002 Topps

The complete set of 2002 Topps consists of 718 cards issued in two separate series. The first series of 364 cards was distributed in November, 2001 and the second series of 354 cards followed up in April, 2002. Please note, the first series is numbered 1-365, but card number seven does not exist (the number was "retired" in 1996 by Topps to honor Mickey Mantle). Similar to the 1999 McGwire and Sosa home run cards, Barry Bonds is featured on card number 365 with 73 different versions to commemorate each of the homers he smashed during the 2001 season. The first series set is considered complete with any "one" of these variations. The cards were issued either in 10 card hobby/retail packs with an SRP of $1.29 or 37 card HTA packs with an SRP of $5 per pack. The hobby packs were issued 36 to a box and 12 boxes to a case. The HTA packs were issued 12 to a box and eight to a case. Cards numbered 277-305 feature managers; cards numbered 307-325/671-690 feature leading prospects; cards numbered 326-331/691-695 feature 2001 draft picks; cards numbered 332-336 feature leading highlights of the 2001 season; cards numbered 337-348 feature league leaders; cards numbered 349-356 feature the eight teams which made the playoffs; cards numbered 357-364 feature major league baseball's stirring tribute to the events of September 11, 2001; cards 641-670 feature Team Cards; 696-713 are Gold Glove subsets, 714-715 are Cy Young subsets, 716-717 are MVP subsets and 718-719 are Rookie of the Year subsets. Notable Rookie Cards include Joe Mauer and Kazhuisa Ishii. Also, Topps repurchased more than 21,000 actual vintage Topps cards and randomly seeded them into packs as follows - Ser.1 Home Team Advantage 1:169, ser.1 retail 1:tbd, ser.2 hobby 1:431, ser.2 Home Team Advantage 1:113 and ser.2 retail 1:331. Brown-boxed hobby factory sets were issued in May, 2002 containing the full 718-card basic set and five Topps Archives Reprints inserts. Green-boxed retail factory sets were issued in late August, 2002 containing the full 718-card basic set and cards 1-5 of a 10-card Draft Picks set. There has been a recently discovered variation of card 160 in which there is a correct back picture for Albert Pujols (#160). While Topps has confirmed this variation, it is unknown what percent of the print run has the correct back photo.

COMPLETE SET (718) 25.00 60.00
COMP.FACT.BROWN SET (723) 40.00 80.00
COMP.FACT.GREEN SET (723) 40.00 80.00
COMPLETE SERIES 1 (364) 12.50 30.00
COMPLETE SERIES 2 (354) 12.50 30.00
COMMON CARD (1-6/8-719) .07 .20
COMMON (307-331/671-695) .20 .50
COMMON CARD (332-364) .20 .50
CARD NUMBER 7 DOES NOT EXIST
CARD 365 AVAIL. IN 73 VARIATIONS
SER.1 SET INCLUDES 1 CARD 365 VARIATION
BUYBACK SER.1 ODDS 1:616 HOB
BUYBACK SER.1 ODDS 1:169 HTA, 1:484 RET
BUYBACK SER.2 ODDS 1:431 HOB
BUYBACK SER.2 ODDS 1:113 HTA, 1:331 RET
1 Pedro Martinez .10 .30
2 Mike Stanton .07 .20
3 Brad Penny .07 .20
4 Mike Matheny .07 .20
5 Johnny Damon .10 .30
6 Bret Boone .07 .20
8 Chris Truby .07 .20
9 B.J. Surhoff .07 .20
10 Mike Hampton .07 .20
11 Juan Pierre .07 .20
12 Mark Buehrle .07 .20
13 Bob Abreu .07 .20
14 David Cone .07 .20
15 Aaron Sele .07 .20
16 Fernando Tatis .07 .20
17 Bobby Jones .07 .20
18 Rick Helling .07 .20
19 Dmitri Young .07 .20
20 Mike Mussina .10 .30
21 Mike Sweeney .07 .20
22 Cristian Guzman .07 .20
23 Ryan Kohlmeier .07 .20
24 Adam Kennedy .07 .20
25 Larry Walker .07 .20
26 Eric Davis .07 .20
27 Jason Tyner .07 .20
28 Eric Young .07 .20
29 Jason Marquis .07 .20
30 Luis Gonzalez .07 .20
31 Kevin Tapani .07 .20
32 Orlando Cabrera .07 .20
33 Marty Cordova .07 .20
34 Brad Ausmus .07 .20
35 Livan Hernandez .07 .20
36 Alex Gonzalez .07 .20
37 Edgar Renteria .07 .20
38 Bengie Molina .07 .20
39 Frank Menechino .07 .20
40 Rafael Palmeiro .10 .30
41 Brad Fullmer .07 .20
42 Julio Zuleta .07 .20
43 Darren Dreifort .07 .20
44 Trot Nixon .07 .20
45 Trevor Hoffman .07 .20
46 Vladimir Nunez .07 .20
47 Mark Kotsay .07 .20
48 Kenny Rogers .07 .20
49 Ben Petrick .07 .20
50 Jeff Bagwell .10 .30
51 Juan Encarnacion .07 .20
52 Ramiro Mendoza .07 .20
53 Brian Meadows .07 .20
54 Chad Curtis .07 .20
55 Aramis Ramirez .07 .20
56 Mark McLemore .07 .20
57 Dante Bichette .07 .20
58 Scott Schoeneweis .07 .20
59 Jose Cruz Jr. .07 .20
60 Roger Clemens .40 1.00
61 Jose Guillen .07 .20
62 Darren Oliver .07 .20
63 Chris Reitsma .07 .20
64 Jeff Abbott .07 .20
65 Robin Ventura .07 .20
66 Denny Neagle .07 .20
67 Al Martin .07 .20
68 Benito Santiago .07 .20
69 Roy Oswalt .07 .20
70 Juan Gonzalez .07 .20
71 Garret Anderson .07 .20
72 Bobby Bonilla .07 .20
73 Danny Bautista .07 .20
74 J.T. Snow .07 .20
75 Derek Jeter .50 1.25
76 John Olerud .07 .20
77 Kevin Appier .07 .20
78 Phil Nevin .07 .20
79 Sean Casey .07 .20
80 Troy Glaus .07 .20
81 Joe Randa .07 .20
82 Jose Valentin .07 .20
83 Ricky Bottalico .07 .20
84 Todd Zeile .07 .20
85 Barry Larkin .10 .30
86 Bob Wickman .07 .20
87 Jeff Shaw .07 .20
88 Greg Vaughn .07 .20
89 Fernando Vina .07 .20
90 Mark Mulder .07 .20
91 Paul Bako .07 .20
92 Aaron Boone .07 .20
93 Esteban Loaiza .07 .20
94 Richie Sexson .07 .20
95 Alfonso Soriano .07 .20
96 Tony Womack .07 .20
97 Paul Shuey .07 .20
98 Melvin Mora .07 .20
99 Tony Gwynn .25 .60
100 Vladimir Guerrero .20 .50
101 Keith Osik .07 .20
102 Bud Smith .07 .20
103 Scott Williamson .07 .20
104 Daryle Ward .07 .20
105 Doug Mientkiewicz .07 .20
106 Stan Javier .07 .20
107 Russ Ortiz .07 .20
108 Wade Miller .07 .20
109 Luke Prokopec .07 .20
110 Andruw Jones .10 .30
111 Ron Coomer .07 .20
112 Dan Wilson .07 .20
113 Luis Castillo .07 .20
114 Derek Bell .07 .20
115 Gary Sheffield .07 .20
116 Ruben Rivera .07 .20
117 Paul O'Neill .10 .30
118 Craig Paquette .07 .20
119 Kelvim Escobar .07 .20
120 Brad Radke .07 .20
121 Jorge Fabregas .07 .20
122 Randy Winn .07 .20
123 Tom Goodwin .07 .20
124 Jaret Wright .07 .20
125 Manny Ramirez .10 .30
126 Al Leiter .07 .20
127 Ben Davis .07 .20
128 Frank Catalanotto .07 .20
129 Jose Cabrera .07 .20
130 Magglio Ordonez .07 .20
131 Jose Macias .07 .20
132 Ted Lilly .07 .20
133 Chris Holt .07 .20
134 Eric Milton .07 .20
135 Shannon Stewart .07 .20
136 Omar Olivares .07 .20
137 David Segui .07 .20
138 Jeff Nelson .07 .20
139 Matt Williams .07 .20
140 Ellis Burks .07 .20
141 Jason Bere .07 .20
142 Jimmy Haynes .07 .20
143 Ramon Hernandez .07 .20
144 Craig Counsell .07 .20
145 John Smoltz .10 .30
146 Homer Bush .07 .20
147 Quilvio Veras .07 .20
148 Esteban Yan .07 .20
149 Ramon Ortiz .07 .20
150 Carlos Delgado .07 .20
151 Lee Stevens .07 .20
152 Wil Cordero .07 .20
153 Mike Bordick .07 .20
154 John Flaherty .07 .20
155 Omar Daal .07 .20
156 Todd Ritchie .07 .20
157 Carl Everett .07 .20
158 Scott Sullivan .07 .20
159 Deivi Cruz .07 .20
160 Albert Pujols .40 1.00
161 Royce Clayton .07 .20
162 Jeff Suppan .07 .20
163 C.C. Sabathia .07 .20
164 Jimmy Rollins .07 .20
165 Rickey Henderson .20 .50
166 Rey Ordonez .07 .20
167 Shawn Estes .07 .20
168 Reggie Sanders .07
169 Jon Lieber .07
170 Armando Benitez .07
171 Mike Remlinger .07
172 Billy Wagner .07
173 Troy Percival .07
174 Devon White .07
175 Ivan Rodriguez .10
176 Dustin Hermanson .07
177 Brian Anderson .07
178 Graeme Lloyd .07
179 Russell Branyan .07
180 Bobby Higginson .07
181 Alex Gonzalez .07
182 John Franco .07
183 Sidney Ponson .07
184 Jose Mesa .07
185 Todd Hollandsworth .07
186 Kevin Young .07
187 Tim Wakefield .07
188 Craig Biggio .10
189 Jason Isringhausen .07
190 Mark Quinn .07
191 Glendon Rusch .07
192 Damian Miller .07
193 Sandy Alomar Jr. .07
194 Scott Brosius .07
195 Dave Martinez .07
196 Danny Graves .07
197 Shea Hillenbrand .07
198 Jimmy Anderson .07
199 Travis Lee .07
200 Randy Johnson .20
201 Carlos Beltran .07
202 Jerry Hairston .07
203 Jesus Sanchez .07
204 Eddie Taubensee .07
205 David Wells .07
206 Russ Davis .07
207 Michael Barrett .07
208 Marquis Grissom .07
209 Byung-Hyun Kim .07
210 Hideo Nomo .20
211 Ryan Rupe .07
212 Ricky Gutierrez .07
213 Darryl Kile .07
214 Rico Brogna .07
215 Terrence Long .07
216 Mike Jackson .07
217 Jamey Wright .07
218 Adrian Beltre .07
219 Benny Agbayani .07
220 Chuck Knoblauch .07
221 Randy Wolf .07
222 Andy Ashby .07
223 Corey Koskie .07
224 Roger Cedeno .07
225 Ichiro Suzuki .40 1
226 Keith Foulke .07
227 Ryan Minor .07
228 Shawon Dunston .07
229 Alex Cora .07
230 Jeromy Burnitz .07
231 Mark Grace .10
232 Aubrey Huff .07
233 Jeffrey Hammonds .07
234 Olmedo Saenz .07
235 Brian Jordan .07
236 Jeremy Giambi .07
237 Joe Girardi .07
238 Eric Gagne .07
239 Masato Yoshii .07
240 Greg Maddux .30
241 Bryan Rekar .07
242 Ray Durham .07
243 Torii Hunter .07
244 Derrek Lee .10
245 Jim Edmonds .07
246 Einar Diaz .07
247 Brian Bohanon .07
248 Ron Belliard .07
249 Mike Lowell .07
250 Sammy Sosa .20
251 Richard Hidalgo .07
252 Bartolo Colon .07
253 Jorge Posada .10
254 LaTroy Hawkins .07
255 Paul LoDuca .07
256 Carlos Febles .07
257 Nelson Cruz .07
258 Edgardo Alfonzo .07
259 Joey Hamilton .07
260 Cliff Floyd .07
261 Wes Helms .07
262 Jay Bell .07
263 Mike Cameron .07
264 Paul Konerko .07
265 Jeff Kent .07
266 Robert Fick .07
267 Allen Levrault .07
268 Placido Polanco .07
269 Marlon Anderson .07
270 Mariano Rivera .20
271 Chan Ho Park .07
272 Jose Vizcaino .07
273 Jeff D'Amico .07
274 Mark Gardner .07
275 Travis Fryman .07
276 Darren Lewis .07
277 Bruce Bochy MG .07
278 Jerry Manuel MG .07
279 Bob Brenly MG .07
280 Don Baylor MG .07

1 Davey Lopes MG	.07	.20
2 Jerry Narron MG	.07	.20
3 Tony Muser MG	.07	.20
4 Hal McRae MG	.07	.20
5 Bobby Cox MG	.07	.20
6 Larry Dierker MG	.07	.20
7 Phil Garner MG	.07	.20
8 Joe Kerrigan MG	.07	.20
9 Bobby Valentine MG	.07	.20
0 Dusty Baker MG	.07	.20
1 Lloyd McClendon MG	.07	.20
2 Mike Scioscia MG	.07	.20
3 Buck Martinez MG	.07	.20
4 Larry Bowa MG	.07	.20
5 Tony LaRussa MG	.07	.20
6 Jeff Torborg MG	.07	.20
7 Tom Kelly MG	.07	.20
8 Mike Hargrove MG	.07	.20
9 Art Howe MG	.07	.20
0 Lou Piniella MG	.07	.20
1 Charlie Manuel MG	.07	.20
2 Buddy Bell MG	.07	.20
3 Tony Perez MG	.07	.20
4 Bob Boone MG	.07	.20
5 Joe Torre MG	.10	.30
6 Jim Tracy MG	.07	.20
7 Jason Lane PROS	.20	.50
8 Chris George PROS	.20	.50
9 Hank Blalock PROS	.40	1.00
0 Joe Borchard PROS	.20	.50
1 Marlon Byrd PROS	.20	.50
2 Raymond Cabrera PROS RC	.20	.50
3 Freddy Sanchez PROS RC	.75	2.00
4 Scott Wiggins PROS RC	.20	.50
5 Jason Maule PROS RC	.20	.50
6 Dionys Cesar PROS RC	.20	.50
7 Boof Bonser PROS	.20	.50
8 Juan Tolentino PROS RC	.20	.50
9 Earl Snyder PROS RC	.20	.50
20 Travis Wade PROS RC	.20	.50
21 Napoleon Calzado PROS RC	.20	.50
22 Eric Glaser PROS RC	.20	.50
23 Craig Kuzmic PROS RC	.20	.50
24 Nic Jackson PROS RC	.20	.50
25 Mike Rivera PROS	.20	.50
26 Jason Bay PROS RC	1.50	4.00
27 Chris Smith DP	.20	.50
28 Jake Gautreau DP	.20	.50
29 Gabe Gross DP	.20	.50
30 Kenny Baugh DP	.20	.50
31 J.D. Martin DP	.20	.50
32 Barry Bonds HL	.50	1.25
33 Rickey Henderson HL	.20	.50
34 Bud Smith HL	.20	.50
35 Rickey Henderson HL	.20	.50
36 Barry Bonds HL	.50	1.25
37 Ichiro Giambi Alomar LL	.20	.50
38 A.Rod Ichiro Boone LL	.15	.40
39 A.Rod Thome Palmeiro LL	.15	.40
40 Boone J.Gonz A.Rod LL	.15	.40
41 Garcia Mussina Mays LL	.20	.50
42 Nomo Mussina Clemens LL	.20	.50
43 Walker Helton Alou Berk LL	.20	.50
44 Sosa Helton Bonds LL	.30	.75
45 Bonds Sosa L.Gonz LL	.30	.75
46 Sosa Helton L.Gonz LL	.20	.50
47 R.John Schilling Burkett LL	.20	.50
48 R.John Schilling Park LL	.20	.50
49 Seattle Mariners PB	.20	.50
50 Oakland Athletics PB	.20	.50
51 New York Yankees PB	.20	.50
52 Cleveland Indians PB	.20	.50
53 Arizona Diamondbacks PB	.20	.50
54 Atlanta Braves PB	.20	.50
55 St. Louis Cardinals PB	.20	.50
56 Houston Astros PB	.20	.50
57 Diamondbacks-Astros UWS	.20	.50
58 Mike Piazza UWS	.20	.50
59 Braves-Phillies UWS	.20	.50
60 Curt Schilling UWS	.20	.50
61 R.Clemens L.Mazzilli UWS	.20	.50
62 Sammy Sosa UWS	.10	.30
63 Lampkin Ichiro Boone UWS	.20	.50
64 B.Bonds J.Bagwell UWS	.30	.75

365 Barry Bonds HR 1	6.00	15.00
365 Barry Bonds HR 2	4.00	10.00
365 Barry Bonds HR 3	4.00	10.00
365 Barry Bonds HR 4	4.00	10.00
365 Barry Bonds HR 5	4.00	10.00
365 Barry Bonds HR 6	4.00	10.00
365 Barry Bonds HR 7	4.00	10.00
365 Barry Bonds HR 8	4.00	10.00
365 Barry Bonds HR 9	4.00	10.00
365 Barry Bonds HR 10	4.00	10.00
365 Barry Bonds HR 11	4.00	10.00
365 Barry Bonds HR 12	4.00	10.00
365 Barry Bonds HR 13	4.00	10.00
365 Barry Bonds HR 14	4.00	10.00
365 Barry Bonds HR 15	4.00	10.00
365 Barry Bonds HR 16	4.00	10.00
365 Barry Bonds HR 17	4.00	10.00
365 Barry Bonds HR 18	4.00	10.00
365 Barry Bonds HR 19	4.00	10.00
365 Barry Bonds HR 20	4.00	10.00
365 Barry Bonds HR 21	4.00	10.00
365 Barry Bonds HR 22	4.00	10.00
365 Barry Bonds HR 23	4.00	10.00
365 Barry Bonds HR 24	4.00	10.00
365 Barry Bonds HR 25	4.00	10.00
365 Barry Bonds HR 26	4.00	10.00
365 Barry Bonds HR 27	4.00	10.00
365 Barry Bonds HR 28	4.00	10.00
365 Barry Bonds HR 29	4.00	10.00
365 Barry Bonds HR 30	4.00	10.00
365 Barry Bonds HR 31	4.00	10.00
365 Barry Bonds HR 32	4.00	10.00
365 Barry Bonds HR 33	4.00	10.00
365 Barry Bonds HR 34	4.00	10.00
365 Barry Bonds HR 35	4.00	10.00
365 Barry Bonds HR 36	4.00	10.00
365 Barry Bonds HR 37	4.00	10.00
365 Barry Bonds HR 38	4.00	10.00
365 Barry Bonds HR 39	4.00	10.00
365 Barry Bonds HR 40	4.00	10.00
365 Barry Bonds HR 41	4.00	10.00
365 Barry Bonds HR 42	4.00	10.00
365 Barry Bonds HR 43	4.00	10.00
365 Barry Bonds HR 44	4.00	10.00
365 Barry Bonds HR 45	4.00	10.00
365 Barry Bonds HR 46	4.00	10.00
365 Barry Bonds HR 47	4.00	10.00
365 Barry Bonds HR 48	4.00	10.00
365 Barry Bonds HR 49	4.00	10.00
365 Barry Bonds HR 50	4.00	10.00
365 Barry Bonds HR 51	4.00	10.00
365 Barry Bonds HR 52	4.00	10.00
365 Barry Bonds HR 53	4.00	10.00
365 Barry Bonds HR 54	4.00	10.00
365 Barry Bonds HR 55	4.00	10.00
365 Barry Bonds HR 56	4.00	10.00
365 Barry Bonds HR 57	4.00	10.00
365 Barry Bonds HR 58	4.00	10.00
365 Barry Bonds HR 59	4.00	10.00
365 Barry Bonds HR 60	4.00	10.00
365 Barry Bonds HR 61	6.00	15.00
365 Barry Bonds HR 62	4.00	10.00
365 Barry Bonds HR 63	4.00	10.00
365 Barry Bonds HR 64	4.00	10.00
365 Barry Bonds HR 65	4.00	10.00
365 Barry Bonds HR 66	4.00	10.00
365 Barry Bonds HR 67	4.00	10.00
365 Barry Bonds HR 68	4.00	10.00
365 Barry Bonds HR 69	4.00	10.00
365 Barry Bonds HR 70	6.00	15.00
365 Barry Bonds HR 71	4.00	10.00
365 Barry Bonds HR 72	4.00	10.00
365 Barry Bonds HR 73	5.00	12.00
366 Pat Meares	.07	.20
367 Mike Lieberthal	.07	.20
368 Larry Bigbie	.07	.20
369 Ron Gant	.07	.20
370 Moises Alou	.07	.20
371 Chad Kreuter	.07	.20
372 Willis Roberts	.07	.20
373 Toby Hall	.07	.20
374 Miguel Batista	.07	.20
375 John Burkett	.07	.20
376 Cory Lidle	.07	.20
377 Nick Neugebauer	.07	.20
378 Jay Payton	.07	.20
379 Steve Karsay	.07	.20
380 Eric Chavez	.07	.20
381 Kelly Stinnett	.07	.20
382 Jarrod Washburn	.07	.20
383 Rick White	.07	.20
384 Jeff Conine	.07	.20
385 Fred McGriff	.10	.30
386 Marvin Benard	.07	.20
387 Joe Crede	.07	.20
388 Dennis Cook	.07	.20
389 Rick Reed	.07	.20
390 Tom Glavine	.10	.30
391 Rondell White	.07	.20
392 Matt Morris	.07	.20
393 Pat Rapp	.07	.20
394 Robert Person	.07	.20
395 Omar Vizquel	.10	.30
396 Jeff Cirillo	.07	.20
397 Dave Mlicki	.07	.20
398 Jose Ortiz	.07	.20
399 Ryan Dempster	.07	.20
400 Curt Schilling	.07	.20
401 Peter Bergeron	.07	.20
402 Kyle Lohse	.07	.20
403 Craig Wilson	.07	.20
404 David Justice	.07	.20
405 Darin Erstad	.07	.20

406 Jose Mercedes	.07	.20
407 Carl Pavano	.07	.20
408 Albie Lopez	.07	.20
409 Alex Ochoa	.07	.20
410 Chipper Jones	.20	.50
411 Tyler Houston	.07	.20
412 Dean Palmer	.07	.20
413 Damian Jackson	.07	.20
414 Josh Towers	.07	.20
415 Rafael Furcal	.07	.20
416 Mike Morgan	.07	.20
417 Herb Perry	.07	.20
418 Mike Sirotka	.07	.20
419 Mark Wohlers	.07	.20
420 Nomar Garciaparra	.30	.75
421 Felipe Lopez	.07	.20
422 Joe McEwing	.07	.20
423 Jacque Jones	.07	.20
424 Julio Franco	.07	.20
425 Frank Thomas	.20	.50
426 So Taguchi RC	.30	.75
427 Kazuhisa Ishii RC	.20	.50
428 D'Angelo Jimenez	.07	.20
429 Chris Stynes	.07	.20
430 Kerry Wood	.07	.20
431 Chris Singleton	.07	.20
432 Erubiel Durazo	.07	.20
433 Matt Lawton	.07	.20
434 Bill Mueller	.07	.20
435 Jose Canseco	.10	.30
436 Ben Grieve	.07	.20
437 Terry Mulholland	.07	.20
438 David Bell	.07	.20
439 A.J. Pierzynski	.07	.20
440 Adam Dunn	.07	.20
441 Jon Garland	.07	.20
442 Jeff Fassero	.07	.20
443 Julio Lugo	.07	.20
444 Carlos Guillen	.07	.20
445 Orlando Hernandez	.07	.20
446 M.Loretta UER Leskanic	.07	.20
447 Scott Spiezio	.07	.20
448 Kevin Millwood	.07	.20
449 Jamie Moyer	.07	.20
450 Todd Helton	.10	.30
451 Todd Walker	.07	.20
452 Jose Lima	.07	.20
453 Brook Fordyce	.07	.20
454 Aaron Rowand	.07	.20
455 Barry Zito	.07	.20
456 Eric Owens	.07	.20
457 Charles Nagy	.07	.20
458 Raul Ibanez	.07	.20
459 Joe Mays	.07	.20
460 Jim Thome	.10	.30
461 Adam Eaton	.07	.20
462 Felix Martinez	.07	.20
463 Vernon Wells	.07	.20
464 Donnie Sadler	.07	.20
465 Tony Clark	.07	.20
466 Jose Hernandez	.07	.20
467 Ramon Martinez	.07	.20
468 Rusty Greer	.07	.20
469 Rod Barajas	.07	.20
470 Lance Berkman	.07	.20
471 Brady Anderson	.07	.20
472 Pedro Astacio	.07	.20
473 Shane Halter	.07	.20
474 Bret Prinz	.07	.20
475 Edgar Martinez	.10	.30
476 Steve Trachsel	.07	.20
477 Gary Matthews Jr.	.07	.20
478 Ismael Valdes	.07	.20
479 Juan Uribe	.07	.20
480 Shawn Green	.07	.20
481 Kirk Rueter	.07	.20
482 Damion Easley	.07	.20
483 Chris Carpenter	.07	.20
484 Kris Benson	.07	.20
485 Antonio Alfonseca	.07	.20
486 Kyle Farnsworth	.07	.20
487 Brandon Lyon	.07	.20
488 Hideki Irabu	.07	.20
489 David Ortiz	.20	.50
490 Mike Piazza	.30	.75
491 Derek Lowe	.07	.20
492 Chris Gomez	.07	.20
493 Mark Johnson	.07	.20
494 John Rocker	.07	.20
495 Eric Karros	.07	.20
496 Bill Haselman	.07	.20
497 Dave Veres	.07	.20
498 Pete Harnisch	.07	.20
499 Tomokazu Ohka	.07	.20
500 Barry Bonds	.50	1.25
501 David Dellucci	.07	.20
502 Wendell Magee	.07	.20
503 Tom Gordon	.07	.20
504 Javier Vazquez	.07	.20
505 Ben Sheets	.07	.20
506 Wilton Guerrero	.07	.20
507 John Halama	.07	.20
508 Mark Redman	.07	.20
509 Jack Wilson	.07	.20
510 Bernie Williams	.10	.30
511 Miguel Cairo	.07	.20
512 Denny Hocking	.07	.20
513 Tony Batista	.07	.20
514 Mark Grudzielanek	.07	.20
515 Jose Vidro	.07	.20
516 Sterling Hitchcock	.07	.20
517 Billy Koch	.07	.20
518 Matt Clement	.07	.20

519 Bruce Chen	.07	.20
520 Roberto Alomar	.10	.30
521 Orlando Palmeiro	.07	.20
522 Steve Finley	.07	.20
523 Danny Patterson	.07	.20
524 Terry Adams	.07	.20
525 Tino Martinez	.10	.30
526 Tony Armas Jr.	.07	.20
527 Geoff Jenkins	.07	.20
528 Kerry Robinson	.07	.20
529 Corey Patterson	.07	.20
530 Brian Giles	.07	.20
531 Jose Jimenez	.07	.20
532 Joe Kennedy	.07	.20
533 Armando Rios	.07	.20
534 Osvaldo Fernandez	.07	.20
535 Ruben Sierra	.07	.20
536 Octavio Dotel	.07	.20
537 Luis Sojo	.07	.20
538 Brent Butler	.07	.20
539 Pablo Ozuna	.07	.20
540 Freddy Garcia	.07	.20
541 Chad Durbin	.07	.20
542 Orlando Merced	.07	.20
543 Michael Tucker	.07	.20
544 Roberto Hernandez	.07	.20
545 Pat Burrell	.07	.20
546 A.J. Burnett	.07	.20
547 Bubba Trammell	.07	.20
548 Scott Elarton	.07	.20
549 Mike Darr	.07	.20
550 Ken Griffey Jr.	.40	1.00
551 Ugueth Urbina	.07	.20
552 Todd Jones	.07	.20
553 Delino Deshields	.07	.20
554 Adam Piatt	.07	.20
555 Jason Kendall	.07	.20
556 Hector Ortiz	.07	.20
557 Turk Wendell	.07	.20
558 Rob Bell	.07	.20
559 Sun Woo Kim	.07	.20
560 Raul Mondesi	.07	.20
561 Brent Abernathy	.07	.20
562 Seth Etherton	.07	.20
563 Shawn Wooten	.07	.20
564 Jay Buhner	.07	.20
565 Andres Galarraga	.07	.20
566 Shane Reynolds	.07	.20
567 Rod Beck	.07	.20
568 Dee Brown	.07	.20
569 Pedro Feliz	.07	.20
570 Ryan Klesko	.07	.20
571 John Vander Wal	.07	.20
572 Nick Bierbrodt	.07	.20
573 Joe Nathan	.07	.20
574 James Baldwin	.07	.20
575 J.D. Drew	.07	.20
576 Greg Colbrunn	.07	.20
577 Doug Glanville	.07	.20
578 Brandon Duckworth	.07	.20
579 Shawn Chacon	.07	.20
580 Rich Aurilia	.07	.20
581 Chuck Finley	.07	.20
582 Abraham Nunez	.07	.20
583 Kenny Lofton	.07	.20
584 Brian Daubach	.07	.20
585 Miguel Tejada	.07	.20
586 Nate Cornejo	.07	.20
587 Kazuhiro Sasaki	.07	.20
588 Chris Richard	.07	.20
589 Armando Reynoso	.07	.20
590 Tim Hudson	.07	.20
591 Neifi Perez	.07	.20
592 Steve Cox	.07	.20
593 Henry Blanco	.07	.20
594 Ricky Ledee	.07	.20
595 Tim Salmon	.10	.30
596 Luis Rivas	.07	.20
597 Jeff Zimmerman	.07	.20
598 Matt Stairs	.07	.20
599 Preston Wilson	.07	.20
600 Mark McGwire	.50	1.25
601 Timo Perez	.07	.20
602 Matt Anderson	.07	.20
603 Todd Hundley	.07	.20
604 Rick Ankiel	.07	.20
605 Tsuyoshi Shinjo	.07	.20
606 Woody Williams	.07	.20
607 Jason LaRue	.07	.20
608 Carlos Lee	.07	.20
609 Russ Johnson	.07	.20
610 Scott Rolen	.10	.30
611 Brent Mayne	.07	.20
612 Darrin Fletcher	.07	.20
613 Ray Lankford	.07	.20
614 Troy O'Leary	.07	.20
615 Javier Lopez	.07	.20
616 Randy Velarde	.07	.20
617 Vinny Castilla	.07	.20
618 Milton Bradley	.07	.20
619 Ruben Mateo	.07	.20
620 Jason Giambi Yankees	.07	.20
621 Andy Benes	.07	.20
622 Joe Mauer RC	4.00	10.00
623 Andy Pettitte	.10	.30
624 Jose Offerman	.07	.20
625 Mo Vaughn	.07	.20
626 Steve Sparks	.07	.20
627 Mike Matthews	.07	.20
628 Robb Nen	.07	.20
629 Kip Wells	.07	.20
630 Kevin Brown	.07	.20
631 Arthur Rhodes	.07	.20

632 Gabe Kapler	.07	.20
633 Jermaine Dye	.07	.20
634 Josh Beckett	.07	.20
635 Pokey Reese	.07	.20
636 Benji Gil	.07	.20
637 Marcus Giles	.07	.20
638 Julian Tavarez	.07	.20
639 Jason Schmidt	.07	.20
640 Alex Rodriguez	.25	.60
641 Anaheim Angels TC	.07	.20
642 Arizona Diamondbacks TC	.10	.30
643 Atlanta Braves TC	.07	.20
644 Baltimore Orioles TC	.07	.20
645 Boston Red Sox TC	.07	.20
646 Chicago Cubs TC	.07	.20
647 Chicago White Sox TC	.07	.20
648 Cincinnati Reds TC	.07	.20
649 Cleveland Indians TC	.07	.20
650 Colorado Rockies TC	.07	.20
651 Detroit Tigers TC	.07	.20
652 Florida Marlins TC	.07	.20
653 Houston Astros TC	.07	.20
654 Kansas City Royals TC	.07	.20
655 Los Angeles Dodgers TC	.07	.20
656 Milwaukee Brewers TC	.07	.20
657 Minnesota Twins TC	.07	.20
658 Montreal Expos TC	.07	.20
659 New York Mets TC	.07	.20
660 New York Yankees TC	.20	.50
661 Oakland Athletics TC	.07	.20
662 Philadelphia Phillies TC	.07	.20
663 Pittsburgh Pirates TC	.07	.20
664 San Diego Padres TC	.07	.20
665 San Francisco Giants TC	.07	.20
666 Seattle Mariners TC	.10	.30
667 St. Louis Cardinals TC	.07	.20
668 Tampa Bay Devil Rays TC	.07	.20
669 Texas Rangers TC	.07	.20
670 Toronto Blue Jays TC	.07	.20
671 Juan Cruz PROS	.20	.50
672 Kevin Cash PROS RC	.20	.50
673 Jimmy Gobble PROS RC	.20	.50
674 Mike Hill PROS RC	.20	.50
675 Taylor Buchholz PROS RC	.20	.50
676 Bill Hall PROS	.20	.50
677 Brett Roneberg PROS RC	.20	.50
678 Royce Huffman PROS RC	.20	.50
679 Chris Tritle PROS RC	.20	.50
680 Nate Espy PROS RC	.20	.50
681 Nick Alvarez PROS RC	.20	.50
682 Jason Botts PROS RC	.20	.50
683 Ryan Gripp PROS RC	.20	.50
684 Dan Phillips PROS RC	.20	.50
685 Pablo Arias PROS RC	.20	.50
686 John Rodriguez PROS RC	.20	.50
687 Rich Harden PROS RC	1.25	3.00
688 Neal Frendling PROS RC	.20	.50
689 Rich Thompson PROS RC	.20	.50
690 Greg Montalbano PROS RC	.20	.50
691 Len Dinardo DP RC	.20	.50
692 Ryan Raburn DP RC	.40	1.00
693 Josh Barfield DP RC	1.00	2.50
694 David Bacani DP RC	.20	.50
695 Dan Johnson DP RC	.40	1.00
696 Mike Mussina GG	.07	.20
697 Ivan Rodriguez GG	.10	.30
698 Doug Mientkiewicz GG	.07	.20
699 Roberto Alomar GG	.07	.20
700 Eric Chavez GG	.07	.20
701 Omar Vizquel GG	.07	.20
702 Mike Cameron GG	.07	.20
703 Torii Hunter GG	.07	.20
704 Ichiro Suzuki GG	.20	.50
705 Greg Maddux GG	.20	.50
706 Brad Ausmus GG	.07	.20
707 Todd Helton GG	.07	.20
708 Fernando Vina GG	.07	.20
709 Scott Rolen GG	.07	.20
710 Orlando Cabrera GG	.07	.20
711 Andruw Jones GG	.07	.20
712 Jim Edmonds GG	.07	.20
713 Larry Walker GG	.07	.20
714 Roger Clemens CY	.20	.50
715 Randy Johnson CY	.10	.30
716 Ichiro Suzuki MVP	.20	.50
717 Barry Bonds MVP	.30	.75
718 Ichiro Suzuki ROY	.20	.50
719 Albert Pujols ROY	.20	.50

2002 Topps Gold

*GOLD 1-306/366-670: 8X TO 20X BASIC
*GOLD 307-330/671-695: 1.5X TO 4X BASIC
*GOLD 426-427: 1.5X TO 4X BASIC
SER.1 ODDS 1:19 HOB, 1:5 HTA, 1:15 RET
SER.2 ODDS 1:12 HOB, 1:3 HTA, 1:9 RET
STATED PRINT RUN 2002 SERIAL #'d SETS

622 Joe Mauer	10.00	25.00

2002 Topps Home Team Advantage

COMP.FACT.SET (718)	40.00	80.00

*HTA: .75X TO 2X BASIC
*BONDS HR 70: .2X TO .5X BASIC HR 70
DISTRIBUTED IN FACT.SET FORM
HTA FACT.SET IS BLUE BOXED

2002 Topps Limited

COMP.FACT.SET (790)	60.00	150.00

*LTD STARS: 1.5X TO 4X BASIC CARDS
*307-331/426-427/622/671-695: 1.5X TO 4X
*BONDS HR: .2X TO .5X BASIC BONDS HR
DISTRIBUTED ONLY IN FACTORY SET FORM
STATED PRINT RUN 1950 SETS

622 Joe Mauer	30.00	60.00

2002 Topps '52 Reprints

Inserted at a rate of one in 25 hobby, one in five HTA packs and one in 16 retail packs, these nineteen reprint cards feature players who participated in the 1952 World Series which was won by the New York Yankees.

COMPLETE SET (19)	20.00	50.00
COMPLETE SERIES 1 (9)	10.00	25.00
COMPLETE SERIES 2 (10)	10.00	25.00

SER.1 ODDS 1:25 HOB, 1:5 HTA, 1:16 RET
SER.2 ODDS 1:25 HOB, 1:5 HTA, 1:16 RET

52R1 Roy Campanella	2.00	5.00
52R2 Duke Snider	1.50	4.00
52R3 Carl Erskine	1.50	4.00
52R4 Andy Pafko	1.50	4.00
52R5 Johnny Mize	1.50	4.00
52R6 Billy Martin	1.50	4.00
52R7 Phil Rizzuto	2.00	5.00
52R8 Gil McDougald	1.50	4.00
52R9 Allie Reynolds	1.50	4.00
52R10 Jackie Robinson	2.00	5.00
52R11 Preacher Roe	1.50	4.00
52R12 Gil Hodges	2.00	5.00
52R13 Billy Cox	1.50	4.00
52R14 Yogi Berra	2.00	5.00
52R15 Gene Woodling	1.50	4.00
52R16 Johnny Sain	1.50	4.00
52R17 Ralph Houk	1.50	4.00
52R18 Joe Collins	1.50	4.00
52R19 Hank Bauer	1.50	4.00

2002 Topps '52 Reprints Autographs

Inserted in series one packs at a rate of one in 10,268 hobby packs, one in 2826 HTA packs and one in 8,005 retail packs and series two packs at a rate of 1:7524 hobby, one in 1985 HTA packs and one in 5839 retail packs these eleven cards feature signed copies of the 1952 reprints. Phil Rizzuto did not return his cards in time for inclusion in this product and those cards could be redeemed until December 1st, 2003. Due to scarcity, no pricing is provided for these cards. These cards were released in different series and we have notated that information next to the player's name in our checklist.

SER.1 ODDS 1:10,268 H, 1:2826 HTA, 1:8005 R
SER.2 ODDS 1:7524 H, 1:1985 HTA, 1:5839 R
SER.1 EXCH. DEADLINE 12/01/03

APA Andy Pafko S1	100.00	175.00
CEA Carl Erskine S1	50.00	100.00
DSA Duke Snider S1	25.00	60.00
GMA Gil McDougald S1	30.00	60.00
HBA Hank Bauer S2	15.00	60.00
JBA Joe Black S1	50.00	100.00
JSA Johnny Sain S2	12.00	30.00
PRA Preacher Roe S2	30.00	60.00
PRA Phil Rizzuto S1	40.00	100.00
RHA Ralph Houk S2	50.00	100.00
YBA Yogi Berra S2	60.00	120.00

2002 Topps '52 World Series Highlights

Inserted in first and second series packs at a rate of one in 25 hobby, one in five HTA and one in 16 retail packs, these eleven cards feature highlights of the 1952 World Series. Next to the card, we have notated whether they were released in the first or second series.

COMPLETE SET (7)	4.00	10.00
COMPLETE SERIES 1 (3)	1.50	4.00
COMPLETE SERIES 2 (4)	2.50	6.00

SER.1 ODDS 1:25 HOB, 1:5 HTA, 1:16 RET
SER.2 ODDS 1:25 HOB, 1:5 HTA, 1:16 RET

52WS1 Dodgers Line Up 1	.75	2.00
52WS2 Billy Martin's Homer 2	.75	2.00
52WS3 Dodgers Celebrate 1	.75	2.00
52WS4 Yanks Slip Dodgers 2	.75	2.00
52WS5 Carl Erskine 1	.75	2.00
52WS6 Stengel Reynolds 2	.75	2.00
52WS7 Reynolds Relieves 2	.75	2.00

2002 Topps 5-Card Stud Aces Relics

Inserted into second series packs at a rate of one in 1180 hobby, one in 293 HTA and one in 966 retail, these five cards feature some of the best pitchers in baseball along with a game jersey swatch "relic".

SER.2 ODDS 1:1180 H, 1:293 HTA, 1:966 R

5AGM Greg Maddux Jsy	12.50	30.00
5AMH Mike Hampton Jsy	10.00	25.00
5AMM Mark Mulder Jsy	10.00	25.00
5APM Pedro Martinez Jsy	15.00	40.00
5ARJ Randy Johnson Jsy	15.00	40.00

2002 Topps 5-Card Stud Deuces are Wild Relics

Inserted into second series packs at an overall rate of one in 1962 hobby, one in 487 HTA and one in 1609 retail, these five cards feature memorabilia game bat and game jersey relics from two of the stars from the same team. These cards were issued in different odds depending on which series they were from and we have notated which group next to the card in the checklist.

SER.2 A ODDS 1:3078 H, 1:796 HTA, 1:2422 R
SER.2 B ODDS 1:5410 H, 1:1254 HTA, 1:4827 R
SER.2 ODDS 1:1962 H, 1:487 HTA, 1:1609 R

5DBG B.Boone/F.Garcia A	15.00	40.00
5DBK B.Bonds/J.Kent A	40.00	80.00
5DJG R.Johnson/L.Gonzalez B	15.00	40.00
5DTA J.Thome/R.Alomar B	30.00	60.00
5DWH L.Walker/T.Helton B	30.00	60.00

2002 Topps 5-Card Stud Jack of All Trades Relics

Inserted into second series packs at an overall rate of one in 1350 Hobby packs, one in 333 HTA packs and one on 1119 retail packs, these five cards feature some of the best five-tool players in the field along with a game-used memorabilia relic from their career. These cards were issued at different odds depending on the player and we have notated that information in our checklist.

SER.2 A ODDS 1:1454 H, 1:357 HTA, 1:1211 R
SER.2B ODDS 1:18883 H,1:4943 HTA,1:14736 R
SER.2 ODDS 1:1350 H, 1:333 HTA, 1:1119

5JAJ Andruw Jones A 10.00 25.00
5JBB Barry Bonds A 10.00 25.00
5JBW Bernie Williams A 10.00 25.00
5JIR Ivan Rodriguez A 10.00 25.00
5JRO Roberto Alomar B 10.00 25.00

2002 Topps 5-Card Stud Kings of the Clubhouse Relics

Inserted into packs at an overall rate of one in 1449 hobby packs, one in 334 HTA packs and one in 1119 retail packs, these five cards feature some of the most effective and highly driven clubhouse leaders along with a game-used memorabilia relic from their career. Depending on the player, these cards were issued in two groups and we have notated that information in our checklist.

SER.2 A ODDS 1:1570 H, 1:358 HTA, 1:1211 R
SER.2B ODDS 1:18883 H,1:4943 HTA,1:14736 R
SER.2 ODDS 1:1449 H, 1:334 HTA, 1:1119 R
5KEM Edgar Martinez A 6.00 15.00
5KPO Paul O'Neill B 6.00 15.00
5KRJ Randy Johnson A 6.00 15.00
5KTG Tom Glavine A 6.00 15.00
5KTH Todd Helton A 6.00 15.00

2002 Topps 5-Card Stud Three of a Kind Relics

Inserted into packs at an overall rate of one in 2039 Hobby packs, one in 524 HTA packs and one in retail 1609 packs, these five cards feature memorabilia relics from three stars from the same team. Depending on the card, these cards were issued as part of two groups, and we have notated that information next to the card in our checklist

SER.2 A ODDS 1:3078 H, 1:796 HTA, 1:2422 R
SER.2 B ODDS 1:6043 H, 1:1532 HTA, 1:4827 R
SER.2 ODDS 1:2039 H, 1:524 HTA, 1:1609 R
5TBDB Burnett/Demp/Beckett A 30.00 60.00
5TFBJ Furcal/Betemit/A.Jones B 30.00 60.00
5TLOC Lee/Ordonez/Canseco B 30.00 60.00
5TPSW Posada/Soriano/Will B 30.00 60.00
5TSPA Shinjo/Piazza/Alfonzo A 30.00 60.00

2002 Topps All-World Team

Inserted into second series packs at a rate of one in 12 packs and one in 4 HTA packs, these 25 cards feature an international mix of upper-echelon stars. These cards are extremely thick as well.

COMPLETE SET (25) 30.00 60.00
SER.2 STATED ODDS 1:12 HOB/RET, 1:4 HTA
AW1 Ichiro Suzuki 1.50 4.00
AW2 Barry Bonds 2.00 5.00
AW3 Pedro Martinez .60 1.50
AW4 Juan Gonzalez .60 1.50
AW5 Larry Walker .60 1.50
AW6 Sammy Sosa .75 2.00
AW7 Mariano Rivera .75 2.00
AW8 Vladimir Guerrero .75 2.00
AW9 Alex Rodriguez 1.00 2.50
AW10 Albert Pujols 1.50 4.00
AW11 Luis Gonzalez .60 1.50
AW12 Ken Griffey Jr. 1.50 4.00
AW13 Kazuhiro Sasaki .60 1.50
AW14 Bob Abreu .60 1.50
AW15 Todd Helton .60 1.50
AW16 Nomar Garciaparra 1.25 3.00
AW17 Miguel Tejada .60 1.50
AW18 Roger Clemens 1.50 4.00
AW19 Mike Piazza 1.25 3.00
AW20 Carlos Delgado .60 1.50
AW21 Derek Jeter 2.00 5.00
AW22 Hideo Nomo .75 2.00
AW23 Randy Johnson .75 2.00
AW24 Ivan Rodriguez .60 1.50
AW25 Chan Ho Park .60 1.50

2002 Topps Autographs

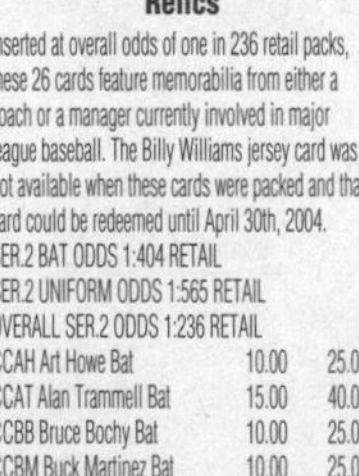

Inserted at varying odds, these 40 cards feature authentic autographs. Alex Rodriguez, Barry Bonds and Xavier Nady did not return their cards in time for series one packout, thus exchange cards were seeded into packs. Those cards could be redeemed until December 1st, 2003. First series cards have a numerical card number on back (i.e. TA-1) and series two cards have card numbering based on player's initials (i.e. TA-AB).

C1 MINOR STARS 10.00 25.00
SER.1 A 1:15,402 H, 1:4256 HTA, 1:12,008 R
SER.2 A 1:10,071 H, 1:2404, 1:7702 R
SER.1 B 1:49,599 H, 1:12,312 HTA, 1:46,944 R
SER.2 B 1:1867 H, 1:487 HTA, 1:1449 R
SER.1 C 1:4104 H, 1:1130 HTA, 1:3238 R
SER.2 C 1:10,071 H, 1:2646 HTA, 1:7702 R
SER.1 D 1:9853 H, 1:2714 HTA, 1:7284 R
SER.2 D 1:1885 H, 1:496 HTA, 1:1449 R
SER.1 E 1:4104 H, 1:1130 HTA, 1:3238 R
SER.2 E 1:5023 H, 1:1323 HTA, 1:3851 R
SER.1 F 1:985 H, 1:271 HTA, 1:776 R
SER.2 F 1:940 H, 1:247 HTA, 1:725 R
SER.2 G 1:3017 H, 1:794 HTA, 1:2327 R
SER.2 EXCHANGE DEADLINE 12/01/03
NO A1 PRICING DUE TO SCARCITY
TA1 Carlos Delgado B1 6.00 15.00
TA3 Miguel Tejada C1 4.00 15.00
TA4 Geoff Jenkins E1 6.00 15.00
TA6 Tim Hudson C1 6.00 15.00
TA7 Terrence Long E1 4.00 10.00
TA8 Gabe Kapler C1 10.00 25.00
TA9 Magglio Ordonez C1 6.00 15.00
TA11 Pat Burrell C1 10.00 25.00
TA13 Eric Valent F1 4.00 10.00
TA14 Xavier Nady F1 4.00 10.00
TA15 Cristian Guerrero F1 4.00 10.00
TA16 Ben Sheets F1 6.00 15.00
TA17 Corey Patterson C1 6.00 15.00
TA18 Carlos Pena F1 4.00 10.00
TA19 Alex Rodriguez D1-A2 20.00 50.00
TAAB Adrian Beltre B2 6.00 15.00
TAAE Alex Escobar F2 4.00 10.00
TABG Brian Giles B2 6.00 15.00
TABW Brad Wilkerson G2 4.00 10.00
TACF Cliff Floyd C2 4.00 10.00
TACG Cristian Guzman B2 6.00 15.00
TAJD Jermaine Dye D2 4.00 10.00
TAJH Josh Hamilton 10.00 25.00
TAJO Jose Ortiz D2 6.00 15.00
TAJR Jimmy Rollins D2 10.00 25.00
TAJW Justin Wayne D2 6.00 15.00
TAKG Keith Ginter F2 4.00 10.00
TAMS Mike Sweeney B2 12.50 30.00
TANJ Nick Johnson F2 6.00 15.00
TARF Rafael Furcal B2 6.00 15.00
TARK Ryan Klesko B2 12.50 30.00
TARO Roy Oswalt F2 4.00 10.00
TARP Rafael Palmeiro A2 15.00 40.00
TARS Richie Sexson B2 12.50 30.00
TATG Troy Glaus A2 8.00 20.00
TABGR Ben Grieve B2 8.00 20.00

2002 Topps Coaches Collection Relics

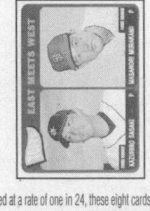

Inserted at overall odds of one in 236 retail packs, these 26 cards feature memorabilia from either a coach or a manager currently involved in major league baseball. The Billy Williams jersey card was not available when these cards were packed and that card could be redeemed until April 30th, 2004.

SER.2 BAT ODDS 1:404 RETAIL
SER.2 UNIFORM ODDS 1:565 RETAIL
OVERALL SER.2 ODDS 1:236 RETAIL
CCAH Art Howe Bat 10.00 25.00
CCAT Alan Trammell Bat 15.00 40.00
CCBB Bruce Bochy Bat 10.00 25.00
CCBM Buck Martinez Bat 10.00 25.00
CCBV Bobby Valentine Bat 15.00 40.00
CCBW Billy Williams Jsy 15.00 40.00
CCBBE Buddy Bell Bat 15.00 40.00
CCBBR Bob Brenly Bat 15.00 40.00
CCDB Dusty Baker Bat 15.00 40.00
CCDL Davey Lopes Bat 15.00 40.00
CCDBA Don Baylor Bat 15.00 40.00
CCEH Elrod Hendricks Bat 10.00 25.00
CCEM Eddie Murray Bat 30.00 60.00
CCFW Frank White Bat 15.00 40.00
CCHM Hal McRae Jsy 4.00 10.00
CCJT Joe Torre Jsy 6.00 15.00
CCKG Ken Griffey Sr. Jsy 4.00 10.00
CCLB Larry Bowa Bat 15.00 40.00
CCLP Lance Parrish Bat 15.00 40.00
CCMH Mike Hargrove Bat 15.00 40.00
CCMS Mike Scioscia Bat 15.00 40.00
CCMW Mookie Wilson Bat 15.00 40.00
CCPG Phil Garner Bat 15.00 40.00
CCPM Paul Molitor Bat 15.00 40.00
CCTP Tony Perez Jsy 4.00 10.00
CCWR Willie Randolph Bat 15.00 40.00

2002 Topps Draft Picks

This 10-card set was distributed in two separate cello-wrapped five-card packets. Cards 1-5 were distributed in late August, 2002 as a bonus in green-boxed 2002 Topps retail factory sets. Cards 6-10 were distributed in November, 2002 within 2002 Topps Holiday factory sets. The cards are designed in the same manner as the Draft Picks and Prospects subsets from the basic 2002 Topps set and feature a selection of players chosen in the 2002 MLB Draft.

COMPLETE SET (10) 15.00 40.00
COMP.SERIES 1 SET (5) 6.00 15.00
COMP.SERIES 2 SET (5) 10.00 25.00
1-5 DIST.IN 02 TOPPS GREEN FACTORY SET
6-10 DIST.IN 02 TOPPS BLUE FACTORY SET
1 Scott Moore 2.00 5.00
2 Val Majewski 1.50 4.00
3 Brian Slocum 1.50 4.00
4 Chris Gruler 1.50 4.00
5 Mark Schramek 1.50 4.00
6 Joe Saunders 3.00 8.00
7 Jeff Francis 3.00 8.00
8 Royce Ring 1.50 4.00
9 Greg Miller 1.50 4.00
10 Brandon Weeden 1.50 4.00

2002 Topps East Meets West

Issued at a rate of one in 24, these eight cards feature Masanori Murakami along with eight other Japanese players who have also played in the major leagues.

COMPLETE SET (8) 6.00 15.00
SER.1 STATED ODDS 1:24 HOB/HTA/RET
EWHI H.Irabu .75 2.00
M.Murakami
EWHN H.Nomo .75 2.00
M.Murakami
EWKS K.Sasaki .75 2.00
M.Murakami
EWMS M.Suzuki .75 2.00
M.Murakami
EWMY M.Yoshii .75 2.00
M.Murakami
EWSH S.Hasegawa .75 2.00
M.Murakami
EWTO T.Ohka .75 2.00
M.Murakami
EWTS T.Shinjo .75 2.00
M.Murakami

2002 Topps East Meets West Relics

Inserted in packs at different odds depending on whether it is a bat or jersey card, these three cards feature game-used relics from Japanese born players.

SR1 BAT 1:12296 H,1:3380 HTA,1:9606 R
SER.1 JSY 1:3419 H, 1:939 HTA, 1:2685 R
EWRHN Hideo Nomo Jsy 20.00 50.00
EWRKS Kazuhiro Sasaki Jsy 10.00 25.00
EWRTS Tsuyoshi Shinjo Bat 10.00 25.00

2002 Topps Ebbets Field Seat Relics

Inserted at a rate of one in 9,116 hobby packs, one in 2516 HTA packs and one in 7,222 retail packs, these nine cards feature not only the player but a slice of a seat used at Brooklyn's Ebbetts Field.

SER.1 ODDS 1:9116 H, 1:2516 HTA, 1:7222 R
EFRAP Andy Pafko 75.00 150.00
EFRBC Billy Cox 200.00 300.00
EFRCF Carl Furillo 75.00 150.00
EFRDS Duke Snider 150.00 250.00
EFRGH Gil Hodges 150.00 250.00
EFRJB Joe Black 75.00 150.00
EFRJR Jackie Robinson 200.00 300.00
EFRRC Roy Campanella 200.00 300.00
EFRPWR Pee Wee Reese 200.00 300.00

2002 Topps Hall of Fame Vintage BuyBacks AutoProofs

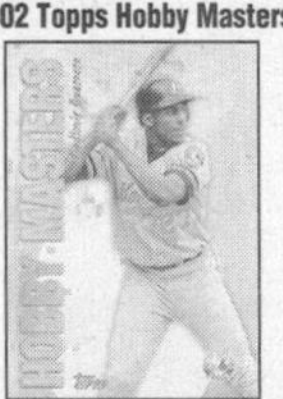

In one of the most ambitious efforts put forth by a manufacturer in hobby history, Topps went into the secondary market and bought more than 3,500 vintage Topps cards (including an amazing selection from the 1950's and 1960's) featuring almost two dozen Hall of Famers (including stars such as Nolan Ryan, Yogi Berra and Carl Yastrzemski) for this far-reaching AutoProofs promotion. In most cases, 100 count lots of each vintage card were used (a staggering figure considering the scarcity of many of the 1950's and 1960's cards) with a few of the more common cards from the early 1980's tallying 200 or 300 count lots. After repurchase, each card was signed by the featured athlete, serial-numbered to a specific amount (exact print runs provided in our checklist) and affixed with a Topps hologram of authenticity on back. The cards were distributed across many 2002 Topps products - starting off with 2002 Topps series one baseball in November, 2001. Odds for finding these cards in packs is as follows: series 1 - 1:2341 hobby and 1:1841 retail; series 2 - 1:2341 hobby, 1:1841 retail.

SER.1 ODDS 1:2,341 H, 1:643 HTA, 1:1841 R
SER.2 ODDS 1:2,431 H, 1:641 HTA, 1:1866 R
SEE BECKETT.COM FOR CHECKLIST
SEEDED IN MANY 2002 TOPPS BRANDS
BW1 Billy Williams 74 AS/100 20.00 50.00
BW2 Billy Williams 76/100 20.00 50.00
EW8 Earl Weaver 83/100 6.00 15.00
JP3 Jim Palmer 82 IA/100 10.00 25.00
OC2 Orl Cepeda 82 KM/200 10.00 25.00
SA1 Sparky Anderson 85/100 15.00 40.00
SC7 Steve Carlton 84 LL V/100 10.00 25.00
SC8 Steve Carlton 85/200 10.00 25.00
BR17 B.Robinson 82 KM/200 15.00 40.00
EW10 Earl Weaver 87/100 10.00 25.00
FJ33 Fergie Jenkins 84/100 10.00 25.00
GP21 Gaylord Perry 79/100 8.00 20.00
GP26 Gaylord Perry 82/100 10.00 25.00
GP29 Gaylord Perry 83/100 6.00 15.00
GP30 Gaylord Perry 83 SV/200 10.00 25.00
RF14 Rollie Fingers 80/100 6.00 15.00
RF15 Rollie Fingers 81/300 10.00 25.00
RF16 Rollie Fingers 81 LL/100 10.00 25.00
RF18 Rollie Fingers 82/100 10.00 25.00
RF19 Rollie Fingers 82 IA/200 10.00 25.00
RF21 Rollie Fingers 82 KM/300 10.00 25.00
RF22 Rollie Fingers 83/200 6.00 15.00
RF24 Rollie Fingers 84/200 10.00 25.00
RF27 Rollie Fingers 85/300 10.00 25.00
RF28 Rollie Fingers 86/100 10.00 25.00
SC10 Steve Carlton 87/200 10.00 25.00

2002 Topps Hobby Masters

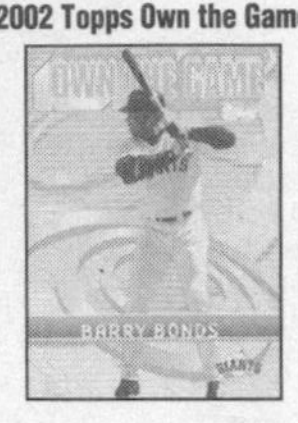

Inserted at a rate of one in 25 hobby and one in 16 retail packs, these 20 cards feature some of the leading players in the game.

COMPLETE SET (20) 30.00 80.00
SER.1 ODDS 1:25 HOBBY, 1:5 HTA 1:16 RETAIL
HM1 Mark McGwire 3.00 8.00
HM2 Derek Jeter 3.00 8.00
HM3 Chipper Jones 1.25 3.00
HM4 Roger Clemens 2.50 6.00
HM5 Vladimir Guerrero 1.25 3.00
HM6 Ichiro Suzuki 2.50 6.00
HM7 Todd Helton 1.25 3.00
HM8 Alex Rodriguez 1.50 4.00
HM9 Albert Pujols 2.50 6.00
HM10 Sammy Sosa 1.25 3.00
HM11 Ken Griffey Jr. 2.50 6.00
HM12 Randy Johnson 1.25 3.00
HM13 Nomar Garciaparra 2.00 5.00
HM14 Ivan Rodriguez 1.25 3.00
HM15 Manny Ramirez 1.25 3.00
HM16 Barry Bonds 3.00 8.00
HM17 Mike Piazza 2.00 5.00
HM18 Pedro Martinez 1.25 3.00
HM19 Jeff Bagwell 1.25 3.00
HM20 Luis Gonzalez 1.25 3.00

2002 Topps Like Father Like Son Relics

These combination memorabilia cards feature famous baseball families with two generations of fathers and sons. The card designs are each based upon the original Topps design of the father's rookie card season (aka The Boone Family card features a 1973 Topps style to honor the year Bob Boone had his Rookie Card issued). The cards were seeded exclusively into retail packs at a rate of 1:1304.

COMMON CARD 10.00 25.00
SER.1 GROUP A ODDS 1:6259 RETAIL
SER.1 GROUP B ODDS 1:6259 RETAIL
SER.1 GROUP C ODDS 1:2235 RETAIL
SER.1 OVERALL ODDS 1:1304 RETAIL
FSAL The Alomar Family A 40.00 80.00
FSBE The Berra Family C 10.00 25.00
FSBON The Bonds Family C 12.50 30.00
FSBOO The Boone Family A 10.00 25.00
FSCR The Cruz Family B 10.00 25.00

2002 Topps Own the Game

Issued at a rate of one in 12 hobby packs and one in eight retail packs, these 30 cards feature players who are among the league leaders for their position.

COMPLETE SET (30) 15.00 40.00
SER.1 ODDS 1:12 HOBBY, 1:4 HTA, 1:8 RETAIL
OG1 Moises Alou .40 1.00
OG2 Roberto Alomar .60 1.50
OG3 Luis Gonzalez .40 1.00
OG4 Bret Boone .40 1.00
OG5 Barry Bonds 2.50 6.00
OG6 Jim Thome .60 1.50
OG7 Jimmy Rollins .40 1.00
OG8 Cristian Guzman .40 1.00
OG9 Lance Berkman .40 1.00
OG10 Mike Sweeney .40 1.00
OG11 Rich Aurilia .40 1.00
OG12 Ichiro Suzuki 2.00 5.00
OG13 Luis Gonzalez .40 1.00
OG14 Ichiro Suzuki 2.00 5.00
OG15 Jimmy Rollins .40 1.00
OG16 Roger Cedeno .40 1.00
OG17 Barry Bonds 2.50 6.00
OG18 Jim Thome .60 1.50
OG19 Curt Schilling .40 1.00
OG20 Roger Clemens 2.00 5.00
OG21 Curt Schilling .40 1.00
OG22 Brad Radke .40 1.00
OG23 Greg Maddux 1.50 4.00
OG24 Mark Mulder .40 1.00
OG25 Jeff Shaw .40 1.00
OG26 Mariano Rivera 1.00 2.50
OG27 Randy Johnson 1.00 2.50
OG28 Pedro Martinez .60 1.50
OG29 John Burkett .40 1.00
OG30 Tim Hudson .40 1.00

2002 Topps Prime Cuts Autograph Relics

Inserted into first series packs at a rate of one in 88,678 hobby and one in 24,624 HTA and second series packs at one in 8927 hobby and one in 2360 HTA packs, these eight cards feature both a memorabilia relic from the player's career as well as their autograph. Cards from series one were issued to a stated print run of 60 serial numbered sets while cards from series two were issued to a stated print run of 50 serial numbered sets. We have notated next to the players name which series the card was issued in.

PCAAE Alex Escobar S2 12.50 30.00
PCABB Barry Bonds S1 400.00 600.00
PCAJH Josh Hamilton 50.00 100.00
PCANJ Nick Johnson S2 15.00 40.00
PCATH Toby Hall S2 15.00 40.00
PCAWB Wilson Betemit S2 15.00 40.00
PCAXN Xavier Nady S2 10.00 25.00
PCACPE Carlos Pena S2 15.00 40.00

2002 Topps Prime Cuts Barrel Relics

Inserted in second series packs at a rate of one in 7824 hobby packs and one in 2063 HTA packs, these eight cards feature a piece from the selected player bat barrel. These cards were issued to a stated print run of 50 serial numbered sets.

PCAAD Adam Dunn 8.00 20.00
PCAAG Alexis Gomez 8.00 20.00
PCAAR Aaron Rowand 10.00 25.00
PCACP Corey Patterson 8.00 20.00
PCAJC Joe Crede 8.00 20.00
PCAMG Marcus Giles
PCARS Ruben Salazar
PCASB Sean Burroughs 8.00 20.00

2002 Topps Prime Cuts Pine Tar Relics

Inserted in packs at stated odds of one in 4,420 hobby packs and one in 1214 HTA packs for first series packs and one in 1043 hobby and one in 275 HTA packs for second series packs, these 20 cards feature pieces from the pine tar section of the player's bat. We have notated which series the player was issued in next to his name in our checklist. These cards have a stated print run of 200 serial numbered sets.

SER.1 ODDS 1:4420 HOBBY, 1:1214 HTA
SER.2 ODDS 1:1043 HOBBY, 1:275 HTA
STATED PRINT RUN 200 SERIAL #'d SETS
PCPAD Adam Dunn 2 5.00 12.00
PCPAE Alex Escobar 2 5.00 12.00
PCPAG Alexis Gomez 2 5.00 12.00
PCPAP Albert Pujols 1 10.00 25.00
PCPAR Aaron Rowand 2 6.00 15.00
PCPBB Barry Bonds 1 10.00 25.00
PCPCP Corey Patterson 2 5.00 12.00
PCPJC Joe Crede 2 5.00 12.00
PCPJH Josh Hamilton 8.00 25.00
PCPLG Luis Gonzalez 1 6.00 15.00
PCPMG Marcus Giles 2 5.00 12.00
PCPNJ Nick Johnson 2 5.00 12.00
PCPRS Ruben Salazar 2 5.00 12.00
PCPSB Sean Burroughs 2 5.00 12.00
PCPTG Tony Gwynn 1 6.00 15.00
PCPTH Todd Helton 1 8.00 20.00
PCPTH Toby Hall 2 5.00 12.00
PCPWB Wilson Betemit 2 5.00 12.00
PCPXN Xavier Nady 2 5.00 12.00
PCPCPE Carlos Pena 2 6.00 15.00

2002 Topps Prime Cuts Trademark Relics

Issued in first series packs at a rate of one in 8,868 hobby and one in 2428 HTA packs and second series packs at a rate of one in 2087 hobby and one in 549 HTA packs, these cards feature a slice of bat taken from the trademark section of a game used bat. Only 100 serial numbered copies of each card were produced. First and second series distribution information is detailed after the player's name in our set checklist.

SER.1 ODDS 1:8868 HOBBY, 1:2428 HTA
SER.2 ODDS 1:2087 HOBBY, 1:549 HTA
STATED PRINT RUN 100 SERIAL #'d SETS
PCTAD Adam Dunn 2 10.00 25.00
PCTAE Alex Escobar 2 10.00 25.00
PCTAG Alexis Gomez 2 10.00 25.00
PCTAP Albert Pujols 1 15.00 40.00
PCTAR Aaron Rowand 2 10.00 25.00
PCTBB Barry Bonds 1 20.00 50.00
PCTCP Corey Patterson 2 10.00 25.00
PCTJC Joe Crede 2 10.00 25.00
PCTJH Josh Hamilton 15.00 40.00
PCTLG Luis Gonzalez 1 10.00 25.00
PCTMG Marcus Giles 2 10.00 25.00
PCTNJ Nick Johnson 2 10.00 25.00
PCTRS Ruben Salazar 2 10.00 25.00
PCTSB Sean Burroughs 2 10.00 25.00
PCTTG Tony Gwynn 1 10.00 25.00
PCTTH Todd Helton 1 10.00 25.00
PCTTH Toby Hall 2 10.00 25.00
PCTWB Wilson Betemit 2 10.00 25.00
PCTXN Xavier Nady 2 10.00 25.00
PCTCPE Carlos Pena 2 10.00 25.00

2002 Topps Ring Masters

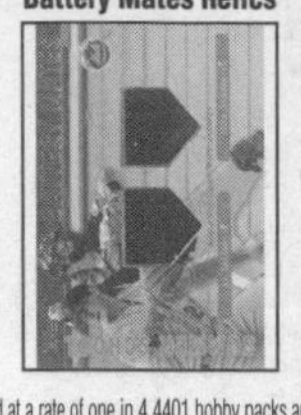

Issued at a rate of one in 25 hobby packs and one in 16 retail packs, these 10 cards feature players who have earned World Series rings in their career.

COMPLETE SET (10) 10.00 25.00
SER.1 ODDS 1:25 HOBBY, 1:5 HTA 1:16 RETAIL
RM1 Derek Jeter 2.00 5.00
RM2 Mark McGwire 2.00 5.00
RM3 Mariano Rivera .75 2.00
RM4 Gary Sheffield .60 1.50
RM5 Al Leiter .60 1.50
RM6 Chipper Jones .75 2.[...]
RM7 Roger Clemens 1.50 4.[...]
RM8 Greg Maddux 1.25 3.[...]
RM9 Roberto Alomar .60 1.[...]
RM10 Paul O'Neill .60 1.[...]

2002 Topps Summer School Battery Mates Relics

Issued at a rate of one in 4,4401 hobby packs and one in 3,477 retail packs, these two cards feature a[...] pitcher and catcher from the same team.

SER.1 ODDS 1:4401 H, 1:1210 HTA, 1:3477 R
BMLP A.Leiter/M.Piazza 6.00 15.[...]
BMML G.Maddux/J.Lopez 10.00 25.[...]

2002 Topps Summer School Heart of the Order Relics

Issued at an overall rate of one in 4,247 hobby pac[...] and one in 3,325 retail packs, these four cards feature relics from three key players from a team's lineup.

SER.1 A 1:8,220 H, 1:2253 HTA, 1:6452 R
SER.1 B 1:8,778 H, 1:2411 HTA, 1:6862 R
SER.1 ODDS 1:4,247 H, 1:1165 HTA, 1:3325 R
HTOARB Abreu/Rolen/Burrell A 40.00 80.[...]
HTOKBA Kent/Bonds/Aurilia A 50.00 100.[...]
HTOOWM O'Neill/B.Will/Tino A 40.00 80.[...]
HTOTGA Thome/Gonz/Alom B 40.00 80.[...]

2002 Topps Summer School Hi[...] and Run Relics

Issued at an overall rate of one in 4,241 hobby pac[...] and one in 3,325 retail packs, these three cards feature relics from some of the leading young stars baseball.

SER.1 A 1:24591 H, 1:6760 HTA, 1:19649 R
SER.1 B 1:12296 H, 1:3380 HTA, 1:9606 R
SER.1 C 1:8788 H, 1:2411 HTA, 1:6862 R
SER.1 ODDS 1:4241 H, 1:1165 HTA, 1:3325 R
HRRDE Darin Erstad Bat B 6.00 15.[...]
HRRJD Johnny Damon Bat A 10.00 25.[...]
HRRRF Rafael Furcal Jsy C 6.00 15.[...]

2002 Topps Summer School Turn Two Relics

Issued at a rate of one in 4,401 hobby packs and on[...] in 3,477 retail packs, these two cards feature relics from two of the best double play combination in baseball's history.

SER.1 ODDS 1:4401 H, 1:1210 HTA, 1:3477 R
TTRTW A.Trammell/L.Whitaker 10.00 25.[...]
TTRVA O.Vizquel/R.Alomar 10.00 25.[...]

2002 Topps Summer School Tw[...] Bagger Relics

Issued at an overall rate of one in 3,733 hobby pack[...] and one in 2,941 retail packs, these three cards feature game-used relics from leading hitters in the game.

SER.1 A 1:4401 H, 1:1210 HTA, 1:3477 R
SER.1 B 1:24591 H,1:6760 HTA,1:19649 R

R.1 ODDS 1:3733 H, 1:1026 HTA, 1:2941 R
SR Scott Rolen Jsy A 10.00 25.00
TG Tony Gwynn Bat B 10.00 25.00
TH Todd Helton Jsy A 10.00 25.00

2002 Topps Yankee Stadium Seat Relics

serted into second series packs at a stated rate of e in 579 Hobby, one in 1472 HTA and one in 4313 tail, these nine cards feature retired Yankee greats ng with a piece of a seat used in the originaly nkee Stadium.

R.2 ODDS 1:5579 H, 1:1472 HTA, 1:4313 R
RAR Allie Reynolds 20.00 50.00
RBM Billy Martin 30.00 60.00
RGM Gil McDougald 12.50 30.00
RGW Gene Woodling 10.00 25.00
RHB Hank Bauer 10.00 25.00
RJC Joe Collins 15.00 40.00
RJM Johnny Mize 40.00 80.00
RPR Phil Rizzuto 40.00 80.00
RYB Yogi Berra 10.00 25.00

2002 Topps Traded

is 275 card set was released in October, 2002. ese cards were issued in 10 card hobby packs ich were issued 24 packs to a box and 12 boxes to case with an SRP of $3 per pack. In addition, this oduct was also issued in 35 count HTA packs. rds numbered 1 to 100 were issued one per pack. rds from previous traded sets were repurchased by pps and were issued at a stated rate of one in 24 bby and Retail Packs and one in 10 HTA packs. wever, there is no way of being able to identify that ese cards are anything but original cards as no arking or stamping is on these cards.

OMPLETE SET (275) 150.00 300.00
OMMON CARD (T1-T110) 1.00 2.50
110 ODDS ONE PER PACK
OMMON CARD (T111-T275) .15 .40
EPURCHASED ODDS 1:24 H/R, 1:10 HTA
Jeff Weaver 1.00 2.50
Jay Powell 1.00 2.50
Alex Gonzalez 1.00 2.50
Jason Isringhausen 1.00 2.50
5 Tyler Houston 1.00 2.50
6 Ben Broussard 1.00 2.50
Chuck Knoblauch 1.00 2.50
8 Brian L. Hunter 1.00 2.50
9 Dustan Mohr 1.00 2.50
0 Eric Hinske 1.00 2.50
1 Roger Cedeno 1.00 2.50
2 Eddie Perez 1.00 2.50
3 Jeromy Burnitz 1.00 2.50
4 Bartolo Colon 1.00 2.50
5 Rick Helling 1.00 2.50
6 Dan Plesac 1.00 2.50
7 Scott Strickland 1.00 2.50
8 Antonio Alfonseca 1.00 2.50
9 Ricky Gutierrez 1.00 2.50
20 John Valentin 1.00 2.50
21 Raul Mondesi 1.00 2.50
22 Ben Davis 1.00 2.50
23 Nelson Figueroa 1.00 2.50
24 Earl Snyder 1.00 2.50
25 Robin Ventura 1.00 2.50
26 Jimmy Haynes 1.00 2.50
27 Kenny Kelly 1.00 2.50
28 Morgan Ensberg 1.00 2.50
29 Reggie Sanders 1.00 2.50
30 Shigetoshi Hasegawa 1.00 2.50
31 Mike Timlin 1.00 2.50
32 Russell Branyan 1.00 2.50
33 Alan Embree 1.00 2.50
34 D'Angelo Jimenez 1.00 2.50
35 Kent Mercker 1.00 2.50
36 Jesse Orosco 1.00 2.50
37 Gregg Zaun 1.00 2.50
38 Reggie Taylor 1.00 2.50
39 Andres Galarraga 1.50 4.00
40 Chris Truby 1.00 2.50
41 Bruce Chen 1.00 2.50
42 Darren Lewis 1.00 2.50
43 Ryan Kohlmeier 1.00 2.50
44 John McDonald 1.00 2.50
45 Omar Daal 1.00 2.50
46 Matt Clement 1.00 2.50
47 Glendon Rusch 1.00 2.50
48 Chan Ho Park 1.50 4.00
49 Benny Agbayani 1.00 2.50
50 Juan Gonzalez 1.00 2.50
51 Carlos Baerga 1.00 2.50
52 Tim Raines 1.50 4.00
53 Kevin Appier 1.00 2.50
54 Marty Cordova 1.00 2.50
55 Jeff D'Amico 1.00 2.50
56 Dmitri Young 1.00 2.50
57 Roosevelt Brown 1.00 2.50
58 Dustin Hermanson 1.00 2.50
T59 Jose Rijo 1.00 2.50
T60 Todd Ritchie 1.00 2.50
T61 Lee Stevens 1.00 2.50
T62 Placido Polanco 1.00 2.50
T63 Eric Young 1.00 2.50
T64 Chuck Finley 1.00 2.50
T65 Dicky Gonzalez 1.00 2.50
T66 Jose Macias 1.00 2.50
T67 Gabe Kapler 1.00 2.50
T68 Sandy Alomar Jr. 1.00 2.50
T69 Henry Blanco 1.00 2.50
T70 Julian Tavarez 1.00 2.50
T71 Paul Bako 1.00 2.50
T72 Scott Rolen 1.50 4.00
T73 Brian Jordan 1.00 2.50
T74 Rickey Henderson 2.50 6.00
T75 Kevin Mench 1.00 2.50
T76 Hideo Nomo 2.50 6.00
T77 Jeremy Giambi 1.00 2.50
T78 Brad Fullmer 1.00 2.50
T79 Carl Everett 1.00 2.50
T80 David Wells 1.00 2.50
T81 Aaron Sele 1.00 2.50
T82 Todd Hollandsworth 1.00 2.50
T83 Vicente Padilla 1.00 2.50
T84 Kenny Lofton 1.00 2.50
T85 Corky Miller 1.00 2.50
T86 Josh Fogg 1.00 2.50
T87 Cliff Floyd 1.00 2.50
T88 Craig Paquette 1.00 2.50
T89 Jay Payton 1.00 2.50
T90 Carlos Pena 1.50 4.00
T91 Juan Encarnacion 1.00 2.50
T92 Rey Sanchez 1.00 2.50
T93 Ryan Dempster 1.00 2.50
T94 Mario Encarnacion 1.00 2.50
T95 Jorge Julio 1.00 2.50
T96 John Mabry 1.00 2.50
T97 Todd Zeile 1.00 2.50
T98 Johnny Damon Sox 1.50 4.00
T99 Deivi Cruz 1.00 2.50
T100 Gary Sheffield 1.00 2.50
T101 Ted Lilly 1.00 2.50
T102 Todd Van Poppel 1.00 2.50
T103 Shawn Estes 1.00 2.50
T104 Cesar Izturis 1.00 2.50
T105 Ron Coomer 1.00 2.50
T106 Grady Little MG RC 1.00 2.50
T107 Jimy Williams MG 1.00 2.50
T108 Tony Pena MG 1.00 2.50
T109 Frank Robinson MG 1.50 4.00
T110 Ron Gardenhire MG 1.00 2.50
T111 Dennis Tankersley .15 .40
T112 Alejandro Cadena RC .15 .40
T113 Justin Reid RC .15 .40
T114 Nate Field RC .15 .40
T115 Rene Reyes RC .15 .40
T116 Nelson Castro RC .15 .40
T117 Miguel Olivo .15 .40
T118 David Espinosa .15 .40
T119 Chris Bootcheck RC .15 .40
T120 Rob Henkel RC .15 .40
T121 Steve Bechler RC .15 .40
T122 Mark Outlaw RC .15 .40
T123 Henry Pichardo RC .15 .40
T124 Michael Floyd RC .15 .40
T125 Richard Lane RC .15 .40
T126 Pete Zamora RC .15 .40
T127 Javier Colina .15 .40
T128 Greg Sain RC .15 .40
T129 Ronnie Merrill .15 .40
T130 Gavin Floyd RC .40 1.00
T131 Josh Bonifay RC .15 .40
T132 Tommy Marx RC .15 .40
T133 Gary Cates Jr. RC .15 .40
T134 Neal Cotts RC .40 1.00
T135 Angel Berroa .15 .40
T136 Elio Serrano RC .15 .40
T137 J.J. Putz RC .20 .50
T138 Ruben Gotay RC .20 .50
T139 Eddie Rogers .15 .40
T140 Wily Mo Pena .15 .40
T141 Tyler Yates RC .15 .40
T142 Colin Young RC .15 .40
T143 Chance Caple .15 .40
T144 Ben Howard RC .15 .40
T145 Ryan Bukvich RC .15 .40
T146 Cliff Bartosh RC .15 .40
T147 Brandon Claussen .15 .40
T148 Cristian Guerrero .15 .40
T149 Derrick Lewis .15 .40
T150 Eric Miller RC .15 .40
T151 Justin Huber RC .30 .75
T152 Adrian Gonzalez .15 .40
T153 Brian West RC .15 .40
T154 Chris Baker RC .15 .40
T155 Drew Henson .15 .40
T156 Scott Hairston RC .20 .50
T157 Jason Simontacchi RC .15 .40
T158 Jason Arnold RC .15 .40
T159 Brandon Phillips .15 .40
T160 Adam Roller RC .15 .40
T161 Scotty Layfield RC .15 .40
T162 Freddie Money RC .15 .40
T163 Noochie Varner RC .15 .40
T164 Terrance Hill RC .15 .40
T165 Jeremy Hill RC .15 .40
T166 Carlos Cabrera RC .15 .40
T167 Jose Morban RC .15 .40
T168 Kevin Frederick RC .15 .40
T169 Mark Teixeira .60 1.50
T170 Brian Rogers .15 .40
T171 Anastacio Martinez RC .15 .40
T172 Bobby Jenks RC .60 1.50
T173 David Gil RC .15 .40
T174 Andres Torres .15 .40
T175 James Barrett RC .15 .40
T176 Jimmy Journell .15 .40
T177 Brett Kay RC .15 .40
T178 Jason Young RC .15 .40
T179 Mark Hamilton RC .15 .40
T180 Jose Bautista RC 2.00 5.00
T181 Blake McGinley RC .15 .40
T182 Ryan Mottl RC .15 .40
T183 Jeff Austin RC .15 .40
T184 Xavier Nady .15 .40
T185 Kyle Kane RC .15 .40
T186 Travis Foley RC .15 .40
T187 Nathan Kaup RC .15 .40
T188 Eric Cyr .15 .40
T189 Josh Cisneros RC .15 .40
T190 Brad Nelson RC .15 .40
T191 Clint Weibl RC .15 .40
T192 Ron Calloway RC .15 .40
T193 Jung Bong .15 .40
T194 Rolando Viera RC .15 .40
T195 Jason Bulger RC .15 .40
T196 Chone Figgins RC .60 1.50
T197 Jimmy Alvarez RC .15 .40
T198 Joel Crump RC .15 .40
T199 Ryan Doumit RC .25 .60
T200 Demetrius Heath RC .15 .40
T201 John Ennis RC .15 .40
T202 Doug Sessions RC .15 .40
T203 Clinton Hosford RC .15 .40
T204 Chris Narveson RC .15 .40
T205 Ross Peeples RC .15 .40
T206 Alex Requena RC .15 .40
T207 Matt Erickson RC .15 .40
T208 Brian Forystek RC .15 .40
T209 Dewon Brazelton .15 .40
T210 Nathan Haynes .15 .40
T211 Jack Cust .15 .40
T212 Jesse Foppert RC .20 .50
T213 Jesus Cota RC .15 .40
T214 Juan M. Gonzalez RC .15 .40
T215 Tim Kalita RC .15 .40
T216 Manny Delcarmen RC .20 .50
T217 Jim Kavourias RC .15 .40
T218 C.J. Wilson RC .50 1.25
T219 Edwin Yan RC .15 .40
T220 Andy Van Hekken .15 .40
T221 Michael Cuddyer .15 .40
T222 Jeff Verplancke RC .15 .40
T223 Mike Wilson RC .15 .40
T224 Corwin Malone RC .15 .40
T225 Chris Snelling RC .25 .60
T226 Joe Rogers RC .15 .40
T227 Jason Bay 1.50 4.00
T228 Ezequiel Astacio RC .15 .40
T229 Joey Hammond RC .15 .40
T230 Chris Duffy RC .20 .50
T231 Mark Prior .60 1.50
T232 Hansel Izquierdo RC .15 .40
T233 Franklyn German RC .15 .40
T234 Alexis Gomez .15 .40
T235 Jorge Padilla RC .15 .40
T236 Ryan Snare RC .15 .40
T237 Deivis Santos .15 .40
T238 Taggert Bozied RC .20 .50
T239 Mike Peeples RC .15 .40
T240 Ronald Acuna RC .15 .40
T241 Koyie Hill .15 .40
T242 Garrett Guzman RC .15 .40
T243 Ryan Church RC .40 1.00
T244 Tony Fontana RC .15 .40
T245 Keto Anderson RC .15 .40
T246 Brad Bouras RC .15 .40
T247 Jason Dubois RC .20 .50
T248 Angel Guzman RC .30 .75
T249 Joel Hanrahan RC .15 .40
T250 Joe Jiannetti RC .15 .40
T251 Sean Pierce RC .15 .40
T252 Jake Mauer RC .15 .40
T253 Marshall McDougall RC .15 .40
T254 Edwin Almonte RC .15 .40
T255 Shawn Riggans RC .15 .40
T256 Steven Shell RC .15 .40
T257 Kevin Hooper RC .15 .40
T258 Michael Frick RC .15 .40
T259 Travis Chapman RC .15 .40
T260 Tim Hummel RC .15 .40
T261 Adam Morrissey RC .15 .40
T262 Dontrelle Willis RC 1.25 3.00
T263 Justin Sherrod RC .15 .40
T264 Gerald Smiley RC .15 .40
T265 Tony Miller RC .15 .40
T266 Nolan Ryan WW 1.00 2.50
T267 Reggie Jackson WW .25 .60
T268 Steve Garvey WW .15 .40
T269 Wade Boggs WW .25 .60
T270 Sammy Sosa WW .40 1.00
T271 Curt Schilling WW .15 .40
T272 Mark Grace WW .25 .60
T273 Jason Giambi WW .15 .40
T274 Ken Griffey Jr. WW .75 2.00
T275 Roberto Alomar WW .25 .60

2002 Topps Traded Gold

*GOLD 1-110: .6X TO 1.5X BASIC
*GOLD 111-275: 2.5X TO 6X BASIC
*GOLD RC'S 111-275: 1.5X TO 4X BASIC
STATED ODDS 1:3 HOBBY/RETAIL, 1:1 HTA
STATED PRINT RUN 2002 SERIAL #'D SETS

2002 Topps Traded Farewell Relic

Inserted at a stated rate of one in 590 Hobby, one in 169 HTA and in 595 Retail packs, this one card set features one-time MVP Jose Canseco along with a game-used bat piece from his career. Canseco had announced his retirement during the 2002 season in an failed attempt to return to the majors.

STATED ODDS 1:590 H, 1:160 HTA, 1:595 R
FWJC Jose Canseco Bat 6.00 15.00

2002 Topps Traded Hall of Fame Relic

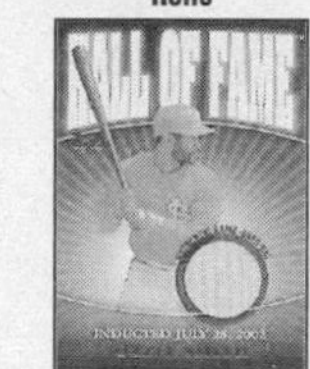

Inserted at a stated rate of one in 1533 Hobby Packs, one in 439 HTA packs and one in 1574 Retail packs, this one card set features Ozzie Smith along with a game-used bat piece from his career. Ozzie Smith was inducted into the HOF in 2002.

STATED ODDS 1:1533 H,1:439 HTA,1:1574 R
HOFOS Ozzie Smith Bat 12.50 30.00

2002 Topps Traded Signature Moves

Inserted at overall odds of one in 91 Hobby or Retail packs and one in 26 HTA packs, these 26 cards feature a mix of basically prospects along with a couple of stars who moved to new teams for 2002 and signed these cards for inclusion in the Topps Traded set. Since there were nine different insertion odds for these cards we have notated both the insertion odds for each group along with which group the player belong to.

A ODDS 1:15,292 H, 1:4288 HTA, 1:22,032 R
B ODDS 1:3846 H, 1:1105 HTA, 1:3840 R
C ODDS 1:6147 H, 1:1778 HTA, 1:6418 R
D ODDS 1:1917 H, 1:548 HTA, 1:1953 R
E ODDS 1:341 H, 1:97 HTA, 1:342 R
F ODDS 1:2247 H, 1:645 HTA, 1:2261 R
G ODDS 1:568 H, 1:162 HTA, 1:571 R
GROUP H ODDS 1:256 H/R, 1:73 HTA
I ODDS 1:1023 H, 1:293 HTA, 1:1025 R
OVERALL ODDS 1:91 HOB/RET, 1:26 HTA
AC Antoine Cameron D 4.00 10.00
AM Andy Morales H 3.00 8.00
BB Boof Bonser E 4.00 10.00
BC Brandon Claussen E 4.00 10.00
CS Chris Smith G 3.00 8.00
CU Chase Utley E 30.00 60.00
CW Corwin Malone H 3.00 8.00
DT Dennis Tankersley F 4.00 10.00
FJ Forrest Johnson E 4.00 10.00
JD Johnny Damon Sox B 8.00 20.00
JD Jeff DaVanon I 3.00 8.00
JM Jake Mauer G 6.00 15.00
JM Justin Morneau H 6.00 15.00
JP Juan Pena E 4.00 10.00
JS Juan Silvestre D 4.00 10.00
JW Justin Wayne E 4.00 10.00
KI Kazuhisa Ishii A 15.00 40.00
MC Matt Cooper E 4.00 10.00
MO Moises Alou B 6.00 15.00
MT Marcus Thames G 5.00 12.00
RA Roberto Alomar C 10.00 25.00
RH Ryan Hannaman E 4.00 10.00
RM Ramon Moreta H 4.00 10.00
TB Tony Blanco E 4.00 10.00
TL Todd Linden H 4.00 10.00
VD Victor Diaz H 4.00 10.00

2002 Topps Traded Tools of the Trade Dual Relics

Inserted at overall odds of one in 539 Hobby, one in 155 HTA and one in 542 Retail packs, these three cards feature two game-used relics from the featured players. As these cards were issued in different insertion ratios, we have notated that information as to the player's specific group next to their name in our checklist.

A ODDS 1:3407 H, 1:972 HTA, 1:3672 R
B ODDS 1:639 H, 1:183 HTA, 1:642 R
OVERALL ODDS 1:539 H, 1:155 HTA, 1:542 R
DTRRCP Chan Ho Park Jsy-Jsy B 6.00 15.00
DTRRHN Hideo Nomo Jsy-Jsy A 15.00 40.00
DTRRMO Moises Alou Jsy-Jsy B 6.00 15.00

2002 Topps Traded Tools of the Trade Relics

Inserted at overall odds for bats of one in 34 Hobby and Retail and one in 10 HTA and for jerseys at one in 426 Hobby, one in 122 HTA and one in 427 retail, these 35 cards feature players who switched teams for the 2002 season along with a game-used memorabilia piece. We have notated in our checklist what type of memorabilia piece on each player's card. In addition, since the bat cards were inserted at three different odds, we have notated that information as to the card's group next to their name in our checklist.

BAT A 1:1203 H, 1:344 HTA, 1:1224 R
BAT B 1:1807 H, 1:517 HTA, 1:1836 R
BAT C 1:35 H/R, 1:10 HTA
OVERALL BAT RELIC 1:34 H/R, 1:10 HTA
JERSEY ODDS 1:426 H, 1:122 HTA, 1:427 R
AB Roberto Alomar Bat C 4.00 10.00
AG Andres Galarraga Bat C 3.00 8.00
BF Brad Fullmer Bat C 3.00 8.00
BJ Brian Jordan Bat C 3.00 8.00
CE Carl Everett Bat C 3.00 8.00
CK Chuck Knoblauch Bat C 3.00 8.00
CP Carlos Pena Bat A 4.00 10.00
DB David Bell Bat C 3.00 8.00
DJ Dave Justice Bat C 3.00 8.00
EY Eric Young Bat C 3.00 8.00
GS Gary Sheffield Bat C 3.00 8.00
HB Rickey Henderson Bat C 4.00 10.00
JBU Jeromy Burnitz Bat C 3.00 8.00
JCI Jeff Cirillo Bat B 3.00 8.00
JDB Johnny Damon Sox Bat C 4.00 10.00
JG Juan Gonzalez Jsy 3.00 8.00
JP Josh Phelps Jsy 3.00 8.00
JV John Vander Wal Bat C 3.00 8.00
KL Kenny Lofton Bat C 3.00 8.00
MA Moises Alou Bat C 3.00 8.00
MLB Matt Lawton Bat C 3.00 8.00
MT Michael Tucker Bat C 3.00 8.00
MVB Mo Vaughn Bat C 3.00 8.00
MVJ Mo Vaughn Jsy 3.00 8.00
PP Placido Polanco Bat A 4.00 10.00
RS Reggie Sanders Bat C 3.00 8.00
RV Robin Ventura Bat C 3.00 8.00
RW Rondell White Bat C 3.00 8.00
SI Ruben Sierra Bat C 3.00 8.00
SR Scott Rolen Bat A 10.00 25.00
TC Tony Clark Bat C 3.00 8.00
TM Tino Martinez Bat C 4.00 10.00
TR Tim Raines Bat C 3.00 8.00
TS Tsuyoshi Shinjo Bat C 3.00 8.00
VC Vinny Castilla Bat C 3.00 8.00

2003 Topps

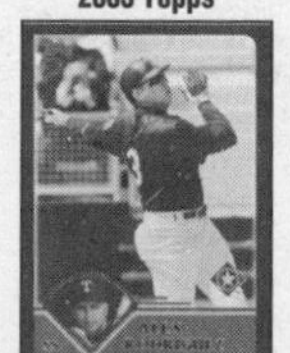

The first series of 366 cards was released in November, 2002. The second series of 354 cards were released in April, 2003. The set was issued either in 10 card hobby packs or 36 card HTA packs. The regular packs were issued 36 packs to a box and 12 boxes to a case with an SRP of $1.59. The HTA packs were issued 12 packs to a box and eight boxes to a case with an SRP of $5 per pack. The following subsets were issued in the first series: 262 through 291 basically featured current managers, cards numbered 292 through 321 featured players in their first year on a Topps card, cards numbered 322 through 331 featured two players who were expected to be major rookies during the 2003 season, cards numbered 332 through 336 honored players who achieved major feats during 2002, cards numbered 337 through 352 featured league leaders, cards 354 and 355 had post season highlights and cards 356 through 367 honored the best players in the American League. Second series subsets included Team Checklists (630-659); Draft Picks (660-674); Prospects (675-684); Award Winners (685-708) All-Stars (709-719) and World Series (720-721). As has been Topps tradition since 1997, there was no card number 7 issued in honor of the memory of Mickey Mantle.

COMPLETE SET (720) 30.00 60.00
COMP.FACT.BLUE SET (725) 40.00 80.00
COMP.FACT.RED SET (725) 40.00 80.00
COMPLETE SERIES 1 (366) 12.50 30.00
COMPLETE SERIES 2 (354) 12.50 30.00
COMMON CARD (1-6/8-721) .07 .20
COMMON (292-331/660-684) .20 .50
CARD 7 DOES NOT EXIST
1 Alex Rodriguez .25 .60
2 Dan Wilson .07 .20
3 Jimmy Rollins .12 .30
4 Jermaine Dye .07 .20
5 Steve Karsay .07 .20
6 Timo Perez .07 .20
8 Jose Vidro .07 .20
9 Eddie Guardado .07 .20
10 Mark Prior .12 .30
11 Curt Schilling .12 .30
12 Dennis Cook .07 .20
13 Andruw Jones .07 .20
14 David Segui .07 .20
15 Trot Nixon .07 .20
16 Kerry Wood .07 .20
17 Magglio Ordonez .12 .30
18 Jason LaRue .07 .20
19 Danys Baez .07 .20
20 Todd Helton .12 .30
21 Denny Neagle .07 .20
22 Dave Mlicki .07 .20
23 Roberto Hernandez .07 .20
24 Odalis Perez .07 .20
25 Nick Neugebauer .07 .20
26 David Ortiz .20 .50
27 Andres Galarraga .12 .30
28 Edgardo Alfonzo .07 .20
29 Chad Bradford .07 .20
30 Jason Giambi .07 .20
31 Brian Giles .07 .20
32 Deivi Cruz .07 .20
33 Robb Nen .07 .20
34 Jeff Nelson .07 .20
35 Edgar Renteria .07 .20
36 Aubrey Huff .07 .20
37 Brandon Duckworth .07 .20
38 Juan Gonzalez .07 .20
39 Sidney Ponson .07 .20
40 Eric Hinske .07 .20
41 Kevin Appier .07 .20
42 Danny Bautista .07 .20
43 Javier Lopez .07 .20
44 Jeff Conine .07 .20
45 Carlos Baerga .07 .20
46 Ugueth Urbina .07 .20
47 Mark Buehrle .12 .30
48 Aaron Boone .07 .20
49 Jason Simontacchi .07 .20
50 Sammy Sosa .20 .50
51 Jose Jimenez .07 .20
52 Bobby Higginson .07 .20
53 Luis Castillo .07 .20
54 Orlando Merced .07 .20
55 Brian Jordan .07 .20
56 Eric Young .07 .20
57 Bobby Kielty .07 .20
58 Luis Rivas .07 .20
59 Brad Wilkerson .07 .20
60 Roberto Alomar .12 .30
61 Roger Clemens .25 .60
62 Scott Hatteberg .07 .20
63 Andy Ashby .07 .20
64 Mike Williams .07 .20
65 Ron Gant .07 .20
66 Benito Santiago .07 .20
67 Bret Boone .07 .20
68 Matt Morris .07 .20
69 Troy Glaus .07 .20
70 Austin Kearns .07 .20
71 Jim Thome .12 .30
72 Rickey Henderson .20 .50
73 Luis Gonzalez .07 .20
74 Brad Fullmer .07 .20
75 Herbert Perry .07 .20
76 Randy Wolf .07 .20
77 Miguel Tejada .12 .30
78 Jimmy Anderson .07 .20
79 Ramon Martinez .07 .20
80 Ivan Rodriguez .12 .30
81 John Flaherty .07 .20
82 Shannon Stewart .07 .20
83 Orlando Palmeiro .07 .20
84 Rafael Furcal .07 .20
85 Kenny Rogers .07 .20
86 Terry Adams .07 .20
87 Mo Vaughn .07 .20
88 Jose Cruz Jr. .07 .20
89 Mike Matheny .07 .20
90 Alfonso Soriano .12 .30
91 Orlando Cabrera .07 .20
92 Jeffrey Hammonds .07 .20
93 Hideo Nomo .20 .50
94 Carlos Febles .07 .20
95 Billy Wagner .07 .20
96 Alex Gonzalez .07 .20
97 Todd Zeile .07 .20
98 Omar Vizquel .12 .30
99 Jose Rijo .07 .20
100 Ichiro Suzuki .25 .60
101 Steve Cox .07 .20
102 Hideki Irabu .07 .20
103 Roy Halladay .12 .30
104 David Eckstein .07 .20
105 Greg Maddux .25 .60
106 Jay Gibbons .07 .20
107 Travis Driskill .07 .20
108 Fred McGriff .12 .30
109 Frank Thomas .20 .50
110 Shawn Green .07 .20
111 Ruben Quevedo .07 .20
112 Jacque Jones .07 .20
113 Tomo Ohka .07 .20
114 Joe McEwing .07 .20
115 Ramiro Mendoza .07 .20
116 Mark Mulder .07 .20
117 Mike Lieberthal .07 .20
118 Jack Wilson .07 .20
119 Randall Simon .07 .20
120 Bernie Williams .12 .30
121 Marvin Benard .07 .20
122 Jamie Moyer .07 .20
123 Andy Benes .07 .20
124 Tino Martinez .07 .20
125 Esteban Yan .07 .20
126 Juan Uribe .07 .20
127 Jason Isringhausen .07 .20
128 Chris Carpenter .12 .30
129 Mike Cameron .07 .20
130 Gary Sheffield .07 .20
131 Geronimo Gil .07 .20
132 Brian Daubach .07 .20
133 Corey Patterson .07 .20
134 Aaron Rowand .07 .20
135 Chris Reitsma .07 .20
136 Bob Wickman .07 .20
137 Cesar Izturis .07 .20
138 Jason Jennings .07 .20
139 Brandon Inge .07 .20
140 Larry Walker .12 .30
141 Ramon Santiago .07 .20
142 Vladimir Nunez .07 .20
143 Jose Vizcaino .07 .20
144 Mark Quinn .07 .20
145 Michael Tucker .07 .20
146 Darren Dreifort .07 .20
147 Ben Sheets .07 .20
148 Corey Koskie .07 .20
149 Tony Armas Jr. .07 .20
150 Kazuhisa Ishii .07 .20
151 Al Leiter .07 .20
152 Steve Trachsel .07 .20
153 Mike Stanton .07 .20
154 David Justice .07 .20
155 Marlon Anderson .07 .20
156 Jason Kendall .07 .20
157 Brian Lawrence .07 .20
158 J.T. Snow .07 .20
159 Edgar Martinez .12 .30
160 Pat Burrell .07 .20
161 Kerry Robinson .07 .20
162 Greg Vaughn .07 .20
163 Carl Everett .07 .20
164 Vernon Wells .07 .20
165 Jose Mesa .07 .20
166 Troy Percival .07 .20
167 Erubiel Durazo .07 .20
168 Jason Marquis .07 .20
169 Jerry Hairston Jr. .07 .20
170 Vladimir Guerrero .12 .30
171 Byung-Hyun Kim .07 .20
172 Marcus Giles .07 .20
173 Johnny Damon .12 .30
174 Jon Lieber .07 .20
175 Terrence Long .07 .20
176 Sean Casey .07 .20
177 Adam Dunn .12 .30
178 Juan Pierre .07 .20
179 Wendell Magee .07 .20
180 Barry Zito .12 .30
181 Aramis Ramirez .07 .20
182 Pokey Reese .07 .20
183 Jeff Kent .07 .20
184 Russ Ortiz .07 .20
185 Ruben Sierra .07 .20
186 Brent Abernathy .07 .20
187 Ismael Valdes .07 .20
188 Tom Wilson .07 .20
189 Craig Counsell .07 .20
190 Mike Mussina .12 .30
191 Ramon Hernandez .07 .20
192 Adam Kennedy .07 .20
193 Tony Womack .07 .20
194 Wes Helms .07 .20
195 Tony Batista .07 .20

196 Rolando Arrojo .07 .20
197 Kyle Farnsworth .07 .20
198 Gary Bennett .07 .20
199 Scott Sullivan .07 .20
200 Albert Pujols .25 .60
201 Kirk Rueter .07 .20
202 Phil Nevin .07 .20
203 Kip Wells .07 .20
204 Ron Coomer .07 .20
205 Jeromy Burnitz .07 .20
206 Kyle Lohse .07 .20
207 Mike DeJean .07 .20
208 Paul Lo Duca .07 .20
209 Carlos Beltran .12 .30
210 Roy Oswalt .12 .30
211 Mike Lowell .07 .20
212 Robert Fick .07 .20
213 Todd Jones .07 .20
214 C.C. Sabathia .12 .30
215 Danny Graves .07 .20
216 Todd Hundley .07 .20
217 Tim Wakefield .12 .30
218 Derek Lowe .07 .20
219 Kevin Millwood .07 .20
220 Jorge Posada .12 .30
221 Bobby J. Jones .07 .20
222 Carlos Guillen .07 .20
223 Fernando Vina .07 .20
224 Ryan Rupe .07 .20
225 Kelvim Escobar .07 .20
226 Ramon Ortiz .07 .20
227 Junior Spivey .07 .20
228 Juan Cruz .07 .20
229 Melvin Mora .07 .20
230 Lance Berkman .12 .30
231 Brent Butler .07 .20
232 Shane Halter .07 .20
233 Derrek Lee .07 .20
234 Matt Lawton .07 .20
235 Chuck Knoblauch .07 .20
236 Eric Gagne .07 .20
237 Alex Sanchez .07 .20
238 Denny Hocking .07 .20
239 Eric Milton .07 .20
240 Rey Ordonez .07 .20
241 Orlando Hernandez .07 .20
242 Robert Person .07 .20
243 Sean Burroughs .07 .20
244 Jeff Cirillo .07 .20
245 Mike Lamb .07 .20
246 Jose Valentin .07 .20
247 Ellis Burks .07 .20
248 Shawn Chacon .07 .20
249 Josh Beckett .07 .20
250 Nomar Garciaparra .12 .30
251 Craig Biggio .12 .30
252 Joe Randa .07 .20
253 Mark Grudzielanek .07 .20
254 Glendon Rusch .07 .20
255 Michael Barrett .07 .20
256 Omar Daal .07 .20
257 Elmer Dessens .07 .20
258 Wade Miller .07 .20
259 Adrian Beltre .20 .50
260 Vicente Padilla .07 .20
261 Kazuhiro Sasaki .07 .20
262 Mike Scioscia MG .07 .20
263 Bobby Cox MG .07 .20
264 Mike Hargrove MG .07 .20
265 Grady Little MG RC .07 .20
266 Alex Gonzalez .07 .20
267 Jerry Manuel MG .07 .20
268 Bob Boone MG .07 .20
269 Joel Skinner MG .07 .20
270 Clint Hurdle MG .07 .20
271 Miguel Batista .07 .20
272 Bob Brenly MG .07 .20
273 Jeff Torborg MG .07 .20
274 Jimy Williams MG .07 .20
275 Tony Pena MG .07 .20
276 Jim Tracy MG .07 .20
277 Jerry Royster MG .07 .20
278 Ron Gardenhire MG .07 .20
279 Frank Robinson MG .12 .30
280 John Halama .07 .20
281 Joe Torre MG .12 .30
282 Art Howe MG .07 .20
283 Larry Bowa MG .07 .20
284 Lloyd McClendon MG .07 .20
285 Bruce Bochy MG .12 .30
286 Dusty Baker MG .07 .20
287 Lou Piniella MG .07 .20
288 Tony LaRussa MG .12 .30
289 Todd Walker .07 .20
290 Jerry Narron MG .07 .20
291 Carlos Tosca MG .07 .20
292 Chris Duncan FY RC .60 1.50
293 Franklin Gutierrez FY RC .50 1.25
294 Adam LaRoche FY .20 .50
295 Manuel Ramirez FY RC .20 .50
296 Il Kim FY RC .20 .50
297 Wayne Lydon FY RC .20 .50
298 Daryl Clark FY RC .20 .50
299 Sean Pierce FY .20 .50
300 Andy Marte FY RC .20 .50
301 Matthew Peterson FY RC .20 .50
302 Gonzalo Lopez FY RC .20 .50
303 Bernie Castro FY RC .20 .50
304 Cliff Lee FY 1.25 3.00
305 Jason Perry FY RC .20 .50
306 Jaime Bubela FY RC .20 .50
307 Alexis Rios FY .20 .50
308 Brendan Harris FY RC .20 .50
309 Ramon Nivar-Martinez FY RC .20 .50
310 Terry Tiffee FY RC .20 .50
311 Kevin Youkilis FY RC 1.25 3.00
312 Ruddy Lugo FY RC .20 .50
313 C.J. Wilson FY 1.50 4.00
314 Mike McNutt FY RC .20 .50
315 Jeff Clark FY RC .20 .50
316 Mark Malaska FY RC .20 .50
317 Doug Waechter FY RC .20 .50
318 Derell McCall FY RC .20 .50
319 Scott Tyler FY RC .20 .50
320 Craig Brazell FY RC .20 .50
321 Walter Young FY .20 .50
322 M.Byrd .20 .50
J.Padilla FS
323 C.Snelling .30 .75
S.Choo FS
324 H.Blalock .30 .75
M.Teixeira FS
325 Josh Hamilton .30 .75
326 O.Hudson .20 .50
J.Phelps FS
327 J.Cust .20 .50
R.Reyes FS
328 A.Berroa .20 .50
A.Gomez FS
329 M.Cuddyer .20 .50
M.Restovich FS
330 J.Rivera .20 .50
M.Thames FS
331 B.Puffer .20 .50
J.Bong FS
332 Mike Cameron SH .07 .20
333 Shawn Green SH .07 .20
334 Oakland A's SH .07 .20
335 Jason Giambi SH .07 .20
336 Derek Lowe SH .07 .20
337 AL Batting Average LL .20 .50
338 AL Runs Scored LL .50 1.25
339 AL Home Runs LL .25 .60
340 AL RBI's LL .25 .60
341 AL ERA LL .12 .30
342 AL Strikeouts LL .25 .60
343 NL Batting Average LL .12 .30
344 NL Runs Scored LL .25 .60
345 NL Home Runs LL .20 .50
346 NL RBI's LL .25 .60
347 NL ERA LL .25 .60
348 NL Strikeouts LL .20 .50
349 AL Division Angels .12 .30
350 AL .10 .30
NL Division Twins
Cards
351 AL .10 .30
NL Division Angels
Giants
352 NL Division Cardinals .12 .30
353 Adam Kennedy ALCS .07 .20
354 J.T. Snow WS .07 .20
355 David Bell NLCS .07 .20
356 Jason Giambi AS .07 .20
357 Alfonso Soriano AS .12 .30
358 Alex Rodriguez AS .25 .60
359 Eric Chavez AS .07 .20
360 Torii Hunter AS .07 .20
361 Bernie Williams AS .12 .30
362 Garret Anderson AS .07 .20
363 Jorge Posada AS .12 .30
364 Derek Lowe AS .07 .20
365 Barry Zito AS .12 .30
366 Manny Ramirez AS .20 .50
367 Mike Scioscia AS .07 .20
368 Francisco Rodriguez .12 .30
369 Chris Hammond .07 .20
370 Chipper Jones .20 .50
371 Chris Singleton .07 .20
372 Cliff Floyd .07 .20
373 Bobby Hill .07 .20
374 Antonio Osuna .07 .20
375 Barry Larkin .12 .30
376 Charles Nagy .07 .20
377 Denny Stark .07 .20
378 Dean Palmer .07 .20
379 Eric Owens .07 .20
380 Randy Johnson .20 .50
381 Jeff Suppan .07 .20
382 Eric Karros .07 .20
383 Luis Vizcaino .07 .20
384 Johan Santana .12 .30
385 Javier Vazquez .07 .20
386 John Thomson .07 .20
387 Nick Johnson .07 .20
388 Mark Ellis .07 .20
389 Doug Glanville .07 .20
390 Ken Griffey Jr. .40 1.00
391 Bubba Trammell .07 .20
392 Livan Hernandez .07 .20
393 Desi Relaford .07 .20
394 Eli Marrero .07 .20
395 Jared Sandberg .07 .20
396 Barry Bonds .30 .75
397 Esteban Loaiza .07 .20
398 Aaron Sele .07 .20
399 Geoff Blum .07 .20
400 Derek Jeter .50 1.25
401 Eric Byrnes .07 .20
402 Mike Timlin .07 .20
403 Mark Kotsay .07 .20
404 Rich Aurilia .07 .20
405 Joel Pineiro .07 .20
406 Chuck Finley .07 .20
407 Bengie Molina .07 .20
408 Steve Finley .07 .20
409 Julio Franco .07 .20
410 Marty Cordova .07 .20
411 Shea Hillenbrand .07 .20
412 Mark Bellhorn .07 .20
413 Jon Garland .07 .20
414 Reggie Taylor .07 .20
415 Milton Bradley .07 .20
416 Carlos Pena .12 .30
417 Andy Fox .07 .20
418 Brad Ausmus .07 .20
419 Brent Mayne .07 .20
420 Paul Quantrill .07 .20
421 Carlos Delgado .07 .20
422 Kevin Mench .07 .20
423 Joe Kennedy .07 .20
424 Mike Crudale .07 .20
425 Mark McLemore .07 .20
426 Bill Mueller .07 .20
427 Rob Mackowiak .07 .20
428 Ricky Ledee .07 .20
429 Ted Lilly .07 .20
430 Sterling Hitchcock .07 .20
431 Scott Strickland .07 .20
432 Damion Easley .07 .20
433 Torii Hunter .07 .20
434 Brad Radke .07 .20
435 Geoff Jenkins .07 .20
436 Paul Byrd .07 .20
437 Morgan Ensberg .07 .20
438 Mike Maroth .07 .20
439 Mike Hampton .07 .20
440 Adam Hyzdu .07 .20
441 Vance Wilson .07 .20
442 Todd Ritchie .07 .20
443 Tom Gordon .07 .20
444 John Burkett .07 .20
445 Rodrigo Lopez .07 .20
446 Tim Spooneybarger .07 .20
447 Quinton Mccracken .07 .20
448 Tim Salmon .07 .20
449 Jarrod Washburn .07 .20
450 Pedro Martinez .12 .30
451 Dustan Mohr .07 .20
452 Julio Lugo .07 .20
453 Scott Stewart .07 .20
454 Armando Benitez .07 .20
455 Raul Mondesi .07 .20
456 Robin Ventura .07 .20
457 Bobby Abreu .07 .20
458 Josh Fogg .07 .20
459 Ryan Klesko .07 .20
460 Tsuyoshi Shinjo .07 .20
461 Jim Edmonds .12 .30
462 Cliff Politte .07 .20
463 Chan Ho Park .12 .30
464 John Mabry .07 .20
465 Woody Williams .07 .20
466 Jason Michaels .07 .20
467 Scott Schoeneweis .07 .20
468 Brian Anderson .07 .20
469 Brett Tomko .07 .20
470 Scott Erickson .07 .20
471 Kevin Millar Sox .07 .20
472 Danny Wright .07 .20
473 Jason Schmidt .07 .20
474 Scott Williamson .07 .20
475 Einar Diaz .07 .20
476 Jay Payton .07 .20
477 Juan Acevedo .07 .20
478 Ben Grieve .07 .20
479 Raul Ibanez .12 .30
480 Richie Sexson .07 .20
481 Rick Reed .07 .20
482 Pedro Astacio .07 .20
483 Adam Piatt .07 .20
484 Bud Smith .07 .20
485 Tomas Perez .07 .20
486 Adam Eaton .07 .20
487 Rafael Palmeiro .12 .30
488 Jason Tyner .07 .20
489 Scott Rolen .12 .30
490 Randy Winn .07 .20
491 Ryan Jensen .07 .20
492 Trevor Hoffman .12 .30
493 Craig Wilson .07 .20
494 Jeremy Giambi .07 .20
495 Daryle Ward .07 .20
496 Shane Spencer .07 .20
497 Andy Pettitte .12 .30
498 John Franco .07 .20
499 Felipe Lopez .07 .20
500 Mike Piazza .20 .50
501 Cristian Guzman .07 .20
502 Jose Hernandez .07 .20
503 Octavio Dotel .07 .20
504 Brad Penny .07 .20
505 Dave Veres .07 .20
506 Ryan Dempster .07 .20
507 Joe Crede .07 .20
508 Chad Hermansen .07 .20
509 Gary Matthews Jr. .07 .20
510 Matt Franco .07 .20
511 Ben Weber .07 .20
512 Dave Berg .07 .20
513 Michael Young .07 .20
514 Frank Catalanotto .07 .20
515 Darin Erstad .07 .20
516 Matt Williams .07 .20
517 B.J. Surhoff .07 .20
518 Kerry Ligtenberg .07 .20
519 Mike Bordick .07 .20
520 Arthur Rhodes .07 .20
521 Joe Girardi .12 .30
522 D'Angelo Jimenez .07 .20
523 Paul Konerko .12 .30
524 Jose Macias .07 .20
525 Joe Mays .07 .20
526 Marquis Grissom .07 .20
527 Neifi Perez .07 .20
528 Preston Wilson .07 .20
529 Jeff Weaver .07 .20
530 Eric Chavez .07 .20
531 Placido Polanco .07 .20
532 Matt Mantei .07 .20
533 James Baldwin .07 .20
534 Toby Hall .07 .20
535 Brendan Donnelly .07 .20
536 Benji Gil .07 .20
537 Damian Moss .07 .20
538 Jorge Julio .07 .20
539 Matt Clement .07 .20
540 Brian Moehler .07 .20
541 Lee Stevens .07 .20
542 Jimmy Haynes .07 .20
543 Terry Mulholland .07 .20
544 Dave Roberts .12 .30
545 J.C. Romero .07 .20
546 Bartolo Colon .07 .20
547 Roger Cedeno .07 .20
548 Mariano Rivera .25 .60
549 Billy Koch .07 .20
550 Manny Ramirez .20 .50
551 Travis Lee .07 .20
552 Oliver Perez .07 .20
553 Tim Worrell .07 .20
554 Rafael Soriano .07 .20
555 Damian Miller .07 .20
556 John Smoltz .20 .50
557 Willis Roberts .07 .20
558 Tim Hudson .12 .30
559 Moises Alou .07 .20
560 Gary Glover .07 .20
561 Corky Miller .07 .20
562 Ben Broussard .07 .20
563 Gabe Kapler .07 .20
564 Chris Woodward .07 .20
565 Paul Wilson .07 .20
566 Todd Hollandsworth .07 .20
567 So Taguchi .07 .20
568 John Olerud .07 .20
569 Reggie Sanders .07 .20
570 Jake Peavy .07 .20
571 Kris Benson .07 .20
572 Todd Pratt .07 .20
573 Ray Durham .07 .20
574 Boomer Wells .07 .20
575 Chris Widger .07 .20
576 Shawn Wooten .07 .20
577 Tom Glavine .12 .30
578 Antonio Alfonseca .07 .20
579 Keith Foulke .07 .20
580 Shawn Estes .07 .20
581 Mark Grace .12 .30
582 Dmitri Young .07 .20
583 A.J. Burnett .07 .20
584 Richard Hidalgo .07 .20
585 Mike Sweeney .07 .20
586 Alex Cora .12 .30
587 Matt Stairs .07 .20
588 Doug Mientkiewicz .07 .20
589 Fernando Tatis .07 .20
590 David Weathers .07 .20
591 Cory Lidle .07 .20
592 Dan Plesac .07 .20
593 Jeff Bagwell .12 .30
594 Steve Sparks .07 .20
595 Sandy Alomar Jr. .07 .20
596 John Lackey .12 .30
597 Rick Helling .07 .20
598 Mark DeRosa .07 .20
599 Carlos Lee .07 .20
600 Garret Anderson .07 .20
601 Vinny Castilla .07 .20
602 Ryan Drese .07 .20
603 LaTroy Hawkins .07 .20
604 David Bell .07 .20
605 Freddy Garcia .07 .20
606 Miguel Cairo .07 .20
607 Scott Spiezio .07 .20
608 Mike Remlinger .07 .20
609 Tony Graffanino .07 .20
610 Russell Branyan .07 .20
611 Chris Magruder .07 .20
612 Jose Contreras RC .20 .50
613 Carl Pavano .07 .20
614 Kevin Brown .07 .20
615 Tyler Houston .07 .20
616 A.J. Pierzynski .07 .20
617 Tony Fiore .07 .20
618 Peter Bergeron .07 .20
619 Rondell White .07 .20
620 Brett Myers .07 .20
621 Kevin Young .07 .20
622 Kenny Lofton .07 .20
623 Ben Davis .07 .20
624 J.D. Drew .07 .20
625 Chris Gomez .07 .20
626 Karim Garcia .07 .20
627 Ricky Gutierrez .07 .20
628 Mark Redman .07 .20
629 Juan Encarnacion .07 .20
630 Anaheim Angels TC .10 .30
631 Arizona Diamondbacks TC .07 .20
632 Atlanta Braves TC .07 .20
633 Baltimore Orioles TC .07 .20
634 Boston Red Sox TC .07 .20
635 Chicago Cubs TC .07 .20
636 Chicago White Sox TC .07 .20
637 Cincinnati Reds TC .07 .20
638 Cleveland Indians TC .07 .20
639 Colorado Rockies TC .07 .20
640 Detroit Tigers TC .07 .20
641 Florida Marlins TC .07 .20
642 Houston Astros TC .07 .20
643 Kansas City Royals TC .07 .20
644 Los Angeles Dodgers TC .07 .20
645 Milwaukee Brewers TC .07 .20
646 Minnesota Twins TC .07 .20
647 Montreal Expos TC .07 .20
648 New York Mets TC .07 .20
649 New York Yankees TC .10 .30
650 Oakland Athletics TC .07 .20
651 Philadelphia Phillies TC .07 .20
652 Pittsburgh Pirates TC .07 .20
653 San Diego Padres TC .07 .20
654 San Francisco Giants TC .07 .20
655 Seattle Mariners TC .07 .20
656 St. Louis Cardinals TC .07 .20
657 Tampa Bay Devil Rays TC .07 .20
658 Texas Rangers TC .07 .20
659 Toronto Blue Jays TC .07 .20
660 Bryan Bullington DP RC .20 .50
661 Jeremy Guthrie DP .20 .50
662 Joey Gomes DP RC .20 .50
663 Evel Bastida-Martinez DP RC .20 .50
664 Brian Wright DP RC .20 .50
665 B.J. Upton DP .30 .75
666 Jeff Francis DP .20 .50
667 Drew Meyer DP .20 .50
668 Jeremy Hermida DP .30 .75
669 Khalil Greene DP .30 .75
670 Darrell Rasner DP RC .20 .50
671 Cole Hamels DP .60 1.50
672 James Loney DP .30 .75
673 Sergio Santos DP .20 .50
674 Jason Pridie DP .20 .50
675 B.Phillips .30 .75
V.Martinez
676 H.Choi .20 .50
N.Jackson
677 D.Willis .20 .50
J.Stokes
678 C.Tracy .20 .50
L.Overbay
679 J.Borchard .20 .50
C.Malone
680 J.Mauer .50 1.25
J.Morneau
681 D.Henson .20 .50
B.Claussen
682 C.Utley .30 .75
G.Floyd
683 T.Bozied .20 .50
X.Nady
684 A.Heilman .50 1.25
J.Reyes
685 Kenny Rogers AW .07 .20
686 Bengie Molina AW .07 .20
687 John Olerud AW .07 .20
688 Bret Boone AW .07 .20
689 Eric Chavez AW .07 .20
690 Alex Rodriguez AW .25 .60
691 Darin Erstad AW .07 .20
692 Ichiro Suzuki AW .25 .60
693 Torii Hunter AW .07 .20
694 Greg Maddux AW .25 .60
695 Brad Ausmus AW .07 .20
696 Todd Helton AW .12 .30
697 Fernando Vina AW .07 .20
698 Scott Rolen AW .12 .30
699 Edgar Renteria AW .07 .20
700 Andruw Jones AW .07 .20
701 Larry Walker AW .12 .30
702 Jim Edmonds AW .12 .30
703 Barry Zito AW .12 .30
704 Randy Johnson AW .20 .50
705 Miguel Tejada AW .12 .30
706 Barry Bonds AW .30 .75
707 Eric Hinske AW .07 .20
708 Jason Jennings AW .07 .20
709 Todd Helton AS .12 .30
710 Jeff Kent AS .07 .20
711 Edgar Renteria AS .07 .20
712 Scott Rolen AS .12 .30
713 Barry Bonds AS .30 .75
714 Sammy Sosa AS .20 .50
715 Vladimir Guerrero AS .12 .30
716 Mike Piazza AS .20 .50
717 Curt Schilling AS .12 .30
718 Randy Johnson AS .20 .50
719 Bobby Cox AS .07 .20
720 Anaheim Angels WS .10 .30
721 Anaheim Angels WS .20 .50

2003 Topps Black

COM 1-291/368-659/685-721 6.00 15.00
SEMIS 1-291/368-659/685-721 10.00 25.00
UNL 1-291/368-659/685-721 15.00 40.00
COM. 292-331/660-684 6.00 15.00
SEMIS 292-331/660-684 10.00 25.00
UNL 292-331/660-684 15.00 40.00
COM. 292-331/612/660-684 6.00 15.00
SEMIS 292-331/612/660-684 10.00 25.00
UNL 92-331/612/660-684 15.00 40.00
SERIES 1 STATED ODDS 1:16 HTA
SERIES 2 STATED ODDS 1:10 HTA
STATED PRINT RUN 52 SERIAL #'d SETS
CARD 7 DOES NOT EXIST
1 Alex Rodriguez 20.00 50.00
61 Roger Clemens 20.00 50.00
100 Ichiro Suzuki 20.00 50.00
105 Greg Maddux 20.00 50.00
200 Albert Pujols 20.00 50.00
292 Chris Duncan FY 20.00 50.00
304 Cliff Lee FY 40.00 100.00
311 Kevin Youkilis FY 40.00 100.00
313 C.J. Wilson FY 50.00 125.00
390 Ken Griffey Jr. 30.00 80.00
396 Barry Bonds 25.00 60.00
400 Derek Jeter 40.00 100.00
671 Cole Hamels DP 20.00 50.00
690 Alex Rodriguez AW 20.00 50.00
692 Ichiro Suzuki AW 20.00 50.00
694 Greg Maddux AW 20.00 50.00
706 Barry Bonds AW 25.00 60.00
713 Barry Bonds AS 25.00 60.00

2003 Topps Box Bottoms

A-Rod/Schill/Helt/L.Gonz 1.50 4.00
Sosa/Soriano/Ishii/Pujols 2.00 5.00
*BOX BOTTOM CARDS: 1X TO 2.5X BASIC
ONE 4-CARD SHEET PER HTA BOX
1 Alex Rodriguez 1 .60 1.50
10 Mark Prior 4 .30 .75
11 Curt Schilling 1 .30 .75
20 Todd Helton 1 .30 .75
50 Sammy Sosa 2 .50 1.25
73 Luis Gonzalez 1 .20 .50
77 Miguel Tejada 4 .30 .75
80 Ivan Rodriguez 4 .30 .75
90 Alfonso Soriano 2 .30 .75
150 Kazuhisa Ishii 2 .20 .50
160 Pat Burrell 4 .20 .50
177 Adam Dunn 3 .30 .75
180 Barry Zito 3 .30 .75
200 Albert Pujols 2 .60 1.50
230 Lance Berkman 3 .30 .75
250 Nomar Garciaparra 3 .30 .75
368 Francisco Rodriguez 5 .30 .75
370 Chipper Jones 8 .50 1.25
380 Randy Johnson 8 .50 1.25
387 Nick Johnson 7 .20 .50
390 Ken Griffey Jr. 6 1.00 2.50
396 Barry Bonds 5 .75 2.00
433 Torii Hunter 5 .20 .50
450 Pedro Martinez 6 .30 .75
489 Scott Rolen 8 .30 .75
500 Mike Piazza 6 .50 1.25
530 Eric Chavez 6 .20 .50
550 Manny Ramirez 7 .50 1.25
558 Tim Hudson 7 .30 .75
585 Mike Sweeney 8 .20 .50
593 Jeff Bagwell 5 .30 .75
600 Garret Anderson 7 .20 .50

2003 Topps Gold

*GOLD 1-291/368-659/685-721: 6X TO 15X
*GOLD: 292-331/660-684: 2.5X TO 6X
*GOLD RC's: 292-331/612/660-684: 6X TO 15X
SERIES 1 STATED ODDS 1:16 H, 1:5 HTA
SERIES 2 STATED ODDS 1:7 H, 1:2 HTA, 1:5 R
STATED PRINT RUN 2003 SERIAL #'d SETS
CARD 7 DOES NOT EXIST

2003 Topps Home Team Advantage

COMP.FACT.SET (720) 40.00 80.
*HTA: .75X TO 2X BASIC
DISTRIBUTED IN FACTORY SET FORM
CARD 7 DOES NOT EXIST

2003 Topps Trademark Variations

SER.1 ODDS 1:8852 H, 1:2665 HTA
SER.2 ODDS 1:4487 H, 1:1277 HTA, 1:3763 R
NO PRICING DUE TO SCARCITY
SKIP-NUMBERED 45-CARD SET

2003 Topps All-Stars

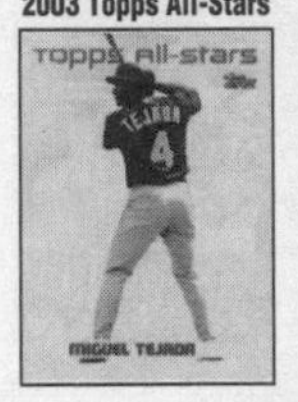

Issued at a stated rate of one in 15 second series hobby packs and one in five second series HTA packs, this 20 card set features most of the leading players in baseball.
COMPLETE SET (20) 12.50 30.
SERIES 2 ODDS 1:15 HOBBY, 1:5 HTA
1 Alfonso Soriano .60 1.5
2 Barry Bonds 1.50 4.0
3 Ichiro Suzuki 1.25 3.0
4 Alex Rodriguez 1.25 3.0
5 Miguel Tejada .60 1.
6 Nomar Garciaparra .60 1.
7 Jason Giambi .40 1.
8 Manny Ramirez 1.00 2.5
9 Derek Jeter 2.50 6.
10 Garret Anderson .40 1.
11 Barry Zito .60 1.5
12 Sammy Sosa 1.00 2.
13 Adam Dunn .60 1.
14 Vladimir Guerrero .60 1.5
15 Mike Piazza 1.00 2.5
16 Shawn Green .40 1.
17 Luis Gonzalez .40 1.0
18 Todd Helton .60 1.
19 Torii Hunter .40 1.
20 Curt Schilling .60 1.5

2003 Topps Autographs

Issued at varying stated odds, these 38 cards featu a mix of prospect and starts who signed cards for inclusion in the 2003 Topps product. The following players did not return their cards in time for inclus in series 1 packs and these cards could be redeem until November 30, 2004: Darin Erstad and Scott Rolen.
GROUP A1 SER.1 1:8910 H, 1: 2533 HTA
GROUP B1 SER.1 1:24,710 H, 1:7037 HTA
GROUP C1 SER.1 1:11,097 H, 1:3167 HTA
GROUP D1 SER.1 1:20,144 H, 1:5758 HTA
GROUP E1 SER.1 1:11,730 H, 1:3333 HTA
GROUP F1 SER.1 1:2209 H, 1:395 HTA
GROUP G1 SER.1 1:3471 H, 1:460 HTA
GROUP A2 1:31,408 H, 1:8808 HTA, 1:26,208 R
GROUP B2 1:5188 H, 1:1460 HTA, 1:4368 R
GROUP C2 1:864 H, 1:232 HTA, 1:708 R
GROUP D2 1:790 H, 1:214 HTA, 1:647 R
SERIES 1 EXCH.DEADLINE 11/30/04
AJ Andruw Jones A1 10.00 25.
AK1 Austin Kearns F1 4.00 10.0
AK2 Austin Kearns C2 4.00 10.0
AP Albert Pujols B2 50.00 120.
AS Alfonso Soriano A1 30.00 60.0
BH Brad Hawpe D2 8.00 20.
BS Ben Sheets E1 6.00 15.0
BU B.J. Upton D2 4.00 10.0
BZ Barry Zito C2 4.00 10.0
CE Clint Everts D2 4.00 10.0
CF Cliff Floyd C2 6.00 15.0
DE Darin Erstad B1 6.00 15.0
DW Dontrelle Willis D2 4.00 10.0
EC Eric Chavez A1 8.00 20.0
EH Eric Hinske C2 6.00 15.0
EM Eric Milton C1 6.00 15.0
HB Hank Blalock F1 10.00 25.0
JB Josh Beckett C2 6.00 15.0
JDM J.D. Martin G1 4.00 10.0

Jason Lane G1 6.00 15.00
M Joe Mauer F1 20.00 50.00
PH Josh Phelps C2 6.00 15.00
V Jose Vidro C2 6.00 15.00
B Lance Berkman A2 6.00 15.00
MB Mark Buehrle C1 6.00 15.00
MO Magglio Ordonez B2 4.00 10.00
MP Mark Prior F1 10.00 25.00
MTE Mark Teixeira F1 6.00 15.00
MTH Marcus Thames G1 4.00 10.00
MT1 Miguel Tejada A1 6.00 15.00
MT2 Miguel Tejada C2 15.00 40.00
N Nick Neugebauer D1 6.00 15.00
OH Orlando Hudson G1 4.00 10.00
K Paul Konerko C2 6.00 15.00
L1 Paul Lo Duca F1 6.00 15.00
L2 Paul Lo Duca C2 10.00 25.00
R Scott Rolen A1 30.00 60.00
H Torii Hunter C2 6.00 15.00

2003 Topps Blue Backs

Issued in the style of the 1951 Topps Blue Back set, these 40 cards were inserted into first series packs at a stated rate of one in 12 hobby packs and one in four HTA packs.

COMPLETE SET (40) 20.00 50.00
SERIES 1 STATED ODDS 1:12 HOB, 1:4 HTA
BB1 Albert Pujols 1.25 3.00
BB2 Ichiro Suzuki 1.25 3.00
BB3 Sammy Sosa 1.00 2.50
BB4 Kazuhisa Ishii .40 1.00
BB5 Alex Rodriguez 1.25 3.00
BB6 Derek Jeter 2.50 6.00
BB7 Vladimir Guerrero .60 1.50
BB8 Ken Griffey Jr. 2.00 5.00
BB9 Jason Giambi .40 1.00
BB10 Todd Helton .60 1.50
BB11 Mike Piazza 1.00 2.50
BB12 Nomar Garciaparra .60 1.50
BB13 Chipper Jones 1.00 2.50
BB14 Ivan Rodriguez .60 1.50
BB15 Luis Gonzalez .40 1.00
BB16 Pat Burrell .40 1.00
BB17 Mark Prior .60 1.50
BB18 Adam Dunn .60 1.50
BB19 Jeff Bagwell .60 1.50
BB20 Austin Kearns .40 1.00
BB21 Alfonso Soriano .60 1.50
BB22 Jim Thome .60 1.50
BB23 Bernie Williams .60 1.50
BB24 Pedro Martinez .60 1.50
BB25 Lance Berkman .60 1.50
BB26 Randy Johnson 1.00 2.50
BB27 Rafael Palmeiro .60 1.50
BB28 Richie Sexson .40 1.00
BB29 Troy Glaus .40 1.00
BB30 Shawn Green .40 1.00
BB31 Larry Walker .60 1.50
BB32 Eric Hinske .40 1.00
BB33 Andruw Jones .40 1.00
BB34 Barry Bonds 1.50 4.00
BB35 Curt Schilling .60 1.50
BB36 Greg Maddux 1.25 3.00
BB37 Jimmy Rollins .60 1.50
BB38 Eric Chavez .40 1.00
BB39 Scott Rolen .60 1.50
BB40 Mike Sweeney .40 1.00

2003 Topps Blue Chips Autographs

SEEDED IN VARIOUS 03-06 TOPPS BRANDS
AH Aubrey Huff 6.00 15.00
BC Bobby Crosby 6.00 15.00
BEP Brandon Phillips 4.00 10.00
BF Ben Fritz 4.00 10.00
BS Brian Slocum 4.00 10.00
CCE Clint Everts 4.00 10.00
CH Cole Hamels 15.00 40.00
CN Clint Nageotte 4.00 10.00
CT Chad Tracy 4.00 10.00
JG Jay Gibbons 4.00 10.00
JHA J.J. Hardy 4.00 10.00
JHU Justin Huber 4.00 10.00
JR Jeremy Reed 4.00 10.00
JRB Jason Bay 6.00 15.00
KH Kris Honel 4.00 10.00
MB Milton Bradley 4.00 10.00
OH Orlando Hudson 4.00 10.00
RN Ramon Nivar 4.00 10.00
VM Val Majewski 4.00 10.00
ZG Zack Greinke 20.00 50.00

2003 Topps Draft Picks

COMPLETE SET (10) 50.00 100.00
COMPLETE SERIES 1 (5) 30.00 60.00
COMPLETE SERIES 2 (5) 20.00 40.00
COMMON CARD (1-10) .75 2.00
1-5 ISSUED IN RETAIL SETS
6-10 DISTRIBUTED IN HOLIDAY SETS
1 Brandon Wood 5.00 12.00
2 Ryan Wagner .75 2.00
3 Sean Rodriguez 1.25 3.00
4 Chris Lubanski .75 2.00
5 Chad Billingsley 4.00 10.00
6 Javi Herrera .75 2.00
7 Brian McFall .75 2.00
8 Nick Markakis 6.00 15.00
9 Adam Miller 3.00 8.00
10 Daric Barton 1.25 3.00

2003 Topps Farewell to Riverfront Stadium Relics

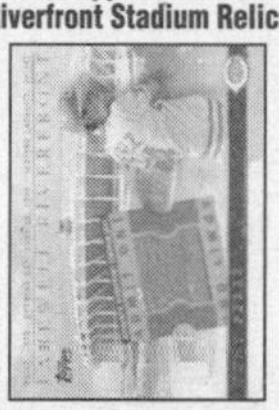

Issued at a stated rate of one in 37 second series HTA packs, this 10 card set featured leading current and retired Cincinnati Reds players since 1970 as well as a piece of Riverfront Stadium.

SERIES 2 STATED ODDS 1:37 HTA
AD Adam Dunn 10.00 25.00
AK Austin Kearns 10.00 25.00
BL Barry Larkin 15.00 40.00
DC Dave Concepcion 12.00 30.00
JB Johnny Bench 15.00 40.00
JM Joe Morgan 20.00 50.00
KG Ken Griffey Jr. 20.00 50.00
PO Paul O'Neill 10.00 25.00
TP Tony Perez 15.00 40.00
TS Tom Seaver 15.00 40.00

2003 Topps First Year Player Bonus

Issued as five card bonus "packs" these 10 cards featured players in their first year on a Topps card. Cards number 1 through 5 were issued in a sealed clear cello pack within the "red" hobby factory sets while cards number 6-10 were issued in the "blue" Sears/JC Penney factory sets.

1-5 ISSUED IN RED HOBBY SETS
6-10 ISSUED IN BLUE SEARS/JC PENNEY SETS
1 Ismael Castro .40 1.00
2 Branden Florence .40 1.00
3 Michael Garciaparra .40 1.00
4 Pete LaForest .40 1.00
5 Hanley Ramirez 3.00 8.00
6 Rajai Davis .40 1.00
7 Gary Schneidmiller .40 1.00
8 Corey Shafer .40 1.00
9 Thomari Story-Harden .40 1.00
10 Bryan Grace .40 1.00

2003 Topps Flashback

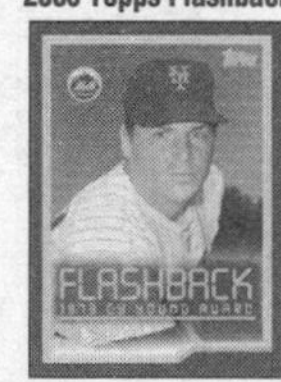

This set, featuring basically retired players, was inserted at a stated rate of one in 12 HTA first series packs. Only Mike Piazza and Randy Johnson were active at the time this set was issued.

SERIES 1 STATED ODDS 1:12 HTA
AR Al Rosen .75 2.00
BM Bill Madlock .75 2.00
CY Carl Yastrzemski 3.00 8.00
DM Dale Murphy 2.00 5.00
EM Eddie Mathews 2.00 5.00
GB George Brett 4.00 10.00
HK Harmon Killebrew 2.00 5.00
JP Jim Palmer 1.25 3.00
LD Lenny Dykstra .75 2.00
MP Mike Piazza 2.00 5.00
NR Nolan Ryan 6.00 15.00
RJ Randy Johnson 2.00 5.00
RR Robin Roberts 1.25 3.00
TS Tom Seaver 1.25 3.00
WS Warren Spahn 1.25 3.00

2003 Topps Hit Parade

Issued at a stated rate of one in 15 hobby packs, one in 5 HTA packs and one in 10 retail packs, this 30 card set feature active players in the top 10 of home runs, runs batted in or hits.

COMPLETE SET (30) 15.00 40.00
SERIES 2 ODDS 1:15 HOB, 1:5 HTA, 1:10 RET
1 Barry Bonds 1.50 4.00
2 Sammy Sosa 1.00 2.50
3 Rafael Palmeiro .60 1.50
4 Fred McGriff .60 1.50
5 Ken Griffey Jr. 2.00 5.00
6 Juan Gonzalez .40 1.00
7 Andres Galarraga .60 1.50
8 Jeff Bagwell .60 1.50
9 Frank Thomas 1.00 2.50
10 Matt Williams .40 1.00
11 Barry Bonds 1.50 4.00
12 Rafael Palmeiro .60 1.50
13 Fred McGriff .60 1.50
14 Andres Galarraga .60 1.50
15 Ken Griffey Jr. 2.00 5.00
16 Sammy Sosa 1.00 2.50
17 Jeff Bagwell .60 1.50
18 Juan Gonzalez .40 1.00
19 Frank Thomas 1.00 2.50
20 Matt Williams .40 1.00
21 Rickey Henderson 1.00 2.50
22 Rafael Palmeiro .60 1.50
23 Roberto Alomar .60 1.50
24 Barry Bonds 1.50 4.00
25 Craig Biggio .60 1.50
26 Fred McGriff .60 1.50
27 Julio Franco .40 1.00
28 Craig Biggio .60 1.50
29 Andres Galarraga .60 1.50
30 Barry Larkin .60 1.50

2003 Topps Hobby Masters

Inserted into first series packs at stated odds of one in 18 Hobby packs and one in six HTA packs, these 20 cards feature some of the most popular players in the hobby.

COMPLETE SET (20) 12.50 30.00
SERIES 1 STATED ODDS 1:18 HOB, 1:6 HTA
HM1 Ichiro Suzuki 1.25 3.00
HM2 Kazuhisa Ishii .40 1.00
HM3 Derek Jeter 2.50 6.00
HM4 Sammy Sosa 1.00 2.50
HM5 Alex Rodriguez 1.25 3.00
HM6 Mike Piazza 1.00 2.50
HM7 Chipper Jones 1.00 2.50
HM8 Vladimir Guerrero .60 1.50
HM9 Nomar Garciaparra .60 1.50
HM10 Todd Helton .60 1.50
HM11 Jason Giambi .40 1.00
HM12 Ken Griffey Jr. 2.00 5.00
HM13 Albert Pujols 1.25 3.00
HM14 Ivan Rodriguez .60 1.50
HM15 Mark Prior .60 1.50
HM16 Adam Dunn .60 1.50
HM17 Randy Johnson 1.00 2.50
HM18 Barry Bonds 1.50 4.00
HM19 Alfonso Soriano .60 1.50
HM20 Pat Burrell .40 1.00

2003 Topps Own the Game

Inserted into first series packs at stated odds of one in 12 hobby and one in four HTA, these 30 cards feature players who put up big numbers during the 2002 season.

COMPLETE SET (30) 15.00 40.00
SERIES 1 STATED ODDS 1:12 HOB, 1:4 HTA
OG1 Ichiro Suzuki 1.25 3.00
OG2 Todd Helton .60 1.50
OG3 Larry Walker .60 1.50
OG4 Mike Sweeney .40 1.00
OG5 Sammy Sosa 1.00 2.50
OG6 Lance Berkman .60 1.50
OG7 Alex Rodriguez 1.25 3.00
OG8 Jim Thome .60 1.50
OG9 Shawn Green .40 1.00
OG10 Nomar Garciaparra .60 1.50
OG11 Miguel Tejada .60 1.50
OG12 Jason Giambi .40 1.00
OG13 Magglio Ordonez .60 1.50
OG14 Manny Ramirez 1.00 2.50
OG15 Alfonso Soriano .60 1.50
OG16 Johnny Damon .60 1.50
OG17 Derek Jeter 2.50 6.00
OG18 Albert Pujols 1.25 3.00
OG19 Luis Castillo .40 1.00
OG20 Barry Bonds 1.50 4.00
OG21 Garret Anderson .40 1.00
OG22 Jimmy Rollins .60 1.50
OG23 Curt Schilling .60 1.50
OG24 Barry Zito .60 1.50
OG25 Randy Johnson 1.00 2.50
OG26 Tom Glavine .60 1.50
OG27 Roger Clemens 1.25 3.00
OG28 Pedro Martinez .60 1.50
OG29 Derek Lowe .40 1.00
OG30 John Smoltz 1.00 2.50

2003 Topps Prime Cuts Relics

Inserted into first series packs at a stated rate of one in 37,066 hobby packs and one in 5067 HTA packs and second series packs at a rate of one in 116,208 hobby, one in 1480 HTA and one in 4368 retail packs, these 31 cards featured game-used bat pieces taken from the barrel of the bat. Each of these cards were issued to a stated print run of 50 serial numbered sets.

SER.1 ODDS 1:37,066 H, 1:5067 HTA
SER.2 ODDS 1:116,208 H,1:1480 HTA,1:4368 R
STATED PRINT RUN 50 SERIAL #'d SETS
NO PRICING DUE TO SCARCITY
AD1 Adam Dunn 1 50.00 100.00
AD2 Adam Dunn 2 50.00 100.00
AP Albert Pujols 1 60.00 120.00
AR1 Alex Rodriguez 1 50.00 100.00
AR2 Alex Rodriguez 2 50.00 100.00
AS Alfonso Soriano 2 20.00 50.00
BBO Barry Bonds 2 50.00 100.00
BW Bernie Williams 1 20.00 50.00
CD Carlos Delgado 2 30.00 60.00
EC Eric Chavez 2 30.00 60.00
EM Edgar Martinez 2 40.00 80.00
FT Frank Thomas 1 60.00 120.00
HB Hank Blalock 2 20.00 50.00
IR Ivan Rodriguez 1 50.00 100.00
JG Juan Gonzalez 1 50.00 100.00
JP Jorge Posada 2 40.00 80.00
LB Lance Berkman 1 20.00 50.00
LG Luis Gonzalez 2 20.00 50.00
MP Mark Prior 2 60.00 120.00
MP Mike Piazza 1 60.00 120.00
MV Mo Vaughn 1 50.00 100.00
NG1 Nomar Garciaparra 1 30.00 60.00
NG2 Nomar Garciaparra 2 30.00 60.00
RA1 Roberto Alomar 1 20.00 50.00
RA2 Roberto Alomar 2 20.00 50.00
RH Rickey Henderson 2 60.00 120.00
RJ Randy Johnson 2 20.00 50.00
RP Rafael Palmeiro 2 40.00 80.00
TG Tony Gwynn 2 60.00 120.00
TH Todd Helton 1 30.00 60.00
TM Tino Martinez 2 20.00 50.00

2003 Topps Prime Cuts Autograph Relics

Inserted into first series packs at stated odds of one in 27,661 hobby and one in 7,917 HTA packs or second series packs at stated odds of one in 232,416 hobb packs, one in 8808 HTA packs or one in 28,598 retail packs, these ten cards feature players who signed the relics cut from the barrel of the bat they used in a game. These cards were issued to a stated print run of 50 serial numbered sets.

SER.1 ODDS 1:27,661 H, 1:7917 HTA
SER2 ODDS 1:232,416H,1:8808HTA,1:28,598R
STATED PRINT RUN 50 SERIAL #'d SETS
NO PRICING DUE TO SCARCITY
AJ Andruw Jones 1 60.00 120.00
CJ Chipper Jones 1 30.00 60.00
DE Darin Erstad 1 30.00 60.00
EC Eric Chavez 1 30.00 60.00
LB Lance Berkman 2 60.00 120.00
MO Magglio Ordonez 2 60.00 120.00
MT Miguel Tejada 1 30.00 60.00
SR Scott Rolen 1 30.00 60.00

2003 Topps Prime Cuts Pine Tar Relics

Inserted into first series packs at a stated rate of one in 9266 hobby packs and one in 1267 HTA packs and second series packs at a rate of one in 4288 hobby, one in 587 HTA and one in 928 retail, these 42 cards featured game-used bat pieces taken from the handle of the bat. Each of these cards were issued to a stated print run of 200 serial numbered sets.

SER.1 ODDS 1:9266 H, 1:1267 HTA
SER.2 ODDS 1:4288 H, 1:587 HTA, 1:928 R
STATED PRINT RUN 200 SERIAL #'d SETS
AD1 Adam Dunn 1 6.00 15.00
AD2 Adam Dunn 2 6.00 15.00
AJ Andruw Jones 1 6.00 15.00
AP1 Albert Pujols 1 30.00 60.00
AP2 Albert Pujols 2 30.00 60.00
AR1 Alex Rodriguez 1 10.00 25.00
AR2 Alex Rodriguez 2 10.00 25.00
AS1 Alfonso Soriano 1 6.00 15.00
AS2 Alfonso Soriano 2 6.00 15.00
BBO Barry Bonds 2 60.00 120.00
BW Bernie Williams 1 6.00 15.00
CD Carlos Delgado 2 6.00 15.00
CJ Chipper Jones 1 6.00 15.00
DE Darin Erstad 1 6.00 15.00
EC1 Eric Chavez 1 6.00 15.00
EC2 Eric Chavez 2 6.00 15.00
EM Edgar Martinez 2 6.00 15.00
FT Frank Thomas 1 6.00 15.00
HB Hank Blalock 2 6.00 15.00
IR Ivan Rodriguez 1 6.00 15.00
JG Juan Gonzalez 1 6.00 15.00
JP Jorge Posada 2 6.00 15.00
LB1 Lance Berkman 1 6.00 15.00
LB2 Lance Berkman 2 6.00 15.00
LG Luis Gonzalez 2 6.00 15.00
MO Magglio Ordonez 2 6.00 15.00
MP Mark Prior 2 6.00 15.00
MP Mike Piazza 1 6.00 15.00
MT Miguel Tejada 1 6.00 15.00
MV Mo Vaughn 1 6.00 15.00
NG1 Nomar Garciaparra 1 6.00 15.00
NG2 Nomar Garciaparra 2 6.00 15.00
RA1 Roberto Alomar 1 6.00 15.00
RA2 Roberto Alomar 2 6.00 15.00
RH Rickey Henderson 2 6.00 15.00
RJ Randy Johnson 2 6.00 15.00
RP1 Rafael Palmeiro 1 10.00 25.00
RP2 Rafael Palmeiro 2 10.00 25.00
SR Scott Rolen 1 6.00 15.00
TG Tony Gwynn 2 40.00 80.00
TH Todd Helton 1 6.00 15.00
TM Tino Martinez 2 6.00 15.00

2003 Topps Prime Cuts Trademark Relics

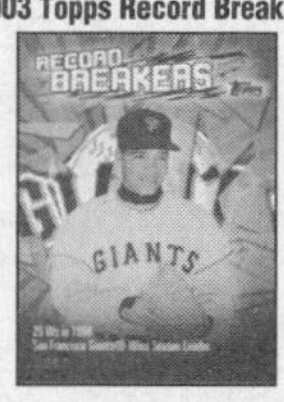

Inserted into first series packs at a stated rate of one in 18,533 hobby packs and one in 2533 HTA packs or second series packs at a rate of one in 12,912 hobby, one in 881 HTA or one in 1857 retail; these 42 cards featured game-used bat pieces taken from the middle of the bat. Each of these cards were issued to a stated print run of 100 serial numbered sets.

SER.1 ODDS 1:18,533 H, 1:2533 HTA
SER.2 ODDS 1:12,912 H, 1:881 HTA, 1:1857 R
STATED PRINT RUN 100 SERIAL #'d SETS
AD1 Adam Dunn 1 40.00 80.00
AD2 Adam Dunn 2 40.00 80.00
AJ Andruw Jones 1 50.00 100.00
AP1 Albert Pujols 1 75.00 150.00
AP2 Albert Pujols 2 75.00 150.00
AR1 Alex Rodriguez 1 60.00 120.00
AR2 Alex Rodriguez 2 60.00 120.00
AS1 Alfonso Soriano 1 50.00 100.00
AS2 Alfonso Soriano 2 50.00 100.00
BBO Barry Bonds 2 75.00 150.00
BW Bernie Williams 1 50.00 100.00
CD Carlos Delgado 2 40.00 80.00
CJ Chipper Jones 1 50.00 100.00
DE Darin Erstad 1 40.00 80.00
EC1 Eric Chavez 1 40.00 80.00
EC2 Eric Chavez 2 40.00 80.00
EM Edgar Martinez 2 50.00 100.00
FT Frank Thomas 1 50.00 100.00
HB Hank Blalock 2 40.00 80.00
IR Ivan Rodriguez 1 50.00 100.00
JG Juan Gonzalez 1 40.00 80.00
JP Jorge Posada 2 50.00 100.00
LB1 Lance Berkman 1 40.00 80.00
LB2 Lance Berkman 2 40.00 80.00
LG Luis Gonzalez 2 40.00 80.00
MO Magglio Ordonez 2 40.00 80.00
MP Mark Prior 2 50.00 100.00
MP Mike Piazza 1 50.00 100.00
MT Miguel Tejada 1 40.00 80.00
MV Mo Vaughn 1 40.00 80.00
NG1 Nomar Garciaparra 1 50.00 100.00
NG2 Nomar Garciaparra 2 50.00 100.00
RA1 Roberto Alomar 1 10.00 25.00
RA2 Roberto Alomar 2 10.00 25.00
RH Rickey Henderson 2 50.00 100.00
RJ Randy Johnson 2 50.00 100.00
RP1 Rafael Palmeiro 1 50.00 100.00
RP2 Rafael Palmeiro 2 50.00 100.00
SR Scott Rolen 1 20.00 50.00
TG Tony Gwynn 2 50.00 100.00
TH Todd Helton 1 50.00 100.00
TM Tino Martinez 2 50.00 100.00

2003 Topps Record Breakers

Inserted into packs at a stated rate of one in six hobby, one in two HTA and one in four retail, these 101 cards feature a mix of active and retired players who hold some sort of season, team, league or major league record.

COMPLETE SET (100) 75.00 150.00
COMPLETE SERIES 1 (50) 40.00 80.00
COMPLETE SERIES 2 (50) 40.00 80.00
SERIES 1 ODDS 1:6 HOB, 1:2 HTA
SERIES 2 ODDS 1:6 HOB, 1:2 HTA, 1:4 RET
AG Andres Galarraga 1 .60 1.50
AR1 Alex Rodriguez 1 1.25 3.00
AR2 Alex Rodriguez 2 1.25 3.00
BB1 Barry Bonds 1 1.50 4.00
BB2 Barry Bonds 2 1.50 4.00
BF Bob Feller 2 .60 1.50
BG Bob Gibson 1 .60 1.50
CB Craig Biggio 2 .60 1.50
CD1 Carlos Delgado 1 .40 1.00
CD2 Carlos Delgado 2 .40 1.00
CF Cliff Floyd 1 .40 1.00
CJ Chipper Jones 1 1.00 2.50
CK Chuck Klein 1 .40 1.00
CS Curt Schilling 1 .60 1.50
DE Darin Erstad 2 .40 1.00
DG Dwight Gooden 2 .40 1.00
DM Don Mattingly 1 2.00 5.00
EM Edgar Martinez 2 .60 1.50
EM Eddie Mathews 1 1.00 2.50
FJ Fergie Jenkins 1 .60 1.50
FM Fred McGriff 1 .60 1.50
FR1 Frank Robinson 1 .60 1.50
FR2 Frank Robinson 2 .60 1.50
FT Frank Thomas 2 1.00 2.50
GA Garret Anderson 2 .40 1.00
GB1 George Brett 1 2.00 5.00
GB2 George Brett 2 2.00 5.00
GF1 George Foster 1 .40 1.00
GF2 George Foster 2 .40 1.00
GM Greg Maddux 2 1.25 3.00
GS Gary Sheffield 1 .40 1.00
HG Hank Greenberg 1 1.00 2.50
HK Harmon Killebrew 1 1.00 2.50
HW Hack Wilson 1 .60 1.50
IS Ichiro Suzuki 2 1.25 3.00
JB1 Jeff Bagwell 1 .60 1.50
JB2 Jeff Bagwell 2 .60 1.50
JD Johnny Damon 2 .60 1.50
JG Jason Giambi 1 .40 1.00
JK Jeff Kent 2 .40 1.00
JME Jose Mesa 2 .40 1.00
JM1 Juan Marichal 1 .60 1.50
JM2 Juan Marichal 2 .60 1.50
JO John Olerud 1 .40 1.00
JP Jim Palmer 2 .60 1.50
JR Jim Rice 2 .60 1.50
JS John Smoltz 2 1.00 2.50
JT Jim Thome 2 .60 1.50
KG1 Ken Griffey Jr. 1 2.00 5.00
KG2 Ken Griffey Jr. 2 2.00 5.00
LA Luis Aparicio 2 .60 1.50
LBR1 Lou Brock 1 .60 1.50
LBR2 Lou Brock 2 .60 1.50
LB1 Lance Berkman 1 .60 1.50
LB2 Lance Berkman 2 .60 1.50
LC Luis Castillo 1 .40 1.00
LD Lenny Dykstra 2 .40 1.00
LG1 Luis Gonzalez 1 .40 1.00
LG2 Luis Gonzalez 2 .40 1.00
LW Larry Walker 2 .60 1.50
MP Mike Piazza 1 1.00 2.50
MR Manny Ramirez 2 1.00 2.50
MS Mike Sweeney 1 .40 1.00
MSC Mike Schmidt 1 1.50 4.00
NG Nomar Garciaparra 2 .60 1.50
NR Nolan Ryan 1 3.00 8.00
PM Pedro Martinez 1 .60 1.50
PM Paul Molitor 2 1.00 2.50
PW Preston Wilson 1 .40 1.00
RA Roberto Alomar 2 .60 1.50
RC Roger Clemens 1 1.25 3.00
RCA Rod Carew 1 .60 1.50
RG Ron Guidry 1 .40 1.00
RH1 Rickey Henderson 1 1.00 2.50
RH2 Rickey Henderson 2 1.00 2.50
RJ1 Randy Johnson 1 1.00 2.50
RJ2 Randy Johnson 2 1.00 2.50
RP Rafael Palmeiro 1 .60 1.50
RS1 Richie Sexson 1 .40 1.00
RS2 Richie Sexson 2 .40 1.00
RY1 Robin Yount 1 1.00 2.50
RY2 Robin Yount 2 1.00 2.50
SG1 Shawn Green 1 .40 1.00
SG2 Shawn Green 2 .40 1.00
SS1 Sammy Sosa 1 1.00 2.50
SS2 Sammy Sosa 2 1.00 2.50
TG Troy Glaus 1 .40 1.00
TG1 Tony Gwynn 1 1.00 2.50
TG2 Tony Gwynn 2 1.00 2.50
TH1 Todd Helton 1 .60 1.50
TH2 Todd Helton 2 .60 1.50
TK Ted Kluszewski 2 .60 1.50
TR Tim Raines 2 .60 1.50
TS1 Tom Seaver 1 .60 1.50
TS2 Tom Seaver 2 .60 1.50
VG1 Vladimir Guerrero 1 .60 1.50
VG2 Vladimir Guerrero 2 .60 1.50
WB Wade Boggs 2 .60 1.50
WM Willie Mays 2 2.00 5.00
WS Willie Stargell 2 .60 1.50

2003 Topps Record Breakers Autographs

This 19 card set partially parallels the Record Breaker insert set. Most of the cards, except for Luis Gonzalez, were inserted into first series packs at a stated rate of one in 6941 hobby packs and one in 1178 HTA packs. The second series cards were issued at a stated rate of one in 2218 hobby, one in 634 HTA and one in 1850 retail packs.

GROUP A1 SER.1 1:6941 H, 1:1178 HTA
GROUP B1 SER.1 1:34,320 H, 1:9744 HTA
GRP 2 SER.2 1:2218 H,1:634 HTA,1:1850 R
CF Cliff Floyd A1 8.00 20.00
CJ Chipper Jones A1 30.00 60.00
DM Don Mattingly 2 50.00 120.00
FJ Fergie Jenkins A1 8.00 20.00
GF George Foster 2 8.00 20.00
HK Harmon Killebrew A1 20.00 50.00
JM Juan Marichal 2 8.00 20.00
LA Luis Aparicio 2 10.00 25.00
LB Lance Berkman 2 10.00 25.00
LBR Lou Brock 2 12.00 30.00
LG Luis Gonzalez B1 8.00 20.00
MS Mike Schmidt A1 25.00 60.00
RP Rafael Palmeiro A1 8.00 20.00
RS Richie Sexson A1 8.00 20.00
RY Robin Yount A1 40.00 80.00
SG Shawn Green A1 30.00 60.00
SW Mike Sweeney A1 8.00 20.00
WM Willie Mays 2 50.00 120.00

2003 Topps Record Breakers Relics

This 40 card set partially parallels the Record Breaker insert set. These cards, depending on the group they belonged to, were inserted into first and second series packs at different rates and we have noted all that information in our headers.

BAT B1/BAT 2/UNI B2 MINORS 4.00 10.00
BAT B1/BAT 2/UNI B2 SEMIS 6.00 15.00
BAT A1 SER.1 ODDS 1:13,528 H, 1:4872 HTA
BAT B1 SER.1 ODDS 1:9058 H, 1:1689 HTA
BAT C1 SER.1 ODDS 1:743 H, 1:90 HTA
UNI A1 SER.1 ODDS 1:6178 H, 1:700 HTA
UNI B1 SER.1 ODDS 1:355 H, 1:51 HTA
BAT 2 SER.2 ODDS 1:191 H, 1:59 HTA
UNI A2 SER.2 ODDS 1:5235, 1:400 HTA
UNI B2 SER.2 ODDS 1:418, 1:176 HTA
UNI C2 SER.2 ODDS 1:1151, 1:87 HTA
AR1 Alex Rodriguez Uni B1 6.00 15.00
AR2 Alex Rodriguez Uni B2 6.00 15.00
CD1 Carlos Delgado Uni B1 4.00 10.00
CD2 Carlos Delgado Uni B2 4.00 10.00
CJ Chipper Jones Uni B1 6.00 15.00
DE Darin Erstad Uni A2 4.00 10.00
DG Dwight Gooden Uni B2 4.00 10.00
DM Don Mattingly Bat C1 10.00 25.00
EM Edgar Martinez Bat 2 6.00 15.00
FR1 Frank Robinson Bat C1 6.00 15.00
FR2 Frank Robinson Bat 2 6.00 15.00
FT Frank Thomas Bat 2 6.00 15.00
GB1 George Brett Bat C1 10.00 25.00

Card	Low	High
GB2 George Brett Bat 2	10.00	25.00
HG Hank Greenberg Bat B1	10.00	25.00
HW Hack Wilson Bat A1	15.00	40.00
JB Jeff Bagwell Uni B1	6.00	15.00
JR Jim Rice Uni B2	4.00	10.00
LBE Lance Berkman Bat C1	4.00	10.00
LC Luis Castillo Bat C1	4.00	10.00
LG Luis Gonzalez Bat 2	4.00	10.00
LGO Luis Gonzalez Uni B1	4.00	10.00
MP Mike Piazza Bat C1	10.00	25.00
MS Mike Sweeney Bat C1	4.00	10.00
NR Nolan Ryan Uni A1	20.00	50.00
NRA Nolan Ryan Uni C2	20.00	50.00
PM Pedro Martinez Uni B1	6.00	15.00
RH Rickey Henderson Bat C1	6.00	15.00
RHO Rogers Hornsby Bat 2	10.00	25.00
RS Richie Sexson Uni C2	4.00	10.00
RY1 Robin Yount Uni B1	10.00	25.00
RY2 Robin Yount Bat 2	10.00	25.00
SG Shawn Green Uni B1	4.00	10.00
TG Tony Gwynn 2B Bat 2	6.00	15.00
TG2 Tony Gwynn Avg Bat 2	6.00	15.00
TH1 Todd Helton Uni B1	6.00	15.00
TH2 Todd Helton Uni B2	6.00	15.00
TK Ted Kluszewski Bat 2	6.00	15.00
TR Tim Raines Bat 2	4.00	10.00
WB Wade Boggs Bat 2	6.00	15.00

2003 Topps Record Breakers Nolan Ryan

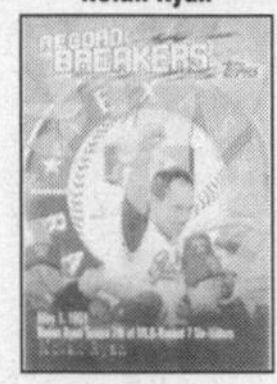

Inserted at a stated rate of one in two HTA packs, this seven card set features all-time strikeout king Nolan Ryan. Each of these cards commemorate one of his record setting seven no-hitters.

Card	Low	High
COMPLETE SET (7)	30.00	60.00
COMMON CARD (NR1-NR7)	4.00	10.00
SER.2 RB CUMULATIVE ODDS 1:2 HTA		

2003 Topps Record Breakers Nolan Ryan Autographs

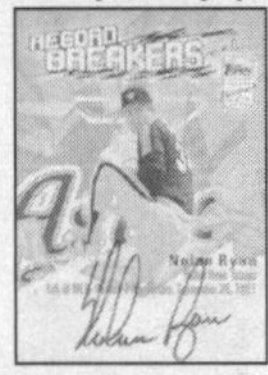

Inserted at a stated rate of one in 1894 HTA packs, this three card set honors Nolan Ryan and the teams he tossed no-hitters for.

Card	Low	High
COMMON CARD	125.00	200.00
SERIES 2 STATED ODDS 1:1894 HTA		

2003 Topps Red Backs

Inserted in second series packs at a stated rate of one in 12 hobby and one in eight retail; this 40-card set features leading players in the style of the 1951 Topps Red Back set.

Card	Low	High
COMPLETE SET (40)	30.00	60.00
SERIES 2 ODDS 1:12 HOBBY, 1:8 RETAIL		
1 Nomar Garciaparra	.60	1.50
2 Ichiro Suzuki	1.25	3.00
3 Alex Rodriguez	1.25	3.00
4 Sammy Sosa	1.00	2.50
5 Barry Bonds	1.50	4.00
6 Vladimir Guerrero	.60	1.50
7 Derek Jeter	2.50	6.00
8 Miguel Tejada	.60	1.50
9 Alfonso Soriano	.60	1.50
10 Manny Ramirez	1.00	2.50
11 Adam Dunn	.60	1.50
12 Jason Giambi	.40	1.00
13 Mike Piazza	1.00	2.50
14 Scott Rolen	.60	1.50
15 Shawn Green	.40	1.00
16 Randy Johnson	1.00	2.50
17 Todd Helton	.60	1.50
18 Garret Anderson	.40	1.00
19 Curt Schilling	.60	1.50
20 Albert Pujols	1.25	3.00
21 Chipper Jones	1.00	2.50
22 Luis Gonzalez	.40	1.00
23 Mark Prior	.60	1.50
24 Jim Thome	.60	1.50
25 Ivan Rodriguez	.60	1.50
26 Torii Hunter	.40	1.00
27 Lance Berkman	.60	1.50
28 Troy Glaus	.40	1.00
29 Andruw Jones	.40	1.00
30 Barry Zito	.60	1.50
31 Jeff Bagwell	.60	1.50
32 Magglio Ordonez	.60	1.50
33 Pat Burrell	.40	1.00
34 Mike Sweeney	.40	1.00
35 Rafael Palmeiro	.60	1.50
36 Larry Walker	.60	1.50
37 Carlos Delgado	.40	1.00
38 Brian Giles	.40	1.00
39 Pedro Martinez	.60	1.50
40 Greg Maddux	1.25	3.00

2003 Topps Turn Back the Clock Autographs

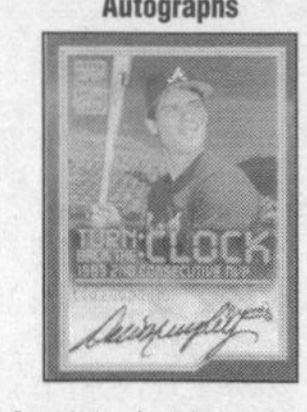

This five card set was inserted at a stated rate of one in 134 HTA packs except for Bill Madlock who signed fewer cards and his card was inserted at a stated rate of one in 268 HTA packs.

Card	Low	High
GROUP A SER.1 ODDS 1:134 HTA		
GROUP B SER.1 ODDS 1:268 HTA		
BM Bill Madlock B	6.00	15.00
DM Dale Murphy A	10.00	25.00
JP Jim Palmer A	8.00	20.00
LD Lenny Dykstra A	8.00	20.00

2003 Topps Vintage Embossed

These 19,878 vintage "buy-back" cards were inserted into first series and second packs at stated odds of one in 940 series one hobby and one in 318 series one HTA packs. Each card, for the first time since Topps began inserting "buy-back" cards into packs, was given a special embossing to notate it as a distinct insert from the 2003 product. Though the cards lack serial-numbering, representatives at Topps have provided specific print runs for each card.

2003 Topps Traded

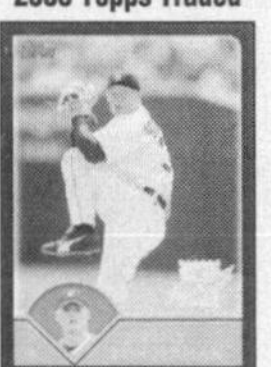

This 275 card-set was released in October, 2003. The set was issued in 10 card packs with an $3 SRP which came 24 packs to a box and 12 boxes to a case. Cards numbered 1 through 115 feature veterans who were traded while cards 116 through 120 feature managers. Cards numbered 121 through 165 featured prospects and cards 166 through 275 feature Rookie Cards. All of these cards were issued with a "T" prefix.

Card	Low	High
COMPLETE SET (275)	25.00	60.00
COMMON CARD (T1-T120)	.07	.20
COMMON CARD (121-165)	.15	.40
COMMON CARD (166-275)	.15	.40
T1 Juan Pierre	.07	.20
T2 Mark Grudzielanek	.07	.20
T3 Tanyon Sturtze	.07	.20
T4 Greg Vaughn	.07	.20
T5 Greg Myers	.07	.20
T6 Randall Simon	.07	.20
T7 Todd Hundley	.07	.20
T8 Marlon Anderson	.07	.20
T9 Jeff Reboulet	.07	.20
T10 Alex Sanchez	.07	.20
T11 Mike Rivera	.07	.20
T12 Todd Walker	.07	.20
T13 Ray King	.07	.20
T14 Shawn Estes	.07	.20
T15 Gary Matthews Jr.	.07	.20
T16 Jaret Wright	.07	.20
T17 Edgardo Alfonzo	.07	.20
T18 Omar Daal	.07	.20
T19 Ryan Rupe	.07	.20
T20 Tony Clark	.07	.20
T21 Jeff Suppan	.07	.20
T22 Mike Stanton	.07	.20
T23 Ramon Martinez	.07	.20
T24 Armando Rios	.07	.20
T25 Johnny Estrada	.07	.20
T26 Joe Girardi	.12	.30
T27 Ivan Rodriguez	.12	.30
T28 Robert Fick	.07	.20
T29 Rick White	.07	.20
T30 Robert Person	.07	.20
T31 Alan Benes	.07	.20
T32 Chris Carpenter	.12	.30
T33 Chris Widger	.07	.20
T34 Travis Hafner	.07	.20
T35 Mike Venafro	.07	.20
T36 Jon Lieber	.07	.20
T37 Orlando Hernandez	.07	.20
T38 Aaron Myette	.07	.20
T39 Paul Bako	.07	.20
T40 Erubiel Durazo	.07	.20
T41 Mark Guthrie	.07	.20
T42 Steve Avery	.07	.20
T43 Damian Jackson	.07	.20
T44 Rey Ordonez	.07	.20
T45 John Flaherty	.07	.20
T46 Byung-Hyun Kim	.07	.20
T47 Tom Goodwin	.07	.20
T48 Elmer Dessens	.07	.20
T49 Al Martin	.07	.20
T50 Gene Kingsale	.07	.20
T51 Lenny Harris	.07	.20
T52 David Ortiz Sox	.20	.50
T53 Jose Lima	.07	.20
T54 Mike Difelice	.07	.20
T55 Jose Hernandez	.07	.20
T56 Todd Zeile	.07	.20
T57 Roberto Hernandez	.07	.20
T58 Albie Lopez	.07	.20
T59 Roberto Alomar	.12	.30
T60 Russ Ortiz	.07	.20
T61 Brian Daubach	.07	.20
T62 Carl Everett	.07	.20
T63 Jeromy Burnitz	.07	.20
T64 Mark Bellhorn	.07	.20
T65 Ruben Sierra	.07	.20
T66 Mike Fetters	.07	.20
T67 Armando Benitez	.07	.20
T68 Deivi Cruz	.07	.20
T69 Jose Cruz Jr.	.07	.20
T70 Jeremy Fikac	.07	.20
T71 Jeff Kent	.07	.20
T72 Andres Galarraga	.12	.30
T73 Rickey Henderson	.20	.50
T74 Royce Clayton	.07	.20
T75 Troy O'Leary	.07	.20
T76 Ron Coomer	.07	.20
T77 Greg Colbrunn	.07	.20
T78 Wes Helms	.07	.20
T79 Kevin Millwood	.07	.20
T80 Damion Easley	.07	.20
T81 Bobby Kielty	.07	.20
T82 Keith Osik	.07	.20
T83 Ramiro Mendoza	.07	.20
T84 Shea Hillenbrand	.07	.20
T85 Shannon Stewart	.07	.20
T86 Eddie Perez	.07	.20
T87 Ugueth Urbina	.07	.20
T88 Orlando Palmeiro	.07	.20
T89 Graeme Lloyd	.07	.20
T90 John Vander Wal	.07	.20
T91 Gary Bennett	.07	.20
T92 Shane Reynolds	.07	.20
T93 Steve Parris	.07	.20
T94 Julio Lugo	.07	.20
T95 John Halama	.07	.20
T96 Carlos Baerga	.07	.20
T97 Jim Parque	.07	.20
T98 Mike Williams	.07	.20
T99 Fred McGriff	.12	.30
T100 Kenny Rogers	.07	.20
T101 Matt Herges	.07	.20
T102 Jay Bell	.07	.20
T103 Esteban Yan	.07	.20
T104 Eric Owens	.07	.20
T105 Aaron Fultz	.07	.20
T106 Rey Sanchez	.07	.20
T107 Jim Thome	.12	.30
T108 Aaron Boone	.07	.20
T109 Raul Mondesi	.07	.20
T110 Kenny Lofton	.07	.20
T111 Jose Guillen	.07	.20
T112 Aramis Ramirez	.07	.20
T113 Sidney Ponson	.07	.20
T114 Scott Williamson	.07	.20
T115 Robin Ventura	.07	.20
T116 Dusty Baker MG	.07	.20
T117 Felipe Alou MG	.07	.20
T118 Buck Showalter MG	.07	.20
T119 Jack McKeon MG	.07	.20
T120 Art Howe MG	.07	.20
T121 Bobby Crosby PROS	.15	.40
T122 Adrian Gonzalez PROS	.30	.75
T123 Kevin Cash PROS	.15	.40
T124 Shin-Soo Choo PROS	.25	.60
T125 Chin-Feng Chen PROS	.15	.40
T126 Miguel Cabrera PROS	2.00	5.00
T127 Jason Young PROS	.15	.40
T128 Alex Herrera PROS	.15	.40
T129 Jason Dubois PROS	.15	.40
T130 Jeff Mathis PROS	.15	.40
T131 Casey Kotchman PROS	.15	.40
T132 Ed Rogers PROS	.15	.40
T133 Wilson Betemit PROS	.15	.40
T134 Jim Kavourias PROS	.15	.40
T135 Taylor Buchholz PROS	.15	.40
T136 Adam LaRoche PROS	.15	.40
T137 Dallas McPherson PROS	.15	.40
T138 Jesus Cota PROS	.15	.40
T139 Clint Nageotte PROS	.15	.40
T140 Boof Bonser PROS	.15	.40
T141 Walter Young PROS	.15	.40
T142 Joe Crede PROS	.15	.40
T143 Denny Bautista PROS	.15	.40
T144 Victor Diaz PROS	.15	.40
T145 Chris Narveson PROS	.15	.40
T146 Gabe Gross PROS	.15	.40
T147 Jimmy Journell PROS	.15	.40
T148 Rafael Soriano PROS	.15	.40
T149 Jerome Williams PROS	.15	.40
T150 Aaron Cook PROS	.15	.40
T151 Anastacio Martinez PROS	.15	.40
T152 Scott Hairston PROS	.15	.40
T153 John Buck PROS	.15	.40
T154 Ryan Ludwick PROS	.15	.40
T155 Chris Bootcheck PROS	.15	.40
T156 John Rheinecker PROS	.15	.40
T157 Jason Lane PROS	.15	.40
T158 Shelley Duncan PROS	.15	.40
T159 Adam Wainwright PROS	.25	.60
T160 Jason Arnold PROS	.15	.40
T161 Jonny Gomes PROS	.15	.40
T162 James Loney PROS	.25	.60
T163 Mike Fontenot PROS	.15	.40
T164 Khalil Greene PROS	.25	.60
T165 Sean Burnett PROS	.15	.40
T166 David Martinez FY RC	.15	.40
T167 Felix Pie FY RC	.25	.60
T168 Joe Valentine FY RC	.15	.40
T169 Brandon Webb FY RC	.50	1.25
T170 Matt Diaz FY RC	.25	.60
T171 Lew Ford FY RC	.15	.40
T172 Jeremy Griffiths FY RC	.15	.40
T173 Matt Hensley FY RC	.15	.40
T174 Charlie Manning FY RC	.15	.40
T175 Elizardo Ramirez FY RC	.15	.40
T176 Greg Aquino FY RC	.15	.40
T177 Felix Sanchez FY RC	.15	.40
T178 Kelly Shoppach FY RC	.25	.60
T179 Bubba Nelson FY RC	.15	.40
T180 Mike O'Keefe FY RC	.15	.40
T181 Hanley Ramirez FY RC	1.25	3.00
T182 Todd Wellemeyer FY RC	.15	.40
T183 Dustin Moseley FY RC	.15	.40
T184 Eric Crozier FY RC	.15	.40
T185 Ryan Shealy FY RC	.15	.40
T186 Jeremy Bonderman FY RC	.60	1.50
T187 T.Story-Harden FY RC	.15	.40
T188 Dusty Brown FY RC	.15	.40
T189 Rob Hammock FY RC	.15	.40
T190 Jorge Piedra FY RC	.15	.40
T191 Chris De La Cruz FY RC	.15	.40
T192 Eli Whiteside FY RC	.15	.40
T193 Jason Kubel FY RC	.50	1.25
T194 Jon Schuerholz FY RC	.15	.40
T195 Stephen Randolph FY RC	.15	.40
T196 Andy Sisco FY RC	.15	.40
T197 Sean Smith FY RC	.15	.40
T198 Jon-Mark Sprowl FY RC	.15	.40
T199 Matt Kata FY RC	.15	.40
T200 Robinson Cano FY RC	8.00	20.00
T201 Nook Logan FY RC	.15	.40
T202 Ben Francisco FY RC	.15	.40
T203 Arnie Munoz FY RC	.15	.40
T204 Ozzie Chavez FY RC	.15	.40
T205 Eric Riggs FY RC	.15	.40
T206 Beau Kemp FY RC	.15	.40
T207 Travis Wong FY RC	.15	.40
T208 Dustin Yount FY RC	.15	.40
T209 Brian McCann FY RC	1.25	3.00
T210 Wilton Reynolds FY RC	.15	.40
T211 Matt Bruback FY RC	.15	.40
T212 Andrew Brown FY RC	.15	.40
T213 Edgar Gonzalez FY RC	.15	.40
T214 Eider Torres FY RC	.15	.40
T215 Aquilino Lopez FY RC	.15	.40
T216 Bobby Basham FY RC	.15	.40
T217 Tim Olson FY RC	.15	.40
T218 Nathan Panther FY RC	.15	.40
T219 Bryan Grace FY RC	.15	.40
T220 Dusty Gomon FY RC	.15	.40
T221 Wil Ledezma FY RC	.15	.40
T222 Josh Willingham FY RC	.50	1.25
T223 David Cash FY RC	.15	.40
T224 Oscar Villarreal FY RC	.15	.40
T225 Jeff Duncan FY RC	.15	.40
T226 Kade Johnson FY RC	.15	.40
T227 Luke Steidlmayer FY RC	.15	.40
T228 Brandon Watson FY RC	.15	.40
T229 Jose Morales FY RC	.15	.40
T230 Mike Gallo FY RC	.15	.40
T231 Tyler Adamczyk FY RC	.15	.40
T232 Adam Stern FY RC	.15	.40
T233 Brennan King FY RC	.15	.40
T234 Dan Haren FY RC	.75	2.00
T235 Michel Hernandez FY RC	.15	.40
T236 Ben Fritz FY RC	.15	.40
T237 Clay Hensley FY RC	.15	.40
T238 Tyler Johnson FY RC	.15	.40
T239 Pete LaForest FY RC	.15	.40
T240 Tyler Martin FY RC	.15	.40
T241 J.D. Durbin FY RC	.15	.40
T242 Shane Victorino FY RC	.50	1.25
T243 Rajai Davis FY RC	.15	.40
T244 Ismael Castro FY RC	.15	.40
T245 Chien-Ming Wang FY RC	.60	1.50
T246 Travis Ishikawa FY RC	.40	1.00
T247 Corey Shafer FY RC	.15	.40
T248 Gary Schneidmiller FY RC	.15	.40
T249 Dave Pember FY RC	.15	.40
T250 Keith Stamler FY RC	.15	.40
T251 Tyson Graham FY RC	.15	.40
T252 Ryan Cameron FY RC	.15	.40
T253 Eric Eckenstahler FY	.15	.40
T254 Matthew Peterson FY RC	.15	.40
T255 Dustin McGowan FY RC	.15	.40
T256 Prentice Redman FY RC	.15	.40
T257 Haj Turay FY RC	.15	.40
T258 Carlos Guzman FY RC	.15	.40
T259 Matt DeMarco FY RC	.15	.40
T260 Derek Michaelis FY RC	.15	.40
T261 Brian Burgamy FY RC	.15	.40
T262 Jay Sitzman FY RC	.15	.40
T263 Chris Fallon FY RC	.15	.40
T264 Mike Adams FY RC	.25	.60
T265 Clint Barmes FY RC	.40	1.00
T266 Eric Reed FY RC	.15	.40
T267 Willie Eyre FY RC	.15	.40
T268 Carlos Duran FY RC	.15	.40
T269 Nick Trzesniak FY RC	.15	.40
T270 Ferdin Tejeda FY RC	.15	.40
T271 Michael Garciaparra FY RC	.15	.40
T272 Michael Hinckley FY RC	.15	.40
T273 Branden Florence FY RC	.15	.40
T274 Trent Oeltjen FY RC	.15	.40
T275 Mike Neu FY RC	.15	.40

2003 Topps Traded Gold

*GOLD 1-120: 3X TO 8X BASIC
*GOLD 121-165: 1.5X TO 4X BASIC
*GOLD 166-275: 1.5X TO 4X BASIC
STATED ODDS 1:2 HOB/RET, 1:1 HTA
STATED PRINT RUN 2003 SERIAL #'d SETS

2003 Topps Traded Future Phenoms Relics

Card	Low	High
GROUP A ODDS 1:2330 HOB/RET, 1:669 HTA		
GROUP B ODDS 1:505 HOB/RET, 1:144 HTA		
GROUP C ODDS 1:101 HOB/RET, 1:29 HTA		
BP Brandon Phillips Bat B	3.00	8.00
CC Chin-Feng Chen Jsy C	10.00	25.00
CDC Carl Crawford Bat C	3.00	8.00
CS Chris Snelling Bat C	3.00	8.00
HB Hank Blalock Bat C	3.00	8.00
JM Justin Morneau Bat C	3.00	8.00
JT Joe Thurston Jsy C	3.00	8.00
MB Marlon Byrd Bat C	3.00	8.00
MR Michael Restovich Bat B	3.00	8.00
MT Mark Teixeira Bat B	4.00	10.00
RB Rocco Baldelli Bat B	3.00	8.00
TAH Trey Hodges Jsy C	3.00	8.00
TH Travis Hafner Bat C	3.00	8.00
WB Wilson Betemit Bat C	3.00	8.00
WPB Willie Bloomquist Bat A	6.00	15.00

2003 Topps Traded Hall of Fame Relics

Card	Low	High
STATED ODDS 1:1009 HOB/RET, 1:289 HTA		
EM Eddie Murray Bat	10.00	25.00
GC Gary Carter Uni	6.00	15.00

2003 Topps Traded Hall of Fame Dual Relic

Card	Low	High
STATED ODDS 1:2015 HOB/RET, 1:578 HTA		
CM G.Carter Uni/E.Murray Bat	12.50	30.00

2003 Topps Traded Signature Moves Autographs

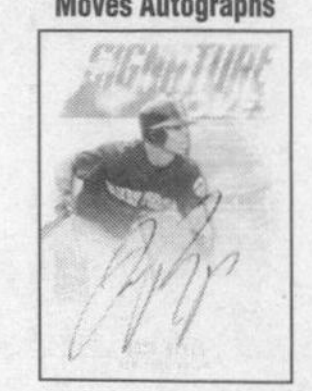

Card	Low	High
GROUP A ODDS 1:280 HOB/RET, 1:80 HTA		
GROUP B ODDS 1:114 HOB/RET, 1:33 HTA		
BC Bartolo Colon A	6.00	15.00
BU B.J. Upton B	6.00	15.00
CF Cliff Floyd A	6.00	15.00
DB David Bell A	6.00	15.00
EA Erick Almonte B	4.00	10.00
ER Elizardo Ramirez B	4.00	10.00
FP Felix Pie B	6.00	15.00
IR Robert Fick A	4.00	10.00
JB Joe Borchard B	4.00	10.00
JC Jose Cruz Jr. A	4.00	10.00
JF Jesse Foppert B	4.00	10.00
JG Joey Gomes B	4.00	10.00
JJC Jack Cust A	4.00	10.00
JL James Loney B	6.00	15.00
JR Jose Reyes B	4.00	10.00
JS Jason Stokes A	4.00	10.00
KG Khalil Greene A	10.00	25.00
MT Mark Teixeira A	4.00	10.00
VM Victor Martinez B	6.00	15.00
WY Walter Young B	4.00	10.00

2003 Topps Traded Transactions Bat Relics

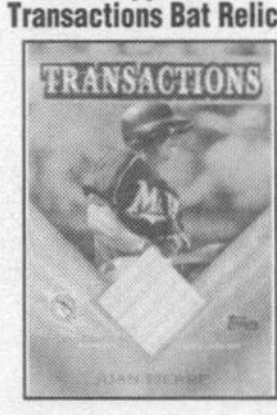

Card	Low	High
GROUP A ODDS 1:168 HOB/RET, 1:48 HTA		
GROUP B ODDS 1:78 HOB/RET, 1:22 HTA		
AG Andres Galarraga A	3.00	8.00
CF Cliff Floyd B	3.00	8.00
DB David Bell B	3.00	8.00
EA Edgardo Alfonzo B	3.00	8.00
ED Erubiel Durazo B	3.00	8.00
EK Eric Karros B	3.00	8.00
FL Felipe Lopez A	3.00	8.00
FM Fred McGriff B	4.00	10.00
JC Jose Cruz Jr. B	3.00	8.00
JG Jeremy Giambi A	3.00	8.00
JK Jeff Kent B	3.00	8.00
JP Juan Pierre B	3.00	8.00
JT Jim Thome A	4.00	10.00
KL Kenny Lofton A	4.00	10.00
KM Kevin Millar Sox B	4.00	10.00
PW Preston Wilson A	3.00	8.00
RD Ray Durham A	3.00	8.00
RF Robert Fick A	3.00	8.00
RO Rey Ordonez B	3.00	8.00
RS Ruben Sierra A	3.00	8.00
RW Rondell White B	3.00	8.00
SH Tsuyoshi Shinjo B	3.00	8.00
SS Shane Spencer A	3.00	8.00
TG Tom Glavine A	4.00	10.00
TZ Todd Zeile A	3.00	8.00

2003 Topps Traded Transactions Dual Relics

Card	Low	High
STATED ODDS 1:421 HOB/RET, 1:120 HTA		
IR Ivan Rodriguez Marlins-Rgr	8.00	20.00
JT Jim Thome Phils-Indians	8.00	20.00
KM Kevin Millwood Phils-Braves	6.00	15.00

2004 Topps

This 366-card standard-size first series was released in November, 2003. In addition, a 366-card second series was released in April, 2004. The cards were issued in 10-card hobby or retail packs with an $1.59 SRP which came 36 packs to a box and 12 boxes to a case. In addition, these cards were also issued in 35-card HTA packs with an $5 SRP which came 12 packs to a box and eight boxes to a case. Please nc that insert cards were issued in different rates in re packs as they were in hobby packs. In addition, to continuing honoring the memory of Mickey Mantle there was no card number 7 issued in this set. Both cards numbered 267 and 274 are numbered as 267 and thus no card number 274 exists. Please note th following subsets were issued: Managers (268-296 First Year Cards (297-326); Future Stars (327-331) Highlights (332-336); League Leaders (337-348); Post-Season Play (349-355); American League All-Stars (356-367). The second series had the followi subsets: Team Card (638-667), Draft Picks (668-687), Prospects (688-692), Combo Cards (693-69 Gold Gloves (696-713), Award Winners (714-718), National League All-Stars (719-729) and World Series Highlights (730-733).

Card	Low	High
COMP.HOBBY SET (737)	25.00	60.0
COMP.HOLIDAY SET (742)	25.00	60.0
COMP.RETAIL SET (737)	25.00	60.C
COMP.ASTROS SET (737)	25.00	60.0
COMP.CUBS SET (737)	25.00	60.0
COMP.RED SOX SET (737)	25.00	60.0
COMP.YANKEES SET (737)	25.00	60.0
COMPLETE SET (732)	20.00	50.0
COMPLETE SERIES 1 (366)	10.00	25.0
COMPLETE SERIES 2 (366)	10.00	25.0
COMMON CARD (1-6/8-732)	.07	.2
COMMON (297-326/668-687)	.20	.5
COMMON (327-331/688-692)	.20	.5
CARDS 7 AND 274 DO NOT EXIST		
SCIOSCIA AND J.CASTRO NUMBERED 267		
1 Jim Thome	.12	.3
2 Reggie Sanders	.07	.2
3 Mark Kotsay	.07	.2
4 Edgardo Alfonzo	.07	.2
5 Ben Davis	.07	.2
6 Mike Matheny	.07	.2
8 Marlon Anderson	.07	.2
9 Chan Ho Park	.12	.3
10 Ichiro Suzuki	.25	.6
11 Kevin Millwood	.07	.2
12 Bengie Molina	.07	.2
13 Tom Glavine	.12	.3
14 Junior Spivey	.07	.2
15 Marcus Giles	.07	.2
16 David Segui	.07	.2
17 Kevin Millar	.07	.2
18 Corey Patterson	.07	.2
19 Aaron Rowand	.07	.2
20 Derek Jeter	.50	1.2
21 Jason LaRue	.07	.2
22 Chris Hammond	.07	.2
23 Jay Payton	.07	.2
24 Bobby Higginson	.07	.2
25 Lance Berkman	.12	.3
26 Juan Pierre	.07	.2
27 Brent Mayne	.07	.2
28 Fred McGriff	.07	.2
29 Richie Sexson	.07	.2
30 Tim Hudson	.12	.3
31 Mike Piazza	.20	.5
32 Brad Radke	.07	.2
33 Jeff Weaver	.07	.2
34 Ramon Hernandez	.07	.2
35 David Bell	.07	.2
36 Craig Wilson	.07	.2
37 Jake Peavy	.07	.2
38 Tim Worrell	.07	.2
39 Gil Meche	.07	.2
40 Albert Pujols	.25	.6
41 Michael Young	.07	.2
42 Josh Phelps	.07	.2
43 Brendan Donnelly	.07	.2
44 Steve Finley	.07	.2
45 John Smoltz	.20	.5
46 Jay Gibbons	.07	.2
47 Trot Nixon	.07	.2
48 Carl Pavano	.07	.2
49 Frank Thomas	.20	.5
50 Mark Prior	.12	.3
51 Danny Graves	.07	.2
52 Milton Bradley UER	.07	.2
53 Jose Jimenez	.07	.2
54 Shane Halter	.07	.2
55 Mike Lowell	.07	.2
56 Geoff Blum	.07	.2
57 Michael Tucker UER	.07	.2
58 Paul Lo Duca	.07	.2
59 Vicente Padilla	.07	.2
60 Jacque Jones	.07	.2
61 Fernando Tatis	.07	.2
62 Ty Wigginton	.07	.2
63 Pedro Astacio	.07	.2
64 Andy Pettitte	.12	.3
65 Terrence Long	.07	.2
66 Cliff Floyd	.07	.2
67 Mariano Rivera	.25	.6
68 Carlos Silva	.07	.2
69 Marlon Byrd	.07	.2
70 Mark Mulder	.07	.2
71 Kerry Ligtenberg	.07	.2
72 Carlos Guillen	.07	.2
73 Fernando Vina	.07	.2
74 Lance Carter	.07	.2
75 Hank Blalock	.07	.2
76 Jimmy Rollins	.12	.3
77 Francisco Rodriguez	.12	.3
78 Javy Lopez	.07	.2
79 Jerry Hairston Jr.	.07	.2
80 Andruw Jones	.07	.2
81 Rodrigo Lopez	.07	.2
82 Johnny Damon	.12	.3

83 Hee Seop Choi .07 .20
84 Miguel Olivo .07 .20
85 Jon Garland .07 .20
86 Matt Lawton .07 .20
87 Juan Uribe .07 .20
88 Steve Sparks .07 .20
89 Tim Spooneybarger .07 .20
90 Jose Vidro .07 .20
91 Luis Rivas .07 .20
92 Hideo Nomo .20 .50
93 Javier Vazquez .07 .20
94 Al Leiter .07 .20
95 Darren Dreifort .07 .20
96 Alex Cintron .07 .20
97 Zach Day .07 .20
98 Jorge Posada .12 .30
99 John Halama .07 .20
100 Alex Rodriguez .25 .60
101 Orlando Palmeiro .07 .20
102 Dave Berg .07 .20
103 Brad Fullmer .07 .20
104 Mike Hampton .07 .20
105 Willis Roberts .07 .20
106 Ramiro Mendoza .07 .20
107 Juan Cruz .07 .20
108 Esteban Loaiza .07 .20
109 Russell Branyan .07 .20
110 Todd Helton .12 .30
111 Braden Looper .07 .20
112 Octavio Dotel .07 .20
113 Mike MacDougal .07 .20
114 Cesar Izturis .07 .20
115 Johan Santana .12 .30
116 Jose Contreras .07 .20
117 Placido Polanco .07 .20
118 Jason Phillips .07 .20
119 Adam Eaton .07 .20
120 Vernon Wells .07 .20
121 Ben Grieve .07 .20
122 Randy Winn .07 .20
123 Ismael Valdes .07 .20
124 Eric Owens .07 .20
125 Curt Schilling .12 .30
126 Russ Ortiz .07 .20
127 Mark Buehrle .12 .30
128 Danys Baez .07 .20
129 Dmitri Young .07 .20
130 Kazuhisa Ishii .07 .20
131 A.J. Pierzynski .07 .20
132 Michael Barrett .07 .20
133 Joe McEwing .07 .20
134 Alex Cora .12 .30
135 Tom Wilson .07 .20
136 Carlos Zambrano .12 .30
137 Brett Tomko .07 .20
138 Shigetoshi Hasegawa .07 .20
139 Jarrod Washburn .07 .20
140 Greg Maddux .25 .60
141 Craig Counsell .07 .20
142 Reggie Taylor .07 .20
143 Omar Vizquel .12 .30
144 Alex Gonzalez .07 .20
145 Billy Wagner .07 .20
146 Brian Jordan .07 .20
147 Wes Helms .07 .20
148 Kyle Lohse .07 .20
149 Timo Perez .07 .20
150 Jason Giambi .07 .20
151 Erubiel Durazo .07 .20
152 Mike Lieberthal .07 .20
153 Jason Kendall .07 .20
154 Xavier Nady .07 .20
155 Kirk Rueter .07 .20
156 Mike Cameron .07 .20
157 Miguel Cairo .07 .20
158 Woody Williams .07 .20
159 Toby Hall .07 .20
160 Bernie Williams .12 .30
161 Darin Erstad .07 .20
162 Matt Mantei .07 .20
163 Geronimo Gil .07 .20
164 Bill Mueller .07 .20
165 Damian Miller .07 .20
166 Tony Graffanino .07 .20
167 Sean Casey .07 .20
168 Brandon Phillips .07 .20
169 Mike Remlinger .07 .20
170 Adam Dunn .12 .30
171 Carlos Lee .07 .20
172 Juan Encarnacion .07 .20
173 Angel Berroa .07 .20
174 Desi Relaford .07 .20
175 Paul Quantrill .07 .20
176 Ben Sheets .07 .20
177 Eddie Guardado .07 .20
178 Rocky Biddle .07 .20
179 Mike Stanton .07 .20
180 Eric Chavez .07 .20
181 Jason Michaels .07 .20
182 Terry Adams .07 .20
183 Kip Wells .07 .20
184 Brian Lawrence .07 .20
185 Bret Boone .07 .20
186 Tino Martinez .12 .30
187 Aubrey Huff .07 .20
188 Kevin Mench .07 .20
189 Tim Salmon .07 .20
190 Carlos Delgado .07 .20
191 John Lackey .12 .30
192 Oscar Villarreal .07 .20
193 Luis Matos .07 .20
194 Derek Lowe .07 .20
195 Mark Grudzielanek .07 .20
196 Tom Gordon .07 .20
197 Matt Clement .07 .20
198 Byung-Hyun Kim .07 .20
199 Brandon Inge .07 .20
200 Nomar Garciaparra .12 .30
201 Antonio Osuna .07 .20
202 Jose Mesa .07 .20
203 Bo Hart .07 .20
204 Jack Wilson .07 .20
205 Ray Durham .07 .20
206 Freddy Garcia .07 .20
207 J.D. Drew .07 .20
208 Einar Diaz .07 .20
209 Roy Halladay .12 .30
210 David Eckstein UER .07 .20
211 Jason Marquis .07 .20
212 Jorge Julio .07 .20
213 Tim Wakefield .12 .30
214 Moises Alou .07 .20
215 Bartolo Colon .07 .20
216 Jimmy Haynes .07 .20
217 Preston Wilson .07 .20
218 Luis Castillo .07 .20
219 Richard Hidalgo .07 .20
220 Manny Ramirez .20 .50
221 Mike Mussina .12 .30
222 Randy Wolf .07 .20
223 Kris Benson .07 .20
224 Ryan Klesko .07 .20
225 Rich Aurilia .07 .20
226 Kelvim Escobar .07 .20
227 Francisco Cordero .07 .20
228 Kazuhiro Sasaki .07 .20
229 Danny Bautista .07 .20
230 Rafael Furcal .07 .20
231 Travis Driskill .07 .20
232 Kyle Farnsworth .07 .20
233 Jose Valentin .07 .20
234 Felipe Lopez .07 .20
235 C.C. Sabathia .12 .30
236 Brad Penny .07 .20
237 Brad Ausmus .07 .20
238 Raul Ibanez .12 .30
239 Adrian Beltre .20 .50
240 Rocco Baldelli .07 .20
241 Orlando Hudson .07 .20
242 Dave Roberts .12 .30
243 Doug Mientkiewicz .07 .20
244 Brad Wilkerson .07 .20
245 Scott Strickland .07 .20
246 Ryan Franklin .07 .20
247 Chad Bradford .07 .20
248 Gary Bennett .07 .20
249 Jose Cruz Jr. .07 .20
250 Jeff Kent .07 .20
251 Josh Beckett .07 .20
252 Ramon Ortiz .07 .20
253 Miguel Batista .07 .20
254 Jung Bong .07 .20
255 Deivi Cruz .07 .20
256 Alex Gonzalez .07 .20
257 Shawn Chacon .07 .20
258 Runelvys Hernandez .07 .20
259 Joe Mays .07 .20
260 Eric Gagne .07 .20
261 Dustan Mohr .07 .20
262 Tomokazu Ohka .07 .20
263 Eric Byrnes .07 .20
264 Frank Catalanotto .07 .20
265 Cristian Guzman .07 .20
266 Orlando Cabrera .07 .20
267A Juan Castro .07 .20
267B Mike Scioscia MG UER 274 .07 .20
268 Bob Brenly MG .07 .20
269 Bobby Cox MG .07 .20
270 Mike Hargrove MG .07 .20
271 Grady Little MG .07 .20
272 Dusty Baker MG .07 .20
273 Jerry Manuel MG .07 .20
275 Eric Wedge MG .07 .20
276 Clint Hurdle MG .07 .20
277 Alan Trammell MG .12 .30
278 Jack McKeon MG .07 .20
279 Jimy Williams MG .07 .20
280 Tony Pena MG .07 .20
281 Jim Tracy MG .07 .20
282 Ned Yost MG .07 .20
283 Ron Gardenhire MG .07 .20
284 Frank Robinson MG .12 .30
285 Art Howe MG .07 .20
286 Joe Torre MG .12 .30
287 Ken Macha MG .07 .20
288 Larry Bowa MG .07 .20
289 Lloyd McClendon MG .07 .20
290 Bruce Bochy MG .12 .30
291 Felipe Alou MG .07 .20
292 Bob Melvin MG .07 .20
293 Tony LaRussa MG .12 .30
294 Lou Piniella MG .07 .20
295 Buck Showalter MG .07 .20
296 Carlos Tosca MG .07 .20
297 Anthony Acevedo FY RC .20 .50
298 Anthony Lerew FY RC .20 .50
299 Blake Hawksworth FY RC .20 .50
300 Brayan Pena FY RC .20 .50
301 Casey Myers FY RC .20 .50
302 Craig Ansman FY RC .20 .50
303 David Murphy FY RC .30 .75
304 Dave Crouthers FY RC .20 .50
305 Dioner Navarro FY RC .30 .75
306 Donald Levinski FY RC .20 .50
307 Jesse Roman FY RC .20 .50
308 Sung Jung FY RC .20 .50
309 Jon Knott FY RC .20 .50
310 Josh Labandeira FY RC .20 .50
311 Kenny Perez FY RC .20 .50
312 Khalid Ballouli FY RC .20 .50
313 Kyle Davies FY RC .20 .50
314 Marcus McBeth FY RC .20 .50
315 Matt Creighton FY RC .20 .50
316 Chris O'Riordan FY RC .20 .50
317 Mike Gosling FY RC .20 .50
318 Nic Ungs FY RC .20 .50
319 Omar Falcon FY RC .20 .50
320 Rodney Choy Foo FY RC .20 .50
321 Tim Frend FY RC .20 .50
322 Todd Self FY RC .20 .50
323 Tydus Meadows FY RC .20 .50
324 Yadier Molina FY RC 10.00 25.00
325 Zach Duke FY RC .30 .75
326 Zach Miner FY RC .30 .75
327 B.Castro .30 .75
K.Greene FS
328 R.Madson .20 .50
E.Ramirez FS
329 R.Harden .20 .50
B.Crosby FS
330 Z.Greinke .50 1.25
J.Gobble FS
331 B.Jenks .20 .50
C.Kotchman FS
332 Sammy Sosa HL .20 .50
333 Kevin Millwood HL .07 .20
334 Rafael Palmeiro HL .12 .30
335 Roger Clemens HL .25 .60
336 Eric Gagne HL .07 .20
337 Mueller .50 1.25
Manny
Jeter LL
338 V.Wells .25 .60
Ichiro
M.Young LL
339 A-Rod .25 .60
Thomas
Delgado LL
340 Delgado .25 .60
A-Rod
Boone LL
341 Pedro .12 .30
Hudson
Loaiza LL
342 Loaiza .12 .30
Pedro
Halladay LL
343 Pujols .25 .60
Helton
Renteria LL
344 Pujols .25 .60
Helton
Pierre LL
345 Thome .12 .30
Sexson
J.Lopez LL
346 P.Wilson .12 .30
Sheff
Thome LL
347 Schmidt .12 .30
K.Brown
Prior LL
348 Wood .12 .30
Prior
Vazquez LL
349 R.Clemens .25 .60
D.Wells ALDS
350 K.Wood .12 .30
M.Prior NLDS
351 Beckett .20 .50
Cabrera
I.Rod NLCS
352 Giambi .25 .60
Rivera
Boone ALCS
353 D.Lowe .12 .30
I.Rod AL
NLDS
354 Pedro .25 .60
Posa
Clemens ALCS
355 Juan Pierre WS .07 .20
356 Carlos Delgado AS .07 .20
357 Bret Boone AS .07 .20
358 Alex Rodriguez AS .25 .60
359 Bill Mueller AS .07 .20
360 Vernon Wells AS .07 .20
361 Garret Anderson AS .07 .20
362 Magglio Ordonez AS .12 .30
363 Jorge Posada AS .12 .30
364 Roy Halladay AS .12 .30
365 Andy Pettitte AS .12 .30
366 Frank Thomas AS .20 .50
367 Jody Gerut AS .07 .20
368 Sammy Sosa .20 .50
369 Joe Crede .07 .20
370 Gary Sheffield .07 .20
371 Coco Crisp .07 .20
372 Torii Hunter .07 .20
373 Derrek Lee .07 .20
374 Adam Everett .07 .20
375 Miguel Tejada .12 .30
376 Jeremy Affeldt .07 .20
377 Robin Ventura .07 .20
378 Scott Podsednik .07 .20
379 Matthew LeCroy .07 .20
380 Vladimir Guerrero .12 .30
381 Tike Redman .07 .20
382 Jeff Nelson .07 .20
383 Cliff Lee .12 .30
384 Bobby Abreu .07 .20
385 Josh Fogg .07 .20
386 Trevor Hoffman .12 .30
387 Jesse Foppert .07 .20
388 Edgar Martinez .12 .30
389 Edgar Renteria .07 .20
390 Chipper Jones .20 .50
391 Eric Munson .07 .20
392 Dewon Brazelton .07 .20
393 John Thomson .07 .20
394 Chris Woodward .07 .20
395 Adam LaRoche .07 .20
396 Elmer Dessens .07 .20
397 Johnny Estrada .07 .20
398 Damian Moss .07 .20
399 Gabe Kapler .07 .20
400 Dontrelle Willis .07 .20
401 Troy Glaus .07 .20
402 Raul Mondesi .07 .20
403 Shane Reynolds .07 .20
404 Kurt Ainsworth .07 .20
405 Pedro Martinez .12 .30
406 Eric Karros .07 .20
407 Billy Koch .07 .20
408 Scott Schoeneweis .07 .20
409 Paul Wilson .07 .20
410 Mike Sweeney .07 .20
411 Jason Bay .12 .30
412 Mark Redman .07 .20
413 Jason Jennings .07 .20
414 Rondell White .07 .20
415 Todd Hundley .07 .20
416 Shannon Stewart .07 .20
417 Jae Weong Seo .07 .20
418 Livan Hernandez .07 .20
419 Mark Ellis .07 .20
420 Pat Burrell .07 .20
421 Mark Loretta .07 .20
422 Robb Nen .07 .20
423 Joel Pineiro .07 .20
424 Jason Simontacchi .07 .20
425 Sterling Hitchcock .07 .20
426 Rey Ordonez .07 .20
427 Greg Myers .07 .20
428 Shane Spencer .07 .20
429 Carlos Baerga .07 .20
430 Garret Anderson .07 .20
431 Horacio Ramirez .07 .20
432 Brian Roberts .07 .20
433 Damian Jackson .07 .20
434 Doug Glanville .07 .20
435 Brian Daubach .07 .20
436 Alex Escobar .07 .20
437 Alex Sanchez .07 .20
438 Jeff Bagwell .12 .30
439 Darrell May .07 .20
440 Shawn Green .07 .20
441 Geoff Jenkins .07 .20
442 Endy Chavez .07 .20
443 Nick Johnson .07 .20
444 Jose Guillen .07 .20
445 Tomas Perez .07 .20
446 Phil Nevin .07 .20
447 Jason Schmidt .07 .20
448 Julio Mateo .07 .20
449 So Taguchi .07 .20
450 Randy Johnson .20 .50
451 Paul Byrd .07 .20
452 Chone Figgins .07 .20
453 Larry Bigbie .07 .20
454 Scott Williamson .07 .20
455 Ramon Martinez .07 .20
456 Roberto Alomar .12 .30
457 Ryan Dempster .07 .20
458 Ryan Ludwick .07 .20
459 Ramon Santiago .07 .20
460 Jeff Conine .07 .20
461 Brad Lidge .07 .20
462 Ken Harvey .07 .20
463 Guillermo Mota .07 .20
464 Rick Reed .07 .20
465 Joey Eischen .07 .20
466 Wade Miller .07 .20
467 Steve Karsay .07 .20
468 Chase Utley .12 .30
469 Matt Stairs .07 .20
470 Yorvit Torrealba .07 .20
471 Joe Kennedy .07 .20
472 Reed Johnson .07 .20
473 Victor Zambrano .07 .20
474 Jeff Davanon .07 .20
475 Luis Gonzalez .07 .20
476 Eli Marrero .07 .20
477 Ray King .07 .20
478 Jack Cust .07 .20
479 Omar Daal .07 .20
480 Todd Walker .07 .20
481 Shawn Estes .07 .20
482 Chris Reitsma .07 .20
483 Jake Westbrook .07 .20
484 Jeremy Bonderman .07 .20
485 A.J. Burnett .07 .20
486 Roy Oswalt .12 .30
487 Kevin Brown .07 .20
488 Eric Milton .07 .20
489 Claudio Vargas .07 .20
490 Roger Cedeno .07 .20
491 David Wells .07 .20
492 Scott Hatteberg .07 .20
493 Ricky Ledee .07 .20
494 Eric Young .07 .20
495 Armando Benitez .07 .20
496 Dan Haren .07 .20
497 Carl Crawford .12 .30
498 Laynce Nix .07 .20
499 Eric Hinske .07 .20
500 Ivan Rodriguez .12 .30
501 Scot Shields .07 .20
502 Brandon Webb .07 .20
503 Mark DeRosa .07 .20
504 Jhonny Peralta .07 .20
505 Adam Kennedy .07 .20
506 Tony Batista .07 .20
507 Jeff Suppan .07 .20
508 Kenny Lofton .07 .20
509 Scott Sullivan .07 .20
510 Ken Griffey Jr. .40 1.00
511 Billy Traber .07 .20
512 Larry Walker .12 .30
513 Mike Maroth .07 .20
514 Todd Hollandsworth .07 .20
515 Kirk Saarloos .07 .20
516 Carlos Beltran .12 .30
517 Juan Rivera .07 .20
518 Roger Clemens .25 .60
519 Karim Garcia .07 .20
520 Jose Reyes .12 .30
521 Brandon Duckworth .07 .20
522 Brian Giles .07 .20
523 J.T. Snow .07 .20
524 Jamie Moyer .07 .20
525 Jason Isringhausen .07 .20
526 Julio Lugo .07 .20
527 Mark Teixeira .12 .30
528 Cory Lidle .07 .20
529 Lyle Overbay .07 .20
530 Troy Percival .07 .20
531 Robby Hammock .07 .20
532 Robert Fick .07 .20
533 Jason Johnson .07 .20
534 Brandon Lyon .07 .20
535 Antonio Alfonseca .07 .20
536 Tom Goodwin .07 .20
537 Paul Konerko .12 .30
538 D'Angelo Jimenez .07 .20
539 Ben Broussard .07 .20
540 Magglio Ordonez .12 .30
541 Ellis Burks .07 .20
542 Carlos Pena .12 .30
543 Chad Fox .07 .20
544 Jeriome Robertson .07 .20
545 Travis Hafner .07 .20
546 Joe Randa .07 .20
547 Wil Cordero .07 .20
548 Brady Clark .07 .20
549 Ruben Sierra .07 .20
550 Barry Zito .12 .30
551 Brett Myers .07 .20
552 Oliver Perez .07 .20
553 Trey Hodges .07 .20
554 Benito Santiago .07 .20
555 David Ross .07 .20
556 Ramon Vazquez .07 .20
557 Joe Nathan .07 .20
558 Dan Wilson .07 .20
559 Joe Mauer .15 .40
560 Jim Edmonds .12 .30
561 Shawn Wooten .07 .20
562 Matt Kata .07 .20
563 Vinny Castilla .07 .20
564 Marty Cordova .07 .20
565 Aramis Ramirez .07 .20
566 Carl Everett .07 .20
567 Ryan Freel .07 .20
568 Jason Davis .07 .20
569 Mark Bellhorn Sox .07 .20
570 Craig Monroe .07 .20
571 Roberto Hernandez .07 .20
572 Tim Redding .07 .20
573 Kevin Appier .07 .20
574 Jeromy Burnitz .07 .20
575 Miguel Cabrera .20 .50
576 Ramon Nivar .07 .20
577 Casey Blake .07 .20
578 Aaron Boone .07 .20
579 Jermaine Dye .07 .20
580 Jerome Williams .07 .20
581 John Olerud .07 .20
582 Scott Rolen .12 .30
583 Bobby Kielty .07 .20
584 Travis Lee .07 .20
585 Jeff Cirillo .07 .20
586 Scott Spiezio .07 .20
587 Stephen Randolph .07 .20
588 Melvin Mora .07 .20
589 Mike Timlin .07 .20
590 Kerry Wood .07 .20
591 Tony Womack .07 .20
592 Jody Gerut .07 .20
593 Franklyn German .07 .20
594 Morgan Ensberg .07 .20
595 Odalis Perez .07 .20
596 Michael Cuddyer .07 .20
597 Jon Lieber .07 .20
598 Mike Williams .07 .20
599 Jose Hernandez .07 .20
600 Alfonso Soriano .12 .30
601 Marquis Grissom .07 .20
602 Matt Morris .07 .20
603 Damian Rolls .07 .20
604 Juan Gonzalez .07 .20
605 Aquilino Lopez .07 .20
606 Jose Valverde .07 .20
607 Kenny Rogers .07 .20
608 Joe Borowski .07 .20
609 Josh Bard .07 .20
610 Austin Kearns .07 .20
611 Chin-Hui Tsao .07 .20
612 Wil Ledezma .07 .20
613 Aaron Guiel .07 .20
614 LaTroy Hawkins .07 .20
615 Tony Armas Jr. .07 .20
616 Steve Trachsel .07 .20
617 Ted Lilly .07 .20
618 Todd Pratt .07 .20
619 Sean Burroughs .07 .20
620 Rafael Palmeiro .12 .30
621 Jeremi Gonzalez .07 .20
622 Quinton McCracken .07 .20
623 David Ortiz .20 .50
624 Randall Simon .07 .20
625 Wily Mo Pena .07 .20
626 Nate Cornejo .07 .20
627 Brian Anderson .07 .20
628 Corey Koskie .07 .20
629 Keith Foulke Sox .07 .20
630 Rheal Cormier .07 .20
631 Sidney Ponson .07 .20
632 Gary Matthews Jr. .07 .20
633 Herbert Perry .07 .20
634 Shea Hillenbrand .07 .20
635 Craig Biggio .12 .30
636 Barry Larkin .12 .30
637 Arthur Rhodes .07 .20
638 Anaheim Angels TC .07 .20
639 Arizona Diamondbacks TC .07 .20
640 Atlanta Braves TC .07 .20
641 Baltimore Orioles TC .07 .20
642 Boston Red Sox TC .10 .30
643 Chicago Cubs TC .07 .20
644 Chicago White Sox TC .07 .20
645 Cincinnati Reds TC .07 .20
646 Cleveland Indians TC .07 .20
647 Colorado Rockies TC .07 .20
648 Detroit Tigers TC .07 .20
649 Florida Marlins TC .07 .20
650 Houston Astros TC .07 .20
651 Kansas City Royals TC .07 .20
652 Los Angeles Dodgers TC .07 .20
653 Milwaukee Brewers TC .07 .20
654 Minnesota Twins TC .07 .20
655 Montreal Expos TC .07 .20
656 New York Mets TC .07 .20
657 New York Yankees TC .20 .50
658 Oakland Athletics TC .07 .20
659 Philadelphia Phillies TC .07 .20
660 Pittsburgh Pirates TC .07 .20
661 San Diego Padres TC .07 .20
662 San Francisco Giants TC .07 .20
663 Seattle Mariners TC .07 .20
664 St. Louis Cardinals TC .07 .20
665 Tampa Bay Devil Rays TC .07 .20
666 Texas Rangers TC .07 .20
667 Toronto Blue Jays TC .07 .20
668 Kyle Sleeth DP RC .20 .50
669 Bradley Sullivan DP RC .20 .50
670 Carlos Quentin DP RC .75 2.00
671 Conor Jackson DP RC .60 1.50
672 Jeffrey Allison DP RC .20 .50
673 Matthew Moses DP RC .30 .75
674 Tim Stauffer DP RC .30 .75
675 Estee Harris DP RC .20 .50
676 David Aardsma DP RC .20 .50
677 Omar Quintanilla DP RC .20 .50
678 Aaron Hill DP .20 .50
679 Tony Richie DP RC .20 .50
680 Lastings Milledge DP RC .30 .75
681 Brad Snyder DP RC .20 .50
682 Jason Hirsh DP RC .20 .50
683 Logan Kensing DP RC .20 .50
684 Chris Lubanski DP .20 .50
685 Ryan Harvey DP .20 .50
686 Ryan Wagner DP .20 .50
687 Rickie Weeks DP .20 .50
688 G.Sizemore .30 .75
J.Guthrie
689 E.Jackson .20 .50
G.Miller
690 J.Reed .20 .50
N.Cotts
691 A.Loewen .40 1.00
N.Markakis
692 B.Upton .30 .75
D.Young
693 A.Rodriguez .50 1.25
D.Jeter
694 I.Suzuki .25 .60
A.Pujols
695 J.Thome .30 .75
M.Schmidt
696 Mike Mussina GG .12 .30
697 Bengie Molina GG .07 .20
698 John Olerud GG .07 .20
699 Bret Boone GG .07 .20
700 Eric Chavez GG .07 .20
701 Alex Rodriguez GG .25 .60
702 Mike Cameron GG .07 .20
703 Ichiro Suzuki GG .25 .60
704 Torii Hunter GG .07 .20
705 Mike Hampton GG .07 .20
706 Mike Matheny GG .07 .20
707 Derrek Lee GG .07 .20
708 Luis Castillo GG .07 .20
709 Scott Rolen GG .12 .30
710 Edgar Renteria GG .07 .20
711 Andruw Jones GG .07 .20
712 Jose Cruz Jr. GG .07 .20
713 Jim Edmonds GG .12 .30
714 Roy Halladay CY .12 .30
715 Eric Gagne CY .07 .20
716 Alex Rodriguez MVP .25 .60
717 Angel Berroa ROY .07 .20
718 Dontrelle Willis ROY .07 .20
719 Todd Helton AS .12 .30
720 Marcus Giles AS .07 .20
721 Edgar Renteria AS .07 .20
722 Scott Rolen AS .12 .30
723 Albert Pujols AS .25 .60
724 Gary Sheffield AS .07 .20
725 Javy Lopez AS .07 .20
726 Eric Gagne AS .07 .20
727 Randy Wolf AS .07 .20
728 Bobby Cox AS .07 .20
729 Scott Podsednik AS .07 .20
730 Alex Gonzalez WS .07 .20
731 Brad Penny WS .07 .20
732 Beckett .12 .30
I.Rod
A.Gonz WS
733 Josh Beckett WS MVP .07 .20

2004 Topps Black

COM. (1-6/8-331/368-695) 6.00 15.00
SEMIS 1-296/368-667/693-695 10.00 25.00
UNL 1-296/368-667/693-695 20.00 40.00
COM. 297-326/668-687 6.00 15.00
SEMIS 297-326/668-687 10.00 25.00
UNL 297-326/668-687 15.00 40.00
COM. 327-331/688-692 6.00 15.00
SEMIS 327-331/688-692 10.00 25.00
UNL 327-331/688-692 20.00 40.00
SERIES 1 ODDS 1:13 HTA
SERIES 2 ODDS 1:12 HTA
STATED PRINT RUN 53 SERIAL #'d SETS
CARDS 7 AND 274 DO NOT EXIST
SCIOSCIA AND J.CASTRO NUMBERED 267
10 Ichiro Suzuki 20.00 50.00
20 Derek Jeter 40.00 100.00
40 Albert Pujols 20.00 50.00
100 Alex Rodriguez 20.00 50.00
140 Greg Maddux 20.00 50.00
510 Ken Griffey Jr. 30.00 80.00
518 Roger Clemens 20.00 50.00
670 Carlos Quentin DP 25.00 60.00
671 Conor Jackson DP 20.00 50.00
680 Lastings Milledge DP 10.00 25.00
693 A.Rodriguez 40.00 100.00
D.Jeter
694 I.Suzuki 20.00 50.00
A.Pujols
695 J.Thome 25.00 60.00
M.Schmidt

2004 Topps Box Bottoms

A-Rod/Piazza/Andruw/Manny 1.50 4.00
*BOX BOTTOM CARDS: 1X TO 2.5X BASIC
ONE 4-CARD SHEET PER HTA BOX

2004 Topps Gold

*GOLD 1-296/368-667/693-695: 6X TO 15X
*GOLD 297-326/668-687: 1.25X TO 3X
*GOLD 327-331/688-692: 6X TO 15X
SERIES 1 ODDS 1:11 HOB, 1:3 HTA, 1:10 RET
SERIES 2 ODDS 1:8 HOB, 1:2 HTA, 1:8 RET
STATED PRINT RUN 2004 SERIAL #'d SETS
CARDS 7 AND 274 DO NOT EXIST
SCIOSCIA AND J.CASTRO NUMBERED 267

2004 Topps All-Star Patch Relics

SER.2 ODDS 1:7698 H, 1:2208 HTA, 1:7819 R
STATED PRINT RUN 15 SETS
CARDS ARE NOT SERIAL-NUMBERED
PRINT RUN INFO PROVIDED BY TOPPS
NO PRICING DUE TO SCARCITY

2004 Topps 1st Edition

*1st.ED 1-296/332-667/693-732: 1.25X TO 3X
*1st.ED 297-326/668-687: 1.25X TO 3X
*1st.ED 327-331/688-692: 1.25X TO 3X
DISTRIBUTED IN 1ST EDITION BOXES
CARDS 7 AND 274 DO NOT EXIST
SCIOSCIA AND J.CASTRO NUMBERED 267

2004 Topps All-Star Stitches Jersey Relics

SERIES 1 ODDS 1:137 HOB/RET, 1:39 HTA
AB Aaron Boone 4.00 10.00
AJ Andruw Jones 4.00 10.00
AR Alex Rodriguez 6.00 15.00
BD Brendan Donnelly 4.00 10.00
BW Billy Wagner 4.00 10.00
CE Carl Everett 4.00 10.00
EG Eddie Guardado 4.00 10.00
EGA Eric Gagne 4.00 10.00
EL Esteban Loaiza 4.00 10.00
EM Edgar Martinez 4.00 10.00
ER Edgar Renteria 4.00 10.00
HB Hank Blalock 4.00 10.00
JL Javy Lopez 4.00 10.00
JM Jamie Moyer 4.00 10.00
JP Jorge Posada 4.00 10.00
JS Jason Schmidt 4.00 10.00
JV Jose Vidro 4.00 10.00
KF Keith Foulke 4.00 10.00
KW Kerry Wood 4.00 10.00
ML Mike Lowell 4.00 10.00
MM Mark Mulder 4.00 10.00
MMO Melvin Mora 4.00 10.00
NG Nomar Garciaparra 6.00 15.00
PL Paul Lo Duca 4.00 10.00
PW Preston Wilson 4.00 10.00
RF Rafael Furcal 4.00 10.00
RH Ramon Hernandez 4.00 10.00
RO Russ Ortiz 4.00 10.00
RW Randy Wolf 4.00 10.00
RWH Rondell White 4.00 10.00
SH Shigetoshi Hasegawa 4.00 10.00
SR Scott Rolen 4.00 10.00
TG Troy Glaus 4.00 10.00
TH Todd Helton 4.00 10.00
VW Vernon Wells 4.00 10.00
WW Woody Williams 4.00 10.00

2004 Topps All-Stars

COMPLETE SET (20) 8.00 20.00
SERIES 2 ODDS 1:16 H, 1:4 HTA
TAS1 Jason Giambi .40 1.00
TAS2 Ichiro Suzuki 1.25 3.00
TAS3 Alex Rodriguez 1.25 3.00
TAS4 Albert Pujols 1.25 3.00
TAS5 Alfonso Soriano .60 1.50
TAS6 Nomar Garciaparra .60 1.50
TAS7 Andruw Jones .40 1.00
TAS8 Carlos Delgado .40 1.00
TAS9 Gary Sheffield .40 1.00
TAS10 Jorge Posada .60 1.50
TAS11 Magglio Ordonez .60 1.50
TAS12 Kerry Wood .40 1.00
TAS13 Garret Anderson .40 1.00
TAS14 Bret Boone .40 1.00
TAS15 Hank Blalock .40 1.00
TAS16 Mike Lowell .40 1.00
TAS17 Todd Helton .60 1.50
TAS18 Vernon Wells .40 1.00
TAS19 Roger Clemens 1.25 3.00
TAS20 Scott Rolen .60 1.50

2004 Topps Autographs

Please note Josh Beckett, Mike Lowell, Mark Prior, Ivan Rodriguez and Scott Rolen did not return their cards in time for inclusion into packs and the exchange date for these cards were November 30th, 2005 for Series one exchange cards and April 30th, 2006 for Series two exchange cards. Cards issued in first series packs carry a "1" and cards from series 2 carry a "2" after their group seeding notes within our checklist.

SER.1 A 1:18,502 H, 1:4735 HTA, 1:18,432 R
SER.1 B 1:7362 H, 1:1911 HTA, 1:7472 R
SER.1 C 1:10,900 H, 1:2741 HTA, 1:11,059 R
SER.1 D 1:1053 H, 1:273 HTA, 1:1055 R
SER.1 E 1:6278 H, 1:1640 HTA, 1:6284 R
SER.1 F 1:1229 H, 1:318 HTA, 1:1229 R
SER.1 G 1:2340 H, 1:668 HTA, 1:1881 R
SER.1 H 1:1167 H, 1:351 HTA, 1:1229 R
SER.2 A 1:10,530 H, 1:2848 HTA, 1:9774 R
SER.2 B 1:1504 H, 1:391 HTA, 1:1422 R
SER.2 C 1:1319 H, 1:333 HTA, 1:1303 R
SER.1 EXCH.DEADLINE 11/30/05
SER.2 EXCH.DEADLINE 04/30/06
AB Aaron Boone B2 12.00 30.00
AH Aubrey Huff B2 6.00 15.00
AK Austin Kearns B1 6.00 15.00
BB Bobby Brownlie C2 10.00 25.00
BS Benito Santiago D1 10.00 25.00
BU B.J. Upton F1 6.00 15.00
CF Cliff Floyd D1 6.00 15.00
DM Dustin McGowan C2 4.00 10.00
DW Dontrelle Willis B2 4.00 10.00
EH Eric Hinske H1 4.00 10.00
ER Elizardo Ramirez H1 4.00 10.00
GA Garret Anderson B2 6.00 15.00
HB Hank Blalock D1 6.00 15.00
IR Ivan Rodriguez B2 10.00 25.00
JB Josh Beckett B1 4.00 10.00
JG Jay Gibbons A1 6.00 15.00
JP1 Josh Phelps G1 4.00 10.00
JP2 Jorge Posada B2 20.00 50.00
JV Jose Vidro F1 4.00 10.00
KG Khalil Greene H1 4.00 10.00
LB Lance Berkman A2 10.00 25.00
MC Miguel Cabrera C2 25.00 60.00
ML Mike Lowell F1 6.00 15.00
MO Magglio Ordonez F1 6.00 15.00
MP Mark Prior D1 6.00 15.00
MS Mike Sweeney D1 6.00 15.00
MT Mark Teixeira D1 6.00 15.00
PK Paul Konerko G1 6.00 15.00
PL Paul Lo Duca E1 6.00 15.00
SP Scott Podsednik B2 10.00 25.00
TH Torii Hunter C1 8.00 20.00
VM Victor Martinez D1 6.00 15.00
ZG Zack Greinke C2 4.00 10.00

2004 Topps Derby Digs Jersey Relics

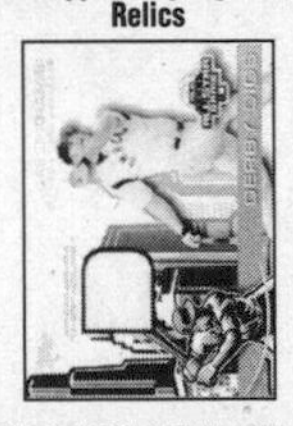

SERIES 1 ODDS 1:585 H, 1:167 HTA, 1:586 R
AP Albert Pujols 10.00 25.00
BB Bret Boone 4.00 10.00
CD Carlos Delgado 4.00 10.00
GA Garret Anderson 4.00 10.00
JE Jim Edmonds 4.00 10.00
JG Jason Giambi 4.00 10.00
RS Richie Sexson 4.00 10.00

2004 Topps Draft Pick Bonus

COMPLETE SET (10) 10.00 25.00
COMP.RETAIL SET (5) 6.00 15.00
COMP.HOLIDAY SET (10) 4.00 10.00
1-5 ISSUED IN BLUE RETAIL FACT.SET
6-15 ISSUED IN GREEN HOLIDAY FACT.SET
1 Josh Johnson .50 1.25
2 Donny Lucy .50 1.25
3 Greg Golson .50 1.25
4 K.C. Herren .50 1.25
5 Jeff Marquez .50 1.25
6 Mark Rogers .75 2.00
7 Eric Hurley .50 1.25
8 Gio Gonzalez .75 2.00
9 Thomas Diamond .50 1.25
10 Matt Bush .75 2.00
11 Kyle Waldrop .50 1.25
12 Neil Walker 2.50 6.00
13 Mike Ferris .50 1.25
14 Ray Liotta .50 1.25
15 Philip Hughes 1.25 3.00

2004 Topps Fall Classic Covers

COMPLETE SET (99) 60.00 120.00
COMPLETE SERIES 1 (48) 30.00 60.00
COMPLETE SERIES 2 (51) 30.00 60.00
COMMON CARD 1.50 4.00
SERIES 1 ODDS 1:12 HOB/RET, 1:4 HTA
SERIES 2 ODDS 1:12 HOB/RET, 1:5 HTA
EVEN YEARS DISTRIBUTED IN SERIES 1
ODD YEARS DISTRIBUTED IN SERIES 2

2004 Topps First Year Player Bonus

COMPLETE SET (10) 8.00 20.00
COMPLETE SERIES 1 (5) 4.00 10.00
COMPLETE SERIES 2 (5) 4.00 10.00
1-5 ISSUED IN BROWN HOBBY FACT.SETS
6-10 ISSUED IN JC PENNEY FACT.SETS
1 Travis Blackley .50 1.25
2 Rudy Guillen .50 1.25
3 Ervin Santana 1.25 3.00
4 Wanell Severino .50 1.25
5 Kevin Kouzmanoff 3.00 8.00
6 Alberto Callaspo 1.25 3.00
7 Bobby Brownlie .50 1.25
8 Travis Hanson .50 1.25
9 Joaquin Arias 1.25 3.00
10 Merkin Valdez .50 1.25

2004 Topps Hit Parade

COMPLETE SET (30) 12.50 30.00
SERIES 2 ODDS 1:7 HOB, 1:2 HTA, 1:9 RET
HP1 Sammy Sosa HR 1.00 2.50
HP2 Rafael Palmeiro HR .60 1.50
HP3 Fred McGriff HR .40 1.00
HP4 Ken Griffey Jr. HR 2.00 5.00
HP5 Juan Gonzalez HR .40 1.00
HP6 Frank Thomas HR 1.00 2.50
HP7 Andres Galarraga HR .60 1.50
HP8 Jim Thome HR .60 1.50
HP9 Jeff Bagwell HR .60 1.50
HP10 Gary Sheffield HR .40 1.00
HP11 Rafael Palmeiro RBI .60 1.50
HP12 Sammy Sosa RBI 1.00 2.50
HP13 Fred McGriff RBI .40 1.00
HP14 Andres Galarraga RBI .60 1.50
HP15 Juan Gonzalez RBI .40 1.00
HP16 Frank Thomas RBI 1.00 2.50
HP17 Jeff Bagwell RBI .60 1.50
HP18 Ken Griffey Jr. RBI 2.00 5.00
HP19 Ruben Sierra RBI .40 1.00
HP20 Gary Sheffield RBI .40 1.00
HP21 Rafael Palmeiro Hits .60 1.50
HP22 Roberto Alomar Hits .60 1.50
HP22A Roberto Alomar Hits .60 1.50
White Card Number
HP23 Julio Franco Hits .40 1.00
HP24 Andres Galarraga Hits .60 1.50
HP25 Fred McGriff Hits .40 1.00
HP26 Craig Biggio Hits .60 1.50
HP27 Barry Larkin Hits .60 1.50
HP28 Steve Finley Hits .40 1.00
HP29 B.J. Surhoff Hits .40 1.00
HP30 Jeff Bagwell Hits .60 1.50

2004 Topps Hobby Masters

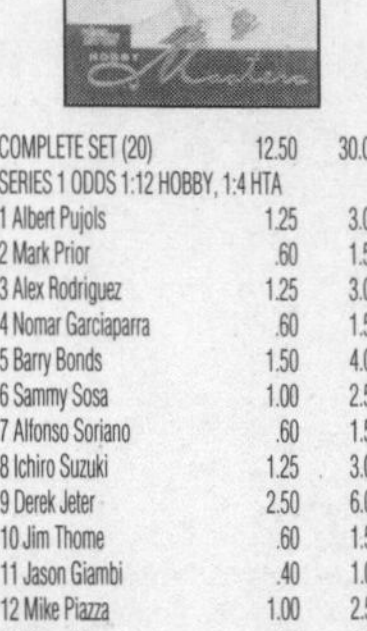

COMPLETE SET (20) 12.50 30.00
SERIES 1 ODDS 1:12 HOBBY, 1:4 HTA
1 Albert Pujols 1.25 3.00
2 Mark Prior .60 1.50
3 Alex Rodriguez 1.25 3.00
4 Nomar Garciaparra .60 1.50
5 Barry Bonds 1.50 4.00
6 Sammy Sosa 1.00 2.50
7 Alfonso Soriano .60 1.50
8 Ichiro Suzuki 1.25 3.00
9 Derek Jeter 2.50 6.00
10 Jim Thome .60 1.50
11 Jason Giambi .40 1.00
12 Mike Piazza 1.00 2.50
13 Barry Zito .60 1.50
14 Randy Johnson 1.00 2.50
15 Adam Dunn .60 1.50
16 Vladimir Guerrero .60 1.50
17 Gary Sheffield .40 1.00
18 Carlos Delgado .40 1.00
19 Chipper Jones 1.00 2.50
20 Dontrelle Willis .40 1.00

2004 Topps Own the Game

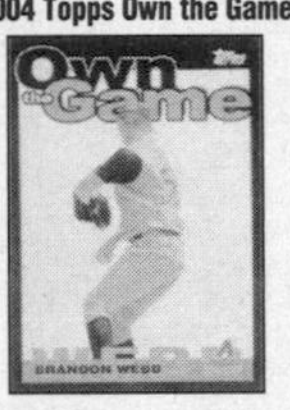

COMPLETE SET (30) 15.00 40.00
SERIES 1 ODDS 1:18 HOB/RET, 1:6 HTA
1 Jim Thome .60 1.50
2 Albert Pujols 1.25 3.00
3 Alex Rodriguez 1.25 3.00
4 Barry Bonds 1.50 4.00
5 Ichiro Suzuki 1.25 3.00
6 Derek Jeter 2.50 6.00
7 Nomar Garciaparra .60 1.50
8 Alfonso Soriano .60 1.50
9 Gary Sheffield .40 1.00
10 Jason Giambi .40 1.00
11 Todd Helton .60 1.50
12 Garret Anderson .40 1.00
13 Carlos Delgado .40 1.00
14 Manny Ramirez 1.00 2.50
15 Richie Sexson .40 1.00
16 Vernon Wells .40 1.00
17 Preston Wilson .40 1.00
18 Frank Thomas 1.00 2.50
19 Shawn Green .40 1.00
20 Rafael Furcal .40 1.00
21 Juan Pierre .40 1.00
22 Javy Lopez .40 1.00
23 Edgar Renteria .40 1.00
24 Mark Prior .60 1.50
25 Pedro Martinez .60 1.50
26 Kerry Wood .40 1.00
27 Curt Schilling .60 1.50
28 Roy Halladay .60 1.50
29 Eric Gagne .60 1.50
30 Brandon Webb .40 1.00

2004 Topps Presidential First Pitch Seat Relics

SERIES 2 ODDS 1:592 H, 1:169 HTA, 1:592 R
BC Bill Clinton 20.00 50.00
CC Calvin Coolidge 10.00 25.00
DE Dwight Eisenhower 10.00 25.00
FR Franklin D. Roosevelt 15.00 40.00
GB George W. Bush 15.00 40.00
GF Gerald Ford 15.00 40.00
HH Herbert Hoover 10.00 25.00
HT Harry Truman 10.00 25.00
JK John F. Kennedy 12.00 30.00
LJ Lyndon B. Johnson 10.00 25.00
RN Richard Nixon 12.00 30.00
RR Ronald Reagan 12.00 30.00
WH Warren Harding 10.00 25.00
WT William Taft 10.00 25.00
WW Woodrow Wilson 10.00 25.00
GHB George H.W. Bush 15.00 40.00

2004 Topps Presidential Pastime

COMPLETE SET (42) 50.00 100.00
SERIES 2 ODDS 1:6 HOB, 1:2 HTA, 1:6 RET
PP1 George Washington 2.00 5.00
PP2 John Adams 1.25 3.00
PP3 Thomas Jefferson 2.00 5.00
PP4 James Madison 1.25 3.00
PP5 James Monroe 1.25 3.00
PP6 John Quincy Adams 1.25 3.00
PP7 Andrew Jackson 1.25 3.00
PP8 Martin Van Buren 1.25 3.00
PP9 William Harrison 1.25 3.00
PP10 John Tyler 1.25 3.00
PP11 James Polk 1.25 3.00
PP12 Zachary Taylor 1.25 3.00
PP13 Millard Fillmore 1.25 3.00
PP14 Franklin Pierce 1.25 3.00
PP15 James Buchanan 1.25 3.00
PP16 Abraham Lincoln 2.00 5.00
PP17 Andrew Johnson 1.25 3.00
PP18 Ulysses S. Grant 1.50 4.00
PP19 Rutherford B. Hayes 1.25 3.00
PP20 James Garfield 1.25 3.00
PP21 Chester Arthur 1.25 3.00
PP22 Grover Cleveland 1.25 3.00
PP23 Benjamin Harrison 1.25 3.00
PP24 William McKinley 1.25 3.00
PP25 Theodore Roosevelt 1.50 4.00
PP26 William Taft 1.25 3.00
PP27 Woodrow Wilson 1.25 3.00
PP28 Warren Harding 1.25 3.00
PP29 Calvin Coolidge 1.25 3.00
PP30 Herbert Hoover 1.25 3.00
PP31 Franklin D. Roosevelt 1.50 4.00
PP32 Harry Truman 1.25 3.00
PP33 Dwight Eisenhower 1.25 3.00
PP34 John F. Kennedy 1.50 4.00
PP35 Lyndon B. Johnson 1.25 3.00
PP36 Richard Nixon 1.50 4.00
PP37 Gerald Ford 1.50 4.00
PP38 Jimmy Carter 1.25 3.00
PP39 Ronald Reagan 4.00 10.00
PP40 George H.W. Bush 1.50 4.00
PP41 Bill Clinton 2.00 5.00
PP42 George W. Bush 2.00 5.00

2004 Topps Team Set Prospect Bonus

COMP.ASTROS SET (5) 3.00 8.00
COMP.CUBS SET (5) 3.00 8.00
COMP.RED SOX SET (5) 3.00 8.00
COMP.YANKEES SET (5) 3.00 8.00
A1-A5 ISSUED IN ASTROS FACTORY SET
C1-C5 ISSUED IN CUBS FACTORY SET
R1-R5 ISSUED IN RED SOX FACTORY SET
Y1-Y5 ISSUED IN YANKEES FACTORY SET
A1 Brooks Conrad .75 2.00
A2 Hector Gimenez .75 2.00
A3 Kevin Davidson .75 2.00
A4 Chris Burke .75 2.00
A5 John Buck .75 2.00
C1 Bobby Brownlie .75 2.00
C2 Felix Pie .75 2.00
C3 Jon Connolly .75 2.00
C4 David Kelton .75 2.00
C5 Ricky Nolasco 1.25 3.00
R1 David Murphy 1.25 3.00
R2 Kevin Youkilis .75 2.00
R3 Juan Cedeno .75 2.00
R4 Matt Murton .75 2.00
R5 Kenny Perez .75 2.00
Y1 Rudy Guillen .75 2.00
Y2 David Parrish .75 2.00
Y3 Brad Halsey .75 2.00
Y4 Hector Made .75 2.00
Y5 Robinson Cano 2.50 6.00

2004 Topps Series Seats Relics

SERIES 2 ODDS 1:316 HOB/RET, 1:89 HTA
AK Al Kaline 10.00 25.00
BF Bob Feller 6.00 15.00
BM Bill Mazeroski 10.00 25.00
BP Boog Powell 6.00 15.00
BR Brooks Robinson 6.00 15.00
FR Frank Robinson 6.00 15.00
HK Harmon Killebrew 10.00 25.00
JP Jim Palmer 6.00 15.00
LA Luis Aparicio 6.00 15.00
LP Lou Piniella 6.00 15.00
PM Paul Molitor 6.00 15.00
RJ Reggie Jackson 6.00 15.00
RY Robin Yount 10.00 25.00
WM Willie Mays 15.00 40.00
WS Warren Spahn 10.00 25.00

2004 Topps Series Stitches Relics

SER.2 GROUP A 1:829 H, 1:236 HTA, 1:832 R
SER.2 GROUP B 1:980 H, 1:280 HTA, 1:984 R
SER.2 GROUP C 1:686 H, 1:196 HTA, 1:686 R
AS Alfonso Soriano Bat B 6.00 15.00
CJ Chipper Jones Jsy C 6.00 15.00
DG Dwight Gooden Jsy A 4.00 10.00
DJ David Justice Bat B 6.00 15.00
FR Frank Robinson Bat A 6.00 15.00
GB George Brett Bat A 15.00 40.00
GC Gary Carter Jkt C 4.00 10.00
HK Harmon Killebrew Bat A 15.00 40.00
JB Johnny Bench Bat A 10.00 25.00
JBE Josh Beckett Jsy C 4.00 10.00
JC Joe Carter Bat B 6.00 15.00
JCA Jose Canseco Bat C 10.00 25.00
KG Kirk Gibson Bat B 6.00 15.00
KP Kirby Puckett Bat B 10.00 25.00
LD Lenny Dykstra Bat A 6.00 15.00
MS Mike Schmidt Uni A 15.00 40.00
PO Paul O'Neill Bat A 10.00 25.00
RC Roger Clemens Uni C 8.00 20.00
RJ Randy Johnson Jsy A 6.00 15.00
RJA Reggie Jackson Bat B 10.00 25.00
RY Robin Yount Uni A 6.00 15.00
SG Steve Garvey Bat B 6.00 15.00
TS Tom Seaver Uni A 6.00 15.00
WM Willie Mays Bat A 15.00 40.00

2004 Topps Legends Autographs

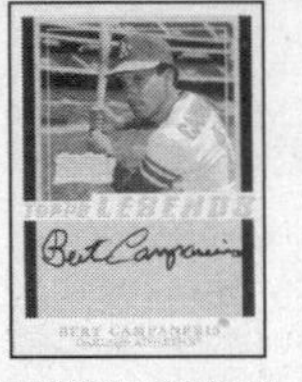

ISSUED IN VARIOUS 03-05 TOPPS BRANDS
SER.1 ODDS 1:1399 H, 1:421 HTA, 1:1494 R
SER.2 ODDS 1:766 H, 1:216 HTA, 1:802 R
AD Andre Dawson 8.00 20.00
BC Bert Campaneris 6.00 15.00
BP Boog Powell 6.00 15.00
CE Carl Erskine 6.00 15.00
DE Dwight Evans 8.00 20.00
DJ Davey Johnson 6.00 15.00
JP Jim Piersall 6.00 15.00
JP Johnny Podres 6.00 15.00
JR Joe Rudi 6.00 15.00
NR Nolan Ryan 125.00 300.00
SA Sparky Anderson 8.00 20.00
SG Steve Garvey 6.00 15.00
WM Willie Mays 100.00 200.00

2004 Topps World Series Highlights

COMPLETE SET (30) 15.00 40.00
COMPLETE SERIES 1 (15) 8.00 20.00
COMPLETE SERIES 2 (15) 8.00 20.00
SERIES 1 ODDS 1:18 HOB/RET, 1:6 HTA
SERIES 2 ODDS 1:18 HOB/RET, 1:7 HTA
AJ Andruw Jones 2 .40 1.00
AK Al Kaline 2 1.00 2.50
BM Bill Mazeroski 1 .60 1.50
BR Brooks Robinson 1 .60 1.50
BT Bobby Thomson 2 .60 1.50
CF Carlton Fisk 1 .60 1.50
CY Carl Yastrzemski 1 1.00 2.50
DB Dusty Baker 2 .40 1.00
DJ David Justice 2 .40 1.00
DL Don Larsen 1 .40 1.00
DS Duke Snider 2 .60 1.50
FR Frank Robinson 2 .60 1.50
JB Johnny Bench 2 1.00 2.50
JC Joe Carter 2 .40 1.00
JCA Jose Canseco 2 .60 1.50
JP1 Jim Palmer 1 .60 1.50
JP2 Johnny Podres 2 .40 1.00
KG Kirk Gibson 1 .40 1.00
KP Kirby Puckett 1 1.00 2.50
LB Lou Brock 1 .60 1.50
LG Luis Gonzalez 2 .40 1.00
MS Mike Schmidt 1 1.50 4.00
OS Ozzie Smith 2 1.25 3.00
RJ Reggie Jackson 1 .60 1.50
RY Robin Yount 1 1.00 2.50
SM Stan Musial 1 1.50 4.00
TS Tom Seaver 1 .60 1.50
WF Whitey Ford 2 .60 1.50
WM1 Willie Mays 1 2.00 5.00
WM2 Willie McCovey 2 .60 1.50

2004 Topps World Series Highlights Autographs

SERIES 1 ODDS 1:74 HTA
SERIES 2 ODDS 1:69 HTA
AK Al Kaline 2 20.00 50.00
BM Bill Mazeroski 1 15.00 40.00
BR Brooks Robinson 1 15.00 40.00
BT Bobby Thomson 2 12.00 30.00
CF Carlton Fisk 1 40.00 80.00
DB Dusty Baker 2 10.00 25.00
DJ David Justice 2 15.00 40.00
DL Don Larsen 1 10.00 25.00
DS Duke Snider 2 15.00 40.00
HK Harmon Killebrew 1 20.00 50.00
JB Johnny Bench 2 30.00 80.00
JP1 Jim Palmer 1 10.00 25.00
JP2 Johnny Podres 2 10.00 25.00
KG Kirk Gibson 1 30.00 80.00
LB Lou Brock 1 15.00 40.00
MS Mike Schmidt 1 30.00 80.00
RJ Reggie Jackson 2 20.00 50.00
RY Robin Yount 1 15.00 40.00
SM Stan Musial 2 40.00 80.00
WF Whitey Ford 2 20.00 50.00

2004 Topps Traded

This 220-card set was released in October, 2004. The set was issued in 11-card hobby and retail packs (including one puzzle piece) which had an $3 SRP and which came 24 packs to a box and 12 boxes to a case. Cards numbered 1-65 feature players who were traded, while cards numbered 66 through 70 feature managers who took over teams after the basic set was issued and cards 71 through 90 are high draft picks, cards numbered 91 through 110 are prospect cards and cards numbered 111-220 feature Rookie Cards. Please note, an additional card (#T221) featuring Barry Bonds was distributed by Topps directly to hobby shop accounts enrolled in the Home Team Advantage program in early January, 2005. Collectors could obtain the card by purchasing a pack of 2005 Topps series 1 baseball. The program was limited to one card per customer.

COMPLETE SET (220) 20.00 50.00
COMMON CARD (1-70) .07 .20
COMMON CARD (71-90) .20 .50
COMMON CARD (91-110) .20 .50
COMMON CARD (111-220) .20 .50
BONDS AVAIL VIA HTA SHOP EXCHANGE
PLATE ODDS 1:1151 H, 1:1173 R, 1:327 HTA
PLATE PRINT RUN 1 SET PER COLOR
BLACK-CYAN-MAGENTA-YELLOW ISSUED
NO PLATE PRICING DUE TO SCARCITY
T1 Pokey Reese .07 .20
T2 Tony Womack .07 .20
T3 Richard Hidalgo .07 .20
T4 Juan Uribe .07 .20
T5 J.D. Drew .07 .20
T6 Alex Gonzalez .07 .20
T7 Carlos Guillen .07 .20
T8 Doug Mientkiewicz .07 .20
T9 Fernando Vina .07 .20
T10 Milton Bradley .07 .20
T11 Kelvim Escobar .07 .20
T12 Ben Grieve .07 .20
T13 Brian Jordan .07 .20
T14 A.J. Pierzynski .07 .20
T15 Billy Wagner .07 .20
T16 Terrence Long .07 .20
T17 Carlos Beltran .12 .30
T18 Carl Everett .07 .20
T19 Reggie Sanders .07 .20
T20 Javy Lopez .07 .20

T21 Jay Payton .07 .20
T22 Octavio Dotel .07 .20
T23 Eddie Guardado .07 .20
T24 Andy Pettitte .12 .30
T25 Richie Sexson .07 .20
T26 Ronnie Belliard .07 .20
T27 Michael Tucker .07 .20
T28 Brad Fullmer .07 .20
T29 Freddy Garcia .07 .20
T30 Bartolo Colon .07 .20
T31 Larry Walker Cards .12 .30
T32 Mark Kotsay .07 .20
T33 Jason Marquis .07 .20
T34 Dustan Mohr .07 .20
T35 Javier Vazquez .07 .20
T36 Nomar Garciaparra .12 .30
T37 Tino Martinez .12 .30
T38 Hee Seop Choi .07 .20
T39 Damian Miller .07 .20
T40 Jose Lima .07 .20
T41 Ty Wigginton .07 .20
T42 Raul Ibanez .12 .30
T43 Danys Baez .07 .20
T44 Tony Clark .07 .20
T45 Greg Maddux .25 .60
T46 Victor Zambrano .07 .20
T47 Orlando Cabrera Sox .07 .20
T48 Jose Cruz Jr. .07 .20
T49 Kris Benson .07 .20
T50 Alex Rodriguez .25 .60
T51 Steve Finley .07 .20
T52 Ramon Hernandez .07 .20
T53 Esteban Loaiza .07 .20
T54 Ugueth Urbina .07 .20
T55 Jeff Weaver .07 .20
T56 Flash Gordon .07 .20
T57 Jose Contreras .07 .20
T58 Paul Lo Duca .07 .20
T59 Junior Spivey .07 .20
T60 Curt Schilling .12 .30
T61 Brad Penny .07 .20
T62 Braden Looper .07 .20
T63 Miguel Cairo .07 .20
T64 Juan Encarnacion .07 .20
T65 Miguel Batista .07 .20
T66 Terry Francona MG .07 .20
T67 Lee Mazzilli MG .07 .20
T68 Al Pedrique MG .07 .20
T69 Ozzie Guillen MG .07 .20
T70 Phil Garner MG .07 .20
T71 Matt Bush DP RC .30 .75
T72 Homer Bailey DP RC .30 .75
T73 Greg Golson DP RC .20 .50
T74 Kyle Waldrop DP RC .20 .50
T75 Richie Robnett DP RC .20 .50
T76 Jay Rainville DP RC .20 .50
T77 Bill Bray DP RC .20 .50
T78 Philip Hughes DP RC .50 1.25
T79 Scott Elbert DP RC .20 .50
T80 Josh Fields DP RC .30 .75
T81 Justin Orenduff DP RC .30 .75
T82 Dan Putnam DP RC .20 .50
T83 Chris Nelson DP RC .20 .50
T84 Blake DeWitt DP RC .30 .75
T85 J.P. Howell DP RC .20 .50
T86 Huston Street DP RC .30 .75
T87 Kurt Suzuki DP RC .30 .75
T88 Erick San Pedro DP RC .20 .50
T89 Matt Tuiasosopo DP RC .50 1.25
T90 Matt Macri DP RC .30 .75
T91 Chad Tracy PROS .20 .50
T92 Scott Hairston PROS .20 .50
T93 Jonny Gomes PROS .20 .50
T94 Chin-Feng Chen PROS .20 .50
T95 Chien-Ming Wang PROS .75 2.00
T96 Dustin McGowan PROS .20 .50
T97 Chris Burke PROS .20 .50
T98 Denny Bautista PROS .20 .50
T99 Preston Larrison PROS .20 .50
T100 Kevin Youkilis PROS .20 .50
T101 John Maine PROS .20 .50
T102 Guillermo Quiroz PROS .20 .50
T103 Dave Krynzel PROS .20 .50
T104 David Kelton PROS .20 .50
T105 Edwin Encarnacion PROS .50 1.25
T106 Chad Gaudin PROS .20 .50
T107 Sergio Mitre PROS .20 .50
T108 Laynce Nix PROS .20 .50
T109 David Parrish PROS .20 .50
T110 Brandon Claussen PROS .20 .50
T111 Frank Francisco FY RC .20 .50
T112 Brian Dallimore FY RC .20 .50
T113 Jim Crowell FY RC .20 .50
T114 Andres Blanco FY RC .20 .50
T115 Eduardo Villacis FY RC .20 .50
T116 Kazuhito Tadano FY RC .20 .50
T117 Aarom Baldiris FY RC .20 .50
T118 Justin Germano FY RC .20 .50
T119 Joey Gathright FY RC .20 .50
T120 Franklyn Gracesqui FY RC .20 .50
T121 Chin-Lung Hu FY RC .20 .50
T122 Scott Olsen FY RC .20 .50
T123 Tyler Davidson FY RC .20 .50
T124 Fausto Carmona FY RC .30 .75
T125 Tim Hutting FY RC .20 .50
T126 Ryan Meaux FY RC .20 .50
T127 Jon Connolly FY RC .20 .50
T128 Hector Made FY RC .20 .50
T129 Jamie Brown FY RC .20 .50
T130 Paul McAnulty FY RC .20 .50
T131 Chris Saenz FY RC .20 .50
T132 Marland Williams FY RC .20 .50
T133 Mike Huggins FY RC .20 .50
T134 Jesse Crain FY RC .30 .75
T135 Chad Bentz FY RC .20 .50
T136 Kazuo Matsui FY RC .30 .75
T137 Paul Maholm FY RC .30 .75
T138 Brock Jacobsen FY RC .20 .50
T139 Casey Daigle FY RC .20 .50
T140 Nyjer Morgan FY RC .20 .50
T141 Tom Mastny FY RC .20 .50
T142 Kody Kirkland FY RC .20 .50
T143 Jose Capellan FY RC .20 .50
T144 Felix Hernandez FY RC 3.00 8.00
T145 Shawn Hill FY RC .20 .50
T146 Danny Gonzalez FY RC .20 .50
T147 Scott Dohmann FY RC .20 .50
T148 Tommy Murphy FY RC .20 .50
T149 Akinori Otsuka FY RC .20 .50
T150 Miguel Perez FY RC .20 .50
T151 Mike Rouse FY RC .20 .50
T152 Ramon Ramirez FY RC .20 .50
T153 Luke Hughes FY RC .50 1.25
T154 Howie Kendrick FY RC 1.00 2.50
T155 Ryan Budde FY RC .20 .50
T156 Charlie Zink FY RC .20 .50
T157 Warner Madrigal FY RC .20 .50
T158 Jason Szuminski FY RC .20 .50
T159 Chad Chop FY RC .20 .50
T160 Shingo Takatsu FY RC .20 .50
T161 Matt Lemanczyk FY RC .20 .50
T162 Wardell Starling FY RC .20 .50
T163 Nick Gorneault FY RC .20 .50
T164 Scott Proctor FY RC .20 .50
T165 Brooks Conrad FY RC .20 .50
T166 Hector Gimenez FY RC .20 .50
T167 Kevin Howard FY RC .20 .50
T168 Vince Perkins FY RC .20 .50
T169 Brock Peterson FY RC .20 .50
T170 Chris Shelton FY RC .20 .50
T171 Erick Aybar FY RC .50 1.25
T172 Paul Bacot FY RC .20 .50
T173 Matt Capps FY RC .20 .50
T174 Kory Casto FY RC .20 .50
T175 Juan Cedeno FY RC .20 .50
T176 Vito Chiaravalloti FY RC .20 .50
T177 Alec Zumwalt FY RC .20 .50
T178 J.J. Furmaniak FY RC .20 .50
T179 Lee Gwaltney FY RC .20 .50
T180 Donald Kelly FY RC .30 .75
T181 Benji DeQuin FY RC .20 .50
T182 Brant Colamarino FY RC .20 .50
T183 Juan Gutierrez FY RC .20 .50
T184 Carl Loadenthal FY RC .20 .50
T185 Ricky Nolasco FY RC .30 .75
T186 Jeff Salazar FY RC .20 .50
T187 Rob Tejeda FY RC .20 .50
T188 Alex Romero FY RC .20 .50
T189 Yoann Torrealba FY RC .20 .50
T190 Carlos Sosa FY RC .20 .50
T191 Tim Bittner FY RC .20 .50
T192 Chris Aguila FY RC .20 .50
T193 Jason Frasor FY RC .20 .50
T194 Reid Gorecki FY RC .20 .50
T195 Dustin Nippert FY RC .20 .50
T196 Javier Guzman FY RC .20 .50
T197 Harvey Garcia FY RC .20 .50
T198 Ivan Ochoa FY RC .20 .50
T199 David Wallace FY RC .20 .50
T200 Joel Zumaya FY RC .75 2.00
T201 Casey Kopitzke FY RC .20 .50
T202 Lincoln Holdzkom FY RC .20 .50
T203 Chad Santos FY RC .20 .50
T204 Brian Pilkington FY RC .20 .50
T205 Terry Jones FY RC .20 .50
T206 Jerome Gamble FY RC .20 .50
T207 Brad Eldred FY RC .20 .50
T208 David Pauley FY RC .30 .75
T209 Kevin Davidson FY RC .20 .50
T210 Damaso Espino FY RC .20 .50
T211 Tom Farmer FY RC .20 .50
T212 Michael Mooney FY RC .20 .50
T213 James Tomlin FY RC .20 .50
T214 Greg Thissen FY RC .20 .50
T215 Calvin Hayes FY RC .20 .50
T216 Fernando Cortez FY RC .20 .50
T217 Sergio Silva FY RC .20 .50
T218 Jon de Vries FY RC .20 .50
T219 Don Sutton FY RC .20 .50
T220 Leo Nunez FY RC .20 .50
T221 Barry Bonds HTA 1.50 4.00

2004 Topps Traded Gold

*GOLD 1-70: 6X TO 15X BASIC
*GOLD 71-90: 1.2X TO 3X BASIC
*GOLD 91-110: 1.2X TO 3X BASIC
*GOLD 111-220: 1.2X TO 3X BASIC
STATED ODDS 1:2 HOB/RET, 1:1 HTA
STATED PRINT RUN 2004 SERIAL #'d SETS

2004 Topps Traded Future Phenoms Relics

GROUP A ODDS 1:184 H/R, 1:53 HTA
GROUP B ODDS 1:65 H/R, 1:27 HTA
AG Adrian Gonzalez Bat A 3.00 8.00
BC Bobby Crosby Bat A 4.00 10.00
BU B.J. Upton Bat A 6.00 15.00
DN Dioner Navarro Bat B 3.00 8.00
DY Delmon Young Bat A 6.00 15.00
ED Eric Duncan Bat B 2.00 5.00
EJ Edwin Jackson Jsy B 2.00 5.00
JH J.J. Hardy Bat B 6.00 15.00
JM Justin Morneau Bat A 4.00 10.00
JW Jayson Werth Bat A 6.00 15.00
KC Kevin Cash Bat B 2.00 5.00
KM Kazuo Matsui Bat A 4.00 10.00
LM Lastings Milledge Bat B 4.00 10.00
MM Mark Malaska Jsy A 3.00 8.00
NG Nick Green Bat A 3.00 8.00
RN Ramon Nivar Bat A 3.00 8.00
VM Victor Martinez Bat A 4.00 10.00

2004 Topps Traded Hall of Fame Relics

A ODDS 1:3388 H, 1:3518 R, 1:966 HTA
B ODDS 1:1011 H, 1:1026 R, 1:289 HTA
DE Dennis Eckersley Jsy B 6.00 15.00
PM Paul Molitor Bat A 6.00 15.00

2004 Topps Traded Hall of Fame Dual Relic

ODDS 1:3388 H, 1:3518 R, 1:966 HTA
ME Molitor Bat/Eckersley Jsy 10.00 25.00

2004 Topps Traded Puzzle

COMPLETE PUZZLE (110) 25.00 50.00
COMMON PIECE (1-110) .20 .50
ONE PER PACK
1 Puzzle Piece 1 .20 .50
2 Puzzle Piece 2 .20 .50
3 Puzzle Piece 3 .20 .50
4 Puzzle Piece 4 .20 .50
5 Puzzle Piece 5 .20 .50
6 Puzzle Piece 6 .20 .50
7 Puzzle Piece 7 .20 .50
8 Puzzle Piece 8 .20 .50
9 Puzzle Piece 9 .20 .50
10 Puzzle Piece 10 .20 .50
11 Puzzle Piece 11 .20 .50
12 Puzzle Piece 12 .20 .50
13 Puzzle Piece 13 .20 .50
14 Puzzle Piece 14 .20 .50
15 Puzzle Piece 15 .20 .50
16 Puzzle Piece 16 .20 .50
17 Puzzle Piece 17 .20 .50
18 Puzzle Piece 18 .20 .50
19 Puzzle Piece 19 .20 .50
20 Puzzle Piece 20 .20 .50
21 Puzzle Piece 21 .20 .50
22 Puzzle Piece 22 .20 .50
23 Puzzle Piece 23 .20 .50
24 Puzzle Piece 24 .20 .50
25 Puzzle Piece 25 .20 .50
26 Puzzle Piece 26 .20 .50
27 Puzzle Piece 27 .20 .50
28 Puzzle Piece 28 .20 .50
29 Puzzle Piece 29 .20 .50
30 Puzzle Piece 30 .20 .50
31 Puzzle Piece 31 .20 .50
32 Puzzle Piece 32 .20 .50
33 Puzzle Piece 33 .20 .50
34 Puzzle Piece 34 .20 .50
35 Puzzle Piece 35 .20 .50
36 Puzzle Piece 36 .20 .50
37 Puzzle Piece 37 .20 .50
38 Puzzle Piece 38 .20 .50
39 Puzzle Piece 39 .20 .50
40 Puzzle Piece 40 .20 .50
41 Puzzle Piece 41 .20 .50
42 Puzzle Piece 42 .20 .50
43 Puzzle Piece 43 .20 .50
44 Puzzle Piece 44 .20 .50
45 Puzzle Piece 45 .20 .50
46 Puzzle Piece 46 .20 .50
47 Puzzle Piece 47 .20 .50
48 Puzzle Piece 48 .20 .50
49 Puzzle Piece 49 .20 .50
50 Puzzle Piece 50 .20 .50
51 Puzzle Piece 51 .20 .50
52 Puzzle Piece 52 .20 .50
53 Puzzle Piece 53 .20 .50
54 Puzzle Piece 54 .20 .50
55 Puzzle Piece 55 .20 .50
56 Puzzle Piece 56 .20 .50
57 Puzzle Piece 57 .20 .50
58 Puzzle Piece 58 .20 .50
59 Puzzle Piece 59 .20 .50
60 Puzzle Piece 60 .20 .50
61 Puzzle Piece 61 .20 .50
62 Puzzle Piece 62 .20 .50
63 Puzzle Piece 63 .20 .50
64 Puzzle Piece 64 .20 .50
65 Puzzle Piece 65 .20 .50
66 Puzzle Piece 66 .20 .50
67 Puzzle Piece 67 .20 .50
68 Puzzle Piece 68 .20 .50
69 Puzzle Piece 69 .20 .50
70 Puzzle Piece 70 .20 .50
71 Puzzle Piece 71 .20 .50
72 Puzzle Piece 72 .20 .50
73 Puzzle Piece 73 .20 .50
74 Puzzle Piece 74 .20 .50
75 Puzzle Piece 75 .20 .50
76 Puzzle Piece 76 .20 .50
77 Puzzle Piece 77 .20 .50
78 Puzzle Piece 78 .20 .50
79 Puzzle Piece 79 .20 .50
80 Puzzle Piece 80 .20 .50
81 Puzzle Piece 81 .20 .50
82 Puzzle Piece 82 .20 .50
83 Puzzle Piece 83 .20 .50
84 Puzzle Piece 84 .20 .50
85 Puzzle Piece 85 .20 .50
86 Puzzle Piece 86 .20 .50
87 Puzzle Piece 87 .20 .50
88 Puzzle Piece 88 .20 .50
89 Puzzle Piece 89 .20 .50
90 Puzzle Piece 90 .20 .50
91 Puzzle Piece 91 .20 .50
92 Puzzle Piece 92 .20 .50
93 Puzzle Piece 93 .20 .50
94 Puzzle Piece 94 .20 .50
95 Puzzle Piece 95 .20 .50
96 Puzzle Piece 96 .20 .50
97 Puzzle Piece 97 .20 .50
98 Puzzle Piece 98 .20 .50
99 Puzzle Piece 99 .20 .50
100 Puzzle Piece 100 .20 .50
101 Puzzle Piece 101 .20 .50
102 Puzzle Piece 102 .20 .50
103 Puzzle Piece 103 .20 .50
104 Puzzle Piece 104 .20 .50
105 Puzzle Piece 105 .20 .50
106 Puzzle Piece 106 .20 .50
107 Puzzle Piece 107 .20 .50
108 Puzzle Piece 108 .20 .50
109 Puzzle Piece 109 .20 .50
110 Puzzle Piece 110 .20 .50

2004 Topps Traded Signature Moves

A ODDS 1:675 H, 1:684 R, 1:193 HTA
B ODDS 1:169 H/R, 1:48 HTA
EXCHANGE DEADLINE 10/31/06
AR Alex Rodriguez A 40.00 80.00
AW Adam Wainwright B 12.50 30.00
EM Eli Marrero B 4.00 10.00
FV Fernando Vina B 4.00 10.00
JV Javier Vazquez A 6.00 15.00
MB Milton Bradley B 6.00 15.00
MK Mark Kotsay B 6.00 15.00
MN Mike Neu B 4.00 10.00

2004 Topps Traded Transactions Relics

STATED ODDS 1:106 H, 1:107 R, 1:30 HTA
AP Andy Pettitte Bat 4.00 10.00
AR Alex Rodriguez Yanks Jsy 10.00 25.00
BJ Brian Jordan Bat 3.00 8.00
CE Carl Everett Bat 3.00 8.00
GS Gary Sheffield Bat 4.00 10.00
HC Hee Seop Choi Bat 3.00 8.00
IR Ivan Rodriguez Bat 4.00 10.00
JB Jeromy Burnitz Bat 3.00 8.00
JG Juan Gonzalez Bat 3.00 8.00
JL Javy Lopez Bat 3.00 8.00
KL Kenny Lofton Bat 3.00 8.00
KM Kazuo Matsui Bat 3.00 8.00
MT Miguel Tejada Bat 3.00 8.00
RA Roberto Alomar Bat 4.00 10.00
RC Roger Clemens Bat 6.00 15.00
RLS Richie Sexson Bat 3.00 8.00
RP Rafael Palmeiro Bat 4.00 10.00
RS Reggie Sanders Bat 3.00 8.00
RW Rondell White Bat 3.00 8.00
VG Vladimir Guerrero Bat 4.00 10.00

2004 Topps Traded Transactions Dual Relics

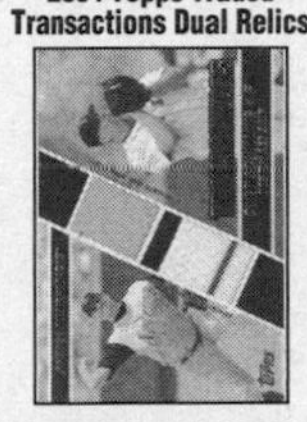

STATED ODDS 1:562 H, 1:563 R, 1:160 HTA
AR Alex Rodriguez Rgr-Yanks 10.00 25.00
CS Curt Schilling D'backs-Sox 6.00 15.00
RP Rafael Palmeiro O's-Rgr 6.00 15.00

2005 Topps

This 367-card first series was released in November, 2004 while the 366 card second series was issued in April. The set was issued in 10-card hobby/retail packs with a $2 SRP which came 36 packs to a box and 12 boxes to a case. These cards were also issued in 35-card HTA packs with a $5 SRP which came 20 packs to a box and two boxes to a case. Please note that card number 7 was not issued. In addition, the following subsets were issued in the first series: Managers (267-296); First year cards (297-326); Prospects (327-331); Season Highlights (332-336); League Leaders (337-348); Post-Season (349-355); AL All-Stars (356-367). In addition, card number 368, which was not on the original checklist, honored the Boston Red Sox World Championship. Subsets in the second series included Team Cards (638-667); First Year players (668-687); Multi player prospect cards (688-694); Award Winners (695-718); NL All-Stars (719-730) and World Series Cards (731-734).

COMP.HOBBY SET (737) 40.00 80.00
COMP.HOLIDAY SET (742) 40.00 80.00
COMP.CUBS SET (737) 40.00 80.00
COMP.GIANTS SET (737) 40.00 80.00
COMP.NATIONALS SET (737) 40.00 80.00
COMP.RED SOX SET (737) 40.00 80.00
COMP.TIGERS SET (737) 40.00 80.00
COMP.YANKEES SET (737) 40.00 80.00
COMPLETE SET (732) 40.00 80.00
COMPLETE SERIES 1 (366) 20.00 40.00
COMPLETE SERIES 2 (366) 20.00 40.00
COMMON CARD (1-6/8-734) .07 .20
COMMON (297-326/668-687) .20 .50
COMMON (327-331/688-692) .20 .50
COM (349-355/368/731-734) .20 .50
CARD NUMBER 7 DOES NOT EXIST
OVERALL PLATE SER.1 ODDS 1:154 HTA
OVERALL PLATE SER.2 ODDS 1:112 HTA
PLATE PRINT RUN 1 SET PER COLOR
BLACK-CYAN-MAGENTA-YELLOW ISSUED
NO PLATE PRICING DUE TO SCARCITY
1 Alex Rodriguez .25 .60
2 Placido Polanco .07 .20
3 Torii Hunter .07 .20
4 Lyle Overbay .07 .20
5 Johnny Damon .12 .30
6 Johnny Estrada .07 .20
8 Francisco Rodriguez .12 .30
9 Jason LaRue .07 .20
10 Sammy Sosa .20 .50
11 Randy Wolf .07 .20
12 Jason Bay .07 .20
13 Tom Glavine .12 .30
14 Michael Tucker .07 .20
15 Brian Giles .07 .20
16 Dan Wilson .07 .20
17 Jim Edmonds .12 .30
18 Danys Baez .07 .20
19 Roy Halladay .12 .30
20 Hank Blalock .07 .20
21 Darin Erstad .07 .20
22 Robby Hammock .07 .20
23 Mike Hampton .07 .20
24 Mark Bellhorn .07 .20
25 Jim Thome .12 .30
26 Scott Schoeneweis .07 .20
27 Jody Gerut .07 .20
28 Vinny Castilla .07 .20
29 Luis Castillo .07 .20
30 Ivan Rodriguez .12 .30
31 Craig Biggio .12 .30
32 Joe Randa .07 .20
33 Adrian Beltre .20 .50
34 Scott Podsednik .07 .20
35 Cliff Floyd .07 .20
36 Livan Hernandez .07 .20
37 Eric Byrnes .07 .20
38 Gabe Kapler .07 .20
39 Jack Wilson .07 .20
40 Gary Sheffield .07 .20
41 Chan Ho Park .12 .30
42 Carl Crawford .12 .30
43 Miguel Batista .07 .20
44 David Bell .07 .20
45 Jeff DaVanon .07 .20
46 Brandon Webb .12 .30
47 Bronson Arroyo .07 .20
48 Melvin Mora .07 .20
49 David Ortiz .20 .50
50 Andruw Jones .07 .20
51 Chone Figgins .07 .20
52 Danny Graves .07 .20
53 Preston Wilson .07 .20
54 Jeremy Bonderman .07 .20
55 Chad Fox .07 .20
56 Dan Miceli .07 .20
57 Jimmy Gobble .07 .20
58 Darren Dreifort .07 .20
59 Matt LeCroy .07 .20
60 Jose Vidro .07 .20
61 Al Leiter .07 .20
62 Javier Vazquez .07 .20
63 Erubiel Durazo .07 .20
64 Doug Glanville .07 .20
65 Scot Shields .07 .20
66 Edgardo Alfonzo .07 .20
67 Ryan Franklin .07 .20
68 Francisco Cordero .07 .20
69 Brett Myers .07 .20
70 Curt Schilling .12 .30
71 Matt Kata .07 .20
72 Mark DeRosa .07 .20
73 Rodrigo Lopez .07 .20
74 Tim Wakefield .12 .30
75 Frank Thomas .20 .50
76 Jimmy Rollins .12 .30
77 Barry Zito .12 .30
78 Hideo Nomo .20 .50
79 Brad Wilkerson .07 .20
80 Adam Dunn .12 .30
81 Billy Traber .07 .20
82 Fernando Vina .07 .20
83 Nate Robertson .07 .20
84 Brad Ausmus .07 .20
85 Mike Sweeney .07 .20
86 Kip Wells .07 .20
87 Chris Reitsma .07 .20
88 Zach Day .07 .20
89 Tony Clark .07 .20
90 Bret Boone .07 .20
91 Mark Loretta .07 .20
92 Jerome Williams .07 .20
93 Randy Winn .07 .20
94 Marlon Anderson .07 .20
95 Aubrey Huff .07 .20
96 Kevin Mench .07 .20
97 Frank Catalanotto .07 .20
98 Flash Gordon .07 .20
99 Scott Hatteberg .07 .20
100 Albert Pujols .25 .60
101 Jose
Bengie Molina .07 .20
102 Oscar Villarreal .07 .20
103 Jay Gibbons .07 .20
104 Byung-Hyun Kim .07 .20
105 Joe Borowski .07 .20
106 Mark Grudzielanek .07 .20
107 Mark Buehrle .12 .30
108 Paul Wilson .07 .20
109 Ronnie Belliard .07 .20
110 Reggie Sanders .07 .20
111 Tim Redding .07 .20
112 Brian Lawrence .07 .20
113 Darrell May .07 .20
114 Jose Hernandez .07 .20
115 Ben Sheets .07 .20
116 Johan Santana .12 .30
117 Billy Wagner .07 .20
118 Mariano Rivera .25 .60
119 Steve Trachsel .07 .20
120 Akinori Otsuka .07 .20
121 Bobby Kielty .07 .20
122 Orlando Hernandez .07 .20
123 Raul Ibanez .12 .30
124 Mike Matheny .07 .20
125 Vernon Wells .07 .20
126 Jason Isringhausen .07 .20
127 Jose Guillen .07 .20
128 Danny Bautista .07 .20
129 Marcus Giles .07 .20
130 Javy Lopez .07 .20
131 Kevin Millar .07 .20
132 Kyle Farnsworth .07 .20
133 Carl Pavano .07 .20
134 D'Angelo Jimenez .07 .20
135 Casey Blake .07 .20
136 Matt Holliday .20 .50
137 Bobby Higginson .07 .20
138 Nate Field .07 .20
139 Alex Gonzalez .07 .20
140 Jeff Kent .07 .20
141 Aaron Guiel .07 .20
142 Shawn Green .07 .20
143 Bill Hall .07 .20
144 Shannon Stewart .07 .20
145 Juan Rivera .07 .20
146 Coco Crisp .07 .20
147 Mike Mussina .12 .30
148 Eric Chavez .07 .20
149 Jon Lieber .07 .20
150 Vladimir Guerrero .12 .30
151 Alex Cintron .07 .20
152 Horacio Ramirez .07 .20
153 Sidney Ponson .07 .20
154 Trot Nixon .07 .20
155 Greg Maddux .25 .60
156 Edgar Renteria .07 .20
157 Ryan Freel .07 .20
158 Matt Lawton .07 .20
159 Shawn Chacon .07 .20
160 Josh Beckett .07 .20
161 Ken Harvey .07 .20
162 Juan Cruz .07 .20
163 Juan Encarnacion .07 .20
164 Wes Helms .07 .20
165 Brad Radke .07 .20
166 Claudio Vargas .07 .20
167 Mike Cameron .07 .20
168 Billy Koch .07 .20
169 Bobby Crosby .07 .20
170 Mike Lieberthal .07 .20
171 Rob Mackowiak .07 .20
172 Sean Burroughs .07 .20
173 J.T. Snow Jr. .07 .20
174 Paul Konerko .12 .30
175 Luis Gonzalez .07 .20
176 John Lackey .12 .30
177 Antonio Alfonseca .07 .20
178 Brian Roberts .07 .20
179 Bill Mueller .07 .20
180 Carlos Lee .07 .20
181 Corey Patterson .07 .20
182 Sean Casey .07 .20
183 Cliff Lee .12 .30
184 Jason Jennings .07 .20
185 Dmitri Young .07 .20
186 Juan Uribe .07 .20
187 Andy Pettitte .12 .30
188 Juan Gonzalez .07 .20
189 Pokey Reese .07 .20
190 Jason Phillips .07 .20
191 Rocky Biddle .07 .20
192 Lew Ford .07 .20
193 Mark Mulder .07 .20
194 Bobby Abreu .07 .20
195 Jason Kendall .07 .20
196 Terrence Long .07 .20
197 A.J. Pierzynski .07 .20
198 Eddie Guardado .07 .20
199 So Taguchi .07 .20
200 Jason Giambi .07 .20
201 Tony Batista .07 .20
202 Kyle Lohse .07 .20
203 Trevor Hoffman .12 .30
204 Tike Redman .07 .20
205 Matt Herges .07 .20
206 Gil Meche .07 .20
207 Chris Carpenter .12 .30
208 Ben Broussard .07 .20
209 Eric Young .07 .20
210 Doug Waechter .07 .20
211 Jarrod Washburn .07 .20
212 Chad Tracy .07 .20
213 John Smoltz .20 .50
214 Jorge Julio .07 .20
215 Todd Walker .07 .20
216 Shingo Takatsu .07 .20
217 Jose Acevedo .07 .20
218 David Riske .07 .20
219 Shawn Estes .07 .20
220 Lance Berkman .12 .30
221 Carlos Guillen .07 .20
222 Jeremy Affeldt .07 .20
223 Cesar Izturis .07 .20
224 Scott Sullivan .07 .20
225 Kazuo Matsui .07 .20
226 Josh Fogg .07 .20
227 Jason Schmidt .07 .20
228 Jason Marquis .07 .20
229 Scott Spiezio .07 .20
230 Miguel Tejada .12 .30
231 Bartolo Colon .07 .20
232 Jose Valverde .07 .20
233 Derrek Lee .07 .20
234 Scott Williamson .07 .20

235 Joe Crede .07 .20
236 John Thomson .07 .20
237 Mike MacDougal .07 .20
238 Eric Gagne .07 .20
239 Alex Sanchez .07 .20
240 Miguel Cabrera .20 .50
241 Luis Rivas .07 .20
242 Adam Everett .07 .20
243 Jason Johnson .07 .20
244 Travis Hafner .07 .20
245 Jose Valentin .07 .20
246 Stephen Randolph .07 .20
247 Rafael Furcal .07 .20
248 Adam Kennedy .07 .20
249 Luis Matos .07 .20
250 Mark Prior .12 .30
251 Angel Berroa .07 .20
252 Phil Nevin .07 .20
253 Oliver Perez .07 .20
254 Orlando Hudson .07 .20
255 Braden Looper .07 .20
256 Khalil Greene .07 .20
257 Tim Worrell .07 .20
258 Carlos Zambrano .12 .30
259 Odalis Perez .07 .20
260 Gerald Laird .07 .20
261 Jose Cruz Jr. .07 .20
262 Michael Barrett .07 .20
263 Michael Young UER .07 .20
264 Toby Hall .07 .20
265 Woody Williams .07 .20
266 Rich Harden .07 .20
267 Mike Scioscia MG .07 .20
268 Al Pedrique MG .07 .20
269 Bobby Cox MG .07 .20
270 Lee Mazzilli MG .07 .20
271 Terry Francona MG .12 .30
272 Dusty Baker MG .07 .20
273 Ozzie Guillen MG .07 .20
274 Dave Miley MG .07 .20
275 Eric Wedge MG .07 .20
276 Clint Hurdle MG .07 .20
277 Alan Trammell MG .12 .30
278 Jack McKeon MG .07 .20
279 Phil Garner MG .07 .20
280 Tony Pena MG .07 .20
281 Jim Tracy MG .07 .20
282 Ned Yost MG .07 .20
283 Ron Gardenhire MG .07 .20
284 Frank Robinson MG .12 .30
285 Art Howe MG .07 .20
286 Joe Torre MG .12 .30
287 Ken Macha MG .07 .20
288 Larry Bowa MG .07 .20
289 Lloyd McClendon MG .07 .20
290 Bruce Bochy MG .12 .30
291 Felipe Alou MG .07 .20
292 Bob Melvin MG .07 .20
293 Tony LaRussa MG .12 .30
294 Lou Piniella MG .07 .20
295 Buck Showalter MG .07 .20
296 John Gibbons MG .07 .20
297 Steve Doetsch FY RC .20 .50
298 Melky Cabrera FY RC .60 1.50
299 Luis Ramirez FY RC .20 .50
300 Chris Seddon FY RC .20 .50
301 Nate Schierholtz FY .20 .50
302 Ian Kinsler FY RC .40 1.00
303 Brandon Moss FY RC .75 2.00
304 Chadd Blasko FY RC .30 .75
305 Jeremy West FY RC .20 .50
306 Sean Marshall FY RC .50 1.25
307 Matt DeSalvo FY RC .20 .50
308 Ryan Sweeney FY RC .30 .75
309 Matthew Lindstrom FY RC .20 .50
310 Ryan Goleski FY RC .20 .50
311 Brett Harper FY RC .20 .50
312 Chris Roberson FY RC .20 .50
313 Andre Ethier FY RC 1.50 4.00
314 Chris Denorfia FY RC .20 .50
315 Ian Bladergroen FY RC .20 .50
316 Darren Fenster FY RC .20 .50
317 Kevin West FY RC .20 .50
318 Chaz Lytle FY RC .30 .75
319 James Jurries FY RC .20 .50
320 Matt Rogelstad FY RC .20 .50
321 Wade Robinson FY RC .20 .50
322 Jake Dittler FY .20 .50
323 Brian Stavisky FY RC .20 .50
324 Kole Strayhorn FY RC .20 .50
325 Jose Vaquedano FY RC .20 .50
326 Elvys Quezada FY RC .20 .50
327 J.Maine V.Majewski FS .20 .50
328 R.Weeks J.Hardy FS .20 .50
329 G.Gross G.Quiroz FS .20 .50
330 D.Wright C.Brazell FS .40 1.00
331 D.McPherson J.Mathis FS .30 .75
332 Randy Johnson SH .20 .50
333 Randy Johnson SH .20 .50
334 Ichiro Suzuki SH .25 .60
335 Ken Griffey Jr. SH .40 1.00
336 Greg Maddux SH .25 .60
337 Ichiro Mora Guerrero LL .25 .60
338 Ichiro Young Guerrero LL .25 .60
339 Manny Konerko Ortiz LL .20 .50
340 Tejada Ortiz Manny LL .20 .50
341 Johan Schill West LL .12 .30
342 Johan Pedro Schill LL .12 .30
343 Helton Loretta Beltre LL .20 .50
344 Pierre Loretta Wilson LL .07 .20
345 Beltre Dunn Pujols LL .25 .60
346 Castilla Rolen Pujols LL .25 .60
347 Peavy Johnson Sheets LL .20 .50
348 Johnson Sheets Schmidt LL .20 .50
349 A.Rodriguez R.Sierra ALDS .60 1.50
350 L.Walker A.Pujols NLDS .60 1.50
351 C.Schilling D.Ortiz ALDS .50 1.25
352 Curt Schilling WS2 .30 .75
353 Sox Celeb Ortiz-Schil ALCS .50 1.25
354 Cards Celeb Puj-Edm NLCS .60 1.50
355 Mark Bellhorn WS1 .20 .50
356 Paul Konerko AS .12 .30
357 Alfonso Soriano AS .12 .30
358 Miguel Tejada AS .12 .30
359 Melvin Mora AS .07 .20
360 Vladimir Guerrero AS .12 .30
361 Ichiro Suzuki AS .25 .60
362 Manny Ramirez AS .20 .50
363 Ivan Rodriguez AS .12 .30
364 Johan Santana AS .12 .30
365 Paul Konerko AS .12 .30
366 David Ortiz AS .20 .50
367 Bobby Crosby AS .07 .20
368 Sox Celeb Ram-Lowe WS4 .50 1.25
369 Garret Anderson .07 .20
370 Randy Johnson .20 .50
371 Charles Thomas .07 .20
372 Rafael Palmeiro .12 .30
373 Kevin Youkilis .07 .20
374 Freddy Garcia .07 .20
375 Magglio Ordonez .12 .30
376 Aaron Harang .07 .20
377 Grady Sizemore .12 .30
378 Chin-Hui Tsao .07 .20
379 Eric Munson .07 .20
380 Juan Pierre .07 .20
381 Brad Lidge .07 .20
382 Brian Anderson .07 .20
383 Alex Cora .12 .30
384 Brady Clark .07 .20
385 Todd Helton .12 .30
386 Chad Cordero .07 .20
387 Kris Benson .07 .20
388 Brad Halsey .07 .20
389 Jermaine Dye .07 .20
390 Manny Ramirez .20 .50
391 Daryle Ward .07 .20
392 Adam Eaton .07 .20
393 Brett Tomko .07 .20
394 Bucky Jacobsen .07 .20
395 Dontrelle Willis .07 .20
396 B.J. Upton .12 .30
397 Rocco Baldelli .07 .20
398 Ted Lilly .07 .20
399 Ryan Drese .07 .20
400 Ichiro Suzuki .25 .60
401 Brendan Donnelly .07 .20
402 Brandon Lyon .07 .20
403 Nick Green .07 .20
404 Jerry Hairston Jr. .07 .20
405 Mike Lowell .07 .20
406 Kerry Wood .07 .20
407 Carl Everett .07 .20
408 Hideki Matsui .30 .75
409 Omar Vizquel .12 .30
410 Joe Kennedy .07 .20
411 Carlos Pena .12 .30
412 Armando Benitez .07 .20
413 Carlos Beltran .12 .30
414 Kevin Appier .07 .20
415 Jeff Weaver .07 .20
416 Chad Moeller .07 .20
417 Joe Mays .07 .20
418 Termel Sledge .07 .20
419 Richard Hidalgo .07 .20
420 Kenny Lofton .07 .20
421 Justin Duchscherer .07 .20
422 Eric Milton .07 .20
423 Jose Mesa .07 .20
424 Ramon Hernandez .07 .20
425 Jose Reyes .12 .30
426 Joel Pineiro .07 .20
427 Matt Morris .07 .20
428 John Halama .07 .20
429 Gary Matthews Jr. .07 .20
430 Ryan Madson .07 .20
431 Mark Kotsay .07 .20
432 Carlos Delgado .07 .20
433 Casey Kotchman .07 .20
434 Greg Aquino .07 .20
435 Eli Marrero .07 .20
436 David Newhan .07 .20
437 Mike Timlin .07 .20
438 LaTroy Hawkins .07 .20
439 Jose Contreras .07 .20
440 Ken Griffey Jr. .40 1.00
441 C.C. Sabathia .12 .30
442 Brandon Inge .07 .20
443 Pete Munro .07 .20
444 John Buck .07 .20
445 Hee Seop Choi .07 .20
446 Chris Capuano .07 .20
447 Jesse Crain .07 .20
448 Geoff Jenkins .07 .20
449 Brian Schneider .07 .20
450 Mike Piazza .20 .50
451 Jorge Posada .12 .30
452 Nick Swisher .12 .30
453 Kevin Millwood .07 .20
454 Mike Gonzalez .07 .20
455 Jake Peavy .07 .20
456 Dustin Hermanson .07 .20
457 Jeremy Reed .07 .20
458 Julian Tavarez .07 .20
459 Geoff Blum .07 .20
460 Alfonso Soriano .12 .30
461 Alexis Rios .07 .20
462 David Eckstein .07 .20
463 Shea Hillenbrand .07 .20
464 Russ Ortiz .07 .20
465 Kurt Ainsworth .07 .20
466 Orlando Cabrera .07 .20
467 Carlos Silva .07 .20
468 Ross Gload .07 .20
469 Josh Phelps .07 .20
470 Marquis Grissom .07 .20
471 Mike Maroth .07 .20
472 Guillermo Mota .07 .20
473 Chris Burke .07 .20
474 David DeJesus .07 .20
475 Jose Lima .07 .20
476 Cristian Guzman .07 .20
477 Nick Johnson .07 .20
478 Victor Zambrano .07 .20
479 Rod Barajas .07 .20
480 Damian Miller .07 .20
481 Chase Utley .12 .30
482 Todd Pratt .07 .20
483 Sean Burnett .07 .20
484 Boomer Wells .07 .20
485 Dustan Mohr .07 .20
486 Bobby Madritsch .07 .20
487 Ray King .07 .20
488 Reed Johnson .07 .20
489 R.A. Dickey .12 .30
490 Scott Kazmir .20 .50
491 Tony Womack .07 .20
492 Tomas Perez .07 .20
493 Esteban Loaiza .07 .20
494 Tomo Ohka .07 .20
495 Mike Lamb .07 .20
496 Ramon Ortiz .07 .20
497 Richie Sexson .07 .20
498 J.D. Drew .07 .20
499 David Segui .07 .20
500 Barry Bonds .30 .75
501 Aramis Ramirez .07 .20
502 Wily Mo Pena .07 .20
503 Jeromy Burnitz .07 .20
504 Craig Monroe .07 .20
505 Nomar Garciaparra .12 .30
506 Brandon Backe .07 .20
507 Marcus Thames .07 .20
508 Derek Lowe .07 .20
509 Doug Davis .07 .20
510 Joe Mauer .15 .40
511 Endy Chavez .07 .20
512 Bernie Williams .12 .30
513 Mark Redman .07 .20
514 Jason Michaels .07 .20
515 Craig Wilson .07 .20
516 Ryan Klesko .07 .20
517 Ray Durham .07 .20
518 Jose Lopez .07 .20
519 Jeff Suppan .07 .20
520 Julio Lugo .07 .20
521 Mike Wood .07 .20
522 David Bush .07 .20
523 Juan Rincon .07 .20
524 Paul Quantrill .07 .20
525 Marlon Byrd .07 .20
526 Roy Oswalt .12 .30
527 Rondell White .07 .20
528 Troy Glaus .07 .20
529 Scott Hairston .07 .20
530 Chipper Jones .20 .50
531 Daniel Cabrera .07 .20
532 Doug Mientkiewicz .07 .20
533 Glendon Rusch .07 .20
534 Jon Garland .07 .20
535 Austin Kearns .07 .20
536 Jake Westbrook .07 .20
537 Aaron Miles .07 .20
538 Omar Infante .07 .20
539 Paul Lo Duca .07 .20
540 Morgan Ensberg .07 .20
541 Tony Graffanino .07 .20
542 Milton Bradley .07 .20
543 Keith Ginter .07 .20
544 Justin Morneau .12 .30
545 Tony Armas Jr. .07 .20
546 Mike Stanton .07 .20
547 Kevin Brown .07 .20
548 Marco Scutaro .12 .30
549 Tim Hudson .12 .30
550 Pat Burrell .07 .20
551 Ty Wigginton .07 .20
552 Jeff Cirillo .07 .20
553 Jim Brower .07 .20
554 Jamie Moyer .07 .20
555 Larry Walker .12 .30
556 Dewon Brazelton .07 .20
557 Brian Jordan .07 .20
558 Josh Towers .07 .20
559 Shigetoshi Hasegawa .07 .20
560 Octavio Dotel .07 .20
561 Travis Lee .07 .20
562 Michael Cuddyer .07 .20
563 Junior Spivey .07 .20
564 Zack Greinke .20 .50
565 Roger Clemens .25 .60
566 Chris Shelton .07 .20
567 Ugueth Urbina .07 .20
568 Rafael Betancourt .07 .20
569 Willie Harris .07 .20
570 Todd Hollandsworth .07 .20
571 Keith Foulke .07 .20
572 Larry Bigbie .07 .20
573 Paul Byrd .07 .20
574 Troy Percival .07 .20
575 Pedro Martinez .12 .30
576 Matt Clement .07 .20
577 Ryan Wagner .07 .20
578 Jeff Francis .07 .20
579 Jeff Conine .07 .20
580 Wade Miller .07 .20
581 Matt Stairs .07 .20
582 Gavin Floyd .07 .20
583 Kazuhisa Ishii .07 .20
584 Victor Santos .07 .20
585 Jacque Jones .07 .20
586 Sunny Kim .07 .20
587 Dan Kolb .07 .20
588 Cory Lidle .07 .20
589 Jose Castillo .07 .20
590 Alex Gonzalez .07 .20
591 Kirk Rueter .07 .20
592 Jolbert Cabrera .07 .20
593 Erik Bedard .07 .20
594 Ben Grieve .07 .20
595 Ricky Ledee .07 .20
596 Mark Hendrickson .07 .20
597 Laynce Nix .07 .20
598 Jason Frasor .07 .20
599 Kevin Gregg .07 .20
600 Derek Jeter .50 1.25
601 Luis Terrero .07 .20
602 Jaret Wright .07 .20
603 Edwin Jackson .07 .20
604 Dave Roberts .12 .30
605 Moises Alou .07 .20
606 Aaron Rowand .07 .20
607 Kazuhito Tadano .07 .20
608 Luis A. Gonzalez .07 .20
609 A.J. Burnett .07 .20
610 Jeff Bagwell .12 .30
611 Brad Penny .07 .20
612 Craig Counsell .07 .20
613 Corey Koskie .07 .20
614 Mark Ellis .07 .20
615 Felix Rodriguez .07 .20
616 Jay Payton .07 .20
617 Hector Luna .07 .20
618 Miguel Olivo .07 .20
619 Rob Bell .07 .20
620 Scott Rolen .12 .30
621 Ricardo Rodriguez .07 .20
622 Eric Hinske .07 .20
623 Tim Salmon .07 .20
624 Adam LaRoche .07 .20
625 B.J. Ryan .07 .20
626 Roberto Alomar .12 .30
627 Steve Finley .07 .20
628 Joe Nathan .07 .20
629 Scott Linebrink .07 .20
630 Vicente Padilla .07 .20
631 Raul Mondesi .07 .20
632 Yadier Molina .20 .50
633 Tino Martinez .12 .30
634 Mark Teixeira .12 .30
635 Kelvim Escobar .07 .20
636 Pedro Feliz .07 .20
637 Rich Aurilia .07 .20
638 Los Angeles Angels TC .07 .20
639 Arizona Diamondbacks TC .07 .20
640 Atlanta Braves TC .12 .30
641 Baltimore Orioles TC .07 .20
642 Boston Red Sox TC .20 .50
643 Chicago Cubs TC .12 .30
644 Chicago White Sox TC .07 .20
645 Cincinnati Reds TC .07 .20
646 Cleveland Indians TC .07 .20
647 Colorado Rockies TC .07 .20
648 Detroit Tigers TC .07 .20
649 Florida Marlins TC .07 .20
650 Houston Astros TC .07 .20
651 Kansas City Royals TC .07 .20
652 Los Angeles Dodgers TC .07 .20
653 Milwaukee Brewers TC .07 .20
654 Minnesota Twins TC .07 .20
655 Montreal Expos TC .07 .20
656 New York Mets TC .07 .20
657 New York Yankees TC .20 .50
658 Oakland Athletics TC .07 .20
659 Philadelphia Phillies TC .07 .20
660 Pittsburgh Pirates TC .07 .20
661 San Diego Padres TC .07 .20
662 San Francisco Giants TC .07 .20
663 Seattle Mariners TC .07 .20
664 St. Louis Cardinals TC .12 .30
665 Tampa Bay Devil Rays TC .07 .20
666 Texas Rangers TC .07 .20
667 Toronto Blue Jays TC .07 .20
668 Billy Butler FY RC 1.00 2.50
669 Wes Swackhamer FY RC .20 .50
670 Matt Campbell FY RC .20 .50
671 Ryan Webb FY .20 .50
672 Glen Perkins FY RC .20 .50
673 Michael Rogers FY RC .20 .50
674 Kevin Melillo FY RC .20 .50
675 Erik Cordier FY RC .20 .50
676 Landon Powell FY RC .20 .50
677 Justin Verlander FY RC 15.00 40.00
678 Eric Nielsen FY RC .20 .50
679 Alexander Smit FY RC .20 .50
680 Ryan Garko FY RC .20 .50
681 Bobby Livingston FY RC .20 .50
682 Jeff Niemann FY RC .50 1.25
683 Wladimir Balentien FY RC .30 .75
684 Chip Cannon FY RC .20 .50
685 Yorman Bazardo FY RC .20 .50
686 Mike Bourn FY RC .50 1.25
687 Andy LaRoche FY RC .20 .50
688 F.Hernandez J.Leone .60 1.50
689 R.Howard C.Hamels .60 1.50
690 M.Cain M.Valdez 1.25 3.00
691 A.Marte J.Francoeur .50 1.25
692 C.Billingsley J.Guzman .20 .50
693 J.Hairston Jr. S.Hairston .07 .20
694 M.Tejada L.Berkman .12 .30
695 Kenny Rogers GG .07 .20
696 Ivan Rodriguez GG .12 .30
697 Darin Erstad GG .07 .20
698 Bret Boone GG .07 .20
699 Eric Chavez GG .07 .20
700 Derek Jeter GG .50 1.25
701 Vernon Wells GG .07 .20
702 Ichiro Suzuki GG .25 .60
703 Torii Hunter GG .07 .20
704 Greg Maddux GG .25 .60
705 Mike Matheny GG .07 .20
706 Todd Helton GG .12 .30
707 Luis Castillo GG .07 .20
708 Scott Rolen GG .12 .30
709 Cesar Izturis GG .07 .20
710 Jim Edmonds GG .12 .30
711 Andruw Jones GG .07 .20
712 Steve Finley GG .07 .20
713 Johan Santana CY .12 .30
714 Roger Clemens CY .25 .60
715 Vladimir Guerrero MVP .12 .30
716 Barry Bonds MVP .30 .75
717 Bobby Crosby ROY .07 .20
718 Jason Bay ROY .07 .20
719 Albert Pujols AS .25 .60
720 Mark Loretta AS .07 .20
721 Edgar Renteria AS .07 .20
722 Scott Rolen AS .12 .30
723 J.D. Drew AS .07 .20
724 Jim Edmonds AS .12 .30
725 Johnny Estrada AS .07 .20
726 Jason Schmidt AS .07 .20
727 Chris Carpenter AS .12 .30
728 Eric Gagne AS .07 .20
729 Jason Bay AS .07 .20
730 Bobby Cox MG AS .07 .20
731 D.Ortiz M.Bellhorn WS1 .50 1.25
732 Curt Schilling WS2 .30 .75
733 M.Ramirez P.Martinez WS3 .50 1.25
734 Sox Win Damon Lowe WS4 .30 .75

2005 Topps 1st Edition

*1st ED 1-296/332-348/356-367: 1.25X TO 3X
*1st ED 369-667/693-730: 1.25X TO 3X
*1st ED 297-326/668-687: .6X TO 1.5X
*1st ED 327-331/688-692: .6X TO 1.5X
*1st ED 349-355/368/731-734: 1.25X TO 3X
ISSUED IN SER.1 & 2 1ST EDITION BOXES
CARD NUMBER 7 DOES NOT EXIST

2005 Topps Black

COMMON (1-6/8-331/369-734) 8.00 20.00
COMMON 297-326/668-687 8.00 20.00
COMMON 327-331/688-692 8.00 20.00
COMMON 731-734 8.00 20.00
SERIES 1 ODDS 1:13 HTA
SERIES 2 ODDS 1:9 HTA
STATED PRINT RUN 54 SERIAL #'d SETS
CARD NUMBER 7 DOES NOT EXIST
1 Alex Rodriguez 25.00 60.00
2 Placido Polanco 8.00 20.00
3 Torii Hunter 8.00 20.00
4 Lyle Overbay 8.00 20.00
5 Johnny Damon 12.00 30.00
6 Johnny Estrada 8.00 20.00
8 Francisco Rodriguez 12.00 30.00
9 Jason LaRue 8.00 20.00
10 Sammy Sosa 20.00 50.00
11 Randy Wolf 8.00 20.00
12 Jason Bay 8.00 20.00
13 Tom Glavine 12.00 30.00
14 Michael Tucker 8.00 20.00
15 Brian Giles 8.00 20.00
16 Dan Wilson 8.00 20.00
17 Jim Edmonds 12.00 30.00
18 Danys Baez 8.00 20.00
19 Roy Halladay 12.00 30.00
20 Hank Blalock 8.00 20.00
21 Darin Erstad 8.00 20.00
22 Robby Hammock 8.00 20.00
23 Mike Hampton 8.00 20.00
24 Mark Bellhorn 8.00 20.00
25 Jim Thome 12.00 30.00
26 Scott Schoeneweis 8.00 20.00
27 Jody Gerut 8.00 20.00
28 Vinny Castilla 8.00 20.00
29 Luis Castillo 8.00 20.00
30 Ivan Rodriguez 12.00 30.00
31 Craig Biggio 12.00 30.00
32 Joe Randa 8.00 20.00
33 Adrian Beltre 20.00 50.00
34 Scott Podsednik 8.00 20.00
35 Cliff Floyd 8.00 20.00
36 Livan Hernandez 8.00 20.00
37 Eric Byrnes 8.00 20.00
38 Gabe Kapler 8.00 20.00
39 Jack Wilson 8.00 20.00
40 Gary Sheffield 8.00 20.00
41 Chan Ho Park 12.00 30.00
42 Carl Crawford 12.00 30.00
43 Miguel Batista 8.00 20.00
44 David Bell 8.00 20.00
45 Jeff DaVanon 8.00 20.00
46 Brandon Webb 12.00 30.00
47 Bronson Arroyo 8.00 20.00
48 Melvin Mora 8.00 20.00
49 David Ortiz 20.00 50.00
50 Andruw Jones 8.00 20.00
51 Chone Figgins 8.00 20.00
52 Danny Graves 8.00 20.00
53 Preston Wilson 8.00 20.00
54 Jeremy Bonderman 8.00 20.00
55 Chad Fox 8.00 20.00
56 Dan Miceli 8.00 20.00
57 Jimmy Gobble 8.00 20.00
58 Darren Dreifort 8.00 20.00
59 Matt LeCroy 8.00 20.00
60 Jose Vidro 8.00 20.00
61 Al Leiter 8.00 20.00
62 Javier Vazquez 8.00 20.00
63 Erubiel Durazo 8.00 20.00
64 Doug Glanville 8.00 20.00
65 Scot Shields 8.00 20.00
66 Edgardo Alfonzo 8.00 20.00
67 Ryan Franklin 8.00 20.00
68 Francisco Cordero 8.00 20.00
69 Brett Myers 8.00 20.00
70 Curt Schilling 12.00 30.00
71 Matt Kata 8.00 20.00
72 Mark DeRosa 8.00 20.00
73 Rodrigo Lopez 8.00 20.00
74 Tim Wakefield 12.00 30.00
75 Frank Thomas 20.00 50.00
76 Jimmy Rollins 12.00 30.00
77 Barry Zito 12.00 30.00
78 Hideo Nomo 20.00 50.00
79 Brad Wilkerson 8.00 20.00
80 Adam Dunn 12.00 30.00
81 Billy Traber 8.00 20.00
82 Fernando Vina 8.00 20.00
83 Nate Robertson 8.00 20.00
84 Brad Ausmus 8.00 20.00
85 Mike Sweeney 8.00 20.00
86 Kip Wells 8.00 20.00
87 Chris Reitsma 8.00 20.00
88 Zach Day 8.00 20.00
89 Tony Clark 8.00 20.00
90 Bret Boone 8.00 20.00
91 Mark Loretta 8.00 20.00
92 Jerome Williams 8.00 20.00
93 Randy Winn 8.00 20.00
94 Marlon Anderson 8.00 20.00
95 Aubrey Huff 8.00 20.00
96 Kevin Mench 8.00 20.00
97 Frank Catalanotto 8.00 20.00
98 Flash Gordon 8.00 20.00
99 Scott Hatteberg 8.00 20.00
100 Albert Pujols 25.00 60.00
101 Jose Bengie Molina 8.00 20.00
102 Oscar Villarreal 8.00 20.00
103 Jay Gibbons 8.00 20.00
104 Byung-Hyun Kim 8.00 20.00
105 Joe Borowski 8.00 20.00
106 Mark Grudzielanek 8.00 20.00
107 Mark Buehrle 12.00 30.00
108 Paul Wilson 8.00 20.00
109 Ronnie Belliard 8.00 20.00
110 Reggie Sanders 8.00 20.00
111 Tim Redding 8.00 20.00
112 Brian Lawrence 8.00 20.00
113 Darrell May 8.00 20.00
114 Jose Hernandez 8.00 20.00
115 Ben Sheets 8.00 20.00
116 Johan Santana 12.00 30.00
117 Billy Wagner 8.00 20.00
118 Mariano Rivera 25.00 60.00
119 Steve Trachsel 8.00 20.00
120 Akinori Otsuka 8.00 20.00
121 Bobby Kielty 8.00 20.00
122 Orlando Hernandez 8.00 20.00
123 Raul Ibanez 12.00 30.00
124 Mike Matheny 8.00 20.00
125 Vernon Wells 8.00 20.00
126 Jason Isringhausen 8.00 20.00
127 Jose Guillen 8.00 20.00
128 Danny Bautista 8.00 20.00
129 Marcus Giles 8.00 20.00
130 Javy Lopez 8.00 20.00
131 Kevin Millar 8.00 20.00
132 Kyle Farnsworth 8.00 20.00
133 Carl Pavano 8.00 20.00
134 D'Angelo Jimenez 8.00 20.00
135 Casey Blake 8.00 20.00
136 Matt Holliday 20.00 50.00
137 Bobby Higginson 8.00 20.00
138 Nate Field 8.00 20.00
139 Alex Gonzalez 8.00 20.00
140 Jeff Kent 8.00 20.00
141 Aaron Guiel 8.00 20.00
142 Shawn Green 8.00 20.00
143 Bill Hall 8.00 20.00
144 Shannon Stewart 8.00 20.00
145 Juan Rivera 8.00 20.00
146 Coco Crisp 8.00 20.00
147 Mike Mussina 12.00 30.00
148 Eric Chavez 8.00 20.00
149 Jon Lieber 8.00 20.00
150 Vladimir Guerrero 12.00 30.00
151 Alex Cintron 8.00 20.00
152 Horacio Ramirez 8.00 20.00
153 Sidney Ponson 8.00 20.00
154 Trot Nixon 8.00 20.00
155 Greg Maddux 25.00 60.00
156 Edgar Renteria 8.00 20.00
157 Ryan Freel 8.00 20.00
158 Matt Lawton 8.00 20.00
159 Shawn Chacon 8.00 20.00
160 Josh Beckett 8.00 20.00
161 Ken Harvey 8.00 20.00
162 Juan Cruz 8.00 20.00
163 Juan Encarnacion 8.00 20.00
164 Wes Helms 8.00 20.00
165 Brad Radke 8.00 20.00
166 Claudio Vargas 8.00 20.00
167 Mike Cameron 8.00 20.00
168 Billy Koch 8.00 20.00
169 Bobby Crosby 8.00 20.00
170 Mike Lieberthal 8.00 20.00
171 Rob Mackowiak 8.00 20.00
172 Sean Burroughs 8.00 20.00
173 J.T. Snow Jr. 8.00 20.00
174 Paul Konerko 12.00 30.00
175 Luis Gonzalez 8.00 20.00
176 John Lackey 12.00 30.00
177 Antonio Alfonseca 8.00 20.00
178 Brian Roberts 8.00 20.00
179 Bill Mueller 8.00 20.00
180 Carlos Lee 8.00 20.00
181 Corey Patterson 8.00 20.00
182 Sean Casey 8.00 20.00
183 Cliff Lee 12.00 30.00
184 Jason Jennings 8.00 20.00
185 Dmitri Young 8.00 20.00
186 Juan Uribe 8.00 20.00
187 Andy Pettitte 12.00 30.00
188 Juan Gonzalez 8.00 20.00
189 Pokey Reese 8.00 20.00
190 Jason Phillips 8.00 20.00
191 Rocky Biddle 8.00 20.00
192 Lew Ford 8.00 20.00
193 Mark Mulder 8.00 20.00
194 Bobby Abreu 8.00 20.00
195 Jason Kendall 8.00 20.00
196 Terrence Long 8.00 20.00
197 A.J. Pierzynski 8.00 20.00
198 Eddie Guardado 8.00 20.00
199 So Taguchi 8.00 20.00
200 Jason Giambi 8.00 20.00
201 Tony Batista 8.00 20.00
202 Kyle Lohse 8.00 20.00
203 Trevor Hoffman 12.00 30.00
204 Tike Redman 8.00 20.00
205 Matt Herges 8.00 20.00

6 Gil Meche 8.00 20.00
7 Chris Carpenter 12.00 30.00
8 Ben Broussard 8.00 20.00
9 Eric Young 8.00 20.00
0 Doug Waechter 8.00 20.00
1 Jarrod Washburn 8.00 20.00
2 Chad Tracy 8.00 20.00
3 John Smoltz 20.00 50.00
4 Jorge Julio 8.00 20.00
5 Todd Walker 8.00 20.00
6 Shingo Takatsu 8.00 20.00
7 Jose Acevedo 8.00 20.00
18 David Riske 8.00 20.00
19 Shawn Estes 8.00 20.00
20 Lance Berkman 12.00 30.00
21 Carlos Guillen 8.00 20.00
22 Jeremy Affeldt 8.00 20.00
23 Cesar Izturis 8.00 20.00
24 Scott Sullivan 8.00 20.00
25 Kazuo Matsui 8.00 20.00
26 Josh Fogg 8.00 20.00
27 Jason Schmidt 8.00 20.00
28 Jason Marquis 8.00 20.00
29 Scott Spiezio 8.00 20.00
30 Miguel Tejada 12.00 30.00
31 Bartolo Colon 8.00 20.00
32 Jose Valverde 8.00 20.00
33 Derrek Lee 8.00 20.00
34 Scott Williamson 8.00 20.00
35 Joe Crede 8.00 20.00
36 John Thomson 8.00 20.00
37 Mike MacDougal 8.00 20.00
38 Eric Gagne 8.00 20.00
239 Alex Sanchez 8.00 20.00
40 Miguel Cabrera 20.00 50.00
41 Luis Rivas 8.00 20.00
42 Adam Everett 8.00 20.00
43 Jason Johnson 8.00 20.00
44 Travis Hafner 8.00 20.00
45 Jose Valentin 8.00 20.00
246 Stephen Randolph 8.00 20.00
247 Rafael Furcal 8.00 20.00
248 Adam Kennedy 8.00 20.00
249 Luis Matos 8.00 20.00
250 Mark Prior 12.00 30.00
251 Angel Berroa 8.00 20.00
252 Phil Nevin 8.00 20.00
253 Oliver Perez 8.00 20.00
254 Orlando Hudson 8.00 20.00
255 Braden Looper 8.00 20.00
256 Khalil Greene 8.00 20.00
257 Tim Worrell 8.00 20.00
258 Carlos Zambrano 12.00 30.00
259 Odalis Perez 8.00 20.00
260 Gerald Laird 8.00 20.00
261 Jose Cruz Jr. 8.00 20.00
262 Michael Barrett 8.00 20.00
263 Michael Young UER 8.00 20.00
264 Toby Hall 8.00 20.00
265 Woody Williams 8.00 20.00
266 Rich Harden 8.00 20.00
267 Mike Scioscia MG 8.00 20.00
268 Al Pedrique MG 8.00 20.00
269 Bobby Cox MG 8.00 20.00
270 Lee Mazzilli MG 8.00 20.00
271 Terry Francona MG 12.00 30.00
272 Dusty Baker MG 8.00 20.00
273 Ozzie Guillen MG 8.00 20.00
274 Dave Miley MG 8.00 20.00
275 Eric Wedge MG 8.00 20.00
276 Clint Hurdle MG 8.00 20.00
277 Alan Trammell MG 12.00 30.00
278 Jack McKeon MG 8.00 20.00
279 Phil Garner MG 8.00 20.00
280 Tony Pena MG 8.00 20.00
281 Jim Tracy MG 8.00 20.00
282 Ned Yost MG 8.00 20.00
283 Ron Gardenhire MG 8.00 20.00
284 Frank Robinson MG 12.00 30.00
285 Art Howe MG 8.00 20.00
286 Joe Torre MG 12.00 30.00
287 Ken Macha MG 8.00 20.00
288 Larry Bowa MG 8.00 20.00
289 Lloyd McClendon MG 8.00 20.00
290 Bruce Bochy MG 12.00 30.00
291 Felipe Alou MG 8.00 20.00
292 Bob Melvin MG 8.00 20.00
293 Tony LaRussa MG 12.00 30.00
294 Lou Piniella MG 8.00 20.00
295 Buck Showalter MG 8.00 20.00
296 John Gibbons MG 8.00 20.00
297 Steve Doetsch FY 8.00 20.00
298 Melky Cabrera FY 25.00 60.00
299 Luis Ramirez FY 8.00 20.00
300 Chris Seddon FY 8.00 20.00
301 Nate Schierholtz FY 8.00 20.00
302 Ian Kinsler FY 40.00 100.00
303 Brandon Moss FY 30.00 80.00
304 Chadd Blasko FY 12.00 30.00
305 Jeremy West FY 8.00 20.00
306 Sean Marshall FY 20.00 50.00
307 Matt DeSalvo FY 8.00 20.00
308 Ryan Sweeney FY 12.00 30.00
309 Matthew Lindstrom FY 8.00 20.00
310 Ryan Goleski FY 8.00 20.00
311 Brett Harper FY 8.00 20.00
312 Chris Roberson FY 8.00 20.00
313 Andre Ethier FY 60.00 150.00
314 Chris Denorfia FY 8.00 20.00
315 Ian Bladergroen FY 8.00 20.00
316 Darren Fenster FY 8.00 20.00
317 Kevin West FY 8.00 20.00
318 Chaz Lytle FY 12.00 30.00
319 James Jurries FY 8.00 20.00
320 Matt Rogelstad FY 8.00 20.00
321 Wade Robinson FY 8.00 20.00
322 Jake Dittler FY 8.00 20.00
323 Brian Stavisky FY 8.00 20.00
324 Kole Strayhorn FY 8.00 20.00
325 Jose Vaquedano FY 8.00 20.00
326 Elvys Quezada FY 8.00 20.00
327 J.Maine 8.00 20.00
V.Majewski FS
328 R.Weeks 8.00 20.00
J.Hardy FS
329 G.Gross 8.00 20.00
G.Quiroz FS
330 D.Wright 15.00 40.00
C.Brazell FS
331 D.McPherson 12.00 30.00
J.Mathis FS
369 Garret Anderson 8.00 20.00
370 Randy Johnson 20.00 50.00
371 Charles Thomas 8.00 20.00
372 Rafael Palmeiro 12.00 30.00
373 Kevin Youkilis 8.00 20.00
374 Freddy Garcia 8.00 20.00
375 Magglio Ordonez 12.00 30.00
376 Aaron Harang 8.00 20.00
377 Grady Sizemore 12.00 30.00
378 Chin-Hui Tsao 8.00 20.00
379 Eric Munson 8.00 20.00
380 Juan Pierre 8.00 20.00
381 Brad Lidge 8.00 20.00
382 Brian Anderson 8.00 20.00
383 Alex Cora 12.00 30.00
384 Brady Clark 8.00 20.00
385 Todd Helton 12.00 30.00
386 Chad Cordero 8.00 20.00
387 Kris Benson 8.00 20.00
388 Brad Halsey 8.00 20.00
389 Jermaine Dye 8.00 20.00
390 Manny Ramirez 20.00 50.00
391 Daryle Ward 8.00 20.00
392 Adam Eaton 8.00 20.00
393 Brett Tomko 8.00 20.00
394 Bucky Jacobsen 8.00 20.00
395 Dontrelle Willis 8.00 20.00
396 B.J. Upton 12.00 30.00
397 Rocco Baldelli 8.00 20.00
398 Ted Lilly 8.00 20.00
399 Ryan Drese 8.00 20.00
400 Ichiro Suzuki 25.00 60.00
401 Brendan Donnelly 8.00 20.00
402 Brandon Lyon 8.00 20.00
403 Nick Green 8.00 20.00
404 Jerry Hairston Jr. 8.00 20.00
405 Mike Lowell 8.00 20.00
406 Kerry Wood 8.00 20.00
407 Carl Everett 8.00 20.00
408 Hideki Matsui 30.00 80.00
409 Omar Vizquel 12.00 30.00
410 Joe Kennedy 8.00 20.00
411 Carlos Pena 12.00 30.00
412 Armando Benitez 8.00 20.00
413 Carlos Beltran 12.00 30.00
414 Kevin Appier 8.00 20.00
415 Jeff Weaver 8.00 20.00
416 Chad Moeller 8.00 20.00
417 Joe Mays 8.00 20.00
418 Termel Sledge 8.00 20.00
419 Richard Hidalgo 8.00 20.00
420 Kenny Lofton 8.00 20.00
421 Justin Duchscherer 8.00 20.00
422 Eric Milton 8.00 20.00
423 Jose Mesa 8.00 20.00
424 Ramon Hernandez 8.00 20.00
425 Jose Reyes 12.00 30.00
426 Joel Pineiro 8.00 20.00
427 Matt Morris 8.00 20.00
428 John Halama 8.00 20.00
429 Gary Matthews Jr. 8.00 20.00
430 Ryan Madson 8.00 20.00
431 Mark Kotsay 8.00 20.00
432 Carlos Delgado 8.00 20.00
433 Casey Kotchman 8.00 20.00
434 Greg Aquino 8.00 20.00
435 Eli Marrero 8.00 20.00
436 David Newhan 8.00 20.00
437 Mike Timlin 8.00 20.00
438 LaTroy Hawkins 8.00 20.00
439 Jose Contreras 8.00 20.00
440 Ken Griffey Jr. 40.00 100.00
441 C.C. Sabathia 12.00 30.00
442 Brandon Inge 8.00 20.00
443 Pete Munro 8.00 20.00
444 John Buck 8.00 20.00
445 Hee Seop Choi 8.00 20.00
446 Chris Capuano 8.00 20.00
447 Jesse Crain 8.00 20.00
448 Geoff Jenkins 8.00 20.00
449 Brian Schneider 8.00 20.00
450 Mike Piazza 20.00 50.00
451 Jorge Posada 12.00 30.00
452 Nick Swisher 12.00 30.00
453 Kevin Millwood 8.00 20.00
454 Mike Gonzalez 8.00 20.00
455 Jake Peavy 8.00 20.00
456 Dustin Hermanson 8.00 20.00
457 Jeremy Reed 8.00 20.00
458 Julian Tavarez 8.00 20.00
459 Geoff Blum 8.00 20.00
460 Alfonso Soriano 12.00 30.00
461 Alexis Rios 8.00 20.00
462 David Eckstein 8.00 20.00
463 Shea Hillenbrand 8.00 20.00
464 Russ Ortiz 8.00 20.00
465 Kurt Ainsworth 8.00 20.00
466 Orlando Cabrera 8.00 20.00
467 Carlos Silva 8.00 20.00
468 Ross Gload 8.00 20.00
469 Josh Phelps 8.00 20.00
470 Marquis Grissom 8.00 20.00
471 Mike Maroth 8.00 20.00
472 Guillermo Mota 8.00 20.00
473 Chris Burke 8.00 20.00
474 David DeJesus 8.00 20.00
475 Jose Lima 8.00 20.00
476 Cristian Guzman 8.00 20.00
477 Nick Johnson 8.00 20.00
478 Victor Zambrano 8.00 20.00
479 Rod Barajas 8.00 20.00
480 Damian Miller 8.00 20.00
481 Chase Utley 12.00 30.00
482 Todd Pratt 8.00 20.00
483 Sean Burnett 8.00 20.00
484 Boomer Wells 8.00 20.00
485 Dustan Mohr 8.00 20.00
486 Bobby Madritsch 8.00 20.00
487 Ray King 8.00 20.00
488 Reed Johnson 8.00 20.00
489 R.A. Dickey 12.00 30.00
490 Scott Kazmir 20.00 50.00
491 Tony Womack 8.00 20.00
492 Tomas Perez 8.00 20.00
493 Esteban Loaiza 8.00 20.00
494 Tomo Ohka 8.00 20.00
495 Mike Lamb 8.00 20.00
496 Ramon Ortiz 8.00 20.00
497 Richie Sexson 8.00 20.00
498 J.D. Drew 8.00 20.00
499 David Segui 8.00 20.00
500 Barry Bonds 30.00 80.00
501 Aramis Ramirez 8.00 20.00
502 Wily Mo Pena 8.00 20.00
503 Jeromy Burnitz 8.00 20.00
504 Craig Monroe 8.00 20.00
505 Nomar Garciaparra 12.00 30.00
506 Brandon Backe 8.00 20.00
507 Marcus Thames 8.00 20.00
508 Derek Lowe 8.00 20.00
509 Doug Davis 8.00 20.00
510 Joe Mauer 15.00 40.00
511 Endy Chavez 8.00 20.00
512 Bernie Williams 12.00 30.00
513 Mark Redman 8.00 20.00
514 Jason Michaels 8.00 20.00
515 Craig Wilson 8.00 20.00
516 Ryan Klesko 8.00 20.00
517 Ray Durham 8.00 20.00
518 Jose Lopez 8.00 20.00
519 Jeff Suppan 8.00 20.00
520 Julio Lugo 8.00 20.00
521 Mike Wood 8.00 20.00
522 David Bush 8.00 20.00
523 Juan Rincon 8.00 20.00
524 Paul Quantrill 8.00 20.00
525 Marlon Byrd 8.00 20.00
526 Roy Oswalt 12.00 30.00
527 Rondell White 8.00 20.00
528 Troy Glaus 8.00 20.00
529 Scott Hairston 8.00 20.00
530 Chipper Jones 20.00 50.00
531 Daniel Cabrera 8.00 20.00
532 Doug Mientkiewicz 8.00 20.00
533 Glendon Rusch 8.00 20.00
534 Jon Garland 8.00 20.00
535 Austin Kearns 8.00 20.00
536 Jake Westbrook 8.00 20.00
537 Aaron Miles 8.00 20.00
538 Omar Infante 8.00 20.00
539 Paul Lo Duca 8.00 20.00
540 Morgan Ensberg 8.00 20.00
541 Tony Graffanino 8.00 20.00
542 Milton Bradley 8.00 20.00
543 Keith Ginter 8.00 20.00
544 Justin Morneau 12.00 30.00
545 Tony Armas Jr. 8.00 20.00
546 Mike Stanton 8.00 20.00
547 Kevin Brown 8.00 20.00
548 Marco Scutaro 12.00 30.00
549 Tim Hudson 12.00 30.00
550 Pat Burrell 8.00 20.00
551 Ty Wigginton 8.00 20.00
552 Jeff Cirillo 8.00 20.00
553 Jim Brower 8.00 20.00
554 Jamie Moyer 8.00 20.00
555 Larry Walker 12.00 30.00
556 Dewon Brazelton 8.00 20.00
557 Brian Jordan 8.00 20.00
558 Josh Towers 8.00 20.00
559 Shigetoshi Hasegawa 8.00 20.00
560 Octavio Dotel 8.00 20.00
561 Travis Lee 8.00 20.00
562 Michael Cuddyer 8.00 20.00
563 Junior Spivey 8.00 20.00
564 Zack Greinke 20.00 50.00
565 Roger Clemens 25.00 60.00
566 Chris Shelton 8.00 20.00
567 Ugueth Urbina 8.00 20.00
568 Rafael Betancourt 8.00 20.00
569 Willie Harris 8.00 20.00
570 Todd Hollandsworth 8.00 20.00
571 Keith Foulke 8.00 20.00
572 Larry Bigbie 8.00 20.00
573 Paul Byrd 8.00 20.00
574 Troy Percival 8.00 20.00
575 Pedro Martinez 12.00 30.00
576 Matt Clement 8.00 20.00
577 Ryan Wagner 8.00 20.00
578 Jeff Francis 8.00 20.00
579 Jeff Conine 8.00 20.00
580 Wade Miller 8.00 20.00
581 Matt Stairs 8.00 20.00
582 Gavin Floyd 8.00 20.00
583 Kazuhisa Ishii 8.00 20.00
584 Victor Santos 8.00 20.00
585 Jacque Jones 8.00 20.00
586 Sunny Kim 8.00 20.00
587 Dan Kolb 8.00 20.00
588 Cory Lidle 8.00 20.00
589 Jose Castillo 8.00 20.00
590 Alex Gonzalez 8.00 20.00
591 Kirk Rueter 8.00 20.00
592 Jolbert Cabrera 8.00 20.00
593 Erik Bedard 8.00 20.00
594 Ben Grieve 8.00 20.00
595 Ricky Ledee 8.00 20.00
596 Mark Hendrickson 8.00 20.00
597 Laynce Nix 8.00 20.00
598 Jason Frasor 8.00 20.00
599 Kevin Gregg 8.00 20.00
600 Derek Jeter 50.00 125.00
601 Luis Terrero 8.00 20.00
602 Jaret Wright 8.00 20.00
603 Edwin Jackson 8.00 20.00
604 Dave Roberts 12.00 30.00
605 Moises Alou 8.00 20.00
606 Aaron Rowand 8.00 20.00
607 Kazuhito Tadano 8.00 20.00
608 Luis A. Gonzalez 8.00 20.00
609 A.J. Burnett 8.00 20.00
610 Jeff Bagwell 12.00 30.00
611 Brad Penny 8.00 20.00
612 Craig Counsell 8.00 20.00
613 Corey Koskie 8.00 20.00
614 Mark Ellis 8.00 20.00
615 Felix Rodriguez 8.00 20.00
616 Jay Payton 8.00 20.00
617 Hector Luna 8.00 20.00
618 Miguel Olivo 8.00 20.00
619 Rob Bell 8.00 20.00
620 Scott Rolen 12.00 30.00
621 Ricardo Rodriguez 8.00 20.00
622 Eric Hinske 8.00 20.00
623 Tim Salmon 8.00 20.00
624 Adam LaRoche 8.00 20.00
625 B.J. Ryan 8.00 20.00
626 Roberto Alomar 12.00 30.00
627 Steve Finley 8.00 20.00
628 Joe Nathan 8.00 20.00
629 Scott Linebrink 8.00 20.00
630 Vicente Padilla 8.00 20.00
631 Raul Mondesi 8.00 20.00
632 Yadier Molina 20.00 50.00
633 Tino Martinez 12.00 30.00
634 Mark Teixeira 12.00 30.00
635 Kelvim Escobar 8.00 20.00
636 Pedro Feliz 8.00 20.00
637 Rich Aurilia 8.00 20.00
638 Los Angeles Angels TC 8.00 20.00
639 Arizona Diamondbacks TC 8.00 20.00
640 Atlanta Braves TC 12.00 30.00
641 Baltimore Orioles TC 8.00 20.00
642 Boston Red Sox TC 20.00 50.00
643 Chicago Cubs TC 12.00 30.00
644 Chicago White Sox TC 8.00 20.00
645 Cincinnati Reds TC 8.00 20.00
646 Cleveland Indians TC 8.00 20.00
647 Colorado Rockies TC 8.00 20.00
648 Detroit Tigers TC 8.00 20.00
649 Florida Marlins TC 8.00 20.00
650 Houston Astros TC 8.00 20.00
651 Kansas City Royals TC 8.00 20.00
652 Los Angeles Dodgers TC 8.00 20.00
653 Milwaukee Brewers TC 8.00 20.00
654 Minnesota Twins TC 8.00 20.00
655 Montreal Expos TC 8.00 20.00
656 New York Mets TC 8.00 20.00
657 New York Yankees TC 20.00 50.00
658 Oakland Athletics TC 8.00 20.00
659 Philadelphia Phillies TC 8.00 20.00
660 Pittsburgh Pirates TC 8.00 20.00
661 San Diego Padres TC 8.00 20.00
662 San Francisco Giants TC 8.00 20.00
663 Seattle Mariners TC 8.00 20.00
664 St. Louis Cardinals TC 12.00 30.00
665 Tampa Bay Devil Rays TC 8.00 20.00
666 Texas Rangers TC 8.00 20.00
667 Toronto Blue Jays TC 8.00 20.00
668 Billy Butler FY 40.00 100.00
669 Wes Swackhamer FY 8.00 20.00
670 Matt Campbell FY 8.00 20.00
671 Ryan Webb FY 8.00 20.00
672 Glen Perkins FY 8.00 20.00
673 Michael Rogers FY 8.00 20.00
674 Kevin Melillo FY 8.00 20.00
675 Erik Cordier FY 8.00 20.00
676 Landon Powell FY 8.00 20.00
677 Justin Verlander FY 150.00 400.00
678 Eric Nielsen FY 8.00 20.00
679 Alexander Smit FY 8.00 20.00
680 Ryan Garko FY 8.00 20.00
681 Bobby Livingston FY 8.00 20.00
682 Jeff Niemann FY 20.00 50.00
683 Wladimir Balentien FY 12.00 30.00
684 Chip Cannon FY 8.00 20.00
685 Yorman Bazardo FY 8.00 20.00
686 Mike Bourn FY 20.00 50.00
687 Andy LaRoche FY 8.00 20.00
688 F.Hernandez 25.00 60.00
J.Leone
689 R.Howard 25.00 60.00
C.Hamels
690 M.Cain 50.00 125.00
M.Valdez
691 A.Marte 20.00 50.00
J.Francoeur
692 C.Billingsley 8.00 20.00
J.Guzman
693 J.Hairston Jr. 8.00 20.00
S.Hairston
694 M.Tejada 12.00 30.00
L.Berkman
695 Kenny Rogers GG 8.00 20.00
696 Ivan Rodriguez GG 12.00 30.00
697 Darin Erstad GG 8.00 20.00
698 Bret Boone GG 8.00 20.00
699 Eric Chavez GG 8.00 20.00
700 Derek Jeter GG 50.00 125.00
701 Vernon Wells GG 8.00 20.00
702 Ichiro Suzuki GG 25.00 60.00
703 Torii Hunter GG 8.00 20.00
704 Greg Maddux GG 25.00 60.00
705 Mike Matheny GG 8.00 20.00
706 Todd Helton GG 12.00 30.00
707 Luis Castillo GG 8.00 20.00
708 Scott Rolen GG 12.00 30.00
709 Cesar Izturis GG 8.00 20.00
710 Jim Edmonds GG 12.00 30.00
711 Andruw Jones GG 8.00 20.00
712 Steve Finley GG 8.00 20.00
713 Johan Santana CY 12.00 30.00
714 Roger Clemens CY 25.00 60.00
715 Vladimir Guerrero MVP 12.00 30.00
716 Barry Bonds MVP 30.00 80.00
717 Bobby Crosby ROY 8.00 20.00
718 Jason Bay ROY 8.00 20.00
719 Albert Pujols AS 25.00 60.00
720 Mark Loretta AS 8.00 20.00
721 Edgar Renteria AS 8.00 20.00
722 Scott Rolen AS 12.00 30.00
723 J.D. Drew AS 8.00 20.00
724 Jim Edmonds AS 12.00 30.00
725 Johnny Estrada AS 8.00 20.00
726 Jason Schmidt AS 8.00 20.00
727 Chris Carpenter AS 12.00 30.00
728 Eric Gagne AS 8.00 20.00
729 Jason Bay AS 8.00 20.00
730 Bobby Cox MG AS 8.00 20.00
731 D.Ortiz 20.00 50.00
M.Bellhorn WS1
732 Curt Schilling WS2 12.00 30.00
733 M.Ramirez 20.00 50.00
P.Martinez WS3
734 Sox Win Damon 12.00 30.00
Lowe WS4

2005 Topps Box Bottoms

ONE 4-CARD SHEET PER HTA BOX
1 Alex Rodriguez 1 .60 1.50
10 Sammy Sosa 1 .50 1.25
20 Hank Blalock 2 .20 .50
25 Jim Thome 2 .30 .75
30 Ivan Rodriguez 3 .30 .75
40 Gary Sheffield 1 .20 .50
78 Hideo Nomo 4 .50 1.25
80 Adam Dunn 2 .30 .75
100 Albert Pujols 3 .60 1.50
120 Akinori Otsuka 4 .20 .50
150 Vladimir Guerrero 1 .30 .75
200 Jason Giambi 2 .20 .50
216 Shingo Takatsu 4 .20 .50
225 Kazuo Matsui 4 .20 .50
230 Miguel Tejada 3 .30 .75
240 Miguel Cabrera 3 .50 1.25
369 Garret Anderson 8 .20 .50
385 Todd Helton 6 .30 .75
390 Manny Ramirez 7 .50 1.25
395 Dontrelle Willis 7 .20 .50
406 Kerry Wood 5 .20 .50
431 Mark Kotsay 6 .20 .50
450 Mike Piazza 5 .50 1.25
455 Jake Peavy 8 .20 .50
460 Alfonso Soriano 6 .30 .75
500 Barry Bonds 5 .75 2.00
505 Nomar Garciaparra 7 .30 .75
510 Joe Mauer 7 .40 1.00
526 Roy Oswalt 6 .30 .75
530 Chipper Jones 5 .50 1.25
550 Pat Burrell 8 .20 .50
620 Scott Rolen 8 .30 .75

2005 Topps Gold

*GOLD 1-296/369-667/693-730: 6X TO 15X
*GOLD 297-326/668-687: 2X TO 5X
*GOLD 327-331/688-692: 2X TO 5X
*GOLD 731-734: 3X TO 8X
SERIES 1 ODDS 1:8 HOB, 1:3 HTA, 1:10 RET
SERIES 2 ODDS 1:5 HOB, 1:2 HTA, 1:6 RET
STATED PRINT RUN 2005 SERIAL #'d SETS
CARD NUMBER 7 DOES NOT EXIST

2005 Topps A-Rod Spokesman

COMPLETE SET (4) 4.00 10.00
SER.2 ODDS 1:24 HOB, 1:8 HTA, 1:24 RET
1 Alex Rodriguez 1994 1.00 2.50
2 Alex Rodriguez 1995 1.00 2.50
3 Alex Rodriguez 1996 1.00 2.50
4 Alex Rodriguez 1997 1.00 2.50

2005 Topps A-Rod Spokesman Autographs

SER.2 ODDS 1:22,279 H, 1:6749 HTA
SER.2 ODDS 1:24,439 R
PRINT RUNS B/WN 1-200 COPIES PER
NO PRICING ON QTY OF 25 OR LESS
3 Alex Rodriguez 1996/100 75.00 150.00
4 Alex Rodriguez 1997/200 25.00 60.00

2005 Topps A-Rod Spokesman Jersey Relics

SER.2 ODDS 1:3550 H, 1:1015 HTA, 1:3564 R
PRINT RUNS B/WN 1-800 COPIES PER
NO PRICING ON QTY OF 1
2 Alex Rodriguez 1995/50 30.00 60.00
3 Alex Rodriguez 1996/300 8.00 20.00
4 Alex Rodriguez 1997/800 6.00 15.00

2005 Topps All-Star Stitches Relics

SERIES 1 ODDS 1:96 H, 1:27 HTA, 1:80 R
AP Albert Pujols 8.00 20.00
AS Alfonso Soriano 4.00 10.00
BA Bobby Abreu 4.00 10.00
BL Barry Larkin 4.00 10.00
BS Ben Sheets 4.00 10.00
CB Carlos Beltran 4.00 10.00
CC Carl Crawford 4.00 10.00
CP Carl Pavano 4.00 10.00
CS C.C. Sabathia 4.00 10.00
CZ Carlos Zambrano 4.00 10.00
DK Danny Kolb 4.00 10.00
DO David Ortiz 4.00 10.00
EL Esteban Loaiza 4.00 10.00
ER Edgar Renteria 4.00 10.00
FG Tom Gordon 4.00 10.00
FR Francisco Rodriguez 4.00 10.00
GS Gary Sheffield 4.00 10.00
HB Hank Blalock 4.00 10.00
IR Ivan Rodriguez 4.00 10.00
JE Johnny Estrada 4.00 10.00
JG Jason Giambi 4.00 10.00
JK Jeff Kent 4.00 10.00
JN Joe Nathan 4.00 10.00
JT Jim Thome 4.00 10.00
JW Jack Wilson 4.00 10.00
KH Ken Harvey 4.00 10.00
LB Lance Berkman 4.00 10.00
MA Moises Alou 4.00 10.00
MC Miguel Cabrera 4.00 10.00
ML Mike Lowell 4.00 10.00
MLA Matt Lawton 4.00 10.00
MLO Mark Loretta 4.00 10.00
MM Mark Mulder 4.00 10.00
MP Mike Piazza 4.00 10.00
MR Manny Ramirez 4.00 10.00
MRI Mariano Rivera 6.00 15.00
MT Miguel Tejada 4.00 10.00
MY Michael Young 4.00 10.00
PL Paul Lo Duca 4.00 10.00
RB Ronnie Belliard 4.00 10.00
SR Scott Rolen 4.00 10.00
SS Sammy Sosa 4.00 10.00
TG Tom Glavine 4.00 10.00
TH Todd Helton 4.00 10.00
TL Ted Lilly 4.00 10.00
VG Vladimir Guerrero 4.00 10.00
VM Victor Martinez 4.00 10.00

2005 Topps All-Stars

COMPLETE SET (15) 10.00 25.00
SER.2 ODDS 1:9 HOBBY, 1:3 HTA
1 Todd Helton .60 1.50
2 Albert Pujols 1.25 3.00
3 Vladimir Guerrero .60 1.50
4 Ichiro Suzuki 1.25 3.00
5 Randy Johnson 1.00 2.50
6 Manny Ramirez 1.00 2.50
7 Sammy Sosa 1.00 2.50
8 Alfonso Soriano .60 1.50
9 Jim Thome .60 1.50
10 Barry Bonds 1.50 4.00
11 Roger Clemens 1.25 3.00
12 Mike Piazza 1.00 2.50
13 Derek Jeter 2.50 6.00
14 Alex Rodriguez 1.25 3.00
15 Carlos Beltran .60 1.50

2005 Topps Autographs

Carlos Beltran and Zack Greinke did not return their cards in time to be included within first series packs, thus exchange cards with a deadline redemption date of November 30th, 2006 were placed into packs in their place.
SER.1 A 1:2683 H, 1:767 HTA, 1:2238 R
SER.1 B 1:3950 H, 1:1129 HTA, 1:3300 R
SER.1 C 1:305 H, 1:87 HTA, 1:254 R
SER.1 D 1:2913 H, 1:833 HTA, 1:2432 R
SER.2 A 1:178,234H,1:51,744HTA,1:171,072R
SER.2 B 1:89,117 H, 1:22,176 HTA, 1:85,536 R
SER.2 C 1:2751 H, 1:780 HTA, 1:2715 R
SER.2 D 1:1367 H, 1:390 HTA, 1:1369 R
SER.2 E 1:2039 H, 1:586 HTA, 1:2061 R
SER.2 F 1:285 H, 1:129 HTA, 1:301 R
SER.2 GROUP A PRINT RUN 25 COPIES
SER.2 GROUP B PRINT RUN 50 COPIES
SER.2 GROUP A-B ARE NOT SERIAL #'d
PRINT RUN INFO PROVIDED BY TOPPS
SER.1 EXCH.DEADLINE 11/30/06
SER.2 EXCH.DEADLINE 04/30/07
NO GROUP A2 PRICING DUE TO SCARCITY
AR Alex Rodriguez A1 60.00 150.00
AR2 Alex Rodriguez B2/50 * 30.00 80.00
ARI Alexis Rios C1 4.00 10.00
BB Billy Butler E2 6.00 15.00
CB Carlos Beltran A1 8.00 20.00
CB2 Carlos Beltran C2 8.00 20.00
CC Carl Crawford D2 10.00 25.00
CK Casey Kotchman C1 4.00 10.00
CT Chad Tracy C1 4.00 10.00
CW Craig Wilson D2 6.00 15.00
DD David DeJesus C1 4.00 10.00
DM Dallas McPherson D1 4.00 10.00
DW David Wright C1 8.00 20.00
EC Eric Chavez A1 10.00 25.00
EC2 Eric Chavez C2 10.00 25.00
ECO Erik Cordier F2 4.00 10.00
EG Eric Gagne C2 15.00 40.00
FH Felix Hernandez D2 10.00 25.00
GP Glen Perkins F2 6.00 15.00
IR Ivan Rodriguez C2 12.00 30.00
JB Jason Bay D2 10.00 25.00
JC Jose Capellan B1 4.00 10.00
JM Justin Morneau C1 6.00 15.00

JMA John Maine C1 6.00 15.00
JS Johan Santana C2 8.00 20.00
JSM Jeff Mathis C1 4.00 10.00
LP Landon Powell F2 6.00 15.00
MB Milton Bradley D2 10.00 25.00
MC Miguel Cabrera C1 15.00 40.00
MCA Matt Campbell F2 4.00 10.00
MH Matt Holliday C1 6.00 15.00
ML Mark Loretta D2 6.00 15.00
MR Michael Rogers F2 4.00 10.00
SK Scott Kazmir C2 10.00 25.00
TH Torii Hunter A1 10.00 25.00
TS Termel Sledge E2 4.00 10.00
VW Vernon Wells A1 10.00 25.00
ZG Zack Greinke C1 5.00 12.00

2005 Topps Barry Bonds Chase to 715

COMMON CARD 15.00 40.00
SER.2 ODDS 1:2539 H, 1:722 HTA, 1:2516 R
STATED PRINT RUN 1 SERIAL #'d SET

2005 Topps Barry Bonds Home Run History

COMP.SERIES 3 (48) 20.00 50.00
COMP.06 UPDATE (26) 10.00 25.00
COMP.07 UPDATE (22) 20.00 50.00
COMMON CARD (1-754) 1.25 3.00
COMMON HR 1 15.00 40.00
COMMON HR 100/200/300/400 6.00 15.00
COMMON HR 500/600 6.00 15.00
COMMON HR 661/700 3.00 8.00
COMMON HR 755-762 2.00 5.00
05 SER.2 ODDS 1:4 H, 1:1 HTA, 1:4 R
05 UPDATE ODDS 1:4 H, 1:1 HTA, 1:4 R
06 SER.1 ODDS 1:4 HOB, 1:4 MINI, 1:4 RET
06 SER.1 ODDS 1:2 RACK
06 UPDATE ODDS 1:6 HOB,1:6 RET
07 UPDATE ODDS 1:12 HOBBY
05 SER.2 EXCH ODDS 1:178,234 HOB
05 SER.2 EXCH ODDS 1:51,744 HTA
05 SER.2 EXCH ODDS 1:171,072 RET
07 UPDATE ODDS 1:12 H,1:3 HTA,1:12 R
EXCH CARD PRINT RUN 25 COPIES
EXCH.CARD PRINT RUN INFO FROM TOPPS
NO EXCH CARD PRICING DUE TO SCARCITY
1-330 ISSUED IN 05 SERIES 2 PACKS
331-660 ISSUED IN 05 UPDATE PACKS
661-708 ISSUED IN 06 SERIES 1 PACKS
709-734 ISSUED IN 06 UPDATE PACKS
735-575 ISSUED IN 07 UPDATE PACKS
1/100/200/300/400/500/600 ARE GOLD FOIL
661/700/755/766 ARE SILVER FOIL

2005 Topps Barry Bonds MVP

SER.2 ODDS 1:2613 H, 1:743 HTA, 1:2592 R
PRINT RUNS B/WN 25-500 COPIES PER
NO PRICING ON QTY OF 25
3 Barry Bonds 1993/100 10.00 25.00
4 Barry Bonds 2001/200 8.00 20.00
5 Barry Bonds 2002/300 8.00 20.00
6 Barry Bonds 2003/400 6.00 15.00
7 Barry Bonds 2004/500 6.00 15.00

2005 Topps Barry Bonds MVP Jersey Relics

SER.2 ODDS 1:2613 H, 1:743 HTA, 1:2592 R
PRINT RUNS B/WN 25-500 COPIES PER
NO PRICING ON QTY OF 25
3 Barry Bonds 1993/100 50.00 100.00
4 Barry Bonds 2001/200 30.00 60.00
5 Barry Bonds 2002/300 20.00 50.00
6 Barry Bonds 2003/400 15.00 40.00
7 Barry Bonds 2004/500 12.50 30.00

2005 Topps Celebrity Threads Jersey Relics

SERIES 1 ODDS 1:562 H, 1:161 HTA, 1:468 R
RELICS ARE FROM CELEBRITY AS EVENT
CC Cesar Cedeno 4.00 10.00
CF Cecil Fielder 6.00 15.00
DW Dave Winfield 4.00 10.00
GG Goose Gossage 4.00 10.00
HR Harold Reynolds 4.00 10.00
MS Mike Scott 4.00 10.00
OS Ozzie Smith 8.00 20.00
RF Rollie Fingers 4.00 10.00

2005 Topps Dem Bums

COMPLETE SET (21) 20.00 50.00
SERIES 1 ODDS 1:12 H, 1:4 HTA, 1:12 R
BB Bob Borkowski 1.25 3.00
CE Carl Erskine 1.25 3.00
CF Carl Furillo 1.25 3.00
CL Clem Labine 1.25 3.00
DH Don Hoak 1.25 3.00
DN Don Newcombe 1.25 3.00
DS Duke Snider 2.00 5.00
DZ Don Zimmer 1.25 3.00
ER Ed Roebuck 1.25 3.00
GS George Shuba 1.25 3.00
JB Joe Black 1.25 3.00
JG Jim Gilliam 1.25 3.00
JH Jim Hughes 1.25 3.00
JP Johnny Podres 1.25 3.00
JR Jackie Robinson 2.00 5.00
KS Karl Spooner 1.25 3.00
RC Roy Campanella 2.00 5.00
RCR Roger Craig 1.25 3.00
RM Russ Meyer 1.25 3.00
RW Rube Walker 1.25 3.00
WA Walter Alston 2.00 5.00

2005 Topps Dem Bums Autographs

SERIES 1 ODDS 1:150 HTA
SERIES 2 ODDS 1:182 HTA
SER.2 EXCH.DEADLINE 04/30/07
CE Carl Erskine 15.00 40.00
CL Clem Labine 15.00 40.00
DN Don Newcombe 20.00 50.00
DS Duke Snider 20.00 50.00
DZ Don Zimmer 20.00 50.00
ER Ed Roebuck 20.00 50.00
JP Johnny Podres 15.00 40.00
RC Roger Craig 15.00 40.00

2005 Topps Derby Digs Jersey Relics

SER.1 ODDS 1:11,208 HOBBY, 1:3232 HTA
SER.1 ODDS 1:9630 RETAIL
STATED PRINT RUN 100 SERIAL #'d SETS
DO David Ortiz 15.00 40.00
HB Hank Blalock 10.00 25.00
JT Jim Thome 15.00 40.00
LB Lance Berkman 10.00 25.00
MT Miguel Tejada 10.00 25.00
SS Sammy Sosa 15.00 40.00

2005 Topps Factory Set Draft Picks Bonus

COMPLETE SET (5) 10.00 20.00
ONE SET PER FACTORY SET
1 Beau Jones 2.00 5.00
2 Cliff Pennington .75 2.00
3 Chris Volstad 2.00 5.00
4 Ricky Romero 1.25 3.00
5 Jay Bruce 6.00 15.00

2005 Topps Factory Set First Year Draft Bonus

COMPLETE SET (10) 15.00 30.00
ONE SET PER GREEN HOLIDAY FACT.SET
1 Nick Webber .75 2.00
2 Aaron Thompson 1.25 3.00
3 Matt Garza 1.25 3.00
4 Tyler Greene .75 2.00
5 Ryan Braun 6.00 15.00
6 C.J. Henry 1.25 3.00
7 Ryan Zimmerman 4.00 10.00
8 John Mayberry Jr. 2.00 5.00
9 Cesar Carrillo 1.25 3.00
10 Mark McCormick .75 2.00

2005 Topps Factory Set First Year Player Bonus

COMPLETE SERIES 1 (5) 6.00 15.00
1-5 ISSUED IN RED HOBBY SETS
1 Bill McCarthy .75 2.00
2 John Hudgins .75 2.00
3 Kyle Nichols .75 2.00
4 Thomas Pauly .75 2.00
5 Philip Humber 2.00 5.00

2005 Topps Factory Set Team Bonus

Issued five per selected Topps factory sets, these cards feature leading prospects from seven-different organizations.

COMP.CUBS SET (5) 6.00 15.00
COMP.GIANTS SET (5) 6.00 15.00
COMP.NATIONALS SET (5) 6.00 15.00
COMP.RED SOX SET (5) 6.00 15.00
COMP.TIGERS SET (5) 6.00 15.00
COMP.YANKEES SET (5) 6.00 15.00
C1-C5 ISSUED IN CUBS FACTORY SET
G1-G5 ISSUED IN GIANTS FACTORY SET
N1-N5 ISSUED IN NATIONALS FACTORY SET
R1-R5 ISSUED IN RED SOX FACTORY SET
T1-T5 ISSUED IN TIGERS FACTORY SET
Y1-Y5 ISSUED IN YANKEES FACTORY SET
C1 Casey McGehee 1.25 3.00
C2 Andy Santana .75 2.00
C3 Buck Coats .75 2.00
C4 Kevin Collins .75 2.00
C5 Brandon Sing .75 2.00
G1 Pat Misch .75 2.00
G2 J.B. Thurmond .75 2.00
G3 Billy Sadler .75 2.00
G4 Jonathan Sanchez 3.00 8.00
G5 Fred Lewis 1.25 3.00
N1 Daryl Thompson .75 2.00
N2 Ender Chavez .75 2.00
N3 Ryan Church .75 2.00
N4 Brendan Harris .75 2.00
N5 Darrell Rasner .75 2.00
R1 Stefan Bailie .75 2.00
R2 Willy Mota .75 2.00
R3 Matt Van Der Bosch .75 2.00
R4 Mike Garber .75 2.00
R5 Dustin Pedroia 2.50 6.00
T1 Eulogio de la Cruz .75 2.00
T2 Humberto Sanchez 1.25 3.00
T3 Danny Zell .75 2.00
T4 Kyle Sleeth .75 2.00
T5 Curtis Granderson 1.50 4.00
Y1 T.J. Beam .75 2.00
Y2 Ben Jones .75 2.00
Y3 Robinson Cano 2.50 6.00
Y4 Steven White .75 2.00
Y5 Philip Hughes 2.00 5.00

2005 Topps Grudge Match

COMPLETE SET (10) 5.00 12.00
SERIES 1 ODDS 1:24 H, 1:8 HTA, 1:18 R
1 J.Posada .60 1.50
P.Martinez
2 M.Piazza 1.25 3.00
R.Clemens
3 M.Rivera 1.25 3.00
L.Gonzalez
4 J.Edmonds .60 1.50
C.Zambrano
5 A.Boone .60 1.50
T.Wakefield
6 M.Ramirez 1.25 3.00
R.Clemens
7 M.Tucker .40 1.00
E.Gagne
8 I.Rodriguez .60 1.50
J.Snow
9 A.Rodriguez 1.25 3.00
B.Arroyo
10 C.Miller 1.00 2.50
S.Sosa

2005 Topps Hit Parade

COMPLETE SET (30) 30.00 60.00
SER.2 ODDS 1:12 H, 1:4 HTA, 1:12 R
HR1 Barry Bonds HR 1.50 4.00
HR2 Sammy Sosa HR 1.00 2.50
HR3 Rafael Palmeiro HR .60 1.50
HR4 Ken Griffey Jr. HR 2.00 5.00
HR5 Jeff Bagwell HR .60 1.50
HR6 Frank Thomas HR 1.00 2.50
HR7 Juan Gonzalez HR .40 1.00
HR8 Jim Thome HR .60 1.50
HR9 Gary Sheffield HR .40 1.00
HR10 Manny Ramirez HR 1.00 2.50
HIT1 Rafael Palmeiro HIT .60 1.50
HIT2 Barry Bonds HIT 1.50 4.00
HIT3 Roberto Alomar HIT .60 1.50
HIT4 Craig Biggio HIT .60 1.50
HIT5 Julio Franco HIT .40 1.00
HIT6 Steve Finley HIT .40 1.00
HIT7 Jeff Bagwell HIT .60 1.50
HIT8 B.J. Surhoff HIT .40 1.00
HIT9 Marquis Grissom HIT .40 1.00
HIT10 Sammy Sosa HIT 1.00 2.50
RBI1 Barry Bonds RBI 1.50 4.00
RBI2 Rafael Palmeiro RBI .60 1.50
RBI3 Sammy Sosa RBI 1.00 2.50
RBI4 Jeff Bagwell RBI .60 1.50
RBI5 Ken Griffey Jr. RBI 2.00 5.00
RBI6 Frank Thomas RBI 1.00 2.50
RBI7 Juan Gonzalez RBI .40 1.00
RBI8 Gary Sheffield RBI .40 1.00
RBI9 Ruben Sierra RBI .40 1.00
RBI10 Manny Ramirez RBI 1.00 2.50

2005 Topps Hobby Masters

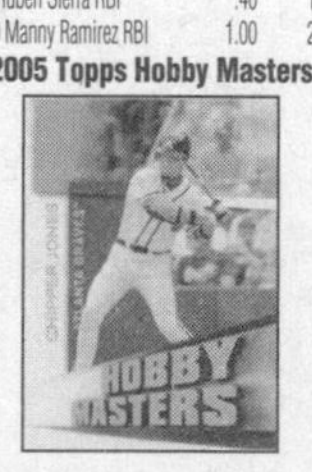

COMPLETE SET (20) 12.50 30.00
SERIES 1 ODDS 1:18 HOBBY, 1:6 HTA
1 Alex Rodriguez 1.25 3.00
2 Sammy Sosa 1.00 2.50
3 Ichiro Suzuki 1.25 3.00
4 Albert Pujols 1.25 3.00
5 Derek Jeter 2.50 6.00
6 Jim Thome .60 1.50
7 Vladimir Guerrero .60 1.50
8 Nomar Garciaparra .60 1.50
9 Mike Piazza 1.00 2.50
10 Jason Giambi .40 1.00
11 Ivan Rodriguez .60 1.50
12 Alfonso Soriano .60 1.50
13 Dontrelle Willis .40 1.00
14 Chipper Jones 1.00 2.50
15 Mark Prior .60 1.50
16 Todd Helton .60 1.50
17 Randy Johnson 1.00 2.50
18 Hank Blalock .40 1.00
19 Ken Griffey Jr. 2.00 5.00
20 Roger Clemens 1.25 3.00

2005 Topps On Deck Circle Relics

SER.2 ODDS 1:1493 H, 1:425 HTA, 1:1488 R
STATED PRINT RUN 275 SETS
CARDS ARE NOT SERIAL-NUMBERED
PRINT RUN INFO PROVIDED BY TOPPS
AP Albert Pujols 15.00 40.00
AR Alex Rodriguez 15.00 40.00
AS Alfonso Soriano 4.00 10.00
CB Carlos Beltran 4.00 10.00
HB Hank Blalock 4.00 10.00
IR Ivan Rodriguez 6.00 15.00
JT Jim Thome 6.00 15.00
SR Scott Rolen 6.00 15.00
SS Sammy Sosa 6.00 15.00
TH Todd Helton 6.00 15.00

2005 Topps Own the Game

COMPLETE SET (30) 12.50 30.00
SERIES 1 ODDS 1:12 H, 1:4 HTA, 1:12 R
1 Ichiro Suzuki 1.25 3.00
2 Todd Helton .60 1.50
3 Adrian Beltre 1.00 2.50
4 Albert Pujols 1.25 3.00
5 Adam Dunn .60 1.50
6 Jim Thome .60 1.50
7 Miguel Tejada .60 1.50
8 David Ortiz 1.00 2.50
9 Manny Ramirez 1.00 2.50
10 Scott Rolen .60 1.50
11 Gary Sheffield .40 1.00
12 Vladimir Guerrero .60 1.50
13 Jim Edmonds .60 1.50
14 Ivan Rodriguez .60 1.50
15 Lance Berkman .60 1.50
16 Michael Young .40 1.00
17 Juan Pierre .40 1.00
18 Craig Biggio .60 1.50
19 Johnny Damon .60 1.50
20 Jimmy Rollins .60 1.50
21 Scott Podsednik .40 1.00
22 Bobby Abreu .40 1.00
23 Lyle Overbay .40 1.00
24 Carl Crawford .60 1.50
25 Mark Loretta .40 1.00
26 Vinny Castilla .40 1.00
27 Curt Schilling .60 1.50
28 Johan Santana .60 1.50
29 Randy Johnson 1.00 2.50
30 Pedro Martinez .60 1.50

2005 Topps Spokesman Jersey Relic

SER.1 ODDS 1:5627 H, 1:1604 HTA, 1:4692 R
RELIC IS EVENT WORN
AR Alex Rodriguez 20.00 50.00

2005 Topps Team Topps Autographs

These cards were issued in some late season 2005 Topps products.

BOWMAN DRAFT ODDS 1:697 H
TOP.UP.ODDS 1:5374H,1:1537 HTA,1:5347R
BH Ben Hendrickson BD 4.00 10.00
JK Josh Kroeger BD 4.00 10.00
KS Kurt Suzuki TU 4.00 10.00

2005 Topps World Champions Red Sox Relics

SER.2 A ODDS 1:649 H, 1:185 HTA, 1:648 R
SER.2 B ODDS 1:311 H, 1:89 HTA, 1:310 R
BM Bill Mueller Bat A 6.00 15.00
BM2 Bill Mueller Jsy B 6.00 15.00
CS Curt Schilling Jsy B 6.00 15.00
DL Derek Lowe Jsy B 6.00 15.00
DMI Doug Mientkiewicz Bat B 6.00 15.00
DO David Ortiz Bat B 15.00 40.00
DO2 David Ortiz Jsy B 8.00 20.00
DR Dave Roberts Bat A 8.00 20.00
JD Johnny Damon Bat A 6.00 15.00
JD2 Johnny Damon Jsy B 6.00 15.00
KM Kevin Millar Bat B 12.00 30.00
KY Kevin Youkilis Bat A 4.00 10.00
MR Manny Ramirez Bat A 6.00 15.00
MR2 Manny Ramirez Home Jsy B 6.00 15.00
MR3 Manny Ramirez Road Jsy B 6.00 15.00
OC Orlando Cabrera Bat A 6.00 15.00
OC2 Orlando Cabrera Jsy B 6.00 15.00
PM Pedro Martinez Uni A 6.00 15.00
PR Pokey Reese Bat B 4.00 10.00
TN Trot Nixon Bat A 6.00 15.00

2005 Topps Update

This 330-card set was released in November, 2005. The set was issued in 10-card packs with a $1.50 SRP which came 36 packs to a box and eight boxes to a case. It is also important to note that a factory set consisting of just the base set (no inserts) was also included in the sealed hobby cases. The basic set consists of cards 1-84 featuring either players who were traded/signed as free agents after the original 2005 Topps set was released. Cards numbered 85-89 feature managers with new teams. Cards numbered 90-110 feature prospects, who previously had cards, who made an impact in baseball in 2005. Cards numbered 111 through 115 feature players who set records in 2005. Cards numbered 116 through 134 feature post-season highlights. Cards numbered 135 through 146 feature 2005 league leaders. Cards numbered 147 through 194 feature a mix of award winners and 2005 All-Stars. Cards numbered 195 through 202 feature players who were in the 2005 All-Star Home Run Derby. Cards numbered 203 through 220 feature players with tremendous futures. Cards numbered 221 through 310 feature Rookie Cards of players who had not been on Topps cards previously. Cards 311 through 330 feature some of the leading players selected in the 2005 amateur draft.

COMPLETE SET (330) 15.00 40.00
COMP.FACT.SET (330) 25.00 40.00
COMMON CARD (1-330) .07 .20
COM (90-110/203-220) .40 1.00
COMMON (116-134) .20 .50
COM (14/66/221-310) .40 1.00
COMMON (311-330) .40 1.00
PLATE ODDS 1:2009 H, 1:582 HTA, 1:2009 R
PLATE PRINT RUN 1 SET PER COLOR
BLACK-CYAN-MAGENTA-YELLOW ISSUED
NO PLATE PRICING DUE TO SCARCITY
1 Sammy Sosa .20 .50
2 Jeff Francoeur .20 .50
3 Tony Clark .07 .20
4 Michael Tucker .07 .20
5 Mike Matheny .07 .20
6 Eric Young .07 .20
7 Jose Valentin .07 .20
8 Matt Lawton .07 .20
9 Juan Rivera .07 .20
10 Shawn Green .07 .20
11 Aaron Boone .07 .20
12 Woody Williams .07 .20
13 Brad Wilkerson .07 .20
14 Anthony Reyes RC .60 1.50
15 Russ Adams .07 .20
16 Gustavo Chacin .07 .20
17 Michael Restovich .07 .20
18 Humberto Quintero .07 .20
19 Matt Ginter .07 .20
20 Scott Podsednik .07 .20
21 Byung-Hyun Kim .07 .20
22 Orlando Hernandez .07 .20
23 Mark Grudzielanek .07 .20
24 Jody Gerut .07 .20
25 Adrian Beltre .20 .50
26 Scott Schoeneweis .07 .20
27 Marlon Anderson .07 .20
28 Jason Vargas .07 .20
29 Claudio Vargas .07 .20
30 Jason Kendall .07 .20
31 Aaron Small .07 .20
32 Juan Cruz .07 .20
33 Placido Polanco .07 .20
34 Jorge Sosa .07 .20
35 John Olerud .07 .20
36 Ryan Langerhans .07 .20
37 Randy Winn .07 .20
38 Zach Duke .07 .20
39 Garrett Atkins .07 .20
40 Al Leiter .07 .20
41 Shawn Chacon .07 .20
42 Mark DeRosa .07 .20
43 Miguel Ojeda .07 .20
44 A.J. Pierzynski .07 .20
45 Carlos Lee .07 .20
46 LaTroy Hawkins .07 .20
47 Nick Green .07 .20
48 Shawn Estes .07 .20
49 Eli Marrero .07 .20
50 Jeff Kent .07 .20
51 Joe Randa .07 .20
52 Jose Hernandez .07 .20
53 Joe Blanton .07 .20
54 Huston Street .07 .20
55 Marlon Byrd .07 .20
56 Alex Sanchez .07 .20
57 Livan Hernandez .07 .20
58 Chris Young .12 .30
59 Brad Eldred .07 .20
60 Terrence Long .07 .20
61 Phil Nevin .07 .20
62 Kyle Farnsworth .07 .20
63 Jon Lieber .07 .20
64 Antonio Alfonseca .07 .20
65 Tony Graffanino .07 .20
66 Tadahito Iguchi RC .60 1.50
67 Brad Thompson .07 .20
68 Jose Vidro .07 .20
69 Jason Phillips .07 .20
70 Carl Pavano .07 .20
71 Pokey Reese .07 .20
72 Jerome Williams .07 .20
73 Kazuhisa Ishii .07 .20
74 Zach Day .07 .20
75 Edgar Renteria .07 .20
76 Mike Myers .07 .20
77 Jeff Cirillo .07 .20
78 Endy Chavez .07 .20
79 Jose Guillen .07 .20
80 Ugueth Urbina .07 .20
81 Vinny Castilla .07 .20
82 Javier Vazquez .07 .20
83 Willy Taveras .07 .20
84 Mark Mulder .07 .20
85 Mike Hargrove MG .07 .20
86 Buddy Bell MG .07 .20
87 Charlie Manuel MG .07 .20
88 Willie Randolph MG .07 .20
89 Bob Melvin MG .07 .20
90 Chris Lambert PROS .40 1.00
91 Homer Bailey PROS .40 1.00
92 Ervin Santana PROS .40 1.00
93 Bill Bray PROS .40 1.00
94 Thomas Diamond PROS .40 1.00
95 Trevor Plouffe PROS 1.00 2.50
96 James Houser PROS .40 1.00
97 Jake Stevens PROS .40 1.00
98 Anthony Whittington PROS .40 1.00
99 Philip Hughes PROS 1.00 2.50
100 Greg Golson PROS .40 1.00
101 Paul Maholm PROS .40 1.00
102 Carlos Quentin PROS .60 1.50
103 Dan Johnson PROS .40 1.00
104 Mark Rogers PROS .40 1.00
105 Neil Walker PROS .60 1.50
106 Omar Quintanilla PROS .40 1.00
107 Blake DeWitt PROS .60 1.50
108 Taylor Tankersley PROS .40 1.00
109 David Murphy PROS .60 1.50
110 Felix Hernandez PROS 1.25 3.00
111 Craig Biggio HL .12 .30
112 Greg Maddux HL .25 .60
113 Bobby Abreu HL .07 .20
114 Alex Rodriguez HL .25 .60
115 Trevor Hoffman HL .12 .30
116 A.Pierzynski .20 .50
T.Iguchi ALDS
117 Reggie Sanders NLDS .12 .30
118 B.Molina .12 .30
E.Santana ALDS
119 Burke .20 .50
Berkman
LaR NLDS
120 Garret Anderson ALCS .12 .30
121 A.J. Pierzynski ALCS .12 .30
122 Paul Konerko ALCS .20 .50
123 Joe Crede ALCS .12 .30
124 M.Buehrle .20 .50
J.Garland ALCS
125 F.Garcia .12 .30
J.Contreras ALCS
126 Reggie Sanders NLCS .12 .30
127 Roy Oswalt NLCS .20 .50
128 Roger Clemens NLCS .40 1.00
129 Albert Pujols NLCS .40 1.00
130 Roy Oswalt NLCS .20 .50
131 J.Crede .12 .30
B.Jenks WS
132 P.Konerko .20 .50
S.Podsed WS
133 Geoff Blum WS .12 .30

4 White Sox Sweep WS	.12	.30
5 ARod Ortiz Manny AL HR	.25	.60
6 Young ARod Vlad AL BA	.25	.60
7 Ortiz Teix Manny AL RBI	.20	.50
8 Colon Garland Lee AL W	.12	.30
9 Mill Johan Buehrle AL ERA	.12	.30
40 Johan Randy Lackey AL K	.20	.50
41 Andruw Lee Pujols NL HR	.25	.60
42 Lee Pujols Cabrera NL BA	.25	.60
43 Andruw Pujols Burr NL RBI	.25	.60
44 Willis Carp Oswalt NL W	.12	.30
45 Roger Andy Willis NL ERA	.25	.60
46 Peavy Carp Pedro NL K	.12	.30
47 Mark Teixeira AS	.12	.30
48 Brian Roberts AS	.07	.20
49 Michael Young AS	.07	.20
50 Alex Rodriguez AS	.25	.60
51 Johnny Damon AS	.12	.30
52 Vladimir Guerrero AS	.12	.30
153 Manny Ramirez AS	.20	.50
154 David Ortiz AS	.20	.50
155 Mariano Rivera AS	.25	.60
156 Joe Nathan AS	.07	.20
157 Albert Pujols AS	.25	.60
158 Jeff Kent AS	.07	.20
159 Felipe Lopez AS	.07	.20
160 Morgan Ensberg AS	.07	.20
161 Miguel Cabrera AS	.20	.50
162 Ken Griffey Jr. AS	.40	1.00
163 Andruw Jones AS	.07	.20
164 Paul Lo Duca AS	.07	.20
165 Chad Cordero AS	.07	.20
166 Ken Griffey Jr. Comeback	.40	1.00
167 Jason Giambi Comeback	.07	.20
168 Willy Taveras ROY	.07	.20
169 Huston Street ROY	.07	.20
170 Chris Carpenter AS	.12	.30
171 Bartolo Colon AS	.07	.20
172 Bobby Cox AS MG	.07	.20
173 Ozzie Guillen AS MG	.07	.20
174 Andruw Jones POY	.07	.20
175 Johnny Damon AS	.12	.30
176 Alex Rodriguez AS	.25	.60
177 David Ortiz AS	.20	.50
178 Manny Ramirez AS	.20	.50
179 Miguel Tejada AS	.12	.30
180 Vladimir Guerrero AS	.12	.30
181 Mark Teixeira AS	.12	.30
182 Ivan Rodriguez AS	.12	.30
183 Brian Roberts AS	.07	.20
184 Mark Buehrle AS	.12	.30
185 Bobby Abreu AS	.07	.20
186 Carlos Beltran AS	.12	.30
187 Albert Pujols AS	.25	.60
188 Derrek Lee AS	.07	.20
189 Jim Edmonds AS	.12	.30
190 Aramis Ramirez AS	.07	.20
191 Mike Piazza AS	.20	.50
192 Jeff Kent AS	.07	.20
193 David Eckstein AS	.07	.20
194 Chris Carpenter AS	.12	.30
195 Bobby Abreu HR	.07	.20
196 Ivan Rodriguez HR	.12	.30
197 Carlos Lee HR	.07	.20
198 David Ortiz HR	.20	.50
199 Hee-Seop Choi HR	.07	.20
200 Andruw Jones HR	.07	.20
201 Mark Teixeira HR	.12	.30
202 Jason Bay HR	.07	.20
203 Hanley Ramirez FUT	.60	1.50
204 Shin-Soo Choo FUT	.60	1.50
205 Justin Huber FUT	.40	1.00
206 Nelson Cruz FUT RC	3.00	8.00
207 Edwin Encarnacion FUT	1.00	2.50
208 Miguel Montero FUT RC	1.25	3.00
209 William Bergolla FUT	.40	1.00
210 Luis Montanez FUT	.40	1.00
211 Francisco Liriano FUT	1.00	2.50
212 Kevin Thompson FUT	.40	1.00
213 B.J. Upton FUT	.60	1.50
214 Conor Jackson FUT	.60	1.50
215 Delmon Young FUT	1.00	2.50
216 Andy LaRoche FUT	.40	1.00
217 Ryan Garko FUT	.40	1.00
218 Josh Barfield FUT	.60	1.50
219 Chris B.Young FUT	1.25	3.00
220 Justin Verlander FUT	8.00	20.00
221 Drew Anderson FY RC	.40	1.00
222 Luis Hernandez FY RC	.40	1.00
223 Jim Burt FY RC	.40	1.00
224 Mike Morse FY RC	1.25	3.00
225 Elliot Johnson FY RC	.40	1.00
226 C.J. Smith FY RC	.40	1.00
227 Casey McGehee FY RC	.60	1.50
228 Brian Miller FY RC	.40	1.00
229 Chris Vines FY RC	.40	1.00
230 D.J. Houlton FY RC	.40	1.00
231 Chuck Tiffany FY RC	1.00	2.50
232 Humberto Sanchez FY RC	.60	1.50
233 Baltazar Lopez FY RC	.40	1.00
234 Russ Martin FY RC	1.25	3.00
235 Dana Eveland FY RC	.40	1.00
236 Johan Silva FY RC	.40	1.00
237 Adam Harben FY RC	.40	1.00
238 Brian Bannister FY RC	.60	1.50
239 Adam Boeve FY RC	.40	1.00
240 Thomas Oldham FY RC	.40	1.00
241 Cody Haerther FY RC	.40	1.00
242 Dan Santin FY RC	.40	1.00
243 Daniel Haigwood FY RC	.40	1.00
244 Craig Tatum FY RC	.40	1.00
245 Martin Prado FY RC	2.50	6.00
246 Errol Simonitsch FY RC	.40	1.00
247 Lorenzo Scott FY RC	.40	1.00
248 Hayden Penn FY RC	.40	1.00
249 Heath Totten FY RC	.40	1.00
250 Nick Masset FY RC	.40	1.00
251 Pedro Lopez FY RC	.40	1.00
252 Ben Harrison FY	.40	1.00
253 Mike Spidale FY RC	.40	1.00
254 Jeremy Harts FY RC	.40	1.00
255 Danny Zell FY RC	.40	1.00
256 Kevin Collins FY RC	.40	1.00
257 Tony Arnerich FY RC	.40	1.00
258 Matt Albers FY RC	.40	1.00
259 Ricky Barrett FY RC	.40	1.00
260 Hernan Iribarren FY RC	.40	1.00
261 Sean Tracey FY RC	.40	1.00
262 Jerry Owens FY RC	.40	1.00
263 Steve Nelson FY RC	.40	1.00
264 Brandon McCarthy FY RC	.60	1.50
265 David Shepard FY RC	.40	1.00
266 Steven Bondurant FY RC	.40	1.00
267 Billy Sadler FY RC	.40	1.00
268 Ryan Feierabend FY RC	.40	1.00
269 Stuart Pomeranz FY RC	.40	1.00
270 Shaun Marcum FY	1.00	2.50
271 Erik Schindewolf FY RC	.40	1.00
272 Stefan Bailie FY RC	.40	1.00
273 Mike Esposito FY RC	.40	1.00
274 Buck Coats FY RC	.40	1.00
275 Andy Sides FY RC	.40	1.00
276 Micah Schnurstein FY RC	.40	1.00
277 Jesse Gutierrez FY RC	.40	1.00
278 Jake Postlewait FY RC	.40	1.00
279 Willy Mota FY RC	.40	1.00
280 Ryan Speier FY RC	.40	1.00
281 Frank Mata FY RC	.40	1.00
282 Jair Jurrjens FY RC	2.00	5.00
283 Nick Touchstone FY RC	.40	1.00
284 Matthew Kemp FY RC	2.00	5.00
285 Vinny Rottino FY RC	.40	1.00
286 J.B. Thurmond FY RC	.40	1.00
287 Kelvin Pichardo FY RC	.40	1.00
288 Scott Mitchinson FY RC	.40	1.00
289 Darwinson Salazar FY RC	.40	1.00
290 George Kottaras FY RC	.60	1.50
291 Kenny Durost FY RC	.40	1.00
292 Jonathan Sanchez FY RC	1.50	4.00
293 Brandon Moorhead FY RC	.40	1.00
294 Kennard Bibbs FY RC	.40	1.00
295 David Gassner FY RC	.40	1.00
296 Micah Furtado FY RC	.40	1.00
297 Ismael Ramirez FY RC	.40	1.00
298 Carlos Gonzalez FY RC	3.00	8.00
299 Brandon Sing FY RC	.40	1.00
300 Jason Motte FY RC	.60	1.50
301 Chuck James FY RC	1.00	2.50
302 Andy Santana FY RC	.40	1.00
303 Manny Parra FY RC	1.00	2.50
304 Chris B.Young FY RC	1.25	3.00
305 Juan Senreiso FY RC	.40	1.00
306 Franklin Morales FY RC	.60	1.50
307 Jared Gothreaux FY RC	.40	1.00
308 Jayce Tingler FY RC	.40	1.00
309 Matt Brown FY RC	.40	1.00
310 Frank Diaz FY RC	.40	1.00
311 Stephen Drew DP RC	1.25	3.00
312 Jered Weaver DP RC	2.00	5.00
313 Ryan Braun DP RC	3.00	8.00
314 John Mayberry Jr. DP RC	1.00	2.50
315 Aaron Thompson DP RC	.60	1.50
316 Cesar Carrillo DP RC	.60	1.50
317 Jacoby Ellsbury DP RC	3.00	8.00
318 Matt Garza DP RC	.60	1.50
319 Cliff Pennington DP RC	.40	1.00
320 Colby Rasmus DP RC	1.00	2.50
321 Chris Volstad DP RC	1.00	2.50
322 Ricky Romero DP RC	.60	1.50
323 Ryan Zimmerman DP RC	2.00	5.00
324 C.J. Henry DP RC	.60	1.50
325 Jay Bruce DP RC	3.00	8.00
326 Beau Jones DP RC	1.00	2.50
327 Mark McCormick DP RC	.40	1.00
328 Eli Iorg DP RC	.40	1.00
329 Andrew McCutchen DP RC	5.00	12.00
330 Mike Costanzo DP RC	.40	1.00

2005 Topps Update Box Bottoms

*BOX BOTTOM: 1X TO 2.5X BASIC
*BOX BOTTOM: .6X TO 1.5X BASIC RC
ONE FOUR-CARD SHEET PER HTA BOX
CL: 1/10/20/22/25/45/50/57/70/84/110
CL: 224/264/311-313

2005 Topps Update Gold

*GOLD 1-89: 3X TO 8X BASIC
*GOLD 90-110: 2X TO 5X BASIC
*GOLD 111-115/135-202: 3X TO 8X BASIC
*GOLD: 116-134: 1.5X TO 4X BASIC
*GOLD: 203-220: 2X TO 5X BASIC
*GOLD 14/66/221-310: 2X TO 5X BASIC
*GOLD 311-330: .6X TO 1.5X BASIC
STATED ODDS 1:4 H, 1:1 HTA, 1:4 R
STATED PRINT RUN 2005 SERIAL #'d SETS

2005 Topps Update All-Star Patches

STATED ODDS 1:910 H, 1:268 HTA, 1:910 R
PRINT RUNS B/WN 20-70 COPIES PER
NO PRICING ON QTY OF 25 OR LESS

AJ Andruw Jones/70	12.50	30.00
AP Albert Pujols/35	30.00	60.00
AR Alex Rodriguez/50	15.00	40.00
ARA Aramis Ramirez/60	10.00	25.00
BA Bobby Abreu/65	10.00	25.00
BC Bartolo Colon/60	10.00	25.00
BL Brad Lidge/65	10.00	25.00
BW Billy Wagner/50	10.00	25.00
CB Carlos Beltran/60	10.00	25.00
CC Chris Carpenter/70	10.00	25.00
CCO Chad Cordero/65	6.00	15.00
CL Carlos Lee/65	10.00	25.00
DE David Eckstein/65	12.50	30.00
DL Derrek Lee/65	12.50	30.00
DO David Ortiz/70	12.50	30.00
DW Dontrelle Willis/60	10.00	25.00
FL Felipe Lopez/35	8.00	20.00
GS Gary Sheffield/50	10.00	25.00
IS Ichiro Suzuki/50	20.00	50.00
JB Jason Bay/50	10.00	25.00
JD Johnny Damon/60	12.50	30.00
JE Jim Edmonds/50	10.00	25.00
JG Jon Garland/70	12.50	30.00
JI Jason Isringhausen/65	10.00	25.00
JK Jeff Kent/65	10.00	25.00
JN Joe Nathan/65	6.00	15.00
JP Jake Peavy/60	10.00	25.00
JS Johan Santana/60	12.50	30.00
JSM John Smoltz/65	12.50	30.00
KR Kenny Rogers/50	6.00	15.00
LC Luis Castillo/70	10.00	25.00
LH Livan Hernandez/50	10.00	25.00
MA Moises Alou/65	6.00	15.00
MB Mark Buehrle/60	10.00	25.00
MC Miguel Cabrera/70	12.50	30.00
MCL Matt Clement/70	10.00	25.00
ME Morgan Ensberg/60	10.00	25.00
MM Melvin Mora/30	12.50	30.00
MP Mike Piazza/50	15.00	40.00
MR Manny Ramirez/65	12.50	30.00
MRI Mariano Rivera/65	15.00	40.00
MT Miguel Tejada/60	10.00	25.00
MTE Mark Teixeira/60	12.50	30.00
MY Michael Young/50	10.00	25.00
PK Paul Konerko/70	10.00	25.00
RO Roy Oswalt/60	10.00	25.00
SP Scott Podsednik/65	10.00	25.00

2005 Topps Update All-Star Stitches

GROUP A ODDS 1:131 H, 1:81 HTA, 1:127 R
GROUP B ODDS 1:91 H, 1:45 HTA, 1:91 R
GROUP C ODDS 1:100 H, 1:41 HTA, 1:100 R
GROUP D ODDS 1:109 H, 1:34 HTA, 1:109 R
GROUP E ODDS 1:98 H, 1:29 HTA, 1:98 R
GROUP F ODDS 1:272 H, 1:89 HTA, 1:272 R

AJ Andruw Jones C	4.00	10.00
AP Albert Pujols E	8.00	20.00
AR Alex Rodriguez D	6.00	15.00
ARA Aramis Ramirez E	3.00	8.00
BA Bobby Abreu B	3.00	8.00
BC Bartolo Colon D	3.00	8.00
BL Brad Lidge D	3.00	8.00
BR Brian Roberts C	3.00	8.00
BW Billy Wagner C	3.00	8.00
CB Carlos Beltran D	3.00	8.00
CC Chris Carpenter E	4.00	10.00
CCO Chad Cordero D	3.00	8.00
CL Carlos Lee E	3.00	8.00
DE David Eckstein B	6.00	15.00
DL Derrek Lee F	4.00	10.00
DO David Ortiz E	4.00	10.00
DW Dontrelle Willis F	3.00	8.00
FL Felipe Lopez B	3.00	8.00
GS Gary Sheffield D	3.00	8.00
IR Ivan Rodriguez A	4.00	10.00
IS Ichiro Suzuki A	8.00	20.00
JB Jason Bay C	3.00	8.00
JD Johnny Damon B	4.00	10.00
JE Jim Edmonds A	3.00	8.00
JG Jon Garland E	4.00	10.00
JI Jason Isringhausen E	3.00	8.00
JK Jeff Kent C	3.00	8.00
JN Joe Nathan D	3.00	8.00
JP Jake Peavy D	3.00	8.00
JS Johan Santana C	4.00	10.00
JSM John Smoltz D	4.00	10.00
KR Kenny Rogers A	3.00	8.00
LC Luis Castillo B	3.00	8.00
LG Luis Gonzalez C	3.00	8.00
LH Livan Hernandez F	3.00	8.00
MA Moises Alou C	3.00	8.00
MB Mark Buehrle B	3.00	8.00
MC Miguel Cabrera E	4.00	10.00
MCL Matt Clement B	3.00	8.00
ME Morgan Ensberg B	3.00	8.00
MM Melvin Mora B	3.00	8.00
MP Mike Piazza E	4.00	10.00
MR Manny Ramirez E	4.00	10.00
MRI Mariano Rivera B	4.00	10.00
MT Miguel Tejada B	3.00	8.00
MTE Mark Teixeira C	3.00	8.00
MY Michael Young A	3.00	8.00
PK Paul Konerko A	3.00	8.00
RO Roy Oswalt A	3.00	8.00
SP Scott Podsednik A	6.00	15.00

2005 Topps Update Derby Digs Jersey Relics

STATED ODDS 1:3320 H,1:637 HTA,1:3320 R
STATED PRINT RUN 100 SERIAL #'d SETS

AJ Andruw Jones	10.00	25.00
BA Bobby Abreu	10.00	25.00
CL Carlos Lee	6.00	15.00
DO David Ortiz	10.00	25.00
IR Ivan Rodriguez	10.00	25.00
JB Jason Bay	6.00	15.00
MT Mark Teixeira	10.00	25.00

2005 Topps Update Hall of Fame Bat Relics

A ODDS 1:6406 H, 1:2012 HTA, 1:6406 R
B ODDS 1:1860 H, 1:548 HTA, 1:1860 R

RS Ryne Sandberg B	8.00	20.00
WB Wade Boggs A	6.00	15.00

2005 Topps Update Hall of Fame Dual Bat Relic

ODDS 1:13,392 H, 1:3815 HTA, 1:13,392 R
STATED PRINT RUN 200 SERIAL #'d CARDS

BS W.Boggs/R.Sandberg	12.50	30.00

2005 Topps Update Legendary Sacks Relics

Please note that while the cards say "Game-Used Jersey" the material embedded in the cards look to be game-used base material.
STATED ODDS 1:965 H, 1:281 HTA, 1:965 R
STATED PRINT RUN 300 SERIAL #'d SETS
CARDS FEATURE CELEBRITY JSY SWATCH

AD Andre Dawson	6.00	15.00
BJ Bo Jackson	10.00	25.00
DW Dave Winfield	6.00	15.00
HR Harold Reynolds	6.00	15.00
JA Jim Abbott	6.00	15.00
LW Lou Whitaker	6.00	15.00
MF Mark Fidrych	10.00	25.00
OS Ozzie Smith	10.00	25.00
RF Rollie Fingers	6.00	15.00

2005 Topps Update Midsummer Covers Ball Relics

STATED ODDS 1:524 H, 1:512 HTA
STATED PRINT RUN 150 SERIAL #'d SETS

AP Albert Pujols	20.00	50.00
AR Alex Rodriguez	12.00	30.00
BR Brian Roberts	10.00	25.00
CB Carlos Beltran	10.00	25.00
DL Derrek Lee	15.00	40.00
DW Dontrelle Willis	10.00	25.00
IS Ichiro Suzuki	12.00	30.00
MT Miguel Tejada	10.00	25.00
RC Roger Clemens	15.00	40.00
VG Vladimir Guerrero	15.00	40.00

2005 Topps Update Signature Moves

A ODDS 1:317,088H,1:103,008HTA,1:40,176R
B ODDS 1:126,836 H,1:51,504 HTA,1:40,176 R
C ODDS 1:1220 H, 1:339 HTA, 1:1220 R
D ODDS 1:1128 H, 1:323 HTA, 1:1128 R
E ODDS 1:916 H, 1:262 HTA, 1:916 R
GROUP A PRINT RUN 15 #'d CARDS
GROUP B PRINT RUN 25 #'d CARDS
GROUP C PRINT RUN 275 #'d SETS
GROUP D PRINT RUN 475 #'d SETS
NO GROUP A-B PRICING DUE TO SCARCITY
RED ODDS 1:6676 H, 1:1908 HTA, 1:6676 R
RED FOIL PRINT RUN 25 SERIAL #'d SETS
NO RED FOIL PRICING DUE TO SCARCITY

BL Bobby Livingston D/475	6.00	15.00
BS Benito Santiago E	12.50	30.00
CJS C.J. Smith D/475	6.00	15.00
GK George Kottaras D/475	8.00	20.00
GP Glen Perkins C/275	8.00	20.00
HS Humberto Sanchez E	10.00	25.00
JP Jake Postlewait C/275	6.00	15.00
JV Justin Verlander C/275	50.00	100.00
KI Kazuhisa Ishii C/275	10.00	25.00
MA Matt Albers D/475	6.00	15.00
MM Mark Mulder C/275	10.00	25.00
RS Richie Sexson C/275	10.00	25.00
TC Travis Chick D/475	6.00	15.00
TG Troy Glaus C/275	10.00	25.00
TH Tim Hudson C/275	10.00	25.00
TW Tony Womack E	6.00	15.00

2005 Topps Update Touch Em All Base Relics

STATED ODDS 1:238 H, 1:77 HTA, 1:238 R
STATED PRINT RUN 1000 SERIAL #'d SETS

AP Albert Pujols	12.50	30.00
AR Alex Rodriguez	8.00	20.00
DL Derrek Lee	6.00	15.00
DO David Ortiz	6.00	15.00
GS Gary Sheffield	4.00	10.00
IR Ivan Rodriguez	6.00	15.00
IS Ichiro Suzuki	10.00	25.00
MR Manny Ramirez	6.00	15.00
MT Miguel Tejada	4.00	10.00
VG Vladimir Guerrero	6.00	15.00

2005 Topps Update Washington Nationals Inaugural Lineup

COMPLETE SET (10)	2.50	6.00
STATED ODDS 1:10 H, 1:4 HTA, 1:10 R		
BS Brian Schneider	.40	1.00
BW Brad Wilkerson	.40	1.00
CG Cristian Guzman	.40	1.00
JG Jose Guillen	.40	1.00
JV Jose Vidro	.40	1.00
LH Livan Hernandez	.40	1.00
NJ Nick Johnson	.40	1.00
TS Termel Sledge	.40	1.00
VC Vinny Castilla	.40	1.00
TEAM Team Photo	.40	1.00

2005 Topps 1955 National

Each collector who purchased a VIP ticket for the 2005 Sports Collectors National Convention in Chicago received this four-card set of 1955 stars who were not issued in the original set. The card numbers assigned matched those numbers not used in the original 1955 Topps set and the card size matches the original 1955 measurements.

COMPLETE SET (4)	8.00	20.00
175 Stan Musial	6.00	15.00
186 Whitey Ford	2.50	6.00
203 Bob Feller	2.50	6.00
209 Herb Score	1.50	4.00

2005 Topps XXL Cubs

COMPLETE SET (4)	2.00	5.00
ONE 4 CARD SET PER PACK		
1 Derrek Lee	.40	1.00
2 Mark Prior	.60	1.50
3 Nomar Garciaparra	.60	1.50
4 Greg Maddux	1.25	3.00

2005 Topps XXL Red Sox

COMPLETE SET (4)	2.00	5.00
ONE 4-CARD SET PER PACK		
1 David Ortiz	1.00	2.50
2 Manny Ramirez	1.00	2.50
3 Johnny Damon	.60	1.50
4 Curt Schilling	.60	1.50

2005 Topps XXL Yankees

COMPLETE SET (4)	4.00	10.00
ONE 4-CARD SET PER PACK		
1 Alex Rodriguez	1.25	3.00
2 Derek Jeter	2.50	6.00
3 Hideki Matsui	1.50	4.00
4 Randy Johnson	1.00	2.50

2006 Topps Pre-Production

COMPLETE SET (3)	.75	2.00
3-CARD SETS MAILED TO HOBBY DEALERS		
PP1 Ichiro Suzuki	.60	1.50
PP2 Alex Rodriguez	.60	1.50
PP3 Albert Pujols	.60	1.50

2006 Topps

This 659-card set was issued over two series. The first series was released in February, 2006 and the second series was released in June, 2006. The cards were issued in a myriad of forms including 10-card hobby packs with an $1.59 SRP which came 36 packs to a box and 10 boxes to a case. Retail packs consisted of 12-card packs with an $1.99 SRP and those cards came 24 packs to a box and 20 boxes to a case. There were also rack packs which had 18 cards and a $2.99 SRP and those packs came 24 packs to a box and three boxes to a case. There were also special packs issued for Target and Walmart. Card number 297, Alex Gordon, was pulled from circulation almost immediately, although a few copies in various forms of production were located in packs. In addition, Pete Mackanin and John Koronka cards were changed for the factory sets. This product has many sub sets including Award Winners (243-265); Managers/Team Cards (266-295, 586-615); Rookies (296-330), 616-645), Team Stars (326-330). Assorted Multi-Player Cards (646-660). A few Alay Soler cards were inserted into series two packs unannounced and those cards are very scarce.

COMP.HOBBY SET (664)	50.00	80.00
COMP.HOLIDAY SET (659)	50.00	80.00
COMP.CARDINALS SET (664)	50.00	80.00
COMP.CUBS SET (664)	50.00	80.00
COMP.PIRATES SET (664)	50.00	80.00
COMP.RED SOX SET (664)	50.00	80.00
COMP.YANKEES SET (664)	50.00	80.00
COMPLETE SET (659)	30.00	80.00
COMPLETE SERIES 1 (329)	15.00	40.00
COMPLETE SERIES 2 (330)	15.00	40.00
COMMON CARD (1-660)	.07	.20
COMP.SER.1 SET EXCLUDES CARD 297		
CARD 297 NOT INTENDED FOR RELEASE		
CARDS 287b AND 312b ISSUED IN FACT.SET		
2 TICKETS EXCH.CARD RANDOM IN PACKS		
OVERALL PLATE SER.1 ODDS 1:246 HTA		
OVERALL PLATE SER.2 ODDS 1:193 HTA		
PLATE PRINT RUN 1 SET PER COLOR		
BLACK-CYAN-MAGENTA-YELLOW ISSUED		
NO PLATE PRICING DUE TO SCARCITY		
1 Alex Rodriguez	.25	.60
2 Jose Valentin	.07	.20
3 Garrett Atkins	.07	.20
4 Scott Hatteberg	.07	.20
5 Carl Crawford	.12	.30
6 Armando Benitez	.07	.20
7 Mickey Mantle	.60	1.50
8 Mike Morse	.07	.20
9 Damian Miller	.07	.20
10 Clint Barmes	.07	.20
11 Michael Barrett	.07	.20
12 Coco Crisp	.07	.20
13 Tadahito Iguchi	.07	.20
14 Chris Snyder	.07	.20
15 Brian Roberts	.07	.20
16 David Wright	.15	.40
17 Victor Santos	.07	.20
18 Trevor Hoffman	.12	.30
19 Jeremy Reed	.07	.20
20 Bobby Abreu	.07	.20
21 Lance Berkman	.12	.30
22 Zach Day	.07	.20
23 Jonny Gomes	.07	.20
24 Jason Marquis	.07	.20
25 Chipper Jones	.20	.50
26 Scott Hairston	.07	.20
27 Ryan Dempster	.07	.20
28 Brandon Inge	.07	.20
29 Aaron Harang	.07	.20
30 Jon Garland	.07	.20
31 Pokey Reese	.07	.20
32 Mike MacDougal	.07	.20
33 Mike Lieberthal	.07	.20
34 Cesar Izturis	.07	.20
35 Brad Wilkerson	.07	.20
36 Jeff Suppan	.07	.20
37 Adam Everett	.07	.20
38 Bengie Molina	.07	.20
39 Rickie Weeks	.07	.20
40 Jorge Posada	.12	.30

41 Rheal Cormier .07 .20
42 Reed Johnson .07 .20
43 Laynce Nix .07 .20
44 Carl Everett .07 .20
45 Greg Maddux .25 .60
46 Jeff Francis .07 .20
47 Felipe Lopez .07 .20
48 Dan Johnson .07 .20
49 Humberto Cota .07 .20
50 Manny Ramirez .20 .50
51 Juan Uribe .07 .20
52 Jaret Wright .07 .20
53 Tomo Ohka .07 .20
54 Mike Matheny .07 .20
55 Joe Mauer .12 .30
56 Jarrod Washburn .07 .20
57 Randy Winn .07 .20
58 Pedro Feliz .07 .20
59 Kenny Rogers .07 .20
60 Rocco Baldelli .07 .20
61 Eric Hinske .07 .20
62 Damaso Marte .07 .20
63 Desi Relaford .07 .20
64 Juan Encarnacion .07 .20
65 Nomar Garciaparra .12 .30
66 Shawn Estes .07 .20
67 Brian Jordan .07 .20
68 Steve Kline .07 .20
69 Braden Looper .07 .20
70 Carlos Lee .07 .20
71 Tom Glavine .12 .30
72 Craig Biggio .12 .30
73 Steve Finley .07 .20
74 David Newhan .07 .20
75 Eric Gagne .07 .20
76 Tony Graffanino .07 .20
77 Dallas McPherson .07 .20
78 Nick Punto .07 .20
79 Mark Kotsay .07 .20
80 Kerry Wood .07 .20
81 Kyle Farnsworth .07 .20
82 Huston Street .07 .20
83 Endy Chavez .07 .20
84 So Taguchi .07 .20
85 Hank Blalock .07 .20
86 Brad Radke .07 .20
87 Chien-Ming Wang .12 .30
88 B.J. Surhoff .07 .20
89 Glendon Rusch .07 .20
90 Mark Buehrle .12 .30
91 Rafael Betancourt .07 .20
92 Lance Cormier .07 .20
93 Alex Gonzalez .07 .20
94 Matt Stairs .07 .20
95 Andy Pettitte .12 .30
96 Jesse Crain .07 .20
97 Kenny Lofton .07 .20
98 Geoff Blum .07 .20
99 Mark Redman .07 .20
100 Barry Bonds .30 .75
101 Chad Orvella .07 .20
102 Xavier Nady .07 .20
103 Junior Spivey .07 .20
104 Bernie Williams .12 .30
105 Victor Martinez .12 .30
106 Nook Logan .07 .20
107 Mark Teahen .07 .20
108 Mike Lamb .07 .20
109 Jayson Werth .12 .30
110 Mariano Rivera .25 .60
111 Erubiel Durazo .07 .20
112 Ryan Vogelsong .07 .20
113 Bobby Madritsch .07 .20
114 Travis Lee .07 .20
115 Adam Dunn .12 .30
116 David Riske .07 .20
117 Troy Percival .07 .20
118 Chad Tracy .07 .20
119 Andy Marte .07 .20
120 Edgar Renteria .07 .20
121 Jason Giambi .07 .20
122 Justin Morneau .12 .30
123 J.T. Snow .07 .20
124 Danys Baez .07 .20
125 Carlos Delgado .07 .20
126 John Buck .07 .20
127 Shannon Stewart .07 .20
128 Mike Cameron .07 .20
129 Joe McEwing .07 .20
130 Richie Sexson .07 .20
131 Rod Barajas .07 .20
132 Russ Adams .07 .20
133 J.D. Closser .07 .20
134 Ramon Ortiz .07 .20
135 Josh Beckett .07 .20
136 Ryan Freel .07 .20
137 Victor Zambrano .07 .20
138 Ronnie Belliard .07 .20
139 Jason Michaels .07 .20
140 Brian Giles .07 .20
141 Randy Wolf .07 .20
142 Robinson Cano .12 .30
143 Joe Blanton .07 .20
144 Esteban Loaiza .07 .20
145 Troy Glaus .07 .20
146 Matt Clement .07 .20
147 Geoff Jenkins .07 .20
148 John Thomson .07 .20
149 A.J. Pierzynski .07 .20
150 Pedro Martinez .12 .30
151 Roger Clemens .25 .60
152 Jack Wilson .07 .20
153 Ray King .07 .20
154 Ryan Church .07 .20
155 Paul Lo Duca .07 .20
156 Dan Wheeler .07 .20
157 Carlos Zambrano .12 .30
158 Mike Timlin .07 .20
159 Brandon Claussen .07 .20
160 Travis Hafner .07 .20
161 Chris Shelton .07 .20
162 Rafael Furcal .07 .20
163 Tom Gordon .07 .20
164 Noah Lowry .07 .20
165 Larry Walker .12 .30
166 Dave Roberts .12 .30
167 Scott Schoeneweis .07 .20
168 Julian Tavarez .07 .20
169 Jhonny Peralta .07 .20
170 Vernon Wells .07 .20
171 Jorge Cantu .07 .20
172 Todd Greene .07 .20
173 Willy Taveras .07 .20
174 Corey Patterson .07 .20
175 Ivan Rodriguez .12 .30
176 Bobby Kielty .07 .20
177 Jose Reyes .12 .30
178 Barry Zito .12 .30
179 Deivi Cruz .07 .20
180 Mark Teixeira .12 .30
181 Chone Figgins .07 .20
182 Aaron Rowand .07 .20
183 Tim Wakefield .12 .30
184 Mike Maroth .07 .20
185 Johnny Damon .12 .30
186 Vicente Padilla .07 .20
187 Ryan Klesko .07 .20
188 Gary Matthews .07 .20
189 Jose Mesa .07 .20
190 Nick Johnson .07 .20
191 Freddy Garcia .07 .20
192 Larry Bigbie .07 .20
193 Chris Ray .07 .20
194 Torii Hunter .07 .20
195 Mike Sweeney .07 .20
196 Brad Penny .07 .20
197 Jason Frasor .07 .20
198 Kevin Mench .07 .20
199 Adam Kennedy .07 .20
200 Albert Pujols .25 .60
201 Jody Gerut .07 .20
202 Luis Gonzalez .07 .20
203 Zack Greinke .12 .30
204 Miguel Cairo .07 .20
205 Jimmy Rollins .12 .30
206 Edgardo Alfonzo .07 .20
207 Billy Wagner .07 .20
208 B.J. Ryan .07 .20
209 Orlando Hudson .07 .20
210 Preston Wilson .07 .20
211 Melvin Mora .07 .20
212 Bill Mueller .07 .20
213 Javy Lopez .07 .20
214 Wilson Betemit .07 .20
215 Garret Anderson .07 .20
216 Russell Branyan .07 .20
217 Jeff Weaver .07 .20
218 Doug Mientkiewicz .07 .20
219 Mark Ellis .07 .20
220 Jason Bay .07 .20
221 Adam LaRoche .07 .20
222 C.C. Sabathia .12 .30
223 Humberto Quintero .07 .20
224 Bartolo Colon .07 .20
225 Ichiro Suzuki .25 .60
226 Brett Tomko .07 .20
227 Corey Koskie .07 .20
228 David Eckstein .07 .20
229 Cristian Guzman .07 .20
230 Jeff Kent .07 .20
231 Chris Capuano .07 .20
232 Rodrigo Lopez .07 .20
233 Jason Phillips .07 .20
234 Luis Rivas .07 .20
235 Cliff Floyd .07 .20
236 Gil Meche .07 .20
237 Adam Eaton .07 .20
238 Matt Morris .07 .20
239 Kyle Davies .07 .20
240 David Wells .07 .20
241 John Smoltz .20 .50
242 Felix Hernandez .12 .30
243 Kenny Rogers GG .07 .20
244 Mark Teixeira GG .12 .30
245 Orlando Hudson GG .07 .20
246 Derek Jeter GG .50 1.25
247 Eric Chavez GG .07 .20
248 Torii Hunter GG .07 .20
249 Vernon Wells GG .07 .20
250 Ichiro Suzuki GG .25 .60
251 Greg Maddux GG .25 .60
252 Mike Matheny GG .07 .20
253 Derrek Lee GG .07 .20
254 Luis Castillo GG .07 .20
255 Omar Vizquel GG .12 .30
256 Mike Lowell GG .07 .20
257 Andruw Jones GG .07 .20
258 Jim Edmonds GG .12 .30
259 Bobby Abreu GG .07 .20
260 Bartolo Colon CY .07 .20
261 Chris Carpenter CY .12 .30
262 Alex Rodriguez MVP .25 .60
263 Albert Pujols MVP .25 .60
264 Huston Street ROY .07 .20
265 Ryan Howard ROY .15 .40
266 Bob Melvin MG .07 .20
267 Bobby Cox MG .07 .20
268 Baltimore Orioles TC .07 .20
269 Boston Red Sox TC .12 .30
270 Chicago White Sox TC .07 .20
271 Dusty Baker MG .07 .20
272 Jerry Narron MG .07 .20
273 Cleveland Indians TC .07 .20
274 Clint Hurdle MG .07 .20
275 Detroit Tigers TC .07 .20
276 Jack McKeon MG .07 .20
277 Phil Garner MG .07 .20
278 Kansas City Royals TC .07 .20
279 Jim Tracy MG .07 .20
280 Los Angeles Angels TC .07 .20
281 Milwaukee Brewers TC .07 .20
282 Minnesota Twins TC .07 .20
283 Willie Randolph MG .07 .20
284 New York Yankees TC .12 .30
285 Oakland Athletics TC .07 .20
286 Charlie Manuel MG .07 .20
287a Pete Mackanin MG ERR .07 .20
287b Pete Mackanin MG COR .07 .20
288 Bruce Bochy MG .12 .30
289 Felipe Alou MG .07 .20
290 Seattle Mariners TC .07 .20
291 Tony LaRussa MG .12 .30
292 Tampa Bay Devil Rays TC .07 .20
293 Texas Rangers TC .07 .20
294 Toronto Blue Jays TC .07 .20
295 Frank Robinson MG .12 .30
296 Anderson Hernandez (RC) .20 .50
297A Alex Gordon (RC) Full 150.00 250.00
297B Alex Gordon Cut Out 30.00 60.00
297C Alex Gordon Blank Gold 20.00 50.00
297D Alex Gordon Blank Silver
298 Jason Botts (RC) .20 .50
299 Jeff Mathis (RC) .20 .50
300 Ryan Garko (RC) .20 .50
301 Charlton Jimerson (RC) .20 .50
302 Chris Denorfia (RC) .20 .50
303 Anthony Reyes (RC) .20 .50
304 Bryan Bullington (RC) .20 .50
305 Chuck James (RC) .20 .50
306 Danny Sandoval RC .20 .50
307 Walter Young (RC) .20 .50
308 Fausto Carmona (RC) .20 .50
309 Francisco Liriano (RC) .50 1.25
310 Hong-Chih Kuo (RC) .50 1.25
311 Joe Saunders (RC) .20 .50
312a John Koronka Cubs (RC) .20 .50
312b John Koronka Rangers (RC) .20 .50
313 Robert Andino RC .20 .50
314 Shaun Marcum (RC) .20 .50
315 Tom Gorzelanny (RC) .20 .50
316 Craig Breslow RC .20 .50
317 Chris DeMaria RC .20 .50
318 Brayan Pena (RC) .20 .50
319 Rich Hill (RC) .50 1.25
320 Rick Short (RC) .20 .50
321 C.J. Wilson (RC) .30 .75
322 Marshall McDougall (RC) .20 .50
323 Darrell Rasner (RC) .20 .50
324 Brandon Watson (RC) .20 .50
325 Paul McAnulty (RC) .20 .50
326 D.Jeter .50 1.25
A.Rodriguez TS
327 M.Tejada .12 .30
M.Mora TS
328 M.Giles .20 .50
C.Jones TS
329 M.Ramirez .20 .50
D.Ortiz TS
330 M.Barrett .25 .60
G.Maddux TS
331 Matt Holliday .20 .50
332 Orlando Cabrera .07 .20
333 Ryan Langerhans .07 .20
334 Lew Ford .07 .20
335 Mark Prior .12 .30
336 Ted Lilly .07 .20
337 Michael Young .07 .20
338 Livan Hernandez .07 .20
339 Yadier Molina .20 .50
340 Eric Chavez .07 .20
341 Miguel Batista .07 .20
342 Bruce Chen .07 .20
343 Sean Casey .07 .20
344 Doug Davis .07 .20
345 Andruw Jones .07 .20
346 Hideki Matsui .20 .50
347 Joe Randa .07 .20
348 Reggie Sanders .07 .20
349 Jason Jennings .07 .20
350 Joe Nathan .07 .20
351 Jose Lopez .07 .20
352 John Lackey .12 .30
353 Claudio Vargas .07 .20
354 Grady Sizemore .12 .30
355 Jon Papelbon (RC) 1.00 2.50
356 Luis Matos .07 .20
357 Orlando Hernandez .07 .20
358 Jamie Moyer .07 .20
359 Chase Utley .12 .30
360 Moises Alou .07 .20
361 Chad Cordero .07 .20
362 Brian McCann .07 .20
363 Jermaine Dye .07 .20
364 Ryan Madson .07 .20
365 Aramis Ramirez .07 .20
366 Matt Treanor .07 .20
367 Ray Durham .07 .20
368 Khalil Greene .07 .20
369 Mike Hampton .07 .20
370 Mike Mussina .12 .30
371 Brad Hawpe .07 .20
372 Marlon Byrd .07 .20
373 Woody Williams .07 .20
374 Victor Diaz .07 .20
375 Brady Clark .07 .20
376 Luis Gonzalez .07 .20
377 Raul Ibanez .12 .30
378 Tony Clark .07 .20
379 Shawn Chacon .07 .20
380 Marcus Giles .07 .20
381 Odalis Perez .07 .20
382 Steve Trachsel .07 .20
383 Russ Ortiz .07 .20
384 Toby Hall .07 .20
385 Bill Hall .07 .20
386 Luke Hudson .07 .20
387 Ken Griffey Jr. .40 1.00
388 Tim Hudson .12 .30
389 Brian Moehler .07 .20
390 Jake Peavy .07 .20
391 Casey Blake .07 .20
392 Sidney Ponson .07 .20
393 Brian Schneider .07 .20
394 J.J. Hardy .07 .20
395 Austin Kearns .07 .20
396 Pat Burrell .07 .20
397 Jason Vargas .07 .20
398 Ryan Howard .15 .40
399 Joe Crede .07 .20
400 Vladimir Guerrero .12 .30
401 Roy Halladay .12 .30
402 David Dellucci .07 .20
403 Brandon Webb .12 .30
404 Marlon Anderson .07 .20
405 Miguel Tejada .12 .30
406 Ryan Doumit .07 .20
407 Kevin Youkilis .07 .20
408 Jon Lieber .07 .20
409 Edwin Encarnacion .20 .50
410 Miguel Cabrera .20 .50
411 A.J. Burnett .07 .20
412 David Bell .07 .20
413 Gregg Zaun .07 .20
414 Lance Niekro .07 .20
415 Shawn Green .07 .20
416 Roberto Hernandez .07 .20
417 Jay Gibbons .07 .20
418 Johnny Estrada .07 .20
419 Omar Vizquel .12 .30
420 Gary Sheffield .07 .20
421 Brad Halsey .07 .20
422 Aaron Cook .07 .20
423 David Ortiz .20 .50
424 Tony Womack .07 .20
425 Joe Kennedy .07 .20
426 Dustin McGowan .07 .20
427 Carl Pavano .07 .20
428 Nick Green .07 .20
429 Francisco Cordero .07 .20
430 Octavio Dotel .07 .20
431 Julio Franco .07 .20
432 Brett Myers .07 .20
433 Casey Kotchman .07 .20
434 Frank Catalanotto .07 .20
435 Paul Konerko .12 .30
436 Keith Foulke .07 .20
437 Juan Rivera .07 .20
438 Todd Pratt .07 .20
439 Ben Broussard .07 .20
440 Scott Kazmir .12 .30
441 Rich Aurilia .07 .20
442 Craig Monroe .07 .20
443 Danny Kolb .07 .20
444 Curtis Granderson .15 .40
445 Jeff Francoeur .20 .50
446 Dustin Hermanson .07 .20
447 Jacque Jones .07 .20
448 Bobby Crosby .07 .20
449 Jason LaRue .07 .20
450 Derrek Lee .07 .20
451 Curt Schilling .12 .30
452 Jake Westbrook .07 .20
453 Daniel Cabrera .07 .20
454 Bobby Jenks .07 .20
455 Dontrelle Willis .07 .20
456 Brad Lidge .07 .20
457 Shea Hillenbrand .07 .20
458 Luis Castillo .07 .20
459 Mark Hendrickson .07 .20
460 Randy Johnson .20 .50
461 Placido Polanco .07 .20
462 Aaron Boone .07 .20
463 Todd Walker .07 .20
464 Nick Swisher .12 .30
465 Joel Pineiro .07 .20
466 Jay Payton .07 .20
467 Cliff Lee .12 .30
468 Johan Santana .12 .30
469 Josh Willingham .12 .30
470 Jeremy Bonderman .07 .20
471 Runelvys Hernandez .07 .20
472 Duaner Sanchez .07 .20
473 Jason Lane .07 .20
474 Trot Nixon .07 .20
475 Ramon Hernandez .07 .20
476 Mike Lowell .07 .20
477 Chan Ho Park .12 .30
478 Doug Waechter .07 .20
479 Carlos Silva .07 .20
480 Jose Contreras .07 .20
481 Vinny Castilla .07 .20
482 Chris Reitsma .07 .20
483 Jose Guillen .07 .20
484 Aaron Hill .07 .20
485 Kevin Millwood .07 .20
486 Wily Mo Pena .07 .20
487 Rich Harden .07 .20
488 Chris Carpenter .12 .30
489 Jason Bartlett .07 .20
490 Magglio Ordonez .12 .30
491 John Rodriguez .07 .20
492 Bob Wickman .07 .20
493 Eddie Guardado .07 .20
494 Kip Wells .07 .20
495 Adrian Beltre .20 .50
496 Jose Capellan (RC) .20 .50
497 Scott Podsednik .07 .20
498 Brad Thompson .07 .20
499 Aaron Heilman .07 .20
500 Derek Jeter .50 1.25
501 Emil Brown .07 .20
502 Morgan Ensberg .07 .20
503 Nate Bump .07 .20
504 Phil Nevin .07 .20
505 Jason Schmidt .07 .20
506 Michael Cuddyer .07 .20
507 John Patterson .07 .20
508 Danny Haren .07 .20
509 Freddy Sanchez .07 .20
510 J.D. Drew .07 .20
511 Dmitri Young .07 .20
512 Eric Milton .07 .20
513 Ervin Santana .07 .20
514 Mark Loretta .07 .20
515 Mark Grudzielanek .07 .20
516 Derrick Turnbow .07 .20
517 Denny Bautista .07 .20
518 Lyle Overbay .07 .20
519 Julio Lugo .07 .20
520 Carlos Beltran .12 .30
521 Jose Cruz Jr. .07 .20
522 Jason Isringhausen .07 .20
523 Bronson Arroyo .07 .20
524 Ben Sheets .07 .20
525 Zach Duke .07 .20
526 Ryan Wagner .07 .20
527 Jose Vidro .07 .20
528 Doug Mirabelli .07 .20
529 Kris Benson .07 .20
530 Carlos Guillen .07 .20
531 Juan Pierre .07 .20
532 Scot Shields .07 .20
533 Scott Hatteberg .07 .20
534 Tim Stauffer .07 .20
535 Jim Edmonds .12 .30
536 Scot Eyre .07 .20
537 Ben Johnson .07 .20
538 Mark Mulder .07 .20
539 Juan Rincon .07 .20
540 Gustavo Chacin .07 .20
541 Oliver Perez .07 .20
542 Chris Young .07 .20
543 Edinson Volquez .07 .20
544 Mark Bellhorn .07 .20
545 Kelvim Escobar .07 .20
546 Andy Sisco .07 .20
547 Derek Lowe .07 .20
548 Sean Burroughs .07 .20
549 Erik Bedard .07 .20
550 Alfonso Soriano .12 .30
551 Matt Murton .07 .20
552 Eric Byrnes .07 .20
553 Chris Duffy .07 .20
554 Kazuo Matsui .07 .20
555 Scott Rolen .12 .30
556 Rob Mackowiak .07 .20
557 Chris Burke .07 .20
558 Jeromy Burnitz .07 .20
559 Jerry Hairston Jr. .07 .20
560 Jim Thome .12 .30
561 Miguel Olivo .07 .20
562 Jose Castillo .07 .20
563 Brad Ausmus .07 .20
564 Yorvit Torrealba .07 .20
565 David DeJesus .07 .20
566 Paul Byrd .07 .20
567 Brandon Backe .07 .20
568 Aubrey Huff .07 .20
569 Mike Jacobs .07 .20
570 Todd Helton .12 .30
571 Angel Berroa .07 .20
572 Todd Jones .07 .20
573 Jeff Bagwell .12 .30
574 Darin Erstad .07 .20
575 Roy Oswalt .12 .30
576 Rondell White .07 .20
577 Alex Rios .07 .20
578 Wes Helms .07 .20
579 Javier Vazquez .07 .20
580 Frank Thomas .20 .50
581 Brian Fuentes .07 .20
582 Francisco Rodriguez .12 .30
583 Craig Counsell .07 .20
584 Jorge Sosa .07 .20
585 Mike Piazza .20 .50
586 Mike Scioscia MG .07 .20
587 Joe Torre MG .12 .30
588 Ken Macha MG .07 .20
589 John Gibbons MG .07 .20
590 Joe Maddon MG .07 .20
591 Eric Wedge MG .07 .20
592 Mike Hargrove MG .07 .20
593 Sam Perlozzo MG .07 .20
594 Buck Showalter MG .07 .20
595 Terry Francona MG .07 .20
596 Buddy Bell MG .07 .20
597 Jim Leyland MG .07 .20
598 Ron Gardenhire MG .07 .20
599 Ozzie Guillen MG .07 .20
600 Ned Yost MG .07 .20
601 Atlanta Braves TC .07 .20
602 Philadelphia Phillies TC .07 .20
603 New York Mets TC .12 .30
604 Washington Nationals TC .07 .20
605 Florida Marlins TC .07 .20
606 Houston Astros TC .07 .20
607 Chicago Cubs TC .07 .20
608 St. Louis Cardinals TC .12 .30
609 Pittsburgh Pirates TC .07 .20
610 Cincinnati Reds TC .07 .20
611 Colorado Rockies TC .07 .20
612 Los Angeles Dodgers TC .12 .30
613 San Francisco Giants TC .07 .20
614 San Diego Padres TC .07 .20
615 Arizona Diamondbacks TC .07 .20
616 Kenji Johjima RC .50 1.25
617 Ryan Zimmerman (RC) .60 1.50
618 Craig Hansen RC .50 1.25
619 Joey Devine RC .20 .50
620 Hanley Ramirez (RC) .30 .75
621 Scott Olsen (RC) .20 .50
622 Jason Bergmann RC .20 .50
623 Geovany Soto (RC) .50 1.25
624 J.J. Furmaniak (RC) .20 .50
625 Jeremy Accardo RC .20 .50
626 Mark Woodyard (RC) .20 .50
627 Matt Capps (RC) .20 .50
628 Tim Corcoran RC .20 .50
629 Ryan Jorgensen RC .20 .50
630 Ronny Paulino (RC) .20 .50
631 Dan Uggla (RC) .30 .75
632 Ian Kinsler (RC) .60 1.50
633 Josh Barfield (RC) .20 .50
634 Reggie Abercrombie (RC) .20 .50
635 Joel Zumaya (RC) .50 1.25
636 Matt Cain (RC) 1.25 3.00
637 Conor Jackson (RC) .30 .75
638 Brian Anderson (RC) .20 .50
639 Prince Fielder (RC) 1.00 2.50
640 Jeremy Hermida (RC) .20 .50
641 Justin Verlander (RC) 4.00 10.00
642 Brian Bannister (RC) .20 .50
643 Willie Eyre (RC) .20 .50
644 Ricky Nolasco (RC) .20 .50
645 Paul Maholm (RC) .20 .50
646 J.Damon .12 .30
J.Giambi
647 R.White .07 .20
L.Ford
648 O.Hernandez .07 .20
O.Hudson
649 A.Dunn .40 1.00
K.Griffey Jr.
650 P.Burrell .07 .20
M.Lieberthal
651 J.Reyes .12 .30
K.Matsui
652 H.Blalock .07 .20
M.Young
653 P.Fielder .40 1.00
R.Weeks
654 T.Lee .07 .20
R.Baldelli
655 D.Lee .07 .20
A.Ramirez
656 G.Sizemore .12 .30
A.Boone
657 Gonzalez .07 .20
Green
Hill
658 I.Rodriguez .12 .30
C.Guillen
659 A.Rodriguez .25 .60
G.Sheffield
660 E.Santana .12 .30
F.Rodriguez
RC1 Alay Soler 15.00 40.00

2006 Topps Black

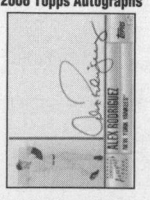

COMMON CARD (1-660) 6.00 15.00
SEMISTARS 10.00 25.00
UNLISTED STARS 50.00 40.00
SERIES 1 ODDS 1:18 HTA
SERIES 2 ODDS 1:14 HTA
STATED PRINT RUN 55 SERIAL #'d SETS
CARD 297 DOES NOT EXIST

2006 Topps Box Bottoms

A.Rod/Wright/Abreu/Lee 1.50 4.00
Young/Tejada/Johan/Fielder 1.50 4.00
ONE 4-CARD SHEET PER HTA BOX
1 Alex Rodriguez .60 1.50
16 David Wright .40 1.00
20 Bobby Abreu .20 .50
25 Chipper Jones .50 1.25
50 Manny Ramirez .50 1.25
70 Carlos Lee .20 .50
90 Mark Buehrle .30 .75
100 Barry Bonds .75 2.00
115 Adam Dunn .30 .75
125 Carlos Delgado .20 .50
150 Pedro Martinez .30 .75
151 Roger Clemens .60 1.50
180 Mark Teixeira .30 .75
194 Torii Hunter .20 .50
200 Albert Pujols .60 1.50
225 Ichiro Suzuki .60 1.50
337 Michael Young .20 .50
345 Andruw Jones .20 .50
357 Orlando Hernandez .20 .50
390 Jake Peavy .20 .50
405 Miguel Tejada .30 .75
423 David Ortiz .50 1.25
450 Derrek Lee .20 .50
468 Johan Santana .30 .75
550 Alfonso Soriano .30 .75
560 Jim Thome .30 .75
570 Todd Helton .30 .75
599 Ozzie Guillen MG .20 .50
616 Kenji Johjima .50 1.25
637 Conor Jackson .30 .75
639 Prince Fielder 1.00 2.50
659 A.Rodriguez/G.Sheffield .60 1.50

2006 Topps Gold

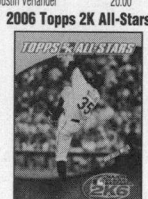

*GOLD 1-295/326-615/646-660: 6X TO 15X
*GOLD 296-325/616-645: 2.5X TO 6X
SER.1 ODDS 1:15 HOB, 1:4 HTA, 1:26 MINI
SER.1 ODDS 1:8 RACK, 1:14 RET
SER.2 ODDS 1:11 HOB, 1:4 HTA, 1:21 MINI
SER.2 ODDS 1:6 RACK, 1:11 RET
STATED PRINT RUN 2006 SERIAL #'d SETS
CARD 297 DOES NOT EXIST
641 Justin Verlander 20.00 50.00

2006 Topps 2K All-Stars

SER.1 ODDS 1:18 H, 1:18 HTA, 1:18 MINI
SER.1 ODDS 1:6 RACK, 1:18 RETAIL
1-6 ISSUED IN 2K ALL-STAR GAMES
7-11 ISSUED IN SER.1 TOPPS PACKS
1 Derek Jeter 4.00 10.00
2 Andruw Jones .60 1.50
3 Miguel Cabrera 1.50 4.00
4 Derrek Lee .60 1.50
5 Mariano Rivera 2.00 5.00
6 Ivan Rodriguez 1.00 2.50
7 Vladimir Guerrero 1.00 2.50
8 Albert Pujols 2.00 5.00
9 Alex Rodriguez 2.00 5.00
10 Alfonso Soriano 1.00 2.50
11 Dontrelle Willis .60 1.50

2006 Topps Autographs

SER.1 A 1:681,120 HOBBY, 1:152,750 HTA
SER.1 A 1:220,032 RACK
SER.1 B 1:14500 H,1:2932 HTA,1:26,900 MINI
SER.1 B 1:7124 RACK, 1:11,500 RETAIL

ER.1 C 1:17400 H,1:4966 HTA, 1:28,622 MINI
ER.1 C 1:8400 RACK, 1:14,000 RET
ER.1 D 1:42,570 H, 1:11,841 HTA
ER.1 D 1:70,000 MINI, 1:20,000 RACK
ER.1 D 1:33,000 RETAIL
ER.1 E 1:3451 H, 1:980 HTA, 1:5800 MINI
ER.1 E 1:1650 RACK, 1:2900 RET
ER.1 F 1:2090 H, 1:560 HTA, 1:3480 MINI
ER.1 F 1:995 RACK, 1:1750 RETAIL
ER.1 G 1:3481 H, 1:944 HTA, 1:5800 MINI
ER.1 G 1:1660 RACK, 1:2900 RETAIL
ER.1 H 1:430 H, 1:121 HTA, 1:725 MINI
ER.1 H 1:207 RACK, 1:363 RETAIL
VERALL SER.1 AU-GU ODDS 1:137 H/R
VERALL SER.1 AU-GU ODDS 1:47 HTA
ROUP A PRINT RUN 10 #'d CARDS
ROUP B PRINT RUN 100 #'d SETS
ROUP C PRINT RUN 200 #'d SETS
ROUP D PRINT RUN 250 #'d CARDS
O GROUP A PRICING DUE TO SCARCITY
.LIVINGSTON ISSUED IN SER.2 PACKS
XCHANGE DEADLINE 02/28/08
G Alex Gordon H 5.00 12.00
L Anthony Lerew H 4.00 10.00
R Alex Rodriguez B/100 75.00 200.00
RE Anthony Reyes H 10.00 25.00
C Brian Cashman B/100 50.00 120.00
BL Bobby Livingston F2 4.00 10.00
BW Brad Wilkerson E 6.00 15.00
CB Craig Breslow H 4.00 10.00
CG Carlos Guillen E 12.00 30.00
CJ Chuck James G 15.00 40.00
DD Doug DeVore H 4.00 10.00
DO David Ortiz B/100 40.00 100.00
DP Dustin Pedrioa 10.00 25.00
DR Darrell Rasner H 4.00 10.00
DW Dave Winfield B/100 60.00 150.00
EC Eric Chavez C/200 10.00 25.00
FC Fausto Carmona H 4.00 10.00
FL Francisco Liriano H 4.00 10.00
GN Graig Nettles E 6.00 15.00
GS Gary Sheffield C/200 20.00 50.00
HR Horacio Ramirez F 4.00 10.00
JB Jason Botts H 4.00 10.00
JJ Josh Johnson H 6.00 15.00
JM Jeff Mathis F 4.00 10.00
LC Lance Cormier E 6.00 15.00
LH Livan Hernandez F 6.00 15.00
MB Milton Bradley C/200 15.00 40.00
MY Michael Young E 10.00 25.00
NC Nelson Cruz G 6.00 15.00
RG Ryan Garko F 6.00 15.00
RH Rich Hill H 3.00 8.00
RO Roy Oswalt F 6.00 15.00
RS Ryne Sandberg B/100 50.00 120.00
SO Scott Olsen H 4.00 10.00
TS Termel Sledge E 6.00 15.00
WB Wade Boggs D/250 15.00 40.00

2006 Topps Autographs Green

SER.2 A 1:160,000 HOBBY, 1:48,000 HTA
SER.2 A 1:350,000 MINI, 1:90,000 RACK
SER.2 A 1:150,000 RETAIL
SER.2 B 1:70,000 HOBBY, 1:12,000 HTA
SER.2 B 1:125,000 MINI, 1:33,000 RACK
SER.2 B 1:80,000 RETAIL
SER.2 C 1:4060 H, 1:1150 HTA, 1:6800 MINI
SER.2 C 1:1400 R, 1:1940 RACK
SER.2 D 1:4750 H, 1:1000 HTA, 1:6500 MINI
SER.2 D 1:4750 R, 1:2000 RACK
SER.2 E 1:2030 H, 1:575 HTA, 1:3390 MINI
SER.2 E 1:2025 R, 1:966 RACK
SER.2 F 1:510 H, 1:190 HTA, 1:1125 MINI
SER.2 F 1:506 R, 1:325 RACK
GROUP A PRINT RUN 50 CARDS
GROUP B PRINT RUN 120 CARDS
GROUP C PRINT RUN 250 SETS
A-C ARE NOT SERIAL-NUMBERED
A-C PRINT RUNS PROVIDED BY TOPPS
NO GROUP A PRICING DUE TO SCARCITY
EXCHANGE DEADLINE 06/30/08
AJ Andruw Jones C/250 * 20.00 50.00
BB Barry Bonds B/120 * 100.00 250.00
BC Brandon Claussen F 4.00 10.00
BM Brandon McCarthy E 6.00 15.00
BR Brian Roberts C/250 * 10.00 25.00
CB Clint Barmes E 6.00 15.00
CO Chad Orvella F 4.00 10.00
CV Claudio Vargas F 4.00 10.00
DD Doug Drabek C/250 * 6.00 15.00
DJ Dan Johnson D 6.00 15.00
DS Darryl Strawberry C/250 * 25.00 60.00
DSN Duke Snider C/250 * 15.00 40.00
GA Garrett Atkins D 6.00 15.00
GC Gary Carter C/250 * 6.00 15.00
JB Jose Bautista F 6.00 15.00
JF Jeff Francis D 6.00 15.00
JP Jonathan Papelbon F 6.00 15.00
RC Robinson Cano E 10.00 25.00
RZ Ryan Zimmerman E 8.00 20.00
SK Scott Kazmir D 4.00 10.00
WP Wily Mo Pena C/250 * 15.00 40.00

2006 Topps Barry Bonds Chase to 715

COMMON CARD 20.00 50.00
SER.1 ODDS 1:4800 HOBBY, 1:5400 HTA
SER.1 ODDS 1:10,900 MINI, 1:3076 RACK
SER.1 ODDS 1:5,300 RETAIL
STATED PRINT RUN 1 SERIAL #'d SET

2006 Topps United States Constitution

COMPLETE SET (42) 30.00 60.00
SER.2 ODDS 1:8 HOBBY, 1:2 HTA, 1:16 MINI
SER.2 ODDS 1:8 RETAIL, 1:4 RACK
AB Abraham Baldwin .75 2.00
AH Alexander Hamilton .75 2.00
BF Benjamin Franklin 1.25 3.00
CP Charles Pinckney .75 2.00
DB David Brearly .75 2.00
DC Daniel Carroll .75 2.00
DJ Daniel of St. Thomas Jenifer .75 2.00
GB Gunning Bedford Jr. .75 2.00
GC George Clymer .75 2.00
GM Gouverneur Morris .75 2.00
GR George Read .75 2.00
GW George Washington 1.25 3.00
HW Hugh Williamson .75 2.00
JB John Blair .75 2.00
JD Jonathan Dayton .75 2.00
JI Jared Ingersoll .75 2.00
JL John Langdon .75 2.00
JM James Madison .75 2.00
JR John Rutledge .75 2.00
JW James Wilson .75 2.00
NG Nicholas Gilman .75 2.00
PB Pierce Butler .75 2.00
RB Richard Bassett .75 2.00
RK Rufus King .75 2.00
RM Robert Morris .75 2.00
RS Roger Sherman .75 2.00
TF Thomas Fitzsimons .75 2.00
TM Thomas Mifflin .75 2.00
WB William Blount .75 2.00
WF William Few .75 2.00
WJ William Samuel Johnson .75 2.00
WI William Livingston .75 2.00
WP William Paterson .75 2.00
CCP Charles Cotesworth Pinckney .75 2.00
JBR Jacob Broom .75 2.00
JDI John Dickinson .75 2.00
JMC James McHenry .75 2.00
NGO Nathaniel Gorham .75 2.00
RDS Richard Dobbs Spaight .75 2.00
HDR1 Header Card 1 .75 2.00
HDR2 Header Card 2 .75 2.00
HDR3 Header Card 3 .75 2.00

2006 Topps Declaration of Independence

COMPLETE SET (56) 70.00 120.00
SER.1 ODDS 1:8 HOBBY, 1:4 HTA, 1:12 MINI
SER.1 ODDS 1:4 RACK, 1:6 RETAIL
AC Abraham Clark 1.25 3.00
AM Arthur Middleton 1.25 3.00
BF Benjamin Franklin 2.00 5.00
BG Button Gwinnett 1.25 3.00
BH Benjamin Harrison 1.25 3.00
BR Benjamin Rush 1.25 3.00
CB Carter Braxton 1.25 3.00
CC Charles Carroll 1.25 3.00
CR Caesar Rodney 1.25 3.00
EG Elbridge Gerry 1.25 3.00
ER Edward Rutledge 1.25 3.00
FH Francis Hopkinson 1.25 3.00
FL Francis Lewis 1.25 3.00
FLL Francis Lightfoot Lee 1.25 3.00
GC George Clymer 1.25 3.00
GR George Ross 1.25 3.00
GRE George Read 1.25 3.00
GT George Taylor 1.25 3.00
GW George Walton 1.25 3.00
GWY George Wythe 1.25 3.00
JA John Adams 1.25 3.00
JB Josiah Bartlett 1.25 3.00
JH John Hancock 2.00 5.00
JHA John Hart 1.25 3.00
JHE Joseph Hewes 1.25 3.00
JM John Morton 1.25 3.00
JP John Penn 1.25 3.00
JS James Smith 1.25 3.00
JW James Wilson 1.25 3.00
JWI John Witherspoon 1.25 3.00
LH Lyman Hall 1.25 3.00
LM Lewis Morris 1.25 3.00
MT Matthew Thornton 1.25 3.00
OW Oliver Wolcott 1.25 3.00
PL Philip Livingston 1.25 3.00
RHL Richard Henry Lee 1.25 3.00
RM Robert Morris 1.25 3.00
RS Roger Sherman 1.25 3.00
RST Richard Stockton 1.25 3.00
RTP Robert Treat Paine 1.25 3.00
SA Samuel Adams 2.00 5.00
SC Samuel Chase 1.25 3.00
SH Stephen Hopkins 1.25 3.00
SHU Samuel Huntington 1.25 3.00
TH Thomas Heyward Jr. 1.25 3.00
TJ Thomas Jefferson 2.00 5.00
TL Thomas Lynch Jr. 1.25 3.00
TM Thomas McKean 1.25 3.00
TN Thomas Nelson Jr. 1.25 3.00
TS Thomas Stone 1.25 3.00
WE William Ellery 1.25 3.00
WF William Floyd 1.25 3.00
WH William Hooper 1.25 3.00
WP William Paca 1.25 3.00
WW William Whipple 1.25 3.00
WWI William Williams 1.25 3.00

2006 Topps Factory Set Rookie Bonus

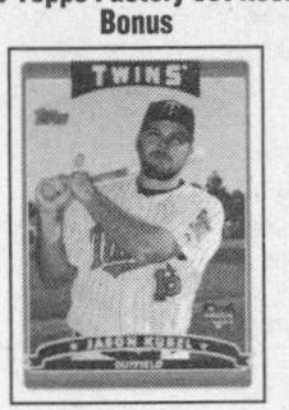

COMP.RETAIL SET (5) 6.00 15.00
COMP.HOBBY SET (5) 6.00 15.00
COMP.HOLIDAY SET (10) 10.00 25.00
1-5 ISSUED IN RETAIL FACTORY SETS
6-10 ISSUED IN HOBBY FACTORY SETS
11-20 ISSUED IN HOLIDAY FACTORY SETS
1 Nick Markakis .75 2.00
2 Kelly Shoppach .40 1.00
3 Jordan Tata .40 1.00
4 Ruddy Lugo .40 1.00
5 Josh Wilson .40 1.00
6 Fernando Nieve .40 1.00
7 Sendy Rleal .40 1.00
8 Jason Kubel .40 1.00
9 James Loney .60 1.50
10 Fabio Castro .40 1.00
11 Jonathan Broxton .40 1.00
12 Eliezer Alfonzo .40 1.00
13 Jason Hirsh .40 1.00
14 Rajai Davis .40 1.00
15 Henry Owens .40 1.00
16 Kevin Frandsen .40 1.00
17 Matt Garza .40 1.00
18 Chris Duncan .60 1.50
19 Chris Coste 1.00 2.50
20 Jeff Karstens .40 1.00

2006 Topps Factory Set Team Bonus

COMP.CARDINALS SET (5) 6.00 15.00
COMP.CUBS SET (5) 6.00 15.00
COMP.PIRATES SET (5) 6.00 15.00
COMP.RED SOX SET (5) 10.00 25.00
COMP.YANKEES SET (5) 8.00 20.00
BRS1-5 ISSUED IN RED SOX FACTORY SET
CC1-5 ISSUED IN CUBS FACTORY SET
NYY1-5 ISSUED IN YANKEES FACTORY SET
PP1-5 ISSUED IN PIRATES FACTORY SET
SLC1-5 ISSUED IN CARDINALS FACTORY SET
BRS1 Jonathan Papelbon 2.00 5.00
BRS2 Manny Ramirez 1.00 2.50
BRS3 David Ortiz 1.00 2.50
BRS4 Josh Beckett .40 1.00
BRS5 Curt Schilling .60 1.50
CC1 Sean Marshall .40 1.00
CC2 Freddie Bynum .40 1.00
CC3 Derrek Lee .40 1.00
CC4 Juan Pierre .40 1.00
CC5 Carlos Zambrano .60 1.50
NYY1 Wil Nieves .40 1.00
NYY2 Alex Rodriguez 1.25 3.00
NYY3 Derek Jeter 2.50 6.00
NYY4 Mariano Rivera 1.25 3.00
NYY5 Randy Johnson 1.00 2.50
PP1 Matt Capps .40 1.00
PP2 Paul Maholm .40 1.00
PP3 Nate McLouth .40 1.00
PP4 John Van Benschoten .40 1.00
PP5 Jason Bay .40 1.00
SLC1 Adam Wainwright .60 1.50
SLC2 Skip Schumaker .40 1.00
SLC3 Albert Pujols 1.25 3.00
SLC4 Jim Edmonds .60 1.50
SLC5 Scott Rolen .60 1.50

2006 Topps Hit Parade

COMPLETE SET (30) 35.00 60.00
SER.2 ODDS 1:18 H, 1:6 HTA, 1:27 MINI
SER.2 ODDS 1:18 R, 1:9 RACK
HR1 Barry Bonds HR 2.50 6.00
HR2 Ken Griffey Jr HR 3.00 8.00
HR3 Jeff Bagwell HR 1.00 2.50
HR4 Gary Sheffield HR .60 1.50
HR5 Frank Thomas HR 1.50 4.00
HR6 Manny Ramirez HR 1.50 4.00
HR7 Jim Thome HR 1.00 2.50
HR8 Alex Rodriguez HR 2.00 5.00
HR9 Mike Piazza HR 1.50 4.00
HIT1 Craig Biggio HIT 1.00 2.50
HIT2 Barry Bonds HIT 2.50 6.00
HIT3 Julio Franco HIT .60 1.50
HIT4 Steve Finley HIT .60 1.50
HIT5 Gary Sheffield HIT .60 1.50
HIT6 Jeff Bagwell HIT 1.00 2.50
HIT7 Ken Griffey Jr HIT 3.00 8.00
HIT8 Omar Vizquel HIT 1.00 2.50
HIT9 Marquis Grissom HIT .60 1.50
HR10 Carlos Delgado HR .60 1.50
RBI1 Barry Bonds RBI 2.50 6.00
RBI2 Ken Griffey Jr RBI 3.00 8.00
RBI3 Jeff Bagwell RBI 1.00 2.50
RBI4 Gary Sheffield RBI .60 1.50
RBI5 Frank Thomas RBI 1.50 4.00
RBI6 Manny Ramirez RBI 1.50 4.00
RBI7 Ruben Sierra RBI .60 1.50
RBI8 Jeff Kent RBI .60 1.50
RBI9 Luis Gonzalez RBI .60 1.50
HIT10 Bernie Williams HIT 1.00 2.50
RBI10 Alex Rodriguez RBI 2.00 5.00

2006 Topps Hobby Masters

COMPLETE SET (20) 8.00 20.00
SER.1 ODDS 1:18 HOBBY, 1:6 HTA
HM1 Derrek Lee .40 1.00
HM2 Albert Pujols 1.25 3.00
HM3 Nomar Garciaparra .60 1.50
HM4 Alfonso Soriano .60 1.50
HM5 Derek Jeter 2.50 6.00
HM6 Miguel Tejada .60 1.50
HM7 Alex Rodriguez 1.25 3.00
HM8 Jim Edmonds UER .60 1.50
HM9 Mark Prior .60 1.50
HM10 Roger Clemens 1.25 3.00
HM11 Randy Johnson 1.00 2.50
HM12 Manny Ramirez 1.00 2.50
HM13 Curt Schilling .60 1.50
HM14 Vladimir Guerrero .60 1.50
HM15 Barry Bonds 1.50 4.00
HM16 Ichiro Suzuki 1.25 3.00
HM17 Pedro Martinez .60 1.50
HM18 Carlos Beltran .60 1.50
HM19 David Ortiz 1.00 2.50
HM20 Andruw Jones .40 1.00

2006 Topps Mantle Collection

COMPLETE SET (10) 60.00 120.00
SER.1 ODDS 1:36 HOB, 1:36 HTA, 1:36 MINI
SER.1 ODDS 1:12 RACK, 1:36 RETAIL
BLACK SER.1 ODDS 1:4,665 HTA
BLACK PRINT RUN 7 SERIAL #'d SETS
NO BLACK PRICING DUE TO SCARCITY
*GOLD p/r 477-977: 1.25X TO 3X BASIC
*GOLD p/r 277-377: 1.5X TO 4X BASIC
*GOLD p/r 177: 2X TO 5X BASIC
*GOLD p/r 77: 4X TO 10X BASIC
GOLD SER.1 ODDS 1:1500 HOB, 1:2332 HTA
GOLD SER.1 ODDS 1:3376 MINI, 1:970 RACK
GOLD SER.1 ODDS 1:1500 RETAIL
GOLD PRINT RUNS B/WN 77-977 PER
1996 Mickey Mantle 96 6.00 15.00
1997 Mickey Mantle 97 6.00 15.00
1998 Mickey Mantle 98 6.00 15.00
1999 Mickey Mantle 99 6.00 15.00
2000 Mickey Mantle 00 6.00 15.00
2001 Mickey Mantle 01 6.00 15.00
2002 Mickey Mantle 02 6.00 15.00
2003 Mickey Mantle 03 6.00 15.00
2004 Mickey Mantle 04 6.00 15.00
2005 Mickey Mantle 05 6.00 15.00

2006 Topps Mantle Collection Bat Relics

SER.1 ODDS 1:4540 HOBBY, 1:8552 HTA
SER.1 ODDS 1:14,000 MINI, 1:6500 RETAIL
PRINT RUNS B/WN 77-167 COPIES PER
BLACK SER.1 ODDS 1:4,665 HTA
BLACK PRINT RUN 7 SERIAL #'d SETS
NO BLACK PRICING DUE TO SCARCITY
1996 Mickey Mantle 96/77 15.00 40.00
1997 Mickey Mantle 97/87 15.00 40.00
1998 Mickey Mantle 98/97 15.00 40.00
1999 Mickey Mantle 99/107 15.00 40.00
2000 Mickey Mantle 00/117 15.00 40.00
2001 Mickey Mantle 01/127 15.00 40.00
2002 Mickey Mantle 02/137 15.00 40.00
2003 Mickey Mantle 03/147 15.00 40.00
2004 Mickey Mantle 04/157 15.00 40.00
2005 Mickey Mantle 05/167 15.00 40.00

2006 Topps Mantle Home Run History

COMPLETE SET (501) 500.00 900.00
COMP.06 SERIES 1-2 SET (1-101) 60.00 120.00
COMP.06 UPDATE (102-201) 60.00 120.00
COMP.07 SERIES 1 SET (202-301) 75.00 150.00
COMP.07 SERIES 2 SET (302-401) 125.00 250.00
COMP.07 UPDATE (402-501) 125.00 250.00
COMP.08 TOPPS (502-536) 20.00 50.00
COMMON CARD (1-201) .40 1.00
COMMON CARD (202-301) 1.00 2.50
COMMON CARD (302-536) .75 2.00
SER.1 ODDS 1:4 HOBBY, 1:1 HTA, 1:4 MINI
SER.1 ODDS 1:2 RACK, 1:4 RETAIL
SER.2 ODDS 1:4 HOBBY, 1:1 HTA, 1:8 MINI
SER.2 ODDS 1:2 RACK, 1:4 RETAIL
UPDATE ODDS 1:4 HOB,1:4 RET
07 SER.1 ODDS 1:9 H, 1:2 HTA, 1:9 K-MART
07 SER.1 ODDS 1:9 RACK, 1:9 TARGET
07 SER.1 ODDS 1:9 WAL-MART
07 SER.2 ODDS 1:9 HOBBY
07 UPDATE ODDS 1:9 HOB, 1:9 RET
08 SER.1 ODDS 1:9 HOB, 1:9 RET
CARD 1 ISSUED IN SERIES 1 PACKS
CARDS 2-101 ISSUED IN SERIES 2 PACKS
CARDS 102-201 ISSUED IN UPDATE PACKS
CARDS 202-301 ISSUED IN 07 SERIES 1
CARDS 302-401 ISSUED IN 07 SERIES 2
CARDS 402-501 ISSUED IN 07 UPDATE
CARDS 502-537 ISSUED IN 08 SERIES 1

2006 Topps Mantle Home Run History Bat Relics

COMMON CARD (R1-R536) 40.00 80.00
SER.1 ODDS 1:681,120 H, 1:102,624 HTA
SER.2 ODDS 1:6250 H, 1:16,000 HTA
SER.2 ODDS 1:21,000 MINI, 1:1575 R
UPD ODDS 1:5100 H,1:1859 HTA,1:5800 R
07 SER.1 ODDS 1:14,618 H, 1:494 HTA
07 SER.1 ODDS 1:32,000 K-MART
07 SER.1 ODDS 1:16,225 RACK
07 SER.1 ODDS 1:32,00 WAL-MART
07 SER.2 ODDS 1:12,106 HOBBY, 1:693 HTA
07 UPD. ODDS 1:5,550 HOBBY
07 UPD. ODDS 1:1,475 HTA
07 UPD. ODDS 1:5,550 RETAIL
08 SER.1 ODDS 1:29,331 H,1:1492 HTA
08 SER.1 ODDS 1:207,000 RETAIL
1 ISSUED IN SERIES 1 PACKS
2-101 ISSUED IN SERIES 2 PACKS
102-201 ISSUED IN UPDATE PACKS
202-301 ISSUED IN 07 SERIES 1 PACKS
302-401 ISSUED IN 07 SERIES 2 PACKS
402-501 ISSUED IN 07 UPDATE
502-536 ISSUED IN 08 SERIES 1
STATED PRINT RUN 7 SERIAL #'d SETS

2006 Topps Opening Day Team vs. Team

COMPLETE SET (15) 6.00 15.00
SER.2 ODDS 1:12 HOBBY, 1:3 HTA, 1:24 MINI
SER.2 ODDS 1:6 RACK, 1:12 RETAIL
AM Houston Astros vs. Marlins .60 1.50
AY Oakland Athletics vs. Yankees .60 1.50
BP Milwaukee Brewers vs. Pirates .60 1.50
DB Los Angeles Dodgers vs. Braves .60 1.50
JT Toronto Blue Jays vs. Twins .60 1.50
MA Seattle Mariners vs. Angels .60 1.50
MN New York Mets vs. Nationals .60 1.50
OD Baltimore Orioles vs. Devil Rays .60 1.50
PC Philadelphia Phillies vs. Cardinals.60 1.50
PG San Diego Padres vs. Giants .60 1.50
RC Cincinnati Reds vs. Cubs .60 1.50
RD Colorado Rockies vs. Diamondbacks.60 1.50
RR Texas Rangers vs. Red Sox .60 1.50
RT Kansas City Royals vs. Tigers .60 1.50
WI Chicago White Sox vs. Indians .60 1.50

2006 Topps Opening Day Team vs. Team Relics

SER.2 A ODDS 1:8800 H, 1:22,000 HTA
SER.2 A ODDS 1:25,000 MINI, 1:2100 R
SER.2 B ODDS 1:810 H, 1:2850 HTA
SER.2 B ODDS 1:3075 MINI, 1:1200 R
GROUP A PRINT RUN 50 SERIAL #'d SETS
NO GROUP A PRICING DUE TO SCARCITY
EXCHANGE DEADLINE 06/30/08
AY Oakland Athletics Base B 6.00 15.00
OD Baltimore Orioles Base B 6.00 15.00
RD Colorado Rockies Base B 6.00 15.00
RT Kansas City Royals Base B 10.00 25.00

2006 Topps Own the Game

COMPLETE SET (30) 20.00 50.00
SER.1 ODDS 1:12 HOB, 1:4 HTA, 1:12 MINI
SER.1 ODDS 1:6 RACK, 1:8 RETAIL
OG1 Derrek Lee .40 1.00
OG2 Michael Young .40 1.00
OG3 Albert Pujols 1.25 3.00
OG4 Roger Clemens 1.25 3.00
OG5 Andy Pettitte .60 1.50
OG6 Dontrelle Willis .40 1.00
OG7 Michael Young .40 1.00
OG8 Ichiro Suzuki 1.25 3.00
OG9 Derek Jeter 2.50 6.00
OG10 Andruw Jones .40 1.00
OG11 Alex Rodriguez 1.25 3.00
OG12 David Ortiz 1.00 2.50
OG13 David Ortiz 1.00 2.50
OG14 Manny Ramirez 1.00 2.50
OG15 Mark Teixeira .60 1.50
OG16 Albert Pujols 1.25 3.00
OG17 Alex Rodriguez 1.25 3.00
OG18 Derek Jeter 2.50 6.00
OG19 Chad Cordero .40 1.00
OG20 Francisco Rodriguez .60 1.50
OG21 Mariano Rivera 1.25 3.00
OG22 Chone Figgins .40 1.00
OG23 Jose Reyes .60 1.50
OG24 Scott Podsednik .40 1.00
OG25 Jake Peavy .40 1.00
OG26 Johan Santana .60 1.50
OG27 Pedro Martinez .60 1.50
OG28 Dontrelle Willis .40 1.00
OG29 Chris Carpenter .60 1.50
OG30 Bartolo Colon .40 1.00

2006 Topps Rookie of the Week

COMPLETE SET (25) 15.00 40.00
COMMON CARD (1-13) .50 1.25
ISSUED ONE PER WEEK VIA HTA SHOPS
1 Mickey Mantle 52 4.00 10.00
2 Barry Bonds 87 2.00 5.00
3 Roger Clemens 85 1.50 4.00
4 Ernie Banks 54 1.25 3.00
5 Nolan Ryan 68 4.00 10.00
6 Albert Pujols 01 1.50 4.00
7 Roberto Clemente 55 3.00 8.00
8 Frank Robinson 57 .75 2.00
9 Brooks Robinson 57 .75 2.00
10 Harmon Killebrew 55 1.25 3.00
11 Reggie Jackson 69 .75 2.00
12 George Brett 75 2.50 6.00
13 Ichiro Suzuki 01 1.50 4.00
14 Cal Ripken 82 4.00 10.00
15 Tom Seaver 68 .75 2.00
16 Johnny Bench 68 1.25 3.00
17 Mike Schmidt 73 2.00 5.00
18 Derek Jeter 93 3.00 8.00
19 Bob Gibson 59 .75 2.00
20 Ozzie Smith 79 1.50 4.00
21 Rickey Henderson 80 1.25 3.00
22 Tony Gwynn 83 1.25 3.00
23 Wade Boggs 83 .75 2.00
24 Ryne Sandberg 83 2.50 6.00
25 Mickey Mantle TBD 4.00 10.00

2006 Topps Stars

COMPLETE SET (15) 6.00 15.00
SER.2 ODDS 1:12 HOBBY, 1:4 HTA
AP Albert Pujols 1.00 2.50
AR Alex Rodriguez 1.00 2.50
AS Alfonso Soriano .50 1.25
BB Barry Bonds 1.25 3.00
DJ Derek Jeter 2.00 5.00
DO David Ortiz .75 2.00
HM Hideki Matsui .75 2.00
IS Ichiro Suzuki 1.00 2.50
MC Miguel Cabrera .75 2.00
MR Manny Ramirez .75 2.00
MT Miguel Tejada .50 1.25
PM Pedro Martinez .50 1.25
RC Roger Clemens 1.00 2.50
TH Todd Helton .50 1.25
VG Vladimir Guerrero .50 1.25

2006 Topps Target Factory Set Mantle Memorabilia

The card was packaged exclusively with 2006 Topps Factory sets sold in Target stores. Each factory set contained the complete Series 1 and Series 2 sets as well as the Mantle 1952 Topps reprint relic card. The original set SRP was $59.99.

MMR52 Mickey Mantle 52T 20.00 50.00

2006 Topps Team Topps Autographs

ISSUED IN VARIOUS 06 TOPPS PRODUCTS
SEE '03 TOPPS BLUE CHIPS FOR ADD'L INFO
BF Bob Feller 10.00 25.00
CS Chris Snyder 4.00 10.00
DD Doug Drabek 6.00 15.00
DS Duke Snider 15.00 40.00
DZ Don Zimmer 8.00 20.00
ED Eric Davis 6.00 15.00
JF Josh Fields 6.00 15.00
JL Jim Leyritz 4.00 10.00
JP Johnny Podres 6.00 15.00
JPI Jimmy Piersall 6.00 15.00
MC Mike Cuellar 6.00 15.00
MP Manny Parra 4.00 10.00
MR Mickey Rivers 6.00 15.00
RS Ryan Sweeney 4.00 10.00
SE Scott Elbert 4.00 10.00
TJ Tommy John 6.00 15.00

2006 Topps Trading Places

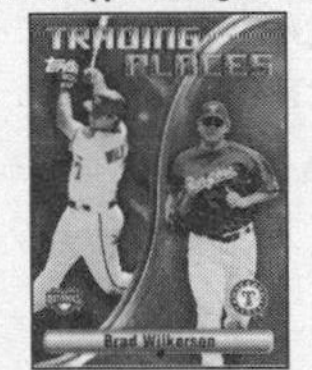

COMPLETE SET (20) 10.00 25.00
SER.2 ODDS 1:18 H, 1:4 HTA, 1:32 MINI
SER.2 ODDS 1:18 R, 1:8 RACK
AS Alfonso Soriano 1.00 2.50
BM Bill Mueller .60 1.50
BW Brad Wilkerson .60 1.50
CC Coco Crisp .60 1.50
CD Carlos Delgado .60 1.50
CP Corey Patterson .60 1.50
ER Edgar Renteria .60 1.50
FT Frank Thomas 1.50 4.00
JD Johnny Damon 1.00 2.50
JP Juan Pierre .60 1.50
JT Jim Thome 1.00 2.50
KL Kenny Lofton .60 1.50
MB Milton Bradley .60 1.50
NG Nomar Garciaparra 1.00 2.50
PW Preston Wilson .60 1.50
RF Rafael Furcal .60 1.50
RH Ramon Hernandez .60 1.50
TG Troy Glaus .60 1.50
JDN Juan Encarnacion .60 1.50
MJP Mike Piazza 1.50 4.00

2006 Topps Wal-Mart

These cards were issued in three-card cello packs within sealed series one Wal-Mart Bonus Boxes. Each Bonus Box carried a $9.97 suggested retail price and contained ten mini packs of series one cards plus the aforementioned three-card cello pack. The mini packs each contained six cards, thus each sealed Bonus Box contained 63 cards in all.

COMPLETE SERIES 1 (18) 12.50 30.00
COMPLETE SERIES 2 (18) 50.00 100.00
THREE PER WAL-MART BLASTER BOX
S1 CARDS ISSUED IN SERIES 1 PACKS
S2 CARDS ISSUED IN SERIES 2 PACKS
WM1 Stan Musial 52 S1 2.00 5.00
WM2 Ted Williams 87 S1 2.50 6.00
WM3 Yogi Berra 54 S2 8.00 20.00
WM4 Joe Mauer 96 UPD .75 2.00
WM5 Mickey Mantle 02 S1 4.00 10.00
WM6 Mickey Mantle 57 S2 6.00 15.00
WM7 Alex Rodriguez 58 S2 5.00 12.00
WM8 Carlos Zambrano 92 UPD .75 2.00
WM9 Gary Carter 60 S2 12.50 30.00
WM10 Roy Oswalt 61 S2 10.00 25.00
WM11 Mickey Mantle 70 UPD 8.00 20.00
WM12 Randy Johnson 62 UPD 1.25 3.00
WM13 Carlos Lee 64 S1 .50 1.25
WM14 Johan Santana 65 S2 8.00 20.00
WM15 Roberto Clemente 66 S2 6.00 15.00
WM16 Carl Yastrzemski 67 S2 6.00 15.00
WM17 Chase Utley 63 UPD .75 2.00
WM18 Pedro Martinez 68 UPD .75 2.00
WM19 Jason Bay 69 UPD .50 1.25
WM20 Alex Rodriguez 59 UPD 1.50 4.00
WM21 Chipper Jones 72 S2 12.50 30.00
WM22 Ichiro Suzuki 01 S1 1.50 4.00
WM23 Bobby Abreu 94 S1 .50 1.25
WM24 Tom Seaver 95 S1 .75 2.00
WM25 Alfonso Soriano 76 S2
WM26 Andruw Jones 92 S1 .50 1.25
WM27 Hanley Ramirez 71 UPD .75 2.00
WM28 Adam Dunn 91 S1 .75 2.00
WM29 Carl Crawford 00 UPD .75 2.00
WM30 Mark Teixeira 81 S1 .75 2.00
WM31 Albert Pujols 82 S2 3.00 8.00
WM32 Cal Ripken 83 S2 5.00 12.00
WM33 Ryne Sandberg 84 S1 2.50 6.00
WM34 Don Mattingly 85 S1 2.50 6.00
WM35 Roger Clemens 86 S1 1.50 4.00
WM36 Jose Reyes 53 S2 5.00 12.00
WM37 Curt Schilling 80 UPD .75 2.00
WM38 Derrek Lee 56 S2 6.00 15.00
WM39 Miguel Cabrera 73 S2 5.00 12.00
WM40 Manny Ramirez 88 UPD 1.25 3.00
WM41 Barry Bonds 89 S1 2.00 5.00
WM42 Barry Bonds 74 S2 5.00 12.00
WM43 Jeff Francoeur 98 UPD 1.25 3.00
WM44 Livan Hernandez 75 S2 6.00 15.00
WM45 Derek Jeter 77 S2 10.00 25.00
WM46 David Ortiz 97 S1 1.25 3.00
WM47 Carlos Delgado 78 UPD .50 1.25
WM48 Ivan Rodriguez 99 S1 .75 2.00
WM49 Todd Helton 05 UPD .75 2.00
WM50 Barry Bonds 79 UPD 2.00 5.00
WM51 Miguel Tejada 55 UPD .75 2.00
WM52 Alex Rodriguez 03 S1 1.50 4.00
WM53 Vladimir Guerrero 04 S1 .75 2.00
WM54 Paul Konerko 90 UPD .75 2.00

2006 Topps Trading Places Autographs

SER.2 A ODDS 1:110,000 HOBBY
SER.2 A ODDS 1:28,000 HTA
SER.2 A ODDS 1:250,000 MINI
SER.2 A ODDS 1:160,000 RACK
SER.2 A ODDS 1:150,000 RETAIL
SER.2 B ODDS 1:18,000 H, 1:5100 HTA
SER.2 B ODDS 1:30,000 MINI, 1:17,000 R
SER.2 B ODDS 1:8700 RACK
SER.2 C ODDS 1:4280 H, 1:1175 HTA
SER.2 C ODDS 1:7200 MINI, 1:4200 R
SER.2 C ODDS 1:2040 RACK
GROUP A PRINT RUN 75 CARDS
GROUP B PRINT RUN 225 SETS
A-B ARE NOT SERIAL-NUMBERED
A-B PRINT RUNS PROVIDED BY TOPPS
BR B.J. Ryan B 15.00 40.00
BW Billy Wagner C 5.00 12.00
JE Johnny Estrada C 4.00 10.00
KJ Kenji Johjima A 20.00 50.00
ML Mike Lowell C 10.00 25.00
PL Paul LoDuca B 15.00 40.00
TS Termel Sledge C 4.00 10.00

2006 Topps Trading Places Relics

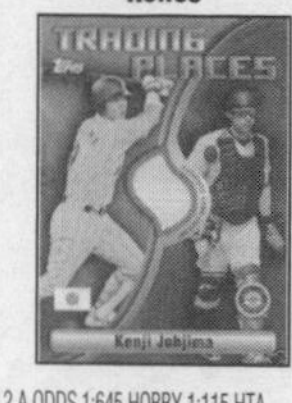

SER.2 A ODDS 1:645 HOBBY 1:115 HTA
SER.2 A ODDS 1:1355 MINI, 1:810 RETAIL
SER.2 B ODDS 1:410 HOBBY 1:120 HTA
SER.2 B ODDS 1:903 MINI, 1:500 RETAIL
AS Alfonso Soriano Bat A 3.00 8.00
BM Bill Mueller Bat A 3.00 8.00
BR B.J. Ryan Jsy B 3.00 8.00
CP Corey Patterson Bat A 3.00 8.00
ER Edgar Renteria Bat A 3.00 8.00
JD Johnny Damon Jsy B 6.00 15.00
JE Johnny Estrada Bat B 3.00 8.00
JP Juan Pierre Bat A 3.00 8.00
JT Jim Thome Bat A 6.00 15.00
KJ Kenji Johjima Bat B 6.00 15.00
KL Kenny Lofton Bat B 3.00 8.00
MB Milton Bradley Bat B 3.00 8.00
ML Mike Lowell Bat A 3.00 8.00
NG Nomar Garciaparra Bat A 4.00 10.00
PL Paul Lo Duca Bat A 3.00 8.00
PW Preston Wilson Bat A 3.00 8.00
RH Ramon Hernandez Bat B 3.00 8.00
TS Termel Sledge Bat B 3.00 8.00
BW1 Billy Wagner Jsy B 3.00 8.00
BW2 Brad Wilkerson Bat B 3.00 8.00

2006 Topps World Series Champion Relics

SER.1 A ODDS 1:23,755 H, 1:9329 HTA
SER.1 A ODDS 1:55,000 MINI, 1:27,000 R
SER.1 B ODDS 1:11,289 H, 1:2544 HTA
SER.1 B ODDS 1:24,000 MINI, 1:11,500 R
SER.1 C ODDS 1:1941 H, 1:880 HTA
SER.1 C ODDS 1:5100 MINI, 1:2500 R
SER.1 D ODDS 1:3144 H, 1:2168 HTA
SER.1 D ODDS 1:9200 MINI, 1:4700 R
SER.1 E ODDS 1:4984 H, 1:3346 HTA
SER.1 E ODDS 1:14,500 MINI, 1:7200 R
SER.1 F ODDS 1:1006 H, 1:617 HTA
SER.1 F ODDS 1:2800 MINI, 1:1430 R
SER.1 G ODDS 1:1396 H, 1:465 HTA
SER.1 G ODDS 1:3500 MINI, 1:1750 R
OVERALL SER.1 AU-GU ODDS 1:137 H/R
OVERALL SER.1 AU-GU ODDS 1:47 HTA
GROUP A PRINT RUN 100 SETS
GROUP A ARE NOT SERIAL-NUMBERED
GROUP A PRINT RUN PROVIDED BY TOPPS
AP A.J. Pierzynski Bat E 15.00 40.00
AR Aaron Rowand Bat D 10.00 25.00
BJ Bobby Jenks Glv A/100 * 250.00 350.00
CEB Carl Everett Bat F 6.00 15.00
CEU Carl Everett Uni A/100 * 6.00 15.00
FT Frank Thomas Uni F 12.50 30.00
JC Joe Crede Bat D 15.00 40.00
JD Jermaine Dye Bat C 30.00 60.00
JG Jon Garland Uni F 12.50 30.00
JU Juan Uribe Bat B 12.50 30.00
MB Mark Buehrle Glv A/100 * 150.00 250.00
PKB Paul Konerko Bat G 10.00 25.00
PKU Paul Konerko Uni G 10.00 25.00
SP Scott Podsednik Bat C 15.00 40.00
TI Tadahito Iguchi Bat C 20.00 50.00
TP Timo Perez Bat C 10.00 25.00
WH Willie Harris Bat F 4.00 10.00

2006 Topps Update

This 330-card set was released in November, 2006. This set was issued in 12-card packs with an $2 SRP and those packs came 36 to a box and 12 boxes to a case. The first 132 cards in this set feature players who were either new to their team in 2006 or made an unexpected impact and were not in the first two Topps series. Cards numbered 133-170 feature 2006 Rookies while cards numbered 171-181 are Season Highlights. Cards number 182-201 are a Postseason Highlight subset, cards 202-217 are an League Leader subset while cards 218-282 form an All-Star subset. Cards numbered 283-290 celebrate players who participated in the Home Run Derby, cards 291-320 were Team Leader cards and the set concluded with Classic Duos (321-330). Cory Lidle, who perished in a plane crash while this set was in production, was issued as an "in memoriam" card.

COMPLETE SET (330) 20.00 50.00
COMMON CARD (1-132) .07 .20
COMMON ROOKIE (133-170) .40 1.00
COMMON CARD (171-330) .12 .30
UNLISTED STARS 171-330 .30 .75
1-330 PLATE ODDS 1:85 HTA
PLATE PRINT RUN 1 SET PER COLOR
BLACK-CYAN-MAGENTA-YELLOW ISSUED
NO PLATE PRICING DUE TO SCARCITY
1 Austin Kearns .07 .20
2 Adam Eaton .07 .20
3 Juan Encarnacion .07 .20
4 Jarrod Washburn .07 .20
5 Alex Gonzalez .07 .20
6 Toby Hall .07 .20
7 Preston Wilson .07 .20
8 Ramon Ortiz .07 .20
9 Jason Michaels .07 .20
10 Jeff Weaver .07 .20
11 Russell Branyan .07 .20
12 Brett Tomko .07 .20
13 Doug Mientkiewicz .07 .20
14 David Wells .07 .20
15 Corey Koskie .07 .20
16 Russ Ortiz .07 .20
17 Carlos Pena .12 .30
18 Mark Hendrickson .07 .20
19 Julian Tavarez .07 .20
20 Jeff Conine .07 .20
21 Dioner Navarro .07 .20
22 Bob Wickman .07 .20
23 Felipe Lopez .07 .20
24 Eddie Guardado .07 .20
25 David Dellucci .07 .20
26 Ryan Wagner .07 .20
27 Nick Green .07 .20
28 Gary Majewski .07 .20
29 Shea Hillenbrand .07 .20
30 Jae Seo .07 .20
31 Royce Clayton .07 .20
32 Dave Riske .07 .20
33 Joey Gathright .07 .20
34 Robinson Tejada .07 .20
35 Edwin Jackson .07 .20
36 Aubrey Huff .07 .20
37 Akinori Otsuka .07 .20
38 Juan Castro .07 .20
39 Zach Day .07 .20
40 Jeremy Accardo .07 .20
41 Shawn Green .07 .20
42 Kazuo Matsui .07 .20
43 J.J. Putz .07 .20
44 David Ross .07 .20
45 Scott Williamson .07 .20
46 Joe Borchard .07 .20
47 Elmer Dessens .07 .20
48 Odalis Perez .07 .20
49 Kelly Shoppach .07 .20
50 Brandon Phillips .07 .20
51 Guillermo Mota .07 .20
52 Alex Cintron .07 .20
53 Denny Bautista .07 .20
54 Josh Bard .07 .20
55 Julio Lugo .07 .20
56 Doug Mirabelli .07 .20
57 Kip Wells .07 .20
58 Adrian Gonzalez .15 .40
59 Shawn Chacon .07 .20
60 Marcus Thames .07 .20
61 Craig Wilson .07 .20
62 Cory Sullivan .07 .20
63 Ben Broussard .07 .20
64 Todd Walker .07 .20
65 Greg Maddux .25 .60
66 Xavier Nady .07 .20
67 Oliver Perez .07 .20
68 Sean Casey .07 .20
69 Kyle Lohse .07 .20
70 Carlos Lee .07 .20
71 Rheal Cormier .07 .20
72 Ronnie Belliard .07 .20
73 Cory Lidle .07 .20
74 David Bell .07 .20
75 Wilson Betemit .07 .20
76 Danys Baez .07 .20
77 Mike Stanton .07 .20
78 Kevin Mench .07 .20
79 Sandy Alomar Jr. .07 .20
80 Cesar Izturis .07 .20
81 Jeremy Affeldt .07 .20
82 Matt Stairs .07 .20
83 Hector Luna .07 .20
84 Tony Graffanino .07 .20
85 J.P. Howell .07 .20
86 Bengie Molina .07 .20
87 Maicer Izturis .07 .20
88 Marco Scutaro .12 .30
89 Daryle Ward .07 .20
90 Sal Fasano .07 .20
91 Oscar Villarreal .07 .20
92 Gabe Gross .07 .20
93 Phil Nevin .07 .20
94 Damon Hollins .07 .20
95 Juan Cruz .07 .20
96 Marlon Anderson .07 .20
97 Jason Davis .07 .20
98 Ryan Shealy .07 .20
99 Francisco Cordero .07 .20
100 Bobby Abreu .07 .20
101 Roberto Hernandez .07 .20
102 Gary Bennett .07 .20
103 Aaron Sele .07 .20
104 Nook Logan .07 .20
105 Alfredo Amezaga .07 .20
106 Chris Woodward .07 .20
107 Kevin Jarvis .07 .20
108 B.J. Upton .07 .20
109 Alan Embree .07 .20
110 Milton Bradley .07 .20
111 Pete Orr .07 .20
112 Jeff Cirillo .07 .20
113 Corey Patterson .07 .20
114 Josh Paul .07 .20
115 Fernando Rodney .07 .20
116 Jerry Hairston Jr. .07 .20
117 Scott Proctor .07 .20
118 Ambiorix Burgos .07 .20
119 Jose Bautista .20 .50
120 Livan Hernandez .07 .20
121 John McDonald .07 .20
122 Ronny Cedeno .07 .20
123 Nate Robertson .07 .20
124 Jamey Carroll .07 .20
125 Alex Escobar .07 .20
126 Endy Chavez .07 .20
127 Jorge Julio .07 .20
128 Kenny Lofton .07 .20
129 Matt Diaz .07 .20
130 Dave Bush .07 .20
131 Jose Molina .07 .20
132 Mike MacDougal .07 .20
133 Ben Zobrist (RC) 2.00 5.00
134 Shane Komine RC .60 1.50
135 Casey Janssen RC .40 1.00
136 Kevin Frandsen (RC) .40 1.00
137 John Rheinecker (RC) .40 1.00
138 Matt Kemp (RC) 1.00 2.50
139 Scott Mathieson (RC) .40 1.00
140 Jered Weaver (RC) 1.25 3.00
141 Joel Guzman (RC) .40 1.00
142 Anibal Sanchez (RC) .40 1.00
143 Melky Cabrera (RC) .60 1.50
144 Howie Kendrick (RC) .75 2.00
145 Cole Hamels (RC) 1.25 3.00
146 Willy Aybar (RC) .40 1.00
147 Jamie Shields RC 1.25 3.00
148 Kevin Thompson (RC) .40 1.00
149 Jon Lester RC 1.50 4.00
150 Stephen Drew (RC) .75 2.00
151 Andre Ethier (RC) 1.25 3.00
152 Jordan Tata RC .40 1.00
153 Mike Napoli RC .60 1.50
154 Kason Gabbard (RC) .40 1.00
155 Lastings Milledge (RC) .40 1.00
156 Erick Aybar (RC) .40 1.00
157 Fausto Carmona (RC) .40 1.00
158 Russ Martin (RC) .60 1.50
159 David Pauley (RC) .40 1.00
160 Andy Marte (RC) .40 1.00
161 Carlos Quentin (RC) .60 1.50
162 Franklin Gutierrez (RC) .40 1.00
163 Taylor Buchholz (RC) .40 1.00
164 Josh Johnson (RC) 1.00 2.50
165 Chad Billingsley (RC) .60 1.50
166 Kendry Morales (RC) 1.00 2.50
167 Adam Loewen (RC) .40 1.00
168 Yusmeiro Petit (RC) .40 1.00
169 Matt Albers (RC) .40 1.00
170 John Maine (RC) .60 1.50
171 Alex Rodriguez SH .30 .75
172 Mike Piazza SH .30 .75
173 Cory Sullivan SH .12 .30
174 Anibal Sanchez SH .12 .30
175 Trevor Hoffman SH .20 .50
176 Barry Bonds SH .50 1.25
177 Derek Jeter SH .75 2.00
178 Jose Reyes SH .20 .50
179 Manny Ramirez SH .30 .75
180 Vladimir Guerrero SH .20 .50
181 Mariano Rivera SH .40 1.00
182 Mark Kotsay PH .12 .30
183 Derek Jeter PH .75 2.00
184 Carlos Delgado PH .12 .30
185 Frank Thomas PH .30 .75
186 Albert Pujols PH .40 1.00
187 Magglio Ordonez PH .12 .30
188 Carlos Delgado PH .12 .30
189 Kenny Rogers PH .12 .30
190 Tom Glavine PH .20 .50
191 P.Polanco .12 .30
J.Suppan PH
192 Jose Reyes PH .20 .50
193 E.Chavez .30 .75
Y.Molina PH
194 Craig Monroe PH .12 .30
195 J.Verlander 1.00 2.50
J.Zumaya PH
196 P.LoDuca .20 .50
C.Beltran PH
197 A.Pujols .40 1.00
J.Edmonds
S.Rolen PH
198 Anthony Reyes PH .12 .30
199 Chris Carpenter PH .20 .50
200 David Eckstein PH .12 .30
201 Jered Weaver PH .40 1.00
202 D.Ortiz .30 .75
J.Dye
T.Hafner LL
203 J.Mauer .75 2.00
D.Jeter
R.Cano LL
204 D.Ortiz .30 .75
J.Morneau
R.Ibanez LL
205 Crawford/Figgins/Ichiro LL .40 1.00
206 J.Santana .20 .50
C.Wang
J.Garland LL
207 J.Santana .20 .50
R.Halladay
C.Sabathia LL
208 J.Santana .20 .50
J.Bonderman
J.Lackey LL
209 F.Rodriguez .20 .50
B.Jenks
B.Ryan LL
210 R.Howard .40 1.00
A.Pujols
A.Soriano LL
211 Sanch./Cabrera/Pujols LL .40 1.00
212 Howard/Pujols/Berk.LL .40 1.00
213 J.Reyes .20 .50
J.Pierre
H.Ramirez LL
214 D.Lowe .20 .50
B.Webb
C.Zambrano LL
215 R.Oswalt .20 .50
C.Carpenter
B.Webb LL
216 A.Harang .30 .75
J.Peavy
J.Smoltz LL
217 T.Hoffman .20 .50
B.Wagner
J.Borowski LL
218 Ichiro Suzuki AS .40 1.00
219 Derek Jeter AS .75 2.00
220 Alex Rodriguez AS .40 1.00
221 David Ortiz AS .30 .75
222 Vladimir Guerrero AS .20 .50
223 Ivan Rodriguez AS .20 .50
224 Vernon Wells AS .12 .30
225 Mark Loretta AS .12 .30
226 Kenny Rogers AS .12 .30
227 Alfonso Soriano AS .20 .50
228 Carlos Beltran AS .20 .50
229 Albert Pujols AS .40 1.00
230 Jason Bay AS .12 .30
231 Edgar Renteria AS .12 .30
232 David Wright AS .25 .60
233 Chase Utley AS .20 .50
234 Paul LoDuca AS .12 .30
235 Brad Penny AS .12 .30
236 Derrick Turnbow AS .12 .30
237 Mark Redman AS .12 .30
238 Francisco Liriano AS .30 .75
239 A.J. Pierzynski AS .12 .30
240 Grady Sizemore AS .20 .50
241 Jose Contreras AS .12 .30
242 Jermaine Dye AS .12 .30
243 Jason Schmidt AS .12 .30
244 Nomar Garciaparra AS .20 .50
245 Scott Kazmir AS .20 .50
246 Johan Santana AS .20 .50
247 Chris Capuano AS .12 .30
248 Magglio Ordonez AS .20 .50
249 Gary Matthews Jr. AS .12 .30
250 Carlos Lee AS .12 .30
251 David Eckstein AS .12 .30
252 Michael Young AS .12 .30
253 Matt Holliday AS .30 .75
254 Lance Berkman AS .20 .50
255 Scott Rolen AS .20 .50
256 Bronson Arroyo AS .12 .30
257 Barry Zito AS .20 .50
258 Brian McCann AS .12 .30
259 Jose Lopez AS .12 .30
260 Chris Carpenter AS .20 .50
261 Roy Halladay AS .20 .50
262 Jim Thome AS .20 .50
263 Dan Uggla AS .20 .50
264 Mariano Rivera AS .40 1.00
265 Roy Oswalt AS .20 .50
266 Tom Gordon AS .12 .30
267 Troy Glaus AS .12 .30
268 Bobby Jenks AS .12 .30
269 Freddy Sanchez AS .12 .30
270 Paul Konerko AS .20 .50
271 Joe Mauer AS .20 .50
272 B.J. Ryan AS .12 .30
273 Ryan Howard AS .25 .60
274 Brian Fuentes AS .12 .30
275 Miguel Cabrera AS .30 .75
276 Brandon Webb AS .20 .50
277 Mark Buehrle AS .20 .50
278 Trevor Hoffman AS .20 .50
279 Jonathan Papelbon AS .60 1.50
280 Andruw Jones AS .12 .30
281 Miguel Tejada AS .20 .50
282 Carlos Zambrano AS .20 .50
283 Ryan Howard HRD .25 .60
284 David Wright HRD .25 .60
285 Miguel Cabrera HRD .30 .75
286 David Ortiz HRD .30 .75
287 Jermaine Dye HRD .12 .30
288 Miguel Tejada HRD .20 .50
289 Lance Berkman HRD .20 .50
290 Troy Glaus HRD .12 .30
291 D.Wright .25 .60
T.Glavine TL
292 R.Howard .25 .60
T.Gordon TL
293 M.Cabrera .30 .75
D.Willis TL
294 A.Jones .30 .75
J.Smoltz TL
295 A.Soriano .20 .50
A.Soriano TL
296 A.Pujols .40 1.00
C.Carpenter TL
297 A.Dunn .20 .50
B.Arroyo TL
298 L.Berkman .20 .50
R.Oswalt TL
299 C.Capuano .60 1.50
P.Fielder TL
300 F.Sanchez .12 .30
J.Bay TL
301 C.Zambrano .20 .50
J.Pierre TL
302 A.Gonzalez .25 .60
T.Hoffman TL
303 D.Lowe .12 .30
R.Furcal TL
304 O.Vizquel .20 .50
J.Schmidt TL
305 B.Webb .20 .50
C.Tracy TL
306 M.Holliday .30 .75
G.Atkins TL
307 A.Rodriguez .40 1.00
C.Wang TL
308 C.Schilling .30 .75
D.Ortiz TL
309 R.Halladay .20 .50
V.Wells TL
310 M.Tejada .20 .50
E.Bedard TL
311 C.Crawford .20 .50
S.Kazmir TL
312 J.Bonderman .20 .50
M.Ordonez TL
313 J.Morneau .20 .50
J.Santana TL
314 J.Garland .12 .30
J.Dye TL
315 T.Hafner .20 .50
C.Sabathia TL
316 E.Brown .12 .30
M.Grudzielanek TL
317 F.Thomas .30 .75
B.Zito TL
318 J.Weaver .40 1.00
V.Guerrero TL
319 M.Young .12 .30
G.Matthews TL
320 I.Suzuki .40 1.00
J.Putz TL
321 D.Jeter .75 2.00
R.Cano CD
322 C.Carpenter .20 .50
M.Mulder CD
323 J.Schmidt .20 .50
T.Hoffman CD
324 D.Wright .25 .60
P.LoDuca CD
325 L.Berkman .20 .50
R.Oswalt CD
326 D.Jeter .75 2.00
J.Reyes CD
327 C.Floyd .25 .60
D.Wright CD
328 F.Liriano .30 .75
J.Santana CD
329 J.Drew .25 .60
S.Drew CD
330 J.Weaver .40 1.00
J.Weaver CD

2006 Topps Update 1st Edition

*1ST ED 1-132: 3X TO 8X BASIC
*1ST ED 133-170: .6X TO 1.5X BASIC RC
*1ST ED 171-330: 2X TO 5X BASIC
STATED ODDS 1:36 HOB, 1:12 HTA

2006 Topps Update Black

*BLACK 1-132: 20X TO 50X BASIC
*BLACK RC: 4X TO 10X BASIC
*BLACK 171-330: 12X TO 30X BASIC
STATED ODDS 1:7 HTA
STATED PRINT RUN 55 SER.#'d SETS

2006 Topps Update Gold

*GOLD 1-132: 2X TO 5X BASIC
*GOLD 133-170: .4X TO 1X BASIC RC
*GOLD 171-330: 1.2X TO 3X BASIC
STATED ODDS 1:4 HOB, 1:2 HTA, 1:6 RET
STATED PRINT RUN 2006 SER.#'d SETS

2006 Topps Update All Star Stitches

STATED ODDS 1:43 H,1:15 HTA,1:53 R
PATCH ODDS 1:2300 HOBBY,1:377 HTA
PATCH PRINT RUN 10 SER. #'d SETS
NO PATCH PRICING DUE TO SCARCITY
AJ Andruw Jones Jsy 5.00 12.00
AJP A.J. Pierzynski Jsy 4.00 10.00
AP Albert Pujols Jsy 12.50 30.00
AR Alex Rodriguez Jsy 6.00 15.00
AS Alfonso Soriano Jsy 5.00 12.00
BA Bronson Arroyo Jsy 5.00 12.00
BF Brian Fuentes Jsy 3.00 8.00
BJ Bobby Jenks Jsy 4.00 10.00
BM Brian McCann Jsy 6.00 15.00
BP Brad Penny Jsy 4.00 10.00
BR B.J. Ryan Jsy 4.00 10.00
BW Brandon Webb Jsy 5.00 12.00
CB Carlos Beltran Jsy 4.00 10.00
CC Chris Carpenter Jsy 5.00 12.00
CFC Chris Capuano Jsy 3.00 8.00
CL Carlos Lee Jsy 4.00 10.00
CU Chase Utley Jsy 5.00 12.00
CZ Carlos Zambrano Jsy 4.00 10.00
DE David Eckstein Jsy 6.00 15.00
DO David Ortiz Jsy 6.00 15.00
DT Derrick Turnbow Jsy 3.00 8.00
DU Dan Uggla Jsy 4.00 10.00
DW David Wright Jsy 8.00 20.00
ER Edgar Renteria Jsy 4.00 10.00
FS Freddy Sanchez Jsy 5.00 12.00
GM Gary Matthews Jr. Jsy 3.00 8.00
GS Grady Sizemore Jsy 5.00 12.00
IR Ivan Rodriguez Jsy 5.00 12.00
JB Jason Bay Jsy 6.00 15.00
JC Jose Contreras Jsy 4.00 10.00
JD Jermaine Dye Jsy 4.00 10.00
JDS Jason Schmidt Jsy 4.00 10.00
JL Jose Lopez Jsy 3.00 8.00
JM Joe Mauer Jsy 5.00 12.00
JP Jonathan Papelbon Jsy 8.00 20.00
JR Jose Reyes Jsy 3.00 8.00
JS Johan Santana Jsy 4.00 10.00
JT Jim Thome Jsy 5.00 12.00
KR Kenny Rogers Jsy 4.00 10.00
LB Lance Berkman Jsy 4.00 10.00
MAR Mark Redman Jsy 4.00 10.00
MB Mark Buehrle Jsy 4.00 10.00
MC Miguel Cabrera Jsy 5.00 12.00
MH Matt Holliday Jsy 5.00 12.00
ML Mark Loretta Jsy 4.00 10.00
MO Magglio Ordonez Jsy 4.00 10.00
MR Mariano Rivera Jsy 5.00 12.00
MT Miguel Tejada Jsy 3.00 8.00
MY Michael Young Jsy 3.00 8.00
PK Paul Konerko Jsy 4.00 10.00
PL Paul LoDuca Jsy 3.00 8.00
RC Robinson Cano Jsy 6.00 15.00
RH Roy Halladay Jsy 4.00 10.00
RJH Ryan Howard Jsy 12.50 30.00
RO Roy Oswalt Jsy 3.00 8.00
SK Scott Kazmir Jsy 4.00 10.00
SR Scott Rolen Jsy 5.00 12.00
TEG Troy Glaus Jsy 3.00 8.00
TG Tom Gordon Jsy 4.00 10.00
TH Trevor Hoffman Jsy 3.00 8.00
TMG Tom Glavine Jsy 5.00 12.00
VG Vladimir Guerrero Jsy 4.00 10.00
VW Vernon Wells Jsy 4.00 10.00

2006 Topps Update All Star Stitches Dual

STATED ODDS 1:2550 HOBBY,1:752 HTA
STATED PRINT RUN 50 SER.#'d SETS

A.Jones/M.Cabrera 10.00 25.00
J.Santana/R.Halladay 10.00 25.00
J.Thome Jsy/R.Howard Jsy 20.00 50.00
M J.Mauer/B.McCann 10.00 25.00
V D.Wright/A.Pujols 30.00 60.00
M.Rivera Jsy/T.Hoffman Jsy 30.00 60.00
D.Ortiz/A.Rodriguez 20.00 50.00
I.Suzuki/A.Soriano 20.00 50.00
M.Tejada/V.Guerrero 10.00 25.00
S G.Sizemore Jsy/V.Wells Jsy 12.50 30.00

006 Topps Update Barry Bonds 715

TATED ODDS 1:36 H,1:36 HTA,1:36 R
B Barry Bonds 1.50 4.00

2006 Topps Update Barry Bonds 715 Relics

DDS 1:5000 H,1:1827 HTA,1:5950 R
STATED PRINT RUN 715 SER.#'d SETS
B Barry Bonds Jsy 20.00 50.00

2006 Topps Update Box Bottoms

HTA1 Shawn Green .20 .50
HTA2 Austin Kearns .20 .50
HTA3 Brandon Phillips .20 .50
HTA4 Jered Weaver .60 1.50
HTA5 Carlos Lee .20 .50
HTA6 Bobby Abreu .20 .50
HTA7 Shea Hillenbrand .20 .50
HTA8 Cole Hamels .60 1.50
HTA9 Greg Maddux .60 1.50
HTA10 B.J. Upton .20 .50
HTA11 Aubrey Huff .20 .50
HTA12 Stephen Drew .40 1.00
HTA13 Sean Casey .20 .50
HTA14 Jeff Conine .20 .50
HTA15 Johan Santana .50 1.25
Francisco Liriano
HTA16 Melky Cabrera .30 .75

2006 Topps Update Rookie Debut

COMPLETE SET (45) 15.00 40.00
STATED ODDS 1:4 HOB, 1:4 RET
RD1 Joel Zumaya 1.00 2.50
RD2 Ian Kinsler 1.25 3.00
RD3 Kenji Johjima 1.00 2.50
RD4 Josh Barfield .40 1.00
RD5 Nick Markakis .75 2.00
RD6 Dan Uggla .60 1.50
RD7 Eric Reed .40 1.00
RD8 Carlos Martinez .40 1.00
RD9 Angel Pagan .40 1.00
RD10 Jason Childers .40 1.00
RD11 Ruddy Lugo .40 1.00
RD12 James Loney .60 1.50
RD13 Fernando Nieve .40 1.00
RD14 Reggie Abercrombie .40 1.00
RD15 Boone Logan .40 1.00
RD16 Brian Bannister .40 1.00
RD17 Ricky Nolasco .40 1.00
RD18 Willie Eyre .40 1.00
RD19 Fabio Castro .40 1.00
RD20 Jordan Tata .40 1.00
RD21 Taylor Buchholz .40 1.00
RD22 Sean Marshall .40 1.00
RD23 John Rheinecker .40 1.00
RD24 Casey Janssen .40 1.00
RD25 Russ Martin .60 1.50
RD26 Yusmeiro Petit .40 1.00
RD27 Kendry Morales 1.00 2.50
RD28 Alay Soler .40 1.00
RD29 Jered Weaver 1.25 3.00
RD30 Matt Kemp 1.00 2.50
RD31 Enrique Gonzalez .40 1.00
RD32 Lastings Milledge .40 1.00
RD33 Jamie Shields 1.25 3.00
RD34 David Pauley .40 1.00
RD35 Zach Jackson .40 1.00
RD36 Zach Minor .40 1.00
RD37 Jon Lester 1.50 4.00
RD38 Chad Billingsley .60 1.50
RD39 Scott Thorman .40 1.00
RD40 Anibal Sanchez .40 1.00
RD41 Mike Thompson .40 1.00
RD42 T.J. Beam .40 1.00
RD43 Stephen Drew .75 2.00
RD44 Joe Saunders .40 1.00
RD45 Carlos Quentin .60 1.50

2006 Topps Update Rookie Debut Autographs

A ODDS 1:10,600 H,1:4416 HTA,1:15,500 R
B ODDS 1:5600 H, 1:2163 HTA,1:7500 R
C ODDS 1:2200 H, 1:815 HTA,1:2650 R
D ODDS 1:1180 H, 1:415 HTA,1:1500 R
NO GROUP A PRICING DUE TO SCARCITY
AL Adam Loewen B 6.00 15.00
BL Bobby Livingston C 6.00 15.00
EF Emiliano Fruto C 6.00 15.00
FC Fausto Carmona C 6.00 15.00
JL Jon Lester D 8.00 20.00
JS Jeremy Sowers B 6.00 15.00
MN Mike Napoli D 12.50 30.00
MP Martin Prado D 8.00 20.00
RN Ricky Nolasco D 6.00 15.00
ST Scott Thorman C 6.00 15.00
YP Yusmeiro Petit D 6.00 15.00

2006 Topps Update Touch 'Em All Base Relics

STATED ODDS 1:610 HOBBY,1:90 HTA
AP Albert Pujols 12.50 30.00
AR Alex Rodriguez 10.00 25.00
CB Carlos Beltran 5.00 12.00
DO David Ortiz 8.00 20.00
DW David Wright 10.00 25.00
IS Ichiro Suzuki 10.00 25.00
JM Joe Mauer 6.00 15.00
MT Miguel Tejada 5.00 12.00
MY Michael Young 5.00 12.00
RH Ryan Howard 10.00 25.00

2006 Topps All-Star FanFest

1 Ichiro Suzuki 1.25 3.00
2 Roberto Clemente 2.50 6.00
3 Albert Pujols 1.25 3.00
4 Mickey Mantle 3.00 8.00
5 Alex Rodriguez 1.25 3.00

2006 Topps National 1955-56 VIP Promos

211 Mickey Mantle 55 6.00 15.00
341 Frank Robinson 56 1.25 3.00
342 Duke Snider 56 HR 1.25 3.00
343 Brooks Robinson 56 1.25 3.00
344 Mickey Mantle 56 TC 6.00 15.00

2007 Topps

COMP.HOBBY SET (661) 40.00 80.00
COMP.HOLIDAY SET (661) 40.00 80.00
COMP.CARDINALS SET (661) 40.00 80.00
COMP.CUBS SET (661) 40.00 80.00
COMP.DODGERS SET (661) 40.00 80.00
COMP.RED SOX SET (661) 40.00 80.00
COMP.YANKEES SET (661) 40.00 80.00
COMP.SET w/o VAR. (661) 40.00 80.00
COMPLETE SERIES 1 (330) 15.00 40.00
COMP.SERIES 1 w/o #40 (329) 10.00 25.00
COMPLETE SERIES 2 (331) 25.00 50.00
COMMON CARD (1-330) .07 .20
COMMON RC .20 .50
SER.1 VAR. ODDS 1:3700 WAL-MART
SER.2 VAR.ODDS 1:30 HOBBY
NO SER.1 VAR.PRICING DUE TO SCARTIY
OVERALL PLATE SER.1 ODDS 1:98 HTA
OVERALL PLATE SER.2 ODDS 1:139 HTA
PLATE PRINT RUN 1 SET PER COLOR
BLACK-CYAN-MAGENTA-YELLOW ISSUED
NO PLATE PRICING DUE TO SCARCITY
1 John Lackey .12 .30
2 Nick Swisher .12 .30
3 Brad Lidge .07 .20
4 Bengie Molina .07 .20
5 Bobby Abreu .07 .20
6 Edgar Renteria .07 .20
7 Mickey Mantle .60 1.50
8 Preston Wilson .07 .20
9 Ryan Zimmerman .07 .20
10 C.C. Sabathia .12 .30
11 Julio Lugo .07 .20
12 J.D. Drew .07 .20
13 Miguel Batista .07 .20
14 Eliezer Alfonzo .07 .20
15a Andrew Miller RC .75 2.00
15b A.Miller Posed RC .75 2.00
16 Jason Varitek .20 .50
17 Saul Rivera .07 .20
18 Orlando Hernandez .07 .20
19 Alfredo Amezaga .07 .20
20a D.Young Face Right (RC) .30 .75
20b D.Young Face Left (RC) .30 .75
21 Chris Britton .07 .20
22 Corey Patterson .07 .20
23 Josh Bard .07 .20
24 Tom Gordon .07 .20
25 Gary Matthews .07 .20
26 Jason Jennings .07 .20
27 Joey Gathright .07 .20
28 Brandon Inge .07 .20
29 Pat Neshek .40 1.00
30 Bronson Arroyo .07 .20
31 Jay Payton .07 .20
32 Andy Pettitte .12 .30
33 Ervin Santana .07 .20
34 Paul Konerko .12 .30
35 Joel Zumaya .07 .20
36 Gregg Zaun .07 .20
37 Tony Gwynn Jr. .07 .20
38 Adam LaRoche .07 .20
39 Jim Edmonds .12 .30
40a D.Jeter w Mantle/Bush 5.00 12.00
40b Derek Jeter .50 1.25
41 Rich Hill .07 .20
42 Livan Hernandez .07 .20
43 Aubrey Huff .07 .20
44 Todd Greene .07 .20
45 Andre Ethier .12 .30
46 Jeremy Sowers .07 .20
47 Ben Broussard .07 .20
48 Darren Oliver .07 .20
49 Nook Logan .07 .20
50 Miguel Cabrera .20 .50
51 Carlos Lee .07 .20
52 Jose Castillo .07 .20
53 Mike Piazza .20 .50
54 Daniel Cabrera .07 .20
55 Cole Hamels .15 .40
56 Mark Loretta .07 .20
57 Brian Fuentes .07 .20
58 Todd Coffey .07 .20
59 Brent Clevlen .07 .20
60 John Smoltz .20 .50
61 Jason Grilli .07 .20
62 Dan Wheeler .07 .20
63 Scott Proctor .07 .20
64 Bobby Kielty .07 .20
65 Dan Uggla .07 .20
66 Lyle Overbay .07 .20
67 Geoff Jenkins .07 .20
68 Michael Barrett .07 .20
69 Casey Fossum .07 .20
70 Ivan Rodriguez .12 .30
71 Jose Lopez .07 .20
72 Jake Westbrook .07 .20
73 Moises Alou .07 .20
74 Jose Valverde .07 .20
75 Jered Weaver .12 .30
76 Lastings Milledge .12 .30
77 Austin Kearns .07 .20
78 Adam Loewen .07 .20
79 Josh Barfield .07 .20
80 Johan Santana .12 .30
81 Ian Kinsler .12 .30
82 Ian Snell .07 .20
83 Mike Lowell .07 .20
84 Elizardo Ramirez .07 .20
85 Scott Rolen .12 .30
86 Shannon Stewart .07 .20
87 Alexis Gomez .07 .20
88 Jimmy Gobble .07 .20
89 Jamey Carroll .07 .20
90 Chipper Jones .20 .50
91 Carlos Silva .07 .20
92 Joe Crede .07 .20
93 Mike Napoli .07 .20
94 Willy Taveras .07 .20
95 Rafael Furcal .07 .20
96 Phil Nevin .07 .20
97 Dave Bush .07 .20
98 Marcus Giles .07 .20
99 Joe Blanton .07 .20
100 Dontrelle Willis .07 .20
101 Scott Kazmir .12 .30
102 Jeff Kent .07 .20
103 Pedro Feliz .07 .20
104 Johnny Estrada .07 .20
105 Travis Hafner .07 .20
106 Ryan Garko .07 .20
107 Rafael Soriano .07 .20
108 Wes Helms .07 .20
109 Billy Wagner .07 .20
110 Aaron Rowand .07 .20
111 Felipe Lopez .07 .20
112 Jeff Conine .07 .20
113 Nick Markakis .15 .40
114 John Koronka .07 .20
115 B.J. Ryan .07 .20
116 Tim Wakefield .12 .30
117 David Ross .07 .20
118 Emil Brown .07 .20
119 Michael Cuddyer .07 .20
120 Jason Giambi .07 .20
121 Alex Cintron .07 .20
122 Luke Scott .07 .20
123 Chone Figgins .07 .20
124 Huston Street .07 .20
125 Carlos Delgado .07 .20
126 Daryle Ward .07 .20
127 Chris Duncan .07 .20
128 Damian Miller .07 .20
129 Aramis Ramirez .07 .20
130 Albert Pujols .25 .60
131 Chris Snyder .07 .20
132 Ray Durham .07 .20
133 Gary Sheffield .07 .20
134 Mike Jacobs .07 .20
135a Troy Tulowitzki (RC) .60 1.50
135b T.Tulowitzki Throw (RC) .60 1.50
136 Jon Rauch .07 .20
137 Jay Gibbons .07 .20
138 Adrian Gonzalez .15 .40
139 Prince Fielder .12 .30
140 Freddy Sanchez .07 .20
141 Rich Aurilia .07 .20
142 Trot Nixon .07 .20
143 Vicente Padilla .07 .20
144 Jack Wilson .07 .20
145 Jake Peavy .07 .20
146 Luke Hudson .07 .20
147 Javier Vazquez .07 .20
148 Scott Podsednik .07 .20
149 M.Ordonez .12 .30
I.Rodriguez CC
150 Todd Helton .12 .30
151 Kendry Morales .07 .20
152 Adam Everett .07 .20
153 Bob Wickman .07 .20
154 Bill Hall .07 .20
155 Jeremy Bonderman .07 .20
156 Ryan Theriot .07 .20
157 Rocco Baldelli .07 .20
158 Noah Lowry .07 .20
159 Jason Michaels .07 .20
160 Justin Verlander .20 .50
161 Eduardo Perez .07 .20
162 Chris Ray .07 .20
163 Dave Roberts .12 .30
164 Zach Duke .07 .20
165 Mark Buehrle .12 .30
166 Hank Blalock .07 .20
167 Royce Clayton .07 .20
168 Mark Teahen .07 .20
169 Todd Jones .07 .20
170 Chien-Ming Wang .12 .30
171 Nick Punto .07 .20
172 Morgan Ensberg .07 .20
173 Rob Mackowiak .07 .20
174 Frank Catalanotto .07 .20
175 Matt Murton .07 .20
176 A.Soriano .12 .30
C.Beltran CC
177 Francisco Cordero .07 .20
178 Jason Marquis .07 .20
179 Joe Nathan .07 .20
180 Roy Halladay .12 .30
181 Melvin Mora .07 .20
182 Ramon Ortiz .07 .20
183 Jose Valentin .07 .20
184 Gil Meche .07 .20
185 B.J. Upton .07 .20
186 Grady Sizemore .12 .30
187 Matt Cain .12 .30
188 Eric Byrnes .07 .20
189 Carl Crawford .12 .30
190 J.J. Putz .07 .20
191 Cla Meredith .07 .20
192 Matt Capps .07 .20
193 Rod Barajas .07 .20
194 Edwin Encarnacion .20 .50
195 James Loney .07 .20
196 Johnny Damon .12 .30
197 Freddy Garcia .07 .20
198 Mike Redmond .07 .20
199 Ryan Shealy .07 .20
200 Carlos Beltran .12 .30
201 Chuck James .07 .20
202 Mark Ellis .07 .20
203 Brad Ausmus .07 .20
204 Juan Rivera .07 .20
205 Cory Sullivan .07 .20
206 Ben Sheets .07 .20
207 Mark Mulder .07 .20
208 Carlos Quentin .07 .20
209 Jonathan Broxton .07 .20
210 Kazuo Matsui .07 .20
211 Armando Benitez .07 .20
212 Richie Sexson .07 .20
213 Josh Johnson .20 .50
214 Brian Schneider .07 .20
215 Craig Monroe .07 .20
216 Chris Duffy .07 .20
217 Chris Coste .07 .20
218 Clay Hensley .07 .20
219 Chris Gomez .07 .20
220 Hideki Matsui .20 .50
221 Robinson Tejeda .07 .20
222 Scott Hatteberg .07 .20
223 Jeff Francis .07 .20
224 Matt Thornton .07 .20
225 Robinson Cano .12 .30
226 Chicago White Sox .07 .20
227 Oakland Athletics .07 .20
228 St. Louis Cardinals .07 .20
229 New York Mets .07 .20
230 Barry Zito .12 .30
231 Baltimore Orioles .07 .20
232 Seattle Mariners .07 .20
233 Houston Astros .07 .20
234 Pittsburgh Pirates .07 .20
235 Reed Johnson .07 .20
236 Boston Red Sox .20 .50
237 Cincinnati Reds .07 .20
238 Philadelphia Phillies .07 .20
239 New York Yankees .20 .50
240 Chris Carpenter .12 .30
241 Atlanta Braves .07 .20
242 San Francisco Giants .07 .20
243 Joe Torre MG .12 .30
244 Tampa Bay Devil Rays .07 .20
245 Chad Tracy .07 .20
246 Clint Hurdle MG .07 .20
247 Mike Scioscia MG .07 .20
248 Ron Gardenhire MG .07 .20
249 Tony LaRussa MG .12 .30
250 Anibal Sanchez .07 .20
251 Charlie Manuel MG .07 .20
252 John Gibbons MG .07 .20
253 Jim Tracy MG .07 .20
254 Jerry Narron MG .07 .20
255 Brad Penny .07 .20
256 Bobby Cox MG .07 .20
257 Bob Melvin MG .07 .20
258 Mike Hargrove MG .07 .20
259 Phil Garner MG .07 .20
260 David Wright .15 .40
261 Vinny Rottino (RC) .20 .50
262 Ryan Braun RC .20 .50
263 Kevin Kouzmanoff (RC) .20 .50
264 David Murphy (RC) .20 .50
265 Jimmy Rollins .12 .30
266 Joe Maddon MG .12 .30
267 Grady Little MG .07 .20
268 Ryan Sweeney (RC) .20 .50
269 Fred Lewis (RC) .30 .75
270 Alfonso Soriano .12 .30
271a Delwyn Young (RC) .20 .50
271b D.Young Swing (RC) .20 .50
272 Jeff Salazar (RC) .20 .50
273 Miguel Montero (RC) .20 .50
274 Shawn Riggans (RC) .20 .50
275 Greg Maddux .25 .60
276 Brian Stokes (RC) .20 .50
277 Philip Humber (RC) .20 .50
278 Scott Moore (RC) .20 .50
279 Adam Lind (RC) .20 .50
280 Curt Schilling .12 .30
281 Chris Narveson (RC) .20 .50
282 Oswaldo Navarro RC .20 .50
283 Drew Anderson RC .20 .50
284 Jerry Owens (RC) .20 .50
285 Stephen Drew .07 .20
286 Joaquin Arias (RC) .20 .50
287 Jose Garcia RC .20 .50
288 Shane Youman RC .20 .50
289 Brian Burres (RC) .20 .50
290 Matt Holliday .20 .50
291 Ryan Feierabend (RC) .20 .50
292a Josh Fields (RC) .20 .50
292b J.Fields Running (RC) .20 .50
293 Glen Perkins (RC) .20 .50
294 Mike Rabelo RC .20 .50
295 Jorge Posada .12 .30
296 Ubaldo Jimenez (RC) .60 1.50
297 Brad Ausmus GG .07 .20
298 Eric Chavez GG .07 .20
299 Orlando Hudson GG .07 .20
300 Vladimir Guerrero .12 .30
301 Derek Jeter GG .50 1.25
302 Scott Rolen GG .12 .30
303 Mark Grudzielanek GG .07 .20
304 Kenny Rogers GG .07 .20
305 Frank Thomas .20 .50
306 Mike Cameron GG .07 .20
307 Torii Hunter GG .07 .20
308 Albert Pujols GG .25 .60
309 Mark Teixeira GG .12 .30
310 Jonathan Papelbon .20 .50
311 Greg Maddux GG .25 .60
312 Carlos Beltran GG .12 .30
313 Ichiro Suzuki GG .25 .60
314 Andruw Jones GG .07 .20
315 Manny Ramirez .20 .50
316 Vernon Wells GG .07 .20
317 Omar Vizquel GG .12 .30
318 Ivan Rodriguez GG .12 .30
319 Brandon Webb CY .12 .30
320 Magglio Ordonez .12 .30
321 Johan Santana CY .12 .30
322 Ryan Howard MVP .15 .40
323 Justin Morneau MVP .12 .30
324 Hanley Ramirez ROY .12 .30
325 Joe Mauer .15 .40
326 Justin Verlander ROY .20 .50
327 B.Abreu .50 1.25
D.Jeter CC
328 C.Delgado .15 .40
D.Wright CC
329 Y.Molina .25 .60
A.Pujols CC
330 Ryan Howard .15 .40
331 Kelly Johnson .07 .20
332 Chris Young .07 .20
333 Mark Kotsay .07 .20
334 A.J. Burnett .07 .20
335 Brian McCann .07 .20
336 Woody Williams .07 .20
337 Jason Isringhausen .07 .20
338 Juan Pierre .07 .20
339 Jonny Gomes .07 .20
340 Roger Clemens .25 .60
341 Akinori Iwamura RC .50 1.25
342 Bengie Molina .07 .20
343 Shin-Soo Choo .12 .30
344 Kenji Johjima .20 .50
345 Joe Borowski .07 .20
346 Shawn Green .07 .20
347 Chicago Cubs .07 .20
348 Rodrigo Lopez .07 .20
349 Brian Giles .07 .20
350 Chase Utley .12 .30
351 Mark DeRosa .07 .20
352 Carl Pavano .07 .20
353 Kyle Lohse .07 .20
354 Chris Iannetta .07 .20
355 Oliver Perez .07 .20
356 Curtis Granderson .15 .40
357 Sean Casey .07 .20
358 Jason Tyner .07 .20
359 Jon Garland .07 .20
360 David Ortiz .20 .50
361 Adam Kennedy .07 .20
362 Chris Burke .07 .20
363 Bobby Crosby .07 .20
364 Conor Jackson .07 .20
365 Tim Hudson .12 .30
366 Rickie Weeks .07 .20
367 Cristian Guzman .07 .20
368 Mark Prior .12 .30
369 Ben Zobrist .12 .30
370 Troy Glaus .07 .20
371 Kenny Lofton .07 .20
372 Shane Victorino .07 .20
373 Cliff Lee .12 .30
374 Adrian Beltre .20 .50
375 Miguel Olivo .07 .20
376 Endy Chavez .07 .20
377 Zack Segovia (RC) .20 .50
378 Ramon Hernandez .07 .20
379 Chris Young .07 .20
380 Jason Schmidt .07 .20
381 Ronny Paulino .07 .20
382 Kevin Millwood .07 .20
383 Jon Lester .12 .30
384 Alex Gonzalez .07 .20
385 Brad Hawpe .07 .20
386 Placido Polanco .07 .20
387 Nate Robertson .07 .20
388 Torii Hunter .07 .20
389 Gavin Floyd .07 .20
390 Roy Oswalt .12 .30
391 Kelvim Escobar .07 .20
392 Craig Wilson .07 .20
393 Milton Bradley .07 .20
394 Aaron Hill .07 .20
395 Matt Diaz .07 .20
396 Chris Capuano .07 .20
397 Juan Encarnacion .07 .20
398 Jacque Jones .07 .20
399 James Shields .07 .20
400 Ichiro Suzuki .25 .60
401 Matt Kemp .15 .40
402 Matt Morris .07 .20
403 Casey Blake .07 .20
404 Corey Hart .07 .20
405 Josh Willingham .12 .30
406 Ryan Madson .07 .20
407 Nick Johnson .07 .20
408 Kevin Millar .07 .20
409 Khalil Greene .07 .20
410 Tom Glavine .12 .30
411a Jason Bay .12 .30
411b Jason Bay No Sig 2.00 5.00
412 Gerald Laird .07 .20
413 Coco Crisp .07 .20
414 Brandon Phillips .07 .20
415 Aaron Cook .07 .20
416 Mark Redman .07 .20
417 Mike Maroth .07 .20
418 Boof Bonser .07 .20
419 Jorge Cantu .07 .20
420 Jeff Weaver .07 .20
421 Melky Cabrera .07 .20
422 Francisco Rodriguez .12 .30
423 Mike Lamb .07 .20
424 Dan Haren .07 .20
425 Tomo Ohka .07 .20
426 Jeff Francoeur .20 .50
427 Randy Wolf .07 .20
428 So Taguchi .07 .20
429 Carlos Zambrano .12 .30
430 Justin Morneau .12 .30
431 Luis Gonzalez .07 .20
432 Takashi Saito .07 .20
433 Brandon Morrow RC 1.00 2.50
434 Victor Martinez .12 .30
435 Felix Hernandez .12 .30
436 Ricky Nolasco .07 .20
437a Paul LoDuca .07 .20
437b Paul LoDuca No Sig 2.00 5.00
438 Chad Cordero .07 .20
439 Miguel Tejada .12 .30
440 Mark Teixeira .12 .30
441 Pat Burrell .07 .20
442 Paul Maholm .07 .20
443 Mike Cameron .07 .20
444 Josh Beckett .07 .20
445 Pablo Ozuna .07 .20
446 Jaret Wright .07 .20
447 Angel Berroa .07 .20
448 Fernando Rodney .07 .20
449 Francisco Liriano .07 .20
450 Ken Griffey Jr. .40 1.00
451 Bobby Jenks .07 .20
452 Mike Mussina .12 .30
453 Howie Kendrick .07 .20
454 Milwaukee Brewers .07 .20
455 Dan Johnson .07 .20
456 Ted Lilly .07 .20
457 Mike Hampton .07 .20
458 J.J. Hardy .07 .20
459 Jeff Suppan .07 .20
460 Jose Reyes .12 .30
461 Jae Seo .07 .20
462 Edgar Gonzalez .07 .20
463 Russell Martin .07 .20
464 Omar Vizquel .12 .30
465 Jhonny Peralta .07 .20
466 Raul Ibanez .12 .30
467 Hanley Ramirez .12 .30
468 Kerry Wood .07 .20
469 Ryan Church .07 .20
470 Gary Sheffield .07 .20
471 David Wells .07 .20
472 David Dellucci .07 .20
473 Xavier Nady .07 .20
474 Michael Young .07 .20
475 Kevin Youkilis .07 .20
476 Aaron Harang .07 .20
477 Brian Lawrence .07 .20
478 Octavio Dotel .07 .20
479 Chris Shelton .07 .20
480 Matt Garza .07 .20
481a Jim Thome .12 .30
481b Jim Thome No Sig 2.00 5.00
482 Jose Contreras .07 .20
483 Kris Benson .07 .20
484 John Maine .07 .20
485 Tadahito Iguchi .07 .20
486 Wandy Rodriguez .07 .20
487 Eric Chavez .07 .20
488 Vernon Wells .07 .20
489 Doug Davis .07 .20
490 Andruw Jones .07 .20
491 David Eckstein .07 .20
492a Michael Barrett .07 .20
492b John Buck 2.00 5.00
493 Greg Norton .07 .20
494 Orlando Hudson .07 .20
495 Wilson Betemit .07 .20
496 Ryan Klesko .07 .20
497 Fausto Carmona .07 .20
498 Jarrod Washburn .07 .20
499 Aaron Boone .07 .20
500 Pedro Martinez .12 .30
501 Mike O'Connor .07 .20
502 Brian Roberts .07 .20
503 Jeff Cirillo .07 .20
504 Brett Myers .07 .20
505 Jose Bautista .12 .30
506 Akinori Otsuka .07 .20
507 Shea Hillenbrand .07 .20
508 Ryan Langerhans .07 .20
509 Josh Fogg .07 .20
510 Alex Rodriguez .25 .60
511 Kenny Rogers .07 .20
512 Jason Kubel .07 .20
513 Jermaine Dye .07 .20
514 Mark Grudzielanek .07 .20
515 Josh Phelps .07 .20
516 Bartolo Colon .07 .20
517 Craig Biggio .12 .30
518 Esteban Loaiza .07 .20
519 Alex Rios .07 .20
520 Adam Dunn .12 .30
521 Derrick Turnbow .07 .20
522 Anthony Reyes .07 .20
523 Derrek Lee .07 .20
524 Ty Wigginton .07 .20
525 Jeremy Hermida .07 .20
526 Derek Lowe .07 .20
527 Randy Winn .07 .20
528 Paul Byrd .07 .20
529 Chris Snelling .07 .20
530 Brandon Webb .12 .30
531 Julio Franco .07 .20
532 Jose Vidro .07 .20
533 Erik Bedard .07 .20
534 Termel Sledge .07 .20
535 Jon Lieber .07 .20
536 Tom Gorzelanny .07 .20
537 Kip Wells .07 .20
538 Wily Mo Pena .07 .20
539 Eric Milton .07 .20
540 Chad Billingsley .12 .30
541 David DeJesus .07 .20
542 Omar Infante .07 .20
543 Rondell White .07 .20
544 Juan Uribe .07 .20
545 Miguel Cairo .07 .20
546 Orlando Cabrera .07 .20
547 Byung-Hyun Kim .07 .20
548 Jason Kendall .07 .20
549 Horacio Ramirez .07 .20
550 Trevor Hoffman .12 .30
551 Ronnie Belliard .07 .20
552 Chris Woodward .07 .20
553 Ramon Martinez .07 .20
554 Elizardo Ramirez .07 .20

555 Andy Marte .07 .20
556 John Patterson .07 .20
557 Scott Olsen .07 .20
558 Steve Trachsel .07 .20
559 Doug Mientkiewicz .07 .20
560 Randy Johnson .20 .50
561 Chan Ho Park .12 .30
562 Jamie Moyer .07 .20
563 Mike Gonzalez .07 .20
564 Nelson Cruz .20 .50
565 Alex Cora .12 .30
566 Ryan Freel .07 .20
567 Chris Stewart RC .20 .50
568 Carlos Guillen .07 .20
569 Jason Bartlett .07 .20
570 Mariano Rivera .25 .60
571 Norris Hopper .07 .20
572 Alex Escobar .07 .20
573 Gustavo Chacin .07 .20
574 Brandon McCarthy .07 .20
575 Seth McClung .07 .20
576 Yuniesky Betancourt .07 .20
577 Jason LaRue .07 .20
578 Dustin Pedroia .15 .40
579 Taylor Tankersley .07 .20
580 Garret Anderson .07 .20
581 Mike Sweeney .07 .20
582 Scott Thorman .07 .20
583 Joe Inglett .07 .20
584 Clint Barmes .07 .20
585 Willie Bloomquist .07 .20
586 Willy Aybar .07 .20
587 Brian Bannister .07 .20
588 Jose Guillen UER .07 .20
589 Brad Wilkerson .07 .20
590 Lance Berkman .12 .30
591 Toronto Blue Jays .07 .20
592 Florida Marlins .07 .20
593 Washington Nationals .07 .20
594 Los Angeles Angels .07 .20
595 Cleveland Indians .07 .20
596 Texas Rangers .07 .20
597 Detroit Tigers .07 .20
598 Arizona Diamondbacks .07 .20
599 Kansas City Royals .07 .20
600 Ryan Zimmerman .12 .30
601 Colorado Rockies .07 .20
602 Minnesota Twins .07 .20
603 Los Angeles Dodgers .07 .20
604 San Diego Padres .07 .20
605 Bruce Bochy MG .12 .30
606 Ron Washington MG .07 .20
607 Manny Acta MG .07 .20
608 Sam Perlozzo MG .07 .20
609 Terry Francona MG .12 .30
610 Jim Leyland MG .07 .20
611 Eric Wedge MG .07 .20
612 Ozzie Guillen MG .07 .20
613 Buddy Bell MG .07 .20
614 Bob Geren MG .07 .20
615 Lou Piniella MG .07 .20
616 Fredi Gonzalez MG .07 .20
617 Ned Yost MG .07 .20
618 Willie Randolph MG .07 .20
619 Bud Black MG .07 .20
620 Garrett Atkins .07 .20
621 Alexi Casilla RC .30 .75
622 Matt Chico (RC) .20 .50
623 Alejandro De Aza RC .30 .75
624 Jeremy Brown .07 .20
625 Josh Hamilton (RC) .60 1.50
626 Doug Slaten RC .20 .50
627 Andy Cannizaro RC .20 .50
628 Juan Salas (RC) .20 .50
629 Levale Speigner RC .20 .50
630a D.Matsuzaka English RC .75 2.00
630b D.Matsuzaka Japanese 1.50 4.00
630c Daisuke Matsuzaka No Sig 1.50 4.00
631 Elijah Dukes RC .30 .75
632 Kevin Cameron RC .20 .50
633 Juan Perez RC .20 .50
634a Alex Gordon RC .60 1.50
634b A.Gordon No Sig 2.00 5.00
635 Juan Lara RC .20 .50
636a Mike Rabelo RC .20 .50
636b Billy Butler (RC)
637 Justin Hampson (RC) .20 .50
638 Cesar Jimenez RC .20 .50
639 Joe Smith RC .20 .50
640 Kei Igawa RC .50 1.25
641 Hideki Okajima RC 1.00 2.50
642 Sean Henn (RC) .20 .50
643 Jay Marshall RC .20 .50
644 Jared Burton RC .20 .50
645 Angel Sanchez RC .20 .50
646 Devern Hansack RC .20 .50
647 Juan Morillo (RC) .20 .50
648 Hector Gimenez (RC) .20 .50
649 Brian Barden RC .20 .50
650 A.Rodriguez .25 .60
J.Giambi CC
651 J.Michaels .07 .20
T.Hafner CC
652 J.Johnson .20 .50
M.Olivo CC
653 S.Casey .07 .20
P.Polanco CC
654 I.Rodriguez .12 .30
F.Rodney CC
655 D.Uggla .12 .30
H.Ramirez CC
656 C.Beltran .12 .30
J.Reyes CC
657 A.Rodriguez .50 1.25
D.Jeter CC
658 A.Rowand .12 .30
J.Rollins CC
659 A.Berroa .07 .20
A.Blanco CC
660a Yadier Molina .20 .50
660b Yadier Molina No Sig 2.00 5.00
661 Barry Bonds 3.00 8.00

2007 Topps 1st Edition

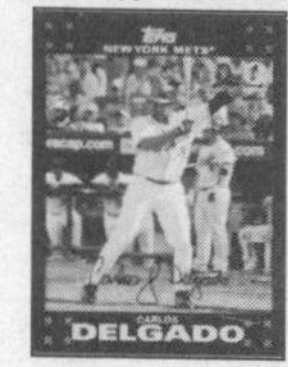

*1st ED: 3X TO 8X BASIC
*1st ED RC: 1.25X TO 3X BASIC
SER.1 ODDS 1:36 HOBBY, 1:5 HTA
SER.2 ODDS 1:36 HOBBY, 1:5 HTA

2007 Topps Copper

COMMON CARD (1-660) 6.00 15.00
UNLISTED STARS 10.00 25.00
SER.1 ODDS 1:7 HTA
SER.2 ODDS 1:10 HTA
STATED PRINT RUN 56 SERIAL #'d SETS
7 Mickey Mantle 75.00 150.00
15 Andrew Miller 100.00 150.00
29 Pat Neshek 30.00 60.00
40 D.Jeter w Mantle/Bush 400.00 800.00
53 Mike Piazza 15.00 40.00
58 Todd Coffey 10.00 25.00
130 Albert Pujols 30.00 60.00
170 Chien-Ming Wang 30.00 60.00
236 Boston Red Sox CL 6.00 15.00
239 New York Yankees CL 10.00 25.00
260 David Wright 15.00 40.00
275 Greg Maddux 15.00 40.00
301 Derek Jeter GG 40.00 80.00
305 Frank Thomas 15.00 40.00
308 Albert Pujols GG 30.00 60.00
311 Greg Maddux GG 15.00 40.00
313 Ichiro Suzuki GG 15.00 40.00
322 Ryan Howard MVP 15.00 40.00
327 B.Abreu 20.00 50.00
D.Jeter CC
328 C.Delgado 15.00 40.00
D.Wright CC
329 Y.Molina 10.00 25.00
A.Pujols CC
330 Ryan Howard 15.00 40.00
340 Roger Clemens 20.00 50.00
341 Akinori Iwamura 15.00 40.00
360 David Ortiz 20.00 50.00
362 Chris Burke 10.00 25.00
400 Ichiro Suzuki 12.50 30.00
403 Casey Blake 15.00 40.00
413 Coco Crisp 10.00 25.00
444 Josh Beckett 10.00 25.00
450 Ken Griffey Jr. 30.00 80.00
460 Jose Reyes 10.00 25.00
475 Kevin Youkilis 10.00 25.00
510 Alex Rodriguez 20.00 50.00
625 Josh Hamilton 30.00 60.00
630 Daisuke Matsuzaka 100.00 150.00
634 Alex Gordon 15.00 40.00
641 Hideki Okajima 20.00 50.00
650 A.Rodriguez 15.00 40.00
J.Giambi CC
657 A.Rodriguez 20.00 50.00
D.Jeter CC

2007 Topps Gold

*GOLD: 6X TO 15X BASIC
*GOLD RC: 2.5X TO 6X BASIC RC
SER.1 ODDS 1:11 H, 1:3 HTA, 1:24 K-MART
SER.1 ODDS 1:6 RACK, 1:11 TARGET
SER.1 ODDS 1:24 WAL-MART
SER.2 ODDS 1:11 HOBBY, 1:2 HTA
STATED PRINT RUN 2007 SER.#'d SETS
40 D.Jeter w Mantle/Bush 125.00 250.00

2007 Topps Red Back

COMP.SERIES 1 (330) 40.00 80.00
COMP.SERIES 2 (330) 40.00 80.00
*RED: 1X TO 2.5X BASIC
*RED RC: .5X TO 1.2X BASIC RC
SER.1 ODDS 2:1 H, 10:1 HTA, 3:1 RACK
40 Jeter/Mantle/Bush 10.00 25.00

2007 Topps '52 Mantle Reprint Relic

SER.1 ODDS 1:158,700 H, 1:8721 HTA
SER.1 ODDS 1:602,600 K-MART
SER.1 ODDS 1:127,100 TARGET
SER 1 ODDS 1:602,600 WAL-MART
STATED PRINT RUN 52 SERIAL #'d SETS
NO PRICING DUE TO SCARCITY
52MM Mickey Mantle Bat 125.00 250.00

2007 Topps Alex Rodriguez Road to 500

COMMON CARD (1-75/101-425) 1.00 2.50
COMMON CARD (76-100) 12.00 30.00
COMMON CARD (401-425) 5.00 12.00
COMMON CARD (451-475) 3.00 8.00
COMMON CARD (476-499) 3.00 8.00
SER.1 ODDS 1:36 H, 1:5 HTA, 1:36 K-MART
SER.1 ODDS 1:36 RACK, 1:36 TARGET
SER.1 ODDS 1:36 WAL-MART
FINEST ODDS TWO PER AROD BOX TOPPER
HERITAGE ODDS 1:24 HOBBY/RETAIL
OPENING DAY ODDS 1:36 H, 1:36 R
MOMENTS ODDS TWO PER BOX TOPPER
CO-SIG ODDS TWO PER AROD BOX TOPPER
BOWMAN ODDS 1:6 HOBBY, 1:2 HTA
SER.2 ODDS 1:36 HOBBY, 1:5 HTA
T.CHROME ODDS TWO PER BOX TOPPER
ALLEN AND GINTER ODDS 1:24 H, 1:24 R
BOW.CHR. ODDS 1:9 HOBBY
TURKEY RED ODDS 1:24 HOBBY/RETAIL
BOW.HER ODDS TWO PER BOX TOPPER
UPDATE ODDS 1:36 H, 1:5 HTA, 1:36 R
TOPPS 52 ODDS 1:20 H, 1:20 R
CARDS 1-25 ISSUED IN SERIES 1
CARDS 26-50 ISSUED IN FINEST
CARDS 51-75 ISSUED IN HERITAGE
CARDS 76-100 ISSUED IN OPENING DAY
CARDS 101-125 ISSUED IN MOMENTS
CARDS 126-175 ISSUED IN BOWMAN
CARDS 176-200 ISSUED IN CO-SIGNERS
CARDS 201-225 ISSUED IN SERIES 2
CARDS 226-250 ISSUED IN TOP.CHROME
CARDS 251-275 ISSUED IN ALLEN GINTER
CARDS 276-300 ISSUED IN BOW.CHR.
CARDS 301-325 ISSUSED IN TUR.RED
CARDS 326-350 ISSUED IN 08 FINEST
CARDS 351-375 ISSUED IN BOW.HER.
CARDS 376-400 ISSUED IN UPDATE
CARDS 401-425 ISSUED IN BOW.BEST
CARDS 426-450 ISSUED IN BOW.DRAFT
CARDS 451-475 ISSUED IN BOW.STERL.
CARDS 476-500 ISSUED IN TOPPS 52
ARHR500 Alex Rodriguez 500HR 8.00 20.00

2007 Topps All Stars

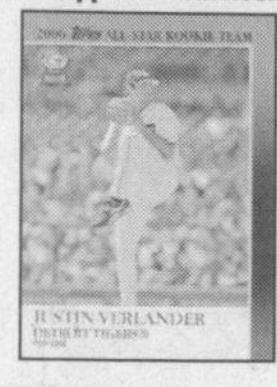

COMPLETE SET (12) 6.00 15.00
SER.1 ODDS ONE PER RACK PACK
AS1 Alfonso Soriano .60 1.50
AS2 Paul Konerko .60 1.50
AS3 Carlos Beltran .60 1.50
AS4 Troy Glaus .40 1.00
AS5 Jason Bay .60 1.50
AS6 Vladimir Guerrero .60 1.50
AS7 Chase Utley .60 1.50
AS8 Michael Young .40 1.00
AS9 David Wright .75 2.00
AS10 Gary Matthews .40 1.00
AS11 Brad Penny .40 1.00
AS12 Roy Halladay .60 1.50

2007 Topps All Star Rookies

COMPLETE SET (10) 6.00 15.00
SER.1 ODDS ONE PER RACK PACK
ASR1 Prince Fielder .60 1.50
ASR2 Dan Uggla .40 1.00
ASR3 Ryan Zimmerman .60 1.50
ASR4 Hanley Ramirez .60 1.50
ASR5 Melky Cabrera .40 1.00
ASR6 Andre Ethier .60 1.50
ASR7 Nick Markakis .75 2.00
ASR8 Justin Verlander 1.00 2.50
ASR9 Francisco Liriano .40 1.00
ASR10 Russell Martin .40 1.00

2007 Topps DiMaggio Streak

COMPLETE SET (56) 20.00 50.00
COMMON CARD .60 1.50
SER.2 ODDS 1:9 HOBBY

2007 Topps DiMaggio Streak Before the Streak

COMPLETE SET (61) 12.50 30.00
COMMON CARD .60 1.50
SER.2 ODDS 1:9 HOBBY

2007 Topps Distinguished Service

COMPLETE SET (30) 10.00 25.00
COMP.SERIES 1 (1-20) 6.00 15.00
COMP.SERIES 2 (21-30) 5.00 12.00
SER.1 ODDS 1:12 H, 1:12 HTA, 1:12 K-MART
SER.1 ODDS 1:12 RACK, 1:12 WAL-MART
SER.2 ODDS 1:12 HOBBY, 1:2 HTA
DS1 Duke Snider .60 1.50
DS2 Yogi Berra 1.00 2.50
DS3 Bob Feller .60 1.50
DS4 Bobby Doerr .60 1.50
DS5 Monte Irvin .60 1.50
DS6 Dwight D. Eisenhower .40 1.00
DS7 George Marshall .40 1.00
DS8 Franklin D. Roosevelt .40 1.00
DS9 Harry Truman .40 1.00
DS10 Douglas MacArthur .40 1.00
DS11 Ralph Kiner .60 1.50
DS12 Hank Sauer .40 1.00
DS13 Elmer Valo .40 1.00
DS14 Sibby Sisti .40 1.00
DS15 Hoyt Wilhelm .60 1.50
DS16 James Doolittle .40 1.00
DS17 Curtis Lemay .40 1.00
DS18 Omar Bradley .40 1.00
DS19 Chester Nimitz .40 1.00
DS20 Mark Clark .40 1.00
DS21 Joe DiMaggio 2.00 5.00
DS22 Warren Spahn .60 1.50
DS23 Stan Musial 1.50 4.00
DS24 Red Schoendienst .60 1.50
DS25 Ted Williams 2.00 5.00
DS26 Winston Churchill .40 1.00
DS27 Charles de Gaulle .40 1.00
DS28 George Bush .40 1.00
DS29 John F. Kennedy 1.50 4.00
DS30 Richard Bong .40 1.00

2007 Topps Distinguished Service Autographs

SER.1 ODDS 1:20,000 H, 1:830 HTA
SER.1 ODDS 1:41,225 K-MART, 1:9200 RACK
SER.1 ODDS 1:20,000 TARGET
SER.1 ODDS 1:41,225 WAL-MART
BD Bobby Doerr 15.00 40.00
BF Bob Feller 20.00 50.00
DS Duke Snider 20.00 50.00
MI Monte Irvin 30.00 60.00
RK Ralph Kiner 10.00 25.00

2007 Topps Factory Set All Star Bonus

1 Alex Rodriguez 1.25 3.00
2 David Wright .75 2.00
3 David Ortiz 1.00 2.50
4 Ichiro Suzuki 1.25 3.00
5 Ryan Howard .75 2.00

2007 Topps Factory Set Cardinals Team Bonus

1 Skip Schumaker .40 1.00
2 Josh Hancock .40 1.00
3 Tyler Johnson .40 1.00
4 Randy Keisler .40 1.00
5 Randy Flores .40 1.00

2007 Topps Factory Set Cubs Team Bonus

1 Ronny Cedeno .40 1.00
2 Cesar Izturis .40 1.00
3 Neal Cotts .40 1.00
4 Wade Miller .40 1.00
5 Michael Wuertz .40 1.00

2007 Topps Factory Set Dodgers Team Bonus

1 Chin-Hui Tsao .60 1.50
2 Olmedo Saenz .40 1.00
3 Brett Tomko .40 1.00
4 Marlon Anderson .40 1.00
5 Brady Clark .40 1.00

2007 Topps Factory Set Red Sox Team Bonus

1 Daisuke Matsuzaka 1.50 4.00
2 Eric Hinske .40 1.00
3 Brendan Donnelly .40 1.00
4 Hideki Okajima 2.00 5.00
5 J.C. Romero .40 1.00

2007 Topps Factory Set Rookie Bonus

COMPLETE SET (20) 12.50 30.00
1 Felix Pie .40 1.00
2 Rick Vanden Hurk .40 1.00
3 Jeff Baker .40 1.00
4 Don Kelly .40 1.00
5 Matt Lindstrom .40 1.00
6 Chase Wright 1.00 2.50
7 Jon Coutlangus .40 1.00
8 Lee Gardner .40 1.00
9 Gustavo Molina .40 1.00
10 Kory Casto .40 1.00
11 Daisuke Matsuzaka 1.50 4.00
12 Tim Lincecum 2.00 5.00
13 Phil Hughes 1.00 2.50
14 Ryan Braun 2.00 5.00
15 Billy Butler .60 1.50
16 Jarrod Saltalamacchia .60 1.50
17 Hideki Okajima 2.00 5.00
18 Akinori Iwamura 1.00 2.50
19a Joba Chamberlain .60 1.50
19b Joba Chamberlain
Houston Astros UER .60 1.50
20 Hunter Pence 1.25 3.00

2007 Topps Factory Set Yankees Team Bonus

1 Darrell Rasner .40 1.00
2 Phil Hughes 1.00 2.50
3 Wil Nieves .40 1.00
4 Kei Igawa 1.00 2.50
5 Kevin Thompson .40 1.00

2007 Topps Flashback Fridays

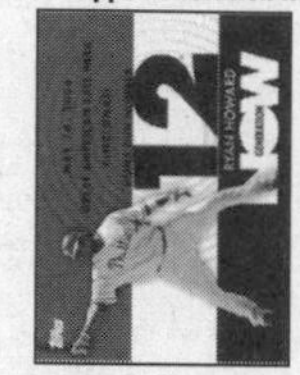

COMPLETE SET (25) 6.00 15.00
ISSUED VIA HTA SHOPS
FF1 Ryan Howard .40 1.00
FF2 Derek Jeter 1.25 3.00
FF3 Ken Griffey Jr 1.00 2.50
FF4 Miguel Tejada .30 .75
FF5 David Wright .40 1.00
FF6 Alfonso Soriano .30 .75
FF7 Matt Holliday .50 1.25
FF8 Jason Bay .30 .75
FF9 Ryan Zimmerman .30 .75
FF10 Alex Rodriguez .60 1.50
FF11 Jermaine Dye .20 .50
FF12 Miguel Cabrera .50 1.25
FF13 Johan Santana .30 .75
FF14 Brandon Webb .30 .75
FF15 Ivan Rodriguez .30 .75
FF16 Ichiro Suzuki .60 1.50
FF17 Michael Young .20 .50
FF18 David Ortiz .50 1.25
FF19 Roger Clemens .60 1.50
FF20 Frank Thomas .50 1.25
FF21 Trevor Hoffman .30 .75
FF22 Gary Matthews .20 .50
FF23 Rafael Furcal .20 .50
FF24 Chipper Jones .50 1.25
FF25 Albert Pujols .60 1.50

2007 Topps Generation Now

SER.1 ODDS 1:4 H, 1:4 K-MART, 1:4 RACK
SER.1 ODDS 1:4 TARGET, 1:4 WAL-MART
SER.2 ODDS 1:4 HOBBY
UPDATE ODDS 1:4 HOB, 1:4 RET
CARDS OF SAME PLAYER EQUALLY PRICED
GN1 Ryan Howard .60 1.50
GN51 Chase Utley .50 1.25
GN85 Chien-Ming Wang .50 1.25
GN103 Mike Napoli .30 .75
GN117 Justin Morneau .50 1.25
GN147 David Wright .60 1.50
GN187 Jered Weaver .50 1.25
GN195 Andre Ethier .50 1.25
GN219 Ryan Zimmerman .50 1.25
GN279 Russell Martin .30 .75
GN283 Justin Verlander .75 2.00
GN299 Hanley Ramirez .50 1.25
GN350 Nick Markakis .60 1.50
GN360 Nick Swisher .50 1.25
GN397 Prince Fielder .50 1.25
GN425 Ian Kinsler .50 1.25
GN452 Kenji Johjima .75 2.00
GN481 Jonathan Papelbon .75 2.00
GN516 Jose Reyes .50 1.25
GN520 Curtis Granderson .60 1.50
GN551 Josh Barfield .30 .75

2007 Topps Generation Now Vintage

RANDOM INSERTS IN K-MART PACKS
1-18 ISSUED IN SER.1 PACKS
19-36 ISSUED IN SER.2 PACKS
37-54 ISSUED IN 07 UPDATE PACKS
GNV1 Ryan Howard .40 1.00
GNV2 Jeff Francoeur .50 1.25
GNV3 Nick Swisher .30 .75
GNV4 Joey Gathright .20 .50
GNV5 Jhonny Peralta .20 .50
GNV6 Willy Taveras .20 .50
GNV7 Cory Sullivan .20 .50
GNV8 Chris Young .20 .50
GNV9 Jered Weaver .30 .75
GNV10 Jonathan Papelbon .50 1.25
GNV11 Russell Martin .20 .50
GNV12 Hanley Ramirez .30 .75
GNV13 Justin Verlander .50 1.25
GNV14 Matt Cain .30 .75
GNV15 Kenji Johjima .50 1.25
GNV16 Angel Pagan .20 .50
GNV17 Brandon Phillips .20 .50
GNV18 Mark Teahen .20 .50
GNV19 Stephen Drew .20 .50
GNV20 Nick Markakis .40 1.00
GNV21 Anibal Sanchez .20 .50
GNV22 Jeremy Hermida .20 .50
GNV23 James Loney .20 .50
GNV24 Prince Fielder .30 .75
GNV25 Josh Barfield .20 .50
GNV26 Ian Kinsler .30 .75
GNV27 Ryan Zimmerman .30 .75
GNV28 David Wright .40 1.00
GNV29 Jose Reyes .30 .75
GNV30 Delmon Young .30 .75
GNV31 Zach Duke .20 .50
GNV32 Brian McCann .20 .50
GNV33 Bobby Jenks .20 .50
GNV34 Robinson Cano .30 .75
GNV35 Jose Lopez .20 .50
GNV36 Daisuke Matsuzaka .75 2.00
GNV37 Alex Rios .20 .50
GNV38 Cole Hamels .40 1.00
GNV39 Matt Kemp .40 1.00
GNV40 Dan Uggla .20 .50
GNV41 Scott Kazmir .30 .75
GNV42 J.J. Hardy .20 .50
GNV43 Hunter Pence .60 1.50
GNV44 Jason Bay .30 .75
GNV45 James Shields .20 .50
GNV46 Chase Utley .30 .75
GNV47 Justin Morneau .30 .75
GNV48 Chien-Ming Wang .30 .75
GNV49 Troy Tulowitski .60 1.50
GNV50 Joe Mauer .40 1.00
GNV51 Brandon Webb .30 .75
GNV52 Matt Holliday .50 1.25
GNV53 Grady Sizemore .30 .75
GNV54 Homer Bailey .30 .75

2007 Topps Gibson Home Run History

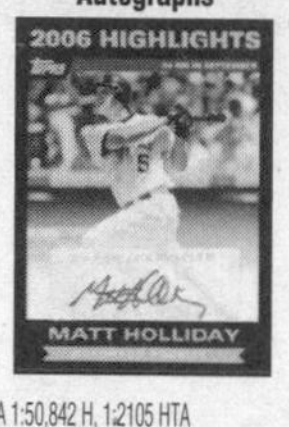

COMPLETE SET (110) 60.00 120.00
COMMON GIBSON .60 1.50
SER.1 ODDS 1:9 H, 1:2 HTA, 1:9 K-MART
SER.1 ODDS 1:9 RACK, 1:9 TARGET
SER.1 ODDS 1:9 WAL-MART
CARDS 1-110 ISSUED IN SERIES 1 PACKS

2007 Topps Highlights Autographs

SER.1 A 1:50,842 H, 1:2105 HTA
SER.1 A 1:101,000 K-MART, 1:18,396 RACK
SER.1 A 1:50,842 TARGET
SER.1 A 1:101,000 WAL-MART
SER.2 A 1:37,162 HOBBY, 1:523 HTA
SER.1 B 1:24,150 H, 1:1034 HTA
SER.1 B 1:51,800 K-MART, 1:12,264 RACK
SER.1 B 1:25,420 TARGET
SER.1 B 1:51,800 WAL-MART
SER.2 B 1:7330 HOBBY, 1:105 HTA
SER.1 C 1:13,000 H, 1:555 HTA
SER.1 C 1:27,300 K-MART, 1:7350 RACK
SER.1 C 1:13,600 TARGET
SER.1 C 1:27,300 WAL-MART
SER.2 C 1:7330 HOBBY, 1:105 HTA
SER.1 D 1:4916 H, 1:208 HTA
SER.1 D 1:10,250 K-MART, 1:2628 RACK
SER.1 D 1:5100 TARGET, 1:10,250 WAL-MART
SER.2 D 1:12,198 HOBBY, 1:174 HTA
SER.1 E 1:2460 H, 1:52 HTA, 1:5125 K-MART
SER.1 E 1:1314 RACK, 1:2550 TARGET
SER.1 E 1:5125 WAL-MART
SER.2 E 1:1410 HOBBY, 1:20 HTA
SER.1 F 1:1256 H, 1:52 HTA, 1:2564 K-MART
SER.1 F 1:657 RACK, 1:1277 TARGET
SER.1 F 1:2564 WAL-MART
SER.1 G 1:376 H, 1:16 HTA, 1:789 K-MART
SER.1 G 1:203 RACK, 1:393 TARGET
SER.1 G 1:789 WAL-MART
GROUP A1 PRINT RUN B/WN 25-50 PER
GROUP B1 PRINT RUN 100 SETS
GROUP C1 PRINT RUN 250 SETS
A1-C1 ARE NOT SERIAL-NUMBERED
A1-C1 PRINT RUNS PROVIDED BY TOPPS
NO GROUP A1 PRICING DUE TO SCARCITY
EXCH * = PARTIAL EXCHANGE
EXCHANGE DEADLINE 02/28/09
AB Aaron Boone E2 4.00 10.00
AJ Andruw Jones B2 12.00 30.00
AM Andrew Miller G 4.00 10.00
AP Albert Pujols A2 60.00 150.00
APA Angel Pagan G 4.00 10.00
AR Anthony Reyes E2 6.00 15.00
AGS A.Soriano B/100 * 8.00 20.00
AS Anibal Sanchez G 4.00 10.00
CG Curtis Granderson B2 4.00 10.00
CQ Carlos Quentin F 4.00 10.00
CW Chien-Ming Wang B/100 * 30.00 80.00
CW Craig Wilson E2 6.00 15.00
DO David Ortiz B2 20.00 50.00
DO David Ortiz B/100 * 60.00 120.00
DT Derrick Turnbow D2 6.00 15.00
DU Dan Uggla E2 4.00 10.00
DW David Wright C2 10.00 25.00
DW David Wright D 10.00 25.00
DWW Dontrelle Willis E 10.00 25.00
DWW Dontrelle Willis C2 6.00 15.00
DY Delmon Young E 4.00 10.00
EC Endy Chavez B2 10.00 25.00
EF Emiliano Fruto G 4.00 10.00
ES Ervin Santana E2 4.00 10.00
HR Hanley Ramirez G 4.00 10.00
JAS John Smoltz C/250 * 20.00 50.00
JD Johnny Damon B2 12.00 30.00
JEM Justin Morneau E 10.00 25.00
JF Josh Fields F 3.00 8.00
JG Jon Garland E2 4.00 10.00
JH John Hattig G 4.00 10.00
JL James Loney G 4.00 10.00
JM John Maine F. 4.00 10.00
JS Johan Santana C/250 * 12.00 30.00
JT Jim Thome A2 25.00 60.00
JV Justin Verlander B2 15.00 40.00

Joel Zumaya E2 3.00 8.00
Kelvin Escobar C2 6.00 15.00
M Kendry Morales B2 4.00 10.00
M Kevin Mench D 4.00 10.00
M Lastings Milledge E2 4.00 10.00
C Melky Cabrera E2 4.00 10.00
C Miguel Cabrera C/250 * 20.00 50.00
G Matt Garza F 4.00 10.00
H Matt Holliday G 6.00 15.00
N Mike Napoli G 6.00 15.00
P Mike Piazza A/50 * 90.00 150.00
TC Matt Cain D2 4.00 10.00
L Paul LoDuca B2 12.00 30.00
C Robinson Cano E2 6.00 15.00
H Ryan Howard A2 20.00 50.00
H Ryan Howard B/100 * 75.00 150.00
M Russell Martin C2 10.00 25.00
Z Ryan Zimmerman C2 6.00 15.00
Z Ryan Zimmerman E 6.00 15.00
C Shawn Chacon E2 4.00 10.00
P Scott Podsednik E2 4.00 10.00
R Shawn Riggans E2 4.00 10.00
SC Shin-Soo Choo B2 12.00 30.00
T Steve Trachsel A2 10.00 25.00
G Tom Glavine B2 8.00 20.00
H Travis Hafner D 10.00 25.00
T Troy Tulowitzki G 6.00 15.00
G Vladimir Guerrero A2 6.00 15.00

2007 Topps Highlights Relics

SER.1 A 1:933 H, 1:33 HTA, 1:2160 K-MART
SER.1 A 1:1070 TARGET, 1:2160 WAL-MART
SER.2 A 1:2435 HOBBY, 1:138 HTA
SER.1 B 1:726 H, 1:19 HTA, 1:1270 K-MART
SER.1 B 1:631 TARGET, 1:1270 WAL-MART
SER.2 B 1:609 HOBBY, 1:35 HTA
SER.1 C 1:2468 H, 1:87 HTA, 1:5675 K-MART
SER.1 C 1:2825 TARGET, 1:5675 WAL-MART
SER.2 C 1:1420 HOBBY, 1:80 HTA
SER.2 D 1:533 HOBBY, 1:30 HTA
SER.2 E 1:1705 HOBBY, 1:96 HTA
AB Adrian Beltre B2 3.00 8.00
AER Alex Rodriguez C2 8.00 20.00
AJ Andruw Jones E2 3.00 8.00
ALR Anthony Reyes B2 4.00 10.00
AP Albert Pujols B2 8.00 20.00
AP Albert Pujols Pants B 8.00 20.00
AP2 Albert Pujols Jsy B 8.00 20.00
AR Aramis Ramirez D2 3.00 8.00
AR Alex Rodriguez Jsy B 8.00 20.00
AR2 Alex Rodriguez Bat A 8.00 20.00
AS Alfonso Soriano A2 4.00 10.00
AS Alfonso Soriano Bat A 4.00 10.00
BM Brian McCann Bat A 3.00 8.00
CB Craig Biggio Pants A 4.00 10.00
CD Carlos Delgado Bat B 3.00 8.00
CIB Carlos Beltran Jsy B 3.00 8.00
CJ Chipper Jones B2 3.00 8.00
CQ Carlos Quentin Bat A 3.00 8.00
CS Curt Schilling Jsy A 3.00 8.00
DE David Eckstein A2 5.00 12.00
DO David Ortiz D2 4.00 10.00
DO David Ortiz Bat B 4.00 10.00
DW Dontrelle Willis Jsy B 4.00 10.00
DW David Wright D2 5.00 12.00
DW2 Dontrelle Willis Pants B 4.00 10.00
DWW Dontrelle Willis E2 4.00 10.00
ER Edgar Renteria Bat B 3.00 8.00
FT Frank Thomas Bat B 4.00 10.00
GA Garrett Atkins A2 3.00 8.00
GS Grady Sizemore A2 5.00 12.00
GS Gary Sheffield Bat B 3.00 8.00
IR Ivan Rodriguez Bat C 3.00 8.00
IS Ichiro Suzuki Bat A 6.00 15.00
JAS John Smoltz Pants A 3.00 8.00
JB Jason Bay Jsy A 3.00 8.00
JB2 Jason Bay Bat A 3.00 8.00
JD Jermaine Dye C2 3.00 8.00
JDD Johnny Damon A2 4.00 10.00
JM Justin Morneau Bat B 3.00 8.00
JPM Joe Mauer Bat A 4.00 10.00
JR Jose Reyes Jsy A 3.00 8.00
JS Johan Santana Jsy A 4.00 10.00
JT Jim Thome B2 5.00 12.00
JV Justin Verlander A2 5.00 12.00
LB Lance Berkman C2 3.00 8.00
MAR Manny Ramirez Jsy B 3.00 8.00
MAR2 Manny Ramirez Bat C 3.00 8.00
MC Matt Cain B2 3.00 8.00
MCT Mark Teixeira B2 3.00 8.00
MEC Melky Cabrera B2 4.00 10.00
MO Magglio Ordonez Bat B 4.00 10.00
MR Mariano Rivera Jsy A 4.00 10.00
MR Manny Ramirez D2 3.00 8.00
MT Miguel Tejada B2 3.00 8.00
MT Miguel Tejada Bat A 3.00 8.00
NS Nick Swisher D2 4.00 10.00
PK Paul Konerko B2 3.00 8.00
PK Paul Konerko Bat A 3.00 8.00
PM Pedro Martinez D2 3.00 8.00
RC Robinson Cano B2 4.00 10.00
RC Robinson Cano Pants A 4.00 10.00
RH Ryan Howard Bat B 6.00 15.00
RH Roy Halladay B2 3.00 8.00
RJH Ryan Howard B2 6.00 15.00
RO Roy Oswalt Jsy A 3.00 8.00
SK Scott Kazmir Jsy B 3.00 8.00
SK Scott Kazmir C2 3.00 8.00
SR Scott Rolen Jsy A 4.00 10.00
TG Tom Glavine A2 4.00 10.00
TG1 Tom Glavine Jsy A 4.00 10.00
TG2 Troy Glaus Bat B 3.00 8.00
VG Vladimir Guerrero D2 4.00 10.00
VW Vernon Wells D2 3.00 8.00
VW Vernon Wells Bat A 3.00 8.00

2007 Topps Hit Parade

SER.2 ODDS 1:9 HOBBY, 1:2 HTA
HP1 Barry Bonds 1.50 4.00
HP2 Ken Griffey Jr. 2.00 5.00
HP3 Frank Thomas 1.00 2.50
HP4 Jim Thome .60 1.50
HP5 Manny Ramirez 1.00 2.50
HP6 Alex Rodriguez 1.25 3.00
HP7 Gary Sheffield .40 1.00
HP8 Mike Piazza 1.00 2.50
HP9 Carlos Delgado .40 1.00
HP10 Chipper Jones 1.00 2.50
HP11 Barry Bonds 1.50 4.00
HP12 Ken Griffey Jr. 2.00 5.00
HP13 Frank Thomas 1.00 2.50
HP14 Manny Ramirez 1.00 2.50
HP15 Gary Sheffield .40 1.00
HP16 Jeff Kent .40 1.00
HP17 Alex Rodriguez 1.25 3.00
HP18 Luis Gonzalez .40 1.00
HP19 Jim Thome .60 1.50
HP20 Mike Piazza 1.00 2.50
HP21 Craig Biggio .60 1.50
HP22 Barry Bonds 1.50 4.00
HP23 Julio Franco .40 1.00
HP24 Steve Finley .40 1.00
HP25 Omar Vizquel .60 1.50
HP26 Ken Griffey Jr. 2.00 5.00
HP27 Gary Sheffield .40 1.00
HP28 Luis Gonzalez .40 1.00
HP29 Ivan Rodriguez .60 1.50
HP30 Bernie Williams .60 1.50

2007 Topps Hobby Masters

COMPLETE SET (20) 10.00 25.00
SER.1 ODDS 1:6 H, 1:4 HTA
HM1 David Wright .75 2.00
HM2 Albert Pujols 1.25 3.00
HM3 David Ortiz 1.00 2.50
HM4 Ryan Howard .75 2.00
HM5 Alfonso Soriano .60 1.50
HM6 Delmon Young .60 1.50
HM7 Jered Weaver .60 1.50
HM8 Derek Jeter 2.50 6.00
HM9 Freddy Sanchez .40 1.00
HM10 Alex Rodriguez 1.25 3.00
HM11 Johan Santana .60 1.50
HM12 Ichiro Suzuki 1.25 3.00
HM13 Andruw Jones .40 1.00
HM14 Vladimir Guerrero .60 1.50
HM15 Miguel Cabrera 1.00 2.50
HM16 Todd Helton .60 1.50
HM17 Manny Ramirez 1.00 2.50
HM18 Carlos Beltran .60 1.50
HM19 Justin Morneau .60 1.50
HM20 Francisco Liriano .40 1.00

2007 Topps Homerun Derby Contest

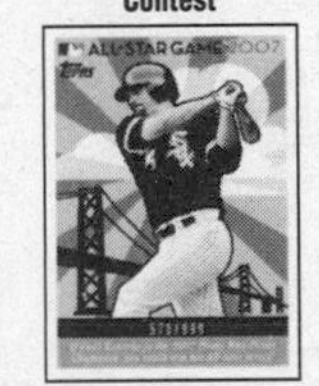

RANDOM INSERTS IN SER.2 PACKS
STATED ODDS 999 SER.#'d SETS
AB Adrian Beltre 1.50 4.00
AD Adam Dunn 1.00 2.50
AER Alex Rodriguez 2.00 5.00
AJ Andruw Jones .60 1.50
AL Adam LaRoche .60 1.50
AP Albert Pujols 2.00 5.00
AR Aramis Ramirez .60 1.50
AS Alfonso Soriano 1.00 2.50
BH Bill Hall .60 1.50
CB Carlos Beltran 1.00 2.50
CD Carlos Delgado .60 1.50
CL Carlos Lee .60 1.50
CM Craig Monroe .60 1.50
CU Chase Utley 1.00 2.50
DO David Ortiz 1.50 4.00
DU Dan Uggla .60 1.50
DW David Wright 1.25 3.00
DY Delmon Young 1.00 2.50
FT Frank Thomas 1.50 4.00
GA Garrett Atkins .60 1.50
GS Grady Sizemore 1.00 2.50
JB Jason Bay 1.00 2.50
JC Joe Crede .60 1.50
JD Jermaine Dye .60 1.50
JDD Johnny Damon 1.00 2.50
JF Jeff Francoeur 1.50 4.00
JG Jason Giambi .60 1.50
JM Justin Morneau 1.00 2.50
JT Jim Thome 1.00 2.50
KG Ken Griffey Jr 3.00 8.00
LB Lance Berkman 1.00 2.50
MC Miguel Cabrera 1.50 4.00
MH Matt Holliday 1.50 4.00
MMT Marcus Thames .60 1.50
MOT Miguel Tejada 1.00 2.50
MP Mike Piazza 1.50 4.00
MR Manny Ramirez 1.50 4.00
MT Mark Teixeira 1.00 2.50
NS Nick Swisher 1.00 2.50
PB Pat Burrell .60 1.50
PF Prince Fielder 1.00 2.50
PK Paul Konerko 1.00 2.50
RH Ryan Howard 1.25 3.00
RI Raul Ibanez 1.00 2.50
RS Richie Sexson .60 1.50
TG Troy Glaus .60 1.50
TH Travis Hafner .60 1.50
TKH Torii Hunter .60 1.50
VG Vladimir Guerrero 1.00 2.50
VW Vernon Wells .60 1.50

2007 Topps In the Name Letter Relics

SER.1 ODDS 1:8292 H, 1:488 HTA
STATED PRINT RUN 1 SERIAL #'d SET
NO PRICING DUE TO SCARCITY

2007 Topps Mickey Mantle Story

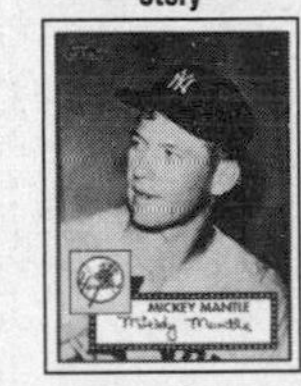

COMPLETE SET (57) 50.00 100.00
COMP.SERIES 1 (1-15) 8.00 20.00
COMP.SERIES 2 (16-30) 8.00 20.00
COMP.UPD.SET (31-45) 12.50 30.00
COMP.08 SER.1 SET (46-57) 6.00 15.00
COMP.08 SER.2 SET (58-67) 6.00 15.00
COMP.08 UPD SET (68-77) 6.00 15.00
COMMON MANTLE (1-77) .75 2.00
SER.1 ODDS 1:18 H, 1:18 HTA, 1:18 K-MART
SER.1 ODDS 1:18 RACK, 1:18 TARGET
SER.1 ODDS 1:18 WAL-MART
SER.2 ODDS 1:18 H,1:3 HTA,1:18 R
UPDATE ODDS 1:18 H, 1:3 HTA, 1:18 R
08 SER.1 ODDS 1:18 H,1:3 HTA
08 SER.2 ODDS 1:18 H,1:3 HTA, 1:18 R
08 UPD.ODDS 1:18 HOBBY
1-15 ISSUED IN SERIES 1
16-30 ISSUED IN SERIES 2
31-45 ISSUED IN UPDATE
46-57 ISSUED IN 08 SERIES 1
58-65 ISSUED IN 08 SERIES 2
66-77 ISSUED IN 08 UPDATE

2007 Topps Opening Day Team vs. Team

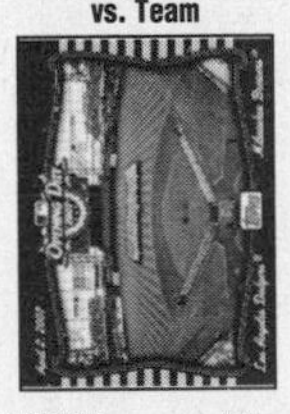

COMPLETE SET (15) 6.00 15.00
SER.2 ODDS 1:12 HOBBY, 1:3 HTA
OD1 New York Mets/St. Louis Cardinals .40 1.00
OD2 Atlanta Braves/Philadelphia Phillies .40 1.00
OD3 Florida Marlins
Washington Nationals .40 1.00
OD4 Tampa Bay Devil Rays
New York Yankees 1.00 2.50
OD5 Toronto Blue Jays/Detroit Tigers .40 1.00
OD6 Cleveland Indians
Chicago White Sox .40 1.00
OD7 Los Angeles Dodgers
Milwaukee Brewers .40 1.00
OD8 Chicago Cubs/Cincinnati Reds .60 1.50
OD9 Arizona Diamondbacks
Colorado Rockies .40 1.00
OD10 Boston Red Sox
Kansas City Royals 1.00 2.50
OD11 Oakland Athletics/Seattle Mariners .40 1.00
OD12 Baltimore Orioles
Minnesota Twins .40 1.00
OD13 Pittsburgh Pirates/Houston Astros .40 1.00
OD14 Texas Rangers
Los Angeles Angels .40 1.00
OD15 San Diego Padres
San Francisco Giants .40 1.00

2007 Topps Own the Game

COMPLETE SET (25) 10.00 25.00
SER.1 ODDS 1:6 H, 1:2 HTA, 1:6 K-MART
SER.1 ODDS 1:6 RACK, 1:6 TARGET
SER.1 ODDS 1:6 WAL-MART
OTG1 Ryan Howard .75 2.00
OTG2 David Ortiz 1.00 2.50
OTG3 Alfonso Soriano .60 1.50
OTG4 Albert Pujols 1.25 3.00
OTG5 Lance Berkman .60 1.50
OTG6 Jermaine Dye .40 1.00
OTG7 Travis Hafner .40 1.00
OTG8 Jim Thome .60 1.50
OTG9 Carlos Beltran .60 1.50
OTG10 Adam Dunn .60 1.50
OTG11 Ryan Howard .75 2.00
OTG12 David Ortiz 1.00 2.50
OTG13 Albert Pujols 1.25 3.00
OTG14 Lance Berkman .60 1.50
OTG15 Justin Morneau .60 1.50
OTG16 Andruw Jones .40 1.00
OTG17 Jermaine Dye .40 1.00
OTG18 Travis Hafner .40 1.00
OTG19 Alex Rodriguez 1.25 3.00
OTG20 David Wright .75 2.00
OTG21 Johan Santana .60 1.50
OTG22 Chris Carpenter .60 1.50
OTG23 Brandon Webb .60 1.50
OTG24 Roy Oswalt .60 1.50
OTG25 Roy Halladay .60 1.50

2007 Topps Rookie Stars

COMPLETE SET (10) 6.00 15.00
SER.2 ODDS 1:9 HOBBY
RS1 Daisuke Matsuzaka 1.25 3.00
RS2 Kevin Kouzmanoff .30 .75
RS3 Elijah Dukes .50 1.25
RS4 Andrew Miller 1.25 3.00
RS5 Kei Igawa .75 2.00
RS6 Troy Tulowitzki 1.00 2.50
RS7 Ubaldo Jimenez 1.00 2.50
RS8 Alex Gordon 1.00 2.50
RS9 Josh Hamilton 1.00 2.50
RS10 Delmon Young .50 1.25

2007 Topps Stars

COMPLETE SET (15) 6.00 15.00
SER.2 ODDS 1:9 HOBBY
TS1 Ryan Howard .60 1.50
TS2 Alfonso Soriano .50 1.25
TS3 Todd Helton .50 1.25
TS4 Johan Santana .50 1.25
TS5 David Wright .60 1.50
TS6 Albert Pujols 1.00 2.50
TS7 Daisuke Matsuzaka 1.25 3.00
TS8 Miguel Cabrera .75 2.00
TS9 David Ortiz .75 2.00
TS10 Alex Rodriguez 1.00 2.50
TS11 Vladimir Guerrero .50 1.25
TS12 Ichiro Suzuki 1.00 2.50
TS13 Derek Jeter 2.00 5.00
TS14 Lance Berkman .50 1.25
TS15 Ryan Zimmerman .50 1.25

2007 Topps Target Factory Set Mantle Memorabilia

COMMON MANTLE MEMORABILIA 1.50 30.00
DISTRIBUTED WITH TOPPS TARGET FACT.SETS
MMR53 Mickey Mantle 53T 15.00 40.00
MMR56 Mickey Mantle 56T 15.00 40.00
MMR57 Mickey Mantle 57T 15.00 40.00

2007 Topps Target Factory Set Red Backs

1 Mickey Mantle 3.00 8.00
2 Ted Williams 2.00 5.00

2007 Topps Trading Places

COMPLETE SET (25) 6.00 15.00
SER.2 ODDS 1:9 HOBBY
TP1 Jeff Weaver .40 1.00
TP2 Frank Thomas 1.00 2.50
TP3 Mike Piazza 1.00 2.50
TP4 Alfonso Soriano .60 1.50
TP5 Freddy Garcia .40 1.00
TP6 Jason Marquis .40 1.00
TP7 Ted Lilly .40 1.00
TP8 Mark Loretta .40 1.00
TP9 Marcus Giles .40 1.00
TP10 Barry Zito .60 1.50
TP11 Andy Pettitte .60 1.50
TP12 J.D. Drew .40 1.00
TP13 Gary Matthews .40 1.00
TP14 Jay Payton .40 1.00
TP15 Aubrey Huff .40 1.00
TP16 Brian Bannister .40 1.00
TP17 Jeff Conine .40 1.00
TP18 Gary Sheffield .40 1.00
TP19 Shea Hillenbrand .40 1.00
TP20 Wes Helms .40 1.00
TP21 Frank Catalanotto .40 1.00
TP22 Adam LaRoche .40 1.00
TP23 Mike Gonzalez .40 1.00
TP24 Greg Maddux 1.25 3.00
TP25 Jason Schmidt .40 1.00

2007 Topps Trading Places Autographs

SER.2 ODDS 1:3,055 HOBBY, 1:44 HTA
AH Aubrey Huff 6.00 15.00
AL Adam LaRoche 4.00 10.00
BB Brian Bannister 5.00 12.00
FC Frank Catalanotto 4.00 10.00
FG Freddy Garcia 6.00 15.00
GS Gary Sheffield 6.00 15.00
JS Jason Schmidt 6.00 15.00
MG Mike Gonzalez 4.00 10.00
SH Shea Hillenbrand 4.00 10.00
WH Wes Helms 4.00 10.00

2007 Topps Trading Places Relics

SER.2 ODDS 1:2,435 HOBBY, 1:137 HTA
AP Andy Pettitte 5.00 12.00
AS Alfonso Soriano 5.00 12.00
BZ Barry Zito 4.00 10.00
FT Frank Thomas 5.00 12.00
GM Greg Maddux 5.00 12.00
GS Gary Sheffield 5.00 12.00
JW Jeff Weaver 4.00 10.00
MG Marcus Giles 4.00 10.00
ML Mark Loretta 4.00 10.00
MP Mike Piazza 6.00 15.00

2007 Topps Unlock the Mick

COMPLETE SET (5) 3.00 8.00
COMMON MANTLE 1.00 2.50
SER.1 ODDS 1:18 H, 1:18 HTA, 1:18 K-MART
SER.1 ODDS 1:18 RACK, 1:18 TARGET
SER.1 ODDS 1:18 WAL-MART

2007 Topps Wal-Mart

COMP.SERIES 1 (18) 15.00 40.00
STATED ODDS 1:4 WAL-MART
SER.1 ODDS 3 PER $9.99 WAL-MART BOX
SER.1 ODDS 6 PER $19.99 WAL-MART BOX
1-18 ISSUED IN SERIES 1
19-36 ISSUED IN SERIES 2
37-54 ISSUED IN UPDATE
WM1 Frank Thomas 41 PB 1.00 2.50
WM2 Mike Piazza 34 DS 1.00 2.50
WM3 Ivan Rodriguez 22 Caramel .60 1.50
WM4 David Ortiz T207 1.00 2.50
WM5 David Wright 1887 AG .75 2.00
WM6 Greg Maddux 52T 1.25 3.00
WM7 Mickey Mantle 51T 3.00 8.00
WM8 Jose Reyes 65T .60 1.50
WM9 John Smoltz T205 1.00 2.50
WM10 Jim Edmonds 56T .60 1.50
WM11 Ryan Howard 58T .75 2.00
WM12 Miguel Cabrera T206 1.00 2.50
WM13 Carlos Delgado 10 Turkey .40 1.00
WM14 Miguel Tejada 55B .60 1.50
WM15 Ichiro Suzuki 33 DeLong 1.25 3.00
WM16 Albert Pujols 49B 1.25 3.00
WM17 Derek Jeter 91 SC 2.50 6.00
WM18 Vladimir Guerrero 61 Baz .60 1.50
WM19 Lance Berkman .60 1.50
WM20 Chase Utley .60 1.50
WM21 Gary Matthews .40 1.00
WM22 Johan Santana .60 1.50
WM23 Todd Helton .60 1.50
WM24 Carlos Beltran .60 1.50
WM25 Alex Rodriguez 1.25 3.00
WM26 Cole Hamels .75 2.00
WM27 Daisuke Matsuzaka 1.50 4.00
WM28 Kei Igawa 1.00 2.50
WM29 Hanley Ramirez .60 1.50
WM30 Joe Mauer .75 2.00
WM31 Brandon Webb .60 1.50
WM32 Michael Young .40 1.00
WM33 Nick Swisher .60 1.50
WM34 Jason Bay .60 1.50
WM35 Manny Ramirez 1.00 2.50
WM36 Ryan Zimmerman .60 1.50
WM37 Grady Sizemore .60 1.50
WM38 Matt Holliday 1.00 2.50
WM39 Jimmy Rollins .60 1.50
WM40 Magglio Ordonez .60 1.50
WM41 Prince Fielder .60 1.50
WM42 Jorge Posada .60 1.50
WM43 Hideki Okajima 2.00 5.00
WM44 Dan Uggla .40 1.00
WM45 Jake Peavy .40 1.00
WM46 Carlos Lee .40 1.00
WM47 C.C. Sabathia .60 1.50
WM48 Gary Sheffield .40 1.00
WM49 Tim Lincecum 2.00 5.00
WM50 J.J. Putz .40 1.00
WM51 Justin Verlander 1.00 2.50
WM52 Akinori Iwamura 1.00 2.50
WM53 Adam LaRoche .40 1.00
WM54 Alfonso Soriano .60 1.50

2007 Topps Williams 406

COMPLETE SET (36) 12.50 30.00
COMP.SERIES 1 (18) 6.00 15.00
COMP.SERIES 2 (18) 6.00 15.00
COMMON WILLIAMS .60 1.50
SER.1 ODDS 1:4 TARGET

2007 Topps World Champion Relics

SER.1 ODDS 1:7550 H, 1:226 HTA
SER.1 ODDS 1:14,750 K-MART
SER.1 ODDS 1:7550 TARGET
SER.1 ODDS 1:14,750 WAL-MART
STATED PRINT RUN 100 SETS
CARDS ARE NOT SERIAL NUMBERED
PRINT RUNS PROVIDED BY TOPPS
WCR1 Jeff Weaver Jsy/100 * 15.00 40.00
WCR2 Chris Duncan Jsy/100 * 40.00 80.00
WCR3 Chris Carpenter Jsy/100 * 20.00 50.00
WCR4 Yadier Molina Jsy/100 * 60.00 120.00
WCR5 Albert Pujols Bat/100 * 75.00 150.00
WCR6 Jim Edmonds Jsy/100 * 40.00 80.00
WCR7 Ronnie Belliard Bat/100 * 40.00 80.00
WCR8 So Taguchi Bat/100 * 60.00 120.00
WCR9 Juan Encarnacion Bat/100 * 15.00 40.00
WCR10 Scott Rolen Jsy/100 * 15.00 40.00
WCR11 Anthony Reyes Jsy/100 * 40.00 80.00
WCR12 Preston Wilson Bat/100 * 50.00 100.00
WCR13 Jeff Suppan Jsy/100 * 25.00 60.00
WCR14 Adam Wainwright Jsy/100 * 40.00 80.00
WCR15 David Eckstein Bat/100 * 15.00 40.00

2007 Topps World Domination

WD1 Ryan Howard .75 2.00
WD2 Justin Morneau .60 1.50
WD3 Ivan Rodriguez .60 1.50
WD4 Albert Pujols 1.25 3.00
WD5 Jorge Cantu .40 1.00
WD6 Johan Santana .60 1.50
WD7 Ichiro Suzuki 1.25 3.00
WD8 Chien-Ming Wang .60 1.50
WD9 Mariano Rivera 1.25 3.00
WD10 Andruw Jones .40 1.00

2007 Topps Update

This 334-card set was released in October, 2007. The set was issued through both hobby and retail channels. The hobby packs were created in two forms: 10-card wax packs with an $1.59 SRP which came 36 packs to a box and 12 boxes per case. The other form were the 50-card HTA pack with an $10 SRP which came 10 packs per box and six boxes per case. While a few rookies were interspersed throughout the set, most of the 2007 rookies were issued betwwen cards 147-202. The other subset is a Classic Combos grouping (275-284).

COMP.SET w/o SPs (330) 15.00 40.00
COMMON CARD (1-330) .12 .30
COMMON ROOKIE (1-330) .40 1.00
1-330 PLATE ODDS 1:54 HTA
PLATE PRINT RUN 1 SET PER COLOR
BLACK-CYAN-MAGENTA-YELLOW ISSUED
NO PLATE PRICING DUE TO SCARCITY
1 Tony Armas Jr. .12 .30
2 Shannon Stewart .12 .30
3 Jason Marquis .12 .30
4 Josh Wilson .12 .30
5 Steve Trachsel .12 .30
6 J.D. Drew .12 .30
7 Ronnie Belliard .12 .30
8 Trot Nixon .12 .30
9 Adam LaRoche .12 .30
10 Mark Loretta .12 .30
11 Matt Morris .12 .30
12 Marlon Anderson .12 .30
13 Jorge Julio .12 .30
14 Brady Clark .12 .30
15 David Wells .12 .30
16 Francisco Rosario .12 .30
17 Jason Ellison .12 .30
18 Adam Jones .20 .50
19 Russell Branyan .12 .30
20 Rob Bowen .12 .30
21 J.D. Durbin .12 .30
22 Jeff Salazar .12 .30
23 Tadahito Iguchi .12 .30
24 Brad Hennessey .12 .30
25 Mark Hendrickson .12 .30
26 Kameron Loe .12 .30
27 Yusmeiro Petit .12 .30
28 Olmedo Saenz .12 .30
29 Carlos Silva .12 .30
30 Kevin Frandsen .12 .30
31 Tony Pena .12 .30
32 Russ Ortiz .12 .30
33 Hong-Chih Kuo .12 .30
34 Paul McAnulty .12 .30
35 Hiram Bocachica .12 .30
36 Justin Germano .12 .30
37 Jason Simontacchi .12 .30
38 Jose Cruz .12 .30
39 Wilfredo Ledezma .12 .30
40 Chris Denorfia UER .12 .30
41 Ryan Langerhans .12 .30
42 Chris Snelling .12 .30
43 Ubaldo Jimenez .40 1.00
44 Scott Spiezio .12 .30
45 Byung-Hyun Kim .12 .30
46 Brandon Lyon .12 .30
47 Scott Hairston .12 .30
48 Chad Durbin .12 .30
49 Sammy Sosa .30 .75
50 Jason Smith .12 .30
51 Zack Greinke .20 .50
52 Armando Benitez .12 .30
53 Randy Messenger .12 .30
54 Mark Teixeira .20 .50
55 Mike Maroth .12 .30
56 Jamie Burke .12 .30
57 Carlos Marmol .20 .50

58 David Weathers .12 .30
59 Ryan Doumit .12 .30
60 Michael Barrett .12 .30
61 Shawn Chacon .12 .30
62 Mike Fontenot .12 .30
63 Cesar Izturis .12 .30
64 Cliff Floyd .12 .30
65 Angel Pagan .12 .30
66 Aaron Miles .12 .30
67 Tony Graffanino .12 .30
68 Kevin Mench .12 .30
69 Claudio Vargas .12 .30
70 Jose Capellan .12 .30
71 A.J. Pierzynski .12 .30
72 Darin Erstad .12 .30
73 Boone Logan .12 .30
74 Luis Castillo .12 .30
75 Marcus Thames .12 .30
76 Neifi Perez .12 .30
77 Esteban German .12 .30
78 Tony Pena .12 .30
79 Adam Wainwright .20 .50
80 Reggie Sanders .12 .30
81 Kelly Shoppach .12 .30
82 Rafael Betancourt .12 .30
83 Tom Mastny .12 .30
84 Kyle Farnsworth .12 .30
85 Rick Ankiel .12 .30
86 Kevin Thompson .12 .30
87 Jeff Karstens .12 .30
88 Eric Hinske .12 .30
89 Doug Mirabelli .12 .30
90 Julian Tavarez .12 .30
91 Carlos Pena .20 .50
92 Brendan Harris .12 .30
93 Chris Sampson .12 .30
94 Al Reyes .12 .30
95 Dmitri Young .12 .30
96 Jason Bergmann .12 .30
97 Shawn Hill .12 .30
98 Greg Dobbs .12 .30
99 Carlos Ruiz .12 .30
100a Abraham Nunez .12 .30
100b Jacoby Ellsbury (RC) 6.00 15.00
101 Jayson Werth .20 .50
102 Adam Eaton .12 .30
103 Antonio Alfonseca .12 .30
104 Jorge Sosa .12 .30
105 Ramon Castro .12 .30
106 Ruben Gotay .12 .30
107 Damion Easley .12 .30
108 David Newhan .12 .30
109 Jason Wood .12 .30
110 Reggie Abercrombie .12 .30
111 Kevin Gregg .12 .30
112 Henry Owens .12 .30
113 Willie Harris .12 .30
114 Pete Orr .12 .30
115 Casey Janssen .12 .30
116 Jason Frasor .12 .30
117 Jeremy Accardo .12 .30
118 John McDonald .12 .30
119 Matt Stairs .12 .30
120 Jason Phillips .12 .30
121 Justin Duchscherer .12 .30
122 Rich Harden .12 .30
123 Jack Cust .12 .30
124 Lenny DiNardo .12 .30
125 Joe Kennedy .12 .30
126 Chad Gaudin .12 .30
127 Marco Scutaro .20 .50
128 Brad Thompson .12 .30
129 Dustin Moseley .12 .30
130 Eric Gagne .12 .30
131 Marlon Byrd .12 .30
132 Scot Shields .12 .30
133 Victor Diaz .12 .30
134 Reggie Willits .12 .30
135 Jose Molina .12 .30
136 Ramon Vazquez .12 .30
137 Erick Aybar .12 .30
138 Sean Marshall .12 .30
139 Casey Kotchman .12 .30
140 Ryan Spilborghs .12 .30
141 Cameron Maybin RC .60 1.50
142 Jeremy Guthrie .12 .30
143 Jeff Baker .12 .30
144 Edwin Jackson .12 .30
145 Macay McBride .12 .30
146 Freddie Bynum .12 .30
147 Eric Patterson .40 1.00
148 Dustin McGowan .12 .30
149 Homer Bailey (RC) .60 1.50
150 Ryan Braun (RC) 2.00 5.00
151 Tony Abreu RC 1.00 2.50
152 Tyler Clippard (RC) .60 1.50
153 Mark Reynolds RC 1.25 3.00
154 Jesse Litsch RC .60 1.50
155 Carlos Gomez RC .75 2.00
156 Matt DeSalvo (RC) .40 1.00
157 Andy LaRoche (RC) .40 1.00
158 Tim Lincecum RC 2.00 5.00
159 Jarrod Saltalamacchia (RC) .60 1.50
160 Hunter Pence (RC) 1.25 3.00
161 Brandon Wood (RC) .40 1.00
162 Phil Hughes (RC) 1.00 2.50
163 Rocky Cherry RC 1.00 2.50
164 Chase Wright RC 1.00 2.50
165 Dallas Braden RC 2.50 6.00
166 Felix Pie (RC) .40 1.00
167 Zach McClellan RC .40 1.00
168 Rick Vanden Hurk RC .40 1.00
169 Micah Owings (RC) .40 1.00
170 Jon Coutlangus (RC) .40 1.00
171 Andy Sonnanstine RC .40 1.00
172 Yunel Escobar (RC) .40 1.00
173 Kevin Slowey (RC) 1.00 2.50
174 Curtis Thigpen (RC) .40 1.00
175 Masumi Kuwata RC .40 1.00
176 Kurt Suzuki (RC) .40 1.00
177 Travis Buck (RC) .40 1.00
178 Matt Lindstrom (RC) .40 1.00
179 Jesus Flores RC .40 1.00
180 Joakim Soria RC .40 1.00
181 Nathan Haynes (RC) .40 1.00
182 Matt Brown (RC) .40 1.00
183 Travis Metcalf RC .60 1.50
184 Yovani Gallardo (RC) 1.00 2.50
185 Nate Schierholtz (RC) .40 1.00
186 Kyle Kendrick RC 1.00 2.50
187 Kevin Melillo (RC) .40 1.00
188 Ryan Rowland-Smith .12 .30
189 Lee Gronkiewicz RC .40 1.00
190 Eulogio De La Cruz (RC) .60 1.50
191 Brett Carroll RC .40 1.00
192 Terry Evans RC .40 1.00
193 Chase Headley (RC) .40 1.00
194 Guillermo Rodriguez RC .40 1.00
195 Marcus McBeth (RC) .40 1.00
196 Brian Wolfe (RC) .40 1.00
197 Troy Cate RC .40 1.00
198 Mike Zagurski RC .40 1.00
199 Yoel Hernandez RC .40 1.00
200 Brad Salmon RC .40 1.00
201 Alberto Arias RC .40 1.00
202 Danny Putnam (RC) .40 1.00
203 Jamie Vermilyea RC .40 1.00
204 Kyle Lohse .12 .30
205 Sammy Sosa .30 .75
206 Tom Glavine .20 .50
207 Prince Fielder .20 .50
208 Mark Buehrle .20 .50
209 Troy Tulowitzki .40 1.00
210 Daisuke Matsuzaka RC 1.50 4.00
211 Randy Johnson .30 .75
212 Justin Verlander .30 .75
213 Trevor Hoffman .20 .50
214 Alex Rodriguez .40 1.00
215 Ivan Rodriguez .20 .50
216 David Ortiz .30 .75
217 Placido Polanco .12 .30
218 Derek Jeter .75 2.00
219 Alex Rodriguez .40 1.00
220 Vladimir Guerrero .20 .50
221 Magglio Ordonez .20 .50
222 Ichiro Suzuki .40 1.00
223 Russell Martin .12 .30
224 Prince Fielder .20 .50
225 Chase Utley .20 .50
226 Jose Reyes .20 .50
227 David Wright .25 .60
228 Carlos Beltran .20 .50
229 Barry Bonds .50 1.25
230 Ken Griffey Jr. .60 1.50
231 Torii Hunter .12 .30
232 Jonathan Papelbon .30 .75
233 J.J. Putz .12 .30
234 Francisco Rodriguez .20 .50
235 C.C. Sabathia .20 .50
236 Johan Santana .20 .50
237 Justin Verlander .30 .75
238 Francisco Cordero .12 .30
239 Mike Lowell .12 .30
240 Cole Hamels .25 .60
241 Trevor Hoffman .20 .50
242 Manny Ramirez .30 .75
243 Jake Peavy .12 .30
244 Brad Penny .12 .30
245 Takashi Saito .12 .30
246 Ben Sheets .12 .30
247 Hideki Okajima .60 1.50
248 Roy Oswalt .20 .50
249 Billy Wagner .12 .30
250 Carl Crawford .20 .50
251 Chris Young .12 .30
252 Brian McCann .12 .30
253 Derrek Lee .12 .30
254 Albert Pujols .40 1.00
255 Dmitri Young .12 .30
256 Orlando Hudson .12 .30
257 J.J. Hardy .12 .30
258 Miguel Cabrera .30 .75
259 Freddy Sanchez .12 .30
260 Matt Holliday .30 .75
261 Carlos Lee .12 .30
262 Aaron Rowand .12 .30
263 Alfonso Soriano .20 .50
264 Victor Martinez .20 .50
265 Jorge Posada .20 .50
266 Justin Morneau .20 .50
267 Brian Roberts .12 .30
268 Carlos Guillen .12 .30
269 Grady Sizemore .20 .50
270 Josh Beckett .12 .30
271 Dan Haren .12 .30
272 Bobby Jenks .12 .30
273 John Lackey .20 .50
274 Gil Meche .12 .30
275 M.Fontenot/K.Greene .12 .30
276 A.Rodriguez/R.Martin .40 1.00
277 T.Tulowitzki/J.Reyes .40 1.00
278 Posada/Jeter/ARod .75 2.00
279 C.Utley/Ichiro .40 1.00
280 C.Crawford/C.Guillen .20 .50
281 C.Hamels/R.Martin .25 .60
282 J.Papelbon/J.Posada .30 .75
283 C.Crawford/V.Martinez .20 .50
284 A.Soriano/J.Hardy .20 .50
285 Justin Morneau .20 .50
286 Prince Fielder .20 .50
287 Alex Rios .12 .30
288 Vladimir Guerrero .20 .50
289 Albert Pujols .40 1.00
290 Ryan Howard .25 .60
291 Magglio Ordonez .20 .50
292 Matt Holliday .30 .75
293 Wilson Betemit .12 .30
294 Todd Wellemeyer .12 .30
295 Scott Baker .12 .30
296 Edgar Gonzalez .12 .30
297 J.P. Howell .12 .30
298 Shaun Marcum .12 .30
299 Edinson Volquez .12 .30
300 Kason Gabbard .12 .30
301 Bob Howry .12 .30
302 J.A. Happ .50 1.25
303 Scott Feldman .20 .50
304 D'Angelo Jimenez .12 .30
305 Orlando Palmeiro .12 .30
306 Paul Bako .12 .30
307 Kyle Davies .12 .30
308 Gabe Gross .12 .30
309 John Wasdin .12 .30
310 Jon Knott .12 .30
311 Josh Phelps .12 .30
312a J.Chamberlain RC .60 1.50
312b J.Chamberlain Rev.Neg 30.00 80.00
312c J.Chamberlain Hou UER
313 Octavio Dotel .12 .30
314 Craig Monroe .12 .30
315 Edward Mujica .12 .30
316 Brandon Watson .12 .30
317 Chris Schroder .12 .30
318 Scott Proctor .12 .30
319 Ty Wigginton .12 .30
320 Troy Percival .12 .30
321 Scott Linebrink .12 .30
322 David Murphy .12 .30
323 Jorge Cantu .12 .30
324 Dan Wheeler .12 .30
325 Jason Kendall .12 .30
326 Milton Bradley .12 .30
327 Justin Upton RC 1.25 3.00
328 Kenny Lofton .12 .30
329 Roger Clemens .40 1.00
330 Brian Burres .12 .30
SQ1 Poley Walnuts 10.00 25.00

2007 Topps Update 1st Edition

*1ST ED VET: 2X TO 5X BASIC
*1ST ED RC: .6X TO 1.5X BASIC RC
STATED ODDS 1:36 HOB, 1:5 HTA

2007 Topps Update Gold

*GOLD VET: 2.5X TO 6X BASIC
*GOLD RC: .75X TO 2X BASIC RC
STATED ODDS 1:4 HOB, 1:4 RET
STATED PRINT RUN 2007 SER.#'d SETS

2007 Topps Update Red Back

COMPLETE SET (330) 30.00 60.00
*RED VET: .5X TO 1.2X BASIC
*RED RC: .5X TO 1.2X BASIC RC
STATED ODDS XXX

2007 Topps Update 2007 Highlights Autographs

GROUP A ODDS 1:14,900 H, 1:252 HTA
GROUP A ODDS 1:14,900 RETAIL
GROUP B ODDS 1:925 H, 19 HTA
GROUP B ODDS 1:1,165 RETAIL
GROUP C ODDS 1:10,100 H, 1:165 HTA
GROUP C ODDS 1:9,700 RETAIL
GROUP D ODDS 1:22,000 H,1:68 HTA
GROUP D ODDS 1:18,400 RETAIL
GROUP E ODDS 1:7,200 H, 1:125 HTA
GROUP E ODDS 1:7,605 RETAIL
GROUP F ODDS 1:7,000 H, 1:123 HTA
GROUP F ODDS 1:7,352 RETAIL
GROUP G ODDS 1:5,025 H, 1:105 HTA
GROUP G ODDS 1:6,563 RETAIL
AC Asdrubal Cabrera G 12.50 30.00
AE Andre Ethier B 6.00 15.00
AG Alex Gordon B 10.00 25.00
AH Aaron Heilman B 4.00 10.00
AJ Andruw Jones A 10.00 25.00
AL Anthony Lerew B 4.00 10.00
AP Albert Pujols A 150.00 200.00
AR Alex Rodriguez A 100.00 175.00
BB Brian Bruney B 4.00 10.00
CJ Conor Jackson B 4.00 10.00
CS C.C. Sabathia B 8.00 20.00
DE Damion Easley F 4.00 10.00
DW David Wright A 15.00 40.00
FC Francisco Cordero B 4.00 10.00
GS Gary Sheffield B 6.00 15.00
JR Jimmy Rollins B 12.50 30.00
JS Jarrod Saltalamacchia B 4.00 10.00
JT Jim Thome A 30.00 60.00
MC Miguel Cairo E 4.00 10.00
PF Prince Fielder B 8.00 20.00
RB Rod Barajas C 4.00 10.00
RC Robinson Cano B 15.00 40.00
RH Ryan Howard A 40.00 80.00
RW Ron Washington D 6.00 15.00
TT Troy Tulowitzki B 4.00 10.00

2007 Topps Update All-Star Stitches

PRINCE FIELDER
MILWAUKEE BREWERS
07
ALL-STAR GAME

STATED ODDS 1:45 H,1:10 HTA,1:55 R
AIR Alex Rios 3.00 8.00
AP Albert Pujols 8.00 20.00
AR Alex Rodriguez 6.00 15.00
ARR Aaron Rowand 3.00 8.00
BF Brian Fuentes 3.00 8.00
BJ Bobby Jenks 3.00 8.00
BM Brian McCann 5.00 12.00
BR Brian Roberts 3.00 8.00
BS Ben Sheets 3.00 8.00
BW Brandon Webb 3.00 8.00
CB Carlos Beltran 3.00 8.00
CC Carl Crawford 3.00 8.00
CH Cole Hamels 4.00 10.00
CL Carlos Lee 3.00 8.00
CS C.C. Sabathia 5.00 12.00
CU Chase Utley 5.00 12.00
CY Chris Young 3.00 8.00
DO David Ortiz 6.00 15.00
DW David Wright 6.00 15.00
DY Dmitri Young 3.00 8.00
FC Francisco Cordero 3.00 8.00
FR Francisco Rodriguez 3.00 8.00
FS Freddy Sanchez 3.00 8.00
GM Gil Meche 3.00 8.00
GS Grady Sizemore 5.00 12.00
HO Hideki Okajima 5.00 12.00
IR Ivan Rodriguez 5.00 12.00
IS Ichiro Suzuki 10.00 25.00
JB Josh Beckett 5.00 12.00
JEP Jake Peavy 3.00 8.00
JH J.J. Hardy 3.00 8.00
JL John Lackey 3.00 8.00
JM Justin Morneau 3.00 8.00
JP J.J. Putz 3.00 8.00
JR Jose Reyes 5.00 12.00
JRP Jorge Posada 5.00 12.00
JRV Jose Valverde 3.00 8.00
JS Johan Santana 5.00 12.00
JV Justin Verlander 6.00 15.00
MH Matt Holliday 5.00 12.00
ML Mike Lowell 5.00 12.00
MR Manny Ramirez 5.00 12.00
OH Orlando Hudson 3.00 8.00
PF Prince Fielder 5.00 12.00
RH Ryan Howard 6.00 15.00
RM Russell Martin 5.00 12.00
RO Roy Oswalt 3.00 8.00
TH Torii Hunter 3.00 8.00
TS Takashi Saito 5.00 12.00
TWH Trevor Hoffman 3.00 8.00
VM Victor Martinez 3.00 8.00

2007 Topps Update Barry Bonds 756

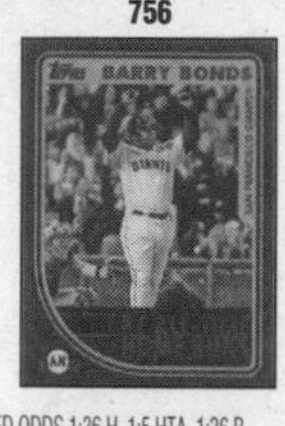

STATED ODDS 1:36 H, 1:5 HTA, 1:36 R
HRK Barry Bonds 1.00 2.50

2007 Topps Update Barry Bonds 756 Relic

STATED ODDS 1:5,145 H,1:1,400 HTA
STATED ODDS 1:5,145 RETAIL
STATED PRINT RUN 756 SER.#'d SETS
HRKR Barry Bonds 12.00 30.00

2007 Topps Update Chrome

STATED ODDS XXX
STATED PRINT RUN 415 SER.#'d SETS
TRC1 Homer Bailey 2.50 6.00
TRC2 Ryan Braun 8.00 20.00
TRC3 Tony Abreu 4.00 10.00
TRC4 Tyler Clippard 2.50 6.00
TRC5 Mark Reynolds 5.00 12.00
TRC6 Jesse Litsch 2.50 6.00
TRC7 Carlos Gomez 3.00 8.00
TRC8 Matt DeSalvo 1.50 4.00
TRC9 Andy LaRoche 1.50 4.00
TRC10 Tim Lincecum 8.00 20.00
TRC11 Jarrod Saltalamacchia 2.50 6.00
TRC12 Hunter Pence 5.00 12.00
TRC13 Brandon Wood 1.50 4.00
TRC14 Phil Hughes 4.00 10.00
TRC15 Rocky Cherry 4.00 10.00
TRC16 Chase Wright 4.00 10.00
TRC17 Dallas Braden 10.00 25.00
TRC18 Felix Pie 1.50 4.00
TRC19 Zach McClellan 1.50 4.00
TRC20 Rick VandenHurk 1.50 4.00
TRC21 Micah Owings 1.50 4.00
TRC22 Jon Coutlangus 1.50 4.00
TRC23 Andy Sonnanstine 1.50 4.00
TRC24 Yunel Escobar 1.50 4.00
TRC25 Kevin Slowey 4.00 10.00
TRC26 Curtis Thigpen 1.50 4.00
TRC27 Masumi Kuwata 1.50 4.00
TRC28 Kurt Suzuki 1.50 4.00
TRC29 Travis Buck 1.50 4.00
TRC30 Matt Lindstrom 1.50 4.00
TRC31 Jesus Flores 1.50 4.00
TRC32 Joakim Soria 1.50 4.00
TRC33 Nathan Haynes 1.50 4.00
TRC34 Matthew Brown 1.50 4.00
TRC35 Travis Metcalf 2.50 6.00
TRC36 Yovani Gallardo 4.00 10.00
TRC37 Nate Schierholtz 1.50 4.00
TRC38 Kyle Kendrick 4.00 10.00
TRC39 Kevin Melillo 1.50 4.00
TRC40 Cameron Maybin 2.50 6.00
TRC41 Lee Gronkiewicz 1.50 4.00
TRC42 Eulogio De La Cruz 2.50 6.00
TRC43 Brett Carroll 1.50 4.00
TRC44 Terry Evans 1.50 4.00
TRC45 Chase Headley 1.50 4.00
TRC46 Guillermo Rodriguez 1.50 4.00
TRC47 Marcus McBeth 1.50 4.00
TRC48 Brian Wolfe 1.50 4.00
TRC49 Troy Cate 1.50 4.00
TRC50 Justin Upton 5.00 12.00
TRC51 Joba Chamberlain 2.50 6.00
TRC52 Brad Salmon 1.50 4.00
TRC53 Alberto Arias 1.50 4.00
TRC54 Danny Putnam 1.50 4.00
TRC55 Jamie Vermilyea 1.50 4.00

2007 Topps Update Target

COMMON CARD .75 2.00
STATED ODDS XXX

2007 Topps Update World Series Watch

COMPLETE SET (15) 8.00 20.00
STATED ODDS 1:36 H, 1:5 HTA, 1:36 R
WSW1 New York Mets .75 2.00
WSW2 Detroit Tigers .75 2.00
WSW3 Boston Red Sox 2.00 5.00
WSW4 Milwaukee Brewers .75 2.00
WSW5 Cleveland Indians .75 2.00
WSW6 Los Angeles Angels .75 2.00
WSW7 San Diego Padres .75 2.00
WSW8 Los Angeles Dodgers .75 2.00
WSW9 Philadelphia Phillies .75 2.00
WSW10 Chicago Cubs .75 2.00
WSW11 St. Louis Cardinals .75 2.00
WSW12 Arizona Diamondbacks .75 2.00
WSW13 New York Yankees 2.00 5.00
WSW14 Seattle Mariners .75 2.00
WSW15 Atlanta Braves .75 2.00

2008 Topps

This 330-card first series was released in February, 2008. The set was issued in myriad forms both in and outside the hobby. The packs were issued into the hobby in 10-card packs, with an $1.59 SRP, which came 36 packs to a box and 12 boxes to a case. The HTA packs had 46-cards (44 cards if a relic card was inserted), with an $10 SRP, which came 10 packs to a box and six boxes to a case. Card number 234, which featured the Boston Red Sox celebrating their 2007 World Series victory was issued in a regular version and in a photoshopped version in which Presidential Candidate (and noted Yankee fan) Rudy Giuliani was placed into the celebration. The Guiliani card was issued at an officially announced stated rate of one in two of the earliest boxes.

COMP.HOBBY SET (660) 30.00 60.00
COMP.CUBS SET (660) 30.00 60.00
COMP.DODGERS SET (660) 30.00 60.00
COMP.METS SET (660) 30.00 60.00
COMP.RED SOX SET (660) 30.00 60.00
COMP.TIGERS SET (660) 30.00 60.00
COMP.YANKEES SET (660) 30.00 60.00
COMP.SET w/o VAR (660) 30.00 60.00
COMP.SERIES 1 (331) 12.50 30.00
COMP.SERIES 2 (330) 12.50 30.00
COMMON CARD (1-660) .12 .30
COMMON RC (1-660) .25 .60
SERIES 1 SET DOES NOT INCLUDE FS1
SERIES 1 SET DOES NOT INCLUDE #234C
SER.2 SET DOES NOT INCLUDE #661
SER.2 SET DOES NOT INCLUDE NNO CARDS
1 Alex Rodriguez .40 1.00
2 Barry Zito .20 .50
3 Jeff Suppan .12 .30
4 Rick Ankiel .12 .30
5 Scott Kazmir .20 .50
6 Felix Pie .12 .30
7 Mickey Mantle 1.00 2.50
8 Stephen Drew .12 .30
9 Randy Wolf .12 .30
10 Miguel Cabrera .30 .75
11 Yorvit Torrealba .12 .30
12 Jason Bartlett .12 .30
13 Kendry Morales .12 .30
14 Lenny DiNardo .20 .50
15 Ordon/Suzuki/Polan .40 1.00
16 Kevin Gregg .12 .30
17 Cristian Guzman .12 .30
18 J.D. Durbin .12 .30
19 Robinson Tejeda .12 .30
20 Daisuke Matsuzaka .20 .50
21 Edwin Encarnacion .30 .75
22 Ron Washington MG .12 .30
23 Chin-Lung Hu (RC) .25 .60
24 ARod/Ordon/Vlad .40 1.00
25 Kaz Matsui .12 .30
26 Manny Ramirez .30 .75
27 Bob Melvin MG .12 .30
28 Kyle Kendrick .12 .30
29 Anibal Sanchez .12 .30
30 Jimmy Rollins .20 .50
31 Ronny Paulino .12 .30
32 Howie Kendrick .12 .30
33 Joe Mauer .25 .60
34 Aaron Cook .12 .30
35 Cole Hamels .25 .60
36 Brendan Harris .12 .30
37 Jason Marquis .12 .30
38 Preston Wilson .12 .30
39 Yovanni Gallardo .12 .30
40 Miguel Tejada .20 .50
41 Rich Aurilia .12 .30
42 Corey Hart .12 .30
43 Ryan Dempster .12 .30
44 Jonathan Broxton .12 .30
45 Dontrelle Willis .12 .30
46 Zack Greinke .20 .50
47 Orlando Cabrera .20 .50
48 Zach Duke .12 .30
49 Orlando Hernandez .12 .30
50 Jake Peavy .12 .30
51 Erik Bedard .12 .30
52 Trevor Hoffman .20 .50
53 Hank Blalock .12 .30
54 Victor Martinez .20 .50
55 Chris Young .12 .30
56 Seth Smith (RC) .25 .60
57 Wladimir Balentien (RC) .25 .60
58 Holliday/Howard/Mig.Cabrera .30 .75
59 Grady Sizemore .20 .50
60 Jose Reyes .20 .50
61 ARod/Pena/Ortiz .40 1.00
62 Rich Thompson RC .40 1.00
63 Jason Michaels .12 .30
64 Mike Lowell .12 .30
65 Billy Wagner .12 .30
66 Brad Wilkerson .12 .30
67 Wes Helms .12 .30
68 Kevin Millar .12 .30
69 Bobby Cox MG .12 .30
70 Dan Uggla .12 .30
71 Jarrod Washburn .12 .30
72 Mike Piazza .30 .75
73 Mike Napoli .20 .50
74 Garrett Atkins .12 .30
75 Felix Hernandez .20 .50
76 Ivan Rodriguez .20 .50
77 Angel Guzman .12 .30
78 Radhames Liz RC .40 1.00
79 Omar Vizquel .20 .50
80 Alex Rios .12 .30
81 Ray Durham .12 .30
82 So Taguchi .12 .30
83 Mark Reynolds .12 .30
84 Brian Fuentes .12 .30
85 Jason Bay .20 .50
86 Scott Podsednik .12 .30
87 Maicer Izturis .12 .30
88 Jack Cust .12 .30
89 Josh Willingham .20 .50
90 Vladimir Guerrero .20 .50
91 Marcus Giles .12 .30
92 Ross Detwiler RC .40 1.00
93 Kenny Lofton .12 .30
94 Bud Black MG .12 .30
95 John Lackey .20 .50
96 Sam Fuld RC .75 2.00
97 Clint Sammons (RC) .25 .60
98 R.Howard/C.Utley .20 .50
99 D.Ortiz/M.Ramirez .30 .75
100 Ryan Howard .20 .50
101 Ryan Braun ROY .20 .50
102 Ross Ohlendorf RC .40 1.00
103 Jonathan Albaladejo RC .40 1.00
104 Kevin Youkilis .12 .30
105 Roger Clemens .40 1.00
106 Josh Bard .12 .30
107 Shawn Green .12 .30
108 B.J. Ryan .12 .30
109 Joe Nathan .12 .30
110 Justin Morneau .20 .50
111 Ubaldo Jimenez .12 .30
112 Jacque Jones .12 .30
113 Kevin Frandsen .12 .30
114 Mike Fontenot .12 .30
115 Johan Santana .20 .50
116 Chuck James .12 .30
117 Boof Bonser .12 .30
118 Marco Scutaro .20 .50
119 Jeremy Hermida .12 .30
120 Andruw Jones .12 .30
121 Mike Cameron .12 .30
122 Jason Varitek .30 .75
123 Terry Francona MG .20 .50
124 Bob Geren MG .12 .30
125 Tim Hudson .20 .50
126 Brandon Jones RC .60 1.50
127 Steve Pearce RC 1.25 3.00
128 Kenny Lofton .12 .30
129 Kevin Hart (RC) .25 .60
130 Justin Upton .20 .50
131 Norris Hopper .12 .30
132 Ramon Vazquez .12 .30
133 Mike Bacsik .12 .30
134 Matt Stairs .12 .30
135 Brad Penny .12 .30
136 Robinson Cano .20 .50
137 Jamey Carroll .12 .30
138 Dan Wheeler .12 .30
139 Johnny Estrada .12 .30
140 Brandon Webb .20 .50
141 Ryan Klesko .12 .30
142 Chris Duncan .12 .30
143 Willie Harris .12 .30
144 Jerry Owens .12 .30
145 Magglio Ordonez .20 .50
146 Aaron Hill .12 .30
147 Marlon Anderson .12 .30
148 Gerald Laird .12 .30
149 Luke Hochevar RC .40 1.00
150 Alfonso Soriano .20 .50
151 Adam Loewen .12 .30
152 Bronson Arroyo .12 .30

153 Luis Mendoza (RC) .25 .60
154 David Ross .12 .30
155 Carlos Zambrano .20 .50
156 Brandon McCarthy .12 .30
157 Tim Redding .12 .30
158 Jose Bautista UER .20 .50
159 Luke Scott .12 .30
160 Ben Sheets .12 .30
161 Matt Garza .12 .30
162 Andy Laroche .12 .30
163 Doug Davis .12 .30
164 Nate Schierholtz .12 .30
165 Tim Lincecum .20 .50
166 Andy Sonnanstine .12 .30
167 Jason Hirsh .12 .30
168 Phil Hughes .12 .30
169 Adam Lind .12 .30
170 Scott Rolen .20 .50
171 John Maine .12 .30
172 Chris Ray .12 .30
173 Jamie Moyer .12 .30
174 Julian Tavarez .12 .30
175 Delmon Young .20 .50
176 Troy Patton (RC) .25 .60
177 Josh Anderson (RC) .25 .60
178 Dustin Pedroia ROY .20 .50
179 Chris Young .12 .30
180 Jose Valverde .12 .30
181 Borowski/Jenks/Putz .12 .30
182 Billy Buckner (RC) .25 .60
183 Paul Byrd .12 .30
184 Tadahito Iguchi .12 .30
185 Yunel Escobar .12 .30
186 Lastings Milledge .12 .30
187 Dustin McGowan .12 .30
188 Kei Igawa .12 .30
189 Esteban German .12 .30
190 Russell Martin .12 .30
191 Orlando Hudson .12 .30
192 Jim Edmonds .20 .50
193 J.J. Hardy .12 .30
194 Chad Billingsley .20 .50
195 Todd Helton .20 .50
196 Ross Gload .12 .30
197 Melky Cabrera .12 .30
198 Shannon Stewart .12 .30
199 Adrian Beltre .30 .75
200 Manny Ramirez .30 .75
201 Matt Capps .12 .30
202 Mike Lamb .12 .30
203 Jason Tyner .12 .30
204 Rafael Furcal .12 .30
205 Gil Meche .12 .30
206 Geoff Jenkins .12 .30
207 Jeff Kent .12 .30
208 David DeJesus .12 .30
209 Andy Phillips .12 .30
210 Mark Teahen .12 .30
211 Lyle Overbay .12 .30
212 Moises Alou .12 .30
213 Michael Barrett .12 .30
214 C.J. Wilson .12 .30
215 Bobby Jenks .12 .30
216 Ryan Garko .12 .30
217 Josh Beckett .12 .30
218 Clint Hurdle MG .12 .30
219 Kevin Kouzmanoff .12 .30
220 Hoy Uswalt .20 .50
221 Ian Snell .12 .30
222 Mark Grudzielanek .12 .30
223 Odalis Perez .12 .30
224 Mark Buehrle .20 .50
225 Hunter Pence .20 .50
226 Kurt Suzuki .12 .30
227 Alfredo Amezaga .12 .30
228 Geoff Blum .12 .30
229 Dustin Pedroia .20 .50
230 Roy Halladay .20 .50
231 Casey Blake .12 .30
232 Clay Buchholz (RC) .40 1.00
233 Jimmy Rollins MVP .20 .50
234a Boston Red Sox .50 1.25
234b Red Sox w/Giuliani 3.00 8.00
234c Red Sox w/Giuliani Red 30.00 60.00
235 Rich Harden .12 .30
236 Joe Koshansky (RC) .25 .60
237 Eric Wedge MG .12 .30
238 Shane Victorino .12 .30
239 Richie Sexson .12 .30
240 Jim Thome .20 .50
241 Ervin Santana .12 .30
242 Manny Acta .12 .30
243 Akinori Iwamura .12 .30
244 Adam Wainwright .20 .50
245 Dan Haren .12 .30
246 Jason Isringhausen .12 .30
247 Edgar Gonzalez .12 .30
248 Jose Contreras .12 .30
249 Chris Sampson .12 .30
250 Jonathan Papelbon .20 .50
251 Dan Johnson .12 .30
252 Dmitri Young .12 .30
253 Bronson Sardinha (RC) .25 .60
254 David Murphy .12 .30
255 Brandon Phillips .12 .30
256 A.Rodriguez MVP .40 1.00
257 A.Kearns/D.Young .12 .30
258 M.Ramirez/K.Youkilis .30 .75
259 Emilio Bonifacio RC .60 1.50
260 Chad Cordero .12 .30
261 Josh Barfield .12 .30
262 Brett Myers .12 .30
263 Nook Logan .12 .30
264 Byung-Hyun Kim .12 .30
265 Fredi Gonzalez .12 .30
266 Ryan Doumit .12 .30
267 Chris Burke .12 .30
268 Daric Barton (RC) .25 .60
269 James Loney .12 .30
270 C.C. Sabathia .20 .50
271 Chad Tracy .12 .30
272 Anthony Reyes .12 .30
273 Rafael Soriano .12 .30
274 Jermaine Dye .12 .30
275 C.C. Sabathia .20 .50
276 Brad Ausmus .12 .30
277 Aubrey Huff .12 .30
278 Xavier Nady .12 .30
279 Damion Easley .12 .30
280 Willie Randolph MG .12 .30
281 Carlos Ruiz .12 .30
282 Jon Lester .20 .50
283 Jorge Sosa .12 .30
284 Lance Broadway (RC) .25 .60
285 Tony LaRussa MG .12 .30
286 Jeff Clement (RC) .40 1.00
287 Morneau/Santana/Mauer .25 .60
288 I.Rodriguez/J.Verlander .30 .75
289 Justin Ruggiano RC .40 1.00
290 Edgar Renteria .12 .30
291 Eugenio Velez RC .25 .60
292 Mark Loretta .20 .50
293 Gavin Floyd .12 .30
294 Brian McCann .20 .50
295 Tim Wakefield .20 .50
296 Paul Konerko .20 .50
297 Jorge Posada .20 .50
298 Fielder/Howard/Dunn .20 .50
299 Cesar Izturis .12 .30
300 Chien-Ming Wang .20 .50
301 Chris Duffy .12 .30
302 Horacio Ramirez .12 .30
303 Jose Lopez .12 .30
304 Jose Vidro .12 .30
305 Carlos Delgado .20 .50
306 Scott Olsen .12 .30
307 Shawn Hill .12 .30
308 Felipe Lopez .12 .30
309 Ryan Church .12 .30
310 Kelvim Escobar .20 .50
311 Jeremy Guthrie .12 .30
312 Ramon Hernandez .12 .30
313 Kameron Loe .12 .30
314 Ian Kinsler .20 .50
315 David Weathers .12 .30
316 Scott Hatteberg .12 .30
317 Cliff Lee .20 .50
318 Ned Yost MG .12 .30
319 Joey Votto (RC) 1.00 2.50
320 Ichiro Suzuki .40 1.00
321 J.R. Towles RC .40 1.00
322 Kazmir/Santana/Bedard .20 .50
323 Valverde/Cordero/Hoffman .20 .50
324 Jake Peavy .12 .30
325 Jim Leyland MG .12 .30
326 Holliday/Chipper/Hanley .30 .75
327 Peavy/Harang/Smoltz .30 .75
328 Nyjer Morgan (RC) .25 .60
329 Lou Piniella MG .12 .30
330 Curtis Granderson .20 .50
331 Dave Roberts .12 .30
332 Grady Sizemore/Jhonny Peralta .20 .50
333 Jayson Nix (RC) .25 .60
334 Oliver Perez .12 .30
335 Eric Byrnes .12 .30
336 Jhonny Peralta .12 .30
337 Livan Hernandez .12 .30
338 Matt Diaz .12 .30
339 Troy Percival .12 .30
340 David Wright .20 .50
341 Daniel Cabrera .12 .30
342 Matt Belisle .12 .30
343 Kason Gabbard .12 .30
344 Mike Rabelo .12 .30
345 Carl Crawford .20 .50
346 Adam Everett .12 .30
347 Chris Capuano .12 .30
348 Craig Monroe .12 .30
349 Mike Mussina .20 .50
350 Mark Teixeira .20 .50
351 Bobby Crosby .12 .30
352 Miguel Batista .12 .30
353 Brendan Ryan .12 .30
354 Edwin Jackson .12 .30
355 Brian Roberts .12 .30
356 Manny Corpas .12 .30
357 Jeremy Accardo .20 .50
358 John Patterson .12 .30
359 Evan Meek RC .25 .60
360 David Ortiz .30 .75
361 Wesley Wright RC .25 .60
362 Fernando Hernandez RC .25 .60
363 Brian Barton RC .40 1.00
364 Al Reyes .12 .30
365 Derrek Lee .12 .30
366 Jeff Weaver .12 .30
367 Khalil Greene .12 .30
368 Michael Bourn .12 .30
369 Luis Castillo .12 .30
370 Adam Dunn .20 .50
371 Rickie Weeks .12 .30
372 Matt Kemp .25 .60
373 Casey Kotchman .12 .30
374 Jason Jennings .12 .30
375 Fausto Carmona .12 .30
376 Willy Taveras .12 .30
377 Jake Westbrook .12 .30
378 Ozzie Guillen .12 .30
379 Hideki Okajima .12 .30
380 Grady Sizemore .20 .50
381 Jeff Francoeur .20 .50
382 Micah Owings .12 .30
383 Jered Weaver .20 .50
384 Carlos Quentin .12 .30
385 Troy Tulowitzki .30 .75
386 Julio Lugo .12 .30
387 Sean Marshall .12 .30
388 Jorge Cantu .12 .30
389 Callix Crabbe (RC) .25 .60
390 Troy Glaus .20 .50
391 Nick Markakis .25 .60
392 Joey Gathright .12 .30
393 Michael Cuddyer .12 .30
394 Mark Ellis .12 .30
395 Lance Berkman .20 .50
396 Randy Johnson .30 .75
397 Brian Wilson .30 .75
398 Kenji Johjima .12 .30
399 Jarrod Saltalamacchia .12 .30
400 Matt Holliday .30 .75
401 Scott Hairston .12 .30
402 Taylor Buchholz .12 .30
403 Nate Robertson .12 .30
404 Cecil Cooper .12 .30
405 Travis Hafner .12 .30
406 Takashi Saito .12 .30
407 Johnny Damon .20 .50
408 Edinson Volquez .12 .30
409 Jason Giambi .12 .30
410 Alex Gordon .20 .50
411 Jason Kubel .12 .30
412 Joel Zumaya .12 .30
413 Wandy Rodriguez .12 .30
414 Andrew Miller .20 .50
415 Derek Lowe .12 .30
416 Elijah Dukes .12 .30
417 Brian Bass (RC) .25 .60
418 Dioner Navarro .12 .30
419 Bengie Molina .12 .30
420 Nick Swisher .20 .50
421 Brandon Backe .12 .30
422 Erick Aybar .12 .30
423 Mike Scioscia MG .12 .30
424 Aaron Harang .12 .30
425 Hanley Ramirez .20 .50
426 Franklin Gutierrez .12 .30
427 Carlos Guillen .12 .30
428 Jair Jurrjens .12 .30
429 Billy Butler .12 .30
430 Ryan Braun .20 .50
431 Delwyn Young .12 .30
432 Jason Kendall .12 .30
433 Carlos Silva .12 .30
434 Ron Gardenhire MG .12 .30
435 Torii Hunter .12 .30
436 Joe Blanton .12 .30
437 Brandon Wood .12 .30
438 Jay Payton .12 .30
439 Josh Hamilton .20 .50
440 Pedro Martinez .20 .50
441 Miguel Olivo .12 .30
442 Luis Gonzalez .12 .30
443 Greg Dobbs .12 .30
444 Jack Wilson .12 .30
445 Hideki Matsui .30 .75
446 Randor Bierd RC .25 .60
447 Chipper Jones/Mark Teixeira .30 .75
448 Cameron Maybin .12 .30
449 Braden Looper .12 .30
450 Prince Fielder .20 .50
451 Brian Giles .12 .30
452 Kevin Slowey .12 .30
453 Josh Fogg .12 .30
454 Mike Hampton .12 .30
455 Derek Jeter .75 2.00
456 Chone Figgins .12 .30
457 Josh Fields .12 .30
458 Brad Hawpe .12 .30
459 Mike Sweeney .12 .30
460 Chase Utley .20 .50
461 Jacoby Ellsbury .25 .60
462 Freddy Sanchez .12 .30
463 John McLaren .12 .30
464 Rocco Baldelli .12 .30
465 Huston Street .12 .30
466 Miguel Cabrera/Ivan Rodriguez .30 .75
467 Nick Blackburn RC .40 1.00
468 Gregor Blanco (RC) .25 .60
469 Brian Bocock RC .25 .60
470 Tom Gorzelanny .12 .30
471 Brian Schneider .12 .30
472 Shaun Marcum .12 .30
473 Joe Maddon .12 .30
474 Yuniesky Betancourt .12 .30
475 Adrian Gonzalez .20 .50
476 Johnny Cueto RC .60 1.50
477 Ben Broussard .12 .30
478 Geovany Soto .30 .75
479 Bobby Abreu .12 .30
480 Matt Cain .20 .50
481 Manny Parra .12 .30
482 Kazuo Fukumori RC .40 1.00
483 Mike Jacobs .12 .30
484 Todd Jones .12 .30
485 J.J. Putz .12 .30
486 Javier Vazquez .12 .30
487 Corey Patterson .12 .30
488 Mike Gonzalez .12 .30
489 Joakim Soria .12 .30
490 Albert Pujols .40 1.00
491 Cliff Floyd .12 .30
492 Harvey Garcia (RC) .25 .60
493 Steve Holm RC .25 .60
494 Paul Maholm .12 .30
495 James Shields .12 .30
496 Brad Lidge .12 .30
497 Cla Meredith .12 .30
498 Matt Chico .12 .30
499 Milton Bradley .12 .30
500 Chipper Jones .30 .75
501 Elliot Johnson (RC) .25 .60
502 Alex Cora .12 .30
503 Jeremy Bonderman .20 .50
504 Conor Jackson .12 .30
505 B.J. Upton .20 .50
506 Jay Gibbons .12 .30
507 Mark DeRosa .12 .30
508 John Danks .12 .30
509 Alex Gonzalez .12 .30
510 Justin Verlander .30 .75
511 Jeff Francis .12 .30
512 Placido Polanco .12 .30
513 Rick Vanden Hurk .12 .30
514 Tony Pena .12 .30
515 A.J. Burnett .12 .30
516 Jason Schmidt .12 .30
517 Bill Hall .12 .30
518 Ian Stewart .12 .30
519 Travis Buck .20 .50
520 Vernon Wells .12 .30
521 Jayson Werth .20 .50
522 Nate McLouth .12 .30
523 Noah Lowry .12 .30
524 Raul Ibanez .20 .50
525 Gary Matthews .12 .30
526 Juan Encarnacion .12 .30
527 Marlon Byrd .12 .30
528 Paul Lo Duca .12 .30
529 Masahide Kobayashi RC .40 1.00
530 Ryan Zimmerman .20 .50
531 Hiroki Kuroda RC .60 1.50
532 Tim Lahey RC .25 .60
533 Kyle McClellan RC .25 .60
534 Matt Tupman RC .25 .60
535 Francisco Rodriguez .20 .50
536 A.Pujols/P.Fielder .40 1.00
537 Scott Moore .12 .30
538 Alex Romero (RC) .40 1.00
539 Clete Thomas RC .40 1.00
540 John Smoltz .30 .75
541 Adam Jones .20 .50
542 Adam Kennedy .12 .30
543 Carlos Lee .12 .30
544 Chad Gaudin .20 .50
545 Chris Young .12 .30
546 Francisco Liriano .12 .30
547 Fred Lewis .12 .30
548 Garrett Olson .12 .30
549 Gregg Zaun .12 .30
550 Curt Schilling .20 .50
551 Erick Threets (RC) .25 .60
552 J.D. Drew .12 .30
553 Jo-Jo Reyes .12 .30
554 Joe Borowski .12 .30
555 Josh Beckett .12 .30
556 John Gibbons .12 .30
557 John McDonald .12 .30
558 John Russell .12 .30
559 Jonny Gomes .12 .30
560 Aramis Ramirez .12 .30
561 Matt Tolbert RC .40 1.00
562 Ronnie Belliard .12 .30
563 Ramon Troncoso RC .25 .60
564 Frank Catalanotto .12 .30
565 A.J. Pierzynski .12 .30
566 Kevin Millwood .12 .30
567 David Eckstein .12 .30
568 Jose Guillen .12 .30
569 Brad Hennessey .12 .30
570 Homer Bailey .20 .50
571 Eric Gagne .12 .30
572 Adam Eaton .12 .30
573 Tom Gordon .12 .30
574 Scott Baker .12 .30
575 Ty Wigginton .20 .50
576 Dave Bush .12 .30
577 John Buck .12 .30
578 Ricky Nolasco .12 .30
579 Jesse Litsch .20 .50
580 Ken Griffey Jr. .60 1.50
581 Kazuo Matsui .12 .30
582 Dusty Baker .12 .30
583 Nick Punto .12 .30
584 Ryan Theriot .12 .30
585 Brian Bannister .12 .30
586 Coco Crisp .12 .30
587 Chris Snyder .12 .30
588 Tony Gwynn .12 .30
589 Dave Trembley .12 .30
590 Mariano Rivera .40 1.00
591 Rico Washington (RC) .25 .60
592 Matt Morris .12 .30
593 Randy Wells RC .40 1.00
594 Mike Morse .12 .30
595 Francisco Cordero .12 .30
596 Joba Chamberlain .12 .30
597 Kyle Davies .12 .30
598 Bruce Bochy .20 .50
599 Austin Kearns .12 .30
600 Tom Glavine .20 .50
601 Felipe Paulino RC .40 1.00
602 Lyle Overbay/Vernon Wells .12 .30
603 Blake DeWitt (RC) .40 1.00
604 Wily Mo Pena .12 .30
605 Andre Ethier .20 .50
606 Jason Bergmann .12 .30
607 Ryan Spilborghs .12 .30
608 Brian Burres .12 .30
609 Ted Lilly .12 .30
610 Carlos Beltran .20 .50
611 Garret Anderson .12 .30
612 Kelly Johnson .12 .30
613 Melvin Mora .12 .30
614 Rich Hill .12 .30
615 Pat Burrell .12 .30
616 Jon Garland .12 .30
617 Asdrubal Cabrera .20 .50
618 Pat Neshek .20 .50
619 Sergio Mitre .12 .30
620 Gary Sheffield .12 .30
621 Denard Span .20 .50
622 Jorge De La Rosa .12 .30
623 Trey Hillman MG .12 .30
624 Joe Torre MG .12 .30
625 Greg Maddux .40 1.00
626 Mike Redmond .12 .30
627 Mike Pelfrey .12 .30
628 Andy Pettitte .20 .50
629 Eric Chavez .12 .30
630 Chris Carpenter .20 .50
631 Joe Girardi MG .20 .50
632 Charlie Manuel MG .12 .30
633 Adam LaRoche .12 .30
634 Kenny Rogers .12 .30
635 Michael Young .12 .30
636 Rafael Betancourt .12 .30
637 Jose Castillo .12 .30
638 Juan Pierre .12 .30
639 Juan Uribe .12 .30
640 Carlos Pena .20 .50
641 Marcus Thames .12 .30
642 Mark Kotsay .12 .30
643 Matt Murton .12 .30
644 Reggie Willits .12 .30
645 Andy Marte .12 .30
646 Rajai Davis .12 .30
647 Randy Winn .12 .30
648 Ryan Freel .12 .30
649 Joe Crede .12 .30
650 Frank Thomas .30 .75
651 Martin Prado .12 .30
652 Rod Barajas .12 .30
653 Endy Chavez .12 .30
654 Willy Aybar .12 .30
655 Aaron Rowand .12 .30
656 Darin Erstad .12 .30
657 Jeff Keppinger .12 .30
658 Kerry Wood .12 .30
659 Vicente Padilla .12 .30
660 Yadier Molina .30 .75
661 Johan Santana NoNo 125.00 250.00
FS1 Kazuo Uzuki .75 2.00
NNO Alexei Ramirez 15.00 40.00
NNO Kosuke Fukudome 20.00 50.00
NNO Yasuhiko Yabuta 40.00 80.00

2008 Topps Black

SER.1 ODDS 1:95 HOBBY
SER.2 ODDS 1:63 HOBBY
STATED PRINT RUN 57 SER.#'d SETS
1 Alex Rodriguez 12.00 30.00
2 Barry Zito 6.00 15.00
3 Jeff Suppan 6.00 15.00
4 Rick Ankiel 6.00 15.00
5 Scott Kazmir 6.00 15.00
6 Felix Pie 6.00 15.00
7 Mickey Mantle 60.00 120.00
8 Stephen Drew 6.00 15.00
9 Randy Wolf 6.00 15.00
10 Miguel Cabrera 10.00 25.00
11 Yorvit Torrealba 6.00 15.00
12 Jason Bartlett 6.00 15.00
13 Kendry Morales 6.00 15.00
14 Lenny DiNardo 6.00 15.00
15 Ordonez/Ichiro/Polanco 12.00 30.00
16 Kevin Gregg 6.00 15.00
17 Cristian Guzman 6.00 15.00
18 J.D. Durbin 6.00 15.00
19 Robinson Tejeda 6.00 15.00
20 Daisuke Matsuzaka 6.00 15.00
21 Edwin Encarnacion 6.00 15.00
22 Ron Washington MG 6.00 15.00
23 Chin-Lung Hu 30.00 60.00
24 A.Rod/Ordonez/Vlad 12.00 30.00
25 Kaz Matsui 6.00 15.00
26 Manny Ramirez 10.00 25.00
27 Bob Melvin MG 6.00 15.00
28 Kyle Kendrick 6.00 15.00
29 Anibal Sanchez 6.00 15.00
30 Jimmy Rollins 10.00 25.00
31 Ronny Paulino 6.00 15.00
32 Howie Kendrick 6.00 15.00
33 Joe Mauer 10.00 25.00
34 Aaron Cook 6.00 15.00
35 Cole Hamels 10.00 25.00
36 Brendan Harris 6.00 15.00
37 Jason Marquis 6.00 15.00
38 Preston Wilson 6.00 15.00
39 Yovanni Gallardo 6.00 15.00
40 Miguel Tejada 6.00 15.00
41 Rich Aurilia 6.00 15.00
42 Corey Hart 6.00 15.00
43 Ryan Dempster 6.00 15.00
44 Jonathan Broxton 6.00 15.00
45 Dontrelle Willis 6.00 15.00
46 Zack Greinke 6.00 15.00
47 Orlando Cabrera 6.00 15.00
48 Zach Duke 6.00 15.00
49 Orlando Hernandez 6.00 15.00
50 Jake Peavy 10.00 25.00
51 Erik Bedard 6.00 15.00
52 Trevor Hoffman 6.00 15.00
53 Hank Blalock 6.00 15.00
54 Victor Martinez 6.00 15.00
55 Chris Young 6.00 15.00
56 Seth Smith 6.00 15.00
57 Wladimir Balentien 6.00 15.00
58 Holliday/Howard/Cabrera 10.00 25.00
59 Grady Sizemore 10.00 25.00
60 Jose Reyes 10.00 25.00
61 A.Rod/C.Pena/Ortiz 12.00 30.00
62 Rich Thompson 6.00 15.00
63 Jason Michaels 6.00 15.00
64 Mike Lowell 10.00 25.00
65 Billy Wagner 6.00 15.00
66 Brad Wilkerson 6.00 15.00
67 Wes Helms 6.00 15.00
68 Kevin Millar 6.00 15.00
69 Bobby Cox MG 6.00 15.00
70 Dan Uggla 6.00 15.00
71 Jarrod Washburn 6.00 15.00
72 Mike Piazza 20.00 50.00
73 Mike Napoli 6.00 15.00
74 Garrett Atkins 6.00 15.00
75 Felix Hernandez 10.00 25.00
76 Ivan Rodriguez 10.00 25.00
77 Angel Guzman 6.00 15.00
78 Radhames Liz 10.00 25.00
79 Omar Vizquel 6.00 15.00
80 Alex Rios 6.00 15.00
81 Ray Durham 6.00 15.00
82 So Taguchi 6.00 15.00
83 Mark Reynolds 6.00 15.00
84 Brian Fuentes 6.00 15.00
85 Jason Bay 10.00 25.00
86 Scott Podsednik 6.00 15.00
87 Maicer Izturis 6.00 15.00
88 Jack Cust 6.00 15.00
89 Josh Willingham 6.00 15.00
90 Vladimir Guerrero 10.00 25.00
91 Marcus Giles 6.00 15.00
92 Ross Detwiler 10.00 25.00
93 Kenny Lofton 6.00 15.00
94 Bud Black MG 6.00 15.00
95 John Lackey 6.00 15.00
96 Sam Fuld 6.00 15.00
97 Clint Sammons 6.00 15.00
98 R.Howard/C.Utley 12.50 30.00
99 D.Ortiz/M.Ramirez 12.50 30.00
100 Ryan Howard 12.50 30.00
101 Ryan Braun ROY 12.50 30.00
102 Ross Ohlendorf 10.00 25.00
103 Jonathan Albaladejo 6.00 15.00
104 Kevin Youkilis 10.00 25.00
105 Roger Clemens 12.00 30.00
106 Josh Bard 6.00 15.00
107 Shawn Green 6.00 15.00
108 B.J. Ryan 6.00 15.00
109 Joe Nathan 6.00 15.00
110 Justin Morneau 6.00 15.00
111 Ubaldo Jimenez 6.00 15.00
112 Jacque Jones 6.00 15.00
113 Kevin Frandsen 6.00 15.00
114 Mike Fontenot 6.00 15.00
115 Johan Santana 12.50 30.00
116 Chuck James 6.00 15.00
117 Boof Bonser 6.00 15.00
118 Marco Scutaro 6.00 15.00
119 Jeremy Hermida 6.00 15.00
120 Andruw Jones 6.00 15.00
121 Mike Cameron 6.00 15.00
122 Jason Varitek 10.00 25.00
123 Terry Francona MG 6.00 15.00
124 Bob Geren MG 6.00 15.00
125 Tim Hudson 6.00 15.00
126 Brandon Jones 6.00 15.00
127 Steve Pearce 15.00 40.00
128 Kenny Lofton 6.00 15.00
129 Kevin Hart 6.00 15.00
130 Justin Upton 10.00 25.00
131 Norris Hopper 6.00 15.00
132 Ramon Vazquez 6.00 15.00
133 Mike Bacsik 6.00 15.00
134 Matt Stairs 6.00 15.00
135 Brad Penny 6.00 15.00
136 Robinson Cano 10.00 25.00
137 Jamey Carroll 6.00 15.00
138 Dan Wheeler 6.00 15.00
139 Johnny Estrada 6.00 15.00
140 Brandon Webb 6.00 15.00
141 Ryan Klesko 6.00 15.00
142 Chris Duncan 6.00 15.00
143 Willie Harris 6.00 15.00
144 Jerry Owens 6.00 15.00
145 Magglio Ordonez 10.00 25.00
146 Aaron Hill 6.00 15.00
147 Marlon Anderson 6.00 15.00
148 Gerald Laird 6.00 15.00
149 Luke Hochevar 10.00 25.00
150 Alfonso Soriano 10.00 25.00
151 Adam Loewen 6.00 15.00
152 Bronson Arroyo 6.00 15.00
153 Luis Mendoza 6.00 15.00
154 David Ross 6.00 15.00
155 Carlos Zambrano 6.00 15.00
156 Brandon McCarthy 6.00 15.00
157 Tim Redding 6.00 15.00
158 Jose Bautista UER 6.00 15.00
Wrong photo
159 Luke Scott 6.00 15.00
160 Ben Sheets 6.00 15.00
161 Matt Garza 6.00 15.00
162 Andy Laroche 6.00 15.00
163 Doug Davis 6.00 15.00
164 Nate Schierholtz 6.00 15.00
165 Tim Lincecum 10.00 25.00
166 Andy Sonnanstine 6.00 15.00
167 Jason Hirsh 6.00 15.00
168 Phil Hughes 12.50 30.00
169 Adam Lind 6.00 15.00
170 Scott Rolen 10.00 25.00
171 John Maine 6.00 15.00
172 Chris Ray 6.00 15.00
173 Jamie Moyer 6.00 15.00
174 Julian Tavarez 6.00 15.00
175 Delmon Young 10.00 25.00
176 Troy Patton 6.00 15.00
177 Josh Anderson 6.00 15.00
178 Dustin Pedroia ROY 10.00 25.00
179 Chris Young 6.00 15.00
180 Jose Valverde 6.00 15.00
181 Joe Borowski/Bobby Jenks/J.J. Putz 6.00 15.00
182 Billy Buckner 6.00 15.00
183 Paul Byrd 6.00 15.00
184 Tadahito Iguchi 6.00 15.00
185 Yunel Escobar 6.00 15.00
186 Lastings Milledge 6.00 15.00
187 Dustin McGowan 6.00 15.00
188 Kei Igawa 6.00 15.00
189 Esteban German 6.00 15.00
190 Russell Martin 6.00 15.00
191 Orlando Hudson 6.00 15.00
192 Jim Edmonds 6.00 15.00
193 J.J. Hardy 6.00 15.00
194 Chad Billingsley 6.00 15.00
195 Todd Helton 10.00 25.00
196 Ross Gload 6.00 15.00
197 Melky Cabrera 6.00 15.00
198 Shannon Stewart 6.00 15.00
199 Adrian Beltre 6.00 15.00
200 Manny Ramirez 10.00 25.00
201 Matt Capps 6.00 15.00
202 Mike Lamb 6.00 15.00
203 Jason Tyner 6.00 15.00
204 Rafael Furcal 6.00 15.00
205 Gil Meche 6.00 15.00
206 Geoff Jenkins 6.00 15.00
207 Jeff Kent 6.00 15.00
208 David DeJesus 6.00 15.00
209 Andy Phillips 6.00 15.00
210 Mark Teahen 6.00 15.00
211 Lyle Overbay 6.00 15.00
212 Moises Alou 6.00 15.00
213 Michael Barrett 6.00 15.00
214 C.J. Wilson 6.00 15.00
215 Bobby Jenks 6.00 15.00
216 Ryan Garko 6.00 15.00
217 Josh Beckett 15.00 40.00
218 Clint Hurdle MG 6.00 15.00
219 Kevin Kouzmanoff 6.00 15.00
220 Hoy Uswalt 6.00 15.00
221 Ian Snell 6.00 15.00
222 Mark Grudzielanek 6.00 15.00
223 Odalis Perez 6.00 15.00
224 Mark Buehrle 6.00 15.00
225 Hunter Pence 12.50 30.00
226 Kurt Suzuki 6.00 15.00
227 Alfredo Amezaga 6.00 15.00
228 Geoff Blum 6.00 15.00
229 Dustin Pedroia 12.50 30.00
230 Roy Halladay 6.00 15.00
231 Casey Blake 6.00 15.00
232 Clay Buchholz 30.00 60.00
233 Jimmy Rollins MVP 10.00 25.00
234 Boston Red Sox 30.00 60.00
235 Rich Harden 6.00 15.00
236 Joe Koshansky 6.00 15.00
237 Eric Wedge MG 6.00 15.00
238 Shane Victorino 6.00 15.00
239 Richie Sexson 6.00 15.00
240 Jim Thome 10.00 25.00
241 Ervin Santana 6.00 15.00
242 Manny Acta 6.00 15.00
243 Akinori Iwamura 6.00 15.00
244 Adam Wainwright 6.00 15.00
245 Dan Haren 6.00 15.00
246 Jason Isringhausen 6.00 15.00
247 Edgar Gonzalez 6.00 15.00
248 Jose Contreras 6.00 15.00
249 Chris Sampson 6.00 15.00
250 Jonathan Papelbon 12.50 30.00
251 Dan Johnson 6.00 15.00
252 Dmitri Young 6.00 15.00
253 Bronson Sardinha 6.00 15.00
254 David Murphy 6.00 15.00
255 Brandon Phillips 6.00 15.00
256 Alex Rodriguez MVP 12.00 30.00
257 Austin Kearns/Dimitri Young 6.00 15.00
258 Manny Ramirez/Kevin Youkilis 10.00 25.00
259 Emilio Bonifacio 6.00 15.00

260 Chad Cordero 6.00 15.00
261 Josh Barfield 6.00 15.00
262 Brett Myers 6.00 15.00
263 Nook Logan 6.00 15.00
264 Byung-Hyun Kim 6.00 15.00
265 Fredi Gonzalez 6.00 15.00
266 Ryan Doumit 6.00 15.00
267 Chris Burke 6.00 15.00
268 Daric Barton 6.00 15.00
269 James Loney 12.50 30.00
270 C.C. Sabathia 6.00 15.00
271 Chad Tracy 6.00 15.00
272 Anthony Reyes 6.00 15.00
273 Rafael Soriano 6.00 15.00
274 Jermaine Dye 6.00 15.00
275 C.C. Sabathia 6.00 15.00
276 Brad Ausmus 6.00 15.00
277 Aubrey Huff 6.00 15.00
278 Xavier Nady 6.00 15.00
279 Damion Easley 6.00 15.00
280 Willie Randolph MG 6.00 15.00
281 Carlos Ruiz 6.00 15.00
282 Jon Lester 10.00 25.00
283 Jorge Sosa 6.00 15.00
284 Lance Broadway 6.00 15.00
285 Tony LaRussa MG 6.00 15.00
286 Jeff Clement 6.00 15.00
287 Morneau/Santana/Mauer 12.50 30.00
288 IRod/Verlander 10.00 25.00
289 Justin Ruggiano 6.00 15.00
290 Edgar Renteria 6.00 15.00
291 Eugenio Velez 6.00 15.00
292 Mark Loretta 6.00 15.00
293 Gavin Floyd 6.00 15.00
294 Brian McCann 6.00 15.00
295 Tim Wakefield 6.00 15.00
296 Paul Konerko 6.00 15.00
297 Jorge Posada 10.00 25.00
298 Prince Fielder/Ryan Howard/Adam Dunn 10.00 25.00
299 Cesar Izturis 6.00 15.00
300 Chien-Ming Wang 12.50 30.00
301 Chris Duffy 6.00 15.00
302 Horacio Ramirez 6.00 15.00
303 Jose Lopez 6.00 15.00
304 Jose Vidro 6.00 15.00
305 Carlos Delgado 6.00 15.00
306 Scott Olsen 6.00 15.00
307 Shawn Hill 6.00 15.00
308 Felipe Lopez 6.00 15.00
309 Ryan Church 6.00 15.00
310 Kelvim Escobar 6.00 15.00
311 Jeremy Guthrie 6.00 15.00
312 Ramon Hernandez 6.00 15.00
313 Kameron Loe 6.00 15.00
314 Ian Kinsler 6.00 15.00
315 David Weathers 6.00 15.00
316 Scott Hatteberg 6.00 15.00
317 Cliff Lee 6.00 15.00
318 Ned Yost MG 6.00 15.00
319 Joey Votto 10.00 25.00
320 Ichiro Suzuki 20.00 50.00
321 J.R. Towles 10.00 25.00
322 Scott Kazmir/Johan Santana/Erik Bedard 10.00 25.00
323 Jose Valverde/Francisco Cordero/Trevor Hoffman 6.00 15.00
324 Jake Peavy 10.00 25.00
325 Jim Leyland MG 6.00 15.00
326 Matt Holliday/Chipper Jones Hanley Ramirez 10.00 25.00
327 Jake Peavy/Aaron Harang John Smoltz 10.00 25.00
328 Nyjer Morgan 6.00 15.00
329 Lou Piniella 6.00 15.00
330 Curtis Granderson 10.00 25.00
331 Dave Roberts 6.00 15.00
332 Grady Sizemore/Jhonny Peralta 10.00 25.00
333 Jayson Nix 6.00 15.00
334 Oliver Perez 6.00 15.00
335 Eric Byrnes 6.00 15.00
336 Jhonny Peralta 6.00 15.00
337 Livan Hernandez 6.00 15.00
338 Matt Diaz 6.00 15.00
339 Troy Percival 6.00 15.00
340 David Wright 12.50 30.00
341 Daniel Cabrera 6.00 15.00
342 Matt Belisle 6.00 15.00
343 Kason Gabbard 6.00 15.00
344 Mike Rabelo 6.00 15.00
345 Carl Crawford 6.00 15.00
346 Adam Everett 6.00 15.00
347 Chris Capuano 6.00 15.00
348 Craig Monroe 6.00 15.00
349 Mike Mussina 6.00 15.00
350 Mark Teixeira 10.00 25.00
351 Bobby Crosby 6.00 15.00
352 Miguel Batista 6.00 15.00
353 Brendan Ryan 15.00 40.00
354 Edwin Jackson 6.00 15.00
355 Brian Roberts 6.00 15.00
356 Manny Corpas 6.00 15.00
357 Jeremy Accardo 6.00 15.00
358 John Patterson 6.00 15.00
359 Evan Meek 6.00 15.00
360 David Ortiz 12.50 30.00
361 Wesley Wright 10.00 25.00
362 Fernando Hernandez 6.00 15.00
363 Brian Barton 12.50 30.00
364 Al Reyes 6.00 15.00
365 Derrek Lee 6.00 15.00
366 Jeff Weaver 6.00 15.00
367 Khalil Greene 6.00 15.00
368 Michael Bourn 6.00 15.00
369 Luis Castillo 6.00 15.00
370 Adam Dunn 6.00 15.00
371 Rickie Weeks 6.00 15.00
372 Matt Kemp 6.00 15.00
373 Casey Kotchman 6.00 15.00
374 Jason Jennings 6.00 15.00
375 Fausto Carmona 6.00 15.00
376 Willy Taveras 6.00 15.00
377 Jake Westbrook 6.00 15.00
378 Ozzie Guillen 6.00 15.00
379 Hideki Okajima 10.00 25.00
380 Grady Sizemore 10.00 25.00
381 Jeff Francoeur 10.00 25.00
382 Micah Owings 10.00 25.00
383 Jered Weaver 6.00 15.00
384 Carlos Quentin 6.00 15.00
385 Troy Tulowitzki 10.00 25.00
386 Julio Lugo 6.00 15.00
387 Sean Marshall 6.00 15.00
388 Jorge Cantu 6.00 15.00
389 Callix Crabbe 6.00 15.00
390 Troy Glaus 6.00 15.00
391 Nick Markakis 10.00 25.00
392 Joey Gathright 6.00 15.00
393 Michael Cuddyer 6.00 15.00
394 Mark Ellis 6.00 15.00
395 Lance Berkman 6.00 15.00
396 Randy Johnson 10.00 25.00
397 Brian Wilson 6.00 15.00
398 Kenji Johjima 6.00 15.00
399 Jarrod Saltalamacchia 6.00 15.00
400 Matt Holliday 6.00 15.00
401 Scott Hairston 6.00 15.00
402 Taylor Buchholz 6.00 15.00
403 Nate Robertson 6.00 15.00
404 Cecil Cooper 6.00 15.00
405 Travis Hafner 6.00 15.00
406 Takashi Saito 10.00 25.00
407 Johnny Damon 6.00 15.00
408 Edinson Volquez 10.00 25.00
409 Jason Giambi 10.00 25.00
411 Jason Kubel 6.00 15.00
412 Joel Zumaya 6.00 15.00
413 Wandy Rodriguez 6.00 15.00
414 Andrew Miller 6.00 15.00
415 Derek Lowe 10.00 25.00
416 Elijah Dukes 6.00 15.00
417 Brian Bass 10.00 25.00
418 Dioner Navarro 6.00 15.00
419 Bengie Molina 6.00 15.00
420 Nick Swisher 6.00 15.00
421 Brandon Backe 6.00 15.00
422 Erick Aybar 6.00 15.00
423 Mike Scioscia 6.00 15.00
424 Aaron Harang 6.00 15.00
425 Hanley Ramirez 10.00 25.00
426 Franklin Gutierrez 6.00 15.00
427 Carlos Guillen 6.00 15.00
428 Jair Jurrjens 6.00 15.00
429 Billy Butler 6.00 15.00
430 Ryan Braun 15.00 40.00
431 Delwyn Young 6.00 15.00
432 Jason Kendall 6.00 15.00
433 Carlos Silva 6.00 15.00
434 Ron Gardenhire MG 6.00 15.00
435 Torii Hunter 6.00 15.00
436 Joe Blanton 6.00 15.00
437 Brandon Wood 6.00 15.00
438 Jay Payton 6.00 15.00
439 Josh Hamilton 30.00 60.00
440 Pedro Martinez 10.00 25.00
441 Miguel Olivo 6.00 15.00
442 Luis Gonzalez 6.00 15.00
443 Greg Dobbs 6.00 15.00
444 Jack Wilson 6.00 15.00
445 Hideki Matsui 12.50 30.00
446 Randor Bierd 6.00 15.00
447 Chipper Jones/Mark Teixeira 10.00 25.00
448 Cameron Maybin 12.50 30.00
449 Braden Looper 6.00 15.00
450 Prince Fielder 12.50 30.00
451 Brian Giles 6.00 15.00
452 Kevin Slowey 10.00 25.00
453 Josh Fogg 6.00 15.00
454 Mike Hampton 6.00 15.00
455 Derek Jeter 40.00 80.00
456 Chone Figgins 6.00 15.00
457 Josh Fields 6.00 15.00
458 Brad Hawpe 6.00 15.00
459 Mike Sweeney 6.00 15.00
460 Chase Utley 12.50 30.00
461 Jacoby Ellsbury 20.00 50.00
462 Freddy Sanchez 6.00 15.00
463 John McLaren 6.00 15.00
464 Rocco Baldelli 6.00 15.00
465 Huston Street 6.00 15.00
466 M.Cabrera/I.Rodriguez 10.00 25.00
467 Nick Blackburn 15.00 40.00
468 Gregor Blanco 6.00 15.00
469 Brian Bocock 10.00 25.00
470 Tom Gorzelanny 6.00 15.00
471 Brian Schneider 6.00 15.00
472 Shaun Marcum 6.00 15.00
473 Joe Maddon 6.00 15.00
474 Yuniesky Betancourt 6.00 15.00
475 Adrian Gonzalez 6.00 15.00
476 Johnny Cueto 12.50 30.00
477 Ben Broussard 6.00 15.00
478 Geovany Soto 15.00 40.00
479 Bobby Abreu 6.00 15.00
480 Matt Cain 6.00 15.00
481 Manny Parra 6.00 15.00
482 Kazuo Fukumori 10.00 25.00
483 Mike Jacobs 6.00 15.00
484 Todd Jones 6.00 15.00
485 J.J. Putz 6.00 15.00
486 Javier Vazquez 6.00 15.00
487 Corey Patterson 6.00 15.00
488 Mike Gonzalez 6.00 15.00
489 Joakim Soria 6.00 15.00
490 Albert Pujols 20.00 50.00
491 Cliff Floyd 6.00 15.00
492 Harvey Garcia 6.00 15.00
493 Steve Holm 6.00 15.00
494 Paul Maholm 6.00 15.00
495 James Shields 6.00 15.00
496 Brad Lidge 6.00 15.00
497 Cla Meredith 6.00 15.00
498 Matt Chico 6.00 15.00
499 Milton Bradley 6.00 15.00
500 Chipper Jones 12.50 30.00
501 Elliot Johnson 6.00 15.00
502 Alex Cora 6.00 15.00
503 Jeremy Bonderman 10.00 25.00
504 Conor Jackson 6.00 15.00
505 B.J. Upton 6.00 15.00
506 Jay Gibbons 6.00 15.00
507 Mark DeRosa 6.00 15.00
508 John Danks 6.00 15.00
509 Alex Gonzalez 6.00 15.00
510 Justin Verlander 10.00 25.00
511 Jeff Francis 6.00 15.00
512 Placido Polanco 6.00 15.00
513 Rick Vanden Hurk 6.00 15.00
514 Tony Pena 6.00 15.00
515 A.J. Burnett 6.00 15.00
516 Jason Schmidt 6.00 15.00
517 Bill Hall 6.00 15.00
518 Ian Stewart 6.00 15.00
519 Travis Buck 6.00 15.00
520 Vernon Wells 6.00 15.00
521 Jayson Werth 6.00 15.00
522 Nate McLouth 15.00 40.00
523 Noah Lowry 6.00 15.00
524 Raul Ibanez 6.00 15.00
525 Gary Matthews 6.00 15.00
526 Juan Encarnacion 6.00 15.00
527 Marlon Byrd 6.00 15.00
528 Paul Lo Duca 6.00 15.00
529 Masahide Kobayashi 10.00 25.00
530 Ryan Zimmerman 10.00 25.00
531 Hiroki Kuroda 12.50 30.00
532 Tim Lahey 6.00 15.00
533 Kyle McClellan 6.00 15.00
534 Matt Tupman 6.00 15.00
535 Francisco Rodriguez 6.00 15.00
536 Albert Pujols/Prince Fielder 12.50 30.00
537 Scott Moore 6.00 15.00
538 Alex Romero 6.00 15.00
539 Clete Thomas 6.00 15.00
540 John Smoltz 10.00 25.00
541 Adam Jones 6.00 15.00
542 Adam Kennedy 6.00 15.00
543 Carlos Lee 6.00 15.00
544 Chad Gaudin 6.00 15.00
545 Chris Young 6.00 15.00
546 Francisco Liriano 6.00 15.00
547 Fred Lewis 6.00 15.00
548 Garrett Olson 6.00 15.00
549 Gregg Zaun 6.00 15.00
550 Curt Schilling 10.00 25.00
551 Erick Threets 6.00 15.00
552 J.D. Drew 6.00 15.00
553 Jo-Jo Reyes 6.00 15.00
554 Joe Borowski 6.00 15.00
555 Josh Beckett 10.00 25.00
556 John Gibbons 6.00 15.00
557 John McDonald 6.00 15.00
558 John Russell 6.00 15.00
559 Jonny Gomes 6.00 15.00
560 Aramis Ramirez 6.00 15.00
561 Matt Tolbert 10.00 25.00
562 Ronnie Belliard 6.00 15.00
563 Ramon Troncoso 6.00 15.00
564 Frank Catalanotto 6.00 15.00
565 A.J. Pierzynski 6.00 15.00
566 Kevin Millwood 6.00 15.00
567 David Eckstein 6.00 15.00
568 Jose Guillen 6.00 15.00
569 Brad Hennessey 6.00 15.00
570 Homer Bailey 6.00 15.00
571 Eric Gagne 6.00 15.00
572 Adam Eaton 6.00 15.00
573 Tom Gordon 6.00 15.00
574 Scott Baker 6.00 15.00
575 Ty Wigginton 6.00 15.00
576 Dave Bush 6.00 15.00
577 John Buck 6.00 15.00
578 Ricky Nolasco 6.00 15.00
579 Jesse Litsch 6.00 15.00
580 Ken Griffey Jr. 25.00 60.00
581 Kazuo Matsui 6.00 15.00
582 Dusty Baker 6.00 15.00
583 Nick Punto 6.00 15.00
584 Ryan Theriot 6.00 15.00
585 Brian Bannister 10.00 25.00
586 Coco Crisp 10.00 25.00
587 Chris Snyder 6.00 15.00
588 Tony Gwynn 6.00 15.00
589 Dave Trembley 6.00 15.00
590 Mariano Rivera 12.50 30.00
591 Rico Washington 6.00 15.00
592 Matt Morris 6.00 15.00
593 Randy Wells 6.00 15.00
594 Mike Morse 6.00 15.00
595 Francisco Cordero 6.00 15.00
596 Joba Chamberlain 20.00 50.00
597 Kyle Davies 6.00 15.00
598 Bruce Bochy 6.00 15.00
599 Austin Kearns 6.00 15.00
600 Tom Glavine 10.00 25.00
601 Felipe Paulino 6.00 15.00
602 Lyle Overbay/Vernon Wells 6.00 15.00
603 Blake DeWitt 15.00 40.00
604 Wily Mo Pena 6.00 15.00
605 Andre Ethier 10.00 25.00
606 Jason Bergmann 6.00 15.00
607 Ryan Spilborghs 6.00 15.00
608 Brian Burres 6.00 15.00
609 Ted Lilly 6.00 15.00
610 Carlos Beltran 6.00 15.00
611 Garret Anderson 6.00 15.00
612 Kelly Johnson 6.00 15.00
613 Melvin Mora 6.00 15.00
614 Rich Hill 6.00 15.00
615 Pat Burrell 6.00 15.00
616 Jon Garland 6.00 15.00
617 Asdrubal Cabrera 6.00 15.00
618 Pat Neshek 6.00 15.00
619 Sergio Mitre 6.00 15.00
620 Gary Sheffield 6.00 15.00
621 Denard Span 6.00 15.00
622 Jorge De La Rosa 6.00 15.00
623 Trey Hillman MG 6.00 15.00
624 Joe Torre MG 12.50 30.00
625 Greg Maddux 15.00 40.00
626 Mike Redmond 6.00 15.00
627 Mike Pelfrey 6.00 15.00
628 Andy Pettitte 10.00 25.00
629 Eric Chavez 6.00 15.00
630 Chris Carpenter 6.00 15.00
631 Joe Girardi MG 6.00 15.00
632 Charlie Manuel MG 6.00 15.00
633 Adam LaRoche 6.00 15.00
634 Kenny Rogers 6.00 15.00
635 Michael Young 6.00 15.00
636 Rafael Betancourt 6.00 15.00
637 Jose Castillo 6.00 15.00
638 Juan Pierre 6.00 15.00
639 Juan Uribe 6.00 15.00
640 Carlos Pena 6.00 15.00
641 Marcus Thames 6.00 15.00
642 Mark Kotsay 6.00 15.00
643 Matt Murton 6.00 15.00
644 Reggie Willits 6.00 15.00
645 Andy Marte 6.00 15.00
646 Rajai Davis 6.00 15.00
647 Randy Winn 6.00 15.00
648 Ryan Freel 6.00 15.00
649 Joe Crede 6.00 15.00
650 Frank Thomas 12.50 30.00
651 Martin Prado 6.00 15.00
652 Rod Barajas 6.00 15.00
653 Endy Chavez 6.00 15.00
654 Willy Aybar 6.00 15.00
655 Aaron Rowand 6.00 15.00
656 Darin Erstad 6.00 15.00
657 Jeff Keppinger 6.00 15.00
658 Kerry Wood 6.00 15.00
659 Vicente Padilla 6.00 15.00
660 Yadier Molina 6.00 15.00

2008 Topps Gold Border

*GOLD: 3X TO 8X BASIC
*GOLD RC: 2X TO 5X BASIC RC
SER.1 ODDS 1:9 H,1:3 HTA,1:13 R
SER.2 ODDS 1:5 H,1:2 HTA,1:12 R
STATED PRINT RUN 2008 SER.#'d SETS
234b Red Sox w/Giuliani 60.00 120.00

2008 Topps Gold Foil

*GOLD FOIL: 1X TO 2.5X BASIC
*GOLD FOIL RC: .6X TO 1.5X BASIC RC
RANDOM INSERTS IN PACKS
234b Red Sox w/Giuliani 4.00 10.00

2008 Topps 1956 Reprint Relic

SER.2 ODDS 1:43,030 HOBBY
SER.2 ODDS 1:5249 HTA
STATED PRINT RUN 56 SER.#'d SETS
56MM Mickey Mantle 90.00 150.00

2008 Topps 50th Anniversary All Rookie Team

COMPLETE SET (110) 50.00 100.00
COMP.SER.1 SET (55) 20.00 50.00
COMP.SER.2 SET (55) 20.00 50.00
SER.1 ODDS 1:5 HOB, 1:5 RET
SER.2 ODDS 1:5 H,1:5 HTA,1:5 RET
AR1 Darryl Strawberry .40 1.00
AR2 Gary Sheffield .40 1.00
AR3 Dwight Gooden .40 1.00
AR4 Melky Cabrera .40 1.00
AR5 Gary Carter .60 1.50
AR6 Lou Piniella .40 1.00
AR7 Dave Justice .40 1.00
AR8 Andre Dawson .60 1.50
AR9 Mark Ellis .40 1.00
AR10 Dave Johnson .40 1.00
AR11 Jermaine Dye .40 1.00
AR12 Dan Johnson .40 1.00
AR13 Alfonso Soriano .60 1.50
AR14 Prince Fielder .60 1.50
AR15 Hanley Ramirez .60 1.50
AR16 Matt Holliday 1.00 2.50
AR17 Justin Verlander 1.00 2.50
AR18 Mark Teixeira .60 1.50
AR19 Julio Franco .40 1.00
AR20 Ivan Rodriguez .60 1.50
AR21 Jason Bay .60 1.50
AR22 Brandon Webb .60 1.50
AR23 Dontrelle Willis .40 1.00
AR24 Brad Wilkerson .40 1.00
AR25 Dan Uggla .40 1.00
AR26 Ozzie Smith 1.25 3.00
AR27 Andruw Jones .40 1.00
AR28 Garret Anderson .40 1.00
AR29 Jimmy Rollins .60 1.50
AR30 Brian McCann .60 1.50
AR31 Scott Podsednik .40 1.00
AR32 Garrett Atkins .40 1.00
AR33 Billy Wagner .40 1.00
AR34 Chipper Jones 1.00 2.50
AR35 Roger McDowell .40 1.00
AR36 Austin Kearns .40 1.00
AR37 Boog Powell .40 1.00
AR38 Ron Swoboda .40 1.00
AR39 Roy Oswalt .60 1.50
AR40 Mike Piazza 1.00 2.50
AR41 Albert Pujols 1.25 3.00
AR42 Ichiro Suzuki 1.25 3.00
AR43 C.C. Sabathia .60 1.50
AR44 Todd Helton .60 1.50
AR45 Scott Rolen .60 1.50
AR46 Derek Jeter 2.50 6.00
AR47 Shawn Green .40 1.00
AR48 Manny Ramirez 1.00 2.50
AR49 Tom Seaver UER .60 1.50
AR50 Kenny Lofton .40 1.00
AR51 Francisco Liriano .40 1.00
AR52 Ryan Zimmerman .60 1.50
AR53 Jeff Francoeur .60 1.50
AR54 Joe Mauer .75 2.00
AR55 Magglio Ordonez .60 1.50
AR56 Carlos Beltran .60 1.50
AR57 Andre Ethier .60 1.50
AR58 Brian Bannister .40 1.00
AR59 Chris Young .40 1.00
AR60 Troy Tulowitzki 1.00 2.50
AR61 Hideki Okajima .40 1.00
AR62 Delmon Young .60 1.50
AR63 Craig Wilson .40 1.00
AR64 Hunter Pence .60 1.50
AR65 Tadahito Iguchi .40 1.00
AR66 Mark Kotsay .40 1.00
AR67 Nick Markakis .75 2.00
AR68 Russ Adams .40 1.00
AR69 Russ Martin .40 1.00
AR70 James Loney .40 1.00
AR71 Ryan Braun .60 1.50
AR72 Jonny Gomes .40 1.00
AR73 Carlos Ruiz .40 1.00
AR74 Willy Taveras .40 1.00
AR75 Joe Torre .60 1.50
AR76 Jeff Kent .40 1.00
AR77 Huston Street .60 1.50
AR78 Dustin Pedroia .60 1.50
AR79 Gustavo Chacin .40 1.00
AR80 Adam Dunn .60 1.50
AR81 Pat Burrell .40 1.00
AR82 Rocco Baldelli .40 1.00
AR83 Chad Tracy .40 1.00
AR84 Adam LaRoche .40 1.00
AR85 Aaron Miles .40 1.00
AR86 Khalil Greene .40 1.00
AR87 Daniel Cabrera .40 1.00
AR88 Mike Gonzalez .40 1.00
AR89 Ty Wigginton .60 1.50
AR90 Angel Berroa .40 1.00
AR91 Moises Alou .40 1.00
AR92 Miguel Olivo .40 1.00
AR93 Nick Johnson .40 1.00
AR94 Eric Hinske .40 1.00
AR95 Ramon Santiago .40 1.00
AR96 Jason Jennings .40 1.00
AR97 Adam Kennedy .40 1.00
AR98 Mike Lamb .40 1.00
AR99 Rafael Furcal .40 1.00
AR100 Jay Payton .40 1.00
AR101 Bengie Molina .40 1.00
AR102 Mark Redman .40 1.00
AR103 Alex Gonzalez .40 1.00
AR104 Ray Durham .40 1.00
AR105 Miguel Cairo .40 1.00
AR106 Kerry Wood .40 1.00
AR107 Dmitri Young .40 1.00
AR108 Jose Cruz .40 1.00
AR109 Jose Guillen .40 1.00
AR110 Scott Hatteberg .40 1.00

2008 Topps 50th Anniversary All Rookie Team Gold

COMMON CARD 5.00 12.00
SEMISTARS 8.00 20.00
UNLISTED STARS 12.50 30.00
SER.1 ODDS 1:1290 H,1:1100 HTA
SER.1 ODDS 1:1290 RETAIL
SER.2 ODDS 1:740 HOB,1:505 HTA
SER.2 ODDS 1:1100 RETAIL
STATED PRINT RUN 99 SER.#'d SETS
AR1 Darryl Strawberry 5.00 12.00
AR2 Gary Sheffield 5.00 12.00
AR3 Dwight Gooden 5.00 12.00
AR4 Melky Cabrera 5.00 12.00
AR5 Gary Carter 8.00 20.00
AR6 Lou Piniella 5.00 12.00
AR7 Dave Justice 5.00 12.00
AR8 Andre Dawson 8.00 20.00
AR9 Mark Ellis 5.00 12.00
AR10 Dave Johnson 5.00 12.00
AR11 Jermaine Dye 5.00 12.00
AR12 Dan Johnson 5.00 12.00
AR13 Alfonso Soriano 8.00 20.00
AR14 Prince Fielder 8.00 20.00
AR15 Hanley Ramirez 8.00 20.00
AR16 Matt Holliday 12.00 30.00
AR17 Justin Verlander 12.00 30.00
AR18 Mark Teixeira 8.00 20.00
AR19 Julio Franco 5.00 12.00
AR20 Ivan Rodriguez 8.00 20.00
AR21 Jason Bay 8.00 20.00
AR22 Brandon Webb 8.00 20.00
AR23 Dontrelle Willis 5.00 12.00
AR24 Brad Wilkerson 5.00 12.00
AR25 Dan Uggla 5.00 12.00
AR26 Ozzie Smith 15.00 40.00
AR27 Andruw Jones 5.00 12.00
AR28 Garret Anderson 5.00 12.00
AR29 Jimmy Rollins 8.00 20.00
AR30 Brian McCann 8.00 20.00
AR31 Scott Podsednik 5.00 12.00
AR32 Garrett Atkins 5.00 12.00
AR33 Billy Wagner 5.00 12.00
AR34 Chipper Jones 12.00 30.00
AR35 Roger McDowell 5.00 12.00
AR36 Austin Kearns 5.00 12.00
AR37 Boog Powell 5.00 12.00
AR38 Ron Swoboda 5.00 12.00
AR39 Roy Oswalt 8.00 20.00
AR40 Mike Piazza 12.00 30.00
AR41 Albert Pujols 20.00 50.00
AR42 Ichiro Suzuki 15.00 40.00
AR43 C.C. Sabathia 8.00 20.00
AR44 Todd Helton 8.00 20.00
AR45 Scott Rolen 8.00 20.00
AR46 Derek Jeter 20.00 50.00
AR47 Shawn Green 5.00 12.00
AR48 Manny Ramirez 12.00 30.00
AR49 Tom Seaver 8.00 20.00
AR50 Kenny Lofton 5.00 12.00
AR51 Francisco Liriano 5.00 12.00
AR52 Ryan Zimmerman 8.00 20.00
AR53 Jeff Francoeur 8.00 20.00
AR54 Joe Mauer 10.00 25.00
AR55 Magglio Ordonez 8.00 20.00
AR56 Carlos Beltran 8.00 20.00
AR57 Andre Ethier 8.00 20.00
AR58 Brian Bannister 5.00 12.00
AR59 Chris Young 5.00 12.00
AR60 Troy Tulowitzki 12.00 30.00
AR61 Hideki Okajima 5.00 12.00
AR62 Delmon Young 8.00 20.00
AR63 Craig Wilson 15.00 40.00
AR64 Hunter Pence 8.00 20.00
AR65 Tadahito Iguchi 5.00 12.00
AR66 Mark Kotsay 5.00 12.00
AR67 Nick Markakis 10.00 25.00
AR68 Russ Adams 5.00 12.00
AR69 Russ Martin 10.00 25.00
AR70 James Loney 5.00 12.00
AR71 Ryan Braun 12.50 30.00
AR72 Jonny Gomes 5.00 12.00
AR73 Carlos Ruiz 5.00 12.00
AR74 Willy Taveras 5.00 12.00
AR75 Joe Torre 8.00 20.00
AR76 Jeff Kent 5.00 12.00
AR77 Huston Street 8.00 20.00
AR78 Dustin Pedroia 8.00 20.00
AR79 Gustavo Chacin 5.00 12.00
AR80 Adam Dunn 8.00 20.00
AR81 Pat Burrell 5.00 12.00
AR82 Rocco Baldelli 5.00 12.00
AR83 Chad Tracy 5.00 12.00
AR84 Adam LaRoche 5.00 12.00
AR85 Aaron Miles 5.00 12.00
AR86 Khalil Greene 5.00 12.00
AR87 Daniel Cabrera 5.00 12.00
AR88 Mike Gonzalez 5.00 12.00
AR89 Ty Wigginton 8.00 20.00
AR90 Angel Berroa 5.00 12.00
AR91 Moises Alou 5.00 12.00
AR92 Miguel Olivo 5.00 12.00
AR93 Nick Johnson 5.00 12.00
AR94 Eric Hinske 5.00 12.00
AR95 Ramon Santiago 5.00 12.00
AR96 Jason Jennings 5.00 12.00
AR97 Adam Kennedy 8.00 20.00
AR98 Mike Lamb 5.00 12.00
AR99 Rafael Furcal 5.00 12.00
AR100 Jay Payton 5.00 12.00
AR101 Bengie Molina 5.00 12.00
AR102 Mark Redman 5.00 12.00
AR103 Alex Gonzalez 5.00 12.00
AR104 Ray Durham 5.00 12.00
AR105 Miguel Cairo 5.00 12.00
AR106 Kerry Wood 5.00 12.00
AR107 Dmitri Young 10.00 25.00
AR108 Jose Cruz 5.00 12.00
AR109 Jose Guillen 5.00 12.00
AR110 Scott Hatteberg 5.00 12.00

2008 Topps 50th Anniversary All Rookie Team Relics

SER.1 ODDS 1:7178 H, 1:366 HTA
SER.1 ODDS 1:50,700 RETAIL
SER.2 ODDS 1:2378 H,1:290 HTA
STATED PRINT RUN 50 SER.#'d SETS
AD Adam Dunn 12.50 30.00
AD Andre Dawson 30.00 60.00
AE Andre Ethier 20.00 50.00
AJ Andruw Jones 12.50 30.00
AS Alfonso Soriano 12.50 30.00
BM Brian McCann 10.00 25.00
BW Brandon Webb 15.00 40.00
CJ Chipper Jones 15.00 40.00
CS C.C. Sabathia 12.50 30.00
DG Dwight Gooden 10.00 25.00
DJ Dave Justice 12.50 30.00
DS Darryl Strawberry 20.00 50.00
DU Dan Uggla 12.50 30.00
DW Dontrelle Willis 12.50 30.00
FL Francisco Liriano 15.00 40.00
GA Garret Anderson 10.00 25.00
GC Gary Carter 20.00 50.00
GS Gary Sheffield 30.00 60.00
HR Hanley Ramirez 10.00 25.00
IR Ivan Rodriguez 12.50 30.00
IS Ichiro Suzuki 30.00 60.00
JB Jason Bay 30.00 60.00
JM Joe Mauer 8.00 20.00
JR Jimmy Rollins 15.00 40.00
JV Justin Verlander 15.00 40.00
MH Matt Holliday 20.00 50.00
MO Magglio Ordonez 20.00 50.00
MP Mike Piazza 20.00 50.00
MT Mark Teixeira 15.00 40.00
NJ Nick Johnson 30.00 60.00
NM Nick Markakis 10.00 25.00
OS Ozzie Smith 15.00 40.00
PB Pat Burrell 12.50 30.00
PF Prince Fielder 15.00 40.00
RB Rocco Baldelli 12.50 30.00
RO Roy Oswalt 10.00 25.00
TH Todd Helton 10.00 25.00
TS Tom Seaver 12.50 30.00

2008 Topps Back to School

TB1 Miguel Cabrera 6.00 15.00
TB2 Albert Pujols 8.00 20.00
TB3 Grady Sizemore 4.00 10.00
TB4 Ken Griffey Jr 20.00 50.00
TB5 David Wright 4.00 10.00
TB6 Ichiro Suzuki 12.00 30.00
TB7 Alex Rodriguez 8.00 20.00
TB8 Chipper Jones 6.00 15.00

2008 Topps Campaign 2008

COMPLETE SET (12) 12.50 30.00
STATED ODDS 1:9 H,1:2 HTA,1:9 R
GOLD ODDS 1:5 HTA
AG Al Gore
AS Arnold Schwarzenegger
BO Barack Obama 6.00 15.00
BR Bill Richardson .60 1.50
DK Dennis Kucinich .60 1.50
FT Fred Thompson .60 1.50
HC Hillary Clinton 2.00 5.00
JB Joseph Biden 2.00 5.00
JE John Edwards 1.00 2.50
JM John McCain 2.00 5.00
MH Mike Huckabee 1.00 2.50
MR Mitt Romney 1.00 2.50
RG Rudy Giuliani 1.00 2.50
RP Ron Paul .60 1.50
SP Sarah Palin 6.00 15.00
SP Sarah Palin Pageant 10.00 25.00

2008 Topps Campaign 2008 Gold

COMPLETE SET 50.00 100.00
*GOLD: .75X TO 2X BASIC
STATED ODDS 1:5 HTA

2008 Topps Campaign 2008 Letter Patches

SER.2 ODDS 1:2642 H,1:322 HTA
STATED PRINT RUN 50 SER.#'d SETS
BO Barack Obama O 60.00 120.00
BO Barack Obama B 60.00 120.00
BO Barack Obama A 60.00 120.00
BO Barack Obama M 60.00 120.00
BO Barack Obama A 60.00 120.00
HC Hillary Clinton C 30.00 60.00
HC Hillary Clinton L 30.00 60.00
HC Hillary Clinton I 30.00 60.00
HC Hillary Clinton N 30.00 60.00
HC Hillary Clinton T 30.00 60.00
HC Hillary Clinton O 30.00 60.00
HC Hillary Clinton N 30.00 60.00
JM John McCain M 10.00 25.00
JM John McCain c 10.00 25.00
JM John McCain C 10.00 25.00
JM John McCain A 10.00 25.00
JM John McCain I 10.00 25.00
JM John McCain N 10.00 25.00

2008 Topps Commemorative Patch Relics

SER.2 ODDS 1:792 HOB,1:97 HTA
STATED PRINT RUN 100 SER.#'d SETS
AP Andy Pettitte 30.00 60.00
AR Alex Rodriguez 50.00 100.00
BA Bobby Abreu 20.00 50.00
BS Brian Schneider 10.00 25.00
BW Billy Wagner 10.00 25.00
CB Carlos Beltran 10.00 25.00
CD Carlos Delgado 10.00 25.00
CMW Chien-Ming Wang 50.00 100.00
DJ Derek Jeter 20.00 50.00
DW David Wright 20.00 50.00
EC Endy Chavez 8.00 20.00
HM Hideki Matsui 15.00 40.00
JC Joba Chamberlain 50.00 100.00
JD Johnny Damon 30.00 60.00
JG Jason Giambi 40.00 80.00
JM John Maine 10.00 25.00
JP Jorge Posada 20.00 50.00
JR Jose Reyes 12.50 30.00
LC Luis Castillo 8.00 20.00
MA Moises Alou 8.00 20.00
MC Melky Cabrera 20.00 50.00
MM Mike Mussina 40.00 80.00
MP Mike Pelfrey 12.50 30.00
MR Mariano Rivera 20.00 50.00
OH Orlando Hernandez 8.00 20.00
OP Oliver Perez 8.00 20.00
PH Phil Hughes 20.00 50.00
PM Pedro Martinez 10.00 25.00
RC Robinson Cano 30.00 60.00
RMC Ryan Church 10.00 25.00

2008 Topps Dick Perez

WMDP1 Manny Ramirez .60 1.50
WMDP2 Cameron Maybin .25 .60
WMDP3 Ryan Howard .40 1.00
WMDP4 David Ortiz .60 1.50
WMDP5 Tim Lincecum .40 1.00
WMDP6 David Wright .40 1.00
WMDP7 Mickey Mantle 2.00 5.00
WMDP8 Joba Chamberlain .25 .60
WMDP9 Ichiro Suzuki .75 2.00
WMDP10 Prince Fielder .40 1.00
WMDP11 Jacoby Ellsbury .50 1.25
WMDP12 Jake Peavy .25 .60
WMDP13 Miguel Cabrera .60 1.50
WMDP14 Josh Beckett .25 .60
WMDP15 Jimmy Rollins .40 1.00
WMDP16 Torii Hunter .25 .60
WMDP17 Alfonso Soriano .40 1.00
WMDP18 Jose Reyes .40 1.00
WMDP19 C.C. Sabathia .40 1.00
WMDP20 Alex Rodriguez .75 2.00
WMDP21 Ryan Braun .40 1.00
WMDP22 Johan Santana .40 1.00
WMDP23 Matt Holliday .60 1.50
WMDP24 Ervin Santana .25 .60
WMDP25 Daisuke Matsuzaka .40 1.00
WMDP26 Josh Hamilton .40 1.00
WMDP27 Chipper Jones .60 1.50
WMDP28 Lance Berkman .40 1.00
WMDP29 Hanley Ramirez .40 1.00
WMDP30 Mariano Rivera .75 2.00

2008 Topps Factory Set Mickey Mantle Blue

MMR52 Mickey Mantle 52T 8.00 20.00
MMR53 Mickey Mantle 53T 8.00 20.00
MMR54 Mickey Mantle 54T 8.00 20.00

2008 Topps Factory Set Mickey Mantle Gold

MMR52 Mickey Mantle 52T 10.00 25.00
MMR53 Mickey Mantle 53T 10.00 25.00
MMR54 Mickey Mantle 54T 10.00 25.00

2008 Topps Highlights Autographs

SER.1 A ODDS 1:32,000 H,1:1463 HTA
SER.1 A ODDS 1:159,000 RETAIL
SER.2 A ODDS 1:28,927 H,1:965 HTA
SER.2 A ODDS 1:76,245 RETAIL
UPD.A ODDS 1:38,362 HOBBY
SER.1 B ODDS 1:4792 H,1:244 HTA
SER.1 B ODDS 1:33,333 RETAIL
SER.2 B ODDS 1:923 H,1:31 HTA
SER.2 B ODDS 1:2451 RETAIL
UPD.B ODDS 1:11,066 HOBBY
SER.1 C ODDS 1:958 H,1:49 HTA
SER.1 C ODDS 1:6470 RETAIL
SER.2 C ODDS 1:651 H,1:87 HTA
SER.2 C ODDS 1:6862 RETAIL
UPD.C ODDS 1:4082 HOBBY
SER.1 D ODDS 1:1425 H,1:70 HTA
SER.1 D ODDS 1:14,250 RETAIL
SER.2 D ODDS 1:15,370 H,1:181 HTA
SER.2 D ODDS 1:14,296 RETAIL
UPD.D ODDS 1:5587 HOBBY
SER.1 E ODDS 1:1075 H,1:117 HTA
SER.1 E ODDS 1:880 RETAIL
SER.2 E ODDS 1:814 H,1:27 HTA
SER.2 E ODDS 1:2144 RETAIL
UPD.E ODDS 1:6851 HOBBY
SER.1 F ODDS 1:895 H,1:23 HTA
SER.1 F ODDS 1:1370 RETAIL
SER.2 F ODDS 1:3254 H,1:108 HTA
SER.2 F ODDS 1:8578 RETAIL
UPD.F ODDS 1:1116 HOBBY
SER.1 G ODDS 1:3070 H,1:224 HTA
SER.1 G ODDS 1:4055 RETAIL
UPD.G ODDS 1:1109 HOBBY
UPD.H ODDS 1:1985 HOBBY
NO GROUP A PRICING AVAILABLE
NO GROUP A2 PRICING AVAILABLE
AC Asdrubal Cabrera C UPD 6.00 15.00
AG Armando Galarraga D UPD 4.00 10.00
AH Aaron Heilman B2 6.00 15.00
AK Austin Kearns F2 4.00 10.00
AL Adam Lind C 4.00 10.00
BB Billy Butler C UPD 10.00 25.00
BC Bobby Crosby B2 6.00 15.00
BD Blake DeWitt C UPD 12.00 30.00
BDB Brian Barton F UPD 4.00 10.00
BP Brandon Phillips B UPD 4.00 10.00
BP Brad Penny B 10.00 25.00
BR B.J. Ryan D UPD 4.00 10.00
CB Clay Buchholz C 4.00 10.00
CC Carl Crawford B2 8.00 20.00
CF Chone Figgins B2 6.00 15.00
CG Carlos Gomez C UPD 4.00 10.00
CK Clayton Kershaw B UPD 40.00 80.00
CM Craig Monroe B2 6.00 15.00
CMW Chien-Ming Wang B 100.00 150.00
CP Carlos Pena C 4.00 10.00
CR Carlos Ruiz F UPD 4.00 10.00
CV Carlos Villanueva F 4.00 10.00
CV Claudio Vargas C2 4.00 10.00
CW Chase Wright E2 4.00 10.00
DB Dallas Braden C2 12.00 30.00
DB Daric Barton G 4.00 10.00
DE Darin Erstad B2 4.00 10.00
DH Dan Haren B 4.00 10.00
DM Dustin McGowan UPD 6.00 15.00
DM Dustin Moseley F 4.00 10.00
DW David Wright B 30.00 60.00
DY Delwyn Young E2 4.00 10.00
EC Eric Chavez B2 4.00 10.00
ED Eulogio De La Cruz C 4.00 10.00
ES Ervin Santana C 4.00 10.00
ES Ervin Santana E2 4.00 10.00
EV Edinson Volquez D UPD 8.00 20.00
FC Fausto Carmona E2 4.00 10.00
FC Fausto Carmona C 6.00 15.00
FL Francisco Liriano B2 6.00 15.00
FS Freddy Sanchez C 6.00 15.00
GS Gary Sheffield B 10.00 25.00
HCK Hong-Chih Kuo C2 6.00 15.00
HK Howie Kendrick D 4.00 10.00
HR Hanley Ramirez B 6.00 15.00
JA Josh Anderson E 4.00 10.00
JAB Jason Bartlett D2 4.00 10.00
JAR Jo-Jo Reyes C2 4.00 10.00
JB Jeremy Bonderman B2 6.00 15.00
JBR John Buck D 4.00 10.00
JBR Jose Reyes B 30.00 60.00
JC Joba Chamberlain B2 10.00 25.00
JEM Justin Morneau B 10.00 25.00
JF Josh Fields C 4.00 10.00
JH Josh Hamilton B UPD 30.00 60.00
JKM John Maine B2 6.00 15.00
JL John Lackey C 5.00 12.00
JLC Jorge Cantu C2 4.00 10.00
JM Jose Molina D 4.00 10.00
JP Jake Peavy D 5.00 12.00
JR Jo-Jo Reyes E UPD 4.00 10.00
JR Jimmy Rollins B 40.00 80.00
JS Jeff Salazar G UPD 4.00 10.00
JTD Jermaine Dye B 4.00 10.00
JTD Jermaine Dye B2 4.00 10.00
JV Joey Votto C UPD 20.00 50.00
JV Jason Varitek B 40.00 80.00
JW Josh Willingham B2 6.00 15.00
JZ Joel Zumaya B2 4.00 10.00
KM Kendry Morales B2 4.00 10.00
LB Lance Broadway E 4.00 10.00
LC Luis Castillo C 4.00 10.00
MB Mike Bacsik F 4.00 10.00
MC Melky Cabrera B2 10.00 25.00
ME Mark Ellis F 4.00 10.00
MG Matt Garza C 4.00 10.00
MG Matt Garza B2 4.00 10.00
MK Masa Kobayashi C UPD 6.00 15.00
MMT Marcus Thames B2 4.00 10.00
MS Max Scherzer B UPD 60.00 150.00
MW Mark Worrell H UPD 4.00 10.00
MY Michael Young B 6.00 15.00
NJM Nyjer Morgan E 4.00 10.00
NM Nick Markakis B UPD 10.00 25.00
NM Nick Markakis C 6.00 15.00
NM Nick Markakis B2 6.00 15.00
NR Nate Robertson B2 4.00 10.00
PF Prince Fielder B2 15.00 40.00
PF Prince Fielder B 30.00 60.00
PH Philip Humber D2 4.00 10.00
PJF Pedro Feliciano B2 6.00 15.00
RB Ryan Braun A UPD 60.00 120.00
RB Ryan Braun B2 20.00 50.00
RC Robinson Cano B2 12.00 30.00
RC Ramon Castro D 4.00 10.00
RH Rich Hill D 6.00 15.00
RJC Robinson Cano B 15.00 40.00
RJM Randy Messenger F 4.00 10.00
RM Russell Martin C 6.00 15.00
RM Russ Martin B2 6.00 15.00
RN Ricky Nolasco B2 4.00 10.00
RP Ronny Paulino E2 4.00 10.00
RR Ryan Roberts E2 4.00 10.00
SF Sam Fuld E 4.00 10.00
SH Steve Holm F UPD 4.00 10.00
SM Scott Moore F 4.00 10.00
SS Seth Smith G UPD 4.00 10.00
SS Seth Smith E 4.00 10.00
SV Shane Victorino B2 8.00 20.00
TG Tom Gorzelanny E2 4.00 10.00
TG Tom Gorzelanny F 4.00 10.00
TT Taylor Tankersley B2 4.00 10.00
UJ Ubaldo Jimenez F 6.00 15.00
WN Wil Nieves C 4.00 10.00
YG Yovani Gallardo C 8.00 20.00
ZG Zack Greinke C UPD 10.00 25.00
ZG Zack Greinke E2 10.00 25.00

2008 Topps Highlights Relics

SER.1 A ODDS 1:3597 H,1:183 HTA
SER.1 A ODDS 1:25,000 RETAIL
SER.2 A ODDS 1:85 H,1:11 HTA
SER.1 B ODDS 1:21,250 H,1:958 HTA
SER.1 B ODDS 1:7500 RETAIL
SER.2 B ODDS 1:108 H, 1:14 HTA
SER.1 C ODDS 1:1725 H,1:705 HTA
SER.1 C ODDS 1:3050 RETAIL
SER.2 C ODDS 1:651 H, 1:80 HTA
SER.1 D ODDS 1:244 RETAIL
SER.1 D ODDS 1:1965 H,1:33 HTA
AG Alex Gordon B2 5.00 12.00
AP Albert Pujols B2 6.00 15.00
AP Albert Pujols D 6.00 15.00
AR Aramis Ramirez B2 3.00 8.00
BP Brandon Phillips B2 3.00 8.00
BU B.J. Upton C2 3.00 8.00
BW Brandon Webb C2 3.00 8.00
CB Carlos Beltran Bat C 3.00 8.00
CC Carl Crawford D 3.00 8.00
CC Carl Crawford Pants B2 3.00 8.00
CM Cameron Maybin Bat C2 3.00 8.00
CM Cameron Maybin D 3.00 8.00
CMW Chien-Ming Wang Jsy B2 8.00 20.00
CS Curt Schilling Jsy D 4.00 10.00
CU Chase Utley Jsy B2 5.00 12.00
DL Derrek Lee B2 3.00 8.00
DO David Ortiz D 4.00 10.00
DO1 David Ortiz B2 4.00 10.00
DO2 David Ortiz B2 4.00 10.00
DU Dan Uggla Jsy B2 3.00 8.00
DW David Wright Jsy C2 5.00 12.00
DW David Wright D 5.00 12.00
DWW Dontrelle Willis D 3.00 8.00
DY Delmon Young Jsy B2 3.00 8.00
EC Eric Chavez D 3.00 8.00
HR Hanley Ramirez B2 3.00 8.00
IR Ivan Rodriguez D 5.00 12.00
IS Ichiro Suzuki D 6.00 15.00
IS Ichiro Suzuki C2 6.00 15.00
JB Jeremy Bonderman B2 3.00 8.00
JL James Loney B2 3.00 8.00
JP Jake Peavy B2 3.00 8.00
JR Jose Reyes A2 5.00 12.00
JR Jose Reyes A 5.00 12.00
JT Jim Thome C2 3.00 8.00
JV Justin Verlander D 5.00 12.00
LB Lance Berkman C 3.00 8.00
MH Matt Holliday B 3.00 8.00
MR Manny Ramirez D 4.00 10.00
MT Miguel Tejada D 3.00 8.00
PF Prince Fielder A 4.00 10.00
PF Prince Fielder B2 4.00 10.00
RB Ryan Braun B2 6.00 15.00
RF Rafael Furcal C2 3.00 8.00
RH Ryan Howard B2 5.00 12.00
RO Roy Oswalt A2 3.00 8.00
RZ Ryan Zimmerman B2 3.00 8.00
ST Scott Thorman B2 3.00 8.00
TH Todd Helton D 3.00 8.00
VG Vladimir Guerrero 4.00 10.00
IBB A
VG Vladimir Guerrero 4.00 10.00
Silver Slugger B2

2008 Topps Historical Campaign Match-Ups

COMPLETE SET (55) 30.00 60.00
SER.2 ODDS 1:6 HOB,1:6 HTA,1:6 RET
1792 G.Washington/J.Adams 1.00 2.50
1796 J.Adams/T.Jefferson 1.00 2.50
1800 T.Jefferson/A.Burr .75 2.00
1804 T.Jefferson/C.Pinckney .75 2.00
1808 James Madison/Charles Pinckney .60 1.50
1812 James Madison/DeWitt Clinton .60 1.50
1816 James Monroe/Rufus King .60 1.50
1820 James Monroe/
John Quincy Adams .60 1.50
1824 John Quincy Adams/
Andrew Jackson .60 1.50
1828 Andrew Jackson/
John Quincy Adams .60 1.50
1832 Andrew Jackson/Henry Clay .40 1.00
1836 Martin Van Buren/
William Henry Harrison .40 1.00
1840 William Henry Harrison/
Martin Van Buren .50 1.25
1844 James K. Polk/Henry Clay .40 1.00
1848 Zachary Taylor/Lewis Cass .40 1.00
1852 Franklin Pierce/Winfield Scott .40 1.00
1856 James Buchanan/John C. Fremont .50 1.25
1860 A.Lincoln/J.Breckinridge .75 2.00
1864 A.Lincoln/G.McClellan .75 2.00
1868 Ulysses S. Grant/Horatio Seymour .50 1.25
1872 Ulysses S. Grant/Horace Greeley .50 1.25
1876 Rutherford B. Hayes/
Samuel J. Tilden .40 1.00
1880 James Garfield/
Winfield Scott Hancock .40 1.00
1884 Grover Cleveland/James G. Blaine .40 1.00
1888 Benjamin Harrison/
Grover Cleveland .40 1.00
1892 Grover Cleveland/
Benjamin Harrison .40 1.00
1896 William McKinley/
William Jennings Bryan .50 1.25
1900 William McKinley/
William Jennings Bryan .40 1.00
1904 Theodore Roosevelt/
Alton B. Parker .60 1.50
1908 William H. Taft/
William Jennings Bryan .50 1.25
1912 Woodrow Wilson/
Theodore Roosevelt .60 1.50
1916 Woodrow Wilson/
Charles Evans Hughes .40 1.00
1920 Warren G. Harding/James M. Cox .40 1.00
1924 Calvin Coolidge/John W. Davis .40 1.00
1928 Herbert Hoover/Al Smith .40 1.00
1932 Franklin D. Roosevelt/
Herbert Hoover .60 1.50
1936 Franklin D. Roosevelt/Alf Landon .50 1.25
1940 Franklin D. Roosevelt/
Wendell Willkie .60 1.50
1944 Franklin D. Roosevelt/
Thomas E. Dewey .50 1.25
1948 Harry S Truman/Thomas E. Dewey .50 1.25
1952 Dwight D. Eisenhower/
Adlai Stevenson .60 1.50
1956 Dwight D. Eisenhower/
Adlai Stevenson .60 1.50
1960 J.Kennedy/R.Nixon 1.25 3.00
1964 Lyndon B. Johnson/
Barry Goldwater .60 1.50
1968 Richard Nixon/
Hubert H. Humphrey .40 1.00
1972 Richard Nixon/George McGovern .60 1.50
1976 J.Carter/G.Ford .75 2.00
1980 R.Reagan/J.Carter 1.25 3.00
1984 R.Reagan/W.Mondale .75 2.00
1988 George Bush/Michael Dukakis .60 1.50
1992 B.Clinton/G.Bush .75 2.00
1996 B.Clinton/B.Dole .75 2.00
2000 G.Bush/A.Gore .75 2.00
2004 G.Bush/J.Kerry .75 2.00
2008D H.Clinton/B.Obama 1.50 4.00

2008 Topps K-Mart

COMPLETE SET (30) 15.00 40.00
RANDOM INSERTS IN KMART PACKS
RV1 Chin Lung Hu .75 2.00
RV2 Steve Pearce 4.00 10.00
RV3 Luke Hochevar 1.25 3.00
RV4 Joey Votto 3.00 8.00
RV5 Clay Buchholz 1.25 3.00
RV6 Emilio Bonifacio 2.00 5.00
RV7 Daric Barton .75 2.00
RV8 Eugenio Velez .75 2.00
RV9 J.R. Towles 1.25 3.00
RV10 Wladimir Balentien .75 2.00
RV11 Ross Detwiler 1.25 3.00
RV12 Troy Patton .75 2.00
RV13 Brandon Jones 2.00 5.00
RV14 Billy Buckner .75 2.00
RV15 Ross Ohlendorf 1.25 3.00
RV16 Nick Blackburn 1.25 3.00
RV17 Masahide Kobayashi 1.25 3.00
RV18 Jayson Nix .75 2.00
RV19 Blake DeWitt 1.25 3.00
RV20 Hiroki Kuroda 2.00 5.00
RV21 Matt Tolbert 1.25 3.00
RV22 Brian Bass .75 2.00
RV23 Fernando Hernandez .75 2.00
RV24 Kazuo Fukumori 1.25 3.00
RV25 Brian Barton 1.25 3.00
RV26 Clete Thomas 1.25 3.00
RV27 Rico Washington .75 2.00
RV28 Erick Threets .75 2.00
RV29 Callix Crabbe .75 2.00
RV30 Johnny Cueto 2.00 5.00

2008 Topps of the Class

RANDOM INSERTS IN PACKS
NNO David Wright .60 1.50

2008 Topps Own the Game

COMPLETE SET (25) 6.00 15.00
STATED ODDS 1:6 HOB, 1:6 RET
OTG1 Alex Rodriguez 1.00 2.50
OTG2 Prince Fielder .50 1.25
OTG3 Ryan Howard .50 1.25
OTG4 Carlos Pena .50 1.25
OTG5 Adam Dunn .50 1.25
OTG6 Matt Holliday .75 2.00
OTG7 David Ortiz .75 2.00
OTG8 Jim Thome .50 1.25
OTG9 Lance Berkman .50 1.25
OTG10 Miguel Cabrera .75 2.00
OTG11 Alex Rodriguez 1.00 2.50
OTG12 Magglio Ordonez .50 1.25
OTG13 Matt Holliday .75 2.00
OTG14 Ryan Howard .50 1.25
OTG15 Vladimir Guerrero .50 1.25
OTG16 Carlos Pena .50 1.25
OTG17 Mike Lowell .30 .75
OTG18 Miguel Cabrera .75 2.00
OTG19 Prince Fielder .50 1.25
OTG20 Carlos Lee .30 .75
OTG21 Jake Peavy .30 .75
OTG22 John Lackey .50 1.25
OTG23 Brandon Webb .50 1.25
OTG24 Brad Penny .30 .75
OTG25 Fausto Carmona .30 .75

2008 Topps Presidential Stamp Collection

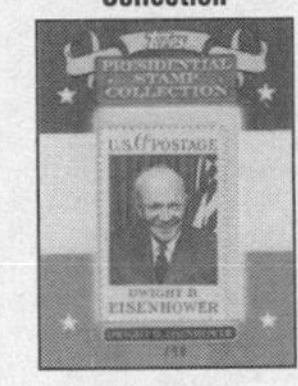

SER.1 ODDS 1:1950 H, 1:1240 HTA
SER.1 ODDS 1:3300 RETAIL
SER.2 ODDS 1:1600 H,1:700 HTA
SER.2 ODDS 1:2000 RETAIL
STATED PRINT RUN 90 SER.#'d SETS
ALL VERSIONS PRICED EQUALLY
AJ1 Andrew Jackson 40.00 80.00
AJO1 Andrew Johnson 20.00 50.00
AL1 Abraham Lincoln 10.00 25.00
AL2 Abraham Lincoln 10.00 25.00
AL3 Abraham Lincoln 10.00 25.00
AL4 Abraham Lincoln 10.00 25.00
AL5 Abraham Lincoln 10.00 25.00
AL6 Abraham Lincoln 10.00 25.00
BH1 Benjamin Harrison 30.00 60.00
CAA1 Chester A. Arthur 50.00 100.00
DDE1 Dwight D. Eisenhower 40.00 80.00
FDR1 Franklin Delano Roosevelt 30.00 60.00
FP1 Franklin Pierce 30.00 60.00
GC1 Grover Cleveland 10.00 25.00
GW1 George Washington 10.00 25.00
GW2 George Washington 10.00 25.00
GW3 George Washington 10.00 25.00
GW4 George Washington 10.00 25.00
GW5 George Washington 10.00 25.00
GW6 George Washington 10.00 25.00
GW7 George Washington 10.00 25.00
GW8 George Washington 10.00 25.00
GW9 George Washington 10.00 25.00
GW10 George Washington 10.00 25.00
GW11 George Washington 10.00 25.00
GW12 George Washington 10.00 25.00
GW13 George Washington 10.00 25.00
HH1 Herbert Hoover 20.00 50.00
HST1 Harry S. Truman 30.00 60.00
JB1 James Buchanan 50.00 100.00
JFK1 John F. Kennedy 12.00 30.00
JFK2 John F. Kennedy 12.00 30.00
JG1 James Garfield 10.00 25.00
JG2 James Garfield 10.00 25.00
JKP1 James K. Polk 50.00 100.00
JM1 James Monroe 10.00 25.00
JM2 James Monroe 10.00 25.00
JMA1 James Madison 50.00 100.00
JMA2 James Madison 50.00 100.00
JQA1 John Quincy Adams 12.00 30.00
JT1 John Tyler 20.00 50.00
LBJ1 Lyndon B. Johnson 12.50 30.00
MF1 Millard Fillmore 30.00 60.00
MVB1 Martin Van Buren 30.00 60.00
RBH1 Rutherford B. Hayes 50.00 100.00
RBH2 Rutherford B. Hayes 50.00 100.00
RN1 Richard Nixon 30.00 60.00
RR1 Ronald Reagan 30.00 60.00
TJ1 Thomas Jefferson 15.00 40.00
TJ2 Thomas Jefferson 15.00 40.00
TJ3 Thomas Jefferson 15.00 40.00
TJ4 Thomas Jefferson 15.00 40.00
TR1 Teddy Roosevelt 30.00 60.00
TR2 Theodore Roosevelt 10.00 25.00
TR3 Theodore Roosevelt 10.00 25.00
USG1 Ulysses S. Grant 10.00 25.00
USG2 Ulysses S. Grant 10.00 25.00
WGH1 Warren G. Harding 50.00 100.00
WGH2 Warren G. Harding 50.00 100.00
WHH1 William Henry Harrison 30.00 60.00
WHT1 William Howard Taft 30.00 60.00
WM1 William McKinley 20.00 50.00
WW1 Woodrow Wilson 10.00 25.00
WW2 Woodrow Wilson 10.00 25.00
ZT1 Zachary Taylor 20.00 50.00

2008 Topps Red Hot Rookie Redemption

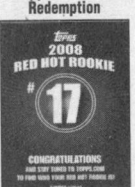

COMMON EXCH 6.00 15.00
RANDOM INSERTS IN SER.2 PACKS
EXCHANGE DEADLINE 5/30/2010
1 Jay Bruce AU 8.00 20.00
2 Justin Masterson 3.00 8.00
3 John Bowker 1.25 3.00
4 Kosuke Fukudome 4.00 10.00
5 Mike Aviles 2.00 5.00
6 Chris Davis 8.00 20.00
7 Chris Volstad 1.25 3.00
8 Jeff Samardzija 4.00 10.00
9 Brad Ziegler 6.00 15.00
10 Gio Gonzalez 2.00 5.00
11 Clayton Kershaw 40.00 100.00
12 Daniel Murphy 5.00 12.00
13 Chris Dickerson 2.00 5.00
14 Pablo Sandoval 5.00 12.00
15 Nick Evans 1.25 3.00
16 Clayton Richard 1.25 3.00
17 Evan Longoria AU 20.00 50.00
18 Taylor Teagarden 2.00 5.00
19 Collin Balester 1.25 3.00
20 Lou Montanez 1.25 3.00

2008 Topps Replica Mini Jerseys

STATED ODDS 1:412 H,1:19 HTA
STATED ODDS 1:8300 RETAIL
PRINT RUNS B/WN 379-539 COPIES PER
AIR Alex Rios/539 5.00 12.00
AP Albert Pujols 10.00 25.00
AR Alex Rodriguez/539 10.00 25.00
BW Brandon Webb 5.00 12.00
CC Carl Crawford/539 5.00 12.00
CH Cole Hamels 6.00 15.00
CMS Curt Schilling 6.00 15.00
CS C.C. Sabathia/539 5.00 12.00
CU Chase Utley 6.00 15.00
DAO David Ortiz 8.00 20.00
DO David Ortiz 8.00 20.00
DP Dustin Pedroia 10.00 25.00
DW David Wright 8.00 20.00
GS Grady Sizemore/539 6.00 15.00
HO Hideki Okajima 8.00 20.00
IS Ichiro Suzuki 10.00 25.00
JAV Jason Varitek 6.00 15.00
JB Josh Beckett 10.00 25.00
JCL Julio Lugo 6.00 15.00
JDD J.D. Drew 6.00 15.00
JE Jacoby Ellsbury 15.00 40.00
JL Jon Lester 8.00 20.00
JM Justin Morneau/539 5.00 12.00
JP Jake Peavy 6.00 15.00
JR Jose Reyes 6.00 15.00
JRP Jonathan Papelbon 8.00 20.00
JV Justin Verlander/539 6.00 15.00
KY Kevin Youkilis 6.00 15.00
MH Matt Holliday 6.00 15.00
ML Mike Lowell 10.00 25.00
MR Manny Ramirez 10.00 25.00
MT Mike Timlin 6.00 15.00
PF Prince Fielder 8.00 20.00
RH Ryan Howard/379 8.00 20.00
RM Russell Martin 5.00 12.00

2008 Topps Retail Relics

ONE PER RETAIL BLASTER BOX
*GOLD UPD/99: .5X TO 1.2X BASIC
*BLACK UPD/25: .6X TO 1.5X BASIC
AB Angel Berroa UPD 2.00 5.00
AC Asdrubal Cabrera UPD 3.00 8.00
AD Adam Dunn 3.00 8.00
AER Alex Rodriguez UPD 6.00 15.00
AH Aaron Harang 2.00 5.00
AL Adam LaRoche 2.00 5.00
AR Aramis Ramirez UPD 2.00 5.00
AR Aaron Rowand 2.00 5.00
BA Bronson Arroyo 2.00 5.00
BC Bobby Crosby 2.00 5.00
BG Brian Giles 2.00 5.00
BH Brad Hawpe 2.00 5.00
BJ Bobby Jenks 2.00 5.00
BKA Bobby Abreu 2.00 5.00
BP Brad Penny 2.00 5.00
BS Ben Sheets 2.00 5.00
BW Brandon Webb 3.00 8.00
CB Carlos Beltran 3.00 8.00
CC Coco Crisp UPD 2.00 5.00
CC Chris Capuano 2.00 5.00
CD Carlos Delgado 2.00 5.00
CDC Carl Crawford 3.00 8.00
CG Curtis Granderson UPD 3.00 8.00
CJC Chris Carpenter 3.00 8.00
CK Casey Kotchman 2.00 5.00
DE Darin Erstad 2.00 5.00
DN Dioner Navarro UPD 2.00 5.00
DP Dustin Pedroia UPD 3.00 8.00
DW David Wright UPD 3.00 8.00
EB Erik Bedard UPD 2.00 5.00
EC Eric Chavez UPD 2.00 5.00
EC Eric Chavez 2.00 5.00
EE Edwin Encarnacion 5.00 12.00
FL Fred Lewis 2.00 5.00
FR Francisco Rodriguez 3.00 8.00
GA Garrett Atkins 2.00 5.00
HB Hank Blalock 2.00 5.00
HK Hong-Chih Kuo UPD 2.00 5.00
IK Ian Kinsler UPD 3.00 8.00
IR Ivan Rodriguez 3.00 8.00
IS Ian Snell 2.00 5.00
JB Jason Bay 3.00 8.00
JD Jermaine Dye 2.00 5.00
JE Johnny Estrada UPD 2.00 5.00

Card	Low	High
JE Jim Edmonds	3.00	8.00
JF Jeff Francis UPD	2.00	5.00
JJH J.J. Hardy	3.00	8.00
JL Jon Lester UPD	3.00	8.00
JL Jon Lester	3.00	8.00
JM John Maine UPD	2.00	5.00
JP Jake Peavy	2.00	5.00
JR Justin Ruggiano UPD	3.00	8.00
JR Jimmy Rollins	3.00	8.00
JRH Rich Harden	2.00	5.00
KG Khalil Greene	2.00	5.00
KH Kevin Hart UPD	2.00	5.00
KM Kendry Morales	2.00	5.00
KW Kerry Wood UPD	2.00	5.00
KW Kerry Wood	2.00	5.00
LB Lance Berkman	3.00	8.00
LB1 Lance Broadway	2.00	5.00
LH Livan Hernandez	2.00	5.00
LM Lastings Milledge UPD	2.00	5.00
MB Mark Buehrle	3.00	8.00
MH Mike Hampton	2.00	5.00
MK Matt Kemp UPD	4.00	10.00
MM Mark Mulder UPD	2.00	5.00
MM Melvin Mora	2.00	5.00
MMM Mike Mussina	3.00	8.00
MS Mike Sweeney	2.00	5.00
MT Mark Teahen	2.00	5.00
MY Michael Young	2.00	5.00
OG Ozzie Guillen UPD	2.00	5.00
OG Ozzie Guillen	2.00	5.00
PB Pat Burrell	2.00	5.00
PM Pedro Martinez	3.00	8.00
RB Rocco Baldelli UPD	2.00	5.00
RF Rafael Furcal UPD	2.00	5.00
RF Rafael Furcal	2.00	5.00
RH Roy Halladay	3.00	8.00
RW Rickie Weeks	2.00	5.00
SC Sean Casey UPD	2.00	5.00
SK Scott Kazmir	3.00	8.00
TG Troy Glaus	3.00	8.00
TH Todd Helton UPD	3.00	8.00
TH Todd Helton	3.00	8.00
TP Tony Pena	2.00	5.00
VW Vernon Wells	2.00	5.00
ZG Zack Greinke	3.00	8.00

2008 Topps Silk Collection

SER.2 ODDS 1:300 HOB, 1:139 RET
STATED PRINT RUN 100 SER.#'d SETS
1-100 FOUND IN SERIES 2
UPD ODDS 1:246 HOBBY
STATED PRINT RUN 100 SER.#'d SETS
101-200 FOUND IN UPDATE

Card	Low	High
SC1 Alex Rodriguez	12.00	30.00
SC2 Scott Kazmir	6.00	15.00
SC3 Ivan Rodriguez	6.00	15.00
SC4 Joe Mauer	8.00	20.00
SC5 Ken Griffey Jr.	20.00	50.00
SC6 Nick Markakis	8.00	20.00
SC7 Mickey Mantle	30.00	80.00
SC8 Erik Bedard	4.00	10.00
SC9 Derrek Lee	4.00	10.00
SC10 Miguel Cabrera	10.00	25.00
SC11 Yovani Gallardo	4.00	10.00
SC12 Victor Martinez	6.00	15.00
SC13 Curtis Granderson	6.00	15.00
SC14 Chris Young	4.00	10.00
SC15 Jimmy Rollins	6.00	15.00
SC16 Dan Uggla	4.00	10.00
SC17 Felix Hernandez	6.00	15.00
SC18 Alex Rios	4.00	10.00
SC19 Jason Bay	6.00	15.00
SC20 Jose Reyes	6.00	15.00
SC21 Mike Lowell	4.00	10.00
SC22 Carl Crawford	6.00	15.00
SC23 Chipper Jones	10.00	25.00
SC24 Troy Glaus	6.00	15.00
SC25 Cole Hamels	8.00	20.00
SC26 Chris Young	4.00	10.00
SC27 Torii Hunter	4.00	10.00
SC28 Hideki Matsui	10.00	25.00
SC29 Freddy Sanchez	4.00	10.00
SC30 Josh Beckett	4.00	10.00
SC31 Mark Buehrle	6.00	15.00
SC32 Brian Bannister	4.00	10.00
SC33 Carlos Beltran	6.00	15.00
SC34 Dontrelle Willis	4.00	10.00
SC35 Vladimir Guerrero	6.00	15.00
SC36 Matt Holliday	10.00	25.00
SC37 Adam Dunn	6.00	15.00
SC38 Gary Matthews	4.00	10.00
SC39 Travis Hafner	4.00	10.00
SC40 Chase Utley	6.00	15.00
SC41 Vernon Wells	4.00	10.00
SC42 Lance Berkman	6.00	15.00
SC43 Jeff Francis	4.00	10.00
SC44 Curt Schilling	6.00	15.00
SC45 Alfonso Soriano	6.00	15.00
SC46 Jarrod Saltalamacchia	4.00	10.00
SC47 Hideki Okajima	4.00	10.00
SC48 Pedro Martinez	6.00	15.00
SC49 Jorge Posada	6.00	15.00
SC50 Justin Upton	6.00	15.00
SC51 Tom Gorzelanny	4.00	10.00
SC52 Carlos Delgado	4.00	10.00
SC53 Edgar Renteria	4.00	10.00
SC54 Chien-Ming Wang	6.00	15.00
SC55 C.C. Sabathia	6.00	15.00
SC56 B.J. Upton	6.00	15.00
SC57 Delmon Young	6.00	15.00
SC58 Tim Lincecum	6.00	15.00
SC59 Carlos Zambrano	6.00	15.00
SC60 Magglio Ordonez	6.00	15.00
SC61 Brandon Webb	6.00	15.00
SC62 Ben Sheets	4.00	10.00
SC63 Brad Penny	4.00	10.00
SC64 John Lackey	6.00	15.00
SC65 Hanley Ramirez	6.00	15.00
SC66 Gary Sheffield	4.00	10.00
SC67 Ubaldo Jimenez	4.00	10.00
SC68 Barry Zito	6.00	15.00
SC69 Daisuke Matsuzaka	6.00	15.00
SC70 Justin Morneau	6.00	15.00
SC71 Jacoby Ellsbury	8.00	20.00
SC72 John Smoltz	10.00	25.00
SC73 Chris Carpenter	6.00	15.00
SC74 Ryan Braun	6.00	15.00
SC75 Prince Fielder	6.00	15.00
SC76 Carlos Lee	4.00	10.00
SC77 Ryan Zimmerman	6.00	15.00
SC78 Troy Tulowitzki	10.00	25.00
SC79 Michael Young	4.00	10.00
SC80 Johan Santana	6.00	15.00
SC81 Hunter Pence	6.00	15.00
SC82 Adrian Gonzalez	6.00	15.00
SC83 Jake Peavy	4.00	10.00
SC84 Derek Jeter	25.00	60.00
SC85 Ichiro Suzuki	12.00	30.00
SC86 Miguel Tejada	6.00	15.00
SC87 Trevor Hoffman	6.00	15.00
SC88 Kevin Youkilis	4.00	10.00
SC89 David Wright	6.00	15.00
SC90 Albert Pujols	12.00	30.00
SC91 Todd Helton	6.00	15.00
SC92 Rich Harden	4.00	10.00
SC93 Fausto Carmona	4.00	10.00
SC94 Mark Teixeira	6.00	15.00
SC95 Justin Verlander	10.00	25.00
SC96 Tim Hudson	6.00	15.00
SC97 Jeff Francoeur	6.00	15.00
SC98 Manny Ramirez	10.00	25.00
SC99 David Ortiz	10.00	25.00
SC100 Ryan Howard	6.00	15.00
SC101 Johan Santana	6.00	15.00
SC102 Cristian Guzman	4.00	10.00
SC103 Brendan Harris	4.00	10.00
SC104 Randy Wolf	4.00	10.00
SC105 Cliff Lee	6.00	15.00
SC106 Roy Halladay	6.00	15.00
SC107 Dustin Pedroia	6.00	15.00
SC108 Chris Iannetta	4.00	10.00
SC109 Kerry Wood	6.00	15.00
SC110 Jim Edmonds	6.00	15.00
SC111 Jon Rauch	4.00	10.00
SC112 Ryan Sweeney	4.00	10.00
SC113 Ryan Ludwick	4.00	10.00
SC114 George Sherrill	4.00	10.00
SC115 Matt Garza	4.00	10.00
SC116 Nate McLouth	4.00	10.00
SC117 Eric Hinske	4.00	10.00
SC118 Adrian Gonzalez	6.00	15.00
SC119 Carlos Marmol	6.00	15.00
SC120 Jose Valverde	4.00	10.00
SC121 Shane Victorino	4.00	10.00
SC122 Brad Wilkerson	4.00	10.00
SC123 Dana Eveland	4.00	10.00
SC124 Luke Scott	4.00	10.00
SC125 Mike Cameron	4.00	10.00
SC126 Ervin Santana	4.00	10.00
SC127 Ryan Dempster	4.00	10.00
SC128 Geoff Jenkins	4.00	10.00
SC129 Billy Wagner	4.00	10.00
SC130 Pedro Feliz	4.00	10.00
SC131 Stephen Drew	4.00	10.00
SC132 Mark Hendrickson	4.00	10.00
SC133 Orlando Hudson	4.00	10.00
SC134 Pat Burrell	4.00	10.00
SC135 Russ Martin	4.00	10.00
SC136 James Loney	4.00	10.00
SC137 Justin Masterson	10.00	25.00
SC138 Matt Kemp	8.00	20.00
SC139 Hiroki Kuroda	10.00	25.00
SC140 Joe Crede	4.00	10.00
SC141 Joakim Soria	4.00	10.00
SC142 Armando Galarraga	6.00	15.00
SC143 Jason Varitek	10.00	25.00
SC144 Aaron Cook	4.00	10.00
SC145 Orlando Cabrera	6.00	15.00
SC146 Ian Kinsler	6.00	15.00
SC147 Carlos Gomez	4.00	10.00
SC148 Mike Aviles	6.00	15.00
SC149 Carlos Guillen	4.00	10.00
SC150 Erik Bedard	4.00	10.00
SC151 J.D. Drew	4.00	10.00
SC152 Marco Scutaro	6.00	15.00
SC153 James Shields	4.00	10.00
SC154 Cesar Izturis	4.00	10.00
SC155 Akinori Iwamura	4.00	10.00
SC156 Aramis Ramirez	4.00	10.00
SC157 Joe Mauer	8.00	20.00
SC158 Brad Lidge	4.00	10.00
SC159 Milton Bradley	4.00	10.00
SC160 Jay Bruce	12.00	30.00
SC161 Andrew Miller	6.00	15.00
SC162 Mark Reynolds	4.00	10.00
SC163 Johnny Damon	6.00	15.00
SC164 Michael Bourn	4.00	10.00
SC165 Andre Ethier	6.00	15.00
SC166 Carlos Pena	6.00	15.00
SC167 Joe Nathan	4.00	10.00
SC168 Cody Ross	4.00	10.00
SC169 Joba Chamberlain	4.00	10.00
SC170 Clayton Kershaw	10.00	25.00
SC171 Francisco Rodriguez	6.00	15.00
SC172 Mark DeRosa	4.00	10.00
SC173 Ben Sheets	4.00	10.00
SC174 Brian Wilson	10.00	25.00
SC175 Emil Brown	4.00	10.00
SC176 Geovany Soto	10.00	25.00
SC177 Jason Giambi	4.00	10.00
SC178 Shaun Marcum	4.00	10.00
SC179 Edinson Volquez	4.00	10.00
SC180 Max Scherzer	50.00	120.00
SC181 Kelly Johnson	4.00	10.00
SC182 Mariano Rivera	12.00	30.00
SC183 Chris Perez	6.00	15.00
SC184 Jose Guillen	4.00	10.00
SC185 Kyle Lohse	4.00	10.00
SC186 Kosuke Fukudome	12.00	30.00
SC187 Takashi Saito	4.00	10.00
SC188 Mike Mussina	6.00	15.00
SC189 J.J. Putz	4.00	10.00
SC190 Evan Longoria	20.00	50.00
SC191 Jered Weaver	6.00	15.00
SC192 Grady Sizemore	6.00	15.00
SC193 Carlos Gonzalez	10.00	25.00
SC194 Brian McCann	6.00	15.00
SC195 Jonathan Papelbon	6.00	15.00
SC196 Dioner Navarro	4.00	10.00
SC197 Bobby Abreu	4.00	10.00
SC198 Carlos Quentin	4.00	10.00
SC199 Josh Hamilton	6.00	15.00
SC200 Dan Haren	4.00	10.00

2008 Topps Stars

Card	Low	High
COMPLETE SET (25)	8.00	20.00
SER.2 ODDS 1:6 HOB, 1:6 RET		
TS1 Alex Rodriguez	1.00	2.50
TS2 Magglio Ordonez	.50	1.25
TS3 Justin Morneau	.50	1.25
TS4 Josh Beckett	.30	.75
TS5 David Wright	.50	1.25
TS6 Jimmy Rollins	.50	1.25
TS7 Ichiro Suzuki	1.00	2.50
TS8 Chipper Jones	.75	2.00
TS9 Brandon Webb	.50	1.25
TS10 Ryan Howard	.50	1.25
TS11 Derek Jeter	2.00	5.00
TS12 Vladimir Guerrero	.50	1.25
TS13 Manny Ramirez	.75	2.00
TS14 Jake Peavy	.30	.75
TS15 David Ortiz	.75	2.00
TS16 Jose Reyes	.50	1.25
TS17 Miguel Cabrera	.75	2.00
TS18 Victor Martinez	.50	1.25
TS19 C.C. Sabathia	.50	1.25
TS20 Prince Fielder	.50	1.25
TS21 Alfonso Soriano	.50	1.25
TS22 Grady Sizemore	.50	1.25
TS23 Albert Pujols	1.00	2.50
TS24 Pedro Martinez	.50	1.25
TS25 Matt Holliday	.75	2.00

2008 Topps Trading Card History

Card	Low	High
COMPLETE SET (75)	20.00	50.00
SER.1 ODDS 1:12 HOBBY		
SER.2 ODDS 1:6 HOBBY		
TCH1 Jacoby Ellsbury	.75	2.00
TCH2 Joba Chamberlain	.40	1.00
TCH3 Daisuke Matsuzaka	.60	1.50
TCH4 Price Fielder	.60	1.50
TCH5 Clay Buchholz	.60	1.50
TCH6 Alex Rodriguez	1.25	3.00
TCH7 Mickey Mantle	2.50	6.00
TCH8 Ryan Braun	.60	1.50
TCH9 Albert Pujols	1.25	3.00
TCH10 Joe Mauer	.75	2.00
TCH11 Jose Reyes	.60	1.50
TCH12 Joey Votto	1.50	4.00
TCH13 Johan Santana	.60	1.50
TCH14 Hunter Pence	.60	1.50
TCH15 Hideki Okajima	.40	1.00
TCH16 Cameron Maybin	.40	1.00
TCH17 Roger Clemens	1.25	3.00
TCH18 Tim Lincecum	.60	1.50
TCH19 Mark Teixeira/Jeff Francoeur	.60	1.50
TCH20 Justin Upton	.60	1.50
TCH21 Alfonso Soriano	.60	1.50
TCH22 Pedro Martinez	.60	1.50
TCH23 Chien-Ming Wang	.60	1.50
TCH24 Ichiro Suzuki	1.25	3.00
TCH25 Grady Sizemore	.60	1.50
TCH26 Ryan Howard	.60	1.50
TCH27 David Wright	.60	1.50
TCH28 Chin-Lung Hu	.40	1.00
TCH29 Jimmy Rollins	.60	1.50
TCH30 Ken Griffey Jr	2.00	5.00
TCH31 Chipper Jones	1.00	2.50
TCH32 Justin Verlander	1.00	2.50
TCH33 Manny Ramirez	1.00	2.50
TCH34 Chase Utley	.60	1.50
TCH35 Ivan Rodriguez	.60	1.50
TCH36 Josh Beckett	.40	1.00
TCH37 Tom Glavine	.60	1.50
TCH38 Vladimir Guerrero	.60	1.50
TCH39 Lance Berkman	.60	1.50
TCH40 Gary Sheffield	.40	1.00
TCH41 Luke Hochevar	.60	1.50
TCH42 David Ortiz	1.00	2.50
TCH43 Miguel Cabrera	1.00	2.50
TCH44 Andruw Jones	.40	1.00
TCH45 Hideki Matsui	1.00	2.50
TCH46 C.C. Sabathia	.60	1.50
TCH47 Magglio Ordonez	.60	1.50
TCH48 Pedro Martinez	.60	1.50
TCH49 Curtis Granderson	.60	1.50
TCH50 Derek Jeter	2.50	6.00
TCH51 Victor Martinez	.60	1.50
TCH52 Hanley Ramirez	.60	1.50
TCH53 Jake Peavy	.40	1.00
TCH54 Brandon Webb	.60	1.50
TCH55 Matt Holliday	1.00	2.50
TCH56 Hiroki Kuroda	1.00	2.50
TCH57 Mike Lowell	.40	1.00
TCH58 Carlos Lee	.40	1.00
TCH59 Nick Markakis	.75	2.00
TCH60 Carlos Beltran	.60	1.50
TCH61 Francisco Rodriguez	.60	1.50
TCH62 Troy Tulowitzki	1.00	2.50
TCH63 Russ Martin	.40	1.00
TCH64 Justin Morneau	.60	1.50
TCH65 Phil Hughes	.40	1.00
TCH66 Torii Hunter	.40	1.00
TCH67 Adam Dunn	.60	1.50
TCH68 Raul Ibanez	.60	1.50
TCH69 Robinson Cano	.60	1.50
TCH70 Brad Hawpe	.40	1.00
TCH71 Michael Young	.40	1.00
TCH72 Jim Thome	.60	1.50
TCH73 Chris Young	.40	1.00
TCH74 Carlos Zambrano	.60	1.50
TCH75 Felix Hernandez	.60	1.50

2008 Topps World Champion Relics

Card	Low	High
STATED ODDS 1:4792 H, 1:244 HTA		
STATED ODDS 1:33,333 RETAIL		
STATE PRINT RUN 100 SER.#'d SETS		
WCR1 Josh Beckett	20.00	50.00
WCR2 Hideki Okajima	10.00	25.00
WCR3 Curt Schilling	6.00	15.00
WCR4 Jason Varitek	15.00	40.00
WCR5 Mike Lowell	12.00	30.00
WCR6 Jacoby Ellsbury	40.00	80.00
WCR7 Dustin Pedroia	15.00	40.00
WCR8 Jonathan Papelbon	8.00	20.00
WCR9 Julio Lugo	12.00	30.00
WCR10 Manny Ramirez	12.00	30.00
WCR11 David Ortiz	10.00	25.00
WCR12 Eric Gagne	6.00	15.00
WCR13 Jon Lester	30.00	60.00
WCR14 J.D. Drew	6.00	15.00
WCR15 Kevin Youkilis	15.00	40.00

2008 Topps World Champion Relics Autographs

Card	Low	High
STATED ODDS 1:14,417 H, 1:732 HTA		
STATED ODDS 1:99,000 RETAIL		
PRINT RUNS B/WN 25-50 COPIES PER		
NO PRICING ON MOST DUE TO SCARCITY		
WCAR10 Manny Ramirez/50	100.00	200.00

2008 Topps Year in Review

Card	Low	High
COMPLETE SET (178)	50.00	100.00
COMP.SER.1 SET (60)	12.50	30.00
COMP.SER.2 SET (60)	12.50	30.00
COMP.UPD SET (58)	12.50	30.00
SER.1 ODDS 1:6 HOB, 1:6 RET		
SER.2 ODDS 1:6 HOB, 1:6 RET		
UPD ODDS 1:6 HOBBY		
YR1 Paul Lo Duca	.30	.75
YR2 Felix Hernandez	.50	1.25
YR3 Ian Snell	.30	.75
YR4 Carlos Beltran	.50	1.25
YR5 Daisuke Matsuzaka	.50	1.25
YR6 Jose Reyes	.50	1.25
YR7 Alex Rodriguez	1.00	2.50
YR8 Scott Kazmir	.50	1.25
YR9 Adam Everett	.30	.75
YR10 J.Beckett/J.Hamilton	.50	1.25
YR11 Craig Monroe	.30	.75
YR12 Justin Morneau	.50	1.25
YR13 Roy Halladay	.50	1.25
YR14 Jeff Suppan	.30	.75
YR15 Marco Scutaro	.50	1.25
YR16 Ivan Rodriguez	.50	1.25
YR17 Dimtri Young	.30	.75
YR18 Mark Buehrle	.50	1.25
YR19 Alex Rodriguez	1.00	2.50
YR20 Joe Saunders	.30	.75
YR21 Russell Martin	.30	.75
YR22 Manny Ramirez	.75	2.00
YR23 Chase Utley	.50	1.25
YR24 Travis Hafner	.30	.75
YR25 Jake Peavy	.30	.75
YR26 Shawn Hill	.30	.75
YR27 Daisuke Matsuzaka	.50	1.25
YR28 Matt Belisle	.30	.75
YR29 Troy Tulowitzki	.75	2.00
YR30 Andruw Jones	.30	.75
YR31 Phil Hughes	.30	.75
YR32 Derrek Lee	.30	.75
YR33 Ichiro Suzuki	1.00	2.50
YR34 Julio Franco	.30	.75
YR35 Chien-Ming Wang	.50	1.25
YR36 Hideki Matsui	.75	2.00
YR37 Brad Penny	.30	.75
YR38 Jack Wilson	.30	.75
YR39 Francisco Cordero	.30	.75
YR40 Omar Vizquel	.50	1.25
YR41 Tim Lincecum	.50	1.25
YR42 Bartolo Colon	.30	.75
YR43 Fred Lewis	.30	.75
YR44 Jeff Kent	.30	.75
YR45 Randy Johnson	.75	2.00
YR46 Rafael Furcal	.30	.75
YR47 Delmon Young	.50	1.25
YR48 Andrew Miller	.50	1.25
YR49 D.Ortiz/M.Lowell	.75	2.00
YR50 Justin Verlander	.75	2.00
YR51 C.C. Sabathia	.50	1.25
YR52 Felipe Lopez	.30	.75
YR53 Oliver Perez	.30	.75
YR54 John Smoltz	.75	2.00
YR55 Mark Reynolds	.30	.75
YR56 Jeremy Accardo	.50	1.25
YR57 Todd Helton	.50	1.25
YR58 Adrian Beltre	.75	2.00
YR59 Carlos Delgado	.30	.75
YR60 Chris Young	.30	.75
YR61 Roy Halladay	.50	1.25
YR62 Kevin Youkilis	.30	.75
YR63 Joe Blanton	.30	.75
YR64 Chad Gaudin	.50	1.25
YR65 Derek Lowe	.30	.75
YR66 C.C. Sabathia	.50	1.25
YR67 Luis Castillo	.30	.75
YR68 Curt Schilling	.50	1.25
YR69 Pedro Feliz	.30	.75
YR70 James Shields	.30	.75
YR71 Masumi Kuwata	.30	.75
YR72 Raul Ibanez	.50	1.25
YR73 Justin Verlander	.75	2.00
YR74 Tim Lincecum	.50	1.25
YR75 Hideki Matsui	.75	2.00
YR76 Julio Franco	.30	.75
YR77 Russell Branyan	.30	.75
YR78 Chipper Jones	.75	2.00
YR79 Chone Figgins	.30	.75
YR80 Chris Young	.30	.75
YR81 Sammy Sosa	.75	2.00
YR82 Miguel Tejada	.50	1.25
YR83 Wil Ledezma	.30	.75
YR84 Victor Martinez	.50	1.25
YR85 Dustin McGowan	.30	.75
YR86 Mike Fontenot	.30	.75
YR87 Mark Ellis	.30	.75
YR88 Ryan Howard	.50	1.25
YR89 Frank Thomas	.75	2.00
YR90 Aubrey Huff	.30	.75
YR91 Jake Peavy	.30	.75
YR92 Dan Haren	.30	.75
YR93 Damian Miller	.30	.75
YR94 Billy Butler	.30	.75
YR95 Dmitri Young	.30	.75
YR96 Chipper Jones	.75	2.00
YR97 Justin Morneau	.50	1.25
YR98 Erik Bedard	.30	.75
YR99 Scott Hatteberg	.30	.75
YR100 Vladimir Guerrero	.50	1.25
YR101 Ichiro Suzuki	1.00	2.50
YR102 Jose Reyes	.50	1.25
YR103 Ryan Garko	.30	.75
YR104 Jeff Francoeur	.50	1.25
YR105 Joe Mauer	.60	1.50
YR106 Manny Ramirez	.75	2.00
YR107 Chase Utley	.50	1.25
YR108 Magglio Ordonez	.50	1.25
YR109 Chris Young	.30	.75
YR110 B.J. Upton	.50	1.25
YR111 Willie Harris	.30	.75
YR112 Shelley Duncan	.30	.75
YR113 Jon Lester	.50	1.25
YR114 Travis Buck	.30	.75
YR115 Ryan Raburn	.30	.75
YR116 Eric Byrnes	.30	.75
YR117 Kenny Lofton	.30	.75
YR118 Jason Isringhausen	.30	.75
YR119 Todd Helton	.50	1.25
YR120 Carl Crawford	.50	1.25
YR121 Mark Teixeira	.50	1.25
YR122 Alex Gordon	.50	1.25
YR123 Jermaine Dye	.30	.75
YR124 Vladimir Guerrero	.50	1.25
YR125 Alex Rodriguez	1.00	2.50
YR126 Tom Glavine	.50	1.25
YR127 Scott Rolen	.50	1.25
YR128 Billy Wagner	.30	.75
YR129 Rick Ankiel	.30	.75
YR130 Jack Cust	.30	.75
YR131 Mike Mussina	.50	1.25
YR132 Magglio Ordonez	.50	1.25
YR133 Placido Polanco	.30	.75
YR134 Russell Branyan	.30	.75
YR135 David Price	.60	1.50
YR136 Mike Cameron	.30	.75
YR137 Brandon Webb	.50	1.25
YR138 Cameron Maybin	.30	.75
YR139 Johan Santana	.50	1.25
YR140 Bobby Jenks	.30	.75
YR141 Garret Anderson	.30	.75
YR142 Jarrod Saltalamacchia	.30	.75
YR143 Adrian Gonzalez	.50	1.25
YR144 Carlos Guillen	.30	.75
YR145 Tom Shearn	.30	.75
YR146 John Lackey	.50	1.25
YR147 Jayson Werth	.50	1.25
YR148 Aaron Harang	.30	.75
YR149 Chien-Ming Wang	.50	1.25
YR150 Scott Baker	.30	.75
YR151 Clay Buchholz	.50	1.25
YR152 Tom Glavine	.50	1.25
YR153 Pedro Martinez	.50	1.25
YR154 Doug Davis	.30	.75
YR155 Brandon Phillips	.30	.75
YR156 Jason Varitek	.75	2.00
YR157 Jim Thome	.50	1.25
YR158 Alex Rodriguez	1.00	2.50
YR159 Curtis Granderson	.50	1.25
YR160 Scott Kazmir	.50	1.25
YR161 Marlon Byrd	.30	.75
YR162 David Ortiz	.75	2.00
YR163 Greg Maddux	1.00	2.50
YR164 Johnny Damon	.50	1.25
YR165 Carlos Lee	.30	.75
YR166 Jim Thome	.50	1.25
YR167 Frank Thomas	.75	2.00
YR168 Greg Maddux	1.00	2.50
YR169 Matt Holliday	.75	2.00
YR170 J.R. Towles	.50	1.25
YR171 Lance Berkman	.50	1.25
YR172 Melky Cabrera	.30	.75
YR173 Vladimir Guerrero	.50	1.25
YR174 Nick Markakis	.60	1.50
YR175 Prince Fielder	.50	1.25
YR176 Moises Alou	.30	.75
YR177 Micah Owings	.30	.75
YR178 Carlos Zambrano	.50	1.25

2008 Topps Update

This set was released on October 22, 2008. The base set consists of 330 cards.

Card	Low	High
COMP.SET w/o VAR (330)	20.00	50.00
COMMON CARD (1-330)	.12	.30
COMMON ROOKIE (1-330)	.40	1.00
1-330 PLATE ODDS 1:457 HOBBY		
PLATE PRINT RUN 1 SET PER COLOR		
BLACK-CYAN-MAGENTA-YELLOW ISSUED		
NO PLATE PRICING DUE TO SCARCITY		
UH1A Kosuke Fukudome RC	1.25	3.00
UH1B Kosuke Fukudome VAR	15.00	40.00
UH2 Sean Casey	.12	.30
UH3 Freddie Bynum	.12	.30
UH4 Brent Lillibridge (RC)	.40	1.00
UH5 Chipper Jones AS	.30	.75
UH6 Yamid Haad	.12	.30
UH7 Josh Anderson	.12	.30
UH8 Jeff Mathis	.12	.30
UH9 Shawn Riggans	.12	.30
UH10A Evan Longoria RC	2.00	5.00
UH10B Evan Longoria VAR	10.00	25.00
UH11 Matt Holliday AS	.30	.75
UH12 Trot Nixon	.12	.30
UH13 Geoff Blum	.12	.30
UH14 Bartolo Colon	.12	.30
UH15 Kevin Cash	.12	.30
UH16 Paul Janish (RC)	.40	1.00
UH17 Russell Martin AS	.12	.30
UH18 Andy Phillips	.12	.30
UH19 Johnny Estrada	.12	.30
UH20 Justin Masterson RC	1.00	2.50
UH21 Darrell Rasner	.12	.30
UH22 Brian Moehler	.12	.30
UH23 Cristian Guzman AS	.12	.30
UH24 Tony Armas Jr.	.12	.30
UH25 Lance Berkman AS	.20	.50
UH26 Chris Iannetta	.12	.30
UH27 Reid Brignac	.20	.50
UH28 Miguel Tejada AS	.20	.50
UH29 Ryan Ludwick AS	.12	.30
UH30 Brendan Harris	.12	.30
UH31 Marco Scutaro	.20	.50
UH32 Cody Ross	.12	.30
UH33 Carlos Marmol	.20	.50
UH34 Nate McLouth AS	.12	.30
UH35 Hanley Ramirez AS	.20	.50
UH36 Xavier Nady	.12	.30
UH37 Connor Robertson	.12	.30
UH38 Carlos Villanueva	.12	.30
UH39 Jose Molina	.12	.30
UH40 Jon Rauch	.12	.30
UH41 Joe Mauer AS	.25	.60
UH42 Chip Ambres	.12	.30
UH43 Jason Bartlett	.12	.30
UH44 Ryan Sweeney	.12	.30
UH45 Eric Hurley (RC)	.40	1.00
UH46 Kevin Youkilis AS	.12	.30
UH47 Dustin Pedroia AS	.20	.50
UH48 Grant Balfour	.12	.30
UH49 Ryan Ludwick	.12	.30
UH50 Matt Garza	.12	.30
UH51 Fernando Tatis	.12	.30
UH52 Derek Jeter AS	.75	2.00
UH53 Justin Duchscherer AS	.12	.30
UH54 Matt Ginter	.12	.30
UH55 Cesar Izturis	.12	.30
UH56 Roy Halladay AS	.20	.50
UH57 Ramon Castro	.12	.30
UH58 Scott Kazmir AS	.20	.50
UH59 Cliff Lee AS	.20	.50
UH60 Jim Edmonds	.20	.50
UH61 Randy Wolf	.12	.30
UH62 Matt Albers	.12	.30
UH63 Eric Bruntlett	.12	.30
UH64 Joe Nathan AS	.12	.30
UH65 Alex Rodriguez AS	.40	1.00
UH66 Robinson Cancel	.12	.30
UH67 Jamey Carroll	.12	.30
UH68 Jonathan Papelbon AS	.20	.50
UH69 Chad Moeller	.12	.30
UH70 George Sherrill	.12	.30
UH71 Mariano Rivera AS	.40	1.00
UH72 Pete Orr	.12	.30
UH73 Jonathan Albaladejo RC	.60	1.50
UH74 Corey Patterson	.12	.30
UH75 Matt Treanor	.12	.30
UH76 Francisco Rodriguez AS	.20	.50
UH77 Ervin Santana AS	.12	.30
UH78 Dallas Braden	.20	.50
UH79 Willie Harris	.12	.30
UH80 Erik Bedard	.12	.30
UH81 J.C. Romero	.12	.30
UH82 Joe Saunders AS	.12	.30
UH83 George Sherrill AS	.12	.30
UH84 Julian Tavarez	.12	.30
UH85 Chad Gaudin	.20	.50
UH86 David Aardsma	.12	.30
UH87 Ryan Langerhans	.12	.30
UH88 Dan Haren Russell Martin	.12	.30
UH89 Joakim Soria AS	.12	.30
UH90 Dan Haren	.12	.30
UH91 Billy Buckner	.12	.30
UH92 Eric Hinske	.12	.30
UH93 Chris Coste	.12	.30
UH94 Edinson Volquez Russell Martin	.12	.30
UH95 Ichiro Suzuki AS	.40	1.00
UH96 Vladimir Nunez	.12	.30
UH97 Sean Gallagher	.12	.30
UH98 Denny Bautista	.12	.30
UH99 Hanley Ramirez/David Ortiz	.30	.75
UH100 Jay Bruce (RC)	1.25	3.00
UH100B Jay Bruce VAR	20.00	50.00
UH101 Dioner Navarro AS	.12	.30
UH102 Matt Murton	.12	.30
UH103 Chris Burke	.12	.30
UH104 Omar Infante	.12	.30
UH105 Dan Giese (RC)	.40	1.00
UH106 C.Guillen/J.Hamilton	.20	.50
UH107 Jason Varitek AS	.30	.75
UH108 Shin- Soo Choo	.20	.50
UH109 Alberto Callaspo	.12	.30
UH110 Jose Valverde	.12	.30
UH111 Brandon Boggs (RC)	.60	1.50
UH112 J.Hamilton/J.Drew	.20	.50
UH113 Justin Morneau AS	.20	.50
UH114 Billy Traber	.12	.30

UH115 Mike Lamb .12 .30
UH116 Odalis Perez .12 .30
UH117 Jed Lowrie (RC) .40 1.00
UH118 Justin Morneau/David Ortiz .30 .75
UH119 Ken Griffey Jr. HL .60 1.50
UH120 Angel Berroa .12 .30
UH121 Jacque Jones .12 .30
UH122 DeWayne Wise .12 .30
UH123 Matt Joyce RC 1.00 2.50
UH124 A.Rodriguez/E.Longoria .60 1.50
UH125 John Smoltz HL .30 .75
UH126 Morgan Ensberg .12 .30
UH127 M.Young/D.Jeter .75 2.00
UH128 LaTroy Hawkins .12 .30
UH129 Nick Adenhart (RC) .40 1.00
UH130 Mike Cameron .12 .30
UH131 Manny Ramirez HL .30 .75
UH132 Jorge De La Rosa .12 .30
UH133 Tadahito Iguchi .12 .30
UH134 Joey Devine .12 .30
UH135 Jose Arredondo RC .60 1.50
UH136 H.Ramirez/A.Pujols .40 1.00
UH137 Evan Longoria HL .60 1.50
UH138 T.J. Beam .12 .30
UH139 Jon Lieber .12 .30
UH140 Dana Eveland .12 .30
UH141 Michael Aubrey RC .60 1.50
UH142 Adrian Gonzalez/Matt Holliday .30 .75
UH143 Chipper Jones HL .30 .75
UH144 Robinson Tejeda .12 .30
UH145 Kip Wells .12 .30
UH146 Carlos Gonzalez (RC) 1.00 2.50
UH147 Josh Banks (RC) .40 1.00
UH148 David Wright AS .20 .50
UH149 Paul Hoover .12 .30
UH150 Jon Lester HL .20 .50
UH151 Darin Erstad .12 .30
UH152 Steve Trachsel .12 .30
UH153 Armando Galarraga RC .60 1.50
UH154 Grady Sizemore HRD .20 .50
UH155 Jay Bruce HL .40 1.00
UH156 Juan Rincon .12 .30
UH157 Mark Hendrickson .12 .30
UH158 Chad Durbin .12 .30
UH159 Mike Aviles RC .60 1.50
UH160 Orlando Cabrera .20 .50
UH161 Asdrubal Cabrera HL .20 .50
UH162 Eric Stults .12 .30
UH163 Miguel Cairo .12 .30
UH164 Jason LaRue .12 .30
UH165 Burke Badenhop RC .60 1.50
UH166 Ryan Braun HRD .20 .50
UH167 Justin Morneau HRD .20 .50
UH168 Ben Zobrist .20 .50
UH169 Eulogio De La Cruz .12 .30
UH170 Greg Smith (RC) .40 1.00
UH171 Brian Bixler (RC) .40 1.00
UH172 Evan Longoria HRD .60 1.50
UH173 Randy Johnson HL .30 .75
UH174 D.J. Carrasco .12 .30
UH175 Luis Vizcaino .12 .30
UH176 Brad Wilkerson .12 .30
UH177 Emmanuel Burriss RC .60 1.50
UH178 Lance Berkman HRD .20 .50
UH179 Johnny Damon HL .20 .50
UH180 Scott Rolen .20 .50
UH181 Runelvys Hernandez .12 .30
UH182 Sidney Ponson .12 .30
UH183 Greg Reynolds RC .60 1.50
UH184 Chase Utley HRD .20 .50
UH185 Joey Votto HL .50 1.25
UH186 Wes Littleton .12 .30
UH187 Rod Barajas .12 .30
UH188 Ray Durham .12 .30
UH189 Micah Hoffpauir RC 1.25 3.00
UH190 Manny Ramirez AS .30 .75
UH191 Ian Kinsler AS .20 .50
UH192 Craig Hansen .12 .30
UH193 Jeremy Affeldt .12 .30
UH194 Gary Bennett .12 .30
UH195 Chris Carter (RC) .60 1.50
UH196 Dan Uggla HRD .12 .30
UH197 Michael Young AS .12 .30
UH198 Andy LaRoche .12 .30
UH199 Lance Cormier .12 .30
UH200 Luke Scott .12 .30
UH201 Travis Denker RC .60 1.50
UH202 Josh Hamilton .20 .50
UH203 Joe Crede AS .12 .30
UH204 Franquelis Osoria .12 .30
UH205 Octavio Dotel .12 .30
UH206 Russell Branyan .12 .30
UH207 Alberto Gonzalez RC .60 1.50
UH208 Kerry Wood AS .12 .30
UH209 Carlos Guillen AS .12 .30
UH210 Joe Saunders .12 .30
UH211 Brett Tomko .12 .30
UH212 Guillermo Mota .12 .30
UH213 German Duran RC .60 1.50
UH214 Carlos Zambrano AS .20 .50
UH215 Josh Hamilton AS .20 .50
UH216 Jason Bay .20 .50
UH217 Willy Aybar .12 .30
UH218 Salomon Torres .12 .30
UH219 Damaso Marte .12 .30
UH220 Geoff Jenkins .12 .30
UH221 J.D. Drew AS .12 .30
UH222 Dave Borkowski .12 .30
UH223 Jeff Ridgway RC .60 1.50
UH224 Angel Pagan .12 .30
UH225 Ryan Tucker (RC) .40 1.00
UH226 Brian McCann AS .20 .50
UH227 Carlos Quentin AS .12 .30
UH228 Joe Blanton .12 .30
UH229 Adrian Gonzalez AS .20 .50
UH230 Jason Jennings .12 .30
UH231 Chris Davis RC .75 2.00
UH232 Geovany Soto AS .30 .75
UH233 Grady Sizemore AS .20 .50
UH234 Carl Pavano .12 .30
UH235 Eddie Guardado .12 .30
UH236 Chris Snelling .12 .30
UH237 Manny Ramirez .30 .75
UH238 Dan Uggla AS .12 .30
UH239 Milton Bradley AS .12 .30
UH240 Clayton Kershaw RC 50.00 120.00
UH241 Chase Utley AS .20 .50
UH242 Raul Chavez .12 .30
UH243 Joe Mather RC .60 1.50
UH244 Brandon Webb AS .20 .50
UH245 Ryan Braun .20 .50
UH246 Kelvin Jimenez .12 .30
UH247 Scott Podsednik .12 .30
UH248 Doug Mientkiewicz .12 .30
UH249 Chris Volstad (RC) .40 1.00
UH250 Pedro Feliz .12 .30
UH251 Mark Redman .12 .30
UH252 Tony Clark .12 .30
UH253 Josh Johnson .20 .50
UH254 Jose Castillo .12 .30
UH255 Brian Horwitz RC .40 1.00
UH256 Aramis Ramirez AS .12 .30
UH257 Casey Blake .12 .30
UH258 Arthur Rhodes .12 .30
UH259 Aaron Boone .20 .50
UH260 Emil Brown .12 .30
UH261 Matt Macri (RC) .40 1.00
UH262 Brian Wilson AS .30 .75
UH263 Eric Patterson .12 .30
UH264 David Ortiz .30 .75
UH265 Tony Abreu .12 .30
UH266 Rob Mackowiak .12 .30
UH267 Gregorio Petit RC .60 1.50
UH268 Alfonso Soriano AS .20 .50
UH269 Robert Andino .12 .30
UH270 Justin Duchscherer .12 .30
UH271 Brad Thompson .12 .30
UH272 Guillermo Quiroz .12 .30
UH273 Chris Perez RC .60 1.50
UH274 Albert Pujols AS .40 1.00
UH275 Rich Harden .12 .30
UH276 Corey Hart AS .12 .30
UH277 John Rheinecker .12 .30
UH278 So Taguchi .12 .30
UH279 Alex Hinshaw RC .60 1.50
UH280 Max Scherzer RC 20.00 50.00
UH281 Chris Aguila .12 .30
UH282 Carlos Marmol AS .20 .50
UH283 Alex Cintron .12 .30
UH284 Curtis Thigpen .12 .30
UH285 Kosuke Fukudome AS .40 1.00
UH286 Aaron Cook AS .12 .30
UH287 Chase Headley .12 .30
UH288 Evan Longoria AS .60 1.50
UH289 Chris Gomez .12 .30
UH290 Carlos Gomez .12 .30
UH291 Jonathan Herrera RC .60 1.50
UH292 Ryan Dempster AS .12 .30
UH293 Adam Dunn .20 .50
UH294 Mark Teixeira .20 .50
UH295 Aaron Miles .12 .30
UH296 Gabe Gross .12 .30
UH297 Cory Wade (RC) .40 1.00
UH298 Dan Haren AS .12 .30
UH299 Jolbert Cabrera .12 .30
UH300 C.C. Sabathia .20 .50
UH301 Tony Pena .12 .30
UH302 Brandon Moss .12 .30
UH303 Taylor Teagarden RC .60 1.50
UH304 Brad Lidge AS .12 .30
UH305 Ben Francisco .12 .30
UH306 Casey Kotchman .12 .30
UH307 Greg Norton .12 .30
UH308 Shelley Duncan .12 .30
UH309 John Bowker (RC) .40 1.00
UH310 Kyle Lohse .12 .30
UH311 Oscar Salazar .12 .30
UH312 Ivan Rodriguez .20 .50
UH313 Tim Lincecum AS .20 .50
UH314 Wilson Betemit .12 .30
UH315 Sean Rodriguez (RC) .40 1.00
UH316 Ben Sheets AS .12 .30
UH317 Brian Buscher .12 .30
UH318 Kyle Farnsworth .12 .30
UH319 Ruben Gotay .12 .30
UH320 Heath Bell .12 .30
UH321 Jeff Niemann (RC) .40 1.00
UH322 Edinson Volquez AS .12 .30
UH323 Jorge Velandia .12 .30
UH324 Ken Griffey Jr. .60 1.50
UH325 Clay Hensley .12 .30
UH326 Kevin Mench .12 .30
UH327 Hernan Iribarren (RC) .60 1.50
UH328 Billy Wagner AS .12 .30
UH329 Jeremy Sowers .12 .30
UH330 Johan Santana .20 .50

2008 Topps Update Black

COMMON CARD (1-330) 4.00 10.00
STATED ODDS 1:59 HOBBY
STATED PRINT RUN 57 SER.#'d SETS
UH1 Kosuke Fukudome 12.00 30.00
UH2 Sean Casey 10.00 25.00
UH3 Freddie Bynum 4.00 10.00
UH4 Brent Lillibridge 4.00 10.00
UH5 Chipper Jones AS 6.00 15.00
UH6 Yamid Haad 4.00 10.00
UH7 Josh Anderson 4.00 10.00
UH8 Jeff Mathis 4.00 10.00
UH9 Shawn Riggans 4.00 10.00
UH10 Evan Longoria 20.00 50.00
UH11 Matt Holliday AS 10.00 25.00
UH12 Trot Nixon 4.00 10.00
UH13 Geoff Blum 4.00 10.00
UH14 Bartolo Colon 4.00 10.00
UH15 Kevin Cash 4.00 10.00
UH16 Paul Janish 4.00 10.00
UH17 Russ Martin AS 15.00 40.00
UH18 Andy Phillips 4.00 10.00
UH19 Johnny Estrada 4.00 10.00
UH20 Justin Masterson 30.00 60.00
UH21 Darrell Rasner 4.00 10.00
UH22 Brian Moehler 4.00 10.00
UH23 Cristian Guzman AS 4.00 10.00
UH24 Tony Armas Jr. 4.00 10.00
UH25 Lance Berkman AS 6.00 15.00
UH26 Chris Iannetta 4.00 10.00
UH27 Reid Brignac 6.00 15.00
UH28 Miguel Tejada AS 6.00 15.00
UH29 Ryan Ludwick AS 6.00 15.00
UH30 Brendan Harris 4.00 10.00
UH31 Marco Scutaro 6.00 15.00
UH32 Cody Ross 4.00 10.00
UH33 Carlos Marmol 6.00 15.00
UH34 Nate McLouth AS 12.50 30.00
UH35 Hanley Ramirez AS 6.00 15.00
UH36 Xavier Nady 4.00 10.00
UH37 Connor Robertson 4.00 10.00
UH38 Carlos Villanueva 4.00 10.00
UH39 Jose Molina 4.00 10.00
UH40 Jon Rauch 4.00 10.00
UH41 Joe Mauer AS 8.00 20.00
UH42 Chip Ambres 4.00 10.00
UH43 Jason Bartlett 4.00 10.00
UH44 Ryan Sweeney 4.00 10.00
UH45 Eric Hurley 4.00 10.00
UH46 Kevin Youkilis AS 10.00 25.00
UH47 Dustin Pedroia AS 10.00 25.00
UH48 Grant Balfour 4.00 10.00
UH49 Ryan Ludwick 6.00 15.00
UH50 Matt Garza 4.00 10.00
UH51 Fernando Tatis 4.00 10.00
UH52 Derek Jeter AS 25.00 60.00
UH53 Justin Duchscherer AS 4.00 10.00
UH54 Matt Ginter 4.00 10.00
UH55 Cesar Izturis 4.00 10.00
UH56 Roy Halladay AS 6.00 15.00
UH57 Ramon Castro 4.00 10.00
UH58 Scott Kazmir AS 6.00 15.00
UH59 Cliff Lee AS 6.00 15.00
UH60 Jim Edmonds 6.00 15.00
UH61 Randy Wolf 4.00 10.00
UH62 Matt Albers 4.00 10.00
UH63 Eric Bruntlett 4.00 10.00
UH64 Joe Nathan AS 4.00 10.00
UH65 Alex Rodriguez AS 10.00 25.00
UH66 Robinson Cancel 4.00 10.00
UH67 Jamey Carroll 4.00 10.00
UH68 Jonathan Papelbon AS 6.00 15.00
UH69 Chad Moeller 4.00 10.00
UH70 George Sherrill 4.00 10.00
UH71 Mariano Rivera AS 12.00 30.00
UH72 Pete Orr 4.00 10.00
UH73 Jonathan Albaladejo 6.00 15.00
UH74 Corey Patterson 4.00 10.00
UH75 Matt Treanor 4.00 10.00
UH76 Francisco Rodriguez AS 6.00 15.00
UH77 Ervin Santana AS 4.00 10.00
UH78 Dallas Braden 6.00 15.00
UH79 Willie Harris 4.00 10.00
UH80 Erik Bedard 4.00 10.00
UH81 J.C. Romero 4.00 10.00
UH82 Joe Saunders AS 4.00 10.00
UH83 George Sherrill AS 4.00 10.00
UH84 Julian Tavarez 4.00 10.00
UH85 Chad Gaudin 6.00 15.00
UH86 David Aardsma 4.00 10.00
UH87 Ryan Langerhans 4.00 10.00
UH88 Dan Haren/Russ Martin 4.00 10.00
UH89 Joakim Soria AS 4.00 10.00
UH90 Dan Haren 4.00 10.00
UH91 Billy Buckner 4.00 10.00
UH92 Eric Hinske 4.00 10.00
UH93 Chris Coste 4.00 10.00
UH94 Edinson Volquez/Russ Martin 4.00 10.00
UH95 Ichiro Suzuki AS 20.00 50.00
UH96 Vladimir Nunez 4.00 10.00
UH97 Sean Gallagher 4.00 10.00
UH98 Denny Bautista 4.00 10.00
UH99 Hanley Ramirez/David Ortiz 10.00 25.00
UH100 Jay Bruce 10.00 25.00
UH101 Dioner Navarro AS 4.00 10.00
UH102 Matt Murton 4.00 10.00
UH103 Chris Burke 4.00 10.00
UH104 Omar Infante 4.00 10.00
UH105 Dan Giese 4.00 10.00
UH106 Carlos Guillen/Josh Hamilton 12.50 30.00
UH107 Jason Varitek AS 10.00 25.00
UH108 Shin- Soo Choo 6.00 15.00
UH109 Alberto Callaspo 4.00 10.00
UH110 Jose Valverde 4.00 10.00
UH111 Brandon Boggs 6.00 15.00
UH112 Josh Hamilton/J.D. Drew 12.50 30.00
UH113 Justin Morneau AS 6.00 15.00
UH114 Billy Traber 4.00 10.00
UH115 Mike Lamb 4.00 10.00
UH116 Odalis Perez 4.00 10.00
UH117 Jed Lowrie 4.00 10.00
UH118 Justin Morneau/David Ortiz 10.00 25.00
UH119 Ken Griffey Jr. HL 20.00 50.00
UH120 Angel Berroa 4.00 10.00
UH121 Jacque Jones 4.00 10.00
UH122 DeWayne Wise 4.00 10.00
UH123 Matt Joyce 10.00 25.00
UH124 Alex Rodriguez/Evan Longoria 20.00 50.00
UH125 John Smoltz HL 10.00 25.00
UH126 Morgan Ensberg 4.00 10.00
UH127 Michael Young/Derek Jeter 25.00 60.00
UH128 LaTroy Hawkins 4.00 10.00
UH129 Nick Adenhart 10.00 25.00
UH130 Mike Cameron 4.00 10.00
UH131 Manny Ramirez HL 12.50 30.00
UH132 Jorge De La Rosa 4.00 10.00
UH133 Tadahito Iguchi 4.00 10.00
UH134 Joey Devine 4.00 10.00
UH135 Jose Arredondo 6.00 15.00
UH136 Hanley Ramirez/Albert Pujols 12.00 30.00
UH137 Evan Longoria HL 15.00 40.00
UH138 T.J. Beam 4.00 10.00
UH139 Jon Lieber 4.00 10.00
UH140 Dana Eveland 4.00 10.00
UH141 Michael Aubrey 6.00 15.00
UH142 Adrian Gonzalez/Matt Holliday 10.00 25.00
UH143 Chipper Jones HL 6.00 15.00
UH144 Robinson Tejeda 4.00 10.00
UH145 Kip Wells 4.00 10.00
UH146 Carlos Gonzalez 10.00 25.00
UH147 Josh Banks 4.00 10.00
UH148 David Wright AS 12.50 30.00
UH149 Paul Hoover 4.00 10.00
UH150 Jon Lester HL 12.50 30.00
UH151 Darin Erstad 4.00 10.00
UH152 Steve Trachsel 4.00 10.00
UH153 Armando Galarraga 6.00 15.00
UH154 Grady Sizemore HRD 6.00 15.00
UH155 Jay Bruce HL 10.00 25.00
UH156 Juan Rincon 4.00 10.00
UH157 Mark Hendrickson 4.00 10.00
UH158 Chad Durbin 4.00 10.00
UH159 Mike Aviles 6.00 15.00
UH160 Orlando Cabrera 6.00 15.00
UH161 Asdrubal Cabrera HL 6.00 15.00
UH162 Eric Stults 4.00 10.00
UH163 Miguel Cairo 4.00 10.00
UH164 Jason LaRue 4.00 10.00
UH165 Burke Badenhop 6.00 15.00
UH166 Ryan Braun HRD 12.50 30.00
UH167 Justin Morneau HRD 6.00 15.00
UH168 Ben Zobrist 6.00 15.00
UH169 Eulogio De La Cruz 4.00 10.00
UH170 Greg Smith 4.00 10.00
UH171 Brian Bixler 4.00 10.00
UH172 Evan Longoria HRD 15.00 40.00
UH173 Randy Johnson HL 10.00 25.00
UH174 D.J. Carrasco 4.00 10.00
UH175 Luis Vizcaino 4.00 10.00
UH176 Brad Wilkerson 4.00 10.00
UH177 Emmanuel Burriss 6.00 15.00
UH178 Lance Berkman HRD 6.00 15.00
UH179 Johnny Damon HL 6.00 15.00
UH180 Scott Rolen 6.00 15.00
UH181 Runelvys Hernandez 4.00 10.00
UH182 Sidney Ponson 4.00 10.00
UH183 Greg Reynolds 6.00 15.00
UH184 Chase Utley HRD 6.00 15.00
UH185 Joey Votto HL 15.00 40.00
UH186 Wes Littleton 4.00 10.00
UH187 Rod Barajas 4.00 10.00
UH188 Ray Durham 4.00 10.00
UH189 Micah Hoffpauir 12.00 30.00
UH190 Manny Ramirez AS 10.00 25.00
UH191 Ian Kinsler AS 6.00 15.00
UH192 Craig Hansen 4.00 10.00
UH193 Jeremy Affeldt 4.00 10.00
UH194 Gary Bennett 4.00 10.00
UH195 Chris Carter 6.00 15.00
UH196 Dan Uggla HRD 4.00 10.00
UH197 Michael Young AS 4.00 10.00
UH198 Andy LaRoche 4.00 10.00
UH199 Lance Cormier 4.00 10.00
UH200 Luke Scott 4.00 10.00
UH201 Travis Denker 6.00 15.00
UH202 Josh Hamilton 12.50 30.00
UH203 Joe Crede AS 4.00 10.00
UH204 Franquelis Osoria 4.00 10.00
UH205 Octavio Dotel 4.00 10.00
UH206 Russell Branyan 4.00 10.00
UH207 Alberto Gonzalez 6.00 15.00
UH208 Kerry Wood AS 4.00 10.00
UH209 Carlos Guillen AS 4.00 10.00
UH210 Joe Saunders 4.00 10.00
UH211 Brett Tomko 4.00 10.00
UH212 Guillermo Mota 4.00 10.00
UH213 German Duran 6.00 15.00
UH214 Carlos Zambrano AS 6.00 15.00
UH215 Josh Hamilton AS 12.50 30.00
UH216 Jason Bay 12.50 30.00
UH217 Willy Aybar 4.00 10.00
UH218 Salomon Torres 4.00 10.00
UH219 Damaso Marte 4.00 10.00
UH220 Geoff Jenkins 4.00 10.00
UH221 J.D. Drew AS 4.00 10.00
UH222 Dave Borkowski 4.00 10.00
UH223 Jeff Ridgway 6.00 15.00
UH224 Angel Pagan 4.00 10.00
UH225 Ryan Tucker 4.00 10.00
UH226 Brian McCann AS 6.00 15.00
UH227 Carlos Quentin AS 4.00 10.00
UH228 Joe Blanton 4.00 10.00
UH229 Adrian Gonzalez AS 6.00 15.00
UH230 Jason Jennings 4.00 10.00
UH231 Chris Davis 10.00 25.00
UH232 Geovany Soto AS 10.00 25.00
UH233 Grady Sizemore AS 6.00 15.00
UH234 Carl Pavano 4.00 10.00
UH235 Eddie Guardado 4.00 10.00
UH236 Chris Snelling 4.00 10.00
UH237 Manny Ramirez 20.00 50.00
UH238 Dan Uggla AS 4.00 10.00
UH239 Milton Bradley AS 4.00 10.00
UH240 Clayton Kershaw 300.00 800.00
UH241 Chase Utley AS 6.00 15.00
UH242 Raul Chavez 4.00 10.00
UH243 Joe Mather 6.00 15.00
UH244 Brandon Webb AS 6.00 15.00
UH245 Ryan Braun 12.50 30.00
UH246 Kelvin Jimenez 4.00 10.00
UH247 Scott Podsednik 4.00 10.00
UH248 Doug Mientkiewicz 4.00 10.00
UH249 Chris Volstad 4.00 10.00
UH250 Pedro Feliz 4.00 10.00
UH251 Mark Redman 4.00 10.00
UH252 Tony Clark 4.00 10.00
UH253 Josh Johnson 6.00 15.00
UH254 Jose Castillo 4.00 10.00
UH255 Brian Horwitz 4.00 10.00
UH256 Aramis Ramirez AS 4.00 10.00
UH257 Casey Blake 10.00 25.00
UH258 Arthur Rhodes 4.00 10.00
UH259 Aaron Boone 6.00 15.00
UH260 Emil Brown 4.00 10.00
UH261 Matt Macri 4.00 10.00
UH262 Brian Wilson AS 10.00 25.00
UH263 Eric Patterson 4.00 10.00
UH264 David Ortiz 10.00 25.00
UH265 Tony Abreu 4.00 10.00
UH266 Rob Mackowiak 4.00 10.00
UH267 Gregorio Petit 6.00 15.00
UH268 Alfonso Soriano AS 6.00 15.00
UH269 Robert Andino 4.00 10.00
UH270 Justin Duchscherer 4.00 10.00
UH271 Brad Thompson 4.00 10.00
UH272 Guillermo Quiroz 4.00 10.00
UH273 Chris Perez 6.00 15.00
UH274 Albert Pujols AS 12.50 30.00
UH275 Rich Harden 4.00 10.00
UH276 Corey Hart AS 4.00 10.00
UH277 John Rheinecker 4.00 10.00
UH278 So Taguchi 4.00 10.00
UH279 Alex Hinshaw 6.00 15.00
UH280 Max Scherzer 300.00 600.00
UH281 Chris Aguila 4.00 10.00
UH282 Carlos Marmol AS 6.00 15.00
UH283 Alex Cintron 4.00 10.00
UH284 Curtis Thigpen 4.00 10.00
UH285 Kosuke Fukudome AS 10.00 25.00
UH286 Aaron Cook AS 4.00 10.00
UH287 Chase Headley 4.00 10.00
UH288 Evan Longoria AS 15.00 40.00
UH289 Chris Gomez 4.00 10.00
UH290 Carlos Gomez 6.00 15.00
UH291 Jonathan Herrera 6.00 15.00
UH292 Ryan Dempster AS 6.00 15.00
UH293 Adam Dunn 6.00 15.00
UH294 Mark Teixeira 6.00 15.00
UH295 Aaron Miles 4.00 10.00
UH296 Gabe Gross 4.00 10.00
UH297 Cory Wade 4.00 10.00
UH298 Dan Haren AS 4.00 10.00
UH299 Jolbert Cabrera 4.00 10.00
UH300 C.C. Sabathia 6.00 15.00
UH301 Tony Pena 4.00 10.00
UH302 Brandon Moss 4.00 10.00
UH303 Taylor Teagarden 6.00 15.00
UH304 Brad Lidge AS 4.00 10.00
UH305 Ben Francisco 4.00 10.00
UH306 Casey Kotchman 4.00 10.00
UH307 Greg Norton 4.00 10.00
UH308 Shelley Duncan 4.00 10.00
UH309 John Bowker 4.00 10.00
UH310 Kyle Lohse 4.00 10.00
UH311 Oscar Salazar 4.00 10.00
UH312 Ivan Rodriguez 4.00 10.00
UH313 Tim Lincecum AS 6.00 15.00
UH314 Wilson Betemit 4.00 10.00
UH315 Sean Rodriguez 4.00 10.00
UH316 Ben Sheets AS 4.00 10.00
UH317 Brian Buscher 4.00 10.00
UH318 Kyle Farnsworth 4.00 10.00
UH319 Ruben Gotay 4.00 10.00
UH320 Heath Bell 4.00 10.00
UH321 Jeff Niemann 4.00 10.00
UH322 Edinson Volquez AS 4.00 10.00
UH323 Jorge Velandia 4.00 10.00
UH324 Ken Griffey Jr. 20.00 50.00
UH325 Clay Hensley 4.00 10.00
UH326 Kevin Mench 4.00 10.00
UH327 Hernan Iribarren 6.00 15.00
UH328 Billy Wagner AS 4.00 10.00
UH329 Jeremy Sowers 4.00 10.00
UH330 Johan Santana 6.00 15.00

2008 Topps Update Gold Border

*GLD BDR VET: 2X TO 5X BASIC
*GLD BDR RC: .6X TO 1.5X BASIC RC
STATED ODDS 1:5 HOBBY
STATED PRINT RUN 2008 SER.#'d SETS
UH240 Clayton Kershaw 125.00 300.00

2008 Topps Update Gold Foil

*GLD FOIL VET: 1.2X TO 3X BASIC
*GLD FOIL RC: .4X TO 1X BASIC RC
STATED ODDS 1:2 HOBBY
UH240 Clayton Kershaw 50.00 120.00

2008 Topps Update 1957 Mickey Mantle Reprint Relic

STATED ODDS 17,982 HOBBY
STATED PRINT RUN 57 SER.#'d SETS
MMR57 Mickey Mantle Uni/57 60.00 120.00

2008 Topps Update 2008 Presidential Picks

STATED ODDS 1:15,984 HOBBY
STATED PRINT RUN 100 SER.#'d SETS
BO Barack Obama EXCH 150.00 250.00
JM John McCain EXCH 40.00 80.00
OPBO Barack Obama Patch/100

2008 Topps Update All-Star Stitches

STATED ODDS 1:44 HOBBY
AC Aaron Cook 3.00 8.00
AER Alex Rodriguez 6.00 15.00
AG Adrian Gonzalez 3.00 8.00
AP Albert Pujols 6.00 15.00
AR Aramis Ramirez 3.00 8.00
AS Alfonso Soriano 3.00 8.00
BL Brad Lidge 5.00 12.00
BM Brian McCann 4.00 10.00
BS Ben Sheets 3.00 8.00
BTW Brandon Webb 3.00 8.00
CAG Carlos Guillen 3.00 8.00
CG Cristian Guzman 3.00 8.00
CH Corey Hart 3.00 8.00
CJ Chipper Jones 4.00 10.00
CL Cliff Lee 4.00 10.00
CM Carlos Marmol 3.00 8.00
CQ Carlos Quentin 3.00 8.00
CU Chase Utley 4.00 10.00
CZ Carlos Zambrano 4.00 10.00
DH Dan Haren 3.00 8.00
DN Dioner Navarro 4.00 10.00
DO David Ortiz 4.00 10.00
DP Dustin Pedroia 5.00 12.00
DU Dan Uggla 3.00 8.00
DW David Wright 5.00 12.00
EL Evan Longoria 12.50 30.00
ES Ervin Santana 3.00 8.00
EV Edinson Volquez 3.00 8.00
FR Francisco Rodriguez 4.00 10.00
GFS George Sherrill 3.00 8.00
GPS Geovany Soto 5.00 12.00
GS Grady Sizemore 4.00 10.00
HR Hanley Ramirez 3.00 8.00
IK Ian Kinsler 3.00 8.00
IS Ichiro Suzuki 8.00 20.00
JC Joe Crede 3.00 8.00
JCD Justin Duchscherer 4.00 10.00
JD J.D. Drew 4.00 10.00
JEM Justin Morneau 4.00 10.00
JH Josh Hamilton 8.00 20.00
JM Joe Mauer 4.00 10.00
JN Joe Nathan 3.00 8.00
JP Jonathan Papelbon 4.00 10.00
JS Joakim Soria 3.00 8.00
JV Jason Varitek 4.00 10.00
KF Kosuke Fukudome 10.00 25.00
KW Kerry Wood 3.00 8.00
KY Kevin Youkilis 3.00 8.00
LB Lance Berkman 4.00 10.00
MB Milton Bradley 3.00 8.00
MH Matt Holliday 3.00 8.00
MR Manny Ramirez 4.00 10.00
MSR Mariano Rivera 4.00 10.00
MT Miguel Tejada 3.00 8.00
MY Michael Young 3.00 8.00
NM Nate McLouth 5.00 12.00
RB Ryan Braun 4.00 10.00
RD Ryan Dempster 3.00 8.00
RH Roy Halladay 3.00 8.00
RL Ryan Ludwick 5.00 12.00
RM Russ Martin 3.00 8.00
SK Scott Kazmir 3.00 8.00
TL Tim Lincecum 12.50 30.00
WW Billy Wagner 3.00 8.00

2008 Topps Update All-Star Stitches Gold

*GOLD: .75X TO 2X BASIC
STATED ODDS 1:373 HOBBY
STATED PRINT RUN 50 SER.#'d SETS
AER Alex Rodriguez 30.00 60.00
EL Evan Longoria 20.00 50.00
IS Ichiro Suzuki 20.00 50.00
KY Kevin Youkilis 30.00 60.00

2008 Topps Update All-Star Stitches Autographs

STATED ODDS 1:6394 HOBBY
STATED PRINT RUN 25 SER.#'d SETS
CJ Chipper Jones 100.00 200.00
DP Dustin Pedroia 75.00 150.00
DU Dan Uggla 10.00 25.00
EV Edinson Volquez 30.00 60.00
HR Hanley Ramirez 30.00 60.00
JH Josh Hamilton 60.00 120.00
JV Jason Varitek 50.00 100.00
RB Ryan Braun 40.00 80.00
RM Russ Martin 20.00 50.00
TL Tim Lincecum 100.00 200.00

2008 Topps Update All-Star Stitches Dual

STATED ODDS 1:5994
STATED PRINT RUN 25 SER.#'d SETS
NO PRICING ON FEW DUE TO SCARCITY
FL K.Fukudome/I.Suzuki 40.00 80.00
HB J.Hamilton/R.Braun 30.00 60.00
LS C.Lee/B.Sheets 10.00 25.00
IV T.Lincecum/E.Volquez 12.50 30.00
RR M.Rivera/F.Rodriguez 30.00 60.00
RT H.Ramirez/M.Tejada 8.00 20.00
UU C.Utley/D.Uggla 20.00 50.00

2008 Topps Update All-Star Stitches Triple

STATED ODDS 1:5994 HOBBY
STATED PRINT RUN 25 SER.#'d SETS
NO PRICING ON FEW DUE TO SCARCITY
HFB Holliday/Fukudome/Braun 20.00 50.00
HRS Hamilton/Manny/Ichiro 30.00 60.00
KHY Kinsler/Bradley/Young 8.00 20.00
MNM Martin/Navarro/McCann 40.00 80.00
PDY Pedroia/Drew/Ortiz 20.00 50.00
PGB Pujols/Gonzalez/Berkman 30.00 60.00
RSS KRod/E.Santana/Saunders 50.00 100.00
RWJ ARod/Wright/Chipper 40.00 80.00
WLW Wood/Lidge/Wagner 20.00 50.00
ZSD Zambrano/Aramis/Dempster 50.00 100.00

2008 Topps Update Chrome

ONE PER BOX TOPPER
CHR1 Jay Bruce 6.00 15.00
CHR2 Dan Giese 2.00 5.00
CHR3 Brandon Boggs 3.00 8.00
CHR4 Jed Lowrie 2.00 5.00
CHR5 Matt Joyce 5.00 12.00
CHR6 Nick Adenhart 2.00 5.00
CHR7 Jose Arredondo 3.00 8.00
CHR8 Michael Aubrey 3.00 8.00
CHR9 Josh Banks 2.00 5.00
CHR10 Armando Galarraga 3.00 8.00
CHR11 Mike Aviles 3.00 8.00
CHR12 Burke Badenhop 3.00 8.00
CHR13 Reid Brignac 3.00 8.00
CHR14 Emmanuel Burriss 3.00 8.00
CHR15 Greg Reynolds 3.00 8.00
CHR16 Chris Volstad 2.00 5.00
CHR17 Brian Bixler 2.00 5.00
CHR18 Chris Carter 3.00 8.00
CHR19 Travis Denker 3.00 8.00
CHR20 Alberto Gonzalez 3.00 8.00
CHR21 Robinzon Diaz 2.00 5.00
CHR22 Brett Gardner 5.00 12.00
CHR23 Micah Hoffpauir 6.00 15.00
CHR24 Hernan Iribarren 3.00 8.00
CHR25 Greg Smith 2.00 5.00
CHR26 German Duran 3.00 8.00
CHR27 Kosuke Fukudome 6.00 15.00
CHR28 Ryan Tucker 2.00 5.00
CHR29 Paul Janish 2.00 5.00
CHR30 Clayton Kershaw 400.00 900.00
CHR31 Chris Davis 4.00 10.00
CHR32 Joe Mather 3.00 8.00
CHR33 Nick Hundley 2.00 5.00
CHR34 Brian Horwitz 2.00 5.00
CHR35 Carlos Gonzalez 5.00 12.00
CHR36 Matt Macri 2.00 5.00
CHR37 Gregorio Petit 3.00 8.00
CHR38 Chris Perez 3.00 8.00
CHR39 Alex Hinshaw 3.00 8.00
CHR40 Max Scherzer 150.00 400.00
CHR41 Jonathan Van Every 2.00 5.00
CHR42 Jonathan Herrera 3.00 8.00
CHR43 Cory Wade 2.00 5.00
CHR44 Max Ramirez 2.00 5.00
CHR45 John Bowker 2.00 5.00
CHR46 Sean Rodriguez 2.00 5.00
CHR47 Jeff Niemann 2.00 5.00
CHR48 Taylor Teagarden 3.00 8.00
CHR49 Mark Worrell 2.00 5.00
CHR50 Evan Longoria 10.00 25.00
CHR51 Chris Smith 2.00 5.00
CHR52 Brent Lillibridge 2.00 5.00
CHR53 Colt Morton 3.00 8.00
CHR54 Eric Hurley 2.00 5.00
CHR55 Justin Masterson 5.00 12.00

2008 Topps Update First Couples

COMPLETE SET (41) 15.00 40.00
STATED ODDS 1:6 HOBBY
FC1 G.Washington/M.Washington .75 2.00
FC2 John Adams/Abagail Adams .60 1.50
FC3 Thomas Jefferson/Martha Jefferson.60 1.50
FC4 James Madison/Dolley Madison .40 1.00
FC5 James Monroe
Elizabeth Kotright Monroe .40 1.00
FC6 John Quincy Adams
Louisa Catherine Adams .40 1.00
FC7 Andrew Jackson/Rachel Jackson .40 1.00
FC8 Martin Van Buren
Hannah Van Buren .40 1.00
FC9 William Henry Harrison
Anna Harrison .40 1.00
FC10 John Tyler/Julia Tyler .40 1.00
FC11 James K. Polk /Sarah Polk .40 1.00
FC12 Zachary Taylor/Margaret Taylor .40 1.00
FC13 Millard Fillmore/Abigail Fillmore.40 1.00
FC14 Franklin Pierce/Jane M. Pierce .40 1.00
FC15 A.Lincoln/M.Lincoln .75 2.00
FC16 Andrew Johnson/Eliza Johnson .40 1.00
FC17 Ulysses S. Grant/Julia Grant .40 1.00
FC18 Rutherford B. Hayes/ Lucy Hayes.40 1.00
FC19 James A. Garfield/Lucretia Garfield.40 1.00
FC20 Chester A. Arthur/Ellen Arthur .40 1.00
FC21 Grover Cleveland
Frances Cleveland .40 1.00
FC22 Benjamin Harrison
Caroline Harrison .40 1.00
FC23 William McKinley/Ida McKinley .40 1.00
FC24 Theodore Roosevelt
Edith Roosevelt .60 1.50
FC25 William H. Taft/Helen Taft .40 1.00
FC26 Woodrow Wilson/Edith Wilson .40 1.00
FC27 Warren G. Harding
Florence Harding .40 1.00
FC28 Calvin Coolidge/Grace Coolidge.40 1.00
FC29 Herbert Hoover/Lou Hoover .40 1.00
FC30 Franklin D. Roosevelt
Eleanor Roosevelt .60 1.50
FC31 Harry S. Truman /Bess Truman .40 1.00
FC32 Dwight D. Eisenhower
Mamie Eisenhower .60 1.50
FC33 J.Kennedy/J.Kennedy 1.00 2.50
FC34 Lyndon B. Johnson
Lady Bird Johnson .60 1.50
FC35 Richard M. Nixon /Pat Nixon .60 1.50
FC36 Gerald R. Ford /Betty Ford .60 1.50
FC37 Jimmy Carter /Rosalynn Carter .60 1.50
FC38 R.Reagan /N.Reagan 1.00 2.50
FC39 George Bush /Barbara Bush .60 1.50
FC40 B.Clinton /H.Clinton .75 2.00
FC41 G.Bush /L.Bush .75 2.00

2008 Topps Update Ring of Honor 1986 New York Mets

COMPLETE SET (10) 5.00 12.00
STATED ODDS 1:18 HOBBY
GOLD ODDS 1:11,743 HOBBY
GOLD PRINT RUN 25 SER.#'d SETS
NO GOLD PRICING AVAILABLE
DG Dwight Gooden .60 1.50
DJ Davey Johnson .60 1.50
DS Darryl Strawberry .60 1.50
GC Gary Carter 1.00 2.50
HJ Howard Johnson .60 1.50
JO Jesse Orosco .60 1.50
KH Keith Hernandez .60 1.50
KM Kevin Mitchell .60 1.50
RD Ron Darling .60 1.50
RK Ray Knight .60 1.50

2008 Topps Update Ring of Honor 1986 New York Mets Autographs

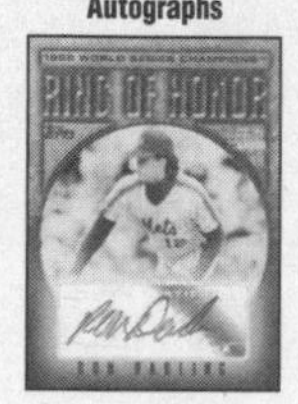

STATED ODDS 1:2849 HOBBY
DG Dwight Gooden 30.00 60.00
DJ Davey Johnson 10.00 25.00
DS Darryl Strawberry 15.00 40.00
GC Gary Carter 20.00 50.00
HJ Howard Johnson 12.50 30.00
JO Jesse Orosco 15.00 40.00
KH Keith Hernandez 10.00 25.00
KM Kevin Mitchell 10.00 25.00
RD Ron Darling 10.00 25.00
RK Ray Knight 12.50 30.00

2008 Topps Update Ring of Honor World Series Champions

COMPLETE SET (10) 5.00 12.00
STATED ODDS 1:18 HOBBY
GOLD ODDS 1:11,743 HOBBY
GOLD PRINT RUN 25 SER.#'d SETS
NO GOLD PRICING AVAILABLE
BS Bruce Sutter 1.00 2.50
DC David Cone COR .60 1.50
DC1 David Cone UER .60 1.50
DJ David Justice .60 1.50
DS Duke Snider 1.00 2.50
JP Johnny Podres .60 1.50
LA Luis Aparicio 1.00 2.50
MI Monte Irvin 1.00 2.50
ML Mike Lowell .60 1.50
OC Orlando Cepeda 1.00 2.50
RK Ray Knight .60 1.50
WF Whitey Ford 1.00 2.50

2008 Topps Update Ring of Honor World Series Champions Autographs

STATED ODDS 1:2569 HOBBY
BS Bruce Sutter 15.00 40.00
DC David Cone 30.00 60.00
DJ David Justice 15.00 40.00
DS Duke Snider 15.00 40.00
JP Johnny Podres 15.00 40.00
LA Luis Aparició 15.00 40.00
MI Monte Irvin 50.00 100.00
ML-Mike Lowell 20.00 50.00
OC Orlando Cepeda 30.00 60.00
WF Whitey Ford 30.00 60.00

2008 Topps Update Take Me Out To The Ballgame

STATED ODDS 1:72 HOBBY
BG 100th Anniversary .75 2.00

2008 Topps Update World Baseball Classic Preview

COMPLETE SET (25) 8.00 20.00
STATED ODDS 1:9 HOBBY
WBC1 Daisuke Matsuzaka .40 1.00
WBC2 Alexei Ramirez .75 2.00
WBC3 Derrek Lee .25 .60
WBC4 Akinori Iwamura .25 .60
WBC5 Chase Utley .40 1.00
WBC6 Jose Reyes .40 1.00
WBC7 Jake Peavy .25 .60
WBC8 Justin Huber .25 .60
WBC9 Justin Morneau .40 1.00
WBC10 Ichiro Suzuki .75 2.00
WBC11 Adrian Gonzalez .40 1.00
WBC12 Carlos Zambrano .40 1.00
WBC13 Miguel Cabrera .60 1.50
WBC14 Carlos Beltran .40 1.00
WBC15 Albert Pujols .75 2.00
WBC16 Paul Bell .25 .60
WBC17 Frank Catalanotto .25 .60
WBC18 Jason Varitek .60 1.50
WBC19 Andruw Jones .25 .60
WBC20 Johan Santana .40 1.00
WBC21 Carlos Lee .25 .60
WBC22 David Ortiz .60 1.50
WBC23 Francisco Rodriguez .40 1.00
WBC24 Chin-Lung Hu .25 .60
WBC25 Kosuke Fukudome .75 2.00

2009 Topps

This set was released on February 4, 2009. The base set consists of 349 cards.
COMP.HOBBY SET (660) 40.00 80.00
COMP.HOLIDAY SET (660) 40.00 80.00
COMP.ALLSTAR.SET (660) 40.00 80.00
COMP.CUBS SET (660) 40.00 80.00
COMP.METS SET (660) 40.00 80.00
COMP.RED SOX SET (660) 40.00 80.00
COMP.YANKEES SET (660) 40.00 80.00
COMP.SET w/o SP's (660) 40.00 80.00
COMP.SER.1 SET w/o SP's (330) 15.00 40.00
COMP.SER.2 SET w/o SP's (330) 15.00 40.00
COMMON CARD (1-696) .15 .40
SER.1 SP VAR ODDS 1:95 HOBBY
SER.2 SP VAR ODDS 1:82 HOBBY
COMMON RC (1-696) .30 .75
SER.1 PLATE ODDS 1:925 HOBBY
SER.2 PLATE ODDS 1:1056 HOBBY
PLATE PRINT RUN 1 SET PER COLOR
BLACK-CYAN-MAGENTA-YELLOW ISSUED
NO PLATE PRICING DUE TO SCARCITY
1a Alex Rodriguez .50 1.25
1b Babe Ruth SP 10.00 25.00
2a Omar Vizquel .25 .60
2b Pee Wee Reese SP 6.00 15.00
3 Andy Marte .15 .40
4 Chipper/Pujols/Holliday LL .50 1.25
5 John Lackey .25 .60
6 Raul Ibanez .25 .60
7 Mickey Mantle 1.25 3.00
8 Terry Francona MG .25 .60
9 Dallas McPherson .15 .40
10a Dan Uggla .15 .40
10b Rogers Hornsby SP 6.00 15.00
11 Fernando Tatis .15 .40
12 Andrew Carpenter RC .50 1.25
13 Ryan Langerhans .15 .40
14 Jon Rauch .15 .40
15 Nate McLouth .15 .40
16 Evan Longoria HL .25 .60
17 Bobby Cox MG .15 .40
18 George Sherrill .15 .40
19 Edgar Gonzalez .15 .40
20 Brad Lidge .15 .40
21 Jack Wilson .15 .40
22 E.Longoria/D.Price CC .30 .75
23 Gerald Laird .15 .40
24 Frank Thomas .40 1.00
25 Jon Lester .25 .60
26 Jason Giambi .15 .40
27 Jonathon Niese RC .50 1.25
28 Mike Lowell .15 .40
29 Jerry Hairston .15 .40
30a Ken Griffey Jr. .75 2.00
30b Jackie Robinson SP 8.00 20.00
31 Ian Stewart .15 .40
32 Daric Barton .15 .40
33 Jose Guillen .15 .40
34 Brandon Inge .15 .40
35 David Price RC .60 1.50
36 Kevin Slowey .25 .60
37 Erick Aybar .15 .40
38 Eric Wedge MG .15 .40
39 Stephen Drew .15 .40
40 Carl Crawford .25 .60
41 Mike Mussina .25 .60
42 Jeff Francoeur .25 .60
43 Mauer/Ped/Brad LL .30 .75
44a Geoff Jenkins .15 .40
44b Barack Obama SP 6.00 15.00
45 Aubrey Huff .15 .40
46 Brad Ziegler .15 .40
47 Jose Valverde .15 .40
48 Mike Napoli .15 .40
49 Kazuo Matsui .15 .40
50 David Ortiz .40 1.00
51 Will Venable RC .30 .75
52 Marco Scutaro .25 .60
53 Jonathan Sanchez .15 .40
54 Dusty Baker MG .15 .40
55 J.J. Hardy .15 .40
56 Edwin Encarnacion .40 1.00
57 Jo-Jo Reyes .15 .40
58 Travis Snider RC .50 1.25
59 Eric Gagne .15 .40
60a Mariano Rivera .50 1.25
60b Cy Young SP 5.00 12.00
61 Lance Berkman/Carlos Lee CC .25 .60
62 Brian Barton .15 .40
63 Josh Outman RC .50 1.25
64 Miguel Montero .15 .40
65 Mike Pelfrey .15 .40
66a Dustin Pedroia .30 .75
66b Ty Cobb SP 12.50 30.00
67 Andruw Jones .15 .40
68 Kyle Lohse .15 .40
69 Rich Aurilia .15 .40
70 Jermaine Dye .15 .40
71 Mat Gamel RC .75 2.00
72 David Dellucci .15 .40
73 Shane Victorino .15 .40
74 Trey Hillman MG .15 .40
75 Rich Harden .15 .40
76 Marcus Thames .15 .40
77 Jed Lowrie .15 .40
78 Tim Lincecum .25 .60
79 David Eckstein .15 .40
80 Brian McCann .25 .60
81 Howard/Dunn/Delgado LL .30 .75
82 Miguel Cairo .15 .40
83 Ryan Garko .15 .40
84 Rod Barajas .15 .40
85 Justin Verlander .40 1.00
86 Kila Kaaihue (RC) .50 1.25
87 Brad Hawpe .15 .40
88 Fredi Gonzalez MG .15 .40
89 Jon Lester .25 .60
Jason Bay HL
90 Justin Morneau .25 .60
91 Cody Ross .15 .40
92 Luis Castillo .15 .40
93 James Parr (RC) .30 .75
94 Adam Lind .15 .40
95 Andrew Miller .25 .60
96 Dexter Fowler (RC) .50 1.25
97 Willie Harris .15 .40
98 Akinori Iwamura .15 .40
99 Juan Castro .15 .40
100 David Wright .30 .75
101 Nick Hundley .15 .40
102 Garrett Atkins .15 .40
103 Kyle Kendrick .15 .40
104 Brandon Moss .15 .40
105 Francisco Liriano .15 .40
106 Marlon Byrd .15 .40
107 Pedro Feliz .15 .40
108 Alcides Escobar RC .50 1.25
109 Tom Gorzelanny .15 .40
110 Hideki Matsui .40 1.00
111 Troy Percival .15 .40
112 Hideki Okajima .15 .40
113 Chris Young .15 .40
114 Chris Dickerson .15 .40
115a Kevin Youkilis .15 .40
115b George Sisler SP 8.00 20.00
116 Omar Infante .15 .40
117 Ron Gardenhire MG .15 .40
118 Josh Johnson .25 .60
119 Craig Counsell .15 .40
120 Mark Teixeira .25 .60
121 Greg Golson (RC) .30 .75
122 Joe Mather .15 .40
123 Casey Blake .15 .40
124 Reed Johnson .15 .40
125 Roy Oswalt .25 .60
126 Orlando Hudson .15 .40
127 M.Cabrera/Quentin/ARod LL .50 1.25
128 Johnny Cueto .25 .60
129 Angel Berroa .15 .40
130 Vladimir Guerrero .25 .60
131 Joe Torre MG .25 .60
132 Juan Pierre .15 .40
133 Brandon Jones .15 .40
134 Evan Longoria .25 .60
135 Carlos Delgado .15 .40
136 Tim Hudson .25 .60
137 Angel Salome (RC) .30 .75
138 Ubaldo Jimenez .15 .40
139 Matt Stairs HL .15 .40
140 Brandon Webb .25 .60
141 Mark Teahen .15 .40
142 Brad Penny .15 .40
143 Matt Joyce .15 .40
144 Matt Tuiasosopo (RC) .30 .75
145 Alex Gordon .25 .60
146 Glen Perkins .15 .40
147 Howard/Wright/A.Gonzalez LL .30 .75
148 Ty Wigginton .25 .60
149 Juan Uribe .15 .40
150 Kosuke Fukudome .25 .60
151 Carl Pavano .15 .40
152 Cody Ransom .15 .40
153 Lastings Milledge .15 .40
154 A.J. Pierzynski .15 .40
155 Roy Halladay .25 .60
156 Carlos Pena .25 .60
157 Brandon Webb/Dan Haren CC .25 .60
158 Ray Durham .15 .40
159 Matt Antonelli RC .50 1.25
160 Evan Longoria .25 .60
161 Brendan Harris .15 .40
162 Mike Cameron .15 .40
163 Ross Gload .15 .40
164 Bob Geren MG .15 .40
165 Matt Kemp .30 .75
166 Jeff Baker .15 .40
167 Aaron Harang .15 .40
168 Mark DeRosa .25 .60
169 Juan Miranda RC .50 1.25
170a CC Sabathia .25 .60
170b Sabathia Yanks SP 5.00 12.00
171 Jeff Bailey .15 .40
172 Yadier Molina .40 1.00
173 Manny Delcarmen .15 .40
174 James Shields .15 .40
175 Jeff Samardzija .25 .60
176 Ham/Morneau/Cabrera .40 1.00
177 Eric Hinske .15 .40
178 Frank Catalanotto .15 .40
179 Rafael Furcal .15 .40
180 Cliff Lee .25 .60
181 Jerry Manuel MG .15 .40
182 Daniel Murphy RC 1.25 3.00
183 Jason Michaels .15 .40
184 Bobby Parnell RC .50 1.25
185 Randy Johnson .40 1.00
186 Ryan Madson .15 .40
187 Jon Garland .15 .40
188 Josh Bard .15 .40
189 Jay Payton .15 .40
190 Chien-Ming Wang .25 .60
191 Shane Victorino HL .15 .40
192 Collin Balester .15 .40
193 Zack Greinke .25 .60
194 Jeremy Guthrie .15 .40
195a Tim Lincecum .25 .60
195b Christy Mathewson SP 8.00 20.00
196 Jason Motte (RC) .50 1.25
197 Ronnie Belliard .15 .40
198 Conor Jackson .15 .40
199 Ramon Castro .15 .40
200a Chase Utley .25 .60
200b Jimmie Foxx SP 6.00 15.00
201 Jarrod Saltalamacchia
Josh Hamilton CC .25 .60
202 Gaby Sanchez RC .50 1.25
203 Jair Jurrjens .15 .40
204 Andy Sonnanstine .15 .40
205a Miguel Tejada .25 .60
205b Honus Wagner SP 8.00 20.00
206 Santana/Lince/Peavy LL .25 .60
207 Joe Blanton .15 .40
208 James McDonald RC .75 2.00
209 Alfredo Amezaga .15 .40
210a Geovany Soto .25 .60
210b Roy Campanella SP 10.00 25.00
211 Ryan Rowland-Smith .15 .40
212 Denard Span .15 .40
213 Jeremy Sowers .15 .40
214 Scott Elbert (RC) .30 .75
215 Ian Kinsler .25 .60
216 Joe Maddon MG .15 .40
217 Albert Pujols .50 1.25
218 Emmanuel Burriss .15 .40
219 Shin-Soo Choo .25 .60
220 Jay Bruce .25 .60
221 C.Lee/Halladay/Matsuzaka LL .25 .60
222 Mark Sweeney .15 .40
223 Dave Roberts .25 .60
224 Max Scherzer .40 1.00
225 Aaron Cook .15 .40
226 Neal Cotts .15 .40
227 Freddy Sandoval (RC) .30 .75
228 Scott Rolen .25 .60
229 Cesar Izturis .15 .40
230 Justin Upton .25 .60
231 Xavier Nady .15 .40
232 Gabe Kapler .15 .40
233 Erik Bedard .15 .40
234 John Russell MG .15 .40
235 Chad Billingsley .25 .60
236 Kelly Johnson .15 .40
237 Aaron Cunningham RC .30 .75
238 Jorge Cantu .15 .40
239 Brandon League .15 .40
240a Ryan Braun .25 .60
240b Mel Ott SP 8.00 20.00
241 David Newhan .15 .40
242 Ricky Nolasco .15 .40
243 Chase Headley .15 .40
244 Sean Rodriguez .15 .40
245 Pat Burrell .15 .40
246 B.Upton/Crawford/Longoria HL .25 .60
247 Yuniesky Betancourt .15 .40
248 Scott Lewis (RC) .30 .75
249 Jack Hannahan .15 .40
250 Josh Hamilton .25 .60
251 Greg Smith .15 .40
252 Brandon Wood .15 .40
253 Edgar Renteria .15 .40
254 Cito Gaston MG .15 .40
255 Joe Crede .25 .60
256 Reggie Abercrombie .15 .40
257 George Kottaras (RC) .30 .75
258 Casey Kotchman .15 .40
259 Lince/Haren/Santana LL .25 .60
260 Manny Ramirez .40 1.00
261 Jose Bautista .25 .60
262 Mike Gonzalez .15 .40
263 Elijah Dukes .15 .40
264 Dave Bush .15 .40
265 Carlos Zambrano .25 .60
266 Todd Wellemeyer .15 .40
267 Michael Bowden (RC) .30 .75
268 Chris Burke .15 .40
269 Hunter Pence .25 .60
270a Grady Sizemore .25 .60
270b Tris Speaker SP 8.00 20.00
271 Cliff Lee .25 .60
272 Chan Ho Park .25 .60
273 Brian Roberts .15 .40
274 Alex Hinshaw .15 .40
275 Alex Rios .15 .40
276 Geovany Soto .25 .60
277 Asdrubal Cabrera .25 .60
278 Philadelphia Phillies HL .15 .40
279 Ryan Church .15 .40
280 Joe Saunders .15 .40
281 Tug Hulett .15 .40
282 Chris Lambert (RC) .30 .75
283 John Baker .15 .40
284 Luis Ayala .15 .40
285 Justin Duchscherer .15 .40
286 Odalis Perez .15 .40
287a Greg Maddux .50 1.25
287b Walter Johnson SP 6.00 15.00
288 Guillermo Quiroz .15 .40
289 Josh Banks .15 .40
290a Albert Pujols .50 1.25
290b Lou Gehrig SP 12.50 30.00
291 Chris Coste .15 .40
292 Francisco Cervelli RC .75 2.00
293 Brian Bixler .15 .40
294 Brandon Boggs .15 .40
295 Derrek Lee .15 .40
296 Reid Brignac .15 .40
297 Bud Black MG .15 .40
298 Jonathan Van Every .15 .40
299 Cole Hamels HL .30 .75
300 Ichiro Suzuki .50 1.25
301 Clint Barmes .15 .40
302 Brian Giles .15 .40
303 Zach Duke .15 .40
304 Jason Kubel .15 .40
305a Ivan Rodriguez .25 .60
305b Thurman Munson SP 6.00 15.00
306 Javier Vazquez .15 .40
307 A.J. Burnett/Ervin Santana
Roy Halladay LL .25 .60
308 Chris Duncan .15 .40
309 Humberto Sanchez (RC) .30 .75
310 Johan Santana .25 .60
311 Kelly Shoppach .15 .40
312 Ryan Sweeney .15 .40
313 Jamey Carroll .15 .40
314 Matt Treanor .15 .40
315 Hiroki Kuroda .15 .40
316 Brian Stokes .15 .40
317 Jarrod Saltalamacchia .15 .40
318 Manny Acta MG .15 .40
319 Brian Fuentes .15 .40
320a Miguel Cabrera .40 1.00
320b Johnny Mize SP 8.00 20.00
321 S.Kazmir/D.Price CC .30 .75
322 John Buck .15 .40
323 Vicente Padilla .15 .40
324 Mark Reynolds .15 .40
325 Dustin McGowan .15 .40
326 Manny Ramirez HL .40 1.00
327 Phil Coke RC .50 1.25
328 Doug Mientkiewicz .15 .40
329 Gil Meche .15 .40
330 Daisuke Matsuzaka .25 .60
331 Luke Scott .15 .40
332 Chone Figgins .15 .40
333 Jeremy Sowers/Aaron Laffey .15 .40
334 Blake DeWitt .15 .40
335 Chris Young .15 .40
336 Jordan Schafer (RC) .50 1.25
337 Bobby Jenks .15 .40
338 Daniel Cabrera .15 .40
339 Jim Leyland MG .15 .40
340a Joe Mauer .30 .75
340b Wade Boggs SP 10.00 25.00
341 Willy Taveras .15 .40
342 Gerald Laird .15 .40
343 Ian Snell .15 .40
344 J.R. Towles .15 .40
345 Stephen Drew .15 .40
346 Mike Cameron .15 .40
347 Jason Bartlett .15 .40
348 Tony Pena .15 .40
349 Justin Masterson .15 .40
350a Dustin Pedroia .30 .75
350b Ryne Sandberg SP 10.00 25.00
351 Chris Snyder .15 .40
352 Gregor Blanco .15 .40
353a Derek Jeter 1.00 2.50
353b Cal Ripken Jr. SP 6.00 15.00
354 Mike Aviles .15 .40
355a John Smoltz .40 1.00
355b Jim Palmer SP 5.00 12.00
356 Ervin Santana .15 .40
357 Huston Street .15 .40
358 Chad Tracy .15 .40
359 Jason Varitek .40 1.00
360 Jorge Posada .25 .60
361 Alex Rios/Vernon Wells .15 .40
362 Luke Montz RC .30 .75
363 Jhonny Peralta .15 .40
364 Kevin Millwood .15 .40
365 Mark Buehrle .25 .60
366 Alexi Casilla .15 .40
367 Bobby Abreu .15 .40
368 Trevor Hoffman .25 .60
369 Matt Harrison .15 .40
370 Victor Martinez .25 .60
371 Jeff Francis .15 .40
372 Rickie Weeks .15 .40
373 Joe Martinez RC .50 1.25
374 Kevin Kouzmanoff .15 .40
375 Carlos Quentin .15 .40
376 Rajai Davis .15 .40
377 Trevor Crowe RC .30 .75
378 Mark Hendrickson .15 .40
379 Howie Kendrick .15 .40
380 Aramis Ramirez .15 .40
381 Sharon Martis RC .50 1.25
382 Wily Mo Pena .15 .40
383 Everth Cabrera RC .50 1.25
384 Bob Melvin MG .15 .40
385 Mike Jacobs .15 .40
386 Jonathan Papelbon .25 .60
387 Adam Everett .15 .40
388 Humberto Quintero .15 .40
389 Garrett Olson .15 .40
390 Joey Votto .40 1.00
391 Dan Haren .15 .40
392 Brandon Phillips .15 .40

393 Alex Cintron .15 .40
394 Barry Zito .25 .60
395 Magglio Ordonez .25 .60
396 Alex Cora .25 .60
397 Carlos Ruiz .15 .40
398 Cameron Maybin .15 .40
399 Wandy Rodriguez .15 .40
400a Alfonso Soriano .25 .60
400b Frank Robinson SP 6.00 15.00
401 Tony La Russa MG .25 .60
402 Nick Blackburn .15 .40
403 Trevor Cahill RC .75 2.00
404 Matt Capps .15 .40
405 Todd Helton .25 .60
406 Mark Ellis .15 .40
407 Dave Trembley MG .15 .40
408 Ronny Paulino .15 .40
409 Jesse Chavez RC .30 .75
410 Lou Piniella MG .15 .40
411 Troy Tulowitzki .40 1.00
412 Taylor Teagarden .15 .40
413 Ruben Gotay .15 .40
414 Cha Seung Baek .15 .40
415a Josh Beckett .15 .40
415b Bob Gibson SP 10.00 25.00
416 Josh Whitesell RC .50 1.25
417 Jason Marquis .15 .40
418 Andy Pettitte .25 .60
419 Braden Looper .15 .40
420 Scott Baker .15 .40
421 B.J. Ryan .15 .40
422 Hank Blalock .15 .40
423 Melvin Mora .15 .40
424 Jorge Campillo .15 .40
425 Curtis Granderson .30 .75
426 Pablo Sandoval .30 .75
427 Brian Duensing RC .50 1.25
428 Jamie Moyer .15 .40
429 Mike Hampton .15 .40
430 Francisco Rodriguez .25 .60
431 Ramon Hernandez .15 .40
432 Wladimir Balentien .15 .40
433 Coco Crisp .15 .40
434 C.Guillen/M.Cabrera .40 1.00
435 Carlos Lee .15 .40
436 Ryan Theriot .15 .40
437 Austin Kearns .15 .40
438 Mark Loretta .15 .40
439 Ryan Spilborghs .15 .40
440 Fausto Carmona .15 .40
441 Andrew Bailey RC .75 2.00
442 Cliff Pennington .15 .40
443 Gavin Floyd .15 .40
444 Jody Gerut .15 .40
445 Joe Nathan .15 .40
446 Matt Holliday .40 1.00
447 Freddy Sanchez .15 .40
448 Jeff Clement .15 .40
449 Mike Fontenot .15 .40
450 Hanley Ramirez .25 .60
451 Ryan Perry RC .75 2.00
452 Orlando Cabrera .15 .40
453 Javier Valentin .15 .40
454 Carlos Silva .15 .40
455 Adam Jones .25 .60
456 Jason Kendall .15 .40
457 John Maine .15 .40
458 Jeremy Bonderman .15 .40
459 Brian Bannister .15 .40
460 Nick Markakis .30 .75
461 Mike Scioscia MG .15 .40
462 James Loney .15 .40
463 Brian Wilson .40 1.00
464 Bobby Crosby .15 .40
465 Troy Glaus .15 .40
466 Wilson Betemit .15 .40
467 Chris Volstad .15 .40
468 Derek Lowe .15 .40
469 Michael Cuddyer .15 .40
470 Lance Berkman .25 .60
471 Kerry Wood .15 .40
472 Bill Hall .15 .40
473 Jered Weaver .25 .60
474 Franklin Gutierrez .15 .40
475a Chipper Jones .40 1.00
475b Mike Schmidt SP 6.00 15.00
476a Edinson Volquez .15 .40
476b Juan Marichal SP 5.00 12.00
477 Josh Willingham .25 .60
478 Jose Molina .15 .40
479 Brad Nelson (RC) .30 .75
480 Prince Fielder .25 .60
481 Nyjer Morgan .15 .40
482 Jason Jaramillo (RC) .30 .75
483 John Lannan .15 .40
484 Chris Carpenter .25 .60
485 Aaron Rowand .15 .40
486 J.J. Putz .15 .40
487 Travis Hafner .15 .40
488 Ozzie Guillen MG .15 .40
489 Matt Guerrier .15 .40
490a Joba Chamberlain .15 .40
490b Nolan Ryan SP 8.00 20.00
491 Paul Bako .15 .40
492 Andre Ethier .25 .60
493 Ramiro Pena RC .50 1.25
494 Gary Matthews .15 .40
495a Eric Chavez .15 .40
495b Brooks Robinson SP 6.00 15.00
496 Charlie Manuel MG .15 .40
497 Clint Hurdle MG .15 .40
498 Kyle Davies .15 .40
499 Edwin Moreno (RC) .30 .75
500 Ryan Howard .30 .75
501 Jeff Suppan .15 .40
502 Yovani Gallardo .15 .40
503 Carlos Gonzalez .25 .60
504 Felix Pie .15 .40
505 Scott Olsen .15 .40
506 Paul Konerko .25 .60
507 Melky Cabrera .15 .40
508 Kenji Johjima .25 .60
509 Lou Montanez .15 .40
510 Ryan Ludwick .25 .60
511 Chad Qualls .15 .40
512 Steve Pearce .40 1.00
513 Bronson Arroyo .15 .40
514 Nick Hundley .15 .40
515a Gary Sheffield .15 .40
515b Reggie Jackson SP 10.00 25.00
516 Brian Anderson .15 .40
517 Kevin Frandsen .15 .40
518 Chris Perez .15 .40
519 Dioner Navarro .15 .40
520a Adrian Gonzalez .30 .75
520b Tony Gwynn SP 6.00 15.00
521 Dana Eveland .15 .40
522 Gio Gonzalez .25 .60
523 Brandon Morrow .15 .40
524 Andy LaRoche .15 .40
525 Jimmy Rollins .25 .60
526 Bruce Bochy MG .25 .60
527 Jason Isringhausen .15 .40
528 Nick Swisher .25 .60
529 Fernando Rodney .15 .40
530 Felix Hernandez .25 .60
531 Frank Francisco .15 .40
532 Garret Anderson .15 .40
533 Darin Erstad .15 .40
534 Skip Schumaker .15 .40
535 Ryan Doumit .15 .40
536 Khalil Greene .15 .40
537 Anthony Reyes .15 .40
538 Carlos Guillen .15 .40
539 Miguel Olivo .15 .40
540 Russell Martin .15 .40
541 Jason Bay .25 .60
542 Chris Ray .15 .40
543 Travis Ishikawa .15 .40
544 Pat Neshek .25 .60
545 Matt Garza .15 .40
546 Matt Cain .25 .60
547 Jack Cust .15 .40
548 John Danks .15 .40
549 Randy Winn .15 .40
550 Carlos Beltran .25 .60
551 Tim Redding .15 .40
552 Eric Byrnes .15 .40
553 Jeff Karstens .15 .40
554 Adam LaRoche .15 .40
555 Joe Girardi MG .25 .60
556 Brendan Ryan .15 .40
557 Jayson Werth .25 .60
558 Edgar Renteria .15 .40
559 Esteban German .15 .40
560 Adrian Beltre .40 1.00
561 Ryan Freel .15 .40
562 Cecil Cooper MG .15 .40
563 Francisco Cordero .15 .40
564 Jesus Flores .15 .40
565 Jose Lopez .15 .40
566 Dontrelle Willis .15 .40
567 Willy Aybar .15 .40
568 Greg Reynolds .15 .40
569 Ted Lilly .15 .40
570 David DeJesus .15 .40
571 Noah Lowry .15 .40
572 Michael Bourn .15 .40
573 Adam Wainwright .25 .60
574 Nate Schierholtz .15 .40
575 Clayton Kershaw .75 2.00
576 Don Wakamatsu MG .15 .40
577 Jose Contreras .15 .40
578 Adam Kennedy .15 .40
579 Rocco Baldelli .15 .40
580 Scott Kazmir .25 .60
581 David Purcey .15 .40
582 Yunel Escobar .15 .40
583 Brett Anderson RC .50 1.25
584 Ron Washington MG .15 .40
585 Alexei Ramirez .25 .60
586 Nelson Cruz .40 1.00
587 Adam Dunn .25 .60
588 Jorge De La Rosa .15 .40
589 Rickey Romero (RC) .50 1.25
590 Johnny Damon .25 .60
591 Elvis Andrus RC .75 2.00
592 Fred Lewis .15 .40
593 Kenshin Kawakami RC .50 1.25
594 Milton Bradley .15 .40
595a Vernon Wells .15 .40
595b Robin Yount SP 6.00 15.00
596 Radhames Liz .15 .40
597 Randy Wolf .15 .40
598 Micah Owings .15 .40
599 Placido Polanco .15 .40
600a Jake Peavy .15 .40
600b Greg Maddux SP 20.00 50.00
601 Ryan Howard/Jimmy Rollins .30 .75
602 Carlos Gomez .15 .40
603 Jose Reyes .25 .60
604 Gregg Zaun .15 .40
605 Rick Ankiel .15 .40
606 Nick Johnson .15 .40
607 Jarrod Washburn .15 .40
608 Cristian Guzman .15 .40
609 Juan Rivera .15 .40
610a Michael Young .15 .40
610b Paul Molitor SP 10.00 25.00
611 Jeremy Hermida .15 .40
612 Joel Pineiro .15 .40
613 Kendry Morales .15 .40
614 David Murphy .15 .40
615 Robinson Cano .25 .60
616 Koji Uehara RC .75 2.00
617 Shaun Marcum .15 .40
618 Brandon Backe .15 .40
619 Chris Carter .15 .40
620 Ryan Zimmerman .25 .60
621 Oliver Perez .15 .40
622 Kurt Suzuki .15 .40
623 Aaron Hill .15 .40
624 Ben Francisco .15 .40
625 Jim Thome .25 .60
626 Scott Hairston .15 .40
627 Billy Butler .15 .40
628 Justin Upton/Chris Young .15 .40
629 Lyle Overbay .15 .40
630 A.J. Burnett .15 .40
631 Colby Rasmus (RC) .50 1.25
632 Brett Myers .15 .40
633 David Patton RC .50 1.25
634 Chris Davis .25 .60
635 Joakim Soria .15 .40
636 Armando Galarraga .15 .40
637 Donald Veal RC .50 1.25
638 Eugenio Velez .15 .40
639 Corey Hart .15 .40
640 B.J. Upton .25 .60
641 Jesse Litsch .15 .40
642 Ken Macha MG .15 .40
643 David Freese RC 1.00 2.50
644 Alfredo Aceves RC .50 1.25
645 Paul Maholm .15 .40
646 Chris Iannetta .15 .40
647 Manny Parra .15 .40
648 J.D. Drew .15 .40
649 Luke Hochevar .15 .40
650a Cole Hamels .30 .75
650b Steve Carlton SP 10.00 25.00
651 Jake Westbrook .15 .40
652 Doug Davis .15 .40
653 Nick Evans .15 .40
654 Brian Schneider .15 .40
655 Bengie Molina .15 .40
656 Delmon Young .25 .60
657 Aaron Heilman .15 .40
658 Rick Porcello RC 1.00 2.50
659 Torii Hunter .15 .40
660a Jacoby Ellsbury .30 .75
660b Carl Yastrzemski SP 10.00 25.00

2009 Topps Gold Border

*GOLD VET: 2X TO 5X BASIC
*GOLD RC: 1X TO 2.5X BASIC RC
SER.1 ODDS 1:7 HOBBY
SER.2 ODDS 1:5 HOBBY
STATED PRINT RUN 2009 SER.#'d SETS
7 Mickey Mantle 8.00 20.00
658 Rick Porcello 5.00 12.00

2009 Topps Target

*VETS: .5X TO 1.2X BASIC TOPPS CARDS
*RC: .5X TO 1.2X BASIC TOPPS RC CARDS

2009 Topps Target Legends Gold

*GOLD: .6X TO 1.5X BASIC
RANDOM INSERTS IN TARGET PACKS

2009 Topps Wal-Mart Black Border

*VETS: .5X TO 1.2X BASIC TOPPS CARDS
*RC: .5X TO 1.2X BASIC TOPPS RC CARDS

2009 Topps 1952 Autographs

STATED ODDS 1:60,000 HOBBY
NNO Billy Crystal 100.00 175.00

2009 Topps Career Best Autographs

GROUP A1 ODDS 1:6708 HOBBY
GROUP A2 ODDS 1:3140 HOBBY
GROUP B1 ODDS 1:416 HOBBY
GROUP B2 ODDS 1:613 HOBBY
UPDATE ODDS 1:352 HOBBY
MOST GROUP A PRICING NOT AVAILABLE
AE Andre Ethier UPD 6.00 15.00
AG Armando Galarraga B1 3.00 8.00
AI Akinori Iwamura B1 5.00 12.00
AI Akinori Iwamura B2 5.00 12.00
AJ Andruw Jones UPD 5.00 12.00
AK Austin Kearns B2 3.00 8.00
AMS Andy Sonnanstine A2 3.00 8.00
AR Alex Rodriguez A2 75.00 150.00
AR Aramis Ramirez A1 6.00 15.00
ASO Alfonso Soriano A2 10.00 25.00
BD Blake DeWitt B2 3.00 8.00
BM Brandon Moss A2 3.00 8.00
BZ Ben Zobrist UPD 10.00 25.00
CD Chris Dickerson B2 3.00 8.00
CF Chone Figgins A2 3.00 8.00
CG Carlos Gomez B2 6.00 15.00
CG Curtis Granderson B1 6.00 15.00
CK Clayton Kershaw A1 20.00 50.00
CK Clayton Kershaw B2 20.00 50.00
CV Chris Volstad B2 3.00 8.00
CW C.J. Wilson B1 4.00 10.00
DM Dallas McPherson B1 3.00 8.00
DMM Dustin McGowan B1 3.00 8.00
DO David Ortiz A1 20.00 50.00
DP David Price A2 20.00 50.00
EK Eddie Kunz B1 3.00 8.00
EL Evan Longoria A2 10.00 25.00
FC Fausto Carmona B2 3.00 8.00
FH Felix Hernandez A2 12.00 30.00
FL Fred Lewis B2 3.00 8.00
GA Garrett Atkins B1 3.00 8.00
GS Greg Smith B1 3.00 8.00
GS Gary Sheffield UPD 10.00 25.00
GTS Greg Smith B2 3.00 8.00
HB Heath Bell UPD 3.00 8.00
HR Hanley Ramirez A1 12.00 30.00
IR Ivan Rodriguez UPD 12.00 30.00
JB Jay Bruce A1 20.00 50.00
JB Jeff Baker B2 3.00 8.00
JCH Joba Chamberlain A2 15.00 40.00
JD Johnny Damon A2 30.00 60.00
JG Jason Giambi UPD 15.00 40.00
JH Josh Hamilton A2 20.00 50.00
JH Josh Hamilton A1 20.00 50.00
JL Jon Lester A2 10.00 25.00
JN Jeff Niemann A2 3.00 8.00
JN Jayson Nix UPD 3.00 8.00
JS Jeff Samardzija A2 8.00 20.00
KG Kevin Gregg UPD 3.00 8.00
KK Kevin Kouzmanoff A2 6.00 15.00
LB Lance Berkman A2 10.00 25.00
LH Luke Hochevar B1 4.00 10.00
MB Milton Bradley UPD 4.00 10.00
MG Mat Gamel B1 6.00 15.00
MH Matt Holliday UPD 20.00 50.00
NM Nick Markakis A1 10.00 25.00
NM Nate McLouth UPD 12.00 30.00
OH Orlando Hudson UPD 5.00 12.00
PF Prince Fielder A1 10.00 25.00
PF Prince Fielder B2 10.00 25.00
PM Peter Moylan UPD 3.00 8.00
PN Pat Neshek B1 3.00 8.00
RC Robinson Cano B2 10.00 25.00
RH Ryan Howard A2 75.00 150.00
RH Rich Hill UPD 3.00 8.00
RI Raul Ibanez UPD 8.00 20.00
RO Roy Oswalt A2 10.00 25.00
RO Roy Oswalt UPD 6.00 15.00
RP Ronny Paulino B1 3.00 8.00
SP Steve Pearce B1 5.00 12.00
SR Sean Rodriguez B1 12.00 30.00
SV Shane Victorino B1 8.00 20.00
TS Travis Snider B1 6.00 15.00
VG Vladimir Guerrero UPD 6.00 15.00
YG Yovani Gallardo B1 6.00 15.00
YG Yovani Gallardo A2 6.00 15.00
ZG Zack Greinke B1 10.00 25.00

2009 Topps Career Best Relics

GROUP A1 ODDS 1:70 HOBBY
GROUP A2 ODDS 1:344 HOBBY
GROUP B1 ODDS 1:146 HOBBY
GROUP B2 ODDS 1:92 HOBBY
AB Angel Berroa Bat B2 2.50 6.00
AE Andre Ethier Jsy B2 3.00 8.00
AER Alex Rodriguez Bat A1 6.00 15.00
AG Alex Gordon Jsy A1 4.00 10.00
AG Alex Gordon Jsy B2 2.50 6.00
AP Albert Pujols Jsy A1 6.00 15.00
AR Aramis Ramirez Jsy B1 2.50 6.00
AR Alex Rodriguez Jsy A2 6.00 15.00
BM Brian McCann Bat A1 2.50 6.00
CB Carlos Beltran Pants B2 2.50 6.00
CG Curtis Granderson Jsy B2 3.00 8.00
CG Curtis Granderson Jsy A1 3.00 8.00
CGG Cristian Guzman Bat A1 2.50 6.00
CH Cole Hamels Jsy B2 4.00 10.00
CJ Conor Jackson Jsy B2 2.50 6.00
CJ Conor Jackson Bat A1 2.50 6.00
CM Cameron Maybin Bat B1 2.50 6.00
DM Daisuke Matsuzaka Jsy A1 4.00 10.00
DO David Ortiz Bat A1 4.00 10.00
DW David Wright Bat A1 5.00 12.00
DW David Wright Bat A2 5.00 12.00
EC Eric Chavez Bat B2 2.50 6.00
FS Freddy Sanchez Jsy A1 2.50 6.00
GA Garret Anderson Jsy A2 4.00 10.00
HO Hideki Okajima Jsy B1 2.50 6.00
IK Ian Kinsler Jsy B1 2.50 6.00
IS Ichiro Suzuki Jsy A1 10.00 25.00
JA Josh Anderson Jsy A1 3.00 8.00
JB Jeremy Bonderman Jsy A1 2.50 6.00
JB Jay Bruce Bat A2 4.00 10.00
JC Jorge Cantu Bat A2 2.50 6.00
JC Johnny Cueto Jsy A1 3.00 8.00
JD Jermaine Dye Jsy A1 2.50 6.00
JD J.D. Drew Bat A2 3.00 8.00
JE Jacoby Ellsbury Jsy A1 8.00 20.00
JH Jeremy Hermida Jsy A1 2.50 6.00
JM Justin Morneau Bat A1 2.50 6.00
JP Jonathan Papelbon Jsy B1 2.50 6.00
JR Jose Reyes Jsy A1 3.00 8.00
LG Luis Gonzalez Bat A2 2.50 6.00
MA Mike Aviles Jsy B1 2.50 6.00
MC Miguel Cabrera Bat A2 4.00 10.00
MK Matt Kemp Jsy B2 4.00 10.00
MO Magglio Ordonez Bat A2 4.00 10.00
OD Octavio Dotel Jsy B2 2.50 6.00
PF Prince Fielder Jsy A2 3.00 8.00
PF Prince Fielder Jsy A1 3.00 8.00
RB Ryan Braun Jsy B1 4.00 10.00
RC Robinson Cano Bat B2 3.00 8.00
RD Ray Durham Bat A2 2.50 6.00
RF Rafael Furcal Bat A2 3.00 8.00
RG Ryan Garko Jsy A1 2.50 6.00
RH Ryan Howard Jsy A1 5.00 12.00
RH Ryan Howard Bat B2 5.00 12.00
SK Scott Kazmir Jsy A1 2.50 6.00
VM Victor Martinez Bat A1 2.50 6.00
VM Victor Martinez Jsy B2 2.50 6.00
ARA Aramis Ramirez Jsy B2 2.50 6.00
JBE Josh Beckett Jsy B2 3.00 8.00
JCU Johnny Cueto Jsy A2 2.50 6.00
RBA Rocco Baldelli Bat B2 2.50 6.00
RBR Ryan Braun Jsy A2 4.00 10.00

2009 Topps Career Best Relics Silver

*SILVER 99: .6X TO 1.5X BASIC
STATED ODDS 1:1033 HOBBY
STATED PRINT RUN 99 SER.#'d SETS

2009 Topps Career Best Relic Autographs

SER.1 ODDS 1:2210 HOBBY
SER.2 ODDS 1:2845 HOBBY
STATED PRINT RUN 50 SER.#'d SETS
AER Alex Rodriguez Bat 100.00 200.00
AI Akinori Iwamura 8.00 20.00
AK Austin Kearns 12.50 30.00
AR Aramis Ramirez Jsy 8.00 20.00
BD Blake DeWitt 10.00 25.00
CC Carl Crawford Jsy 8.00 20.00
DP Dustin Pedroia Jsy 50.00 100.00
DW David Wright Bat 20.00 50.00
EL Evan Longoria 20.00 50.00
FC Fausto Carmona 10.00 25.00
FH Felix Hernandez 20.00 50.00
FL Fred Lewis 8.00 20.00
HR Hanley Ramirez Jsy 20.00 50.00
JC Joba Chamberlain 20.00 50.00
JH Josh Hamilton 12.50 30.00
JH Josh Hamilton Jsy 12.50 30.00
JL Jon Lester 20.00 50.00
JR Jose Reyes Jsy 30.00 60.00
NM Nick Markakis Jsy 8.00 20.00
PF Prince Fielder Jsy 15.00 40.00
RB Ryan Braun Jsy 20.00 50.00

2009 Topps Career Best Relics Dual

STATED ODDS 1:472 HOBBY
STATED PRINT RUN 99 SER.#'d SETS
BL Braun Jsy/Longoria Jsy 12.50 30.00
CP Cabrera Bat/Pujols Jsy 12.50 30.00
EP Ellsbury Jsy/Pedroia Jsy 15.00 40.00
FH Fielder Bat/Howard Jsy 6.00 15.00
GJ Tom Glavine Jsy 6.00 15.00
Randy Johnson Jsy
GO Guerrero Jsy/Ortiz Jsy 20.00 50.00
HB Hamilton Jsy/Braun Jsy 12.50 30.00
HC Howard Jsy/Cabrera Bat 6.00 15.00
HR Howard Jsy/Rodriguez Bat 10.00 25.00
HU Ryan Howard Jsy 10.00 25.00
Chase Utley Jsy
LC Tim Lincecum Jsy 10.00 25.00
Matt Cain Jsy
LS Longoria Jsy/Soto Jsy 8.00 20.00
MM Joe Mauer Jsy 8.00 20.00
Brian McCann Jsy
OL Magglio Ordonez Bat 6.00 15.00
Carlos Lee Bat
OP Roy Oswalt Jsy 6.00 15.00
Jake Peavy Jsy
OR Ortiz Bat/Rodriguez Bat 12.50 30.00
PB Pence Bat/Braun Jsy 12.50 30.00
PK Dustin Pedroia Jsy 8.00 20.00
Ian Kinsler Jsy
RB Alex Rios Jsy 10.00 25.00
Carlos Beltran Pants
RR Jimmy Rollins Jsy 6.00 15.00
Jose Reyes Jsy
RU Hanley Ramirez Jsy 6.00 15.00
Dan Uggla Jsy
SM Suzuki Jsy/Matsuzaka Jsy 30.00 60.00
TS Jim Thome Jsy 6.00 15.00
Gary Sheffield Bat
UU Justin Upton Bat 6.00 15.00
B.J. Upton Bat
VP Jason Varitek Bat 6.00 15.00
Jorge Posada Uni
WJ Wright Pants/Jones Jsy 10.00 25.00
WL Wright Jsy/Longoria Jsy 12.50 30.00
ZL Zimm Jsy/Longoria Jsy 8.00 20.00
OPU Ortiz Bat/Pujols Jsy 8.00 20.00
RRA Rollins Jsy/Ramirez Jsy 6.00 15.00

2009 Topps Factory Set JCPenney Bonus

COMPLETE SET (5) 3.00 8.00
JCP1 Rick Porcello 1.25 3.00
JCP2 David Price .75 2.00
JCP3 Koji Uehara 1.00 2.50
JCP4 Colby Rasmus .60 1.50
JCP5 Jordan Schafer .60 1.50

2009 Topps Factory Set Rookie Bonus

COMPLETE SET (20) 8.00 20.00
1 David Price .75 2.00
2 Rick Porcello 1.25 3.00
3 Ryan Perry 1.00 2.50
4 Brett Anderson .60 1.50
5 David Freese 1.25 3.00
6 Koji Uehara 1.00 2.50
7 Elvis Andrus 1.00 2.50
8 Trevor Cahill 1.00 2.50
9 Andrew Bailey 1.00 2.50
10 Jordan Schafer .60 1.50
11 Colby Rasmus .60 1.50
12 Kenshin Kawakami .60 1.50
13 Michael Bowden .40 1.00
14 Edwin Moreno .40 1.00
15 Ricky Romero .60 1.50
16 Tommy Hanson 1.00 2.50
17 Ramiro Pena .60 1.50
18 Freddy Sandoval .40 1.00
19 Andrew McCutchen 2.00 5.00
20 George Kottaras .40 1.00

2009 Topps Factory Set Target Ruth Chrome Gold Refractors

COMPLETE SET (3) 15.00 40.00
1 Babe Ruth 8.00 20.00
2 Babe Ruth 8.00 20.00
3 Babe Ruth 8.00 20.00

2009 Topps Legendary Letters Commemorative Patch

STATED ODDS 1:630 HOBBY
EACH LETTER SER.#'d TO 50
COMBINED PRINT RUNS LISTED BELOW
BG Bob Gibson/300 * 10.00 25.00
BR Babe Ruth/200 * 12.50 30.00
CM C.Mathewson/450 * 8.00 20.00
CMY C.Yastrzemski/550 * 8.00 20.00
CR C.Ripken Jr./300 * 12.50 30.00
CY Cy Young/250 * 12.50 30.00
GS George Sisler/300 * 4.00 10.00
HW H.Wagner/300 * 8.00 20.00
JF Jimmie Foxx/200 * 4.00 10.00
JM Johnny Mize/200 * 6.00 15.00
JR J.Robinson/400 * 8.00 20.00
LG Lou Gehrig/300 * 12.50 30.00
MM M.Mantle/300 * 8.00 20.00
MO Mel Ott/150 * 4.00 10.00
NR Nolan Ryan/200 * 12.50 30.00
PWR Pee Wee Reese/250 * 8.00 20.00
RC R.Campanella/500 * 8.00 20.00
RH R.Hornsby/350 * 4.00 10.00
TC Ty Cobb/200 * 12.50 30.00
TM T.Munson/300 * 10.00 25.00
TS Tris Speaker/350 * 5.00 12.00
WJ W.Johnson/350 * 5.00 12.00

2009 Topps Legends Chrome Target Cereal

COMPLETE SET (30) 30.00 60.00
RANDOM INSERTS IN TARGET CEREAL PACKS
GR1 Ted Williams 3.00 8.00
GR2 Bob Gibson 1.00 2.50
GR3 Babe Ruth 4.00 10.00
GR4 Roy Campanella 1.50 4.00
GR5 Ty Cobb 2.50 6.00
GR6 Cy Young 1.50 4.00
GR7 Mickey Mantle 5.00 12.00
GR8 Walter Johnson 1.50 4.00
GR9 Roberto Clemente 4.00 10.00
GR10 Jimmie Foxx 1.50 4.00
GR11 Christy Mathewson 1.50 4.00
GR12 Jackie Robinson 1.50 4.00
GR13 Ty Cobb 2.50 6.00
GR14 Honus Wagner 1.50 4.00
GR15 Lou Gehrig 3.00 8.00
GR16 Nolan Ryan 5.00 12.00
GR17 Cal Ripken Jr 5.00 12.00
GR18 Thurman Munson 1.50 4.00
GR19 Rogers Hornsby 1.00 2.50
GR20 George Sisler 1.00 2.50
LLG21 Rickey Henderson 1.50 4.00
LLG22 Ozzie Smith 2.00 5.00
LLG23 Babe Ruth 4.00 10.00
LLG24 Roger Maris 2.50 6.00
LLG25 Nolan Ryan 5.00 12.00
LLG26 Reggie Jackson 1.00 2.50
LLG27 Frank Robinson 1.00 2.50
LLG28 Ryne Sandberg 3.00 8.00
LLG29 Steve Carlton 1.00 2.50
LLG30 Johnny Bench 1.50 4.00

2009 Topps Legends Chrome Target Cereal Refractors

*REF: .5X TO 1.2X BASIC
RANDOM INSERTS IN TARGET PACKS

2009 Topps Legends Chrome Target Cereal Gold Refractors

*GOLD REF: .75X TO 2X BASIC
RANDOM INSERTS IN TARGET PACKS

2009 Topps Legends Chrome Wal-Mart Cereal

RANDOM INSERTS IN WALMART CEREAL PACKS
PR1 Ted Williams 3.00 8.00
PR2 Jackie Robinson 1.50 4.00
PR3 Babe Ruth 4.00 10.00
PR4 Honus Wagner 1.50 4.00
PR5 Lou Gehrig 3.00 8.00
PR6 Nolan Ryan 5.00 12.00
PR7 Mickey Mantle 5.00 12.00
PR8 Thurman Munson 1.50 4.00
PR9 Cal Ripken Jr. 5.00 12.00
PR10 George Sisler 1.00 2.50
PR11 Mel Ott 1.50 4.00
PR12 Bob Gibson 1.00 2.50
PR13 Jackie Robinson 1.50 4.00
PR14 Roy Campanella 1.50 4.00
PR15 Ty Cobb 2.50 6.00
PR16 Cy Young 1.50 4.00
PR17 Cal Ripken Jr 5.00 12.00
PR18 Walter Johnson 1.50 4.00
PR19 Lou Gehrig 3.00 8.00
PR20 Jimmie Foxx 1.50 4.00
PR21 Babe Ruth 4.00 10.00
PR22 Rogers Hornsby 1.00 2.50
PR23 Johnny Mize 1.00 2.50
PR24 Ty Cobb 2.50 6.00
PR25 Tris Speaker 1.00 2.50
PR26 Rickey Henderson 1.50 4.00
PR27 Ozzie Smith 2.00 5.00
PR28 Nolan Ryan 5.00 12.00
PR29 Reggie Jackson 1.00 2.50
PR30 Frank Robinson 1.00 2.50

2009 Topps Legends Chrome Wal-Mart Cereal Refractors

*REF: .5X TO 1.2X BASIC
RANDOM INSERTS IN TARGET PACKS

2009 Topps Legends Chrome Wal-Mart Cereal Gold Refractors

*GOLD REF: .75X TO 2X BASIC
RANDOM INSERTS IN TARGET PACKS

2009 Topps Legends Commemorative Patch

SERIES 1 ODDS 1:343 HOBBY
UPDATE RANDOMLY INSERTED
1-100 ISSUED IN SERIES 1
101-150 ISSUED IN UPDATE
LPR1 B.Ruth 1921 WS 8.00 20.00
LPR2 B.Ruth 1927 WS 8.00 20.00
LPR3 L.Gehrig 1928 WS 6.00 15.00
LPR4 L.Gehrig 1933 ASG 6.00 15.00
LPR5 Jimmie Foxx 1934 ASG 8.00 20.00
LPR6 Mel Ott 1934 ASG 4.00 10.00
LPR7 T.Williams 1946 ASG 6.00 15.00
LPR8 T.Williams 1949 ASG 6.00 15.00
LPR9 J.Robinson 1949 ASG 8.00 20.00
LPR10 Campy 1949 ASG 12.50 30.00
LPR11 M.Mantle 1951 WS 12.50 30.00
LPR12 M.Mantle 1952 WS 12.50 30.00
LPR13 T.Williams 1953 ASG 6.00 15.00
LPR14 Campy 1953 ASG 4.00 10.00
LPR15 T.Williams 1954 ASG 6.00 15.00
LPR16 M.Mantle 1954 ASG 6.00 15.00
LPR17 Duke Snider 1954 ASG 10.00 25.00
LPR18 Whitey Ford 1954 ASG 6.00 15.00
LPR19 J.Robinson 1955 WS 8.00 20.00
LPR20 M.Mantle 1956 WS 6.00 15.00
LPR21 Don Larsen 1956 WS 4.00 10.00
LPR22 T.Williams 1960 ASG 6.00 15.00
LPR23 E.Banks 1960 ASG 8.00 20.00
LPR24 Clemente 1961 ASG 10.00 25.00
LPR25 Clemente 1962 ASG 10.00 25.00
LPR26 Clemente 1962 ASG 10.00 25.00
LPR27 E.Banks 1962 ASG 8.00 20.00
LPR28 M.Mantle 1962 WS 12.50 30.00
LPR29 Clemente 1963 ASG 10.00 25.00
LPR30 N.Ryan 1969 WS 6.00 15.00
LPR31 Tom Seaver 1969 WS 10.00 25.00
LPR32 Clemente 1971 ASG 10.00 25.00
LPR33 T.Munson 1971 ASG 6.00 15.00
LPR34 Carl Yastrzemski 1971 ASG 10.00 25.00
LPR35 N.Ryan 1972 ASG 6.00 15.00
LPR36 Bob Gibson 1972 ASG 8.00 20.00
LPR37 Carl Yastrzemski 1972 ASG 10.00 25.00
LPR38 N.Ryan 1973 ASG 6.00 15.00
LPR39 Tom Seaver 1973 ASG 10.00 25.00
LPR40 Reggie Jackson 1973 WS 10.00 25.00
LPR41 Reggie Jackson 1977 WS 10.00 25.00
LPR42 T.Munson 1978 WS 8.00 20.00
LPR43 C.Ripken 1983 ASG 12.50 30.00
LPR44 M.Schmidt 1983 ASG 10.00 25.00
LPR45 C.Ripken 1983 WS 12.50 30.00
LPR46 N.Ryan 1985 ASG 6.00 15.00
LPR47 C.Ripken 1985 ASG 12.50 30.00
LPR48 N.Ryan 1989 ASG 6.00 15.00
LPR49 C.Ripken 1989 ASG 12.50 30.00
LPR50 C.Ripken 2001 ASG 12.50 30.00
LPR51 Cy Young 10.00 25.00
LPR52 Christy Mathewson 6.00 15.00
LPR53 Honus Wagner 6.00 15.00
LPR54 Walter Johnson 6.00 15.00
LPR55 Rogers Hornsby 10.00 25.00
LPR56 Lou Gehrig 6.00 15.00
LPR57 Babe Ruth 8.00 20.00
LPR58 Jimmie Foxx 8.00 20.00
LPR59 Jimmie Foxx 8.00 20.00
LPR60 Babe Ruth 8.00 20.00
LPR61 Lou Gehrig 6.00 15.00
LPR62 Johnny Mize 10.00 25.00
LPR63 Pee Wee Reese 6.00 15.00
LPR64 Jackie Robinson 8.00 20.00
LPR65 Johnny Mize 10.00 25.00
LPR66 Mickey Mantle 6.00 15.00
LPR67 Jackie Robinson 8.00 20.00
LPR68 Roy Campanella 12.50 30.00
LPR69 Mickey Mantle 12.50 30.00
LPR70 Brooks Robinson 6.00 15.00
LPR71 Bill Mazeroski 6.00 15.00
LPR72 Frank Robinson 10.00 25.00
LPR73 Carl Yastrzemski 10.00 25.00
LPR74 Juan Marichal 10.00 25.00
LPR75 Brooks Robinson 6.00 15.00

LPR76 Frank Robinson 10.00 25.00
LPR77 Steve Carlton 8.00 20.00
LPR78 Jim Palmer 8.00 20.00
LPR79 Frank Robinson 10.00 25.00
LPR80 Jim Palmer 8.00 20.00
LPR81 Reggie Jackson 10.00 25.00
LPR82 Thurman Munson 8.00 20.00
LPR83 Mike Schmidt 10.00 25.00
LPR84 Robin Yount 10.00 25.00
LPR85 Robin Yount 10.00 25.00
LPR86 Ryne Sandberg 10.00 25.00
LPR87 Tony Gwynn 8.00 20.00
LPR88 Mike Schmidt 10.00 25.00
LPR89 Paul Molitor 4.00 10.00
LPR90 Frank Thomas 4.00 410.00
LPR91 Chipper Jones 10.00 25.00
LPR92 John Smoltz 10.00 25.00
LPR93 Wade Boggs 10.00 25.00
LPR94 Greg Maddux 12.50 30.00
LPR95 Tony Gwynn 8.00 20.00
LPR96 Mariano Rivera 5.00 12.00
LPR97 Manny Ramirez 10.00 25.00
LPR98 Albert Pujols 6.00 15.00
LPR99 Ichiro Suzuki 12.50 30.00
LPR100 Alex Rodriguez 10.00 25.00
LPR101 Babe Ruth 8.00 20.00
LPR102 Babe Ruth 8.00 20.00
LPR103 Lou Gehrig 6.00 15.00
LPR104 Hank Greenberg 10.00 25.00
LPR105 Jimmie Foxx 8.00 20.00
LPR106 Lou Gehrig 6.00 15.00
LPR107 Stan Musial 15.00 40.00
LPR108 Hank Greenberg 10.00 25.00
LPR109 Pee Wee Reese 6.00 15.00
LPR110 Johnny Mize 10.00 25.00
LPR111 Jackie Robinson 8.00 20.00
LPR112 Roy Campanella 12.50 30.00
LPR113 Whitey Ford 6.00 15.00
LPR114 Robin Roberts 4.00 10.00
LPR115 Roy Campanella 12.50 30.00
LPR116 Johnny Mize 10.00 25.00
LPR117 Jackie Robinson 8.00 20.00
LPR118 Mickey Mantle 12.50 30.00
LPR119 Ernie Banks 8.00 20.00
LPR120 Duke Snider 10.00 25.00
LPR121 Mickey Mantle 12.50 30.00
LPR122 Brooks Robinson 6.00 15.00
LPR123 Mickey Mantle 12.50 30.00
LPR124 Whitey Ford 6.00 15.00
LPR125 Duke Snider 10.00 25.00
LPR126 Bob Gibson 8.00 20.00
LPR127 Ernie Banks 8.00 20.00
LPR128 Frank Robinson 10.00 25.00
LPR129 Jim Palmer 8.00 20.00
LPR130 Bob Gibson 8.00 20.00
LPR131 Steve Carlton 8.00 20.00
LPR132 Reggie Jackson 10.00 25.00
LPR133 Willie McCovey 10.00 25.00
LPR134 Carl Yastrzemski 10.00 25.00
LPR135 Tom Seaver 10.00 25.00
LPR136 Brooks Robinson 6.00 15.00
LPR137 Frank Robinson 10.00 25.00
LPR138 Thurman Munson 8.00 20.00
LPR139 Thurman Munson 8.00 20.00
LPR140 Carl Yastrzemski 10.00 25.00
LPR141 Nolan Ryan 6.00 15.00
LPR142 Robin Yount 10.00 25.00
LPR143 Reggie Jackson 10.00 25.00
LPR144 Cal Ripken 6.00 15.00
LPR145 Wade Boggs 10.00 25.00
LPR146 Mike Schmidt 6.00 15.00
LPR147 Ryne Sandberg 10.00 25.00
LPR148 Paul Molitor 10.00 25.00
LPR149 Cal Ripken 12.50 30.00
LPR150 Tony Gwynn 8.00 20.00

2009 Topps Legends of the Game

COMPLETE SET (75) 40.00 80.00
COMP.UPD.SET (25) 8.00 20.00
STATED ODDS 1:6 HOBBY
1-25 ISSUED IN TOPPS 1
26-50 ISSUED IN TOPPS 2
51-75 ISSUED IN UPDATE
*GOLD: 1.5X TO 4X BASIC
GOLD SER.1 ODDS 1:1975 HOBBY
GOLD SER.2 ODDS 1:1725 HOBBY
GOLD UPD.ODDS 1:950 HOBBY
GOLD PRINT RUN 99 SER.#'d SETS
*PLATINUM: 4X TO 10X BASIC
PLAT.SER.1 ODDS 1:8200 HOBBY
PLAT.SER.2 ODDS 1:6900 HOBBY
PLAT.UPD.ODDS 1:3800 HOBBY
PLATINUM PRINT RUN 25 SER.#'d SETS
LG1 Cy Young .75 2.00
LG2 Honus Wagner .75 2.00
LG3 Christy Mathewson .75 2.00
LG4 Ty Cobb 1.25 3.00
LG5 Walter Johnson .75 2.00
LG6 Tris Speaker .50 1.25
LG7 Babe Ruth 2.00 5.00
LG8 George Sisler .50 1.25
LG9 Rogers Hornsby .50 1.25
LG10 Jimmie Foxx .75 2.00
LG11 Lou Gehrig 1.50 4.00
LG12 Mel Ott .75 2.00
LG13 Jackie Robinson .75 2.00
LG14 Johnny Mize .50 1.25
LG15 Pee Wee Reese .50 1.25
LG16 Roy Campanella .75 2.00
LG17 Ted Williams 1.50 4.00
LG18 Roger Maris .75 2.00
LG19 Bob Gibson .50 1.25
LG20 Mickey Mantle 2.50 6.00
LG21 Roberto Clemente 2.00 5.00
LG22 Thurman Munson .75 2.00
LG23 Carl Yastrzemski 1.25 3.00
LG24 Nolan Ryan 2.50 6.00
LG25 Cal Ripken Jr. 2.50 6.00
LGAP Albert Pujols 1.00 2.50
LGAR Alex Rodriguez 1.00 2.50
LGBR Brooks Robinson .50 1.25
LGCJ Chipper Jones .75 2.00
LGFR Frank Robinson .50 1.25
LGFT Frank Thomas .75 2.00
LGGM Greg Maddux 1.00 2.50
LGIS Ichiro Suzuki 1.00 2.50
LGJM Juan Marichal .50 1.25
LGJP Jim Palmer .50 1.25
LGJS John Smoltz .75 2.00
LGMR Mariano Rivera 1.00 2.50
LGMS Mike Schmidt 1.25 3.00
LGPM Paul Molitor .75 2.00
LGRJ Reggie Jackson .50 1.25
LGRS Ryne Sandberg 1.50 4.00
LGRY Robin Yount .50 1.25
LGSC Steve Carlton .50 1.25
LGTG Tony Gwynn .75 2.00
LGTH Trevor Hoffman .50 1.25
LGVG Vladimir Guerrero .50 1.25
LGWB Wade Boggs .50 1.25
LGMRA Manny Ramirez .75 2.00
LGRJO Randy Johnson .75 2.00
LGTGL Tom Glavine .50 1.25
LGU01 Cy Young .75 2.00
LGU02 Honus Wagner .75 2.00
LGU03 Christy Mathewson .75 2.00
LGU04 Ty Cobb 1.25 3.00
LGU05 Tris Speaker .50 1.25
LGU06 Babe Ruth 2.00 5.00
LGU07 George Sisler .50 1.25
LGU08 Rogers Hornsby .50 1.25
LGU09 Jimmie Foxx .75 2.00
LGU10 Johnny Mize .50 1.25
LGU11 Nolan Ryan 2.50 6.00
LGU12 Juan Marichal .50 1.25
LGU13 Steve Carlton .50 1.25
LGU14 Reggie Jackson .50 1.25
LGU15 Frank Robinson .50 1.25
LGU16 Wade Boggs .50 1.25
LGU17 Paul Molitor .75 2.00
LGU18 Babe Ruth 2.00 5.00
LGU19 Nolan Ryan 2.50 6.00
LGU20 Frank Robinson .50 1.25
LGU21 Reggie Jackson .50 1.25
LGU22 Wade Boggs .50 1.25
LGU23 Rogers Hornsby .50 1.25
LGU24 Paul Molitor .75 2.00
LGU25 Johnny Mize .50 1.25

2009 Topps Legends of the Game Career Best

RANDOM INSERTS IN PACKS
BR Babe Ruth 2.50 6.00
CY Cy Young 1.00 2.50
GS George Sisler .60 1.50
HW Honus Wagner 1.00 2.50
JF Jimmie Foxx 1.00 2.50
JR Jackie Robinson 1.00 2.50
LG Lou Gehrig 2.00 5.00
MM Mickey Mantle 3.00 8.00
MO Mel Ott 1.00 2.50
RC Roy Campanella 1.00 2.50
RH Rogers Hornsby .60 1.50
TC Ty Cobb 1.50 4.00
TS Tris Speaker .60 1.50
WJ Walter Johnson 1.00 2.50
CZM Christy Mathewson 1.00 2.50

2009 Topps Legends of the Game Nickname Letter Patch

RANDOM INSERTS IN PACKS
EACH LETTER SER.#'D TO 50
COMBINED PRINT RUNS LISTED BELOW
BG Bob Gibson/250 * 10.00 25.00
BO B.Obama/600 * 10.00 25.00
BR Babe Ruth/350 * 6.00 15.00
BR Brooks Robinson/650 * 4.00 10.00
CM C.Mathewson/300 * 4.00 10.00
CMY Yastrzemski/150 * 10.00 25.00
CR C.Ripken Jr./350 * 15.00 40.00
CY Cy Young/350 * 4.00 10.00
FR Frank Robinson/400 * 6.00 15.00
GM Greg Maddux/300 * 10.00 25.00
GS George Sisler/400 * 4.00 10.00
HW H.Wagner/400 * 10.00 25.00
JB Joe Biden/650 * 6.00 15.00
JF Jimmie Foxx/400 * 4.00 10.00
JM Johnny Mize/450 * 4.00 10.00
JM Juan Marichal/700 * 4.00 10.00
JR J.Robinson/300 * 12.50 30.00
LG Lou Gehrig/450 * 12.50 30.00
MIO M.Obama/450 * 12.50 30.00
MM M.Mantle/350 * 15.00 40.00
MM M.Mantle/650 * 15.00 40.00
MO Mel Ott/300 * 6.00 15.00
NR Nolan Ryan/700 * 6.00 15.00
PM Paul Molitor/350 * 6.00 15.00
PWR P.Reese/300 * 6.00 15.00
RC Campanella/250 * 10.00 25.00
RCW R.Clemente/300 * 20.00 50.00
RH R.Hornsby/250 * 4.00 10.00
RJ Reggie Jackson/500 * 6.00 15.00
RM Roger Maris/700 * 10.00 25.00
TC Ty Cobb/350 * 6.00 15.00
TM T.Munson/350 * 10.00 25.00
TS Tris Speaker/450 * 4.00 10.00
TW T.Williams/650 * 12.50 30.00
WB Wade Boggs/500 * 5.00 12.00
WJ W.Johnson/400 * 8.00 20.00

2009 Topps Legends of the Game Framed Stamps

SERIES 1 ODDS 1:1555 HOBBY
SERIES 2 ODDS 1:9400 HOBBY
SERIES 1 PRINT RUN 95 SER.#'d SETS
SERIES 2 PRINT RUN 90 SER.#'d SETS
BR1 Babe Ruth 20.00 50.00
BR2 Babe Ruth 20.00 50.00
BR3 Babe Ruth 20.00 50.00
BR4 Babe Ruth 20.00 50.00
BR5 Babe Ruth 20.00 50.00
BR6 Babe Ruth 20.00 50.00
BR7 Babe Ruth 20.00 50.00
BR8 Babe Ruth 20.00 50.00
BR9 Babe Ruth 20.00 50.00
CM1 Christy Mathewson 12.50 30.00
CY1 Cy Young 12.50 30.00
GS1 George Sisler 4.00 10.00
HW1 Honus Wagner 20.00 50.00
JF1 Jimmie Foxx 12.50 30.00
JR1 Jackie Robinson 10.00 25.00
JR2 Jackie Robinson 10.00 25.00
JR3 Jackie Robinson 10.00 25.00
JR4 Jackie Robinson 10.00 25.00
JR5 Jackie Robinson 10.00 25.00
JR6 Jackie Robinson 10.00 25.00
JR7 Jackie Robinson 10.00 25.00
LG1 Lou Gehrig 30.00 60.00
LG2 Lou Gehrig 30.00 60.00
LG3 Lou Gehrig 30.00 60.00
MM1 Mickey Mantle 15.00 40.00
MM2 Mickey Mantle 15.00 40.00
RC1 Roberto Clemente 30.00 60.00
RH1 Rogers Hornsby 12.50 30.00
TC1 Ty Cobb 15.00 40.00
TS1 Tris Speaker 10.00 25.00
WJ1 Walter Johnson 15.00 40.00

2009 Topps Red Hot Rookie Redemption

In mid-June 2009, it was announced that 10 percent of the Gordon Beckham redemptions (#RHR2) would feature a certified autograph.

COMPLETE SET (10) 15.00 40.00
COMMON EXCHANGE 6.00 15.00
STATED ODDS 1:36 HOBBY
1:10 G.BECKHAM CARDS ARE SIGNED
EXCHANGE DEADLINE 6/30/2010
RHR1 Fernando Martinez 3.00 8.00
RHR2A Gordon Beckham 2.00 5.00
RHR3 Andrew McCutchen 6.00 15.00
RHR4 Tommy Hanson 3.00 8.00
RHR5 Nolan Reimold 1.25 3.00
RHR6 Neftali Feliz 2.00 5.00
RHR7 Mat Latos 4.00 10.00
RHR8 Julio Borbon 1.25 3.00
RHR9 Jhoulys Chacin 2.00 5.00
RHR10 Chris Coghlan 3.00 8.00

2009 Topps Ring Of Honor

COMPLETE SET (100) 30.00 60.00
COMP.UPD SET (25) 6.00 15.00
STATED ODDS 1:6 HOBBY
101-125 ISSUED IN UPDATE
RH1 David Justice .40 1.00
RH2 Whitey Ford .60 1.50
RH3 Orlando Cepeda .60 1.50
RH4 Cole Hamels .75 2.00
RH5 Darryl Strawberry .40 1.00
RH6 Johnny Bench 1.00 2.50
RH7 David Ortiz 1.00 2.50
RH8 Derek Jeter 2.50 6.00
RH9 Dwight Gooden .40 1.00
RH10 Brooks Robinson .60 1.50
RH11 Ivan Rodriguez .60 1.50
RH12 David Eckstein .40 1.00
RH13 Derek Jeter 2.50 6.00
RH14 Paul Molitor 1.00 2.50
RH15 Don Zimmer .40 1.00
RH16 Jermaine Dye .40 1.00
RH17 Gary Sheffield .40 1.00
RH18 Bob Gibson .60 1.50
RH19 Pedro Martinez .60 1.50
RH20 Manny Ramirez 1.00 2.50
RH21 Johnny Podres .40 1.00
RH22 Johnny Podres .40 1.00
RH23 Mariano Rivera 1.25 3.00
RH24 Curt Schilling .60 1.50
RH25 Lou Piniella .40 1.00
RH26 Roberto Clemente 2.50 6.00
RH27 Kevin Mitchell .40 1.00
RH28 Frank Robinson .60 1.50
RH29 Francisco Rodriguez .60 1.50
RH30 Troy Glaus .40 1.00
RH31 Tony LaRussa .60 1.50
RH32 Mike Schmidt 1.50 4.00
RH33 Brad Lidge .40 1.00
RH34 Randy Johnson 1.00 2.50
RH35 Duke Snider .60 1.50
RH36 Rollie Fingers .60 1.50
RH37 Luis Gonzalez .40 1.00
RH38 Josh Beckett .40 1.00
RH39 Gary Carter .60 1.50
RH40 Bob Gibson .60 1.50
RH41 Andy Pettitte .60 1.50
RH42 Reggie Jackson .60 1.50
RH43 Jim Leyland .40 1.00
RH44 Mariano Rivera 1.25 3.00
RH45 Albert Pujols 1.25 3.00
RH46 Don Larsen .40 1.00
RH47 Roger Clemens 1.25 3.00
RH48 Tom Glavine .60 1.50
RH49 Ryan Howard .75 2.00
RH50 Reggie Jackson .60 1.50
RH51 Carlos Ruiz .40 1.00
RH52 Tyler Johnson .40 1.00
RH53 Jason Varitek 1.00 2.50
RH54 Darryl Strawberry .40 1.00
RH55 Dusty Baker .40 1.00
RH56 Dustin Pedroia .75 2.00
RH57 Jayson Werth .60 1.50
RH58 Garret Anderson .40 1.00
RH59 Dontrelle Willis .40 1.00
RH60 David Justice .40 1.00
RH61 Luis Aparicio .60 1.50
RH62 John Smoltz 1.00 2.50
RH63 Miguel Cabrera 1.00 2.50
RH64 Yadier Molina 1.00 2.50
RH65 Jacoby Ellsbury .75 2.00
RH66 Mark Buehrle .60 1.50
RH67 Johnny Damon .60 1.50
RH68 Brad Penny .40 1.00
RH69 Joe Torre .60 1.50
RH70 Chris Carpenter .60 1.50
RH71 Bobby Cox .40 1.00
RH72 Jonathan Papelbon .60 1.50
RH73 Joe Girardi .60 1.50
RH74 Aaron Rowand .40 1.00
RH75 Daisuke Matzusaka .60 1.50
RH76 Babe Ruth 2.50 6.00
RH77 Jackie Robinson 1.00 2.50
RH78 Chris Duncan .40 1.00
RH79 Christy Mathewson 1.00 2.50
RH80 Cy Young 1.00 2.50
RH81 Jermaine Dye .40 1.00
RH82 Honus Wagner 1.00 2.50
RH83 Chone Figgins .40 1.00
RH84 Walter Johnson 1.00 2.50
RH85 Jon Garland .40 1.00
RH86 Mel Ott 1.00 2.50
RH87 Jimmie Foxx 1.00 2.50
RH88 Hideki Okajima .40 1.00
RH89 Johnny Mize .60 1.50
RH90 Rogers Hornsby .60 1.50
RH91 Miguel Cabrera 1.00 2.50
RH92 Pee Wee Reese .60 1.50
RH93 Darin Erstad .40 1.00
RH94 Tris Speaker .60 1.50
RH95 Steve Garvey .40 1.00
RH96 Lou Gehrig 2.00 5.00
RH97 Babe Ruth 2.50 6.00
RH98 David Ortiz 1.00 2.50
RH99 Thurman Munson 1.00 2.50
RH100 Roy Campanella 1.00 2.50

2009 Topps Silk Collection

SER.1 ODDS 1:241 HOBBY
SER.2 ODDS 1:280 HOBBY
UPDATE ODDS 1:163 HOBBY
STATED PRINT RUN 50 SER.#'d SETS
1-100 ISSUED IN SERIES 1
101-200 ISSUED IN SERIES 2
201-300 ISSUED IN UPDATE
S1 David Wright 8.00 20.00
S2 Nate McLouth 4.00 10.00
S3 Brandon Jones 4.00 10.00
S4 Mike Mussina 6.00 15.00
S5 Kevin Youkilis 4.00 10.00
S6 Kyle Lohse 4.00 10.00
S7 Rich Aurilia 4.00 10.00
S8 Rich Harden 4.00 10.00
S9 Chase Headley 4.00 10.00
S10 Vladimir Guerrero 6.00 15.00
S11 Denard Span 4.00 10.00
S12 Andrew Miller 6.00 15.00
S13 Justin Upton 6.00 15.00
S14 Aaron Cook 4.00 10.00
S15 Travis Snider 6.00 15.00
S16 Scott Rolen 6.00 15.00
S17 Chad Billingsley 6.00 15.00
S18 Brandon Wood 4.00 10.00
S19 Brad Lidge 4.00 10.00
S20 Dexter Fowler 6.00 15.00
S21 Ian Kinsler 6.00 15.00
S22 Joe Crede 6.00 15.00
S23 Jay Bruce 6.00 15.00
S24 Frank Thomas 10.00 25.00
S25 Roy Halladay 6.00 15.00
S26 Justin Duchscherer 4.00 10.00
S27 Carl Crawford 6.00 15.00
S28 Jeff Francoeur 6.00 15.00
S29 Mike Napoli 4.00 10.00
S30 Ryan Braun 6.00 15.00
S31 Yuniesky Betancourt 4.00 10.00
S32 James Shields 4.00 10.00
S33 Hunter Pence 6.00 15.00
S34 Ian Stewart 4.00 10.00
S35 David Price 8.00 20.00
S36 Hideki Okajima 4.00 10.00
S37 Brad Penny 4.00 10.00
S38 Ivan Rodriguez 6.00 15.00
S39 Chris Duncan 4.00 10.00
S40 Johan Santana 6.00 15.00
S41 Joe Saunders 4.00 10.00
S42 Jose Valverde 4.00 10.00
S43 Tim Lincecum 6.00 15.00
S44 Miguel Tejada 6.00 15.00
S45 Geovany Soto 6.00 15.00
S46 Mark DeRosa 6.00 15.00
S47 Yadier Molina 10.00 25.00
S48 Collin Balester 4.00 10.00
S49 Zack Greinke 6.00 15.00
S50 Manny Ramirez 10.00 25.00
S51 Brian Giles 4.00 10.00
S52 J.J. Hardy 4.00 10.00
S53 Jarrod Saltalamacchia 4.00 10.00
S54 Aubrey Huff 4.00 10.00
S55 Carlos Zambrano 6.00 15.00
S56 Ken Griffey Jr. 20.00 50.00
S57 Daric Barton 4.00 10.00
S58 Randy Johnson 10.00 25.00
S59 Jon Garland 4.00 10.00
S60 Daisuke Matsuzaka 6.00 15.00
S61 Miguel Cabrera 10.00 25.00
S62 Orlando Hudson 4.00 10.00
S63 Johnny Cueto 6.00 15.00
S64 Omar Vizquel 6.00 15.00
S65 Derrek Lee 4.00 10.00
S66 Brad Ziegler 4.00 10.00
S67 Shane Victorino 4.00 10.00
S68 Roy Oswalt 6.00 15.00
S69 Cliff Lee 6.00 15.00
S70 Ichiro Suzuki 12.00 30.00
S71 Casey Blake 4.00 10.00
S72 Kelly Shoppach 4.00 10.00
S73 Ryan Sweeney 4.00 10.00
S74 Carlos Pena 6.00 15.00
S75 Carlos Delgado 4.00 10.00
S76 Tim Hudson 6.00 15.00
S77 Brandon Webb 6.00 15.00
S78 Adam Lind 4.00 10.00
S79 Akinori Iwamura 4.00 10.00
S80 Mariano Rivera 12.00 30.00
S81 Pat Burrell 4.00 10.00
S82 Mark Teixeira 6.00 15.00
S83 Matt Kemp 8.00 20.00
S84 Jeff Samardzija 6.00 15.00
S85 Kosuke Fukudome 6.00 15.00
S86 Aaron Harang 4.00 10.00
S87 Conor Jackson 4.00 10.00
S88 Andy Sonnanstine 4.00 10.00
S89 Joe Blanton 4.00 10.00
S90 CC Sabathia 6.00 15.00
S91 Greg Maddux 12.00 30.00
S92 Gabe Kapler 4.00 10.00
S93 Garrett Atkins 4.00 10.00
S94 Hideki Matsui 10.00 25.00
S95 Chien-Ming Wang 6.00 15.00
S96 Josh Johnson 6.00 15.00
S97 Dustin McGowan 4.00 10.00
S98 Gil Meche 4.00 10.00
S99 Justin Morneau 6.00 15.00
S100 Evan Longoria 6.00 15.00
S101 Joe Mauer 8.00 20.00
S102 Derek Jeter 25.00 60.00
S103 Jorge Posada 6.00 15.00
S104 Victor Martinez 6.00 15.00
S105 Carlos Quentin 4.00 10.00
S106 Jonathan Papelbon 6.00 15.00
S107 Brandon Phillips 4.00 10.00
S108 Alfonso Soriano 6.00 15.00
S109 Carlos Lee 4.00 10.00
S110 Joe Nathan 4.00 10.00
S111 Jeremy Bonderman 4.00 10.00
S112 Nick Markakis 8.00 20.00
S113 Troy Glaus 4.00 10.00
S114 Travis Hafner 4.00 10.00
S115 Joba Chamberlain 4.00 10.00
S116 Melky Cabrera 4.00 10.00
S117 Kenji Johjima 6.00 15.00
S118 Carlos Guillen 4.00 10.00
S119 Matt Cain 6.00 15.00
S120 Clayton Kershaw 20.00 50.00
S121 Yunel Escobar 4.00 10.00
S122 Michael Young 4.00 10.00
S123 Stephen Drew 4.00 10.00
S124 Justin Masterson 4.00 10.00
S125 Mike Aviles 4.00 10.00
S126 Josh Beckett 4.00 10.00
S127 Fausto Carmona 4.00 10.00
S128 Gavin Floyd 4.00 10.00
S129 Hanley Ramirez 6.00 15.00
S130 Adam Jones 6.00 15.00
S131 Jered Weaver 6.00 15.00
S132 Edinson Volquez 4.00 10.00
S133 Prince Fielder 6.00 15.00
S134 Adrian Gonzalez 8.00 20.00
S135 Jimmy Rollins 6.00 15.00
S136 Felix Hernandez 6.00 15.00
S137 Ryan Doumit 4.00 10.00
S138 Russell Martin 4.00 10.00
S139 Carlos Beltran 6.00 15.00
S140 Nelson Cruz 10.00 25.00
S141 Jeremy Hermida 4.00 10.00
S142 Robinson Cano 6.00 15.00
S143 Armando Galarraga 4.00 10.00
S144 Luke Hochevar 4.00 10.00
S145 Delmon Young 6.00 15.00
S146 Chris Young 4.00 10.00
S147 Dustin Pedroia 8.00 20.00
S148 Ervin Santana 4.00 10.00
S149 Jhonny Peralta 4.00 10.00
S150 Alexi Casilla 4.00 10.00
S151 Kevin Kouzmanoff 4.00 10.00
S152 Aramis Ramirez 4.00 10.00
S153 Joey Votto 10.00 25.00
S154 Barry Zito 6.00 15.00
S155 Cameron Maybin 4.00 10.00
S156 Todd Helton 6.00 15.00
S157 Curtis Granderson 8.00 20.00
S158 Jamie Moyer 4.00 10.00
S159 Wladimir Balentien 4.00 10.00
S160 John Maine 4.00 10.00
S161 Chris Carpenter 6.00 15.00
S162 Andre Ethier 6.00 15.00
S163 Yovani Gallardo 4.00 10.00
S164 Nick Hundley 4.00 10.00
S165 Brandon Morrow 4.00 10.00
S166 Jason Bay 6.00 15.00
S167 Randy Winn 4.00 10.00
S168 Willy Aybar 4.00 10.00
S169 David DeJesus 4.00 10.00
S170 Scott Kazmir 4.00 10.00
S171 Johnny Damon 6.00 15.00
S172 Carlos Gomez 4.00 10.00
S173 Jose Reyes 6.00 15.00
S174 Rick Ankiel 4.00 10.00
S175 Ryan Zimmerman 6.00 15.00
S176 Jim Thome 6.00 15.00
S177 Chris Davis 6.00 15.00
S178 Paul Maholm 4.00 10.00
S179 Manny Parra 4.00 10.00
S180 Rickie Weeks 4.00 10.00
S181 Dan Haren 4.00 10.00
S182 Magglio Ordonez 6.00 15.00
S183 Troy Tulowitzki 10.00 25.00
S184 Freddy Sanchez 4.00 10.00
S185 James Loney 4.00 10.00
S186 Michael Cuddyer 4.00 10.00
S187 Lance Berkman 6.00 15.00
S188 Chipper Jones 10.00 25.00
S189 Eric Chavez 4.00 10.00
S190 Ryan Howard 8.00 20.00
S191 Gary Sheffield 4.00 10.00
S192 Eric Byrnes 4.00 10.00
S193 Jayson Werth 6.00 15.00
S194 Adrian Beltre 10.00 25.00
S195 Fred Lewis 4.00 10.00
S196 Vernon Wells 4.00 10.00
S197 Jake Peavy 4.00 10.00
S198 Joakim Soria 4.00 10.00
S199 B.J. Upton 6.00 15.00
S200 J.D. Drew 4.00 10.00
S201 Ivan Rodriguez 6.00 15.00
S202 Felipe Lopez 4.00 10.00
S203 David Hernandez 4.00 10.00
S204 Brian Fuentes 4.00 10.00
S205 Jonathan Broxton 4.00 10.00
S206 Tommy Hanson 10.00 25.00
S207 Daniel Schlereth 4.00 10.00
S208 Gordon Beckham 12.00 30.00
S209 Sean O'Sullivan 4.00 10.00
S210 Gabe Gross 4.00 10.00
S211 Orlando Hudson 4.00 10.00
S212 Matt Murton 4.00 10.00
S213 Rich Hill 4.00 10.00
S214 J.A. Happ 6.00 15.00
S215 Kris Medlen 10.00 25.00
S216 Daniel Bard 4.00 10.00
S217 Laynce Nix 4.00 10.00
S218 Jake Fox 6.00 15.00
S219 Carl Pavano 4.00 10.00
S220 Clayton Richard 4.00 10.00
S221 Edwin Jackson 4.00 10.00
S222 Gary Sheffield 4.00 10.00
S223 Kyle Blanks 6.00 15.00
S224 Vin Mazzaro 4.00 10.00
S225 Juan Uribe 4.00 10.00
S226 David Ross 4.00 10.00
S227 Russell Branyan 4.00 10.00
S228 David Eckstein 4.00 10.00
S229 Wilkin Ramirez 4.00 10.00
S230 John Mayberry Jr. 6.00 15.00
S231 Sean West 6.00 15.00
S232 Matt Lindstrom 4.00 10.00
S233 Jermey Reed 4.00 10.00
S234 Emilio Bonifacio 4.00 10.00
S235 Gerardo Parra 6.00 15.00
S236 Joe Crede 6.00 15.00
S237 Tony Gwynn 4.00 10.00
S238 Kevin Gregg 4.00 10.00
S239 CC Sabathia 6.00 15.00
S240 Nick Green 4.00 10.00
S241 Anthony Swarzak 4.00 10.00
S242 Livan Hernandez 4.00 10.00
S243 Chris Coghlan 10.00 25.00
S244 Jeff Weaver 4.00 10.00
S245 Alfredo Figaro 4.00 10.00
S246 Aaron Poreda 4.00 10.00
S247 Delwyn Young 6.00 15.00
S248 Fernando Martinez 10.00 25.00
S249 Gaby Sanchez 6.00 15.00
S250 Derek Holland 6.00 15.00
S251 Jayson Nix 4.00 10.00
S252 Raul Ibanez 6.00 15.00
S253 Andrew McCutchen 20.00 50.00
S254 Edgar Renteria 4.00 10.00
S255 Chris Perez 4.00 10.00
S256 Maicer Izturis 4.00 10.00
S257 Mark Kotsay 4.00 10.00
S258 Jason Giambi 4.00 10.00
S259 Tyler Greene 4.00 10.00
S260 Omar Vizquel 6.00 15.00
S261 Diory Hernandez 4.00 10.00
S262 Ben Zobrist 6.00 15.00
S263 Landon Powell 4.00 10.00
S264 Ty Wigginton 6.00 15.00
S265 Randy Johnson 10.00 25.00
S266 Jordan Zimmermann 10.00 25.00
S267 Victor Martinez 6.00 15.00
S268 Andruw Jones 4.00 10.00
S269 Jason Vargas 4.00 10.00
S270 Brad Bergesen 4.00 10.00
S271 Craig Stammen 4.00 10.00
S272 Matt LaPorta 6.00 15.00
S273 Takashi Saito 4.00 10.00
S274 Kevin Millar 4.00 10.00
S275 Randy Wells 4.00 10.00
S276 Javier Vazquez 4.00 10.00
S277 Mark Teixeira 6.00 15.00
S278 Cesar Izturis 4.00 10.00
S279 Omir Santos 4.00 10.00
S280 Jeff Niemann 4.00 10.00
S281 Chris Getz 4.00 10.00
S282 Brad Penny 4.00 10.00
S283 Mark DeRosa 6.00 15.00
S284 Jon Garland 4.00 10.00
S285 Matt Holliday 10.00 25.00
S286 Casey McGehee 4.00 10.00
S287 Brett Cecil 4.00 10.00
S288 Ryan Langerhans 4.00 10.00
S289 Endy Chavez 4.00 10.00
S290 Heath Bell 4.00 10.00
S291 Scott Podsednik 4.00 10.00
S292 Scott Richmond 4.00 10.00
S293 David Huff 4.00 10.00
S294 Ramon Castro 4.00 10.00
S295 Sean Marshall 4.00 10.00
S296 Ramon Ramirez 4.00 10.00
S297 Nolan Reimold 4.00 10.00
S298 Nate McLouth 4.00 10.00
S299 Matt Palmer 4.00 10.00
S300 Ken Griffey Jr. 20.00 50.00

2009 Topps Target Legends

RANDOM INSERTS IN TARGET PACKS
LLG1 Ted Williams 2.00 5.00
LLG2 Jackie Robinson 1.00 2.50
LLG3 Babe Ruth 2.50 6.00
LLG4 Honus Wagner 1.00 2.50
LLG5 Lou Gehrig 2.00 5.00
LLG6 Nolan Ryan 3.00 8.00
LLG7 Mickey Mantle 3.00 8.00
LLG8 Thurman Munson 1.00 2.50
LLG9 Cal Ripken Jr. 3.00 8.00
LLG10 George Sisler .60 1.50
LLG11 Mel Ott 1.00 2.50
LLG12 Bob Gibson .60 1.50
LLG13 Babe Ruth 2.50 6.00
LLG14 Roy Campanella 1.00 2.50
LLG15 Ty Cobb 1.50 4.00
LLG16 Cy Young 1.25 3.00
LLG17 Mickey Mantle 3.00 8.00
LLG18 Walter Johnson 1.00 2.50
LLG19 Pee Wee Reese .60 1.50
LLG20 Jimmie Foxx 1.00 2.50
LLG21 Rickey Henderson 1.00 2.50
LLG22 Ozzie Smith 1.25 3.00
LLG23 Babe Ruth 2.50 6.00
LLG24 Roger Maris 1.00 2.50
LLG25 Nolan Ryan 3.00 8.00
LLG26 Reggie Jackson .60 1.50
LLG27 Frank Robinson .60 1.50
LLG28 Ryne Sandberg 2.00 5.00
LLG29 Steve Carlton .60 1.50
LLG30 Johnny Bench 1.00 2.50

2009 Topps Topps Town

COMPLETE SET (75) 15.00 40.00
COMP.UPD.SET (25) 5.00 12.00
RANDOM INSERTS IN PACKS
UPDATE ODDS 1:9 HOBBY
1-50 ISSUED IN TOPPS
51-75 ISSUED IN UPDATE
COMP.GOLD SET (50) 40.00 80.00
COMP.UPD.GLD.SET (25) 8.00 20.00
*GOLD: 1X TO 2.5X BASIC
GOLD RANDOMLY INSERTED
TTT1 Alex Rodriguez .60 1.50
TTT2 Roy Halladay .30 .75
TTT3 Grady Sizemore .30 .75
TTT4 Brandon Webb .30 .75
TTT5 Evan Longoria .30 .75
TTT6 Johan Santana .30 .75
TTT7 Hanley Ramirez .30 .75
TTT8 Alex Gordon .30 .75
TTT9 Ryan Howard .40 1.00
TTT10 Jake Peavy .20 .50
TTT11 Nick Markakis .40 1.00
TTT12 Justin Morneau .30 .75
TTT13 Albert Pujols .60 1.50

TTT14 CC Sabathia .30 .75
TTT15 Alfonso Soriano .30 .75
TTT16 Ichiro Suzuki .60 1.50
TTT17 Francisco Rodriguez .30 .75
TTT18 Miguel Cabrera .50 1.25
TTT19 Carlos Quentin .20 .50
TTT20 Lance Berkman .30 .75
TTT21 Chipper Jones .50 1.25
TTT22 Tim Lincecum .30 .75
TTT23 Josh Hamilton .30 .75
TTT24 Jay Bruce .30 .75
TTT25 Daisuke Matsuzaka .30 .75
TTT26 Joe Mauer .40 1.00
TTT27 David Ortiz .50 1.25
TTT28 Jimmy Rollins .30 .75
TTT29 Derek Jeter 1.25 3.00
TTT30 Ryan Braun .30 .75
TTT31 Vladimir Guerrero .30 .75
TTT32 David Wright .40 1.00
TTT33 Carlos Lee .20 .50
TTT34 Dustin Pedroia .40 1.00
TTT35 Prince Fielder .30 .75
TTT36 Ian Kinsler .30 .75
TTT37 Justin Upton .30 .75
TTT38 Kosuke Fukudome .30 .75
TTT39 Carlos Zambrano .30 .75
TTT40 Nate McLouth .20 .50
TTT41 Manny Ramirez .50 1.25
TTT42 Kevin Youkilis .20 .50
TTT43 Curtis Granderson .40 1.00
TTT44 Todd Helton .30 .75
TTT45 Alex Rios .20 .50
TTT46 Roy Oswalt .30 .75
TTT47 Carlos Beltran .30 .75
TTT48 Mark Teixeira .30 .75
TTT49 Daisuke Matsuzaka .30 .75
TTT50 Chase Utley .30 .75
TTT51 Mariano Rivera .60 1.50
TTT52 Torii Hunter .20 .50
TTT53 Felix Hernandez .30 .75
TTT54 Adam Jones .30 .75
TTT55 Vernon Wells .20 .50
TTT56 Josh Beckett .30 .75
TTT57 Joey Votto .50 1.25
TTT58 Adrian Gonzalez .40 1.00
TTT59 Justin Verlander .50 1.25
TTT60 Dan Uggla .20 .50
TTT61 Zack Greinke .30 .75
TTT62 Russell Martin .20 .50
TTT63 Jose Reyes .30 .75
TTT64 Jorge Posada .30 .75
TTT65 Raul Ibanez .30 .75
TTT66 Chris Carpenter .30 .75
TTT67 Carl Crawford .30 .75
TTT68 Michael Young .20 .50
TTT69 Victor Martinez .20 .50
TTT70 Hunter Pence .30 .75
TTT71 Troy Tulowitzki .50 1.25
TTT72 Jacoby Ellsbury .40 1.00
TTT73 Matt Cain .30 .75
TTT74 Brian McCann .30 .75
TTT75 Alexei Ramirez .30 .75

2009 Topps Turkey Red

COMPLETE SET (150) 75.00 150.00
COMP.UPD.SET (50) 20.00 50.00
STATED ODDS 1:4 HOBBY
UPDATE ODDS 1:4 HOBBY
1-100 ISSUED IN TOPPS
101-150 ISSUED IN UPDATE
TR1 Babe Ruth 2.50 6.00
TR2 Evan Longoria .60 1.50
TR3 Jimmie Foxx 1.00 2.50
TR4 Alex Rios .40 1.00
TR5 Nick Markakis .75 2.00
TR6 Ian Kinsler .60 1.50
TR7 Andre Ethier .60 1.50
TR8 Ryan Ludwick .60 1.50
TR9 Tim Lincecum .60 1.50
TR10 Jackie Robinson 1.00 2.50
TR11 Bengie Molina .40 1.00
TR12 Jermaine Dye .40 1.00
TR13 Brian Giles .40 1.00
TR14 Chase Utley .60 1.50
TR15 David Ortiz 1.00 2.50
TR16 Joe Mauer .75 2.00
TR17 Conor Jackson .40 1.00
TR18 Jose Lopez .40 1.00
TR19 Brian McCann .60 1.50
TR20 George Sisler .60 1.50
TR21 Garret Anderson .40 1.00
TR22 Cliff Lee .60 1.50
TR23 Garrett Atkins .40 1.00
TR24 Curtis Granderson .75 2.00
TR25 Alex Rodriguez 1.25 3.00
TR26 Cristian Guzman .40 1.00
TR27 Aubrey Huff .40 1.00
TR28 Delmon Young .60 1.50
TR29 Carlos Quentin .40 1.00
TR30 Christy Mathewson 1.00 2.50
TR31 Justin Upton .60 1.50
TR32 Shane Victorino .40 1.00
TR33 Joey Votto 1.00 2.50
TR34 Kelly Johnson .40 1.00
TR35 David Wright .75 2.00
TR36 Jacoby Ellsbury .75 2.00
TR37 Kevin Kouzmanoff .40 1.00
TR38 Hunter Pence .60 1.50
TR39 Corey Hart .40 1.00
TR40 Kosuke Fukudome .60 1.50
TR41 Cole Hamels .75 2.00
TR42 Geovany Soto .60 1.50
TR43 Torii Hunter .40 1.00
TR44 Ervin Santana .40 1.00
TR45 Miguel Cabrera 1.00 2.50
TR46 Josh Johnson .60 1.50
TR47 Carlos Gomez .40 1.00
TR48 Nate McLouth .40 1.00
TR49 Ben Sheets .40 1.00
TR50 Tris Speaker .60 1.50
TR51 Josh Hamilton .60 1.50
TR52 Rich Harden .40 1.00
TR53 Francisco Rodriguez .60 1.50
TR54 Alex Gordon .60 1.50
TR55 Manny Ramirez 1.00 2.50
TR56 Carlos Zambrano .60 1.50
TR57 Brandon Webb .60 1.50
TR58 Alfonso Soriano .60 1.50
TR59 Mel Ott 1.00 2.50
TR60 Carlos Lee .40 1.00
TR61 Lou Gehrig 2.00 5.00
TR62 Adam Jones .60 1.50
TR63 Josh Beckett .40 1.00
TR64 Prince Fielder .60 1.50
TR65 Jimmy Rollins .60 1.50
TR66 Justin Morneau .60 1.50
TR67 Dan Uggla .40 1.00
TR68 Lance Berkman .60 1.50
TR69 Chipper Jones 1.00 2.50
TR70 Jon Lester .60 1.50
TR71 Albert Pujols 1.25 3.00
TR72 Ryan Braun .60 1.50
TR73 Grady Sizemore .60 1.50
TR74 Carlos Beltran .60 1.50
TR75 Hanley Ramirez .60 1.50
TR76 Jay Bruce .60 1.50
TR77 Derek Jeter 2.50 6.00
TR78 Matt Cain .60 1.50
TR79 Roy Campanella 1.00 2.50
TR80 Rogers Hornsby .60 1.50
TR81 Ryan Zimmerman .60 1.50
TR82 Dustin Pedroia .75 2.00
TR83 B.J. Upton .60 1.50
TR84 Jose Reyes .60 1.50
TR85 Johnny Mize .60 1.50
TR86 Magglio Ordonez .60 1.50
TR87 Ty Cobb 1.50 4.00
TR88 Michael Young .40 1.00
TR89 Todd Helton .60 1.50
TR90 Walter Johnson 1.00 2.50
TR91 Matt Kemp .75 2.00
TR92 Adrian Gonzalez .75 2.00
TR93 Pee Wee Reese .60 1.50
TR94 Ryan Doumit .40 1.00
TR95 Ryan Howard .75 2.00
TR96 Ichiro Suzuki 1.25 3.00
TR97 Cy Young 1.00 2.50
TR98 Mark Teixeira .60 1.50
TR99 Vladimir Guerrero .60 1.50
TR100 Honus Wagner 1.00 2.50
TR101 Ty Cobb 1.50 4.00
TR102 David Price .75 2.00
TR103 Jorge Posada .60 1.50
TR104 Brian Roberts .40 1.00
TR105 Tris Speaker .60 1.50
TR106 John Lackey .60 1.50
TR107 Miguel Tejada .60 1.50
TR108 Dan Haren .40 1.00
TR109 Troy Tulowitzki 1.00 2.50
TR110 Yunel Escobar .40 1.00
TR111 Koji Uehara 1.00 2.50
TR112 Vernon Wells .40 1.00
TR113 Jimmie Foxx 1.00 2.50
TR114 CC Sabathia .60 1.50
TR115 Alexei Ramirez .60 1.50
TR116 Rick Porcello 1.25 3.00
TR117 Gary Sheffield .40 1.00
TR118 Ryan Dempster .40 1.00
TR119 Shin-Soo Choo .60 1.50
TR120 Adam Dunn .60 1.50
TR121 Edinson Volquez .40 1.00
TR122 Kevin Youkilis .40 1.00
TR123 Roy Halladay .60 1.50
TR124 Justin Verlander 1.00 2.50
TR125 Max Scherzer 1.00 2.50
TR126 Jorge Cantu .40 1.00
TR127 Roy Oswalt .60 1.50
TR128 Tommy Hanson 1.00 2.50
TR129 Raul Ibanez .60 1.50
TR130 Johan Santana .60 1.50
TR131 Jermaine Dye .40 1.00
TR132 Mariano Rivera 1.25 3.00
TR133 Rogers Hornsby .60 1.50
TR134 Daisuke Matsuzaka .60 1.50
TR135 Andrew McCutchen 2.00 5.00
TR136 Jake Peavy .40 1.00
TR137 Jason Bay .60 1.50
TR138 Ken Griffey 2.00 5.00
TR139 Chris Carpenter .60 1.50
TR140 Carl Crawford .60 1.50
TR141 Victor Martinez .60 1.50
TR142 Brad Hawpe .40 1.00
TR143 Aaron Hill .40 1.00
TR144 Randy Johnson 1.00 2.50
TR145 Gordon Beckham .60 1.50
TR146 Jordan Zimmermann 1.00 2.50
TR147 Freddy Sanchez .40 1.00
TR148 Carlos Pena .60 1.50
TR149 Johnny Cueto .60 1.50
TR150 Babe Ruth 2.50 6.00

2009 Topps Wal-Mart Legends

RANDOM INSERTS IN WALMART PACKS
LLP1 Ted Williams 2.00 5.00
LLP2 Bob Gibson .60 1.50
LLP3 Babe Ruth 2.50 6.00
LLP4 Roy Campanella 1.00 2.50
LLP5 Ty Cobb 1.50 4.00
LLP6 Cy Young 1.00 2.50
LLP7 Mickey Mantle 3.00 8.00
LLP8 Walter Johnson 1.00 2.50
LLP9 Roberto Clemente 2.50 6.00
LLP10 Jimmie Foxx 1.00 2.50
LLP11 Johnny Mize .60 1.50
LLP11 Johnny Mize .60 1.50
LLP12 Jackie Robinson 1.00 2.50
LLP12 Jackie Robinson 1.00 2.50
LLP13 Babe Ruth 2.50 6.00
LLP13 Babe Ruth 2.50 6.00
LLP14 Honus Wagner 1.00 2.50
LLP14 Honus Wagner 1.00 2.50
LLP15 Lou Gehrig 2.00 5.00
LLP15 Lou Gehrig 2.00 5.00
LLP16 Nolan Ryan 3.00 8.00
LLP16 Nolan Ryan 3.00 8.00
LLP17 Mickey Mantle 3.00 8.00
LLP17 Mickey Mantle 3.00 8.00
LLP18 Thurman Munson 1.00 2.50
LLP18 Thurman Munson 1.00 2.50
LLP19 Christy Mathewson 1.00 2.50
LLP19 Christy Mathewson 1.00 2.50
LLP20 George Sisler .60 1.50
LLP20 George Sisler .60 1.50
LLP21 Babe Ruth 2.50 6.00
LLP22 Rickey Henderson 1.00 2.50
LLP23 Roger Maris 1.00 2.50
LLP24 Nolan Ryan 3.00 8.00
LLP25 Reggie Jackson .60 1.50
LLP26 Steve Carlton .60 1.50
LLP27 Tony Gwynn 1.00 2.50
LLP28 Paul Molitor 1.00 2.50
LLP29 Brooks Robinson .60 1.50
LLP30 Wade Boggs .60 1.50

2009 Topps Wal-Mart Legends Gold

*GOLD: .6X TO 1.5X BASIC
RANDOM INSERTS IN WAL MART PACKS

2009 Topps WBC Autographs

COMMON CARD 10.00 25.00
STATED ODDS 1:1418 HOBBY
STATED PRINT RUN 100 SER.#'d SETS
BM Brian McCann 10.00 25.00
CD Carlos Delgado 12.50 30.00
CG Curtis Granderson 10.00 25.00
CR Carlos Ruiz 10.00 25.00
DO David Ortiz 75.00 200.00
DP Dustin Pedroia 25.00 60.00
DW David Wright 75.00 150.00
JR Jose Reyes 10.00 25.00
RB Ryan Braun 12.00 30.00
AIR Alex Rios 10.00 25.00

2009 Topps WBC Autograph Relics

STATED ODDS 1:14,200 HOBBY
STATED PRINT RUN 50 SER.#'d SETS
CR Carlos Ruiz 15.00 40.00
JR Jose Reyes 12.50 30.00

2009 Topps WBC Stars

COMPLETE SET (25) 12.50 30.00
STATED ODDS 1:12 HOBBY
BCS1 David Wright .75 2.00
BCS2 Jin Young Kee .60 1.50
BCS3 Yulieski Gourriel 1.25 3.00
BCS4 Hiroyuki Nakajima .60 1.50
BCS5 Ichiro Suzuki 1.25 3.00
BCS6 Jose Reyes .60 1.50
BCS7 Yu Darvish 1.50 4.00
BCS8 Carlos Lee .40 1.00
BCS9 Fu-Te Ni .40 1.00
BCS10 Derek Jeter 2.50 6.00
BCS11 Adrian Gonzalez .75 2.00
BCS12 Dylan Lindsay .60 1.50
BCS13 Greg Halman .60 1.50
BCS14 Miguel Cabrera 1.00 2.50
BCS15 Chris Denorfia .40 1.00
BCS16 Aroldis Chapman 2.00 5.00
BCS17 Alex Rios .40 1.00
BCS18 Luke Hughes .40 1.00
BCS19 Gregor Blanco .40 1.00
BCS20 Bernie Williams .60 1.50
BCS21 Phillippe Aumont .60 1.50
BCS22 Shuichi Murata .60 1.50
BCS23 Frederich Cepeda .60 1.50
BCS24 Dustin Pedroia .75 2.00
BCS25 David Ortiz 1.00 2.50

2009 Topps WBC Stars Relics

STATED ODDS 1:219 HOBBY
AC Aroldis Chapman 8.00 20.00
BW Bernie Williams 4.00 10.00
DL Dylan Lindsay 3.00 8.00
FC Frederich Cepeda 3.00 8.00
GH Greg Halman 3.00 8.00
HR Hanley Ramirez 4.00 10.00
MO Magglio Ordonez 3.00 8.00
PA Phillippe Aumont 4.00 10.00
RM Russell Martin 4.00 10.00
FTN Fu-Te Ni 4.00 10.00
JRO Jimmy Rollins 5.00 12.00
LJY Jin Young Lee 3.00 8.00

2009 Topps WBC Stamp Collection

STATED ODDS 1:9400 HOBBY
STATED PRINT RUN 90 SER.#'d SETS
WBC1 Pro Baseball 10.00 25.00
WBC2 Baseball Centennial 15.00 40.00
WBC3 Take Me Out 10.00 25.00
WBC4 USA 12.50 30.00

2009 Topps World Baseball Classic Rising Star Redemption

COMPLETE SET (10) 8.00 20.00
1 Lee Jin Young .60 1.50
2 Derek Jeter 4.00 10.00
3 Gift Ngoepe .60 1.50
4 Ubaldo Jimenez .60 1.50
5 Sidney De Jong .60 1.50
6 Yoennis Cespedes 6.00 15.00
7 Yu Darvish 12.50 30.00
8 Dae Ho Lee .60 1.50
9 Jung Keun Bong .60 1.50
10 Daisuke Matsuzaka 1.00 2.50

2009 Topps World Champion Autographs

STATED ODDS 1:20,000 HOBBY
CR Carlos Ruiz 60.00 120.00
JW Jayson Werth 60.00 120.00
SV Shane Victorino 100.00 200.00

2009 Topps World Champion Relics

STATED ODDS 1:5600 HOBBY
STATED PRINT RUN 100 SER.#'d SETS
CH Cole Hamels Jsy 30.00 60.00
CU Chase Utley Jsy 40.00 80.00
JR Jimmy Rollins Jsy 30.00 60.00
PB Pat Burrell Bat 20.00 50.00
RH Ryan Howard Jsy 50.00 100.00

2009 Topps World Champion Relics Autographs

STATED ODDS 1:11,400 HOBBY
PRINT RUNS B/WN 8-50 COPIES PER
NO HAMELS PRICING AVAILABLE
JR Jimmy Rollins Jsy 75.00 150.00
RH Ryan Howard Jsy 200.00 400.00

2009 Topps Update

COMP.SET w/o VAR (330) 20.00 50.00
COMMON CARD (1-330) .12 .30
COMMON SP VAR (1-330) 5.00 12.00
SP VAR ODDS 1:32 HOBBY
COMMON RC (1-330) 4.00 1.00
PRINTING PLATE ODDS 1:615 HOBBY
PLATE PRINT RUN 1 SET PER COLOR
BLACK-CYAN-MAGENTA-YELLOW ISSUED
NO PLATE PRICING DUE TO SCARCITY
UH1 Ivan Rodriguez .20 .50
UH2 Felipe Lopez .12 .30
UH3 Michael Saunders RC 1.00 2.50
UH4 David Hernandez RC .40 1.00
UH5 Brian Fuentes .12 .30
UH6 Josh Barfield .12 .30
UH7 Brayan Pena .12 .30
UH8 Lance Broadway .12 .30
UH9 Jonathan Broxton .12 .30
UH10 Tommy Hanson RC 1.00 2.50
UH11 Daniel Schlereth RC .40 1.00
UH12 Edwin Maysonet .12 .30
UH13 Scott Hairston .12 .30
UH14 Yadier Molina .30 .75
UH15 Jacoby Ellsbury .25 .60
UH16 Brian Buscher .12 .30
UH17 D.Jeter/D.Wright .75 2.00
UH18 John Grabow .12 .30
UH19 Nelson Cruz .30 .75
UH20 Gordon Beckham RC .60 1.50
UH21 Matt Diaz .12 .30
UH22 Brett Gardner .20 .50
UH23 Sean O'Sullivan RC .40 1.00
UH24 Gabe Gross .12 .30
UH25 Orlando Hudson .12 .30
UH26 Ryan Howard .25 .60
UH27 Josh Reddick RC .60 1.50
UH28 Matt Murton .12 .30
UH29 Rich Hill .12 .30
UH30 J.A. Happ .20 .50
UH31 Adam Jones .20 .50
UH32 Kris Medlen RC 1.00 2.50
UH33 Daniel Bard RC .40 1.00
UH34 Laynce Nix .12 .30
UH35 Tom Gorzelanny .12 .30
UH36 Paul Konerko/Jermaine Dye .20 .50
UH37 Adam Kennedy .12 .30
UH38 Justin Upton .20 .50
UH39 Jake Fox .20 .50
UH40 Carl Pavano .12 .30
UH41 Xavier Paul (RC) .40 1.00
UH42 Eric Hinske .12 .30
UH43 Koyie Hill .12 .30
UH44 Seth Smith .12 .30
UH45 Brad Ausmus .12 .30
UH46 Clayton Richard .12 .30
UH47a Carlos Beltran .20 .50
UH47b D.Snider SP 6.00 15.00
UH48a Albert Pujols .40 1.00
UH48b R.Maris SP 6.00 15.00
UH49 Edwin Jackson .12 .30
UH50 Gary Sheffield .12 .30
UH51 Jesus Guzman RC .40 1.00
UH52a Kyle Blanks RC .60 1.50
UH52b Bo Jackson SP 5.00 12.00
UH53 Clete Thomas .12 .30
UH54 Vin Mazzaro RC .40 1.00
UH55 Ben Zobrist .20 .50
UH56 Wes Helms .12 .30
UH57 Juan Uribe .12 .30
UH58 Omar Quintanilla .12 .30
UH59 David Ross .12 .30
UH60 Brandon Inge .12 .30
UH61 Jamie Hoffmann RC .40 1.00
UH62 Russell Branyan .12 .30
UH63 Mark Rzepczynski RC .60 1.50
UH64 Alex Gonzalez .12 .30
UH65a Joe Mauer .25 .60
UH65b Paul Molitor SP 5.00 12.00
UH66 Jhoulys Chacin RC .60 1.50
UH67 Brandon McCarthy .12 .30
UH68 David Eckstein .12 .30
UH69 J.Girardi/D.Jeter .75 2.00
UH70 Wilkin Ramirez RC .40 1.00
UH71a Chase Utley .20 .50
UH71b Rogers Hornsby SP 5.00 12.00
UH71c R.Sandberg SP 6.00 15.00
UH72 John Mayberry Jr. (RC) .60 1.50
UH73 Sean West (RC) .60 1.50
UH74 Mitch Maier .12 .30
UH75 Matt Lindstrom .12 .30
UH76 Scott Rolen .20 .50
UH77 Jeremy Reed .12 .30
UH78 LaTroy Hawkins .12 .30
UH79 Robert Andino .12 .30
UH80 Matt Stairs .12 .30
UH81 Mark Teixeira .20 .50
UH82 David Wright .25 .60
UH83 Emilio Bonifacio .12 .30
UH84 Gerardo Parra RC .60 1.50
UH85 Joe Crede .20 .50
UH86 Carlos Pena .20 .50
UH87 Jake Peavy .12 .30
UH88 Jim Leyland/Tony La Russa .12 .30
UH89 Phil Hughes .12 .30
UH90 Orlando Cabrera .12 .30
UH91 Anderson Hernandez .12 .30
UH92 Edwin Encarnacion .30 .75
UH93 Pedro Martinez .20 .50
UH94 Jarrod Washburn .12 .30
UH95 Ryan Freel .12 .30
UH96 Tony Gwynn .12 .30
UH97 Juan Castro .12 .30
UH98a Hanley Ramirez .20 .50
UH98b Honus Wagner SP 5.00 12.00
UH99 Kevin Gregg .12 .30
UH100 CC Sabathia .20 .50
UH101 Nick Green .20 .50
UH102 Brett Hayes (RC) .40 1.00
UH103a Evan Longoria .20 .50
UH103b Wade Boggs SP 5.00 12.00
UH104 Geoff Blum .12 .30
UH105 Luis Valbuena .20 .50
UH106 Jonny Gomes .12 .30
UH107 Anthony Swarzak (RC) .40 1.00
UH108 Chris Tillman RC .60 1.50
UH109 Orlando Hudson .12 .30
UH110 Justin Masterson .12 .30
UH111 Livan Hernandez .12 .30
UH112 Kyle Farnsworth .12 .30
UH113 Francisco Rodriguez .20 .50
UH114 Chris Coghlan RC 1.00 2.50
UH115 Jeff Weaver .12 .30
UH116 Alfredo Figaro RC .40 1.00
UH117 Alex Rios .12 .30
UH118 Blake Hawksworth (RC) .40 1.00
UH119 Bud Norris RC .40 1.00
UH120 Aaron Poreda RC .40 1.00
UH121 Brandon Inge .12 .30
UH122 Youk/Wright/Jeter/Vict .75 2.00
UH123 Ryan Braun .20 .50
UH124 Delwyn Young .20 .50
UH125 Fernando Martinez RC 1.00 2.50
UH126 Matt Tolbert .12 .30
UH127 Shane Robinson RC .40 1.00
UH128 Chone Figgins .12 .30
UH129 Shane Victorino .12 .30
UH130 Randy Johnson .30 .75
UH131 Derek Jeter .75 2.00
UH132 Joe Thurston .12 .30
UH133 Graham Taylor RC .60 1.50
UH134 Derek Holland RC .60 1.50
UH135 R.Perry/R.Porcello .40 1.00
UH136 Raul Ibanez .20 .50
UH137 Ross Ohlendorf .12 .30
UH138 Ryan Church .12 .30
UH139 Brian Moehler .12 .30
UH140 Jack Wilson .12 .30
UH141 Jason Hammel .12 .30
UH142 Jorge Posada .20 .50
UH143 Matt Maloney (RC) .40 1.00
UH144 Ronny Cedeno .12 .30
UH145 Micah Hoffpauir .12 .30
UH146 Juan Cruz .12 .30
UH147 Jayson Nix .12 .30
UH148a Jason Bay .20 .50
UH148b Tris Speaker SP 5.00 12.00
UH149 Joel Hanrahan .20 .50
UH150a Raul Ibanez .20 .50
UH150b Ty Cobb SP 5.00 12.00
UH151 Jayson Werth .20 .50
UH152 Barbaro Canizares RC .40 1.00
UH153a Ichiro Suzuki .40 1.00
UH153b George Sisler SP 5.00 12.00
UH154 Gerardo Parra .20 .50
UH155 Andrew McCutchen (RC) 2.00 5.00
UH156 Heath Bell .12 .30
UH157 Josh Hamilton .20 .50
UH158 Wilson Valdez .12 .30
UH159 Chad Billingsley .20 .50
UH160 Edgar Renteria .12 .30
UH161 Andrew Bailey .30 .75
UH162 Chris Perez .12 .30
UH163 Alejandro De Aza .12 .30
UH164 Brett Tomko .12 .30
UH165 Maicer Izturis .12 .30
UH166 Mike Redmond .12 .30
UH167 Julio Borbon RC .40 1.00
UH168 Paul Phillips .12 .30
UH169 Mark Kotsay .12 .30
UH170 Jason Giambi .12 .30
UH171 Trevor Hoffman .20 .50
UH172 Tyler Greene (RC) .40 1.00
UH173 David Robertson .12 .30
UH174 Omar Vizquel .20 .50
UH175 Jody Gerut .12 .30
UH176 Diory Hernandez RC .40 1.00
UH177 Neftali Feliz RC .60 1.50
UH178 Josh Beckett .12 .30
UH179 Carl Crawford .20 .50
UH180 Mariano Rivera .40 1.00
UH181 Zach Duke .12 .30
UH182 Mark Buehrle .20 .50
UH183 Guillermo Quiroz .12 .30
UH184 Francisco Cordero .12 .30
UH185 Kevin Correia .12 .30
UH186a Zack Greinke .20 .50
UH186b Christy Mathewson SP 5.00 12.00
UH187 Ryan Franklin .20 .50
UH188 Jeff Francouer .20 .50
UH189 Michael Young
Josh Hamilton/Ian Kinsler .20 .50
UH190 Ken Griffey Jr. .60 1.50
UH191 Ben Zobrist .20 .50
UH192 Prince Fielder .20 .50
UH193 Landon Powell (RC) .40 1.00
UH194 Ty Wigginton .20 .50
UH195 P.J. Walters RC .40 1.00
UH196 Brian Fuentes .12 .30
UH197 Dan Haren .12 .30
UH198a Roy Halladay .20 .50
UH198b Cy Young SP 5.00 12.00
UH199 Mike Rivera .12 .30
UH200 Randy Johnson .30 .75
UH201 Jordan Zimmermann RC 1.00 2.50
UH202 Angel Berroa .12 .30
UH203 Ben Francisco .12 .30
UH204 Brian Barden .12 .30
UH205 Dallas Braden .20 .50
UH206 Chris Burke .12 .30
UH207 Garrett Jones .20 .50
UH208 Chad Gaudin .12 .30
UH209 Andruw Jones .12 .30
UH210 Jason Vargas .12 .30
UH211 Brad Bergesen (RC) .40 1.00
UH212 Ian Kinsler .20 .50
UH213 Josh Johnson .20 .50
UH214 Jason Grilli .12 .30
UH215 Felix Hernandez .20 .50
UH216 Mat Latos RC 1.25 3.00
UH217 Craig Stammen RC .40 1.00
UH218 Cliff Lee .20 .50
UH219 Ken Takahashi RC .60 1.50
UH220 Matt LaPorta RC .60 1.50
UH221 Adrian Gonzalez .25 .60
UH222 Ted Lilly .12 .30
UH223 Jack Hannahan .12 .30
UH224 Takashi Saito .12 .30
UH225 Gregorio Petit .12 .30
UH226 Kevin Hart .12 .30
UH227 Edwin Jackson .12 .30
UH228 Jason LaRue .12 .30
UH229 Kevin Millar .12 .30
UH230 Freddy Sanchez .12 .30
UH231 Josh Bard .12 .30
UH232a Tim Lincecum .20 .50
UH232b N.Ryan CAL SP 6.00 15.00
UH232c N.Ryan NYM SP 6.00 15.00
UH233 Ramon Santiago .12 .30
UH234 Mike Sweeney .12 .30
UH235 Joe Nathan .12 .30
UH236 Kris Benson .12 .30
UH237 Dustin Pedroia .25 .60
UH238 Kevin Cash .12 .30
UH239 George Sherrill .12 .30
UH240 Jason Marquis .12 .30
UH241 Dewayne Wise .12 .30
UH242 Randy Wells .12 .30
UH243 Jonathan Papelbon .20 .50
UH244 Johan Santana .20 .50
UH245 Mariano Rivera .40 1.00
UH246 Javier Vazquez .12 .30
UH247 Lastings Milledge .12 .30
UH248 Chan Ho Park .20 .50
UH249 Brian McCann .20 .50
UH250a Mark Teixeira .20 .50
UH250c Johnny Mize NYG SP 5.00 12.00
UH250b Johnny Mize NYY SP 5.00 12.00
UH251 Ian Snell .12 .30
UH252 Justin Verlander .30 .75
UH253a Prince Fielder .20 .50
UH253b Reggie Jackson CAL SP 5.00 12.00
UH253c Reggie Jackson OAK SP 5.00 12.00
UH254 Cesar Izturis .12 .30
UH255 Omir Santos RC .40 1.00
UH256 Tim Wakefield .20 .50
UH257 Adrian Gonzalez .25 .60
UH258 Nyjer Morgan .12 .30
UH259 Victor Martinez .20 .50
UH260a Ryan Howard .25 .60
UH260b Willie McCovey SP 5.00 12.00
UH261 Aaron Bates RC .40 1.00
UH262 Jeff Niemann .12 .30
UH263 Matt Holliday .30 .75
UH264 Adam LaRoche .12 .30
UH265 Justin Morneau .20 .50
UH266 Jonathan Broxton .12 .30
UH267 Miguel Cairo .12 .30
UH268 Chris Getz .12 .30
UH269 Cliff Floyd .12 .30
UH270 D.Ortiz/A.Rodriguez .40 1.00
UH271 Frank Catalanotto .12 .30
UH272 Carlos Pena .20 .50
UH273 Mark Lowe .12 .30
UH274 Joe Mauer .25 .60
UH275 Ryan Garko .12 .30
UH276 Brad Penny .12 .30
UH277 Orlando Hudson .12 .30
UH278 Gaby Sanchez RC .60 1.50
UH279 Ross Detwiler .12 .30
UH280 Mark DeRosa .20 .50
UH281a Kevin Youkilis .12 .30
UH281b Jimmie Foxx SP 5.00 12.00
UH282 Victor Martinez .20 .50
UH283 Freddy Sanchez .12 .30
UH284 Mark Melancon RC .40 1.00
UH285 Ryan Franklin .20 .50
UH286 Sidney Ponson .12 .30
UH287 Matt Joyce .12 .30
UH288 Jon Garland .12 .30
UH289 Nick Johnson .12 .30
UH290 Jason Michaels .12 .30
UH291 Ross Gload .12 .30
UH292 Yuniesky Betancourt .12 .30
UH293 Aaron Hill .12 .30
UH294 Josh Anderson .12 .30
UH295 Miguel Tejada .20 .50
UH296 Casey McGehee .12 .30
UH297 Brett Cecil RC .40 1.00
UH298 Jason Bartlett .12 .30
UH299 Ryan Langerhans .12 .30
UH300 Albert Pujols .40 1.00
UH301 Ryan Zimmerman .20 .50
UH302 Casey Kotchman .12 .30
UH303 Luke French (RC) .40 1.00
UH304 Nick Swisher/Johnny Damon .20 .50
UH305 Michael Young .12 .30
UH306 Endy Chavez .12 .30
UH307 Heath Bell .12 .30
UH308 Matt Cain .20 .50
UH309 Scott Podsednik .12 .30
UH310 Scott Richmond .12 .30
UH311 David Huff RC .40 1.00
UH312 Ryan Hanigan .12 .30
UH313 Jeff Baker .12 .30
UH314 Brad Hawpe .12 .30
UH315 Jerry Hairston Jr. .12 .30
UH316 H.Pence/R.Braun .20 .50
UH317 Nelson Cruz .30 .75
UH318a Carl Crawford .20 .50
UH318b Rickey Henderson SP 5.00 12.00
UH319 Ramon Castro .12 .30
UH320 Mark Schlereth/Daniel Schlereth .12 .30
UH321 Hunter Pence .20 .50
UH322 Sean Marshall .12 .30
UH323 Ramon Ramirez .12 .30
UH324 Nolan Reimold (RC) .40 1.00
UH325a Torii Hunter .12 .30
UH325b Frank Robinson SP 5.00 12.00
UH326 Nate McLouth .12 .30
UH327 Julio Lugo .12 .30
UH328 Matt Palmer .12 .30
UH329 Curtis Granderson .25 .60
UH330a Ken Griffey Jr. .60 1.50
UH330b B.Ruth Braves SP 8.00 20.00
UH330c B.Ruth Sox SP 8.00 20.00

2009 Topps Update Black

STATED ODDS 1:44 HOBBY
STATED PRINT RUN 58 SER.#'d SETS
UH1 Ivan Rodriguez 6.00 15.00
UH2 Felipe Lopez 4.00 10.00
UH3 Michael Saunders 10.00 25.00
UH4 David Hernandez 4.00 10.00
UH5 Brian Fuentes 4.00 10.00
UH6 Josh Barfield 4.00 10.00
UH7 Brayan Pena 4.00 10.00
UH8 Lance Broadway 4.00 10.00
UH9 Jonathan Broxton 4.00 10.00
UH10 Tommy Hanson 10.00 25.00
UH11 Daniel Schlereth 4.00 10.00
UH12 Edwin Maysonet 4.00 10.00
UH13 Scott Hairston 4.00 10.00
UH14 Yadier Molina 10.00 25.00
UH15 Jacoby Ellsbury 8.00 20.00
UH16 Brian Buscher 4.00 10.00
UH17 D.Jeter/D.Wright 25.00 60.00
UH18 John Grabow 4.00 10.00
UH19 Nelson Cruz 10.00 25.00
UH20 Gordon Beckham 6.00 15.00
UH21 Matt Diaz 4.00 10.00
UH22 Brett Gardner 6.00 15.00
UH23 Sean O'Sullivan 4.00 10.00
UH24 Gabe Gross 4.00 10.00
UH25 Orlando Hudson 4.00 10.00
UH26 Ryan Howard 8.00 20.00
UH27 Josh Reddick 6.00 15.00
UH28 Matt Murton 4.00 10.00
UH29 Rich Hill 4.00 10.00
UH30 J.A. Happ 6.00 15.00
UH31 Adam Jones 6.00 15.00
UH32 Kris Medlen 10.00 25.00
UH33 Daniel Bard 4.00 10.00
UH34 Laynce Nix 4.00 10.00
UH35 Tom Gorzelanny 4.00 10.00

UH36 Paul Konerko/Jermaine Dye 6.00 15.00
UH37 Adam Kennedy 4.00 10.00
UH38 Justin Upton 6.00 15.00
UH39 Jake Fox 6.00 15.00
UH40 Carl Pavano 4.00 10.00
UH41 Xavier Paul 4.00 10.00
UH42 Eric Hinske 4.00 10.00
UH43 Koyie Hill 4.00 10.00
UH44 Seth Smith 4.00 10.00
UH45 Brad Ausmus 4.00 10.00
UH46 Clayton Richard 4.00 10.00
UH47 Carlos Beltran 6.00 15.00
UH48 Albert Pujols 12.00 30.00
UH49 Edwin Jackson 4.00 10.00
UH50 Gary Sheffield 4.00 10.00
UH51 Jesus Guzman 4.00 10.00
UH52 Kyle Blanks 6.00 15.00
UH53 Clete Thomas 4.00 10.00
UH54 Vin Mazzaro 4.00 10.00
UH55 Ben Zobrist 6.00 15.00
UH56 Wes Helms 4.00 10.00
UH57 Juan Uribe 4.00 10.00
UH58 Omar Quintanilla 4.00 10.00
UH59 David Ross 4.00 10.00
UH60 Brandon Inge 4.00 10.00
UH61 Jamie Hoffmann 4.00 10.00
UH62 Russell Branyan 4.00 10.00
UH63 Mark Rzepczynski 6.00 15.00
UH64 Alex Gonzalez 4.00 10.00
UH65 Joe Mauer 8.00 20.00
UH66 Jhoulys Chacin 6.00 15.00
UH67 Brandon McCarthy 4.00 10.00
UH68 David Eckstein 4.00 10.00
UH69 J.Girardi/D.Jeter 25.00 60.00
UH70 Wilkin Ramirez 4.00 10.00
UH71 Chase Utley 6.00 15.00
UH72 John Mayberry Jr. 6.00 15.00
UH73 Sean West 6.00 15.00
UH74 Mitch Maier 4.00 10.00
UH75 Matt Lindstrom 4.00 10.00
UH76 Scott Rolen 6.00 15.00
UH77 Jeremy Reed 4.00 10.00
UH78 LaTroy Hawkins 4.00 10.00
UH79 Robert Andino 4.00 10.00
UH80 Matt Stairs 4.00 10.00
UH81 Mark Teixeira 6.00 15.00
UH82 David Wright 8.00 20.00
UH83 Emilio Bonifacio 4.00 10.00
UH84 Gerardo Parra 6.00 15.00
UH85 Joe Crede 6.00 15.00
UH86 Carlos Pena 6.00 15.00
UH87 Jake Peavy 4.00 10.00
UH88 Jim Leyland/Tony La Russa 4.00 10.00
UH89 Phil Hughes 4.00 10.00
UH90 Orlando Cabrera 4.00 10.00
UH91 Anderson Hernandez 4.00 10.00
UH92 Edwind Encarnacion 10.00 25.00
UH93 Pedro Martinez 6.00 15.00
UH94 Jarrod Washburn 4.00 10.00
UH95 Ryan Freel 4.00 10.00
UH96 Tony Gwynn 4.00 10.00
UH97 Juan Castro 4.00 10.00
UH98 Hanley Ramirez 6.00 15.00
UH99 Kevin Gregg 4.00 10.00
UH100 CC Sabathia 6.00 15.00
UH101 Nick Green 4.00 10.00
UH102 Brett Hayes 4.00 10.00
UH103 Evan Longoria 6.00 15.00
UH104 Geoff Blum 4.00 10.00
UH105 Luis Valbuena 6.00 15.00
UH106 Jonny Gomes 4.00 10.00
UH107 Anthony Swarzak 4.00 10.00
UH108 Chris Tillman 6.00 15.00
UH109 Orlando Hudson 4.00 10.00
UH110 Justin Masterson 4.00 10.00
UH111 Livan Hernandez 4.00 10.00
UH112 Kyle Farnsworth 4.00 10.00
UH113 Francisco Rodriguez 6.00 15.00
UH114 Chris Coghlan 10.00 25.00
UH115 Jeff Weaver 4.00 10.00
UH116 Alfredo Figaro 4.00 10.00
UH117 Alex Rios 4.00 10.00
UH118 Blake Hawksworth 4.00 10.00
UH119 Bud Norris 4.00 10.00
UH120 Aaron Poreda 4.00 10.00
UH121 Brandon Inge 4.00 10.00
UH122 Youk/Wrig/Jet/Vict 25.00 60.00
UH123 Ryan Braun 6.00 15.00
UH124 Delwyn Young 6.00 15.00
UH125 Fernando Martinez 10.00 25.00
UH126 Matt Tolbert 4.00 10.00
UH127 Shane Robinson 4.00 10.00
UH128 Chone Figgins 4.00 10.00
UH129 Shane Victorino 4.00 10.00
UH130 Randy Johnson 10.00 25.00
UH131 Derek Jeter 25.00 60.00
UH132 Joe Thurston 4.00 10.00
UH133 Graham Taylor 6.00 15.00
UH134 Derek Holland 6.00 15.00
UH135 R.Perry/R.Porcello 12.00 30.00
UH136 Raul Ibanez 6.00 15.00
UH137 Ross Ohlendorf 4.00 10.00
UH138 Ryan Church 4.00 10.00
UH139 Brian Moehler 4.00 10.00
UH140 Jack Wilson 4.00 10.00
UH141 Jason Hammel 4.00 10.00
UH142 Jorge Posada 6.00 15.00
UH143 Matt Maloney 4.00 10.00
UH144 Ronny Cedeno 4.00 10.00
UH145 Micah Hoffpauir 4.00 10.00
UH146 Juan Cruz 4.00 10.00
UH147 Jayson Nix 4.00 10.00
UH148 Jason Bay 6.00 15.00
UH149 Joel Hanrahan 6.00 15.00
UH150 Raul Ibanez 6.00 15.00
UH151 Jayson Werth 6.00 15.00
UH152 Barbaro Canizares 4.00 10.00
UH153 Ichiro Suzuki 12.00 30.00
UH154 Gerardo Parra 6.00 15.00
UH155 Andrew McCutchen 20.00 50.00
UH156 Heath Bell 4.00 10.00
UH157 Josh Hamilton 6.00 15.00
UH158 Wilson Valdez 4.00 10.00
UH159 Chad Billingsley 6.00 15.00
UH160 Edgar Renteria 4.00 10.00
UH161 Andrew Bailey 10.00 25.00
UH162 Chris Peréz 4.00 10.00
UH163 Alejandro De Aza 4.00 10.00
UH164 Brett Tomko 4.00 10.00
UH165 Maicer Izturis 4.00 10.00
UH166 Mike Redmond 4.00 10.00
UH167 Julio Borbon 4.00 10.00
UH168 Paul Phillips 4.00 10.00
UH169 Mark Kotsay 4.00 10.00
UH170 Jason Giambi 4.00 10.00
UH171 Trevor Hoffman 6.00 15.00
UH172 Tyler Greene 4.00 10.00
UH173 David Robertson 4.00 10.00
UH174 Omar Vizquel 6.00 15.00
UH175 Jody Gerut 4.00 10.00
UH176 Diory Hernandez 4.00 10.00
UH177 Neftali Feliz 6.00 15.00
UH178 Josh Beckett 4.00 10.00
UH179 Carl Crawford 6.00 15.00
UH180 Mariano Rivera 12.00 30.00
UH181 Zach Duke 4.00 10.00
UH182 Mark Buehrle 6.00 15.00
UH183 Guillermo Quiroz 4.00 10.00
UH184 Francisco Cordero 4.00 10.00
UH185 Kevin Correia 4.00 10.00
UH186 Zack Greinke 6.00 15.00
UH187 Ryan Franklin 6.00 15.00
UH188 Jeff Francoeur 6.00 15.00
UH189 Young/Hamil/Kinsler 6.00 15.00
UH190 Ken Griffey Jr. 20.00 50.00
UH191 Ben Zobrist 6.00 15.00
UH192 Prince Fielder 6.00 15.00
UH193 Landon Powell 4.00 10.00
UH194 Ty Wigginton 4.00 10.00
UH195 P.J. Walters 4.00 10.00
UH196 Brian Fuentes 4.00 10.00
UH197 Dan Haren 4.00 10.00
UH198 Roy Halladay 6.00 15.00
UH199 Mike Rivera 4.00 10.00
UH200 Randy Johnson 10.00 25.00
UH201 Jordan Zimmermann 10.00 25.00
UH202 Angel Berroa 4.00 10.00
UH203 Ben Francisco 4.00 10.00
UH204 Brian Barden 4.00 10.00
UH205 Dallas Braden 6.00 15.00
UH206 Chris Burke 4.00 10.00
UH207 Garrett Jones 6.00 15.00
UH208 Chad Gaudin 4.00 10.00
UH209 Andruw Jones 4.00 10.00
UH210 Jason Vargas 4.00 10.00
UH211 Brad Bergesen 4.00 10.00
UH212 Ian Kinsler 6.00 15.00
UH213 Josh Johnson 6.00 15.00
UH214 Jason Grilli 4.00 10.00
UH215 Felix Hernandez 6.00 15.00
UH216 Mat Latos 12.00 30.00
UH217 Craig Stammen 4.00 10.00
UH218 Cliff Lee 6.00 15.00
UH219 Ken Takahashi 6.00 15.00
UH220 Matt LaPorta 6.00 15.00
UH221 Adrian Gonzalez 8.00 20.00
UH222 Ted Lilly 4.00 10.00
UH223 Jack Hannahan 4.00 10.00
UH224 Takashi Saito 4.00 10.00
UH225 Gregorio Petit 4.00 10.00
UH226 Kevin Hart 4.00 10.00
UH227 Edwin Jackson 4.00 10.00
UH228 Jason LaRue 4.00 10.00
UH229 Kevin Millar 4.00 10.00
UH230 Freddy Sanchez 4.00 10.00
UH231 Josh Bard 4.00 10.00
UH232 Tim Lincecum 6.00 15.00
UH233 Ramon Santiago 4.00 10.00
UH234 Mike Sweeney 4.00 10.00
UH235 Joe Nathan 4.00 10.00
UH236 Kris Benson 4.00 10.00
UH237 Dustin Pedroia 8.00 20.00
UH238 Kevin Cash 4.00 10.00
UH239 George Sherrill 4.00 10.00
UH240 Jason Marquis 4.00 10.00
UH241 Dewayne Wise 4.00 10.00
UH242 Randy Wells 4.00 10.00
UH243 Jonathan Papelbon 6.00 15.00
UH244 Johan Santana 6.00 15.00
UH245 Mariano Rivera 12.00 30.00
UH246 Javier Vazquez 4.00 10.00
UH247 Lastings Milledge 4.00 10.00
UH248 Chan Ho Park 6.00 15.00
UH249 Brian McCann 6.00 15.00
UH250 Mark Teixeira 6.00 15.00
UH251 Ian Snell 4.00 10.00
UH252 Justin Verlander 10.00 25.00
UH253 Prince Fielder 6.00 15.00
UH254 Cesar Izturis 4.00 10.00
UH255 Omir Santos 4.00 10.00
UH256 Tim Wakefield 6.00 15.00
UH257 Adrian Gonzalez 8.00 20.00
UH258 Nyjer Morgan 4.00 10.00
UH259 Victor Martinez 6.00 15.00
UH260 Ryan Howard 8.00 20.00
UH261 Aaron Bates 4.00 10.00
UH262 Jeff Niemann 4.00 10.00
UH263 Matt Holliday 10.00 25.00
UH264 Adam LaRoche 4.00 10.00
UH265 Justin Morneau 6.00 15.00
UH266 Jonathan Broxton 4.00 10.00
UH267 Miguel Cairo 4.00 10.00
UH268 Chris Getz 4.00 10.00
UH269 Cliff Floyd 4.00 10.00
UH270 D.Ortiz/A.Rodriguez 12.00 30.00
UH271 Frank Catalanotto 4.00 10.00
UH272 Carlos Pena 6.00 15.00
UH273 Mark Lowe 4.00 10.00
UH274 Joe Mauer 8.00 20.00
UH275 Ryan Garko 4.00 10.00
UH276 Brad Penny 4.00 10.00
UH277 Orlando Hudson 4.00 10.00
UH278 Gaby Sanchez 6.00 15.00
UH279 Ross Detwiler 4.00 10.00
UH280 Mark DeRosa 6.00 15.00
UH281 Kevin Youkilis 6.00 15.00
UH282 Victor Martinez 6.00 15.00
UH283 Freddy Sanchez 4.00 10.00
UH284 Mark Melancon 4.00 10.00
UH285 Ryan Franklin 6.00 15.00
UH286 Sidney Ponson 4.00 10.00
UH287 Matt Joyce 4.00 10.00
UH288 Jon Garland 4.00 10.00
UH289 Nick Johnson 4.00 10.00
UH290 Jason Michaels 4.00 10.00
UH291 Ross Gload 4.00 10.00
UH292 Yuniesky Betancourt 4.00 10.00
UH293 Aaron Hill 4.00 10.00
UH294 Josh Anderson 4.00 10.00
UH295 Miguel Tejada 6.00 15.00
UH296 Casey McGehee 4.00 10.00
UH297 Brett Cecil 4.00 10.00
UH298 Jason Bartlett 4.00 10.00
UH299 Ryan Langerhans 4.00 10.00
UH300 Albert Pujols 12.00 30.00
UH301 Ryan Zimmerman 6.00 15.00
UH302 Casey Kotchman 4.00 10.00
UH303 Luke French 4.00 10.00
UH304 Nick Swisher/Johnny Damon 6.00 15.00
UH305 Michael Young 4.00 10.00
UH306 Endy Chavez 4.00 10.00
UH307 Heath Bell 4.00 10.00
UH308 Matt Cain 6.00 15.00
UH309 Scott Podsednik 4.00 10.00
UH310 Scott Richmond 4.00 10.00
UH311 David Huff 4.00 10.00
UH312 Ryan Hanigan 4.00 10.00
UH313 Jeff Baker 4.00 10.00
UH314 Brad Hawpe 4.00 10.00
UH315 Jerry Hairston Jr. 4.00 10.00
UH316 H.Pence/R.Braun 6.00 15.00
UH317 Nelson Cruz 10.00 25.00
UH318 Carl Crawford 6.00 15.00
UH319 Ramon Castro 4.00 10.00
UH320 Mark Schlereth/Daniel Schlereth 4.00 10.00
UH321 Hunter Pence 6.00 15.00
UH322 Sean Marshall 4.00 10.00
UH323 Ramon Ramirez 4.00 10.00
UH324 Nolan Reimold 4.00 10.00
UH325 Torii Hunter 4.00 10.00
UH326 Nate McLouth 4.00 10.00
UH327 Julio Lugo 4.00 10.00
UH328 Matt Palmer 4.00 10.00
UH329 Curtis Granderson 8.00 20.00
UH330 Ken Griffey Jr. 20.00 50.00

2009 Topps Update Gold Border

*GOLD VET: 2.5X TO 6X BASIC
*GOLD RC: .75X TO 2X BASIC RC
STATED ODDS 1:3 HOBBY
STATED PRINT RUN 2009 SER.#'d SETS

2009 Topps Update Target

*VETS: .5X TO 1.2X BASIC TOPPS CARDS
*RC: .5X TO 1.2X BASIC TOPSP RC CARDS

2009 Topps Update All-Star Stitches

STATED ODDS 1:58 HOBBY
AST1 Chase Utley 5.00 12.00
AST2 Nelson Cruz 3.00 8.00
AST3 Adam Jones 6.00 15.00
AST4 Justin Upton 3.00 8.00
AST5 Albert Pujols 15.00 40.00
AST6 Ben Zobrist 4.00 10.00
AST7 Joe Mauer 6.00 15.00
AST8 Yadier Molina 3.00 8.00
AST9 Mark Teixeira 5.00 12.00
AST10 David Wright 5.00 12.00
AST11 Carlos Pena 3.00 8.00
AST12 Hanley Ramirez 4.00 10.00
AST13 Adrian Gonzalez 4.00 10.00
AST14 Francisco Rodriguez 4.00 10.00
AST15 Evan Longoria 6.00 15.00
AST16 Brandon Inge 5.00 12.00
AST17 Shane Victorino 5.00 12.00
AST18 Raul Ibanez 5.00 12.00
AST19 Jason Bay 4.00 10.00
AST20 Jayson Werth 6.00 15.00
AST21 Ichiro Suzuki 10.00 25.00
AST22 Heath Bell 3.00 8.00
AST23 Andrew Bailey 3.00 8.00
AST24 Chad Billingsley 3.00 8.00
AST25 Josh Hamilton 5.00 12.00
AST26 Trevor Hoffman 3.00 8.00
AST27 Josh Beckett 4.00 10.00
AST28 Zach Duke 4.00 10.00
AST29 Mark Buehrle 3.00 8.00
AST30 Zack Greinke 5.00 12.00
AST31 Francisco Cordero 3.00 8.00
AST32 Ryan Franklin 12.50 30.00
AST33 Brian Fuentes 3.00 8.00
AST34 Dan Haren 3.00 8.00
AST35 Roy Halladay 4.00 10.00
AST36 Josh Johnson 3.00 8.00
AST37 Felix Hernandez 4.00 10.00
AST38 Ted Lilly 3.00 8.00
AST39 Edwin Jackson 4.00 10.00
AST40 Tim Lincecum 6.00 15.00
AST41 Joe Nathan 4.00 10.00
AST42 Jason Marquis 3.00 8.00
AST43 Jonathan Papelbon 3.00 8.00
AST44 Johan Santana 4.00 10.00
AST45 Mariano Rivera 4.00 10.00
AST46 Brian McCann 4.00 10.00
AST47 Justin Verlander 5.00 12.00
AST48 Prince Fielder 4.00 10.00
AST49 Tim Wakefield 4.00 10.00
AST50 Ryan Braun 4.00 10.00
AST51 Victor Martinez 3.00 8.00
AST52 Ryan Zimmerman 4.00 10.00
AST53 Orlando Hudson 3.00 8.00
AST54 Kevin Youkilis 3.00 8.00
AST55 Freddy Sanchez 3.00 8.00
AST56 Aaron Hill 4.00 10.00
AST57 Miguel Tejada 3.00 8.00
AST58 Jason Bartlett 3.00 8.00
AST59 Ryan Howard 8.00 20.00
AST60 Michael Young 3.00 8.00
AST61 Brad Hawpe 3.00 8.00
AST62 Carl Crawford 3.00 8.00
AST63 Hunter Pence 3.00 8.00
AST64 Curtis Granderson 4.00 10.00
AST65 Jonathan Broxton 3.00 8.00
AST66 Matt Cain 3.00 8.00

2009 Topps Update All-Star Stitches Gold

*GOLD: .75X TO 2X BASIC
STATED ODDS 1:616 HOBBY
STATED PRINT RUN 50 SER.#'d SETS

2009 Topps Update Career Quest Autographs

STATED ODDS 1:546 HOBBY
AM Andrew McCutchen 10.00 25.00
DH David Hernandez 3.00 8.00
DS Daniel Schlereth 3.00 8.00
GB Gordon Beckham 4.00 10.00
JZ Jordan Zimmermann 4.00 10.00
KU Koji Uehara 8.00 20.00
MG Mat Gamel 4.00 10.00
RB Reid Brignac 4.00 10.00
RP Ryan Perry 4.00 10.00
TH Tommy Hanson 5.00 12.00
VM Vin Mazzaro 4.00 10.00
RPO Rick Porcello 4.00 10.00

2009 Topps Update Chrome Rookie Refractors

ONE PER BOX TOPPER
CHR1 Michael Saunders 5.00 12.00
CHR2 David Hernandez 2.00 5.00
CHR3 Tommy Hanson 5.00 12.00
CHR4 Daniel Schlereth 2.00 5.00
CHR5 Nolan Reimold 4.00 10.00
CHR6 Sean O'Sullivan 2.00 5.00
CHR7 Josh Reddick 3.00 8.00
CHR8 Kris Medlen 5.00 12.00
CHR9 Daniel Bard 2.00 5.00
CHR10 Xavier Paul 2.00 5.00
CHR11 Jesus Guzman 2.00 5.00
CHR12 Kyle Blanks 3.00 8.00
CHR13 Vin Mazzaro 2.00 5.00
CHR14 Jamie Hoffmann 2.00 5.00
CHR15 Mark Rzepczynski 3.00 8.00
CHR16 Jhoulys Chacin 3.00 8.00
CHR17 Wilkin Ramirez 2.00 5.00
CHR18 John Mayberry Jr. 3.00 8.00
CHR19 Sean West 3.00 8.00
CHR20 Gerardo Parra 3.00 8.00
CHR21 Brett Hayes 2.00 5.00
CHR22 Anthony Swarzak 2.00 5.00
CHR23 Chris Tillman 3.00 8.00
CHR24 Chris Coghlan 5.00 12.00
CHR25 Alfredo Figaro 2.00 5.00
CHR26 Blake Hawksworth 2.00 5.00
CHR27 Bud Norris 2.00 5.00
CHR28 Aaron Poreda 2.00 5.00
CHR29 Fernando Martinez 5.00 12.00
CHR30 Shane Robinson 2.00 5.00
CHR31 Graham Taylor 3.00 8.00
CHR32 Derek Holland 3.00 8.00
CHR33 Matt Maloney 2.00 5.00
CHR34 Barbaro Canizares 2.00 5.00
CHR35 Andrew McCutchen 10.00 25.00
CHR36 Julio Borbon 2.00 5.00
CHR37 Tyler Greene 2.00 5.00
CHR38 Diory Hernandez 2.00 5.00
CHR39 Neftali Feliz 3.00 8.00
CHR40 Landon Powell 2.00 5.00
CHR41 P.J. Walters 2.00 5.00
CHR42 Jordan Zimmermann 5.00 12.00
CHR43 Brad Bergesen 2.00 5.00
CHR44 Mat Latos 6.00 15.00
CHR45 Craig Stammen 2.00 5.00
CHR46 Ken Takahashi 2.00 5.00
CHR47 Matt LaPorta 3.00 8.00
CHR48 Omir Santos 2.00 5.00
CHR49 Aaron Bates 2.00 5.00
CHR50 Gaby Sanchez 3.00 8.00
CHR51 Mark Melancon 2.00 5.00
CHR52 Brett Cecil 2.00 5.00
CHR53 Luke French 2.00 5.00
CHR54 David Huff 2.00 5.00
CHR55 Nolan Reimold 2.00 5.00

2009 Topps Update Legends of the Game Team Name Letter Patch

STATED ODDS 1:408 HOBBY
STATED PRINT RUN 50 SER.#'d SETS
BR Babe Ruth/50 * 10.00 25.00
CM Christy Mathewson/50 * 4.00 10.00
CY Cy Young/50 * 4.00 10.00
GS George Sisler/50 * 4.00 10.00
HW Honus Wagner/50 * 6.00 15.00
JF Jimmie Foxx/50 * 8.00 20.00
JM Johnny Mize/50 * 4.00 10.00
JR Jackie Robinson/50 * 6.00 15.00
LG Lou Gehrig/50 * 12.50 30.00
MM Mickey Mantle/50 * 12.50 30.00
PR Pee Wee Reese/50 * 6.00 15.00
RC Roy Campanella/50 * 10.00 25.00
RH Rogers Hornsby/50 * 12.50 30.00
TC Ty Cobb/50 * 10.00 25.00
TM Thurman Munson/50 * 10.00 25.00
TS Tris Speaker/50 * 4.00 10.00
WJ Walter Johnson/50 * 8.00 20.00
BR2 Babe Ruth/50 * 10.00 25.00

2009 Topps Update Propaganda

COMPLETE SET (30) 8.00 20.00
STATED ODDS 1:6 HOBBY
PP01 Adam Dunn .50 1.25
PP02 Adrian Gonzalez .60 1.50
PP03 Albert Pujols 1.00 2.50
PP04 Andrew McCutchen 1.50 4.00
PP05 Alfonso Soriano .50 1.25
PP06 Carlos Quentin .30 .75
PP07 Chipper Jones .75 2.00
PP08 David Wright .60 1.50
PP09 Dustin Pedroia .60 1.50
PP10 Evan Longoria .50 1.25
PP11 Grady Sizemore .50 1.25
PP12 Hanley Ramirez .50 1.25
PP13 Hunter Pence .50 1.25
PP14 Ichiro Suzuki 1.00 2.50
PP15 Andrew Bailey .75 2.00
PP16 Jay Bruce .50 1.25
PP17 Joe Mauer .60 1.50
PP18 Josh Hamilton .50 1.25
PP19 Justin Upton .50 1.25
PP20 Manny Ramirez .75 2.00
PP21 Mark Teixeira .50 1.25
PP22 Miguel Cabrera .75 2.00
PP23 Nick Markakis .60 1.50
PP24 Roy Halladay .50 1.25
PP25 Ryan Braun .50 1.25
PP26 Ryan Howard .60 1.50
PP27 Tim Lincecum .50 1.25
PP28 Todd Helton .50 1.25
PP29 Vladimir Guerrero .50 1.25
PP30 Zack Greinke .50 1.25

2009 Topps Update Stadium Stamp Collection

STATED ODDS 1:2280 HOBBY
STATED PRINT RUN 90 SER.#'d SETS
SSC1 Polo Grounds 12.50 30.00
SSC2 Forbes Field 10.00 25.00
SSC3 Wrigley Field 12.50 30.00
SSC4 Yankee Stadium 15.00 40.00
SSC5 Tiger Stadium 12.50 30.00
SSC6 Shibe Park 10.00 25.00
SSC7 Crosley Field 10.00 25.00
SSC8 Comiskey Park 10.00 25.00
SSC9 Fenway Park 12.50 30.00
SSC10 Ebbets Field 10.00 25.00

2010 Topps

COMP.HOBBY.SET (661) 40.00 80.00
COMP.ALLSTAR.SET (661) 40.00 80.00
COMP.PHILLIES SET (661) 40.00 80.00
COMP.RED SOX SET (661) 40.00 80.00
COMP.YANKEES SET (661) 40.00 80.00
COMP.SET w/o SPs (660) 30.00 60.00
COMP.SER. 1 SET w/o SPs (330) 12.50 30.00
COMP.SER. 2 SET w/o SPs (330) 12.50 30.00
COMMON CARD (1-660) .15 .40
COMMON RC (1-660) .25 .60
COMMON SP VAR (1-660) 5.00 12.00
COMMON PIE SP (1-660) 15.00 40.00
SER. 1 PRINTING PLATE ODDS 1:1417 HOBBY
SER. 2 PRINTING PLATE ODDS 1:1642 HOBBY
661B ISSUED IN FACTORY SETS
1A Prince Fielder .25 .60
1B H.Greenberg SP 6.00 15.00
2 Buster Posey RC 5.00 12.00
3 Derrek Lee .15 .40
4 Hanley/Pablo/Pujols .50 1.25
5 Texas Rangers .15 .40
6 Chicago White Sox .15 .40
7 Mickey Mantle 1.25 3.00
8 Mauer/Ichiro/Jeter 1.00 2.50
9 T.Lincecum NL CY .25 .60
10 Clayton Kershaw .75 2.00
11 Orlando Cabrera .15 .40
12 Doug Davis .15 .40
13A Melvin Mora COR .15 .40
Mora pictured on back
13B Melvin Mora ERR
Adam Jones pictured on back
14 Ted Lilly .15 .40
15 Bobby Abreu .15 .40
16 Johnny Cueto .25 .60
17 Dexter Fowler .25 .60
18 Tim Stauffer .15 .40
19 Felipe Lopez .15 .40
20A Tommy Hanson .15 .40
20B Warren Spahn SP 5.00 12.00
21 Cristian Guzman .15 .40
22 Anthony Swarzak .15 .40
23 Shane Victorino .25 .60
24 John Maine .15 .40
25 Adam Jones .25 .60
26 Zach Duke .15 .40
27 Lance Berkman/Mike Hampton .25 .60
28 Jonathan Sanchez .15 .40
29 Aubrey Huff .15 .40
30 Victor Martinez .25 .60
31 Jason Grilli .15 .40
32 Cincinnati Reds .15 .40
33 Adam Moore RC .25 .60
34 Michael Dunn RC .25 .60
35 Rick Porcello .25 .60
36 Tobi Stoner RC .40 1.00
37 Garret Anderson .15 .40
38 Houston Astros .15 .40
39 Jeff Baker .15 .40
40 Josh Johnson .25 .60
41 Los Angeles Dodgers .25 .60
42 Prince/Howard/Pujols .50 1.25
43 Marco Scutaro .25 .60
44 Howie Kendrick .15 .40
45 David Hernandez .15 .40
46 Chad Tracy .15 .40
47 Brad Penny .15 .40
48 Joey Votto .40 1.00
49 Jorge De La Rosa .15 .40
50A Zack Greinke .25 .60
50B C.Young SP 5.00 12.00
51 Eric Young Jr .15 .40
52 Billy Butler .15 .40
53 Craig Counsell .15 .40
54 John Lackey .25 .60
55 Manny Ramirez .40 1.00
56A Andy Pettitte .25 .60
56B W.Ford SP 6.00 15.00
57 CC Sabathia .25 .60
58 Kyle Blanks .15 .40
59 Kevin Gregg .15 .40
60 David Wright .30 .75
61 Skip Schumaker .15 .40
62 Kevin Millwood .15 .40
63 Josh Bard .15 .40
64 Drew Stubbs RC .60 1.50
65A Nick Swisher .25 .60
65B N.Swisher Pie 100.00 200.00
66 Kyle Phillips RC .25 .60
67 Matt LaPorta .15 .40
68 Brandon Inge .25 .60
69 Kansas City Royals .15 .40
70 Cole Hamels .30 .75
71 Mike Hampton .15 .40
72 Milwaukee Brewers .15 .40
73 Adam Wainwright
Chris Carpenter/Jorge De La Rosa .25 .60
74 Casey Blake .15 .40
75 Adrian Gonzalez .30 .75
76 Joe Saunders .15 .40
77 Kenshin Kawakami .25 .60
78 Cesar Izturis .15 .40
79 Francisco Cordero .15 .40
80A Tim Lincecum .25 .60
80B C.Mathewson SP 6.00 15.00
81 Ryan Theriot .15 .40
82 Jason Marquis .15 .40
83 Mark Teahen .15 .40
84 Nate Robertson .15 .40
85A Ken Griffey Jr. .75 2.00
85B J.Robinson SP 6.00 15.00
86 Gil Meche .15 .40
87 Darin Erstad .15 .40
88A Jerry Hairston Jr. .15 .40
88B J.Hairston Jr. Pie 15.00 40.00
89 J.A. Happ .25 .60
90A Ian Kinsler .25 .60
90B R.Hornsby SP 6.00 15.00
91 Erik Bedard .15 .40
92 David Eckstein .15 .40
93 Joe Nathan .15 .40
94A Ivan Rodriguez .25 .60
94B C.Fisk SP 6.00 15.00
95A Carl Crawford .25 .60
95B R.Henderson SP 6.00 15.00
96 Jon Garland .15 .40
97 Luis Durango RC .25 .60
98 Cesar Ramos (RC) .25 .60
99 Garrett Jones .25 .60
100A Albert Pujols .50 1.25
100B S.Musial SP 6.00 15.00
101 Scott Baker .15 .40
102 Minnesota Twins .15 .40
103 Daniel Murphy .30 .75
104 New York Mets .15 .40
105 Madison Bumgarner RC 2.00 5.00
106 Carp/Lince/Jurrjens .25 .60
107 Scott Hairston .15 .40
108 Erick Aybar .15 .40
109 Justin Masterson .15 .40
110A Andrew McCutchen .40 1.00
110B W.Stargell SP 6.00 15.00
111 Ty Wigginton .15 .40
112 Kevin Correia .15 .40
113 Willy Taveras .15 .40
114 Chris Iannetta .15 .40
115 Gordon Beckham .15 .40
116A Carlos Gomez .15 .40
116B R.Yount SP 6.00 15.00
117 David DeJesus .15 .40
118 Brandon Morrow .15 .40
119 Wilkin Ramirez .15 .40
120A Jorge Posada .25 .60
120B J.Posada Pie 30.00 60.00
121 Brett Anderson .15 .40
122 Carlos Ruiz .15 .40
123A Jeff Samardzija .15 .40
123B Samardzija Abe SP 75.00 150.00
124 Rickie Weeks .15 .40
125A Ichiro Suzuki .50 1.25
125B G.Sisler SP 5.00 12.00
126 John Smoltz .40 1.00
127 Hank Blalock .15 .40
128 Garrett Mock .15 .40
129 Reid Gorecki (RC) .40 1.00
130A Vladimir Guerrero .25 .60
130B R.Jackson SP 5.00 12.00
131 Dustin Richardson RC .25 .60
132 Cliff Lee .25 .60
133 Freddy Sanchez .15 .40
134 Philadelphia Phillies .15 .40
135A Ryan Dempster .15 .40
135B Dempster Abe SP 75.00 150.00
136 Adam Wainwright .25 .60
137 A's/R.Henderson .40 1.00
138 Carlos Pena
Mark Teixeira/Jason Bay .25 .60
139 Frank Francisco .15 .40
140 Matt Holliday .40 1.00
141 Chone Figgins .15 .40
142 Tim Hudson .25 .60
143 Omar Vizquel .25 .60
144 Rich Harden .15 .40
145 Justin Upton .25 .60
146 Yunel Escobar .15 .40
147 Huston Street .15 .40
148 Cody Ross .15 .40
149 Jose Guillen .15 .40
150 Joe Mauer .30 .75
151 Mat Gamel .15 .40
152 Nyjer Morgan .15 .40
153 Justin Duchscherer .15 .40
154 Pedro Feliz .15 .40
155 Zack Greinke AL CY .25 .60
156 Tony Gwynn Jr. .15 .40
157 Mike Sweeney .15 .40
158 Jeff Niemann .15 .40
159 Vernon Wells .15 .40
160 Miguel Tejada .25 .60
161 Denard Span .15 .40
162 Wade Davis (RC) .40 1.00
163 Josh Butler RC .25 .60
164 Carlos Carrasco (RC) .60 1.50
165A Brandon Phillips .15 .40
165B J.Morgan SP 5.00 12.00
166 Eric Byrnes .15 .40
167 San Diego Padres .15 .40
168 Brad Kilby RC .25 .60
169 Pittsburgh Pirates .15 .40
170 Jason Bay .25 .60
171 Felix/CC/Verland .40 1.00
172 Joe Mauer AL MVP .30 .75
173 Kendry Morales .15 .40
174 Mike Gonzalez .15 .40
175A Josh Hamilton .25 .60
175B R.Maris SP 6.00 15.00
176 Yovani Gallardo .15 .40
177 Adam Lind .25 .60
178 Kerry Wood .15 .40
179 Ryan Spilborghs .15 .40
180 Jayson Nix .15 .40
181 Nick Johnson .15 .40
182 Coco Crisp .15 .40
183 Jonathan Papelbon .25 .60
184 Jeff Francoeur .25 .60
185A Hideki Matsui .40 1.00
185B H.Matsui Pie 40.00 80.00
186 Andrew Bailey .15 .40
187 Will Venable .15 .40
188 Joe Blanton .15 .40
189 Adrian Beltre .40 1.00
190 Pablo Sandoval .25 .60
191 Mat Latos .25 .60
192 Andruw Jones .15 .40
193 Shairon Martis .15 .40
194 Neill Walker (RC) .40 1.00
195 James Shields .15 .40
196 Ian Desmond (RC) .40 1.00
197 Cleveland Indians .15 .40
198 Florida Marlins .15 .40
199 Seattle Mariners .15 .40
200A Roy Halladay .25 .60
200B W.Johnson SP 6.00 15.00
201 Detroit Tigers .15 .40
202 San Francisco Giants .15 .40
203 Zack Greinke/Felix Hernandez
Roy Halladay .25 .60
204 Elvis Andrus/Ian Kinsler .25 .60
205 Chris Coghlan .15 .40
206 Pujols/Prince/Howard .50 1.25
207 Colby Rasmus .25 .60
208 Tim Wakefield .25 .60
209 Alexei Ramirez .25 .60
210 Josh Beckett .25 .60
211 Kelly Shoppach .15 .40
212 Magglio Ordonez .25 .60
213 Ricky Nolasco .15 .40
214 Matt Kemp .30 .75
215 Max Scherzer .40 1.00
216 Mike Cameron .15 .40
217 Gio Gonzalez .25 .60
218 Fernando Martinez .15 .40
219 Kevin Hart .15 .40
220 Randy Johnson .40 1.00
221 Russell Branyan .15 .40
222A Curtis Granderson .30 .75
Tigers

222B Granderson SP Yanks 10.00 25.00
223 Ryan Church .15 .40
224 Rod Barajas .15 .40
225A David Price .30 .75
225B D.Price Pie 12.50 30.00
226 Juan Rivera .15 .40
227 Josh Thole RC .40 1.00
228 Chris Pettit RC .25 .60
229 Daniel McCutchen RC .40 1.00
230 Jonathan Broxton .15 .40
231 Luke Scott .15 .40
232 St. Louis Cardinals .25 .60
233 Mark Teixeira/Jason Bay/Adam Lind.25 .60
234 Tampa Bay Rays .15 .40
235 Neftali Feliz .15 .40
236 Andrew Bailey AL ROY .15 .40
237 R.Braun/P.Fielder .25 .60
238 Ian Stewart .15 .40
239 Juan Uribe .15 .40
240 Ricky Romero .15 .40
241 Rocco Baldelli .15 .40
242 Bobby Jenks .15 .40
243 Asdrubal Cabrera .25 .60
244 Barry Zito .25 .60
245 Lance Berkman .25 .60
246 Leo Nunez .15 .40
247 Andre Ethier .25 .60
248 Jason Kendall .15 .40
249 Jon Niese .15 .40
250A Mark Teixeira .25 .60
250B M.Teixeira Pie 30.00 60.00
250C L.Gehrig SP 8.00 20.00
251 John Lannan .15 .40
252 Ronny Cedeno .15 .40
253 Bengie Molina .15 .40
254 Edwin Jackson .15 .40
255 Chris Davis .25 .60
256 Akinori Iwamura .15 .40
257 Bobby Crosby .15 .40
258 Edwin Encarnacion .40 1.00
259 Daniel Hudson RC .40 1.00
260 New York Yankees .40 1.00
261 Matt Carson (RC) .25 .60
262 Homer Bailey .15 .40
263 Placido Polanco .15 .40
264 Arizona Diamondbacks .15 .40
265 Los Angeles Angels .15 .40
266 Humberto Quintero .15 .40
267 Toronto Blue Jays .15 .40
268 Juan Pierre .15 .40
269 ARod/Jeter/Cano 1.00 2.50
270 Michael Brantley RC .40 1.00
271 Jermaine Dye .15 .40
272 Jair Jurrjens .15 .40
273 Pat Neshek .15 .40
274 Stephen Drew .15 .40
275 Chris Coghlan NL ROY .15 .40
276 Matt Lindstrom .15 .40
277 Jarrod Washburn .15 .40
278 Carlos Delgado .15 .40
279 Randy Wolf .15 .40
280 Mark DeRosa .15 .40
281 Braden Looper .15 .40
282 Washington Nationals .15 .40
283 Adam Kennedy .15 .40
284 Ross Ohlendorf .15 .40
285 Kurt Suzuki .15 .40
286 Javier Vazquez .15 .40
287 Jhonny Peralta .15 .40
288 Boston Red Sox .25 .60
289 Lyle Overbay .15 .40
290 Orlando Hudson .15 .40
291 Austin Kearns .15 .40
292 Tommy Manzella (RC) .25 .60
293 Brent Dlugach (RC) .25 .60
294A Adam Dunn .25 .60
294B B.Ruth SP 10.00 25.00
295 Kevin Youkilis .15 .40
296 Atlanta Braves .15 .40
297 Ben Zobrist .25 .60
298 Baltimore Orioles .15 .40
299 Gary Sheffield .15 .40
300A Chase Utley .25 .60
300B R.Sandberg SP 6.00 15.00
301 Jack Cust .15 .40
302 Kevin Youkilis/David Ortiz .40 1.00
303 Chris Snyder .15 .40
304 Adam LaRoche .15 .40
305 Juan Francisco RC .40 1.00
306A Milton Bradley .25 .60
306B M.Bradley Abe SP 60.00 120.00
307 Henry Rodriguez RC .25 .60
308 Robinzon Diaz .15 .40
309 Gerald Laird .15 .40
310 Elvis Andrus .25 .60
311 Jose Valverde .15 .40
312 Tyler Flowers RC .40 1.00
313 Jason Kubel .15 .40
314 Angel Pagan .15 .40
315 Scott Kazmir .15 .40
316 Chris Young .15 .40
317 Ryan Doumit .15 .40
318 Nate Schierholtz .15 .40
319 Ryan Franklin .15 .40
320 Brian McCann .25 .60
321 Pat Burrell .15 .40
322 Travis Buck .15 .40
323 Jim Thome .25 .60
324 Alex Rios .15 .40
325 Julio Lugo .15 .40
326A Tyler Colvin RC .40 1.00
326B Colvin Abe SP 60.00 120.00
327 A.Pujols NL MVP .50 1.25
328 Chicago Cubs .25 .60
329 Colorado Rockies .15 .40
330 Brandon Allen (RC) .25 .60
331A Ryan Braun .25 .60
331B Eddie Mathews SP 6.00 15.00
332 Brad Hawpe .15 .40
333 Ryan Ludwick .15 .40
334 Jayson Werth .25 .60
335 Jordan Norberto RC .25 .60
336 C.J. Wilson .15 .40
337 Carlos Zambrano .25 .60
338 Brett Cecil .15 .40
339 Jose Reyes .25 .60
340 John Buck .15 .40
341 Texas Rangers .15 .40
342 Melky Cabrera .15 .40
343 Brian Bruney .15 .40
344 Brett Myers .15 .40
345 Chris Volstad .15 .40
346 Taylor Teagarden .15 .40
347 Aaron Harang .15 .40
348 Jordan Zimmermann .25 .60
349 Felix Pie .15 .40
350 Prince Fielder/Ryan Braun .25 .60
351 Koji Uehara .25 .60
352 Cameron Maybin .15 .40
353A Jason Heyward RC 1.00 2.50
353B J.Heyward Pie 8.00 20.00
354A Evan Longoria .25 .60
354B Johnny Mize SP 5.00 12.00
355 James Russell RC .60 1.50
356 Los Angeles Angels .15 .40
357 Scott Downs .15 .40
358 Mark Buehrle .25 .60
359 Aramis Ramirez .15 .40
360 Justin Morneau .25 .60
361 Washington Nationals .15 .40
362 Travis Snider .15 .40
363 Joba Chamberlain .15 .40
364 Trevor Hoffman .25 .60
365 Logan Ondrusek RC .25 .60
366 Hiroki Kuroda .15 .40
367 Wandy Rodriguez .15 .40
368 Wade LeBlanc .15 .40
369a David Ortiz .40 1.00
369b Jimmie Foxx SP 6.00 15.00
370A Robinson Cano .25 .60
370B R.Cano Pie 30.00 60.00
370C R.Cano Pie 30.00 60.00
370D Mel Ott SP 6.00 15.00
371 Nick Hundley .15 .40
372 Philadelphia Phillies .15 .40
373 Clint Barmes .15 .40
374 Scott Feldman .15 .40
375 Mike Leake RC .75 2.00
376 Esmil Rogers RC .25 .60
377A Felix Hernandez .25 .60
377B Tom Seaver SP 6.00 15.00
378 George Sherrill .15 .40
379 Phil Hughes .15 .40
380 J.D. Drew .15 .40
381 Miguel Montero .15 .40
382 Kyle Davies .15 .40
383 Derek Lowe .15 .40
384 Chris Johnson RC .40 1.00
385 Torii Hunter .15 .40
386 Dan Haren .15 .40
387 Josh Fields .15 .40
388 Joel Pineiro .15 .40
389 Troy Tulowitzki .40 1.00
390 Ervin Santana .15 .40
391 Manny Parra .15 .40
392 Carlos Monasterios RC .40 1.00
393 Jason Frasor .15 .40
394 Luis Castillo .15 .40
395 Jenrry Mejia RC .40 1.00
396 Jake Westbrook .15 .40
397 Colorado Rockies .15 .40
398 Carlos Gonzalez .25 .60
399A Matt Garza .15 .40
399B M.Garza UPD Pie 12.50 30.00
400A Alex Rodriguez .50 1.25
400B A.Rodriguez Pie 75.00 150.00
400C A.Rodriguez Pie 50.00 100.00
400D Frank Robinson SP 6.00 15.00
401 Chad Billingsley .25 .60
402 J.P. Howell .15 .40
403A Jimmy Rollins .25 .60
403B Ozzie Smith SP 6.00 15.00
404 Mariano Rivera .50 1.25
405 Dustin McGowan .15 .40
406 Jeff Francis .15 .40
407 Nick Punto .15 .40
408 Detroit Tigers .15 .40
409A Kosuke Fukudome .25 .60
409B Richie Ashburn SP 10.00 25.00
410 Oakland Athletics .15 .40
411 Jack Wilson .15 .40
412 San Francisco Giants .15 .40
413 J.J. Hardy .15 .40
414 Sean West .15 .40
415 Cincinnati Reds .15 .40
416 Ruben Tejada RC .40 1.00
417 Dallas Braden .25 .60
418 Aaron Laffey .15 .40
419 David Aardsma .15 .40
420 Shin-Soo Choo .25 .60
421 Doug Fister RC .40 1.00
422A Vin Mazzaro .15 .40
422B F.Cervelli Pie 30.00 60.00
423 Brad Bergesen .15 .40
424 David Herndon RC .25 .60
425 Dontrelle Willis .15 .40
426 Mark Reynolds .15 .40
427 Brandon Webb .25 .60
428 Baltimore Orioles .15 .40
429 Seth Smith .15 .40
430 Kazuo Matsui .15 .40
431 John Raynor RC .25 .60
432 A.J. Burnett .15 .40
433 Julio Borbon .15 .40
434 Kevin Slowey .15 .40
435A Nelson Cruz .40 1.00
435B N.Cruz Pie 15.00 30.00
436 New York Mets .25 .60
437 Luke Hochevar .15 .40
438 Jason Bartlett .15 .40
439 Emilio Bonifacio .15 .40
440 Willie Harris .15 .40
441 Clete Thomas .15 .40
442 Dan Runzler RC .40 1.00
443 Jason Hammel .25 .60
444 Yuniesky Betancourt .15 .40
445 Miguel Olivo .15 .40
446 Gavin Floyd .15 .40
447 Jeremy Guthrie .15 .40
448 Joakim Soria .15 .40
449 Ryan Sweeney .15 .40
450A Omir Santos .15 .40
450B O.Santos UPD Cup SP 15.00 40.00
451 Michael Saunders .25 .60
452 Allen Craig RC .60 1.50
453 Jesse English (RC) .25 .60
454 James Loney .15 .40
455 St. Louis Cardinals .25 .60
456 Clayton Richard .15 .40
457 Kanekoa Texeira RC .25 .60
458 Todd Wellemeyer .15 .40
459 Joel Zumaya .15 .40
460 Aaron Cunningham .15 .40
461 Tyson Ross RC .25 .60
462 Alcides Escobar .25 .60
463 Carlos Marmol .25 .60
464 Francisco Liriano .15 .40
465 Chien-Ming Wang .25 .60
466 Jered Weaver .25 .60
467A Fausto Carmona .15 .40
467B M.Talbot Pie 15.00 30.00
468 Delmon Young .25 .60
469 Alex Burnett RC .25 .60
470 New York Yankees .40 1.00
471 Drew Butera (RC) .25 .60
472 Toronto Blue Jays .15 .40
473 Jason Varitek .40 1.00
474 Kyle Kendrick .15 .40
475A Johnny Damon .25 .60
475B J.Damon Pie 20.00 50.00
476A Yadier Molina .40 1.00
476B Thurman Munson SP 6.00 15.00
477 Nate McLouth .15 .40
478 Conor Jackson .15 .40
479A Chris Carpenter .25 .60
479B Dizzy Dean SP 6.00 15.00
480 Boston Red Sox .25 .60
481 Scott Rolen .25 .60
482 Mike McCoy RC .25 .60
483 Daisuke Matsuzaka .25 .60
484 Mike Fontenot .15 .40
485 Jesus Flores .15 .40
486 Raul Ibanez .25 .60
487 Dan Uggla .15 .40
488 Delwyn Young .15 .40
489A Russell Martin .15 .40
489B Roy Campanella SP 6.00 15.00
490 Michael Bourn .15 .40
491 Rafael Furcal .15 .40
492 Brian Wilson .40 1.00
493A Travis Ishikawa .15 .40
493B T.Ishikawa UPD CUP SP 12.00 30.00
494 Andrew Miller .25 .60
495 Carlos Pena .25 .60
496 Rajai Davis .15 .40
497 Edgar Renteria .15 .40
498 Sergio Santos (RC) .25 .60
499 Michael Bowden .15 .40
500 Brad Lidge .15 .40
501 Jake Peavy .15 .40
502 Jhoulys Chacin .15 .40
503 Austin Jackson RC .40 1.00
504 Jeff Mathis .15 .40
505 Andy Marte .15 .40
506 Jose Lopez .15 .40
507 Francisco Rodriguez .25 .60
508A Chris Getz .15 .40
508B C.Getz UPD Cup SP 10.00 25.00
509A Todd Helton .25 .60
509B I.Davis Pie 20.00 50.00
510 Justin Upton/Mark Reynolds .25 .60
511 Chicago Cubs .25 .60
512 Scot Shields .15 .40
513 Scott Sizemore RC .40 1.00
514 Rafael Soriano .15 .40
515 Seattle Mariners .15 .40
516 Marlon Byrd .15 .40
517 Cliff Pennington .15 .40
518 Corey Hart .15 .40
519 Alexi Casilla .15 .40
520 Randy Wells .15 .40
521 Jeremy Bonderman .15 .40
522 Jordan Schafer .15 .40
523 Phil Coke .15 .40
524 Dusty Hughes RC .25 .60
525 David Huff .15 .40
526 Carlos Guillen .15 .40
527 Brandon Wood .15 .40
528 Brian Bannister .15 .40
529 Carlos Lee .15 .40
530 Steve Pearce .40 1.00
531 Matt Cain .25 .60
532A Hunter Pence .25 .60
532B Dale Murphy SP 6.00 15.00
533 Gary Matthews Jr. .15 .40
534 Hideki Okajima .15 .40
535 Andy Sonnanstine .15 .40
536 Matt Palmer .15 .40
537 Michael Cuddyer .15 .40
538 Travis Hafner .15 .40
539 Arizona Diamondbacks .15 .40
540 Sean Rodriguez .15 .40
541 Jason Motte .15 .40
542 Heath Bell .15 .40
543 Adam Jones/Nick Markakis .30 .75
544 Kevin Kouzmanoff .15 .40
545 Fred Lewis .15 .40
546 Bud Norris .15 .40
547 Brett Gardner .25 .60
548 Minnesota Twins .15 .40
549A Derek Jeter 1.00 2.50
549B Pee Wee Reese SP 6.00 15.00
550 Freddy Garcia .15 .40
551 Everth Cabrera .15 .40
552 Chris Tillman .15 .40
553 Florida Marlins .15 .40
554 Ramon Hernandez .15 .40
555 B.J. Upton .25 .60
556 Chicago White Sox .15 .40
557 Aaron Hill .15 .40
558 Ronny Paulino .15 .40
559A Nick Markakis .30 .75
559B Eddie Murray SP 6.00 15.00
560 Ryan Rowland-Smith .15 .40
561 Ryan Zimmerman .25 .60
562 Carlos Quentin .15 .40
563 Bronson Arroyo .15 .40
564 Houston Astros .15 .40
565 Franklin Morales .15 .40
566 Maicer Izturis .15 .40
567 Mike Pelfrey .25 .60
568 Jarrod Saltalamacchia .15 .40
569A Jacoby Ellsbury .30 .75
569B Tris Speaker SP 6.00 15.00
570 Josh Willingham .25 .60
571 Brandon Lyon .15 .40
572 Clay Buchholz .15 .40
573 Johan Santana .25 .60
574 Milwaukee Brewers .15 .40
575 Ryan Perry .15 .40
576 Paul Maholm .15 .40
577 Jason Jaramillo .15 .40
578 Aaron Rowand .15 .40
579A Trevor Cahill .15 .40
579B J.Miranda Pie 15.00 40.00
580 Ian Snell .15 .40
581 Chris Dickerson .15 .40
582 Martin Prado .15 .40
583 Anibal Sanchez .15 .40
584 Matt Capps .15 .40
585 Dioner Navarro .15 .40
586 Roy Oswalt .25 .60
587 David Murphy .15 .40
588 Landon Powell .15 .40
589 Edinson Volquez .15 .40
590A Ryan Howard .30 .75
590B Ernie Banks SP 6.00 15.00
591 Fernando Rodney .15 .40
592 Brian Roberts .15 .40
593 Derek Holland .15 .40
594 Andy LaRoche .15 .40
595 Mike Lowell .15 .40
596 Brendan Ryan .15 .40
597 J.R. Towles .15 .40
598 Alberto Callaspo .15 .40
599 Jay Bruce .25 .60
600A Hanley Ramirez .25 .60
600B Honus Wagner SP 6.00 15.00
601 Blake DeWitt .15 .40
602 Kansas City Royals .15 .40
603 Gerardo Parra .15 .40
604 Atlanta Braves .15 .40
605 A.J. Pierzynski .15 .40
606 Chad Qualls .15 .40
607 Ubaldo Jimenez .15 .40
608 Pittsburgh Pirates .15 .40
609 Jeff Suppan .15 .40
610 Alex Gordon .25 .60
611 Josh Outman .15 .40
612 Lastings Milledge .15 .40
613 Eric Chavez .15 .40
614 Kelly Johnson .15 .40
615A Justin Verlander .40 1.00
615B Nolan Ryan SP 8.00 20.00
616 Franklin Gutierrez .15 .40
617 Luis Valbuena .15 .40
618 Jorge Cantu .15 .40
619 Mike Napoli .15 .40
620 Geovany Soto .25 .60
621 Aaron Cook .15 .40
622 Cleveland Indians .15 .40
623 Miguel Cabrera .40 1.00
624 Carlos Beltran .25 .60
625 Grady Sizemore .25 .60
626 Glen Perkins .15 .40
627 Jeremy Hermida .15 .40
628 Ross Detwiler .15 .40
629 Oliver Perez .15 .40
630 Ben Francisco .15 .40
631 Marc Rzepczynski .15 .40
632 Daric Barton .15 .40
633 Daniel Bard .15 .40
634 Casey Kotchman .15 .40
635 Carl Pavano .15 .40
636 Evan Longoria/B.J. Upton .25 .60
637 Babe Ruth/Lou Gehrig 1.00 2.50
638 Paul Konerko .25 .60
639 Los Angeles Dodgers .25 .60
640 Matt Diaz .15 .40
641 Chase Headley .15 .40
642 San Diego Padres .15 .40
643 Michael Young .15 .40
644 David Purcey .15 .40
645 Texas Rangers .15 .40
646 Trevor Crowe .15 .40
647 Alfonso Soriano .25 .60
648 Brian Fuentes .15 .40
649 Casey McGehee .15 .40
650A Dustin Pedroia .30 .75
650B Ty Cobb SP 6.00 15.00
651 Mike Aviles .15 .40
652A Chipper Jones .40 1.00
652B Mickey Mantle SP 8.00 20.00
653A Nolan Reimold .15 .40
653B N.Reimold UPD Cup SP 10.00 25.00
654 Collin Balester .15 .40
655 Ryan Madson .15 .40
656 Jon Lester .25 .60
657 Chris Young .15 .40
658 Tommy Hunter .15 .40
659 Nick Blackburn .15 .40
660 Brandon McCarthy .15 .40
661A S.Strasburg MCG 10.00 25.00
661B S.Strasburg FS 5.00 12.00
661C Strasburg MCG AU/299 75.00 200.00
661D S.Strasburg UPD 4.00 10.00
661E S.Strasburg UPD SP VAR 25.00 60.00
661F S.Strasburg UPD Pie 40.00 100.00
661G B.Gibson UPD SP VAR 6.00 15.00

2010 Topps Black

SER.1 ODDS 1:96 HOBBY
SER.2 ODDS 1:112 HOBBY
STATED PRINT RUN 59 SER.#'d SETS
1 Prince Fielder 5.00 12.00
2 Buster Posey 25.00 60.00
3 Derrek Lee 4.00 10.00
4 Hanley/Pablo/Pujols 10.00 25.00
5 Texas Rangers 5.00 12.00
6 Chicago White Sox 5.00 12.00
7 Mickey Mantle 25.00 60.00
8 Mauer/Ichiro/Jeter 20.00 50.00
9 T.Lincecum NL CY 5.00 12.00
10 Clayton Kershaw 15.00 40.00
11 Orlando Cabrera 5.00 12.00
12 Doug Davis 5.00 12.00
13 Melvin Mora 5.00 12.00
14 Ted Lilly 5.00 12.00
15 Bobby Abreu 5.00 12.00
16 Johnny Cueto 8.00 20.00
17 Dexter Fowler 8.00 20.00
18 Tim Stauffer 5.00 12.00
19 Felipe Lopez 5.00 12.00
20 Tommy Hanson 4.00 10.00
21 Cristian Guzman 5.00 12.00
22 Anthony Swarzak 5.00 12.00
23 Shane Victorino 6.00 15.00
24 John Maine 5.00 12.00
25 Adam Jones 6.00 15.00
26 Zach Duke 5.00 12.00
27 Lance Berkman/Mike Hampton 6.00 15.00
28 Jonathan Sanchez 5.00 12.00
29 Aubrey Huff 5.00 12.00
30 Victor Martinez 6.00 15.00
31 Jason Grilli 5.00 12.00
32 Cincinnati Reds 5.00 12.00
33 Adam Moore 5.00 12.00
34 Michael Dunn 5.00 12.00
35 Rick Porcello 5.00 12.00
36 Tobi Stoner 6.00 15.00
37 Garret Anderson 5.00 12.00
38 Houston Astros 5.00 12.00
39 Jeff Baker 5.00 12.00
40 Josh Johnson 6.00 15.00
41 Los Angeles Dodgers 6.00 15.00
42 Prince/Howard/Pujols 10.00 25.00
43 Marco Scutaro 8.00 20.00
44 Howie Kendrick 5.00 12.00
45 David Hernandez 5.00 12.00
46 Chad Tracy 5.00 12.00
47 Brad Penny 5.00 12.00
48 Joey Votto 8.00 20.00
49 Jorge De La Rosa 5.00 12.00
50 Zack Greinke 5.00 12.00
51 Eric Young Jr 5.00 12.00
52 Billy Butler 5.00 12.00
53 Craig Counsell 5.00 12.00
54 John Lackey 8.00 20.00
55 Manny Ramirez 8.00 20.00
56 Andy Pettitte 6.00 15.00
57 CC Sabathia 6.00 15.00
58 Kyle Blanks 5.00 12.00
59 Kevin Gregg 5.00 12.00
60 David Wright 6.00 15.00
61 Skip Schumaker 5.00 12.00
62 Kevin Millwood 5.00 12.00
63 Josh Bard 5.00 12.00
64 Drew Stubbs 8.00 20.00
65 Nick Swisher 6.00 15.00
66 Kyle Phillips 5.00 12.00
67 Matt LaPorta 3.00 8.00
68 Brandon Inge 6.00 15.00
69 Kansas City Royals 5.00 12.00
70 Cole Hamels 6.00 15.00
71 Mike Hampton 5.00 12.00
72 Milwaukee Brewers 5.00 12.00
73 Adam Wainwright
Chris Carpenter/Jorge De La Rosa 6.00 15.00
74 Casey Blake 5.00 12.00
75 Adrian Gonzalez 8.00 20.00
76 Joe Saunders 5.00 12.00
77 Kenshin Kawakami 6.00 15.00
78 Cesar Izturis 5.00 12.00
79 Francisco Cordero 5.00 12.00
80 Tim Lincecum 5.00 12.00
81 Ryan Theriot 5.00 12.00
82 Jason Marquis 5.00 12.00
83 Mark Teahen 5.00 12.00
84 Nate Robertson 5.00 12.00
85 Ken Griffey Jr. 15.00 40.00
86 Gil Meche 5.00 12.00
87 Darin Erstad 5.00 12.00
88 Jerry Hairston Jr. 5.00 12.00
89 J.A. Happ 6.00 15.00
90 Ian Kinsler 6.00 15.00
91 Erik Bedard 5.00 12.00
92 David Eckstein 5.00 12.00
93 Joe Nathan 5.00 12.00
94 Ivan Rodriguez 6.00 15.00
95 Carl Crawford 6.00 15.00
96 Jon Garland 5.00 12.00
97 Luis Durango 5.00 12.00
98 Cesar Ramos 5.00 12.00
99 Garrett Jones 5.00 12.00
100 Albert Pujols 10.00 25.00
101 Scott Baker 5.00 12.00
102 Minnesota Twins 5.00 12.00
103 Daniel Murphy 10.00 25.00
104 New York Mets 6.00 15.00
105 Madison Bumgarner 25.00 60.00
106 Carp/Linc/Jurrjens 5.00 12.00
107 Scott Hairston 5.00 12.00
108 Erick Aybar 5.00 12.00
109 Justin Masterson 5.00 12.00
110 Andrew McCutchen 8.00 20.00
111 Ty Wigginton 5.00 12.00
112 Kevin Correia 5.00 12.00
113 Willy Taveras 5.00 12.00
114 Chris Iannetta 5.00 12.00
115 Gordon Beckham 4.00 10.00
116 Carlos Gomez 5.00 12.00
117 David DeJesus 5.00 12.00
118 Brandon Morrow 5.00 12.00
119 Wilkin Ramirez 5.00 12.00
120 Jorge Posada 6.00 15.00
121 Brett Anderson 5.00 12.00
122 Carlos Ruiz 5.00 12.00
123 Jeff Samardzija 5.00 12.00
124 Rickie Weeks 5.00 12.00
125 Ichiro Suzuki 10.00 25.00
126 John Smoltz 8.00 20.00
127 Hank Blalock 5.00 12.00
128 Garrett Mock 5.00 12.00
129 Reid Gorecki 6.00 15.00
130 Vladimir Guerrero 5.00 12.00
131 Dustin Richardson 5.00 12.00
132 Cliff Lee 6.00 15.00
133 Freddy Sanchez 5.00 12.00
134 Philadelphia Phillies 5.00 12.00
135 Ryan Dempster 5.00 12.00
136 Adam Wainwright 6.00 15.00
137 Oakland Athletics 5.00 12.00
138 Carlos Pena/Mark Teixeira
Jason Bay 5.00 12.00
139 Frank Francisco 5.00 12.00
140 Matt Holliday 8.00 20.00
141 Chone Figgins 5.00 12.00
142 Tim Hudson 8.00 20.00
143 Omar Vizquel 6.00 15.00
144 Rich Harden 5.00 12.00
145 Justin Upton 6.00 15.00
146 Yunel Escobar 5.00 12.00
147 Huston Street 5.00 12.00
148 Cody Ross 5.00 12.00
149 Jose Guillen 5.00 12.00
150 Joe Mauer 6.00 15.00
151 Mat Gamel 5.00 12.00
152 Nyjer Morgan 5.00 12.00
153 Justin Duchscherer 5.00 12.00
154 Pedro Feliz 5.00 12.00
155 Zack Greinke AL CY 5.00 12.00
156 Tony Gwynn Jr. 5.00 12.00
157 Mike Sweeney 5.00 12.00
158 Jeff Niemann 5.00 12.00
159 Vernon Wells 5.00 12.00
160 Miguel Tejada 6.00 15.00
161 Denard Span 5.00 12.00
162 Wade Davis 8.00 20.00
163 Josh Butler 5.00 12.00
164 Carlos Carrasco 8.00 20.00
165 Brandon Phillips 5.00 12.00
166 Eric Byrnes 5.00 12.00
167 San Diego Padres 5.00 12.00
168 Brad Kilby 5.00 12.00
169 Pittsburgh Pirates 5.00 12.00
170 Jason Bay 6.00 15.00
171 King Felix/Sabathia/Verlander 10.00 25.00
172 Joe Mauer AL MVP 6.00 15.00
173 Kendry Morales 5.00 12.00
174 Mike Gonzalez 5.00 12.00
175 Josh Hamilton 5.00 12.00
176 Yovani Gallardo 5.00 12.00
177 Adam Lind 6.00 15.00
178 Kerry Wood 5.00 12.00
179 Ryan Spilborghs 5.00 12.00
180 Jayson Nix 5.00 12.00
181 Nick Johnson 5.00 12.00
182 Coco Crisp 5.00 12.00
183 Jonathan Papelbon 6.00 15.00
184 Jeff Francoeur 6.00 15.00
185 Hideki Matsui 8.00 20.00
186 Andrew Bailey 5.00 12.00
187 Will Venable 5.00 12.00
188 Joe Blanton 5.00 12.00
189 Adrian Beltre 12.00 30.00
190 Pablo Sandoval 6.00 15.00
191 Mat Latos 8.00 20.00
192 Andruw Jones 5.00 12.00
193 Shairon Martis 5.00 12.00
194 Neil Walker 8.00 20.00
195 James Shields 5.00 12.00
196 Ian Desmond 8.00 20.00
197 Cleveland Indians 5.00 12.00
198 Florida Marlins 5.00 12.00
199 Seattle Mariners 5.00 12.00
200 Roy Halladay 5.00 12.00
201 Detroit Tigers 5.00 12.00
202 San Francisco Giants 5.00 12.00
203 Zack Greinke/Felix
Hernandez/Roy Halladay 5.00 12.00
204 Elvis Andrus/Ian Kinsler 6.00 15.00
205 Chris Coghlan 4.00 10.00
206 Pujols/Prince/Howard 10.00 25.00
207 Colby Rasmus 5.00 12.00
208 Tim Wakefield 8.00 20.00
209 Alexei Ramirez 8.00 20.00
210 Josh Beckett 4.00 10.00
211 Kelly Shoppach 5.00 12.00
212 Magglio Ordonez 6.00 15.00
213 Ricky Nolasco 5.00 12.00
214 Matt Kemp 8.00 20.00
215 Max Scherzer 12.00 30.00
216 Mike Cameron 5.00 12.00
217 Gio Gonzalez 8.00 20.00
218 Fernando Martinez 5.00 12.00
219 Kevin Hart 5.00 12.00
220 Randy Johnson 10.00 25.00
221 Russell Branyan 5.00 12.00
222 Curtis Granderson 8.00 20.00
223 Ryan Church 5.00 12.00
224 Rod Barajas 5.00 12.00
225 David Price 6.00 15.00
226 Juan Rivera 5.00 12.00
227 Josh Thole 6.00 15.00
228 Chris Pettit 5.00 12.00
229 Daniel McCutchen 6.00 15.00
230 Jonathan Broxton 5.00 12.00
231 Luke Scott 5.00 12.00
232 St. Louis Cardinals 5.00 12.00
233 Mark Teixeira/Jason Bay/Adam Lind 5.00 12.00
234 Tampa Bay Rays 5.00 12.00
235 Neftali Feliz 4.00 10.00
236 Andrew Bailey AL ROY 5.00 12.00
237 Braun/Prince 5.00 12.00
238 Ian Stewart 5.00 12.00
239 Juan Uribe 5.00 12.00
240 Ricky Romero 5.00 12.00
241 Rocco Baldelli 5.00 12.00
242 Bobby Jenks 5.00 12.00
243 Asdrubal Cabrera 8.00 20.00
244 Barry Zito 8.00 20.00
245 Lance Berkman 6.00 15.00
246 Leo Nunez 5.00 12.00
247 Andre Ethier 6.00 15.00
248 Jason Kendall 5.00 12.00
249 Jon Niese 5.00 12.00
250 Mark Teixeira 5.00 12.00
251 John Lannan 5.00 12.00
252 Ronny Cedeno 5.00 12.00
253 Bengie Molina 5.00 12.00
254 Edwin Jackson 5.00 12.00
255 Chris Davis 8.00 20.00
256 Akinori Iwamura 5.00 12.00
257 Bobby Crosby 5.00 12.00
258 Edwin Encarnacion 12.00 30.00
259 Daniel Hudson 6.00 15.00
260 New York Yankees 8.00 20.00
261 Matt Carson 5.00 12.00
262 Homer Bailey 5.00 12.00
263 Placido Polanco 5.00 12.00
264 Arizona Diamondbacks 5.00 12.00
265 Los Angeles Angels 5.00 12.00
266 Humberto Quintero 5.00 12.00
267 Toronto Blue Jays 5.00 12.00
268 Juan Pierre 5.00 12.00
269 A.Rod/Jeter/Cano 20.00 50.00
270 Michael Brantley 8.00 20.00
271 Jermaine Dye 5.00 12.00
272 Jair Jurrjens 5.00 12.00
273 Pat Neshek 5.00 12.00
274 Stephen Drew 4.00 10.00
275 Chris Coghlan NL ROY 4.00 10.00
276 Matt Lindstrom 5.00 12.00
277 Jarrod Washburn 5.00 12.00
278 Carlos Delgado 5.00 12.00
279 Randy Wolf 5.00 12.00
280 Mark DeRosa 5.00 12.00
281 Braden Looper 5.00 12.00
282 Washington Nationals 5.00 12.00
283 Adam Kennedy 5.00 12.00
284 Ross Ohlendorf 5.00 12.00
285 Kurt Suzuki 5.00 12.00
286 Javier Vazquez 5.00 12.00
287 Jhonny Peralta 5.00 12.00
288 Boston Red Sox 6.00 15.00
289 Lyle Overbay 5.00 12.00
290 Orlando Hudson 5.00 12.00
291 Austin Kearns 5.00 12.00
292 Tommy Manzella 5.00 12.00
293 Brent Dlugach 5.00 12.00
294 Adam Dunn 8.00 20.00

295 Kevin Youkilis 4.00 10.00
296 Atlanta Braves 5.00 12.00
297 Ben Zobrist 8.00 20.00
298 Baltimore Orioles 5.00 12.00
299 Gary Sheffield 5.00 12.00
300 Chase Utley 5.00 12.00
301 Jack Cust 5.00 12.00
302 Kevin Youkilis/David Ortiz 10.00 25.00
303 Chris Snyder 5.00 12.00
304 Adam LaRoche 5.00 12.00
305 Juan Francisco 6.00 15.00
306 Milton Bradley 5.00 12.00
307 Henry Rodriguez 5.00 12.00
308 Robinzon Diaz 5.00 12.00
309 Gerald Laird 5.00 12.00
310 Elvis Andrus 6.00 15.00
311 Jose Valverde 5.00 12.00
312 Tyler Flowers 6.00 15.00
313 Jason Kubel 5.00 12.00
314 Angel Pagan 5.00 12.00
315 Scott Kazmir 5.00 12.00
316 Chris Young 5.00 12.00
317 Ryan Doumit 5.00 12.00
318 Nate Schierholtz 5.00 12.00
319 Ryan Franklin 5.00 12.00
320 Brian McCann 6.00 15.00
321 Pat Burrell 5.00 12.00
322 Travis Buck 5.00 12.00
323 Jim Thome 6.00 15.00
324 Alex Rios 4.00 10.00
325 Julio Lugo 5.00 12.00
326 Tyler Colvin 6.00 15.00
327 A.Pujols NL MVP 10.00 25.00
328 Chicago Cubs 6.00 15.00
329 Colorado Rockies 5.00 12.00
330 Brandon Allen 5.00 12.00
331 Ryan Braun 5.00 12.00
332 Brad Hawpe 5.00 12.00
333 Ryan Ludwick 5.00 12.00
334 Jayson Werth 8.00 20.00
335 Jordan Norberto 5.00 12.00
336 C.J. Wilson 5.00 12.00
337 Carlos Zambrano 6.00 15.00
338 Brett Cecil 5.00 12.00
339 Jose Reyes 6.00 15.00
340 John Buck 5.00 12.00
341 Texas Rangers 5.00 12.00
342 Melky Cabrera 5.00 12.00
343 Brian Bruney 5.00 12.00
344 Brett Myers 5.00 12.00
345 Chris Volstad 5.00 12.00
346 Taylor Teagarden 5.00 12.00
347 Aaron Harang 5.00 12.00
348 Jordan Zimmermann 8.00 20.00
349 Felix Pie 5.00 12.00
350 Prince Fielder/Ryan Braun 5.00 12.00
351 Koji Uehara 4.00 10.00
352 Cameron Maybin 4.00 10.00
353 Jason Heyward 100.00 175.00
354 Evan Longoria 5.00 12.00
355 James Russell 8.00 20.00
356 Los Angeles Angels 5.00 12.00
357 Scott Downs 5.00 12.00
358 Mark Buehrle 8.00 20.00
359 Aramis Ramirez 5.00 12.00
360 Justin Morneau 6.00 15.00
361 Washington Nationals 5.00 12.00
362 Travis Snider 5.00 12.00
363 Joba Chamberlain 4.00 10.00
364 Trevor Hoffman 8.00 20.00
365 Logan Ondrusek 5.00 12.00
366 Hiroki Kuroda 5.00 12.00
367 Wandy Rodriguez 5.00 12.00
368 Wade LeBlanc 5.00 12.00
369 David Ortiz 10.00 25.00
370 Robinson Cano 6.00 15.00
371 Nick Hundley 5.00 12.00
372 Philadelphia Phillies 5.00 12.00
373 Clint Barmes 5.00 12.00
374 Scott Feldman 5.00 12.00
375 Mike Leake 10.00 25.00
376 Esmil Rogers 5.00 12.00
377 Felix Hernandez 6.00 15.00
378 George Sherrill 5.00 12.00
379 Phil Hughes 5.00 12.00
380 J.D. Drew 5.00 12.00
381 Miguel Montero 5.00 12.00
382 Kyle Davies 5.00 12.00
383 Derek Lowe 5.00 12.00
384 Chris Johnson 8.00 20.00
385 Torii Hunter 5.00 12.00
386 Dan Haren 5.00 12.00
387 Josh Fields 5.00 12.00
388 Joel Pineiro 5.00 12.00
389 Troy Tulowitzki 10.00 25.00
390 Ervin Santana 5.00 12.00
391 Manny Parra 5.00 12.00
392 Carlos Monasterios 6.00 15.00
393 Jason Frasor 5.00 12.00
394 Luis Castillo 5.00 12.00
395 Jenrry Mejia 8.00 20.00
396 Jake Westbrook 5.00 12.00
397 Colorado Rockies 5.00 12.00
398 Carlos Gonzalez 8.00 20.00
399 Matt Garza 5.00 12.00
400 Alex Rodriguez 10.00 25.00
401 Chad Billingsley 8.00 20.00
402 J.P. Howell 5.00 12.00
403 Jimmy Rollins 6.00 15.00
404 Mariano Rivera 10.00 25.00
405 Dustin McGowan 5.00 12.00
406 Jeff Francis 5.00 12.00
407 Nick Punto 5.00 12.00
408 Detroit Tigers 5.00 12.00
409 Kosuke Fukudome 5.00 12.00
410 Oakland Athletics 5.00 12.00
411 Jack Wilson 5.00 12.00
412 San Francisco Giants 5.00 12.00
413 J.J. Hardy 5.00 12.00
414 Sean West 5.00 12.00
415 Cincinnati Reds 5.00 12.00
416 Ruben Tejada 6.00 15.00
417 Dallas Braden 6.00 15.00
418 Aaron Laffey 5.00 12.00
419 David Aardsma 5.00 12.00
420 Shin-Soo Choo 8.00 20.00
421 Doug Fister 5.00 12.00
422 Vin Mazzaro 5.00 12.00
423 Brad Bergesen 5.00 12.00
424 David Herndon 5.00 12.00
425 Dontrelle Willis 5.00 12.00
426 Mark Reynolds 5.00 12.00
427 Brandon Webb 6.00 15.00
428 Baltimore Orioles 5.00 12.00
429 Seth Smith 5.00 12.00
430 Kazuo Matsui 5.00 12.00
431 John Raynor 5.00 12.00
432 A.J. Burnett 4.00 10.00
433 Julio Borbon 5.00 12.00
434 Kevin Slowey 5.00 12.00
435 Nelson Cruz 12.00 30.00
436 New York Mets 6.00 15.00
437 Luke Hochevar 5.00 12.00
438 Jason Bartlett 5.00 12.00
439 Emilio Bonifacio 5.00 12.00
440 Willie Harris 5.00 12.00
441 Clete Thomas 5.00 12.00
442 Dan Runzler 6.00 15.00
443 Jason Hammel 8.00 20.00
444 Yuniesky Betancourt 5.00 12.00
445 Miguel Olivo 5.00 12.00
446 Gavin Floyd 5.00 12.00
447 Jeremy Guthrie 5.00 12.00
448 Joakim Soria 5.00 12.00
449 Ryan Sweeney 5.00 12.00
450 Omir Santos 5.00 12.00
451 Michael Saunders 8.00 20.00
452 Allen Craig 12.00 30.00
453 Jesse English 5.00 12.00
454 James Loney 4.00 10.00
455 St. Louis Cardinals 6.00 15.00
456 Clayton Richard 5.00 12.00
457 Kanekoa Texeira 5.00 12.00
458 Todd Wellemeyer 5.00 12.00
459 Joel Zumaya 5.00 12.00
460 Aaron Cunningham 5.00 12.00
461 Tyson Ross 5.00 12.00
462 Alcides Escobar 6.00 15.00
463 Carlos Marmol 8.00 20.00
464 Francisco Liriano 5.00 12.00
465 Chien-Ming Wang 5.00 12.00
466 Jered Weaver 8.00 20.00
467 Fausto Carmona 5.00 12.00
468 Delmon Young 6.00 15.00
469 Alex Burnett 5.00 12.00
470 New York Yankees 8.00 20.00
471 Drew Butera 5.00 12.00
472 Toronto Blue Jays 5.00 12.00
473 Jason Varitek 8.00 20.00
474 Kyle Kendrick 5.00 12.00
475 Johnny Damon 6.00 15.00
476 Yadier Molina 10.00 25.00
477 Nate McLouth 5.00 12.00
478 Conor Jackson 5.00 12.00
479 Chris Carpenter 6.00 15.00
480 Boston Red Sox 6.00 15.00
481 Scott Rolen 6.00 15.00
482 Mike McCoy 5.00 12.00
483 Daisuke Matsuzaka 5.00 12.00
484 Mike Fontenot 5.00 12.00
485 Jesus Flores 5.00 12.00
486 Raul Ibanez 6.00 15.00
487 Dan Uggla 4.00 10.00
488 Delwyn Young 5.00 12.00
489 Russell Martin 4.00 10.00
490 Michael Bourn 5.00 12.00
491 Rafael Furcal 5.00 12.00
492 Brian Wilson 12.00 30.00
493 Travis Ishikawa 5.00 12.00
494 Andrew Miller 8.00 20.00
495 Carlos Pena 6.00 15.00
496 Rajai Davis 5.00 12.00
497 Edgar Renteria 5.00 12.00
498 Sergio Santos 5.00 12.00
499 Michael Bowden 5.00 12.00
500 Brad Lidge 5.00 12.00
501 Jake Peavy 4.00 10.00
502 Jhoulys Chacin 5.00 12.00
503 Austin Jackson 5.00 12.00
504 Jeff Mathis 5.00 12.00
505 Andy Marte 5.00 12.00
506 Jose Lopez 5.00 12.00
507 Francisco Rodriguez 6.00 15.00
508 Chris Getz 5.00 12.00
509 Todd Helton 6.00 15.00
510 Justin Upton/Mark Reynolds 6.00 15.00
511 Chicago Cubs 6.00 15.00
512 Scott Shields 5.00 12.00
513 Scott Sizemore 6.00 15.00
514 Rafael Soriano 5.00 12.00
515 Seattle Mariners 5.00 12.00
516 Marlon Byrd 5.00 12.00
517 Cliff Pennington 5.00 12.00
518 Corey Hart 5.00 12.00
519 Alexi Casilla 5.00 12.00
520 Randy Wells 5.00 12.00
521 Jeremy Bonderman 5.00 12.00
522 Jordan Schafer 5.00 12.00
523 Phil Coke 5.00 12.00
524 Dusty Hughes 5.00 12.00
525 David Huff 5.00 12.00
526 Carlos Guillen 5.00 12.00
527 Brandon Wood 5.00 12.00
528 Brian Bannister 5.00 12.00
529 Carlos Lee 5.00 12.00
530 Steve Pearce 12.00 30.00
531 Matt Cain 6.00 15.00
532 Hunter Pence 6.00 15.00
533 Gary Matthews Jr. 5.00 12.00
534 Hideki Okajima 5.00 12.00
535 Andy Sonnanstine 5.00 12.00
536 Matt Palmer 5.00 12.00
537 Michael Cuddyer 5.00 12.00
538 Travis Hafner 5.00 12.00
539 Arizona Diamondbacks 5.00 12.00
540 Sean Rodriguez 5.00 12.00
541 Jason Motte 5.00 12.00
542 Heath Bell 5.00 12.00
543 Adam Jones/Nick Markakis 8.00 20.00
544 Kevin Kouzmanoff 5.00 12.00
545 Fred Lewis 5.00 12.00
546 Bud Norris 5.00 12.00
547 Brett Gardner 8.00 20.00
548 Minnesota Twins 5.00 12.00
549 Derek Jeter 20.00 50.00
550 Freddy Garcia 5.00 12.00
551 Everth Cabrera 5.00 12.00
552 Chris Tillman 5.00 12.00
553 Florida Marlins 5.00 12.00
554 Ramon Hernandez 5.00 12.00
555 B.J. Upton 6.00 15.00
556 Chicago White Sox 5.00 12.00
557 Aaron Hill 5.00 12.00
558 Ronny Paulino 5.00 12.00
559 Nick Markakis 8.00 20.00
560 Ryan Rowland-Smith 5.00 12.00
561 Ryan Zimmerman 6.00 15.00
562 Carlos Quentin 4.00 10.00
563 Bronson Arroyo 5.00 12.00
564 Houston Astros 5.00 12.00
565 Franklin Morales 5.00 12.00
566 Maicer Izturis 5.00 12.00
567 Mike Pelfrey 5.00 12.00
568 Jarrod Saltalamacchia 5.00 12.00
569 Jacoby Ellsbury 6.00 15.00
570 Josh Willingham 8.00 20.00
571 Brandon Lyon 5.00 12.00
572 Clay Buchholz 4.00 10.00
573 Johan Santana 5.00 12.00
574 Milwaukee Brewers 5.00 12.00
575 Ryan Perry 5.00 12.00
576 Paul Maholm 5.00 12.00
577 Jason Jaramillo 5.00 12.00
578 Aaron Rowand 5.00 12.00
579 Trevor Cahill 5.00 12.00
580 Ian Snell 5.00 12.00
581 Chris Dickerson 5.00 12.00
582 Martin Prado 5.00 12.00
583 Anibal Sanchez 5.00 12.00
584 Matt Capps 5.00 12.00
585 Dioner Navarro 5.00 12.00
586 Roy Oswalt 6.00 15.00
587 David Murphy 5.00 12.00
588 Landon Powell 5.00 12.00
589 Edinson Volquez 5.00 12.00
590 Ryan Howard 6.00 15.00
591 Fernando Rodney 5.00 12.00
592 Brian Roberts 5.00 12.00
593 Derek Holland 5.00 12.00
594 Andy LaRoche 5.00 12.00
595 Mike Lowell 5.00 12.00
596 Brendan Ryan 5.00 12.00
597 J.R. Towles 5.00 12.00
598 Alberto Callaspo 5.00 12.00
599 Jay Bruce 6.00 15.00
600 Hanley Ramirez 5.00 12.00
601 Blake DeWitt 5.00 12.00
602 Kansas City Royals 5.00 12.00
603 Gerardo Parra 5.00 12.00
604 Atlanta Braves 5.00 12.00
605 A.J. Pierzynski 5.00 12.00
606 Chad Qualls 5.00 12.00
607 Ubaldo Jimenez 4.00 10.00
608 Pittsburgh Pirates 5.00 12.00
609 Jeff Suppan 5.00 12.00
610 Alex Gordon 6.00 15.00
611 Josh Outman 5.00 12.00
612 Lastings Milledge 5.00 12.00
613 Eric Chavez 5.00 12.00
614 Kelly Johnson 5.00 12.00
615 Justin Verlander 10.00 25.00
616 Franklin Gutierrez 5.00 12.00
617 Luis Valbuena 5.00 12.00
618 Jorge Cantu 5.00 12.00
619 Mike Napoli 5.00 12.00
620 Geovany Soto 6.00 15.00
621 Aaron Cook 5.00 12.00
622 Cleveland Indians 5.00 12.00
623 Miguel Cabrera 10.00 25.00
624 Carlos Beltran 8.00 20.00
625 Grady Sizemore 6.00 15.00
626 Glen Perkins 5.00 12.00
627 Jeremy Hermida 5.00 12.00
628 Ross Detwiler 5.00 12.00
629 Oliver Perez 5.00 12.00
630 Ben Francisco 5.00 12.00
631 Marc Rzepczynski 5.00 12.00
632 Daric Barton 5.00 12.00
633 Daniel Bard 5.00 12.00
634 Casey Kotchman 5.00 12.00
635 Carl Pavano 5.00 12.00
636 Evan Longoria/B.J. Upton 5.00 12.00
637 Babe Ruth/Lou Gehrig 20.00 50.00
638 Paul Konerko 8.00 20.00
639 Los Angeles Dodgers 6.00 15.00
640 Matt Diaz 5.00 12.00
641 Chase Headley 5.00 12.00
642 San Diego Padres 5.00 12.00
643 Michael Young 4.00 10.00
644 David Purcey 5.00 12.00
645 Texas Rangers 5.00 12.00
646 Trevor Crowe 5.00 12.00
647 Alfonso Soriano 6.00 15.00
648 Brian Fuentes 5.00 12.00
649 Casey McGehee 5.00 12.00
650 Dustin Pedroia 6.00 15.00
651 Mike Aviles 5.00 12.00
652 Chipper Jones 8.00 20.00
653 Nolan Reimold 4.00 10.00
654 Collin Balester 5.00 12.00
655 Ryan Madson 5.00 12.00
656 Jon Lester 6.00 15.00
657 Chris Young 5.00 12.00
658 Tommy Hunter 5.00 12.00
659 Nick Blackburn 5.00 12.00
660 Brandon McCarthy 5.00 12.00

2010 Topps Copper

*COPPER VET: 4X TO 10X BASIC
*COPPER RC: 2.5X TO 6X BASIC RC
STATED ODDS 1:11 WM RETAIL
STATED PRINT RUN 399 SER.#'d SETS

2010 Topps Gold Border

*GOLD VET: 2X TO 5X BASIC
*GOLD RC: 1.2X TO 3X BASIC RC
STATED ODDS 1:6 HOBBY
STATED PRINT RUN 2010 SER.#'d SETS
1-330 ISSUED IN SERIES 1
331-660 ISSUE IN SERIES 2

2010 Topps Target

*VETS: .5X TO 1.2X BASIC TOPPS CARDS
*RC: .5X TO 1.2X BASIC TOPPS RC CARDS

2010 Topps Wal-Mart Black Border

*VETS: .5X TO 1.2X BASIC TOPPS CARDS
*RC: .5X TO 1.2X BASIC TOPPS RC CARDS

2010 Topps 2020

COMPLETE SET (20) 6.00 15.00
STATED ODDS 1:6 HOBBY
T1 Ryan Braun .50 1.25
T2 Gordon Beckham .30 .75
T3 Andre Ethier .50 1.25
T4 David Price .60 1.50
T5 Justin Upton .50 1.25
T6 Hunter Pence .50 1.25
T7 Ryan Howard .60 1.50
T8 Buster Posey 2.50 6.00
T9 Madison Bumgarner 2.50 6.00
T10 Evan Longoria .50 1.25
T11 Joe Mauer .60 1.50
T12 Chris Coghlan .30 .75
T13 Andrew McCutchen .75 2.00
T14 Ubaldo Jimenez .30 .75
T15 Pablo Sandoval .50 1.25
T16 David Wright .60 1.50
T17 Tommy Hanson .30 .75
T18 Clayton Kershaw 1.50 4.00
T19 Zack Greinke .50 1.25
T20 Matt Kemp .60 1.50

2010 Topps Blue Back

INSERTED IN WAL MART PACKS
31-45 ISSUED IN UPD WM PACKS
1 Babe Ruth 2.50 6.00
2 Stan Musial 1.50 4.00
3 George Sisler .60 1.50
4 Tim Lincecum .60 1.50
5 Ichiro Suzuki 1.25 3.00
6 Roy Halladay .60 1.50
7 Walter Johnson 1.00 2.50
8 Nolan Ryan 3.00 8.00
9 Hanley Ramirez .60 1.50
10 Derek Jeter 2.50 6.00
11 Tom Seaver .60 1.50
12 Roger Maris 1.00 2.50
13 Honus Wagner 1.00 2.50
14 Vladimir Guerrero .60 1.50
15 Mel Ott 1.00 2.50
16 Mickey Mantle 3.00 8.00
17 Cal Ripken Jr. 3.00 8.00
18 Cy Young 1.00 2.50
19 Jackie Robinson 1.00 2.50
20 Jimmie Foxx 1.00 2.50
21 Lou Gehrig 2.00 5.00
22 Rogers Hornsby .60 1.50
23 Ty Cobb 1.50 4.00
24 Dizzy Dean .60 1.50
25 Reggie Jackson .60 1.50
26 Warren Spahn .60 1.50
27 Albert Pujols 1.25 3.00
28 Chipper Jones 1.00 2.50
29 Mariano Rivera 1.25 3.00
30 David Wright .75 2.00
31 Babe Ruth 2.50 6.00
32 Jimmie Foxx 1.00 2.50
33 Rogers Hornsby .60 1.50
34 Ty Cobb 1.50 4.00
35 Dizzy Dean .60 1.50
36 Reggie Jackson .60 1.50
37 Nolan Ryan 3.00 8.00
38 Tom Seaver .60 1.50
39 Roger Maris 1.00 2.50
40 Vladimir Guerrero .60 1.50
41 Roy Campanella 1.00 2.50
42 Johnny Mize .60 1.50
43 Christy Mathewson 1.00 2.50
44 Carl Yastrzemski 1.50 4.00
45 Joe Mauer .75 2.00

2010 Topps Cards Your Mom Threw Out

COMPLETE SET (174) 40.00 100.00
SER.1 ODDS 1:3 HOBBY
SER.2 ODDS 1:3 HOBBY
UPD ODDS 1:3 HOBBY
CMT1 Mickey Mantle 52 3.00 8.00
CMT2 Jackie Robinson 1.00 2.50
CMT3 Ernie Banks 1.00 2.50
CMT4 Duke Snider .60 1.50
CMT5 Luis Aparicio .60 1.50
CMT6 Frank Robinson .60 1.50
CMT7 Orlando Cepeda .60 1.50
CMT8 Bob Gibson .60 1.50
CMT9 Carl Yastrzemski 1.50 4.00
CMT10 Roger Maris 1.00 2.50
CMT11 Mickey Mantle 3.00 8.00
CMT12 Stan Musial 1.50 4.00
CMT13 Brooks Robinson .60 1.50
CMT14 Juan Marichal .60 1.50
CMT15 Jim Palmer .60 1.50
CMT16 Willie McCovey .60 1.50
CMT17 Mickey Mantle 3.00 8.00
CMT18 Reggie Jackson .60 1.50
CMT19 Steve Carlton .60 1.50
CMT20 Thurman Munson 1.00 2.50
CMT21 Tom Seaver .60 1.50
CMT22 Johnny Bench 1.00 2.50
CMT23 Dave Winfield .60 1.50
CMT24 Robin Yount 1.00 2.50
CMT25 Mike Schmidt 1.50 4.00
CMT26 Reggie Jackson .60 1.50
CMT27 Nolan Ryan 3.00 8.00
CMT28 Ozzie Smith 1.25 3.00
CMT29 Rickey Henderson 1.00 2.50
CMT30 Eddie Murray .60 1.50
CMT31 Paul Molitor 1.00 2.50
CMT32 Ryne Sandberg 2.00 5.00
CMT33 Don Mattingly 2.00 5.00
CMT34 Dwight Gooden .40 1.00
CMT35 Tony Gwynn 1.00 2.50
CMT36 Bo Jackson 1.00 2.50
CMT37 Nolan Ryan 3.00 8.00
CMT38 Gary Sheffield .40 1.00
CMT39 Frank Thomas 1.00 2.50
CMT40 Chipper Jones 1.00 2.50
CMT41 Manny Ramirez 1.00 2.50
CMT42 Derek Jeter 2.50 6.00
CMT43 Tony Gwynn 1.00 2.50
CMT44 Mike Piazza 1.00 2.50
CMT45 Cal Ripken 3.00 8.00
CMT46 Pedro Martinez .60 1.50
CMT47 Alex Rodriguez 1.25 3.00
CMT48 Ivan Rodriguez .60 1.50
CMT49 Randy Johnson 1.00 2.50
CMT50 Ichiro Suzuki 1.25 3.00
CMT51 Albert Pujols 1.25 3.00
CMT52 Kevin Youkilis .40 1.00
CMT53 Alfonso Soriano .60 1.50
CMT54 R.Howard/C.Hamels .75 2.00
CMT55 Alex Gordon .60 1.50
CMT56 Dustin Pedroia .75 2.00
CMT57 Tim Lincecum .60 1.50
CMT58 Evan Longoria .60 1.50
CMT59 Phil Rizzuto .60 1.50
CMT60 Mickey Mantle 3.00 8.00
CMT61 Al Kaline 1.00 2.50
CMT62 Yogi Berra 1.00 2.50
CMT63 Ernie Banks 1.00 2.50
CMT64 Whitey Ford .60 1.50
CMT65 Duke Snider .60 1.50
CMT66 Warren Spahn .60 1.50
CMT67 Willie McCovey .60 1.50
CMT68 Brooks Robinson .60 1.50
CMT69 Roger Maris 1.00 2.50
CMT70 Harmon Killebrew 1.00 2.50
CMT71 Eddie Mathews 1.00 2.50
CMT72 Carl Yastrzemski 1.50 4.00
CMT73 Gaylord Perry .60 1.50
CMT74 Jim Bunning .60 1.50
CMT75 Rod Carew .60 1.50
CMT76 Nolan Ryan 3.00 8.00
CMT77 Johnny Bench 1.00 2.50
CMT78 Frank Robinson .60 1.50
CMT79 Juan Marichal .60 1.50
CMT80 Reggie Jackson .60 1.50
CMT81 Willie McCovey .60 1.50
CMT82 George Brett 2.00 5.00
CMT83 Dennis Eckersley .60 1.50
CMT84 Tom Seaver .60 1.50
CMT85 Eddie Murray .60 1.50
CMT86 Paul Molitor 1.00 2.50
CMT87 Joe Morgan .60 1.50
CMT88 Rickey Henderson 1.00 2.50
CMT89 Steve Carlton .60 1.50
CMT90 Tony Gwynn 1.00 2.50
CMT91 Ryne Sandberg 2.00 5.00
CMT92 Robin Yount 1.00 2.50
CMT93 Mike Schmidt 1.50 4.00
CMT94 Don Mattingly 2.00 5.00
CMT95 Darryl Strawberry .40 1.00
CMT96 Randy Johnson 1.00 2.50
CMT97 Frank Thomas 1.00 2.50
CMT98 Ken Griffey Jr. 2.00 5.00
CMT99 Cal Ripken 3.00 8.00
CMT100 Ozzie Smith 1.25 3.00
CMT101 Bo Jackson 1.00 2.50
CMT102 Babe Ruth 2.50 6.00
CMT103 Manny Ramirez 1.00 2.50
CMT104 John Smoltz 1.00 2.50
CMT105 Derek Jeter 2.50 6.00
CMT106 Alex Rodriguez 1.25 3.00
CMT107 Chipper Jones 1.00 2.50
CMT108 Mariano Rivera 1.25 3.00
CMT109 Joe Mauer .75 2.00
CMT110 Cole Hamels .75 2.00
CMT111 I.Suzuki/A.Pujols 1.25 3.00
CMT112 Andre Ethier .60 1.50
CMT113 Justin Verlander 1.00 2.50
CMT114 Derek Jeter 2.50 6.00
CMT115 Ryan Zimmerman .60 1.50
CMT116 Rick Porcello .60 1.50
CMT117 Eddie Mathews 1.00 2.50
CMT118 John Podres .40 1.00
CMT119 Tom Lasorda .60 1.50
CMT120 Harmon Killebrew 1.00 2.50
CMT121 Jackie Robinson 1.00 2.50
CMT122 Y.Berra/M.Mantle 3.00 8.00
CMT123 Roger Maris 1.00 2.50
CMT124 Lew Burdette .40 1.00
CMT125 Roger Maris 1.00 2.50
CMT126 Carl Yastrzemski 1.50 4.00
CMT127 Lou Brock .60 1.50
CMT128 Willie McCovey .60 1.50
CMT129 Willie Stargell .60 1.50
CMT130 Ernie Banks 1.00 2.50
CMT131 Robin Roberts .60 1.50
CMT132 Brooks Robinson .60 1.50
CMT133 Tom Seaver .60 1.50
CMT134 Mickey Mantle 3.00 8.00
CMT135 Nolan Ryan 3.00 8.00
CMT136 Steve Garvey .40 1.00
CMT137 Frank Robinson .60 1.50
CMT138 Luis Aparicio .60 1.50
CMT139 Nolan Ryan 3.00 8.00
CMT140 Yogi Berra 1.00 2.50
Roy Campanella
CMT141 Reggie Jackson .60 1.50
CMT142 Mark Fidrych .40 1.00
CMT143 Andre Dawson .60 1.50
CMT144 Dale Murphy 1.00 2.50
CMT145 L.Brock/C.Yastrzemski 1.50 4.00
CMT146 Ozzie Smith 1.25 3.00
CMT147 Rickey Henderson 1.00 2.50
CMT148 Wade Boggs .60 1.50
CMT149 Darryl Strawberry .40 1.00
CMT150 Dave Winfield .60 1.50
CMT151 Paul Molitor 1.00 2.50
CMT152 Barry Larkin .60 1.50
CMT153 Eddie Murray .60 1.50
CMT154 Craig Biggio .60 1.50
CMT155 Larry Walker .60 1.50
CMT156 Nolan Ryan 3.00 8.00
CMT157 Don Mattingly 2.00 5.00
CMT158 Frank Thomas 1.00 2.50
CMT159 Billy Wagner .40 1.00
CMT160 Derek Jeter 2.50 6.00
CMT161 Chipper Jones 1.00 2.50
CMT162 Derek Jeter 2.50 6.00
CMT163 Mike Piazza/Ken Griffey Jr. 2.00 5.00
CMT164 A.Rod/Nomar/Jeter 2.50 6.00
CMT165 Barry Zito .60 1.50
Ben Sheets
CMT166 Vladimir Guerrero .60 1.50
CMT167 Jason Bay .60 1.50
CMT168 Josh Hamilton .60 1.50
Carl Crawford
CMT169 J.Thome/M.Schmidt 1.50 4.00
CMT170 Ian Kinsler .60 1.50
CMT171 Ryan Zimmerman .60 1.50
CMT172 Ubaldo Jimenez .40 1.00
CMT173 Joey Votto 1.00 2.50
CMT174 David Price .75 2.00

2010 Topps Cards Your Mom Threw Out Original Back

*ORIG: .6X TO 1.5X BASIC
STATED ODDS 1:36 HOBBY

2010 Topps Commemorative Patch

1-50 ISSUED IN SERIES 1
51-100 ISSUED IN SERIES 2
101-150 ISSUED IN UPDATE
MCP1 Tris Speaker 8.00 20.00
MCP2 Babe Ruth 12.50 30.00
MCP3 Babe Ruth 12.50 30.00
MCP4 Mel Ott 4.00 10.00
MCP5 Dizzy Dean 8.00 20.00
MCP6 Jimmie Foxx 4.00 10.00
MCP7 Hank Greenberg 4.00 10.00
MCP8 Lou Gehrig 6.00 15.00
MCP9 Lou Gehrig 6.00 15.00
MCP10 Ralph Kiner 4.00 10.00
MCP11 Johnny Mize 4.00 10.00
MCP12 Robin Roberts 4.00 10.00
MCP13 Monte Irvin 4.00 10.00
MCP14 Duke Snider 5.00 12.00
MCP15 Eddie Mathews 5.00 12.00
MCP16 Mickey Mantle 8.00 20.00
MCP17 Roger Maris 6.00 15.00
MCP18 Johnny Podres 4.00 10.00
MCP19 Bob Gibson 4.00 10.00
MCP20 Juan Marichal 4.00 10.00
MCP21 Orlando Cepeda 4.00 10.00
MCP22 Al Kaline 4.00 10.00
MCP23 Frank Robinson 4.00 10.00
MCP24 Bobby Murcer 8.00 20.00
MCP25 Willie Stargell 8.00 20.00
MCP26 Johnny Bench 10.00 25.00
MCP27 Ozzie Smith 5.00 12.00
MCP28 Eddie Murray 4.00 10.00
MCP29 Gary Carter 4.00 10.00
MCP30 Dennis Eckersley 4.00 10.00
MCP31 Ryne Sandberg 4.00 10.00
MCP32 Gary Sheffield 4.00 10.00
MCP33 Frank Thomas 5.00 12.00
MCP34 Vladimir Guerrero 4.00 10.00
MCP35 Ichiro Suzuki 5.00 10.00
MCP36 Curt Schilling 4.00 10.00
MCP37 Chipper Jones 4.00 10.00
MCP38 Ryan Zimmerman 4.00 10.00
MCP39 Roy Halladay 5.00 12.00
MCP40 Grady Sizemore 4.00 10.00
MCP41 Manny Ramirez 4.00 10.00
MCP42 Tim Lincecum 10.00 25.00
MCP43 Evan Longoria 8.00 20.00
MCP44 David Wright 5.00 12.00
MCP45 Chase Utley 5.00 12.00
MCP46 Mariano Rivera 8.00 20.00
MCP47 Joe Mauer 8.00 20.00
MCP48 Albert Pujols 6.00 15.00
MCP49 Ichiro Suzuki 8.00 20.00
MCP50 Mark Teixeira 5.00 12.00
MCP51 Richie Ashburn 10.00 25.00
MCP52 Johnny Bench 10.00 25.00
MCP53 Yogi Berra 4.00 10.00
MCP54 Rod Carew 8.00 20.00
MCP55 Orlando Cepeda 4.00 10.00
MCP56 Rickey Henderson 5.00 12.00
MCP57 Bob Feller 5.00 12.00
MCP58 Rollie Fingers 5.00 12.00
MCP60 Catfish Hunter 5.00 12.00
MCP61 Monte Irvin 4.00 10.00
MCP62 Reggie Jackson 4.00 10.00
MCP63 Fergie Jenkins 4.00 10.00
MCP64 Al Kaline 4.00 10.00
MCP65 George Kell 5.00 12.00
MCP66 Harmon Killebrew 8.00 20.00
MCP67 Ralph Kiner 4.00 10.00
MCP68 Juan Marichal 4.00 10.00
MCP69 Eddie Mathews 5.00 12.00
MCP70 Bill Mazeroski 4.00 10.00
MCP71 Willie McCovey 4.00 10.00
MCP72 Joe Morgan 5.00 12.00
MCP73 Eddie Murray 4.00 10.00
MCP74 Ryne Sandberg 4.00 10.00
MCP75 Tom Seaver 8.00 20.00
MCP76 Hal Newhouser 5.00 12.00
MCP79 Tony Perez 5.00 12.00
MCP80 Phil Rizzuto 5.00 12.00
MCP81 Robin Roberts 4.00 10.00
MCP82 Brooks Robinson 4.00 10.00
MCP83 Mike Schmidt 5.00 12.00
MCP84 Red Schoendienst 5.00 12.00
MCP85 Ozzie Smith 5.00 12.00
MCP86 Warren Spahn 8.00 20.00
MCP87 Willie Stargell 8.00 20.00
MCP88 Hoyt Wilhelm 4.00 10.00
MCP89 Jimmie Foxx 4.00 10.00
MCP90 Mickey Mantle 8.00 20.00
MCP91 Jackie Robinson 4.00 10.00
MCP92 Lou Gehrig 5.00 12.00
MCP93 Babe Ruth 10.00 25.00
MCP94 Albert Pujols 6.00 15.00
MCP95 David Wright 5.00 12.00
MCP96 Mariano Rivera 10.00 25.00
MCP97 Ryan Howard 6.00 15.00
MCP98 Ryan Braun 5.00 12.00
MCP99 Joe Mauer 8.00 20.00
MCP100 CC Sabathia 5.00 12.00
MCP101 Tris Speaker 8.00 20.00
MCP102 Dizzy Dean 6.00 15.00
MCP103 Lou Gehrig 5.00 12.00
MCP104 Jimmie Foxx 4.00 10.00
MCP105 Hank Greenberg 4.00 10.00
MCP106 Bob Feller 5.00 12.00
MCP107 Mel Ott 4.00 10.00
MCP108 Johnny Mize 4.00 10.00
MCP109 Phil Rizzuto 5.00 12.00
MCP110 Enos Slaughter 5.00 12.00
MCP111 Pee Wee Reese 5.00 12.00
MCP112 Stan Musial 10.00 25.00
MCP113 Hal Newhouser 5.00 12.00
MCP114 Red Schoendienst 5.00 12.00
MCP115 Yogi Berra 6.00 15.00
MCP116 Larry Doby 6.00 15.00
MCP117 Richie Ashburn 10.00 25.00
MCP119 Johnny Podres 4.00 10.00
MCP120 Duke Snider 5.00 12.00
MCP121 Roger Maris 8.00 20.00
MCP122 Lou Brock 6.00 15.00
MCP123 Luis Aparicio 5.00 12.00
MCP124 Eddie Mathews 5.00 12.00
MCP125 Rollie Fingers 5.00 12.00
MCP126 Reggie Jackson 4.00 10.00
MCP127 Joe Morgan 5.00 12.00
MCP128 Johnny Bench 10.00 25.00
MCP129 Steve Carlton 4.00 10.00
MCP130 Barry Larkin 8.00 20.00
MCP131 Roberto Alomar 5.00 12.00
MCP132 Greg Maddux 4.00 10.00

MCP133 Derek Jeter 12.50 30.00
MCP135 Derek Jeter 10.00 25.00
MCP136 Chipper Jones 4.00 10.00
MCP137 Alex Rodriguez 5.00 12.00
MCP138 Roy Halladay 5.00 12.00
MCP139 Josh Beckett 5.00 12.00
MCP140 Hideki Matsui 12.50 30.00
MCP142 Ryan Braun 5.00 12.00
MCP143 Andre Ethier 4.00 10.00
MCP144 Justin Morneau 5.00 12.00
MCP145 Joe Mauer 8.00 20.00
MCP146 Chase Utley 5.00 12.00
MCP147 Vladimir Guerrero 4.00 10.00
MCP148 Evan Longoria 8.00 20.00
MCP149 Derek Jeter 10.00 25.00
MCP150 Albert Pujols 6.00 15.00

2010 Topps Factory Set All Star Bonus

COMPLETE SET (5) 1.25 3.00
AS1 Hideki Matsui 1.00 2.50
AS2 Kendry Morales .40 1.00
AS3 Torii Hunter .40 1.00
AS4 Scott Kazmir .40 1.00
AS5 Bobby Abreu .40 1.00

2010 Topps Factory Set Phillies Team Bonus

COMPLETE SET (5) 2.50 6.00
PHI1 Roy Halladay .60 1.50
PHI2 Ryan Howard .75 2.00
PHI3 Chase Utley .60 1.50
PHI4 Jimmy Rollins .60 1.50
PHI5 Jayson Werth .60 1.50

2010 Topps Factory Set Red Sox Team Bonus

COMPLETE SET (5) 3.00 8.00
BOS1 Dustin Pedroia .75 2.00
BOS2 Jacoby Ellsbury .75 2.00
BOS3 Victor Martinez .60 1.50
BOS4 John Lackey .60 1.50
BOS5 Daisuke Matsuzaka .60 1.50

2010 Topps Factory Set Retail Bonus

COMPLETE SET (5) 6.00 15.00
RS1 Ryan Howard .75 2.00
RS2 Ichiro Suzuki 1.25 3.00
RS3 Hanley Ramirez .60 1.50
RS4 Derek Jeter 2.50 6.00
RS5 Albert Pujols 1.25 3.00

2010 Topps Factory Set Target Ruth Chrome Gold Refractors

COMPLETE SET (3) 15.00 40.00
COMMON RUTH 8.00 20.00
1 Babe Ruth 8.00 20.00
2 Babe Ruth 8.00 20.00
3 Babe Ruth 8.00 20.00

2010 Topps Factory Set Wal-Mart Mantle Chrome Gold Refractors

COMPLETE SET (3) 20.00 50.00
COMMON MANTLE 10.00 25.00
1 Mickey Mantle 10.00 25.00
2 Mickey Mantle 10.00 25.00
3 Mickey Mantle 10.00 25.00

2010 Topps Factory Set Yankees Team Bonus

COMPLETE SET (5) 4.00 10.00
NYY1 Derek Jeter 2.50 6.00
NYY2 Alex Rodriguez 1.25 3.00
NYY3 Mariano Rivera 1.25 3.00
NYY4 Mark Teixeira .60 1.50
NYY5 Curtis Granderson .75 2.00

2010 Topps History of the Game

STATED ODDS 1:6 HOBBY
HOG1 Alexander Cartwright .40 1.00
Baseball Invented
HOG2 First Professional Baseball Game .40 1.00
HOG3 National League Created .40 1.00
HOG4 American League Elevated .40 1.00
to Major League Status
HOG5 First World Series Game Played .40 1.00
HOG6 William H. Taft .40 1.00
Taft Attends Opening Day
HOG7 Ruth Sold 1.25 3.00
HOG8 Baseball hits the Airwaves .40 1.00
HOG9 Gehrig Replaces Pipp 1.00 2.50
HOG10 Ruth Sets HR Mark 1.25 3.00
HOG11 Babe Ruth
BabeFirst MLB All-Star Game
HOG12 Babe Ruth
First Night Game Played
HOG13 Ruth Retires 1.25 3.00
HOG14 1st Hall of Fame Class Inducted .40 1.00
HOG15 Robinson Plays MLB 1.00 2.50
HOG16 First Televised Game .40 1.00
HOG17 Dodgers & Giants move to CA .40 1.00
HOG18 Maris HR Record .75 2.00
HOG19 Johnny Bench
First MLB Draft
HOG20 F.Robinson MVP .40 1.00
HOG21 DH rule created .40 1.00
HOG22 Ryan 7th No-Hitter 1.50 4.00
HOG23 Ripken Breaks Streak 1.50 4.00
HOG24 Interleague Play Introduced .40 1.00
HOG25 1st MLB game played in Japan .40 1.00

2010 Topps History of the World Series

COMPLETE SET (25) 8.00 20.00
STATED ODDS 1:6 HOBBY
HWS1 Christy Mathewson .75 2.00
HWS2 Walter Johnson .75 2.00
HWS3 Babe Ruth 2.00 5.00
HWS4 Rogers Hornsby .50 1.25
HWS5 Babe Ruth 2.00 5.00
HWS6 Mickey Mantle 2.50 6.00
HWS7 Mel Ott .75 2.00
HWS8 Enos Slaughter .50 1.25
HWS9 Bob Feller .50 1.25
HWS10 Whitey Ford .50 1.25
HWS11 Johnny Podres .30 .75
HWS12 Yogi Berra .75 2.00
HWS13 Yogi Berra .75 2.00
HWS14 Jim Palmer .50 1.25
HWS15 Bob Gibson .50 1.25
HWS16 Brooks Robinson .50 1.25
HWS17 Dennis Eckersley .50 1.25
HWS18 Paul Molitor .75 2.00
HWS19 Jason Varitek .75 2.00
HWS20 Edgar Renteria .30 .75
HWS21 Derek Jeter 2.00 5.00
HWS22 Alex Gonzalez .30 .75
HWS23 Cole Hamels .60 1.50
HWS24 Chase Utley .50 1.25
HWS25 New York Yankees .75 2.00

2010 Topps Legendary Lineage

Please note that it was discovered that the Cal Ripken/Hanley Ramirez card exists as both card number LL38 and LR38.
STATED ODDS 1:4 HOBBY
UPDATE ODDS 1:8 HOBBY
1-30 ISSUED IN SERIES 1
31-60 ISSUED IN SERIES 2
61-75 ISSUED IN UPDATE
LL1 W.McCovey/R.Howard .60 1.50
LL2 M.Mantle/C.Jones 2.50 6.00
LL3 B.Ruth/A.Rodriguez 2.00 5.00
LL4 L.Gehrig/M.Teixeira 1.50 4.00
LL5 T.Cobb/C.Granderson 1.25 3.00
LL6 Jimmie Foxx/Manny Ramirez .75 2.00
LL7 G.Sisler/I.Suzuki 1.00 2.50
LL8 Tris Speaker/Grady Sizemore .50 1.25
LL9 Honus Wagner/Hanley Ramirez .75 2.00
LL10 Johnny Bench/Ivan Rodriguez .75 2.00
LL11 M.Schmidt/E.Longoria 1.25 3.00
LL12 O.Smith/J.Reyes 1.00 2.50
LL13 Reggie Jackson/Adam Dunn .50 1.25
LL14 Warren Spahn/Tommy Hanson .50 1.25
LL15 Duke Snider/Andre Ethier .50 1.25
LL16 S.Musial/A.Pujols 1.25 3.00
LL17 C.Ripken/D.Jeter 2.50 6.00
LL18 G.Carter/D.Wright .60 1.50
LL19 Whitey Ford/CC Sabathia .50 1.25
LL20 Frank Thomas/Prince Fielder .75 2.00
LL21 H.Greenberg/R.Braun .75 2.00
LL22 Frank Robinson/Vladimir Guerrero .50 1.25
LL23 Jackie Robinson/Matt Kemp .75 2.00
LL24 B.Gibson/T.Lincecum .50 1.25
LL25 Tom Seaver/Roy Halladay .50 1.25
LL26 D.Eckersley/M.Rivera 1.00 2.50
LL27 Tony Gwynn/Joe Mauer .75 2.00
LL28 N.Ryan/Z.Greinke 2.50 6.00
LL29 C.Yaz/K.Youkilis 1.25 3.00
LL30 Rickey Henderson/Carl Crawford .75 2.00
LL31 Joe Mauer/Johnny Bench .50 1.25
LL32 Orlando Cepeda/Pablo Sandoval .50 1.25
LL33 Carlton Fisk/Victor Martinez .50 1.25
LL34 Eddie Mathews/Chipper Jones .75 2.00
LL35 A.Kaline/M.Cabrera .75 2.00
LL36 Andre Dawson/Alfonso Soriano .50 1.25
LL37 J.Robinson/I.Suzuki 1.00 2.50
LL38 C.Ripken Jr./H.Ramirez 2.50 6.00
LL39 P.Rizzuto/D.Jeter 2.00 5.00
LL40 Harmon Killebrew/Justin Morneau .75 2.00
LL41 Jimmie Foxx/Prince Fielder .75 2.00
LL42 L.Gehrig/A.Pujols 1.50 4.00
LL43 M.Schmidt/A.Rodriguez 1.25 3.00
LL44 Bo Jackson/Justin Upton .75 2.00
LL45 B.Ruth/R.Howard 2.00 5.00
LL46 Luis Aparicio/Alexei Ramirez .50 1.25
LL47 F.Robinson/R.Braun .50 1.25
LL48 S.Musial/M.Holliday 1.25 3.00
LL49 Lou Brock/Carl Crawford .50 1.25
LL50 Tris Speaker/Jacoby Ellsbury .60 1.50
LL51 J.Marichal/T.Lincecum .50 1.25
LL52 Dale Murphy/Matt Kemp .75 2.00
LL53 N.Ryan/J.Verlander 2.50 6.00
LL54 O.Smith/E.Andrus 1.00 2.50
LL55 Rickey Henderson/B.J. Upton .75 2.00
LL56 Brooks Robinson
Ryan Zimmerman .50 1.25
LL57 Yogi Berra/Jorge Posada .75 2.00
LL58 H.Wagner/A.McCutchen .75 2.00
LL59 M.Mantle/M.Teixeira 2.50 6.00
LL60 R.Sandberg/C.Utley 1.50 4.00
LL61 D.Winfield/J.Heyward 1.25 3.00
LL62 W.Johnson/S.Strasburg 2.50 6.00
LL63 V.Martinez/C.Santana 1.00 2.50
LL64 Rod Carew/Robinson Cano .50 1.25
LL65 Bob Gibson/Ubaldo Jimenez .50 1.25
LL66 M.Cabrera/M.Stanton 2.50 6.00
LL67 H.Greenberg/I.Davis .75 2.00
LL68 Mark Teixeira/Logan Morrison .50 1.25
LL69 T.Seaver/M.Leake 1.00 2.50
LL70 E.Banks/S.Castro .75 2.00
LL71 J.Palmer/B.Matusz .75 2.00
LL72 Larry Walker/Justin Morneau .50 1.25
LL73 Steve Carlton/Jon Lester .50 1.25
LL74 J.Bench/B.Posey 2.50 6.00
LL75 Joe Nathan/Drew Storen .50 1.25
LR38 C.Ripken Jr./H.Ramirez

2010 Topps Legendary Lineage Relics

SER.1 ODDS 1:7540 HOBBY
SER.2 ODDS 1:6075 HOBBY
STATED PRINT RUN 50 SER.#'d SETS
BC L.Brock/C.Crawford 10.00 25.00
BM Y.Berra/J.Posada 25.00 60.00
CR Johnny Bench/Ivan Rodriguez 12.50 30.00
CS O.Cepeda/P.Sandoval 15.00 40.00
CW G.Carter/D.Wright 15.00 40.00
ER Eckersley/Rivera 40.00 80.00
FR J.Foxx/M.Ramirez 30.00 60.00
GB H.Greenberg/R.Braun 30.00 60.00
HU R.Henderson/B.Upton 30.00 60.00
KC A.Kaline/M.Cabrera 30.00 60.00
KM H.Killebrew/J.Morneau 10.00 25.00
MH W.McCovey/R.Howard 12.50 30.00
MJ M.Mantle/C.Jones 60.00 120.00
MJ E.Mathews/C.Jones 60.00 120.00
MK D.Murphy/M.Kemp 10.00 25.00
MP S.Musial/A.Pujols 75.00 150.00
MT M.Mantle/M.Teixeira 75.00 150.00
RB F.Robinson/R.Braun 10.00 25.00
RH B.Ruth/R.Howard 30.00 80.00
RR C.Ripken Jr/H.Ramirez 20.00 50.00
SE D.Snider/A.Ethier 12.50 30.00
SH W.Spahn/T.Hanson 60.00 120.00
SL M.Schmidt/E.Longoria 20.00 50.00
SR M.Schmidt/A.Rodriguez 30.00 60.00
SS G.Sisler/I.Suzuki 60.00 120.00
SU R.Sandberg/C.Utley 12.50 30.00
TF F.Thomas/P.Fielder 60.00 120.00
WR H.Wagner/H.Ramirez 50.00 100.00
BMA J.Bench/J.Mauer 40.00 80.00
SSI T.Speaker/G.Sizemore 20.00 50.00

2010 Topps Legends Gold Chrome Target Cereal

INSERTED IN TARGET PACKS
GC1 Babe Ruth 6.00 15.00
GC2 Honus Wagner 2.50 6.00
GC3 Ichiro Suzuki 3.00 8.00
GC4 Nolan Ryan 8.00 20.00
GC5 Jackie Robinson 2.50 6.00
GC6 Tom Seaver 1.50 4.00
GC7 Derek Jeter 6.00 15.00
GC8 George Sisler 1.50 4.00
GC9 Roger Maris 2.50 6.00
GC10 Lou Gehrig 5.00 12.00
GC11 Mickey Mantle 8.00 20.00
GC12 Willie McCovey 1.50 4.00
GC13 Ty Cobb 4.00 10.00
GC14 Warren Spahn 1.50 4.00
GC15 Albert Pujols 3.00 8.00
GC16 Lou Gehrig 5.00 12.00
GC17 Mariano Rivera 3.00 8.00
GC18 Jimmie Foxx 2.50 6.00
GC19 Babe Ruth 6.00 15.00
GC20 Honus Wagner 2.50 6.00

2010 Topps Legends Platinum Chrome Wal-Mart Cereal

INSERTED IN WAL MART PACKS
PC1 Mickey Mantle 8.00 20.00
PC2 Jackie Robinson 2.50 6.00
PC3 Ty Cobb 4.00 10.00
PC4 Warren Spahn 1.50 4.00
PC5 Albert Pujols 3.00 8.00
PC6 Lou Gehrig 5.00 12.00
PC7 Mariano Rivera 3.00 8.00
PC8 Jimmie Foxx 2.50 6.00
PC9 Cy Young 2.50 6.00
PC10 Honus Wagner 2.50 6.00
PC11 Babe Ruth 6.00 15.00
PC12 Mickey Mantle 8.00 20.00
PC13 Ichiro Suzuki 3.00 8.00
PC14 Nolan Ryan 8.00 20.00
PC15 Jackie Robinson 2.50 6.00
PC16 Tom Seaver 1.50 4.00
PC17 Derek Jeter 6.00 15.00
PC18 Ty Cobb 4.00 10.00
PC19 Roger Maris 2.50 6.00
PC20 Lou Gehrig 5.00 12.00

2010 Topps Logoman HTA

DISTRIBUTED IN HTA STORES
1 Albert Pujols .75 2.00
2 Hanley Ramirez .40 1.00
3 Mike Schmidt 1.00 2.50
4 CC Sabathia .40 1.00
5 Babe Ruth 1.50 4.00
6 George Sisler .40 1.00
7 Gordon Beckham .25 .60
8 Tris Speaker .40 1.00
9 Ryan Braun .40 1.00
10 Jackie Robinson .60 1.50
11 Stan Musial 1.00 2.50
12 Ichiro Suzuki .75 2.00
13 Manny Ramirez .60 1.50
14 Ty Cobb 1.00 2.50
15 Tommy Hanson .25 .60
16 Joe Mauer .50 1.25
17 David Ortiz .60 1.50
18 Tim Lincecum .40 1.00
19 Andrew McCutchen .60 1.50
20 Reggie Jackson .40 1.00
21 Nolan Ryan 2.00 5.00
22 Evan Longoria .40 1.00
23 Johan Santana .40 1.00
24 Mark Teixeira .40 1.00
25 Pablo Sandoval .40 1.00
26 Jimmie Foxx .60 1.50
27 Roy Halladay .40 1.00
28 Lou Gehrig 1.25 3.00
29 Alex Rodriguez .75 2.00
30 Thurman Munson .60 1.50
31 Mel Ott .60 1.50
32 Mickey Mantle 2.00 5.00
33 Johnny Mize .40 1.00
34 Rogers Hornsby .40 1.00
35 Chase Utley .40 1.00
36 Walter Johnson .60 1.50
37 Zack Greinke .40 1.00
38 Honus Wagner .60 1.50
39 Roy Campanella .60 1.50
40 Prince Fielder .40 1.00
41 Cal Ripken Jr. 2.00 5.00
42 Carl Yastrzemski 1.00 2.50
43 David Wright .50 1.25
44 Tom Seaver .40 1.00
45 Cy Young .60 1.50
46 Christy Mathewson .60 1.50
47 Justin Morneau .40 1.00
48 Ryan Howard .50 1.25
49 Rick Porcello .40 1.00
50 Nolan Reimold .25 .60

2010 Topps Manufactured Hat Logo Patch

SER.1 ODDS 1:432 HOBBY
SER.2 ODDS 1:420 HOBBY
STATED PRINT RUN 99 SER.#'d SETS
1-186 ISSUED IN SERIES 1
187-416 ISSUED IN SERIES 2
VAR.OF SAME PLAYER EQUALLY PRICED
MHR1 Babe Ruth 10.00 25.00
MHR2 Babe Ruth 10.00 25.00
MHR3 George Sisler 8.00 20.00
MHR4 George Sisler 8.00 20.00
MHR5 Honus Wagner 10.00 25.00
MHR6 Jackie Robinson 10.00 25.00
MHR7 Jimmie Foxx 8.00 20.00
MHR8 Jimmie Foxx 8.00 20.00
MHR9 Johnny Mize 5.00 12.00
MHR10 Johnny Mize 5.00 12.00
MHR11 Johnny Mize 5.00 12.00
MHR12 Lou Gehrig 8.00 20.00
MHR13 Mel Ott 10.00 25.00
MHR14 Rogers Hornsby 4.00 10.00
MHR15 Rogers Hornsby 4.00 10.00
MHR16 Roy Campanella 10.00 25.00
MHR17 Thurman Munson 10.00 25.00
MHR18 Tris Speaker 10.00 25.00
MHR19 Ty Cobb 10.00 25.00
MHR20 Ty Cobb 10.00 25.00
MHR21 Mickey Mantle 12.50 30.00
MHR22 Richie Ashburn 10.00 25.00
MHR23 Bo Jackson 8.00 20.00
MHR24 Bo Jackson 8.00 20.00
MHR25 Paul Molitor 10.00 25.00
MHR26 Paul Molitor 10.00 25.00
MHR27 Paul Molitor 10.00 25.00
MHR28 Tony Gwynn 6.00 15.00
MHR29 Tony Gwynn 6.00 15.00
MHR30 Tony Gwynn 6.00 15.00
MHR31 Al Kaline 8.00 20.00
MHR32 Andre Dawson 6.00 15.00
MHR33 Andre Dawson 6.00 15.00
MHR34 Bob Feller 6.00 15.00
MHR35 Bob Gibson 8.00 20.00
MHR36 Bobby Murcer 6.00 15.00
MHR37 Carl Erskine 10.00 25.00
MHR38 Carl Erskine 10.00 25.00
MHR39 Curt Schilling 6.00 15.00
MHR40 Curt Schilling 6.00 15.00
MHR41 Curt Schilling 6.00 15.00
MHR42 Dale Murphy 10.00 25.00
MHR43 Dale Murphy 10.00 25.00
MHR44 Dizzy Dean 6.00 15.00
MHR45 Dizzy Dean 6.00 15.00
MHR46 Duke Snider 8.00 20.00
MHR47 Duke Snider 8.00 20.00
MHR48 Duke Snider 8.00 20.00
MHR49 Dwight Gooden 6.00 15.00
MHR50 Dwight Gooden 6.00 15.00
MHR51 Eddie Mathews 10.00 25.00
MHR52 Eddie Mathews 10.00 25.00
MHR53 Eddie Murray 10.00 25.00
MHR54 Eddie Murray 10.00 25.00
MHR55 Eddie Murray 10.00 25.00
MHR56 Eddie Murray 10.00 25.00
MHR57 Fergie Jenkins 8.00 20.00
MHR58 Fergie Jenkins 8.00 20.00
MHR59 Frank Robinson 8.00 20.00
MHR60 Frank Robinson 8.00 20.00
MHR61 Frank Thomas 10.00 25.00
MHR62 Frank Thomas 10.00 25.00
MHR63 Frank Thomas 10.00 25.00
MHR64 Gary Carter 10.00 25.00
MHR65 Gary Carter 10.00 25.00
MHR66 George Kell 8.00 20.00
MHR67 Hank Greenberg 6.00 15.00
MHR68 Jim Palmer 6.00 15.00
MHR69 Jim Palmer 6.00 15.00
MHR70 Jim Palmer 6.00 15.00
MHR71 Jimmy Piersall 12.50 30.00
MHR72 Johnny Bench 10.00 25.00
MHR73 Johnny Bench 10.00 25.00
MHR74 Johnny Podres 12.50 30.00
MHR75 Johnny Podres 12.50 30.00
MHR76 Juan Marichal 8.00 20.00
MHR77 Juan Marichal 8.00 20.00
MHR78 Monte Irvin 6.00 15.00
MHR79 Nolan Ryan 20.00 50.00
MHR80 Nolan Ryan 20.00 50.00
MHR81 Nolan Ryan 20.00 50.00
MHR82 Nolan Ryan 20.00 50.00
MHR83 Orlando Cepeda 4.00 10.00
MHR84 Orlando Cepeda 4.00 10.00
MHR85 Ozzie Smith 15.00 40.00
MHR86 Ozzie Smith 15.00 40.00
MHR87 Ralph Kiner 6.00 15.00
MHR88 Reggie Jackson 15.00 40.00
MHR89 Reggie Jackson 15.00 40.00
MHR90 Reggie Jackson 15.00 40.00
MHR91 Reggie Jackson 15.00 40.00
MHR92 Reggie Jackson 15.00 40.00
MHR93 Robin Roberts 12.50 30.00
MHR94 Robin Yount 12.50 30.00
MHR95 Robin Yount 12.50 30.00
MHR96 Roger Maris 12.50 30.00
MHR97 Roger Maris 12.50 30.00
MHR98 Roger Maris 12.50 30.00
MHR99 Stan Musial 12.50 30.00
MHR100 Steve Carlton 8.00 20.00
MHR101 Steve Carlton 8.00 20.00
MHR102 Tom Seaver 8.00 20.00
MHR103 Tom Seaver 8.00 20.00
MHR104 Tony Perez 6.00 15.00
MHR105 Warren Spahn 10.00 25.00
MHR106 Warren Spahn 10.00 25.00
MHR107 Willie McCovey 6.00 15.00
MHR108 Willie McCovey 6.00 15.00
MHR109 Willie Stargell 12.50 30.00
MHR110 Rickey Henderson 12.50 30.00
MHR111 Rickey Henderson 12.50 30.00
MHR112 Rickey Henderson 12.50 30.00
MHR113 Rickey Henderson 12.50 30.00
MHR114 Carlton Fisk 8.00 20.00
MHR115 Carlton Fisk 8.00 20.00
MHR116 Dennis Eckersley 8.00 20.00
MHR117 Dennis Eckersley 8.00 20.00
MHR118 Ryne Sandberg 15.00 40.00
MHR119 Ryne Sandberg 15.00 40.00
MHR120 Lou Brock 8.00 20.00
MHR121 Carl Yastrzemski 10.00 25.00
MHR122 Ernie Banks 10.00 25.00
MHR123 Mike Schmidt 12.50 30.00
MHR124 Alex Rodriguez 12.50 30.00
MHR125 Alex Rodriguez 12.50 30.00
MHR126 Alex Rodriguez 12.50 30.00
MHR127 Kevin Youkilis 10.00 25.00
MHR128 Vladimir Guerrero 10.00 25.00
MHR129 Vladimir Guerrero 10.00 25.00
MHR130 Chipper Jones 8.00 20.00
MHR131 Dustin Pedroia 12.50 30.00
MHR132 Ian Kinsler 4.00 10.00
MHR133 Dustin Pedroia 12.50 30.00
MHR134 Ryan Howard 12.50 30.00
MHR135 Prince Fielder 8.00 20.00
MHR136 David Wright 10.00 25.00
MHR137 Carl Crawford 6.00 15.00
MHR138 Justin Upton 10.00 25.00
MHR139 Dan Haren 4.00 10.00
MHR140 Randy Johnson 10.00 25.00
MHR141 Randy Johnson 10.00 25.00
MHR142 Randy Johnson 10.00 25.00
MHR143 Randy Johnson 10.00 25.00
MHR144 Randy Johnson 10.00 25.00
MHR145 Randy Johnson 10.00 25.00
MHR146 David Ortiz 10.00 25.00
MHR147 Roy Halladay 10.00 25.00
MHR148 Tim Lincecum 20.00 50.00
MHR149 Pablo Sandoval 10.00 25.00
MHR150 Albert Pujols 30.00 60.00
MHR151 Hanley Ramirez 6.00 15.00
MHR152 Nick Markakis 8.00 20.00
MHR153 Ichiro Suzuki 20.00 50.00
MHR154 Adam Jones 4.00 10.00
MHR155 Evan Longoria 10.00 25.00
MHR156 Joe Mauer 12.50 30.00
MHR157 Matt Kemp 8.00 20.00
MHR158 Justin Verlander 12.50 30.00
MHR159 Zack Greinke 8.00 20.00
MHR160 Miguel Cabrera 8.00 20.00
MHR161 Chase Utley 12.50 30.00
MHR162 Adam Dunn 6.00 15.00
MHR163 Manny Ramirez 10.00 25.00
MHR164 Manny Ramirez 10.00 25.00
MHR165 Grady Sizemore 12.50 30.00
MHR166 Felix Hernandez 12.50 30.00
MHR167 Mark Teixeira 10.00 25.00
MHR168 Joey Votto 15.00 40.00
MHR169 Ryan Braun 12.50 30.00
MHR170 Mariano Rivera 12.50 30.00
MHR171 Tommy Hanson 6.00 15.00
MHR172 Matt Cain 8.00 20.00
MHR173 Josh Johnson 6.00 15.00
MHR174 Clayton Kershaw 4.00 10.00
MHR175 Jon Lester 10.00 25.00
MHR176 Elvis Andrus 5.00 12.00
MHR177 Dexter Fowler 5.00 12.00
MHR178 Rick Porcello 6.00 15.00
MHR179 Andrew McCutchen 8.00 20.00
MHR180 Colby Rasmus 10.00 25.00
MHR181 Chris Coghlan 4.00 10.00
MHR182 Nolan Reimold 5.00 12.00
MHR183 Buster Posey 40.00 80.00
MHR184 Koji Uehara 6.00 15.00
MHR185 Madison Bumgarner 12.50 30.00
MHR186 Neftali Feliz 6.00 15.00
MHR187 Mark Teixeira 10.00 25.00
MHR188 Vladimir Guerrero 10.00 25.00
MHR189 Joe Mauer 12.50 30.00
MHR190 Max Scherzer 4.00 10.00
MHR191 Adrian Gonzalez 4.00 10.00
MHR192 Josh Beckett 10.00 25.00
MHR193 Jose Reyes 10.00 25.00
MHR194 Ryan Braun 12.50 30.00
MHR195 Cliff Lee 4.00 10.00
MHR196 Kendry Morales 5.00 12.00
MHR197 Tim Lincecum 20.00 50.00
MHR198 Prince Fielder 8.00 20.00
MHR199 Ichiro Suzuki 20.00 50.00
MHR200 Chipper Jones 8.00 20.00
MHR201 Chase Utley 12.50 30.00
MHR202 Felix Hernandez 12.50 30.00
MHR203 Nolan Reimold 5.00 12.00
MHR204 Albert Pujols 30.00 60.00
MHR205 Torii Hunter 6.00 15.00
MHR206 Evan Longoria 12.50 30.00
MHR207 CC Sabathia 8.00 20.00
MHR208 Mariano Rivera 12.50 30.00
MHR209 B.J. Upton 6.00 15.00
MHR210 Justin Upton 10.00 25.00
MHR211 Ivan Rodriguez 6.00 15.00
MHR212 Curtis Granderson 5.00 12.00
MHR213 Josh Hamilton 8.00 20.00
MHR214 Tim Hudson 8.00 20.00
MHR215 Neftali Feliz 6.00 15.00
MHR216 Babe Ruth 10.00 25.00
MHR217 Adam Lind 4.00 10.00
MHR218 David Price 8.00 20.00
MHR219 Tommy Hanson 6.00 15.00
MHR220 Andrew McCutchen 8.00 20.00
MHR221 Adam Dunn 6.00 15.00
MHR222 Victor Martinez 5.00 12.00
MHR223 Pablo Sandoval 10.00 25.00
MHR224 Ricky Romero 5.00 12.00
MHR225 Brian McCann 4.00 10.00
MHR226 Jered Weaver 5.00 12.00
MHR227 Andrew Bailey 4.00 10.00
MHR228 Joe Saunders 4.00 10.00
MHR229 Colby Rasmus 10.00 25.00
MHR230 Nick Markakis 8.00 20.00
MHR231 Mark Reynolds 5.00 12.00
MHR232 Ryan Howard 12.50 30.00
MHR233 Stephen Drew 4.00 10.00
MHR234 David Ortiz 10.00 25.00
MHR235 Kenshin Kawakami 6.00 15.00
MHR236 Michael Young 4.00 10.00
MHR237 Jayson Werth 8.00 20.00
MHR238 John Lackey 4.00 10.00
MHR239 Dustin Pedroia 12.50 30.00
MHR240 Travis Snider 6.00 15.00
MHR241 Rajai Davis 8.00 20.00
MHR242 Edgar Renteria 4.00 10.00
MHR243 Justin Morneau 10.00 25.00
MHR244 Jimmy Rollins 8.00 20.00
MHR245 Elvis Andrus 5.00 12.00
MHR246 David Wright 10.00 25.00
MHR247 Javier Vazquez 6.00 15.00
MHR248 Jorge Posada 6.00 15.00
MHR249 Carlos Beltran 8.00 20.00
MHR250 Jonathan Broxton 4.00 10.00
MHR251 Adam Jones 8.00 20.00
MHR252 Alex Rodriguez 12.50 30.00
MHR253 Koji Uehara 5.00 12.00
MHR254 Brandon Webb 6.00 15.00
MHR255 Kevin Kouzmanoff 8.00 20.00
MHR256 Ryan Zimmerman 12.50 30.00
MHR257 Brian Roberts 5.00 12.00
MHR258 Alfonso Soriano 4.00 10.00
MHR259 Jason Varitek 8.00 20.00
MHR260 Aramis Ramirez 4.00 10.00
MHR261 Jeremy Guthrie 6.00 15.00
MHR262 Johnny Cueto 5.00 12.00
MHR263 Jacoby Ellsbury 10.00 25.00
MHR264 Carlos Quentin 4.00 10.00
MHR265 Kosuke Fukudome 6.00 15.00
MHR266 Grady Sizemore 12.50 30.00
MHR267 Troy Tulowitzki 8.00 20.00
MHR268 Alexei Ramirez 4.00 10.00
MHR269 Jeff Francis 4.00 10.00
MHR270 Jay Bruce 4.00 10.00
MHR271 Rick Porcello 6.00 15.00
MHR272 Gordon Beckham 6.00 15.00
MHR273 Justin Verlander 12.50 30.00
MHR274 Magglio Ordonez 8.00 20.00
MHR275 Miguel Cabrera 8.00 20.00
MHR276 Jake Peavy 4.00 10.00
MHR277 Ryan Ludwick 4.00 10.00
MHR278 Todd Helton 6.00 15.00
MHR279 Carlos Lee 4.00 10.00
MHR280 Mark Buehrle 6.00 15.00
MHR281 Billy Butler 6.00 15.00
MHR282 Chris Coghlan 4.00 10.00
MHR283 Brett Anderson 8.00 20.00
MHR284 Lance Berkman 6.00 15.00
MHR285 Chone Figgins 4.00 10.00
MHR286 Ubaldo Jimenez 5.00 12.00
MHR287 Jason Kubel 6.00 15.00
MHR288 Manny Ramirez 8.00 20.00
MHR289 Joe Nathan 5.00 12.00
MHR290 Jimmie Foxx 8.00 20.00
MHR291 J.J. Hardy 8.00 20.00
MHR292 Mike Cameron 4.00 10.00
MHR293 Roy Oswalt 4.00 10.00
MHR294 Carlos Delgado 5.00 12.00
MHR295 Rogers Hornsby 4.00 10.00
MHR296 Hunter Pence 4.00 10.00
MHR297 Scott Kazmir 8.00 20.00
MHR298 Tris Speaker 10.00 25.00
MHR299 Jhoulys Chacin 4.00 10.00
MHR300 Michael Cuddyer 8.00 20.00
MHR301 Zack Greinke 8.00 20.00
MHR302 Jeff Francoeur 4.00 10.00
MHR303 Matt Kemp 8.00 20.00
MHR304 Dan Haren 4.00 10.00
MHR305 Andy Pettitte 4.00 10.00
MHR306 David DeJesus 4.00 10.00
MHR307 A.J. Burnett 5.00 12.00
MHR308 Ty Cobb 10.00 25.00
MHR309 Johnny Mize 5.00 12.00
MHR310 Joakim Soria 6.00 15.00
MHR311 Chris Carpenter 6.00 15.00
MHR312 Asdrubal Cabrera 10.00 25.00
MHR313 Shane Victorino 12.50 30.00
MHR314 Andre Ethier 6.00 15.00
MHR315 Kurt Suzuki 6.00 15.00
MHR316 Honus Wagner 10.00 25.00
MHR317 Clayton Kershaw 4.00 10.00
MHR318 Zach Duke 4.00 10.00
MHR319 Shin-Soo Choo 10.00 25.00
MHR320 Matt Cain 6.00 15.00
MHR321 Russell Martin 5.00 12.00
MHR322 Joba Chamberlain 6.00 15.00
MHR323 Jason Bay 5.00 12.00
MHR324 Delmon Young 6.00 15.00
MHR325 Matt Holliday 6.00 15.00
MHR326 Scott Rolen 8.00 20.00
MHR327 Adam Wainwright 5.00 12.00
MHR328 Hanley Ramirez 6.00 15.00
MHR329 Cal Ripken Jr. 10.00 25.00
MHR330 Mickey Mantle 12.50 30.00
MHR331 Chase Headley 4.00 10.00
MHR332 Rich Harden 4.00 10.00
MHR333 Garrett Jones 5.00 12.00
MHR334 Dexter Fowler 5.00 12.00
MHR335 Ian Kinsler 4.00 10.00
MHR336 Raul Ibanez 6.00 15.00
MHR337 Roy Halladay 10.00 25.00
MHR338 Ryan Spilborghs 6.00 15.00
MHR339 Cole Hamels 10.00 25.00
MHR340 Thurman Munson 10.00 25.00
MHR341 Robinson Cano 6.00 15.00
MHR342 Matt LaPorta 5.00 12.00
MHR343 Travis Hafner 5.00 12.00
MHR344 Lou Gehrig 8.00 20.00
MHR345 Nelson Cruz 6.00 15.00
MHR346 Derrek Lee 6.00 15.00
MHR347 Juan Marichal 8.00 20.00
MHR348 Rollie Fingers 5.00 12.00
MHR349 Carl Yastrzemski 10.00 25.00
MHR350 Frank Robinson 8.00 20.00
MHR351 Joe Morgan 6.00 15.00
MHR352 Steve Carlton 8.00 20.00
MHR353 Catfish Hunter 10.00 25.00
MHR354 Willie Stargell 12.50 30.00
MHR355 Early Wynn 5.00 12.00
MHR356 Larry Doby 5.00 12.00
MHR357 Bill Mazeroski 6.00 15.00
MHR358 Carlton Fisk 8.00 20.00
MHR359 Dave Winfield 5.00 12.00
MHR360 Enos Slaughter 10.00 25.00
MHR361 Ernie Banks 10.00 25.00
MHR362 Joe Morgan 6.00 15.00
MHR363 Rollie Fingers 5.00 12.00
MHR364 Phil Rizzuto 8.00 20.00
MHR365 Bo Jackson 8.00 20.00
MHR366 Dave Winfield 5.00 12.00
MHR367 Babe Ruth 10.00 5.00
MHR368 Luis Aparicio 5.00 12.00
MHR369 Duke Snider 8.00 20.00
MHR370 Richie Ashburn 10.00 25.00
MHR371 Early Wynn 5.00 12.00
MHR372 Yogi Berra 10.00 25.00
MHR373 Lou Brock 8.00 20.00
MHR374 Roger Maris 12.50 30.00
MHR375 Orlando Cepeda 4.00 10.00
MHR376 Catfish Hunter 10.00 25.00
MHR377 Ralph Kiner 6.00 15.00
MHR378 Bob Gibson 8.00 20.00
MHR379 Robin Yount 12.50 30.00
MHR380 Harmon Killebrew 10.00 25.00
MHR381 Orlando Cepeda 4.00 10.00
MHR382 Steve Carlton 8.00 20.00
MHR383 Bob Feller 6.00 15.00
MHR384 Dennis Eckersley 8.00 20.00
MHR385 Robin Roberts 12.50 30.00
MHR386 Willie McCovey 6.00 15.00
MHR387 Hank Greenberg 5.00 12.00
MHR388 Johnny Bench 10.00 25.00
MHR389 Eddie Murray 12.50 30.00
MHR390 Red Schoendienst 5.00 12.00
MHR391 Roger Maris 12.50 30.00
MHR392 Tris Speaker 10.00 25.00
MHR393 Dale Murphy 10.00 25.00
MHR394 Fergie Jenkins 6.00 15.00
MHR395 Frank Robinson 8.00 20.00
MHR396 Willie McCovey 6.00 15.00
MHR397 George Kell 8.00 20.00
MHR398 Dave Winfield 5.00 12.00
MHR399 Ozzie Smith 15.00 40.00
MHR400 Rogers Hornsby 4.00 10.00
MHR401 Jim Palmer 6.00 15.00
MHR402 Carlton Fisk 8.00 20.00
MHR403 Duke Snider 8.00 20.00
MHR404 Gary Carter 10.00 25.00
MHR405 Luis Aparicio 5.00 12.00
MHR406 Andre Dawson 6.00 15.00
MHR407 Hal Newhouser 8.00 20.00
MHR408 Al Kaline 8.00 20.00

MHR409 Bo Jackson 8.00 20.00
MHR410 Johnny Mize 5.00 12.00
MHR411 Mike Schmidt 12.50 30.00
MHR412 Jim Bunning 6.00 15.00
MHR413 Tony Perez 6.00 15.00
MHR414 Dizzy Dean 6.00 15.00
MHR415 Frank Thomas 12.00 30.00
MHR416 Stan Musial 12.50 30.00

2010 Topps Manufactured MLB Logoman Patch

RANDOM INSERTS IN VARIOUS 2010 PRODUCTS
STATED PRINT RUN 50 SER.#'d SETS
LM1 Albert Pujols 12.00 30.00
LM2 Hanley Ramirez 6.00 15.00
LM3 Mike Schmidt 15.00 40.00
LM4 Nick Markakis 8.00 20.00
LM5 CC Sabathia 6.00 15.00
LM6 Babe Ruth 25.00 60.00
LM7 George Sisler 6.00 15.00
LM8 Gordon Beckham 4.00 10.00
LM9 Adrian Gonzalez 8.00 20.00
LM10 Ozzie Smith 12.00 30.00
LM11 Yogi Berra 10.00 25.00
LM12 Tris Speaker 6.00 15.00
LM13 Ryan Braun 6.00 15.00
LM14 Juan Marichal 6.00 15.00
LM21 Joe Mauer 8.00 20.00
LM22 David Ortiz 10.00 25.00
LM23 Tim Lincecum 6.00 15.00
LM25 Miguel Cabrera 10.00 25.00
LM27 Lou Gehrig 20.00 50.00
LM28 Stan Musial 15.00 40.00
LM29 Whitey Ford 6.00 15.00
LM30 Ty Cobb 15.00 40.00
LM31 Dustin Pedroia 8.00 20.00
LM32 Evan Longoria 6.00 15.00
LM33 Clayton Kershaw 12.00 30.00
LM35 Mark Teixeira 6.00 15.00
LM36 Frank Robinson 6.00 15.00
LM37 Johnny Bench 10.00 25.00
LM38 Ryne Sandberg 20.00 50.00
LM39 Reggie Jackson 6.00 15.00
LM40 Nolan Ryan 30.00 80.00
LM41 Steve Carlton 6.00 15.00
LM42 Johnny Podres 4.00 10.00
LM43 Jim Palmer 6.00 15.00
LM44 Jimmie Foxx 10.00 25.00
LM45 Robin Yount 10.00 25.00
LM46 Justin Upton 6.00 15.00
LM47 Alfonso Soriano 6.00 15.00
LM48 Grady Sizemore 6.00 15.00
LM49 Matt Kemp 8.00 20.00
LM50 B.J. Upton 6.00 15.00
LM52 Roy Halladay 6.00 15.00
LM54 Chipper Jones 10.00 25.00
LM55 Alex Rodriguez 12.00 30.00
LM56 Andre Dawson 6.00 15.00
LM57 Tony Gwynn 10.00 25.00
LM58 Mickey Mantle 30.00 80.00
LM59 Johnny Mize 6.00 15.00
LM61 Walter Johnson 10.00 25.00
LM62 Honus Wagner 10.00 25.00
LM63 Bob Gibson 6.00 15.00
LM64 Warren Spahn 6.00 15.00
LM65 Dizzy Dean 6.00 15.00
LM66 Roy Campanella 10.00 25.00
LM67 Cal Ripken Jr. 30.00 80.00
LM68 Carl Yastrzemski 15.00 40.00
LM69 Mel Ott 10.00 25.00
LM70 Roger Maris 10.00 25.00
LM72 Justin Verlander 10.00 25.00
LM73 Aaron Hill 4.00 10.00
LM74 Josh Beckett 4.00 10.00
LM75 Adam Wainwright 6.00 15.00
LM77 Derrek Lee 4.00 10.00
LM78 Chase Utley 6.00 15.00
LM79 Zack Greinke 6.00 15.00
LM81 Tom Seaver 6.00 15.00
LM82 Cy Young 10.00 25.00
LM83 Christy Mathewson 10.00 25.00
LM84 Thurman Munson 10.00 25.00
LM85 Eddie Mathews 10.00 25.00
LM87 Willie McCovey 6.00 15.00
LM88 Willie Stargell 6.00 15.00
LM90 Ernie Banks 10.00 25.00
LM91 Felix Hernandez 6.00 15.00
LM92 Prince Fielder 6.00 15.00
LM93 David Wright 8.00 20.00
LM94 Kevin Youkilis 4.00 10.00
LM95 Justin Morneau 6.00 15.00
LM96 Ryan Howard 8.00 20.00
LM97 Todd Helton 6.00 15.00
LM98 Rick Porcello 6.00 15.00
LM99 Nolan Reimold 4.00 10.00
LM100 Dan Haren 4.00 10.00

2010 Topps Mickey Mantle Reprint Relics

SERIES 1 ODDS 1:88,000
UPDATE ODDS 1:60,000 HOBBY
SER.1 PRINT RUN 61 SER.#'d SETS
SER.2 PRINT RUN 62 SER.#'d SETS
UPD PRINT RUN 63 SER.#'d SETS
MMR61 M.Mantle Bat/61 150.00 400.00
MMR66 M.Mantle Bat/63 90.00 150.00

2010 Topps Mickey Mouse All-Stars

COMPLETE SET (10) 20.00 50.00
COMP.FANFEST SET (5) 10.00 25.00
COMP.UPDATE SET (5) 10.00 25.00
MM1 All Star Game 2.50 6.00
MM2 American League 2.50 6.00
MM3 National League 2.50 6.00
MM4 Los Angeles Angels 2.50 6.00
MM5 Los Angeles Dodgers 2.50 6.00
MM6 Atlanta Braves 2.50 6.00
MM7 Chicago Cubs 2.50 6.00
MM8 New York Mets 2.50 6.00
MM9 New York Yankees 4.00 10.00
MM10 San Francisco Giants 2.50 6.00

2010 Topps Million Card Giveaway

COMMON CARD 1.50 4.00
RANDOM INSERTS IN VAR.TOPPS PRODUCTS
TMC1 Roy Campanella 1.50 4.00
TMC2 Gary Carter 1.50 4.00
TMC3 Bob Gibson 1.50 4.00
TMC4 Ichiro Suzuki 1.50 4.00
TMC5 Mickey Mantle 1.50 4.00
TMC6 Mickey Mantle 1.50 4.00
TMC7 Roger Maris 1.50 4.00
TMC8 Thurman Munson 1.50 4.00
TMC9 Mike Schmidt 1.50 4.00
TMC10 Carl Yastrzemski 1.50 4.00
TMC11 Roy Campanella 1.50 4.00
TMC12 Gary Carter 1.50 4.00
TMC13 Bob Gibson 1.50 4.00
TMC14 Ichiro Suzuki 1.50 4.00
TMC15 Mickey Mantle 1.50 4.00
TMC16 Mickey Mantle 1.50 4.00
TMC17 Roger Maris 1.50 4.00
TMC18 Thurman Munson 1.50 4.00
TMC19 Mike Schmidt 1.50 4.00
TMC20 Carl Yastrzemski 1.50 4.00
TMC21 Roy Campanella 1.50 4.00
TMC22 Gary Carter 1.50 4.00
TMC23 Bob Gibson 1.50 4.00
TMC24 Ichiro Suzuki 1.50 4.00
TMC25 Mickey Mantle 1.50 4.00
TMC26 Roger Maris 1.50 4.00
TMC27 Thurman Munson 1.50 4.00
TMC28 Mike Schmidt 1.50 4.00
TMC29 Carl Yastrzemski 1.50 4.00
TMC30 Mickey Mantle 1.50 4.00

2010 Topps Peak Performance

STATED ODDS 1:4 HOBBY
UPDATE ODDS 1:8 HOBBY
1-50 ISSUED IN SERIES 1
51-100 ISSUED IN SERIES 2
101-125 ISSUED IN UPDATE
1 Albert Pujols 1.00 2.50
2 Tim Lincecum .50 1.25
3 Honus Wagner .75 2.00
4 Walter Johnson .75 2.00
5 Babe Ruth 2.00 5.00
6 Steve Carlton .50 1.25
7 Grady Sizemore .50 1.25
8 Justin Morneau .50 1.25
9 Bob Gibson .50 1.25
10 Christy Mathewson .75 2.00
11 Mel Ott .75 2.00
12 Lou Gehrig 1.50 4.00
13 Mariano Rivera 1.00 2.50
14 Raul Ibanez .50 1.25
15 Alex Rodriguez 1.00 2.50
16 Vladimir Guerrero .50 1.25
17 Reggie Jackson .50 1.25
18 Mickey Mantle 2.50 6.00
19 Tris Speaker .50 1.25
20 Mark Teixeira .50 1.25
21 Jimmie Foxx .75 2.00
22 George Sisler .50 1.25
23 Stan Musial 1.25 3.00
24 Willie Stargell .50 1.25
25 Chase Utley .50 1.25
26 Joe Mauer .60 1.50
27 Tom Seaver .50 1.25
28 Johnny Mize .50 1.25
29 Roy Campanella .75 2.00
30 Prince Fielder .50 1.25
31 Manny Ramirez .75 2.00
32 Ryan Howard .60 1.50
33 Cy Young .75 2.00
34 Ichiro Suzuki 1.00 2.50
35 Miguel Cabrera .50 1.25
36 Dizzy Dean .50 1.25
37 Hanley Ramirez .50 1.25
38 David Ortiz .75 2.00
39 Chipper Jones .75 2.00
40 Alfonso Soriano .50 1.25
41 David Wright .60 1.50
42 Ryan Braun .50 1.25
43 Dustin Pedroia .50 1.25
44 Roy Halladay .50 1.25
45 Jackie Robinson .75 2.00
46 Rogers Hornsby .50 1.25
47 Roger Maris .75 2.00
48 Curt Schilling .50 1.25
49 Evan Longoria .50 1.25
50 Ty Cobb 1.25 3.00
51 Luis Aparicio .50 1.25
52 Lance Berkman .50 1.25
53 Ubaldo Jimenez .30 .75
54 Ian Kinsler .50 1.25
55 George Kell .50 1.25
56 Felix Hernandez .50 1.25
57 Max Scherzer .75 2.00
58 Magglio Ordonez .50 1.25
59 Derek Jeter 2.00 5.00
60 Mike Schmidt 1.25 3.00
61 Hunter Pence .50 1.25
62 Jason Bay .50 1.25
63 Clay Buchholz .30 .75
64 Josh Hamilton .50 1.25
65 Willie McCovey .50 1.25
66 Aaron Hill .30 .75
67 Derrek Lee .30 .75
68 Andre Ethier .50 1.25
69 Ryan Zimmerman .50 1.25
70 Joe Morgan .50 1.25
71 Carlos Lee .30 .75
72 Chad Billingsley .50 1.25
73 Adam Dunn .50 1.25
74 Dan Uggla .30 .75
75 Jermaine Dye .30 .75
76 Monte Irvin .50 1.25
77 Curtis Granderson .60 1.50
78 Mark Reynolds .30 .75
79 Matt Kemp .60 1.50
80 Ozzie Smith 1.00 2.50
81 Brandon Phillips .30 .75
82 Yogi Berra .75 2.00
83 Bobby Abreu .30 .75
84 Catfish Hunter .50 1.25
85 Justin Upton .50 1.25
86 Justin Verlander .75 2.00
87 Troy Tulowitzki .75 2.00
88 Phil Rizzuto .50 1.25
89 B.J. Upton .50 1.25
90 Richie Ashburn .50 1.25
91 Matt Cain .50 1.25
92 Joey Votto .75 2.00
93 Robin Roberts .50 1.25
94 Nick Markakis .60 1.50
95 Al Kaline .75 2.00
96 Dan Haren .30 .75
97 Thurman Munson .75 2.00
98 Victor Martinez .50 1.25
99 Brian McCann .50 1.25
100 Zack Greinke .50 1.25
101 Stephen Strasburg 2.50 6.00
102 Vladimir Guerrero .50 1.25
103 Hideki Matsui .75 2.00
104 Chone Figgins .30 .75
105 John Lackey .50 1.25
106 Max Scherzer .75 2.00
107 Carlos Pena .50 1.25
108 Ubaldo Jimenez .30 .75
109 Colby Rasmus .50 1.25
110 Jered Weaver .50 1.25
111 Ryan Zimmerman .50 1.25
112 Jason Heyward 1.25 3.00
113 Carlos Santana 1.00 2.50
114 Mike Leake 1.00 2.50
115 Ike Davis .60 1.50
116 Starlin Castro .75 2.00
117 Mike Stanton 2.50 6.00
118 Austin Jackson .50 1.25
119 Dustin Pedroia .60 1.50
120 Tyler Colvin .50 1.25
121 Brennan Boesch .75 2.00
122 Dallas Braden .50 1.25
123 Edwin Jackson .30 .75
124 Daniel Nava .30 .75
125 Roy Halladay .50 1.25

2010 Topps Peak Performance Autographs

SER.1 A ODDS 1:19,950 HOBBY
SER.2 A ODDS 1:6800 HOBBY
UPD A ODDS 1:9310 HOBBY
SER.1 B ODDS 1:1125 HOBBY
SER.2 B ODDS 1:626 HOBBY
UPD B ODDS 1:914 HOBBY
SER.1 C ODDS 1:600 HOBBY
SER.2 C ODDS 1:526 HOBBY
UPD C ODDS 1:1775 HOBBY
SER.1 D ODDS 1:1850 HOBBY
AB Andrew Bailey B2 8.00 20.00
AC Andrew Carpenter 3.00 8.00
AD Jason Donald UPD 3.00 8.00
AE Andre Ethier B2 4.00 10.00
AE Andre Ethier UPD B 10.00 25.00
AES Alcides Escobar UPD B 5.00 12.00
AG A.Gonzalez UPD A 10.00 25.00
AH Aaron Hill B2 6.00 15.00
AL Adam Lind UPD B 3.00 8.00
AM A.McCutchen UPD B 12.00 30.00
BM Peter Moylan 3.00 8.00
BP Buster Posey B1 60.00 150.00
BPA Bobby Parnell C1 3.00 8.00
CB Collin Balester C1 3.00 8.00
CB Clay Buchholz B2 6.00 15.00
CBI Chad Billingsley C2 5.00 12.00
CC Chris Coghlan UPD B 4.00 10.00
CCR Carl Crawford UPD A 8.00 20.00
CF Chone Figgins UPD B 4.00 10.00
CGE Chris Getz C2 3.00 8.00
CGO Carlos Gomez B2 3.00 8.00
CK Clayton Kershaw C1 30.00 80.00
CM Cameron Maybin C2 3.00 8.00
CP Carlos Pena UPD B 4.00 10.00
CPE Cliff Pennington 3.00 8.00
CR Carlos Ruiz C2 10.00 25.00
CR Colby Rasmus UPD B 3.00 8.00
CV Chris Volstad C2 3.00 8.00
CY Chris Young C1 3.00 8.00
DB Daniel Bard B1 8.00 20.00
DB Dallas Braden C2 5.00 12.00
DM Daniel Murphy B2 10.00 25.00
DMC Dustin McGowan B2 3.00 8.00
DP Dustin Pedroia B2 15.00 40.00
DP Dustin Pedroia B1 15.00 40.00
DS Daniel Schlereth C1 3.00 8.00
DS Denard Span B2 4.00 10.00
DS Daniel Stange 3.00 8.00
DS Drew Stubbs UPD B 3.00 8.00
DW David Wright UPD A 15.00 40.00
EC Everth Cabrera C2 3.00 8.00
ES Ervin Santana UPD B 4.00 10.00
EV Edinson Volquez B2 3.00 8.00
FC Fausto Carmona B2 4.00 10.00
FC F.Carmona UPD B 4.00 10.00
FM Franklin Morales D1 3.00 8.00
FP Felipe Paulino 6.00 15.00
GB Gordon Beckham B1 6.00 15.00
GC Gary Carter B1 15.00 40.00
GG Gio Gonzalez C2 3.00 8.00
GK George Kell B2 12.50 30.00
GP Glen Perkins 3.00 8.00
GP Gerardo Parra 3.00 8.00
HB Heath Bell UPD C 3.00 8.00
HK Howie Kendrick B2 4.00 10.00
HR Hanley Ramirez B1 5.00 12.00
JB Jay Bruce C1 4.00 10.00
JB Jason Bartlett B2 4.00 10.00
JB J.Bautista UPD C 6.00 15.00
JC Johnny Cueto C1 4.00 10.00
JC Johnny Cueto UPD B 4.00 10.00
JD Jermaine Dye B2 6.00 15.00
JDE Joey Devine C2 3.00 8.00
JFR Jeff Francis B2 4.00 10.00
JH Joel Hanrahan 3.00 8.00
JJ Josh Johnson 6.00 15.00
JL Jon Lester B2 4.00 10.00
JL John Lackey UPD A 6.00 15.00
JLM Jason Motte C2 5.00 12.00
JM Joe Morgan A2 20.00 50.00
JM J.Masterson UPD B 4.00 10.00
JMI Jose Mijares D1 3.00 8.00
JO Josh Outman B2 3.00 8.00
JP Jhonny Peralta B2 5.00 12.00
JR Juan Rivera B2 4.00 10.00
JRE Josh Reddick C2 4.00 10.00
JS Joe Saunders B2 5.00 12.00
JSO Joakim Soria B2 3.00 8.00
JU Justin Upton UPD A 8.00 20.00
KG Kevin Gregg UPD B 4.00 10.00
KK K.Kouzmanoff UPD B 4.00 10.00
KS Kurt Suzuki 3.00 8.00
LM Lou Marson C2 3.00 8.00
MB Milton Bradley B1 4.00 10.00
MC Matt Capps UPD B 4.00 10.00
MCA Matt Cain UPD B 4.00 10.00
MG Mat Gamel C1 4.00 10.00
MN Mike Napoli B2 8.00 20.00
MS Max Scherzer B1 12.00 30.00
MS Max Scherzer UPD B 12.00 30.00
MSC Max Scherzer B2 12.00 30.00
MT Matt Tolbert 3.00 8.00
NE Nick Evans C2 3.00 8.00
NF Neftali Feliz UPD B 6.00 15.00
NM Nyjer Morgan UPD B 3.00 8.00
NS Nick Swisher B2 10.00 25.00
PF Prince Fielder UPD A 6.00 15.00
PH Phil Hughes B1 8.00 20.00
PH Phil Hughes B2 10.00 25.00
PP P.Polanco UPD B 3.00 8.00
PS P.Sandoval UPD B 8.00 20.00
RB Ryan Braun B1 20.00 50.00
RB Ryan Braun UPD A 10.00 25.00
RB Reid Brignac 3.00 8.00
RC Robinson Cano B1 12.50 30.00
RC R.Cano UPD A 10.00 25.00
RH Ryan Howard UPD A 30.00 60.00
RN Ricky Nolasco UPD B 3.00 8.00
RP Ryan Perry C1 4.00 10.00
RP Ryan Perry C2 3.00 8.00
RR Randy Ruiz B1 6.00 15.00
RR R.Romero UPD C 3.00 8.00
RW Randy Wells UPD C 3.00 8.00
SP Steve Pearce 5.00 12.00
SR Sean Rodriguez UPD B 3.00 8.00
SV Shane Victorino C1 3.00 8.00
TC Trevor Cahill B2 4.00 10.00
TC Trevor Cahill UPD B 5.00 12.00
TH Tommy Hanson B1 10.00 25.00
TH T.Hanson UPD B 8.00 20.00
TS Travis Snider B2 5.00 12.00
TT Troy Tulowitzki B1 6.00 15.00
TW Tim Wood UPD C 3.00 8.00
UJ Ubaldo Jimenez B2 12.50 30.00
UJ U.Jimenez UPD B 6.00 15.00
VW Vernon Wells UPD A 10.00 25.00
WD Wade Davis B2 5.00 12.00
WD Wade Davis B1 10.00 25.00

2010 Topps Peak Performance Autograph Relics

SERIES 1 ODDS 1:3740 HOBBY
SERIES 2ODDS 1:4350 HOBBY
STATED PRINT RUN 50 SER.#'d SETS
CG Curtis Granderson 15.00 40.00
DO David Ortiz 30.00 60.00
DW David Wright 30.00 60.00
GB Gordon Beckham 75.00 150.00
HP Hunter Pence S2 12.50 30.00
HR Hanley Ramirez S2 6.00 15.00
JJ Josh Johnson 12.50 30.00
JM Justin Morneau S2 20.00 50.00
JU Justin Upton S2 15.00 40.00
MK Matt Kemp S2 12.50 30.00
PF Prince Fielder S2 12.50 30.00
PF Prince Fielder 12.50 30.00
RB Ryan Braun 20.00 50.00
RH Ryan Howard 40.00 80.00
RH Ryan Howard S2 50.00 100.00
TT Troy Tulowitzki S2 15.00 40.00

2010 Topps Peak Performance Dual Relics

STATED ODDS 1:6315 HOBBY
STATED PRINT RUN 50 SER.#'d SETS
BR G.Beckham/A.Ramirez 30.00 60.00
GY A.Gonzalez/K.Youkilis 12.00 30.00
HJ F.Hernandez/U.Jimenez 8.00 20.00
IF I.Suzuki/K.Fukudome 30.00 60.00
KE M.Kemp/A.Ethier 10.00 25.00
LB Carlos Lee/Lance Berkman 8.00 20.00
LS T.Lincecum/P.Sandoval 40.00 80.00
RTU H.Ramirez/T.Tulowitzki 30.00 60.00
SU R.Sandberg/C.Utley 20.00 50.00
UU B.Upton/J.Upton 8.00 20.00
WL D.Wright/E.Longoria 20.00 50.00

2010 Topps Peak Performance Relics

SER.1 A ODDS 1:1555 HOBBY
SER.1 B ODDS 1:71 HOBBY
SER.1 C ODDS 1:153 HOBBY
SER.2 ODDS 1:49 HOBBY
AC Asdrubal Cabrera B 3.00 8.00
AE Alcides Escobar C 3.00 8.00
AG Adrian Gonzalez S2 4.00 10.00
AH Aaron Hill S2 2.00 5.00
AH1 Aaron Hill Bat B 2.00 5.00
AH2 Aaron Hill Jsy B 2.00 5.00
AJ Adam Jones B 3.00 8.00
AJ Adam Jones S2 3.00 8.00
AK Al Kaline S2 5.00 12.00
AL Adam LaRoche A 2.00 5.00
AM Andrew McCutchen S2 5.00 12.00
AP Albert Pujols B 6.00 15.00
AP Andy Pettitte S2 3.00 8.00
AR Alexei Ramirez S2 3.00 8.00
AR Aramis Ramirez C 2.00 5.00
ARA Aramis Ramirez S2 2.00 5.00
AS Alfonso Soriano S2 3.00 8.00
BG Bob Gibson A 8.00 20.00
BM Brian McCann C 3.00 8.00
BP Buster Posey S2 10.00 25.00
BR Brad Lidge B 2.00 5.00
BRU Babe Ruth A 150.00 300.00
CC Chris Coghlan S2 2.00 5.00
CF Carlton Fisk A 8.00 20.00
CH Cole Hamels B 4.00 10.00
CJ Chipper Jones B 5.00 12.00
CJ Chipper Jones S2 5.00 12.00
CL Cliff Lee B 3.00 8.00
CR Cal Ripken Jr. B 8.00 20.00
CR Colby Rasmus S2 3.00 8.00
CS CC Sabathia S2 3.00 8.00
CU Chase Utley B 3.00 8.00
CZ Carlos Zambrano S2 3.00 8.00
DE Dennis Eckersley B 3.00 8.00
DG Dwight Gooden B 3.00 8.00
DH Dan Haren S2 2.00 5.00
DL Derrek Lee S2 2.00 5.00
DL Derrek Lee B 2.00 5.00
DM Daniel Murphy A 4.00 10.00
DO David Ortiz B 5.00 12.00
DO David Ortiz S2 5.00 12.00
DP David Price S2 4.00 10.00
DP Dustin Pedroia B 4.00 10.00
DU Dan Uggla B 2.00 5.00
DU Dan Uggla S2 2.00 5.00
DW Dave Winfield C 3.00 8.00
DW David Wright C 4.00 10.00
DY Delmon Young B 3.00 8.00
EL Evan Longoria B 3.00 8.00
FC Fausto Carmona B 2.00 5.00
FH Felix Hernandez B 3.00 8.00
FH Felix Hernandez S2 3.00 8.00
GB Gordon Beckham S2 2.00 5.00
GK George Kell S2 3.00 8.00
GS Grady Sizemore S2 3.00 8.00
GS Gary Sheffield A 2.00 5.00
GSI George Sisler A 15.00 40.00
GSI George Sisler S2 15.00 40.00
GSO Geovany Soto S2 3.00 8.00
GSO Geovany Soto C 3.00 8.00
HG Hank Greenberg B 8.00 20.00
HM Hideki Matsui B 5.00 12.00
HR Hanley Ramirez S2 3.00 8.00
HW Honus Wagner S2 40.00 100.00
HW Honus Wagner A 40.00 100.00
IK Ian Kinsler S2 3.00 8.00
IS Ichiro Suzuki S2 6.00 15.00
IS Ichiro Suzuki B 6.00 15.00
JB Jason Bulger B 2.00 5.00
JBO Jeremy Bonderman B 2.00 5.00
JC Johnny Cueto S2 EXCH 3.00 8.00
JD J.D. Drew B 2.00 5.00
JE Jacoby Ellsbury B 4.00 10.00
JG Jody Gerut B 2.00 5.00
JH Jeremy Hermida B 2.00 5.00
JH Josh Hamilton S2 3.00 8.00
JM Justin Morneau S2 3.00 8.00
JM Johnny Mize A 12.00 30.00
JMI Johnny Mize S2 3.00 8.00
JP Willie Stargell S2 3.00 8.00
JP Jonathan Papelbon B 3.00 8.00
JPO Jorge Posada B 3.00 8.00
JR Jose Reyes B 3.00 8.00
JS Joakim Soria B 2.00 5.00
JV Joey Votto S2 5.00 12.00
JV1 Joey Votto Bat B 5.00 12.00
JV2 Joey Votto Jsy B 5.00 12.00
JW Jayson Werth A 3.00 8.00
JWI Josh Willingham B 3.00 8.00
JZ Jordan Zimmermann B 3.00 8.00
KF Kosuke Fukudome B 3.00 8.00
KF Kosuke Fukudome S2 3.00 8.00
KJ Kenji Johjima B 2.00 5.00
KK Kenshin Kawakami S2 3.00 8.00
KY1 Kevin Youkilis Bat B 2.00 5.00
KY2 Kevin Youkilis Jsy C 2.00 5.00
LB Lance Berkman S2 3.00 8.00
MC Matt Cain S2 3.00 8.00
MC Matt Cain B 3.00 8.00
MCA Melky Cabrera B 2.00 5.00
MF Mike Fontenot S2 2.00 5.00
MG Matt Gamel C 2.00 5.00
MK Matt Kemp C 4.00 10.00
MM Melvin Mora B 2.00 5.00
MMA Mickey Mantle A 125.00 250.00
MO Mel Ott A 15.00 40.00
MO Mel Ott S2 15.00 40.00
MP Manny Parra C 2.00 5.00
MS Mike Schmidt A 8.00 20.00
MT Mark Teixeira S2 3.00 8.00
MY Michael Young B 2.00 5.00
NF Neftali Feliz S2 2.00 5.00
NM Nick Markakis S2 4.00 10.00
NS Nick Swisher S2 3.00 8.00
NS Nick Swisher C 3.00 8.00
OS Ozzie Smith S2 6.00 15.00
PF Prince Fielder S2 3.00 8.00
PF Prince Fielder B 3.00 8.00
PH Phil Hughes S2 2.00 5.00
PM Paul Molitor B 5.00 12.00
PS Pablo Sandoval S2 EXCH 3.00 8.00
PWR Pee Wee Reese A 12.00 30.00
PWR Pee Wee Reese S2 15.00 40.00
RA Richie Ashburn S2 15.00 40.00
RA Rick Ankiel B 2.00 5.00
RB Ryan Braun B 3.00 8.00
RC Roy Campanella S2 10.00 25.00
RCA Robinson Cano S2 3.00 8.00
RD Ryan Dempster S2 2.00 5.00
RH Ryan Howard S2 4.00 10.00
RH Rich Harden B 2.00 5.00
RHE Rickey Henderson B 10.00 25.00
RHO Ryan Howard B 4.00 10.00
RHO Rogers Hornsby S2 15.00 40.00
RP Rick Porcello S2 3.00 8.00
RR Robin Roberts S2 12.00 30.00
RT Ryan Theriot S2 2.00 5.00
RW Rickie Weeks C 2.00 5.00
SC Shin-Soo Choo B 3.00 8.00
SK1 Scott Kazmir Rays Jsy B 2.00 5.00
SK2 Scott Kazmir LAA Jsy C 2.00 5.00
TG Tony Gwynn B 5.00 12.00
TH Tim Hudson B 3.00 8.00
THA Tommy Hanson B 2.00 5.00
TL Ted Lilly S2 2.00 5.00
TM Thurman Munson S2 12.00 30.00
TM Thurman Munson A 12.00 30.00
TS Tris Speaker A 10.00 25.00
TS Tris Speaker S2 15.00 40.00
TT Troy Tulowitzki S2 5.00 12.00
TT Troy Tulowitzki B 5.00 12.00
UJ Ubaldo Jimenez S2 2.00 5.00
YB Yogi Berra S2 6.00 15.00
YG Yovani Gallardo S2 2.00 5.00
YG Yovani Gallardo B 2.00 5.00
ZG Zack Greinke S2 3.00 8.00

2010 Topps Peak Performance Relics Blue

*BLUE: .6X TO 1.5X BASIC
RANDOM INSERTS IN SER.2 PACKS
STATED PRINT RUN 99 SER.#'d SETS
CH Catfish Hunter S2 10.00 25.00

2010 Topps Red Back

INSERTED IN TARGET PACKS
31-45 ISSUED IN UPD TARGET PACKS
1 Mickey Mantle 3.00 8.00
2 Rogers Hornsby .60 1.50
3 Warren Spahn .60 1.50
4 Jackie Robinson 1.00 2.50
5 Ty Cobb 1.50 4.00
6 Cy Young 1.00 2.50
7 Albert Pujols 1.25 3.00
8 Mariano Rivera 1.25 3.00
9 Jimmie Foxx 1.00 2.50
10 Reggie Jackson .60 1.50
11 Lou Gehrig 2.00 5.00
12 Dizzy Dean .60 1.50
13 Chipper Jones 1.00 2.50
14 Cal Ripken Jr. 3.00 8.00
15 David Wright .75 2.00
16 Babe Ruth 2.50 6.00
17 Honus Wagner 1.00 2.50
18 Ichiro Suzuki 1.25 3.00
19 Nolan Ryan 3.00 8.00
20 Stan Musial 1.50 4.00
21 Tom Seaver .60 1.50
22 Derek Jeter 2.50 6.00
23 Roy Halladay .60 1.50
24 Mel Ott 1.00 2.50
25 George Sisler .60 1.50
26 Roger Maris 1.00 2.50
27 Walter Johnson 1.00 2.50
28 Vladimir Guerrero .60 1.50
29 Tim Lincecum .60 1.50
30 Hanley Ramirez .60 1.50
31 Babe Ruth 2.50 6.00
32 Jimmie Foxx 1.00 2.50
33 Rogers Hornsby .60 1.50
34 Warren Spahn .60 1.50
35 Reggie Jackson .60 1.50
36 Nolan Ryan 3.00 8.00
37 Tom Seaver .60 1.50
38 George Sisler .60 1.50
39 Roger Maris 1.00 2.50
40 Vladimir Guerrero .60 1.50
41 Thurman Munson 1.00 2.50
42 Johnny Mize .60 1.50
43 Pee Wee Reese .60 1.50
44 Hank Greenberg 1.00 2.50
45 Ryan Braun .60 1.50

2010 Topps Red Hot Rookie Redemption

COMPLETE SET (10) 15.00 40.00
STATED ODDS 1:36 HOBBY
RHR1 Carlos Santana 2.00 5.00
RHR2 Jose Tabata 1.00 2.50
RHR3 Brennan Boesch 1.50 4.00
RHR4 Mike Stanton 12.00 30.00
RHR5 Starlin Castro 1.50 4.00
RHR6 Logan Morrison 1.00 2.50
RHR7 Dominic Brown 2.50 6.00
RHR8 Stephen Strasburg 5.00 12.00
RHR9 Mike Minor 1.00 2.50
RHR10A Brett Wallace 1.50 4.00
RHR10B Brett Wallace AU 6.00 15.00

2010 Topps Series 2 Attax Code Cards

COMPLETE SET (27) 5.00 12.00
1 Jason Bay .50 1.25
2 Lance Berkman .50 1.25
3 Billy Butler .30 .75
4 Stephen Drew .30 .75
5 Yunel Escobar .30 .75
6 Yovani Gallardo .30 .75
7 Zack Greinke .50 1.25
8 Felix Hernandez .50 1.25
9 Matt Holliday .75 2.00
10 Torii Hunter .30 .75
11 Josh Johnson .50 1.25
12 Matt Kemp .60 1.50
13 Ian Kinsler .50 1.25
14 Derrek Lee .30 .75
15 Jon Lester .50 1.25
16 Tim Lincecum .50 1.25
17 Justin Morneau .50 1.25
18 Alexei Ramirez .50 1.25
19 Alex Rodriguez 1.00 2.50
20 Pablo Sandoval .50 1.25
21 Max Scherzer .75 2.00
22 Grady Sizemore .50 1.25
23 B.J. Upton .50 1.25
24 Chase Utley .50 1.25
25 Justin Verlander .75 2.00
26 Joey Votto .75 2.00
27 Ryan Zimmerman .50 1.25

2010 Topps Silk Collection

SER.1 ODDS 1:373 HOBBY
SER.2 ODDS 1:431 HOBBY
UPDATE ODDS 1:412 HOBBY
STATED PRINT RUN 50 SER.#'d SETS
1-50 ISSUED IN SERIES 1
51-100 ISSUED IN SERIES 2
101-200 ISSUED IN UPDATE
S1 Prince Fielder 6.00 15.00
S3 Derrek Lee 4.00 10.00
S4 Mickey Mantle 30.00 80.00
S5 Clayton Kershaw 20.00 50.00
S6 Bobby Abreu 4.00 10.00
S7 Johnny Cueto 6.00 15.00
S8 Dexter Fowler 6.00 15.00
S9 Felipe Lopez 4.00 10.00
S10 Tommy Hanson 4.00 10.00
S11 Shane Victorino 6.00 15.00
S12 Adam Jones 6.00 15.00
S13 Victor Martinez 6.00 15.00
S14 Rick Porcello 6.00 15.00
S15 Garret Anderson 4.00 10.00
S16 Josh Johnson 6.00 15.00
S17 Marco Scutaro 6.00 15.00
S18 Howie Kendrick 4.00 10.00
S19 Joey Votto 10.00 25.00
S20 Jorge De La Rosa 4.00 10.00
S21 Zack Greinke 6.00 15.00
S23 Billy Butler 4.00 10.00
S24 John Lackey 6.00 15.00
S25 Manny Ramirez 10.00 25.00
S26 CC Sabathia 6.00 15.00
S27 David Wright 8.00 20.00
S28 Nick Swisher 6.00 15.00
S29 Matt LaPorta 4.00 10.00
S30 Brandon Inge 6.00 15.00
S31 Cole Hamels 8.00 20.00
S32 Adrian Gonzalez 8.00 20.00
S33 Joe Saunders 4.00 10.00
S34 Tim Lincecum 6.00 15.00
S35 Ken Griffey Jr. 20.00 50.00

S36 J.A. Happ 6.00 15.00
S37 Ian Kinsler 6.00 15.00
S38 Ivan Rodriguez 6.00 15.00
S39 Carl Crawford 6.00 15.00
S40 Jon Garland 4.00 10.00
S41 Albert Pujols 12.00 30.00
S43 Andrew McCutchen 10.00 25.00
S44 Gordon Beckham 4.00 10.00
S45 Jorge Posada 6.00 15.00
S46 Ichiro Suzuki 12.00 30.00
S47 Vladimir Guerrero 6.00 15.00
S48 Cliff Lee 6.00 15.00
S49 Freddy Sanchez 4.00 10.00
S50 Ryan Dempster 4.00 10.00
S51 Adam Wainwright 6.00 15.00
S52 Matt Holliday 10.00 25.00
S53 Chone Figgins 4.00 10.00
S54 Tim Hudson 6.00 15.00
S55 Rich Harden 4.00 10.00
S56 Justin Upton 6.00 15.00
S57 Joe Mauer 8.00 20.00
S58 Vernon Wells 4.00 10.00
S59 Miguel Tejada 6.00 15.00
S60 Denard Span 4.00 10.00
S61 Brandon Phillips 4.00 10.00
S62 Jason Bay 6.00 15.00
S63 Kendry Morales 4.00 10.00
S64 Josh Hamilton 6.00 15.00
S65 Yovani Gallardo 4.00 10.00
S66 Adam Lind 6.00 15.00
S67 Hideki Matsui 10.00 25.00
S68 Will Venable 4.00 10.00
S69 Joe Blanton 4.00 10.00
S70 Adrian Beltre 10.00 25.00
S71 Pablo Sandoval 6.00 15.00
S72 Roy Halladay 6.00 15.00
S73 Chris Coghlan 4.00 10.00
S74 Colby Rasmus 6.00 15.00
S75 Alexei Ramirez 6.00 15.00
S76 Josh Beckett 4.00 10.00
S77 Matt Kemp 8.00 20.00
S78 Max Scherzer 10.00 25.00
S79 Randy Johnson 10.00 25.00
S80 Curtis Granderson 8.00 20.00
S81 David Price 8.00 20.00
S82 Neftali Feliz 4.00 10.00
S83 Ricky Romero 4.00 10.00
S84 Lance Berkman 6.00 15.00
S85 Andre Ethier 6.00 15.00
S86 Mark Teixeira 6.00 15.00
S87 Edwin Jackson 4.00 10.00
S88 Akinori Iwamura 4.00 10.00
S90 Jair Jurrjens 4.00 10.00
S91 Stephen Drew 4.00 10.00
S92 Javier Vazquez 4.00 10.00
S93 Orlando Hudson 4.00 10.00
S94 Adam Dunn 6.00 15.00
S95 Kevin Youkilis 4.00 10.00
S96 Chase Utley 6.00 15.00
S98 Brian McCann 6.00 15.00
S99 Jim Thome 6.00 15.00
S100 Alex Rios 4.00 10.00
S101 Geovany Soto 6.00 15.00
S102 Joakim Soria 4.00 10.00
S103 Chad Billingsley 6.00 15.00
S104 Jacoby Ellsbury 8.00 20.00
S105 Justin Morneau 6.00 15.00
S106 Jeff Francis 4.00 10.00
S107 Francisco Rodriguez 6.00 15.00
S108 Torii Hunter 4.00 10.00
S109 A.J Burnett 4.00 10.00
S110 Chris Young 4.00 10.00
S111 Bud Norris 4.00 10.00
S112 Todd Helton 6.00 15.00
S113 Shin-Soo Choo 6.00 15.00
S114 Matt Cain 6.00 15.00
S115 Jered Weaver 6.00 15.00
S116 Jason Bartlett 4.00 10.00
S117 Chris Carpenter 6.00 15.00
S118 Kosuke Fukudome 6.00 15.00
S119 Roy Oswalt 6.00 15.00
S120 Alex Rodriguez 12.00 30.00
S121 Dan Haren 4.00 10.00
S122 Hiroki Kuroda 4.00 10.00
S123 Hunter Pence 6.00 15.00
S124 Jeremy Guthrie 4.00 10.00
S125 Grady Sizemore 6.00 15.00
S126 Mark Reynolds 4.00 10.00
S127 Johnny Damon 6.00 15.00
S128 Aaron Rowand 4.00 10.00
S129 Carlos Beltran 6.00 15.00
S130 Alfonso Soriano 6.00 15.00
S131 Nelson Cruz 10.00 25.00
S132 Edinson Volquez 4.00 10.00
S133 Jayson Werth 6.00 15.00
S134 Mariano Rivera 12.00 30.00
S135 Brandon Webb 6.00 15.00
S136 Jordan Zimmermann 6.00 15.00
S137 Michael Young 4.00 10.00
S138 Daisuke Matsuzaka 6.00 15.00
S139 Ubaldo Jimenez 4.00 10.00
S140 Evan Longoria 6.00 15.00
S141 Brad Lidge 4.00 10.00
S142 Carlos Zambrano 6.00 15.00
S143 Heath Bell 4.00 10.00
S144 Trevor Cahill 4.00 10.00
S145 Carlos Gonzalez 6.00 15.00
S146 Jose Reyes 6.00 15.00
S147 Ian Snell 4.00 10.00
S148 Manny Parra 4.00 10.00
S149 Michael Cuddyer 4.00 10.00
S150 Melky Cabrera 4.00 10.00
S151 Justin Verlander 10.00 25.00
S152 Delmon Young 6.00 15.00
S153 Kelly Johnson 4.00 10.00
S154 Derek Lowe 4.00 10.00
S155 Derek Jeter 25.00 60.00
S156 Paul Maholm 4.00 10.00
S157 Mike Napoli 4.00 10.00
S158 Aramis Ramirez 4.00 10.00
S159 Alex Gordon 6.00 15.00
S160 Jorge Cantu 4.00 10.00
S161 Brad Hawpe 4.00 10.00
S162 Troy Tulowitzki 10.00 25.00
S163 Casey Kotchman 4.00 10.00
S164 Carlos Guillen 4.00 10.00
S165 J.D. Drew 4.00 10.00
S166 Dustin Pedroia 8.00 20.00
S167 Francisco Liriano 4.00 10.00
S168 Jimmy Rollins 6.00 15.00
S169 Wade LeBlanc 4.00 10.00
S170 Miguel Cabrera 10.00 25.00
S171 Jeremy Hermida 4.00 10.00
S172 Koji Uehara 4.00 10.00
S173 Tommy Hunter 4.00 10.00
S174 Dustin McGowan 4.00 10.00
S175 Corey Hart 4.00 10.00
S176 Jake Peavy 4.00 10.00
S177 Jason Varitek 10.00 25.00
S178 Chris Dickerson 4.00 10.00
S179 Robinson Cano 6.00 15.00
S180 Michael Bourn 4.00 10.00
S181 Chris Volstad 4.00 10.00
S182 Mark Buehrle 6.00 15.00
S183 Jarrod Saltalamacchia 4.00 10.00
S184 Aaron Hill 4.00 10.00
S185 Carlos Pena 6.00 15.00
S186 Luke Hochevar 4.00 10.00
S187 Derek Holland 4.00 10.00
S188 Carlos Quentin 4.00 10.00
S189 J.J. Hardy 4.00 10.00
S190 Ryan Zimmerman 6.00 15.00
S191 Travis Snider 4.00 10.00
S192 Russell Martin 4.00 10.00
S193 Brian Roberts 4.00 10.00
S194 Ryan Ludwick 4.00 10.00
S195 Aaron Cook 4.00 10.00
S196 Jay Bruce 6.00 15.00
S197 Kevin Slowey 4.00 10.00
S198 Johan Santana 6.00 15.00
S199 Carlos Lee 4.00 10.00
S200 David Ortiz 10.00 25.00
S201 Doug Davis 4.00 10.00
S202 Coco Crisp 4.00 10.00
S203 Jason Kendall 4.00 10.00
S204 Jason Bay 6.00 15.00
S205 Jim Thome 6.00 15.00
S206 Omar Vizquel 6.00 15.00
S207 Jose Valverde 4.00 10.00
S208 Adam Kennedy 4.00 10.00
S209 Kelly Shoppach 4.00 10.00
S210 Akinori Iwamura 4.00 10.00
S211 Brad Penny 4.00 10.00
S212 Kevin Millwood 4.00 10.00
S213 Cliff Lee 6.00 15.00
S214 Andruw Jones 4.00 10.00
S215 Rod Barajas 4.00 10.00
S216 Pedro Feliz 4.00 10.00
S218 Placido Polanco 4.00 10.00
S219 Jhan Marinez 4.00 10.00
S220 Bobby Wilson 4.00 10.00
S221 Kris Medlen 6.00 15.00
S222 Aaron Heilman 4.00 10.00
S223 Shaun Marcum 4.00 10.00
S224 Alfredo Simon 4.00 10.00
S225 Matt Thornton 4.00 10.00
S226 Billy Wagner 4.00 10.00
S227 Troy Glaus 4.00 10.00
S228 Jesus Feliciano 4.00 10.00
S229 Dana Eveland 4.00 10.00
S230 Scott Olsen 4.00 10.00
S231 Corey Patterson 4.00 10.00
S232 Livan Hernandez 4.00 10.00
S233 Bill Hall 4.00 10.00
S234 Josh Reddick 4.00 10.00
S235 Xavier Nady 4.00 10.00
S236 Koyie Hill 4.00 10.00
S237 Tom Gorzelanny 4.00 10.00
S238 Kevin Frandsen 4.00 10.00
S239 Mark Kotsay 4.00 10.00
S240 Arthur Rhodes 4.00 10.00
S241 Micah Owings 4.00 10.00
S242 Shelley Duncan 4.00 10.00
S243 Mike Redmond 4.00 10.00
S244 Chris Perez 4.00 10.00
S245 Don Kelly 4.00 10.00
S246 Alex Avila 6.00 15.00
S247 Geoff Blum 4.00 10.00
S248 Mitch Maier 4.00 10.00
S249 Roy Halladay 6.00 15.00
S250 Matt Daley 4.00 10.00
S251 Vicente Padilla 4.00 10.00
S252 Kila Ka'aihue 6.00 15.00
S253 Dave Bush 4.00 10.00
S254 Jody Gerut 4.00 10.00
S255 George Kottaras 4.00 10.00
S256 LaTroy Hawkins 4.00 10.00
S257 Brendan Harris 4.00 10.00
S258 Alex Cora 6.00 15.00
S259 Randy Winn 4.00 10.00
S260 Matt Harrison 4.00 10.00
S261 Pat Burrell 4.00 10.00
S262 Mark Ellis 4.00 10.00
S263 Conor Jackson 4.00 10.00
S264 Matt Downs 4.00 10.00
S265 Jeff Clement 4.00 10.00
S266 Joel Hanrahan 6.00 15.00
S267 John Jaso 4.00 10.00
S268 John Danks 4.00 10.00
S269 Eugenio Velez 4.00 10.00
S270 Jason Vargas 4.00 10.00
S271 Rob Johnson 4.00 10.00
S272 Gabe Gross 4.00 10.00
S273 David Freese 6.00 15.00
S274 Jamie Garcia 6.00 15.00
S275 Gabe Kapler 4.00 10.00
S276 Colby Lewis 6.00 15.00
S277 Carlos Santana 12.00 30.00
S278 Cole Gillespie 4.00 10.00
S279 Jonny Venters 4.00 10.00
S280 Jeff Suppan 4.00 10.00
S281 Lance Zawadzki 4.00 10.00
S282 Mike Leake 12.00 30.00
S283 John Ely 4.00 10.00
S284 Mike Stanton 30.00 80.00
S285 Rhyne Hughes 4.00 10.00
S286 Jeanmar Gomez 6.00 15.00
S287 Brennan Boesch 10.00 25.00
S288 Austin Jackson 6.00 15.00
S289 Alex Sanabia 4.00 10.00
S290 Jason Donald 4.00 10.00
S291 Andrew Cashner 4.00 10.00
S292 Josh Bell 4.00 10.00
S293 Travis Wood 6.00 15.00
S294 Mike Stanton 12.00 30.00
S295 Jose Tabata 6.00 15.00
S296 Jake Arrieta 10.00 25.00
S297 Carlos Santana 12.00 30.00
S298 Sam Demel 4.00 10.00
S299 Felix Doubront 4.00 10.00
S300 Stephen Strasburg 12.00 30.00

2010 Topps Tales of the Game

STATED ODDS 1:6 HOBBY
TOG1 Spikes Up .75 2.00
TOG2 The Curse of the Bambino 1.25 3.00
TOG3 Ruth Calls His Shot 1.25 3.00
TOG4 Topps Dumps 1952 Cards in the River .40 1.00
TOG5 Jackie Robinson Steals Home in World Series .75 2.00
TOG6 Let's Play Two .75 2.00
TOG7 Mazeroski Hits World Series Walk-Off .60 1.50
TOG8 Maris Chases #61 .75 2.00
TOG9 Mantle HR Off Facade 1.50 4.00
TOG10 Piersall Runs Backwards for HR #100 .40 1.00
TOG11 1969 Amazin' Mets .60 1.50
TOG12 Reggie has Light Tower Power .60 1.50
TOG13 Carlton Fisk: The Wave .60 1.50
TOG14 Reggie's World Series HR Hat Trick .60 1.50
TOG15 Ozzie Smith Flips Out .60 1.50
TOG16 Bo Knows Wall Climbing .75 2.00
TOG17 Wade Boggs Who You Calling Chicken? .60 1.50
TOG18 Prince: BP HR at Age 12 .50 1.25
TOG19 Old Cal Clutch 1.50 4.00
TOG20 Jeter: The Flip 1.25 3.00
TOG21 Schilling's Bloody Sock .60 1.50
TOG22 Pesky's Pole .40 1.00
TOG23 Manny Being Manny .75 2.00
TOG24 The Great Ham-Bino .50 1.25
TOG25 Yankees Dig Up Ortiz' Jersey 1.00 2.50

2010 Topps Topps Town

RANDOM INSERTS IN PACKS
TTT1 Joe Mauer .40 1.00
TTT2 David Wright .40 1.00
TTT3 Hanley Ramirez .30 .75
TTT4 Adrian Gonzalez .40 1.00
TTT5 Evan Longoria .30 .75
TTT6 Ichiro Suzuki .60 1.50
TTT7 Josh Hamilton .30 .75
TTT8 Zack Greinke .30 .75
TTT9 Roy Halladay .30 .75
TTT10 Tim Lincecum .30 .75
TTT11 Brian McCann .30 .75
TTT12 Miguel Tejada .30 .75
TTT13 Ryan Howard .40 1.00
TTT14 Albert Pujols .60 1.50
TTT15 Miguel Cabrera .50 1.25
TTT16 Kevin Youkilis .20 .50
TTT17 Todd Helton .30 .75
TTT18 Vladimir Guerrero .30 .75
TTT19 Justin Upton .30 .75
TTT20 Adam Jones .30 .75
TTT21 Adam Dunn .30 .75
TTT22 Andrew McCutchen .50 1.25
TTT23 CC Sabathia .30 .75
TTT24 Ryan Braun .30 .75
TTT25 Manny Ramirez .50 1.25

2010 Topps Topps Town Gold

*GOLD: .75X TO 2X BASIC
RANDOM INSERTS IN PACKS

2010 Topps Turkey Red

STATED ODDS 1:4 HOBBY
1-50 ISSUED IN SERIES 1
51-100 ISSUED IN SERIES 2
101-150 ISSUED IN UPDATE
TR1 Ryan Howard .60 1.50
TR2 Miguel Tejada .50 1.25
TR3 Nolan Ryan 2.50 6.00
TR4 Albert Pujols 1.00 2.50
TR5 Josh Beckett .30 .75
TR6 Justin Upton .50 1.25
TR7 Andre Ethier .50 1.25
TR8 Tommy Hanson .30 .75
TR9 Josh Johnson .50 1.25
TR10 Jonathan Papelbon .50 1.25
TR11 Cole Hamels .60 1.50
TR12 Manny Ramirez .75 2.00
TR13 Yovani Gallardo .50 1.25
TR14 Kevin Youkilis .30 .75
TR15 Hank Greenberg .75 2.00
TR16 Ozzie Smith 1.00 2.50
TR17 Derrek Lee .30 .75
TR18 Ryan Braun .50 1.25
TR19 Cal Ripken Jr. 2.50 6.00
TR20 CC Sabathia .50 1.25
TR21 Johnny Bench .75 2.00
TR22 Tim Lincecum .50 1.25
TR23 Mike Schmidt 1.25 3.00
TR24 Clayton Kershaw 1.50 4.00
TR25 Ernie Banks .75 2.00
TR26 Dexter Fowler .50 1.25
TR27 Edwin Jackson .30 .75
TR28 Mickey Mantle 2.50 6.00
TR29 Gordon Beckham .30 .75
TR30 Victor Martinez .50 1.25
TR31 Mel Ott .75 2.00
TR32 Zack Greinke .75 2.00
TR33 Roy Halladay .50 1.25
TR34 David Wright .60 1.50
TR35 Stephen Drew .30 .75
TR36 Matt Holliday .75 2.00
TR37 Chase Utley .50 1.25
TR38 Rick Porcello .50 1.25
TR39 Vladimir Guerrero .50 1.25
TR40 Mark Teixeira .50 1.25
TR41 Evan Longoria .50 1.25
TR42 Ian Kinsler .50 1.25
TR43 Adrian Gonzalez .60 1.50
TR44 Matt Kemp .60 1.50
TR45 Ryne Sandberg 1.50 4.00
TR46 Babe Ruth 2.00 5.00
TR47 Curtis Granderson .60 1.50
TR48 Willie McCovey .50 1.25
TR49 Josh Hamilton .50 1.25
TR50 Pablo Sandoval .50 1.25
TR51 Torii Hunter .30 .75
TR52 Adam Dunn .50 1.25
TR53 Alexei Ramirez .50 1.25
TR54 Andrew McCutchen .75 2.00
TR55 Aaron Hill .30 .75
TR56 Alcides Escobar .50 1.25
TR57 Jimmie Foxx .75 2.00
TR58 Joey Votto .75 2.00
TR59 Jose Reyes .50 1.25
TR60 Al Kaline .75 2.00
TR61 Felix Hernandez .50 1.25
TR62 Troy Tulowitzki .75 2.00
TR63 Nate McLouth .30 .75
TR64 Justin Morneau .50 1.25
TR65 Prince Fielder .50 1.25
TR66 Nelson Cruz .75 2.00
TR67 Grady Sizemore .50 1.25
TR68 Hanley Ramirez .50 1.25
TR69 Brooks Robinson .50 1.25
TR70 Jackie Robinson .75 2.00
TR71 Nick Markakis .60 1.50
TR72 Roy Oswalt .50 1.25
TR73 Chad Billingsley .50 1.25
TR74 Tom Seaver .50 1.25
TR75 B.J. Upton .50 1.25
TR76 Chris Coghlan .30 .75
TR77 Luis Aparicio .50 1.25
TR78 Dan Haren .30 .75
TR79 Raul Ibanez .50 1.25
TR80 Kosuke Fukudome .50 1.25
TR81 Denard Span .30 .75
TR82 Joe Morgan .50 1.25
TR83 Yogi Berra .75 2.00
TR84 Dustin Pedroia .60 1.50
TR85 Lou Gehrig 1.50 4.00
TR86 Billy Butler .30 .75
TR87 Jake Peavy .30 .75
TR88 Eddie Mathews .75 2.00
TR89 Ubaldo Jimenez .30 .75
TR90 Johan Santana .50 1.25
TR91 Buster Posey 2.50 6.00
TR92 George Sisler .50 1.25
TR93 Ian Desmond .50 1.25
TR94 Kurt Suzuki .30 .75
TR95 Ty Cobb 1.25 3.00
TR96 Magglio Ordonez .50 1.25
TR97 Chase Headley .30 .75
TR98 Hunter Pence .50 1.25
TR99 Ryan Ludwick .30 .75
TR100 Derek Jeter 2.00 5.00
TR101 Hideki Matsui .75 2.00
TR102 Kelly Johnson .30 .75
TR103 Jason Heyward 1.25 3.00
TR104 Adam Jones .50 1.25
TR105 John Lackey .50 1.25
TR106 Roy Campanella .75 2.00
TR107 Aramis Ramirez .30 .75
TR108 Carlos Quentin .30 .75
TR109 Brandon Phillips .30 .75
TR110 Shin-Soo Choo .50 1.25
TR111 Ian Stewart .30 .75
TR112 Miguel Cabrera .75 2.00
TR113 Josh Johnson .50 1.25
TR114 Carlos Lee .30 .75
TR115 Joakim Soria .30 .75
TR116 Jonathan Broxton .30 .75
TR117 Carlos Gomez .30 .75
TR118 Joe Mauer .60 1.50
TR119 Jason Bay .50 1.25
TR120 Curtis Granderson .60 1.50
TR121 A.J. Burnett .30 .75
TR122 Ben Sheets .30 .75
TR123 Roy Halladay .50 1.25
TR124 Ryan Doumit .30 .75
TR125 Kyle Blanks .30 .75
TR126 Matt Cain .50 1.25
TR127 Ichiro Suzuki 1.00 2.50
TR128 Chris Carpenter .50 1.25
TR129 Matt Garza .30 .75
TR130 Vladimir Guerrero .50 1.25
TR131 Vernon Wells .30 .75
TR132 Ryan Zimmerman .50 1.25
TR133 Lou Brock .50 1.25
TR134 Rod Carew .50 1.25
TR135 Orlando Cepeda .50 1.25
TR136 Rogers Hornsby .50 1.25
TR137 Walter Johnson .75 2.00
TR138 Christy Mathewson .75 2.00
TR139 Johnny Mize .50 1.25
TR140 Thurman Munson .75 2.00
TR141 Pee Wee Reese .50 1.25
TR142 Tris Speaker .50 1.25
TR143 Honus Wagner .75 2.00
TR144 Cy Young .75 2.00
TR145 Robin Yount .75 2.00
TR146 Duke Snider .50 1.25
TR147 Frank Robinson .50 1.25
TR148 Stephen Strasburg 2.50 6.00
TR149 Mike Stanton 2.50 6.00
TR150 Starlin Castro .50 1.25

2010 Topps Vintage Legends Collection

COMPLETE SET (50) 15.00 40.00
COM.UPDATE SET (25) 5.00 12.00
STATED ODDS 1:4 HOBBY
26-50 ISSUED IN UPDATE
VLC1 Lou Gehrig 1.50 4.00
VLC2 Johnny Mize .50 1.25
VLC3 Reggie Jackson .50 1.25
VLC4 Tris Speaker .50 1.25
VLC5 George Sisler .50 1.25
VLC6 Willie McCovey .50 1.25
VLC7 Tom Seaver .50 1.25
VLC8 Walter Johnson .75 2.00
VLC9 Ozzie Smith 1.00 2.50
VLC10 Babe Ruth 2.00 5.00
VLC11 Christy Mathewson .75 2.00
VLC12 Jackie Robinson .75 2.00
VLC13 Eddie Murray .50 1.25
VLC14 Mel Ott .75 2.00
VLC15 Jimmie Foxx .75 2.00
VLC16 Thurman Munson .75 2.00
VLC17 Mike Schmidt 1.25 3.00
VLC18 Johnny Bench .75 2.00
VLC19 Rogers Hornsby .50 1.25
VLC20 Ty Cobb 1.25 3.00
VLC21 Nolan Ryan 2.50 6.00
VLC22 Roy Campanella .75 2.00
VLC23 Cy Young .75 2.00
VLC24 Pee Wee Reese .50 1.25
VLC25 Honus Wagner .75 2.00
VLC26 Johnny Mize .50 1.25
VLC27 Cy Young .75 2.00
VLC28 Ozzie Smith 1.00 2.50
VLC29 Nolan Ryan 2.50 6.00
VLC30 George Sisler .50 1.25
VLC31 Babe Ruth 2.00 5.00
VLC32 Reggie Jackson .50 1.25
VLC33 Christy Mathewson .75 2.00
VLC34 Mike Schmidt 1.25 3.00
VLC35 Mel Ott .75 2.00
VLC36 Ty Cobb 1.25 3.00
VLC37 Eddie Murray .50 1.25
VLC38 Lou Gehrig 1.50 4.00
VLC39 Roy Campanella .75 2.00
VLC40 Tom Seaver .50 1.25
VLC41 Honus Wagner .75 2.00
VLC42 Jackie Robinson .75 2.00
VLC43 Johnny Bench .75 2.00
VLC44 Pee Wee Reese .50 1.25
VLC45 Thurman Munson .75 2.00
VLC46 Rogers Hornsby .50 1.25
VLC47 Jimmie Foxx .75 2.00
VLC48 Willie McCovey .50 1.25
VLC49 Tris Speaker .50 1.25
VLC50 Walter Johnson .75 2.00

2010 Topps When They Were Young

STATED ODDS 1:6 HOBBY
AP Aaron Poreda .40 1.00
AR Alex Rodriguez 1.25 3.00
BR Brian Roberts .40 1.00
CM Charlie Morton 1.00 2.50
CR Cody Ross .40 1.00
CS Clint Sammons .40 1.00
DM Daniel McCutchen .60 1.50
DO David Ortiz 1.00 2.50
DW David Wright .75 2.00
GB Gordon Beckham .40 1.00
JB Jason Berken .40 1.00
JD Johnny Damon .60 1.50
JV Justin Verlander 1.00 2.50
RD Ryan Doumit .40 1.00
RM Russell Martin .40 1.00
RN Ricky Nolasco .40 1.00
SO Scott Olsen .40 1.00
YM Yadier Molina 1.00 2.50

2010 Topps World Champion Autograph Relics

STATED ODDS 1:7,500 HOBBY
STATED PRINT RUN 50 SER.#'d SETS
AR Alex Rodriguez 100.00 200.00
CS CC Sabathia 40.00 100.00
MC Melky Cabrera 30.00 60.00
MR Mariano Rivera 125.00 250.00
RC Robinson Cano 100.00 200.00

2010 Topps World Champion Autographs

STATED ODDS 1:22,600 HOBBY
STATED PRINT RUN 50 SER.#'d SETS
AR Alex Rodriguez 125.00 250.00
CS CC Sabathia 125.00 250.00
MC Melky Cabrera 20.00 50.00
MR Mariano Rivera 100.00 200.00
RC Robinson Cano 50.00 100.00

2010 Topps World Champion Relics

STATED ODDS 1:3750 HOBBY
STATED PRINT RUN 100 SER.#'d SETS
AP Andy Pettitte 20.00 50.00
AR Alex Rodriguez 30.00 60.00
BG Brett Gardner 10.00 25.00
CS CC Sabathia 20.00 50.00
EH Eric Hinske 15.00 40.00
HM Hideki Matsui 40.00 80.00
JD Johnny Damon 20.00 50.00
JG Joe Girardi 15.00 40.00
JH Jerry Hairston Jr. 30.00 60.00
JP Jorge Posada 20.00 50.00
MC Melky Cabrera 15.00 40.00
MR Mariano Rivera 25.00 60.00
MT Mark Teixeira 30.00 60.00
NS Nick Swisher 15.00 40.00
RC Robinson Cano 30.00 60.00

2010 Topps Update

COMP.SET w/o SP's (330) 15.00 40.00
COMMON CARD (1-330) .12 .30
COMMON SP VAR (1-330) 6.00 15.00
COMMON RC (1-330) .40 1.00
PRINTING PLATE ODDS 1:1550 HOBBY
US1 Vladimir Guerrero .20 .50
US2 Dayan Viciedo RC .60 1.50
US3 Sam Demel RC .40 1.00
US4 Alex Cora .20 .50
US5 Troy Glaus .12 .30
US6 Adam Ottavino RC .40 1.00
US7 Sam LeCure (RC) .40 1.00
US8 Fred Lewis .12 .30
US9 Danny Worth RC .40 1.00
US10 Hideki Matsui .30 .75
US11 Vernon Wells .12 .30
US12 Jason Michaels .12 .30
US13 Max Scherzer .30 .75
US14 Ike Davis .25 .60
US15A Ike Davis RC .75 2.00
US15B Willie McCovey VAR SP 6.00 15.00
US16 Felipe Paulino .12 .30
US17 Marlon Byrd .12 .30
US18 Omar Beltre (RC) .40 1.00
US19 Russell Branyan .12 .30
US20 Jason Bay .20 .50
US21 Roy Oswalt .20 .50
US22 Ty Wigginton .12 .30
US23 Andy Pettitte .20 .50
US24 V.Guerrero/M.Cabrera .30 .75
US25A Andrew Bailey .12 .30
US25B Philadelphia Athletics VAR SP 6.00 15.00
US26 Jesus Feliciano RC .40 1.00
US27 Koyie Hill .12 .30
US28 Bill Hall .12 .30
US29 Livan Hernandez .12 .30
US30 Roy Halladay .20 .50
US31 Corey Patterson .12 .30
US32 Doug Davis .12 .30
US33 Matt Capps .12 .30
US34 Shaun Marcum .12 .30
US35 Ryan Braun .20 .50
US36 Omar Vizquel .20 .50
US37 Alex Avila .20 .50
US38 Chris Young .12 .30
US39 Kila Ka'aihue .20 .50
US40 Evan Longoria .20 .50
US41 Anthony Slama RC .40 1.00
US42 Conor Jackson .12 .30
US43 Brennan Boesch .30 .75
US44 Scott Rolen .20 .50
US45A David Price .25 .60
US45B Steve Carlton VAR SP 6.00 15.00
US46 Colby Lewis .12 .30
US47 Jody Gerut .12 .30
US48 Geoff Blum .12 .30
US49 Bobby Wilson .12 .30
US50A Mike Stanton RC 8.00 20.00
US50B Reggie Jackson VAR SP 6.00 15.00
US51 Tom Gorzelanny .12 .30
US52 Andy Oliver RC .40 1.00
US53 Jordan Smith RC .40 1.00
US54 Akinori Iwamura .12 .30
US55 Stephen Strasburg 1.00 2.50
US56 Matt Holliday .30 .75
US57 Derek Jeter/Elvis Andrus .75 2.00
US58A Brian Wilson .30 .75
US58B New York Giants VAR SP 6.00 15.00
US59A Jeanmar Gomez RC .60 1.50
US59B J.Gomez Pie SP 10.00 25.00
US60 Miguel Tejada .20 .50
US61 Alfredo Simon .12 .30
US62 Chris Narveson .12 .30
US63 David Ortiz .30 .75
US64 Jose Valverde .12 .30
US65 Victor Martinez/Robinson Cano .20 .50
US66 Ronnie Belliard .12 .30
US67 Kyle Farnsworth .12 .30
US68 John Danks .12 .30
US69 Lance Cormier .12 .30
US70 Jonathan Broxton .12 .30
US71 Jason Giambi .12 .30
US72 Milton Bradley .12 .30
US73 Torii Hunter .12 .30
US74 Ryan Church .12 .30
US75 Jason Heyward .50 1.25
US76 Jose Tabata .20 .50
US77 John Axford RC .40 1.00
US78 Jon Link RC .40 1.00
US79 Jonny Gomes .12 .30
US80 David Ortiz .30 .75
US81 Rich Harden .12 .30
US82 Emmanuel Burriss .12 .30
US83 Jeff Suppan .12 .30
US84 Melvin Mora .12 .30
US85A Starlin Castro RC 1.00 2.50
US85B Andre Dawson VAR SP 6.00 15.00
US86 Matt Guerrier .12 .30
US87 Trevor Plouffe (RC) 1.00 2.50
US88 Lance Berkman .20 .50
US89 Frank Herrmann RC .40 1.00
US90 Rafael Furcal .12 .30
US91 Nick Johnson .12 .30
US92 Pedro Feliciano .12 .30
US93 Jon Rauch .12 .30
US94 Reid Brignac .12 .30
US95 Jamie Moyer .12 .30
US96 John Bowker .12 .30
US97 Troy Tulowitzki/Matt Holliday .30 .75
US98 Yunel Escobar .12 .30
US99 Jose Bautista .20 .50
US100A Roy Halladay .20 .50
US100B Robin Roberts VAR SP 6.00 15.00
US101 Jake Westbrook .12 .30
US102 Chris Carter RC .60 1.50
US103 Matt Tuiasosopo .12 .30
US104 Paul Konerko .20 .50
US105 Chone Figgins .12 .30
US106 Orlando Cabrera .12 .30
US107 Matt Capps .12 .30
US108 John Buck .12 .30
US109 Luke Hughes (RC) .40 1.00
US110 Curtis Granderson .25 .60
US111 Willie Bloomquist .12 .30
US112 Chad Qualls .12 .30
US113 Brad Ziegler .12 .30
US114 Kenley Jansen RC 1.25 3.00
US115 Brad Lincoln RC .60 1.50
US116 Brandon Morrow .12 .30
US117 Martin Prado .12 .30
US118 Jose Bautista .20 .50
US119 Adam LaRoche .12 .30
US120 Brennan Boesch RC 1.00 2.50
US121 J.A. Happ .20 .50
US122 Darnell McDonald .12 .30
US123 Alberto Callaspo .12 .30
US124 Chris Young .12 .30
US125 Adam Wainwright .20 .50
US126 Elvis Andrus .20 .50
US127 Nick Swisher .20 .50
US128 Reed Johnson .12 .30
US129 Gregor Blanco .12 .30
US130 Ichiro Suzuki .40 1.00
US131 Takashi Saito .12 .30
US132 Corey Hart .12 .30
US133 Javier Vazquez .12 .30
US134 Rick Ankiel .12 .30
US135 Starlin Castro .30 .75
US136 Jarrod Saltalamacchia .12 .30
US137 Austin Kearns .12 .30
US138 Brandon League .12 .30
US139 Jorge Cantu .12 .30
US140 Josh Hamilton .20 .50
US141 Phil Hughes .12 .30
US142 Mike Cameron .12 .30
US143 Jonathan Lucroy RC 1.00 2.50
US144 Eric Patterson .12 .30
US145 Adrian Beltre .30 .75
US146 Peter Bourjos RC .60 1.50
US147 Argenis Diaz RC .60 1.50
US148 J.J. Putz .12 .30
US149A Kevin Russo RC .40 1.00
US149B B.Ruth VAR SP 10.00 25.00
US150 Hanley Ramirez .20 .50
US151 Kerry Wood .12 .30
US152 Ian Kennedy .12 .30
US153 Brian McCann .20 .50
US154 Jose Guillen .12 .30
US155 Ivan Rodriguez .20 .50
US156 Matt Thornton .12 .30
US157 Jason Marquis .12 .30

US158 CC Sabathia/Carl Crawford .20 .50
US159 Octavio Dotel .12 .30
US160 Josh Johnson .20 .50
US161 Matt Holliday .30 .75
US162 Hong-Chih Kuo .12 .30
US163 Marco Scutaro .20 .50
US164 Gaby Sanchez .12 .30
US165 Omar Infante .12 .30
US166 Jon Garland .12 .30
US167 Ramon Santiago .12 .30
US168 Wilson Ramos RC 1.00 2.50
US169 Ryan Ludwick .12 .30
US170 Carl Crawford .20 .50
US171 Cristian Guzman .12 .30
US172 Josh Donaldson RC 2.00 5.00
US173 Lorenzo Cain RC 1.00 2.50
US174 Matt Lindstrom .12 .30
US175A Drew Storen RC .60 1.50
US175B Bruce Sutter VAR SP 6.00 15.00
US176 Felipe Lopez .12 .30
US177 Chris Heisey RC .60 1.50
US178 Jim Edmonds .20 .50
US179 Juan Pierre .12 .30
US180 David Wright .25 .60
US181 J.P. Arencibia RC .75 2.00
US182 Randy Wolf .12 .30
US183 Luis Atilano RC .40 1.00
US184 Blake DeWitt .12 .30
US185A Brian Matusz RC 1.00 2.50
US185B Jim Palmer VAR SP 6.00 15.00
US186 Scott Hairston .12 .30
US187 Phil Hughes/David Price .25 .60
US188 Orlando Hudson .12 .30
US189 Derrek Lee .12 .30
US190 John Lackey .20 .50
US191 Danny Valencia RC 2.50 6.00
US192 Daniel Nava RC .40 1.00
US193 Ryan Theriot .12 .30
US194 Vernon Wells .12 .30
US195 Mark DeRosa .12 .30
US196 Aubrey Huff .12 .30
US197 Sean Marshall .12 .30
US198 Francisco Cervelli .12 .30
US199 Jhonny Peralta .12 .30
US200A Albert Pujols .40 1.00
US200B St. Louis Browns VAR SP 6.00 15.00
US201 Jeffrey Marquez RC .60 1.50
US202 Mitch Moreland RC .60 1.50
US203A Jon Jay RC .60 1.50
US203B Tony Gwynn VAR SP 6.00 15.00
US204 Carlos Silva .12 .30
US205 Ben Sheets .12 .30
US206 Garret Anderson .12 .30
US207 Jerry Hairston Jr. .12 .30
US208 Jeff Keppinger .12 .30
US209 Bengie Molina .12 .30
US210 Ubaldo Jimenez .12 .30
US211 Daniel Hudson .20 .50
US212 Mitch Talbot .12 .30
US213 Alex Gonzalez .12 .30
US214A Jason Heyward .50 1.25
US214B Dave Winfield VAR SP 6.00 15.00
US215 Albert Pujols/Ryan Braun .40 1.00
US216 John Baker .12 .30
US217 Yorvit Torrealba .12 .30
US218 Kevin Gregg .12 .30
US219 Bobby Crosby .12 .30
US220A Jon Lester .20 .50
US220B Boston Americans VAR SP 6.00 15.00
US221 Heath Bell .12 .30
US222 Ted Lilly .12 .30
US223 Henry Blanco .12 .30
US224 Scott Olsen .12 .30
US225A Josh Bell (RC) .40 1.00
US225B Brooks Robinson VAR SP 6.00 15.00
US226 Scott Podsednik .12 .30
US227 Mark Kotsay .12 .30
US228 Brandon Phillips/Martin Prado .12 .30
US229 Joe Saunders .12 .30
US230 Robinson Cano .20 .50
US231 Gabe Kapler .12 .30
US232 Jason Kendall .12 .30
US233 Brendan Harris .12 .30
US234 Matt Downs RC .40 1.00
US235 Jose Tabata RC .60 1.50
US236 Matt Daley .12 .30
US237 Jhan Marinez RC .40 1.00
US238 Mark Ellis .12 .30
US239 Gabe Gross .12 .30
US240 Adrian Gonzalez .25 .60
US241 Joey Votto .30 .75
US242 Shelley Duncan .12 .30
US243 Michael Bourn .12 .30
US244 Mike Redmond .12 .30
US245 Placido Polanco .12 .30
US246 LaTroy Hawkins .12 .30
US247 Nick Swisher .20 .50
US248 Matt Harrison .12 .30
US249 Rafael Soriano .12 .30
US250 Miguel Cabrera .30 .75
US251A Jake Arrieta RC 1.00 2.50
US251B J.Arrieta Pie SP 15.00 40.00
US252 Jim Thome .20 .50
US253 Mike Minor RC .60 1.50
US254 Chris Perez .12 .30
US255 Kevin Millwood .12 .30
US256 Mike Gonzalez .12 .30
US257 Joel Hanrahan .20 .50
US258 Dana Eveland .12 .30
US259 Yadier Molina .30 .75
US260A Andre Ethier .20 .50
US260B Brooklyn Dodgers VAR SP 6.00 15.00
US261 Jason Vargas .12 .30
US262 Rob Johnson .12 .30
US263 Randy Winn .12 .30
US264 Vicente Padilla .12 .30
US265 Ryan Howard .25 .60
US266 Billy Wagner .12 .30
US267 Eugenio Velez .12 .30
US268 Logan Morrison RC .60 1.50
US269 Dave Bush .12 .30
US270 Vladimir Guerrero .20 .50
US271 Travis Wood (RC) .60 1.50
US272 Brian Stokes .12 .30
US273 John Jaso .12 .30
US274 S.Strasburg/I.Rodriguez 1.00 2.50
US275 Hong-Chih Kuo .12 .30
US276A Austin Jackson .20 .50
US276B Rickey Henderson VAR SP 6.00 15.00
US277 Micah Owings .12 .30
US278 Brad Penny .12 .30
US279 Hanley Ramirez .20 .50
US280 Alex Rodriguez .40 1.00
US281 Jose Valverde .12 .30
US282 Rhyne Hughes RC .40 1.00
US283 Kevin Frandsen .12 .30
US284 Josh Reddick .12 .30
US285 Jaime Garcia .20 .50
US286 Arthur Rhodes .12 .30
US287 Alex Sanabia RC .40 1.00
US288 Jonny Venters RC .40 1.00
US289 Adam Kennedy .12 .30
US290 Justin Verlander .30 .75
US291 Corey Hart .12 .30
US292 Kelly Shoppach .12 .30
US293 Pat Burrell .12 .30
US294 Aaron Heilman .12 .30
US295 Andrew Cashner RC .40 1.00
US296 Lance Zawadzki RC .40 1.00
US297 Don Kelly (RC) .40 1.00
US298 David Freese .20 .50
US299 Xavier Nady .12 .30
US300 Cliff Lee .20 .50
US301 Jeff Clement .12 .30
US302 Pedro Feliz .12 .30
US303 Brandon Phillips .12 .30
US304 Kris Medlen .20 .50
US305 Cliff Lee .20 .50
US306 Dan Haren .12 .30
US307 Carlos Santana .40 1.00
US308 Matt Thornton .12 .30
US309 Andruw Jones .12 .30
US310 Derek Jeter .75 2.00
US311 Felix Doubront RC .40 1.00
US312 Coco Crisp .12 .30
US313 Mitch Maier .12 .30
US314 Cole Gillespie RC .40 1.00
US315A Edwin Jackson .12 .30
US315B E.Jackson Pie SP 10.00 25.00
US316 Rod Barajas .12 .30
US317A Mike Leake .40 1.00
US317B B.Ruth VAR SP 8.00 20.00
US318A Domonic Brown RC 1.50 4.00
US318B Bo Jackson VAR SP 6.00 15.00
US319 Josh Tomlin RC 1.00 2.50
US320A Joe Mauer .25 .60
US320B Washington Senators VAR SP 6.00 15.00
US321 Jason Donald RC .40 1.00
US322 John Ely RC .40 1.00
US323 Ryan Kalish RC .60 1.50
US324 George Kottaras .12 .30
US325 Ian Kinsler .20 .50
US326 Miguel Cabrera .30 .75
US327 Mike Stanton 1.00 2.50
US328 Adrian Beltre .30 .75
US329 Jose Reyes/Hanley Ramirez .20 .50
US330A Carlos Santana RC 1.25 3.00
US330B Cleveland Naps VAR SP 6.00 15.00
US330C Johnny Bench VAR SP 6.00 15.00

2010 Topps Update Black

STATED ODDS 1:105 HOBBY
STATED PRINT RUN 59 SER.#'d SETS
US1 Vladimir Guerrero 8.00 20.00
US2 Dayan Viciedo 8.00 20.00
US3 Sam Demel 5.00 12.00
US4 Alex Cora 8.00 20.00
US5 Troy Glaus 5.00 12.00
US6 Adam Ottavino 5.00 12.00
US7 Sam LeCure 5.00 12.00
US8 Fred Lewis 5.00 12.00
US9 Danny Worth 5.00 12.00
US10 Hideki Matsui 10.00 25.00
US11 Vernon Wells 5.00 12.00
US12 Jason Michaels 5.00 12.00
US13 Max Scherzer 12.00 30.00
US14 Ike Davis 8.00 20.00
US15 Ike Davis 8.00 20.00
US16 Felipe Paulino 5.00 12.00
US17 Marlon Byrd 5.00 12.00
US18 Omar Beltre 5.00 12.00
US19 Russell Branyan 5.00 12.00
US20 Jason Bay 8.00 20.00
US21 Roy Oswalt 8.00 20.00
US22 Ty Wigginton 5.00 12.00
US23 Andy Pettitte 8.00 20.00
US24 V.Guerrero/M.Cabrera 10.00 25.00
US25 Andrew Bailey 5.00 12.00
US26 Jesus Feliciano 5.00 12.00
US27 Koyie Hill 5.00 12.00
US28 Bill Hall 5.00 12.00
US29 Livan Hernandez 5.00 12.00
US30 Roy Halladay 6.00 15.00
US31 Corey Patterson 5.00 12.00
US32 Doug Davis 5.00 12.00
US33 Matt Capps 5.00 12.00
US34 Shaun Marcum 5.00 12.00
US35 Ryan Braun 6.00 15.00
US36 Omar Vizquel 8.00 20.00
US37 Alex Avila 8.00 20.00
US38 Chris Young 5.00 12.00
US39 Kila Ka'aihue 8.00 20.00
US40 Evan Longoria 6.00 15.00
US41 Anthony Slama 5.00 12.00
US42 Conor Jackson 5.00 12.00
US43 Brennan Boesch 10.00 25.00
US44 Scott Rolen 8.00 20.00
US45 David Price 8.00 20.00
US46 Colby Lewis 5.00 12.00
US47 Jody Gerut 5.00 12.00
US48 Geoff Blum 5.00 12.00
US49 Bobby Wilson 5.00 12.00
US50 Mike Stanton 30.00 80.00
US51 Tom Gorzelanny 5.00 12.00
US52 Andy Oliver 5.00 12.00
US53 Jordan Smith 5.00 12.00
US54 Akinori Iwamura 5.00 12.00
US55 Stephen Strasburg 15.00 40.00
US56 Matt Holliday 10.00 25.00
US57 Derek Jeter/Elvis Andrus 25.00 60.00
US58 Brian Wilson 12.00 30.00
US59 Jeanmar Gomez 6.00 15.00
US60 Miguel Tejada 8.00 20.00
US61 Alfredo Simon 5.00 12.00
US62 Chris Narveson 5.00 12.00
US63 David Ortiz 12.00 30.00
US64 Jose Valverde 5.00 12.00
US65 Victor Martinez/Robinson Cano 6.00 15.00
US66 Ronnie Belliard 5.00 12.00
US67 Kyle Farnsworth 5.00 12.00
US68 John Danks 5.00 12.00
US69 Lance Cormier 5.00 12.00
US70 Jonathan Broxton 5.00 12.00
US71 Jason Giambi 5.00 12.00
US72 Milton Bradley 5.00 12.00
US73 Torii Hunter 5.00 12.00
US74 Ryan Church 5.00 12.00
US75 Jason Heyward 15.00 40.00
US76 Jose Tabata 6.00 15.00
US77 John Axford 5.00 12.00
US78 Jon Link 5.00 12.00
US79 Jonny Gomes 5.00 12.00
US80 David Ortiz 12.00 30.00
US81 Rich Harden 5.00 12.00
US82 Emmanuel Burriss 5.00 12.00
US83 Jeff Suppan 5.00 12.00
US84 Melvin Mora 5.00 12.00
US85 Starlin Castro 10.00 25.00
US86 Matt Guerrier 5.00 12.00
US87 Trevor Plouffe 12.00 30.00
US88 Lance Berkman 8.00 20.00
US89 Frank Herrmann 5.00 12.00
US90 Rafael Furcal 5.00 12.00
US91 Nick Johnson 5.00 12.00
US92 Pedro Feliciano 5.00 12.00
US93 Jon Rauch 5.00 12.00
US94 Reid Brignac 5.00 12.00
US95 Jamie Moyer 5.00 12.00
US96 John Bowker 5.00 12.00
US97 Troy Tulowitzki/Matt Holliday 10.00 25.00
US98 Yunel Escobar 5.00 12.00
US99 Jose Bautista 8.00 20.00
US100 Roy Halladay 6.00 15.00
US101 Jake Westbrook 5.00 12.00
US102 Chris Carter 8.00 20.00
US103 Matt Tuiasosopo 5.00 12.00
US104 Paul Konerko 8.00 20.00
US105 Chone Figgins 5.00 12.00
US106 Orlando Cabrera 5.00 12.00
US107 Matt Capps 5.00 12.00
US108 John Buck 5.00 12.00
US109 Luke Hughes 5.00 12.00
US110 Curtis Granderson 10.00 25.00
US111 Willie Bloomquist 5.00 12.00
US112 Chad Qualls 5.00 12.00
US113 Brad Ziegler 5.00 12.00
US114 Kenley Jansen 15.00 40.00
US115 Brad Lincoln 8.00 20.00
US116 Brandon Morrow 5.00 12.00
US117 Martin Prado 5.00 12.00
US118 Jose Bautista 8.00 20.00
US119 Adam LaRoche 5.00 12.00
US120 Brennan Boesch 10.00 25.00
US121 J.A. Happ 8.00 20.00
US122 Darnell McDonald 5.00 12.00
US123 Alberto Callaspo 5.00 12.00
US124 Chris Young 5.00 12.00
US125 Adam Wainwright 8.00 20.00
US126 Elvis Andrus 8.00 20.00
US127 Nick Swisher 8.00 20.00
US128 Reed Johnson 5.00 12.00
US129 Gregor Blanco 5.00 12.00
US130 Ichiro Suzuki 12.00 30.00
US131 Takashi Saito 5.00 12.00
US132 Corey Hart 5.00 12.00
US133 Javier Vazquez 5.00 12.00
US134 Rick Ankiel 5.00 12.00
US135 Starlin Castro 10.00 25.00
US136 Jarrod Saltalamacchia 5.00 12.00
US137 Austin Kearns 5.00 12.00
US138 Brandon League 5.00 12.00
US139 Jorge Cantu 5.00 12.00
US140 Josh Hamilton 6.00 15.00
US141 Phil Hughes 5.00 12.00
US142 Mike Cameron 5.00 12.00
US143 Jonathan Lucroy 12.00 30.00
US144 Eric Patterson 5.00 12.00
US145 Adrian Beltre 12.00 30.00
US146 Peter Bourjos 8.00 20.00
US147 Argenis Diaz 8.00 20.00
US148 J.J. Putz 5.00 12.00
US149 Kevin Russo 5.00 12.00
US150 Hanley Ramirez 6.00 15.00
US151 Kerry Wood 5.00 12.00
US152 Ian Kennedy 5.00 12.00
US153 Brian McCann 8.00 20.00
US154 Jose Guillen 5.00 12.00
US155 Ivan Rodriguez 8.00 20.00
US156 Matt Thornton 5.00 12.00
US157 Jason Marquis 5.00 12.00
US158 CC Sabathia/Carl Crawford 8.00 20.00
US159 Octavio Dotel 5.00 12.00
US160 Josh Johnson 6.00 15.00
US161 Matt Holliday 10.00 25.00
US162 Hong-Chih Kuo 5.00 12.00
US163 Marco Scutaro 8.00 20.00
US164 Gaby Sanchez 5.00 12.00
US165 Omar Infante 5.00 12.00
US166 Jon Garland 5.00 12.00
US167 Ramon Santiago 5.00 12.00
US168 Wilson Ramos 12.00 30.00
US169 Ryan Ludwick 5.00 12.00
US170 Carl Crawford 8.00 20.00
US171 Cristian Guzman 5.00 12.00
US172 Josh Donaldson 25.00 60.00
US173 Lorenzo Cain 12.00 30.00
US174 Matt Lindstrom 5.00 12.00
US175 Drew Storen 8.00 20.00
US176 Felipe Lopez 5.00 12.00
US177 Chris Heisey 6.00 15.00
US178 Jim Edmonds 8.00 20.00
US179 Juan Pierre 5.00 12.00
US180 David Wright 8.00 20.00
US181 J.P. Arencibia 10.00 25.00
US182 Randy Wolf 5.00 12.00
US183 Luis Atilano 5.00 12.00
US184 Blake DeWitt 5.00 12.00
US185 Brian Matusz 10.00 25.00
US186 Scott Hairston 5.00 12.00
US187 Phil Hughes/David Price 8.00 20.00
US188 Orlando Hudson 5.00 12.00
US189 Derrek Lee 5.00 12.00
US190 John Lackey 8.00 20.00
US191 Danny Valencia 25.00 60.00
US192 Daniel Nava 4.00 10.00
US193 Ryan Theriot 5.00 12.00
US194 Vernon Wells 5.00 12.00
US195 Mark DeRosa 5.00 12.00
US196 Aubrey Huff 5.00 12.00
US197 Sean Marshall 5.00 12.00
US198 Francisco Cervelli 5.00 12.00
US199 Jhonny Peralta 5.00 12.00
US200 Albert Pujols 12.00 30.00
US201 Jeffrey Marquez 8.00 20.00
US202 Mitch Moreland 6.00 15.00
US203 Jon Jay 6.00 15.00
US204 Carlos Silva 5.00 12.00
US205 Ben Sheets 5.00 12.00
US206 Garret Anderson 5.00 12.00
US207 Jerry Hairston Jr. 5.00 12.00
US208 Jeff Keppinger 5.00 12.00
US209 Bengie Molina 5.00 12.00
US210 Ubaldo Jimenez 4.00 10.00
US211 Daniel Hudson 6.00 15.00
US212 Mitch Talbot 5.00 12.00
US213 Alex Gonzalez 5.00 12.00
US214 Jason Heyward 15.00 40.00
US215 Albert Pujols/Ryan Braun 12.00 30.00
US216 John Baker 5.00 12.00
US217 Yorvit Torrealba 5.00 12.00
US218 Kevin Gregg 5.00 12.00
US219 Bobby Crosby 5.00 12.00
US220 Jon Lester 8.00 20.00
US221 Heath Bell 5.00 12.00
US222 Ted Lilly 5.00 12.00
US223 Henry Blanco 5.00 12.00
US224 Scott Olsen 5.00 12.00
US225 Josh Bell 5.00 12.00
US226 Scott Podsednik 5.00 12.00
US227 Mark Kotsay 5.00 12.00
US228 Brandon Phillips/Martin Prado 5.00 12.00
US229 Joe Saunders 5.00 12.00
US230 Robinson Cano 6.00 15.00
US231 Gabe Kapler 5.00 12.00
US232 Jason Kendall 5.00 12.00
US233 Brendan Harris 5.00 12.00
US234 Matt Downs 5.00 12.00
US235 Jose Tabata 6.00 15.00
US236 Matt Daley 5.00 12.00
US237 Jhan Marinez 5.00 12.00
US238 Mark Ellis 5.00 12.00
US239 Gabe Gross 5.00 12.00
US240 Adrian Gonzalez 10.00 25.00
US241 Joey Votto 10.00 25.00
US242 Shelley Duncan 5.00 12.00
US243 Michael Bourn 5.00 12.00
US244 Mike Redmond 5.00 12.00
US245 Placido Polanco 5.00 12.00
US246 LaTroy Hawkins 5.00 12.00
US247 Nick Swisher 8.00 20.00
US248 Matt Harrison 5.00 12.00
US249 Rafael Soriano 5.00 12.00
US250 Miguel Cabrera 10.00 25.00
US251 Jake Arrieta 12.00 30.00
US252 Jim Thome 8.00 20.00
US253 Mike Minor 6.00 15.00
US254 Chris Perez 5.00 12.00
US255 Kevin Millwood 5.00 12.00
US256 Mike Gonzalez 5.00 12.00
US257 Joel Hanrahan 8.00 20.00
US258 Dana Eveland 5.00 12.00
US259 Yadier Molina 12.00 30.00
US260 Andre Ethier 6.00 15.00
US261 Jason Vargas 5.00 12.00
US262 Rob Johnson 5.00 12.00
US263 Randy Winn 5.00 12.00
US264 Vicente Padilla 5.00 12.00
US265 Ryan Howard 8.00 20.00
US266 Billy Wagner 5.00 12.00
US267 Eugenio Velez 5.00 12.00
US268 Logan Morrison 8.00 20.00
US269 Dave Bush 5.00 12.00
US270 Vladimir Guerrero 6.00 15.00
US271 Travis Wood 6.00 15.00
US272 Brian Stokes 5.00 12.00
US273 John Jaso 5.00 12.00
US274 S.Strasburg/I.Rodriguez 15.00 40.00
US275 Hong-Chih Kuo 5.00 12.00
US276 Austin Jackson 6.00 15.00
US277 Micah Owings 5.00 12.00
US278 Brad Penny 5.00 12.00
US279 Hanley Ramirez 6.00 15.00
US280 Alex Rodriguez 12.00 30.00
US281 Jose Valverde 5.00 12.00
US282 Rhyne Hughes 5.00 12.00
US283 Kevin Frandsen 5.00 12.00
US284 Josh Reddick 5.00 12.00
US285 Jaime Garcia 8.00 20.00
US286 Arthur Rhodes 5.00 12.00
US287 Alex Sanabia 5.00 12.00
US288 Jonny Venters 5.00 12.00
US289 Adam Kennedy 5.00 12.00
US290 Justin Verlander 12.00 30.00
US291 Corey Hart 5.00 12.00
US292 Kelly Shoppach 5.00 12.00
US293 Pat Burrell 5.00 12.00
US294 Aaron Heilman 5.00 12.00
US295 Andrew Cashner 5.00 12.00
US296 Lance Zawadzki 5.00 12.00
US297 Don Kelly 5.00 12.00
US298 David Freese 8.00 20.00
US299 Xavier Nady 5.00 12.00
US300 Cliff Lee 8.00 20.00
US301 Jeff Clement 5.00 12.00
US302 Pedro Feliz 5.00 12.00
US303 Brandon Phillips 5.00 12.00
US304 Kris Medlen 8.00 20.00
US305 Cliff Lee 8.00 20.00
US306 Dan Haren 5.00 12.00
US307 Carlos Santana 12.00 30.00
US308 Matt Thornton 5.00 12.00
US309 Andruw Jones 5.00 12.00
US310 Derek Jeter 25.00 60.00
US311 Felix Doubront 5.00 12.00
US312 Coco Crisp 5.00 12.00
US313 Mitch Maier 5.00 12.00
US314 Cole Gillespie 5.00 12.00
US315 Edwin Jackson 5.00 12.00
US316 Rod Barajas 5.00 12.00
US317 Mike Leake 12.00 30.00
US318 Domonic Brown 15.00 40.00
US319 Josh Tomlin 12.00 30.00
US320 Joe Mauer 8.00 20.00
US321 Jason Donald 5.00 12.00
US322 John Ely 5.00 12.00
US323 Ryan Kalish 6.00 15.00
US324 George Kottaras 5.00 12.00
US325 Ian Kinsler 8.00 20.00
US326 Miguel Cabrera 12.00 30.00
US327 Mike Stanton 30.00 80.00
US328 Adrian Beltre 12.00 30.00
US329 Jose Reyes/Hanley Ramirez 6.00 15.00
US330 Carlos Santana 12.00 30.00

2010 Topps Update Gold

*GOLD VET: 2X TO 5X BASIC
*GOLD RC: .6X TO 1.5X BASIC RC
STATED ODDS 1:6 HOBBY
STATED PRINT RUN 2010 SER.#'d SETS
US55 Stephen Strasburg 4.00 10.00
US274 S.Strasburg/I.Rodriguez 4.00 10.00

2010 Topps Update Target

*VETS: .5X TO 1.2X BASIC TOPPS UPD CARDS
*RC: .5X TO 1.2X BASIC TOPPS UPD RC CARDS

2010 Topps Update Wal-Mart Black Border

*VETS: .5X TO 1.2X BASIC TOPPS UPD CARDS
*RC: .5X TO 1.2X BASIC TOPPS UPD RC CARDS

2010 Topps Update All-Star Stitches

STATED ODDS 1:53 HOBBY
AB Andrew Bailey 3.00 8.00
AE Andre Ethier 3.00 8.00
AG Adrian Gonzalez 3.00 8.00
AP Andy Pettitte 5.00 12.00
AR Alex Rodriguez 5.00 12.00
AW Adam Wainwright 4.00 10.00
BM Brian McCann 4.00 10.00
BP Brandon Phillips 3.00 8.00
BW Brian Wilson 5.00 12.00
CB Clay Buchholz 3.00 8.00
CC Carl Crawford 3.00 8.00
CH Corey Hart 3.00 8.00
CL Cliff Lee 4.00 10.00
CY Chris Young 3.00 8.00
DJ Derek Jeter 10.00 25.00
DO David Ortiz 3.00 8.00
DP David Price 4.00 10.00
DW David Wright 3.00 8.00
EA Elvis Andrus 4.00 10.00
EL Evan Longoria 5.00 12.00
EM Evan Meek 3.00 8.00
FC Fausto Carmona 3.00 8.00
HB Heath Bell 4.00 10.00
HR Hanley Ramirez 3.00 8.00
IK Ian Kinsler 3.00 8.00
IS Ichiro Suzuki 10.00 25.00
JB Jose Bautista 4.00 10.00
JH Josh Hamilton 4.00 10.00
JJ Josh Johnson 3.00 8.00
JL Jon Lester 3.00 8.00
JM Joe Mauer 5.00 12.00
JR Jose Reyes 4.00 10.00
JS Joakim Soria 3.00 8.00
JV Justin Verlander 3.00 8.00
JW Jered Weaver 3.00 8.00
MB Marlon Byrd 4.00 10.00
MC Miguel Cabrera 4.00 10.00
MH Matt Holliday 4.00 10.00
MP Martin Prado 3.00 8.00
MT Matt Thornton 3.00 8.00
NF Neftali Feliz 4.00 10.00
OI Omar Infante 3.00 8.00
PH Phil Hughes 4.00 10.00
PK Paul Konerko 3.00 8.00
RB Ryan Braun 3.00 8.00
RC Robinson Cano 5.00 12.00
RF Rafael Furcal 3.00 8.00
RH Roy Halladay 5.00 12.00
RS Rafael Soriano 3.00 8.00
SR Scott Rolen 4.00 10.00
TC Trevor Cahill 3.00 8.00
TH Torii Hunter 3.00 8.00
TL Tim Lincecum 8.00 20.00
TT Troy Tulowitzki 4.00 10.00
TW Ty Wigginton 4.00 10.00
UJ Ubaldo Jimenez 3.00 8.00
VG Vladimir Guerrero 3.00 8.00
VM Victor Martinez 3.00 8.00
VW Vernon Wells 3.00 8.00
YG Yovani Gallardo 3.00 8.00
YM Yadier Molina 4.00 10.00
ABE Adrian Beltre 4.00 10.00
APU Albert Pujols 8.00 20.00
ARH Arthur Rhodes 3.00 8.00
CCA Chris Carpenter 4.00 10.00
CCS CC Sabathia 3.00 8.00
DPE Dustin Pedroia 4.00 10.00
HCK Hong-Chih Kuo 4.00 10.00
JBR Jonathan Broxton 3.00 8.00
JBU John Buck 3.00 8.00
JHE Jason Heyward 6.00 15.00
JVO Joey Votto 5.00 12.00
MBO Michael Bourn 3.00 8.00
MCA Matt Capps 3.00 8.00
RHO Ryan Howard 4.00 10.00
THU Tim Hudson 3.00 8.00

2010 Topps Update All-Star Stitches Gold

*GOLD: .6X TO 1.5X BASIC
STATED ODDS 1:1047 HOBBY
STATED PRINT RUN 50 SER.#'d SETS

2010 Topps Update Attax Code Cards

28 Jered Weaver .50 1.25
29 Hideki Matsui .75 2.00
30 Mark Reynolds .30 .75
31 Justin Upton .50 1.25
32 Jason Heyward 1.25 3.00
33 Brian McCann .50 1.25
34 Adam Jones .50 1.25
35 Nick Markakis .60 1.50
36 Kevin Youkilis .30 .75
37 Victor Martinez .50 1.25
38 John Lackey .50 1.25
39 Starlin Castro .75 2.00
40 Alfonso Soriano .50 1.25
41 Jake Peavy .30 .75
42 Paul Konerko .50 1.25
43 Carlos Santana 1.00 2.50
44 Shin-Soo Choo .50 1.25
45 Mike Leake 1.00 2.50
46 Ubaldo Jimenez .30 .75
47 Miguel Cabrera .75 2.00
48 Austin Jackson .50 1.25
49 Hanley Ramirez .50 1.25
50 Mike Stanton 2.50 6.00
51 Hunter Pence .50 1.25
52 Joakim Soria .30 .75
53 Andre Ethier .50 1.25
54 Clayton Kershaw 1.50 4.00
55 Ryan Braun .50 1.25
56 Joe Mauer .60 1.50
57 Francisco Liriano .30 .75
58 Ike Davis .60 1.50
59 David Wright .60 1.50
60 Robinson Cano .50 1.25
61 Derek Jeter 2.00 5.00
62 Kurt Suzuki .30 .75
63 Roy Halladay .50 1.25
64 Ryan Howard .60 1.50
65 Andrew McCutchen .75 2.00
66 Albert Pujols 1.00 2.50
67 Adam Wainwright .50 1.25
68 Adrian Gonzalez .60 1.50
69 Buster Posey 2.50 6.00
70 Matt Cain .50 1.25
71 Ichiro Suzuki 1.00 2.50
72 Evan Longoria .50 1.25
73 David Price .60 1.50
74 Josh Hamilton .50 1.25
75 Vernon Wells .30 .75
76 Stephen Strasburg 2.50 6.00
77 Adam Dunn .50 1.25

2010 Topps Update Chrome Rookie Refractors

CHR01 Stephen Strasburg 8.00 20.00
CHR02 Wilson Ramos 2.50 6.00
CHR03 Lance Zawadzki 1.00 2.50
CHR04 Jesus Feliciano 1.00 2.50
CHR05 Logan Morrison 1.50 4.00
CHR06 Josh Donaldson 5.00 12.00
CHR07 Travis Wood 1.50 4.00
CHR08 Cole Gillespie 1.00 2.50
CHR09 Ryan Kalish 1.50 4.00
CHR10 Domonic Brown 4.00 10.00
CHR11 Jason Donald 1.00 2.50
CHR12 Jeffrey Marquez 1.50 4.00
CHR13 Adam Ottavino 1.00 2.50
CHR14 Luke Hughes 1.00 2.50
CHR15 Jose Tabata 1.50 4.00
CHR16 Josh Bell 1.00 2.50
CHR17 Jon Link 1.00 2.50
CHR18 John Ely 1.00 2.50
CHR19 Jeanmar Gomez 1.50 4.00
CHR20 Mike Stanton 8.00 20.00
CHR21 Luis Atilano 1.00 2.50
CHR22 Chris Heisey 1.50 4.00
CHR23 Jake Arrieta 2.50 6.00
CHR24 Jonathan Lucroy 2.50 6.00
CHR25 Andrew Cashner 1.00 2.50
CHR26 Sam LeCure 1.00 2.50
CHR27 Danny Valencia 6.00 15.00
CHR28 Rhyne Hughes 1.00 2.50
CHR29 Kenley Jansen 3.00 8.00
CHR30 Ike Davis 2.00 5.00
CHR31 Lorenzo Cain 2.50 6.00
CHR32 Jonny Venters 1.00 2.50
CHR33 Andy Oliver 1.00 2.50
CHR34 Jon Jay 1.50 4.00
CHR35 Drew Storen 1.50 4.00
CHR36 Omar Beltre 1.00 2.50
CHR37 Alex Sanabia 1.00 2.50
CHR38 Jordan Smith 1.00 2.50
CHR39 Trevor Plouffe 2.50 6.00
CHR40 Starlin Castro 2.50 6.00
CHR41 Jhan Marinez 1.00 2.50
CHR42 Brad Lincoln 1.50 4.00
CHR43 Kevin Russo 1.00 2.50
CHR44 Frank Herrmann 1.00 2.50
CHR45 Brennan Boesch 2.50 6.00
CHR46 Daniel Nava 1.00 2.50
CHR47 Sam Demel 1.00 2.50
CHR48 Dayan Viciedo 1.50 4.00
CHR49 Felix Doubront 1.00 2.50
CHR50 Carlos Santana 3.00 8.00
CHR51 Josh Tomlin 2.50 6.00
CHR52 Anthony Slama 1.00 2.50
CHR53 Chris Carter 1.50 4.00
CHR54 J.P. Arencibia 2.00 5.00
CHR55 Mitch Moreland 1.50 4.00
CHR56 Peter Bourjos 1.50 4.00
CHR57 Argenis Diaz 1.50 4.00
CHR58 Mike Minor 1.50 4.00
CHR59 Brian Matusz 2.50 6.00
CHR60 Jason Heyward 4.00 10.00
CHR61 Mike Stanton 8.00 20.00
CHR62 Ike Davis 2.00 5.00
CHR63 Carlos Santana 3.00 8.00
CHR64 Austin Jackson 1.50 4.00
CHR65 Mike Leake 3.00 8.00
CHR66 Brennan Boesch 2.50 6.00
CHR67 Stephen Strasburg 8.00 20.00
CHR68 Jose Tabata 1.50 4.00
CHR69 Starlin Castro 2.50 6.00
CHR70 Danny Worth 1.00 2.50

2010 Topps Update Manufactured Bat Barrel

STATED ODDS 1:380 HOBBY
STATED PRINT RUN 99 SER.#'d SETS
BLACK ODDS 1:1960 HOBBY
BLACK PRINT RUN 25 SER.#'d SETS
PINK ODDS 1:44,000 HOBBY
PINK PRINT RUN 1 SER.#'d SET
MB1 Ryan Braun 5.00 12.00
MB2 Derek Jeter 20.00 50.00

MB3 Torii Hunter 3.00 8.00
MB4 Chase Utley 5.00 12.00
MB5 Justin Upton 5.00 12.00
MB6 David Wright 6.00 15.00
MB7 Troy Tulowitzki 8.00 20.00
MB8 Kevin Youkilis 3.00 8.00
MB9 Jose Reyes 5.00 12.00
MB10 Albert Pujols 10.00 25.00
MB11 Jimmy Rollins 5.00 12.00
MB12 Victor Martinez 5.00 12.00
MB13 Shane Victorino 5.00 12.00
MB14 Matt Holliday 8.00 20.00
MB15 Prince Fielder 5.00 12.00
MB16 Hideki Matsui 8.00 20.00
MB17 Nick Markakis 6.00 15.00
MB18 Alfonso Soriano 5.00 12.00
MB19 Shin-Soo Choo 5.00 12.00
MB20 Evan Longoria 5.00 12.00
MB21 Joey Votto 8.00 20.00
MB22 Andrew McCutchen 8.00 20.00
MB23 Mark Reynolds 3.00 8.00
MB24 Andre Ethier 5.00 12.00
MB25 Robinson Cano 5.00 12.00
MB26 Casey McGehee 3.00 8.00
MB27 Paul Konerko 5.00 12.00
MB28 Adam Lind 5.00 12.00
MB29 Dustin Pedroia 6.00 15.00
MB30 Jason Heyward 12.00 30.00
MB31 Billy Butler 3.00 8.00
MB32 Justin Morneau 5.00 12.00
MB33 Aaron Hill 3.00 8.00
MB34 Pablo Sandoval 5.00 12.00
MB35 Miguel Cabrera 8.00 20.00
MB36 Ryan Zimmerman 5.00 12.00
MB37 Hunter Pence 5.00 12.00
MB38 Adrian Gonzalez 6.00 15.00
MB39 Adam Dunn 5.00 12.00
MB40 Vladimir Guerrero 5.00 12.00
MB41 Jason Bay 5.00 12.00
MB42 Matt Kemp 6.00 15.00
MB43 Dan Uggla 3.00 8.00
MB44 Brandon Phillips 3.00 8.00
MB45 Alex Rodriguez 10.00 25.00
MB46 Manny Ramirez 8.00 20.00
MB47 Nick Swisher 5.00 12.00
MB48 Vernon Wells 3.00 8.00
MB49 Corey Hart 3.00 8.00
MB50 Joe Mauer 6.00 15.00
MB51 David Ortiz 8.00 20.00
MB52 Josh Hamilton 5.00 12.00
MB53 Kendry Morales 3.00 8.00
MB54 Colby Rasmus 5.00 12.00
MB55 Chipper Jones 8.00 20.00
MB56 Lance Berkman 5.00 12.00
MB57 James Loney 3.00 8.00
MB58 Ian Kinsler 5.00 12.00
MB59 Carl Crawford 5.00 12.00
MB60 Hanley Ramirez 5.00 12.00
MB61 Buster Posey 25.00 60.00
MB62 Ike Davis 6.00 15.00
MB63 Adam Jones 5.00 12.00
MB64 Brian McCann 5.00 12.00
MB65 Mark Teixeira 5.00 12.00
MB66 Kurt Suzuki 3.00 8.00
MB67 Mike Stanton 20.00 50.00
MB68 Jayson Werth 5.00 12.00
MB69 Nelson Cruz 8.00 20.00
MB70 Ryan Howard 6.00 15.00
MB71 Martin Prado 3.00 8.00
MB72 Michael Young 3.00 8.00
MB73 Ben Zobrist 5.00 12.00
MB74 Carlos Lee 3.00 8.00
MB75 Ichiro Suzuki 10.00 25.00
MB76 Carlos Quentin 3.00 8.00
MB77 B.J. Upton 5.00 12.00
MB78 Alex Rios 3.00 8.00
MB79 Magglio Ordonez 5.00 12.00
MB80 Jose Bautista 5.00 12.00
MB81 Garrett Jones 3.00 8.00
MB82 Carlos Pena 5.00 12.00
MB83 Jay Bruce 5.00 12.00
MB84 Austin Jackson 5.00 12.00
MB85 Chris Young 3.00 8.00
MB86 Alexei Ramirez 5.00 12.00
MB87 Carlos Gonzalez 5.00 12.00
MB88 Howie Kendrick 3.00 8.00
MB89 Ryan Ludwick 3.00 8.00
MB90 Miguel Tejada 5.00 12.00
MB91 Derrek Lee 3.00 8.00
MB92 Adrian Beltre 8.00 20.00
MB93 Gordon Beckham 3.00 8.00
MB94 Yadier Molina 8.00 20.00
MB95 Starlin Castro 8.00 20.00
MB96 Stephen Drew 3.00 8.00
MB97 Carlos Santana 10.00 25.00
MB98 Bobby Abreu 3.00 8.00
MB99 Ty Wigginton 3.00 8.00
MB100 Scott Rolen 5.00 12.00
MB101 Grady Sizemore 5.00 12.00
MB102 Miguel Montero 3.00 8.00
MB103 Todd Helton 5.00 12.00
MB104 Chris Coghlan 3.00 8.00
MB105 Curtis Granderson 6.00 15.00
MB106 Troy Glaus 3.00 8.00
MB107 Placido Polanco 3.00 8.00
MB108 Elvis Andrus 5.00 12.00
MB109 Aramis Ramirez 3.00 8.00
MB110 Jose Tabata 5.00 12.00
MB111 Ian Desmond 5.00 12.00
MB112 Craig Biggio 5.00 12.00
MB113 Bernie Williams 5.00 12.00
MB114 Frank Robinson 5.00 12.00
MB115 Babe Ruth 20.00 50.00
MB116 Jimmie Foxx 8.00 20.00
MB117 Yogi Berra 8.00 20.00
MB118 Lou Gehrig 15.00 40.00
MB119 Tris Speaker 5.00 12.00
MB120 Roy Campanella 8.00 20.00
MB121 Bobby Murcer 3.00 8.00
MB122 Jimmy Piersall 3.00 8.00
MB123 Bo Jackson 8.00 20.00
MB124 Frank Thomas 8.00 20.00
MB125 Rogers Hornsby 5.00 12.00
MB126 Lou Brock 5.00 12.00
MB127 Richie Ashburn 5.00 12.00
MB128 Steve Garvey 3.00 8.00
MB129 Larry Doby 5.00 12.00
MB130 Jackie Robinson 8.00 20.00
MB131 Andre Dawson 5.00 12.00
MB132 Tony Gwynn 8.00 20.00
MB133 Don Mattingly 15.00 40.00
MB134 Carl Yastrzemski 12.00 30.00
MB135 Hank Greenberg 8.00 20.00
MB136 Dale Murphy 8.00 20.00
MB137 Paul Molitor 8.00 20.00
MB138 Eddie Murray 5.00 12.00
MB139 Mike Piazza 8.00 20.00
MB140 Ty Cobb 12.00 30.00
MB141 Al Kaline 8.00 20.00
MB142 Joe Morgan 5.00 12.00
MB143 Willie McCovey 5.00 12.00
MB144 Bill Mazeroski 5.00 12.00
MB145 George Sisler 5.00 12.00
MB146 Carlton Fisk 5.00 12.00
MB147 Sal Bando 3.00 8.00
MB148 Rod Carew 5.00 12.00
MB149 Orlando Cepeda 5.00 12.00
MB150 Mickey Mantle 25.00 60.00
MB151 Mike Schmidt 12.00 30.00
MB152 Rickey Henderson 8.00 20.00
MB153 Monte Irvin 5.00 12.00
MB154 George Kell 5.00 12.00
MB155 Pee Wee Reese 5.00 12.00
MB156 Robin Yount 8.00 20.00
MB157 Tony Perez 5.00 12.00
MB158 Ryne Sandberg 15.00 40.00
MB159 Luis Aparicio 5.00 12.00
MB160 Honus Wagner 8.00 20.00
MB161 Roger Maris 8.00 20.00
MB162 Duke Snider 5.00 12.00
MB163 Willie Stargell 5.00 12.00
MB164 Dave Winfield 5.00 12.00
MB165 Johnny Mize 5.00 12.00
MB166 Phil Rizzuto 5.00 12.00
MB167 Johnny Bench 8.00 20.00
MB168 Ozzie Smith 10.00 25.00
MB169 Reggie Jackson 5.00 12.00
MB170 Thurman Munson 8.00 20.00
MB171 Harmon Killebrew 8.00 20.00
MB172 Eddie Mathews 8.00 20.00
MB173 Ralph Kiner 5.00 12.00
MB174 Brooks Robinson 5.00 12.00
MB175 Mel Ott 8.00 20.00

2010 Topps Update Manufactured Rookie Logo Patch

STATED ODDS 1:1125 HOBBY
STATED PRINT RUN 500 SER.#'d SETS
AJ Austin Jackson 5.00 12.00
JH Jason Heyward 8.00 20.00
SS Stephen Strasburg 12.00 30.00

2010 Topps Update More Tales of the Game

STATED ODDS 1:6 HOBBY
1 Joel Youngblood .40 1.00
2 Triple Billing .40 1.00
3 Seven Touchdowns .40 1.00
4 Eddie Mathews .75 2.00
5 Babe Ruth 1.25 3.00
6 Intracity Sweep .40 1.00
7 Mike Schmidt .75 2.00
8 Mile-High Humidor .40 1.00
9 Andre Dawson/Alex Rodriguez .60 1.50
10 Walter Johnson .75 2.00
11 Warren Spahn .60 1.50
12 There's No Tying in Baseball .40 1.00
13 Harry Truman .40 1.00
14 Stephen Strasburg 1.50 4.00
15 Roy Halladay .50 1.25

2010 Topps Update Peek Performance Autographs

GROUP A ODDS 1:2450 HOBBY
GROUP B ODDS 1:834 HOBBY
TCO Tyler Colvin A 5.00 12.00
AC Andrew Cashner B 3.00 8.00
AJ Austin Jackson A 8.00 20.00
AO Adam Ottavino B 4.00 10.00
AOL Andy Oliver B 5.00 12.00
BB Brennan Boesch B 4.00 10.00
BL Brad Lincoln A 4.00 10.00
BP Buster Posey A 50.00 100.00
CS Carlos Santana A 8.00 20.00
DST Drew Storen A 4.00 10.00
ID Ike Davis A 6.00 15.00
JCA Jason Castro B 4.00 10.00
JD Jason Donald B 3.00 8.00
JE John Ely B 3.00 8.00
JH Jason Heyward A 12.00 30.00
JT Jose Tabata A 8.00 20.00
JV Jonny Venters B 8.00 20.00
LA Luis Atilano B 3.00 8.00
ML Mike Leake A 8.00 20.00
MST Mike Stanton A 30.00 60.00
SC Starlin Castro A 10.00 25.00
SS Stephen Strasburg A 40.00 80.00

2011 Topps

COMP.FACT.HOBBY SET (660) 30.00 60.00
COMP.ALLSTAR SET (660) 30.00 60.00
COMP.FACT.BLUE SET (660) 30.00 60.00
COMP.FACT.HOLIDAY SET (660) 30.00 60.00
COMP.FACT.ORANGE SET (660) 30.00 60.00
COMP.FACT.RED SET (660) 30.00 60.00
COMP.SET w/o SP's (660) 30.00 60.00
COMP.SER.1 w/o SP's (330) 12.50 30.00
COMP.SER.2 w/o SP's (330) 12.50 30.00
COMMON CARD (1-660) .15 .40
COMMON RC (1-660) .25 .60
COMMON SP VAR (1-660) 6.00 15.00
SER.1 PLATE ODDS 1:1500 HOBBY
PLATE PRINT RUN 1 SET PER COLOR
BLACK-CYAN-MAGENTA-YELLOW ISSUED
NO PLATE PRICING DUE TO SCARCITY
1 Ryan Braun .25 .60
2 Jake Westbrook .15 .40
3 Jon Lester .25 .60
4 Jason Kubel .15 .40
5A Joey Votto .40 1.00
5B Lou Gehrig SP 10.00 25.00
6 Neftali Feliz .15 .40
7 Mickey Mantle 1.25 3.00
8 Julio Borbon .15 .40
9 Gil Meche .15 .40
10 Stephen Strasburg .40 1.00
11 Roy Halladay/Adam Wainwright
Ubaldo Jimenez LL .25 .60
12 Carlos Marmol .25 .60
13 Billy Wagner .15 .40
14 Randy Wolf .15 .40
15 David Wright .30 .75
16 Aramis Ramirez .15 .40
17 Mark Ellis .15 .40
18 Kevin Millwood .15 .40
19 Derek Lowe .15 .40
20 Hanley Ramirez .25 .60
21 Michael Cuddyer .15 .40
22 Barry Zito .25 .60
23 Jaime Garcia .25 .60
24 Neil Walker .25 .60
25A Carl Crawford .25 .60
25B Crawford Red Sox SP 10.00 25.00
25C Carl Yastrzemski SP 6.00 15.00
26 Neftali Feliz .15 .40
27 Ben Zobrist .25 .60
28 Carlos Carrasco .25 .60
29 Josh Hamilton .25 .60
30 Gio Gonzalez .25 .60
31 Erick Aybar .15 .40
32 Chris Johnson .15 .40
33 Max Scherzer .40 1.00
34 Rick Ankiel .15 .40
35 Shin-Soo Choo .25 .60
36 Ted Lilly .15 .40
37 Vicente Padilla .15 .40
38 Ryan Dempster .15 .40
39 Ian Kennedy .15 .40
40 Justin Upton .25 .60
41 Freddy Garcia .15 .40
42 Mariano Rivera .50 1.25
43 Brendan Ryan .15 .40
44A Martin Prado .15 .40
44B Rogers Hornsby SP 6.00 15.00
45 Hunter Pence .25 .60
46 Hong-Chih Kuo .15 .40
47 Kevin Correia .15 .40
48 Andrew Cashner .15 .40
49 Los Angeles Angels TC .15 .40
50A Alex Rodriguez .50 1.25
50B Mike Schmidt SP 8.00 20.00
51 David Eckstein .15 .40
52 Tampa Bay Rays TC .15 .40
53 Arizona Diamondbacks TC .15 .40
54 Brian Fuentes .15 .40
55 Matt Joyce .15 .40
56 Johan Santana .25 .60
57 Mark Trumbo (RC) .60 1.50
58 Edgar Renteria .15 .40
59 Gaby Sanchez .15 .40
60 Andrew McCutchen .40 1.00
61 David Price .30 .75
62 Jonathan Papelbon .25 .60
63 Edinson Volquez .15 .40
64 Yorvit Torrealba .15 .40
65 Chris Sale RC 1.50 4.00
66 R.A. Dickey .25 .60
67 Vladimir Guerrero .25 .60
68 Cleveland Indians TC .15 .40
69 Brett Gardner .25 .60
70 Kyle Drabek RC .40 1.00
71 Trevor Hoffman .25 .60
72 Jair Jurrjens .15 .40
73 James McDonald .15 .40
74 Tyler Clippard .15 .40
75 Jered Weaver .25 .60
76 Tom Gorzelanny .15 .40
77 Tim Hudson .25 .60
78 Mike Stanton .40 1.00
79 Kurt Suzuki .15 .40
80A Desmond Jennings RC .40 1.00
80B Jackie Robinson SP 8.00 20.00
81 Omar Infante .15 .40
82 Josh Johnson/Adam Wainwright
Roy Halladay LL .25 .60
83 Greg Halman RC .40 1.00
84 Roger Bernadina .15 .40
85 Jack Wilson .15 .40
86 Carlos Silva .15 .40
87 Daniel Descalso RC .25 .60
88 Brian Bogusevic (RC) .25 .60
89 Placido Polanco .15 .40
90A Yadier Molina .40 1.00
90B Yogi Berra SP 8.00 20.00
91 Lucas May RC .25 .60
92 Chris Narveson .15 .40
93A Paul Konerko .25 .60
93B Frank Thomas SP 6.00 15.00
94 Ryan Raburn .15 .40
95 Pedro Alvarez RC .50 1.25
96 Zach Duke .15 .40
97 Carlos Gomez .15 .40
98 Bronson Arroyo .15 .40
99 Ben Revere RC .40 1.00
100A Albert Pujols .50 1.25
100B Stan Musial SP 10.00 25.00
101 Gregor Blanco .15 .40
102A CC Sabathia .25 .60
102B Christy Mathewson SP 6.00 15.00
103 Cliff Lee .25 .60
104 Ian Stewart .15 .40
105 Jonathan Lucroy .25 .60
106 Felix Pie .15 .40
107 Aubrey Huff .15 .40
108 Zack Greinke .25 .60
109 Hamilton/Cabrera/Mauer LL .40 1.00
110 Aroldis Chapman RC .75 2.00
111 Kevin Gregg .15 .40
112 Jorge Cantu .15 .40
113 Arthur Rhodes .15 .40
114 Russell Martin .15 .40
115 Jason Varitek .40 1.00
116 Russell Branyan .15 .40
117 Brett Sinkbeil RC .25 .60
118 Howie Kendrick .15 .40
119 Jason Bay .25 .60
120 Mat Latos .25 .60
121 Brandon Inge .15 .40
122 Bobby Jenks .15 .40
123 Mike Lowell .15 .40
124 CC Sabathia/Jon Lester
David Price LL .30 .75
125 Evan Meek .15 .40
126 San Diego Padres TC .15 .40
127 Chris Volstad .15 .40
128 Manny Ramirez .40 1.00
129 Lucas Duda RC .60 1.50
130 Robinson Cano .25 .60
131 Kevin Kouzmanoff .15 .40
132 Brian Duensing .15 .40
133 Miguel Tejada .25 .60
134 Carlos Gonzalez/Joey Votto
Omar Infante LL .40 1.00
135A Mike Stanton .40 1.00
135B Dale Murphy SP 6.00 15.00
136 Jason Marquis .15 .40
137 Xavier Nady .15 .40
138 Pujols/Gonzalez/Votto LL .50 1.25
139 Eric Young Jr. .15 .40
140 Brett Anderson .15 .40
141 Ubaldo Jimenez .15 .40
142 Johnny Cueto .25 .60
143 Jeremy Jeffress RC .25 .60
144 Lance Berkman .25 .60
145 Freddie Freeman RC 4.00 10.00
146 Roy Halladay .25 .60
147 Jon Niese .15 .40
148 Ricky Romero .15 .40
149 David Aardsma .15 .40
150A Miguel Cabrera .40 1.00
150B Hank Greenberg SP 6.00 15.00
151 Fausto Carmona .15 .40
152 Baltimore Orioles TC .15 .40
153 A.J. Pierzynski .15 .40
154 Marlon Byrd .15 .40
155 Alex Rodriguez .50 1.25
156 Josh Thole .15 .40
157 New York Mets TC .25 .60
158 Casey Blake .15 .40
159 Chris Perez .15 .40
160 Josh Willingham .15 .40
161 Chicago White Sox TC .15 .40
162 Ronny Cedeno .15 .40
163 Carlos Pena .25 .60
164 Koji Uehara .15 .40
165 Jeremy Hellickson RC .60 1.50
166 Josh Johnson .25 .60
167 Clay Hensley .15 .40
168 Felix Hernandez .25 .60
169 Chipper Jones .40 1.00
170 David DeJesus .15 .40
171 Garrett Jones .15 .40
172 Lyle Overbay .15 .40
173 Jose Lopez .15 .40
174 Roy Oswalt .25 .60
175 Brennan Boesch .25 .60
176 Daniel Hudson .15 .40
177 Brian Matusz .15 .40
178 Heath Bell .15 .40
179 Armando Galarraga .15 .40
180 Paul Maholm .15 .40
181 Magglio Ordonez .25 .60
182 Jeremy Bonderman .15 .40
183 Stephen Strasburg .40 1.00
184 Brandon Morrow .15 .40
185 Peter Bourjos .25 .60
186 Carl Pavano .15 .40
187 Milwaukee Brewers TC .15 .40
188 Pablo Sandoval .25 .60
189 Kerry Wood .15 .40
190 Coco Crisp .15 .40
191 Jay Bruce .25 .60
192 Cincinnati Reds TC .15 .40
193 Cory Luebke RC .25 .60
194 Andres Torres .15 .40
195 Nick Markakis .30 .75
196 Jose Ceda RC .25 .60
197 Aaron Hill .15 .40
198A Buster Posey .50 1.25
198B Johnny Bench SP 8.00 20.00
199A Jimmy Rollins .25 .60
199B Ozzie Smith SP 6.00 15.00
200A Ichiro Suzuki .50 1.25
200B Ty Cobb SP 8.00 20.00
201 Mike Napoli .15 .40
202 Bautista/Konerko/Cabrera LL .40 1.00
203 Dillon Gee RC .40 1.00
204 Oakland Athletics TC .15 .40
205 Ty Wigginton .15 .40
206 Chase Headley .15 .40
207 Angel Pagan .15 .40
208 Clay Buchholz .15 .40
209A Carlos Santana .40 1.00
209B Roy Campanella SP 6.00 15.00
20B Honus Wagner SP 6.00 15.00
210 Brian Wilson .40 1.00
211 Joey Votto .40 1.00
212 Pedro Feliz .15 .40
213 Brandon Snyder (RC) .25 .60
214 Chase Utley .25 .60
215 Edwin Encarnacion .40 1.00
216 Jose Bautista .25 .60
217 Yunel Escobar .15 .40
218 Victor Martinez .25 .60
219A Carlos Ruiz .15 .40
219B Thurman Munson SP 6.00 15.00
220 Todd Helton .25 .60
221 Scott Hairston .15 .40
222 Matt Lindstrom .25 .60
223 Gregory Infante RC .25 .60
224 Milton Bradley .15 .40
225 Josh Willingham .25 .60
226 Jose Guillen .15 .40
227 Nate McLouth .15 .40
228 Scott Rolen .25 .60
229 Jonathan Sanchez .15 .40
230 Aaron Cook .15 .40
231 Mark Buehrle .25 .60
232 Jamie Moyer .15 .40
233 Ramon Hernandez .15 .40
234 Miguel Montero .15 .40
235 Felix Hernandez/Clay Buchholz
David Price LL .30 .75
236 Nelson Cruz .40 1.00
237 Jason Vargas .15 .40
238 Pedro Ciriaco RC .40 1.00
239 Jhoulys Chacin .15 .40
240 Andre Ethier .25 .60
241 Wandy Rodriguez .15 .40
242 Brad Lidge .15 .40
243 Omar Vizquel .25 .60
244 Mike Aviles .15 .40
245 Neil Walker .25 .60
246 John Lannan .15 .40
247A Starlin Castro .25 .60
247B Ernie Banks SP 6.00 15.00
248 Wade LeBlanc .15 .40
249 Aaron Harang .15 .40
250A Carlos Gonzalez .25 .60
250B Mel Ott SP 6.00 15.00
251 Alcides Escobar .25 .60
252 Michael Saunders .25 .60
253 Jim Thome .25 .60
254 Lars Anderson RC .40 1.00
255 Torii Hunter .15 .40
256 Tyler Colvin .15 .40
257 Travis Hafner .15 .40
258 Rafael Soriano .15 .40
259 Kyle Davies .15 .40
260 Freddy Sanchez .15 .40
261 Alexei Ramirez .25 .60
262 Alex Gordon .25 .60
263 Joel Pineiro .15 .40
264 Ryan Perry .15 .40
265 John Danks .15 .40
266 Rickie Weeks .15 .40
267 Jose Contreras .15 .40
268 Jake McGee (RC) .25 .60
269 Stephen Drew .15 .40
270 Ubaldo Jimenez .15 .40
271A Adam Dunn .25 .60
271B Babe Ruth SP 10.00 25.00
272 J.J. Hardy .15 .40
273 Derrek Lee .15 .40
274 Michael Brantley .15 .40
275 Clayton Kershaw .75 2.00
276 Miguel Olivo .15 .40
277 Trevor Hoffman .25 .60
278 Marco Scutaro .25 .60
279 Nick Swisher .25 .60
280 Andrew Bailey .15 .40
281 Kevin Slowey .15 .40
282 Buster Posey .50 1.25
283 Colorado Rockies TC .15 .40
284 Reid Brignac .15 .40
285 Hank Conger RC .40 1.00
286 Melvin Mora .15 .40
287 Scott Cousins RC .25 .60
288 Matt Capps .15 .40
289 Yuniesky Betancourt .15 .40
290 Ike Davis .15 .40
291 Juan Gutierrez .15 .40
292 Darren Ford RC .25 .60
293A Justin Morneau .25 .60
293B Harmon Killebrew SP 6.00 15.00
294 Luke Scott .15 .40
295 Jon Jay .15 .40
296 John Buck .15 .40
297 Jason Jaramillo .15 .40
298 Jeff Keppinger .15 .40
299 Chris Carpenter .25 .60
300A Roy Halladay .25 .60
300B Walter Johnson SP 6.00 15.00
301 Seth Smith .15 .40
302 Adrian Beltre .40 1.00
303 Emilio Bonifacio .15 .40
304 Jim Thome .25 .60
305 James Loney .15 .40
306 Cabrera/ARod/Bautista LL .50 1.25
307 Alex Rios .15 .40
308 Ian Desmond .15 .40
309 Chicago Cubs TC .25 .60
310 Alex Gonzalez .15 .40
311 James Shields .15 .40
312 Gaby Sanchez .15 .40
313 Chris Coghlan .15 .40
314 Ryan Kalish .25 .60
315A David Ortiz .40 1.00
315B Jimmie Foxx SP 6.00 15.00
316 Chris Young .15 .40
317 Yonder Alonso RC .40 1.00
318 Pujols/Dunn/Votto LL .50 1.25
319 Atlanta Braves TC .15 .40
320 Michael Young .15 .40
321 Jeremy Guthrie .15 .40
322 Brent Morel RC .25 .60
323 C.J. Wilson .15 .40
324 Boston Red Sox TC .25 .60
325 Jayson Werth .25 .60
326 Ozzie Martinez RC .25 .60
327 Christian Guzman .15 .40
328 David Price .30 .75
329 Brett Wallace .15 .40
330A Derek Jeter 1.00 2.50
330B Phil Rizzuto SP 6.00 15.00
331 Carlos Guillen .15 .40
332 Melky Cabrera .15 .40
333 Tom Wilhelmsen RC .25 .60
334 St. Louis Cardinals .25 .60
335 Buster Posey .50 1.25
336 Chris Heisey .15 .40
337 Jordan Walden .15 .40
338 Jason Hammel .25 .60
339 Alexi Casilla .15 .40
340 Evan Longoria .25 .60
341 Kyle Kendrick .15 .40
342 Jorge De La Rosa .15 .40
343 Mason Tobin RC .25 .60
344 Michael Kohn RC .25 .60
345 Austin Jackson .15 .40
346 Jose Bautista .25 .60
347 Darwin Barney RC .75 2.00
348 Landon Powell .15 .40
349 Drew Stubbs .15 .40
350A Francisco Liriano .15 .40
350B Gonzalez Red Sox SP 10.00 25.00
351 Jacoby Ellsbury .30 .75
352 Colby Lewis .15 .40
353 Cliff Pennington .15 .40
354 Scott Baker .15 .40
355A Justin Verlander .40 1.00
355B Bob Feller SP 6.00 15.00
356 Alfonso Soriano .25 .60
357 Mike Cameron .15 .40
358 Paul Janish .15 .40
359 Roy Halladay .25 .60
360 Ivan Rodriguez .25 .60
361 Florida Marlins .15 .40
362 Doug Fister .15 .40
363 Aaron Rowand .15 .40
364 Tim Wakefield .25 .60
365 Adam Lind .15 .40
366 Joe Nathan .15 .40
367 Hiroki Kuroda .15 .40
368 Brian Broderick RC .25 .60
369 Wilson Betemit .15 .40
370 Matt Garza .15 .40
371 Taylor Teagarden .15 .40
372 Jarrod Saltalamacchia .15 .40
373 Trever Miller .15 .40
374 Washington Nationals .15 .40
375A Matt Kemp .30 .75
375B Andre Dawson SP 6.00 15.00
376 Clayton Richard .15 .40
377 Esmil Rogers .15 .40
378 Mark Reynolds .15 .40
379 Ben Francisco .15 .40
380 Jose Reyes .25 .60
381 Michael Gonzalez .15 .40
382 Travis Snider .15 .40
383 Ryan Ludwick .15 .40
384 Nick Hundley .15 .40
385 Ichiro Suzuki .50 1.25
386 Barry Enright RC .15 .40
387 Danny Valencia .25 .60
388 Kenley Jansen .25 .60
389 Carlos Quentin .15 .40
390 Danny Valencia .25 .60
391 Phil Coke .15 .40
392 Kris Medlen .25 .60
393A Jake Arrieta .30 .75
393B Jim Palmer SP 6.00 15.00
394 Austin Jackson .15 .40
395 Tyler Flowers .15 .40
396 Adam Jones .25 .60
397 Sean Rodriguez .15 .40
398 Pittsburgh Pirates .15 .40
399 Adam Moore .15 .40
400 Troy Tulowitzki .40 1.00
401 Michael Crotta RC .25 .60
402 Jack Cust .15 .40
403 Felix Hernandez .25 .60
404 Chris Capuano .15 .40
405A Ian Kinsler .25 .60
405B Ryne Sandberg SP 6.00 15.00
406 John Lackey .25 .60
407 Jonathan Broxton .15 .40
408 Denard Span .15 .40
409 Vin Mazzaro .15 .40
410A Prince Fielder .25 .60
410B Reggie Jackson SP 6.00 15.00
411 Josh Bell .15 .40
412 Samuel Deduno RC .25 .60
413 Derek Holland .15 .40
414 Jose Molina .15 .40
415 Brian McCann .25 .60
416 Everth Cabrera .15 .40
417 Miguel Cairo .15 .40
418 Zach Britton RC .60 1.50
419 Kelly Johnson .15 .40
420 Ryan Howard .30 .75
421 Domonic Brown .30 .75
422 Juan Pierre .15 .40
423 Hideki Okajima .15 .40
424 New York Yankees .25 .60
425A Adrian Gonzalez .30 .75
425B Johnny Mize SP 6.00 15.00
426 Travis Buck .15 .40
427 Brad Emaus RC .25 .60
428 Brett Myers .15 .40
429 Skip Schumaker .15 .40
430 Trevor Crowe .15 .40
431 Marcos Mateo RC .40 1.00
432 Matt Harrison .15 .40
433 Curtis Granderson .30 .75
434 Mark DeRosa .15 .40
435A Elvis Andrus .25 .60
435B Pee Wee Reese SP 6.00 15.00
436 Trevor Cahill .15 .40
437 Jordan Schafer .15 .40
438 Ryan Theriot .15 .40
439 Ervin Santana .15 .40
440 Grady Sizemore .25 .60
441 Rafael Furcal .15 .40
442 Brad Bergesen .15 .40
443 Brian Roberts .15 .40
444 Brett Cecil .15 .40
445 Mitch Talbot .15 .40
446 Brandon Beachy RC .60 1.50
447 Toronto Blue Jays .15 .40
448 Colby Rasmus .25 .60
449 Austin Kearns .15 .40
450A Mark Teixeira .25 .60
450B Mickey Mantle SP 10.00 25.00
451 Livan Hernandez .15 .40
452 David Freese .15 .40
453 Joe Saunders .15 .40
454 Alberto Callaspo .15 .40
455 Logan Morrison .15 .40
456 Ryan Doumit .15 .40
457 Brandon Allen .15 .40
458 Javier Vazquez .15 .40
459 Frank Francisco .15 .40
460A Cole Hamels .30 .75
460B Robin Roberts SP 6.00 15.00
461 Eric Sogard RC .25 .60
462 Daric Barton .15 .40
463 Will Venable .15 .40
464 Daniel Bard .15 .40
465 Yovani Gallardo .15 .40
466 Johnny Damon .25 .60
467 Wade Davis .15 .40
468 Chone Figgins .15 .40
469 Joe Blanton .15 .40
470 Billy Butler .15 .40
471 Tim Collins RC .25 .60
472 Jason Kendall .15 .40
473 Chad Billingsley .25 .60
474 Jeff Mathis .15 .40
475 Phil Hughes .15 .40
476 Matt LaPorta .15 .40
477 Franklin Gutierrez .15 .40
478 Mike Minor .15 .40
479 Justin Duchscherer .15 .40
480A Dustin Pedroia .30 .75
480B Roberto Alomar SP 6.00 15.00
481 Randy Wells .15 .40
482 Eric Hinske .15 .40
483 Justin Smoak RC .25 .60
484 Gerardo Parra .15 .40
485 Delmon Young .25 .60
486 Francisco Rodriguez .25 .60
487 Chris Snyder .15 .40
488 Brayan Villarreal RC .25 .60
489 Marc Rzepczynski .15 .40
490A Matt Holliday .40 1.00
490B Duke Snider SP 6.00 15.00
491 Fernando Abad RC .25 .60
492 A.J. Burnett .15 .40
493 Ryan Sweeney .15 .40
494 Drew Storen .15 .40

495 Shane Victorino .25 .60
496 Gavin Floyd .15 .40
497 Alex Avila .25 .60
498 Scott Feldman .15 .40
499 J.A. Happ .25 .60
500 Kevin Youkilis .15 .40
501 Tsuyoshi Nishioka RC .75 2.00
502 Jeff Baker .15 .40
503 Nathan Adcock RC .25 .60
504 Jhonny Peralta .15 .40
505A Tommy Hanson .15 .40
505B Greg Maddux SP 6.00 15.00
506 Aneury Rodriguez RC .25 .60
507 Huston Street .15 .40
508 Homer Bailey .15 .40
509 Michael Bourn .15 .40
510A Jason Heyward .30 .75
510B Hank Aaron SP 8.00 20.00
511 Philadelphia Phillies .15 .40
512 Octavio Dotel .15 .40
513 Adam LaRoche .15 .40
514 Kelly Shoppach .15 .40
515 Carlos Beltran .25 .60
516A Mike Leake .25 .60
516B Tom Seaver SP 6.00 15.00
517 Fred Lewis .15 .40
518 Michael Morse .15 .40
519 Corey Hart .15 .40
520 Jorge Posada .25 .60
521 Joaquin Benoit .15 .40
522 Asdrubal Cabrera .25 .60
523 Mike Nickeas (RC) .25 .60
524 Michael Martinez RC .40 1.00
525 Vernon Wells .15 .40
526 Jason Donald .15 .40
527 Kila Ka'aihue .15 .40
528 Bobby Abreu .15 .40
529 Maicer Izturis .15 .40
530A Felix Hernandez .25 .60
530B Sandy Koufax SP 10.00 25.00
531 Juan Rivera .15 .40
532 Erik Bedard .15 .40
533 Lorenzo Cain .15 .40
534 Bud Norris .15 .40
535 Rich Harden .15 .40
536 Tony Sipp .15 .40
537 Jake Peavy .15 .40
538 Jason Motte .15 .40
539 Brandon Lyon .15 .40
540 Joakim Soria .15 .40
541 John Jaso .15 .40
542 Mike Pelfrey .15 .40
543 Texas Rangers .15 .40
544 Justin Masterson .15 .40
545 Jose Tabata .15 .40
546 Pat Burrell .15 .40
547 Albert Pujols .50 1.25
548 Ryan Franklin .15 .40
549 Jayson Nix .15 .40
550 Joe Mauer .30 .75
551 Marcus Thames .15 .40
552 San Francisco Giants .15 .40
553 Kyle Lohse .15 .40
554 Cedric Hunter RC .25 .60
555 Madison Bumgarner .30 .75
556 B.J. Upton .25 .60
557 Wes Helms .15 .40
558 Carlos Zambrano .25 .60
559 Reggie Willits .15 .40
560 Chris Iannetta .15 .40
561 Luke Gregerson .15 .40
562 Gordon Beckham .15 .40
563 Josh Rodriguez RC .25 .60
564 Jeff Samardzija .15 .40
565 Mark Teahen .15 .40
566 Jordan Zimmermann .25 .60
567 Dallas Braden .15 .40
568 Kansas City Royals .15 .40
569 Cameron Maybin .15 .40
570A Matt Cain .25 .60
570B Bert Blyleven SP 6.00 15.00
571 Jeremy Affeldt .15 .40
572 Brad Hawpe .15 .40
573 Nyjer Morgan .15 .40
574 Brandon Kintzler RC .25 .60
575 Rod Barajas .15 .40
576 Jed Lowrie .15 .40
577 Mike Fontenot .15 .40
578 Willy Aybar .15 .40
579 Jeff Niemann .15 .40
580 Chris Young .15 .40
581 Fernando Rodney .15 .40
582 Kosuke Fukudome .25 .60
583 Ryan Spilborghs .15 .40
584 Jason Bartlett .15 .40
585 Dan Johnson .15 .40
586 Carlos Lee .15 .40
587 J.P. Arencibia .15 .40
588 Rajai Davis .15 .40
589 Seattle Mariners .15 .40
590A Tim Lincecum .25 .60
590B Juan Marichal SP 6.00 15.00
591 John Axford .15 .40
592 Dayan Viciedo .15 .40
593 Francisco Cordero .15 .40
594 Jose Valverde .15 .40
595 Michael Pineda RC .60 1.50
596 Anibal Sanchez .15 .40
597 Rick Porcello .25 .60
598 Jonny Gomes .15 .40
599 Travis Ishikawa .15 .40
600A Neftali Feliz .15 .40
600B John Smoltz SP 6.00 15.00
601 J.J. Putz .15 .40
602 Ivan DeJesus RC .25 .60
603 David Murphy .15 .40
604 Joe Paterson RC .40 1.00
605 Brandon Belt RC .60 1.50
606 Juan Miranda .15 .40
607 Daniel Murphy .30 .75
608 Casey McGehee .15 .40
609 Juan Francisco .15 .40
610 Josh Beckett .15 .40
611 Geovany Soto .25 .60
612 Detroit Tigers .15 .40
613 Dexter Fowler .25 .60
614 Minnesota Twins .15 .40
615 Shaun Marcum .15 .40
616 Ross Ohlendorf .15 .40
617 Joel Zumaya .15 .40
618 Josh Lueke RC .25 .60
619 Jonny Venters .15 .40
620 Luke Hochevar .15 .40
621 Omar Beltre .15 .40
622 Matt Thornton .15 .40
623 Leo Nunez .15 .40
624 Luke French .15 .40
625 Ruben Tejada .15 .40
626A Dan Haren .15 .40
626B Nolan Ryan SP 10.00 25.00
627 Kyle Blanks .15 .40
628 Blake DeWitt .15 .40
629 Ivan Nova .25 .60
630A Brandon Phillips .15 .40
630B Joe Morgan SP 6.00 15.00
631 Houston Astros .15 .40
632 Scott Kazmir .15 .40
633 Aaron Crow RC .40 1.00
634 Mitch Moreland .15 .40
635 Jason Heyward .30 .75
636 Chris Tillman .15 .40
637 Ricky Nolasco .15 .40
638 Ryan Madson .15 .40
639 Pedro Beato RC .25 .60
640A Dan Uggla .15 .40
640B Eddie Mathews SP 6.00 15.00
641 Travis Wood .15 .40
642 Jason Hammel .25 .60
643 Jaime Garcia .25 .60
644 Joel Hanrahan .25 .60
645A Adam Wainwright .25 .60
645B Bob Gibson SP 6.00 15.00
646 Los Angeles Dodgers .25 .60
647 Jeanmar Gomez .15 .40
648 Cody Ross .15 .40
649 Joba Chamberlain .15 .40
650A Josh Hamilton .25 .60
650B Frank Robinson SP 6.00 15.00
651A Kendrys Morales .15 .40
651B Eddie Murray SP 6.00 15.00
652 Edwin Jackson .15 .40
653 J.D. Drew .15 .40
654 Chris Getz .15 .40
655 Starlin Castro .25 .60
656 Raul Ibanez .25 .60
657 Nick Blackburn .15 .40
658 Mitch Maier .15 .40
659 Clint Barmes .15 .40
660A Ryan Zimmerman .25 .60
660B Brooks Robinson SP 6.00 15.00

2011 Topps Black

SER.1 ODDS 1:100 HOBBY
STATED PRINT RUN 60 SER.#'d SETS

1 Ryan Braun 6.00 15.00
2 Jake Westbrook 6.00 15.00
3 Jon Lester 6.00 15.00
4 Jason Kubel 6.00 15.00
5 Joey Votto 10.00 25.00
6 Neftali Feliz 6.00 15.00
7 Mickey Mantle 50.00 120.00
8 Julio Borbon 6.00 15.00
9 Gil Meche 6.00 15.00
10 Stephen Strasburg 10.00 25.00
11 Roy Halladay/Adam Wainwright
Ubaldo Jimenez LL 6.00 15.00
12 Carlos Marmol 8.00 20.00
13 Billy Wagner 6.00 15.00
14 Randy Wolf 6.00 15.00
15 David Wright 8.00 20.00
16 Aramis Ramirez 6.00 15.00
17 Mark Ellis 6.00 15.00
18 Kevin Millwood 6.00 15.00
19 Derek Lowe 6.00 15.00
20 Hanley Ramirez 6.00 15.00
21 Michael Cuddyer 6.00 15.00
22 Barry Zito 10.00 25.00
23 Jaime Garcia 8.00 20.00
24 Neil Walker 10.00 25.00
25 Carl Crawford 8.00 20.00
26 Neftali Feliz 6.00 15.00
27 Ben Zobrist 10.00 25.00
28 Carlos Carrasco 10.00 25.00
29 Josh Hamilton 6.00 15.00
30 Gio Gonzalez 10.00 25.00
31 Erick Aybar 6.00 15.00
32 Chris Johnson 6.00 15.00
33 Max Scherzer 15.00 40.00
34 Rick Ankiel 6.00 15.00
35 Shin-Soo Choo 6.00 15.00
36 Ted Lilly 6.00 15.00
37 Vicente Padilla 6.00 15.00
38 Ryan Dempster 6.00 15.00
39 Ian Kennedy 6.00 15.00
40 Justin Upton 10.00 25.00
41 Freddy Garcia 6.00 15.00
42 Mariano Rivera 12.00 30.00
43 Brendan Ryan 6.00 15.00
44 Martin Prado 6.00 15.00
45 Hunter Pence 8.00 20.00
46 Hong-Chih Kuo 6.00 15.00
47 Kevin Correia 6.00 15.00
48 Andrew Cashner 6.00 15.00
49 Los Angeles Angels TC 6.00 15.00
50 Alex Rodriguez 12.00 30.00
51 David Eckstein 6.00 15.00
52 Tampa Bay Rays TC 6.00 15.00
53 Arizona Diamondbacks TC 6.00 15.00
54 Brian Fuentes 6.00 15.00
55 Matt Joyce 6.00 15.00
56 Johan Santana 6.00 15.00
57 Mark Trumbo 12.00 30.00
58 Edgar Renteria 6.00 15.00
59 Gaby Sanchez 6.00 15.00
60 Andrew McCutchen 12.00 30.00
61 David Price 8.00 20.00
62 Jonathan Papelbon 8.00 20.00
63 Edinson Volquez 6.00 15.00
64 Yorvit Torrealba 6.00 15.00
65 Chris Sale 25.00 60.00
66 R.A. Dickey 10.00 25.00
67 Vladimir Guerrero 6.00 15.00
68 Cleveland Indians TC 6.00 15.00
69 Brett Gardner 10.00 25.00
70 Kyle Drabek 6.00 15.00
71 Trevor Hoffman 8.00 20.00
72 Jair Jurrjens 6.00 15.00
73 James McDonald 6.00 15.00
74 Tyler Clippard 6.00 15.00
75 Jered Weaver 10.00 25.00
76 Tom Gorzelanny 6.00 15.00
77 Tim Hudson 8.00 20.00
78 Mike Stanton 12.00 30.00
79 Kurt Suzuki 6.00 15.00
80 Desmond Jennings 6.00 15.00
81 Omar Infante 6.00 15.00
82 Josh Johnson
Adam Wainwright/Roy Halladay LL 6.00 15.00
83 Greg Halman 6.00 15.00
84 Roger Bernadina 6.00 15.00
85 Jack Wilson 6.00 15.00
86 Carlos Silva 6.00 15.00
87 Daniel Descalso 6.00 15.00
88 Brian Bogusevic 6.00 15.00
89 Placido Polanco 6.00 15.00
90 Yadier Molina 12.00 30.00
91 Lucas May 6.00 15.00
92 Chris Narveson 6.00 15.00
93 Paul Konerko 10.00 25.00
94 Ryan Raburn 6.00 15.00
95 Pedro Alvarez 10.00 25.00
96 Zach Duke 6.00 15.00
97 Carlos Gomez 6.00 15.00
98 Bronson Arroyo 6.00 15.00
99 Ben Revere 8.00 20.00
100 Albert Pujols 12.00 30.00
101 Gregor Blanco 6.00 15.00
102 CC Sabathia 8.00 20.00
103 Cliff Lee 6.00 15.00
104 Ian Stewart 6.00 15.00
105 Jonathan Lucroy 10.00 25.00
106 Felix Pie 6.00 15.00
107 Aubrey Huff 6.00 15.00
108 Zack Greinke 8.00 20.00
109 Hamilton/Cabrera/Mauer LL 10.00 25.00
110 Aroldis Chapman 12.00 30.00
111 Kevin Gregg 6.00 15.00
112 Jorge Cantu 6.00 15.00
113 Arthur Rhodes 6.00 15.00
114 Russell Martin 6.00 15.00
115 Jason Varitek 10.00 25.00
116 Russell Branyan 6.00 15.00
117 Brett Sinkbeil 6.00 15.00
118 Howie Kendrick 6.00 15.00
119 Jason Bay 8.00 20.00
120 Mat Latos 10.00 25.00
121 Brandon Inge 6.00 15.00
122 Bobby Jenks 6.00 15.00
123 Mike Lowell 6.00 15.00
124 CC Sabathia/Jon Lester
David Price LL 8.00 20.00
125 Evan Meek 6.00 15.00
126 San Diego Padres TC 6.00 15.00
127 Chris Volstad 6.00 15.00
128 Manny Ramirez 10.00 25.00
129 Lucas Duda 15.00 40.00
130 Robinson Cano 6.00 15.00
131 Kevin Kouzmanoff 6.00 15.00
132 Brian Duensing 6.00 15.00
133 Miguel Tejada 8.00 20.00
134 Carlos Gonzalez/Joey Votto
Omar Infante LL 10.00 25.00
135 Mike Stanton 12.00 30.00
136 Jason Marquis 6.00 15.00
137 Xavier Nady 6.00 15.00
138 Pujols/Gonzalez/Votto LL 12.00 30.00
139 Eric Young Jr. 6.00 15.00
140 Brett Anderson 5.00 12.00
141 Ubaldo Jimenez 5.00 12.00
142 Johnny Cueto 10.00 25.00
143 Jeremy Jeffress 6.00 15.00
144 Lance Berkman 8.00 20.00
145 Freddie Freeman 125.00 300.00
146 Roy Halladay 6.00 15.00
147 Jon Niese 6.00 15.00
148 Ricky Romero 6.00 15.00
149 David Aardsma 6.00 15.00
150 Miguel Cabrera 10.00 25.00
151 Fausto Carmona 6.00 15.00
152 Baltimore Orioles TC 6.00 15.00
153 A.J. Pierzynski 6.00 15.00
154 Marlon Byrd 6.00 15.00
155 Alex Rodriguez 12.00 30.00
156 Josh Thole 6.00 15.00
157 New York Mets TC 8.00 20.00
158 Casey Blake 6.00 15.00
159 Chris Perez 6.00 15.00
160 Josh Tomlin 6.00 15.00
161 Chicago White Sox TC 6.00 15.00
162 Ronny Cedeno 6.00 15.00
163 Carlos Pena 8.00 20.00
164 Koji Uehara 6.00 15.00
165 Jeremy Hellickson 10.00 25.00
166 Josh Johnson 8.00 20.00
167 Clay Hensley 6.00 15.00
168 Felix Hernandez 6.00 15.00
169 Chipper Jones 10.00 25.00
170 David DeJesus 6.00 15.00
171 Garrett Jones 6.00 15.00
172 Lyle Overbay 6.00 15.00
173 Jose Lopez 6.00 15.00
174 Roy Oswalt 8.00 20.00
175 Brennan Boesch 8.00 20.00
176 Daniel Hudson 6.00 15.00
177 Brian Matusz 4.00 10.00
178 Heath Bell 6.00 15.00
179 Armando Galarraga 6.00 15.00
180 Paul Maholm 6.00 15.00
181 Magglio Ordonez 8.00 20.00
182 Jeremy Bonderman 6.00 15.00
183 Stephen Strasburg 10.00 25.00
184 Brandon Morrow 6.00 15.00
185 Peter Bourjos 8.00 20.00
186 Carl Pavano 6.00 15.00
187 Milwaukee Brewers TC 6.00 15.00
188 Pablo Sandoval 8.00 20.00
189 Kerry Wood 6.00 15.00
190 Coco Crisp 6.00 15.00
191 Jay Bruce 8.00 20.00
192 Cincinnati Reds TC 6.00 15.00
193 Cory Luebke 6.00 15.00
194 Andres Torres 6.00 15.00
195 Nick Markakis 8.00 20.00
196 Jose Ceda 5.00 12.00
197 Aaron Hill 6.00 15.00
198 Buster Posey 12.00 30.00
199 Jimmy Rollins 8.00 20.00
200 Ichiro Suzuki 12.00 30.00
201 Mike Napoli 6.00 15.00
202 Bautista/Konerko/Cabrera LL 10.00 25.00
203 Dillon Gee 10.00 25.00
204 Oakland Athletics TC 6.00 15.00
205 Ty Wigginton 6.00 15.00
206 Chase Headley 6.00 15.00
207 Angel Pagan 6.00 15.00
208 Clay Buchholz 5.00 12.00
209 Carlos Santana 10.00 25.00
210 Brian Wilson 10.00 25.00
211 Joey Votto 10.00 25.00
212 Pedro Feliz 6.00 15.00
213 Brandon Snyder 6.00 15.00
214 Chase Utley 6.00 15.00
215 Edwin Encarnacion 15.00 40.00
216 Jose Bautista 8.00 20.00
217 Yunel Escobar 6.00 15.00
218 Victor Martinez 8.00 20.00
219 Carlos Ruiz 6.00 15.00
220 Todd Helton 8.00 20.00
221 Scott Hairston 6.00 15.00
222 Matt Lindstrom 6.00 15.00
223 Gregory Infante 6.00 15.00
224 Milton Bradley 6.00 15.00
225 Josh Willingham 10.00 25.00
226 Jose Guillen 6.00 15.00
227 Nate McLouth 6.00 15.00
228 Scott Rolen 8.00 20.00
229 Jonathan Sanchez 6.00 15.00
230 Aaron Cook 6.00 15.00
231 Mark Buehrle 8.00 20.00
232 Jamie Moyer 6.00 15.00
233 Ramon Hernandez 6.00 15.00
234 Miguel Montero 6.00 15.00
235 Felix Hernandez
Clay Buchholz/David Price LL 8.00 20.00
236 Nelson Cruz 12.00 30.00
237 Jason Vargas 6.00 15.00
238 Pedro Ciriaco 10.00 25.00
239 Jhoulys Chacin 6.00 15.00
240 Andre Ethier 8.00 20.00
241 Wandy Rodriguez 6.00 15.00
242 Brad Lidge 6.00 15.00
243 Omar Vizquel 8.00 20.00
244 Mike Aviles 6.00 15.00
245 Neil Walker 10.00 25.00
246 John Lannan 6.00 15.00
247 Starlin Castro 6.00 15.00
248 Wade LeBlanc 6.00 15.00
249 Aaron Harang 6.00 15.00
250 Carlos Gonzalez 8.00 20.00
251 Alcides Escobar 10.00 25.00
252 Michael Saunders 10.00 25.00
253 Jim Thome 8.00 20.00
254 Lars Anderson 8.00 20.00
255 Torii Hunter 6.00 15.00
256 Tyler Colvin 5.00 12.00
257 Travis Hafner 6.00 15.00
258 Rafael Soriano 6.00 15.00
259 Kyle Davies 6.00 15.00
260 Freddy Sanchez 6.00 15.00
261 Alexei Ramirez 10.00 25.00
262 Alex Gordon 8.00 20.00
263 Joel Pineiro 6.00 15.00
264 Ryan Perry 6.00 15.00
265 John Danks 6.00 15.00
266 Rickie Weeks 5.00 12.00
267 Jose Contreras 6.00 15.00
268 Jake McGee 6.00 15.00
269 Stephen Drew 6.00 15.00
270 Ubaldo Jimenez 5.00 12.00
271 Adam Dunn 8.00 20.00
272 J.J. Hardy 6.00 15.00
273 Derrek Lee 6.00 15.00
274 Michael Brantley 6.00 15.00
275 Clayton Kershaw 20.00 50.00
276 Miguel Olivo 6.00 15.00
277 Trevor Hoffman 8.00 20.00
278 Marco Scutaro 10.00 25.00
279 Nick Swisher 6.00 15.00
280 Andrew Bailey 6.00 15.00
281 Kevin Slowey 6.00 15.00
282 Buster Posey 12.00 30.00
283 Colorado Rockies TC 6.00 15.00
284 Reid Brignac 6.00 15.00
285 Hank Conger 8.00 20.00
286 Melvin Mora 6.00 15.00
287 Scott Cousins 6.00 15.00
288 Matt Capps 6.00 15.00
289 Yuniesky Betancourt 6.00 15.00
290 Ike Davis 5.00 12.00
291 Juan Gutierrez 6.00 15.00
292 Darren Ford 6.00 15.00
293 Justin Morneau 6.00 15.00
294 Luke Scott 6.00 15.00
295 Jon Jay 6.00 15.00
296 John Buck 6.00 15.00
297 Jason Jaramillo 6.00 15.00
298 Jeff Keppinger 6.00 15.00
299 Chris Carpenter 6.00 15.00
300 Roy Halladay 6.00 15.00
301 Seth Smith 6.00 15.00
302 Adrian Beltre 15.00 40.00
303 Emilio Bonifacio 6.00 15.00
304 Jim Thome 8.00 20.00
305 James Loney 5.00 12.00
306 Cabrera/ARod/Bautista LL 12.00 30.00
307 Alex Rios 5.00 12.00
308 Ian Desmond 5.00 12.00
309 Chicago Cubs TC 8.00 20.00
310 Alex Gonzalez 6.00 15.00
311 James Shields 6.00 15.00
312 Gaby Sanchez 6.00 15.00
313 Chris Coghlan 6.00 15.00
314 Ryan Kalish 8.00 20.00
315 David Ortiz 12.00 30.00
316 Chris Young 6.00 15.00
317 Yonder Alonso 6.00 15.00
318 Pujols/Dunn/Votto LL 12.00 30.00
319 Atlanta Braves TC 6.00 15.00
320 Michael Young 6.00 15.00
321 Jeremy Guthrie 6.00 15.00
322 Brent Morel 6.00 15.00
323 C.J. Wilson 6.00 15.00
324 Boston Red Sox TC 8.00 20.00
325 Jayson Werth 8.00 20.00
326 Ozzie Martinez 6.00 15.00
327 Christian Guzman 6.00 15.00
328 David Price 8.00 20.00
329 Brett Wallace 6.00 15.00
330 Derek Jeter 25.00 60.00
331 Carlos Guillen 6.00 15.00
332 Melky Cabrera 6.00 15.00
333 Tom Wilhelmsen 20.00 50.00
334 St. Louis Cardinals 15.00 40.00
335 Buster Posey 12.00 30.00
336 Chris Heisey 6.00 15.00
337 Jordan Walden 15.00 40.00
338 Jason Hammel 10.00 25.00
339 Alexi Casilla 6.00 15.00
340 Evan Longoria 6.00 15.00
341 Kyle Kendrick 6.00 15.00
342 Jorge De La Rosa 6.00 15.00
343 Mason Tobin 6.00 15.00
344 Michael Kohn 6.00 15.00
345 Austin Jackson 6.00 15.00
346 Jose Bautista 6.00 15.00
347 Darwin Barney 12.00 30.00
348 Landon Powell 6.00 15.00
349 Drew Stubbs 6.00 15.00
350 Francisco Liriano 6.00 15.00
351 Jacoby Ellsbury 15.00 40.00
352 Colby Lewis 6.00 15.00
353 Cliff Pennington 6.00 15.00
354 Scott Baker 6.00 15.00
355 Justin Verlander 12.00 30.00
356 Alfonso Soriano 8.00 20.00
357 Mike Cameron 6.00 15.00
358 Paul Janish 6.00 15.00
359 Roy Halladay 6.00 15.00
360 Ivan Rodriguez 8.00 20.00
361 Florida Marlins 6.00 15.00
362 Doug Fister 6.00 15.00
363 Aaron Rowand 6.00 15.00
364 Tim Wakefield 10.00 25.00
365 Adam Lind 8.00 20.00
366 Joe Nathan 12.00 30.00
367 Hiroki Kuroda 15.00 40.00
368 Brian Broderick 6.00 15.00
369 Wilson Betemit 6.00 15.00
370 Matt Garza 6.00 15.00
371 Taylor Teagarden 6.00 15.00
372 Jarrod Saltalamacchia 6.00 15.00
373 Trever Miller 6.00 15.00
374 Washington Nationals 6.00 15.00
375 Matt Kemp 10.00 25.00
376 Clayton Richard 6.00 15.00
377 Esmil Rogers 6.00 15.00
378 Mark Reynolds 6.00 15.00
379 Ben Francisco 6.00 15.00
380 Jose Reyes 8.00 20.00
381 Michael Gonzalez 6.00 15.00
382 Travis Snider 6.00 15.00
383 Ryan Ludwick 6.00 15.00
384 Nick Hundley 6.00 15.00
385 Ichiro Suzuki 12.00 30.00
386 Barry Enright 6.00 15.00
387 Danny Valencia 8.00 20.00
388 Kenley Jansen 10.00 25.00
389 Carlos Quentin 5.00 12.00
390 Danny Valencia 12.00 30.00
391 Phil Coke 6.00 15.00
392 Kris Medlen 10.00 25.00
393 Jake Arrieta 6.00 15.00
394 Austin Jackson 6.00 15.00
395 Tyler Flowers 6.00 15.00
396 Adam Jones 8.00 20.00
397 Sean Rodriguez 6.00 15.00
398 Pittsburgh Pirates 30.00 80.00
399 Adam Moore 6.00 15.00
400 Troy Tulowitzki 20.00 50.00
401 Michael Crotta 6.00 15.00
402 Jack Cust 6.00 15.00
403 Felix Hernandez 6.00 15.00
404 Chris Capuano 6.00 15.00
405 Ian Kinsler 8.00 20.00
406 John Lackey 10.00 25.00
407 Jonathan Broxton 6.00 15.00
408 Denard Span 6.00 15.00
409 Vin Mazzaro 6.00 15.00
410 Prince Fielder 6.00 15.00
411 Josh Bell 6.00 15.00
412 Samuel Deduno 6.00 15.00
413 Derek Holland 6.00 15.00
414 Jose Molina 6.00 15.00
415 Brian McCann 8.00 20.00
416 Everth Cabrera 6.00 15.00
417 Miguel Cairo 6.00 15.00
418 Zach Britton 10.00 25.00
419 Kelly Johnson 6.00 15.00
420 Ryan Howard 8.00 20.00
421 Domonic Brown 8.00 20.00
422 Juan Pierre 6.00 15.00
423 Hideki Okajima 6.00 15.00
424 New York Yankees 12.00 30.00
425 Adrian Gonzalez 10.00 25.00
426 Travis Buck 6.00 15.00
427 Brad Emaus 6.00 15.00
428 Brett Myers 6.00 15.00
429 Skip Schumaker 6.00 15.00
430 Trevor Crowe 6.00 15.00
431 Marcos Mateo 12.00 30.00
432 Matt Harrison 6.00 15.00
433 Curtis Granderson 10.00 25.00
434 Mark DeRosa 6.00 15.00
435 Elvis Andrus 8.00 20.00
436 Trevor Cahill 6.00 15.00
437 Jordan Schafer 6.00 15.00
438 Ryan Theriot 6.00 15.00
439 Ervin Santana 6.00 15.00
440 Grady Sizemore 8.00 20.00
441 Rafael Furcal 6.00 15.00
442 Brad Bergesen 6.00 15.00
443 Brian Roberts 6.00 15.00
444 Brett Cecil 6.00 15.00
445 Mitch Talbot 6.00 15.00
446 Brandon Beachy 10.00 25.00
447 Toronto Blue Jays 6.00 15.00
448 Colby Rasmus 6.00 15.00
449 Austin Kearns 6.00 15.00
450 Mark Teixeira 6.00 15.00
451 Livan Hernandez 6.00 15.00
452 David Freese 6.00 15.00
453 Joe Saunders 12.00 30.00
454 Alberto Callaspo 6.00 15.00
455 Logan Morrison 6.00 15.00
456 Ryan Doumit 6.00 15.00
457 Brandon Allen 6.00 15.00
458 Javier Vazquez 6.00 15.00
459 Frank Francisco 6.00 15.00
460 Cole Hamels 8.00 20.00
461 Eric Sogard 6.00 15.00
462 Daric Barton 6.00 15.00
463 Will Venable 6.00 15.00
464 Daniel Bard 6.00 15.00
465 Yovani Gallardo 6.00 15.00
466 Johnny Damon 8.00 20.00
467 Wade Davis 6.00 15.00
468 Chone Figgins 6.00 15.00
469 Joe Blanton 6.00 15.00
470 Billy Butler 6.00 15.00
471 Tim Collins 5.00 12.00
472 Jason Kendall 6.00 15.00
473 Chad Billingsley 10.00 25.00
474 Jeff Mathis 6.00 15.00
475 Phil Hughes 6.00 15.00
476 Matt LaPorta 6.00 15.00
477 Franklin Gutierrez 6.00 15.00
478 Mike Minor 6.00 15.00
479 Justin Duchscherer 6.00 15.00
480 Dustin Pedroia 8.00 20.00
481 Randy Wells 6.00 15.00
482 Eric Hinske 6.00 15.00
483 Justin Smoak 25.00 60.00
484 Gerardo Parra 6.00 15.00
485 Delmon Young 8.00 20.00
486 Francisco Rodriguez 8.00 20.00
487 Chris Snyder 12.00 30.00
488 Brayan Villarreal 6.00 15.00
489 Marc Rzepczynski 6.00 15.00
490 Matt Holliday 10.00 25.00
491 Fernando Abad 5.00 12.00
492 A.J. Burnett 5.00 12.00
493 Ryan Sweeney 6.00 15.00
494 Drew Storen 6.00 15.00
495 Shane Victorino 8.00 20.00
496 Gavin Floyd 6.00 15.00
497 Alex Avila 12.00 30.00
498 Scott Feldman 6.00 15.00
499 J.A. Happ 8.00 20.00
500 Kevin Youkilis 5.00 12.00
501 Tsuyoshi Nishioka 12.00 30.00
502 Jeff Baker 6.00 15.00
503 Nathan Adcock 6.00 15.00
504 Jhonny Peralta 6.00 15.00
505 Tommy Hanson 5.00 12.00
506 Aneury Rodriguez 5.00 12.00
507 Huston Street 6.00 15.00
508 Homer Bailey 6.00 15.00
509 Michael Bourn 6.00 15.00
510 Jason Heyward 8.00 20.00
511 Philadelphia Phillies 12.00 30.00
512 Octavio Dotel 6.00 15.00
513 Adam LaRoche 6.00 15.00
514 Kelly Shoppach 6.00 15.00
515 Carlos Beltran 10.00 25.00
516 Mike Leake 8.00 20.00
517 Fred Lewis 6.00 15.00
518 Michael Morse 6.00 15.00
519 Corey Hart 6.00 15.00
520 Jorge Posada 15.00 40.00
521 Joaquin Benoit 6.00 15.00
522 Asdrubal Cabrera 10.00 25.00
523 Mike Nickeas 6.00 15.00
524 Michael Martinez 20.00 50.00
525 Vernon Wells 6.00 15.00
526 Jason Donald 6.00 15.00
527 Kila Ka'aihue 6.00 15.00
528 Bobby Abreu 6.00 15.00
529 Maicer Izturis 6.00 15.00
530 Felix Hernandez 6.00 15.00
531 Juan Rivera 6.00 15.00
532 Erik Bedard 6.00 15.00
533 Lorenzo Cain 6.00 15.00
534 Bud Norris 6.00 15.00
535 Rich Harden 6.00 15.00
536 Tony Sipp 15.00 40.00
537 Jake Peavy 6.00 15.00
538 Jason Motte 6.00 15.00
539 Brandon Lyon 6.00 15.00
540 Joakim Soria 6.00 15.00
541 John Jaso 6.00 15.00
542 Mike Pelfrey 6.00 15.00
543 Texas Rangers 6.00 15.00
544 Justin Masterson 6.00 15.00
545 Jose Tabata 5.00 12.00
546 Pat Burrell 6.00 15.00
547 Albert Pujols 30.00 80.00
548 Ryan Franklin 6.00 15.00
549 Jayson Nix 6.00 15.00
550 Joe Mauer 8.00 20.00
551 Marcus Thames 6.00 15.00
552 San Francisco Giants 6.00 15.00
553 Kyle Lohse 6.00 15.00
554 Cedric Hunter 6.00 15.00
555 Madison Bumgarner 12.00 30.00
556 B.J. Upton 8.00 20.00
557 Wes Helms 6.00 15.00
558 Carlos Zambrano 8.00 20.00
559 Reggie Willits 6.00 15.00
560 Chris Iannetta 6.00 15.00
561 Luke Gregerson 6.00 15.00
562 Gordon Beckham 5.00 12.00
563 Josh Rodriguez 6.00 15.00
564 Jeff Samardzija 12.00 30.00
565 Mark Teahen 6.00 15.00
566 Jordan Zimmermann 10.00 25.00
567 Dallas Braden 6.00 15.00
568 Kansas City Royals 6.00 15.00
569 Cameron Maybin 5.00 12.00
570 Matt Cain 8.00 20.00
571 Jeremy Affeldt 6.00 15.00
572 Brad Hawpe 6.00 15.00
573 Nyjer Morgan 6.00 15.00
574 Brandon Kintzler 6.00 15.00
575 Rod Barajas 6.00 15.00
576 Jed Lowrie 5.00 12.00
577 Mike Fontenot 6.00 15.00
578 Willy Aybar 6.00 15.00
579 Jeff Niemann 6.00 15.00
580 Chris Young 6.00 15.00
581 Fernando Rodney 6.00 15.00
582 Kosuke Fukudome 6.00 15.00
583 Ryan Spilborghs 6.00 15.00
584 Jason Bartlett 6.00 15.00
585 Dan Johnson 6.00 15.00
586 Carlos Lee 6.00 15.00
587 J.P. Arencibia 15.00 40.00
588 Rajai Davis 6.00 15.00
589 Seattle Mariners 25.00 60.00
590 Tim Lincecum 6.00 15.00
591 John Axford 6.00 15.00

592 Dayan Viciedo 6.00 15.00
593 Francisco Cordero 6.00 15.00
594 Jose Valverde 6.00 15.00
595 Michael Pineda 10.00 25.00
596 Anibal Sanchez 6.00 15.00
597 Rick Porcello 10.00 25.00
598 Jonny Gomes 6.00 15.00
599 Travis Ishikawa 6.00 15.00
600 Neftali Feliz 6.00 15.00
601 J.J. Putz 6.00 15.00
602 Ivan DeJesus 6.00 15.00
603 David Murphy 6.00 15.00
604 Joe Paterson 10.00 25.00
605 Brandon Belt 10.00 25.00
606 Juan Miranda 6.00 15.00
607 Daniel Murphy 12.00 30.00
608 Casey McGehee 6.00 15.00
609 Juan Francisco 6.00 15.00
610 Josh Beckett 5.00 12.00
611 Geovany Soto 8.00 20.00
612 Detroit Tigers 6.00 15.00
613 Dexter Fowler 10.00 25.00
614 Minnesota Twins 6.00 15.00
615 Shaun Marcum 6.00 15.00
616 Ross Ohlendorf 6.00 15.00
617 Joel Zumaya 6.00 15.00
618 Josh Lueke 6.00 15.00
619 Jonny Venters 6.00 15.00
620 Luke Hochevar 6.00 15.00
621 Omar Beltre 6.00 15.00
622 Matt Thornton 6.00 15.00
623 Leo Nunez 6.00 15.00
624 Luke French 6.00 15.00
625 Ruben Tejada 6.00 15.00
626 Dan Haren 6.00 15.00
627 Kyle Blanks 6.00 15.00
628 Blake DeWitt 6.00 15.00
629 Ivan Nova 10.00 25.00
630 Brandon Phillips 6.00 15.00
631 Houston Astros 6.00 15.00
632 Scott Kazmir 6.00 15.00
633 Aaron Crow 8.00 20.00
634 Mitch Moreland 6.00 15.00
635 Jason Heyward 25.00 60.00
636 Chris Tillman 6.00 15.00
637 Ricky Nolasco 6.00 15.00
638 Ryan Madson 6.00 15.00
639 Pedro Beato 4.00 10.00
640 Dan Uggla 5.00 12.00
641 Travis Wood 6.00 15.00
642 Jason Hammel 10.00 25.00
643 Jaime Garcia 30.00 80.00
644 Joel Hanrahan 10.00 25.00
645 Adam Wainwright 8.00 20.00
646 Los Angeles Dodgers 8.00 20.00
647 Jeanmar Gomez 6.00 15.00
648 Cody Ross 6.00 15.00
649 Joba Chamberlain 5.00 12.00
650 Josh Hamilton 6.00 15.00
651 Kendrys Morales 6.00 15.00
652 Edwin Jackson 6.00 15.00
653 J.D. Drew 6.00 15.00
654 Chris Getz 6.00 15.00
655 Starlin Castro 15.00 40.00
656 Raul Ibanez 8.00 20.00
657 Nick Blackburn 6.00 15.00
658 Mitch Maier 6.00 15.00
659 Clint Barmes 6.00 15.00
660 Ryan Zimmerman 8.00 20.00

2011 Topps Cognac Diamond Anniversary

*COGNAC VET: 1.5X TO 4X BASIC
*COGNAC RC: 1X TO 2.5X BASIC RC
*COGNAC SP: .2X TO .5X BASIC SP
STATED ODDS 1:2 UPDATE HOBBY
STATED SP ODDS 1:41 UPDATE HOBBY
145 Freddie Freeman 40.00 100.00

2011 Topps Diamond Anniversary

*DIAMOND VET: 2X TO 5X BASIC
*DIAMOND RC: 1.2X TO 3X BASIC RC
*DIAMOND SP: .3X TO .8X BASIC SP
SER.1 STATED ODDS 1:4 HOBBY
145 Freddie Freeman 25.00 60.00

2011 Topps Diamond Anniversary Factory Set Limited Edition

COMPLETE SET (660) 30.00 80.00
*FACT.SET LTD: .5X TO 1.2X BASIC
145 Freddie Freeman 40.00 100.00

2011 Topps Diamond Anniversary HTA

COMPLETE SET (25) 5.00 12.00
HTA1 Hank Aaron 1.00 2.50
HTA2 Ichiro Suzuki .60 1.50
HTA3 Babe Ruth 1.25 3.00
HTA4 Evan Longoria .30 .75
HTA5 Josh Hamilton .30 .75
HTA6 Jason Heyward .40 1.00
HTA7 Mickey Mantle 1.50 4.00
HTA8 Ryan Braun .30 .75
HTA9 Joey Votto .50 1.25
HTA10 Sandy Koufax 1.00 2.50
HTA11 David Wright .40 1.00
HTA12 Troy Tulowitzki .50 1.25
HTA13 Derek Jeter 1.25 3.00
HTA14 Tim Lincecum .30 .75
HTA15 Joe Mauer .40 1.00
HTA16 Mike Schmidt .75 2.00
HTA17 Ryan Howard .40 1.00
HTA18 Robinson Cano .30 .75
HTA19 Carl Crawford .30 .75
HTA20 Albert Pujols .60 1.50
HTA21 Roy Halladay .30 .75
HTA22 Miguel Cabrera .50 1.25
HTA23 Buster Posey .60 1.50
HTA24 Jackie Robinson .50 1.25
HTA25 Felix Hernandez .30 .75

2011 Topps Factory Set Red Border

*RED VET: 4X TO 10X BASIC
*RED RC: 2.5X TO 6X BASIC RC
ONE PACK OF FIVE RED PER FACT.SET
STATED PRINT RUN 245 SER.#'d SETS
145 Freddie Freeman 50.00 120.00

2011 Topps Gold

*GOLD VET: 2X TO 5X BASIC
*GOLD RC: 1.2X TO 3X BASIC RC
SER.1 ODDS 1:8 HOBBY
STATED PRINT RUN 2011 SER.#'d SETS
145 Freddie Freeman 25.00 60.00

2011 Topps Hope Diamond Anniversary

*HOPE VET: 8X TO 20X BASIC
*HOPE RC: 5X TO 12X BASIC RC
*HOPE SP: X TO X BASIC SP
STATED ODDS 1:35 UPDATE HOBBY
STATED SP ODDS 1:1340 UPDATE HOBBY
STATED PRINT RUN 60 SER.#'d SETS
145 Freddie Freeman 100.00 250.00

2011 Topps Sparkle

APPX.ODDDS ONE PER HOBBY CASE
1 Ryan Braun 12.50 30.00
3 Jon Lester 15.00 40.00
5 Joey Votto 12.50 30.00
15 David Wright 20.00 50.00
20 Hanley Ramirez 8.00 20.00
23 Jaime Garcia 8.00 20.00
25 Carl Crawford 20.00 50.00
35 Shin-Soo Choo 20.00 50.00
40 Justin Upton 10.00 25.00
42 Mariano Rivera 15.00 40.00
44 Martin Prado 10.00 25.00
50 Alex Rodriguez 20.00 50.00
60 Andrew McCutchen 12.50 30.00
61 David Price 8.00 20.00
67 Vladimir Guerrero 15.00 40.00
70 Kyle Drabek 12.50 30.00
75 Jered Weaver 10.00 25.00
78 Mike Stanton 12.50 30.00
80 Desmond Jennings 10.00 25.00
100 Albert Pujols 30.00 60.00
102 CC Sabathia 15.00 40.00
108 Zack Greinke 10.00 25.00
110 Aroldis Chapman 15.00 40.00
120 Mat Latos 10.00 25.00
128 Manny Ramirez 12.50 30.00
140 Brett Anderson 10.00 25.00
150 Miguel Cabrera 10.00 25.00
165 Jeremy Hellickson 10.00 25.00
166 Josh Johnson 10.00 25.00
169 Chipper Jones 12.50 30.00
177 Roy Oswalt 12.50 30.00
187 Brian Matusz 10.00 25.00
195 Nick Markakis 20.00 50.00
200 Ichiro Suzuki 12.50 30.00
208 Clay Buchholz 10.00 25.00
209 Carlos Santana 12.50 30.00
210 Brian Wilson 12.50 30.00
214 Chase Utley 12.50 30.00
216 Jose Bautista 12.50 30.00
218 Victor Martinez 10.00 25.00
236 Nelson Cruz 8.00 20.00
240 Andre Ethier 10.00 25.00
241 Wandy Rodriguez 12.50 30.00
247 Starlin Castro 20.00 50.00
250 Carlos Gonzalez 8.00 20.00
255 Torii Hunter 10.00 25.00
269 Stephen Drew 10.00 25.00
270 Ubaldo Jimenez 12.50 30.00
271 Adam Dunn 10.00 25.00
275 Clayton Kershaw 8.00 20.00
290 Ike Davis 12.50 30.00
293 Justin Morneau 12.50 30.00
294 Luke Scott 12.50 30.00
299 Chris Carpenter 8.00 20.00
300 Roy Halladay 20.00 50.00
307 Alex Rios 10.00 25.00
315 David Ortiz 10.00 25.00
320 Michael Young 12.50 30.00
322 Brent Morel 8.00 20.00
330 Derek Jeter 40.00 80.00
335 Buster Posey 12.50 30.00
340 Evan Longoria 10.00 25.00
345 Austin Jackson 12.50 30.00
350 Francisco Liriano 8.00 20.00
351 Jacoby Ellsbury 12.50 30.00
355 Justin Verlander 12.50 30.00
356 Alfonso Soriano 8.00 20.00
375 Matt Kemp 10.00 25.00
378 Mark Reynolds 10.00 25.00
380 Jose Reyes 10.00 25.00
389 Carlos Quentin 8.00 20.00
396 Adam Jones 8.00 20.00
400 Troy Tulowitzki 10.00 25.00
405 Ian Kinsler 10.00 25.00
407 Jonathan Broxton 8.00 20.00
410 Prince Fielder 15.00 40.00
415 Brian McCann 10.00 25.00
419 Kelly Johnson 8.00 20.00
420 Ryan Howard 10.00 25.00
425 Adrian Gonzalez 10.00 25.00
435 Elvis Andrus 8.00 20.00
436 Trevor Cahill 12.50 30.00
441 Rafael Furcal 10.00 25.00
450 Mark Teixeira 12.50 30.00
455 Logan Morrison 8.00 20.00
460 Cole Hamels 10.00 25.00
465 Yovani Gallardo 8.00 20.00
470 Billy Butler 8.00 20.00
473 Chad Billingsley 12.50 30.00
478 Mike Minor 8.00 20.00
480 Dustin Pedroia 10.00 25.00
485 Delmon Young 10.00 25.00
490 Matt Holliday 8.00 20.00
500 Kevin Youkilis 8.00 20.00
505 Tommy Hanson 10.00 25.00
510 Jason Heyward 10.00 25.00
519 Corey Hart 12.50 30.00
520 Jorge Posada 10.00 25.00
525 Vernon Wells 10.00 25.00
530 Felix Hernandez 10.00 25.00
545 Jose Tabata 12.50 30.00
550 Joe Mauer 12.50 30.00
555 Madison Bumgarner 12.50 30.00
560 Chris Iannetta 12.50 30.00
562 Gordon Beckham 12.50 30.00
567 Dallas Braden 10.00 25.00
570 Matt Cain 12.50 30.00
586 Carlos Lee 15.00 40.00
590 Tim Lincecum 20.00 50.00
610 Josh Beckett 12.50 30.00
613 Dexter Fowler 12.50 30.00
626 Dan Haren 10.00 25.00
627 Kyle Blanks 8.00 20.00
630 Brandon Phillips 10.00 25.00
640 Dan Uggla 8.00 20.00
645 Adam Wainwright 10.00 25.00
650 Josh Hamilton 12.50 30.00
651 Kendrys Morales 8.00 20.00
652 Edwin Jackson 8.00 20.00
660 Ryan Zimmerman 10.00 25.00

2011 Topps Target

*VETS: .5X TO 1.2X BASIC TOPPS CARDS
*RC: .5X TO 1.2X BASIC TOPPS RC CARDS
145 Freddie Freeman 10.00 25.00

2011 Topps Wal-Mart Black Border

*VETS: .5X TO 1.2X BASIC TOPPS CARDS
*RC: .5X TO 1.2X BASIC TOPPS RC CARDS
145 Freddie Freeman 10.00 25.00

2011 Topps 60

COMPLETE SET (150) 30.00 80.00
COMP.SER.1 SET (50) 10.00 25.00
COMP.SER.2 SET (50) 10.00 25.00
COMP.UPD.SET (50) 10.00 25.00
SER.1 ODDS 1:4 HOBBY
UPD.ODDS 1:4 HOBBY
1-50 ISSUED IN SERIES 1
51-100 ISSUED IN SERIES 2
101-150 ISSUED IN UPDATE
1 Ryan Howard .60 1.50
2 Andre Dawson .50 1.25
3 Babe Ruth 2.00 5.00
4 Gary Carter .50 1.25
5 Lou Gehrig 1.50 4.00
6 Robinson Cano .50 1.25
7 Mickey Mantle 2.50 6.00
8 Felix Hernandez .50 1.25
9 Ian Kinsler .50 1.25
10 Alex Rodriguez 1.00 2.50
11 Troy Tulowitzki .75 2.00
12 Prince Fielder .50 1.25
13 Jonathan Papelbon .50 1.25
14 Barry Larkin .50 1.25
15 Jason Heyward .60 1.50
16 Carl Crawford .50 1.25
17 Dale Murphy .75 2.00
18 Keith Hernandez .30 .75
19 Andre Ethier .50 1.25
20 Manny Ramirez .75 2.00
21 Tommy Hanson .30 .75
22 Clay Buchholz .30 .75
23 Neftali Feliz .30 .75
24 Josh Johnson .50 1.25
25 Orlando Cepeda .50 1.25
26 Derek Jeter 2.00 5.00
27 David Wright .60 1.50
28 Billy Butler .30 .75
29 Ryan Zimmerman .50 1.25
30 Nick Markakis .60 1.50
31 Justin Upton .50 1.25
32 Adam Dunn .50 1.25
33 Johan Santana .50 1.25
34 Mark Reynolds .30 .75
35 Frank Thomas .75 2.00
36 Adam Jones .50 1.25
37 Stephen Strasburg .75 2.00
38 Ryan Braun .50 1.25
39 Adam Wainwright .50 1.25
40 Michael Young .30 .75
41 Shin-Soo Choo .50 1.25
42 Mat Latos .50 1.25
43 Chipper Jones .75 2.00
44 Duke Snider .50 1.25
45 Hanley Ramirez .50 1.25
46 Ike Davis .30 .75
47 Nolan Ryan 2.50 6.00
48 Buster Posey 1.00 2.50
49 Josh Hamilton .50 1.25
50 Miguel Cabrera .75 2.00
51 Walter Johnson .75 2.00
52 Felix Hernandez .50 1.25
53 Jose Bautista .50 1.25
54 Ryan Zimmerman .50 1.25
55 Mariano Rivera 1.00 2.50
56 Roberto Alomar .50 1.25
57 Sandy Koufax 1.50 4.00
58 Hank Aaron 1.50 4.00
59 Roy Campanella .75 2.00
60 Mel Ott .75 2.00
61 Tom Seaver .50 1.25
62 Mike Stanton .75 2.00
63 Evan Longoria .50 1.25
64 Jorge Posada .50 1.25
65 Don Mattingly 1.50 4.00
66 Paul Molitor .75 2.00
67 Andrew McCutchen .75 2.00
68 Joey Votto .75 2.00
69 David Price .60 1.50
70 Chris Carpenter .50 1.25
71 Willie Stargell .50 1.25
72 Eddie Mathews .75 2.00
73 Nelson Cruz .75 2.00
74 Chase Utley .50 1.25
75 CC Sabathia .50 1.25
76 Joe Mauer .60 1.50
77 Dave Winfield .50 1.25
78 Francisco Liriano .30 .75
79 Rickey Henderson .75 2.00
80 Thurman Munson .75 2.00
81 Brian McCann .50 1.25
82 Shane Victorino .50 1.25
83 Hunter Pence .50 1.25
84 Starlin Castro .50 1.25
85 Johnny Bench .75 2.00
86 Dustin Pedroia .60 1.50
87 Clayton Kershaw 1.50 4.00
88 Mark Teixeira .50 1.25
89 Jered Weaver .50 1.25
90 Greg Maddux 1.00 2.50
91 David Ortiz .75 2.00
92 Alfonso Soriano .50 1.25
93 Carlos Gonzalez .50 1.25
94 Torii Hunter .30 .75
95 Jon Lester .50 1.25
96 Tim Lincecum .50 1.25
97 Jackie Robinson .75 2.00
98 Marlon Byrd .30 .75
99 Jacoby Ellsbury .60 1.50
100 Albert Pujols 1.00 2.50
101 Joe DiMaggio 1.50 4.00
102 Hank Aaron 1.50 4.00
103 Alex Rodriguez 1.00 2.50
104 Alex Rodriguez 1.00 2.50
105 Rogers Hornsby .50 1.25
106 Jimmie Foxx .75 2.00
107 Johnny Mize .50 1.25
108 Babe Ruth 2.00 5.00
109 Luis Aparicio .50 1.25
110 Carlton Fisk .50 1.25
111 Reggie Jackson .50 1.25
112 Reggie Jackson .50 1.25
113 Willie McCovey .50 1.25
114 Nolan Ryan 2.50 6.00
115 Nolan Ryan 2.50 6.00
116 Nolan Ryan 2.50 6.00
117 Fergie Jenkins .50 1.25
118 Joe Morgan .50 1.25
119 Tom Seaver .50 1.25
120 Ozzie Smith 1.00 2.50
121 Pee Wee Reese .50 1.25
122 Roberto Alomar .50 1.25
123 Andre Dawson .50 1.25
124 Rickey Henderson .75 2.00
125 Paul Molitor .75 2.00
126 Frank Robinson .50 1.25
127 Duke Snider .50 1.25
128 Frank Thomas .75 2.00
129 Ty Cobb 1.25 3.00
130 Lou Gehrig 1.50 4.00
131 Christy Mathewson .75 2.00
132 George Sisler .50 1.25
133 Tris Speaker .50 1.25
134 Honus Wagner .75 2.00
135 Cy Young .75 2.00
136 Bert Blyleven .50 1.25
137 Steve Garvey .30 .75
138 Roger Maris .75 2.00
139 Dan Uggla .30 .75
140 Eric Hosmer 2.00 5.00
141 Danny Duffy .50 1.25
142 Tyler Chatwood .30 .75
143 Lance Berkman .50 1.25
144 Zach Britton .75 2.00
145 Michael Pineda .75 2.00
146 Freddie Freeman 5.00 12.00
147 Kyle Drabek .50 1.25
148 Craig Kimbrel .75 2.00
149 Drew Storen .30 .75
150 Sandy Koufax 1.50 4.00

2011 Topps 60 Autograph Relics

COMMON CARD 6.00 15.00
SER.1 ODDS 1:3970 HOBBY
STATED PRINT RUN 50 SER.#'d SETS
AC Aroldis Chapman S2 15.00 40.00
AD Andre Dawson 50.00 100.00
AG Adrian Gonzalez S2 50.00 100.00
AK Al Kaline 20.00 50.00
BM Brian Matusz 6.00 15.00
BW Bernie Williams S2 50.00 100.00
CF Carlton Fisk S2 50.00 100.00
DP David Price S2 10.00 25.00
DS Duke Snider 10.00 25.00
FH Felix Hernandez 25.00 60.00
GC Gary Carter 20.00 50.00
HR Hanley Ramirez 6.00 15.00
IK Ian Kinsler 12.50 30.00
JH Jason Heyward S2 50.00 100.00
JV Joey Votto S2 20.00 50.00
RC Robinson Cano 50.00 100.00
RH Ryan Howard 20.00 50.00
RO Roy Oswalt S2 40.00 80.00
RS Ryne Sandberg S2 40.00 80.00
TS Tom Seaver S2 60.00 150.00

2011 Topps 60 Autographs

SER.1 ODDS 1:342 HOBBY
UPD.ODDS 1:620 HOBBY
EXCHANGE DEADLINE 1/31/2014
EXCH * IS PARTIAL EXCHANGE
AC Andrew Cashner S2 6.00 15.00
AC Andrew Cashner UPD 3.00 8.00
ACA Asdrubal Cabrera S2 5.00 12.00
AD Andre Dawson 10.00 25.00
AE Andre Ethier 8.00 20.00
AG Alex Gordon 6.00 15.00
AG Adrian Gonzalez UPD 8.00 20.00
AJ Adam Jones 6.00 15.00
AK Al Kaline EXCH * 12.00 30.00
AM Andrew McCutchen 20.00 50.00
AP Albert Pujols S2 100.00 200.00
AP Albert Pujols UPD 100.00 200.00
APA Angel Pagan S2 5.00 12.00
APA Angel Pagan UPD 5.00 12.00
AR Alex Rodriguez 60.00 120.00
AT Andres Torres S2 5.00 12.00
BA Brett Anderson UPD 4.00 10.00
BC Brett Cecil UPD 3.00 8.00
BD Blake DeWitt 8.00 20.00
BDU Brian Duensing 4.00 10.00
BJU B.J. Upton 5.00 12.00
BL Barry Larkin 30.00 60.00
BL Brandon League UPD 3.00 8.00
BM Brian McCann 6.00 15.00
BMA Brian Matusz 5.00 12.00
BP Buster Posey S2 30.00 80.00
CB Clay Buchholz 6.00 15.00
CB Clay Buchholz UPD 6.00 15.00
CC Carl Crawford 8.00 20.00
CCO Chris Coghlan 3.00 8.00
CD Chris Dickerson 8.00 20.00
CF Chone Figgins 4.00 10.00
CG Chris Getz 4.00 10.00
CH Chris Heisey UPD 5.00 12.00
CL Cliff Lee 10.00 25.00
CL Cliff Lee S2 10.00 25.00
CP Carlos Pena S2 5.00 12.00
CR Colby Rasmus UPD 10.00 25.00
CT Chris Tillman 6.00 15.00
CU Chase Utley S2 20.00 50.00
CV Chris Volstad EXCH * 3.00 8.00
CY Chris B. Young UPD 4.00 10.00
DB Domonic Brown 10.00 25.00
DB Daniel Bard UPD 6.00 15.00
DBA Daric Barton 3.00 8.00
DG Dwight Gooden S2 8.00 20.00
DM Daniel McCutchen UPD 3.00 8.00
DS Duke Snider 15.00 40.00
DS Darryl Strawberry S2 8.00 20.00
DS Drew Stubbs UPD 5.00 12.00
DSN Drew Storen EXCH 6.00 15.00
DST Drew Stubbs 6.00 15.00
DW David Wright S2 20.00 50.00
DW David Wright UPD 15.00 40.00
FCA Fausto Carmona EXCH 3.00 8.00
FD Felix Doubront 6.00 15.00
FF Freddie Freeman S2 15.00 40.00
FH Felix Hernandez S2 12.50 30.00
FH Felix Hernandez UPD 12.00 30.00
FR Fernando Rodney UPD 3.00 8.00
GB Gordon Beckham 5.00 12.00
GC Gary Carter 20.00 50.00
GC Gary Carter UPD 20.00 50.00
GG Gio Gonzalez S2 4.00 10.00
GP Glen Perkins 4.00 10.00
GS Gaby Sanchez S2 5.00 12.00
GS Gaby Sanchez UPD 3.00 8.00
HA Hank Aaron UPD 125.00 250.00
HP Hunter Pence 8.00 20.00
HR Hanley Ramirez 8.00 20.00
IK Ian Kinsler 3.00 8.00
IK Ian Kinsler S2 5.00 12.00
JB Jose Bautista S2 10.00 25.00
JB Jose Bautista UPD 10.00 25.00
JBR Jay Bruce UPD 6.00 15.00
JC Joba Chamberlain 3.00 8.00
JF Jeff Francis 3.00 8.00
JH Jason Heyward 10.00 25.00
JH Josh Hamilton UPD 20.00 50.00
JJ Josh Johnson 5.00 12.00
JJ Josh Johnson UPD 4.00 10.00
JJA Jon Jay UPD 4.00 10.00
JN Jon Niese UPD 4.00 10.00
JNI Jeff Niemann UPD 3.00 8.00
JP Jonathan Papelbon 3.00 8.00
JP Jhonny Peralta S2 4.00 10.00
JT Josh Tomlin 5.00 12.00
JT Josh Tomlin S2 5.00 12.00
JT Josh Thole UPD EXCH 4.00 10.00
JZ Jordan Zimmermann UPD EXCH 4.00 10.00
KD Kyle Drabek S2 3.00 8.00
KH Keith Hernandez 8.00 20.00
KJ Kevin Jepsen 3.00 8.00
KU Koji Uehara 8.00 20.00
LC Lorenzo Cain S2 8.00 20.00
LM Logan Morrison S2 3.00 8.00
LMA Lou Marson 15.00 40.00
MB Marlon Byrd 3.00 8.00
MB Madison Bumgarner S2 20.00 50.00
MC Miguel Cabrera UPD 75.00 150.00
MF Mark Fidrych 20.00 50.00
MH Matt Harrison 3.00 8.00
ML Mike Leake S2 3.00 8.00
MN Mike Napoli 5.00 12.00
MR Manny Ramirez 20.00 50.00
MR Mark Reynolds S2 3.00 8.00
MSC Max Scherzer 12.00 30.00
NW Neil Walker 5.00 12.00
OC Orlando Cepeda 6.00 15.00
PB Peter Bourjos EXCH 15.00 40.00
PF Prince Fielder 12.50 30.00
PS Pablo Sandoval UPD 10.00 25.00
RC Robinson Cano 12.00 30.00
RC Robinson Cano S2 12.00 30.00
RK Ryan Kalish 3.00 8.00
RK Ralph Kiner S2 15.00 40.00
RP Rick Porcello S2 5.00 12.00
RW Randy Wells 4.00 10.00
RZ Ryan Zimmerman S2 6.00 15.00
SC Starlin Castro S2 8.00 20.00
SK Sandy Koufax UPD 200.00 400.00
SSC Shin-Soo Choo S2 10.00 25.00
SV Shane Victorino S2 8.00 20.00
TB Taylor Buchholz S2 5.00 12.00
TC Tyler Colvin 8.00 20.00
TC Trevor Cahill S2 3.00 8.00
TH Tommy Hanson 8.00 20.00
TH Tim Hudson UPD 10.00 25.00
TT Troy Tulowitzki 12.50 30.00
TW Travis Wood 5.00 12.00
TW Travis Wood UPD 3.00 8.00
VM Vin Mazzaro 3.00 8.00
WD Wade Davis 4.00 10.00
WL Wade LeBlanc S2 3.00 8.00
WV Will Venable 6.00 15.00

2011 Topps 60 Dual Relics

STATED PRINT RUN 50 SER.#'d SETS
1 Josh Hamilton 6.00 15.00
2 J.Votto/M.Cabrera 20.00 50.00
3 R.Cano/D.Pedroia 20.00 50.00
4 J.Lester/C.Kershaw 15.00 40.00
5 B.Posey/J.Heyward 30.00 60.00
6 R.Alomar/B.Blyleven 15.00 40.00
7 H.Aaron/C.Jones 30.00 60.00
8 L.Gehrig/C.Ripken Jr. 100.00 175.00
9 B.Gibson/A.Wainwright 20.00 50.00
10 J.Morgan/C.Utley 20.00 50.00
11 Ichiro Suzuki 12.50 30.00
Torii Hunter
12 M.Teixeira/J.Posada 50.00 100.00
13 Mariano Rivera 12.50 30.00
Carlos Marmol
14 Josh Beckett 6.00 15.00
John Lackey
15 Josh Johnson 10.00 25.00
Clay Buchholz

2011 Topps 60 Relics

SER.1 ODDS 1:47 HOBBY
AD Andre Dawson 2.50 6.00
AG Adrian Gonzalez 3.00 8.00
AJ Adam Jones S2 2.50 6.00
AR Aramis Ramirez 1.50 4.00
AR Aramis Ramirez S2 1.50 4.00
AS Alfonso Soriano S2 2.50 6.00
BL Barry Larkin 2.50 6.00
BR Babe Ruth 250.00 400.00
CB Carlos Beltran 2.50 6.00
CK Clayton Kershaw S2 8.00 20.00
CM Carlos Marmol 2.50 6.00
CM Carlos Marmol S2 2.50 6.00
CS Curt Schilling 2.50 6.00
CU1 Chase Utley Bat S2 2.50 6.00
CU2 Chase Utley Jsy S2 2.50 6.00
CZ Carlos Zambrano 2.50 6.00
DB Daniel Bard S2 1.50 4.00
DJ Derek Jeter 8.00 25.00
DJ Derek Jeter S2 8.00 20.00
DM Don Mattingly 6.00 15.00
DO David Ortiz S2 4.00 10.00
DP Dustin Pedroia 3.00 8.00
DW Dave Winfield 2.50 6.00
EL Evan Longoria 4.00 10.00
FC Fausto Carmona 1.50 4.00
FH Felix Hernandez 2.50 6.00
GC Gary Carter 2.50 6.00
GG Goose Gossage 2.50 6.00
GS Geovany Soto 2.50 6.00
GS Geovany Soto S2 2.50 6.00
HA Hank Aaron S2 12.00 30.00
HJ Howard Johnson 1.50 4.00
IK Ian Kinsler S2 2.50 6.00
IS Ichiro Suzuki 8.00 20.00
JA Jonathan Albaladejo 1.50 4.00
JB Josh Beckett S2 1.50 4.00
JC Joba Chamberlain 1.50 4.00
JE Jacoby Ellsbury 3.00 8.00
JH Josh Hamilton 2.50 6.00
JH Jason Heyward S2 3.00 8.00
JL Jon Lester S2 2.50 6.00
JM Joe Morgan 2.50 6.00
JR Jimmy Rollins 2.50 6.00
JR Jackie Robinson S2 8.00 20.00
JU Justin Upton 2.50 6.00
JW Jered Weaver 2.50 6.00
KF Kosuke Fukudome 2.50 6.00
LB Lew Burdette 1.50 4.00
MB Marlon Byrd S2 1.50 4.00
MG Matt Garza 1.50 4.00
MH Matt Holliday 4.00 10.00
MK Matt Kemp 3.00 8.00
ML Mat Latos S2 2.50 6.00
MP Mike Piazza 4.00 10.00
MR Manny Ramirez 4.00 10.00
MR Mark Reynolds S2 1.50 4.00
MS Marco Scutaro S2 2.50 6.00
MT Mark Teixeira 2.50 6.00
MT Mark Teixeira S2 2.50 6.00
MY Michael Young S2 1.50 4.00
NR Nolan Ryan 4.00 10.00
NS Nick Swisher S2 2.50 6.00
OS Ozzie Smith 5.00 12.00
PF Prince Fielder 2.50 6.00
PF Prince Fielder S2 2.50 6.00
PH Phil Hughes S2 1.50 4.00
PS Pablo Sandoval S2 2.50 6.00
RA Roberto Alomar 2.50 6.00
RC Roy Campanella S2 10.00 25.00
RD Ryan Dempster S2 1.50 4.00
RH Ryan Howard 3.00 8.00
RH Rickey Henderson S2 4.00 10.00
RI Raul Ibanez 2.50 6.00
RR Robin Roberts 6.00 15.00
RZ Ryan Zimmerman S2 2.50 6.00
SB Sal Bando 1.50 4.00
SC Starlin Castro S2 2.50 6.00
SG Steve Garvey 1.50 4.00
SV Shane Victorino S2 2.50 6.00
TC Tyler Colvin 1.50 4.00
TC Tyler Colvin S2 1.50 4.00
TG Tony Gwynn 4.00 10.00
TH Torii Hunter 1.50 4.00
TT Troy Tulowitzki 1.50 4.00
VG Vladimir Guerrero S2 2.50 6.00
VM Victor Martinez 2.50 6.00
WB Wade Boggs 2.50 6.00
YB Yogi Berra 8.00 20.00
ABE Adrian Beltre 4.00 10.00

AGO Alex Gordon 2.50 6.00
AJB A.J. Burnett 1.50 4.00
APE Andy Pettitte 2.50 6.00
ARO Alex Rodriguez 5.00 12.00
BGA Brett Gardner 2.50 6.00
BGA Brett Gardner S2 2.50 6.00
CCS CC Sabathia 2.50 6.00
DLE Derrek Lee 1.50 4.00
DMC Daniel McCutchen 1.50 4.00
DWR David Wright 3.00 8.00
JCH Joba Chamberlain S2 1.50 4.00
JDA Johnny Damon 2.50 6.00
JDD J.D. Drew 1.50 4.00
JDD J.D. Drew S2 1.50 4.00
JLA John Lackey S2 2.50 6.00
JLO Jed Lowrie S2 1.50 4.00
JPA Jonathan Papelbon 2.50 6.00
JPO Jorge Posada 2.50 6.00
MBY Marlon Byrd 1.50 4.00
MRI Mariano Rivera 5.00 12.00
PHU Phil Hughes 1.50 4.00
PWR Pee Wee Reese 8.00 20.00
RCA Robinson Cano 2.50 6.00
RCA Robinson Cano S2 2.50 6.00
RHE Rickey Henderson 4.00 10.00
RWE Randy Wells S2 1.50 4.00
SCA Starlin Castro 2.50 6.00
SSC Shin-Soo Choo 2.50 6.00

2011 Topps 60 Relics Diamond Anniversary

*DA: .75X TO 2X BASIC
STATED PRINT RUN 99 SER.#'d SETS
DJ Derek Jeter S2 20.00 50.00
HA Hank Aaron S2 15.00 40.00
RH Rickey Henderson S2 15.00 40.00

2011 Topps 60 Years of Topps

COMPLETE SET (118) 30.00 60.00
COMP.SER.1 SET (59) 12.50 30.00
COMP.SER.2 SET (59) 12.50 30.00
SER.1 ODDS 1:3 HOBBY
1-59 ISSUED IN SER.1
59-118 ISSUED IN SER.2
*ORIGINAL BACK: .6X TO 1.5X BASIC
ORIGINAL ODDS 1:36 HOBBY
1 Jackie Robinson .75 2.00
2 Roy Campanella .75 2.00
3 Monte Irvin .50 1.25
4 Ernie Banks .75 2.00
5 Phil Rizzuto .50 1.25
6 Mickey Mantle 2.50 6.00
7 Pee Wee Reese .50 1.25
8 Roger Maris .75 2.00
9 Stan Musial 1.25 3.00
10 Juan Marichal .50 1.25
11 Gaylord Perry .50 1.25
12 Frank Robinson .50 1.25
13 Bob Gibson .50 1.25
14 Lou Brock .50 1.25
15 Al Kaline .75 2.00
16 Tony Perez .50 1.25
17 Frank Robinson/Brooks Robinson .50 1.25
18 Tom Seaver .50 1.25
19 Reggie Jackson .50 1.25
20 Nolan Ryan 2.50 6.00
21 Rod Carew .50 1.25
22 Carlton Fisk .50 1.25
23 Mike Schmidt 1.25 3.00
24 Carl Yastrzemski 1.25 3.00
25 Robin Yount .75 2.00
26 Bruce Sutter .50 1.25
27 P.Niekro/N.Ryan 2.50 6.00
28 Eddie Murray .50 1.25
29 Paul Molitor .75 2.00
30 Andre Dawson .50 1.25
31 Jim Palmer .50 1.25
32 Ozzie Smith 1.00 2.50
33 Tony Gwynn .75 2.00
34 Steve Garvey .30 .75
35 Dave Winfield .50 1.25
36 Dennis Eckersley .50 1.25
37 Greg Maddux 1.00 2.50
38 Bo Jackson .75 2.00
39 Bernie Williams .50 1.25
40 Roberto Alomar .50 1.25
41 Frank Thomas .75 2.00
42 Jim Edmonds .50 1.25
43 Mike Piazza .75 2.00
44 Barry Larkin .50 1.25
45 Mickey Mantle 2.50 6.00
46 Mariano Rivera 1.00 2.50
47 Bob Abreu .30 .75
48 Mike Piazza/Ivan Rodriguez/Jason Kendall .75 2.00
49 Alex Rodriguez 1.00 2.50
50 Manny Ramirez .75 2.00
51 Vladimir Guerrero .50 1.25
52 Cliff Lee .50 1.25
53 Mark Teixeira .50 1.25
54 Justin Verlander .75 2.00
55 Ryan Howard .60 1.50
56 Troy Tulowitzki .75 2.00
57 Johnny Cueto .50 1.25
58 Joe Mauer .60 1.50
59 Albert Pujols 1.00 2.50
60 Yogi Berra .75 2.00
61 Warren Spahn .50 1.25
62 Jackie Robinson .75 2.00
63 Ed Mathews .75 2.00
64 Mickey Mantle 2.50 6.00
65 Brooks Robinson .50 1.25
66 Luis Aparicio .50 1.25
67 Richie Ashburn .50 1.25
68 Harmon Killebrew .75 2.00
69 Stan Musial 1.25 3.00
70 Orlando Cepeda .50 1.25
71 Duke Snider .50 1.25
72 Carl Yastrzemski 1.25 3.00
73 Frank Robinson .50 1.25
74 Roger Maris .75 2.00
75 Steve Carlton .50 1.25
76 Ernie Banks .75 2.00
77 Johnny Bench .75 2.00
78 Tom Seaver .50 1.25
79 Gaylord Perry .50 1.25
80 Nolan Ryan 2.50 6.00
81 Rich Gossage .50 1.25
82 Dave Parker .30 .75
83 Reggie Jackson .50 1.25
84 Dave Winfield .50 1.25
85 Don Sutton .50 1.25
86 Gary Carter .50 1.25
87 Eddie Murray .50 1.25
88 Ron Guidry .30 .75
89 Jim Palmer .50 1.25
90 Steve Garvey .30 .75
91 Cal Ripken Jr. 2.50 6.00
92 Rickey Henderson .75 2.00
93 Andre Dawson .50 1.25
94 Don Mattingly 1.50 4.00
95 Ozzie Smith 1.00 2.50
96 Dale Murphy .75 2.00
97 Paul Molitor .75 2.00
98 Curt Schilling .50 1.25
99 Larry Walker .50 1.25
100 Wade Boggs .50 1.25
101 Craig Biggio .50 1.25
102 Manny Ramirez .75 2.00
103 Frank Thomas .75 2.00
104 Derek Jeter 2.00 5.00
105 Tony Gwynn .75 2.00
106 Mariano Rivera 1.00 2.50
107 Roy Halladay .50 1.25
108 Chris Carpenter .50 1.25
109 David Ortiz .75 2.00
110 Josh Beckett .30 .75
111 Albert Pujols 1.00 2.50
112 A.Rodriguez/D.Jeter 2.00 5.00
113 Billy Butler .30 .75
114 Hanley Ramirez .50 1.25
115 Josh Hamilton .50 1.25
116 Ryan Braun .50 1.25
117 E.Longoria/D.Price .60 1.50
118 Buster Posey 1.00 2.50

2011 Topps 60 Years of Topps Original Back

*ORIGINAL BACK: .6X TO 1.5X BASIC
SER.1 ODDS 1:36 HOBBY
1-59 ISSUED IN SER.1
60-118 ISSUED IN SER.2

2011 Topps 60th Anniversary Reprint Autographs

SER.1 ODDS 1:14,750 HOBBY
EXCHANGE DEADLINE 1/31/2014
AK Al Kaline S2 60.00 150.00
BG Bob Gibson 40.00 100.00
'59 Topps/60
BR Brooks Robinson 40.00 80.00
EB Ernie Banks EXCH 40.00 80.00
EM Eddie Murray S2 60.00 120.00
FR Frank Robinson EXCH 40.00 80.00
HA Henry Aaron S2 250.00 350.00
MS Mike Schmidt S2 30.00 60.00
PM Paul Molitor S2 50.00 100.00
RJ Reggie Jackson 100.00 200.00
RS Ryne Sandberg 75.00 150.00
SK Sandy Koufax S2 200.00 400.00
SM Stan Musial S2 250.00 350.00
TG Tony Gwynn S2 50.00 100.00
TS Tom Seaver EXCH 60.00 150.00
WB Wade Boggs S2 50.00 100.00

2011 Topps 60th Anniversary Reprint Relics

SER.1 ODDS 1:7817 HOBBY
STATED PRINT RUN 60 SER.#'d SETS
AD Andre Dawson S2 60.00 120.00
AK Al Kaline S2 10.00 25.00
AR Alex Rodriguez 30.00 60.00
BB Bert Blyleven S2 10.00 25.00
BG Bob Gibson 25.00 60.00
BR Brooks Robinson 40.00 80.00
CF Carlton Fisk S2 10.00* 25.00
CY Carl Yastrzemski 15.00 40.00
DJ Derek Jeter 75.00 150.00
DM Dale Murphy S2 10.00 25.00
DW Dave Winfield S2 30.00 60.00
EB Ernie Banks 50.00 100.00
EM Eddie Murray S2 10.00 25.00
FR Frank Robinson 10.00 25.00
FT Frank Thomas S2 30.00 60.00
HA Henry Aaron S2 10.00 25.00
HK Harmon Killebrew S2 10.00 25.00
JB Johnny Bench 30.00 60.00
JM Joe Mauer 12.00 30.00
JM Joe Morgan S2 50.00 100.00
JR Jackie Robinson 10.00 25.00
LB Lou Brock S2 10.00 25.00
MS Mike Schmidt S2 40.00 80.00
NR Nolan Ryan 10.00 25.00
NR Nolan Ryan S2 10.00 25.00
PM Paul Molitor S2 30.00 60.00
RA Roberto Alomar S2 10.00 25.00
RC Roy Campanella 10.00 25.00
RH Rickey Henderson 30.00 60.00
RJ Reggie Jackson 10.00 25.00
RS Ryne Sandberg 30.00 60.00
SK Sandy Koufax S2 50.00 100.00
SM Stan Musial S2 30.00 60.00
TG Tony Gwynn S2 40.00 80.00
TM Thurman Munson 10.00 25.00
TS Tom Seaver 40.00 80.00
WB Wade Boggs S2 10.00 25.00
WM Willie McCovey 30.00 60.00
YB Yogi Berra 10.00 25.00

2011 Topps Before There Was Topps

COMPLETE SET (7) 4.00 10.00
COMMON CARD .75 2.00
BTT1 American Tobacco 1909 T206 .75 2.00
BTT2 American Tobacco 1911 T205 .75 2.00
BTT3 American Tobacco 1911 T201 .75 2.00
BTT4 Exhibit Supply Company 1921 .75 2.00
BTT5 Goudey 1933 .75 2.00
BTT6 Gum Inc 1939 Play Ball .75 2.00
BTT7 Bowman 1948-1955 .75 2.00

2011 Topps Black Diamond Wrapper Redemption

COMPLETE SET (60) 60.00 120.00
1 Cliff Lee 1.25 3.00
2 Roy Halladay 1.25 3.00
3 Zack Greinke 1.25 3.00
4 David Wright 1.50 4.00
5 Justin Upton 1.25 3.00
6 Joey Votto 2.00 5.00
7 CC Sabathia 1.25 3.00
8 Ichiro Suzuki 2.50 6.00
9 Jered Weaver 1.25 3.00
10 Adrian Gonzalez 1.50 4.00
11 Albert Pujols 2.50 6.00
12 Joe Mauer 1.50 4.00
13 Adam Dunn 1.25 3.00
14 Ryan Zimmerman 1.25 3.00
15 Adam Jones 1.25 3.00
16 Tim Lincecum 1.25 3.00
17 Carlos Gonzalez 1.25 3.00
18 Mark Teixeira 1.25 3.00
19 Mat Latos 1.25 3.00
20 Ubaldo Jimenez .75 2.00
21 Prince Fielder 1.25 3.00
22 Victor Martinez 1.25 3.00
23 Ian Kinsler 1.25 3.00
24 Dan Uggla .75 2.00
25 Justin Morneau 1.25 3.00
26 Brian McCann 1.25 3.00
27 Josh Johnson 1.25 3.00
28 Roy Oswalt 1.25 3.00
29 Chase Utley 1.25 3.00
30 Jose Reyes 1.25 3.00
31 Felix Hernandez 1.25 3.00
32 Alex Rodriguez 2.50 6.00
33 Troy Tulowitzki 2.00 5.00
34 Dustin Pedroia 1.50 4.00
35 Adam Wainwright 1.25 3.00
36 David Price 1.50 4.00
37 Jon Lester 1.25 3.00
38 Josh Hamilton 1.25 3.00
39 Aroldis Chapman 2.50 6.00
40 Jason Heyward 1.50 4.00
41 Ryan Braun 1.25 3.00
42 Matt Holliday 2.00 5.00
43 Buster Posey 2.50 6.00
44 Nick Markakis 1.50 4.00
45 Kevin Youkilis .75 2.00
46 Clayton Kershaw 4.00 10.00
47 Evan Longoria 1.25 3.00
48 Andre Ethier 1.25 3.00
49 Hanley Ramirez 1.25 3.00
50 Robinson Cano 1.25 3.00
51 Andrew McCutchen 2.00 5.00
52 Martin Prado .75 2.00
53 Carl Crawford 1.25 3.00
54 Derek Jeter 5.00 12.00
55 Torii Hunter .75 2.00
56 Mark Reynolds .75 2.00
57 Miguel Cabrera 2.00 5.00
58 Mike Stanton 2.00 5.00
59 Starlin Castro 1.25 3.00
60 Ryan Howard 1.50 4.00

2011 Topps Black Diamond Wrapper Redemption Autographs

STATED PRINT RUN 60 SER.#'d SETS
RA1 Monte Irvin 50.00 100.00
RA2 Irv Noren 12.50 30.00
RA3 Roy Sievers 15.00 40.00
RA4 Vernon Law 30.00 60.00
RA5 Bill Pierce 75.00 150.00
RA6 Eddie Yost 12.00 30.00
RA7 John Antonelli 30.00 60.00
RA8 Charlie Silvera 50.00 100.00
RA9 Roy Smalley 12.50 30.00
RA10 Curt Simmons 125.00 250.00
RA11 Ned Garver 40.00 80.00
RA12 Bobby Shantz 30.00 60.00
RA13 Joe Presko 75.00 150.00
RA14 Bob Friend 20.00 50.00
RA15 Jerry Coleman 100.00 200.00
RA16 Virgil Trucks 75.00 150.00
RA17 Chuck Diering 10.00 25.00
RA18 Lou Brissie 10.00 25.00
RA19 Joe DeMaestri 10.00 25.00
RA20 Randy Jackson 12.00 30.00
RA21 Ivan Delock 30.00 60.00
RA22 Bob DelGreco 75.00 150.00
RA23 Dick Groat 30.00 60.00
RA24 Johnny Groth 20.00 50.00
RA25 Eddie Robinson 12.50 30.00
RA26 Cloyd Boyer 20.00* 50.00
RA29 Joe Astroth 10.00 25.00
RA30 Del Crandall 20.00 50.00
RA31 Ralph Branca 40.00 80.00
RA32 Red Schoendienst 25.00 60.00
RA33 Yogi Berra 60.00 150.00
RA34 Joe Garagiola 20.00 50.00

2011 Topps CMG Reprints

COMPLETE SET (30) 12.50 30.00
STATED ODDS 1:8 HOBBY
CMGR1 Babe Ruth 2.00 5.00
CMGR2 Babe Ruth 2.00 5.00
CMGR3 Hank Greenberg .75 2.00
CMGR4 Babe Ruth 2.00 5.00
CMGR5 Babe Ruth 2.00 5.00
CMGR6 Christy Mathewson .75 2.00
CMGR7 Jackie Robinson .75 2.00
CMGR8 Cy Young .75 2.00
CMGR9 George Sisler .50 1.25
CMGR10 Honus Wagner .75 2.00
CMGR11 Honus Wagner .75 2.00
CMGR12 Honus Wagner .75 2.00
CMGR13 Honus Wagner .75 2.00
CMGR14 Jackie Robinson .75 2.00
CMGR15 Jimmie Foxx .75 2.00
CMGR16 Jimmie Foxx .75 2.00
CMGR17 Jimmie Foxx .75 2.00
CMGR18 Johnny Mize/Enos Slaughter .50 1.25
CMGR19 Walter Johnson .75 2.00
CMGR20 Lou Gehrig 1.50 4.00
CMGR21 Lou Gehrig 1.50 4.00
CMGR22 Mel Ott .75 2.00
CMGR23 Rogers Hornsby .50 1.25
CMGR24 Lou Gehrig 1.50 4.00
CMGR25 Ty Cobb 1.25 3.00
CMGR26 Ty Cobb 1.25 3.00
CMGR27 Ty Cobb 1.25 3.00
CMGR28 Ty Cobb 1.25 3.00
CMGR29 Ty Cobb 1.25 3.00
CMGR30 Walter Johnson .75 2.00

2011 Topps Commemorative Patch

RANDOM INSERTS IN PACKS
AC Aroldis Chapman S2 5.00 12.00
AE Andre Ethier 4.00 10.00
AG Adrian Gonzalez 6.00 15.00
AG Adrian Gonzalez S2 6.00 15.00
AJ Adam Jones 5.00 12.00
AK Al Kaline UPD 10.00 25.00
AM Andrew McCutchen 5.00 12.00
AM Andrew McCutchen S2 5.00 12.00
AP Albert Pujols 8.00 20.00
AP Albert Pujols S2 8.00 20.00
AW Adam Wainwright 5.00 12.00
BA Brett Anderson S2 4.00 10.00
BB Brandon Belt UPD 8.00 20.00
BF Bob Feller S2 5.00 12.00
BG Bob Gibson UPD 8.00 20.00
BL Barry Larkin UPD 8.00 20.00
BM Brandon Morrow 4.00 10.00
BM Brian McCann S2 6.00 15.00
BM Bill Mazeroski UPD 8.00 20.00
BP Buster Posey 6.00 15.00
BP Buster Posey S2 6.00 15.00
BR Brian Roberts S2 5.00 12.00
BR Babe Ruth UPD 8.00 15.00
BW Brian Wilson S2 5.00 12.00
CB Chad Billingsley S2 5.00 12.00
CF Carlton Fisk UPD 6.00 15.00
CH Cole Hamels 5.00 12.00
CK Clayton Kershaw 5.00 12.00
CL Cliff Lee S2 6.00 15.00
CR Cal Ripken Jr. S2 8.00 20.00
CS Carlos Santana 5.00 12.00
CU Chase Utley 8.00 20.00
DG Dee Gordon UPD 5.00 12.00
DJ Derek Jeter 10.00 25.00
DL Derrek Lee S2 5.00 12.00
DO David Ortiz 6.00 15.00
DP David Price UPD 5.00 12.00
DW David Wright 5.00 12.00
DW David Wright S2 5.00 12.00
EH Eric Hosmer UPD 10.00 25.00
EL Evan Longoria 6.00 15.00
EM Eddie Murray UPD 4.00 10.00
FF Freddie Freeman UPD 8.00 20.00
FH Felix Hernandez 5.00 12.00
FH Felix Hernandez S2 5.00 12.00
FJ Fergie Jenkins UPD 5.00 12.00
FR Frank Robinson UPD 5.00 12.00
FT Frank Thomas UPD 8.00 20.00
GG Gio Gonzalez 4.00 10.00
GP Gaylord Perry UPD 5.00 12.00
GS Grady Sizemore S2 5.00 12.00
HA Hank Aaron S2 12.50 30.00
HA Hank Aaron UPD 8.00 20.00
HP Hunter Pence 5.00 12.00
ID Ian Desmond 4.00 10.00
IK Ian Kinsler S2 4.00 10.00
IS Ichiro Suzuki 8.00 20.00
IS Ichiro Suzuki S2 8.00 20.00
JB Josh Bell 4.00 10.00
JB Jose Bautista S2 6.00 15.00
JB Johnny Bench UPD 5.00 12.00
JF Jimmie Foxx UPD 6.00 15.00
JH Jason Heyward 6.00 15.00
JM Joe Mauer 6.00 15.00
JM Juan Marichal UPD 5.00 12.00
JP Jim Palmer S2 6.00 15.00
JR Jose Reyes 6.00 15.00
JR Jose Reyes S2 6.00 15.00
JS John Smoltz UPD 5.00 12.00
JU Justin Upton 4.00 10.00
JV Joey Votto 6.00 15.00
JW Jered Weaver S2 5.00 12.00
KS Kurt Suzuki 4.00 10.00
KU Koji Uehara 4.00 10.00
LA Luis Aparicio UPD 10.00 25.00
MB Madison Bumgarner S2 5.00 12.00
MC Miguel Cabrera 5.00 12.00
MG Matt Garza S2 5.00 12.00
MH Matt Holliday 4.00 10.00
MI Monte Irvin UPD 6.00 15.00
MK Matt Kemp S2 5.00 12.00
ML Mat Latos 4.00 10.00
ML Mat Latos S2 4.00 10.00
MP Martin Prado S2 5.00 12.00
MP Michael Pineda UPD 5.00 12.00
MR Manny Ramirez 4.00 10.00
MR Mark Reynolds S2 5.00 12.00
MS Mike Schmidt S2 8.00 20.00
MS Mike Schmidt UPD 8.00 20.00
NM Nick Markakis 5.00 12.00
NR Nolan Ryan S2 10.00 25.00
NR Nolan Ryan UPD 12.50 30.00
OS Ozzie Smith UPD 10.00 25.00
PA Pedro Alvarez S2 5.00 12.00
PF Prince Fielder S2 5.00 12.00
PM Paul Molitor UPD 6.00 15.00
PO Paul O'Neill UPD 4.00 10.00
PS Pablo Sandoval 4.00 10.00
RA Roberto Alomar S2 6.00 15.00
RA Roberto Alomar UPD 6.00 15.00
RB Ryan Braun S2 6.00 15.00
RB Ryan Braun UPD 5.00 12.00
RC Robinson Cano S2 6.00 15.00
RF Rollie Fingers UPD 6.00 15.00
RH Roy Halladay 6.00 15.00
RH Rickey Henderson S2 6.00 15.00
RH Rickey Henderson UPD 6.00 15.00
RJ Reggie Jackson S2 6.00 15.00
RJ Reggie Jackson UPD 10.00 25.00
RM Roger Maris UPD 8.00 20.00
RS Ryne Sandberg UPD 12.50 30.00
RZ Ryan Zimmerman 5.00 12.00
RZ Ryan Zimmerman S2 5.00 12.00
SC Starlin Castro 5.00 12.00
SD Stephen Drew S2 4.00 10.00
SG Steve Garvey UPD 12.50 30.00
SS Stephen Strasburg 6.00 15.00
TC Trevor Cahill 4.00 10.00
TG Tony Gwynn S2 6.00 15.00
TH Torii Hunter 4.00 10.00
TL Tim Lincecum 6.00 15.00
TS Tom Seaver S2 6.00 15.00
TS Tom Seaver UPD 6.00 15.00
VW Vernon Wells 4.00 10.00
WM Willie McCovey UPD 4.00 10.00
ZB Zach Britton UPD 4.00 10.00
BMA Brian Matusz 6.00 15.00
CFI Carlton Fisk UPD 6.00 15.00
CLE Carlos Lee S2 4.00 10.00
FJE Fergie Jenkins UPD 5.00 12.00
IDA Ike Davis 4.00 10.00
ISU Ichiro Suzuki 4.00 10.00
ISU Ichiro Suzuki S2 4.00 10.00
JBA Jose Bautista UPD 4.00 10.00
JHA Josh Hamilton 8.00 20.00
JMI Johnny Mize UPD 8.00 20.00
JMO Joe Morgan UPD 5.00 12.00
JWE Jayson Werth S2 5.00 12.00
JWR Jayson Werth UPD 5.00 12.00
NRY Nolan Ryan S2 10.00 25.00
NRY Nolan Ryan UPD 12.50 30.00
PMO Paul Molitor UPD 6.00 15.00
RAL Roberto Alomar S2 6.00 15.00
RAL Roberto Alomar UPD 6.00 15.00
RED Red Schoendienst UPD 8.00 20.00
RHO Ryan Howard 6.00 15.00
RJA Reggie Jackson UPD 10.00 25.00
RZI Ryan Zimmerman S2 5.00 12.00
SSC Shin-Soo Choo 6.00 15.00
THA Tommy Hanson 4.00 10.00

2011 Topps Diamond Anniversary Autographs

SOME HARPER ISSUED IN 2010 BOW.STER.
STATED PRINT RUN 60 SER.#'d SETS
60AAK Al Kaline 25.00 50.00
60ANR Nolan Ryan 50.00 100.00
60AAC Andrew Cashner 40.00 80.00
60AAD1 Andre Dawson 50.00 100.00
60AAD2 Andre Dawson Expos 20.00 50.00
60AAE Andre Ethier 20.00 50.00
60AAJ Adam Jones 40.00 80.00
60ABG Bob Gibson 60.00 120.00
60ABH Bryce Harper 150.00 300.00
60ABM Brian McCann 75.00 150.00
60ABR Brooks Robinson 40.00 80.00
60ACB Clay Buchholz 20.00 50.00
60ACF Carlton Fisk 40.00 80.00
60ACG Carlos Gonzalez 10.00 25.00
60ACJ Chipper Jones 75.00 150.00
60ACR Cal Ripken Jr. 100.00 200.00
60ACS Charlie Sheen 250.00 500.00
60ACU Chase Utley 50.00 100.00
60ACY Carl Yastrzemski 75.00 150.00
60ADM Don Mattingly 75.00 150.00
60ADM Dale Murphy 20.00 50.00
60ADO David Ortiz 50.00 100.00
60ADW David Wright 60.00 120.00
60AEB Ernie Banks 75.00 150.00
60AEL Evan Longoria 30.00 60.00
60AEM Eddie Murray 60.00 120.00
60AFJ Fergie Jenkins 12.00 30.00
60AFR Frank Robinson 25.00 60.00
60AFT Frank Thomas 200.00 300.00
60AGB Gordon Beckham 10.00 25.00
60AGC Gary Carter Expos 30.00 60.00
60AGC Gary Carter 20.00 50.00
60AHA Hank Aaron 100.00 200.00
60AHR Hanley Ramirez 20.00 50.00
60AIK Ian Kinsler 30.00 60.00
60AJB Johnny Bench 40.00 80.00
60AJH Jason Heyward 20.00 40.00
60AJH Josh Hamilton 125.00 250.00
60AJJ Josh Johnson 30.00 60.00
60AJM Joe Morgan 40.00 80.00
60AJM Juan Marichal 15.00 40.00
60AJU Justin Upton 20.00 50.00
60AKO Keith Olbermann 40.00 80.00
60ALA Luis Aparicio 30.00 60.00
60AMK Matt Kemp 30.00 60.00
60AMR Mariano Rivera 100.00 200.00
60AMS Mike Schmidt 75.00 150.00
60AMS Mike Stanton 150.00 300.00
60ANC Nelson Cruz 12.00 30.00
60ANM Nick Markakis 20.00 50.00
60AOC Orlando Cepeda 20.00 50.00
60APG Peter Gammons 50.00 100.00
60APM Paul Molitor 20.00 50.00
60APS Pablo Sandoval 20.00 50.00
60ARA Roberto Alomar 50.00 100.00
60ARJ Reggie Jackson A's 30.00 60.00
60ARJ Reggie Jackson Yankees 30.00 60.00
60ARK Ralph Kiner 150.00 250.00
60ARO Ryan O'Hara 150.00 250.00
60ARS Ryne Sandberg 60.00 120.00
60ASB Sy Berger 75.00 150.00
60ASM Stan Musial 200.00 350.00
60ASS Stephen Strasburg 175.00 350.00
60ATG Tony Gwynn 40.00 80.00
60ATP Tony Perez 30.00 60.00

2011 Topps Diamond Die Cut

DDC1 Ryan Braun 3.00 8.00
DDC2 Mickey Mantle 15.00 40.00
DDC3 Aaron Hill 2.00 5.00
DDC4 Tim Hudson 3.00 8.00
DDC5 CC Sabathia 3.00 8.00
DDC6 Shin-Soo Choo 3.00 8.00
DDC7 Andrew McCutchen 5.00 12.00
DDC8 Hank Aaron 10.00 25.00
DDC9 Max Scherzer 5.00 12.00
DDC10 Miguel Cabrera 5.00 12.00
DDC11 Brian Matusz 2.00 5.00
DDC12 Jackie Robinson 5.00 12.00
DDC13 Chipper Jones 5.00 12.00
DDC14 Johan Santana 3.00 8.00
DDC15 Andre Ethier 3.00 8.00
DDC16 Justin Upton 3.00 8.00
DDC17 Johnny Cueto 3.00 8.00
DDC18 Gordon Beckham 2.00 5.00
DDC19 Alex Rios 2.00 5.00
DDC20 Nolan Ryan 15.00 40.00
DDC21 Rickey Henderson 5.00 12.00
DDC22 Carlos Marmol 3.00 8.00
DDC23 Matt Cain 3.00 8.00
DDC24 Adam Wainwright 3.00 8.00
DDC25 Vladimir Guerrero 3.00 8.00
DDC26 Mike Minor 2.00 5.00
DDC27 Ricky Romero 2.00 5.00
DDC28 Delmon Young 3.00 8.00
DDC29 Brett Anderson 2.00 5.00
DDC30 Evan Longoria 3.00 8.00
DDC31 Brett Wallace 2.00 5.00
DDC32 Cal Ripken Jr. 15.00 40.00
DDC33 Tommy Hanson 2.00 5.00
DDC34 Mark Buehrle 3.00 8.00
DDC35 Mariano Rivera 6.00 15.00
DDC36 Stephen Drew 2.00 5.00
DDC37 Ubaldo Jimenez 2.00 5.00
DDC38 Alexei Ramirez 3.00 8.00
DDC39 Thurman Munson 5.00 12.00
DDC40 Felix Hernandez 3.00 8.00
DDC41 Adrian Beltre 5.00 12.00
DDC42 Ian Kinsler 3.00 8.00
DDC43 Billy Butler 2.00 5.00
DDC44 Carlos Ruiz 2.00 5.00
DDC45 Stephen Strasburg 5.00 12.00
DDC46 Vernon Wells 2.00 5.00
DDC47 Ian Desmond 2.00 5.00
DDC48 Matt Holliday 5.00 12.00
DDC49 Ike Davis 2.00 5.00
DDC50 Ryan Howard 6.00 15.00
DDC51 Andrew Bailey 2.00 5.00
DDC52 David Ortiz 5.00 12.00
DDC53 Jimmy Rollins 3.00 8.00
DDC54 Ernie Banks 5.00 12.00
DDC55 Ryan Zimmerman 3.00 8.00
DDC56 Alex Rodriguez 6.00 15.00
DDC57 Brian McCann 3.00 8.00
DDC58 Tim Lincecum 3.00 8.00
DDC59 Freddie Freeman 30.00 80.00
DDC60 David Wright 4.00 10.00
DDC61 Carlos Quentin 2.00 5.00
DDC62 Adam Jones 3.00 8.00
DDC63 Brandon Morrow 2.00 5.00
DDC64 Chris Sale 12.00 30.00
DDC65 Reggie Jackson 3.00 8.00
DDC66 Carl Yastrzemski 8.00 20.00
DDC67 Sandy Koufax 10.00 25.00
DDC68 Nick Markakis 4.00 10.00
DDC69 Jair Jurrjens 2.00 5.00
DDC70 Josh Hamilton 3.00 8.00
DDC71 Prince Fielder 3.00 8.00
DDC72 Cole Hamels 4.00 10.00
DDC73 Kelly Johnson 2.00 5.00
DDC74 Colby Rasmus 3.00 8.00
DDC75 Tony Gwynn 5.00 12.00
DDC76 Hank Greenberg 5.00 12.00
DDC77 Tom Seaver 3.00 8.00
DDC78 Bob Gibson 3.00 8.00
DDC79 Fausto Carmona 2.00 5.00
DDC80 Joe Mauer 4.00 10.00
DDC81 Jose Bautista 3.00 8.00
DDC82 Yunel Escobar 2.00 5.00
DDC83 Jeremy Hellickson 5.00 12.00
DDC84 Josh Beckett 2.00 5.00
DDC85 Hanley Ramirez 3.00 8.00
DDC86 Yadier Molina 5.00 12.00
DDC87 Corey Hart 2.00 5.00
DDC88 Hunter Pence 3.00 8.00
DDC89 Roger Maris 5.00 12.00
DDC90 Ichiro Suzuki 6.00 15.00
DDC91 Martin Prado 2.00 5.00
DDC92 Starlin Castro 3.00 8.00
DDC93 Kendry Morales 2.00 5.00
DDC94 Marlon Byrd 2.00 5.00
DDC95 Domonic Brown 4.00 10.00
DDC96 Dave Winfield 3.00 8.00
DDC97 Wade Boggs 3.00 8.00
DDC98 Heath Bell 2.00 5.00
DDC99 Dan Haren 2.00 5.00
DDC100 Albert Pujols 6.00 15.00
DDC101 Nelson Cruz 5.00 12.00
DDC102 Yovani Gallardo 2.00 5.00
DDC103 Howie Kendrick 2.00 5.00
DDC104 Desmond Jennings 3.00 8.00
DDC105 Troy Tulowitzki 5.00 12.00
DDC106 Gaby Sanchez 2.00 5.00
DDC107 Joakim Soria 2.00 5.00
DDC108 Clayton Kershaw 10.00 25.00
DDC109 Mike Schmidt 8.00 20.00
DDC110 Roy Halladay 3.00 8.00
DDC111 Jered Weaver 3.00 8.00
DDC112 Babe Ruth 12.00 30.00
DDC113 Wandy Rodriguez 2.00 5.00
DDC114 Torii Hunter 2.00 5.00
DDC115 Josh Johnson 3.00 8.00
DDC116 Justin Verlander 5.00 12.00
DDC117 Clay Buchholz 2.00 5.00
DDC118 Danny Valencia 3.00 8.00
DDC119 Kurt Suzuki 2.00 5.00
DDC120 David Price 4.00 10.00
DDC121 Daniel Hudson 2.00 5.00
DDC122 Neftali Feliz 2.00 5.00
DDC123 Michael Young 2.00 5.00
DDC124 Jose Reyes 3.00 8.00
DDC125 Robinson Cano 3.00 8.00
DDC126 Billy Wagner 2.00 5.00
DDC127 Miguel Montero 2.00 5.00
DDC128 Kevin Youkilis 2.00 5.00
DDC129 Austin Jackson 2.00 5.00
DDC130 Chase Utley 3.00 8.00
DDC131 Rickie Weeks 2.00 5.00
DDC132 Manny Ramirez 5.00 12.00
DDC133 Carlos Santana 5.00 12.00
DDC134 Aramis Ramirez 2.00 5.00
DDC135 Jason Heyward 4.00 10.00
DDC136 Chris Young 2.00 5.00
DDC137 Tyler Colvin 2.00 5.00
DDC138 Jon Jay 2.00 5.00
DDC139 Nick Swisher 3.00 8.00
DDC140 Mark Teixeira 3.00 8.00
DDC141 Jose Tabata 2.00 5.00
DDC142 Francisco Liriano 2.00 5.00

DDC143 Mike Stanton 5.00 12.00
DDC144 Grady Sizemore 3.00 8.00
DDC145 Justin Morneau 3.00 8.00
DDC146 Jon Lester 3.00 8.00
DDC147 Chris Carpenter 3.00 8.00
DDC148 Mark Reynolds 2.00 5.00
DDC149 Scott Rolen 3.00 8.00
DDC150 Carlos Gonzalez 3.00 8.00
DDC151 Derek Jeter 12.00 30.00
DDC152 Lou Gehrig 10.00 25.00
DDC153 Ryne Sandberg 10.00 25.00
DDC154 Jay Bruce 3.00 8.00
DDC155 Eric Hosmer 12.00 30.00

2011 Topps Diamond Die Cut Black

*BLACK: 1X TO 2.5X BASIC
ISSUED VIA ONLINE REDEMPTION
STATED PRINT RUN 60 SER.#'D SETS

2011 Topps Diamond Duos

COMPLETE SET (30) 6.00 15.00
STATED ODDS 1:4 HOBBY
BD R.Braun/I.Davis .40 1.00
BW Lance Berkman/Brett Wallace .40 1.00
BY Wade Boggs/Kevin Youkilis .40 1.00
CC T.Cobb/M.Cabrera 1.00 2.50
CS Steve Carlton/CC Sabathia .40 1.00
GT Carlos Gonzalez/Troy Tulowitzki .60 1.50
HF J.Heyward/F.Freeman 4.00 10.00
HG Josh Hamilton/Vladimir Guerrero .40 1.00
HH R.Howard/J.Heyward .50 1.25
HJ Rickey Henderson
Desmond Jennings .60 1.50
HM Tommy Hanson/Mike Minor .25 .60
JC D.Jeter/R.Cano 1.50 4.00
JJ Reggie Jackson/Adam Jones .40 1.00
KA Ian Kinsler/Elvis Andrus .40 1.00
KL C.Kershaw/M.Latos 1.25 3.00
KT Harmon Killebrew/Jim Thome .60 1.50
LJ B.Larkin/D.Jeter 1.50 4.00
LZ E.Longoria/R.Zimmerman .40 1.00
MH G.Maddux/J.Hellickson .75 2.00
MP J.Mauer/B.Posey .75 2.00
PC A.Pujols/M.Cabrera .75 2.00
PG David Price/Matt Garza .50 1.25
RS Ramirez/Stanton .60 1.50
SC T.Seaver/A.Chapman .75 2.00
TR Frank Thomas/Manny Ramirez .60 1.50
TU Hisanori Takahashi/Koji Uehara .25 .60
UR Chase Utley/Jimmy Rollins .40 1.00
US Upton/Stanton .60 1.50
VG Joey Votto/Adrian Gonzalez .60 1.50
HHO Rogers Hornsby/Matt Holliday .60 1.50

2011 Topps Diamond Duos Series 2

COMPLETE SET (30) 6.00 15.00
DD1 Roy Halladay/Roy Oswalt .40 1.00
DD2 Chase Utley/Robinson Cano .40 1.00
DD3 Cliff Lee/Zack Greinke .40 1.00
DD4 Adrian Gonzalez/Carl Crawford .50 1.25
DD5 D.Uggla/J.Heyward .50 1.25
DD6 R.Braun/C.Gonzalez .40 1.00
DD7 Frank Thomas/Adam Dunn .60 1.50
DD8 Zack Greinke/Yovani Gallardo .40 1.00
DD9 Adrian Beltre/Elvis Andrus .60 1.50
DD10 Adrian Gonzalez/Kevin Youkilis .50 1.25
DD11 Carl Crawford/Jacoby Ellsbury .50 1.25
DD12 Troy Tulowitzki/Hanley Ramirez .60 1.50
DD13 A.Chapman/C.Sale 1.50 4.00
DD14 Ryan Zimmerman/Jayson Werth .40 1.00
DD15 T.Lincecum/B.Wilson .60 1.50
DD16 Josh Hamilton/Joey Votto .60 1.50
DD17 B.Posey/N.Feliz .75 2.00
DD18 Roy Halladay/Felix Hernandez .40 1.00
DD19 M.Cabrera/V.Martinez .60 1.50
DD20 Kershaw/Bumgarner 1.25 3.00
DD21 David Price/Jon Lester .50 1.25
DD22 Troy Tulowitzki/Ubaldo Jimenez .60 1.50
DD23 Cliff Lee/CC Sabathia .40 1.00
DD24 A.McCutchen/P.Alvarez .60 1.50
DD25 Mark Teixeira/Adrian Gonzalez .50 1.25
DD26 A.Rodriguez/E.Longoria .75 2.00
DD27 Johnson/Verlander .60 1.50
DD28 A.Pujols/M.Holliday .75 2.00
DD29 H.Aaron/J.Heyward 1.25 3.00
DD30 S.Koufax/C.Kershaw 1.25 3.00

2011 Topps Diamond Duos Relics

STATED ODDS 1:12,500 HOBBY
STATED PRINT RUN 50 SER.#'d SETS
DDR1 D.Jeter/R.Cano 12.00 30.00
DDR2 J.Mauer/B.Posey 50.00 100.00
DDR3 A.Pujols/M.Cabrera 30.00 60.00
DDR4 R.Howard/J.Heyward 40.00 80.00
DDR5 J.Hamilton/V.Guerrero 20.00 50.00
DDR6 E.Longoria/R.Zimmerman 10.00 25.00
DDR7 C.Utley/J.Rollins 30.00 60.00
DDR8 J.Votto/A.Gonzalez 10.00 25.00
DDR9 H.Ramirez/M.Stanton 15.00 40.00
DDR10 B.Larkin/D.Jeter 50.00 100.00
DDR11 R.Jackson/A.Jones 30.00 60.00
DDR12 T.Cobb/M.Cabrera 30.00 60.00
DDR13 W.Boggs/K.Youkilis 30.00 60.00
DDR14 C.Kershaw/M.Latos 30.00 60.00
DDR15 J.Upton/M.Stanton 10.00 25.00

2011 Topps Diamond Duos Relics Series 2

STATED PRINT RUN 50 SER.#'d SETS
DDR1 C.Utley/R.Cano 10.00 25.00
DDR2 H.Aaron/J.Heyward 40.00 80.00
DDR3 M.Cabrera/V.Martinez 12.50 30.00
DDR5 R.Braun/C.Gonzalez 12.50 30.00
DDR6 J.Lester/K.Youkilis 20.00 50.00
DDR7 R.Alomar/R.Cano 30.00 60.00
DDR8 I.Kinsler/N.Cruz 10.00 25.00
DDR9 T.Lincecum/B.Posey 50.00 100.00
DDR10 J.Hamilton/J.Votto 10.00 25.00
DDR11 B.Posey/N.Feliz 20.00 50.00
DDR12 R.Halladay/F.Hernandez 12.50 30.00
DDR13 A.Rodriguez/E.Longoria 40.00 80.00
DDR14 J.Johnson/J.Verlander 10.00 25.00
DDR15 A.Pujols/M.Holliday 20.00 50.00

2011 Topps Diamond Giveaway

COMPLETE SET (30) 40.00 100.00
COMP.SER.1 SET (10) 12.50 30.00
COMP.SER.2 SET (10) 12.50 30.00
COMP.UPD.SET (10) 12.50 30.00
APPX.SER.1 ODDS 1:9 HOBBY
TDG1 Mickey Mantle 2.00 5.00
TDG2 Jackie Robinson 2.00 5.00
TDG3 Reggie Jackson 2.00 5.00
TDG4 Albert Pujols 2.00 5.00
TDG5 Derek Jeter 2.00 5.00
TDG6 Roy Halladay 2.00 5.00
TDG7 Derek Jeter 2.00 5.00
TDG8 Albert Pujols 2.00 5.00
TDG9 Ryan Howard 2.00 5.00
TDG10 Tim Lincecum 2.00 5.00
TDG11 Tony Gwynn 2.00 5.00
TDG12 Mike Schmidt 2.00 5.00
TDG13 Nolan Ryan 2.00 5.00
TDG14 Jason Heyward 2.00 5.00
TDG15 Troy Tulowitzki 2.00 5.00
TDG16 Buster Posey 2.00 5.00
TDG17 Ryan Braun 2.00 5.00
TDG18 Evan Longoria 2.00 5.00
TDG19 Joe Mauer 2.00 5.00
TDG20 Kevin Youkilis 2.00 5.00
TDG21 Mickey Mantle 2.00 5.00
TDG22 Sandy Koufax 2.00 5.00
TDG23 Cal Ripken Jr. 2.00 5.00
TDG24 Adrian Gonzalez 2.00 5.00
TDG25 Adrian Beltre 2.00 5.00
TDG26 Carl Crawford 2.00 5.00
TDG27 Victor Martinez 2.00 5.00
TDG28 Cliff Lee 2.00 5.00
TDG29 Jose Bautista 2.00 5.00
TDG30 Prince Fielder 2.00 5.00

2011 Topps Diamond Stars

COMPLETE SET (25) 10.00 25.00
DS1 Evan Longoria .40 1.00
DS2 Troy Tulowitzki .60 1.50
DS3 Joe Mauer .50 1.25
DS4 Adrian Gonzalez .50 1.25
DS5 Joey Votto .60 1.50
DS6 Buster Posey .75 2.00
DS7 Chase Utley .40 1.00
DS8 David Wright .50 1.25
DS9 Hanley Ramirez .40 1.00
DS10 Albert Pujols .75 2.00
DS11 Roy Halladay .40 1.00
DS12 Alex Rodriguez .75 2.00
DS13 Jason Heyward .50 1.25
DS14 Miguel Cabrera .60 1.50
DS15 Cliff Lee .40 1.00
DS16 Felix Hernandez .40 1.00
DS17 Matt Holliday .60 1.50
DS18 Robinson Cano .40 1.00
DS19 Josh Hamilton .40 1.00
DS20 Ichiro Suzuki .75 2.00
DS21 Carl Crawford .40 1.00
DS22 Ryan Howard .50 1.25
DS23 Josh Johnson .40 1.00
DS24 Ryan Braun .40 1.00
DS25 Carlos Gonzalez .40 1.00

2011 Topps Factory Set All Star Bonus

COMPLETE SET (5) 3.00 8.00
1 Albert Pujols 1.25 3.00
2 Ichiro Suzuki 1.25 3.00
3 Roy Halladay .60 1.50
4 Tim Lincecum .60 1.50
5 Adrian Gonzalez .75 2.00

2011 Topps Factory Set Bonus

*BONUS: 5X TO 12X BASIC
*BONUS RC: 3X TO 8X BASIC
STATED PRINT RUN 75 SER.#'d SETS
145 Freddie Freeman 60.00 150.00

2011 Topps Factory Set Mantle Chrome Gold Refractors

200 Mickey Mantle 1963 Topps 6.00 15.00
200 Mickey Mantle 1962 Topps 6.00 15.00
300 Mickey Mantle 1961 Topps 6.00 15.00

2011 Topps Factory Set Mantle World Series Medallion

1 Mickey Mantle 1953 6.00 15.00
2 Mickey Mantle 1956 6.00 15.00
3 Mickey Mantle 1961 6.00 15.00

2011 Topps Glove Manufactured Leather Nameplates

SER.1 ODDS 1:461 HOBBY
BLACK: .5X TO 1.2X BASIC
SER.1 BLACK ODDS 1:1815 HOBBY
UPD.BLACK ODDS 1:935 HOBBY
BLACK PRINT RUN 99 SER.#'d SETS
SER.1 NICKNAME ODDS 1:200,000 HOBBY
UPD.NICKNAME ODDS 1:87,500 HOBBY
NICKNAME PRINT RUN 1 SER.#'d SET
NO NICKNAME PRICING AVAILABLE
AD Andre Dawson S2 4.00 10.00
AD Andre Dawson UPD 4.00 10.00
AE Andre Ethier 4.00 10.00
AG Adrian Gonzalez 4.00 10.00
AM Andrew McCutchen 4.00 10.00
AP Albert Pujols 8.00 20.00
AR Alex Rodriguez 5.00 12.00
AR Alex Rodriguez UPD 5.00 12.00
AW Adam Wainwright 6.00 15.00
BB Billy Butler 4.00 10.00
BB Brandon Belt UPD 4.00 10.00
BF Bob Feller S2 6.00 15.00
BG Bob Gibson S2 8.00 20.00
BM Bill Mazeroski S2 5.00 12.00
BP Buster Posey 10.00 25.00
BR Babe Ruth S2 10.00 25.00
BR Babe Ruth UPD 10.00 25.00
BW Brian Wilson UPD 4.00 10.00
BZ Ben Zobrist UPD 4.00 10.00
CC Carl Crawford 4.00 10.00
CF Carlton Fisk S2 4.00 10.00
CF Carlton Fisk UPD 4.00 10.00
CG Carlos Gonzalez 5.00 12.00
CH Cole Hamels UPD 4.00 10.00
CK Clayton Kershaw 4.00 10.00
CR Cal Ripken Jr. S2 5.00 12.00
CU Chase Utley 6.00 15.00
CY Carl Yastrzemski S2 6.00 15.00
DD Danny Duffy UPD 4.00 10.00
DJ Derek Jeter 10.00 25.00
DM Don Mattingly S2 6.00 15.00
DP David Price 4.00 10.00
DS Duke Snider UPD 4.00 10.00
DW David Wright 8.00 20.00
EH Eric Hosmer UPD 6.00 15.00
EL Evan Longoria 6.00 15.00
EM Eddie Murray S2 8.00 20.00
FH Felix Hernandez 4.00 10.00
FJ Fergie Jenkins S2 4.00 10.00
FJ Fergie Jenkins UPD 4.00 10.00
FR Frank Robinson S2 4.00 10.00
FR Frank Robinson UPD 4.00 10.00
FT Frank Thomas S2 4.00 10.00
FT Frank Thomas UPD 4.00 10.00
GM Greg Maddux S2 6.00 15.00
HA Hank Aaron S2 4.00 10.00
HA Hank Aaron UPD 4.00 10.00
HG Hank Greenberg S2 5.00 12.00
HK Harmon Killebrew S2 8.00 20.00
HP Hunter Pence 4.00 10.00
HR Hanley Ramirez 4.00 10.00
IS Ichiro Suzuki 8.00 20.00
JB Johnny Bench S2 8.00 20.00
JB Jose Bautista UPD 5.00 12.00
JD Joe DiMaggio UPD 6.00 15.00
JF Jimmie Foxx S2 4.00 10.00
JF Jimmie Foxx UPD 4.00 10.00
JH Josh Hamilton 6.00 15.00
JH Jim Hunter S2 4.00 10.00
JJ Josh Johnson 4.00 10.00
JL Jon Lester 5.00 12.00
JM Joe Mauer 8.00 20.00
JM Johnny Mize S2 4.00 10.00
JM Johnny Mize UPD 4.00 10.00
JP Jim Palmer S2 6.00 15.00
JS James Shields UPD 4.00 10.00
JT Julio Teheran UPD 4.00 10.00
JU Justin Upton 4.00 10.00
JV Joey Votto 8.00 20.00
JW Jayson Werth UPD 4.00 10.00
KY Kevin Youkilis UPD 4.00 10.00
LA Luis Aparicio S2 4.00 10.00
LA Luis Aparicio UPD 4.00 10.00
LB Lance Berkman UPD 4.00 10.00
LG Lou Gehrig S2 8.00 20.00
MC Miguel Cabrera 4.00 10.00
MC Miguel Cabrera UPD 4.00 10.00
MH Matt Holliday 6.00 15.00
MI Monte Irvin S2 5.00 12.00
MK Matt Kemp UPD 4.00 10.00
ML Mat Latos 4.00 10.00
MM Mickey Mantle S2 12.50 30.00
MO Mel Ott S2 5.00 12.00
MP Martin Prado 4.00 10.00
MP Michael Pineda UPD 5.00 12.00
MS Mike Stanton 5.00 12.00
MS Mike Schmidt S2 8.00 20.00
MS Max Scherzer UPD 4.00 10.00
MT Mark Teixeira 5.00 12.00
NC Nelson Cruz 6.00 15.00
NM Nick Markakis 6.00 15.00
NR Nolan Ryan S2 8.00 20.00
NR Nolan Ryan UPD 8.00 20.00
OC Orlando Cepeda S2 5.00 12.00
OS Ozzie Smith S2 4.00 10.00
OS Ozzie Smith UPD 4.00 10.00
PM Paul Molitor UPD 4.00 10.00
PN Phil Niekro S2 6.00 15.00
PR Phil Rizzuto S2 6.00 15.00
RA Richie Ashburn S2 5.00 12.00
RA Roberto Alomar UPD 4.00 10.00
RB Ryan Braun 5.00 12.00
RC Robinson Cano 6.00 15.00
RC Roy Campanella S2 5.00 12.00
RH Ryan Howard 8.00 20.00
RH Rogers Hornsby S2 4.00 10.00
RH Rogers Hornsby UPD 4.00 10.00
RJ Reggie Jackson S2 4.00 10.00
RJ Reggie Jackson UPD 4.00 10.00
RS Ryne Sandberg S2 6.00 15.00
RZ Ryan Zimmerman 4.00 10.00
SC Starlin Castro 6.00 15.00
SK Sandy Koufax S2 10.00 25.00
SM Stan Musial S2 10.00 25.00
SS Stephen Strasburg 10.00 25.00
TC Trevor Cahill 4.00 10.00
TG Tony Gwynn S2 5.00 12.00
TH Torii Hunter 4.00 10.00
TH Travis Hafner UPD 4.00 10.00
TL Tim Lincecum 8.00 20.00
TM Thurman Munson S2 6.00 15.00
TN Tsuyoshi Nishioka UPD 5.00 12.00
TS Tom Seaver S2 5.00 12.00
TS Tom Seaver UPD 5.00 12.00
UJ Ubaldo Jimenez 4.00 10.00
VM Victor Martinez 4.00 10.00
WF Whitey Ford S2 5.00 12.00
WM Willie McCovey S2 4.00 10.00
WM Willie McCovey UPD 4.00 10.00
WS Willie Stargell S2 5.00 12.00
ZB Zach Britton UPD 4.00 10.00
ADU Adam Dunn UPD 4.00 10.00
ARO Alex Rodriguez UPD 5.00 12.00
BRO Brooks Robinson S2 8.00 20.00
CCS CC Sabathia 5.00 12.00
DMU Dale Murphy S2 6.00 15.00
JAS Jerry Sands UPD 4.00 10.00
JHE Jason Heyward 10.00 25.00
JMA Juan Marichal S2 6.00 15.00
JMO Joe Morgan UPD 4.00 10.00
JVE Justin Verlander 5.00 12.00
JWE Jered Weaver UPD 4.00 10.00
NOR Nolan Ryan UPD 8.00 20.00
NRY Nolan Ryan UPD 8.00 20.00
PWR Pee Wee Reese UPD 4.00 10.00
RHA Roy Halladay 6.00 15.00
RHE Rickey Henderson S2 4.00 10.00
RHE Rickey Henderson UPD 4.00 10.00
RJA Reggie Jackson UPD 4.00 10.00
SSC Shin-Soo Choo 6.00 15.00

2011 Topps History of Topps

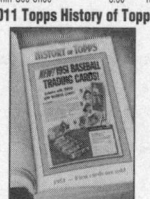

COMPLETE SET (10) 3.00 8.00
STATED ODDS 1:18 HOBBY

2011 Topps Kimball Champions

COMPLETE SET (150) 40.00 100.00
COMP.SER.1 SET (50) 12.50 30.00
COMP.SER.2 SET (50) 12.50 30.00
COMP.UPD SET (50) 12.50 30.00
SER.1 ODDS 1:4 HOBBY
UPD.ODDS 1:4 HOBBY
KC1 Ubaldo Jimenez .25 .60
KC2 Derek Jeter 1.50 4.00
KC3 Carlos Santana .60 1.50
KC4 Johan Santana .40 1.00
KC5 Carlos Gonzalez .40 1.00
KC6 Clay Buchholz .25 .60
KC7 Mickey Mantle 2.00 5.00
KC8 Ryan Braun .40 1.00
KC9 Chase Utley .40 1.00
KC10 Ichiro Suzuki .75 2.00
KC11 Starlin Castro .40 1.00
KC12 Torii Hunter .25 .60
KC13 Ty Cobb 1.00 2.50
KC14 Clayton Kershaw 1.25 3.00
KC15 David Price .50 1.25
KC16 Aroldis Chapman .75 2.00
KC17 Chris Carpenter .40 1.00
KC18 Andrew McCutchen .60 1.50
KC19 Brandon Morrow .25 .60
KC20 Roy Halladay .40 1.00
KC21 Shin-Soo Choo .40 1.00
KC22 Victor Martinez .40 1.00
KC23 Mat Latos .40 1.00
KC24 Josh Johnson .40 1.00
KC25 Vladimir Guerrero .40 1.00
KC26 Justin Morneau .40 1.00
KC27 Nick Markakis .50 1.25
KC28 Mike Stanton .60 1.50
KC29 Jered Weaver .40 1.00
KC30 David Wright .50 1.25
KC31 Nelson Cruz .60 1.50
KC32 Alex Rios .25 .60
KC33 Martin Prado .25 .60
KC34 Joey Votto .60 1.50
KC35 Jon Lester .40 1.00
KC36 Hanley Ramirez .40 1.00
KC37 Stephen Strasburg .60 1.50
KC38 Roy Oswalt .40 1.00
KC39 CC Sabathia .40 1.00
KC40 Albert Pujols .75 2.00
KC41 Pablo Sandoval .40 1.00
KC42 Mariano Rivera .75 2.00
KC43 Pee Wee Reese .40 1.00
KC44 Hunter Pence .40 1.00
KC45 David Ortiz .60 1.50
KC46 Mel Ott .60 1.50
KC47 Brett Anderson .25 .60
KC48 Justin Upton .40 1.00
KC49 Jose Bautista .40 1.00
KC50 Miguel Cabrera .60 1.50
KC51 Hank Aaron 1.25 3.00
KC52 Sandy Koufax 1.25 3.00
KC53 Carlton Fisk .40 1.00
KC54 Nolan Ryan 2.00 5.00
KC55 Stan Musial 1.00 2.50
KC56 Steve Carlton .40 1.00
KC57 Tom Seaver .40 1.00
KC58 Mel Ott .60 1.50
KC59 Tony Gwynn .60 1.50
KC60 Johnny Bench .60 1.50
KC61 Greg Maddux .75 2.00
KC62 Luis Aparicio .40 1.00
KC63 Juan Marichal .40 1.00
KC64 Jackie Robinson .60 1.50
KC65 Bob Gibson .40 1.00
KC66 Yogi Berra .60 1.50
KC67 Pee Wee Reese .40 1.00
KC68 Reggie Jackson .40 1.00
KC69 Robin Roberts .40 1.00
KC70 Roy Campanella .60 1.50
KC71 Brooks Robinson .40 1.00
KC72 Ernie Banks .60 1.50
KC73 Phil Rizzuto .40 1.00
KC74 Eddie Murray .40 1.00
KC75 Bob Feller .40 1.00
KC76 Lou Brock .40 1.00
KC77 Frank Robinson .40 1.00
KC78 Eddie Mathews .60 1.50
KC79 Barry Larkin .40 1.00
KC80 Roger Maris .60 1.50
KC81 Craig Biggio .40 1.00
KC82 Mike Schmidt 1.00 2.50
KC83 Don Mattingly 1.25 3.00
KC84 Ryne Sandberg 1.25 3.00
KC85 Willie McCovey .40 1.00
KC86 Whitey Ford .40 1.00
KC87 Andre Dawson .40 1.00
KC88 Jim Palmer .40 1.00
KC89 Duke Snider .40 1.00
KC90 Hank Greenberg .60 1.50
KC91 Dale Murphy .60 1.50
KC92 Frank Thomas .60 1.50
KC93 Wade Boggs .40 1.00
KC94 Carl Yastrzemski 1.00 2.50
KC95 Lou Gehrig 1.25 3.00
KC96 Cal Ripken Jr. 2.00 5.00
KC97 Paul Molitor .60 1.50
KC98 Gary Carter .40 1.00
KC99 Ty Cobb 1.00 2.50
KC100 Babe Ruth 1.50 4.00
KC101 Babe Ruth 1.50 4.00
KC102 Willie McCovey .40 1.00
KC103 Zach Britton .60 1.50
KC104 Jimmie Foxx .60 1.50
KC105 Honus Wagner .60 1.50
KC106 Gary Carter .40 1.00
KC107 Dan Uggla .25 .60
KC108 Lance Berkman .40 1.00
KC109 Trevor Cahill .25 .60
KC110 Hank Aaron 1.25 3.00
KC111 Tris Speaker .40 1.00
KC112 Cole Hamels .50 1.25
KC113 Alex Rodriguez .75 2.00
KC114 Felix Hernandez .40 1.00
KC115 Ty Cobb 1.00 2.50
KC116 Johnny Mize .40 1.00
KC117 Curtis Granderson .50 1.25
KC118 Cliff Lee .40 1.00
KC119 Matt Holliday .60 1.50
KC120 Frank Robinson .40 1.00
KC121 Luis Aparicio .40 1.00
KC122 Christy Mathewson .60 1.50
KC123 Bert Blyleven .40 1.00
KC124 Frank Thomas .60 1.50
KC125 Nolan Ryan 2.00 5.00
KC126 Danny Duffy .40 1.00
KC127 Justin Verlander .60 1.50
KC128 Carlton Fisk .40 1.00
KC129 George Sisler .40 1.00
KC130 Adrian Gonzalez .50 1.25
KC131 Adam Dunn .40 1.00
KC132 Tom Seaver .40 1.00
KC133 Ozzie Smith .75 2.00
KC134 Miguel Cabrera .60 1.50
KC135 Carl Crawford .40 1.00
KC136 Paul Molitor .60 1.50
KC137 Joe Morgan .40 1.00
KC138 Rogers Hornsby .40 1.00
KC139 James Shields .25 .60
KC140 Michael Pineda .60 1.50
KC141 Andre Dawson .40 1.00
KC142 Ryan Howard .50 1.25
KC143 Kyle Drabek .40 1.00
KC144 Reggie Jackson .40 1.00
KC145 Eric Hosmer 1.50 4.00
KC146 Vladimir Guerrero .40 1.00
KC147 Mark Teixeira .40 1.00
KC148 Jose Reyes .40 1.00
KC149 Cy Young .60 1.50
KC150 Joe DiMaggio 1.25 3.00

2011 Topps Lost Cards

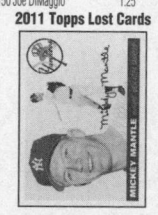

COMPLETE SET (10) 6.00 15.00
STATED ODDS 1:12 HOBBY
*ORIGINAL BACK: .6X TO 1.5X BASIC
ORIGINAL ODDS 1:108 HOBBY
LC1 Stan Musial 53T 1.25 3.00
LC2 Duke Snider 53T .50 1.25
LC3 Mickey Mantle 54T 2.50 6.00
LC4 Roy Campanella 54T .75 2.00
LC5 Stan Musial 55T 1.25 3.00
LC6 Whitey Ford 55T .50 1.25
LC7 Bob Feller 55T .50 1.25
LC8 Mickey Mantle 55T 2.50 6.00
LC9 Stan Musial 56T 1.25 3.00
LC10 Stan Musial 57T 1.25 3.00

2011 Topps Mickey Mantle Reprint Relics

SER.1 ODDS 1:115,000 HOBBY
UPD.ODDS 1:52,500 HOBBY
PRINT RUNS B/WN 64-66 COPIES PER
MMRR2 Mickey Mantle Bat/65 30.00 60.00
MMRR1 Mickey Mantle Jsy/64 30.00 60.00
MMRR3 Mickey Mantle Jsy/66 30.00 60.00

2011 Topps Prime 9 Player of the Week Refractors

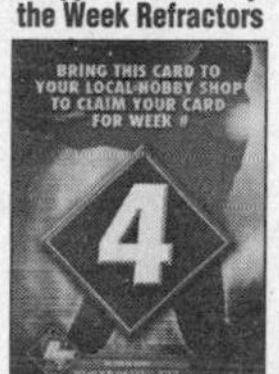

COMPLETE SET (9) 10.00 25.00
PNR1 Johnny Bench 1.00 2.50
PNR2 Albert Pujols 1.25 3.00
PNR3 Jackie Robinson 1.00 2.50
PNR4 Derek Jeter 2.50 6.00
PNR5 Mike Schmidt 1.50 4.00
PNR6 Hank Aaron 2.00 5.00
PNR7 Mickey Mantle 3.00 8.00
PNR8 Ichiro Suzuki 1.25 3.00
PNR9 Sandy Koufax 2.00 5.00

2011 Topps Silk Collection

SER.1 ODDS 1:396 HOBBY
UPD.ODDS 1:221 HOBBY
STATED PRINT RUN 50 SER.#'d SETS
1 Ryan Kalish 6.00 15.00
2 Jose Bautista 6.00 15.00
3 Carlos Gonzalez 6.00 15.00
4 Justin Upton 6.00 15.00
5 Chipper Jones 10.00 25.00
6 Ubaldo Jimenez 4.00 10.00
7 Brett Wallace 4.00 10.00
8 Roy Oswalt 6.00 15.00
9 Brennan Boesch 6.00 15.00
10 Albert Pujols 12.00 30.00
11 Jaime Garcia 6.00 15.00
12 Kevin Kouzmanoff 4.00 10.00
13 Brett Anderson 4.00 10.00
14 Ian Desmond 4.00 10.00
15 Adam Dunn 6.00 15.00
16 David Wright 8.00 20.00
17 Andrew Bailey 4.00 10.00
18 Torii Hunter 4.00 10.00
19 Max Scherzer 10.00 25.00
20 Carl Crawford 6.00 15.00
21 Michael Young 6.00 15.00
22 Chris Carpenter 6.00 15.00
23 Chase Utley 6.00 15.00
24 Clay Buchholz 4.00 10.00
25 Stephen Drew 4.00 10.00
26 Alex Gordon 6.00 15.00
27 Shin-Soo Choo 6.00 15.00
28 Miguel Cabrera 10.00 25.00
29 Andrew McCutchen 10.00 25.00
30 Victor Martinez 6.00 15.00
31 Jered Weaver 6.00 15.00
32 Clayton Kershaw 10.00 25.00
33 Ichiro Suzuki 12.00 30.00
34 Mike Stanton 10.00 25.00
35 Vladimir Guerrero 4.00 10.00
36 Cliff Lee 6.00 15.00
37 Miguel Montero 4.00 10.00
38 Howie Kendrick 4.00 10.00
39 Jon Lester 6.00 15.00
40 Nick Swisher 6.00 15.00
41 Magglio Ordonez 6.00 15.00
42 Carlos Santana 10.00 25.00
43 Ryan Braun 6.00 15.00
44 Carlos Pena 6.00 15.00
45 Tim Hudson 6.00 15.00
46 Alex Rodriguez 12.00 30.00
47 Aaron Hill 4.00 10.00
48 Chris Young 4.00 10.00
49 Johan Santana 6.00 15.00
50 James Shields 4.00 10.00
51 C.J. Wilson 4.00 10.00
52 Mariano Rivera 15.00 40.00
53 Marlon Byrd 4.00 10.00
54 Martin Prado 4.00 10.00
55 Joey Votto 10.00 25.00
56 Paul Konerko 6.00 15.00
57 Mark Buehrle 6.00 15.00
58 Fausto Carmona 4.00 10.00
59 Nelson Cruz 10.00 25.00
60 Wandy Rodriguez 4.00 10.00
61 Derrek Lee 4.00 10.00
62 Ricky Romero 4.00 10.00
63 Carlos Marmol 6.00 15.00
64 Johnny Cueto 6.00 15.00
65 Starlin Castro 6.00 15.00
66 Zack Greinke 6.00 15.00
67 Scott Rolen 6.00 15.00
68 Nick Markakis 8.00 20.00
69 Jimmy Rollins 6.00 15.00
70 John Danks 4.00 10.00
71 Ike Davis 4.00 10.00
72 Brandon Morrow 4.00 10.00
73 Derek Jeter 25.00 60.00
74 Peter Bourjos 6.00 15.00
75 Roy Halladay 6.00 15.00
76 Alex Rios 4.00 10.00
77 Hanley Ramirez 6.00 15.00
78 Jon Jay 4.00 10.00
79 Justin Morneau 6.00 15.00
80 Aramis Ramirez 4.00 10.00
81 Todd Helton 6.00 15.00
82 Andre Ethier 6.00 15.00
83 Stephen Strasburg 10.00 25.00
84 Adrian Beltre 10.00 25.00
85 Brian Wilson 10.00 25.00
86 Kurt Suzuki 4.00 10.00
87 David Price 8.00 20.00
88 Jason Kubel 4.00 10.00
89 Hunter Pence 6.00 15.00
90 Alexei Ramirez 6.00 15.00
91 Billy Wagner 4.00 10.00
92 Michael Cuddyer 4.00 10.00
93 Jeremy Hellickson 10.00 25.00
94 CC Sabathia 6.00 15.00
95 Josh Johnson 6.00 15.00
96 Brian Matusz 4.00 10.00
97 Mat Latos 6.00 15.00
98 Rickie Weeks 4.00 10.00
99 Heath Bell 4.00 10.00
100 David Ortiz 10.00 25.00
101 Trevor Cahill 4.00 10.00
102 Felix Hernandez 6.00 15.00
103 Shane Victorino 6.00 15.00
104 Michael Bourn 4.00 10.00
105 Josh Hamilton 6.00 15.00
106 Corey Hart 4.00 10.00
107 John Lackey 6.00 15.00
108 Kevin Youkilis 4.00 10.00
109 Daric Barton 4.00 10.00
110 Danny Valencia 6.00 15.00
111 Edwin Jackson 4.00 10.00
112 Jason Bartlett 4.00 10.00
113 Matt Cain 6.00 15.00
114 Rick Porcello 6.00 15.00
115 Huston Street 4.00 10.00
116 Dan Uggla 4.00 10.00
117 Ryan Ludwick 4.00 10.00
118 Elvis Andrus 6.00 15.00
119 Ivan Rodriguez 6.00 15.00
120 Casey McGehee 4.00 10.00
121 Adam Wainwright 6.00 15.00
122 Dustin Pedroia 8.00 20.00
123 Travis Snider 4.00 10.00
124 Jason Heyward 8.00 20.00
125 Phil Hughes 4.00 10.00
126 Dan Haren 4.00 10.00
127 J.P. Arencibia 4.00 10.00
128 Matt Kemp 8.00 20.00
129 Denard Span 4.00 10.00
130 Drew Storen 4.00 10.00
131 Jonathan Broxton 4.00 10.00
132 Adrian Gonzalez 8.00 20.00
133 Adam Jones 6.00 15.00
134 Joba Chamberlain 6.00 15.00
135 Carlos Beltran 6.00 15.00
136 Evan Longoria 6.00 15.00
137 Adam Lind 6.00 15.00
138 Joe Mauer 8.00 20.00
139 Brian McCann 6.00 15.00
140 Francisco Liriano 6.00 15.00
141 Chris Tillman 4.00 10.00
142 Troy Tulowitzki 10.00 25.00
143 Grady Sizemore 6.00 15.00
144 Jose Tabata 4.00 10.00
145 Drew Stubbs 4.00 10.00
146 Austin Jackson 4.00 10.00
147 Franklin Gutierrez 4.00 10.00
148 Kendrys Morales 4.00 10.00

- 149 Carlos Quentin 4.00 10.00
- 150 Wade Davis 4.00 10.00
- 151 Jose Valverde 4.00 10.00
- 152 Logan Morrison 4.00 10.00
- 153 Delmon Young 6.00 15.00
- 154 Alfonso Soriano 6.00 15.00
- 155 Colby Rasmus 6.00 15.00
- 156 Mike Minor 4.00 10.00
- 157 Yovani Gallardo 4.00 10.00
- 158 Chris Iannetta 4.00 10.00
- 159 Cody Ross 4.00 10.00
- 160 Jorge Posada 6.00 15.00
- 161 Dallas Braden 4.00 10.00
- 162 Dexter Fowler 6.00 15.00
- 163 Shaun Marcum 4.00 10.00
- 164 Kyle Blanks 4.00 10.00
- 165 B.J. Upton 6.00 15.00
- 166 Matt Holliday 10.00 25.00
- 167 Joakim Soria 4.00 10.00
- 168 Jake Arrieta 8.00 20.00
- 169 Ryan Doumit 4.00 10.00
- 170 Curtis Granderson 8.00 20.00
- 171 Madison Bumgarner 8.00 20.00
- 172 Buster Posey 12.00 30.00
- 173 Kelly Johnson 4.00 10.00
- 174 Chad Billingsley 6.00 15.00
- 175 Cole Hamels 8.00 20.00
- 176 Justin Verlander 10.00 25.00
- 177 Domonic Brown 8.00 20.00
- 178 Billy Butler 4.00 10.00
- 179 Jacoby Ellsbury 8.00 20.00
- 180 Will Venable 4.00 10.00
- 181 Ian Kinsler 6.00 15.00
- 182 Tommy Hanson 4.00 10.00
- 183 Kosuke Fukudome 6.00 15.00
- 184 Ryan Zimmerman 6.00 15.00
- 185 Geovany Soto 6.00 15.00
- 186 Matt Garza 4.00 10.00
- 187 Prince Fielder 6.00 15.00
- 188 Mark Reynolds 4.00 10.00
- 189 Mark Teixeira 6.00 15.00
- 190 Carlos Lee 4.00 10.00
- 191 Brian Roberts 4.00 10.00
- 192 Kila Ka'aihue 4.00 10.00
- 193 Brett Myers 4.00 10.00
- 194 Vernon Wells 4.00 10.00
- 195 Jose Reyes 6.00 15.00
- 196 Brandon Phillips 4.00 10.00
- 197 Josh Beckett 4.00 10.00
- 198 Gordon Beckham 4.00 10.00
- 199 Tim Lincecum 6.00 15.00
- 200 Jeff Niemann 4.00 10.00
- 201 Adrian Gonzalez 8.00 20.00
- 202 Josh Willingham 6.00 15.00
- 203 Jose Iglesias 6.00 15.00
- 204 Mike Napoli 4.00 10.00
- 205 Conor Jackson 4.00 10.00
- 206 Tim Stauffer 4.00 10.00
- 207 Carlos Pena 6.00 15.00
- 208 Rick Ankiel 4.00 10.00
- 209 Russell Martin 4.00 10.00
- 210 Zach Britton 10.00 25.00
- 211 Brian Fuentes 4.00 10.00
- 212 Angel Sanchez 4.00 10.00
- 213 Andruw Jones 4.00 10.00
- 214 Jerry Sands 10.00 25.00
- 215 Brandon Belt 10.00 25.00
- 216 Jonathan Herrera 4.00 10.00
- 217 Yuniesky Betancourt 4.00 10.00
- 218 Mitchell Boggs 4.00 10.00
- 219 Andy Dirks 10.00 25.00
- 220 Zack Greinke 6.00 15.00
- 221 Jeff Francis 4.00 10.00
- 222 Nolan Reimold 4.00 10.00
- 223 Freddy Garcia 4.00 10.00
- 224 Aaron Harang 4.00 10.00
- 225 Kerry Wood 4.00 10.00
- 226 Orlando Cabrera 4.00 10.00
- 227 Lyle Overbay 4.00 10.00
- 228 Scott Downs 4.00 10.00
- 229 Sean Burnett 4.00 10.00
- 230 Victor Martinez 6.00 15.00
- 231 Logan Forsythe 4.00 10.00
- 232 Brandon McCarthy 4.00 10.00
- 233 Joe Mather 4.00 10.00
- 234 Edgar Renteria 4.00 10.00
- 235 Scott Sizemore 4.00 10.00
- 236 Jeff Francoeur 6.00 15.00
- 237 Kyle Farnsworth 4.00 10.00
- 238 Jon Rauch 4.00 10.00
- 239 Brad Penny 4.00 10.00
- 240 Fernando Salas 6.00 15.00
- 241 Doug Davis 4.00 10.00
- 242 Pete Kozma 10.00 25.00
- 243 Alfredo Amezaga 4.00 10.00
- 244 Mark Melancon 4.00 10.00
- 245 Rafael Soriano 4.00 10.00
- 246 Alex White 4.00 10.00
- 247 Bartolo Colon 4.00 10.00
- 248 Trystan Magnuson 4.00 10.00
- 249 Omar Infante 4.00 10.00
- 250 Carl Crawford 6.00 15.00
- 251 Matt Guerrier 4.00 10.00
- 252 Alexi Amarista 4.00 10.00
- 253 Humberto Quintero 4.00 10.00
- 254 Reed Johnson 4.00 10.00
- 255 Darren Oliver 4.00 10.00
- 256 Alex Cobb 4.00 10.00
- 257 Josh Collmenter 4.00 10.00
- 258 Michael Pineda 10.00 25.00
- 259 Jon Garland 4.00 10.00
- 260 Lance Berkman 6.00 15.00
- 261 Eduardo Sanchez 6.00 15.00
- 262 John Mayberry 4.00 10.00
- 263 Brendan Ryan 4.00 10.00
- 264 Bruce Chen 4.00 10.00
- 265 Alexi Ogando 10.00 25.00
- 266 Brad Ziegler 4.00 10.00
- 267 Jason Giambi 4.00 10.00
- 268 Charlie Furbush 4.00 10.00
- 269 Julio Teheran 6.00 15.00
- 270 Vladimir Guerrero 6.00 15.00
- 271 Xavier Nady 4.00 10.00
- 272 Kevin Gregg 4.00 10.00
- 273 Jason Bourgeois 4.00 10.00
- 274 Derrek Lee 4.00 10.00
- 275 Adrian Beltre 10.00 25.00
- 276 Daniel Moskos 4.00 10.00
- 277 Carlos Peguero 6.00 15.00
- 278 Tyler Chatwood 4.00 10.00
- 279 Orlando Hudson 4.00 10.00
- 280 Jayson Werth 6.00 15.00
- 281 Philip Humber 4.00 10.00
- 282 Brandon League 4.00 10.00
- 283 J.P. Howell 4.00 10.00
- 284 Michael Dunn 4.00 10.00
- 285 Miguel Tejada 6.00 15.00
- 286 Jamey Carroll 4.00 10.00
- 287 Arthur Rhodes 4.00 10.00
- 288 Bill Hall 4.00 10.00
- 289 David DeJesus 4.00 10.00
- 290 Adam Dunn 6.00 15.00
- 291 Charlie Morton 10.00 25.00
- 292 J.J. Hardy 4.00 10.00
- 293 Kevin Correia 4.00 10.00
- 294 Alcides Escobar 6.00 15.00
- 295 Danny Duffy 6.00 15.00
- 296 Justin Turner 8.00 20.00
- 297 John Buck 4.00 10.00
- 298 Sergio Santos 4.00 10.00
- 299 Todd Frazier 12.00 30.00
- 300 Cliff Lee 6.00 15.00

2011 Topps Target Hanger Pack Exlcusives

ONE PER TARGET HANGER PACK

- THP1 Albert Pujols 1.50 4.00
- THP2 Derek Jeter 3.00 8.00
- THP3 Mat Latos .75 2.00
- THP4 Hanley Ramirez .75 2.00
- THP5 Miguel Cabrera 1.25 3.00
- THP6 Aroldis Chapman 1.50 4.00
- THP7 Chase Utley .75 2.00
- THP8 Ryan Braun .75 2.00
- THP9 David Price 1.00 2.50
- THP10 Joey Votto 1.25 3.00
- THP11 David Wright 1.00 2.50
- THP12 Carlos Gonzalez .75 2.00
- THP13 David Ortiz 1.25 3.00
- THP14 Andre Ethier .75 2.00
- THP15 Roy Halladay .75 2.00
- THP16 Cliff Lee .75 2.00
- THP17 Dan Uggla .50 1.25
- THP18 Mark Teixeira .75 2.00
- THP19 Felix Hernandez .75 2.00
- THP20 Buster Posey 1.50 4.00
- THP21 Ryan Zimmerman .75 2.00
- THP22 Ian Kinsler .75 2.00
- THP23 Mike Stanton 1.25 3.00
- THP24 Troy Tulowitzki 1.25 3.00
- THP25 Zack Greinke .75 2.00
- THP26 Pedro Alvarez 1.00 2.50
- THP27 Jon Lester .75 2.00
- THP28 Justin Upton .75 2.00
- THP29 Clayton Kershaw 2.50 6.00
- THP30 Carl Crawford .75 2.00

2011 Topps Target Red Diamond

COMPLETE SET (30) 40.00 80.00
RANDOM INSERTS IN TARGET PACKS

- RDT1 Babe Ruth 3.00 8.00
- RDT2 Derek Jeter 3.00 8.00
- RDT3 Ty Cobb 2.00 5.00
- RDT4 Josh Hamilton .75 2.00
- RDT5 Albert Pujols 1.50 4.00
- RDT6 Jason Heyward 1.00 2.50
- RDT7 Mickey Mantle 4.00 10.00
- RDT8 Ryan Braun .75 2.00
- RDT9 Honus Wagner 1.25 3.00
- RDT10 Jackie Robinson 1.25 3.00
- RDT11 Roy Halladay .75 2.00
- RDT12 Carlos Gonzalez .75 2.00
- RDT13 Ichiro Suzuki 1.50 4.00
- RDT14 Roy Campanella 1.25 3.00
- RDT15 Miguel Cabrera 1.25 3.00
- RDT16 Adrian Gonzalez 1.00 2.50
- RDT17 CC Sabathia .75 2.00
- RDT18 Ryan Howard 1.00 2.50
- RDT19 Adrian Beltre 1.25 3.00
- RDT20 Sandy Koufax 2.50 6.00
- RDT21 Evan Longoria .75 2.00
- RDT22 Robinson Cano .75 2.00
- RDT23 Adam Dunn .75 2.00
- RDT24 Joe Mauer 1.00 2.50
- RDT25 Tim Lincecum .75 2.00
- RDT26 Victor Martinez .75 2.00
- RDT27 Ubaldo Jimenez .50 1.25
- RDT28 Matt Holliday 1.25 3.00
- RDT29 Josh Johnson .75 2.00
- RDT30 Hank Aaron 2.50 6.00

2011 Topps Topps Town

COMPLETE SET (50) 6.00 15.00
STATED ODDS 1:1 HOBBY

- TT1 Miguel Cabrera .50 1.25
- TT2 Dan Haren .20 .50
- TT3 Brett Wallace .20 .50
- TT4 Brett Anderson .20 .50
- TT5 Roy Halladay .30 .75
- TT6 Vernon Wells .20 .50
- TT7 Joe Mauer .40 1.00
- TT8 Jose Reyes .30 .75
- TT9 Adam Jones .30 .75
- TT10 Josh Hamilton .30 .75
- TT11 Chris Young .20 .50
- TT12 Mat Latos .30 .75
- TT13 Chase Utley .30 .75
- TT14 Shin-Soo Choo .30 .75
- TT15 David Wright .40 1.00
- TT16 Nick Markakis .40 1.00
- TT17 Aroldis Chapman .75 2.00
- TT18 Ryan Zimmerman .30 .75
- TT19 Andrew McCutchen .50 1.25
- TT20 Ichiro Suzuki .60 1.50
- TT21 Starlin Castro .30 .75
- TT22 Jason Heyward .40 1.00
- TT23 Evan Longoria .30 .75
- TT24 Josh Johnson .30 .75
- TT25 Ryan Howard .40 1.00
- TT26 Matt Garza .20 .50
- TT27 Andre Ethier .30 .75
- TT28 David Ortiz .50 1.25
- TT29 Carlos Gonzalez .30 .75
- TT30 Ryan Braun .30 .75
- TT31 Manny Ramirez .50 1.25
- TT32 Mike Stanton .50 1.25
- TT33 Victor Martinez .30 .75
- TT34 Felix Hernandez .30 .75
- TT35 David Price .40 1.00
- TT36 Robinson Cano .30 .75
- TT37 Billy Butler .20 .50
- TT38 Justin Verlander .50 1.25
- TT39 Adrian Gonzalez .40 1.00
- TT40 Buster Posey .60 1.50
- TT41 Carlos Santana .50 1.25
- TT42 Kevin Youkilis .20 .50
- TT43 Vladimir Guerrero .30 .75
- TT44 Ubaldo Jimenez .20 .50
- TT45 Hanley Ramirez .30 .75
- TT46 Joey Votto .50 1.25
- TT47 Dustin Pedroia .40 1.00
- TT48 Troy Tulowitzki .50 1.25
- TT49 CC Sabathia .30 .75
- TT50 Albert Pujols .60 1.50

2011 Topps Topps Town Series 2

COMPLETE SET (50) 6.00 15.00

- TT1 Tim Lincecum .30 .75
- TT2 Mark Reynolds .20 .50
- TT3 Cliff Lee .30 .75
- TT4 Logan Morrison .20 .50
- TT5 Grady Sizemore .20 .50
- TT6 Todd Helton .30 .75
- TT7 Adrian Gonzalez .40 1.00
- TT8 Ryan Ludwick .20 .50
- TT9 Dan Uggla .20 .50
- TT10 Justin Upton .30 .75
- TT11 Kendrys Morales .20 .50
- TT12 Justin Morneau .30 .75
- TT13 Zack Greinke .30 .75
- TT14 Derek Jeter 1.25 3.00
- TT15 Jose Bautista .30 .75
- TT16 Adam Wainwright .30 .75
- TT17 Nelson Cruz .50 1.25
- TT18 Brandon Phillips .20 .50
- TT19 Victor Martinez .30 .75
- TT20 Clayton Kershaw 1.00 2.50
- TT21 Adam Dunn .30 .75
- TT22 Chone Figgins .20 .50
- TT23 Matt Holliday .50 1.25
- TT24 Neftali Feliz .20 .50
- TT25 Pedro Alvarez .40 1.00
- TT26 Trevor Cahill .20 .50
- TT27 Mark Teixeira .30 .75
- TT28 Aramis Ramirez .20 .50
- TT29 Chris Coghlan .20 .50
- TT30 Carl Crawford .30 .75
- TT31 Jon Lester .30 .75
- TT32 Cole Hamels .40 1.00
- TT33 Austin Jackson .20 .50
- TT34 Ike Davis .20 .50
- TT35 Ian Kinsler .30 .75
- TT36 Hunter Pence .30 .75
- TT37 Jeremy Hellickson .50 1.25
- TT38 Brian Matusz .20 .50
- TT39 Clay Buchholz .20 .50
- TT40 Lance Berkman .30 .75
- TT41 Angel Pagan .20 .50
- TT42 Torii Hunter .20 .50
- TT43 Chris Carpenter .30 .75
- TT44 B.J. Upton .30 .75
- TT45 Martin Prado .20 .50
- TT46 Roy Oswalt .30 .75
- TT47 Jay Bruce .30 .75
- TT48 Joakim Soria .20 .50
- TT49 Jayson Werth .30 .75
- TT50 Phil Hughes .20 .50

2011 Topps Toys R Us Purple Diamond

COMPLETE SET (10) 12.50 30.00
RANDOM INSERTS IN TRU PACKS

- PDC1 Buster Posey 6.00 15.00
- PDC2 Troy Tulowitzki 1.25 3.00
- PDC3 Evan Longoria .75 2.00
- PDC4 Tim Lincecum .75 2.00
- PDC5 Alex Rodriguez 1.50 4.00
- PDC6 CC Sabathia .75 2.00
- PDC7 Joe Mauer 1.00 2.50
- PDC8 Robinson Cano .75 2.00
- PDC9 Starlin Castro .75 2.00
- PDC10 Ryan Howard 1.00 2.50

2011 Topps Value Box Chrome Refractors

COMPLETE SET (3) 4.00 10.00
ONE PER $14.99 RETAIL VALUE BOX

- MBC1 Mickey Mantle 2.50 6.00
- MBC2 Jackie Robinson .75 2.00
- MBC3 Babe Ruth 2.00 5.00

2011 Topps Wal-Mart Blue Diamond

COMPLETE SET (30) 30.00 60.00
RANDOM INSERTS IN WAL MART PACKS

- BDW1 Albert Pujols 1.50 4.00
- BDW2 Derek Jeter 3.00 8.00
- BDW3 Mat Latos .75 2.00
- BDW4 Hanley Ramirez .75 2.00
- BDW5 Miguel Cabrera 1.25 3.00
- BDW6 Aroldis Chapman 1.50 4.00
- BDW7 Chase Utley .75 2.00
- BDW8 Ryan Braun .75 2.00
- BDW9 David Price 1.00 2.50
- BDW10 Joey Votto 1.25 3.00
- BDW11 David Wright 1.00 2.50
- BDW12 Carlos Gonzalez .75 2.00
- BDW13 David Ortiz 1.25 3.00
- BDW14 Andre Ethier .75 2.00
- BDW15 Roy Halladay .75 2.00
- BDW16 Cliff Lee .75 2.00
- BDW17 Dan Uggla .50 1.25
- BDW18 Mark Teixeira .75 2.00
- BDW19 Felix Hernandez .75 2.00
- BDW20 Buster Posey 1.50 4.00
- BDW21 Ryan Zimmerman .75 2.00
- BDW22 Ian Kinsler .75 2.00
- BDW23 Mike Stanton 1.25 3.00
- BDW24 Troy Tulowitzki 1.25 3.00
- BDW25 Zack Greinke .75 2.00
- BDW26 Pedro Alvarez 1.00 2.50
- BDW27 Jon Lester .75 2.00
- BDW28 Justin Upton .75 2.00
- BDW29 Clayton Kershaw 2.50 6.00
- BDW30 Carl Crawford .75 2.00

2011 Topps Wal-Mart Hanger Pack Exclusives

ONE PER WAL MART HANGER PACK

- WHP1 Babe Ruth 6.00 15.00
- WHP2 Derek Jeter 6.00 15.00
- WHP3 Ty Cobb 4.00 10.00
- WHP4 Josh Hamilton 1.50 4.00
- WHP5 Albert Pujols 3.00 8.00
- WHP6 Jason Heyward 2.00 5.00
- WHP7 Mickey Mantle 8.00 20.00
- WHP8 Ryan Braun 1.50 4.00
- WHP9 Honus Wagner 2.50 6.00
- WHP10 Jackie Robinson 2.50 6.00
- WHP11 Roy Halladay 1.50 4.00
- WHP12 Carlos Gonzalez 1.50 4.00
- WHP13 Ichiro Suzuki 3.00 8.00
- WHP14 Roy Campanella 2.50 6.00
- WHP15 Miguel Cabrera 2.50 6.00
- WHP16 Adrian Gonzalez 2.00 5.00
- WHP17 CC Sabathia 1.50 4.00
- WHP18 Ryan Howard 2.00 5.00
- WHP19 Adrian Beltre 2.50 6.00
- WHP20 Sandy Koufax 5.00 12.00
- WHP21 Evan Longoria 1.50 4.00
- WHP22 Robinson Cano 1.50 4.00
- WHP23 Adam Dunn 1.50 4.00
- WHP24 Joe Mauer 2.00 5.00
- WHP25 Tim Lincecum 1.50 4.00
- WHP26 Victor Martinez 1.50 4.00
- WHP27 Ubaldo Jimenez 1.00 2.50
- WHP28 Matt Holliday 2.50 6.00
- WHP29 Josh Johnson 1.50 4.00
- WHP30 Hank Aaron 5.00 12.00

2011 Topps World Champion Autograph Relics

STATED ODDS 1:7941 HOBBY
STATED PRINT RUN 50 SER.#'d SETS
EXCHANGE DEADLINE 1/31/2014

- BP Buster Posey 300.00 600.00
- CR Cody Ross EXCH 150.00 250.00
- FS Freddy Sanchez EXCH 125.00 250.00
- MB Madison Bumgarner 100.00 200.00
- PS Pablo Sandoval 75.00 150.00

2011 Topps World Champion Autographs

STATED ODDS 1:33,000 HOBBY
STATED PRINT RUN 50 SER.#'d SETS
EXCHANGE DEADLINE 1/31/2014

- WCA1 Buster Posey 175.00 350.00
- WCA2 Madison Bumgarner 100.00 200.00
- WCA3 Pablo Sandoval 100.00 200.00
- WCA4 Cody Ross 100.00 200.00
- WCA5 Freddy Sanchez 100.00 200.00

2011 Topps World Champion Relics

STATED ODDS 1:6250 HOBBY
STATED PRINT RUN 100 SER.#'d SETS
EXCHANGE DEADLINE 1/31/2014

- WCR1 Buster Posey 100.00 200.00
- WCR2 Madison Bumgarner 60.00 120.00
- WCR3 Pablo Sandoval 50.00 100.00
- WCR4 Cody Ross EXCH 75.00 150.00
- WCR5 Freddy Sanchez 40.00 80.00
- WCR6 Tim Lincecum 125.00 250.00
- WCR7 Matt Cain 40.00 80.00
- WCR8 Jonathan Sanchez EXCH 75.00 150.00
- WCR9 Brian Wilson 75.00 150.00
- WCR10 Juan Uribe EXCH 40.00 80.00
- WCR11 Aubrey Huff EXCH 60.00 120.00
- WCR12 Edgar Renteria 50.00 100.00
- WCR13 Andres Torres EXCH 40.00 80.00
- WCR14 Pat Burrell 60.00 120.00
- WCR15 Mike Fontenot 40.00 80.00

2011 Topps Update

COMP.SET w/o SP's (330) 400.00 1000.00
COMMON CARD (1-330) .12 .30
COMMON SP VAR (1-330) 5.00 12.00
COMMON RC (1-330) .40 1.00
PRINTING PLATE ODDS 1:846 HOBBY
PLATE PRINT RUN 1 SET PER COLOR
BLACK-CYAN-MAGENTA-YELLOW ISSUED
NO PLATE PRICING DUE TO SCARCITY

- US1 Adrian Gonzalez .25 .60
- US2 Ty Wigginton .12 .30
- US3 Blake Beavan .20 .50
- US5 Josh Willingham .20 .50
- US6 Prince Fielder .20 .50
- US7 Nate Schierholtz .12 .30
- US8 David Robertson .12 .30
- US9 Jose Iglesias RC .60 1.50
- US11 Jason Pridie .12 .30
- US12 Greg Dobbs .12 .30
- US13 Koyie Hill .12 .30
- US14 Alex Avila .20 .50
- US15 Aaron Heilman .12 .30
- US16 Wellington Castillo .12 .30
- US17 Craig Gentry .12 .30
- US18A Robinson Cano .20 .50
- US18B Joe DiMaggio SP 12.50 30.00
- US19 Mike Napoli .12 .30
- US20 Adrian Gonzalez .25 .60
- US22 Randall Delgado RC .60 1.50
- US23 Chance Ruffin RC .40 1.00
- US24 Rex Brothers RC .40 1.00
- US25 Tim Stauffer .12 .30
- US26 Jered Weaver .20 .50
- US27 Joey Devine .12 .30
- US28 Adam Kennedy .12 .30
- US29 Mike MacDougal .12 .30
- US30 Dustin Ackley RC .60 1.50
- US32 Matt Stairs .12 .30
- US33 Jayson Nix .12 .30
- US34 David Ross .12 .30
- US35 Eduardo Nunez RC 1.00 2.50
- US36 Josh Judy RC .40 1.00
- US37 Rick Ankiel .12 .30
- US38A Josh Hamilton .20 .50
- US38B Roger Maris SP 5.00 12.00
- US39 Eduardo Sanchez RC .60 1.50
- US40 Brian Fuentes .12 .30
- US41 Lou Marson .12 .30
- US42A David Ortiz .30 .75
- US42B Frank Thomas SP 5.00 12.00
- US43 Carlos Quentin .12 .30
- US44 Matt Treanor .12 .30
- US45 Peter Moylan .12 .30
- US46 Angel Sanchez .12 .30
- US47 Paul Goldschmidt RC 6.00 15.00
- US48 Scott Hairston .12 .30
- US49 Rickie Weeks .12 .30
- US4A Brian McCann .20 .50
- US4B Carlton Fisk SP 5.00 12.00
- US50A Jered Weaver .20 .50
- US50B Nolan Ryan SP 8.00 20.00
- US51 Andruw Jones .12 .30
- US52 Lance Berkman .20 .50
- US53 Koji Uehara .12 .30
- US54 Jerry Sands RC 1.00 2.50
- US55 Anthony Rizzo RC 8.00 20.00
- US56 Ryan Adams RC .40 1.00
- US57 Tony Campana RC 1.00 2.50
- US58A Tim Lincecum .20 .50
- US58B Bert Blyleven SP 5.00 12.00
- US59A Matt Kemp .25 .60
- US59B Rickey Henderson SP 5.00 12.00
- US60 Heath Bell .12 .30
- US61 Nick Masset .12 .30
- US62 Jason Marquis .12 .30
- US63 Doug Fister .12 .30
- US64 J.C. Romero .12 .30
- US65 Mitchell Boggs .12 .30
- US66 Andy Dirks RC 1.00 2.50
- US67 Miguel Olivo .12 .30
- US68 Tyler Clippard .12 .30
- US69 Gerald Laird .12 .30
- US70 Michael Wuertz .12 .30
- US71 Jeff Francis .12 .30
- US72 Colby Rasmus .20 .50
- US73 Juan Nicasio .12 .30
- US74 Henry Blanco .12 .30
- US75 Gio Gonzalez .20 .50
- US76 Nolan Reimold .12 .30
- US77 Freddy Garcia .12 .30
- US78 David Ortiz .30 .75
- US79 Chris Dickerson .12 .30
- US80 Jose Bautista .20 .50
- US81 Aaron Harang .12 .30
- US82 Mark Ellis .12 .30
- US83 Brandon Belt .30 .75
- US84 Pablo Sandoval .20 .50
- US85A Roy Halladay .20 .50
- US85B Tom Seaver SP 5.00 12.00
- US86 Rafael Furcal .12 .30
- US87 Clayton Mortensen .12 .30
- US88 Orlando Cabrera .12 .30
- US89 Sean O'Sullivan .12 .30
- US90 James Russell .12 .30
- US91 Brandon League .12 .30
- US92 Hunter Pence .20 .50
- US93 Matt Downs .12 .30
- US94 Ryan Vogelsong .12 .30
- US95 Lyle Overbay .12 .30
- US96 Ryan Hanigan .12 .30
- US97 Cody Eppley RC .40 1.00
- US98 Alexi Ogando .30 .75
- US99 Carlos Villanueva .12 .30
- US100 Cliff Lee .20 .50
- US101 Scott Downs .12 .30
- US102 Sean Burnett .12 .30
- US103 Josh Collmenter RC .40 1.00
- US104 Logan Forsythe RC .40 1.00
- US105 Joel Hanrahan .20 .50
- US106 Ryan Ludwick .12 .30
- US107 Brandon McCarthy .12 .30
- US108 Ubaldo Jimenez .12 .30
- US109 Jair Jurrjens .12 .30
- US10A Jose Bautista .20 .50
- US10B Hank Aaron SP 6.00 15.00
- US110 Edgar Renteria .12 .30
- US111 Scott Sizemore .12 .30
- US112 Lonnie Chisenhall RC .60 1.50
- US113 Chris Perez .12 .30
- US114 Lance Lynn RC 1.00 2.50
- US115 Kerry Wood .12 .30
- US116 Shawn Camp .12 .30
- US117 Michael Stutes RC .60 1.50
- US118 Michael Pineda .30 .75
- US119 Jeff Francoeur .20 .50
- US120 Bobby Parnell .12 .30
- US121 Jon Rauch .12 .30
- US122 Alfredo Aceves .12 .30
- US123 Brad Penny .12 .30
- US124 Xavier Paul .12 .30
- US125 Joel Peralta .12 .30
- US126 Adrian Gonzalez .25 .60
- US127 Rickie Weeks .12 .30
- US128 Mariano Rivera .40 1.00
- US129 Brooks Conrad .12 .30
- US130 David Robertson .12 .30
- US131 Jeff Keppinger .12 .30
- US132 Jose Altuve RC 12.00 30.00
- US133 Fernando Salas .20 .50
- US134 Michael Bourn .12 .30
- US135 Grant Balfour .12 .30
- US136 Brandon Crawford .20 .50
- US137 Willie Bloomquist .12 .30
- US138A Michael Young .12 .30
- US138B Paul Molitor SP 5.00 12.00
- US139 Rafael Soriano .12 .30
- US140A Clayton Kershaw .60 1.50
- US140B Sandy Koufax SP 6.00 15.00
- US141 Mike Cameron .12 .30
- US142 Alex White RC .40 1.00
- US143 Craig Kimbrel .30 .75
- US144 Kevin Youkilis .12 .30
- US145 Bartolo Colon .12 .30
- US146 Jordan Walden .12 .30
- US147 C.J. Wilson .12 .30
- US148 Alex Presley RC .60 1.50
- US149 Omar Infante .12 .30
- US150 Adrian Beltre .30 .75
- US151 Cory Gearrin RC .40 1.00
- US152 Julio Teheran RC .60 1.50
- US153 Matt Guerrier .12 .30
- US154A Cliff Lee .20 .50
- US154B Babe Ruth SP 6.00 15.00
- US155 Eric Hosmer RC 2.50 6.00
- US156 Humberto Quintero .12 .30
- US157 Reed Johnson .12 .30
- US158 Darren Oliver .12 .30
- US159 Alex Cobb RC .40 1.00
- US160 Victor Martinez .20 .50
- US161 Conor Jackson .12 .30
- US162 Troy Tulowitzki .30 .75
- US163 Adrian Beltre .30 .75
- US164 Hector Noesi .60 1.50
- US165 Al Albuquerque RC .40 1.00
- US166 David Ortiz .30 .75
- US167 Brandan Ryan .12 .30
- US168 Bruce Chen .12 .30
- US169 Ezequiel Carrera RC .40 1.00
- US170 Brad Ziegler .12 .30
- US171 Matt Lindstrom .12 .30
- US172 Jonny Venters .12 .30
- US173 Charlie Furbush RC .40 1.00
- US174 Jacob Turner RC 1.50 4.00
- US175 Mike Trout RC 600.00 1200.00
- US176 Xavier Nady .12 .30
- US177 Rene Tosoni RC .40 1.00
- US178 Jason Bourgeois .12 .30
- US179 Michael Pineda .30 .75
- US180 Daniel Moskos RC .40 1.00
- US181 Jo Jo Reyes .12 .30
- US182 Ronny Paulino .12 .30
- US183 Carlos Peguero RC .60 1.50
- US184 Tyler Chatwood RC .40 1.00
- US185 Orlando Hudson .12 .30
- US186 J.D. Martinez RC 4.00 10.00
- US187 Bobby Wilson .12 .30
- US188 Eric Hosmer .75 2.00
- US189 Wilson Valdez .12 .30
- US190 Alexi Ogando .30 .75
- US191 Andy Sonnanstine .12 .30
- US192 Mike Moustakas RC 1.00 2.50
- US193 Lonnie Chisenhall .20 .50
- US194 Jason Kipnis RC 1.25 3.00
- US195A Joey Votto .30 .75
- US195B Larry Walker SP 5.00 12.00
- US196 Philip Humber .12 .30
- US197 Brandon League .12 .30
- US198 Kevin Jepsen .12 .30
- US199 Micah Owings .12 .30
- US200 Vladimir Guerrero .20 .50
- US201 Hisanori Takahashi .12 .30
- US202 Derrek Lee .12 .30
- US203 Juan Nicasio RC .40 1.00
- US204 Brian Wilson .30 .75
- US205 D.J. LeMahieu RC 10.00 25.00
- US206 J.P. Howell .12 .30
- US207A Jay Bruce .20 .50
- US207B Frank Robinson SP 5.00 12.00
- US208 Javier Lopez .12 .30
- US209 Rubby De La Rosa RC 1.00 2.50
- US210 Jayson Werth .20 .50
- US211 Dustin Moseley .12 .30
- US212 Pat Neshek .12 .30
- US213 Louis Coleman RC .40 1.00
- US214 Matt Daley .12 .30
- US215 Michael Dunn .12 .30
- US216 Takashi Saito .12 .30
- US217 Elliot Johnson .12 .30
- US218 Matt Kemp .25 .60
- US219 George Sherrill .12 .30
- US21A Prince Fielder .20 .50
- US21B Willie McCovey SP 5.00 12.00
- US220 Adam Dunn .20 .50
- US221 Jamey Carroll .12 .30
- US222 Chris Gimenez .12 .30
- US223 Arthur Rhodes .12 .30
- US224 Bill Hall .12 .30
- US225 David DeJesus .12 .30
- US226 Steve Pearce .30 .75
- US227 Kosuke Fukudome .20 .50
- US228 Zach Britton .30 .75
- US229A Asdrubal Cabrera .20 .50
- US229B Roberto Alomar SP 8.00 20.00
- US230A Miguel Cabrera .30 .75
- US230B Al Kaline SP 5.00 12.00
- US231 Charlie Blackmon RC 8.00 20.00
- US232 Miguel Tejada .20 .50
- US233 John McDonald .12 .30
- US234 Brandon Crawford RC .60 1.50
- US235 Charlie Morton .30 .75
- US236 Jose Morales .12 .30
- US237 Ryan Roberts .12 .30
- US238A Carlos Beltran .20 .50
- US238B Darryl Strawberry SP 5.00 12.00
- US239 J.J. Hardy .12 .30
- US240 Blake Tekotte RC .40 1.00
- US241 Brandon Wood .12 .30
- US242 Matt Holliday .30 .75
- US243 Chris Denorfia .12 .30
- US244 Francisco Rodriguez .20 .50
- US245 Kevin Correia .12 .30
- US246 Alcides Escobar .20 .50
- US247 Zack Cozart RC 1.00 2.50
- US248 Octavio Dotel .12 .30
- US249A Starlin Castro .20 .50
- US249B Ozzie Smith SP 5.00 12.00
- US250 Zack Greinke .20 .50
- US251 Justin Turner .25 .60
- US252 Derek Jeter .75 2.00
- US253 Scott Linebrink .12 .30
- US254 Dustin Ackley .20 .50
- US255 Allen Craig .25 .60
- US256 Mark Kotsay .12 .30
- US257 Erik Bedard .12 .30
- US258A Andre Ethier .20 .50
- US258B Monte Irvin SP 5.00 12.00
- US259 Andre Ethier .20 .50
- US260A Matt Holliday .30 .75
- US260B Ty Cobb SP 5.00 12.00
- US261 John Buck .12 .30
- US262 Javy Guerra (RC) .60 1.50
- US263 Chad Qualls .12 .30
- US264 Alex White .12 .30
- US265 Willie Harris .12 .30
- US266 Jason Isringhausen .12 .30
- US267 Sam Fuld .12 .30
- US268 Yadier Molina .30 .75
- US269 Sergio Santos .12 .30
- US270 Todd Frazier RC 1.25 3.00
- US271 Eric O'Flaherty .12 .30
- US272 Jorge Cantu .12 .30
- US273 Miguel Montero .12 .30
- US274 Jeff Karstens .12 .30
- US275 Michael Cuddyer .12 .30
- US276 Yuniesky Betancourt .12 .30
- US277 Sam LeCure .12 .30

US278A Jacoby Ellsbury .25 .60
US278B Tris Speaker SP 5.00 12.00
US279 Trevor Plouffe .12 .30
US280 Kyle Farnsworth .12 .30
US281 Mark Melancon .12 .30
US282 Brad Hand RC .40 1.00
US283 Latroy Hawkins .12 .30
US284 Laynce Nix .12 .30
US285 David Purcey .12 .30
US286 Rich Thompson .12 .30
US287 Matt Joyce .12 .30
US288 Eric Thames RC 2.00 5.00
US289 Eric Chavez .12 .30
US290 Sean Burroughs .12 .30
US291A Andrew McCutchen .30 .75
US291B Andre Dawson SP 5.00 12.00
US292 Mike Adams .12 .30
US293 Howie Kendrick .12 .30
US294 Edwin Jackson .12 .30
US295 Wilson Ramos .12 .30
US296 Bobby Jenks .12 .30
US297 Chase D'Arnaud RC .40 1.00
US298 Yorvit Torrealba .12 .30
US299 Robinson Cano .20 .50
US300 Carl Crawford .20 .50
US301 Tom Gorzelanny .12 .30
US302 Alex Torres RC .40 1.00
US303 Juan Uribe .12 .30
US304 Hunter Pence .20 .50
US305 Carlos Beltran .20 .50
US306 Brandon Phillips .12 .30
US307 Casey Coleman .12 .30
US308 Kyle Seager RC 1.00 2.50
US309A Paul Konerko .20 .50
US309B Jimmie Foxx SP 5.00 12.00
US310 Scott Rolen .20 .50
US311 Drew Butera .12 .30
US312 Danny Duffy RC .60 1.50
US313 Tyson Ross .12 .30
US314 Armando Galarraga .12 .30
US315 Carlos Pena .20 .50
US316 Justin Upton .20 .50
US317 Craig Counsell .12 .30
US318 Brayan Pena .12 .30
US319 Corey Patterson .12 .30
US31A Curtis Granderson .25 .60
US31B Paul O'Neill SP 5.00 12.00
US320 Russell Martin .12 .30
US321 Gaby Sanchez .12 .30
US322 Fernando Martinez .12 .30
US323 Jhonny Peralta .12 .30
US324 Melvin Mora .12 .30
US325 Jason Giambi .12 .30
US326 Trevor Bell .12 .30
US327 Blake Beavan RC .60 1.50
US328 Kevin Gregg .12 .30
US329 Dee Gordon RC .60 1.50
US330 Lance Berkman .20 .50

2011 Topps Update Cognac Diamond Anniversary

*COGNAC VET: 2X TO 5X BASIC
*COGNAC RC: .6X TO 1.5X BASIC RC
*COGNAC SP: .25X TO .6X BASIC SP
STATED ODDS 1:3 HOBBY
STATED SP ODDS 1:81 HOBBY
US47 Paul Goldschmidt 15.00 40.00
US55 Anthony Rizzo 20.00 50.00
US132 Jose Altuve 50.00 120.00
US175 Mike Trout 1500.00 2500.00
US186 J.D. Martinez 15.00 40.00

2011 Topps Update Black

*BLACK: 12X TO 30X BASIC
*BLACK RC: 4X TP 10X BASIC
STATED ODDS 1:58 HOBBY
STATED PRINT RUN 60 SER.#'d SETS
US47 Paul Goldschmidt 200.00 500.00
US55 Anthony Rizzo 75.00 200.00
US132 Jose Altuve 1000.00 1500.00
US175 Mike Trout 8000.00 12000.00
US186 J.D. Martinez 125.00 300.00

2011 Topps Update Diamond Anniversary

*DIAMOND VET: 2X TO 5X BASIC
*DIAMOND RC: .6X TO 1.5X BASIC RC
*DIAMOND SP: .25X TO .6X BASIC SP
STATED ODDS 1:4 HOBBY
STATED SP ODDS 1:79 HOBBY
US47 Paul Goldschmidt 15.00 40.00
US55 Anthony Rizzo 20.00 50.00
US132 Jose Altuve 50.00 120.00
US175 Mike Trout 1500.00 2500.00

2011 Topps Update Gold

*GOLD VET: 2X TO 5X BASIC
*GOLD RC: .6X TO 1.5X BASIC RC
STATED ODDS 1:3 HOBBY
STATED PRINT RUN 2011 SER.#'d SETS
US47 Paul Goldschmidt 15.00 40.00
US55 Anthony Rizzo 20.00 50.00
US132 Jose Altuve 50.00 120.00
US175 Mike Trout 1500.00 2500.00
US186 J.D. Martinez 15.00 40.00

2011 Topps Update Hope Diamond Anniversary

*HOPE VET: 12X TO 30X BASIC
*HOPE RC: 4X TO 10X BASIC RC
*HOPE SP: .75X TO 2X BASIC SP
STATED ODDS 1:68 HOBBY
STATED SP ODDS 1:2627 HOBBY
STATED PRINT RUN 60 SER.#'d SETS
US47 Paul Goldschmidt 200.00 500.00
US55 Anthony Rizzo 75.00 200.00
US132 Jose Altuve 1000.00 1500.00
US175 Mike Trout 7000.00 12000.00

2011 Topps Update Target Red Border

*TARGET: 2X TO 5X BASIC
*TARGET RC: .6X TO 1.5X BASIC RC
FOUND IN TARGET RETAIL PACKS
US47 Paul Goldschmidt 15.00 40.00
US55 Anthony Rizzo 20.00 50.00
US132 Jose Altuve 150.00 400.00
US175 Mike Trout 1500.00 2500.00
US186 J.D. Martinez 15.00 40.00

2011 Topps Update Wal-Mart Blue Border

*WM: 2X TO 5X BASIC
*WM RC: .6X TO 1.5X BASIC RC
FOUND IN WAL MART RETAIL PACKS
US47 Paul Goldschmidt 15.00 40.00
US55 Anthony Rizzo 20.00 50.00
US132 Jose Altuve 75.00 200.00
US175 Mike Trout 1500.00 2500.00
US186 J.D. Martinez 15.00 40.00

2011 Topps Update All-Star Stitches

STATED ODDS 1:51 HOBBY
AS1 Jose Bautista 4.00 10.00
AS2 Alex Avila 4.00 10.00
AS3 Robinson Cano 5.00 12.00
AS4 Adrian Gonzalez 4.00 10.00
AS5 Curtis Granderson 4.00 10.00
AS6 Josh Hamilton 5.00 12.00
AS7 David Ortiz 4.00 10.00
AS8 Carlos Quentin 3.00 8.00
AS9 Jered Weaver 3.00 8.00
AS10 Tim Lincecum 5.00 12.00
AS11 Gio Gonzalez 3.00 8.00
AS12 Brandon League 3.00 8.00
AS13 Alexi Ogando 3.00 8.00
AS14 Chris Perez 4.00 10.00
AS15 Justin Verlander 5.00 12.00
AS16 David Robertson 4.00 10.00
AS17 Michael Young 3.00 8.00
AS18 Kevin Youkilis 3.00 8.00
AS19 Josh Beckett 4.00 10.00
AS20 C.J. Wilson 3.00 8.00
AS21 Adrian Beltre 3.00 8.00
AS22 Asdrubal Cabrera 4.00 10.00
AS23 Miguel Cabrera 5.00 12.00
AS24 Michael Cuddyer 4.00 10.00
AS25 Jacoby Ellsbury 4.00 10.00
AS26 Matt Joyce 4.00 10.00
AS27 Howie Kendrick 3.00 8.00
AS28 Paul Konerko 3.00 8.00
AS29 Justin Upton 4.00 10.00
AS30 Jhonny Peralta 4.00 10.00
AS31 Brian McCann 3.00 8.00
AS32 Prince Fielder 4.00 10.00
AS33 Rickie Weeks 3.00 8.00
AS34 Lance Berkman 3.00 8.00
AS35 Matt Kemp 5.00 12.00
AS36 Heath Bell 3.00 8.00
AS37 Tyler Clippard 3.00 8.00
AS38 Pablo Sandoval 4.00 10.00
AS39 Roy Halladay 5.00 12.00
AS40 Joel Hanrahan 4.00 10.00
AS41 Jair Jurrjens 4.00 10.00
AS42 Clayton Kershaw 5.00 12.00
AS43 Craig Kimbrel 5.00 12.00
AS44 Cliff Lee 5.00 12.00
AS45 Troy Tulowitzki 3.00 8.00
AS46 Jonny Venters 4.00 10.00
AS47 Joey Votto 4.00 10.00
AS48 Brian Wilson 5.00 12.00
AS49 Jay Bruce 4.00 10.00
AS50 Carlos Beltran 3.00 8.00
AS51 Starlin Castro 5.00 12.00
AS52 Andre Ethier 3.00 8.00
AS53 Matt Holliday 4.00 10.00
AS54 Yadier Molina 4.00 10.00
AS55 Miguel Montero 4.00 10.00
AS56 Andrew McCutchen 4.00 10.00
AS57 Hunter Pence 4.00 10.00
AS58 Brandon Phillips 4.00 10.00
AS59 Scott Rolen 4.00 10.00
AS60 Gaby Sanchez 3.00 8.00
AS61 Kevin Correia 4.00 10.00
AS62 Russell Martin 4.00 10.00
AS63 Jose Valverde 4.00 10.00
AS64 Jose Reyes 5.00 12.00
AS65 Ryan Braun 4.00 10.00
AS66 Felix Hernandez 3.00 8.00
AS67 Jon Lester 4.00 10.00
AS68 David Price 4.00 10.00
AS69 James Shields 3.00 8.00
AS70 Matt Cain 4.00 10.00
AS71 Cole Hamels 4.00 10.00
AS72 Ryan Vogelsong 4.00 10.00
AS73 Placido Polanco 4.00 10.00
AS74 Shane Victorino 4.00 10.00
AS75 Ricky Romero 3.00 8.00

2011 Topps Update All-Star Stitches Diamond Anniversary

*DIAMOND: .75X TO 2X BASIC
STATED ODDS 1:759 HOBBY
STATED PRINT RUN 60 SER.#'d SETS

2011 Topps Update Diamond Duos

COMPLETE SET (30) 6.00 15.00
STATED ODDS 1:8 HOBBY
DD1 F.Hernanez/M.Pineda .60 1.50
DD2 Andre Ethier/Matt Kemp .50 1.25
DD3 Jered Weaver/Dan Haren .40 1.00
DD4 A.Pujols/L.Berkman .75 2.00
DD5 E.Hosmer/B.Belt 1.50 4.00
DD6 Brett Anderson/Trevor Cahill .25 .60
DD7 S.Castro/D.Barney .75 2.00
DD8 Joey Votto/Jay Bruce .60 1.50
DD9 Zack Greinke/Shaun Marcum .40 1.00
DD10 M.Pineda/Z.Britton .60 1.50
DD11 Adam Dunn/Paul Konerko .40 1.00
DD12 Matt Holliday/Colby Rasmus .60 1.50
DD13 Stanton/Morrison .60 1.50
DD14 Jose Bautista/Adam Lind .40 1.00
DD15 J.DiMaggio/D.Jeter 1.50 4.00
DD16 E.Hosmer/D.Duffy 1.50 4.00
DD17 C.Kimbrel/J.Teheran .60 1.50
DD18 Adrian Gonzalez/Jose Bautista .50 1.25
DD19 J.Verlander/M.Scherzer .60 1.50
DD20 H.Aaron/J.Bautista 1.25 3.00
DD21 David Price/James Shields .50 1.25
DD22 Ricky Romero/Kyle Drabek .40 1.00
DD23 David Ortiz/Vladimir Guerrero .60 1.50
DD24 E.Longoria/B.Zobrist .40 1.00
DD25 E.Hosmer/F.Freeman 4.00 10.00
DD26 B.Posey/B.McCann .75 2.00
DD27 Grady Sizemore/Shin-Soo Choo .40 1.00
DD28 Brandon Phillips/Howie Kendrick .25 .60
DD29 M.Kemp/J.Sands .60 1.50
DD30 S.Koufax/R.Braun 1.25 3.00

2011 Topps Update Diamond Duos Dual Relics

STATED ODDS 1:4650 HOBBY
STATED PRINT RUN 50 SER.#'d SETS
DD1 F.Hernanez/M.Pineda 15.00 40.00
DD2 A.Ethier/M.Kemp 20.00 50.00
DD3 J.Weaver/D.Haren 20.00 50.00
DD4 A.Pujols/L.Berkman 40.00 80.00
DD5 E.Hosmer/B.Belt 50.00 100.00
DD6 B.Anderson/T.Cahill 6.00 15.00
DD7 S.Castro/D.Barney 30.00 60.00
DD8 J.Votto/J.Bruce 15.00 40.00
DD9 Z.Greinke/S.Marcum 15.00 40.00
DD10 M.Pineda/Z.Britton 15.00 40.00
DD11 A.Dunn/P.Konerko 20.00 50.00
DD12 M.Holliday/C.Rasmus 10.00 25.00
DD13 M.Stanton/L.Morrison 12.50 30.00
DD14 J.Bautista/A.Lind 15.00 40.00
DD15 J.DiMaggio/D.Jeter 100.00 175.00

2011 Topps Update Next 60 Autographs

STATED ODDS 1:566 HOBBY
EXCHANGE DEADLINE 9/30/2014
AC Aroldis Chapman 20.00 50.00
AJ Austin Jackson 6.00 15.00
AO Alexi Ogando 4.00 10.00
BB Brandon Belt 4.00 10.00
BW Brett Wallace 4.00 10.00
CK Craig Kimbrel 12.00 30.00
CS Chris Sale 8.00 20.00
DA Dustin Ackley 12.50 30.00
DD Danny Duffy 4.00 10.00
DH Daniel Hudson 3.00 8.00
EH Eric Hosmer 60.00 120.00
FF Freddie Freeman 10.00 25.00
JH Jeremy Hellickson 5.00 12.00
JJ Jeremy Jeffress 3.00 8.00
JS Jerry Sands 4.00 10.00
JW Jordan Walden 4.00 10.00
KD Kyle Drabek 3.00 8.00
MM Mike Moustakas 8.00 20.00
MP Michael Pineda 8.00 20.00
MS Mike Stanton 60.00 120.00
MT Mark Trumbo 8.00 20.00
NF Neftali Feliz 4.00 10.00
SC Starlin Castro 40.00 80.00
JT1 Jose Tabata 5.00 12.00
JT2 Julio Teheran 4.00 10.00

2011 Topps Update Topps Town

STATED ODDS 1:8 HOBBY
TTU1 Eric Hosmer 1.25 3.00
TTU2 Francisco Liriano .20 .50
TTU3 Prince Fielder .30 .75
TTU4 Carlos Beltran .30 .75
TTU5 Ricky Romero .20 .50
TTU6 Vernon Wells .20 .50
TTU7 Rickie Weeks .20 .50
TTU8 Brian Wilson .50 1.25
TTU9 Colby Rasmus .30 .75
TTU10 Zach Britton .50 1.25
TTU11 Wandy Rodriguez .20 .50
TTU12 Gaby Sanchez .20 .50
TTU13 Shane Victorino .30 .75
TTU14 Matt Garza .20 .50
TTU15 Francisco Rodriguez .30 .75
TTU16 Drew Stubbs .20 .50
TTU17 James Shields .20 .50
TTU18 Heath Bell .20 .50
TTU19 Fausto Carmona .20 .50
TTU20 Freddie Freeman 3.00 8.00
TTU21 Chad Billingsley .30 .75
TTU22 Stephen Drew .30 .75
TTU23 Jimmy Rollins .30 .75
TTU24 Vladimir Guerrero .30 .75
TTU25 Gio Gonzalez .30 .75
TTU26 Curtis Granderson .40 1.00
TTU27 Neil Walker .30 .75
TTU28 Alfonso Soriano .30 .75
TTU29 Michael Young .20 .50
TTU30 Paul Konerko .30 .75
TTU31 Adam Lind .30 .75
TTU32 Ben Zobrist .30 .75
TTU33 Travis Hafner .20 .50
TTU34 Jhoulys Chacin .20 .50
TTU35 Jaime Garcia .30 .75
TTU36 Jered Weaver .30 .75
TTU37 Max Scherzer .50 1.25
TTU38 Alex Rodriguez .60 1.50
TTU39 Jacoby Ellsbury .40 1.00
TTU40 Matt Kemp .40 1.00
TTU41 Michael Bourn .20 .50
TTU42 Kurt Suzuki .20 .50
TTU43 Brian McCann .30 .75
TTU44 CC Sabathia .30 .75
TTU45 Josh Beckett .20 .50
TTU46 Adrian Beltre .50 1.25
TTU47 Drew Storen .20 .50
TTU48 Ian Desmond .20 .50
TTU49 Matt Cain .30 .75
TTU50 Michael Pineda .50 1.25

2012 Topps

COMP.FACT.HOBBY.SET (661) 40.00 80.00
COMP.FACT.ALLSTAR.SET (661) 40.00 80.00
COMP.FACT.FENWAY SET(661) 40.00 80.00
COMP.FACT.HOLIDAY SET(661) 40.00 80.00
COMP.SER.1 w/o SP's (330) 12.50 30.00
COMP.SER.1 w/o SP's (330) 12.50 30.00
COMMON CARD (1-660) .15 .40
COMMON RC (1-660) .25 .60
COMMON SP VAR (1-660) 5.00 12.00
SER.1 PLATE ODDS 1:2331 HOBBY
SER.2 PLATE ODDS 1:1624 HOBBY
PLATE PRINT RUN 1 SET PER COLOR
BLACK-CYAN-MAGENTA-YELLOW ISSUED
NO PLATE PRICING DUE TO SCARCITY
1A Ryan Braun .15 .40
1B Ryan Braun VAR SP 5.00 12.00
2 Trevor Cahill .15 .40
3 Jaime Garcia .20 .50
4 Jeremy Guthrie .15 .40
5 Desmond Jennings .20 .50
6 Nick Hagadone RC .25 .60
7A Mickey Mantle .75 2.00
7B Mickey Mantle UER .75 2.00
8 Mike Adams .15 .40
9 Jesus Montero RC .25 .60
10 Jon Lester .15 .40
11 Hong-Chih Kuo .15 .40
12 Wilson Ramos .15 .40
13 Vernon Wells .15 .40
14 Jesus Guzman .15 .40
15 Melky Cabrera .15 .40
16 Desmond Jennings .20 .50
17 Alex Rios .20 .50
18 Colby Lewis .15 .40
19 Yonder Alonso .15 .40
20 Craig Kimbrel .20 .50
21 Chris Iannetta .15 .40
22 Alfredo Simon .15 .40
23 Cory Luebke .15 .40
24 Ike Davis .15 .40
25 Neil Walker .20 .50
26 Kyle Lohse .15 .40
27 John Buck .15 .40
28 Placido Polanco .15 .40
29 Livan Hernandez/Roy Oswalt
Randy Wolf LDR .20 .50
30A Derek Jeter .60 1.50
30B Derek Jeter VAR SP 12.00 30.00
30C J.DiMaggio VAR SP 8.00 20.00
31 Brent Morel .15 .40
32 Detroit Tigers PS HL .15 .40
33 Curtis Granderson/Robinson Cano
Adrian Gonzalez LL .20 .50
34 Derek Holland .15 .40
35A Eric Hosmer .20 .50
35B Hosmer VAR Gatorade SP 5.00 12.00
35C Hosmer VAR Dugout SP 5.00 12.00
36 Michael Taylor RC .25 .60
37 Mike Napoli .15 .40
38 Felipe Paulino .15 .40
39 James Loney .15 .40
40 Tom Milone RC .25 .60
41 Devin Mesoraco RC .25 .60
42 Drew Pomeranz RC .25 .60
43 Brett Wallace .15 .40
44 Edwin Jackson .15 .40
45 Jhoulys Chacin .15 .40
46 Peter Bourjos .15 .40
47 Luke Hochevar .15 .40
48 Wade Davis .20 .50
49 Jon Niese .15 .40
50 Adrian Gonzalez .20 .50
51 Alcides Escobar .20 .50
52 Verland/Weaver/Shields LL .25 .60
53 St. Louis Cardinals WS HL .25 .60
54 Jhonny Peralta .15 .40
55 Michael Young .15 .40
56 Geovany Soto .15 .40
57 Yuniesky Betancourt .15 .40
58 Tim Hudson .20 .50
59 Texas Rangers PS HL .15 .40
60 Hanley Ramirez .20 .50
61 Daniel Bard .15 .40
62 Ben Revere .20 .50
63 Nate Schierholtz .15 .40
64 Michael Martinez .15 .40
65 Delmon Young .20 .50
66 Nyjer Morgan .15 .40
67 Aaron Crow .15 .40
68 Jason Hammel .20 .50
69 Dee Gordon .15 .40
70 Brett Pill RC .40 1.00
71 Jeff Karstens .15 .40
72 Rex Brothers .15 .40
73 Brandon McCarthy .15 .40
74 Kevin Correia .15 .40
75 Jordan Zimmermann .20 .50
76A Ian Kennedy .15 .40
76B Ian Kennedy VAR SP 5.00 12.00
77 Kemp/Prince/Pujols LL .30 .75
78 Erick Aybar .15 .40
79 Austin Romine RC .25 .60
80A David Price .20 .50
80B David Price VAR SP 5.00 12.00
With trophy
81 Liam Hendriks RC .25 .60
82 Rick Porcello .15 .40
83 Bobby Parnell .15 .40
84 Brian Matusz .15 .40
85A Jason Heyward .20 .50
85B Jason Heyward VAR SP 5.00 12.00
Throwback jersey
86 Brett Cecil .15 .40
87 Craig Kimbrel .20 .50
88 Javy Guerra .15 .40
89 Dontrelle Willis .15 .40
90 Adron Chambers RC .40 1.00
91 ARodr/Thome/Giambi LDR .30 .75
92 Tim Lincecum/Chris Carpenter
Roy Oswalt LDR .20 .50
93A Skip Schumaker .15 .40
93B Schumaker Squirrel SP 30.00 80.00
94 Logan Forsythe .15 .40
95 Chris Parmelee RC .25 .60
96 Grady Sizemore .20 .50
97 Jim Thome RB .20 .50
98 Domonic Brown .20 .50
99 Michael McKenry .15 .40
100 Jose Bautista .20 .50
101 David Hernandez .15 .40
102 Chase d'Arnaud .15 .40
103 Madison Bumgarner .20 .50
104 Brett Anderson .15 .40
105 Paul Konerko .15 .40
106 Mark Trumbo .15 .40
107 Luke Scott .15 .40
108 Albert Pujols WS HL .30 .75
109 Mariano Rivera RB .30 .75
110 Mark Teixeira .20 .50
111 Kevin Slowey .15 .40
112 Juan Nicasio .15 .40
113 Craig Kimbrel RB .20 .50
114 Matt Garza .15 .40
115 Tommy Hanson .15 .40
116 A.J. Pierzynski .15 .40
117 Carlos Ruiz .15 .40
118 Miguel Olivo .15 .40
119 Ichiro/Mauer/Vlad LDR .30 .75
120 Hunter Pence .20 .50
121 Josh Bell .15 .40
122 Ted Lilly .15 .40
123 Scott Downs .15 .40
124 Pujols/Vlad/Helton LDR .30 .75
125 Adam Jones .20 .50
126 Eduardo Nunez .15 .40
127 Eli Whiteside .15 .40
128 Lucas Duda .20 .50
129A Matt Moore RC .40 1.00
129B Moore Leg Up FS .40 1.00
130 Asdrubal Cabrera .20 .50
131 Ian Desmond .15 .40
132 Will Venable .15 .40
133 Ivan Nova .20 .50
134 Stephen Lombardozzi RC .25 .60
135 Johnny Cueto .20 .50
136 Casey McGehee .15 .40
137 Jarrod Saltalamacchia .15 .40
138 Pedro Alvarez .15 .40
139 Scott Sizemore .15 .40
140 Troy Tulowitzki .25 .60
141 Brandon Belt .20 .50
142 Travis Wood .15 .40
143 George Kottaras .15 .40
144 Marlon Byrd .15 .40
145A Billy Butler .15 .40
145B Billy Butler VAR SP 5.00 12.00
146 Carlos Gomez .15 .40
147 Orlando Hudson .15 .40
148 Chris Getz .15 .40
149 Chris Sale .25 .60
150 Roy Halladay .20 .50
151 Chris Davis .15 .40
152 Chad Billingsley .15 .40
153 Mark Melancon .15 .40
154 Ty Wigginton .15 .40
155 Matt Cain .20 .50
156 Kenn/Kershaw/Halladay LL .50 1.25
157 Anibal Sanchez .15 .40
158A Josh Reddick .15 .40
158B Josh Reddick VAR SP 5.00 12.00
Rookie Cup
159 Chipper/Pujols/Helton LDR .30 .75
160 Kevin Youkilis .25 .60
161 Dee Gordon .15 .40
162 Max Scherzer .25 .60
163 Justin Turner .20 .50
164 Carl Pavano .15 .40
165A Michael Morse .15 .40
165B Michael Morse VAR SP 5.00 12.00
166 Brennan Boesch .15 .40
167 Starlin Castro RB .20 .50
168 Blake Beavan .15 .40
169 Brett Myers .15 .40
170 Jacoby Ellsbury .20 .50
171 Koji Uehara .15 .40
172 Reed Johnson .15 .40
173A Ryan Roberts .15 .40
173B Ryan Roberts VAR SP 5.00 12.00
174 Yadier Molina .25 .60
175 Jared Hughes RC .25 .60
176 Nolan Reimold .15 .40
177 Josh Thole .15 .40
178 Edward Mujica .15 .40
179 Denard Span .15 .40
180 Mariano Rivera .30 .75
181 Reyes/Braun/Kemp LL .20 .50
182 Michael Brantley .15 .40
183 Addison Reed RC .25 .60
184 Wilin Rosario RC .25 .60
185A Pablo Sandoval .20 .50
185B Pablo Sandoval VAR SP 5.00 12.00
185C Pablo Sandoval VAR SP 5.00 12.00
186 John Lannan .15 .40
187 Jose Altuve .20 .50
188A Bobby Abreu .15 .40
188B Bobby Abreu VAR SP 5.00 12.00
189 Alberto Callaspo .15 .40
190 Cole Hamels .20 .50
191 Angel Pagan .15 .40
192 Chipper/Pujols/Jones LDR .30 .75
193 Kelly Shoppach .15 .40
194 Danny Duffy .15 .40
195 Ben Zobrist .20 .50
196 Matt Joyce .15 .40
197 Brendan Ryan .15 .40
198 Matt Dominguez RC .30 .75
199 Adam Dunn .20 .50
200 Miguel Cabrera .25 .60
201 Doug Fister .15 .40
202 Andrew Carignan RC .25 .60
203 Jeff Niemann .15 .40
204 Tom Gorzelanny .15 .40
205 Justin Masterson .15 .40
206 David Robertson .15 .40
207A J.P. Arencibia .15 .40
207B J.P. Arencibia VAR SP 5.00 12.00
Rookie Cup
208 Mark Reynolds .15 .40
209 A.J. Burnett .15 .40
210 Zack Greinke .20 .50
211 Kelvin Herrera RC .25 .60
212 Tim Wakefield/CC Sabathia
Mark Buehrle LDR .20 .50
213 Alex Avila .20 .50
214 Mike Pelfrey .15 .40
215A Freddie Freeman .30 .75
215B Freddie Freeman VAR SP 5.00 12.00
216 Jason Kipnis .20 .50
217 Texas Rangers PS HL .15 .40
218 Kyle Hudson RC .25 .60
219 Jordan Pacheco RC .25 .60
220 Jay Bruce .20 .50
221 Luke Gregerson .15 .40
222 Chris Coghlan .15 .40
223 Joe Saunders .15 .40
224 Kemp/Prince/Howard LL .30 .75
225 Michael Pineda .15 .40
226 Ryan Hanigan .15 .40
227 Mike Minor .15 .40
228 Brent Lillibridge .15 .40
229 Yunel Escobar .20 .50
230 Justin Morneau .20 .50
231 Dexter Fowler .20 .50
232 Rivera/Johan/Felix LDR .30 .75
233 St. Louis Cardinals PS HL .25 .60
234 Mark Teixeira RB .20 .50
235 Joe Benson RC .25 .60
236 Jose Tabata .15 .40
237 Russell Martin .15 .40
238 Emilio Bonifacio .15 .40
239 Cabrera/Young/Gonzalez .25 .60
240 David Wright .20 .50
241 James McDonald .15 .40
242 Eric Young .15 .40
243 Justin De Fratus RC .25 .60
244 Sergio Santos .15 .40
245 Adam Lind .20 .50
246 Bud Norris .15 .40
247 Clay Buchholz .15 .40
248 Stephen Drew .15 .40
249 Trevor Plouffe .15 .40
250 Jered Weaver .20 .50
251 Jason Bay .20 .50
252 Dellin Betances RC .40 1.00
253 Tim Federowicz RC .25 .60
254 Philip Humber .15 .40
255 Scott Rolen .20 .50
256A Mat Latos .20 .50
256B Mat Latos VAR SP 5.00 12.00
257 Seth Smith .15 .40
258 Jon Jay .25 .60
259 Michael Stutes .15 .40
260 Brian Wilson .25 .60
261 Kyle Blanks .15 .40
262 Shaun Marcum .15 .40
263 Steve Delabar RC .25 .60
264 Chris Carpenter PS HL .20 .50
265 Aroldis Chapman .25 .60
266 Carlos Corporan .15 .40
267 Joel Pineiro .15 .40
268 Miguel Cairo .15 .40
269 Jason Vargas .15 .40
270A Starlin Castro .20 .50
270B Starlin Castro VAR SP 5.00 12.00
271 John Jaso .15 .40
272 Nyjer Morgan PS HL .15 .40
273A David Freese .20 .50
273B David Freese VAR SP 8.00 20.00
273C S.Musial VAR SP 6.00 15.00
274 Alex Liddi RC .25 .60
275 Brad Peacock RC .25 .60
276 Scott Baker .15 .40
277 Jeremy Moore RC .25 .60
278 Randy Wells .15 .40
279 R.A. Dickey .20 .50
280A Ryan Howard .20 .50
280B Ryan Howard VAR SP 8.00 20.00
Back of jersey
281 Mark Trumbo .15 .40
282 Ryan Raburn .15 .40
283 Brandon Allen .15 .40
284 Tony Gwynn .15 .40
285 Drew Storen .15 .40
286 Franklin Gutierrez .15 .40
287 Antonio Bastardo .15 .40
288 Miguel Montero .15 .40
289 Casey Kotchman .15 .40
290 Curtis Granderson .20 .50
291 David Freese WS HL .20 .50
292 Ben Revere .20 .50
293 Eric Thames .20 .50
294 John Axford .15 .40
295 Jayson Werth .20 .50
296 Brayan Pena .15 .40
297 Kershaw/Halladay/Lee LL .50 1.25
298 Jeff Keppinger .15 .40
299 Mitch Moreland .15 .40
300 Josh Hamilton .20 .50
301 Alexi Ogando .15 .40
302 Jose Bautista/Curtis Granderson
Mark Teixeira LL .20 .50
303 Danny Valencia .20 .50
304 Brandon Morrow .15 .40
305 Chipper Jones .25 .60
306 Ubaldo Jimenez .15 .40
307 Vance Worley .20 .50
308A Mike Leake .15 .40
308B Mike Leake VAR SP 5.00 12.00
309 Kurt Suzuki .15 .40
310 Adrian Beltre .25 .60
311 John Danks .15 .40
312 Nick Hundley .15 .40
313 Phil Hughes .15 .40
314 Matt LaPorta .15 .40
315 Dustin Ackley .15 .40
316 Nick Blackburn .15 .40
317 Tyler Chatwood .15 .40
318 Erik Bedard .15 .40
319 Verland/CC/Weaver LL .25 .60
320 Matt Holliday .25 .60
321 Jason Bourgeois .15 .40
322 Ricky Nolasco .15 .40
323 Jason Isringhausen .15 .40
324 ARod/Thme/Gmbi LDR .30 .75
325 Chris Schwinden RC .30 .75
326 Kevin Gregg .15 .40
327 Mark Kotsay .15 .40
328 John Lackey .20 .50
329 Allen Craig WS HL .20 .50
330A Matt Kemp .20 .50
330B Matt Kemp VAR SP 6.00 15.00
330C W.Mays VAR SP 6.00 15.00
331A A.Pujols w/Glove SP 40.00 80.00
331B Albert Pujols .30 .75
Swinging
331C Pujols Wearing suit SP 8.00 20.00
331D Babe Ruth VAR SP 8.00 20.00
332A Jose Reyes .15 .40
332B Jose Reyes SP 30.00 60.00
333 Roger Bernadina .15 .40
334 Anthony Rizzo .40 1.00
335 Josh Satin RC .30 .75
336 Gavin Floyd .15 .40
337 Glen Perkins .15 .40
338 Jose Constanza RC .25 .60
339 Clayton Richard .15 .40
340 Adam LaRoche .15 .40
341 Edwin Encarnacion .25 .60
342 Kosuke Fukudome .20 .50
343 Salvador Perez .20 .50
344 Nelson Cruz .25 .60
345 Jonathan Papelbon .20 .50
346 Dillon Gee .15 .40
347 Craig Gentry .15 .40
348 Alfonso Soriano .20 .50
349 Tim Lincecum .20 .50
350A Evan Longoria .20 .50
350B Evan Longoria VAR SP 5.00 12.00
With fans
351 Corey Hart .15 .40
352 Julio Teheran .20 .50
353 John Mayberry .15 .40
354 Jeremy Hellickson .15 .40
355 Mark Buehrle .20 .50
356 Endy Chavez .15 .40
357 Aaron Harang .15 .40
358 Jacob Turner .20 .50
359 Danny Espinosa .15 .40
360 Nelson Cruz RB .25 .60
361 Chase Utley .20 .50
362 Dayan Viciedo .15 .40
363 Fernando Salas .15 .40
364 Brandon Beachy .15 .40
365 Aramis Ramirez .15 .40
366 Jose Molina .15 .40
367 Chris Volstad .15 .40
368 Carl Crawford .20 .50
369 Huston Street .15 .40
370 Lyle Overbay .15 .40
371 Jim Thome .20 .50
372 Daniel Descalso .15 .40
373 Carlos Gonzalez .20 .50
374 Coco Crisp .15 .40
375 Drew Stubbs .15 .40
376 Carlos Quentin .15 .40

377 Brandon Inge .15 .40
378 Brandon League .15 .40
379 Sergio Romo RC .30 .75
380 Daniel Murphy .20 .50
381 David DeJesus .15 .40
382 Wandy Rodriguez .15 .40
383 Andre Ethier .20 .50
384 Sean Marshall .15 .40
385 David Murphy .15 .40
386 Ryan Zimmerman .20 .50
387 Joakim Soria .15 .40
388 Chase Headley .15 .40
389 Alexi Casilla .15 .40
390 Taylor Green RC .25 .60
391 Rod Barajas .20 .50
392 Cliff Lee .20 .50
393 Manny Ramirez .25 .60
394 Bryan LaHair .15 .40
395A Jonathan Lucroy .20 .50
395B Rod Barajas .20 .50
396A Yoenis Cespedes RC .60 1.50
396B Cespedes Grey Jsy FS .60 1.50
397 Hector Noesi .15 .40
398A Buster Posey .30 .75
398B Buster Posey VAR SP 8.00 20.00
399 Brian McCann .20 .50
400A Robinson Cano VAR SP 5.00 12.00
400B Robinson Cano .20 .50
401 Kenley Jansen .20 .50
402 Allen Craig .20 .50
403 Bronson Arroyo .15 .40
404 Jonathan Sanchez .15 .40
405 Nathan Eovaldi .20 .50
406 Juan Rivera .15 .40
407 Torii Hunter .20 .50
408 Jonny Venters .15 .40
409 Greg Holland RC .30 .75
410 Jeff Locke RC .40 1.00
411A T.Nishioka VAR SP 5.00 12.00
411B Tsuyoshi Nishioka .20 .50
412 Don Kelly .15 .40
413 Frank Francisco .15 .40
414 Ryan Vogelsong .15 .40
415 Rafael Furcal .15 .40
416 Todd Helton .20 .50
417 Carlos Pena .20 .50
418 Jarrod Parker RC .30 .75
419 Cameron Maybin .15 .40
420 Barry Zito .20 .50
421A Heath Bell VAR SP 5.00 12.00
421B Heath Bell .15 .40
422 Austin Jackson .20 .50
423 Colby Rasmus .20 .50
424 Vladimir Guerrero RB .20 .50
425 Carlos Zambrano .20 .50
426 Eric Hinske .15 .40
427 Rafael Dolis RC .30 .75
428 Jordan Schafer .15 .40
429 Michael Bourn .15 .40
430A Felix Hernandez .20 .50
430B Felix Hernandez VAR SP 5.00 12.00
Wearing glasses
431 Guillermo Moscoso .20 .50
432 Wei-Yin Chen RC .60 1.50
433 Nate McLouth .15 .40
434 Jason Motte .15 .40
435 Jeff Baker .15 .40
436 Chris Perez .15 .40
437 Yoshinori Tateyama RC .30 .75
438 Juan Uribe .15 .40
439 Elvis Andrus .20 .50
440 Chien-Ming Wang .20 .50
441 Mike Aviles .15 .40
442 Johnny Giavotella .15 .40
443 B.J. Upton .20 .50
444 Rafael Betancourt .15 .40
445 Ramon Santiago .15 .40
446 Mike Trout 6.00 15.00
447 Jair Jurrjens .15 .40
448 Dustin Moseley .15 .40
449 Shane Victorino .20 .50
450B Justin Upton .20 .50
450A Justin Upton VAR SP 5.00 12.00
451 Jeff Francoeur .20 .50
452 Robert Andino .15 .40
453 Garrett Jones .15 .40
454 Michael Cuddyer .15 .40
455 Jed Lowrie .15 .40
456 Omar Infante .15 .40
457 J.D. Martinez .25 .60
458 Kyle Kendrick .15 .40
459 Eric Surkamp RC .40 1.00
460 Thomas Field RC .25 .60
461 Victor Martinez .20 .50
462A Brett Lawrie RC .30 .75
462B Brett Lawrie VAR SP 5.00 12.00
462C B.Lawrie Fielding FS .30 .75
463 Francisco Cordero .15 .40
464 Joe Savery RC .30 .75
465 Michael Schwimer RC .30 .75
466 Lance Berkman .20 .50
467 Juan Francisco .20 .50
468 Nick Markakis .20 .50
469 Vinnie Pestano .15 .40
470A Howie Kendrick VAR SP 5.00 12.00
470B Howie Kendrick .15 .40
471 James Shields .15 .40
472 Mat Gamel .15 .40
473 Evan Meek .15 .40
474 Mitch Maier .15 .40
475 Chris Dickerson .15 .40
476 Ramon Hernandez .15 .40
477 Edinson Volquez .15 .40
478 Rajai Davis .15 .40
479 Johan Santana .20 .50
480 J.J. Putz .15 .40
481 Matt Harrison .15 .40
482 Chris Capuano .15 .40
483 Alex Gordon .20 .50
484 Hisashi Iwakuma RC .50 1.25
485 Carlos Marmol .15 .40
486 Jerry Sands .15 .40
487 Eric Sogard .15 .40
488 Nick Swisher .20 .50
489 Andres Torres .15 .40
490 Chris Carpenter .20 .50
491 Jose Valverde RB .20 .50
492 Rickie Weeks .15 .40
493 Ryan Madson .15 .40
494 Darwin Barney .15 .40
495 Adam Wainwright .20 .50
496 Jorge De La Rosa .15 .40
497A Andrew McCutchen .25 .60
497B Andrew McCutchen VAR SP 5.00 12.00
497C R.Clemente VAR SP 8.00 20.00
498 Joey Votto .25 .60
499 Francisco Rodriguez .20 .50
500 Alex Rodriguez .30 .75
501 Matt Capps .15 .40
502 Collin Cowgill RC .25 .60
503 Tyler Clippard .15 .40
504 Ryan Dempster .15 .40
505 Fautino De Los Santos .15 .40
506 David Ortiz .25 .60
507 Norichika Aoki RC .30 .75
508 Brandon Phillips .15 .40
509 Travis Snider .15 .40
510 Randall Delgado .15 .40
511 Ervin Santana .15 .40
512 Josh Willingham .20 .50
513 Gaby Sanchez .20 .50
514 Brian Roberts .15 .40
515 Willie Bloomquist .15 .40
516 Charlie Morton .25 .60
517 Francisco Liriano .15 .40
518 Jake Peavy .15 .40
519 Gio Gonzalez .20 .50
520 Ryan Adams .15 .40
521 Ruben Tejada .15 .40
522 Matt Downs .15 .40
523 Jim Johnson .15 .40
524 Martin Prado .15 .40
525 Paul Maholm .15 .40
526 Casper Wells .15 .40
527 Aaron Hill .15 .40
528 Bryan Petersen .15 .40
529 Luke Hughes .15 .40
530 Cliff Pennington .15 .40
531 Joel Hanrahan .15 .40
532 Tim Stauffer .15 .40
533 Ian Stewart .15 .40
534 Hector Gomez RC .25 .60
535 Joe Mauer .20 .50
536 Kendrys Morales .15 .40
537A Ichiro Suzuki .30 .75
537B I.Suzuki VAR SP 6.00 15.00
538 Wilson Betemit .15 .40
539 Andrew Bailey .15 .40
540A Dustin Pedroia .20 .50
540B D.Pedroia VAR SP 6.00 15.00
541 Jack Hannahan .15 .40
542 Jeff Samardzija .15 .40
543 Josh Johnson .20 .50
544 Josh Collmenter .20 .50
545 Randy Wolf .15 .40
546 Matt Thornton .15 .40
547 Jason Giambi .15 .40
548 Charlie Furbush .15 .40
549 Kelly Johnson .15 .40
550 Ian Kinsler .20 .50
551 Joe Blanton .15 .40
552 Kyle Drabek .15 .40
553 James Darnell RC .25 .60
554 Raul Ibanez .20 .50
555 Alex Presley .15 .40
556 Stephen Strasburg .25 .60
557 Zack Cozart .15 .40
558 Wade Miley RC .30 .75
559 Brandon Dickson RC .30 .75
560 J.A. Happ .20 .50
561 Freddy Sanchez .25 .60
562 Henderson Alvarez .15 .40
563 Alex White .15 .40
564 Jose Valverde .20 .50
565 Dan Uggla .20 .50
566 Jason Donald .15 .40
567 Mike Stanton .25 .60
568 Jason Castro .15 .40
569 Travis Hafner .15 .40
570 Zach McAllister RC .30 .75
571 J.J. Hardy .15 .40
572 Hiroki Kuroda .15 .40
573 Kyle Farnsworth .20 .50
574 Kerry Wood .15 .40
575 Garrett Richards RC .40 1.00
576 Jonathan Herrera .15 .40
577 Dallas Braden .15 .40
578 Wade Davis .20 .50
579 Dan Uggla RB .20 .50
580 Tony Campana .15 .40
581 Jason Kubel .15 .40
582 Shin-Soo Choo .20 .50
583 Josh Tomlin .15 .40
584 Daric Barton .15 .40
585 Jimmy Paredes .15 .40
586 Daisuke Matsuzaka .20 .50
587 Chris Johnson .15 .40
588 Mark Ellis .15 .40
589 Alex Gonzalez .15 .40
590 Humberto Quintero .15 .40
591 Aubrey Huff .15 .40
592 Carlos Lee .15 .40
593 Marco Scutaro .20 .50
594 Ricky Romero .15 .40
595 David Carpenter RC .30 .75
596 Freddy Garcia .15 .40
597 Hank Conger .15 .40
598 Reid Brignac .15 .40
599 Zach Britton .20 .50
600A Clayton Kershaw .50 1.25
600B Clayton Kershaw VAR SP 5.00 12.00
Brooklyn jersey
601 Dan Haren .15 .40
602 Alejandro De Aza .15 .40
603 Lonnie Chisenhall .15 .40
604 Juan Abreu RC .30 .75
605 Jason Bartlett .15 .40
606 Mike Carp .15 .40
607 CC Sabathia .20 .50
608 Paul Goldschmidt .25 .60
609 Lorenzo Cain .15 .40
610 Cody Ross .15 .40
611 Neftali Feliz .15 .40
612 Carlos Beltran .20 .50
613 C.J. Wilson .15 .40
614 Andruw Jones .15 .40
615 Luis Marte RC .25 .60
616 Tyler Pastornicky RC .25 .60
617 Jimmy Rollins .20 .50
618 Eric Chavez .15 .40
619 Tyler Greene .15 .40
620 Trayvon Robinson .15 .40
621 Scott Hairston .15 .40
622 Daniel Hudson .15 .40
623 Clint Barmes .15 .40
624 Gerardo Parra .15 .40
625 Tommy Hunter .15 .40
626 Alexei Ramirez .20 .50
627 Justin Smoak .20 .50
628 Sean Rodriguez .15 .40
629 Gordon Beckham .15 .40
630 Logan Morrison .15 .40
631 Ryan Kalish .15 .40
632 Joe Nathan .15 .40
633 Chris Narveson .15 .40
634 Jose Contreras .15 .40
635 Brett Gardner .20 .50
636 Chris Heisey .15 .40
637 Brad Brach RC .25 .60
638 Derek Lowe .15 .40
639A Justin Verlander .25 .60
639B J.Verlander VAR SP 6.00 15.00
640 Jemile Weeks RC .15 .40
641 Derek Jeter RB .60 1.50
642 Mike Moustakas .20 .50
643 Chris Young .15 .40
644 Andy Dirks .15 .40
645 Kyle Seager .15 .40
646 Francisco Cervelli .15 .40
647 Bruce Chen .15 .40
648 Josh Beckett .15 .40
649 Brandon Crawford .15 .40
650A Prince Fielder .20 .50
650B Prince Fielder VAR SP 5.00 12.00
651 Ryan Sweeney .15 .40
652 Grant Balfour .15 .40
653 Jordan Walden .15 .40
654 Yovani Gallardo .20 .50
655 Ryan Doumit .15 .40
656 Carlos Santana .20 .50
657 Dave Sappelt RC .30 .75
658 Juan Pierre .15 .40
659 Homer Bailey .15 .40
660A Yu Darvish RC .60 1.50
660B Darvish Left Hand SP 5.00 12.00
660C Darvish Gray jsy SP .60 1.50
661A Bryce Harper SP RC 300.00 600.00
661B Bryce Harper AU 600.00 1000.00
661C B.Harper Leg up FS 8.00 20.00
661D B.Harper Yelling FS 8.00 20.00
NNO Fenway Park Dirt 8.00 20.00

2012 Topps Black

*BLACK VET: 10X TO 25X BASIC
*BLACK RC: 6X TO 15X BASIC RC
SER.1 ODDS 1:150 HOBBY
SER.2 ODDS 1:108 HOBBY
STATED PRINT RUN 61 SER.#'d SETS
7 Mickey Mantle 60.00 120.00
30 Derek Jeter 60.00 120.00
41 Devin Mesoraco 15.00 40.00
44 Edwin Jackson 30.00 60.00
53 St. Louis Cardinals WS HL 20.00 50.00
93 Skip Schumaker 12.50 30.00
97 Jim Thome RB 20.00 50.00
129 Matt Moore 40.00 80.00
164 Carl Pavano 6.00 15.00
179 Denard Span 15.00 40.00
305 Chipper Jones 20.00 50.00
307 Vance Worley 10.00 25.00
329 Allen Craig WS HL 12.50 30.00
330 Matt Kemp 15.00 40.00
377 Brandon Inge 10.00 25.00
380 Daniel Murphy 8.00 20.00
418 Jarrod Parker 8.00 20.00
432 Wei-Yin Chen 30.00 60.00
438 Juan Uribe 12.50 30.00
441 Mike Aviles 8.00 20.00
462 Brett Lawrie 12.50 30.00
475 Chris Dickerson 6.00 15.00
482 Chris Capuano 15.00 40.00
501 Matt Capps 6.00 15.00
518 Jake Peavy 6.00 15.00
531 Joel Hanrahan 8.00 20.00
539 Andrew Bailey 8.00 20.00
561 Freddy Sanchez 8.00 20.00
610 Cody Ross 6.00 15.00
613 C.J. Wilson 10.00 25.00
614 Andruw Jones 6.00 15.00
617 Jimmy Rollins 10.00 25.00
634 Jose Contreras 8.00 20.00
636 Chris Heisey 8.00 20.00
644 Andy Dirks 6.00 15.00
648 Josh Beckett 10.00 25.00
658 Juan Pierre 8.00 20.00

2012 Topps Factory Set Orange

*RED VET: 4X TO 10X BASIC
*RED RC: 2.5X TO 6X BASIC RC
ONE PACK OF FIVE RED PER FACT.SET
STATED PRINT RUN 190 SER.#'d SETS
661 Bryce Harper 30.00 60.00

2012 Topps Gold

*GOLD VET: 1X TO 2.5X BASIC
*GOLD RC: .6X TO 1.5X BASIC RC
STATED ODDS 1:3 UPD.HOBBY
STATED PRINT RUN 2012 SER.#'d SETS
446 Mike Trout 60.00 150.00

2012 Topps Gold Sparkle

*GOLD VET: 1.5X TO 4X BASIC
*GOLD RC: 1X TO 2.5X BASIC RC
STATED ODDS 1:4 HOBBY
660 Yu Darvish 8.00 20.00

2012 Topps Target Red Border

*TARGET RED: 1.25X TO 3X BASIC
*TARGET RED RC: .75X TO 2X BASIC RC
FOUND IN TARGET RETAIL PACKS
446 Mike Trout 60.00 150.00

2012 Topps Toys R Us Purple Border

*TRU PURPLE: 1.2X TO 3X BASIC
*TRU PURPLE RC: .75X TO 2X BASIC RC
FOUND IN TOYS R US RETAIL PACKS

2012 Topps Wal-Mart Blue Border

*WM BLUE: 1.25X TO 3X BASIC
*WM BLUE RC: .75X TO 2X BASIC RC
FOUND IN WALMART RETAIL PACKS

2012 Topps 1987 Topps Minis

COMPLETE SET (150) 50.00 100.00
COMP.SER 1 SET (50) 12.50 30.00
COMP.SER 2 SET (50) 15.00 40.00
COMP.UPD SET (50) 12.50 30.00
STATED ODDS 1:4 HOBBY
UPDATE ODDS 1:4 UPDATE
1-50 ISSUED IN SERIES 1
51-100 ISSUED IN SERIES 2
101-150 ISSUED IN UPDATE
TM1 Ryan Braun .40 1.00
TM2 Mike Stanton .60 1.50
TM3 Eric Hosmer .50 1.25
TM4 Michael Young .40 1.00
TM5 Howie Kendrick .40 1.00
TM6 Dustin Ackley .40 1.00
TM7 Joey Votto .60 1.50
TM8 Ian Kinsler .50 1.25
TM9 Jason Heyward .50 1.25
TM10 Roy Halladay .50 1.25
TM11 Ubaldo Jimenez .40 1.00
TM12 Shin-Soo Choo .50 1.25
TM13 Jayson Werth .50 1.25
TM14 Ichiro Suzuki .75 2.00
TM15 Robinson Cano .50 1.25
TM16 Derek Jeter 1.50 4.00
TM17 Craig Kimbrel .50 1.25
TM18 Michael Bourn .40 1.00
TM19 Lance Berkman .50 1.25
TM20 Evan Longoria .50 1.25
TM21 Matt Holliday .60 1.50
TM22 Brett Gardner .50 1.25
TM23 Dustin Pedroia .50 1.25
TM24 Dan Uggla .50 1.25
TM25 Hanley Ramirez .50 1.25
TM26 David Wright .50 1.25
TM27 Ryan Howard .50 1.25
TM28 Buster Posey .75 2.00
TM29 Adam Jones .50 1.25
TM30 Andre Ethier .50 1.25
TM31 Brandon Phillips .40 1.00
TM32 Tommy Hanson .40 1.00
TM33 Adrian Gonzalez .50 1.25
TM34 Josh Johnson .50 1.25
TM35 Zack Greinke .50 1.25
TM36 Mariano Rivera .75 2.00
TM37 CC Sabathia .50 1.25
TM38 Chase Utley .50 1.25
TM39 Jay Bruce .50 1.25
TM40 Andrew McCutchen .60 1.50
TM41 James Shields .40 1.00
TM42 Josh Hamilton .50 1.25
TM43 Mat Latos .50 1.25
TM44 Troy Tulowitzki .60 1.50
TM45 Shane Victorino .50 1.25
TM46 David Price .50 1.25
TM47 Starlin Castro .50 1.25
TM48 Paul Konerko .40 1.00
TM49 Jered Weaver .50 1.25
TM50 Curtis Granderson .50 1.25
TM51 Albert Pujols .75 2.00
TM52 Miguel Cabrera .60 1.50
TM53 Matt Kemp .50 1.25
TM54 Justin Upton .50 1.25
TM55 Justin Verlander .60 1.50
TM56 Jose Bautista .50 1.25
TM57 Jacoby Ellsbury .50 1.25
TM58 Prince Fielder .50 1.25
TM59 Cliff Lee .50 1.25
TM60 Clayton Kershaw 1.25 3.00
TM61 Carlos Gonzalez .50 1.25
TM62 Tim Lincecum .50 1.25
TM63 Felix Hernandez .50 1.25
TM64 Jose Reyes .40 1.00
TM65 Mark Teixeira .50 1.25
TM66 Cole Hamels .50 1.25
TM67 Adrian Beltre .60 1.50
TM68 Dan Haren .40 1.00
TM69 Ryan Zimmerman .50 1.25
TM70 Jon Lester .40 1.00
TM71 Carlos Santana .50 1.25
TM72 Hunter Pence .50 1.25
TM73 Alex Gordon .50 1.25
TM74 Nelson Cruz .60 1.50
TM75 Alex Rodriguez .75 2.00
TM76 Rickie Weeks .40 1.00
TM77 Mike Napoli .40 1.00
TM78 Brian McCann .50 1.25
TM79 Brian Wilson .60 1.50
TM80 Pablo Sandoval .50 1.25
TM81 David Price .50 1.25
TM82 Josh Beckett .40 1.00
TM83 Joe Mauer .50 1.25
TM84 Stephen Strasburg .60 1.50
TM85 Michael Pineda .40 1.00
TM86 Bob Gibson .40 1.00
TM87 Stan Musial 1.00 2.50
TM88 Brooks Robinson .40 1.00
TM89 Frank Robinson .40 1.00
TM90 Babe Ruth 1.50 4.00
TM91 Tom Seaver .40 1.00
TM92 Sandy Koufax 1.25 3.00
TM93 Warren Spahn .40 1.00
TM94 Jim Palmer .40 1.00
TM95 Roger Maris .60 1.50
TM96 Mickey Mantle 2.00 5.00
TM97 Ken Griffey Jr. 1.25 3.00
TM98 Joe DiMaggio 1.25 3.00
TM99 Roberto Clemente 1.50 4.00
TM100 Johnny Bench .60 1.50
TM101 Paul Goldschmidt .60 1.50
TM102 Reggie Jackson .40 1.00
TM103 Lance Lynn .40 1.00
TM104 Chipper Jones .60 1.50
TM105 Ichiro Suzuki .75 2.00
TM106 Al Kaline .60 1.50
TM107 Madison Bumgarner .50 1.25
TM108 Jesus Montero .40 1.00
TM109 Carl Yastrzemski 1.00 2.50
TM110 Asdrubal Cabrera .50 1.25
TM111 Andy Pettitte .50 1.25
TM112 Yu Darvish 1.00 2.50
TM113 Billy Butler .40 1.00
TM114 Jonathan Papelbon .50 1.25
TM115 Carlos Beltran .50 1.25
TM116 Ian Kennedy .40 1.00
TM117 Gary Carter .40 1.00
TM118 Austin Jackson .50 1.25
TM119 Gio Gonzalez .50 1.25
TM120 Matt Cain .50 1.25
TM121 Mat Latos .50 1.25
TM122 Yonder Alonso .40 1.00
TM123 C.J. Wilson .40 1.00
TM124 Yoenis Cespedes 1.00 2.50
TM125 Lou Gehrig 1.25 3.00
TM126 Jackie Robinson .60 1.50
TM127 Mike Trout 4.00 10.00
TM128 Freddie Freeman .75 2.00
TM129 Elvis Andrus .50 1.25
TM130 Ty Cobb 1.00 2.50
TM131 Jimmy Rollins .50 1.25
TM132 Jim Rice .40 1.00
TM133 Will Middlebrooks .50 1.25
TM134 Bryan LaHair .40 1.00
TM135 Mike Moustakas .50 1.25
TM136 Brandon Beachy .40 1.00
TM137 Cal Ripken Jr. 2.00 5.00
TM138 Ryan Dempster .40 1.00
TM139 Matt Moore .60 1.50
TM140 Don Mattingly 1.25 3.00
TM141 Nolan Ryan 2.00 5.00
TM142 Albert Belle .25 .60
TM143 R.A. Dickey .50 1.25
TM144 Mark Trumbo .40 1.00
TM145 Chris Sale .60 1.50
TM146 Brett Lawrie .50 1.25
TM147 Johan Santana .50 1.25
TM148 Justin Morneau .50 1.25
TM149 Giancarlo Stanton .60 1.50
TM150 Bryce Harper 4.00 10.00

2012 Topps A Cut Above

COMPLETE SET (25) 6.00 15.00
STATED ODDS 1:6 HOBBY
ACA1 Prince Fielder .50 1.25
ACA2 Albert Pujols .75 2.00
ACA3 Justin Verlander .60 1.50
ACA4 Ken Griffey Jr. 1.25 3.00
ACA5 Ryan Braun .40 1.00
ACA6 Evan Longoria .50 1.25
ACA7 Dustin Pedroia .50 1.25
ACA8 Hanley Ramirez .50 1.25
ACA9 Cal Ripken Jr. 2.00 5.00
ACA10 Miguel Cabrera .60 1.50
ACA11 Nolan Ryan 2.00 5.00
ACA12 Stan Musial 1.00 2.50
ACA13 Mike Schmidt 1.00 2.50
ACA14 Willie Mays 1.25 3.00
ACA15 Jose Bautista .50 1.25
ACA16 Sandy Koufax 1.25 3.00
ACA17 Tim Lincecum .50 1.25
ACA18 Roy Halladay .50 1.25
ACA19 Robinson Cano .50 1.25
ACA20 Johnny Bench .60 1.50
ACA21 Hank Aaron 1.25 3.00
ACA22 Jackie Robinson .60 1.50
ACA23 Matt Kemp .50 1.25
ACA24 Mickey Mantle 2.00 5.00
ACA25 Troy Tulowitzki .60 1.50

2012 Topps A Cut Above Relics

STATED ODDS 1:9525 HOBBY
STATED PRINT RUN 50 SER.#'d SETS
AP Albert Pujols 15.00 40.00
EL Evan Longoria 8.00 20.00
HA Hank Aaron 30.00 60.00
HR Hanley Ramirez 4.00 10.00
JB Johnny Bench 12.50 30.00
JR Jackie Robinson 12.00 30.00
JV Justin Verlander 12.50 30.00
NR Nolan Ryan 30.00 60.00
RB Ryan Braun 12.50 30.00
TL Tim Lincecum 10.00 25.00
WM Willie Mays 40.00 80.00

2012 Topps Babe Ruth Commemorative Rings

BR1 Babe Ruth 6.00 15.00
1923 World Series
BR2 Babe Ruth 6.00 15.00
1927 World Series
BR3 Babe Ruth 6.00 15.00
1928 World Series
BR4 Babe Ruth 6.00 15.00
1932 World Series
BR5 Babe Ruth 6.00 15.00
1918 World Series

2012 Topps Career Day

COMPLETE SET (25) 6.00 15.00
STATED ODDS 1:6 HOBBY
CD1 Albert Pujols .75 2.00
CD2 Ken Griffey Jr. 1.25 3.00
CD3 Al Kaline .60 1.50
CD4 Stan Musial 1.00 2.50
CD5 Sandy Koufax 1.25 3.00
CD6 Joe DiMaggio 1.25 3.00
CD7 Frank Robinson .40 1.00
CD8 Mike Schmidt 1.00 2.50
CD9 Johnny Bench .60 1.50
CD10 Ryan Braun .40 1.00
CD11 Miguel Cabrera .60 1.50
CD12 Reggie Jackson .40 1.00
CD13 Evan Longoria .50 1.25
CD14 Dustin Pedroia .50 1.25
CD15 Willie Mays 1.25 3.00
CD16 Ryan Howard .50 1.25
CD17 Joey Votto .60 1.50
CD18 Robinson Cano .50 1.25
CD19 Jackie Robinson .60 1.50
CD20 Josh Hamilton .50 1.25
CD21 Matt Kemp .50 1.25
CD22 Mickey Mantle 2.00 5.00
CD23 Roberto Clemente 1.50 4.00
CD24 Troy Tulowitzki .60 1.50
CD25 Yogi Berra .60 1.50

2012 Topps Classic Walk-Offs

COMPLETE SET (15) 5.00 12.00
STATED ODDS 1:8 HOBBY
CW1 Bill Mazeroski .40 1.00
CW2 Carlton Fisk .40 1.00
CW3 Johnny Bench .60 1.50
CW4 David Ortiz .60 1.50
CW5 Jay Bruce .50 1.25
CW6 Mark Teixeira .50 1.25
CW7 Mickey Mantle 2.00 5.00
CW8 Alfonso Soriano .50 1.25
CW9 Rafael Furcal .40 1.00
CW10 Jim Thome .50 1.25
CW11 Magglio Ordonez .40 1.00
CW12 Alex Gonzalez .40 1.00
CW13 Scott Podsednik .25 .60
CW14 David Ortiz .60 1.50
CW15 Derek Jeter 1.50 4.00

2012 Topps Classic Walk-Offs Relics

STATED ODDS 1:20,200 HOBBY
STATED PRINT RUN 50 SER.#'d SETS
BM Bill Mazeroski 40.00 80.00
CF Carlton Fisk 40.00 80.00
DJ Derek Jeter 50.00 100.00
DO David Ortiz 10.00 25.00
JB Johnny Bench 10.00 25.00
JB Jay Bruce 10.00 25.00
JT Jim Thome 10.00 25.00
MM Mickey Mantle 60.00 120.00
MT Mark Teixeira 30.00 60.00

2012 Topps Gold Futures

COMPLETE SET (50) 10.00 25.00
COMP.SER 1 SET (25) 5.00 12.00
COMP.SER 2 SET (25) 5.00 12.00
STATED ODDS 1:6 HOBBY
1-25 ISSUED IN SERIES 1
26-50 ISSUED IN SERIES 2
GF1 Michael Pineda .40 1.00
GF2 Zach Britton .50 1.25
GF3 Brandon Belt .50 1.25
GF4 Freddie Freeman .75 2.00
GF5 Eric Hosmer .50 1.25
GF6 Dustin Ackley .40 1.00
GF7 Starlin Castro .50 1.25
GF8 Aroldis Chapman .60 1.50
GF9 Jeremy Hellickson .40 1.00
GF10 Craig Kimbrel .50 1.25
GF11 Julio Teheran .50 1.25
GF12 J.P. Arencibia .40 1.00
GF13 Anthony Rizzo 1.00 2.50
GF14 Mike Stanton .60 1.50
GF15 Mark Trumbo .40 1.00
GF16 Mike Trout 6.00 15.00
GF17 Dee Gordon .40 1.00
GF18 Alexi Ogando .40 1.00
GF19 Jose Tabata .40 1.00
GF20 Mike Moustakas .50 1.25
GF21 Arodys Vizcaino .25 .60
GF22 Ryan Lavarnway .40 1.00
GF23 Ivan Nova .50 1.25
GF24 Paul Goldschmidt .60 1.50
GF25 Jason Kipnis .50 1.25
GF26 Jesus Montero .40 1.00
GF27 Matt Moore .60 1.50
GF28 Buster Posey .75 2.00
GF29 Chris Sale .60 1.50
GF30 Carlos Santana .50 1.25
GF31 Desmond Jennings .50 1.25
GF32 Drew Storen .40 1.00
GF33 Madison Bumgarner .50 1.25
GF34 Brandon Beachy .40 1.00
GF35 Randall Delgado .40 1.00
GF36 Brad Peacock .40 1.00
GF37 Jordan Walden .40 1.00
GF38 Domonic Brown .50 1.25
GF39 Drew Pomeranz .40 1.00
GF40 Jason Heyward .50 1.25
GF41 Neftali Feliz .40 1.00
GF42 Yonder Alonso .40 1.00
GF43 Stephen Strasburg .60 1.50
GF44 Matt Dominguez .50 1.25
GF45 Lonnie Chisenhall .40 1.00
GF46 Jemile Weeks .40 1.00
GF47 Jacob Turner .50 1.25
GF48 Dellin Betances .60 1.50
GF49 Liam Hendriks .40 1.00
GF50 Corey Luebke .40 1.00

2012 Topps Gold Futures Coins

SER.2 ODDS 1:8,487 HOBBY
UPDATE ODDS 1:9725 HOBBY
PRINT RUNS B/WN 5-58 COPIES PER
NO PRICING ON QTY 5 OR LESS
BH Bryce Harper/34 UPD 100.00 200.00
EH Eric Hosmer/35 12.50 30.00
JH Jeremy Hellickson/58 10.00 25.00
MM Matt Moore/55 12.50 30.00
MP Michael Pineda/36 12.50 30.00
MT Mike Trout/27 125.00 300.00
SS Stephen Strasburg/37 40.00 80.00
YC Yoenis Cespedes/52 UPD 12.00 30.00

2012 Topps Gold Futures Relics

SER.1 ODDS 1:13,400 HOBBY
SER.2 ODDS 1:9525 HOBBY
STATED PRINT RUN 50 SER.#'d SETS
AR Anthony Rizzo 10.00 25.00
BB Brandon Beachy S2 6.00 15.00
BB Brandon Belt 6.00 15.00
BP Buster Posey S2 12.50 30.00
CK Craig Kimbrel 5.00 12.00
CS Chris Sale S2 12.50 30.00
DA Dustin Ackley 30.00 60.00
DG Dee Gordon 6.00 15.00
DJ Desmond Jennings S2 5.00 12.00
DP Drew Pomeranz S2 10.00 25.00
DS Drew Storen S2 10.00 25.00
EH Eric Hosmer 10.00 25.00
JA J.P. Arencibia 8.00 20.00
JH Jeremy Hellickson 6.00 15.00
JM Jesus Montero S2 10.00 25.00
JT Julio Teheran 5.00 12.00
JW Jordan Walden S2 10.00 25.00
MB Madison Bumgarner S2 12.50 30.00
MM Matt Moore S2 8.00 20.00

Michael Pineda 10.00 25.00
Mike Stanton 10.00 25.00
Mark Trumbo 10.00 25.00
Starlin Castro 8.00 20.00
Zach Britton 8.00 20.00
Mike Trout 75.00 200.00

2012 Topps Gold Rush Wrapper Redemption

MPLETE SET (100) 125.00 250.00
Albert Pujols 1.50 4.00
Adrian Gonzalez 1.00 2.50
Albert Belle .50 1.25
Allen Craig 1.00 2.50
Aroldis Chapman 1.25 3.00
Brandon Phillips .75 2.00
Brandon Belt 1.00 2.50
Brett Gardner 1.00 2.50
Nelson Cruz 1.25 3.00
Carl Yastrzemski 2.00 5.00
Carlos Gonzalez 1.00 2.50
Jay Bruce 1.00 2.50
Chris Young .75 2.00
Clayton Kershaw 2.50 6.00
Dan Uggla 1.00 2.50
Daniel Hudson .75 2.00
Danny Espinosa .75 2.00
Edgar Martinez .75 2.00
Felix Hernandez 1.00 2.50
Willie Mays 2.50 6.00
Frank Thomas 1.25 3.00
Jordan Zimmermann 1.00 2.50
Ian Kinsler 1.00 2.50
Tony Gwynn 1.25 3.00
Jason Motte .75 2.00
Jemile Weeks .75 2.00
Jered Weaver 1.00 2.50
Jesus Montero .75 2.00
Joe Mauer 1.00 2.50
Mariano Rivera 1.50 4.00
Jhonny Peralta .75 2.00
Tommy Hanson .75 2.00
Josh Hamilton 1.00 2.50
Andre Ethier 1.00 2.50
John Smoltz 1.25 3.00
Matt Kemp 1.00 2.50
Miguel Cabrera 1.25 3.00
Mitch Moreland .75 2.00
Roy Halladay 1.00 2.50
Ryan Braun .75 2.00
Dennis Eckersley .75 2.00
Ryne Sandberg 2.50 6.00
Salvador Perez 1.00 2.50
Starlin Castro 1.00 2.50
Tim Hudson 1.00 2.50
Tim Lincecum 1.00 2.50
Sandy Koufax 2.50 6.00
Warren Spahn .75 2.00
Yovani Gallardo 1.00 2.50
Hank Aaron 2.50 6.00
Harmon Killebrew 1.25 3.00
Stan Musial 2.00 5.00
Ken Griffey Jr. 2.50 6.00
Cal Ripken Jr. 4.00 10.00
Duke Snider .75 2.00
Evan Longoria 1.00 2.50
Justin Upton 1.00 2.50
Brett Lawrie 1.00 2.50
Jon Niese .75 2.00
Bryce Harper 10.00 25.00
Giancarlo Stanton 1.25 3.00
Ricky Romero .75 2.00
Rickie Weeks .75 2.00
Brian McCann 1.00 2.50
Ike Davis .75 2.00
Yonder Alonso .75 2.00
Alex Gordon 1.00 2.50
Aramis Ramirez .75 2.00
J.P. Arencibia .75 2.00
Ivan Nova 1.00 2.50
Pablo Sandoval 1.00 2.50
Matt Garza .75 2.00
Joe Saunders .75 2.00
Gio Gonzalez 1.00 2.50
Dee Gordon .75 2.00
Jeremy Hellickson .75 2.00
Derek Holland .75 2.00
Ervin Santana .75 2.00
Adam Lind 1.00 2.50
Nick Markakis 1.00 2.50
Billy Butler .75 2.00
Adam Jones 1.00 2.50
Rick Porcello .75 2.00
Brennan Boesch .75 2.00
David Price 1.00 2.50
Madison Bumgarner 1.00 2.50
Clay Buchholz .75 2.00
Yu Darvish 2.00 5.00
Mike Trout 75.00 200.00
Eric Hosmer 1.00 2.50
Craig Kimbrel 1.00 2.50
Elvis Andrus 1.00 2.50
Juan Marichal .75 2.00
Johnny Bench 1.25 3.00
Ozzie Smith 1.50 4.00
Willie Mays 2.50 6.00
Bob Gibson .75 2.00
Don Mattingly 2.50 6.00
Paul O'Neill .75 2.00
Gary Carter .75 2.00

2012 Topps Gold Rush Wrapper Redemption Autographs

PRINT RUNS B/WN 25-150 COPIES PER
2 Adrian Gonzalez/50 50.00 100.00
3 Albert Belle/50 12.50 30.00
4 Allen Craig/50 30.00 60.00
5 Aroldis Chapman/50 12.50 30.00
6 Brandon Phillips/50 20.00 50.00
7 Brandon Belt/50 10.00 25.00
8 Brett Gardner/50 10.00 25.00
9 Nelson Cruz/50 12.50 30.00
11 Carlos Gonzalez/50 30.00 60.00
12 Jay Bruce/50 30.00 60.00
13 Chris Young/50 12.50 30.00
15 Dan Uggla/50 6.00 15.00
16 Daniel Hudson/50 50.00 100.00
17 Danny Espinosa/50 10.00 25.00
22 Jordan Zimmermann/50 10.00 25.00
25 Jason Motte/50 10.00 25.00
27 Jered Weaver/50 20.00 50.00
28 Jesus Montero/50 15.00 40.00
34 Andre Ethier/50 30.00 60.00
36 Matt Kemp/50 100.00 200.00
38 Mitch Moreland/50 10.00 25.00
41 Dennis Eckersley/50 10.00 25.00
43 Salvador Perez/50 40.00 100.00
44 Starlin Castro/50 50.00 100.00
45 Tim Hudson/50 6.00 15.00
52 Stan Musial/50 50.00 100.00
55 Duke Snider/75 10.00 25.00
56 Evan Longoria/50 50.00 100.00
58 Brett Lawrie/80 20.00 50.00
59 Jon Niese/100 6.00 15.00
61 Giancarlo Stanton/70 25.00 60.00
62 Ricky Romero/135 6.00 15.00
63 Rickie Weeks/150 6.00 15.00
65 Ike Davis/100 6.00 15.00
66 Yonder Alonso/150 6.00 15.00
67 Alex Gordon/100 6.00 15.00
68 Aramis Ramirez/100 10.00 25.00
69 J.P. Arencibia/100 6.00 15.00
70 Ivan Nova/150 15.00 40.00
71 Pablo Sandoval/75 20.00 50.00
72 Matt Garza/100 6.00 15.00
73 Joe Saunders/100 6.00 15.00
74 Gio Gonzalez/100 12.50 30.00
75 Dee Gordon/100 6.00 15.00
76 Jeremy Hellickson/100 10.00 25.00
77 Derek Holland/100 12.50 30.00
78 Ervin Santana/100 10.00 25.00
79 Adam Lind/50 6.00 15.00
80 Nick Markakis/80 6.00 15.00
81 Billy Butler/100 6.00 15.00
87 Clay Buchholz/100 20.00 50.00
91 Craig Kimbrel/30 20.00 50.00
92 Elvis Andrus/100 10.00 25.00

2012 Topps Gold Standard

COMPLETE SET (50) 12.50 30.00
COMP.SER 1 SET (25) 6.00 15.00
COMP.SER 2 SET (25) 6.00 15.00
STATED ODDS 1:6 HOBBY
1-25 ISSUED IN SERIES 1
26-50 ISSUED IN SERIES 2
GS1 Nolan Ryan 2.00 5.00
GS2 Stan Musial 1.00 2.50
GS3 Paul Molitor .60 1.50
GS4 Cal Ripken Jr. 2.00 5.00
GS5 Bob Gibson .40 1.00
GS6 Mike Schmidt 1.00 2.50
GS7 Frank Robinson .40 1.00
GS8 Ernie Banks .60 1.50
GS9 Willie McCovey .40 1.00
GS10 Reggie Jackson .40 1.00
GS11 Tom Seaver .40 1.00
GS12 Al Kaline .60 1.50
GS13 Alex Rodriguez .75 2.00
GS14 Frank Thomas .60 1.50
GS15 Ty Cobb 1.00 2.50
GS16 John Smoltz .60 1.50
GS17 Jim Thome .50 1.25
GS18 Joe DiMaggio 1.25 3.00
GS19 Andre Dawson .40 1.00
GS20 Derek Jeter 1.50 4.00
GS21 Chipper Jones .60 1.50
GS22 Nolan Ryan 2.00 5.00
GS23 Tom Seaver .40 1.00
GS24 Mickey Mantle 2.00 5.00
GS25 Willie Mays 1.25 3.00
GS26 Andre Dawson .40 1.00
GS27 Jim Thome .50 1.25
GS28 Stan Musial 1.00 2.50
GS29 Cal Ripken Jr. 2.00 5.00
GS30 Willie Mays 1.25 3.00
GS31 Hank Aaron 1.25 3.00
GS32 Ernie Banks .60 1.50
GS33 Bob Gibson .40 1.00
GS34 Reggie Jackson .40 1.00
GS35 Chipper Jones .60 1.50
GS36 Al Kaline .60 1.50
GS37 Willie McCovey .40 1.00
GS38 Paul Molitor .60 1.50
GS39 Frank Robinson .40 1.00
GS40 Nolan Ryan 2.00 5.00
GS41 Mike Schmidt 1.00 2.50
GS42 John Smoltz .60 1.50
GS43 Tom Seaver .40 1.00
GS44 Alex Rodriguez .75 2.00
GS45 Derek Jeter 1.50 4.00
GS46 Joe DiMaggio 1.25 3.00
GS47 Mickey Mantle 2.00 5.00
GS48 Lou Gehrig 1.25 3.00
GS49 Roberto Clemente 1.50 4.00
GS50 Ty Cobb 1.00 2.50

2012 Topps Gold Standard Relics

SER.1 ODDS 1:20,200 HOBBY
SER.2 ODDS 1:9250 HOBBY
STATED PRINT RUN 50 SER.#'d SETS
EXCHANGE DEADLINE 12/31/2014
AD Andre Dawson S2 5.00 12.00
AR Alex Rodriguez 20.00 50.00
CR Cal Ripken Jr. S2 30.00 60.00
CR Cal Ripken Jr. 30.00 60.00
DJ Derek Jeter S2 40.00 80.00
DJ Derek Jeter 40.00 80.00
EB Ernie Banks 20.00 50.00
FR Frank Robinson S2 20.00 50.00
HA Hank Aaron S2 20.00 50.00
JD Joe DiMaggio S2 30.00 60.00
JD Joe DiMaggio 30.00 60.00
LG Lou Gehrig S2 40.00 80.00
MM Mickey Mantle S2 40.00 80.00
MM Mickey Mantle 40.00 80.00
MS Mike Schmidt S2 20.00 50.00
NR Nolan Ryan S2 30.00 60.00
NR Nolan Ryan 30.00 60.00
PM Paul Molitor S2 12.50 30.00
RC Roberto Clemente S2 30.00 60.00
TC Ty Cobb S2 30.00 60.00
TC Ty Cobb EXCH 30.00 60.00
TS Tom Seaver S2 10.00 25.00
TS Tom Seaver 10.00 25.00
WM Willie Mays S2 12.50 30.00
WM Willie Mays 12.50 30.00

2012 Topps Gold Team Coin Autographs

STATED PRINT RUN 30 SER.#'d SETS
KG Ken Griffey Jr./30 150.00 300.00
WM Willie Mays/30 150.00 300.00

2012 Topps Gold World Series Champion Pins

SER.1 ODDS 1:1000 HOBBY
SER.2 ODDS 1:1160 HOBBY
SER.1 PRINT RUN 736 SER.#'d SETS
AP Albert Pujols S2 8.00 20.00
AP Albert Pujols 10.00 25.00
BG Bob Gibson 8.00 20.00
BL Barry Larkin S2 8.00 20.00
BM Bill Mazeroski S2 10.00 25.00
BR Babe Ruth S2 12.50 30.00
BRO Brooks Robinson 8.00 20.00
CH Cole Hamels 8.00 20.00
CJ Chipper Jones 10.00 25.00
CR Cal Ripken Jr. S2 12.50 30.00
DJ Derek Jeter 10.00 25.00
DO David Ortiz 6.00 15.00
DP Dustin Pedroia 6.00 15.00
DS Darryl Strawberry S2 6.00 15.00
FR Frank Robinson 6.00 15.00
HA Hank Aaron S2 8.00 20.00
JR Johnny Bench 8.00 20.00
JD Joe DiMaggio S2 8.00 20.00
JR Jackie Robinson S2 6.00 15.00
LG Lou Gehrig 10.00 25.00
MC Miguel Cabrera S2 6.00 15.00
MM Mickey Mantle S2 12.50 30.00
MR Mariano Rivera S2 8.00 20.00
MS Mike Schmidt 10.00 25.00
OS Ozzie Smith S2 8.00 20.00
PM Paul Molitor 5.00 12.00
RA Roberto Alomar S2 6.00 15.00
RC Roberto Clemente 12.00 30.00
RH Rickey Henderson S2 10.00 25.00
RJ Reggie Jackson S2 6.00 15.00
RJ Reggie Jackson 6.00 15.00
SG Steve Garvey S2 5.00 12.00
SK Sandy Koufax S2 10.00 25.00
SK Sandy Koufax 10.00 25.00
SM Stan Musial 10.00 25.00
TL Tim Lincecum 10.00 25.00
TS Tom Seaver 8.00 20.00
WB Wade Boggs S2 6.00 15.00
WM Willie Mays 10.00 25.00
YB Yogi Berra S2 8.00 20.00

2012 Topps Golden Giveaway Code Cards

STATED ODDS 1:6 HOBBY
PRICING FOR UNUSED CODES
GGC1 Ryan Braun 1.00 2.50
GGC2 Troy Tulowitzki 1.00 2.50
GGC3 Miguel Cabrera 1.00 2.50
GGC4 Roy Halladay 1.00 2.50
GGC5 Matt Kemp 1.00 2.50
GGC6 Albert Pujols 1.00 2.50
GGC7 Willie Mays 1.00 2.50
GGC8 Roberto Clemente 1.00 2.50
GGC9 Ichiro Suzuki 1.00 2.50
GGC10 Sandy Koufax 1.00 2.50
GGC11 Albert Pujols 1.00 2.50
GGC12 Felix Hernandez 1.00 2.50
GGC13 Buster Posey 1.00 2.50
GGC14 Clayton Kershaw 1.00 2.50
GGC15 Carlos Gonzalez 1.00 2.50
GGC16 Johnny Bench 1.00 2.50
GGC17 Tim Lincecum 1.00 2.50
GGC18 Cal Ripken Jr. 1.00 2.50
GGC19 Derek Jeter 1.00 2.50
GGC20 Ken Griffey Jr. 1.25 3.00
GGC21 Bob Gibson 1.00 2.50
GGC22 Nolan Ryan 1.00 2.50
GGC23 Tony Gwynn 1.00 2.50
GGC24 Steve Carlton 1.00 2.50
GGC25 Warren Spahn 1.00 2.50
GGC26 Bryce Harper 1.00 2.50
GGC27 Trevor Bauer 1.00 2.50
GGC28 Yu Darvish 1.00 2.50
GGC29 Yoenis Cespedes 1.00 2.50
GGC30 Will Middlebrooks 1.00 2.50

2012 Topps Golden Greats

COMPLETE SET (100) 40.00 80.00
STATED ODDS 1:4 HOBBY
UPDATE ODDS 1:6 HOBBY
ALL VERSIONS PRICED EQUALLY
GG1 Lou Gehrig 1.00 2.50
GG2 Lou Gehrig 1.00 2.50
GG3 Lou Gehrig 1.00 2.50
GG4 Lou Gehrig 1.00 2.50
GG5 Lou Gehrig 1.00 2.50
GG6 Nolan Ryan 1.50 4.00
GG7 Nolan Ryan 1.50 4.00
GG8 Nolan Ryan 1.50 4.00
GG9 Nolan Ryan 1.50 4.00
GG10 Nolan Ryan 1.50 4.00
GG11 Willie Mays 1.00 2.50
GG12 Willie Mays 1.00 2.50
GG13 Willie Mays 1.00 2.50
GG14 Willie Mays 1.00 2.50
GG15 Willie Mays 1.00 2.50
GG16 Ty Cobb .75 2.00
GG17 Ty Cobb .75 2.00
GG18 Ty Cobb .75 2.00
GG19 Ty Cobb .75 2.00
GG20 Ty Cobb .75 2.00
GG21 Joe DiMaggio 1.00 2.50
GG22 Joe DiMaggio 1.00 2.50
GG23 Joe DiMaggio 1.00 2.50
GG24 Joe DiMaggio 1.00 2.50
GG25 Joe DiMaggio 1.00 2.50
GG26 Derek Jeter 1.25 3.00
GG27 Derek Jeter 1.25 3.00
GG28 Derek Jeter 1.25 3.00
GG29 Derek Jeter 1.25 3.00
GG30 Derek Jeter 1.25 3.00
GG31 Mickey Mantle 1.50 4.00
GG32 Mickey Mantle 1.50 4.00
GG33 Mickey Mantle 1.50 4.00
GG34 Mickey Mantle 1.50 4.00
GG35 Mickey Mantle 1.50 4.00
GG36 Roberto Clemente 1.25 3.00
GG37 Roberto Clemente 1.25 3.00
GG38 Roberto Clemente 1.25 3.00
GG39 Roberto Clemente 1.25 3.00
GG40 Roberto Clemente 1.25 3.00
GG41 Cal Ripken Jr. 1.50 4.00
GG42 Cal Ripken Jr. 1.50 4.00
GG43 Cal Ripken Jr. 1.50 4.00
GG44 Cal Ripken Jr. 1.50 4.00
GG45 Cal Ripken Jr. 1.50 4.00
GG46 Sandy Koufax 1.00 2.50
GG47 Sandy Koufax 1.00 2.50
GG48 Sandy Koufax 1.00 2.50
GG49 Sandy Koufax 1.00 2.50
GG50 Sandy Koufax 1.00 2.50
GG51 Hank Aaron 1.00 2.50
GG52 Hank Aaron 1.00 2.50
GG53 Hank Aaron 1.00 2.50
GG54 Hank Aaron 1.00 2.50
GG55 Hank Aaron 1.00 2.50
GG56 Tom Seaver .30 .75
GG57 Tom Seaver .30 .75
GG58 Tom Seaver .30 .75
GG59 Tom Seaver .30 .75
GG60 Tom Seaver .30 .75
GG61 Jackie Robinson .50 1.25
GG62 Jackie Robinson .50 1.25
GG63 Jackie Robinson .50 1.25
GG64 Jackie Robinson .50 1.25
GG65 Jackie Robinson .50 1.25
GG66 Albert Pujols .60 1.50
GG67 Albert Pujols .60 1.50
GG68 Albert Pujols .60 1.50
GG69 Albert Pujols .60 1.50
GG70 Albert Pujols .60 1.50
GG71 Babe Ruth 1.25 3.00
GG72 Babe Ruth 1.25 3.00
GG73 Babe Ruth 1.25 3.00
GG74 Babe Ruth 1.25 3.00
GG75 Babe Ruth 1.25 3.00
GG76 Andre Dawson .30 .75
GG77 Bob Gibson .30 .75
GG78 Brooks Robinson .30 .75
GG79 Dave Winfield .30 .75
GG80 Don Mattingly 1.00 2.50
GG81 Ernie Banks .50 1.25
GG82 Gary Carter .30 .75
GG83 Harmon Killebrew .50 1.25
GG84 Jim Palmer .30 .75
GG85 Joe Morgan .30 .75
GG86 John Smoltz .50 1.25
GG87 Johnny Bench .50 1.25
GG88 Ken Griffey Jr. 1.00 2.50
GG89 Lou Brock .30 .75
GG90 Mike Schmidt .75 2.00
GG91 Ozzie Smith .60 1.50
GG92 Reggie Jackson .30 .75
GG93 Rickey Henderson .50 1.25
GG94 Stan Musial .75 2.00
GG95 Tony Gwynn .50 1.25
GG96 Tony Perez .30 .75
GG97 Wade Boggs .30 .75
GG98 Warren Spahn .30 .75
GG99 Willie Stargell .30 .75
GG100 Yogi Berra .50 1.25

2012 Topps Golden Greats Autographs

STATED ODDS 1:39,990 HOBBY
UPDATE ODDS 1:34,350 HOBBY
STATED PRINT RUN 10 SER.#'d SETS
ALL VERSIONS EQUALLY PRICED
NO PRICING ON MOST DUE TO SCARCITY
EXCHANGE DEADLINE 12/31/2014
UPD.EXCH.DEADLINE 9/30/2015
SK1 Sandy Koufax 250.00 350.00
SK2 Sandy Koufax 250.00 350.00
SK3 Sandy Koufax 250.00 350.00
SK4 Sandy Koufax 250.00 350.00
SK5 Sandy Koufax 250.00 350.00
WM1 Willie Mays EXCH 150.00 250.00
WM2 Willie Mays EXCH 150.00 250.00
WM3 Willie Mays EXCH 150.00 250.00
WM4 Willie Mays EXCH 150.00 250.00
WM5 Willie Mays EXCH 150.00 250.00

2012 Topps Golden Greats Coins

SER.1 ODDS 1:52,700 HOBBY
SER.2 ODDS 1:15,560 HOBBY
PRINT RUNS B/WN 2-44 COPIES PER
NO PRICING ON QTY 24 OR LESS
HA Hank Aaron/44 75.00 150.00
JR Jackie Robinson/42 40.00 80.00
NR Nolan Ryan/34 100.00 200.00
RJ Reggie Jackson/44 S2 40.00 80.00
SK Sandy Koufax/32 150.00 250.00
TS Tom Seaver/41 40.00 80.00

2012 Topps Golden Greats Relics

STATED ODDS 1:13,400 HOBBY
UPDATE ODDS 1:22,400 HOBBY
STATED PRINT RUN 10 SER.#'d SETS
ALL VERSIONS EQUALLY PRICED
NO UPDATE CARD PRICING AVAILABLE
EXCHANGE DEADLINE 12/31/2014
GGR1 Lou Gehrig 40.00 80.00
GGR2 Lou Gehrig 40.00 80.00
GGR3 Lou Gehrig 40.00 80.00
GGR4 Lou Gehrig 40.00 80.00
GGR5 Lou Gehrig 40.00 80.00
GGR6 Nolan Ryan EXCH 60.00 120.00
GGR7 Nolan Ryan EXCH 60.00 120.00
GGR8 Nolan Ryan EXCH 60.00 120.00
GGR9 Nolan Ryan EXCH 60.00 120.00
GGR10 Nolan Ryan EXCH 60.00 120.00
GGR11 Willie Mays 40.00 80.00
GGR12 Willie Mays 40.00 80.00
GGR13 Willie Mays 40.00 80.00
GGR14 Willie Mays 40.00 80.00
GGR15 Willie Mays 40.00 80.00
GGR16 Ty Cobb EXCH 50.00 100.00
GGR17 Ty Cobb EXCH 50.00 100.00
GGR18 Ty Cobb EXCH 50.00 100.00
GGR19 Ty Cobb EXCH 50.00 100.00
GGR20 Ty Cobb EXCH 50.00 100.00
GGR21 Joe DiMaggio 40.00 80.00
GGR22 Joe DiMaggio 40.00 80.00
GGR23 Joe DiMaggio 40.00 80.00
GGR24 Joe DiMaggio 40.00 80.00
GGR25 Joe DiMaggio 40.00 80.00
GGR26 Derek Jeter 150.00 250.00
GGR27 Derek Jeter 150.00 250.00
GGR28 Derek Jeter 150.00 250.00
GGR29 Derek Jeter 150.00 250.00
GGR30 Derek Jeter 150.00 250.00
GGR31 Mickey Mantle 60.00 120.00
GGR32 Mickey Mantle 60.00 120.00
GGR33 Mickey Mantle 60.00 120.00
GGR34 Mickey Mantle 60.00 120.00
GGR35 Mickey Mantle 60.00 120.00
GGR36 Roberto Clemente 50.00 100.00
GGR37 Roberto Clemente 50.00 100.00
GGR38 Roberto Clemente 50.00 100.00
GGR39 Roberto Clemente 50.00 100.00
GGR40 Roberto Clemente 50.00 100.00
GGR41 Cal Ripken Jr. 75.00 150.00
GGR42 Cal Ripken Jr. 75.00 150.00
GGR43 Cal Ripken Jr. 75.00 150.00
GGR44 Cal Ripken Jr. 75.00 150.00
GGR45 Cal Ripken Jr. 75.00 150.00
GGR46 Sandy Koufax EXCH 75.00 150.00
GGR47 Sandy Koufax EXCH 75.00 150.00
GGR48 Sandy Koufax EXCH 75.00 150.00
GGR49 Sandy Koufax EXCH 75.00 150.00
GGR50 Sandy Koufax EXCH 75.00 150.00
GGR51 Hank Aaron 40.00 80.00
GGR52 Hank Aaron 40.00 80.00
GGR53 Hank Aaron 40.00 80.00
GGR54 Hank Aaron 40.00 80.00
GGR55 Hank Aaron 40.00 80.00
GGR56 Tom Seaver 40.00 80.00
GGR57 Tom Seaver 40.00 80.00
GGR58 Tom Seaver 40.00 80.00
GGR59 Tom Seaver 40.00 80.00
GGR60 Tom Seaver 40.00 80.00
GGR61 Jackie Robinson 30.00 60.00
GGR62 Jackie Robinson 30.00 60.00
GGR63 Jackie Robinson 30.00 60.00
GGR64 Jackie Robinson 30.00 60.00
GGR65 Jackie Robinson 30.00 60.00
GGR66 Albert Pujols 75.00 150.00
GGR67 Albert Pujols 75.00 150.00
GGR68 Albert Pujols 75.00 150.00
GGR69 Albert Pujols 75.00 150.00
GGR70 Albert Pujols 75.00 150.00
GGR71 Babe Ruth 100.00 200.00
GGR72 Babe Ruth 100.00 200.00
GGR73 Babe Ruth 100.00 200.00
GGR74 Babe Ruth 100.00 200.00
GGR75 Babe Ruth 100.00 200.00

2012 Topps Golden Moments

COMPLETE SET (50) 8.00 20.00
STATED ODDS 1:4 HOBBY
GM1 Tom Seaver .40 1.00
GM2 Jose Bautista .50 1.25
GM3 Derek Jeter 1.50 4.00
GM4 Josh Hamilton .50 1.25
GM5 Adrian Gonzalez .50 1.25
GM6 Red Schoendienst .40 1.00
GM7 Clayton Kershaw 1.25 3.00
GM8 Andre Dawson .40 1.00
GM9 Justin Verlander .60 1.50
GM10 Prince Fielder .50 1.25
GM11 Edgar Martinez .40 1.00
GM12 Andrew McCutchen .60 1.50
GM13 Don Mattingly 1.25 3.00
GM14 Felix Hernandez .50 1.25
GM15 Ryan Braun .40 1.00
GM16 Jim Rice .40 1.00
GM17 Jered Weaver .50 1.25
GM18 Barry Larkin .40 1.00
GM19 Andy Pettitte .50 1.25
GM20 Ryne Sandberg 1.25 3.00
GM21 Albert Belle .25 .60
GM22 Willie McCovey .40 1.00
GM23 Dennis Eckersley .40 1.00
GM24 Justin Upton .50 1.25
GM25 Ichiro Suzuki .75 2.00
GM26 Paul O'Neill .40 1.00
GM27 Lance Berkman .50 1.25
GM28 George Foster .25 .60
GM29 Albert Pujols .75 2.00
GM30 Jacoby Ellsbury .50 1.25
GM31 CC Sabathia .50 1.25
GM32 Roger Maris .60 1.50
GM33 Troy Tulowitzki .60 1.50
GM34 Brooks Robinson .40 1.00
GM35 Frank Thomas .60 1.50
GM36 John Smoltz .60 1.50
GM37 Asdrubal Cabrera .50 1.25
GM38 Matt Kemp .50 1.25
GM39 Robinson Cano .50 1.25
GM40 Miguel Cabrera .60 1.50
GM41 Joey Votto .60 1.50
GM42 Al Kaline .60 1.50
GM43 Curtis Granderson .50 1.25
GM44 Jim Thome .50 1.25
GM45 Joe Morgan .40 1.00
GM46 Dustin Pedroia .50 1.25
GM47 Carlton Fisk .40 1.00
GM48 Luis Aparicio .40 1.00
GM49 James Shields .40 1.00
GM50 Roy Halladay .50 1.25

2012 Topps Golden Moments Series 2

COMPLETE SET (50) 12.50 30.00
STATED ODDS 1:4 HOBBY
GM1 Adam Jones .50 1.25
GM2 Buster Posey .75 2.00
GM3 Eric Hosmer .50 1.25
GM4 Evan Longoria .50 1.25
GM5 Johnny Bench .60 1.50
GM6 Jose Bautista .50 1.25
GM7 Pablo Sandoval .50 1.25
GM8 Paul Molitor .60 1.50
GM9 Ryan Howard .50 1.25
GM10 Ryan Zimmerman .50 1.25
GM11 Stan Musial 1.00 2.50
GM12 Tim Lincecum .50 1.25
GM13 Alex Rodriguez .75 2.00
GM14 Cal Ripken Jr. 2.00 5.00
GM15 Carl Yastrzemski 1.00 2.50
GM16 Carlos Gonzalez .50 1.25
GM17 Cliff Lee .50 1.25
GM18 Cole Hamels .50 1.25
GM19 Craig Kimbrel .50 1.25
GM20 Dave Winfield .40 1.00
GM21 David Ortiz .60 1.50
GM22 David Wright .50 1.25
GM23 Don Mattingly 1.25 3.00
GM24 George Brett 1.25 3.00
GM25 Hanley Ramirez .50 1.25
GM26 Ian Kinsler .50 1.25
GM27 Jim Palmer .40 1.00
GM28 Joe Mauer .50 1.25
GM29 Mariano Rivera .75 2.00
GM30 Mark Teixeira .50 1.25
GM31 Giancarlo Stanton .60 1.50
GM32 Ozzie Smith .75 2.00
GM33 Reggie Jackson .40 1.00
GM34 Rickey Henderson .60 1.50
GM35 Starlin Castro .50 1.25
GM36 Stephen Strasburg .60 1.50
GM37 Tony Gwynn .40 1.00
GM38 Wade Boggs .40 1.00
GM39 Willie Mays 1.25 3.00
GM40 Adrian Gonzalez .50 1.25
GM41 Andre Dawson .40 1.00
GM42 Chase Utley .50 1.25
GM43 Gary Carter .40 1.00
GM44 Josh Hamilton .50 1.25
GM45 Miguel Cabrera .60 1.50
GM46 Mike Schmidt 1.00 2.50
GM47 Prince Fielder .50 1.25
GM48 Ryne Sandberg 1.25 3.00
GM49 Steve Garvey .25 .60
GM50 Ken Griffey Jr. 1.25 3.00

2012 Topps Golden Moments 24K Gold Embedded

STATED ODDS 1:147,500 HOBBY
STATED PRINT RUN 1 SER.#'d SET
NO PRICING DUE TO SCARCITY
EXCHANGE DEADLINE 12/31/2014

2012 Topps Golden Moments Die Cuts

GMDC1 Babe Ruth 8.00 20.00
GMDC2 Lou Gehrig 6.00 15.00
GMDC3 Ty Cobb 5.00 12.00
GMDC4 Stan Musial 5.00 12.00
GMDC5 Joe DiMaggio 6.00 15.00
GMDC6 Willie Mays 6.00 15.00
GMDC7 Mickey Mantle 10.00 25.00
GMDC8 Warren Spahn 2.00 5.00
GMDC9 Bob Gibson 2.00 5.00
GMDC10 Johnny Bench 3.00 8.00
GMDC11 Sandy Koufax 6.00 15.00
GMDC12 Frank Robinson 2.00 5.00
GMDC13 Tom Seaver 2.00 5.00
GMDC14 Roberto Clemente 8.00 20.00
GMDC15 Steve Carlton 2.00 5.00
GMDC16 Yogi Berra 3.00 8.00
GMDC17 Jim Thome 2.50 6.00
GMDC18 Jackie Robinson 3.00 8.00
GMDC19 Ken Griffey Jr. 6.00 15.00
GMDC20 Rickey Henderson 3.00 8.00
GMDC21 Nolan Ryan 10.00 25.00
GMDC22 Eddie Mathews 3.00 8.00
GMDC23 Cal Ripken Jr. 10.00 25.00
GMDC24 Tony Gwynn 2.00 5.00
GMDC25 Ichiro Suzuki 4.00 10.00
GMDC26 Carl Yastrzemski 5.00 12.00
GMDC27 Joe Mauer 2.50 6.00
GMDC28 Josh Hamilton 2.50 6.00
GMDC29 Ozzie Smith 4.00 10.00
GMDC30 Ryan Braun 2.00 5.00
GMDC31 Willie McCovey 2.00 5.00
GMDC32 Jim Palmer 2.00 5.00
GMDC33 Rod Carew 2.00 5.00
GMDC34 Derek Jeter 8.00 20.00
GMDC35 Duke Snider 2.00 5.00
GMDC36 Al Kaline 3.00 8.00
GMDC37 Alex Rodriguez 4.00 10.00
GMDC38 Harmon Killebrew 3.00 8.00
GMDC39 Reggie Jackson 2.00 5.00
GMDC40 Vladimir Guerrero 2.50 6.00
GMDC41 Albert Pujols 4.00 10.00
GMDC42 Robin Yount 3.00 8.00
GMDC43 Roy Halladay 2.50 6.00
GMDC44 Wade Boggs 2.00 5.00
GMDC45 Eddie Murray 2.00 5.00
GMDC46 Johan Santana 2.50 6.00
GMDC47 Mariano Rivera 4.00 10.00
GMDC48 Hanley Ramirez 2.50 6.00
GMDC49 Robinson Cano 2.50 6.00
GMDC50 Carlton Fisk 2.00 5.00
GMDC51 Don Mattingly 6.00 15.00
GMDC52 Justin Upton 2.50 6.00
GMDC53 Buster Posey 4.00 10.00
GMDC54 Clayton Kershaw 6.00 15.00
GMDC55 Matt Kemp 2.50 6.00
GMDC56 Ryne Sandberg 6.00 15.00
GMDC57 Joey Votto 3.00 8.00
GMDC58 Carlos Gonzalez 2.50 6.00
GMDC59 Craig Kimbrel 2.50 6.00
GMDC60 Stephen Strasburg 3.00 8.00
GMDC61 David Wright 2.50 6.00
GMDC62 Eric Hosmer 2.50 6.00
GMDC63 Evan Longoria 2.50 6.00
GMDC64 Mark Teixeira 2.50 6.00
GMDC65 Mike Stanton 3.00 8.00
GMDC66 CC Sabathia 2.50 6.00
GMDC67 Dustin Pedroia 2.50 6.00

GMDC68 Justin Verlander 3.00 8.00
GMDC69 David Price 2.50 6.00
GMDC70 Jered Weaver 2.50 6.00
GMDC71 Cliff Lee 2.50 6.00
GMDC72 Ian Kinsler 2.50 6.00
GMDC73 Roberto Alomar 2.00 5.00
GMDC74 Pablo Sandoval 2.50 6.00
GMDC75 Troy Tulowitzki 3.00 8.00
GMDC76 Felix Hernandez 2.50 6.00
GMDC77 Mike Trout 100.00 250.00
GMDC78 Starlin Castro 2.50 6.00
GMDC79 Brooks Robinson 2.00 5.00
GMDC80 Jacob Ellsbury 3.00 8.00
GMDC81 Jose Bautista 2.50 6.00
GMDC82 Tim Lincecum 2.50 6.00
GMDC83 Miguel Cabrera 3.00 8.00
GMDC84 Ryan Zimmerman 2.50 6.00
GMDC85 Nelson Cruz 3.00 8.00
GMDC86 Ryan Howard 2.50 6.00
GMDC87 Jason Heyward 2.50 6.00
GMDC88 David Ortiz 3.00 8.00
GMDC89 Adrian Gonzalez 2.50 6.00
GMDC90 Brian Wilson 3.00 8.00
GMDC91 Chris Carpenter 2.50 6.00
GMDC92 David Freese 2.00 5.00
GMDC93 Josh Johnson 2.50 6.00
GMDC94 Adam Jones 2.50 6.00
GMDC95 Jay Bruce 2.50 6.00
GMDC96 Shin-Soo Choo 2.50 6.00
GMDC97 Chase Utley 2.50 6.00
GMDC98 Mike Napoli 2.00 5.00
GMDC99 Jose Reyes 2.00 5.00
GMDC100 Jon Lester 2.00 5.00
GMDC101 Yoenis Cespedes 2.50 6.00
GMDC102 Yu Darvish 4.00 10.00
GMDC103 Bryce Harper 50.00 100.00

2012 Topps Golden Moments Die Cuts Gold

*GOLD: 1X TO 2.5X BASIC
PRINT RUNS B/WN 99-100 COPIES PER
GMDC101 Yoenis Cespedes/100 6.00 15.00
GMDC102 Yu Darvish/100 10.00 25.00
GMDC103 Bryce Harper/100 100.00 200.00

2012 Topps Golden Moments Autographs

SER.1 ODDS 1:322 HOBBY
SER.2 ODDS 1:335 HOBBY
UPDATE ODDS 1:531 HOBBY
SER.1 EXCH DEADLINE 12/31/2014
SER.2 EXCH DEADLINE 04/30/2015
UPD.EXCH DEADLINE 9/30/2015
AB Albert Belle S2 10.00 25.00
AB Antonio Bastardo UPD 4.00 10.00
AC Alex Cobb S2 5.00 12.00
AC Andrew Carignan UPD 3.00 8.00
ACA Andrew Carignan S2 5.00 12.00
AD Andre Dawson S2 6.00 15.00
AE Andre Ethier S2 5.00 12.00
AE Andre Ethier 5.00 12.00
AE A.J. Ellis UPD 5.00 12.00
AG Adrian Gonzalez 8.00 20.00
AG Adrian Gonzalez S2 8.00 20.00
AJ Adam Jones S2 6.00 15.00
AJ Adam Jones 6.00 15.00
AJA Austin Jackson S2 6.00 15.00
AL Adam Lind 3.00 8.00
AL Tyler Pastornicky UPD 3.00 8.00
AO Alexi Ogando 4.00 10.00
AP Andy Pettitte S2 50.00 100.00
AR Aramis Ramirez S2 4.00 10.00
BG Bob Gibson S2 30.00 60.00
BG Brett Gardner 8.00 20.00
BH Bryce Harper UPD 125.00 250.00
BL Brett Lawrie UPD 6.00 15.00
BM Brian McCann 4.00 10.00
BP Brandon Phillips 10.00 25.00
BP Brad Peacock S2 3.00 8.00
BPO Buster Posey S2 50.00 100.00
BS Bruce Sutter UPD 10.00 25.00
BU B.J. Upton S2 6.00 15.00
CB Clay Buchholz S2 10.00 25.00
CB Chad Billingsley 3.00 8.00
CC Chris Coghlan 4.00 10.00
CC Chris Coghlan S2 3.00 8.00
CG Carlos Gonzalez 6.00 15.00
CJ Chipper Jones 25.00 60.00
CK Clayton Kershaw 15.00 40.00
CR Cody Ross S2 10.00 25.00
CR Cody Ross UPD 8.00 20.00
CS Carlos Santana S2 3.00 8.00
CS Chris Sale 8.00 20.00
CU Chase Utley S2 20.00 50.00
CY Chris Young S2 5.00 12.00
CY Chris Young 4.00 10.00
DB Domonic Brown S2 8.00 20.00
DB Daniel Bard UPD 3.00 8.00
DG Dee Gordon S2 3.00 8.00
DGO Dwight Gooden S2 15.00 40.00
DH Derek Holland UPD 6.00 15.00
DJ David Justice S2 30.00 60.00
DP Drew Pomeranz S2 6.00 15.00
DP Dustin Pedroia 15.00 40.00
DS Drew Stubbs 5.00 12.00
DS Darryl Strawberry S2 6.00 15.00
DSN Duke Snider S2 12.00 30.00
DST Drew Storen S2 3.00 8.00
EA Elvis Andrus S2 5.00 12.00
EA Elvis Andrus 5.00 12.00
EH Eric Hosmer S2 5.00 12.00
EK Ed Kranepool UPD 3.00 8.00
EL Evan Longoria S2 15.00 40.00
EM Edgar Martinez 10.00 25.00
FF Freddie Freeman S2 8.00 20.00
FH Felix Hernandez 6.00 15.00
GB Gordon Beckham 6.00 15.00
GB Gordon Beckham S2 6.00 15.00
GC Gary Carter S2 20.00 50.00
GG Gio Gonzalez S2 6.00 15.00
GG Gio Gonzalez 6.00 15.00
GS Gary Sheffield S2 10.00 25.00
HR Hanley Ramirez 8.00 20.00
IK Ian Kinsler 10.00 30.00
IK Ian Kennedy S2 5.00 12.00
IKE Ian Kennedy 4.00 10.00
JA Jose Altuve S2 15.00 40.00
JB Johnny Bench S2 40.00 80.00
JB Jose Bautista 10.00 25.00
JBA Jose Bautista S2 15.00 40.00
JBR Jay Bruce 5.00 12.00
JC Johnny Cueto 8.00 20.00
JDM J.D. Martinez UPD 10.00 25.00
JG Jason Grilli UPD 3.00 8.00
JH Josh Hamilton 15.00 40.00
JH Jason Heyward S2 8.00 20.00
JH Joel Hanrahan UPD 4.00 10.00
JHA Josh Hamilton S2 60.00 120.00
JM Jason Motte S2 3.00 8.00
JM Jesus Montero UPD 6.00 15.00
JMO Jesus Montero S2 6.00 15.00
JN Jeff Niemann UPD 3.00 8.00
JP Jarrod Parker S2 5.00 12.00
JPO Johnny Podres S2 5.00 12.00
JS John Smoltz S2 40.00 80.00
JT Justin Turner UPD 5.00 12.00
JTA Jose Tabata S2 4.00 10.00
JV Justin Verlander UPD 20.00 50.00
JW Jordan Walden S2 3.00 8.00
JW Jered Weaver 5.00 12.00
JW Jordan Walden UPD 8.00 20.00
JZ Jordan Zimmermann 6.00 15.00
JZ Jordan Zimmermann S2 6.00 15.00
LA Luis Aparicio 40.00 80.00
LH Liam Hendriks S2 3.00 8.00
MB Madison Bumgarner S2 20.00 50.00
MB Madison Bumgarner 20.00 50.00
MBY Marlon Byrd 5.00 12.00
MC Miguel Cabrera 40.00 80.00
MC Miguel Cabrera S2 60.00 120.00
MG Matt Garza 3.00 8.00
MH Mark Hamburger UPD 3.00 8.00
MK Matt Kemp 8.00 20.00
MM Matt Moore S2 6.00 15.00
MM Matt Moore UPD 6.00 15.00
MMI Mike Minor S2 3.00 8.00
MMO Mike Morse S2 10.00 25.00
MP Michael Pineda UPD 8.00 20.00
MR Manny Ramirez UPD 60.00 150.00
MS Mike Schmidt S2 20.00 50.00
MT Mike Trout S2 200.00 500.00
NF Neftali Feliz S2 5.00 12.00
NF Neftali Feliz 6.00 15.00
NW Neil Walker 5.00 12.00
OC Orlando Cepeda S2 10.00 25.00
PF Prince Fielder S2 30.00 60.00
PM Paul Molitor S2 12.50 30.00
PO Paul O'Neill S2 10.00 25.00
PO Paul O'Neill 10.00 25.00
PS Pablo Sandoval 8.00 20.00
PS Pablo Sandoval S2 8.00 20.00
RB Ryan Braun 10.00 25.00
RD Randall Delgado S2 3.00 8.00
RD Rafael Dolis UPD 3.00 8.00
RH Ryan Howard S2 30.00 60.00
RK Ralph Kiner S2 10.00 25.00
RK Ralph Kiner UPD 10.00 25.00
RP Rick Porcello S2 5.00 12.00
RS Ryne Sandberg S2 30.00 60.00
RW Rickie Weeks UPD 4.00 10.00
RZ Ryan Zimmerman S2 6.00 15.00
RZ Ryan Zimmerman 6.00 15.00
SG Steve Garvey S2 8.00 20.00
SM Stan Musial S2 20.00 50.00
SP Salvador Perez UPD 10.00 25.00
SV Shane Victorino S2 8.00 20.00
TB Trevor Bauer UPD 12.00 30.00
TC Trevor Cahill S2 4.00 10.00
TC Trevor Cahill 5.00 12.00
TH Tommy Hanson 10.00 25.00
UJ Ubaldo Jimenez 6.00 15.00
UJ Ubaldo Jimenez S2 12.50 30.00
WM Willie McCovey S2 20.00 50.00
WM Will Middlebrooks UPD 30.00 60.00
WR Wilin Rosario S2 3.00 8.00
YD Yu Darvish S2 60.00 150.00
ZC Zack Cozart UPD 5.00 12.00

2012 Topps Golden Moments Dual Relics

STATED ODDS 1:9525 HOBBY
STATED PRINT 50 SER.#'d SETS
GBG J.Bruce/K.Griffey Jr. 20.00 50.00
GBM J.Bench/D.Mesoraco 12.00 30.00
GBP J.Bench/B.Posey 20.00 50.00
GCM R.Clemente/A.McCutchen 75.00 150.00
GDB A.Dawson/E.Banks 20.00 50.00
GHL J.Hellickson/E.Longoria 15.00 40.00
GIG I.Suzuki/K.Griffey Jr. 50.00 100.00
GJS C.Jones/M.Schmidt 20.00 50.00
GKV S.Koufax/J.Verlander 60.00 120.00
GML P.Molitor/A.Lind 10.00 25.00
GMM M.Mantle/R.Maris 75.00 150.00
GMP W.McCovey/B.Posey 60.00 120.00
GPF D.Pedroia/C.Fisk 20.00 50.00
GPM A.Pujols/S.Musial 50.00 100.00
GYE C.Yastrzemski/J.Ellsbury 30.00 60.00

2012 Topps Golden Moments Relics

SER.1 ODDS 1:47 HOBBY
SER.2 ODDS 1:50 HOBBY
I Ichiro Suzuki S2 6.00 15.00
AA Alex Avila S2 3.00 8.00
AA Alex Avila 3.00 8.00
AB A.J. Burnett S2 3.00 8.00
AC Asdrubal Cabrera 4.00 10.00
AD Adam Dunn 4.00 10.00
AG Adrian Gonzalez 4.00 10.00
AJ Austin Jackson 4.00 10.00
AL Adam Lind S2 4.00 10.00
AM Andrew McCutchen S2 5.00 12.00
AM Andrew McCutchen 5.00 12.00
AP Albert Pujols S2 12.00 30.00
AP Albert Pujols 12.00 30.00
BA Bobby Abreu S2 3.00 8.00
BA Brett Anderson 3.00 8.00
BB Billy Butler S2 3.00 8.00
BL Barry Larkin S2 6.00 15.00
BL Barry Larkin 6.00 15.00
BM Bengie Molina S2 2.00 5.00
BM Brian McCann 4.00 10.00
BP Brandon Phillips S2 3.00 8.00
BP Buster Posey 6.00 15.00
BU B.J. Upton S2 4.00 10.00
BU B.J. Upton 4.00 10.00
BW Brian Wilson S2 5.00 12.00
BW Brian Wilson 5.00 12.00
CB Clay Buchholz S2 3.00 8.00
CB Chad Billingsley 3.00 8.00
CG Curtis Granderson 4.00 10.00
CH Corey Hart S2 3.00 8.00
CH Corey Hart 3.00 8.00
CI Chris Iannetta S2 3.00 8.00
CJ Chipper Jones S2 5.00 12.00
CJ Chipper Jones 5.00 12.00
CL Carlos Lee S2 3.00 8.00
CM Casey McGehee S2 3.00 8.00
CM Casey McGehee 3.00 8.00
CP Carlos Pena S2 4.00 10.00
CP Carlos Pena 4.00 10.00
CQ Carlos Quentin 3.00 8.00
CS CC Sabathia 4.00 10.00
CS Chris Sale 5.00 12.00
CZ Carlos Zambrano S2 4.00 10.00
DD David DeJesus S2 3.00 8.00
DD Daniel Descalso 3.00 8.00
DG Dillon Gee S2 3.00 8.00
DH Daniel Hudson 3.00 8.00
DJ Derek Jeter 10.00 25.00
DM Don Mattingly S2 10.00 25.00
DM Don Mattingly 10.00 25.00
DO David Ortiz S2 5.00 12.00
DO David Ortiz 5.00 12.00
DP David Price 4.00 10.00
DS Drew Stubbs S2 3.00 8.00
DS Drew Stubbs 3.00 8.00
DU Dan Uggla S2 4.00 10.00
DU Dan Uggla 4.00 10.00
DW David Wright S2 4.00 10.00
DW David Wright 4.00 10.00
EA Elvis Andrus 4.00 10.00
EB Ernie Banks 8.00 20.00
EL Evan Longoria S2 4.00 10.00
With bat
EL Evan Longoria 4.00 10.00
EM Evan Meek S2 3.00 8.00
FR Frank Robinson 5.00 12.00
FT Frank Thomas S2 5.00 12.00
GB Gordon Beckham S2 3.00 8.00
GB Gordon Beckham 3.00 8.00
GC Gary Carter 4.00 10.00
GS Geovany Soto S2 4.00 10.00
HB Heath Bell S2 3.00 8.00
HC Hank Conger S2 3.00 8.00
HR Hanley Ramirez 4.00 10.00
ID Ian Desmond S2 3.00 8.00
ID Ivan DeJesus 2.00 5.00
IK Ian Kinsler S2 4.00 10.00
JA J.P. Arencibia S2 3.00 8.00
JA John Axford 3.00 8.00
JB Jay Bruce S2 4.00 10.00
JB Jose Bautista 4.00 10.00
JC Johnny Cueto S2 4.00 10.00
JC Jhoulys Chacin 3.00 8.00
JD Johnny Damon S2 4.00 10.00
JD Johnny Damon 4.00 10.00
JG Jaime Garcia S2 4.00 10.00
JH Jeremy Hellickson S2 4.00 10.00
JH Josh Hamilton 4.00 10.00
JJ Josh Johnson S2 4.00 10.00
JL James Loney S2 3.00 8.00
JL Jon Lester 3.00 8.00
JN Jon Niese 3.00 8.00
JP Jhonny Peralta S2 3.00 8.00
JP Jhonny Peralta 3.00 8.00
JR Jose Reyes 3.00 8.00
JU Justin Upton S2 4.00 10.00
JV Justin Verlander 5.00 12.00
JW Jayson Werth S2 4.00 10.00
JW Jered Weaver 4.00 10.00
JZ Jordan Zimmermann S2 4.00 10.00
KM Kendrys Morales 3.00 8.00
KS Kurt Suzuki 3.00 8.00
KY Kevin Youkilis 5.00 12.00
MB Marlon Byrd S2 3.00 8.00
MB Madison Bumgarner 4.00 10.00
MC Melky Cabrera S2 3.00 8.00
MC Miguel Cabrera 6.00 15.00
MH Matt Holliday 5.00 12.00
MK Matt Kemp 4.00 10.00
ML Mat Latos S2 4.00 10.00
ML Mat Latos 4.00 10.00
MM Mitch Moreland S2 3.00 8.00
MP Martin Prado 3.00 8.00
MR Mark Reynolds S2 3.00 8.00
MS Max Scherzer S2 5.00 12.00
MS Mike Schmidt 6.00 15.00
MT Mark Teixeira 4.00 10.00
NM Nick Markakis S2 4.00 10.00
NM Nick Markakis 4.00 10.00
PB Pat Burrell 2.00 5.00
PF Prince Fielder S2 4.00 10.00
PF Prince Fielder 4.00 10.00
PM Paul Molitor S2 5.00 12.00
PM Paul Molitor 5.00 12.00
PO Paul O'Neill S2 3.00 8.00
RA Roberto Alomar S2 3.00 8.00
RB Ryan Braun S2 3.00 8.00
RB Ryan Braun 3.00 8.00
RC Robinson Cano 4.00 10.00
RH Roy Halladay 4.00 10.00
RJ Reggie Jackson 3.00 8.00
RM Roger Maris S2 12.00 30.00
RM Roger Maris 12.00 30.00
RP Rick Porcello S2 3.00 8.00
RR Ricky Romero S2 3.00 8.00
RZ Ryan Zimmerman S2 4.00 10.00
RZ Ryan Zimmerman 4.00 10.00
SC Shin-Soo Choo S2 4.00 10.00
SC Starlin Castro 4.00 10.00
SM Shaun Marcum 3.00 8.00
SR Scott Rolen 4.00 10.00
SS Stephen Strasburg S2 8.00 20.00
SS Sergio Santos 3.00 8.00
TC Trevor Cahill 3.00 8.00
TH Torii Hunter S2 4.00 10.00
TH Tommy Hanson 3.00 8.00
TL Tim Lincecum 4.00 10.00
TT Troy Tulowitzki 5.00 12.00
TW Travis Wood 3.00 8.00
UJ Ubaldo Jimenez S2 3.00 8.00
UJ Ubaldo Jimenez 3.00 8.00
VM Victor Martinez S2 4.00 10.00
VW Vernon Wells S2 3.00 8.00
WB Wade Boggs S2 3.00 8.00
YG Yovani Gallardo S2 4.00 10.00
YG Yovani Gallardo 4.00 10.00
ZG Zack Greinke S2 4.00 10.00
AGR Alex Gordon 4.00 10.00
APA Angel Pagan S2 3.00 8.00
BMC Brian McCann S2 4.00 10.00
BWA Brett Wallace 3.00 8.00
CGE Craig Gentry 3.00 8.00
CGO Carlos Gonzalez 4.00 10.00
CZA Carlos Zambrano S2 4.00 10.00
DDE David DeJesus S2 3.00 8.00
DME Devin Mesoraco S2 3.00 8.00
DPE Dustin Pedroia 4.00 10.00
DST Drew Stubbs S2 3.00 8.00
ELO Evan Longoria S2 4.00 10.00
HCO Hank Conger S2 3.00 8.00
IDA Ike Davis S2 3.00 8.00
JCU Johnny Cueto 4.00 10.00
JJA Jon Jay S2 5.00 12.00
JLO Jed Lowrie S2 3.00 8.00
JLU Jonathan Lucroy 4.00 10.00
JPA Jonathan Papelbon S2 4.00 10.00
JPA Jonathan Papelbon 4.00 10.00
JPE Jake Peavy S2 3.00 8.00
JPO Jorge Posada S2 3.00 8.00
JVO Joey Votto 5.00 12.00
JWA Jordan Walden S2 3.00 8.00
JWE Jayson Werth 4.00 10.00
JZI Jordan Zimmermann S2 4.00 10.00
MBO Michael Bourn S2 3.00 8.00
MCA Melky Cabrera S2 3.00 8.00
MCA Matt Cain 4.00 10.00
MCB Miguel Cabrera S2 6.00 15.00
MLA Matt LaPorta 3.00 8.00
MSC Max Scherzer 5.00 12.00
MST Mike Stanton 5.00 12.00
RAL Roberto Alomar S2 3.00 8.00
RMA Russell Martin S2 3.00 8.00
SCA Starlin Castro S2 4.00 10.00
SMU Stan Musial 6.00 15.00
SST Stephen Strasburg 8.00 20.00
THU Tim Hudson 4.00 10.00
UJI Ubaldo Jimenez S2 3.00 8.00
VWE Vernon Wells S2 3.00 8.00
ZGR Zack Greinke S2 4.00 10.00

2012 Topps Golden Moments Relics Gold Sparkle

*GOLD: .6X TO 1.5X BASIC
STATED ODDS 1:953 HOBBY
STATED PRINT RUN 99 SER.#'d SETS
CY Carl Yastrzemski S2 10.00 25.00

2012 Topps Historical Stitches

RANDOM INSERTS IN RETAIL PACKS
I Ichiro Suzuki S2 3.00 8.00
AB Albert Belle S2 1.00 2.50
AD Andre Dawson S2 1.50 4.00
AK Al Kaline 2.50 6.00
AP Albert Pujols S2 3.00 8.00
AR Alex Rodriguez S2 3.00 8.00
BG Bob Gibson 1.50 4.00
CF Carlton Fisk 1.50 4.00
CJ Chipper Jones S2 2.50 6.00
CR Cal Ripken Jr. S2 8.00 20.00
CY Carl Yastrzemski S2 4.00 10.00
DJ Derek Jeter S2 12.50 30.00
DM Don Mattingly 5.00 12.00
FR Frank Robinson 1.50 4.00
GC Gary Carter S2 1.50 4.00
HA Hank Aaron 5.00 12.00
HK Harmon Killebrew S2 2.50 6.00
IR Ivan Rodriguez S2 1.50 4.00
JB Johnny Bench 2.50 6.00
JD Joe DiMaggio 5.00 12.00
JH Josh Hamilton S2 2.00 5.00
JM Juan Marichal S2 1.50 4.00
JM Joe Morgan 1.50 4.00
JR Jackie Robinson 2.50 6.00
JR Jim Rice S2 1.50 4.00
JS John Smoltz S2 2.50 6.00
JV Justin Verlander S2 2.50 6.00
KG Ken Griffey Jr. S2 12.50 30.00
LA Luis Aparicio 1.50 4.00
LG Lou Gehrig 5.00 12.00
MM Mickey Mantle 8.00 20.00
MR Mariano Rivera S2 3.00 8.00
MS Mike Schmidt 4.00 10.00
NR Nolan Ryan 8.00 20.00
NR Nolan Ryan S2 8.00 20.00
PM Paul Molitor S2 2.50 6.00
RC Roberto Clemente 10.00 25.00
RJ Reggie Jackson 1.50 4.00
RM Roger Maris 2.50 6.00
RM Roger Maris S2 2.50 6.00
RS Ryne Sandberg 5.00 12.00
SK Sandy Koufax 5.00 12.00
SM Stan Musial 4.00 10.00
TC Ty Cobb 4.00 10.00
TS Tom Seaver 1.50 4.00
VG Vladimir Guerrero S2 2.00 5.00
WM Willie Mays 5.00 12.00
WMC Willie McCovey 1.50 4.00
WS Warren Spahn S2 1.50 4.00
YB Yogi Berra S2 2.50 6.00

2012 Topps Mickey Mantle Reprint Relics

STATED ODDS 1:147,600 HOBBY
PRINT RUNS B/WN 67-69 COPIES PER
MMR67 Mickey Mantle/67 50.00 100.00
MMR68 Mickey Mantle/68 50.00 100.00
MMR69 Mickey Mantle/69 50.00 100.00

2012 Topps Mound Dominance

COMPLETE SET (15) 6.00 15.00
STATED ODDS 1:8 HOBBY
MD1 Tom Seaver .40 1.00
MD2 Justin Verlander .60 1.50
MD3 Sandy Koufax 1.25 3.00
MD4 Jim Palmer .40 1.00
MD5 Dennis Eckersley .40 1.00
MD6 Bob Gibson .40 1.00
MD7 Roy Halladay .50 1.25
MD8 Nolan Ryan 2.00 5.00
MD9 Phil Niekro .40 1.00
MD10 Armando Galarraga .25 .60
MD11 Warren Spahn .40 1.00
MD12 Bob Feller .40 1.00
MD13 Jon Lester .40 1.00
MD14 John Smoltz .60 1.50
MD15 Dwight Gooden .25 .60

2012 Topps Mound Dominance Relics

STATED ODDS 1:9525 HOBBY
STATED PRINT 50 SER.#'d SETS
CB Clay Buchholz 10.00 25.00
DE Dennis Eckersley 20.00 50.00
FH Felix Hernandez 5.00 12.00
JP Jim Palmer 6.00 15.00
JS John Smoltz 12.50 30.00
JV Justin Verlander 15.00 40.00
MG Matt Garza 4.00 10.00
NR Nolan Ryan 15.00 40.00
RH Roy Halladay 10.00 25.00
SC Steve Carlton 15.00 40.00
SK Sandy Koufax 20.00 50.00
TS Tom Seaver 15.00 40.00
UJ Ubaldo Jimenez 4.00 10.00

2012 Topps Prime Nine Home Run Legends

COMPLETE SET (9) 6.00 15.00
COMMON EXCHANGE 1.50 4.00
STATED ODDS 1:18 HOBBY
HRL1 Hank Aaron 1.50 4.00
HRL2 Babe Ruth 2.00 5.00
HRL3 Willie Mays 1.50 4.00
HRL4 Reggie Jackson .50 1.25
HRL5 Alex Rodriguez 1.00 2.50
HRL6 Mickey Mantle 2.50 6.00
HRL7 Ernie Banks .75 2.00
HRL8 Frank Robinson .50 1.25
HRL9 Albert Pujols 1.00 2.50

2012 Topps Retail Refractors

COMPLETE SET (3) 4.00 10.00
MBC1 Mickey Mantle 3.00 8.00
MBC2 Willie Mays 2.00 5.00
MBC3 Ken Griffey Jr. 2.00 5.00

2012 Topps Retired Number Patches

RANDOM INSERTS IN RETAIL PACKS
AD Andre Dawson 1.25 3.00
AK Al Kaline 2.00 5.00
BF Bob Feller S2 1.25 3.00
BG Bob Gibson 1.25 3.00
BR Brooks Robinson S2 1.25 3.00
CF Carlton Fisk S2 1.25 3.00
CF Carlton Fisk 1.25 3.00
CH Catfish Hunter S2 1.25 3.00
CR Cal Ripken Jr. 6.00 15.00
DW Dave Winfield S2 1.25 3.00
EB Ernie Banks S2 2.00 5.00
FR Frank Robinson 1.25 3.00
FT Frank Thomas 2.00 5.00
GB George Brett S2 4.00 10.00
GC Gary Carter S2 1.25 3.00
HA Hank Aaron S2 4.00 10.00
HA Hank Aaron 4.00 10.00
JB Johnny Bench 2.00 5.00
JD Joe DiMaggio 4.00 10.00
JM Joe Morgan 1.25 3.00
JP Jim Palmer S2 1.25 3.00
JR Jackie Robinson 2.00 5.00
JRI Jim Rice 1.25 3.00
LB Lou Boudreau S2 1.25 3.00
LG Lou Gehrig 4.00 10.00
MM Mickey Mantle 6.00 15.00
MS Mike Schmidt 3.00 8.00
NR Nolan Ryan 6.00 15.00
NR Nolan Ryan S2 6.00 15.00
PN Phil Niekro S2 1.25 3.00
PR Phil Rizzuto S2 1.25 3.00
RC Rod Carew S2 1.25 3.00
RC Roberto Clemente 5.00 12.00
RH Rickey Henderson S2 2.00 5.00
RJ Reggie Jackson S2 1.25 3.00
RJ Reggie Jackson 1.25 3.00
RJA Reggie Jackson 1.25 3.00
RM Roger Maris 2.00 5.00
RS Ryne Sandberg S2 4.00 10.00
RY Robin Yount S2 2.00 5.00
SA Sparky Anderson S2 1.25 3.00
SK Sandy Koufax 4.00 10.00
SM Stan Musial 3.00 8.00
TG Tony Gwynn S2 1.25 3.00
TL Tommy Lasorda S2 1.25 3.00
TS Tom Seaver 1.25 3.00
WB Wade Boggs S2 1.25 3.00
WM Willie Mays 4.00 10.00
WS Willie Stargell S2 1.25 3.00
YB Yogi Berra S2 2.00 5.00

2012 Topps Retired Rings

STATED ODDS 1:759 HOBBY
STATED PRINT RUN 736 SER.#'d SETS
BR Babe Ruth 12.00 30.00
CF Carlton Fisk 4.00 10.00
CR Cal Ripken Jr. 10.00 25.00
DM Don Mattingly 10.00 25.00
FR Frank Robinson 4.00 10.00
FRO Frank Robinson 4.00 10.00
FT Frank Thomas 6.00 15.00
HA Hank Aaron 10.00 25.00
JB Johnny Bench 6.00 15.00
JD Joe DiMaggio 10.00 25.00
JM Joe Morgan 4.00 10.00
JR Jackie Robinson 10.00 25.00
LA Luis Aparicio 4.00 10.00
LG Lou Gehrig 10.00 25.00
MM Mickey Mantle 20.00 50.00
MS Mike Schmidt 10.00 25.00
NR Nolan Ryan 12.00 30.00
NRY Nolan Ryan 12.00 30.00
RC Roberto Clemente 15.00 40.00
RJ Reggie Jackson 4.00 10.00
RM Roger Maris 10.00 25.00
RS Ryne Sandberg 10.00 25.00
SK Sandy Koufax 10.00 25.00
SM Stan Musial 10.00 25.00
TS Tom Seaver 4.00 10.00
WM Willie Mays 10.00 25.00

2012 Topps Silk Collection

SER.2 ODDS 1:425 HOBBY
UPDATE ODDS 1:240 HOBBY
STATED PRINT RUN 50 SER.#'d SETS
SC1 Ryan Braun 6.00 15.00
SC2 Jaime Garcia 8.00 20.00
SC3 Desmond Jennings 8.00 20.00
SC4 Mickey Mantle 40.00 100.00
SC5 Jon Lester 6.00 15.00
SC6 Vernon Wells 6.00 15.00
SC7 Melky Cabrera 6.00 15.00
SC8 Craig Kimbrel 8.00 20.00
SC9 Chris Iannetta 6.00 15.00
SC10 Ike Davis 6.00 15.00
SC11 Derek Jeter 25.00 60.00
SC12 Eric Hosmer 8.00 20.00
SC13 Mike Napoli 6.00 15.00
SC14 Jhoulys Chacin 6.00 15.00
SC15 Adrian Gonzalez 8.00 20.00
SC16 Michael Young 6.00 15.
SC17 Geovany Soto 8.00 20.
SC18 Hanley Ramirez 8.00 20.
SC19 Jordan Zimmermann 8.00 20.
SC20 Ian Kennedy 6.00 15.
SC21 David Price 8.00 20.
SC22 Jason Heyward 8.00 20.
SC23 Jose Bautista 8.00 20.
SC24 Madison Bumgarner 8.00 20.
SC25 Brett Anderson 6.00 15.
SC26 Paul Konerko 6.00 15.
SC27 Mark Teixeira 8.00 20.
SC28 Matt Garza 6.00 15.
SC29 Tommy Hanson 6.00 15.
SC30 Hunter Pence 8.00 20.
SC31 Adam Jones 8.00 20.
SC32 Asdrubal Cabrera 8.00 20.
SC33 Johnny Cueto 8.00 20.
SC34 Troy Tulowitzki 10.00 25.
SC35 Brandon Belt 8.00 20.
SC36 Roy Halladay 8.00 20.
SC37 Matt Cain 8.00 20.
SC38 Kevin Youkilis 10.00 25.
SC39 Jacoby Ellsbury 8.00 20.
SC40 Mariano Rivera 12.00 30.
SC41 Pablo Sandoval 8.00 20.
SC42 Cole Hamels 8.00 20.
SC43 Ben Zobrist 8.00 20.
SC44 Miguel Cabrera 10.00 25.
SC45 Justin Masterson 6.00 15.
SC46 David Robertson 6.00 15.
SC47 Zack Greinke 8.00 20.
SC48 Alex Avila 6.00 15.
SC49 Freddie Freeman 12.00 30.
SC50 Jason Kipnis 8.00 20.
SC51 Jay Bruce 8.00 20.
SC52 Ubaldo Jimenez 6.00 15.
SC53 Mike Minor 6.00 15.
SC54 Justin Morneau 8.00 20.
SC55 David Wright 8.00 20.
SC56 Adam Lind 8.00 20.
SC57 Stephen Drew 6.00 15.
SC58 Jered Weaver 8.00 20.
SC59 Mat Latos 8.00 20.
SC60 Brian Wilson 10.00 25.
SC61 Kyle Blanks 6.00 15.
SC62 Shaun Marcum 6.00 15.
SC63 Aroldis Chapman 10.00 25.
SC64 Starlin Castro 8.00 20.
SC65 Dexter Fowler 8.00 20.
SC66 David Freese 6.00 15.
SC67 Scott Baker 6.00 15.
SC68 Sergio Santos 6.00 15.
SC69 R.A. Dickey 8.00 20.
SC70 Ryan Howard 8.00 20.
SC71 Mark Trumbo 6.00 15.
SC72 Delmon Young 8.00 20.
SC73 Erick Aybar 6.00 15.
SC74 Tony Gwynn 6.00 15.
SC75 Drew Storen 6.00 15.
SC76 Antonio Bastardo 6.00 15.
SC77 Miguel Montero 6.00 15.
SC78 Casey Kotchman 6.00 15.
SC79 Curtis Granderson 8.00 20.
SC80 Eric Thames 8.00 20.
SC81 John Axford 6.00 15.
SC82 Jayson Werth 8.00 20.
SC83 Mitch Moreland 6.00 15.
SC84 Josh Hamilton 8.00 20.
SC85 Alexi Ogando 6.00 15.
SC86 Danny Valencia 6.00 15.
SC87 Brandon Morrow 6.00 15.
SC88 Chipper Jones 10.00 25.
SC89 Emilio Bonifacio 6.00 15.
SC90 Vance Worley 8.00 20.
SC91 Mike Leake 6.00 15.
SC92 Kurt Suzuki 6.00 15.
SC93 Adrian Beltre 10.00 25.
SC94 John Danks 6.00 15.
SC95 Phil Hughes 6.00 15.
SC96 Matt LaPorta 6.00 15.
SC97 Tim Hudson 6.00 15.
SC98 Erik Bedard 6.00 15.
SC99 Matt Holliday 10.00 25.
SC100 Matt Kemp 8.00 20.
SC101 Brett Lawrie 8.00 20.
SC102 Michael Cuddyer 6.00 15.
SC103 Martin Prado 6.00 15.
SC104 Anthony Rizzo 15.00 40.
SC105 Victor Martinez 8.00 20.
SC106 Michael Bourn 6.00 15.
SC107 Elvis Andrus 8.00 20.
SC108 Chris Carpenter 8.00 20.
SC109 Joey Votto 10.00 25.
SC110 Carlos Lee 6.00 15.
SC111 Rickie Weeks 6.00 15.
SC112 Todd Helton 8.00 20.
SC113 Josh Johnson 8.00 20.
SC114 Dustin Pedroia 8.00 20.
SC115 J.J. Hardy 6.00 15.
SC116 Brett Gardner 8.00 20.
SC117 Gio Gonzalez 8.00 20.
SC118 Dayan Viciedo 6.00 15.
SC119 Albert Pujols 12.00 30.
SC120 Cameron Maybin 6.00 15.
SC121 Cliff Lee 8.00 20.
SC122 Carlos Quentin 6.00 15.
SC123 James Shields 6.00 15.
SC124 Yovani Gallardo 8.00 20.
SC125 Shin-Soo Choo 8.00 20.
SC126 Darwin Barney 6.00 15.
SC127 Alex Rodriguez 12.00 30.
SC128 Carlos Santana 8.00 20.

SC129 Chris Young 6.00 15.00
SC130 Travis Hafner 6.00 15.00
SC131 Ichiro Suzuki 12.00 30.00
SC132 David Ortiz 10.00 25.00
SC133 Corey Hart 6.00 15.00
SC134 Carl Crawford 8.00 20.00
SC135 Logan Morrison 6.00 15.00
SC136 Josh Beckett 6.00 15.00
SC137 Brandon Beachy 6.00 15.00
SC138 Ian Kinsler 8.00 20.00
SC139 Dan Haren 6.00 15.00
SC140 Felix Hernandez 8.00 20.00
SC141 Brandon Phillips 6.00 15.00
SC142 Evan Longoria 8.00 20.00
SC143 Nelson Cruz 10.00 25.00
SC144 Joe Mauer 8.00 20.00
SC145 Andrew McCutchen 10.00 25.00
SC146 Carlos Zambrano 8.00 20.00
SC147 Stephen Strasburg 10.00 25.00
SC148 Justin Verlander 10.00 25.00
SC149 Jose Valverde 8.00 20.00
SC150 CC Sabathia 8.00 20.00
SC151 Kerry Wood 6.00 15.00
SC152 Jeff Francoeur 8.00 20.00
SC153 Andrew Bailey 6.00 15.00
SC154 Alex Gordon 8.00 20.00
SC155 Howie Kendrick 6.00 15.00
SC156 Nick Markakis 8.00 20.00
SC157 Jimmy Rollins 8.00 20.00
SC158 Brian McCann 8.00 20.00
SC159 Jeremy Hellickson 6.00 15.00
SC160 Dan Uggla 8.00 20.00
SC161 Adam Wainwright 8.00 20.00
SC162 Ricky Romero 6.00 15.00
SC163 Daniel Hudson 6.00 15.00
SC164 Wandy Rodriguez 6.00 15.00
SC165 Andre Ethier 8.00 20.00
SC166 Lance Berkman 8.00 20.00
SC167 Alexei Ramirez 8.00 20.00
SC168 Mike Moustakas 8.00 20.00
SC169 Chase Utley 8.00 20.00
SC170 C.J. Wilson 6.00 15.00
SC171 Ervin Santana 6.00 15.00
SC172 Jair Jurrjens 6.00 15.00
SC173 Robinson Cano 8.00 20.00
SC174 Clayton Kershaw 20.00 50.00
SC175 Jose Reyes 6.00 15.00
SC176 Tsuyoshi Nishioka 8.00 20.00
SC177 Mike Stanton 10.00 25.00
SC178 Drew Stubbs 6.00 15.00
SC179 Jemile Weeks 6.00 15.00
SC180 Justin Upton 8.00 20.00
SC181 Carlos Beltran 8.00 20.00
SC182 Carlos Marmol 6.00 15.00
SC183 Shane Victorino 8.00 20.00
SC184 Nick Swisher 8.00 20.00
SC185 Tim Lincecum 8.00 20.00
SC186 Ryan Zimmerman 8.00 20.00
SC187 Aramis Ramirez 6.00 15.00
SC188 Jim Thome 8.00 20.00
SC189 Torii Hunter 8.00 20.00
SC190 Mike Trout 300.00 800.00
SC191 Paul Goldschmidt 10.00 25.00
SC192 Yu Darvish 15.00 40.00
SC193 Hiroki Kuroda 6.00 15.00
SC194 Johan Santana 8.00 20.00
SC195 Carlos Gonzalez 8.00 20.00
SC196 Prince Fielder 8.00 20.00
SC197 J.J. Putz 6.00 15.00
SC198 Neftali Feliz 6.00 15.00
SC199 Buster Posey 12.00 30.00
SC200 Alfonso Soriano 8.00 20.00
SC201 Bryce Harper 40.00 100.00
SC202 Jamey Carroll 6.00 15.00
SC203 Matt Treanor 6.00 15.00
SC204 Darren Oliver 6.00 15.00
SC205 Miguel Batista 6.00 15.00
SC206 Trevor Bauer 20.00 50.00
SC207 Luke Scott 6.00 15.00
SC208 Matt Lindstrom 6.00 15.00
SC209 A.J. Ellis 6.00 15.00
SC210 Giancarlo Stanton 10.00 25.00
SC211 Yu Darvish 15.00 40.00
SC212 Travis Ishikawa 6.00 15.00
SC213 Brian Duensing 6.00 15.00
SC214 Jonny Gomes 6.00 15.00
SC215 Gerald Laird 6.00 15.00
SC216 Ross Detwiler 6.00 15.00
SC217 Johnny Damon 8.00 20.00
SC218 Hector Santiago 8.00 20.00
SC219 Ernesto Frieri 6.00 15.00
SC220 Joel Peralta 6.00 15.00
SC221 Adam Kennedy 6.00 15.00
SC222 Jason Hammel 8.00 20.00
SC223 Javier Lopez 6.00 15.00
SC224 Ty Wigginton 6.00 15.00
SC225 Matt Moore 10.00 25.00
SC226 Kevin Millwood 6.00 15.00
SC227 Lucas Harrell 6.00 15.00
SC228 Chris Nelson 6.00 15.00
SC229 Erik Bedard 6.00 15.00
SC230 Fernando Rodney 6.00 15.00
SC231 Tom Milone 6.00 15.00
SC232 Brad Ziegler 6.00 15.00
SC233 Joe Smith 6.00 15.00
SC234 Casey Kotchman 6.00 15.00
SC235 Andrew Cashner 6.00 15.00
SC236 Drew Hutchison 8.00 20.00
SC237 Brandon Inge 6.00 15.00
SC238 Todd Frazier 8.00 20.00
SC239 Xavier Nady 6.00 15.00
SC240 Will Middlebrooks 8.00 20.00
SC241 Jason Grilli 6.00 15.00
SC242 Trevor Cahill 6.00 15.00
SC243 Greg Dobbs 6.00 15.00
SC244 Ryan Theriot 20.00 50.00
SC245 Takashi Saito 6.00 15.00
SC246 Austin Kearns 6.00 15.00
SC247 Santiago Casilla 6.00 15.00
SC248 Manny Acosta 6.00 15.00
SC249 Edwin Jackson 6.00 15.00
SC250 Yoenis Cespedes 15.00 40.00
SC251 Matt Albers 6.00 15.00
SC252 Felix Doubront 6.00 15.00
SC253 Octavio Dotel 6.00 15.00
SC254 Rick Ankiel 6.00 15.00
SC255 Andy Pettitte 8.00 20.00
SC256 Brad Peacock 6.00 15.00
SC257 Phil Coke 6.00 15.00
SC258 Josh Harrison 8.00 20.00
SC259 Kyle McClellan 6.00 15.00
SC260 Rafael Soriano 6.00 15.00
SC261 Michael Saunders 8.00 20.00
SC262 Lance Lynn 6.00 15.00
SC263 Jesus Montero 6.00 15.00
SC264 Jose Arredondo 6.00 15.00
SC265 J.P. Howell 6.00 15.00
SC266 Maicer Izturis 6.00 15.00
SC267 Drew Smyly 6.00 15.00
SC268 Yuniesky Betancourt 6.00 15.00
SC269 A.J. Burnett 6.00 15.00
SC270 Casey McGehee 6.00 15.00
SC271 Mitchell Boggs 6.00 15.00
SC272 Michael Pineda 6.00 15.00
SC273 Dan Wheeler 6.00 15.00
SC274 Alfredo Aceves 6.00 15.00
SC275 Angel Pagan 6.00 15.00
SC276 Steve Cishek 6.00 15.00
SC277 Jack Wilson 6.00 15.00
SC278 Randy Choate 6.00 15.00
SC279 Joaquin Benoit 6.00 15.00
SC280 Bobby Abreu 6.00 15.00
SC281 A.J. Pollock 10.00 25.00
SC282 Will Ohman 6.00 15.00
SC283 Jonathan Broxton 6.00 15.00
SC284 Matt Diaz 6.00 15.00
SC285 Ryan Ludwick 6.00 15.00
SC286 Jerry Hairston 6.00 15.00
SC287 Brian Fuentes 6.00 15.00
SC288 Chone Figgins 6.00 15.00
SC289 Cesar Izturis 6.00 15.00
SC290 Eric Chavez 6.00 15.00
SC291 Mark Derosa 6.00 15.00
SC292 Jason Marquis 6.00 15.00
SC293 Jake Westbrook 6.00 15.00
SC294 Kevin Slowey 6.00 15.00
SC295 Alfredo Simon 6.00 15.00
SC296 John McDonald 6.00 15.00
SC297 Mat Latos 8.00 20.00
SC298 Henry Rodriguez 6.00 15.00
SC299 Sergio Santos 6.00 15.00
SC300 Melky Cabrera 6.00 15.00

2012 Topps Team Rings

SER.2 ODDS 1:774 HOBBY
BF Bob Feller 2.00 5.00
CJ Chipper Jones 3.00 8.00
CR Cal Ripken Jr. 10.00 25.00
CY Carl Yastrzemski 5.00 12.00
EB Ernie Banks 3.00 8.00
EL Evan Longoria 2.50 6.00
FT Frank Thomas 3.00 8.00
GB George Brett 6.00 15.00
HK Harmon Killebrew 3.00 8.00
HR Hanley Ramirez 2.50 6.00
JB Johnny Bench 3.00 8.00
JBA Jose Bautista 2.50 6.00
JH Josh Hamilton 2.50 6.00
JU Justin Upton 2.50 6.00
KG Ken Griffey Jr. 6.00 15.00
MM Mickey Mantle 10.00 25.00
MS Mike Schmidt 5.00 12.00
NR Nolan Ryan 10.00 25.00
RC Rod Carew 2.00 5.00
RCL Roberto Clemente 8.00 20.00
RH Rickey Henderson 3.00 8.00
RY Robin Yount 3.00 8.00
SK Sandy Koufax 6.00 15.00
SM Stan Musial 5.00 12.00
SS Stephen Strasburg 3.00 8.00
TC Ty Cobb 5.00 12.00
TG Tony Gwynn 2.00 5.00
TH Todd Helton 2.50 6.00
TS Tom Seaver 2.00 5.00
WM Willie Mays 6.00 15.00

2012 Topps Timeless Talents

COMPLETE SET (25) 5.00 12.00
STATED ODDS 1:6 HOBBY
TT1 P.Molitor/R.Braun .60 1.50
TT2 Chase Utley/Dustin Ackley .50 1.25
TT3 D.Mattingly/E.Hosmer 1.25 3.00
TT4 W.Mays/M.Kemp 1.25 3.00
TT5 N.Ryan/J.Verlander 2.00 5.00
TT6 Felix Hernandez/Michael Pineda .50 1.25
TT7 Frank Thomas/Paul Konerko .50 1.25
TT8 Frank Robinson/Jose Bautista .50 1.25
TT9 John Smoltz/Craig Kimbrel .60 1.50
TT10 R.Sandberg/D.Uggla 1.25 3.00
TT11 Johnny Bench/Brian McCann .60 1.50
TT12 Andy Pettitte/Cliff Lee .50 1.25
TT13 Barry Larkin/Asdrubal Cabrera .50 1.25
TT14 N.Ryan/J.Weaver 2.00 5.00
TT15 Bob Gibson/Roy Halladay .50 1.25
TT16 Andre Dawson/Justin Upton .50 1.25
TT17 Joe Morgan/Brandon Phillips .40 1.00
TT18 Albert Belle/Mike Stanton .60 1.50
TT19 S.Musial/L.Berkman 1.00 2.50
TT20 Ernie Banks/Troy Tulowitzki .60 1.50
TT21 Dennis Eckersley/Andrew Bailey .40 1.00
TT22 Luis Aparicio/Starlin Castro .50 1.25
TT23 Edgar Martinez/David Ortiz .60 1.50
TT24 Roger Maris/Curtis Granderson .60 1.50
TT25 C.Ripken/D.Jeter 2.00 5.00

2012 Topps Timeless Talents Dual Relics

STATED ODDS 1:17,000 HOBBY
STATED PRINT RUN 50 SER.#'d SETS
BM J.Bench/B.McCann 30.00 60.00
DU A.Dawson/J.Upton 30.00 60.00
HP Felix Hernandez 10.00 25.00
Michael Pineda
MK W.Mays/M.Kemp 50.00 100.00
RJ C.Ripken/D.Jeter 50.00 100.00
RV Ryan/Verlander EXCH 50.00 100.00
RW Ryan/Weaver 20.00 50.00
SU R.Sandberg/D.Uggla 20.00 50.00
MTT R.Maris/C.Granderson 40.00 80.00
TTH Gibson/Halladay EXCH 50.00 100.00

2012 Topps World Champion Autograph Relics

STATED ODDS 1:12,300 HOBBY
STATED PRINT RUN 50 SER.#'d SETS
EXCHANGE DEADLINE 12/31/2014
AC Allen Craig 100.00 200.00
AP Albert Pujols 125.00 250.00
JG Jaime Garcia 90.00 150.00
JM Jason Motte 50.00 100.00
MH Matt Holliday 100.00 200.00

2012 Topps World Champion Autographs

STATED ODDS 1:39,990 HOBBY
STATED PRINT RUN 50 SER.#'d SETS
EXCHANGE DEADLINE 12/31/2014
AC Allen Craig 60.00 120.00
AP Albert Pujols 150.00 300.00
JG Jaime Garcia 75.00 150.00
JM Jason Motte 60.00 120.00
MH Matt Holliday 60.00 120.00

2012 Topps World Champion Relics

STATED ODDS 1:6700 HOBBY
STATED PRINT RUN 100 SER.#'d SETS
EXCHANGE DEADLINE 12/31/2014
AC Allen Craig 40.00 80.00
AP Albert Pujols 75.00 150.00
CC Chris Carpenter 50.00 100.00
DD Daniel Descalso 40.00 80.00
DF David Freese 90.00 150.00
EJ Edwin Jackson 10.00 25.00
JG Jaime Garcia 40.00 80.00
JJ Jon Jay 50.00 100.00
JM Jason Motte 40.00 80.00
LB Lance Berkman 75.00 150.00
MH Matt Holliday 50.00 100.00
RF Rafael Furcal 40.00 80.00
RT Ryan Theriot 10.00 25.00
SS Skip Schumaker EXCH 60.00 120.00
YM Yadier Molina 75.00 150.00

2012 Topps Update

COMP.SET w/o SPs (330) 20.00 50.00
COMMON CARD (1-330) .12 .30
COMMON VAR SP (1-330) 1.50 4.00
COMMON RC (1-330) .40 1.00
PRINTING PLATE ODDS 1:911 HOBBY
PLATE PRINT RUN 1 SET PER COLOR
BLACK-CYAN-MAGENTA-YELLOW ISSUED
NO PLATE PRICING DUE TO SCARCITY
US1A Francisco Liriano .12 .30
US1B A.Gonzalez LAD SP 100.00 200.00
US2A Kris Medlen .12 .30
US2B C.Crawford LAD SP 40.00 80.00
US3A Adam Kennedy .12 .30
US3B J.Beckett LAD SP 60.00 120.00
US4A Matt Treanor .12 .30
US4B N.Punto LAD SP 75.00 150.00
US5A Wade Miley .15 .40
US5B J.Loney BOS SP 40.00 100.00
US6A Carlos Gonzalez .15 .40
US6B K.Youkilis CHI SP 20.00 50.00
US7A Joe Mauer .15 .40
US7B J.Thome BAL SP 75.00 150.00
US8 Luis Perez .12 .30
US9 Andrew McCutchen .20 .50
US10A Mark Trumbo .12 .30
US10B Mark Trumbo 1.50 4.00
With teammates SP
US11 Rick Ankiel .12 .30
US12 Jake Westbrook .12 .30
US13 Matt Lindstrom .12 .30
US14 Jeremy Hefner RC .40 1.00
US15A Justin Verlander .20 .50
US15B J.Verlander 2.50 6.00
ASG SP
US16 Patrick Corbin RC .50 1.25
US17 Joe Smith .12 .30
US18 Tom Wilhelmsen .12 .30
US19 Jonathan Broxton .12 .30
US20 Christian Friedrich RC .40 1.00
US21 Buster Posey .25 .60
US22 Chris Nelson .12 .30
US23 Matt Harvey RC 2.50 6.00
US24 J.P. Howell .12 .30
US25 Joe Mather .12 .30
US26 Santiago Casilla .12 .30
US27 Cesar Izturis .12 .30
US28 Matt Albers .12 .30
US29 Jonathan Sanchez .12 .30
US30 Jonny Gomes .12 .30
US31 Esmil Rogers .12 .30
US32 Adam Jones .15 .40
US33 Nathan Eovaldi .15 .40
US34 A.J. Griffin RC .50 1.25
US35 Craig Breslow .12 .30
US36 Juan Cruz .12 .30
US37A Billy Butler .12 .30
US37B Billy Butler 5.00 12.00
With George Brett SP
US37C George Brett SP 5.00 12.00
US38 Elian Herrera RC .60 1.50
US39 Cory Wade .12 .30
US40 Jose Bautista .15 .40
US41 Juan Francisco .15 .40
US42 Yoenis Cespedes RC 1.00 2.50
US43 Michael Bowden .12 .30
US44 Jeremy Hermida .12 .30
US45 Eric Chavez .12 .30
US46 Jamie Moyer .12 .30
US47 Yuniesky Betancourt .12 .30
US48 Asdrubal Cabrera .15 .40
US49 A.J. Burnett .12 .30
US50 C.J. Wilson .12 .30
US51 Manny Parra .12 .30
US52A Clayton Kershaw .40 1.00
US52B Kershaw w/Kemp SP 5.00 12.00
US53 Omar Infante .12 .30
US54 Phil Coke .12 .30
US55 Austin Kearns .12 .30
US56 Matt Diaz .12 .30
US57 Hanley Ramirez .15 .40
US58 Manny Acosta .12 .30
US59 Jerome Williams .12 .30
US60 Edwin Jackson .12 .30
US61 Alfredo Simon .12 .30
US62A CC Sabathia .15 .40
US62B CC Sabathia 2.00 5.00
With Kemp SP
US63 Gerald Laird .12 .30
US64 Matt Moore .20 .50
US65 Derek Norris RC .40 1.00
US66 James Russell .12 .30
US67 Jamey Carroll .12 .30
US68 Fernando Rodney .12 .30
US69 Brett Jackson RC .60 1.50
US70 Will Middlebrooks RC .50 1.25
US71 Brett Myers .12 .30
US72 Carlos Beltran .15 .40
US73 Joel Peralta .12 .30
US74 Starlin Castro .15 .40
US75 Rafael Furcal .15 .40
US76 Adam Dunn .15 .40
US77 Miguel Batista .12 .30
US78 Chad Durbin .12 .30
US79 Mike Baxter RC .40 1.00
US80 Jered Weaver .15 .40
US81 Lou Marson .12 .30
US82 Ty Wigginton .12 .30
US83 Carlos Lee .12 .30
US84 Eric Thames .15 .40
US85 Jacob Diekman RC .50 1.25
US86 Anibal Sanchez .12 .30
US87A Andrew McCutchen .20 .50
US87B Andrew McCutchen 2.50 6.00
In Suit SP
US88 Will Ohman .12 .30
US89 Andrew Cashner .12 .30
US90 Michael Saunders .15 .40
US91 Jonathan Papelbon .15 .40
US92 Chone Figgins .12 .30
US93 Chris Iannetta .12 .30
US94 Kevin Slowey .12 .30
US95 Edward Mujica .12 .30
US96 Jose Mijares .12 .30
US97 Shelley Duncan .12 .30
US98 Hector Santiago RC .50 1.25
US99 Chris Johnson .12 .30
US100 Ryan Dempster .12 .30
US101 Casey McGehee .12 .30
US102 Brandon League .12 .30
US103 Jack Wilson .12 .30
US104 Yasmani Grandal RC .40 1.00
US105 Mat Latos .15 .40
US106 Pedro Strop .12 .30
US107 Randy Choate .12 .30
US108 Kameron Loe .12 .30
US109 Starling Marte RC .50 1.25
US110 Robinson Cano .15 .40
US111 Clay Rapada .12 .30
US112 Eduardo Escobar RC .50 1.25
US113 Scott Elbert .12 .30
US114 Jeremy Guthrie .12 .30
US115 Jason Grilli .12 .30
US116 Chris Denorfia .12 .30
US117 Chris Resop .12 .30
US118 David Freese .12 .30
US119 Derek Jeter .50 1.25
US120A Robinson Cano .15 .40
US120B Robinson Cano 2.00 5.00
In Suit SP
US121 Johnny Damon .15 .40
US122 Logan Ondrusek .12 .30
US123 Jamie Moyer .12 .30
US124 Brad Peacock .12 .30
US125 Mark Lowe .12 .30
US126 John McDonald .12 .30
US127 Josh Harrison RC .50 1.25
US128 Dan Straily RC .40 1.00
US129 Giancarlo Stanton .20 .50
US130 Laynce Nix .12 .30
US131 Mitchell Boggs .12 .30
US132 Tommy Milone .12 .30
US133A Matt Kemp .15 .40
US133B Matt Kemp 2.00 5.00
In Suit SP
US134 Ramon Ramirez .12 .30
US135 Clay Hensley .12 .30
US136 Reed Johnson .12 .30
US137A Josh Hamilton .15 .40
US137B Josh Hamilton 2.00 5.00
With teammates SP
US138 Ernesto Frieri .12 .30
US139 Zack Greinke .15 .40
US140 Brian Duensing .12 .30
US141 R.A. Dickey .15 .40
US142 Erik Bedard .12 .30
US143 Jose Veras .12 .30
US144A Mike Trout 25.00 60.00
US144B M.Trout w/team SP 6.00 15.00
US145 Joey Devine .12 .30
US146 Casey Kotchman .12 .30
US147 Steve Delabar .12 .30
US148 Paul Konerko .12 .30
US149 Octavio Dotel .12 .30
US150 Jake Arrieta .15 .40
US151 Jordany Valdespin RC .50 1.25
US152 Jim Thome .15 .40
US153 Paul Maholm .12 .30
US154 Giancarlo Stanton .20 .50
US155 Franklin Morales .12 .30
US156 Troy Patton .12 .30
US157 Kole Calhoun RC .50 1.25
US158 Jared Burton .12 .30
US159 Ben Sheets .12 .30
US160 Marco Scutaro .15 .40
US161 Brian Dozier RC 1.25 3.00
US162A Yu Darvish RC 1.00 2.50
US162B Darvish Dress shirt SP 5.00 12.00
US163 Scott Diamond RC .40 1.00
US164 Melky Cabrera .12 .30
US165 Jacob Turner .15 .40
US166A Chipper Jones .20 .50
US166B C.Jones w/sign SP 5.00 12.00
US167 Trevor Cahill .12 .30
US168 Yu Darvish .30 .75
US169 Steve Cishek .12 .30
US170 Jerry Hairston .12 .30
US171 Rhiner Cruz RC .40 1.00
US172 Wilson Valdez .12 .30
US173 Jose Bautista .15 .40
US174 Javier Lopez .12 .30
US175 Tim Byrdak .12 .30
US176 Brad Ziegler .12 .30
US177 Mike Napoli .12 .30
US178 Lance Lynn .12 .30
US179 Matt Adams RC .50 1.25
US180 Roy Oswalt .15 .40
US181 Takashi Saito .12 .30
US182 Pablo Sandoval .15 .40
US183 Bryce Harper RC 12.00 30.00
US184 Stephen Strasburg .20 .50
US185 Donovan Solano RC 3.00 8.00
US186 Jason Hammel .15 .40
US187 John Jaso .12 .30
US188 Dallas Keuchel RC 2.00 5.00
US189 Melky Cabrera .12 .30
US190 Francisco Cordero .12 .30
US191 Bobby Abreu .12 .30
US192 Josh Hamilton .15 .40
US193 Henry Blanco .12 .30
US194 Brad Lincoln .12 .30
US195 Chad Qualls .12 .30
US196 Seth Smith .12 .30
US197 Cody Ransom .12 .30
US198 Michael Pineda .12 .30
US199 Nate Schierholtz .12 .30
US200 Chris Perez .12 .30
US201 Jason Frasor .12 .30
US202 Mark Trumbo .12 .30
US203 Fernando Rodney .12 .30
US204 Jesus Montero RC .40 1.00
US205 Travis Ishikawa .12 .30
US206 Cole Hamels .15 .40
US207 Greg Dobbs .12 .30
US208 Tyler Moore RC .40 1.00
US209 Yasmani Grandal .12 .30
US210 Tyler Chatwood .12 .30
US211 Matt Cain .15 .40
US212 Trevor Bauer .40 1.00
US213 Trevor Bauer RC 2.50 6.00
US214 Jeremy Affeldt .12 .30
US215 Brian Bogusevic .12 .30
US216 Matt Cain .15 .40
US217 Matt Guerrier .12 .30
US218 Alfredo Aceves .12 .30
US219 Brian Fuentes .12 .30
US220 Adrian Beltre .20 .50
US221 Drew Smyly RC .40 1.00
US222 Jairo Asencio .12 .30
US223 Boone Logan .12 .30
US224 Matt Belisle .12 .30
US225 Josh Lindblom .12 .30
US226 Rafael Soriano .12 .30
US227 Mark DeRosa .12 .30
US228 Aaron Cunningham .12 .30
US229 Quintin Berry RC .60 1.50
US230 Xavier Nady .12 .30
US231 Tim Dillard .12 .30
US232 Andrelton Simmons RC .60 1.50
US233 Jose Arredondo .12 .30
US234 Jeff Keppinger .12 .30
US235 Marc Rzepczynski .12 .30
US236 Lucas Luetge RC .40 1.00
US237 Prince Fielder .15 .40
US238 Shawn Camp .12 .30
US239 Luke Scott .12 .30
US240 Ronny Paulino .12 .30
US241A Curtis Granderson .15 .40
US241B Curtis Granderson 2.00 5.00
In suit SP
US242 Joe Kelly RC .60 1.50
US243 Brandon Inge .12 .30
US244 Matt Downs .12 .30
US245 Erasmo Ramirez RC .40 1.00
US246 Miguel Cabrera .20 .50
US247 Ryan Ludwick .12 .30
US248 Felix Doubront .12 .30
US249 Angel Pagan .12 .30
US250 Cristhian Martinez .12 .30
US251 Kyle McClellan .12 .30
US252 Chad Gaudin .12 .30
US253 Ryan Webb .12 .30
US254 Jason Marquis .12 .30
US255A Joey Votto .20 .50
US255B Joey Votto 2.50 6.00
With teammates SP
US256 Joe Nathan .12 .30
US257 Jose Quintana RC .40 1.00
US258 Josh Vitters RC .50 1.25
US259A Carlos Gonzalez .15 .40
US259B Carlos Gonzalez 2.00 5.00
In suit SP
US260 Ryan Cook RC .40 1.00
US261 Darren Oliver .12 .30
US262 Matt Kemp .15 .40
US263 Travis Snider .12 .30
US264 Josh Edgin RC .40 1.00
US265 Will Middlebrooks .15 .40
US266 Brandon Lyon .12 .30
US267 Darren O'Day .12 .30
US268A Craig Kimbrel .15 .40
US268B Craig Kimbrel 2.00 5.00
Dress shirt SP
US269 Drew Hutchison RC .50 1.25
US270 Luis Ayala .12 .30
US271A Ryan Braun .12 .30
US271B Ryan Braun 1.50 4.00
With teammates SP
US272A Ichiro Suzuki .25 .60
US272B Ichiro Bowing SP 10.00 25.00
US273 Yadier Molina .20 .50
US274 Jeff Gray .12 .30
US275 Todd Frazier .15 .40
US276 Matt Harvey 2.50 6.00
US277 Ben Francisco .12 .30
US278 Andy Pettitte .15 .40
US279 Ryan Cook RC .40 1.00
US280A David Wright .15 .40
US280B David Wright 2.00 5.00
With R.A. Dickey SP
US281 Matt Reynolds RC .40 1.00
US282 Darnell McDonald .12 .30
US283 Elvis Andrus .15 .40
US284 R.A. Dickey .15 .40
US285 Ian Kinsler .15 .40
US286 J.A. Happ .15 .40
US287 Dan Wheeler .12 .30
US288 Maicer Izturis .12 .30
US289A Prince Fielder .15 .40
US289B Prince Fielder 2.00 5.00
In suit SP
US290 Joaquin Benoit .12 .30
US291 Jesus Montero .40 1.00
US292A David Ortiz .20 .50
US292B David Ortiz 2.50 6.00
With teammates SP
US293 Shane Victorino .15 .40
US294 Sergio Santos .12 .30
US295 Carlos Ruiz .12 .30
US296 Henry Rodriguez .12 .30
US297 Hunter Pence .15 .40
US298 Gaby Sanchez .15 .40
US299A Bryce Harper 6.00 15.00
US299B B.Harper Suit SP 10.00 25.00
US299C Harper w/Chipper SP 10.00 25.00
US300 Mark Kotsay .12 .30
US301 Carlos Beltran .15 .40
US302 Lucas Harrell .12 .30
US303 Kevin Millwood .12 .30
US304 A.J. Ellis .15 .40
US305 David Price .15 .40
US306 Joe Wieland RC .40 1.00
US307 Ryan Roberts .12 .30
US308 Jay Bruce .15 .40
US309 Chris Heisey .12 .30
US310 Kelly Shoppach .12 .30
US311 Dan Uggla .15 .40
US312 Craig Stammen .12 .30
US313 Wandy Rodriguez .12 .30
US314 Eric O'Flaherty .12 .30
US315 Ross Detwiler .12 .30
US316 Ryan Theriot .40 1.00
US317 Marco Estrada RC .40 1.00
US318 Anthony Bass .12 .30
US319 A.J. Pollock RC 1.00 2.50
US320 Xavier Avery RC .40 1.00
US321 David Carpenter RC .50 1.25
US322 Jordan Danks RC .60 1.50
US323 Fernando Abad .12 .30
US324 Jamey Wright .12 .30
US325 Joel Hanrahan .12 .30
US326 Gio Gonzalez .15 .40
US327A Chris Sale .30 .75
US327B Sale w/Team SP 2.50 6.00
US328 Geovany Soto .25 .60
US329 Jason Isringhausen .20 .50
US330 Alex Burnett .12 .30

2012 Topps Update Black

*BLACK: 12X TO 30X BASIC
*BLACK RC: 4X TO 10X BASIC
STATED ODDS 1:59 HOBBY
STATED PRINT RUN 61 SER.#'d SETS
US144 Mike Trout 600.00 1500.00
US162 Yu Darvish 12.50 30.00
US168 Yu Darvish 12.50 30.00
US183 Bryce Harper 500.00 1200.00
US299 Bryce Harper 40.00 100.00

2012 Topps Update Gold

*GOLD VET: 1.5X TO 4X BASIC
*GOLD RC: .5X TO 1.2X BASIC RC
STATED ODDS 1:5 HOBBY
STATED PRINT RUN 2012 SER.#'d SETS
US183 Bryce Harper 40.00 100.00

2012 Topps Update Gold Sparkle

*GLD SPARKLE VET: 1.2X TO 3X BASIC
*GLD SPARKLE RC: .4X TO 1X BASIC RC
STATED ODDS 1:4 HOBBY
US299 Bryce Harper 10.00 25.00

2012 Topps Update Orange

*GOLD VET: 5X TO 12X BASIC
*GOLD RC: 1.5X TO 4X BASIC RC
STATED PRINT RUN 210 SER.#'d SETS
US183 Bryce Harper 100.00 250.00

2012 Topps Update Target Red Border

*TARGET: 1.5X TO 4X BASIC
*TARGET RC: .5X TO 1.2X BASIC RC
FOUND IN TARGET RETAIL PACKS
US183 Bryce Harper 125.00 300.00
US299 Bryce Harper 10.00 25.00

2012 Topps Update Wal-Mart Blue Border

*WM: 1.5X TO 4X BASIC
*WM RC: .5X TO 1.2X BASIC RC
FOUND IN WAL MART RETAIL PACKS
US183 Bryce Harper 50.00 120.00
US299 Bryce Harper 8.00 20.00

2012 Topps Update All-Star Stitches

STATED ODDS 1:49 HOBBY
AB Adrian Beltre 3.00 8.00
AJ Adam Jones 4.00 10.00
AM Andrew McCutchen 5.00 12.00
BB Billy Butler 4.00 10.00
BH Bryce Harper 12.50 30.00
BP Buster Posey 6.00 15.00
CAG Carlos Gonzalez 3.00 8.00
CB Carlos Beltran 4.00 10.00
CCS CC Sabathia 3.00 8.00
CH Cole Hamels 3.00 8.00
CHS Chris Sale 3.00 8.00
CJ Chipper Jones 8.00 20.00
CLK Clayton Kershaw 4.00 10.00
CP Chris Perez 3.00 8.00
CR Carlos Ruiz 4.00 10.00
CRK Craig Kimbrel 4.00 10.00
CUG Curtis Granderson 4.00 10.00
CW C.J. Wilson 3.00 8.00
DJ Derek Jeter 10.00 25.00
DO David Ortiz 3.00 8.00
DP David Price 3.00 8.00
DU Dan Uggla 3.00 8.00
DW David Wright 4.00 10.00
EA Elvis Andrus 3.00 8.00
FH Felix Hernandez 3.00 8.00
FR Fernando Rodney 3.00 8.00
GG Gio Gonzalez 3.00 8.00
IK Ian Kinsler 3.00 8.00
JAB Jay Bruce 4.00 10.00
JHM Josh Hamilton 5.00 12.00
JM Joe Mauer 4.00 10.00
JN Joe Nathan 3.00 8.00
JOB Jose Bautista 4.00 10.00
JOP Jonathan Papelbon 3.00 8.00
JOV Joey Votto 5.00 12.00
JW Jered Weaver 3.00 8.00
MAC Matt Cain 4.00 10.00
MAH Matt Harrison 3.00 8.00
MAT Mark Trumbo 4.00 10.00
MEC Melky Cabrera 4.00 10.00
MHO Matt Holliday 4.00 10.00
MIC Miguel Cabrera 6.00 15.00
MIT Mike Trout 25.00 60.00
MK Matt Kemp 4.00 10.00
MN Mike Napoli 3.00 8.00
PF Prince Fielder 4.00 10.00
PK Paul Konerko 3.00 8.00
PS Pablo Sandoval 4.00 10.00
RB Ryan Braun 4.00 10.00
RD R.A. Dickey 5.00 12.00
RF Rafael Furcal 3.00 8.00
ROC Robinson Cano 4.00 10.00
SC Starlin Castro 4.00 10.00
SS Stephen Strasburg 6.00 15.00
YD Yu Darvish 10.00 25.00

2012 Topps Update All-Star Stitches Gold Sparkle

*GOLD: 1X TO 2.5X BASIC
STATED ODDS 1:1216 HOBBY
STATED PRINT RUN 50 SER.#'d SETS

2012 Topps Update Award Winners Gold Rings

STATED ODDS 1:940 HOBBY
I Ichiro Suzuki 8.00 20.00
AD Andre Dawson 6.00 15.00
AP Albert Pujols 10.00 25.00
BR Babe Ruth 12.50 30.00
CF Carlton Fisk 6.00 15.00

CR Cal Ripken Jr. 12.50 30.00
CY Carl Yastrzemski 8.00 20.00
DJ Derek Jeter 15.00 40.00
FR Frank Robinson 6.00 15.00
JB Johnny Bench 6.00 15.00
JR Jackie Robinson 10.00 25.00
JV Justin Verlander 8.00 20.00
KG Ken Griffey Jr. 12.50 30.00
LG Lou Gehrig 12.50 30.00
MM Mickey Mantle 25.00 50.00
MS Mike Schmidt 8.00 20.00
RB Ryan Braun 6.00 15.00
RC Roberto Clemente 15.00 40.00
RH Roy Halladay 6.00 15.00
RJ Reggie Jackson 6.00 15.00
SK Sandy Koufax 8.00 20.00
SM Stan Musial 10.00 25.00
TL Tim Lincecum 6.00 15.00
TS Tom Seaver 6.00 15.00
WM Willie Mays 10.00 25.00

2012 Topps Update Blockbusters

COMPLETE SET (30) 6.00 15.00
STATED ODDS 1:4 HOBBY
BB1 Albert Pujols .75 2.00
BB2 CC Sabathia .50 1.25
BB3 Frank Robinson .40 1.00
BB4 Gary Carter .40 1.00
BB5 Hanley Ramirez .50 1.25
BB6 Jay Buhner .25 .60
BB7 Ken Griffey Jr. 1.25 3.00
BB8 Miguel Cabrera .60 1.50
BB9 Nolan Ryan 2.00 5.00
BB10 Prince Fielder .50 1.25
BB11 Rickey Henderson .60 1.50
BB12 Tom Seaver .40 1.00
BB13 Yoenis Cespedes 1.00 2.50
BB14 Yu Darvish 1.00 2.50
BB15 Babe Ruth 1.50 4.00
BB16 Ivan Rodriguez .40 1.00
BB17 Catfish Hunter .40 1.00
BB18 Carlton Fisk .40 1.00
BB19 Ryne Sandberg 1.25 3.00
BB20 David Ortiz .60 1.50
BB21 Roy Halladay .50 1.25
BB22 Josh Beckett .40 1.00
BB23 Ichiro Suzuki .75 2.00
BB24 Steve Carlton .40 1.00
BB25 Alex Rodriguez .75 2.00
BB26 Bruce Sutter .40 1.00
BB27 Carlos Gonzalez .50 1.25
BB28 Johan Santana .50 1.25
BB29 Manny Ramirez .60 1.50
BB30 Jose Bautista .50 1.25

2012 Topps Update Blockbusters Commemorative Hat Logo Patch

BP1 Albert Pujols 2.50 6.00
BP2 CC Sabathia 1.50 4.00
BP3 Frank Robinson 1.25 3.00
BP4 Gary Carter 1.25 3.00
BP5 Hanley Ramirez 1.50 4.00
BP6 Jay Buhner .75 2.00
BP7 Ken Griffey Jr. 4.00 10.00
BP8 Miguel Cabrera 2.00 5.00
BP9 Nolan Ryan 6.00 15.00
BP10 Prince Fielder 1.50 4.00
BP11 Rickey Henderson 2.00 5.00
BP12 Tom Seaver 1.25 3.00
BP13 Yoenis Cespedes 3.00 8.00
BP14 Yu Darvish 3.00 8.00
BP15 Babe Ruth 5.00 12.00
BP16 Ivan Rodriguez 1.25 3.00
BP17 Catfish Hunter 1.25 3.00
BP18 Carlton Fisk 1.25 3.00
BP19 Ryne Sandberg 4.00 10.00
BP20 David Ortiz 2.00 5.00
BP21 Roy Halladay 1.50 4.00
BP22 Josh Beckett 1.25 3.00
BP23 Ichiro Suzuki 2.50 6.00
BP24 Steve Carlton 1.25 3.00
BP25 Alex Rodriguez 2.50 6.00
BP26 Johan Santana 1.50 4.00
BP27 Carlos Gonzalez 1.50 4.00
BP28 John Smoltz 2.00 5.00
BP29 Jose Reyes 1.25 3.00
BP30 Jose Bautista 1.50 4.00

2012 Topps Update Blockbusters Relics

STATED ODDS 1:6700 HOBBY
STATED PRINT RUN 50 SER.#'d SETS
AP Albert Pujols 10.00 25.00
BR Babe Ruth 75.00 150.00
GC Gary Carter 15.00 40.00
HR Hanley Ramirez 10.00 25.00
JB Jose Bautista 30.00 60.00
KG Ken Griffey Jr. 30.00 60.00
MC Miguel Cabrera 15.00 40.00
NR Nolan Ryan 12.00 30.00
RH Roy Halladay 10.00 25.00
YD Yu Darvish 20.00 50.00

2012 Topps Update General Manager Autographs

STATED ODDS 1:1345 HOBBY
AF Andrew Friedman 6.00 15.00
DM Dayton Moore 10.00 25.00
DO Dan O'Dowd 6.00 15.00
FW Frank Wren 10.00 25.00
JB Josh Byrnes 8.00 20.00
JD Jon Daniels 8.00 20.00
JL Jeff Luhnow 10.00 25.00
JZ Jack Zduriencik 6.00 15.00
MR Mike Rizzo 12.00 30.00
NC Ned Colletti 20.00 50.00
NH Neal Huntington 8.00 20.00
SA Sandy Alderson 20.00 50.00
TR Terry Ryan 15.00 40.00
JDI Jerry Dipoto 10.00 25.00

2012 Topps Update Gold Engravings

STATED ODDS 1:8053 HOBBY
BR Brooks Robinson 50.00 100.00
DS Duke Snider 12.00 30.00
HA Hank Aaron 100.00 200.00

2012 Topps Update Gold Hall of Fame Plaque

STATED ODDS 1:940 HOBBY
HOFBR Babe Ruth 10.00 25.00
HOFCR Cal Ripken Jr. 12.50 30.00
HOFCY Carl Yastrzemski 10.00 25.00
HOFGB George Brett 8.00 20.00
HOFGC Gary Carter 6.00 15.00
HOFJB Johnny Bench 10.00 25.00
HOFJP Jim Palmer 6.00 15.00
HOFJR Jackie Robinson 10.00 25.00
HOFLG Lou Gehrig 12.50 30.00
HOFMM Mickey Mantle 20.00 50.00
HOFMS Mike Schmidt 8.00 20.00
HOFNR Nolan Ryan 10.00 25.00
HOFOS Ozzie Smith 8.00 20.00
HOFRC Roberto Clemente 15.00 40.00
HOFRH Rickey Henderson 8.00 20.00
HOFRJ Reggie Jackson 8.00 20.00
HOFRS Ryne Sandberg 12.50 30.00
HOFSK Sandy Koufax 15.00 40.00
HOFSM Stan Musial 6.00 15.00
HOFTC Ty Cobb 8.00 20.00
HOFTS Tom Seaver 6.00 15.00
HOFWB Wade Boggs 6.00 15.00
HOFWM Willie Mays 8.00 20.00
HOFWS Warren Spahn 6.00 15.00
HOFYB Yogi Berra 12.50 30.00

2012 Topps Update Golden Debut Autographs

STATED ODDS 1:915 HOBBY
AR Anthony Rizzo 40.00 100.00
BB Brandon Belt 6.00 15.00
DM Devin Mesoraco 6.00 15.00
HI Hisashi Iwakuma 15.00 40.00
JP Jordan Pacheco 3.00 8.00
JPA Jarrod Parker 8.00 20.00
JW Jemile Weeks 4.00 10.00
LH Liam Hendriks 4.00 10.00
MH Mark Hamburger 3.00 8.00
MM Matt Moore 5.00 12.00
NE Nathan Eovaldi 3.00 8.00
PG Paul Goldschmidt 12.00 30.00
TB Trevor Bauer 15.00 40.00
TM Tom Milone 3.00 8.00
TP Tyler Pastornicky 3.00 8.00
WM Will Middlebrooks 5.00 12.00
WR Wilin Rosario 3.00 8.00
YA Yonder Alonso 8.00 20.00
YC Yoenis Cespedes 12.00 30.00
YD Yu Darvish 100.00 200.00

2012 Topps Update Golden Moments

COMPLETE SET (50) 10.00 25.00
STATED ODDS 1:4 HOBBY
GMU1 Bryce Harper 6.00 15.00
GMU2 Mike Trout 20.00 50.00
GMU3 Jered Weaver .50 1.25
GMU4 Josh Hamilton .50 1.25
GMU5 Johan Santana .50 1.25
GMU6 Adam Jones .50 1.25
GMU7 Philip Humber .40 1.00
GMU8 Ian Kennedy .40 1.00
GMU9 Miguel Cabrera .60 1.50
GMU10 Justin Verlander .60 1.50
GMU11 Yu Darvish 1.00 2.50
GMU12 Curtis Granderson .50 1.25
GMU13 Matt Cain .50 1.25
GMU14 Yoenis Cespedes 1.00 2.50
GMU15 Starlin Castro .50 1.25
GMU16 Andre Ethier .50 1.25
GMU17 David Price .50 1.25
GMU18 Bob Feller .40 1.00
GMU19 Joey Votto .60 1.50
GMU20 David Ortiz .60 1.50
GMU21 Ernie Banks .60 1.50
GMU22 Albert Belle .25 .60
GMU23 Nolan Ryan 2.00 5.00
GMU24 Giancarlo Stanton .60 1.50
GMU25 Ryan Braun .40 1.00
GMU26 Robin Yount .60 1.50
GMU27 Matt Kemp .50 1.25
GMU28 Harmon Killebrew .60 1.50
GMU29 David Wright .50 1.25
GMU30 Cal Ripken Jr. 2.00 5.00
GMU31 Reggie Jackson .40 1.00
GMU32 Mike Schmidt 1.00 2.50
GMU33 Roy Halladay .50 1.25
GMU34 Andrew McCutchen .60 1.50
GMU35 Eric Hosmer .50 1.25
GMU36 Matt Holliday .60 1.50
GMU37 Tony Gwynn .60 1.50
GMU38 Tim Lincecum .50 1.25
GMU39 Ryan Zimmerman .50 1.25
GMU40 Johnny Bench .60 1.50
GMU41 Derek Jeter 1.50 4.00
GMU42 Billy Butler .40 1.00
GMU43 Jose Bautista .50 1.25
GMU44 Jake Peavy .40 1.00
GMU45 Troy Tulowitzki .60 1.50
GMU46 Jon Lester .40 1.00
GMU47 George Brett 1.25 3.00
GMU48 Madison Bumgarner .50 1.25
GMU49 Edgar Martinez .40 1.00
GMU50 Al Kaline .60 1.50

2012 Topps Update Ichiro Yankees Commemorative Logo Patch

STATED ODDS 1:23,400 HOBBY
STATED PRINT RUN 200 SER.#'d SETS
MPR1 Ichiro Suzuki 20.00 50.00

2012 Topps Update Obama Presidential Predictor

COMMON OBAMA 2.00 5.00
STATED ODDS 1:81 HOBBY
PRICING FOR CARDS W/UNUSED CODES
PP1 Barack Obama/50 40.00 80.00

2012 Topps Update Romney Presidential Predictor

COMMON ROMNEY 2.00 5.00
STATED ODDS 1:81 HOBBY
PRICING FOR CARDS W/UNUSED CODES

2013 Topps

COMP.FACT.HOBBY.SET (660) 40.00 80.00
COMP.FACT.RUTH.SET (660) 40.00 80.00
COMP.FACT.ROBINSON.SET (660) 40.00 80.00
COMP.FACT.ALLSTAR.SET (660) 40.00 80.00
COMP.FACT.AARON.SET (660) 40.00 80.00
COMP.SET w/o SP's (660) 30.00 60.00
COMP.SER.1 SET w/o SP's (330) 12.50 30.00
COMP.SER.2 SET w/o SP's (330) 12.50 30.00
SERIES 1 PLATE ODDS 1:2323 HOBBY
SERIES 2 PLATE ODDS 1:1578 HOBBY
PLATE PRINT RUN 1 SET PER COLOR
BLACK-CYAN-MAGENTA-YELLOW ISSUED
NO PLATE PRICING DUE TO SCARCITY
1A Bryce Harper .40 1.00
1B Bryce Harper SP 8.00 20.00
1C Bryce Harper SP 10.00 25.00
2A Derek Jeter .60 1.50
2B Jeter SP w/Award 30.00 80.00
3 Hunter Pence .20 .50
4 Yadier Molina .25 .60
5 Carlos Gonzalez .20 .50
6A Ryan Howard .20 .50
6B Ryan Howard SP 4.00 10.00
8 Ryan Braun .20 .50
9 Dee Gordon .15 .40
10A Adam Jones .20 .50
10B Adam Jones SP 4.00 10.00
11A Yu Darvish .25 .60
11B Yu Darvish SP 4.00 10.00
11C Yu Darvish SP 4.00 10.00
12 A.J. Pierzynski .15 .40
13A Brett Lawrie .20 .50
13B Brett Lawrie SP 4.00 10.00
14A Paul Konerko .20 .50
14B Paul Konerko SP 4.00 10.00
15 Dustin Pedroia .20 .50
16A Andre Ethier .20 .50
16B Andre Ethier SP 4.00 10.00
17 Shin-Soo Choo .20 .50
18 Mitch Moreland .15 .40
19 Joey Votto .25 .60
20A Kevin Youkilis .15 .40
20B Kevin Youkilis SP 4.00 10.00
21 Lucas Duda .20 .50
22A Clayton Kershaw .50 1.25
22B Clayton Kershaw SP 4.00 10.00
23 Jemile Weeks .15 .40
24 Dan Haren .15 .40
25 Mark Teixeira .20 .50
26A Chase Utley .20 .50
26B Chase Utley SP 4.00 10.00
27A Mike Trout 2.00 5.00
27B Mike Trout SP 8.00 20.00
27C Mike Trout SP 8.00 20.00
27D Mike Trout SP 8.00 20.00
28A Prince Fielder .20 .50
28B Prince Fielder SP 4.00 10.00
29 Adrian Beltre .25 .60
30 Neftali Feliz .15 .40
31 Jose Tabata .15 .40
32 Craig Breslow .15 .40
33 Cliff Lee .20 .50
34A Felix Hernandez .20 .50
34B Felix Hernandez SP 4.00 10.00
35 Justin Verlander .25 .60
36 Jered Weaver .20 .50
37 Max Scherzer .25 .60
38 Brian Wilson .25 .60
39 Scott Feldman .15 .40
40 Chien-Ming Wang .20 .50
41 Daniel Hudson .15 .40
42 Detroit Tigers .15 .40
43 R.A. Dickey .20 .50
44A Anthony Rizzo .40 1.00
44B Anthony Rizzo SP 4.00 10.00
45 Travis Ishikawa .15 .40
46 Craig Kimbrel .20 .50
47 Howie Kendrick .15 .40
48 Ryan Cook .15 .40
49 Chris Sale .25 .60
50 Adam Wainwright .20 .50
51 Jonathan Broxton .15 .40
52 CC Sabathia .20 .50
53 Alex Cobb .15 .40
54 Jaime Garcia .20 .50
55A Tim Lincecum .20 .50
55B Tim Lincecum SP 4.00 10.00
56 Joe Blanton .15 .40
57 Mark Lowe .15 .40
58 Jeremy Hellickson .15 .40
59 John Axford .15 .40
60 Jon Rauch .15 .40
61 Trevor Bauer .25 .60
62 Tommy Hunter .15 .40
63 Justin Masterson .15 .40
64 Will Middlebrooks .15 .40
65 J.P. Howell .15 .40
66 Daniel Nava .15 .40
67 San Francisco Giants .15 .40
68 Colby Rasmus .20 .50
69 Marco Scutaro .20 .50
70A Todd Frazier .20 .50
70B Todd Frazier SP 4.00 10.00
71A Kyle Kendrick .15 .40
71B KendrickClose up 20.00 50.00
72 Gerardo Parra .15 .40
73 Brandon Crawford .20 .50
74 Kenley Jansen .20 .50
75 Barry Zito .20 .50
76 Brandon Inge .15 .40
77 Dustin Moseley .15 .40
78A Dylan Bundy RC .60 1.50
78B Dylan Bundy SP 4.00 10.00
79 Adam Eaton RC .40 1.00
80 Ryan Zimmerman .20 .50
81 Kershaw/Cueto/Dickey .50 1.25
82 Jason Vargas .15 .40
83 Darin Ruf RC .50 1.25
84 Adeiny Hechavarria (RC) .30 .75
85 Sean Doolittle RC .15 .40
86 Henry Rodriguez RC .25 .60
87 Mike Olt RC .30 .75
88 Jamey Carroll .15 .40
89 Johan Santana .20 .50
90 Andy Pettitte .20 .50
91 Alfredo Aceves .15 .40
92 Clint Barmes .15 .40
93 Austin Kearns .15 .40
94 Verland/Price/Weaver .25 .60
95 Matt Harrison .20 .50
David Price
Jered Weaver
96 Edward Mujica .15 .40
97 Danny Espinosa .15 .40
98 Gaby Sanchez .15 .40
99 Paco Rodriguez RC .40 1.00
100A Mike Moustakas .20 .50
100B Mike Moustakas SP 4.00 10.00
101 Bryan Shaw .15 .40
102 Denard Span. .15 .40
103 Evan Longoria .20 .50
104 Jed Lowrie .15 .40
105A Freddie Freeman .30 .75
105B Freddie Freeman SP 4.00 10.00
106 Drew Stubbs .15 .40
107A Joe Mauer .20 .50
107B Joe Mauer SP 4.00 10.00
108 Kendrys Morales .15 .40
109 Kirk Nieuwenhuis .15 .40
110A Justin Upton .20 .50
110B Justin Upton SP 4.00 10.00
111 Casey Kelly RC .30 .75
112A Mark Reynolds .15 .40
112B Mark Reynolds SP 4.00 10.00
113 Starlin Castro .15 .40
114 Casey McGehee .15 .40
115 Tim Hudson .20 .50
116 Brian McCann .20 .50
117 Aubrey Huff .15 .40
118 Daisuke Matsuzaka .20 .50
119 Chris Davis .20 .50
120 Ian Desmond .15 .40
121 Delmon Young .20 .50
122A Andrew McCutchen .25 .60
122B Andrew McCutchen SP 6.00 15.00
122C Andrew McCutchen SP 5.00 12.00
123 Rickie Weeks .15 .40
124 Ricky Romero .15 .40
125 Matt Holliday .25 .60
126 Dan Uggla .15 .40
127A Giancarlo Stanton .25 .60
127B Giancarlo Stanton SP 4.00 10.00
128A Buster Posey .30 .75
128B Buster Posey SP 5.00 12.00
129 Ike Davis .15 .40
130 Jason Motte .15 .40
131 Ian Kennedy .15 .40
132 Ryan Vogelsong .15 .40
133 James Shields .15 .40
134 Jake Arrieta .20 .50
135A Eric Hosmer .20 .50
135B Eric Hosmer SP 4.00 10.00
136 Tyler Clippard .15 .40
137 Edinson Volquez .15 .40
138 Michael Morse .15 .40
139 Bobby Parnell .15 .40
140 Wade Davis .15 .40
141 Carlos Santana .20 .50
142 Tony Cingrani RC .50 1.25
143 Jim Johnson .15 .40
144 Jason Bay .20 .50
145 Anthony Bass .15 .40
146 Kyle McClellan .15 .40
147 Ivan Nova .20 .50
148 L.J. Hoes RC .30 .75
149 Yovani Gallardo .15 .40
150 John Danks .15 .40
151 Alex Rios .20 .50
152 Jose Contreras .15 .40
153 Cabrera/Hamilton/Granderson .25 .60
154 Sergio Romo .15 .40
155 Mat Latos .20 .50
156 Dillon Gee .15 .40
157 Carter Capps RC .25 .60
158 Chad Billingsley .20 .50
159 Felipe Paulino .15 .40
160 Stephen Drew .15 .40
161 Bronson Arroyo .15 .40
162 Kyle Seager .15 .40
163 J.A. Happ .20 .50
164 Lucas Harrell .15 .40
165 Ramon Hernandez .15 .40
166 Logan Ondrusek .15 .40
167 Luke Hochevar .15 .40
168 Kyle Farnsworth .15 .40
169 Brad Ziegler .15 .40
170 Eury Perez RC .30 .75
171 Brock Holt RC .30 .75
172 Nyjer Morgan .15 .40
173 Tyler Skaggs RC .40 1.00
174 Jason Grilli .15 .40
175 A.J. Ramos RC .30 .75
176 Robert Andino .15 .40
177 Elliot Johnson .15 .40
178 Justin Maxwell .15 .40
179 Detroit Tigers .15 .40
180 Casey Kotchman .15 .40
181 Jeff Keppinger .15 .40
182 Randy Choate .25 .60
183 Drew Hutchison .20 .50
184 Geovany Soto .20 .50
185 Rob Scahill RC .25 .60
186 Jordan Pacheco .15 .40
187 Nick Maronde RC .30 .75
188 Brian Fuentes .15 .40
189 Posey/McCutch/Braun .30 .75
190 Daniel Descalso .15 .40
191 Chris Capuano .15 .40
192 Javier Lopez .20 .50
193 Matt Carpenter .25 .60
194 Encarn/Cabrera/Hamilton .25 .60
195 Chris Heisey .15 .40
196 Ryan Vogelsong .15 .40
197 Tyler Cloyd RC .30 .75
198 Chris Coghlan .15 .40
199 Avisail Garcia RC .30 .75
200 Scott Downs .15 .40
201 Jonny Venters .15 .40
202 Zack Cozart .15 .40
203 Wilson Ramos .15 .40
204A Alex Gordon .20 .50
204B Alex Gordon SP 4.00 10.00
205 Ryan Theriot .15 .40
206 Jimmy Rollins .20 .50
207 Matt Holliday .25 .60
208 Kurt Suzuki .15 .40
209 David DeJesus .15 .40
210 Vernon Wells .15 .40
211 Jarrod Parker .15 .40
212 Eric Chavez .15 .40
213A Alex Rodriguez .30 .75
213B Alex Rodriguez SP 4.00 10.00
214 Curtis Granderson .20 .50
215 Gordon Beckham .15 .40
216A Josh Willingham .20 .50
216B Josh Willingham SP 4.00 10.00
217 Brian Matusz .15 .40
218 Ben Zobrist .20 .50
219 Josh Beckett .15 .40
220 Octavio Dotel .15 .40
221 Heath Bell .15 .40
222 Jason Heyward .20 .50
223 Yonder Alonso .15 .40
224 Jon Jay .15 .40
225 Will Venable .15 .40
226 Derek Lowe .15 .40
227 Jose Altuve .20 .50
228A Adrian Gonzalez .20 .50
228B Adrian Gonzalez SP 4.00 10.00
229 Jeff Samardzija .15 .40
230 David Robertson .15 .40
231 Melky Mesa RC .30 .75
232 Jake Odorizzi RC .30 .75
233 Edwin Jackson .15 .40
234 A.J. Burnett .15 .40
235 Jake Westbrook .15 .40
236 Joe Nathan .15 .40
237 Brandon Lyon .15 .40
238 Carlos Zambrano .20 .50
239 Ramon Santiago .15 .40
240 J.J. Putz .15 .40
241 Jacoby Ellsbury .20 .50
242A Matt Kemp .20 .50
242B Matt Kemp SP 4.00 10.00
242C Matt Kemp SP 4.00 10.00
243 Aaron Crow .15 .40
244 Lucas Luetge .15 .40
245 Jason Isringhausen .15 .40
246 Braun/Stanton/Bruce .25 .60
247 Luis Perez .15 .40
248 Colby Lewis .15 .40
249 Vance Worley .20 .50
250 Jonathon Niese .15 .40
251 Sean Marshall .15 .40
252 Dustin Ackley .15 .40
253 Adam Greenberg (RC) .30 .75
254 Sean Burnett .15 .40
255 Josh Johnson .20 .50
256 Madison Bumgarner .20 .50
257 Mike Minor .15 .40
258 Doug Fister .15 .40
259 Bartolo Colon .15 .40
260 San Francisco Giants .15 .40
261 Trevor Rosenthal (RC) .50 1.25
262 Kevin Correia .15 .40
263 Ted Lilly .15 .40
264 Roy Halladay .20 .50
265 Tyler Colvin .15 .40
266 Albert Pujols .30 .75
267 Jason Kipnis .20 .50
268 David Lough RC .25 .60
269 St. Louis Cardinals .25 .60
270A Manny Machado RC 1.50 4.00
270B Machado SP Blk jsy 25.00 60.00
271 Jeurys Familia RC .40 1.00
272 Ryan Braun .20 .50
Alfonso Soriano
Chase Headley
273 Dexter Fowler .20 .50
274 Miguel Montero .15 .40
275 Johnny Cueto .20 .50
276 Luis Ayala .15 .40
277 Brendan Ryan .15 .40
278 Christian Garcia (RC) .25 .60
279 Vicente Padilla .15 .40
280 Rafael Dolis .15 .40
281 David Hernandez .15 .40
282A Russell Martin .15 .40
282B Russell Martin SP 4.00 10.00
283 CC Sabathia .20 .50
284 Angel Pagan .15 .40
285 Addison Reed .15 .40
286A Jurickson Profar RC .30 .75
286B Profar SP Blue jsy 20.00 50.00
287 Johnny Cueto .20 .50
Gio Gonzalez
R.A. Dickey
288 Starling Marte .20 .50
289 Jeremy Guthrie .15 .40
290 Tom Layne RC .25 .60
291 Ryan Sweeney .15 .40
292 Matt Thornton .15 .40
293 Jeff Karstens .15 .40
294 Trout/Beltre/Miggy 2.00 5.00
295 Brandon League .15 .40
296 Didi Gregorius RC 1.00 2.50
297 Michael Saunders .20 .50
298 Pablo Sandoval .20 .50
299 Darwin Barney .15 .40
300 Daniel Murphy .20 .50
301 Jarrod Saltalamacchia .15 .40
302 Aaron Hill .15 .40
303 Alex Rodriguez .30 .75
304 Kyle Drabek .15 .40
305A Shelby Miller RC .60 1.50
305B Miller SP Blue cap 20.00 50.00
306 Jerry Hairston .15 .40
307 Norichika Aoki .15 .40
308 Desmond Jennings .20 .50
309 Endy Chavez .15 .40
310 Edwin Encarnacion .25 .60
311A Rajai Davis .15 .40
311B Rajai Davis SP 4.00 10.00
312 Scott Hairston .15 .40
313 Maicer Izturis .15 .40
314 A.J. Ellis .15 .40
315 Rafael Furcal .15 .40
316A Josh Reddick .15 .40
316B Josh Reddick SP 4.00 10.00
317 Baltimore Orioles .15 .40
318 Hiroki Kuroda .15 .40
319 Brian Bogusevic .15 .40
320 Michael Young .15 .40
321 Allen Craig .20 .50
322 Alex Gonzalez .15 .40
323 Michael Brantley .15 .40
324A Cameron Maybin .15 .40
324B Cameron Maybin SP 4.00 10.00
325 Kevin Millwood .15 .40
326 Andruw Jones .15 .40
327 Jhonny Peralta .15 .40
328 Jayson Werth .20 .50
329 Rafael Soriano .15 .40
330 Ryan Raburn .15 .40
331A Jose Reyes .20 .50
331B Jose Reyes SP 4.00 10.00
332 Cole Hamels .20 .50
333 Santiago Casilla .15 .40
334 Derek Norris .15 .40
335 Chris Herrmann RC .25 .60
336 Hank Conger .15 .40
337 Chris Iannetta .15 .40
338 Mike Trout 2.00 5.00
339 Nick Swisher .20 .50
340 Franklin Gutierrez .15 .40
341 Lonnie Chisenhall .15 .40
342 Matt Dominguez .15 .40
343 Alex Avila .20 .50
344 Kris Medlen .20 .50
345 Jenrry Mejia .15 .40
346 Aaron Hicks RC .40 1.00
347 Brett Anderson .15 .40
348 Jonny Gomes .15 .40
349 Ernesto Frieri .15 .40
350A Albert Pujols .30 .75
350B Albert Pujols SP 6.00 15.00
351 Asdrubal Cabrera .20 .50
352 Tommy Hanson .15 .40
353 Bud Norris .15 .40
354 Casey Janssen .15 .40
355 Carlos Marmol .15 .40
356 Greg Dobbs .15 .40
357 Juan Francisco .15 .40
358 Henderson Alvarez .15 .40
359 CC Sabathia .20 .50
360 Khristopher Davis RC .75 2.00
361 Erik Kratz .15 .40
362A Yoenis Cespedes .25 .60
362B Yoenis Cespedes SP 4.00 10.0
363 Sergio Santos .15 .4
364 Carlos Pena .20 .5
365 Mike Baxter .15 .4
366 Ervin Santana .15 .4
367 Carlos Ruiz .15 .4
368 Chris Young .15 .4
369 Bryce Harper .40 1.0
370 A.J. Griffin .15 .4
371 Jeremy Affeldt .15 .4
372 Jeff Locke .15 .4
373 Derek Jeter .60 1.5
374 Miguel Cabrera .25 .6
375 Wilin Rosario .15 .4
376 Juan Pierre .15 .4
377 J.D. Martinez .25 .6
378 Joe Kelly .15 .4
379 Madison Bumgarner .20 .5
380 Juan Nicasio .15 .4
381 Wily Peralta .15 .4
382 Jackie Bradley Jr. RC .60 1.5
383 Matt Harrison .15 .4
384 Jake McGee .15 .4
385 Brandon Belt .20 .5
386 Brandon Phillips .15 .4
387 Jean Segura .20 .5
388 Justin Turner .20 .5
389 Phil Hughes .15 .4
390 James McDonald .15 .4
391 Travis Wood .15 .4
392 Tom Koehler RC .25 .6
393 Andres Torres .15 .4
394 Ubaldo Jimenez .15 .4
395 Alexei Ramirez .20 .5
396 Aroldis Chapman .25 .6
397 Mike Aviles .15 .4
398 Mike Fiers .15 .4
399 Shane Victorino .20 .5
400A David Wright .20 .5
400B David Wright SP 6.00 15.0
401 Ryan Dempster .15 .4
402 Tom Wilhelmsen .15 .4
403 Hisashi Iwakuma .20 .5
404 Ryan Madson .15 .4
405 Hector Sanchez .15 .4
406 Brandon McCarthy .15 .4
407 Juan Pierre .15 .4
408 Coco Crisp .15 .4
409 Logan Morrison .15 .4
410 Roy Halladay .20 .5
411 Jesus Guzman .15 .4
412 Everth Cabrera .15 .4
413 Brett Gardner .20 .5
414 Mark Buehrle .20 .5
415 Leonys Martin .15 .4
416 Jordan Lyles .15 .4
417 Logan Forsythe .15 .4
418 Evan Gattis RC .50 1.2
419 Matt Moore .20 .5
420 Rick Porcello .20 .5
421 Jordy Mercer RC .25 .6
422 Alfredo Marte RC .25 .6
423 Miguel Gonzalez RC .15 .4
424 Steven Lerud (RC) .25 .6
425 Josh Donaldson .20 .5
426 Vinnie Pestano .15 .4
427 Chris Nelson .15 .4
428 Kyle McPherson RC .25 .6
429 David Price .20 .5
430 Josh Harrison .15 .4
431 Blake Beavan .15 .4
432 Jose Iglesias .20 .5
433 Andrew Werner RC .25 .6
434 Wei-Yin Chen .15 .4
435 Brandon Maurer RC .30 .7
436 Elvis Andrus .20 .5
437 Dayan Viciedo .15 .4
438 Yasmani Grandal .15 .4
439 Marco Estrada .15 .4
440 Ian Kinsler .20 .5
441 Jose Bautista .20 .5
442 Mike Leake .15 .4
443 Lou Marson .15 .4
444 Jordan Walden .15 .4
445 Joe Thatcher .15 .4
446 Chris Parmelee .15 .4
447 Jacob Turner .20 .5
448 Tim Hudson .20 .5
449 Michael Cuddyer .15 .4
450A Jay Bruce .20 .5
450B Jay Bruce SP 6.00 15.0
451 Pedro Florimon .15 .4
452 Raul Ibanez .20 .5
453 Troy Tulowitzki .25 .6
454 Paul Goldschmidt .25 .6
455 Buster Posey .30 .7
456A Pablo Sandoval .20 .5
456B Pablo Sandoval SP 4.00 10.0
457 Nate Schierholtz .15 .4
458 Jake Peavy .15 .4
459 Jesus Montero .15 .4
460 Ryan Doumit .15 .4
461 Drew Pomeranz .20 .5
462 Eduardo Nunez .15 .4
463 Jason Hammel .20 .5
464 Luis Jimenez RC .25 .6
465 Placido Polanco .15 .4
466 Jerome Williams .15 .4
467 Brian Duensing .15 .4
468 Anthony Gose .15 .4
469 Adam Warren RC .25 .6
470 Jeff Francoeur .20 .5
471 Trevor Cahill .15 .4

472 John Mayberry .15 .40
473 Josh Johnson .20 .50
474 Brian Omogrosso RC .25 .60
475 Garrett Jones .15 .40
476 John Buck .20 .50
477 Paul Maholm .15 .40
478 Gavin Floyd .15 .40
479 Kelly Johnson .15 .40
480 Lance Berkman .20 .50
481 Justin Wilson RC .25 .60
482 Emilio Bonifacio .15 .40
483 Jordany Valdespin .15 .40
484 Johan Santana .20 .50
485 Ruben Tejada .15 .40
486 Jason Kubel .15 .40
487 Hanley Ramirez .20 .50
488 Ryan Wheeler RC .25 .60
489 Erick Aybar .15 .40
490 Cody Ross .15 .40
491 Clayton Richard .15 .40
492 Jose Molina .15 .40
493 Johnny Giavotella .15 .40
494 Alberto Callaspo .15 .40
495 Joaquin Benoit .15 .40
496 Scott Sizemore .15 .40
497 Brett Myers .15 .40
498 Martin Prado .15 .40
499 Billy Butler .15 .40
500 Stephen Strasburg .25 .60
501 Tommy Milone .15 .40
502 Patrick Corbin .20 .50
503 Clay Buchholz .15 .40
504 Michael Bourn .15 .40
505 Ross Detwiler .15 .40
506 Andy Pettitte .20 .50
507 Lance Lynn .15 .40
508 Felix Doubront .15 .40
509 Brennan Boesch .15 .40
510 Nate McLouth .15 .40
511 Rob Brantly RC .25 .60
512 Justin Smoak .15 .40
513 Zach McAllister .15 .40
514 Jonathan Papelbon .20 .50
515 Brian Roberts .15 .40
516 Omar Infante .15 .40
517 Pedro Alvarez .15 .40
518 Nolan Reimold .15 .40
519 Zack Greinke .20 .50
520 Peter Bourjos .15 .40
521 Evan Scribner RC .25 .60
522 Dallas Keuchel .15 .40
523 Wandy Rodriguez .15 .40
524 Wade LeBlanc .15 .40
525 J.P. Arencibia .15 .40
526 Tyler Flowers .15 .40
527 Carlos Beltran .20 .50
528 Darin Mastroianni .15 .40
529 Collin McHugh RC .25 .60
530 Wade Miley .15 .40
531 Craig Gentry .15 .40
532 Todd Helton .20 .50
533 J.J. Hardy .15 .40
534 Alberto Cabrera RC .25 .60
535 Philip Humber .15 .40
536 Mike Trout 2.00 5.00
537 Neil Walker .20 .50
538 Brett Wallace .15 .40
539 Phil Coke .15 .40
540 Michael Bourn .15 .40
541 Jon Lester .20 .50
542 Jeff Niemann .15 .40
543 Donovan Solano .25 .60
544 Tyler Chatwood .15 .40
545 Alex Presley .15 .40
546 Carlos Quentin .15 .40
547 Glen Perkins .15 .40
548 John Lackey .20 .50
549 Huston Street .15 .40
550 Matt Joyce .15 .40
551 Wellington Castillo .15 .40
552 Francisco Cervelli .15 .40
553 Josh Rutledge .15 .40
554 R.A. Dickey .20 .50
555 Joel Hanrahan .15 .40
556 Nick Hundley .15 .40
557 Adam Lind .20 .50
558 David Murphy .15 .40
559 Travis Snider .15 .40
560 Yunel Escobar .15 .40
561 Josh Vitters .20 .50
562 Jason Marquis .15 .40
563 Nate Eovaldi .20 .50
564 Francisco Peguero RC .25 .60
565 Torii Hunter .15 .40
566 C.J. Wilson .15 .40
567 Alfonso Soriano .20 .50
568 Steve Lombardozzi .15 .40
569 Ryan Ludwick .15 .40
570 Devin Mesoraco .15 .40
571 Melky Cabrera .15 .40
572 Lorenzo Cain .15 .40
573 Ian Stewart .15 .40
574 Corey Hart .15 .40
575 Justin Morneau .20 .50
576 Julio Teheran .20 .50
577 Matt Harvey .20 .50
578 Brett Jackson .15 .40
579 Adam LaRoche .15 .40
580 Jordan Danks .15 .40
581 Andrelton Simmons .15 .40
582 Seth Smith .15 .40
583 Alejandro De Aza .15 .40
584 Alfonso Soriano .20 .50
585 Homer Bailey .15 .40
586 Jose Quintana .15 .40
587 Matt Cain .20 .50
588 Jordan Zimmermann .20 .50
589A Jose Fernandez RC .60 1.50
589B Fernandez SP w/Miggy 25.00 60.00
590 Liam Hendriks .15 .40
591 Derek Holland .15 .40
592 Nick Markakis .20 .50
593 James Loney .20 .50
594 Carl Crawford .20 .50
595A David Ortiz .25 .60
595B David Ortiz SP 25.00 60.00
596 Brian Dozier .20 .50
597 Marco Scutaro .20 .50
598 Fernando Martinez .15 .40
599 Carlos Carrasco .15 .40
600 Mariano Rivera .30 .75
601 Brandon Moss .15 .40
602 Anibal Sanchez .15 .40
603 Chris Perez .15 .40
604 Rafael Betancourt .15 .40
605 Aramis Ramirez .15 .40
606 Mark Trumbo .15 .40
607 Chris Carter .15 .40
608 Ricky Nolasco .15 .40
609 Scott Baker .15 .40
610 Brandon Beachy .15 .40
611 Drew Storen .25 .60
612 Robinson Cano .20 .50
613 Jhoulys Chacin .15 .40
614 B.J. Upton .20 .50
615 Mark Ellis .15 .40
616 Grant Balfour .15 .40
617 Fernando Rodney .15 .40
618 Koji Uehara .15 .40
619 Carlos Gomez .15 .40
620 Hector Santiago .15 .40
621 Steve Cishek .15 .40
622 Alcides Escobar .20 .50
623 Alexi Ogando .15 .40
624 Justin Ruggiano .15 .40
625 Domonic Brown .20 .50
626 Gio Gonzalez .20 .50
627 David Price .20 .50
628 Martin Maldonado (RC) .25 .60
629 Trevor Plouffe .15 .40
630 Andy Dirks .15 .40
631 Chris Carpenter .20 .50
632 R.A. Dickey .20 .50
633 Victor Martinez .20 .50
634 Drew Smyly .15 .40
635 Jedd Gyorko RC .30 .75
636 Cole De Vries RC .25 .60
637 Ben Revere .15 .40
638 Andrew Cashner .15 .40
639 Josh Hamilton .20 .50
640 Jason Castro .15 .40
641 Bruce Chen .15 .40
642 Austin Jackson .15 .40
643 Matt Garza .15 .40
644 Ryan Lavarnway .15 .40
645 Luis Cruz .15 .40
646 Phillippe Aumont RC .25 .60
647 Adam Dunn .20 .50
648 Dan Straily .15 .40
649 Ryan Hanigan .15 .40
650 Nelson Cruz .25 .60
651 Gregor Blanco .15 .40
652 Jonathan Lucroy .20 .50
653 Chase Headley .15 .40
654 Brandon Barnes RC .25 .60
655 Salvador Perez .20 .50
656 Scott Diamond .15 .40
657 Jorge De La Rosa .15 .40
658 David Freese .15 .40
659 Mike Napoli .15 .40
660A Miguel Cabrera .25 .60
660B Miguel Cabrera SP 5.00 12.00
661A Hyun-Jin Ryu RC .60 1.50
661B Hyun-Jin Ryu SP 4.00 10.00
661C Ryu SP Grey jsy 20.00 50.00
661D Ryu SP Batting 20.00 50.00

2013 Topps Black

*BLACK VET: 8X TO 20X BASIC
*BLACK RC: 5X TO 12X BASIC RC
SERIES 1 ODDS 1:150 HOBBY
SERIES 2 ODDS 1:104 HOBBY
STATED PRINT RUN 62 SER.#'d SETS
16 Andre Ethier 10.00 25.00
19 Joey Votto 15.00 40.00
28 Prince Fielder 10.00 25.00
67 San Francisco Giants 20.00 50.00
78 Dylan Bundy 30.00 80.00
122 Andrew McCutchen 20.00 50.00
128 Buster Posey 30.00 60.00
154 Sergio Romo 10.00 25.00
188 Brian Fuentes 10.00 25.00
190 Daniel Descalso 10.00 25.00
205 Ryan Theriot 10.00 25.00
224 Jon Jay 8.00 20.00
261 Trevor Rosenthal 15.00 40.00
294 Trout/Beltre/Cabrera 15.00 40.00
645 Luis Cruz 5.00 12.00
660 Miguel Cabrera 15.00 40.00
661 Hyun-Jin Ryu 30.00 60.00

2013 Topps Camo

*CAMO VET: 10X TO 25X BASIC
*CAMO RC: 6X TO 15X BASIC RC
SERIES 1 ODDS 1:286 HOBBY
SERIES 2 ODDS 1:195 HOBBY
STATED PRINT RUN 99 SER.#'d SETS
2 Derek Jeter 60.00 120.00
16 Andre Ethier 8.00 20.00
19 Joey Votto 12.50 30.00
27 Mike Trout 20.00 50.00
28 Prince Fielder 8.00 20.00
122 Andrew McCutchen 15.00 40.00
154 Sergio Romo 8.00 20.00
205 Ryan Theriot 8.00 20.00
266 Albert Pujols 10.00 25.00
270 Manny Machado 30.00 60.00
294 Trout/Beltre/Cabrera 12.50 30.00
317 Baltimore Orioles 10.00 25.00
338 Mike Trout 20.00 50.00
350 Albert Pujols 10.00 25.00
362 Yoenis Cespedes 10.00 25.00
536 Mike Trout 20.00 50.00

2013 Topps Emerald

COMPLETE SET (660) 200.00 500.00
*EMERALD VET: 1.2X TO 3X BASIC
*EMERALD RC: .75X TO 2X BASIC RC
STATED ODDS 1:6 HOBBY

2013 Topps Factory Set Orange

*ORANGE VET: 5X TO 12X BASIC
*ORANGE RC: 3X TO 8X BASIC RC
INSERTED IN FACTORY SETS
STATED PRINT RUN 230 SER.#'d SETS

2013 Topps Gold

COMPLETE SET (660) 250.00 500.00
*GOLD VET: 1.2X TO 3X BASIC
*GOLD RC: .75X TO 2X BASIC RC
SERIES 1 ODDS 1:9 HOBBY
SERIES 2 ODDS 1:7 HOBBY
STATED PRINT RUN 2013 SER.#'d SETS

2013 Topps Pink

*PINK VET: 6X TO 15X BASIC
*PINK RC: 4X TO 10X BASIC RC
SERIES 1 ODDS 1:566 HOBBY
SERIES 2 ODDS 1:391 HOBBY
STATED PRINT RUN 50 SER.#'d SETS
2 Derek Jeter 60.00 120.00
16 Andre Ethier 10.00 25.00
19 Joey Votto 15.00 40.00
28 Prince Fielder 10.00 25.00
67 San Francisco Giants 20.00 50.00
78 Dylan Bundy 30.00 60.00
122 Andrew McCutchen 20.00 50.00
128 Buster Posey 30.00 60.00
154 Sergio Romo 10.00 25.00
188 Brian Fuentes 10.00 25.00
190 Daniel Descalso 10.00 25.00
205 Ryan Theriot 10.00 25.00
224 Jon Jay 8.00 20.00
261 Trevor Rosenthal 15.00 40.00
294 Trout/Beltre/Cabrera 15.00 40.00
645 Luis Cruz 20.00 50.00
660 Miguel Cabrera 15.00 40.00
661 Hyun-Jin Ryu 30.00 60.00

2013 Topps Silver Slate Blue Sparkle Wrapper Redemption

*SLATE VET: 2.5X TO 6X BASIC
*SLATE RC: 1.5X TO 4X BASIC RC
1 Bryce Harper 25.00 60.00
2 Derek Jeter 10.00 25.00
294 Trout/Beltre/Cabrera 6.00 15.00

2013 Topps Silver Slate Wrapper Redemption Autographs

PRINT RUNS B/WN 5-170 COPIES PER
AG Adrian Gonzalez/35 30.00 60.00
BB Brandon Beachy/24 15.00 40.00
CC Chris Carpenter/50 20.00 50.00
CK Clayton Kershaw/35 30.00 60.00
DB Dylan Bundy/50 15.00 40.00
JN Jeff Niemann/114 4.00 10.00
JV Josh Vitters/102 4.00 10.00
MD Matt Dominguez/37 8.00 20.00
MM Manny Machado/50 75.00 150.00
NM Nick Markakis/100 10.00 25.00
RD R.A. Dickey/35 30.00 60.00
SP Salvador Perez/100 10.00 25.00
SV Shane Victorino/48 15.00 40.00
TS Tyler Skaggs/50 6.00 15.00
WR Wilin Rosario/170 6.00 15.00
YE Yunel Escobar/100 6.00 15.00

2013 Topps Target Red Border

*TARGET RED: .75X TO 2X BASIC
*TARGET RED RC: .5X TO 1.2X BASIC RC
FOUND IN TARGET RETAIL PACKS

2013 Topps Toys R Us Purple Border

*TRU PURPLE: 3X TO 8X BASIC
*TRU PURPLE RC: 2X TO 5X BASIC RC
FOUND IN TOYS R US RETAIL PACKS
2 Derek Jeter 20.00 50.00
234 A.J. Burnett 5.00 12.00

2013 Topps Wal-Mart Blue Border

*WM BLUE: .75X TO 2X BASIC
*WM BLUE RC: .5X TO 1.2X BASIC RC
FOUND IN WAL MART RETAIL PACKS

2013 Topps '72 Topps Minis

COMPLETE SET (100) 40.00 80.00
COMP.SERIES 1 SET (1-50) 12.50 30.00
COMP.SERIES 2 SET (51-100) 15.00 40.00
STATED ODDS 1:4 HOBBY
TM1 Buster Posey .75 2.00
TM2 Dan Haren .40 1.00
TM3 Jered Weaver .50 1.25
TM4 Mike Trout 5.00 12.00
TM5 Ian Kennedy .40 1.00
TM6 Trevor Bauer .60 1.50
TM7 Craig Kimbrel .50 1.25
TM8 Dan Uggla .40 1.00
TM9 Adam Jones .50 1.25
TM10 Adrian Gonzalez .50 1.25
TM11 Dustin Pedroia .50 1.25
TM12 Anthony Rizzo 1.00 2.50
TM13 Starlin Castro .40 1.00
TM14 Chris Sale .60 1.50
TM15 Paul Konerko .50 1.25
TM16 Joey Votto .60 1.50
TM17 Johnny Cueto .50 1.25
TM18 Carlos Santana .50 1.25
TM19 Carlos Gonzalez .50 1.25
TM20 Justin Verlander .60 1.50
TM21 Prince Fielder .50 1.25
TM22 Andre Ethier .50 1.25
TM23 Clayton Kershaw 1.25 3.00
TM24 Giancarlo Stanton .60 1.50
TM25 Jose Reyes .50 1.25
TM26 Ryan Braun .50 1.25
TM27 R.A. Dickey .50 1.25
TM28 Alex Rodriguez .75 2.00
TM29 CC Sabathia .50 1.25
TM30 Curtis Granderson .50 1.25
TM31 Mark Teixeira .50 1.25
TM32 Josh Reddick .40 1.00
TM33 Cliff Lee .50 1.25
TM34 Andrew McCutchen .60 1.50
TM35 Felix Hernandez .50 1.25
TM36 Matt Holliday .60 1.50
TM37 Evan Longoria .50 1.25
TM38 Adrian Beltre .60 1.50
TM39 Yu Darvish .60 1.50
TM40 Colby Rasmus .50 1.25
TM41 Bryce Harper 1.00 2.50
TM42 Willie Mays 1.25 3.00
TM43 Tony Gwynn .60 1.50
TM44 Nolan Ryan 2.00 5.00
TM45 Cal Ripken Jr. 2.00 5.00
TM46 Jim Rice .50 1.25
TM47 Roberto Clemente 1.50 4.00
TM48 Lou Gehrig 1.25 3.00
TM49 Matt Kemp .50 1.25
TM50 Ted Williams 1.25 3.00
TM51 Ken Griffey Jr. 1.25 3.00
TM52 David Freese .40 1.00
TM53 Gio Gonzalez .50 1.25
TM54 Roy Halladay .50 1.25
TM55 Miguel Cabrera .60 1.50
TM56 David Wright .50 1.25
TM57 Albert Pujols .75 2.00
TM58 James Shields .40 1.00
TM59 Shelby Miller 1.00 2.50
TM60 Yoenis Cespedes .60 1.50
TM61 Brooks Robinson .50 1.25
TM62 Paul O'Neill .50 1.25
TM63 Yogi Berra .60 1.50
TM64 David Price .50 1.25
TM65 Manny Machado 2.50 6.00
TM66 Troy Tulowitzki .60 1.50
TM67 Tim Lincecum .50 1.25
TM68 Matt Cain .50 1.25
TM69 Robin Yount .60 1.50
TM70 Justin Upton .50 1.25
TM71 Reggie Jackson .50 1.25
TM72 Brandon Phillips .40 1.00
TM73 Dylan Bundy 1.00 2.50
TM74 Johan Santana .50 1.25
TM75 Willie Stargell .50 1.25
TM76 Jose Altuve .50 1.25
TM77 Fred Lynn .40 1.00
TM78 R.A. Dickey .50 1.25
TM79 Josh Hamilton .50 1.25
TM80 Johnny Bench .60 1.50
TM81 Eric Davis .40 1.00
TM82 Gary Sheffield .40 1.00
TM83 Don Mattingly 1.25 3.00
TM84 Ryan Howard .50 1.25
TM85 Matt Williams .40 1.00
TM86 George Brett 1.25 3.00
TM87 Jurickson Profar .50 1.25
TM88 Jose Bautista .50 1.25
TM89 Will Middlebrooks .40 1.00
TM90 Joe Morgan .50 1.25
TM91 Stephen Strasburg .60 1.50
TM92 Cole Hamels .50 1.25
TM93 Robinson Cano .50 1.25
TM94 David Ortiz .60 1.50
TM95 B.J. Upton .50 1.25
TM96 Jason Heyward .50 1.25
TM97 Josh Johnson .50 1.25
TM98 Ernie Banks .60 1.50
TM99 Ozzie Smith .75 2.00
TM100 Eddie Mathews .60 1.50

2013 Topps Calling Cards

COMPLETE SET (15) 4.00 10.00
STATED ODDS 1:8 HOBBY
CC1 Prince Fielder .50 1.25
CC2 Brandon Phillips .40 1.00
CC3 Felix Hernandez .50 1.25
CC4 David Ortiz .60 1.50
CC5 Jonathan Papelbon .50 1.25
CC6 Willie Stargell .50 1.25
CC7 Mark Teixeira .50 1.25
CC8 CC Sabathia .50 1.25
CC9 R.A. Dickey .50 1.25
CC10 Tim Lincecum .50 1.25
CC11 Reggie Jackson .50 1.25
CC12 Kevin Youkilis .40 1.00
CC13 Aroldis Chapman .60 1.50
CC14 Pablo Sandoval .50 1.25
CC15 Albert Pujols .75 2.00

2013 Topps Chasing History

COMPLETE SET (100) 25.00 60.00
COMP.SER 1 SET (1-50) 8.00 20.00
COMP.SER 2 SET (51-100) 8.00 20.00
COMP UPDATE SET (101-150) 8.00 20.00
STATED ODDS 1:4 HOBBY
CH1 Roy Halladay .40 1.00
CH2 Roberto Clemente 1.25 3.00
CH3 Ian Kinsler .40 1.00
CH4 Cal Ripken Jr. 1.50 4.00
CH5 Yogi Berra .50 1.25
CH6 Rod Carew .40 1.00
CH7 Carlos Santana .40 1.00
CH8 Rickey Henderson .50 1.25
CH9 Mariano Rivera .60 1.50
CH10 Lou Gehrig 1.00 2.50
CH11 Babe Ruth 1.25 3.00
CH12 Evan Longoria .40 1.00
CH13 Don Mattingly 1.00 2.50
CH14 Lou Brock .40 1.00
CH15 Willie McCovey .40 1.00
CH16 Lance Berkman .40 1.00
CH17 R.A. Dickey .40 1.00
CH18 Ken Griffey Jr. 1.00 2.50
CH19 Harmon Killebrew .50 1.25
CH20 Reggie Jackson .40 1.00
CH21 Frank Robinson .40 1.00
CH22 Matt Kemp .40 1.00
CH23 George Brett 1.00 2.50
CH24 David Wright .40 1.00
CH25 Frank Thomas .50 1.25
CH26 Chipper Jones .50 1.25
CH27 Nolan Ryan 1.50 4.00
CH28 Tony Gwynn .50 1.25
CH29 Stan Musial .75 2.00
CH30 Adam Dunn .40 1.00
CH31 Warren Spahn .40 1.00
CH32 Brian Wilson .50 1.25
CH33 Ted Williams 1.00 2.50
CH34 Robin Yount .50 1.25
CH35 Hank Aaron 1.00 2.50
CH36 Kerry Wood .30 .75
CH37 Derek Jeter 1.25 3.00
CH38 Tom Seaver .40 1.00
CH39 Jim Thome .30 .75
CH40 Mike Schmidt .75 2.00
CH41 Johan Santana .40 1.00
CH42 Alex Rodriguez .60 1.50
CH43 CC Sabathia .40 1.00
CH44 Mark Buehrle .40 1.00
CH45 Bob Feller .40 1.00
CH46 Hanley Ramirez .40 1.00
CH47 Willie Mays 1.00 2.50
CH48 Paul Konerko .40 1.00
CH49 Jackie Robinson .50 1.25
CH50 Sandy Koufax 1.00 2.50
CH51 Jason Kipnis .40 1.00
CH52 Gary Sheffield .30 .75
CH53 Jered Weaver .40 1.00
CH54 Anthony Rizzo .75 2.00
CH55 Ken Griffey Jr. 1.00 2.50
CH56 Matt Holliday .50 1.25
CH57 Cal Ripken Jr. 1.50 4.00
CH58 Rickey Henderson .50 1.25
CH59 Fred Lynn .30 .75
CH60 Derek Jeter 1.25 3.00
CH61 David Price .40 1.00
CH62 Willie McCovey .40 1.00
CH63 Jordan Zimmermann .40 1.00
CH64 Mike Trout 4.00 10.00
CH65 Gary Carter .40 1.00
CH66 Adrian Gonzalez .40 1.00
CH67 Stephen Strasburg .50 1.25
CH68 John Smoltz .50 1.25
CH69 Sandy Koufax 1.00 2.50
CH70 Miguel Cabrera .50 1.25
CH71 Buster Posey .60 1.50
CH72 Carlos Gonzalez .40 1.00
CH73 Robinson Cano .40 1.00
CH74 Stan Musial .75 2.00
CH75 Dustin Pedroia .40 1.00
CH76 Tony Gwynn .50 1.25
CH77 Roberto Clemente 1.25 3.00
CH78 Mark Trumbo .30 .75
CH79 Hank Aaron 1.00 2.50
CH80 Yu Darvish .50 1.25
CH81 Cliff Lee .40 1.00
CH82 Felix Hernandez .40 1.00
CH83 Willie Mays 1.00 2.50
CH84 Mariano Rivera .60 1.50
CH85 Tim Lincecum .40 1.00
CH86 Roy Halladay .40 1.00
CH87 Lance Lynn .30 .75
CH88 Justin Verlander .50 1.25
CH89 Darryl Strawberry .30 .75
CH90 Prince Fielder .40 1.00
CH91 Joey Votto .50 1.25
CH92 Mike Schmidt .75 2.00
CH93 Manny Machado 2.00 5.00
CH94 Ty Cobb .75 2.00
CH95 Matt Cain .40 1.00
CH96 Dylan Bundy .75 2.00
CH97 Troy Tulowitzki .50 1.25
CH98 Carl Crawford .40 1.00
CH99 David Wright .40 1.00
CH100 Phil Niekro .40 1.00
CH101 Jackie Bradley Jr. .75 2.00
CH102 Reggie Jackson .40 1.00
CH103 Anthony Rizzo .75 2.00
CH104 Nomar Garciaparra .40 1.00
CH105 Carlos Santana .40 1.00
CH106 Edwin Encarnacion .50 1.25
CH107 Babe Ruth 1.25 3.00
CH108 Shelby Miller .75 2.00
CH109 Jurickson Profar .40 1.00
CH110 Ted Williams 1.00 2.50
CH111 Bo Jackson .50 1.25
CH112 Johnny Podres .20 .50
CH113 Ozzie Smith .60 1.50
CH114 Tom Seaver .40 1.00
CH115 Paul Goldschmidt .50 1.25
CH116 Mike Zunino .50 1.25
CH117 Anthony Rendon 1.50 4.00
CH118 Mike Mussina .40 1.00
CH119 Pedro Martinez .40 1.00
CH120 Miguel Cabrera .50 1.25
CH121 Mike Trout 4.00 10.00
CH122 Roberto Clemente 1.25 3.00
CH123 Robinson Cano .40 1.00
CH124 Joey Votto .50 1.25
CH125 Justin Upton .40 1.00
CH126 Andrew McCutchen .50 1.25
CH127 Prince Fielder .40 1.00
CH128 Troy Tulowitzki .50 1.25
CH129 Clayton Kershaw 1.00 2.50
CH130 Jackie Robinson .50 1.25
CH131 Hyun-Jin Ryu .75 2.00
CH132 Justin Verlander .50 1.25
CH133 Dustin Pedroia .40 1.00
CH134 Tony Cingrani .60 1.50
CH135 Bret Saberhagen .20 .50
CH136 Zack Wheeler .60 1.50
CH137 Wade Boggs .40 1.00
CH138 David Ortiz .50 1.25
CH139 Buster Posey .60 1.50
CH140 Wil Myers .40 1.00
CH141 Marcell Ozuna .75 2.00
CH142 Matt Harvey .40 1.00
CH143 Craig Biggio .40 1.00
CH144 Yasiel Puig 1.25 3.00
CH145 Jim Palmer .40 1.00
CH146 Joe Morgan .40 1.00
CH147 Bob Feller .40 1.00
CH148 Manny Machado 2.00 5.00
CH149 Tony Gwynn .50 1.25
CH150 Jose Fernandez .75 2.00

2013 Topps Chasing History Holofoil

*HOLOFOIL: .75X TO 2X BASIC

2013 Topps Chasing History Holofoil Gold

*GOLD: 1X TO 2.5X BASIC

2013 Topps Chasing History Autographs

SERIES 1 ODDS 1:498 HOBBY
SERIES 2 ODDS 1:435 HOBBY
UPDATE ODDS 1:384 HOBBY
SERIES 1 EXCH DEADLINE 01/31/2016
SERIES 2 EXCH DEADLINE 06/30/2016
UPDATE EXHC DEADLINE 09/30/2016
AC Alex Cobb S2 3.00 8.00
AE Adam Eaton S2 4.00 10.00
AE Adam Eaton UPD 3.00 8.00
AG Adrian Gonzalez S2 30.00 60.00
AR Anthony Rizzo 20.00 50.00
BH Brock Holt S2 12.00 30.00
BH Brock Holt UPD 12.00 30.00
BJ Bo Jackson UPD
BM Brandon Maurer UPD 3.00 8.00
BR Bruce Rondon UPD 4.00 10.00
BS Bret Sabherhagen UPD 5.00 12.00
BT Bob Tewksbury UPD 4.00 10.00
CA Chris Archer UPD 4.00 10.00
CA Chris Archer S2 4.00 10.00
CB Craig Biggio UPD
CC Collin Cowgill UPD 3.00 8.00
CC Collin Cowgill S2 4.00 10.00
CCS CC Sabathia 10.00 25.00
CD Cole De Vries S2 4.00 10.00
CRJ Cal Ripken Jr. 150.00 250.00
CSA Chris Sale 8.00 20.00
CST Carlos Santana 4.00 10.00
DB Dylan Bundy S2 10.00 25.00
DBA Don Baylor UPD 6.00 15.00
DC David Cooper S2 3.00 8.00
DG Dwight Gooden 6.00 15.00
DG Didi Gregorius S2 8.00 20.00
DG Didi Gregorius UPD 4.00 10.00
DGO Dee Gordon 5.00 12.00
DJ David Justice 8.00 20.00
DM Don Mattingly 60.00 120.00
DM Don Mattingly S2 60.00 120.00
DS Duke Snider 10.00 25.00
DW David Wright 12.00 30.00
EL Evan Longoria 20.00 50.00
FL Fred Lynn S2 8.00 20.00
FR Fernando Rodney 4.00 10.00
FT Frank Thomas 40.00 80.00
GC Gary Carter 12.50 30.00
GC Gary Carter S2 12.50 30.00
GC Gerrit Cole UPD 8.00 20.00
GR Garrett Richards UPD 3.00 8.00
GS Gary Sheffield 5.00 12.00
GS Gary Sheffield S2 8.00 20.00
GST Giancarlo Stanton 30.00 80.00
HA Hank Aaron 100.00 250.00
HJ Howard Johnson UPD 5.00 12.00
HR Hanley Ramirez 10.00 25.00
IN Ivan Nova 4.00 10.00
JA Jose Altuve 15.00 40.00
JB Jose Bautista 8.00 20.00
JB Jay Bruce S2 10.00 25.00
JBA Jose Bautista S2 8.00 20.00
JG Jason Grilli S2 6.00 15.00
JH Joel Hanrahan 4.00 10.00
JK Jason Kipnis S2 5.00 12.00
JP Jarrod Parker 3.00 8.00
JP Jim Palmer S2 10.00 25.00
JPO Johnny Podres 6.00 15.00
JPO Johnny Podres S2 6.00 15.00
JPR Jurickson Profar S2 5.00 12.00
JS James Shields S2 6.00 15.00
JW Jered Weaver S2 10.00 25.00
KGJ Ken Griffey Jr. 100.00 200.00
KH Kelvin Herrera UPD 4.00 10.00
LB Larry Bowa UPD 6.00 15.00
MA Matt Adams UPD 8.00 20.00
MAM Matt Moore 5.00 12.00
MAT Mark Trumbo 8.00 20.00
MC Miguel Cabrera S2 75.00 150.00
MIT Mike Trout 100.00 200.00
MM Manny Machado S2 60.00 120.00
MM Mike Mussina UPD
MM Matt Magill UPD 3.00 8.00
MS Mike Schmidt 50.00 100.00
MS Mike Schmidt S2 40.00 80.00
MT Mark Trumbo S2 6.00 15.00
MTR Mike Trout S2 75.00 150.00
MZ Mike Zunino UPD 4.00 10.00
NM Nick Maronde UPD 3.00 8.00
NM Nick Maronde S2 4.00 10.00
NR Nolan Ryan 60.00 120.00
OC Orlando Cepeda 15.00 40.00
PF Prince Fielder S2 20.00 50.00
PM Pedro Martinez UPD
PR Paco Rodriguez S2 4.00 10.00
RD Rafael Dolis UPD 3.00 8.00
RH Rickey Henderson 75.00 150.00
RJ Reggie Jackson 50.00 100.00
RP Ryan Pressly UPD 3.00 8.00
RS Ruben Sierra UPD 4.00 10.00
SC Starlin Castro 5.00 12.00
SD Scott Diamond S2 3.00 8.00
SG Steve Garvey S2 20.00 50.00
SK Sandy Koufax EXCH 200.00 400.00
SM Stan Musial 15.00 40.00
SM Starling Marte S2 6.00 15.00
SMA Shaun Marcum S2 4.00 10.00
TC Tony Cingrani UPD 3.00 8.00
TG Tony Gwynn 50.00 100.00
TG Tony Gwynn S2 EXCH 15.00 40.00
TS Tyler Skaggs S2 4.00 10.00
WB Wade Boggs S2 30.00 60.00
WF Whitey Ford 30.00 60.00
WP Wily Peralta S2 4.00 10.00
WR Wilin Rosario S2 4.00 10.00
YG Yan Gomes UPD 6.00 15.00
ZC Zack Cozart S2 4.00 10.00
ZW Zack Wheeler UPD 8.00 20.00

2013 Topps Chasing History Dual Relics

STATED ODDS 1:7650 HOBBY
STATED PRINT RUN 50 SER.#'d SETS
CB S.Castro/E.Banks 20.00 50.00
CC R.Clemente/T.Cobb 100.00 250.00
DR Jose Reyes/R.A. Dickey 10.00 25.00
JH R.Henderson/R.Jackson 30.00 60.00
KM J.Morneau/H.Killebrew 20.00 50.00
MB R.Braun/P.Molitor 10.00 25.00
PT Albert Pujols/Mike Trout
RD Y.Darvish/N.Ryan 40.00 80.00
RJ C.Ripken/D.Jeter 60.00 120.00
RR A.Rodriguez/M.Rivera 12.50 30.00
SB G.Brett/M.Schmidt 30.00 60.00
SS G.Sheffield/G.Stanton 10.00 25.00
UU B.J. Upton/Justin Upton
VP J.Verlander/D.Price 20.00 50.00
WS Tom Seaver/David Wright

2013 Topps Chasing History Relics

SERIES 1 ODDS 1:70 HOBBY
SERIES 2 ODDS 1:68 HOBBY
AB Albert Belle 3.00 8.00
AB Adrian Beltre S2 5.00 12.00
AC Aroldis Chapman 5.00 12.00
AC Asdrubal Cabrera S2 4.00 10.00
AD Adam Dunn 4.00 10.00
AE Andre Ethier 4.00 10.00
AG Alex Gordon S2 4.00 10.00
AGO Adrian Gonzalez S2 4.00 10.00
AJ Adam Jones 4.00 10.00
AJA Austin Jackson 3.00 8.00
AM Andrew McCutchen 5.00 12.00
AP Andy Pettitte S2 4.00 10.00
AR Anthony Rizzo 4.00 10.00
AR Alex Rodriguez S2 5.00 12.00
AS Alfonso Soriano S2 4.00 10.00
BB Billy Butler S2 3.00 8.00
BM Brian McCann S2 4.00 10.00
BP Brandon Phillips S2 3.00 8.00
BPO Buster Posey S2 6.00 15.00
BS Bruce Sutter 4.00 10.00
BW Brian Wilson 5.00 12.00
CB Chad Billingsley S2 4.00 10.00
CC Carl Crawford S2 4.00 10.00
CF Carlton Fisk S2 4.00 10.00
CG Curtis Granderson 4.00 10.00
CG Carlos Gonzalez S2 4.00 10.00
CGO Carlos Gonzalez 4.00 10.00
CJW C.J. Wilson 3.00 8.00
CK Clayton Kershaw 5.00 12.00
CL Cliff Lee 4.00 10.00
CL Cliff Lee S2 4.00 10.00
CR Colby Rasmus S2 4.00 10.00

CRJ Cal Ripken Jr. 10.00 25.00
CS Carlos Santana 4.00 10.00
CSA Chris Sale 5.00 12.00
DG Dwight Gooden 3.00 8.00
DJ Derek Jeter S2 6.00 15.00
DM Don Mattingly S2 10.00 25.00
DO David Ortiz 5.00 12.00
DP David Price S2 4.00 10.00
DW David Wright 4.00 10.00
Facing left
DW David Wright S2 4.00 10.00
Facing right
EA Elvis Andrus S2 4.00 10.00
EL Evan Longoria 4.00 10.00
FH Felix Hernandez S2 4.00 10.00
FJ Fergie Jenkins S2 4.00 10.00
FT Frank Thomas 10.00 25.00
GB George Brett 10.00 25.00
GS Gary Sheffield S2 3.00 8.00
HK Harmon Killebrew 10.00 25.00
HP Hunter Pence 4.00 10.00
HP Hunter Pence S2 4.00 10.00
HR Hanley Ramirez 4.00 10.00
IK Ian Kinsler 4.00 10.00
IKE Ian Kennedy 3.00 8.00
JA John Axford S2 3.00 8.00
JAH Jason Heyward 4.00 10.00
JB Jose Bautista 4.00 10.00
JC Johnny Cueto 4.00 10.00
JH Joel Hanrahan 3.00 8.00
JH Josh Hamilton S2 4.00 10.00
JHA Josh Hamilton 4.00 10.00
JK Jason Kipnis S2 4.00 10.00
JOV Joey Votto 5.00 12.00
JS Johan Santana 4.00 10.00
JS James Shields S2 3.00 8.00
JSM John Smoltz S2 5.00 12.00
JUV Justin Verlander 5.00 12.00
JV Justin Verlander S2 5.00 12.00
JVO Joey Votto S2 5.00 12.00
JW Jered Weaver 4.00 10.00
JZ Jordan Zimmermann S2 4.00 10.00
KGJ Ken Griffey Jr. 8.00 20.00
LB Lance Berkman 4.00 10.00
LL Lance Lynn S2 3.00 8.00
MAM Matt Moore 4.00 10.00
MAT Mark Trumbo 3.00 8.00
MC Matt Cain S2 4.00 10.00
MEC Melky Cabrera 3.00 8.00
MH Matt Holliday S2 5.00 12.00
MIC Miguel Cabrera 5.00 12.00
MIM Mike Moustakas 4.00 10.00
MIT Mike Trout 12.00 30.00
MK Matt Kemp 4.00 10.00
MR Mariano Rivera S2 8.00 20.00
MS Mike Schmidt 5.00 12.00
MS Max Scherzer S2 5.00 12.00
NC Nelson Cruz S2 5.00 12.00
NR Nolan Ryan 10.00 25.00
OC Orlando Cepeda S2 5.00 12.00
PF Prince Fielder S2 4.00 10.00
PK Paul Konerko 4.00 10.00
PK Paul Konerko S2 4.00 10.00
PN Phil Niekro S2 4.00 10.00
PS Pablo Sandoval S2 4.00 10.00
RC Roberto Clemente S2 20.00 50.00
RH Rickey Henderson 5.00 12.00
RHA Roy Halladay 4.00 10.00
RHA Roy Halladay S2 4.00 10.00
RHO Ryan Howard S2 4.00 10.00
RJ Reggie Jackson 4.00 10.00
RZ Ryan Zimmerman S2 4.00 10.00
SC Starlin Castro 3.00 8.00
SC Starlin Castro S2 3.00 8.00
SM Stan Musial 12.00 30.00
SM Stan Musial S2 12.00 30.00
SR Scott Rolen S2 4.00 10.00
SS Stephen Strasburg S2 5.00 12.00
TC Ty Cobb S2 20.00 50.00
TG Tony Gwynn 5.00 12.00
TL Tim Lincecum S2 5.00 12.00
TT Troy Tulowitzki 5.00 12.00
TT Troy Tulowitzki S2 5.00 12.00
VW Vernon Wells S2 3.00 8.00
WM Willie McCovey S2 8.00 20.00
WMA Willie Mays S2 15.00 40.00
YB Yogi Berra S2 5.00 12.00
YG Yovani Gallardo 3.00 8.00

2013 Topps Chasing History Relics Gold

*GOLD: .6X TO 1.5X BASIC
STATED ODDS 1:969 HOBBY
STATED PRINT RUN 99 SER.#'d SETS

2013 Topps Chase It Down

COMPLETE SET (15) 5.00 12.00
STATED ODDS 1:8 HOBBY
CD1 Mike Trout 4.00 10.00
CD2 Pablo Sandoval .40 1.00
CD3 Ryan Zimmerman .40 1.00
CD4 Jason Heyward .40 1.00
CD5 Adam Jones .40 1.00
CD6 Mike Moustakas .40 1.00
CD7 Bryce Harper .75 2.00
CD8 Chase Headley .30 .75
CD9 Josh Reddick .30 .75
CD10 Jon Jay .30 .75
CD11 Alex Gordon .40 1.00
CD12 Carlos Gonzalez .40 1.00
CD13 Manny Machado 2.00 5.00
CD14 Cameron Maybin .30 .75
CD15 Giancarlo Stanton .50 1.25

2013 Topps Chasing the Dream

COMPLETE SET (25) 6.00 15.00
STATED ODDS 1:6 HOBBY
CD1 Bryce Harper 1.00 2.50
CD2 Mike Trout 5.00 12.00
CD3 Will Middlebrooks .40 1.00
CD4 Trevor Bauer .60 1.50
CD5 Matt Moore .50 1.25
CD6 Anthony Rizzo 1.00 2.50
CD7 Jesus Montero .40 1.00
CD8 Josh Reddick .40 1.00
CD9 Devin Mesoraco .40 1.00
CD10 Giancarlo Stanton .60 1.50
CD11 Jacob Turner .50 1.25
CD12 Casey Kelly .50 1.25
CD13 Drew Hutchison .50 1.25
CD14 Drew Pomeranz .50 1.25
CD15 Jonathon Niese .40 1.00
CD16 Yonder Alonso .40 1.00
CD17 Addison Reed .40 1.00
CD18 Chris Sale .60 1.50
CD19 Yu Darvish .60 1.50
CD20 Tommy Milone .40 1.00
CD21 Jarrod Parker .40 1.00
CD22 Drew Smyly .40 1.00
CD23 Jose Altuve .50 1.25
CD24 Brett Lawrie .50 1.25
CD25 Mike Moustakas .50 1.25

2013 Topps Chasing The Dream Autographs

STATED ODDS 1:996 HOBBY
EXCHANGE DEADLINE 01/31/2016
AR Anthony Rizzo 20.00 50.00
BH Bryce Harper 300.00 400.00
BL Brett Lawrie 6.00 15.00
BP Brad Peacock 4.00 10.00
CS Chris Sale 6.00 15.00
DG Dee Gordon 5.00 12.00
DH Drew Hutchison 4.00 10.00
EA Elvis Andrus 3.00 8.00
FD Felix Doubront 4.00 10.00
GS Giancarlo Stanton 20.00 50.00
JP Jarrod Parker 4.00 10.00
MAM Matt Moore 5.00 12.00
MB Madison Bumgarner 12.00 30.00
MT Mike Trout 75.00 150.00
PG Paul Goldschmidt 12.00 30.00
TB Trevor Bauer 8.00 20.00
TM Tommy Milone 4.00 10.00
WP Wily Peralta 4.00 10.00
YA Yonder Alonso 5.00 12.00
YD Yu Darvish 75.00 150.00

2013 Topps Chasing The Dream Relics

STATED ODDS 1:210 HOBBY
AR Anthony Rizzo 5.00 12.00
BH Bryce Harper 10.00 25.00
BIB Billy Butler 4.00 10.00
BL Brett Lawrie 5.00 12.00
BP Buster Posey 10.00 25.00
BRB Brandon Beachy 4.00 10.00
CS Chris Sale 4.00 10.00
DA Dustin Ackley 4.00 10.00
DF David Freese 4.00 10.00
DG Dee Gordon 4.00 10.00
DH Derek Holland 5.00 12.00
DJ Desmond Jennings 4.00 10.00
DP Drew Pomeranz 4.00 10.00
EA Elvis Andrus 4.00 10.00
GG Gio Gonzalez 4.00 10.00
JAP Jarrod Parker 4.00 10.00
JM Jesus Montero 4.00 10.00
JPA J.P. Arencibia 4.00 10.00
JR Josh Reddick 4.00 10.00
JSM Justin Smoak 4.00 10.00
JT Jacob Turner 4.00 10.00
JZ Jordan Zimmermann 5.00 12.00
LL Lance Lynn 4.00 10.00
MA Matt Adams 4.00 10.00
MAM Matt Moore 4.00 10.00
MAT Mark Trumbo 4.00 10.00
MB Madison Bumgarner 6.00 15.00
MIM Mike Morse 4.00 10.00
MIT Mike Trout 10.00 25.00
MMO Mike Moustakas 4.00 10.00
NF Neftali Feliz 4.00 10.00
PG Paul Goldschmidt 4.00 10.00
TM Tommy Milone 4.00 10.00
WM Will Middlebrooks 6.00 15.00
WMI Wade Miley 4.00 10.00
WR Wilin Rosario 4.00 10.00
YA Yonder Alonso 4.00 10.00
YC Yoenis Cespedes 6.00 15.00
YD Yu Darvish 6.00 15.00

2013 Topps Cut To The Chase

COMPLETE SET (48) 40.00 80.00
COMP.SERIES 1 SET (23) 15.00 40.00
COMP.SERIES 2 SET (25) 15.00 40.00
SERIES 1 ODDS 1:14 HOBBY
SERIES 2 ODDS 1:12 HOBBY
CTC1 Mike Trout 8.00 20.00
CTC2 Ken Griffey Jr. 2.00 5.00
CTC3 Derek Jeter 2.50 6.00
CTC4 Babe Ruth 2.50 6.00
CTC5 Paul Molitor 1.00 2.50
CTC6 Carlos Gonzalez .75 2.00
CTC7 Stan Musial 1.50 4.00
CTC8 Ryan Braun .75 2.00
CTC9 Ted Williams 2.00 5.00
CTC10 Adam Jones .75 2.00
CTC11 Yu Darvish 1.00 2.50
CTC12 Lance Berkman .75 2.00
CTC13 Brett Lawrie .75 2.00
CTC14 David Price .75 2.00
CTC15 Dustin Pedroia .75 2.00
CTC16 Nelson Cruz 1.00 2.50
CTC17 Matt Cain .75 2.00
CTC18 Tony Gwynn 1.00 2.50
CTC19 Mike Schmidt 1.50 4.00
CTC20 Roberto Clemente 2.50 6.00
CTC21 Andrew McCutchen 1.00 2.50
CTC22 Ryne Sandberg 2.00 5.00
CTC23 Willie Mays 2.00 5.00
CTC24 Buster Posey 1.25 3.00
CTC25 Josh Hamilton .75 2.00
CTC26 Albert Belle .60 1.50
CTC27 Ralph Kiner .60 1.50
CTC28 Al Kaline 1.00 2.50
CTC29 Tom Seaver .75 2.00
CTC30 Rickey Henderson 1.00 2.50
CTC31 Matt Holliday 1.00 2.50
CTC32 Harmon Killebrew 1.00 2.50
CTC33 Jered Weaver .75 2.00
CTC34 Ernie Banks 1.00 2.50
CTC35 Chris Sale 1.00 2.50
CTC36 Joe Morgan .75 2.00
CTC37 Albert Pujols 1.25 3.00
CTC38 Prince Fielder .75 2.00
CTC39 Yoenis Cespedes 1.00 2.50
CTC40 Cal Ripken Jr. 3.00 8.00
CTC41 Stephen Strasburg 1.00 2.50
CTC42 R.A. Dickey .75 2.00
CTC43 Miguel Cabrera 1.00 2.50
CTC44 Manny Machado 4.00 10.00
CTC45 Bryce Harper 1.50 4.00
CTC46 Duke Snider .75 2.00
CTC47 Alex Rodriguez 1.25 3.00
CTC48 Sandy Koufax 2.00 5.00

2013 Topps Cy Young Award Winners Trophy

STATED ODDS 1:1396 HOBBY
BC Bartolo Colon 6.00 15.00
BG Bob Gibson 10.00 25.00
BW Brandon Webb 6.00 15.00
BZ Barry Zito 6.00 15.00
CC Chris Carpenter 10.00 25.00
CH Catfish Hunter 8.00 20.00
CK Clayton Kershaw 8.00 20.00
CL Cliff Lee 6.00 15.00
CS CC Sabathia 8.00 20.00
DE Dennis Eckersley 6.00 15.00
DG Dwight Gooden 6.00 15.00
FH Felix Hernandez 8.00 20.00
FJ Fergie Jenkins 6.00 15.00
JP Jim Palmer 8.00 20.00
JPE Jake Peavy 6.00 15.00
JS Johan Santana 6.00 15.00
JSM John Smoltz 8.00 20.00
JV Justin Verlander 6.00 15.00
PM1 Pedro Martinez 8.00 20.00
PM2 Pedro Martinez 8.00 20.00
RH1 Roy Halladay 8.00 20.00
RH2 Roy Halladay 8.00 20.00
SK Sandy Koufax 12.50 30.00
TL Tim Lincecum 10.00 25.00
TS Tom Seaver 12.50 30.00
VB Vida Blue 6.00 15.00
WF Whitey Ford 10.00 25.00
WS Warren Spahn 10.00 25.00
ZG Zack Greinke 6.00 15.00

2013 Topps Making Their Mark

COMPLETE SET (25) 5.00 12.00
STATED ODDS 1:6 HOBBY
MM1 Yoenis Cespedes .50 1.25
MM2 Mike Trout 4.00 10.00
MM3 Andrelton Simmons .30 .75
MM4 Jason Kipnis .40 1.00
MM5 Jeremy Hellickson .30 .75
MM6 Ike Davis .30 .75
MM7 Mike Olt .40 1.00
MM8 Kris Medlen .40 1.00
MM9 Tyler Skaggs .50 1.25
MM10 Wilin Rosario .30 .75
MM11 Trevor Bauer .50 1.25
MM12 Zack Cozart .30 .75
MM13 Matt Moore .40 1.00
MM14 Lance Lynn .30 .75
MM15 Salvador Perez .40 1.00
MM16 Will Middlebrooks .30 .75
MM17 Anthony Rizzo .75 2.00
MM18 Wade Miley .30 .75
MM19 Bryce Harper .75 2.00
MM20 Dylan Bundy .75 2.00
MM21 Jurickson Profar .40 1.00
MM22 Yu Darvish .50 1.25
MM23 Todd Frazier .40 1.00
MM24 Manny Machado 2.00 5.00
MM25 Stephen Strasburg .50 1.25
MM26 Jean Segura .40 1.00
MM27 Zack Wheeler .60 1.50
MM28 Nick Franklin .40 1.00
MM29 Marcell Ozuna .75 2.00
MM30 Wei-Yin Chen .30 .75
MM31 Mike Zunino .50 1.25
MM32 Matt Harvey .40 1.00
MM33 Starling Marte .40 1.00
MM34 Nolan Arenado 1.50 4.00
MM35 Aaron Hicks .50 1.25
MM36 Carlos Martinez .50 1.25
MM37 Matt Adams .30 .75
MM38 Yasiel Puig 1.25 3.00
MM39 Kevin Gausman .50 1.25
MM40 Jackie Bradley Jr. .75 2.00
MM41 Shelby Miller .75 2.00
MM42 Wil Myers .40 1.00
MM43 Jose Fernandez .75 2.00
MM44 Jedd Gyorko .40 1.00
MM45 Evan Gattis .60 1.50
MM46 Hyun-Jin Ryu .75 2.00
MM47 Tony Cingrani .60 1.50
MM48 Craig Kimbrel .40 1.00
MM49 Kyle Gibson .50 1.25
MM50 Patrick Corbin .40 1.00

2013 Topps Making Their Mark Autographs

SERIES 2 ODDS 1:1638 HOBBY
UPDATE ODDS 1:2525
SERIES 2 EXCH DEADLINE 06/30/2016
UPDATE EXCH DEADLINE 09/30/2016
AH Aaron Hicks UPD 5.00 12.00
BR Bruce Rondon UPD 5.00 12.00
BR Bruce Rondon 5.00 12.00
CM Carlos Martinez UPD 10.00 25.00
DB Dylan Bundy 30.00 60.00
EG Evan Gattis UPD 15.00 40.00
JG Jedd Gyorko UPD
KG Kevin Gausman UPD 20.00 50.00
MA Matt Adams UPD 6.00 15.00
MM Manny Machado 50.00 100.00
MO Mike Olt 5.00 12.00
TC Tony Cingrani UPD 5.00 12.00
TS Tyler Skaggs 5.00 10.00
WM Wade Miley 5.00 10.00
WMI Will Middlebrooks 8.00 20.00
YC Yoenis Cespedes 8.00 20.00
YD Yu Darvish 60.00 120.00
YP Yasiel Puig UPD 125.00 250.00

2013 Topps Making Their Mark Relics

STATED ODDS 1:176 HOBBY
AS Andrelton Simmons 4.00 10.00
BH Bryce Harper 6.00 15.00
DB Darwin Barney 4.00 10.00
JH Jeremy Hellickson 4.00 10.00
JK Jason Kipnis 4.00 10.00
JPR Jurickson Profar 4.00 10.00
LL Lance Lynn 4.00 10.00
MO Mike Olt 4.00 10.00
PG Paul Goldschmidt 5.00 12.00
SC Starlin Castro 4.00 10.00
SS Stephen Strasburg 5.00 12.00
WR Wilin Rosario 4.00 10.00
YC Yoenis Cespedes 4.00 10.00
YD Yu Darvish 5.00 12.00
ZC Zack Cozart 4.00 10.00

2013 Topps Manufactured Commemorative Patch

CP1 Adam Jones 2.50 6.00
CP2 Dustin Pedroia 2.50 6.00
CP3 Mike Trout 25.00 60.00
CP4 Felix Hernandez 2.50 6.00
CP5 Yu Darvish 3.00 8.00
CP6 Jose Bautista 2.50 6.00
CP7 Trevor Bauer 3.00 8.00
CP8 Jason Heyward 2.50 6.00
CP9 Nolan Ryan 10.00 25.00
CP10 Adrian Gonzalez 2.50 6.00
CP11 Giancarlo Stanton 3.00 8.00
CP12 David Wright 2.50 6.00
CP13 Yonder Alonso 2.00 5.00
CP14 Matt Holliday 3.00 8.00
CP15 Bryce Harper 5.00 12.00
CP16 Billy Butler 2.00 5.00
CP17 Ryan Braun 2.50 6.00
CP18 Yoenis Cespedes 3.00 8.00
CP19 Will Clark 2.50 6.00
CP20 Chipper Jones 3.00 8.00
CP21 Anthony Rizzo 5.00 12.00
CP22 Chris Sale 3.00 8.00
CP23 Mike Schmidt 5.00 12.00
CP24 Stephen Strasburg 3.00 8.00
CP25 Joey Votto 3.00 8.00
CP26 Cal Ripken Jr. 10.00 25.00
CP27 Babe Ruth 8.00 20.00
CP28 Frank Thomas 3.00 8.00
CP29 Bob Feller 2.50 6.00
CP30 Miguel Cabrera 3.00 8.00
CP31 Josh Hamilton 2.50 6.00
CP32 Joe Mauer 2.50 6.00
CP33 Yogi Berra 3.00 8.00
CP34 Rickey Henderson 3.00 8.00
CP35 Ken Griffey Jr. 6.00 15.00
CP36 Evan Longoria 2.50 6.00
CP37 Ian Kinsler 2.50 6.00
CP38 Jose Reyes 2.50 6.00
CP39 Justin Upton 2.50 6.00
CP40 Ernie Banks 3.00 8.00
CP41 Johnny Bench 3.00 8.00
CP42 Carlos Gonzalez 2.50 6.00
CP43 Sandy Koufax 6.00 15.00
CP44 Jackie Robinson 3.00 8.00
CP45 Tom Seaver 2.50 6.00
CP46 Ryan Howard 2.50 6.00
CP47 Roberto Clemente 8.00 20.00
CP48 Andrew McCutchen 3.00 8.00
CP49 Buster Posey 4.00 10.00
CP50 Stan Musial 5.00 12.00

2013 Topps Manufactured Commemorative Rookie Patch

RCP1 Willie Mays 10.00 25.00
RCP2 Ernie Banks 6.00 15.00
RCP3 Roberto Clemente 10.00 25.00
RCP4 Sandy Koufax 10.00 25.00
RCP5 Bob Gibson 6.00 15.00
RCP6 Willie McCovey 6.00 15.00
RCP7 Reggie Jackson 5.00 12.00
RCP8 Ryne Sandberg 6.00 15.00
RCP9 George Brett 8.00 20.00
RCP10 Eddie Murray 5.00 12.00
RCP11 Ozzie Smith 6.00 15.00
RCP12 Rickey Henderson 6.00 15.00
RCP13 Jim Palmer 5.00 12.00
RCP14 Tony Gwynn 5.00 12.00
RCP15 Wade Boggs 6.00 15.00
RCP16 Don Mattingly 8.00 20.00
RCP17 Darryl Strawberry 5.00 12.00
RCP18 Dwight Gooden 5.00 12.00
RCP19 Ken Griffey Jr. 12.50 30.00
RCP20 Chipper Jones 10.00 25.00
RCP21 Derek Jeter 12.50 30.00
RCP22 Albert Pujols 8.00 20.00
RCP23 Mike Trout 15.00 40.00
RCP24 Bryce Harper 10.00 25.00
RCP25 Yu Darvish 5.00 12.00

2013 Topps Manufactured Patch

MCP1 Jackie Robinson 6.00 15.00
MCP2 Willie Mays 10.00 25.00
MCP3 Jackie Robinson 6.00 15.00
MCP4 Hank Aaron 8.00 20.00
MCP5 Willie Mays 10.00 25.00
MCP6 Ted Williams 10.00 25.00
MCP7 Al Kaline 8.00 20.00
MCP8 Ted Williams 10.00 25.00
MCP9 Roberto Clemente 10.00 25.00
MCP10 Sandy Koufax 10.00 25.00
MCP11 Ted Williams 10.00 25.00
MCP12 Sandy Koufax 10.00 25.00
MCP13 Stan Musial 8.00 20.00
MCP14 Nolan Ryan 10.00 25.00
MCP15 Roberto Clemente 10.00 25.00
MCP16 Joe Morgan 5.00 12.00
MCP17 Mike Schmidt 8.00 20.00
MCP18 Reggie Jackson 6.00 15.00
MCP19 Prince Fielder 5.00 12.00
MCP20 Frank Thomas 6.00 15.00
MCP21 Joe Mauer 5.00 12.00
MCP22 Justin Verlander 6.00 15.00
MCP23 Derek Jeter 10.00 25.00
MCP24 Buster Posey 12.50 30.00
MCP25 Yoenis Cespedes 5.00 12.00

2013 Topps MVP Award Winners Trophy

SERIES 1 ODDS 1:1396 HOBBY
SERIES 2 ODDS 1:3800 HOBBY
AP Albert Pujols 8.00 20.00
AR Alex Rodriguez 8.00 20.00
BP Buster Posey S2 12.50 30.00
BR Babe Ruth 12.50 30.00
CJ Chipper Jones 10.00 25.00
CR Cal Ripken Jr. 12.50 30.00
DE Dennis Eckersley 6.00 15.00
DM Dale Murphy 8.00 20.00
DMA Don Mattingly 10.00 25.00
DP Dustin Pedroia 8.00 20.00
EB Ernie Banks S2 6.00 15.00
FT Frank Thomas 8.00 20.00
GB George Brett 8.00 20.00
HK Harmon Killebrew 8.00 20.00
JB Johnny Bench 8.00 20.00
JH Josh Hamilton 10.00 25.00
JR Jackie Robinson 8.00 20.00
JR Jackie Robinson S2 8.00 20.00
JRO Jimmy Rollins 6.00 15.00
JV Justin Verlander 10.00 25.00
JV Joey Votto S2 6.00 15.00
JVO Joey Votto 8.00 20.00
KG Ken Griffey Jr. 12.50 30.00
KG Ken Griffey Jr. S2 12.50 30.00
LB Lou Boudreau S2 6.00 15.00
MC Miguel Cabrera S2 10.00 25.00
MS Mike Schmidt 10.00 25.00
RB Ryan Braun 6.00 15.00
RC Roberto Clemente 12.50 30.00
RH Ryan Howard 8.00 20.00
RJ Reggie Jackson 6.00 15.00
SK Sandy Koufax 8.00 20.00
SM Stan Musial 8.00 20.00
SM Stan Musial S2 8.00 20.00
TW Ted Williams S2 10.00 25.00
VG Vladimir Guerrero 6.00 15.00
WM Willie Mays 10.00 25.00
WS Willie Stargell 8.00 20.00
YB Yogi Berra 10.00 25.00
YB Yogi Berra S2 6.00 15.00

2013 Topps Proven Mettle Coins Copper

SERIES 1 ODDS 1:5622 HOBBY
SERIES 2 ODDS 1:1685 HOBBY
STATED PRINT RUN 99 SER.#'d SETS
AG Adrian Gonzalez S2 12.50 30.00
AM Andrew McCutchen S2 15.00 40.00
AP Albert Pujols 20.00 50.00
BH Bryce Harper S2 20.00 50.00
BR Babe Ruth 40.00 80.00
BR Babe Ruth S2 20.00 50.00
BRO Brooks Robinson S2 20.00 50.00
CK Clayton Kershaw 12.50 30.00
CL Cliff Lee 10.00 25.00
CR Cal Ripken Jr. S2 15.00 40.00
CS CC Sabathia S2 12.50 30.00
DJ Derek Jeter 15.00 40.00
DW David Wright S2 15.00 40.00
EL Evan Longoria 10.00 25.00
GB George Brett S2 20.00 50.00
HA Hank Aaron 15.00 40.00
HK Harmon Killebrew S2 12.50 30.00
JB Johnny Bench S2 10.00 25.00
JF Jimmie Foxx S2 15.00 40.00
JH Josh Hamilton 12.50 30.00
JH Josh Hamilton S2 12.50 30.00
JM Joe Morgan 12.50 30.00
JR Jackie Robinson 12.50 30.00
JV Justin Verlander 15.00 40.00
JV Joey Votto S2 12.00 30.00
JVO Joey Votto 12.00 30.00
KGJ Ken Griffey Jr. 25.00 60.00
LG Lou Gehrig 15.00 40.00
MC Miguel Cabrera 10.00 25.00
MK Matt Kemp 10.00 25.00
MM Manny Machado S2 10.00 25.00
MT Mike Trout S2 25.00 60.00
NR Nolan Ryan S2 20.00 50.00
OS Ozzie Smith S2 20.00 50.00
PF Prince Fielder S2 12.50 30.00
RB Ryan Braun 10.00 25.00
RC Roberto Clemente 30.00 60.00
RIH Rickey Henderson 12.50 30.00
RJ Reggie Jackson S2 10.00 25.00
ROC Robinson Cano 12.50 30.00
ROH Roy Halladay 10.00 25.00
SK Sandy Koufax 15.00 40.00
SM Stan Musial 15.00 40.00
TC Ty Cobb 15.00 40.00
TS Tom Seaver S2 15.00 40.00
TW Ted Williams S2 10.00 25.00
WM Willie Mays 15.00 40.00
WS Willie Stargell S2 10.00 25.00
WSP Warren Spahn S2 10.00 25.00
YD Yu Darvish S2 10.00 25.00

2013 Topps Proven Mettle Coins Wrought Iron

*IRON: .5X TO 1.2X BASIC
SERIES 1 ODDS 1:11,126 HOBBY
SERIES 2 ODDS 1:2850 HOBBY
STATED PRINT RUN 50 SER.#'d SETS

2013 Topps ROY Award Winners Trophy

STATED ODDS 1:1575 HOBBY
AD Andre Dawson 6.00 15.00
AP Albert Pujols 8.00 20.00
BH Bryce Harper 10.00 25.00
BP Buster Posey 8.00 20.00
BW Billy Williams 5.00 12.00
CF Carlton Fisk 5.00 12.00
CK Craig Kimbrel 6.00 15.00
CR Cal Ripken Jr. 12.50 30.00
DG Dwight Gooden 6.00 15.00
DJ Derek Jeter 15.00 40.00
DJU David Justice 5.00 12.00
DP Dustin Pedroia 6.00 15.00
DS Darryl Strawberry 5.00 12.00
EL Evan Longoria 5.00 12.00
EM Eddie Murray 6.00 15.00
FL Fred Lynn 5.00 12.00
HR Hanley Ramirez 5.00 12.00
JB Johnny Bench 8.00 20.00
JH Jeremy Hellickson 5.00 12.00
JR Jackie Robinson 8.00 20.00
JV Justin Verlander 6.00 15.00
LA Luis Aparicio 5.00 12.00
MT Mike Trout 10.00 25.00
RB Ryan Braun 5.00 12.00
RC Rod Carew 5.00 12.00
RH Ryan Howard 5.00 12.00
SR Scott Rolen 5.00 12.00
TS Tom Seaver 6.00 15.00
WM Willie Mays 8.00 20.00
WMC Willie McCovey 8.00 20.00

2013 Topps Spring Fever

COMPLETE SET (50) 10.00 25.00
SF1 Wally Joyner .30 .75
SF2 Dan Haren .30 .75
SF3 Mike Trout 4.00 10.00
SF4 Tyler Skaggs .50 1.25
SF5 Orlando Cepeda .40 1.00
SF6 Tommy Hanson .30 .75
SF7 Jason Heyward .40 1.00
SF8 Nick Markakis .40 1.00
SF9 Manny Machado 2.00 5.00
SF10 Cal Ripken Jr. 1.50 4.00
SF11 Dustin Pedroia .40 1.00
SF12 Will Middlebrooks .30 .75
SF13 Josh Vitters .40 1.00
SF14 Anthony Rizzo .75 2.00
SF15 Andre Dawson .40 1.00
SF16 Jake Peavy .30 .75
SF17 Todd Frazier .40 1.00
SF18 Devin Mesoraco .30 .75
SF19 Prince Fielder .40 1.00
SF20 Miguel Cabrera .50 1.25
SF21 Salvador Perez .40 1.00
SF22 A.J. Ellis .30 .75
SF23 Adrian Gonzalez .40 1.00
SF24 Nate Eovaldi .40 1.00
SF25 Jean Segura .40 1.00
SF26 David Wright .40 1.00
SF27 Boone Logan .30 .75
SF28 Jeurys Familia .50 1.25
SF29 Raul Ibanez .40 1.00
SF30 Robinson Cano .40 1.00
SF31 Don Mattingly 1.00 2.50
SF32 Rickey Henderson .50 1.25
SF33 Starling Marte .40 1.00
SF34 Will Clark .40 1.00
SF35 Ken Griffey Jr. 1.00 2.50
SF36 Stan Musial .75 2.00
SF37 Jeff Niemann .30 .75
SF38 Fernando Rodney .30 .75
SF39 Carlos Pena .40 1.00
SF40 Evan Longoria .40 1.00
SF41 Mike Olt .40 1.00
SF42 Jurickson Profar .40 1.00
SF43 Josh Hamilton .40 1.00
SF44 Jose Bautista .40 1.00
SF45 Bryce Harper .75 2.00
SF46 Ted Williams 1.00 2.50
SF47 Joey Votto .50 1.25
SF48 Matt Kemp .40 1.00
SF49 Ryan Braun .40 1.00
SF50 Buster Posey .60 1.50

2013 Topps Spring Fever Autographs

PRINT RUNS B/WN 10-451 COPIES PER
NO PRICING ON QTY 15 OR LESS
AD Andre Dawson/51 20.00 50.00
AE A.J. Ellis/155 8.00 20.00
AG Adrian Gonzalez/51 4.00 10.00
AR Anthony Rizzo/68 15.00 40.00
BL Boone Logan/151 8.00 20.00
CP Carlos Pena/138 6.00 15.00
CR Cal Ripken Jr./26 75.00 150.00
DP Dustin Pedroia/101 12.00 30.00
EL Evan Longoria/51 40.00 80.00
FR Fernando Rodney/174 6.00 15.00
JB Jose Bautista/101 20.00 50.00
JF Jeurys Familia/152 6.00 15.00
JH Josh Hamilton/51 30.00 60.00
JN Jeff Niemann/192 6.00 15.00
JP Jake Peavy/51 6.00 15.00
JS Jean Segura/316 6.00 15.00
JV Josh Vitters/451 8.00 20.00
MM Manny Machado/72 40.00 80.00
MT Mike Trout/51 100.00 200.00
NM Nick Markakis/345 8.00 20.00
OC Orlando Cepeda/176 10.00 25.00
RC Robinson Cano/58 12.50 30.00
RH Rickey Henderson/26 30.00 80.00
RI Raul Ibanez/113 8.00 20.00
SM Starling Marte/29 15.00 40.00
SMU Stan Musial/26
SP Salvador Perez/169 12.50 30.00
TH Tommy Hanson/151 12.50 30.00
TS Tyler Skaggs/110 8.00 20.00
WC Will Clark/44 20.00 50.00

2013 Topps Silk Collection

SERIES 1 ODDS 1:614 HOBBY
UPDATE ODDS 1:313 HOBBY
STATED PRINT RUN 50 SER.#'d SETS
CARDS LISTED ALPHABETICALLY
SC1 Dustin Ackley S1 6.00 15.00
SC2 Matt Adams UPD 6.00 15.00
SC3 Mike Adams UPD 6.00 15.00
SC4 Al Alburquerque UPD 6.00 15.00
SC5 Yonder Alonso S1 6.00 15.00
SC6 Jose Altuve S1 8.00 20.00
SC7 Pedro Alvarez S2 6.00 15.00
SC8 Robert Andino UPD 6.00 15.00
SC9 Elvis Andrus S2 8.00 20.00
SC10 Nolan Arenado UPD 30.00 80.00
SC11 Dylan Axelrod UPD 6.00 15.00
SC12 John Axford S1 6.00 15.00
SC13 Andrew Bailey UPD 6.00 15.00
SC14 Grant Balfour S2 6.00 15.00
SC15 Daniel Bard UPD 6.00 15.00
SC16 Trevor Bauer S1 10.00 25.00
SC17 Trevor Bauer UPD 10.00 25.00
SC18 Jose Bautista S2 8.00 20.00
SC19 Jason Bay UPD 8.00 20.00
SC20 Josh Beckett S1 6.00 15.00
SC21 Erik Bedard UPD 6.00 15.00
SC22 Brandon Belt S2 8.00 20.00
SC23 Carlos Beltran S2 8.00 20.00
SC24 Adrian Beltre S1 10.00 25.00
SC25 Quintin Berry UPD 4.00 10.00
SC26 Wilson Betemit UPD 6.00 15.00
SC27 Chad Billingsley S1 8.00 20.00
SC28 Kyle Blanks UPD 6.00 15.00
SC29 Joe Blanton UPD 6.00 15.00
SC30 Willie Bloomquist UPD 6.00 15.00
SC31 Mitchell Boggs UPD 6.00 15.00
SC32 Ryan Braun S1 8.00 20.00
SC33 Zach Britton UPD 8.00 20.00
SC34 Jay Bruce S2 8.00 20.00
SC35 Mark Buehrle S2 8.00 20.00
SC36 Madison Bumgarner S2 8.00 20.00
SC37 Billy Butler S2 6.00 15.00
SC38 Asdrubal Cabrera S2 8.00 20.00
SC39 Melky Cabrera S2 6.00 15.00
SC40 Miguel Cabrera S2 10.00 25.00
SC41 Matt Cain S2 8.00 20.00
SC42 Robinson Cano S2 8.00 20.00
SC43 Chris Carpenter S2 8.00 20.00
SC44 Chris Carter UPD 6.00 15.00
SC45 Starlin Castro S1 8.00 20.00
SC46 Yoenis Cespedes S2 10.00 25.00
SC47 Joba Chamberlain UPD 6.00 15.00
SC48 Aroldis Chapman S2 10.00 25.00
SC49 Endy Chavez UPD 6.00 15.00
SC50 Eric Chavez UPD 6.00 15.00
SC51 Randy Choate UPD 10.00 25.00
SC52 Shin-Soo Choo S1 8.00 20.00
SC53 Shin-Soo Choo UPD 8.00 20.00
SC54 Tyler Clippard S1 6.00 15.00
SC55 Tim Collins UPD 6.00 15.00
SC56 Ryan Cook S1 6.00 15.00
SC57 Kevin Correia UPD 6.00 15.00
SC58 Carl Crawford S2 8.00 20.00
SC59 Nelson Cruz S2 10.00 25.00
SC60 Johnny Cueto S1 8.00 20.00
SC61 Yu Darvish S1 10.00 25.00
SC62 Wade Davis UPD 6.00 15.00

SC63 Ryan Dempster S2 6.00 15.00
SC64 Ian Desmond S1 6.00 15.00
SC65 Scott Diamond S2 6.00 15.00
SC66 R.A. Dickey S1 8.00 20.00
SC67 R.A. Dickey S2 8.00 20.00
SC68 Stephen Drew UPD 6.00 15.00
SC69 Danny Duffy UPD 6.00 15.00
SC70 Adam Dunn S2 8.00 20.00
SC71 Jacoby Ellsbury S1 8.00 20.00
SC72 Edwin Encarnacion S1 10.00 25.00
SC73 Andre Ethier S1 8.00 20.00
SC74 Scott Feldman UPD 6.00 15.00
SC75 Neftali Feliz S1 6.00 15.00
SC76 Prince Fielder S1 8.00 20.00
SC77 Nick Franklin UPD 8.00 20.00
SC78 Freddie Freeman S1 12.00 30.00
SC79 David Freese S2 6.00 15.00
SC80 Christian Friedrich UPD 6.00 15.00
SC81 Rafael Furcal S1 6.00 15.00
SC82 Yovani Gallardo S1 6.00 15.00
SC83 Mat Gamel UPD 4.00 10.00
SC84 Jaime Garcia S1 8.00 20.00
SC85 Matt Garza S2 6.00 15.00
SC86 Kevin Gausman UPD 10.00 25.00
SC87 Jason Giambi UPD 6.00 15.00
SC88 Paul Goldschmidt S2 10.00 25.00
SC89 Adrian Gonzalez S1 8.00 20.00
SC90 Carlos Gonzalez S1 8.00 20.00
SC91 Gio Gonzalez S2 8.00 20.00
SC92 Alex Gordon S1 8.00 20.00
SC93 Yasmani Grandal S2 6.00 15.00
SC94 Curtis Granderson S1 8.00 20.00
SC95 Kevin Gregg UPD 6.00 15.00
SC96 Didi Gregorius UPD 25.00 60.00
SC97 Zack Greinke S2 8.00 20.00
SC98 Justin Grimm UPD 6.00 15.00
SC99 Travis Hafner UPD 6.00 15.00
SC100 Scott Hairston UPD 6.00 15.00
SC101 Roy Halladay S2 8.00 20.00
SC102 Cole Hamels S2 8.00 20.00
SC103 Josh Hamilton S2 8.00 20.00
SC104 Aaron Harang UPD 6.00 15.00
SC105 Dan Haren S1 6.00 15.00
SC106 Dan Haren UPD 6.00 15.00
SC107 Bryce Harper S1 15.00 40.00
SC108 Corey Hart S2 6.00 15.00
SC109 Matt Harvey S2 8.00 20.00
SC110 Chase Headley S2 6.00 15.00
SC111 Adeiny Hechavarria UPD 8.00 20.00
SC112 Jeremy Hellickson S1 6.00 15.00
SC113 Todd Helton S2 8.00 20.00
SC114 Jim Henderson UPD 8.00 20.00
SC115 Felix Hernandez S1 8.00 20.00
SC116 Kolvin Herrera UPD 6.00 15.00
SC117 Jason Heyward S1 8.00 20.00
SC118 Greg Holland UPD 6.00 15.00
SC119 Matt Holliday S1 10.00 25.00
SC120 Eric Hosmer S1 8.00 20.00
SC121 Ryan Howard S1 8.00 20.00
SC122 Tim Hudson S1 8.00 20.00
SC123 Torii Hunter S2 6.00 15.00
SC124 Hisashi Iwakuma S2 8.00 20.00
SC125 Maicer Izturis UPD 6.00 15.00
SC126 Austin Jackson S2 6.00 15.00
SC127 Edwin Jackson S1 6.00 15.00
SC128 Edwin Jackson UPD 6.00 15.00
SC129 Desmond Jennings S1 8.00 20.00
SC130 Ubaldo Jimenez S2 6.00 15.00
SC131 Chris Johnson UPD 6.00 15.00
SC132 Elliot Johnson UPD 6.00 15.00
SC133 Jim Johnson S1 6.00 15.00
SC134 Josh Johnson S1 8.00 20.00
SC135 Josh Johnson S2 8.00 20.00
SC136 Adam Jones S1 8.00 20.00
SC137 Garrett Jones S2 6.00 15.00
SC138 Ryan Kalish UPD 6.00 15.00
SC139 Scott Kazmir UPD 6.00 15.00
SC140 Don Kelly UPD 6.00 15.00
SC141 Ian Kennedy S1 6.00 15.00
SC142 Clayton Kershaw S1
SC143 Craig Kimbrel S1 8.00 20.00
SC144 Ian Kinsler S2 8.00 20.00
SC145 Paul Konerko S1 8.00 20.00
SC146 Casey Kotchman UPD 6.00 15.00
SC147 Hiroki Kuroda S1 6.00 15.00
SC148 Mat Latos S1 8.00 20.00
SC149 Brett Lawrie S1 8.00 20.00
SC150 Cliff Lee S1 8.00 20.00
SC151 Jon Lester S2 8.00 20.00
SC152 Tim Lincecum S1 8.00 20.00
SC153 Francisco Liriano UPD 6.00 15.00
SC154 Kyle Lohse UPD 6.00 15.00
SC155 Evan Longoria S1 8.00 20.00
SC156 Jed Lowrie UPD 6.00 15.00
SC157 Jonathan Lucroy S2 8.00 20.00
SC158 Lance Lynn S2 6.00 15.00
SC159 Ryan Madson S2 6.00 15.00
SC160 Shaun Marcum UPD 6.00 15.00
SC161 Nick Markakis S2 8.00 20.00
SC162 Russell Martin UPD 6.00 15.00
SC163 Carlos Martinez UPD 10.00 25.00
SC164 J.D. Martinez S2 10.00 25.00
SC165 Justin Masterson S1 6.00 15.00
SC166 Daisuke Matsuzaka UPD 8.00 20.00
SC167 Brian McCann S1 8.00 20.00
SC168 Andrew McCutchen S1 10.00 25.00
SC169 James McDonald S2 6.00 15.00
SC170 Kris Medlen S2 8.00 20.00
SC171 Will Middlebrooks S1 6.00 15.00
SC172 Wade Miley S2 6.00 15.00
SC173 Tommy Milone S2 6.00 15.00
SC174 Yadier Molina S1 10.00 25.00
SC175 Jesus Montero S2 6.00 15.00
SC176 Matt Moore S2 8.00 20.00
SC177 Kendrys Morales S1 6.00 15.00
SC178 Kendrys Morales UPD 6.00 15.00
SC179 Justin Morneau S2 8.00 20.00
SC180 Logan Morrison S2 6.00 15.00
SC181 Brandon Morrow UPD 6.00 15.00
SC182 Michael Morse UPD 6.00 15.00
SC183 Charlie Morton UPD 10.00 25.00
SC184 Mike Moustakas S1 8.00 20.00
SC185 Joe Nathan S1 6.00 15.00
SC186 Laynce Nix UPD 6.00 15.00
SC187 Derek Norris S2 6.00 15.00
SC188 Ivan Nova S1 8.00 20.00
SC189 Miguel Olivo UPD 4.00 10.00
SC190 David Ortiz S2 10.00 25.00
SC191 Marcell Ozuna UPD 15.00 40.00
SC192 Jonathan Papelbon S2 8.00 20.00
SC193 Jake Peavy S2 6.00 15.00
SC194 Dustin Pedroia S1 8.00 20.00
SC195 Carlos Pena S2 8.00 20.00
SC196 Hunter Pence S1 8.00 20.00
SC197 Cliff Pennington UPD 6.00 15.00
SC198 Wily Peralta S2 6.00 15.00
SC199 Chris Perez S2 6.00 15.00
SC200 Salvador Perez S2 8.00 20.00
SC201 Andy Pettitte S2 8.00 20.00
SC202 Brandon Phillips S2 6.00 15.00
SC203 A.J. Pierzynski UPD 6.00 15.00
SC204 Trevor Plouffe S2 6.00 15.00
SC205 Buster Posey S1 12.00 30.00
SC206 David Price S2 8.00 20.00
SC207 Yasiel Puig UPD 25.00 60.00
SC208 Albert Pujols S2 12.00 30.00
SC209 Nick Punto UPD 6.00 15.00
SC210 Carlos Quentin S2 6.00 15.00
SC211 Ryan Raburn UPD 6.00 15.00
SC212 Aramis Ramirez S2 6.00 15.00
SC213 Hanley Ramirez S2 8.00 20.00
SC214 Colby Rasmus S1 8.00 20.00
SC215 Jon Rauch UPD 6.00 15.00
SC216 Josh Reddick S1 6.00 15.00
SC217 Anthony Rendon UPD 30.00 80.00
SC218 Ben Revere S2 6.00 15.00
SC219 Jose Reyes S1 8.00 20.00
SC220 Mark Reynolds S1 6.00 15.00
SC221 Mariano Rivera S2 12.00 30.00
SC222 Anthony Rizzo S1 15.00 40.00
SC223 Ryan Roberts UPD 6.00 15.00
SC224 Fernando Rodney S2 6.00 15.00
SC225 Alex Rodriguez S1 12.00 30.00
SC226 Jimmy Rollins S1 8.00 20.00
SC227 Bruce Rondon UPD 6.00 15.00
SC228 Wilin Rosario S2 6.00 15.00
SC229 Cody Ross S2 6.00 15.00
SC230 Carlos Ruiz S2 6.00 15.00
SC231 James Russell UPD 6.00 15.00
SC232 Hyun-Jin Ryu S2 15.00 40.00
SC233 CC Sabathia S1 8.00 20.00
SC234 Chris Sale S1 10.00 25.00
SC235 Jarrod Saltalamacchia S1 6.00 15.00
SC236 Jeff Samardzija S1 6.00 15.00
SC237 Alex Sanabia UPD 6.00 15.00
SC238 Anibal Sanchez S2 6.00 15.00
SC239 Jonathan Sanchez UPD 4.00 10.00
SC240 Pablo Sandoval S2 8.00 20.00
SC241 Carlos Santana S1 8.00 20.00
SC242 Ervin Santana S2 6.00 15.00
SC243 Johan Santana S2 8.00 20.00
SC244 Skip Schumaker UPD 6.00 15.00
SC245 Luke Scott UPD 6.00 15.00
SC246 Marco Scutaro S2 8.00 20.00
SC247 Jean Segura S2 8.00 20.00
SC248 James Shields S1 6.00 15.00
SC249 James Shields UPD 6.00 15.00
SC250 Andrelton Simmons S2 6.00 15.00
SC251 Eric Sogard UPD 6.00 15.00
SC252 Rafael Soriano S1 6.00 15.00
SC253 Rafael Soriano UPD 6.00 15.00
SC254 Denard Span UPD 6.00 15.00
SC255 Giancarlo Stanton S1 10.00 25.00
SC256 Stephen Strasburg S2 10.00 25.00
SC257 Huston Street S2 6.00 15.00
SC258 Drew Stubbs UPD 6.00 15.00
SC259 Nick Swisher S2 8.00 20.00
SC260 Mark Teixeira S1 8.00 20.00
SC261 Miguel Tejada UPD 6.00 15.00
SC262 Chris Tillman UPD 6.00 15.00
SC263 Mike Trout S1 80.00 200.00
SC264 Mark Trumbo S2 8.00 20.00
SC265 Troy Tulowitzki S2 10.00 25.00
SC266 Jacob Turner S2 8.00 20.00
SC267 Dan Uggla S1 6.00 15.00
SC268 B.J. Upton S2 6.00 15.00
SC269 Justin Upton S1 8.00 20.00
SC270 Justin Upton UPD 8.00 20.00
SC271 Juan Uribe UPD 6.00 15.00
SC272 Chase Utley S1 8.00 20.00
SC273 Jason Vargas UPD 6.00 15.00
SC274 Jose Veras UPD 6.00 15.00
SC275 Justin Verlander S1 10.00 25.00
SC276 Shane Victorino S2 8.00 20.00
SC277 Edinson Volquez S1 6.00 15.00
SC278 Joey Votto S1 10.00 25.00
SC279 Adam Wainwright S1 8.00 20.00
SC280 Neil Walker S2 8.00 20.00
SC281 Jered Weaver S1 8.00 20.00
SC282 Rickie Weeks S1 6.00 15.00
SC283 Vernon Wells UPD 6.00 15.00
SC284 Jayson Werth S1 8.00 20.00
SC285 Ty Wigginton UPD 6.00 15.00
SC286 Brian Wilson S1 10.00 25.00
SC287 C.J. Wilson S2 6.00 15.00
SC288 Dewayne Wise UPD 6.00 15.00
SC289 Vance Worley UPD 8.00 20.00
SC290 David Wright S2 8.00 20.00
SC291 Kevin Youkilis S1 6.00 15.00
SC292 Kevin Youkilis UPD 6.00 15.00
SC293 Delmon Young S1 8.00 20.00
SC294 Delmon Young UPD 8.00 20.00
SC295 Michael Young S1 6.00 15.00
SC296 Michael Young UPD 6.00 15.00
SC297 Ryan Zimmerman S1 8.00 20.00
SC298 Jordan Zimmermann S2 8.00 20.00
SC299 Barry Zito S1 8.00 20.00
SC300 Ben Zobrist S1 8.00 20.00

2013 Topps Silver Slugger Award Winners Trophy

STATED ODDS 1:1674 HOBBY
AB Adrian Beltre 6.00 15.00
ABE Albert Belle 4.00 10.00
AD Andre Dawson 5.00 12.00
AR Alex Rodriguez 8.00 20.00
CF Carlton Fisk 5.00 12.00
CG Curtis Granderson 5.00 12.00
CGO Carlos Gonzalez 5.00 12.00
DM Dale Murphy 6.00 15.00
DMA Don Mattingly 12.00 30.00
DO David Ortiz 6.00 15.00
DS Darryl Strawberry 4.00 10.00
EM Eddie Murray 5.00 12.00
JB Jose Bautista 5.00 12.00
JR Jim Rice 5.00 12.00
KG Ken Griffey Jr. 12.00 30.00
MK Matt Kemp 5.00 12.00
MR Manny Ramirez 4.00 10.00
MS Mike Schmidt 10.00 25.00
PF Prince Fielder 5.00 12.00
RH Ryan Howard 5.00 12.00
RY Robin Yount 6.00 15.00
TG Tony Gwynn 6.00 15.00
TH Todd Helton 5.00 12.00
TT Troy Tulowitzki 6.00 15.00
WB Wade Boggs 5.00 12.00

2013 Topps The Elite

COMPLETE SET (20) 10.00 25.00
STATED ODDS 1:18 HOBBY
TE1 Miguel Cabrera .75 2.00
TE2 Ryan Braun .60 1.50
TE3 Josh Hamilton .60 1.50
TE4 Tom Seaver .60 1.50
TE5 Sandy Koufax 1.50 4.00
TE6 Nolan Ryan 2.50 6.00
TE7 Reggie Jackson .60 1.50
TE8 Rickey Henderson .75 2.00
TE9 Johnny Bench .75 2.00
TE10 Ernie Banks .75 2.00
TE11 Ozzie Smith 1.00 2.50
TE12 Bob Gibson .60 1.50
TE13 Joe Morgan .60 1.50
TE14 Buster Posey 1.00 2.50
TE15 Willie Mays 1.50 4.00
TE16 Mike Schmidt 1.25 3.00
TE17 Babe Ruth 2.00 5.00
TE18 Ted Williams 1.50 4.00
TE19 Jackie Robinson .75 2.00
TE20 Lou Gehrig 1.50 4.00

2013 Topps The Elite Gold

*GOLD: 2.5X TO 6X BASIC
STATED ODDS 1:1050 HOBBY
STATED PRINT RUN 99 SER.#'d SETS

2013 Topps The Elite Red

*RED: 3X TO 8X BASIC
STATED PRINT RUN 50 SER.#'d SETS

2013 Topps The Greatest Chase Relic

STATED ODDS 1:119,550 HOBBY
STATED PRINT RUN 50 SER.#'d SETS
TW Ted Williams 50.00 100.00

2013 Topps The Greats

COMPLETE SET (30) 50.00 100.00
STATED ODDS 1:18 HOBBY
TG1 Roberto Clemente 2.50 6.00
TG2 Willie Mays 2.00 5.00
TG3 Babe Ruth 2.50 6.00
TG4 Ernie Banks 1.00 2.50
TG5 Ted Williams 2.00 5.00
TG6 Jimmie Foxx 1.00 2.50
TG7 Ken Griffey Jr. 2.00 5.00
TG8 Mike Schmidt 1.50 4.00
TG9 Rickey Henderson 1.00 2.50
TG10 Nolan Ryan 3.00 8.00
TG11 John Smoltz 1.00 2.50
TG12 Johnny Bench 1.00 2.50
TG13 Reggie Jackson .75 2.00
TG14 Stan Musial 1.50 4.00
TG15 Bob Gibson .75 2.00
TG16 Tom Seaver .75 2.00
TG17 Chipper Jones 1.00 2.50
TG18 Tony Gwynn 1.00 2.50
TG19 Willie McCovey .75 2.00
TG20 Tom Glavine .60 1.50
TG21 Joe Morgan .75 2.00
TG22 Hank Aaron 2.00 5.00
TG23 Yogi Berra 1.00 2.50
TG24 Sandy Koufax 2.00 5.00
TG25 Albert Pujols 1.25 3.00
TG26 Derek Jeter 2.50 6.00
TG27 Alex Rodriguez 1.25 3.00
TG28 Roy Halladay .75 2.00
TG29 Mariano Rivera 1.25 3.00
TG30 Cal Ripken Jr. 3.00 8.00

2013 Topps The Greats Gold

*GOLD: 2X TO 5X BASIC
STATED ODDS 1:1034 HOBBY
STATED PRINT RUN 99 SER.#'d SETS

2013 Topps The Greats Red

*RED: 3X TO 8X BASIC
STATED PRINT RUN 50 SER.#'d SETS

2013 Topps Triple Crown Relics

COMMON CARD 20.00 50.00
STATED ODDS 1:432 HOBBY
EXCHANGE DEADLINE 01/31/2016

2013 Topps WBC Stars

COMPLETE SET (15) 5.00 12.00
STATED ODDS 1:8
WBC1 Jose Reyes .40 1.00
WBC2 Anthony Rizzo .75 2.00
WBC3 Joey Votto .50 1.25
WBC4 Robinson Cano .40 1.00
WBC5 Hanley Ramirez .40 1.00
WBC6 Giancarlo Stanton .50 1.25
WBC7 Adrian Gonzalez .40 1.00
WBC8 Justin Morneau .40 1.00
WBC9 Carlos Beltran .40 1.00
WBC10 Miguel Cabrera .50 1.25
WBC11 Pablo Sandoval .40 1.00
WBC12 Carlos Gonzalez .40 1.00
WBC13 Joe Mauer .40 1.00
WBC14 David Wright .40 1.00
WBC15 Ryan Braun .40 1.00

2013 Topps World Champion Autograph Relics

STATED ODDS 1:12,247 HOBBY
STATED PRINT RUN 50 SER.#'d SETS
EXCHANGE DEADLINE 01/31/2016
BC Brandon Crawford EXCH 100.00 175.00
BP Buster Posey 250.00 400.00
MB Madison Bumgarner 75.00 200.00
MC Matt Cain EXCH 100.00 175.00
PS Pablo Sandoval 125.00 250.00

2013 Topps World Champion Autographs

STATED ODDS 1:23,579 HOBBY
STATED PRINT RUN 50 SER.#'d SETS
EXCHANGE DEADLINE 01/31/2016
BC Brandon Crawford EXCH 60.00 120.00
BP Buster Posey 150.00 300.00
MB Madison Bumgarner 75.00 150.00
MC Matt Cain 100.00 200.00
PS Pablo Sandoval EXCH 60.00 150.00

2013 Topps World Champion Relics

STATED ODDS 1:3940 HOBBY
STATED PRINT RUN 100 SER.#'d SETS
EXCHANGE DEADLINE 01/31/2016
AP Angel Pagan 20.00 50.00
BB Brandon Belt 30.00 60.00
BC Brandon Crawford EXCH 60.00 120.00
BP Buster Posey 75.00 150.00
BW Brian Wilson 20.00 50.00
BZ Barry Zito 12.50 30.00
HP Hunter Pence 30.00 60.00
MB Madison Bumgarner 40.00 80.00
MC Matt Cain 15.00 40.00
MS Marco Scutaro 20.00 50.00
PS Pablo Sandoval 60.00 120.00
RT Ryan Theriot 20.00 50.00
RV Ryan Vogelsong 12.50 30.00
TL Tim Lincecum 60.00 120.00
XN Xavier Nady 12.50 30.00

2013 Topps World Series MVP Award Winners Trophy

STATED ODDS 1:2300 HOBBY
BG Bob Gibson 8.00 20.00
BR Brooks Robinson 8.00 20.00
CH Cole Hamels 6.00 15.00
DF David Freese 6.00 15.00
DJ Derek Jeter 10.00 25.00
MR Mariano Rivera 8.00 20.00
MS Mike Schmidt 8.00 20.00
PM Paul Molitor 6.00 15.00
PS Pablo Sandoval 8.00 20.00
RC Roberto Clemente 12.50 30.00
RJ Reggie Jackson 6.00 15.00
RJA Reggie Jackson 6.00 15.00
SK Sandy Koufax 10.00 25.00
WF Whitey Ford 6.00 15.00
WS Willie Stargell 6.00 15.00

2013 Topps Update

COMPLETE SET w/o SP's (330) 15.00 40.00
PRINTING PLATE ODDS 1:1182 HOBBY
PLATE PRINT RUN 1 SET PER COLOR
BLACK-CYAN-MAGENTA-YELLOW ISSUED
NO PLATE PRICING DUE TO SCARCITY
US1A Matt Harvey .20 .50
US1B Harvey SP AS Jsy 4.00 10.00
US1C Tom Seaver SP 30.00 80.00
US2 Trevor Bauer .25 .60
US3 Chad Qualls .15 .40
US4 Matt Adams .15 .40
US5 Chris Sale .25 .60
US6 Joel Peralta .15 .40
US7A Yoenis Cespedes .25 .60
US7B Cespedes SP High five 4.00 10.00
US7C Cespedes SP Group pic 4.00 10.00
US8 Anthony Rendon RC 6.00 15.00
US9 Cody Allen RC .25 .60
US10 Kevin Youkilis .15 .40
US11 Joakim Soria .15 .40
US12 Brandon Phillips .15 .40
US13 Jose Fernandez .40 1.00
US14 Joe Saunders .15 .40
US15 DJ LeMahieu .25 .60
US16A Alex Gordon .20 .50
US16B Bo Jackson SP 4.00 10.00
US17 Justin Grimm RC .25 .60
US18 Ross Ohlendorf .15 .40
US19 Johnny Hellweg RC .25 .60
US20 Carlos Gomez .15 .40
US21 Junior Lake RC .25 .60
US22 Carlos Beltran .20 .50
US23 Mike Olt RC .30 .75
US24 Ryan Raburn .15 .40
US25 Wade Davis .15 .40
US26 Wil Myers .20 .50
US27 Eric Hinske .15 .40
US28 Pedro Alvarez .15 .40
US29 Scott Van Slyke RC .30 .75
US30 Mike Adams .15 .40
US31 Edwin Encarnacion .25 .60
US32 Adeiny Hechavarria RC .30 .75
US33 Garrett Richards .20 .50
US34 A.J. Pollock .20 .50
US35A Andrew McCutchen .25 .60
US35B McCutch SP Horizontal 4.00 10.00
US36 Daisuke Matsuzaka .20 .50
US37 Cliff Pennington .15 .40
US38 Denard Span .15 .40
US39 Shin-Soo Choo .20 .50
US40 Tim Collins .15 .40
US41 Dan Haren .15 .40
US42 Rafael Betancourt .15 .40
US43 Luke Putkonen .15 .40
US44 Jason Bay .20 .50
US45 Joey Terdoslavich RC .25 .60
US46 Yasiel Puig .60 1.50
US47 Matt Garza .15 .40
US48 Vance Worley .20 .50
US49 Marlon Byrd .15 .40
US50 Zack Wheeler RC .50 1.25
US51 Brett Marshall RC .30 .75
US52 Chris Davis .20 .50
US53A Craig Kimbrel .20 .50
US53B Kimbrel SP In dugout 4.00 10.00
US53C Hank Aaron SP 15.00 40.00
US53D Chipper Jones SP 4.00 10.00
US54 Jason Giambi .15 .40
US55 Pete Kozma .15 .40
US56 Kyuji Fujikawa RC .40 1.00
US57 Dayan Viciedo .15 .40
US58 Kevin Frandsen .15 .40
US59 Hisashi Iwakuma .20 .50
US60 Chris Tillman .15 .40
US61 Rafael Soriano .15 .40
US62 Carlos Villanueva .15 .40
US63 Clay Buchholz .15 .40
US64 Mark Reynolds .15 .40
US65 Ryan Roberts .15 .40
US66 James Russell .15 .40
US67 Kyle McClellan .15 .40
US68 Nick Franklin RC .30 .75
US69 Martin Perez .20 .50
US70 Joe Mauer .20 .50
US71 Cody Asche RC .40 1.00
US72 Adam Jones .20 .50
US73A Buster Posey .30 .75
US73B Will Clark SP 40.00 80.00
US73C Willie Mays SP 40.00 80.00
US74 Kyle Blanks .15 .40
US75 Ty Wigginton .15 .40
US76 Roy Oswalt .20 .50
US77 Kelvin Herrera .15 .40
US78 Francisco Rodriguez .20 .50
US79A Yu Darvish .25 .60
US79B Darvish SP Glasses on 4.00 10.00
US80 Zoilo Almonte RC .30 .75
US81 Casey Kotchman .15 .40
US82 Bryan Petersen .15 .40
US83 Alex Sanabia .15 .40
US84 Stephen Drew .15 .40
US85 Pedro Strop .15 .40
US86 Chad Gaudin .15 .40
US87 Evan Gattis .30 .75
US88A Troy Tulowitzki .25 .60
US88B Tulo SP w/Teammates 4.00 10.00
US89 Michael Pineda .15 .40
US90 Michael Young .15 .40
US91 Prince Fielder .20 .50
US92 Jeanmar Gomez .15 .40
US93 Adam Wainwright .20 .50
US94 Joba Chamberlain .15 .40
US95 Eric Chavez .15 .40
US96 Mark DeRosa .15 .40
US97 Alexi Amarista .15 .40
US98 Salvador Perez .20 .50
US99 Derrick Robinson RC .25 .60
US100 Bryce Harper .40 1.00
US101 Jonathan Villar RC .40 1.00
US102 Christian Friedrich .15 .40
US103 Michael Morse .15 .40
US104 Matt Carpenter .25 .60
US105 Corey Kluber RC .75 2.00
US106 Clayton Kershaw .50 1.25
US107 Andrew Bailey .15 .40
US108 Ryan Kalish .15 .40
US109 Jose Dominguez RC .25 .60
US110 Kole Calhoun .15 .40
US111 Scott Hairston .15 .40
US112 Luke Gregerson .15 .40
US113 Samuel Deduno .15 .40
US114A Dustin Pedroia .20 .50
US114B Nomar Garciaparra SP 4.00 10.00
US114C Wade Boggs SP 40.00 80.00
US115 Drew Stubbs .15 .40
US116 Mike Kickham RC .25 .60
US117 Willie Bloomquist .15 .40
US118 Joe Blanton .15 .40
US119A Felix Hernandez .20 .50
US119B Griffey Jr. SP Blk jsy 6.00 15.00
US119C Griffey Jr. SP Red jsy 20.00 50.00
US120 Matt Tuiasosopo .15 .40
US121 Jason Frasor .15 .40
US122 Danny Duffy .15 .40
US123 Tom Gorzelanny .15 .40
US124 Jason Kipnis .20 .50
US125 J.J. Hardy .15 .40
US126 Mike Zunino RC .40 1.00
US127 David Phelps .15 .40
US128 Bartolo Colon .15 .40
US129 David Wright .20 .50
US130 Jesse Chavez .15 .40
US131 Josh Phegley RC .25 .60
US132 Ronald Belisario .15 .40
US133 Jose Fernandez .40 1.00
US134A Justin Verlander .25 .60
US134B Verland SP Blue jsy 4.00 10.00
US135 Dewayne Wise .15 .40
US136 Travis Hafner .15 .40
US137 Yoervis Medina RC .25 .60
US138 Danny Salazar RC .50 1.25
US139 John Jaso .15 .40
US140A Justin Upton .20 .50
US140B Tony Gwynn SP 30.00 60.00
US141 Chris Carter .15 .40
US142A Yadier Molina .25 .60
US142B Molina SP Orange jsy 5.00 12.00
US143 Tim Lincecum .20 .50
US144 Drake Britton RC .30 .75
US145 Michael Cuddyer .15 .40
US146 Didi Gregorius RC 1.00 2.50
US147 Charlie Morton .25 .60
US148 Ben Zobrist .20 .50
US149 Daniel Bard .15 .40
US150A Gerrit Cole RC 1.50 4.00
US150B G.Cole SP Blk jsy 40.00 80.00
US151 Shawn Kelley .15 .40
US152 Randy Choate .25 .60
US153 Jeff Francoeur .20 .50
US154 Kyle Gibson RC .40 1.00
US155 J.B. Shuck RC .25 .60
US156 Laynce Nix .15 .40
US157 Marco Scutaro .20 .50
US158 Erasmo Ramirez .15 .40
US159 Donald Lutz RC .25 .60
US160 Lyle Overbay .20 .50
US161 Jim Henderson RC .30 .75
US162 Mark Melancon .15 .40
US163 Chris Davis .20 .50
US164 Robert Andino .15 .40
US165 A.J. Pierzynski .15 .40
US166 Kevin Gregg .15 .40
US167 Randall Delgado .15 .40
US168 Michael Wacha RC .30 .75
US169 Ezequiel Carrera .15 .40
US170 Miguel Tejada .15 .40
US171 Nick Punto .15 .40
US172 Blake Parker .15 .40
US173 Reed Johnson .15 .40
US174 Jose Mijares .15 .40
US175 Carlos Martinez RC .40 1.00
US176 Matt Lindstrom .15 .40
US177 David Ortiz .25 .60
US178 Derek Dietrich RC .30 .75
US179 Joe Smith .20 .50
US180A Bryce Harper .40 1.00
US180B Harper SP Group pic 4.00 10.00
US181 Oliver Perez .15 .40
US182 Luis Valbuena .15 .40
US183 Jeff Bianchi .15 .40
US184 Dioner Navarro .15 .40
US185 Daniel Nava .15 .40
US186 Jake Elmore .15 .40
US187 Wilson Betemit .15 .40
US188A Cliff Lee .20 .50
US188B John Kruk SP 15.00 40.00
US189 Kyle Lohse .15 .40
US190 Steve Delabar .15 .40
US191 Ricky Nolasco .15 .40
US192 Hyun-Jin Ryu .40 1.00
US193A Max Scherzer .25 .60
US193B Scherz SP Blue jsy 4.00 10.00
US194 Xavier Paul .15 .40
US195 Chris Johnson .15 .40
US196 Brayan Pena .15 .40
US197 Josh Collmenter .15 .40
US198 Brian Bogusevic .15 .40
US199 Juan Lagares RC .30 .75
US200A Wil Myers RC .30 .75
US200B Myers SP Group pic 40.00 80.00
US201 Adam Ottavino .15 .40
US202 Yoenis Cespedes .25 .60
US203 Russell Martin .15 .40
US204 Mike Pelfrey .15 .40
US205A Prince Fielder .20 .50
US205B Prince George SP 40.00 80.00
US206 Reid Brignac .15 .40
US207 Matt Thornton .15 .40
US208 Juan Uribe .15 .40
US209 Anthony Swarzak .15 .40
US210 Matt Albers .15 .40
US211 Jarred Cosart RC .30 .75
US212 Alfonso Soriano .20 .50
US213 Matt Adams .15 .40
US214 Jean Segura .20 .50
US215 Travis Blackley .15 .40
US216A Manny Machado 1.00 2.50
US216B Ripken SP White jsy 40.00 80.00
US216C Ripken SP Blk jsy 6.00 15.00
US217 Elliot Johnson .15 .40
US218A Miguel Cabrera .25 .60
US218B Cabrera SP Group pic 4.00 10.00
US219 Pedro Alvarez .15 .40
US220 Zack Wheeler .30 .75
US221 Allen Craig .20 .50
US222 Erik Bedard .15 .40
US223 Jose Valverde .15 .40
US224 Brad Miller RC .30 .75
US225 Chris Getz .15 .40
US226 Michael Cuddyer .15 .40
US227 Carlos Gonzalez .20 .50
US228 Matt Moore .20 .50
US229 Jason Vargas .15 .40
US230 Scott Kazmir .15 .40
US231 Scott Feldman .15 .40
US232 Al Alburquerque .15 .40
US233 Anthony Rendon .75 2.00
US234 Jurickson Profar .20 .50
US235 Jose Iglesias .20 .50
US236 Shaun Marcum .15 .40
US237 Mariano Rivera .30 .75
US238 Eric Young Jr. .15 .40
US239 Justin Masterson .15 .40
US240 Paul Goldschmidt .25 .60
US241 Alberto Callaspo .15 .40
US242 Delmon Young .20 .50
US243 Marwin Gonzalez .15 .40
US244 Glen Perkins .15 .40
US245 James Shields .15 .40
US246 Don Kelly .15 .40
US247 Casper Wells .15 .40
US248 Jason Grilli .15 .40
US249 Madison Bumgarner .20 .50
US250A Yasiel Puig RC 1.00 2.50
US250B Puig SP Arms up 50.00 100.00
US250C Puig SP Big glove 12.00 30.00
US250D Puig SP Sliding 75.00 150.00
US251 Aaron Harang .15 .40
US252 Preston Claiborne .15 .40
US253 Shelby Miller .40 1.00
US254 Brian Wilson .25 .60
US255 Alex Wood RC .30 .75
US256 Luke Scott .15 .40
US257 Bryan Shaw .15 .40
US258 Jose Bautista .20 .50
US259 Nolan Arenado RC 15.00 40.00
US260 Darren O'Day .15 .40
US261 Skip Schumaker .15 .40
US262 Jayson Nix .15 .40
US263 Austin Romine .15 .40
US264 Nate Freiman RC .25 .60
US265 Gerrit Cole 1.00 2.50
US266 Jed Lowrie .15 .40
US267 Nick Tepesch RC .20 .50
US268A Joey Votto .25 .60
US268B Votto SP Group pic 4.00 10.00
US268C Teddy Kremer SP 100.00 200.00
US269 Kendrys Morales .15 .40
US270 Edwin Jackson .15 .40
US271 Francisco Liriano .15 .40
US272 Josh Thole .15 .40
US273 Jeff Keppinger .15 .40
US274 Kevin Gausman RC .40 1.00
US275 Bud Norris .15 .40
US276A Torii Hunter .15 .40
US276B Hunter SP Group pic 4.00 10.00
US277 Sonny Gray RC .40 1.00
US278 Jose Alvarez RC .25 .60
US279 Marcell Ozuna RC .60 1.50
US280 John Lannan .15 .40
US281 Jonathan Pettibone RC .40 1.00
US282 Brock Peterson (RC) .30 .75
US283 Conor Gillaspie .20 .50
US284 Stephen Pryor .15 .40
US285A David Ortiz .25 .60
US285B Ortiz SP Group pic 5.00 12.00
US286 Aroldis Chapman .25 .60
US287 Brandon Morrow .15 .40
US288 Maicer Izturis .15 .40
US289 Kevin Correia .15 .40
US290 Christian Yelich RC 20.00 50.00
US291 Logan Schafer .15 .40
US292 Zach Britton .20 .50
US293 Robinson Cano .20 .50
US294 Chris Denorfia .15 .40
US295 Sean Burnett .15 .40
US296 Joe Nathan .15 .40
US297 Chris Narveson .15 .40
US298 Luis Avilan RC .25 .60
US299 Ian Kennedy .15 .40
US300A Mike Trout 2.00 5.00
US300B Trout SP w/Cano 5.00 12.00
US301 Juan Francisco .15 .40
US302 Yan Gomes .20 .50
US303 Jose Veras .15 .40
US304 Patrick Corbin .20 .50
US305 Dylan Axelrod .15 .40
US306 Pat Neshek .15 .40
US307 Mike Carp .15 .40
US308 J.P. Howell .15 .40
US309 Domonic Brown .20 .50
US310 Boone Logan .15 .40
US311 Craig Stammen .15 .40
US312 Nate Jones .15 .40
US313A Mariano Rivera .30 .75
US313B Rivera SP Running 5.00 12.00
US313C Rivera SP Out of pen 50.00 100.00
US314 Junichi Tazawa .15 .40
US315 Bruce Rondon RC .25 .60
US316A David Wright .20 .50
US316B Wright SP Group pic 4.00 10.00
US317 Oswaldo Arcia RC .25 .60

US318 Greg Holland .15 .40
US319 Jordan Schafer .15 .40
US320 Chris Archer .15 .40
US321 Grant Green RC .40 1.00
US322 Brandon Inge .15 .40
US323A Robinson Cano .20 .50
US323B Cano SP Glasses 4.00 10.00
US323C Don Mattingly SP 60.00 120.00
US323D Lou Gehrig SP 40.00 80.00
US324 Chris Colabello RC .40 1.00
US325 Vernon Wells .15 .40
US326 Jake Peavy .15 .40
US327 Endy Chavez .15 .40
US328 Eric Sogard .15 .40
US329 Henry Urrutia RC .30 .75
US330 Yasiel Puig .60 1.50

2013 Topps Update Black

*BLACK: 10X TO 25X BASIC
*BLACK RC: 3X TO 8X BASIC
STATED ODDS 1:77 HOBBY
STATED PRINT RUN 62 SER.#'d SETS
US46 Yasiel Puig 30.00 80.00
US205 Prince Fielder 12.50 30.00
US250 Yasiel Puig 30.00 80.00
US259 Nolan Arenado 250.00 600.00
US290 Christian Yelich 300.00 800.00
US330 Yasiel Puig 30.00 80.00

2013 Topps Update Boston Strong

15 Dustin Pedroia 40.00 80.00
32 Craig Breslow 20.00 50.00
64 Will Middlebrooks 15.00 40.00
241 Jacoby Ellsbury 20.00 50.00
301 Jarrod Saltalamacchia 50.00 100.00
348 Jonny Gomes 15.00 40.00
382 Jackie Bradley Jr. 12.50 30.00
399 Shane Victorino 20.00 50.00
401 Ryan Dempster 15.00 40.00
503 Clay Buchholz 10.00 25.00
508 Felix Doubront 12.50 30.00
541 Jon Lester 15.00 40.00
548 John Lackey 12.00 30.00
555 Joel Hanrahan 12.00 30.00
595 David Ortiz 75.00 150.00
618 Koji Uehara 20.00 50.00
644 Ryan Lavarnway 10.00 25.00
659 Mike Napoli 40.00 80.00
US84 Stephen Drew 10.00 25.00
US107 Andrew Bailey 10.00 25.00
US108 Ryan Kalish 10.00 25.00
US144 Drake Britton 30.00 60.00
US149 Daniel Bard 10.00 25.00
US185 Daniel Nava 50.00 100.00
US207 Matt Thornton 10.00 25.00
US307 Mike Carp 20.00 50.00
US314 Junichi Tazawa 10.00 25.00

2013 Topps Update Camo

*CAMO VET: 8X TO 20X BASIC
*CAMO RC: 1.5X TO 4X BASIC RC
STATED ODDS 1:125 HOBBY
STATED PRINT RUN 99 SER.#'d SETS
US35 Andrew McCutchen 12.00 30.00
US46 Yasiel Puig 25.00 60.00
US250 Yasiel Puig 25.00 60.00
US259 Nolan Arenado 200.00 500.00
US290 Christian Yelich 250.00 600.00

2013 Topps Update Emerald

*EMERALD VET: 1.2X TO 3X BASIC
*EMERALD RC: .4X TO 1X BASIC RC
STATED ODDS 1:6 HOBBY
US259 Nolan Arenado 50.00 120.00
US290 Christian Yelich 60.00 150.00

2013 Topps Update Gold

*GOLD VET: 1.2X TO 3X BASIC
*GOLD RC: .4X TO 1X BASIC RC
STATED ODDS 1:6 HOBBY
STATED PRINT RUN 2013 SER.#'d SETS
US259 Nolan Arenado 60.00 150.00
US290 Christian Yelich 75.00 200.00

2013 Topps Update Pink

*PINK VET: 8X TO 20X BASIC
*PINK RC: 2.5X TO 6X BASIC RC
STATED ODDS 1:250 HOBBY
STATED PRINT RUN 50 SER.#'d SETS
US35 Andrew McCutchen 30.00 60.00
US259 Nolan Arenado 200.00 500.00
US290 Christian Yelich 250.00 600.00

2013 Topps Update Target Red Border

*TARGET VET: 1.2X TO 3X BASIC
*TARGET RC: .4X TO 1X BASIC
US259 Nolan Arenado 60.00 150.00
US290 Christian Yelich 75.00 200.00

2013 Topps Update Wal-Mart Blue Border

*WM VET: 1.2X TO 3X BASIC
*WM RC: .4X TO 1X BASIC
US259 Nolan Arenado 30.00 80.00
US290 Christian Yelich 60.00 150.00

2013 Topps Update '71 Topps Minis

COMPLETE SET (50) 20.00 50.00
1 Bryce Harper 1.00 2.50
2 Babe Ruth 1.50 4.00
3 Derek Jeter 1.50 4.00
4 Bo Jackson .60 1.50
5 Ken Griffey Jr. 1.25 3.00
6 Miguel Cabrera .60 1.50
7 Mike Trout 5.00 12.00
8 Joe Mauer .50 1.25
9 Robinson Cano .50 1.25
10 Joey Votto .60 1.50
11 Justin Upton .50 1.25
12 Andrew McCutchen .60 1.50
13 Prince Fielder .50 1.25
14 Troy Tulowitzki .60 1.50
15 Clayton Kershaw 1.25 3.00
16 Jackie Robinson .60 1.50
17 Hyun-Jin Ryu 1.00 2.50
18 Justin Verlander .60 1.50
19 Dustin Pedroia .50 1.25
20 David Wright .50 1.25
21 Ian Kinsler .50 1.25
22 Evan Longoria .50 1.25
23 Adam Jones .50 1.25
24 Greg Maddux .75 2.00
25 Shelby Miller 1.00 2.50
26 Mariano Rivera .75 2.00
27 Stan Musial 1.00 2.50
28 Johnny Bench .60 1.50
29 Mike Schmidt 1.00 2.50
30 Cal Ripken Jr. 2.00 5.00
31 Yasiel Puig 1.50 4.00
32 Carlos Gonzalez .50 1.25
33 Buster Posey .75 2.00
34 Yu Darvish .60 1.50
35 Paul Goldschmidt .60 1.50
36 Felix Hernandez .50 1.25
37 David Ortiz .60 1.50
38 Will Clark .50 1.25
39 Giancarlo Stanton .60 1.50
40 Nomar Garciaparra .50 1.25
41 Yoenis Cespedes .60 1.50
42 Roberto Clemente 1.50 4.00
43 Frank Thomas .60 1.50
44 Wil Myers .50 1.25
45 Stephen Strasburg .60 1.50
46 George Brett 1.25 3.00
47 Don Mattingly 1.25 3.00
48 Jay Bruce .50 1.25
49 Matt Harvey .50 1.25
50 Manny Machado 2.50 6.00

2013 Topps Update All Star Game MVP Commemorative Patches

1 Willie Mays 8.00 20.00
2 Juan Marichal 4.00 10.00
3 Brooks Robinson 5.00 12.00
4 Tony Perez 4.00 10.00
5 Willie McCovey 4.00 10.00
6 Frank Robinson 4.00 10.00
7 Joe Morgan 4.00 10.00
8 Don Sutton 4.00 10.00
9 Gary Carter 4.00 10.00
10 Bo Jackson 4.00 10.00
11 Ken Griffey Jr. 6.00 15.00
12 Fred McGriff 4.00 10.00
13 Pedro Martinez 6.00 15.00
14 Derek Jeter 8.00 20.00
15 Cal Ripken Jr. 6.00 15.00

2013 Topps Update All Star Stitches

STATED ODDS 1:49 HOBBY
AC Allen Craig 5.00 12.00
ACH Aroldis Chapman 3.00 8.00
AG Alex Gordon 5.00 12.00
AJ Adam Jones 4.00 10.00
AW Adam Wainwright 5.00 12.00
BC Bartolo Colon 3.00 8.00
BH Bryce Harper 10.00 25.00
BP Buster Posey 6.00 15.00
BPH Brandon Phillips 4.00 10.00
BZ Ben Zobrist 3.00 8.00
CB Carlos Beltran 5.00 12.00
CBU Clay Buchholz 4.00 10.00
CD Chris Davis 6.00 15.00
CG Carlos Gonzalez 3.00 8.00
CK Clayton Kershaw 5.00 12.00
CKI Craig Kimbrel 4.00 10.00
CL Cliff Lee 5.00 12.00
CS Chris Sale 3.00 8.00
DB Domonic Brown 4.00 10.00
DO David Ortiz 5.00 12.00
DP Dustin Pedroia 5.00 12.00
DW David Wright 10.00 25.00
EE Edwin Encarnacion 3.00 8.00
FH Felix Hernandez 3.00 8.00
GP Glen Perkins 3.00 8.00
HI Hisashi Iwakuma 4.00 10.00
JB Jose Bautista 4.00 10.00
JF Jose Fernandez 5.00 12.00
JG Jason Grilli 4.00 10.00
JH J.J. Hardy 4.00 10.00
JK Jason Kipnis 4.00 10.00
JM Justin Masterson 4.00 10.00
JMA Joe Mauer 4.00 10.00
JN Joe Nathan 3.00 8.00
JP Jhonny Peralta 3.00 8.00
JS Jean Segura 4.00 10.00
JV Justin Verlander 6.00 15.00
JVO Joey Votto 5.00 12.00
JZ Jordan Zimmermann 4.00 10.00
MB Madison Bumgarner 6.00 15.00
MC Miguel Cabrera 6.00 15.00
MCA Matt Carpenter 4.00 10.00
MH Matt Harvey 8.00 20.00
MM Manny Machado 10.00 25.00
MMO Matt Moore 3.00 8.00
MR Mariano Rivera 10.00 25.00
MS Max Scherzer 5.00 12.00
MSC Marco Scutaro 4.00 10.00
MT Mike Trout 12.50 30.00
NC Nelson Cruz 3.00 8.00
PA Pedro Alvarez 4.00 10.00
PC Patrick Corbin 3.00 8.00
PF Prince Fielder 4.00 10.00
PG Paul Goldschmidt 3.00 8.00
RC Robinson Cano 4.00 10.00
SP Salvador Perez 4.00 10.00
TH Torii Hunter 4.00 10.00
TT Troy Tulowitzki 4.00 10.00
YD Yu Darvish 5.00 12.00
YM Yadier Molina 6.00 15.00

2013 Topps Update All-Star Stitches Chrome

ASRAC Allen Craig 5.00 12.00
ASRBH Bryce Harper 15.00 40.00
ASRBP Buster Posey
ASRCB Carlos Beltran 12.50 30.00
ASRCD Chris Davis 6.00 15.00
ASRCG Carlos Gonzalez
ASRCK Clayton Kershaw
ASRCL Cliff Lee
ASRDO David Ortiz 4.00 10.00
ASRDW David Wright 8.00 20.00
ASRFH Felix Hernandez 4.00 10.00
ASRJF Jose Fernandez
ASRJV Justin Verlander 10.00 25.00
ASRMC Miguel Cabrera
ASRMH Matt Harvey 12.50 30.00
ASRMM Manny Machado 10.00 25.00
ASRMR Mariano Rivera
ASRMT Mike Trout 15.00 40.00
ASRPF Prince Fielder
ASRPG Paul Goldschmidt 4.00 10.00
ASRRC Robinson Cano 4.00 10.00
ASRTT Troy Tulowitzki 6.00 15.00
ASRYM Yadier Molina 4.00 10.00
ASRJVO Joey Votto 10.00 25.00

2013 Topps Update All Star Stitches Gold

*GOLD: 1X TO 2.5X BASIC
STATED ODDS 1:1139 HOBBY
STATED PRINT RUN 50 SER.#'d SETS

2013 Topps Update Franchise Forerunners

COMPLETE SET (10) 5.00 12.00
1 H.J.Ryu/S.Koufax 1.25 3.00
2 Y.Puig/M.Kemp 1.50 4.00
3 C.Ripken/M.Machado 2.00 5.00
4 A.McCutchen/G.Cole 2.50 6.00
5 E.Longoria/W.Myers .50 1.25
6 B.Gibson/S.Miller .50 1.25
7 D.Wright/M.Harvey .50 1.25
8 Y.Darvish/N.Ryan 2.00 5.00
9 R.Henderson/Y.Cespedes .60 1.50
10 J.Fernandez/G.Stanton 1.00 2.50

2013 Topps Update League Leaders Pins

STATED ODDS 1:713 HOBBY
BG Bob Gibson 1.50 4.00
BP Buster Posey 2.50 6.00
BR Babe Ruth 5.00 12.00
CR Cal Ripken Jr. 6.00 15.00
DJ Derek Jeter 5.00 12.00
FH Felix Hernandez 1.50 4.00
JB Johnny Bench 2.00 5.00
JP Jim Palmer 1.50 4.00
JV Joey Votto 2.00 5.00
KG Ken Griffey Jr. 4.00 10.00
LG Lou Gehrig 4.00 10.00
MC Miguel Cabrera 2.00 5.00
MK Matt Kemp 1.50 4.00
MS Mike Schmidt 3.00 8.00
MT Mike Trout 15.00 40.00
NG Nomar Garciaparra 1.50 4.00
NR Nolan Ryan 6.00 15.00
RC Rod Carew 1.50 4.00
TC Ty Cobb 3.00 8.00
TW Ted Williams 4.00 10.00

2013 Topps Update Pennant Coins Copper

STATED ODDS 1:6300 HOBBY
STATED PRINT RUN 99 SER.#'d SETS
BR Brooks Robinson 12.50 30.00
BR Babe Ruth 10.00 25.00
DJ Derek Jeter 20.00 50.00
DO David Ortiz 8.00 20.00
GB George Brett 12.50 30.00
MR Mariano Rivera 15.00 40.00
OS Ozzie Smith 12.50 30.00
RC Roberto Clemente 20.00 50.00
RH Rickey Henderson 12.50 30.00
RY Robin Yount 8.00 20.00
SK Sandy Koufax 20.00 50.00
SM Stan Musial 20.00 50.00
TG Tom Glavine 8.00 20.00
TW Ted Williams 20.00 50.00
WM Willie Mays 15.00 40.00

2013 Topps Update Pennant Coins Wrought Iron

*WROUGHT IRON: .5X TO 1.2X BASIC
STATED ODDS 1: 12,250 HOBBY
STATED PRINT RUN 50 SER.#'d SETS

2013 Topps Update Postseason Heroes

COMPLETE SET (20) 6.00 15.00
1 David Freese .40 1.00
2 Justin Verlander .60 1.50
3 George Brett 1.25 3.00
4 John Smoltz .60 1.50
5 Greg Maddux .75 2.00
6 Sandy Koufax 1.25 3.00
7 Reggie Jackson .50 1.25
8 Derek Jeter 1.50 4.00
9 Mariano Rivera .75 2.00
10 Bob Gibson .50 1.25
11 Buster Posey .75 2.00
12 Deion Sanders .40 1.00
13 David Ortiz .60 1.50
14 Roy Halladay .50 1.25
15 Evan Longoria .50 1.25
16 Nolan Ryan 2.00 5.00
17 Miguel Cabrera .60 1.50
18 Bret Saberhagen .25 .60
19 Jim Palmer .50 1.25
20 David Wright .50 1.25

2013 Topps Update Postseason Heroes Chrome

PH1 David Freese .60 1.50
PH2 Justin Verlander 1.00 2.50
PH3 George Brett 2.00 5.00
PH4 John Smoltz 1.00 2.50
PH5 Greg Maddux 1.25 3.00
PH6 Sandy Koufax 2.00 5.00
PH7 Reggie Jackson .75 2.00
PH8 Derek Jeter 2.50 6.00
PH9 Mariano Rivera 1.25 3.00
PH10 Bob Gibson .75 2.00
PH11 Buster Posey 1.25 3.00
PH12 Deion Sanders .60 1.50
PH13 David Ortiz 1.00 2.50
PH14 Roy Halladay .75 2.00
PH15 Evan Longoria .75 2.00
PH16 Nolan Ryan 3.00 8.00
PH17 Miguel Cabrera 1.00 2.50
PH18 Bret Saberhagen .40 1.00
PH19 Jim Palmer .75 2.00
PH20 David Wright .75 2.00

2013 Topps Update Record Holder Rings

STATED ODDS 1:1460 HOBBY
BR Babe Ruth 10.00 25.00
CR Cal Ripken Jr. 10.00 25.00
GB George Brett 10.00 25.00
NR Nolan Ryan 10.00 25.00
OS Ozzie Smith 8.00 20.00
RH Rickey Henderson 8.00 20.00
TC Ty Cobb 8.00 20.00
TW Ted Williams 10.00 25.00
WM Willie McCovey 6.00 15.00
YB Yogi Berra 8.00 20.00

2013 Topps Update Rookie Commemorative Patches

1 Cal Ripken Jr. 10.00 25.00
2 Will Clark 4.00 10.00
3 CC Sabathia 4.00 10.00
4 Josh Hamilton 4.00 10.00
5 Miguel Cabrera 5.00 12.00
6 Adrian Gonzalez 4.00 10.00
7 Robinson Cano 5.00 12.00
8 Felix Hernandez 4.00 10.00
9 Carl Crawford 4.00 10.00
10 Matt Kemp 4.00 10.00
11 Tim Lincecum 4.00 10.00
12 Ryan Zimmerman 4.00 10.00
13 Jose Reyes 4.00 10.00
14 Clayton Kershaw 4.00 10.00
15 Yasiel Puig 10.00 25.00

2014 Topps

COMP.ALLSTAR.FACT SET (660) 30.00 80.00
COMP.BLUE.RET.FACT SET (660) 30.00 80.00
COMP.GREEN.RET.FACT SET (660) 30.00 80.00
COMP.PURP.RET.FACT SET (660) 30.00 80.00
COMP.RED.HOB.FACT SET (660) 30.00 80.00
COMPLETE SET w/o SP's (660) 25.00 60.00
COMP.SERIES 1 SET w/o SP's (330) 12.00 30.00
COMP.SERIES 2 SET w/o SP's (330) 12.00 30.00
SER.1 PLATE ODDS 1:1610 HOBBY
SER.2 PLATE ODDS 1:874 HOBBY
PLATE PRINT RUN 1 SET PER COLOR
BLACK-CYAN-MAGENTA-YELLOW ISSUED
NO PLATE PRICING DUE TO SCARCITY
1A Mike Trout 1.25 3.00
1B Trout SP Gatorade 12.00 30.00
1C Trout SP Fut Star 12.00 30.00
1D Trout SP SABR 12.00 30.00
2 Jhonny Peralta .15 .40
3 Jarrod Dyson .15 .40
4 Cody Asche .20 .50
5 Lance Lynn .15 .40
6 Josh Beckett .15 .40
8 Coco Crisp .15 .40
9 Dustin Ackley .15 .40
10 Junior Lake .15 .40
11 Mike Carp .15 .40
12 Aaron Hicks .20 .50
13 Juan Nicasio .15 .40
14A Yoenis Cespedes .25 .60
14B Yoenis Cespedes SP 5.00 12.00
Celebrating
15A Paul Goldschmidt .25 .60
15B Paul Goldschmidt SP 2.50 6.00
Future Stars
15C Paul Goldschmidt SP 2.50 6.00
SABRmetrics
16 Johnny Cueto .20 .50
17 Todd Helton .20 .50
18A Jurickson Profar FS .20 .50
18B Jurickson Profar SP 2.00 5.00
Future Stars
19 Joey Votto .25 .60
20 Charlie Blackmon .25 .60
21 Alfredo Simon .15 .40
22 Mike Napoli WS .15 .40
23 Chris Heisey .15 .40
24A Manny Machado FS .25 .60
24B Manny Machado SP 2.50 6.00
Future Stars
24C Machado SP SABR 2.50 6.00
25A Troy Tulowitzki .25 .60
25B Troy Tulowitzki SP 2.50 6.00
SABRmetrics
26 Josh Phegley .15 .40
27 Michael Choice RC .25 .60
28 Brayan Pena .15 .40
29 Dvis/Cbrra/Encrncn LL .25 .60
30 Mark Buehrle .20 .50
31 Victor Martinez .20 .50
32 Reymond Fuentes RC .25 .60
33A Matt Harvey .20 .50
33B Pedro Alvarez SP 1.50 4.00
Future Stars
33C Pedro Alvarez SP 1.50 4.00
SABRmetrics
34 Buddy Boshers RC .25 .60
35 Trevor Cahill .15 .40
36A Billy Hamilton RC .30 .75
36B Hamilton SP Fut Star 2.00 5.00
36C Hamilton Swing FS 2.00 5.00
37 Nick Hundley .15 .40
38 Alvrz/Gldsmdt/Brce LL .25 .60
39 David Murphy .15 .40
40A Hyun-Jin Ryu .20 .50
40B Hyun-Jin Ryu SP 4.00 10.00
Celebrating
41 Adeiny Hechavarria .15 .40
42 Mariano Rivera .30 .75
43 Mark Trumbo .15 .40
44A Matt Carpenter .25 .60
44B Matt Carpenter SP 2.50 6.00
SABRmetrics
45 Jake Marisnick RC .25 .60
46A Kolten Wong RC .30 .75
46B K.Wong SP FS 2.00 5.00
47 Chris Davis HL .15 .40
48 Jarrod Saltalamacchia .15 .40
49 Enny Romero RC .25 .60
50A Buster Posey .30 .75
50B Posey SP SABR 3.00 8.00
51 Kyle Lohse .15 .40
52 Jim Adduci RC .25 .60
53 Clay Buchholz .15 .40
54 Andrew Lambo RC .25 .60
55 Chia-Jen Lo RC .25 .60
56A Taijuan Walker RC .25 .60
56B Taijuan Walker SP 1.50 4.00
Future Stars
57A Yadier Molina .25 .60
57B Yadier Molina SP 5.00 12.00
Celebrating
57C Yadier Molina SP 2.50 6.00
SABRmetrics
58 Dan Straily .15 .40
59 Nate Schierholtz .15 .40
60 Jon Niese .15 .40
61 Nick Markakis .20 .50
62 Joe Kelly .15 .40
63 Tyler Skaggs FS .15 .40
64 Will Venable .15 .40
65 Hisashi Iwakuma .20 .50
66 Kris Medlen .20 .50
67 Yasmani Grandal .15 .40
68 Sean Burnett .15 .40
69 Jhoulys Chacin .15 .40
70 Marcell Ozuna .25 .60
71 Anthony Rizzo .40 1.00
72 Michael Young .15 .40
73 Kyle Seager .15 .40
74 John Mayberry .15 .40
75 Brandon Barnes .15 .40
76 Mike Aviles .15 .40
77 Aroldis Chapman .25 .60
78 Bronson Arroyo .15 .40
79 Garrett Jones .15 .40
80 Jack Hannahan .15 .40
81A Anibal Sanchez .15 .40
81B Anibal Sanchez SP 1.50 4.00
SABRmetrics
82A Leonys Martin .15 .40
82B Leonys Martin SP 1.50 4.00
SABRmetrics
83 Jonathan Schoop RC .25 .60
84 Todd Redmond .15 .40
85 Matt Joyce .15 .40
86 Wilmer Flores RC .30 .75
87 Tyson Ross .15 .40
88 Oswaldo Arcia .15 .40
89 Jarred Cosart FS .15 .40
90 Ethan Martin RC .25 .60
91 Starling Marte FS .20 .50
92 Martin Perez FS .20 .50
93 Ryan Sweeney .15 .40
94 Mitch Moreland .15 .40
95 Brandon Morrow .15 .40
96 Wily Peralta .15 .40
97A Alex Gordon .20 .50
97B Starling Marte SP 2.00 5.00
SABRmetrics
98 Edwin Encarnacion .25 .60
99 Melky Cabrera .15 .40
100A Bryce Harper .40 1.00
100B Harper SP Fut Star 4.00 10.00
101 Chris Nelson .15 .40
102 Matt Lindstrom .15 .40
103 Cbrra/Mauer/Trout LL 1.25 3.00
104 Kurt Suzuki .15 .40
105 Ryan Howard .20 .50
106 Shin-Soo Choo .20 .50
107 Jordan Zimmermann .20 .50
108 J.D. Martinez .25 .60
109 David Freese .15 .40
110A Wil Myers .15 .40
110B Wil Myers SP 1.50 4.00
Future Stars
111 Mark Ellis .15 .40
112 Torii Hunter .15 .40
113 Krshw/Frnndz/Hrvey LL .50 1.25
114 Francisco Liriano .15 .40
115 Brett Oberholtzer .15 .40
116 Hiroki Kuroda .15 .40
117 Snchz/Clon/Iwkma LL .20 .50
118A Ian Desmond .15 .40
118B Ian Desmond SP 1.50 4.00
SABRmetrics
119 Brandon Crawford .20 .50
120 Kevin Correia .15 .40
121 Franklin Gutierrez .15 .40
122 Jonathan Papelbon .20 .50
123 James Paxton RC .40 1.00
124A Jay Bruce .20 .50
124B Jay Bruce SP 2.00 5.00
SABRmetrics
125A Joe Mauer .20 .50
125B Joe Mauer SP 2.00 5.00
SABRmetrics
125C Joe Mauer SP 6.00 15.00
Snoopy
126 David DeJesus .15 .40
127 Yusmeiro Petit .15 .40
128 Erasmo Ramirez .15 .40
129 Yonder Alonso .15 .40
130 Scooter Gennett .20 .50
131 Junichi Tazawa .15 .40
132 Henderson Alvarez HL .15 .40
133A Xander Bogaerts RC .75 2.00
133B Bogaerts SP Fut Star 5.00 12.00
133C Bogaerts Gry Jsy FS 2.00 5.00
134A Josh Donaldson .20 .50
134B Josh Donaldson SP 2.00 5.00
SABRmetrics
135 Eric Sogard .15 .40
136A Will Middlebrooks FS .15 .40
136B Will Middlebrooks SP 1.50 4.00
Future Stars
137 Boone Logan .15 .40
138 Wei-Yin Chen .15 .40
139 Rafael Betancourt .15 .40
140 Jonathan Broxton .15 .40
141 Chris Tillman .15 .40
142 Zack Greinke .20 .50
143 Gldsmdt/Brce/Frman LL .30 .75
144 Joakim Soria .15 .40
145 Jason Castro .15 .40
146 Jonny Gomes WS .15 .40
147 Jason Frasor .15 .40
148 Chris Sale .25 .60
148B Sale SABR SP 2.50 6.00
149 Miguel Cabrera HL .25 .60
150A Andrew McCutchen .25 .60
150B McCutch SP Blk jsy 8.00 20.00
150C McCutch SP SABR 2.50 6.00
151 Bruce Chen .15 .40
152 Jonathan Herrera .15 .40
153 Dvis/Cbrra/Jones LL .25 .60
154 Chris Iannetta .15 .40
155 Daniel Murphy .20 .50
156 Kendrys Morales .15 .40
157 Matt Adams .15 .40
158 Nate McLouth .15 .40
159 Jason Grilli .15 .40
160 Bruce Rondon .15 .40
161A Adrian Beltre .25 .60
161B Adrian Beltre SP 2.50 6.00
SABRmetrics
162 Josmil Pinto RC .25 .60
163 Matt Shoemaker RC .40 1.00
164 Jaime Garcia .20 .50
165 Rajai Davis .15 .40
166A Dustin Pedroia .25 .60
166B Dustin Pedroia SP 5.00 12.00
In dugout
166C Dustin Pedroia SP 2.50 6.00
SABRmetrics
167 Jeremy Guthrie .15 .40
168 Alex Rodriguez .30 .75
169 Nick Franklin FS .15 .40
170 Wade Miley .15 .40
171 Trevor Rosenthal .20 .50
172 Rickie Weeks .15 .40
173 Brandon League .15 .40
174 Bobby Parnell .15 .40
175 Casey Janssen .15 .40
176 Alex Cobb .15 .40
177 Esmil Rogers .15 .40
178 Erik Johnson RC .25 .60
179A Gerrit Cole FS .25 .60
179B Gerrit Cole SP 2.50 6.00
Future Stars
180 Ben Revere .15 .40
181 Jim Henderson .15 .40
182 Carlos Ruiz .15 .40
183 Darwin Barney .15 .40
184 Yunel Escobar .15 .40
185 Howie Kendrick .15 .40
186 Clayton Richard .15 .40
187 Justin Turner .20 .50
188 Mark Melancon .15 .40
189 Adam LaRoche .15 .40
190 Kevin Gausman FS .20 .50
191 Chris Perez .15 .40
192A Pedro Alvarez .15 .4
192B Matt Harvey SP 2.00 5.0
Future Stars
192B Matt Harvey SP 2.00 5.0
SABRmetrics
193 Ricky Nolasco .15 .4
194 Joel Hanrahan .15 .4
195A Nick Castellanos RC .75 2.0
195B Castellanos SP Fut Star 5.00 12.0
195C Castellanos Gry Jsy FS 2.00 5.0
196 Cole Hamels .20 .5
197 Onelki Garcia RC .25 .6
198A Nick Swisher .20 .5
198B Nick Swisher SP 4.00 10.0
Celebrating
199 Matt Davidson RC .30 .7
200 Derek Jeter .60 1.5
201 Alex Rios .20 .5
202 Jeremy Hellickson .15 .4
203 Cliff Pennington .15 .4
204A Adrian Gonzalez .20 .5
204B Adrian Gonzalez SP 4.00 10.0
Celebrating
205 Seth Smith .15 .4
206 Jon Lester WS .20 .5
207 Jonathan Villar .15 .4
208 Dayan Viciedo .15 .4
209 Carlos Quentin .15 .4
210 Jose Altuve .20 .5
211 Dioner Navarro .15 .4
212A Jason Heyward .20 .5
212B Jason Heyward SP 4.00 10.0
High-five
212C Jason Heyward SP 2.00 5.0
Future Stars
213 Justin Smoak .15 .4
214 James Shields .15 .4
215 Jean Segura FS .20 .5
216 Ubaldo Jimenez .15 .4
217A Giancarlo Stanton .25 .6
217B Giancarlo Stanton SP 2.50 6.0
SABRmetrics
218 Matt Dominguez .15 .4
219 Charlie Morton .25 .6
220 Ryan Doumit .15 .4
221 Brian Dozier .20 .5
222 Vernon Wells .15 .4
223 Joaquin Benoit .15 .4
224 Michael Saunders .20 .5
225 Brian McCann .20 .5
226 Sean Doolittle .15 .4
227 Andrew Cashner .15 .4
228A Jayson Werth .20 .5
228B Jayson Werth SP 2.00 5.0
SABRmetrics
229A Justin Upton .20 .5
229B Justin Upton SP 4.00 10.0
High-five
230 Andre Rienzo RC .25 .6
231 J.R. Murphy RC .25 .6
232 Chris Owings RC .25 .6
233 Rafael Soriano .15 .4
234 Eric Stults .15 .4
235A Jason Kipnis .20 .5
235B Jason Kipnis SP 2.00 5.0
Future Stars
235C Jason Kipnis SP 2.00 5.0
SABRmetrics
236 Joel Peralta .15 .4
237 Cddyer/Jhnsn/Frman LL .30 .7
238 Alberto Callaspo .15 .4
239 Jeff Samardzija .15 .4
240 Ernesto Frieri .15 .4
241 Henderson Alvarez .15 .4
242 David Holmberg RC .25 .6
243 Ryan Cook .15 .4
244 Danny Farquhar .15 .4
245 Ross Detwiler .15 .4
246 Eduardo Nunez .15 .4
247 Anthony Gose .15 .4
248 Travis d'Arnaud RC .30 .7
249 Heath Hembree RC .50 1.2
250A Miguel Cabrera .25 .6
250B Miggy SP Look Up 5.00 12.0
250C Cabrera SP SABR 2.50 6.0
251 Sergio Romo .15 .4
252 Kevin Pillar RC .25 .6
253 Todd Helton HL .20 .5
254 Brett Gardner .20 .5
255 Billy Butler .15 .4
256 Abraham Almonte RC .25 .6
257 C.J. Wilson .15 .4
258 Jon Lester .20 .5
259 David Ortiz WS .25 .6
260 Zoilo Almonte .20 .5
261 Michael Brantley .20 .5
262 Jeff Keppinger .15 .4
263 Doug Fister .15 .4
264 Huston Street .15 .4
265 Yordano Ventura RC .30 .7
266 Zack Wheeler FS .20 .5
267 Ryan Vogelsong .15 .4
268 Don Kelly .15 .4
269 Joe Blanton .15 .4
270 Gregor Blanco .15 .4
271 Justin Ruggiano .15 .4
272A Carlos Villanueva .15 .4
272B Joey Votto SP 2.50 6.0
SABRmetrics
273 Mark DeRosa .15 .4
274 Jonny Gomes .15 .4
275A Nolan Arenado .30 .7
275B Nolan Arenado SP 3.00 8.0

Future Stars
275C Nolan Arenado SP 3.00 8.00
SABRmetrics
276 Alfonso Soriano .20 .50
277 Mike Leake .15 .40
278 Tommy Medica RC .25 .60
279 Corey Kluber .20 .50
280 Everth Cabrera .15 .40
281 Robbie Erlin RC .25 .60
282 Rex Brothers .15 .40
283A Andrelton Simmons FS .15 .40
283B Andrelton Simmons SP 1.50 4.00
SABRmetrics
284 Brandon Belt .20 .50
285 Jonathan Lucroy .20 .50
286 Josh Fields RC .25 .60
287 Miguel Montero .15 .40
288A Julio Teheran FS .20 .50
288B Julio Teheran SP 2.00 5.00
Future Stars
289 Matt Thornton .15 .40
290 Chad Bettis RC .25 .60
291 Brandon McCarthy .15 .40
292 Aaron Hill .15 .40
293 Mike Zunino FS .15 .40
294 Wnwrght/Zmmrmnn/Krshw LL .50 1.25
295 Matt Tuiasosopo .15 .40
296 Domonic Brown .20 .50
297A Max Scherzer .25 .60
297B Max Scherzer SP 5.00 12.00
Celebrating
297C Max Scherzer SP 2.50 6.00
SABRmetrics
298 Chris Getz .15 .40
299 Schrzr/Clon/Moore LL .25 .60
300A Yu Darvish .25 .60
300B Yu Darvish SP 2.50 6.00
SABRmetrics
301A Shane Victorino .20 .50
301B Shane Victorino SP 2.00 5.00
SABRmetrics
302A Carlos Gomez .15 .40
302B Carlos Gomez SP 1.50 4.00
SABRmetrics
303 Andres Torres .15 .40
304 Juan Lagares .15 .40
305 Steve Cishek .15 .40
306 Garrett Richards .20 .50
307 Jake Peavy .15 .40
308 Alexei Ramirez .20 .50
309 Drew Stubbs .15 .40
310 Neftali Feliz .15 .40
311 Chris Young .15 .40
312 Jimmy Rollins .20 .50
313 Brad Peacock .15 .40
314A Hanley Ramirez .20 .50
314B Hanley Ramirez SP 4.00 10.00
Celebrating
315 Jose Quintana .15 .40
316 Mike Minor .15 .40
317 Lonnie Chisenhall .15 .40
318 Luis Valbuena .15 .40
319 Ryan Goins RC .30 .75
320 Hector Santiago .15 .40
321 Mariano Rivera HL .30 .75
322 Emilio Bonifacio .15 .40
323A Jose Bautista .20 .50
323B Jose Bautista SP 2.00 5.00
SABRmetrics
324 Elvis Andrus .20 .50
325 Trevor Plouffe .15 .40
326 Khris Davis .25 .60
327 Pablo Sandoval .20 .50
328 James Loney .15 .40
329A Matt Holliday .25 .60
329B Matt Holliday SP 2.50 6.00
SABRmetrics
330A Evan Longoria .20 .50
330B Evan Longoria SP 4.00 10.00
Celebrating
330C Evan Longoria SP 2.00 5.00
SABRmetrics
331A Yasiel Puig .25 .60
331B Puig SP FS 8.00 20.00
331C Puig SP Hands hips 8.00 20.00
332 Stephen Strasburg .25 .60
333 Wil Myers ERR .15 .40
Name spelled Will on back
334 Andy Dirks .15 .40
335 Miguel Cabrera .25 .60
336A Ben Zobrist .20 .50
336B Ben Zobrist SP 2.00 5.00
SABRmetrics
337 Zach Walters RC .25 .60
338 Carlos Santana .20 .50
339 Cody Ross .15 .40
340 Casey McGehee .15 .40
341 Mike Moustakas .20 .50
342 Brad Miller .20 .50
343 Nate Freiman .15 .40
344 Kevin Siegrist (RC) .25 .60
345 Darin Ruf .20 .50
346 Derek Norris .15 .40
347 Matt Cain .20 .50
348 Salvador Perez .20 .50
349 Martin Prado .15 .40
350 Carlos Gonzalez .20 .50
351 Matt Garza .15 .40
352 Ryan Wheeler .15 .40
353 A.J. Ramos .15 .40
354 Donnie Murphy .15 .40
355 Jarrod Parker .15 .40
356 Jose Reyes .20 .50
357 Lorenzo Cain .15 .40
358A Christian Yelich .30 .75
358B Yelich SP FS 3.00 8.00
359 Sean Rodriguez .15 .40
360 Russell Martin .15 .40
361 Edwin Jackson .15 .40
362 Daniel Nava .15 .40
363 David Hale RC .25 .60
364 Mike Trout 1.25 3.00
365 Dan Uggla .15 .40
366 Zack Cozart .15 .40
367 Brian Wilson .25 .60
368 Kyuji Fujikawa .20 .50
369 Erick Aybar .15 .40
370 Jerry Blevins .15 .40
371 Scott Kazmir .15 .40
372 Austin Jackson .15 .40
373 Kyle Drabek .15 .40
374 Taylor Jordan (RC) .15 .40
375A Adam Wainwright .20 .50
375AB Adam Wainwright SP 4.00 10.00
In front of fans
375C Adam Wainwright SP 4.00 10.00
Celebrating
375D Adam Wainwright SP 2.00 5.00
SABRmetrics
376 Jeurys Familia .20 .50
377 J.J. Hardy .15 .40
378 Ryan Zimmerman .20 .50
379 Gerardo Parra .15 .40
380 Tyler Chatwood .15 .40
381 Drew Smyly .15 .40
382 Michael Bourn .15 .40
383 Chris Archer .15 .40
384 Rick Porcello .20 .50
385 Josh Willingham .20 .50
386 Mike Olt .15 .40
387 Ed Lucas .15 .40
388 Yovani Gallardo .15 .40
389 Geovany Soto .20 .50
390 Bryce Harper .40 1.00
391 Blake Parker .15 .40
392 Jacob Turner .20 .50
393 Devin Mesoraco .15 .40
394 Sean Halton .15 .40
395 John Danks .15 .40
396 Brian Roberts .15 .40
397 Tim Lincecum .20 .50
398A Adam Jones .20 .50
398B Adam Jones SP 2.00 5.00
SABRmetrics
399 Hector Sanchez .15 .40
400 Clayton Kershaw .50 1.25
400A Kershaw SP Throw 10.00 25.00
400B Kershaw SP Celebrate 10.00 25.00
400C Kershaw SP SABR 5.00 12.00
401A Felix Hernandez .20 .50
401B Felix Hernandez SP 2.00 5.00
SABRmetrics
402 J.J. Putz .15 .40
403 Gordon Beckham .15 .40
404 C.C. Lee RC .25 .60
405 Jason Kubel .15 .40
406 Ramon Santiago .15 .40
407 John Jaso .15 .40
408 Joey Terdoslavich .15 .40
409 Ian Kennedy .15 .40
410 A.J. Griffin .15 .40
411 Josh Rutledge .15 .40
412A Hunter Pence .20 .50
412B Hunter Pence SP 2.00 5.00
SABRmetrics
413 Jose Fernandez .25 .60
414 Michael Wacha .20 .50
415 Andre Ethier .20 .50
416A Josh Reddick .15 .40
416B Josh Reddick SP 1.50 4.00
Future Stars
416C Josh Reddick SP 1.50 4.00
SABRmetrics
417 Chase Headley .15 .40
418 Jordy Mercer .15 .40
419 Lucas Harrell .15 .40
420 Lucas Duda .20 .50
421 R.A. Dickey .20 .50
422 Alexi Ogando .15 .40
423 Marco Scutaro .20 .50
424 Jose Ramirez RC 4.00 10.00
425A Craig Kimbrel .20 .50
425B Craig Kimbrel SP 4.00 10.00
Making fist
426 Koji Uehara .15 .40
427 Cameron Maybin .15 .40
428 Skip Schumaker .15 .40
429 Marcus Semien RC .25 .60
430 Roger Kieschnick RC .25 .60
431 Brett Anderson .15 .40
432 Dillon Gee .15 .40
433 Omar Infante .15 .40
434 Miguel Gonzalez .15 .40
435 Ryan Braun .20 .50
436 Eric Young Jr. .15 .40
437 Alex Wood .15 .40
438 Jake Arrieta .20 .50
439 Jackie Bradley Jr. .25 .60
440 Ryan Raburn .15 .40
441 Mike Pelfrey .15 .40
442 Angel Pagan .15 .40
443 Jeff Kobernus RC .25 .60
444 Robbie Grossman .15 .40
445 Sean Marshall .15 .40
446 Tim Hudson .20 .50
447 Christian Bethancourt RC .25 .60
448 Brett Lawrie .20 .50
449 Jedd Gyorko .15 .40
450A Justin Verlander .25 .60
450B Verlander SP Celebrate 5.00 12.00
450C Verlander SP SABR 2.50 6.00
451 Luis Garcia RC .25 .60
452 Andrew McCutchen .25 .60
453 Nelson Cruz .25 .60
454 Brandon Beachy .15 .40
455 Danny Espinosa .15 .40
456 Eury De La Rosa RC .25 .60
457 CC Sabathia .20 .50
458 Vinnie Pestano .15 .40
459 Eric Hosmer .20 .50
460 Matt Kemp .20 .50
461 Steve Delabar .15 .40
462 J.A. Happ .20 .50
463 Samuel Deduno .15 .40
464 Evan Gattis .15 .40
465 Justin Morneau .20 .50
466 Ryan Dempster .15 .40
467 Scott Feldman .15 .40
468 Wilin Rosario .15 .40
469 Jesse Crain .15 .40
470 Kole Calhoun .15 .40
471 Brandon Moss .15 .40
472 Caleb Gindl .15 .40
473A Mike Napoli .15 .40
473B Mike Napoli SP 1.50 4.00
SABRmetrics
474 Carlos Martinez .20 .50
475A David Ortiz .25 .60
475B David Ortiz SP 5.00 12.00
Goggles on face
475C David Ortiz SP 5.00 12.00
Goggles on head
475D David Ortiz SP 2.50 6.00
SABRmetrics
476 D.J. LeMahieu .25 .60
477 Craig Gentry .15 .40
478 Billy Hamilton .20 .50
479 Ivan Nova .20 .50
480 Peter Bourjos .15 .40
481 Allen Craig .20 .50
482 Dallas Keuchel .20 .50
483 Shane Robinson .15 .40
484 Marlon Byrd .15 .40
485 Gonzalez Germen RC .30 .75
486 Drew Hutchison .15 .40
487 Jim Johnson .15 .40
488 Brian Duensing .15 .40
489 David Price .20 .50
490 Logan Morrison .15 .40
491 Felix Doubront .15 .40
492 Glen Perkins .15 .40
493 Ruben Tejada .15 .40
494 Rob Wooten RC .25 .60
495 John Axford .15 .40
496A Jose Abreu RC 2.00 5.00
496B Abreu Look left FS 4.00 10.00
497 Fernando Rodney .15 .40
498 Steve Susdorf RC .25 .60
499 Craig Kimbrel .20 .50
500 Robinson Cano .20 .50
501 Carlos Carrasco .15 .40
502 Chase Utley .20 .50
503 Kyle Kendrick .15 .40
504 Kelly Johnson .15 .40
505 Homer Bailey .15 .40
506 Rafael Furcal .15 .40
507 Justin Masterson .15 .40
508 Sonny Gray FS .20 .50
509A Brandon Phillips .15 .40
509B Brandon Phillips SP 1.50 4.00
SABRmetrics
510 Matt den Dekker RC .30 .75
511 Travis Wood .15 .40
512 Neil Walker .20 .50
513 Jordan Pacheco .15 .40
514 Alcides Escobar .20 .50
515 Curtis Granderson .20 .50
516 Mike Belfiore RC .25 .60
517 Norichika Aoki .15 .40
518 Chris Parmelee .15 .40
519 A.J. Ellis .15 .40
520 Jorge De La Rosa .15 .40
521 Anthony Rendon .25 .60
522 Wandy Rodriguez .15 .40
523 Gio Gonzalez .20 .50
524 Brian Bogusevic .15 .40
525A Chris Davis .15 .40
525B Chris Davis SP 1.50 4.00
SABRmetrics
526 Avisail Garcia .20 .50
527 Travis Snider .15 .40
528A Shelby Miller .20 .50
528B Shelby Miller SP 2.00 5.00
USA Jersey
529 Jesus Montero .15 .40
530 Danny Salazar .20 .50
531A Dylan Bundy .20 .50
531B Dylan Bundy SP 2.00 5.00
USA Jersey
532 Danny Duffy .15 .40
533 Jose Veras .15 .40
534 Ian Kinsler .20 .50
535 Juan Francisco .15 .40
536 Matt Harrison .15 .40
537 Madison Bumgarner .20 .50
538 Jon Jay .15 .40
539 Trevor Bauer .25 .60
540 Ike Davis .15 .40
541 Phil Hughes .15 .40
542 Josh Zeid RC .25 .60
543 Bud Norris .15 .40
544 Jason Vargas .15 .40
545 Jeremy Affeldt .15 .40
546 Heath Bell .15 .40
547 Brian Matusz .15 .40
548 Jered Weaver .20 .50
549 Hank Conger .15 .40
550A Prince Fielder .20 .50
550B Prince Fielder SP 4.00 10.00
Postseason sweatshirt
551 Addison Reed .15 .40
552 Yasiel Puig .25 .60
553 Michael Pineda .15 .40
554 Maicer Izturis .15 .40
555 Adam Eaton .15 .40
556 Brad Ziegler .15 .40
557 Vic Black RC .40 1.00
558 Nolan Reimold .15 .40
559 Asdrubal Cabrera .20 .50
560 Aramis Ramirez .15 .40
561 Wellington Castillo .15 .40
562 Didi Gregorius .20 .50
563 Colt Hynes RC .25 .60
564 Alejandro De Aza .15 .40
565 Roy Halladay .20 .50
566 Carl Crawford .20 .50
567 Donovan Solano .25 .60
568 Pedro Florimon .15 .40
569 Michael Morse .15 .40
570 Nathan Eovaldi .20 .50
571A Colby Rasmus .20 .50
571B Colby Rasmus SP 2.00 5.00
SABRmetrics
572 Tommy Milone .15 .40
573 Adam Lind .20 .50
574 Tyler Clippard .15 .40
575 Josh Hamilton .20 .50
576 David Robertson .15 .40
577 Steve Ames RC .25 .60
578 Tyler Thornburg .15 .40
579A Freddie Freeman .30 .75
579B Freeman SP SABR 3.00 8.00
580A Todd Frazier .20 .50
580B Todd Frazier SP 2.00 5.00
SABRmetrics
581 Tony Cingrani .20 .50
582 Desmond Jennings .20 .50
583 Ryan Ludwick .15 .40
584 Tyler Flowers .15 .40
585 Stephen Drew .15 .40
586 Luke Hochevar .15 .40
587 Dee Gordon .15 .40
588 Matt Moore .20 .50
589 Chris Carter .15 .40
590 Brett Cecil .15 .40
591 Jenrry Mejia .15 .40
592 Simon Castro RC .25 .60
593 Carlos Beltran .20 .50
594 Justin Maxwell .15 .40
595 A.J. Pierzynski .15 .40
596 Juan Uribe .15 .40
597 Mat Latos .20 .50
598 Marco Estrada .15 .40
599 Jason Motte .15 .40
600 David Wright .20 .50
601 Jason Hammel .20 .50
602 Tanner Roark RC .25 .60
603 Starlin Castro .15 .40
604 Clayton Kershaw .50 1.25
605 Tim Beckham RC .40 1.00
606 Kenley Jansen .20 .50
607 Jed Lowrie .15 .40
608 Jeff Locke .15 .40
609 Jonathan Pettibone .15 .40
610 Paul Konerko .20 .50
611 Patrick Corbin .20 .50
612 Jake Petricka RC .25 .60
613 Mark Teixeira .20 .50
614 Moises Sierra .15 .40
615 Drew Storen .15 .40
616 Zach McAllister .15 .40
617 Greg Holland .15 .40
618 Adam Dunn .20 .50
619 Chris Johnson .15 .40
620 Yan Gomes .15 .40
621 B.J. Upton .20 .50
622 Dexter Fowler .20 .50
623 Chad Billingsley .20 .50
624 Alex Presley .15 .40
625 Albert Pujols .30 .75
626 Tommy Hanson .10 .25
627 J.P. Arencibia .15 .40
628 Joe Nathan .15 .40
629A Cliff Lee .20 .50
629B Cliff Lee SP 2.00 5.00
SABRmetrics
630 Max Scherzer .25 .60
631 Bartolo Colon .15 .40
632 John Lackey .20 .50
633 Alex Avila .20 .50
634 Gaby Sanchez .15 .40
635 Josh Johnson .20 .50
636 Santiago Casilla .15 .40
637 Freddy Galvis .15 .40
638 Michael Cuddyer .15 .40
639 Conor Gillaspie .20 .50
640 Kyle Blanks .15 .40
641 A.J. Burnett .15 .40
642 Brandon Kintzler .15 .40
643 Alex Guerrero RC .30 .75
644 Grant Green .15 .40
645 Wilson Ramos .15 .40
646 Dan Haren .15 .40
647 L.J. Hoes .15 .40
648 A.J. Pollock .20 .50
649 Jordan Danks .15 .40
650 Jacoby Ellsbury .20 .50
651 Denard Span .15 .40
652 Edinson Volquez .15 .40
653 Jose Iglesias .20 .50
654 Jose Tabata .15 .40
655 Derek Holland .15 .40
656 Grant Balfour .15 .40
657 Corey Hart .15 .40
658 Wade Davis .15 .40
659 Ervin Santana .15 .40
660A Jose Fernandez .25 .60
660B Jose Fernandez SP 2.50 6.00
Future Stars
661A Masahiro Tanaka RC .75 2.00
661B Tanaka SP Press Conf 10.00 25.00
661C Tanaka Blue Jsy FS 1.50 4.00

2014 Topps Black

*BLACK VET: 10X TO 25X BASIC
*BLACK RC: 6X TO 15X BASIC RC
SERIES ONE ODDS 1:104 HOBBY
SERIES TWO ODDS 1:56 HOBBY
STATED PRINT RUN 63 SER.#'d SETS
42 Mariano Rivera 20.00 50.00
57 Yadier Molina 12.00 30.00
103 Cbrra/Mauer/Trout LL 10.00 25.00
133 Xander Bogaerts 40.00 100.00
150 Andrew McCutchen 20.00 50.00
179 Gerrit Cole FS 10.00 25.00
200 Derek Jeter 40.00 80.00
204 Adrian Gonzalez 12.50 30.00
248 Travis d'Arnaud 8.00 20.00
259 David Ortiz WS 10.00 25.00
274 Jonny Gomes 5.00 12.00

2014 Topps Camo

*CAMO VET: 8X TO 20X BASIC
*CAMO RC: 5X TO 12X BASIC RC
SERIES ONE ODDS 1:250 HOBBY
SERIES TWO ODDS 1:123 HOBBY
STATED PRINT RUN 99 SER.#'d SETS
19 Joey Votto 10.00 25.00
42 Mariano Rivera 20.00 50.00
44 Matt Carpenter 10.00 25.00
50 Buster Posey 15.00 40.00
56 Taijuan Walker 10.00 25.00
57 Yadier Molina 10.00 25.00
91 Starling Marte FS 8.00 20.00
105 Ryan Howard 8.00 20.00
110 Wil Myers 10.00 25.00
119 Brandon Crawford 8.00 20.00
125 Joe Mauer 12.00 30.00
133 Xander Bogaerts 30.00 60.00
146 Jonny Gomes WS 4.00 10.00
150 Andrew McCutchen 20.00 50.00
179 Gerrit Cole FS 8.00 20.00
192 Pedro Alvarez 6.00 15.00
200 Derek Jeter 30.00 60.00
259 David Ortiz WS 8.00 20.00
274 Jonny Gomes 4.00 10.00
283 Andrelton Simmons FS 6.00 15.00
321 Mariano Rivera HL 20.00 50.00
329 Matt Holliday 8.00 20.00

2014 Topps Factory Set Orange Border

*ORANGE VET: 6X TO 15X BASIC
*ORANGE RC: 4X TO 10X BASIC RC
INSERTED IN FACTORY SETS
STATED PRINT RUN 199 SER.#'d SETS
200 Derek Jeter 50.00 100.00

2014 Topps Gold

*GOLD VET: 1.5X TO 4X BASIC
*GOLD RC: .6X TO 1.5X BASIC RC
SERIES ONE ODDS 1:9 HOBBY
SERIES TWO ODDS 1:4 HOBBY
STATED PRINT RUN 2014 SER.#'d SETS

2014 Topps Green

*GREEN VET: 2.5X TO 6X BASIC
*GREEN RC: 1.5X TO 4X BASIC RC
42 Mariano Rivera 6.00 15.00
200 Derek Jeter 15.00 40.00
321 Mariano Rivera HL 6.00 15.00

2014 Topps Orange

*ORANGE VET: 4X TO 10X BASIC
*ORANGE RC: 2.5X TO 6X BASIC RC
496 Jose Abreu 8.00 20.00

2014 Topps Pink

*PINK VET: 12X TO 30X BASIC
*PINK RC: 8X TO 20X BASIC RC
SERIES ONE ODDS 1:501 HOBBY
SERIES TWO ODDS 1:501 HOBBY
STATED PRINT RUN 50 SER.#'d SETS
4 Cody Asche 15.00 40.00
12 Aaron Hicks 8.00 20.00
19 Joey Votto 10.00 25.00
42 Mariano Rivera 20.00 50.00
50 Buster Posey 20.00 50.00
55 Chia-Jen Lo 8.00 20.00
57 Yadier Molina 12.00 30.00
91 Starling Marte FS 10.00 25.00
105 Ryan Howard 10.00 25.00
110 Wil Myers 12.00 30.00
125 Joe Mauer 10.00 25.00
146 Jonny Gomes WS 12.50 30.00
150 Andrew McCutchen 20.00 50.00
179 Gerrit Cole FS 10.00 25.00
183 Darwin Barney 10.00 25.00
192 Pedro Alvarez 8.00 20.00
195 Nick Castellanos 15.00 40.00
200 Derek Jeter 40.00 80.00
206 Jon Lester WS 8.00 20.00
258 Jon Lester 8.00 20.00
259 David Ortiz WS 12.50 30.00
274 Jonny Gomes 12.50 30.00
283 Andrelton Simmons FS 8.00 20.00
321 Mariano Rivera HL 20.00 50.00
329 Matt Holliday 10.00 25.00

2014 Topps Red Foil

*RED FOIL VET: 1.5X TO 4X BASIC
*RED FOIL RC: 1X TO 2.5X BASIC RC
STATED ODDS 1:6 HOBBY

2014 Topps Sparkle

1 Mike Trout 30.00 80.00
14 Yoenis Cespedes 6.00 15.00
15 Paul Goldschmidt 6.00 15.00
18 Jurickson Profar FS 5.00 12.00
19 Joey Votto 25.00 60.00
24 Manny Machado FS 30.00 80.00
25 Troy Tulowitzki 6.00 15.00
33 Matt Harvey 5.00 12.00
36 Billy Hamilton 25.00 60.00
40 Hyun-Jin Ryu 5.00 12.00
42 Mariano Rivera 40.00 100.00
44 Matt Carpenter 25.00 60.00
50 Buster Posey 20.00 50.00
56 Taijuan Walker 12.00 30.00
57 Yadier Molina 20.00 50.00
71 Anthony Rizzo 10.00 25.00
77 Aroldis Chapman 6.00 15.00
97 Alex Gordon 15.00 40.00
100 Bryce Harper 10.00 25.00
106 Shin-Soo Choo 5.00 12.00
110 Wil Myers 4.00 10.00
124 Jay Bruce 5.00 12.00
125 Joe Mauer 25.00 60.00
133 Xander Bogaerts 30.00 80.00
148 Chris Sale 6.00 15.00
150 Andrew McCutchen 20.00 50.00
161 Adrian Beltre 6.00 15.00
166 Dustin Pedroia 20.00 50.00
179 Gerrit Cole FS 30.00 80.00
192 Pedro Alvarez 4.00 10.00
195 Nick Castellanos 12.00 30.00
196 Cole Hamels 5.00 12.00
204 Adrian Gonzalez 5.00 12.00
212 Jason Heyward 5.00 12.00
217 Giancarlo Stanton 6.00 15.00
229 Justin Upton 5.00 12.00
235 Jason Kipnis 12.00 30.00
250 Miguel Cabrera 20.00 50.00
251 Sergio Romo 4.00 10.00
266 Zack Wheeler FS 20.00 50.00
276 Alfonso Soriano 5.00 12.00
296 Domonic Drown 5.00 12.00
297 Max Scherzer 6.00 15.00
300 Yu Darvish 6.00 15.00
314 Hanley Ramirez 5.00 12.00
323 Jose Bautista 12.00 30.00
327 Pablo Sandoval 5.00 12.00
329 Matt Holliday 25.00 60.00
330 Evan Longoria 5.00 12.00
331 Yasiel Puig 6.00 15.00
332 Stephen Strasburg 6.00 15.00
338 Carlos Santana 12.00 30.00
347 Matt Cain 5.00 12.00
350 Carlos Gonzalez 5.00 12.00
356 Jose Reyes 5.00 12.00
358 Christian Yelich 8.00 20.00
375 Adam Wainwright 5.00 12.00
378 Ryan Zimmerman 5.00 12.00
383 Chris Archer 4.00 10.00
388 Yovani Gallardo 4.00 10.00
397 Tim Lincecum 8.00 20.00
398 Adam Jones 15.00 40.00
400 Clayton Kershaw 12.00 30.00
401 Felix Hernandez 5.00 12.00
412 Hunter Pence 20.00 50.00
414 Michael Wacha 5.00 12.00
421 R.A. Dickey 5.00 12.00
425 Craig Kimbrel 5.00 12.00
435 Ryan Braun 5.00 12.00
450 Justin Verlander 6.00 15.00
457 CC Sabathia 5.00 12.00
460 Matt Kemp 5.00 12.00
464 Evan Gattis 15.00 40.00
473 Mike Napoli 15.00 40.00
475 David Ortiz 20.00 50.00
481 Allen Craig 5.00 12.00
489 David Price 5.00 12.00
500 Robinson Cano 5.00 12.00
502 Chase Utley 30.00 80.00
509 Brandon Phillips 15.00 40.00
521 Anthony Rendon 6.00 15.00
525 Chris Davis 4.00 10.00
528 Shelby Miller 20.00 50.00
534 Ian Kinsler 5.00 12.00
537 Madison Bumgarner 8.00 20.00
548 Jered Weaver 5.00 12.00
550 Prince Fielder 5.00 12.00
555 Adam Eaton 4.00 10.00
579 Freddie Freeman 8.00 20.00
581 Tony Cingrani 5.00 12.00
597 Mat Latos 5.00 12.00
600 David Wright 15.00 40.00
613 Mark Teixeira 20.00 50.00
621 B.J. Upton 5.00 12.00
625 Albert Pujols 12.00 30.00
629 Cliff Lee 5.00 12.00
638 Michael Cuddyer 4.00 10.00
650 Jacoby Ellsbury 20.00 50.00
660 Jose Fernandez 6.00 15.00

2014 Topps Target Red Border

*TARGET RED VET: 1.2X TO 3X BASIC
*TARGET RED RC: .75X TO 2X BASIC RC
200 Derek Jeter 4.00 10.00

2014 Topps Toys R Us Purple Border

*TRU PURPLE VET: 4X TO 10X BASIC
*TRU PURPLE RC: 2.5X TO 6X BASIC RC
200 Derek Jeter 15.00 40.00

2014 Topps Wal-Mart Blue Border

*WALMART BLUE VET: 1.2X TO 3X BASIC
*WALMART BLUE RC: .75X TO 2X BASIC RC

2014 Topps Yellow

*YELLOW VET: 5X TO 12X BASIC
*YELLOW RC: 3X TO 8X BASIC RC
24 Manny Machado FS 8.00 20.00
42 Mariano Rivera 8.00 20.00
57 Yadier Molina 8.00 20.00
133 Xander Bogaerts 15.00 40.00
200 Derek Jeter 12.00 30.00
321 Mariano Rivera HL 8.00 20.00

2014 Topps '89 Topps Die Cut Mini Relics

SERIES ONE ODDS 1:19,275 HOBBY
SERIES TWO ODDS 1:9765 HOBBY
UPDATE ODDS 1:7334 HOBBY
STATED PRINT RUN 25 SER.#'d SETS
TMRAB Adrian Beltre S2 20.00 50.00
TMRAD Andre Dawson 15.00 40.00
TMRAM Andrew McCutchen UPD 20.00 50.00
TMRAR Alexei Ramirez UPD 15.00 40.00
TMRBH Bryce Harper S2 12.00 30.00
TMRBH Bryce Harper UPD 30.00 80.00
TMRBJ Bo Jackson 20.00 50.00
TMRCR Cal Ripken Jr. 75.00 150.00
TMRDM Don Mattingly 40.00 100.00
TMRDMU Dale Murphy 20.00 50.00
TMRDO David Ortiz S2 20.00 50.00
TMRFM Fred McGriff 15.00 40.00
TMRGM Greg Maddux 15.00 40.00
TMRGM Greg Maddux UPD 25.00 60.00
TMRIR Ivan Rodriguez UPD 15.00 40.00
TMRJH Jason Heyward UPD 15.00 40.00
TMRJR Jim Rice 15.00 40.00
TMRJV Joey Votto UPD 20.00 50.00
TMRMC Matt Cain UPD 15.00 40.00
TMRMM Mark McGwire S2 60.00 120.00
TMRMS Mike Schmidt 30.00 80.00
TMRMS Max Scherzer UPD 20.00 50.00
TMRSC Steve Carlton S2 15.00 40.00
TMRSM Shelby Miller S2 40.00 80.00
TMRTG Tom Glavine S2 15.00 40.00
TMRTG Tom Glavine 12.00 30.00
TMRTO Tony Gwynn 20.00 50.00
TMRTT Troy Tulowitzki S2 20.00 50.00
TMRVG Vladimir Guerrero UPD 15.00 40.00
TMRVM Victor Martinez UPD 15.00 40.00
TMRWB Wade Boggs 60.00 120.00
TMRYS Yangervis Solarte UPD 12.00 30.00
TMRBHA Billy Hamilton S2 15.00 40.00
TMRDJT Derek Jeter UPD 40.00 100.00
TMRGSP George Springer UPD 12.00 30.00
TMRGST Giancarlo Stanton UPD 20.00 50.00
TMRSMA Starling Marte S2 15.00 40.00

2014 Topps '89 Topps Die Cut Minis

STATED ODDS 1:8 HOBBY
TM1 Yasiel Puig .50 1.25
TM2 Clayton Kershaw 1.00 2.50
TM3 Fred Lynn .30 .75
TM4 Tony Gwynn .50 1.25
TM5 Tim Raines .40 1.00
TM6 Bo Jackson .50 1.25
TM7 Sandy Koufax 1.00 2.50
TM8 Babe Ruth 1.25 3.00
TM9 Nolan Ryan 1.50 4.00
TM10 Rickey Henderson .50 1.25
TM11 Fred McGriff .40 1.00
TM12 Lee Smith .30 .75
TM13 Don Mattingly 1.00 2.50
TM14 Wade Boggs .40 1.00
TM15 Andre Dawson .40 1.00
TM16 Mike Schmidt .75 2.00
TM17 Tom Glavine .40 1.00
TM18 George Brett 1.00 2.50
TM19 Lou Gehrig 1.00 2.50
TM20 Yogi Berra .50 1.25
TM21 Ted Williams 1.00 2.50
TM22 Jimmie Foxx .50 1.25
TM23 Roberto Clemente 1.25 3.00
TM24 Ozzie Smith .60 1.50
TM25 Greg Maddux .60 1.50
TM26 Jim Rice .40 1.00
TM27 Cal Ripken Jr. 1.50 4.00
TM28 Mike Trout 2.50 6.00
TM29 Josh Hamilton .40 1.00
TM30 Paul Goldschmidt .50 1.25
TM31 Manny Machado .50 1.25
TM32 Chris Davis .30 .75
TM33 Dustin Pedroia .50 1.25
TM34 David Ortiz .50 1.25
TM35 Ernie Banks .50 1.25
TM36 Randy Johnson .50 1.25
TM37 Joey Votto .50 1.25
TM38 Johnny Bench .50 1.25
TM39 Joe Morgan .40 1.00
TM40 Miguel Cabrera .50 1.25
TM41 Justin Verlander .50 1.25
TM42 Buster Posey .60 1.50
TM43 Joe Mauer .40 1.00

- TM44 Matt Harvey .40 1.00
- TM45 Felix Hernandez .40 1.00
- TM46 Andrew McCutchen .50 1.25
- TM47 Adam Wainwright .40 1.00
- TM48 Yu Darvish .50 1.25
- TM49 Bryce Harper .75 2.00
- TM50 Robinson Cano .40 1.00
- TM51 Ken Griffey Jr. 1.00 2.50
- TM52 Mariano Rivera .60 1.50
- TM53 Jose Canseco .40 1.00
- TM54 Steve Carlton .40 1.00
- TM55 Evan Longoria .40 1.00
- TM56 Troy Tulowitzki .50 1.25
- TM57 Deion Sanders .40 1.00
- TM58 Mark McGwire 1.00 2.50
- TM59 Chris Sale .50 1.25
- TM60 Shelby Miller .40 1.00
- TM61 Hanley Ramirez .40 1.00
- TM62 Billy Hamilton .40 1.00
- TM63 Juan Gonzalez .30 .75
- TM64 Nomar Garciaparra .40 1.00
- TM65 Ryan Braun .40 1.00
- TM66 Max Scherzer .50 1.25
- TM67 Freddie Freeman .60 1.50
- TM68 Adam Jones .40 1.00
- TM69 Giancarlo Stanton .50 1.25
- TM70 Starlin Castro .30 .75
- TM71 Jason Kipnis .40 1.00
- TM72 Cliff Lee .40 1.00
- TM73 Justin Upton .40 1.00
- TM74 Carlos Gonzalez .40 1.00
- TM75 Stephen Strasburg .50 1.25
- TM76 Jose Altuve .40 1.00
- TM77 Billy Butler .30 .75
- TM78 Ivan Rodriguez .40 1.00
- TM79 Albert Pujols .60 1.50
- TM80 Jose Fernandez .50 1.25
- TM81 Jean Segura .40 1.00
- TM82 Robin Yount .50 1.25
- TM83 David Wright .40 1.00
- TM84 Derek Jeter 1.25 3.00
- TM85 Yoenis Cespedes .50 1.25
- TM86 Domonic Brown .40 1.00
- TM87 Craig Kimbrel .40 1.00
- TM88 Matt Kemp .40 1.00
- TM89 Ryan Zimmerman .40 1.00
- TM90 Hyun-Jin Ryu .40 1.00
- TM91 Gerrit Cole .50 1.25
- TM92 Wil Myers .30 .75
- TM93 Prince Fielder .40 1.00
- TM94 Jose Bautista .40 1.00
- TM95 Jordan Zimmermann .40 1.00
- TM96 Mark Teixeira .40 1.00
- TM97 Darryl Strawberry .30 .75
- TM98 Ryne Sandberg 1.00 2.50
- TM99 Jorge Posada .40 1.00
- TMAB Adrian Beltre UPD .50 1.25
- TMAG Adrian Gonzalez UPD .40 1.00
- TMAJ Adam Jones UPD .40 1.00
- TMAM Andrew McCutchen UPD .50 1.25
- TMAR Alexei Ramirez UPD .40 1.00
- TMBB Billy Butler UPD .30 .75
- TMBH Bryce Harper UPD .75 2.00
- TMCB Clay Buchholz UPD .30 .75
- TMCD Chris Davis UPD .30 .75
- TMCG Carlos Gonzalez UPD .40 1.00
- TMDC David Cone UPD .30 .75
- TMDO David Ortiz UPD .50 1.25
- TMDW David Wright UPD .40 1.00
- TMEE Edwin Encarnacion UPD .50 1.25
- TMEL Evan Longoria UPD .40 1.00
- TMGM Greg Maddux UPD .60 1.50
- TMHK Hiroki Kuroda UPD .30 .75
- TMHR Hanley Ramirez UPD .40 1.00
- TMIK Ian Kinsler UPD .40 1.00
- TMIR Ivan Rodriguez UPD .40 1.00
- TMJA Jose Abreu UPD 2.50 6.00
- TMJC Jarred Cosart UPD .30 .75
- TMJE Jacoby Ellsbury UPD .40 1.00
- TMJF Jose Fernandez UPD .50 1.25
- TMJH Jason Heyward UPD .40 1.00
- TMJM Joe Mauer UPD .40 1.00
- TMJV Joey Votto UPD .50 1.25
- TMLG Luis Gonzalez UPD .30 .75
- TMOV Omar Vizquel UPD .40 1.00
- TMPF Prince Fielder UPD .40 1.00
- TMPG Paul Goldschmidt UPD .50 1.25
- TMRA Roberto Alomar UPD .40 1.00
- TMRB Ryan Braun UPD .40 1.00
- TMRC Robinson Cano UPD .40 1.00
- TMRH Roy Halladay UPD .40 1.00
- TMTT Troy Tulowitzki UPD .50 1.25
- TMVG Vladimir Guerrero UPD .40 1.00
- TMVM Victor Martinez UPD .40 1.00
- TMYD Yu Darvish UPD .50 1.25
- TMYS Yangervis Solarte UPD .30 .75
- TM100 Will Clark .40 1.00
- TMCKE Clayton Kershaw UPD 1.00 2.50
- TMCKI Craig Kimbrel UPD .40 1.00
- TMDJE Desmond Jennings UPD .40 1.00
- TMDJT Derek Jeter UPD 1.25 3.00
- TMGSP George Springer UPD 1.25 3.00
- TMGST Giancarlo Stanton UPD .50 1.25
- TMMCA Miguel Cabrera UPD .50 1.25
- TMMCI Matt Cain UPD .40 1.00
- TMMSC Max Scherzer UPD .50 1.25
- TMMST Mel Stottlemyre UPD .30 .75

2014 Topps 50 Years of the Draft

- COMPLETE SET (10) 5.00 12.00
- STATED ODDS 1:18 HOBBY
- 50YD1 Joe Mauer .40 1.00
- 50YD2 Gerrit Cole .50 1.25
- 50YD3 David Price .40 1.00
- 50YD4 Don Mattingly 1.00 2.50
- 50YD5 Adrian Gonzalez .40 1.00
- 50YD6 Josh Hamilton .40 1.00
- 50YD7 Derek Jeter 1.25 3.00
- 50YD8 Ken Griffey Jr. 1.00 2.50
- 50YD9 Darryl Strawberry .30 .75
- 50YD10 Johnny Bench .50 1.25

2014 Topps All Rookie Cup

- COMPLETE SET (10) 5.00 12.00
- STATED ODDS 1:18 HOBBY
- RCT1 Tom Seaver .40 1.00
- RCT2 Willie McCovey .40 1.00
- RCT3 Joe Morgan .40 1.00
- RCT4 Albert Pujols .60 1.50
- RCT5 Derek Jeter 1.25 3.00
- RCT6 Jim Rice .40 1.00
- RCT7 Mike Trout 2.50 6.00
- RCT8 Ken Griffey Jr. 1.00 2.50
- RCT9 Johnny Bench .50 1.25
- RCT10 CC Sabathia .40 1.00

2014 Topps All Rookie Cup Team Autograph Relics

- STATED ODDS 1:17,170 HOBBY
- STATED PRINT RUN 25 SER.#'d SETS
- EXCHANGE DEADLINE 1/31/2017
- RCTARCS CC Sabathia EXCH 25.00 60.00
- RCTARJR Jim Rice 25.00 60.00
- RCTARKG Ken Griffey Jr. 100.00 200.00
- RCTARMT Mike Trout 150.00 300.00

2014 Topps All Rookie Cup Team Autographs

- STATED ODDS 1:29,500 HOBBY
- STATED PRINT RUN 50 SER.#'d SETS
- EXCHANGE DEADLINE 1/31/2017
- RCTACS CC Sabathia 20.00 50.00
- RCTAJB Johnny Bench 25.00 60.00
- RCTAKG Ken Griffey Jr. 75.00 150.00
- RCTAMT Mike Trout 125.00 250.00

2014 Topps All Rookie Cup Team Commemorative

- STATED ODDS 1:10,700 HOBBY
- STATED PRINT RUN 99 SER.#'d SETS
- TARC1 Tom Seaver 15.00 40.00
- TARC2 Willie McCovey 10.00 25.00
- TARC3 Joe Morgan 10.00 25.00
- TARC4 Albert Pujols 15.00 40.00
- TARC5 Derek Jeter 25.00 60.00
- TARC6 Jim Rice 8.00 20.00
- TARC7 Mike Trout 12.00 30.00
- TARC8 Ken Griffey Jr. 30.00 60.00
- TARC9 Johnny Bench 10.00 25.00
- TARC10 CC Sabathia 8.00 20.00

2014 Topps All Rookie Cup Team Commemorative Vintage

- *VINTAGE: .75X TO 2X BASIC
- STATED ODDS 1:42,925 HOBBY
- STATED PRINT RUN 25 SER.#'d SETS
- TARC8 Ken Griffey Jr. 75.00 150.00

2014 Topps All Rookie Cup Team Relics

- STATED ODDS 1:14,750 HOBBY
- STATED PRINT RUN 99 SER.#'d SETS
- RCTRCK Craig Kimbrel 10.00 25.00
- RCTRCS CC Sabathia 8.00 20.00
- RCTRDJ Derek Jeter 15.00 40.00
- RCTRJB Johnny Bench 15.00 40.00
- RCTRJR Jim Rice 8.00 20.00

2014 Topps Before They Were Great

- COMPLETE SET (30) 40.00 100.00
- STATED ODDS 1:18 HOBBY
- BG1 Johnny Bench .60 1.50
- BG2 George Brett 1.25 3.00
- BG3 Nomar Garciaparra .50 1.25
- BG4 Bob Gibson .50 1.25
- BG5 Tom Glavine .50 1.25
- BG6 Ken Griffey Jr. 1.25 3.00
- BG7 Tony Gwynn .60 1.50
- BG8 Rickey Henderson .60 1.50
- BG9 Reggie Jackson .50 1.25
- BG10 Randy Johnson .60 1.50
- BG11 Sandy Koufax 1.25 3.00
- BG12 Greg Maddux .75 2.00
- BG13 Pedro Martinez .60 1.50
- BG14 Don Mattingly 1.25 3.00
- BG15 Willie Mays 1.25 3.00
- BG16 Mike Mussina .50 1.25
- BG17 Jim Rice .50 1.25
- BG18 Cal Ripken Jr. 2.00 5.00
- BG19 Nolan Ryan 2.00 5.00
- BG20 Mike Schmidt 1.00 2.50
- BG21 Steve Carlton .50 1.25
- BG22 Ted Williams 1.25 3.00
- BG23 Jimmie Foxx .60 1.50
- BG24 Roberto Clemente 1.50 4.00
- BG25 Ty Cobb 1.00 2.50
- BG26 Joe DiMaggio 1.25 3.00
- BG27 Tom Seaver .50 1.25
- BG28 Derek Jeter 1.50 4.00
- BG29 Miguel Cabrera .60 1.50
- BG30 Joe Morgan .50 1.25

2014 Topps Before They Were Great Gold

- *GOLD: 2X TO 5X BASIC
- STATED ODDS 1:715 HOBBY
- STATED PRINT RUN 99 SER.#'d SETS

2014 Topps Before They Were Great Relics

- STATED ODDS 1:3400 HOBBY
- STATED PRINT RUN 25 SER.#'d SETS
- EXCHANGE DEADLINE 1/31/2017
- BGRBG Bob Gibson 12.00 30.00
- BGRDJ Derek Jeter 30.00 60.00
- BGRGM Greg Maddux 20.00 50.00
- BGRJB Johnny Bench 15.00 40.00
- BGRJM Joe Morgan 12.00 30.00
- BGRJR Jim Rice 15.00 40.00
- BGRKG Ken Griffey Jr. 40.00 100.00
- BGRMC Miguel Cabrera 20.00 50.00
- BGRMM Mike Mussina 12.00 30.00
- BGRMS Mike Schmidt 10.00 25.00
- BGRNG Nomar Garciaparra 12.00 30.00
- BGRNR Nolan Ryan 40.00 80.00
- BGRPM Pedro Martinez 20.00 50.00
- BGRRC Roberto Clemente 75.00 150.00
- BGRRH Rickey Henderson 20.00 50.00
- BGRRJ Randy Johnson 15.00 40.00
- BGRRJA Reggie Jackson 20.00 50.00
- BGRSC Steve Carlton 12.00 30.00
- BGRTG Tom Glavine 12.00 30.00
- BGRTGW Tony Gwynn 20.00 50.00
- BGRTS Tom Seaver EXCH 12.00 30.00
- BGRTW Ted Williams 40.00 80.00
- BGRWM Willie Mays 40.00 80.00

2014 Topps Breakout Moments

- BM1 Buster Posey .75 2.00
- BM2 Luis Gonzalez .40 1.00
- BM3 Mark McGwire 1.25 3.00
- BM4 Tony Gwynn .60 1.50
- BM5 Zack Wheeler .50 1.25
- BM6 Jayson Werth .50 1.25
- BM7 Jean Segura .50 1.25
- BM8 Clayton Kershaw 1.25 3.00
- BM9 Max Scherzer .60 1.50
- BM10 James Shields .40 1.00
- BM11 Cal Ripken Jr. 2.00 5.00
- BM12 Ivan Rodriguez .50 1.25
- BM13 Adam Jones .50 1.25
- BM14 Wil Myers .40 1.00
- BM15 Tim Raines .50 1.25
- BM16 Randy Johnson .60 1.50
- BM17 Jeff Bagwell .50 1.25
- BM18 Bryce Harper 1.00 2.50
- BM19 Yoenis Cespedes .60 1.50
- BM20 Matt Harvey .50 1.25
- BM21 Shelby Miller .50 1.25
- BM22 Michael Wacha .50 1.25
- BM23 Derek Jeter 1.50 4.00
- BM24 Ken Griffey Jr. 1.25 3.00
- BM25 Robin Yount .60 1.50

2014 Topps Breakout Moments Relics

- STATED PRINT RUN 25 SER.#'d SETS
- BMRAJ Adam Jones 8.00 20.00
- BMRBP Buster Posey 12.00 30.00
- BMRCK Clayton Kershaw 40.00 80.00
- BMRCR Cal Ripken Jr. 30.00 80.00
- BMRJSH James Shields 6.00 15.00
- BMRMM Mark McGwire 20.00 50.00
- BMRYP Yasiel Puig 10.00 25.00
- BMRZW Zack Wheeler 6.00 15.00

2014 Topps Class Rings Gold

- *GOLD: .75X TO 2X BASIC
- SERIES ONE ODDS 1:4375 HOBBY
- SERIES TWO ODDS 1:2200 HOBBY
- STATED PRINT RUN 99 SER.#'d SETS
- CR3 Derek Jeter 20.00 50.00
- CR8 Lou Gehrig 12.00 30.00

2014 Topps Class Rings Gold Gems

- *GOLD GEMS: 2.5X TO 6X BASIC
- SERIES ONE ODDS 1:17,200 HOBBY
- SERIES TWO ODDS 1:9410 HOBBY
- STATED PRINT RUN 25 SER.#'d SETS
- CR3 Derek Jeter 60.00 150.00

2014 Topps Class Rings Silver

- SERIES ONE ODDS 1:610 HOBBY
- SERIES TWO ODDS 1:1050 HOBBY
- CR1 Sandy Koufax 6.00 15.00
- CR2 Willie Mays 6.00 15.00
- CR3 Derek Jeter 12.00 30.00
- CR4 Randy Johnson 4.00 10.00
- CR5 Ted Williams 4.00 10.00
- CR6 Ty Cobb 4.00 10.00
- CR7 Babe Ruth 6.00 15.00
- CR8 Lou Gehrig 6.00 15.00
- CR9 Roberto Clemente 6.00 15.00
- CR10 Yogi Berra 4.00 10.00
- CR11 Harmon Killebrew 4.00 10.00
- CR12 Reggie Jackson 3.00 8.00
- CR13 Cal Ripken Jr. 8.00 20.00
- CR14 Rickey Henderson 4.00 10.00
- CR15 Nolan Ryan 8.00 20.00
- CR16 George Brett 4.00 10.00
- CR17 Tony Gwynn 4.00 10.00
- CR18 Jackie Robinson 4.00 10.00
- CR19 Stan Musial 5.00 12.00
- CR20 Miguel Cabrera 4.00 10.00
- CR21 Mike Trout 10.00 25.00
- CR22 Bryce Harper 6.00 15.00
- CR23 Ken Griffey Jr. 8.00 20.00
- CR24 Clayton Kershaw 8.00 20.00
- CR25 Justin Verlander 4.00 10.00
- CR26 Mike Schmidt 6.00 15.00
- CR27 Tom Seaver 5.00 12.00
- CR28 Buster Posey 5.00 12.00
- CR29 Albert Pujols 5.00 12.00
- CR30 Greg Maddux 5.00 12.00
- CR31 Pedro Martinez 5.00 12.00
- CR32 Johnny Bench 5.00 12.00
- CR33 Steve Carlton 4.00 10.00
- CR34 Ivan Rodriguez 3.00 8.00
- CR35 Jeff Bagwell 4.00 10.00
- CR36 Robin Yount 4.00 10.00
- CR37 Deion Sanders 4.00 10.00
- CR38 Mark McGwire 6.00 15.00
- CR39 Rafael Palmeiro 4.00 10.00
- CR40 Jose Canseco 4.00 10.00
- CR41 Luis Gonzalez 4.00 10.00
- CR42 Juan Gonzalez 4.00 10.00
- CR43 Craig Biggio 4.00 10.00
- CR44 Andre Dawson 3.00 8.00
- CR45 Yoenis Cespedes 4.00 10.00
- CR46 Ozzie Smith 5.00 12.00
- CR47 Rod Carew 3.00 8.00
- CR48 Jim Palmer 3.00 8.00
- CR49 Eddie Murray 3.00 8.00
- CR50 Joe Morgan 3.00 8.00

2014 Topps Factory Set All-Star Game Exclusive

- AS1 Andrew McCutchen 4.00 10.00
- AS2 Derek Jeter 10.00 25.00
- AS3 Miguel Cabrera 4.00 10.00
- AS4 Joe Mauer 3.00 8.00
- AS5 Mike Trout 20.00 50.00

2014 Topps Factory Set Sandy Koufax Refractors

- *GOLD REF: .75X TO 2X BASIC
- 79 Sandy Koufax 6.00 15.00
  1956 Topps
- 187 Sandy Koufax 6.00 15.00
  1958 Topps
- 302 Sandy Koufax 6.00 15.00
  1957 Topps

2014 Topps Factory Set Ted Williams Refractors

- *GOLD REF: .75X TO 2X BASIC
- 1 Ted Williams 6.00 15.00
  1954 Topps
- 66 Ted Williams 6.00 15.00
  1954 Bowman
- 165 Ted Williams 6.00 15.00
  1951 Bowman

2014 Topps Future Stars That Never Were

- STATED ODDS 1:18 HOBBY
- FS1 Mike Schmidt 2.50 6.00
- FS2 Jose Canseco 1.25 3.00
- FS3 Eddie Murray 1.25 3.00
- FS4 Robin Yount 1.50 4.00
- FS5 Ozzie Smith 2.00 5.00
- FS6 Joey Votto 1.50 4.00
- FS7 Buster Posey 2.00 5.00
- FS8 Evan Longoria 1.25 3.00
- FS9 Jeff Bagwell 1.25 3.00
- FS10 Mike Trout 8.00 20.00
- FS11 Bryce Harper 2.50 6.00
- FS12 Yoenis Cespedes 1.50 4.00
- FS13 Mark McGwire 3.00 8.00
- FS14 Randy Johnson 1.50 4.00
- FS15 Hank Aaron 3.00 8.00
- FS16 Willie Mays 3.00 8.00
- FS17 Sandy Koufax 3.00 8.00
- FS18 Greg Maddux 2.00 5.00
- FS19 Steve Carlton 1.25 3.00
- FS20 Chris Sale 1.50 4.00
- FS21 Willie Stargell 1.25 3.00
- FS22 R.A. Dickey 1.25 3.00
- FS23 Tony Gwynn 1.50 4.00
- FS24 Rickey Henderson 1.50 4.00
- FS25 Ken Griffey Jr. 3.00 8.00
- FS26 Stephen Strasburg 1.50 4.00
- FS27 Wade Boggs 1.25 3.00
- FS28 Darryl Strawberry 1.00 2.50
- FS29 Don Mattingly 3.00 8.00
- FS30 George Brett 3.00 8.00

2014 Topps Future Stars That Never Were Gold

- *GOLD: 1X TO 2.5X BASIC
- STATED ODDS 1:387 HOBBY
- STATED PRINT RUN 99 SER.#'d SETS

2014 Topps Future Stars That Never Were Relics

- STATED ODDS 1:1848 HOBBY
- STATED PRINT RUN 25 SER.#'d SETS
- FSRBH Bryce Harper 20.00 50.00
- FSRBP Buster Posey 50.00 100.00
- FSRCS Chris Sale 10.00 25.00
- FSRDM Don Mattingly 50.00 100.00
- FSRDS Darryl Strawberry 15.00 40.00
- FSREL Evan Longoria 8.00 20.00
- FSRGM Greg Maddux 12.00 30.00
- FSRJB Jeff Bagwell 12.00 30.00
- FSRJC Jose Canseco 15.00 40.00
- FSRJS John Smoltz 15.00 40.00
- FSRJV Joey Votto 15.00 40.00
- FSRKG Ken Griffey Jr. 40.00 80.00
- FSRMM Mark McGwire 50.00 100.00
- FSRMS Mike Schmidt 15.00 40.00
- FSRMT Mike Trout 50.00 100.00
- FSRPO Paul O'Neill 8.00 20.00
- FSRRD R.A. Dickey 8.00 20.00
- FSRRH Rickey Henderson 20.00 50.00
- FSRRY Robin Yount 30.00 60.00
- FSRSC Steve Carlton 15.00 40.00
- FSRSS Stephen Strasburg 10.00 25.00
- FSRTG Tony Gwynn 20.00 50.00
- FSRWB Wade Boggs 40.00 80.00
- FSRYC Yoenis Cespedes 10.00 25.00

2014 Topps Gold Label

- STATED ODDS 1:575 HOBBY
- UPDATE ODDS 1:1005 HOBBY
- STATED PRINT RUN 99 SER.#'d SETS
- GL1 Greg Maddux 10.00 25.00
- GL2 Rickey Henderson 8.00 20.00
- GL3 Albert Pujols 10.00 25.00
- GL4 Mike Schmidt 12.00 30.00
- GL5 Joe Morgan 15.00 40.00
- GL6 Randy Johnson 8.00 20.00
- GL7 Tom Seaver 10.00 25.00
- GL8 Steve Carlton 8.00 20.00
- GL9 Johnny Bench 8.00 20.00
- GL10 George Brett 15.00 40.00
- GL11 Cal Ripken Jr. 20.00 50.00
- GL12 Derek Jeter 40.00 80.00
- GL13 Roberto Clemente 20.00 50.00
- GL14 Ken Griffey Jr. 15.00 40.00
- GL15 Nolan Ryan 30.00 60.00
- GL16 Mike Trout 40.00 100.00
- GL17 Andrew McCutchen 15.00 40.00
- GL18 Miguel Cabrera 8.00 20.00
- GL19 Clayton Kershaw 15.00 40.00
- GL20 Joey Votto 15.00 40.00
- GL21 Max Scherzer 8.00 20.00
- GL22 Manny Machado 8.00 20.00
- GL23 Felix Hernandez 6.00 15.00
- GL24 Dustin Pedroia 8.00 20.00
- GL25 Robinson Cano 6.00 15.00
- GL26 Derek Jeter UPD 20.00 50.00
- GL27 Mike Trout UPD 40.00 100.00
- GL28 Bryce Harper UPD 20.00 50.00
- GL29 Prince Fielder UPD 6.00 15.00
- GL30 Andrew McCutchen UPD 8.00 20.00
- GL31 Miguel Cabrera UPD 12.00 30.00
- GL32 Yasiel Puig UPD 8.00 20.00
- GL33 Albert Pujols UPD 12.00 30.00
- GL34 Frank Thomas UPD 8.00 20.00
- GL35 Jose Abreu UPD 20.00 50.00
- GL36 Masahiro Tanaka UPD 20.00 50.00
- GL37 Sandy Koufax UPD 15.00 40.00
- GL38 Mark McGwire UPD 15.00 40.00
- GL39 Roberto Clemente UPD 10.00 25.00
- GL40 Cal Ripken Jr. UPD 20.00 50.00

2014 Topps Jackie Robinson Reprints Framed Black

- COMMON CARD 8.00 20.00
- STATED ODDS 1:2844 HOBBY

2014 Topps Jackie Robinson Reprints Framed Silver

- *SILVER: .5X TO 1.2X BASIC
- STATED ODDS 1:4750 HOBBY
- STATED PRINT RUN 50 SER.#'d SETS

2014 Topps Manufactured Commemorative All Rookie Cup Patch

- RCMPAM Andrew McCutchen 2.50 6.00
- RCMPAP Albert Pujols 3.00 8.00
- RCMPBP Buster Posey 3.00 8.00
- RCMPCR Cal Ripken Jr. 8.00 20.00
- RCMPDJ Derek Jeter 6.00 15.00
- RCMPDS Darryl Strawberry 1.50 4.00
- RCMPEM Eddie Murray 2.00 5.00
- RCMPGC Gary Carter 2.00 5.00
- RCMPJB Johnny Bench 2.50 6.00
- RCMPJBA Jeff Bagwell 2.00 5.00
- RCMPJC Jose Canseco 2.00 5.00
- RCMPJM Joe Morgan 2.00 5.00
- RCMPJV Joey Votto 2.50 6.00
- RCMPJVE Justin Verlander 2.50 6.00
- RCMPKG Ken Griffey Jr. 5.00 12.00
- RCMPMM Mark McGwire 5.00 12.00
- RCMPMR Manny Ramirez 2.50 6.00
- RCMPMT Mike Trout 12.00 30.00
- RCMPOS Ozzie Smith 3.00 8.00
- RCMPRC Rod Carew 2.00 5.00
- RCMPSS Stephen Strasburg 2.50 6.00
- RCMPTS Tom Seaver 2.00 5.00
- RCMPTT Troy Tulowitzki 2.50 6.00
- RCMPWM Willie McCovey 2.00 5.00
- RCMPYP Yasiel Puig 2.50 6.00

2014 Topps Manufactured Commemorative Team Logo Patch

- CP1 Chris Davis 2.50 6.00
- CP2 David Ortiz 4.00 10.00
- CP3 Prince Fielder 3.00 8.00
- CP4 Miguel Cabrera 4.00 10.00
- CP5 Allen Craig 3.00 8.00
- CP6 Bryce Harper 6.00 15.00
- CP7 Mike Trout 20.00 50.00
- CP8 Joe Mauer 3.00 8.00
- CP9 Mariano Rivera 5.00 12.00
- CP10 Derek Jeter 10.00 25.00
- CP11 Felix Hernandez 3.00 8.00
- CP12 David Price 3.00 8.00
- CP13 Yu Darvish 4.00 10.00
- CP14 Jose Bautista 3.00 8.00
- CP15 Stephen Strasburg 4.00 10.00
- CP16 Troy Tulowitzki 4.00 10.00
- CP17 Yasiel Puig 4.00 10.00
- CP18 Clayton Kershaw 8.00 20.00
- CP19 Jose Fernandez 4.00 10.00
- CP20 Anthony Rizzo 6.00 15.00
- CP21 Matt Harvey 3.00 8.00
- CP22 David Wright 3.00 8.00
- CP23 Chase Utley 3.00 8.00
- CP24 Buster Posey 5.00 12.00
- CP25 Adam Wainwright 3.00 8.00
- CP26 Chris Davis 2.50 6.00
- CP27 David Ortiz 4.00 10.00
- CP28 Chris Sale 4.00 10.00
- CP29 Paul Goldschmidt 4.00 10.00
- CP30 Freddie Freeman 5.00 12.00
- CP31 Starlin Castro 2.50 6.00
- CP32 Mike Trout 20.00 50.00
- CP33 Jean Segura 3.00 8.00
- CP34 Joe Mauer 3.00 8.00
- CP35 Yoenis Cespedes 4.00 10.00
- CP36 Domonic Brown 3.00 8.00
- CP37 Jedd Gyorko 2.50 6.00
- CP38 Buster Posey 5.00 12.00
- CP39 Evan Longoria 3.00 8.00
- CP40 David Wright 3.00 8.00
- CP41 Jason Kipnis 3.00 8.00
- CP42 Troy Tulowitzki 4.00 10.00
- CP43 Jose Altuve 3.00 8.00
- CP44 Alex Gordon 3.00 8.00
- CP45 Hyun-Jin Ryu 3.00 8.00
- CP46 Giancarlo Stanton 4.00 10.00
- CP47 Andrew McCutchen 4.00 10.00
- CP48 Felix Hernandez 3.00 8.00
- CP49 Ryan Braun 3.00 8.00
- CP50 Joey Votto 4.00 10.00

2014 Topps Manufactured Commemorative Rookie Card Patch

- RCP1 Al Kaline 1.50 4.00
- RCP2 Ernie Banks 1.50 4.00
- RCP3 Sandy Koufax 3.00 8.00
- RCP4 Harmon Killebrew 1.50 4.00
- RCP5 Roberto Clemente 4.00 10.00
- RCP6 Bill Mazeroski 1.25 3.00
- RCP7 Frank Robinson 1.25 3.00
- RCP8 Brooks Robinson 1.25 3.00
- RCP9 George Brett 3.00 8.00
- RCP10 Robin Yount 1.50 4.00
- RCP11 Wade Boggs 1.25 3.00
- RCP12 Ryne Sandberg 3.00 8.00
- RCP13 Tony Gwynn 1.50 4.00
- RCP14 Greg Maddux 2.00 5.00
- RCP15 Bryce Harper 2.50 6.00
- RCP16 Yu Darvish 1.50 4.00
- RCP17 Yoenis Cespedes 1.50 4.00
- RCP18 Matt Harvey 1.25 3.00
- RCP19 Don Mattingly 3.00 8.00
- RCP20 Dwight Gooden 1.00 2.50
- RCP21 Randy Johnson 1.50 4.00
- RCP22 Clayton Kershaw 3.00 8.00
- RCP23 Joey Votto 1.50 4.00
- RCP25 John Smoltz 1.50 4.00

2014 Topps Postseason Performance Autograph Relics

- STATED ODDS 1:4250 HOBBY
- STATED PRINT RUN 50 SER.#'d SETS
- EXCHANGE DEADLINE 1/31/2017
- PPARAS Anibal Sanchez EXCH 20.00 50.00
- PPARCK Clayton Kershaw 60.00 150.00
- PPARDO David Ortiz 60.00 150.00
- PPAREL Evan Longoria 10.00 25.00
- PPARMC Miguel Cabrera 60.00 150.00
- PPARMH Matt Holliday EXCH 40.00 100.00
- PPARMW Michael Wacha 100.00 200.00
- PPARWM Wil Myers 8.00 20.00
- PPARYC Yoenis Cespedes 12.00 30.00
- PPARYP Yasiel Puig EXCH 75.00 200.00

2014 Topps Postseason Performance Autographs

- STATED ODDS 1:14,250 HOBBY
- STATED PRINT RUN 50 SER.#'d SETS
- EXCHANGE DEADLINE 1/31/2017
- PPAAS Anibal Sanchez EXCH 12.00 30.00
- PPACK Clayton Kershaw 75.00 150.00
- PPADF David Freese 40.00 80.00
- PPADO David Ortiz EXCH 75.00 150.00
- PPAFF Freddie Freeman 30.00 60.00
- PPAMH Matt Holliday EXCH 30.00 60.00
- PPAMW Michael Wacha 60.00 120.00
- PPAWM Wil Myers 12.00 30.00
- PPAYC Yoenis Cespedes 40.00 80.00

2014 Topps Postseason Performance Relics

- STATED ODDS 1:2900 HOBBY
- STATED PRINT RUN 100 SER.#'d SETS
- EXCHANGE DEADLINE 1/31/2017
- PPRAM Andrew McCutchen 12.00 30.00
- PPRAS Anibal Sanchez 15.00 40.00
- PPRCK Clayton Kershaw 10.00 25.00
- PPRCKI Craig Kimbrel 10.00 25.00
- PPRDF David Freese 10.00 25.00
- PPRDO David Ortiz 12.00 30.00
- PPRDP Dustin Pedroia 15.00 40.00
- PPREL Evan Longoria 6.00 15.00
- PPRFF Freddie Freeman 20.00 50.00
- PPRHR Hanley Ramirez 12.00 30.00
- PPRJE Jacoby Ellsbury 8.00 20.00
- PPRJU Justin Upton 12.00 30.00
- PPRJV Justin Verlander 8.00 20.00
- PPRMC Miguel Cabrera 20.00 50.00
- PPRMH Matt Holliday 20.00 50.00
- PPRMW Michael Wacha 15.00 40.00
- PPRPA Pedro Alvarez 15.00 40.00
- PPRPF Prince Fielder 12.00 30.00
- PPRVM Victor Martinez 12.00 30.00
- PPRWMY Wil Myers 15.00 40.00
- PPRXB Xander Bogaerts 40.00 80.00
- PPRYC Yoenis Cespedes 12.00 30.00
- PPRYM Yadier Molina 50.00 100.00
- PPRYP Yasiel Puig 20.00 50.00
- PPRZG Zack Greinke 10.00 25.00

2014 Topps Power Players

- STATED ODDS 1:12 HOBBY
- PP1 Bryce Harper 1.50 4.00
- PP2 Cole Hamels .75 2.00
- PP3 Wade Miley .60 1.50
- PP4 Troy Tulowitzki 1.00 2.50
- PP5 Andrew McCutchen 1.00 2.50
- PP6 Nick Swisher .75 2.00
- PP7 Aaron Hill .60 1.50
- PP8 Alex Rios .75 2.00
- PP9 Ernesto Frieri .60 1.50
- PP10 Ben Revere .60 1.50
- PP11 Chris Tillman .60 1.50
- PP12 Clay Buchholz .60 1.50
- PP13 Charlie Blackmon 1.00 2.50
- PP14 Garrett Jones .60 1.50
- PP15 Garrett Richards .75 2.00
- PP16 Lonnie Chisenhall .60 1.50
- PP17 Kolten Wong .75 2.00
- PP18 Chris Perez .60 1.50
- PP19 Matt Adams .60 1.50
- PP20 Jason Heyward .75 2.00
- PP21 Doug Fister .60 1.50
- PP22 Jose Quintana .60 1.50
- PP23 Mike Minor .60 1.50
- PP24 Matt Holliday 1.00 2.50
- PP25 Lance Lynn .60 1.50
- PP26 Jon Lester .75 2.00
- PP27 Onelki Garcia .60 1.50
- PP28 Giancarlo Stanton 1.00 2.50
- PP29 Kevin Pillar .60 1.50
- PP30 Chad Bettis .60 1.50
- PP31 Joe Blanton .60 1.50
- PP32 Jason Kipnis .75 2.00
- PP33 Ian Desmond .60 1.50
- PP34 Adam LaRoche .60 1.50
- PP35 David Freese .60 1.50
- PP36 Martin Perez .75 2.00
- PP37 Chris Iannetta .60 1.50
- PP38 Sean Burnett .60 1.50
- PP39 Adrian Gonzalez .75 2.00
- PP40 Manny Machado 1.00 2.50
- PP41 Matt Lindstrom .60 1.50
- PP42 Matt Thornton .60 1.50
- PP43 Trevor Cahill .60 1.50
- PP44 Junior Lake .60 1.50
- PP45 Johnny Cueto .75 2.00
- PP46 Wei-Yin Chen .60 1.50
- PP47 Carlos Villanueva .60 1.50
- PP48 Max Scherzer 1.00 2.50
- PP49 C.J. Wilson .60 1.50
- PP50 Chris Owings .60 1.50
- PP51 Shin-Soo Choo .75 2.00
- PP52 Yadier Molina 1.00 2.50
- PP53 Yonder Alonso .60 1.50
- PP54 Ryan Howard .75 2.00
- PP55 Jason Grilli .60 1.50
- PP56 Zack Greinke .75 2.00
- PP57 Justin Upton .75 2.00
- PP58 Chris Sale 1.00 2.50
- PP59 Yu Darvish 1.00 2.50
- PP60 Carlos Gomez .60 1.50
- PP61 Joey Votto 1.00 2.50
- PP62 Pablo Sandoval .75 2.00
- PP63 Matt Davidson .75 2.00
- PP64 Jordan Zimmermann .75 2.00
- PP65 Ethan Martin .60 1.50
- PP66 Brandon McCarthy .60 1.50
- PP67 Cliff Pennington .60 1.50
- PP68 Torii Hunter .60 1.50
- PP69 Dustin Pedroia 1.00 2.50
- PP70 Mark Trumbo .60 1.50
- PP71 Mike Zunino .60 1.50
- PP72 Michael Brantley .75 2.00
- PP73 Paul Goldschmidt 1.00 2.50
- PP74 Erik Johnson .60 1.50
- PP75 Marcell Ozuna 1.00 2.50
- PP76 Mike Leake .60 1.50
- PP77 Derek Jeter 2.50 6.00
- PP78 Jake Peavy .60 1.50
- PP79 Shane Victorino .75 2.00
- PP80 Aroldis Chapman 1.00 2.50
- PP81 Miguel Montero .60 1.50
- PP82 Julio Teheran .75 2.00
- PP83 Wilmer Flores .75 2.00
- PP84 Alexei Ramirez .75 2.00
- PP85 Melky Cabrera .60 1.50
- PP86 Jhonny Peralta .60 1.50
- PP87 Dayan Viciedo .60 1.50
- PP88 Hiroki Kuroda .60 1.50
- PP89 Brandon Belt .75 2.00
- PP90 Brandon Crawford .75 2.00
- PP91 Hector Santiago .60 1.50
- PP92 Elvis Andrus .75 2.00
- PP93 Jeff Samardzija .60 1.50
- PP94 Kyle Lohse .60 1.50
- PP95 James Shields .60 1.50
- PP96 Darwin Barney .60 1.50
- PP97 Nate McLouth .60 1.50
- PP98 Tyler Skaggs .60 1.50
- PP99 Jay Bruce .75 2.00
- PP100 Hanley Ramirez .75 2.00
- PP101 Brian McCann .75 2.00
- PP102 Jurickson Profar .75 2.00
- PP103 Jose Altuve .75 2.00
- PP104 Joe Mauer .75 2.00
- PP105 Carlos Ruiz .60 1.50
- PP106 Edwin Encarnacion 1.00 2.50
- PP107 Sergio Romo .60 1.50
- PP108 Buster Posey 1.25 3.00

PP109 James Paxton 1.00 2.50
PP110 Chris Nelson .60 1.50
PP111 Matt Kemp .75 2.00
PP112 David Price .75 2.00
PP113 Evan Gattis .60 1.50
PP114 Nelson Cruz 1.00 2.50
PP115 Patrick Corbin .75 2.00
PP116 Colby Rasmus .75 2.00
PP117 Adam Wainwright .75 2.00
PP118 Brad Miller .75 2.00
PP119 Shelby Miller .75 2.00
PP120 Koji Uehara .60 1.50
PP121 Michael Bourn .60 1.50
PP122 Brad Ziegler .60 1.50
PP123 Scott Kazmir .60 1.50
PP124 Trevor Bauer 1.00 2.50
PP125 Aramis Ramirez .60 1.50
PP126 Jackie Bradley Jr. 1.00 2.50
PP127 Addison Reed .60 1.50
PP128 Ben Zobrist .75 2.00
PP129 Carlos Martinez .75 2.00
PP130 Martin Prado .60 1.50
PP131 Adam Eaton .60 1.50
PP132 Todd Frazier .75 2.00
PP133 Derek Holland .60 1.50
PP134 Carlos Santana .75 2.00
PP135 Marcus Semien .60 1.50
PP136 Masahiro Tanaka 4.00 10.00
PP137 Ryan Braun .75 2.00
PP138 Brandon Phillips .60 1.50
PP139 Ian Kennedy .60 1.50
PP140 Danny Salazar .75 2.00
PP141 CC Sabathia .75 2.00
PP142 Christian Yelich 1.25 3.00
PP143 Mat Latos .75 2.00
PP144 Stephen Strasburg 1.00 2.50
PP145 Ian Kinsler .75 2.00
PP146 Kyuji Fujikawa .75 2.00
PP147 Drew Storen .60 1.50
PP148 Mike Napoli .60 1.50
PP149 Prince Fielder .75 2.00
PP150 David Wright .75 2.00
PP151 Matt Cain .75 2.00
PP152 Justin Verlander 1.00 2.50
PP153 Jose Fernandez 1.00 2.50
PP154 Tim Hudson .75 2.00
PP155 Josh Reddick .60 1.50
PP156 Starlin Castro .60 1.50
PP157 Carlos Beltran .75 2.00
PP158 Ryan Zimmerman .75 2.00
PP159 Adam Dunn .75 2.00
PP160 Jose Reyes .75 2.00
PP161 Norichika Aoki .60 1.50
PP162 Albert Pujols 1.25 3.00
PP163 Wilin Rosario .60 1.50
PP164 Brian Wilson 1.00 2.50
PP165 Peter Bourjos .60 1.50
PP166 Jed Lowrie .60 1.50
PP167 Cliff Lee .75 2.00
PP168 Anthony Rendon 1.00 2.50
PP169 Freddie Freeman 1.25 3.00
PP170 Yovani Gallardo .60 1.50
PP171 Phil Hughes .60 1.50
PP172 Allen Craig .75 2.00
PP173 Gerardo Parra .60 1.50
PP174 Adam Jones .75 2.00
PP175 Jedd Gyorko .60 1.50
PP176 Chris Archer .60 1.50
PP177 Paul Konerko .75 2.00
PP178 Mike Moustakas .75 2.00
PP179 Chase Headley .60 1.50
PP180 Tim Lincecum .75 2.00
PP181 Dan Uggla .60 1.50
PP182 Corey Hart .60 1.50
PP183 Sonny Gray .75 2.00
PP184 Dylan Bundy .75 2.00
PP185 Jarrod Parker .60 1.50
PP186 Gio Gonzalez .75 2.00
PP187 J.J. Hardy .60 1.50
PP188 Michael Cuddyer .60 1.50
PP189 Madison Bumgarner .75 2.00
PP190 Rick Porcello .75 2.00
PP191 Salvador Perez .75 2.00
PP192 Ivan Nova .75 2.00
PP193 Jose Iglesias .75 2.00
PP194 Jacoby Ellsbury .75 2.00
PP195 Bartolo Colon .60 1.50
PP196 Carl Crawford .75 2.00
PP197 Christian Bethancourt .60 1.50
PP198 Matt Garza .60 1.50
PP199 Matt Moore .75 2.00
PP200 Clayton Kershaw 2.00 5.00
PP201 Mark Teixeira .75 2.00
PP202 Tony Cingrani .75 2.00
PP203 Hunter Pence .75 2.00
PP204 Michael Wacha .75 2.00
PP205 Curtis Granderson .75 2.00
PP206 Joe Nathan .60 1.50
PP207 B.J. Upton .75 2.00
PP208 Michael Pineda .60 1.50
PP209 Chris Davis .60 1.50
PP210 Andre Ethier .75 2.00
PP211 Jered Weaver .75 2.00
PP212 Brandon Beachy .60 1.50
PP213 Alex Wood .60 1.50
PP214 Felix Hernandez .75 2.00
PP215 Josh Hamilton .75 2.00
PP216 Homer Bailey .60 1.50
PP217 Glen Perkins .60 1.50
PP218 Chase Utley .75 2.00
PP219 Eric Hosmer .75 2.00
PP220 Jose Abreu 3.00 8.00

2014 Topps Power Players Autographs

UPDATE ODDS 1:7334 HOBBY
PRINT RUNS B/WN 15-40 COPIES PER
NO PRICING ON QTY 15
UPD EXCH DEADLINE 9/30/2017
PPAAG Adrian Gonzalez/25 UPD 50.00 100.00
PPAAJ Adam Jones/25 UPD 25.00 60.00
PPAAM A.McCutchen/25 UPD 60.00 120.00
PPAAR Anthony Rizzo/25 UPD 30.00 80.00
PPAGS Giancarlo Stanton/25 UPD 20.00 50.00
PPAJA J.Abreu/25 UPD EXCH 100.00 200.00
PPAJB Jose Bautista/25 UPD 15.00 40.00
PPAJL Junior Lake/40 12.00 30.00
PPAMS Max Scherzer/25 UPD 30.00 80.00
PPAPG Paul Goldschmidt/25 UPD 20.00 50.00
PPARC Robinson Cano/25 UPD 15.00 40.00
PPATT Troy Tulowitzki/25 UPD 20.00 50.00
PPAYV Yordano Ventura/25 UPD 15.00 40.00
PPACGN Carlos Gonzalez/25 UPD 15.00 40.00

2014 Topps Rookie Cup All Stars Commemorative

STATED ODDS 1:4375 HOBBY
STATED PRINT RUN 99 SER.#'d SETS
RCAS1 Cal Ripken Jr. 25.00 60.00
RCAS2 Tony Perez 12.00 30.00
RCAS3 Rod Carew 10.00 25.00
RCAS4 Carlton Fisk 10.00 25.00
RCAS5 Gary Carter 12.50 30.00
RCAS6 Andre Dawson 8.00 20.00
RCAS7 Paul Molitor 10.00 25.00
RCAS8 Ozzie Smith 10.00 25.00
RCAS9 Ryne Sandberg 12.00 30.00
RCAS10 Darryl Strawberry 8.00 20.00
RCAS11 Dwight Gooden 8.00 20.00
RCAS12 Nomar Garciaparra 10.00 25.00
RCAS13 Joe Mauer 12.50 30.00
RCAS14 Justin Verlander 8.00 20.00
RCAS15 Troy Tulowitzki 8.00 20.00
RCAS16 Ryan Braun 6.00 15.00
RCAS17 Dustin Pedroia 12.00 30.00
RCAS18 Joey Votto 8.00 20.00
RCAS19 Evan Longoria 6.00 15.00
RCAS20 Andrew McCutchen 12.00 30.00
RCAS21 Buster Posey 10.00 25.00
RCAS22 Stephen Strasburg 8.00 20.00
RCAS23 Bryce Harper 12.00 30.00
RCAS24 Yu Darvish 10.00 25.00
RCAS25 Fred Lynn 10.00 25.00

2014 Topps Rookie Cup All Stars Commemorative Vintage

*VINTAGE: .6X TO 1.5X BASIC
STATED ODDS 1:17,200 HOBBY
STATED PRINT RUN 25 SER.#'d SETS

2014 Topps Rookie Reprints Framed Black

STATED ODDS 1:428 HOBBY
STATED PRINT RUN 199 SER.#'d SETS
RCF1 Willie Mays 12.00 30.00
RCF2 Ernie Banks 10.00 25.00
RCF3 Sandy Koufax 12.00 30.00
RCF4 Roberto Clemente 12.00 30.00
RCF5 Brooks Robinson 8.00 20.00
RCF6 Frank Robinson 8.00 20.00
RCF7 Bob Gibson 8.00 20.00
RCF8 Willie McCovey 8.00 20.00
RCF9 Reggie Jackson 8.00 20.00
RCF10 Robin Yount 10.00 25.00
RCF11 George Brett 10.00 25.00
RCF12 Eddie Murray 8.00 20.00
RCF13 Ozzie Smith 10.00 25.00
RCF14 Rickey Henderson 10.00 25.00
RCF15 Cal Ripken Jr. 15.00 40.00
RCF16 Tony Gwynn 8.00 20.00
RCF17 Wade Boggs 8.00 20.00
RCF18 Don Mattingly 10.00 25.00
RCF19 Ken Griffey Jr. 10.00 25.00
RCF20 Derek Jeter 15.00 40.00
RCF21 Miguel Cabrera 10.00 25.00
RCF22 Justin Verlander 10.00 25.00
RCF23 Buster Posey 10.00 25.00
RCF24 Mike Trout 15.00 40.00
RCF25 Bryce Harper 15.00 40.00

2014 Topps Rookie Reprints Framed Gold

*GOLD: 1X TO 2.5X BASIC
STATED ODDS 1:3400 HOBBY
STATED PRINT RUN 25 SER.#'d SETS
RCF1 Willie Mays 75.00 150.00
RCF8 Willie McCovey 30.00 80.00
RCF9 Reggie Jackson 75.00 150.00
RCF14 Rickey Henderson 75.00 150.00
RCF15 Cal Ripken Jr. 60.00 120.00
RCF19 Ken Griffey Jr. 90.00 150.00
RCF20 Derek Jeter 100.00 200.00
RCF23 Buster Posey 90.00 150.00
RCF24 Mike Trout 90.00 150.00
RCF25 Bryce Harper 90.00 150.00

2014 Topps Rookie Reprints Framed Silver

*SILVER: .5X TO 1.2X BASIC
STATED ODDS 1:859 HOBBY
STATED PRINT RUN 99 SER.#'d SETS

2014 Topps Saber Stars

COMPLETE SET (25) 5.00 12.00
STATED ODDS 1:8 HOBBY
SST1 Mike Trout 2.00 5.00
SST2 Clayton Kershaw .75 2.00
SST3 Carlos Gomez .25 .60
SST4 Andrew McCutchen .40 1.00
SST5 Josh Donaldson .30 .75
SST6 Matt Carpenter .40 1.00
SST7 Robinson Cano .30 .75
SST8 Miguel Cabrera .40 1.00
SST9 Paul Goldschmidt .40 1.00
SST10 Evan Longoria .30 .75
SST11 Joe Mauer .30 .75
SST12 Michael Cuddyer .25 .60
SST13 Chris Davis .25 .60
SST14 Joey Votto .40 1.00
SST15 Freddie Freeman .50 1.25
SST16 Allen Craig .30 .75
SST17 Jacoby Ellsbury .30 .75
SST18 Juan Uribe .25 .60
SST19 Manny Machado .40 1.00
SST20 Shane Victorino .30 .75
SST21 Andrelton Simmons .25 .60
SST22 Matt Harvey .30 .75
SST23 Anibal Sanchez .25 .60
SST24 Adam Wainwright .30 .75
SST25 Felix Hernandez .30 .75

2014 Topps Saber Stars Autograph Relics

STATED ODDS 1:4620 HOBBY
STATED PRINT RUN 25 SER.#'d SETS
EXCHANGE DEADLINE 5/31/2017
SSTARAC Allen Craig 15.00 40.00
SSTARAS Andrelton Simmons EXCH 12.00 30.00
SSTARCK Clayton Kershaw 60.00 150.00
SSTAREL Evan Longoria 20.00 50.00
SSTARJV Joey Votto 40.00 100.00
SSTARMC Michael Cuddyer 12.00 30.00
SSTARMCA Miguel Cabrera 150.00 250.00
SSTARMM Manny Machado 60.00 150.00
SSTARMT Mike Trout EXCH 150.00 300.00
SSTARPG Paul Goldschmidt 20.00 50.00

2014 Topps Saber Stars Autographs

STATED ODDS 1:7290 HOBBY
STATED PRINT RUN 50 SER.#'d SETS
EXCHANGE DEADLINE 5/31/2017
SSTAAC Allen Craig 20.00 50.00
SSTAAS Andrelton Simmons EXCH 10.00 25.00
SSTACK Clayton Kershaw 60.00 150.00
SSTAEL Evan Longoria EXCH 12.00 30.00
SSTAFF Freddie Freeman 20.00 50.00
SSTAJV Joey Votto 20.00 50.00
SSTAMC Michael Cuddyer 10.00 25.00
SSTAMM Manny Machado 15.00 40.00
SSTAMT Mike Trout 150.00 250.00
SSTAPG Paul Goldschmidt 15.00 40.00

2014 Topps Saber Stars Relics

STATED ODDS 1:3697 HOBBY
STATED PRINT RUN 99 SER.#'d SETS
SSTRAC Allen Craig 25.00 60.00
SSTRCK Clayton Kershaw 25.00 60.00
SSTREL Evan Longoria 4.00 10.00
SSTRFF Freddie Freeman 6.00 15.00
SSTRJE Jacoby Ellsbury 10.00 25.00
SSTRJV Joey Votto 5.00 12.00
SSTRMC Michael Cuddyer 25.00 60.00
SSTRMM Manny Machado 5.00 12.00
SSTRMT Mike Trout 25.00 60.00
SSTRPG Paul Goldschmidt 5.00 12.00

2014 Topps Silk Collection

SERIES ONE ODDS 1:424 HOBBY
SERIES TWO ODDS 1:232 HOBBY
STATED PRINT RUN 50 SER.#'d SETS
CARDS LISTED ALPHABETICALLY
1 Matt Adams 4.00 10.00
2 Yonder Alonso 4.00 10.00
3 Jose Altuve 5.00 12.00
4 Pedro Alvarez 4.00 10.00
5 Elvis Andrus 5.00 12.00
6 Norichika Aoki S2 4.00 10.00
7 Chris Archer S2 4.00 10.00
8 Nolan Arenado 8.00 20.00
9 Homer Bailey S2 4.00 10.00
10 Jose Bautista 5.00 12.00
11 Brandon Beachy S2 4.00 10.00
12 Brandon Belt 5.00 12.00
13 Carlos Beltran S2 5.00 12.00
14 Adrian Beltre 6.00 15.00
15 Michael Bourn S2 4.00 10.00
16 Ryan Braun S2 5.00 12.00
17 Domonic Brown 5.00 12.00
18 Madison Bumgarner S2 5.00 12.00
19 Asdrubal Cabrera S2 5.00 12.00
20 Melky Cabrera 4.00 10.00
21 Miguel Cabrera 6.00 15.00
22 Matt Cain S2 5.00 12.00
23 Robinson Cano S2 5.00 12.00
24 Starlin Castro S2 4.00 10.00
25 Yoenis Cespedes 6.00 15.00
26 Aroldis Chapman 6.00 15.00
27 Shin-Soo Choo 5.00 12.00
28 Tony Cingrani S2 5.00 12.00
29 Gerrit Cole 6.00 15.00
30 Patrick Corbin S2 5.00 12.00
31 Allen Craig S2 5.00 12.00
32 Brandon Crawford 5.00 12.00
33 Carl Crawford S2 5.00 12.00
34 Michael Cuddyer S2 4.00 10.00
35 Johnny Cueto 5.00 12.00
36 Yu Darvish 6.00 15.00
37 Chris Davis S2 4.00 10.00
38 Ian Desmond 4.00 10.00
39 R.A. Dickey S2 5.00 12.00
40 Josh Donaldson 5.00 12.00
41 Adam Dunn S2 5.00 12.00
42 Adam Eaton S2 4.00 10.00
43 Jacoby Ellsbury S2 5.00 12.00
44 Edwin Encarnacion 6.00 15.00
45 Jose Fernandez S2 6.00 15.00
46 Prince Fielder S2 5.00 12.00
47 Doug Fister 4.00 10.00
48 Nick Franklin 4.00 10.00
49 Todd Frazier S2 5.00 12.00
50 Freddie Freeman S2 8.00 20.00
51 David Freese 4.00 10.00
52 Yovani Gallardo S2 4.00 10.00
53 Evan Gattis S2 4.00 10.00
54 Kevin Gausman 5.00 12.00
55 Paul Goldschmidt 6.00 15.00
56 Carlos Gomez 4.00 10.00
57 Adrian Gonzalez 5.00 12.00
58 Carlos Gonzalez S2 5.00 12.00
59 Gio Gonzalez S2 5.00 12.00
60 Curtis Granderson S2 5.00 12.00
61 Sonny Gray S2 5.00 12.00
62 Zack Greinke 5.00 12.00
63 Jason Grilli 4.00 10.00
64 Jedd Gyorko S2 4.00 10.00
65 Roy Halladay S2 5.00 12.00
66 Cole Hamels 5.00 12.00
67 Josh Hamilton S2 5.00 12.00
68 J.J. Hardy S2 4.00 10.00
69 Bryce Harper 10.00 25.00
70 Matt Harvey 5.00 12.00
71 Chase Headley S2 4.00 10.00
72 Jeremy Hellickson 4.00 10.00
73 Felix Hernandez S2 5.00 12.00
74 Jason Heyward 5.00 12.00
75 Aaron Hicks 5.00 12.00
76 Derek Holland S2 4.00 10.00
77 Greg Holland S2 4.00 10.00
78 Matt Holliday 6.00 15.00
79 Eric Hosmer S2 5.00 12.00
80 Ryan Howard 5.00 12.00
81 Torii Hunter 4.00 10.00
82 Jose Iglesias S2 5.00 12.00
83 Austin Jackson S2 4.00 10.00
84 Kenley Jansen S2 5.00 12.00
85 Desmond Jennings S2 5.00 12.00
86 Derek Jeter 15.00 40.00
87 Chris Johnson S2 4.00 10.00
88 Adam Jones S2 5.00 12.00
89 Garrett Jones 4.00 10.00
90 Joe Kelly 4.00 10.00
91 Matt Kemp S2 5.00 12.00
92 Clayton Kershaw S2 12.00 30.00
93 Craig Kimbrel S2 5.00 12.00
94 Ian Kinsler S2 5.00 12.00
95 Jason Kipnis 5.00 12.00
96 Paul Konerko S2 5.00 12.00
97 Hiroki Kuroda 4.00 10.00
98 John Lackey S2 5.00 12.00
99 Adam LaRoche 4.00 10.00
100 Mat Latos S2 5.00 12.00
101 Brett Lawrie S2 5.00 12.00
102 Mike Leake 4.00 10.00
103 Cliff Lee S2 5.00 12.00
104 Jon Lester 5.00 12.00
105 Tim Lincecum S2 5.00 12.00
106 Kyle Lohse 4.00 10.00
107 Evan Longoria 5.00 12.00
108 Jed Lowrie S2 4.00 10.00
109 Lance Lynn 4.00 10.00
110 Manny Machado 6.00 15.00
111 Nick Markakis 5.00 12.00
112 Starling Marte 5.00 12.00
113 Carlos Martinez S2 5.00 12.00
114 Victor Martinez 5.00 12.00
115 Justin Masterson S2 4.00 10.00
116 Joe Mauer 5.00 12.00
117 Brian McCann 5.00 12.00
118 Andrew McCutchen 6.00 15.00
119 Kris Medlen 5.00 12.00
120 Wade Miley 4.00 10.00
121 Shelby Miller S2 5.00 12.00
122 Yadier Molina 6.00 15.00
123 Matt Moore S2 5.00 12.00
124 Wil Myers 4.00 10.00
125 Mike Napoli S2 5.00 12.00
126 Joe Nathan S2 5.00 12.00
127 Ivan Nova S2 5.00 12.00
128 David Ortiz S2 6.00 15.00
129 Marcell Ozuna 6.00 15.00
130 Jarrod Parker S2 4.00 10.00
131 Dustin Pedroia 6.00 15.00
132 Hunter Pence S2 5.00 12.00
133 Jhonny Peralta 4.00 10.00
134 Chris Perez 4.00 10.00
135 Salvador Perez S2 5.00 12.00
136 Glen Perkins S2 4.00 10.00
137 Brandon Phillips S2 4.00 10.00
138 Buster Posey 8.00 20.00
139 Martin Prado S2 4.00 10.00
140 David Price S2 5.00 12.00
141 Jurickson Profar 5.00 12.00
142 Yasiel Puig 6.00 15.00
143 Albert Pujols S2 8.00 20.00
144 Aramis Ramirez S2 4.00 10.00
145 Hanley Ramirez 5.00 12.00
146 Colby Rasmus S2 5.00 12.00
147 Josh Reddick S2 4.00 10.00
148 Addison Reed S2 4.00 10.00
149 Anthony Rendon S2 6.00 15.00
150 Ben Revere 4.00 10.00
151 Jose Reyes S2 5.00 12.00
152 Anthony Rizzo 6.00 15.00
153 Jimmy Rollins 5.00 12.00
154 Sergio Romo 4.00 10.00
155 Wilin Rosario S2 4.00 10.00
156 Trevor Rosenthal 5.00 12.00
157 Carlos Ruiz 4.00 10.00
158 Hyun-Jin Ryu 5.00 12.00
159 CC Sabathia S2 5.00 12.00
160 Danny Salazar S2 5.00 12.00
161 Chris Sale 6.00 15.00
162 Jeff Samardzija 4.00 10.00
163 Pablo Sandoval 5.00 12.00
164 Carlos Santana S2 5.00 12.00
165 Max Scherzer 6.00 15.00
166 Kyle Seager 4.00 10.00
167 Jean Segura 5.00 12.00
168 James Shields 4.00 10.00
169 Tyler Skaggs 4.00 10.00
170 Rafael Soriano 4.00 10.00
171 Giancarlo Stanton 6.00 15.00
172 Stephen Strasburg S2 6.00 15.00
173 Nick Swisher 5.00 12.00
174 Julio Teheran 5.00 12.00
175 Mark Teixeira S2 5.00 12.00
176 Mike Trout 30.00 80.00
177 Mark Trumbo 4.00 10.00
178 Troy Tulowitzki 6.00 15.00
179 Koji Uehara S2 4.00 10.00
180 B.J. Upton S2 5.00 12.00
181 Justin Upton 5.00 12.00
182 Chase Utley S2 5.00 12.00
183 Justin Verlander S2 6.00 15.00
184 Shane Victorino 5.00 12.00
185 Joey Votto 6.00 15.00
186 Michael Wacha S2 5.00 12.00
187 Adam Wainwright S2 5.00 12.00
188 Neil Walker S2 5.00 12.00
189 Jered Weaver S2 5.00 12.00
190 Jayson Werth 5.00 12.00
191 Zack Wheeler 5.00 12.00
192 Brian Wilson S2 6.00 15.00
193 C.J. Wilson 4.00 10.00
194 Alex Wood S2 4.00 10.00
195 David Wright S2 5.00 12.00
196 Christian Yelich S2 8.00 20.00
197 Ryan Zimmerman S2 5.00 12.00
198 Jordan Zimmermann 5.00 12.00
199 Ben Zobrist S2 5.00 12.00
200 Mike Zunino 4.00 10.00

2014 Topps Spring Fever

COMPLETE SET (50) 12.00 30.00
SF1 Evan Longoria .25 .60
SF2 Mike Trout 1.50 4.00
SF3 Robinson Cano .25 .60
SF4 Miguel Cabrera .30 .75
SF5 Carlos Gonzalez .25 .60
SF6 Chris Davis .20 .50
SF7 Adam Jones .25 .60
SF8 Adrian Beltre .30 .75
SF9 Jose Bautista .25 .60
SF10 Clayton Kershaw .60 1.50
SF11 Hanley Ramirez .25 .60
SF12 Prince Fielder .25 .60
SF13 Adam Wainwright .25 .60
SF14 Felix Hernandez .25 .60
SF15 Ryan Braun .25 .60
SF16 Freddie Freeman .40 1.00
SF17 Billy Hamilton .25 .60
SF18 Giancarlo Stanton .30 .75
SF19 Mariano Rivera .40 1.00
SF20 Jose Fernandez .30 .75
SF21 Chris Sale .30 .75
SF22 Buster Posey .40 1.00
SF23 Joe Mauer .25 .60
SF24 Justin Verlander .30 .75
SF25 Yasiel Puig .30 .75
SF26 Albert Pujols .40 1.00
SF27 Jose Reyes .25 .60
SF28 Justin Upton .25 .60
SF29 David Ortiz .30 .75
SF30 Yoenis Cespedes .30 .75
SF31 Michael Wacha .25 .60
SF32 Xander Bogaerts .60 1.50
SF33 Max Scherzer .25 .60
SF34 Bryce Harper .50 1.25
SF35 Yu Darvish .30 .75
SF36 Andrew McCutchen .30 .75
SF37 Josh Hamilton .25 .60
SF38 Wil Myers .20 .50
SF39 Paul Goldschmidt .30 .75
SF40 Jason Heyward .25 .60
SF41 Craig Kimbrel .25 .60
SF42 Dustin Pedroia .30 .75
SF43 CC Sabathia .25 .60
SF44 Edwin Encarnacion .30 .75
SF45 Joey Votto .30 .75
SF46 Jason Kipnis .25 .60
SF47 Troy Tulowitzki .30 .75
SF48 Stephen Strasburg .30 .75
SF49 Adrian Gonzalez .25 .60
SF50 Derek Jeter 2.00 5.00

2014 Topps Spring Fever Autographs

PRINT RUNS B/WN 5-600 COPIES PER
NO PRICING ON QTY 10 OR LESS
SFAAW Allen Webster/150 10.00 25.00
SFABM Brad Miller/600 5.00 12.00
SFADB Domonic Brown/150 10.00 25.00
SFADS Duke Snider/20
SFAJK Joe Kelly/300 4.00 10.00
SFAJP Johnny Podres/30 20.00 50.00
SFANE Nate Eovaldi/300 5.00 12.00
SFASD Steve Delabar/300 4.00 10.00
SFATC Tony Cingrani/150 8.00 20.00
SFADBU Dylan Bundy/150 5.00 12.00

2014 Topps Strata Autograph Relics

SERIES ONE ODDS 1:3400 HOBBY
SERIES TWO ODDS 1:1850 HOBBY
UPDATE ODDS 1:26,002 HOBBY
STATED PRINT RUN 25 SER.#'d SETS
SER.1 EXCH DEADLINE 1/31/2017
SER.2 EXCH DEADLINE 5/31/2017
UPD EXCH DEADLINE 9/30/2017
SSRAJ A.Jones UPD EXCH 30.00 80.00
SSRBJ B.Jackson UPD EXCH 50.00 120.00
SSRBP Posey EXCH 200.00 300.00
SSRCB Craig Biggio S2 50.00 100.00
SSRCG Gonzalez EXCH 50.00 120.00
SSRCK Kershaw UPD EXCH 125.00 250.00
SSRCR Ripken Jr. S2 EXCH 150.00 250.00
SSRCS Chris Sale UPD 30.00 80.00
SSRDM Dale Murphy UPD 50.00 100.00
SSRDO David Ortiz S2 75.00 150.00
SSRDP Pedroia S2 EXCH 75.00 150.00
SSRDP Dustin Pedroia 200.00 400.00
SSRDPR Price EXCH 30.00 60.00
SSRDW Wright EXCH 200.00 300.00
SSRDW Wright S2 EXCH 75.00 150.00
SSREB Banks S2 EXCH 150.00 250.00
SSREL Longoria UPD EXCH 25.00 60.00
SSREM Edgar Martinez UPD 50.00 100.00
SSRFF Freddie Freeman UPD 30.00 80.00
SSRGG Gonzalez EXCH 75.00 150.00
SSRGM Maddux S2 EXCH 60.00 150.00
SSRGS Stanton EXCH 75.00 150.00
SSRHA Aaron S2 EXCH 200.00 300.00
SSRIR Rodriguez S2 EXCH 60.00 120.00
SSRIR Rodriguez EXCH 75.00 150.00
SSRJB Bautista EXCH 40.00 100.00
SSRJB Bench S2 EXCH 40.00 100.00
SSRJC Canseco EXCH 75.00 150.00
SSRJD Josh Donaldson UPD 25.00 60.00
SSRJF Fernandez EXCH 175.00 350.00
SSRJG Juan Gonzalez UPD 25.00 60.00
SSRJH Josh Hamilton 75.00 150.00
SSRJP Posada UPD EXCH 50.00 100.00
SSRJS Segura EXCH 60.00 120.00
SSRJT Teheran UPD EXCH 30.00 80.00
SSRJV Joey Votto UPD 30.00 80.00
SSRKG Griffey Jr. S2 EXCH 250.00 350.00
SSRKW Kolten Wong UPD 100.00 200.00
SSRLG L.Gonzalez UPD EXCH 20.00 50.00
SSRMC Cabrera S2 EXCH 150.00 250.00
SSRMC Cabrera EXCH 150.00 250.00
SSRMCA Cain EXCH 60.00 120.00
SSRMM Manny Machado 250.00 400.00
SSRMM McGwire UPD EXCH 100.00 200.00
SSRMR Rivera S2 EXCH 150.00 250.00
SSRMS Schmidt S2 EXCH 75.00 150.00
SSRMT Trout S2 EXCH 175.00 350.00
SSRNG Garciaparra UPD EXCH 30.00 80.00
SSRNR Nolan Ryan S2 75.00 200.00
SSROS Smith S2 EXCH 60.00 120.00
SSROS Smith EXCH 150.00 300.00
SSRPF Fielder EXCH 30.00 80.00
SSRPG Paul Goldschmidt 150.00 250.00
SSRPM Martinez S2 EXCH 75.00 150.00
SSRRB Ryan Braun UPD 25.00 60.00
SSRRC Cano UPD EXCH 50.00 100.00
SSRRH Rickey Henderson S2 30.00 80.00
SSRRJA Reggie Jackson S2 25.00 60.00
SSRSM Miller EXCH 100.00 200.00
SSRTD d'Arnaud EXCH 100.00 200.00
SSRTG Gwynn EXCH 75.00 150.00
SSRTG Tony Gwynn S2 75.00 150.00
SSRTR Raines UPD EXCH 25.00 60.00
SSRTS Tom Seaver S2 60.00 150.00
SSRTT Tulowitzki EXCH 30.00 80.00
SSRWB Boggs S2 EXCH 60.00 120.00
SSRWM Mays S2 EXCH 250.00 350.00
SSRWM Myers EXCH 100.00 200.00
SSRYD Darvish EXCH 300.00 400.00
SSRYM Yadier Molina UPD 75.00 150.00
SSRZW Zack Wheeler UPD 75.00 150.00
SSRJBA Bagwell S2 EXCH 40.00 100.00

2014 Topps Super Veteran

COMPLETE SET (15) 10.00 25.00
SV1 Albert Pujols .75 2.00
SV2 Miguel Cabrera .60 1.50
SV3 Derek Jeter 1.50 4.00
SV4 Adrian Beltre .60 1.50
SV5 Torii Hunter .40 1.00
SV6 David Ortiz .60 1.50
SV7 Carlos Beltran .50 1.25
SV8 Jimmy Rollins .50 1.25
SV9 Barry Zito .50 1.25
SV10 Andy Pettitte .50 1.25
SV11 Matt Holliday .60 1.50
SV12 Adam Wainwright .50 1.25
SV13 CC Sabathia .50 1.25
SV14 Roy Halladay .50 1.25
SV15 Mariano Rivera .75 2.00

2014 Topps Super Veteran Relics

STATED PRINT RUN 25 SER.#'d SETS
SVRAPE Andy Pettitte 12.00 30.00
SVRBZ Barry Zito 12.00 30.00
SVRCB Carlos Beltran 12.00 30.00
SVRDO David Ortiz 30.00 60.00
SVRJR Jimmy Rollins 20.00 50.00
SVRMC Miguel Cabrera 15.00 40.00
SVRMH Matt Holliday 40.00 80.00

2014 Topps The Future is Now

STATED ODDS 1:4 HOBBY
FN1 Shelby Miller .25 .60
FN2 Shelby Miller .25 .60
FN3 Shelby Miller .25 .60
FN4 Jurickson Profar .25 .60
FN5 Jurickson Profar .25 .60
FN6 Jurickson Profar .25 .60
FN7 Jean Segura .25 .60
FN8 Jean Segura .25 .60
FN9 Jean Segura .25 .60
FN10 Zack Wheeler .25 .60
FN11 Zack Wheeler .25 .60
FN12 Zack Wheeler .25 .60
FN13 Yoenis Cespedes .30 .75
FN14 Yoenis Cespedes .30 .75
FN15 Hyun-Jin Ryu .25 .60
FN16 Hyun-Jin Ryu .25 .60
FN17 Wil Myers .20 .50
FN18 Wil Myers .20 .50
FN19 Mike Trout 1.50 4.00
FN20 Mike Trout 1.50 4.00
FN21 Jose Fernandez .30 .75
FN22 Jose Fernandez .30 .75
FN23 Manny Machado .30 .75
FN24 Manny Machado .30 .75
FN25 Yasiel Puig .30 .75
FN26 Yasiel Puig .30 .75
FN27 Yu Darvish .30 .75
FN28 Yu Darvish .30 .75
FN29 Bryce Harper .50 1.25
FN30 Bryce Harper .50 1.25
FN31 Michael Wacha .25 .60
FN32 Michael Wacha .25 .60
FN33 Michael Wacha .25 .60
FN34 Billy Hamilton .25 .60
FN35 Billy Hamilton .25 .60
FN36 Billy Hamilton .25 .60
FN37 Kolten Wong .25 .60
FN38 Kolten Wong .25 .60
FN39 Kolten Wong .25 .60
FN40 Xander Bogaerts .60 1.50
FN41 Xander Bogaerts .60 1.50
FN42 Xander Bogaerts .60 1.50
FN43 Taijuan Walker .20 .50
FN44 Taijuan Walker .20 .50
FN45 Taijuan Walker .20 .50
FN46 Sonny Gray .25 .60
FN47 Sonny Gray .25 .60
FN48 Sonny Gray .25 .60
FN49 Jarrod Parker .20 .50
FN50 Jarrod Parker .20 .50
FN51 Jarrod Parker .20 .50
FN52 Freddie Freeman .40 1.00
FN53 Freddie Freeman .40 1.00
FN54 Freddie Freeman .40 1.00
FN55 Dylan Bundy .25 .60
FN56 Dylan Bundy .25 .60
FN57 Dylan Bundy .25 .60
FN58 Kevin Gausman .25 .60
FN59 Kevin Gausman .25 .60
FN60 Kevin Gausman .25 .60
FNCY1 Christian Yelich UPD UER .40 1.00
FNCY2 Christian Yelich UPD .40 1.00
FNCY3 Christian Yelich UPD .40 1.00
FNGP1 Gregory Polanco UPD .30 .75
FNGP2 Gregory Polanco UPD .30 .75
FNGP3 Gregory Polanco UPD .30 .75
FNGS1 George Springer UPD .75 2.00
FNGS2 George Springer UPD .75 2.00
FNGS3 George Springer UPD .75 2.00
FNJA1 Jose Abreu UPD 1.50 4.00
FNJA2 Jose Abreu UPD 1.50 4.00
FNJA3 Jose Abreu UPD 1.50 4.00
FNJS1 Jon Singleton UPD .25 .60
FNJS2 Jon Singleton UPD .25 .60
FNJS3 Jon Singleton UPD .25 .60
FNMB1 Mookie Betts UPD 4.00 10.00
FNMB2 Mookie Betts UPD 4.00 10.00
FNMB3 Mookie Betts UPD 4.00 10.00
FNMW1 Michael Wacha UPD .25 .60
FNMW2 Michael Wacha UPD .25 .60
FNMW3 Michael Wacha UPD .25 .60
FNNC1 Nick Castellanos UPD .60 1.50
FNNC2 Nick Castellanos UPD .60 1.50
FNNC3 Nick Castellanos UPD .60 1.50
FNOT1 Oscar Taveras UPD .25 .60
FNOT2 Oscar Taveras UPD .25 .60
FNOT3 Oscar Taveras UPD .25 .60
FNYV1 Yordano Ventura UPD .25 .60
FNYV2 Yordano Ventura UPD .25 .60
FNYV3 Yordano Ventura UPD .25 .60

2014 Topps The Future is Now Autographs

SERIES ONE ODDS 1:9736 HOBBY
SERIES TWO ODDS 1:4880 HOBBY
UPDATE ODDS 1:3667 HOBBY
STATED PRINT RUN 25 SER.#'d SETS
SER.1 EXCH DEADLINE 1/31/2017
SER.2 EXCH DEADLINE 5/31/2017
EXCHANGE DEADLINE 9/30/2017
ALL VERSIONS EQUALLY PRICED
FNAAA1 Arismendy Alcantara UPD 10.00 25.00
FNAAA2 Arismendy Alcantara UPD 10.00 25.00
FNAAA3 Arismendy Alcantara UPD 10.00 25.00
FNABH1 Bryce Harper 100.00 200.00
FNABH2 Bryce Harper 100.00 200.00
FNACY1 Christian Yelich UPD UER 25.00 60.00
FNACY2 Christian Yelich UPD 25.00 60.00
FNACY3 Christian Yelich UPD 25.00 60.00
FNADB1 Dylan Bundy S2 15.00 40.00
FNADB2 Dylan Bundy S2 15.00 40.00
FNADB3 Dylan Bundy S2 15.00 40.00
FNAFF1 Freddie Freeman S2 15.00 40.00
FNAFF2 Freddie Freeman S2 15.00 40.00
FNAFF3 Freddie Freeman S2 15.00 40.00

FNAGP1 Gregory Polanco UPD 25.00 60.00
FNAGP2 Gregory Polanco UPD 25.00 60.00
FNAGP3 Gregory Polanco UPD 25.00 60.00
FNAGS1 George Springer UPD 25.00 60.00
FNAGS2 George Springer UPD 25.00 60.00
FNAGS3 George Springer UPD 25.00 60.00
FNAJA1 Jose Abreu UPD 75.00 150.00
FNAJA2 Jose Abreu UPD 75.00 150.00
FNAJA3 Jose Abreu UPD 75.00 150.00
FNAJP1 Jurickson Profar 20.00 50.00
FNAJP1 Jarrod Parker S2 10.00 25.00
FNAJP2 Jurickson Profar 20.00 50.00
FNAJP2 Jarrod Parker S2 10.00 25.00
FNAJP3 Jurickson Profar 20.00 50.00
FNAJP3 Jarrod Parker S2 10.00 25.00
FNAJS1 Jean Segura EXCH 6.00 15.00
FNAJS1 Jon Singleton UPD 12.00 30.00
FNAJS2 Jean Segura EXCH 6.00 15.00
FNAJS2 Jon Singleton UPD 12.00 30.00
FNAJS3 Jean Segura EXCH 6.00 15.00
FNAJS3 Jon Singleton UPD 12.00 30.00
FNAJT1 Julio Teheran 30.00 60.00
FNAJT1 Julio Teheran S2 15.00 40.00
FNAJT2 Julio Teheran 30.00 60.00
FNAJT2 Julio Teheran S2 15.00 40.00
FNAJT3 Julio Teheran S2 15.00 40.00
FNAKG1 Kevin Gausman S2 20.00 50.00
FNAKG2 Kevin Gausman S2 20.00 50.00
FNAKG3 Kevin Gausman S2 20.00 50.00
FNAKW1 Kolten Wong S2 20.00 50.00
FNAKW2 Kolten Wong S2 20.00 50.00
FNAKW3 Kolten Wong S2 20.00 50.00
FNAMB1 Mookie Betts UPD 40.00 100.00
FNAMB2 Mookie Betts UPD 40.00 100.00
FNAMB3 Mookie Betts UPD 40.00 100.00
FNAMM1 Manny Machado 50.00 100.00
FNAMM2 Manny Machado 50.00 100.00
FNAMT1 Mike Trout 100.00 250.00
FNAMT2 Mike Trout 100.00 250.00
FNAMW1 Michael Wacha S2 20.00 50.00
FNAMW2 Michael Wacha S2 20.00 50.00
FNAMW3 Michael Wacha S2 20.00 50.00
FNAOT1 Oscar Taveras UPD 40.00 100.00
FNAOT2 Oscar Taveras UPD 40.00 100.00
FNAOT3 Oscar Taveras UPD 40.00 100.00
FNASG1 Sonny Gray S2 12.00 30.00
FNASG2 Sonny Gray S2 12.00 30.00
FNASG3 Sonny Gray S2 12.00 30.00
FNASM1 Shelby Miller EXCH 12.50 30.00
FNASM2 Shelby Miller EXCH 12.50 30.00
FNASM3 Shelby Miller EXCH 12.50 30.00
FNATW1 Taijuan Walker S2 15.00 40.00
FNATW2 Taijuan Walker S2 15.00 40.00
FNATW3 Taijuan Walker S2 15.00 40.00
FNAWM1 Wil Myers 40.00 80.00
FNAWM2 Wil Myers 40.00 80.00
FNAXB1 Xander Bogaerts S2 25.00 60.00
FNAXB2 Xander Bogaerts S2 25.00 60.00
FNAXB3 Xander Bogaerts S2 25.00 60.00
FNAYC1 Yoenis Cespedes 20.00 50.00
FNAYC2 Yoenis Cespedes 20.00 50.00
FNAYD1 Yu Darvish 50.00 100.00
FNAYD2 Yu Darvish 50.00 100.00
FNAYS1 Yangervis Solarte UPD 12.00 30.00
FNAYS2 Yangervis Solarte UPD 12.00 30.00
FNAYS3 Yangervis Solarte UPD 12.00 30.00
FNAYV1 Yordano Ventura UPD 15.00 40.00
FNAYV2 Yordano Ventura UPD 15.00 40.00
FNAYV3 Yordano Ventura UPD 15.00 40.00
FNAZW1 Zack Wheeler 20.00 50.00
FNAZW2 Zack Wheeler 20.00 50.00
FNAZW3 Zack Wheeler 20.00 50.00

2014 Topps The Future is Now National Promos

1 Mike Trout 6.00 15.00
2 Yasiel Puig 1.25 3.00
3 Xander Bogaerts 2.50 6.00
4 Yoenis Cespedes 1.25 3.00
5 Billy Hamilton 1.00 2.50
6 Bryce Harper 2.00 5.00

2014 Topps The Future is Now Relics

SERIES ONE ODDS 1:2425 HOBBY
SERIES TWO ODDS 1:1232 HOBBY
UPDATE ODDS 1:2777 HOBBY
STATED PRINT RUN 99 SER.#'d SETS
FNRBH1 Billy Hamilton 5.00 12.00
FNRBH1 Bryce Harper 10.00 25.00
FNRBH2 Bryce Harper 10.00 25.00
FNRBH2 Billy Hamilton 5.00 12.00
FNRBH3 Billy Hamilton 5.00 12.00
FNRCY1 Christian Yelich UPD 8.00 20.00
FNRDB1 Dylan Bundy 5.00 12.00
FNRDB2 Dylan Bundy 5.00 12.00
FNRDB3 Dylan Bundy 5.00 12.00
FNRFF1 Freddie Freeman 8.00 20.00
FNRFF2 Freddie Freeman 8.00 20.00
FNRFF3 Freddie Freeman 8.00 20.00
FNRGS1 George Springer UPD 8.00 20.00
FNRHR1 Hyun-Jin Ryu 5.00 12.00
FNRHR2 Hyun-Jin Ryu 5.00 12.00
FNRJF1 Jose Fernandez 6.00 15.00
FNRJF2 Jose Fernandez 6.00 15.00
FNRJP1 Jurickson Profar 5.00 12.00
FNRJP1 Jarrod Parker 4.00 10.00
FNRJP1 James Paxton UPD 6.00 15.00
FNRJP2 Jarrod Parker 4.00 10.00
FNRJP2 Jurickson Profar 5.00 12.00
FNRJP3 Jurickson Profar 5.00 12.00
FNRJP3 Jarrod Parker 4.00 10.00
FNRJS1 Jean Segura 5.00 12.00
FNRJS1 Jon Singleton UPD 5.00 12.00
FNRJS2 Jean Segura 5.00 12.00
FNRJS3 Jean Segura 5.00 12.00
FNRKG1 Kevin Gausman 5.00 12.00
FNRKG2 Kevin Gausman 5.00 12.00
FNRKG3 Kevin Gausman 5.00 12.00
FNRKW1 Kolten Wong 5.00 12.00
FNRKW2 Kolten Wong 5.00 12.00
FNRKW3 Kolten Wong 5.00 12.00
FNRMM1 Manny Machado 6.00 15.00
FNRMM2 Manny Machado 6.00 15.00
FNRMT1 Mike Trout 12.00 30.00
FNRMT2 Mike Trout 12.00 30.00
FNRMW1 Michael Wacha UPD 8.00 20.00
FNRNC1 Nick Castellanos UPD 12.00 30.00
FNROT1 Oscar Taveras UPD 15.00 40.00
FNRSG1 Sonny Gray 5.00 12.00
FNRSG2 Sonny Gray 5.00 12.00
FNRSG3 Sonny Gray 5.00 12.00
FNRSM1 Shelby Miller 8.00 20.00
FNRSM2 Shelby Miller 8.00 20.00
FNRSM3 Shelby Miller 8.00 20.00
FNRTD1 Travis d'Arnaud UPD 5.00 12.00
FNRTS1 Tyler Skaggs UPD 4.00 10.00
FNRTW1 Taijuan Walker 4.00 10.00
FNRTW2 Taijuan Walker 4.00 10.00
FNRTW3 Taijuan Walker 4.00 10.00
FNRWM1 Wil Myers 8.00 20.00
FNRWM2 Wil Myers 8.00 20.00
FNRWR1 Wilin Rosario 4.00 10.00
FNRWR2 Wilin Rosario 4.00 10.00
FNRWR3 Wilin Rosario 4.00 10.00
FNRXB1 Xander Bogaerts 12.00 30.00
FNRXB2 Xander Bogaerts 12.00 30.00
FNRXB3 Xander Bogaerts 12.00 30.00
FNRYC1 Yoenis Cespedes 6.00 15.00
FNRYC2 Yoenis Cespedes 6.00 15.00
FNRYD1 Yu Darvish 12.00 30.00
FNRYD2 Yu Darvish 12.00 30.00
FNRYP1 Yasiel Puig 15.00 40.00
FNRYP2 Yasiel Puig 15.00 40.00
FNRYV1 Yordano Ventura UPD 6.00 15.00
FNRZW1 Zack Wheeler 5.00 12.00
FNRZW2 Zack Wheeler 5.00 12.00
FNRZW3 Zack Wheeler 5.00 12.00

2014 Topps Trajectory Autographs

SERIES ONE ODDS 1:568 HOBBY
SERIES TWO ODDS 1:585 HOBBY
UPDATE ODDS 1:575 HOBBY
SER.1 EXCH.DEADLINE 1/31/2017
SER.2 EXCH DEADLINE 5/31/2017
UPDATE EXCH DEADLINE 9/30/2017
TAAA Arismendy Alcantara UPD 3.00 8.00
TAAC Allen Craig S2 30.00 60.00
TAAE Adam Eaton S2 3.00 8.00
TAAGO Anthony Gose S2 3.00 8.00
TAAH Adeiny Hechavarria S2 3.00 8.00
TAAL Andrew Lambo 3.00 8.00
TAAR Andre Rienzo 3.00 8.00
TABBU Bill Buckner 5.00 12.00
TABH Bryce Harper 50.00 120.00
TABJ Bo Jackson 30.00 60.00
TACA Chris Archer 3.00 8.00
TACB Christian Bethancourt S2 3.00 8.00
TACB Cam Bedrosian UPD 3.00 8.00
TACBL Charlie Blackmon UPD 5.00 12.00
TACC Chris Colabello UPD 3.00 8.00
TACCR C.J. Cron UPD 3.00 8.00
TACF Cliff Floyd S2 3.00 8.00
TACO Chris Owings S2 3.00 8.00
TACO Chris Owings UPD 3.00 8.00
TACR Cal Ripken Jr. EXCH 60.00 120.00
TACS Carlos Santana S2 4.00 10.00
TACW Chase Whitley UPD 3.00 8.00
TACY Christian Yelich 20.00 50.00
TADB Dave Buchanan UPD 3.00 8.00
TADB Dusty Baker S2 3.00 8.00
TADD Derek Dietrich UPD 4.00 10.00
TADG Didi Gregorius 4.00 10.00
TADM Dale Murphy S2 10.00 25.00
TADN Daniel Nava S2 3.00 8.00
TADS Deion Sanders 20.00 50.00
TADW David Wright EXCH 15.00 40.00
TAEA Erisbel Arruebarrena UPD 3.00 8.00
TAEB Ernie Banks 20.00 50.00
TAED Eric Davis S2 3.00 8.00
TAEG Evan Gattis 3.00 8.00
TAFF Freddie Freeman S2 6.00 15.00
TAFM Fred McGriff S2 6.00 15.00
TAFV Fernando Valenzuela S2 25.00 60.00
TAGM Greg Maddux EXCH 40.00 80.00
TAGS George Springer UPD 6.00 15.00
TAHA Hank Aaron 100.00 200.00
TAHA Henderson Alvarez S2 3.00 8.00
TAIR Ivan Rodriguez EXCH 10.00 25.00
TAJA Jose Abreu S2 60.00 150.00
TAJA Jose Abreu UPD 40.00 80.00
TAJB Johnny Bench S2 40.00 80.00
TAJD Jake Diekman UPD 3.00 8.00
TAJDE Jacob deGrom UPD 20.00 50.00
TAJG Jason Grilli S2 3.00 8.00
TAJH Jason Heyward S2 8.00 20.00
TAJK Jason Kipnis 5.00 12.00
TAJK Joe Kelly UPD 3.00 8.00
TAJM Jake Marisnick 3.00 8.00
TAJR Junior Lake S2 3.00 8.00
TAJS Jean Segura S2 4.00 10.00
TAJS Jonathan Schoop UPD 3.00 8.00
TAJSI Jon Singleton UPD 6.00 15.00
TAKG Ken Griffey Jr. 75.00 150.00
TAKM Kris Medlen 4.00 10.00
TAKP Kyle Parker UPD 4.00 10.00
TAKS Kevin Siegrist S2 3.00 8.00
TAKW Kolten Wong 4.00 10.00
TAKW Kolten Wong S2 4.00 10.00
TALA Luis Aparicio 10.00 25.00
TALH Livan Hernandez S2 3.00 8.00
TAMA Matt Adams 3.00 8.00
TAMBE Mookie Betts UPD 50.00 120.00
TAMC Matt Cain EXCH 12.00 30.00
TAMD Matt Davidson 4.00 10.00
TAMM Mark McGwire S2 40.00 100.00
TAMMA Manny Machado S2 20.00 50.00
TAMMI Mike Minor S2 3.00 8.00
TAMN Mike Napoli S2 8.00 20.00
TAMS Marcus Stroman UPD 5.00 12.00
TAMT Mike Trout 100.00 200.00
TANG Nomar Garciaparra 12.50 30.00
TANM Nick Martinez UPD 3.00 8.00
TAOS Ozzie Smith S2 10.00 25.00
TAOT Oscar Taveras UPD 12.00 30.00
TAPB Peter Bourjos S2 3.00 8.00
TAPG Paul Goldschmidt 8.00 20.00
TAPG Paul Goldschmidt S2 8.00 20.00
TAPM Pedro Martinez 60.00 120.00
TARB Rex Brothers UPD 3.00 8.00
TARE Roenis Elias UPD 3.00 8.00
TARK Ralph Kiner S2 15.00 40.00
TARM Rafael Montero UPD 3.00 8.00
TARN Ricky Nolasco 3.00 8.00
TARO Rougned Odor UPD 8.00 20.00
TASC Steve Cishek S2 3.00 8.00
TASK Sandy Koufax 150.00 300.00
TASM Starling Marte S2 4.00 10.00
TASMI Shelby Miller S2 15.00 40.00
TASS Steven Souza UPD 4.00 10.00
TATC Tyler Chatwood S2 3.00 8.00
TATD Travis d'Arnaud 4.00 10.00
TATG Tom Glavine 20.00 50.00
TATK Tom Koehler UPD 3.00 8.00
TATL Tommy La Stella UPD 3.00 8.00
TATR Tim Raines S2 10.00 25.00
TATT Troy Tulowitzki S2 8.00 20.00
TATW Taijuan Walker 3.00 8.00
TAWM Wil Myers 3.00 8.00
TAWMI Wade Miley 3.00 8.00
TAYC Yoenis Cespedes 8.00 20.00
TAYD Yu Darvish EXCH 40.00 80.00
TAYS Yangervis Solarte UPD 3.00 8.00
TAZA Zoilo Almonte S2 4.00 10.00

2014 Topps Trajectory Jumbo Relics

STATED ODDS 1:2625 HOBBY
UPDATE ODDS 1:11,001 HOBBY
PRINT RUNS B/WN 25-99 COPIES PER
TJRAC Alex Cobb/99 10.00 25.00
TJRAW Adam Wainwright/99 25.00 60.00
TJRBH Billy Hamilton/99 20.00 50.00
TJRBHA Billy Hamilton/99 20.00 50.00
TJRBM Brian McCann/25 UPD 12.00 30.00
TJRBP Buster Posey/25 UPD 20.00 50.00
TJRBZ Ben Zobrist/99 8.00 20.00
TJRCC CC Sabathia/25 UPD 20.00 50.00
TJRCD Chris Davis/99 6.00 15.00
TJRCG Carlos Gonzalez/25 UPD 25.00 60.00
TJRCK Craig Kimbrel/99 8.00 20.00
TJRCS Chris Sale/99 10.00 25.00
TJRCS Chris Sale/25 UPD 15.00 40.00
TJRCW C.J. Wilson/99 10.00 25.00
TJRDF David Freese/99 6.00 15.00
TJRDG Didi Gregorius/99 8.00 20.00
TJRDJ Derek Jeter/25 UPD 40.00 100.00
TJRDM Devin Mesoraco/99 6.00 15.00
TJRDO David Ortiz/99 12.00 30.00
TJRDW David Wright/99 10.00 25.00
TJREE Edwin Encarnacion/99 10.00 25.00
TJREL Evan Longoria/99 8.00 20.00
TJREL Evan Longoria/25 UPD 12.00 30.00
TJREL1 Evan Longoria/99 8.00 20.00
TJREM Eddie Murray/99 10.00 25.00
TJRFF Freddie Freeman/99 12.00 30.00
TJRFH Felix Hernandez/99 8.00 20.00
TJRFH Felix Hernandez/25 UPD 12.00 30.00
TJRHR Hanley Ramirez/25 UPD 60.00 120.00
TJRJB Jay Bruce/25 UPD 8.00 20.00
TJRJC Jose Canseco/99 15.00 40.00
TJRJM Joe Morgan/99 10.00 25.00
TJRJM Joe Mauer/25 UPD 60.00 120.00
TJRJP Jorge Posada/25 UPD 12.00 30.00
TJRJS Justin Smoak/99 6.00 15.00
TJRJSE Jean Segura/99 8.00 20.00
TJRJT Julio Teheran/99 8.00 20.00
TJRJV Joey Votto/25 UPD 15.00 40.00
TJRJW Jayson Werth/99 8.00 20.00
TJRJWE Jayson Werth/99 8.00 20.00
TJRJZ Jordan Zimmermann/99 8.00 20.00
TJRKG Ken Griffey Jr./99 20.00 50.00
TJRMA Matt Adams/99 6.00 15.00
TJRMB Madison Bumgarner/99 12.00 30.00
TJRMCA Matt Cain/25 UPD 30.00 80.00
TJRMH Matt Holliday/99 8.00 20.00
TJRML Mike Leake/99 8.00 20.00
TJRMM Mike Minor/99 10.00 25.00
TJRMMC Mark McGwire/99 15.00 40.00
TJRMS Max Scherzer/99 10.00 25.00
TJRMT Mike Trout/99 40.00 80.00
TJRMT Mike Trout/25 UPD 30.00 80.00
TJRMTA Masahiro Tanaka/25 UPD 90.00 150.00
TJRNG Nomar Garciaparra/25 UPD 40.00 100.00
TJROT Oscar Taveras/99 8.00 20.00
TJRPA Pedro Alvarez/99 10.00 25.00
TJRPK Paul Konerko/99 8.00 20.00
TJRRZ Ryan Zimmerman/99 8.00 20.00
TJRSC Starlin Castro/99 8.00 20.00
TJRSC Shin-Soo Choo/25 UPD 12.00 30.00
TJRSCA Steve Carlton/99 10.00 25.00
TJRSM Shelby Miller/99 15.00 40.00
TJRSS Stephen Strasburg/99 10.00 25.00
TJRSV Shane Victorino/25 UPD 12.00 30.00
TJRTD Travis d'Arnaud/99 6.00 15.00
TJRTG Tom Glavine/99 12.00 30.00
TJRTGW Tony Gwynn/99 10.00 25.00
TJRTL Tim Lincecum/25 UPD 25.00 60.00
TJRTT Troy Tulowitzki/99 8.00 20.00
TJRVG Vladimir Guerrero/25 UPD 12.00 30.00
TJRWM Wil Myers/25 UPD 10.00 25.00
TJRWM Willie McCovey/99 15.00 40.00
TJRWMA Wade Miley/99 6.00 15.00
TJRWMI Will Middlebrooks/99 6.00 15.00
TJRWR Wilin Rosario/99 6.00 15.00
TJRXB Xander Bogaerts/99 20.00 50.00
TJRYA Yonder Alonso/99 6.00 15.00
TJRYP Yasiel Puig/25 UPD 15.00 40.00

2014 Topps Trajectory Relics

SERIES ONE ODDS 1:50 HOBBY
SERIES TWO ODDS 1:51 HOBBY
TRAB Adrian Beltre S2 3.00 8.00
TRAC Alex Cobb S2 2.00 5.00
TRAH Aaron Hicks S2 2.50 6.00
TRAP Andy Pettitte 2.50 6.00
TRAR Alex Rodriguez 4.00 10.00
TRARA Alexei Ramirez 2.50 6.00
TRAS Andrelton Simmons 2.00 5.00
TRAW Adam Wainwright S2 2.50 6.00
TRBB Brennan Boesch S2 2.00 5.00
TRBBE Brandon Belt 2.50 6.00
TRBG Brett Gardner S2 2.50 6.00
TRBH Bryce Harper 12.00 30.00
TRBM Brandon Morrow S2 2.00 5.00
TRBP Buster Posey 4.00 10.00
TRBR Babe Ruth 60.00 120.00
TRBRO Bruce Rondon 2.00 5.00
TRBS Bruce Sutter 2.00 5.00
TRBZ Ben Zobrist 2.50 6.00
TRCC CC Sabathia S2 2.50 6.00
TRCS Carlos Santana 2.50 6.00
TRCSA Chris Sale 3.00 8.00
TRDJ1 Derek Jeter Bat 20.00 50.00
TRDJ2 Derek Jeter Jsy 15.00 40.00
TRDPR David Price 2.50 6.00
TRDS Don Sutton 2.50 6.00
TREA Elvis Andrus 2.50 6.00
TREB Ernie Banks 10.00 25.00
TRGB Gordon Beckham S2 2.00 5.00
TRGS Gary Sheffield 2.00 5.00
TRHA Hank Aaron 40.00 80.00
TRHAL Henderson Alvarez 2.00 5.00
TRHW Hoyt Wilhelm 10.00 25.00
TRID Ian Desmond 2.00 5.00
TRID Ike Davis S2 2.00 5.00
TRIR Ivan Rodriguez S2 2.50 6.00
TRIR Ivan Rodriguez 2.50 6.00
TRJE Jacoby Ellsbury S2 2.50 6.00
TRJP Jorge Posada S2 2.50 6.00
TRJPE Jhonny Peralta 2.00 5.00
TRJR Jose Reyes 2.50 6.00
TRJS Jean Segura 2.50 6.00
TRJSH James Shields 2.00 5.00
TRJT Julio Teheran 2.50 6.00
TRJV Joey Votto S2 3.00 8.00
TRJVO Joey Votto 3.00 8.00
TRJW Jayson Werth 2.50 6.00
TRJZ Jordan Zimmermann 2.50 6.00
TRML Mike Leake S2 2.00 5.00
TRMM Mike Minor S2 2.00 5.00
TRMS Max Scherzer S2 3.00 8.00
TRMS Mike Schmidt 6.00 15.00
TRMT Mike Trout 12.00 30.00
TRMTE Mark Teixeira 2.50 6.00
TRMY Michael Young 2.00 5.00
TRNF Neftali Feliz S2 2.00 5.00
TRPA Pedro Alvarez 2.00 5.00
TRPF Prince Fielder 2.50 6.00
TRPS Pablo Sandoval 2.50 6.00
TRPS Pablo Sandoval S2 2.50 6.00
TRRC Roberto Clemente 40.00 80.00
TRRH Ryan Howard S2 2.50 6.00
TRRP Rick Porcello 2.50 6.00
TRRS Red Schoendienst 10.00 25.00
TRRW Rickie Weeks 2.00 5.00
TRRY Robin Yount 15.00 40.00
TRSC Starlin Castro S2 2.00 5.00
TRSM Shelby Miller S2 2.50 6.00
TRSP Salvador Perez 2.50 6.00
TRSS Stephen Strasburg 3.00 8.00
TRTL Tim Lincecum S2 2.50 6.00
TRTT Troy Tulowitzki 3.00 8.00
TRTW Ted Williams 40.00 80.00
TRVG Vladimir Guerrero S2 2.50 6.00
TRVM Victor Martinez S2 2.50 6.00
TRWM Willie Mays 25.00 60.00
TRWR Wilin Rosario 2.00 5.00
TRYA Yonder Alonso 2.00 5.00
TRYA Yonder Alonso S2 2.00 5.00
TRYP Yasiel Puig 10.00 25.00
TRZW Zack Wheeler 2.50 6.00
TRJPA Jordan Pacheco S2 2.00 5.00
TRJPR Jarrod Parker S2 2.00 5.00
TRMCA Matt Carpenter S2 3.00 8.00
TRMMA Manny Machado S2 3.00 8.00
TRMMO Mitch Moreland S2 2.00 5.00
TRSC1 Starlin Castro S2 2.00 5.00

2014 Topps Trajectory Relics Gold

*GOLD: .6X TO 1.5X BASIC
SERIES TWO ODDS 1:1155 HOBBY
STATED PRINT RUN 99 SER.#'d SETS

2014 Topps Upper Class

COMPLETE SET (50) 10.00 25.00
STATED ODDS 1:4 HOBBY
UC1 Bryce Harper .50 1.25
UC2 Mike Trout 1.50 4.00
UC3 Yu Darvish .30 .75
UC4 Yoenis Cespedes .30 .75
UC5 Matt Harvey .25 .60
UC6 Craig Kimbrel .25 .60
UC7 Freddie Freeman .40 1.00
UC8 Sandy Koufax .60 1.50
UC9 Roberto Clemente .75 2.00
UC10 Buster Posey .40 1.00
UC11 David Freese .20 .50
UC12 Giancarlo Stanton .30 .75
UC13 Stephen Strasburg .30 .75
UC14 Madison Bumgarner .25 .60
UC15 Evan Longoria .25 .60
UC16 Joey Votto .30 .75
UC17 Jay Bruce .25 .60
UC18 Ryan Braun .25 .60
UC19 Troy Tulowitzki .30 .75
UC20 Dustin Pedroia .30 .75
UC21 Hanley Ramirez .25 .60
UC22 Matt Cain .25 .60
UC23 Prince Fielder .25 .60
UC24 Justin Verlander .30 .75
UC25 Jered Weaver .25 .60
UC26 Ryan Howard .25 .60
UC27 Robinson Cano .25 .60
UC28 Brian McCann .25 .60
UC29 Felix Hernandez .25 .60
UC30 Matt Holliday .30 .75
UC31 David Wright .25 .60
UC32 Yadier Molina .30 .75
UC33 Randy Johnson .30 .75
UC34 Gary Sheffield .20 .50
UC35 Ken Griffey Jr. .60 1.50
UC36 Albert Belle .20 .50
UC37 Jim Abbott .20 .50
UC38 Tom Glavine .20 .50
UC39 Greg Maddux .40 1.00
UC40 Bo Jackson .30 .75
UC41 Jacoby Ellsbury .25 .60
UC42 Jim Rice .25 .60
UC43 Fred Lynn .20 .50
UC44 Gary Carter .25 .60
UC45 Ryne Sandberg .60 1.50
UC46 Wade Boggs .25 .60
UC47 Cal Ripken Jr. 1.00 2.50
UC48 Hank Aaron .60 1.50
UC49 Al Kaline .30 .75
UC50 Ernie Banks .30 .75

2014 Topps Upper Class Autograph Relics

STATED ODDS 1:3400 HOBBY
STATED PRINT RUN 25 SER.#'d SETS
EXCHANGE DEADLINE 1/31/2017
UCARAB Albert Belle 12.00 30.00
UCARBH Bryce Harper 125.00 250.00
UCARBJ Bo Jackson 100.00 200.00
UCARDF David Freese 20.00 50.00
UCARDP Dustin Pedroia EXCH 60.00 120.00
UCAREB Ernie Banks EXCH 60.00 120.00
UCARFF Freddie Freeman 40.00 80.00
UCARFL Fred Lynn 12.00 30.00
UCARGC Gary Carter 40.00 80.00
UCARGS Giancarlo Stanton 75.00 150.00
UCARGSH Gary Sheffield 12.00 30.00
UCARHR Hanley Ramirez EXCH 15.00 40.00
UCARJH Jeremy Hellickson EXCH 12.00 30.00
UCARJR Jim Rice 12.00 30.00
UCARMB Madison Bumgarner 50.00 100.00
UCARMC Matt Cain 30.00 60.00
UCARMT Mike Trout 100.00 200.00
UCARMTR Mark Trumbo 20.00 50.00
UCARRB Ryan Braun 15.00 40.00
UCARRP Rafael Palmeiro EXCH 20.00 50.00
UCARTG Tom Glavine 20.00 50.00
UCARTT Troy Tulowitzki EXCH 20.00 50.00
UCARYC Yoenis Cespedes 20.00 50.00
UCARYD Yu Darvish EXCH 60.00 120.00
UCARYM Yadier Molina 20.00 50.00

2014 Topps Upper Class Autographs

STATED ODDS 1:5829 HOBBY
STATED PRINT RUN 50 SER.#'d SETS
EXCHANGE DEADLINE 1/31/2017
UCAAB Albert Belle EXCH 6.00 15.00
UCAAK Al Kaline 25.00 50.00
UCABH Bryce Harper 60.00 120.00
UCABP Buster Posey 75.00 200.00
UCADF David Freese 6.00 15.00
UCADP Dustin Pedroia EXCH 20.00 50.00
UCAEB Ernie Banks EXCH 60.00 120.00
UCAFF Freddie Freeman 30.00 60.00
UCAFL Fred Lynn 6.00 15.00
UCAGC Gary Carter 12.00 30.00
UCAGS Giancarlo Stanton 10.00 25.00
UCAGSH Gary Sheffield 6.00 15.00
UCAHR Hanley Ramirez EXCH 8.00 20.00
UCAJA Jim Abbott 6.00 15.00
UCAJH Jeremy Hellickson EXCH 6.00 15.00
UCAJR Jim Rice 15.00 40.00
UCAMB Madison Bumgarner 8.00 20.00
UCAMC Matt Cain EXCH 8.00 20.00
UCAMT Mike Trout 100.00 200.00
UCAMTR Mark Trumbo 10.00 25.00
UCARP Rafael Palmeiro 10.00 25.00
UCATG Tom Glavine 15.00 40.00
UCATT Troy Tulowitzki EXCH 10.00 25.00
UCAYC Yoenis Cespedes 10.00 25.00
UCAYD Yu Darvish EXCH 50.00 100.00

2014 Topps Upper Class Relics

STATED ODDS 1:2425 HOBBY
STATED PRINT RUN 99 SER.#'d SETS
UCRBP Buster Posey 15.00 40.00
UCRCK Craig Kimbrel 10.00 25.00
UCRCR Cal Ripken Jr. 40.00 80.00
UCRDF David Freese 6.00 15.00
UCREL Evan Longoria 4.00 10.00
UCRGM Greg Maddux 10.00 25.00
UCRGS Giancarlo Stanton 5.00 12.00
UCRHR Hanley Ramirez 4.00 10.00
UCRJB Jay Bruce 10.00 25.00
UCRJH Jeremy Hellickson 3.00 8.00
UCRJV Justin Verlander 8.00 20.00
UCRJVO Joey Votto 12.00 30.00
UCRMB Madison Bumgarner 15.00 40.00
UCRMC Matt Cain 6.00 15.00
UCRMH Matt Harvey 8.00 20.00
UCRMHO Matt Holliday 5.00 12.00
UCRMTR Mark Trumbo 3.00 8.00
UCRPF Prince Fielder 4.00 10.00
UCRRC Roberto Clemente 40.00 80.00
UCRRCA Robinson Cano 4.00 10.00
UCRRH Ryan Howard 4.00 10.00
UCRSS Stephen Strasburg 6.00 15.00
UCRTT Troy Tulowitzki 5.00 12.00
UCRYC Yoenis Cespedes 5.00 12.00
UCRYM Yadier Molina 5.00 12.00

2014 Topps World Champion Autograph Relics

STATED ODDS 1:8500 HOBBY
STATED PRINT RUN 50 SER.#'d SETS
EXCHANGE DEADLINE 1/31/2017
WCARDO David Ortiz EXCH 75.00 150.00
WCARDP Dustin Pedroia EXCH 75.00 150.00
WCARFD Felix Doubront 75.00 150.00
WCARMN Mike Napoli 100.00 200.00
WCARWM Will Middlebrooks 15.00 40.00

2014 Topps World Champion Autographs

STATED ODDS 1:29,500 HOBBY
STATED PRINT RUN 50 SER.#'d SETS
EXCHANGE DEADLINE 1/31/2017
WCADO David Ortiz 150.00 300.00
WCADP Dustin Pedroia EXCH 75.00 150.00
WCAFD Felix Doubront 30.00 80.00
WCAMN Mike Napoli 50.00 100.00
WCAWM Will Middlebrooks 50.00 100.00

2014 Topps World Champion Relics

STATED ODDS 1:4825 HOBBY
STATED PRINT RUN 100 SER.#'d SETS
EXCHANGE DEADLINE 1/31/2017
WCRCB Clay Buchholz 10.00 25.00
WCRDO David Ortiz 15.00 40.00
WCRDP Dustin Pedroia 15.00 40.00
WCRFD Felix Doubront 10.00 25.00
WCRJE Jacoby Ellsbury 12.00 30.00
WCRJG Jonny Gomes EXCH 30.00 80.00
WCRJL Jon Lester 20.00 50.00
WCRJLA John Lackey 12.00 30.00
WCRJP Jake Peavy 50.00 100.00
WCRJS Jarrod Saltalamacchia 10.00 25.00
WCRKU Koji Uehara 20.00 50.00
WCRMN Mike Napoli 20.00 50.00
WCRSD Stephen Drew EXCH 10.00 25.00
WCRSV Shane Victorino 20.00 50.00
WCRXB Xander Bogaerts 40.00 80.00

2014 Topps Update

COMPLETE SET w/o SP's (330) 15.00 40.00
PRINTING PLATE ODDS 1:970 HOBBY
PLATE PRINT RUN 1 SET PER COLOR
BLACK-CYAN-MAGENTA-YELLOW ISSUED
NO PLATE PRICING DUE TO SCARCITY
US1 Albert Pujols .25 .60
US2 Derek Jeter .50 1.25
US3 Tom Wilhelmsen .12 .30
US4 Mark Reynolds .12 .30
US5 Jair Jurrjens .12 .30
US6A Jose Molina .12 .30
US6B Jose Molina SP 1.50 4.00
White jersey
US7 David Price .15 .40
US8 Josh Harrison .12 .30
US9 Francisco Rodriguez .15 .40
US10A George Springer RC 1.50 4.00
US10B Springer SP Fldng 6.00 15.00
US11 Robbie Ross Jr. .12 .30
US12A Brian McCann .15 .40
US12B Brian McCann SP 2.00 5.00
With glove
US12C Brian McCann SP 2.00 5.00
SABRmetrics
US13 Andrew Heaney RC .40 1.00
US14 Justin Grimm .12 .30
US15A Joba Chamberlain .12 .30
US15B Joba Chamberlain SP 1.50 4.00
With teammate
US15C Joba Chamberlain SP 1.50 4.00
SABRmetrics
US16 Andrew Brown .12 .30
US17A Yangervis Solarte RC .40 1.00
US17B Yangervis Solarte SP 1.50 4.00
Blue jersey
US18 Aramis Ramirez .12 .30
US19A Bronson Arroyo .12 .30
US19B Bronson Arroyo SP 1.50 4.00
SABRmetrics
US20 Gregory Polanco RC .60 1.50
US22A Kendrys Morales .12 .30
US22B Kendrys Morales SP 1.50 4.00
SABRmetrics
US23A Ubaldo Jimenez .12 .30
US23B Ubaldo Jimenez SP 1.50 4.00
SABRmetrics
US24 Tony Sanchez RC .40 1.00
US25 Masahiro Tanaka RC 1.25 3.00
US26A Mookie Betts RC 25.00 60.00
US26B Betts SP In dugout 30.00 80.00
US27A Shin-Soo Choo .15 .40
US27B Shin-Soo Choo SP 2.00 5.00
In dugout
US27C Shin-Soo Choo SP 2.00 5.00
SABRmetrics
US28A David Freese .12 .30
US28B David Freese SP 1.50 4.00
SABRmetrics
US29 Tyler Skaggs .12 .30
US30 Elian Herrera .12 .30
US31 Francisco Rodriguez .15 .40
US32A Mark Trumbo .12 .30
US32B Mark Trumbo SP 1.50 4.00
SABRmetrics
US33 Grady Sizemore .15 .40
US34 Gavin Floyd .12 .30
US35 Marcus Stroman RC .60 1.50
US36 Vance Worley .12 .30
US37 Leury Garcia .12 .30
US38A Jason Giambi .12 .30
US38B Jason Giambi SP 1.50 4.00
With bat
US38C Jason Giambi SP 1.50 4.00
SABRmetrics
US39 Brock Holt .12 .30
US40 Stephen Vogt RC .50 1.25
US41A Drew Stubbs .12 .30
US41B Drew Stubbs SP 1.50 4.00
SABRmetrics
US42 J.D. Martinez .20 .50
US43 Pat Neshek .12 .30
US44 Jesus Guzman .12 .30
US45 Pedro Ciriaco .12 .30
US46 Jake Marisnick .12 .30
US47 Steve Tolleson .12 .30
US48A Scott Hairston .12 .30
US48B Scott Hairston SP 1.50 4.00
Red jersey
US49 Willie Bloomquist .12 .30
US50A Jacob deGrom RC 6.00 15.00
US50B deGrom SP Wht Jsy 10.00 25.00
US51 Brandon Guyer RC .40 1.00
US52 Chase Anderson RC .40 1.00
US53 Miguel Cabrera .20 .50
US54 Mike Trout 1.00 2.50
US55 Jon Lester .15 .40
US56A Huston Street .12 .30
US56B Huston Street SP 1.50 4.00
SABRmetrics
US57 Jacob deGrom .75 2.00
US58 Raul Ibanez .15 .40
US59 Brandon McCarthy .12 .30
US60 David Ross .12 .30
US61 Ryan Kalish .12 .30
US62A Adam Eaton .12 .30
US62B Adam Eaton SP 1.50 4.00
With glove
US62C Adam Eaton SP 1.50 4.00
SABRmetrics
US63A David Murphy .12 .30
US63B David Murphy SP 1.50 4.00
SABRmetrics
US64 LaTroy Hawkins .12 .30
US65 Chad Qualls .12 .30
US66 Marc Krauss .12 .30
US67 Scott Van Slyke .12 .30
US68 Justin Turner .15 .40
US69A Dellin Betances .15 .40
US69B Dellin Betances SP 2.00 5.00
SABRmetrics
US70A Jarrod Saltalamacchia .12 .30
US70B Jarrod Saltalamacchia SP 1.50 4.00
Tossing bat
US70C Jarrod Saltalamacchia SP 1.50 4.00
SABRmetrics
US71 Justin Masterson .12 .30
US72A Chris Young .12 .30
US72B Chris Young SP 1.50 4.00
SABRmetrics
US73A Francisco Cervelli .12 .30
US73B Francisco Cervelli SP 1.50 4.00
SABRmetrics
US74 Antonio Bastardo .12 .30
US75 Nick Punto .12 .30
US76 Daric Barton .12 .30
US77 Wil Nieves .12 .30
US78 Reid Brignac .12 .30
US79 Clint Barmes .12 .30
US80A Josh Harrison .12 .30
US80B Josh Harrison SP 1.50 4.00
SABRmetrics
US81 Seth Smith .12 .30
US82A Joaquin Arias .12 .30
US82B Joaquin Arias SP 1.50 4.00
SABRmetrics
US83 Brandon Hicks .12 .30
US84 Brandon Maurer .12 .30
US85 Daniel Descalso .12 .30
US86 Cesar Ramos .12 .30

US87 Allen Craig .15 .40
US88 Jon Singleton RC .50 1.25
US89 Stephen Drew .12 .30
US90 Steve Lombardozzi .12 .30
US91A Nate McLouth .12 .30
US91B Nate McLouth SP 1.50 4.00
In dugout
US92 Jeff Samardzija .12 .30
US93 Troy Patton .12 .30
US94 Tuffy Gosewisch RC .40 1.00
US95 Vidal Nuno RC .40 1.00
US96 Eugenio Suarez RC 1.50 4.00
US97 Salvador Perez .15 .40
US98 Anthony Rizzo .30 .75
US99 Scott Kazmir .12 .30
US100 Jose Abreu RC 3.00 8.00
US101 Kyle Blanks .12 .30
US102 Daniel Murphy .15 .40
US103 Starlin Castro .12 .30
US104 Luis Sardinas RC .40 1.00
US105 Ehire Adrianza RC .40 1.00
US106A Collin Cowgill .12 .30
US106B Collin Cowgill SP 1.50 4.00
SABRmetrics
US107A Josh Collmenter .12 .30
US107B Josh Collmenter SP 1.50 4.00
SABRmetrics
US108 Ryan Doumit .12 .30
US109 David Lough .12 .30
US110 Jackie Bradley Jr. .20 .50
US111A Emilio Bonifacio .12 .30
US111B Emilio Bonifacio SP 1.50 4.00
SABRmetrics
US112 Alfredo Simon .12 .30
US113 Oscar Taveras RC .50 1.25
US114 Jeff Francis .12 .30
US115 Nyjer Morgan .12 .30
US116 Brett Anderson .12 .30
US117A John Lackey .15 .40
US117B Bryan Holaday .12 .30
US117C John Lackey SP 2.00 5.00
SABRmetrics
US118 Collin McHugh .12 .30
US119 Mike Dunn RC .40 1.00
US120 Randy Wolf .12 .30
US121 Kyle Crockett RC .50 1.25
US122 Jeff Baker .12 .30
US123 Lyle Overbay .12 .30
US124 Nick Tepesch .12 .30
US125 Jason Bartlett .12 .30
US126 Omar Quintanilla .12 .30
US127 David Phelps .12 .30
US128 Luke Gregerson .12 .30
US129 Mike Adams .12 .30
US130 Tony Watson .12 .30
US131 Chris Denorfia .12 .30
US132A Tyler Colvin .12 .30
US132B Tyler Colvin SP 1.50 4.00
SABRmetrics
US133 Chris Young .12 .30
US134 Tony Cruz .12 .30
US135A Jake Odorizzi .12 .30
US135B Jake Odorizzi SP 1.50 4.00
SABRmetrics
US136 Dioner Navarro .12 .30
US137A Doug Fister .12 .30
US137B Doug Fister SP 1.50 4.00
SABRmetrics
US138 Asdrubal Cabrera .15 .40
US139 Jason Hammel .15 .40
US140 Nick Hundley .12 .30
US141 Chris Dickerson .12 .30
US142 Jon Lester .15 .40
US143A Jake Peavy .12 .30
US143B Jake Peavy SP 1.50 4.00
SABRmetrics
US144 Hector Rondon RC .40 1.00
US145 A.J. Pierzynski .12 .30
US146 Neftali Soto RC .40 1.00
US147 James Jones RC .40 1.00
US148 Kyle Parker RC .50 1.25
US149 C.J. Cron RC .40 1.00
US150A Jon Singleton RC .50 1.25
US150B Jon Singleton SP 2.00 5.00
Orange jersey
US151 Robinson Cano .15 .40
US152 Josh Donaldson .15 .40
US153 Kurt Suzuki .12 .30
US154 Yu Darvish .20 .50
US155 Devin Mesoraco .12 .30
US156 Ronald Belisario .12 .30
US157 Joe Smith .12 .30
US158A Eric Chavez .12 .30
US158B Eric Chavez SP 1.50 4.00
SABRmetrics
US159 Tyler Pastornicky .12 .30
US160A Delmon Young .15 .40
US160B Delmon Young SP 2.00 5.00
SABRmetrics
US161 Edward Mujica .12 .30
US162 Yoenis Cespedes .20 .50
US163 Ramon Santiago .12 .30
US164A Joe Kelly .12 .30
US164B Josh Tomlin .12 .30
US164C Joe Kelly SP 1.50 4.00
SABRmetrics
US165A Justin Morneau .15 .40
US165B Justin Morneau SP 2.00 5.00
SABRmetrics
US166 Andrew Romine .12 .30
US167 Jeff Francoeur .15 .40
US168 Austin Jackson .12 .30
US169A Chone Figgins .12 .30
US169B Chone Figgins SP 1.50 4.00
SABRmetrics
US170 Matt Davidson RC .50 1.25
US171A Chase Whitley RC .40 1.00
US171B Chase Whitley SP 1.50 4.00
Grey jersey
US172 Tucker Barnhart RC .40 1.00
US173 Jose Bautista .15 .40
US174 Jace Peterson RC .40 1.00
US175 Oscar Taveras .15 .40
US176 Michael Brantley .15 .40
US177 Dee Gordon .12 .30
US178 Clayton Kershaw .40 1.00
US179 John Baker .12 .30
US180 Chris Taylor RC 2.00 5.00
US181A Tony Gwynn Jr. .12 .30
US181B Tony Gwynn Jr. SP 1.50 4.00
SABRmetrics
US182 Chris Colabello .12 .30
US183 Kelly Johnson .12 .30
US184 Danny Santana RC .50 1.25
US185A Juan Francisco .12 .30
US185B Juan Francisco SP 1.50 4.00
SABRmetrics
US186 Arismendy Alcantara RC .40 1.00
US187 Jonathan Herrera .12 .30
US188 Paul Maholm .12 .30
US189 Brandon Cumpton RC .40 1.00
US190 Jose Altuve .15 .40
US191 Yoenis Cespedes .20 .50
US192 Pat Neshek .12 .30
US193 Robinson Chirinos .12 .30
US194A Hector Santiago .12 .30
US194B Hector Santiago SP 1.50 4.00
SABRmetrics
US195A Gerald Laird .12 .30
US195B Gerald Laird SP 1.50 4.00
SABRmetrics
US196A Erisbel Arruebarrena RC .40 1.00
US196B Erisbel Arruebarrena SP 1.50 4.00
Fielding
US197A Marcus Stroman .20 .50
US197B Marcus Stroman SP 2.50 6.00
Looking up
US198 Adam Jones .15 .40
US199 Julio Teheran .15 .40
US200 Masahiro Tanaka .40 1.00
US201 Derek Norris .12 .30
US202 Rubby De La Rosa (RC) .40 1.00
US203 Cole Figueroa RC .40 1.00
US204A Chris Capuano .12 .30
US204B Chris Capuano SP 1.50 4.00
SABRmetrics
US205 Reed Johnson .12 .30
US206 Chris Perez .12 .30
US207A Rajai Davis .12 .30
US207B Rajai Davis SP 1.50 4.00
SABRmetrics
US208 Joakim Soria .12 .30
US209 Roger Bernadina .12 .30
US210 George Springer .50 1.25
US211 Jordan Schafer .12 .30
US212 Randy Choate .12 .30
US213A Stefen Romero RC .40 1.00
US213B Stefen Romero SP 1.50 4.00
Fielding
US214 Tommy La Stella RC .40 1.00
US215 Paul Goldschmidt .20 .50
US216 Andrew McCutchen .20 .50
US217 Charlie Furbush .12 .30
US218 David Carpenter .12 .30
US219A Mike Olt .12 .30
US219B Mike Olt SP 1.50 4.00
SABRmetrics
US220A Roenis Elias RC .40 1.00
US220B Roenis Elias SP 1.50 4.00
With water
US221A Gregory Polanco .20 .50
US221B Polanco SP Blk Jsy 2.50 6.00
US222 Brandon Moss .12 .30
US223 Yasiel Puig .20 .50
US224 Jared Burton .12 .30
US225A Luis Avilan .12 .30
US225B Luis Avilan SP 1.50 4.00
SABRmetrics
US226 Chris Coghlan .12 .30
US227 Ryan Wheeler .12 .30
US228 Aaron Crow .12 .30
US229A Sam Fuld .12 .30
US229B Sam Fuld SP 1.50 4.00
SABRmetrics
US230 Kurt Suzuki .12 .30
US231 Brendan Ryan .12 .30
US232 Scott Carroll RC .40 1.00
US233 Nelson Cruz .20 .50
US234 Felix Hernandez .15 .40
US235A Tommy Hunter .12 .30
US235B Tommy Hunter SP 1.50 4.00
SABRmetrics
US236 Jerome Williams .12 .30
US237 Jorge Polanco RC .40 1.00
US238 Giancarlo Stanton .20 .50
US239 Jose Abreu 1.00 2.50
US240 Aaron Sanchez RC .40 1.00
US241A Michael Choice RC .40 1.00
US241B Michael Choice SP 1.50 4.00
Blue jersey
US242 Javier Lopez .12 .30
US243 Jesse Chavez .12 .30
US244A Daisuke Matsuzaka .15 .40
US244B Daisuke Matsuzaka SP 2.00 5.00
White jersey
US244C Daisuke Matsuzaka SP 2.00 5.00
SABRmetrics
US245A Andrew Heaney .12 .30
US245B Andrew Heaney SP 1.50 4.00
Black jersey
US246 Erick Aybar .12 .30
US247 Tony Watson .12 .30
US248 Brayan Pena .12 .30
US249 Eduardo Nunez .12 .30
US250 Yu Darvish .20 .50
US251 Ike Davis .12 .30
US252 Adrian Nieto RC .40 1.00
US253 Kevin Kiermaier RC .60 1.50
US254 Adrian Beltre .20 .50
US255 Jonathan Lucroy .15 .40
US256 Garrett Jones .12 .30
US257 Eduardo Escobar .12 .30
US258 Matt Carpenter .20 .50
US259 Craig Kimbrel .15 .40
US260A Jhonny Peralta .12 .30
US260B Jhonny Peralta SP 1.50 4.00
SABRmetrics
US261 Rene Rivera .12 .30
US262 Eddie Butler RC .40 1.00
US263 Kyle Seager .12 .30
US264 Freddie Freeman .25 .60
US265 Yoervis Medina .12 .30
US266 Drew Smyly .12 .30
US267 Jonathan Diaz RC .40 1.00
US268 Matt Shoemaker RC .60 1.50
US269 Max Scherzer .20 .50
US270 Hunter Pence .15 .40
US271 Juan Perez RC .40 1.00
US272A Mark Ellis .12 .30
US272B Mark Ellis SP 1.50 4.00
SABRmetrics
US273 Martin Prado .12 .30
US274 Chris Withrow .12 .30
US275 Boone Logan .12 .30
US276 Rougned Odor RC .75 2.00
US277 Chris Sale .20 .50
US278A Rafael Montero RC .40 1.00
US278B Rafael Montero SP 1.50 4.00
Throwing underhand
US279 Kevin Frandsen .12 .30
US280 Cole Gillespie .12 .30
US281 David Buchanan RC .40 1.00
US282 Glen Perkins .12 .30
US283 Tyson Ross .12 .30
US284 Robbie Ray RC .40 1.00
US285 Cody Allen .12 .30
US286 Brandon Barnes .12 .30
US287 Mike Bolsinger RC .40 1.00
US288 Aroldis Chapman .20 .50
US289 Adam Wainwright .15 .40
US290 Cam Bedrosian RC .40 1.00
US291 Jake McGee .12 .30
US292 Chase Utley .15 .40
US293 Tom Koehler .12 .30
US294 Chris Martin RC .40 1.00
US295 Greg Holland .12 .30
US296 Tyler Moore .12 .30
US297 Zack Greinke .15 .40
US298A Bobby Abreu .12 .30
US298B Bobby Abreu SP 1.50 4.00
On deck
US299 Charlie Blackmon .20 .50
US300 Miguel Cabrera .20 .50
US301 Mookie Betts 2.50 6.00
US302 Tom Gorzelanny .12 .30
US303 Jarred Cosart .12 .30
US304 Nick Martinez RC .40 1.00
US305 Sean Doolittle .12 .30
US306 Logan Forsythe .12 .30
US307 Santiago Casilla .12 .30
US308 Zelous Wheeler RC .40 1.00
US309 Alexei Ramirez .15 .40
US310 Troy Tulowitzki .20 .50
US312 Matt Thornton .12 .30
US313 Derek Dietrich .15 .40
US314 Corey Dickerson .12 .30
US315 Carlos Gomez .12 .30
US316 Ian Krol .12 .30
US317 Marwin Gonzalez .12 .30
US318 Logan Schafer .12 .30
US319A Ricky Nolasco .12 .30
US319B Ricky Nolasco SP 1.50 4.00
SABRmetrics
US320 Koji Uehara .12 .30
US321 Josh Satin .12 .30
US322A Drew Pomeranz .15 .40
US322B Drew Pomeranz SP 2.00 5.00
SABRmetrics
US323A Chase Headley .12 .30
US323B Chase Headley SP 1.50 4.00
SABRmetrics
US324 Alexi Amarista .12 .30
US325 Jose Abreu 1.00 2.50
US326A Joaquin Benoit .12 .30
US326B Joaquin Benoit SP 1.50 4.00
SABRmetrics
US327 Jonny Gomes .12 .30
US328A Dustin Ackley .12 .30
US328B Dustin Ackley SP 1.50 4.00
SABRmetrics
US329 Todd Frazier .15 .40
US330 Daniel Webb RC .40 1.00

2014 Topps Update Black

*BLACK: 8X TO 20X BASIC
*BLACK RC: 2.5X TO 6X BASIC RC
STATED ODDS 1:62 HOBBY
STATED PRINT RUN 63 SER.#'d SETS
US2 Derek Jeter 25.00 60.00
US54 Mike Trout 20.00 50.00
US100 Jose Abreu 15.00 40.00
US178 Clayton Kershaw 20.00 50.00
US223 Yasiel Puig 15.00 40.00
US239 Jose Abreu 15.00 40.00
US325 Jose Abreu 15.00 40.00

2014 Topps Update Camo

*CAMO VET: 8X TO 20X BASIC
*CAMO RC: 2.5X TO 6X BASIC RC
STATED ODDS 1:103 HOBBY
STATED PRINT RUN 99 SER.#'d SETS
US2 Derek Jeter 25.00 60.00
US54 Mike Trout 20.00 50.00
US100 Jose Abreu 15.00 40.00
US178 Clayton Kershaw 20.00 50.00
US223 Yasiel Puig 15.00 40.00
US239 Jose Abreu 15.00 40.00
US325 Jose Abreu 15.00 40.00

2014 Topps Update Gold

*GOLD VET: 1.2X TO 3X BASIC
*GOLD RC: .4X TO 1X BASIC RC
STATED ODDS 1:3 HOBBY
STATED PRINT RUN 2014 SER.#'d SETS

2014 Topps Update Pink

*PINK VET: 10X TO 25X BASIC
*PINK RC: 3X TO 8X BASIC RC
STATED ODDS 1:203 HOBBY
STATED PRINT RUN 50 SER.#'d SETS
US2 Derek Jeter 30.00 80.00
US54 Mike Trout 25.00 60.00
US100 Jose Abreu 20.00 50.00
US178 Clayton Kershaw 25.00 60.00
US223 Yasiel Puig 20.00 50.00
US239 Jose Abreu 20.00 50.00
US325 Jose Abreu 20.00 50.00

2014 Topps Update Red Hot Foil

*RED FOIL VET: 1.5X TO 4X BASIC
*RED FOIL RC: .4X TO 1X BASIC RC
STATED ODDS 1:6 HOBBY

2014 Topps Update Sparkle

RANDOM INSERTS IN PACKS
US10 George Springer 15.00 40.00
US23 Ubaldo Jimenez 6.00 15.00
US37 Leury Garcia 6.00 15.00
US45 Pedro Ciriaco 6.00 15.00
US59 Brandon McCarthy 6.00 15.00
US63 David Murphy 6.00 15.00
US64 LaTroy Hawkins 6.00 15.00
US70 Jarrod Saltalamacchia 6.00 15.00
US95 Vidal Nuno 6.00 15.00
US106 Collin Cowgill 6.00 15.00
US107 Josh Collmenter 6.00 15.00
US109 David Lough 6.00 15.00
US114 Jeff Francis 6.00 15.00
US115 Nyjer Morgan 6.00 15.00
US116 Brett Anderson 6.00 15.00
US120 Randy Wolf 6.00 15.00
US122 Jeff Baker 6.00 15.00
US124 Nick Tepesch 6.00 15.00
US137 Doug Fister 6.00 15.00
US142 Jon Lester 8.00 20.00
US148 Kyle Parker 8.00 20.00
US157 Joe Smith 6.00 15.00
US161 Edward Mujica 6.00 15.00
US163 Ramon Santiago 6.00 15.00
US166 Andrew Romine 6.00 15.00
US169 Chone Figgins 6.00 15.00
US170 Matt Davidson 8.00 20.00
US188 Paul Maholm 6.00 15.00
US194 Hector Santiago 6.00 15.00
US203 Cole Figueroa 6.00 15.00
US205 Reed Johnson 6.00 15.00
US206 Chris Perez 6.00 15.00
US214 Tommy La Stella 6.00 15.00
US226 Chris Coghlan 6.00 15.00
US237 Jorge Polanco 6.00 15.00
US271 Juan Perez 6.00 15.00
US275 Boone Logan 6.00 15.00
US276 Rougned Odor 12.00 30.00
US278 Rafael Montero 6.00 15.00
US281 David Buchanan 6.00 15.00
US284 Robbie Ray 6.00 15.00
US287 Mike Bolsinger 6.00 15.00
US290 Cam Bedrosian 6.00 15.00
US291 Jake McGee 6.00 15.00
US302 Tom Gorzelanny 6.00 15.00
US316 Ian Krol 6.00 15.00
US317 Marwin Gonzalez 6.00 15.00
US328 Dustin Ackley 6.00 15.00
US330 Daniel Webb 6.00 15.00

2014 Topps Update Target Red Border

*TARGET VET: 1.2X TO 3X BASIC
*TARGET RC: .4X TO 1X BASIC

2014 Topps Update Wal-Mart Blue Border

*WM VET: 1.2X TO 3X BASIC
*WM RC: .4X TO 1X BASIC

2014 Topps Update All Star Access

RANDOM INSERTS IN PACKS
ASAAC Aroldis Chapman 2.50 6.00
ASAAJ Adam Jones 2.00 5.00
ASAAM Andrew McCutchen 2.50 6.00
ASAARA Alexei Ramirez 2.00 5.00
ASAARI Anthony Rizzo 4.00 10.00
ASABM Brandon Moss 1.50 4.00
ASADG Dee Gordon 1.50 4.00
ASADJ Derek Jeter 6.00 15.00
ASADM Daniel Murphy 2.00 5.00
ASAEA Erick Aybar 1.50 4.00
ASAFH Felix Hernandez 2.00 5.00
ASAGS Giancarlo Stanton 2.50 6.00
ASAJB Jose Bautista 2.00 5.00
ASAJS Jeff Samardzija 1.50 4.00
ASAKU Koji Uehara 1.50 4.00
ASAMCA Miguel Cabrera 2.50 6.00
ASAMCR Matt Carpenter 2.50 6.00
ASAMS Max Scherzer 2.50 6.00
ASAMT Mike Trout 12.00 30.00
ASARC Robinson Cano 2.00 5.00
ASASP Salvador Perez 2.00 5.00
ASATT Troy Tulowitzki 2.50 6.00
ASAYC Yoenis Cespedes 2.50 6.00
ASAYD Yu Darvish 2.50 6.00
ASAYP Yasiel Puig 2.50 6.00

2014 Topps Update All Star Access Autographs

RANDOM INSERTS IN PACKS
STATED PRINT RUN 25 SER.#'d SETS
EXCHANGE DEADLINE 9/30/2017
AAAJA Jose Abreu 100.00 200.00
AAANC Nelson Cruz 30.00 80.00
AAARC Robinson Cano 25.00 60.00
AAATF Todd Frazier 25.00 60.00

2014 Topps Update All Star Access Relics

RANDOM INSERTS IN PACKS
STATED PRINT RUN 99 SER.#'d SETS
ASARAM Andrew McCutchen 20.00 50.00
ASARCK Clayton Kershaw 15.00 40.00
ASARDJ Derek Jeter 25.00 60.00
ASARJB Jose Bautista 6.00 15.00
ASARMTT Mike Trout 40.00 100.00
ASARRC Robinson Cano 6.00 15.00
ASARTT Troy Tulowitzki 8.00 20.00
ASARYC Yoenis Cespedes 12.00 30.00
ASARYD Yu Darvish 8.00 20.00
ASARYP Yasiel Puig 12.00 30.00

2014 Topps Update All Star Stitches

STATED ODDS 1:52 HOBBY
*GOLD/50: .75X TO 2X BASIC
ASRAJ Adam Jones 3.00 8.00
ASRAM Andrew McCutchen 4.00 10.00
ASRARI Anthony Rizzo 6.00 15.00
ASRARR Aramis Ramirez 2.50 6.00
ASRAW Adam Wainwright 3.00 8.00
ASRCB Charlie Blackmon 4.00 10.00
ASRCG Carlos Gomez 2.50 6.00
ASRCKE Clayton Kershaw 5.00 12.00
ASRCKI Craig Kimbrel 3.00 8.00
ASRCS Chris Sale 4.00 10.00
ASRCU Chase Utley 3.00 8.00
ASRDG Dee Gordon 2.50 6.00
ASRDJ Derek Jeter 10.00 25.00
ASRDME Devin Mesoraco 2.50 6.00
ASRDMU Daniel Murphy 3.00 8.00
ASRFF Freddie Freeman 5.00 12.00
ASRFH Felix Hernandez 3.00 8.00
ASRFR Francisco Rodriguez 3.00 8.00
ASRGP Glen Perkins 2.50 6.00
ASRGS Giancarlo Stanton 4.00 10.00
ASRHP Hunter Pence 3.00 8.00
ASRJA Jose Abreu 6.00 15.00
ASRJB Jose Bautista 3.00 8.00
ASRJD Josh Donaldson 3.00 8.00
ASRJLU Jonathan Lucroy 3.00 8.00
ASRKSE Kyle Seager 2.50 6.00
ASRKU Koji Uehara 2.50 6.00
ASRMCA Matt Carpenter 4.00 10.00
ASRMCR Miguel Cabrera 5.00 12.00
ASRMS Max Scherzer 4.00 10.00
ASRMT Mike Trout 20.00 50.00
ASRNC Nelson Cruz 4.00 10.00
ASRPG Paul Goldschmidt 4.00 10.00
ASRRC Robinson Cano 3.00 8.00
ASRSC Starlin Castro 2.50 6.00
ASRTR Tyson Ross 2.50 6.00
ASRTT Troy Tulowitzki 4.00 10.00
ASRYC Yoenis Cespedes 4.00 10.00
ASRYD Yu Darvish 4.00 10.00
ASRYP Yasiel Puig 5.00 12.00

2014 Topps Update All Star Stitches Autographs

STATED ODDS 1:4146 HOBBY
STATED PRINT RUN 25 SER.#'d SETS
EXCHANGE DEADLINE 9/30/2017
ASTARAJ Adam Jones 30.00 80.00
ASTARBM Brandon Moss 20.00 50.00
ASTARCB Charlie Blackmon 30.00 80.00
ASTARGP Glen Perkins 25.00 60.00
ASTARGS Giancarlo Stanton 40.00 100.00
ASTARJA Jose Abreu 100.00 200.00
ASTARJD Josh Donaldson 30.00 80.00
ASTARJH Josh Harrison EXCH 30.00 80.00
ASTARJL Jonathan Lucroy 30.00 80.00
ASTARKS Kyle Seager 25.00 60.00
ASTARMC Matt Carpenter 30.00 80.00
ASTARMS Max Scherzer 50.00 120.00
ASTARNC Nelson Cruz 30.00 80.00
ASTARPG Paul Goldschmidt 30.00 80.00
ASTARTT Troy Tulowitzki 30.00 80.00

2014 Topps Update All Star Stitches Dual

STATED ODDS 1:11,001 HOBBY
STATED PRINT RUN 25 SER.#'d SETS
ASDAR J.Abreu/A.Ramirez 30.00 80.00
ASDBT T.Tulowitzki/C.Blackmon 20.00 50.00
ASDCD Y.Cespedes/J.Donaldson 20.00 50.00
ASDCG Cabrera/Goldschmidt 20.00 50.00
ASDGR A.Ramirez/C.Gomez 12.00 30.00
ASDJT Tulowitzki/Jeter 50.00 125.00
ASDKP Y.Puig/C.Kershaw 40.00 100.00
ASDMJ D.Murphy/D.Jeter 40.00 100.00
ASDTP M.Trout/Y.Puig 100.00 250.00

2014 Topps Update All Star Stitches Triple

STATED ODDS 1:5108 HOBBY
STATED PRINT RUN 25 SER.#'d SETS
ASTRACY McCtchn/Puig/Gmz 40.00 100.00
ASTRAJY McCtchn/Puig/Hrrsn 40.00 100.00
ASTRAYG McCtchn/Stntn/Puig 40.00 100.00
ASTRCJA Gomez/Ramirez/Lucroy 25.00 60.00
ASTRCYD Kershaw/Puig/Gordon 50.00 120.00
ASTRJCA Sale/Ramirez/Abreu 25.00 60.00
ASTRJMA Bautista/Trout/Jones 50.00 120.00
ASTRMIM Cbrr/Knslr/Schrzr 30.00 80.00
ASTRRKF Hernandez/Cano/Seager 25.00 60.00
ASTRYJB Moss/Cespedes/Donaldson 30.00 80.00

2014 Topps Update Fond Farewells

COMPLETE SET (15) 4.00 10.00
STATED ODDS 1:8 HOBBY
FFAK Al Kaline .40 1.00
FFCR Cal Ripken Jr. 1.25 3.00
FFDJ Derek Jeter 1.00 2.50
FFGB George Brett .75 2.00
FFJS John Smoltz .40 1.00
FFMM Mark McGwire .75 2.00
FFMR Mariano Rivera .50 1.25
FFOV Omar Vizquel .30 .75
FFPK Paul Konerko .30 .75
FFRC Rod Carew .30 .75
FFRH Roy Halladay .30 .75
FFRY Robin Yount .40 1.00
FFTH Todd Helton .30 .75
FFWS Willie Stargell .30 .75

2014 Topps Update Fond Farewells Autographs

STATED ODDS 1:22,002 HOBBY
STATED PRINT RUN 25 SER.#'d SETS
EXCHANGE DEADLINE 9/30/2017
FFAAK Al Kaline 30.00 80.00
FFAJS John Smoltz 40.00 100.00
FFAOV Omar Vizquel 150.00 250.00
FFAPM Paul Molitor 25.00 60.00

2014 Topps Update Fond Farewells Relics

STATED ODDS 1:2777 HOBBY
STATED PRINT RUN 99 SER.#'d SETS
FFRCR Cal Ripken Jr. 15.00 40.00
FFRDJ Derek Jeter 25.00 60.00
FFRJS John Smoltz 8.00 20.00
FFRMM Mark McGwire 15.00 40.00
FFRMR Mariano Rivera 10.00 25.00
FFRPK Paul Konerko 6.00 15.00
FFRPM Paul Molitor 8.00 20.00
FFRRH Roy Halladay 6.00 15.00
FFRRY Robin Yount 8.00 20.00
FFRTH Todd Helton 6.00 15.00

2014 Topps Update Framed Derek Jeter Reprints Black

STATED ODDS 1:1211 HOBBY
STATED PRINT RUN 75 SER.#'d SETS
*SILVER: .5X TO 1.2X BASIC
SILVER ODDS 1:2848 HOBBY
SILVER PRINT RUN 25 SER.#'d SETS
*GOLD: 1X TO 2.5X BASIC
GOLD ODDS 1:7067 HOBBY
SILVER PRINT RUN 10 SER.#'d SETS
1994 Derek Jeter 15.00 40.00
1995 Derek Jeter 15.00 40.00
1996 Derek Jeter 15.00 40.00
1997 Derek Jeter 15.00 40.00
1998 Derek Jeter 15.00 40.00
1999 Derek Jeter 15.00 40.00
2000 Derek Jeter 15.00 40.00
2001 Derek Jeter 15.00 40.00
2002 Derek Jeter 15.00 40.00
2003 Derek Jeter 15.00 40.00
2004 Derek Jeter 15.00 40.00
2005 Derek Jeter 15.00 40.00
2006 Derek Jeter 15.00 40.00
2007 Derek Jeter 15.00 40.00
2008 Derek Jeter 15.00 40.00
2009 Derek Jeter 15.00 40.00
2010 Derek Jeter 15.00 40.00
2011 Derek Jeter 15.00 40.00
2012 Derek Jeter 15.00 40.00
2013 Derek Jeter 15.00 40.00
2014 Derek Jeter 15.00 40.00

2014 Topps Update Power Players

COMPLETE SET (25) 4.00 10.00
STATED ODDS 1:6 HOBBY
PPAAG Adrian Gonzalez .30 .75
PPAAJ Adam Jones .30 .75
PPAAM Andrew McCutchen .40 1.00
PPAAP Albert Pujols .50 1.25
PPAAR Anthony Rizzo .60 1.50
PPAAW Adam Wainwright .30 .75
PPACK Clayton Kershaw .75 2.00
PPAFH Felix Hernandez .30 .75
PPAGS Giancarlo Stanton .40 1.00
PPAHR Hanley Ramirez .30 .75
PPAJA Jose Abreu 2.00 5.00
PPAJB Jose Bautista .30 .75
PPAJE Jacoby Ellsbury .30 .75
PPAJU Justin Upton .30 .75
PPAMC Miguel Cabrera .40 1.00
PPAMS Max Scherzer .40 1.00
PPAPG Paul Goldschmidt .40 1.00
PPARC Robinson Cano .30 .75
PPASR Sergio Romo .25 .60
PPATT Troy Tulowitzki .40 1.00
PPAYV Yordano Ventura .30 .75
PPACGN Carlos Gonzalez .30 .75
PPACGM Carlos Gomez .25 .60
PPAMTA Masahiro Tanaka .75 2.00
PPAMTR Mike Trout 2.00 5.00

2014 Topps Update Power Players Relics

STATED ODDS 1:2777 HOBBY
STATED PRINT RUN 99 SER.#'d SETS
PPRAP Albert Pujols 6.00 15.00
PPRAR Anthony Rizzo 8.00 20.00
PPRCGM Carlos Gomez 3.00 8.00
PPRCGN Carlos Gonzalez 4.00 10.00
PPRGS Giancarlo Stanton 5.00 12.00
PPRJB Jose Bautista 4.00 10.00
PPRMTA Masahiro Tanaka 10.00 25.00
PPRMTR Mike Trout 25.00 60.00
PPRPG Paul Goldschmidt 5.00 12.00
PPRTT Troy Tulowitzki 5.00 12.00

2014 Topps Update World Series Championship Trophies

STATED ODDS 1:2712 HOBBY
WSCTAP Albert Pujols 12.00 30.00
WSCTBRO Brooks Robinson 8.00 20.00
WSCTBRU Babe Ruth 15.00 40.00
WSCTCH Cole Hamels 8.00 20.00
WSCTCR Cal Ripken Jr. 15.00 40.00
WSCTDF David Freese 6.00 15.00
WSCTDJ Derek Jeter 20.00 50.00
WSCTDO David Ortiz 12.00 30.00
WSCTGB George Brett 10.00 25.00
WSCTGM Greg Maddux 12.00 30.00
WSCTJB Johnny Bench 10.00 25.00
WSCTJM Joe Morgan 8.00 20.00
WSCTJP Johnny Podres 6.00 15.00
WSCTMC Miguel Cabrera 10.00 25.00
WSCTMR Manny Ramirez 10.00 25.00
WSCTPM Pedro Martinez 8.00 20.00
WSCTPS Pablo Sandoval 8.00 20.00
WSCTRC Roberto Clemente 20.00 50.00
WSCTRJ Randy Johnson 10.00 25.00
WSCTSC Steve Carlton 8.00 20.00
WSCTSK Sandy Koufax 12.00 30.00
WSCTSM Stan Musial 15.00 40.00
WSCTTS Tom Seaver 12.00 30.00
WSCTWF Whitey Ford 8.00 20.00
WSCTWS Willie Stargell 8.00 20.00

2014 Topps Update World Series Heroes

STATED ODDS 1:8 HOBBY
WSHAP Albert Pujols .75 2.00
WSHBM Bill Mazeroski .50 1.25
WSHBR Brooks Robinson .50 1.25
WSHBSA Bret Saberhagen .40 1.00
WSHBSU Bruce Sutter .40 1.00
WSHCC Chris Carpenter .50 1.25
WSHCH Cole Hamels .50 1.25
WSHCS Chris Sabo .40 1.00
WSHDC David Cone .40 1.00
WSHDE David Eckstein .40 1.00
WSHDF David Freese .40 1.00
WSHDJ Derek Jeter 1.50 4.00
WSHDO David Ortiz .60 1.50
WSHDS Duke Snider .50 1.25
WSHEM Eddie Murray .50 1.25
WSHFV Fernando Valenzuela .40 1.00
WSHGB George Brett 1.25 3.00
WSHGC Gary Carter .50 1.25
WSHGS Gary Sheffield .40 1.00
WSHHA Hank Aaron 1.25 3.00
WSHIR Ivan Rodriguez .50 1.25
WSHJB Josh Beckett .40 1.00
WSHJBE Johnny Bench .60 1.50
WSHJL John Lackey .50 1.25
WSHJM Joe Morgan .50 1.25
WSHJP Jonathan Papelbon .50 1.25
WSHJS John Smoltz .60 1.50
WSHLH Livan Hernandez .50 1.25
WSHMRA Manny Ramirez .60 1.50
WSHMRI Mariano Rivera .75 2.00
WSHMS Mike Schmidt 1.00 2.50
WSHMW Mookie Wilson .40 1.00
WSHOH Orlando Hernandez .40 1.00
WSHPMA Pedro Martinez .50 1.25
WSHPMO Paul Molitor .60 1.50
WSHPS Pablo Sandoval .50 1.25
WSHRA Roberto Alomar .50 1.25
WSHRC Roberto Clemente 1.50 4.00
WSHRH Rickey Henderson .60 1.50
WSHRJ Reggie Jackson .50 1.25
WSHRJA Reggie Jackson .50 1.25
WSHRJO Randy Johnson .60 1.50
WSHSC Steve Carlton .50 1.25
WSHSK Sandy Koufax 1.25 3.00
WSHTG Tom Glavine .50 1.25
WSHTL Tim Lincecum .50 1.25
WSHTS Tom Seaver .50 1.25
WSHWF Whitey Ford .50 1.25
WSHWS Willie Stargell .50 1.25

2014 Topps Update World Series Heroes Autographs

STATED ODDS 1:4401 HOBBY
PRINT RUNS B/WN 25-200 COPIES PER
EXCHANGE DEADLINE 9/30/2017
WSHACS Chris Sabo/200 15.00 40.00
WSHADC David Cone/25 15.00 40.00
WSHADE David Eckstein/25 100.00 200.00
WSHAGC Gary Carter/25 25.00 60.00
WSHAJS John Smoltz/25 40.00 100.00
WSHALH Livan Hernandez/25 15.00 40.00

WSHAMW Mookie Wilson/200 15.00 40.00
WSHAOH Orlando Hernandez/25 25.00 60.00
WSHABSA Bret Saberhagen/50 15.00 40.00

2014 Topps Update World Series Heroes Relics

STATED ODDS 1:2777 HOBBY
STATED PRINT RUN 99 SER.#'d SETS
WSHRAP Albert Pujols 8.00 20.00
WSHRDJ Derek Jeter 15.00 40.00
WSHRDO David Ortiz 20.00 50.00
WSHRIR Ivan Rodriguez 5.00 12.00
WSHRJM Joe Morgan 5.00 12.00
WSHRMRI Mariano Rivera 8.00 20.00
WSHRMS Mike Schmidt 12.00 30.00
WSHRPS Pablo Sandoval 5.00 12.00
WSHRRA Roberto Alomar 5.00 12.00
WSHRTG Tom Glavine 5.00 12.00

2014 Topps Update World Series MVP Patches

RANDOM INSERTS IN PACKS
WSPBR Brooks Robinson 5.00 12.00
WSPBS Bret Saberhagen 4.00 10.00
WSPCH Cole Hamels 5.00 12.00
WSPDE David Eckstein 4.00 10.00
WSPDF David Freese 4.00 10.00
WSPDJ Derek Jeter 10.00 25.00
WSPDO David Ortiz 6.00 15.00
WSPJB Johnny Bench 6.00 15.00
WSPJBE Josh Beckett 4.00 10.00
WSPJP Johnny Podres 4.00 10.00
WSPLH Livan Hernandez 4.00 10.00
WSPMR Mariano Rivera 6.00 15.00
WSPMRA Manny Ramirez 6.00 15.00
WSPMS Mike Schmidt 6.00 15.00
WSPPM Paul Molitor 6.00 15.00
WSPPS Pablo Sandoval 5.00 12.00
WSPRC Roberto Clemente 10.00 25.00
WSPRF Rollie Fingers 5.00 12.00
WSPRJ Reggie Jackson 5.00 12.00
WSPRJA Reggie Jackson 5.00 12.00
WSPRJO Randy Johnson 6.00 15.00
WSPSK Sandy Koufax 8.00 20.00
WSPTG Tom Glavine 5.00 12.00
WSPWF Whitey Ford 5.00 12.00
WSPWS Willie Stargell 5.00 12.00

2014 Topps Update World Series Rings Gold Gems

*GOLD GEM: 2X TO 5X BASIC
STATED ODDS 1:10,794 HOBBY
STATED PRINT RUN 25 SER.#'d SETS

2014 Topps Update World Series Rings Silver

STATED ODDS 1:756 HOBBY
*GOLD: .6X TO 1.5X BASIC
GOLD STATED ODDS 1:2712 HOBBY
GOLD PRINT RUN 99 SER.#'d SETS
*GOLD GEM: 2X TO 5X BASIC
GOLD GEM STATED ODDS 1:10,794 HOBBY
GOLD GEM PRINT RUN 25 SER.#'d SETS
WSRBF Bob Feller 5.00 12.00
WSRBR Babe Ruth 10.00 25.00
WSRBS Bret Saberhagen 4.00 10.00
WSRDO David Ortiz 6.00 15.00
WSREM Eddie Murray 5.00 12.00
WSRFR Frank Robinson 5.00 12.00
WSRHA Hank Aaron 6.00 15.00
WSRJB Johnny Bench 6.00 15.00
WSRJF Jimmie Foxx 6.00 15.00
WSRJP Johnny Podres 4.00 10.00
WSRMR Mariano Rivera 6.00 15.00
WSRMS Mike Schmidt 5.00 12.00
WSROC Orlando Cepeda 5.00 12.00
WSROS Ozzie Smith 6.00 15.00
WSRRC Roberto Clemente 10.00 25.00
WSRRH Rickey Henderson 6.00 15.00
WSRRJA Reggie Jackson 5.00 12.00
WSRRJO Randy Johnson 6.00 15.00
WSRRM Roger Maris 6.00 15.00
WSRSK Sandy Koufax 6.00 15.00
WSRSM Stan Musial 8.00 20.00
WSRTG Tom Glavine 5.00 12.00
WSRWF Whitey Ford 5.00 12.00
WSRWS Willie Stargell 5.00 12.00
WSRYB Yogi Berra 6.00 15.00

2015 Topps

COMPLETE SET (755) 25.00 60.00
COMP.RED.HOB.FACT SET (700) 30.00 80.00
COMP.BLUE.RET.FACT SET (700) 30.00 80.00
COMP.PURP.RET.FACT SET (700) 30.00 80.00
COMP.SER.1 SET w/o SP's (350) 12.00 30.00
COMP.SER.2 SET w/o SP's (350) 12.00 30.00
SER.1 VAR RANDOMLY INSERTED
FIVE RC VAR PER FACTORY SET
SER.2 VAR STATED ODDS 1:67 HOBBY
SER.1 PLATE ODDS 1:1721 HOBBY
SER.2 PLATE ODDS 1:926 HOBBY
PLATE PRINT RUN 1 SET PER COLOR
BLACK-CYAN-MAGENTA-YELLOW ISSUED
NO PLATE PRICING DUE TO SCARCITY
1A Derek Jeter 1.50 4.00
1B Jeter SP Tipping cap 60.00 80.00-
2 Altuve/Martinez/Brantley LL .20 .50
3 Rene Rivera .15 .40
4 Curtis Granderson .20 .50
5A Josh Donaldson .20 .50
5B Josh Donaldson Gatorade 3.00 8.00
6 Jayson Werth .20 .50
8 Miguel Gonzalez .15 .40
9 Hunter Pence WSH .20 .50
10 Cole Hamels .20 .50
11 Jon Jay .15 .40
12 James McCann RC .40 1.00
13 Toronto Blue Jays .15 .40
14 Kendall Graveman RC .25 .60
15 Joey Votto .25 .60
16 David DeJesus .15 .40
17 Brian McCann .20 .50
18 Cody Allen .15 .40
19 Baltimore Orioles .15 .40
20A Madison Bumgarner .20 .50
20B Bumgarner SP Batting 3.00 8.00
21 Brett Gardner .20 .50
22 Tyler Flowers .15 .40
23 Michael Bourn .15 .40
24 New York Mets .15 .40
25A Jose Bautista .20 .50
25B Jose Bautista Standing 3.00 8.00
26 Bryce Brentz RC .25 .60
27 Kendrys Morales .15 .40
28 Alex Cobb .15 .40
29 Brandon Belt BH .20 .50
30 Tanner Roark FS .15 .40
31 Nick Tropeano RC .25 .60
32 Carlos Quentin .15 .40
33 Oakland Athletics .15 .40
34 Charlie Blackmon .25 .60
35 Brandon Moss .15 .40
36 Julio Teheran .20 .50
37 Arismendy Alcantara FS .15 .40
38 Jordan Zimmermann .20 .50
39A Salvador Perez .20 .50
39B Salvador Perez Celebrating 3.00 8.00
40 Joakim Soria .15 .40
41 Chris Colabello .15 .40
42 Todd Frazier .20 .50
43 Starlin Castro .15 .40
44 Gio Gonzalez .20 .50
45 Carlos Beltran .20 .50
46A Wilson Ramos .15 .40
46B Wilson Ramos Gatorade 2.50 6.00
47 Anthony Rizzo .40 1.00
48 John Axford .15 .40
49 Dominic Leone RC .25 .60
50A Yu Darvish .25 .60
50B Yu Darvish Batting 4.00 10.00
51 Ryan Howard .20 .50
52 Fernando Rodney .15 .40
53 Nathan Eovaldi .20 .50
54 Joe Nathan .15 .40
55 Trevor May RC .25 .60
56 Matt Garza .15 .40
57 Lyle Overbay .15 .40
58 Evan Gattis FS .15 .40
59 Jake Odorizzi .15 .40
60 Michael Wacha .20 .50
61 Cto/Krshw/Wnwrght LL .50 1.25
62 Nolan Arenado .30 .75
63 Chris Owings FS .15 .40
64 Atlanta Braves .15 .40
65 Alexei Ramirez .20 .50
66 Vance Worley .15 .40
67 Hunter Pence .20 .50
68 Lonnie Chisenhall .15 .40
69 Justin Upton .20 .50
70 Charlie Furbush .15 .40
71 Adrian Beltre BH .25 .60
72 Jordan Lyles .15 .40
73 Freddie Freeman .30 .75
74 Tyler Skaggs .15 .40
75 Dustin Pedroia .25 .60
76 Ian Kennedy .15 .40
77 Edwin Escobar RC .25 .60
78 Yordano Ventura .20 .50
79 Starling Marte .20 .50
80 Adam Wainwright .20 .50
81 Chris Young .15 .40
82 Nick Tepesch .15 .40
83 David Wright .20 .50
84 Jonathan Schoop .15 .40
85 Wnwrght/Cto/Krshw LL .50 1.25
86 Tim Hudson .20 .50
87 Eric Sogard .15 .40
88 Madison Bumgarner WSH .20 .50
89 Michael Choice .15 .40
90 Marcus Stroman FS .20 .50
91 Corey Dickerson .20 .50
92A Ian Kinsler .20 .50
92B Ian Kinsler Facing right 3.00 8.00
93 Andre Ethier .20 .50
94 Tommy Kahnle RC .25 .60
95 Junior Lake .15 .40
96 Sergio Santos .15 .40
97 Dalton Pompey RC .30 .75
98 Trt/Crz/Cbrra LL 1.25 3.00
99 Yonder Alonso .15 .40
100A Clayton Kershaw .50 1.25
100B Kershaw SP Bubble 8.00 20.00
101 Scooter Gennett .20 .50
102 Gordon Beckham .15 .40
103 Guilder Rodriguez RC .25 .60
104 Bud Norris .15 .40
105 Jeff Baker .15 .40
106 Pedro Alvarez .15 .40
107 James Loney .15 .40
108A Jorge Soler RC .40 1.00
108B J.Soler No bat FS 1.50 4.00
109 Doug Fister .15 .40
110 Tony Sipp .15 .40
111 Trevor Bauer .25 .60
112 Daniel Nava .15 .40
113 Jason Castro .15 .40
114 Mike Zunino .15 .40
115 Khris Davis .25 .60
116 Vidal Nuno .15 .40
117 Sean Doolittle .15 .40
118 Domonic Brown .20 .50
119 Anibal Sanchez .20 .50
120 Yoenis Cespedes .20 .50
121 Garrett Jones .15 .40
122 Corey Kluber .20 .50
123 Ben Revere .15 .40
124 Mark Melancon .15 .40
125 Troy Tulowitzki .25 .60
126 Detroit Tigers .15 .40
127 McCtchn/Mrn/Hrrsn LL .25 .60
128 Anthony Swarzak .15 .40
129 Jacob deGrom FS .25 .60
130 Mike Napoli .15 .40
131 Edward Mujica .15 .40
132 Michael Taylor RC .25 .60
133 Daisuke Matsuzaka .20 .50
134A Brett Lawrie .20 .50
134B Brett Lawrie Baseballs in air 3.00 8.00
135 Matt Dominguez .15 .40
136A Manny Machado .25 .60
136B Machado SP w/Trout 6.00 15.00
137 Alcides Escobar .20 .50
138 Tim Lincecum .20 .50
139 Gary Brown RC .25 .60
140 Alex Avila .20 .50
141 Cory Spangenberg RC .25 .60
142 Masahiro Tanaka FS .20 .50
143 Jonathan Papelbon .20 .50
144 Rusney Castillo RC .30 .75
145 Jesse Hahn .15 .40
146 Tony Watson .15 .40
147 Andrew Heaney FS .15 .40
148 J.D. Martinez .25 .60
149 Daniel Murphy .20 .50
150A Giancarlo Stanton .25 .60
150B Giancarlo Stanton Celebrating 4.00 10.00
151 C.J. Cron FS .15 .40
152 Michael Pineda .15 .40
153 Josh Reddick .15 .40
154 Brandon Finnegan RC .25 .60
155 Jesse Chavez .15 .40
156 Santiago Casilla .15 .40
157 Ubaldo Jimenez .15 .40
158 Kevin Kiermaier FS .20 .50
159 Brandon Crawford .20 .50
160 Washington Nationals .15 .40
161 Howie Kendrick .15 .40
162 Drew Pomeranz .20 .50
163A Chase Utley .20 .50
163B Utley SP Dugout 3.00 8.00
164 Brian Schlitter RC .25 .60
165 John Jaso .15 .40
166 Jenrry Mejia .15 .40
167 Matt Cain .20 .50
168 Colorado Rockies .15 .40
169A Adam Jones .20 .50
169B Adam Jones (Bubble 3.00 8.00
170 Tommy Medica .15 .40
171 Mike Foltynewicz RC .25 .60
172 Didi Gregorius .20 .50
173 Carlos Torres .15 .40
174 Jesus Guzman .15 .40
175 Adrian Beltre .25 .60
176 Jose Abreu FS .25 .60
177A Paul Konerko .20 .50
177B Paul Konerko With fans 3.00 8.00
178 Christian Yelich .30 .75
179 Jason Vargas .15 .40
180 Steve Pearce .25 .60
181A Jason Heyward .20 .50
181B Jason Heyward Waving 3.00 8.00
182 Devin Mesoraco .15 .40
183 Craig Gentry .15 .40
184 B.J. Upton .20 .50
185 Ricky Nolasco .15 .40
186 Rex Brothers .15 .40
187 Marlon Byrd .15 .40
188 Madison Bumgarner WSH .15 .40
189 Dustin Ackley .15 .40
190 Zach Britton .20 .50
191 Yimi Garcia RC .25 .60
192A Joc Pederson RC .50 1.25
192B Pederson Running FS 2.00 5.00
193 Buck Farmer RC .25 .60
194 David Murphy .15 .40
195 Garrett Richards .20 .50
196 Chicago Cubs .15 .40
197 Glen Perkins .15 .40
198 Alexi Ogando .15 .40
199 Eric Young Jr. .15 .40
200A Miguel Cabrera .25 .60
200B Miggy SP Celebration 4.00 10.00
201 Tommy La Stella .15 .40
202 Mike Minor .15 .40
203 Paul Goldschmidt .25 .60
204 Eduardo Escobar .15 .40
205 Josh Harrison .15 .40
206 Rick Porcello .20 .50
207A Bryce Harper .40 1.00
207B Harper SP Scream 6.00 15.00
208 Wilin Rosario .15 .40
209 Daniel Corcino .25 .60
210 Salvador Perez BH .20 .50
211 Clay Buchholz .15 .40
212 Cliff Lee .20 .50
213 Jered Weaver .20 .50
214 Kluber/Scherzer/Weaver LL .25 .60
215 Alejandro De Aza .15 .40
216A Greg Holland .15 .40
216B Greg Holland Gatorade 2.50 6.00
217 Daniel Norris RC .25 .60
218 David Buchanan .20 .50
219A Kennys Vargas .15 .40
219B Kennys Vargas Flexing 2.50 6.00
220 Shelby Miller .20 .50
221A Jason Kipnis .20 .50
221B Jason Kipnis Sliding 3.00 8.00
222 Antonio Bastardo .15 .40
223 Los Angeles Angels .15 .40
224 Bryan Mitchell RC .25 .60
225 Jacoby Ellsbury .20 .50
226 Dioner Navarro .15 .40
227 Madison Bumgarner WSH .20 .50
228 Jake Peavy .15 .40
229 Bryan Morris .15 .40
230 Jean Segura .20 .50
231 Andrew Cashner .15 .40
232 Andrew Susac .15 .40
233 Carlos Ruiz .15 .40
234 Brandon Belt .20 .50
235 Jeremy Guthrie .15 .40
236 Zack Wheeler .20 .50
237 Lucas Duda .20 .50
238 Hyun-Jin Ryu .20 .50
239 Jose Iglesias .20 .50
240 Anthony Ranaudo RC .25 .60
241 Dilson Herrera RC .30 .75
242 Edwin Encarnacion .25 .60
243 Al Alburquerque .15 .40
244 Bartolo Colon .15 .40
245 Tyler Colvin .15 .40
246 Chris Carter .15 .40
247 Aaron Hill .15 .40
248 Addison Reed .15 .40
249 Jose Reyes .20 .50
250A Evan Longoria .20 .50
250B Evan Longoria No cap 3.00 8.00
251 Anthony Rendon .25 .60
252 Travis Wood .15 .40
253 Gregory Polanco FS .20 .50
254 Steve Cishek .15 .40
255 James Russell .15 .40
256 Adam Eaton .15 .40
257 Jarrod Saltalamacchia .15 .40
258 Kansas City Royals .15 .40
259 Brian Dozier .20 .50
260 David Peralta RC .25 .60
261 Lance Lynn .15 .40
262 Ryan Braun .20 .50
263 Dillon Gee .15 .40
264 Tony Cingrani .20 .50
265 Arizona Diamondbacks .15 .40
266 Brandon Phillips .15 .40
267 Zack Greinke .20 .50
268 Aroldis Chapman .25 .60
269 Jordy Mercer .15 .40
270 Steven Moya RC .30 .75
271 Pittsburgh Pirates .15 .40
272 Matt Kemp .20 .50
273 Brandon Hicks .15 .40
274 Ryan Zimmerman .20 .50
275 Buster Posey .30 .75
276 Conor Gillaspie .20 .50
277 Cincinnati Reds .15 .40
278 David Phelps .15 .40
279 Coco Crisp .15 .40
280 Miguel Montero .15 .40
281A Elvis Andrus .20 .50
281B Andrus SP w/Jeter 6.00 15.00
282 Alex Presley .15 .40
283 Chris Johnson .15 .40
284 Brandon League .15 .40
285 Crtr/Trt/Crz LL 1.25 3.00
286 Trevor Rosenthal .20 .50
287 Everth Cabrera .15 .40
288 Chris Parmelee .15 .40
289 Matt Joyce .15 .40
290 David Lough .15 .40
291 Mark Reynolds .15 .40
292 Neil Walker .20 .50
293 Zach Duke .15 .40
294 Aaron Sanchez FS .20 .50
295 Erick Aybar .20 .50
296 Charlie Morton .15 .40
297 Scott Kazmir .20 .50
298 Rymer Liriano RC .25 .60
299 Joaquin Arias .15 .40
300 Mike Trout 1.25 3.00
301 Zack Cozart .15 .40
302A Martin Prado .20 .50
302B Martin Prado Gatorade 2.50 6.00
303 Ike Davis .15 .40
304 Shawn Kelley .15 .40
305 Sonny Gray .20 .50
306 Juan Lagares FS .20 .50
307 Mark Teixeira .20 .50
308 Carl Crawford .20 .50
309 Maikel Franco RC .30 .75
310 Jake Lamb RC .40 1.00
311 Jhonny Peralta .15 .40
312 Kyle Lobstein RC .25 .60
313 Rizzo/Stntn/Duda LL .40 1.00
314 Jackie Bradley Jr. .25 .60
315 Javier Baez RC 2.00 5.00
316 R.A. Dickey .20 .50
317 Clayton Kershaw BH .50 1.25
318A George Springer FS .20 .50
318B George Springer Gatorade 3.00 8.00
319 Derek Jeter BH 1.50 4.00
320 Shin-Soo Choo .20 .50
321 Josh Hamilton .20 .50
322 Phil Hughes .15 .40
323 Eric Hosmer .20 .50
324 Chris Archer .15 .40
325 Felix Hernandez .20 .50
326 C.J. Wilson .15 .40
327 Xander Bogaerts FS .25 .60
328 Adrian Gonzalez .20 .50
329 Logan Forsythe .15 .40
330 Brian Duensing .15 .40
331 Danny Espinosa .15 .40
332 Kyle Seager .15 .40
333 Billy Hamilton FS .20 .50
334 Gerardo Parra .15 .40
335 Matt Barnes RC .25 .60
336 Matt Carpenter .25 .60
337 Jedd Gyorko .15 .40
338 Yasmani Grandal .15 .40
339 Austin Jackson .15 .40
340 Carlos Gomez .15 .40
341 Kluber/Sale/Hernandez LL .25 .60
342 San Diego Padres .15 .40
343 Shane Greene .15 .40
344 Manny Parra .15 .40
345 Brandon Cumpton .15 .40
346 Trevor Cahill .15 .40
347 Dexter Fowler .20 .50
348 Carlos Santana .15 .40
349 Upton/Gnzlz/Stntn LL .25 .60
350 Yasiel Puig .25 .60
351 Tom Koehler .15 .40
352 Jaime Garcia .15 .40
353 Mike Leake .15 .40
354 Kyle Hendricks .25 .60
355 Travis Snider .15 .40
356 Marcus Semien .15 .40
357 Derek Holland .15 .40
358 Jon Singleton FS .20 .50
359 Robinson Chirinos .15 .40
360 Adam LaRoche .15 .40
361 Matt Holliday .25 .60
362 Jason Bourgeois .15 .40
363 Avisail Garcia .20 .50
364A Travis Ishikawa .15 .40
364B Ishikawa Dugout 2.50 6.00
365 L.J. Hoes .15 .40
366 Jhoulys Chacin .15 .40
367 Sam Fuld .15 .40
368 David Robertson .20 .50
369 Aaron Loup .15 .40
370 Marcell Ozuna FS .25 .60
371 Koji Uehara .15 .40
372 Matt Adams .15 .40
373 Kurt Suzuki .15 .40
374 Nick Martinez .15 .40
375A Johnny Cueto .20 .50
375B Cueto Batting 3.00 8.00
376A Chris Sale .25 .60
376B Sale Dugout 4.00 10.00
377 Tommy Hunter .15 .40
378 Danny Duffy .15 .40
379 Phil Gosselin RC .25 .60
380 Hector Noesi .15 .40
381 Stephen Drew .15 .40
382 Ivan Nova .20 .50
383 Delmon Young .20 .50
384 Justin Ruggiano .15 .40
385 James Paxton FS .20 .50
386 Ben Zobrist .20 .50
387A Jacob deGrom ROY .25 .60
387B deGrom Glasses 4.00 10.00
388 Francisco Liriano .15 .40
389A Mookie Betts FS .40 1.00
389B Betts Sliding 6.00 15.00
390 Cody Ross .15 .40
391 Hisashi Iwakuma .20 .50
392 Brandon Guyer .15 .40
393 Danny Salazar .20 .50
394 Marco Scutaro .15 .40
395 Chris Taylor .20 .50
396 Alex Colome .15 .40
397 Mike Aviles .15 .40
398 Jordan Zimmermann HL .20 .50
399 Josmil Pinto .15 .40
400A Andrew McCutchen .25 .60
400B McCutchen w/pic 4.00 10.00
401 Chris Coghlan .15 .40
402 Jeurys Familia .20 .50
403 Leury Garcia .15 .40
404 Tanner Scheppers .15 .40
405 Ross Detwiler .15 .40
406 Jon Lester .20 .50
407 Jed Lowrie .15 .40
408 Jake Smolinski .15 .40
409 Juan Uribe .15 .40
410 Kyle Lohse .15 .40
411 Nelson Cruz .25 .60
412 Hector Rondon .15 .40
413 Anthony Gose .15 .40
414 J.A. Happ .15 .40
415 Ervin Santana .15 .40
416 Francisco Cervelli .15 .40
417 Leonys Martin .15 .40
418 Jung Ho Kang RC .25 .60
419 Omar Infante .15 .40
420 Cody Asche .20 .50
421 Joe Kelly .15 .40
422 Prince Fielder .20 .50
423 Javy Guerra .15 .40
424 Michael Saunders .20 .50
425 Bryan Shaw .15 .40
426 Trevor Plouffe .15 .40
427 Raisel Iglesias RC .30 .75
428 Jon Niese .15 .40
429 A.J. Ellis .15 .40
430 Jarred Cosart .15 .40
431 Brandon McCarthy .15 .40
432 Alex Rios .20 .50
433 Justin Masterson .15 .40
434 Carlos Frias RC .40 1.00
435 Mike Fiers .15 .40
436 Russell Martin .15 .40
437 Jake Marisnick .15 .40
438 DJ LeMahieu .25 .60
439 Kenley Jansen .20 .50
440 Denard Span .20 .50
442 Tyler Matzek .15 .40
443 Maicer Izturis .15 .40
444 Lonnie Chisenhall HL .15 .40
445 Christian Vazquez .15 .40
446 Nick Franklin .15 .40
447 Jose Ramirez .20 .50
448 Ryan Hanigan .15 .40
449 Joe Panik HL .20 .50
450A Robinson Cano .20 .50
450B Cano Signing 3.00 8.00
451 Clayton Kershaw AW .50 1.25
452 Drew Smyly .15 .40
453 Elian Herrera .15 .40
454 Wade Davis .15 .40
455 Adam Lind .20 .50
456 Alex Gordon .20 .50
457 Aaron Hicks .20 .50
458 Junichi Tazawa .15 .40
459 Tuffy Gosewisch .15 .40
461A Mike Moustakas .15 .40
461B Moustakas w/fans 3.00 8.00
462 Shae Simmons RC .25 .60
463 Justin Verlander .25 .60
464 Brett Cecil .15 .40
465 Seattle Mariners .15 .40
466 A.J. Burnett .15 .40
467 Mat Latos .20 .50
468A CC Sabathia .20 .50
468B Sabathia w/Jeter 5.00 12.00
469 James Shields .15 .40
470 Mark Trumbo .15 .40
471 Pat Neshek .15 .40
472 T.J. House .15 .40
473 Ryan Raburn .15 .40
474 Alexi Amarista .15 .40
475 Juan Perez .15 .40
476 Jose Lobaton .15 .40
477 Dallas Keuchel .20 .50
478 Los Angeles Dodgers .15 .40
479A Carlos Gonzalez .20 .50
479B Gonzalez Glasses 3.00 8.00
480 Matt Harvey FS .20 .50
481 Freddy Galvis .15 .40
482 Joaquin Benoit .15 .40
483 Randal Grichuk .15 .40
484 Melvin Mercedes RC .25 .60
485 Daniel Hudson .15 .40
486 Erik Goeddel RC .30 .75
487A Corey Kluber AW .20 .50
487B Kluber High five 3.00 8.00
488 John Lackey .20 .50
489 Jeremy Hellickson .15 .40
490 Gavin Floyd .15 .40
491 Rougned Odor FS .20 .50
492 Brandon Barnes .15 .40
493 Alex Rodriguez .30 .75
494 James Jones .15 .40
495 Christian Colon .15 .40
496 Houston Astros .15 .40
497 Hunter Strickland RC .25 .60
498 Anthony Desclafani .15 .40
499 Eduardo Nunez .15 .40
500 David Ortiz .25 .60
501 Will Venable .15 .40
502 Kevin Frandsen .15 .40
503 Joe Panik FS .20 .50
503B Panik Smiling 3.00 8.00
504 Minnesota Twins .15 .40
505 Arodys Vizcaino .15 .40
506 Chase Anderson .15 .40
507 A.J. Pierzynski .15 .40
508 Collin McHugh .15 .40
509 Danny Santana FS .15 .40
510 Mike Trout MVP 1.25 3.00
511 Asdrubal Cabrera .20 .50
512 Jay Bruce .20 .50
513 Michael Cuddyer .15 .40
514 Will Smith .15 .40
515 Victor Martinez .20 .50
516A Lorenzo Cain .15 .40
516B Cain High five 2.50 6.00
517 Yusmeiro Petit .15 .40
518 Rajai Davis .15 .40
519A Archie Bradley RC .25 .60
519B Bradley Drk jsy FS 1.00 2.50
520 Brayan Pena .15 .40
521 Nick Castellanos FS .25 .60
522 Sam Tuivailala RC .25 .60
523 Christian Bethancourt FS .15 .40
524 John Danks .15 .40
525 Luke Gregerson .15 .40
526 Will Middlebrooks .15 .40
527 Carlos Martinez FS .20 .50
528 Brad Ziegler .15 .40
529 Ryan Flaherty RC .15 .40
530 Chris Heston RC .25 .60
531 Drew Hutchison .15 .40
532 Dellin Betances FS .20 .50
533 Marwin Gonzalez .15 .40
534 Chris Capuano .15 .40
535 Erik Cordier RC .25 .60
536 Logan Morrison .15 .40
537 Steven Souza Jr. .20 .50
538 Brad Boxberger RC .25 .60
539 Jimmy Nelson FS .15 .40
540 Drew Stubbs .15 .40
541 Homer Bailey .15 .40
542 Yasmany Tomas RC .30 .75
543 Alberto Callaspo .15 .40
544 Travis d'Arnaud FS .20 .50
545 Clayton Kershaw MVP .50 1.25
546 Tyler Clippard .15 .40
547 Kristopher Negron RC .25 .60
548 Cleveland Indians .15 .40
549 Christian Walker RC .50 1.25
550 David Price .20 .50
551 Corey Hart .15 .40
552 Yovani Gallardo .15 .40
553 Grady Sizemore .20 .50
554 A.J. Griffin .15 .40
555 Jake Arrieta .20 .50
556 Jake McGee .15 .40
557 Nick Markakis .20 .50
558 Patrick Corbin .20 .50
559 Dee Gordon .15 .40
560 Jerome Williams .15 .40
561 Ken Giles .15 .40
562 Wilmer Flores .20 .50
563 J.J. Hardy .15 .40
564 Jose Quintana .15 .40
565 Michael Morse .15 .40
566 Chris Davis .15 .40
567 Brennan Boesch .15 .40
568 Chris Tillman .15 .40
569 Marco Estrada .15 .40
570 Jarrod Dyson .15 .40
571A Devon Travis RC .25 .60
571B Travis Wht Jsy FS 1.00 2.50
572 A.J. Pollock .20 .50
573 Ryan Rua RC .25 .60
574 Mitch Moreland .15 .40
575 Kris Medlen .20 .50
576 Chase Headley .15 .40
577 Henderson Alvarez .15 .40
578 Ender Inciarte RC .25 .60
579 Jason Hammel .15 .40
580 Chris Bassitt RC .25 .60
581 John Holdzkom RC .25 .60
582 Wei-Yin Chen .15 .40
583 Jose Abreu ROY .25 .60
584 Danny Farquhar .15 .40
585 Matt Moore .20 .50
586A Max Scherzer .25 .60
586B Scherzer Red jrsy 4.00 10.00
587 Daniel Descalso .15 .40
588A Kolten Wong FS .20 .50
588B Wong Waving 3.00 8.00
589 Jeff Locke .15 .40
590 Torii Hunter .15 .40
591 Josh Collmenter .15 .40
592 Martin Maldonado .15 .40
593 Ruben Tejada .15 .40
594 Jose Pirela RC .25 .60
595A Craig Kimbrel .20 .50
595B Kimbrel Bullpen 3.00 8.00
596 Bronson Arroyo .15 .40
597 Matt Shoemaker FS .20 .50
598 Nick Swisher .20 .50
599A Michael Brantley .20 .50
599B Brantley Leg up 3.00 8.00
600A Albert Pujols .30 .75
600B Pujols Laughing 5.00 12.00
601 Wade Miley .15 .40
602 Drew Storen .15 .40
603A Jose Fernandez FS .25 .60
603B Fernandez Ornge jrsy 4.00 10.00
604 Jordan Schafer .15 .40
605 Huston Street .15 .40
606 Ian Desmond .15 .40
607 Jarrod Parker .15 .40
608 Justin Smoak .15 .40
609 Luke Hochevar .15 .40
610 David Freese .15 .40
611 Gregor Blanco .15 .40
612 Caleb Joseph RC .25 .60
613 Josh Beckett HL .15 .40
614 Jordan Walden .15 .40
615 Carlos Sanchez .15 .40
616A Kris Bryant RC 10.00 25.00
616B Bryant Face Left FS 15.00 40.00
617 Terrance Gore RC .25 .60
618 Billy Butler .15 .40
619 Kevin Gausman .15 .40
620 Jose Altuve .20 .50
621 Luis Valbuena .15 .40
622A Yan Gomes .15 .40
622B Gomes Dugout 2.50 6.00
623 Melky Cabrera .15 .40
624 Miguel Alfredo Gonzalez RC .25 .60
625 Mark Buehrle .20 .50
626 Hanley Ramirez .20 .50

627 Jason Grilli .15 .40
628 Peter Bourjos .15 .40
629 Robbie Grossman .15 .40
630 Carlos Carrasco .15 .40
631 Chris Iannetta .15 .40
632 Kyle Gibson .20 .50
633 Skip Schumaker .15 .40
634 Roenis Elias FS .15 .40
635 Scott Feldman .15 .40
636 Micah Johnson RC .25 .60
637 Matt Szczur RC .30 .75
638 Jimmy Rollins .20 .50
639 Cameron Maybin .15 .40
640 Matt Clark RC .25 .60
641 Yorman Rodriguez RC .25 .60
642 Alex Wood .15 .40
643 Oswaldo Arcia .15 .40
644 Chicago White Sox .15 .40
645A Neftali Feliz .15 .40
645B Feliz Hugging 2.50 6.00
646 Aramis Ramirez .15 .40
647A Yadier Molina .25 .60
647B Molina Celebrating 4.00 10.00
648 St. Louis Cardinals BB .15 .40
649 Emilio Bonifacio .15 .40
650 Pablo Sandoval .20 .50
651A Andrelton Simmons .15 .40
651B Simmons w/fans 2.50 6.00
652 Stephen Vogt .20 .50
653 Rafael Montero FS .15 .40
654 Alfredo Simon .15 .40
655 Taylor Hill .15 .40
656 Adeiny Hechavarria FS .15 .40
657 Justin Morneau .20 .50
658 Tsuyoshi Wada .15 .40
659 Jimmy Rollins HL .20 .50
660 Roberto Osuna RC .25 .60
661 Grant Balfour .15 .40
662 Darin Hut .15 .40
663 Jake Diekman .15 .40
664 Hector Santiago .15 .40
665 Stephen Strasburg .25 .60
666 Jonathan Broxton .15 .40
667 Kole Calhoun .15 .40
668 Jatro Diaz RC .25 .60
669 Tampa Bay Rays .15 .40
670 Darren O'Day .15 .40
671 Gerrit Cole .25 .60
672 Wily Peralta .15 .40
673 Brett Oberholtzer .15 .40
674 Desmond Jennings .20 .50
675A Jonathan Lucroy .20 .50
675B Lucroy High five 3.00 8.00
676 Nate McLouth .15 .40
677 Ryan Goins .15 .40
678 Sam Freeman .15 .40
679 Jorge De La Rosa .15 .40
680 Nick Hundley .15 .40
681 Zoilo Almonte .15 .40
682 Christian Bergman .15 .40
683 LaTroy Hawkins .15 .40
684 Wil Myers .15 .40
685 Yangervis Solarte .15 .40
686 Tyson Ross .15 .40
687 Odubol Herrera RC .40 1.00
688 Angel Pagan .15 .40
689 R.J. Alvarez RC .25 .60
690 Brett Bochy RC .25 .60
691 Lisalverto Bonilla RC .25 .60
692 Andrew Chafin RC .25 .60
693 Jason Rogers RC .25 .60
694 Xavier Scruggs RC .25 .60
695 Rafael Ynoa RC .25 .60
696 Boston Red Sox .15 .40
697 New York Yankees .15 .40
698 Texas Rangers .15 .40
699 Miami Marlins .15 .40
700A Joe Mauer .20 .50
700B Mauer Dugout 3.00 8.00
701 Milwaukee Brewers .15 .40

2015 Topps Black

*BLACK: 10X TO 25X BASIC
*BLACK RC: 6X TO 15X BASIC RC
SER.1STATED ODDS 1:108 HOBBY
SER.2 STATED ODDS 1:58 HOBBY
STATED PRINT RUN 64 SER.#'d SETS
1 Derek Jeter 15.00 40.00
98 Trout/Cruz/Cabrera LL 30.00 80.00
285 Carter/Trout/Cruz LL 30.00 80.00
319 Derek Jeter BH 15.00 40.00
400 Andrew McCutchen 15.00 40.00
530 Chris Heston 20.00 50.00
545 Clayton Kershaw 15.00 40.00
588 Kolten Wong 10.00 25.00
647 Yadier Molina 12.00 30.00

2015 Topps Factory Set Sparkle Foil

*SPARKLE: 8X TO 20X BASIC
*SPARKLE RC: 5X TO 12X BASIC RC
STATED PRINT RUN 179 SER.#'d SETS

2015 Topps Framed

*FRAMED: 20X TO 50X BASIC
*FRAMED RC: 12X TO 30X BASIC RC
SER.1 STATED ODDS 1:427 HOBBY
SER.2 STATED ODDS 1:186 HOBBY
STATED PRINT RUN 20 SER.#'d SETS
1 Derek Jeter 125.00 250.00
12 James McCann 15.00 40.00
15 Joey Votto 15.00 40.00
20 Madison Bumgarner 20.00 50.00
43 Starlin Castro 15.00 40.00
51 Ryan Howard 15.00 40.00
61 Cto/Krshw/Wnwrght LL 25.00 60.00
75 Dustin Pedroia 15.00 40.00
83 David Wright 15.00 40.00
85 Wnwrght/Cto/Krshw LL 25.00 60.00
88 Madison Bumgarner WSH 20.00 50.00
90 Marcus Stroman FS 15.00 40.00
97 Dalton Pompey 15.00 40.00
98 Trt/Crz/Cbrra LL 25.00 60.00
100 Clayton Kershaw 25.00 60.00
108 Jorge Soler 40.00 100.00
125 Troy Tulowitzki 15.00 40.00
127 McCtchn/Mrn/Hrrsn LL 15.00 40.00
129 Jacob deGrom FS 20.00 50.00
136 Manny Machado 15.00 40.00
144 Rusney Castillo 30.00 80.00
150 Giancarlo Stanton 15.00 40.00
176 Jose Abreu FS 25.00 60.00
188 Madison Bumgarner WSH 20.00 50.00
192 Joc Pederson 20.00 50.00
200 Miguel Cabrera 25.00 60.00
203 Paul Goldschmidt 15.00 40.00
207 Bryce Harper 50.00 120.00
219 Kennys Vargas 15.00 40.00
227 Madison Bumgarner WSH 20.00 50.00
253 Gregory Polanco FS 15.00 40.00
275 Buster Posey 25.00 60.00
285 Carter/Trout/Cruz LL 25.00 60.00
300 Mike Trout 50.00 120.00
309 Maikel Franco 20.00 50.00
313 Rzzo/Stntn/Dda LL 15.00 40.00
315 Javier Baez 15.00 40.00
317 Clayton Kershaw BH 25.00 60.00
318 George Springer FS 15.00 40.00
319 Derek Jeter BH 125.00 250.00
327 Xander Bogaerts FS 20.00 50.00
333 Billy Hamilton FS 20.00 50.00
336 Matt Carpenter 15.00 40.00
349 Uptn/Gnzlz/Stntn LL 15.00 40.00
350 Yasiel Puig 25.00 60.00
400 Andrew McCutchen 25.00 60.00
530 Chris Heston 20.00 50.00
588 Kolten Wong 15.00 40.00

2015 Topps Gold

*GOLD: 2X TO 5X BASIC
*GOLD RC: 1.2X TO 3X BASIC RC
SER.1 STATED ODDS 1:10 HOBBY
SER.2 STATED ODDS 1:4 HOBBY
STATED PRINT RUN 2015 SER.#'d SETS
1 Derek Jeter 12.00 30.00
319 Derek Jeter BH 12.00 30.00

2015 Topps Limited

*LIMITED: .75X TO 2X BASIC
*LIMITED RC: .75X TO 2X BASIC RC
ISSUED VIA TOPPS.COM
REPORTEDLY LESS THAN 1000 SETS MADE
616 Kris Bryant 8.00 20.00

2015 Topps Pink

*PINK: 10X TO 25X BASIC
*PINK RC: 6X TO 15X BASIC RC
SER.1 STATED ODDS 1:527 HOBBY
SER.2 STATED ODDS 1:284 HOBBY
STATED PRINT RUN 50 SER.#'d SETS
1 Derek Jeter 75.00 200.00
98 Trout/Cruz/Cabrera LL 12.00 30.00
285 Carter/Trout/Cruz LL 12.00 30.00
319 Derek Jeter BH 75.00 200.00
400 Andrew McCutchen 20.00 50.00
530 Chris Heston 15.00 40.00
588 Kolten Wong 12.00 30.00

2015 Topps Rainbow Foil

*RAINBOW: 2X TO 5X BASIC
*RAINBOW RC: 1.2X TO 6X BASIC RC
SER.1 STATED ODDS 1:10 HOBBY
SER.2 STATED ODDS 1:10 HOBBY

2015 Topps Snow Camo

*SNOW CAMO: 8X TO 20X BASIC
*SNOW CAMO RC: 5X TO 12X BASIC RC
SER.1 STATED ODDS 1:266 HOBBY
SER.2 STATED ODDS 1:144 HOBBY
STATED PRINT RUN 99 SER.#'d SETS
1 Derek Jeter 25.00 60.00
98 Trout/Cruz/Cabrera LL 10.00 25.00
285 Carter/Trout/Cruz LL 10.00 25.00
319 Derek Jeter BH 25.00 60.00

2015 Topps Sparkle

SER.1 RANDOMLY INSERTED
SER.2 STATED ODDS 1:331 HOBBY
5 Josh Donaldson 6.00 15.00
6 Jayson Werth 6.00 15.00
15 Joey Votto 8.00 20.00
20 Madison Bumgarner 6.00 15.00
25 Jose Bautista 6.00 15.00
34 Charlie Blackmon 8.00 20.00
42 Todd Frazier 6.00 15.00
43 Starlin Castro 5.00 12.00
47 Anthony Rizzo 12.00 30.00
50 Yu Darvish 8.00 20.00
60 Michael Wacha 6.00 15.00
62 Nolan Arenado 10.00 25.00
67 Hunter Pence 6.00 15.00
73 Freddie Freeman 20.00 50.00
75 Dustin Pedroia 20.00 50.00
80 Adam Wainwright 6.00 15.00
83 David Wright 6.00 15.00
92 Ian Kinsler 6.00 15.00
100 Clayton Kershaw 15.00 40.00
109 Doug Fister 5.00 12.00
120 Yoenis Cespedes 6.00 15.00
125 Troy Tulowitzki 8.00 20.00
136 Manny Machado 8.00 20.00
144 Rusney Castillo 40.00 100.00
149 Daniel Murphy 6.00 15.00
150 Giancarlo Stanton 8.00 20.00
163 Chase Utley 6.00 15.00
169 Adam Jones 6.00 15.00
175 Adrian Beltre 8.00 20.00
181 Jason Heyward 6.00 15.00
192 Joc Pederson 10.00 25.00
200 Miguel Cabrera 8.00 20.00
203 Paul Goldschmidt 8.00 20.00
205 Josh Harrison 5.00 12.00
207 Bryce Harper 12.00 30.00
225 Jacoby Ellsbury 6.00 15.00
242 Edwin Encarnacion 8.00 20.00
250 Evan Longoria 6.00 15.00
251 Anthony Rendon 8.00 20.00
262 Ryan Braun 6.00 15.00
272 Matt Kemp 6.00 15.00
275 Buster Posey 10.00 25.00
300 Mike Trout 40.00 100.00
315 Javier Baez 20.00 50.00
320 Shin-Soo Choo 6.00 15.00
321 Josh Hamilton 6.00 15.00
325 Felix Hernandez 6.00 15.00
336 Matt Carpenter 8.00 20.00
348 Carlos Santana 15.00 40.00
350 Yasiel Puig 8.00 20.00
360 Adam LaRoche 5.00 12.00
361 Matt Holliday 8.00 20.00
363 Avisail Garcia 6.00 15.00
372 Matt Adams 5.00 12.00
383 Delmon Young 6.00 15.00
386 Ben Zobrist 6.00 15.00
391 Hisashi Iwakuma 6.00 15.00
393 Danny Salazar 6.00 15.00
407 Jed Lowrie 5.00 12.00
411 Nelson Cruz 8.00 20.00
415 Ervin Santana 5.00 12.00
421 Joe Kelly 5.00 12.00
422 Prince Fielder 6.00 15.00
436 Russell Martin 5.00 12.00
438 DJ LeMahieu 8.00 20.00
445 Christian Vazquez 5.00 12.00
452 Drew Smyly 5.00 12.00
461 Mike Moustakas 6.00 15.00
463 Justin Verlander 8.00 20.00
468 CC Sabathia 6.00 15.00
469 James Shields 5.00 12.00
470 Mark Trumbo 5.00 12.00
475 Juan Perez 5.00 12.00
493 Alex Rodriguez 10.00 25.00
497 Hunter Strickland 5.00 12.00
507 A.J. Pierzynski 5.00 12.00
513 Michael Cuddyer 5.00 12.00
526 Will Middlebrooks 5.00 12.00
555 Jake Arrieta 6.00 15.00
557 Nick Markakis 6.00 15.00
568 Chris Tillman 5.00 12.00
579 Jason Hammel 6.00 15.00
586 Max Scherzer 8.00 20.00
590 Torii Hunter 5.00 12.00
596 Bronson Arroyo 5.00 12.00
606 Ian Desmond 5.00 12.00
610 David Freese 5.00 12.00
618 Billy Butler 5.00 12.00
620 Jose Altuve 6.00 15.00
624 Miguel Alfredo Gonzalez 5.00 12.00
638 Jimmy Rollins 6.00 15.00
645 Neftali Feliz 5.00 12.00
657 Justin Morneau 6.00 15.00
664 Hector Santiago 5.00 12.00
665 Stephen Strasburg 8.00 20.00
671 Gerrit Cole 8.00 20.00
674 Desmond Jennings 6.00 15.00
684 Wil Myers 5.00 12.00
690 Brott Bochy 5.00 12.00
691 Lisalverto Bonilla 5.00 12.00

2015 Topps Throwback Variations

RANDOM INSERT IN UPD PACKS
15 Joey Votto 3.00 8.00
23 Michael Bourn 2.00 5.00
42 Todd Frazier 2.50 6.00
43 Starlin Castro 2.00 5.00
47 Anthony Rizzo 5.00 12.00
78 Yordano Ventura 2.50 6.00
92 Ian Kinsler 2.50 6.00
200 Miguel Cabrera 3.00 8.00
239 Jose Iglesias 2.50 6.00
266 Brandon Phillips 2.00 5.00
286 Trevor Rosenthal 2.50 6.00
300 Mike Trout 15.00 40.00
301 Zack Cozart 2.00 5.00
311 Jhonny Peralta 2.00 5.00
318 George Springer FS 2.50 6.00
325 Felix Hernandez 2.50 6.00
326 C.J. Wilson 2.00 5.00
327 Xander Bogaerts FS 3.00 8.00
333 Billy Hamilton FS 2.50 6.00
336 Matt Carpenter 3.00 8.00
348 Carlos Santana 2.50 6.00
371 Koji Uehara 2.00 5.00
389 Mookie Betts FS 5.00 12.00
401 Chris Coghlan 2.00 5.00
406 Jon Lester 2.50 6.00
412 Hector Rondon 2.00 5.00
450 Robinson Cano 2.50 6.00
456 Alex Gordon 2.50 6.00
458 Junichi Tazawa 2.00 5.00
477 Dallas Keuchel 2.50 6.00
500 David Ortiz 3.00 8.00
515 Victor Martinez 2.50 6.00
518 Rajai Davis 2.00 5.00
525 Luke Gregerson 2.00 5.00
599 Michael Brantley 2.50 6.00
620 Jose Altuve 2.50 6.00
626 Hanley Ramirez 2.50 6.00
654 Alfredo Simon 2.00 5.00

2015 Topps Toys R Us Purple Border

*PURPLE: 5X TO 12X BASIC
*PURPLE RC: 3X TO 8X BASIC RC
INSERTED IN TOYS R US PACKS
1 Derek Jeter 25.00 60.00
98 Trout/Cruz/Cabrera LL 5.00 12.00
285 Carter/Trout/Cruz LL 5.00 12.00
319 Derek Jeter BH 15.00 40.00

2015 Topps 2632

COMPLETE SET (10) 20.00 50.00
RANDOM INSERTS IN RETAIL PACKS
26321 Cal Ripken Jr. 2.00 5.00
26322 Cal Ripken Jr. 2.00 5.00
26323 Cal Ripken Jr. 2.00 5.00
26324 Cal Ripken Jr. 2.00 5.00
26325 Cal Ripken Jr. 2.00 5.00
26326 Cal Ripken Jr. 2.00 5.00
26327 Cal Ripken Jr. 2.00 5.00
26328 Cal Ripken Jr. 2.00 5.00
26329 Cal Ripken Jr. 2.00 5.00
263210 Cal Ripken Jr. 2.00 5.00

2015 Topps Archetypes

COMPLETE SET (25) 8.00 20.00
STATED ODDS 1:6 HOBBY
A1 Rickey Henderson .50 1.25
A2 Mariano Rivera .60 1.50
A3 Steve Carlton .40 1.00
A4 Mike Trout 2.50 6.00
A5 Yasiel Puig .50 1.25
A6 Yoenis Cespedes .40 1.00
A7 Paul Goldschmidt .50 1.25
A8 Giancarlo Stanton .50 1.25
A9 Buster Posey .60 1.50
A10 Babe Ruth 1.25 3.00
A11 Mark McGwire .75 2.00
A12 Derek Jeter 1.25 3.00
A13 Cal Ripken Jr. 1.50 4.00
A14 Nolan Ryan 1.50 4.00
A15 Mike Piazza .50 1.25
A16 Johnny Bench .50 1.25
A17 Tony Gwynn .50 1.25
A18 Ted Williams 1.00 2.50
A19 Albert Pujols .60 1.50
A20 Greg Maddux .60 1.50
A21 Jackie Robinson .50 1.25
A22 Hank Aaron 1.00 2.50
A23 Willie Mays 1.00 2.50
A24 Ty Cobb .75 2.00
A25 Ken Griffey Jr. 1.00 2.50

2015 Topps Archetypes Autographs

STATED ODDS 1:31,455 HOBBY
STATED PRINT RUN 25 SER.#'d SETS
EXCHANGE DEADLINE 1/31/2018
AAMM Mark McGwire 100.00 200.00
AAMP Mike Piazza EXCH 60.00 150.00
AAYC Yoenis Cespedes 20.00 50.00

2015 Topps Archetypes Relics

STATED ODDS 1:5270 HOBBY
STATED PRINT RUN 99 SER.#'d SETS
ARAM Andrew McCutchen 10.00 25.00
ARAP Albert Pujols 10.00 25.00
ARBP Buster Posey 15.00 40.00
ARCK Clayton Kershaw 15.00 40.00
ARDJ Derek Jeter 30.00 80.00
ARGM Greg Maddux 10.00 25.00
ARGS Giancarlo Stanton 8.00 20.00
ARMM Mark McGwire 15.00 40.00
ARMP Mike Piazza 8.00 20.00
ARMR Mariano Rivera 10.00 25.00
ARMT Mike Trout 20.00 50.00
ARPG Paul Goldschmidt 8.00 20.00
ARRH Rickey Henderson 8.00 20.00
ARSC Steve Carlton 6.00 15.00
ARYP Yasiel Puig 8.00 20.00

2015 Topps Baseball History

COMPLETE SET (30) 8.00 20.00
STATED ODDS 1:8 HOBBY
1A Geneva Conference Begins .30 .75
1B Hank Aaron 1.00 2.50
2A Polio Vaccine Announced As Safe .30 .75
2B Robin Roberts .40 1.00
3A American Debuts .30 .75
3B Red Schoendienst .40 1.00
4A Nixon-Kennedy Debate .30 .75
4B Ted Williams 1.00 2.50
5A MLK Leads March On Washington .30 .75
5B Warren Spahn .40 1.00
6A Apollo 11 .30 .75
6B Tom Seaver .40 1.00
7A Top 40 Countdown Premiers .30 .75
7B Hank Aaron 1.00 2.50
8A Gerald Ford Sworn In As Of USA .30 .75
8B Nolan Ryan 1.50 4.00
9A Apple Founded .30 .75
9B Reggie Jackson .40 1.00
10A ESPN's First Broadcast .30 .75
10B Bruce Sutter .40 1.00
11A CNN Begins Broadcasting .30 .75
11B Darryl Strawberry .30 .75
12A Space Shuttle Columbia Launches .30 .75
12B Fernando Valenzuela .30 .75
13A Sandra Day O'Connor Sworn In .30 .75
13B Steve Carlton .40 1.00
14A Live Aid Concert .30 .75
14B Nolan Ryan 1.50 4.00
15A Clinton Earns
Democratic Nomination .30 .75
15B Ken Griffey Jr. 1.00 2.50

2015 Topps Baseball Royalty

COMPLETE SET (25) 60.00 120.00
STATED ODDS 1:18 HOBBY
BR1 Babe Ruth 3.00 8.00
BR2 Sandy Koufax 2.50 6.00
BR3 Ted Williams 2.50 6.00
BR4 Joe DiMaggio 2.50 6.00
BR5 Jackie Robinson 1.25 3.00
BR6 Willie Mays 2.50 6.00
BR7 Hank Aaron 2.50 6.00
BR8 Mike Piazza 1.25 3.00
BR9 Roger Clemens 1.50 4.00
BR10 Cal Ripken Jr. 4.00 10.00
BR11 Greg Maddux 1.50 4.00
BR12 Ken Griffey Jr. 2.50 6.00
BR13 Randy Johnson 1.25 3.00
BR14 Nolan Ryan 4.00 10.00
BR15 Reggie Jackson 1.00 2.50
BR16 Ozzie Smith 1.50 4.00
BR17 Mark McGwire 2.00 5.00
BR18 Mariano Rivera 1.50 4.00
BR19 Frank Thomas 1.25 3.00
BR20 Miguel Cabrera 1.25 3.00
BR21 David Ortiz 1.25 3.00
BR22 Chipper Jones 1.25 3.00
BR23 Albert Pujols 1.50 4.00
BR24 Derek Jeter 3.00 8.00
BR25 John Smoltz 1.25 3.00

2015 Topps Baseball Royalty Silver

*SILVER: 1.2X TO 3X BASIC
STATED ODDS 1:524 HOBBY
STATED PRINT RUN 99 SER.#'d SETS
BR24 Derek Jeter 12.00 30.00

2015 Topps Birth Year Coin and Stamps Quarter

SER.1 ODDS 1:10,271 HOBBY
SER.2 ODDS 1:4935 HOBBY
UPD ODDS 1:11,193 HOBBY
STATED PRINT RUN 50 SER.#'d SETS
*PENNY/50: .4X TO 1X QUARTER
*NICKEL/50: .4X TO 1X QUARTER
*DIME/50: .4X TO 1X QUARTER
BYBB Brandon Belt UPD 10.00 25.00
BYCB Craig Biggio UPD 10.00 25.00
BYEE Edwin Encarnacion UPD 12.00 30.00
BYFF Freddie Freeman UPD 15.00 40.00
BYJD Jacob deGrom UPD 12.00 30.00
BYJL Jon Lester UPD 10.00 25.00
BYJS John Smoltz UPD 12.00 30.00
BYRC Rusney Castillo UPD 12.00 30.00
BYRJ Randy Johnson UPD 12.00 30.00
BYYT Yasmany Tomas UPD 12.00 30.00
CS01 Hank Aaron 25.00 60.00
CS02 Javier Baez 60.00 150.00
CS03 Madison Bumgarner 10.00 25.00
CS04 Miguel Cabrera 25.00 60.00
CS05 Roberto Clemente 30.00 80.00
CS06 Josh Donaldson 10.00 25.00
CS07 Lou Gehrig 60.00 150.00
CS08 Tom Glavine 10.00 25.00
CS09 Bo Jackson 25.00 60.00
CS10 Reggie Jackson 25.00 60.00
CS11 Derek Jeter 50.00 120.00
CS12 Sandy Koufax 25.00 60.00
CS13 Mike Piazza 12.00 30.00
CS14 Yasiel Puig 25.00 60.00
CS15 Albert Pujols 25.00 60.00
CS16 Jim Rice 20.00 50.00
CS17 Babe Ruth 60.00 150.00
CS18 Nolan Ryan 50.00 120.00
CS19 Chris Sale 12.00 30.00
CS20 Max Scherzer 12.00 30.00
CS21 Ozzie Smith 30.00 80.00
CS23 Julio Teherán 10.00 25.00
CS24 Mike Trout 40.00 100.00
CS25 David Wright 10.00 25.00
CS26 Jose Abreu 12.00 30.00
CS27 Jeff Bagwell 20.00 50.00
CS28 Mookie Betts 20.00 50.00
CS29 Wade Boggs 20.00 50.00
CS30 Paul Goldschmidt 20.00 50.00
CS31 Clayton Kershaw 25.00 60.00
CS32 Mark McGwire 20.00 50.00
CS33 Anthony Rizzo 20.00 50.00
CS34 Mike Schmidt 20.00 50.00
CS35 Giancarlo Stanton 12.00 30.00
CS36 Buster Posey 15.00 40.00
CS38 Roger Maris 30.00 80.00
CS39 Jorge Soler 12.00 30.00
CS40 Joc Pederson 30.00 80.00
CS41 Kennys Vargas 8.00 20.00
CS42 Evan Longoria 10.00 25.00
CS43 Yu Darvish 15.00 40.00
CS44 Cal Ripken Jr. 40.00 100.00
CS45 Tom Seaver 30.00 80.00
CS46 Lonnie Chisenhall 8.00 20.00
CS47 Ken Griffey Jr. 25.00 60.00
CS48 Andrew McCutchen 30.00 80.00
CS49 Felix Hernandez 15.00 40.00
CS50 Ted Williams 25.00 60.00

2015 Topps Bunt Player Code Cards

STATED ODDS 1:917 HOBBY
UPDATE ODDS 1:1030 HOBBY
STATED PRINT RUN 25 SER.#'d SETS
AC Aroldis Chapman 75.00 150.00
AM Andrew McCutchen 125.00 250.00
AR Anthony Rizzo 100.00 200.00
BH Bryce Harper 150.00 300.00
BP Buster Posey UPD 75.00 200.00
CG Carlos Gonzalez UPD 50.00 120.00
CG Carlos Gomez 75.00 150.00
CH Chris Heston UPD 15.00 40.00
CK Craig Kimbrel 75.00 150.00
CK Clayton Kershaw 150.00 300.00
CS Chris Sale 100.00 200.00
DG Dee Gordon UPD 12.00 30.00
DO David Ortiz 75.00 150.00
DP David Price 75.00 150.00
FH Felix Hernandez 100.00 200.00
GH Greg Holland 60.00 120.00
GS Giancarlo Stanton 100.00 200.00
JC Johnny Cueto 100.00 200.00
JE Jacoby Ellsbury 100.00 200.00
JK Jason Kipnis UPD 15.00 40.00
JL Jon Lester 75.00 150.00
KB Kris Bryant UPD 25.00 60.00
MB Madison Bumgarner 125.00 250.00
MH Matt Harvey 100.00 200.00
MH Matt Harvey UPD 40.00 100.00
MT Mike Trout UPD 50.00 120.00
MT Mark Teixeira UPD 8.00 20.00
MT Mike Trout 150.00 300.00
PF Prince Fielder UPD 12.00 30.00
RC Robinson Cano 100.00 200.00
SG Sonny Gray UPD 20.00 50.00
SS Stephen Strasburg 75.00 150.00
TT Troy Tulowitzki 50.00 120.00
YP Yasiel Puig 150.00 300.00
ZG Zack Greinke UPD 12.00 30.00

2015 Topps Career High Autographs

SER.1 STATED ODDS 1:405 HOBBY
SER.2 STATED ODDS 1:405 HOBBY
UPD STATED ODDS 1:253 HOBBY
SER.1 EXCH DEADLINE 1/31/2018
SER.2 EXCH DEADLINE 1/31/2018
UPD EXCH DEADLINE 9/30/2017
CHAA Arismendy Alcantara 3.00 8.00
CHAC Allen Craig 3.00 8.00
CHAD Andre Dawson 4.00 10.00
CHAE A.J. Ellis 3.00 8.00
CHAJ Adam Jones 4.00 10.00
CHARA Anthony Ranaudo 3.00 8.00
CHAS Aaron Sanchez 4.00 10.00
CHBC Brett Cecil 3.00 8.00
CHCB Charlie Blackmon 5.00 12.00
CHCC C.J. Cron 3.00 8.00
CHCJ Chipper Jones 25.00 60.00
CHCO Chris Owings 3.00 8.00
CHCS Carlos Santana 4.00 10.00
CHCSA Chris Sale 6.00 15.00
CHCSP Cory Spangenberg 3.00 8.00
CHCY Christian Yelich 20.00 50.00
CHDB Dellin Betances 4.00 10.00
CHDC David Cone 10.00 25.00
CHDM Daisuke Matsuzaka 6.00 15.00
CHDS Duke Snider 12.00 30.00
CHED Eric Davis 3.00 8.00
CHEF Erik Cordier 3.00 8.00
CHEL Evan Longoria 4.00 10.00
CHFJ Fergie Jenkins 4.00 10.00
CHGB Grant Balfour 3.00 8.00
CHGP Gregory Polanco 4.00 10.00
CHGS George Springer 10.00 25.00
CHGST Giancarlo Stanton 12.00 30.00
CHHA Hank Aaron 125.00 250.00
CHHI Hisashi Iwakuma 6.00 15.00
CHHK Hiroki Kuroda 50.00 120.00
CHIK Ian Kinsler 4.00 10.00
CHJB Javier Baez 8.00 20.00
CHJD Jacob deGrom 10.00 25.00
CHJH John Holdzkom 3.00 8.00
CHJJ John Jaso 3.00 8.00
CHJL Juan Lagares 6.00 15.00
CHJM J.D. Martinez 12.00 30.00
CHJP Johnny Podres 10.00 25.00
CHJPA Joe Panik 10.00 25.00
CHJPO Jorge Posada 15.00 40.00
CHJS Jonathan Schoop 3.00 8.00
CHJSM John Smoltz 12.00 30.00
CHJSO Jorge Soler 10.00 25.00
CHJT Julio Teheran 4.00 10.00
CHKW Kolten Wong 4.00 10.00
CHMA Mike Adams 3.00 8.00
CHMAD Matt Adams 3.00 8.00
CHMM Mike Minor 3.00 8.00
CHMT Mike Trout 100.00 200.00
CHMZ Mike Zunino 3.00 8.00
CHRC Rusney Castillo 12.00 30.00
CHRH Ryan Howard 4.00 10.00
CHSK Sandy Koufax 150.00 300.00
CHSM Shelby Miller 4.00 10.00
CHSMA Starling Marte 4.00 10.00
CHSS Scott Sizemore 3.00 8.00
CHST Sam Tuivailala 3.00 8.00
CHUJ Ubaldo Jimenez 3.00 8.00
CHYP Yasiel Puig 15.00 40.00
CHYV Yordano Ventura 8.00 20.00
CHAAB Archie Bradley S2 3.00 8.00
CHAAN Aaron Northcraft S2 3.00 8.00
CHAAR Anthony Ranaudo S2 6.00 15.00
CHAAS Andrew Susac UPD 3.00 8.00
CHABB Byron Buxton UPD 20.00 50.00
CHABH Brock Holt UPD 4.00 10.00
CHABS Blake Swihart UPD 4.00 10.00
CHABW Bernie Williams UPD 10.00 25.00
CHACC Carlos Correa UPD 75.00 200.00
CHACJ Chris Johnson S2 3.00 8.00
CHACM Carlos Martinez UPD 6.00 15.00
CHACR Carlos Rodon S2 5.00 12.00
CHACW Christian Walker S2 10.00 25.00
CHADG Dee Gordon UPD 3.00 8.00
CHADH Dilson Herrera S2 4.00 10.00
CHADL DJ LeMahieu UPD 10.00 25.00
CHADN Daniel Norris S2 3.00 8.00
CHADP David Peralta UPD 3.00 8.00
CHADP Dalton Pompey S2 4.00 10.00
CHADT Devon Travis UPD 3.00 8.00
CHAEC Eric Campbell UPD 3.00 8.00
CHAEC Erik Cordier S2 3.00 8.00
CHAEE Edwin Escobar S2 3.00 8.00
CHAFJ Fergie Jenkins S2 8.00 20.00
CHAFL Francisco Lindor UPD 8.00 20.00
CHAGB Gary Brown S2 3.00 8.00
CHAGS George Springer S2 8.00 20.00
CHAHK Hiroki Kuroda S2 50.00 120.00
CHAHS Hector Santiago UPD 3.00 8.00
CHAHS Hector Santiago S2 3.00 8.00
CHAIK Ian Kinsler S2 4.00 10.00
CHAJB Javier Baez S2 25.00 60.00
CHAJC Jose Canseco S2 30.00 80.00
CHAJJ Jon Jay S2 3.00 8.00
CHAJP Jose Pirela UPD 3.00 8.00
CHAJR Jason Rogers UPD 3.00 8.00
CHAJR Jason Rogers S2 3.00 8.00
CHAJS Jorge Soler S2 8.00 20.00
CHAJT Junichi Tazawa S2 3.00 8.00
CHAJW Josh Willingham S2 3.00 8.00
CHAKB Kris Bryant UPD 75.00 200.00
CHAKB Kris Bryant S2 75.00 200.00
CHAKG Kendall Graveman S2 3.00 8.00
CHAKL Kyle Lobstein UPD 3.00 8.00
CHAKP Kevin Plawecki UPD 3.00 8.00
CHAKS Kyle Seager UPD 3.00 8.00
CHALD Lucas Duda S2 4.00 10.00
CHALS Luis Sardinas UPD 3.00 8.00
CHAMB Matt Barnes UPD 3.00 8.00
CHAMT Michael Taylor S2 3.00 8.00
CHANC Nick Castellanos S2 5.00 12.00
CHANS Noah Syndergaard UPD 12.00 30.00
CHARC Rusney Castillo S2 12.00 30.00
CHARD Rubby De La Rosa S2 3.00 8.00
CHARP Rafael Palmeiro UPD 6.00 15.00
CHASG Shane Greene UPD 3.00 8.00
CHASH Slade Heathcott UPD 6.00 15.00
CHASM Steven Matz UPD 20.00 50.00
CHASP Spencer Patton UPD 3.00 8.00
CHATC Tyler Chatwood S2 3.00 8.00
CHATH T.J. House UPD 3.00 8.00
CHATM Trevor May S2 3.00 8.00
CHATP Tommy Pham S2 4.00 10.00
CHAWP Wily Peralta UPD 3.00 8.00
CHAYV Yordano Ventura S2 6.00 15.00
CHAZW Zach Walters UPD 3.00 8.00
CHAACL Alex Colome UPD 3.00 8.00
CHAAJC A.J. Cole UPD 3.00 8.00
CHABFA Buck Farmer S2 3.00 8.00
CHABFI Brandon Finnegan S2 3.00 8.00
CHACSA Carlos Santana S2 4.00 10.00
CHACSP Cory Spangenberg S2 3.00 8.00
CHAJGA Joey Gallo UPD 8.00 20.00
CHAJGR J.R. Graham UPD 3.00 8.00
CHAJHO John Holdzkom S2 3.00 8.00
CHAJLG Juan Lagares S2 3.00 8.00
CHAJMC James McCann S2 5.00 12.00
CHAJMR Jake Marisnick S2 3.00 8.00
CHAJPA Joe Panik S2 10.00 25.00
CHAJPE Joc Pederson S2 6.00 15.00
CHAJPO Johnny Podres S2 3.00 8.00
CHAMAN Matt Andriese UPD 3.00 8.00
CHAMBR Matt Barnes S2 3.00 8.00
CHAMCL Matt Clark S2 3.00 8.00
CHAMFO Mike Foltynewicz S2 3.00 8.00
CHAMFR Maikel Franco S2 4.00 10.00
CHAMSE Marcus Semien UPD 3.00 8.00
CHAYGA Yimi Garcia S2 3.00 8.00

2015 Topps Career High Relics

SER.1 STATED ODDS 1:49 HOBBY
SER.2 STATED ODDS 1:52 HOBBY
CHRAC Allen Craig S2 2.00 5.00
CHRAG Adrian Gonzalez S2 2.50 6.00
CHRAJ Adam Jones S2 2.50 6.00
CHRAS Andrelton Simmons S2 2.00 5.00
CHRBH Billy Hamilton S2 2.50 6.00
CHRCBI Craig Biggio S2 4.00 10.00
CHRCBL Charlie Blackmon S2 3.00 8.00
CHRCR Cal Ripken Jr. S2 12.00 30.00
CHRCU Chase Utley S2 2.50 6.00
CHRDJ Derek Jeter S2 8.00 20.00
CHRDM Don Mattingly S2 6.00 15.00
CHRDN Daniel Norris S2 2.00 5.00
CHRDW David Wright S2 2.50 6.00
CHREL Evan Longoria S2 2.50 6.00
CHRGC Gerrit Cole S2 3.00 8.00
CHRHP Hunter Pence S2 2.50 6.00
CHRHR Hanley Ramirez S2 2.50 6.00
CHRJA Jose Abreu S2 3.00 8.00
CHRJBA Jose Bautista S2 2.50 6.00
CHRJBR Javier Baez S2 15.00 40.00
CHRJH Josh Hamilton S2 2.50 6.00
CHRJM Joe Mauer S2 2.50 6.00
CHRJS Jon Singleton S2 2.50 6.00
CHRJVE Justin Verlander S2 3.00 8.00
CHRLL Lance Lynn S2 2.00 5.00
CHRMBU Madison Bumgarner S2 2.50 6.00
CHRMC Miguel Cabrera S2 3.00 8.00
CHRMH Matt Holliday S2 3.00 8.00
CHRMMC Mark McGwire S2 10.00 25.00
CHRMS Max Scherzer S2 3.00 8.00
CHRNC Nick Castellanos S2 3.00 8.00

CHRPS Pablo Sandoval S2 2.50 6.00
CHRRB Ryan Braun S2 2.50 6.00
CHRRC Roger Clemens S2 6.00 15.00
CHRRJ Randy Johnson S2 3.00 8.00
CHRRZ Ryan Zimmerman S2 2.50 6.00
CHRSC Shin-Soo Choo S2 2.50 6.00
CHRSS Stephen Strasburg S2 3.00 8.00
CHRVG Vladimir Guerrero S2 2.50 6.00
CHRVM Victor Martinez S2 2.50 6.00
CHRWB Wade Boggs S2 4.00 10.00
CHRYD Yu Darvish S2 3.00 8.00
CHRYP Yasiel Puig S2 3.00 8.00
CRHAC Allen Craig 2.00 5.00
CRHAJ Adam Jones 2.50 6.00
CRHAM Andrew McCutchen 6.00 15.00
CRHAP Albert Pujols 15.00 40.00
CRHAR Anthony Rizzo 5.00 12.00
CRHAW Adam Wainwright 5.00 12.00
CRHBH Bryce Harper 8.00 20.00
CRHBP Buster Posey 4.00 10.00
CRHCG Carlos Gomez 2.00 5.00
CRHCK Clayton Kershaw 6.00 15.00
CRHCS Carlos Santana 2.50 6.00
CRHDM Daisuke Matsuzaka 2.50 6.00
CRHDO David Ortiz 3.00 8.00
CRHDPA Dustin Pedroia 3.00 8.00
CRHDPE David Price 2.50 6.00
CRHDW David Wright 2.50 6.00
CRHEL Evan Longoria 2.50 6.00
CRHFF Freddie Freeman 4.00 10.00
CRHFH Felix Hernandez 2.50 6.00
CRHGP Gregory Polanco 2.50 6.00
CRHGSN Giancarlo Stanton 3.00 8.00
CRHGSR George Springer 2.50 6.00
CRHHI Hisashi Iwakuma 2.50 6.00
CRHHR Hanley Ramirez 2.50 6.00
CRHIK Ian Kinsler 2.50 6.00
CRHJA Jose Abreu 8.00 20.00
CRHJBA Jose Bautista 2.50 6.00
CRHJBZ Javier Baez 6.00 15.00
CRHJC Johnny Cueto 2.50 6.00
CRHJD Josh Donaldson 2.50 6.00
CRHJE Jacoby Ellsbury 2.50 6.00
CRHJT Julio Teheran 2.50 6.00
CRHMA Matt Adams 2.00 5.00
CRHMB Mookie Betts 5.00 12.00
CRHMC Miguel Cabrera 3.00 8.00
CRHMM Manny Machado 3.00 8.00
CRHMS Max Scherzer 3.00 8.00
CRHMTA Masahiro Tanaka 12.00 30.00
CRHMTT Mike Trout 15.00 40.00
CRHPG Paul Goldschmidt 3.00 8.00
CRHRB Ryan Braun 2.50 6.00
CRHRC Robinson Cano 2.50 6.00
CRHTT Troy Tulowitzki 3.00 8.00
CRHXB Xander Bogaerts 3.00 8.00
CRHYD Yu Darvish 3.00 8.00
CRHYM Yadier Molina 4.00 10.00
CRHYP Yasiel Puig 3.00 8.00

2015 Topps Commemorative Bat Knobs

STATED ODDS 1:10,956 HOBBY
*BLACK/99: .5X TO 1.2X BASIC
*PINK/25: .75X TO 2X BASIC
CBK01 Willie Mays 15.00 40.00
CBK02 Mike Trout 20.00 50.00
CBK03 Buster Posey 12.00 30.00
CBK04 Babe Ruth 20.00 50.00
CBK05 Mark McGwire 15.00 40.00
CBK06 Derek Jeter 20.00 50.00
CBK07 Jose Abreu 10.00 25.00
CBK08 Ty Cobb 10.00 25.00
CBK09 Jackie Robinson 12.00 30.00
CBK10 Yasiel Puig 10.00 25.00
CBK11 Albert Pujols 10.00 25.00
CBK12 Ken Griffey Jr. 15.00 40.00
CBK13 Giancarlo Stanton 10.00 25.00
CBK14 Andrew McCutchen 15.00 40.00
CBK15 Robinson Cano 8.00 20.00
CBK16 David Ortiz 10.00 25.00
CBK17 Ted Williams 12.00 30.00
CBK18 Adam Jones 10.00 25.00
CBK19 Jacoby Ellsbury 8.00 20.00
CBK20 Miguel Cabrera 12.00 30.00
CBK21 Hunter Pence 8.00 20.00
CBK22 Ryan Braun 8.00 20.00
CBK23 Prince Fielder 8.00 20.00
CBK24 Rusney Castillo 8.00 20.00
CBK25 Jorge Soler 8.00 20.00

2015 Topps Commemorative Patch Pins

STATED ODDS 1:1154 HOBBY
STATED PRINT RUN 199 SER.#'d SETS
CPP01 Ken Griffey Jr. 8.00 20.00
CPP02 Derek Jeter 10.00 25.00
CPP03 Greg Maddux 5.00 12.00
CPP04 Cal Ripken Jr. 12.00 30.00
CPP05 Roger Clemens 5.00 12.00
CPP06 David Ortiz 4.00 10.00
CPP07 Dustin Pedroia 4.00 10.00
CPP08 Frank Thomas 10.00 25.00
CPP09 Nolan Ryan 12.00 30.00
CPP10 George Brett 8.00 20.00
CPP11 Rod Carew 5.00 12.00
CPP12 Clayton Kershaw 8.00 20.00
CPP13 Ivan Rodriguez 3.00 8.00
CPP14 Joe Mauer 3.00 8.00
CPP15 Dwight Gooden 2.50 6.00
CPP16 David Wright 3.00 8.00
CPP17 Mariano Rivera 10.00 25.00
CPP18 Mark McGwire 6.00 15.00
CPP19 Tony Gwynn 4.00 10.00
CPP20 Johnny Bench 6.00 15.00
CPP21 Ted Williams 8.00 20.00
CPP22 Bob Feller 3.00 8.00
CPP23 Brooks Robinson 8.00 20.00
CPP24 Alex Rodriguez 5.00 12.00
CPP25 Don Mattingly 10.00 25.00

2015 Topps Eclipsing History

COMPLETE SET (10) 4.00 10.00
STATED ODDS 1:10 HOBBY
EH1 L.Brock/R.Henderson .50 1.25
EH2 S.Musial/H.Aaron 1.00 2.50
EH3 S.Koufax/N.Ryan 1.50 4.00
EH4 O.Smith/O.Vizquel .60 1.50
EH5 T.Seaver/D.Gooden .40 1.00
EH6 W.Ford/M.Rivera .60 1.50
EH7 R.Carew/M.Trout 2.50 6.00
EH8 J.Rice/N.Garciaparra .40 1.00
EH9 D.Jeter/L.Gehrig 1.25 3.00
EH10 D.Strawberry/D.Wright .40 1.00

2015 Topps Eclipsing History Dual Relics

STATED ODDS 1:17,118 HOBBY
STATED PRINT RUN 50 SER.#'d SETS
EHRGS T.Seaver/D.Gooden 10.00 25.00
EHRTC R.Carew/M.Trout 25.00 60.00
EHRVS O.Smith/O.Vizquel 20.00 50.00

2015 Topps Factory Set All Star Bonus

AS1 Clayton Kershaw 1.00 2.50
AS2 Buster Posey .60 1.50
AS3 Mike Trout 2.50 6.00
AS4 Jose Abreu .50 1.25
AS5 Miguel Cabrera .50 1.25

2015 Topps First Home Run

COMPLETE SET (40) 20.00 50.00
*GOLD: .5X TO 1.2X BASIC
*SILVER: .5X TO 1.2X BASIC
RANDOM INSERT IN RETAIL PACKS
FHR01 Jorge Soler .75 2.00
FHR02 Andrew McCutchen .75 2.00
FHR03 David Wright .60 1.50
FHR04 Robinson Cano .60 1.50
FHR05 Derek Jeter 2.00 5.00
FHR06 Bryce Harper 1.25 3.00
FHR07 Mike Moustakas .60 1.50
FHR08 Eric Hosmer .60 1.50
FHR09 Matt Carpenter .75 2.00
FHR10 Chipper Jones .75 2.00
FHR11 Anthony Rizzo 1.25 3.00
FHR12 Jason Heyward .60 1.50
FHR13 Javier Baez 4.00 10.00
FHR14 Yasiel Puig .75 2.00
FHR15 Alex Rodriguez 1.00 2.50
FHR16 Matt Adams .50 1.25
FHR17 Adam Dunn .60 1.50
FHR18 Buster Posey 1.00 2.50
FHR19 Paul Konerko .60 1.50
FHR20 Adrian Gonzalez .60 1.50
FHR21 Jose Bautista .60 1.50
FHR22 Josh Hamilton .60 1.50
FHR23 Chase Utley .60 1.50
FHR24 Ryan Howard .60 1.50
FHR25 Joey Votto .75 2.00
FHR26 Adam Jones .60 1.50
FHR27 Chris Davis .50 1.25
FHR28 Don Mattingly 1.50 4.00
FHR29 Joe Mauer .60 1.50
FHR30 Jose Abreu .75 2.00
FHR31 Yoenis Cespedes .60 1.50
FHR32 Paul Goldschmidt .75 2.00
FHR33 Freddie Freeman 1.00 2.50
FHR34 Mike Trout 4.00 10.00
FHR35 Evan Longoria .60 1.50
FHR36 Victor Martinez .60 1.50
FHR37 Mike Piazza .75 2.00
FHR38 Troy Tulowitzki .75 2.00
FHR39 Dustin Pedroia .75 2.00
FHR40 Deion Sanders .60 1.50

2015 Topps First Home Run Series 2

COMPLETE SET (40) 20.00 50.00
*GOLD: .5X TO 1.2X BASIC
*SILVER: .5X TO 1.2X BASIC
RANDOM INSERT IN RETAIL PACKS
FHR1 Eddie Murray .60 1.50
FHR2 Cal Ripken Jr. 2.50 6.00
FHR3 Brooks Robinson .60 1.50
FHR4 Babe Ruth 2.00 5.00
FHR5 Ted Williams 1.50 4.00
FHR6 Frank Thomas .75 2.00
FHR7 Johnny Bench .75 2.00
FHR8 Tony Perez .60 1.50
FHR9 Ty Cobb 1.25 3.00
FHR10 Miguel Cabrera .75 2.00
FHR11 Giancarlo Stanton .75 2.00
FHR12 Hunter Pence .60 1.50
FHR13 Reggie Jackson .60 1.50
FHR14 Carlos Beltran .60 1.50
FHR15 Bo Jackson .75 2.00
FHR16 David Ortiz .75 2.00
FHR17 Mark McGwire 1.25 3.00
FHR18 Tony Gwynn .75 2.00
FHR19 Jayson Werth .60 1.50
FHR20 Harmon Killebrew .75 2.00
FHR21 Clayton Kershaw 1.50 4.00
FHR22 Rusney Castillo .60 1.50
FHR23 Dwight Gooden .50 1.25
FHR24 Greg Maddux 1.00 2.50
FHR25 Pedro Alvarez .50 1.25
FHR26 Ryan Braun .60 1.50
FHR27 Albert Pujols 1.00 2.50
FHR28 Matt Kemp .60 1.50
FHR29 Prince Fielder .60 1.50
FHR30 Nelson Cruz .75 2.00
FHR31 Cliff Floyd .50 1.25
FHR32 Pablo Sandoval .60 1.50
FHR33 Yadier Molina .75 2.00
FHR34 Alex Gordon .60 1.50
FHR35 Lucas Duda .60 1.50

2015 Topps First Home Run Medallions

RANDOM INSERT IN RETAIL PACKS
FHRMAD Adam Dunn 2.50 6.00
FHRMAG Adrian Gonzalez 2.50 6.00
FHRMAG Alex Gordon S2 2.50 6.00
FHRMAJ Adam Jones 2.50 6.00
FHRMAM Andrew McCutchen 3.00 8.00
FHRMAP Albert Pujols S2 4.00 10.00
FHRMARI Anthony Rizzo 5.00 12.00
FHRMARO Alex Rodriguez 4.00 10.00
FHRMBH Bryce Harper 5.00 12.00
FHRMBJ Bo Jackson S2 3.00 8.00
FHRMBP Buster Posey 4.00 10.00
FHRMCB Carlos Beltran S2 2.50 6.00
FHRMCD Chris Davis 2.00 5.00
FHRMCF Cliff Floyd S2 2.00 5.00
FHRMCJ Chipper Jones 3.00 8.00
FHRMCK Clayton Kershaw S2 6.00 15.00
FHRMCR Cal Ripken Jr. S2 10.00 25.00
FHRMCU Chase Utley 2.50 6.00
FHRMDG Dwight Gooden S2 2.00 5.00
FHRMDJ Derek Jeter 8.00 20.00
FHRMDM Don Mattingly 6.00 15.00
FHRMDO David Ortiz S2 3.00 8.00
FHRMDP Dustin Pedroia 3.00 8.00
FHRMDS Deion Sanders 2.50 6.00
FHRMDW David Wright 2.50 6.00
FHRMEH Eric Hosmer 2.50 6.00
FHRMEL Evan Longoria 2.50 6.00
FHRMEM Eddie Murray S2 2.50 6.00
FHRMFF Freddie Freeman 4.00 10.00
FHRMFT Frank Thomas S2 3.00 8.00
FHRMGM Greg Maddux S2 4.00 10.00
FHRMGS Giancarlo Stanton S2 3.00 8.00
FHRMHK Harmon Killebrew S2 3.00 8.00
FHRMHP Hunter Pence S2 2.50 6.00
FHRMJA Jose Abreu 3.00 8.00
FHRMJB Johnny Bench S2 3.00 8.00
FHRMJBA Javier Baez 15.00 40.00
FHRMJBU Jose Bautista 2.50 6.00
FHRMJHA Josh Hamilton 2.50 6.00
FHRMJHE Jason Heyward 2.50 6.00
FHRMJM Joe Mauer 2.50 6.00
FHRMJS Jorge Soler 3.00 8.00
FHRMJV Joey Votto 3.00 8.00
FHRMJW Jayson Werth S2 2.50 6.00
FHRMLD Lucas Duda S2 2.50 6.00
FHRMMA Matt Adams 2.00 5.00
FHRMMC Matt Carpenter 3.00 8.00
FHRMMC Miguel Cabrera S2 3.00 8.00
FHRMMK Matt Kemp S2 2.50 6.00
FHRMMM Mark McGwire S2 5.00 12.00
FHRMMM Mike Moustakas 2.50 6.00
FHRMMP Mike Piazza 3.00 8.00
FHRMMT Mike Trout 15.00 40.00
FHRMNC Nelson Cruz S2 3.00 8.00
FHRMPA Pedro Alvarez S2 2.00 5.00
FHRMPF Prince Fielder S2 2.50 6.00
FHRMPG Paul Goldschmidt 3.00 8.00
FHRMPK Paul Konerko 2.50 6.00
FHRMPS Pablo Sandoval S2 2.50 6.00
FHRMRB Ryan Braun S2 2.50 6.00
FHRMRC Rusney Castillo S2 2.50 6.00
FHRMRC Robinson Cano 2.50 6.00
FHRMRH Ryan Howard 2.50 6.00
FHRMRJ Reggie Jackson S2 2.50 6.00
FHRMTC Ty Cobb S2 5.00 12.00
FHRMTG Tony Gwynn S2 3.00 8.00
FHRMTP Tony Perez S2 2.50 6.00
FHRMTT Troy Tulowitzki 3.00 8.00
FHRMTW Ted Williams S2 6.00 15.00
FHRMVM Victor Martinez 2.50 6.00
FHRMYC Yoenis Cespedes 2.50 6.00
FHRMYM Yadier Molina S2 3.00 8.00
FHRMYP Yasiel Puig 3.00 8.00
FHRMBRO Brooks Robinson S2 2.50 6.00
FHRMBRU Babe Ruth S2 8.00 20.00

2015 Topps First Home Run Relics

RANDOM INSERT IN RETAIL PACKS
STATED PRINT RUN 99 SER.#'d SETS
FHRRAD Adam Dunn 8.00 20.00
FHRRAG Adrian Gonzalez 8.00 20.00
FHRRAG Alex Gordon S2 5.00 12.00
FHRRAJ Adam Jones 5.00 12.00
FHRRAM Andrew McCutchen 15.00 40.00
FHRRAP Albert Pujols S2 8.00 20.00
FHRRBH Bryce Harper 12.00 30.00
FHRRCK Clayton Kershaw S2 6.00 15.00
FHRRDJ Derek Jeter 50.00 100.00
FHRRDO David Ortiz S2 6.00 15.00
FHRRDP Dustin Pedroia 30.00 80.00
FHRREH Eric Hosmer 5.00 12.00
FHRRFF Freddie Freeman 10.00 25.00
FHRRGS Giancarlo Stanton S2 6.00 15.00
FHRRHP Hunter Pence S2 6.00 15.00
FHRRJB Jose Bautista 5.00 12.00
FHRRJHA Josh Hamilton 8.00 20.00
FHRRJHE Jason Heyward 5.00 12.00
FHRRJV Joey Votto 10.00 25.00
FHRRMC Miguel Cabrera S2 6.00 15.00
FHRRMT Mike Trout 20.00 50.00
FHRRNC Nelson Cruz S2 6.00 15.00
FHRRPA Pedro Alvarez S2 10.00 25.00
FHRRPF Prince Fielder S2 5.00 12.00
FHRRPG Paul Goldschmidt 10.00 25.00
FHRRPS Pablo Sandoval S2 5.00 12.00
FHRRRB Ryan Braun S2 5.00 12.00
FHRRRC Rusney Castillo S2 5.00 12.00
FHRRRJ Reggie Jackson S2 10.00 25.00
FHRRTG Tony Gwynn S2 15.00 40.00
FHRRTT Troy Tulowitzki 6.00 15.00
FHRRYM Yadier Molina S2 6.00 15.00

2015 Topps First Pitch

COMPLETE SET (25) 10.00 25.00
SER.1 STATED ODDS 1:8 HOBBY
SER.2 STATED ODDS 1:8 HOBBY
FP01 Jeff Bridges .75 2.00
FP02 Jack White 1.25 3.00
FP03 McKayla Maroney .75 2.00
FP04 Eddie Vedder 1.50 4.00
FP05 Biz Markie .75 2.00
FP06 Agnes McKee .75 2.00
FP07 Austin Mahone .75 2.00
FP08 Jermaine Jones .75 2.00
FP09 Tom Willis .75 2.00
FP10 Graham Elliot .75 2.00
FP11 Tom Morello .75 2.00
FP12 Macklemore .75 2.00
FP13 Suzy 1.25 3.00
FP14 50 Cent .75 2.00
FP15 Meb Keflezighi .75 2.00
FP16 Kelsey Grammer .75 2.00
FP17 Chris Pratt .75 2.00
FP18 Jon Hamm .75 2.00
FP19 Melissa McCarthy .75 2.00
FP20 Chelsea Handler .75 2.00
FP21 Stan Lee .75 2.00
FP22 Lars Ulrich .75 2.00
FP23 Kevin Hart .75 2.00
FP24 Bill Kreutzmann .75 2.00
Mickey Hart
FP25 Gabriel Iglesias .75 2.00

2015 Topps Free Agent 40

COMPLETE SET (15) 5.00 12.00
STATED ODDS 1:8 HOBBY
F401 Albert Pujols .60 1.50
F402 Robinson Cano .40 1.00
F403 CC Sabathia .40 1.00
F404 Nolan Ryan 1.50 4.00
F405 Goose Gossage .40 1.00
F406 David Ortiz .50 1.25
F407 Andre Dawson .40 1.00
F408 Greg Maddux .60 1.50
F409 Alex Rodriguez .60 1.50
F4010 Randy Johnson .50 1.25
F4011 Reggie Jackson .40 1.00
F4012 Carlton Fisk .40 1.00
F4013 David Cone .30 .75
F4014 Roger Clemens .60 1.50
F4015 Ivan Rodriguez .40 1.00

2015 Topps Free Agent 40 Relics

STATED ODDS 1:31,455 HOBBY
STATED PRINT RUN 50 SER.#'d SETS
F40RAP Albert Pujols 20.00 50.00
F40RCS CC Sabathia 6.00 15.00
F40RRJ Reggie Jackson 10.00 25.00

2015 Topps Future Stars Pin

STATED ODDS 1:1896 HOBBY
*VINTAGE/99: .75X TO 2X BASIC
FS01 Xander Bogaerts 3.00 8.00
FS02 Billy Hamilton 2.50 6.00
FS03 George Springer 2.50 6.00
FS04 Gregory Polanco 2.50 6.00
FS05 Arismendy Alcantara 2.00 5.00
FS06 Jacob deGrom 3.00 8.00
FS07 Masahiro Tanaka 2.50 6.00
FS08 Dellin Betances 2.50 6.00
FS09 Tanner Roark 2.00 5.00
FS10 Jose Abreu 3.00 8.00

2015 Topps Gallery of Greats

COMPLETE SET (25) 40.00 100.00
STATED ODDS 1:18 HOBBY
GG1 Clayton Kershaw 2.50 6.00
GG2 Frank Thomas 1.25 3.00
GG3 Derek Jeter 3.00 8.00
GG4 Ken Griffey Jr. 3.00 8.00
GG5 Tom Glavine 1.00 2.50
GG6 Mike Piazza 1.25 3.00
GG7 Mark McGwire 2.00 5.00
GG8 Roger Clemens 1.50 4.00
GG9 Miguel Cabrera 1.25 3.00
GG10 Cal Ripken Jr. 4.00 10.00
GG11 Yasiel Puig 1.25 3.00
GG12 Steve Carlton 1.00 2.50
GG13 Hanley Ramirez 1.00 2.50
GG14 Willie Mays 2.50 6.00
GG15 Sandy Koufax 2.50 6.00
GG16 Hank Aaron 2.50 6.00
GG17 Albert Pujols 1.50 4.00
GG18 Bryce Harper 2.00 5.00
GG19 Mariano Rivera 1.50 4.00
GG20 Jackie Robinson 1.25 3.00
GG21 Joe DiMaggio 2.50 6.00
GG22 Babe Ruth 3.00 8.00
GG23 Roberto Clemente 3.00 8.00
GG24 Nolan Ryan 4.00 10.00
GG25 Tony Gwynn 1.25 3.00

2015 Topps Gallery of Greats Gold

*GOLD: 1.2X TO 3X BASIC
STATED ODDS 1:974 HOBBY
STATED PRINT RUN 99 SER.#'d SETS
GG3 Derek Jeter 20.00 50.00

2015 Topps Gallery of Greats Relics

STATED ODDS 1:6452 HOBBY
STATED PRINT RUN 25 SER.#'d SETS
GGRAP Albert Pujols 20.00 50.00
GGRCK Clayton Kershaw 10.00 25.00
GGRDJ Derek Jeter 25.00 60.00
GGRFT Frank Thomas 20.00 50.00
GGRHR Hanley Ramirez 20.00 50.00
GGRKG Ken Griffey Jr. 25.00 60.00
GGRMM Mark McGwire 60.00 150.00
GGRMP Mike Piazza 25.00 60.00
GGRRC Roger Clemens 10.00 25.00
GGRTG Tom Glavine 40.00 100.00
GGRYP Yasiel Puig 15.00 40.00

2015 Topps Hall of Fame Class of '14 Triple Autograph

ISSUED AS EXCH IN '14 SER.1
STATED PRINT RUN 50 SER.#'d SETS
HOF14 Thomas/Gravine/Maddux 125.00 300.00

2015 Topps Heart of the Order

COMPLETE SET (20) 5.00 12.00
STATED ODDS 1:6 HOBBY
HOR1 Ted Williams 1.00 2.50
HOR2 Mike Piazza .50 1.25
HOR3 Hank Aaron 1.00 2.50
HOR4 Ken Griffey Jr. 1.00 2.50
HOR5 Jose Canseco .40 1.00
HOR6 Yasiel Puig .50 1.25
HOR7 Mike Trout 2.50 6.00
HOR8 Gary Carter .40 1.00
HOR9 Chipper Jones .50 1.25
HOR10 Giancarlo Stanton .50 1.25
HOR11 Tony Gwynn .50 1.25
HOR12 Hanley Ramirez .40 1.00
HOR13 Prince Fielder .40 1.00
HOR14 Ryan Howard .40 1.00
HOR15 Matt Adams .30 .75
HOR16 Jeff Bagwell .40 1.00
HOR17 Edgar Martinez .40 1.00
HOR18 Freddie Freeman .60 1.50
HOR19 Paul Goldschmidt .50 1.25
HOR20 Adam Jones .40 1.00

2015 Topps Heart of the Order Relics

STATED ODDS 1:4280 HOBBY
STATED PRINT RUN 99 SER.#'d SETS
HTORCJ Chipper Jones 10.00 25.00
HTORDO David Ortiz 8.00 20.00
HTORGC Gary Carter 10.00 25.00
HTORGS Giancarlo Stanton 8.00 20.00
HTORHA Hank Aaron 15.00 40.00
HTORKG Ken Griffey Jr. 30.00 80.00
HTORMT Mike Trout 40.00 100.00
HTORTG Tony Gwynn 30.00 80.00
HTORTW Ted Williams 25.00 60.00
HTORYP Yasiel Puig 15.00 40.00

2015 Topps Hot Streak

COMPLETE SET (20) 12.00 30.00
RANDOM INSERTS IN RETAIL PACKS
HS1 Yasiel Puig .60 1.50
HS2 Jim Palmer .75 2.00
HS3 Sandy Koufax 2.00 5.00
HS4 Max Scherzer .60 1.50
HS5 Don Mattingly 2.00 5.00
HS6 Chipper Jones 1.00 2.50
HS7 Vinny Castilla .60 1.50
HS8 Nomar Garciaparra .75 2.00
HS9 Frank Robinson .75 2.00
HS10 Clayton Kershaw 2.00 5.00
HS11 Roger Clemens 1.25 3.00
HS12 Randy Johnson 1.00 2.50
HS13 Pablo Sandoval .75 2.00
HS14 George Brett 2.00 5.00
HS15 Ozzie Smith 1.25 3.00
HS16 David Cone .60 1.50
HS17 Corey Kluber .75 2.00
HS18 Livan Hernandez .60 1.50
HS19 Albert Pujols 1.25 3.00
HS20 Luis Gonzalez .60 1.50

2015 Topps Hot Streak Relics

RANDOM INSERTS IN PACKS
STATED PRINT RUN 50 SER.#'d SETS
HSRCK Clayton Kershaw 30.00 80.00
HSRDM Don Mattingly 20.00 50.00
HSRFR Frank Robinson 12.00 30.00
HSRJP Jim Palmer 12.00 30.00
HSRTS Tom Seaver 12.00 30.00
HSRYP Yasiel Puig 20.00 50.00

2015 Topps Highlight of the Year

COMPLETE SET (90) 15.00 40.00
SER.1 STATED ODDS 1:4 HOBBY
SER.2 STATED ODDS 1:4 HOBBY
UPD STATED ODDS 1:4 HOBBY
H1 Lou Gehrig 1.00 2.50
H2 Babe Ruth 1.25 3.00
H3 Babe Ruth 1.25 3.00
H4 Bob Feller .40 1.00
H5 Stan Musial .75 2.00
H6 Ted Williams 1.00 2.50
H7 New York Giants .30 .75
H8 Ted Williams 1.00 2.50
H9 Enos Slaughter .40 1.00
H10 Ernie Banks .50 1.25
H11 Roger Maris .50 1.25
H12 Roger Maris .50 1.25
H13 Warren Spahn .40 1.00
H14 Brooks Robinson .40 1.00
H15 Juan Marichal .40 1.00
H16 Catfish Hunter .40 1.00
H17 Nolan Ryan 1.50 4.00
H18 Willie McCovey .40 1.00
H19 Mike Schmidt .75 2.00
H20 Fergie Jenkins .40 1.00
H21 Fernando Valenzuela .30 .75
H22 Nolan Ryan 1.50 4.00
H23 Jose Canseco .40 1.00
H24 Derek Jeter 1.25 3.00
H25 Mark McGwire .75 2.00
H26 Nomar Garciaparra .40 1.00
H27 Cal Ripken Jr. 1.50 4.00
H28 Josh Beckett .30 .75
H29 Justin Verlander .50 1.25
H30 Miguel Cabrera .50 1.25
H31 Ty Cobb .75 2.00
H32 Babe Ruth 1.25 3.00
H33 Babe Ruth 1.25 3.00
H34 Babe Ruth 1.25 3.00
H35 Babe Ruth 1.25 3.00
H36 Enos Slaughter .40 1.00
H37 Lou Gehrig 1.00 2.50
H38 Ted Williams 1.00 2.50
H39 Bobby Doerr .40 1.00
H40 Jackie Robinson .50 1.25
H41 Joe DiMaggio 1.00 2.50
H42 Bob Feller .40 1.00
H43 Willie Mays 1.00 2.50
H44 Roberto Clemente 1.25 3.00
H45 Hank Aaron 1.00 2.50
H46 Sandy Koufax 1.00 2.50
H47 Jim Palmer .40 1.00
H48 Tom Seaver .40 1.00
H49 Rickey Henderson .50 1.25
H50 Andre Dawson .40 1.00
H51 Roger Clemens .60 1.50
H52 Don Mattingly 1.00 2.50
H53 Mark McGwire .75 2.00
H54 Nolan Ryan 1.50 4.00
H55 Ozzie Smith .60 1.50
H56 Cal Ripken Jr. 1.50 4.00
H57 Edgar Martinez .40 1.00
H58 Greg Maddux .60 1.50
H59 Mariano Rivera .60 1.50
H60 Clayton Kershaw 1.00 2.50
H61 Babe Ruth UPD 1.25 3.00
H62 Lou Gehrig UPD 1.00 2.50
H63 Babe Ruth UPD 1.25 3.00
H64 Joe DiMaggio UPD 1.00 2.50
H65 Bob Feller UPD .40 1.00
H66 Ted Williams UPD 1.00 2.50
H67 Red Schoendienst UPD .40 1.00
H68 Bob Lemon UPD .40 1.00
H69 Hank Aaron UPD 1.00 2.50
H70 Hoyt Wilhelm UPD .40 1.00
H71 Sandy Koufax UPD 1.00 2.50
H72 Tom Seaver UPD .40 1.00
H73 Tom Seaver UPD .40 1.00
H74 Harmon Killebrew UPD .50 1.25
H75 Willie Mays UPD 1.00 2.50
H76 Hank Aaron UPD 1.00 2.50
H77 Reggie Jackson UPD .40 1.00
H78 Lou Brock UPD .40 1.00
H79 Dwight Gooden UPD .30 .75
H80 Fernando Valenzuela UPD .30 .75
H81 Robin Yount UPD .50 1.25
H82 Ken Griffey Jr. UPD 1.00 2.50
H83 Jackie Robinson UPD .50 1.25
H84 Randy Johnson UPD .50 1.25
H85 John Smoltz UPD .50 1.25
H86 David Ortiz UPD .50 1.25
H87 Ivan Rodriguez UPD .40 1.00
H88 Ubaldo Jimenez UPD .30 .75
H89 Albert Pujols UPD .60 1.50
H90 Yasiel Puig UPD .50 1.25

2015 Topps Highlight of the Year Autographs

STATED ODDS 1:31,455 HOBBY
UPD ODDS 1:10,614 HOBBY
STATED PRINT RUN 25 SER.#'d SETS
EXCHANGE DEADLINE 1/31/2018
UPD.EXCHANGE 9/30/2017
HYAAD Andre Dawson S2 8.00 20.00
HYACK Clayton Kershaw S2 30.00 80.00
HYACR Cal Ripken Jr. S2 50.00 120.00
HYACR Cal Ripken Jr. 50.00 120.00
HYADM Don Mattingly S2 25.00 60.00
HYADO David Ortiz UPD 40.00 100.00
HYAEB Ernie Banks 50.00 120.00
HYAEM Edgar Martinez S2 20.00 50.00
HYAJC Jose Canseco 40.00 100.00
HYAJP Jim Palmer S2 12.00 30.00
HYAJS John Smoltz UPD 20.00 50.00
HYAKG Ken Griffey Jr. UPD 75.00 200.00
HYALB Lou Brock UPD 60.00 150.00
HYAMC Miguel Cabrera 60.00 150.00
HYAMM Mark McGwire 50.00 120.00
HYAMS Mike Schmidt 25.00 60.00
HYANG Nomar Garciaparra 60.00 150.00
HYANR Nolan Ryan S2 60.00 150.00
HYAOS Ozzie Smith S2 20.00 50.00
HYARC Roger Clemens S2 30.00 80.00
HYARH Rickey Henderson S2 30.00 80.00
HYARJ Reggie Jackson UPD 30.00 80.00
HYASM Stan Musial 60.00 150.00

2015 Topps Highlight of the Year Relics

SER.1 STATED ODDS 1:5270 HOBBY
SER.2 STATED ODDS 1:4280 HOBBY
STATED PRINT RUN 99 SER.#'d SETS
HYRAD Andre Dawson S2 4.00 10.00
HYRBR Brooks Robinson 10.00 25.00
HYRCH Catfish Hunter 4.00 10.00
HYRCR Cal Ripken Jr. 15.00 40.00
HYRCR Cal Ripken Jr. S2 15.00 40.00
HYRDJ Derek Jeter 25.00 60.00
HYRDM Don Mattingly S2 15.00 40.00
HYREB Ernie Banks 12.00 30.00
HYRFJ Fergie Jenkins 4.00 10.00
HYRFV Fernando Valenzuela 10.00 25.00
HYRJM Juan Marichal 4.00 10.00
HYRJP Jim Palmer S2 8.00 20.00
HYRJV Justin Verlander 5.00 12.00
HYRMC Miguel Cabrera 5.00 12.00
HYRMM Mark McGwire 15.00 40.00
HYRMM Mark McGwire S2 8.00 20.00
HYRMS Mike Schmidt 15.00 40.00
HYRNG Nomar Garciaparra 4.00 10.00
HYRNR Nolan Ryan S2 15.00 40.00
HYRNRC Nolan Ryan 15.00 40.00
HYRNRH Nolan Ryan 15.00 40.00
HYROS Ozzie Smith S2 6.00 15.00
HYRRC Roger Clemens S2 6.00 15.00
HYRRH Rickey Henderson S2 5.00 12.00
HYRTS Tom Seaver S2 4.00 10.00

2015 Topps Inspired Play Dual Relics

STATED ODDS 1:31,455 HOBBY
STATED PRINT RUN 50 SER.#'d SETS
IRCG R.Cano/K.Griffey Jr. 20.00 50.00
IRFM F.McGriff/F.Freeman 12.00 30.00
IRHC C.Hamels/S.Carlton 25.00 60.00
IRMR M.Machado/C.Ripken Jr. 40.00 100.00

2015 Topps Inspired Play

COMPLETE SET (15) 5.00 12.00
STATED ODDS 1:8 HOBBY
I1 M.Machado/C.Ripken Jr. 1.50 4.00
I2 K.Griffey Jr./R.Cano 1.00 2.50
I3 D.Mattingly/M.Teixeira 1.00 2.50
I4 A.Kaline/M.Cabrera .50 1.25
I5 S.Carlton/C.Hamels .40 1.00
I6 R.Carew/J.Mauer .40 1.00
I7 C.Kershaw/F.Valenzuela 1.00 2.50
I8 J.Rice/Y.Cespedes .40 1.00
I9 S.Musial/M.McGwire .75 2.00
I10 F.McGriff/F.Freeman .60 1.50
I11 T.Seaver/M.Harvey .40 1.00
I12 J.Abreu/F.Thomas .50 1.25
I13 C.Kimbrel/J.Smoltz .50 1.25
I14 R.Johnson/F.Hernandez .50 1.25
I15 McCutchen/Stargell .50 1.25

2015 Topps Logoman Pin

STATED ODDS 1:758 HOBBY
MSBL01 Yu Darvish 5.00 12.00
MSBL02 Bryce Harper 8.00 20.00
MSBL03 David Wright 4.00 10.00
MSBL04 David Ortiz 6.00 15.00
MSBL05 Albert Pujols 8.00 20.00
MSBL06 Buster Posey 8.00 20.00
MSBL07 Dustin Pedroia 5.00 12.00
MSBL08 Mike Trout 8.00 20.00
MSBL09 Yasiel Puig 8.00 20.00
MSBL10 Miguel Cabrera 8.00 20.00
MSBL11 Andrew McCutchen 5.00 12.00
MSBL12 Freddie Freeman 6.00 15.00
MSBL13 Robinson Cano 4.00 10.00
MSBL14 Masahiro Tanaka 8.00 20.00
MSBL15 Anthony Rizzo 8.00 20.00
MSBL16 Manny Machado 5.00 12.00
MSBL17 Yadier Molina 5.00 12.00
MSBL18 Javier Baez 25.00 60.00
MSBL19 Clayton Kershaw 8.00 20.00
MSBL20 Giancarlo Stanton 5.00 12.00
MSBL21 Jose Abreu 8.00 20.00
MSBL22 Jose Bautista 4.00 10.00
MSBL23 David Price 4.00 10.00
MSBL24 Adam Wainwright 4.00 10.00
MSBL25 Jacoby Ellsbury 4.00 10.00

2015 Topps Postseason Performance Autograph Relics

STATED ODDS 1:4840 HOBBY
STATED PRINT RUN 50 SER.#'d SETS
EXCHANGE DEADLINE 1/31/2018
PPARBH Bryce Harper EXCH 100.00 200.00
PPARCK Clayton Kershaw 60.00 150.00
PPARMC Matt Carpenter 30.00 80.00
PPARSP Salvador Perez 25.00 60.00
PPARYV Yordano Ventura 40.00 100.00
PPARJSC Jonathan Schoop 20.00 50.00

2015 Topps Postseason Performance Autographs

STATED ODDS 1:15,728 HOBBY
STATED PRINT RUN 50 SER.#'d SETS
EXCHANGE DEADLINE 1/31/2018
PPABH Bryce Harper EXCH 100.00 200.00
PPACK Clayton Kershaw 100.00 200.00
PPACT Chris Tillman 15.00 40.00
PPAMA Matt Adams 40.00 80.00
PPAMC Matt Carpenter 10.00 25.00
PPASP Salvador Perez 15.00 40.00
PPAYV Yordano Ventura 8.00 20.00
PPAJSC Jonathan Schoop 6.00 15.00

2015 Topps Postseason Performance Relics

STATED ODDS 1:3126 HOBBY
STATED PRINT RUN 100 SER.#'d SETS
PPRAE A.J. Ellis 4.00 10.00
PPRAGN Adrian Gonzalez 5.00 12.00
PPRAGO Alex Gordon 12.00 30.00
PPRAJ Adam Jones 5.00 12.00
PPRAR Anthony Rendon 6.00 15.00

PRBBU Billy Butler 4.00 10.00
PRBH Bryce Harper 12.00 30.00
PRDG Dee Gordon 4.00 10.00
PRDS Drew Storen 4.00 10.00
PREH Eric Hosmer 20.00 50.00
PRJJ Jon Jay 4.00 10.00
PRJS Jonathan Schoop 4.00 10.00
PRKW Kolten Wong 25.00 60.00
PRLL Lance Lynn 15.00 40.00
PRMH Matt Holliday 25.00 60.00
PRMK Matt Kemp 5.00 12.00
PRMM Mike Moustakas 5.00 12.00
PRNC Nelson Cruz 6.00 15.00
PRNM Nick Markakis 5.00 12.00
PRSM Shelby Miller 5.00 12.00
PRSP Salvador Perez 5.00 12.00
PRWC Wei-Yin Chen 20.00 50.00
PRYM Yadier Molina 25.00 60.00
PRYV Yordano Ventura 20.00 50.00
PRZG Zack Greinke 5.00 12.00

2015 Topps Robbed

COMPLETE SET (15) 12.00 30.00
RANDOM INSERTS IN RETAIL PACKS
R1 Dustin Ackley .50 1.25
R2 Alexi Amarista .50 1.25
R3 Jacoby Ellsbury .60 1.50
R4 Carlos Gomez .50 1.25
R5 Josh Hamilton .60 1.50
R6 Jason Heyward .60 1.50
R7 Ryan Ludwick .50 1.25
R8 Michael Morse .50 1.25
R9 Yasiel Puig .75 2.00
R10 Colby Rasmus .60 1.50
R11 Ben Revere .50 1.25
R12 George Springer .60 1.50
R13 Giancarlo Stanton .75 2.00
R14 Mike Trout 4.00 10.00
R15 Mookie Betts 1.25 3.00

2015 Topps Robbed Relics

RANDOM INSERTS IN RETAIL PACKS
STATED PRINT RUN 25 SER.#'d SETS
RRDA Dustin Ackley 12.00 30.00
RRGSN Giancarlo Stanton 15.00 40.00
RRJHD Jason Heyward 20.00 50.00

2015 Topps Spring Fever

COMPLETE SET (50) 10.00 25.00
SF1 Albert Pujols .40 1.00
SF2 Mike Trout 1.50 4.00
SF3 Freddie Freeman .40 1.00
SF4 Adam Jones .25 .60
SF5 David Ortiz .30 .75
SF6 Dustin Pedroia .30 .75
SF7 Anthony Rizzo .50 1.25
SF8 Javier Baez 1.50 4.00
SF9 Jose Abreu .30 .75
SF10 Miguel Cabrera .30 .75
SF11 Max Scherzer .30 .75
SF12 Yasiel Puig .30 .75
SF13 Clayton Kershaw .60 1.50
SF14 Giancarlo Stanton .30 .75
SF15 David Wright .25 .60
SF16 Masahiro Tanaka .25 .60
SF17 Jacoby Ellsbury .25 .60
SF18 Andrew McCutchen .30 .75
SF19 Buster Posey .40 1.00
SF20 Robinson Cano .25 .60
SF21 Yadier Molina .30 .75
SF22 Adam Wainwright .25 .60
SF23 Yu Darvish .30 .75
SF24 Jose Bautista .25 .60
SF25 Bryce Harper .50 1.25
SF26 Chris Sale .30 .75
SF27 Felix Hernandez .25 .60
SF28 Adrian Beltre .30 .75
SF29 Ryan Braun .25 .60
SF30 Billy Hamilton .25 .60
SF31 Jose Altuve .25 .60
SF32 Ian Desmond .20 .50
SF33 Madison Bumgarner .25 .60
SF34 Edwin Encarnacion .30 .75
SF35 Stephen Strasburg .30 .75
SF36 Josh Donaldson .25 .60
SF37 Evan Longoria .25 .60
SF38 Jon Lester .25 .60
SF39 Michael Brantley .25 .60
SF40 Alex Gordon .25 .60
SF41 Jason Kipnis .25 .60
SF42 Adrian Gonzalez .25 .60
SF43 Prince Fielder .25 .60
SF44 Paul Goldschmidt .30 .75
SF45 Jason Heyward .25 .60
SF46 Joey Votto .30 .75
SF47 Troy Tulowitzki .30 .75
SF48 Hanley Ramirez .25 .60
SF49 Chase Utley .25 .60
SF50 Hunter Pence .25 .60

2015 Topps Spring Fever Autographs

PRINT RUNS B/WN 10-225 COPIES PER
NO PRICING ON QTY 10
EXCHANGE DEADLINE 1/31/2018
SFACB Charlie Blackmon/99 6.00 15.00
SFACC C.J. Cron/199 4.00 10.00
SFACOW Chris Owings/199 4.00 10.00
SFACSP Cory Spangenberg/199 4.00 10.00
SFADH Dilson Herrera/48 5.00 12.00
SFAFJ Fergie Jenkins/25 12.00 30.00
SFAIK Ian Kinsler/25 20.00 50.00
SFAJB Javier Baez/50 30.00 80.00
SFAJD Jacob deGrom/75 25.00 60.00
SFAJPA Joe Panik/75 30.00 80.00
SFAJPE Joc Pederson/99 6.00 15.00
SFAJPO Johnny Podres/50 8.00 20.00
SFAJS Jorge Soler/99 15.00 40.00
SFAKV Kennys Vargas/199 10.00 25.00
SFAMAA Mike Adams/200 10.00 25.00
SFAMAD Matt Adams/99 10.00 25.00
SFAMB Mookie Betts/225 40.00 100.00
SFAMFO Mike Foltynewicz/112 4.00 10.00
SFAMFR Maikel Franco/199 5.00 12.00
SFAMS Max Scherzer/25 30.00 80.00
SFARO Rougned Odor/92 10.00 25.00
SFASM Shelby Miller/50 20.00 50.00
SFAYS Yangervis Solarte/202 4.00 10.00

2015 Topps Stepping Up

COMPLETE SET (20) 5.00 12.00
STATED ODDS 1:6 HOBBY
SU1 Reggie Jackson .40 1.00
SU2 Duke Snider .40 1.00
SU3 Sandy Koufax 1.00 2.50
SU4 Johnny Podres .30 .75
SU5 David Ortiz .50 1.25
SU6 Mariano Rivera .60 1.50
SU7 Miguel Cabrera .50 1.25
SU8 Joey Votto .50 1.25
SU9 Adrian Gonzalez .40 1.00
SU10 Randy Johnson .50 1.25
SU11 Madison Bumgarner .40 1.00
SU12 Albert Pujols .60 1.50
SU13 Ryan Howard .40 1.00
SU14 Hunter Pence .40 1.00
SU15 Luis Gonzalez .30 .75
SU16 Mookie Wilson .30 .75
SU17 Fernando Valenzuela .30 .75
SU18 Corey Kluber .40 1.00
SU19 Joe Panik .40 1.00
SU20 Jacob deGrom .50 1.25

2015 Topps Stepping Up Relics

STATED ODDS 1:4280 HOBBY
STATED PRINT RUN 99 SER.#'d SETS
SURAG Adrian Gonzalez 8.00 20.00
SURDO David Ortiz 8.00 20.00
SURDS Duke Snider 8.00 20.00
SURJV Joey Votto 8.00 20.00
SURMB Madison Bumgarner 6.00 15.00
SURMC Miguel Cabrera 8.00 20.00
SURMR Mariano Rivera 10.00 25.00
SURRH Ryan Howard 6.00 15.00
SURRJA Reggie Jackson 10.00 25.00
SURRJO Randy Johnson 8.00 20.00

2015 Topps Strata Signature Relics

STATED ODDS 1:3857 HOBBY
STATED PRINT RUN 25 SER.#'d SETS
EXCHANGE DEADLINE 1/31/2018
SSRAJ Adam Jones 30.00 80.00
SSRBH Bryce Harper EXCH 150.00 300.00
SSRBP Buster Posey S2 100.00 250.00
SSRCG Carlos Gonzalez EXCH 30.00 80.00
SSRCK Clayton Kershaw EXCH 100.00 250.00
SSRCS CC Sabathia EXCH 30.00 80.00
SSRCS Chris Sale S2 30.00 80.00
SSREE Edwin Encarnacion S2 25.00 60.00
SSREL Evan Longoria EXCH 25.00 60.00
SSRFF Freddie Freeman 60.00 150.00
SSRGP Gregory Polanco EXCH 50.00 120.00
SSRGS George Springer EXCH 75.00 200.00
SSRGST Giancarlo Stanton EXCH 75.00 200.00
SSRHR Hanley Ramirez EXCH 25.00 60.00
SSRJA Jose Abreu EXCH 150.00 250.00
SSRJB Jay Bruce EXCH 25.00 60.00
SSRJB Javier Baez S2 40.00 100.00
SSRJG Juan Gonzalez S2 20.00 50.00
SSRJH Jason Heyward S2 40.00 100.00
SSRJV Joey Votto EXCH 40.00 100.00
SSRKU Koji Uehara S2 20.00 50.00
SSRMC Miguel Cabrera EXCH 150.00 250.00
SSRMM Mike Minor S2 20.00 50.00
SSRMP Mike Piazza EXCH 75.00 200.00
SSRMR Mariano Rivera 200.00 300.00
SSRMS Max Scherzer EXCH 75.00 200.00
SSRMT Mark Teixeira S2 50.00 120.00
SSRPF Prince Fielder S2 20.00 50.00
SSRPG Paul Goldschmidt EXCH 50.00 120.00
SSRRB Ryan Braun EXCH 15.00 40.00
SSRRC Robinson Cano EXCH 50.00 120.00
SSRRP Rafael Palmeiro S2 40.00 100.00
SSRSC Steve Carlton EXCH 50.00 120.00
SSRVG Vladimir Guerrero S2 40.00 100.00
SSRYC Yoenis Cespedes EXCH 40.00 100.00
SSRYP Yasiel Puig EXCH 75.00 200.00
SSRJDE Jacob deGrom S2 75.00 200.00
SSRJSO Jorge Soler S2 30.00 80.00

2015 Topps Sultan of Swat

COMPLETE SET (10) 15.00 40.00
RANDOM INSERTS IN TARGET PACKS
RUTH1 Babe Ruth 1.50 4.00
RUTH2 Babe Ruth 1.50 4.00
RUTH3 Babe Ruth 1.50 4.00
RUTH4 Babe Ruth 1.50 4.00
RUTH5 Babe Ruth 1.50 4.00
RUTH6 Babe Ruth 1.50 4.00
RUTH7 Babe Ruth 1.50 4.00
RUTH8 Babe Ruth 1.50 4.00
RUTH9 Babe Ruth 1.50 4.00
RUTH10 Babe Ruth 1.50 4.00

2015 Topps The Babe Ruth Story

COMPLETE SET (10) 10.00 25.00
RANDOM INSERTS IN WAL-MART PACKS
BR1 St. Mary's Industrial School Student 1.50 4.00
BR2 Hometown Hero Baltimore 1.50 4.00
BR3 Red Sox Double Threat 1.50 4.00
BR4 Postseason Pitching Phenom 1.50 4.00
BR5 From Hurler To Hitter 1.50 4.00
BR6 The Home Run King 1.50 4.00
BR7 MVP In '23 1.50 4.00
BR8 Murderer's Row Member 1.50 4.00
BR9 The Called Shot 1.50 4.00
BR10 The Babe Becomes A Media Star 1.50 4.00

2015 Topps The Jackie Robinson Story

COMPLETE SET (10) 15.00 40.00
RANDOM INSERTS IN TARGET PACKS
JR1 Two-Sport College Star 2.00 5.00
JR2 Serving His Country 2.00 5.00
JR3 .387 With Kansas City 2.00 5.00
JR4 Robinson Signs With The Dodgers 2.00 5.00
JR5 Robinson Travels North 2.00 5.00
JR6 Breaking The MLB Color Barrier 2.00 5.00
JR7 NL MVP In 1949 2.00 5.00
JR8 World Series Title In 1955 2.00 5.00
JR9 Call To The Hall 2.00 5.00
JR10 Number 42 Retired Across MLB 2.00 5.00

2015 Topps The Pennant Chase

STATED ODDS 1:6138 HOBBY
ANNOUNCED PRINT RUN OF 50 EACH
EXCHANGE DEADLINE 11/1/2015
1 Arizona Diamondbacks 10.00 25.00
2 Atlanta Braves 20.00 50.00
3 Boston Red Sox 20.00 50.00
4 Chicago Cubs 10.00 25.00
5 Chicago White Sox 10.00 25.00
6 Cincinnati Reds 10.00 25.00
7 Cleveland Indians 10.00 25.00
8 Colorado Rockies BB 10.00 25.00
9 Houston Astros 10.00 25.00
10 Miami Marlins 10.00 25.00
11 Milwaukee Brewers 10.00 25.00
12 Minnesota Twins 10.00 25.00
13 New York Mets 10.00 25.00
14 New York Yankees 40.00 100.00
15 Philadelphia Phillies 10.00 25.00
16 San Diego Padres 10.00 25.00
17 Seattle Mariners 10.00 25.00
18 Tampa Bay Rays 10.00 25.00
19 Texas Rangers 10.00 25.00
20 Toronto Blue Jays 10.00 25.00
21 Kansas City Royals 10.00 25.00
22 Oakland Athletics 10.00 25.00
23 Pittsburgh Pirates 10.00 25.00
24 San Francisco Giants 20.00 50.00
25 Baltimore Orioles 10.00 25.00
26 Detroit Tigers 40.00 100.00
27 Los Angeles Dodgers 40.00 100.00
28 St. Louis Cardinals BB 40.00 100.00
29 Los Angeles Angels 10.00 25.00
30 Washington Nationals 40.00 100.00

2015 Topps Til It's Over

COMPLETE SET (15) 4.00 10.00
STATED ODDS 1:8 HOBBY
TIO1 David Ortiz .50 1.25
TIO2 Ken Griffey Jr. 1.00 2.50
TIO3 Troy Tulowitzki .50 1.25
TIO4 Evan Longoria .40 1.00
TIO5 Omar Vizquel .40 1.00
TIO6 Joe Mauer .40 1.00
TIO7 Lou Brock .40 1.00
TIO8 Nolan Ryan 1.50 4.00
TIO9 Craig Biggio .40 1.00
TIO10 Tom Seaver .40 1.00
TIO11 Ivan Rodriguez .40 1.00
TIO12 Matt Cain .40 1.00
TIO13 Willie Mays 1.00 2.50
TIO14 David Freese .30 .75
TIO15 Salvador Perez .40 1.00

2015 Topps World Champion Autograph Relics

STATED ODDS 1:9678 HOBBY
STATED PRINT RUN 50 SER.#'d SETS
EXCHANGE DEADLINE 1/31/2018
WCARBC Brandon Crawford 150.00 300.00
WCARBP Buster Posey 75.00 200.00
WCARHP Hunter Pence 150.00 300.00
WCARJP Joe Panik 150.00 300.00

2015 Topps World Champion Autographs

STATED ODDS 1:31,455 HOBBY
STATED PRINT RUN 50 SER.#'d SETS
EXCHANGE DEADLINE 1/31/2018
WCARBC Brandon Crawford 150.00 250.00
WCARJP Joe Panik 200.00 300.00

2015 Topps World Champion Relics

STATED ODDS 1:5215 HOBBY
STATED PRINT RUN 100 SER.#'d SETS
WCRBB Brandon Belt 50.00 120.00
WCRBC Brandon Crawford 40.00 100.00
WCRBP Buster Posey 100.00 200.00
WCRGB Gregor Blanco 40.00 100.00
WCRHP Hunter Pence 75.00 200.00
WCRJPA Joe Panik 30.00 80.00
WCRJPE Juan Perez 50.00 120.00
WCRMB Madison Bumgarner 60.00 150.00
WCRMM Michael Morse 40.00 100.00
WCRPS Pablo Sandoval 75.00 200.00
WCRRV Ryan Vogelsong 20.00 50.00
WCRSR Sergio Romo 40.00 80.00
WCRTH Tim Hudson 50.00 120.00
WCRTI Travis Ishikawa 40.00 100.00
WCRTL Tim Lincecum 50.00 120.00

2015 Topps Update

COMPLETE SET w/o SP's (400) 15.00 40.00
PHOTO VAR ODDS 1:45 HOBBY
PRINTING PLATE ODDS 1:758 HOBBY
PLATE PRINT RUN 1 SET PER COLOR
BLACK-CYAN-MAGENTA-YELLOW ISSUED
NO PLATE PRICING DUE TO SCARCITY
US1 Aaron Thompson .12 .30
US2 Wilmer Difo RC .40 1.00
US3 Tyler Wilson RC .40 1.00
US4 Jean Machi .12 .30
US5 Ryan Vogelsong .12 .30
US6 David DeJesus .12 .30
US7A Brad Miller .15 .40
US8 Alex Claudio RC .40 1.00
US9 Shane Greene FS .12 .30
US10 Bobby Parnell .12 .30
US11A Evan Gattis FS .12 .30
US12 Travis Ishikawa .12 .30
US13 Tommy Pham RC .50 1.25
US14 Joey Gallo RD .25 .60
US15 McCutchen/Harrison .20 .50
US16 John Axford .12 .30
US17 Manny Machado .20 .50
US18 Michael Blazek .12 .30
US19 Erasmo Ramirez .12 .30
US20 Cole Hamels .15 .40
US21 Posey/Bumgardner .25 .60
US22 Jake Diekman .12 .30
US23 Kevin Plawecki RC .40 1.00
US24 Chris Young .12 .30
US25 Byron Buxton RC .60 1.50
US26 Jack Leathersich RC .40 1.00
US27 Nathan Eovaldi .15 .40
US28 Miguel Cabrera .20 .50
US29 Ben Paulsen RC .40 1.00
US30 David Phelps .12 .30
US31 Gordon Beckham .12 .30
US32A Blake Swihart RC .50 1.25
US32B Blake Swihart SP VAR 1.50 4.00
Taking off mask
US33 Alex Rodriguez .25 .60
US34 Matt Andriese RC .40 1.00
US35 Justin Bour RC .60 1.50
US36 Roberto Perez RC .12 .30
US37 Luis Avilan .12 .30
US38 Michael Lorenzen RC .40 1.00
US39 Potent Padres .15 .40
Matt Kemp
Justin Upton
Wil Myers
US40 Sam Dyson RC .40 1.00
US41 T.Shaw RC/A.Dykstra RC .40 1.00
US42 Madison Bumgarner .15 .40
US43 Randall Delgado .12 .30
US44 Tim Cooney RC .40 1.00
US45 Ryan Lavarnway .12 .30
US46 David Price .15 .40
US47 Jeremy Jeffress .12 .30
US48 Carlos Perez RC .40 1.00
US49 Mark Canha RC .60 1.50
US50 Alex Guerrero .15 .40
US51 Yasmani Grandal .12 .30
US52 C.Anderson RC/P.Klein RC .40 1.00
US53 Daniel Norris RC .40 1.00
US54 Ldndrf RC/Muncy RC 2.00 5.00
US55 Hank Conger .12 .30
US56 Kevin Siegrist .12 .30
US57 Nick Ahmed .12 .30
US58 Josh Donaldson .15 .40
US59 R.Martin RC/M.Grace RC .40 1.00
US60 Branden Pinder RC .60 1.50
US61 Dallas Keuchel .15 .40
US62 Brian Dozier .15 .40
US63 Kelvin Herrera .12 .30
US64 David Price .15 .40
US65 Todd Frazier .15 .40
US66 Neftali Feliz .12 .30
US67 Leonel Campos RC .40 1.00
US68 Albert Pujols .25 .60
US69A Zach McAllister .12 .30
US70 Vance Worley .12 .30
US71 Joakim Soria .12 .30
US72 Brett Gardner .15 .40
US73 Tyler Saladino RC .50 1.25
US74 Giovanny Urshela RC 4.00 10.00
US75 Ross Detwiler .12 .30
US76 Lorenzo Cain .12 .30
US77 Joe Smith .12 .30
US78 Kris Bryant RC 2.50 6.00
US79 Bryant/Russell .75 2.00
US80 Juan Uribe .12 .30
US81 Pat Venditte RC .40 1.00
US82 Francisco Lindor RC 10.00 25.00
US83 Mason Williams RC .50 1.25
US84 Sean O'Sullivan .12 .30
US85 Justin Nicolino RC .40 1.00
US86 Chris Colabello .12 .30
US87 Zack Greinke .15 .40
US88 Marc Rzepczynski .12 .30
US89 Kendall Graveman .12 .30
US90 Jacob deGrom .20 .50
US91 Brad Boxberger .12 .30
US92A Justin Upton .12 .30
US92B Justin Upton SP VAR 1.50 4.00
With bats
US93 Sonny Gray .15 .40
US94 Shane Victorino .15 .40
US95 Elvis Araujo RC .40 1.00
US96 Ben Zobrist .15 .40
US97 Josh Ravin RC .60 1.50
US98 Josh Fields .12 .30
US99 Daniel Fields RC .40 1.00
US100 Andrew McCutchen .20 .50
US101 Jumbo Diaz RC .40 1.00
US102 Chi Chi Gonzalez RC .60 1.50
US103A Joey Gallo RC .75 2.00
US103B J.Gallo Smiling 2.50 6.00
US104 Steve Cishek .12 .30
US105 Brandon Moss .12 .30
US106 Shelby Miller .15 .40
US107 Carlos Gomez .12 .30
US108 A.Garcia RC/J.Marte RC .40 1.00
US109 Anthony Ranaudo RC .40 1.00
US110 A.McKirahan RC/S.Marimon RC .40 1.00
US111 Todd Cunningham .12 .30
US112 Conor Gillaspie .15 .40
US113 Eric Campbell .15 .40
US114 J.Garcia RC/S.Copeland RC .40 1.00
US115 Stephen Vogt .15 .40
US116 Miguel Castro RC .40 1.00
US117 Enrique Hernandez RC 2.50 6.00
US118 Jason Frasor .12 .30
US119 Jacob Lindgren RC .50 1.25
US120 Brandon Cunniff RC .40 1.00
US121 Alexi Ogando .12 .30
US122 Marlon Byrd .20 .50
US123 Felix Hernandez .15 .40
US124 Preston Tucker RC .60 1.50
US125 Ben Revere .12 .30
US126 Tyler Olson RC .40 1.00
US127A Eduardo Rodriguez RC .40 1.00
US127B E.Rod High-five 1.25 3.00
US128 Brock Holt .12 .30
US129A David Ross .12 .30
US130 Jonathan Villar .12 .30
US131 Jordan Pacheco .12 .30
US132 Gerardo Parra .12 .30
US133 Vinnie Pestano .12 .30
US134 Steven Matz RD RC .60 1.50
US135A Jason Heyward .15 .40
US135B J.Hywrd Laughing 1.50 4.00
US136 Byron Buxton RD .20 .50
US137 Andrew Romine .12 .30
US138 Dellin Betances .15 .40
US139 Mike Moustakas .15 .40
US140 Mark Melancon .12 .30
US141 Glen Perkins .12 .30
US142 Kendrys Morales .12 .30
US143 Tommy Hunter .12 .30
US144 Delino DeShields Jr. RC .40 1.00
US145 Yasmany Tomas RD .15 .40
US146 Aaron Harang .12 .30
US147 Chris Archer .12 .30
US148 Taylor Featherston RC .40 1.00
US149 Thomas Field .12 .30
US150 Eric Sogard .12 .30
US151A Colby Lewis .12 .30
US151B Lewis Rubbing ball 1.25 3.00
US152 J.R. Graham RC .40 1.00
US153 Archie Bradley RD .12 .30
US154 Paul Goldschmidt .20 .50
US155A Yoenis Cespedes .15 .40
US155B Cespedes Batting cage 6.00 15.00
US156 Amazing Astros .15 .40
Colby Rasmus
George Springer
Jake Marisnick
US157A Noah Syndergaard RC .75 2.00
US157B Syndergaard Batting 2.50 6.00
US158 Jason Kipnis .15 .40
US159 Darren O'Day .12 .30
US160 Slade Heathcott RC .50 1.25
US161A Jeff Samardzija .12 .30
US161B Samardzija In dugout 1.25 3.00
US162 Jorge Soler RD .20 .50
US163 Andrew Heaney .12 .30
US164 Johnny Giavotella .12 .30
US165 Seth Maness .12 .30
US166 Severino Gonzalez RC .40 1.00
US167A Derek Norris .12 .30
US167B D.Norris Finger up 1.25 3.00
US168 George Kontos RC .50 1.25
US169 Max Scherzer .20 .50
US170 Mike Foltynewicz RC .40 1.00
US171 Jhonny Peralta .12 .30
US172 Adrian Gonzalez .15 .40
US173 Salvador Perez .15 .40
US174A Carlos Correa RC 2.00 5.00
US174B C.Correa In dugout 12.00 30.00
US175 Edinson Volquez .12 .30
US176 Austin Hedges RC .40 1.00
US177 Matt Holliday .20 .50
US178 Zach Duke .12 .30
US179 Adam Liberatore RC .50 1.25
US180 Tyler Collins .12 .30
US181 Jimmy Paredes FS .12 .30
US182 Scott Van Slyke .12 .30
US183 Justin Turner .15 .40
US184 Sean Rodriguez .12 .30
US185 David Murphy .12 .30
US186 A.J. Pollock .15 .40
US187 Heart of the Order .15 .40
Jose Bautista
Josh Donaldson
Devon Travis
US188 deGrom/Harvey .20 .50
US189 Adam Warren .12 .30
US190A Shelby Miller .15 .40
US190B S.Miller Black jersey 1.50 4.00
US191 Royals Crush .15 .40
Eric Hosmer
Kendrys Morales
Mike Moustakas
US192 Albert Pujols .25 .60
US193 A.Castro RC/A.Leon RC .40 1.00
US194 C.Rearick RC/C.Mazzoni RC .40 1.00
US195 A.J. Ramos .12 .30
US196 Paulo Orlando RC .60 1.50
US197 Wandy Rodriguez .12 .30
US198 Brett Anderson .12 .30
US199 Troy Tulowitzki .20 .50
US200 Adam Jones .15 .40
US201 Jose Altuve .15 .40
US202 Manny Machado .20 .50
US203 Jesse Hahn .12 .30
US204 Jeff Francoeur .15 .40
US205 Andres Blanco .12 .30
US206 Mike Pelfrey .12 .30
US207 Chris Young .12 .30
US208 Addison Russell RD .40 1.00
US209 Prince Fielder .15 .40
US210 Yunel Escobar .12 .30
US211 Tommy Milone .12 .30
US212 Scott Carroll .12 .30
US213 Pujols/Trout 1.00 2.50
US214 Yadier Molina .20 .50
US215 Jonathan Papelbon .15 .40
US216 Carlos Peguero .12 .30
US217 Franklin Morales .12 .30
US218 Pedro Ciriaco .12 .30
US219 Michael Morse .12 .30
US220A Addison Russell RC 1.25 3.00
US220B A.Rssll Signing autos 4.00 10.00
US221 Francisco Rodriguez .15 .40
US222 Arquimedes Caminero .12 .30
US223 Kevin Jepsen .12 .30
US224 Ezequiel Carrera .12 .30
US225 Keone Kela RC .50 1.25
US226 Josh Donaldson .15 .40
US227 Mike Trout 1.00 2.50
US228 Geovany Soto .15 .40
US229 Hector Gomez .12 .30
US230 Shawn Tolleson .12 .30
US231 Felipe Rivero RC .60 1.50
US232 Hansel Robles RC .40 1.00
US233 Danny Muno RC .40 1.00
US234 Noah Syndergaard RD .25 .60
US235 Anthony Rizzo .30 .75
US236 Angel Nesbitt RC .40 1.00
US237A Craig Kimbrel .15 .40
US237B Kimbrel Shaking hands 1.50 4.00
US238 A.J. Cole RC .40 1.00
US239 Michael McKenry .12 .30
US240 Jonathan Papelbon .15 .40
US241 Sluggers Supreme .20 .50
David Ortiz
Pablo Sandoval
Hanley Ramirez
US242 Kris Bryant .75 2.00
US243 Austin Adams .12 .30
US244 Colby Rasmus .15 .40
US245 Rubby De La Rosa .12 .30
US246 Blaine Hardy RC .40 1.00
US247 Ryan Braun .15 .40
US248 Lance McCullers RC .40 1.00
US249 Anthony Rizzo .30 .75
US250 Danny Valencia .15 .40
US251 Carlos Correa RD .60 1.50
US252 Francisco Rodriguez .15 .40
US253 Trevor Rosenthal .15 .40
US254 Billy Burns .12 .30
US255 Sean Gilmartin RC .40 1.00
US256 D.Ceciliani RC/D.Dorn RC .40 1.00
US257 Josh Hamilton .15 .40
US258 V.Velasquez RC/R.O'Rourke RC .60 1.50
US259 John Jaso .12 .30
US260A Andrew Miller .15 .40
US260B A.Miller In dugout 1.50 4.00
US261 R.J. Alvarez RC .40 1.00
US262 Eric Young Jr. .12 .30
US263 Pedro Strop .12 .30
US264 Brock Holt FS .12 .30
US265A Brett Lawrie .15 .40
US265B Lawrie Hands together 1.50 4.00
US266 Ike Davis .12 .30
US267 Joe Ross RC .40 1.00
US268 Troy Tulowitzki .20 .50
US269 Burke Badenhop .12 .30
US270 Craig Breslow .12 .30
US271 Mike Leake .12 .30
US272 Matt Duffy FS RC .50 1.25
US273 Justin Upton .15 .40
US274 Tucker Barnhart .12 .30
US275 Casey McGehee .12 .30
US276 Alex Wilson .12 .30
US277 Yasmani Grandal .12 .30
US278 Rene Rivera .12 .30
US279 Juan Nicasio .12 .30
US280 Mike Bolsinger FS .12 .30
US281 Manny Banuelos RC .60 1.50
US282 Jose Iglesias .15 .40
US283 Kris Bryant RD .75 2.00
US284 Matt Wisler RC .40 1.00
US285 Josh Rutledge .12 .30
US286 Francisco Lindor RD .75 2.00
US287 Jim Johnson .12 .30
US288 Matt Joyce .12 .30
US289 Williams Perez RC .50 1.25
US290 Zach Britton .15 .40
US291 Eddie Butler FS .12 .30
US292 Chad Qualls .12 .30
US293 Cesar Ramos .12 .30
US294 Mark Trumbo .12 .30
US295 Russell Martin .12 .30
US296 J.B. Shuck .12 .30
US297 Wade Davis .12 .30
US298 R.Navarro RC/D.Coleman RC .40 1.00
US299 Mikie Mahtook RC .40 1.00
US300 Max Scherzer .20 .50
US301 Carlos Villanueva .12 .30
US302 Chris Sale .20 .50
US303 Asher Wojciechowski RC .40 1.00
US304 Johnny Cueto .15 .40
US305 Ryan Tepera RC .40 1.00
US306 Vidal Nuno .12 .30
US307 Hector Santiago .12 .30
US308 Joey Butler .12 .30
US309A Howie Kendrick .12 .30
US309B H.Kendrick No hat 1.25 3.00
US310 Clayton Kershaw .40 1.00
US311 Carlos Martinez .15 .40
US312 S.Oberg RC/D.Guerra RC .40 1.00
US313 Jose Urena RC .40 1.00
US314 Rafael Betancourt .12 .30
US315 Kyle Kendrick .12 .30
US316 Tyler Clippard .12 .30
US317 Luis Sardinas .12 .30
US318A Phillippe Aumont .12 .30
US318B Aumont Rally squirrel 5.00 12.00
US319 Will Harris FS RC .40 1.00
US320 Josh Donaldson .15 .40
US321 Chris Heston RC .40 1.00
US322 Mat Latos .15 .40
US323 Joc Pederson RC .75 2.00
US324A Carlos Rodon RC .60 1.50
US324B Rodon Wearing jacket 2.00 5.00
US325A Matt Kemp .15 .40
US325B M.Kemp In dugout 1.50 4.00
US326 Jonathan Herrera .12 .30
US327 Ryan Webb .12 .30
US328 Brandon Morrow .12 .30
US329 J.D. Martinez .20 .50
US330 Nate Karns .12 .30
US331 Orlando Calixte RC .40 1.00
US332 Matt Boyd RC .40 1.00
US333 Mark Reynolds .12 .30
US334 Clint Barmes .12 .30
US335A Norichika Aoki .12 .30
US335B Aoki In on deck circle 1.25 3.00
US336 Mark Teixeira .15 .40
US337A Martin Prado .12 .30
US337B M.Prado w/fans 1.25 3.00
US338 Pete Kozma .12 .30
US339 Jose Alvarez .12 .30
US340 Fernando Salas .12 .30
US341 Eddie Rosario RC .75 2.00
US342 Todd Frazier .15 .40
US343 A.J. Burnett .12 .30
US344 Aramis Ramirez .12 .30
US345 Blaine Boyer .12 .30
US346 Brandon Crawford .15 .40
US347 Joe Blanton .12 .30
US348 Jonathan Broxton .12 .30
US349 DJ LeMahieu .20 .50
US350A Didi Gregorius .15 .40
US350B Gregorius Throwing 1.50 4.00
US351 Mike Fiers .12 .30
US352 Jose Reyes .15 .40
US353 Michael Wacha .15 .40
US354 Brandon Finnegan RC .40 1.00
US355 Gerrit Cole .20 .50
US356 Miguel Montero .12 .30
US357 Joe Panik .15 .40
US358 Nolan Arenado .25 .60
US359 E.Burgos RC/O.Hernandez RC .40 1.00
US360 Joc Pederson .25 .60
US361 LaTroy Hawkins .12 .30
US362 Rick Porcello .15 .40
US363 Chasen Shreve RC .40 1.00
US364 Mike Trout 1.00 2.50
US365 J.P. Howell .12 .30
US366 Kelly Johnson .12 .30
US367 Frank Garces RC .40 1.00
US368 Aroldis Chapman .20 .50
US369 Cory Rasmus .12 .30
US370 Prince Fielder .15 .40
US371 Carson Smith RC .40 1.00
US372 Alex Wood .12 .30
US373 Mitch Harris RC .50 1.25
US374 Tyler Moore .12 .30
US375 Mark Lowe .12 .30
US376 Joc Pederson RD .25 .60
US377 Taijuan Walker FS .12 .30
US378 Devon Travis RD .12 .30
US379 Cameron Maybin .12 .30
US380 Buster Posey .25 .60
US381 Sergio Romo .12 .30
US382 Dan Uggla .12 .30
US383 Nelson Cruz .20 .50
US384 Melvin Upton Jr. .15 .40
US385 Collin Cowgill .12 .30
US386 Alcides Escobar .15 .40
US387 Jonny Gomes .12 .30
US388 Kevin Pillar FS .12 .30
US389 Seth Smith .12 .30
US390 Donovan Solano .20 .50
US391 Clayton Richard .12 .30
US392 Odrisamer Despaigne FS .12 .30
US393 Dan Haren .12 .30
US394 Scott Kazmir .12 .30
US395A Dexter Fowler .15 .40
US395B Fowler Holding cap 1.50 4.00
US396A Ichiro Suzuki .25 .60
US396B Ichiro In on deck circle 2.50 6.00
US397 Bryce Harper .30 .75
US398 J.T. Realmuto RC 2.50 6.00
US399 Jace Peterson .12 .30
US400 Logan Verrett RC .50 1.25

2015 Topps Update Black

*BLACK: 10X TO 25X BASIC
*BLACK RC: 3X TO 8X BASIC RC
STATED ODDS 1:48 HOBBY
STATED PRINT RUN 64 SER.#'d SETS
US25 Byron Buxton 15.00 40.00

US32 Blake Swihart 8.00 20.00
US82 Francisco Lindor 125.00 300.00
US90 Jacob deGrom 8.00 20.00
US100 Andrew McCutchen 10.00 25.00
US134 Steven Matz RD 20.00 50.00
US136 Byron Buxton RD 15.00 40.00
US155 Yoenis Cespedes 8.00 20.00
US157 Noah Syndergaard 12.00 30.00
US174 Carlos Correa 60.00 150.00
US234 Noah Syndergaard RD 12.00 30.00
US251 Carlos Correa RD 25.00 60.00
US310 Clayton Kershaw 10.00 25.00
US341 Eddie Rosario 10.00 25.00
US380 Buster Posey 6.00 15.00

2015 Topps Update Gold

*GOLD: 1.2X TO 3X BASIC
*GOLD RC: .4X TO 1X BASIC RC
STATED ODDS 1:3 HOBBY
STATED PRINT RUN 2015 SER.#'d SETS
US25 Byron Buxton 1.50 4.00
US78 Kris Bryant 10.00 258.00
US82 Francisco Lindor 30.00 80.00
US100 Andrew McCutchen 1.25 3.00
US157 Noah Syndergaard 1.50 4.00
US174 Carlos Correa 10.00 25.00
US234 Noah Syndergaard RD 1.50 4.00
US242 Kris Bryant 6.00 15.00
US251 Carlos Correa RD 8.00 20.00
US283 Kris Bryant RD 6.00 15.00

2015 Topps Update No Logo

*NO LOGO: 1.2X TO 3X BASIC
*NO LOGO RC: .75X TO 2X BASIC RC
RANDOM INSERTS IN RETAIL PACKS
CARDS MISSING THE TOPPS LOGO
US82 Francisco Lindor 25.00 60.00

2015 Topps Update Pink

*PINK: 12X TO 30X BASIC
*PINK RC: 4X TO 10X BASIC RC
STATED ODDS 1:169 HOBBY
STATED PRINT RUN 50 SER.#'d SETS
US25 Byron Buxton 20.00 50.00
US32 Blake Swihart 10.00 25.00
US82 Francisco Lindor 150.00 400.00
US90 Jacob deGrom 10.00 25.00
US100 Andrew McCutchen 12.00 30.00
US134 Steven Matz RD 25.00 60.00
US136 Byron Buxton RD 20.00 50.00
US155 Yoenis Cespedes 10.00 25.00
US157 Noah Syndergaard 15.00 40.00
US174 Carlos Correa 75.00 200.00
US234 Noah Syndergaard RD 15.00 40.00
US251 Carlos Correa RD 30.00 80.00
US310 Clayton Kershaw 12.00 30.00
US341 Eddie Rosario 12.00 30.00
US380 Buster Posey 8.00 20.00

2015 Topps Update Rainbow Foil

*FOIL: 2.5X TO 6X BASIC
*FOIL RC: 1.5X TO 4X BASIC RC
STATED ODDS 1:10 HOBBY
US25 Byron Buxton 3.00 8.00
US100 Andrew McCutchen 2.50 6.00
US157 Noah Syndergaard 3.00 8.00
US174 Carlos Correa 12.00 30.00
US234 Noah Syndergaard RD 3.00 8.00
US251 Carlos Correa RD 10.00 25.00

2015 Topps Update Sparkle

STATED ODDS 1:225 HOBBY
US16 John Axford 4.00 10.00
US23 Kevin Plawecki 4.00 10.00
US25 Byron Buxton 15.00 40.00
US31 Gordon Beckham 4.00 10.00
US32 Blake Swihart 10.00 25.00
US35 Justin Bour 10.00 25.00
US46 David Price 5.00 12.00
US49 Mark Canha 6.00 15.00
US50 Alex Guerrero 10.00 25.00
US51 Yasmani Grandal 8.00 20.00
US82 Francisco Lindor 150.00 400.00
US92 Justin Upton 5.00 12.00
US99 Daniel Fields 8.00 20.00
US122 Marlon Byrd 4.00 10.00
US124 Preston Tucker 6.00 15.00
US130 Jonathan Villar 4.00 10.00
US135 Jason Heyward 10.00 25.00
US148 Taylor Featherston 4.00 10.00
US155 Yoenis Cespedes 10.00 25.00
US157 Noah Syndergaard 15.00 40.00
US160 Slade Heathcott 5.00 12.00
US161 Jeff Samardzija 4.00 10.00
US167 Derek Norris 4.00 10.00
US170 Mike Foltynewicz 10.00 25.00
US176 Austin Hedges 4.00 10.00
US190 Shelby Miller 10.00 25.00
US203 Jesse Hahn 4.00 10.00
US224 Ezequiel Carrera 4.00 10.00
US228 Geovany Soto 5.00 12.00
US237 Craig Kimbrel 5.00 12.00
US244 Colby Rasmus 5.00 12.00
US245 Rubby De La Rosa 4.00 10.00
US257 Josh Hamilton 5.00 12.00
US260 Andrew Miller 10.00 25.00
US284 Matt Wisler 15.00 40.00
US315 Kyle Kendrick 4.00 10.00
US317 Luis Sardinas 4.00 10.00
US320 Josh Donaldson 10.00 25.00
US325 Matt Kemp 10.00 25.00
US335 Norichika Aoki 4.00 10.00
US341 Eddie Rosario 8.00 20.00
US350 Didi Gregorius
US356 Miguel Montero 8.00 20.00
US362 Rick Porcello 5.00 12.00
US374 Tyler Moore 6.00 15.00
US379 Cameron Maybin
US384 Melvin Upton Jr. 6.00 15.00
US387 Jonny Gomes 6.00 15.00
US395 Dexter Fowler 5.00 12.00
US396 Ichiro Suzuki 8.00 20.00

2015 Topps Update Snow Camo

*SNOW CAMO: 10X TO 25X BASIC
*SNOW CAMO RC: 6X TO 15X BASIC RC
STATED ODDS 1:86 HOBBY
STATED PRINT RUN 99 SER.#'d SETS
US25 Byron Buxton 12.00 30.00
US82 Francisco Lindor 125.00 300.00
US100 Andrew McCutchen 10.00 25.00
US134 Steven Matz RD 10.00 25.00
US155 Yoenis Cespedes 8.00 20.00
US157 Noah Syndergaard 12.00 30.00
US174 Carlos Correa 50.00 120.00
US234 Noah Syndergaard RD 12.00 30.00
US251 Carlos Correa RD 20.00 50.00
US310 Clayton Kershaw 10.00 25.00
US380 Buster Posey 6.00 15.00

2015 Topps Update Stat Back Variations

STATED ODDS 1:68 HOBBY
US17 Manny Machado 2.00 5.00
US42 Madison Bumgarner 1.50 4.00
US58 Josh Donaldson 1.50 4.00
US61 Dallas Keuchel 1.50 4.00
US64 David Price 1.50 4.00
US68 Albert Pujols 2.50 6.00
US72 Brett Gardner 1.50 4.00
US76 Lorenzo Cain 1.25 3.00
US87 Zack Greinke 1.50 4.00
US90 Jacob deGrom 2.00 5.00
US93 Sonny Gray 1.50 4.00
US100 Andrew McCutchen 2.00 5.00
US115 Stephen Vogt 1.50 4.00
US123 Felix Hernandez 1.50 4.00
US139 Mike Moustakas 1.50 4.00
US141 Glen Perkins 1.25 3.00
US147 Chris Archer 1.25 3.00
US154 Paul Goldschmidt 2.00 5.00
US158 Jason Kipnis 1.50 4.00
US171 Jhonny Peralta 1.25 3.00
US172 Adrian Gonzalez 1.50 4.00
US173 Salvador Perez 1.50 4.00
US186 A.J. Pollock 1.50 4.00
US199 Troy Tulowitzki 2.00 5.00
US200 Adam Jones 1.50 4.00
US201 Jose Altuve 1.50 4.00
US214 Yadier Molina 2.00 5.00
US240 Jonathan Papelbon 1.50 4.00
US247 Ryan Braun 1.50 4.00
US249 Anthony Rizzo 3.00 8.00
US252 Francisco Rodriguez 1.50 4.00
US273 Justin Upton 1.50 4.00
US295 Russell Martin 1.25 3.00
US300 Max Scherzer 2.00 5.00
US302 Chris Sale 2.00 5.00
US310 Clayton Kershaw 4.00 10.00
US336 Mark Teixeira 1.50 4.00
US342 Todd Frazier 1.50 4.00
US343 A.J. Burnett 1.25 3.00
US346 Brandon Crawford 1.50 4.00
US349 DJ LeMahieu 2.00 5.00
US353 Michael Wacha 1.50 4.00
US355 Gerrit Cole 2.00 5.00
US358 Nolan Arenado 2.50 6.00
US364 Mike Trout 10.00 25.00
US370 Prince Fielder 1.50 4.00
US380 Buster Posey 2.50 6.00
US383 Nelson Cruz 2.00 5.00
US386 Alcides Escobar 1.50 4.00
US397 Bryce Harper 3.00 8.00

2015 Topps Update Throwback Variations

RANDOM INSERTS IN PACKS
US7 Brad Miller 2.50 6.00
US11 Evan Gattis FS 2.00 5.00
US32 Blake Swihart 2.50 6.00
US69 Zach McAllister 2.00 5.00
US129 David Ross 2.00 5.00
US161 Jeff Samardzija 2.00 5.00
US362 Rick Porcello 2.50 6.00
US395 Dexter Fowler 2.50 6.00

2015 Topps Update All Star Access

COMPLETE SET (25) 30.00 80.00
INSERTED IN RETAIL PACKS
MLB1 Mike Trout 5.00 12.00
MLB2 Albert Pujols 1.25 3.00
MLB3 Brock Holt .60 1.50
MLB4 Yadier Molina 1.00 2.50
MLB5 Madison Bumgarner 1.25 3.00
MLB6 Joc Pederson 1.25 3.00
MLB7 Joe Panik .75 2.00
MLB8 Kris Bryant 3.00 8.00
MLB9 Jacob deGrom 1.00 2.50
MLB10 Adam Jones .75 2.00
MLB11 Manny Machado 1.00 2.50
MLB12 Zack Greinke .75 2.00
MLB13 Andrew McCutchen 1.00 2.50
MLB14 Anthony Rizzo 1.50 4.00
MLB15 Clayton Kershaw 2.00 5.00
MLB16 Sonny Gray .75 2.00
MLB17 Prince Fielder .75 2.00
MLB18 Max Scherzer 1.00 2.50
MLB19 Todd Frazier .75 2.00
MLB20 Lorenzo Cain .60 1.50
MLB21 Alcides Escobar .75 2.00
MLB22 Nelson Cruz 1.00 2.50
MLB23 Jose Altuve .75 2.00
MLB24 Josh Donaldson .75 2.00
MLB25 Bryce Harper 1.50 4.00

2015 Topps Update All Star Access Autographs

INSERTED IN RETAIL PACKS
STATED PRINT RUN 25 SER.#'d SETS
EXCHANGE DEADLINE 9/30/2017
MLBAJA Jose Altuve 25.00 60.00
MLBASP Salvador Perez 25.00 60.00
MLBATF Todd Frazier 25.00 60.00

2015 Topps Update All Star Stitches

STATED ODDS 1:53 HOBBY
*GOLD/50: .75X TO 2X BASIC
STITAB A.J. Burnett 2.00 5.00
STITAC Aroldis Chapman 3.00 8.00
STITAE Alcides Escobar 2.50 6.00
STITAGN Adrian Gonzalez 2.50 6.00
STITAJ Adam Jones 2.50 6.00
STITAM Andrew McCutchen 3.00 8.00
STITAPO A.J. Pollock 2.50 6.00
STITAPU Albert Pujols 4.00 10.00
STITAR Anthony Rizzo 5.00 12.00
STITBB Brad Boxberger 2.00 5.00
STITBC Brandon Crawford 2.50 6.00
STITBD Brian Dozier 2.50 6.00
STITBG Brett Gardner 2.50 6.00
STITBHA Bryce Harper 8.00 20.00
STITBHO Brock Holt 2.00 5.00
STITBP Buster Posey 4.00 10.00
STITCA Chris Archer 2.00 5.00
STITCK Clayton Kershaw 6.00 15.00
STITCM Carlos Martinez 2.50 6.00
STITCS Chris Sale 3.00 8.00
STITDB Dellin Betances 2.50 6.00
STITDK Dallas Keuchel 2.50 6.00
STITDL DJ LeMahieu 3.00 8.00
STITDO Darren O'Day 2.00 5.00
STITDP David Price 2.50 6.00
STITFH Felix Hernandez 2.50 6.00
STITGC Gerrit Cole 3.00 8.00
STITGP Glen Perkins 2.00 5.00
STITJA Jose Altuve 2.50 6.00
STITJDE Jacob deGrom 3.00 8.00
STITJDO Josh Donaldson 2.50 6.00
STITJK Jason Kipnis 2.50 6.00
STITJM J.D. Martinez 3.00 8.00
STITJPA Joe Panik 2.50 6.00
STITJPD Joc Pederson 4.00 10.00
STITJPE Jhonny Peralta 2.00 5.00
STITJU Justin Upton 2.50 6.00
STITKB Kris Bryant 15.00 40.00
STITKH Kelvin Herrera 2.00 5.00
STITLC Lorenzo Cain 2.00 5.00
STITMB Madison Bumgarner 2.50 6.00
STITMMA Manny Machado 3.00 8.00
STITMME Mark Melancon 2.00 5.00
STITMTE Mark Teixeira 2.50 6.00
STITMTR Mike Trout 15.00 40.00
STITNA Nolan Arenado 4.00 10.00
STITNC Nelson Cruz 3.00 8.00
STITPF Prince Fielder 2.50 6.00
STITPG Paul Goldschmidt 3.00 8.00
STITRM Russell Martin 2.00 5.00
STITSM Shelby Miller 2.50 6.00
STITSP Salvador Perez 2.50 6.00
STITSV Stephen Vogt 2.50 6.00
STITTF Todd Frazier 2.50 6.00
STITTT Troy Tulowitzki 3.00 8.00
STITWD Wade Davis 2.00 5.00
STITYG Yasmani Grandal 2.00 5.00
STITYM Yadier Molina 3.00 8.00
STITZB Zach Britton 2.50 6.00
STITZG Zack Greinke 2.50 6.00

2015 Topps Update All Star Stitches Autographs

STATED ODDS 1:6996 HOBBY
STATED PRINT RUN 25 SER.#'d SETS
EXCHANGE DEADLINE 9/30/2017
ASTARAE Alcides Escobar 30.00 80.00
ASTARBC Brandon Crawford 30.00 80.00
ASTARBH Brock Holt 25.00 60.00
ASTARDL DJ LeMahieu 50.00 120.00
ASTARDP David Price 30.00 80.00
ASTARGC Gerrit Cole 40.00 100.00
ASTARJA Jose Altuve 30.00 80.00
ASTARJK Jason Kipnis 30.00 80.00
ASTARJM J.D. Martinez 40.00 100.00
ASTARPG Paul Goldschmidt 40.00 100.00
ASTARSP Salvador Perez 30.00 80.00
ASTARTF Todd Frazier 30.00 80.00
ASTARJPD Joc Pederson 50.00 125.00
ASTARJPR Jhonny Peralta 30.00 80.00

2015 Topps Update All Star Stitches Dual

STATED ODDS 1:10,800 HOBBY
STATED PRINT RUN 25 SER.#'d SETS
ASDCG L.Cain/M.Moustakas 15.00 40.00
ASDFC A.Chapman/T.Frazier 20.00 50.00
ASDGP J.Pederson/A.Gonzalez 15.00 40.00
ASDHP Peralta/Martinez 25.00 60.00
ASDHS Pederson/Harper 25.00 60.00
ASDMJ A.Jones/M.Machado 20.00 50.00
ASDPB Bumgarner/Posey 25.00 60.00
ASDRB Rizzo/Bryant 40.00 100.00

2015 Topps Update All Star Stitches Triple

STATED ODDS 1:4848 HOBBY
STATED PRINT RUN 25 SER.#'d SETS
ASTDPH Prz/Hrva/Dvs 25.00 60.00
ASTGGP Pdrsn/Gnzlz/Grndl 30.00 80.00
ASTHMU Hrpr/Pdrsn/McCtchn 30.00 80.00
ASTMJB Jns/Brttn/Mchdo 20.00 50.00
ASTPBC Bmgrnr/Crwfrd/Psy 25.00 60.00
ASTPCG Cain/Prz/Mstks 50.00 120.00
ASTRMW Wcha/Rsnthl/Mlna 40.00 100.00

2015 Topps Update Career High Jumbo Relics

STATED ODDS 1:11,193 HOBBY
STATED PRINT RUN 25 SER.#'d SETS
CHJRAG Alex Gordon 15.00 40.00
CHJRAJ Adam Jones 12.00 30.00
CHJRAM Andrew McCutchen 60.00 150.00
CHJRBP Buster Posey 15.00 40.00
CHJRCB Clay Buchholz 15.00 40.00
CHJRCG Carlos Gomez 8.00 20.00
CHJRDJ Derek Jeter 25.00 60.00
CHJRFH Felix Hernandez 10.00 25.00
CHJRJBA Jose Bautista 10.00 25.00
CHJRJBZ Javier Baez 8.00 20.00
CHJRJE Jacoby Ellsbury 10.00 25.00
CHJRJM Joe Mauer 15.00 40.00
CHJRJPE Joc Pederson 15.00 40.00
CHJRMB Madison Bumgarner 20.00 50.00
CHJRMC Miguel Cabrera 30.00 80.00
CHJRMH Matt Harvey 20.00 50.00
CHJRMP Mike Piazza 20.00 50.00
CHJRMTE Mark Teixeira 10.00 25.00
CHJRRC Robinson Cano 8.00 20.00
CHJRYM Yadier Molina 20.00 50.00

2015 Topps Update Chrome

RANDOM INSERTS IN HOLIDAY MEGA BOXES
*GOLD/250: 2.5X TO 6X BASIC
*BLACK/99: 4X TO 10X BASIC
US9 Shane Greene .50 1.25
US11 Evan Gattis .50 1.25
US16 John Axford .50 1.25
US23 Kevin Plawecki RC .50 1.25
US32 Blake Swihart RC .60 1.50
US46 David Price .60 1.50
US102 Chi Chi Gonzalez RC .75 2.00
US103 Joey Gallo RC 1.00 2.50
US119 Jacob Lindgren RC .60 1.50
US127 Eduardo Rodriguez RC .75 2.00
US135 Jason Heyward .60 1.50
US136 Byron Buxton RD .75 2.00
US144 Delino DeShields Jr. RC .50 1.25
US151 Colby Lewis .50 1.25
US155 Yoenis Cespedes .60 1.50
US157 Noah Syndergaard RC 1.00 2.50
US161 Jeff Samardzija .50 1.25
US170 Mike Foltynewicz RC .50 1.25
US174 Carlos Correa RC 6.00 15.00
US181 Jimmy Paredes .50 1.25
US190 Shelby Miller .60 1.50
US208 Addison Russell RD 1.50 4.00
US220 Addison Russell RC 1.50 4.00
US225 Keone Kela .60 1.50
US237 Craig Kimbrel .60 1.50
US238 A.J. Cole .50 1.25
US257 Josh Hamilton .60 1.50
US264 Brock Holt .60 1.50
US272 Matt Duffy .60 1.50
US280 Mike Bolsinger .50 1.25
US283 Kris Bryant RD 3.00 8.00
US286 Francisco Lindor RD 3.00 8.00
US291 Eddie Butler .50 1.25
US294 Mark Trumbo .50 1.25
US308 Joey Butler .50 1.25
US309 Howie Kendrick .50 1.25
US319 Will Harris .50 1.25
US320 Josh Donaldson .60 1.50
US324 Carlos Rodon RC .75 2.00
US325 Matt Kemp .60 1.50
US341 Eddie Rosario RC 1.00 2.50
US350 Didi Gregorius .60 1.50
US362 Rick Porcello .60 1.50
US376 Joc Pederson RD 1.00 2.50
US377 Taijuan Walker .50 1.25
US388 Kevin Pillar .50 1.25
US392 Odrisamer Despaigne .50 1.25
US395 Dexter Fowler .60 1.50
US396 Ichiro 1.00 2.50
US398 J.T. Realmuto 3.00 8.00

2015 Topps Update Chrome All Star Stiches

RANDOM INSERTS IN HOLIDAY MEGA BOXES
ASCRAE Alcides Escobar 4.00 10.00
ASCRAJ Adam Jones 4.00 10.00
ASCRAM Andrew McCutchen 5.00 12.00
ASCRAP Albert Pujols 6.00 15.00
ASCRBH Bryce Harper 10.00 25.00
ASCRBP Buster Posey 10.00 25.00
ASCRCS Chris Sale 8.00 20.00
ASCRJA Jose Altuve 4.00 10.00
ASCRKB Kris Bryant 25.00 60.00
ASCRLC Lorenzo Cain 8.00 20.00
ASCRMB Madison Bumgarner 4.00 10.00
ASCRMM Manny Machado 10.00 25.00
ASCRNC Nelson Cruz 5.00 12.00
ASCRPF Prince Fielder 4.00 10.00
ASCRPG Paul Goldschmidt 8.00 20.00
ASCRSM Shelby Miller 5.00 12.00
ASCRSP Salvador Perez 4.00 10.00
ASCRTF Todd Frazier 12.00 30.00
ASCRZG Zack Greinke 6.00 15.00
ASCRJDE Jacob deGrom 10.00 25.00
ASCRJDO Josh Donaldson 4.00 10.00
ASCRJPD Joc Pederson 6.00 15.00
ASCRJPR Jhonny Peralta 3.00 8.00
ASCRMTE Mark Teixeira 4.00 10.00
ASCRMTR Mike Trout 25.00 60.00

2015 Topps Update Chrome All Star Stiches Autographs

RANDOM INSERTS IN HOLIDAY MEGA BOXES
STATED PRINT RUN 25 SER.#'d SETS
ASCARAG Adrian Gonzalez 20.00 50.00
ASCARBP Buster Posey 150.00 250.00
ASCARDP David Price 30.00 80.00
ASCARJA Jose Altuve 20.00 50.00
ASCARJD Jacob deGrom 75.00 200.00
ASCARMM Manny Machado 150.00 250.00
ASCARMT Mike Trout 200.00 400.00
ASCARPG Paul Goldschmidt 60.00 150.00
ASCARSP Salvador Perez 20.00 50.00

2015 Topps Update Chrome Rookie Sensations

RANDOM INSERTS IN PACKS
RSC1 Hanley Ramirez .75 2.00
RSC2 Ichiro 1.25 3.00
RSC3 Mike Trout 5.00 12.00
RSC4 Mike Piazza 1.00 2.50
RSC5 Carlton Fisk .75 2.00
RSC6 Nomar Garciaparra .75 2.00
RSC7 Troy Tulowitzki 1.00 2.50
RSC8 Jose Fernandez 1.00 2.50
RSC9 Jacob deGrom 1.00 2.50
RSC10 Fernando Valenzuela .60 1.50
RSC11 Dwight Gooden .60 1.50
RSC12 Ted Williams 2.00 5.00
RSC13 Jeff Bagwell .75 2.00
RSC14 Jose Abreu 1.00 2.50
RSC15 Dustin Pedroia 1.00 2.50
RSC16 Jackie Robinson 1.00 2.50
RSC17 Cal Ripken Jr. 3.00 8.00
RSC18 Derek Jeter 2.50 6.00
RSC19 Neftali Feliz .60 1.50
RSC20 Tom Seaver .75 2.00
RSC21 Albert Pujols 1.25 3.00
RSC22 Bryce Harper 1.50 4.00
RSC23 Buster Posey 1.25 3.00
RSC24 Livan Hernandez .60 1.50
RSC25 Mark McGwire 1.50 4.00

2015 Topps Update Etched in History

STATED ODDS 1:621 HOBBY
*GOLD/50: 1.5X TO 4X BASIC
EIH1 Nolan Ryan 6.00 15.00
EIH2 Hank Aaron 4.00 10.00
EIH3 Rickey Henderson 2.00 5.00
EIH4 Ted Williams 4.00 10.00
EIH5 Babe Ruth 5.00 12.00
EIH6 Ichiro Suzuki 2.50 6.00
EIH7 Mariano Rivera 2.50 6.00
EIH8 Nolan Ryan 6.00 15.00
EIH9 Francisco Rodriguez 1.50 4.00
EIH10 Roger Clemens 2.50 6.00
EIH11 Alex Rodriguez 2.50 6.00
EIH12 Cal Ripken Jr. 6.00 15.00
EIH13 Nomar Garciaparra 1.50 4.00
EIH14 Roger Maris 2.00 5.00
EIH15 Ozzie Smith 2.50 6.00

2015 Topps Update First Home Run

COMPLETE SET (30) 20.00 50.00
*GOLD: .5X TO 1.2X BASIC
*SILVER: .5X TO 1.2X BASIC
*WHITE: .5X TO 1.2X BASIC
RANDOM INSERT IN RETAIL PACKS
FHR1 Ernie Banks .60 1.50
FHR2 Brandon Belt .50 1.25
FHR3 Adrian Beltre .60 1.50
FHR4 Craig Biggio .50 1.25
FHR5 Wade Boggs .50 1.25
FHR6 Kole Calhoun .40 1.00
FHR7 Roberto Clemente 2.00 5.00
FHR8 Jacoby Ellsbury .50 1.25
FHR9 Edwin Encarnacion .60 1.50
FHR10 Nomar Garciaparra .50 1.25
FHR11 Carlos Gomez .40 1.00
FHR12 Ken Griffey Jr. 1.25 3.00
FHR13 Jonathan Lucroy .50 1.25
FHR14 Starling Marte .50 1.25
FHR15 Edgar Martinez .50 1.25
FHR16 Willie Mays 1.25 3.00
FHR17 Devin Mesoraco .40 1.00
FHR18 Paul O'Neill .50 1.25
FHR19 Brandon Phillips .40 1.00
FHR20 Dalton Pompey .50 1.25
FHR21 Hanley Ramirez .50 1.25
FHR22 Jackie Robinson .60 1.50
FHR23 Ryne Sandberg 1.25 3.00
FHR24 Mike Schmidt 1.00 2.50
FHR25 Mark Teixeira .50 1.25
FHR26 Kennys Vargas .40 1.00
FHR27 Kolten Wong .50 1.25
FHR28 Mike Zunino .40 1.00
FHR29 Ichiro Suzuki .75 2.00
FHR30 Kris Bryant 3.00 8.00

2015 Topps Update First Home Run Medallions

RANDOM INSERT IN RETAIL PACKS
FHRM1 Brandon Phillips 2.00 5.00
FHRM2 Kolten Wong 2.50 6.00
FHRM3 Kole Calhoun 2.00 5.00
FHRM4 Craig Biggio 2.50 6.00
FHRM5 Mike Zunino 2.00 5.00
FHRM6 Devin Mesoraco 2.00 5.00
FHRM7 Kennys Vargas 2.00 5.00
FHRM8 Edwin Encarnacion 3.00 8.00
FHRM9 Wade Boggs 2.50 6.00
FHRM10 Edgar Martinez 2.50 6.00
FHRM11 Brandon Belt 2.50 6.00
FHRM12 Paul O'Neill 2.50 6.00
FHRM13 Jackie Robinson 6.00 15.00
FHRM14 Roberto Clemente 10.00 25.00
FHRM15 Willie Mays 6.00 15.00
FHRM16 Ernie Banks 5.00 12.00
FHRM17 Ken Griffey Jr. 6.00 15.00
FHRM18 Mike Schmidt 5.00 12.00
FHRM19 Ryne Sandberg 6.00 15.00
FHRM20 Nomar Garciaparra 2.50 6.00
FHRM21 Hanley Ramirez 2.50 6.00
FHRM22 Carlos Gomez 2.00 5.00
FHRM23 Adrian Beltre 3.00 8.00
FHRM24 Dalton Pompey 2.50 6.00
FHRM25 Jacoby Ellsbury 2.50 6.00
FHRM26 Starling Marte 2.50 6.00
FHRM27 Jonathan Lucroy 2.50 6.00
FHRM28 Mark Teixeira 2.50 6.00
FHRM29 Ichiro Suzuki 4.00 10.00
FHRM30 Kris Bryant 12.00 30.00

2015 Topps Update First Home Run Relics

INSERTED IN RETAIL PACKS
STATED PRINT RUN 99 SER.#'d SETS
FHRRAB Adrian Beltre 15.00 40.00
FHRRBB Brandon Belt 6.00 15.00
FHRRBP Brandon Phillips 6.00 15.00
FHRRCB Craig Biggio 8.00 20.00
FHRRDM Devin Mesoraco 6.00 15.00
FHRREB Ernie Banks 12.00 30.00
FHRRHR Hanley Ramirez 5.00 12.00
FHRRJE Jacoby Ellsbury 12.00 30.00
FHRRKB Kris Bryant 20.00 50.00
FHRRKC Kole Calhoun 10.00 25.00
FHRRMS Mike Schmidt 12.00 30.00
FHRRMT Mark Teixeira 5.00 12.00
FHRRMZ Mike Zunino 10.00 25.00
FHRRNG Nomar Garciaparra 10.00 25.00
FHRRPO Paul O'Neill 8.00 20.00

2015 Topps Update Pride and Perseverance

COMPLETE SET (12) 4.00 10.00
STATED ODDS 1:10 HOBBY
PP1 Buddy Carlyle .40 1.00
PP2 Curtis Pride .40 1.00
PP3 George Springer .50 1.25
PP4 Jake Peavy .40 1.00
PP5 Jason Johnson .40 1.00
PP6 Jim Abbott .40 1.00
PP7 Jim Eisenreich .40 1.00
PP8 Jon Lester .50 1.25
PP9 Pete Wyshner Gray .40 1.00
PP10 Sam Fuld .40 1.00
PP11 William Hoy .40 1.00
PP12 Anthony Rizzo 1.00 2.50

2015 Topps Update Rarities

COMPLETE SET (15) 5.00 12.00
STATED ODDS 1:8 HOBBY
R1 Frank Robinson .30 .75
R2 Shawn Green .25 .60
R3 Daniel Nava .25 .60
R4 Ted Williams .75 2.00
R5 Roberto Clemente 1.00 2.50
R6 Mariano Rivera .50 1.25
R7 Anibal Sanchez .25 .60
R8 Mike Mussina .30 .75
R9 George Brett .75 2.00
R10 Rod Carew .30 .75
R11 Asdrubal Cabrera .30 .75
R12 Don Mattingly .75 2.00
R13 Randy Johnson .40 1.00
R14 Ken Griffey Jr. .75 2.00
R15 Billy Williams .30 .75

2015 Topps Update Rarities Autographs

STATED ODDS 1:21,228 HOBBY
STATED PRINT RUN 25 SER.#'d SETS
EXCHANGE DEADLINE 9/30/2017
RADM Don Mattingly 30.00 80.00
RARC Rod Carew 40.00 100.00
RARJ Randy Johnson EXCH 75.00 200.00
RASG Shawn Green 10.00 25.00

2015 Topps Update Rookie Sensations

COMPLETE SET (25) 5.00 12.00
STATED ODDS 1:6 HOBBY
RS1 Hanley Ramirez .30 .75
RS2 Ichiro Suzuki .50 1.25
RS3 Mike Trout 2.00 5.00
RS4 Mike Piazza .40 1.00
RS5 Carlton Fisk .30 .75
RS6 Nomar Garciaparra .30 .75
RS7 Troy Tulowitzki .40 1.00
RS8 Jose Fernandez .40 1.00
RS9 Jacob deGrom .40 1.00
RS10 Fernando Valenzuela .25 .60
RS11 Dwight Gooden .25 .60
RS12 Ted Williams .75 2.00
RS13 Jeff Bagwell .30 .75
RS14 Jose Abreu .40 1.00
RS15 Dustin Pedroia .40 1.00
RS16 Jackie Robinson .40 1.00
RS17 Cal Ripken Jr. 1.25 3.00
RS18 Derek Jeter 1.00 2.50
RS19 Neftali Feliz .25 .60
RS20 Tom Seaver .30 .75
RS21 Albert Pujols .50 1.25
RS22 Bryce Harper .60 1.50
RS23 Buster Posey .50 1.25
RS24 Livan Hernandez .25 .60
RS25 Mark McGwire .60 1.50

2015 Topps Update Rookie Sensations Autographs

STATED ODDS 1:6996 HOBBY
STATED PRINT RUN 25 SER.#'d SETS
EXCHANGE DEADLINE 9/30/2017
RSACF Carlton Fisk 25.00 60.00
RSADP Dustin Pedroia 25.00 60.00
RSAFV Fernando Valenzuela 40.00 100.00
RSAJB Jeff Bagwell 40.00 100.00
RSAJF Jose Fernandez 15.00 40.00
RSALH Livan Hernandez 10.00 25.00
RSAMH Matt Harvey EXCH 30.00 80.00
RSANG Nomar Garciaparra 20.00 50.00
RSATT Troy Tulowitzki 25.00 60.00

2015 Topps Update Tape Measure Blasts

COMPLETE SET (15) 5.00 12.00
STATED ODDS 1:8 HOBBY
TMB1 Jose Canseco .30 .75
TMB2 Andres Galarraga .30 .75
TMB3 Mark McGwire .60 1.50
TMB4 Reggie Jackson .30 .75
TMB5 Mike Trout 2.00 5.00
TMB6 Ryan Howard .30 .75
TMB7 Giancarlo Stanton .40 1.00
TMB8 Adam Dunn .30 .75
TMB9 Bo Jackson .40 1.00
TMB10 David Ortiz .40 1.00
TMB11 Mark McGwire .60 1.50
TMB12 Roberto Clemente 1.00 2.50
TMB13 Albert Pujols .50 1.25
TMB14 Ted Williams .75 2.00
TMB15 Josh Gibson .40 1.00

2015 Topps Update Tape Measure Blasts Autographs

STATED ODDS 1:21,228 HOBBY
STATED PRINT RUN 25 SER.#'d SETS
EXCHANGE DEADLINE 9/30/2017
TMBAAG Andres Galarraga 12.00 30.00
TMBAJC Jose Canseco 20.00 50.00
TMBAMMC Mark McGwire 100.00 200.00
TMBARH Ryan Howard 12.00 30.00

2015 Topps Update Whatever Works

COMPLETE SET (15) 4.00 10.00
STATED ODDS 1:8 HOBBY
WW1 Mark Teixeira .30 .75
WW2 Tim Lincecum .30 .75
WW3 Wade Boggs .30 .75
WW4 Nomar Garciaparra .30 .75
WW5 Craig Biggio .30 .75
WW6 Max Scherzer .40 1.00
WW7 Joe DiMaggio .75 2.00
WW8 Roger Clemens .50 1.25
WW9 Richie Ashburn .30 .75
WW10 Jim Palmer .30 .75
WW11 Mike Napoli .25 .60
WW12 Justin Verlander .40 1.00
WW13 David Ortiz .40 1.00
WW14 Chipper Jones .40 1.00
WW15 Alex Gordon .30 .75

2015 Topps Update Whatever Works Autographs

STATED ODDS 1:21,228 HOBBY
STATED PRINT RUN 25 SER.#'d SETS
EXCHANGE DEADLINE 9/30/2017
WWAAG Alex Gordon 20.00 50.00
WWACB Craig Biggio 30.00 80.00
WWAMN Mike Napoli 20.00 50.00
WWAMT Mark Teixeira 40.00 100.00

2016 Topps

COMP.RED.HOB.FACT SET (700) 30.00 80.00
COMP.BLUE.RET.FACT SET (700) 30.00 80.00
COMP.SER.1 SET w/o SP's (350) 12.00 30.00
COMP.SER.2 SET w/o SP's (350) 12.00 30.00
CAMO ODDS 1:125 HOBBY; 1:25 JUMBO
42 SP ODDS 1:69 HOBBY
SER.1 VAR ODDS 1:1247 H; 1:250 JUMBO
SER.2 VAR ODDS 1:683 HOBBY
SER.1 PLATE ODDS 1:1350 HOBBY
SER.2 PLATE ODDS 1:803 HOBBY
PLATE PRINT RUN 1 SET PER COLOR
BLACK-CYAN-MAGENTA-YELLOW ISSUED
NO PLATE PRICING DUE TO SCARCITY
1A Mike Trout 1.25 3.00
1B Trout SP Camo 15.00 40.00
1C Trout SP Pointing bat 125.00 250.00
2 Jerad Eickhoff RC .40 1.00
3 Richie Shaffer RC .25 .60
4A Sonny Gray .20 .50
4B Sonny Gray SP Sunglasses 40.00 100.00
5 Kyle Seager .15 .40
6 Jimmy Paredes .15 .40
8A Michael Brantley .20 .50
8B Michael Brantley SP Sunglasses 40.00 100.00
9 Eric Hosmer .20 .50
10 Nelson Cruz .25 .60
11 Andre Ethier .20 .50
12A Nolan Arenado .30 .75
12B Nolan Arenado SP Camo 5.00 12.00
13 Craig Kimbrel .20 .50
14 Chris Davis .15 .40
15 Ryan Howard .20 .50
16 Rougned Odor .20 .50
17 Billy Butler .15 .40
18 Francisco Rodriguez .20 .50
19 Delino DeShields Jr. FS .15 .40
20 Andrew McCutchen .25 .60
21 Mike Moustakas WSH .20 .50

22 John Hicks RC .25 .60
23 Jeff Francoeur .20 .50
24 Clayton Kershaw .50 1.25
25 Brad Ziegler .15 .40
26 Dvs/Trt/Cruz LL 1.25 3.00
27 Alec Asher RC .25 .60
28A Brian McCann .20 .50
28B Brian McCann SP Camo 3.00 8.00
29 Altve/Cbrra/Bgrts LL .25 .60
30 Yan Gomes .15 .40
31 Travis d'Arnaud .20 .50
32 Zack Greinke .20 .50
33 Edinson Volquez .15 .40
34 Omar Infante .15 .40
35 Luke Hochevar .15 .40
36 Miguel Montero .15 .40
37 C.J. Cron .15 .40
38 Jed Lowrie .15 .40
39 Mark Trumbo .15 .40
40 Jedd Gyorko .15 .40
41 Josh Harrison .15 .40
42 A.J. Ramos .15 .40
43 Noah Syndergaard FS .20 .50
44 David Freese .15 .40
45 Ryan Zimmerman .20 .50
46A Jhonny Peralta .15 .40
46B Jhonny Peralta SP Camo 2.50 6.00
47 Gio Gonzalez .20 .50
48 J.J. Hoover .15 .40
49 Ike Davis .15 .40
50A Salvador Perez .20 .50
50B Salvador Perez SP Camo 3.00 8.00
51 Dustin Garneau RC .25 .60
52 Julio Teheran .20 .50
53A George Springer .20 .50
53B George Springer SP Camo 3.00 8.00
54 Jung Ho Kang FS .15 .40
55 Jesus Montero .15 .40
56 Salvador Perez WSH .20 .50
57 Adam Lind .20 .50
58 Grnke/Krshw/Arrta LL .50 1.25
59 John Lamb RC .25 .60
60 Shelby Miller .20 .50
61 Johnny Cueto WSH .20 .50
62 Trayce Thompson RC .40 1.00
63 Zach Britton .20 .50
64 Corey Kluber .20 .50
65 Pittsburgh Pirates .15 .40
66A Kyle Schwarber RC .75 2.00
66B Schwarber Gry jrsy Fctry
67 Matt Harvey .20 .50
68 Odubel Herrera FS .20 .50
69 Anibal Sanchez .15 .40
70 Kendrys Morales .15 .40
71 John Danks .15 .40
72 Chris Young .15 .40
73 Ketel Marte RC .50 1.25
74 Troy Tulowitzki .25 .60
75 Rusney Castillo .15 .40
76 Glen Perkins .15 .40
77 Clay Buchholz .15 .40
78A Miguel Sano RC .40 1.00
78B Sano SP Dugout 75.00 200.00
78C Sano Drk jrsy Fctry
79 Seattle Mariners .15 .40
80 Carson Smith .15 .40
81 Alexei Ramirez .20 .50
82 Michael Bourn .15 .40
83 Starling Marte .20 .50
84A Mookie Betts .40 1.00
84B Betts SP Camo 6.00 15.00
85A Corey Seager RC 6.00 15.00
85B Seagr Fldng Fctry
86A Wilmer Flores .20 .50
86B Wilmer Flores SP Camo 3.00 8.00
87 Jorge De La Rosa .15 .40
88 Ubaldo Jimenez .15 .40
89 Edwin Encarnacion .25 .60
90 Koji Uehara .15 .40
91 Yasmani Grandal FS .15 .40
92 Darren O'Day .15 .40
93 Charlie Blackmon .25 .60
94 Miguel Cabrera .25 .60
95 Kole Calhoun FS .15 .40
96 Jose Bautista .20 .50
97 Ender Inciarte FS .15 .40
98 Garrett Richards .20 .50
99 Taijuan Walker .15 .40
100A Bryce Harper .40 1.00
100B Harper SP Camo 10.00 25.00
101 Justin Turner .20 .50
102 Doug Fister .15 .40
103 Trea Turner RC .75 2.00
104 Jeremy Hellickson .15 .40
105 Marcus Semien .15 .40
106 Jordan Walden .15 .40
107 Kevin Siegrist .15 .40
108 Ben Paulsen .15 .40
109 Henry Owens RC .30 .75
110 J.D. Martinez FS .25 .60
111 Coco Crisp .15 .40
112 Matt Kemp .20 .50
113 Aaron Sanchez .20 .50
114 Brett Lawrie .20 .50
115 Aaron Harang .15 .40
116 Brett Gardner .20 .50
117 Liam Hendriks .15 .40
118 Jose Fernandez .25 .60
119 Sean Doolittle .15 .40
120 Alcides Escobar WSH .20 .50
121 Roberto Osuna FS .15 .40
122 Melky Cabrera .15 .40
123 J.P. Howell .15 .40
124 Melvin Upton Jr. .20 .50
125 Grnke/Krshw/Arrta LL .50 1.25
126 David Ortiz .30 .75
Albert Pujols
127 Zach Lee RC .25 .60
128 Eddie Rosario .20 .50
129 Kendall Graveman .15 .40
130 A.J. Pollock .15 .40
131 Adam LaRoche .15 .40
132A Joe Ross FS .15 .40
132B Joe Ross FS SP 30.00 80.00
Sunglasses
133A Aaron Nola RC .50 1.25
133B Nola SP Dugout 50.00 125.00
134A Yadier Molina .25 .60
134B Yadier Molina SP 50.00 125.00
Glove out
135 Colby Rasmus .20 .50
136 Michael Cuddyer .15 .40
137 Joe Panik .20 .50
138 Francisco Liriano .15 .40
139A Yasiel Puig .25 .60
139B Puig SP w/bat 50.00 125.00
140 Carlos Carrasco FS .15 .40
141 Colin Rea RC .25 .60
142 CC Sabathia .20 .50
143 Oliver Perez .15 .40
144 Jose Iglesias .20 .50
145 Jon Niese .15 .40
146 Stephen Piscotty RC .40 1.00
147 Dee Gordon .15 .40
148 Yangervis Solarte .15 .40
149 Chad Bettis .15 .40
150A Clayton Kershaw .50 1.25
150B Kershaw SP W/bat 100.00 250.00
151 Jon Lester .20 .50
152 Kyle Lohse .15 .40
153 Jason Hammel .20 .50
154A Hunter Pence .20 .50
154B Hunter Pence SP Camo 3.00 8.00
155 New York Yankees .15 .40
156 Cameron Maybin .15 .40
157 Darnell Sweeney RC .25 .60
158 Henry Urrutia .15 .40
159 Erick Aybar .15 .40
160 Chris Sale .25 .60
161 Phil Hughes .15 .40
162 Bautista/Donaldson/Davis LL .20 .50
163 Joaquin Benoit .15 .40
164 Andrew Heaney .15 .40
165 Adam Eaton .15 .40
166 Gldschmdt/Rizzo/Arndo LL .40 1.00
167 Jacoby Ellsbury .20 .50
168 Nathan Eovaldi .20 .50
169 Charlie Morton .25 .60
170 Carlos Gomez .15 .40
171 Matt Cain .20 .50
172 Carter Capps .15 .40
173A Jose Abreu .25 .60
173B Abreu SP Camo 4.00 10.00
173C Abreu SP Blk jsy 40.00 100.00
174 Jered Weaver .20 .50
175A Manny Machado .25 .60
175B Manny Machado SP Camo 4.00 10.00
176 Brandon Phillips .15 .40
177 Gregor Blanco .15 .40
178 Rob Refsnyder RC .30 .75
179 Jose Peraza RC .30 .75
180 Kevin Gausman .15 .40
181 Minnesota Twins .15 .40
182 Kevin Pillar .15 .40
183 Andrelton Simmons .15 .40
184 Travis Jankowski RC .25 .60
185 Keuchel/Gray/Price LL .20 .50
186 Yasmany Tomas FS .15 .40
187 Keuchel/McHugh/Price LL .20 .50
188A Greg Bird RC .30 .75
188B Greg Bird SP 40.00 100.00
Tipping cap
189 Jake McGee .15 .40
190 Jeurys Familia .20 .50
191 Brian Johnson RC .25 .60
192 John Jaso .15 .40
193 Trevor Bauer .25 .60
194 Chase Headley .15 .40
195A Jason Kipnis .20 .50
195B Jason Kipnis SP Camo 3.00 8.00
196 Hunter Strickland .15 .40
197 Neil Walker .20 .50
198 Oakland Athletics .15 .40
199 Jay Bruce .20 .50
200A Josh Donaldson .20 .50
200B Josh Donaldson SP Camo 3.00 8.00
201 Adam Jones .20 .50
202 Colorado Rockies .15 .40
203 Aaron Hill .15 .40
204 Mark Teixeira .20 .50
205 Taylor Jungmann FS .15 .40
206A Alex Gordon .20 .50
206B Alex Gordon SP Camo 3.00 8.00
207 Maikel Franco FS .20 .50
208 Kurt Suzuki .15 .40
209 Max Scherzer .25 .60
210 Mike Zunino .15 .40
211 Nick Ahmed .15 .40
212 Starlin Castro .15 .40
213 Matt Shoemaker .20 .50
214 Chris Colabello .15 .40
215 Adrian Gonzalez .20 .50
216 Logan Forsythe .15 .40
217 Lance Lynn .15 .40
218 Andrew Miller .20 .50
219 Hector Olivera RC .30 .75
220 GreinkeCole/Arrieta LL .25 .60
221 Ryan LaMarre RC .25 .60
222 Homer Bailey .15 .40
223 Christian Yelich .30 .75
224 Billy Burns FS .15 .40
225 Scooter Gennett .20 .50
226 Brian Ellington RC .25 .60
227 David Murphy .15 .40
228 Matt Garza .15 .40
229 Jesse Hahn .15 .40
230 Ryan Vogelsong .15 .40
231 Chris Coghlan .15 .40
232A Michael Conforto RC .30 .75
232B Conforto SP Camo 10.00 25.00
232C Cnfrto Fldng Fctry
233 J.J. Hardy .15 .40
234 David Robertson .15 .40
235 Blaine Boyer .15 .40
236 Juan Lagares .15 .40
237 Carlos Ruiz .15 .40
238 Baltimore Orioles .15 .40
239 Huston Street .15 .40
240 Nick Markakis .20 .50
241 Freddie Freeman .30 .75
242 Matt Wisler FS .15 .40
243 Luke Gregerson .15 .40
244A Matt Carpenter .25 .60
244B Matt Carpenter SP Camo 4.00 10.00
245 Tommy Kahnle .15 .40
246 Dustin Pedroia .25 .60
247 Yunel Escobar .15 .40
248 Atlanta Braves .15 .40
249 Carlos Gomez .15 .40
250A Miguel Cabrera .25 .60
250B Cabrera SP Glasses 50.00 125.00
251 Silvino Bracho RC .25 .60
252 Jorge Soler .25 .60
253A Nick Castellanos .25 .60
253B Nick Castellanos SP 50.00 125.00
Blowing bubble
254 Matt Holliday .25 .60
255 Justin Verlander .25 .60
256 C.J. Wilson .15 .40
257 Jake Marisnick .15 .40
258 Devon Travis FS .15 .40
259A Paul Goldschmidt .25 .60
259B Paul Goldschmidt SP 40.00 100.00
Ceremony
260 Ryan Hanigan .15 .40
261A Russell Martin .15 .40
261B Russell Martin SP Camo 2.50 6.00
261C Russell Martin SP 30.00 80.00
Catcher's gear
262 Ervin Santana .15 .40
263 Joc Pederson FS .20 .50
264A Jake Arrieta .20 .50
264B Jake Arrieta SP 40.00 100.00
Blue jersey
265A Luis Severino RC .30 .75
265B Svrno Gry jrsy Fcty
266 Jonathan Papelbon .20 .50
267 Chris Heston FS .15 .40
268A Robinson Cano .20 .50
268B Robinson Cano SP 40.00 100.00
With base
269A Giancarlo Stanton .25 .60
269B Giancarlo Stanton SP Camo 4.00 10.00
270 Pat Neshek .15 .40
271 Kevin Kiermaier .20 .50
272 Denard Span .15 .40
273 New York Mets .15 .40
274 Ryan Goins .15 .40
275A Ian Kinsler .20 .50
275B Ian Kinsler SP Camo 3.00 8.00
276 Francisco Cervelli .15 .40
277 Elvis Andrus .20 .50
278 Evan Gattis .15 .40
279 Alex Guerrero FS .20 .50
280 Brock Holt .15 .40
281 Alex Dickerson RC .25 .60
282 Scott Feldman .15 .40
283 Felix Hernandez .20 .50
284 Jon Gray RC .25 .60
285 Pablo Sandoval .20 .50
286A Joe Mauer .20 .50
286B Joe Mauer SP Camo 3.00 8.00
286C Joe Mauer SP 40.00 100.00
On deck
287 Alcides Escobar .20 .50
288 Jake Lamb FS .20 .50
289 Nick Hundley .15 .40
290 Zack Godley RC .25 .60
291 Asdrubal Cabrera .20 .50
292A Todd Frazier .20 .50
292B Todd Frazier SP Camo 3.00 8.00
293 Hyun-Jin Ryu .20 .50
294 Chicago White Sox .15 .40
295 Jonathan Schoop .15 .40
296 Yordano Ventura .20 .50
297 Detroit Tigers .15 .40
298A Ryan Braun .20 .50
298B Ryan Braun SP 40.00 100.00
In dugout
299 Angel Pagan .15 .40
300A Buster Posey .30 .75
300B Posey SP Running 75.00 200.00
301 Wade Miley .15 .40
302 Houston Astros .15 .40
303 Steve Pearce .25 .60
304 Charlie Furbush .15 .40
305 Colby Lewis .15 .40
306 Jarrod Saltalamacchia .15 .40
307 Wade Davis .15 .40
308 Brian Dozier .20 .50
309 Shin-Soo Choo .20 .50
310 David Wright .20 .50
311 Dariel Alvarez RC .25 .60
312A Curtis Granderson .20 .50
312B Grndrsn SP Lckr room 60.00 150.00
313 Martin Maldonado .15 .40
314 Kyle Hendricks .25 .60
315 San Diego Padres .15 .40
316 Jake Odorizzi FS .15 .40
317A Jose Altuve .20 .50
317B Altuve SP Camo 3.00 8.00
317C Altuve SP Clap 40.00 100.00
318 Washington Nationals .15 .40
319 Adam Wainwright .20 .50
320 Jake Peavy .15 .40
321A Hanley Ramirez .20 .50
321B Hanley Ramirez SP 40.00 100.00
With glove
322 Kelby Tomlinson RC .25 .60
323 Jacob deGrom .25 .60
324 Steven Souza Jr. .20 .50
325 Kaleb Cowart RC .25 .60
326 Kevin Plawecki FS .15 .40
327A Anthony Rizzo .40 1.00
327B Rizzo SP Dugout 80.00 200.00
328 Anthony DeSclafani .15 .40
329 Alex Rodriguez .30 .75
330 Edward Mujica .15 .40
331 Will Harris .15 .40
332 Toronto Blue Jays .15 .40
333 Keyvius Sampson RC .25 .60
334 Brandon McCarthy .15 .40
335 Mitch Moreland .15 .40
336 Mark Melancon .15 .40
337 Arndo/Hrpr/Gnzlz LL .40 1.00
338 Gldschmdt/Grdn/Hrpr LL .40 1.00
339 Carlos Santana .20 .50
340 Victor Martinez .20 .50
341A Josh Hamilton .20 .50
341B Josh Hamilton SP Camo 3.00 8.00
342 Jayson Werth .20 .50
343 Drew Hutchison .15 .40
344 Jonathan Lucroy .20 .50
345 Yonder Alonso .15 .40
346 Kluber/Keuchel/Estrada LL .20 .50
347 Jason Grilli .15 .40
348 Seth Smith .15 .40
349 Ben Revere .15 .40
350A Kris Bryant FS .30 .75
350B Bryant FS SP Camo 15.00 40.00
350C Bryant FS SP Dugout 125.00 250.00
351 Chase Utley .20 .50
352 Carson Blair RC .25 .60
353 Joey Gallo .20 .50
354A Tyson Ross .15 .40
354B Tyson Ross SP 20.00 50.00
w/Catcher
355 Avisail Garcia .20 .50
356 Odrisamer Despaigne .15 .40
357 Jace Peterson .15 .40
358 Chris Young .15 .40
359 Christian Colon .15 .40
360 Eduardo Escobar .15 .40
361 Jeff Locke .15 .40
362 Cory Spangenberg .15 .40
363 Brett Cecil .15 .40
364 Keon Broxton RC .25 .60
365 James Pazos RC .30 .75
366 Scott Alexander RC .25 .60
367 Pedro Alvarez .15 .40
368A Xander Bogaerts .25 .60
368B Xander Bogaerts SP 3.00 8.00
42 jersey
Fielding
369 Dellin Betances .20 .50
370 Bud Norris .15 .40
371 Jason Heyward .20 .50
372 Zack Cozart .15 .40
373 Tucker Barnhart .15 .40
374 Zach McAllister .15 .40
375 Jordan Lyles .15 .40
376 Brandon Barnes .15 .40
377 Scott Kazmir .15 .40
378 Jeff Mathis .20 .50
379 Wei-Yin Chen .15 .40
380 Michael Blazek .15 .40
381 Bartolo Colon .15 .40
382 David Ortiz .25 .60
David Price
Winning Formula
383 Andres Blanco .15 .40
384 Michael Morse .15 .40
385 Jon Jay .15 .40
386 Nori Aoki .15 .40
387 Kansas City Clutch .15 .40
388 Evan Longoria .20 .50
389 Sam Dyson .15 .40
390 Danny Espinosa .15 .40
391 Matt Boyd FS .15 .40
392 Jon Singleton .20 .50
393 Kelvin Herrera .15 .40
394 Abel De Los Santos RC .25 .60
395 Raul Mondesi RC .30 .75
396 Matt Reynolds RC .25 .60
397 Mac Williamson RC .25 .60
398 Cleveland Indians .15 .40
399 Kansas City Royals .15 .40
400A David Ortiz .25 .60
400B David Ortiz SP 30.00 80.00
Hand goggles
401 Peter O'Brien RC .25 .60
402 Daniel Norris FS .15 .40
403 David Peralta .15 .40
404 Miami Marlins .15 .40
405A Ruben Tejada .15 .40
405B Ruben Tejada SP 30.00 80.00
No glasses
406 Marwin Gonzalez .15 .40
407A Yoenis Cespedes .25 .60
407B Yoenis Cespedes SP 30.00 80.00
w/Horse
408 Jason Castro .15 .40
409 Jean Segura .20 .50
410A Mike Moustakas .20 .50
410B Mike Moustakas SP 2.50 6.00
42 jersey
411 Brian Matusz .15 .40
412 Mark Lowe .15 .40
413 David Phelps .15 .40
414A Wily Peralta .15 .40
414B Wily Peralta SP 1.50 4.00
42 jersey
415 Brett Wallace .15 .40
416 Johnny Cueto .20 .50
417 Brad Boxberger .15 .40
418 Yu Darvish .25 .60
419 Aaron Altherr RC .25 .60
420 Pedro Severino RC .25 .60
421A Cesar Hernandez .15 .40
421B Cesar Hernandez SP 2.00 5.00
42 jersey
422 Miguel Gonzalez .15 .40
423A Carl Crawford .20 .50
423B Carl Crawford SP 2.50 6.00
42 jersey
White jersey
424 Brandon Belt .20 .50
425 Jackie Bradley Jr. .25 .60
426A Joey Votto .25 .60
426B Joey Votto SP 3.00 8.00
42 jersey
Diving
426C Joey Votto SP 30.00 80.00
All Star patch on sleeve
427 Travis Shaw .15 .40
428 Gregory Polanco .20 .50
429 Kenta Maeda RC .50 1.25
430 Ariel Pena RC .25 .60
431 Philadelphia Phillies .15 .40
432A Cameron Rupp .15 .40
432B Cameron Rupp SP 2.00 5.00
42 jersey
433 Trevor Brown RC .30 .75
434 Matt Adams .15 .40
435 Enrique Hernandez .20 .50
436 Raudel Lazo RC .25 .60
437 Michael Lorenzen .15 .40
438 Paulo Orlando .15 .40
439 Francisco Lindor FS .25 .60
440A Tommy Pham FS .15 .40
440B Tommy Pham SP 20.00 50.00
Batting
441 David Ross .15 .40
442A Brandon Crawford .20 .50
442B Brandon Crawford SP 25.00 60.00
Black shirt
443A Prince Fielder .20 .50
443B Prince Fielder SP 25.00 60.00
In dugout
444 Jordan Zimmermann .20 .50
445 Robbie Ray .15 .40
446 Tom Murphy RC .25 .60
447 Ben Zobrist .20 .50
448 St. Louis Cardinals .15 .40
449 J.A. Happ .20 .50
450A David Price .20 .50
450B Price SPw/Dog 40.00 100.00
451 Jose Reyes .20 .50
452A Gerrit Cole .25 .60
452B Gerrit Cole SP 30.00 80.00
No cap
453 A.Rizzo/K.Bryant .40 1.00
454 Greg Holland .15 .40
455 Preston Tucker .15 .40
456 Gordon Beckham .15 .40
457 Nick Swisher .20 .50
458 Kenley Jansen .20 .50
459 James Loney .15 .40
460 Danny Salazar .20 .50
461 Freddy Galvis .15 .40
462 Jumbo Diaz .15 .40
463 Boston Red Sox .15 .40
464A Robinson Chirinos .15 .40
464B Robinson Chirinos SP 20.00 50.00
Red shirt
465 Jesse Chavez .15 .40
466 Marco Estrada .15 .40
467 Giovanny Urshela .25 .60
468 Rajai Davis .15 .40
469 Logan Morrison .15 .40
470 John Lackey .20 .50
471A Kolten Wong .20 .50
471B Kolten Wong SP 25.00 60.00
Wearing hoodie
472 Josh Reddick .15 .40
473 Robbie Erlin .15 .40
474 Chicago Cubs .15 .40
475 Max Kepler RC .40 1.00
476 Hisashi Iwakuma .20 .50
477 Chris Tillman .15 .40
478A Cody Asche .15 .40
478B Cody Asche SP 2.00 5.00
42 jersey
479A Marcus Stroman .20 .50
479B Marcus Stroman SP 25.00 60.00
w/Bobblehead
480 Mike Foltynewicz .15 .40
481 Hector Rondon .15 .40
482 Drew Smyly .15 .40
483 Erasmo Ramirez .15 .40
484A Trevor Rosenthal .20 .50
484B Trevor Rosenthal SP 2.50 6.00
42 jersey
Pitching
485 James Paxton .20 .50
486 Chris Rusin .15 .40
487 Martin Prado .15 .40
488 Colton Murray RC .25 .60
489A Adeiny Hechavarria .15 .40
489B Adeiny Hechavarria SP 2.00 5.00
42 jersey
w/Teammate
490 Guido Knudson RC .25 .60
491 Rich Hill .15 .40
492 Yadier Molina .15 .40
Randal Grichuk
Many Healthy Returns
493 R.A. Dickey .20 .50
494 Luis Avilan .15 .40
495 Luke Maile RC .25 .60
496A Brett Anderson .15 .40
496B Brett Anderson SP 2.00 5.00
42 jersey
497 Devin Mesoraco .15 .40
498 Steve Cishek .15 .40
499 Carlos Perez .15 .40
500A Albert Pujols .30 .75
500B Pujols SP 42 jersey 4.00 10.00
501 Alex Rios .20 .50
502 Austin Hedges .15 .40
503 Luis Valbuena .15 .40
504 Elias Diaz RC .25 .60
505 Frankie Montas RC .30 .75
506 Stephen Vogt .20 .50
507A Travis Wood .15 .40
507B Travis Wood SP 2.00 5.00
42 jersey
Mound meeting
508 Jaime Garcia .15 .40
509 Mark Canha .15 .40
510 Tony Watson .15 .40
511 Manny Banuelos .25 .60
512 Ryan Madson .15 .40
513 Caleb Joseph .15 .40
514 Michael Taylor .15 .40
515 Ryan Flaherty .15 .40
516 Steve Johnson .15 .40
517 Corey Knebel .15 .40
518A Matt Duffy .15 .40
518B Duffy SP 42 jersey 2.00 5.00
519 Kyle Barraclough RC .25 .60
520 Anthony Rendon .25 .60
521A Chris Archer .15 .40
521B Chris Archer SP 20.00 50.00
No cap
522 Alex Avila .20 .50
523 Blake Swihart FS .20 .50
524 Justin Nicolino FS .15 .40
525 Jurickson Profar .20 .50
526 T.J. McFarland .15 .40
527 Jordy Mercer .15 .40
528 Byron Buxton FS .20 .50
529 Zack Wheeler .20 .50
530 Caleb Cotham RC .30 .75
531 Cody Allen .15 .40
532 Matt Marksberry RC .25 .60
533 Jonathan Villar .15 .40
534 Eduardo Nunez .15 .40
535 Ivan Nova .20 .50
536 Alex Wood .15 .40
537 Tampa Bay Rays .15 .40
538 Michael Reed RC .25 .60
539 Nate Karns .15 .40
540 Curt Casali .15 .40
541 James Shields .15 .40
542A Scott Van Slyke .15 .40
542B Scott Van Slyke SP 2.00 5.00
42 jersey
543 Carlos Rodon FS .25 .60
544 Jeremy Jeffress .15 .40
545A Hector Santiago .15 .40
545B Hector Santiago SP 2.00 5.00
42 jersey
546 Ricky Nolasco .15 .40
547 Nick Goody RC .30 .75
548A Lucas Duda .15 .40
548B Lucas Duda SP 2.50 6.00
42 jersey
Entering dugout
548C Lucas Duda SP 30.00 80.00
Blue jersey
549 Luke Jackson RC .25 .60
550A Dallas Keuchel .20 .50
550B Dallas Keuchel SP 25.00 60.00
Jacket on shoulder
551 Steven Matz FS .20 .50
552 Texas Rangers .15 .40
553 Adrian Houser RC .25 .60
554A Daniel Murphy .20 .50
554B Murphy SP Press conf 60.00 150.00
555 Franklin Gutierrez .15 .40
556 Abraham Almonte .15 .40
557 Alexi Amarista .15 .40
558 Sean Rodriguez .15 .40
559 Cliff Pennington .15 .40
560 Kennys Vargas .15 .40
561 Kyle Gibson .20 .50
562 Addison Russell FS .25 .60
563 Lance McCullers FS .15 .40
564 Tanner Roark .15 .40
565 Matt den Dekker .15 .40
566 Alex Rodriguez .30 .75
567 Carlos Beltran .20 .50
568 Arizona Diamondbacks .15 .40
569 Los Angeles Dodgers .15 .40
570 Corey Dickerson .15 .40
571 Mark Reynolds .15 .40
572 Marcell Ozuna .25 .60
573 Tom Koehler .15 .40
574 Ryan Dull RC .25 .60
575 Ryan Strausborger RC .25 .60
576 Tyler Duffey RC .25 .60
577 Jason Gurka RC .25 .60
578 Mike Leake .15 .40
579A Michael Wacha .20 .50
579B Michael Wacha SP 25.00 60.00
Hand goggles
580 Socrates Brito RC .25 .60
581 Zach Davies RC .30 .75
582 Jose Quintana .15 .40
583A Didi Gregorius .20 .50
583B Didi Gregorius SP 25.00 60.00
Golden sky
584 Adam Duvall RC .75 2.00
585 Raisel Iglesias FS .20 .50
586 Chris Stewart .15 .40
587 Neftali Feliz .15 .40
588 Cole Hamels .20 .50
589 Derek Holland .15 .40
590 Anthony Gose .15 .40
591 Trevor Plouffe .15 .40
592 Adrian Beltre .25 .60
593 Alex Cobb .15 .40
594 Lonnie Chisenhall .15 .40
595 Mike Napoli .15 .40
596 Sergio Romo .15 .40
597 Chi Chi Gonzalez .15 .40
598 Khris Davis .25 .60
599 Domingo Santana .20 .50
600A Madison Bumgarner .20 .50
600B Bmgrnr SP Hoodie 30.00 80.00
601 Leonys Martin .15 .40
602 Keith Hessler RC .25 .60
603 Shawn Armstrong RC .25 .60
604 Jeff Samardzija .15 .40
605 Santiago Casilla .15 .40
606 Miguel Almonte RC .25 .60
607 Brandon Drury RC .40 1.00
608 Rick Porcello .20 .50
609A Billy Hamilton .20 .50
609B Billy Hamilton SP 30.00 80.00
w/Bat
610 Adam Morgan .15 .40
611 Darin Ruf .15 .40
612 Cincinnati Reds .15 .40
613 Milwaukee Brewers .15 .40
614 Dalton Pompey .20 .50
615 Miguel Castro .15 .40
616 Keone Kela .15 .40
617 Justin Smoak .15 .40
618 Desmond Jennings .20 .50
619 Dustin Ackley .15 .40
620 Daniel Hudson .15 .40
621 Zach Duke .15 .40
622 Ken Giles .15 .40
623 Tyler Saladino .15 .40
624 Tommy Milone .15 .40
625A Wil Myers .15 .40
625B Wil Myers SP 2.00 5.00
42 jersey
626 Danny Valencia .20 .50
627 Mike Fiers .15 .40
628 Wellington Castillo .15 .40
629 Patrick Corbin .20 .50
630 Michael Saunders .20 .50
631 Chris Reed RC .25 .60
632 Ramon Cabrera RC .25 .60
633 Martin Perez .20 .50
634 Jorge Lopez RC .25 .60
635 A.J. Pierzynski .15 .40
636 Arodys Vizcaino .15 .40
637 Stephen Strasburg .25 .60
638 Michael Pineda .15 .40
639 Rubby De La Rosa .15 .40
640 Carl Edwards Jr. RC .30 .75
641 Vidal Nuno .15 .40
642 Mike Pelfrey .15 .40
643 Yoenis Cespedes .25 .60
David Wright
Elite Meet and Greet
644 Los Angeles Angels .15 .40
645 Danny Santana .15 .40
646 Brad Miller .20 .50
647 Eduardo Rodriguez FS .15 .40
648 San Francisco Giants .15 .40
649 Aroldis Chapman .25 .60
650 Carlos Correa FS .25 .60
651 Dioner Navarro .15 .40
652A Collin McHugh .15 .40
652B Collin McHugh SP 2.00 5.00
42 jersey
653 Chris Iannetta .15 .40
654 Brandon Guyer .15 .40
655 Domonic Brown .20 .50
656 Randal Grichuk FS .15 .40
657 Johnny Giavotella .15 .40
658A Wilson Ramos .15 .40
658B Wilson Ramos SP 2.00 5.00
42 jersey
659 Adonis Garcia .15 .40
660 John Axford .15 .40

661A DJ LeMahieu .25 .60
661B DJ LeMahieu SP 3.00 8.00
42 jersey
Facing right
661C DJ LeMahieu SP 30.00 80.00
Black hoodie
662 Masahiro Tanaka .20 .50
663 Jake Petricka .15 .40
664 Mikie Mahtook .15 .40
665A Jared Hughes .15 .40
665B Jared Hughes SP 2.00 5.00
42 jersey
666 J.T. Realmuto FS .25 .60
667 James McCann FS .20 .50
668 Javier Baez FS .30 .75
669 Tyler Skaggs .15 .40
670 Will Smith .15 .40
671 Tony Cingrani .20 .50
672 Shane Peterson .15 .40
673A Justin Upton .20 .50
673B Justin Upton SP 30.00 80.00
w/Microphone
674 Tyler Chatwood .15 .40
675 Gary Sanchez RC .75 2.00
676 Jarred Cosart .15 .40
677 Derek Norris .15 .40
678A Carlos Martinez .20 .50
678B Carlos Martinez SP 30.00 80.00
Hands together
679 Nate Jones .15 .40
680 Tuffy Gosewisch .15 .40
681 Joe Smith .15 .40
682 Danny Duffy .15 .40
683A Carlos Gonzalez .20 .50
683B Carlos Gonzalez SP 2.50 6.00
42 jersey
Batting
684 Jarrod Dyson .15 .40
685 Kyle Waldrop RC .30 .75
686 Brandon Finnegan FS .15 .40
687 Chris Owings .15 .40
688 Shawn Tolleson .15 .40
689 Eugenio Suarez .20 .50
690 Jimmy Nelson .15 .40
691 Kris Medlen .20 .50
692 Giovanni Soto RC .30 .75
693 Josh Tomlin .15 .40
694 Scott McGough RC .25 .60
695 Kyle Crockett .15 .40
696A Lorenzo Cain .15 .40
696B Lorenzo Cain SP 2.00 5.00
42 jersey
696C Lorenzo Cain SP 20.00 50.00
Parade
697 Andrew Cashner .15 .40
698 Matt Moore .20 .50
699 Justin Bour FS .20 .50
700A Ichiro Suzuki .30 .75
700B Ichiro SP 42 jersey 4.00 10.00
701 Tyler Flowers .15 .40

2016 Topps Black

*BLACK: 10X TO 25X BASIC
*BLACK RC: 6X TO 15X BASIC RC
SER.1 ODDS 1:83 HOBBY; 1:17 JUMBO
SER.2 ODDS 1:50 HOBBY
STATED PRINT RUN 64 SER.#'d SETS
1 Mike Trout 30.00 80.00
2 Jerad Eickhoff 12.00 30.00
20 Andrew McCutchen 15.00 40.00
24 Clayton Kershaw 12.00 30.00
26 Dvs/Trt/Cruz LL 12.00 30.00
54 Jung Ho Kang FS 10.00 25.00
56 Salvador Perez WSH 10.00 25.00
66 Kyle Schwarber 30.00 80.00
78 Miguel Sano 25.00 60.00
100 Bryce Harper 15.00 40.00
134 Yadier Molina 12.00 30.00
137 Joe Panik 10.00 25.00
175 Manny Machado 8.00 20.00
254 Matt Holliday 10.00 25.00
255 Justin Verlander 6.00 15.00
337 Arndo/Hrpr/Gnzlz LL 6.00 15.00
338 Gldschmdt/Grdn/Hrpr LL 6.00 15.00
350 Kris Bryant FS 25.00 60.00
453 A.Rizzo/K.Bryant 8.00 20.00

2016 Topps Black and White Negative

*BW NEGATIVE: 8X TO 20X BASIC
*BW NEGATIVE RC: 5X TO 12X BASIC
SER.1 ODDS 1:1108 HOBBY, 1:22 J
SER.2 ODDS 1:65 HOBBY
1 Mike Trout 25.00 60.00
24 Clayton Kershaw 12.00 30.00
26 Dvs/Trt/Cruz LL 12.00 30.00
54 Jung Ho Kang FS 10.00 25.00
56 Salvador Perez WSH 10.00 25.00
78 Miguel Sano 20.00 50.00
100 Bryce Harper 15.00 40.00
134 Yadier Molina 12.00 30.00
137 Joe Panik 10.00 25.00
150 Clayton Kershaw 12.00 30.00
175 Manny Machado 6.00 15.00
254 Matt Holliday 10.00 25.00
255 Justin Verlander 6.00 15.00
337 Arndo/Hrpr/Gnzlz LL 6.00 15.00
338 Gldschmdt/Grdn/Hrpr LL 6.00 15.00
350 Kris Bryant FS 20.00 50.00
453 A.Rizzo/K.Bryant 6.00 15.00

2016 Topps Factory Set Sparkle Foil

*SPARKLE: 8X TO 20X BASIC
*SPARKLE RC: 5X TO 12X BASIC RC
STATED PRINT RUN 177 SER.#'d SETS
1 Mike Trout 25.00 60.00
24 Clayton Kershaw 10.00 25.00
26 Dvs/Trt/Cruz LL 10.00 25.00
54 Jung Ho Kang FS 8.00 20.00
56 Salvador Perez WSH 8.00 20.00
78 Miguel Sano 20.00 50.00
100 Bryce Harper 12.00 30.00
134 Yadier Molina 10.00 25.00
150 Clayton Kershaw 10.00 25.00
175 Manny Machado 6.00 15.00
254 Matt Holliday 8.00 20.00
255 Justin Verlander 5.00 12.00
337 Arndo/Hrpr/Gnzlz LL 5.00 12.00
338 Gldschmdt/Grdn/Hrpr LL 5.00 12.00
350 Kris Bryant FS 20.00 50.00
453 A.Rizzo/K.Bryant 6.00 15.00

2016 Topps Gold

*GOLD: 2X TO 5X BASIC
*GOLD RC: 1.2X TO 3X BASIC RC
SER.1 ODDS 1:11 HOBBY, 1:3 JUMBO
SER.2 ODDS 1:6 HOBBY
146 Stephen Piscotty 6.00 15.00

2016 Topps Limited

COMPLETE SET (700) 90.00 150.00
1 Mike Trout 5.00 12.00
2 Jerad Eickhoff 1.00 2.50
3 Richie Shaffer .60 1.50
4 Sonny Gray .75 2.00
5 Kyle Seager .60 1.50
6 Jimmy Paredes .60 1.50
8 Michael Brantley .75 2.00
9 Eric Hosmer .75 2.00
10 Nelson Cruz 1.00 2.50
11 Andre Ethier .75 2.00
12 Nolan Arenado 1.25 3.00
13 Craig Kimbrel .75 2.00
14 Chris Davis .60 1.50
15 Ryan Howard .75 2.00
16 Rougned Odor .75 2.00
17 Billy Butler .60 1.50
18 Francisco Rodriguez .75 2.00
19 Delino DeShields Jr. FS .60 1.50
20 Andrew McCutchen 1.00 2.50
21 Mike Moustakas WSH .75 2.00
22 John Hicks .60 1.50
23 Jeff Francoeur .75 2.00
24 Clayton Kershaw 2.00 5.00
25 Brad Ziegler .60 1.50
26 Chris Davis 5.00 12.00
Mike Trout
Nelson Cruz LL
27 Alec Asher .60 1.50
28 Brian McCann .75 2.00
29 Altuve/Cabrera/Bogaerts 1.00 2.50
30 Yan Gomes .60 1.50
31 Travis d'Arnaud .75 2.00
32 Zack Greinke .75 2.00
33 Edinson Volquez .60 1.50
34 Omar Infante .60 1.50
35 Luke Hochevar .60 1.50
36 Miguel Montero .60 1.50
37 C.J. Cron .60 1.50
38 Jed Lowrie .60 1.50
39 Mark Trumbo .60 1.50
40 Jedd Gyorko .60 1.50
41 Josh Harrison .60 1.50
42 A.J. Ramos .60 1.50
43 Noah Syndergaard FS .75 2.00
44 David Freese .60 1.50
45 Ryan Zimmerman .75 2.00
46 Jhonny Peralta .60 1.50
47 Gio Gonzalez .75 2.00
48 J.J. Hoover .60 1.50
49 Ike Davis .60 1.50
50 Salvador Perez .75 2.00
51 Dustin Garneau .60 1.50
52 Julio Teheran .75 2.00
53 George Springer .75 2.00
54 Jung Ho Kang FS .60 1.50
55 Jesus Montero .60 1.50
56 Salvador Perez WSH .75 2.00
57 Adam Lind .75 2.00
58 Zack Greinke 2.00 5.00
Clayton Kershaw
Jake Arrieta LL
59 John Lamb .60 1.50
60 Shelby Miller .75 2.00
61 Johnny Cueto WSH .75 2.00
62 Trayce Thompson 1.00 2.50
63 Zach Britton .75 2.00
64 Corey Kluber .75 2.00
65 Pittsburgh Pirates .60 1.50
66 Kyle Schwarber 2.00 5.00
67 Matt Harvey .75 2.00
68 Odubel Herrera FS .75 2.00
69 Anibal Sanchez .60 1.50
70 Kendrys Morales .60 1.50
71 John Danks .60 1.50
72 Chris Young .60 1.50
73 Ketel Marte 1.25 3.00
74 Troy Tulowitzki 1.00 2.50
75 Rusney Castillo .60 1.50
76 Glen Perkins .60 1.50
77 Clay Buchholz .60 1.50
78 Miguel Sano 1.00 2.50
79 Seattle Mariners .60 1.50
80 Carson Smith .60 1.50
81 Alexei Ramirez .75 2.00
82 Michael Bourn .60 1.50
83 Starling Marte .75 2.00
84 Mookie Betts 1.50 4.00
85 Corey Seager 15.00 40.00
86 Wilmer Flores .75 2.00
87 Jorge De La Rosa .60 1.50
88 Ubaldo Jimenez .60 1.50
89 Edwin Encarnacion 1.00 2.50
90 Koji Uehara .60 1.50
91 Yasmani Grandal FS .60 1.50
92 Darren O'Day .60 1.50
93 Charlie Blackmon 1.00 2.50
94 Miguel Cabrera 1.00 2.50
95 Kole Calhoun FS .60 1.50
96 Jose Bautista .75 2.00
97 Ender Inciarte FS .60 1.50
98 Garrett Richards .75 2.00
99 Taijuan Walker .60 1.50
100 Bryce Harper 1.50 4.00
101 Justin Turner .75 2.00
102 Doug Fister .60 1.50
103 Trea Turner 2.00 5.00
104 Jeremy Hellickson .60 1.50
105 Marcus Semien .60 1.50
106 Jordan Walden .60 1.50
107 Kevin Siegrist .60 1.50
108 Ben Paulsen .60 1.50
109 Henry Owens .75 2.00
110 J.D. Martinez FS 1.00 2.50
111 Coco Crisp .60 1.50
112 Matt Kemp .75 2.00
113 Aaron Sanchez .75 2.00
114 Brett Lawrie .75 2.00
115 Aaron Harang .60 1.50
116 Brett Gardner .75 2.00
117 Liam Hendriks .60 1.50
118 Jose Fernandez 1.00 2.50
119 Sean Doolittle .60 1.50
120 Alcides Escobar WSH .75 2.00
121 Roberto Osuna FS .60 1.50
122 Melky Cabrera .60 1.50
123 J.P. Howell .60 1.50
124 Melvin Upton Jr. .75 2.00
125 Zack Greinke 2.00 5.00
Clayton Kershaw
Jake Arrieta LL
126 David Ortiz 1.25 3.00
Albert Pujols
127 Zach Lee .60 1.50
128 Eddie Rosario .75 2.00
129 Kendall Graveman .60 1.50
130 A.J. Pollock .60 1.50
131 Adam LaRoche .60 1.50
132 Joe Ross FS .60 1.50
133 Aaron Nola 1.25 3.00
134 Yadier Molina 1.00 2.50
135 Colby Rasmus .75 2.00
136 Michael Cuddyer .60 1.50
137 Joe Panik .75 2.00
138 Francisco Liriano .60 1.50
139 Yasiel Puig 1.00 2.50
140 Carlos Carrasco FS .60 1.50
141 Colin Rea .60 1.50
142 CC Sabathia .75 2.00
143 Oliver Perez .60 1.50
144 Jose Iglesias .75 2.00
145 Jon Niese .60 1.50
146 Stephen Piscotty 1.00 2.50
147 Dee Gordon .60 1.50
148 Yangervis Solarte .60 1.50
149 Chad Bettis .60 1.50
150 Clayton Kershaw 2.00 5.00
151 Jon Lester .75 2.00
152 Kyle Lohse .60 1.50
153 Jason Hammel .75 2.00
154 Hunter Pence .75 2.00
155 New York Yankees .60 1.50
156 Cameron Maybin .60 1.50
157 Darnell Sweeney .60 1.50
158 Henry Urrutia .60 1.50
159 Erick Aybar .60 1.50
160 Chris Sale 1.00 2.50
161 Phil Hughes .60 1.50
162 Jose Bautista .75 2.00
Josh Donaldson
Chris Davis LL
163 Joaquin Benoit .60 1.50
164 Andrew Heaney .60 1.50
165 Adam Eaton .60 1.50
166 Gldschmdt/Rizzo/Arndo LL 1.50 4.00
167 Jacoby Ellsbury .75 2.00
168 Nathan Eovaldi .75 2.00
169 Charlie Morton 1.00 2.50
170 Carlos Gomez .60 1.50
171 Matt Cain .75 2.00
172 Carter Capps .60 1.50
173 Jose Abreu 1.00 2.50
174 Jered Weaver .75 2.00
175 Manny Machado 1.00 2.50
176 Brandon Phillips .60 1.50
177 Gregor Blanco .60 1.50
178 Rob Refsnyder .75 2.00
179 Jose Peraza .75 2.00
180 Kevin Gausman .60 1.50
181 Minnesota Twins .60 1.50
182 Kevin Pillar .60 1.50
183 Andrelton Simmons .60 1.50
184 Travis Jankowski .60 1.50
185 Dallas Keuchel .75 2.00
Sonny Gray
David Price LL
186 Yasmany Tomas FS .60 1.50
187 Dallas Keuchel .75 2.00
Collin McHugh
David Price LL
188 Greg Bird .75 2.00
189 Jake McGee .60 1.50
190 Jeurys Familia .75 2.00
191 Brian Johnson .60 1.50
192 John Jaso .60 1.50
193 Trevor Bauer 1.00 2.50
194 Chase Headley .60 1.50
195 Jason Kipnis .75 2.00
196 Hunter Strickland .60 1.50
197 Neil Walker .75 2.00
198 Oakland Athletics .60 1.50
199 Jay Bruce .75 2.00
200 Josh Donaldson .75 2.00
201 Adam Jones .75 2.00
202 Colorado Rockies .60 1.50
203 Aaron Hill .60 1.50
204 Mark Teixeira .75 2.00
205 Taylor Jungmann FS .60 1.50
206 Alex Gordon .75 2.00
207 Maikel Franco FS .75 2.00
208 Kurt Suzuki .60 1.50
209 Max Scherzer 1.00 2.50
210 Mike Zunino .60 1.50
211 Nick Ahmed .60 1.50
212 Starlin Castro .60 1.50
213 Matt Shoemaker .75 2.00
214 Chris Colabello .60 1.50
215 Adrian Gonzalez .75 2.00
216 Logan Forsythe .60 1.50
217 Lance Lynn .60 1.50
218 Andrew Miller .75 2.00
219 Hector Olivera .75 2.00
220 Zack Greinke 1.00 2.50
Gerrit Cole
Jake Arrieta LL
221 Ryan LaMarre .60 1.50
222 Homer Bailey .60 1.50
223 Christian Yelich 1.25 3.00
224 Billy Burns FS .60 1.50
225 Scooter Gennett .75 2.00
226 Brian Ellington .60 1.50
227 David Murphy .60 1.50
228 Matt Garza .60 1.50
229 Jesse Hahn .60 1.50
230 Ryan Vogelsong .60 1.50
231 Chris Coghlan .60 1.50
232 Michael Conforto .75 2.00
233 J.J. Hardy .60 1.50
234 David Robertson .60 1.50
235 Blaine Boyer .60 1.50
236 Juan Lagares .60 1.50
237 Carlos Ruiz .60 1.50
238 Baltimore Orioles .60 1.50
239 Huston Street .60 1.50
240 Nick Markakis .75 2.00
241 Freddie Freeman 1.25 3.00
242 Matt Wisler FS .60 1.50
243 Luke Gregerson .60 1.50
244 Matt Carpenter 1.00 2.50
245 Tommy Kahnle .60 1.50
246 Dustin Pedroia 1.00 2.50
247 Yunel Escobar .60 1.50
248 Atlanta Braves .60 1.50
249 Carlos Gomez .60 1.50
250 Miguel Cabrera 1.00 2.50
251 Silvino Bracho .60 1.50
252 Jorge Soler 1.00 2.50
253 Nick Castellanos 1.00 2.50
254 Matt Holliday .60 1.50
255 Justin Verlander 1.00 2.50
256 C.J. Wilson .60 1.50
257 Jake Marisnick .60 1.50
258 Devon Travis FS .60 1.50
259 Paul Goldschmidt 1.00 2.50
260 Ryan Hanigan .60 1.50
261 Russell Martin .60 1.50
262 Ervin Santana .60 1.50
263 Joc Pederson FS .60 1.50
264 Jake Arrieta .75 2.00
265 Luis Severino .75 2.00
266 Jonathan Papelbon .75 2.00
267 Chris Heston FS .60 1.50
268 Robinson Cano .75 2.00
269 Giancarlo Stanton 1.00 2.50
270 Pat Neshek .60 1.50
271 Kevin Kiermaier .75 2.00
272 Denard Span .60 1.50
273 New York Mets .60 1.50
274 Ryan Goins .60 1.50
275 Ian Kinsler .75 2.00
276 Francisco Cervelli .60 1.50
277 Elvis Andrus .75 2.00
278 Evan Gattis .60 1.50
279 Alex Guerrero FS .75 2.00
280 Brock Holt .60 1.50
281 Alex Dickerson .60 1.50
282 Scott Feldman .60 1.50
283 Felix Hernandez .75 2.00
284 Jon Gray .60 1.50
285 Pablo Sandoval .75 2.00
286 Joe Mauer .75 2.00
287 Alcides Escobar .60 1.50
288 Jake Lamb FS .75 2.00
289 Nick Hundley .60 1.50
290 Zack Godley .60 1.50
291 Asdrubal Cabrera .75 2.00
292 Todd Frazier .75 2.00
293 Hyun-Jin Ryu .60 1.50
294 Chicago White Sox .60 1.50
295 Jonathan Schoop .60 1.50
296 Yordano Ventura .75 2.00
297 Detroit Tigers .60 1.50
298 Ryan Braun .75 2.00
299 Angel Pagan .60 1.50
300 Buster Posey 1.25 3.00
301 Wade Miley .60 1.50
302 Houston Astros .60 1.50
303 Steve Pearce 1.00 2.50
304 Charlie Furbush .60 1.50
305 Colby Lewis .60 1.50
306 Jarrod Saltalamacchia .60 1.50
307 Wade Davis .60 1.50
308 Brian Dozier .75 2.00
309 Shin-Soo Choo .75 2.00
310 David Wright .75 2.00
311 Dariel Alvarez .60 1.50
312 Curtis Granderson .75 2.00
313 Martin Maldonado .60 1.50
314 Kyle Hendricks 1.00 2.50
315 San Diego Padres .60 1.50
316 Jake Odorizzi FS .60 1.50
317 Jose Altuve .75 2.00
318 Washington Nationals .60 1.50
319 Adam Wainwright .75 2.00
320 Jake Peavy .60 1.50
321 Hanley Ramirez .75 2.00
322 Kelby Tomlinson .60 1.50
323 Jacob deGrom 1.00 2.50
324 Steven Souza Jr. .75 2.00
325 Kaleb Cowart .60 1.50
326 Kevin Plawecki FS .60 1.50
327 Anthony Rizzo 1.50 4.00
328 Anthony DeSclafani .60 1.50
329 Alex Rodriguez 1.25 3.00
330 Edward Mujica .60 1.50
331 Will Harris .60 1.50
332 Toronto Blue Jays .60 1.50
333 Keyvius Sampson .60 1.50
334 Brandon McCarthy .60 1.50
335 Mitch Moreland .60 1.50
336 Mark Melancon .60 1.50
337 Nolan Arenado 1.50 4.00
Bryce Harper
Carlos Gonzalez LL
338 Paul Goldschmidt 1.50 4.00
Dee Gordon
Bryce Harper LL
339 Carlos Santana .75 2.00
340 Victor Martinez .75 2.00
341 Josh Hamilton .75 2.00
342 Jayson Werth .75 2.00
343 Drew Hutchison .60 1.50
344 Jonathan Lucroy .75 2.00
345 Yonder Alonso .60 1.50
346 Corey Kluber .75 2.00
Dallas Keuchel
Marco Estrada LL
347 Jason Grilli .60 1.50
348 Seth Smith .60 1.50
349 Ben Revere .60 1.50
350 Kris Bryant FS 1.25 3.00
351 Chase Utley .75 2.00
352 Carson Blair .60 1.50
353 Joey Gallo .75 2.00
354 Tyson Ross .60 1.50
355 Avisail Garcia .75 2.00
356 Odrisamer Despaigne .60 1.50
357 Jace Peterson .60 1.50
358 Chris Young .60 1.50
359 Christian Colon .60 1.50
360 Eduardo Escobar .60 1.50
361 Jeff Locke .60 1.50
362 Cory Spangenberg .60 1.50
363 Brett Cecil .60 1.50
364 Keon Broxton .60 1.50
365 James Pazos .75 2.00
366 Scott Alexander .60 1.50
367 Pedro Alvarez .60 1.50
368 Xander Bogaerts 1.00 2.50
369 Dellin Betances .75 2.00
370 Bud Norris .60 1.50
371 Jason Heyward .75 2.00
372 Zack Cozart .60 1.50
373 Tucker Barnhart .60 1.50
374 Zach McAllister .60 1.50
375 Jordan Lyles .60 1.50
376 Brandon Barnes .60 1.50
377 Scott Kazmir .60 1.50
378 Jeff Mathis .75 2.00
379 Wei-Yin Chen .60 1.50
380 Michael Blazek .60 1.50
381 Bartolo Colon .60 1.50
382 David Ortiz 1.00 2.50
David Price
Winning Formula
383 Andres Blanco .60 1.50
384 Michael Morse .60 1.50
385 Jon Jay .60 1.50
386 Nori Aoki .60 1.50
387 Kansas City Clutch .60 1.50
388 Evan Longoria .75 2.00
389 Sam Dyson .60 1.50
390 Danny Espinosa .60 1.50
391 Matt Boyd FS .60 1.50
392 Jon Singleton .75 2.00
393 Kelvin Herrera .60 1.50
394 Abel De Los Santos .60 1.50
395 Raul Mondesi .75 2.00
396 Matt Reynolds .60 1.50
397 Mac Williamson .60 1.50
398 Cleveland Indians .60 1.50
399 Kansas City Royals .60 1.50
400 David Ortiz 1.00 2.50
401 Peter O'Brien .60 1.50
402 Daniel Norris FS .60 1.50
403 David Peralta .60 1.50
404 Miami Marlins .60 1.50
405 Ruben Tejada .60 1.50
406 Marwin Gonzalez .60 1.50
407 Yoenis Cespedes 1.00 2.50
408 Jason Castro .60 1.50
409 Jean Segura .75 2.00
410 Mike Moustakas .75 2.00
411 Brian Matusz .60 1.50
412 Mark Lowe .60 1.50
413 David Phelps .60 1.50
414 Wily Peralta .60 1.50
415 Brett Wallace .60 1.50
416 Johnny Cueto .75 2.00
417 Brad Boxberger .60 1.50
418 Yu Darvish 1.00 2.50
419 Aaron Altherr .60 1.50
420 Pedro Severino .60 1.50
421 Cesar Hernandez .60 1.50
422 Miguel Gonzalez .60 1.50
423 Carl Crawford .75 2.00
424 Brandon Belt .75 2.00
425 Jackie Bradley Jr. 1.00 2.50
426 Joey Votto 1.00 2.50
427 Travis Shaw .60 1.50
428 Gregory Polanco .75 2.00
429 Kenta Maeda 1.25 3.00
430 Ariel Pena .60 1.50
431 Philadelphia Phillies .60 1.50
432 Cameron Rupp .60 1.50
433 Trevor Brown .75 2.00
434 Matt Adams .60 1.50
435 Enrique Hernandez .75 2.00
436 Raudel Lazo .60 1.50
437 Michael Lorenzen .60 1.50
438 Paulo Orlando .60 1.50
439 Francisco Lindor FS 1.00 2.50
440 Tommy Pham FS .60 1.50
441 David Ross .60 1.50
442 Brandon Crawford .75 2.00
443 Prince Fielder .75 2.00
444 Jordan Zimmermann .75 2.00
445 Robbie Ray .60 1.50
446 Tom Murphy .60 1.50
447 Ben Zobrist .75 2.00
448 St. Louis Cardinals .60 1.50
449 J.A. Happ .75 2.00
450 David Price .75 2.00
451 Jose Reyes .75 2.00
452 Gerrit Cole 1.00 2.50
453 Rizzo/Bryant 1.50 4.00
454 Greg Holland .60 1.50
455 Preston Tucker .60 1.50
456 Gordon Beckham .60 1.50
457 Nick Swisher .75 2.00
458 Kenley Jansen .75 2.00
459 James Loney .60 1.50
460 Danny Salazar .75 2.00
461 Freddy Galvis .60 1.50
462 Jumbo Diaz .60 1.50
463 Boston Red Sox .60 1.50
464 Robinson Chirinos .60 1.50
465 Jesse Chavez .60 1.50
466 Marco Estrada .60 1.50
467 Giovanny Urshela 1.00 2.50
468 Rajai Davis .60 1.50
469 Logan Morrison .60 1.50
470 John Lackey .75 2.00
471 Kolten Wong .75 2.00
472 Josh Reddick .60 1.50
473 Robbie Erlin .60 1.50
474 Chicago Cubs .60 1.50
475 Max Kepler 1.00 2.50
476 Hisashi Iwakuma .75 2.00
477 Chris Tillman .60 1.50
478 Cody Asche .60 1.50
479 Marcus Stroman .75 2.00
480 Mike Foltynewicz .60 1.50
481 Hector Rondon .60 1.50
482 Drew Smyly .60 1.50
483 Erasmo Ramirez .60 1.50
484 Trevor Rosenthal .75 2.00
485 James Paxton .75 2.00
486 Chris Rusin .60 1.50
487 Martin Prado .60 1.50
488 Colton Murray .60 1.50
489 Adeiny Hechavarria .60 1.50
490 Guido Knudson .60 1.50
491 Rich Hill .60 1.50
492 Yadier Molina 1.00 2.50
Randal Grichuk
Many Healthy Returns
493 R.A. Dickey .75 2.00
494 Luis Avilan .60 1.50
495 Luke Maile .60 1.50
496 Brett Anderson .60 1.50
497 Devin Mesoraco .60 1.50
498 Steve Cishek .60 1.50
499 Carlos Perez .60 1.50
500 Albert Pujols 1.25 3.00
501 Alex Rios .75 2.00
502 Austin Hedges .60 1.50
503 Luis Valbuena .60 1.50
504 Elias Diaz .60 1.50
505 Frankie Montas .75 2.00
506 Stephen Vogt .60 1.50
507 Travis Wood .60 1.50
508 Jaime Garcia .60 1.50
509 Mark Canha .60 1.50
510 Tony Watson .60 1.50
511 Manny Banuelos 1.00 2.50
512 Ryan Madson .60 1.50
513 Caleb Joseph .60 1.50
514 Michael Taylor .60 1.50
515 Ryan Flaherty .60 1.50
516 Steve Johnson .60 1.50
517 Corey Knebel .60 1.50
518 Matt Duffy .60 1.50
519 Kyle Barraclough .60 1.50
520 Anthony Rendon 1.00 2.50
521 Chris Archer .60 1.50
522 Alex Avila .75 2.00
523 Blake Swihart FS .75 2.00
524 Justin Nicolino FS .60 1.50
525 Jurickson Profar .75 2.00
526 T.J. McFarland .60 1.50
527 Jordy Mercer .60 1.50
528 Byron Buxton FS .75 2.00
529 Zack Wheeler .75 2.00
530 Caleb Cotham .75 2.00
531 Cody Allen .60 1.50
532 Matt Marksberry .60 1.50
533 Jonathan Villar .60 1.50
534 Eduardo Nunez .60 1.50
535 Ivan Nova .75 2.00
536 Alex Wood .60 1.50
537 Tampa Bay Rays .60 1.50
538 Michael Reed .60 1.50
539 Nate Karns .60 1.50
540 Curt Casali .60 1.50
541 James Shields .60 1.50
542 Scott Van Slyke .60 1.50
543 Carlos Rodon FS 1.00 2.50
544 Jeremy Jeffress .60 1.50
545 Hector Santiago .60 1.50
546 Ricky Nolasco .60 1.50
547 Nick Goody .75 2.00
548 Lucas Duda .75 2.00
549 Luke Jackson .60 1.50
550 Dallas Keuchel .75 2.00
551 Steven Matz FS .75 2.00
552 Texas Rangers .60 1.50
553 Adrian Houser .60 1.50
554 Daniel Murphy .75 2.00
555 Franklin Gutierrez .60 1.50
556 Abraham Almonte .60 1.50
557 Alexi Amarista .60 1.50
558 Sean Rodriguez .60 1.50
559 Cliff Pennington .60 1.50
560 Kennys Vargas .60 1.50
561 Kyle Gibson .75 2.00
562 Addison Russell FS 1.00 2.50
563 Lance McCullers FS .60 1.50
564 Tanner Roark .60 1.50
565 Matt den Dekker .60 1.50
566 Alex Rodriguez 1.25 3.00
567 Carlos Beltran .75 2.00
568 Arizona Diamondbacks .60 1.50
569 Los Angeles Dodgers .60 1.50
570 Corey Dickerson .60 1.50
571 Mark Reynolds .60 1.50
572 Marcell Ozuna 1.00 2.50
573 Tom Koehler .60 1.50
574 Ryan Dull .60 1.50
575 Ryan Strausborger .60 1.50
576 Tyler Duffey .60 1.50
577 Jason Gurka .60 1.50
578 Mike Leake .60 1.50
579 Michael Wacha .75 2.00
580 Socrates Brito .60 1.50
581 Zach Davies .75 2.00
582 Jose Quintana .60 1.50
583 Didi Gregorius .75 2.00
584 Adam Duvall 2.00 5.00
585 Raisel Iglesias FS .75 2.00
586 Chris Stewart .60 1.50
587 Neftali Feliz .60 1.50
588 Cole Hamels .75 2.00
589 Derek Holland .60 1.50
590 Anthony Gose .60 1.50
591 Trevor Plouffe .60 1.50
592 Adrian Beltre 1.00 2.50
593 Alex Cobb .60 1.50
594 Lonnie Chisenhall .60 1.50
595 Mike Napoli .60 1.50
596 Sergio Romo .60 1.50
597 Chi Chi Gonzalez .60 1.50
598 Khris Davis 1.00 2.50
599 Domingo Santana .75 2.00
600 Madison Bumgarner .75 2.00
601 Leonys Martin .60 1.50
602 Keith Hessler .60 1.50
603 Shawn Armstrong .60 1.50
604 Jeff Samardzija .60 1.50
605 Santiago Casilla .60 1.50
606 Miguel Almonte .60 1.50
607 Brandon Drury 1.00 2.50
608 Rick Porcello .75 2.00
609 Billy Hamilton .75 2.00
610 Adam Morgan .60 1.50
611 Darin Ruf .60 1.50
612 Cincinnati Reds .60 1.50
613 Milwaukee Brewers .60 1.50
614 Dalton Pompey .75 2.00
615 Miguel Castro .60 1.50
616 Keone Kela .60 1.50
617 Justin Smoak .60 1.50
618 Desmond Jennings .75 2.00
619 Dustin Ackley .60 1.50
620 Daniel Hudson .60 1.50
621 Zach Duke .60 1.50
622 Ken Giles .60 1.50
623 Tyler Saladino .60 1.50
624 Tommy Milone .60 1.50

625 Wil Myers .60 1.50
626 Danny Valencia .75 2.00
627 Mike Fiers .60 1.50
628 Wellington Castillo .60 1.50
629 Patrick Corbin .75 2.00
630 Michael Saunders .75 2.00
631 Chris Reed .60 1.50
632 Ramon Cabrera .60 1.50
633 Martin Perez .75 2.00
634 Jorge Lopez .60 1.50
635 A.J. Pierzynski .60 1.50
636 Arodys Vizcaino .60 1.50
637 Stephen Strasburg 1.00 2.50
638 Michael Pineda .60 1.50
639 Rubby De La Rosa .60 1.50
640 Carl Edwards Jr. .75 2.00
641 Vidal Nuno .60 1.50
642 Mike Pelfrey .60 1.50
643 Yoenis Cespedes 1.00 2.50
David Wright
Elite Meet and Greet
644 Los Angeles Angels .60 1.50
645 Danny Santana .60 1.50
646 Brad Miller .75 2.00
647 Eduardo Rodriguez FS .60 1.50
648 San Francisco Giants .60 1.50
649 Aroldis Chapman 1.00 2.50
650 Carlos Correa FS 1.00 2.50
651 Dioner Navarro .60 1.50
652 Collin McHugh .60 1.50
653 Chris Iannetta .60 1.50
654 Brandon Guyer .60 1.50
655 Domonic Brown .75 2.00
656 Randal Grichuk FS .60 1.50
657 Johnny Giavotella .60 1.50
658 Wilson Ramos .60 1.50
659 Adonis Garcia .60 1.50
660 John Axford .60 1.50
661 DJ LeMahieu 1.00 2.50
662 Masahiro Tanaka .75 2.00
663 Jake Petricka .60 1.50
664 Mikie Mahtook .60 1.50
665 Jared Hughes .60 1.50
666 J.T. Realmuto FS 1.00 2.50
667 James McCann FS .75 2.00
668 Javier Baez FS 1.25 3.00
669 Tyler Skaggs .60 1.50
670 Will Smith .60 1.50
671 Tony Cingrani .75 2.00
672 Shane Peterson .60 1.50
673 Justin Upton .75 2.00
674 Tyler Chatwood .60 1.50
675 Gary Sanchez 2.00 5.00
676 Jarrod Cosart .60 1.50
677 Derek Norris .60 1.50
678 Carlos Martinez .75 2.00
679 Nate Jones .60 1.50
680 Tuffy Gosewisch .60 1.50
681 Joe Smith .60 1.50
682 Danny Duffy .60 1.50
683 Carlos Gonzalez .75 2.00
684 Jarrod Dyson .60 1.50
685 Kyle Waldrop .75 2.00
686 Brandon Finnegan FS .60 1.50
687 Chris Owings .60 1.50
688 Shawn Tolleson .60 1.50
689 Eugenio Suarez .75 2.00
690 Jimmy Nelson .60 1.50
691 Kris Medlen .75 2.00
692 Giovanni Soto .75 2.00
693 Josh Tomlin .60 1.50
694 Scott McGough .60 1.50
695 Kyle Crockett .60 1.50
696 Lorenzo Cain .60 1.50
697 Andrew Cashner .60 1.50
698 Matt Moore .75 2.00
699 Justin Bour FS .75 2.00
700 Ichiro Suzuki 1.25 3.00
701 Tyler Flowers .60 1.50

2016 Topps Pink

*PINK: 10X TO 25X BASIC
*PINK RC: 6X TO 15X BASIC RC
SER.1 ODDS 1:535 HOBBY; 1:107 JUMBO
SER.2 ODDS 1:293 HOBBY
STATED PRINT RUN 50 SER.#'d SETS
1 Mike Trout 30.00 80.00
20 Andrew McCutchen 15.00 40.00
24 Clayton Kershaw 12.00 30.00
26 Dvs/Trt/Cruz LL 12.00 30.00
54 Jung Ho Kang FS 10.00 25.00
56 Salvador Perez WSH 10.00 25.00
66 Kyle Schwarber 30.00 80.00
78 Miguel Sano 25.00 60.00
100 Bryce Harper 15.00 40.00
134 Yadier Molina 12.00 30.00
137 Joe Panik 10.00 25.00
150 Clayton Kershaw 12.00 30.00
175 Manny Machado 8.00 20.00
254 Matt Holliday 10.00 25.00
255 Justin Verlander 6.00 15.00
337 Arndo/Hrpr/Gnzlz LL 6.00 15.00
338 Gldschmdt/Grdn/Hrpr LL 6.00 15.00
350 Kris Bryant FS 25.00 60.00
453 A.Rizzo/K.Bryant 8.00 20.00

2016 Topps Rainbow Foil

*RAINBOW: 2X TO 5X BASIC
*RAINBOW RC: 1.2X TO 3X BASIC RC
SER.1 ODDS 1:10 HOBBY, 1:2 JUMBO
SER.2 ODDS 1:10 HOBBY

2016 Topps Toys R Us Purple

*PURPLE: 5X TO 12X BASIC
*PURPLE RC: 3X TO 8X BASIC RC
INSERTED IN TRU PACKS

2016 Topps Vintage Stock

*VINTAGE: 8X TO 20X BASIC
*VINTAGE RC: 5X TO 12X BASIC RC
SER.1 ODDS 1:270 HOBBY, 1:54 JUMBO
SER.2 ODDS 1:148 HOBBY
STATED PRINT RUN 99 SER.#'d SETS
1 Mike Trout 25.00 60.00
24 Clayton Kershaw 10.00 25.00
26 Dvs/Trt/Cruz LL 10.00 25.00
54 Jung Ho Kang FS 8.00 20.00
56 Salvador Perez WSH 8.00 20.00
78 Miguel Sano 20.00 50.00
100 Bryce Harper 12.00 30.00
134 Yadier Molina 10.00 25.00
150 Clayton Kershaw 10.00 25.00
175 Manny Machado 6.00 15.00
254 Matt Holliday 8.00 20.00
255 Justin Verlander 5.00 12.00
337 Arndo/Hrpr/Gnzlz LL 5.00 12.00
338 Gldschmdt/Grdn/Hrpr LL 5.00 12.00
350 Kris Bryant FS 20.00 50.00
453 A.Rizzo/K.Bryant 6.00 15.00

2016 Topps 100 Years at Wrigley Field

COMPLETE SET (50) 15.00 40.00
SER.1 ODDS 1:8 HOBBY; 1:2 JUMBO
SER.2 ODDS 1:8 HOBBY
WRIG1 Kris Bryant .60 1.50
WRIG2 Ryne Sandberg 1.00 2.50
WRIG3 Greg Maddux .60 1.50
WRIG4 Mark Grace .40 1.00
WRIG5 Jake Arrieta .40 1.00
WRIG6 Mark Prior .40 1.00
WRIG7 Bruce Sutter .40 1.00
WRIG8 Fergie Jenkins .40 1.00
WRIG9 Goose Gossage .40 1.00
WRIG10 Stan Musial .75 2.00
WRIG11 Andre Dawson .40 1.00
WRIG12 Anthony Rizzo .75 2.00
WRIG13 Addison Russell .50 1.25
WRIG14 Wrigley Field Marquee Installed .30 .75
WRIG15 Cubs Park
Becomes Wrigley Field .30 .75
WRIG16 Maddux/Jenkins .60 1.50
WRIG17 Jimmie Foxx .50 1.25
WRIG18 William Wrigley Jr. becomes majority
shareholder of the Cubs .30 .75
WRIG19 Babe Ruth 1.25 3.00
WRIG20 Aramis Ramirez .30 .75
WRIG21 Cole Hamels .40 1.00
WRIG22 Rafael Palmeiro .40 1.00
WRIG23 Ted Williams 1.00 2.50
WRIG24 Clark .30 .75
Mascot
WRIG25 Kyle Schwarber 1.00 2.50
WRIG26 Mark Grace .40 1.00
WRIG27 Billy Williams .40 1.00
WRIG28 Fergie Jenkins .40 1.00
WRIG29 Anthony Rizzo .75 2.00
WRIG30 Mark Prior .40 1.00
WRIG31 Jorge Soler .50 1.25
WRIG32 Kyle Schwarber 1.00 2.50
WRIG33 Rafael Palmeiro .40 1.00
WRIG34 Andre Dawson .40 1.00
WRIG35 Kris Bryant .60 1.50
WRIG36 Ryne Sandberg 1.00 2.50
WRIG37 Ron Santo .40 1.00
WRIG38 Greg Maddux .60 1.50
WRIG39 Addison Russell .50 1.25
WRIG40 Jason Heyward .40 1.00
WRIG41 Jon Lester .40 1.00
WRIG42 Bruce Sutter .40 1.00
WRIG43 Tom Glavine .40 1.00
WRIG44 Bricks and Ivy .30 .75
WRIG45 Jackie Robinson .50 1.25
WRIG46 Weeghman Park .30 .75
WRIG47 Ronald Reagan .30 .75
WRIG48 The Friendly Confines .30 .75
WRIG49 Hal Newhouser .40 1.00
WRIG50 Lou Gehrig 1.00 2.50

2016 Topps 100 Years at Wrigley Field Autographs

SER.1 ODDS 1:30,058 HOBBY; 1:5942 JUMBO
SER.2 ODDS 1:16,848 HOBBY
STATED PRINT RUN 25 SER.#'d SETS
SER.1 EXCH DEADLINE 1/31/2018
WRIGAAD Andre Dawson S2 60.00 150.00
WRIGAARI Anthony Rizzo S2 75.00 200.00
WRIGABS Bruce Sutter 10.00 25.00
WRIGABW Billy Williams S2 25.00 60.00
WRIGAEB Ernie Banks 60.00 150.00
WRIGAFJ Fergie Jenkins
WRIGAFJ Fergie Jenkins S2 15.00 40.00
WRIGAGG Goose Gossage 25.00 60.00
WRIGAGM Greg Maddux
WRIGAJS Jorge Soler S2 40.00 100.00
WRIGAKB Kris Bryant 200.00 300.00
WRIGAKB Bryant S2 Celebrate 200.00 300.00
WRIGAKS Kyle Schwarber S2
WRIGAMG Mark Grace 30.00 80.00
WRIGAMG Grace S2 Face left 30.00 80.00
WRIGAMP Mark Prior 20.00 50.00
WRIGARP Rafael Palmeiro S2
WRIGARS Ryne Sandberg 60.00 150.00
WRIGARSN Ron Santo S2 60.00 150.00
WRIGASM Stan Musial 60.00 150.00

2016 Topps 100 Years at Wrigley Field Relics

SER.1 ODDS 1:5075 HOBBY; 1:1015 JUMBO
SER.2 ODDS 1:2856 HOBBY
STATED PRINT RUN 99 SER.#'d SETS
WRIGRAD Andre Dawson 8.00 20.00
Fully body
WRIGRAD Andre Dawson S2 8.00 20.00
Waist up
WRIGRAR Anthony Rizzo 15.00 40.00
w/Fan
WRIGRARA Aramis Ramirez 6.00 15.00
WRIGRARI Anthony Rizzo S2 15.00 40.00
Batting
WRIGRARU Addison Russell 10.00 25.00
Batting
WRIGRARU Addison Russell S2 10.00 25.00
Dugout
WRIGRBS Bruce Sutter 8.00 20.00
WRIGRCH Cole Hamels 12.00 30.00
WRIGRFJ Fergie Jenkins 8.00 20.00
WRIGRGG Goose Gossage 8.00 20.00
WRIGRGM Maddux Microphone 12.00 30.00
WRIGRGM Maddux Pitching 12.00 30.00
WRIGRJA Jake Arrieta S2 12.00 30.00
WRIGRJH Jason Heyward S2 8.00 20.00
WRIGRJL Jon Lester S2 8.00 20.00
WRIGRJS Jorge Soler S2 15.00 40.00
WRIGRKB Bryant Face left 20.00 50.00
WRIGRKB Bryant Celebrate 20.00 50.00
WRIGRKS Kyle Schwarber S2 12.00 30.00
WRIGRMG Mark Grace 10.00 25.00
Facing right
WRIGRMG Mark Grace S2 10.00 25.00
Facing left
WRIGRRP Rafael Palmeiro 8.00 20.00
Running
WRIGRRP Rafael Palmeiro S2 8.00 20.00
Batting
WRIGRRS Sandberg Whte jsy 15.00 40.00
WRIGRRSA Sandberg Blue jsy 15.00 40.00
WRIGRRSN Ron Santo S2 20.00 50.00
WRIGRSC Starlin Castro 6.00 15.00
WRIGRTG Tom Glavine S2 8.00 20.00
WRIGRTMO Greg Maddux 6.00 15.00
Fergie Jekins
Take Me Out to the Ballgame Tradition Begins

2016 Topps Amazing Milestones

COMPLETE SET (10) 10.00 25.00
RANDOM INSERTS IN PACKS
AM01 Warren Spahn .50 1.25
AM02 Alex Rodriguez .75 2.00
AM03 Carl Yastrzemski 1.00 2.50
AM04 Ted Williams 1.25 3.00
AM05 Nolan Ryan 2.00 5.00
AM06 Hank Aaron 1.25 3.00
AM07 Babe Ruth 1.50 4.00
AM08 Greg Maddux .75 2.00
AM09 Rickey Henderson .60 1.50
AM10 Willie Mays 1.25 3.00

2016 Topps Back to Back

COMPLETE SET (15) 3.00 8.00
STATED ODDS 1:8 HOBBY; 1:2 JUMBO
B2B1 R.Braun/P.Fielder .30 .75
B2B2 K.Bryant/A.Rizzo .60 1.50
B2B3 B.Posey/B.Belt .50 1.25
B2B4 Griffey Jr./Martinez .75 2.00
B2B5 B.Phillips/J.Votto .40 1.00
B2B6 J.Pederson/A.Gonzalez .30 .75
B2B7 J.Bagwell/C.Biggio .30 .75
B2B8 P.Molitor/R.Yount .40 1.00
B2B9 Schoendienst/.Musial .60 1.50
B2B10 Martinez/Cabrera .40 1.00
B2B11 Pujols/Trout 2.00 5.00
B2B12 Ruth/Gehrig 1.00 2.50
B2B13 Doerr/Williams .75 2.00
B2B14 Murray/Ripken Jr. 1.25 3.00
B2B15 Tulowitzki/Donaldson .40 1.00

2016 Topps Back to Back Autographs

STATED ODDS 1:60,115 HOBBY; 1:12,233 JUMBO
STATED PRINT RUN 25 SER.#'d SETS
EXCHANGE DEADLINE 1/31/2018
B2BAFB R.Braun/P.Fielder
B2BAMG Martinez/Griffey Jr. 100.00 250.00
B2BAPB B.Belt/B.Posey 60.00 150.00
B2BARB K.Bryant/A.Rizzo
B2BAVP J.Votto/B.Phillips 50.00 120.00

2016 Topps Back to Back Relics

STATED ODDS 1:15,324 HOBBY; 1:3059 JUMBO
STATED PRINT RUN 99 SER.#'d SETS
B2BRFB P.Fielder/R.Braun 5.00 12.00
B2BRMG E.Martinez/K.Griffey Jr. 15.00 40.00
B2BRPB B.Posey/B.Belt 8.00 20.00
B2BRRB A.Rizzo/K.Bryant 30.00 80.00
B2BRVP J.Votto/B.Phillips 6.00 15.00

2016 Topps Berger's Best

COMPLETE SET (65) 25.00 60.00
STATED ODDS 1:4 HOBBY
BB1 Willie Mays .75 2.00
BB2 Satchel Paige .40 1.00
BB3 Henry Aaron .75 2.00
BB4 Sandy Koufax .75 2.00
BB5 Jackie Robinson .40 1.00
BB6 Ted Williams .75 2.00
BB7 Roger Maris .40 1.00
BB8 Roberto Clemente 1.00 2.50
BB9 Willie McCovey .30 .75
BB10 Bill Mazeroski .30 .75
BB11 Roger Maris .40 1.00
BB12 Brooks Robinson .30 .75
BB13 Whitey Ford .30 .75
BB14 Hank Aaron .75 2.00
BB15 Jim Palmer .30 .75
BB16 Steve Carlton .30 .75
BB17 Rod Carew .30 .75
BB18 Reggie Jackson .30 .75
BB19 Johnny Bench .40 1.00
BB20 Nolan Ryan 1.25 3.00
BB21 Tom Seaver .30 .75
BB22 Joe Morgan .30 .75
BB23 Dave Winfield .30 .75
BB24 George Brett .75 2.00
BB25 Dennis Eckersley .30 .75
BB26 Robin Yount .40 1.00
BB27 Eddie Murray .30 .75
BB28 Ozzie Smith .50 1.25
BB29 Rickey Henderson .40 1.00
BB30 Harold Baines .30 .75
BB31 Cal Ripken Jr. 1.25 3.00
BB32 Tony Gwynn .40 1.00
BB33 Don Mattingly .75 2.00
BB34 Dwight Gooden .25 .60
BB35 Roger Clemens .50 1.25
BB36 Bo Jackson .40 1.00
BB37 Wade Boggs .30 .75
BB38 Ken Griffey Jr. .75 2.00
BB39 George Brett .75 2.00
BB40 Frank Thomas .40 1.00
BB41 Cal Ripken Jr. 1.25 3.00
BB42 Randy Johnson .40 1.00
BB43 Mike Piazza .40 1.00
BB44 Barry Larkin .30 .75
BB45 John Smoltz .40 1.00
BB46 Livan Hernandez .25 .60
BB47 Alex Rodriguez .50 1.25
BB48 Josh Hamilton .30 .75
BB49 Miguel Cabrera .40 1.00
BB50 Albert Pujols .50 1.25
BB51 Joe Mauer .30 .75
BB52 Robinson Cano .30 .75
BB53 Yadier Molina .40 1.00
BB54 Justin Verlander .40 1.00
BB55 Hanley Ramirez .30 .75
BB56 Daisuke Matsuzaka .30 .75
BB57 Clayton Kershaw .75 2.00
BB58 David Price .30 .75
BB59 Stephen Strasburg .40 1.00
BB60 Mike Trout 2.00 5.00
BB61 Bryce Harper .60 1.50
BB62 Mike Trout 2.00 5.00
BB63 Masahiro Tanaka .30 .75
BB64 Kris Bryant .50 1.25
BB65 Buster Posey .50 1.25

2016 Topps Berger's Best Series 2

COMPLETE SET (65) 25.00 60.00
STATED ODDS 1:4 HOBBY
BB21952 Eddie Mathews .40 1.00
BB21953 Willie Mays .75 2.00
BB21954 Al Kaline .40 1.00
BB21955 Roberto Clemente 1.00 2.50
BB21956 Ted Williams .75 2.00
BB21957 Hank Aaron .75 2.00
BB21958 Roberto Clemente 1.00 2.50
BB21959 Sandy Koufax .75 2.00
BB21960 Carl Yastrzemski .60 1.50
BB21961 Roger Maris .30 .75
BB21962 Lou Brock .30 .75
BB21963 Stan Musial .60 1.50
BB21964 H.Aaron/W.Mays .75 2.00
BB21965 Willie Mays .75 2.00
BB21966 Frank Robinson .30 .75
BB21967 Tony Perez .30 .75
BB21968 Tom Seaver .30 .75
BB21969 Johnny Bench .40 1.00
BB21970 Reggie Jackson .30 .75
BB21971 Bert Blyleven .30 .75
BB21972 Hank Aaron .75 2.00
BB21973 Rich Gossage .30 .75
BB21974 Hank Aaron .75 2.00
BB21975 Robin Yount .40 1.00
BB21976 Nolan Ryan 1.25 3.00
BB21977 Bruce Sutter .30 .75
BB21978 Brooks Robinson .30 .75
BB21979 Rollie Fingers .30 .75
BB21980 Ozzie Smith .50 1.25
BB21981 Fernando Valenzuela .25 .60
BB21982 Reggie Jackson .30 .75
BB21983 Wade Boggs .30 .75
BB21984 Dwight Gooden .25 .60
BB21985 Roger Clemens .50 1.25
BB21986 Cal Ripken Jr. 1.25 3.00
BB21987 Jose Canseco .30 .75
BB21988 Tom Glavine .30 .75
BB21989 Randy Johnson .40 1.00
BB21990 Bernie Williams .30 .75
BB21991 Nolan Ryan 1.25 3.00
BB21992 Ken Griffey Jr. .75 2.00
BB21993 Mike Piazza .40 1.00
BB21994 Ryne Sandberg .75 2.00
BB21995 Nomar Garciaparra .30 .75
BB21996 Cal Ripken Jr. 1.25 3.00
BB21997 Ken Griffey Jr. .75 2.00
BB21998 Greg Maddux .50 1.25
BB21999 Mark McGwire .60 1.50
BB22000 Adrian Gonzalez .30 .75
BB22001 Ichiro Suzuki .50 1.25
BB22002 Jose Bautista .30 .75
BB22003 Albert Pujols .50 1.25
BB22004 David Ortiz .40 1.00
BB22005 Andrew McCutchen .40 1.00
BB22006 Ryan Howard .30 .75
BB22007 Alex Gordon .30 .75
BB22008 Evan Longoria .30 .75
BB22009 Tim Lincecum .30 .75
BB22010 Buster Posey .50 1.25
BB22011 Eric Hosmer .30 .75
BB22012 Yu Darvish .40 1.00
BB22013 Yasiel Puig .40 1.00
BB22014 Jose Abreu .40 1.00
BB22015 Carlos Correa .40 1.00
BB22016 Kyle Schwarber .75 2.00

2016 Topps Berger's Best Autographs

SER.1 ODDS 1:30,058 HOBBY; 1:5942 JUMBO
SER.2 ODDS 1:16,848 HOBBY
STATED PRINT RUN 25 SER.#'d SETS
SER.1 EXCH DEADLINE 1/31/2018
BBABJ Bo Jackson 40.00 100.00
BBADM Don Mattingly 75.00 200.00
BBAHR Hanley Ramirez 50.00 120.00
BBAJS John Smoltz 60.00 150.00
BBAKB Kris Bryant 60.00 150.00
BBAOS Ozzie Smith 30.00 80.00
BBARY Robin Yount
BBASC Steve Carlton 30.00 80.00
BBARCN Robinson Cano
BBARCR Rod Carew 20.00 50.00
BB2A1957 Hank Aaron
BB2A1963 Stan Musial
BB2A1966 Frank Robinson 30.00 80.00
BB2A1981 Fernando Valenzuela
BB2A1990 Bernie Williams 15.00 40.00
BB2A1994 Ryne Sandberg
BB2A1995 Nomar Garciaparra 50.00 120.00
BB2A2008 Evan Longoria 15.00 40.00
BB2A2014 Jose Abreu 12.00 30.00
BB2A2015 Carlos Correa 150.00 250.00

2016 Topps Berger's Best Relics

SER.1 ODDS 1:3794 HOBBY; 1:759 JUMBO
SER.2 ODDS 1:2142 HOBBY
STATED PRINT RUN 99 SER.#'d SETS
BBRAP Albert Pujols 12.00 30.00
BBRBH Bryce Harper 8.00 20.00
BBRBP Buster Posey 12.00 30.00
BBRCK Clayton Kershaw 12.00 30.00
BBRDE Dennis Eckersley 10.00 25.00
BBRDP David Price 4.00 10.00
BBREM Eddie Murray 10.00 25.00
BBRHR Hanley Ramirez 4.00 10.00
BBRJM Joe Mauer 8.00 20.00
BBRJV Justin Verlander 10.00 25.00
BBRKB Kris Bryant 20.00 50.00
BBRKG Ken Griffey Jr. 12.00 30.00
BBRMC Miguel Cabrera 12.00 30.00
BBRMP Mike Piazza 5.00 12.00
BBRSC Steve Carlton 12.00 30.00
BBRSS Stephen Strasburg 5.00 12.00
BBRTG Tony Gwynn 12.00 30.00
BBRYM Yadier Molina 20.00 50.00
BBRRCA Robinson Cano 4.00 10.00
BBRRCL Roger Clemens 12.00 30.00
BB2R1957 Hank Aaron 12.00 30.00
BB2R1960 Carl Yastrzemski 10.00 25.00
BB2R1966 Frank Robinson 10.00 25.00
BB2R1975 Robin Yount 8.00 20.00
BB2R1981 Fernando Valenzuela 8.00 20.00
BB2R1983 Wade Boggs 10.00 25.00
BB2R1989 Randy Johnson 5.00 12.00
BB2R1990 Bernie Williams 4.00 10.00
BB2R1991 Nolan Ryan 25.00 60.00
BB2R1994 Ryne Sandberg 10.00 25.00
BB2R1995 Nomar Garciaparra 6.00 15.00
BB2R1997 Ken Griffey Jr. 10.00 25.00
BB2R1999 Mark McGwire 8.00 20.00
BB2R2003 Albert Pujols 6.00 15.00
BB2R2004 David Ortiz 10.00 25.00
BB2R2005 Andrew McCutchen 10.00 25.00
BB2R2008 Evan Longoria
BB2R2010 Buster Posey 6.00 15.00
BB2R2012 Yu Darvish 5.00 12.00
BB2R2014 Jose Abreu 8.00 20.00

2016 Topps Bunt Player Code Cards

SER.1 ODDS 1:3740 HOBBY; 1:519 JUMBO
SER.2 ODDS 1:8152 HOBBY
STATED PRINT RUN 25 SER.#'d SETS
AM Andrew McCutchen 50.00 120.00
MC Miguel Cabrera 60.00 150.00
FH Felix Hernandez 40.00 100.00
TF Todd Frazier 60.00 150.00
MT Mike Trout 75.00 200.00
KB Kris Bryant 75.00 200.00
AG Alex Gordon S2
CK Clayton Kershaw
MB Madison Bumgarner 60.00 150.00
AP A.J. Pollock S2 60.00 150.00
DO David Ortiz 60.00 150.00
AR Alex Rodriguez S2 60.00 150.00
AR Anthony Rizzo 60.00 150.00
KS Kyle Schwarber
CS Corey Seager 60.00 150.00
JD Josh Donaldson 40.00 100.00
TT Troy Tulowitzki 75.00 200.00
DG Dee Gordon S2 25.00 60.00
IS Ichiro Suzuki
DW David Wright 60.00 150.00
CC Carlos Correa 150.00 300.00
EH Eric Hosmer S2 60.00 150.00
EL Evan Longoria S2 60.00 150.00
FF Freddie Freeman S2
DP Dustin Pedroia 50.00 120.00
GC Gerrit Cole S2 75.00 200.00
GS Giancarlo Stanton S2 50.00 120.00
AG Adrian Gonzalez
BH Bryce Harper
JA Jake Arrieta S2
HP Hunter Pence
JF Jose Fernandez S2 60.00 150.00
JP Joe Panik S2 50.00 120.00
JV Joey Votto S2
MH Matt Harvey 75.00 200.00
BP Buster Posey
LS Luis Severino S2
AP Albert Pujols 60.00 150.00
YM Yadier Molina
MC Miguel Cabrera S2 150.00 300.00
MM Manny Machado S2 125.00 300.00
MSA Miguel Sano S2 50.00 120.00
MSC Max Scherzer S2
NA Nolan Arenado S2 50.00 120.00
NS Noah Syndergaard S2 125.00 250.00
PF Prince Fielder S2 50.00 120.00
PG Paul Goldschmidt S2
RB Ryan Braun S2 100.00 250.00
SG Sonny Gray S2
XB Xander Bogaerts S2 125.00 250.00

2016 Topps Celebrating 65 Years

COMPLETE SET (10) 20.00 50.00
INSERTED IN RETAIL PACKS
651952 Jackie Robinson .60 1.50
651953 Satchel Paige .60 1.50
651954 Ted Williams 1.25 3.00
651955 Willie Mays 1.25 3.00
651973 Roberto Clemente 1.50 4.00
651977 Reggie Jackson .50 1.25
651980 Rickey Henderson .60 1.50
651989 Ken Griffey Jr. 1.25 3.00
652011 Mike Trout 3.00 8.00
652012 Matt Harvey .50 1.25

2016 Topps Changing of the Guard

COMPLETE SET (10) 20.00 50.00
INSERTED IN RETAIL PACKS
CTG1 Mike Trout 3.00 8.00
CTG2 Kris Bryant .75 2.00
CTG3 Bryce Harper 1.00 2.50
CTG4 Buster Posey .75 2.00
CTG5 Carlos Correa .60 1.50
CTG6 Kyle Schwarber 1.25 3.00
CTG7 Giancarlo Stanton .60 1.50
CTG8 Manny Machado .60 1.50
CTG9 Madison Bumgarner .50 1.25
CTG10 Jose Fernandez .60 1.50

2016 Topps Chasing 3000

COMMON CARD .60 1.50
STATED ODDS 1:9 HOBBY

2016 Topps Chasing 3000 Relics

COMMON CARD 25.00 60.00
STATED ODDS 1:14,040 HOBBY
STATED PRINT RUN 10 SER.#'d SETS

2016 Topps First Pitch

COMPLETE SET (40) 12.00 30.00
SER.1 ODDS 1:8 HOBBY; 1:2 JUMBO
SER.2 ODDS 1:8 HOBBY
FP1 Abby Wambach .75 2.00
FP1 Tim McGraw S2 .75 2.00
FP2 Gabrielle Giffords .75 2.00
FP2 Jimmy Kimmel S2 .75 2.00
FP3 Don Cherry .75 2.00
FP3 Rosie Rios S2 .75 2.00
FP4 Mo'ne Davis .75 2.00
FP4 Billy Joe Armstrong S2 .75 2.00
FP5 Evelyn Jones .75 2.00
FP5 Nina Agdal S2 .75 2.00
FP6 Bree Morse .75 2.00
FP6 Jeff Tweedy S2 .75 2.00
FP7 Jordan Spieth .75 2.00
FP7 Jim Harbaugh S2 3.00 8.00
FP8 Kristaps Porzingis .75 2.00
FP8 Jim Breuer S2 .75 2.00
FP9 Victor Espinoza .75 2.00
FP9 Spencer Stone S2 .75 2.00
FP10 Johnny Knoxville .75 2.00
FP10 Kyle Larson S2 .75 2.00
FP11 James Taylor .75 2.00
FP11 Miguel Cotto S2 .75 2.00
FP12 Bud Selig .75 2.00
FP12 Tom Watson S2 .75 2.00
FP13 LeVar Burton .75 2.00
FP13 Edward Burns S2 .75 2.00
FP14 Hayley Atwell .75 2.00
FP14 Geoff Britten S2 .75 2.00
FP15 Bill Withers .75 2.00
FP15 Lea Thompson S2 .75 2.00
FP16 Steve Aoki .75 2.00
FP16 Jim Caviezel S2 .75 2.00
FP17 Carrie Brownstein .75 2.00
FP17 George H. W. Bush S2 .75 2.00
FP18 Rebekah Gregory .75 2.00
FP18 J.K. Simmons S2 .75 2.00
FP19 Tony Hawk .75 2.00
FP19 Kendrick Lamar S2 .75 2.00
FP20 Iron E Singleton .75 2.00
FP20 David Hearn S2 .75 2.00

2016 Topps Futures Game Pins

STATED ODDS 1:1620 HOBBY
FGPAM Andrew McCutchen 3.00 8.00
FGPBH Bryce Harper 5.00 12.00
FGPCC Carlos Correa 3.00 8.00
FGPCK Clayton Kershaw 6.00 15.00
FGPDW David Wright 2.50 6.00
FGPFH Felix Hernandez 2.50 6.00
FGPGS Giancarlo Stanton 2.50 6.00
FGPJA Jose Altuve 2.50 6.00
FGPJM Joe Mauer 2.50 6.00
FGPKB Kris Bryant 4.00 10.00
FGPKS Kyle Schwarber 6.00 15.00
FGPMB Madison Bumgarner 2.50 6.00
FGPMC Michael Conforto 2.50 6.00
FGPMT Mike Trout 15.00 40.00
FGPNS Noah Syndergaard 2.50 6.00

2016 Topps Futures Game Pins Autographs

STATED ODDS 1:9360 HOBBY
STATED PRINT RUN 25 SER.#'d SETS
FGPABH Bryce Harper
FGPACC Carlos Correa
FGPACK Clayton Kershaw 75.00 150.00
FGPADW David Wright 30.00 80.00
FGPAJA Jose Altuve 40.00 100.00
FGPAKB Kris Bryant 250.00 350.00
FGPAKS Kyle Schwarber 30.00 80.00
FGPAMT Mike Trout 200.00 300.00
FGPANS Noah Syndergaard 50.00 120.00

2016 Topps Hallowed Highlights

COMPLETE SET (15) 4.00 10.00
STATED ODDS 1:8 HOBBY
HH1 Stan Musial .60 1.50
HH2 Ozzie Smith .50 1.25
HH3 John Smoltz .40 1.00
HH4 Frank Thomas .40 1.00
HH5 Sandy Koufax .75 2.00
HH6 Mark McGwire .60 1.50
HH7 Willie Mays .75 2.00
HH8 Cal Ripken Jr. 1.25 3.00
HH9 Nolan Ryan 1.25 3.00
HH10 Ken Griffey Jr. .75 2.00
HH11 Don Mattingly .75 2.00
HH12 Tony Gwynn .40 1.00
HH13 Robin Yount .40 1.00
HH14 Wade Boggs .30 .75
HH15 Greg Maddux .50 1.25

2016 Topps Hallowed Highlights Relics

STATED ODDS 1:33,696 HOBBY
STATED PRINT RUN 25 SER.#'d SETS
HHKG Ken Griffey Jr.
HHMM Mark McGwire
HHNR Nolan Ryan 40.00 100.00
HHTG Tony Gwynn 25.00 60.00
HHWM Willie Mays

2016 Topps Laser

SER.1 ODDS 1:736 HOBBY; 1:153 JUMBO
SER.2 ODDS 1:454 HOBBY
TL1 Mike Trout 20.00 50.00
TL2 Paul Goldschmidt 8.00 20.00
TL3 Kyle Schwarber 20.00 50.00
TL4 David Ortiz 8.00 20.00
TL5 Hanley Ramirez 6.00 15.00
TL6 Kris Bryant 10.00 25.00
TL7 Jose Abreu 8.00 20.00
TL8 Ichiro Suzuki 12.00 30.00
TL9 Clayton Kershaw 15.00 40.00
TL10 Ryan Braun 6.00 15.00
TL11 Matt Harvey 6.00 15.00
TL12 Buster Posey 12.00 30.00
TL13 Robinson Cano 6.00 15.00
TL14 Prince Fielder 6.00 15.00
TL15 Jason Heyward 6.00 15.00
TL16 Bryce Harper 25.00 60.00
TL17 Miguel Cabrera 12.00 30.00
TL18 Eric Hosmer 6.00 15.00
TL19 Yasiel Puig 12.00 30.00
TL20 Giancarlo Stanton 8.00 20.00
TL21 Masahiro Tanaka 6.00 15.00
TL22 Andrew McCutchen 8.00 20.00
TL23 Madison Bumgarner 6.00 15.00
TL24 Yadier Molina 15.00 40.00
TL25 Jose Bautista 6.00 15.00
TLAG Adrian Gonzalez S2 6.00 15.00
TLAP Albert Pujols S2 10.00 25.00
TLARI Anthony Rizzo S2 15.00 40.00
TLARO Alex Rodriguez S2 10.00 25.00
TLCC Carlos Correa S2 10.00 25.00
TLCD Chris Davis S2 5.00 12.00
TLCS Corey Seager S2 40.00 100.00
TLDK Dallas Keuchel S2 6.00 15.00
TLDP Dustin Pedroia S2 8.00 20.00
TLDW David Wright S2 6.00 15.00
TLFF Freddie Freeman S2 12.00 30.00
TLFH Felix Hernandez S2 6.00 15.00
TLHOL Hector Olivera S2 6.00 15.00
TLHOW Henry Owens S2 6.00 15.00
TLHP Hunter Pence S2 6.00 15.00
TLJA Jake Arrieta S2 6.00 15.00
TLJDE Jacob deGrom S2 8.00 20.00
TLJDO Josh Donaldson S2 6.00 15.00
TLLC Lorenzo Cain S2 5.00 12.00
TLMSA Miguel Sano S2 8.00 20.00
TLMSC Max Scherzer S2 8.00 20.00
TLNS Noah Syndergaard S2 8.00 20.00
TLTF Todd Frazier S2 8.00 20.00
TLTT Trea Turner S2 15.00 40.00
TLYD Yu Darvish S2 8.00 20.00

2016 Topps Laser Autographs

SER.1 ODDS 1:7515 HOBBY; 1:1497 JUMBO
SER.2 ODDS 1:4680 HOBBY
STATED PRINT RUN 25 SER.#'d SETS
SER.1 EXCH DEADLINE 1/31/2018
TLAAG Adrian Gonzalez S2 25.00 60.00
TLACC Carlos Correa S2 100.00 200.00
TLACS Corey Seager S2 150.00 400.00
TLADK Dallas Keuchel S2 25.00 60.00
TLADO David Ortiz 125.00 250.00

TLADP Dustin Pedroia S2 60.00 150.00
TLADW David Wright S2 25.00 60.00
TLAFF Freddie Freeman S2 30.00 80.00
TLAHOL Hector Olivera S2 25.00 60.00
TLAHR Hanley Ramirez 25.00 60.00
TLAIC Ichiro Suzuki 200.00 400.00
TLAJA Jose Abreu 30.00 80.00
TLAKB Kris Bryant 75.00 200.00
TLAKS Kyle Schwarber
TLAMH Matt Harvey EXCH 60.00 150.00
TLAMT Mike Trout 175.00 350.00
TLANS Noah Syndergaard S2 50.00 120.00
TLAPG Paul Goldschmidt 30.00 80.00
TLARB Ryan Braun 25.00 60.00

2016 Topps Laser Relics

SER.1 ODDS 1:1271 HOBBY; 1:255 JUMBO
SER.2 ODDS 1:798 HOBBY
STATED PRINT RUN 99 SER.#'d SETS
TLRAG Adrian Gonzalez S2 8.00 20.00
TLRAM Andrew McCutchen 20.00 50.00
TLRBP Buster Posey 12.00 30.00
TLRCK Clayton Kershaw 20.00 50.00
TLRCS Corey Seager S2 50.00 125.00
TLRDK Dallas Keuchel S2 8.00 20.00
TLRDO David Ortiz 20.00 50.00
TLRDP Dustin Pedroia S2 20.00 50.00
TLRDW David Wright S2 12.00 30.00
TLRFF Freddie Freeman S2 6.00 15.00
TLRHP Hunter Pence S2 8.00 20.00
TLRJA Jose Abreu 10.00 25.00
TLRKB Kris Bryant 50.00 120.00
TLRKS Kyle Schwarber 10.00 25.00
TLRLC Lorenzo Cain S2 6.00 15.00
TLRMB Madison Bumgarner 8.00 20.00
TLRMC Miguel Cabrera 20.00 50.00
TLRMH Matt Harvey 30.00 80.00
TLRMT Mike Trout 50.00 125.00
TLRPF Prince Fielder 8.00 20.00
TLRYD Yu Darvish S2 10.00 25.00
TLRYM Yadier Molina 25.00 60.00
TLRHOL Hector Olivera S2 8.00 20.00
TLRHOW Henry Owens S2 8.00 20.00
TLRJDE Jacob deGrom S2 15.00 40.00
TLRJDO Josh Donaldson S2 10.00 25.00
TLRMSA Miguel Sano S2 10.00 25.00
TLRMTA Masahiro Tanaka 8.00 20.00
TLRNSY Noah Syndergaard S2 20.00 50.00

2016 Topps MLB Debut Bronze

RANDOM INSERTS IN PACKS
*SILVER: .5X TO 1.2X BASIC
*GOLD: .6X TO 1.5X BASIC
MLBD1 Hank Aaron .75 2.00
MLBD2 Ryan Braun .30 .75
MLBD3 Kris Bryant .50 1.25
MLBD4 Miguel Cabrera .40 1.00
MLBD5 Robinson Cano .30 .75
MLBD6 Starlin Castro .25 .60
MLBD7 Yoenis Cespedes .40 1.00
MLBD8 Nelson Cruz .40 1.00
MLBD9 Yu Darvish .40 1.00
MLBD10 Josh Donaldson .30 .75
MLBD11 Jacoby Ellsbury .30 .75
MLBD12 Paul Goldschmidt .40 1.00
MLBD13 Adrian Gonzalez .30 .75
MLBD14 Dwight Gooden .25 .60
MLBD15 Matt Harvey .30 .75
MLBD16 Jason Heyward .30 .75
MLBD17 Ryan Howard .30 .75
MLBD18 Sandy Koufax .75 2.00
MLBD19 Evan Longoria .30 .75
MLBD20 Victor Martinez .30 .75
MLBD21 Joe Mauer .30 .75
MLBD22 Willie Mays .75 2.00
MLBD23 Andrew McCutchen .40 1.00
MLBD24 Satchel Paige .40 1.00
MLBD25 Mike Piazza .40 1.00
MLBD26 Buster Posey .50 1.25
MLBD27 Albert Pujols .50 1.25
MLBD28 Cal Ripken Jr. 1.25 3.00
MLBD29 Brooks Robinson .30 .75
MLBD30 Jackie Robinson .40 1.00
MLBD31 Alex Rodriguez .50 1.25
MLBD32 Babe Ruth 1.00 2.50
MLBD33 Nolan Ryan 1.25 3.00
MLBD34 Giancarlo Stanton .40 1.00
MLBD35 Mike Trout 2.00 5.00
MLBD36 Troy Tulowitzki .40 1.00
MLBD37 Justin Upton .30 .75
MLBD38 Fernando Valenzuela .25 .60
MLBD39 Jayson Werth .30 .75
MLBD40 Bernie Williams .30 .75
MLBD2-1 Carl Yastrzemski .60 1.50
MLBD2-2 Johnny Bench .40 1.00
MLBD2-3 Wade Boggs .30 .75
MLBD2-4 George Brett .75 2.00
MLBD2-5 Tony Gwynn .40 1.00
MLBD2-6 Ken Griffey Jr. .75 2.00
MLBD2-7 Tom Seaver .30 .75
MLBD2-8 Paul Molitor .40 1.00
MLBD2-9 Robin Yount .40 1.00
MLBD2-10 Warren Spahn .30 .75
MLBD2-11 Duke Snider .30 .75
MLBD2-12 Bill Mazeroski .30 .75
MLBD2-13 Madison Bumgarner .30 .75
MLBD2-14 Clayton Kershaw .75 2.00
MLBD2-15 David Ortiz .40 1.00
MLBD2-16 Anthony Rizzo .60 1.50
MLBD2-17 Dustin Pedroia .40 1.00
MLBD2-18 Felix Hernandez .30 .75
MLBD2-19 David Wright .30 .75
MLBD2-20 Jake Arrieta .30 .75
MLBD2-21 Carlos Correa .40 1.00
MLBD2-22 Rob Refsnyder .30 .75
MLBD2-23 Don Mattingly .75 2.00
MLBD2-24 David Price .30 .75
MLBD2-25 Jose Abreu .40 1.00
MLBD2-26 Ichiro Suzuki .50 1.25
MLBD2-27 Hanley Ramirez .30 .75
MLBD2-28 Mark McGwire .60 1.50
MLBD2-29 Rod Carew .30 .75
MLBD2-30 Jeff Bagwell .30 .75
MLBD2-31 Alex Gordon .30 .75
MLBD2-32 Mike Moustakas .30 .75
MLBD2-33 Noah Syndergaard .30 .75
MLBD2-34 Manny Machado .40 1.00
MLBD2-35 Carlos Gonzalez .30 .75
MLBD2-36 Zack Greinke .30 .75
MLBD2-37 Joey Votto .40 1.00
MLBD2-38 Starling Marte .30 .75
MLBD2-39 Sonny Gray .30 .75
MLBD2-40 Tom Glavine .30 .75

2016 Topps MLB Debut Medallion

RANDOM INSERTS IN PACKS
MDMAG Adrian Gonzalez 1.50 4.00
MDMAM Andrew McCutchen 2.00 5.00
MDMAP Albert Pujols 2.50 6.00
MDMAR Alex Rodriguez 2.50 6.00
MDMBP Buster Posey 2.50 6.00
MDMBR Brooks Robinson 1.50 4.00
MDMBW Bernie Williams 1.50 4.00
MDMCR Cal Ripken Jr. 6.00 15.00
MDMDG Dwight Gooden 1.25 3.00
MDMEL Evan Longoria 1.50 4.00
MDMFV Fernando Valenzuela 1.25 3.00
MDMGS Giancarlo Stanton 2.00 5.00
MDMHA Hank Aaron 4.00 10.00
MDMJD Josh Donaldson 1.50 4.00
MDMJE Jacoby Ellsbury 1.50 4.00
MDMJH Jason Heyward 1.50 4.00
MDMJM Joe Mauer 1.50 4.00
MDMJR Jackie Robinson 2.00 5.00
MDMJU Justin Upton 1.50 4.00
MDMJW Jayson Werth 1.50 4.00
MDMKB Kris Bryant 2.50 6.00
MDMMC Miguel Cabrera 2.00 5.00
MDMMH Matt Harvey 1.50 4.00
MDMMP Mike Piazza 2.00 5.00
MDMMT Mike Trout 10.00 25.00
MDMNC Nelson Cruz 2.00 5.00
MDMNR Nolan Ryan 6.00 15.00
MDMPG Paul Goldschmidt 2.00 5.00
MDMRB Ryan Braun 1.50 4.00
MDMRC Robinson Cano 1.50 4.00
MDMRH Ryan Howard 1.50 4.00
MDMSC Starlin Castro 1.25 3.00
MDMSK Sandy Koufax 4.00 10.00
MDMSP Satchel Paige 2.00 5.00
MDMTT Troy Tulowitzki 2.00 5.00
MDMVM Victor Martinez 1.50 4.00
MDMWM Willie Mays 4.00 10.00
MDMYC Yoenis Cespedes 2.00 5.00
MDMYD Yu Darvish 2.00 5.00
MDMBRU Babe Ruth 5.00 12.00
MLBDM21 Carl Yastrzemski S2 3.00 8.00
MLBDM22 Johnny Bench S2 2.00 5.00
MLBDM23 Wade Boggs S2 1.50 4.00
MLBDM24 George Brett S2 4.00 10.00
MLBDM25 Tony Gwynn S2 2.00 5.00
MLBDM26 Ken Griffey Jr. S2 4.00 10.00
MLBDM27 Tom Seaver S2 1.50 4.00
MLBDM28 Paul Molitor S2 2.00 5.00
MLBDM29 Robin Yount S2 2.00 5.00
MLBDM210 Warren Spahn S2 1.50 4.00
MLBDM211 Duke Snider S2 1.50 4.00
MLBDM212 Bill Mazeroski S2 1.50 4.00
MLBDM213 Madison Bumgarner S2 1.50 4.00
MLBDM214 Clayton Kershaw S2 4.00 10.00
MLBDM215 David Ortiz S2 2.00 5.00
MLBDM216 Anthony Rizzo S2 3.00 8.00
MLBDM217 Dustin Pedroia S2 2.00 5.00
MLBDM218 Felix Hernandez S2 1.50 4.00
MLBDM219 David Wright S2 1.50 4.00
MLBDM220 Jake Arrieta S2 1.50 4.00
MLBDM221 Carlos Correa S2 2.00 5.00
MLBDM222 Rob Refsnyder S2 1.50 4.00
MLBDM223 Don Mattingly S2 4.00 10.00
MLBDM224 David Price S2 1.50 4.00
MLBDM225 Jose Abreu S2 2.00 5.00
MLBDM226 Ichiro Suzuki S2 2.50 6.00
MLBDM227 Hanley Ramirez S2 1.50 4.00
MLBDM228 Mark McGwire S2 3.00 8.00
MLBDM229 Rod Carew S2 1.50 4.00
MLBDM230 Jeff Bagwell S2 1.50 4.00
MLBDM231 Alex Gordon S2 1.50 4.00
MLBDM232 Mike Moustakas S2 1.50 4.00
MLBDM233 Noah Syndergaard S2 1.50 4.00
MLBD2M34 Manny Machado S2 2.00 5.00
MLBDM235 Carlos Gonzalez S2 1.50 4.00
MLBDM236 Zack Greinke S2 1.50 4.00
MLBDM237 Joey Votto S2 2.00 5.00
MLBDM238 Starling Marte S2 1.50 4.00
MLBDM239 Sonny Gray S2 1.50 4.00
MLBDM240 Tom Glavine S2 1.50 4.00

2016 Topps MLB Debut Relics

RANDOM INSERTS IN PACKS
STATED PRINT RUN 99 SER.#'d SETS
MDRAG Adrian Gonzalez
MDRAM Andrew McCutchen 6.00 15.00
MDRAP Albert Pujols 5.00 12.00
MDREL Evan Longoria
MDRJD Josh Donaldson 10.00 25.00
MDRJE Jacoby Ellsbury 5.00 12.00
MDRJH Jason Heyward 8.00 20.00
MDRJM Joe Mauer 8.00 20.00
MDRKB Kris Bryant 30.00 80.00
MDRMC Miguel Cabrera
MDRMH Matt Harvey
MDRNC Nelson Cruz 6.00 15.00
MDRPG Paul Goldschmidt 15.00 40.00
MDRRB Ryan Braun 5.00 12.00
MDRRC Robinson Cano 5.00 12.00
MDRRH Ryan Howard 5.00 12.00
MDRSC Starlin Castro 4.00 10.00
MDRVM Victor Martinez 5.00 12.00
MDRYC Yoenis Cespedes 6.00 15.00
MDRYD Yu Darvish 6.00 15.00
MLBD2RAG Alex Gordon S2 5.00 12.00
MLBD2RAR Anthony Rizzo S2 10.00 25.00
MLBD2RCG Carlos Gonzalez S2 5.00 12.00
MLBD2RCK Clayton Kershaw S2 12.00 30.00
MLBD2RDO David Ortiz S2 20.00 50.00
MLBD2RDPE Dustin Pedroia S2 15.00 40.00
MLBD2RDPR David Price S2 15.00 40.00
MLBD2RDW David Wright S2 5.00 12.00
MLBD2RFH Felix Hernandez S2
MLBD2RHR Hanley Ramirez S2
MLBD2RJA Jose Abreu S2
MLBD2RJV Joey Votto S2
MLBD2RMMA Manny Machado S2 12.00 30.00
MLBD2RMMO Mike Moustakas S2 5.00 12.00
MLBD2RNS Noah Syndergaard S2 5.00 12.00
MLBD2RPM Paul Molitor S2 15.00 40.00
MLBD2RRR Rob Refsnyder S2 5.00 12.00
MLBD2RSM Starling Marte S2 12.00 30.00
MLBD2RTGW Tony Gwynn S2 6.00 15.00
MLBD2RZG Zack Greinke S2 5.00 12.00

2016 Topps MLB Wacky Promos

COMPLETE SET (6) 2.00 5.00
RANDOM INSERTS IN PACKS
MLBW1 Giants .40 1.00
Magic Beans
MLBW2 Mets .40 1.00
Deli Meat
MLBW3 Royals .40 1.00
Blue Cheese
MLBW4 Dodgers .40 1.00
Sushi
MLBW5 Red Sox .40 1.00
Tea Bags
MLBW6 Cardinals .40 1.00
Eggs

2016 Topps No Hitter Pins

STATED ODDS 1:1826 HOBBY; 1:43 JUMBO
NHPBF Bob Feller 4.00 10.00
NHPCK Clayton Kershaw 10.00 25.00
NHPFV Fernando Valenzuela 3.00 8.00
NHPHB Homer Bailey 3.00 8.00
NHPJL Jon Lester 4.00 10.00
NHPJP Jim Palmer 4.00 10.00
NHPJS Johan Santana 4.00 10.00
NHPJZ Jordan Zimmermann 4.00 10.00
NHPMC Matt Cain 4.00 10.00
NHPNR Nolan Ryan 8.00 20.00
NHPPN Phil Niekro 4.00 10.00
NHPRJ Randy Johnson 5.00 12.00
NHPSK Sandy Koufax 6.00 15.00
NHPTS Tom Seaver 4.00 10.00
NHPWS Warren Spahn 4.00 10.00

2016 Topps No Hitter Pins Autographs

STATED ODDS 1:78,148 HOBBY; 1:1857 JUMBO
STATED PRINT RUN 25 SER.#'d SETS
EXCHANGE DEADLINE 1/31/2018
NHPCK Clayton Kershaw 125.00 250.00
NHPJL Jon Lester 75.00 150.00
NHPNR Nolan Ryan 125.00 250.00
NHPRJ Randy Johnson EXCH 125.00 250.00
NHPSK Sandy Koufax EXCH 200.00 300.00

2016 Topps Perspectives

COMPLETE SET (25) 5.00 12.00
STATED ODDS 1:4 HOBBY
P1 Andrew McCutchen .40 1.00
P2 Adrian Gonzalez .30 .75
P3 Robinson Cano .30 .75
P4 Bryce Harper .60 1.50
P5 Rusney Castillo .25 .60
P6 Byron Buxton .30 .75
P7 Yasiel Puig .40 1.00
P8 Troy Tulowitzki .40 1.00
P9 Jhonny Peralta .25 .60
P10 Jung Ho Kang .25 .60
P11 Kris Bryant .50 1.25
P12 David Ortiz .40 1.00
P13 Ichiro Suzuki .50 1.25
P14 Justin Upton .30 .75
P15 Yadier Molina .40 1.00
P16 Gregory Polanco .30 .75
P17 Evan Longoria .30 .75
P18 Mark Teixeira .30 .75
P19 Ryan Braun .30 .75
P20 Ryan Howard .30 .75
P21 Cal Ripken Jr. 1.25 3.00
P22 Randy Johnson .40 1.00
P23 Craig Biggio .30 .75
P24 Nolan Ryan 1.25 3.00
P25 Ozzie Smith .50 1.25

2016 Topps Postseason Performance Autograph Relics

STATED ODDS 1:14,746 HOBBY; 1:746 JUMBO
STATED PRINT RUN 50 SER.#'d SETS
EXCHANGE DEADLINE 1/31/2018
PPARARI Anthony Rizzo 50.00 120.00
PPARARU Addison Russell 40.00 100.00
PPARDW David Wright 40.00 100.00
PPARJD Jacob deGrom 50.00 120.00
PPARJF Jeurys Familia 30.00 80.00
PPARJLE Jon Lester 25.00 60.00
PPARLD Lucas Duda 25.00 60.00
PPARMS Marcus Stroman 25.00 60.00
PPARNS Noah Syndergaard 50.00 120.00
PPARWF Wilmer Flores 25.00 60.00

2016 Topps Postseason Performance Autographs

STATED ODDS 1:14,746 HOBBY; 1:3014 JUMBO
STATED PRINT RUN 50 SER.#'d SETS
EXCHANGE DEADLINE 1/31/2018
PPAJB Javier Baez 30.00 80.00
PPAJD Jacob deGrom 20.00 50.00
PPAJF Jeurys Familia 25.00 60.00
PPAKP Kevin Pillar 15.00 40.00
PPALD Lucas Duda 20.00 50.00
PPAMS Marcus Stroman 20.00 50.00
PPANS Noah Syndergaard 50.00 120.00
PPAWF Wilmer Flores
PPAARU Addison Russell
PPAJLE Jon Lester 20.00 50.00

2016 Topps Postseason Performance Relics

STATED ODDS 1:2506 HOBBY; 1:501 JUMBO
STATED PRINT RUN 100 SER.#'d SETS
PPRARI Anthony Rizzo 15.00 40.00
PPRARU Addison Russell 10.00 25.00
PPRAS Aaron Sanchez 12.00 30.00
PPRBC Bartolo Colon 10.00 25.00
PPRDF Dexter Fowler 8.00 20.00
PPRDM Daniel Murphy 20.00 50.00
PPRDP David Price 20.00 50.00
PPRDW David Wright 20.00 50.00
PPREE Edwin Encarnacion 10.00 25.00
PPRJBA Jose Bautista 8.00 20.00
PPRJBE Javier Baez 12.00 30.00
PPRJDE Jacob deGrom 20.00 50.00
PPRJDO Josh Donaldson 8.00 20.00
PPRJF Jeurys Familia 20.00 50.00
PPRJLA Juan Lagares 25.00 60.00
PPRJLE Jon Lester 8.00 20.00
PPRKB Kris Bryant 12.00 30.00
PPRKS Kyle Schwarber 20.00 50.00
PPRLD Lucas Duda 8.00 20.00
PPRMH Matt Harvey 40.00 100.00
PPRNS Noah Syndergaard 20.00 50.00
PPRRD R.A. Dickey 10.00 25.00
PPRRM Russell Martin 20.00 50.00
PPRRO Roberto Osuna 6.00 15.00
PPRSC Starlin Castro 6.00 15.00
PPRSM Steven Matz 40.00 100.00
PPRTD Travis d'Arnaud 25.00 60.00
PPRTT Troy Tulowitzki 25.00 60.00
PPRWF Wilmer Flores 15.00 40.00
PPRYC Yoenis Cespedes 20.00 50.00

2016 Topps Pressed Into Service

COMPLETE SET (10) 2.00 5.00
STATED ODDS 1:8 HOBBY; 1:2 JUMBO
PIS1 Mitch Moreland .25 .60
PIS2 Wade Boggs .30 .75
PIS3 Jose Canseco .30 .75
PIS4 Michael Cuddyer .25 .60
PIS5 Paul O'Neill .30 .75
PIS6 Stan Musial .60 1.50
PIS7 Josh Harrison .25 .60
PIS8 Garrett Jones .25 .60
PIS9 Ichiro Suzuki .50 1.25
PIS10 Nick Swisher .30 .75

2016 Topps Pressed Into Service Autographs

STATED ODDS 1:60,115 HOBBY; 1:12,233 JUMBO
STATED PRINT RUN 25 SER.#'d SETS
EXCHANGE DEADLINE 1/31/2018
PSAJC Jose Canseco
PSAMC Michael Cuddyer
PSAPO Paul O'Neill
PSASM Stan Musial
PSAWB Wade Boggs EXCH 40.00 100.00

2016 Topps Pressed Into Service Relics

STATED ODDS 1:30,058 HOBBY; 1:5942 JUMBO
STATED PRINT RUN 50 SER.#'d SETS
PISRI Ichiro Suzuki 15.00 40.00
PISRJC Jose Canseco 10.00 25.00
PISRMC Michael Cuddyer 15.00 40.00
PISRPO Paul O'Neill 20.00 50.00
PISRWB Wade Boggs 12.00 30.00

2016 Topps Record Setters

COMPLETE SET (15) 20.00 50.00
INSERTED IN RETAIL PACKS
RS1 Mike Trout 3.00 8.00
RS2 Adrian Gonzalez .50 1.25
RS3 David Ortiz .60 1.50
RS4 Carlos Correa .60 1.50
RS5 Max Scherzer .60 1.50
RS6 Steven Matz .50 1.25
RS7 Dallas Keuchel .50 1.25
RS8 Chris Sale .60 1.50
RS9 Alex Rodriguez .75 2.00
RS10 Chris Heston .40 1.00
RS11 Edwin Encarnacion .60 1.50
RS12 Bryce Harper 1.00 2.50
RS13 Kris Bryant .75 2.00
RS14 Josh Donaldson .50 1.25
RS15 Jose Altuve .50 1.25

2016 Topps Record Setters Relics

INSERTED IN RETAIL PACKS
STATED PRINT RUN 25 SER.#'d SETS
RSRAG Adrian Gonzalez
RSRAR Alex Rodriguez
RSRCS Chris Sale
RSRDK Dallas Keuchel
RSRDO David Ortiz
RSREE Edwin Encarnacion
RSREH Eric Hosmer
RSRJD Josh Donaldson 15.00 40.00
RSRKB Kris Bryant 15.00 40.00
RSRMT Mike Trout

2016 Topps Scouting Report Autographs

SER.1 ODDS 1:293 HOBBY; 1:11 JUMBO
SER.2 ODDS 1:313 HOBBY
SER.1 EXCH DEADLINE 1/31/2018
UPD EXCH DEADLINE 9/30/2018
SRAAA Albert Almora UPD 10.00 25.00
SRAAB Archie Bradley 3.00 8.00
SRAAB Aaron Blair UPD 3.00 8.00
SRAAC Adam Conley UPD 3.00 8.00
SRAAD Aledmys Diaz UPD 25.00 60.00
SRAAH Alen Hanson UPD 4.00 10.00
SRAAK Al Kaline 15.00 40.00
SRAAN Aaron Nola 6.00 15.00
SRAAN Aaron Nola S2 6.00 15.00
SRAARE A.J. Reed UPD 3.00 8.00
SRAAW Alex Wood S2 3.00 8.00
SRABC Brandon Crawford 15.00 40.00
SRABD Brandon Drury S2 5.00 12.00
SRABH Brock Holt UPD 3.00 8.00
SRABHA Bryce Harper 50.00 120.00
SRABHO Brock Holt 5.00 12.00
SRABJ Brian Johnson 3.00 8.00
SRABJ Brian Johnson S2 3.00 8.00
SRABM Brian McCann 15.00 40.00
SRABP Byung-Ho Park S2 20.00 50.00
SRABP Byung-Ho Park UPD 4.00 10.00
SRABPO Buster Posey 30.00 80.00
SRABS Blake Snell UPD 4.00 10.00
SRABSN Blake Snell S2 4.00 10.00
SRACC Carlos Correa 30.00 80.00
SRACE Carl Edwards Jr. S2 4.00 10.00
SRACH Cody Hall S2 3.00 8.00
SRACR Cal Ripken Jr. 25.00 60.00
SRACR Cody Reed UPD 3.00 8.00
SRACRE Colin Rea S2 3.00 8.00
SRACRO Carlos Rodon S2 5.00 12.00
SRACRO Carlos Rodon UPD 5.00 12.00
SRACS Corey Seager 40.00 100.00
SRACS Corey Seager S2 40.00 100.00
SRACV Christian Vazquez UPD 4.00 10.00
SRADF Doug Fister 3.00 8.00
SRADG Didi Gregorius 5.00 12.00
SRADK Dallas Keuchel 10.00 25.00
SRADM Devin Mesoraco 3.00 8.00
SRADS Duke Snider 6.00 15.00
SRAEG Erik Goeddel S2 3.00 8.00
SRAEI Ender Inciarte 3.00 8.00
SRAER Eddie Rosario UPD 4.00 10.00
SRAFL Francisco Lindor UPD 20.00 50.00
SRAFM Frankie Montas S2 4.00 10.00
SRAGB Greg Bird S2 4.00 10.00
SRAGS George Springer 10.00 25.00
SRAGS George Springer S2 10.00 25.00
SRAHO Henry Owens 4.00 10.00
SRAHOL Hector Olivera 4.00 10.00
SRAHOL Hector Olivera S2 4.00 10.00
SRAHOW Henry Owens S2 4.00 10.00
SRAJBE Jose Berrios S2 4.00 10.00
SRAJF Jose Fernandez 10.00 25.00
SRAJG Jon Gray 3.00 8.00
SRAJG Jon Gray S2 3.00 8.00
SRAJH Jeremy Hazelbaker UPD 4.00 10.00
SRAJHM Jason Hammel 4.00 10.00
SRAJHR Josh Harrison 5.00 12.00
SRAJM James McCann 4.00 10.00
SRAJP Jose Peraza UPD 4.00 10.00
SRAJP Jose Peraza S2 4.00 10.00
SRAJR J.T. Realmuto 15.00 40.00
SRAJR Joey Rickard UPD 5.00 12.00
SRAJT Jameson Taillon UPD 4.00 10.00
SRAJU Julio Urias UPD EXCH 15.00 40.00
SRAKC Kole Calhoun 3.00 8.00
SRAKG Ken Giles UPD 3.00 8.00
SRAKH Kelvin Herrera UPD 4.00 10.00
SRAKK Kevin Kiermaier UPD 4.00 10.00
SRAKM Ketel Marte 4.00 10.00
SRAKM Kenta Maeda UPD 20.00 50.00
SRAKME Kenta Maeda S2 40.00 100.00
SRAKS Kyle Schwarber S2 30.00 80.00
SRAKSC Kyle Schwarber 30.00 80.00
SRAKSU Kurt Suzuki 3.00 8.00
SRAKW Kyle Waldrop 4.00 10.00
SRAKW Kyle Waldrop S2 4.00 10.00
SRALG Lucas Giolito UPD 5.00 12.00
SRALJ Luke Jackson S2 3.00 8.00
SRALS Luis Severino 10.00 25.00
SRALS Luis Severino S2 10.00 25.00
SRALS Luis Severino UPD 4.00 10.00
SRAMAL Miguel Almonte S2 3.00 8.00
SRAMB Mike Bolsinger UPD 4.00 10.00
SRAMC Mike Clevinger UPD 6.00 15.00
SRAMCA Matt Cain 4.00 10.00
SRAMCO Michael Conforto 20.00 50.00
SRAMCO Michael Conforto S2 20.00 50.00
SRAMDF Matt Duffy SF S2 20.00 50.00
SRAMDU Matt Duffy HOU S2 3.00 8.00
SRAMF Michael Fulmer UPD 8.00 20.00
SRAMG Mychal Givens S2 3.00 8.00
SRAMK Max Kepler S2 6.00 15.00
SRAMK Max Kepler UPD 5.00 12.00
SRAMP Mark Prior 4.00 10.00
SRAMRE Michael Reed S2 3.00 8.00
SRAMRY Matt Reynolds S2 3.00 8.00
SRAMS Miguel Sano 10.00 25.00
SRAMS Miguel Sano S2 10.00 25.00
SRAMT Mike Trout 100.00 200.00
SRAMW Matt Wisler 3.00 8.00
SRAMW Mac Williamson S2 3.00 8.00
SRANK Nate Karns S2 3.00 8.00
SRANM Nomar Mazara UPD 5.00 12.00
SRANV Nick Vincent UPD 3.00 8.00
SRAPM Paul Molitor 8.00 20.00
SRAPO Peter O'Brien S2 3.00 8.00
SRAPS Pablo Sandoval 6.00 15.00
SRAPV Pat Venditte UPD 3.00 8.00
SRARCR Rod Carew 15.00 40.00
SRARM Raul Mondesi S2
SRARR Rob Refsnyder 4.00 10.00
SRARR Rob Refsnyder S2 4.00 10.00
SRARS Richie Shaffer S2 3.00 8.00
SRARS Robert Stephenson UPD 3.00 8.00
SRARST Ross Stripling UPD 3.00 8.00
SRARY Robin Yount 20.00 50.00
SRASB Socrates Brito UPD 3.00 8.00
SRASK Sandy Koufax 150.00 250.00
SRASMA Steven Matz 4.00 10.00
SRASP Stephen Piscotty 8.00 20.00
SRASP Stephen Piscotty S2 8.00 20.00
SRATD Tyler Duffey S2 3.00 8.00
SRATH T.J. House S2 3.00 8.00
SRATJ Taylor Jungmann 3.00 8.00
SRATJ Tyrell Jenkins UPD 8.00 20.00
SRATM Tom Murphy S2 3.00 8.00
SRATN Tyler Naquin UPD 4.00 10.00
SRATP Tommy Pham UPD 3.00 8.00
SRATP Tommy Pham S2 3.00 8.00
SRATS Trevor Story UPD 6.00 15.00
SRATT Trea Turner 12.00 30.00
SRATT Trea Turner S2 12.00 30.00
SRATW Tyler White UPD 3.00 8.00
SRAWM Wil Myers 3.00 8.00
SRAYD Yu Darvish 30.00 80.00
SRAYG Yan Gomes 3.00 8.00
SRAZL Zach Lee 3.00 8.00
SRAZL Zach Lee S2 3.00 8.00

2016 Topps Scouting Report Relics

SER.1 ODDS 1:54 HOBBY; 1:12 JUMBO
SER.2 ODDS 1:61 HOBBY
SRRAG Adrian Gonzalez 2.50 6.00
SRRAJ Adam Jones S2 2.50 6.00
SRRAM Andrew McCutchen 5.00 12.00
SRRAPU Albert Pujols 4.00 10.00
SRRAPU Albert Pujols S2 4.00 10.00
SRRAR Anthony Rizzo 4.00 10.00
SRRARI Anthony Rizzo S2 5.00 12.00
SRRARU Addison Russell S2 3.00 8.00
SRRBH Bryce Harper 6.00 15.00
SRRBP Buster Posey 4.00 10.00
SRRCD Chris Davis 2.00 5.00
SRRCGM Carlos Gomez S2 2.00 5.00
SRRCGN Carlos Gonzalez S2 2.50 6.00
SRRCK Craig Kimbrel S2 2.50 6.00
SRRCKE Clayton Kershaw 6.00 15.00
SRRCKL Corey Kluber 2.50 6.00
SRRCS Corey Seager S2 5.00 12.00
SRRCSA CC Sabathia 2.50 6.00
SRRDG Dee Gordon S2 2.00 5.00
SRRDK Dallas Keuchel S2 2.50 6.00
SRRDO David Ortiz 4.00 10.00
SRRDP Dustin Pedroia S2 2.50 6.00
SRRDPR David Price 2.50 6.00
SRRDW David Wright S2 2.50 6.00
SRREE Edwin Encarnacion S2 2.50 6.00
SRREH Eric Hosmer S2 2.50 6.00
SRREL Evan Longoria S2 2.50 6.00
SRRFF Freddie Freeman 4.00 10.00
SRRFH Felix Hernandez 2.50 6.00
SRRGC Gerrit Cole S2 2.50 6.00
SRRGS Giancarlo Stanton 3.00 8.00
SRRGSP George Springer S2 2.50 6.00
SRRGST Giancarlo Stanton S2 3.00 8.00
SRRHR Hanley Ramirez 2.50 6.00
SRRI Ichiro Suzuki 4.00 10.00
SRRJAB Jose Abreu S2 3.00 8.00
SRRJC Johnny Cueto 2.50 6.00
SRRJDE Jacob deGrom 3.00 8.00
SRRJDO Josh Donaldson 2.50 6.00
SRRJF Jose Fernandez S2 3.00 8.00
SRRJH Jason Heyward S2 2.50 6.00
SRRJK Jason Kipnis S2 2.50 6.00
SRRJM Joe Mauer 2.50 6.00
SRRJP Joc Pederson 2.50 6.00
SRRJS Jorge Soler S2 3.00 8.00
SRRJU Justin Upton S2 2.50 6.00
SRRJV Joey Votto S2 3.00 8.00
SRRJVE Justin Verlander 3.00 8.00
SRRJVE Justin Verlander S2 3.00 8.00
SRRKB Kris Bryant S2 4.00 10.00
SRRKP Kevin Plawecki 2.00 5.00
SRRKS Kyle Schwarber S2 5.00 12.00
SRRLC Lorenzo Cain S2 2.00 5.00
SRRLM Leonys Martin 2.00 5.00
SRRMA Matt Adams 2.00 5.00
SRRMB Madison Bumgarner 2.50 6.00
SRRMBR Michael Brantley 2.50 6.00
SRRMC Miguel Cabrera 4.00 10.00
SRRMCA Miguel Cabrera S2 3.00 8.00
SRRMH Matt Harvey S2 2.50 6.00
SRRMHA Matt Harvey 2.50 6.00
SRRMHO Matt Holliday 3.00 8.00
SRRMK Matt Kemp S2 2.50 6.00
SRRMM Manny Machado S2 5.00 12.00
SRRMS Max Scherzer 3.00 8.00
SRRMSA Miguel Sano S2 3.00 8.00
SRRMT Mark Teixeira 2.50 6.00
SRRMT Mike Trout S2 12.00 30.00
SRRMW Michael Wacha 2.50 6.00
SRRNC Nelson Cruz 3.00 8.00
SRRNS Noah Syndergaard 2.50 6.00
SRRPF Prince Fielder 2.50 6.00
SRRPF Prince Fielder S2 2.50 6.00
SRRPG Paul Goldschmidt S2 3.00 8.00
SRRRB Ryan Braun S2
SRRRC Robinson Cano S2 2.50 6.00
SRRRP Rick Porcello 2.50 6.00
SRRSMA Starling Marte 2.50 6.00
SRRTT Troy Tulowitzki S2 3.00 8.00
SRRWM Wil Myers S2 2.00 5.00
SRRYC Yoenis Cespedes 3.00 8.00
SRRYD Yu Darvish 3.00 8.00
SRRYM Yadier Molina 3.00 8.00
SRRYP Yasiel Puig 3.00 8.00
SRRYT Yasmany Tomas 2.00 5.00
SRRZG Zack Greinke 2.50 6.00

2016 Topps Spring Fever

COMPLETE SET (50) 10.00 25.00
SF1 Mike Trout 1.50 4.00
SF2 Buster Posey .40 1.00
SF3 Jason Heyward .25 .60
SF4 Todd Frazier .25 .60
SF5 David Price .25 .60
SF6 Zack Greinke .25 .60
SF7 Yu Darvish .30 .75
SF8 Salvador Perez .25 .60
SF9 Johnny Cueto .25 .60
SF10 Jacob deGrom .30 .75
SF11 Joey Votto .30 .75
SF12 Robinson Cano .25 .60
SF13 Josh Donaldson .25 .60
SF14 Madison Bumgarner .25 .60
SF15 Kris Bryant .40 1.00
SF16 Clayton Kershaw .60 1.50
SF17 Hunter Pence .25 .60
SF18 Matt Harvey .25 .60
SF19 David Ortiz .30 .75
SF20 Anthony Rizzo .50 1.25
SF21 Dustin Pedroia .30 .75
SF22 Yadier Molina .30 .75
SF23 Miguel Cabrera .30 .75
SF24 Felix Hernandez .25 .60
SF25 Andrew McCutchen .30 .75
SF26 David Wright .25 .60
SF27 Albert Pujols .40 1.00
SF28 Max Scherzer .30 .75
SF29 Bryce Harper .50 1.25
SF30 Adrian Gonzalez .25 .60
SF31 Kyle Schwarber .60 1.50
SF32 Corey Seager 1.50 4.00
SF33 Jon Gray .20 .50
SF34 Luis Severino .25 .60
SF35 Miguel Sano .30 .75
SF36 Trea Turner .60 1.50
SF37 Aaron Nola .40 1.00
SF38 Hector Olivera .25 .60
SF39 Stephen Piscotty .30 .75
SF40 Joe Mauer .25 .60
SF41 Ichiro Suzuki .40 1.00
SF42 Giancarlo Stanton .30 .75
SF43 Carlos Correa .30 .75
SF44 Masahiro Tanaka .25 .60
SF45 Jose Bautista .25 .60
SF46 Jake Arrieta .25 .60
SF47 Paul Goldschmidt .30 .75
SF48 Francisco Lindor .30 .75
SF49 Dee Gordon .20 .50
SF50 Manny Machado .30 .75

2016 Topps Team Glove Leather Autographs

SER.1 ODDS 1:2995 HOBBY; 1:598 JUMBO
SER.2 ODDS 1:1872 HOBBY
STATED PRINT RUN 25 SER.#'d SETS
SER.1 EXCH DEADLINE 1/31/2018
GLAAGA Andres Galarraga S2 20.00 50.00
GLAAGO Alex Gordon S2 40.00 100.00
GLAAK Al Kaline 75.00 200.00
GLAAN Aaron Nola EXCH 40.00 100.00
GLABH Bryce Harper EXCH 100.00 250.00
GLABJ Bo Jackson S2 40.00 100.00
GLABM Brian McCann EXCH 50.00 120.00
GLABP Buster Posey EXCH 200.00 300.00
GLACC Carlos Correa 75.00 200.00
GLACJ Chipper Jones 60.00 150.00
GLACK Clayton Kershaw S2 75.00 200.00
GLACL Roger Clemens EXCH 60.00 150.00
GLACN Robinson Cano EXCH 40.00 100.00
GLACR Cal Ripken Jr. 200.00 300.00
GLACRA Rod Carew 25.00 60.00
GLACS Chris Sale EXCH 40.00 100.00
GLACS Corey Seager S2 40.00 100.00
GLACY Carl Yastrzemski S2 50.00 120.00
GLADK Dallas Keuchel S2 20.00 50.00
GLADW David Wright S2
GLAFM Frankie Montas S2 10.00 25.00
GLAFT Frank Thomas 200.00 300.00
GLAFV Fernando Valenzuela S2 40.00 100.00
GLAGR Ken Griffey Jr. 250.00 400.00
GLAHO Henry Owens S2 15.00 40.00
GLAI Ichiro Suzuki 300.00 500.00
GLAJA Jose Abreu S2 25.00 60.00
GLAJC Jose Canseco S2 40.00 100.00

LAJF Jeurys Familia S2 20.00 50.00
LAJG Jon Gray 25.00 60.00
LAJP Joc Pederson S2 25.00 60.00
LAJS Jorge Soler S2 40.00 100.00
LALS Luis Severino 12.00 30.00
LAMC Michael Conforto EXCH 150.00 300.00
LAMC Matt Cain S2 40.00 100.00
LAMP Mike Piazza 60.00 150.00
LAMS Miguel Sano S2 12.00 30.00
LAMT Mike Trout 250.00 400.00
LANS Noah Syndergaard S2 50.00 120.00
LAPM Paul Molitor
LAPS Pablo Sandoval 40.00 100.00
LARJ Randy Johnson S2 60.00 150.00
LARY Robin Yount S2 30.00 80.00
LASC Kyle Schwarber 200.00 300.00
LASC Steve Carlton S2 20.00 50.00
LASK Sandy Koufax 300.00 400.00
LASP Stephen Piscotty S2 50.00 120.00
LATT Troy Tulowitzki S2 30.00 80.00
LAVG Vladimir Guerrero S2 60.00 150.00
LAWM Wil Myers 8.00 20.00

2016 Topps Team Logo Pins

SER.1 ODDS 1:897 HOBBY; 1:19 JUMBO
SER.2 ODDS 1:1412 HOBBY
TLPI Ichiro Suzuki 3.00 8.00
TLPAD Andre Dawson 2.00 5.00
TLPAM Andrew McCutchen 2.50 6.00
TLPAN Aaron Nola 3.00 8.00
TLPAP Albert Pujols 3.00 8.00
TLPARI Anthony Rizzo 4.00 10.00
TLPARO Alex Rodriguez 3.00 8.00
TLPBH Bryce Harper 4.00 10.00
TLPBP Buster Posey 3.00 8.00
TLPBR Babe Ruth 6.00 15.00
TLPCA Chris Archer 1.50 4.00
TLPCC Carlos Correa 2.50 6.00
TLPCD Chris Davis 1.50 4.00
TLPCK Clayton Kershaw 5.00 12.00
TLPCR Cal Ripken Jr. 8.00 20.00
TLPCS Chris Sale 2.50 6.00
TLPCSE Corey Seager 12.00 30.00
TLPDK Dallas Keuchel 2.00 5.00
TLPDO David Ortiz 2.50 6.00
TLPDPE Dustin Pedroia 2.50 6.00
TLPDPR David Price 2.00 5.00
TLPDW Dave Winfield 2.00 5.00
TLPDW David Wright 2.00 5.00
TLPFF Freddie Freeman 3.00 8.00
TLPFH Felix Hernandez 2.00 5.00
TLPFL Francisco Lindor 2.50 6.00
TLPGB George Brett 5.00 12.00
TLPGM Greg Maddux 3.00 8.00
TLPGS Giancarlo Stanton 2.50 6.00
TLPHA Hank Aaron 5.00 12.00
TLPHP Hunter Pence 2.00 5.00
TLPJA Jose Abreu 2.50 6.00
TLPJA Jake Arrieta 2.00 5.00
TLPJB Jose Bautista 2.00 5.00
TLPJBE Johnny Bench 2.50 6.00
TLPJD Josh Donaldson 2.00 5.00
TLPJR Jackie Robinson 2.50 6.00
TLPJVE Justin Verlander 2.50 6.00
TLPJVO Joey Votto 2.50 6.00
TLPKB Kris Bryant 3.00 8.00
TLPKG Ken Griffey Jr. 5.00 12.00
TLPKS Kyle Schwarber 5.00 12.00
TLPLC Lorenzo Cain 1.50 4.00
TLPMB Madison Bumgarner 2.00 5.00
TLPMC Miguel Cabrera 2.50 6.00
TLPMH Matt Harvey 2.00 5.00
TLPMM Mark McGwire 4.00 10.00
TLPMS Miguel Sano 2.50 6.00
TLPMTA Masahiro Tanaka 2.00 5.00
TLPMTR Mike Trout 12.00 30.00
TLPNA Nolan Arenado 3.00 8.00
TLPNC Nelson Cruz 2.50 6.00
TLPNR Nolan Ryan 8.00 20.00
TLPOS Ozzie Smith 3.00 8.00
TLPPF Prince Fielder 2.00 5.00
TLPPG Paul Goldschmidt 2.50 6.00
TLPRC Roberto Clemente 6.00 15.00
TLPRJ Randy Johnson 2.50 6.00
TLPRY Robin Yount 2.50 6.00
TLPSC Steve Carlton 2.00 5.00
TLPSK Sandy Koufax 5.00 12.00
TLPSM Shelby Miller 2.00 5.00
TLPTF Todd Frazier 2.00 5.00
TLPTG Tony Gwynn 2.50 6.00
TLPTT Troy Tulowitzki 2.50 6.00
TLPTW Ted Williams 5.00 12.00
TLPWM Willie Mays 5.00 12.00
TLPYD Yu Darvish 2.50 6.00
TLPYM Yadier Molina 2.50 6.00

2016 Topps Team Logo Pins Autographs

SER.1 ODDS 1:42,131 HOBBY; 1:929 JUMBO
SER.2 ODDS 1:4680 HOBBY
STATED PRINT RUN 25 SER.#'d SETS
SER.1 EXCH DEADLINE 1/31/2018
TLPTT Troy Tulowitzki EXCH 100.00 250.00
TLPCK Clayton Kershaw 100.00 250.00
TLPCR Cal Ripken Jr. 150.00 300.00
TLPJA Jose Abreu EXCH 60.00 150.00
TLPKB Kris Bryant 150.00 300.00
TLPKS Kyle Schwarber 125.00 250.00
TLPMS Miguel Sano 40.00 100.00
TLPMTR Mike Trout 300.00 500.00
TLPNR Nolan Ryan 100.00 200.00
TLPRJ Randy Johnson EXCH 60.00 150.00
TLPABH Bryce Harper 150.00 250.00
TLPADK Dallas Keuchel 25.00 60.00
TLPADO David Ortiz 150.00 300.00
TLPADP Dustin Pedroia 60.00 150.00
TLPADW David Wright 12.00 30.00
TLPAGM Greg Maddux 150.00 250.00
TLPAMM Mark McGwire 100.00 250.00
TLPASC Steve Carlton 50.00 120.00

2016 Topps The Greatest Streaks

COMPLETE SET (10) 10.00 25.00
RANDOM INSERTS IN PACKS
GS01 Cal Ripken Jr. 2.00 5.00
GS02 Ken Griffey Jr. 1.25 3.00
GS03 Zack Greinke .50 1.25
GS04 Ichiro Suzuki .75 2.00
GS05 Babe Ruth 1.50 4.00
GS06 Chris Sale .60 1.50
GS07 Tom Seaver .50 1.25
GS08 Nolan Ryan 2.00 5.00
GS09 Ted Williams 1.25 3.00
GS10 Lou Gehrig 1.25 3.00

2016 Topps Tribute to the Kid

COMMON CARD .75 2.00
STATED ODDS 1:8 HOBBY

2016 Topps Tribute to the Kid Relics

COMMON CARD 12.00 30.00
STATED ODDS 1:2824 HOBBY
STATED PRINT RUN 50 SER.#'d SETS

2016 Topps Walk Off Wins

COMPLETE SET (15) 12.00 30.00
RANDOM INSERTS IN PACKS
WOW1 Luis Gonzalez 1.00 2.50
WOW2 David Ortiz 1.25 3.00
WOW3 Evan Longoria 1.00 2.50
WOW4 Bill Mazeroski 1.00 2.50
WOW5 David Freese .75 2.00
WOW6 Manny Machado 1.25 3.00
WOW7 Wilmer Flores 1.00 2.50
WOW8 Allen Craig .75 2.00
WOW9 Nomar Garciaparra 1.00 2.50
WOW10 Jose Abreu 1.25 3.00
WOW11 Todd Frazier 1.00 2.50
WOW12 Starling Marte 1.00 2.50
WOW13 Ozzie Smith 1.50 4.00
WOW14 Carlton Fisk 1.00 2.50
WOW15 Henry Urrutia .75 2.00

2016 Topps Walk Off Wins Autographs

RANDOM INSERTS IN PACKS
STATED PRINT RUN 25 SER.#'d SETS
EXCHANGE DEADLINE 1/31/2018
WOWABM Bill Mazeroski
WOWADO David Ortiz
WOWAEL Evan Longoria
WOWALG Luis Gonzalez
WOWAWF Wilmer Flores

2016 Topps Walk Off Wins Relics

RANDOM INSERTS IN PACKS
STATED PRINT RUN 25 SER.#'d SETS
WOWRAC Allen Craig
WOWRDF David Freese 15.00 40.00
WOWRDO David Ortiz
WOWREL Evan Longoria
WOWRJA Jose Abreu 15.00 40.00
WOWRLG Luis Gonzalez
WOWRMMA Manny Machado 12.00 30.00
WOWRNG Nomar Garciaparra
WOWRTF Todd Frazier 15.00 40.00
WOWRWF Wilmer Flores 25.00 60.00

2016 Topps World Champion Autograph Relics

STATED ODDS 1:7515 HOBBY; 1:1497 JUMBO
STATED PRINT RUN 50 SER.#'d SETS
EXCHANGE DEADLINE 1/31/2018
WCARAE Alcides Escobar 25.00 60.00
WCARAG Alex Gordon 60.00 120.00
WCARKM Kendrys Morales 40.00 80.00
WCARSP Salvador Perez 50.00 100.00

2016 Topps World Champion Autographs

STATED ODDS 1:30,058 HOBBY; 1:5942 JUMBO
STATED PRINT RUN 50 SER.#'d SETS
EXCHANGE DEADLINE 1/31/2018
WCAAE Alcides Escobar 40.00 80.00
WCAAG Alex Gordon 60.00 120.00
WCAKH Kelvin Herrera EXCH 40.00 80.00
WCAKM Kendrys Morales EXCH 25.00 60.00
WCASP Salvador Perez 40.00 80.00

2016 Topps World Champion Coin and Stamps Quarter

SER.1 ODDS 1:8057 HOBBY; 1:188 JUMBO
SER.2 ODDS 1:1921 HOBBY
SER.1 PRINT RUN 50 SER.#'d SETS
SER.2 PRINT RUN 25 SER.#'d SETS
*DIME/50: .4X TO 1X QUARTER
*NICKEL/50: .4X TO 1X QUARTER
*PENNY/50: .4X TO 1X QUARTER
WCCSAK Al Kaline 20.00 50.00
WCCSBL Barry Larkin 15.00 40.00
WCCSBP Buster Posey 15.00 40.00
WCCSBR Babe Ruth 60.00 150.00
WCCSCH Cole Hamels 10.00 25.00
WCCSCR Cal Ripken Jr. 20.00 50.00
WCCSCS CC Sabathia 10.00 25.00
WCCSDF David Freese 10.00 25.00
WCCSDO David Ortiz 15.00 40.00
WCCSDP Dustin Pedroia 20.00 50.00
WCCSGB George Brett 25.00 60.00
WCCSGC Gary Carter 12.00 30.00
WCCSLG Lou Gehrig 25.00 60.00
WCCSLGO Luis Gonzalez 10.00 25.00
WCCSMB Madison Bumgarner 10.00 25.00
WCCSOS Ozzie Smith 20.00 50.00
WCCSPM Paul Molitor 12.00 30.00
WCCSPS Pablo Sandoval 10.00 25.00
WCCSSK Sandy Koufax 25.00 60.00
WCCSTG Tom Glavine 10.00 25.00
WCCSTL Tommy Lasorda 10.00 25.00
WCCSWM Willie Mays 30.00 80.00
WCCSWS Warren Spahn 10.00 25.00
WCCSWST Willie Stargell 15.00 40.00
WCCSYM Yadier Molina 12.00 30.00
WCCSRAP Albert Pujols 20.00 50.00
WCCSRAR Alex Rodriguez 30.00 80.00
WCCSRBM Bill Mazeroski 30.00 80.00
WCCSRDG Dwight Gooden 8.00 20.00
WCCSRDO David Ortiz 25.00 60.00
WCCSRDP Dustin Pedroia 12.00 30.00
WCCSRDW Dave Winfield 20.00 50.00
WCCSRHP Hunter Pence 25.00 60.00
WCCSRHW Honus Wagner 75.00 200.00
WCCSRJB Johnny Bench 25.00 60.00
WCCSRJC Jose Canseco 30.00 80.00
WCCSRJE Jacoby Ellsbury 15.00 40.00
WCCSRJP Joe Panik 30.00 80.00
WCCSRMA Moises Alou 15.00 40.00
WCCSRMC Matt Cain 20.00 50.00
WCCSRMT Mark Teixeira 30.00 80.00
WCCSRNR Nolan Ryan 40.00 100.00
WCCSRPR Phil Rizzuto 25.00 60.00
WCCSRRC Roberto Clemente 30.00 80.00
WCCSRRF Rollie Fingers 10.00 25.00
WCCSRRJ Reggie Jackson 25.00 60.00
WCCSRSK Sandy Koufax 40.00 100.00
WCCSRTP Tony Perez 20.00 50.00
WCCSRBRO Brooks Robinson 20.00 50.00
WCCSRBRU Babe Ruth 100.00 250.00

2016 Topps World Champion Relics

STATED ODDS 1:7515 HOBBY; 1:1005 JUMBO
STATED PRINT RUN 100 SER.#'d SETS
WCRAE Alcides Escobar 8.00 20.00
WCRAG Alex Gordon 8.00 20.00
WCREH Eric Hosmer 30.00 80.00
WCRJC Johnny Cueto 25.00 60.00
WCRKM Kendrys Morales 6.00 15.00
WCRLC Lorenzo Cain 20.00 50.00
WCRMM Mike Moustakas 8.00 20.00
WCRSP Salvador Perez 20.00 50.00
WCRYV Yordano Ventura 25.00 60.00

2016 Topps Update

COMPLETE SET w/o SP's (300) 20.00 50.00
PLATE PRINT RUN 1 SET PER COLOR
BLACK-CYAN-MAGENTA-YELLOW ISSUED
NO PLATE PRICING DUE TO SCARCITY
US1A Manny Machado AS .20 .50
US2 Dean Kiekhefer RC .40 1.00
US3 C.Mullee/C.Green .40 1.00
US4 Jake Arrieta AS .15 .40
US5 B.Gamel/J.Barbato .50 1.25
US6 Chris Herrmann .12 .30
US7 Blaine Boyer .12 .30
US8 Pedro Alvarez .12 .30
US9 Ross Stripling RC .40 1.00
US10 John Jaso .12 .30
US11 Erick Aybar .12 .30
US12 Matt Szczur .15 .40
US13A Sean Manaea RC .40 1.00
US13B Sean Manaea SP 1.00 2.50
w/Catcher
US14 Chris Capuano .12 .30
US15 Wilson Ramos AS .12 .30
US16 Alexei Ramirez .15 .40
US17 Pat Dean RC .40 1.00
US18 Luis Cessa RC .40 1.00
US19 Max Scherzer AS .20 .50
US20 Junichi Tazawa .12 .30
US21 Austin Barnes RC .60 1.50
US22 Neil Walker .15 .40
US23 Ian Desmond AS .12 .30
US24 Jett Bandy RC .40 1.00
US25 Hyun-Soo Kim RD .20 .50
US26 Jose Lobaton .12 .30
US27 C.Correa/J.Altuve .20 .50
US28 Alfredo Simon .12 .30
US29 Jon Moscot RC .40 1.00
US30 J.Harrison/A.McCutchen .20 .50
US31 Eduardo Nunez AS .12 .30
US32 Juan Uribe .12 .30
US33 Aledmys Diaz AS .20 .50
US34A Cody Reed RC .40 1.00
US34B Cody Reed SP 1.00 2.50
Batting
US35 Joaquin Benoit .12 .30
US36 Yonder Alonso .12 .30
US37 Jon Niese .12 .30
US38 Cole Hamels AS .12 .30
US39 Tommy Joseph RC .75 2.00
US40 Blake Snell RD .15 .40
US41 Mark Melancon .12 .30
US42 Andrew Miller .15 .40
US43 Michael Conforto RD .15 .40
US44 Aledmys Diaz RD .20 .50
US45A Julio Urias RC 1.25 3.00
US45B Julio Urias SP 3.00 8.00
US46 Steven Wright .12 .30
US47 Austin Romine .12 .30
US48 Kelvin Herrera AS .12 .30
US49 Ivan Nova .12 .30
US50 Ben Zobrist AS .15 .40
US51 Steve Pearce .20 .50
US52A Wil Myers AS .12 .30
US53 H.Cervenka/J.Gant .12 .30
US54 Adam Duvall AS .40 1.00
US55 Vince Velasquez .12 .30
US56 Corey Kluber AS .15 .40
US57 B.Nicholas/D.Lee .60 1.50
US58A Jameson Taillon RC .50 1.25
US58B Jameson Taillon SP 1.25 3.00
Bullpen
US59 Steven Brault RC .40 1.00
US60 Daniel Hudson .12 .30
US61 Jed Lowrie .12 .30
US62 Jake Arrieta HL .15 .40
US63 G.Mahle/A.Triggs .40 1.00
US64 Steve Pearce .20 .50
US65A Byung-Ho Park RC .50 1.25
US65B Byung-Ho Park SP 1.25 3.00
In dugout
US66 Fernando Rodney .12 .30
US67A Blake Snell RC .50 1.25
US67B Blake Snell SP 1.25 3.00
In dugout
US68 Adam Duvall HRD .40 1.00
US69A Mike Clevinger RC .75 2.00
US69B Mike Clevinger SP 2.00 5.00
Batting
US70 Brandon Belt AS .15 .40
US71 Kelly Johnson .12 .30
US72 Derek Law RC .50 1.25
US73 Scott Schebler RC .60 1.50
US74 Brandon Nimmo RC .60 1.50
US75 Alex Colome .12 .30
US76 Yunel Escobar .12 .30
US77 Wade Miley .12 .30
US78 Jay Bruce .15 .40
US79A Josh Donaldson AS .15 .40
US80 Aaron Hill .12 .30
US81 Jeimer Candelario RC .50 1.25
US82 Chad Qualls .12 .30
US83 Bud Norris .12 .30
US84 Marcell Ozuna AS .20 .50
US85 Shawn Morimando RC .40 1.00
US86 Stephen Vogt AS .15 .40
US87 Asdrubal Cabrera .15 .40
US88 Tyrell Jenkins RC .40 1.00
US89 A.J. Reed RD .12 .30
US90 Jake McGee .12 .30
US91 Dan Jennings RC .40 1.00
US92A A.J. Reed RC .40 1.00
US92B A.J. Reed SP 1.00 2.50
Running
US93 Addison Russell AS .20 .50
US94 Adam Lind .15 .40
US95 Hector Neris .12 .30
US96 Chad Kuhl RC .40 1.00
US97 Cameron Maybin .12 .30
US98 Mike Bolsinger .12 .30
US99A Jeremy Hazelbaker RC .50 1.25
US99B Jeremy Hazelbaker SP 1.25 3.00
Dugout
US100 Andrew Cashner .12 .30
US101 Brad Brach AS .12 .30
US102 Aaron Hicks .15 .40
US103 Matt Purke RC .40 1.00
US104 Matt Wieters .20 .50
US105 Joey Rickard RC .40 1.00
US106 Ji-Man Choi RC .50 1.25
US107 Rene Rivera .12 .30
US108 Keon Broxton RC .40 1.00
US109 Shelby Miller .15 .40
US110 Bryan Shaw .12 .30
US111 Josh Reddick .12 .30
US112 Ben Revere .12 .30
US113 Steven Wright AS .12 .30
US114 Trevor Story HL .50 1.25
US115 Xander Bogaerts AS .20 .50
US116 Jake Diekman .12 .30
US117A Tyler Naquin RC .50 1.25
US117B Tyler Naquin SP 1.25 3.00
Dugout
US118 Mark Trumbo HRD .12 .30
US119 Stephen Piscotty RD .20 .50
US120 C.Davis/M.Machado .20 .50
US121 Ender Inciarte .12 .30
US122 Oswaldo Arcia .12 .30
US123 J.Blash/L.Perdomo .40 1.00
US124 Junior Guerra RC .50 1.25
US125A Daniel Murphy AS .15 .40
US126 Bartolo Colon HL .12 .30
US127 Brad Ziegler .12 .30
US128 Denard Span .12 .30
US129 Peter Bourjos .12 .30
US130 Ryan Rua .12 .30
US131 Tyler Flowers .12 .30
US132 Jose Reyes .15 .40
US133 Odubel Herrera AS .15 .40
US134 Luis Severino RD .15 .40
US135 Tony Barnette RC .40 1.00
US136 Julio Urias RD .40 1.00
US137 Dexter Fowler .15 .40
US138 Kyle Schwarber RD .40 1.00
US139 Albert Almora RD .15 .40
US140 Eduardo Nunez .12 .30
US141 Buster Posey AS .25 .60
US142 Andrelton Simmons .12 .30
US143 Drew Stubbs .12 .30
US144 Giancarlo Stanton HRD .20 .50
US145 Aroldis Chapman .20 .50
US146 Alen Hanson RC .50 1.25
US147 T.Guerrero/M.Buschmann .40 1.00
US148 Matt Moore .15 .40
US149 Matt Bowman RC .40 1.00
US150 Trevor Story RD .50 1.25
US151 Taylor Motter RC .40 1.00
US152A Michael Fulmer RC .60 1.50
US152B Michael Fulmer SP 1.50 4.00
US153 Zach Duke .12 .30
US154 Trevor Cahill .12 .30
US155 Nolan Reimold .12 .30
US156 Geovany Soto .12 .30
US157 Jameson Taillon RD .15 .40
US158A Nomar Mazara RC .60 1.50
US158B Nomar Mazara SP 1.50 4.00
US159 Edwin Encarnacion AS .20 .50
US160 Jon Lester AS .15 .40
US161A Bartolo Colon AS .12 .30
US162 Drew Pomeranz .15 .40
US163 Matt Wieters AS .20 .50
US164 Todd Frazier HRD .15 .40
US165 Drew Butera .12 .30
US166 Starling Marte AS .15 .40
US167A Corey Seager AS 1.00 2.50
US168 Robbie Grossman .12 .30
US169 Max Scherzer HL .20 .50
US170 Addison Reed .12 .30
US171 Miguel Sano RD .20 .50
US172 Kenley Jansen AS .15 .40
US173 Fernando Rodney AS .12 .30
US174 Starlin Castro .12 .30
US175A Mike Trout AS 1.00 2.50
US176A Jose Berrios RC .50 1.25
US176B Jose Berrios SP 1.25 3.00
In Dugout
US177 Matt Joyce .12 .30
US178A Albert Almora RC .50 1.25
US178B Albert Almora SP 1.25 3.00
Gray jersey
US179 Ezequiel Carrera .12 .30
US180 Matt Andriese .15 .40
US181 Andrew Miller AS .15 .40
US182A Hyun-Soo Kim RC .60 1.50
US182B Hyun-Soo Kim SP 1.50 4.00
w/Fans
US183 Todd Frazier .15 .40
US184 Yovani Gallardo .12 .30
US185 Jeremy Hellickson .12 .30
US186 Melvin Upton Jr. .15 .40
US187 Justin Wilson .12 .30
US188 Shawn Kelley .12 .30
US189 Jonathan Lucroy .15 .40
US190A Trayce Thompson RC .60 1.50
US190B Trayce Thompson SP 1.50 4.00
Fielding
US191 Mark Trumbo AS .12 .30
US192 Jackie Bradley Jr. AS .20 .50
US193 Joakim Soria .12 .30
US194A Eric Hosmer AS .15 .40
US195 Carlos Beltran .15 .40
US196 Mark Trumbo .12 .30
US197 Brad Brach .12 .30
US198A Carlos Gonzalez AS .15 .40
US199 Brandon Moss .12 .30
US200 Alex Colome AS .12 .30
US201A Mookie Betts AS .30 .75
US202 Jose Ramirez .15 .40
US203 Tony Kemp RC .40 1.00
US204 Michael Fulmer RD .20 .50
US205 Corey Seager HRD 1.00 2.50
US206A Salvador Perez AS .15 .40
US207 Jarrod Cosart .12 .30
US208 Pedro Strop .12 .30
US209 Tyler Clippard .12 .30
US210 James Shields .12 .30
US211A Tyler White RC .40 1.00
US211B Tyler White SP 1.00 2.50
In dugout
US212 Ian Kennedy .12 .30
US213 Lucas Giolito RD .20 .50
US214 Edwin Diaz RC .75 2.00
US215 Kirby Yates RC .60 1.50
US216A Robert Stephenson RC .40 1.00
US216B Robert Stephenson SP 1.00 2.50
Bunting
US217 J.Martinez/M.Cabrera .20 .50
US218 Carlos Gonzalez HRD .15 .40
US219 Tim Adleman RC .40 1.00
US220A Colin Moran RC .40 1.00
US220B Colin Moran SP 1.00 2.50
w/Bat
US221 D.Gregorius/S.Castro .15 .40
US222A Zach Britton AS .15 .40
US223A Jose Fernandez AS .20 .50
US224 Albert Suarez RC .40 1.00
US225 Tim Lincecum .15 .40
US226A Trevor Story RC 4.00 10.00
US226B Trevor Story SP 20.00 50.00
US227 Aaron Sanchez AS .15 .40
US228 Jose Berrios RD .15 .40
US229A Lucas Giolito RC .60 1.50
US229B Lucas Giolito SP 1.50 4.00
Batting
US230 Zack Greinke .15 .40
US231 Austin Jackson .12 .30
US232A Clayton Kershaw AS .40 1.00
US233A Chris Sale AS .20 .50
US234 Carlos Beltran AS .15 .40
US235 Matt Bush (RC) .50 1.25
US236 Drew Pomeranz AS .15 .40
US237 Ian Desmond .12 .30
US238 Alejandro de Aza .12 .30
US239 Matt Kemp .15 .40
US240 Rickie Weeks Jr. .12 .30
US241 Jose Quintana AS .12 .30
US242 Joe Biagini RC .40 1.00
US243 Drew Storen .12 .30
US244A Mallex Smith RC .40 1.00
US244B Mallex Smith SP 1.00 2.50
No helmet
US245 Howie Kendrick .12 .30
US246 Jay Bruce AS .15 .40
US247 Tyler Goeddel RC .40 1.00
US248 Sam Dyson .12 .30
US249 Tony Wolters RC .40 1.00
US250 Jonathan Lucroy AS .15 .40
US251 Craig Kimbrel .15 .40
US252A Johnny Cueto AS .15 .40
US253 A.J. Ramos AS .12 .30
US254A David Ortiz AS .20 .50
US255 Adam Conley .12 .30
US256A Nolan Arenado AS .25 .60
US257 Jedd Gyorko .12 .30
US258A Seung-Hwan Oh RC 1.00 2.50
US258B Seung-Hwan Oh SP 2.50 6.00
US259 Chris Young .12 .30
US260 Ichiro Suzuki HL .25 .60
US261 Jarrod Saltalamacchia .12 .30
US262A Robinson Cano AS .15 .40
US263 Kirk Nieuwenhuis .12 .30
US264 Cody Anderson .12 .30
US265 Doug Fister .12 .30
US266 Willson Contreras RC 2.50 6.00
US267 Michael Saunders AS .15 .40
US268 Wil Myers HRD .12 .30
US269 Francisco Rodriguez .15 .40
US270 Chris Devenski RC .40 1.00
US271 Jeff Francoeur .15 .40
US272 Brett Lawrie .15 .40
US273 Paul Goldschmidt AS .20 .50
US274 Chris Coghlan .12 .30
US275 Francisco Lindor AS .20 .50
US276 Justin Grimm .12 .30
US277 Derek Dietrich .15 .40
US278 Mark Melancon AS .12 .30
US279 Corey Seager RD 2.50 6.00
US280 Robinson Cano HRD .15 .40
US281A Anthony Rizzo AS .30 .75
US282 Will Harris AS .12 .30
US283 David Freese .12 .30
US284 Aaron Nola RD .25 .60
US285 Kenta Maeda RD .25 .60
US286 Gerardo Parra .12 .30
US287A Tim Anderson RC 5.00 12.00
US287B Tim Anderson SP 50.00 120.00
Dugout
US288A Jose Altuve AS .15 .40
US289 Cesar Vargas RC .40 1.00
US290A Miguel Cabrera AS .20 .50
US291A Dellin Betances AS .15 .40
US292A Aledmys Diaz RC .60 1.50
US292B Aledmys Diaz SP 1.50 4.00
Tipping cap
US293 Hansel Robles .12 .30
US294A Kris Bryant AS .25 .60
US295 Nomar Mazara RD .20 .50
US296 Jeurys Familia AS .15 .40
US297A Bryce Harper AS .30 .75
US298 Jhoulys Chacin .12 .30
US299 Julio Teheran AS .15 .40
US300 A.J. Ellis .12 .30

2016 Topps Update Black

*BLACK: 10X TO 25X BASIC
*BLACK RC: 3X TO 8X BASIC RC
STATED PRINT RUN 65 SER.#'d SETS
US33 Aledmys Diaz AS 15.00 40.00
US44 Aledmys Diaz RD 15.00 40.00
US167 Corey Seager AS 20.00 50.00
US205 Corey Seager HRD 20.00 50.00
US232 Clayton Kershaw AS 20.00 50.00
US292 Aledmys Diaz 15.00 40.00
US294 Kris Bryant AS 15.00 40.00

2016 Topps Update Black and White Negative

*BW NEGATIVE: 6X TO 15X BASIC
*BW NEGATIVE RC: 2X TO 5X BASIC
US33 Aledmys Diaz AS 8.00 20.00
US44 Aledmys Diaz RD 8.00 20.00
US141 Buster Posey AS 10.00 25.00
US175 Mike Trout AS 15.00 40.00
US232 Clayton Kershaw AS 10.00 25.00
US266 Willson Contreras 8.00 20.00
US292 Aledmys Diaz 8.00 20.00

2016 Topps Update Gold

*GOLD: 2X TO 5X BASIC
*GOLD RC: .6X TO 1.5X BASIC RC
STATED PRINT RUN 2016 SER.#'d SETS

2016 Topps Update Pink

*PINK: 12X TO 30X BASIC
*PINK RC: 4X TO 10X BASIC RC
STATED PRINT RUN 50 SER.#'d SETS
US33 Aledmys Diaz AS 20.00 50.00
US44 Aledmys Diaz RD 20.00 50.00
US167 Corey Seager AS 25.00 60.00
US205 Corey Seager HRD 25.00 60.00
US232 Clayton Kershaw AS 25.00 60.00
US292 Aledmys Diaz 20.00 50.00
US294 Kris Bryant AS 20.00 50.00

2016 Topps Update Rainbow Foil

*FOIL: 3X TO 8X BASIC
*FOIL RC: 1X TO 2.5X BASIC RC

2016 Topps Update 3000 Hits Club

COMPLETE SET (20) 4.00 10.00
3000H1 Carl Yastrzemski .75 2.00
3000H2 Ty Cobb .75 2.00
3000H3 Hank Aaron 1.00 2.50
3000H4 Stan Musial .75 2.00
3000H5 Honus Wagner .75 2.00
3000H6 Paul Molitor .50 1.25
3000H7 Willie Mays 1.00 2.50
3000H8 Eddie Murray .40 1.00
3000H9 Cal Ripken Jr. 1.50 4.00
3000H10 George Brett 1.00 2.50
3000H11 Robin Yount .50 1.25
3000H12 Tony Gwynn .50 1.25
3000H13 Ichiro Suzuki .60 1.50
3000H14 Craig Biggio .40 1.00
3000H15 Rickey Henderson
3000H16 Rod Carew .40 1.00
3000H17 Lou Brock .40 1.00
3000H18 Wade Boggs .40 1.00
3000H19 Roberto Clemente 1.25 3.00
3000H20 Al Kaline .50 1.25

2016 Topps Update 3000 Hits Club Autographs

STATED PRINT RUN 25 SER.#'d SETS
EXCHANGE DEADLINE 9/30/2018
3000AI Ichiro Suzuki 200.00 400.00
3000AAK Al Kaline 25.00 50.00
3000ACB Craig Biggio
3000ACR Cal Ripken Jr. 40.00 100.00
3000ACY Carl Yastrzemski 30.00 80.00
3000APM Paul Molitor 20.00 50.00
3000ARC Rod Carew
3000ARH Rickey Henderson
3000AWB Wade Boggs

2016 Topps Update 3000 Hits Club Medallions

*GOLD/50: 1.2X TO 3X BASIC
3000M1 Ty Cobb 2.00 5.00
3000M2 Hank Aaron 2.50 6.00
3000M3 Stan Musial 2.00 5.00
3000M4 Honus Wagner 1.25 3.00
3000M5 Carl Yastrzemski 2.00 5.00
3000M6 Paul Molitor 1.25 3.00
3000M7 Willie Mays 2.50 6.00
3000M8 Eddie Murray 1.00 2.50
3000M9 Cal Ripken Jr. 4.00 10.00
3000M10 George Brett 2.50 6.00
3000M11 Robin Yount 1.25 3.00
3000M12 Tony Gwynn 1.25 3.00
3000M13 Alex Rodriguez 1.50 4.00
3000M14 Craig Biggio 1.00 2.50
3000M15 Rickey Henderson 1.25 3.00
3000M16 Rod Carew 1.00 2.50
3000M17 Lou Brock 1.00 2.50
3000M18 Wade Boggs 1.00 2.50
3000M19 Roberto Clemente 3.00 8.00
3000M20 Al Kaline 1.25 3.00

2016 Topps Update 500 Home Run Club Stamps

PRINT RUNS B/WN 220-375 COPIES PER
500SCAP Albert Pujols/375 20.00 50.00
500SCAR Alex Rodriguez/375 6.00 15.00
500SCBR Babe Ruth/375 12.00 30.00
500SCDO David Ortiz/375 8.00 20.00
500SCEM Eddie Murray/375 4.00 10.00
500SCFT Frank Thomas/375 8.00 20.00
500SCHA Hank Aaron/375 10.00 25.00
500SCHK Harmon Killebrew/375 5.00 12.00
500SCKG Ken Griffey Jr./375 10.00 25.00
500SCRJ Reggie Jackson/375 4.00 10.00
500SCRP Rafael Palmeiro/375 4.00 10.00
500SCTW Ted Williams/375 10.00 25.00
500SCWM Willie McCovey/375 4.00 10.00
500SCMMC Mark McGwire/220 8.00 20.00
500SCWMA Willie Mays/375 10.00 25.00

2016 Topps Update 500 HR Futures Club

COMPLETE SET (20) 10.00 25.00
*GOLD: .5X TO 1.2X BASIC
*SILVER: .5X TO 1.2X BASIC
5001 Miguel Cabrera .60 1.50
5002 Prince Fielder .50 1.25
5003 Ryan Braun .50 1.25
5004 Giancarlo Stanton .60 1.50
5005 Mike Trout 3.00 8.00
5006 Bryce Harper 1.00 2.50
5007 Adam Jones .50 1.25
5008 Nolan Arenado .75 2.00
5009 Adrian Gonzalez .50 1.25
50010 Jose Bautista .50 1.25
50011 Josh Donaldson .50 1.25
50012 Paul Goldschmidt .60 1.50
50013 Carlos Gonzalez .50 1.25
50014 Justin Upton .50 1.25
50015 Kyle Schwarber 1.25 3.00
50016 Chris Davis .40 1.00
50017 Anthony Rizzo 1.00 2.50
50018 Carlos Correa .60 1.50
50019 Joc Pederson .50 1.25
50020 Miguel Sano .60 1.50

2016 Topps Update 500 HR Futures Club Medallions

*GOLD/50: 1X TO 2.5X BASIC
500M1 Miguel Cabrera 4.00 10.00
500M2 Prince Fielder 3.00 8.00
500M3 Ryan Braun 3.00 8.00
500M4 Giancarlo Stanton 4.00 10.00
500M5 Mike Trout 6.00 15.00
500M6 Bryce Harper 5.00 12.00
500M7 Adam Jones 3.00 8.00
500M8 Nolan Arenado 5.00 12.00
500M9 Adrian Gonzalez 3.00 8.00
500M10 Jose Bautista 3.00 8.00
500M11 Josh Donaldson 3.00 8.00
500M12 Paul Goldschmidt 4.00 10.00
500M13 Carlos Gonzalez 3.00 8.00
500M14 Justin Upton 3.00 8.00
500M15 Kyle Schwarber 6.00 15.00

500M16 Chris Davis 2.50 6.00
500M17 Anthony Rizzo 6.00 15.00
500M18 Carlos Correa 4.00 10.00
500M19 Joc Pederson 3.00 8.00
500M20 Miguel Sano 4.00 10.00

2016 Topps Update 500 HR Futures Club Relics

STATED PRINT RUN 99 SER.#'d SETS
500RAG Adrian Gonzalez 12.00 30.00
500RAJ Adam Jones 5.00 12.00
500RAR Anthony Rizzo 10.00 25.00
500RBH Bryce Harper 10.00 25.00
500RCC Carlos Correa 6.00 15.00
500RGS Giancarlo Stanton 6.00 15.00
500RJU Justin Upton 5.00 12.00
500RKS Kyle Schwarber 10.00 25.00
500RMC Miguel Cabrera 6.00 15.00
500RMS Miguel Sano 6.00 15.00
500RMT Mike Trout 30.00 80.00
500RNA Nolan Arenado 8.00 20.00
500RPF Prince Fielder 5.00 12.00
500RPG Paul Goldschmidt 6.00 15.00
500RRB Ryan Braun 5.00 12.00

2016 Topps Update All-Star Game Access

COMPLETE SET (25) 25.00 60.00
MLB1 Clayton Kershaw 2.00 5.00
MLB2 Manny Machado 1.00 2.50
MLB3 Anthony Rizzo 1.50 4.00
MLB4 Nolan Arenado 1.25 3.00
MLB5 Kris Bryant 1.25 3.00
MLB6 Chris Sale 1.00 2.50
MLB7 Jose Altuve .75 2.00
MLB8 Mike Trout 5.00 12.00
MLB9 Robinson Cano .75 2.00
MLB10 Bryce Harper 1.50 4.00
MLB11 David Ortiz 1.00 2.50
MLB12 Buster Posey 1.25 3.00
MLB13 Corey Seager 5.00 12.00
MLB14 Wil Myers .60 1.50
MLB15 Dellin Betances .75 2.00
MLB16 Zach Britton .75 2.00
MLB17 Miguel Cabrera 1.00 2.50
MLB18 Bartolo Colon .60 1.50
MLB19 Johnny Cueto .75 2.00
MLB20 Josh Donaldson .75 2.00
MLB21 Edwin Encarnacion 1.00 2.50
MLB22 Carlos Gonzalez .75 2.00
MLB23 Eric Hosmer .75 2.00
MLB24 Daniel Murphy .75 2.00
MLB25 Salvador Perez .75 2.00

2016 Topps Update All-Star Stitches

*GOLD/50: .75X TO 2X BASIC
ASTITAD Adam Duvall 6.00 15.00
ASTITADI Aledmys Diaz 8.00 20.00
ASTITAM Andrew Miller 5.00 12.00
ASTITARI Anthony Rizzo 5.00 12.00
ASTITARU Addison Russell 5.00 12.00
ASTITAS Aaron Sanchez 4.00 10.00
ASTITBBE Brandon Belt 4.00 10.00
ASTITBC Bartolo Colon 4.00 10.00
ASTITBH Bryce Harper 5.00 12.00
ASTITBP Buster Posey 4.00 10.00
ASTITBZ Ben Zobrist 5.00 12.00
ASTITCB Carlos Beltran 4.00 10.00
ASTITCH Cole Hamels 2.50 6.00
ASTITCK Clayton Kershaw 6.00 15.00
ASTITCKL Corey Kluber 5.00 12.00
ASTITCS Corey Seager 10.00 25.00
ASTITCSA Chris Sale 3.00 8.00
ASTITDB Dellin Betances 4.00 10.00
ASTITDF Dexter Fowler 4.00 10.00
ASTITDM Daniel Murphy 4.00 10.00
ASTITDO David Ortiz 8.00 20.00
ASTITDP Drew Pomeranz 2.50 6.00
ASTITDS Danny Salazar 2.50 6.00
ASTITEE Edwin Encarnacion 4.00 10.00
ASTITEH Eric Hosmer 2.50 6.00
ASTITFL Francisco Lindor 8.00 20.00
ASTITID Ian Desmond 2.00 5.00
ASTITJA Jake Arrieta 4.00 10.00
ASTITJAL Jose Altuve 4.00 10.00
ASTITJB Jackie Bradley Jr. 4.00 10.00
ASTITJBR Jay Bruce 2.50 6.00
ASTITJC Johnny Cueto 2.50 6.00
ASTITJD Josh Donaldson 2.50 6.00
ASTITJF Jose Fernandez 6.00 15.00
ASTITJL Jon Lester 4.00 10.00
ASTITJT Julio Teheran 4.00 10.00
ASTITKB Kris Bryant 4.00 10.00
ASTITMB Madison Bumgarner 2.50 6.00
ASTITMBE Mookie Betts 5.00 12.00
ASTITMC Matt Carpenter 3.00 8.00
ASTITMCA Miguel Cabrera 5.00 12.00
ASTITMMA Manny Machado 5.00 12.00
ASTITMO Marcell Ozuna 3.00 8.00
ASTITMS Michael Saunders 2.50 6.00
ASTITMSC Max Scherzer 3.00 8.00
ASTITMT Mark Trumbo 3.00 8.00
ASTITMTR Mike Trout 15.00 40.00
ASTITMW Matt Wieters 3.00 8.00
ASTITNA Nolan Arenado 4.00 10.00
ASTITNS Noah Syndergaard 5.00 12.00
ASTITPG Paul Goldschmidt 4.00 10.00
ASTITRC Robinson Cano 2.50 6.00
ASTITSM Starling Marte 2.50 6.00
ASTITSP Salvador Perez 4.00 10.00
ASTITSS Stephen Strasburg 3.00 8.00
ASTITSV Stephen Vogt 2.50 6.00
ASTITSW Steven Wright 5.00 12.00
ASTITTF Todd Frazier 2.50 6.00
ASTITWR Wilson Ramos 4.00 10.00
ASTITXB Xander Bogaerts 5.00 12.00
ASTITZB Zach Britton 2.50 6.00

2016 Topps Update All-Star Stitches Autographs

STATED PRINT RUN 25 SER.#'d SETS
EXCHANGE DEADLINE 9/30/2018
ASAPAR Anthony Rizzo 100.00 250.00
ASAPBH Bryce Harper 125.00 300.00
ASAPBP Buster Posey 125.00 300.00
ASAPCK Clayton Kershaw 125.00 300.00
ASAPDO David Ortiz 100.00 250.00
ASAPJAR Jake Arrieta 100.00 250.00
ASAPKB Kris Bryant 150.00 400.00
ASAPMM Manny Machado 100.00 250.00
ASAPMT Mike Trout 150.00 400.00
ASAPNA Nolan Arenado 60.00 150.00
ASAPNS Noah Syndergaard 50.00 120.00
ASAPRC Robinson Cano 30.00 80.00

2016 Topps Update All-Star Stitches Dual

STATED PRINT RUN 25 SER.#'d SETS
ASDAR Rizzo/Arrieta 25.00 60.00
ASDBBR Bogaerts/Betts 25.00 60.00
ASDBC Cueto/Bumgarner 8.00 20.00
ASDBO Ortiz/Betts 30.00 80.00
ASDBR Rizzo/Bryant 30.00 80.00
ASDDE Encarnacion/Donaldson 25.00 60.00
ASDHS Strasburg/Harper 25.00 60.00
ASDHT Trout/Harper 40.00 100.00
ASDPB Bumgarner/Posey 30.00 80.00
ASDPH Hosmer/Perez 30.00 80.00

2016 Topps Update All-Star Stitches Triple

STATED PRINT RUN 25 SER.#'d SETS
ASTABR Brnt/Arrta/Rzzo 30.00 80.00
ASTBBB Bgrts/Btts/Brdly Jr. 30.00 80.00
ASTBOB Btts/Bgrts/Ortiz 30.00 80.00
ASTBRR Rzzo/Brnt/Rssll 40.00 100.00
ASTFSS Strsbrg/Sndrgrd/Frnndz 30.00 80.00
ASTHTB Brnt/Trt/Hrpr 100.00 250.00
ASTMAD Dnldsn/Mchdo/Arndo 30.00 80.00
ASTMTW Trumbo/Machado/Wieters 20.00 50.00
ASTPBC Clo/Psy/Bmgrnr 25.00 60.00
ASTRLS Rssll/Sgr/Lndr 30.00 80.00

2016 Topps Update Fire

COMPLETE SET (15) 4.00 10.00
F1 Kenta Maeda .60 1.50
F2 Michael Conforto .40 1.00
F3 Bryce Harper .75 2.00
F4 Mike Trout 2.50 6.00
F5 Carlos Correa .50 1.25
F6 Ken Griffey Jr. 1.00 2.50
F7 Clayton Kershaw 1.00 2.50
F8 Noah Syndergaard .40 1.00
F9 Kris Bryant .60 1.50
F10 Anthony Rizzo .75 2.00
F11 Corey Seager 2.50 6.00
F12 Miguel Sano .50 1.25
F13 Andrew McCutchen .50 1.25
F14 Josh Donaldson .40 1.00
F15 Giancarlo Stanton .50 1.25

2016 Topps Update Fire Autographs

STATED PRINT RUN 25 SER.#'d SETS
EXCHANGE DEADLINE 9/30/2018
FA1 Kenta Maeda 40.00 100.00
FA5 Carlos Correa 60.00 150.00
FA7 Clayton Kershaw
FA8 Noah Syndergaard 40.00 100.00
FA9 Kris Bryant 125.00 300.00
FA10 Anthony Rizzo 30.00 80.00
FA11 Corey Seager EXCH 75.00 200.00
FA12 Miguel Sano 20.00 50.00

2016 Topps Update First Pitch

COMPLETE SET (20) 3.00 8.00
FP1 Jeff Bauman .75 2.00
FP2 Jake Gyllenhaal .75 2.00
FP3 Warren G .75 2.00
FP4 Brady Kahle .75 2.00
FP5 Keith Urban .75 2.00
FP6 Aubrey Plaza .75 2.00
FP7 Chance the Rapper .75 2.00
FP8 Burke Waldron .75 2.00
FP9 Craig Sager .75 2.00
FP10 JoJo Fletcher .75 2.00

2016 Topps Update First Pitch Relics

STATED PRINT RUN 25 SER.#'d SETS
FPRAP Aubrey Plaza 20.00 50.00
FPRBW Burke Waldron 20.00 50.00
FPRCS Craig Sager 20.00 50.00
FPRCTR Chance the Rapper 20.00 50.00
FPRJF JoJo Fletcher 20.00 50.00
FPRKU Keith Urban 20.00 50.00
FPRWG Warren G 20.00 50.00

2016 Topps Update Target Exclusive Rookies

TAR1 Luis Severino 1.50 4.00
TAR2 Trea Turner 4.00 10.00
TAR3 Jose Berrios 1.50 4.00
TAR4 Trevor Story 5.00 12.00
TAR5 Nomar Mazara 2.00 5.00
TAR6 Julio Urias 4.00 10.00
TAR7 Blake Snell 1.50 4.00
TAR8 Jameson Taillon 1.50 4.00
TAR9 Hyun-Soo Kim 2.00 5.00
TAR10 Lucas Giolito 2.00 5.00
TAR11 Michael Fulmer 2.00 5.00
TAR12 Byung-Ho Park 1.50 4.00
TAR13 Michael Conforto 1.50 4.00
TAR14 Jon Gray 1.25 3.00
TAR15 Kenta Maeda 2.50 6.00
TAR16 Peter O'Brien 1.25 3.00
TAR17 Stephen Piscotty 2.00 5.00
TAR18 Miguel Sano 2.00 5.00
TAR19 Kyle Schwarber 4.00 10.00
TAR20 Corey Seager 10.00 25.00

2016 Topps Update Team Franklin

COMPLETE SET (20) 4.00 10.00
TF1 Miguel Cabrera .50 1.25
TF2 Yadier Molina .50 1.25
TF3 Robinson Cano .40 1.00
TF4 Salvador Perez .40 1.00
TF5 Paul Goldschmidt .50 1.25
TF6 Jose Altuve .40 1.00
TF7 Evan Longoria .40 1.00
TF8 Justin Upton .40 1.00
TF9 Joey Votto .50 1.25
TF10 Yoenis Cespedes .50 1.25
TF11 Hunter Pence .40 1.00
TF12 Dustin Pedroia .50 1.25
TF13 Ryan Braun .40 1.00
TF14 Starling Marte .40 1.00
TF15 Jose Abreu .50 1.25
TF16 Edwin Encarnacion .50 1.25
TF17 Hanley Ramirez .40 1.00
TF18 Miguel Sano .50 1.25
TF19 Josh Reddick .30 .75
TF20 Ben Zobrist .40 1.00

2016 Topps Update Team Franklin Autographs

STATED PRINT RUN 25 SER.#'d SETS
EXCHANGE DEADLINE 9/30/2018
TFADP Dustin Pedroia 20.00 50.00
TFAEL Evan Longoria
TFAHR Hanley Ramirez 10.00 25.00
TFAMS Miguel Sano 20.00 50.00
TFARC Robinson Cano 20.00 50.00

2016 Topps Update Walmart Exclusive Rookies

W1 Aaron Nola 2.50 6.00
W2 Henry Owens 1.50 4.00
W3 Jose Berrios 1.50 4.00
W4 Trevor Story 5.00 12.00
W5 Nomar Mazara 2.00 5.00
W6 Julio Urias 4.00 10.00
W7 Blake Snell 1.50 4.00
W8 Jameson Taillon 1.50 4.00
W9 Hyun-Soo Kim 2.00 5.00
W10 Lucas Giolito 2.00 5.00
W11 Michael Fulmer 2.00 5.00
W12 Byung-Ho Park 1.50 4.00
W13 Michael Conforto 1.50 4.00
W14 Jon Gray 1.25 3.00
W15 Kenta Maeda 2.50 6.00
W16 Peter O'Brien 1.25 3.00
W17 Stephen Piscotty 2.00 5.00
W18 Miguel Sano 2.00 5.00
W19 Kyle Schwarber 4.00 10.00
W20 Corey Seager 10.00 25.00

2016 Topps Walmart Holiday Snowflake

HMW1 Mike Trout 1.50 4.00
HMW2 Jose Berrios RC .25 .60
HMW3 Paul Goldschmidt .30 .75
HMW4 Jason Heyward .25 .60
HMW5 CC Sabathia .25 .60
HMW6 Starling Marte .25 .60
HMW7 George Springer .25 .60
HMW8 Jaime Garcia .20 .50
HMW9 Justin Upton .25 .60
HMW10 Brett Gardner .25 .60
HMW11 Jose Abreu .30 .75
HMW12 Dallas Keuchel .25 .60
HMW13 Aroldis Chapman .30 .75
HMW14 Andrelton Simmons .20 .50
HMW15 Adam Jones .25 .60
HMW16 Matt Holliday .30 .75
HMW17 Jacoby Ellsbury .25 .60
HMW18 Wade Davis .20 .50
HMW19 Joe Panik .25 .60
HMW20 Alex Rodriguez .40 1.00
HMW21 Matt Andriese .25 .60
HMW22 Byung-Ho Park RC .25 .60
HMW23 Carlos Gonzalez .25 .60
HMW24 Manny Machado .30 .75
HMW25 Noah Syndergaard .25 .60
HMW26 Julio Urias RC .60 1.50
HMW27 Dustin Pedroia .30 .75
HMW28 Jackie Bradley Jr. .30 .75
HMW29 Nelson Cruz .30 .75
HMW30 Jonathan Lucroy .25 .60
HMW31 Corey Kluber .25 .60
HMW32 Adeiny Hechavarria .20 .50
HMW33 Seung-Hwan Oh RC .50 1.25
HMW34 Michael Fulmer RC .30 .75
HMW35 Andrew Miller .25 .60
HMW36 Shelby Miller .25 .60
HMW37 Raisel Iglesias .25 .60
HMW38 Nori Aoki .20 .50
HMW39 Anthony Rizzo .50 1.25
HMW40 Byron Buxton .25 .60
HMW41 Jake Odorizzi .20 .50
HMW42 Madison Bumgarner .25 .60
HMW43 Masahiro Tanaka .25 .60
HMW44 Curtis Granderson .25 .60
HMW45 Aaron Nola RC .40 1.00
HMW46 Tyler White RC .20 .50
HMW47 Johnny Cueto .25 .60
HMW48 Andrew McCutchen .30 .75
HMW49 Francisco Rodriguez .25 .60
HMW50 Asdrubal Cabrera .25 .60
HMW51 Luis Severino RC .25 .60
HMW52 Marcell Ozuna .30 .75
HMW53 Vince Velasquez .20 .50
HMW54 Melvin Upton Jr. .25 .60
HMW55 Lorenzo Cain .20 .50
HMW56 David Price .25 .60
HMW57 Michael Conforto RC .25 .60
HMW58 Kris Bryant .40 1.00
HMW59 Kole Calhoun .20 .50
HMW60 Freddie Freeman .40 1.00
HMW61 Brandon Crawford .25 .60
HMW62 Aledmys Diaz RC .30 .75
HMW63 Ryan Howard .25 .60
HMW64 Giancarlo Stanton .30 .75
HMW65 Mark Teixeira .25 .60
HMW66 Marco Estrada .20 .50
HMW67 Mallex Smith RC .20 .50
HMW68 Mark Trumbo .20 .50
HMW69 Zack Greinke .25 .60
HMW70 Matt Wieters .30 .75
HMW71 Jon Lester .25 .60
HMW72 Jeremy Hazelbaker RC .25 .60
HMW73 Jacob deGrom .30 .75
HMW74 Clayton Kershaw .60 1.50
HMW75 Max Scherzer .25 .60
HMW76 David Ortiz .30 .75
HMW77 Evan Gattis .20 .50
HMW78 Ichiro .40 1.00
HMW79 J.D. Martinez .30 .75
HMW80 Josh Donaldson .25 .60
HMW81 Kyle Schwarber RC .60 1.50
HMW82 Justin Verlander .30 .75
HMW83 Evan Longoria .25 .60
HMW84 Ian Desmond .20 .50
HMW85 Neil Walker .25 .60
HMW86 Matt Harvey .25 .60
HMW87 Steven Matz .25 .60
HMW88 Matt Adams .20 .50
HMW89 Hyun-Soo Kim RC .30 .75
HMW90 Dexter Fowler .25 .60
HMW91 Prince Fielder .25 .60
HMW92 Elvis Andrus .25 .60
HMW93 Cole Hamels .25 .60
HMW94 Albert Almora RC .25 .60
HMW95 Tanner Roark .20 .50
HMW96 Gerrit Cole .30 .75
HMW97 Matt Carpenter .30 .75
HMW98 Jason Kipnis .25 .60
HMW99 Miguel Cabrera .30 .75
HMW100 Carlos Martinez .25 .60
HMW101 Eric Hosmer .25 .60
HMW102 Maikel Franco .25 .60
HMW103 Jason Hammel .25 .60
HMW104 Xander Bogaerts .30 .75
HMW105 Dellin Betances .25 .60
HMW106 Hanley Ramirez .25 .60
HMW107 Joe Mauer .25 .60
HMW108 R.A. Dickey .25 .60
HMW109 Russell Martin .20 .50
HMW110 Bryce Harper .50 1.25
HMW111 Daniel Murphy .25 .60
HMW112 Bartolo Colon .20 .50
HMW113 Denard Span .20 .50
HMW114 Yu Darvish .30 .75
HMW115 Todd Frazier .20 .50
HMW116 Sonny Gray .20 .50
HMW117 Trayce Thompson RC .30 .75
HMW118 Adrian Beltre .30 .75
HMW119 Yunel Escobar .20 .50
HMW120 Trevor Rosenthal .25 .60
HMW121 James Shields .20 .50
HMW122 Joc Pederson .25 .60
HMW123 Josh Reddick .20 .50
HMW124 Doug Fister .20 .50
HMW125 Gregory Polanco .25 .60
HMW126 Henry Owens RC .25 .60
HMW127 Jose Bautista .25 .60
HMW128 Robert Stephenson RC .20 .50
HMW129 Corey Seager RC 1.50 4.00
HMW130 Eugenio Suarez .25 .60
HMW131 Tyler Naquin RC .30 .75
HMW132 Carlos Correa .30 .75
HMW133 Michael Brantley .25 .60
HMW134 Stephen Strasburg .30 .75
HMW135 Justin Bour .25 .60
HMW136 Trevor Story RC .75 2.00
HMW137 Josh Harrison .20 .50
HMW138 Stephen Piscotty RC .30 .75
HMW139 Cameron Maybin .20 .50
HMW140 Yovani Gallardo .20 .50
HMW141 Mookie Betts .50 1.25
HMW142 Michael Pineda .20 .50
HMW143 Adam Wainwright .25 .60
HMW144 Erick Aybar .20 .50
HMW145 Odubel Herrera .25 .60
HMW146 Addison Russell .30 .75
HMW147 Michael Wacha .25 .60
HMW148 Francisco Lindor .30 .75
HMW149 Kenta Maeda RC .40 1.00
HMW150 Yasiel Puig .30 .75
HMW151 Jeremy Hellickson .20 .50
HMW152 DJ LeMahieu .30 .75
HMW153 Adrian Gonzalez .25 .60
HMW154 Miguel Sano RC .30 .75
HMW155 Nomar Mazara RC .30 .75
HMW156 Jon Jay .20 .50
HMW157 Hunter Pence .25 .60
HMW158 Edwin Encarnacion .30 .75
HMW159 Didi Gregorius .25 .60
HMW160 Chris Archer .20 .50
HMW161 Buster Posey .40 1.00
HMW162 Salvador Perez .25 .60
HMW163 Felix Hernandez .25 .60
HMW164 Albert Pujols .40 1.00
HMW165 Mike Moustakas .25 .60
HMW166 Roberto Osuna .20 .50
HMW167 Craig Kimbrel .25 .60
HMW168 Jeff Samardzija .20 .50
HMW169 Jed Lowrie .20 .50
HMW170 Ian Kinsler .25 .60
HMW171 Jake Arrieta .25 .60
HMW172 Blake Snell RC .25 .60
HMW173 Ross Stripling RC .20 .50
HMW174 Martin Prado .20 .50
HMW175 Troy Tulowitzki .30 .75
HMW176 Ryan Braun .25 .60
HMW177 Chris Sale .30 .75
HMW178 Matt Duffy .20 .50
HMW179 Ender Inciarte .20 .50
HMW180 Wil Myers .20 .50
HMW181 Nolan Arenado .40 1.00
HMW182 Starlin Castro .20 .50
HMW183 Yadier Molina .30 .75
HMW184 Javier Baez .40 1.00
HMW185 Carlos Rodon .30 .75
HMW186 Christian Yelich .40 1.00
HMW187 Stephen Vogt .25 .60
HMW188 Robinson Cano .25 .60
HMW189 Brandon Belt .25 .60
HMW190 Danny Salazar .25 .60
HMW191 Victor Martinez .25 .60
HMW192 Joey Votto .30 .75
HMW193 Rougned Odor .25 .60
HMW194 Kyle Seager .20 .50
HMW195 Marcus Stroman .25 .60
HMW196 Kenley Jansen .25 .60
HMW197 Jameson Taillon RC .25 .60
HMW198 David Wright .25 .60
HMW199 Yoenis Cespedes .30 .75
HMW200 Nick Castellanos .30 .75

2016 Topps Walmart Holiday Snowflake Metallic

*METALLIC: 1.5X TO 4X BASIC

2016 Topps Walmart Holiday Snowflake Relics

RAB Aaron Blair 2.50 6.00
RAC Aroldis Chapman 4.00 10.00
RAG Adrian Gonzalez 3.00 8.00
RAJ Adam Jones 3.00 8.00
RAN Aaron Nola 5.00 12.00
RBS Blake Snell 3.00 8.00
RCA Chris Archer 2.50 6.00
RCD Corey Dickerson 2.50 6.00
RCK Corey Kluber 3.00 8.00
RCM Colin Moran 2.50 6.00
RCR Carlos Rodon 4.00 10.00
RCS Chris Sale 4.00 10.00
RDP Dustin Pedroia 4.00 10.00
RDW David Wright 3.00 8.00
REH Eric Hosmer 3.00 8.00
REL Evan Longoria 3.00 8.00
RFF Freddie Freeman 5.00 12.00
RGC Gerrit Cole 4.00 10.00
RGS Giancarlo Stanton 4.00 10.00
RHR Hanley Ramirez 3.00 8.00
RIK Ian Kinsler 3.00 8.00
RJD Jacob deGrom 4.00 10.00
RJR Joey Rickard 2.50 6.00
RJS Jorge Soler 4.00 10.00
RJU Justin Upton 3.00 8.00
RKC Kole Calhoun 2.50 6.00
RKK Kevin Kiermaier 3.00 8.00
RLS Luis Severino 3.00 8.00
RMC Miguel Cabrera 4.00 10.00
RMD Matt Duffy 2.50 6.00
RMP Michael Pineda 2.50 6.00
RNM Nomar Mazara 4.00 10.00
RNS Noah Syndergaard 3.00 8.00
RRB Ryan Braun 3.00 8.00
RRC Robinson Cano 3.00 8.00
RSD Sean Doolittle 2.50 6.00
RSG Sonny Gray 3.00 8.00
RTT Troy Tulowitzki 4.00 10.00
RYC Yoenis Cespedes 4.00 10.00
RYP Yasiel Puig 4.00 10.00
RARI Anthony Rizzo 6.00 15.00
RARU Addison Russell 4.00 10.00
RCMA Carlos Martinez 3.00 8.00
RDPR David Price 3.00 8.00
RGSP George Springer 3.00 8.00
RJAB Jose Abreu 4.00 10.00
RJHE Jason Heyward 3.00 8.00
RJPE Joc Pederson 3.00 8.00
RMSA Miguel Sano 4.00 10.00
RSMA Starling Marte 3.00 8.00
RTWA Taijuan Walker 2.50 6.00

2016 Topps Walmart Holiday Snowflake Autographs

AAC Alex Cobb/100
AAN Aaron Nola/100
AARE A.J. Reed/100
ABPA Byung-Ho Park/50
ABS Blake Snell/25
ACKL Corey Kluber/100
ACR Carlos Rodon
AFL Francisco Lindor/25
AJB Jose Berrios/50
AJD Jacob deGrom/10
AJE Jerad Eickhoff/95
AJH Jason Heyward
AJP Joe Panik/100
AJS Jorge Soler/25
AJT Jameson Taillon/25
AKB Kris Bryant/10
AKK Kevin Kiermaier/100
AKM Kendrys Morales/100
AKS Kyle Schwarber
ALG Lucas Giolito/50
ALS Luis Severino
AMD Matt Duffy/200
AMF Michael Fulmer/25
AMFR Maikel Franco
AMP Michael Pineda
AMS Miguel Sano/25
ANM Nomar Mazara/25
ANS Noah Syndergaard/10
APO Peter O'Brien/200
ARST Ross Stripling
ASD Sean Doolittle/50
ASP Stephen Piscotty/100
ATS Trevor Story/50
ATT Trea Turner/100
ATW Taijuan Walker

2017 Topps

COMP.RED.HOB.FACT SET (700) 30.00 80.00
COMP.BLUE.RET.FACT SET (700) 30.00 80.00
COMP. SET w/o SP'S (700) 25.00 60.00
SP SER.1 ODDS 1:678 HOBBY
SP SER.1 ODDS 1:136 JUMBO
SP SER.1 ODDS 1:189 FAT PACK
SP SER.1 ODDS 1:566 RETAIL
SP SER.1 ODDS 1:95 ALL HANGERS
SP SER.1 ODDS 1:680 ALL BLASTERS
SP SER.2 ODDS 1:353 HOBBY
SER.1 PLATE ODDS 1:7286 HOBBY
SER.1 PLATE ODDS 1:2020 FAT PACK
SER.1 PLATE ODDS 1:1011 HANGER
SER.1 PLATE ODDS 1:7285 BLASTER
SER.1 PLATE ODDS 1:1454 JUMBO
SER.1 PLATE ODDS 1:6028 TAR. RETAIL
SER.1 PLATE ODDS 1:6042 WM. RETAIL
SER.2 PLATE ODDS 1:3773 WM. HOBBY
PLATE PRINT RUN 1 SET PER COLOR
BLACK-CYAN-MAGENTA-YELLOW ISSUED
NO PLATE PRICING DUE TO SCARCITY
1A Kris Bryant .30 .75
1B Bryant SP Dugout 30.00 80.00
1C Bryant UPD SP 1.25 3.00
2 Jason Hammel .20 .50
3 Chris Capuano .15 .40
4 Mark Reynolds .15 .40
5A Corey Seager .25 .60
5B Seager SP On-deck 25.00 60.00
6 Kevin Pillar .15 .40
7 Gary Sanchez .25 .60
8A Jose Berrios .20 .50
8B Jose Berrios SP red jersey 20.00 50.00
9A Chris Sale .25 .60
9B Sale Blk jkt SP 25.00 60.00
10 Steven Souza Jr. .20 .50
11 Jake Smolinski .15 .40
12 Jerad Eickhoff .15 .40
13 Adeiny Hechavarria .15 .40
14 Travis d'Arnaud .20 .50
15 Braden Shipley RC .25 .60
16 Lance McCullers .15 .40
17 Daniel Descalso .15 .40
18 Jake Arrieta WS HL .20 .50
19 David Wright .20 .50
20A Mike Trout 1.25 3.00
20B Trout SP Dugout 125.00 300.00
20C Trout UPD SP 5.00 12.00
21 Robert Gsellman RC .25 .60
22 Keone Kela .15 .40
23 Marcell Ozuna .25 .60
24 Christian Friedrich .15 .40
25A Giancarlo Stanton .25 .60
25B Giancarlo Stanton SP standing against fence 25.00 60.00
26 David Peralta .15 .40
27 Kurt Suzuki .15 .40
28 Rick Porcello LL .20 .50
29 Marco Estrada .15 .40
30A Josh Bell RC .60 1.50
30B Bell UPD SP 1.50 4.00
30C Bell UPD SP 1.50 4.00
31 Carlos Carrasco .15 .40
32 Syndergaard/Harvey .20 .50
33 Carson Fulmer RC .25 .60
34A Bryce Harper .40 1.00
34B Harper SP On-deck 40.00 100.00
35 Nolan Arenado LL .30 .75
36 Machado/Trumbo/Jones .25 .60
37 Toronto Blue Jays .15 .40
38A Stephen Strasburg .25 .60
38B Stephen Strasburg SP stepping out of dugout 25.00 60.00
39 Aroldis Chapman WS HL .25 .60
40 Jordan Zimmermann .20 .50
41 Paulo Orlando .15 .40
42 Trevor Story .25 .60
43 Tyler Austin RC .40 1.00
44A Paul Goldschmidt .25 .60
44B Paul Goldschmidt SP Double Bubble Bath 25.00 60.00
45 Joakim Soria .15 .40
46 Will Middlebrooks .15 .40
47 Gregor Blanco .15 .40
48 Brian McCann .20 .50
49 Scooter Gennett .20 .50
50A Clayton Kershaw .50 1.25
50B Krshw SP Cap on chest 40.00 100.00
51 Jake Barrett .15 .40
52 Neftali Feliz .15 .40
53A Ryon Healy RC .30 .75
53B Ryon Healy UPD SP green jersey .75 2.00
53C Ryon Healy UPD SP throwing helmet .75 2.00
54 Dellin Betances .20 .50
55 Mark Trumbo LL .15 .40
56 Danny Salazar .20 .50
57 C.J. Cron .15 .40
58 Starling Marte .20 .50
59 Carlos Rodon .20 .50
60A Jose Bautista .20 .50
60B Jose Bautista SP pointing fingers 20.00 50.00
61 Xander Bogaerts .25 .60
62 Daniel Murphy .20 .50
63 Mike Moustakas .20 .50
64 Adam Eaton .25 .60
65A Madison Bumgarner .20 .50
65B Bmgrnr SP Cap at chest 20.00 50.00
66 Aaron Altherr .15 .40
67 Teoscar Hernandez RC .75 2.00
68 Zach Britton .20 .50
69 Henry Owens .15 .40
70 Wily Peralta .15 .40
71 Matt Shoemaker .20 .50
72 Chicago Cubs .15 .40
73 Kyle Schwarber .25 .60
74 Brett Lawrie .20 .50
75A Carlos Correa .25 .60
75B Correa SP Celebrate 25.00 60.00
76 Andre Ethier .20 .50
77 Austin Jackson .15 .40
78 Addison Russell WS HL .25 .60
79 Gabriel Ynoa RC .25 .60
80 Ivan Nova .20 .50
81 DJ LeMahieu LL .25 .60
82 Aaron Sanchez LL .20 .50
83 Anibal Sanchez .15 .40
84 Daniel Murphy LL .20 .50
85 Brandon Finnegan .15 .40
86 Asdrubal Cabrera .20 .50
87A Dansby Swanson RC .60 1.50
87B Swanson SP Red jsy 75.00 200.00
87C Swanson UPD SP 1.50 4.00
88 Freddy Galvis .15 .40
89 Brandon Moss .15 .40
90 Jason Grilli .15 .40
91A Troy Tulowitzki .25 .60
91B Troy Tulowitzki SP blue jersey 25.00 60.00
92 Derek Norris .15 .40
93 Matt Joyce .15 .40
94 Kyle Barraclough .15 .40
95 Chris Davis .15 .40
96 Jose Quintana .15 .40
97 Marcus Semien .15 .40
98 Junior Guerra .15 .40
99 Michael Wacha .20 .50
100 Nate Jones .15 .40
101 Pedro Alvarez .15 .40
102 Cameron Maybin .15 .40
103 Alex Reyes RC .30 .75
104 Dioner Navarro .15 .40
105 Francisco Rodriguez .20 .50
106 Brandon Crawford .20 .50
107 Howie Kendrick .15 .40
108 Nick Hundley .15 .40
109A Nelson Cruz .25 .60
109B Nelson Cruz SP blue hoodie 25.00 60.00
110 Joey Votto LL .25 .60
111 Edinson Volquez .15 .40
112 Angel Pagan .15 .40
113 Kyle Hendricks LL .25 .60
114 Colin Rea .15 .40
115 Joaquin Benoit .15 .40
116 Archie Bradley .15 .40
117 Adrian Gonzalez .20 .50
118 Billy Butler .15 .40
119A Francisco Lindor .25 .60
119B Lindor SP Running 60.00 150.00
120 Reynaldo Lopez RC .25 .60
121 Carlos Santana .20 .50
122 Cleveland Indians .15 .40
123 Jean Segura .20 .50
124 Travis Jankowski .15 .40
125 Yangervis Solarte .15 .40
126A Miguel Sano .20 .50
126B Miguel Sano SP red jersey 20.00 50.00
127 Michael Bourn .15 .40
128 Adam Duvall .25 .60
129 Adonis Garcia .15 .40
130A Dustin Pedroia .25 .60
130B Dustin Pedroia SP in dugout 25.00 60.00
131 J.A. Happ LL .20 .50
132 Randal Grichuk .15 .40
133 Jace Peterson .15 .40
134 Chase Utley .20 .50
135 Jered Weaver .20 .50
136 Matt Reynolds .15 .40
137 Yan Gomes .25 .60
138 Tyson Ross .15 .40
139 JaCoby Jones RC .30 .75
140 Jesse Hahn .15 .40
141 Baltimore Orioles .15 .40
142 Carlos Ruiz .15 .40
143 Nick Noonan .15 .40
144 Jon Lester LL .20 .50
145 Max Scherzer LL .25 .60
146 Chad Pinder RC .25 .60
147 Marcus Stroman .20 .50

148 Tim Anderson .25 .60
149 Gregory Polanco .20 .50
150A Miguel Cabrera .25 .60
150B Cabrera SP Dugout 60.00 150.00
150C Cabrera UPD SP 1.00 2.50
151 Jonathan Villar .15 .40
152 Nolan Arenado LL .30 .75
153 Nori Aoki .15 .40
154 Kevin Kiermaier .20 .50
155A Jacob deGrom .25 .60
155B Jacob deGrom SP 25.00 60.00
in dugout
156 Alex Colome .15 .40
157 Sean Doolittle .15 .40
158 Tommy Pham .15 .40
159 Justin Verlander LL .25 .60
160 Evan Gattis .15 .40
161A Mookie Betts .40 1.00
161B Betts SP Celebrate 40.00 100.00
162 Jon Lester LL .20 .50
163 Adam Conley .15 .40
164 Matt Harvey .20 .50
165 Corey Dickerson .15 .40
166 Jorge Soler .25 .60
167 Lorenzo Cain .15 .40
168 Ryan Zimmerman .20 .50
169 Steve Pearce .25 .60
170 Chris Carter LL .15 .40
171 Seth Smith .15 .40
172 Wilmer Flores .20 .50
173 Chicago White Sox .15 .40
174 Philadelphia Phillies .15 .40
175 Houston Astros .15 .40
176 Jaime Garcia .15 .40
177A Sonny Gray .20 .50
177B Sonny Gray SP 20.00 50.00
yellow jersey
178 Rick Porcello .20 .50
179 Matt Moore .20 .50
180 Jake McGee .15 .40
181 Aaron Hicks .20 .50
182 Keon Broxton .20 .50
183 Wade Miley .15 .40
184 Oswaldo Arcia .15 .40
185 Raisel Iglesias .20 .50
186 Andrew Cashner .15 .40
187 Sean Manaea .15 .40
188 Caleb Cotham .15 .40
189 Los Angeles Angels .15 .40
190 Blake Snell .20 .50
191 Wilson Ramos .15 .40
192 San Diego Padres .15 .40
193 Jimmy Nelson .15 .40
194 A.J. Ramos .15 .40
195 Edwin Encarnacion LL .25 .60
196 Colby Rasmus .20 .50
197 Jacoby Ellsbury .20 .50
198 Francisco Cervelli .15 .40
199A Johnny Cueto .20 .50
199B Johnny Cueto SP 20.00 50.00
blowing bubble
200 Homer Bailey .15 .40
201 Eddie Rosario .20 .50
202 Masahiro Tanaka LL .20 .50
203 Tyler Naquin .15 .40
204 Anthony Rizzo LL .40 1.00
205 Kendrys Morales .15 .40
206 Chicago Cubs WS HL .15 .40
207A Justin Upton .20 .50
207B Justin Upton SP 20.00 50.00
Tigres jersey
208A Masahiro Tanaka .20 .50
208B Tanaka SP Hi Five 40.00 100.00
209 Jon Gray .15 .40
210A Yoan Moncada RC .75 2.00
210B Moncada SP Red jsy 60.00 150.00
211 Noah Syndergaard LL .20 .50
212 Tanner Roark .15 .40
213 Alex Wood .15 .40
214 Jose Altuve LL .20 .50
215 Johnny Giavotella .15 .40
216 Denard Span .15 .40
217 Miami Marlins .15 .40
218 Michael Saunders .20 .50
219 Joe Musgrove RC .25 .60
220A Ryan Braun .20 .50
220B Ryan Braun SP 20.00 50.00
batting cage
221 Adam Wainwright .20 .50
222 Cesar Hernandez .15 .40
223 Jason Heyward .20 .50
224 Hector Rondon .15 .40
225 Wade Davis .15 .40
226 Logan Morrison .15 .40
227A Byron Buxton .20 .50
227B Buxton SP On-deck 50.00 120.00
228 Mike Foltynewicz .15 .40
229 David Ortiz LL .25 .60
230 Tulowitzki/Donaldson .25 .60
231 Rubby De La Rosa .15 .40
232 Geovany Soto .15 .40
233 Nomar Mazara .15 .40
234A Luke Weaver RC .30 .75
234B Luke Weaver UPD SP .75 2.00
head bowed
234C Luke Weaver UPD SP .75 2.00
in dugout
235 San Francisco Giants .15 .40
236 Lucas Duda UER .20 .50
Eric Campbell pictured
237 Joey Gallo .20 .50
238 Ben Zobrist .20 .50
239 Rajai Davis .15 .40
240 Mike Aviles .15 .40
241 Chris Young .15 .40
242 Mookie Betts LL .40 1.00
243A Felix Hernandez .20 .50
243B Felix Hernandez SP 20.00 50.00
hoodie
244A Freddie Freeman .30 .75
244B Freeman SP Water bath 30.00 80.00
244C Frmn UPD SP w/o Hat 1.25 3.00
245 Jackie Bradley Jr. .25 .60
246 Hunter Strickland .15 .40
247 Hector Neris .15 .40
248 Yasmany Tomas .15 .40
249 New York Yankees .15 .40
250 Sean Rodriguez .15 .40
251 Justin Turner .20 .50
252 Clint Robinson .15 .40
253 Tucker Barnhart .15 .40
254 Wade LeBlanc .15 .40
255A Orlando Arcia RC .40 1.00
255B Orlando Arcia UPD SP 1.00 2.50
fists out
255C Orlando Arcia UPD SP 1.00 2.50
in dugout
256 Tony Watson .15 .40
257 Corey Kluber LL .20 .50
258 Matt Adams .15 .40
259 Taijuan Walker .15 .40
260A Stephen Piscotty .20 .50
260B Stephen Piscotty SP 20.00 50.00
with team
261 Nathan Eovaldi .20 .50
262 Liam Hendriks .15 .40
263A Addison Russell .25 .60
263B Addison Russell SP 25.00 60.00
high fives
264 Cory Spangenberg .15 .40
265A Charlie Blackmon .25 .60
265B Charlie Blackmon SP 25.00 60.00
purple jersey
266 Tampa Bay Rays .15 .40
267 Clay Buchholz .15 .40
268 Anthony Gose .15 .40
269 Jose De Leon RC .25 .60
270 Jake Arrieta LL .20 .50
271 Nelson Cruz LL .25 .60
272 Pat Neshek .15 .40
273 A.J. Reed .15 .40
274 Matt Strahm RC .25 .60
275 Dallas Keuchel .20 .50
276 Yelich/Ozuna/Stanton .30 .75
277 Kris Bryant LL .30 .75
278 Julio Teheran .20 .50
279 Leonys Martin .15 .40
280 Adrian Beltre .25 .60
281 Coco Crisp .15 .40
282 Tyler Flowers .15 .40
283A Andrew Benintendi RC .75 2.00
283B Bnntndi SP Inteview 50.00 125.00
283C Bnntndi UPD SP 2.00 5.00
284 Elvis Andrus .20 .50
285 Tyler White .15 .40
286 Drew Pomeranz .20 .50
287A Aaron Judge RC 5.00 12.00
287B Judge SP w/Bat 200.00 500.00
287C Judge UPD SP 10.00 25.00
288A Joey Votto .25 .60
288B Joey Votto SP 25.00 60.00
Gatorade shower
289 Brian Goodwin RC .25 .60
290 Shin-Soo Choo .20 .50
291 Khris Davis LL .25 .60
292 Fernando Rodney .15 .40
293 Aledmys Diaz .20 .50
294 Kole Calhoun .15 .40
295 Matt Kemp LL .20 .50
296 Tyler Clippard .15 .40
297 Anthony DeSclafani .15 .40
298 Story/Arenado .30 .75
299A Yulieski Gurriel RC .40 1.00
299B Yulieski Gurriel SP 25.00 60.00
dark blue jersey
299C Yulieski Gurriel UPD SP 1.00 2.50
no hat
299D Yulieski Gurriel UPD SP 1.00 2.50
orange jersey
300 Arodys Vizcaino .15 .40
301 Jeurys Familia .15 .40
302 David Freese .15 .40
303 Pedro Strop .15 .40
304 Minnesota Twins .15 .40
305 Tyler Duffey .15 .40
306A David Dahl RC .30 .75
306B David Dahl UPD SP .75 2.00
sunglasses on
306C David Dahl UPD SP .75 2.00
lowering bat
307 Zach Duke .15 .40
308 Yovani Gallardo .15 .40
309 Craig Kimbrel .20 .50
310 Scott Schebler .20 .50
311 Tyler Chatwood .15 .40
312 Brandon Guyer .15 .40
313 Robbie Grossman .15 .40
314 Ryan Flaherty .15 .40
315 Carlos Beltran .20 .50
316 Justin Smoak .15 .40
317 Mitch Moreland .15 .40
318 Matt Carasiti RC .25 .60
319 Seth Lugo RC .25 .60
320 Arizona Diamondbacks .15 .40
321 Dustin Pedroia LL .25 .60
322 Albert Pujols LL .30 .75
323 Jameson Taillon .20 .50
324 Ben Revere .15 .40
325 Chris Hatcher .15 .40
326 Chris Archer .15 .40
327 Danny Espinosa .15 .40
328 Adam Lind .20 .50
329 Josh Reddick .15 .40
330 Doug Fister .15 .40
331 Jake Lamb .20 .50
332 Huston Street .15 .40
333 Jarred Cosart .15 .40
334 Drew Smyly .15 .40
335A Jeff Hoffman RC .25 .60
335B Jeff Hoffman UPD SP .60 1.50
high five
336 Hector Santiago .15 .40
337 Scott Van Slyke .15 .40
338 Alcides Escobar .20 .50
339 Daniel Norris .15 .40
340A Aaron Nola .20 .50
340B Nola SP Thrbck 40.00 100.00
341A Alex Bregman RC 1.00 2.50
341B Bregman SP Kneeling 75.00 200.00
341C Bregman UPD SP 2.50 6.00
342 Josh Tomlin .15 .40
343 Mike Zunino .15 .40
344 Jake Thompson RC .25 .60
345 Kevin Gausman .15 .40
346 Jonathan Lucroy .20 .50
347 Brandon Belt .20 .50
348 Jeremy Hellickson .15 .40
349A Tyler Glasnow RC .30 .75
349B Tyler Glasnow UPD SP .75 2.00
black jersey
350A David Ortiz .25 .60
350B Ortiz SP Door 25.00 60.00
350C Ortiz SP Cowboy 25.00 60.00
350D Ortiz SP Dugout 25.00 60.00
350E Ortiz SP Gatorade 25.00 60.00
350F Ortiz SP Tigers 25.00 60.00
350G Ortiz SP Lego 25.00 60.00
350H Ortiz SP Jacket 25.00 60.00
350I Ortiz SP Pujols 25.00 60.00
350J Ortiz SP Dodgers 25.00 60.00
350K Ortiz SP Helmet 25.00 60.00
351 German Marquez RC .40 1.00
352 Cameron Rupp .15 .40
353 Felipe Rivero .20 .50
354 Nick Tropeano .15 .40
355 Shelby Miller .20 .50
356 Brad Miller .20 .50
357 Kelvin Herrera .15 .40
358 Brad Boxberger .15 .40
359A Matt Carpenter .25 .60
359B Matt Carpenter SP 25.00 60.00
no hat
360 Jon Lester .20 .50
361 Dylan Bundy .20 .50
362 John Lackey .20 .50
363 Yunel Escobar .15 .40
364 Koda Glover RC .25 .60
365 Jorge De La Rosa .15 .40
366 Jayson Werth .20 .50
367 Jurickson Profar .20 .50
368 Jhonny Peralta .15 .40
369 Mark Canha .15 .40
370 St. Louis Cardinals .15 .40
371 Chad Bettis .15 .40
372 Ryan Schimpf .15 .40
373A Yadier Molina .25 .60
373B Yadier Molina SP 25.00 60.00
in gear
374 Jim Johnson .15 .40
375A Yasiel Puig .25 .60
375B Jackie Robinson SP 30.00 80.00
376 Chase Anderson .15 .40
377 Adam Rosales .15 .40
378 They Got Hops! .25 .60
Francisco Lindor
Tyler Naquin
379 Phil Hughes .15 .40
380A Albert Pujols .30 .75
380B Pujols SP Thrwng 30.00 80.00
381A Hunter Renfroe RC .30 .75
381B Hunter Renfroe UPD SP .75 2.00
camo jersey
382A Josh Harrison .15 .40
382B Honus Wagner SP 40.00 100.00
383 Adam Frazier .15 .40
384 Welington Castillo .15 .40
385 DJ LeMahieu .25 .60
386 Michael Lorenzen .15 .40
387 Zack Godley .15 .40
388 Yasmani Grandal .15 .40
389A George Springer .20 .50
389B George Springer SP 20.00 50.00
sitting
390A Evan Longoria .20 .50
390B Evan Longoria SP 20.00 50.00
throwback jersey
391 Jonathan Schoop .15 .40
392 Pablo Sandoval .20 .50
393 Koji Uehara .15 .40
394 Detroit Tigers .15 .40
395 Drew Storen .15 .40
396 J.T. Realmuto .25 .60
397 Stephen Cardullo RC .25 .60
398 Blake Treinen RC .40 1.00
399 Ender Inciarte .25 .60
400A Nolan Arenado .30 .75
400B Arenado SP Dugout 40.00 100.00
401A Manny Margot RC .25 .60
401B Manny Margot UPD SP .60 1.50
brown jersey
401C Manny Margot UPD SP .60 1.50
gray jersey
402 Logan Forsythe .15 .40
403 John Axford .15 .40
404A Joe Mauer .20 .50
404B Mauer SP Pine tar 40.00 100.00
405 Max Kepler .20 .50
406 Stephen Vogt .20 .50
407 Eduardo Escobar .15 .40
408 Michael Conforto .20 .50
409 R.A. Dickey .20 .50
410 Jarrett Parker .15 .40
411 Maikel Franco .20 .50
412 Chris Iannetta .15 .40
413 Rob Segedin RC .25 .60
414 Zack Cozart .15 .40
415 Pat Valaika RC .30 .75
416 Neil Walker .20 .50
417 Darren O'Day .15 .40
418 James McCann .20 .50
419 Roberto Perez .15 .40
420 Matt Wisler .15 .40
421 Santiago Casilla .15 .40
422 Andrew Miller .20 .50
423 Sergio Romo .15 .40
424 Derek Dietrich .20 .50
425A Carlos Gonzalez .20 .50
425B Carlos Gonzalez SP 20.00 50.00
pinstripe jersey
426 New York Mets .15 .40
427 Carlos Gomez .15 .40
428 Jay Bruce .20 .50
429 Mark Melancon .15 .40
430 Texas Rangers .15 .40
431 Tommy Joseph .25 .60
432 Lucas Giolito .20 .50
433A Mitch Haniger RC .40 1.00
433B Mitch Haniger UPD SP 1.00 2.50
gray jersey
434 Tyler Saladino .15 .40
435 Robbie Ray .15 .40
436 Cody Allen .15 .40
437 Trevor Rosenthal .20 .50
438 Chris Carter .15 .40
439A Salvador Perez .20 .50
439B Salvador Perez SP 20.00 50.00
sunglasses on
440 Eduardo Rodriguez .15 .40
441 Jose Iglesias .20 .50
442A Javier Baez .30 .75
442B Baez SP In jckt 30.00 80.00
443 Dee Gordon .15 .40
444 Andrew Heaney .15 .40
445 Alex Gordon .20 .50
446 Dexter Fowler .20 .50
447 Scott Kazmir .15 .40
448 Jose Martinez RC .40 1.00
449 Ian Kennedy .15 .40
450A Justin Verlander .25 .60
450B Vrlndr SP Fist bump 40.00 100.00
451 Jharel Cotton RC .25 .60
452 Travis Shaw .15 .40
453 Danny Santana .15 .40
454 Andrew Toles RC .25 .60
455 Mauricio Cabrera RC .25 .60
456 Steve Cishek .15 .40
457 Brett Gardner .20 .50
458 Hernan Perez .15 .40
459A Wil Myers .15 .40
459B Wil Myers SP 15.00 40.00
sunglasses on
460 Alejandro De Aza .15 .40
461 Bruce Maxwell RC .25 .60
462 Rich Hill .15 .40
463 Jeff Samardzija .15 .40
464 Hisashi Iwakuma .20 .50
465 CC Sabathia .20 .50
466 David Robertson .15 .40
467 Adam Ottavino .15 .40
468 Kyle Hendricks .25 .60
469 Francisco Liriano .15 .40
470 Brandon Drury .15 .40
471 Nick Franklin .15 .40
472 Pittsburgh Pirates .15 .40
473 Eugenio Suarez .20 .50
474 Michael Pineda .15 .40
475 Peter O'Brien .15 .40
476 Matt Olson RC .40 1.00
477 Zach Davies .15 .40
478 Rob Zastryzny RC .25 .60
479 Ryan Madson .15 .40
480 Jason Kipnis .20 .50
481 Kansas City Royals .15 .40
482A Didi Gregorius .20 .50
482B Lou Gehrig SP 30.00 80.00
483 Anthony Rendon .25 .60
484 Yonder Alonso .15 .40
485A Greg Bird .20 .50
485B Roger Maris SP 40.00 100.00
486 Aroldis Chapman .25 .60
487 Jose Ramirez .20 .50
488 Jake Odorizzi .15 .40
489 Jarrod Dyson .15 .40
490 Joc Pederson .20 .50
491 Ryan Vogelsong .15 .40
492 Avisail Garcia .20 .50
493 Hunter Dozier RC .25 .60
494 Tom Murphy .15 .40
495 Adam Jones .20 .50
496 Mike Fiers .15 .40
497 Boston Red Sox .15 .40
498 Roman Quinn RC .25 .60
499 Danny Valencia .20 .50
500A Anthony Rizzo .40 1.00
500B Rizzo SP Blue jrsy 30.00 80.00
500C Ernie Banks SP 50.00 120.00
500D Rizzo UPD SP Rnng 1.50 4.00
501 Ian Kinsler .20 .50
502 Willson Contreras .25 .60
503 Jesus Aguilar (RC) .40 1.00
504 Austin Hedges .15 .40
505 Seung-Hwan Oh .30 .75
506 Jose Peraza .20 .50
507 Matt Garza .15 .40
508A Hanley Ramirez .20 .50
508B Hanley Ramirez SP 20.00 50.00
kneeling
508C Ted Williams SP 60.00 150.00
509 Miguel Rojas RC .25 .60
510 Kelby Tomlinson .15 .40
511 Devin Mesoraco .15 .40
512 Mallex Smith .15 .40
513 Tony Kemp .15 .40
514 Jeremy Jeffress .15 .40
515 Nick Castellanos .25 .60
516 Tony Wolters .15 .40
517 Kolten Wong .20 .50
518 Christian Yelich .30 .75
519 Dan Vogelbach RC .40 1.00
520 Andrelton Simmons .15 .40
521 Brandon Phillips .15 .40
522 Edwin Diaz .20 .50
523A Carlos Martinez .20 .50
523B Carlos Martinez SP 20.00 50.00
no hat
524 James Loney .15 .40
525 Curtis Granderson .20 .50
526 Jake Marisnick .15 .40
527 Gio Gonzalez .20 .50
528A Jake Arrieta .20 .50
528B Jake Arrieta SP 20.00 50.00
with bat
529 J.J. Hardy .15 .40
530 Jabari Blash .15 .40
531 Nick Markakis .20 .50
532 Eduardo Nunez .15 .40
533 Trevor Bauer .25 .60
534 Cody Asche .15 .40
535 Lonnie Chisenhall .15 .40
536A Trey Mancini RC .50 1.25
536B Mancini UPD SP 1.25 3.00
537 Gerardo Parra .15 .40
538 Brad Ziegler .15 .40
539A Amir Garrett RC .25 .60
539B Amir Garrett UPD SP .60 1.50
gray jersey
540 Billy Hamilton .20 .50
541 Shawn Kelley .15 .40
542 Trevor Plouffe .15 .40
543 Brian Dozier .25 .60
544 Luis Severino .20 .50
545 Martin Perez .20 .50
546 Addison Reed .15 .40
547 Vince Velasquez .15 .40
548A David Price .20 .50
548B Price SP Dugout 30.00 80.00
549 Miguel Gonzalez .15 .40
550 Mikie Mahtook .15 .40
551 Matt Duffy .15 .40
552 Tom Koehler .15 .40
553 T.J. Rivera RC .40 1.00
554 Jason Castro .15 .40
555A Noah Syndergaard .20 .50
555B Sndrgrd SP Throwback 40.00 100.00
555C Noah Syndergaard UPD SP .75 2.00
bat in hand
556 Starlin Castro .15 .40
557 Milwaukee Brewers .15 .40
558 Oakland Athletics .15 .40
559 Jason Motte .15 .40
560 Zack Greinke .20 .50
561 Ricky Nolasco .15 .40
562 Nick Ahmed .15 .40
563 Marwin Gonzalez .15 .40
564 Washington Nationals .15 .40
565 J.D. Martinez .25 .60
566 Heart of Texas .20 .50
Elvis Andrus
Rougned Odor
567 Devon Travis .15 .40
568 Ryan Pressly .15 .40
569 Jorge Alfaro RC .30 .75
570A Josh Donaldson .20 .50
570B Josh Donaldson SP 20.00 50.00
camo hat
570C Josh Donaldson UPD SP .75 2.00
white jersey
571 J.C. Ramirez .15 .40
572 Atlanta Braves .15 .40
573 Bartolo Colon .15 .40
574 Trayce Thompson .20 .50
575 Chris Owings .15 .40
576 Russell Martin .15 .40
577 Chris Tillman .15 .40
578 Jed Lowrie .15 .40
579 Taylor Jungmann .15 .40
580 Matt Holliday .25 .60
581 Brock Holt .20 .50
582A Julio Urias .25 .60
582B Julio Urias SP 25.00 60.00
sunglasses on
583 Colorado Rockies .15 .40
584 Tater Triumph .40 1.00
Jayson Werth
Bryce Harper
585 Collin McHugh .15 .40
586A Aaron Sanchez .20 .50
586B Aaron Sanchez SP 20.00 50.00
patch on hat
587 Gerrit Cole .25 .60
588 Kirk Nieuwenhuis .15 .40
589 Ian Desmond .15 .40
590 Triplet of Twins .20 .50
Miguel Sano
Byron Buxton
Eduardo Escobar
591 Matt Bush .20 .50
592 Kendall Graveman .15 .40
593A Jose Abreu .25 .60
593B Jose Abreu SP 25.00 60.00
fingers over eye
594 Justin Bour .20 .50
595A Max Scherzer .25 .60
595B Schrzr SP Wht Jrsy 30.00 80.00
596 Ken Giles .15 .40
597A Kenta Maeda .20 .50
597B Kenta Maeda SP 20.00 50.00
warm-up on
597C Sandy Koufax SP 50.00 125.00
598 Michael Taylor .15 .40
599 Cincinnati Reds .15 .40
600A Yoenis Cespedes .25 .60
600B Yoenis Cespedes .25 .60
hands on lips
600C Yoenis Cespedes UPD SP 1.00 2.50
holding glove
601 Khris Davis .25 .60
602 Alex Dickerson .15 .40
603A Eric Thames .20 .50
603B Eric Thames UPD SP .75 2.00
blue and yellow hat
604 Gavin Cecchini RC .25 .60
605 Michael Brantley .20 .50
606 Glen Perkins .15 .40
607 Tyler Thornburg .15 .40
608 Los Angeles Dodgers .15 .40
609 Adalberto Mejia RC .25 .60
610 Ryan Buchter RC .25 .60
611A Victor Martinez .20 .50
611B Ty Cobb SP 75.00 200.00
612 Odubel Herrera .20 .50
613 Jonathan Broxton .15 .40
614 Shawn O'Malley .15 .40
615 John Jaso .15 .40
616 Mark Trumbo .15 .40
617 A.J. Pollock .15 .40
618 Kenley Jansen .20 .50
619 Brad Brach .15 .40
620 Sam Dyson .15 .40
621 Chase Headley .15 .40
622 Steven Wright .15 .40
623 Melvin Upton Jr. .20 .50
624 Brandon Maurer .15 .40
625 Ty Blach RC .25 .60
626 Roberto Osuna .15 .40
627 Zach Putnam .15 .40
628 Domingo Santana .20 .50
629 Jordy Mercer .15 .40
630A Edwin Encarnacion .25 .60
630B Edwin Encarnacion SP 25.00 60.00
standing at fence
631 Zack Wheeler .20 .50
632 Steven Matz .20 .50
633A Hunter Pence .20 .50
633B Pence SP No hat 30.00 80.00
634 Danny Duffy .15 .40
635A Michael Fulmer .15 .40
635B Michael Fulmer SP 15.00 40.00
high five
636 Allegheny Armada .25 .60
Andrew McCutchen
John Jaso
637 Ryan Rua .15 .40
638 Luis Valbuena .15 .40
639A Matt Kemp .20 .50
639B Matt Kemp SP 20.00 50.00
blue jersey
639C Hank Aaron SP 60.00 150.00
640 Cole Hamels .20 .50
641A Robinson Cano .20 .50
641B Robinson Cano SP 20.00 50.00
Albert Pujols pictured
642 Renato Nunez RC .50 1.25
643 Wei-Yin Chen .15 .40
644 Jose Altuve .20 .50
645A Trea Turner .20 .50
645B Turner SP High five 20.00 50.00
645C Turner UPD SP .75 2.00
646 Corey Knebel .15 .40
647 Jose Reyes .20 .50
648 Seattle Mariners .15 .40
649A Manny Machado .25 .60
649B Manny Machado SP 25.00 60.00
black t-shirt
649C Manny Machado UPD SP 1.00 2.50
black hoodie
650A Andrew McCutchen .25 .60
650B McCtchn SP Holding bat 40.00 100.00
650C Roberto Clemente SP 60.00 150.00
651 Jose Lobaton .15 .40
652A Kyle Seager .15 .40
652B Seager SP Teal jrsy 30.00 80.00
653 Cam Bedrosian .15 .40
654 Chris Young .15 .40
655 Garrett Richards .20 .50
656 Todd Frazier .20 .50
657 Kevin Quackenbush RC .25 .60
658 James Paxton .20 .50
659 Melky Cabrera .15 .40
660 Jeanmar Gomez .15 .40
661 Peter Bourjos .15 .40
662 J.A. Happ .20 .50
663 Ketel Marte .20 .50
664 Blake Swihart .20 .50
665 Yu Darvish .25 .60
666A Rougned Odor .20 .50
666B Rougned Odor SP 20.00 50.00
white jersey
667 Alex Cobb .15 .40
668 Jedd Gyorko .15 .40
669 Corey Kluber .20 .50
670 Martin Maldonado .15 .40
671 Joe Ross .15 .40
672 Luke Maile .15 .40
673 Joe Panik .20 .50
674 Martin Prado .15 .40
675A Buster Posey .30 .75
675B Posey SP Hand raised 30.00 80.00
676A Eric Hosmer .20 .50
676B Hosmer SP Glove 30.00 80.00
677 Cheslor Cuthbert .15 .40
678 Ervin Santana .15 .40
679 Jung Ho Kang .15 .40
680 Mike Pelfrey .15 .40
681 Mike Napoli .15 .40
682 James Shields .15 .40
683 Mac Williamson .15 .40
684 Jorge Polanco .15 .40
685 Enrique Hernandez .20 .50
686 Luis Sardinas .15 .40
687 Tyler Collins .15 .40
688 Mike Clevinger .20 .50
689 Jason Vargas .15 .40
690 Andres Blanco .15 .40
691 Richard Bleier RC .25 .60
692 Rob Refsnyder .15 .40
693 Matt Cain .20 .50
694 Matt Wieters .25 .60
695 Jon Jay .15 .40
696 Jeff Mathis .20 .50
697 Christian Bethancourt .15 .40
698 Tony Cingrani .20 .50
699 Ichiro .30 .75
700 Ryan Goins .15 .40

2017 Topps Black

*BLACK: 10X TO 25X BASIC
*BLACK RC: 6X TO 15X BASIC RC
SER.1 ODDS 1:102 HOBBY
SER.1 STATED ODDS 1:20 JUMBO
SER.2 STATED ODDS 1:60 HOBBY
STATED PRINT RUN 66 SER.#'d SETS
7 Gary Sanchez 20.00 50.00
210 Yoan Moncada 30.00 80.00
283 Andrew Benintendi 40.00 100.00
287 Aaron Judge 75.00 200.00
341 Alex Bregman 30.00 80.00

2017 Topps Black and White Negative

*BW NEGATIVE: 8X TO 20X BASIC
*BW NEGATIVE RC: 5X TO 12X BASIC
STATED ODDS 1:135 HOBBY
STATED ODDS 1:26 JUMBO
SER.2 ODDS 1:84 HOBBY
287 Aaron Judge 60.00 150.00

2017 Topps Factory Set Sparkle Foil

*SPARKLE: 8X TO 20X BASIC
*SPARKLE RC: 5X TO 12X BASIC RC
STATED PRINT RUN 175 SER.#'d SETS

2017 Topps Father's Day Blue

*BLUE: 10X TO 25X BASIC
*BLUE RC: 6X TO 15X BASIC RC
STATED ODDS 1:562 HOBBY
STATED ODDS 1:162 FAT PACK
STATED ODDS 1:485 TAR. RETAIL
STATED ODDS 1:81 HANGER
STATED ODDS 1:583 BLASTER
STATED ODDS 1:117 JUMBO
STATED ODDS 1:486 WM RETAIL
SER.2 ODDS 1:303 HOBBY
STATED PRINT RUN 50 SER. #'d SETS
210 Yoan Moncada 30.00 80.00
283 Andrew Benintendi 40.00 100.00
287 Aaron Judge 75.00 200.00
341 Alex Bregman 30.00 80.00

2017 Topps Gold

*GOLD: 2X TO 5X BASIC
*GOLD RC: 1.2X TO 3X BASIC RC
STATED ODDS 1:15 HOBBY
STATED ODDS 1:5 FAT PACK
STATED ODDS 1:13 RETAIL
STATED ODDS 1:2 HANGER
STATED ODDS 1:15 BLASTER
STATED ODDS 1:3 JUMBO
SER.2 ODDS 1:8 HOBBY
STATED PRINT RUN 2017 SER. #'d SETS

2017 Topps Memorial Day Camo

COMPLETE SET (700)
*CAMO: 12X TO 30X BASIC
*CAMO RC: 8X TO 20X BASIC RC
STATED ODDS 1:1165 HOBBY
STATED ODDS 1:324 FAT PACK
STATED ODDS 1:969 TAR.RETAIL
STATED ODDS 1:161 HANGER
STATED ODDS 1:1165 BLASTER
STATED ODDS 1:233 JUMBO
STATED ODDS 1:971 WM RETAIL
SER.2 ODDS 1:605 HOBBY
STATED PRINT RUN 25 SER. #'d SETS

283 Andrew Benintendi 50.00 120.00
287 Aaron Judge 100.00 250.00
341 Alex Bregman 40.00 100.00

2017 Topps Mother's Day Pink

*PINK: 10X TO 25X BASIC
*PINK RC: 6X TO 15X BASIC RC
STATED ODDS 1:562 HOBBY
STATED ODDS 1:162 FAT PACK
STATED ODDS 1:485 TAR. RETAIL
STATED ODDS 1:81 HANGER
STATED ODDS 1:583 BLASTER
STATED ODDS 1:117 JUMBO
STATED ODDS 1:486 WM RETAIL
SER.2 ODDS 1:303 HOBBY
STATED PRINT RUN 50 SER. #'d SETS
283 Andrew Benintendi 40.00 100.00
287 Aaron Judge 75.00 200.00
341 Alex Bregman 30.00 80.00

2017 Topps Rainbow Foil

*RAINBOW: 2X TO 5X BASIC
*RAINBOW RC: 1.2X TO 3X BASIC RC
STATED ODDS 1:10 HOBBY
STATED ODDS 1:4 FAT PACK
STATED ODDS 1:10 RETAIL
STATED ODDS 1:2 HANGER
STATED ODDS 1:10 BLASTER
STATED ODDS 1:2 JUMBO
SER.2 ODDS 1:10 HOBBY
287 Aaron Judge 15.00 40.00

2017 Topps Toys R Us Purple Border

*PURPLE: 5X TO 12X BASIC
*PURPLE RC: 3X TO 8X BASIC RC
287 Aaron Judge 40.00 100.00

2017 Topps Vintage Stock

*VINTAGE: 8X TO 20X BASIC
*VINTAGE RC: 5X TO 12X BASIC RC
STATED ODDS 1:294 HOBBY
STATED ODDS 1:82 FAT PACK
STATED ODDS 1:245 RETAIL
STATED ODDS 1:41 HANGER
STATED ODDS 1:294 BLASTER
STATED ODDS 1:59 JUMBO
SER.2 ODDS 1:153 HOBBY
STATED PRINT RUN 99 SER. #'d SETS
287 Aaron Judge 60.00 150.00

2017 Topps '87 Topps

COMPLETE SET (200) 100.00 250.00
STATED ODDS 1:4 HOBBY
STATED ODDS 1:2 FAT PACK
STATED ODDS 1:4 WM/TAR. RETAIL
STATED ODDS 1:4 BLASTER
SER.2 ODDS 1:4 HOBBY
*RED/25: 6X TO 15X BASIC
871 Carlos Correa .40 1.00
872 Giancarlo Stanton .40 1.00
873 Nomar Mazara .25 .60
874 Carlos Gonzalez .30 .75
875 Kris Bryant .50 1.25
876 Ichiro Suzuki .50 1.25
877 Felix Hernandez .30 .75
878 Stephen Strasburg .40 1.00
879 Sandy Koufax .75 2.00
8710 Francisco Lindor .40 1.00
8711 Ozzie Smith .50 1.25
8712 Yoan Moncada .75 2.00
8713 David Wright .30 .75
8714 Henry Owens .25 .60
8715 Miguel Cabrera .40 1.00
8716 Miguel Sano .30 .75
8717 Anthony Rizzo .60 1.50
8718 Trea Turner .30 .75
8719 Adam Jones .30 .75
8720 Buster Posey .50 1.25
8721 Frank Thomas .40 1.00
8722 Carlos Rodon .30 .75
8723 Luis Severino .30 .75
8724 Yoenis Cespedes .40 1.00
8725 Willson Contreras .40 1.00
8726 Robinson Cano .30 .75
8727 Reggie Jackson .30 .75
8728 Chris Sale .40 1.00
8729 Rickey Henderson .40 1.00
8730 Orlando Arcia .40 1.00
8731 Evan Longoria .30 .75
8732 Bo Jackson .40 1.00
8733 Alex Bregman 1.00 2.50
8734 David Price .30 .75
8735 Wil Myers .25 .60
8736 Josh Bell .60 1.50
8737 Randy Johnson .40 1.00
8738 Nolan Ryan 1.25 3.00
8739 Clayton Kershaw .75 2.00
8740 Corey Seager .40 1.00
8741 Troy Tulowitzki .40 1.00
8742 Nolan Arenado .50 1.25
8743 Hunter Pence .30 .75
8744 Max Scherzer .40 1.00
45 Eric Hosmer .30 .75
8746 Aledmys Diaz .30 .75
8747 Roger Clemens .50 1.25
8748 Cal Ripken Jr. 1.25 3.00
8749 Jake Arrieta .30 .75
8750 Mike Trout 2.00 5.00
8751 Trevor Story .40 1.00
8752 Jose Canseco .30 .75
8753 Yu Darvish .40 1.00
8754 Madison Bumgarner .30 .75
8755 Jose Altuve .30 .75
8756 Hank Aaron .75 2.00
8757 Mike Piazza .40 1.00
8758 Aaron Judge 10.00 25.00
8759 Ken Griffey Jr. .75 2.00
8760 Tyler Glasnow .30 .75
8761 Dustin Pedroia .40 1.00
8762 Aaron Nola .30 .75
8763 Andrew Benintendi .75 2.00
8764 Manny Machado .40 1.00
8765 John Smoltz .40 1.00
8766 Gerrit Cole .40 1.00
8767 Don Mattingly .75 2.00
8768 Masahiro Tanaka .30 .75
8769 Kenta Maeda .30 .75
8770 Julio Urias .40 1.00
8771 Barry Larkin .30 .75
8772 Blake Snell .30 .75
8773 Mookie Betts .60 1.50
8774 Kyle Schwarber .40 1.00
8775 Bryce Harper .60 1.50
8776 David Ortiz .40 1.00
8777 Freddie Freeman .50 1.25
8778 Josh Donaldson .30 .75
8779 Alex Reyes .30 .75
8780 Greg Maddux .50 1.25
8781 Michael Conforto .30 .75
8782 Albert Pujols .50 1.25
8783 Lucas Giolito .30 .75
8784 Andrew McCutchen .40 1.00
8785 Ryne Sandberg .75 2.00
8786 Jacob deGrom .40 1.00
8787 Sonny Gray .30 .75
8788 Aroldis Chapman .40 1.00
8789 Mark McGwire .60 1.50
8790 David Dahl .30 .75
8791 Stephen Piscotty .30 .75
8792 Addison Russell .40 1.00
8793 Xander Bogaerts .40 1.00
8794 Noah Syndergaard .30 .75
8795 Johnny Cueto .30 .75
8796 Chipper Jones .40 1.00
8797 Yulieski Gurriel .40 1.00
8798 Justin Verlander .40 1.00
8799 Joc Pederson .30 .75
87100 Dansby Swanson .60 1.50
87101 Josh Donaldson .30 .75
87102 Manny Margot .25 .60
87103 Corey Seager .40 1.00
87104 Tyler Glasnow .30 .75
87105 Alex Bregman 1.00 2.50
87106 Jose Altuve .30 .75
87107 Braden Shipley .25 .60
87108 Cal Ripken Jr. 1.25 3.00
87109 Matt Carpenter .40 1.00
87110 Gavin Cecchini .25 .60
87111 Chad Pinder .25 .60
87112 Reggie Jackson .30 .75
87113 Josh Bell .60 1.50
87114 Carl Yastrzemski .60 1.50
87115 Max Scherzer .40 1.00
87116 Jake Thompson .25 .60
87117 Kris Bryant .50 1.25
87118 Reynaldo Lopez .25 .60
87119 Buster Posey .50 1.25
87120 Clayton Kershaw .75 2.00
87121 David Ortiz .40 1.00
87122 Raimel Tapia .30 .75
87123 Bo Jackson .40 1.00
87124 Dustin Pedroia .40 1.00
87125 Ken Griffey Jr. .75 2.00
87126 Noah Syndergaard .30 .75
87127 Robert Gsellman .25 .60
87128 Ryne Sandberg .75 2.00
87129 Matt Strahm .25 .60
87130 Jose Canseco .30 .75
87131 Jose De Leon .25 .60
87132 Ivan Rodriguez .30 .75
87133 Francisco Lindor .40 1.00
87134 Miguel Cabrera .40 1.00
87135 Sandy Koufax .75 2.00
87136 Chipper Jones .40 1.00
87137 Yulieski Gurriel .40 1.00
87138 Corey Kluber .30 .75
87139 Dansby Swanson .60 1.50
87140 Jason Varitek .40 1.00
87141 Randy Johnson .40 1.00
87142 Matt Olson .40 1.00
87143 Hank Aaron .75 2.00
87144 Anthony Rizzo .60 1.50
87145 Chris Sale .40 1.00
87146 Omar Vizquel .30 .75
87147 Adam Jones .30 .75
87148 Roger Clemens .50 1.25
87149 Andrew Toles .25 .60
87150 Mike Trout 2.00 5.00
87151 Jorge Alfaro .30 .75
87152 Eric Hosmer .30 .75
87153 Don Mattingly .75 2.00
87154 John Smoltz .40 1.00
87155 Yoan Moncada .75 2.00
87156 Rickey Henderson .40 1.00
87157 Tom Glavine .30 .75
87158 Robinson Cano .30 .75
87159 Nolan Arenado .50 1.25
87160 Seth Lugo .25 .60
87161 David Dahl .30 .75
87162 Carlos Gonzalez .30 .75
87163 Dave Winfield .30 .75
87164 Andrew Benintendi .75 2.00
87165 Alex Reyes .30 .75
87166 German Marquez .40 1.00
87167 Manny Machado .40 1.00
87168 Mike Piazza .40 1.00
87169 Ozzie Smith .50 1.25
87170 Rob Zastryzny .25 .60
87171 Ichiro .50 1.25
87172 Bryce Harper .60 1.50
87173 Renato Nunez .50 1.25
87174 George Brett .75 2.00
87175 Frank Thomas .40 1.00
87176 Greg Maddux .50 1.25
87177 Aaron Judge 10.00 25.00
87178 Hunter Dozier .25 .60
87179 Johnny Damon .30 .75
87180 Andres Galarraga .30 .75
87181 Aledmys Diaz .30 .75
87182 Barry Larkin .30 .75
87183 Dan Vogelbach .40 1.00
87184 Bruce Maxwell .25 .60
87185 Roman Quinn .25 .60
87186 Ty Blach .25 .60
87187 Nolan Ryan 1.25 3.00
87188 Starling Marte .30 .75
87189 Teoscar Hernandez .75 2.00
87190 Mookie Betts .60 1.50
87191 Fernando Valenzuela .25 .60
87192 Dellin Betances .30 .75
87193 Addison Russell .40 1.00
87194 Derek Jeter 1.00 2.50
87195 Mark McGwire .60 1.50
87196 Jeff Hoffman .25 .60
87197 Trey Mancini .50 1.25
87198 Jacob deGrom .40 1.00
87199 JaCoby Jones .30 .75
87200 Jharel Cotton .25 .60

2017 Topps '87 Topps Autographs

STATED ODDS 1:465 HOBBY
STATED ODDS 1:681 FAT PACK
STATED ODDS 1:1770 TAR. RETAIL
STATED ODDS 1:2298 HANGER
STATED ODDS 1:15 JUMBO
STATED ODDS 1:1534 WM RETAIL
SER.2 ODDS 1:588 HOBBY
SER.1 EXCH DEADLINE 12/31/2018
SER.2 EXCH DEADLINE 5/31/2019
*MAPLE/25: .75X TO 2X BASIC
1987AAB Alex Bregman 40.00 100.00
1987AABE Andrew Benintendi 60.00 150.00
1987AABE Andrew Benintendi S2 75.00 200.00
1987AABR Alex Bregman S2 25.00 60.00
1987AAD Aledmys Diaz 15.00 40.00
1987AADI Aledmys Diaz S2 10.00 25.00
1987AAGA Andres Galarraga 15.00 40.00
1987AAGA Andres Galarraga S2 8.00 20.00
1987AAJU Aaron Judge 125.00 300.00
1987AAJU Aaron Judge S2 300.00 600.00
1987AAN Aaron Nola 6.00 15.00
1987AAR Alex Reyes 15.00 40.00
1987AARE Alex Reyes S2 10.00 25.00
1987AARI Anthony Rizzo
1987AARI Anthony Rizzo S2 40.00 100.00
1987AAT Andrew Toles S2 3.00 8.00
1987ABB Barry Bonds 250.00 500.00
1987ABD Brandon Drury 3.00 8.00
1987ABH Bryce Harper
1987ABHA Bryce Harper S2 250.00 400.00
1987ABJ Bo Jackson 60.00 150.00
1987ABJ Bo Jackson S2
1987ABL Barry Larkin 20.00 50.00
1987ABM Bruce Maxwell S2 3.00 8.00
1987ABP Buster Posey S2
1987ABS Blake Snell 4.00 10.00
1987ABS Braden Shipley S2 3.00 8.00
1987ABW Billy Wagner 6.00 15.00
1987ACC Carlos Correa 40.00 100.00
1987ACFU Carson Fulmer 6.00 15.00
1987ACKE Clayton Kershaw S2 100.00 250.00
1987ACM Carlos Martinez 4.00 10.00
1987ACP Chad Pinder S2 3.00 8.00
1987ACR Carlos Rodon 10.00 25.00
1987ACR Cal Ripken Jr. S2 150.00 300.00
1987ACRI Cal Ripken Jr.
1987ACSE Corey Seager 60.00 150.00
1987ACSE Corey Seager S2 60.00 150.00
1987ADD David Dahl 10.00 25.00
1987ADD David Dahl S2 4.00 10.00
1987ADJ Derek Jeter 400.00 800.00
1987ADJ Derek Jeter S2 500.00 800.00
1987ADMA Don Mattingly 100.00 250.00
1987ADO David Ortiz 150.00 300.00
1987ADS Dansby Swanson 60.00 150.00
1987ADST Darryl Strawberry S2
1987ADSW Dansby Swanson S2 40.00 100.00
1987ADV Dan Vogelbach S2 5.00 12.00
1987AFL Francisco Lindor 25.00 60.00
1987AFL Francisco Lindor S2 EXCH 20.00 50.00
1987AFT Frank Thomas 30.00 80.00
1987AFV Fernando Valenzuela 20.00 50.00
1987AGMR German Marquez S2 5.00 12.00
1987AGS George Springer 10.00 25.00
1987AHA Hank Aaron
1987AHA Hank Aaron S2 200.00 400.00
1987AHO Henry Owens 3.00 8.00
1987AHR Hunter Renfroe 12.00 30.00
1987AIR Ivan Rodriguez 20.00 50.00
1987AI Ichiro S2 250.00 500.00
1987AJA Jim Abbott 10.00 25.00
1987AJAF Jorge Alfaro S2 4.00 10.00
1987AJAL Jose Altuve 25.00 60.00
1987AJB Josh Bell 25.00 60.00
1987AJBE Jose Berrios 5.00 12.00
1987AJC Jose Canseco 10.00 25.00
1987AJCA Jose Canseco S2 6.00 15.00
1987AJCO Jharel Cotton S2 3.00 8.00
1987AJDE Jacob deGrom 30.00 80.00
1987AJDL Jose De Leon S2 3.00 8.00
1987AJH Jeremy Hazelbaker 4.00 10.00
1987AJH Jeff Hoffman S2 3.00 8.00
1987AJJ JaCoby Jones S2 4.00 10.00
1987AJMU Joe Musgrove 3.00 8.00
1987AJP Joc Pederson 8.00 20.00
1987AJP Joe Panik S2 4.00 10.00
1987AJT Jake Thompson S2 3.00 8.00
1987AJU Julio Urias 15.00 40.00
1987AKB Kris Bryant 300.00 500.00
1987AKB Kris Bryant S2 150.00 300.00
1987AKG Ken Griffey Jr.
1987AKG Ken Griffey Jr. S2 150.00 300.00
1987AKMA Kenta Maeda 30.00 80.00
1987AKS Kyle Schwarber 40.00 100.00
1987ALS Luis Severino 8.00 20.00
1987AMC Michael Conforto 20.00 50.00
1987AMM Manny Machado S2 75.00 200.00
1987AMMA Manny Machado S2 75.00 200.00
1987AMMC Mark McGwire 75.00 200.00
1987AMMG Mark McGwire S2
1987AMMR Manny Margot S2 6.00 15.00
1987AMO Matt Olson S2 10.00 25.00
1987AMP Mike Piazza S2 60.00 150.00
1987AMS Matt Strahm S2 3.00 8.00
1987AMSA Miguel Sano 10.00 25.00
1987AMSM Mallex Smith 3.00 8.00
1987AMT Mike Trout
1987AMTR Mike Trout S2 200.00 400.00
1987ANA Nolan Arenado 15.00 40.00
1987AND Norman Dale Gene Hackman 250.00 500.00
1987ANM Nomar Mazara 8.00 20.00
1987ANR Nolan Ryan S2 100.00 250.00
1987ANS Noah Syndergaard 30.00 80.00
1987ANS Noah Syndergaard S2 25.00 60.00
1987AOS Ozzie Smith 60.00 150.00
1987AOV Omar Vizquel 15.00 40.00
1987AOV Omar Vizquel S2 10.00 25.00
1987APO Peter O'Brien 3.00 8.00
1987ARG Robert Gsellman S2 3.00 8.00
1987ARH Rickey Henderson 30.00 80.00
1987ARHE Ryon Healy 4.00 10.00
1987ARL Reynaldo Lopez S2 3.00 8.00
1987ARN Renato Nunez S2 6.00 15.00
1987ARQ Roman Quinn S2 3.00 8.00
1987ARTA Raimel Tapia S2 4.00 10.00
1987ARZ Rob Zastryzny S2 3.00 8.00
1987ASK Sandy Koufax EXCH 175.00 350.00
1987ASK Sandy Koufax S2 600.00 800.00
1987ASL Seth Lugo S2 3.00 8.00
1987ASM Starling Marte
1987ASMA Steven Matz 12.00 30.00
1987ASP Stephen Piscotty 10.00 25.00
1987ATA Tyler Austin 8.00 20.00
1987ATA Tyler Austin S2 6.00 15.00
1987ATB Ty Blach S2 3.00 8.00
1987ATG Tyler Glasnow S2 4.00 10.00
1987ATGS Tyler Glasnow S2 4.00 10.00
1987ATGV Tom Glavine S2 25.00 60.00
1987ATH Teoscar Hernandez S2 10.00 25.00
1987ATM Trey Mancini S2 20.00 50.00
1987ATN Tyler Naquin 3.00 8.00
1987ATS Trevor Story 15.00 40.00
1987ATT Trea Turner 10.00 25.00
1987AVG Vladimir Guerrero S2 50.00 120.00
1987AWCO Willson Contreras 30.00 80.00
1987AYG Yulieski Gurriel 30.00 80.00
1987AYG Yulieski Gurriel S2 8.00 20.00
1987AYM Yoan Moncada 150.00 300.00
1987AYM Yoan Moncada S2 60.00 150.00

2017 Topps '87 Topps Silver Pack Chrome

*GREEN/150: 1X TO 2.5X BASIC
*BLUE/99: 1.5X TO 4X BASIC
*ORANGE/75-99: 2X TO 5X BASIC
*GOLD/50: 2.5X TO 6X BASIC
87AB Andrew Benintendi 2.00 5.00
87ABR Alex Bregman 2.50 6.00
87AD Aledmys Diaz S2 .75 2.00
87AE Adam Eaton S2 1.00 2.50
87AJ Aaron Judge 30.00 80.00
87AJ Adam Jones S2 .75 2.00
87AM Andrew McCutchen 1.00 2.50
87AN Aaron Nola .75 2.00
87AR Alex Reyes .75 2.00
87ARI Anthony Rizzo S2 1.50 4.00
87ARU Addison Russell 1.00 2.50
87BB Byron Buxton .75 2.00
87BH Bryce Harper S2 1.50 4.00
87BJ Bo Jackson 1.00 2.50
87BP Buster Posey S2 1.25 3.00
87BR Babe Ruth S2 2.50 6.00
87CC Carlos Correa S2 1.00 2.50
87CK Clayton Kershaw 2.00 5.00
87CK Corey Kluber S2 .75 2.00
87CR Cal Ripken Jr. 3.00 8.00
87CS Chris Sale 1.00 2.50
87CSA Carlos Santana S2 .75 2.00
87CSE Corey Seager S2 1.00 2.50
87DB Dellin Betances S2 .75 2.00
87DD David Dahl .75 2.00
87DJ Derek Jeter S2 2.50 6.00
87DM Don Mattingly S2 2.00 5.00
87DP David Price .75 2.00
87DS Dansby Swanson 1.50 4.00
87EB Ernie Banks S2 1.00 2.50
87EH Eric Hosmer .75 2.00
87EL Evan Longoria .75 2.00
87FF Freddie Freeman 1.25 3.00
87FH Felix Hernandez .75 2.00
87FL Francisco Lindor 1.00 2.50
87FT Frank Thomas S2 1.00 2.50
87GB George Brett S2 2.00 5.00
87GS Gary Sanchez 1.00 2.50
87GS George Springer S2 .75 2.00
87GST Giancarlo Stanton 1.00 2.50
87HA Hank Aaron 2.00 5.00
87HR Hunter Renfroe S2 .75 2.00
87I Ichiro S2 1.25 3.00
87JA Jose Altuve .75 2.00
87JAR Jake Arrieta .75 2.00
87JBA Javier Baez S2 1.25 3.00
87JBE Johnny Bench S2 1.00 2.50
87JBU Jose Bautista S2 .75 2.00
87JD Josh Donaldson .75 2.00
87JDG Jacob deGrom S2 1.00 2.50
87JDL Jose De Leon S2 .60 1.50
87JL Jake Lamb S2 .75 2.00
87JR Jackie Robinson 1.00 2.50
87JS John Smoltz S2 1.00 2.50
87JU Julio Urias 1.00 2.50
87JV Joey Votto 1.00 2.50
87JV Justin Verlander S2 1.00 2.50
87KB Kris Bryant 1.25 3.00
87KG Ken Griffey Jr. 2.00 5.00
87KM Kenta Maeda .75 2.00
87KS Kyle Schwarber S2 1.00 2.50
87LW Luke Weaver .75 2.00
87MB Madison Bumgarner .75 2.00
87MB Mookie Betts S2 1.50 4.00
87MC Miguel Cabrera 1.00 2.50
87MC Matt Carpenter S2 1.00 2.50
87MM Manny Machado 1.00 2.50
87MM Manny Margot S2 .60 1.50
87MMG Mark McGwire S2 1.50 4.00
87MS Max Scherzer 1.00 2.50
87MSA Miguel Sano S2 .75 2.00
87MST Marcus Stroman S2 .75 2.00
87MT Mike Trout 5.00 12.00
87MT Masahiro Tanaka S2 .75 2.00
87NA Nolan Arenado 1.25 3.00
87NR Nolan Ryan 3.00 8.00
87NS Noah Syndergaard .75 2.00
87OA Orlando Arcia 1.00 2.50
87PG Paul Goldschmidt 1.00 2.50
87RCA Robinson Cano S2 .75 2.00
87RCL Roberto Clemente S2 2.50 6.00
87RH Ryon Healy S2 .75 2.00
87RP Rick Porcello S2 .75 2.00
87SG Sonny Gray .75 2.00
87SK Sandy Koufax S2 2.00 5.00
87SMR Starling Marte S2 .75 2.00
87SMZ Steven Matz S2 .75 2.00
87SP Stephen Piscotty S2 .75 2.00
87SS Stephen Strasburg S2 1.00 2.50
87TA Tyler Austin S2 1.00 2.50
87TG Tyler Glasnow .75 2.00
87TM Trey Mancini S2 1.25 3.00
87TS Trevor Story 1.00 2.50
87TT Trea Turner .75 2.00
87TW Ted Williams S2 2.00 5.00
87WM Wil Myers .60 1.50
87YC Yoenis Cespedes 1.00 2.50
87YD Yu Darvish 1.00 2.50
87YG Yulieski Gurriel S2 1.00 2.50
87YM Yoan Moncada S2 2.00 5.00

2017 Topps '87 Topps Silver Pack Chrome Autographs

RANDOM INSERTS IN PACKS
PRINT RUNS B/WN 40-199 COPIES PER
87AI Ichiro S2
87AAB Andrew Benintendi/199 60.00 150.00
87AABR Alex Bregman/199 50.00 125.00
87AAE Adam Eaton S2/99
87AAJ Aaron Judge/199 200.00 400.00
87AAJ Adam Jones S2/20
87AAN Aaron Nola/40 10.00 25.00
87AAR Alex Reyes/199 15.00 40.00
87ABB Byron Buxton/149 15.00 40.00
87ABH Bryce Harper S2
87ACC Carlos Correa S2
87ACK Clayton Kershaw
87ADB Dellin Betances S2/99
87ADD David Dahl/199 15.00 40.00
87ADJ Derek Jeter S2
87ADM Don Mattingly S2
87AFL Francisco Lindor/199 20.00 50.00
87AFT Frank Thomas S2
87AJA Jake Arrieta
87AJAT Jose Altuve/199 25.00 60.00
87AJL Jake Lamb S2/99
87AJS John Smoltz S2
87AKB Kris Bryant/50
87AKM Kenta Maeda/50 15.00 40.00
87ALW Luke Weaver/199 8.00 20.00
87AMC Matt Carpenter S2/50
87AMM Manny Margot S2/50
87AMT Mike Trout
87ANA Nolan Arenado/50 20.00 50.00
87ANS Noah Syndergaard/50 30.00 80.00
87ARP Rick Porcello S2/50
87ASP Stephen Piscotty S2
87ATA Tyler Austin S2/50
87ATG Tyler Glasnow/199 8.00 20.00
87ATS Trevor Story/149 20.00 50.00
87ATT Trea Turner/149 15.00 40.00
87AYC Yoenis Cespedes
87AYG Yulieski Gurriel S2/50
87AYM Yoan Moncada S2
87AARI Anthony Rizzo S2/15
87ACSA Carlos Santana S2/99
87ACSE Corey Seager S2
87AJBA Javier Baez S2/14
87AMMG Mark McGwire S2
87AMST Marcus Stroman S2/99
87ASMZ Steven Matz S2/50

2017 Topps All Star Team Medallions

STATED ODDS 1:1274 HOBBY
STATED ODDS 1:30 JUMBO
*GOLD/99: .5X TO 1.2X BASIC
*BLACK/50: .6X TO 1.5X BASIC
MLBASARI Anthony Rizzo 6.00 15.00
MLBASARU Addison Russell 4.00 10.00
MLBASBH Bryce Harper 6.00 15.00
MLBASBP Buster Posey 5.00 12.00
MLBASCG Carlos Gonzalez 3.00 8.00
MLBASCH Chris Sale 4.00 10.00
MLBASCSA Matt Carpenter 4.00 10.00
MLBASCSE Corey Seager 6.00 15.00
MLBASDO David Ortiz 6.00 15.00
MLBASEE Edwin Encarnacion 4.00 10.00
MLBASEH Eric Hosmer 3.00 8.00
MLBASFL Francisco Lindor 6.00 15.00
MLBASJAL Jose Altuve 3.00 8.00
MLBASJAR Jake Arrieta 3.00 8.00
MLBASJB Jackie Bradley Jr. 4.00 10.00
MLBASJD Josh Donaldson 3.00 8.00
MLBASKB Kris Bryant 10.00 25.00
MLBASMBE Mookie Betts 6.00 15.00
MLBASMBU Madison Bumgarner 3.00 8.00
MLBASMCB Miguel Cabrera 4.00 10.00
MLBASMCP Cole Hamels 3.00 8.00
MLBASMM Manny Machado 4.00 10.00
MLBASMT Mike Trout 10.00 25.00
MLBASNA Nolan Arenado 5.00 12.00
MLBASNS Noah Syndergaard 5.00 12.00
MLBASRC Robinson Cano 3.00 8.00
MLBASSP Salvador Perez 5.00 12.00
MLBASSS Stephen Strasburg 4.00 10.00
MLBASWM Wil Myers 2.50 6.00
MLBASXB Xander Bogaerts 4.00 10.00

2017 Topps All Time All Stars

COMPLETE SET (50) 30.00 80.00
ATAS1 Johnny Bench .60 1.50
ATAS2 Gary Carter .50 1.25
ATAS3 Bryce Harper 1.00 2.50
ATAS4 Reggie Jackson .50 1.25
ATAS5 Edgar Martinez .50 1.25
ATAS6 Cal Ripken Jr. 2.00 5.00
ATAS7 Brooks Robinson .50 1.25
ATAS8 Bob Feller .50 1.25
ATAS9 Buster Posey .75 2.00
ATAS10 Ryne Sandberg 1.25 3.00
ATAS11 Pedro Martinez .50 1.25
ATAS12 Ken Griffey Jr. 1.25 3.00
ATAS13 Rod Carew .50 1.25
ATAS14 Albert Pujols .75 2.00
ATAS15 Harmon Killebrew .60 1.50
ATAS16 Joe Morgan .50 1.25
ATAS17 Nolan Ryan 2.00 5.00
ATAS18 Duke Snider .50 1.25
ATAS19 Don Mattingly 1.25 3.00
ATAS20 Ted Williams 1.25 3.00
ATAS21 Rickey Henderson .60 1.50
ATAS23 Mike Piazza .60 1.50
ATAS24 Roger Clemens .75 2.00
ATAS25 Steve Carlton .50 1.25
ATAS26 Ernie Banks .60 1.50
ATAS27 Clayton Kershaw 1.25 3.00
ATAS28 Derek Jeter 1.50 4.00
ATAS29 Hank Aaron 1.25 3.00
ATAS30 Jimmie Foxx .60 1.50
ATAS31 Wade Boggs .50 1.25
ATAS32 Ichiro .75 2.00
ATAS33 Tom Glavine .50 1.25
ATAS34 Carlton Fisk .50 1.25
ATAS35 George Brett 1.25 3.00
ATAS36 Eddie Mathews .60 1.50
ATAS37 Greg Maddux .75 2.00
ATAS38 Eddie Murray .50 1.25
ATAS39 Lou Gehrig 1.25 3.00
ATAS40 Justin Verlander .60 1.50
ATAS41 Nomar Garciaparra .50 1.25
ATAS42 Juan Marichal .50 1.25
ATAS43 Carl Yastrzemski 1.00 2.50
ATAS44 Al Kaline .60 1.50
ATAS45 Alex Rodriguez .75 2.00
ATAS46 Miguel Cabrera .60 1.50
ATAS47 Chipper Jones .60 1.50
ATAS48 Barry Larkin .50 1.25
ATAS49 John Smoltz .60 1.50
ATAS50 Roberto Alomar .50 1.25
ATAS61 Andre Dawson .50 1.25

2017 Topps All Star MVPs

*BLUE: .5X TO 1.2X BASIC
ASM1 Juan Marichal .50 1.25
ASM2 Brooks Robinson .50 1.25
ASM3 Tony Perez .50 1.25
ASM4 Willie McCovey .50 1.25
ASM5 Carl Yastrzemski 1.00 2.50
ASM6 Frank Robinson .50 1.25
ASM7 Joe Morgan .50 1.25
ASM8 Gary Carter .50 1.25
ASM9 Roger Clemens .75 2.00
ASM10 Bo Jackson .60 1.50
ASM11 Cal Ripken Jr. 2.00 5.00
ASM12 Ken Griffey Jr. 1.25 3.00
ASM13 Mike Piazza .60 1.50
ASM14 Roberto Alomar .50 1.25
ASM15 Pedro Martinez .50 1.25
ASM16 Derek Jeter 1.50 4.00
ASM17 Cal Ripken Jr. 2.00 5.00
ASM18 Ichiro .75 2.00
ASM19 Carl Crawford .50 1.25
ASM20 Brian McCann .50 1.25
ASM21 Prince Fielder .50 1.25
ASM22 Melky Cabrera .40 1.00
ASM23 Mike Trout 3.00 8.00
ASM24 Mike Trout 3.00 8.00
ASM25 Eric Hosmer .50 1.25

2017 Topps Reverence Patch Autographs

STATED ODDS 1:3629 HOBBY
STATED ODDS 1:680 JUMBO
STATED PRINT RUN 25 SER. #'d SETS
EXCHANGE DEADLINE 12/31/2018
TAPABE Andrew Benintendi 100.00 250.00
TAPABR Alex Bregman 75.00 200.00
TAPAP Andy Pettitte EXCH 30.00 80.00
TAPBL Barry Larkin EXCH 30.00 80.00
TAPCC Carlos Correa EXCH 75.00 200.00
TAPCJ Chipper Jones 75.00 200.00
TAPCK Clayton Kershaw 60.00 150.00
TAPCR Cal Ripken Jr. 150.00 400.00
TAPDM Don Mattingly 125.00 250.00
TAPDS Dansby Swanson EXCH 75.00 200.00
TAPFL Francisco Lindor
TAPI Ichiro Suzuki 300.00 500.00
TAPJS John Smoltz 30.00 80.00
TAPMP Mike Piazza 125.00 300.00
TAPMT Mike Trout 200.00 500.00
TAPNS Noah Syndergaard EXCH 30.00 80.00
TAPRH Rickey Henderson 60.00 150.00
TAPTS Trevor Story 30.00 80.00

2017 Topps Bowman Then and Now

COMPLETE SET (20) 5.00 12.00
STATED ODDS 1:8 HOBBY
STATED ODDS 1:3 FAT PACK
STATED ODDS 1:8 RETAIL
STATED ODDS 1:2 HANGER
STATED ODDS 1:8 BLASTER
STATED ODDS 1:2 JUMBO
BOWMAN1 Trout 2.00 5.00
BOWMAN2 Kershaw .75 2.00
BOWMAN3 Bryant .50 1.25
BOWMAN4 Manny Machado .40 1.00
BOWMAN5 Bumgarner .30 .75
BOWMAN6 Harper .60 1.50
BOWMAN7 Posey .50 1.25
BOWMAN8 Felix Hernandez .30 .75
BOWMAN9 Joe Mauer .30 .75
BOWMAN10 Pujols .50 1.25
BOWMAN11 Stephen Strasburg .40 1.00
BOWMAN12 Andrew McCutchen .40 1.00
BOWMAN13 Eric Hosmer .30 .75
BOWMAN14 David Price .30 .75
BOWMAN15 Joey Votto .40 1.00
BOWMAN16 Justin Verlander .40 1.00
BOWMAN17 Robinson Cano .30 .75
BOWMAN18 Correa .40 1.00
BOWMAN19 Seager .40 1.00
BOWMAN20 Cabrera .40 1.00

2017 Topps Factory Set Retail Bonus Rookie Variations

87 Dansby Swanson
210 Yoan Moncada
283 Andrew Benintendi
287 Aaron Judge
341 Alex Bregman

2017 Topps First Pitch

COMPLETE SET (40) 8.00 20.00
SER.1 ODDS 1:8 HOBBY
SER.1 ODDS 1:3 FAT PACK
SER.1 ODDS 1:8 RETAIL
SER.1 ODDS 1:2 HANGER
SER.1 ODDS 1:8 BLASTER
SER.1 ODDS 1:2 JUMBO
SER.2 ODDS 1:8 HOBBY
FP1 William Shatner .60 1.50
FP2 Bob Odenkirk .60 1.50
FP3 Judd Apatow .60 1.50
FP4 Jeremy Piven .60 1.50
FP5 Deshauna Barber .60 1.50
FP6 John Goodman .60 1.50
FP7 Keegan-Michael Key .60 1.50
FP8 Joan Jett .60 1.50
FP9 Joe Mantegna .60 1.50
FP10 Leslie Jordan .60 1.50
FP11 Paul Wall .60 1.50
FP12 Chris Lane .60 1.50
FP13 Luis Coronel .60 1.50
FP14 Brett Eldredge .60 1.50
FP15 Victoria Justice .60 1.50
FP16 Lou Ferrigno .60 1.50
FP17 Bethanie Mattek-Sands .60 1.50
FP21 Jon Lovitz .60 1.50
FP21 Bonnie Hunt .60 1.50
FP22 Stephen Colbert .60 1.50
FP22 Isaiah Mustafa .60 1.50
FP23 Mase .60 1.50
FP23 Ben Higgins .60 1.50
FP24 Gary Busey .60 1.50
FP25 Ben Gibbard .60 1.50
FP26 Josh Duhamel .60 1.50
FP27 Chace Crawford .60 1.50
FP28 Diplo .60 1.50
FP29 Donovan Bailey .60 1.50
FP30 Jabbawockeez .60 1.50
FP31 Morimoto .60 1.50
FP32 Brian Shaw .60 1.50
FP33 Anthony Rapp .60 1.50
FP34 Ty Pennington .60 1.50
FP35 Steve Bowen .60 1.50
FP36 Alex Curry .60 1.50
FP37 Camilla Luddington .60 1.50
FP38 Tom Lehman .60 1.50

FP39 Danny Willett .60 1.50
FP40 Luke Donald .60 1.50

2017 Topps Five Tool
STATED ODDS 1:8 HOBBY
STATED ODDS 1:3 FAT PACK
STATED ODDS 1:8 RETAIL
STATED ODDS 1:2 HANGER
STATED ODDS 1:8 BLASTER
STATED ODDS 1:2 JUMBO
5T1 Mike Trout 2.00 5.00
5T2 Bryce Harper .60 1.50
5T3 Anthony Rizzo .60 1.50
5T4 Manny Machado .40 1.00
5T5 Josh Donaldson .30 .75
5T6 Mookie Betts .60 1.50
5T7 Evan Longoria .30 .75
5T8 Francisco Lindor .40 1.00
5T9 Eric Hosmer .30 .75
5T10 Carlos Correa .40 1.00
5T11 Giancarlo Stanton .40 1.00
5T12 Kris Bryant .50 1.25
5T13 Andrew McCutchen .40 1.00
5T14 Ryan Braun .30 .75
5T15 Buster Posey .50 1.25
5T16 Wil Myers .25 .60
5T17 Nolan Arenado .50 1.25
5T18 Joey Votto .40 1.00
5T19 Paul Goldschmidt .40 1.00
5T20 Corey Seager .40 1.00
5T21 Robinson Cano .30 .75
5T22 Jose Altuve .30 .75
5T23 Yoenis Cespedes .40 1.00
5T24 Addison Russell .40 1.00
5T25 Carlos Gonzalez .30 .75
5T26 Xander Bogaerts .40 1.00
5T27 Ian Kinsler .30 .75
5T28 Dustin Pedroia .40 1.00
5T29 Trevor Story .40 1.00
5T30 George Springer .30 .75
5T31 Miguel Cabrera .40 1.00
5T32 Matt Kemp .30 .75
5T33 Ichiro Suzuki .50 1.25
5T34 Hanley Ramirez .30 .75
5T35 Noah Syndergaard .30 .75
5T36 Madison Bumgarner .30 .75
5T37 Jake Arrieta .30 .75
5T38 Jason Kipnis .30 .75
5T39 Adam Jones .30 .75
5T40 Kyle Seager .25 .60
5T41 Brian Dozier .40 1.00
5T42 Freddie Freeman .50 1.25
5T43 Yoan Moncada .75 2.00
5T44 Hunter Pence .30 .75
5T45 Edwin Encarnacion .40 1.00
5T46 Aaron Judge 3.00 8.00
5T47 Alex Bregman 1.00 2.50
5T48 Dansby Swanson .60 1.50
5T49 Andrew Benintendi .75 2.00
5T50 David Dahl .30 .75

2017 Topps Golden Glove Awards
COMPLETE SET (18) 10.00 25.00
STATED ODDS 1:5 TAR. RETAIL
STATED ODDS 1:5 TAR. BLASTER
GG1 Dallas Keuchel .50 1.25
GG2 Zack Greinke .50 1.25
GG3 Salvador Perez .50 1.25
GG4 Buster Posey .75 2.00
GG5 Mitch Moreland .40 1.00
GG6 Anthony Rizzo 1.00 2.50
GG7 Ian Kinsler .50 1.25
GG8 Joe Panik .50 1.25
GG9 Adrian Beltre .60 1.50
GG10 Nolan Arenado .75 2.00
GG11 Francisco Lindor .60 1.50
GG12 Brandon Crawford .50 1.25
GG13 Brett Gardner .50 1.25
GG14 Starling Marte .50 1.25
GG15 Kevin Kiermaier .50 1.25
GG16 Ender Inciarte .60 1.50
GG17 Mookie Betts 1.00 2.50
GG18 Jason Heyward .50 1.25

2017 Topps Home Run Derby Champions
COMPLETE SET (21) 30.00 80.00
HRD1 Andre Dawson .50 1.25
HRD5 Juan Gonzalez .60 1.50
HRD7 Frank Thomas .60 1.50
HRD10 Luis Gonzalez .40 1.00
HRD11 Bobby Abreu .40 1.00
HRD12 Ryan Howard .50 1.25
HRD13 Justin Morneau .50 1.25
HRD14 Prince Fielder .50 1.25
HRD15 David Ortiz .60 1.50
HRD16 Robinson Cano .50 1.25
HRD17 Prince Fielder .50 1.25
HRD18 Yoenis Cespedes .60 1.50
HRD19 Yoenis Cespedes .60 1.50
HRD20 Todd Frazier .50 1.25
HRD21 Giancarlo Stanton .60 1.50

2017 Topps Independence Day
COMPLETE SET (30) 15.00 40.00
ID1 Miguel Cabrera .60 1.50
ID2 Gregory Polanco .50 1.25
ID3 Evan Longoria .50 1.25
ID4 Jose Abreu .60 1.50
ID5 Khris Davis .60 1.50
ID6 Manny Machado .60 1.50
ID7 Corey Seager .60 1.50
ID8 Nolan Arenado .75 2.00
ID9 Trevor Story .60 1.50
ID10 Kyle Seager .40 1.00
ID11 Kris Bryant .75 2.00
ID12 Giancarlo Stanton .60 1.50
ID13 Miguel Sano .50 1.25
ID14 Anthony Rizzo 1.00 2.50
ID15 Carlos Correa .60 1.50
ID16 Julio Urias .60 1.50
ID17 Matt Carpenter .60 1.50
ID18 Max Scherzer .60 1.50
ID19 Yoenis Cespedes .60 1.50
ID20 Andrew McCutchen .60 1.50
ID21 Freddie Freeman .75 2.00
ID22 Jose Altuve .50 1.25
ID23 David Ortiz .60 1.50
ID24 Bryce Harper 1.00 2.50
ID25 Maikel Franco .50 1.25
ID26 Buster Posey .75 2.00
ID27 Francisco Lindor .60 1.50
ID28 Joe Mauer .50 1.25
ID29 Mookie Betts 1.00 2.50
ID30 Robinson Cano .50 1.25

2017 Topps Independence Day MLB Logo Patch
IDMLAB Adrian Beltre 4.00 10.00
IDMLAD Aledmys Diaz 3.00 8.00
IDMLAJ Adam Jones 3.00 8.00
IDMLAM Andrew McCutchen 4.00 10.00
IDMLAN Aaron Nola 3.00 8.00
IDMLAP Albert Pujols 5.00 12.00
IDMLAR Anthony Rizzo 6.00 15.00
IDMLBB Byron Buxton 3.00 8.00
IDMLBH Bryce Harper 6.00 15.00
IDMLBP Buster Posey 5.00 12.00
IDMLCC Carlos Correa 4.00 10.00
IDMLCK Clayton Kershaw 8.00 20.00
IDMLCS Corey Seager 4.00 10.00
IDMLDO David Ortiz 4.00 10.00
IDMLDP Dustin Pedroia 4.00 10.00
IDMLEH Eric Hosmer 3.00 8.00
IDMLEL Evan Longoria 3.00 8.00
IDMLFF Freddie Freeman 5.00 12.00
IDMLFH Felix Hernandez 3.00 8.00
IDMLFL Francisco Lindor 4.00 10.00
IDMLGS Giancarlo Stanton 4.00 10.00
IDMLJAB Jose Abreu 4.00 10.00
IDMLJAL Jose Altuve 3.00 8.00
IDMLJB Javier Baez 5.00 12.00
IDMLJM Joe Mauer 3.00 8.00
IDMLJU Julio Urias 4.00 10.00
IDMLJVE Justin Verlander 4.00 10.00
IDMLJVO Joey Votto 4.00 10.00
IDMLKB Kris Bryant 5.00 12.00
IDMLKD Khris Davis 4.00 10.00
IDMLKS Kyle Seager 2.50 6.00
IDMLMBE Mookie Betts 6.00 15.00
IDMLMCB Miguel Cabrera 4.00 10.00
IDMLMCR Matt Carpenter 4.00 10.00
IDMLMF Maikel Franco 3.00 8.00
IDMLMM Manny Machado 4.00 10.00
IDMLMSA Miguel Sano 3.00 8.00
IDMLMSC Max Scherzer 4.00 10.00
IDMLMTA Masahiro Tanaka 3.00 8.00
IDMLMTR Mike Trout 15.00 40.00
IDMLNA Nolan Arenado 5.00 12.00
IDMLPG Paul Goldschmidt 4.00 10.00
IDMLRB Ryan Braun 3.00 8.00
IDMLRC Robinson Cano 3.00 8.00
IDMLRO Rougned Odor 3.00 8.00
IDMLTS Trevor Story 4.00 10.00
IDMLWM Wil Myers 2.50 6.00
IDMLYC Yoenis Cespedes 4.00 10.00
IDMLYD Yu Darvish 4.00 10.00
IDMLYM Yadier Molina 4.00 10.00

2017 Topps Jackie Robinson Day
COMPLETE SET (30) 15.00 40.00
STATED ODDS 1:2 BLASTER
*RED/25: 2.5X TO 6X BASIC
JRD1 Manny Machado .60 1.50
JRD2 Josh Donaldson .50 1.25
JRD3 Mookie Betts 1.00 2.50
JRD4 Evan Longoria .50 1.25
JRD5 Masahiro Tanaka .50 1.25
JRD6 Francisco Lindor .60 1.50
JRD7 Miguel Cabrera .60 1.50
JRD8 Todd Frazier .50 1.25
JRD9 Eric Hosmer .50 1.25
JRD10 Joe Mauer .50 1.25
JRD11 Yu Darvish .60 1.50
JRD12 Felix Hernandez .50 1.25
JRD13 Carlos Correa .60 1.50
JRD14 Sonny Gray .50 1.25
JRD15 Mike Trout 3.00 8.00
JRD16 Bryce Harper 1.00 2.50
JRD17 Giancarlo Stanton .60 1.50
JRD18 Miguel Sano .50 1.25
JRD19 Aaron Nola .50 1.25
JRD20 Yoenis Cespedes .60 1.50
JRD21 Kris Bryant .75 2.00
JRD22 Matt Carpenter .60 1.50
JRD23 Andrew McCutchen .60 1.50
JRD24 Ryan Braun .50 1.25
JRD25 Buster Posey .75 2.00
JRD26 Clayton Kershaw 1.25 3.00
JRD27 Wil Myers .40 1.00
JRD28 Nolan Arenado .75 2.00
JRD29 Joey Votto .60 1.50
JRD30 Paul Goldschmidt .60 1.50

2017 Topps Jackie Robinson Logo Patch
STATED ODDS 1:1 PER BLASTER BOX
*GOLD/99: .5X TO 1.2X BASIC
*BLACK/50: .6X TO 1.5X BASIC
JRPCABE Andrew Benintendi 6.00 15.00
JRPCABR Alex Bregman 3.00 8.00
JRPCAJO Adam Jones 3.00 8.00
JRPCAJU Aaron Judge 10.00 25.00
JRPCAM Andrew McCutchen 4.00 10.00
JRPCAN Aaron Nola 3.00 8.00
JRPCARI Anthony Rizzo 6.00 15.00
JRPCARU Addison Russell 4.00 10.00
JRPCBH Bryce Harper 6.00 15.00
JRPCBP Buster Posey 5.00 12.00
JRPCCC Carlos Correa 4.00 10.00
JRPCCG Carlos Gonzalez 3.00 8.00
JRPCCK Clayton Kershaw 5.00 12.00
JRPCCSA Chris Sale 4.00 10.00
JRPCCSE Corey Seager 6.00 15.00
JRPCDPE Dustin Pedroia 4.00 10.00
JRPCDPR David Price 3.00 8.00
JRPCEH Eric Hosmer 3.00 8.00
JRPCEL Evan Longoria 3.00 8.00
JRPCFF Freddie Freeman 5.00 12.00
JRPCFH Felix Hernandez 3.00 8.00
JRPCFL Francisco Lindor 4.00 10.00
JRPCGS Giancarlo Stanton 4.00 10.00
JRPCJA Jose Altuve 3.00 8.00
JRPCJBE Josh Bell 6.00 15.00
JRPCJD Josh Donaldson 3.00 8.00
JRPCJM Joe Mauer 3.00 8.00
JRPCJVE Justin Verlander 4.00 10.00
JRPCJVO Joey Votto 4.00 10.00
JRPCKB Kris Bryant 10.00 25.00
JRPCMBE Mookie Betts 6.00 15.00
JRPCMBU Madison Bumgarner 3.00 8.00
JRPCMCB Miguel Cabrera 4.00 10.00
JRPCMCR Matt Carpenter 4.00 10.00
JRPCMK Matt Kemp 3.00 8.00
JRPCMM Manny Machado 4.00 10.00
JRPCMSA Miguel Sano 3.00 8.00
JRPCMSC Max Scherzer 4.00 10.00
JRPCMTA Masahiro Tanaka 3.00 8.00
JRPCMTR Mike Trout 10.00 25.00
JRPCNA Nolan Arenado 5.00 12.00
JRPCNS Noah Syndergaard 5.00 12.00
JRPCPG Paul Goldschmidt 4.00 10.00
JRPCRB Ryan Braun 3.00 8.00
JRPCRC Robinson Cano 3.00 8.00
JRPCSG Sonny Gray 3.00 8.00
JRPCTF Todd Frazier 3.00 8.00
JRPCWM Wil Myers 2.50 6.00
JRPCYC Yoenis Cespedes 4.00 10.00
JRPCYD Yu Darvish 4.00 10.00

2017 Topps Major League Material Autographs
SER.1 ODDS 1:2387 HOBBY
SER.1 ODDS 1:1987 FAT PACK
SER.1 ODDS 1:5290 TAR. RETAIL
SER.1 ODDS 1:5323 HANGER
SER.1 ODDS 1:332 JUMBO
SER.1 ODDS 1:5317 WM RETAIL
SER.2 ODDS 1:5196 HOBBY
PRINT RUNS B/WN 15-50 COPIES PER
NO PRICING ON QTY 15
SER.1 EXCH DEADLINE 12/31/2018
SER.2 EXCH DEADLINE 5/31/2019
MLMAADI Aledmys Diaz S2
MLMAAG Alex Gordon/50
MLMAAJ Aaron Judge/50 75.00 200.00
MLMAAN Aaron Nola/50 20.00 50.00
MLMAARE Anthony Rendon/50 15.00 40.00
MLMABB Brandon Belt/50 10.00 25.00
MLMACC Carlos Correa/50 30.00 80.00
MLMACKL Corey Kluber/50 15.00 40.00
MLMACR Carlos Rodon/50 15.00 40.00
MLMADB Dellin Betances/25 S2 10.00 25.00
MLMADDU Danny Duffy/50 15.00 40.00
MLMADPO Drew Pomeranz/35 S2 10.00 25.00
MLMADPR David Price/50 20.00 50.00
MLMAFL Francisco Lindor/50 25.00 60.00
MLMAGS George Springer/50 12.00 30.00
MLMAGSA Gary Sanchez/50 60.00 150.00
MLMAHO Henry Owens/50 8.00 20.00
MLMAIK Ian Kinsler/50 12.00 30.00
MLMAJAL Jose Altuve/50 30.00 80.00
MLMAJB Jackie Bradley Jr./50 20.00 50.00
MLMAJBA Javier Baez S2 15.00 40.00
MLMAJD Jacob deGrom/50 20.00 50.00
MLMAJH Jason Hammel/50 10.00 25.00
MLMAJP Joe Panik/35 S2 10.00 25.00
MLMAJPE Joc Pederson/50 20.00 50.00
MLMAJS Jorge Soler/50 12.00 30.00
MLMAKB Kris Bryant/50 75.00 200.00
MLMAKK Kevin Kiermaier/50 10.00 25.00
MLMAKM Kenta Maeda/50 15.00 40.00
MLMAKS Kyle Schwarber/50 30.00 80.00
MLMAKS Kyle Seager/35 S2 8.00 20.00
MLMALS Luis Severino/50 12.00 30.00
MLMAMCA Matt Carpenter/50 15.00 40.00
MLMAMF Maikel Franco/50
MLMAMF Michael Fulmer/35 S2 8.00 20.00
MLMAMSA Miguel Sano/50 15.00 40.00
MLMAMST Marcus Stroman/50
MLMANS Noah Syndergaard/50 20.00 50.00
MLMANS Noah Syndergaard/25 S2 25.00 60.00
MLMASMA Starling Marte/50 10.00 25.00
MLMASMZ Steven Matz/50 8.00 20.00
MLMASMZ Steven Matz/50 S2 10.00 25.00
MLMASP Stephen Piscotty/50 10.00 25.00
MLMATN Tyler Naquin/35 S2 8.00 20.00
MLMATS Trevor Story/50 20.00 50.00
MLMATT Trea Turner/35 S2 10.00 25.00
MLMAWC Willson Contreras/50 12.00 30.00
MLMAWM Wil Myers/50 8.00 20.00

2017 Topps Major League Materials
SER.1 ODDS 1:46 HOBBY
SER.1 ODDS 1:38 FAT PACK
SER.1 ODDS 1:101 WM/TAR. RETAIL
SER.1 ODDS 1:11 JUMBO
SER.1 ODDS 1:101 HANGER
SER.2 ODDS 1:49 HOBBY
*RED/25: .75X TO 2X BASIC
MLMAG Adrian Gonzalez 3.00 8.00
MLMAGO Alex Gordon S2 3.00 8.00
MLMAJ Adam Jones 3.00 8.00
MLMAJ Adam Jones S2 3.00 8.00
MLMAM Andrew McCutchen 4.00 10.00
MLMAM Andrew McCutchen S2 4.00 10.00
MLMAN Aaron Nola 3.00 8.00
MLMAP Albert Pujols 5.00 12.00
MLMAP Albert Pujols S2 5.00 12.00
MLMARI Anthony Rizzo 6.00 15.00
MLMARI Anthony Rizzo S2 6.00 15.00
MLMARU Addison Russell 4.00 10.00
MLMARU Addison Russell S2 4.00 10.00
MLMAW Adam Wainwright 3.00 8.00
MLMAW Adam Wainwright S2 3.00 8.00
MLMBH Bryce Harper S2 6.00 15.00
MLMBHM Billy Hamilton 3.00 8.00
MLMBPH Brandon Phillips 2.50 6.00
MLMBPO Buster Posey S2 5.00 12.00
MLMCA Chris Archer S2 2.50 6.00
MLMCB Carlos Beltran S2 3.00 8.00
MLMCC Carlos Correa S2 4.00 10.00
MLMCG Curtis Granderson 3.00 8.00
MLMCGO Carlos Gonzalez S2 3.00 8.00
MLMCGR Curtis Granderson S2 3.00 8.00
MLMCH Cole Hamels 3.00 8.00
MLMCKE Clayton Kershaw S2 5.00 12.00
MLMCKL Corey Kluber 3.00 8.00
MLMCKL Corey Kluber S2 3.00 8.00
MLMCM Carlos Martinez 3.00 8.00
MLMCSN Carlos Santana 3.00 8.00
MLMCY Christian Yelich 5.00 12.00
MLMCY Christian Yelich S2 5.00 12.00
MLMDB Dellin Betances S2 3.00 8.00
MLMDBE Dellin Betances 3.00 8.00
MLMDO David Ortiz S2 4.00 10.00
MLMDPE Dustin Pedroia 4.00 10.00
MLMDPR David Price 3.00 8.00
MLMDW David Wright 3.00 8.00
MLMDW David Wright S2 3.00 8.00
MLMEE Edwin Encarnacion 4.00 10.00
MLMEH Eric Hosmer 3.00 8.00
MLMEL Evan Longoria 3.00 8.00
MLMEL Evan Longoria S2 3.00 8.00
MLMFF Freddie Freeman 5.00 12.00
MLMFF Freddie Freeman S2 5.00 12.00
MLMFH Felix Hernandez S2 3.00 8.00
MLMGC Gerrit Cole 4.00 10.00
MLMGP Gregory Polanco 3.00 8.00
MLMGP Gregory Polanco S2 3.00 8.00
MLMGSA Gary Sanchez S2 4.00 10.00
MLMGSP George Springer 3.00 8.00
MLMGST Giancarlo Stanton 4.00 10.00
MLMGST Giancarlo Stanton S2 4.00 10.00
MLMHJR Hyun-Jin Ryu 3.00 8.00
MLMHR Hanley Ramirez 3.00 8.00
MLMHR Hanley Ramirez S2 3.00 8.00
MLMIK Ian Kinsler 3.00 8.00
MLMI Ichiro S2 5.00 12.00
MLMJAB Jose Abreu 4.00 10.00
MLMJAR Jake Arrieta 3.00 8.00
MLMJBA Javier Baez 5.00 12.00
MLMJBA Javier Baez S2 5.00 12.00
MLMJBR Jay Bruce S2 3.00 8.00
MLMJDG Jacob deGrom 4.00 10.00
MLMJDG Jacob deGrom S2 4.00 10.00
MLMJDO Josh Donaldson 3.00 8.00
MLMJE Jacoby Ellsbury S2 3.00 8.00
MLMJF Jeurys Familia S2 3.00 8.00
MLMJG Jon Gray S2 2.50 6.00
MLMJHA Josh Harrison 2.50 6.00
MLMJHE Jason Heyward 3.00 8.00
MLMJL Jon Lester 3.00 8.00
MLMJM J.D. Martinez S2 4.00 10.00
MLMJMR J.D. Martinez 4.00 10.00
MLMJPA Joe Panik S2 3.00 8.00
MLMJT Julio Teheran 3.00 8.00
MLMJT Jameson Taillon S2 3.00 8.00
MLMJU Justin Upton 3.00 8.00
MLMJUP Justin Upton S2 3.00 8.00
MLMJV Joey Votto S2 4.00 10.00
MLMJVE Justin Verlander 4.00 10.00
MLMJVO Joey Votto 4.00 10.00
MLMKB Kris Bryant 10.00 25.00
MLMKB Kris Bryant S2 10.00 25.00
MLMKK Kevin Kiermaier S2 3.00 8.00
MLMKS Kyle Seager S2 2.50 6.00
MLMKSC Kyle Schwarber 4.00 10.00
MLMKSE Kyle Seager 2.50 6.00
MLMKW Kolten Wong S2 3.00 8.00
MLMLC Lorenzo Cain 2.50 6.00
MLMLC Lorenzo Cain S2 2.50 6.00
MLMLS Luis Severino S2 3.00 8.00
MLMMBU Madison Bumgarner 3.00 8.00
MLMMCB Miguel Cabrera 4.00 10.00
MLMMCB Miguel Cabrera S2 4.00 10.00
MLMMCO Michael Conforto S2 3.00 8.00
MLMMH Matt Harvey S2 3.00 8.00
MLMMHA Matt Harvey 3.00 8.00
MLMMHO Matt Holliday 4.00 10.00
MLMMM Manny Machado 4.00 10.00
MLMMM Manny Machado S2 4.00 10.00
MLMMP Michael Pineda S2 2.50 6.00
MLMMS Miguel Sano 3.00 8.00
MLMMS Miguel Sano S2 3.00 8.00
MLMMT Mike Trout S2 10.00 25.00
MLMMTA Masahiro Tanaka S2 3.00 8.00
MLMMTE Mark Teixeira S2 3.00 8.00
MLMMTR Mike Trout 10.00 25.00
MLMMW Matt Wieters 4.00 10.00
MLMMW Michael Wacha S2 3.00 8.00
MLMNA Nolan Arenado S2 5.00 12.00
MLMNC Nelson Cruz 4.00 10.00
MLMNC Nelson Cruz S2 4.00 10.00
MLMNS Noah Syndergaard S2 3.00 8.00
MLMPF Prince Fielder 3.00 8.00
MLMPF Prince Fielder S2 3.00 8.00
MLMPG Paul Goldschmidt 4.00 10.00
MLMRB Ryan Braun 3.00 8.00
MLMRB Ryan Braun S2 3.00 8.00
MLMRC Robinson Cano 3.00 8.00
MLMRC Robinson Cano S2 3.00 8.00
MLMRO Rougned Odor 3.00 8.00
MLMRP Rick Porcello 3.00 8.00
MLMSC Starlin Castro S2 2.50 6.00
MLMSG Sonny Gray 3.00 8.00
MLMSM Starling Marte S2 3.00 8.00
MLMSPE Salvador Perez S2 3.00 8.00
MLMTT Troy Tulowitzki S2 4.00 10.00
MLMVM Victor Martinez 3.00 8.00
MLMWM Wil Myers 2.50 6.00
MLMWM Wil Myers S2 2.50 6.00
MLMYC Yoenis Cespedes 4.00 10.00
MLMYC Yoenis Cespedes S2 4.00 10.00
MLMYM Yadier Molina 4.00 10.00
MLMYMO Yadier Molina S2 4.00 10.00
MLMYP Yasiel Puig 4.00 10.00
MLMYT Yasmany Tomas 2.50 6.00
MLMYV Yordano Ventura 3.00 8.00
MLMZG Zack Greinke S2 3.00 8.00

2017 Topps Major League Milestones
COMPLETE SET (20) 6.00 15.00
STATED ODDS 1:8 HOBBY
MLM1 Miguel Cabrera .40 1.00
MLM2 Albert Pujols .50 1.25
MLM3 Trevor Story .40 1.00
MLM4 Adrian Gonzalez .30 .75
MLM5 Jose Bautista .30 .75
MLM6 Corey Seager .40 1.00
MLM7 Alex Rodriguez .50 1.25
MLM8 Miguel Cabrera .40 1.00
MLM9 Ichiro .50 1.25
MLM10 Max Scherzer .40 1.00
MLM11 Adrian Beltre .40 1.00
MLM12 Jake Arrieta .30 .75
MLM13 David Ortiz .40 1.00
MLM14 Justin Verlander .40 1.00
MLM15 Felix Hernandez .30 .75
MLM16 Cole Hamels .30 .75
MLM17 Kris Bryant .50 1.25
MLM18 Mark Teixeira .30 .75
MLM19 Ichiro .50 1.25
MLM20 David Ortiz .40 1.00

2017 Topps Major League Milestones Relics
STATED ODDS 1:1362 HOBBY
STATED PRINT RUN 100 SER.#'d SETS
*RED/25: .6X TO 1.5X BASIC
MLMRAB Adrian Beltre 5.00 12.00
MLMRAG Adrian Gonzalez 4.00 10.00
MLMRAP Albert Pujols 6.00 15.00
MLMRAR Alex Rodriguez 10.00 25.00
MLMRCS Corey Seager 5.00 12.00
MLMRDOR David Ortiz 6.00 15.00
MLMRDOT David Ortiz 6.00 15.00
MLMRFH Felix Hernandez 4.00 10.00
MLMRIC Ichiro 10.00 25.00
MLMRIH Ichiro 10.00 25.00
MLMRJA Jake Arrieta 8.00 20.00
MLMRJB Jose Bautista 4.00 10.00
MLMRJV Justin Verlander 5.00 12.00
MLMRKB Kris Bryant 6.00 15.00
MLMRMCA Miguel Cabrera 5.00 12.00
MLMRMCB Miguel Cabrera 5.00 12.00
MLMRMS Max Scherzer 5.00 12.00
MLMRMT Mark Teixeira 4.00 10.00
MLMRTS Trevor Story 5.00 12.00
MLMRZG Zack Greinke 4.00 10.00

2017 Topps Memorable Moments
COMPLETE SET (50) 10.00 25.00
STATED ODDS 1:8 HOBBY
MM1 Lou Gehrig .75 2.00
MM2 Anthony Rizzo .60 1.50
MM3 Babe Ruth 1.00 2.50
MM4 Steve Carlton .30 .75
MM5 Roger Clemens .50 1.25
MM6 Sandy Koufax .75 2.00
MM7 Roger Maris .40 1.00
MM8 Carlton Fisk .30 .75
MM9 Ted Williams .75 2.00
MM10 Aaron Boone .25 .60
MM11 Ichiro .50 1.25
MM12 Ozzie Smith .50 1.25
MM13 Roberto Clemente 1.00 2.50
MM14 Mark McGwire .60 1.50
MM15 Nolan Ryan 1.25 3.00
MM16 Bill Mazeroski .30 .75
MM17 Jackie Robinson .40 1.00
MM18 Bo Jackson .40 1.00
MM19 Ty Cobb .60 1.50
MM20 Ted Williams .75 2.00
MM21 Luis Gonzalez .25 .60
MM22 Willie Stargell .30 .75
MM23 Mike Piazza .40 1.00
MM24 Derek Jeter 1.00 2.50
MM25 Jackie Robinson .40 1.00
MM26 Jimmie Foxx .40 1.00
MM27 Nolan Ryan 1.25 3.00
MM28 Ken Griffey Jr. .75 2.00
MM29 Carl Yastrzemski .60 1.50
MM30 Miguel Cabrera .40 1.00
MM31 Derek Jeter 1.00 2.50
MM32 Ty Cobb .60 1.50
MM33 Jackie Robinson .40 1.00
MM34 Topps .25 .60
MM35 Lou Gehrig .75 2.00
MM36 Satchel Paige .40 1.00
MM37 Ted Williams .75 2.00
MM38 Brooks Robinson .30 .75
MM39 Fernando Valenzuela .25 .60
MM40 Cal Ripken Jr. 1.25 3.00
MM41 Reggie Jackson .30 .75
MM42 Babe Ruth 1.00 2.50
MM43 Rickey Henderson .40 1.00
MM44 Babe Ruth 1.00 2.50
MM45 Ichiro .50 1.25
MM46 Hank Aaron .75 2.00
MM47 Johnny Damon .30 .75
MM48 Ken Griffey Jr. .75 2.00
MM49 Cal Ripken Jr. 1.25 3.00
MM50 Mike Trout 2.00 5.00

2017 Topps Memorable Moments Autograph Relics
STATED ODDS 1:15,189 HOBBY
PRINT RUNS B/WN 10-35 COPIES PER
NO PRICING ON QTY 10
EXCHANGE DEADLINE 5/31/2019
MMARAD Aledmys Diaz/35 20.00 50.00
MMARCC Carlos Correa
MMARCF Carlton Fisk
MMARFV Fernando Valenzuela
MMARJD Josh Donaldson
MMAROS Ozzie Smith
MMARTN Tyler Naquin/35 12.00 30.00
MMARTS Trevor Story EXCH

2017 Topps Memorable Moments Autographs
STATED ODDS 1:14,809 HOBBY
PRINT RUNS B/WN 10-35 COPIES PER
NO PRICING ON QTY 15 OR LESS
EXCHANGE DEADLINE 5/31/2019
MMAAD Aledmys Diaz/35 20.00 50.00
MMALG Luis Gonzalez
MMATT Trea Turner
MMAKMA Kenta Maeda/15
MMAKMI Kevin Mitchell/25 10.00 25.00

2017 Topps Memorable Moments Relics
STATED ODDS 1:1818 HOBBY
STATED PRINT RUN 100 SER.#'d SETS
*RED/25: .6X TO 1.5X BASIC
MMRAR Anthony Rizzo 10.00 25.00
MMRBC Bartolo Colon 8.00 20.00
MMRCR Cal Ripken Jr. 15.00 40.00
MMRDG Dee Gordon 3.00 8.00
MMRDJ Derek Jeter 25.00 60.00
MMRI Ichiro 10.00 25.00
MMRJD Johnny Damon 6.00 15.00
MMRKGR Ken Griffey Jr. 10.00 25.00
MMRMC Miguel Cabrera 5.00 12.00
MMRMM Mark McGwire 15.00 40.00
MMRMPI Mike Piazza 10.00 25.00
MMRMT Mike Trout 25.00 60.00
MMRNR Nolan Ryan 15.00 40.00
MMROS Ozzie Smith 10.00 25.00
MMRRJ Reggie Jackson 12.00 30.00

2017 Topps MLB All Star Logo Patch
STATED ODDS 1:2219 HOBBY
*GOLD/75: .5X TO 1.2X BASIC
*BLACK/50: .5X TO 1.2X BASIC
ASLBJ Bo Jackson 10.00 25.00
ASLBL Barry Larkin 8.00 20.00
ASLBRO Brooks Robinson 10.00 25.00
ASLBRU Babe Ruth 10.00 25.00
ASLCJ Chipper Jones 8.00 20.00
ASLCR Cal Ripken Jr. 15.00 40.00
ASLCY Carl Yastrzemski 12.00 30.00
ASLDM Don Mattingly 10.00 25.00
ASLGB George Brett 10.00 25.00
ASLGM Greg Maddux 10.00 25.00
ASLHA Hank Aaron 10.00 25.00
ASLHK Harmon Killebrew 8.00 20.00
ASLIR Ivan Rodriguez 4.00 10.00
ASLJB Johnny Bench 5.00 12.00
ASLJM Joe Morgan 5.00 12.00
ASLKG Ken Griffey Jr. 10.00 25.00
ASLLG Lou Gehrig 10.00 25.00
ASLMM Mark McGwire 8.00 20.00
ASLMP Mike Piazza 6.00 15.00
ASLNR Nolan Ryan 15.00 40.00
ASLOS Ozzie Smith 8.00 20.00
ASLOV Omar Vizquel 4.00 10.00
ASLRC Roberto Clemente 12.00 30.00
ASLRCA Rod Carew 5.00 12.00
ASLRCL Roger Clemens 6.00 15.00
ASLRJ Reggie Jackson 10.00 25.00
ASLRS Ryne Sandberg 10.00 25.00
ASLSK Sandy Koufax 10.00 25.00
ASLWF Whitey Ford 4.00 10.00
ASLWS Willie Stargell 10.00 25.00

2017 Topps MLB Awards
COMPLETE SET (14) 8.00 20.00
STATED ODDS 1:4 RETAIL
STATED ODDS 1:4 BLASTER
CBP1 Mark Trumbo .40 1.00
CBP2 Jose Fernandez .60 1.50
CYA1 Rick Porcello .50 1.25
CYA2 Max Scherzer .60 1.50
HA1 David Ortiz .60 1.50
HA2 Kris Bryant .75 2.00
MOY1 Terry Francona .50 1.25
MOY2 Dave Roberts .50 1.25
MVP1 Mike Trout 3.00 8.00
MVP2 Kris Bryant .75 2.00
RLY1 Zach Britton .50 1.25
RLY2 Kenley Jansen .50 1.25
ROY1 Michael Fulmer .40 1.00
ROY2 Corey Seager .60 1.50

2017 Topps MLB Network
COMPLETE SET (29) 25.00 60.00
SER.1 ODDS 1:36 HOBBY
SER.1 ODDS 1:10 FAT PACK
SER.1 ODDS 1:24 RETAIL
SER.1 ODDS 1:24 BLASTER
SER.1 ODDS 1:5 HANGER
SER.1 ODDS 1:10 JUMBO
SER.2 ODDS 1:36 HOBBY
MLBN1 Kevin Millar 1.00 2.50
MLBN2 Mike Lowell 1.00 2.50
MLBN3 Greg Amsinger 1.00 2.50
MLBN4 Ryan Dempster 1.00 2.50
MLBN4 Tim Flannery UPD 1.00 2.50
MLBN5 MLB Tonight 1.00 2.50
MLBN6 Lauren Shehadi 1.00 2.50
MLBN7 Sean Casey 1.00 2.50
MLBN8 Harold Reynolds 1.00 2.50
MLBN8 Christopher Russo UPD 1.00 2.50
MLBN9 John Smoltz 1.50 4.00
MLBN10 Dan Plesac 1.00 2.50
MLBN11 Bob Costas 1.00 2.50
MLBN12 Tom Verducci UPD 1.00 2.50
MLBN13 Joel Sherman UPD 1.00 2.50
MLBN14 Brian Kenny 1.00 2.50
MLBN15 Bill Ripken 1.00 2.50
MLBN16 Carlos Pena 1.25 3.00
MLBN17 Eric Byrnes 1.00 2.50
MLBN20 Robert Flores 1.00 2.50
MLBN21 Matt Yallof UPD 1.00 2.50
MLBN23 Paul Severino UPD 1.00 2.50
MLBN25 Mark DeRosa 1.00 2.50
MLBN26 Scott Braun UPD 1.00 2.50
MLBN27 Kelly Nash 1.00 2.50
MLBN28 Heidi Watney UPD 1.00 2.50
MLBN29 Intentional Talk 1.00 2.50
MLBN30 Ken Rosenthal UPD 1.00 2.50
MLBN31 Peter Gammons 1.00 2.50

2017 Topps Postseason Performance Autograph Relics
STATED ODDS 1:8363 HOBBY
STATED ODDS 1:6976 FAT PACK
STATED ODDS 1:18,515 TAR. RETAIL
STATED ODDS 1:18,187 HANGER
STATED ODDS 1:18,988 WM RETAIL
STATED ODDS 1:1159 JUMBO
STATED PRINT RUN 50 SER. #'d SETS
EXCHANGE DEADLINE 12/31/2018
*RED/25: .5X TO 1.2X BASIC
PPARARU Addison Russell 50.00 120.00
PPARCK Clayton Kershaw 50.00 125.00
PPARCKL Corey Kluber 25.00 60.00
PPARDO David Ortiz
PPAREE Edwin Encarnacion
PPARFL Francisco Lindor 50.00 120.00
PPARJB Javier Baez 30.00 80.00
PPARJP Joe Panik 40.00 100.00
PPARJU Julio Urias EXCH 25.00 60.00
PPARKB Kris Bryant 150.00 300.00
PPARNS Noah Syndergaard
PPARTT Troy Tulowitzki 25.00 60.00

2017 Topps Postseason Performance Autographs
STATED ODDS 1:8363 HOBBY
STATED ODDS 1:6976 FAT PACK
STATED ODDS 1:18,515 TAR. RETAIL
STATED ODDS 1:18,187 HANGER
STATED ODDS 1:18,988 WM RETAIL
STATED ODDS 1:1159 JUMBO
STATED PRINT RUN 50 SER. #'d SETS
EXCHANGE DEADLINE 12/31/2018
*RED/25: .5X TO 1.2X BASIC
PPACKL Corey Kluber 12.00 30.00
PPADF Dexter Fowler 25.00 60.00
PPAFL Francisco Lindor 40.00 100.00
PPAJB Javier Baez 40.00 100.00
PPAJP Joe Panik
PPAJU Julio Urias 25.00 60.00
PPAKB Kris Bryant 125.00 300.00
PPANS Noah Syndergaard

2017 Topps Postseason Performance Relics
STATED ODDS 1:4332 HOBBY
STATED ODDS 1:9726 WM RETAIL
STATED ODDS 1:9600 TAR. RETAIL
STATED ODDS 1:9489 HANGER
STATED ODDS 1:1601 JUMBO
STATED PRINT RUN 100 SER. #'d SETS
*RED/25: .5X TO 1.2X BASIC
PPRAR Anthony Rizzo 12.00 30.00
PPRBP Buster Posey 20.00 50.00
PPRCK Clayton Kershaw 15.00 40.00
PPRCS Corey Seager 8.00 20.00

PPRDO David Ortiz 20.00 50.00
PPREE Edwin Encarnacion 8.00 20.00
PPRFL Francisco Lindor 12.00 30.00
PPRJU Julio Urias 8.00 20.00
PPRKB Kris Bryant 30.00 80.00
PPRMB Madison Bumgarner 20.00 50.00
PPRNS Noah Syndergaard 20.00 50.00

2017 Topps Rediscover Topps

COMPLETE SET (10) 4.00 10.00
STATED ODDS 1:8 HOBBY
STATED ODDS 1:3 FAT PACK
STATED ODDS 1:8 RETAIL
STATED ODDS 1:2 HANGER
STATED ODDS 1:8 BLASTER
STATED ODDS 1:2 JUMBO
RT1 Hank Aaron .75 2.00
RT2 Jackie Robinson .40 1.00
RT3 Reggie Jackson .30 .75
RT4 Nolan Ryan 1.25 3.00
RT5 Roberto Clemente 1.00 2.50
RT6 George Brett .75 2.00
RT7 Don Mattingly .75 2.00
RT8 Mark McGwire .60 1.50
RT9 Ken Griffey Jr. .75 2.00
RT10 Mike Trout 2.00 5.00

2017 Topps Reverance Autograph Patches

STATED ODDS 1:2645 HOBBY
STATED PRINT RUN 25 SER.#'d SETS
EXCHANGE DEADLINE 5/31/2019
TAPAR Anthony Rizzo EXCH 75.00 200.00
TAPARU Addison Russell EXCH 15.00 40.00
TAPBH Bryce Harper 150.00 300.00
TAPBP Buster Posey 75.00 200.00
TAPCS Corey Seager 75.00 200.00
TAPCY Carl Yastrzemski 60.00 150.00
TAPDO David Ortiz 75.00 200.00
TAPDP Dustin Pedroia 30.00 80.00
TAPGM Greg Maddux 75.00 200.00
TAPJAL Jose Altuve 75.00 200.00
TAPJU Julio Urias 20.00 50.00
TAPKM Kenta Maeda 20.00 50.00
TAPKS Kyle Schwarber 20.00 50.00
TAPMM Manny Machado 60.00 150.00
TAPMMG Mark McGwire 75.00 200.00
TAPRC Roger Clemens 40.00 100.00
TAPRJO Randy Johnson 60.00 150.00
TAPTT Troy Tulowitzki 10.00 25.00
TAPYM Yoan Moncada 60.00 150.00

2017 Topps Salute

COMPLETE SET (200) 75.00 200.00
STATED ODDS 1:4 HOBBY
STATED ODDS 1:2 FAT PACK
STATED ODDS 1:4 WM/TAR. RETAIL
STATED ODDS 1:4 BLASTER
SER.2 ODDS 1:4 HOBBY
*RED/25: 6X TO 15X BASIC
S1 Bryce Harper .60 1.50
S2 Miguel Cabrera .40 1.00
S3 Ty Cobb .60 1.50
S4 Paul Goldschmidt .40 1.00
S5 Braden Shipley .25 .60
S6 Jacob deGrom .40 1.00
S7 Johnny Bench .40 1.00
S8 Duke Snider .30 .75
S9 Freddie Freeman .50 1.25
S10 David Price .30 .75
S11 Orlando Arcia .30 .75
S12 Alex Reyes .30 .75
S13 Kyle Seager .25 .60
S14 Francisco Lindor .40 1.00
S15 Al Kaline .40 1.00
S16 Sandy Koufax .75 2.00
S17 Robin Yount .40 1.00
S18 Roberto Clemente 1.00 2.50
S19 Ted Williams .75 2.00
S20 Gregory Polanco .30 .75
S21 Cal Ripken Jr. 1.25 3.00
S22 Addison Russell .40 1.00
S23 Honus Wagner .40 1.00
S24 Joey Votto .40 1.00
S25 Mike Trout 2.00 5.00
S26 Bo Jackson .40 1.00
S27 Jorge Soler .40 1.00
S28 Jose Altuve .30 .75
S29 Tyler Glasnow .30 .75
S30 Matt Shoemaker .30 .75
S31 Frank Robinson .30 .75
S32 Jake Arrieta .30 .75
S33 Anthony Rendon .40 1.00
S34 Buster Posey .50 1.25
S35 Ian Kinsler .30 .75
S36 George Springer .30 .75
S37 Jim Palmer .30 .75
S38 Joe Mauer .30 .75
S39 Jackie Robinson .40 1.00
S40 David Ortiz .40 1.00
S41 Jason Hammel .30 .75
S42 Jose Peraza .30 .75
S43 Brandon Belt .30 .75
S44 Anthony Rizzo .60 1.50
S45 Noah Syndergaard .30 .75
S46 Alex Gordon .30 .75
S47 Trevor Story .40 1.00
S48 Yoenis Cespedes .40 1.00
S49 Luke Weaver .30 .75
S50 Brooks Robinson .30 .75
S51 Mookie Betts .60 1.50
S52 Babe Ruth 1.00 2.50
S53 Carlos Rodon .30 .75
S54 Ryan Braun .30 .75
S55 Tyler Austin .40 1.00
S56 Joe Morgan .30 .75
S57 Stephen Piscotty .30 .75
S58 Josh Donaldson .30 .75
S59 Carlos Gonzalez .30 .75
S60 Andrew McCutchen .40 1.00
S61 Jackie Bradley Jr. .40 1.00
S62 Manny Machado .40 1.00
S63 Willson Contreras .40 1.00
S64 Ken Griffey Jr. .75 2.00
S65 Kenta Maeda .30 .75
S66 Alex Bregman 1.00 2.50
S67 Todd Frazier .30 .75
S68 Josh Bell .60 1.50
S69 Ozzie Smith .50 1.25
S70 Giancarlo Stanton .40 1.00
S71 Justin Verlander .40 1.00
S72 Ichiro Suzuki .50 1.25
S73 Aaron Judge 3.00 8.00
S74 Rickey Henderson .40 1.00
S75 Dansby Swanson .60 1.50
S76 Miguel Sano .30 .75
S77 Ivan Rodriguez .30 .75
S78 Aaron Nola .30 .75
S79 Jameson Taillon .30 .75
S80 Kris Bryant .50 1.25
S81 Corey Seager .40 1.00
S82 Albert Pujols .50 1.25
S83 David Dahl .30 .75
S84 Carlos Correa .40 1.00
S85 Chris Sale .40 1.00
S86 Kendrys Morales .25 .60
S87 Wil Myers .25 .60
S88 Nolan Ryan 1.25 3.00
S89 Yulieski Gurriel .40 1.00
S90 Jose Abreu .40 1.00
S91 Rod Carew .30 .75
S92 Andrew Benintendi .75 2.00
S93 Jose Bautista .30 .75
S94 Brandon Phillips .25 .60
S95 Nolan Arenado .50 1.25
S96 Joe Musgrove .25 .60
S97 Lou Brock .30 .75
S98 Hank Aaron .75 2.00
S99 Stan Musial .60 1.50
S100 Barry Larkin .30 .75
S101 Bobby Abreu .25 .60
S102 Hunter Dozier .25 .60
S103 Addison Russell .40 1.00
S104 Tyler Naquin .25 .60
S105 Steven Matz .30 .75
S106 Jason Kipnis .30 .75
S107 Alex Gordon .30 .75
S108 Eddie Mathews .40 1.00
S109 Dave Winfield .30 .75
S110 Bryce Harper .60 1.50
S111 Aledmys Diaz .30 .75
S112 David Ortiz .40 1.00
S113 Jose Canseco .30 .75
S114 Yoan Moncada .75 2.00
S115 Trey Mancini .50 1.25
S116 Gary Sanchez .40 1.00
S117 Bob Feller .30 .75
S118 Joey Rickard .25 .60
S119 Orlando Cepeda .30 .75
S120 Kris Bryant .50 1.25
S121 Juan Marichal .30 .75
S122 Byron Buxton .30 .75
S123 Matt Olson .40 1.00
S124 Matt Strahm .25 .60
S125 Mike Trout 2.00 5.00
S126 David Dahl .30 .75
S127 Warren Spahn .30 .75
S128 Trey Mancini .50 1.25
S129 Josh Donaldson .30 .75
S130 Carlos Correa .40 1.00
S131 Robert Gsellman .25 .60
S132 Aaron Judge 3.00 8.00
S133 Andrew Toles .25 .60
S134 Fergie Jenkins .30 .75
S135 Jake Thompson .25 .60
S136 Tyler Austin .40 1.00
S137 Gary Carter .30 .75
S138 JaCoby Jones .30 .75
S139 Tim Anderson .30 .75
S140 Todd Frazier .30 .75
S141 Alex Bregman 1.00 2.50
S142 Harmon Killebrew .40 1.00
S143 Brian Dozier .40 1.00
S144 Anthony Rizzo .60 1.50
S145 Ken Griffey Jr. .75 2.00
S146 Noah Syndergaard .30 .75
S147 Jorge Alfaro .30 .75
S148 Tommy Lasorda .30 .75
S149 Jeff Bagwell .30 .75
S150 Clayton Kershaw .75 2.00
S151 Joe Panik .30 .75
S152 Buster Posey .50 1.25
S153 Roberto Alomar .30 .75
S154 Josh Donaldson .30 .75
S155 Jose De Leon .25 .60
S156 Maikel Franco .30 .75
S157 Javier Baez .50 1.25
S158 Willie Stargell .30 .75
S159 Tim Raines .30 .75
S160 Dansby Swanson .60 1.50
S161 Stephen Piscotty .30 .75
S162 Yulieski Gurriel .40 1.00
S163 George Brett .75 2.00
S164 Eddie Murray .30 .75
S165 Jered Weaver .30 .75
S166 Adam Duvall .40 1.00
S167 Joey Votto .40 1.00
S168 Frank Thomas .40 1.00
S169 Jharel Cotton .25 .60
S170 Tyler Glasnow .30 .75
S171 Dan Vogelbach .40 1.00
S172 Ty Blach .25 .60
S173 Duke Snider .30 .75
S174 Willie McCovey .30 .75
S175 Anthony Rizzo .60 1.50
S176 Raimel Tapia .30 .75
S177 Starling Marte .30 .75
S178 Reynaldo Lopez .25 .60
S179 Jacob deGrom .40 1.00
S180 Corey Seager .40 1.00
S181 Anthony Rendon .40 1.00
S182 Manny Margot .25 .60
S183 Mookie Betts .60 1.50
S184 Manny Machado .40 1.00
S185 Braden Shipley .25 .60
S186 Addison Russell .40 1.00
S187 Kenny Lofton .25 .60
S188 Renato Nunez .50 1.25
S189 Alex Reyes .30 .75
S190 Teoscar Hernandez .75 2.00
S191 Jeff Hoffman .25 .60
S192 Francisco Lindor .40 1.00
S193 Aledmys Diaz .30 .75
S194 Josh Bell .60 1.50
S195 Tyler Glasnow .30 .75
S196 Randal Grichuk .25 .60
S197 Gavin Cecchini .25 .60
S198 Gregory Polanco .30 .75
S199 Andrew Benintendi .75 2.00
S200 Derek Jeter 1.00 2.50

2017 Topps Salute Autographs

SER.1 ODDS 1:1987 HOBBY
SER.1 ODDS 1:1567 TAR. RETAIL
SER.1 ODDS 1:1284 HANGER
SER.1 ODDS 1:679 FAT PACK
SER.1 ODDS 1:168 JUMBO
SER.1 ODDS 1:1773 WM RETAIL
SER.2 ODDS 1:951 HOBBY
SER.1 EXCH DEADLINE 12/31/2018
SER.2 EXCH DEADLINE 5/31/2019
*RED/25: .6X TO 1.5X BASIC
TSAAB Alex Bregman 25.00 60.00
TSAABE Andrew Benintendi 75.00 200.00
TSAABE Andrew Benintendi S2 75.00 200.00
TSAABR Alex Bregman S2 25.00 60.00
TSAABR Archie Bradley 3.00 8.00
TSAADA Aledmys Diaz S2 10.00 25.00
TSAADI Aledmys Diaz S2 10.00 25.00
TSAADU Adam Duvall S2 20.00 50.00
TSAAG Andres Galarraga 12.00 30.00
TSAAGO Alex Gordon 20.00 50.00
TSAAGO Alex Gordon S2 20.00 50.00
TSAAJ Aaron Judge S2 125.00 300.00
TSAAJ Aaron Judge 125.00 300.00
TSAAK Al Kaline 25.00 50.00
TSAAN Aaron Nola 4.00 10.00
TSAAR Anthony Rendon 10.00 25.00
TSAARE Alex Reyes 4.00 10.00
TSAARE Anthony Rendon S2 10.00 25.00
TSAARI Anthony Rizzo S2 25.00 60.00
TSAARI Anthony Rizzo 25.00 60.00
TSAARS Addison Russell S2
TSAARU Addison Russell S2
TSAARY Alex Reyes S2 4.00 10.00
TSAAT Andrew Toles S2 3.00 8.00
TSABA Bobby Abreu S2 12.00 30.00
TSABB Byron Buxton S2 10.00 25.00
TSABB Brandon Belt 10.00 25.00
TSABH Bryce Harper
TSABJ Bo Jackson
TSABL Barry Larkin 30.00 80.00
TSABM Bill Mazeroski 20.00 50.00
TSABM Bruce Maxwell S2 3.00 8.00
TSABPH Brandon Phillips 8.00 20.00
TSABRO Brooks Robinson 20.00 50.00
TSABS Braden Shipley 3.00 8.00
TSABS Braden Shipley S2 3.00 8.00
TSACC Carlos Correa 40.00 100.00
TSACFI Carlton Fisk
TSACFU Carson Fulmer 3.00 8.00
TSACL Cliff Lee
TSACP Chad Pinder S2 3.00 8.00
TSACR Cal Ripken Jr.
TSACRO Carlos Rodon 4.00 10.00
TSADB Dellin Betances 6.00 15.00
TSADD David Dahl 3.00 8.00
TSADD David Dahl S2 4.00 10.00
TSADO David Ortiz S2
TSADS Dansby Swanson EXCH 60.00 150.00
TSADSA Danny Salazar 8.00 20.00
TSADSN Duke Snider
TSADSN Duke Snider S2
TSADSW Dansby Swanson S2
TSADV Dan Vogelbach S2 5.00 12.00
TSAEM Edgar Martinez 10.00 25.00
TSAFJ Fergie Jenkins 10.00 25.00
TSAFJ Fergie Jenkins S2 5.00 12.00
TSAFL Francisco Lindor S2 EXCH 20.00 50.00
TSAFL Francisco Lindor 25.00 60.00
TSAFM Fred McGriff
TSAFR Frank Robinson 40.00 100.00
TSAFV Fernando Valenzuela
TSAGCA Gary Carter S2 20.00 50.00
TSAGCE Gavin Cecchini S2 EXCH 3.00 8.00
TSAGG Goose Gossage 10.00 25.00
TSAGM German Marquez S2 5.00 12.00
TSAGP Gregory Polanco S2 4.00 10.00
TSAGPO Gregory Polanco 10.00 25.00
TSAGS George Springer 10.00 25.00
TSAHD Hunter Dozier S2 3.00 8.00
TSAHR Hunter Renfroe 6.00 15.00
TSAHS Hector Santiago 3.00 8.00
TSAIK Ian Kinsler 15.00 40.00
TSAIR Ivan Rodriguez
TSAJA Jose Abreu
TSAJA Jorge Alfaro S2 4.00 10.00
TSAJB Jackie Bradley Jr. 15.00 40.00
TSAJBA Javier Baez 20.00 50.00
TSAJBA Javier Baez S2 6.00 15.00
TSAJBAG Jeff Bagwell 30.00 80.00
TSAJBE Josh Bell 25.00 60.00
TSAJBER Jose Berrios 4.00 10.00
TSAJBL Josh Bell S2 8.00 20.00
TSAJBR Jay Bruce 10.00 25.00
TSAJCA Jose Canseco S2 15.00 40.00
TSAJCO Jharel Cotton S2 3.00 8.00
TSAJDA Johnny Damon
TSAJDE Jacob deGrom
TSAJDG Jacob deGrom S2 30.00 80.00
TSAJDL Jose De Leon S2 3.00 8.00
TSAJDO Josh Donaldson S2
TSAJH Jeff Hoffman S2 3.00 8.00
TSAJH Jason Hammel 10.00 25.00
TSAJJ JaCoby Jones S2 4.00 10.00
TSAJK Jason Kipnis S2 8.00 20.00
TSAJL Jake Lamb 4.00 10.00
TSAJM Joe Mauer
TSAJMA J.D. Martinez 12.00 30.00
TSAJMAR Juan Marichal 12.00 30.00
TSAJMO Joe Morgan
TSAJMU Joe Musgrove 3.00 8.00
TSAJO Jake Odorizzi 3.00 8.00
TSAJP Joe Panik 12.00 30.00
TSAJP Joe Panik S2 12.00 30.00
TSAJPA Jim Palmer 12.00 30.00
TSAJPE Joc Pederson 6.00 15.00
TSAJPER Jose Peraza 12.00 30.00
TSAJR Joey Rickard S2 10.00 25.00
TSAJS Jorge Soler 15.00 40.00
TSAJT Julio Teheran 10.00 25.00
TSAJT Jake Thompson S2 3.00 8.00
TSAJTA Jameson Taillon 4.00 10.00
TSAJTH Jake Thompson 10.00 25.00
TSAJW Jered Weaver S2
TSAKB Kris Bryant
TSAKG Ken Griffey Jr. S2
TSAKL Kenny Lofton S2 12.00 30.00
TSAKM Kendrys Morales 8.00 20.00
TSAKSE Kyle Seager 8.00 20.00
TSALB Lou Brock 25.00 60.00
TSALS Luis Severino 8.00 20.00
TSALW Luke Weaver 6.00 15.00
TSAMF Maikel Franco S2 8.00 20.00
TSAMM Manny Margot S2
TSAMO Matt Olson S2 6.00 15.00
TSAMS Matt Strahm S2 10.00 25.00
TSAMS Matt Shoemaker 4.00 10.00
TSAMSA Miguel Sano 8.00 20.00
TSAMT Mike Trout
TSANS Noah Syndergaard 15.00 40.00
TSAOAR Orlando Arcia 6.00 15.00
TSAOC Orlando Cepeda
TSAOC Orlando Cepeda S2 8.00 20.00
TSAOS Ozzie Smith
TSAPC Patrick Corbin 4.00 10.00
TSAPN Phil Niekro 12.00 30.00
TSAPO Paul O'Neill 12.00 30.00
TSARA Roberto Alomar 25.00 60.00
TSARA Roberto Alomar S2 30.00 80.00
TSARC Rod Carew
TSARF Rollie Fingers 15.00 40.00
TSARGR Randal Grichuk S2
TSARGS Robert Gsellman S2 3.00 8.00
TSARH Ryon Healy 4.00 10.00
TSARL Reynaldo Lopez S2 3.00 8.00
TSARN Renato Nunez S2 6.00 15.00
TSARQ Roman Quinn S2 3.00 8.00
TSARTA Raimel Tapia S2 4.00 10.00
TSARY Robin Yount 30.00 80.00
TSARZ Rob Zastryzny S2
TSASL Seth Lugo S2 10.00 25.00
TSASMR Starling Marte S2 4.00 10.00
TSASMT Steven Matz S2 12.00 30.00
TSASP Stephen Piscotty S2 6.00 15.00
TSASP Stephen Piscotty 8.00 20.00
TSATA Tyler Austin 8.00 20.00
TSATAN Tim Anderson S2 5.00 12.00
TSATAU Tyler Austin S2 8.00 20.00
TSATB Ty Blach S2 12.00 30.00
TSATF Todd Frazier S2
TSATGA Tyler Glasnow S2 EXCH 4.00 10.00
TSATGL Tyler Glasnow S2 EXCH 4.00 10.00
TSATH Teoscar Hernandez S2 10.00 25.00
TSATL Tommy Lasorda S2 12.00 30.00
TSATMA Trey Mancini S2 20.00 50.00
TSATMN Trey Mancini S2 20.00 50.00
TSATN Tyler Naquin S2 3.00 8.00
TSATST Trevor Story 15.00 40.00
TSATW Taijuan Walker 10.00 25.00
TSAVG Vladimir Guerrero S2 40.00 100.00
TSAWC Willson Contreras 15.00 40.00
TSAWD Wade Davis 10.00 25.00
TSAWM Wil Myers
TSAYG Yulieski Gurriel 30.00 80.00
TSAYG Yulieski Gurriel S2 5.00 12.00
TSAYM Yoan Moncada S2

2017 Topps Silver Slugger Awards

STATED ODDS 1:4 WM RETAIL
STATED ODDS 1:5 WM BLASTER
SS1 Salvador Perez .50 1.25
SS2 Wilson Ramos .40 1.00
SS3 Miguel Cabrera .60 1.50
SS4 Anthony Rizzo 1.00 2.50
SS5 Jose Altuve .50 1.25
SS6 Daniel Murphy .50 1.25
SS7 Josh Donaldson .50 1.25
SS8 Nolan Arenado .75 2.00
SS9 Xander Bogaerts .60 1.50
SS10 Corey Seager .60 1.50
SS11 Mike Trout 3.00 8.00
SS12 Charlie Blackmon .60 1.50
SS13 Mark Trumbo .40 1.00
SS14 Christian Yelich .75 2.00
SS15 Mookie Betts 1.00 2.50
SS16 Yoenis Cespedes .60 1.50
SS17 David Ortiz .60 1.50
SS18 Jake Arrieta .50 1.25

2017 Topps Spring Training Logo Patch

STATED ODDS 1:1295 HOBBY
STATED ODDS 1:30 JUMBO
*GOLD/99: .5X TO 1.2X BASIC
*BLACK/50: .6X TO 1.5X BASIC
MLBSTAM Andrew McCutchen 4.00 10.00
MLBSTAN Aaron Nola 3.00 8.00
MLBSTBH Bryce Harper 6.00 15.00
MLBSTBP Buster Posey 5.00 12.00
MLBSTCC Carlos Correa 4.00 10.00
MLBSTCK Clayton Kershaw 5.00 12.00
MLBSTCS Chris Sale 4.00 10.00
MLBSTEH Eric Hosmer 3.00 8.00
MLBSTEL Evan Longoria 3.00 8.00
MLBSTFF Freddie Freeman 5.00 12.00
MLBSTFL Francisco Lindor 4.00 10.00
MLBSTGS Giancarlo Stanton 4.00 10.00
MLBSTGSA Gary Sanchez 6.00 15.00
MLBSTJD Josh Donaldson 3.00 8.00
MLBSTJM Joe Mauer 3.00 8.00
MLBSTJV Joey Votto 4.00 10.00
MLBSTKB Kris Bryant 10.00 25.00
MLBSTMB Mookie Betts 6.00 15.00
MLBSTMC Miguel Cabrera 4.00 10.00
MLBSTMCR Matt Carpenter 4.00 10.00
MLBSTMM Manny Machado 4.00 10.00
MLBSTMT Mike Trout 8.00 20.00
MLBSTNA Nolan Arenado 5.00 12.00
MLBSTNS Noah Syndergaard 5.00 12.00
MLBSTPG Paul Goldschmidt 4.00 10.00
MLBSTRB Ryan Braun 3.00 8.00
MLBSTRC Robinson Cano 3.00 8.00
MLBSTSG Sonny Gray 3.00 8.00
MLBSTWM Wil Myers 2.50 6.00
MLBSTYD Yu Darvish 4.00 10.00

2017 Topps World Champion Autograph Relics

STATED ODDS 1:16,871 HOBBY
STATED ODDS 1:13,952 FAT PACK
STATED ODDS 1:37,029 TAR. RETAIL
STATED ODDS 1:36,374 HANGER
STATED ODDS 1:2328 JUMBO
STATED ODDS 1:36,249 WM RETAIL
STATED PRINT RUN 50 SER. #'d SETS
EXCHANGE DEADLINE 12/31/2018
*RED/25: .75X TO 2X BASIC
WCRAA Albert Almora 40.00 100.00
WCRARU Addison Russell 60.00 150.00
WCRJB Javier Baez
WCRJH Jason Heyward 30.00 80.00
WCRKB Kris Bryant 200.00 400.00
WCRKS Kyle Schwarber 50.00 120.00
WCRWC Willson Contreras 30.00 80.00

2017 Topps World Champion Autographs

STATED ODDS 1:16,871 HOBBY
STATED ODDS 1:13,952 FAT PACK
STATED ODDS 1:37,029 TAR. RETAIL
STATED ODDS 1:36,374 HANGER
STATED ODDS 1:2328 JUMBO
STATED ODDS 1:36,249 RETAIL
STATED PRINT RUN 50 SER. #'d SETS
EXCHANGE DEADLINE 12/31/2018
*RED/25: .5X TO 1.2X BASIC
WCAAA Albert Almora 30.00 80.00
WCAARU Addison Russell 60.00 150.00
WCAJB Javier Baez 25.00 60.00
WCAJH Jason Heyward
WCAKB Kris Bryant 250.00 400.00
WCAKS Kyle Schwarber 60.00 150.00
WCAWC Willson Contreras 40.00 100.00

2017 Topps World Champion Relics

STATED ODDS 1:2888 HOBBY
STATED ODDS 1:2408 FAT PACK
STATED ODDS 1:6400 TAR. RETAIL
STATED ODDS 1:6419 HANGER
STATED ODDS 1:6432 TAR. RETAIL
STATED ODDS 1:401 JUMBO
STATED PRINT RUN 100 SER. #'d SETS
*RED/25: .75X TO 2X BASIC
WCRAA Albert Almora 15.00 40.00
WCRAC Aroldis Chapman 15.00 40.00
WCRARI Anthony Rizzo 20.00 50.00
WCRARU Addison Russell 15.00 40.00
WCRBZ Ben Zobrist 20.00 50.00
WCRDF Dexter Fowler 12.00 30.00
WCRJA Jake Arrieta 15.00 40.00
WCRJB Javier Baez 20.00 50.00
WCRJH Jason Heyward 10.00 25.00
WCRJL Jon Lester 15.00 40.00
WCRJS Jorge Soler 12.00 30.00
WCRKB Kris Bryant 50.00 120.00
WCRKS Kyle Schwarber 12.00 30.00
WCRWC Willson Contreras 15.00 40.00

2017 Topps Update

COMPLETE SET w/o SP's (300) 20.00 50.00
PLATE PRINT RUN 1 SET PER COLOR
BLACK-CYAN-MAGENTA-YELLOW ISSUED
NO PLATE PRICING DUE TO SCARCITY
US1 Aaron Judge HRD 1.50 4.00
US2 Domingo German RC 1.25 3.00
US3 Paul Sewald RC .40 1.00
Tyler Pill RC
US4 Matt Chapman RC .60 1.50
US5 Casey Fien RC .40 1.00
US6 Ramon Torres RC .40 1.00
US7 Willy Garcia RC .40 1.00
Adam Engel RC
US8 Yulieski Gurriel RD .20 .50
US9A George Springer AS .15 .40
US9B George Springer SP .75 2.00
US10A Ian Happ RC .75 2.00
US10B Ernie Banks SP .75 2.00
US10C Ian Happ SP 1.25 3.00
US10D Ian Happ SP
US10E Ryne Sandberg SP 1.50 4.00
US11 Gary Sanchez HRD .20 .50
US12 Lisalverto Bonilla .12 .30
US13 Brian McCann .15 .40
US14 Blast Off! .20 .50
Carlos Correa
Jose Altuve
US15 Kyle Higashioka RC .40 1.00
US16 Rafael Bautista RC .40 1.00
US17 Chris Archer AS .12 .30
US18A Mookie Betts AS .30 .75
US18B Mookie Betts SP 1.50 4.00
US18C Ted Williams SP 1.50 4.00
US19 Eric Skoglund RC .40 1.00
US20 Jason Vargas AS .12 .30
US21 Christian Arroyo RD .20 .50
US22A Hunter Renfroe RD .15 .40
US22B Hunter Renfroe SP .75 2.00
blue jersey
US23 Derek Holland .12 .30
US24 Joe Smith .12 .30
US25A Christian Arroyo RC .60 1.50
US25B Christian Arroyo SP 1.00 2.50
US25C Christian Arroyo SP
US26 Steve Pearce .20 .50
US27A Nolan Arenado AS .25 .60
US27B Nolan Arenado SP 1.25 3.00
US28 Drew Robinson RC .40 1.00
US29 Drew Steckenrider RC .40 1.00
US30 Danny Ortiz RC .40 1.00
US31 Danny Santana .12 .30
US32 Luis Torrens RC .40 1.00
US33A Salvador Perez AS .15 .40
US33B Bo Jackson SP .75 2.00
US33C Salvador Perez SP .75 2.00
US34 Nelson Cruz AS .20 .50
US35 Dinelson Lamet RC .40 1.00
US36 Adam Lind .15 .40
US37 Ian Happ RD .25 .60
US38A Cody Bellinger AS 2.00 5.00
US38B Cody Bellinger SP 5.00 12.00
US39 Charlie Morton .20 .50
US40 Pat Neshek .12 .30
US41A Mitch Haniger RD .20 .50
US41B Mitch Haniger SP
Mariners
US42A Seth Smith .12 .30
US42B Eddie Murray SP .60 1.50
US43A Joey Votto AS .20 .50
US43B Johnny Bench SP .75 2.00
US43C Joey Votto SP 1.00 2.50
US44 Chicago Cubs World
Series Celebration .20 .50
US45 Johan Camargo RC .40 1.00
US46 Dylan Covey RC .40 1.00
US47A Yadier Molina AS .20 .50
US47B Yadier Molina SP 1.00 2.50
US47C Ozzie Smith SP 1.00 2.50
US48 Ariel Hernandez RC .40 1.00
US49 Austin Bibens-Dirkx RC .40 1.00
US50A Cody Bellinger RC 20.00 50.00
US50B Cody Bellinger SP 6.00 15.00
US50C Cody Bellinger SP
gray jersey
US50D Jackie Robinson SP .75 2.00
US51 Jorge Bonifacio RC .40 1.00
US52 Michael Fulmer AS .12 .30
US53 Barrett Astin RC .40 1.00
US54 Ronald Torreyes .12 .30
US55 Luis Severino AS .15 .40
US56 Jake Junis RC .60 1.50
US57 Charged-Up Battery .12 .30
Roberto Osuna
Russell Martin
US58 Ervin Santana .12 .30
US59 Matt Joyce .12 .30
US60 Kyle Freeland RC .50 1.25
US61 Matt Szczur .15 .40
US62 Travis Wood .12 .30
US63 Andrew Cashner .12 .30
US64 Corey Kluber AS .15 .40
US65 Giancarlo Stanton HRD .20 .50
US66 Jose Osuna RC .40 1.00
US67 Avisail Garcia AS .12 .30
US68 Jered Weaver .15 .40
US69 Alex Avila .15 .40
US70 Josh Reddick .12 .30
US71 Junichi Tazawa .12 .30
US72 Joaquin Benoit .12 .30
US73 Jason Grilli .12 .30
US74 Ryne Stanek RC .40 1.00
US75 Jake Buchanan RC .40 1.00
US76 Miguel Montero .12 .30
US77A Mike Moustakas AS .15 .40
US77B George Brett SP 1.50 4.00
US78 Jarlin Garcia RC .40 1.00
US79 Nick Goody .12 .30
US80 Ichiro .25 .60
US81 Clay Buchholz .12 .30
US82 Matt Boyd .12 .30
US83 Carlos Ruiz .12 .30
US84 Michael Brantley AS .15 .40
US85 Tommy Milone .12 .30
US86 Clayton Richard .12 .30
US87A Chris Sale AS .20 .50
US87B Roger Clemens SP 1.00 2.50
US87C Chris Sale SP 1.00 2.50
US88 Jorge Soler .20 .50
US89 Casey Lawrence RC .40 1.00
US90A Derek Fisher RC .50 1.25
US90B Derek Fisher SP .75 2.00
US90C Derek Fisher SP
US91A Jordan Montgomery RC .60 1.50
US91B Jordan Montgomery SP 1.00 2.50
US91C Jordan Montgomery SP
US92 Anthony Alford RC .40 1.00
US93 Jesse Chavez .12 .30
US94 Justin Upton AS .15 .40
US95 Stephen Strasburg AS .20 .50
US96A Brett Phillips RC .50 1.25
US96B Brett Phillips SP .75 2.00
US97 Alexi Amarista .12 .30
US98 Andrew Moore RC .50 1.25
US99A Aaron Judge RD 1.50 4.00
US99B Reggie Jackson SP .60 1.50
US99C Aaron Judge SP 75.00 200.00
US100 Chris Sale .20 .50
US101 Magneuris Sierra RC .60 1.50
US102 Dovydas Neverauskas RC .40 1.00
Gift Ngoepe RC
US103 Matt Adams .12 .30
US104 Sam Gaviglio RC .40 1.00
US105 John Brebbia RC .50 1.25
US106 Kendrys Morales .12 .30
US107 Andrew Bailey .12 .30
US108 Wilson Ramos .12 .30
US109 Ben Revere .12 .30
US110A Corey Seager AS .20 .50
US110B Corey Seager SP 1.00 2.50
US111 Meat of the Mets .15 .40
Wilmer Flores
Michael Conforto
US112A Ryan Zimmerman AS .15 .40
US112B Ryan Zimmerman SP .75 2.00
US113 Franklin Barreto RD .12 .30
US114 Pat Neshek AS .12 .30
US115 M Is For Mashing .30 .75
Manny Machado
Mookie Betts
US116 Tyler Glasnow RD .15 .40
US117 Neftali Feliz .12 .30
US118 Bradley Zimmer RD .15 .40
US119 Greg Holland .12 .30
US120 Carlos Beltran .15 .40
US121A Daniel Murphy AS .15 .40
US121B Daniel Murphy SP .75 2.00
US122 Coming to America .20 .50
Yu Darvish
Nori Aoki
US123 Colby Rasmus .15 .40
US124 Nick Hundley .12 .30
US125 Yoan Moncada RD .40 1.00
US126 Austin Slater RC .40 1.00
US127 Antonio Senzatela RC .40 1.00
US128 Ervin Santana AS .12 .30
US129 Brooks Pounders .12 .30
US130 Zack Greinke AS .15 .40
US131 Doug Fister .12 .30
US132 Dallas Keuchel AS .15 .40
US133 Keynan Middleton RC .60 1.50
US134 Justin Bour HRD .15 .40
US135 Chase De Jong RC .50 1.25
US136A Josh Harrison AS .12 .30
US136B Roberto Clemente SP 2.00 5.00
US137 Daniel Hudson .12 .30
US138 Logan Verrett .12 .30
US139 Luis Castillo RC 1.25 3.00
US140 Sal Romano RC .40 1.00
US141A Bryce Harper AS .30 .75
US141B Bryce Harper SP 1.50 4.00
US142 Tzu-Wei Lin RC .40 1.00
US143 Trevor Cahill .12 .30
US144 Charlie Blackmon AS .20 .50
US145 Dillon Overton RC .40 1.00
US146 David Dahl RD .15 .40
US147 Jose Alvarado RC .40 1.00
Austin Pruitt RC
US148 The Next Dynasty 1.50 4.00
Aaron Judge
Greg Bird
US149 James Pazos .12 .30
US150A Alex Bregman RD .50 1.25
US150B Alex Bregman SP
US151 Yandy Diaz RC .75 2.00
US152A Robinson Cano AS .15 .40
US152B Robinson Cano SP .75 2.00
US152C Ken Griffey Jr. SP 1.50 4.00
US153 Robbie Ray AS .12 .30
US154 Franklin Gutierrez .12 .30
US155 Run and Hit .20 .50
Joey Votto
Billy Hamilton
US156A Yu Darvish AS .20 .50
US156B Yu Darvish SP 1.00 2.50

US156C Yu Darvish SP 1.00 2.50
US156D Nolan Ryan SP 2.50 6.00
US157 Corey Dickerson AS .12 .30
US158 Phillip Ervin RC .40 1.00
US159 JT Riddle RC .40 1.00
US160 Ben Lively RC .40 1.00
Andrew Knapp RC
US161 Justin Haley RC .40 1.00
US162A Sean Newcomb RC .50 1.25
US162B Greg Maddux SP 1.00 2.50
US162C Sean Newcomb SP .75 2.00
in dugout
US162D Sean Newcomb SP
US163 Edinson Volquez .12 .30
US164 Carlos Martinez AS .15 .40
US165 Boone Logan .12 .30
US166A Aaron Judge AS 1.50 4.00
US166B Aaron Judge SP 8.00 20.00
US166C Babe Ruth SP 2.00 5.00
US167 Drew Smyly .12 .30
US168A Michael Conforto AS .15 .40
US168B Michael Conforto .15 .40
pinstripe jersey
US168C Mike Piazza SP .75 2.00
US169 A.J. Ellis .12 .30
US170 Cameron Maybin .12 .30
US171 Brock Stassi RC .50 1.25
US172 Jason Hammel .15 .40
US173 Chris Coghlan .12 .30
US174 Brandon Moss .12 .30
US175A Jose Altuve AS .15 .40
US175B Jose Altuve .15 .40
blue jersey
US176 History Makers .30 .75
Kris Bryant
Anthony Rizzo
US177 Jake Lamb AS .15 .40
US178 Stuart Turner RC .40 1.00
US179 Pierce Johnson RC .40 1.00
US180 Mike Moustakas HRD .15 .40
US181 Emilio Pagan RC .40 1.00
US182A Jaime Garcia .12 .30
US182B John Smoltz SP .75 2.00
US183 Taylor Motter .12 .30
US184 Jean Segura .15 .40
US185 Birds in the Garden
Stephen Piscotty .15 .40
Jason Heyward
Randal Grichuk
US186 Jose De Leon RC .40 1.00
US187 Jaycob Brugman RC .40 1.00
US188 Trevor Plouffe .12 .30
US189 Chad Bell RC .60 1.50
US190 Brad Goldberg RC .40 1.00
US191 Corey Knebel AS .12 .30
US192 Jacob May RC .40 1.00
US193 Orlando Arcia RD .20 .50
US194 Derek Fisher RD .15 .40
US195 Fernando Rodney .12 .30
US196 Brad Hand AS .12 .30
US197 Dellin Betances AS .15 .40
US198 Chih-Wei Hu RC .40 1.00
US199 Brett Cecil .12 .30
US200A Yoan Moncada RC 1.25 3.00
US200B Yoan Moncada SP 2.00 5.00
US200C Yoan Moncada SP
white wrist tape
US201 Nolan Fontana RC .40 1.00
US202 Kenley Jansen AS .15 .40
US203 Joe Blanton .12 .30
US204 Chris Heston .12 .30
US205A Zack Cozart AS .12 .30
US205B Barry Larkin SP .60 1.50
US206 Partners in Pop .15 .40
Eric Thames
Ryan Braun
US207 Kurt Suzuki .12 .30
US208 Randy Rosario RC .40 1.00
US209 Josh Hader RC .40 1.00
US210 Sammy Solis .12 .30
US211 Rookie Davis RC .40 1.00
US212 Jose Quintana .12 .30
US213 Yovani Gallardo .12 .30
US214 Cody Bellinger RD 2.00 5.00
US215 Joe Jimenez RC .40 1.00
US216 J.P. Howell .12 .30
US217 Howie Kendrick .12 .30
US218 Greg Holland AS .12 .30
US219 Paul DeJong RC 1.25 3.00
US220 Jeff Locke .12 .30
US221 Mark Zagunis RC .40 1.00
US222 Jose Ramirez AS .15 .40
US223A Clayton Kershaw AS .40 1.00
US223B Clayton Kershaw SP 2.00 5.00
US223C Sandy Koufax SP 1.50 4.00
US224 Wade Davis AS .12 .30
US225A Andrew Benintendi RD .40 1.00
US225B Andrew Benintendi SP 2.00 5.00
US225C Andrew Benintendi SP
US226A Lewis Brinson RC .60 1.50
US226B Lewis Brinson SP 1.00 2.50
US226C Lewis Brinson SP
US227A Trey Mancini RC .25 .60
US227B Trey Mancini SP 1.25 3.00
US227C Cal Ripken Jr. SP 2.50 6.00
US228 Wade Davis .12 .30
US229 Tyson Ross .12 .30
US230 DJ LeMahieu AS .20 .50
US231 Reynaldo Lopez RC .40 1.00
US232A Marcell Ozuna AS .20 .50
US232B Marcell Ozuna SP 1.00 2.50
US233 Taijuan Walker .12 .30
US234A Francisco Lindor AS .20 .50
US234B Francisco Lindor SP 1.00 2.50
US235 Nick Pivetta RC .50 1.25
Ricardo Pinto RC
US236A Starlin Castro AS .12 .30
US236B Derek Jeter SP 2.00 5.00
US237A Buster Posey AS .25 .60
US237B Buster Posey SP 1.25 3.00
US238 Chris Bostick RC .50 1.25
US239 Neil Ramirez .12 .30
US240A Jacob Faria RC .40 1.00
US240B Jacob Faria SP .60 1.50
US241 Ryon Healy RD .15 .40
US242 Mike Hauschild RC .40 1.00
US243 Hector Velazquez RC .75 2.00
US244 Justin Turner AS .15 .40
US245A Yonder Alonso AS .12 .30
US245B Mark McGwire SP 1.25 3.00
US246 Marc Rzepczynski .12 .30
US247A Dansby Swanson RD .30 .75
US247B Hank Aaron SP 1.50 4.00
US247C Dansby Swanson SP
US248A Ender Inciarte AS .20 .50
US248B Chipper Jones SP .75 2.00
US249 Alex Reyes RD .15 .40
US250 Daniel Robertson RC .40 1.00
US251 Daniel Descalso .12 .30
US252 Mike Dunn .12 .30
US253 Matt Belisle .12 .30
US254 Amir Garrett RD .12 .30
US255 Stefan Crichton RC .40 1.00
US256 Mike Ohlman RC .40 1.00
US257 Alex Wood AS .12 .30
US258 Francis Martes RC .40 1.00
US259A Tyler Austin RD .20 .50
US259B Lou Gehrig SP 1.50 4.00
US260A Carlos Correa AS .20 .50
US260B Carlos Correa SP 1.00 2.50
US261A Max Scherzer AS .20 .50
US261B Max Scherzer SP 1.00 2.50
US262 Fernando Salas .12 .30
US263 Brian Duensing .12 .30
US264 Boog Powell RC .40 1.00
US265 Eric Young Jr. .12 .30
US266 Jett Bandy .12 .30
US267 Jhoulys Chacin .12 .30
US268 Miguel Sano HRD .15 .40
US269A Craig Kimbrel AS .15 .40
US269B Craig Kimbrel SP .75 2.00
US269C Pedro Martinez SP .60 1.50
US270A Gary Sanchez AS .20 .50
US270B Don Mattingly SP 1.50 4.00
US270C Gary Sanchez SP 1.00 2.50
US271A Jesse Winker RC .40 1.00
US271B Jesse Winker SP .60 1.50
US272 Justin Smoak AS .12 .30
US273 Dwight Smith RC .40 1.00
US274 Mitch Moreland .12 .30
US275A Bradley Zimmer .15 .40
US275B Bradley Zimmer SP .75 2.00
US275C Bradley Zimmer SP
US276 Allen Cordoba RC .40 1.00
Franchy Cordero RC
US277A Paul Goldschmidt AS .20 .50
US277B Paul Goldschmidt SP 1.00 2.50
US278 Rajai Davis .12 .30
US279A Franklin Barreto RC .40 1.00
US279B Franklin Barreto SP .60 1.50
US279C Franklin Barreto SP
on dugout steps
US279D Rickey Henderson SP .75 2.00
US280 Brett Anderson .12 .30
US281 Luke Voit RC 8.00 20.00
US282 Michael Martinez .12 .30
US283 Adam Eaton .20 .50
US284 Peter Bourjos .12 .30
US285 Scott Feldman .12 .30
US286 Jeff Hoffman RD .12 .30
US287 Mark Leiter Jr. RC .60 1.50
US288A Miguel Sano AS .15 .40
US288B Miguel Sano SP .75 2.00
US289 Sam Travis RC .40 1.00
US290 Anthony Rendon .20 .50
US291 Andrew Miller AS .15 .40
US292A Jonathan Schoop AS .12 .30
US292B Brooks Robinson SP .60 1.50
US293 Tuffy Gosewisch .12 .30
US294 Bobby Wahl RC .40 1.00
US295 Ben Taylor RC .50 1.25
US296A Giancarlo Stanton AS .20 .50
US296B Giancarlo Stanton SP 1.00 2.50
US297 Reymin Guduan RC .40 1.00
Jordan Jankowski RC
US298 Brett Eibner .12 .30
US299 Charlie Blackmon HRD .20 .50
US300 Cody Bellinger HRD 2.00 5.00

2017 Topps Update Black

*BLACK: 10X TO 25X BASIC
*BLACK RC: 3X TO 8X BASIC RC
STATED PRINT RUN 66 SER.#'d SETS
US50 Cody Bellinger 150.00 400.00
US148 The Next Dynasty 12.00 30.00
Aaron Judge
Greg Bird

2017 Topps Update Black and White Negative

*BW NEGATIVE: 5X TO 12X BASIC
*BW NEGATIVE RC: 1.5X TO 4X BASIC
US50 Cody Bellinger 75.00 200.00
US148 The Next Dynasty 10.00 25.00
Aaron Judge
Greg Bird

2017 Topps Update Father's Day Blue

*BLUE: 10X TO 25X BASIC
*BLUE RC: 3X TO 8X BASIC RC
STATED PRINT RUN 50 SER.#'d SETS
US50 Cody Bellinger 150.00 400.00
US148 The Next Dynasty 15.00 40.00
Aaron Judge
Greg Bird

2017 Topps Update Gold

*GOLD: 2.5X TO 6X BASIC
*GOLD RC: .75X TO 2X BASIC RC
STATED PRINT RUN 2017 SER.#'d SETS
US50 Cody Bellinger 40.00 100.00
US148 The Next Dynasty 4.00 10.00
Aaron Judge
Greg Bird

2017 Topps Update Memorial Day Camo

*CAMO: 12X TO 30X BASIC
*CAMO RC: 4X TO 10X BASIC RC
STATED PRINT RUN 25 SER.#'d SETS
US50 Cody Bellinger 200.00 500.00
US148 The Next Dynasty 20.00 50.00
Aaron Judge
Greg Bird

2017 Topps Update Mother's Day Pink

*PINK: 10X TO 25X BASIC
*PINK RC: 3X TO 8X BASIC RC
STATED PRINT RUN 50 SER.#'d SETS
US50 Cody Bellinger 150.00 400.00
US148 The Next Dynasty 15.00 40.00
Aaron Judge
Greg Bird

2017 Topps Update Rainbow Foil

*FOIL: 2X TO 5X BASIC
*FOIL RC: .6X TO 1.5X BASIC RC
US50 Cody Bellinger 30.00 80.00
US148 The Next Dynasty 3.00 8.00
Aaron Judge
Greg Bird

2017 Topps Update Salute

COMPLETE SET (50) 30.00 80.00
*RED/25: 5X TO 12X BASIC
USS1 Mike Trout 2.50 6.00
USS2 Jose Altuve .40 1.00
USS3 Nelson Cruz .50 1.25
USS4 Francisco Lindor .50 1.25
USS5 Koda Glover .30 .75
USS6 Manny Machado .50 1.25
USS7 Ichiro .60 1.50
USS8 Jesse Winker .50 1.25
USS9 Ian Happ .60 1.50
USS10 Clayton Kershaw 1.00 2.50
USS11 Mitch Haniger .50 1.25
USS12 Mitch Haniger .50 1.25
USS13 Tim Anderson .50 1.25
USS14 Franklin Barreto .30 .75
USS15 Jeff Hoffman .30 .75
USS16 Alex Bregman 1.25 3.00
USS17 George Springer .40 1.00
USS18 Antonio Senzatela .30 .75
USS19 Lewis Brinson .50 1.25
USS20 Chris Sale .50 1.25
USS21 Sean Newcomb .40 1.00
USS22 Manny Margot .30 .75
USS23 Bradley Zimmer .40 1.00
USS24 Javier Baez .60 1.50
USS25 Masahiro Tanaka .40 1.00
USS26 Gerrit Cole .50 1.25
USS27 Kendrys Morales .30 .75
USS28 Max Scherzer .50 1.25
USS29 Andrew Benintendi 1.00 2.50
USS30 Bryce Harper .75 2.00
USS31 Dansby Swanson .75 2.00
USS32 Josh Reddick .30 .75
USS33 Keon Broxton .30 .75
USS34 Amir Garrett .30 .75
USS35 Jordan Montgomery .50 1.25
USS36 Marcell Ozuna .50 1.25
USS37 Starling Marte .40 1.00
USS38 Michael Pineda .30 .75
USS39 Nomar Mazara .30 .75
USS40 Daniel Murphy .40 1.00
USS41 Christian Arroyo .50 1.25
USS42 Billy Hamilton .40 1.00
USS43 Cody Bellinger 5.00 12.00
USS44 Randal Grichuk .30 .75
USS45 Ryan Braun .40 1.00
USS46 Jose Bautista .40 1.00
USS47 Andrew McCutchen .50 1.25
USS48 Mark Trumbo .30 .75
USS49 Kyle Freeland .40 1.00
USS50 Anthony Rizzo .75 2.00

2017 Topps Update Toys R Us Purple

*PURPLE: 5X TO 12X BASIC
*PURPLE RC: 1.5X TO 4X BASIC
US38 Cody Bellinger 12.00 30.00
US50 Cody Bellinger 75.00 200.00
US148 The Next Dynasty 10.00 25.00
Aaron Judge
Greg Bird
US214 Cody Bellinger 12.00 30.00
US300 Cody Bellinger 12.00 30.00

2017 Topps Update Vintage Stock

*VINTAGE: 6X TO 15X BASIC
*VINTAGE RC: 2X TO 5X BASIC RC
STATED PRINT RUN 99 SER.#'d SETS
US38 Cody Bellinger 20.00 50.00
US50 Cody Bellinger 100.00 250.00
US148 The Next Dynasty 12.00 30.00
Aaron Judge
Greg Bird
US214 Cody Bellinger 20.00 50.00
US300 Cody Bellinger 20.00 50.00

2017 Topps Update '87 Topps

COMPLETE SET (50) 30.00 80.00
*RED/25: 5X TO 12X BASIC
US871 Bryce Harper .75 2.00
US872 Amir Garrett .30 .75
US873 Noah Syndergaard .40 1.00
US874 Manny Machado .50 1.25
US875 Adam Eaton .50 1.25
US876 Starlin Castro .30 .75
US877 Dexter Fowler .40 1.00
US878 Dallas Keuchel .40 1.00
US879 Brandon Phillips .30 .75
US8710 Mike Trout 2.50 6.00
US8711 Edwin Diaz .40 1.00
US8712 Dee Gordon .30 .75
US8713 Mitch Haniger .50 1.25
US8714 Koda Glover .30 .75
US8715 Jean Segura .40 1.00
US8716 Jeff Hoffman .30 .75
US8717 Antonio Senzatela .30 .75
US8718 Magneuris Sierra .50 1.25
US8719 Matt Holliday .50 1.25
US8720 Kris Bryant .60 1.50
US8721 Matt Wieters .50 1.25
US8722 Dylan Bundy .40 1.00
US8723 Billy Hamilton .40 1.00
US8724 Orlando Arcia .50 1.25
US8725 Andrew Benintendi 1.00 2.50
US8726 Jake Lamb .40 1.00
US8727 Jesse Winker .30 .75
US8728 Marcell Ozuna .50 1.25
US8729 Chris Sale .50 1.25
US8730 Christian Arroyo .50 1.25
US8731 Edwin Encarnacion .50 1.25
US8732 Yonder Alonso .30 .75
US8733 Jose Ramirez .40 1.00
US8734 Cody Bellinger 5.00 12.00
US8735 Aaron Judge 5.00 12.00
US8736 Eric Thames .40 1.00
US8737 Christian Yelich .60 1.50
US8738 Lucas Giolito .40 1.00
US8739 Corey Seager .50 1.25
US8740 Ian Desmond .30 .75
US8741 Aroldis Chapman .50 1.25
US8742 Jordan Montgomery .50 1.25
US8743 Khris Davis .50 1.25
US8744 Joey Gallo .40 1.00
US8745 Franklin Barreto .30 .75
US8746 Bradley Zimmer .40 1.00
US8747 Lewis Brinson .50 1.25
US8748 Ian Happ .60 1.50
US8749 Sean Newcomb .40 1.00
US8750 Adalberto Mejia .30 .75

2017 Topps Update '87 Topps Autographs

EXCHANGE DEADLINE 9/30/2019
87AAA Anthony Alford 3.00 8.00
87AABE Andrew Benintendi 40.00 100.00
87AABR Alex Bregman 12.00 30.00
87AAG Amir Garrett 3.00 8.00
87AAJ Aaron Judge
87AAS Antonio Senzatela 3.00 8.00
87ABH Bryce Harper
87ABPH Brett Phillips 4.00 10.00
87ABZ Bradley Zimmer 5.00 12.00
87ACA Christian Arroyo 5.00 12.00
87ACB Cody Bellinger 40.00 100.00
87ACE Carl Edwards Jr. 3.00 8.00
87ACSA Chris Sale 30.00 80.00
87ACSE Corey Seager
87ADL Dinelson Lamet 3.00 8.00
87AEE Edwin Encarnacion 75.00 200.00
87AERS Eddie Rosario 4.00 10.00
87AET Eric Thames 12.00 30.00
87AFB Franklin Barreto 3.00 8.00
87AIH Ian Happ 6.00 15.00
87AJBN Jorge Bonifacio 3.00 8.00
87AJJ Joe Jimenez 3.00 8.00
87AJM Jordan Montgomery 8.00 20.00
87AJW Jesse Winker 5.00 12.00
87AKB Kris Bryant
87AKD Khris Davis 5.00 12.00
87AKGL Koda Glover 3.00 8.00
87ALB Lewis Brinson 5.00 12.00
87AMS Magneuris Sierra 15.00 40.00
87AMT Mike Trout 500.00 700.00
87ANS Noah Syndergaard
87APD Paul DeJong 10.00 25.00
87APV Pat Valaika 4.00 10.00
87ARSE Rob Segedin 3.00 8.00
87ASN Sean Newcomb 4.00 10.00
87AST Sam Travis 3.00 8.00
87AYM Yoan Moncada

2017 Topps Update All Rookie Cup

COMPLETE SET (50) 20.00 50.00
ARC1 Chipper Jones .60 1.50
ARC2 Stephen Strasburg .60 1.50
ARC3 Eddie Murray .40 1.00
ARC4 Andre Dawson .50 1.25
ARC5 Mike Trout 3.00 8.00
ARC6 Ichiro .75 2.00
ARC7 Ryan Braun .50 1.25
ARC8 Derek Jeter 1.50 4.00
ARC9 Willie McCovey .50 1.25
ARC10 Joe Mauer .50 1.25
ARC11 Jeff Bagwell .50 1.25
ARC12 Evan Longoria .50 1.25
ARC13 Cal Ripken Jr. 2.00 5.00
ARC14 Cal Ripken Jr. 2.00 5.00
ARC15 Ivan Rodriguez .50 1.25
ARC16 Ryne Sandberg 1.25 3.00
ARC17 Johnny Bench .60 1.50
ARC18 Tom Seaver .50 1.25
ARC19 Andrew McCutchen .60 1.50
ARC20 Yasiel Puig .60 1.50
ARC21 Anthony Rizzo 1.00 2.50
ARC22 Ken Griffey Jr. 1.25 3.00
ARC23 Buster Posey .75 2.00
ARC24 Tony Perez .50 1.25
ARC25 Carlton Fisk .50 1.25
ARC26 Fernando Valenzuela .40 1.00
ARC27 Mike Piazza .60 1.50
ARC28 Dustin Pedroia .60 1.50
ARC29 Tim Raines .50 1.25
ARC30 Noah Syndergaard .50 1.25
ARC31 Billy Williams .50 1.25
ARC32 Joey Votto .60 1.50
ARC33 Justin Verlander .60 1.50
ARC34 George Springer .50 1.25
ARC35 Jose Canseco .50 1.25
ARC36 Nomar Garciaparra .50 1.25
ARC37 Gary Carter .50 1.25
ARC38 Kris Bryant .75 2.00
ARC39 Nolan Arenado .75 2.00
ARC40 Masahiro Tanaka .50 1.25
ARC41 Mark McGwire 1.00 2.50
ARC42 Giancarlo Stanton .60 1.50
ARC43 Ozzie Smith .75 2.00
ARC44 Prince Fielder .50 1.25
ARC45 Bryce Harper 1.00 2.50
ARC46 Yu Darvish .60 1.50
ARC47 Joe Morgan .50 1.25
ARC48 Rod Carew .50 1.25
ARC49 Albert Pujols .75 2.00
ARC50 Carlos Correa .60 1.50

2017 Topps Update All Star Stitches

*GOLD/50: .6X TO 1.5X BASIC
*ORANGE/25: .75X TO 2X BASIC
ASRAG Avisail Garcia 3.00 8.00
ASRAJ Aaron Judge 25.00 60.00
ASRAM Andrew Miller 3.00 8.00
ASRAW Alex Wood 2.50 6.00
ASRBH Bryce Harper 5.00 12.00
ASRBHA Brad Hand 2.50 6.00
ASRBK Brandon Kintzler 2.50 6.00
ASRBP Buster Posey 5.00 12.00
ASRCA Chris Archer 2.50 6.00
ASRCB Cody Bellinger 10.00 25.00
ASRCBL Charlie Blackmon 4.00 10.00
ASRCC Carlos Correa 4.00 10.00
ASRCD Corey Dickerson 2.50 6.00
ASRCK Clayton Kershaw 8.00 20.00
ASRCKI Craig Kimbrel 3.00 8.00
ASRCKL Corey Kluber 3.00 8.00
ASRCKN Corey Knebel 2.50 6.00
ASRCM Carlos Martinez 3.00 8.00
ASRCS Corey Seager 4.00 10.00
ASRCSA Chris Sale 4.00 10.00
ASRDB Dellin Betances 3.00 8.00
ASRDK Dallas Keuchel 3.00 8.00
ASRDL DJ LeMahieu 4.00 10.00
ASRDM Daniel Murphy 3.00 8.00
ASREI Ender Inciarte 3.00 8.00
ASRES Ervin Santana 2.50 6.00
ASRFL Francisco Lindor 4.00 10.00
ASRGH Greg Holland 2.50 6.00
ASRGS Giancarlo Stanton 4.00 10.00
ASRGSA Gary Sanchez 6.00 15.00
ASRGSP George Springer 5.00 12.00
ASRJA Jose Altuve 3.00 8.00
ASRJH Josh Harrison 2.50 6.00
ASRJL Jake Lamb 3.00 8.00
ASRJR Jose Ramirez 3.00 8.00
ASRJS Jonathan Schoop 2.50 6.00
ASRJSM Justin Smoak 2.50 6.00
ASRJT Justin Turner 5.00 12.00
ASRJU Justin Upton 3.00 8.00
ASRJV Jason Vargas 3.00 8.00
ASRJVO Joey Votto 4.00 10.00
ASRKJ Kenley Jansen 3.00 8.00
ASRLM Lance McCullers 2.50 6.00
ASRLS Luis Severino 4.00 10.00
ASRMB Mookie Betts 6.00 15.00
ASRMBR Michael Brantley 3.00 8.00
ASRMC Michael Conforto 3.00 8.00
ASRMF Michael Fulmer 2.50 6.00
ASRMM Mike Moustakas 3.00 8.00
ASRMO Marcell Ozuna 4.00 10.00
ASRMS Max Scherzer 4.00 10.00
ASRMSA Miguel Sano 4.00 10.00
ASRNA Nolan Arenado 5.00 12.00
ASRNC Nelson Cruz 4.00 10.00
ASRPG Paul Goldschmidt 4.00 10.00
ASRRC Robinson Cano 3.00 8.00
ASRRO Roberto Osuna 2.50 6.00
ASRRR Robbie Ray 2.50 6.00
ASRRZ Ryan Zimmerman 3.00 8.00
ASRSC Starlin Castro 2.50 6.00
ASRSP Salvador Perez 3.00 8.00
ASRSS Stephen Strasburg 4.00 10.00
ASRWD Wade Davis 2.50 6.00
ASRYA Yonder Alonso 2.50 6.00
ASRYD Yu Darvish 4.00 10.00
ASRYM Yadier Molina 4.00 10.00
ASRZC Zack Cozart 2.50 6.00
ASRZG Zack Greinke 3.00 8.00

2017 Topps Update All Star Stitches Autographs

STATED PRINT RUN 25 SER.#'d SETS
EXCHANGE DEADLINE 9/30/2019
ASARAJ Aaron Judge
ASARBH Bryce Harper
ASARBP Buster Posey EXCH 30.00 80.00
ASARCB Cody Bellinger EXCH 125.00 300.00
ASARCBL Charlie Blackmon 25.00 60.00
ASARCC Carlos Correa
ASARCK Clayton Kershaw
ASARCS Corey Seager EXCH 60.00 150.00
ASARCSA Chris Sale
ASARFL Francisco Lindor EXCH 40.00 100.00
ASARGS George Springer 20.00 50.00
ASARJA Jose Altuve 20.00 50.00
ASARJV Joey Votto
ASARMC Michael Conforto
ASARMS Miguel Sano 30.00 80.00

2017 Topps Update All Star Stitches Duals

STATED PRINT RUN 25 SER.#'d SETS
ASDAC Altuve/Correa
ASDBS Bellinger/Seager 30.00 80.00
ASDCS Springer/Correa 20.00 50.00
ASDJB Bellinger/Judge 60.00 150.00
ASDJS Sanchez/Judge 80.00 200.00
ASDMC Betts/Sale 20.00 50.00
ASDOS Stanton/Ozuna 10.00 25.00
ASDSS Strasburg/Scherzer

2017 Topps Update All Star Stitches Triples

STATED PRINT RUN 25 SER.#'d SETS
ASTACS Springer/Altuve/Correa 25.00 60.00
ASTCMC Betts/Sale/Kimbrel 20.00 50.00
ASTGGL Goldschmidt Greinke Lamb 12.00 30.00
ASTKBS Bellinger/Kershaw/Seager 40.00 100.00
ASTKLR Ramirez/Kluber/Lindor 25.00 60.00
ASTPHB Posey/Bellinger/Harper 25.00 60.00
ASTSHS Harper/Strasburg/Scherzer 40.00 100.00
ASTSJS Sanchez/Judge/Severino 60.00 150.00
ASTSKS Sale/Scherzer/Kershaw 25.00 60.00
ASTZHM Zimmerman/Murphy/Harper

2017 Topps Update Hank Aaron Award Relics

*GOLD/99: .75X TO 2X BASIC
*BLACK/50: 1X TO 2.5X BASIC
HAAP Albert Pujols 2.00 5.00
HAAR Alex Rodriguez 2.00 5.00
HABH Bryce Harper 2.50 6.00
HABP Buster Posey 2.00 5.00
HADJE Derek Jeter 4.00 10.00
HADJT Derek Jeter 4.00 10.00
HADO David Ortiz 1.50 4.00
HAGS Giancarlo Stanton 1.50 4.00
HAJB Jose Bautista 1.25 3.00
HAJD Josh Donaldson 1.25 3.00
HAJV Joey Votto 1.50 4.00
HAKB Kris Bryant 2.00 5.00
HAMC Miguel Cabrera 1.50 4.00
HAMT Mike Trout 8.00 20.00
HAPG Paul Goldschmidt 1.50 4.00

2017 Topps Update Heroes of Autumn

COMPLETE SET (25) 60.00 150.00
*BLUE/500: .6X TO 1.5X BASIC
*RED/250: .75X TO 2X BASIC
*SILVER/50: 1X TO 2.5X BASIC
PLATE PRINT RUN 1 SET PER COLOR
BLACK-CYAN-MAGENTA-YELLOW ISSUED
NO PLATE PRICING DUE TO SCARCITY
HA1 Randy Johnson 1.25 3.00
HA2 Frank Robinson 1.00 2.50
HA3 Anthony Rizzo 2.00 5.00
HA4 Roberto Alomar 1.00 2.50
HA5 Albert Pujols 1.50 4.00
HA6 Luis Gonzalez .75 2.00
HA7 George Brett 2.50 6.00
HA8 Sandy Koufax 2.50 6.00
HA9 Andy Pettitte 1.00 2.50
HA10 Reggie Jackson 1.00 2.50
HA11 Babe Ruth 3.00 8.00
HA12 Ben Zobrist 1.00 2.50
HA13 Brooks Robinson 1.00 2.50
HA14 Willie Stargell 1.00 2.50
HA15 Dennis Eckersley 1.00 2.50
HA16 Pedro Martinez 1.00 2.50
HA17 Tom Glavine 1.00 2.50
HA18 Buster Posey 1.50 4.00
HA19 Johnny Bench 1.25 3.00
HA20 Rickey Henderson 1.25 3.00
HA21 Derek Jeter 3.00 8.00
HA22 Roger Clemens 1.50 4.00
HA23 John Smoltz 1.25 3.00
HA24 David Ortiz 1.25 3.00
HA25 Jackie Robinson 1.25 3.00

2017 Topps Update MVP Award

COMPLETE SET (30) 15.00 40.00
*RED/25: 5X TO 12X BASIC
MVP1 Mike Trout 2.50 6.00
MVP2 Roger Clemens .60 1.50
MVP3 Rickey Henderson .50 1.25
MVP4 Clayton Kershaw 1.00 2.50
MVP5 Frank Thomas .50 1.25
MVP6 Sandy Koufax 1.00 2.50
MVP7 Chipper Jones .50 1.25
MVP8 Ichiro .60 1.50
MVP9 Roger Maris .50 1.25
MVP10 Kris Bryant .60 1.50
MVP11 Ken Griffey Jr. 1.00 2.50
MVP12 Jackie Robinson .50 1.25
MVP13 Reggie Jackson .40 1.00
MVP14 Joey Votto .50 1.25
MVP15 Cal Ripken Jr. 1.50 4.00
MVP16 Brooks Robinson .40 1.00
MVP17 Babe Ruth 1.25 3.00
MVP18 Bryce Harper .75 2.00
MVP19 Roberto Clemente 1.25 3.00
MVP20 Carl Yastrzemski .75 2.00
MVP21 George Brett 1.00 2.50
MVP22 Josh Donaldson .40 1.00
MVP23 Don Mattingly 1.00 2.50
MVP24 Buster Posey .60 1.50
MVP25 Ty Cobb .75 2.00
MVP26 Ernie Banks .50 1.25
MVP27 Lou Gehrig 1.00 2.50
MVP28 Ted Williams 1.00 2.50
MVP29 Johnny Bench .50 1.25
MVP30 Hank Aaron 1.00 2.50

2017 Topps Update MVP Award Relics

*GOLD/99: .6X TO 1.5X BASIC
*BLACK/50: .75X TO 2X BASIC
MVPRAD Andre Dawson 2.50 6.00
MVPRAM Andrew McCutchen 5.00 12.00
MVPRAP Albert Pujols 6.00 15.00
MVPRAR Alex Rodriguez 6.00 15.00
MVPRBH Bryce Harper 8.00 20.00
MVPRBL Barry Larkin 2.50 6.00
MVPRBP Buster Posey 6.00 15.00
MVPRBRO Brooks Robinson 2.50 6.00
MVPRCJ Chipper Jones 3.00 8.00
MVPRCK Clayton Kershaw 5.00 12.00
MVPRCRI Cal Ripken Jr. 8.00 20.00
MVPRCRJ Cal Ripken Jr. 8.00 20.00
MVPRCY Carl Yastrzemski 5.00 12.00
MVPRDM Don Mattingly 8.00 20.00
MVPREBA Ernie Banks 5.00 12.00
MVPREBN Ernie Banks 5.00 12.00
MVPRFRB Frank Robinson 2.50 6.00
MVPRFRO Frank Robinson 2.50 6.00
MVPRFT Frank Thomas 3.00 8.00
MVPRGB George Brett 6.00 15.00
MVPRHA Hank Aaron 6.00 15.00
MVPRIR Ivan Rodriguez 2.50 6.00
MVPRI Ichiro 6.00 15.00
MVPRJB2 Johnny Bench 3.00 8.00
MVPRJBA Jeff Bagwell 2.50 6.00
MVPRJBE Johnny Bench 3.00 8.00
MVPRJC Jose Canseco 2.50 6.00
MVPRJD Josh Donaldson 2.50 6.00
MVPRJM Joe Morgan 2.50 6.00
MVPRJR Jackie Robinson 3.00 8.00
MVPRJVE Justin Verlander 5.00 12.00
MVPRJVO Joey Votto 5.00 12.00
MVPRKB Kris Bryant 8.00 20.00
MVPRKG Ken Griffey Jr. 8.00 20.00
MVPRMC Miguel Cabrera 3.00 8.00
MVPRMTO Mike Trout 8.00 20.00
MVPRMTR Mike Trout 8.00 20.00
MVPRRCA Rod Carew 2.50 6.00
MVPRRCE Roberto Clemente 10.00 25.00
MVPRRCL Roger Clemens 6.00 15.00
MVPRRH Rickey Henderson 5.00 12.00
MVPRRJ Reggie Jackson 2.50 6.00
MVPRRM Roger Maris 3.00 8.00
MVPRRS Ryne Sandberg 10.00 25.00
MVPRRY Robin Yount 3.00 8.00
MVPRSK Sandy Koufax 8.00 20.00
MVPRTWI Ted Williams 8.00 20.00
MVPRTWI Ted Williams 8.00 20.00
MVPRWM Willie McCovey 2.50 6.00
MVPRWS Willie Stargell 2.50 6.00

2017 Topps Update Postseason Celebration

COMPLETE SET (25) 10.00 25.00
*BLUE/500: .6X TO 1.5X BASIC
*RED/250: .75X TO 2X BASIC
*SILVER/50: 1X TO 2.5X BASIC
PC1 Toronto Blue Jays 1.00 2.50
PC2 San Francisco Giants 1.00 2.50
PC3 Philadelphia Phillies 1.00 2.50
PC4 Detroit Tigers 1.00 2.50
PC5 Chicago White Sox 1.00 2.50
PC6 New York Mets 1.00 2.50
PC7 St. Louis Cardinals 1.00 2.50
PC8 New York Yankees 1.00 2.50
PC9 Oakland Athletics 1.00 2.50
PC10 St. Louis Cardinals 1.00 2.50
PC11 San Francisco Giants 1.00 2.50
PC12 Boston Red Sox 1.00 2.50
PC13 Oakland Athletics 1.00 2.50
PC14 Pittsburgh Pirates 1.00 2.50
PC15 Kansas City Royals 1.00 2.50
PC16 New York Yankees 1.00 2.50
PC17 Chicago Cubs 1.00 2.50
PC18 Los Angeles Angels 1.00 2.50
PC19 Philadelphia Phillies 1.00 2.50
PC20 Boston Red Sox 1.00 2.50
PC21 Boston Red Sox 1.00 2.50
PC22 San Francisco Giants 1.00 2.50
PC23 Pittsburgh Pirates 1.00 2.50
PC24 New York Yankees 1.00 2.50
PC25 Brooklyn Dodgers 1.00 2.50

2017 Topps Update Salute Autographs

EXCHANGE DEADLINE 9/30/2019
SAAB Andrew Benintendi 40.00 100.00
SABE Andrew Benintendi 40.00 100.00
SAABR Alex Bregman 12.00 30.00
SAAG Amir Garrett 3.00 8.00

SAAJ Aaron Judge
SAARI Anthony Rizzo
SAAS Antonio Senzatela 3.00 8.00
SABHM Billy Hamilton 12.00 30.00
SABHR Bryce Harper
SABZ Bradley Zimmer 4.00 10.00
SACA Christian Arroyo 6.00 15.00
SACB Cody Bellinger EXCH 125.00 300.00
SACK Clayton Kershaw
SACS Chris Sale 30.00 80.00
SACSE Corey Seager
SADR Daniel Robertson 3.00 8.00
SAFL Francisco Lindor 60.00 150.00
SAGS George Springer 15.00 40.00
SAIH Ian Happ 12.00 30.00
SAJA Jose Altuve 25.00 60.00
SAJBZ Javier Baez
SAJH Jeff Hoffman 3.00 8.00
SAJJ Joe Jimenez 3.00 8.00
SAJM Jordan Montgomery 10.00 25.00
SAJR Josh Reddick 3.00 8.00
SAJW Jesse Winker 5.00 12.00
SAKM Kendrys Morales 6.00 15.00
SALB Lewis Brinson 5.00 12.00
SAMHN Mitch Haniger 6.00 15.00
SAMMA Manny Machado
SAMMR Manny Margot 8.00 20.00
SAMP Michael Pineda 3.00 8.00
SAMTO Mike Trout 500.00 700.00
SARG Randal Grichuk 3.00 8.00
SASM Starling Marte 4.00 10.00
SASN Sean Newcomb 4.00 10.00

2017 Topps Update Storied World Series

COMPLETE SET (25) 15.00 40.00
SWS1 1907 Chicago Cubs 1.00 2.50
SWS2 1999 New York Yankees 1.00 2.50
SWS3 1963 Los Angeles Dodgers 1.00 2.50
SWS4 1984 Detroit Tigers 1.00 2.50
SWS5 1905 New York Giants 1.00 2.50
SWS6 1967 St. Louis Cardinals 1.00 2.50
SWS7 1979 Pittsburgh Pirates 1.00 2.50
SWS8 2004 Boston Red Sox 1.00 2.50
SWS9 1932 New York Yankees 1.00 2.50
SWS10 1961 New York Yankees 1.00 2.50
SWS11 1995 Atlanta Braves 1.00 2.50
SWS12 1954 New York Giants 1.00 2.50
SWS13 1970 Baltimore Orioles 1.00 2.50
SWS14 2016 Chicago Cubs 1.00 2.50
SWS15 1936 New York Yankees 1.00 2.50
SWS16 1939 New York Yankees 1.00 2.50
SWS17 1989 Oakland Athletics 1.00 2.50
SWS18 1948 Cleveland Indians 1.00 2.50
SWS19 1969 New York Mets 1.00 2.50
SWS20 1986 New York Mets 1.00 2.50
SWS21 1955 Brooklyn Dodgers 1.00 2.50
SWS22 1942 St. Louis Cardinals 1.00 2.50
SWS23 1909 Pittsburgh Pirates 1.00 2.50
SWS24 1998 New York Yankees 1.00 2.50
SWS25 1927 New York Yankees 1.00 2.50

2017 Topps Update Untouchables

COMPLETE SET (30) 6.00 15.00
U1 Pedro Martinez .40 1.00
U2 Jake Arrieta .40 1.00
U3 Warren Spahn .40 1.00
U4 Justin Verlander .50 1.25
U5 Roy Halladay .40 1.00
U6 Tom Glavine .40 1.00
U7 CC Sabathia .40 1.00
U8 Bartolo Colon .30 .75
U9 Felix Hernandez .40 1.00
U10 Sandy Koufax 1.00 2.50
U11 Dallas Keuchel .40 1.00
U12 Greg Maddux .60 1.50
U13 John Smoltz .50 1.25
U14 Tim Lincecum .40 1.00
U15 Roger Clemens .60 1.50
U16 Steve Carlton .40 1.00
U17 Pedro Martinez .40 1.00
U18 Roy Halladay .40 1.00
U19 Randy Johnson .50 1.25
U20 Jim Palmer .40 1.00
U21 Clayton Kershaw 1.00 2.50
U22 Max Scherzer .50 1.25
U23 Tom Seaver .40 1.00
U24 Roger Clemens .60 1.50
U25 Randy Johnson .50 1.25
U26 Rick Porcello .40 1.00
U27 Corey Kluber .40 1.00
U28 Greg Maddux .60 1.50
U29 Whitey Ford .40 1.00
U30 Roger Clemens .60 1.50

2018 Topps

COMPLETE SET (700) 30.00 80.00
COMP.RED.HOB.FACT SET (700) 30.00 80.00
COMP.BLUE.RET.FACT SET (700) 30.00 80.00
COMP.SER.1 SET (350) 12.00 30.00
COMP.SER.2 SET (350) 15.00 40.00
SER.1 PLATE ODDS 1:8716 HOBBY
SER.2 PLATE ODDS 1:4730 HOBBY
PLATE PRINT RUN 1 SET PER COLOR
BLACK-CYAN-MAGENTA-YELLOW ISSUED
NO PLATE PRICING DUE TO SCARCITY
1 Aaron Judge .60 1.50
2 Clayton Kershaw LL .50 1.25
3 Dylan Bundy .20 .50
4 Kevin Pillar .15 .40
5 Chris Tillman .15 .40
6 Dominic Smith RC .25 .60
7 Clint Frazier RC .50 1.25
8 Detroit Tigers .15 .40
9 Jon Gray .15 .40
10 Francisco Lindor .25 .60
11 Aaron Nola .20 .50
12 Joey Gallo LL .20 .50
13 Jay Bruce .20 .50
14 Amir Garrett .15 .40
15 Andrelton Simmons .15 .40
16 Daniel Coulombe RC .40 1.00
17 Robbie Ray .15 .40
18 Rafael Devers RC .75 2.00
19 Garrett Richards .20 .50
20 Chris Sale .25 .60
21 Harrison Bader RC .40 1.00
22 Edinson Volquez .15 .40
23 Jordy Mercer .15 .40
24 Martin Maldonado .15 .40
25 Manny Machado .25 .60
26 Cesar Hernandez .15 .40
27 Josh Tomlin .15 .40
28 Jayson Werth .20 .50
29 Hunter Renfroe .15 .40
30 Carlos Correa .25 .60
31 Corey Kluber LL .20 .50
32 Jose Iglesias .20 .50
33 Dexter Fowler .20 .50
34 Luis Severino LL .20 .50
35 Logan Forsythe .15 .40
36 Anthony Rendon .25 .60
37 Corey Kluber LL .20 .50
38 Danny Salazar .20 .50
39 Alex Bregman WS HL .25 .60
40 Carlos Santana .20 .50
41 Daniel Norris .15 .40
42 Cody Bellinger .50 1.25
43 Eduardo Rodriguez .15 .40
44 Trea Turner .20 .50
45 Giancarlo Stanton LL .25 .60
46 Cam Bedrosian .15 .40
47 Hunter Pence .20 .50
48 Boston Red Sox .15 .40
49 Ervin Santana .15 .40
50 Anthony Rizzo .40 1.00
51 Michael Wacha .20 .50
52 Brad Hand .15 .40
53 Alex Avila .20 .50
54 Chase Anderson .15 .40
55 Raisel Iglesias .20 .50
56 Rougned Odor .20 .50
57 Scott Feldman .15 .40
58 Ryan Zimmerman .20 .50
59 Clayton Kershaw LL .50 1.25
60 Starling Marte .20 .50
61 Keon Broxton .15 .40
62 Austin Hays RC .40 1.00
63 Amed Rosario RC .30 .75
64 Giancarlo Stanton LL .25 .60
65 Alex Wood .15 .40
66 Ian Kennedy .15 .40
67 Aledmys Diaz .20 .50
68 Billy Hamilton .20 .50
69 Jed Lowrie .15 .40
70 Johnny Cueto .20 .50
71 Mike Foltynewicz .15 .40
72 Cheslor Cuthbert .15 .40
73 Miami Marlins .15 .40
74 Roberto Osuna .15 .40
75 Andrew Miller .20 .50
76 Eduardo Nunez .15 .40
77 Martin Prado .15 .40
78 Carlos Carrasco LL .15 .40
79 J.T. Realmuto .25 .60
80 Dellin Betances .20 .50
81 Adam Wainwright .20 .50
82 Justin Smoak .15 .40
83 Howie Kendrick .15 .40
84 Todd Frazier .20 .50
85 Antonio Senzatela .15 .40
86 Eric Hosmer .20 .50
87 Brandon Phillips .15 .40
88 Michael Conforto .20 .50
89 Yasiel Puig .25 .60
90 Miguel Cabrera .25 .60
91 Travis d'Arnaud .20 .50
92 Charlie Blackmon LL .25 .60
93 Jack Flaherty RC .40 1.00
94 Robbie Grossman .15 .40
95 Tyler Mahle RC .30 .75
96 David Dahl .15 .40
97 Dinelson Lamet .15 .40
98 Chicago White Sox .15 .40
99 Greg Allen RC .25 .60
100 Giancarlo Stanton .25 .60
101 Avisail Garcia .20 .50
102 Wil Myers .15 .40
103 Christian Vazquez .15 .40
104 Mitch Moreland .15 .40
105 Daniel Murphy .20 .50
106 Jharel Cotton .15 .40
107 Jorge Polanco .15 .40
108 Justin Turner LL .20 .50
109 Starlin Castro .15 .40
110 Carlos Gonzalez .20 .50
111 Aaron Judge LL .60 1.50
112 Pat Valaika .15 .40
113 Gio Gonzalez .20 .50
114 Cody Bellinger LL .50 1.25
115 Zack Granite RC .25 .60
116 Ariel Miranda RC .40 1.00
117 Kendrys Morales .15 .40
118 Ian Happ .20 .50
119 Los Angeles Angels .15 .40
120 Carlos Carrasco .15 .40
121 Rich Hill .15 .40
122 Chris Owings .15 .40
123 A.J. Ramos .15 .40
124 Julio Urias .25 .60
125 Yoenis Cespedes .25 .60
126 A.Rizzo/B.Harper .40 1.00
127 Byron Buxton .20 .50
128 Jake Marisnick .15 .40
129 Chris Sale LL .25 .60
130 Brian Dozier .20 .50
131 Jonathan Schoop .15 .40
132 Marcell Ozuna .25 .60
133 Nomar Mazara .15 .40
134 Lance Lynn .15 .40
135 Atlanta Braves .15 .40
136 Raudy Read RC .25 .60
137 Michael Lorenzen .15 .40
138 Luiz Gohara RC .25 .60
139 Zach Davies LL .15 .40
140 Mookie Betts .40 1.00
141 Brandon Drury .15 .40
142 Adam Jones .20 .50
143 James Paxton .20 .50
144 Jean Segura .15 .40
145 Michael Fulmer .15 .40
146 Zack Greinke LL .20 .50
147 Randal Grichuk .15 .40
148 Richard Urena RC .25 .60
149 John Jaso .15 .40
150 Nolan Arenado .30 .75
151 Ryan McMahon RC .30 .75
152 Matt Barnes .15 .40
153 Scooter Gennett .20 .50
154 George Springer WS HL .20 .50
155 Matt Joyce .15 .40
156 Milwaukee Brewers .15 .40
157 Ichiro .30 .75
158 Stephen Piscotty .15 .40
159 Joc Pederson .20 .50
160 Masahiro Tanaka .20 .50
161 Matt Moore .20 .50
162 Matt Shoemaker .20 .50
163 Mike Leake .15 .40
164 Adeiny Hechavarria .15 .40
165 Ty Blach .15 .40
166 Victor Robles RC .60 1.50
167 Dansby Swanson .25 .60
168 Ricky Nolasco .15 .40
169 Khris Davis LL .25 .60
170 Christian Yelich .30 .75
171 John Lackey .20 .50
172 Willson Contreras .25 .60
173 Mike Moustakas .20 .50
174 Jimmie Sherfy RC .25 .60
175 Jose Quintana .15 .40
176 Seattle Mariners .15 .40
177 Walker Buehler RC 1.25 3.00
178 Matt Adams .15 .40
179 Brandon Woodruff RC .30 .75
180 Ryan Braun .20 .50
181 Garrett Cooper RC .25 .60
182 Alex Bregman .25 .60
183 Matt Kemp .20 .50
184 Mike Fiers .15 .40
185 Chance Sisco RC .30 .75
186 Luis Perdomo .15 .40
187 Chad Kuhl .15 .40
188 Matt Harvey .20 .50
189 Jedd Gyorko .15 .40
190 Justin Upton .20 .50
191 Chris Archer .15 .40
192 Nolan Arenado LL .30 .75
193 Aaron Judge LL .60 1.50
194 Lonnie Chisenhall .15 .40
195 Avisail Garcia LL .20 .50
196 Orlando Arcia .15 .40
197 Maikel Franco .20 .50
198 Marcus Semien .15 .40
199 Shin-Soo Choo .20 .50
200 Andrew McCutchen .25 .60
201 Gregory Polanco .20 .50
202 Brett Phillips .15 .40
203 Odubel Herrera .20 .50
204 Brett Gardner .20 .50
205 R.Cano/K.Seager .20 .50
206 Nick Markakis .20 .50
207 Jackson Stephens RC .25 .60
208 Andrew Cashner .15 .40
209 Eugenio Suarez .20 .50
210 Brandon Belt .20 .50
211 Btts/Brdly/Bnntndi .40 1.00
212 Lance McCullers WS HL .15 .40
213 J.A. Happ .20 .50
214 Corey Knebel .15 .40
215 Marwin Gonzalez .15 .40
216 A.J. Pollock .15 .40
217 Erick Fedde RC .25 .60
218 Khris Davis LL .25 .60
219 J.P. Crawford RC .25 .60
220 Nelson Cruz .25 .60
221 Steven Matz .20 .50
222 Ivan Nova .20 .50
223 Evan Longoria .20 .50
224 Dillon Peters RC .25 .60
225 Kyle Schwarber .25 .60
226 Nick Williams RC .30 .75
227 Corey Dickerson .15 .40
228 Zack Wheeler .20 .50
229 Texas Rangers .15 .40
230 Trevor Story .25 .60
231 Joe Mauer .20 .50
232 Nate Jones .15 .40
233 Stephen Strasburg .25 .60
234 Brian Anderson RC .30 .75
235 Mark Reynolds .15 .40
236 CC Sabathia .20 .50
237 Mike Clevinger .20 .50
238 Jose Bautista .20 .50
239 Cleveland Indians .15 .40
240 Robinson Cano .20 .50
241 Nick Pivetta .15 .40
242 Craig Kimbrel .20 .50
243 James McCann .20 .50
244 Francisco Mejia RC .30 .75
245 Willie Calhoun RC .30 .75
246 Yangervis Solarte .15 .40
247 Anthony Banda RC .25 .60
248 Jake Lamb .20 .50
249 Christian Arroyo .15 .40
250 Buster Posey .30 .75
251 Aaron Sanchez .20 .50
252 Tim Anderson .25 .60
253 Nelson Cruz LL .25 .60
254 Adrian Beltre .25 .60
255 Zach Davies .15 .40
256 Eric Hosmer LL .20 .50
257 J.D. Martinez .25 .60
258 Tyler Saladino .15 .40
259 Rhys Hoskins RC 1.00 2.50
260 Rick Porcello .20 .50
261 Andrew Stevenson RC .25 .60
262 E.Hosmer/M.Sano .20 .50
263 Chase Utley .20 .50
264 Carlos Rodon .20 .50
265 Javier Baez .30 .75
266 Jon Lester .20 .50
267 Yoan Moncada .25 .60
268 Neil Walker .20 .50
269 Greg Holland .15 .40
270 Jackie Bradley Jr. .25 .60
271 Cam Gallagher RC .25 .60
272 Paul Blackburn RC .25 .60
273 Charlie Blackmon LL .25 .60
274 Jeff Samardzija .15 .40
275 George Springer .20 .50
276 Ozzie Albies RC .75 2.00
277 Aaron Slegers RC .40 1.00
278 Lucas Sims RC .25 .60
279 Jordan Zimmermann .20 .50
280 Jose Abreu .25 .60
281 Alex Verdugo RC .40 1.00
282 Ender Inciarte .15 .40
283 Koji Uehara .15 .40
284 Jose Pirela .15 .40
285 Trey Mancini .20 .50
286 New York Yankees .15 .40
287 Mark Trumbo .15 .40
288 Miguel Sano .20 .50
289 Jonathan Villar .15 .40
290 Salvador Perez .20 .50
291 Marcell Ozuna LL .25 .60
292 Baltimore Orioles .15 .40
293 Felipe Rivero .20 .50
294 Jose Altuve LL .20 .50
295 Zack Godley .15 .40
296 Lewis Brinson .15 .40
297 Kevin Kiermaier .20 .50
298 Y.Gurriel/J.Marisnick .20 .50
299 Luis Santos RC .40 1.00
300 Mike Trout 1.25 3.00
301 Brandon Finnegan .15 .40
302 Troy Tulowitzki .25 .60
303 Luis Severino .20 .50
304 Whit Merrifield .25 .60
305 Miguel Andujar RC 1.00 2.50
306 Nicky Delmonico RC .25 .60
307 Daniel Murphy LL .20 .50
308 Cameron Rupp .15 .40
309 Josh Reddick .15 .40
310 Jason Kipnis .20 .50
311 Yulieski Gurriel .20 .50
312 Carlos Asuaje .15 .40
313 Raimel Tapia .15 .40
314 Colorado Rockies .15 .40
315 Chris Rowley RC .40 1.00
316 Max Fried RC 1.00 2.50
317 Chase Headley .15 .40
318 Danny Duffy .15 .40
319 David Peralta .15 .40
320 Yasmani Grandal .15 .40
321 Edwin Diaz .20 .50
322 Parker Bridwell RC .25 .60
323 Elvis Andrus .20 .50
324 Jake Odorizzi .15 .40
325 Khris Davis .25 .60
326 Joey Gallo .20 .50
327 Jason Vargas LL .15 .40
328 Tyler Flowers .15 .40
329 George Springer WS HL .20 .50
330 Ian Kinsler .20 .50
331 Zack Cozart .15 .40
332 Alex Colome .15 .40
333 Joe Musgrove .15 .40
334 Eddie Rosario .25 .60
335 Stephen Strasburg LL .25 .60
336 Bruce Maxwell .15 .40
337 Nick Ahmed .15 .40
338 Brandon McCarthy .15 .40
339 Philadelphia Phillies .15 .40
340 Gary Sanchez .25 .60
341 J.D. Davis RC .30 .75
342 Sean Manaea .15 .40
343 Kevin Gausman .15 .40
344 Wilmer Flores .20 .50
345 Jose Reyes .20 .50
346 Max Scherzer LL .25 .60
347 Kolten Wong .20 .50
348 Hisashi Iwakuma .20 .50
349 Washington Nationals .15 .40
350 Clayton Kershaw .50 1.25
351 Bryce Harper .40 1.00
352 Cincinnati Reds Team Card .15 .40
353 Yan Gomes .25 .60
354 Robert Stephenson .15 .40
355 Joe Ross .15 .40
356 Jeff Hoffman .15 .40
357 Josh Hader .15 .40
358 Brad Brach .15 .40
359 Wade Miley .15 .40
360 Taijuan Walker .15 .40
361 J.Altuve/C.Correa .25 .60
362 Miguel Rojas .15 .40
363 Bryan Shaw .15 .40
365 Y.Puig/C.Bellinger .50 1.25
365 Mallex Smith .15 .40
366 Tyler Glasnow FS .15 .40
367 Liam Hendriks .15 .40
368 Matt Strahm .15 .40
369 Chris Taylor .20 .50
370 Steven Wright .15 .40
371 Cole Hamels .20 .50
372 Nick Tropeano .15 .40
373 Jorge Bonifacio .15 .40
374 Bradley Zimmer FS .15 .40
375 Evan Gattis .15 .40
376 Kyle McGrath RC .25 .60
377 Domingo Santana .20 .50
378 Aaron Wilkerson RC .25 .60
379 Zimmerman/Werth .20 .50
380 Kelby Tomlinson .15 .40
381 Kole Calhoun .15 .40
382 Brandon Guyer .15 .40
383 JaCoby Jones .20 .50
384 Addison Russell .20 .50
385 Jason Hammel .20 .50
386 James Shields .15 .40
387 Julio Teheran .20 .50
388 Taylor Motter .15 .40
389 Stanton/Judge .60 1.50
390 Jesse Chavez .15 .40
391 Ben Zobrist .20 .50
392 Marcus Stroman .20 .50
393 Corey Kluber .20 .50
394 Chad Pinder .15 .40
395 Martin Perez .20 .50
396 Matt Olson .15 .40
397 Dallas Keuchel .20 .50
398 Sam Dyson .15 .40
399 Chicago Cubs Team Card .15 .40
400 Jose Altuve .20 .50
401 Michael Brantley .20 .50
402 Adam Warren .15 .40
403 Luis Torrens .15 .40
404 Alex Claudio .15 .40
405 T.J. Rivera .15 .40
406 Kelvin Herrera .15 .40
407 Pat Neshek .15 .40
408 Mikie Mahtook .15 .40
409 Scott Kingery RC .40 1.00
410 Felix Jorge RC .25 .60
411 David Price .20 .50
412 Mike Minor .15 .40
413 Trevor Bauer .25 .60
414 Danny Valencia .20 .50
415 Jace Peterson .15 .40
416 Derek Fisher FS .15 .40
417 Yolmer Sanchez .15 .40
418 Jose Ramirez .20 .50
419 Fernando Rodney .15 .40
420 Alex Cobb .15 .40
421 Lorenzo Cain .15 .40
422 Victor Caratini RC .30 .75
423 Houston Astros .15 .40
424 Matt Wieters .25 .60
425 Shelby Miller .20 .50
426 Jacob Faria .15 .40
427 Jordan Montgomery .25 .60
428 Jakob Junis .15 .40
429 Victor Martinez .20 .50
430 Manny Margot FS .15 .40
431 Charlie Blackmon .25 .60
432 Albert Almora .20 .50
433 Anthony Santander RC .25 .60
434 Miguel Montero .15 .40
435 Matt Holliday .25 .60
436 Yu Darvish .25 .60
437 J.J. Hardy .15 .40
438 Stephen Vogt .20 .50
439 Dustin Pedroia .25 .60
440 Troy Scribner RC .25 .60
441 Danny Santana .15 .40
442 Jesus Aguilar .15 .40
443 Gerrit Cole .25 .60
444 Aaron Altherr .15 .40
445 Trevor Cahill .15 .40
446 Lucas Duda .20 .50
447 Carlos Gomez .15 .40
448 Max Kepler .20 .50
449 DJ LeMahieu .25 .60
450 Joey Votto .25 .60
451 Ubaldo Jimenez .15 .40
452 Tucker Barnhart .15 .40
453 Devon Travis .15 .40
454 Kyle Seager .15 .40
455 Hernan Perez .15 .40
456 Jimmy Nelson .15 .40
457 Hanley Ramirez .20 .50
458 Yovani Gallardo .15 .40
459 Breyvic Valera RC .25 .60
460 Robert Gsellman .15 .40
461 Michael Taylor .15 .40
462 Paul DeJong FS .25 .60
463 Cory Spangenberg .15 .40
464 Travis Jankowski .15 .40
465 San Diego Padres .15 .40
466 Tim Locastro RC .25 .60
467 Carlos Ramirez RC .25 .60
468 Tampa Bay Rays .15 .40
469 Sonny Gray .20 .50
470 Alex Mejia RC .25 .60
471 Josh Harrison .15 .40
472 Matt Garza .15 .40
473 Wilmer Difo .15 .40
474 Jeff Mathis .20 .50
475 Aroldis Chapman .25 .60
476 Wilson Ramos .15 .40
477 Logan Morrison .15 .40
478 Brad Miller .20 .50
479 Daniel Descalso .15 .40
480 Aaron Hicks .20 .50
481 Ronald Torreyes .15 .40
482 Delino DeShields .15 .40
483 Drew Pomeranz .15 .40
484 Kenta Maeda .20 .50
485 Kyle Farmer RC .25 .60
486 Tomas Nido RC .25 .60
487 Carl Edwards Jr. .15 .40
488 Joe Panik .20 .50
489 Blake Snell .20 .50
490 Jarrod Dyson .15 .40
491 Andrew Heaney .15 .40
492 Jon Jay .15 .40
493 Kyle Gibson .20 .50
494 Adalberto Mejia .15 .40
495 Aaron Bummer RC .25 .60
496 Leury Garcia .15 .40
497 Chasen Shreve .15 .40
498 Jen-Ho Tseng RC .25 .60
499 Justin Bour .15 .40
500 Kris Bryant .30 .75
501 Clayton Richard .15 .40
502 Xander Bogaerts .25 .60
503 Josh Donaldson .20 .50
504 Scott Schebler .20 .50
505 Taylor Williams RC .25 .60
506 Jose Berrios .20 .50
507 Zack Greinke .20 .50
508 Ryon Healy .15 .40
509 Santiago Casilla .15 .40
510 Freddie Freeman .30 .75
511 Wade Davis .15 .40
512 Mike Napoli .15 .40
513 Mike Zunino .15 .40
514 A.J. Minter RC .30 .75
515 Greg Bird .20 .50
516 Ken Giles .15 .40
517 Phillip Evans RC .25 .60
518 Andrew Toles .15 .40
519 Reyes Moronta RC .25 .60
520 Jim Johnson .15 .40
521 Jose Osuna .15 .40
522 Guillermo Heredia .15 .40
523 Matt Bush .15 .40
524 Steve Pearce .25 .60
525 Johan Camargo .15 .40
526 Tanner Roark .15 .40
527 Francisco Cervelli .15 .40
528 Marco Estrada .15 .40
529 Bryant/Schwarber .30 .75
530 Jason Vargas .15 .40
531 Chris O'Grady RC .25 .60
532 Tim Beckham .20 .50
533 Kennys Vargas .15 .40
534 German Marquez .15 .40
535 Jhoulys Chacin .15 .40
536 San Francisco Giants .15 .40
537 Phil Hughes .15 .40
538 Jason Castro .15 .40
539 Lance McCullers .15 .40
540 Mitch Garver RC .25 .60
541 Dwight Smith Jr. .15 .40
542 Pittsburgh Pirates .15 .40
543 Luis Castillo .20 .50
544 Yadier Molina .25 .60
545 Nicholas Castellanos .25 .60
546 Jordan Luplow RC .25 .60
547 Travis Wood .15 .40
548 Alex Meyer .15 .40
549 Alex Gordon .20 .50
550 Corey Seager .25 .60
551 Yacksel Rios RC .25 .60
552 Kyle Hendricks .25 .60
553 Denard Span .15 .40
554 Yonder Alonso .15 .40
555 Jacob deGrom .25 .60
556 Andrew Benintendi FS .25 .60
557 Jacoby Ellsbury .20 .50
558 Ben Gamel .20 .50
559 Ian Desmond .15 .40
560 Mark Melancon .15 .40
561 Dan Straily .15 .40
562 Brian McCann .20 .50
563 Hector Neris .15 .40
564 Joey Rickard .15 .40
564 New York Mets .15 .40
566 Yasmany Tomas .15 .40
567 Felix Hernandez .20 .50
568 J.C. Ramirez .15 .40
569 Keone Kela .15 .40
570 Trevor Williams .15 .40
571 C.J. Cron .15 .40
572 Dillon Maples RC .25 .60
573 Mark Leiter Jr. .20 .50
574 Jared Hughes .15 .40
575 Adrian Gonzalez .20 .50
576 Didi Gregorius .20 .50
577 Yunel Escobar .15 .40
578 Melky Cabrera .15 .40
579 Carson Fulmer .15 .40
580 Oakland Athletics .15 .40
581 Jesse Winker .15 .40
582 Albert Pujols .30 .75
583 Tommy Joseph .25 .60
584 Toronto Blue Jays Team Card .15 .40
585 Brandon Crawford .20 .50
586 Kyle Freeland .20 .50
587 Chris Davis .15 .40
588 David Wright .20 .50
589 Adam Duvall .25 .60
590 Dee Gordon .15 .40
591 Daniel Nava .15 .40
592 Gorkys Hernandez .15 .40
593 Luke Weaver FS .20 .50
594 Sandy Alcantara RC .25 .60
595 Addison Reed .15 .40
596 Keury Mella RC .25 .60
597 Caleb Joseph .15 .40
598 David Robertson .15 .40
599 Justin Turner .20 .50
600 Noah Syndergaard .20 .50
601 Jose Peraza .20 .50
602 Michael Pineda .15 .40
603 Zach Britton .15 .40
604 Gerardo Parra .15 .40
605 Lucas Giolito .20 .50
606 Jake Arrieta .20 .50
607 Sean Newcomb FS .20 .50
608 Kurt Suzuki .15 .40
609 Austin Hedges .15 .40
610 Scott Kazmir .15 .40
611 Josh Bell FS .20 .50
612 Steven Souza Jr. .20 .50
613 Cory Gearrin .15 .40
614 Minnesota Twins .15 .40
615 Eric Thames .20 .50
616 Greg Garcia .15 .40
617 Doug Fister .15 .40
618 Paul Goldschmidt .25 .60
619 Jeremy Hellickson .15 .40
620 Chris Young .15 .40
621 Jerad Eickhoff .15 .40
622 Ryan Rua .15 .40
623 Josh Fields .15 .40
624 Franklin Barreto .15 .40
625 Los Angeles Dodgers .15 .40
626 Brandon Maurer .15 .40
627 Matthew Boyd .15 .40
628 Vince Velasquez .15 .40
629 Max Scherzer .25 .60
630 Alcides Escobar .20 .50
631 David Freese .15 .40
632 Edwin Encarnacion .25 .60
633 Jameson Taillon .20 .50
634 Carlos Martinez .20 .50
635 Cody Allen .15 .40
636 Freddy Galvis .15 .40
637 Manny Pina .15 .40
638 Travis Shaw .15 .40
639 Niko Goodrum RC .40 1.00
640 Seth Lugo .15 .40
641 Cameron Maybin .15 .40
642 Ben Revere .15 .40
643 Justin Wilson .15 .40
644 Carlos Perez .15 .40
645 Welington Castillo .15 .40
646 Jose de Leon .15 .40
647 Jose Urena .15 .40
648 Derek Holland .15 .40
649 Curtis Granderson .20 .50
650 Justin Verlander .25 .60
651 JT Riddle .15 .40
652 Matt Carpenter .25 .60
653 Jorge Soler .25 .60
654 Trayce Thompson .20 .50
655 Andre Ethier .20 .50
656 Brian Goodwin .15 .40
657 Derek Dietrich .20 .50
658 Tom Koehler .15 .40
659 Arizona Diamondbacks .15 .40
660 Mitch Haniger FS .20 .50
661 Christian Villanueva RC .25 .60
662 Patrick Corbin .20 .50
663 Seth Smith .15 .40
664 Gregor Blanco .15 .40
665 Tommy Pham .15 .40
666 Eric Sogard .15 .40
667 Jonathan Lucroy .20 .50
668 Tyler Anderson .15 .40
669 Matt Chapman .25 .60
670 Asdrubal Cabrera .20 .50
671 Tyler Clippard .15 .40
672 Brandon Nimmo .20 .50
673 Adam Frazier .15 .40
674 Jose Martinez .15 .40
675 Victor Arano RC .25 .60
676 Chad Green .15 .40
677 Brandon Moss .15 .40
678 Chad Bettis .15 .40
679 Tyson Ross .15 .40
680 Enrique Hernandez .20 .50
681 Ehire Adrianza .15 .40
682 Kansas City Royals .15 .40
683 Adam Eaton .25 .60
684 Hunter Strickland .15 .40
685 Russell Martin .15 .40
686 Bud Norris .15 .40

687 Blake Treinen .15 .40
688 Tony Wolters .15 .40
689 Jeurys Familia .20 .50
690 St. Louis Cardinals .15 .40
691 Jason Heyward .20 .50
692 Tony Watson .15 .40
693 Brandon Kintzler .15 .40
694 Anthony DeSclafani .15 .40
695 Matt Davidson .20 .50
696 Kenley Jansen .20 .50
697 Eduardo Escobar .15 .40
698 Ryan Sherriff RC .25 .60
699 Drew Smyly .15 .40
700 Shohei Ohtani RC 1.50 4.00

2018 Topps Black

*BLACK: 10X TO 25X BASIC
*BLACK RC: 6X TO 15X BASIC RC
SER.1 ODDS 1:169 HOBBY
SER.2 ODDS 1:114 HOBBY
STATED PRINT RUN 67 SER. #'d SETS
259 Rhys Hoskins 30.00 80.00
529 Bryant/Schwarber 8.00 20.00
700 Shohei Ohtani 200.00 500.00

2018 Topps Black and White Negative

*BW NEGATIVE: 8X TO 20X BASIC
*BW NEGATIVE RC: 5X TO 12X BASIC
SER.1 ODDS 1:230 HOBBY
SER.2 ODDS 1:155 HOBBY
259 Rhys Hoskins 15.00 40.00
700 Shohei Ohtani 150.00 400.00

2018 Topps Factory Set Foilboard

*FACT.FOIL: 6X TO 15X BASIC
*FACT.FOIL RC: 4X TO 10X BASIC RC
INSERTED IN FACTORY SETS
STATED PRINT RUN 190 SER. #'d SETS
698B Ronald Acuna Jr 1000.00 2000.00

2018 Topps Father's Day Blue

*BLUE: 10X TO 25X BASIC
*BLUE RC: 6X TO 15X BASIC RC
SER.1 ODDS 1:693 HOBBY
SER.2 ODDS 1:380 HOBBY
STATED PRINT RUN 50 SER. #'d SETS
259 Rhys Hoskins 30.00 80.00
529 Bryant/Schwarber 8.00 20.00
700 Shohei Ohtani 200.00 500.00

2018 Topps Gold

*GOLD: 2X TO 5X BASIC
*GOLD RC: 1.2X TO 3X BASIC RC
SER. 1 ODDS 1:18 HOBBY
SER.2 ODDS 1:10 HOBBY
STATED PRINT RUN 2018 SER. #'d SETS

2018 Topps Limited

*LTD: .1.5X TO 4X BASIC
LTD RC: 1X TO 2.5X BASIC RC
ANNCD PRINT RUN OF 1000

2018 Topps Memorial Day Camo

*CAMO: 12X TO 30X BASIC
*CAMO RC: 8X TO 20X BASIC RC
SER.1 ODDS 1:1388 HOBBY
SER.2 ODDS 1:759 HOBBY
STATED PRINT RUN 25 SER. #'d SETS
259 Rhys Hoskins 40.00 100.00
529 Bryant/Schwarber 10.00 25.00
700 Shohei Ohtani 250.00 600.00

2018 Topps Mother's Day Pink

*PINK: 10X TO 25X BASIC
*PINK RC: 6X TO 15X BASIC RC
SER.1 ODDS 1:693 HOBBY
SER.2 ODDS 1:380 HOBBY
STATED PRINT RUN 50 SER. #'d SETS
259 Rhys Hoskins 30.00 80.00
529 Bryant/Schwarber 8.00 20.00
700 Shohei Ohtani 200.00 500.00

2018 Topps Rainbow Foil

*RAINBOW: 2X TO 5X BASIC
*RAINBOW RC: 1.2X TO 3X BASIC RC
SER.1 ODDS 1:10 HOBBY
SER.2 ODDS 1:10 HOBBY
259 Rhys Hoskins 6.00 15.00

2018 Topps Toys R Us Purple

*PURPLE: 5X TO 12X BASIC
*PURPLE RC: 3X TO 8X BASIC RC
SER.1 ODDS 1:XX BLASTER
259 Rhys Hoskins 15.00 40.00

2018 Topps Vintage Stock

*VINTAGE: 8X TO 20X BASIC
*VINTAGE RC: 5X TO 12X BASIC RC
SER.1 ODDS 1:351 HOBBY
SER.2 ODDS 1:192 HOBBY
STATED PRINT RUN 99 SER. #'d SETS
259 Rhys Hoskins 25.00 60.00
529 Bryant/Schwarber 6.00 15.00
700 Shohei Ohtani 150.00 400.00

2018 Topps Base Set Factory Chrome Variations

RANDOMLY INSERTED IN FACTORY SETS
*GOLD/50: 1X TO 2.5X BASIC
*ORANGE/25: 2X TO 5X BASIC
7 Clint Frazier 5.00 12.00
18 Rafael Devers 8.00 20.00
63 Amed Rosario 3.00 8.00
166 Victor Robles 6.00 15.00
259 Rhys Hoskins 10.00 25.00
700 Shohei Ohtani 30.00 80.00

2018 Topps Base Set Photo Variations

SER.1 STATED ODDS 1:57 HOBBY
SER. 1 ODDS ROOKIE SSP 1:1619 HOBBY
SER.2 STATED ODDS 1:30 HOBBY
SER. 2 SSP ODDS SSP 1:886 HOBBY
1A Judge Blue pllvr 25.00 60.00
1B Judge Stripe jrsy 250.00 500.00
6A Dominic Smith 1.50 4.00
Blue and gray shirt
6B Smith Celebrating 75.00 200.00
7A Frazier Blue pllvr 10.00 25.00
7B Frazier Bttng glvs 125.00 300.00
7C Frazier One hand
10A Lindor No helmet 2.50 6.00
10B Lindor White Jrsy 100.00 250.00
11 Aaron Nola 2.00 5.00
Sitting in dugout
18A Devers Red pllvr 12.00 30.00
18B Devers Pointing 100.00 250.00
18C Devers Brwn bat
20A Sale Jckt 2.50 6.00
20B Sale Off mound 40.00 100.00
25A Machado Snglss 6.00 15.00
25B Machado Hand face 75.00 200.00
30A Correa Blue warmup 2.50 6.00
30B Correa White Jrsy 30.00 80.00
33 Dexter Fowler 2.00 5.00
Red pullover
42A Bllngr Blue gray shirt 6.00 15.00
42B Bllngr Gray Jrsy 75.00 200.00
44 Turner Red pllvr 2.00 5.00
50A Anthony Rizzo 4.00 10.00
Blue pullover
50B Rizzo Gray Jrsy 60.00 150.00
58 Ryan Zimmerman 2.00 5.00
Red pullover
63A Rosario Blue pllvr 10.00 25.00
63B Rosario Gray Jrsy 60.00 150.00
63C Rosario Pnstrp Jrsy
68 Hamilton Red hde 6.00 15.00
81 Adam Wainwright 2.00 5.00
Red hoodie
82 Justin Smoak 1.50 4.00
Blue pullover
86 Eric Hosmer 2.00 5.00
Blue shirt
88 Michael Conforto 2.00 5.00
Blue pullover
89 Yasiel Puig 2.50 6.00
Blue shirt
90 Cabrera Blue hde 2.50 6.00
100A Stanton Orange shirt 2.50 6.00
100B Stanton Gray Jrsy 100.00 250.00
102 Wil Myers 1.50 4.00
Blue shirt
105 Daniel Murphy 2.00 5.00
Red shirt
110 Carlos Gonzalez 2.00 5.00
Black pullover
118 Ian Happ 2.00 5.00
Blue pullover
125 Yoenis Cespedes 2.50 6.00
Blue sleeveless shirt, black sleeves under
127 Byron Buxton 2.00 5.00
Blue and gray shirt
130 Brian Dozier 2.00 5.00
Blue pullover
132 Marcell Ozuna 2.50 6.00
Black pullover
140A Betts Blue hde 4.00 10.00
140B Betts On base 60.00 150.00
142 Adam Jones 2.00 5.00
Black and gray shirt
150A Nolan Arenado 3.00 8.00
Black pullover
150B Arndo Stripe Jrsy 75.00 200.00
157A Ichiro Black pllvr 3.00 8.00
157B Ichiro On base
160 Masahiro Tanaka 2.00 5.00
Dark blue pullover
166 Robles Hispanic Logo 15.00 40.00
172 Contreras Blue pllvr 2.50 6.00
173 Mike Moustakas 2.00 5.00
Blue hoodie
180 Ryan Braun 2.00 5.00
Blue pullover
182 Alex Bregman 2.50 6.00
Blue pullover
190 Justin Upton 2.00 5.00
Horziontal, bat next to head
191 Chris Archer 1.50 4.00
Blue sleeveless shirt
196 Orlando Arcia 1.50 4.00
Blue and gray shirt
200A Andrew McCutchen 2.50 6.00
Black pullover
200B McCtchn Gray Jrsy 75.00 200.00
220 Nelson Cruz 2.50 6.00
Blue pullover
223 Evan Longoria 2.00 5.00
Blue and gray shirt
225A Kyle Schwarber 2.50 6.00
Blue and gray shirt
225B Schwarber Point 40.00 100.00
226A Williams Red shirt 2.00 5.00
226B Williams Stripe Jrsy 50.00 120.00
233 Stephen Strasburg 2.50 6.00
Blue and red pullover
238 Jose Bautista 2.00 5.00
Blue shirt
240A Robinson Cano 2.00 5.00
Blue pullover
240B Cano White Jrsy 75.00 200.00
245 Calhoun Red shirt 2.00 5.00
248 Jake Lamb 2.00 5.00
Black pullover
250A Posey Black pllvr 3.00 8.00
250B Posey White Jrsy 60.00 150.00
254 Beltre Blue pllvr 2.50 6.00
257 Martinez Pullover 2.50 6.00
259A Hoskins Red pllvr 15.00 40.00
259B Hoskins Red Jrsy 75.00 200.00
259C Hoskins Look at sky
264 Carlos Rodon 2.00 5.00
Black pullover
265A Baez Blue hde 3.00 8.00
265B Baez Pinstripe Jrsy 50.00 120.00
267 Moncada Black pllvr 2.50 6.00
275 Springer Hispanic Logo 2.00 5.00
276A Albies Blue pllvr 10.00 25.00
276B Albies Blue Jrsy 40.00 100.00
280 Jose Abreu 2.50 6.00
Black pullover
288 Sano Blue hde 2.00 5.00
290 Salvador Perez 2.00 5.00
Blue hoodie
297 Kevin Kiermaier 2.00 5.00
Blue shirt
300A Trout Gray red shirt 12.00 30.00
300B Trout Red Jrsy 250.00 500.00
303 Svrno Blue gray shirt 2.00 5.00
306 Dlmnco Black and gray 1.50 4.00
325 Khris Davis 2.50 6.00
Green pullover
326 Gallo Blue pllvr 2.00 5.00
330 Ian Kinsler 2.00 5.00
Blue pullover
340 Sanchez Blue pllvr 2.50 6.00
350A Kershaw Blue shirt 5.00 12.00
350B Kershaw Gray Jrsy 50.00 120.00
351A Harper Red shirt 4.00 10.00
351B Harper Clapping 60.00 150.00
351C Reggie Jackson 3.00 8.00
351D Ty Cobb 4.00 10.00
369 Chris Taylor 2.00 5.00
Blue shirt
384A Russell Blue pllvr 2.00 5.00
384B Russell Pointing
384C Ernie Banks 2.50 6.00
392 Marcus Stroman 2.00 5.00
Standing behing cage
393A Kluber Red shirt 2.00 5.00
393B Kluber Clench fist 20.00 50.00
397 Dallas Keuchel 2.00 5.00
Blue pullover
400A Altuve Blue shirt 2.00 5.00
400B Altuve Clapping 25.00 60.00
400C Honus Wagner 2.50 6.00
413 Trevor Bauer 2.50 6.00
Blue hoodie
416 Matt Olson 1.50 4.00
Green Pullover
418A Ramirez Hat 2.00 5.00
418B Ramirez Pointing 25.00 60.00
430 Manny Margot 1.50 4.00
Blue hoodie
431A Blackmon Blk hoodie 2.50 6.00
431B Blackmon Hand out 12.00 30.00
431C Rickey Henderson 2.50 6.00
436A Darvish Blue pllvr 2.50 6.00
436B Darvish Streching 15.00 40.00
436C Greg Maddux 3.00 8.00
439A Pedroia Blue pllvr 2.50 6.00
439B Pedroia Hand up 30.00 80.00
450A Votto Red pllvr 2.50 6.00
450B Votto Hands out 30.00 80.00
450C Johnny Bench 4.00 10.00
454 Kyle Seager 1.50 4.00
Blue shirt
462A Paul DeJong 2.50 6.00
Carrying bag
462B Ozzie Smith 3.00 8.00
469A Gray Interview 2.00 5.00
469B Gray Pointing 30.00 80.00
471 Josh Harrison 1.50 4.00
Standing behing cage
484 Kenta Maeda 2.00 5.00
Blue shirt
499 Justin Bour 1.50 4.00
Black shirt
500A Bryant Holding bat 3.00 8.00
500B Bryant Sliding 75.00 200.00
500C Ryne Sandberg 5.00 12.00
502 Xander Bogaerts 2.50 6.00
Red and blue pullover
503A Donaldson Cage 2.00 5.00
503B Donaldson Hand up 20.00 50.00
503C George Brett 5.00 12.00
506 Jose Berrios 2.00 5.00
Blue hoodie
507 Zack Greinke 2.00 5.00
Black shirt
510A Freeman Hat 3.00 8.00
510B Freeman Waving 25.00 60.00
510C Chipper Jones 2.50 6.00
515A Greg Bird 2.00 5.00
Blue shirt
515B Don Mattingly 5.00 12.00
544A Molina Behind cage 2.50 6.00
544B Molina Hands up 30.00 80.00
544C Roberto Clemente 6.00 15.00
545 Nicholas Castellanos 2.50 6.00
Red shirt
550A Cal Ripken Jr. 6.00 15.00
550B Jackie Robinson 2.50 6.00
555A deGrom Blue shirt 2.50 6.00
555B deGrom Helmet 25.00 60.00
556A Benintendi Blue pllvr 2.50 6.00
556B Benintendi Arm up 40.00 100.00
556C C.Seager Blue pllvr 2.50 6.00
556D C.Seager Helmet 30.00 80.00
556E Ted Williams 5.00 12.00
567A Hernandez Gray shirt 2.00 5.00
567B Hernandez Point 20.00 50.00
576A Gregorius Blue pllvr 2.00 5.00
576B Gregorius Pointing 25.00 60.00
576C Derek Jeter 12.00 30.00
582A Pujols Red pllvr 3.00 8.00
582B Pujols Pointing up 50.00 120.00
582C Hank Aaron 5.00 12.00
585A Brandon Crawford 2.00 5.00
Black hat
585B Willie McCovey 2.00 5.00
589 Adam Duvall 2.50 6.00
Red jersey
593 Luke Weaver 2.00 5.00
Red hat
599 Justin Turner 2.00 5.00
Blue pullover
600A Syndrgrd Blue pllvr 2.00 5.00
600B Syndrgrd Fist 75.00 200.00
600C Tom Seaver 2.00 5.00
605A Lucas Giolito 2.00 5.00
No hat
605B Frank Thomas 2.50 6.00
611A Scherzer Red pllvr 2.50 6.00
611B Scherzer Fist 25.00 60.00
615 Eric Thames 2.00 5.00
Blue pullover
618A Gldschmdt Blk pllvr 2.50 6.00
618B Gldschmdt Hand out 30.00 80.00
618C Lou Gehrig 4.00 10.00
629 Sandy Koufax 4.00 10.00
632 Edwin Encarnacion 2.50 6.00
Red and blue pullover
650A Verlander Blue hoodie 3.00 8.00
650B Verlander Hand up 30.00 80.00
650C Bob Gibson 2.00 5.00
652 Matt Carpenter 2.50 6.00
Red shirt
665 Tommy Pham 1.50 4.00
Red shirt
698A Acuna Bat down 300.00 600.00
698B Acuna Bat up 20.00 50.00
699A Torres Both hands 20.00 50.00
699B Torres One hand
700A Ohtani Red pllvr 30.00 80.00
700B Ohtani Hand on hlmt 150.00 400.00
700C Babe Ruth 6.00 15.00
700D Ohtani Red glv

2018 Topps '83 All Stars

STATED ODDS 1:4 HOBBY
*BLUE: 1.2X TO 3X BASIC
*BLACK/299: 1.5X TO 4X BASIC
*GOLD/50: 4X TO 10X BASIC
83AS1 Aaron Judge 1.00 2.50
83AS2 Giancarlo Stanton .40 1.00
83AS3 Carlos Correa .40 1.00
83AS4 Mike Trout 2.00 5.00
83AS5 Jose Altuve .30 .75
83AS6 Chris Sale .40 1.00
83AS7 George Springer .30 .75
83AS8 Francisco Lindor .40 1.00
83AS9 Miguel Sano .30 .75
83AS10 Luis Severino .30 .75
83AS11 Corey Kluber .30 .75
83AS12 Clayton Kershaw .75 2.00
83AS13 Bryce Harper .60 1.50
83AS14 Buster Posey .50 1.25
83AS15 Charlie Blackmon .40 1.00
83AS16 Cody Bellinger .75 2.00
83AS17 Paul Goldschmidt .40 1.00
83AS18 Corey Seager .40 1.00
83AS19 Joey Votto .40 1.00
83AS20 Max Scherzer .40 1.00
83AS21 Stephen Strasburg .40 1.00
83AS22 Mookie Betts .60 1.50
83AS23 Gary Sanchez .40 1.00
83AS24 Robinson Cano .30 .75
83AS25 Yadier Molina .40 1.00
83AS26 Salvador Perez .30 .75
83AS27 Craig Kimbrel .30 .75
83AS28 Jose Ramirez .30 .75
83AS29 Josh Harrison .25 .60
83AS30 Justin Upton .30 .75
83AS31 Justin Verlander .40 1.00
83AS32 Yu Darvish .40 1.00
83AS33 Kris Bryant .50 1.25
83AS34 Anthony Rizzo .60 1.50
83AS35 Addison Russell .40 1.00
83AS36 Yoenis Cespedes .40 1.00
83AS37 Josh Donaldson .30 .75
83AS38 Manny Machado .40 1.00
83AS39 Starling Marte .30 .75
83AS40 Noah Syndergaard .30 .75
83AS41 Andrew McCutchen .40 1.00
83AS42 Adam Jones .30 .75
83AS43 Albert Pujols .50 1.25
83AS44 Brian Dozier .30 .75
83AS45 Miguel Cabrera .40 1.00
83AS46 Ichiro .50 1.25
83AS47 Wade Boggs .30 .75
83AS48 Cal Ripken Jr. 1.25 3.00
83AS49 Ryne Sandberg .75 2.00
83AS50 Rickey Henderson .40 1.00
83AS51 Don Mattingly .75 2.00
83AS52 Chipper Jones .40 1.00
83AS53 John Smoltz .40 1.00
83AS54 Greg Maddux .50 1.25
83AS55 Dwight Gooden .25 .60
83AS56 Darryl Strawberry .25 .60
83AS57 Roger Clemens .50 1.25
83AS58 Mark McGwire .60 1.50
83AS59 Jose Canseco .30 .75
83AS60 Randy Johnson .40 1.00
83AS61 Frank Thomas .40 1.00
83AS62 Mariano Rivera .50 1.25
83AS63 Mike Piazza .40 1.00
83AS64 Derek Jeter 1.00 2.50
83AS65 Pedro Martinez .30 .75
83AS66 Dave Winfield .30 .75
83AS67 Dennis Eckersley .30 .75
83AS68 Ozzie Smith .50 1.25
83AS69 Barry Larkin .30 .75
83AS70 Rod Carew .30 .75
83AS71 Reggie Jackson .30 .75
83AS72 Johnny Bench .40 1.00
83AS73 Gary Carter .30 .75
83AS74 George Brett .75 2.00
83AS75 Hideki Matsui .40 1.00

2018 Topps '83 Rookies

STATED ODDS 1:4 HOBBY
*BLUE: 1.2X TO 3X BASIC
*BLACK/299: 1.5X TO 4X BASIC
*GOLD/50: 4X TO 10X BASIC
831 Shohei Ohtani 5.00 12.00
832 Walker Buehler 1.25 3.00
833 Luiz Gohara .25 .60
834 Tyler Mahle .30 .75
835 Austin Hays .40 1.00
836 Chance Sisco .30 .75
837 Sandy Alcantara .25 .60
838 Jen-Ho Tseng .25 .60
839 Richard Urena .25 .60
8310 Greg Allen .25 .60
8311 Brian Anderson .30 .75
8312 Dillon Peters .25 .60
8313 A.J. Minter .30 .75
8314 Troy Scribner .25 .60
8315 Clint Frazier .50 1.25
8316 Ozzie Albies .75 2.00
8317 Amed Rosario .30 .75
8318 Rhys Hoskins 1.00 2.50
8319 Rafael Devers .75 2.00
8320 Dominic Smith .25 .60
8321 Victor Robles .60 1.50
8322 Dillon Maples .25 .60
8323 Christian Villanueva .25 .60
8324 Nick Williams .30 .75

2018 Topps '83 Topps

COMPLETE SET (100) 60.00 150.00
STATED ODDS 1:4 HOBBY
*BLUE: 2X TO 5X BASIC
*BLACK/299: 3X TO 8X BASIC
*GOLD/50: 4X TO 10X BASIC
831 Ryne Sandberg .75 2.00
832 Hank Aaron .75 2.00
833 Andrew McCutchen .40 1.00
834 Mookie Betts .60 1.50
835 Jacob deGrom .40 1.00
836 Noah Syndergaard .30 .75
837 Frank Thomas .40 1.00
838 Khris Davis .40 1.00
839 Alex Verdugo .40 1.00
8310 Eric Thames .30 .75
8311 Matt Carpenter .40 1.00
8312 Carlos Martinez .30 .75
8313 Mike Trout 2.00 5.00
8314 Rafael Devers .75 2.00
8315 Ian Happ .30 .75
8316 Clayton Kershaw .75 2.00
8317 Dominic Smith .25 .60
8318 Nolan Ryan 1.25 3.00
8319 Nick Williams .30 .75
8320 Alex Wood .25 .60
8321 Jake Arrieta .30 .75
8322 Giancarlo Stanton .40 1.00
8323 Kris Bryant .50 1.25
8324 Aaron Judge 1.00 2.50
8325 Yu Darvish .40 1.00
8326 Brian Dozier .30 .75
8327 Charlie Blackmon .40 1.00
8328 Luis Severino .30 .75
8329 Harrison Bader .40 1.00
8330 Rhys Hoskins 1.00 2.50
8331 Jose Altuve .30 .75
8332 Manny Machado .40 1.00
8333 Michael Fulmer .25 .60
8334 Kyle Seager .25 .60
8335 Nelson Cruz .40 1.00
8336 Stephen Strasburg .40 1.00
8337 Miguel Sano .30 .75
8338 Matt Kemp .30 .75
8339 Cal Ripken Jr. 1.25 3.00
8340 Ozzie Albies .75 2.00
8341 Miguel Cabrera .40 1.00
8342 Yadier Molina .40 1.00
8343 Andrew Benintendi .40 1.00
8344 Roy Halladay .30 .75
8345 Josh Donaldson .30 .75
8346 Dansby Swanson .40 1.00
8347 Jose Berrios .30 .75
8348 Darryl Strawberry .25 .60
8349 Freddie Freeman .50 1.25
8350 Amed Rosario .30 .75
8351 Buster Posey .50 1.25
8352 Jeff Bagwell .40 1.00
8353 Willie Calhoun .30 .75
8354 Anthony Rizzo .60 1.50
8355 Justin Upton .30 .75
8356 Don Mattingly .75 2.00
8357 Barry Larkin .30 .75
8358 Nolan Arenado .50 1.25
8359 Yoan Moncada .40 1.00
8360 Justin Turner .30 .75
8361 Felix Hernandez .30 .75
8362 Sandy Koufax .75 2.00
8363 Kenta Maeda .30 .75
8364 Robinson Cano .30 .75
8365 Edwin Encarnacion .40 1.00
8366 Daniel Murphy .30 .75
8367 Ichiro .50 1.25
8368 Derek Jeter 1.00 2.50
8369 Tom Glavine .30 .75
8370 Clint Frazier .50 1.25
8371 Craig Kimbrel .30 .75
8372 Didi Gregorius .30 .75
8373 Adam Jones .30 .75
8374 Gary Sanchez .40 1.00
8375 Max Scherzer .40 1.00
8376 Ryan McMahon .30 .75
8377 Byron Buxton .30 .75
8378 Masahiro Tanaka .30 .75
8379 Jose Canseco .30 .75
8380 George Springer .30 .75
8381 Kyle Schwarber .40 1.00
8382 Trea Turner .30 .75
8383 Paul Goldschmidt .40 1.00
8384 Bryce Harper .60 1.50
8385 Victor Robles .60 1.50
8386 Javier Baez .50 1.25
8387 Cody Bellinger .75 2.00
8388 John Smoltz .40 1.00
8389 Bo Jackson .40 1.00
8390 J.P. Crawford .25 .60
8391 Eric Hosmer .30 .75
8392 Carlos Correa .40 1.00
8393 Chris Sale .40 1.00
8394 Wil Myers .25 .60
8395 Francisco Lindor .40 1.00
8396 Alex Bregman .40 1.00
8397 Corey Seager .40 1.00
8398 Justin Verlander .40 1.00
8399 Addison Russell .30 .75
83100 Wade Boggs .30 .75

2018 Topps '83 Topps Autographs

SER.1 ODDS 1:809 HOBBY
SER.2 ODDS 1:1233 HOBBY
UPD ODDS 1:1352 HOBBY
SER.1 EXCH.DEADLINE 12/31/2019
SER.2 EXCH.DEADLINE 5/31/2020
UPD EXCH.DEADLINE 9/30/2020
*BLACK/99: .5X TO 1.2X BASIC
*BLACK/50: .6X TO 1.5X BASIC
*BLACK/25: .75X TO 2X BASIC
*GOLD/50: .6X TO 1.5X BASIC
*GOLD/25: .75X TO 2X BASIC
*RED/25: .75X TO 2X BASIC
83AABA Anthony Banda 2.50 6.00
83AABE Andrew Benintendi UPD 40.00 100.00
83AABL Adrian Beltre S2 20.00 50.00
83AABR Alex Bregman 15.00 40.00
83AAC Andrew McCutchen UPD 25.00 60.00
83AADI Aledmys Diaz 3.00 8.00
83AADU Adam Duvall 8.00 20.00
83AAE Austin Meadows UPD 6.00 15.00
83AAGR Amir Garrett S2 2.50 6.00
83AAH Austin Hays S2 6.00 15.00
83AAJN Andruw Jones 10.00 25.00
83AAJO Adam Jones
83AAN A.J. Minter UPD 3.00 8.00
83AAN Aaron Nola 8.00 20.00
83AAO Adam Jones S2
83AAP Andy Pettitte
83AARI Anthony Rizzo UPD
83AARO Amed Rosario EXCH 25.00 60.00
83AARU Addison Russell S2 12.00 30.00
83AAS Amed Rosario S2 10.00 25.00
83AASL Aaron Slegers 6.00 15.00
83AAST Andrew Stevenson 8.00 20.00
83AAV Alex Verdugo 15.00 40.00
83AAW Alex Wood 8.00 20.00
83ABA Brian Anderson S2 8.00 20.00
83ABBU Byron Buxton UPD 6.00 15.00
83ABD Brian Dozier S2
83ABF Brandon Finnegan 2.50 6.00
83ABG Ben Gamel 3.00 8.00
83ABH Bryce Harper S2
83ABJ Bo Jackson S2 60.00 150.00
83ABL Barry Larkin
83ABL Barry Larkin S2 25.00 60.00
83ABP Boog Powell 2.50 6.00
83ABPH Brett Phillips 5.00 12.00
83ABPO Buster Posey UPD
83ABT Blake Treinen UPD 2.50 6.00
83ABW Brandon Woodruff 5.00 12.00
83ACAR Christian Arroyo S2 6.00 15.00
83ACCA Carlos Carrasco 8.00 20.00
83ACCO Carlos Correa S2
83ACF Clint Frazier 25.00 60.00
83ACG Chad Green UPD 6.00 15.00
83ACR Cal Ripken Jr.
83ACR Cal Ripken Jr. S2
83ACS Chris Sale S2 30.00 80.00
83ACS Chris Stratton UPD 2.50 6.00
83ACSA Chris Sale 15.00 40.00
83ACSE Corey Seager 40.00 100.00
83ACY Christian Yelich UPD 40.00 100.00
83ACY Clayton Kershaw S2
83ADA Don Mattingly S2 25.00 60.00
83ADCZ Dylan Cozens UPD 2.50 6.00
83ADD David Dahl 6.00 15.00
83ADE Dennis Eckersley UPD 6.00 15.00
83ADFI Derek Fisher S2 2.50 6.00
83ADFO Dexter Fowler S2
83ADFW Dustin Fowler S2 2.50 6.00
83ADG Dwight Gooden S2 20.00 50.00
83ADGE Domingo German 15.00 40.00
83ADI Dominic Smith S2 6.00 15.00
83ADJ Derek Jeter S2
83ADJE Derek Jeter S2
83ADMA Don Mattingly 100.00 250.00
83ADN Dennis Eckersley S2 15.00 40.00
83ADN Daniel Mengden UPD 4.00 10.00
83ADS Darryl Strawberry S2
83ADSI Dominic Smith 12.00 30.00
83ADSM Drew Smyly 2.50 6.00
83ADST Darryl Strawberry 30.00 80.00
83ADSW Dansby Swanson S2 12.00 30.00
83AED Eric Davis 10.00 25.00
83AET Eric Thames 3.00 8.00
83AFF Freddie Freeman S2 30.00 80.00
83AFH Frank Thomas S2
83AFJ Felix Jorge S2 2.50 6.00
83AFME Francisco Mejia 15.00 40.00
83AFO Fernando Romero UPD 2.50 6.00
83AFP Freddy Peralta UPD 2.50 6.00
83AFR Franmil Reyes UPD 4.00 10.00
83AFT Frank Thomas S2
83AGA Gary Sanchez S2 40.00 100.00
83AGB Greg Bird 3.00 8.00
83AGC Garrett Cooper 2.50 6.00
83AGL Greg Allen S2 2.50 6.00
83AGMA Greg Maddux
83AGO Gleyber Torres UPD 50.00 120.00
83AGS Gary Sanchez 40.00 100.00
83AGT Gleyber Torres S2 100.00 250.00
83AHA Hank Aaron 125.00 300.00
83AHB Harrison Bader 4.00 10.00
83AHR Hunter Renfroe 6.00 15.00
83AIF Ian Kinsler UPD 15.00 40.00
83AIH Ian Happ 12.00 30.00
83AIK Isiah Kiner-Falefa UPD 2.50 6.00
83AJBA Jeff Bagwell 40.00 100.00
83AJBE Johnny Bench S2
83AJBR Jose Berrios 10.00 25.00
83AJBZ Javier Baez 20.00 50.00
83AJC Jose Canseco S2 20.00 50.00
83AJCA Jose Canseco 15.00 40.00
83AJCR J.P. Crawford 8.00 20.00
83AJD J.D. Davis 3.00 8.00
83AJDO Josh Donaldson UPD 20.00 50.00
83AJE Jerad Eickhoff 2.50 6.00
83AJF Jack Flaherty UPD 4.00 10.00
83AJF Jacob Faria 2.50 6.00
83AJHA Josh Hader 6.00 15.00
83AJHO Jeff Hoffman 6.00 15.00
83AJK Jordan Hicks UPD 6.00 15.00
83AJL Joey Lucchesi UPD 6.00 15.00
83AJL Jake Lamb S2
83AJM John Smoltz S2
83AJMO Jordan Montgomery S2 4.00 10.00
83AJR Jose Ramirez S2 25.00 60.00
83AJS Jesse Biddle UPD 3.00 8.00
83AJS Justin Smoak S2 6.00 15.00
83AJSM John Smoltz S2
83AJST Jackson Stephens 2.50 6.00
83AJTH Jim Thome
83AJU Juan Soto UPD 150.00 300.00
83AJU Justin Upton S2
83AJV Joey Votto S2 60.00 150.00
83AJW Jesse Winker 10.00 25.00
83AJY Joey Votto S2 60.00 150.00
83AKB Kris Bryant S2
83AKBO Keon Broxton 2.50 6.00
83AKBR Kris Bryant 60.00 150.00
83AKD Khris Davis 8.00 20.00
83AKGI Ken Giles S2 2.50 6.00
83AKGL Koda Glover 4.00 10.00
83AKSE Kyle Seager 6.00 15.00
83ALC Luis Castillo UPD 3.00 8.00
83ALE Luis Severino S2 30.00 80.00
83ALG Lucas Giolito 8.00 20.00
83ALI Lucas Sims S2 2.50 6.00
83ALU Lourdes Gurriel Jr. UPD 10.00 25.00
83ALW Luke Weaver 3.00 8.00
83AMA Miguel Andujar 50.00 120.00
83AMC Mike Clevinger UPD 3.00 8.00
83AMC Mike Clevinger 4.00 10.00
83AMD Mike Soroka UPD 5.00 12.00
83AMF Michael Fulmer UPD 5.00 12.00
83AMF Max Fried 6.00 15.00
83AMG Mark McGwire S2
83AMK Max Kepler 5.00 12.00
83AML Mark Leiter 3.00 8.00
83AMM Miles Mikolas UPD 6.00 15.00
83AMM Manny Machado S2
83AMMA Manny Machado 60.00 150.00
83AMMG Mark McGwire
83AMMR Manny Margot S2 2.50 6.00
83AMN Miguel Andujar UPD 40.00 100.00
83AMO Marcell Ozuna UPD 10.00 25.00
83AMO Matt Olson 8.00 20.00
83AMO Miguel Gomez S2 2.50 6.00
83AMT Mike Trout S2
83AMTR Mike Trout 250.00 500.00
83AND Nicky Delmonico 8.00 20.00
83ANK Nick Kingham UPD 3.00 8.00
83ANP Nick Pivetta UPD 2.50 6.00
83ANR Nolan Ryan S2
83ANS Noah Syndergaard S2
83AOA Ozzie Albies UPD 20.00 50.00

83AOAL Ozzie Albies 20.00 50.00
83AOS Ozzie Smith S2 60.00 150.00
83AOV Omar Vizquel 25.00 60.00
83APB Paul Blackburn 2.50 6.00
83APBR Parker Bridwell 2.50 6.00
83APD Paul DeJong 10.00 25.00
83APG Paul Goldschmidt S2
83APN Pat Neshek UPD 4.00 10.00
83ARA Ronald Acuna S2 100.00 250.00
83ARD Rafael Devers 50.00 120.00
83ARHO Rhys Hoskins S2 30.00 80.00
83ARM Ryan McMahon 6.00 15.00
83ARR Rod Carew S2
83ARS Ryne Sandberg
83ARS Ryne Sandberg S2
83ARU Ronald Acuna Jr. UPD 100.00 250.00
83ARU Richard Urena S2 5.00 12.00
83ASA Sandy Alcantara S2 2.50 6.00
83ASD Sean Doolittle UPD 2.50 6.00
83ASI Scott Kingery UPD 4.00 10.00
83ASK Sandy Koufax UPD 300.00 600.00
83ASM Starling Marte UPD 5.00 12.00
83ASN Sean Newcomb S2 5.00 12.00
83ASO Shohei Ohtani UPD EXCH 250.00 500.00
83ASO Shohei Ohtani S2 800.00 1200.00
83ASS Steven Souza Jr. 3.00 8.00
83AST Sam Travis S2 3.00 8.00
83ATAN Tim Anderson 10.00 25.00
83ATAU Tyler Austin UPD 4.00 10.00
83ATB Tyler Beede UPD 2.50 6.00
83ATBK Tim Beckham S2 5.00 12.00
83ATGS Tyler Glasnow 5.00 12.00
83ATGV Tom Glavine S2
83ATL Tzu-Wei Lin UPD 3.00 8.00
83ATM Tyler Mahle UPD 3.00 8.00
83ATMA Trey Mancini S2 8.00 20.00
83ATN Tomas Nido S2 2.50 6.00
83ATO Tyler O'Neill UPD EXCH 4.00 10.00
83ATS Trevor Story 5.00 12.00
83ATS Troy Scribner S2 2.50 6.00
83ATU Torii Hunter UPD 6.00 15.00
83ATW Tyler Wade 12.00 30.00
83AVR Victor Robles 40.00 100.00
83AVR Victor Robles S2 20.00 50.00
83AWA Willy Adames UPD EXCH 10.00 25.00
83AWB Wade Boggs 40.00 100.00
83AWB Wade Boggs S2 40.00 100.00
83AWU Walker Buehler UPD 30.00 80.00
83AYM Yadier Molina S2
83AYO Yoan Moncada UPD
83AZG Zack Granite 8.00 20.00

2018 Topps '83 Topps Silver Pack Chrome

COMPLETE SET (150) 100.00 250.00
*BLUE/150: 1.5X TO 4X BASIC
*GREEN/99: 2X TO 5X BASIC
*BLUE WAVE/75: 2X TO 5X BASIC
*PURPLE/75: 2X TO 5X BASIC
*GOLD/50: 2.5X TO 6X BASIC
*ORANGE/25: 3X TO 8X BASIC
1 Derek Jeter 2.00 5.00
2 Mike Trout 4.00 10.00
3 Ichiro 1.00 2.50
4 Brandon Woodruff .60 1.50
5 Mark McGwire 1.25 3.00
6 Cal Ripken Jr. 2.50 6.00
7 Kris Bryant 1.00 2.50
8 Carlos Correa .75 2.00
9 Manny Machado .75 2.00
10 Clayton Kershaw 1.50 4.00
11 Anthony Rizzo 1.25 3.00
12 Nicky Delmonico .50 1.25
13 Aaron Judge 2.00 5.00
14 Jack Flaherty .75 2.00
15 Jose Altuve .60 1.50
16 Cody Bellinger 1.50 4.00
17 Noah Syndergaard .60 1.50
18 Andrew Benintendi .75 2.00
19 Clint Frazier 1.00 2.50
20 Rafael Devers 1.50 4.00
21 Garrett Cooper .50 1.25
22 Javier Baez 1.00 2.50
23 Giancarlo Stanton .75 2.00
24 Amed Rosario .60 1.50
25 Luis Severino .60 1.50
26 Ozzie Albies 1.50 4.00
27 Victor Robles 1.25 3.00
28 Trey Mancini .60 1.50
29 Ian Happ .60 1.50
30 Paul Goldschmidt .75 2.00
31 Harrison Bader .75 2.00
32 Zack Granite .50 1.25
33 Walker Buehler 2.50 6.00
34 Paul DeJong .75 2.00
35 Rhys Hoskins 2.00 5.00
36 Dominic Smith .50 1.25
37 Dustin Fowler .50 1.25
38 Miguel Andujar 2.00 5.00
39 Hank Aaron 1.50 4.00
40 Bryce Harper 1.25 3.00
41 J.P. Crawford .50 1.25
42 Joey Votto .75 2.00
43 Ryne Sandberg 1.50 4.00
44 Ryan McMahon .60 1.50
45 Andrew Stevenson .50 1.25
46 Alex Verdugo .75 2.00
47 Francisco Mejia .60 1.50
48 Wade Boggs .60 1.50
49 Max Fried 2.00 5.00
50 Parker Bridwell .50 1.25
51 Shohei Ohtani 3.00 8.00
52 Kyle Schwarber .75 2.00
53 Sandy Alcantara .50 1.25
54 Mookie Betts 1.25 3.00
55 Charlie Blackmon .75 2.00
56 Ozzie Smith 1.00 2.50
57 Tyler Mahle .60 1.50
58 Will Clark .60 1.50
59 Matt Olson .50 1.25
60 Lucas Sims .50 1.25
61 Nolan Ryan 2.50 6.00
62 Wil Myers .50 1.25
63 Gary Sanchez .75 2.00
64 Yu Darvish .75 2.00
65 Jose Ramirez .60 1.50
66 Rickey Henderson .75 2.00
67 Yadier Molina .75 2.00
68 Anthony Banda .50 1.25
69 Nick Williams .60 1.50
70 Alex Bregman .75 2.00
71 Darryl Strawberry .50 1.25
72 Robinson Cano .60 1.50
73 George Springer .60 1.50
74 Adrian Beltre .75 2.00
75 Don Mattingly 1.50 4.00
76 Chris Sale .75 2.00
77 J.D. Davis .60 1.50
78 Travis Shaw .50 1.25
79 Roberto Clemente 2.00 5.00
80 Francisco Lindor .75 2.00
81 A.J. Minter .60 1.50
82 Whit Merrifield .75 2.00
83 Austin Hays .75 2.00
84 Chance Sisco .60 1.50
85 Josh Donaldson .60 1.50
86 Victor Caratini .60 1.50
87 Trea Turner .60 1.50
88 Troy Scribner .50 1.25
89 Yoan Moncada .75 2.00
90 Justin Upton .60 1.50
91 Michael Conforto .60 1.50
92 Brian Anderson .60 1.50
93 George Brett 1.50 4.00
94 Paul Blackburn .50 1.25
95 Max Scherzer .75 2.00
96 Buster Posey 1.00 2.50
97 Tyler Wade .60 1.50
98 George Springer .75 2.00
99 Byron Buxton .75 2.00
100 Chipper Jones .75 2.00
101 Ronald Acuna Jr. 10.00 25.00
102 Nolan Arenado 1.00 2.50
103 David Ortiz .75 2.00
104 Jacob deGrom .75 2.00
105 Eddie Murray .60 1.50
106 Mike Piazza .75 2.00
107 Ichiro 1.00 2.50
108 Andrew McCutchen .75 2.00
109 Austin Meadows .75 2.00
110 Barry Larkin .60 1.50
111 Fernando Romero .50 1.25
112 Joey Lucchesi .50 1.25
113 Gerrit Cole .75 2.00
114 J.D. Martinez .75 2.00
115 Mike Soroka 1.50 4.00
116 Marcell Ozuna .75 2.00
117 Justin Verlander .75 2.00
118 Jake Lamb .60 1.50
119 Chris Stratton .50 1.25
120 Mariano Rivera 1.00 2.50
121 Corey Kluber .60 1.50
122 Masahiro Tanaka .60 1.50
123 Isiah Kiner-Falefa .60 1.50
124 Todd Frazier .60 1.50
125 Giancarlo Stanton .75 2.00
126 Ernie Banks .75 2.00
127 Bo Jackson .75 2.00
128 Chris Archer .50 1.25
129 Ian Kinsler .60 1.50
130 Dustin Pedroia .75 2.00
131 Freddie Freeman 1.00 2.50
132 Frank Thomas .75 2.00
133 Tyler O'Neill .75 2.00
134 Juan Soto 10.00 25.00
135 Stephen Strasburg .75 2.00
136 Daniel Mengden .50 1.25
137 Randy Johnson .75 2.00
138 Lourdes Gurriel Jr. 1.00 2.50
139 Christian Yelich 1.00 2.50
140 Starling Marte .60 1.50
141 Matt Kemp .60 1.50
142 Jordan Hicks 1.00 2.50
143 Albert Pujols 1.00 2.50
144 Didi Gregorius .60 1.50
145 Shohei Ohtani 3.00 8.00
146 Jackie Robinson .75 2.00
147 Gleyber Torres 5.00 12.00
148 Miles Mikolas .60 1.50
149 Nick Kingham .50 1.25
150 Scott Kingery .75 2.00

2018 Topps '83 Topps Silver Pack Chrome Autographs

RANDOM INSERTS IN SILVER PACKS
PRINT RUNS B/WN 10-199 COPIES PER
NO PRICING ON QTY 10
*ORANGE/25: .6X TO 1.5X BASIC
4 Brandon Woodruff/199 8.00 20.00
12 Nicky Delmonico/199 6.00 15.00
14 Jack Flaherty/199 10.00 25.00
17 Noah Syndergaard/50 12.00 30.00
19 Clint Frazier/99 50.00 120.00
20 Rafael Devers/99 60.00 150.00
21 Garrett Cooper/199 12.00 30.00
22 Javier Baez/50 20.00 50.00
24 Amed Rosario/99 20.00 50.00
25 Luis Severino/30 20.00 50.00
26 Ozzie Albies/99 40.00 100.00
27 Victor Robles/99 40.00 100.00
28 Trey Mancini/99 20.00 50.00
29 Ian Happ/99 15.00 40.00
30 Paul Goldschmidt/30 15.00 40.00
31 Harrison Bader/199 10.00 25.00
32 Zack Granite/199 6.00 15.00
34 Paul DeJong/99 30.00 80.00
36 Dominic Smith/50 12.00 30.00
37 Dustin Fowler/199 6.00 15.00
38 Miguel Andujar/199 60.00 150.00
41 J.P. Crawford/199 6.00 15.00
44 Ryan McMahon/199 8.00 20.00
45 Andrew Stevenson/199 6.00 15.00
46 Alex Verdugo/199 15.00 40.00
49 Max Fried/199 25.00 60.00
50 Parker Bridwell/199 6.00 15.00
51 Shohei Ohtani/25 150.00 400.00
53 Sandy Alcantara/99 6.00 15.00
57 Tyler Mahle/149 8.00 20.00
58 Will Clark/99 30.00 80.00
59 Matt Olson/149 6.00 15.00
68 Anthony Banda/149 6.00 15.00
70 Alex Bregman/50
71 Darryl Strawberry/99 25.00 60.00
73 George Springer/50 20.00 50.00
75 Don Mattingly/25 60.00 150.00
77 J.D. Davis/99 8.00 20.00
78 Travis Shaw/149 6.00 15.00
81 A.J. Minter/99 8.00 20.00
82 Whit Merrifield/149 10.00 25.00
83 Austin Hays/99 10.00 25.00
84 Chance Sisco/149 8.00 20.00
88 Troy Scribner/99 6.00 15.00
90 Justin Upton/50 8.00 20.00
91 Michael Conforto/50 15.00 40.00
92 Brian Anderson/99 8.00 20.00
94 Paul Blackburn/99 6.00 15.00
97 Tyler Wade/99 8.00 20.00
101 Ronald Acuna Jr./99 150.00 400.00
103 David Ortiz
104 Jacob deGrom/30
107 Ichiro
108 Andrew McCutchen/30 20.00 50.00
109 Austin Meadows
110 Barry Larkin/30
111 Fernando Romero/99 6.00 15.00
115 Mike Soroka/99 20.00 50.00
116 Marcell Ozuna/99 10.00 25.00
118 Jake Lamb/99 8.00 20.00
119 Chris Stratton/99 6.00 15.00
120 Mariano Rivera
121 Corey Kluber/30 8.00 20.00
123 Isiah Kiner-Falefa/99 6.00 15.00
127 Bo Jackson
129 Ian Kinsler/99 8.00 20.00
131 Freddie Freeman/30
132 Frank Thomas
134 Juan Soto/99 150.00 400.00
136 Daniel Mengden/99 6.00 15.00
138 Lourdes Gurriel Jr./99 12.00 30.00
139 Christian Yelich/50
145 Shohei Ohtani
147 Gleyber Torres/99 150.00 400.00
148 Miles Mikolas/99 8.00 20.00
149 Nick Kingham/99 6.00 15.00
150 Scott Kingery/99 10.00 25.00

2018 Topps '83 Topps Silver Pack Chrome Autographs Orange Refractors

*ORANGE REF: .6X TO 1.5X BASIC
RANDOM INSERTS IN SILVER PACKS
STATED PRINT RUN 25 SER.#'d SETS

2018 Topps Aaron Judge Highlights

INSERTED IN WALMART PACKS
*BLUE: .5X TO 1.2X BASIC
*BLACK: .6X TO 1.5X BASIC
*GOLD/50: 5X TO 12X BASIC
AJ1 Aaron Judge 1.00 2.50
AJ2 Aaron Judge 1.00 2.50
AJ3 Aaron Judge 1.00 2.50
AJ4 Aaron Judge 1.00 2.50
AJ5 Aaron Judge 1.00 2.50
AJ6 Aaron Judge 1.00 2.50
AJ7 Aaron Judge 1.00 2.50
AJ8 Aaron Judge 1.00 2.50
AJ9 Aaron Judge 1.00 2.50
AJ10 Aaron Judge 1.00 2.50
AJ11 Aaron Judge 1.00 2.50
AJ12 Aaron Judge 1.00 2.50
AJ13 Aaron Judge 1.00 2.50
AJ14 Aaron Judge 1.00 2.50
AJ15 Aaron Judge 1.00 2.50
AJ16 Aaron Judge 1.00 2.50
AJ17 Aaron Judge 1.00 2.50
AJ18 Aaron Judge 1.00 2.50
AJ19 Aaron Judge 1.00 2.50
AJ20 Aaron Judge 1.00 2.50
AJ21 Aaron Judge 1.00 2.50
AJ22 Aaron Judge 1.00 2.50
AJ23 Aaron Judge 1.00 2.50
AJ24 Aaron Judge 1.00 2.50
AJ25 Aaron Judge 1.00 2.50
AJ26 Aaron Judge 1.00 2.50
AJ27 Aaron Judge 1.00 2.50
AJ28 Aaron Judge 1.00 2.50
AJ29 Aaron Judge 1.00 2.50
AJ30 Aaron Judge 1.00 2.50

2018 Topps All Star Medallions

STATED ODDS 1:1537 HOBBY
*BLACK/99: .5X TO 1.2X BASIC
*GOLD/50: .75X TO 2X BASIC
*RED/25: 1X TO 2.5X BASIC
ASTMAJ Aaron Judge 6.00 15.00
ASTMBH Bryce Harper 4.00 10.00
ASTMBP Buster Posey 3.00 8.00
ASTMCB Cody Bellinger 5.00 12.00
ASTMCBL Charlie Blackmon 2.50 6.00
ASTMCC Carlos Correa 2.50 6.00
ASTMCK Clayton Kershaw 5.00 12.00
ASTMCKI Craig Kimbrel 2.00 5.00
ASTMCKL Corey Kluber 2.00 5.00
ASTMCSA Chris Sale 2.50 6.00
ASTMCSE Corey Seager 2.50 6.00
ASTMDM Daniel Murphy 2.00 5.00
ASTMFL Francisco Lindor 2.50 6.00
ASTMGSA Gary Sanchez 2.50 6.00
ASTMGSP George Springer 2.00 5.00
ASTMGST Giancarlo Stanton 2.50 6.00
ASTMJA Jose Altuve 2.00 5.00
ASTMJV Joey Votto 2.50 6.00
ASTMLS Luis Severino 2.00 5.00
ASTMMB Mookie Betts 4.00 10.00
ASTMMC Michael Conforto 2.00 5.00
ASTMMSA Miguel Sano 2.00 5.00
ASTMMSC Max Scherzer 2.50 6.00
ASTMNA Nolan Arenado 3.00 8.00
ASTMPG Paul Goldschmidt 2.50 6.00
ASTMRC Robinson Cano 2.00 5.00
ASTMRZ Ryan Zimmerman 2.00 5.00
ASTMSP Salvador Perez 2.00 5.00
ASTMSS Stephen Strasburg 2.50 6.00
ASTMYM Yadier Molina 2.50 6.00

2018 Topps Cody Bellinger Highlights

INSERTED IN TARGET PACKS
*BLUE: .5X TO 1.2X BASIC
*BLACK: .6X TO 1.5X BASIC
*GOLD/50: 5X TO 12X BASIC
CB1 Cody Bellinger .75 2.00
CB2 Cody Bellinger .75 2.00
CB3 Cody Bellinger .75 2.00
CB4 Cody Bellinger .75 2.00
CB5 Cody Bellinger .75 2.00
CB6 Cody Bellinger .75 2.00
CB7 Cody Bellinger .75 2.00
CB8 Cody Bellinger .75 2.00
CB9 Cody Bellinger .75 2.00
CB10 Cody Bellinger .75 2.00
CB11 Cody Bellinger .75 2.00
CB12 Cody Bellinger .75 2.00
CB13 Cody Bellinger .75 2.00
CB14 Cody Bellinger .75 2.00
CB15 Cody Bellinger .75 2.00
CB16 Cody Bellinger .75 2.00
CB17 Cody Bellinger .75 2.00
CB18 Cody Bellinger .75 2.00
CB19 Cody Bellinger .75 2.00
CB20 Cody Bellinger .75 2.00
CB21 Cody Bellinger .75 2.00
CB22 Cody Bellinger .75 2.00
CB23 Cody Bellinger .75 2.00
CB24 Cody Bellinger .75 2.00
CB25 Cody Bellinger .75 2.00
CB26 Cody Bellinger .75 2.00
CB27 Cody Bellinger .75 2.00
CB28 Cody Bellinger .75 2.00
CB29 Cody Bellinger .75 2.00
CB30 Cody Bellinger .75 2.00

2018 Topps Derek Jeter Highlights

INSERTED IN TARGET PACKS
*BLUE: .5X TO 1.2X BASIC
*BLACK: .6X TO 1.5X BASIC
*GOLD/50: 5X TO 12X BASIC
DJH1 Derek Jeter 1.00 2.50
DJH2 Derek Jeter 1.00 2.50
DJH3 Derek Jeter 1.00 2.50
DJH4 Derek Jeter 1.00 2.50
DJH5 Derek Jeter 1.00 2.50
DJH6 Derek Jeter 1.00 2.50
DJH7 Derek Jeter 1.00 2.50
DJH8 Derek Jeter 1.00 2.50
DJH9 Derek Jeter 1.00 2.50
DJH10 Derek Jeter 1.00 2.50
DJH11 Derek Jeter 1.00 2.50
DJH12 Derek Jeter 1.00 2.50
DJH13 Derek Jeter 1.00 2.50
DJH14 Derek Jeter 1.00 2.50
DJH15 Derek Jeter 1.00 2.50
DJH16 Derek Jeter 1.00 2.50
DJH17 Derek Jeter 1.00 2.50
DJH18 Derek Jeter 1.00 2.50
DJH19 Derek Jeter 1.00 2.50
DJH20 Derek Jeter 1.00 2.50
DJH21 Derek Jeter 1.00 2.50
DJH22 Derek Jeter 1.00 2.50
DJH23 Derek Jeter 1.00 2.50
DJH24 Derek Jeter 1.00 2.50
DJH25 Derek Jeter 1.00 2.50
DJH26 Derek Jeter 1.00 2.50
DJH27 Derek Jeter 1.00 2.50
DJH28 Derek Jeter 1.00 2.50
DJH29 Derek Jeter 1.00 2.50
DJH30 Derek Jeter 1.00 2.50

2018 Topps Future Stars

INSERTED IN RETAIL RELIC BOXES
*BLUE: .5X TO 1.2X BASIC
*BLACK: .75X TO 2X BASIC
*GOLD/50: 4X TO 10X BASIC
FS1 Rhys Hoskins 1.00 2.50
FS2 Victor Robles .60 1.50
FS3 Amed Rosario .30 .75
FS4 Dominic Smith .25 .60
FS5 Shohei Ohtani 1.50 4.00
FS6 Clint Frazier .50 1.25
FS7 Ozzie Albies .75 2.00
FS8 Nick Williams .30 .75
FS9 Alex Verdugo .40 1.00
FS10 Willie Calhoun .30 .75
FS11 J.P. Crawford .25 .60
FS12 Francisco Mejia .30 .75
FS13 Austin Hays .40 1.00
FS14 Chance Sisco .30 .75
FS15 Walker Buehler 1.25 3.00
FS16 Ryan McMahon .30 .75
FS17 Cody Bellinger .75 2.00
FS18 Trey Mancini .30 .75
FS19 Andrew Benintendi .40 1.00
FS20 Manny Margot .25 .60
FS21 Paul DeJong .40 1.00
FS22 Hunter Renfroe .25 .60
FS23 Ian Happ .30 .75
FS24 Matt Olson .25 .60
FS25 Lucas Giolito .30 .75
FS26 Alex Bregman .40 1.00
FS27 Byron Buxton .30 .75
FS28 Dansby Swanson .40 1.00
FS29 Lewis Brinson .25 .60
FS30 Gary Sanchez .40 1.00
FS31 Aaron Judge 1.00 2.50
FS32 Michael Conforto .30 .75
FS33 Addison Russell .30 .75
FS34 Trea Turner .30 .75
FS35 Javier Baez .50 1.25
FS36 Nomar Mazara .25 .60
FS37 Kyle Schwarber .40 1.00
FS38 Aaron Nola .30 .75
FS39 Rougned Odor .30 .75
FS40 Trevor Story .40 1.00
FS41 Franklin Barreto .25 .60
FS42 Jack Flaherty .40 1.00
FS43 Harrison Bader
FS44 Luiz Gohara .25 .60
FS45 Tyler Mahle .30 .75
FS46 Francisco Lindor .40 1.00
FS47 Corey Seager .40 1.00
FS48 Carlos Correa .40 1.00
FS49 Julio Urias .40 1.00
FS50 Matt Chapman .40 1.00

2018 Topps Home Run Challenge

SER.1 ODDS 1:36 HOBBY
GINTER ODDS 1:24 HOBBY
HRCAD Adam Duvall 2.00 5.00
HRCAE Anthony Rendon 2.00 5.00
HRCAJ Aaron Judge 5.00 12.00
HRCAM Andrew McCutchen 2.00 5.00
HRCAO Adam Jones 1.50 4.00
HRCAR Anthony Rizzo 3.00 8.00
HRCBD Brian Dozier 1.50 4.00
HRCBH Bryce Harper 3.00 8.00
HRCCB Cody Bellinger 4.00 10.00
HRCCD Corey Dickerson 1.25 3.00
HRCCL Charlie Blackmon 2.00 5.00
HRCEE Edwin Encarnacion 2.00 5.00
HRCET Eric Thames 1.50 4.00
HRCFF Freddie Freeman 2.50 6.00
HRCGA Gary Sanchez 2.00 5.00
HRCGP George Springer 1.50 4.00
HRCGS Giancarlo Stanton 2.00 5.00
HRCJA Jose Abreu 2.00 5.00
HRCJB Jay Bruce 1.50 4.00
HRCJC Jonathan Schoop 1.25 3.00
HRCJG Joey Gallo 1.50 4.00
HRCJL Jake Lamb 1.50 4.00
HRCJM J.D. Martinez 2.00 5.00
HRCJS Justin Smoak 1.25 3.00
HRCJU Justin Upton 1.50 4.00
HRCJV Joey Votto 2.50 6.00
HRCKB Kris Bryant 2.50 6.00
HRCKD Khris Davis 2.00 5.00
HRCLM Logan Morrison 1.25 3.00
HRCMA Manny Machado 2.00 5.00
HRCMC Michael Conforto 1.50 4.00
HRCMD Matt Davidson 1.50 4.00
HRCMM Mike Moustakas 1.50 4.00
HRCMN Mike Napoli 1.25 3.00
HRCMO Marcell Ozuna 2.00 5.00
HRCMR Mark Reynolds 1.25 3.00
HRCMS Miguel Sano 1.50 4.00
HRCMT Mike Trout 10.00 25.00
HRCNA Nolan Arenado 2.50 6.00
HRCNC Nelson Cruz 2.00 5.00
HRCPG Paul Goldschmidt 2.00 5.00
HRCRO Rougned Odor 1.50 4.00
HRCRZ Ryan Zimmerman 1.50 4.00
HRCSC Scott Schebler 1.50 4.00
HRCSS Steven Souza Jr. 1.50 4.00
HRCTM Trey Mancini 1.50 4.00
HRCTS Travis Shaw 1.25 3.00
HRCWC Willson Contreras 2.00 5.00
HRCWM Wil Myers 1.25 3.00
HRCYA Yonder Alonso 1.25 3.00

2018 Topps Independence Day

*INDPNDNCE: 10X TO 25X BASIC
*INDPNDNCE RC: 6X TO 15X BASIC RC
SER.1 ODDS 1:456 HOBBY
RANDOMLY INSERTED IN SER.2
STATED PRINT RUN 76 SER.#'d SETS
259 Rhys Hoskins 30.00 80.00
529 Bryant/Schwarber 8.00 20.00
700 Shohei Ohtani 200.00 500.00

2018 Topps Instant Impact

STATED ODDS 1:8 HOBBY
*BLUE: 1.2X TO 3X BASIC
*BLACK/299: 1.5X TO 4X BASIC
*GOLD/50: 4X TO 10X BASIC
II1 Ted Williams .75 2.00
II2 Al Kaline .40 1.00
II3 Nomar Garciaparra .30 .75
II4 Ichiro .50 1.25
II5 Mike Trout 2.00 5.00
II6 Albert Pujols .50 1.25
II7 Shohei Ohtani 1.50 4.00
II8 Rafael Devers .75 2.00
II9 Cody Bellinger .75 2.00
II10 Andrew Benintendi .40 1.00
II11 Corey Seager .40 1.00
II12 Aaron Judge 1.00 2.50
II13 Mark McGwire .60 1.50
II14 Dwight Gooden
II15 Mike Piazza .40 1.00
II16 Cal Ripken Jr. 1.25 3.00
II17 Andruw Jones .25 .60
II18 Billy Williams .30 .75
II19 Bryce Harper .60 1.50
II20 Buster Posey .50 1.25
II21 Carlos Correa .40 1.00
II22 Chipper Jones .40 1.00
II23 Carlton Fisk .30 .75
II24 Darryl Strawberry .25 .60
II25 Derek Jeter 1.00 2.50
II26 Dustin Pedroia .40 1.00
II27 Gary Sanchez .40 1.00
II28 Jackie Robinson .40 1.00
II29 Yasiel Puig .40 1.00
II30 Johnny Bench .40 1.00
II31 Jose Abreu .40 1.00
II32 Jose Canseco .30 .75
II33 Justin Verlander .40 1.00
II34 Evan Longoria .40 1.00
II35 Willie McCovey .30 .75
II36 Jeff Bagwell .30 .75
II37 Joey Votto .40 1.00
II38 Masahiro Tanaka .30 .75
II39 Paul DeJong .40 1.00
II40 Trey Mancini .30 .75
II41 Ryan Braun .30 .75
II42 Stephen Strasburg .40 1.00
II43 Rod Carew .30 .75
II44 Tom Seaver .30 .75
II45 Trea Turner .30 .75
II46 Tim Raines .30 .75
II47 Amed Rosario .30 .75
II48 Rhys Hoskins 1.00 2.50
II49 Francisco Lindor .40 1.00
II50 Victor Robles .60 1.50

2018 Topps Instant Impact Autograph Relics

STATED ODDS 1:12,461 HOBBY
STATED PRINT RUN 25 SER.#'d SETS
EXCHANGE DEADLINE 5/31/2020
IARAO Andruw Jones
IARBP Buster Posey
IARCB Cody Bellinger
IARCJ Chipper Jones
IARCR Cal Ripken Jr.
IARDS Darryl Strawberry 40.00 100.00
IARGS Gary Sanchez
IARI Ichiro
IARJB Jeff Bagwell
IARJC Jose Canseco
IARMM Mark McGwire
IARMP Mike Piazza
IARMT Mike Trout
IARNG Nomar Garciaparra
IARPd Paul DeJong
IARRC Rod Carew
IARRD Rafael Devers 40.00 100.00
IARTM Trey Mancini
IARTR Tim Raines
IARVR Victor Robles

2018 Topps Instant Impact Relics

STATED ODDS 1:11,545 HOBBY
STATED PRINT RUN 100 SER.#'d SETS
*RED/25: .6X TO 1.5X BASIC
IIRAB Andrew Benintendi 5.00 12.00
IIRAO Andruw Jones 3.00 8.00
IIRAP Albert Pujols 12.00 30.00
IIRAR Amed Rosario 4.00 10.00
IIRBH Bryce Harper 8.00 20.00
IIRBP Buster Posey 12.00 30.00
IIRCB Cody Bellinger 8.00 20.00
IIRCC Carlos Correa 5.00 12.00
IIRCJ Chipper Jones 8.00 20.00
IIRCR Cal Ripken Jr. 15.00 40.00
IIRCS Corey Seager 8.00 20.00
IIRDJ Derek Jeter 20.00 50.00
IIRGS Gary Sanchez 5.00 12.00
IIRI Ichiro 6.00 15.00
IIRJB Jeff Bagwell 4.00 10.00
IIRJC Jose Canseco 12.00 30.00
IIRJV Joey Votto 5.00 12.00
IIRMK Masahiro Tanaka 4.00 10.00
IIRMM Mark McGwire 8.00 20.00
IIRMP Mike Piazza 8.00 20.00
IIRMT Mike Trout 25.00 60.00
IIRNG Nomar Garciaparra 6.00 15.00
IIRPd Paul DeJong 5.00 12.00
IIRRB Ryan Braun 4.00 10.00
IIRRD Rafael Devers 10.00 25.00
IIRSS Stephen Strasburg 5.00 12.00
IIRTR Tim Raines 4.00 10.00
IIRTT Trea Turner 4.00 10.00
IIRVR Victor Robles 8.00 20.00
IIRYP Yasiel Puig 6.00 15.00

2018 Topps Kris Bryant Highlights

INSERTED IN WALMART PACKS
*BLUE: .5X TO 1.2X BASIC
*BLACK: .6X TO 1.5X BASIC
*GOLD/50: 5X TO 12X BASIC
KB1 Kris Bryant .50 1.25
KB2 Kris Bryant .50 1.25
KB3 Kris Bryant .50 1.25
KB4 Kris Bryant .50 1.25
KB5 Kris Bryant .50 1.25
KB6 Kris Bryant .50 1.25
KB7 Kris Bryant .50 1.25
KB8 Kris Bryant .50 1.25
KB9 Kris Bryant .50 1.25
KB10 Kris Bryant .50 1.25
KB11 Kris Bryant .50 1.25
KB12 Kris Bryant .50 1.25
KB13 Kris Bryant .50 1.25
KB14 Kris Bryant .50 1.25
KB15 Kris Bryant .50 1.25
KB16 Kris Bryant .50 1.25
KB17 Kris Bryant .50 1.25
KB18 Kris Bryant .50 1.25
KB19 Kris Bryant .50 1.25
KB20 Kris Bryant .50 1.25
KB21 Kris Bryant .50 1.25
KB22 Kris Bryant .50 1.25
KB23 Kris Bryant .50 1.25
KB24 Kris Bryant .50 1.25
KB25 Kris Bryant .50 1.25
KB26 Kris Bryant .50 1.25
KB27 Kris Bryant .50 1.25
KB28 Kris Bryant .50 1.25
KB29 Kris Bryant .50 1.25
KB30 Kris Bryant .50 1.25

2018 Topps Legends in the Making

COMPLETE SET (30) 15.00 40.00
STATED ODDS 1:4 BLASTER
*BLUE: .6X TO 1.5X BASIC
*BLACK: 1.2X TO 3X BASIC
*GOLD/50: 2.5X TO 6X BASIC
LTMAB Andrew Benintendi .40 1.00
LTMAJ Aaron Judge 1.00 2.50
LTMAM Andrew McCutchen .40 1.00
LTMAR Anthony Rizzo .60 1.50
LTMBH Bryce Harper .60 1.50
LTMBP Buster Posey .50 1.25
LTMCB Cody Bellinger .75 2.00
LTMCC Carlos Correa .40 1.00
LTMCE Corey Seager .40 1.00
LTMCS Chris Sale .40 1.00
LTMFF Freddie Freeman .50 1.25
LTMFL Francisco Lindor .40 1.00
LTMGS Giancarlo Stanton .40 1.00
LTMJA Jose Altuve .30 .75
LTMJD Josh Donaldson .30 .75
LTMJV Joey Votto .40 1.00
LTMKB Kris Bryant .50 1.25
LTMMB Mookie Betts .60 1.50
LTMMC Miguel Cabrera .40 1.00
LTMMM Manny Machado .40 1.00
LTMMS Miguel Sano .30 .75
LTMMT Mike Trout 2.00 5.00
LTMNA Nolan Arenado .50 1.25
LTMNS Noah Syndergaard .30 .75
LTMPG Paul Goldschmidt .40 1.00
LTMRC Robinson Cano .30 .75
LTMWM Wil Myers .25 .60
LTMYD Yu Darvish .40 1.00
LTMYM Yadier Molina .40 1.00
LTMYO Yoan Moncada .40 1.00

2018 Topps Legends in the Making Series 2

INSERTED IN RETAIL PACKS
*BLUE: .5X TO 1.2X BASIC
*BLACK: .75X TO 2X BASIC
*GOLD/50: 4X TO 10X BASIC
LITM1 Rafael Devers .75 2.00
LITM2 Shohei Ohtani 1.50 4.00
LITM3 Byron Buxton .30 .75
LITM4 Ozzie Albies .75 2.00
LITM5 Kyle Schwarber .40 1.00
LITM6 Addison Russell .30 .75
LITM7 Javier Baez .50 1.25
LITM8 Jose Abreu .40 1.00
LITM9 Charlie Blackmon .40 1.00
LITM10 George Springer .30 .75
LITM11 Alex Bregman .40 1.00
LITM12 Marcell Ozuna .40 1.00
LITM13 Clayton Kershaw .75 2.00
LITM14 Christian Yelich .50 1.25
LITM15 Michael Conforto .30 .75
LITM16 Jacob deGrom .40 1.00
LITM17 Gary Sanchez .40 1.00
LITM18 Luis Severino .30 .75
LITM19 Giancarlo Stanton .40 1.00
LITM20 Rhys Hoskins 1.00 2.50
LITM21 Trea Turner .30 .75
LITM22 Victor Robles .60 1.50
LITM23 Amed Rosario .30 .75
LITM24 Justin Verlander .40 1.00
LITM25 Felix Hernandez .30 .75
LITM26 Corey Kluber .30 .75

LITM27 Adrian Beltre .40 1.00
LITM28 Max Scherzer .40 1.00
LITM29 Albert Pujols .50 1.25
LITM30 Stephen Strasburg .40 1.00

2018 Topps Longball Legends

STATED ODDS 1:8 HOBBY
*BLUE: 1.2X TO 3X BASIC
*BLACK/299: 1.5X TO 4X BASIC
*GOLD/50: 4X TO 10X BASIC
LL1 Aaron Judge 1.00 2.50
LL2 Giancarlo Stanton .40 1.00
LL3 Babe Ruth 1.00 2.50
LL4 Willson Contreras .40 1.00
LL5 Ted Williams .75 2.00
LL6 Darryl Strawberry .25 .60
LL7 Mark McGwire .60 1.50
LL8 Jose Canseco .30 .75
LL9 Mike Piazza .40 1.00
LL10 Cecil Fielder .25 .60
LL11 Jim Thome .30 .75
LL12 Willie Stargell .30 .75
LL13 Reggie Jackson .30 .75
LL14 Joey Gallo .30 .75
LL15 Gary Sanchez .40 1.00
LL16 Charlie Blackmon .40 1.00
LL17 Paul Goldschmidt .40 1.00
LL18 Mark McGwire .60 1.50
LL19 Josh Donaldson .30 .75
LL20 Kris Bryant .50 1.25
LL21 Mike Trout 2.00 5.00
LL22 Harmon Killebrew .40 1.00
LL23 Roberto Clemente 1.00 2.50
LL24 Alex Rodriguez .50 1.25
LL25 Joey Votto .40 1.00
LL26 Anthony Rizzo .60 1.50
LL27 Bryce Harper .60 1.50
LL28 Manny Machado .40 1.00
LL29 Nelson Cruz .40 1.00
LL30 Joc Pederson .30 .75
LL31 Nomar Mazara .25 .60
LL32 Jon Gray .25 .60
LL33 Kyle Schwarber .40 1.00
LL34 Noah Syndergaard .30 .75
LL35 Aaron Judge 1.00 2.50
LL36 Matt Olson .25 .60
LL37 Jake Lamb .30 .75
LL38 Giancarlo Stanton .40 1.00
LL39 Khris Davis .40 1.00
LL40 David Ortiz .40 1.00
LL41 Hank Aaron .75 2.00
LL42 Albert Pujols .50 1.25
LL43 Bo Jackson .40 1.00
LL44 Hank Aaron .75 2.00
LL45 Albert Pujols .50 1.25
LL46 Babe Ruth 1.00 2.50
LL47 Frank Thomas .40 1.00
LL48 Bryce Harper .60 1.50
LL49 Mike Trout 2.00 5.00
LL50 Nolan Arenado .50 1.25

2018 Topps Longball Legends Autograph Relics

STATED ODDS 1:11,091 HOBBY
STATED PRINT RUN 25 SER.#'d SETS
EXCHANGE DEADLINE 5/31/2020
LARAR Anthony Rizzo
LARBJ Bo Jackson
LARDO David Ortiz
LARDS Darryl Strawberry 40.00 100.00
LARFT Frank Thomas
LARGS Gary Sanchez
LARJC Jose Canseco
LARJG Joey Gallo
LARJL Jake Lamb
LARJP Joc Pederson 25.00 60.00
LARJR Jon Gray
LARJT Jim Thome
LARJV Joey Votto
LARKB Kris Bryant EXCH 100.00 250.00
LARKD Khris Davis
LARKS Kyle Schwarber
LARMA Manny Machado
LARMC Mark McGwire
LARMM Mark McGwire
LARMT Mike Trout
LARNS Noah Syndergaard
LARPG Paul Goldschmidt 15.00 40.00
LARRJ Reggie Jackson

2018 Topps Longball Legends Relics

STATED ODDS 1:1353 HOBBY
STATED PRINT RUN 100 SER.#'d SETS
*RED/25: .6X TO 1.5X BASIC
LLRAO Alex Rodriguez 10.00 25.00
LLRAR Anthony Rizzo 8.00 20.00
LLRBA Bryce Harper 8.00 20.00
LLRBH Bryce Harper 8.00 20.00
LLRBJ Bo Jackson 5.00 12.00
LLRCF Cecil Fielder 10.00 25.00
LLRDO David Ortiz 5.00 12.00
LLRFT Frank Thomas 8.00 20.00
LLRGA Gary Sanchez 5.00 12.00
LLRGS Giancarlo Stanton 5.00 12.00
LLRGT Giancarlo Stanton 5.00 12.00
LLRJC Jose Canseco 12.00 30.00
LLRJD Josh Donaldson 4.00 10.00
LLRJG Joey Gallo 4.00 10.00
LLRJP Joc Pederson 8.00 20.00
LLRJR Jon Gray 3.00 8.00
LLRJT Jim Thome 8.00 20.00
LLRJV Joey Votto 5.00 12.00
LLRKB Kris Bryant 10.00 25.00
LLRKS Kyle Schwarber 5.00 12.00
LLRMC Mark McGwire 8.00 20.00
LLRMG Mark McGwire 8.00 20.00
LLRMM Manny Machado 5.00 12.00
LLRMP Mike Piazza 8.00 20.00
LLRMR Mike Trout 25.00 60.00
LLRMT Mike Trout 25.00 60.00
LLRNA Nolan Arenado 6.00 15.00
LLRNS Noah Syndergaard 8.00 20.00
LLRPG Paul Goldschmidt 5.00 12.00
LLRWC Willson Contreras 5.00 12.00

2018 Topps Manufactured All Star Patches

STATED ODDS 1:1001 HOBBY
*BLACK/99: .5X TO 1.2X BASIC
*GOLD/50: .6X TO 1.5X BASIC
*RED/25: .75X TO 2X BASIC
ASPAK Al Kaline 8.00 20.00
ASPBR Brooks Robinson 6.00 15.00
ASPCF Carlton Fisk 8.00 20.00
ASPCJ Cal Ripken Jr. 10.00 25.00
ASPCR Cal Ripken Jr. 10.00 25.00
ASPDB Don Mattingly 10.00 25.00
ASPDG Dwight Gooden 8.00 20.00
ASPDK Duke Snider 8.00 20.00
ASPDM Don Mattingly 10.00 25.00
ASPDS Darryl Strawberry 8.00 20.00
ASPEM Eddie Mathews 6.00 15.00
ASPGR George Brett 12.00 30.00
ASPHA Hank Aaron 10.00 25.00
ASPHH Hank Aaron 10.00 25.00
ASPHK Harmon Killebrew 6.00 15.00
ASPJB Johnny Bench 6.00 15.00
ASPJR Jackie Robinson 8.00 20.00
ASPMM Mark McGwire 8.00 20.00
ASPOS Ozzie Smith 8.00 20.00
ASPRA Ryne Sandberg 6.00 15.00
ASPRC Rod Carew 5.00 12.00
ASPRH Rickey Henderson 8.00 20.00
ASPRJ Reggie Jackson 8.00 20.00
ASPRO Roberto Clemente 10.00 25.00
ASPRS Ryne Sandberg 6.00 15.00
ASPRY Robin Yount 6.00 15.00
ASPSK Sandy Koufax 8.00 20.00
ASPSP Satchel Paige 6.00 15.00
ASPTW Ted Williams 12.00 30.00
ASPWB Wade Boggs 6.00 15.00

2018 Topps Major League Material Autographs

SER.1 ODDS 1:5491 HOBBY
SER.2 ODDS 1:8873 HOBBY
PRINT RUNS B/WN 15-50 COPIES PER
NO PRICING ON QTY 15 OR LESS
SER.1 EXCH.DEADLINE 12/31/2019
SER.2 EXCH.DEADLINE 5/31/2020
*RED/25: .5X TO 1.2X BASIC
MLMAAI Aledmys Diaz/50
MLMAAI Anthony Rizzo S2
MLMAAN Aaron Nola/50 S2 12.00 30.00
MLMAAR Anthony Rizzo/25
MLMAAR Amed Rosario/30 S2 8.00 20.00
MLMAAW Alex Wood/50
MLMABD Brian Dozier S2
MLMABG Ben Gamel/50 8.00 20.00
MLMABH Bryce Harper S2
MLMABZ Bradley Zimmer/50 15.00 40.00
MLMACA Christian Arroyo/50
MLMACB Cody Bellinger EXCH
MLMACF Clint Frazier/50 20.00 50.00
MLMACL Charlie Blackmon/50 10.00 25.00
MLMACS Chris Sale
MLMACS Carlos Santana/30 S2 15.00 40.00
MLMACY Christian Yelich/50 S2 20.00 50.00
MLMADG Didi Gregorius/50
MLMAET Eric Thames/50
MLMAFB Franklin Barreto/50 12.00 30.00
MLMAGB Greg Bird/50 S2 8.00 20.00
MLMAGS George Springer/50
MLMAIH Ian Happ/50 20.00 50.00
MLMAJA Jose Altuve/25 20.00 50.00
MLMAJL Jake Lamb/30 S2 8.00 20.00
MLMAJO Justin Smoak/30 S2 8.00 20.00
MLMAJP Joc Pederson/30 S2 8.00 20.00
MLMAJR Jose Ramirez/30 S2 25.00 60.00
MLMAJS Jean Segura/50
MLMAJU Justin Upton S2
MLMAJV Joey Votto S2
MLMAJZ Javier Baez/50
MLMAKD Khris Davis/50 15.00 40.00
MLMAKE Kyle Seager/50
MLMAKS Kyle Schwarber S2
MLMALS Luis Severino/50
MLMAMT Mike Trout S2
MLMANS Noah Syndergaard/25
MLMAPD Paul DeJong/50 15.00 40.00
MLMARD Rafael Devers/50 20.00 50.00
MLMARG Randal Grichuk/50
MLMARH Ryon Healy/50 6.00 15.00
MLMASM Starling Marte/50 30.00 80.00
MLMATM Trey Mancini/50 20.00 50.00
MLMATP Tommy Pham/50 S2 15.00 40.00
MLMAWC Willson Contreras/50 S2 15.00 40.00
MLMAWM Whit Merrifield/50 S2

2018 Topps Major League Materials

SER.1 STATED ODDS 1:55 HOBBY
SER.2 STATED ODDS 1:68 HOBBY
*BLACK/99: .5X TO 1.2X BASIC
*GOLD/50: .6X TO 1.5X BASIC
*RED/25: .75X TO 2X BASIC
MLMAB Andrew Benintendi 5.00 12.00
MLMAB Andrew Benintendi S2 5.00 12.00
MLMAE Alex Bregman 4.00 10.00
MLMAG Adrian Gonzalez 3.00 8.00
MLMAI Anthony Rizzo S2 6.00 15.00
MLMAJ Adam Jones 3.00 8.00
MLMAJ Adam Jones S2 3.00 8.00
MLMAM Andrew McCutchen 4.00 10.00
MLMAN Aaron Nola S2 3.00 8.00
MLMAP Albert Pujols 5.00 12.00
MLMAP Albert Pujols S2 5.00 12.00
MLMAR Addison Russell 3.00 8.00
MLMAR Amed Rosario S2 3.00 8.00
MLMAU Addison Russell S2 3.00 8.00
MLMAZ Anthony Rizzo 6.00 15.00
MLMBC Brandon Crawford 3.00 8.00
MLMBH Bryce Harper 5.00 12.00
MLMBH Bryce Harper S2 5.00 12.00
MLMBP Buster Posey 5.00 12.00
MLMBP Buster Posey S2 5.00 12.00
MLMBZ Ben Zobrist 3.00 8.00
MLMCA Chris Sale 4.00 10.00
MLMCAR Chris Archer 2.50 6.00
MLMCB Cody Bellinger 5.00 12.00
MLMCB Charlie Blackmon S2 4.00 10.00
MLMCC Carlos Correa 4.00 10.00
MLMCC Carlos Correa S2 4.00 10.00
MLMCE Corey Seager S2 4.00 10.00
MLMCI Craig Kimbrel 3.00 8.00
MLMCK Clayton Kershaw 5.00 12.00
MLMCK Clayton Kershaw S2 5.00 12.00
MLMCL Charlie Blackmon 4.00 10.00
MLMCL Corey Kluber S2 3.00 8.00
MLMCM Carlos Martinez 3.00 8.00
MLMCS Corey Seager 4.00 10.00
MLMCS Carlos Santana S2 3.00 8.00
MLMCU Corey Kluber 3.00 8.00
MLMCY Christian Yelich S2 5.00 12.00
MLMDB Dellin Betances 3.00 8.00
MLMDE Dustin Pedroia 4.00 10.00
MLMDE Dustin Pedroia S2 4.00 10.00
MLMDF Dexter Fowler S2 3.00 8.00
MLMDG Didi Gregorius 3.00 8.00
MLMDG Dee Gordon S2 2.50 6.00
MLMDK Dallas Keuchel 3.00 8.00
MLMDM Daniel Murphy 3.00 8.00
MLMDP David Price 3.00 8.00
MLMDR Didi Gregorius S2 3.00 8.00
MLMDS Dansby Swanson 4.00 10.00
MLMDS Dominic Smith S2 2.50 6.00
MLMEE Edwin Encarnacion 4.00 10.00
MLMEH Eric Hosmer S2 3.00 8.00
MLMEL Evan Longoria 3.00 8.00
MLMEL Evan Longoria S2 3.00 8.00
MLMET Eric Thames 3.00 8.00
MLMFF Freddie Freeman 5.00 12.00
MLMFH Felix Hernandez S2 3.00 8.00
MLMFL Francisco Lindor S2 4.00 10.00
MLMGA Gary Sanchez 5.00 12.00
MLMGB Greg Bird S2 3.00 8.00
MLMGS George Springer 3.00 8.00
MLMGT Giancarlo Stanton 5.00 12.00
MLMHJR Hyun-Jin Ryu 3.00 8.00
MLMHP Hunter Pence S2 3.00 8.00
MLMHR Hanley Ramirez 3.00 8.00
MLMIH Ian Happ 3.00 8.00
MLMIK Ian Kinsler S2 3.00 8.00
MLMI Ichiro 5.00 12.00
MLMI Ichiro S2 5.00 12.00
MLMJA Jose Altuve 3.00 8.00
MLMJA Jose Abreu S2 4.00 10.00
MLMJB Javier Baez 5.00 12.00
MLMJD Josh Donaldson S2 3.00 8.00
MLMJE Josh Bell 3.00 8.00
MLMJE Jason Heyward S2 3.00 8.00
MLMJF Jack Flaherty S2 4.00 10.00
MLMJG Jon Gray 2.50 6.00
MLMJG Joey Gallo S2 3.00 8.00
MLMJH Jason Heyward 3.00 8.00
MLMJI Jose Bautista 3.00 8.00
MLMJJ Jacob deGrom S2 4.00 10.00
MLMJL Justin Verlander 4.00 10.00
MLMJL Jose Altuve S2 3.00 8.00
MLMJM J.D. Martinez 4.00 10.00
MLMJM Joe Mauer S2 3.00 8.00
MLMJO Joey Votto S2 4.00 10.00
MLMJR Jackie Bradley Jr. 4.00 10.00
MLMJT Jameson Taillon 3.00 8.00
MLMJU Justin Upton 3.00 8.00
MLMJU Justin Upton S2 3.00 8.00
MLMJV Joey Votto 4.00 10.00
MLMJV Justin Verlander S2 4.00 10.00
MLMJZ Javier Baez S2 5.00 12.00
MLMKB Kris Bryant 6.00 15.00
MLMKD Khris Davis S2 4.00 10.00
MLMKE Kyle Seager 2.50 6.00
MLMKJ Kenley Jansen S2 3.00 8.00
MLMKK Kevin Kiermaier 3.00 8.00
MLMKM Kenta Maeda 3.00 8.00
MLMKS Kyle Schwarber 4.00 10.00
MLMLE Luis Severino S2 3.00 8.00
MLMLG Lucas Giolito S2 3.00 8.00
MLMLS Luis Severino 3.00 8.00
MLMLW Luke Weaver S2 3.00 8.00
MLMMA Masahiro Tanaka 3.00 8.00
MLMMA Miguel Cabrera S2 4.00 10.00
MLMMB Mookie Betts 6.00 15.00
MLMMC Miguel Cabrera 4.00 10.00
MLMMD Marcus Stroman S2 3.00 8.00
MLMMF Michael Fulmer 2.50 6.00
MLMMH Mitch Haniger S2 3.00 8.00
MLMMK Matt Kemp S2 3.00 8.00
MLMMM Manny Machado 4.00 10.00
MLMMM Manny Machado S2 4.00 10.00
MLMMN Michael Conforto 3.00 8.00
MLMMN Michael Conforto S2 3.00 8.00
MLMMO Marcell Ozuna 4.00 10.00
MLMMO Marcell Ozuna S2 4.00 10.00
MLMMOL Matt Olson 2.50 6.00
MLMMR Masahiro Tanaka S2 3.00 8.00
MLMMS Marcus Stroman 3.00 8.00
MLMMS Miguel Sano S2 3.00 8.00
MLMMT Mike Trout 10.00 25.00
MLMMT Mike Trout S2 10.00 25.00
MLMMX Max Scherzer S2 4.00 10.00
MLMNA Nolan Arenado 5.00 12.00
MLMNA Nolan Arenado S2 5.00 12.00
MLMNC Nelson Cruz 4.00 10.00
MLMNC Nicholas Castellanos S2 4.00 10.00
MLMNR Nelson Cruz S2 4.00 10.00
MLMNS Noah Syndergaard 3.00 8.00
MLMNS Noah Syndergaard S2 3.00 8.00
MLMOA Orlando Arcia 2.50 6.00
MLMPD Paul DeJong S2 4.00 10.00
MLMPG Paul Goldschmidt S2 4.00 10.00
MLMRB Ryan Braun 3.00 8.00
MLMRC Robinson Cano 3.00 8.00
MLMRC Robinson Cano S2 3.00 8.00
MLMRD Rafael Devers S2 5.00 12.00
MLMRZ Ryan Zimmerman 3.00 8.00
MLMSA Starling Marte 3.00 8.00
MLMSC Starlin Castro 2.50 6.00
MLMSG Sonny Gray S2 3.00 8.00
MLMSP Salvador Perez 3.00 8.00
MLMTB Trevor Bauer S2 4.00 10.00
MLMTP Tommy Pham 2.50 6.00
MLMTT Trea Turner 3.00 8.00
MLMTT Trea Turner S2 3.00 8.00
MLMTU Troy Tulowitzki 4.00 10.00
MLMVM Victor Martinez 3.00 8.00
MLMWC Willson Contreras 4.00 10.00
MLMWC Willson Contreras S2 4.00 10.00
MLMWM Wil Myers 2.50 6.00
MLMXB Xander Bogaerts 4.00 10.00
MLMXB Xander Bogaerts S2 4.00 10.00
MLMYC Yoenis Cespedes 4.00 10.00
MLMYC Yoenis Cespedes S2 4.00 10.00
MLMYM Yadier Molina 4.00 10.00
MLMYM Yadier Molina S2 4.00 10.00
MLMYP Yasiel Puig 4.00 10.00

2018 Topps MLB Awards

COMPLETE SET (50) 15.00 40.00
STATED ODDS 1:8
*BLUE: .75X TO 2X BASIC
*BLACK/299: 1.5X TO 4X BASIC
*GOLD/50: 4X TO 10X BASIC
MLBA1 Jose Altuve .30 .75
MLBA2 Giancarlo Stanton .40 1.00
MLBA3 Craig Kimbrel .30 .75
MLBA4 Kenley Jansen .30 .75
MLBA5 Anthony Rizzo .60 1.50
MLBA6 Mike Moustakas .30 .75
MLBA7 Ryan Zimmerman .30 .75
MLBA8 Aaron Judge 1.00 2.50
MLBA9 Cody Bellinger .75 2.00
MLBA10 Corey Kluber .30 .75
MLBA11 Max Scherzer .40 1.00
MLBA12 Jose Altuve .30 .75
MLBA13 Giancarlo Stanton .40 1.00
MLBA14 Martin Maldonado .25 .60
MLBA15 Tucker Barnhart .25 .60
MLBA16 Eric Hosmer .30 .75
MLBA17 Paul Goldschmidt .40 1.00
MLBA18 Brian Dozier .30 .75
MLBA19 DJ LeMahieu .40 1.00
MLBA20 Andrelton Simmons .25 .60
MLBA21 Brandon Crawford .30 .75
MLBA22 Evan Longoria .30 .75
MLBA23 Nolan Arenado .50 1.25
MLBA24 Alex Gordon .30 .75
MLBA25 Marcell Ozuna .40 1.00
MLBA26 Byron Buxton .40 1.00
MLBA27 Ender Inciarte .25 .60
MLBA28 Mookie Betts .60 1.50
MLBA29 Jason Heyward .30 .75
MLBA30 Marcus Stroman .30 .75
MLBA31 Zack Greinke .30 .75
MLBA32 Buster Posey .50 1.25
MLBA33 Gary Sanchez .40 1.00
MLBA34 Eric Hosmer .30 .75
MLBA35 Paul Goldschmidt .40 1.00
MLBA36 Daniel Murphy .30 .75
MLBA37 Jose Altuve .30 .75
MLBA38 Corey Seager .40 1.00
MLBA39 Francisco Lindor .40 1.00
MLBA40 George Springer .30 .75
MLBA41 Justin Upton .30 .75
MLBA42 Aaron Judge 1.00 2.50
MLBA43 Marcell Ozuna .40 1.00
MLBA44 Giancarlo Stanton .40 1.00
MLBA45 Charlie Blackmon .40 1.00
MLBA46 Nolan Arenado .50 1.25
MLBA47 Jose Ramirez .30 .75
MLBA48 Adam Wainwright .30 .75
MLBA49 Nelson Cruz .40 1.00
MLBA50 George Springer .30 .75

2018 Topps Opening Day Insert

COMPLETE SET (30) 15.00 40.00
STATED ODDS 1:2 BLASTER
*BLUE: .75X TO 2X BASIC
*BLACK: 1X TO 2.5X BASIC
*GOLD/50: 3X TO 8X BASIC
*RED/25: .6X TO 1.5X BASIC
OD1 Robinson Cano .30 .75
OD2 Adrian Beltre .40 1.00
OD3 Carlos Correa .40 1.00
OD4 Miguel Sano .30 .75
OD5 Cody Bellinger .75 2.00
OD6 Salvador Perez .30 .75
OD7 Wil Myers .25 .60
OD8 Mike Trout 2.00 5.00
OD9 Noah Syndergaard .30 .75
OD10 Yadier Molina .40 1.00
OD11 Giancarlo Stanton .40 1.00
OD12 Freddie Freeman .50 1.25
OD13 Buster Posey .50 1.25
OD14 Francisco Lindor .40 1.00
OD15 Andrew McCutchen .40 1.00
OD16 Miguel Cabrera .40 1.00
OD17 Kris Bryant .50 1.25
OD18 Josh Donaldson .30 .75
OD19 Nolan Arenado .50 1.25
OD20 Joey Votto .40 1.00
OD21 Evan Longoria .30 .75
OD22 Aaron Judge 1.00 2.50
OD23 Aaron Nola .30 .75
OD24 Khris Davis .40 1.00
OD25 Bryce Harper .60 1.50
OD26 Yoan Moncada .40 1.00
OD27 Andrew Benintendi .40 1.00
OD28 Eric Thames .30 .75
OD29 Manny Machado .40 1.00
OD30 Paul Goldschmidt .40 1.00

2018 Topps Players Weekend Patches

STATED ODDS 1:1 BLASTER
*BLUE/99: .5X TO 1.2X BASIC
*GOLD/50: .75X TO 2X BASIC
*RED/25: 1X TO 2.5X BASIC
PWPABL Adrian Beltre 2.00 5.00
PWPABN Andrew Benintendi 2.00 5.00
PWPAJO Adam Jones 1.50 4.00
PWPAJU Aaron Judge 5.00 12.00
PWPAM Andrew McCutchen 2.00 5.00
PWPAP Albert Pujols 2.50 6.00
PWPAR Amed Rosario 1.50 4.00
PWPARI Anthony Rizzo 3.00 8.00
PWPBB Byron Buxton 1.50 4.00
PWPBP Buster Posey 2.50 6.00
PWPCL Charlie Blackmon 2.00 5.00
PWPCSE Corey Seager 2.00 5.00
PWPDM Daniel Murphy 1.50 4.00
PWPEH Eric Hosmer 1.50 4.00
PWPEL Evan Longoria 1.50 4.00
PWPET Eric Thames 1.50 4.00
PWPFF Freddie Freeman 2.50 6.00
PWPFL Francisco Lindor 2.00 5.00
PWPGSA Gary Sanchez 2.00 5.00
PWPGSP George Springer 1.50 4.00
PWPGST Giancarlo Stanton 2.00 5.00
PWPI Ichiro 2.50 6.00
PWPJA Jose Altuve 1.50 4.00
PWPJB Jose Bautista 1.50 4.00
PWPJD Josh Donaldson 1.50 4.00
PWPJG Jacob deGrom 2.00 5.00
PWPJR Jose Abreu 2.00 5.00
PWPJVO Joey Votto 2.00 5.00
PWPJZ Javier Baez 2.50 6.00
PWPKB Kris Bryant 2.50 6.00
PWPKC Kyle Schwarber 2.00 5.00
PWPKD Khris Davis 2.00 5.00
PWPKS Kyle Seager 1.25 3.00
PWPMA Masahiro Tanaka 1.50 4.00
PWPMB Mookie Betts 3.00 8.00
PWPMCB Miguel Cabrera 2.00 5.00
PWPMK Matt Kemp 1.50 4.00
PWPMM Manny Machado 2.00 5.00
PWPMT Mike Trout 10.00 25.00
PWPNA Nolan Arenado 2.50 6.00
PWPNC Nelson Cruz 2.00 5.00
PWPPC Paul Goldschmidt 2.00 5.00
PWPRC Robinson Cano 1.50 4.00
PWPRD Rafael Devers 4.00 10.00
PWPRH Rhys Hoskins 6.00 15.00
PWPSP Salvador Perez 1.50 4.00
PWPWM Wil Myers 1.25 3.00
PWPYD Yu Darvish 2.00 5.00
PWPYML Yadier Molina 2.00 5.00
PWPYP Yasiel Puig 2.00 5.00

2018 Topps Postseason Performance Autograph Relics

STATED ODDS 1:12024 HOBBY
PRINT RUNS B/WN 35-50 COPIES PER
EXCHANGE DEADLINE 12/31/2019
*RED/25: X TO X BASIC
PSARAB Andrew Benintendi EXCH 75.00 200.00
PSARAR Anthony Rizzo
PSARCB Cody Bellinger EXCH 50.00 120.00
PSARCC Carlos Correa
PSARDG Didi Gregorius
PSARGB Greg Bird/40
PSARGS Gary Sanchez/50 60.00 150.00
PSARJA Jose Altuve/35
PSARJB Javier Baez/50 30.00 80.00
PSARJM J.D. Martinez
PSARJR Jay Bruce/50
PSARLS Luis Severino/50 15.00 40.00
PSARPG Paul Goldschmidt/50 20.00 50.00
PSARRD Rafael Devers/50 75.00 200.00
PSARWC Willson Contreras EXCH 20.00 50.00

2018 Topps Postseason Performance Autographs

STATED ODDS 1:10231 HOBBY
STATED PRINT RUN 50 SER.#'d SETS
EXCHANGE DEADLINE 12/31/2019
*RED/25: .6X TO 1.5X BASIC
PSPACB Cody Bellinger EXCH 50.00 120.00
PSPADG Didi Gregorius
PSPAGB Greg Bird 15.00 40.00
PSPAGS Gary Sanchez
PSPAJB Javier Baez 25.00 60.00
PSPAJL Jake Lamb 15.00 40.00
PSPAJR Jay Bruce 25.00 60.00
PSPAKB Kris Bryant
PSPAPG Paul Goldschmidt
PSPARD Rafael Devers 75.00 200.00

2018 Topps Postseason Performance Relics

STATED ODDS 1:2723 HOBBY
STATED PRINT RUN 100 SER.#'d SETS
*RED/25: .6X TO 1.5X BASIC
PSPAB Andrew Benintendi 12.00 30.00
PSPAC Aroldis Chapman 10.00 25.00
PSPAI Anthony Rizzo 12.00 30.00
PSPAR Addison Russell 6.00 15.00
PSPBH Bryce Harper 8.00 20.00
PSPCC Carlos Correa 8.00 20.00
PSPCK Clayton Kershaw 10.00 25.00
PSPCS Corey Seager 8.00 20.00
PSPDG Didi Gregorius
PSPDK Dallas Keuchel 10.00 25.00
PSPDM Daniel Murphy 6.00 15.00
PSPGS Gary Sanchez 10.00 25.00
PSPJA Jose Altuve 12.00 30.00
PSPJB Javier Baez 10.00 25.00
PSPJM J.D. Martinez
PSPJT Justin Turner 6.00 15.00
PSPJV Justin Verlander 8.00 20.00
PSPKB Kris Bryant 12.00 30.00
PSPLS Luis Severino
PSPMB Mookie Betts 12.00 30.00
PSPMT Masahiro Tanaka 6.00 15.00
PSPPG Paul Goldschmidt 6.00 15.00
PSPRD Rafael Devers 12.00 30.00
PSPTB Trevor Bauer 8.00 20.00
PSPWC Willson Contreras 8.00 20.00
PSPYD Yu Darvish 8.00 20.00
PSPYP Yasiel Puig 6.00 15.00

2018 Topps Salute

COMPLETE SET (100) 50.00 120.00
STATED ODDS 1:4 HOBBY
*BLUE: 1.2X TO 3X BASIC
*BLACK/299: 1.5X TO 4X BASIC
*GOLD/50: 4X TO 10X BASIC
TS1 Bryce Harper .60 1.50
TS2 Carlos Correa .40 1.00
TS3 Joey Votto .40 1.00
TS4 Corey Seager .40 1.00
TS5 Adam Jones .30 .75
TS6 Chris Sale .40 1.00
TS7 Jose Altuve .30 .75
TS8 Dexter Fowler .30 .75
TS9 George Springer .30 .75
TS10 Charlie Blackmon .40 1.00
TS11 Khris Davis .40 1.00
TS12 Trevor Story .40 1.00
TS13 Alex Wood .25 .60
TS14 Domingo Santana .30 .75
TS15 Anthony Rizzo .60 1.50
TS16 Paul Goldschmidt .40 1.00
TS17 Francisco Lindor .40 1.00
TS18 Javier Baez .50 1.25
TS19 Aaron Judge 1.00 2.50
TS20 Ryon Healy .25 .60
TS21 Trey Mancini .30 .75
TS22 Ben Gamel .30 .75
TS23 Mitch Haniger .30 .75
TS24 Matt Carpenter .40 1.00
TS25 Cody Bellinger .75 2.00
TS26 Cal Ripken Jr. 1.25 3.00
TS27 Don Mattingly .75 2.00
TS28 Frank Thomas .40 1.00
TS29 Barry Larkin .30 .75
TS30 John Smoltz .40 1.00
TS31 Brooks Robinson .30 .75
TS32 Craig Biggio .30 .75
TS33 Jim Palmer .30 .75
TS34 Roy Halladay .30 .75
TS35 Ivan Rodriguez .30 .75
TS36 Roberto Alomar .30 .75
TS37 Darryl Strawberry .25 .60
TS38 Johnny Damon .30 .75
TS39 Andres Galarraga .30 .75
TS40 Eric Davis .25 .60
TS41 George Brett .75 2.00
TS42 Willie McCovey .30 .75
TS43 Andre Dawson .30 .75
TS44 Tom Seaver .30 .75
TS45 Jose Canseco .30 .75
TS46 Nolan Arenado .50 1.25
TS47 Kris Bryant .50 1.25
TS48 Miguel Sano .30 .75
TS49 Eric Thames .30 .75
TS50 Kyle Seager .25 .60
TS51 Michael Fulmer .25 .60
TS52 Joe Panik .30 .75
TS53 Jean Segura .25 .60
TS54 Aledmys Diaz .30 .75
TS55 Kevin Kiermaier .30 .75
TS56 Keon Broxton .25 .60
TS57 Bradley Zimmer .25 .60
TS58 Christian Arroyo .25 .60
TS59 Mike Trout 2.00 5.00
TS60 Daniel Murphy .30 .75
TS61 Alex Bregman .40 1.00
TS62 Andrew Benintendi .40 1.00
TS63 Luis Severino .30 .75
TS64 Didi Gregorius .30 .75
TS65 Dellin Betances .30 .75
TS66 Hunter Renfroe .25 .60
TS67 Jose Berrios .30 .75
TS68 Ken Giles .25 .60
TS69 Dansby Swanson .40 1.00
TS70 Ian Happ .30 .75
TS71 Rafael Devers .75 2.00
TS72 Amed Rosario .30 .75
TS73 Nick Williams .30 .75
TS74 Ozzie Albies .75 2.00
TS75 Clint Frazier .50 1.25
TS76 J.P. Crawford .25 .60
TS77 Dominic Smith .25 .60
TS78 Rhys Hoskins 1.00 2.50
TS79 Ryan McMahon .30 .75
TS80 Alex Verdugo .40 1.00
TS81 Willie Calhoun .30 .75
TS82 Victor Robles .60 1.50
TS83 Walker Buehler 1.25 3.00
TS84 Luiz Gohara .25 .60
TS85 Francisco Mejia .30 .75
TS86 Jack Flaherty .40 1.00
TS87 Tyler Mahle .30 .75
TS88 J.D. Davis .30 .75
TS89 Lucas Sims .25 .60
TS90 Max Fried 1.00 2.50
TS91 Brandon Woodruff .30 .75
TS92 Nicky Delmonico .25 .60
TS93 Harrison Bader .40 1.00
TS94 Miguel Andujar 1.00 2.50
TS95 Parker Bridwell .25 .60
TS96 Zack Granite .25 .60
TS97 Andrew Stevenson .25 .60
TS98 Austin Hays .40 1.00
TS99 Chance Sisco .30 .75
TS100 Sandy Alcantara .25 .60

2018 Topps Salute Autographs

SER.1 ODDS 1:1100 HOBBY
SER.2 ODDS 1:1215 HOBBY
UPD ODDS 1:699 HOBBY
SER.1 EXCH.DEADLINE 12/31/2019
SER.2 EXCH.DEADLINE 5/31/2020
UPD EXCH.DEADLINE 9/30/2020
*RED/25: .75X TO 2X BASIC
SAAA Aaron Altherr S2 15.00 40.00
SAAB Alex Bregman S2 15.00 40.00
SAAC Austin Barnes S2 3.00 8.00
SAAD Adam Duvall S2 4.00 10.00
SAADA Andre Dawson
SAADI Aledmys Diaz 3.00 8.00
SAAE Alex Bregman S2 15.00 40.00
SAAE Austin Meadows UPD 5.00 12.00
SAAG Andres Galarraga 3.00 8.00
SAAH Austin Hays 15.00 40.00
SAAH Austin Hays S2 10.00 25.00
SAAI Anthony Rizzo S2
SAAJ Alex Mejia S2 15.00 40.00
SAAJ Aaron Judge UPD
SAAJO Adam Jones
SAAM Andrew McCutchen UPD 20.00 50.00
SAAN Aaron Nola S2
SAAR Amed Rosario S2 8.00 20.00
SAAR Alex Rodriguez UPD
SAARI Anthony Rizzo
SAARO Amed Rosario 20.00 50.00
SAAS Andrew Stevenson 8.00 20.00
SAAS Anthony Santander S2 2.50 6.00
SAAV Alex Verdugo 5.00 12.00
SAAW Alex Wood 4.00 10.00
SABG Ben Gamel 3.00 8.00
SABG Ben Gamel S2 3.00 8.00
SABJ Bo Jackson UPD 40.00 100.00
SABL Barry Larkin
SABP Brett Phillips S2 2.50 6.00
SABRO Brooks Robinson
SABW Brandon Woodruff 6.00 15.00
SABZ Bradley Zimmer 10.00 25.00
SABZ Bradley Zimmer S2 8.00 20.00
SACAR Christian Arroyo 2.50 6.00
SACBE Cody Bellinger EXCH
SACBI Craig Biggio
SACBL Charlie Blackmon 8.00 20.00
SACC Carlos Correa
SACC Carlos Carrasco S2
SACF Clint Frazier 20.00 50.00
SACF Clint Frazier S2 15.00 40.00
SACJ Chipper Jones
SACJ Chipper Jones S2
SACK Corey Kluber S2
SACR Cal Ripken Jr. 100.00 250.00
SACR Clint Frazier S2 15.00 40.00
SACR Cal Ripken Jr. UPD 75.00 200.00
SACS Chance Sisco S2 6.00 15.00
SACSA Chris Sale S2 15.00 40.00
SACSI Chance Sisco 15.00 40.00
SACT Chris Taylor S2 8.00 20.00
SACV Christian Villanueva S2 10.00 25.00
SACV Christian Villanueva UPD 2.50 6.00
SADB Dellin Betances 6.00 15.00
SADB Don Mattingly S2
SADFO Dexter Fowler 20.00 50.00
SADG Didi Gregorius 15.00 40.00
SADG Dwight Gooden UPD 20.00 50.00
SADM Dillon Maples S2 4.00 10.00
SADMA Don Mattingly
SADO David Ortiz
SADR Didi Gregorius UPD 8.00 20.00
SADS Domingo Santana S2 3.00 8.00
SADSA Domingo Santana 6.00 15.00
SADSM Dominic Smith 2.50 6.00
SADST Darryl Strawberry 30.00 80.00
SADSW Dansby Swanson 25.00 60.00
SAED Eric Davis 10.00 25.00
SAEE Edwin Encarnacion S2
SAEH Eric Thames S2 6.00 15.00
SAER Eddie Rosario S2 4.00 10.00
SAET Eric Thames 3.00 8.00

SAET Eric Thames S2 6.00 15.00
SAFB Franklin Barreto S2
SAFI Francisco Lindor S2
SAFL Francisco Lindor S2
SAFL Francisco Lindor UPD 15.00 40.00
SAFM Francisco Mejia 15.00 40.00
SAFM Francisco Mejia S2 6.00 15.00
SAFN Francisco Lindor S2
SAFP Freddy Peralta UPD 2.50 6.00
SAFR Franmil Reyes UPD 6.00 15.00
SAFT Frank Thomas
SAGS George Springer UPD 8.00 20.00
SAGT Gleyber Torres UPD 40.00 100.00
SAHB Harrison Bader 4.00 10.00
SAHR Hunter Renfroe 6.00 15.00
SAHR Hunter Renfroe S2 2.50 6.00
SAIH Ian Happ 3.00 8.00
SAIK Isiah Kiner-Falefa UPD 4.00 10.00
SAIR Ivan Rodriguez
SAJB Jaime Barria UPD 5.00 12.00
SAJB Jose Abreu S2
SAJBR Jose Berrios 10.00 25.00
SAJBZ Javier Baez 20.00 50.00
SAJC J.P. Crawford S2 6.00 15.00
SAJC Johan Camargo UPD 10.00 25.00
SAJCA Jose Canseco 8.00 20.00
SAJCR J.P. Crawford 10.00 25.00
SAJD J.D. Davis 3.00 8.00
SAJDA Johnny Damon 12.00 30.00
SAJE Jean Segura S2 2.50 6.00
SAJF Jack Flaherty S2 4.00 10.00
SAJF Jack Flaherty UPD 4.00 10.00
SAJH Josh Hader S2 6.00 15.00
SAJI Josh Harrison S2 20.00 50.00
SAJL Jack Flaherty 4.00 10.00
SAJL Jose Altuve S2
SAJM Joe Morgan UPD
SAJO Josh Harrison S2 20.00 50.00
SAJPL Jim Palmer 25.00 60.00
SAJPN Joe Panik 3.00 8.00
SAJR Jose Ramirez S2 12.00 30.00
SAJS Juan Soto UPD 40.00 100.00
SAJSE Jean Segura 5.00 12.00
SAJSM John Smoltz
SAJT Jim Thome S2
SAJTH Jim Thome
SAJV Joey Votto
SAKB Keon Broxton S2 2.50 6.00
SAKBO Keon Broxton 2.50 6.00
SAKBR Kris Bryant EXCH
SAKD Khris Davis 8.00 20.00
SAKD Khris Davis S2 4.00 10.00
SAKF Kyle Farmer S2 5.00 12.00
SAKM Keury Mella S2 2.50 6.00
SAKP Kevin Pillar S2
SAKR Keon Broxton S2 2.50 6.00
SAKS Kyle Seager 6.00 15.00
SALG Lourdes Gurriel Jr. UPD 5.00 12.00
SALI Lucas Sims 5.00 12.00
SALS Luis Severino
SAMA Miguel Andujar 40.00 100.00
SAMA Manny Machado S2
SAMC Matt Carpenter
SAMC Mike Clevinger S2 3.00 8.00
SAMF Michael Fulmer 12.00 30.00
SAMH Mitch Haniger 3.00 8.00
SAMH Matt Chapman S2 4.00 10.00
SAMM Manny Machado S2
SAMM Miles Mikolas UPD 6.00 15.00
SAMMU Max Muncy UPD 10.00 25.00
SAMN Manny Margot S2
SAMR Max Fried 10.00 25.00
SAMR Mariano Rivera UPD
SAMT Mike Trout 250.00 500.00
SAMT Mike Trout UPD
SANC Nicholas Castellanos S2 10.00 25.00
SAND Nicky Delmonico 6.00 15.00
SANK Nick Kingham UPD 6.00 15.00
SAOA Ozzie Albies 15.00 40.00
SAOL Ozzie Albies S2 25.00 60.00
SAOS Ozzie Smith S2
SAOV Omar Vizquel 25.00 60.00
SAPB Parker Bridwell 2.50 6.00
SAPd Paul DeJong S2 4.00 10.00
SAPG Paul Goldschmidt 20.00 50.00
SAPM Pedro Martinez UPD
SARA Ronald Acuna Jr. UPD 100.00 250.00
SARA Roberto Alomar
SARB Ryan Braun S2
SARC Rod Carew UPD
SARD Rafael Devers S2
SARD Rafael Devers 30.00 80.00
SARH Rhys Hoskins S2 50.00 120.00
SARH Rhys Hoskins UPD 15.00 40.00
SARHE Ryon Healy 4.00 10.00
SARHO Rhys Hoskins 75.00 200.00
SARJ Ryder Jones S2 4.00 10.00
SARM Ryan McMahon 3.00 8.00
SARO Randy Johnson UPD
SASA Sandy Alcantara 2.50 6.00
SASA Sandy Alcantara S2 2.50 6.00
SASK Scott Kingery UPD 4.00 10.00
SASO Shohei Ohtani UPD 150.00 400.00
SASO Shohei Ohtani S2 125.00 300.00
SATB Tyler Beede UPD 2.50 6.00
SATH Torii Hunter UPD 8.00 20.00
SATH Tommy Pham S2 10.00 25.00
SATH Tyler Mahle 8.00 20.00
SATM Trey Mancini 15.00 40.00
SATM Trey Mancini S2 6.00 15.00
SATP Tommy Pham S2 10.00 25.00
SATR Tim Raines UPD 10.00 25.00
SATS Travis Shaw S2 6.00 15.00
SATW Travis Shaw S2 6.00 15.00
SAVA Victor Arano S2 4.00 10.00
SAVR Victor Robles S2 15.00 40.00
SAVR Victor Robles 30.00 80.00
SAWB Walker Buehler S2 12.00 30.00
SAWC Willie Calhoun 8.00 20.00
SAWM Whit Merrifield S2 4.00 10.00
SAYM Yoan Moncada S2
SAZG Zack Granite S2 3.00 8.00
SAZG Zack Granite 2.50 6.00

2018 Topps Salute Series 2

STATED ODDS 1:4 HOBBY
*BLUE: 1.2X TO 3X BASIC
*BLACK/299: 1.5X TO 4X BASIC
*GOLD/50: 4X TO 10X BASIC
S1 Bryce Harper .60 1.50
S2 Francisco Lindor .40 1.00
S3 Tommy Pham .25 .60
S4 Trey Mancini .30 .75
S5 Manny Machado .40 1.00
S6 Eric Thames .30 .75
S7 Nolan Arenado .50 1.25
S8 Clint Frazier .50 1.25
S9 Franklin Barreto .25 .60
S10 Khris Davis .40 1.00
S11 Miguel Cabrera .40 1.00
S12 Edwin Encarnacion .40 1.00
S13 Josh Harrison .25 .60
S14 Jose Altuve .30 .75
S15 Manny Machado .40 1.00
S16 Alex Bregman .40 1.00
S17 Jose Altuve .30 .75
S18 Travis Shaw .25 .60
S19 Orlando Arcia .25 .60
S20 Adam Duvall .40 1.00
S21 Mike Clevinger .30 .75
S22 Francisco Lindor .40 1.00
S23 Jose Ramirez .30 .75
S24 Edwin Encarnacion .40 1.00
S25 Chris Archer .25 .60
S26 Corey Kluber .30 .75
S27 Francisco Lindor .40 1.00
S28 Yoan Moncada .40 1.00
S29 Jose Abreu .40 1.00
S30 Nick Williams .30 .75
S31 Keon Broxton .25 .60
S32 Eric Thames .30 .75
S33 Aaron Nola .30 .75
S34 Travis Shaw .25 .60
S35 Ryan Braun .30 .75
S36 Domingo Santana .30 .75
S37 Carlos Carrasco .25 .60
S38 Nicholas Castellanos .40 1.00
S39 Nick Williams .30 .75
S40 Elvis Andrus .30 .75
S41 Robinson Cano .30 .75
S42 Josh Reddick .25 .60
S43 Lance McCullers .25 .60
S44 Ben Gamel .30 .75
S45 Alex Bregman .40 1.00
S46 Jean Segura .25 .60
S47 Hunter Renfroe .25 .60
S48 Wil Myers .25 .60
S49 Anthony Rizzo .60 1.50
S50 Addison Russell .30 .75
S51 Josh Bell .30 .75
S52 Josh Harrison .25 .60
S53 Andrew McCutchen .40 1.00
S54 Shohei Ohtani 5.00 12.00
S55 Dillon Maples .25 .60
S56 Rafael Devers .75 2.00
S57 Amed Rosario .30 .75
S58 Clint Frazier .50 1.25
S59 Willie Calhoun .30 .75
S60 Ozzie Albies .75 2.00
S61 Rhys Hoskins 1.00 2.50
S62 J.P. Crawford .25 .60
S63 Francisco Mejia .30 .75
S64 Jack Flaherty .40 1.00
S65 Austin Hays .40 1.00
S66 Sandy Alcantara .25 .60
S67 Christian Villanueva .25 .60
S68 Kyle Farmer .25 .60
S69 Tim Locastro .25 .60
S70 Bob Gibson .30 .75
S71 Chipper Jones .40 1.00
S72 Jim Thome .30 .75
S73 Roberto Clemente 1.00 2.50
S74 Ted Williams .75 2.00
S75 Ernie Banks .40 1.00
S76 Wade Boggs .30 .75
S77 Reggie Jackson .30 .75
S78 Derek Jeter 1.00 2.50
S79 Nolan Ryan 1.25 3.00
S80 Rickey Henderson .40 1.00
S81 Ozzie Smith .50 1.25
S82 Mariano Rivera .50 1.25
S83 Sandy Koufax .75 2.00
S84 Jackie Robinson .40 1.00
S85 Hank Aaron .75 2.00
S86 Aaron Judge 1.00 2.50
S87 Billy Hamilton .30 .75
S88 Jackie Bradley Jr. .40 1.00
S89 Manny Margot .25 .60
S90 Javier Baez .50 1.25
S91 Addison Russell .30 .75
S92 Byron Buxton .30 .75
S93 Kevin Kiermaier .30 .75
S94 Nolan Arenado .50 1.25
S95 Yasiel Puig .40 1.00
S96 Kevin Pillar .25 .60
S98 Chris Taylor .30 .75
S99 Tommy Pham .25 .60
S100 Justin Turner .30 .75

2018 Topps Spring Training Logo Patches

STATED ODDS 1:832 HOBBY
*BLUE/99: .5X TO 1.2X BASIC
*GOLD/50: .75X TO 2X BASIC
*RED/25: 1X TO 2.5X BASIC
STPAB Andrew Benintendi
STPABE Adrian Beltre 2.50 6.00
STPAJ Aaron Judge 6.00 15.00
STPAM Andrew McCutchen 2.50 6.00
STPAN Aaron Nola 2.00 5.00
STPBH Bryce Harper 4.00 10.00
STPBP Buster Posey 3.00 8.00
STPCB Cody Bellinger 5.00 12.00
STPCC Carlos Correa 2.50 6.00
STPEL Evan Longoria 2.00 5.00
STPET Eric Thames 2.00 5.00
STPFF Freddie Freeman 3.00 8.00
STPFL Francisco Lindor 2.50 6.00
STPGS Giancarlo Stanton 2.50 6.00
STPJD Josh Donaldson 2.00 5.00
STPJV Joey Votto 2.50 6.00
STPKB Kris Bryant 3.00 8.00
STPKD Khris Davis 2.50 6.00
STPMCB Miguel Cabrera 2.50 6.00
STPMM Manny Machado 2.50 6.00
STPMS Miguel Sano 2.00 5.00
STPMT Mike Trout 12.00 30.00
STPNA Nolan Arenado 3.00 8.00
STPNS Noah Syndergaard 2.00 5.00
STPPG Paul Goldschmidt 2.50 6.00
STPRC Robinson Cano 2.00 5.00
STPSP Salvador Perez 2.00 5.00
STPWM Wil Myers 1.50 4.00
STPYML Yadier Molina 2.50 6.00
STPYMN Yoan Moncada 2.50 6.00

2018 Topps Superstar Sensations

COMPLETE SET (50) 15.00 40.00
STATED ODDS 1:8
*BLUE: 1.2X TO 3X BASIC
*BLACK/299: 1.5X TO 4X BASIC
*GOLD/50: 3X TO 8X BASIC
SSS1 Mike Trout 2.00 5.00
SSS2 Jose Altuve .30 .75
SSS3 Josh Donaldson .30 .75
SSS4 Addison Russell .30 .75
SSS5 Carlos Correa .40 1.00
SSS6 Corey Seager .40 1.00
SSS7 Jose Bautista .30 .75
SSS8 Wil Myers .25 .60
SSS9 Manny Machado .40 1.00
SSS10 Trea Turner .30 .75
SSS11 Yu Darvish .40 1.00
SSS12 Clayton Kershaw .75 2.00
SSS13 Miguel Sano .30 .75
SSS14 Nelson Cruz .40 1.00
SSS15 Chris Sale .40 1.00
SSS16 Yoan Moncada .40 1.00
SSS17 Miguel Cabrera .40 1.00
SSS18 Felix Hernandez .30 .75
SSS19 Freddie Freeman .50 1.25
SSS20 Noah Syndergaard .30 .75
SSS21 Adam Jones .30 .75
SSS22 Gary Sanchez .40 1.00
SSS23 Nolan Arenado .50 1.25
SSS24 Evan Longoria .30 .75
SSS25 Max Scherzer .40 1.00
SSS26 Justin Verlander .40 1.00
SSS27 Andrew Benintendi .40 1.00
SSS28 Khris Davis .40 1.00
SSS29 Eric Hosmer .30 .75
SSS30 Aaron Judge 1.00 2.50
SSS31 Bryce Harper .60 1.50
SSS32 Yadier Molina .40 1.00
SSS33 Joey Votto .40 1.00
SSS34 Paul Goldschmidt .40 1.00
SSS35 Francisco Lindor .40 1.00
SSS36 Michael Conforto .30 .75
SSS37 Robinson Cano .30 .75
SSS38 Eric Thames .30 .75
SSS39 George Springer .30 .75
SSS40 Cody Bellinger .75 2.00
SSS41 Daniel Murphy .30 .75
SSS42 Kris Bryant .50 1.25
SSS43 Giancarlo Stanton .40 1.00
SSS44 Anthony Rizzo .60 1.50
SSS45 Ichiro .50 1.25
SSS46 Andrew McCutchen .40 1.00
SSS47 Mookie Betts .60 1.50
SSS48 Matt Kemp .30 .75
SSS49 Yoenis Cespedes .40 1.00
SSS50 Buster Posey .50 1.25

2018 Topps Team MVP Medallions

STATED ODDS 1:1001 HOBBY
*BLACK/99: .75X TO 2X BASIC
*GOLD/50: 1X TO 2.5X BASIC
*RED/25: 1.2X TO 3X BASIC
MVPAB Adrian Beltre 2.50 6.00
MVPAJ Aaron Judge 5.00 12.00
MVPBB Byron Buxton 1.50 4.00
MVPBH Bryce Harper 3.00 8.00
MVPBP Buster Posey 2.50 6.00
MVPCA Chris Archer 1.25 3.00
MVPCK Clayton Kershaw 4.00 10.00
MVPFF Freddie Freeman 2.50 6.00
MVPFL Francisco Lindor 2.00 5.00
MVPJA Jose Altuve 1.50 4.00
MVPJB Josh Bell 1.50 4.00
MVPJBO Justin Bour 1.25 3.00
MVPJD Josh Donaldson 1.50 4.00
MVPJR Jose Abreu 2.00 5.00
MVPJV Joey Votto 2.00 5.00
MVPKB Kris Bryant 2.50 6.00
MVPKD Khris Davis 2.00 5.00
MVPMB Mookie Betts 3.00 8.00
MVPMC Miguel Cabrera 2.00 5.00
MVPMM Manny Machado 2.00 5.00
MVPMT Mike Trout 10.00 25.00
MVPNA Nolan Arenado 2.50 6.00
MVPNC Nelson Cruz 2.00 5.00
MVPNS Noah Syndergaard 1.50 4.00
MVPPG Paul Goldschmidt 2.00 5.00
MVPRB Ryan Braun 1.50 4.00
MVPRH Rhys Hoskins 5.00 12.00
MVPSP Salvador Perez 1.50 4.00
MVPWM Wil Myers 1.25 3.00
MVPYM Yadier Molina 2.00 5.00

2018 Topps Top 10 Topps Now Inserts

COMPLETE SET (10) 10.00 25.00
STATED ODDS 1:18
TN1 Aaron Judge 1.00 2.50
TN2 Aaron Judge 1.00 2.50
TN3 Aaron Judge 1.00 2.50
TN4 Aaron Judge 1.00 2.50
TN5 Derek Jeter 1.00 2.50
TN6 Derek Jeter 1.00 2.50
TN7 Cody Bellinger .75 2.00
TN8 Aaron Judge 1.00 2.50
TN9 A.Judge/B.Ruth 1.00 2.50
TN10 Aaron Judge 1.00 2.50

2018 Topps World Series Champions Autograph Relics

STATED ODDS 1:18719 HOBBY
PRINT RUNS B/WN 15-50 COPIES PER
EXCHANGE DEADLINE 12/31/2019
WCARAR Alex Bregman/50 60.00 150.00
WCARCC Carlos Correa/50 50.00 120.00
WCAREG Evan Gattis/15 50.00 120.00
WCARGS George Springer/50 40.00 100.00
WCARJM Joe Musgrove/50 12.00 30.00
WCARYU Yuli Gurriel/50 15.00 40.00

2018 Topps World Series Champions Autograph Relics Red

*RED: .75X TO 2X BASIC
STATED ODDS 1:32945 HOBBY
STATED PRINT RUN 25 SER.#'d SETS
EXCHANGE DEADLINE 12/31/2019
WCAREG Evan Gattis 50.00 120.00

2018 Topps World Series Champions Autographs

STATED ODDS 1:19380 HOBBY
STATED PRINT RUN 50 SER.#'d SETS
EXCHANGE DEADLINE 12/31/2019
*RED/25: .75X TO 2X BASIC
WCAAR Alex Bregman
WCACC Carlos Correa 50.00 120.00
WCAGS George Springer
WCAJM Joe Musgrove 12.00 30.00
WCAKG Ken Giles
WCAYG Yuli Gurriel

2018 Topps World Series Champions Relics

STATED ODDS 1:5821 HOBBY
STATED PRINT RUN 100 SER.#'d SETS
*RED/25: .6X TO 1.5X BASIC
WCRAB Alex Bregman 15.00 40.00
WCRCC Carlos Correa 15.00 40.00
WCRDK Dallas Keuchel 12.00 30.00
WCREG Evan Gattis 10.00 25.00
WCRGS George Springer 12.00 30.00
WCRJA Jose Altuve 12.00 30.00
WCRJM Joe Musgrove 15.00 40.00
WCRJR Josh Reddick 12.00 30.00
WCRJV Justin Verlander 15.00 40.00
WCRKG Ken Giles 10.00 25.00
WCRMG Marwin Gonzalez 20.00 50.00
WCRYG Yuli Gurriel 12.00 30.00

2018 Topps Update

COMPLETE SET (300) 20.00 50.00
PRINTING PLATE ODDS 1:5519 HOBBY
PLATE PRINT RUN 1 SET PER COLOR
BLACK-CYAN-MAGENTA-YELLOW ISSUED
NO PLATE PRICING DUE TO SCARCITY
US1 Shohei Ohtani RC 1.50 4.00
US2 Joe Jimenez .15 .40
US3 Jordan Lyles .15 .40
US4 Jorge Alfaro .15 .40
US5 James Paxton HL .20 .50
US6 Jacob Nottingham RC .25 .60
US7 Giancarlo Stanton .25 .60
US8 Manny Machado .25 .60
US9 Nick Kingham RD .15 .40
US10 Ian Kinsler .20 .50
US11 Adam Engel .15 .40
US12 Miles Mikolas RC .30 .75
US13 P.J. Conlon RC .25 .60
Corey Oswalt RC
US14 Scott Kingery RD .25 .60
US15 Kyle Barraclough .15 .40
US16 Brad Boxberger .15 .40
US17 Jason Vargas .15 .40
US18 Michael Soroka RD .50 1.25
US19 Billy McKinney RC .30 .75
US20 Jeurys Familia .20 .50
US21 Kenley Jansen AS .20 .50
US22 Tyler Chatwood .15 .40
US23 J.D. Martinez AS .25 .60
US24 Pablo Sandoval .20 .50
US25 Willy Adames RD .20 .50
US26 Felipe Vazquez .20 .50
US27 Christian Yelich AS .30 .75
US28 Alex Blandino RC .25 .60
Brandon Dixon RC
US29 David Hess RC .30 .75
Pedro Araujo RC
US30 Jon Lester AS .20 .50
US31 Jose Ramirez AS .20 .50
US32 Cole Hamels .20 .50
US33 Reynaldo Lopez .20 .50
US34 Austin Meadows RC .40 1.00
US35 Dan Otero .15 .40
US36 Mike Gerber RC .25 .60
Grayson Greiner RC
US37 Javier Baez HRD .30 .75
US38 Jose Berrios AS .20 .50
US39 Freddy Peralta RC .25 .60
US40 Jacob Barnes RC .25 .60
US41 Pedro Strop .15 .40
US42 Teoscar Hernandez .25 .60
US43 Albies/Acuna 3.00 8.00
US44 Freddie Freeman AS .30 .75
US45 Bartolo Colon .15 .40
US46 Carlos Gomez .15 .40
US47 Jake Odorizzi .15 .40
US48 Nick Markakis AS .20 .50
US49 Eugenio Suarez AS .20 .50
US50 Andrew Cashner .15 .40
US51 Nathan Eovaldi .20 .50
US52 Michael Hermosillo RC .25 .60
Justin Anderson RC
US53 Seung Hwan Oh .20 .50
US54 Denard Span .15 .40
US55 Mike Moustakas .20 .50
US56 Trevor Oaks RC .25 .60
Eric Stout RC
US57 Ryder Jones RC .25 .60
US58 Jordan Hicks RC .50 1.25
US59 Kyle Schwarber HRD .25 .60
US60 Yadier Molina AS .25 .60
US61 Mike Tauchman RC 1.25 3.00
US62 Mark Reynolds .15 .40
US63 Corey Dickerson .15 .40
US64 Mookie Betts AS .40 1.00
US65 Yelich/Cain .30 .75
US66 J.A. Happ AS .20 .50
US67 Alex Bregman AS .25 .60
US68 Michael Soroka RC .75 2.00
US69 Martinez/Betts .40 1.00
US70 Brad Hand AS .15 .40
US71 Logan Morrison .15 .40
US72 Mike Foltynewicz AS .15 .40
US73 Marcell Ozuna .25 .60
US74 Joey Votto AS .25 .60
US75 J.A. Happ .20 .50
US76 Salvador Perez AS .20 .50
US77 Merandy Gonzalez RC .25 .60
Elieser Hernandez RC
US78 Luis Severino AS .20 .50
US79 Altuve/Judge .60 1.50
US80 Jonathan Villar .15 .40
US81 Sean Doolittle AS .15 .40
US82 Eric Lauer RC .30 .75
US83 Andrew McCutchen .25 .60
US84 Jack Reinheimer RC .30 .75
US85 Josh Hader AS .15 .40
US86 Randal Grichuk .15 .40
US87 Thunder and Lighting .25 .60
Joey Votto
Billy Hamilton
US88 Daniel Mengden RC .25 .60
US89 Justin Verlander HL .25 .60
US90 Ryan Yarbrough RC .40 1.00
US91 Zack Littell RC .25 .60
US92 Jeremy Hellickson .15 .40
US93 Daniel Winkler .15 .40
US94 Willson Contreras AS .25 .60
US95 Dustin Fowler RC .25 .60
US96 Tyler Clippard .15 .40
US97 Charlie Blackmon AS .25 .60
US98 Edwin Diaz AS .20 .50
US99 Gleyber Torres AS 1.50 4.00
US100 Ichiro .30 .75
US101 Chris Sale AS .25 .60
US102 Albert Pujols HL .30 .75
US103 Gerson Bautista .25 .60
Luis Guillorme RC
US104 Juan Soto RD 5.00 12.00
US105 Ronald Guzman RC .25 .60
US106 Jesmuel Valentin RC .25 .60
Mitch Walding RC
US107 Craig Kimbrel AS .20 .50
US108 Sean Rodriguez .15 .40
US109 Patrick Corbin AS .20 .50
US110 Lourdes Gurriel Jr. RC .50 1.25
US111 Jean Segura AS .15 .40
US112 J.T. Realmuto AS .25 .60
US113 Jesus Aguilar AS .15 .40
US114 Ildemaro Vargas RC .25 .60
US115 Eric Hosmer .20 .50
US116 Asdrubal Cabrera .20 .50
US117 Kyle Martin RC .25 .60
US118 Evan Longoria .20 .50
US119 Javier Baez AS .30 .75
US120 Joey Wendle RC .25 .60
US121 George Springer AS .20 .50
US122 Jesus Aguilar HRD .15 .40
US123 Wade LeBlanc .15 .40
US124 Ariel Jurado RC .25 .60
US125 Carlos Santana .20 .50
US126 Joe Musgrove .15 .40
US127 Tyler Skaggs .15 .40
US128 Kingery/Hoskins .60 1.50
US129 Tyson Ross .15 .40
US130 Austin Meadows RD .25 .60
US131 Zach Britton .15 .40
US132 Brandon Crawford AS .20 .50
US133 Devin Mesoraco .15 .40
US134 Brett Phillips .15 .40
US135 Sal Romano .15 .40
US136 Starlin Castro .15 .40
US137 Trevor Bauer AS .25 .60
US138 Junior Guerra .15 .40
US139 John Hicks .15 .40
US140 Clay Buchholz .15 .40
US141 Eduardo Escobar .15 .40
US142 Tyler Beede RC .25 .60
US143 Jeimer Candelario .20 .50
US144 Lou Trivino RC .30 .75
US145 Scooter Gennett AS .20 .50
US146 Blake Treinen AS .15 .40
US147 Matt Moore .20 .50
US148 Michael Brantley AS .20 .50
US149 Leonys Martin .15 .40
US150 Hosmer/Bellinger .50 1.25
US151 Matt Kemp .20 .50
US152 Steve Cishek .15 .40
US153 Ohtani/Ichiro 1.00 2.50
US154 Jaime Barria RC .30 .75
US155 Brad Ziegler .15 .40
US156 Paul Goldschmidt AS .25 .60
US157 Francisco Lindor AS .25 .60
US158 Upton/Ohtani/Trout 1.25 3.00
US159 Nolan Arenado AS .30 .75
US160 Ryan Madson .15 .40
US161 Seranthony Dominguez RC .25 .60
US162 Ozzie Albies AS .50 1.25
US163 Danny Valencia .20 .50
US164 Jefry Marte .15 .40
US165 Matt Kemp AS .20 .50
US166 Juan Lagares .15 .40
US167 Sean Manaea HL .15 .40
US168 Freddie Freeman HRD .30 .75
US169 Jose Castillo RC .25 .60
Walker Lockett RC
US170 Wilson Ramos .15 .40
US171 Adam Duvall .25 .60
US172 Aaron Judge AS .60 1.50
US173 Tyler Wade RC .30 .75
US174 Fernando Romero RC .25 .60
US175 Dylan Cozens RC .25 .60
US176 Mike Trout AS 1.25 3.00
US177 Jacob deGrom AS .25 .60
US178 Danny Farquhar .15 .40
US179 Hyun-Jin Ryu .20 .50
US180 Francisco Liriano .15 .40
US181 Gerson Bautista RC .25 .60
US182 Nelson Cruz AS .25 .60
US183 Mitch Moreland AS .15 .40
US184 Jurickson Profar .20 .50
US185 Corey Kluber AS .20 .50
US186 Lorenzo Cain AS .15 .40
US187 Jonathan Lucroy .20 .50
US188 Nick Gardewine RC .25 .60
US189 Shohei Ohtani HL 1.00 2.50
US190 Mike Montgomery .15 .40
US191 Gleyber Torres RD 1.50 4.00
US192 Daniel Palka RC .25 .60
US193 Christian Arroyo .15 .40
US194 Miguel Gomez RC .25 .60
US195 J.D. Martinez .25 .60
US196 Braxton Lee RC .25 .60
US197 Joe Jimenez AS .15 .40
US198 Shane Bieber RC 3.00 8.00
US199 Ramirez/LIndor .25 .60
US200 Gleyber Torres RC 6.00 15.00
US201 Nick Kingham RC .25 .60
US202 Bryce Harper HRD .40 1.00
US203 Roberto Osuna .15 .40
US204 Zack Cozart .15 .40
US205 Shin-Soo Choo AS .20 .50
US206 Neil Walker .20 .50
US207 Trevor Story AS .25 .60
US208 Brandon Mann RC .25 .60
US209 Bryce Harper AS .40 1.00
US210 Kirby Yates .20 .50
US211 Brandon Morrow .15 .40
US212 Alex Bregman HRD .25 .60
US213 Todd Frazier .20 .50
US214 Max Scherzer AS .25 .60
US215 Archie Bradley .15 .40
US216 Max Stassi .15 .40
US217 Justin Verlander AS .25 .60
US218 Tyler O'Neill RC .40 1.00
US219 Aroldis Chapman AS .25 .60
US220 Robinson Chirinos .15 .40
US221 Jose Bautista .20 .50
US222 Felipe Vazquez AS .20 .50
US223 Dominic Leone .15 .40
US224 Brandon McCarthy .15 .40
US225 Mike Fiers .15 .40
US226 Sean Doolittle .15 .40
US227 Ketel Marte .20 .50
US228 Colin Moran .15 .40
US229 Taylor Davis RC .25 .60
US230 Garrett Cooper RC .25 .60
US231 Jesse Biddle RC .30 .75
US232 Brad Hand .15 .40
US233 Tommy Pham .15 .40
US234 Jose Abreu AS .25 .60
US235 Trevor Cahill .15 .40
US236 Mitch Haniger AS .20 .50
US237 Carson Kelly .15 .40
US238 Matt Harvey .20 .50
US239 Mark Canha .15 .40
US240 Gerrit Cole AS .25 .60
US241 Chris Archer .15 .40
US242 Franmil Reyes RC .40 1.00
US243 Marco Gonzales .15 .40
US244 Daniel Robertson .15 .40
US245 Jose Pirela .15 .40
US246 Tony Kemp .15 .40
US247 Marcus Walden RC .30 .75
US248 Christian Yelich .30 .75
US249 Wander Suero RC .25 .60
US250 Ronald Acuna Jr. RC 30.00 80.00
US251 Aledmys Diaz .20 .50
US252 Ronald Acuna Jr. RD 3.00 8.00
US253 Manny Machado AS .25 .60
US254 Tommy Kahnle .15 .40
US255 Max Muncy HRD .20 .50
US256 Cameron Maybin .15 .40
US257 Chris Stratton RC .25 .60
US258 Lance Lynn .15 .40
US259 Stephen Piscotty .15 .40
US260 Lewis Brinson .15 .40
US261 Andrew Suarez RC .25 .60
US262 Sam Gaviglio .15 .40
US263 Brian Dozier .20 .50
US264 Jaime Garcia .15 .40
US265 Kevin Gausman .15 .40
US266 Austin Gomber RC .30 .75
US267 Alex Colome .15 .40
US268 Rhys Hoskins HRD .60 1.50
US269 Francisco Mejia RC .30 .75
US270 Dereck Rodriguez RC .30 .75
US271 Joey Lucchesi RC .25 .60
US272 Matt Duffy .15 .40
US273 David Bote RC .60 1.50
US274 Yairo Munoz RC .25 .60
US275 Jay Bruce .20 .50
US276 Hector Santiago .15 .40
US277 Ryan Tepera .15 .40
US278 Yan Gomes AS .25 .60
US279 Isiah Kiner-Falefa RC .25 .60
US280 Ross Stripling .15 .40
US281 Willy Adames RC .30 .75
US282 Brian Flynn .15 .40
US283 Daniel Gossett RC .25 .60
US284 Arodys Vizcaino .15 .40
US285 Shohei Ohtani RD 1.00 2.50
US286 Shane Carle RC .30 .75
US287 Jonathan Schoop .15 .40
US288 Jordan Hicks RD .30 .75
US289 Matt Adams .15 .40
US290 Anthony Banda RC .25 .60
US291 Brent Suter .15 .40
US292 Brandon Drury .15 .40
US293 Charlie Culberson .15 .40
US294 Shane Greene .15 .40
US295 Yonny Chirinos RC .25 .60
US296 Aaron Nola AS .20 .50
US297 Luis Valbuena .15 .40
US298 Rajai Davis .15 .40
US299 Jose Altuve AS .20 .50
US300 Juan Soto RC 12.00 30.00

2018 Topps Update Black

*BLACK: 10X TO 25X BASIC
*BLACK RC: 6X TO 15X BASIC RC
STATED ODDS 1:94 HOBBY
STATED PRINT RUN 67 SER. #'d SETS
US250 Ronald Acuna Jr. 2500.00 4000.00
US300 Juan Soto 600.00 1200.00

2018 Topps Update Black and White Negative

*BW NEGATIVE: 8X TO 20X BASIC
*BW NEGATIVE RC: 5X TO 12X BASIC
STATED ODDS 1:137 HOBBY
US250 Ronald Acuna Jr. 600.00 1200.00
US300 Juan Soto 300.00 600.00

2018 Topps Update Father's Day Blue

*BLUE: 10X TO 25X BASIC
*BLUE RC: 6X TO 15X BASIC RC
STATED ODDS 1:442 HOBBY
STATED PRINT RUN 50 SER. #'d SETS
US250 Ronald Acuna Jr. 1200.00 2500.00
US300 Juan Soto 600.00 1200.00

2018 Topps Update Gold

*GOLD: 2X TO 5X BASIC
*GOLD RC: 1.2X TO 3X BASIC RC
STATED ODDS 1:11 HOBBY
STATED PRINT RUN 2018 SER. #'d SETS
US99 Gleyber Torres AS 20.00 50.00
US250 Ronald Acuna Jr. 250.00 600.00
US300 Juan Soto 125.00 300.00

2018 Topps Update Independence Day

*INDPNDNCE: 10X TO 25X BASIC
*INDPNDNCE RC: 6X TO 15X BASIC RC
STATED ODDS 1:291 HOBBY
STATED PRINT RUN 76 SER. #'d SETS
US250 Ronald Acuna Jr. 2000.00 3000.00
US300 Juan Soto 600.00 1200.00

2018 Topps Update Memorial Day Camo

*CAMO: 12X TO 30X BASIC
*CAMO RC: 8X TO 20X BASIC RC
STATED ODDS 1:884 HOBBY
STATED PRINT RUN 25 SER. #'d SETS
US250 Ronald Acuna Jr. 2500.00 4000.00
US300 Juan Soto 1000.00 2000.00

2018 Topps Update Mother's Day Pink

INK: 10X TO 25X BASIC
INK RC: 6X TO 15X BASIC RC
ATED ODDS 1:442 HOBBY
ATED PRINT RUN 50 SER. #'d SETS
S250 Ronald Acuna Jr. 1200.00 2500.00
S300 Juan Soto 600.00 1200.00

2018 Topps Update Rainbow Foil

AINBOW: 2X TO 5X BASIC
AINBOW RC: 1.2X TO 3X BASIC RC
ATED ODDS 1:10 HOBBY
S99 Gleyber Torres AS 15.00 40.00
S250 Ronald Acuna Jr. 250.00 600.00
S300 Juan Soto 125.00 300.00

2018 Topps Update Vintage Stock

INTAGE: 8X TO 20X BASIC
INTAGE RC: 5X TO 12X BASIC RC
TATED ODDS 1:223 HOBBY
TATED PRINT RUN 99 SER. #'d SETS
S250 Ronald Acuna Jr. 600.00 1200.00
S300 Juan Soto 300.00 600.00

2018 Topps Update Photo Variations

P STATED ODDS 1:45 HOBBY
SP STATED ODDS 1:273 HOBBY
S1A Ohtani Red pllvr 10.00 25.00
S1B Ohtani Wht jrsy 40.00 100.00
S1C Ohtani Bttng 40.00 100.00
S1D Nolan Ryan 5.00 12.00
S7A Stanton Blue pllvr 1.50 4.00
S7B Babe Ruth 4.00 10.00
S9 Roberto Clemente 4.00 10.00
S10 Kinsler w/Glv 2.50 6.00
S12A Mikolas Tip cap 1.25 3.00
S12B Mikolas w/ball 20.00 50.00
S14A Kingery Red pllvr 1.50 4.00
S14B Kingery Pnstpe jrsy 15.00 40.00
S20 Don Mattingly 3.00 8.00
S21 Sandy Koufax 3.00 8.00
S23A Wade Boggs 1.25 3.00
S23B Pedro Martinez 1.25 3.00
S31 Chipper Jones 1.50 4.00
S34A Austin Meadows 1.50 4.00
Blue jersey
JS34B Meadows Fldng 12.00 30.00
S38 Torii Hunter 1.00 2.50
JS39 Prlta Frnt jrsy shwn 10.00 25.00
JS44 Hank Aaron 3.00 8.00
JS58A Hicks w/team 2.00 5.00
JS58B Hicks Leg out 15.00 40.00
S64 Ted Williams 3.00 8.00
JS68A Michael Soroka 3.00 8.00
In dugout
JS68B Soroka Hrzntl 12.00 30.00
JS73 Marcell Ozuna 1.50 4.00
Red pullover
JS76 George Brett 3.00 8.00
JS83A Andrew McCutchen 1.50 4.00
Black pullover
JS83B Andrew McCutchen 1.50 4.00
Yankees
JS88 Mengden Hrzntl 8.00 20.00
JS95A Dustin Fowler 1.00 2.50
In dugout
JS95B Fowler Tan bat 12.00 30.00
JS98 Randy Johnson 1.50 4.00
JS100 Ichiro 2.00 5.00
Blue and teal pullover
JS101 Roger Clemens 2.00 5.00
JS107 Rally Goose 25.00 60.00
US110A Gurriel Dugout 2.00 5.00
US110B Gurriel Fldng 12.00 30.00
US111 Bob Gibson 1.25 3.00
US118A Evan Longoria 1.25 3.00
In dugout, leaning on bat rack
US118B Bo Jackson 1.50 4.00
US121 Rickey Henderson 1.50 4.00
US151 Matt Kemp 1.25 3.00
Batting cage, no helmet
US157 Ernie Banks 1.50 4.00
US174A Fernando Romero 1.00 2.50
Looking up
US174B Romero Knee up 12.00 30.00
US175 Cozens Running 12.00 30.00
US177 Mike Piazza 1.50 4.00
US195 Martinez Blue pllvr 1.50 4.00
US197 Will Clark 1.25 3.00
US198 Bieber Ball over head 15.00 40.00
US200A Torres Blk pllvr 10.00 25.00
US200B Torres Gry jrsy 40.00 100.00
US200C Torres Thrwng 40.00 100.00
US200D Lou Gehrig 3.00 8.00
US201A Nick Kingham 1.00 2.50
Walking
US201B Kingham Yllw jrsy 10.00 25.00
US213 Todd Frazier 1.25 3.00
Blue pullover
US217 Trevor Hoffman 1.25 3.00
US218A Tyler O'Neill 1.50 4.00
In dugout
US218B O'Neill Bttng 12.00 30.00
US232 Josh Donaldson 1.25 3.00
US242 Reyes Bttng 12.00 30.00
US248 Yelich Pllvr 2.00 5.00
US250A Acuna Pllvr 150.00 400.00
US250B Acuna bttng 1000.00 2000.00
US250C Acuna Hldng glv 800.00 1500.00
US250D Derek Jeter 4.00 10.00
US253 Cal Ripken Jr. 4.00 10.00
US257 Stratton Blck jrsy 20.00 50.00
US259 Mark McGwire 2.50 6.00
US271 Joey Lucchesi 1.00 2.50
Brown jersey
US281 Adames Vrtcle 12.00 30.00
US300A Soto Dugout 60.00 150.00
US300B Soto Gtrde 400.00 800.00

2018 Topps Update '83 Topps

STATED ODDS 1:4 HOBBY
*BLUE: 1.2X TO 3X BASIC
*BLACK/299: 1.5X TO 4X BASIC
*GOLD/50: 3X TO 8X BASIC
831 Andrew McCutchen .40 1.00
832 Shohei Ohtani 1.50 4.00
833 Scott Kingery .40 1.00
834 Jordan Hicks .50 1.25
835 Joey Lucchesi .25 .60
836 Trevor Hoffman .30 .75
837 Torii Hunter .25 .60
838 Willy Adames .30 .75
839 Steven Souza Jr. .30 .75
8310 Marcell Ozuna .40 1.00
8311 Christian Yelich .50 1.25
8312 Juan Soto 5.00 12.00
8313 Ronald Acuna Jr. 5.00 12.00
8314 Austin Meadows .40 1.00
8315 Tyler O'Neill .40 1.00
8316 Gleyber Torres 2.50 6.00
8317 Lourdes Gurriel Jr. .50 1.25
8318 Mitch Haniger .30 .75
8319 Ian Kinsler .30 .75
8320 Tommy Pham .25 .60
8321 Todd Frazier .30 .75
8322 Matt Chapman .40 1.00
8323 J.D. Martinez .40 1.00
8324 Dee Gordon .25 .60
8325 Lorenzo Cain .25 .60
8326 Joey Gallo .30 .75
8327 Ichiro .50 1.25
8328 Giancarlo Stanton .40 1.00
8329 Patrick Corbin .30 .75
8330 Sean Manaea .25 .60
8331 Gerrit Cole .40 1.00
8332 Johnny Cueto .30 .75
8333 Evan Longoria .30 .75
8334 Sean Doolittle .25 .60
8335 Dylan Bundy .30 .75
8336 Miles Mikolas .30 .75
8337 Jack Flaherty .40 1.00
8338 Jose Bautista .30 .75
8339 Matt Kemp .30 .75
8340 Blake Snell .30 .75
8341 Hyun-Jin Ryu .30 .75
8342 Mike Trout 2.00 5.00
8343 Aaron Judge 1.00 2.50
8344 Kris Bryant .50 1.25
8345 Bryce Harper .60 1.50
8346 Rhys Hoskins 1.00 2.50
8347 Rafael Devers .75 2.00
8348 Michael Soroka .75 2.00
8349 Freddy Peralta .25 .60
8350 Fernando Romero .25 .60

2018 Topps Update All Star Stitches

STATED ODDS 1:59 HOBBY
*SILVER/50: .6X TO 1.5X BASIC
*RED/25: .75X TO 2X BASIC
ASTAB Alex Bregman 4.00 10.00
ASTAC Aroldis Chapman 4.00 10.00
ASTAJ Aaron Judge 10.00 25.00
ASTAN Aaron Nola 3.00 8.00
ASTBC Brandon Crawford 3.00 8.00
ASTBS Blake Snell 3.00 8.00
ASTBT Blake Treinen 2.50 6.00
ASTCB Charlie Blackmon 4.00 10.00
ASTCI Craig Kimbrel 3.00 8.00
ASTCK Corey Kluber 3.00 8.00
ASTCM Charlie Morton 4.00 10.00
ASTCS Chris Sale 4.00 10.00
ASTCY Christian Yelich 5.00 12.00
ASTED Edwin Diaz 3.00 8.00
ASTES Eugenio Suarez 3.00 8.00
ASTFF Freddie Freeman 5.00 12.00
ASTFL Francisco Lindor 4.00 10.00
ASTFV Felipe Vazquez 3.00 8.00
ASTGC Gerrit Cole 4.00 10.00
ASTGS George Springer 3.00 8.00
ASTGT Gleyber Torres 6.00 15.00
ASTJA Jose Abreu 4.00 10.00
ASTJB Javier Baez 5.00 12.00
ASTJD Jacob deGrom 4.00 10.00
ASTJE Jose Berrios 3.00 8.00
ASTJG Jesus Aguilar 2.50 6.00
ASTJH Josh Hader 2.50 6.00
ASTJI Jose Ramirez 3.00 8.00
ASTJL Jon Lester 3.00 8.00
ASTJLO Jed Lowrie 2.50 6.00
ASTJM J.D. Martinez 4.00 10.00
ASTJN Justin Verlander 4.00 10.00
ASTJP J.A. Happ 3.00 8.00
ASTJR J.T. Realmuto 4.00 10.00
ASTJS Jean Segura 2.50 6.00
ASTJT Jose Altuve 3.00 8.00
ASTJV Joey Votto 4.00 10.00
ASTKJ Kenley Jansen 3.00 8.00
ASTKS Kyle Schwarber 4.00 10.00
ASTLC Lorenzo Cain 2.50 6.00
ASTLS Luis Severino 3.00 8.00
ASTMA Manny Machado 4.00 10.00
ASTMB Mookie Betts 6.00 15.00
ASTMF Mike Foltynewicz 2.50 6.00
ASTMH Mitch Haniger 3.00 8.00
ASTMK Matt Kemp 3.00 8.00
ASTMM Max Muncy 3.00 8.00
ASTMO Mitch Moreland 2.50 6.00
ASTMR Michael Brantley 3.00 8.00
ASTMS Max Scherzer 4.00 10.00
ASTMT Mike Trout 10.00 25.00
ASTNA Nolan Arenado 5.00 12.00
ASTNC Nelson Cruz 4.00 10.00
ASTNM Nick Markakis 3.00 8.00
ASTOA Ozzie Albies 5.00 12.00
ASTPC Patrick Corbin 3.00 8.00
ASTPG Paul Goldschmidt 4.00 10.00
ASTRS Ross Stripling 2.50 6.00
ASTSC Shin-Soo Choo 3.00 8.00
ASTSD Sean Doolittle 2.50 6.00
ASTSG Scooter Gennett 3.00 8.00
ASTSP Salvador Perez 3.00 8.00
ASTTB Trevor Bauer 4.00 10.00
ASTTS Trevor Story 4.00 10.00
ASTWC Willson Contreras 4.00 10.00
ASTWR Wilson Ramos 2.50 6.00
ASTYG Yan Gomes 4.00 10.00
ASTYM Yadier Molina 4.00 10.00
ASTZG Zack Greinke 3.00 8.00

2018 Topps Update All Star Stitches Autographs

STATED ODDS 1:10,826 HOBBY
PRINT RUNS B/WN 10-25 COPIES PER
NO PRICING DUE TO SCARCITY
EXCHANGE DEADLINE 9/30/2020
SSAAB Alex Bregman EXCH 50.00 120.00
SSAAJ Aaron Judge
SSACK Corey Kluber 25.00 60.00
SSACS Chris Sale 12.00 30.00
SSAFF Freddie Freeman 25.00 60.00
SSAFL Francisco Lindor 50.00 120.00
SSAGS George Springer 15.00 40.00
SSAGT Gleyber Torres 40.00 100.00
SSAJA Jose Altuve 50.00 120.00
SSAJB Javier Baez EXCH 30.00 80.00
SSAJd Jacob deGrom 30.00 80.00
SSAJV Joey Votto
SSALS Luis Severino 20.00 50.00
SSAMH Mitch Haniger 25.00 60.00
SSAMM Manny Machado 25.00 60.00
SSAOA Ozzie Albies/25
SSAPG Paul Goldschmidt 12.00 30.00
SSAWC Willson Contreras/25 40.00 100.00
SSAYM Yadier Molina EXCH 40.00 100.00

2018 Topps Update All Star Stitches Dual Autographs

STATED ODDS 1:31,274 HOBBY
STATED PRINT RUN 25 SER.#'d SETS
EXHCANGE DEADLINE 9/30/2020
SSDAB Alluve/Bregman EXCH 60.00 150.00
SSDAS Altuve/Springer
SSDBS Story/Blackmon 20.00 50.00
SSDCB Baez/Contereas 50.00 120.00
SSDFA Freeman/Albies 60.00 150.00
SSDJT Torres/Judge
SSDLK Lindor/Kluber 60.00 150.00
SSDTJ Judge/Trout
SSDTS Severino/Torres

2018 Topps Update All Star Stitches Dual Relics

STATED ODDS 1:17,059 HOBBY
STATED PRINT RUN 25 SER.#'d SETS
EXHCANGE DEADLINE 9/30/2020
ASDAB Blackmon/Arenado 20.00 50.00
ASDAL Altuve/Bregman 25.00 60.00
ASDBS Betts/Sale 25.00 60.00
ASDCB Contreras/Baez 50.00 120.00
ASDCY Cain/Yelich 20.00 50.00
ASDFA Albies/Freeman 20.00 50.00
ASDJT Torres/Judge 30.00 80.00
ASDTJ Judge/Trout 60.00 150.00
ASDTS Severino/Torres 25.00 60.00
ASDVC Cole/Verlander 30.00 80.00

2018 Topps Update An International Affair

STATED ODDS 1:8 HOBBY
*BLUE: 1.2X TO 3X BASIC
*BLACK/299: 1.5X TO 4X BASIC
*GOLD/50: 3X TO 8X BASIC
IA1 Xander Bogaerts .40 1.00
IA2 Luiz Gohara .25 .60
IA3 Freddie Freeman .50 1.25
IA4 Joey Votto .40 1.00
IA5 Jose Quintana .25 .60
IA6 Yasiel Puig .40 1.00
IA7 Yoan Moncada .40 1.00
IA8 Yoenis Cespedes .40 1.00
IA9 Aroldis Chapman .40 1.00
IA10 Jose Abreu .40 1.00
IA11 Jonathan Schoop .25 .60
IA12 Ozzie Albies .75 2.00
IA13 Pedro Martinez .30 .75
IA14 Adrian Beltre .40 1.00
IA15 Albert Pujols .50 1.25
IA16 David Ortiz .40 1.00
IA17 Gary Sanchez .40 1.00
IA18 Manny Machado .40 1.00
IA19 Rafael Devers .75 2.00
IA20 Robinson Cano .30 .75
IA21 Victor Robles .60 1.50
IA22 Max Kepler .30 .75
IA23 Shohei Ohtani 2.00 5.00
IA24 Ichiro .50 1.25
IA25 Yu Darvish .40 1.00
IA26 Hideki Matsui .40 1.00
IA27 Masahiro Tanaka .30 .75
IA28 Julio Urias .40 1.00
IA29 Khris Davis .40 1.00
IA30 Didi Gregorius .30 .75
IA31 Mariano Rivera .50 1.25
IA32 Carlos Correa .40 1.00
IA33 Roberto Clemente 1.00 2.50
IA34 Francisco Lindor .40 1.00
IA35 Javier Baez .50 1.25
IA36 Yadier Molina .40 1.00
IA37 Gift Ngoepe .25 .60
IA38 Hyun-Jin Ryu .30 .75
IA39 Aaron Judge 1.00 2.50
IA40 Bryce Harper .60 1.50
IA41 Giancarlo Stanton .40 1.00
IA42 Kris Bryant .50 1.25
IA43 Mike Trout 2.00 5.00
IA44 Buster Posey .50 1.25
IA45 Mookie Betts .60 1.50
IA46 Jose Altuve .30 .75
IA47 Ronald Acuna Jr. 2.00 5.00
IA48 Miguel Cabrera .40 1.00
IA49 Willson Contreras .40 1.00
IA50 Gleyber Torres 2.50 6.00

2018 Topps Update Bryce Harper Highlights

RANDOM INSERTS IN PACKS
BH1 Bryce Harper 1.00 2.50
BH2 Bryce Harper 1.00 2.50
BH3 Bryce Harper 1.00 2.50
BH4 Bryce Harper 1.00 2.50
BH5 Bryce Harper 1.00 2.50
BH6 Bryce Harper 1.00 2.50
BH7 Bryce Harper 1.00 2.50
BH8 Bryce Harper 1.00 2.50
BH9 Bryce Harper 1.00 2.50
BH10 Bryce Harper 1.00 2.50
BH11 Bryce Harper 1.00 2.50
BH12 Bryce Harper 1.00 2.50
BH13 Bryce Harper 1.00 2.50
BH14 Bryce Harper 1.00 2.50
BH15 Bryce Harper 1.00 2.50
BH16 Bryce Harper 1.00 2.50
BH17 Bryce Harper 1.00 2.50
BH18 Bryce Harper 1.00 2.50
BH19 Bryce Harper 1.00 2.50
BH20 Bryce Harper 1.00 2.50

2018 Topps Update Don't Blink

STATED ODDS 1:8 HOBBY
*BLUE: 1.2X TO 3X BASIC
*BLACK/299: 1.5X TO 4X BASIC
*GOLD/50: 3X TO 8X BASIC
DB1 Rickey Henderson .40 1.00
DB2 Tim Raines .30 .75
DB3 Billy Hamilton .30 .75
DB4 Lou Brock .30 .75
DB5 Mike Trout 2.00 5.00
DB6 Byron Buxton .30 .75
DB7 Ichiro .50 1.25
DB8 Dee Gordon .25 .60
DB9 Trea Turner .30 .75
DB10 Jose Altuve .30 .75
DB11 Bo Jackson .40 1.00
DB12 Ozzie Smith .50 1.25
DB13 Honus Wagner .40 1.00
DB14 Lorenzo Cain .25 .60
DB15 Andrew McCutchen .40 1.00
DB16 Jackie Robinson .40 1.00
DB17 Kris Bryant .50 1.25
DB18 Wil Myers .25 .60
DB19 Ty Cobb .60 1.50
DB20 Amed Rosario .30 .75
DB21 Bradley Zimmer .25 .60
DB22 Whit Merrifield .40 1.00
DB23 Kevin Kiermaier .30 .75
DB24 Yoan Moncada .40 1.00
DB25 Mookie Betts .60 1.50

2018 Topps Update Hall of Famer Highlights

RANDOM INSERTS IN PACKS
HFH1 Chipper Jones .60 1.50
HFH2 Chipper Jones .60 1.50
HFH3 Chipper Jones .60 1.50
HFH4 Chipper Jones .60 1.50
HFH5 Chipper Jones .60 1.50
HFH6 Chipper Jones .60 1.50
HFH7 Chipper Jones .60 1.50
HFH8 Vladimir Guerrero .50 1.25
HFH9 Vladimir Guerrero .50 1.25
HFH10 Vladimir Guerrero .50 1.25
HFH11 Vladimir Guerrero .50 1.25
HFH12 Jim Thome .50 1.25
HFH13 Jim Thome .50 1.25
HFH14 Jim Thome .50 1.25
HFH15 Jim Thome .50 1.25
HFH16 Jim Thome .50 1.25
HFH17 Trevor Hoffman .50 1.25
HFH18 Trevor Hoffman .50 1.25
HFH19 Trevor Hoffman .50 1.25
HFH20 Trevor Hoffman .50 1.25

2018 Topps Update Jackie Robinson Commemorative Patches

RANDOM INSERTS IN PACKS
*GOLD/99: .6X TO 1.5X BASIC
*BLUE/50: 1X TO 2.5X BASIC
JRPAB Andrew Benintendi 1.25 3.00
JRPAE Adrian Beltre 1.25 3.00
JRPAJ Aaron Judge 3.00 8.00
JRPAM Andrew McCutchen 1.25 3.00
JRPAP Albert Pujols 1.50 4.00
JRPAR Anthony Rizzo 2.00 5.00
JRPBA Billy Hamilton 1.00 2.50
JRPBD Brian Dozier 1.00 2.50
JRPBH Bryce Harper 2.00 5.00
JRPCA Chris Sale 1.25 3.00
JRPCB Charlie Blackmon 1.25 3.00
JRPCC Carlos Correa 1.25 3.00
JRPCE Cody Bellinger 2.50 6.00
JRPCI Craig Kimbrel 1.00 2.50
JRPCK Clayton Kershaw 2.50 6.00
JRPCM Carlos Martinez 1.00 2.50
JRPCS Corey Seager 1.25 3.00
JRPDG Dee Gordon .75 2.00
JRPFF Freddie Freeman 1.50 4.00
JRPFH Felix Hernandez 1.00 2.50
JRPFL Francisco Lindor 1.25 3.00
JRPGA Gary Sanchez 1.25 3.00
JRPGO Gleyber Torres 8.00 20.00
JRPGS George Springer 1.00 2.50
JRPGT Giancarlo Stanton 1.25 3.00
JRPIK Ian Kinsler 1.00 2.50
JRPJA Jose Altuve 1.00 2.50
JRPJB Josh Bell 1.00 2.50
JRPJD Josh Donaldson 1.00 2.50
JRPJO Joey Votto 1.25 3.00
JRPJR Jose Abreu 1.25 3.00
JRPJU Justin Upton 1.00 2.50
JRPJV Justin Verlander 1.25 3.00
JRPJZ Javier Baez 1.50 4.00
JRPKB Kris Bryant 1.50 4.00
JRPKS Kyle Schwarber 1.25 3.00
JRPMG Miguel Cabrera 1.25 3.00
JRPMK Matt Kemp 1.00 2.50
JRPMM Manny Machado 1.25 3.00
JRPMT Mike Trout 6.00 15.00
JRPNS Noah Syndergaard 1.00 2.50
JRPOA Ozzie Albies 2.50 6.00
JRPPG Paul Goldschmidt 1.25 3.00
JRPRH Rhys Hoskins 3.00 8.00
JRPSP Salvador Perez 1.00 2.50
JRPTS Trevor Story 1.25 3.00
JRPTT Trea Turner 1.00 2.50
JRPYM Yadier Molina 1.25 3.00
JRPYO Yoan Moncada 1.25 3.00
JRPYP Yasiel Puig 1.25 3.00

2018 Topps Update Legends in the Making

INSERTED IN RETAIL PACKS
*BLUE: .5X TO 1.2X BASIC
*BLACK: .75X TO 2X BASIC
*GOLD/50: 3X TO 8X BASIC
LITM1 Ronald Acuna Jr. 5.00 12.00
LITM2 Gleyber Torres 2.50 6.00
LITM3 Scott Kingery .40 1.00
LITM4 Austin Meadows .40 1.00
LITM5 Didi Gregorius .30 .75
LITM6 Matt Chapman .40 1.00
LITM7 Starling Marte .30 .75
LITM8 Juan Soto 5.00 12.00
LITM9 Jameson Taillon .30 .75
LITM10 Gerrit Cole .40 1.00
LITM11 Francisco Mejia .30 .75
LITM12 Justin Upton .30 .75
LITM13 Billy Hamilton .30 .75
LITM14 Lance McCullers .25 .60
LITM15 Ian Happ .30 .75
LITM16 Joey Gallo .30 .75
LITM17 Khris Davis .40 1.00
LITM18 J.D. Martinez .40 1.00
LITM19 Giancarlo Stanton .40 1.00
LITM20 Andrew McCutchen .40 1.00
LITM21 Shohei Ohtani 1.50 4.00
LITM22 Walker Buehler 1.25 3.00
LITM23 Xander Bogaerts .40 1.00
LITM24 Clint Frazier .50 1.25
LITM25 Miguel Sano .30 .75
LITM26 Yu Darvish .40 1.00
LITM27 Paul DeJong .40 1.00
LITM28 Jose Berrios .30 .75
LITM29 Craig Kimbrel .30 .75
LITM30 Luke Weaver .30 .75

2018 Topps Update Postseason Manufactured Relics

STATED ODDS 1:270 HOBBY
*GOLD/99: .6X TO 1.5X BASIC
*BLUE/50: 1X TO 2.5X BASIC
PSLAB Adrian Beltre 1.25 3.00
PSLAJ Aaron Judge 3.00 8.00
PSLAO Alex Rodriguez 1.50 4.00
PSLAP Albert Pujols 1.50 4.00
PSLAR Anthony Rizzo 2.00 5.00
PSLBC Brandon Crawford 1.00 2.50
PSLBH Bryce Harper 2.00 5.00
PSLBP Buster Posey 1.50 4.00
PSLCC Carlos Correa 1.25 3.00
PSLCK Clayton Kershaw 2.50 6.00
PSLCL Corey Kluber 1.00 2.50
PSLDF David Freese .75 2.00
PSLDG Didi Gregorius 1.00 2.50
PSLDJ Derek Jeter 3.00 8.00
PSLEH Eric Hosmer 1.00 2.50
PSLFL Francisco Lindor 1.25 3.00
PSLGS George Springer 1.00 2.50
PSLHM Hideki Matsui 1.25 3.00
PSLJA Jose Altuve 1.00 2.50
PSLJB Jose Bautista 1.00 2.50
PSLJD Josh Donaldson 1.00 2.50
PSLJE Jacob deGrom 1.25 3.00
PSLJV Justin Verlander 1.25 3.00
PSLKB Kris Bryant 1.50 4.00
PSLMC Miguel Cabrera 1.25 3.00
PSLMR Mariano Rivera 1.50 4.00
PSLNS Noah Syndergaard 1.00 2.50
PSLPS Pablo Sandoval 1.00 2.50
PSLSP Salvador Perez 1.00 2.50
PSLYM Yadier Molina 1.25 3.00

2018 Topps Update Postseason Preeminence

INSERTED IN RETAIL PACKS
*BLUE: .5X TO 1.2X BASIC
*BLACK: .75X TO 2X BASIC
*GOLD/50: 3X TO 8X BASIC
PO1 Johnny Bench .40 1.00
PO2 Lou Gehrig .75 2.00
PO3 Roberto Alomar .30 .75
PO4 Derek Jeter 1.00 2.50
PO5 Ozzie Smith .50 1.25
PO6 George Brett .75 2.00
PO7 Brooks Robinson .30 .75
PO8 Buster Posey .50 1.25
PO9 Chipper Jones .40 1.00
PO10 Reggie Jackson .30 .75
PO11 Babe Ruth 1.00 2.50
PO12 Lou Brock .30 .75
PO13 David Ortiz .40 1.00
PO14 Hideki Matsui .40 1.00
PO15 Sandy Koufax .75 2.00
PO16 Bob Gibson .30 .75
PO17 John Smoltz .40 1.00
PO18 Mariano Rivera .50 1.25
PO19 Albert Pujols .50 1.25
PO20 Rickey Henderson .40 1.00
PO21 Justin Verlander .40 1.00
PO22 Jose Altuve .30 .75
PO23 George Springer .30 .75
PO24 Kris Bryant .50 1.25
PO25 Anthony Rizzo .60 1.50
PO26 Corey Kluber .30 .75
PO27 Jackie Robinson .40 1.00
PO28 Jon Lester .30 .75
PO29 Randy Johnson .40 1.00
PO30 Andy Pettitte .30 .75

2018 Topps Update Salute

2018 Topps Update Salute Platinum
*BLUE: 1.2X TO 3X BASIC
*BLACK/299: 1.5X TO 4X BASIC
*GOLD/50: 3X TO 8X BASIC
S1 Babe Ruth 1.00 2.50
S2 Ted Williams .75 2.00
S3 Jackie Robinson .40 1.00
S4 Reggie Jackson .30 .75
S5 Bo Jackson .40 1.00
S6 Pedro Martinez .30 .75
S7 Randy Johnson .40 1.00
S8 Cal Ripken Jr. 1.25 3.00
S9 Torii Hunter .25 .60
S10 Ichiro .50 1.25
S11 Willie McCovey .30 .75
S12 Rod Carew .30 .75
S13 Tim Raines .30 .75
S14 Satchel Paige .40 1.00
S15 Joe Morgan .30 .75
S16 Dwight Gooden .25 .60
S17 Alex Rodriguez .50 1.25
S18 Aaron Judge 1.00 2.50
S19 Mike Trout 2.00 5.00
S20 Mariano Rivera .50 1.25
S21 Ronald Acuna Jr. 5.00 12.00
S22 Gleyber Torres 2.50 6.00
S23 Scott Kingery .40 1.00
S24 Jordan Hicks .50 1.25
S25 Austin Meadows .40 1.00
S26 Tyler O'Neill .40 1.00
S27 Lourdes Gurriel Jr. .50 1.25
S28 Isiah Kiner-Falefa .25 .60
S29 Juan Soto 5.00 12.00
S30 Miles Mikolas .30 .75
S31 Jack Flaherty .40 1.00
S32 Dylan Cozens .25 .60
S33 Mike Soroka .75 2.00
S34 Shane Bieber 3.00 8.00
S35 Daniel Mengden .25 .60
S36 Freddy Peralta .25 .60
S37 Willy Adames .30 .75
S38 Sean Manaea .25 .60
S39 Shohei Ohtani 1.50 4.00
S40 Mookie Betts .60 1.50
S41 Didi Gregorius .30 .75
S42 Giancarlo Stanton .40 1.00
S43 Nick Kingham .25 .60
S44 Justin Verlander .40 1.00
S45 Willson Contreras .40 1.00
S46 George Springer .30 .75
S47 Francisco Lindor .40 1.00
S48 Edwin Encarnacion .40 1.00
S49 James Paxton .30 .75
S50 Andrew McCutchen .40 1.00

2018 Topps Update Storybook Endings

STATED ODDS 1:8 HOBBY
*BLUE: 1.2X TO 3X BASIC
*BLACK/299: 1.5X TO 4X BASIC
*GOLD/50: 3X TO 8X BASIC
SE1 Derek Jeter 1.00 2.50
SE2 David Ortiz .40 1.00
SE3 Sandy Koufax .75 2.00
SE4 Ted Williams .75 2.00
SE5 Jackie Robinson .40 1.00
SE6 Mariano Rivera .50 1.25
SE7 Cal Ripken Jr. 1.25 3.00
SE8 Chipper Jones .40 1.00
SE9 Will Clark .30 .75
SE10 Andy Pettitte .30 .75

2018 Topps Update Triple All Star Stitches

STATED ODDS 1:17,059 HOBBY
STATED PRINT RUN 25 SER.#'d SETS
ASTSABS Altuve/Bregman/Springer 40.00 100.00
ASTSASB Blackmon/Story/Arenado
ASTSAVC Verlander/Altuve/Cole 20.00 50.00
ASTSBMS Martinez/Sale/Betts 50.00 120.00
ASTSCBL Contreras/Baez/Lester
ASTSCYH Hader/Cain/Yelich 25.00 60.00
ASTSFAM Albies/Freeman/Markakis 40.00 100.00
ASTSHCD Cruz/Diaz/Haniger 40.00 100.00
ASTSJTS Judge/Torres/Severino 75.00 200.00
ASTSLRB Ramirez/Lindor/Bauer 20.00 50.00

2019 Topps

COMPLETE SET (702)
SER.1 PLATE ODDS 1:2369 HOBBY
SER.2 PLATE ODDS 1:3060 HOBBY
PLATE PRINT RUN 1 SET PER COLOR
BLACK-CYAN-MAGENTA-YELLOW ISSUED
NO PLATE PRICING DUE TO SCARCITY
1 Ronald Acuna Jr. 1.25 3.00
2 Tyler Anderson .15 .40
3 Eduardo Nunez WSH .15 .40
4 Dereck Rodriguez FS .15 .40
5 Chase Anderson .15 .40
6 Max Scherzer LL .25 .60
7 Gleyber Torres .50 1.25
8 Adam Jones .20 .50
9 Ben Zobrist .20 .50
10 Clayton Kershaw .50 1.25
11 Mike Zunino .15 .40
12 Rizzo/Perez .40 1.00
13 David Price .20 .50
14 Judge/Gregorius .60 1.50
15 J.P. Crawford .15 .40
16 Charlie Blackmon .25 .60
17 Caleb Joseph .15 .40
18 Blake Parker .15 .40
19 Jacob deGrom LL .25 .60
20 Jose Urena .15 .40
21 Jean Segura .25 .60
22 Adalberto Mondesi .30 .75
23 J.D. Martinez LL .25 .60
24 Blake Snell LL .20 .50
25 Chad Green .15 .40
26 Angel Stadium .15 .40
27 Mike Leake .15 .40
28 Betts/Benintendi .40 1.00
29 Eugenio Suarez .20 .50
30 Josh Hader .15 .40
31 Busch Stadium .15 .40
32 Carlos Correa .25 .60
33 Jacob Nix RC .30 .75
34 Josh Donaldson .20 .50
35 Joey Rickard .15 .40
36 Paul Blackburn .15 .40
37 Marcus Stroman .20 .50
38 Kolby Allard RC .40 1.00
39 Richard Urena .15 .40
40 Jon Lester .20 .50
41 Corey Seager .25 .60
42 Edwin Encarnacion .25 .60
43 Nick Burdi RC .25 .60
44 Jay Bruce .20 .50
45 Nick Pivetta .15 .40
46 Jose Abreu .25 .60
47 Yankee Stadium .15 .40
48 PNC Park .15 .40
49 Michael Kopech RC .50 1.25
50 Mookie Betts .40 1.00
51 Michael Brantley .20 .50
52 J.T. Realmuto .25 .60
53 Brandon Crawford .20 .50
54 Rick Porcello .20 .50
55 Yuli Gurriel .20 .50
56 Christian Villanueva .15 .40
57 Justin Verlander .25 .60
58 Carlos Martinez .20 .50
59 Zack Godley .15 .40
60 Kyle Tucker RC .50 1.25
61 Touki Toussaint RC .30 .75
62 Elvis Andrus .20 .50
63 Jake Odorizzi .15 .40
64 Ramon Laureano RC .50 1.25
65 Derek Dietrich .20 .50
66 Stephen Piscotty .15 .40
67 Danny Jansen RC .25 .60
68 Nick Ahmed .15 .40
69 Jorge Polanco .15 .40
70 Nolan Arenado LL .30 .75
71 SunTrust Park .15 .40
72 Chris Taylor .20 .50
73 Jon Gray .15 .40
74 Chad Bettis .15 .40
75 Safeco Field .15 .40
76 J.D. Martinez WSH .25 .60
77 J.D. Martinez .25 .60
78 Francisco Arcia RC .40 1.00
79 Miller Park .15 .40
80 Tim Anderson .25 .60
81 Wade Davis .15 .40
82 Lourdes Gurriel Jr. FS .20 .50
83 Lou Trivino .15 .40
84 Matt Carpenter .25 .60
85 Garrett Hampson RC .25 .60
86 David Bote .20 .50
87 Danny Duffy .15 .40
88 Jonathan Villar .15 .40
89 Corey Dickerson .15 .40
90 Javier Baez LL .30 .75
91 Hector Rondon .15 .40

92 Clayton Richard .15 .40
93 Matthew Boyd .15 .40
94 Corbin Burnes RC .40 1.00
95 Dennis Santana RC .25 .60
96 Trevor Williams .15 .40
97 Harrison Bader .20 .50
98 Chance Adams RC .25 .60
99 Aroldis Chapman .25 .60
100 Mike Trout 1.25 3.00
101 Michael Taylor .15 .40
102 Shin-Soo Choo .20 .50
103 Sean Manaea .15 .40
104 Joe Musgrove .15 .40
105 Jose Quintana .15 .40
106 Adam Ottavino .15 .40
107 Scooter Gennett .20 .50
108 Ian Kennedy .15 .40
109 Michael Conforto .20 .50
110 Trevor Bauer .25 .60
111 Reynaldo Lopez .20 .50
112 Joey Gallo .20 .50
113 Willie Calhoun FS .15 .40
114 Brandon Lowe RC .40 1.00
115 Tyler Glasnow .15 .40
116 Miguel Sano .20 .50
117 Enrique Hernandez .20 .50
118 Julio Teheran .20 .50
119 Willson Contreras .20 .50
120 Robert Gsellman .15 .40
121 Joey Wendle .15 .40
122 Zach Davies .15 .40
123 Jose Martinez .15 .40
124 Jason Kipnis .20 .50
125 Paul DeJong .25 .60
126 Oakland Coliseum .15 .40
127 Seranthony Dominguez .15 .40
128 Yoenis Cespedes .25 .60
129 Kenley Jansen .20 .50
130 Blake Snell .20 .50
131 Mark Trumbo .15 .40
132 Miguel Andujar .25 .60
133 Ryan Zimmerman .20 .50
134 Sean Reid-Foley RC .25 .60
135 Wade LeBlanc .15 .40
136 Brad Peacock .15 .40
137 Carlos Rodon .20 .50
138 Kyle Barraclough .15 .40
139 Mitch Haniger .20 .50
140 Daniel Poncedeleon RC .40 1.00
141 Ryon Healy .15 .40
142 Pedro Strop .15 .40
143 Yan Gomes .25 .60
144 Jake Arrieta .20 .50
145 Harper/ Gennett .40 1.00
146 Jesse Winker .15 .40
147 Blake Treinen .15 .40
148 Brandon Belt .20 .50
149 Khris Davis .25 .60
150 Aaron Judge .60 1.50
151 Pablo Lopez RC .25 .60
152 Teoscar Hernandez .25 .60
153 Hunter Strickland .15 .40
154 Johnny Cueto .20 .50
155 James McCann .20 .50
156 Luis Castillo .20 .50
157 Buster Posey .30 .75
158 Byron Buxton .20 .50
159 Minute Maid Park .15 .40
160 Fenway Park .15 .40
161 Eric Hosmer .20 .50
162 Yasiel Puig .25 .60
163 Aaron Nola .20 .50
164 Billy Hamilton .20 .50
165 Robbie Ray .15 .40
166 Matt Chapman .25 .60
167 Xander Bogaerts .25 .60
168 Salvador Perez .20 .50
169 Charlie Morton .25 .60
170 Manny Margot .15 .40
171 Kyle Hendricks .25 .60
172 Brandon Nimmo .20 .50
173 Michael Fulmer .15 .40
174 Jose Leclerc RC .25 .60
175 Tommy Pham .15 .40
176 Trea Turner .20 .50
177 Kohl Stewart RC .30 .75
178 Jose Altuve .20 .50
179 Jackie Bradley Jr. .25 .60
180 Justin Turner .20 .50
181 Antonio Senzatela .15 .40
182 Archie Bradley .15 .40
183 Freddie Freeman .30 .75
184 Ken Giles .15 .40
185 Matt Duffy .15 .40
186 Franmil Reyes FS .15 .40
187 Citizens Bank Park .15 .40
188 Matt Davidson .20 .50
189 Khris Davis LL .20 .50
190 Steven Duggar RC .30 .75
191 Dansby Swanson .25 .60
192 Luis Urias RC .40 1.00
193 Addison Reed .15 .40
194 Felipe Vazquez .15 .40
195 Brett Phillips .15 .40
196 Adam Engel .15 .40
197 Wrigley Field .15 .40
198 Gregory Polanco .20 .50
199 Mike Clevinger .20 .50
200 Jacob deGrom .25 .60
201 Marcus Semien .15 .40
202 Muncy/Bellinger .50 1.25
203A Will Smith UER .15 .40
Tony Watson pictured
203B Will Smith COR
204 Zack Cozart .15 .40
205 Todd Frazier .20 .50
206 Jaime Barria .15 .40
207 Richard Bleier .15 .40
208 Josh Bell .20 .50
209 Nicholas Castellanos .25 .60
210 Kris Bryant .30 .75
211 Jeimer Candelario .15 .40
212 Brian Anderson FS .15 .40
213 Juan Soto .75 2.00
214 Colin Moran .15 .40
215 Didi Gregorius .20 .50
216 Arenado/Baez .30 .75
217 Joe Jimenez .15 .40
218 Scott Schebler .20 .50
219 Martin Perez .20 .50
220 Alex Colome .15 .40
221 Luis Severino .20 .50
222 Zack Greinke .20 .50
223 Jose Ramirez .20 .50
224 Odubel Herrera .20 .50
225 Yadier Molina .25 .60
226 Albert Almora .15 .40
227 Adolis Garcia RC .25 .60
228 Rafael Devers .30 .75
229 Shane Greene .15 .40
230 Miguel Cabrera .25 .60
231 Joc Pederson .20 .50
232 Kyle Seager .15 .40
233 Dylan Bundy .20 .50
234 Austin Hedges .15 .40
235 Luke Weaver .15 .40
236 Sean Doolittle .15 .40
237 Seth Lugo .15 .40
238 Whit Merrifield .25 .60
239 Christian Yelich LL .30 .75
240 Trey Mancini .20 .50
241 James Paxton .20 .50
242 Anthony Rendon .25 .60
243 Jonathan Loaisiga RC .30 .75
244 Tyler Flowers .15 .40
245 Rogers Centre .15 .40
246 Ryan Borucki RC .25 .60
247 Sam Tuivailala .15 .40
248 Justin Bour .15 .40
249 Jordan Zimmermann .20 .50
250 Shohei Ohtani .30 .75
251 Niko Goodrum .40 1.00
252 Jakob Junis .15 .40
253 Starling Marte .20 .50
254 Dodger Stadium .25 .60
255 Andrelton Simmons .15 .40
256 Cody Allen .15 .40
257 Andrew Heaney .15 .40
258 Eddie Rosario .20 .50
259 Jonathan Schoop .15 .40
260 Aaron Hicks .20 .50
261 Jedd Gyorko .15 .40
262 Mitch Moreland .15 .40
263 Gray/Gregorius .20 .50
264 Avisail Garcia .20 .50
265 Joey Lucchesi FS .15 .40
266 Ohtani/Bregman .30 .75
267 Ross Stripling .15 .40
268 Blake Snell LL .20 .50
269 Francisco Lindor .25 .60
270 Brad Keller RC .25 .60
271 Shane Bieber FS .25 .60
272 Orlando Arcia .15 .40
273 Kole Calhoun .15 .40
274 Francisco Cervelli .15 .40
275 Steve Pearce WSH .25 .60
276 Nolan Arenado .30 .75
277 Mitch Garver .15 .40
278 Mike Minor .15 .40
279 Rhys Hoskins .30 .75
280 Miles Mikolas .25 .60
281 Jeff McNeil RC .60 1.50
282 Tim Beckham .20 .50
283 Rich Hill .15 .40
284 Joey Votto .25 .60
285 Sonny Gray .20 .50
286 Taijuan Walker .15 .40
287 Jesus Aguilar .20 .50
288 Joe Panik .20 .50
289 Matt Olson .15 .40
290 Steven Souza Jr. .20 .50
291 Enyel De Los Santos RC .25 .60
292 Dee Gordon .15 .40
293 Andrew Miller .20 .50
294 Correa/Altuve .25 .60
295 Pujols/Betts .40 1.00
296 Lewis Brinson .15 .40
297 Paul Goldschmidt .25 .60
298 Devon Travis .15 .40
299 Edwin Diaz .20 .50
300 Christian Yelich .30 .75
301 Tanner Roark .15 .40
302 Jose Berrios .20 .50
303 Ranger Suarez RC .25 .60
304 Michael Lorenzen .15 .40
305 Brad Boxberger .15 .40
306 Justus Sheffield RC .40 1.00
307 Jorge Soler .25 .60
308 Yolmer Sanchez .15 .40
309 Randal Grichuk .15 .40
310 Javier Baez .30 .75
311 Jake Bauers RC .40 1.00
312 Mookie Betts LL .40 1.00
313 Robinson Cano .20 .50
314 David Price WSH .20 .50
315 Duane Underwood Jr. RC .25 .60
316 Adam Eaton .25 .60
317 Kevin Gausman .15 .40
318 Cedric Mullins RC .40 1.00
319 Alex Gordon .15 .40
320 Ronald Guzman FS .15 .40
321 Jack Flaherty FS .20 .50
322 Brian McCann .25 .60
323 George Springer .20 .50
324 Logan Morrison .15 .40
325 Dan Straily .15 .40
326 Heath Fillmyer RC .25 .60
327 Maikel Franco .20 .50
328 Yonder Alonso .15 .40
329 Jordan Hicks FS .20 .50
330 Lorenzo Cain .15 .40
331 Cesar Hernandez .15 .40
332 Ryan O'Hearn RC .25 .60
333 Ray Black RC .25 .60
334 Jake Lamb .20 .50
335 Ervin Santana .15 .40
336 Corey Kluber .20 .50
337 Mychal Givens .15 .40
338 Andrew Cashner .15 .40
339 Josh Harrison .15 .40
340 Tyler Skaggs .15 .40
341 Nationals Park .15 .40
342 Wilmer Difo .15 .40
343 Sal Romano .15 .40
344 Max Scherzer .25 .60
345 Justin Upton .15 .40
346 Chris Iannetta .15 .40
347 Kirby Yates .20 .50
348 Russell Martin .15 .40
349 Kyle Schwarber .25 .60
350 Nick Markakis .20 .50
351 Jarrod Dyson .15 .40
352 David Peralta .15 .40
353 Gary Sanchez .25 .60
354 Nomar Mazara .15 .40
355 Stephen Gonsalves RC .25 .60
356 Stephen Strasburg .25 .60
357 Chris Martin .15 .40
358 Leonys Martin .15 .40
359 Noah Syndergaard .20 .50
360 Mark Melancon .15 .40
361 Taylor Davis .15 .40
362 Jeremy Jeffress .15 .40
363 Max Stassi .15 .40
364 Kenta Maeda .20 .50
365 Ketel Marte .20 .50
366 Isiah Kiner-Falefa .15 .40
367 Ohtani/Trout 1.25 3.00
368 Brad Hand .15 .40
369 Charlie Culberson .15 .40
370 Jacoby Ellsbury .20 .50
371 Zack Wheeler .20 .50
372 Yu Darvish .25 .60
373 Christian Vazquez .20 .50
374 Alex Blandino .15 .40
375 Cody Reed .15 .40
376 Framber Valdez RC .25 .60
377 Yoan Moncada .25 .60
378 Brandon Workman .15 .40
379 Tim Hill RC .25 .60
380 Chris Archer .15 .40
381 Juan Lagares .15 .40
382 Daniel Norris .15 .40
383 Adalberto Mejia .15 .40
384 Dominic Leone .15 .40
385 Ender Inciarte .15 .40
386 Ryan Pressly .15 .40
387 Mike Foltynewicz .25 .60
388 Dominic Smith .15 .40
389 Victor Caratini .15 .40
390 Evan Longoria .20 .50
391 Jung Ho Kang .15 .40
392 Cionel Perez RC .25 .60
393 Hunter Renfroe .15 .40
394 Miguel Rojas .15 .40
395 Andrew McCutchen .25 .60
396 Masahiro Tanaka .20 .50
397 Lance McCullers Jr. .25 .60
398 Erick Fedde .15 .40
399 Tyler Mahle .15 .40
400 Bryce Harper .40 1.00
401 Tony Kemp .15 .40
402 Victor Robles FS .30 .75
403 Ivan Nova .20 .50
404 Jace Peterson .15 .40
405 Chaz Roe .15 .40
406 Jason Castro .15 .40
407 Eduardo Nunez .15 .40
408 Sean Newcomb .15 .40
409 Nate Jones .15 .40
410 Fernando Tatis Jr. RC 20.00 50.00
411 Magneuris Sierra .25 .60
412 Clint Frazier FS .20 .50
413 Mike Fiers .30 .75
414 Michael Soroka FS .25 .60
415 Bryan Shaw .15 .40
416 Keon Broxton .15 .40
417 Noel Cuevas RC .25 .60
418 Jason Vargas .15 .40
419 Sandy Leon .15 .40
420 Kevin Kiermaier .15 .40
421 Yoshihisa Hirano .15 .40
422 Matt Barnes .15 .40
423 Ji-Man Choi .15 .40
424 Target Field .40 1.00
425 Steel City Slammers .40 1.00
Corey Dickerson
426 Austin Romine .15 .40
427 Jorge Bonifacio .15 .40
428 Pablo Sandoval .20 .50
429 Wilmer Font .15 .40
430 Roman Quinn .15 .40
431 Lonnie Chisenhall .15 .40
432 Ryan Yarbrough .15 .40
433 Pedro Baez .15 .40
434 Roberto Osuna .15 .40
435 Steven Brault .15 .40
436 Kendrys Morales .15 .40
437 Albert Pujols .30 .75
438 Max Kepler .20 .50
439 Ryan McMahon .15 .40
440 Dustin Pedroia .25 .60
441 Oriole Park at Camden Yards .15 .40
442 Reese McGuire RC .40 1.00
443 Steven Matz .20 .50
444 Judge/Staton .60 1.50
445 Walker Buehler .30 .75
446 Francisco Mejia FS .20 .50
447 Up High, Down Low .20 .50
Jose Altuve
George Springer
448 Willians Astudillo RC .25 .60
449 Matt Moore .20 .50
450 Greg Garcia .15 .40
451 Jorge Alfaro .15 .40
452 Caleb Ferguson RC .30 .75
453 Taylor Rogers .15 .40
454 Matt Kemp .20 .50
455 Zach Eflin .15 .40
456 Austin Barnes .15 .40
457 Nick Ciuffo RC .25 .60
458 Alex Avila .20 .50
459 Trevor Hildenberger .15 .40
460 Trevor Story .25 .60
461 Eduardo Rodriguez .15 .40
462 Luke Voit .40 1.00
463 Wily Peralta .15 .40
464 Alex Wood .15 .40
465 Raisel Iglesias .15 .40
466 Yairo Munoz .15 .40
467 A.J. Minter .20 .50
468 Anthony DeSclafani .15 .40
469 Brandon Morrow .20 .50
470 Peter O'Brien .15 .40
471 Kevin Newman RC .40 1.00
472 Scott Kingery FS .20 .50
473 Kyle Wright RC .40 1.00
474 Carson Kelly .15 .40
475 Pete Alonso RC 5.00 12.00
476 Arodys Vizcaino .15 .40
477 Mikie Mahtook .15 .40
478 Alen Hanson .20 .50
479 Wei-Yin Chen .15 .40
480 Vince Velasquez .15 .40
481 J.A. Happ .20 .50
482 Starlin Castro .15 .40
483 Alex Cobb .15 .40
484 Andrew Chafin .15 .40
485 Wil Myers .15 .40
486 CC Sabathia .20 .50
487 San Diego Sluggers .20 .50
Hunter Renfroe
Eric Hosmer
488 Dexter Fowler .20 .50
489 Joe Ross .15 .40
490 Matt Harvey .20 .50
491 Comerica Park .15 .40
492 Adam Plutko .15 .40
493 JaCoby Jones .20 .50
494 Ian Desmond .15 .40
495 Progressive Field .15 .40
496 Buck Farmer .15 .40
497 Citi Field .15 .40
498 Pablo Reyes RC .25 .60
499 Daniel Murphy .20 .50
500 Manny Machado .25 .60
501 Carlos Carrasco .15 .40
502 Mike Montgomery .15 .40
503 Marcell Ozuna .25 .60
504 Stephen Tarpley RC .30 .75
505 Dellin Betances .15 .40
506 Ben Gamel .20 .50
507 Cody Bellinger .50 1.25
508 Albies/Acuna 1.25 3.00
509 Globe Life Park in Arlington .15 .40
510 Patrick Corbin .20 .50
511 Rougned Odor .20 .50
512 Franklin Barreto .15 .40
513 Brett Gardner .15 .40
514 Greg Allen .20 .50
515 Hyun-Jin Ryu .20 .50
516 Keone Kela .15 .40
517 Shawn Armstrong .15 .40
518 Steven Wright .15 .40
519 Julio Urias .25 .60
520 David Fletcher RC .75 2.00
521 Chase Field .15 .40
522 Brian Johnson .15 .40
523 Marco Gonzales .15 .40
524 Chad Pinder .15 .40
525 Ian Kinsler .20 .50
526 Sandy Alcantara .15 .40
527 Guaranteed Rate Field .15 .40
528 Jon Edwards RC .25 .60
529 Chance Sisco .15 .40
530 Ian Happ .20 .50
531 Josh Reddick .15 .40
532 Lance Lynn .15 .40
533 Matt Shoemaker .20 .50
534 Aaron Altherr .15 .40
535 Tyler Naquin .15 .40
536 Get Up! .25 .60
Yadier Molina
Marcell Ozuna
537 Ronald Torreyes .15 .40
538 Seung-Hwan Oh .20 .50
539 Franchy Cordero .15 .40
540 Cole Hamels .20 .50
541 Michael Wacha .15 .40
542 Chris Davis .15 .40
543 Nick Williams .15 .40
544 Jake Marisnick .15 .40
545 Tyler White .15 .40
546 Brock Holt .15 .40
547 Trevor Richards RC .25 .60
548 Chris Owings .15 .40
549 Sale/Vazquez
550 Adam Cimber RC .25 .60
551 Kolten Wong .20 .50
552 David Hess .15 .40
553 Daniel Mengden .15 .40
554 Corey Knebel .15 .40
555 Marlins Park .15 .40
556 Rowdy Tellez RC .40 1.00
557 Adam Duvall .20 .50
558 Phillip Ervin .15 .40
559 Ildemaro Vargas .15 .40
560 Victor Reyes RC .25 .60
561 Ozzie Albies FS .25 .60
562 Willy Adames .15 .40
563 Keynan Middleton .15 .40
564 Austin Meadows FS .20 .50
565 Andrew Triggs .15 .40
566 Tropicana Field .20 .50
567 Josh Rogers RC .25 .60
568 Giancarlo Stanton .25 .60
569 Carl Edwards Jr. .15 .40
570 Eduardo Escobar .15 .40
571 Bobby Poyner RC .30 .75
572 Gerrit Cole .25 .60
573 Tucker Barnhart .15 .40
574 Jeff Samardzija .15 .40
575 Jimmy Yacabonis RC .25 .60
576 Jake Cave RC .30 .75
577 Nicky Delmonico .15 .40
578 Patrick Wisdom RC .25 .60
579 Andrew Benintendi .25 .60
580 DJ Stewart RC .30 .75
581 Travis Jankowski .15 .40
582 Austin Wynns RC .25 .60
583 Yefry Ramirez RC .25 .60
584 Josh James RC .40 1.00
585 Carlos Santana .20 .50
586 Drew VerHagen RC .25 .60
587 Johan Camargo .15 .40
588 Taylor Ward RC .25 .60
589 Jeurys Familia .20 .50
590 Jose Peraza .20 .50
591 Wilson Ramos .15 .40
592 Eric Lauer .15 .40
593 John Hicks .15 .40
594 Austin Slater .15 .40
595 Yandy Diaz .20 .50
596 Anthony Rizzo .40 1.00
597 Kyle Gibson .20 .50
598 Chris Devenski .15 .40
599 Daniel Palka .15 .40
600 Shohei Ohtani .30 .75
601 David Dahl .15 .40
602 German Marquez .15 .40
603 J.D. Davis .15 .40
604 Coors Field .15 .40
605 Jeffrey Springs RC .25 .60
606 Johnny Field RC .30 .75
607 J.T. Riddle .15 .40
608 Ehire Adrianza .15 .40
609 Kauffman Stadium .15 .40
610 Howie Kendrick .15 .40
611 Chris Shaw RC .40 1.00
612 Mark Canha .15 .40
613 Welington Castillo .15 .40
614 Ryan Braun .20 .50
615 Nick Tropeano .15 .40
616 Oracle Park .15 .40
617 Hernan Perez .15 .40
618 Nick Martini RC .25 .60
619 Tommy Hunter .15 .40
620 Jared Hughes .15 .40
621 Pat Valaika .15 .40
622 Troy Tulowitzki .25 .60
623 Kevin Pillar .15 .40
624 Amed Rosario FS .20 .50
625 Yelich/Arcia .30 .75
626 Robbie Erlin .15 .40
627 Freddy Peralta .25 .60
628 Roenis Elias .15 .40
629 Myles Straw RC .40 1.00
630 Dustin Fowler .15 .40
631 Tyler Austin .25 .60
632 Yusei Kikuchi RC .40 1.00
633 Addison Russell .20 .50
634 John Gant .15 .40
635 Adam Frazier .15 .40
636 Jace Fry RC .25 .60
637 Yusmeiro Petit .15 .40
638 Kristopher Negron .15 .40
639 Roberto Perez .15 .40
640 Brian Goodwin .15 .40
641 Bryse Wilson RC .30 .75
642 Jhoulys Chacin .15 .40
643 Chris Sale .25 .60
644 Delino DeShields .15 .40
645 Steve Cishek .15 .40
646 Jason Heyward .20 .50
647 Kyle Freeland .20 .50
648 Kevin Kramer RC .30 .75
649 Carlos Tocci RC .25 .60
650 Diego Castillo RC .25 .60
651 Jorge Lopez .15 .40
652 Rosell Herrera RC .25 .60
653 Greg Bird .20 .50
654 Kurt Suzuki .15 .40
655 Tyler O'Neill FS .20 .50
656 Jacob Faria .15 .40
657 JC Ramirez .15 .40
658 Max Muncy .20 .50
659 Aramis Garcia RC .25 .60
660 Dawel Lugo RC .40 1.00
661 Zack Greinke .20 .50
662 Jameson Taillon .20 .50
663 Adam Conley .15 .40
664 Lucas Giolito .20 .50
665 David Freese .15 .40
666 Cam Gallagher .15 .40
667 Ronny Rodriguez RC .25 .60
668 Pat Neshek .15 .40
669 Mallex Smith .15 .40
670 Eloy Jimenez RC 4.00 10.00
671 Alex Verdugo FS .20 .50
672 Christin Stewart RC .30 .75
673 Danny Salazar .20 .50
674 Collin McHugh .15 .40
675 Nelson Cruz .25 .60
676 Travis Shaw .15 .40
677 Aaron Sanchez .20 .50
678 Luis Ortiz RC .25 .60
679 Adam Wainwright .20 .50
680 Justin Smoak .15 .40
681 Jeff Mathis .20 .50
682 Petco Park .15 .40
683 Isaac Galloway RC .25 .60
684 Robert Stock RC .25 .60
685 Billy McKinney .15 .40
686 Brandon Drury .15 .40
687 Brandon Woodruff .15 .40
688 Jalen Beeks RC .25 .60
689 Jose Briceno RC .25 .60
690 Hunter Dozier .15 .40
691 Great American Ball Park .15 .40
692 Fernando Rodney .15 .40
693 Ryan Brasier RC .25 .60
694 Steve Pearce .25 .60
695 Eric Thames .15 .40
696 Sam Dyson .15 .40
697 Dakota Hudson RC .30 .75
698 Baez/Contreras .30 .75
699 Felix Hernandez .20 .50
700 Alex Bregman .25 .60
NNO Vladimir Guerrero Jr SP 12.00 30.00

2019 Topps 150th Anniversary

*150TH ANNV: 2X TO 5X BASIC
*150TH ANNV RC: 1.2X TO 3X BASIC RC
SER.1 ODDS 1:6 HOBBY
SER.2 ODDS 1:6 HOBBY
281 Jeff McNeil 8.00 20.00
410 Fernando Tatis Jr. 60.00 150.00
475 Pete Alonso 15.00 40.00

2019 Topps Advanced Stats

*ADV STATS: 6X TO 15X BASIC
*ADV STATS RC: 4X TO 10X BASIC RC
SER.1 ODDS 1:75 HOBBY
SER.2 ODDS 1:89 HOBBY
STATED PRINT RUN 150 SER. #'d SETS
281 Jeff McNeil 12.00 30.00

2019 Topps Black

*BLACK: 10X TO 25X BASIC
*BLACK RC: 6X TO 15X BASIC RC
SER.1 ODDS 1:122 HOBBY
SER.2 ODDS 1:178 HOBBY
STATED PRINT RUN 67 SER. #'d SETS
1 Ronald Acuna Jr. 60.00 150.00
60 Kyle Tucker 40.00 100.00
100 Mike Trout 60.00 150.00
132 Miguel Andujar 25.00 60.00
250 Shohei Ohtani 25.00 60.00
281 Jeff McNeil 25.00 60.00
400 Bryce Harper 25.00 60.00
410 Fernando Tatis Jr. 600.00 1500.00
445 Walker Buehler 30.00 80.00
473 Kyle Wright 12.00 30.00
475 Pete Alonso 200.00 500.00
560 Victor Reyes 8.00 20.00
588 Taylor Ward 6.00 15.00

2019 Topps Father's Day Blue

*BLUE: 10X TO 25X BASIC
*BLUE RC: 6X TO 15X BASIC RC
SER.1 ODDS 1:191 HOBBY
STATED PRINT RUN 50 SER. #'d SETS
1 Ronald Acuna Jr. 60.00 150.00
50 Mookie Betts 20.00 50.00
60 Kyle Tucker 40.00 100.00
100 Mike Trout 60.00 150.00
132 Miguel Andujar 25.00 60.00
250 Shohei Ohtani 25.00 60.00
281 Jeff McNeil 25.00 60.00
400 Bryce Harper 25.00 60.00
410 Fernando Tatis Jr. 600.00 1500.00
445 Walker Buehler 30.00 80.00
473 Kyle Wright 12.00 30.00
475 Pete Alonso 200.00 500.00
560 Victor Reyes 8.00 20.00
588 Taylor Ward 6.00 15.00
632 Yusei Kikuchi 10.00 25.00

2019 Topps Gold

*GOLD: 2X TO 5X BASIC
*GOLD RC: 1.2X TO 3X BASIC RC
SER. 1 ODDS 1:5 HOBBY
SER. 2 ODDS 1:6 HOBBY
STATED PRINT RUN 2019 SER. #'d SETS
281 Jeff McNeil 8.00 20.00
410 Fernando Tatis Jr. 150.00 400.00
475 Pete Alonso 30.00 80.00

2019 Topps Independence Day

*INDPNDNCE: 10X TO 25X BASIC
*INDPNDNCE RC: 6X TO 15X BASIC RC
SER.1 ODDS 1:126 HOBBY
SER.2 ODDS 1:160 HOBBY
STATED PRINT RUN 76 SER. #'d SETS
1 Ronald Acuna Jr. 60.00 150.00
60 Kyle Tucker 40.00 100.00
100 Mike Trout 60.00 150.00
132 Miguel Andujar 25.00 60.00
250 Shohei Ohtani 25.00 60.00
281 Jeff McNeil 25.00 60.00
400 Bryce Harper 25.00 60.00
410 Fernando Tatis Jr. 600.00 1500.00
445 Walker Buehler 30.00 80.00
473 Kyle Wright 12.00 30.00
475 Pete Alonso 200.00 500.00
560 Victor Reyes 8.00 20.00
588 Taylor Ward 6.00 15.00

2019 Topps Meijer Purple

*PURPLE: 5X TO 12X BASIC
*PURPLE RC: 3X TO 8X BASIC RC
281 Jeff McNeil 10.00 25.00

2019 Topps Memorial Day Camo

*CAMO: 12X TO 30X BASIC
*CAMO RC: 8X TO 20X BASIC RC
SER.1 ODDS 1:381 HOBBY
SER.2 ODDS 1:486 HOBBY
STATED PRINT RUN 25 SER. #'d SETS
1 Ronald Acuna Jr. 75.00 200.00
50 Mookie Betts 25.00 60.00
60 Kyle Tucker 50.00 120.00
100 Mike Trout 75.00 200.00
132 Miguel Andujar 30.00 80.00
250 Shohei Ohtani 30.00 80.00
281 Jeff McNeil 30.00 80.00
400 Bryce Harper 30.00 80.00
410 Fernando Tatis Jr. 500.00 1200.00
445 Walker Buehler 40.00 100.00
473 Kyle Wright 15.00 40.00
475 Pete Alonso 250.00 600.00
560 Victor Reyes 10.00 25.00
588 Taylor Ward 8.00 20.00
632 Yusei Kikuchi 12.00 30.00

2019 Topps Mother's Day Pink

*PINK: 10X TO 25X BASIC
*PINK RC: 6X TO 15X BASIC RC
SER.1 ODDS 1:191 HOBBY
STATED PRINT RUN 50 SER. #'d SETS
1 Ronald Acuna Jr. 60.00 150.00
50 Mookie Betts 20.00 50.00
60 Kyle Tucker 40.00 100.00
100 Mike Trout 60.00 150.00
132 Miguel Andujar 25.00 60.00
250 Shohei Ohtani 25.00 60.00
281 Jeff McNeil 25.00 60.00
400 Bryce Harper 25.00 60.00
410 Fernando Tatis Jr. 600.00 1500.00
445 Walker Buehler 30.00 80.00
473 Kyle Wright 12.00 30.00
475 Pete Alonso 200.00 500.00
560 Victor Reyes 8.00 20.00
588 Taylor Ward 6.00 15.00
632 Yusei Kikuchi 10.00 25.00

2019 Topps Rainbow Foil

*RAINBOW: 2X TO 5X BASIC
*RAINBOW RC: 1.2X TO 3X BASIC RC
SER.1 ODDS 1:10 HOBBY
SER.2 ODDS 1:10 HOBBY
281 Jeff McNeil 6.00 15.00
410 Fernando Tatis Jr. 150.00 400.00
475 Pete Alonso 20.00 50.00

2019 Topps Vintage Stock

*VINTAGE: 8X TO 20X BASIC
*VINTAGE RC: 5X TO 12X BASIC RC
SER.1 ODDS 1:97 HOBBY
SER.2 ODDS 1:123 HOBBY
STATED PRINT RUN 99 SER. #'d SETS
250 Shohei Ohtani 20.00 50.00
281 Jeff McNeil 25.00 60.00
410 Fernando Tatis Jr. 500.00 1200.00
475 Pete Alonso 100.00 250.00

2019 Topps Walgreens Yellow

*YELLOW: 3X TO 8X BASIC
*YELLOW RC: 2X TO 5X BASIC RC
INSERTED IN WALGREENS PACKS
1 Ronald Acuna Jr. 20.00 50.00
213 Juan Soto 15.00 40.00

2019 Topps Base Set Legend Variations

SER.1 STATED ODDS 1:444 HOBBY
SER.2 STATED ODDS 1:20 HOBBY
SER.2 SSP ODDS 1:589 HOBBY

) Sandy Koufax 25.00 60.00
1 Ozzie Smith 25.00 60.00
2 Cal Ripken Jr. 30.00 80.00
5 Frank Thomas 20.00 50.00
) Ted Williams 40.00 100.00
7 Nolan Ryan 40.00 100.00
0 Hank Aaron 40.00 100.00
50 Don Mattingly 30.00 80.00
72 Mike Piazza 25.00 60.00
76 Ty Cobb 20.00 50.00
78 Jackie Robinson 30.00 80.00
15 Derek Jeter 40.00 100.00
30 Lou Gehrig 30.00 80.00
38 Rickey Henderson 20.00 50.00
30 Babe Ruth 50.00 120.00
53 Roberto Clemente 50.00 125.00
60 Reggie Jackson 30.00 80.00
62 Wade Boggs 25.00 60.00
76 Brooks Robinson 25.00 60.00
80 Bob Gibson 20.00 50.00
89 Mark McGwire 25.00 60.00
92 Ichiro 25.00 60.00
30 Bo Jackson 40.00 100.00
44 Pedro Martinez 20.00 50.00
50 Carl Yastrzemski 30.00 80.00
70 Lou Brock 2.00 5.00
73 Carlton Fisk 2.00 5.00
74 Joe Morgan 2.00 5.00
77 Roberto Alomar 2.00 5.00
81 Darryl Strawberry 1.50 4.00
85 Dale Murphy 2.50 6.00
87 Warren Spahn 20.00 50.00
28 Will Clark 2.00 5.00
31 Willie Stargell 2.00 5.00
36 Edgar Martinez 2.00 5.00
37 Johnny Mize 15.00 40.00
60 Ernie Banks 20.00 50.00
77 Al Kaline 20.00 50.00
86 Whitey Ford 15.00 40.00
88 Ken Griffey Jr. 5.00 12.00
01 Bob Feller 15.00 40.00
03 Roger Maris 40.00 100.00
05 Mariano Rivera 3.00 8.00
07 Pee Wee Reese 15.00 40.00
14 Tony Gwynn 2.50 6.00
18 Roger Clemens 3.00 8.00
25 Ryne Sandberg 5.00 12.00
29 Frank Robinson 2.00 5.00
42 Eddie Murray 2.00 5.00
45 Jeff Bagwell 2.00 5.00
51 Rogers Hornsby 20.00 50.00
64 Mel Ott 25.00 60.00
65 Catfish Hunter 2.00 5.00
68 Harmon Killebrew 20.00 50.00
73 Johnny Bench 2.50 6.00
74 Christy Mathewson 20.00 50.00
79 Tris Speaker 15.00 40.00
87 Chipper Jones 2.50 6.00
90 Barry Larkin 2.00 5.00
91 Gary Carter 2.00 5.00
94 Monte Irvin 25.00 60.00
22 Honus Wagner 20.00 50.00
23 Stan Musial 30.00 80.00
31 Rod Carew 2.00 5.00
46 Andre Dawson 2.00 5.00
53 Dave Winfield 2.00 5.00
65 Duke Snider 15.00 40.00
75 Vladimir Guerrero Sr. 2.00 5.00
76 Robin Yount 2.50 6.00
76 Eddie Mathews 25.00 60.00
79 Dizzy Dean 20.00 50.00
80 Willie McCovey 25.00 60.00
90 George Brett 5.00 12.00
92 Dennis Eckersley 2.00 5.00
94 David Ortiz 2.50 6.00

2019 Topps Base Set Photo Variations

SER.1 STATED ODDS 1:15 HOBBY
SER.2 STATED ODDS 1:20 HOBBY
SER.2 SSP ODDS 1:589 HOBBY
1 Ronald Acuna Jr. 15.00 40.00
7 Gleyber Torres 5.00 12.00
10 Clayton Kershaw 5.00 12.00
16 Charlie Blackmon 2.50 6.00
32 Carlos Correa 2.50 6.00
34 Josh Donaldson 2.00 5.00
37 Marcus Stroman 2.00 5.00
41 Corey Seager 2.50 6.00
46 Jose Abreu 2.50 6.00
49 Michael Kopech 3.00 8.00
50 Mookie Betts 6.00 15.00
52 J.T. Realmuto 2.50 6.00
53 Brandon Crawford 2.00 5.00
57 Justin Verlander 2.50 6.00
60 Kyle Tucker 15.00 40.00
62 Elvis Andrus 2.00 5.00
77 J.D. Martinez 2.50 6.00
84 Matt Carpenter 2.50 6.00
100 Mike Trout 12.00 30.00
107 Scooter Gennett 2.00 5.00
109 Michael Conforto 2.00 5.00
110 Trevor Bauer 2.50 6.00
112 Joey Gallo 2.00 5.00
119 Willson Contreras 2.00 5.00
125 Paul DeJong 2.50 6.00
128 Yoenis Cespedes 2.50 6.00
130 Blake Snell 2.50 6.00
133 Ryan Zimmerman 2.00 5.00
137 Carlos Rodon 2.00 5.00
139 Mitch Haniger 2.00 5.00
149 Khris Davis 2.50 6.00
150 Aaron Judge 6.00 15.00
157 Buster Posey 3.00 8.00
161 Eric Hosmer 2.00 5.00
163 Aaron Nola 2.00 5.00
166 Matt Chapman 2.50 6.00
168 Salvador Perez 2.00 5.00
176 Trea Turner 2.00 5.00
178 Jose Altuve 2.00 5.00
180 Justin Turner 2.00 5.00
183 Freddie Freeman 3.00 8.00
200 Jacob deGrom 2.50 6.00
209 Nicholas Castellanos 2.50 6.00
210 Kris Bryant 3.00 8.00
213 Juan Soto 8.00 20.00
215 Didi Gregorius 2.00 5.00
221 Luis Severino 2.00 5.00
222 Zack Greinke 2.00 5.00
223 Jose Ramirez 2.00 5.00
225 Yadier Molina 6.00 15.00
228 Rafael Devers 3.00 8.00
230 Miguel Cabrera 2.50 6.00
238 Whit Merrifield 2.50 6.00
250 Shohei Ohtani 10.00 25.00
253 Starling Marte 2.00 5.00
258 Eddie Rosario 2.00 5.00
262 Adam Jones 2.00 5.00
269 Francisco Lindor 5.00 12.00
276 Nolan Arenado 3.00 8.00
279 Rhys Hoskins 3.00 8.00
284 Joey Votto 2.50 6.00
287 Jesus Aguilar 1.50 4.00
292 Dee Gordon 1.50 4.00
297 Paul Goldschmidt 2.50 6.00
300 Christian Yelich 3.00 8.00
302 Jose Berrios 2.00 5.00
306 Justus Sheffield 2.50 6.00
310 Javier Baez 3.00 8.00
311 Jake Bauers 2.50 6.00
313 Robinson Cano 2.00 5.00
323 George Springer 2.00 5.00
330 Lorenzo Cain 1.50 4.00
336 Corey Kluber 2.00 5.00
344 Max Scherzer 2.50 6.00
349 Kyle Schwarber 2.50 6.00
353 Gary Sanchez 2.50 6.00
356 Stephen Strasburg 2.50 6.00
359 Noah Syndergaard 2.00 5.00
372 Yu Darvish 2.50 6.00
380 Chris Archer 1.50 4.00
390 Evan Longoria 2.00 5.00
395 Andrew McCutchen 2.50 6.00
396 Masahiro Tanaka 2.00 5.00
397 Lance McCullers 1.50 4.00
400A Bryce Harper 4.00 10.00
400B Bryce Harper 60.00 150.00
402 Victor Robles 3.00 8.00
410 Fernando Tatis Jr.
412 Clint Frazier 2.00 5.00
437 Albert Pujols 3.00 8.00
440 Dustin Pedroia 2.50 6.00
442 Reese McGuire 2.50 6.00
445 Walker Buehler 3.00 8.00
448 Willians Astudillo 1.50 4.00
460 Trevor Story 2.50 6.00
473 Kyle Wright 5.00 12.00
475 Pete Alonso
485 Wil Myers 1.50 4.00
486 CC Sabathia 2.00 5.00
500A Manny Machado 2.00 5.00
500B Manny Machado 12.00 30.00
503 Marcell Ozuna 2.50 6.00
507 Cody Bellinger 5.00 12.00
515 Hyun-Jin Ryu 2.00 5.00
540 Cole Hamels 2.00 5.00
556 Rowdy Tellez 2.50 6.00
561 Ozzie Albies 4.00 10.00
564 Austin Meadows 2.00 5.00
568 Giancarlo Stanton 2.50 6.00
572 Gerrit Cole 2.50 6.00
579 Andrew Benintendi 2.50 6.00
596A Anthony Rizzo 4.00 10.00
596B Anthony Rizzo 30.00 80.00
618 Nick Martini 1.50 4.00
624 Amed Rosario 2.00 5.00
629 Myles Straw 2.50 6.00
632A Yusei Kikuchi 2.50 6.00
632B Yusei Kikuchi 15.00 40.00
632C Yusei Kikuchi
643 Chris Sale 2.50 6.00
655 Tyler O'Neill 2.00 5.00
658 Max Muncy 2.00 5.00
661 Zack Greinke 2.00 5.00
670 Eloy Jimenez
672 Christin Stewart 2.00 5.00
680 Justin Smoak 1.50 4.00
699 Felix Hernandez 2.00 5.00
700A Alex Bregman 2.50 6.00
700B Alex Bregman 20.00 50.00
700C Vladimir Guerrero Jr
700D Vladimir Guerrero Jr

2019 Topps '18 Topps Now Review

STATED ODDS 1:18 HOBBY
TN1 Aaron Judge 1.00 2.50
TN2 Shohei Ohtani .50 1.25
TN3 Shohei Ohtani .50 1.25
TN4 Gleyber Torres .75 2.00
TN5 Juan Soto 1.25 3.00
TN6 Bryce Harper .60 1.50
TN7 Kyle Schwarber .40 1.00
TN8 Mike Trout 2.00 5.00
TN9 Trout/Pujols/Ohtani 2.00 5.00
TN10 Ronald Acuna Jr. 2.00 5.00

2019 Topps '84 Topps

STATED ODDS 1:4 HOBBY
*150TH/150: 2X TO 5X BASIC
T841 Don Mattingly .75 2.00
T842 Juan Soto 1.25 3.00
T843 Trea Turner .30 .75
T844 Rhys Hoskins .50 1.25
T845 Javier Baez .50 1.25
T846 Carlos Santana .30 .75
T847 Jake Bauers .40 1.00
T848 Max Scherzer .40 1.00
T849 Vladimir Guerrero .30 .75
T8410 J.T. Realmuto .40 1.00
T8411 Luis Urias .40 1.00
T8412 Trevor Hoffman .30 .75
T8413 Luke Weaver .25 .60
T8414 Paul Goldschmidt .40 1.00
T8415 Joey Votto .40 1.00
T8416 Whit Merrifield .40 1.00
T8417 Bob Gibson .30 .75
T8418 Gleyber Torres .75 2.00
T8419 Ronald Acuna Jr. 2.00 5.00
T8420 Mookie Betts .60 1.50
T8421 Andrew Benintendi .40 1.00
T8422 Jose Altuve .30 .75
T8423 Derek Jeter 1.00 2.50
T8424 Wade Boggs .30 .75
T8425 Nick Williams .25 .60
T8426 Luis Severino .30 .75
T8427 Chris Sale .40 1.00
T8428 Ramon Laureano .50 1.25
T8429 Pedro Martinez .30 .75
T8430 Frank Thomas .40 1.00
T8431 Will Clark .30 .75
T8432 Robin Yount .40 1.00
T8433 Dee Gordon .25 .60
T8434 Cody Bellinger .75 2.00
T8435 Ivan Rodriguez .30 .75
T8436 Jacob deGrom .40 1.00
T8437 Touki Toussaint .30 .75
T8438 Charlie Blackmon .40 1.00
T8439 Anthony Rizzo .60 1.50
T8440 Blake Snell .30 .75
T8441 Mike Trout 2.00 5.00
T8442 Clayton Kershaw .75 2.00
T8443 Mike Piazza .40 1.00
T8444 Kris Bryant .50 1.25
T8445 Zack Greinke .30 .75
T8446 Kyle Seager .25 .60
T8447 Trey Mancini .30 .75
T8448 Eric Thames .25 .60
T8449 Dennis Eckersley .25 .60
T8450 Kyle Tucker .50 1.25
T8451 Matt Chapman .40 1.00
T8452 Ozzie Albies .40 1.00
T8453 Joey Gallo .30 .75
T8454 Dale Murphy .40 1.00
T8455 Matt Olson .25 .60
T8456 Starling Marte .30 .75
T8457 Roberto Alomar .30 .75
T8458 Justin Verlander .40 1.00
T8459 Adrian Beltre .40 1.00
T8460 Eric Hosmer .30 .75
T8461 Mark McGwire .60 1.50
T8462 Tom Glavine .30 .75
T8463 Eddie Rosario .30 .75
T8464 Christian Yelich .50 1.25
T8465 Steve Carlton .30 .75
T8466 Jose Ramirez .30 .75
T8467 Buster Posey .50 1.25
T8468 Jesus Aguilar .25 .60
T8469 Shohei Ohtani .50 1.25
T8470 Albert Pujols .50 1.25
T8471 Nolan Arenado .50 1.25
T8472 Matt Carpenter .40 1.00
T8473 Ozzie Smith .50 1.25
T8474 Aaron Nola .30 .75
T8475 Bo Jackson .40 1.00
T8476 Willie McCovey .30 .75
T8477 Jose Abreu .40 1.00
T8478 Ryan O'Hearn .25 .60
T8479 Gary Sanchez .40 1.00
T8480 Jeff McNeil .60 1.50
T8481 Kolby Allard .40 1.00
T8482 Yadier Molina .40 1.00
T8483 Travis Shaw .25 .60
T8484 Jonathan Loaisiga .30 .75
T8485 Bert Blyleven .30 .75
T8486 Jose Berrios .30 .75
T8487 Wil Myers .25 .60
T8488 Brian Anderson .25 .60
T8489 Francisco Lindor .40 1.00
T8490 Noah Syndergaard .30 .75
T8491 Miles Mikolas .40 1.00
T8492 Carlos Correa .40 1.00
T8493 Mitch Haniger .30 .75
T8494 Corey Seager .40 1.00
T8495 Khris Davis .40 1.00
T8496 Nolan Ryan 1.25 3.00
T8497 Chance Adams .25 .60
T8498 David Ortiz .40 1.00
T8499 Trevor Bauer .40 1.00
T84100 Aaron Judge 1.00 2.50

2019 Topps '84 Topps All Star Relics

STATED ODDS 1:207 HOBBY
*150th/150: .6X TO 1.5X BASIC
*GOLD/50: 1X TO 2.5X BASIC
*RED/25: 2X TO 5X BASIC
ASRCF Carlton Fisk 2.00 5.00
ASRCR Cal Ripken Jr. 8.00 20.00
ASRCY Carl Yastrzemski 4.00 10.00
ASRDM Dale Murphy 2.50 6.00
ASRDT Don Mattingly 8.00 20.00
ASRDW Dave Winfield 2.00 5.00
ASRMM Mark McGwire 4.00 10.00
ASRNR Nolan Ryan 8.00 20.00
ASROS Ozzie Smith 3.00 8.00
ASRRA Rod Carew 2.00 5.00
ASRRC Roger Clemens 3.00 8.00
ASRRH Rickey Henderson 2.50 6.00
ASRRJ Reggie Jackson 2.00 5.00
ASRRS Ryne Sandberg 5.00 12.00
ASRRY Robin Yount 2.50 6.00
ASRSC Steve Carlton 2.00 5.00
ASRTG Tony Gwynn 2.50 6.00
ASRTS Tom Seaver 2.00 5.00
ASRWB Wade Boggs 2.00 5.00
ASRWC Will Clark 2.00 5.00

2019 Topps '84 Topps All Stars

84ASI Ichiro .50 1.25
84ASAB Alex Bregman .40 1.00
84ASAD Andre Dawson .30 .75
84ASAJ Aaron Judge 1.00 2.50
84ASBH Bryce Harper .60 1.50
84ASBJ Bo Jackson .40 1.00
84ASCB Charlie Blackmon .40 1.00
84ASCF Carlton Fisk .30 .75
84ASCR Cal Ripkon Jr. 1.25 3.00
84ASCS Chris Sale .40 1.00
84ASCY Christian Yelich .50 1.25
84ASDG Dwight Gooden .25 .60
84ASDJ Derek Jeter 1.00 2.50
84ASDM Dale Murphy .40 1.00
84ASDS Darryl Strawberry .25 .60
84ASDW Dave Winfield .30 .75
84ASFF Freddie Freeman .50 1.25
84ASFL Francisco Lindor .40 1.00
84ASHM Hideki Matsui .40 1.00
84ASJA Jose Altuve .30 .75
84ASJB Javier Baez .50 1.25
84ASJD Jacob deGrom .40 1.00
84ASJM J.D. Martinez .40 1.00
84ASJV Joey Votto .40 1.00
84ASKG Ken Griffey Jr. .75 2.00
84ASLS Luis Severino .30 .75
84ASMB Mookie Betts .60 1.50
84ASMM Manny Machado .40 1.00
84ASMS Max Scherzer .40 1.00
84ASMT Mike Trout 2.00 5.00
84ASOA Ozzie Albies .40 1.00
84ASOS Ozzie Smith .50 1.25
84ASPG Paul Goldschmidt .40 1.00
84ASRC Rod Carew .30 .75
84ASRH Rickey Henderson .40 1.00
84ASRJ Reggie Jackson .30 .75
84ASRS Ryne Sandberg .75 2.00
84ASRY Robin Yount .40 1.00
84ASTG Tony Gwynn .40 1.00
84ASTS Trevor Story .40 1.00
84ASWB Wade Boggs .30 .75
84ASWC Willson Contreras .30 .75
84ASYM Yadier Molina .40 1.00
84ASCYA Carl Yastrzemski .60 1.50
84ASDMA Don Mattingly .75 2.00
84ASJBE Johnny Bench .40 1.00
84ASMAC Mark McGwire .60 1.50
84ASRCL Roger Clemens .50 1.25
84ASTGL Tom Glavine .30 .75
84ASWCL Will Clark .30 .75

2019 Topps '84 Topps All Stars 150th Anniversary

*150th/150: 2X TO 5X BASIC
STATED ODDS 1:284 HOBBY
STATED PRINT RUN 150 SER.#'d SETS
84ASDJ Derek Jeter 8.00 20.00
84ASMT Mike Trout 15.00 40.00

2019 Topps '84 Topps All Stars Black

*BLACK/299: 1.2X TO 3X BASIC
STATED ODDS 1:49 HOBBY
STATED PRINT RUN 299 SER.#'d SETS
84ASDJ Derek Jeter 5.00 12.00
84ASMT Mike Trout 10.00 25.00

2019 Topps '84 Topps All Stars Gold

*GOLD/50: 3X TO 8X BASIC
STATED ODDS 1:294 HOBBY
STATED PRINT RUN 50 SER.#'d SETS
84ASDJ Derek Jeter 12.00 30.00
84ASMT Mike Trout 25.00 60.00

2019 Topps '84 Topps Autographs

SER.1 ODDS 1:740 HOBBY
SER.2 ODDS 1:800 HOBBY
EXCHANGE DEADLINE 12/31/2020
84AAG Adolis Garcia 5.00 12.00
84AAK Al Kaline 15.00 40.00
84AARZ Anthony Rizzo 40.00 100.00
84ABHA Bryce Harper
84ABK Brad Keller 2.50 6.00
84ABL Brandon Lowe 15.00 40.00
84ABN Brandon Nimmo 3.00 8.00
84ABS Blake Snell 6.00 15.00
84ABT Blake Treinen 2.50 6.00
84ACA Chance Adams 5.00 12.00
84ACHE Cesar Hernandez 5.00 12.00
84ACJ Chipper Jones 60.00 150.00
84ACM Colin Moran 3.00 8.00
84ACMU Cedric Mullins 5.00 12.00
84ACR Cal Ripken Jr. 75.00 200.00
84ACT Chris Taylor S2 5.00 12.00
84ADBO David Bote 10.00 25.00
84ADJ Danny Jansen 2.50 6.00
84ADJ Derek Jeter 200.00 500.00
84ADM Daniel Mengden S2 4.00 10.00
84ADMA Don Mattingly 50.00 120.00
84ADMU Dale Murphy 25.00 60.00
84ADRO Dereck Rodriguez 10.00 25.00
84ADST Darryl Strawberry 15.00 40.00
84AEJ Eloy Jimenez S2 25.00 60.00
84AFL Francisco Lindor EXCH 20.00 50.00
84AFP Freddy Peralta 4.00 10.00
84AFR Fernando Romero S2 4.00 10.00
84AFT Fernando Tatis Jr. S2 60.00 150.00
84AFTH Frank Thomas 40.00 100.00
84AFV Felipe Vazquez 5.00 12.00
84AGSA Gary Sanchez 15.00 40.00
84AHA Hank Aaron 125.00 300.00
84AIR Ivan Rodriguez S2 15.00 40.00
84AJA Jose Altuve 30.00 80.00
84AJB Jake Bauers 5.00 12.00
84AJC Johan Camargo S2 6.00 15.00
84AJHA Josh Hader 2.50 6.00
84AJJ Jake Junis 4.00 10.00
84AJMC Jeff McNeil 15.00 40.00
84AJN Jacob Nix S2 4.00 10.00
84AJS Juan Soto 50.00 120.00
84AKA Kolby Allard 6.00 15.00
84AKB Kris Bryant 30.00 80.00
84AKD Khris Davis 8.00 20.00
84AKSC Kyle Schwarber 10.00 25.00
84AKT Kyle Tucker 25.00 60.00
84ALG Lourdes Gurriel Jr. 6.00 15.00
84ALS Luis Severino 3.00 8.00
84AMA Miguel Andujar 12.00 30.00
84AMCL Mike Clevinger 5.00 12.00
84AMF Mike Foltynewicz 4.00 10.00
84AMH Mitch Haniger 6.00 15.00
84AMKO Michael Kopech 15.00 40.00
84AMMG Mark McGwire 60.00 150.00
84AMMU Max Muncy 6.00 15.00
84AMO Matt Olson 6.00 15.00
84ANP Nick Pivetta S2 4.00 10.00
84ANR Nolan Ryan 75.00 200.00
84ANSY Noah Syndergaard 12.00 30.00
84AOS Ozzie Smith 40.00 100.00
84APD Paul DeJong S2 8.00 20.00
84APW Patrick Wisdom 4.00 10.00
84ARA Ronald Acuna Jr. 75.00 200.00
84ARHE Rickey Henderson 50.00 120.00
84ARO Ryan O'Hearn 2.50 6.00
84ARS Ryne Sandberg 40.00 100.00
84ARY Robin Yount 20.00 50.00
84ASD Steven Duggar 4.00 10.00
84ASN Sean Newcomb S2 2.50 6.00
84ASO Shohei Ohtani 125.00 300.00
84ASR Sean Reid-Foley 2.50 6.00
84ATAN Tim Anderson 8.00 20.00
84ATO Tyler O'Neill S2 6.00 15.00
84ATS Travis Shaw 5.00 12.00
84ATST Trevor Story 6.00 15.00
84ATT Touki Toussaint S2 3.00 8.00
84ATW Taylor Ward 2.50 6.00
84AVG Vladimir Guerrero Jr. S2 60.00 150.00
84AVR Victor Robles S2 8.00 20.00
84AWCL Will Clark 30.00 80.00
84AWM Whit Merrifield 6.00 15.00
84AYM Yadier Molina S2 25.00 60.00
84AZG Zack Godley 2.50 6.00
84AARS Amed Rosario S2 5.00 12.00
84AIKF Isiah Kiner-Falefa S2 2.50 6.00
84AJBE Johnny Bench S2 40.00 10.00
84AJBS Jose Berrios S2 3.00 8.00
84AMMI Miles Mikolas S2 5.00 12.00
84ARHY Rhys Hoskins S2 15.00 40.00
84ASAD Andre Dawson S2 15.00 40.00
84ASAJ Aaron Judge S2
84ASBB Bert Blyleven S2 3.00 8.00
84ASBG Bob Gibson S2 50.00 120.00
84ASBI Shane Bieber S2 12.00 30.00
84ASBJ Bo Jackson S2 40.00 100.00
84ASBS Blake Snell S2 6.00 15.00
84ASCF Carlton Fisk S2 20.00 50.00
84ASCK Corey Kluber S2 6.00 15.00
84ASCR Cal Ripken Jr. S2 75.00 200.00
84ASCS Chris Sale S2 10.00 25.00
84ASCY Christian Yelich S2 25.00 60.00
84ASDG Dwight Gooden S2 15.00 40.00
84ASDJ Derek Jeter S2 200.00 500.00
84ASDM Dale Murphy S2 25.00 60.00
84ASDS Darryl Strawberry S2 12.00 30.00
84ASDW Dave Winfield S2 10.00 25.00
84ASFL Francisco Lindor S2 20.00 50.00
84ASHM Hideki Matsui S2 40.00 100.00
84ASJB Johnny Bench S2 40.00 100.00
84ASJd Jacob deGrom S2
84ASJV Joey Votto S2
84ASLS Luis Severino S2 3.00 8.00
84ASMH Mitch Haniger S2 6.00 15.00
84ASMM Mark McGwire S2 30.00 80.00
84ASMT Mike Trout S2
84ASMZ Steven Matz S2 5.00 12.00
84ASOA Ozzie Albies S2 20.00 50.00
84ASOS Ozzie Smith S2 40.00 100.00
84ASPN Phil Niekro S2 10.00 25.00
84ASRC Roger Clemens S2
84ASRH Rickey Henderson S2 50.00 120.00
84ASRJ Reggie Jackson S2
84ASRS Ryne Sandberg S2 40.00 100.00
84ASRY Robin Yount S2 20.00 50.00
84ASTG Tom Glavine S2 25.00 60.00
84ASTR Tim Raines S2 3.00 8.00
84ASWB Wade Boggs S2 3.00 8.00
84ASWC Willson Contreras S2 10.00 25.00
84RAAD Austin Dean S2 2.50 6.00
84RAAG Aramis Garcia S2 2.50 6.00
84RABW Bryse Wilson S2 3.00 8.00
84RACB Corbin Burnes S2 4.00 10.00
84RACS Chris Shaw S2 4.00 10.00
84RADF David Fletcher S2 8.00 20.00
84RADH Dakota Hudson S2 5.00 12.00
84RADP Daniel Poncedeleon S2 4.00 10.00
84RADS Dennis Santana S2 2.50 6.00
84RAFV Framber Valdez S2 8.00 20.00
84RAHF Heath Fillmyer S2 5.00 12.00
84RAJB Jose Briceno S2 5.00 12.00
84RAJC Jake Cave S2 5.00 12.00
84RAJJ Josh James S2 5.00 12.00
84RAKK Kevin Kramer S2 3.00 8.00
84RAKN Kevin Newman S2 5.00 12.00
84RAKW Kyle Wright S2 4.00 10.00
84RAMS Myles Straw S2 8.00 20.00
84RANB Nick Burdi S2 2.50 6.00
84RANM Nick Martini S2 5.00 12.00
84RPA Peter Alonso 60.00 150.00
84RARB Ray Black S2 2.50 6.00
84RART Rowdy Tellez S2 6.00 15.00
84RASG Stephen Gonsalves S2 2.50 6.00
84RAWA Willians Astudillo S2 10.00 25.00
84ASBSU Bruce Sutter S2 10.00 25.00
84ASCYA Carl Yastrzemski S2 50.00 120.00
84ASDMA Don Mattingly S2 50.00 120.00
84ASJAL Jose Altuve S2 15.00 40.00
84ASJRI Jim Rice S2 8.00 20.00
84ASWCL Will Clark S2 30.00 80.00
84RACST Christin Stewart S2 3.00 8.00
84RAJBE Jalen Beeks S2 2.50 6.00
84RARMC Reese McGuire S2 5.00 12.00

2019 Topps '84 Topps Autographs 150th Anniversary

*150TH ANNV/150: .5X TO 1.2X BASIC
SER.1 ODDS 1:2431 HOBBY
SER.2 ODDS 1:1825 HOBBY
STATED PRINT RUN 150 SER.#'d SETS
EXCHANGE DEADLINE 12/31/2020
84AFT Fernando Tatis Jr. S2 125.00 300.00

2019 Topps '84 Topps Autographs Gold

*GOLD/50: .6X TO 1.5X BASIC
SER.1 ODDS 1:3808 HOBBY
SER.2 ODDS 1:5390 HOBBY
STATED PRINT RUN 50 SER.#'d SETS
EXCHANGE DEADLINE 12/31/2020
84ADMA Don Mattingly 100.00 250.00
84AFL Francisco Lindor EXCH 25.00 60.00
84AFT Fernando Tatis Jr. S2 150.00 400.00
84AJA Jose Altuve 50.00 120.00
84AOS Ozzie Smith 40.00 100.00
84ARY Robin Yount 30.00 80.00
84ASBG Bob Gibson S2 75.00 200.00

2019 Topps '84 Topps Autographs Red

*RED/25: .8X TO 2X BASIC
SER.1 ODDS 1:750 HOBBY
SER.2 ODDS 1:6274 HOBBY
STATED PRINT RUN 25 SER.#'d SETS
EXCHANGE DEADLINE 12/31/2020
84AARZ Anthony Rizzo 50.00 120.00
84ACJ Chipper Jones 75.00 200.00
84ACR Cal Ripken Jr. 100.00 250.00
84ADMA Don Mattingly 125.00 300.00
84AFL Francisco Lindor EXCH 30.00 80.00
84AFT Fernando Tatis Jr. S2 200.00 500.00
84AGSA Gary Sanchez 20.00 50.00
84AJA Jose Altuve 60.00 150.00
84AMMG Mark McGwire 75.00 200.00
84AMTR Mike Trout 400.00 800.00
84ANR Nolan Ryan 125.00 300.00
84AOS Ozzie Smith 50.00 120.00
84ARHE Rickey Henderson 60.00 150.00
84ARS Ryne Sandberg 50.00 120.00
84ARY Robin Yount 40.00 100.00
84RPA Peter Alonso 125.00 300.00

2019 Topps '84 Topps Relics

SER.1 ODDS 1:82 HOBBY
SER.2 ODDS 1:149 HOBBY
*150TH/150: .5X TO 1.2X BASIC
*GOLD/50: .6X TO 1.5X BASIC
*RED/25: .75X TO 2X BASIC
84RAB Adrian Beltre 3.00 8.00
84RAB Alex Bregman S2 3.00 8.00
84RABE Andrew Benintendi 3.00 8.00
84RAJ Aaron Judge 8.00 20.00
84RAJ Aaron Judge S2 8.00 20.00
84RAN Aaron Nola S2 2.50 6.00
84RAP Albert Pujols 4.00 10.00
84RAR Anthony Rizzo 5.00 12.00
84RBC Brandon Crawford 2.50 6.00
84RBH Bryce Harper S2 5.00 12.00
84RBP Buster Posey 4.00 10.00
84RCC Carlos Correa 3.00 8.00
84RCH Charlie Blackmon S2 3.00 8.00
84RCK Clayton Kershaw 6.00 15.00
84RCR Cal Ripken Jr. 6.00 15.00
84RCS Corey Seager 3.00 8.00
84RCSA Chris Sale 3.00 8.00
84RDJ Derek Jeter S2 8.00 20.00
84RDM Don Mattingly 8.00 20.00
84RDO David Ortiz S2 3.00 8.00
84REM Eddie Murray 6.00 15.00
84RFF Freddie Freeman 4.00 10.00
84RFL Francisco Lindor 3.00 8.00
84RGS George Springer S2 2.50 6.00
84RJA Jose Abreu 3.00 8.00
84RJAL Jose Altuve 2.50 6.00
84RJB Javier Baez 4.00 10.00
84RJd Jacob deGrom 3.00 8.00
84RJM Joe Mauer 2.50 6.00
84RJM J.D. Martinez S2 3.00 8.00
84RJS Juan Soto S2 4.00 10.00
84RJV Joey Votto 3.00 8.00
84RJVE Justin Verlander 3.00 8.00
84RKB Kris Bryant S2 4.00 10.00
84RKBR Kris Bryant 4.00 10.00
84RKD Khris Davis S2 3.00 8.00
84RMA Miguel Andujar S2 3.00 8.00
84RMB Mookie Betts 8.00 20.00
84RMB Mookie Betts S2 5.00 12.00
84RMC Matt Carpenter S2 3.00 8.00
84RMH Mitch Haniger 2.50 6.00
84RMI Miguel Cabrera S2 3.00 8.00
84RMK Masahiro Tanaka S2 2.50 6.00
84RMO Michael Conforto S2 2.50 6.00
84RMS Max Scherzer 3.00 8.00
84RMT Mike Trout 8.00 20.00
84RMT Mike Trout S2 15.00 40.00
84RNA Nolan Arenado 4.00 10.00
84RNC Nicholas Castellanos 3.00 8.00
84RNR Nolan Ryan 12.00 30.00
84RNS Noah Syndergaard 2.50 6.00
84ROA Ozzie Albies 3.00 8.00
84ROS Ozzie Smith 4.00 10.00
84RPG Paul Goldschmidt 3.00 8.00
84RRA Ronald Acuna Jr. 12.00 30.00
84RRH Rickey Henderson 4.00 10.00
84RRHO Rhys Hoskins 4.00 10.00
84RRJ Reggie Jackson 5.00 12.00
84RRY Robin Yount 3.00 8.00
84RSO Shohei Ohtani 10.00 25.00
84RTM Trey Mancini 2.50 6.00
84RTT Trea Turner 2.50 6.00
84RVR Victor Robles S2 4.00 10.00
04RWB Wade Boggs 5.00 12.00
84RWM Wil Myers 2.00 5.00
84RYM Yadier Molina 3.00 8.00

2019 Topps '84 Topps Rookies

STATED ODDS 1:4 HOBBY
*BLUE: .75X TO 2X BASIC
*BLACK/299: 1.2X TO 3X BASIC
*150th/150: 2X TO 5X BASIC
*GOLD/50: 3X TO 8X BASIC
84RAC Adam Cimber .25 .60
84RAD Austin Dean .25 .60
84RAG Aramis Garcia .25 .60
84RBK Brad Keller .25 .60
84RBL Brandon Lowe .40 1.00
84RBW Bryse Wilson .30 .75
84RCB Corbin Burnes .40 1.00
84RCM Cedric Mullins .40 1.00
84RCP Cionel Perez .25 .60
84RCS Christin Stewart .30 .75
84RCT Carlos Tocci .25 .60
84RDD Dean Deetz .25 .60
84RDF David Fletcher .75 2.00
84RDH Dakota Hudson .30 .75
84RDJ Danny Jansen .25 .60
84RDP Daniel Ponce De Leon .40 1.00
84RDS Dennis Santana .25 .60
84RED Enyel De Los Santos .25 .60
84RFV Framber Valdez .25 .60
84RHF Heath Fillmyer .25 .60
84RJB Jose Briceno .25 .60
84RJC Jake Cave .30 .75
84RJF Johnny Field .30 .75
84RJJ Josh James .40 1.00
84RJS Jeffrey Springs .25 .60
84RKK Kevin Kramer .30 .75
84RKN Kevin Newman .40 1.00
84RKW Kyle Wright .40 1.00
84RMK Michael Kopech .50 1.25
84RMS Myles Straw .40 1.00
84RNB Nick Burdi .25 .60
84RNC Noel Cuevas .25 .60
84RNM Nick Martini .25 .60
84RPL Pablo Lopez .25 .60
84RPW Patrick Wisdom .25 .60
84RRB Ryan Borucki .25 .60
84RRM Reese McGuire .40 1.00
84RRT Rowdy Tellez .40 1.00
84RSD Steven Duggar .30 .75
84RSG Stephen Gonsalves .25 .60
84RSR Sean Reid-Foley .25 .60
84RTR Trevor Richards .25 .60

84RTW Taylor Ward .25 .60
84RWA Willians Astudillo .25 .60
84RYK Yusei Kikuchi .40 1.00
84RCSH Chris Shaw .40 1.00
84RDST DJ Stewart .30 .75
84RJBE Jalen Beeks .25 .60
84RJSH Justus Sheffield .40 1.00
84RRBL Ray Black .25 .60

2019 Topps '84 Topps Silver Pack Chrome

T841 Don Mattingly 1.25 3.00
T842 Mike Trout 3.00 8.00
T843 Ronald Acuna Jr. 3.00 8.00
T844 Javier Baez .75 2.00
T845 Mookie Betts 1.00 2.50
T846 Jackie Robinson .60 1.50
T847 Corey Kluber .50 1.25
T848 Kris Bryant .75 2.00
T849 Francisco Lindor .60 1.50
T8410 Charlie Blackmon .60 1.50
T8411 Jose Altuve .50 1.25
T8412 Noah Syndergaard .50 1.25
T8413 George Springer .50 1.25
T8414 Bo Jackson .60 1.50
T8415 Manny Machado .60 1.50
T8416 Christian Yelich .75 2.00
T8417 Shohei Ohtani .75 2.00
T8418 Aaron Judge 1.50 4.00
T8419 Derek Jeter 1.50 4.00
T8420 Ryne Sandberg 1.25 3.00
T8421 Gleyber Torres 1.25 3.00
T8422 Rickey Henderson .60 1.50
T8423 Rhys Hoskins .75 2.00
T8424 Yadier Molina .60 1.50
T8425 Jake Bauers .60 1.50
T8426 Juan Soto 2.00 5.00
T8427 Buster Posey .75 2.00
T8428 Kyle Schwarber .60 1.50
T8429 Will Clark .50 1.25
T8430 Darryl Strawberry .40 1.00
T8431 John Smoltz .60 1.50
T8432 Cedric Mullins .60 1.50
T8433 Jeff McNeil 1.00 2.50
T8434 Patrick Wisdom .40 1.00
T8435 Brad Keller .40 1.00
T8436 Chance Adams .40 1.00
T8437 Sean Reid-Foley .40 1.00
T8438 Ramon Laureano .75 2.00
T8439 Ryan O'Hearn .40 1.00
T8440 Justus Sheffield .60 1.50
T8441 Kevin Kramer .50 1.25
T8442 Bryse Wilson .50 1.25
T8443 Steven Matz .50 1.25
T8444 Jesus Aguilar .40 1.00
T8445 Jim Rice .50 1.25
T8446 Mark Grace .50 1.25
T8447 Adalberto Mondesi .50 1.25
T8448 Ozzie Smith .75 2.00
T8449 Mark McGwire 1.00 2.50
T8450 Cal Ripken Jr. 2.00 5.00

2019 Topps '84 Topps Silver Pack Chrome Blue Refractors

*BLUE REF: 1.5X TO 4X BASIC
RANDOM INSERTS IN SILVER PACKS
STATED PRINT RUN 150 SER.#'d SETS

2019 Topps '84 Topps Silver Pack Chrome Gold Refractors

*GOLD REF: 5X TO 12X BASIC
RANDOM INSERTS IN SILVER PACKS
STATED PRINT RUN 50 SER.#'d SETS

2019 Topps '84 Topps Silver Pack Chrome Green Refractors

*GREEN REF: 2X TO 5X BASIC
RANDOM INSERTS IN SILVER PACKS
STATED PRINT RUN 150 SER.#'d SETS

2019 Topps '84 Topps Silver Pack Chrome Orange Refractors

*ORANGE REF: 6X TO 15X BASIC
RANDOM INSERTS IN SILVER PACKS
STATED PRINT RUN 25 SER.#'d SETS

2019 Topps '84 Topps Silver Pack Chrome Purple Refractors

*PURPLE REF: 2X TO 5X BASIC
RANDOM INSERTS IN SILVER PACKS
STATED PRINT RUN 75 SER.#'d SETS

2019 Topps '84 Topps Silver Pack Chrome Autographs

RANDOM INSERTS IN SILVER PACKS
PRINT RUNS B/WN 10-299 COPIES PER
NO PRICING ON QTY 10
T84A1 Don Mattingly/30 75.00 200.00
T84A2 Mike Trout
T84A7 Corey Kluber/50 8.00 20.00
T84A11 Jose Altuve/50 20.00 50.00
T84A13 George Springer/50 15.00 40.00
T84A15 Manny Machado/30 25.00 60.00
T84A19 Derek Jeter
T84A20 Ryne Sandberg/30 40.00 100.00
T84A23 Rhys Hoskins/30 30.00 80.00
T84A24 Yadier Molina
T84A25 Jake Bauers/199 5.00 12.00
T84A28 Kyle Schwarber/30 15.00 40.00
T84A29 Will Clark
T84A30 Darryl Strawberry/50 15.00 40.00
T84A31 John Smoltz/50 15.00 40.00
T84A32 Cedric Mullins/199 5.00 12.00
T84A33 Jeff McNeil/299 15.00 40.00
T84A34 Patrick Wisdom/199 3.00 8.00
T84A35 Brad Keller/199 3.00 8.00
T84A36 Chance Adams/199 3.00 8.00
T84A37 Sean Reid-Foley/199 3.00 8.00
T84A38 Ramon Laureano/199 20.00 50.00
T84A39 Ryan O'Hearn/199 3.00 8.00
T84A40 Justus Sheffield/199 5.00 12.00
T84A41 Kevin Kramer/199 4.00 10.00
T84A42 Bryse Wilson/199 4.00 10.00
T84A43 Steven Matz/199 4.00 10.00
T84A44 Jesus Aguilar/199 5.00 12.00
T84A45 Jim Rice/199 10.00 25.00
T84A46 Mark Grace/199 10.00 25.00
T84A47 Adalberto Mondesi/199 10.00 25.00
T84A48 Ozzie Smith/30 30.00 80.00
T84A49 Mark McGwire/30 30.00 80.00

2019 Topps '84 Topps Silver Pack Chrome Autographs Orange Refractors

*ORANGE/25: 1X TO 2.5X p/r 199-299
*ORANGE/25: .75X TO 2X p/r 50
*ORANGE/25: .5X TO 1.2X p/r 30
RANDOM INSERTS IN SILVER PACKS
STATED PRINT RUN 25 SER.#'d SETS
T84A29 Will Clark 40.00 100.00

2019 Topps '84 Topps Silver Pack Chrome Series 2

T841 Clayton Kershaw 1.25 3.00
T842 Ken Griffey Jr. 1.25 3.00
T843 Alex Bregman .60 1.50
T844 Paul Goldschmidt .60 1.50
T845 Robinson Cano .50 1.25
T846 Anthony Rizzo 1.00 2.50
T847 Nolan Ryan 2.00 5.00
T848 Joey Votto .60 1.50
T849 Albert Pujols .75 2.00
T8410 Chipper Jones .60 1.50
T8411 Touki Toussaint .50 1.25
T8412 Kolby Allard .60 1.50
T8413 DJ Stewart .50 1.25
T8414 Wade Boggs .50 1.25
T8415 Chris Sale .60 1.50
T8416 Ernie Banks .60 1.50
T8417 Frank Thomas .60 1.50
T8418 Michael Kopech .75 2.00
T8419 Nolan Arenado .75 2.00
T8420 Eloy Jimenez 1.50 4.00
T8421 Kyle Tucker .75 2.00
T8422 George Brett 1.25 3.00
T8423 Cody Bellinger 1.25 3.00
T8424 Robin Yount .60 1.50
T8425 Willians Astudillo .40 1.00
T8426 Jacob deGrom .60 1.50
T8427 Miguel Andujar .60 1.50
T8428 Jonathan Loaisiga .50 1.25
T8429 Nick Martini .40 1.00
T8430 Khris Davis .60 1.50
T8431 Andrew McCutchen .60 1.50
T8432 Kevin Newman .60 1.50
T8433 Roberto Clemente 1.50 4.00
T8434 Luis Urias .60 1.50
T8435 Tony Gwynn .60 1.50
T8436 Steven Duggar .50 1.25
T8437 Yusei Kikuchi .60 1.50
T8438 Adrian Beltre .60 1.50
T8439 Dakota Hudson .50 1.25
T8440 Manny Machado .60 1.50
T8441 Bryce Harper 1.00 2.50
T8442 Rowdy Tellez .60 1.50
T8443 Danny Jansen .40 1.00
T8444 Roberto Alomar .50 1.25
T8445 Max Scherzer .60 1.50
T8446 Josh James .60 1.50
T8447 Daniel Ponce de Leon .60 1.50
T8448 Myles Straw .60 1.50
T8449 Kohl Stewart .50 1.25
T8450 Mariano Rivera .75 2.00

2019 Topps '84 Topps Silver Pack Chrome Series 2 Black Refractors

*BLACK REF: 1.2X TO 3X BASIC
RANDOM INSERTS IN SILVER PACKS
STATED PRINT RUN 199 SER.#'d SETS

2019 Topps '84 Topps Silver Pack Chrome Series 2 Blue Refractors

*BLUE REF: 1.5X TO 4X BASIC
RANDOM INSERTS IN SILVER PACKS
STATED PRINT RUN 150 SER.#'d SETS

2019 Topps '84 Topps Silver Pack Chrome Series 2 Gold Refractors

*GOLD REF: 5X TO 12X BASIC
RANDOM INSERTS IN SILVER PACKS
STATED PRINT RUN 50 SER.#'d SETS

2019 Topps '84 Topps Silver Pack Chrome Series 2 Green Refractors

*GREEN REF: 2X TO 5X BASIC
RANDOM INSERTS IN SILVER PACKS
STATED PRINT RUN 99 SER.#'d SETS

2019 Topps '84 Topps Silver Pack Chrome Series 2 Orange Refractors

*ORANGE REF: 6X TO 15X BASIC
RANDOM INSERTS IN SILVER PACKS
STATED PRINT RUN 25 SER.#'d SETS

2019 Topps '84 Topps Silver Pack Chrome Series 2 Purple Refractors

*PURPLE REF: 2X TO 5X BASIC
RANDOM INSERTS IN SILVER PACKS
STATED PRINT RUN 75 SER.#'d SETS

2019 Topps '84 Topps Silver Pack Chrome Series 2 Autographs

RANDOM INSERTS IN SILVER PACKS
PRINT RUNS B/WN 10-149 COPIES PER
NO PRICING ON QTY 10
*ORANGE/25: 1X TO 2.5X p/r 149
*ORANGE/25: .75X TO 2X p/r 50-99
T844 Paul Goldschmidt/30 20.00 50.00
T8411 Touki Toussaint/149 4.00 10.00
T8412 Kolby Allard/149 5.00 12.00
T8413 DJ Stewart/149 4.00 10.00
T8414 Wade Boggs
T8418 Michael Kopech/99 10.00 25.00
T8420 Eloy Jimenez/30 60.00 150.00
T8421 Kyle Tucker/50 25.00 60.00
T8425 Willians Astudillo/149 8.00 20.00
T8426 Jacob deGrom/30 20.00 50.00
T8427 Miguel Andujar/30 15.00 40.00
T8428 Jonathan Loaisiga/149 4.00 10.00
T8429 Nick Martini/149 3.00 8.00
T8432 Kevin Newman/149 6.00 15.00
T8436 Steven Duggar/149 4.00 10.00
T8437 Yusei Kikuchi/99 6.00 15.00
T8439 Dakota Hudson/149 5.00 12.00
T8442 Rowdy Tellez/149 5.00 12.00
T8446 Josh James/149 5.00 12.00
T8447 Daniel Ponce de Leon/149 5.00 12.00
T8448 Myles Straw/149 6.00 15.00
T8449 Kohl Stewart/149 4.00 10.00

2019 Topps 150 Years of Professional Baseball

STATED ODDS 1:7 HOBBY
*150TH/150: 2X TO 5X BASIC
*GREEN: .75X TO 2X BASIC
1501 Babe Ruth 1.00 2.50
1502 Babe Ruth 1.00 2.50
1503 Lou Gehrig .75 2.00
1504 Roger Maris .40 1.00
1505 Cal Ripken Jr. 1.25 3.00
1506 Carlton Fisk .30 .75
1507 Reggie Jackson .30 .75
1508 Jackie Robinson .40 1.00
1509 Babe Ruth 1.00 2.50
15010 Nolan Ryan 1.25 3.00
15011 Cal Ripken Jr. 1.25 3.00
15012 Babe Ruth 1.00 2.50
15013 Babe Ruth 1.00 2.50
15014 Ty Cobb 1.25 3.00
15015 Mike Piazza .40 1.00
15016 Nolan Ryan 1.25 3.00
15017 Rickey Henderson .40 1.00
15018 Ichiro .50 1.25
15019 Roberto Clemente 1.00 2.50
15020 David Ortiz .40 1.00
15021 Ty Cobb .60 1.50
15022 Cal Ripken Jr. 1.25 3.00
15023 Jackie Robinson .40 1.00
15024 Mariano Rivera .50 1.25
15025 Ozzie Smith .50 1.25
15026 Derek Jeter 1.00 2.50
15027 The Topps Company .25 .60
15028 Nolan Ryan 1.25 3.00
15029 Lou Brock .30 .75
15030 William Howard Taft .25 .60
15031 Catfish Hunter .30 .75
15032 Ted Williams .75 2.00
15033 Hank Aaron .75 2.00
15034 Ted Williams .75 2.00
15035 Hank Aaron .75 2.00
15036 Wrigley Field .25 .60
15037 Bill Mazeroski .30 .75
15038 Brooks Robinson .30 .75
15039 Phil Niekro .30 .75
15040 Duke Snider .30 .75
15041 Lou Gehrig .75 2.00
15042 Ted Williams .75 2.00
15043 Larry Doby .30 .75
15044 George Brett .75 2.00
15045 Sandy Koufax .75 2.00
15046 Enos Slaughter .30 .75
15047 Sandy Koufax .75 2.00
15048 Ted Williams .75 2.00
15049 Eddie Mathews .40 1.00
15050 Oriole Park at Camden Yards .25 .60
15051 Babe Ruth 1.00 2.50
15052 Jackie Robinson .40 1.00
15053 Lou Gehrig .75 2.00
15054 Clayton Kershaw .75 2.00
15055 Robin Yount .40 1.00
15056 Tom Glavine .30 .75
15057 Vladimir Guerrero .30 .75
15058 Don Mattingly .75 2.00
15059 Reggie Jackson .30 .75
15060 Ivan Rodriguez .30 .75
15061 Roger Maris .40 1.00
15062 Dennis Eckersley .30 .75
15063 Mariano Rivera .50 1.25
15064 Frank Thomas .40 1.00
15065 Adrian Beltre .40 1.00
15066 Justin Verlander .40 1.00
15067 Rod Carew .30 .75
15068 Bryce Harper .60 1.50
15069 Ernie Banks .40 1.00
15070 Mike Piazza .40 1.00
15071 Mark McGwire .60 1.50
15072 Roberto Clemente 1.00 2.50
15073 Derek Jeter 1.00 2.50
15074 Miguel Cabrera .40 1.00
15075 Mike Trout 2.00 5.00
15076 Bob Gibson .30 .75
15077 Al Kaline .40 1.00
15078 Albert Pujols .50 1.25
15079 Wade Boggs .30 .75
15080 David Ortiz .40 1.00
15081 Willie McCovey .30 .75
15082 Tom Seaver .30 .75
15083 Steve Carlton .30 .75
15084 Ty Cobb .60 1.50
15085 Carl Yastrzemski .60 1.50
15086 Pedro Martinez .30 .75
15087 Juan Marichal .30 .75
15088 Nolan Ryan 1.25 3.00
15089 Hank Aaron .75 2.00
15090 Ted Williams .75 2.00
15091 Bob Feller .30 .75
15092 Duke Snider .30 .75
15093 Eddie Mathews .40 1.00
15094 Warren Spahn .30 .75
15095 George Brett .75 2.00
15096 Brooks Robinson .30 .75
15097 Lou Brock .30 .75
15098 Jim Palmer .30 .75
15099 Harmon Killebrew .40 1.00
150100 Ichiro .50 1.25
150101 Ty Cobb .60 1.50
150102 Babe Ruth 1.00 2.50
150103 Jake Arrieta .30 .75
150104 Ichiro .50 1.25
150105 Rickey Henderson .40 1.00
150106 Rickey Henderson .40 1.00
150107 Frank Thomas .40 1.00
150108 Jeff Bagwell .30 .75
150109 Mookie Betts .60 1.50
150110 Albert Pujols .50 1.25
150111 Jacob deGrom .40 1.00
150112 Pedro Martinez .30 .75
150113 Bob Gibson .30 .75
150114 Ichiro .50 1.25
150115 Steve Carlton .30 .75
150116 Carl Yastrzemski .60 1.50
150117 Miguel Cabrera .40 1.00
150118 Lou Gehrig .75 2.00
150119 Tom Seaver .30 .75
150120 Roger Maris .40 1.00
150121 Clayton Kershaw .75 2.00
150122 Jackie Robinson .40 1.00
150123 Sandy Koufax .75 2.00
150124 Ted Williams .75 2.00
150125 Randy Johnson .40 1.00
150126 Juan Marichal .30 .75
150127 Ernie Banks .40 1.00
150128 Mark McGwire .60 1.50
150129 Todd Helton .30 .75
150130 Albert Pujols .50 1.25
150131 Bryce Harper .60 1.50
150132 Mike Trout 2.00 5.00
150133 Joe Morgan .30 .75
150134 Nolan Ryan 1.25 3.00
150135 Hank Aaron .75 2.00
150136 Mark McGwire .60 1.50
150137 Mike Trout 2.00 5.00
150138 Robin Yount .40 1.00
150139 Zack Greinke .30 .75
150140 Nolan Ryan 1.25 3.00
150141 Mike Piazza .40 1.00
150142 Cal Ripken Jr. 1.25 3.00
150143 Willie McCovey .30 .75
150144 Rod Carew .30 .75
150145 Pedro Martinez .30 .75
150146 Babe Ruth 1.00 2.50
150147 Aaron Judge 1.00 2.50
150148 Lou Gehrig .75 2.00
150149 Babe Ruth 1.00 2.50
150150 Jim Rice .30 .75

2019 Topps 150 Years of Professional Baseball Autographs

STATED ODDS 1:13,136 HOBBY
PRINT RUNS B/WN 5-25 COPIES PER
NO PRICING ON QTY 15 OR LESS
EXCHANGE DEADLINE 12/30/2020
1506 Carlton Fisk/25 75.00 200.00
15015 Mike Piazza
15018 Ichiro
15020 David Ortiz
15024 Mariano Rivera
15025 Ozzie Smith/25 25.00 60.00
15037 Bill Mazeroski/25 25.00 60.00
15039 Phil Niekro/25 15.00 40.00
15058 Don Mattingly/25 60.00 150.00
15062 Dennis Eckersley/25 12.00 30.00
15076 Bob Gibson/25 30.00 80.00
15087 Juan Marichal/25 60.00 150.00

2019 Topps 150 Years of Professional Baseball Greatest Moments

STATED ODDS 1:14 HOBBY
*BLUE: .75X TO 2X BASIC
*GREEN: .75X TO 2X BASIC
*BLACK/299: 1.2X TO 3X BASIC
*150th/150: 2X TO 5X BASIC
*GOLD/50: 3X TO 8X BASIC
GM1 Don Larsen .25 .60
GM2 Christy Mathewson .40 1.00
GM3 Mel Ott .40 1.00
GM4 Roger Clemens .50 1.25
GM5 Mark McGwire .60 1.50
GM6 Bob Feller .30 .75
GM7 Ted Williams .75 2.00
GM8 Derek Jeter 1.00 2.50
GM9 Bartolo Colon .25 .60
GM10 Bo Jackson .40 1.00
GM11 Edgar Martinez .30 .75
GM12 Ken Griffey Jr. .75 2.00
GM13 Bob Gibson .30 .75
GM14 Christy Mathewson .40 1.00
GM15 Derek Jeter 1.00 2.50
GM16 Sandy Koufax .75 2.00
GM17 Albert Pujols .50 1.25
GM18 Aaron Judge 1.00 2.50
GM19 Bryce Harper .60 1.50
GM20 Mariano Rivera .50 1.25
GM21 Max Scherzer .40 1.00
GM22 Anthony Rizzo .60 1.50
GM23 Ted Williams .75 2.00
GM24 Edinson Volquez .25 .60
GM25 David Freese .25 .60

2019 Topps 150 Years of Professional Baseball Greatest Moments Autographs

STATED ODDS 1:12,167 HOBBY
PRINT RUNS B/WN 5-25 COPIES PER
NO PRICING ON QTY 15 OR LESS
EXCHANGE DEADLINE 12/31/2020
GM11 Edgar Martinez/25 15.00 40.00
GM18 Aaron Judge

2019 Topps 150 Years of Professional Baseball Greatest Players

STATED ODDS 1:14 HOBBY
*BLUE: .75X TO 2X BASIC
*GREEN: .75X TO 2X BASIC
*BLACK/299: 1.2X TO 3X BASIC
*150th/150: 2X TO 5X BASIC
*GOLD/50: 3X TO 8X BASIC
GP1 Max Scherzer .40 1.00
GP2 Barry Larkin .30 .75
GP3 Joey Votto .40 1.00
GP4 Johnny Bench .40 1.00
GP5 Rickey Henderson .40 1.00
GP6 Cal Ripken Jr. 1.25 3.00
GP7 Yadier Molina .40 1.00
GP8 Buster Posey .50 1.25
GP9 Honus Wagner .40 1.00
GP10 Sandy Koufax .75 2.00
GP11 Stan Musial .60 1.50
GP12 Chipper Jones .40 1.00
GP13 Ryne Sandberg .75 2.00
GP14 Ozzie Smith .50 1.25
GP15 John Smoltz .40 1.00
GP16 Alex Rodriguez .50 1.25
GP17 Jeff Bagwell .30 .75
GP18 Tony Gwynn .40 1.00
GP19 Rogers Hornsby .30 .75
GP20 Mel Ott .40 1.00
GP21 Christy Mathewson .40 1.00
GP22 Johnny Mize .30 .75
GP23 Lefty Grove .30 .75
GP24 Tris Speaker .30 .75
GP25 Dizzy Dean .30 .75
GP26 Don Larsen .25 .60
GP27 Pee Wee Reese .30 .75
GP28 Gil Hodges .30 .75
GP29 Whitey Ford .30 .75
GP30 Billy Williams .30 .75
GP31 Dave Winfield .30 .75
GP32 Tony Perez .30 .75
GP33 Bill Mazeroski .30 .75
GP34 Rollie Fingers .30 .75
GP35 Ken Griffey Jr. .75 2.00
GP36 Frank Robinson .30 .75
GP37 Phil Rizzuto .30 .75
GP38 Joe Morgan .30 .75
GP39 Eddie Murray .30 .75
GP40 Phil Niekro .30 .75
GP41 Red Schoendienst .30 .75
GP42 Enos Slaughter .30 .75
GP43 Willie Stargell .30 .75
GP44 Fergie Jenkins .30 .75
GP45 Ralph Kiner .30 .75
GP46 Catfish Hunter .30 .75
GP47 Monte Irvin .30 .75
GP48 Orlando Cepeda .30 .75
GP49 Larry Doby .30 .75
GP50 Roberto Alomar .30 .75

2019 Topps 150 Years of Professional Baseball Greatest Players Autographs

STATED ODDS 1:12,167 HOBBY
PRINT RUNS B/WN 5-25 COPIES PER
NO PRICING ON QTY 15 OR LESS
EXCHANGE DEADLINE 12/31/2020
GP5 Rickey Henderson
GP8 Buster Posey
GP31 Dave Winfield
GP33 Bill Mazeroski/25 50.00 120.00
GP34 Rollie Fingers/25 10.00 25.00
GP40 Phil Niekro/25 20.00 50.00
GP48 Orlando Cepeda/25 15.00 40.00

2019 Topps 150 Years of Professional Baseball Greatest Seasons

STATED ODDS 1:14 HOBBY
*BLUE: .75X TO 2X BASIC
2019 Topps 150 Years of Professional Baseball Green
*BLACK/299: 1.2X TO 3X BASIC
*150th/150: 2X TO 5X BASIC
*GOLD/50: 3X TO 8X BASIC
GS1 Dwight Gooden .25 .60
GS2 Roger Clemens .50 1.25
GS3 Tony Gwynn .40 1.00
GS4 Christy Mathewson .40 1.00
GS5 Tris Speaker .30 .75
GS6 Mel Ott .40 1.00
GS7 Frank Robinson .30 .75
GS8 David Ortiz .40 1.00
GS9 Roberto Clemente 1.00 2.50
GS10 Mariano Rivera .50 1.25
GS11 Lou Brock .30 .75
GS12 Brooks Robinson .30 .75
GS13 Duke Snider .30 .75
GS14 George Brett .75 2.00
GS15 Eddie Mathews .40 1.00
GS16 Reggie Jackson .30 .75
GS17 Al Kaline .40 1.00
GS18 Bob Feller .30 .75
GS19 Whitey Ford .30 .75
GS20 Stan Musial .60 1.50
GS21 Johnny Mize .30 .75
GS22 Honus Wagner .40 1.00
GS23 Dizzy Dean .30 .75
GS24 Aaron Judge 1.00 2.50
GS25 Ken Griffey Jr. .75 2.00

2019 Topps 150 Years of Professional Baseball Greatest Seasons Autographs

STATED ODDS 1:12,167 HOBBY
PRINT RUNS B/WN 5-25 COPIES PER
NO PRICING ON QTY 15 OR LESS
EXCHANGE DEADLINE 12/31/2020
GS1 Dwight Gooden/25 20.00 50.00
GS11 Lou Brock/25 25.00 60.00

2019 Topps 150th Anniversary Manufactured Medallions

SER.1 ODDS 1:1230 HOBBY
SER.2 ODDS 1:XX HOBBY
*150TH/150: .6X TO 1.5X BASIC
*GOLD/50: .75X TO 2X BASIC
*RED/25: 1.2X TO 3X BASIC
AMMAB Adrian Beltre 2.50 6.00
AMMAD Andre Dawson S2 4.00 10.00
AMMAJ Aaron Judge 6.00 15.00
AMMAK Al Kaline 2.50 6.00
AMMAP Albert Pujols 3.00 8.00
AMMAR Anthony Rizzo 4.00 10.00
AMMBF Bob Feller S2 5.00 12.00
AMMBG Bob Gibson 2.00 5.00
AMMBH Bryce Harper S2 4.00 10.00
AMMBJ Bo Jackson 2.50 6.00
AMMBL Barry Larkin S2 5.00 12.00
AMMBP Buster Posey 3.00 8.00
AMMBR Babe Ruth S2 6.00 15.00
AMMCB Charlie Blackmon S2 2.50 6.00
AMMCF Carlton Fisk S2 3.00 8.00
AMMCJ Chipper Jones S2 5.00 12.00
AMMCK Clayton Kershaw 5.00 12.00
AMMCR Cal Ripken Jr. 6.00 15.00
AMMCS Chris Sale S2 2.50 6.00
AMMCY Carl Yastrzemski 4.00 10.00
AMMCY Christian Yelich S2 5.00 12.00
AMMDE Dennis Eckersley S2 3.00 8.00
AMMDJ Derek Jeter 10.00 25.00
AMMDM Don Mattingly 5.00 12.00
AMMDO David Ortiz 2.50 6.00
AMMDS Duke Snider S2 2.00 5.00
AMMEB Ernie Banks S2 2.00 5.00
AMMEM Eddie Murray S2 5.00 12.00
AMMFF Freddie Freeman S2 3.00 8.00
AMMFH Felix Hernandez 2.00 5.00
AMMFL Francisco Lindor 2.50 6.00
AMMFT Frank Thomas 2.50 6.00
AMMGB George Brett S2 12.00 30.00
AMMHA Hank Aaron S2 10.00 25.00
AMMHW Honus Wagner S2 2.50 6.00
AMMI Ichiro 3.00 8.00
AMMIR Ivan Rodriguez 2.00 5.00
AMMJA Jose Altuve 2.00 5.00
AMMJB Javier Baez S2 3.00 8.00
AMMJd Jacob deGrom S2 2.50 6.00
AMMJM Joe Mauer 2.00 5.00
AMMJM Juan Marichal S2 2.00 5.00
AMMJR Jackie Robinson 2.50 6.00
AMMJR Jose Ramirez S2 2.00 5.00
AMMJS Juan Soto 8.00 20.00
AMMJT Joey Votto 2.50 6.00
AMMJV Justin Verlander 2.50 6.00
AMMKB Kris Bryant 3.00 8.00
AMMLB Lou Brock S2 6.00 15.00
AMMLG Lou Gehrig 5.00 12.00
AMMMB Mookie Betts 4.00 10.00
AMMMC Miguel Cabrera S2 2.50 6.00
AMMMG Mark McGwire 4.00 10.00
AMMMM Manny Machado 2.50 6.00
AMMMO Mel Ott S2 2.50 6.00
AMMMP Mike Piazza 2.50 6.00
AMMMR Mariano Rivera S2 3.00 8.00
AMMMS Max Scherzer 2.50 6.00
AMMMT Mike Trout 12.00 30.00
AMMNA Nolan Arenado 3.00 8.00
AMMNR Nolan Ryan S2 8.00 20.00
AMMOS Ozzie Smith S2 3.00 8.00
AMMPG Paul Goldschmidt 2.50 6.00
AMMPM Pedro Martinez S2 2.00 5.00
AMMRA Roberto Alomar 2.00 5.00
AMMRC Roberto Clemente 10.00 25.00
AMMRC Roger Clemens S2 3.00 8.00
AMMRCA Rod Carew 2.00 5.00
AMMRH Rogers Hornsby S2 3.00 8.00
AMMRJ Reggie Jackson 2.00 5.00
AMMRM Roger Maris S2 2.50 6.00
AMMRO Ronald Acuna Jr. 12.00 30.00
AMMRS Ryne Sandberg S2 5.00 12.00
AMMRY Robin Yount 5.00 12.00
AMMSC Steve Carlton 2.00 5.00
AMMSK Sandy Koufax S2 5.00 12.00
AMMSM Stan Musial S2 8.00 20.00
AMMSO Shohei Ohtani 3.00 8.0
AMMTC Ty Cobb 4.00 10.0
AMMTG Tom Glavine 2.00 5.0
AMMTG Tony Gwynn S2 5.00 12.0
AMMTH Todd Helton S2 4.00 10.0
AMMTS Tom Seaver 2.00 5.0
AMMTW Ted Williams S2 5.00 12.0
AMMVG Vladimir Guerrero 2.00 5.0
AMMVG Vladimir Guerrero S2 2.00 5.0
AMMWB Wade Boggs 2.00 5.0
AMMWC Will Clark S2 4.00 10.0
AMMWM Willie McCovey 2.00 5.0
AMMWS Willie Stargell S2 3.00 8.0
AMMYM Yadier Molina 3.00 8.0
AMMBRO Brooks Robinson S2 6.00 15.0
AMMBRU Babe Ruth S2 6.00 15.0
AMMEMA Eddie Mathews S2 2.50 6.0
AMMJMO Joe Morgan S2 2.00 5.0
AMMNRY Nolan Ryan S2 8.00 20.0
AMMRCA Rod Carew S2 2.00 5.0
AMMRHE Rickey Henderson S2 2.50 6.0
AMMRHO Rhys Hoskins S2 3.00 8.0
AMMWSP Warren Spahn S2 2.00 5.0

2019 Topps 150th Anniversary Manufactured Patches

ONE PER RETAIL BLASTER
*150TH/150: .75X TO 2X BASIC
*GOLD/50: 1X TO 2.5X BASIC
*RED/25: 1.5X TO 4X BASIC
AMPI Ichiro S2 2.00 5.0
AMPAB Alex Bregman 1.50 4.0
AMPAB Adrian Beltre S2 1.50 4.0
AMPABE Andrew Benintendi 1.50 4.0
AMPAJ Aaron Judge S2 4.00 10.0
AMPAK Al Kaline S2 1.50 4.0
AMPAP Andy Pettitte 1.25 3.0
AMPAP Albert Pujols S2 2.00 5.0
AMPAR Anthony Rizzo S2 2.50 6.0
AMPBG Bob Gibson S2 1.25 3.0
AMPBH Bryce Harper S2 2.50 6.0
AMPBJ Bo Jackson S2 1.50 4.0
AMPBL Barry Larkin 1.25 3.0
AMPBP Buster Posey S2 2.00 5.0
AMPBRU Babe Ruth 4.00 10.0
AMPCB Cody Bellinger 3.00 8.0
AMPCBL Charlie Blackmon 1.50 4.0
AMPCC Carlos Correa 1.50 4.0
AMPCJ Chipper Jones S2 1.50 4.0
AMPCK Clayton Kershaw 3.00 8.0
AMPCR Cal Ripken Jr. 5.00 12.0
AMPCS Corey Seager 1.50 4.0
AMPCSA Chris Sale 1.50 4.0
AMPCY Christian Yelich 2.00 5.0
AMPCY Carl Yastrzemski S2 2.50 6.0
AMPDE Dennis Eckersley 1.25 3.0
AMPDJ Derek Jeter S2 4.00 10.0
AMPDM Don Mattingly S2 3.00 8.0
AMPDO David Ortiz S2 1.50 4.0
AMPDP Dustin Pedroia 1.50 4.0
AMPDW David Wright S2 1.25 3.0
AMPEB Ernie Banks S2 1.50 4.0
AMPFF Freddie Freeman 2.00 5.0
AMPFL Francisco Lindor S2 1.50 4.0
AMPFT Frank Thomas S2 1.50 4.0
AMPGB George Brett S2 3.00 8.0
AMPGC Gerrit Cole 1.50 4.0
AMPGS Giancarlo Stanton 1.50 4.0
AMPGSP George Springer 1.25 3.0
AMPGT Gleyber Torres 3.00 8.0
AMPHA Hank Aaron S2 3.00 8.0
AMPHK Harmon Killebrew S2 1.50 4.0
AMPHW Honus Wagner S2 1.50 4.0
AMPIR Ivan Rodriguez S2 1.25 3.0
AMPJA Jose Abreu 1.50 4.0
AMPJA Jose Altuve S2 1.25 3.0
AMPJB Javier Baez 2.00 5.0
AMPJB Jeff Bagwell S2 1.25 3.0
AMPJDE Jacob deGrom 1.50 4.0
AMPJG Juan Gonzalez 1.00 2.5
AMPJR Jose Ramirez 1.25 3.0
AMPJR Jackie Robinson S2 1.50 4.0
AMPJS Juan Soto S2 5.00 12.0
AMPJU Justin Upton 1.25 3.0
AMPJV Justin Verlander S2 1.50 4.0
AMPKB Kris Bryant 2.00 5.0
AMPLG Lou Gehrig S2 3.00 8.0
AMPLS Luis Severino 1.25 3.0
AMPMB Mookie Betts S2 2.50 6.0
AMPMC Miguel Cabrera 1.50 4.0
AMPMM Mark McGwire 2.50 6.0
AMPMM Mark McGwire S2 2.50 6.0
AMPMMC Manny Machado 1.50 4.0
AMPMP Mike Piazza 1.50 4.0
AMPMP Mike Piazza S2 1.50 4.0
AMPMS Max Scherzer 1.50 4.0
AMPMS Max Scherzer S2 1.50 4.0
AMPMT Mike Trout 8.00 20.0
AMPNA Nolan Arenado S2 2.00 5.0
AMPNR Nolan Ryan 5.00 12.0
AMPNS Noah Syndergaard 1.25 3.0
AMPOA Ozzie Albies 1.50 4.0
AMPOS Ozzie Smith 2.00 5.0
AMPPG Paul Goldschmidt 1.50 4.0
AMPPM Pedro Martinez 1.25 3.0
AMPRA Ronald Acuna Jr. 8.00 20.0
AMPRA Roberto Alomar S2 1.25 3.0
AMPRC Roberto Clemente 4.00 10.0
AMPRC Rod Carew S2 1.25 3.0
AMPRCA Rod Carew 1.25 3.0
AMPRH Rhys Hoskins 2.00 5.0
AMPRHE Rickey Henderson 1.50 4.0
AMPRJ Randy Johnson 1.50 4.0

AMPRJ Reggie Jackson S2 1.25 3.00
AMPRM Roger Maris 1.50 4.00
AMPRY Robin Yount S2 1.50 4.00
AMPSC Steve Carlton S2 1.25 3.00
AMPSK Sandy Koufax S2 3.00 8.00
AMPSM Stan Musial S2 2.50 6.00
AMPSO Shohei Ohtani S2 2.00 5.00
AMPSP Salvador Perez 1.25 3.00
AMPTC Ty Cobb 2.50 6.00
AMPTG Tony Gwynn S2 1.50 4.00
AMPTT Trea Turner 1.25 3.00
AMPTW Ted Williams S2 3.00 8.00
AMPVG Vladimir Guerrero S2 1.25 3.00
AMPWS Willie Stargell S2 1.25 3.00
AMPYM Yadier Molina S2 1.50 4.00
AMPJVO Joey Votto S2 1.50 4.00
AMPTGL Tom Glavine S2 1.25 3.00

2019 Topps Aaron Judge Highlights

STATED ODDS 1:4 TAR.BLASTER
*150th/150: 1.25X TO 3X BASIC
AJ1 Aaron Judge 1.00 2.50
AJ2 Aaron Judge 1.00 2.50
AJ3 Aaron Judge 1.00 2.50
AJ4 Aaron Judge 1.00 2.50
AJ5 Aaron Judge 1.00 2.50
AJ6 Aaron Judge 1.00 2.50
AJ7 Aaron Judge 1.00 2.50
AJ8 Aaron Judge 1.00 2.50
AJ9 Aaron Judge 1.00 2.50
AJ10 Aaron Judge 1.00 2.50
AJ11 Aaron Judge 1.00 2.50
AJ12 Aaron Judge 1.00 2.50
AJ13 Aaron Judge 1.00 2.50
AJ14 Aaron Judge 1.00 2.50
AJ15 Aaron Judge 1.00 2.50
AJ16 Aaron Judge 1.00 2.50
AJ17 Aaron Judge 1.00 2.50
AJ18 Aaron Judge 1.00 2.50
AJ19 Aaron Judge 1.00 2.50
AJ20 Aaron Judge 1.00 2.50
AJ21 Aaron Judge 1.00 2.50
AJ22 Aaron Judge 1.00 2.50
AJ23 Aaron Judge 1.00 2.50
AJ24 Aaron Judge 1.00 2.50
AJ25 Aaron Judge 1.00 2.50
AJ26 Aaron Judge 1.00 2.50
AJ27 Aaron Judge 1.00 2.50
AJ28 Aaron Judge 1.00 2.50
AJ29 Aaron Judge 1.00 2.50
AJ30 Aaron Judge 1.00 2.50

2019 Topps Cactus League Legends

*150TH/150: 1.5X TO 4X BASIC
CLL1 Ernie Banks .50 1.25
CLL2 Mike Trout 2.50 6.00
CLL3 Rickey Henderson .50 1.25
CLL4 Juan Marichal .40 1.00
CLL5 Rod Carew .40 1.00
CLL6 Ichiro .60 1.50
CLL7 Clayton Kershaw 1.00 2.50
CLL8 Frank Thomas .50 1.25
CLL9 Reggie Jackson .40 1.00
CLL10 Brooks Robinson .40 1.00
CLL11 Corey Seager .50 1.25
CLL12 Paul Goldschmidt .50 1.25
CLL13 Buster Posey .60 1.50
CLL14 Trevor Hoffman .40 1.00
CLL15 Adrian Beltre .50 1.25
CLL16 Mark McGwire .75 2.00
CLL17 Will Clark .40 1.00
CLL18 Shohei Ohtani .60 1.50
CLL19 Willie McCovey .40 1.00
CLL20 Randy Johnson .50 1.25
CLL21 Fergie Jenkins .40 1.00
CLL22 Albert Pujols .60 1.50
CLL23 Kris Bryant .60 1.50
CLL24 Joey Votto .50 1.25
CLL25 Francisco Lindor .50 1.25
CLL26 Nolan Arenado .60 1.50
CLL27 Charlie Blackmon .50 1.25
CLL28 Khris Davis .50 1.25
CLL29 Robin Yount .50 1.25
CLL30 Cody Bellinger 1.00 2.50

2019 Topps Commemorative Retro Hat Logos

STATED ODDS 1:635 HOBBY
*150TH/150: .6X TO 1.5X BASIC
*GOLD/50: .75X TO 2X BASIC
*RED/25: 1.2X TO 3X BASIC
RHLPAB Alex Bregman 2.00 5.00
RHLPABR Alex Bregman 2.00 5.00
RHLPAN Aaron Nola 1.50 4.00
RHLPAR Anthony Rizzo 3.00 8.00
RHLPBS Blake Snell 1.50 4.00
RHLPCC Carlos Correa 2.00 5.00
RHLPCK Clayton Kershaw 4.00 10.00
RHLPCY Christian Yelich 2.50 6.00
RHLPDP Dustin Pedroia 2.00 5.00
RHLPDS Dansby Swanson 2.00 5.00
RHLPEA Elvis Andrus 1.50 4.00
RHLPFF Freddie Freeman 2.50 6.00
RHLPFL Francisco Lindor 2.00 5.00
RHLPGS George Springer 1.50 4.00
RHLPJAB Jose Abreu 2.00 5.00
RHLPJAL Jose Altuve 1.50 4.00
RHLPJD Jacob deGrom 2.00 5.00
RHLPJM Joe Mauer 1.50 4.00
RHLPJR Jose Ramirez 1.50 4.00
RHLPLC Lorenzo Cain 1.25 3.00
RHLPMB Mookie Betts 3.00 8.00
RHLPMC Michael Conforto 1.50 4.00
RHLPMK Matt Kemp 1.50 4.00
RHLPMT Mike Trout 10.00 25.00
RHLPMTR Mike Trout 10.00 25.00
RHLPNS Noah Syndergaard 1.50 4.00
RHLPOA Ozzie Albies 2.00 5.00
RHLPPG Paul Goldschmidt 2.00 5.00
RHLPRC Robinson Cano 1.50 4.00
RHLPRH Rhys Hoskins 2.50 6.00
RHLPSM Starling Marte 1.50 4.00
RHLPSO Shohei Ohtani 2.50 6.00
RHLPTM Trey Mancini 1.50 4.00
RHLPTS Travis Shaw 1.25 3.00
RHLPWM Wil Myers 1.25 3.00
RHLPXB Xander Bogaerts 2.00 5.00
RHLPYM Yadier Molina 2.00 5.00
RHLPYMO Yoan Moncada 2.00 5.00
RHLPZG Zack Greinke 1.50 4.00

2019 Topps Evolution

STATED ODDS 1:42 HOBBY
*150TH/150: 2X TO 5X BASIC
EO1 Robinson/Kershaw 1.25 3.00
EO2 Aaron/Acuna 3.00 8.00
EO3 Harper/Guerrero 1.00 2.50
EO4 Harmon Killebrew .60 1.50
Joe Mauer
EO5 Blake Snell .50 1.25
Wade Boggs
EO6 Feller/Lindor .60 1.50
EO7 Ruth/Judge 1.50 4.00
EO8 Cobb/Cabrera 1.00 2.50
EO9 Benintendi/Williams 1.25 3.00
EO10 Bryant/Banks .75 2.00
EO11 Fenway Park .40 1.00
Fenway Park
EO12 Wrigley Field .40 1.00
Wrigley Field
EO13 Yankee Stadium .40 1.00
Yankee Stadium
EO14 Candlestick Park .40 1.00
At&t Park
EO15 Ebbets Field .40 1.00
Dodger Stadium
EO16 Forbes Field .40 1.00
PNC Park
EO17 Sportsman's Park .40 1.00
Busch Stadium
EO18 Shea Stadium .40 1.00
Citi Field
EO19 Memorial Stadium .40 1.00
Oriole Park at Camden Yards
EO20 Crosley Field .40 1.00
Great American Ball Park
EO21 Vintage Baseball .40 1.00
Modern Baseball
EO22 Vintage Catcher's Mask .40 1.00
Modern Catcher's Mask
EO23 Vintage Baseball Glove .40 1.00
Modern Baseball Glove
EO24 Vintage Sunglasses .40 1.00
Modern Sunglasses
EO25 Vintage Cleats .40 1.00
Modern Cleats

2019 Topps Evolution of Stadiums

STATED ODDS 1:56 HOBBY
*BLUE: .6X TO 1.5X BASIC
*BLACK/299: 1X TO 2.5X BASIC
*150th/150: 2X TO 5X BASIC
*GOLD/50: 3X TO 8X BASIC
ES1 T-Mobile Park .40 1.00
The Kingdome
ES2 Citizens Bank Park .40 1.00
Veterans Stadium
ES3 Minute Maid Park .40 1.00
Astrodome
ES4 Comerica Park .40 1.00
Tiger Stadium
ES5 Oracle Park .40 1.00
Polo Grounds
ES6 Guaranteed Rate Field .40 1.00
Comiskey Park
ES7 SunTrust Park .40 1.00
Turner Field
ES8 Miller Park .40 1.00
Milwaukee County Stadium
ES9 Municipal Stadium .40 1.00
Kauffman Stadium
ES10 Target Field .40 1.00
Hubert H. Humphrey Metrodome

2019 Topps Evolution of Team Logos

STATED ODDS 1:56 HOBBY
*BLUE: .6X TO 1.5X BASIC
*BLACK/299: 1X TO 2.5X BASIC
*150th/150: 2X TO 5X BASIC
*GOLD/50: 3X TO 8X BASIC
EL1 Yadier Molina .60 1.50
Bob Gibson
EL2 Lewis Brinson .60 1.50
Miguel Cabrera
EL3 Ichiro 1.25 3.00
Ken Griffey Jr.
EL4 Rhys Hoskins .75 2.00
Steve Carlton
EL5 Buster Posey .75 2.00
Mel Ott
EL6 Joey Votto .60 1.50
Johnny Bench
EL7 Mike Trout 3.00 8.00
Rod Carew
EL8 Frank Thomas .60 1.50
Carlton Fisk
EL9 Roberto Clemente 1.50 4.00
Starling Marte
EL10 Jose Altuve 2.00 5.00
Nolan Ryan

2019 Topps Evolution of Technology

STATED ODDS 1:56 HOBBY
*BLUE: .6X TO 1.5X BASIC
*BLACK/299: 1X TO 2.5X BASIC
*150th/150: 2X TO 5X BASIC
*GOLD/50: 3X TO 8X BASIC
ET1 Ticket Stubs .40 1.00
Digital Mobile Ticket
ET2 Jumbotron .40 1.00
Scoreboard
ET3 Instant Replay Review .40 1.00
Field Umpire
ET4 Box Scores .40 1.00
MLB At Bat App
ET5 Television Broadcast .40 1.00
Radio Broadcast

2019 Topps Franchise Feats

STATED ODDS 1:4 BLASTER
*BLUE: .6X TO 1.5X BASIC
*BLACK/299: 1X TO 2.5X BASIC
*150th/150: 1.5X TO 4X BASIC
*GOLD/50: 2.5X TO 6X BASIC
FF1 Hank Aaron 1.25 3.00
FF2 Randy Johnson .60 1.50
FF3 Mike Trout 3.00 8.00
FF4 Cal Ripken Jr. 2.00 5.00
FF5 Ted Williams 1.25 3.00
FF6 Ernie Banks .60 1.50
FF7 Frank Thomas .60 1.50
FF8 Johnny Bench .60 1.50
FF9 Bob Feller .50 1.25
FF10 Todd Helton .50 1.25
FF11 Al Kaline .60 1.50
FF12 Jose Altuve .50 1.25
FF13 George Brett 1.25 3.00
FF14 Sandy Koufax 1.25 3.00
FF15 Giancarlo Stanton .60 1.50
FF16 Robin Yount .60 1.50
FF17 Harmon Killebrew .60 1.50
FF18 Mike Piazza .60 1.50
FF19 Babe Ruth 1.50 4.00
FF20 Rickey Henderson .60 1.50
FF21 Steve Carlton .50 1.25
FF22 Roberto Clemente 1.50 4.00
FF23 Tony Gwynn .60 1.50
FF24 Buster Posey .75 2.00
FF25 Nolan Ryan 2.00 5.00
FF26 Ken Griffey Jr. 1.25 3.00
FF27 Stan Musial 1.00 2.50
FF28 Roberto Alomar .50 1.25
FF29 Max Scherzer .60 1.50
FF30 Evan Longoria .50 1.25

2019 Topps Gary Vee's Top Entrepreneurs in Baseball

STATED ODDS 1:18 HOBBY
*BLUE: .6X TO 1.5X BASIC
*BLACK/299: 1X TO 2.5X BASIC
*150th/150: 1.5X TO 4X BASIC
*GOLD/50: 3X TO 8X BASIC
GV1 Bryce Harper 1.00 2.50
GV2 Marcus Stroman .50 1.25
GV3 Ian Kinsler .50 1.25
GV4 Hunter Pence .50 1.25
GV5 Jose Ramirez .50 1.25
GV6 Alex Bregman .60 1.50
GV7 Chris Iannetta .40 1.00
GV8 Randy Johnson .60 1.50
GV9 Derek Jeter 1.50 4.00
GV10 Trevor May .40 1.00

2019 Topps Gary Vee's Top Entrepreneurs in Baseball 150th Anniversary

*150th/150: 1.5X TO 4X BASIC
STATED ODDS 1:3054 HOBBY
STATED PRINT RUN 150 SER.#'d SETS
GV1 Bryce Harper 8.00 20.00
GV9 Derek Jeter 20.00 50.00

2019 Topps Gary Vee's Top Entrepreneurs in Baseball Black

*BLACK/299: 1X TO 2.5X BASIC
STATED ODDS 1:49 HOBBY
STATED PRINT RUN 299 SER.#'d SETS
GV1 Bryce Harper 6.00 15.00
GV9 Derek Jeter 15.00 40.00

2019 Topps Gary Vee's Top Entrepreneurs in Baseball Gold

*GOLD/50: 3X TO 8X BASIC
STATED ODDS 1:294 HOBBY
STATED PRINT RUN 50 SER.#'d SETS
GV1 Bryce Harper 12.00 30.00
GV9 Derek Jeter 50.00 120.00

2019 Topps Gary Vee's Top Entrepreneurs in Baseball Dual Autographs

STATED ODDS 1:53,533 HOBBY
PRINT RUNS B/WN 5-25 COPIES PER
NO PRICING ON QTY 15 OR LESS
EXCHANGE DEADLINE 12/31/2020
GVIK Ian Kinsler 200.00 500.00
Gary Vaynerchuk/25
GVIR Jose Ramirez 150.00 400.00
Gary Vaynerchuk/25

2019 Topps Gleyber Torres Highlights

*150TH/150: 1.5X TO 4X BASIC
GT1 Gleyber Torres .75 2.00
GT2 Gleyber Torres .75 2.00
GT3 Gleyber Torres .75 2.00
GT4 Gleyber Torres .75 2.00
GT5 Gleyber Torres .75 2.00
GT6 Gleyber Torres .75 2.00
GT7 Gleyber Torres .75 2.00
GT8 Gleyber Torres .75 2.00
GT9 Gleyber Torres .75 2.00
GT10 Gleyber Torres .75 2.00
GT11 Gleyber Torres .75 2.00
GT12 Gleyber Torres .75 2.00
GT13 Gleyber Torres .75 2.00
GT14 Gleyber Torres .75 2.00
GT15 Gleyber Torres .75 2.00
GT16 Gleyber Torres .75 2.00
GT17 Gleyber Torres .75 2.00
GT18 Gleyber Torres .75 2.00
GT19 Gleyber Torres .75 2.00
GT20 Gleyber Torres .75 2.00
GT21 Gleyber Torres .75 2.00
GT22 Gleyber Torres .75 2.00
GT23 Gleyber Torres .75 2.00
GT24 Gleyber Torres .75 2.00
GT25 Gleyber Torres .75 2.00
GT26 Gleyber Torres .75 2.00
GT27 Gleyber Torres .75 2.00
GT28 Gleyber Torres .75 2.00
GT29 Gleyber Torres .75 2.00
GT30 Gleyber Torres .75 2.00

2019 Topps MLB Logo Golden Anniversary Commemorative Patches

STATED ODDS 1:2828 HOBBY
*150th/150: .6X TO 1.5X BASIC
*GOLD/50: .75X TO 2X BASIC
*RED/25: 1.2X TO 3X BASIC
GAPAB Alex Bregman 2.00 5.00
GAPAJ Aaron Judge 5.00 12.00
GAPAR Anthony Rizzo 3.00 8.00
GAPBH Bryce Harper 3.00 8.00
GAPBP Buster Posey 2.50 6.00
GAPBS Blake Snell 1.50 4.00
GAPCC Carlos Correa 2.00 5.00
GAPCS Chris Sale 2.00 5.00
GAPCY Christian Yelich 2.50 6.00
GAPFF Freddie Freeman 2.50 6.00
GAPFL Francisco Lindor 2.00 5.00
GAPGS Giancarlo Stanton 2.00 5.00
GAPGT Gleyber Torres 4.00 10.00
GAPJA Jose Altuve 1.50 4.00
GAPJB Jose Berrios 1.50 4.00
GAPJd Jacob deGrom 2.00 5.00
GAPJG Joey Gallo 1.50 4.00
GAPJM J.D. Martinez 2.00 5.00
GAPJR J.T. Realmuto 2.00 5.00
GAPJS Juan Soto 6.00 15.00
GAPJV Justin Verlander 2.00 5.00
GAPKB Kris Bryant 2.50 6.00
GAPKD Khris Davis 2.00 5.00
GAPMB Mookie Betts 3.00 8.00
GAPMC Matt Carpenter 2.00 5.00
GAPMH Mitch Haniger 1.50 4.00
GAPMS Max Scherzer 2.00 5.00
GAPMT Mike Trout 10.00 25.00
GAPNA Nolan Arenado 2.50 6.00
GAPNS Noah Syndergaard 1.50 4.00
GAPPG Paul Goldschmidt 2.00 5.00
GAPRA Ronald Acuna Jr. 10.00 25.00
GAPRH Rhys Hoskins 2.50 6.00
GAPSM Starling Marte 1.50 4.00
GAPSO Shohei Ohtani 2.50 6.00
GAPSP Salvador Perez 1.50 4.00
GAPTM Trey Mancini 1.50 4.00
GAPTS Trevor Story 2.00 5.00
GAPWM Wil Myers 1.25 3.00
GAPYM Yadier Molina 2.00 5.00
GAPABE Andrew Benintendi 2.00 5.00
GAPCBE Cody Bellinger 4.00 10.00
GAPCKE Clayton Kershaw 4.00 10.00
GAPJAB Jose Abreu 2.00 5.00
GAPJBZ Javier Baez 2.50 6.00
GAPJRA Jose Ramirez 1.50 4.00
GAPJSM Justin Smoak 1.25 3.00
GAPJVO Joey Votto 2.00 5.00
GAPMCA Miguel Cabrera 2.00 5.00
GAPMCH Matt Chapman 2.00 5.00

2019 Topps Grapefruit League Greats

STATED ODDS 1:2 BLASTER
*150TH/150: 1.5X TO 4X BASIC
GLG1 Hank Aaron 1.00 2.50
GLG2 Jackie Robinson .50 1.25
GLG3 Don Mattingly 1.00 2.50
GLG4 Cal Ripken Jr. 1.50 4.00
GLG5 Babe Ruth 1.25 3.00
GLG6 Ted Williams 1.00 2.50
GLG7 Ty Cobb .75 2.00
GLG8 Lou Gehrig 1.00 2.50
GLG9 Sandy Koufax 1.00 2.50
GLG10 Bob Gibson .40 1.00
GLG11 Roberto Clemente 1.25 3.00
GLG12 Nolan Ryan 1.50 4.00
GLG13 George Brett 1.00 2.50
GLG14 Max Scherzer .50 1.25
GLG15 Pedro Martinez .40 1.00
GLG16 Chipper Jones .50 1.25
GLG17 Wade Boggs .40 1.00
GLG18 Derek Jeter 1.25 3.00
GLG19 Carl Yastrzemski .75 2.00
GLG20 Al Kaline .50 1.25
GLG21 David Ortiz .50 1.25
GLG22 Vladimir Guerrero .40 1.00
GLG23 Bo Jackson .50 1.25
GLG24 Jose Altuve .40 1.00
GLG25 Mike Piazza .50 1.25
GLG26 Aaron Judge 1.25 3.00
GLG27 Gleyber Torres 1.00 2.50
GLG28 Mookie Betts .75 2.00
GLG29 Ronald Acuna Jr. 2.50 6.00
GLG30 Yadier Molina .50 1.25

2019 Topps Greatness Returns

STATED ODDS 1:42 HOBBY
*150TH/150: 1.5X TO 4X BASIC
GR1 Ryan/Verlander 2.00 5.00
GR2 Judge/Jeter 1.50 4.00
GR3 Kershaw/Koufax 1.25 3.00
GR4 Stanton/Jackson .60 1.50
GR5 Yount/Yelich .75 2.00
GR6 Benintendi/Yaz 1.00 2.50
GR7 Betts/Williams 1.25 3.00
GR8 Banks/Baez .75 2.00
GR9 Sale/Martinez .60 1.50
GR10 Jacob deGrom .60 1.50
Tom Seaver
GR11 Cobb/Harper 1.00 2.50
GR12 Ohtani/Ryan 2.00 5.00
GR13 Alomar/Lindor .60 1.50
GR14 Trout/Aaron 3.00 8.00
GR15 Ichiro/Ohtani .75 2.00
GR16 Clark/Posey .75 2.00
GR17 Trout/Acuna 3.00 8.00
GR18 Max Scherzer .60 1.50
Bob Gibson
GR19 Sale/Johnson .60 1.50
GR20 Jeter/Torres 1.50 4.00
GR21 Ripken/Correa 2.00 5.00
GR22 Charlie Blackmon .60 1.50
Todd Helton
GR23 Brooks Robinson .75 2.00
Nolan Arenado
GR24 Betts/Henderson 1.00 2.50
GR25 Pujols/Gehrig 1.25 3.00

2019 Topps Historic Homes Stadium Relics

STATED ODDS 1:6121 HOBBY
PRINT RUNS B/WN 40-99 COPIES PER
HHR1 Yankee Stadium/40 200.00 400.00
HHR2 Wrigley Field/99 75.00 200.00
HHR3 Fenway Park/99 75.00 200.00
HHR4 Memorial Stadium/99 75.00 200.00
HHR5 Tiger Stadium/99 60.00 150.00
HHR6 Metropolitan Stadium/99 50.00 120.00
HHR7 Three Rivers Stadium/90 60.00 150.00
HHR8 Atlanta Fulton
County Stadium/99 50.00 120.00
HHR9 Cleveland Municipal Stadium/99 50.00 120.00
HHR10 Milwaukee County Stadium/99 50.00 120.00

2019 Topps Home Run Challenge

SER.1 ODDS 1:24 HOBBY
SER.2 ODDS 1:24 HOBBY
HRC1 Mike Trout 6.00 15.00
HRC2 J.D. Martinez 1.25 3.00
HRC3 Giancarlo Stanton 1.25 3.00
HRC4 Jose Ramirez 1.00 2.50
HRC5 Khris Davis 1.25 3.00
HRC6 Aaron Judge 3.00 8.00
HRC7 Bryce Harper 2.00 5.00
HRC8 Manny Machado 1.25 3.00
HRC9 Nolan Arenado 1.50 4.00
HRC10 Paul Goldschmidt 1.25 3.00
HRC11 Mookie Betts 2.00 5.00
HRC12 Kris Bryant 1.50 4.00
HRC13 Javier Baez 1.50 4.00
HRC14 Alex Bregman 1.50 4.00
HRC15 Francisco Lindor 1.25 3.00
HRC16 Ronald Acuna Jr. 6.00 15.00
HRC17 Rhys Hoskins 1.50 4.00
HRC18 Shohei Ohtani 1.50 4.00
HRC19 Carlos Correa 1.25 3.00
HRC20 Anthony Rizzo 2.00 5.00
HRC21 Gleyber Torres 2.50 6.00
HRC22 Andrew Benintendi 1.25 3.00
HRC23 Ozzie Albies 1.25 3.00
HRC24 Joey Votto 1.25 3.00
HRC25 Trevor Story 1.25 3.00
HRC26 Freddie Freeman 1.50 4.00
HRC27 Jose Altuve 1.00 2.50
HRC28 George Springer 1.00 2.50
HRC29 Matt Carpenter 1.25 3.00
HRC30 Gary Sanchez 1.25 3.00
HRC31 Kyle Schwarber 1.25 3.00
HRC32 Cody Bellinger 2.50 6.00
HRC33 Miguel Andujar 1.25 3.00
HRC34 Christian Yelich 1.50 4.00
HRC35 Juan Soto 4.00 10.00

2019 Topps Iconic Card Reprints

SER.1 ODDS 1:21 HOBBY
SER.2 ODDS 1:9 HOBBY
*150TH/150: 2X TO 5X BASIC
ICR1 Ty Cobb .75 2.00
ICR2 Ty Cobb .75 2.00
ICR3 Babe Ruth 1.25 3.00
ICR4 Babe Ruth 1.25 3.00
ICR5 Lou Gehrig 1.00 2.50
ICR6 Jackie Robinson .50 1.25
ICR7 Al Kaline .50 1.25
ICR8 Roberto Clemente 1.25 3.00
ICR9 Jackie Robinson .50 1.25
ICR10 Roberto Clemente 1.25 3.00
ICR11 Bob Gibson .40 1.00
ICR12 Carl Yastrzemski .75 2.00
ICR13 Rod Carew .40 1.00
ICR14 Robin Yount .50 1.25
ICR15 Don Mattingly 1.00 2.50
ICR16 Jose Canseco .40 1.00
ICR17 Bo Jackson .50 1.25
ICR18 Mike Piazza .50 1.25
ICR19 Derek Jeter 1.25 3.00
ICR20 Miguel Cabrera .50 1.25
ICR21 Albert Pujols .60 1.50
ICR22 Rickey Henderson .50 1.25
ICR23 Justin Verlander .50 1.25
ICR24 Clayton Kershaw 1.00 2.50
ICR25 Cal Ripken Jr. 1.50 4.00
ICR26 Buster Posey .60 1.50
ICR27 Stephen Strasburg .50 1.25
ICR28 Bryce Harper .75 2.00
ICR29 Mike Trout 2.50 6.00
ICR30 Mike Trout 2.50 6.00
ICR31 Mookie Betts .75 2.00
ICR32 Kris Bryant .60 1.50
ICR33 Aaron Judge 1.25 3.00
ICR34 Ichiro .60 1.50
ICR35 Tom Seaver .40 1.00
ICR36 Nolan Ryan 1.50 4.00
ICR37 Wade Boggs .40 1.00
ICR38 Mark McGwire .75 2.00
ICR39 Bob Feller .40 1.00
ICR40 Duke Snider .40 1.00
ICR41 Eddie Mathews .50 1.25
ICR42 Warren Spahn .40 1.00
ICR43 George Brett 1.00 2.50
ICR44 Brooks Robinson .40 1.00
ICR45 Hank Aaron 1.00 2.50
ICR46 Hank Aaron 1.00 2.50
ICR47 Frank Thomas .50 1.25
ICR48 Mariano Rivera .60 1.50
ICR49 Sandy Koufax 1.00 2.50
ICR50 Ted Williams 1.00 2.50
ICR51 Ty Cobb .75 2.00
ICR52 Ty Cobb .75 2.00
ICR53 Lou Gehrig 1.00 2.50
ICR54 Whitey Ford .40 1.00
ICR55 Lou Gehrig 1.00 2.50
ICR56 Monte Irvin .40 1.00
ICR57 Warren Spahn .40 1.00
ICR58 Duke Snider .40 1.00
ICR59 Bob Feller .40 1.00
ICR60 Jackie Robinson .50 1.25
ICR61 Ted Williams 1.00 2.50
ICR62 Ernie Banks .50 1.25
ICR63 Harmon Killebrew .50 1.25
ICR64 Jackie Robinson .50 1.25
ICR65 Roberto Clemente 1.25 3.00
ICR66 Ted Williams 1.00 2.50
ICR67 Sandy Koufax 1.00 2.50
ICR68 Hank Aaron 1.00 2.50
ICR69 Sandy Koufax 1.00 2.50
ICR70 Roger Maris .50 1.25
ICR71 Willie McCovey .40 1.00
ICR72 Carl Yastrzemski .75 2.00
ICR73 Juan Marichal .40 1.00
ICR74 Roger Maris .50 1.25
ICR75 Lou Brock .40 1.00
ICR76 Jim Palmer .40 1.00
ICR77 Joe Morgan .40 1.00
ICR78 Steve Carlton .40 1.00
ICR79 Reggie Jackson .40 1.00
ICR80 Nolan Ryan 1.50 4.00
ICR81 Bert Blyleven .40 1.00
ICR82 Carlton Fisk .40 1.00
ICR83 Roberto Clemente 1.25 3.00
ICR84 Hank Aaron 1.00 2.50
ICR85 Dennis Eckersley .40 1.00
ICR86 Eddie Murray .40 1.00
ICR87 Dale Murphy .50 1.25
ICR88 Ryne Sandberg 1.00 2.50
ICR89 Darryl Strawberry .30 .75
ICR90 Roger Clemens .60 1.50
ICR91 Will Clark .40 1.00
ICR92 Bo Jackson .50 1.25
ICR93 Roberto Alomar .40 1.00
ICR94 Randy Johnson .50 1.25
ICR95 Derek Jeter 1.25 3.00
ICR96 Derek Jeter 1.25 3.00
ICR97 Vladimir Guerrero .40 1.00
ICR98 Bryce Harper .75 2.00
ICR99 Mike Trout 2.50 6.00
ICR100 Manny Machado .50 1.25

2019 Topps Iconic Cards Reprints Autographs

SER.1 ODDS 1:23,858 HOBBY
SER.2 ODDS 1:18,250 HOBBY
PRINT RUNS B/WN 5-25 COPIES PER
NO PRICING ON QTY 15 OR LESS
EXCHANGE DEADLINE 12/31/2020
ICR16 Al Kaline/25 75.00 200.00
ICR17 Sandy Koufax EXCH
ICR23 Bob Gibson/25 60.00 150.00
ICR27 Nolan Ryan
ICR29 Robin Yount
ICR31 Rickey Henderson
ICR32 Cal Ripken Jr.
ICR34 Don Mattingly/25 75.00 200.00
ICR36 Bo Jackson
ICR38 Frank Thomas
ICR40 Mike Piazza
ICR41 Derek Jeter
ICR51 Bryce Harper
ICR56 Aaron Judge
ICR68 Hank Aaron S2
ICR73 Juan Marichal/25 S2
ICR75 Lou Brock/25 S2 25.00 60.00
ICR78 Steve Carlton/25 S2
ICR80 Nolan Ryan S2
ICR82 Carlton Fisk/25 S2 25.00 60.00
ICR84 Hank Aaron S2
ICR85 Dennis Eckersley/25 S2 10.00 25.00
ICR87 Dale Murphy/25 S2 50.00 120.00
ICR89 Darryl Strawberry/25 S2 25.00 60.00
ICR91 Will Clark/25 S2 40.00 100.00
ICR93 Roberto Alomar/25 S2 20.00 50.00
ICR94 Randy Johnson S2
ICR96 Derek Jeter S2
ICR97 Vladimir Guerrero/25 S2 100.00 250.00

2019 Topps Legacy of Baseball Autographs

STATED ODDS 1:1073 HOBBY
EXCHANGE DEADLINE 12/31/2020
LBAAD Aledmys Diaz 2.50 6.00
LBAAG Avisail Garcia 3.00 8.00
LBAAH Alen Hanson 3.00 8.00
LBAAM Adalberto Mondesi 5.00 12.00
LBAAS Antonio Senzatela 2.50 6.00
LBABJ Brian Johnson 2.50 6.00
LBABK Brad Keller 2.50 6.00
LBACMU Cedric Mullins 6.00 15.00
LBADJ Danny Jansen 6.00 15.00
LBADST Dan Straily 2.50 6.00
LBAED Edwin Diaz 6.00 15.00
LBAFM Frankie Montas 2.50 6.00
LBAFV Felipe Vazquez 5.00 12.00
LBAJB Jake Bauers 3.00 8.00
LBAJBO Justin Bour 4.00 10.00
LBAJC Johan Camargo 8.00 20.00
LBAJF Jake Faria 2.50 6.00
LBAJH Josh Hader 5.00 12.00
LBAJM Jeff McNeil 8.00 20.00
LBAJMA Jake Marisnick 2.50 6.00
LBAJP Jose Peraza 4.00 10.00
LBAKA Kolby Allard 4.00 10.00
LBAKB Kris Bryant
LBAKF Kyle Freeland 3.00 8.00
LBALB Lou Brock
LBALH Livan Hernandez 2.50 6.00
LBAMD Matt Duffy 2.50 6.00
LBAMFO Mike Foltynewicz 4.00 10.00
LBAMGO Marwin Gonzalez 2.50 6.00
LBAMI Monte Irvin 15.00 40.00
LBAMM Max Muncy 8.00 20.00
LBAMTR Mike Trout
LBANG Niko Goodrum 6.00 15.00
LBAPN Phil Niekro
LBARO Roy Oswalt 5.00 12.00
LBARS Ross Stripling 2.50 6.00
LBASD Steven Duggar 5.00 12.00
LBASO Shohei Ohtani
LBASR Sean Reid-Foley 2.50 6.00
LBATA Tyler Anderson 2.50 6.00
LBATL Tzu-Wei Lin 2.50 6.00
LBATS Tyler Skaggs 10.00 25.00
LBAYS Yangervis Solarte 2.50 6.00
LBAZG Zack Godley 2.50 6.00

2019 Topps Legacy of Baseball Autographs 150th Anniversary

*150TH ANNV/150: .5X TO 1.2X BASIC
SER.1 ODDS 1:1559 HOBBY
SER.2 ODDS 1:1998 HOBBY
STATED PRINT RUN 150 SER.#'d SETS
EXCHANGE DEADLINE 12/31/2020
LBAAG Adolis Garcia S2 3.00 8.00
LBABW Bryse Wilson S2 4.00 10.00
LBACM Colin Moran 6.00 15.00
LBACS Christin Stewart S2 4.00 10.00
LBACY Carl Yastrzemski S2 8.00 20.00
LBADC David Cone 8.00 20.00
LBADH Dakota Hudson S2 4.00 10.00
LBADP Daniel Ponce de Leon S2 5.00 12.00
LBADR Dereck Rodriguez S2 3.00 8.00
LBAEDA Eric Davis 8.00 20.00
LBAFV Framber Valdez S2 3.00 8.00
LBAHF Heath Fillmyer S2 3.00 8.00
LBAJK John Kruk S2 3.00 8.00
LBAJR Josh Rogers S2 3.00 8.00
LBAKG Ken Giles 3.00 8.00
LBAKK Kevin Kramer S2 4.00 10.00
LBAKS Kohl Stewart S2 4.00 10.00
LBAKT Kyle Tucker 25.00 60.00
LBALV Luke Voit S2 20.00 50.00
LBAMC Matt Chapman 8.00 20.00
LBAMCA Matt Carpenter 8.00 20.00
LBAMG Mark Grace 10.00 25.00
LBANB Nick Burdi S2 3.00 8.00
LBAPW Patrick Wisdom S2 3.00 8.00
LBARA Rick Ankiel 8.00 20.00
LBARL Ramon Laureano S2 8.00 20.00
LBATH Teoscar Hernandez 5.00 12.00
LBAYG Yasmani Grandal 3.00 8.00
LBADSA Dennis Santana S2 3.00 8.00
LBAJSP Jeffrey Springs S2 3.00 8.00

2019 Topps Legacy of Baseball Autographs Gold

*GOLD/50: .6X TO 1.5X BASIC
SER.1 ODDS 1:3897
SER.2 ODDS 1:4838
STATED PRINT RUN 50 SER.#'d SETS
EXCHANGE DEADLINE 12/31/2020
LBABB Bert Blyleven 10.00 25.00
LBABM Bill Mazeroski 25.00 60.00
LBACM Colin Moran 8.00 20.00
LBACR Carlos Rodon 5.00 12.00
LBADC David Cone 10.00 25.00
LBAEDA Eric Davis 10.00 25.00
LBAFT Fernando Tatis Jr. S2 100.00 250.00
LBAJA Jesus Aguilar 8.00 20.00
LBAKG Ken Giles 4.00 10.00

LBAKT Kyle Tucker 30.00 80.00
LBAMC Matt Chapman 10.00 25.00
LBAMCA Matt Carpenter 10.00 25.00
LBAMG Mark Grace 12.00 30.00
LBAPA Pete Alonso S2 75.00 200.00
LBARA Rick Ankiel 10.00 25.00
LBASG Shawn Green 8.00 20.00
LBATH Teoscar Hernandez 6.00 15.00
LBAVC Vinny Castilla 4.00 10.00
LBAYG Yasmani Grandal 4.00 10.00
LBAYK Yusei Kikuchi S2 8.00

2019 Topps Legacy of Baseball Autographs Red

*RED/25: .8X TO 2X BASIC
SER.1 ODDS 1:7794 HOBBY
SER.2 ODDS 1:6864 HOBBY
PRINT RUN BTW 10-25 COPIES PER
NO PRICING QTY 15 OR LESS
EXCHANGE DEADLINE 12/31/2020
LBABA Bobby Abreu 25.00 60.00
LBABB Bert Blyleven 12.00 30.00
LBABG Bob Gibson 50.00 120.00
LBABM Bill Mazeroski 30.00 80.00
LBACK Corey Kluber 25.00 60.00
LBACM Colin Moran 10.00 25.00
LBACR Carlos Rodon 6.00 15.00
LBADC David Cone 12.00 30.00
LBAEDA Eric Davis 12.00 30.00
LBAFJ Fergie Jenkins 15.00 40.00
LBAFT Fernando Tatis Jr. S2 125.00 300.00
LBAGS George Springer 12.00 30.00
LBAJA Jesus Aguilar 10.00 25.00
LBAKG Ken Giles 5.00 12.00
LBAKL Kenny Lofton 25.00 60.00
LBAKT Kyle Tucker 40.00 100.00
LBALS Luis Severino 6.00 15.00
LBAMC Matt Chapman 12.00 30.00
LBAMCA Matt Carpenter 12.00 30.00
LBAMG Mark Grace 15.00 40.00
LBARA Rick Ankiel 12.00 30.00
LBARH Rhys Hoskins 25.00 60.00
LBASG Shawn Green 10.00 25.00
LBATH Teoscar Hernandez 8.00 20.00
LBAVC Vinny Castilla 5.00 12.00
LBAYG Yasmani Grandal 5.00 12.00

2019 Topps Major League Materials

SER.1 ODDS 1:70 HOBBY
SER.2 ODDS 1:111 HOBBY
*150TH/150: .5X TO 1.2X BASIC
*GOLD/50: .6X TO 1.5X BASIC
*RED/25: .75X TO 2X BASIC
MLMAB Adrian Beltre 3.00 8.00
MLMAB Alex Bregman S2 3.00 8.00
MLMABE Andrew Benintendi 3.00 8.00
MLMAJ Aaron Judge 8.00 20.00
MLMAM Andrew McCutchen S2 3.00 8.00
MLMAP Albert Pujols 4.00 10.00
MLMAR Anthony Rizzo S2 5.00 12.00
MLMARI Anthony Rizzo 5.00 12.00
MLMBB Byron Buxton S2 2.50 6.00
MLMBC Brandon Crawford 2.50 6.00
MLMBH Bryce Harper 5.00 12.00
MLMBH Bryce Harper S2 5.00 12.00
MLMBP Buster Posey 4.00 10.00
MLMCA Chris Archer S2 2.00 5.00
MLMCB Cody Bellinger S2 6.00 15.00
MLMCC Carlos Correa 3.00 8.00
MLMCK Clayton Kershaw 6.00 15.00
MLMCK Corey Kluber S2 2.50 6.00
MLMCS Corey Seager 3.00 8.00
MLMCS CC Sabathia S2 2.50 6.00
MLMCSA Chris Sale 3.00 8.00
MLMDG Didi Gregorius S2 2.50 6.00
MLMDO David Ortiz S2 3.00 8.00
MLMDP Dustin Pedroia 3.00 8.00
MLMDP David Price S2 2.50 6.00
MLMDS Dansby Swanson S2 3.00 8.00
MLMEA Elvis Andrus 2.50 6.00
MLMEL Evan Longoria S2 2.50 6.00
MLMFF Freddie Freeman 4.00 10.00
MLMFL Francisco Lindor 3.00 8.00
MLMGS Gary Sanchez 3.00 8.00
MLMGS George Springer S2 2.50 6.00
MLMGT Gleyber Torres 6.00 15.00
MLMJA Jose Altuve 2.50 6.00
MLMJAB Jose Abreu 3.00 8.00
MLMJB Javier Baez 4.00 10.00
MLMJD Josh Donaldson 2.50 6.00
MLMJD Josh Donaldson S2 2.50 6.00
MLMJDE Jacob deGrom 3.00 8.00
MLMJG Joey Gallo S2 2.50 6.00
MLMJH Jason Heyward S2 2.50 6.00
MLMJM Joe Mauer 2.50 6.00
MLMJR Jose Ramirez S2 2.50 6.00
MLMJS Jean Segura 3.00 8.00
MLMJS Justin Smoak S2 2.00 5.00
MLMJT Jameson Taillon S2 2.50 6.00
MLMJV Justin Verlander 3.00 8.00
MLMJVO Joey Votto 3.00 8.00
MLMKB Kris Bryant 4.00 10.00
MLMKS Kyle Schwarber S2 3.00 8.00
MLMLC Lorenzo Cain S2 2.00 5.00
MLMLS Luis Severino S2 2.50 6.00
MLMMA Miguel Andujar S2 3.00 8.00
MLMMB Mookie Betts 6.00 15.00
MLMMC Michael Conforto 2.50 6.00
MLMMCA Miguel Cabrera 3.00 8.00
MLMMH Mitch Haniger 2.50 6.00
MLMMS Max Scherzer 3.00 8.00
MLMMS Miguel Sano S2 2.50 6.00
MLMMT Mike Trout 10.00 25.00
MLMMT Mike Trout S2 15.00 40.00
MLMOA Ozzie Albies 3.00 8.00
MLMPG Paul Goldschmidt 3.00 8.00
MLMPG Paul Goldschmidt S2 3.00 8.00
MLMRA Ronald Acuna Jr. 12.00 30.00
MLMRD Rafael Devers S2 4.00 10.00
MLMRH Rhys Hoskins 4.00 10.00
MLMSG Scooter Gennett S2 2.50 6.00
MLMSO Shohei Ohtani 4.00 10.00
MLMSP Salvador Perez 2.50 6.00
MLMSS Stephen Strasburg S2 3.00 8.00
MLMTM Trey Mancini 2.50 6.00
MLMTS Travis Shaw 2.00 5.00
MLMTS Trevor Story S2 3.00 8.00
MLMTT Trea Turner 2.50 6.00
MLMTT Troy Tulowitzki S2 3.00 8.00
MLMVR Victor Robles S2 4.00 10.00
MLMWC Willson Contreras 2.50 6.00
MLMWM Wil Myers 2.00 5.00
MLMXB Xander Bogaerts S2 3.00 8.00
MLMYM Yoan Moncada 3.00 8.00
MLMYMO Yadier Molina 3.00 8.00
MLMYP Yasiel Puig S2 3.00 8.00
MLMABE Andrew Benintendi S2 3.00 8.00
MLMDPE Dustin Pedroia S2 3.00 8.00
MLMJTO Juan Soto S2 10.00 25.00
MLMMST Marcus Stroman S2 2.50 6.00

2019 Topps Major League Materials Autographs

SER.1 ODDS 1:3808 HOBBY
SER.2 ODDS 1:3432 HOBBY
PRINT RUNS B/WN 10-50 COPIES PER
NO PRICING ON QTY 15 OR LESS
EXCHANGE DEADLINE 12/31/2020
*RED/25: .5X TO 1.2X BASIC
MLARAJ Aaron Judge/10 S2
MLARBB Byron Buxton S2 8.00 20.00
MLARBN Brandon Nimmo S2 8.00 20.00
MLARBS Blake Snell/50
MLARCS Chris Sale EXCH 25.00 60.00
MLARCY Christian Yelich/50 20.00 50.00
MLARDB Dellin Betances S2 8.00 20.00
MLARDG Didi Gregorius/50 8.00 20.00
MLARER Eddie Rosario S2 8.00 20.00
MLARFF Freddie Freeman/50 25.00 60.00
MLARFL Francisco Lindor/30 S2 20.00 50.00
MLARFV Felipe Vazquez S2 6.00 15.00
MLARGS George Springer/50 8.00 20.00
MLARJA Jesus Aguilar/50 6.00 15.00
MLARJA Jose Altuve S2
MLARJd Jacob deGrom/50 20.00 50.00
MLARJF Jack Flaherty S2 8.00 20.00
MLARJH Josh Hader S2 6.00 15.00
MLARJM Jose Martinez S2 6.00 15.00
MLARJS Juan Soto S2 25.00 60.00
MLARJSO Juan Soto/50 60.00 150.00
MLARKB Kris Bryant S2
MLARKD Khris Davis/50
MLARKS Kyle Schwarber/50 15.00 40.00
MLARKT Kyle Tucker/50 40.00 100.00
MLARLS Luis Severino/50 15.00 40.00
MLARMA Miguel Andujar S2 10.00 25.00
MLARMC Matt Carpenter S2 10.00 25.00
MLARMH Mitch Haniger/50 12.00 30.00
MLARMM Manny Machado/30 S2 25.00 60.00
MLARMO Matt Olson/50 10.00 25.00
MLARNS Noah Syndergaard/50 20.00 50.00
MLAROA Ozzie Albies/50 25.00 60.00
MLARPD Paul DeJong S2 10.00 25.00
MLARPG Paul Goldschmidt
MLARRD Rafael Devers S2 25.00 60.00
MLARRH Rhys Hoskins/50 40.00 100.00
MLARRH Rhys Hoskins S2 25.00 60.00
MLARSMA Starling Marte/50 50.00 120.00
MLARSP Salvador Perez/50
MLARTB Trevor Bauer S2 10.00 25.00
MLARTM Trey Mancini S2 10.00 25.00
MLARTP Tommy Pham S2 6.00 15.00
MLARTS Travis Shaw/50
MLARTST Trevor Story/50
MLARVR Victor Robles S2 12.00 30.00
MLARWC Willson Contreras/25 15.00 40.00
MLARWM Whit Merrifield S2 10.00 25.00
MLARYM Yadier Molina/50 50.00 120.00
MLARAMC Andrew McCutchen S2
MLARARO Amed Rosario S2 8.00 20.00
MLARJMC Jeff McNeil S2 15.00 40.00
MLARJSM Justin Smoak S2 6.00 15.00
MLARMMU Max Muncy S2 8.00 20.00
MLARSMA Steven Matz S2 8.00 20.00

2019 Topps Mookie Betts Highlights

STATED ODDS 1:4 WM BLASTER
*150th/150: 1.25X TO 3X BASIC
MB1 Mookie Betts .60 1.50
MB2 Mookie Betts .60 1.50
MB3 Mookie Betts .60 1.50
MB4 Mookie Betts .60 1.50
MB5 Mookie Betts .60 1.50
MB6 Mookie Betts .60 1.50
MB7 Mookie Betts .60 1.50
MB8 Mookie Betts .60 1.50
MB9 Mookie Betts .60 1.50
MB10 Mookie Betts .60 1.50
MB11 Mookie Betts .60 1.50
MB12 Mookie Betts .60 1.50
MB13 Mookie Betts .60 1.50
MB14 Mookie Betts .60 1.50
MB15 Mookie Betts .60 1.50
MB16 Mookie Betts .60 1.50
MB17 Mookie Betts .60 1.50
MB18 Mookie Betts .60 1.50
MB19 Mookie Betts .60 1.50
MB20 Mookie Betts .60 1.50
MB21 Mookie Betts .60 1.50
MB22 Mookie Betts .60 1.50
MB23 Mookie Betts .60 1.50
MB24 Mookie Betts .60 1.50
MB25 Mookie Betts .60 1.50
MB26 Mookie Betts .60 1.50
MB27 Mookie Betts .60 1.50
MB28 Mookie Betts .60 1.50
MB29 Mookie Betts .60 1.50
MB30 Mookie Betts .60 1.50

2019 Topps Mystery Rookie Redemption Autographs

RANDOM INSERTS IN PACKS
EXCHANGE DEADLINE 12/31/2020
MRAA Vladimir Guerrero Jr. 150.00 400.00
MRAB Eloy Jimenez 50.00 120.00

2019 Topps Postseason Performance Autograph Relics

SER.1 ODDS 1:11,809 HOBBY
STATED PRINT RUN 50 SER.#'d SETS
EXCHANGE DEADLINE 12/31/2020
*RED/25: .75X TO 2X BASIC
PPARAR Anthony Rizzo
PPARCC Carlos Correa
PPARCS Chris Sale
PPARFF Freddie Freeman
PPARGS George Springer
PPARJA Jose Altuve 20.00 50.00
PPARJAG Jesus Aguilar
PPARJP Joc Pederson
PPARKF Kyle Freeland 10.00 25.00
PPARMCA Matt Chapman 12.00 30.00
PPARMG Marwin Gonzalez 15.00 40.00
PPARMK Matt Kemp
PPARMT Masahiro Tanaka
PPAROA Ozzie Albies
PPARRA Ronald Acuna Jr.
PPARTS Travis Shaw
PPARTST Trevor Story
PPAYG Yuli Gurriel

2019 Topps Postseason Performance Autographs

STATED ODDS 1:14,798 HOBBY
STATED PRINT RUN 50 SER.#'d SETS
EXCHANGE DEADLINE 12/31/2020
*RED/25: .6X TO 1.5X BASIC
PPAAJ Aaron Judge
PPAAR Anthony Rizzo
PPABW Brandon Woodruff 8.00 20.00
PPACT Chris Taylor EXCH 10.00 25.00
PPACY Christian Yelich
PPAFFR Freddie Freeman
PPAFL Francisco Lindor EXCH
PPAGSP George Springer
PPAJA Jose Altuve 15.00 40.00
PPAJAG Jesus Aguilar 12.00 30.00
PPAJH Josh Hader 15.00 40.00
PPAKD Khris Davis
PPAKF Kyle Freeland 10.00 25.00
PPAMCA Matt Chapman 12.00 30.00
PPAMG Marwin Gonzalez 8.00 20.00
PPAMM Manny Machado
PPAMMU Max Muncy
PPAMT Masahiro Tanaka
PPATS Travis Shaw
PPATST Trevor Story

2019 Topps Postseason Performance Relics

STATED ODDS 1:6058 HOBBY
STATED PRINT RUN 99 SER.#'d SETS
*RED/25: .6X TO 1.5X BASIC
PPRAB Alex Bregman 8.00 20.00
PPRABE Andrew Benintendi 10.00 25.00
PPRAJ Aaron Judge 25.00 60.00
PPRAR Anthony Rizzo 8.00 20.00
PPRCB Charlie Blackmon 5.00 12.00
PPRCC Carlos Correa 5.00 12.00
PPRCK Clayton Kershaw 8.00 20.00
PPRCS Chris Sale 5.00 12.00
PPRFF Freddie Freeman 6.00 15.00
PPRGS George Springer 4.00 10.00
PPRHR Hyun-Jin Ryu 4.00 10.00
PPRJA Jose Altuve 4.00 10.00
PPRJL Jon Lester 4.00 10.00
PPRJM J.D. Martinez 15.00 40.00
PPRJP Joc Pederson 4.00 10.00
PPRJT Justin Turner 6.00 15.00
PPRJV Justin Verlander 5.00 12.00
PPRKB Kris Bryant 6.00 15.00
PPRLS Luis Severino 10.00 25.00
PPRMB Mookie Betts 12.00 30.00
PPRMC Matt Chapman 5.00 12.00
PPRMT Masahiro Tanaka 15.00 40.00
PPROA Ozzie Albies 5.00 12.00
PPRTS Trevor Story 5.00 12.00
PPRXB Xander Bogaerts 10.00 25.00
PPRYP Yasiel Puig 5.00 12.00

2019 Topps Revolution of the Game

STATED ODDS 1:104 HOBBY
*150TH/150: 1.2X TO 3X BASIC
REV2 Kenesaw Mountain Landis .60 1.50
REV3 Casey Stengel .75 2.00
REV5 Albert Spalding .60 1.50
REV6 Tommy Lasorda .75 2.00
REV7 Tony LaRussa .75 2.00
REV7 Henry Chadwick .60 1.50
REV8 Joe Torre .75 2.00
REV9 Bill James .60 1.50
REV10 Branch Rickey .60 1.50
REV11 Happy Chandler .60 1.50

2019 Topps Revolution of the Game Autographs

STATED ODDS 1:13,920 HOBBY
STATED PRINT RUNS B/WN 99-199 COPIES PER
EXCHANGE DEADLINE 12/31/2020
REVBJ Bill James/199 10.00 25.00
REVBS Bud Selig/99 12.00 30.00
REVJT Joe Torre EXCH 25.00 60.00
REVTL Tony LaRussa/99 8.00 20.00
REVTO Tommy Lasorda/99 25.00 60.00

2019 Topps Ronald Acuna Highlights

STATED ODDS 1:4 BLASTER
*150TH/150: 1.5X TO 4X BASIC
RA1 Ronald Acuna Jr. 2.00 5.00
RA2 Ronald Acuna Jr. 2.00 5.00
RA3 Ronald Acuna Jr. 2.00 5.00
RA4 Ronald Acuna Jr. 2.00 5.00
RA5 Ronald Acuna Jr. 2.00 5.00
RA6 Ronald Acuna Jr. 2.00 5.00
RA7 Ronald Acuna Jr. 2.00 5.00
RA8 Ronald Acuna Jr. 2.00 5.00
RA9 Ronald Acuna Jr. 2.00 5.00
RA10 Ronald Acuna Jr. 2.00 5.00
RA11 Ronald Acuna Jr. 2.00 5.00
RA12 Ronald Acuna Jr. 2.00 5.00
RA13 Ronald Acuna Jr. 2.00 5.00
RA14 Ronald Acuna Jr. 2.00 5.00
RA15 Ronald Acuna Jr. 2.00 5.00
RA16 Ronald Acuna Jr. 2.00 5.00
RA17 Ronald Acuna Jr. 2.00 5.00
RA18 Ronald Acuna Jr. 2.00 5.00
RA19 Ronald Acuna Jr. 2.00 5.00
RA20 Ronald Acuna Jr. 2.00 5.00
RA21 Ronald Acuna Jr. 2.00 5.00
RA22 Ronald Acuna Jr. 2.00 5.00
RA23 Ronald Acuna Jr. 2.00 5.00
RA24 Ronald Acuna Jr. 2.00 5.00
RA25 Ronald Acuna Jr. 2.00 5.00
RA26 Ronald Acuna Jr. 2.00 5.00
RA27 Ronald Acuna Jr. 2.00 5.00
RA28 Ronald Acuna Jr. 2.00 5.00
RA29 Ronald Acuna Jr. 2.00 5.00
RA30 Ronald Acuna Jr. 2.00 5.00

2019 Topps Significant Statistics

STATED ODDS 1:56 HOBBY
*BLUE: .6X TO 1.5X BASIC
*BLACK/299: 1X TO 2.5X BASIC
*150th/150: 2X TO 5X BASIC
*GOLD/50: 3X TO 8X BASIC
SS1 Giancarlo Stanton .60 1.50
SS2 Khris Davis .60 1.50
SS3 Aaron Judge 1.50 4.00
SS4 Trevor Story .60 1.50
SS5 Aaron Judge 1.50 4.00
SS6 Manny Machado .60 1.50
SS7 Joey Gallo .50 1.25
SS8 Byron Buxton .50 1.25
SS9 Mookie Betts 1.00 2.50
SS10 Mookie Betts 1.00 2.50
SS11 J.D. Martinez .60 1.50
SS12 Edwin Diaz .50 1.25
SS13 Blake Treinen .40 1.00
SS14 Josh Hader .40 1.00
SS15 Edwin Diaz .50 1.25
SS16 Harrison Bader .50 1.25
SS17 Lorenzo Cain .40 1.00
SS18 J.T. Realmuto .60 1.50
SS19 Jordan Hicks .50 1.25
SS20 Jordan Hicks .50 1.25
SS21 Tyler Glasnow .40 1.00
SS22 Alex Colome .40 1.00
SS23 Kyle Crick .40 1.00
SS24 Jeremy Jeffress .40 1.00
SS25 Jacob deGrom .60 1.50

2019 Topps Significant Statistics Autograph Relics

STATED ODDS 1:10,165 HOBBY
PRINT RUN B/TW 10-50 COPIES PER
NO PRICING QTY 15 OR LESS
EXCHANGE DEADLINE 12/31/2020
*RED/25: .75X TO 2X BASIC
SSARAC Alex Colome/50 5.00 12.00
SSARBB Byron Buxton/30 6.00 15.00
SSARBT Blake Treinen/50 5.00 12.00
SSARHB Harrison Bader/50 6.00 15.00
SSARJH Jordan Hicks/50 6.00 15.00
SSARJJ Jeremy Jeffress/50 5.00 12.00
SSARKD Khris Davis/50 8.00 20.00
SSARJHA Josh Hader/50 5.00 12.00
SSARJHI Jordan Hicks/50 6.00 15.00

2019 Topps Significant Statistics Autograph Relics Red

*RED/25: .75X TO 2X BASIC
STATED ODDS 1:17,845 HOBBY
PRINT RUN B/TW X-25 COPIES PER
NO PRICING QTY 15 OR LESS
EXCHANGE DEADLINE 12/31/2020
SSARJd Jacob deGrom 15.00 40.00

2019 Topps Significant Statistics Autographs

STATED ODDS 1:11,310 HOBBY
STATED PRINT RUN 50 SER.#'d SETS
EXCHANGE DEADLINE 12/31/2020
*RED/25: .6X TO 1.5X BASIC
SSABT Blake Treinen 3.00 8.00
SSAHB Harrison Bader 4.00 10.00
SSAJJ Jeremy Jeffress 3.00 8.00
SSAKD Khris Davis 5.00 12.00
SSAJHA Josh Hader 3.00 8.00
SSAJHI Jordan Hicks 4.00 10.00
SSAJHK Jordan Hicks 4.00 10.00

2019 Topps Significant Statistics Relics

STATED ODDS 1:2760 HOBBY
STATED PRINT RUN 99 SER.#'d SETS
*RED/25: .75X TO 2X BASIC
SSRBB Byron Buxton 2.50 6.00
SSRBT Blake Treinen 2.00 5.00
SSRGS Giancarlo Stanton 3.00 8.00
SSRHB Harrison Bader 2.50 6.00
SSRJd Jacob deGrom 3.00 8.00
SSRJG Joey Gallo 2.50 6.00
SSRJH Josh Hader 2.00 5.00
SSRJM J.D. Martinez 3.00 8.00
SSRJR J.T. Realmuto 3.00 8.00
SSRKD Khris Davis 3.00 8.00
SSRLC Lorenzo Cain 2.00 5.00
SSRMB Mookie Betts 5.00 12.00
SSRMM Manny Machado 5.00 12.00
SSRTS Trevor Story 3.00 8.00
SSRAJD Aaron Judge 8.00 20.00
SSRAJU Aaron Judge 8.00 20.00
SSRJHI Jordan Hicks 2.50 6.00
SSRJHK Jordan Hicks 2.50 6.00
SSRJMA J.D. Martinez 3.00 8.00
SSRMBT Mookie Betts 5.00 12.00

2019 Topps Significant Statistics Relics Red

*RED/25: .75X TO 2X BASIC
STATED ODDS 1:10,429 HOBBY
STATED PRINT RUN 25 SER.#'d SETS
SSRJd Jacob deGrom 15.00 40.00
SSRJM J.D. Martinez 12.00 30.00
SSRMM Manny Machado 12.00 30.00
SSRJMA J.D. Martinez 12.00 30.00

2019 Topps Stars of the Game

INSERTED IN RETAIL PACKS
SSB1 Ronald Acuna Jr. 5.00 12.00
SSB2 Mike Trout 5.00 12.00
SSB3 J.D. Martinez 1.00 2.50
SSB4 Justin Verlander 1.00 2.50
SSB5 Luis Severino .75 2.00
SSB6 Edwin Encarnacion 1.00 2.50
SSB7 Christian Yelich 1.25 3.00
SSB8 Xander Bogaerts 1.00 2.50
SSB9 Eric Hosmer .75 2.00
SSB10 Charlie Blackmon 1.00 2.50
SSB11 Rafael Devers 1.25 3.00
SSB12 Trea Turner .75 2.00
SSB13 Gary Sanchez 1.00 2.50
SSB14 Kris Bryant 1.25 3.00
SSB15 Mookie Betts 1.50 4.00
SSB16 Michael Conforto .75 2.00
SSB17 Nolan Arenado 1.25 3.00
SSB18 Paul Goldschmidt 1.00 2.50
SSB19 Bryce Harper 1.50 4.00
SSB20 Justin Upton .75 2.00
SSB21 Francisco Lindor 1.00 2.50
SSB22 Eddie Rosario .75 2.00
SSB23 Gerrit Cole 1.00 2.50
SSB24 Eugenio Suarez .75 2.00
SSB25 Joey Gallo .75 2.00
SSB26 Andrew Benintendi 1.00 2.50
SSB27 Jose Berrios .75 2.00
SSB28 Rhys Hoskins 1.25 3.00
SSB29 Blake Snell .75 2.00
SSB30 Miguel Andujar 1.00 2.50
SSB31 Shohei Ohtani 1.25 3.00
SSB32 Matt Carpenter 1.00 2.50
SSB33 Anthony Rizzo 1.50 4.00
SSB34 Corey Seager 1.00 2.50
SSB35 Adrian Beltre 1.00 2.50
SSB36 Whit Merrifield 1.00 2.50
SSB37 Alex Bregman 1.00 2.50
SSB38 Max Scherzer 1.00 2.50
SSB39 Nicholas Castellanos 1.00 2.50
SSB40 Adam Jones .75 2.00
SSB41 Stephen Strasburg 1.00 2.50
SSB42 Scooter Gennett .75 2.00
SSB43 Manny Machado 1.00 2.50
SSB44 Lorenzo Cain .60 1.50
SSB45 Wil Myers .60 1.50
SSB46 Javier Baez 1.25 3.00
SSB47 Khris Davis .75 2.00
SSB48 Giancarlo Stanton 1.00 2.50
SSB49 Starling Marte .60 1.50
SSB50 Carlos Correa 1.00 2.50
SSB51 Aaron Nola .75 2.00
SSB52 Yoan Moncada 1.00 2.50
SSB53 Mitch Haniger .75 2.00
SSB54 Dee Gordon .60 1.50
SSB55 Jose Abreu 1.00 2.50
SSB56 Juan Soto 3.00 8.00
SSB57 Jose Altuve .75 2.00
SSB58 Zack Greinke .75 2.00
SSB59 Michael Kopech 1.25 3.00
SSB60 Miguel Cabrera 1.00 2.50
SSB61 Felix Hernandez .75 2.00
SSB62 Jacob deGrom 1.00 2.50
SSB63 Ozzie Albies 1.00 2.50
SSB64 Joey Votto 1.00 2.50
SSB65 Salvador Perez .75 2.00
SSB66 Cody Bellinger 2.00 5.00
SSB67 Trey Mancini .75 2.00
SSB68 Clayton Kershaw 2.00 5.00
SSB69 Trevor Bauer 1.00 2.50
SSB70 Jose Ramirez .75 2.00
SSB71 Kyle Schwarber 1.00 2.50
SSB72 Edwin Diaz .75 2.00
SSB73 Justin Smoak .60 1.50
SSB74 Yoenis Cespedes 1.00 2.50
SSB75 Andrew McCutchen 1.00 2.50
SSB76 Matt Chapman 1.00 2.50
SSB77 Corey Kluber .75 2.00
SSB78 Freddie Freeman 1.25 3.00
SSB79 Robinson Cano .75 2.00
SSB80 Masahiro Tanaka .75 2.00
SSB81 Paul DeJong 1.00 2.50
SSB82 Yadier Molina 1.00 2.50
SSB83 Gleyber Torres 2.00 5.00
SSB84 Jon Lester .75 2.00
SSB85 Marcell Ozuna 1.00 2.50
SSB86 Ichiro 1.25 3.00
SSB87 James Paxton .75 2.00
SSB88 Josh Donaldson .75 2.00
SSB89 Nelson Cruz 1.00 2.50
SSB90 J.T. Realmuto 1.00 2.50
SSB91 Yu Darvish 1.00 2.50
SSB92 Trevor Story 1.00 2.50
SSB93 Albert Pujols 1.25 3.00
SSB94 Noah Syndergaard .75 2.00
SSB95 Aaron Judge 2.50 6.00
SSB96 Daniel Murphy .75 2.00
SSB97 Buster Posey 1.25 3.00
SSB98 George Springer .75 2.00
SSB99 Chris Sale 1.00 2.50
SSB100 Kyle Tucker 1.25 3.00

2019 Topps World Series Champion Autograph Relics

STATED ODDS 1:15,798 HOBBY
STATED PRINT RUN 50 SER.#'d SETS
EXCHANGE DEADLINE 12/31/2020
*RED/25: .6X TO 1.5X BASIC
WCARBH Brock Holt 40.00 100.00
WCARCS Chris Sale 40.00 100.00
WCARCV Christian Vazquez 50.00 120.00
WCARDP David Price 30.00 80.00
WCARER Eduardo Rodriguez 50.00 120.00
WCARMB Matt Barnes
WCARRP Rick Porcello EXCH 40.00 100.00

2019 Topps World Series Champion Autographs

STATED ODDS 1:14,798 HOBBY
STATED PRINT RUN 50 SER.#'d SETS
EXCHANGE DEADLINE 12/31/2020
*RED/25: .6X TO 1.5X BASIC
WCABH Brock Holt EXCH 30.00 80.00
WCABS Blake Swihart 30.00 80.00
WCACS Chris Sale EXCH 40.00 100.00
WCACV Christian Vazquez 40.00 100.00
WCADP David Price
WCAER Eduardo Rodriguez
WCAJB Jackie Bradley Jr.
WCANE Nathan Eovaldi
WCARB Ryan Brasier 40.00 100.00
WCARD Rafael Devers EXCH
WCARP Rick Porcello EXCH 30.00 80.00
WCASP Steve Pearce EXCH 50.00 120.00

2019 Topps World Series Champion Relics

STATED ODDS 1:6058 HOBBY
STATED PRINT RUN 99 SER.#'d SETS
*RED/25: .75X TO 2X BASIC
WCRAN Andrew Benintendi 20.00 50.00
WCRBR Brock Holt 10.00 25.00
WCRCS Chris Sale 12.00 30.00
WCRCV Christian Vazquez 20.00 50.00
WCRDP David Price 15.00 40.00
WCRIK Ian Kinsler 12.00 30.00
WCRJB Jackie Bradley Jr. 25.00 60.00
WCRJM J.D. Martinez 15.00 40.00
WCRKI Craig Kimbrel 12.00 30.00
WCRMB Matt Barnes 15.00 40.00
WCRMO Mookie Betts 30.00 80.00
WCRRD Rafael Devers 20.00 50.00
WCRRP Rick Porcello 20.00 50.00
WCRXB Xander Bogaerts 20.00 50.00

2019 Topps Update

COMPLETE SET (300) 20.00 50.00
PRINTING PLATE ODDS 1:3863 HOBBY
PLATE PRINT RUN 1 SET PER COLOR
BLACK-CYAN-MAGENTA-YELLOW ISSUED
NO PLATE PRICING DUE TO SCARCITY
US1 Vladimir Guerrero Jr. RC 1.50 4.00
US2 Mike Tauchman (RC) .40 1.00
US3 Curt Casali .15 .40
US4 Gary Sanchez AS .25 .60
US5 CC Sabathia HL CL .20 .50
US6 Yonder Alonso .15 .40
US7 Aroldis Chapman AS .25 .60
US8 Walker Buehler AS .30 .75
US9 Masahiro Tanaka AS .20 .50
US10 Jorge Polanco AS .15 .40
US11 Brandon Brennan RC .25 .60
US12 Paul Goldschmidt .25 .60
US13 Yasmani Grandal AS .15 .40
US14 Jose Suarez RC .25 .60
US15 James McCann AS .20 .50
US16 Martin Maldonado .15 .40
US17 Edwin Diaz .20 .50
US18 Christian Walker .20 .50
US19 Zach Plesac RC .60 1.50
US20 Mike Soroka AS .25 .60
US21 Melky Cabrera .15 .40
US22 Ian Kinsler .20 .50
US23 Cal Quantrill RC .25 .60
US24 Lucas Giolito AS .25 .60
US25 Cody Bellinger AS .50 1.25
US26 Mark Reynolds .15 .40
US27 JD Hammer RC .30 .75
US28 Oscar Mercado RC .60 1.50
US29 Tommy La Stella .15 .40
US30 Hanser Alberto RC .15 .40
US31 Joc Pederson HRD .20 .50
US32 Matt Albers .15 .40
US33 Josh Harrison .15 .40
US34 Griffin Canning RD .25 .60
US35 Derek Dietrich .20 .50
US36 Jake Odorizzi AS .15 .40
US37 Tim Beckham .20 .50
US38 Harold Ramirez RC .40 1.00
US39 Cavan Biggio RC 1.25 3.00
US40 Travis Bergen RC .25 .60
US41 Russell Martin .15 .40
US42 David Dahl AS .15 .40
US43 Josh Naylor RC .30 .75
US44 Trevor Story AS .25 .60
US45 Brendan Rodgers RD .25 .60
US46 Tanner Roark .15 .40
US47 Pete Alonso AS 1.25 3.00
US48 Matt Chapman HRD .25 .60
US49 Mike Moustakas AS .20 .50
US50 Nick Senzel RC .75 2.00
US51 Bryan Reynolds RC .75 2.00
US52 Keston Hiura RD 1.50 4.00
US53 P.Markel RC/D.McKay RC .25 .60
US54 Paul DeJong AS .25 .60
US55 Javier Baez AS .30 .75
US56 Fernando Tatis Jr. RD 4.00 10.00
US57 Clayton Richard .15 .40
US58 J.T. Realmuto AS .25 .60
US59 Jared Walsh RC 3.00 8.00
US60 Kyle Barraclough .15 .40
US61 Francisco Liriano .15 .40
US62 Vladimir Guerrero Jr. RD 1.00 2.50
US63 Trent Thornton RC .25 .60
US64 Junior Guerra .15 .40
US65 Brad Hand AS .15 .40
US66 J.T. Realmuto .25 .60
US67 Nick Ramirez RC .25 .60
US68 Yandy Diaz .20 .50
US69 Shed Long RC .40 1.00
US70 A.J. Pollock .15 .40
US71 D.Dietrich/Y.Puig .25 .60
US72 Albert Pujols HL CL .30 .75
US73 Peter Lambert RC .40 1.00
US74 Elvis Luciano RC .40 1.00
US75 Shane Bieber AS .25 .60
US76 Alex Colome .15 .40
US77 Drew Pomeranz .15 .40
US78 Mike Ford RC 1.25 3.00
US79 Jonathan Schoop .15 .40
US80 Kyle Bird RC .25 .60
US81 Jose Iglesias .20 .50
US82 Jose Alvarado .15 .40
US83 Whit Merrifield AS .25 .60
US84 Tommy Edman RC 1.25 3.00
US85 Robbie Grossman .15 .40
US86 Hunter Pence .20 .50
US87 Willson Contreras AS .20 .50
US88 Aaron Brooks RC .25 .60
US89 Carlos Santana AS .20 .50
US90 Blake Parker .15 .40
US91 Ketel Marte AS .20 .50
US92 George Springer AS .20 .50
US93 Michael Brantley .20 .50
US94 Gregory Soto RC .25 .60
US95 Nick Senzel RD .60 1.50
US96 Justin Verlander AS .25 .60
US97 Erik Swanson RC .25 .60
US98 Jones/Dyson/Peralta .20 .50
US99 T.Anderson/J.Harrison .25 .60
US100 Austin Riley RC 1.25 3.00
US101 Joe Kelly .15 .40
US102 Matt Strahm .15 .40
US103 Austin Allen RC .30 .75
US104 Sandy Alcantara AS .15 .40
US105 Luis Rengifo RC .40 1.00
US106 Yasiel Puig .25 .60
US107 Robinson Cano .20 .50
US108 Cole Irvin RC .25 .60
US109 Carter Kieboom RC .40 1.00
US110 Marwin Gonzalez .15 .40
US111 Matt Festa RC .25 .60
US112 Josh Bell HRD .20 .50
US113 Cody Bellinger HL CL .50 1.25
US114 Joey Gallo AS .20 .50
US115 Pedro Avila RC .25 .60
US116 Kelvin Gutierrez RC .40 1.00
US117 DJ LeMahieu AS .25 .60
US118 Freddy Galvis .15 .40
US119 Jesus Sucre .15 .40
US120 Billy Hamilton .20 .50
US121 Asdrubal Cabrera .20 .50
US122 Kris Bryant AS .30 .75
US123 Justus Sheffield RC .40 1.00
US124 Raimel Tapia .15 .40
US125 Braden Bishop RC .30 .75
US126 Luis Castillo AS .20 .50
US127 Kelvin Herrera .15 .40
US128 Gio Urshela .25 .60

US129 Ty France RC .75 2.00
US130 Devin Smeltzer RC .40 1.00
US131 Mike Moustakas .20 .50
US132 Neil Walker .20 .50
US133 Leury Garcia .15 .40
US134 J.D. Martinez AS .25 .60
US135 Will Smith AS .15 .40
US136 Austin Meadows AS .20 .50
US137 Hansel Robles .15 .40
US138 Adam Warren .15 .40
US139 Adam Haseley RC .40 1.00
US140 Michael Pineda .15 .40
US141 Brandon Woodruff AS .15 .40
US142 Shaun Anderson RC .25 .60
US143 Alex Bregman AS .25 .60
US144 Xander Bogaerts AS .25 .60
US145 Nick Anderson RC .25 .60
US146 Mike Trout AS 1.25 3.00
US147 Richie Martin RC .25 .60
US148 Gleyber Torres AS .50 1.25
US149 Corbin Martin RC .40 1.00
US150 Keston Hiura RC 3.00 8.00
US151 Mookie Betts AS .40 1.00
US152 Jordan Lyles .15 .40
US153 Tyler Austin .25 .60
US154 Sonny Gray .20 .50
US155 Charlie Morton .25 .60
US156 Jeurys Familia .20 .50
US157 Matt Chapman AS .25 .60
US158 Brian Dozier .20 .50
US159 Jordan Luplow .15 .40
US160 Jose Abreu AS .25 .60
US161 Tommy Kahnle .15 .40
US162 Scott Alexander .15 .40
US163 Miguel Castro .15 .40
US164 Sergio Romo .15 .40
US165 Dwight Smith Jr. .15 .40
US166 Andrew Miller .20 .50
US167 Nolan Arenado AS .30 .75
US168 Thairo Estrada RC .40 1.00
US169 Taylor Clarke RC .25 .60
US170 Michael Chavis RC .40 1.00
US171 Corbin Martin RD .25 .60
US172 Y.Moncada/Y.Alonso .25 .60
US173 M.Gonzalez/G.Springer .20 .50
US174 Matthew Beaty RC .50 1.25
US175 Derek Holland .15 .40
US176 Anibal Sanchez .15 .40
US177 J.P. Crawford .15 .40
US178 Charlie Blackmon AS .25 .60
US179 Hector Neris .15 .40
US180 Josh VanMeter RC .40 1.00
US181 Scott Oberg .15 .40
US182 Andrew Knizner RC .40 1.00
US183 K.Dowdy/K.Bird
US184 Travis d'Arnaud .20 .50
US185 Christian Yelich AS .30 .75
US186 John Ryan Murphy .15 .40
US187 Curtis Granderson .20 .50
US188 Avisail Garcia .20 .50
US189 M.Trout/S.Ohtani 1.25 3.00
US190 Greg Holland .15 .40
US191 Brad Boxberger .15 .40
US192 Michael Chavis RD .25 .60
US193 Marcus Stroman AS .25 .60
US194 Max Muncy AS .20 .50
US195 Nick Hundley .15 .40
US196 Trevor May .15 .40
US197 Cole Tucker RC .40 1.00
US198 Pete Alonso RD 1.25 3.00
US199 Will Smith RC .60 1.50
US200 Griffin Canning RC .40 1.00
US201 Kevin Pillar .15 .40
US202 Nicky Lopez RC .40 1.00
US203 Wilmer Flores .15 .40
US204 Jason Martin RC .30 .75
US205 Darwinzon Hernandez RC .25 .60
US206 Dylan Moore RC .25 .60
US207 Chris Paddack RD .30 .75
US208 Carter Kieboom RD .25 .60
US209 Justin Bour .15 .40
US210 J.Noll RC/J.Bourque RC .25 .60
US211 Skye Bolt RC .30 .75
US212 Wei-Chieh Huang RC .30 .75
US213 Richard Lovelady RC .25 .60
US214 Zack Britton .15 .40
US215 Frankie Montas .15 .40
US216 Christian Yelich HL CL .30 .75
US217 David Robertson .15 .40
US218 Mitch Keller RC .30 .75
US219 Adrian Sampson RC .25 .60
US220 Ronald Acuna Jr. AS 1.25 3.00
US221 Shelby Miller .20 .50
US222 Martin Perez .20 .50
US223 John Means AS .25 .60
US224 Yasmani Grandal .16 .40
US225 Kevin Plawecki .15 .40
US226 Ryne Harper RC .40 1.00
US227 Lane Thomas RC .40 1.00
US228 Montana DuRapau RC .25 .60
US229 Kyle Dowdy RC .30 .75
US230 Pedro Severino .15 .40
US231 Mike Shawaryn RC .25 .60
US232 Michael Brantley AS .20 .50
US233 DJ LeMahieu .25 .60
US234 Trevor Cahill .15 .40
US235 Alex Jackson RC .40 1.00
US236 Adam Ottavino .15 .40
US237 Domingo Santana .20 .50
US238 T.Bergen/S.Coonrod RC .25 .60
US239 Thomas Pannone RC .40 1.00
US240 Merrill Kelly RC .25 .60
US241 B.Drury/V.Guerrero Jr. .75 2.00
US242 Adam Jones .20 .50
US243 Eloy Jimenez RD .60 1.50
US244 Jon Duplantier RC .25 .60
US245 Mike Yastrzemski RC 1.50 4.00
US246 M.Betts/J.Martinez .40 1.00
US247 Luis Arraez RC 1.00 2.50
US248 Ryan Helsley RC .30 .75
US249 Nick Margevicius RC .25 .60
US250 Jonathan Lucroy .20 .50
US251 Bell/Marte/Cervelli .20 .50
US252 Austin Riley RD .75 2.00
US253 C.J. Cron .15 .40
US254 Shane Greene AS .15 .40
US255 Jurickson Profar .20 .50
US256 Jake Bauers RC .40 1.00
US257 Josh Donaldson .20 .50
US258 Lance Lynn .15 .40
US259 Alex Bregman HRD .25 .60
US260 F.Freeman/B.Harper .40 1.00
US261 Jeff McNeil AS .40 1.00
US262 Pete Alonso HRD 1.25 3.00
US263 Chris Paddack RC .50 1.25
US264 B.Kline RC/M.Wotherspoon RC .40 1.00
US265 Noah Syndergaard HL CL .20 .50
US266 Kevin Cron RC .75 2.00
US267 Jacob deGrom AS .25 .60
US268 Jose Berrios AS .20 .50
US269 Craig Kimbrel .20 .50
US270 Homer Bailey .15 .40
US271 Ronald Acuna Jr. HRD 1.25 3.00
US272 Vladimir Guerrero Jr. HRD 1.00 2.50
US273 Wade Miley .15 .40
US274 Josh Bell AS .20 .50
US275 Brandon Kintzler .15 .40
US276 Spencer Turnbull RC .40 1.00
US277 Luke Weaver .15 .40
US278 Yusei Kikuchi RC .25 .60
US279 Freddie Freeman AS .30 .75
US280 Yan Gomes .25 .60
US281 Tyson Ross .15 .40
US282 Nathan Eovaldi .20 .50
US283 Omar Narvaez RC .30 .75
US284 Clayton Kershaw AS .50 1.25
US285 Dallas Keuchel .20 .50
US286 Luis Cessa .15 .40
US287 Edwin Encarnacion .25 .60
US288 Amir Garrett .15 .40
US289 Mike Zunino .15 .40
US290 Marco Estrada .15 .40
US291 Nate Lowe RC .30 .75
US292 Joe Biagini .15 .40
US293 Francisco Lindor AS .25 .60
US294 Josh Fuentes RC .40 1.00
US295 Cavan Biggio RD .75 2.00
US296 Daniel Vogelbach AS .15 .40
US297 Hyun-Jin Ryu AS .20 .50
US298 Carlos Santana HRD .20 .50
US299 Brendan Rodgers RC .40 1.00
US300 Renato Nunez .20 .50

2019 Topps Update Advanced Stats

*ADV STATS: 5X TO 12X BASIC
*ADV STATS RC: 3X TO 8X BASIC RC
STATED ODDS 1:240 HOBBY
STATED PRINT RUN 150 SER.#'d SETS

2019 Topps Update Black

*BLACK: 8X TO 20X BASIC
*BLACK RC: 5X TO 12X BASIC RC
STATED ODDS 1:102 HOBBY
STATED PRINT RUN 67 SER. #'d SETS
US1 Vladimir Guerrero Jr. 500.00 800.00
US2 Mike Tauchman 12.00 30.00
US28 Oscar Mercado 15.00 40.00
US39 Cavan Biggio 25.00 60.00
US45 Brendan Rodgers RD 8.00 20.00
US50 Nick Senzel 40.00 100.00
US51 Bryan Reynolds 25.00 60.00
US52 Keston Hiura RD 20.00 50.00
US56 Fernando Tatis Jr. RD 75.00 200.00
US59 Jared Walsh 75.00 200.00
US69 Shed Long 8.00 20.00
US84 Tommy Edman 50.00 120.00
US100 Austin Riley 100.00 250.00
US109 Carter Kieboom 75.00 200.00
US130 Devin Smeltzer 12.00 30.00
US139 Adam Haseley 12.00 30.00
US150 Keston Hiura 100.00 250.00
US170 Michael Chavis 60.00 150.00
US182 Andrew Knizner 12.00 30.00
US192 Michael Chavis RD 12.00 30.00
US197 Cole Tucker 8.00 20.00
US198 Pete Alonso RD 60.00 150.00
US199 Will Smith 50.00 120.00
US207 Chris Paddack RD 12.00 30.00
US208 Carter Kieboom RD 15.00 40.00
US218 Mitch Keller 12.00 30.00
US227 Lane Thomas 12.00 30.00
US243 Eloy Jimenez RD 30.00 80.00
US245 Mike Yastrzemski 30.00 80.00
US247 Luis Arraez 50.00 120.00
US252 Austin Riley RD 30.00 80.00
US261 Jeff McNeil AS 12.00 30.00
US263 Chris Paddack 40.00 100.00
US291 Nate Lowe 12.00 30.00
US295 Cavan Biggio RD 25.00 60.00
US299 Brendan Rodgers 50.00 120.00

2019 Topps Update Father's Day Blue

*BLUE: 8X TO 20X BASIC
*BLUE RC: 5X TO 12X BASIC RC
STATED ODDS 1:311 HOBBY
STATED PRINT RUN 50 SER. #'d SETS
US1 Vladimir Guerrero Jr. 200.00 500.00
US2 Mike Tauchman 12.00 30.00
US28 Oscar Mercado 15.00 40.00
US39 Cavan Biggio 25.00 60.00
US45 Brendan Rodgers RD 8.00 20.00
US50 Nick Senzel 40.00 100.00
US51 Bryan Reynolds 25.00 60.00
US52 Keston Hiura RD 20.00 50.00
US56 Fernando Tatis Jr. RD 75.00 200.00
US59 Jared Walsh 75.00 200.00
US69 Shed Long 8.00 20.00
US84 Tommy Edman 50.00 120.00
US100 Austin Riley 100.00 250.00
US109 Carter Kieboom 75.00 200.00
US130 Devin Smeltzer 12.00 30.00
US139 Adam Haseley 12.00 30.00
US150 Keston Hiura 100.00 250.00
US170 Michael Chavis 20.00 50.00
US182 Andrew Knizner 12.00 30.00
US192 Michael Chavis RD 12.00 30.00
US197 Cole Tucker 8.00 20.00
US198 Pete Alonso RD 60.00 150.00
US199 Will Smith 50.00 120.00
US207 Chris Paddack RD 12.00 30.00
US208 Carter Kieboom RD 15.00 40.00
US218 Mitch Keller 12.00 30.00
US227 Lane Thomas 12.00 30.00
US243 Eloy Jimenez RD 30.00 80.00
US245 Mike Yastrzemski 30.00 80.00
US247 Luis Arraez 50.00 120.00
US252 Austin Riley RD 30.00 80.00
US261 Jeff McNeil AS 12.00 30.00
US263 Chris Paddack 12.00 30.00
US291 Nate Lowe 12.00 30.00
US295 Cavan Biggio RD 25.00 60.00
US299 Brendan Rodgers 30.00 80.00

2019 Topps Update Gold

*GOLD: 1.2X TO 3X BASIC
*GOLD RC: .75X TO 2X BASIC RC
STATED ODDS 1:8 HOBBY
STATED PRINT RUN 2018 SER. #'d SETS
US1 Vladimir Guerrero Jr. 50.00 120.00
US28 Oscar Mercado 6.00 15.00
US39 Cavan Biggio 4.00 10.00
US50 Nick Senzel 6.00 15.00
US52 Keston Hiura RD 3.00 8.00
US56 Fernando Tatis Jr. RD 40.00 100.00
US59 Jared Walsh 10.00 25.00
US84 Tommy Edman 8.00 20.00
US100 Austin Riley 6.00 15.00
US109 Carter Kieboom 12.00 30.00
US150 Keston Hiura 30.00 80.00
US192 Michael Chavis RD 2.00 5.00
US198 Pete Alonso RD 10.00 25.00
US199 Will Smith 8.00 20.00
US208 Carter Kieboom RD 2.50 6.00
US227 Lane Thomas 2.00 5.00
US243 Eloy Jimenez RD 5.00 12.00
US247 Luis Arraez 8.00 20.00
US295 Cavan Biggio RD 4.00 10.00
US299 Brendan Rodgers 5.00 12.00

2019 Topps Update Independence Day

*INDPNDNCE: 8X TO 20X BASIC
*INDPNDNCE RC: 5X TO 12X BASIC RC
STATED ODDS 1:205 HOBBY
STATED PRINT RUN 76 SER. #'d SETS
US1 Vladimir Guerrero Jr. 200.00 500.00
US2 Mike Tauchman 12.00 30.00
US28 Oscar Mercado 15.00 40.00
US39 Cavan Biggio 25.00 60.00
US45 Brendan Rodgers RD 8.00 20.00
US50 Nick Senzel 40.00 100.00
US51 Bryan Reynolds 25.00 60.00
US52 Keston Hiura RD 20.00 50.00
US56 Fernando Tatis Jr. RD 75.00 200.00
US59 Jared Walsh 75.00 200.00
US84 Tommy Edman 50.00 120.00
US100 Austin Riley 100.00 250.00
US109 Carter Kieboom 75.00 200.00
US130 Devin Smeltzer 12.00 30.00
US139 Adam Haseley 12.00 30.00
US150 Keston Hiura 100.00 250.00
US170 Michael Chavis 20.00 50.00
US182 Andrew Knizner 12.00 30.00
US192 Michael Chavis RD 12.00 30.00
US197 Cole Tucker 8.00 20.00
US198 Pete Alonso RD 60.00 150.00
US199 Will Smith 50.00 120.00
US207 Chris Paddack RD 12.00 30.00
US208 Carter Kieboom RD 15.00 40.00
US218 Mitch Keller 12.00 30.00
US227 Lane Thomas 12.00 30.00
US243 Eloy Jimenez RD 30.00 80.00
US245 Mike Yastrzemski 30.00 80.00
US247 Luis Arraez 12.00 30.00
US252 Austin Riley RD 30.00 80.00
US261 Jeff McNeil AS 12.00 30.00
US263 Chris Paddack 12.00 30.00
US291 Nate Lowe 12.00 30.00
US295 Cavan Biggio RD 25.00 60.00
US299 Brendan Rodgers 30.00 80.00

2019 Topps Update Memorial Day Camo

*CAMO: 12X TO 30X BASIC
*CAMO RC: 8X TO 20X BASIC RC
STATED ODDS 1:622 HOBBY
STATED PRINT RUN 25 SER. #'d SETS
US1 Vladimir Guerrero Jr. 600.00 1000.00
US28 Oscar Mercado 25.00 60.00
US39 Cavan Biggio 40.00 100.00
US45 Brendan Rodgers RD 12.00 30.00
US50 Nick Senzel 60.00 150.00
US51 Bryan Reynolds 40.00 100.00
US52 Keston Hiura RD 30.00 80.00
US56 Fernando Tatis Jr. RD 125.00 300.00
US59 Jared Walsh 125.00 300.00
US69 Shed Long 12.00 30.00
US84 Tommy Edman 75.00 200.00
US100 Austin Riley 150.00 400.00
US109 Carter Kieboom 125.00 300.00
US130 Devin Smeltzer 20.00 50.00
US139 Adam Haseley 20.00 50.00
US150 Keston Hiura 150.00 400.00
US170 Michael Chavis 100.00 250.00
US182 Andrew Knizner 20.00 50.00
US192 Michael Chavis RD 20.00 50.00
US197 Cole Tucker 12.00 30.00
US198 Pete Alonso RD 100.00 250.00
US199 Will Smith 75.00 200.00
US207 Chris Paddack RD 20.00 50.00
US208 Carter Kieboom RD 25.00 60.00
US218 Mitch Keller 20.00 50.00
US227 Lane Thomas 20.00 50.00
US243 Eloy Jimenez RD 50.00 120.00
US245 Mike Yastrzemski 50.00 120.00
US247 Luis Arraez 75.00 200.00
US252 Austin Riley RD 50.00 120.00
US261 Jeff McNeil AS 20.00 50.00
US263 Chris Paddack 60.00 150.00
US291 Nate Lowe 20.00 50.00
US295 Cavan Biggio RD 40.00 100.00
US299 Brendan Rodgers 75.00 200.00

2019 Topps Update Mother's Day Pink

*PINK: 8X TO 20X BASIC
*PINK RC: 5X TO 12X BASIC RC
STATED ODDS 1:311 HOBBY
STATED PRINT RUN 50 SER. #'d SETS
US1 Vladimir Guerrero Jr. 200.00 500.00
US2 Mike Tauchman 12.00 30.00
US28 Oscar Mercado 15.00 40.00
US39 Cavan Biggio 25.00 60.00
US45 Brendan Rodgers RD 8.00 20.00
US50 Nick Senzel 40.00 100.00
US51 Bryan Reynolds 25.00 60.00
US52 Keston Hiura RD 20.00 50.00
US56 Fernando Tatis Jr. RD 75.00 200.00
US59 Jared Walsh 75.00 200.00
US69 Shed Long 8.00 20.00
US84 Tommy Edman 50.00 120.00
US100 Austin Riley 100.00 250.00
US109 Carter Kieboom 75.00 200.00
US130 Devin Smeltzer 12.00 30.00
US139 Adam Haseley 12.00 30.00
US150 Keston Hiura 100.00 250.00
US170 Michael Chavis 20.00 50.00
US182 Andrew Knizner 12.00 30.00
US192 Michael Chavis RD 12.00 30.00
US197 Cole Tucker 8.00 20.00
US198 Pete Alonso RD 60.00 150.00
US199 Will Smith 50.00 120.00
US207 Chris Paddack RD 12.00 30.00
US208 Carter Kieboom RD 15.00 40.00
US218 Mitch Keller 12.00 30.00
US227 Lane Thomas 12.00 30.00
US243 Eloy Jimenez RD 30.00 80.00
US245 Mike Yastrzemski 30.00 80.00
US247 Luis Arraez 50.00 120.00
US252 Austin Riley RD 30.00 80.00
US261 Jeff McNeil AS 12.00 30.00
US263 Chris Paddack 12.00 30.00
US291 Nate Lowe 12.00 30.00
US295 Cavan Biggio RD 25.00 60.00
US299 Brendan Rodgers 30.00 80.00

2019 Topps Update Photo Variations

VAR STATED ODDS 1:32 HOBBY
RC VAR STATED ODDS 1:622 HOBBY
US1A Guerrero Jr. Point 40.00 100.00
US1B Guerrero Jr. w/Ball 150.00 400.00
US12 Paul Goldschmidt 1.50 4.00
arms streched out
US21 Willie Mays 3.00 8.00
US28A Mercado Crouch 2.50 6.00
US28B Mercado Point 25.00 60.00
US35 Derek Dietrich 1.25 3.00
red tank top
US39A Biggio Interview 5.00 12.00
US39B Biggio Trot 30.00 80.00
US50A Senzel Touch Hat 6.00 15.00
US50B Senzel Gatorade 50.00 120.00
US56 Tony Gwynn 1.50 4.00
US63A Trent Thornton 1.00 2.50
blue jersey
US63B Thornton Gray jrsy 15.00 40.00
US74 Luciano Tossing ball 25.00 60.00
US79 Jackie Robinson 1.50 4.00
US93 Ken Griffey Jr. 3.00 8.00
US100A Riley Jump 10.00 25.00
US100B Riley w/Blooper 40.00 100.00
US105 Rengifo Pullover 10.00 25.00
US106 Yasiel Puig 1.50 4.00
with Indians
US107 Robinson Cano 1.25 3.00
touching chest
US109A Kieboom Thrwng 8.00 20.00
US109B Kieboom Blue jrsy 30.00 80.00
US123A Justus Sheffield 1.50 4.00
Arm up
US123B Sheffield Arm down 15.00 40.00
US128 Thurman Munson 4.00 10.00
US133 Willie Mays 3.00 8.00
US147 Cal Ripken Jr. 4.00 10.00
US149A Corbin Martin 1.50 4.00
tipping hat
US149B Martin Clenched fist 15.00 40.00
US150A Hiura Thrwbck 40.00 100.00
US150B Hiura Hand helmet 40.00 100.00
US165 Eddie Murray 1.25 3.00
US168 Estrada Thrwng 40.00 100.00
US168 Robin Yount 1.50 4.00
US170A Chavis Wht jrsy 4.00 10.00
US170B Chavis Red jrsy 50.00 120.00
US179 Mariano Rivera 2.00 5.00
US182 Johnny Bench 1.50 4.00
US187 Roberto Clemente 4.00 10.00
US197A Cole Tucker 1.50 4.00
wearing costume
US197B Tucker Signs 30.00 80.00
US199A Smith Vertical 5.00 12.00
US199B Smith Horizontal 30.00 80.00
US200A Griffin Canning 1.50 4.00
red pullover
US200B Canning w/Catcher 15.00 40.00
US202 George Brett 3.00 8.00
US206 Ichiro 2.00 5.00
US218 Mitch Keller 1.25 3.00
sitting in dugout
US219 Nolan Ryan 5.00 12.00
US224 Yasmani Grandal 1.00 2.50
running
US227 Thomas w/Ozuna 20.00 50.00
US237 Randy Johnson 1.50 4.00
US242 Adam Jones 1.25 3.00
left foot off ground
US244A Duplantier Gray jrsy 1.00 2.50
US244B Duplantier Wht jrsy 15.00 40.00
US245 Carl Yastrzemski 2.50 6.00
US249A Nick Margevicius 1.00 2.50
brown jersey
US249B Margevicius Full mound 15.00 40.00
US256A Jake Bauers 1.50 4.00
white jersey
US256B Bauers Gray jrsy 15.00 40.00
US257 Josh Donaldson 1.25 3.00
ball visible
US263B Chris Paddack 2.00 5.00
with Machado
US263A Paddack Jckt 30.00 80.00
US266A Cron Dirt 3.00 8.00
US266B Cron Dugout 20.00 50.00
US269 Ryne Sandberg 3.00 8.00
US283 Edgar Martinez 1.25 3.00
US291A Nate Lowe 1.25 3.00
peace sign
US291B Lowe Bttng cage 15.00 40.00
US295 Roy Halladay 1.25 3.00
US299A Brendan Rodgers 1.50 4.00
coming out dugout
US299B Rodgers Barehand 30.00 80.00
US300 Mike Mussina 1.25 3.00

2019 Topps Update Rainbow Foil

*RAINBOW: 1.2X TO 3X BASIC
*RAINBOW RC: .75X TO 2X BASIC RC
STATED ODDS 1:10 HOBBY
US1 Vladimir Guerrero Jr. 30.00 80.00
US28 Oscar Mercado 2.50 6.00
US39 Cavan Biggio 4.00 10.00
US50 Nick Senzel 6.00 15.00
US52 Keston Hiura RD 3.00 8.00
US56 Fernando Tatis Jr. RD 15.00 40.00
US59 Jared Walsh 12.00 30.00
US84 Tommy Edman 4.00 10.00
US100 Austin Riley 6.00 15.00
US109 Carter Kieboom 12.00 30.00
US150 Keston Hiura 30.00 80.00
US192 Michael Chavis RD 2.00 5.00
US198 Pete Alonso RD 10.00 25.00
US199 Will Smith 8.00 20.00
US208 Carter Kieboom RD 2.50 6.00
US227 Lane Thomas 2.00 5.00
US243 Eloy Jimenez RD 5.00 12.00
US247 Luis Arraez 8.00 20.00
US295 Cavan Biggio RD 4.00 10.00
US299 Brendan Rodgers 5.00 12.00

2019 Topps Update Vintage Stock

*VINTAGE: 6X TO 15X BASIC
*VINTAGE RC: 4X TO 10X BASIC RC
STATED ODDS 1:157 HOBBY
STATED PRINT RUN 99 SER. #'d SETS
US1 Vladimir Guerrero Jr. 150.00 400.00
US28 Oscar Mercado 12.00 30.00
US39 Cavan Biggio 20.00 50.00
US45 Brendan Rodgers RD 6.00 15.00
US50 Nick Senzel 30.00 80.00
US51 Bryan Reynolds 20.00 50.00
US52 Keston Hiura RD 15.00 40.00
US56 Fernando Tatis Jr. RD 60.00 150.00
US59 Jared Walsh 50.00 120.00
US84 Tommy Edman 40.00 100.00
US100 Austin Riley 40.00 100.00
US109 Carter Kieboom 60.00 150.00
US139 Adam Haseley 10.00 25.00
US150 Keston Hiura 75.00 200.00
US170 Michael Chavis 15.00 40.00
US182 Andrew Knizner 10.00 25.00
US192 Michael Chavis RD 10.00 25.00
US197 Cole Tucker 6.00 15.00
US198 Pete Alonso RD 50.00 120.00
US199 Will Smith 40.00 100.00
US208 Carter Kieboom RD 12.00 30.00
US218 Mitch Keller 10.00 25.00
US227 Lane Thomas 10.00 25.00
US243 Eloy Jimenez RD 25.00 60.00
US245 Mike Yastrzemski 25.00 60.00
US247 Luis Arraez 40.00 100.00
US252 Austin Riley RD 25.00 60.00
US261 Jeff McNeil AS 10.00 25.00
US263 Chris Paddack 10.00 25.00
US291 Nate Lowe 10.00 25.00
US295 Cavan Biggio RD 20.00 50.00
US299 Brendan Rodgers 25.00 60.00

2019 Topps Update Walgreens Yellow

*YELLOW: 2.5X TO 6X BASIC
*YELLOW RC: 1.5X TO 4X BASIC RC
INSERTED IN WALGREENS PACKS
US1 Vladimir Guerrero Jr. 50.00 120.00
US28 Oscar Mercado 5.00 12.00
US39 Cavan Biggio 8.00 20.00
US50 Nick Senzel 12.00 30.00
US52 Keston Hiura RD 6.00 15.00
US56 Fernando Tatis Jr. RD 40.00 100.00
US59 Jared Walsh 20.00 50.00
US84 Tommy Edman 8.00 20.00
US100 Austin Riley 12.00 30.00
US109 Carter Kieboom 25.00 60.00
US150 Keston Hiura 30.00 80.00
US192 Michael Chavis RD 4.00 10.00
US198 Pete Alonso RD 20.00 50.00
US199 Will Smith 15.00 40.00
US208 Carter Kieboom RD 5.00 12.00
US227 Lane Thomas 4.00 10.00
US243 Eloy Jimenez RD 10.00 25.00
US247 Luis Arraez 15.00 40.00
US295 Cavan Biggio RD 8.00 20.00
US299 Brendan Rodgers 10.00 25.00

2019 Topps Update '84 Oversized Box Toppers

84BT1 Yusei Kikuchi .60 1.50
84BT2 Mike Trout 5.00 12.00
84BT3 Noah Syndergaard .75 2.00
84BT4 Max Scherzer 1.00 2.50
84BT5 Juan Soto 3.00 8.00
84BT6 Aaron Judge 2.50 6.00
84BT7 Jacob deGrom 1.00 2.50
84BT8 Cody Bellinger 2.00 5.00
84BT9 Christian Yelich 1.25 3.00
84BT10 Clayton Kershaw 2.00 5.00
84BT11 Nolan Ryan 3.00 8.00
84BT12 Francisco Lindor 1.00 2.50
84BT13 Kris Bryant 1.25 3.00
84BT14 Mookie Betts 1.50 4.00
84BT15 Ronald Acuna Jr. 5.00 12.00
84BT16 Javier Baez 1.25 3.00
84BT17 Jose Altuve .75 2.00
84BT18 Don Mattingly 2.00 5.00
84BT19 Derek Jeter 2.50 6.00
84BT20 Mark McGwire 1.50 4.00
84BT21 Fernando Tatis Jr. 6.00 15.00
84BT22 Eloy Jimenez 2.50 6.00
84BT23 Vladimir Guerrero Jr. 4.00 10.00
84BT24 Pete Alonso 5.00 12.00
84BT25 Ted Williams 2.00 5.00
84BT26 Nick Senzel 2.00 5.00
84BT27 Carter Kieboom 1.00 2.50
84BT28 Chris Paddack 1.25 3.00
84BT29 Michael Chavis 1.00 2.50
84BT30 Austin Riley 3.00 8.00
84BT31 Keston Hiura 2.00 5.00
84BT32 Brendan Rodgers 1.00 2.50
84BT33 Willie Mays 2.00 5.00
84BT34 Bryce Harper 1.50 4.00
84BT35 Manny Machado 1.00 2.50
84BT36 Paul Goldschmidt 1.00 2.50
84BT37 Mariano Rivera 1.25 3.00
84BT38 Walker Buehler 1.25 3.00
84BT39 Alex Bregman 1.00 2.50
84BT40 Shohei Ohtani 1.25 3.00
84BT41 Roberto Clemente 2.50 6.00
84BT42 Jackie Robinson 1.00 2.50
84BT43 Thurman Munson 1.00 2.50
84BT44 Andrew McCutchen 1.00 2.50
84BT45 Mike Piazza 1.00 2.50
84BT46 Albert Pujols 1.25 3.00
84BT47 Pedro Martinez .75 2.00
84BT48 David Ortiz 1.00 2.50
84BT49 Frank Thomas 1.00 2.50
84BT50 Bo Jackson 1.00 2.50

2019 Topps Update '84 Topps

STATED ODDS 1:4 HOBBY
*BLUE: .6X TO 1.5X
*BLACK/299: 1X TO 2.5X
*150TH/150: 1X TO 2.5X
*GOLD/50: 5X TO 12X
841 Garrett Hampson .25 .60
842 Kerry Wood .25 .60
843 J.D. Martinez .40 1.00
844 Gerrit Cole .40 1.00
845 Xander Bogaerts .40 1.00
846 Miguel Cabrera .40 1.00
847 CC Sabathia .30 .75
848 Fernando Tatis Jr. 2.50 6.00
849 Eloy Jimenez 1.00 2.50
8410 Vladimir Guerrero Jr. 1.50 4.00
8411 Pete Alonso 2.00 5.00
8412 Ted Williams .75 2.00
8413 Nick Senzel .75 2.00
8414 Carter Kieboom .40 1.00
8415 Chris Paddack .50 1.25
8416 Michael Chavis .40 1.00
8417 Nick Margevicius .25 .60
8418 Jon Duplantier .25 .60
8419 Mariano Rivera .50 1.25
8420 Roy Halladay .30 .75
8421 Griffin Canning .40 1.00
8422 Thairo Estrada .40 1.00
8423 Lane Thomas .40 1.00
8424 Cole Tucker .40 1.00
8425 Shohei Ohtani .50 1.25
8426 Corbin Martin .40 1.00
8427 Roberto Clemente 1.00 2.50
8428 Jackie Robinson .40 1.00
8429 Austin Riley 1.25 3.00
8430 Keston Hiura .75 2.00
8431 Willie Mays .75 2.00
8432 Oscar Mercado .60 1.50
8433 Ken Griffey Jr. .75 2.00
8434 Adam Jones .30 .75
8435 Patrick Corbin .30 .75
8436 Brendan Rodgers .40 1.00
8437 Will Smith .60 1.50
8438 Bryce Harper .60 1.50
8439 Manny Machado .40 1.00
8440 Andrew McCutchen .40 1.00
8441 Paul Goldschmidt .40 1.00
8442 Robinson Cano .30 .75
8443 Josh Donaldson .30 .75
8444 Nelson Cruz .40 1.00
8445 Yasmani Grandal .25 .60
8446 Michael Brantley .30 .75
8447 Victor Robles .50 1.25
8448 Walker Buehler .50 1.25
8449 Alex Bregman .40 1.00
8450 Thurman Munson .40 1.00

2019 Topps Update '84 Topps Autographs

STATED ODDS 1:431 HOBBY
EXCHANGE DEADLINE 9/30/2021
84AAME Austin Meadows 5.00 12.00
84ABBX Byron Buxton 8.00 20.00
84ABR Bryan Reynolds 6.00 15.00
84ACK Carter Kieboom 12.00 30.00
84ACP Chris Paddack 10.00 25.00
84ACS CC Sabathia
84ACT Cole Tucker 4.00 10.00
84ADH Darwinzon Hernandez 2.50 6.00
84ADP Dustin Pedroia 20.00 50.00
84AEJ Eloy Jimenez 40.00 100.00
84AEL Elvis Luciano 4.00 10.00
84AFT Fernando Tatis Jr. 125.00 300.00
84AGC Gerrit Cole 20.00 50.00
84AGH Garrett Hampson 2.50 6.00
84AJAG Jesus Aguilar 2.50 6.00
84AJCA Jose Canseco 10.00 25.00
84AJD Jon Duplantier 2.50 6.00
84AJM J.D. Martinez 25.00 60.00
84AJMA Jason Martin 3.00 8.00
84AJME John Means 6.00 15.00
84AJV Joey Votto 20.00 50.00
84AKW Kerry Wood 15.00 40.00
84ALBR Lou Brock 20.00 50.00
84ALT Lane Thomas 8.00 20.00
84AMBE Matthew Beaty 6.00 15.00
84AMC Miguel Cabrera 60.00 150.00
84AMCA Michael Chavis 12.00 30.00
84AMK Merrill Kelly 2.50 6.00
84AMM Mike Mussina 60.00 150.00
84AMS Max Scherzer
84AMS Mike Soroka 10.00 25.00
84ANA Nolan Arenado 30.00 80.00
84ANGA Nomar Garciaparra 25.00 60.00
84ANL Nate Lowe 3.00 8.00
84ANM Nick Margevicius 2.50 6.00
84APA Pete Alonso 60.00 150.00
84APAV Pedro Avila 2.50 6.00
84ARH Ryan Helsley 3.00 8.00
84ARL Richard Lovelady 2.50 6.00
84ASB Skye Bolt 3.00 8.00
84ASL Shed Long 4.00 10.00
84ASP Salvador Perez 8.00 20.00
84ATE Thairo Estrada 10.00 25.00
84ATG Tom Glavine 10.00 25.00
84ATM Trey Mancini 3.00 8.00
84ATT Trent Thornton 2.50 6.00
84AVG Vladimir Guerrero Jr. 75.00 200.00
84AVGU Vladimir Guerrero 20.00 50.00
84RAAR Austin Riley 15.00 40.00

84RJSH Justus Sheffield 4.00 10.00
84RKH Keston Hiura 30.00 80.00
84RRBO Ryan Borucki 2.50 6.00
84RWS Will Smith 12.00 30.00

2019 Topps Update '84 Topps Autographs 150th Anniversary

*150TH ANNV/150: .5X TO 1.2X BASIC
STATED ODDS 1:967 HOBBY
STATED PRINT RUN 150 SER.#'d SETS
EXCHANGE DEADLINE 9/30/2021
84AMKE Mitch Keller 4.00 10.00

2019 Topps Update '84 Topps Autographs Gold

*GOLD/50: .6X TO 1.5X BASIC
STATED ODDS 1:2681 HOBBY
STATED PRINT RUN 50 SER.#'d SETS
EXCHANGE DEADLINE 9/30/2021
84ACB Cavan Biggio EXCH 60.00 150.00
84AMKE Mitch Keller 5.00 12.00
84ANS Nick Senzel EXCH 40.00 100.00

2019 Topps Update '84 Topps Autographs Red

*RED/25: .8X TO 2X BASIC
STATED ODDS 1:637 HOBBY
STATED PRINT RUN 25 SER.#'d SETS
EXCHANGE DEADLINE 9/30/2021
84ACB Cavan Biggio EXCH 75.00 200.00
84AMKE Mitch Keller 6.00 15.00
84ANS Nick Senzel EXCH 50.00 120.00

2019 Topps Update '84 Topps Silver Pack Chrome

T84U1 Mike Trout 3.00 8.00
T84U2 Shohei Ohtani .75 2.00
T84U3 Griffin Canning .60 1.50
T84U4 Randy Johnson .60 1.50
T84U5 Jon Duplantier .40 1.00
T84U6 Ronald Acuna Jr. 3.00 8.00
T84U7 Austin Riley 2.00 5.00
T84U8 Michael Chavis .60 1.50
T84U9 J.D. Martinez .60 1.50
T84U10 Rafael Devers .75 2.00
T84U11 Kerry Wood .40 1.00
T84U12 Eloy Jimenez 1.50 4.00
T84U13 Nick Senzel 1.25 3.00
T84U14 Ken Griffey Jr. 1.25 3.00
T84U15 Trevor Bauer .60 1.50
T84U16 Brendan Rodgers .60 1.50
T84U17 Jeff Bagwell .50 1.25
T84U18 Justin Verlander .60 1.50
T84U19 Corbin Martin .60 1.50
T84U20 Walker Buehler .75 2.00
T84U21 Christian Yelich .75 2.00
T84U22 Keston Hiura 1.25 3.00
T84U23 Byron Buxton .50 1.25
T84U24 Pete Alonso 3.00 8.00
T84U25 Clint Frazier .50 1.25
T84U26 Gary Sanchez .60 1.50
T84U27 Giancarlo Stanton .60 1.50
T84U28 Thairo Estrada .60 1.50
T84U29 Aaron Judge 1.50 4.00
T84U30 Jose Canseco .50 1.25
T84U31 Aaron Nola .50 1.25
T84U32 Bryce Harper 1.00 2.50
T84U33 Cole Tucker .60 1.50
T84U34 Fernando Tatis Jr. 4.00 10.00
T84U35 Chris Paddack .75 2.00
T84U36 Willie Mays 1.25 3.00
T84U37 Edgar Martinez .50 1.25
T84U38 Ichiro Suzuki .75 2.00
T84U39 Will Smith 1.00 2.50
T84U40 Mitch Keller .50 1.25
T84U41 Lane Thomas .60 1.50
T84U42 Brandon Lowe .60 1.50
T84U43 Blake Snell .50 1.25
T84U44 Joey Gallo .50 1.25
T84U45 Cavan Biggio 2.00 5.00
T84U46 Vladimir Guerrero Jr. 2.50 6.00
T84U47 Trent Thornton .40 1.00
T84U48 Carter Kieboom .60 1.50
T84U49 Victor Robles .75 2.00
T84U50 Kevin Cron 1.25 3.00

2019 Topps Update '84 Topps Silver Pack Chrome Black Refractors

*BLACK REF: 1.2X TO 3X BASIC
RANDOM INSERTS IN SILVER PACKS
STATED PRINT RUN 199 SER.#'d SETS

2019 Topps Update '84 Topps Silver Pack Chrome Blue Refractors

*BLUE REF: 1.5X TO 4X BASIC
RANDOM INSERTS IN SILVER PACKS
STATED PRINT RUN 150 SER.#'d SETS

2019 Topps Update '84 Topps Silver Pack Chrome Gold Refractors

*GOLD REF: 5X TO 12X BASIC
RANDOM INSERTS IN SILVER PACKS
STATED PRINT RUN 50 SER.#'d SETS

2019 Topps Update '84 Topps Silver Pack Chrome Green Refractors

*GREEN REF: 2X TO 5X BASIC
RANDOM INSERTS IN SILVER PACKS
STATED PRINT RUN 150 SER.#'d SETS

2019 Topps Update '84 Topps Silver Pack Chrome Orange Refractors

*ORANGE REF: 6X TO 15X BASIC
RANDOM INSERTS IN SILVER PACKS
STATED PRINT RUN 25 SER.#'d SETS

2019 Topps Update '84 Topps Silver Pack Chrome Purple Refractors

*PURPLE REF: 2X TO 5X BASIC
RANDOM INSERTS IN SILVER PACKS
STATED PRINT RUN 75 SER.#'d SETS

2019 Topps Update '84 Topps Silver Pack Chrome Autographs

RANDOM INSERTS IN SILVER PACKS
PRINT RUNS B/WN 8-150 COPIES PER
NO PRICING ON QTY 10 OR LESS
T84U2 Shohei Ohtani
T84U3 Griffin Canning/149 6.00 15.00
T84U4 Randy Johnson
T84U6 Ronald Acuna Jr./25 75.00 200.00
T84U7 Austin Riley/149 30.00 80.00
T84U8 Michael Chavis/149 12.00 30.00
T84U10 Rafael Devers/25 30.00 80.00
T84U11 Kerry Wood/25 15.00 40.00
T84U12 Eloy Jimenez/50 40.00 100.00
T84U15 Trevor Bauer
T84U17 Jeff Bagwell
T84U19 Corbin Martin/150 5.00 12.00
T84U22 Keston Hiura/149 30.00 80.00
T84U23 Byron Buxton
T84U24 Pete Alonso/149 60.00 150.00
T84U25 Clint Frazier
T84U26 Gary Sanchez
T84U28 Thairo Estrada/149 10.00 25.00
T84U30 Jose Canseco
T84U33 Cole Tucker/149 6.00 15.00
T84U34 Fernando Tatis Jr./99 150.00 400.00
T84U35 Chris Paddack/99 20.00 50.00
T84U37 Edgar Martinez/25 20.00 50.00
T84U39 Will Smith/149 10.00 25.00
T84U40 Mitch Keller
T84U41 Lane Thomas/149 8.00 20.00
T84U42 Brandon Lowe/99 10.00 25.00
T84U43 Blake Snell
T84U45 Cavan Biggio
T84U46 Vladimir Guerrero Jr./99 75.00 200.00
T84U47 Trent Thornton
T84U48 Carter Kieboom/149 15.00 40.00
T84U49 Victor Robles

2019 Topps Update '84 Topps Silver Pack Chrome Autographs Orange Refractors

*ORANGE/25: 1X TO 2.5X p/r 149-150
*ORANGE/25: .6X TO 1.5X p/r 50
RANDOM INSERTS IN SILVER PACKS
STATED PRINT RUN 25 SER.#'d SETS
T84U30 Jose Canseco 30.00 80.00
T84U40 Mitch Keller 25.00 60.00
T84U43 Blake Snell 12.00 30.00
T84U45 Cavan Biggio 40.00 100.00
T84U47 Trent Thornton 6.00 15.00
T84U49 Victor Robles 12.00 30.00

2019 Topps Update 150 Years of Baseball

STATED ODDS 1:8 HOBBY
*BLUE: .6X TO 1.5X
*BLACK/299: 1X TO 2.5X
*150TH/150: 1X TO 2.5X
*GOLD/50: 1.5X TO 4X
1501 Gary Carter .30 .75
1502 Willie Mays .75 2.00
1503 Aaron Judge 1.00 2.50
1504 Alex Bregman .40 1.00
1505 Andre Dawson .30 .75
1506 Andy Pettitte .30 .75
1507 Anthony Rizzo .60 1.50
1508 Carlton Fisk .30 .75
1509 Chris Sale .40 1.00
15010 Christian Yelich .60 1.50
15011 Cody Bellinger .75 2.00
15012 Edgar Martinez .30 .75
15013 Eloy Jimenez 1.00 2.50
15014 Fernando Tatis Jr. 2.50 6.00
15015 Francisco Lindor .40 1.00
15016 Freddie Freeman .50 1.25
15017 George Springer .30 .75
15018 Giancarlo Stanton .40 1.00
15019 Gleyber Torres .75 2.00
15020 Jacob deGrom .40 1.00
15021 Javier Baez .50 1.25
15022 Jose Altuve .30 .75
15023 Kris Bryant .50 1.25
15024 Lou Boudreau .30 .75
15025 Manny Machado .40 1.00
15026 Mike Mussina .30 .75
15027 Mookie Betts .60 1.50
15028 Noah Syndergaard .30 .75
15029 Nolan Arenado .50 1.25
15030 Randy Johnson .40 1.00
15031 Pete Alonso 2.00 5.00
15032 Rhys Hoskins .50 1.25
15033 Robinson Cano .30 .75
15034 Roger Clemens .50 1.25
15035 Jim Bunning .30 .75
15036 Ronald Acuna Jr. 2.00 5.00
15037 Roy Halladay .30 .75
15038 Shohei Ohtani .50 1.25
15039 Stephen Strasburg .40 1.00
15040 Thurman Munson .40 1.00
15041 Tim Raines .30 .75
15042 Todd Helton .30 .75
15043 Tony Perez .30 .75
15044 Vladimir Guerrero Jr. 1.50 4.00
15045 Paul Molitor .40 1.00
15046 Luis Aparicio .30 .75
15047 Bert Blyleven .30 .75
15048 Bruce Sutter .30 .75
15049 Jim Thome .30 .75
15050 Goose Gossage .30 .75
15051 Willie Mays .75 2.00
15052 Willie Mays .75 2.00
15053 Babe Ruth 1.00 2.50
15054 Bud Selig .25 .60
15055 Warren Spahn .30 .75
15056 Willie Stargell .30 .75
15057 Sandy Alomar Jr. .25 .60
15058 Bo Jackson .40 1.00
15059 Willie Mays .75 2.00
15060 Chad Bettis .25 .60
15061 Marcus Stroman .30 .75
15062 Luis Gonzalez .25 .60
15063 John Ward .30 .75
15064 Hugh Duffy .30 .75
15065 Jose Canseco .30 .75
15066 Deion Sanders .30 .75
15067 Ken Griffey Jr. .75 2.00
15068 Dwight Gooden .25 .60
15069 Tris Speaker .30 .75
15070 George Springer .30 .75
15071 Casey Stengel .30 .75
15072 Phil Niekro .30 .75
15073 Jim Bunning .30 .75
15074 Randy Johnson .40 1.00
15075 Tom Seaver .30 .75
15076 Rogers Hornsby .30 .75
15077 Willie Mays .75 2.00
15078 Warren Spahn .30 .75
15079 Catfish Hunter .30 .75
15080 Derek Jeter 1.00 2.50
15081 Adrian Beltre .40 1.00
15082 Tom Glavine .30 .75
15083 Vladimir Guerrero .30 .75
15084 Wade Boggs .30 .75
15085 Orlando Cepeda .30 .75
15086 Jose Altuve .30 .75
15087 Johnny Bench .40 1.00
15088 Javier Baez .50 1.25
15089 Jim Palmer .30 .75
15090 Ivan Rodriguez .30 .75
15091 Willie Stargell .30 .75
15092 Max Scherzer .40 1.00
15093 Thurman Munson .40 1.00
15094 Ken Griffey Jr. .75 2.00
15095 Roger Clemens .50 1.25
15096 Jackie Robinson .40 1.00
15097 Sandy Koufax .75 2.00
15098 Randy Johnson .40 1.00
15099 Nolan Ryan 1.25 3.00
150100 David Ortiz .40 1.00

2019 Topps Update 150th Anniversary

*150TH: 1.2X TO 3X BASIC
*150TH RC: .75X TO 2X BASIC RC
STATED ODDS 1:6 HOBBY
US1 Vladimir Guerrero Jr. 12.00 30.00
US28 Oscar Mercado 2.50 6.00
US39 Cavan Biggio 4.00 10.00
US50 Nick Senzel 6.00 15.00
US52 Keston Hiura RD 3.00 8.00
US56 Fernando Tatis Jr. RD 15.00 40.00
US59 Jared Walsh 12.00 30.00
US84 Tommy Edman 4.00 10.00
US100 Austin Riley 6.00 15.00
US109 Carter Kieboom 12.00 30.00
US150 Keston Hiura 30.00 80.00
US192 Michael Chavis RD 2.00 5.00
US198 Pete Alonso RD 10.00 25.00
US199 Will Smith 8.00 20.00
US208 Carter Kieboom RD 2.50 6.00
US227 Lane Thomas 2.00 5.00
US243 Eloy Jimenez RD 5.00 12.00
US247 Luis Arraez 8.00 20.00
US295 Cavan Biggio RD 4.00 10.00
US299 Brendan Rodgers 5.00 12.00

2019 Topps Update 150th Anniversary Manufactured Medallions

STATED ODDS 1:242 HOBBY
*150TH/150: .6X TO 1.5X BASIC
*GOLD/50: 1X TO 2.5X BASIC
*RED/25: 2X TO 5X BASIC
AMMAB Alex Bregman 1.25 3.00
AMMAD Andre Dawson 1.00 2.50
AMMAR Alex Rodriguez 1.50 4.00
AMMBB Bert Blyleven 1.00 2.50
AMMBS Blake Snell 1.00 2.50
AMMCB Cody Bellinger 2.50 6.00
AMMCC Carlos Correa 1.25 3.00
AMMCF Carlton Fisk 2.50 6.00
AMMCM Christy Mathewson 1.25 3.00
AMMDD Dizzy Dean 1.00 2.50
AMMDM Dale Murphy 2.50 6.00
AMMDW David Wright 2.50 6.00
AMMEJ Eloy Jimenez 3.00 8.00
AMMEM Edgar Martinez 1.00 2.50
AMMFR Frank Robinson 1.00 2.50
AMMFT Fernando Tatis Jr. 8.00 20.00
AMMGC Gary Carter 2.50 6.00
AMMGS Giancarlo Stanton 1.25 3.00
AMMHK Harmon Killebrew 2.50 6.00
AMMJB Jeff Bagwell 1.00 2.50
AMMJM J.D. Martinez 1.25 3.00
AMMJP Jim Palmer 2.50 6.00
AMMJS John Smoltz 1.25 3.00
AMMJT Jim Thome 1.00 2.50
AMMKD Khris Davis 1.25 3.00
AMMKG Ken Griffey Jr. 5.00 12.00
AMMMM Manny Machado 1.25 3.00
AMMMP Mike Piazza 2.50 6.00
AMMNS Nick Senzel 3.00 8.00
AMMPA Pete Alonso 6.00 15.00
AMMPG Paul Goldschmidt 1.25 3.00
AMMRC Roger Clemens 2.50 6.00
AMMRH Roy Halladay 1.00 2.50
AMMRJ Reggie Jackson 2.50 6.00
AMMTM Thurman Munson 2.50 6.00
AMMTP Tony Perez 2.50 6.00
AMMTR Tim Raines 1.00 2.50
AMMTS Tris Speaker 1.00 2.50
AMMVG Vladimir Guerrero Jr. 5.00 12.00
AMMVR Victor Robles 1.50 4.00
AMMWF Whitey Ford 2.50 6.00
AMMWM Willie Mays 3.00 8.00
AMMJBE Johnny Bench 2.50 6.00
AMMJBZ Javier Baez 2.50 6.00
AMMJMI Johnny Mize 1.00 2.50
AMMKGE Ken Griffey Jr. 5.00 12.00
AMMMMS Mike Mussina 2.00 5.00
AMMNSY Noah Syndergaard 1.00 2.50
AMMRJO Randy Johnson 1.25 3.00
AMMSSO Sammy Sosa 1.25 3.00

2019 Topps Update 150th Anniversary Manufactured Patches

RANDOM INSERTS IN PACKS
*150TH/150: .5X TO 1.2X BASIC
*GOLD/50: .75X TO 2X BASIC
*RED/25: 1.2X TO 3X BASIC
AMPAD Andre Dawson 1.00 2.50
AMPAR Alex Rodriguez 1.50 4.00
AMPBF Bob Feller 1.00 2.50
AMPBH Bryce Harper 2.00 5.00
AMPBR Brooks Robinson 1.00 2.50
AMPBS Blake Snell 1.00 2.50
AMPCM Christy Mathewson 1.25 3.00
AMPDS Darryl Strawberry .75 2.00
AMPEJ Eloy Jimenez 3.00 8.00
AMPEM Eddie Mathews 1.25 3.00
AMPFR Frank Robinson 1.00 2.50
AMPFT Fernando Tatis Jr. 4.00 10.00
AMPGC Gerrit Cole 1.25 3.00
AMPHM Hideki Matsui 1.25 3.00
AMPJM Joe Morgan 1.00 2.50
AMPJR Jim Rice 1.00 2.50
AMPKG Ken Griffey Jr. 2.50 6.00
AMPLB Lou Brock 1.00 2.50
AMPMC Matt Chapman 1.25 3.00
AMPMM Manny Machado 1.25 3.00
AMPMO Mel Ott 1.25 3.00
AMPMR Mariano Rivera 1.50 4.00
AMPNG Nomar Garciaparra 1.00 2.50
AMPNR Nolan Ryan 4.00 10.00
AMPNS Nick Senzel 2.50 6.00
AMPPA Pete Alonso 5.00 12.00
AMPPG Paul Goldschmidt 1.25 3.00
AMPPR Pee Wee Reese 1.00 2.50
AMPRC Robinson Cano 1.00 2.50
AMPRH Roy Halladay 1.00 2.50
AMPRS Ryne Sandberg 2.50 6.00
AMPSS Sammy Sosa 1.25 3.00
AMPTB Trevor Bauer 1.25 3.00
AMPTM Thurman Munson 1.25 3.00
AMPTS Trevor Story 1.25 3.00
AMPVG Vladimir Guerrero Jr. 6.00 15.00
AMPVR Victor Robles 1.50 4.00
AMPWB Walker Buehler 1.50 4.00
AMPWM Willie Mays 2.50 6.00
AMPWS Warren Spahn 1.00 2.50
AMPYK Yusei Kikuchi 1.25 3.00
AMPEMU Eddie Murray 1.00 2.50
AMPJBE Johnny Bench 1.25 3.00
AMPJMA J.D. Martinez 1.25 3.00
AMPNRY Nolan Ryan 4.00 10.00
AMPRHO Rogers Hornsby 1.00 2.50
AMPTSE Tom Seaver 1.00 2.50
AMPVGU Vladimir Guerrero 1.00 2.50
AMPWME Whit Merrifield 1.25 3.00
AMPWSP Warren Spahn 1.00 2.50

2019 Topps Update All Star Stitches

STATED ODDS 1:42 HOBBY
*GOLD/50: .6X TO 1.5X BASIC
*SILVER/50: .6X TO 1.5X BASIC
*RED/25: .75X TO 2X BASIC
ASSRAB Alex Bregman 3.00 8.00
ASSRAC Aroldis Chapman 3.00 8.00
ASSRAM Austin Meadows 2.50 6.00
ASSRCB Cody Bellinger 6.00 15.00
ASSRCBL Charlie Blackmon 3.00 8.00
ASSRCK Clayton Kershaw 6.00 15.00
ASSRCM Charlie Morton 3.00 8.00
ASSRCS Carlos Santana 2.50 6.00
ASSRCY Christian Yelich 4.00 10.00
ASSRDD David Dahl 2.00 5.00
ASSRDL DJ LeMahieu 3.00 8.00
ASSRDV Daniel Vogelbach 2.00 5.00
ASSRFF Freddie Freeman 4.00 10.00
ASSRFL Francisco Lindor 3.00 8.00
ASSRGC Gerrit Cole 3.00 8.00
ASSRGS Gary Sanchez 3.00 8.00
ASSRGSP George Springer 2.50 6.00
ASSRGT Gleyber Torres 5.00 12.00
ASSRHP Hunter Pence 2.50 6.00
ASSRHR Hyun-Jin Ryu 2.50 6.00
ASSRJA Jose Abreu 3.00 8.00
ASSRJB Javier Baez 4.00 10.00
ASSRJBE Josh Bell 2.50 6.00
ASSRJBR Jose Berrios 2.50 6.00
ASSRJD Jacob deGrom 3.00 8.00
ASSRJEM Jeff McNeil 5.00 12.00
ASSRJG Joey Gallo 2.50 6.00
ASSRJH Josh Hader 2.00 5.00
ASSRJM J.D. Martinez 3.00 8.00
ASSRJMC James McCann 2.50 6.00
ASSRJO Jake Odorizzi 2.00 5.00
ASSRJP Jorge Polanco 2.00 5.00
ASSRJR J.T. Realmuto 3.00 8.00
ASSRJV Justin Verlander 3.00 8.00
ASSRKB Kris Bryant 4.00 10.00
ASSRKM Ketel Marte 2.50 6.00
ASSRKY Kirby Yates 2.50 6.00
ASSRLC Luis Castillo 2.50 6.00
ASSRLG Lucas Giolito 2.50 6.00
ASSRMB Mookie Betts 5.00 12.00
ASSRMBR Michael Brantley 2.50 6.00
ASSRMC Matt Chapman 3.00 8.00
ASSRMMO Mike Moustakas 2.50 6.00
ASSRMMU Max Muncy 2.50 6.00
ASSRMS Max Scherzer 3.00 8.00
ASSRMSO Mike Soroka 3.00 8.00
ASSRMST Marcus Stroman 2.50 6.00
ASSRMT Mike Trout 10.00 25.00
ASSRMTA Masahiro Tanaka 2.50 6.00
ASSRNA Nolan Arenado 4.00 10.00
ASSRPA Pete Alonso 10.00 25.00
ASSRPD Paul DeJong 3.00 8.00
ASSRRA Ronald Acuna Jr. 8.00 20.00
ASSRSB Shane Bieber 3.00 8.00
ASSRSGR Sonny Gray 2.50 6.00
ASSRTS Trevor Story 3.00 8.00
ASSRWB Walker Buehler 5.00 12.00
ASSRWC Willson Contreras 2.50 6.00
ASSRWM Whit Merrifield 3.00 8.00
ASSRYG Yasmani Grandal 2.00 5.00

2019 Topps Update All Star Stitches Autographs

STATED ODDS 1:13,946 HOBBY
STATED PRINT RUN 25 SER.#'d SETS
EXCHANGE DEADLINE 9/30/2021
ASSAAM Austin Meadows 10.00 25.00
ASSACB Charlie Blackmon 12.00 30.00
ASSACS Carlos Santana 20.00 50.00
ASSAFL Francisco Lindor 25.00 60.00
ASSAGC Gerrit Cole 25.00 60.00
ASSAGS Gary Sanchez 20.00 50.00
ASSAGSP George Springer 25.00 60.00
ASSAJH Josh Hader 8.00 20.00
ASSAMS Max Scherzer 40.00 100.00
ASSANA Nolan Arenado 30.00 80.00
ASSAPA Pete Alonso 125.00 300.00
ASSAPD Paul DeJong 12.00 30.00
ASSARA Ronald Acuna Jr. 75.00 200.00
ASSAWB Walker Buehler
ASSAWC Willson Contreras 10.00 25.00
ASSAWM Whit Merrifield 15.00 40.00

2019 Topps Update All Star Stitches Dual Autographs

STATED ODDS 1:41,139 HOBBY
STATED PRINT RUN 25 SER.#'d SETS
EXCHANGE DEADLINE 9/30/2021
ASDARSC G.Sanchez/W.Contreras 25.00 60.00
ASDARSL F.Lindor/C.Santana 40.00 100.00
SADARAD D.Dahl/N.Arenado
SADARAM J.McNeil/P.Alonso 125.00 300.00
SADARCS M.Scherzer/G.Cole 75.00 200.00
SADARDA P.Alonso/J.deGrom 125.00 300.00
SADARMM C.Morton/A.Meadows 25.00 60.00

2019 Topps Update Bryce Harper Welcome to Philly

150TH/150: 2X TO 5X BASIC
*RED/10: 6X TO 15X BASIC
BH1 Bryce Harper .50 1.25
BH2 Bryce Harper .50 1.25
BH3 Bryce Harper .50 1.25
BH4 Bryce Harper .50 1.25
BH5 Bryce Harper .50 1.25
BH6 Bryce Harper .50 1.25
BH7 Bryce Harper .50 1.25
BH8 Bryce Harper .50 1.25
BH9 Bryce Harper .50 1.25
BH10 Bryce Harper .50 1.25
BH11 Bryce Harper .50 1.25
BH12 Bryce Harper .50 1.25
BH13 Bryce Harper .50 1.25
BH14 Bryce Harper .50 1.25
BH15 Bryce Harper .50 1.25
BH16 Bryce Harper .50 1.25
BH17 Bryce Harper .50 1.25
BH18 Bryce Harper .50 1.25
BH19 Bryce Harper .50 1.25
BH20 Bryce Harper .50 1.25

2019 Topps Update Dual All Star Stitches

STATED ODDS 1:21,652 HOBBY
STATED PRINT RUN 25 SER.#'d SETS
ASSDRBB K.Bryant/J.Baez 25.00 60.00
ASSDRBM M.Betts/J.Martinez 40.00 100.00
ASSDRBS G.Springer/A.Bregman 12.00 30.00
ASSDRCV J.Verlander/G.Cole 12.00 30.00
ASSDRDA P.Alonso/J.deGrom
ASSDRFA R.Acuna Jr./F.Freeman 30.00 80.00
ASSDRKB C.Bellinger/C.Kershaw 25.00 60.00
ASSDRLS C.Santana/F.Lindor 40.00 100.00
ASSDRSL G.Sanchez/D.LeMahieu 12.00 30.00
ASSDRTY C.Yelich/M.Trout 20.00 50.00

2019 Topps Update Est 1869

COMPLETE SET (13) 20.00 50.00
STATED ODDS 1:51 HOBBY
*BLUE: .6X TO 1.5X
*BLACK/299: 1X TO 2.5X
*150TH/150: 1X TO 2.5X
*GOLD/50: 5X TO 12X
EST1 Cincinnati Red Stockings .60 1.50
EST2 Joey Votto 1.00 2.50
EST3 Nick Senzel 2.00 5.00
EST4 George Foster .60 1.50
EST5 Frank Robinson .75 2.00
EST6 Joe Morgan .75 2.00
EST7 Johnny Bench 1.00 2.50
EST8 Tony Perez .75 2.00
EST9 Tom Seaver .75 2.00
EST10 Eric Davis .60 1.50
EST11 Tom Browning .60 1.50
EST12 Barry Larkin .75 2.00
EST13 Ken Griffey Jr. 2.00 5.00

2019 Topps Update Est 1869 Autographs

STATED ODDS 1:39,180 HOBBY
PRINT RUNS B/WN 5-25 COPIES PER
NO PRICING ON QTY 10 OR LESS
EXCHANGE DEADLINE 9/30/2021
EST4 George Foster/25 25.00 60.00
EST8 Tony Perez/25 25.00 60.00
EST10 Eric Davis/25 25.00 60.00
EST11 Tom Browning/25 25.00 60.00

2019 Topps Update Iconic Card Reprints

STATED ODDS 1:16 HOBBY
*150 ANN/150: 2.5X TO 6X HOBBY
ICR1 Johnny Bench .40 1.00
ICR2 Ozzie Smith .50 1.25
ICR3 Joey Votto .40 1.00
ICR4 Nolan Ryan 1.25 3.00
ICR5 Honus Wagner .40 1.00
ICR6 Tony Gwynn .40 1.00
ICR7 Ken Griffey Jr. .75 2.00
ICR8 Joe Mauer .30 .75
ICR9 Luis Aparicio .30 .75
ICR10 Frank Robinson .30 .75
ICR11 Orlando Cepeda .30 .75
ICR12 Roger Maris .40 1.00
ICR13 Sandy Koufax .75 2.00
ICR14 Dave Winfield .30 .75
ICR15 Paul Molitor .40 1.00
ICR16 Miguel Cabrera .40 1.00
ICR17 Johnny Mize .30 .75
ICR18 Gil Hodges .30 .75
ICR19 Willie Mays .75 2.00
ICR20 Phil Rizzuto .30 .75
ICR21 Pee Wee Reese .30 .75
ICR22 Stan Musial .60 1.50
ICR23 Stan Musial .60 1.50
ICR24 Stan Musial .60 1.50
ICR25 Bob Clemente 1.00 2.50
ICR26 Bob Gibson .30 .75
ICR27 Billy Williams .30 .75
ICR28 Bob Clemente 1.00 2.50
ICR29 Chipper Jones .40 1.00
ICR30 Tim Raines .30 .75
ICR31 Darryl Strawberry .25 .60
ICR32 Dwight Gooden .25 .60
ICR33 Jeff Bagwell .30 .75
ICR34 Ivan Rodriguez .30 .75
ICR35 Christy Mathewson .40 1.00
ICR36 Tris Speaker .30 .75
ICR37 Willie Stargell .30 .75
ICR38 Gary Carter .30 .75
ICR39 Ralph Kiner .30 .75
ICR40 Enos Slaughter .30 .75
ICR41 Red Schoendienst .30 .75
ICR42 Fergie Jenkins .30 .75
ICR43 Tony Perez .30 .75
ICR44 Ernie Banks .40 1.00
ICR45 Lefty Grove .30 .75
ICR46 Ken Griffey Jr. .75 2.00
ICR47 Mel Ott .40 1.00
ICR48 Frank Thomas .40 1.00
ICR49 Frank Thomas .40 1.00
ICR50 Chipper Jones .40 1.00

2019 Topps Update Iconic Card Reprints Autographs

STATED ODDS 1:24,200 HOBBY
PRINT RUNS B/WN 5-25 COPIES PER
NO PRICING ON QTY 10 OR LESS
EXCHANGE DEADLINE 9/30/2021
ICR1 Johnny Bench
ICR2 Ozzie Smith
ICR7 Ken Griffey Jr.
ICR31 Darryl Strawberry/25 40.00 100.00
ICR33 Jeff Bagwell/25 30.00 80.00
ICR34 Ivan Rodriguez/25 20.00 50.00
ICR43 Tony Perez/25 40.00 100.00
ICR46 Ken Griffey Jr

2019 Topps Update Legacy of Baseball Autographs 150th Anniversary

STATED ODDS 1:2177 HOBBY
STATED PRINT RUN 150 SER.#'d SETS
EXCHANGE DEADLINE 9/30/2021
LBABRE Bryan Reynolds 12.00 30.00
LBADH Darwinzon Hernandez 3.00 8.00
LBAGC Griffin Canning 5.00 12.00
LBAGH Garrett Hampson 3.00 8.00
LBAHRA Harold Ramirez 5.00 12.00
LBAJD Jon Duplantier 3.00 8.00
LBAJH JD Hammer 4.00 10.00
LBAJMA Jason Martin 4.00 10.00
LBALAR Luis Arraez 15.00 40.00
LBALT Lane Thomas 5.00 12.00
LBAMK Merrill Kelly 3.00 8.00
LBANLO Nate Lowe 4.00 10.00
LBARH Ryan Helsley 4.00 10.00
LBASA Shaun Anderson 3.00 8.00
LBASB Skye Bolt 4.00 10.00
LBATT Trent Thornton 3.00 8.00

2019 Topps Update Legacy of Baseball Autographs Gold

*GOLD/50: .6X TO 1.5X BASIC
STATED ODDS 1:3165 HOBBY
STATED PRINT RUN 50 SER.#'d SETS
EXCHANGE DEADLINE 9/30/2021
LBAAR Austin Riley 15.00 40.00
LBACK Carter Kieboom 15.00 40.00
LBACP Chris Paddack 12.00 30.00
LBACT Cole Tucker 20.00 50.00
LBAEJ Eloy Jimenez 20.00 50.00
LBAEL Elvis Luciano 12.00 30.00
LBAFT Fernando Tatis Jr. 75.00 200.00
LBAKH Keston Hiura 25.00 60.00
LBAMC Michael Chavis 10.00 25.00
LBANM Nick Margevicius 4.00 10.00
LBAPA Pete Alonso 75.00 200.00
LBAPC Patrick Corbin
LBATE Thairo Estrada 10.00 25.00
LBAVG Vladimir Guerrero Jr. 50.00 120.00
LBAWS Will Smith 15.00 40.00

2019 Topps Update Legacy of Baseball Autographs Red

*RED/25: .8X TO 2X BASIC
STATED ODDS 1:4472 HOBBY
PRINT RUNS B/WN 5-25 COPIES PER
NO PRICING ON QTY 5
EXCHANGE DEADLINE 9/30/2021
LBAAJ Adam Jones/25 10.00 25.00
LBAAR Austin Riley/25 20.00 50.00
LBACF Cecil Fielder/25 20.00 50.00
LBACFR Clint Frazier/25 6.00 15.00
LBACK Carter Kieboom/25 20.00 50.00
LBACP Chris Paddack/25 15.00 40.00
LBACS CC Sabathia/25
LBACT Cole Tucker/25 25.00 60.00
LBAEJ Eloy Jimenez/25 25.00 60.00
LBAEL Elvis Luciano/25 15.00 40.00
LBAFT Fernando Tatis Jr./25 100.00 250.00
LBAGCO Gerrit Cole/25 40.00 100.00
LBAKG Ken Griffey Jr./25
LBAKH Keston Hiura/25 30.00 80.00
LBAKW Kerry Wood/25 25.00 60.00
LBALM Lance McCullers Jr./25 10.00 25.00
LBAMC Michael Chavis/25 12.00 30.00
LBAMS Max Scherzer/25 40.00 100.00
LBANA Nolan Arenado/25 30.00 80.00
LBANM Nick Margevicius/25 5.00 12.00
LBAPA Pete Alonso/25 100.00 250.00
LBAPC Patrick Corbin/25
LBASC Shin-Soo Choo/25 20.00 50.00
LBATE Thairo Estrada/25 12.00 30.00
LBATM Tino Martinez/25 12.00 30.00
LBAVG Vladimir Guerrero Jr./25 60.00 150.00
LBAWS Will Smith/25 20.00 50.00

2019 Topps Update Major League Materials

STATED ODDS 1:425 HOBBY
*150TH/150: .5X TO 1.2X BASIC
*GOLD/50: .6X TO 1.5X BASIC
*RED/25: .75X TO 2X BASIC
MLMAB Alex Bregman 3.00 8.00
MLMAM Austin Meadows 2.50 6.00
MLMBP Buster Posey 4.00 10.00
MLMBR Brendan Rodgers 3.00 8.00
MLMBS Blake Snell 2.50 6.00
MLMCB Cody Bellinger 6.00 15.00
MLMCC Carlos Correa 3.00 8.00
MLMCR Cal Ripken Jr. 8.00 20.00
MLMCS Chris Sale 3.00 8.00
MLMDG Didi Gregorius 2.50 6.00
MLMFL Francisco Lindor 3.00 8.00
MLMFT Frank Thomas 3.00 8.00
MLMGC Gerrit Cole 3.00 8.00
MLMGS George Springer 2.50 6.00
MLMJB Javier Baez 4.00 10.00
MLMJL Jon Lester 2.50 6.00
MLMJM J.D. Martinez 3.00 8.00
MLMJR J.T. Realmuto 3.00 8.00
MLMJV Joey Votto 3.00 8.00
MLMKG Ken Griffey Jr. 6.00 15.00
MLMKH Keston Hiura 4.00 10.00
MLMLS Luis Severino 2.50 6.00
MLMMB Mookie Betts 4.00 10.00
MLMMC Michael Chavis 3.00 8.00
MLMMO Marcell Ozuna 3.00 8.00
MLMMT Mike Trout 10.00 25.00
MLMNA Nolan Arenado 4.00 10.00
MLMNS Nick Senzel 4.00 10.00
MLMPC Patrick Corbin 2.50 6.00
MLMRD Rafael Devers 4.00 10.00
MLMRH Rickey Henderson 3.00 8.00
MLMRZ Ryan Zimmerman 2.50 6.00
MLMSS Stephen Strasburg 3.00 8.00
MLMTB Trevor Bauer 3.00 8.00
MLMTG Tony Gwynn 3.00 8.00
MLMVG Vladimir Guerrero Jr. 6.00 15.00
MLMABE Andrew Benintendi 4.00 10.00
MLMFTJ Fernando Tatis Jr. 5.00 12.00
MLMGST Giancarlo Stanton 3.00 8.00
MLMRHA Roy Halladay 2.50 6.00

2019 Topps Update Perennial All Stars

PAS1 Babe Ruth 1.00 2.50
PAS2 Ted Williams .75 2.00
PAS3 Jackie Robinson .40 1.00
PAS4 Reggie Jackson .30 .75
PAS5 Pedro Martinez .30 .75
PAS6 Randy Johnson .40 1.00

PAS7 Cal Ripken Jr. 1.25 3.00
PAS8 Ichiro Suzuki .50 1.25
PAS9 Willie Mays .75 2.00
PAS10 Tony Gwynn .40 1.00
PAS11 Carl Yastrzemski .60 1.50
PAS12 Stan Musial .60 1.50
PAS13 Johnny Bench .40 1.00
PAS14 Ozzie Smith .50 1.25
PAS15 Al Kaline .40 1.00
PAS16 Brooks Robinson .30 .75
PAS17 Derek Jeter 1.00 2.50
PAS18 Ken Griffey Jr. .75 2.00
PAS19 George Brett .75 2.00
PAS20 Roberto Clemente 1.00 2.50
PAS21 Mel Ott .40 1.00
PAS22 Alex Rodriguez .50 1.25
PAS23 Ryne Sandberg .75 2.00
PAS24 Mariano Rivera .50 1.25
PAS25 Ernie Banks .40 1.00
PAS26 Mark McGwire .60 1.50
PAS27 Rickey Henderson .40 1.00
PAS28 David Ortiz .40 1.00
PAS29 Aaron Judge 1.00 2.50
PAS30 Mike Trout 2.00 5.00
PAS31 Bryce Harper .60 1.50
PAS32 Chris Sale .40 1.00
PAS33 Justin Verlander .40 1.00
PAS34 Clayton Kershaw .75 2.00
PAS35 Paul Goldschmidt .40 1.00
PAS36 Jose Altuve .30 .75
PAS37 Max Scherzer .40 1.00
PAS38 Buster Posey .50 1.25
PAS39 Vladimir Guerrero .30 .75
PAS40 Roy Halladay .30 .75
PAS41 Sandy Koufax .75 2.00
PAS42 Nolan Ryan 1.25 3.00
PAS43 Yadier Molina .40 1.00
PAS44 Javier Baez .50 1.25
PAS45 Nolan Arenado .50 1.25
PAS46 Francisco Lindor .40 1.00
PAS47 Christian Yelich .50 1.25
PAS48 Jacob deGrom .40 1.00
PAS49 Alex Bregman .40 1.00
PAS50 Mookie Betts .60 1.50

2019 Topps Update Shohei Ohtani Highlights

150TH/150: 2X TO 5X BASIC
*RED/10: 6X TO 15X BASIC
SO1 Shohei Ohtani .40 1.00
SO2 Shohei Ohtani .40 1.00
SO3 Shohei Ohtani .40 1.00
SO4 Shohei Ohtani .40 1.00
SO5 Shohei Ohtani .40 1.00
SO6 Shohei Ohtani .40 1.00
SO7 Shohei Ohtani .40 1.00
SO8 Shohei Ohtani .40 1.00
SO9 Shohei Ohtani .40 1.00
SO10 Shohei Ohtani .40 1.00
SO11 Shohei Ohtani .40 1.00
SO12 Shohei Ohtani .40 1.00
SO13 Shohei Ohtani .40 1.00
SO14 Shohei Ohtani .40 1.00
SO15 Shohei Ohtani .40 1.00
SO16 Shohei Ohtani .40 1.00
SO17 Shohei Ohtani .40 1.00
SO18 Shohei Ohtani .40 1.00
SO19 Shohei Ohtani .40 1.00
SO20 Shohei Ohtani .40 1.00

2019 Topps Update The Family Business

STATED ODDS 1:31 HOBBY
*BLUE: .6X TO 1.5X
*BLACK/299: 1X TO 2.5X
*150TH/150: 1X TO 2.5X
*GOLD/50: 1.5X TO 4X
FB1 Ken Griffey Jr. 1.25 3.00
FB2 Cal Ripken Jr. 1.25 3.00
FB3 Roberto Alomar .30 .75
FB4 Vladimir Guerrero .30 .75
FB5 Ivan Rodriguez .30 .75
FB6 Roger Clemens .50 1.25
FB7 Yadier Molina .40 1.00
FB8 Ronald Acuna Jr. 2.00 5.00
FB9 Cecil Fielder .25 .60
FB10 Mariano Rivera .50 1.25
FB11 Hank Aaron .75 2.00
FB12 Tim Raines .30 .75
FB13 Jose Canseco .30 .75
FB14 Bryce Harper .60 1.50
FB15 Fernando Tatis Jr. 2.50 6.00
FB16 Tony Gwynn .40 1.00
FB17 Corey Seager .40 1.00
FB18 Manny Machado .40 1.00
FB19 Dee Gordon .25 .60
FB20 Nolan Arenado .50 1.25
FB21 Pedro Martinez .30 .75
FB22 Cody Bellinger .75 2.00
FB23 Robinson Cano .30 .75
FB24 Vladimir Guerrero Jr. 1.50 4.00
FB25 Reggie Jackson .30 .75

2019 Topps Update The Family Business Autographs

STATED ODDS 1:34,282 HOBBY
PRINT RUNS B/WN 5-25 COPIES PER
NO PRICING ON QTY 5
EXCHANGE DEADLINE 9/30/2021
FB3 Roberto Alomar
FB4 Vladimir Guerrero
FB8 Ronald Acuna Jr.
FB9 Cecil Fielder/25 25.00 60.00
FB13 Jose Canseco/25 25.00 60.00
FB15 Fernando Tatis Jr./25
FB24 Vladimir Guerrero Jr./25 50.00 120.00

2019 Topps Update Triple All Star Stitches

STATED ODDS 1:21,652 HOBBY
STATED PRINT RUN 25 SER.#'d SETS
ASTRADM Alonso/deGrom/McNeil 50.00 120.00
ASTRBAS Story/Blackmon/Arenado 20.00 50.00
ASTRBCB Baez/Bryant/Contreras 60.00 150.00
ASTRFSA Acuna/Soroka/Freeman 30.00 80.00
ASTRGHY Hader/Grandal/Yelich 25.00 60.00
ASTRKBB Buehler/Kershaw/Bellinger 40.00 100.00
ASTRLHS Santana/Hand/Lindor 50.00 120.00
ASTRSCL LeMahieu/Sanchez/Chapman 12.00 30.00
ASTRSVB Verlander/Springer/Bregman
ASTRTYB Yelich/Trout/Bryant

2020 Topps

COMPLETE SET (700) 30.00 80.00
COMP.SER.1 SET (350) 15.00 40.00
COMP.SER.2 SET (350) 15.00 40.00
SER.1 GOLDEN TICKET ODDS 1:196,245 HOBBY
SER.2 GOLDEN TICKET ODDS 1:236,030 HOBBY
TICKET ANNCD PRINT RUN OF 50
NO TICKET PRICING DUE TO SCARCITY
1 Mike Trout 1.25 3.00
2 Gerrit Cole LL .40 1.00
3 Nicky Lopez .15 .40
4 Robinson Cano .20 .50
5 JaCoby Jones .20 .50
6 Juan Soto WSH .75 2.00
7 Aaron Judge .60 1.50
8 Jonathan Villar .15 .40
9 Trent Grisham RC 1.00 2.50
10 Austin Meadows .20 .50
11 Anthony Rendon LL .25 .60
12 Sam Hilliard RC .40 1.00
13 Miles Mikolas .15 .40
14 Anthony Rendon .25 .60
15 F.Tatis/M.Machado .30 .75
16 Gleyber Torres .50 1.25
17 Franmil Reyes .15 .40
18 Master and Apprentice .25 .60
Nelson Cruz
Mitch Garver
19 Los Angeles Angels TC .15 .40
20 Aristides Aquino RC .50 1.25
21 Shane Greene .15 .40
22 Emilio Pagan .15 .40
23 Christin Stewart .15 .40
24 Kenley Jansen .20 .50
25 Kirby Yates .15 .40
26 Kyle Hendricks .25 .60
27 Milwaukee Brewers TC .15 .40
28 Tim Anderson .25 .60
29 Starlin Castro .15 .40
30 Josh VanMeter .15 .40
31 Close Call .20 .50
Niko Goodrum
Jorge Polanco
32 Brandon Woodruff .15 .40
33 Houston Astros TC .15 .40
34 Ian Kinsler .20 .50
35 Adalberto Mondesi .25 .60
36 Sean Doolittle .15 .40
37 Albert Almora .20 .50
38 Austin Nola RC .40 1.00
39 Tyler O'neill .20 .50
40 Bobby Bradley RC .30 .75
41 Brian Anderson .15 .40
42 Lewis Brinson .15 .40
43 Leury Garcia .15 .40
44 Tommy Edman FS .25 .60
45 Mitch Haniger .20 .50
46 Gary Sanchez .25 .60
47 Dansby Swanson .25 .60
48 Jeff McNeil FS .20 .50
49 Eloy Jimenez CUP .50 1.25
50 Cody Bellinger .50 1.25
51 Anthony Rizzo .40 1.00
52 Yasmani Grandal .15 .40
53 Pete Alonso LL .60 1.50
54 Hunter Dozier .15 .40
55 Jose Martinez .15 .40
56 Andres Munoz RC .30 .75
57 Travis Demeritte RC .30 .75
58 Jesse Winker .15 .40
59 Chris Archer .15 .40
60 Matt Barnes .15 .40
61 C.Biggio/B.Bichette 1.00 2.50
62 Chase Anderson .15 .40
63 Christian Vazquez .15 .40
64 Kyle Lewis RC 2.00 5.00
65 Cleveland Indians TC .15 .40
66 Andrew Heaney .15 .40
67 Tyler Beede .15 .40
68 James Paxton .20 .50
69 Brendan McKay RC .40 1.00
70 Nico Hoerner RC 1.00 2.50
71 Sandy Alcantara .15 .40
72 K.Hiura/B.Gamel .30 .75
73 Oakland Athletics TC .15 .40
74 Bubba Starling RC .50 1.25
75 Michael Conforto .20 .50
76 Stephen Strasburg WSH .25 .60
77 Charlie Culberson .15 .40
78 Bo Bichette RC 2.00 5.00
79 Brad Keller .15 .40
80 Austin Barnes .15 .40
81 Ryan Yarbrough .15 .40
82 Jorge Polanco .20 .50
83 New York Yankees TC .15 .40
84 Ken Giles .15 .40
85 Tim and Yolmer .25 .60
Tim Anderson
Yolmer Sanchez
86 Hyun-Jin Ryu LL .20 .50
87 St. Louis Cardinals TC .15 .40
88 Jorge Alfaro .15 .40
89 Kurt Suzuki .15 .40
90 Brock Holt .15 .40
91 Yolmer Sanchez .15 .40
92 Blake Treinen .15 .40
93 Alex Colome .15 .40
94 Marwin Gonzalez .15 .40
95 Ian Kennedy .15 .40
96 Jose Abreu LL .25 .60
97 Lewis Thorpe RC .25 .60
98 Jesus Aguilar .15 .40
99 Dan Vogelbach .15 .40
100 Alex Bregman .25 .60
101 Brad Hand .15 .40
102 Josh Phegley .15 .40
103 Danny Hultzen RC .30 .75
104 Marco Gonzales .15 .40
105 Niko Goodrum .20 .50
106 Rogelio Armenteros RC .30 .75
107 Luis Castillo .20 .50
108 Josh Rojas RC .25 .60
109 Reese McGuire .20 .50
110 Jesus Luzardo RC .50 1.25
111 Buster Posey .30 .75
112 Max Stassi .15 .40
113 Matt Carpenter .25 .60
114 Ildemaro Vargas .15 .40
115 Matt Thaiss RC .30 .75
116 Daniel Murphy .20 .50
117 Max Kepler .20 .50
118 Clayton Kershaw .50 1.25
119 Kyle Schwarber .25 .60
120 Kenta Maeda .20 .50
121 DJ LeMahieu .25 .60
122 Caleb Smith .15 .40
123 Seth Brown RC .25 .60
124 Jose Berrios .20 .50
125 Shohei Ohtani .30 .75
126 German Marquez .25 .60
127 Matt Chapman .25 .60
128 Steven Matz .20 .50
129 Yoan Moncada .25 .60
130 Michael Chavis FS .20 .50
131 Ketel Marte .20 .50
132 Jay Bruce .20 .50
133 Michael Brosseau RC .50 1.25
134 David Fletcher .25 .60
135 Enrique Hernandez .20 .50
136 Amed Rosario .20 .50
137 Merrill Kelly .15 .40
138 Jackie Bradley Jr. .25 .60
139 Jose Quintana .15 .40
140 Trevor Bauer .25 .60
141 Roberto Osuna .15 .40
142 Tyler Flowers .15 .40
143 Christian Yelich LL .30 .75
144 Jake Arrieta .20 .50
145 Paul Goldschmidt .25 .60
146 Dwight Smith Jr. .15 .40
147 Jake Rogers RC .25 .60
148 Willy Adames .15 .40
149 Orlando Arcia .15 .40
150 Ronald Acuna Jr. 1.00 2.50
151 Tommy La Stella .15 .40
152 Zack Wheeler .20 .50
153 Andrew Cashner .15 .40
154 C.J. Cron .15 .40
155 Jack Flaherty .20 .50
156 Nick Markakis .20 .50
157 G.Torres/D.Gregorius .30 .75
158 Jake Lamb .20 .50
159 Jorge Soler LL .25 .60
160 C.Yelich/N.Arenado .30 .75
161 Aroldis Chapman .25 .60
162 Michel Baez RC .25 .60
163 Ryan Pressly .15 .40
164 Matt Strahm .15 .40
165 Matthew Boyd .15 .40
166 Nick Solak RC .40 1.00
167 Anthony Kay RC .25 .60
168 Fernando Tatis Jr. CUP 1.00 2.50
169 Jacob Waguespack RC .30 .75
170 Gregory Polanco .20 .50
171 Kole Calhoun .15 .40
172 Sonny Gray .20 .50
173 Yadier Molina .25 .60
174 Alex Verdugo .20 .50
175 Lucas Giolito .20 .50
176 Brandon Belt .20 .50
177 Craig Kimbrel .20 .50
178 Mauricio Dubon RC .30 .75
179 Ramon Laureano FS .25 .60
180 Max Scherzer .25 .60
181 Stephen Strasburg LL .25 .60
182 Vladimir Guerrero Jr. CUP .50 1.25
183 Starling Marte .20 .50
184 Mychal Givens .15 .40
185 Johnny Cueto .20 .50
186 Roberto Perez .15 .40
187 Chance Sisco .15 .40
188 Manny Machado .25 .60
189 Mike Moustakas .20 .50
190 Aaron Nola .20 .50
191 Jeremy Jeffress .15 .40
192 Yusei Kikuchi .20 .50
193 Anibal Sanchez .15 .40
194 Liam Hendriks .15 .40
195 Julio Teheran .20 .50
196 Andrew Benintendi .25 .60
197 Raisel Iglesias .15 .40
198 Erick Fedde .15 .40
199 Domingo Santana .20 .50
200 Christian Yelich .30 .75
201 Francisco Lindor .25 .60
202 New York Mets TC .15 .40
203 Joc Pederson .20 .50
204 Hector Neris .15 .40
205 Patrick Sandoval RC .40 1.00
206 Tommy Pham .15 .40
207 Zac Gallen RC .60 1.50
208 Zack Collins RC .30 .75
209 Derek Dietrich .15 .40
210 Mitch Garver .15 .40
211 Trevor Richards .15 .40
212 Mike Fiers .15 .40
213 Minnesota Twins TC .15 .40
214 Trea Turner .20 .50
215 Luke Jackson .15 .40
216 Scott Kingery .20 .50
217 Amir Garrett .15 .40
218 Atlanta Braves TC .15 .40
219 Jean Segura .20 .50
220 J.T. Realmuto .25 .60
221 Nick Pivetta .15 .40
222 Andrew Chafin .15 .40
223 Aaron Civale RC .40 1.00
224 Juan Soto .75 2.00
225 Oscar Mercado FS .20 .50
226 Trent Thornton .15 .40
227 David Peralta .15 .40
228 Logan Allen RC .25 .60
229 Randy Arozarena RC 2.00 5.00
230 Nolan Arenado .30 .75
231 Randal Grichuk .15 .40
232 Justin Verlander LL .25 .60
233 David Dahl .15 .40
234 Cesar Hernandez .15 .40
235 Dustin May RC 1.00 2.50
236 Brandon Crawford .20 .50
237 Luis Garcia .15 .40
238 Freddy Peralta .15 .40
239 Anthony Rendon WSH .25 .60
240 Jameson Taillon .20 .50
241 Mike Clevinger .20 .50
242 Alex Young RC .25 .60
243 Jeimer Candelario .15 .40
244 Chris Paddack FS .25 .60
245 Los Angeles Dodgers TC .15 .40
246 Philadelphia Phillies TC .15 .40
247 Garrett Cooper .15 .40
248 Hunter Renfroe .15 .40
249 Jordan Yamamoto RC .30 .75
250 Bryce Harper .40 1.00
251 A.J. Puk RC .50 1.25
252 Aaron Hicks .20 .50
253 Brandon Drury .15 .40
254 Andrew Miller .20 .50
255 Max Muncy .20 .50
256 Roman Quinn .15 .40
257 Joey Lucchesi .15 .40
258 Max Scherzer WSH .25 .60
259 Jaylin Davis RC .40 1.00
260 Zack Greinke .20 .50
261 Daniel Mengden .15 .40
262 Anthony Santander .15 .40
263 J.P. Crawford .15 .40
264 Abraham Toro RC .30 .75
265 Patrick Corbin .20 .50
266 Austin Riley FS .40 1.00
267 Joey Votto .25 .60
268 Ian Desmond .15 .40
269 J.D. Martinez .25 .60
270 Jose Urena .15 .40
271 Josh Bell .20 .50
272 Carlos Santana .20 .50
273 Bryan Abreu RC .25 .60
274 Boston Red Sox TC .15 .40
275 JT Riddle .15 .40
276 Yordan Alvarez RC 1.25 3.00
277 Dominic Smith .15 .40
278 Isan Diaz RC .40 1.00
279 Masahiro Tanaka .25 .60
280 Tony Gonsolin RC 1.00 2.50
281 Nelson Cruz .25 .60
282 Jake Marisnick .15 .40
283 Robel Garcia RC .25 .60
284 Jason Kipnis .20 .50
285 Tyler Alexander RC .40 1.00
286 Blake Parker .15 .40
287 Jose Peraza .20 .50
288 Jon Gray .15 .40
289 Yuli Gurriel .20 .50
290 Nick Senzel FS .25 .60
291 Tyler Naquin .15 .40
292 Gavin Lux RC 1.50 4.00
293 Wade Davis .15 .40
294 Jordan Zimmermann .20 .50
295 Jeff Samardzija .15 .40
296 Whit Merrifield .25 .60
297 Mike Yastrzemski FS .40 1.00
298 C.Bellinger/A.Verdugo .30 .75
299 David Price .20 .50
300 Javier Baez .30 .75
301 Mike Tauchman .25 .60
302 Tim Anderson LL .25 .60
303 Mallex Smith .15 .40
304 Shane Bieber .25 .60
305 Tyler Glasnow .15 .40
306 Jon Lester .20 .50
307 Daniel Palka .15 .40
308 Carlos Rodon .20 .50
309 Robbie Grossman .15 .40
310 Jose Urquidy RC .30 .75
311 David Bote .20 .50
312 Billy Hamilton .20 .50
313 Melky Cabrera .15 .40
314 Rafael Devers .30 .75
315 Adam Frazier .15 .40
316 Justin Turner .20 .50
317 Sean Murphy RC .40 1.00
318 Omar Narvaez .15 .40
319 Matt Olson .15 .40
320 Austin Hedges .15 .40
321 Eduardo Rodriguez .15 .40
322 Dario Agrazal RC .30 .75
323 Tyler White .15 .40
324 Mike Soroka CUP .25 .60
325 Good-bye, Home Run .25 .60
Kyle Schwarber
326 Dylan Cease RC .50 1.25
327 Cavan Biggio FS .30 .75
328 Chris Davis .15 .40
329 Washington Nationals TC .15 .40
330 George Springer .20 .50
331 Kevin McCarthy RC .25 .60
332 Jacob deGrom .25 .60
333 Evan Longoria .20 .50
334 Kevin Pillar .15 .40
335 Luke Voit .30 .75
336 Miguel Cabrera .25 .60
337 Michael Pineda .15 .40
338 Chicago Cubs TC .15 .40
339 Hansel Robles .15 .40
340 Adbert Alzolay RC .30 .75
341 Hanser Alberto .15 .40
342 Taylor Rogers .15 .40
343 Carson Kelly .15 .40
344 Ben Gamel .20 .50
345 Justin Verlander .25 .60
346 Lourdes Gurriel Jr. .20 .50
347 Ryan Braun .20 .50
348 Adrian Morejon RC .25 .60
349 Carlos Correa .25 .60
350 Pete Alonso CUP .60 1.50
351 Gerrit Cole .40 1.00
352 Tanner Roark .15 .40
353 DJ Stewart .15 .40
354 Luke Weaver .15 .40
355 Max Fried FS .25 .60
356 Franklin Barreto .15 .40
357 Homer Bailey .15 .40
358 Rio Ruiz .15 .40
359 Domingo Leyba RC .30 .75
360 Luis Rengifo .15 .40
361 Zach Eflin .15 .40
362 Chris Shaw .15 .40
363 Shed Long .20 .50
364 Hunter Harvey RC .40 1.00
365 Three's Company .25 .60
Elvis Andrus
Willie Calhoun
Joey Gallo
366 Marcus Semien .15 .40
367 Giancarlo Stanton .25 .60
368 Wade Miley .15 .40
369 Kolten Wong .20 .50
370 Seth Mejias-Brean RC .25 .60
371 Victor Caratini .15 .40
372 Josh Donaldson .20 .50
373 Kevin Cron .25 .60
374 Jose Ramirez .20 .50
375 Jose Osuna .15 .40
376 Shogo Akiyama RC .40 1.00
377 Phillip Ervin .15 .40
378 Nathan Eovaldi .20 .50
379 Ivan Nova .20 .50
380 James Karinchak RC .40 1.00
381 Kyle Garlick RC .40 1.00
382 Archie Bradley .15 .40
383 Steven Brault .15 .40
384 Carlos Carrasco .15 .40
385 Ryan Zimmerman .20 .50
386 Dakota Hudson FS .20 .50
387 Tony Wolters .15 .40
388 Dustin Pedroia .25 .60
389 Ryan O'Hearn .15 .40
390 Emmanuel Clase RC .30 .75
391 Justin Upton .20 .50
392 Luis Robert RC 10.00 25.00
393 Dereck Rodriguez .15 .40
394 Keone Kela .15 .40
395 Scott Oberg .15 .40
396 Miami Marlins TC .15 .40
397 Charlie Blackmon .25 .60
398 Miguel Andujar .25 .60
399 Adrian Houser .15 .40
400 Hyun-Jin Ryu .20 .50
401 Jake Fraley RC .30 .75
402 Vince Velazquez .15 .40
403 Jose Trevino .15 .40
404 Raimel Tapia .15 .40
405 San Francisco Giants TC .15 .40
406 Charlie Morton .25 .60
407 T.J. Zeuch RC .25 .60
408 Brendan Rodgers FS .25 .60
409 Jake Odorizzi .15 .40
410 Luis Urias FS .20 .50
411 Mark Melancon .15 .40
412 Bomba Brothers .25 .60
Nelson Cruz
Miguel Sano
413 Rich Hill .15 .40
414 Gio Gonzalez .20 .50
415 Joey Gallo .25 .60
416 Chris Taylor .20 .50
417 Colorado Rockies TC .15 .40
418 Alex Dickerson .15 .40
419 J.A. Happ .20 .50
420 Mookie Betts .50 1.25
421 Garrett Stubbs RC .25 .60
422 Will Smith .15 .40
423 Andrelton Simmons .15 .40
424 Miguel Sano .20 .50
425 Mike Foltynewicz .15 .40
426 Yoenis Cespedes .25 .60
427 Edwin Diaz .20 .50
428 Jaime Barria .15 .40
429 Joe Musgrove .15 .40
430 Darwinzon Hernandez .15 .40
431 Cincinnati Reds TC .15 .40
432 Walker Buehler .30 .75
433 Noah Syndergaard .20 .50
434 Brusdar Graterol RC .40 1.00
435 Mitch Keller .25 .60
436 Travis d'Arnaud .20 .50
437 Scott Heineman RC .25 .60
438 Danny Duffy .15 .40
439 Dee Gordon .15 .40
440 Carter Kieboom FS .20 .50
441 Nick Wittgren .25 .60
442 Tom Eshelman RC .30 .75
443 Johan Camargo .15 .40
444 Martin Perez .20 .50
445 Spencer Turnbull .15 .40
446 B.Harper/R.Hoskins .40 1.00
447 Griffin Canning FS .25 .60
448 Ian Happ .20 .50
449 Shun Yamaguchi RC .30 .75
450 Jorge Soler .25 .60
451 Justus Sheffield .25 .60
452 Joe Jimenez .15 .40
453 Miguel Rojas .15 .40
454 Austin Voth .15 .40
455 Kris Bryant .30 .75
456 Dom Nunez RC .30 .75
457 Kevin Gausman .15 .40
458 Trey Mancini .25 .60
459 Kwang-Hyun Kim RC .75 2.00
460 Tyler Mahle .15 .40
461 Harrison Bader .20 .50
462 Tony Kemp .15 .40
463 Frankie Montas .15 .40
464 Randy Dobnak RC .50 1.25
465 Eugenio Suarez .20 .50
466 Garrett Hampson .15 .40
467 Andrew McCutchen .25 .60
468 Chad Green .15 .40
469 Kris Bryant .30 .75
470 Yan Gomes .25 .60
471 Lorenzo Cain .15 .40
472 Steven Duggar .15 .40
473 Lance McCullers Jr. .15 .40
474 Mark Canha .15 .40
475 Robert Dugger RC .25 .60
476 James Marvel RC .25 .60
477 Brent Suter .15 .40
478 Cole Tucker .25 .60
479 Dexter Fowler .20 .50
480 Ozzie Albies .25 .60
481 Victor Reyes .20 .50
482 Adam Duvall .25 .60
483 Eddie Rosario .20 .50
484 Brian Goodwin .15 .40
485 Jack Mayfield RC .25 .60
486 Dawel Lugo .15 .40
487 Yandy Diaz .20 .50
488 Reynaldo Lopez .20 .50
489 Colin Moran .15 .40
490 Austin Slater .15 .40
491 Will Smith .30 .75
492 Paul DeJong .25 .60
493 Christian Walker .20 .50
494 Rowan Wick .15 .40
495 Lamonte Wade Jr. RC .40 1.00
496 Lucas Sims .15 .40
497 Albert Pujols .30 .75
498 Brandon Workman .15 .40
499 Sam Tuivailala .15 .40
500 Nick Anderson .15 .40
501 Tampa Bay Rays TC .15 .40
502 Willians Astudillo .15 .40
503 Dylan Bundy .20 .50
504 Pablo Lopez .15 .40
505 Billy McKinney .15 .40
506 Delino DeShields .15 .40
507 Blake Snell .20 .50
508 Carlos Martinez .20 .50
509 Willi Castro RC .40 1.00
510 Michael Lorenzen .15 .40
511 Jordan Hicks .20 .50
512 Josh James .25 .60
513 Michael Brantley .20 .50
514 Logan Webb RC .30 .75
515 Maikel Franco .20 .50
516 Texas Rangers TC .15 .40
517 Dylan Moore .15 .40
518 Shin-Soo Choo .20 .50
519 Didi Gregorius .20 .50
520 Justin Smoak .15 .40
521 Felix Hernandez .20 .50
522 J.D. Davis .15 .40
523 Corey Kluber .20 .50
524 Jurickson Profar .20 .50
525 Jake Cave .20 .50
526 Byron Buxton .20 .50
527 Khris Davis .25 .60
528 Harold Ramirez .15 .40
529 Ender Inciarte .15 .40
530 Xander Bogaerts .25 .60
531 David Bednar RC .25 .60
532 Robbie Ray .15 .40
533 Nick Castellanos .25 .60
534 Michael Wacha .20 .50
535 Avisail Garcia .20 .50
536 Elvis Luciano .15 .40
537 Marcell Ozuna .25 .60
538 O.Albies/R.Acuna .75 2.00
539 Tyrone Taylor RC .25 .60
540 Kean Wong RC .30 .75
541 Danny Mendick RC .30 .75
542 Tom Murphy .15 .40
543 Harold Castro .20 .50
544 Wil Myers .15 .40
545 Kevin Kiermaier .20 .50
546 Ross Stripling .15 .40
547 Victor Robles .30 .75
548 Brian O'Grady RC .25 .60
549 Freddie Freeman .30 .75
550 John Means .15 .40
551 Clint Frazier .20 .50
552 Yu Darvish .25 .60
553 Salvador Perez .20 .50
554 Mike Zunino .15 .40
555 Marcus Stroman .20 .50
556 Josh Naylor .15 .40
557 Adam Ottavino .15 .40
558 Sean Manaea .15 .40
559 Josh Hader .15 .40
560 Chad Pinder .15 .40
561 Trevor Williams .15 .40
562 Gio Urshela .25 .60
563 Danny Jansen .15 .40
564 Matt Beaty .20 .50
565 Jordan Luplow .15 .40
566 Seattle Mariners TC .15 .40
567 Yonathan Daza RC .30 .75
568 Adam Eaton .25 .60
569 E.Jimenez/T.Anderson .50 1.25
570 Manny Pina .15 .40
571 Keston Hiura .30 .75
572 Manuel Margot .15 .40
573 Jason Heyward .20 .50
574 Brandon Lowe FS .20 .50
575 Kyle Seager .15 .40
576 Sergio Romo .15 .40
577 Elvis Andrus .20 .50
578 Chris Bassitt .15 .40
579 Kevin Kramer .15 .40
580 Dellin Betances .15 .40
581 Michael Taylor .15 .40
582 Willie Calhoun .15 .40
583 Josh Staumont RC .25 .60
584 Michael Kopech .30 .75
585 Kyle Tucker FS .20 .50
586 Stevie Wilkerson RC .40 1.00
587 Lou Trivino .15 .40
588 Tommy Kahnle .15 .40
589 Eric Lauer .15 .40
590 Yu Chang RC .40 1.00
591 A.Judge/G.Sanchez .60 1.50
592 Corey Dickerson .20 .50
593 Stephen Piscotty .15 .40
594 Pittsburgh Pirates TC .15 .40
595 Eduardo Escobar .15 .40
596 Daniel Norris .15 .40
597 Jonathan Hernandez RC .25 .60
598 Jacob Stallings .20 .50
599 Ryan McMahon .15 .40
600 Drew Steckenrider .15 .40
601 Tucker Barnhart .15 .40
602 Jose Altuve .20 .50
603 Dinelson Lamet .15 .40
604 Derek Fisher .15 .40
605 Stephen Vogt .20 .50
606 Martin Maldonado .15 .40
607 Cal Quantrill .15 .40
608 Sam Gaviglio .15 .40
609 Ronald Guzman .15 .40
610 Cole Hamels .20 .50
611 Braun/Cain/Yelich .30 .75
612 Luis Arraez FS .30 .75
613 Isiah Kiner-Falefa .15 .40
614 Brett Gardner .20 .50
615 Junior Fernandez RC .25 .60

616 Cam Gallagher .15 .40
617 Bryan Reynolds .20 .50
618 Joey Wendle .15 .40
619 Rick Porcello .20 .50
620 Corey Seager .25 .60
621 Dallas Keuchel .20 .50
622 Brett Phillips .15 .40
623 Mike Ford .25 .60
624 Renato Nunez .20 .50
625 Detroit Tigers TC .15 .40
626 Nate Lowe .15 .40
627 Eric Hosmer .20 .50
628 Julio Urias .25 .60
629 Toronto Blue Jays TC .15 .40
630 Francisco Mejia .20 .50
631 Stephen Strasburg .25 .60
632 Austin Hays .25 .60
633 Lance Lynn .15 .40
634 San Diego Padres TC .15 .40
635 Sean Newcomb .15 .40
636 Jake Bauers .20 .50
637 Trevor Story .25 .60
638 Nomar Mazara .15 .40
639 Kolby Allard .15 .40
640 Rev'd Up .25 .60
Adam Eaton
Howie Kendrick
641 A.J. Pollock .15 .40
642 Ryan Borucki .15 .40
643 Wilson Ramos .15 .40
644 Teoscar Hernandez .25 .60
645 Jeff Mathis .20 .50
646 Kevin Newman FS .20 .50
647 Joe Ross .15 .40
648 Mike Leake .15 .40
649 Jed Lowrie .15 .40
650 Kelvin Herrera .15 .40
651 Arizona Diamondbacks TC .15 .40
652 Pedro Severino .15 .40
653 Zach Plesac .25 .60
654 Tim Lopes RC .30 .75
655 Howie Kendrick .15 .40
656 Alex Cobb .15 .40
657 Rougned Odor .20 .50
658 Chad Wallach RC .25 .60
659 Aledmys Diaz .15 .40
660 Brandon Nimmo .20 .50
661 Justin Dunn RC .30 .75
662 Andrew Knapp .15 .40
663 Chicago White Sox TC .15 .40
664 Yonny Chirinos .15 .40
665 Willson Contreras .25 .60
666 Kyle Freeland .20 .50
667 Adam Haseley .25 .60
668 Kansas City Royals TC .15 .40
669 Luis Severino .20 .50
670 Aaron Barrett RC .25 .60
671 Ryan McBroom RC .30 .75
672 Chris Sale .25 .60
673 Anthony DeSclafani .15 .40
674 Jose Abreu .25 .60
675 David Robertson .15 .40
676 Rangel Ravelo RC .30 .75
677 Ji-Man Choi .15 .40
678 Jose Rodriguez RC .25 .60
679 Glenn Sparkman .15 .40
680 Nick Ahmed .15 .40
681 Edwin Rios RC .60 1.50
682 Ronny Rodriguez .15 .40
683 Jakob Junis .15 .40
684 Mike Minor .15 .40
685 Freddy Galvis .15 .40
686 Josh Reddick .15 .40
687 Rhys Hoskins .30 .75
688 Austin Romine .15 .40
689 James McCann .20 .50
690 Ehire Adrianza .15 .40
691 Brock Burke RC .25 .60
692 Jonathan Schoop .15 .40
693 Jon Berti RC .25 .60
694 Baltimore Orioles TC .15 .40
695 Danny Santana .15 .40
696 G.Torres/F.Lindor .50 1.25
697 Eric Sogard .15 .40
698 Tyler Chatwood .15 .40
699 Sheldon Neuse RC .30 .75
700 Adam Wainwright .20 .50

2020 Topps Advanced Stats
*ADV STATS: 4X TO 10X BASIC
SER.1 STATED ODDS 1:107 HOBBY
SER.2 STATED ODDS 1:65 HOBBY
STATED PRINT RUN 300 SER. #'d SETS
69 Brendan McKay 10.00 25.00
70 Nico Hoerner 20.00 50.00
78 Bo Bichette 75.00 200.00
110 Jesus Luzardo 12.00 30.00
229 Randy Arozarena 20.00 50.00
235 Dustin May 10.00 25.00
276 Yordan Alvarez 40.00 100.00
292 Gavin Lux 60.00 150.00
376 Shogo Akiyama 25.00 60.00
392 Luis Robert 150.00 400.00
459 Kwang-Hyun Kim 6.00 15.00
681 Edwin Rios 6.00 15.00

2020 Topps Black
*BLACK: 10X TO 25X BASIC
*BLACK RC: 6X TO 15X BASIC RC
SER.1 ODDS 1:117 HOBBY
SER.2 ODDS 1:97 HOBBY
STATED PRINT RUN 69 SER. #'d SETS
1 Mike Trout 50.00 120.00
69 Brendan McKay 25.00 60.00
70 Nico Hoerner 50.00 125.00
78 Bo Bichette 200.00 500.00
110 Jesus Luzardo 30.00 80.00
178 Mauricio Dubon 20.00 50.00
229 Randy Arozarena 50.00 120.00
235 Dustin May 25.00 60.00
276 Yordan Alvarez 150.00 400.00
292 Gavin Lux 150.00 400.00
376 Shogo Akiyama 60.00 150.00
392 Luis Robert 300.00 800.00
459 Kwang-Hyun Kim 15.00 40.00
681 Edwin Rios 15.00 40.00

2020 Topps Father's Day Blue
*BLUE: 10X TO 25X BASIC
*BLUE RC: 6X TO 15X BASIC RC
SER.1 STATED ODDS 1:546 HOBBY
SER.2 STATED ODDS 1:358 HOBBY
STATED PRINT RUN 50 SER. #'d SETS
1 Mike Trout 50.00 120.00
69 Brendan McKay 25.00 60.00
70 Nico Hoerner 50.00 125.00
78 Bo Bichette 200.00 500.00
110 Jesus Luzardo 30.00 80.00
178 Mauricio Dubon 20.00 50.00
229 Randy Arozarena 50.00 120.00
235 Dustin May 25.00 60.00
276 Yordan Alvarez 150.00 400.00
292 Gavin Lux 150.00 400.00
376 Shogo Akiyama 30.00 80.00
392 Luis Robert 300.00 800.00
459 Kwang-Hyun Kim 15.00 40.00
681 Edwin Rios 15.00 40.00

2020 Topps Gold
*GOLD: 2X TO 5X BASIC
*GOLD RC: 1.2X TO 3X BASIC RC
SER.1 STATED ODDS 1:14 HOBBY
SER.2 STATED ODDS 1:9 HOBBY
STATED PRINT RUN 2020 SER. #'d SETS
69 Brendan McKay 5.00 12.00
70 Nico Hoerner 10.00 25.00
78 Bo Bichette 40.00 100.00
110 Jesus Luzardo 6.00 15.00
229 Randy Arozarena 10.00 25.00
235 Dustin May 5.00 12.00
276 Yordan Alvarez 20.00 50.00
292 Gavin Lux 30.00 80.00
376 Shogo Akiyama 6.00 15.00
392 Luis Robert 75.00 200.00

2020 Topps Gold Foil
*GOLD FOIL: 2X TO 5X BASIC
*GOLD FOIL RC: 1.2X TO 3X BASIC RC
SER.1 STATED ODDS 1:2 HOBBY JUMBO
SER.2 STATED ODDS 1:2 HOBBY JUMBO
69 Brendan McKay 5.00 12.00
70 Nico Hoerner 10.00 25.00
78 Bo Bichette 40.00 100.00
235 Dustin May 5.00 12.00
276 Yordan Alvarez 20.00 50.00
292 Gavin Lux 30.00 80.00
376 Shogo Akiyama 6.00 15.00
392 Luis Robert 75.00 200.00

2020 Topps Independence Day
*INDPNDNCE: 10X TO 25X BASIC
*INDPNDNCE RC: 6X TO 15X BASIC RC
SER.1 STATED ODDS 1:359 HOBBY
SER.2 STATED ODDS 1:236 HOBBY
STATED PRINT RUN 76 SER. #'d SETS
1 Mike Trout 50.00 120.00
69 Brendan McKay 25.00 60.00
70 Nico Hoerner 50.00 125.00
78 Bo Bichette 200.00 500.00
110 Jesus Luzardo 30.00 80.00
178 Mauricio Dubon 20.00 50.00
229 Randy Arozarena 50.00 120.00
235 Dustin May 25.00 60.00
276 Yordan Alvarez 150.00 400.00
292 Gavin Lux 150.00 400.00
376 Shogo Akiyama 30.00 80.00
392 Luis Robert 300.00 800.00
459 Kwang-Hyun Kim 15.00 40.00
681 Edwin Rios 15.00 40.00

2020 Topps Meijer Purple
*PURPLE: 5X TO 12X BASIC
*PURPLE RC: 3X TO 8X BASIC RC
STATED ODDS TWO PER BLISTER PACK
69 Brendan McKay 12.00 30.00
70 Nico Hoerner 25.00 60.00
78 Bo Bichette 100.00 250.00
110 Jesus Luzardo 15.00 40.00
229 Randy Arozarena 25.00 60.00
235 Dustin May 12.00 30.00
276 Yordan Alvarez 60.00 150.00
292 Gavin Lux 75.00 200.00

2020 Topps Memorial Day Camo
*CAMO: 12X TO 30X BASIC
*CAMO RC: 8X TO 20X BASIC RC
SER.1 STATED ODDS 1:1091 HOBBY
SER.2 STATED ODDS 1:715 HOBBY
STATED PRINT RUN 25 SER. #'d SETS
1 Mike Trout 60.00 150.00
69 Brendan McKay 30.00 80.00
70 Nico Hoerner 60.00 150.00
78 Bo Bichette 250.00 600.00
110 Jesus Luzardo 40.00 100.00
178 Mauricio Dubon 25.00 60.00
229 Randy Arozarena 60.00 150.00
235 Dustin May 30.00 80.00
276 Yordan Alvarez 200.00 500.00
292 Gavin Lux 200.00 500.00
376 Shogo Akiyama 40.00 100.00
392 Luis Robert 400.00 1000.00
459 Kwang-Hyun Kim 20.00 50.00
681 Edwin Rios 20.00 50.00

2020 Topps Mother's Day Pink
*PINK: 10X TO 25X BASIC
*PINK RC: 6X TO 15X BASIC RC
SER.1 STATED ODDS 1:546 HOBBY
SER.2 STATED ODDS 1:358 HOBBY
STATED PRINT RUN 50 SER. #'d SETS
1 Mike Trout 50.00 120.00
69 Brendan McKay 25.00 60.00
70 Nico Hoerner 50.00 125.00
78 Bo Bichette 200.00 500.00
110 Jesus Luzardo 30.00 80.00
178 Mauricio Dubon 20.00 50.00
229 Randy Arozarena 50.00 120.00
235 Dustin May 25.00 60.00
276 Yordan Alvarez 150.00 400.00
292 Gavin Lux 150.00 400.00
376 Shogo Akiyama 30.00 80.00
392 Luis Robert 300.00 800.00
459 Kwang-Hyun Kim 15.00 40.00
681 Edwin Rios 15.00 40.00

2020 Topps Rainbow Foil
*RAINBOW: 2X TO 5X BASIC
*RAINBOW RC: 1.2X TO 3X BASIC RC
SER.1 STATED ODDS 1:10 HOBBY
SER.2 STATED ODDS 1:10 HOBBY
69 Brendan McKay 5.00 12.00
70 Nico Hoerner 10.00 25.00
78 Bo Bichette 40.00 100.00
235 Dustin May 5.00 12.00
276 Yordan Alvarez 20.00 50.00
292 Gavin Lux 30.00 80.00
376 Shogo Akiyama 6.00 15.00
392 Luis Robert 75.00 200.00

2020 Topps Vintage Stock
*VINTAGE: 8X TO 20X BASIC
*VINTAGE RC: 5X TO 12X BASIC RC
SER.1 STATED ODDS 1:186 HOBBY
SER.2 STATED ODDS 1:186 HOBBY
STATED PRINT RUN 99 SER. #'d SETS
1 Mike Trout 40.00 100.00
69 Brendan McKay 20.00 50.00
70 Nico Hoerner 40.00 100.00
78 Bo Bichette 150.00 400.00
110 Jesus Luzardo 25.00 60.00
178 Mauricio Dubon 15.00 40.00
229 Randy Arozarena 40.00 100.00
235 Dustin May 20.00 50.00
276 Yordan Alvarez 100.00 250.00
292 Gavin Lux 125.00 300.00
376 Shogo Akiyama 25.00 60.00
392 Luis Robert 250.00 600.00
459 Kwang-Hyun Kim 12.00 30.00
681 Edwin Rios 12.00 30.00

2020 Topps Walgreens Yellow
69 Brendan McKay 8.00 20.00
70 Nico Hoerner 15.00 40.00
78 Bo Bichette 60.00 150.00
110 Jesus Luzardo 10.00 25.00
229 Randy Arozarena 15.00 40.00
235 Dustin May 8.00 20.00
276 Yordan Alvarez 60.00 150.00
292 Gavin Lux 50.00 120.00

2020 Topps Base Set Photo Variations
SER.1 STATED ODDS 1:43 HOBBY
SER.2 STATED ODDS 1:28 HOBBY
SER.1 STATED SSP ODDS 1:1272 HOBBY
SER.2 STATED SSP ODDS 1:835 HOBBY
1A Trout Signing 10.00 25.00
1B Mike Trout SSP 800.00 1200.00
7A Judge Blue shirt 5.00 12.00
7B Aaron Judge SSP 300.00 600.00
8 Cal Ripken Jr. SSP 20.00 50.00
13 Stan Musial SSP 15.00 40.00
14 Anthony Rendon 2.00 5.00
Expos uniform
20A Aquino Flex 2.50 6.00
20B Aristides Aquino SSP 60.00 150.00
20C Aquino FACTORY 2.50 6.00
35 George Brett 4.00 10.00
46 Sanchez Dugout 3.00 8.00
47 Chipper Jones 3.00 8.00
49 Jimenez w/Ball 4.00 10.00
50A Bellinger Overhead 6.00 15.00
50B Cody Bellinger SSP 30.00 80.00
51 Rizzo Overhead 4.00 10.00
52 Mike Piazza 3.00 8.00
55 Ozzie Smith 3.00 8.00
60 Roger Clemens 2.50 6.00
64 Lewis Dugout 20.00 50.00
68 Gerrit Cole 3.00 8.00
69A McKay Wht jrsy 2.00 5.00
69B Brendan McKay SSP 25.00 60.00
70 Hoerner High-five 10.00 25.00
78A Bichette Wknd uni 60.00 150.00
78B Bo Bichette SSP 150.00 400.00
78C Bichette FACTORY 10.00 25.00
94 Brooks Robinson 1.50 4.00
100A Alex Bregman 2.00 5.00
iPad photo
100B Alex Bregman SSP 25.00 60.00
110 Luzardo Overhead 8.00 20.00
111 Posey Blck pants 3.00 8.00
117 Max Kepler 1.50 4.00
red jersey
118 Kershaw Blue shirt 5.00 12.00
119 Kyle Schwarber 2.00 5.00
pink sleeves
120 Sandy Koufax SSP 20.00 50.00
121 Lou Gehrig SSP 25.00 60.00
124 Randy Johnson 2.00 5.00
125 Ohtani Warmup 2.50 6.00
127 Chapman Wknd uni 2.00 5.00
129 Jackie Robinson SSP 25.00 60.00
138 Ty Cobb SSP 25.00 60.00
140 Trevor Bauer 2.00 5.00
camo hat
145 Goldschmidt Dive 2.50 6.00
149 Robin Yount• 2.00 5.00
150A Acuna Signing 15.00 40.00
150B Ronald Acuna Jr. SSP 100.00 250.00
156 Hank Aaron SSP 40.00 100.00
161 Mariano Rivera 3.00 8.00
168A Tatis Crouching 10.00 25.00
168B Fernando Tatis Jr. SSP 75.00 200.00
170 Roberto Clemente SSP 40.00 100.00
173 Molina Blue chest 2.50 6.00
175 Frank Thomas 3.00 8.00
179 Ramon Laureano 2.00 5.00
in dugout
180 Scherzer Expos 3.00 8.00
182A Guerrero Jr. Red hat 4.00 10.00
182B Vladimir Guerrero Jr. SSP 75.00 200.00
183 Vladimir Guerrero 1.50 4.00
186 Johnny Bench 3.00 8.00
188 Manny Machado 2.00 5.00
sunglasses on
192 Ichiro 3.00 8.00
196 Ted Williams SSP 25.00 60.00
200A Yelich Pinstripe 2.50 6.00
200B Christian Yelich SSP 25.00 60.00
201 Lindor Red carpet 2.50 6.00
206 Reggie Jackson• 1.50 4.00
219 Honus Wagner 3.00 8.00
224 Soto Expos 8.00 20.00
230 Arenado Prpl uni 2.50 6.00
235 May Glasses 10.00 25.00
248 Tony Gwynn 2.00 5.00
250A Harper Gatorade 3.00 8.00
250B Bryce Harper SSP 30.00 80.00
252 Roger Maris 4.00 10.00
253 Ernie Banks 2.50 6.00
260 Nolan Ryan 5.00 12.00
267 Votto Slvlss jrsy 3.00 8.00
269 J.D. Martinez 2.00 5.00
close-up
271 Josh Bell 1.50 4.00
Red Carpet Show
276A Alvarez Wlkng w/bat 40.00 100.00
276B Yordan Alvarez SSP 150.00 400.00
276C Alvarez FACTORY 6.00 15.00
279 Masahiro Tanaka 2.00 5.00
jacket on
289 Mark McGwire 3.00 8.00
292A Lux Jumping 40.00 100.00
292B Gavin Lux SSP 125.00 300.00
292C Gavin Lux 8.00 20.00
gray jsy FACTORY
296 Merrifield Wknd uni 3.00 8.00
299 Pedro Martinez 1.50 4.00
300A Baez Jumping 2.50 6.00
300B Javier Baez SSP 40.00 100.00
303 Ken Griffey Jr. SSP 30.00 80.00
306 Ryne Sandberg 4.00 10.00
309 Rickey Henderson 3.00 8.00
314 Devers Weights 2.50 6.00
317 Murphy Grn jrsy 4.00 10.00
330 George Springer 1.50 4.00
jumping
332 Jacob deGrom 2.50 6.00
batting
334 Willie Mays SSP 25.00 60.00
335A Don Mattingly 5.00 12.00
335B Babe Ruth SSP 40.00 100.00
341 Frank Robinson 1.50 4.00
345 Verlander Orng jrsy 2.00 5.00
349 Carlos Correa 2.00 5.00
blue jersey
350A Alonso Gatorade 3.00 8.00
350B Pete Alonso SSP 600.00 1000.00
351A Cole Blue jrsy 3.00 8.00
351B Cole SSP Pinstripe 40.00 100.00
354 Randy Johnson 2.00 5.00
361 Steve Carlton 1.50 4.00
362 Will Clark 1.50 4.00
363 Ichiro SSP 25.00 60.00
364 Hunter Harvey 2.00 5.00
black jsy
366 Marcus Semien 1.25 3.00
green jsy
367A Giancarlo Stanton 2.00 5.00
gray jsy, fielding
367B Stanton SSP Hggng 20.00 50.00
375A Willie Stargell 1.50 4.00
375B Robert Clemente SSP 40.00 100.00
378 Carl Yastrzemski 3.00 8.00
381 Sandy Koufax SSP 40.00 100.00
388A Carlton Fisk 1.50 4.00
388B Ted Williams SSP 40.00 100.00
392A Robert Snglsss 200.00 500.00
392B Robert SSP Rnnng 500.00 1200.00
392C Bichette/Robert/Alvarez SSP 1000.00 2000.00
392D Luis Robert NNOF 1500.00 3000.00
392E Robert FACTORY 6.00 15.00
397 Charlie Blackmon 2.00 5.00
pinstripe jsy
401 Fraley Hdbnd 1.50 4.00
408 Brendan Rodgers 2.00 5.00
dugout steps
416 Jackie Robinson SSP 25.00 60.00
418 Willie McCovey 1.50 4.00
419 Lou Gehrig SSP 40.00 100.00
420A Betts Hoodie 4.00 10.00
420B Betts SSP Blue jrsy 40.00 100.00
420C Betts SSP Hllywd 300.00 800.00
424 Rod Carew 1.50 4.00
427 Tom Seaver 1.50 4.00
432A Buehler Bttng 2.50 6.00
432B Buehler SSP Run 20.00 50.00
433 Noah Syndergaard 1.50 4.00
wearing helmet
434 Brusdar Graterol 2.00 5.00
white jsy
440 Carter Kieboom 1.50 4.00
red hoodie
455A Bryant Bttng 2.50 6.00
455B Kris Bryant SSP Glv 25.00 60.00
458 Trey Mancini 2.00 5.00
black jsy
461 Lou Brock 1.50 4.00
464 Dobnak Hoodie 2.50 6.00
465 Eugenio Suarez 1.50 4.00
white jsy
467A Andrew McCutchen 20.00 50.00
red jsy
467B McCtchn SSP Pnstrpe jrsy 25.00 60.00
469 Tom Glavine 1.50 4.00
472 Willie Mays SSP 25.00 60.00
480 Ozzie Albies 2.00 5.00
hoodie
482A Eddie Mathews 2.00 5.00
482B Hank Aaron SSP 30.00 80.00
483 Eddie Rosario 1.50 4.00
blue jsy
486 Al Kaline 2.00 5.00
497A Pujols Shkng hnds 2.50 6.00
497B Pujols SSP Cap chest 25.00 60.00
507 Blake Snell 1.50 4.00
wearing shirt
508 Bob Gibson 1.50 4.00
514 Logan Webb 1.50 4.00
batting
517 Ken Griffey Jr. SSP 30.00 80.00
519 Mike Schmidt 3.00 8.00
525A Harmon Killebrew 2.00 5.00
looking forward
525B Killebrew SSP Look up 25.00 60.00
530 Xander Bogaerts 2.00 5.00
tuxedo
533 Nick Castellanos 2.00 5.00
gray jsy
541 Danny Mendick 1.50 4.00
batting
549 Freeman Bttng 2.50 6.00
552 Yu Darvish 2.00 5.00
batting
556 Dave Winfield 1.50 4.00
557 Mariano Rivera SSP 40.00 100.00
558 Dennis Eckersley 1.50 4.00
559 Josh Hader 1.25 3.00
white plyr's wknd jsy
560 Reggie Jackson 1.50 4.00
561 Wade Boggs 1.50 4.00
562 Babe Ruth SSP 60.00 150.00
567 Yonathan Daza 1.50 4.00
jsy#2
571 Hiura Blue jrsy 2.50 6.00
577 Elvis Andrus 1.50 4.00
Gatorade shower
585 Kyle Tucker 1.50 4.00
swinging
586 Cal Ripken Jr. SSP 40.00 100.00
590 Yu Chang 2.00 5.00
wearing a hat
591 Craig Biggio 1.50 4.00
602A Jose Altuve 1.50 4.00
cap on chest
602B Altuve SSP Cage 25.00 60.00
609 Nolan Ryan SSP 30.00 80.00
615 Junior Fernandez 1.25 3.00
with catcher
620 Corey Seager 2.00 5.00
gray jsy
624 Eddie Murray 1.50 4.00
631A Stephen Strasburg 2.00 5.00
bunting
631B Strasburg SSP White House 25.00 60.00
637 Trevor Story 2.00 5.00
purple jsy
649 Gary Carter 1.50 4.00
660 Darryl Strawberry 1.25 3.00
661 Justin Dunn 1.50 4.00
Futures game jsy
665 Willson Contreras 2.00 5.00
in shorts
669 Luis Severino 1.50 4.00
locker room celebration
672 Chris Sale 2.00 5.00
Stars and Stripes hat
674 Jose Abreu 2.00 5.00
throwback jsy
676 Rangel Ravelo 1.50 4.00
in dugout
681 Edwin Rios 3.00 8.00
bat up
685 Frank Robinson 1.50 4.00
686 Jeff Bagwell 1.50 4.00
687A Hoskins Bubble 2.50 6.00
687B Hoskins SSP Sgnng 25.00 60.00
691 Brock Burke 1.25 3.00
blue jsy
699 Sheldon Neuse 1.50 4.00
gray jsy
NNO Rob Manfred SSP 60.00 150.00

2020 Topps '19 Topps Now Review
COMPLETE SET (10) 4.00 10.00
STATED ODDS 1:18 HOBBY
TNR1 Mike Trout 1.50 4.00
TNR2 Vladimir Guerrero Jr. .60 1.50
TNR3 Albert Pujols .40 1.00
TNR4 Yordan Alvarez 1.00 2.50
TNR5 Shohei Ohtani .40 1.00
TNR6 Pete Alonso .75 2.00
TNR7 Mariano Rivera .40 1.00
TNR8 Bryce Harper .50 1.25
TNR9 Pete Alonso .75 2.00
TNR10 Justin Verlander .30 .75

2020 Topps '85 Topps
STATED ODDS 1:4 HOBBY
*BLUE: 1.2X TO 3X BASIC
*BLACK/299: 2X TO 5X BASIC
*GOLD/50: 5X TO 12X BASIC
851 Mike Trout 1.50 4.00
852 Shohei Ohtani .40 1.00
853 Albert Pujols .40 1.00
854 Matt Thaiss .25 .60
855 Alex Young .20 .50
856 Zac Gallen .50 1.25
857 Chipper Jones .30 .75
858 Dale Murphy .30 .75
859 Hank Aaron .60 1.50
8510 Mike Soroka .30 .75
8511 Ozzie Albies .30 .75
8512 Ronald Acuna Jr. 1.25 3.00
8513 Cal Ripken Jr. 1.00 2.50
8514 Mike Mussina .25 .60
8515 Chris Sale .30 .75
8516 J.D. Martinez .30 .75
8517 Rafael Devers .40 1.00
8518 Roger Clemens .40 1.00
8519 Wade Boggs .25 .60
8520 Xander Bogaerts .30 .75
8521 Mookie Betts .60 1.50
8522 Jackie Robinson .30 .75
8523 Rod Carew .25 .60
8524 Anthony Rizzo .50 1.25
8525 Kris Bryant .40 1.00
8526 Kyle Schwarber .30 .75
8527 Ryne Sandberg .60 1.50
8528 Willson Contreras .30 .75
8529 Robel Garcia .20 .50
8530 Dylan Cease .40 1.00
8531 Eloy Jimenez .60 1.50
8532 Frank Thomas .30 .75
8533 Zack Collins .25 .60
8534 Joey Votto .30 .75
8535 Johnny Bench .30 .75
8536 Nick Senzel .30 .75
8537 Trevor Bauer .30 .75
8538 Aristides Aquino .40 1.00
8539 Francisco Lindor .30 .75
8540 Shane Bieber .30 .75
8541 Nolan Arenado .40 1.00
8542 Al Kaline .30 .75
8543 Miguel Cabrera .30 .75
8544 Jake Rogers .20 .50
8545 George Springer .25 .60
8546 Gerrit Cole .50 1.25
8547 Jeff Bagwell .25 .60
8548 Jose Altuve .25 .60
8549 Nolan Ryan 1.00 2.50
8550 Yordan Alvarez 1.00 2.50
8551 Alex Bregman .30 .75
8552 Whit Merrifield .30 .75
8553 George Brett .60 1.50
8554 Clayton Kershaw .50 1.25
8555 Sandy Koufax .60 1.50
8556 Walker Buehler .40 1.00
8557 Dustin May .75 2.00
8558 Jordan Yamamoto .25 .60
8559 Christian Yelich .40 1.00
8560 Keston Hiura .40 1.00
8561 Robin Yount .30 .75
8562 Jose Berrios .25 .60
8563 Max Kepler .25 .60
8564 Vladimir Guerrero .25 .60
8565 Darryl Strawberry .20 .50
8566 Jacob deGrom .30 .75
8567 Noah Syndergaard .25 .60
8568 Pete Alonso .75 2.00
8569 Aaron Judge .75 2.00
8570 Don Mattingly .60 1.50
8571 Luis Severino .25 .60
8572 Mariano Rivera .40 1.00
8573 Reggie Jackson .25 .60
8574 Gleyber Torres .60 1.50
8575 Mark McGwire .50 1.25
8576 Ramon Laureano .30 .75
8577 Rickey Henderson .30 .75
8578 Matt Chapman .30 .75
8579 Bryce Harper .50 1.25
8580 Rhys Hoskins .40 1.00
8581 Roberto Clemente .75 2.00
8582 Manny Machado .30 .75
8583 Chris Paddack .30 .75
8584 Fernando Tatis Jr. 1.25 3.00
8585 Tony Gwynn .30 .75
8586 Will Clark .25 .60
8587 Willie Mays .60 1.50
8588 Ichiro .40 1.00
8589 Ken Griffey Jr. .60 1.50
8590 Paul Goldschmidt .30 .75
8591 Ozzie Smith .40 1.00
8592 Gavin Lux 1.25 3.00
8593 Yadier Molina .30 .75
8594 Blake Snell .25 .60
8595 Nico Hoerner .75 2.00
8596 Brendan McKay .30 .75
8597 Bo Bichette 1.50 4.00
8598 Vladimir Guerrero Jr. .60 1.50
8599 Juan Soto 1.00 2.50
85100 Max Scherzer .30 .75

2020 Topps '85 Topps Series 2
COMPLETE SET (50) 10.00 25.00
STATED ODDS 1:8 HOBBY
*BLUE: 1.2X TO 3X BASIC
*BLACK/299: 2X TO 5X BASIC
*GOLD/50: 5X TO 12X BASIC
85TB1 Anthony Rendon .30 .75
85TB2 Ketel Marte .25 .60
85TB3 Freddie Freeman .40 1.00
85TB4 Austin Riley .50 1.25
85TB5 Trey Mancini .30 .75
85TB6 Andrew Benintendi .30 .75
85TB7 David Ortiz .30 .75
85TB8 Javier Baez .40 1.00
85TB9 Tim Anderson .30 .75
85TB10 Jose Abreu .30 .75
85TB11 Sonny Gray .25 .60
85TB12 Eugenio Suarez .25 .60
85TB13 Barry Larkin .25 .60
85TB14 Mike Clevinger .25 .60
85TB15 Carlos Santana .25 .60
85TB16 Trevor Story .30 .75
85TB17 Charlie Blackmon .30 .75
85TB18 Gerrit Cole .50 1.25
85TB19 Carlos Correa .30 .75
85TB20 Jorge Soler .30 .75
85TB21 Cody Bellinger .60 1.50
85TB22 Corey Seager .30 .75
85TB23 Lorenzo Cain .20 .50
85TB24 Nelson Cruz .30 .75
85TB25 Miguel Sano .25 .60
85TB26 Robinson Cano .25 .60
85TB27 Marcus Stroman .25 .60
85TB28 Masahiro Tanaka .30 .75
85TB29 Giancarlo Stanton .30 .75
85TB30 DJ LeMahieu .30 .75
85TB31 Matt Olson .20 .50
85TB32 Mookie Betts .60 1.50
85TB33 Marcus Semien .20 .50
85TB34 Aaron Nola .30 .75
85TB35 J.T. Realmuto .30 .75
85TB36 Andrew McCutchen .30 .75
85TB37 Josh Bell .25 .60
85TB38 Trent Grisham .75 2.00
85TB39 Buster Posey .40 1.00
85TB40 Mike Yastrzemski .50 1.25
85TB41 Kyle Lewis 1.50 4.00
85TB42 Randy Johnson .30 .75
85TB43 Jack Flaherty .25 .60
85TB44 Jose Canseco .25 .60
85TB45 Tyler Glasnow .20 .50
85TB46 Joey Gallo .30 .75
85TB47 Luis Robert 2.00 5.00
85TB48 Roberto Alomar .25 .60
85TB49 Stephen Strasburg .30 .75
85TB50 Trea Turner .25 .60

2020 Topps '85 Topps All Stars
COMPLETE SET (50) 12.00 30.00
STATED ODDS 1:8 HOBBY
*BLUE: 1.2X TO 3X BASIC
*BLACK/299: 2X TO 5X BASIC
*GOLD/50: 5X TO 12X BASIC
85AS1 Mike Trout 1.50 4.00
85AS2 Aaron Judge .75 2.00
85AS3 Roger Clemens .40 1.00
85AS4 Cal Ripken Jr. 1.00 2.50
85AS5 Reggie Jackson .25 .60
85AS6 Rickey Henderson .30 .75
85AS7 Carl Yastrzemski .50 1.25
85AS8 Mark McGwire .50 1.25
85AS9 Johnny Bench
85AS10 Hideki Matsui .30 .75
85AS11 Bo Jackson .30 .75
85AS12 Ryne Sandberg .60 1.50
85AS13 Andre Dawson .25 .60
85AS14 Chris Sale .30 .75
85AS15 Tom Glavine .25 .60

85AS16 Willson Contreras .30 .75
85AS17 Jacob deGrom .30 .75
85AS18 Francisco Lindor .30 .75
85AS19 Christian Yelich .40 1.00
85AS20 Luis Severino .25 .60
85AS21 Wade Boggs .25 .60
85AS22 Robin Yount .30 .75
85AS23 Don Mattingly .60 1.50
85AS24 Ozzie Smith .40 1.00
85AS25 Jose Altuve .25 .60
85AS26 Bob Gibson .25 .60
85AS27 Carlton Fisk .25 .60
85AS28 Dale Murphy .30 .75
85AS29 Will Clark .25 .60
85AS30 Darryl Strawberry .20 .50
85AS31 Edgar Martinez .25 .60
85AS32 Blake Snell .25 .60
85AS33 Ozzie Albies .30 .75
85AS34 Jim Rice .25 .60
85AS35 Rod Carew .25 .60
85AS36 Paul Goldschmidt .30 .75
85AS37 George Springer .25 .60
85AS38 Max Scherzer .30 .75
85AS39 Ronald Acuna Jr. 1.25 3.00
85AS40 Ken Griffey Jr. .60 1.50
85AS41 Ketel Marte .25 .60
85AS42 Nolan Arenado .40 1.00
85AS43 Gleyber Torres .60 1.50
85AS44 Pete Alonso .75 2.00
85AS45 Jeff McNeil .25 .60
85AS46 Lucas Giolito .25 .60
85AS47 Shane Bieber .25 .60
85AS48 Jose Berrios .25 .60
85AS49 Clayton Kershaw .60 1.50
85AS50 Kris Bryant .40 1.00

2020 Topps '85 Topps All Stars Autographs

STATED ODDS 1:591 HOBBY
EXCHANGE DEADLINE 4/30/2022
85ASAAD Andre Dawson 20.00 50.00
85ASAAJ Aaron Judge
85ASABGI Bob Gibson
85ASABJA Bo Jackson
85ASABS Blake Snell 4.00 10.00
85ASACFI Carlton Fisk 25.00 60.00
85ASACK Clayton Kershaw 40.00 100.00
85ASACRJ Cal Ripken Jr. 60.00 150.00
85ASACS Chris Sale 10.00 25.00
85ASACSA Carlos Santana 15.00 40.00
85ASACY Carl Yastrzemski 50.00 120.00
85ASACYE Christian Yelich 30.00 80.00
85ASADJL DJ LeMahieu 30.00 80.00
85ASADM Don Mattingly 40.00 100.00
85ASADMU Dale Murphy
85ASADS Darryl Strawberry 12.00 30.00
85ASAEM Edgar Martinez 15.00 40.00
85ASAGS George Springer 8.00 20.00
85ASAHM Hideki Matsui
85ASAJAL Jose Altuve 10.00 25.00
85ASAJB Johnny Bench
85ASAJM Jeff McNeil 15.00 40.00
85ASAJME John Means
85ASAKB Kris Bryant
85ASAKGJ Ken Griffey Jr.
85ASAKMA Ketel Marte 12.00 30.00
85ASALG Lucas Giolito 10.00 25.00
85ASAMM Mark McGwire 30.00 80.00
85ASAMMU Max Muncy 8.00 20.00
85ASAMS Max Scherzer 25.00 60.00
85ASAMSO Mike Soroka 15.00 40.00
85ASAMT Mike Trout
85ASANA Nolan Arenado
85ASAOS Ozzie Smith
85ASAPA Pete Alonso 50.00 120.00
85ASAPG Paul Goldschmidt 10.00 25.00
85ASARAJ Ronald Acuna Jr. 60.00 150.00
85ASARC Roger Clemens
85ASARH Rickey Henderson
85ASARJ Reggie Jackson
85ASARS Ryne Sandberg
85ASARYO Robin Yount 25.00 60.00
85ASASB Shane Bieber 20.00 50.00
85ASAWB Wade Boggs 30.00 80.00
85ASAWC Willson Contreras 8.00 20.00
85ASAWCL Will Clark 25.00 60.00

2020 Topps '85 Topps All Stars Autographs Gold

*GOLD: .5X TO 1.2X BASIC
STATED ODDS 1:2032 HOBBY
STATED PRINT RUN 50 SER.#'d SETS
EXCHANGE DEADLINE 4/30/2022

2020 Topps '85 Topps All Stars Autographs Red

*RED: .6X TO 1.5X BASIC
STATED ODDS 1:3216 HOBBY
STATED PRINT RUN 25 SER.#'d SETS
SER.1 EXCH DEADLINE 12/31/2021

2020 Topps '85 Topps All Stars Relics

STATED ODDS 1:74 HOBBY
85ASRAB Alex Bregman 2.50 6.00
85ASRAJ Aaron Judge 6.00 15.00
85ASRAP Albert Pujols 3.00 8.00
85ASRBL Barry Larkin 6.00 15.00
85ASRBP Buster Posey 3.00 8.00
85ASRCB Cody Bellinger 5.00 12.00
85ASRCF Carlton Fisk 6.00 15.00
85ASRCJ Chipper Jones 6.00 15.00
85ASRCK Clayton Kershaw 5.00 12.00
85ASRCR Cal Ripken Jr. 6.00 15.00
85ASRCY Christian Yelich 3.00 8.00
85ASRDM Don Mattingly 12.00 30.00
85ASRDO David Ortiz 4.00 10.00
85ASRDS Darryl Strawberry 6.00 15.00
85ASRDW David Wright 6.00 15.00
85ASRDWI Dave Winfield 4.00 10.00
85ASREM Eddie Murray 6.00 15.00
85ASRFL Francisco Lindor 2.50 6.00
85ASRFT Frank Thomas 4.00 10.00
85ASRGB George Brett 8.00 20.00
85ASRGS George Springer 2.00 5.00
85ASRGT Gleyber Torres 5.00 12.00
85ASRI Ichiro 3.00 8.00
85ASRJA Jose Altuve 2.00 5.00
85ASRJB Javier Baez 3.00 8.00
85ASRJM Joe Mauer 2.00 5.00
85ASRKB Kris Bryant 3.00 8.00
85ASRKG Ken Griffey Jr. 10.00 25.00
85ASRMC Miguel Cabrera 2.50 6.00
85ASRMM Mark McGwire 6.00 15.00
85ASRMS Max Scherzer 2.50 6.00
85ASRMT Masahiro Tanaka 6.00 15.00
85ASRMTR Mike Trout 10.00 25.00
85ASRNR Nolan Ryan 10.00 25.00
85ASROS Ozzie Smith 5.00 12.00
85ASRPA Pete Alonso 6.00 15.00
85ASRPM Paul Molitor
85ASRRA Ronald Acuna Jr. 6.00 15.00
85ASRRC Roger Clemens 5.00 12.00
85ASRRH Rickey Henderson 4.00 10.00
85ASRRS Ryne Sandberg 8.00 20.00
85ASRTG Tony Gwynn 4.00 10.00
85ASRWB Wade Boggs 5.00 12.00
85ASRWC Willson Contreras 2.50 6.00
85ASRWCL Will Clark 6.00 15.00
85ASRYM Yadier Molina 2.50 6.00

2020 Topps '85 Topps All Stars Relics Black

*BLACK: .6X TO 1.5X BASIC
STATED ODDS 1:193 HOBBY
STATED PRINT RUN 199 SER.#'d SETS
85ASRDG Dwight Gooden 6.00 15.00

2020 Topps '85 Topps All Stars Relics Gold

*GOLD: 1X TO 2.5X BASIC
STATED ODDS 1:1259 HOBBY
STATED PRINT RUN 50 SER.#'d SETS
85ASRDG Dwight Gooden 10.00 25.00
85ASRDMU Dale Murphy 10.00 25.00
85ASRJR Jim Rice 8.00 20.00
85ASRTR Tim Raines 5.00 12.00

2020 Topps '85 Topps All Stars Relics Red

*RED: 1.5X TO 4X BASIC
STATED ODDS 1:2517 HOBBY
STATED PRINT RUN 25 SER.#'d SETS
85ASRDG Dwight Gooden 15.00 40.00
85ASRDMU Dale Murphy 15.00 40.00
85ASRJR Jim Rice 12.00 30.00
85ASRTR Tim Raines 8.00 20.00

2020 Topps '85 Topps Autographs

SER.1 STATED ODDS 1:656 HOBBY
SER.2 STATED ODDS 1:591 HOBBY
SER.1 EXCH DEADLINE 12/31/2021
SER.2 EXCH DEADLINE 4/30/2022
85BAAKN Andrew Knizner S2 2.50 6.00
85BADJ Derek Jeter S2 EXCH 200.00 500.00
85BALA Luis Arraez S2 6.00 15.00
85BALTH Lane Thomas S2 5.00 12.00
85BAMBE Matt Beaty S2 3.00 8.00
85BAZP Zach Plesac S2 10.00 25.00
85AAA Adbert Alzolay S2 3.00 8.00
85AAAQ Aristides Aquino
85AAC Aaron Civale 4.00 10.00
85AAD Andre Dawson 20.00 50.00
85AAJ Aaron Judge EXCH 100.00 250.00
85AAJO Andruw Jones S2 8.00 20.00
85AAN Aaron Nola 6.00 15.00
85AAP A.J. Puk
85AARI Austin Riley 20.00 50.00
85AARZ Anthony Rizzo S2 20.00 50.00
85AAT Abraham Toro 3.00 8.00
85AAY Alex Young 2.50 6.00
85ABB Bo Bichette 50.00 120.00
85ABBE Brock Burke 2.50 6.00
85ABBU Byron Buxton S2 6.00 15.00
85ABHA Bryce Harper S2 125.00 300.00
85ABL Brandon Lowe S2 6.00 15.00
85ABM Brendan McKay S2 4.00 10.00
85ABO Bobby Bradley 3.00 8.00
85ACB Cavan Biggio 15.00 40.00
85ACC Carlos Carrasco S2 2.50 6.00
85ACF Carlton Fisk 25.00 60.00
85ACJ Chipper Jones S2 50.00 120.00
85ACK Carter Kieboom 10.00 25.00
85ACKE Clayton Kershaw 60.00 150.00
85ACP Chris Paddack S2 4.00 10.00
85ACR Cal Ripken Jr. 30.00 80.00
85ACY Christian Yelich S2 30.00 80.00
85ADC Dylan Cease 5.00 12.00
85ADE Dennis Eckersley 8.00 20.00
85ADH Dakota Hudson S2 3.00 8.00
85ADHA Darwinzon Hernandez S2 2.50 6.00
85ADJ Danny Jansen S2 2.50 6.00
85ADL DJ LeMahieu 25.00 60.00
85ADM Don Mattingly 50.00 120.00
85ADMA Dustin May 20.00 50.00
85ADMU Dale Murphy S2 12.00 30.00
85ADO David Ortiz 50.00 120.00
85ADPD Dustin Pedroia 20.00 50.00
85ADPE David Peralta S2 2.50 6.00
85ADS Dansby Swanson 12.00 30.00
85ADST Darryl Strawberry 20.00 50.00
85AEJ Eloy Jimenez 15.00 40.00
85AFT Fernando Tatis Jr. 100.00 250.00
85AFTH Frank Thomas 50.00 120.00
85AGC Gerrit Cole 30.00 80.00
85AGCA Griffin Canning S2 4.00 10.00
85AGL Gavin Lux 50.00 120.00
85AHA Hank Aaron 100.00 250.00
85AHH Hunter Harvey 6.00 15.00
85AHM Hideki Matsui 30.00 80.00
85AID Isan Diaz 6.00 15.00
85AJAA Jose Altuve 15.00 40.00
85AJB Jake Bauers S2 3.00 8.00
85AJBN Johnny Bench 25.00 60.00
85AJDA Jaylin Davis S2 4.00 10.00
85AJFE Junior Fernandez 2.50 6.00
85AJFR Jake Fraley S2 3.00 8.00
85AJL Jesus Luzardo S2 12.00 30.00
85AJMA J.D. Martinez S2 12.00 30.00
85AJR Jake Rogers 8.00 20.00
85AJRA Jose Ramirez S2 8.00 20.00
85AJRI Jim Rice S2 15.00 40.00
85AJS Juan Soto 50.00 120.00
85AJSM John Smoltz 20.00 50.00
85AJV Joey Votto 30.00 80.00
85AJVA Jason Varitek 20.00 50.00
85AJY Jordan Yamamoto 3.00 8.00
85AKB Kris Bryant S2 30.00 80.00
85AKHI Keston Hiura 12.00 30.00
85AKL Kyle Lewis 20.00 50.00
85AKT Kyle Tucker S2 8.00 20.00
85AKW Kerry Wood 10.00 25.00
85ALA Logan Allen 2.50 6.00
85ALB Lou Brock S2 25.00 60.00
85ALG Lourdes Gurriel Jr. S2 3.00 8.00
85ALM Lance McCullers Jr. 4.00 10.00
85ALR Luis Robert S2 150.00 400.00
85ALS Luis Severino S2 5.00 12.00
85ALW Logan Webb 3.00 8.00
85AMB Michel Baez S2 2.50 6.00
85AMCL Mike Clevinger 8.00 20.00
85AMD Mauricio Dubon S2 3.00 8.00
85AMG Mark Grace S2 15.00 40.00
85AM Mike Mussina S2 12.00 30.00
85AMMU Max Muncy 8.00 20.00
85AMR Mariano Rivera 100.00 250.00
85AMSO Mike Soroka 12.00 30.00
85AMT Mike Trout 300.00 600.00
85AMTH Matt Thaiss S2 5.00 12.00
85AMU Andres Munoz 3.00 8.00
85ANGA Nomar Garciaparra 30.00 80.00
85ANH Nico Hoerner 20.00 50.00
85ANR Nolan Ryan 100.00 250.00
85ANSE Nick Senzel S2 8.00 20.00
85ANSO Nick Solak 8.00 20.00
85AOS Ozzie Smith 25.00 60.00
85APAL Pete Alonso 40.00 100.00
85APS Patrick Sandoval 4.00 10.00
85ARAC Ronald Acuna Jr. 75.00 200.00
85ARAL Roberto Alomar 20.00 50.00
85ARCL Roger Clemens 60.00 150.00
85ARG Robel Garcia 6.00 15.00
85ARHO Rhys Hoskins S2 12.00 30.00
85ASB Shane Bieber S2 20.00 50.00
85ASB Seth Brown 2.50 6.00
85ASH Sam Hilliard 4.00 10.00
85ASM Sean Murphy 8.00 20.00
85ASO Shohei Ohtani 75.00 200.00
85ATA Tim Anderson 6.00 15.00
85ATB Trevor Bauer S2 8.00 20.00
85ATD Travis Demeritte 6.00 15.00
85ATG Tom Glavine 40.00 100.00
85ATG Trent Grisham S2 12.00 30.00
85ATJZ T.J. Zeuch S2 2.50 6.00
85ATTO Touki Toussaint S2 3.00 8.00
85AVG Vladimir Guerrero Jr. 40.00 100.00
85AVGJ Vladimir Guerrero S2 12.00 30.00
85AWB Wade Boggs 30.00 80.00
85AWBU Walker Buehler S2 20.00 50.00
85AWCA Willi Castro S2 10.00 25.00
85AWCO Willson Contreras 10.00 25.00
85AXB Xander Bogaerts 25.00 60.00
85AYA Yordan Alvarez 75.00 200.00

2020 Topps '85 Topps Autographs Black

*BLACK: .5X TO 1.2X BASIC
SER.1 STATED ODDS 1:1927 HOBBY
SER.2 STATED ODDS 1:765 HOBBY
PRINT RUNS B/WN 112-199 COPIES PER
SER.1 EXCH DEADLINE 12/31/2021
SER.2 EXCH DEADLINE 4/30/2022
85AAP A.J. Puk/199 15.00 40.00

2020 Topps '85 Topps Autographs Gold

*GOLD: .6X TO 1.5X BASIC
SER.1 STATED ODDS 1:6360 HOBBY
SER.2 STATED ODDS 1:2032 HOBBY
STATED PRINT RUN 50 SER.#'d SETS
SER.1 EXCH DEADLINE 12/31/2021
SER.2 EXCH DEADLINE 4/30/2022
85AAAQ Aristides Aquino/50 50.00 120.00
85ABB Bo Bichette/50 100.00 250.00
85ACF Carlton Fisk/50 30.00 80.00
85ADM Don Mattingly/50 60.00 150.00
85ADPD Dustin Pedroia/50 30.00 80.00
85AGC Gerrit Cole/50 40.00 100.00
85AHM Hideki Matsui/50 40.00 100.00
85AJS Juan Soto/50 60.00 150.00
85AJSM John Smoltz/50 25.00 60.00
85AJVA Jason Varitek/50 25.00 60.00
85AOS Ozzie Smith/50 30.00 80.00
85ARAC Ronald Acuna Jr./50 100.00 250.00
85ARAL Roberto Alomar/47 25.00 60.00
85AWCO Willson Contreras/50 15.00 40.00
85AXB Xander Bogaerts/50 30.00 80.00

2020 Topps '85 Topps Autographs Red

*RED: .75X TO 2X BASIC
SER.1 STATED ODDS 1:805 HOBBY
SER.2 STATED ODDS 1:3216 HOBBY
PRINT RUNS B/WN 21-25 COPIES PER
SER.1 EXCH DEADLINE 12/31/2021
SER.2 EXCH DEADLINE 4/30/2022
85AAAQ Aristides Aquino/25 60.00 150.00
85ABB Bo Bichette/25 125.00 300.00
85ABHA Bryce Harper/25 150.00 400.00
85ACF Carlton Fisk/25 40.00 100.00
85ACKE Clayton Kershaw/25 75.00 200.00
85ACR Cal Ripken Jr./25 60.00 150.00
85ADM Don Mattingly/25 75.00 200.00
85ADO David Ortiz/25 60.00 150.00
85ADPD Dustin Pedroia/25 40.00 100.00
85AGC Gerrit Cole/25 50.00 120.00
85AHA Hank Aaron/25 125.00 300.00
85AHM Hideki Matsui/25 50.00 120.00
85AJS Juan Soto/25 75.00 200.00
85AJSM John Smoltz/25 30.00 80.00
85AJVA Jason Varitek/25 30.00 80.00
85AMR Mariano Rivera/25 125.00 300.00
85AMT Mike Trout/25 400.00 800.00
85ANR Nolan Ryan/25 125.00 300.00
85AOS Ozzie Smith/24 40.00 100.00
85ARAC Ronald Acuna Jr./25 125.00 300.00
85ARAL Roberto Alomar/21 30.00 80.00
85ARCL Roger Clemens/25 75.00 200.00
85ASO Shohei Ohtani/25 100.00 250.00
85AWB Wade Boggs/25 40.00 100.00
85AWCO Willson Contreras/25 20.00 50.00
85AXB Xander Bogaerts/25 40.00 100.00

2020 Topps '85 Topps Relics

SER.1 STATED ODDS 1:49 HOBBY
SER.2 STATED ODDS 1:74 HOBBY
85RAB Alex Bregman 2.50 6.00
85RAJ Aaron Judge 6.00 15.00
85RAP Albert Pujols 3.00 8.00
85RBH Bryce Harper 6.00 15.00
85RBL Barry Larkin 6.00 15.00
85RBP Buster Posey 3.00 8.00
85RCB Charlie Blackmon 2.50 6.00
85RCBE Cody Bellinger 5.00 12.00
85RCR Cal Ripken Jr. 6.00 15.00
85RDM Don Mattingly 12.00 30.00
85REM Eddie Murray 6.00 15.00
85RFF Freddie Freeman 3.00 8.00
85RFL Francisco Lindor 2.50 6.00
85RFT Fernando Tatis Jr. 8.00 20.00
85RFTH Frank Thomas 4.00 10.00
85RGB George Brett 8.00 20.00
85RGS George Springer 2.00 5.00
85RGT Gleyber Torres 5.00 12.00
85RHR Hyun-Jin Ryu 2.00 5.00
85RJBZ Javier Baez 3.00 8.00
85RJS Juan Soto 8.00 20.00
85RKB Kris Bryant 3.00 8.00
85RKG Ken Griffey Jr. 10.00 25.00
85RKH Keston Hiura 3.00 8.00
85RMC Miguel Cabrera 2.50 6.00
85RMK Max Kepler 2.00 5.00
85RMM Manny Machado 2.50 6.00
85RMMG Mark McGwire 6.00 15.00
85RMS Max Scherzer 2.50 6.00
85RMT Mike Trout 10.00 25.00
85RNA Nolan Arenado 3.00 8.00
85RNR Nolan Ryan 10.00 25.00
85ROS Ozzie Smith 5.00 12.00
85RPA Pete Alonso 6.00 15.00
85RPG Paul Goldschmidt 2.50 6.00
85RRA Ronald Acuna Jr. 6.00 15.00
85RRC Roger Clemens 5.00 12.00
85RRD Rafael Devers 3.00 8.00
85RRH Rickey Henderson 4.00 10.00
85RRHO Rhys Hoskins 4.00 10.00
85RRJ Reggie Jackson 6.00 15.00
85RRS Ryne Sandberg 8.00 20.00
85RRY Robin Yount 5.00 12.00
85RTG Tony Gwynn 4.00 10.00
85RVG Vladimir Guerrero Jr. 5.00 12.00
85RWB Wade Boggs 5.00 12.00
85RWC Will Clark 6.00 15.00
85RWM Whit Merrifield 2.50 6.00
85RXB Xander Bogaerts 2.50 6.00
85TRAJ Aaron Judge S2 6.00 15.00
85TRAM Andrew McCutchen S2 2.50 6.00
85TRAN Aaron Nola S2 2.50 6.00
85TRAR Anthony Rizzo S2 4.00 10.00
85TRBB Bo Bichette S2 12.00 30.00
85TRCK Clayton Kershaw S2 5.00 12.00
85TRCP Chris Paddack S2 2.50 6.00
85TRCS Corey Seager S2 2.50 6.00
85TRCSA Chris Sale S2 2.50 6.00
85TRCSO Carlos Santana S2 2.00 5.00
85TRCY Christian Yelich S2 3.00 8.00
85TRDV Dan Vogelbach S2 1.50 4.00
85TREA Elvis Andrus S2 2.00 5.00
85TRES Eugenio Suarez S2 2.00 5.00
85TRGS Gary Sanchez S2 2.50 6.00
85TRGSA Giancarlo Stanton S2 2.50 6.00
85TRJA Jose Altuve S2 2.00 5.00
85TRJd Jacob deGrom S2 4.00 10.00
85TRJF Jack Flaherty S2 2.00 5.00
85TRJG Joey Gallo S2 2.50 6.00
85TRJM J.D. Martinez S2 2.50 6.00
85TRJR J.T. Realmuto S2 2.50 6.00
85TRJS Jorge Soler S2 2.50 6.00
85TRJV Joey Votto S2 2.50 6.00
85TRJVE Justin Verlander S2 2.50 6.00
85TRKS Kyle Schwarber S2 2.50 6.00
85TRLC Lorenzo Cain S2 1.50 4.00
85TRLG Lourdes Gurriel Jr. S2 2.00 5.00
85TRLS Luis Severino S2 2.00 5.00
85TRMCO Michael Conforto S2 2.00 5.00
85TRMO Matt Olson S2 1.50 4.00
85TRMS Marcus Semien S2 1.50 4.00
85TRMSA Miguel Sano S2 2.00 5.00
85TRMT Mike Trout S2 10.00 25.00
85TRNS Noah Syndergaard S2 2.00 5.00
85TROA Ozzie Albies S2 2.50 6.00
85TRPD Paul DeJong S2 2.50 6.00
85TRRA Ronald Acuna Jr. S2 6.00 15.00
85TRRC Robinson Cano S2 2.00 5.00
85TRSB Shane Bieber S2 2.50 6.00
85TRSG Sonny Gray S2 2.00 5.00
85TRSO Shohei Ohtani S2 6.00 15.00
85TRSS Stephen Strasburg S2 2.50 6.00
85TRTS Trevor Story S2 2.50 6.00
85TRWB Walker Buehler S2 3.00 8.00
85TRYA Yordan Alvarez S2 6.00 15.00
85TRYM Yadier Molina S2 2.50 6.00

2020 Topps '85 Topps Relics Black

*BLACK: .6X TO 1.5X BASIC
SER.1 STATED ODDS 1:717 HOBBY
SER.2 STATED ODDS 1:193 HOBBY
STATED PRINT RUN 199 SER.#'d SETS
85RMB Mookie Betts 8.00 20.00
85TRER Eddie Rosario S2 3.00 8.00
85TRMY Mike Yastrzemski S2 6.00 15.00

2020 Topps '85 Topps Relics Gold

*GOLD: 1X TO 2.5X BASIC
SER.1 STATED ODDS 1:2856 HOBBY
SER.2 STATED ODDS 1:1259 HOBBY
STATED PRINT RUN 50 SER.#'d SETS
85RMB Mookie Betts 12.00 30.00
85TRER Eddie Rosario S2 5.00 12.00
85TRMY Mike Yastrzemski S2 10.00 25.00
85TRSB Shane Bieber S2 6.00 15.00

2020 Topps '85 Topps Relics Red

*RED: 1.5X TO 4X BASIC
SER.1 STATED ODDS 1:5701 HOBBY
SER.2 STATED ODDS 1:2517 HOBBY
STATED PRINT RUN 25 SER.#'d SETS
85RMB Mookie Betts 20.00 50.00
85TRBB Bo Bichette S2 40.00 100.00
85TRER Eddie Rosario S2 8.00 20.00
85TRMY Mike Yastrzemski S2 15.00 40.00
85TRSB Shane Bieber S2 10.00 25.00

2020 Topps '85 Topps Silver Pack Chrome

85C1 Mike Trout 5.00 12.00
85C2 Shohei Ohtani 1.25 3.00
85C3 Ronald Acuna Jr. 4.00 10.00
85C4 Cal Ripken Jr. 3.00 8.00
85C5 Rafael Devers 1.25 3.00
85C6 Nico Hoerner 2.50 6.00
85C7 Mookie Betts 2.00 5.00
85C8 Kris Bryant 1.25 3.00
85C9 Ryne Sandberg 2.00 5.00
85C10 Dylan Cease 1.25 3.00
85C11 Frank Thomas 1.00 2.50
85C12 Francisco Lindor 1.00 2.50
85C13 Nolan Arenado 1.25 3.00
85C14 Jose Altuve .75 2.00
85C15 Nolan Ryan 3.00 8.00
85C16 Yordan Alvarez 3.00 8.00
85C17 Whit Merrifield 1.00 2.50
85C18 Clayton Kershaw 2.00 5.00
85C19 Dustin May 2.50 6.00
85C20 Jordan Yamamoto .75 2.00
85C21 Christian Yelich 1.25 3.00
85C22 Keston Hiura 1.25 3.00
85C23 Max Kepler .75 2.00
85C24 Darryl Strawberry .60 1.50
85C25 Jacob deGrom 1.00 2.50
85C26 Pete Alonso 2.50 6.00
85C27 Aaron Judge 2.50 6.00
85C28 Don Mattingly 3.00 8.00
85C29 Gleyber Torres 2.00 5.00
85C30 Mark McGwire 1.50 4.00
85C31 Bryce Harper 1.50 4.00
85C32 Manny Machado 1.00 2.50
85C33 Fernando Tatis Jr. 4.00 10.00
85C34 Sean Murphy 1.00 2.50
85C35 Will Clark 2.50 6.00
85C36 Ichiro 1.25 3.00
85C37 Ken Griffey Jr. 3.00 8.00
85C38 Paul Goldschmidt 1.00 2.50
85C39 Kyle Lewis 5.00 12.00
85C40 Brendan McKay 1.00 2.50
85C41 Bo Bichette 5.00 12.00
85C42 Vladimir Guerrero Jr. 2.00 5.00
85C43 Juan Soto 3.00 8.00
85C44 Matt Thaiss .75 2.00
85C45 Zac Gallen 1.50 4.00
85C46 Aristides Aquino 1.25 3.00
85C47 Robel Garcia .60 1.50
85C48 Gavin Lux 4.00 10.00
85C49 Jesus Luzardo 1.25 3.00
85C50 Trent Grisham 2.50 6.00

2020 Topps '85 Topps Silver Pack Chrome Black Refractors

*BLACK REF: .75X TO 2X BASIC
RANDOM INSERTS IN PACKS
STATED PRINT RUN 199 SER.#'d SETS
85C16 Yordan Alvarez 12.00 30.00
85C41 Bo Bichette 15.00 40.00
85C48 Gavin Lux 15.00 40.00

2020 Topps '85 Topps Silver Pack Chrome Blue Refractors

*BLUE REF: 1X TO 2.5X BASIC
RANDOM INSERTS IN PACKS
STATED PRINT RUN 150 SER.#'d SETS
85C16 Yordan Alvarez 15.00 40.00
85C41 Bo Bichette 20.00 50.00
85C48 Gavin Lux 20.00 50.00

2020 Topps '85 Topps Silver Pack Chrome Gold Refractors

*GOLD REF: 2.5X TO 6X BASIC
RANDOM INSERTS IN PACKS
STATED PRINT RUN 50 SER.#'d SETS
85C1 Mike Trout 40.00 100.00
85C16 Yordan Alvarez 40.00 100.00
85C37 Ken Griffey Jr. 30.00 80.00
85C41 Bo Bichette 50.00 120.00
85C48 Gavin Lux 50.00 120.00

2020 Topps '85 Topps Silver Pack Chrome Green Refractors

*GREEN REF: 1.2X TO 3X BASIC
RANDOM INSERTS IN PACKS
STATED PRINT RUN 99 SER.#'d SETS
85C16 Yordan Alvarez 20.00 50.00
85C41 Bo Bichette 25.00 60.00
85C48 Gavin Lux 25.00 60.00

2020 Topps '85 Topps Silver Pack Chrome Orange Refractors

*ORANGE REF: 4X TO 10X BASIC
RANDOM INSERTS IN PACKS
STATED PRINT RUN 25 SER.#'d SETS
85C1 Mike Trout 60.00 150.00
85C16 Yordan Alvarez 60.00 150.00
85C37 Ken Griffey Jr. 50.00 120.00
85C41 Bo Bichette 75.00 200.00
85C48 Gavin Lux 75.00 200.00

2020 Topps '85 Topps Silver Pack Chrome Purple Refractors

*PURPLE REF: 1.2X TO 3X BASIC
RANDOM INSERTS IN PACKS
STATED PRINT RUN 75 SER.#'d SETS
85C16 Yordan Alvarez 20.00 50.00
85C41 Bo Bichette 25.00 60.00
85C48 Gavin Lux 25.00 60.00

2020 Topps '85 Topps Silver Pack Chrome Series 2

85TC1 Ketel Marte .75 2.00
85TC2 Shogo Akiyama 1.00 2.50
85TC3 Chipper Jones 1.00 2.50
85TC4 Ozzie Albies 1.00 2.50
85TC5 Hunter Harvey 1.00 2.50
85TC6 Xander Bogaerts 1.00 2.50
85TC7 Albert Alzolay .75 2.00
85TC8 Anthony Rizzo 1.50 4.00
85TC9 Javier Baez 1.25 3.00
85TC10 Eloy Jimenez 2.00 5.00
85TC11 Zack Collins .75 2.00
85TC12 Joey Votto 1.00 2.50
85TC13 Aaron Civale 1.00 2.50
85TC14 Kwang-Hyun Kim 2.00 5.00
85TC15 Sam Hilliard 1.00 2.50
85TC16 Jake Rogers .60 1.50
85TC17 Alex Bregman 1.00 2.50
85TC18 Justin Verlander 1.00 2.50
85TC19 Abraham Toro .75 2.00
85TC20 Jose Urquidy .75 2.00
85TC21 George Brett 2.00 5.00
85TC22 Jorge Soler 1.00 2.50
85TC23 Cody Bellinger 2.00 5.00
85TC24 Isan Diaz 1.00 2.50
85TC25 Robin Yount 1.00 2.50
85TC26 Noah Syndergaard .75 2.00
85TC27 Shun Yamaguchi .75 2.00
85TC28 Masahiro Tanaka 1.00 2.50
85TC29 A.J. Puk 1.25 3.00
85TC30 Sheldon Neuse .75 2.00
85TC31 Matt Chapman 1.00 2.50
85TC32 Rickey Henderson 1.00 2.50
85TC33 Roberto Clemente 2.50 6.00
85TC34 Tony Gwynn 1.00 2.50
85TC35 Giancarlo Stanton 1.00 2.50
85TC36 Mauricio Dubon .75 2.00
85TC37 Jaylin Davis 1.00 2.50
85TC38 Buster Posey 1.25 3.00
85TC39 Justin Dunn .75 2.00
85TC40 Randy Johnson 1.00 2.50
85TC41 Randy Arozarena 5.00 12.00
85TC42 Yadier Molina 1.00 2.50
85TC43 Brandon Lowe 1.00 2.50
85TC44 Nick Solak 1.00 2.50
85TC45 Josh Rojas .60 1.50
85TC46 Danny Mendick .75 2.00
85TC47 Anthony Kay .60 1.50
85TC48 Luis Robert 15.00 40.00
85TC49 Carter Kieboom .75 2.00
85TC50 Max Scherzer 1.00 2.50

2020 Topps '85 Topps Silver Pack Chrome Series 2 Black Refractors

*BLACK REF: .75X TO 2X BASIC
RANDOM INSERTS IN PACKS
STATED PRINT RUN 199 SER.#'d SETS
85TC2 Shogo Akiyama 10.00 25.00
85TC3 Chipper Jones 5.00 12.00
85TC21 George Brett 6.00 15.00
85TC32 Rickey Henderson 8.00 20.00
85TC33 Roberto Clemente 8.00 20.00
85TC34 Tony Gwynn 6.00 15.00
85TC38 Buster Posey 3.00 8.00
85TC48 Luis Robert 40.00 100.00

2020 Topps '85 Topps Silver Pack Chrome Series 2 Blue Refractors

*BLUE REF: 1X TO 2.5X BASIC
RANDOM INSERTS IN PACKS
STATED PRINT RUN 150 SER.#'d SETS
85TC2 Shogo Akiyama 12.00 30.00
85TC3 Chipper Jones 6.00 15.00
85TC21 George Brett 8.00 20.00
85TC32 Rickey Henderson 10.00 25.00
85TC33 Roberto Clemente 10.00 25.00
85TC34 Tony Gwynn 8.00 20.00
85TC38 Buster Posey 4.00 10.00
85TC48 Luis Robert 50.00 120.00

2020 Topps '85 Topps Silver Pack Chrome Series 2 Gold Refractors

*GOLD REF: 2.5X TO 6X BASIC
RANDOM INSERTS IN PACKS
STATED PRINT RUN 50 SER.#'d SETS
85TC2 Shogo Akiyama 30.00 80.00
85TC3 Chipper Jones 15.00 40.00
85TC21 George Brett 20.00 50.00
85TC32 Rickey Henderson 25.00 60.00
85TC33 Roberto Clemente 25.00 60.00
85TC34 Tony Gwynn 20.00 50.00
85TC38 Buster Posey 10.00 25.00
85TC48 Luis Robert 125.00 300.00

2020 Topps '85 Topps Silver Pack Chrome Series 2 Green Refractors

*GREEN REF: 1.2X TO 3X BASIC
RANDOM INSERTS IN PACKS
STATED PRINT RUN 99 SER.#'d SETS
85TC2 Shogo Akiyama 15.00 40.00
85TC3 Chipper Jones 8.00 20.00
85TC21 George Brett 10.00 25.00
85TC32 Rickey Henderson 12.00 30.00
85TC33 Roberto Clemente 12.00 30.00
85TC34 Tony Gwynn 10.00 25.00
85TC38 Buster Posey 5.00 12.00
85TC48 Luis Robert 60.00 150.00

2020 Topps '85 Topps Silver Pack Chrome Series 2 Orange Refractors

*ORANGE REF: 4X TO 10X BASIC
RANDOM INSERTS IN PACKS
STATED PRINT RUN 25 SER.#'d SETS
85TC2 Shogo Akiyama 50.00 120.00
85TC3 Chipper Jones 25.00 60.00
85TC21 George Brett 30.00 80.00
85TC32 Rickey Henderson 40.00 100.00
85TC33 Roberto Clemente 40.00 100.00
85TC34 Tony Gwynn 30.00 80.00
85TC38 Buster Posey 15.00 40.00
85TC48 Luis Robert 200.00 500.00

2020 Topps '85 Topps Silver Pack Chrome Series 2 Purple Refractors

*PURPLE REF: 1.2X TO 3X BASIC
RANDOM INSERTS IN PACKS
STATED PRINT RUN 75 SER.#'d SETS
85TC2 Shogo Akiyama 15.00 40.00
85TC3 Chipper Jones 8.00 20.00
85TC21 George Brett 10.00 25.00
85TC32 Rickey Henderson 12.00 30.00
85TC33 Roberto Clemente 12.00 30.00
85TC34 Tony Gwynn 10.00 25.00
85TC38 Buster Posey 5.00 12.00
85TC48 Luis Robert 60.00 150.00

2020 Topps '85 Topps Silver Pack Chrome Autographs

RANDOM INSERTS IN SILVER PACKS
PRINT RUNS B/WN 10-299 COPIES PER
NO PRICING ON QTY 15 OR LESS
*ORANGE/25: 1X TO 2.5X p/r 199-299
*ORANGE/25: .75X TO 2X p/r 50
*ORANGE/25: .5X TO 1.2X p/r 30
85C3 Ronald Acuna Jr./30 75.00 200.00
85C5 Rafael Devers/30 30.00 80.00
85C6 Nico Hoerner/299 12.00 30.00
85C10 Dylan Cease/299 15.00 40.00
85C14 Jose Altuve
85C16 Yordan Alvarez/199 75.00 200.00
85C17 Whit Merrifield/50 10.00 25.00
85C19 Dustin May/299 12.00 30.00
85C20 Jordan Yamamoto/199 8.00 20.00
85C22 Keston Hiura/50 30.00 80.00

85C23 Max Kepler/30 15.00 40.00
85C24 Darryl Strawberry/30 25.00 60.00
85C25 Jacob deGrom/30 40.00 100.00
85C26 Pete Alonso/30 60.00 150.00
85C27 Aaron Judge
85C33 Fernando Tatis Jr./30 75.00 200.00
85C34 Sean Murphy/299 5.00 12.00
85C39 Kyle Lewis/299 12.00 30.00
85C40 Brendan McKay/199 10.00 25.00
85C41 Bo Bichette/199 75.00 200.00
85C42 Vladimir Guerrero Jr./30 100.00 250.00
85C43 Juan Soto
85C44 Matt Thaiss/299 10.00 25.00
85C46 Aristides Aquino/299 40.00 100.00
85C47 Robel Garcia/299 3.00 8.00
85C48 Gavin Lux/199 60.00 150.00
85C49 Jesus Luzardo/299 20.00 50.00
85C50 Trent Grisham/299 6.00 15.00

2020 Topps 2030

COMPLETE SET (20) 12.00 30.00
STATED ODDS 1:6 HOBBY
T20301 Mike Trout 1.50 4.00
T20302 Aaron Judge .75 2.00
T20303 Luis Robert 6.00 15.00
T20304 Francisco Lindor .30 .75
T20305 Christian Yelich .40 1.00
T20306 Gavin Lux 1.25 3.00
T20307 Ronald Acuna Jr. 1.25 3.00
T20308 Bo Bichette 4.00 10.00
T20309 Kris Bryant .40 1.00
T203010 Nolan Arenado .40 1.00
T203011 Pete Alonso .75 2.00
T203012 Juan Soto 1.00 2.50
T203013 Fernando Tatis Jr. 1.25 3.00
T203014 Bryce Harper .50 1.25
T203015 Alex Bregman .30 .75
T203016 Mookie Betts .60 1.50
T203017 Cody Bellinger .60 1.50
T203018 Vladimir Guerrero Jr. .60 1.50
T203019 Javier Baez .40 1.00
T203020 Shohei Ohtani .40 1.00

2020 Topps Baseball Stars Autographs

STATED ODDS 1:580 HOBBY
EXCHANGE DEADLINE 12/31/2021
*BLACK/199: .5X TO 1.2X BASIC
*GOLD/50: .6X TO 1.5X BASIC
*RED/25: .75X TO 2X BASIC
BSAAA Adbert Alzolay 3.00 8.00
BSAAAQ Aristides Aquino 15.00 40.00
BSAAC Aaron Civale 4.00 10.00
BSAAM Andres Munoz
BSAAN Austin Nola 4.00 10.00
BSAAR Austin Riley 15.00 40.00
BSAARI Anthony Rizzo 20.00 50.00
BSAAT Abraham Toro 3.00 8.00
BSABA Bryan Abreu 2.50 6.00
BSABB Bobby Bradley 3.00 8.00
BSABBU Brock Burke 2.50 6.00
BSABO Bo Bichette 40.00 100.00
BSABR Bryan Reynolds 3.00 8.00
BSACD Corey Dickerson 3.00 8.00
BSACF Cecil Fielder 15.00 40.00
BSACH Cesar Hernandez 2.50 6.00
BSACK Clayton Kershaw
BSACKE Clayton Kershaw
BSACP Chris Paddack 12.00 30.00
BSACW Christian Walker 3.00 8.00
BSACY Christian Yelich
BSADF David Fletcher 4.00 10.00
BSADM Dustin May 12.00 30.00
BSADM Daniel Mengden 2.50 6.00
BSADME Danny Mendick 3.00 8.00
BSADPD Daniel Ponce de Leon 2.50 6.00
BSADR Dereck Rodriguez 2.50 6.00
BSADSR Darryl Strawberry 20.00 50.00
BSAEE Eduardo Escobar 2.50 6.00
BSAFP Freddy Peralta 2.50 6.00
BSAFT Frank Thomas 30.00 80.00
BSAFT Fernando Tatis Jr. 60.00 150.00
BSAGH Garrett Hampson 2.50 6.00
BSAGL Gavin Lux 40.00 100.00
BSAGL Gavin Lux 40.00 100.00
BSAGS George Springer 8.00 20.00
BSAGU Gio Urshela 12.00 30.00
BSAHH Hunter Harvey
BSAHR Harold Ramirez 2.50 6.00
BSAID Isan Diaz 4.00 10.00
BSAJB Jake Bauers 3.00 8.00
BSAJD Jaylin Davis
BSAJDU Justin Dunn 3.00 8.00
BSAJF Jack Flaherty 10.00 25.00
BSAJF Junior Fernandez
BSAJFR Jake Fraley 3.00 8.00
BSAJRA Jose Ramirez 8.00 20.00
BSAJJ Josh James 4.00 10.00
BSAJL Jesus Luzardo 10.00 25.00
BSAJM Jordan Montgomery 4.00 10.00
BSAJR Jake Rogers 2.50 6.00
BSAJSM John Smoltz 12.00 30.00
BSAJSO Juan Soto 40.00 100.00
BSAJST Josh Staumont
BSAJY Jordan Yamamoto 3.00 8.00
BSAKB Kris Bryant
BSAKB Kris Bryant 50.00 120.00
BSAKGJ Ken Griffey Jr. 100.00 250.00
BSAKH Keston Hiura 10.00 25.00
BSAKK Kwang-Hyun Kim 20.00 50.00
BSAKL Kyle Lewis 30.00 80.00
BSALA Logan Allen 2.50 6.00
BSALAR Luis Arraez 10.00 25.00
BSALGJ Lourdes Gurriel Jr. 3.00 8.00
BSALMJ Lance McCullers Jr. 2.50 6.00
BSALR Luis Robert 100.00 250.00
BSALTH Lewis Thorpe
BSAMB Michael Brosseau 5.00 12.00
BSAMC Michael Chavis 3.00 8.00
BSAMM Mitch Moreland 2.50 6.00
BSAMMA Manny Machado
BSAMMC Mark McGwire
BSAMO Matt Olson 8.00 20.00
BSAMS Max Scherzer 25.00 60.00
BSAMT Mike Trout 125.00 300.00
BSANA Nolan Arenado 20.00 50.00
BSANH Nico Hoerner 20.00 50.00
BSANH Nico Hoerner 20.00 50.00
BSANL Nate Lowe 2.50 6.00
BSANLA Aaron Nola 8.00 20.00
BSANS Noah Syndergaard 12.00 30.00
BSANSO Nick Solak 10.00 25.00
BSAPA Pete Alonso 30.00 80.00
BSAPG Paul Goldschmidt
BSARA Rogelio Armenteros 3.00 8.00
BSARAR Randy Arozarena 40.00 100.00
BSARF Rollie Fingers 6.00 15.00
BSARH Rhys Hoskins 10.00 25.00
BSARMC Ryan McMahon 2.50 6.00
BSARY Ryan Yarbrough 2.50 6.00
BSASA Shogo Akiyama 10.00 25.00
BSASB Seth Brown 2.50 6.00
BSASH Sam Hilliard
BSASL Shed Long
BSASM Sean Murphy 4.00 10.00
BSASMU Sean Murphy 4.00 10.00
BSASN Sheldon Neuse 3.00 8.00
BSASO Shohei Ohtani 75.00 200.00
BSASSC Shin-Soo Choo 10.00 25.00
BSASY Shun Yamaguchi 5.00 12.00
BSATA Tim Anderson 10.00 25.00
BSATB Trevor Bauer
BSATD Travis Demeritte
BSATE Tommy Edman 12.00 30.00
BSATG Trent Grisham 8.00 20.00
BSATG Tony Gonsolin 8.00 20.00
BSATK Tommy Kahnle
BSATM Tino Martinez 15.00 40.00
BSAVG Vladimir Guerrero Jr. EXCH 25.00 60.00
BSAVR Victor Robles 8.00 20.00
BSAWA Willians Astudillo 2.50 6.00
BSAWC Willson Contreras 8.00 20.00
BSAWM Whit Merrifield 6.00 15.00
BSAWS Will Smith 8.00 20.00
BSAYA Yordan Alvarez 30.00 80.00
BSAYA Yordan Alvarez
BSAYC Yu Chang 4.00 10.00

2020 Topps Best of Topps Now

COMPLETE SET (10) 5.00 12.00
STATED ODDS 1:18 HOBBY
BTN1 Juan Soto 1.00 2.50
BTN2 Howie Kendrick .20 .50
BTN3 Juan Soto 1.00 2.50
BTN4 Justin Verlander .30 .75
BTN5 Mike Trout 1.50 4.00
BTN6 Yordan Alvarez 1.00 2.50
Pete Alonso
BTN7 Anthony Rendon .30 .75
BTN8 Gerrit Cole .50 1.25
BTN9 Luis Robert 2.00 5.00
BTN10 Mookie Betts .60 1.50

2020 Topps Decade of Dominance

STATED ODDS 1:35 HOBBY
*BLUE: 1X TO 2.5X BASIC
*BLACK/299: 1.5X TO 4X BASIC
*GOLD/50: 3X TO 8X BASIC
DOD1 Babe Ruth 1.00 2.50
DOD2 Willie Mays .75 2.00
DOD3 Hank Aaron .75 2.00
DOD4 Mark McGwire .60 1.50
DOD5 Ken Griffey Jr. .75 2.00
DOD6 Roger Clemens .50 1.25
DOD7 Sandy Koufax .75 2.00
DOD8 Ty Cobb .60 1.50
DOD9 Mike Trout 2.00 5.00
DOD10 Lou Gehrig .75 2.00
DOD11 Tony Gwynn .40 1.00
DOD12 Ichiro .50 1.25
DOD13 Alex Rodriguez .50 1.25
DOD14 Randy Johnson .40 1.00
DOD15 Mariano Rivera .50 1.25
DOD16 Ted Williams .75 2.00
DOD17 Honus Wagner .40 1.00
DOD18 Nolan Ryan 1.25 3.00
DOD19 Rickey Henderson .40 1.00
DOD20 Johnny Bench .40 1.00

2020 Topps Decade's Next

STATED ODDS 1:24 HOBBY
*BLUE: 1X TO 2.5X BASIC
*BLACK/299: 1.2X TO 3X BASIC
*GOLD/50: 3X TO 8X BASIC
DN1 Vladimir Guerrero Jr. .60 1.50
DN2 Austin Riley .50 1.25
DN3 Fernando Tatis Jr. 1.25 3.00
DN4 Yordan Alvarez 1.00 2.50
DN5 Ronald Acuna Jr. 1.25 3.00
DN6 Gleyber Torres .60 1.50
DN7 Keston Hiura .40 1.00
DN8 Brendan Rodgers .30 .75
DN9 Eloy Jimenez .60 1.50
DN10 Gavin Lux 1.25 3.00
DN11 Pete Alonso .75 2.00
DN12 Juan Soto 1.00 2.50
DN13 Bo Bichette 1.50 4.00
DN14 Kyle Tucker .25 .60
DN15 Nick Senzel .30 .75
DN16 Ozzie Albies .30 .75
DN17 Walker Buehler .40 1.00
DN18 Rafael Devers .40 1.00
DN19 Cody Bellinger .60 1.50
DN20 Victor Robles .40 1.00
DN21 Lucas Giolito .25 .60
DN22 Nico Hoerner .75 2.00
DN23 Shohei Ohtani .40 1.00
DN24 Julio Urias .30 .75
DN25 Chris Paddack .30 .75
DN26 Brendan McKay .30 .75
DN27 Ramon Laureano .30 .75
DN28 Jesus Luzardo .40 1.00
DN29 Carter Kieboom .25 .60
DN30 Mike Soroka .30 .75

2020 Topps Decade's Next Autographs

STATED ODDS 1:23,284 HOBBY
PRINT RUNS B/WN 5-25 COPIES PER
NO PRICING ON QTY 5
EXCHANGE DEADLINE 12/31/2021
DN1 Vladimir Guerrero Jr./25 50.00 120.00
DN2 Austin Riley/25 25.00 60.00
DN3 Fernando Tatis Jr./25 75.00 200.00
DN4 Yordan Alvarez/25 100.00 250.00
DN5 Ronald Acuna Jr./25 100.00 250.00
DN6 Gleyber Torres/25 60.00 150.00
DN7 Keston Hiura/25 30.00 80.00
DN9 Eloy Jimenez/25 20.00 50.00
DN10 Gavin Lux/25 100.00 250.00
DN11 Pete Alonso/25 75.00 200.00
DN12 Juan Soto/25 75.00 200.00
DN13 Bo Bichette/25 100.00 250.00
DN14 Kyle Tucker/25 12.00 30.00
DN16 Ozzie Albies/25 20.00 50.00
DN18 Rafael Devers/25 25.00 60.00
DN20 Victor Robles/25 20.00 50.00
DN21 Lucas Giolito/25 20.00 50.00
DN22 Nico Hoerner/25 30.00 80.00
DN24 Julio Urias/25 15.00 40.00
DN25 Chris Paddack/25 15.00 40.00
DN26 Brendan McKay/25 25.00 60.00
DN27 Ramon Laureano/25 20.00 50.00
DN28 Jesus Luzardo/25 30.00 80.00
DN30 Mike Soroka/25 15.00 40.00

2020 Topps Decades' Best

STATED ODDS 1:7 HOBBY
*BLUE: 1X TO 2.5X BASIC
*CHROME: 1X TO 2.5X BASIC
*BLACK/299: 1.2X TO 3X BASIC
*GREEN: 1.5X TO 4X BASIC
*CHR.GOLD/50: 3X TO 8X BASIC
*GOLD/50: 3X TO 8X BASIC
DB1 Willie Mays .60 1.50
DB2 Ernie Banks .30 .75
DB3 Ernie Banks .30 .75
DB4 Hank Aaron .60 1.50
DB5 Warren Spahn .25 .60
DB6 Willie Mays .60 1.50
DB7 Frank Robinson .25 .60
DB8 Orlando Cepeda .25 .60
DB9 Luis Aparicio .25 .60
DB10 Phil Rizzuto .25 .60
DB11 Larry Doby .25 .60
DB12 Eddie Mathews .30 .75
DB13 Duke Snider .25 .60
DB14 Ted Williams .60 1.50
DB15 Stan Musial .50 1.25
DB16 Jackie Robinson .30 .75
DB17 Willie Mays .60 1.50
DB18 Monte Irvin .25 .60
DB19 Ralph Kiner .25 .60
DB20 Hank Aaron .60 1.50
DB21 Pittsburgh Pirates .20 .50
DB22 New York Yankees .30 .75
DB23 San Francisco Giants .30 .75
DB24 Los Angeles Dodgers .30 .75
DB25 St. Louis Cardinals .30 .75
DB26 Minnesota Twins .20 .50
DB27 Baltimore Orioles .20 .50
DB28 Cincinnati Reds .20 .50
DB29 Detroit Tigers .20 .50
DB30 New York Mets .30 .75
DB31 Bob Gibson .25 .60
DB32 Jim Palmer .25 .60
DB33 Tom Seaver .25 .60
DB34 Fergie Jenkins .25 .60
DB35 Catfish Hunter .25 .60
DB36 Steve Carlton .25 .60
DB37 Nolan Ryan 1.00 2.50
DB38 Bert Blyleven .25 .60
DB39 Don Sutton .25 .60
DB40 Phil Niekro .25 .60
DB41 Wade Boggs .25 .60
DB42 Don Mattingly .60 1.50
DB43 Ryne Sandberg .60 1.50
DB44 Cal Ripken Jr. 1.00 2.50
DB45 Darryl Strawberry .20 .50
DB46 Eddie Murray .25 .60
DB47 Dale Murphy .30 .75
DB48 George Brett .60 1.50
DB49 Robin Yount .30 .75
DB50 Andre Dawson .25 .60
DB51 Ken Griffey Jr. .60 1.50
DB52 Frank Thomas .30 .75
DB53 Sammy Sosa .30 .75
DB54 Mark McGwire .50 1.25
DB55 Jeff Bagwell .25 .60
DB56 Tony Gwynn .30 .75
DB57 Roberto Alomar .25 .60
DB58 Barry Larkin .25 .60
DB59 Chipper Jones .30 .75
DB60 Edgar Martinez .25 .60
DB61 Cal Ripken Jr. 1.00 2.50
DB62 Pedro Martinez .25 .60
DB63 Rickey Henderson .30 .75
DB64 Roger Clemens .40 1.00
DB65 Sammy Sosa .30 .75
DB66 Ken Griffey Jr. .60 1.50
DB67 Chipper Jones .30 .75
DB68 Jeff Bagwell .25 .60
DB69 Barry Larkin .25 .60
DB70 Frank Thomas .30 .75
DB71 Pedro Martinez .25 .60
DB72 Randy Johnson .30 .75
DB73 Andy Pettitte .25 .60
DB74 Roger Clemens .40 1.00
DB75 Mike Mussina .25 .60
DB76 Mariano Rivera .40 1.00
DB77 Tom Glavine .25 .60
DB78 John Smoltz .30 .75
DB79 CC Sabathia .25 .60
DB80 Roy Oswalt .25 .60
DB81 Boston Red Sox .30 .75
DB82 New York Yankees .30 .75
DB83 Chicago Cubs .30 .75
DB84 Houston Astros .20 .50
DB85 Los Angeles Dodgers .30 .75
DB86 Cleveland Indians .20 .50
DB87 San Francisco Giants .30 .75
DB88 St. Louis Cardinals .30 .75
DB89 Texas Rangers .20 .50
DB90 Kansas City Royals .20 .50
DB91 Miguel Cabrera .30 .75
DB92 Shohei Ohtani .40 1.00
DB93 Mike Trout 1.50 4.00
DB94 Kris Bryant .40 1.00
DB95 Jacob DeGrom .30 .75
DB96 Bryce Harper .50 1.25
DB97 Max Scherzer .30 .75
DB98 Felix Hernandez .25 .60
DB99 Mookie Betts .60 1.50
DB100 Aaron Judge .75 2.00

2020 Topps Decades' Best Series 2

STATED ODDS 1:7 HOBBY
*BLUE: 1X TO 2.5X BASIC
*CHROME: 1X TO 2.5X BASIC
*BLACK/299: 1.2X TO 3X BASIC
*GREEN: 1.5X TO 4X BASIC
*CHR.GOLD/50: 3X TO 8X BASIC
*GOLD/50: 3X TO 8X BASIC
DB1 Detroit Tigers .20 .50
DB2 Philadelphia Phillies .20 .50
DB3 St. Louis Cardinals BB .20 .50
DB4 Boston Red Sox .20 .50
DB5 New York Giants .20 .50
DB6 New York Yankees .20 .50
DB7 Brooklyn Dodgers .20 .50
DB8 Milwaukee Braves .20 .50
DB9 Cleveland Indians .20 .50
DB10 Chicago White Sox .20 .50
DB11 Whitey Ford .25 .60
DB12 Juan Marichal .25 .60
DB13 Jim Bunning .25 .60
DB14 Bob Gibson .25 .60
DB15 Sandy Koufax .60 1.50
DB16 Warren Spahn .25 .60
DB17 Hoyt Wilhelm .25 .60
DB18 Fergie Jenkins .25 .60
DB19 Phil Niekro .25 .60
DB20 Don Sutton .25 .60
DB21 Hank Aaron .60 1.50
DB22 Frank Robinson .25 .60
DB23 Brooks Robinson .25 .60
DB24 Carl Yastrzemski .50 1.25
DB25 Harmon Killebrew .30 .75
DB26 Willie Mays .60 1.50
DB27 Willie McCovey .25 .60
DB28 Orlando Cepeda .25 .60
DB29 Roberto Clemente .75 2.00
DB30 Roger Maris .30 .75
DB31 Eddie Murray .25 .60
DB32 Carlton Fisk .25 .60
DB33 Andre Dawson .25 .60
DB34 Johnny Bench .30 .75
DB35 Joe Morgan .25 .60
DB36 Rod Carew .25 .60
DB37 Steve Carlton .25 .60
DB38 Tom Seaver .25 .60
DB39 Jim Palmer .25 .60
DB40 Catfish Hunter .25 .60
DB41 Johnny Bench .30 .75
DB42 Jim Rice .25 .60
DB43 Willie Stargell .25 .60
DB44 Rod Carew .25 .60
DB45 Joe Morgan .25 .60
DB46 Reggie Jackson .25 .60
DB47 Mike Schmidt .50 1.25
DB48 Willie McCovey .25 .60
DB49 George Foster .20 .50
DB50 Hank Aaron .60 1.50
DB51 New York Yankees .20 .50
DB52 Oakland Athletics .20 .50
DB53 St. Louis Cardinals BB .20 .50
DB54 Detroit Tigers .20 .50
DB55 New York Mets .20 .50
DB56 Kansas City Royals .20 .50
DB57 Los Angeles Dodgers .20 .50
DB58 Philadelphia Phillies 5.00 12.00
DB59 Minnesota Twins .20 .50
DB60 Baltimore Orioles .20 .50
DB61 Bert Blyleven .25 .60
DB62 Steve Carlton .25 .60
DB63 Dwight Gooden .20 .50
DB64 Roger Clemens .40 1.00
DB65 Nolan Ryan 1.00 2.50
DB66 Jack Morris .25 .60
DB67 Rollie Fingers .25 .60
DB68 Goose Gossage .25 .60
DB69 Bruce Sutter .25 .60
DB70 Dennis Eckersley .25 .60
DB71 Houston Astros .20 .50
DB72 Montreal Expos .20 .50
DB73 Cleveland Indians .20 .50
DB74 Atlanta Braves .20 .50
DB75 New York Yankees .20 .50
DB76 Toronto Blue Jays .20 .50
DB77 Cincinnati Reds .20 .50
DB78 Pittsburgh Pirates .20 .50
DB79 Texas Rangers .20 .50
DB80 Boston Red Sox .20 .50
DB81 Albert Pujols .40 1.00
DB82 Joe Mauer .25 .60
DB83 Ryan Howard .25 .60
DB84 Alex Rodriguez .40 1.00
DB85 Ichiro .40 1.00
DB86 Albert Pujols .40 1.00
DB87 Randy Johnson .30 .75
DB88 Tim Lincecum .25 .60
DB89 Barry Zito .25 .60
DB90 Pedro Martinez .25 .60
DB91 Justin Verlander .30 .75
DB92 Clayton Kershaw .60 1.50
DB93 Max Scherzer .30 .75
DB94 Stephen Strasburg .30 .75
DB95 Felix Hernandez .25 .60
DB96 Chris Sale .30 .75
DB97 Zack Greinke .25 .60
DB98 Jacob deGrom .30 .75
DB99 Corey Kluber .25 .60
DB100 Jon Lester .25 .60

2020 Topps Decades' Best Autographs

SER.1 STATED ODDS 1:25,440 HOBBY
SER.2 STATED ODDS 1:8808 HOBBY
PRINT RUNS B/WN 5-25 COPIES PER
NO PRICING ON QTY 15 OR LESS
SER.1 EXCH DEADLINE 12/31/2021
SER.2 EXCH DEADLINE 4/30/2022
DB12 Juan Marichal S2 30.00 80.00
DB14 Bob Gibson/25 S2 30.00 80.00
DB20 Don Sutton/25 S2 20.00 50.00
DB28 Orlando Cepeda/25 S2 25.00 60.00
DB32 Carlton Fisk/25 S2 25.00 60.00
DB33 Andre Dawson/25 S2 15.00 40.00
DB37 Steve Carlton/25 S2 25.00 60.00
DB38 Bert Blyleven/25 15.00 40.00
DB39 Don Sutton/25 20.00 50.00
DB42 Jim Rice/25 S2 25.00 60.00
DB45 Darryl Strawberry/25 30.00 80.00
DB47 Dale Murphy/25 30.00 80.00
DB49 George Foster/25 S2 20.00 50.00
DB50 Andre Dawson/25 15.00 40.00
DB57 Roberto Alomar/25 40.00 100.00
DB58 Barry Larkin/25 25.00 60.00
DB60 Edgar Martinez/25 25.00 60.00
DB61 Bert Blyleven/25 S2 15.00 40.00
DB62 Steve Carlton/25 S2 25.00 60.00
DB63 Dwight Gooden/25 S2 25.00 60.00
DB66 Jack Morris/25 S2 30.00 80.00
DB66 Ken Griffey Jr.
DB67 Rollie Fingers/25 S2 15.00 40.00
DB68 Goose Gossage/25 S2 25.00 60.00
DB69 Bruce Sutter/25 S2 10.00 25.00
DB70 Dennis Eckersley/25 S2 15.00 40.00
DB83 Ryan Howard/25 S2 30.00 80.00
DB88 Tim Lincecum/25 S2 60.00 150.00
DB89 Barry Zito/25 S2 15.00 40.00
DB92 Clayton Kershaw S2
DB93 Max Scherzer/25 S2 40.00 100.00
DB95 Jacob DeGrom/25 20.00 50.00
DB96 Chris Sale/25 S2 25.00 60.00
DB97 Max Scherzer/25 40.00 100.00
DB98 Jacob deGrom/25 S2 20.00 50.00
DB99 Corey Kluber/25 S2 20.00 50.00

2020 Topps Draft Day Medallions

STATED ODDS 1:739 HOBBY
*BLACK/50: .75X TO 2X BASIC
*GOLD/25: 1X TO 2.5X BASIC
DDMAB Alex Bregman 2.00 5.00
DDMABE Andrew Benintendi 2.00 5.00
DDMAJ Aaron Judge 5.00 12.00
DDMAR Anthony Rizzo 3.00 8.00
DDMARE Anthony Rendon 2.00 5.00
DDMBB Byron Buxton 1.50 4.00
DDMBBI Bo Bichette 6.00 15.00
DDMBH Bryce Harper 5.00 12.00
DDMBR Brendan Rodgers 2.00 5.00
DDMCB Cody Bellinger 4.00 10.00
DDMCC Carlos Correa 2.00 5.00
DDMCK Clayton Kershaw 3.00 8.00
DDMCKI Carter Kieboom 1.50 4.00
DDMCS Corey Seager 2.00 5.00
DDMCSA Chris Sale 2.00 5.00
DDMCY Christian Yelich 2.50 6.00
DDMDS Dansby Swanson 2.00 5.00
DDMEL Evan Longoria 1.50 4.00
DDMFF Freddie Freeman 2.50 6.00
DDMFL Francisco Lindor 2.00 5.00
DDMGC Gerrit Cole 3.00 8.00
DDMGL Gavin Lux 6.00 15.00
DDMGS Giancarlo Stanton 2.00 5.00
DDMGSA George Springer 1.50 4.00
DDMJB Javier Baez 3.00 8.00
DDMJD Josh Donaldson 1.50 4.00
DDMJdG Jacob deGrom 2.00 5.00
DDMJF Jack Flaherty 1.50 4.00
DDMKB Kris Bryant 2.50 6.00
DDMKL Kyle Lewis 10.00 25.00
DDMKS Kyle Schwarber 2.00 5.00
DDMLG Lucas Giolito 1.50 4.00
DDMMB Mookie Betts 3.00 8.00
DDMMC Michael Conforto 1.50 4.00
DDMMCH Matt Chapman 2.00 5.00
DDMMM Manny Machado 2.00 5.00
DDMMS Max Scherzer 2.00 5.00
DDMMSO Mike Soroka 2.00 5.00
DDMMT Mike Trout 10.00 25.00
DDMNA Nolan Arenado 2.50 6.00
DDMNS Nick Senzel 2.00 5.00
DDMPA Pete Alonso 5.00 12.00
DDMPG Paul Goldschmidt 2.00 5.00
DDMRH Rhys Hoskins 2.50 6.00
DDMSS Stephen Strasburg 2.00 5.00
DDMTA Tim Anderson 2.00 5.00
DDMTL Tim Lincecum 1.50 4.00
DDMTS Trevor Story 2.00 5.00
DDMTT Trea Turner 1.50 4.00
DDMWB Walker Buehler 2.50 6.00

2020 Topps Empire State Award Winners Pete Alonso

COMMON CARD .60 1.50
RANDOM INSERTS IN PACKS
*BLUE: 1.2X TO 3X BASIC
*BLACK/299: 1.5X TO 4X BASIC
*GOLD/50: 3X TO 8X BASIC
*RED/10: 8X TO 20X BASIC

2020 Topps Empire State Award Winners Pete Alonso Autographs

COMMON CARD 75.00 200.00
RANDOM INSERTS IN PACKS
STATED PRINT RUN 5 SER.#'d SETS
EXCHANGE DEADLINE 4/30/2022

2020 Topps Fernando Tatis Jr. Highlights

COMPLETE SET (30) 15.00 40.00
STATED ODDS 1:4 GRAVITY
*BLUE: 1.2X TO 3X BASIC
*BLACK/299: 1.5X TO 4X BASIC
*GOLD/50: 3X TO 8X BASIC
*RED/10: 8X TO 20X BASIC
FTH1 Fernando Tatis Jr. 1.25 3.00
FTH2 Fernando Tatis Jr. 1.25 3.00
FTH3 Fernando Tatis Jr. 1.25 3.00
FTH4 Fernando Tatis Jr. 1.25 3.00
FTH5 Fernando Tatis Jr. 1.25 3.00
FTH6 Fernando Tatis Jr. 1.25 3.00
FTH7 Fernando Tatis Jr. 1.25 3.00
FTH8 Fernando Tatis Jr. 1.25 3.00
FTH9 Fernando Tatis Jr. 1.25 3.00
FTH10 Fernando Tatis Jr. 1.25 3.00
FTH11 Fernando Tatis Jr. 1.25 3.00
FTH12 Fernando Tatis Jr. 1.25 3.00
FTH13 Fernando Tatis Jr. 1.25 3.00
FTH14 Fernando Tatis Jr. 1.25 3.00
FTH15 Fernando Tatis Jr. 1.25 3.00
FTH16 Fernando Tatis Jr. 1.25 3.00
FTH17 Fernando Tatis Jr. 1.25 3.00
FTH18 Fernando Tatis Jr. 1.25 3.00
FTH19 Fernando Tatis Jr. 1.25 3.00
FTH20 Fernando Tatis Jr. 1.25 3.00
FTH21 Fernando Tatis Jr. 1.25 3.00
FTH22 Fernando Tatis Jr. 1.25 3.00
FTH23 Fernando Tatis Jr. 1.25 3.00
FTH24 Fernando Tatis Jr. 1.25 3.00
FTH25 Fernando Tatis Jr. 1.25 3.00
FTH26 Fernando Tatis Jr. 1.25 3.00
FTH27 Fernando Tatis Jr. 1.25 3.00
FTH28 Fernando Tatis Jr. 1.25 3.00
FTH29 Fernando Tatis Jr. 1.25 3.00
FTH30 Fernando Tatis Jr. 1.25 3.00

2020 Topps Fernando Tatis Jr. Highlights Autographs

STATED ODDS 1:5410 GRAVITY
STATED PRINT RUN 5 SER.#'d SETS
EXCHANGE DEADLINE 4/30/2022
FTJHA1 Fernando Tatis Jr. 125.00 300.00
FTJHA2 Fernando Tatis Jr. 125.00 300.00
FTJHA3 Fernando Tatis Jr. 125.00 300.00
FTJHA4 Fernando Tatis Jr. 125.00 300.00
FTJHA5 Fernando Tatis Jr. 125.00 300.00
FTJHA6 Fernando Tatis Jr. 125.00 300.00
FTJHA7 Fernando Tatis Jr. 125.00 300.00
FTJHA8 Fernando Tatis Jr. 125.00 300.00
FTJHA9 Fernando Tatis Jr. 125.00 300.00
FTJHA10 Fernando Tatis Jr. 125.00 300.00
FTJHA11 Fernando Tatis Jr. 125.00 300.00
FTJHA12 Fernando Tatis Jr. 125.00 300.00
FTJHA13 Fernando Tatis Jr. 125.00 300.00
FTJHA14 Fernando Tatis Jr. 125.00 300.00
FTJHA15 Fernando Tatis Jr. 125.00 300.00
FTJHA16 Fernando Tatis Jr. 125.00 300.00
FTJHA17 Fernando Tatis Jr. 125.00 300.00
FTJHA18 Fernando Tatis Jr. 125.00 300.00
FTJHA19 Fernando Tatis Jr. 125.00 300.00
FTJHA20 Fernando Tatis Jr. 125.00 300.00
FTJHA21 Fernando Tatis Jr. 125.00 300.00
FTJHA22 Fernando Tatis Jr. 125.00 300.00
FTJHA23 Fernando Tatis Jr. 125.00 300.00
FTJHA24 Fernando Tatis Jr. 125.00 300.00
FTJHA25 Fernando Tatis Jr. 125.00 300.00
FTJHA26 Fernando Tatis Jr. 125.00 300.00
FTJHA27 Fernando Tatis Jr. 125.00 300.00
FTJHA28 Fernando Tatis Jr. 125.00 300.00
FTJHA29 Fernando Tatis Jr. 125.00 300.00
FTJHA30 Fernando Tatis Jr. 125.00 300.00

2020 Topps Global Game Medallions

STATED ODDS 1:2213 HOBBY
*BLACK/149: .5X TO 1.2X BASIC
*GOLD/50: .6X TO 1.5X BASIC
GGMAB Alex Bregman 2.50 6.00
GGMAC Aroldis Chapman 2.50 6.00
GGMAJ Aaron Judge 6.00 15.00
GGMAP Albert Pujols 3.00 8.00
GGMAV Alex Verdugo 2.00 5.00
GGMBH Bryce Harper 4.00 10.00
GGMBP Buster Posey 3.00 8.00
GGMCB Cody Bellinger 5.00 12.00
GGMCC Carlos Correa 4.00 10.00
GGMCK Clayton Kershaw 5.00 12.00
GGMCY Christian Yelich 3.00 8.00
GGMDG Didi Gregorius 2.00 5.00
GGMDO David Ortiz 2.50 6.00
GGMEJ Eloy Jimenez 5.00 12.00
GGMFF Freddie Freeman 3.00 8.00
GGMFL Francisco Lindor 2.50 6.00
GGMGS Gary Sanchez 2.50 6.00
GGMGT Gleyber Torres 5.00 12.00
GGMHM Hideki Matsui 2.50 6.00
GGMI Ichiro 5.00 12.00
GGMJA Jose Altuve 2.00 5.00
GGMJB Javier Baez 3.00 8.00
GGMJS Juan Soto 8.00 20.00
GGMJT Jameson Taillon 2.00 5.00
GGMJU Julio Urias 2.50 6.00
GGMJV Joey Votto 2.50 6.00
GGMKB Kris Bryant 3.00 8.00
GGMKD Khris Davis 2.50 6.00
GGMKG Ken Griffey Jr. 6.00 15.00
GGMLU Luis Urias 2.00 5.00
GGMMA Masahiro Tanaka 2.50 6.00
GGMMB Mookie Betts 5.00 12.00
GGMMC Miguel Cabrera 2.50 6.00
GGMMM Manny Machado 2.50 6.00
GGMMT Mike Trout 12.00 30.00
GGMOA Ozzie Albies 2.50 6.00
GGMRA Ronald Acuna Jr. 10.00 25.00
GGMRC Roberto Clemente 10.00 25.00
GGMRD Rafael Devers 3.00 8.00
GGMRO Robinson Cano 2.00 5.00
GGMSO Shohei Ohtani 5.00 12.00
GGMVG Vladimir Guerrero Jr. 5.00 12.00
GGMWC Willson Contreras 2.50 6.00
GGMXB Xander Bogaerts 2.50 6.00
GGMYA Yordan Alvarez 8.00 20.00
GGMYD Yu Darvish 2.50 6.00
GGMYG Yasmani Grandal 1.50 4.00
GGMYM Yadier Molina 2.50 6.00
GGMYO Yoan Moncada 2.50 6.00
GGMYP Yasiel Puig 2.50 6.00

2020 Topps Home Run Challenge Code Cards

STATED ODDS 1:24 HOBBY
HRC1 Bryce Harper 1.25 3.00
HRC2 Ronald Acuna Jr. 3.00 8.00
HRC3 J.D. Martinez .75 2.00
HRC4 Freddie Freeman 1.00 2.50
HRC5 Mookie Betts 1.50 4.00
HRC6 Nolan Arenado 1.00 2.50
HRC7 Javier Baez 1.00 2.50
HRC8 Kris Bryant 1.00 2.50
HRC9 Anthony Rizzo 1.00 2.50
HRC10 Francisco Lindor .75 2.00
HRC11 Aaron Judge 2.00 5.00
HRC12 Giancarlo Stanton .75 2.00
HRC13 Vladimir Guerrero Jr. 1.50 4.00
HRC14 George Springer .60 1.50
HRC15 Juan Soto 2.50 6.00
HRC16 Joey Gallo .75 2.00
HRC17 Paul Goldschmidt .75 2.00
HRC18 Manny Machado .75 2.00
HRC19 Fernando Tatis Jr. 3.00 8.00
HRC20 Josh Bell .60 1.50
HRC21 Pete Alonso 2.00 5.00
HRC22 Gleyber Torres 1.50 4.00
HRC23 Christian Yelich 1.00 2.50
HRC24 Mike Trout 4.00 10.00
HRC25 Cody Bellinger 1.50 4.00
HRC26 Alex Bregman .75 2.00
HRC27 Yordan Alvarez 2.50 6.00
HRC28 Max Kepler .60 1.50

HRC29 Max Muncy .60 1.50
HRC30 Rhys Hoskins 1.00 2.50

2020 Topps Home Run Challenge Code Cards Series 2

STATED ODDS 1:24 HOBBY
HRC1 Bryce Harper .75 2.00
HRC2 Ronald Acuna Jr. 2.00 5.00
HRC3 J.D. Martinez .50 1.25
HRC4 Freddie Freeman .60 1.50
HRC5 Mookie Betts 1.00 2.50
HRC6 Nolan Arenado .60 1.50
HRC7 Javier Baez .60 1.50
HRC8 Kris Bryant .60 1.50
HRC9 Anthony Rizzo .75 2.00
HRC10 Francisco Lindor .50 1.25
HRC11 Aaron Judge 1.25 3.00
HRC12 Giancarlo Stanton .50 1.25
HRC13 Vladimir Guerrero Jr. 1.00 2.50
HRC14 George Springer .40 1.00
HRC15 Juan Soto 1.50 4.00
HRC16 Joey Gallo .50 1.25
HRC17 Paul Goldschmidt .50 1.25
HRC18 Manny Machado .50 1.25
HRC19 Fernando Tatis Jr. 2.00 5.00
HRC20 Josh Bell .40 1.00
HRC21 Pete Alonso 1.25 3.00
HRC22 Gleyber Torres 1.00 2.50
HRC23 Christian Yelich .60 1.50
HRC24 Mike Trout 2.50 6.00
HRC25 Cody Bellinger 1.00 2.50
HRC26 Alex Bregman .50 1.25
HRC27 Yordan Alvarez 1.50 4.00
HRC28 Max Kepler .40 1.00
HRC29 Max Muncy .40 1.00
HRC30 Rhys Hoskins .60 1.50

2020 Topps Jumbo Jersey Sleeve Patches

STATED ODDS 1:1963 HOBBY
*BLACK/149: .5X TO 1.2X BASIC
*GOLD/50: .75X TO 2X BASIC
JJSPAA Aristides Aquino 12.00 30.00
JJSPABR Alex Bregman 3.00 8.00
JJSPAM Adalberto Mondesi 3.00 8.00
JJSPAP Albert Pujols 4.00 10.00
JJSPARI Anthony Rizzo 10.00 25.00
JJSPBH Bryce Harper 5.00 12.00
JJSPBM Brendan McKay 4.00 10.00
JJSPBP Buster Posey 4.00 10.00
JJSPBS Blake Snell 2.50 6.00
JJSPCB Cody Bellinger 5.00 12.00
JJSPCK Clayton Kershaw 6.00 15.00
JJSPDV Daniel Vogelbach 2.00 5.00
JJSPEA Elvis Andrus 2.50 6.00
JJSPEJ Eloy Jimenez 6.00 15.00
JJSPFF Freddie Freeman 4.00 10.00
JJSPJB Javier Baez 6.00 15.00
JJSPJBE Josh Bell 2.50 6.00
JJSPJD Jacob deGrom 5.00 12.00
JJSPJG Joey Gallo 3.00 8.00
JJSPJL Jesus Luzardo 4.00 10.00
JJSPJS Juan Soto 10.00 25.00
JJSPJV Justin Verlander 3.00 8.00
JJSPJVO Joey Votto 3.00 8.00
JJSPJY Jordan Yamamoto 2.50 6.00
JJSPKR Kris Bryant 6.00 15.00
JJSPKL Kyle Lewis 15.00 40.00
JJSPKM Ketel Marte 2.50 6.00
JJSPMB Mookie Betts 4.00 10.00
JJSPMC Matt Chapman 3.00 8.00
JJSPMK Max Kepler 2.50 6.00
JJSPMS Max Scherzer 3.00 8.00
JJSPMT Mike Trout 15.00 40.00
JJSPNA Nolan Arenado 4.00 10.00
JJSPOA Ozzie Albies 3.00 8.00
JJSPPA Pete Alonso 10.00 25.00
JJSPRA Ronald Acuna Jr. 10.00 25.00
JJSPRD Rafael Devers 4.00 10.00
JJSPRH Rhys Hoskins 4.00 10.00
JJSPSO Shohei Ohtani 10.00 25.00
JJSPTM Trey Mancini 3.00 8.00
JJSPTS Trevor Story 3.00 8.00
JJSPWB Walker Buehler 4.00 10.00
JJSPWM Whit Merrifield 3.00 8.00
JJSPXB Xander Bogaerts 3.00 8.00
JJSPYA Yordan Alvarez 12.00 30.00
JJSPZG Zac Gallen 5.00 12.00

2020 Topps Major League Material Autographs

SER.1 STATED ODDS 1:8,326 HOBBY
SER.2 STATED ODDS 1:2583 HOBBY
PRINT RUNS B/WN 8-50 COPIES PER
NO PRICING ON QTY 8
SER.1 EXCH DEADLINE 12/31/2021
SER.2 EXCH DEADLINE 4/30/2022
MJMABB Bo Bichette/50 S2 50.00 120.00
MJMABS Blake Snell/50 S2 8.00 20.00
MJMABZ Barry Zito S2
MJMACB Cavan Biggio/50 S2 12.00 30.00
MJMACC Carlos Carrasco S2
MJMACF Clint Frazier/50 S2 8.00 20.00
MJMADL DJ LeMahieu/50 S2 30.00 80.00
MJMADW David Wright/25 S2 20.00 50.00
MJMAEJ Eloy Jimenez/50 S2 20.00 50.00
MJMAFT Fernando Tatis Jr./25 S2 125.00 300.00
MJMAGL Gavin Lux/50 S2 50.00 120.00
MJMAJR J.T. Realmuto/50 S2 15.00 40.00
MJMAJS Juan Soto/25 S2 60.00 150.00
MJMAKH Kyle Hendricks/50 S2 12.00 30.00
MJMAKY Kirby Yates/50 S2 6.00 15.00
MJMALM Lance McCullers Jr./50 S2 10.00 25.00
MJMAMC Michael Chavis/50 S2 8.00 20.00
MJMAMG Mitch Garver/50 S2 10.00 25.00
MJMAMM Miles Mikolas/21 S2 8.00 20.00
MJMAMMU Max Muncy/50 S2 8.00 20.00
MJMAMT Mike Trout/25 S2 250.00 600.00
MJMAMV Mo Vaughn/25 S2 30.00 80.00
MJMAMY Mike Yastrzemski/50 S2 15.00 40.00
MJMANH Nico Hoerner/50 S2 25.00 60.00
MJMANS Nick Solak/50 S2 12.00 30.00
MJMANSE Nick Senzel/50 S2 10.00 25.00
MJMANSY Noah Syndergaard/25 S2 15.00 40.00
MJMAPA Pete Alonso/25 S2 50.00 120.00
MJMAPC Patrick Corbin/50 S2 8.00 20.00
MJMARA Ronald Acuna Jr./25 S2 100.00 250.00
MJMARD Rafael Devers/25 S2 15.00 40.00
MJMARH Ryan Howard/50 S2 12.00 30.00
MJMARHO Rhys Hoskins/25 S2 25.00 60.00
MJMASB Shane Bieber/50 S2 15.00 40.00
MJMASC Shin-Soo Choo/50 S2 15.00 40.00
MJMASM Sean Murphy/50 S2 10.00 25.00
MJMATL Tim Lincecum/50 S2 30.00 80.00
MJMAVG Vladimir Guerrero Jr./25 S2 30.00 80.00
MJMAWC Willson Contreras/50 S2 12.00 30.00
MJMAWCL Will Clark/25 S2 40.00 100.00
MJMAXB Xander Bogaerts S2 10.00 25.00
MLMAAN Aaron Nola/50 15.00 40.00
MLMAAR Austin Riley/50 25.00 60.00
MLMABL Brandon Lowe/50 10.00 25.00
MLMABM Brendan McKay/50 10.00 25.00
MLMABR Brendan Rodgers/50 10.00 25.00
MLMACCS CC Sabathia/30 25.00 60.00
MLMACP Chris Paddack/50 10.00 25.00
MLMACY Christian Yelich/30 30.00 80.00
MLMAFR Franmil Reyes/50 6.00 15.00
MLMAFTJ Fernando Tatis Jr./50 100.00 250.00
MLMAGT Gleyber Torres/30 40.00 100.00
MLMAGU Gio Urshela/50 25.00 60.00
MLMAJA Jose Altuve/30 15.00 40.00
MLMAJB Jose Berrios/50 8.00 20.00
MLMAJDM J.D. Martinez/50 10.00 25.00
MLMAJF Jack Flaherty/50 15.00 40.00
MLMAJS Juan Soto/50 50.00 120.00
MLMAJSH Justus Sheffield/50 10.00 25.00
MLMAKH Keston Hiura/50 10.00 25.00
MLMAKS Kyle Schwarber/50 15.00 40.00
MLMALGJ Lourdes Gurriel Jr./50 10.00 25.00
MLMALV Luke Voit/50 12.00 30.00
MLMAMCH Matt Chapman/50 10.00 25.00
MLMAMCL Mike Clevinger/50 12.00 30.00
MLMAMK Max Kepler/50 10.00 25.00
MLMAMS Max Scherzer/50 20.00 50.00
MLMAMSO Mike Soroka/50 10.00 25.00
MLMANA Nolan Arenado/30 25.00 60.00
MLMAPA Pete Alonso/50 40.00 100.00
MLMARAJ Ronald Acuna Jr./30 75.00 200.00
MLMARH Rhys Hoskins/50 20.00 50.00
MLMAVGJ Vladimir Guerrero Jr./50 25.00 60.00
MLMAVR Victor Robles/50 12.00 30.00
MLMAWA Willians Astudillo/50 10.00 25.00
MLMAYA Yordan Alvarez/50 60.00 150.00

2020 Topps Major League Material Autographs Red

*RED/25: .5X TO 1.2X BASIC
SER.1 STATED ODDS 1:14,932 HOBBY
SER.2 STATED ODDS 1:5341 HOBBY
PRINT RUNS B/WN 10-25 COPIES PER
NO PRICING ON QTY 10
SER.1 EXCH DEADLINE 12/31/2021
SER.2 EXCH DEADLINE 4/30/2022
MJMABZ Barry Zito/25 S2 10.00 25.00
MJMACC Carlos Carrasco/25 S2 15.00 40.00

2020 Topps Major League Materials

SER.1 STATED ODDS 1:136 HOBBY
SER.2 STATED ODDS 1:171 HOBBY
*BLACK/199: .5X TO 1.2X BASIC
*GOLD/50: .6X TO 1.5X BASIC
*RED/25: .75X TO 2X BASIC
MLMAA Aristides Aquino S2 4.00 10.00
MLMAB Andrew Benintendi 3.00 8.00
MLMAB Alex Bregman S2 3.00 8.00
MLMAJ Aaron Judge 8.00 20.00
MLMAM Austin Meadows 2.50 6.00
MLMAR Anthony Rizzo 5.00 12.00
MLMARI Austin Riley 4.00 10.00
MLMARO Amed Rosario 2.50 6.00
MLMBB Byron Buxton 2.50 6.00
MLMBH Bryce Harper S2 6.00 15.00
MLMBP Buster Posey 4.00 10.00
MLMBS Blake Snell 2.50 6.00
MLMCB Charlie Blackmon 3.00 8.00
MLMCBE Cody Bellinger 6.00 15.00
MLMCK Clayton Kershaw S2 6.00 15.00
MLMCP Chris Paddack S2 3.00 8.00
MLMCS Corey Seager 3.00 8.00
MLMCS CC Sabathia S2 2.50 6.00
MLMCSA Carlos Santana 2.50 6.00
MLMCY Christian Yelich S2 4.00 10.00
MLMDD David Dahl 2.00 5.00
MLMDG Didi Gregorius 2.50 6.00
MLMDO David Ortiz S2 3.00 8.00
MLMDS Dansby Swanson 3.00 8.00
MLMDV Daniel Vogelbach 2.00 5.00
MLMEA Elvis Andrus S2 2.50 6.00
MLMEJ Eloy Jimenez S2 6.00 15.00
MLMES Eugenio Suarez S2 2.50 6.00
MLMET Eric Thames 2.00 5.00
MLMFF Freddie Freeman 4.00 10.00
MLMFL Francisco Lindor 3.00 8.00
MLMFT Fernando Tatis Jr. S2 5.00 12.00
MLMGS George Springer 2.50 6.00
MLMGSA Gary Sanchez 3.00 8.00
MLMGT Gleyber Torres S2 5.00 12.00
MLMJA Jose Altuve 2.50 6.00
MLMJB Jose Berrios 2.50 6.00
MLMJB Javier Baez S2 4.00 10.00
MLMJF Jack Flaherty S2 2.50 6.00
MLMJG Joey Gallo 3.00 8.00
MLMJH Josh Hader 2.00 5.00
MLMJR J.T. Realmuto 3.00 8.00
MLMJS Jorge Soler S2 3.00 8.00
MLMJSO Juan Soto S2 5.00 12.00
MLMJV Justin Verlander S2 3.00 8.00
MLMJVO Joey Votto S2 3.00 8.00
MLMKB Kris Bryant S2 4.00 10.00
MLMKH Keston Hiura S2 4.00 10.00
MLMKW Kolten Wong S2 2.50 6.00
MLMLC Lorenzo Cain 2.00 5.00
MLMLG Lourdes Gurriel Jr. 2.50 6.00
MLMLG Lucas Giolito S2 2.50 6.00
MLMLV Luke Voit 4.00 10.00
MLMMB Matthew Boyd 2.00 5.00
MLMMC Miguel Cabrera S2 3.00 8.00
MLMMCO Michael Conforto 2.50 6.00
MLMMK Max Kepler S2 2.50 6.00
MLMMM Manny Machado S2 3.00 8.00
MLMMO Matt Olson S2 2.00 5.00
MLMMS Max Scherzer S2 3.00 8.00
MLMMSA Miguel Sano 2.50 6.00
MLMMSE Marcus Semien S2 2.00 5.00
MLMMT Mike Trout 12.00 30.00
MLMMTA Masahiro Tanaka S2 3.00 8.00
MLMMTR Mike Trout S2 12.00 30.00
MLMNA Nolan Arenado S2 4.00 10.00
MLMNC Nick Castellanos S2 3.00 8.00
MLMNS Nick Senzel 3.00 8.00
MLMNSY Noah Syndergaard 2.50 6.00
MLMOA Ozzie Albies 3.00 8.00
MLMPA Pete Alonso 8.00 20.00
MLMPD Paul DeJong 3.00 8.00
MLMPG Paul Goldschmidt S2 3.00 8.00
MLMRC Robinson Cano S2 2.50 6.00
MLMRH Rhys Hoskins S2 4.00 10.00
MLMSB Shane Bieber S2 3.00 8.00
MLMSG Sonny Gray 2.50 6.00
MLMSO Shohei Ohtani S2 4.00 10.00
MLMSS Stephen Strasburg 3.00 8.00
MLMTA Tim Anderson 3.00 8.00
MLMTM Trey Mancini 3.00 8.00
MLMTS Trevor Story 3.00 8.00
MLMTT Trea Turner 2.50 6.00
MLMVG Vladimir Guerrero Jr. S2 4.00 10.00
MLMWB Walker Buehler 4.00 10.00
MLMWC Willson Contreras 3.00 8.00
MLMWM Whit Merrifield 3.00 8.00
MLMXB Xander Bogaerts 3.00 8.00
MLMYM Yoan Moncada 3.00 8.00
MLMYM Yadier Molina S2 3.00 8.00

2020 Topps Player Medallions

ONE PER BLASTER
*BLACK/199: .6X TO 1.5X BASIC
*GOLD/50: 1X TO 2.5X BASIC
TPMAA Aristides Aquino 2.00 5.00
TPMAB Alex Bregman 1.50 4.00
TPMAJ Aaron Judge 4.00 10.00
TPMAR Anthony Rendon 1.50 4.00
TPMARZ Anthony Rizzo 2.50 6.00
TPMBB Bo Bichette 4.00 10.00
TPMBH Bryce Harper 2.50 6.00
TPMBM Brendan McKay 1.50 4.00
TPMBP Buster Posey 2.00 5.00
TPMCB Cody Bellinger 3.00 8.00
TPMCK Clayton Kershaw 3.00 8.00
TPMCY Christian Yelich 2.00 5.00
TPMEJ Eloy Jimenez 3.00 8.00
TPMFF Freddie Freeman 2.00 5.00
TPMFL Francisco Lindor 1.50 4.00
TPMFT Fernando Tatis Jr. 6.00 15.00
TPMGC Gerrit Cole 2.50 6.00
TPMGL Gavin Lux 4.00 10.00
TPMGT Gleyber Torres 3.00 8.00
TPMJA Jose Altuve 1.25 3.00
TPMJB Josh Bell 1.25 3.00
TPMJBA Javier Baez 2.00 5.00
TPMJd Jacob deGrom 1.50 4.00
TPMJG Joey Gallo 1.50 4.00
TPMJL Jesus Luzardo 2.00 5.00
TPMJS Juan Soto 5.00 12.00
TPMJV Justin Verlander 1.50 4.00
TPMKB Kris Bryant 2.00 5.00
TPMKH Keston Hiura 2.00 5.00
TPMKL Kyle Lewis 8.00 20.00
TPMKM Ketel Marte 1.25 3.00
TPMLR Luis Robert 10.00 25.00
TPMMB Mookie Betts 3.00 8.00
TPMMC Matt Chapman 1.50 4.00
TPMMCA Miguel Cabrera 1.50 4.00
TPMMK Max Kepler 1.25 3.00
TPMMS Max Scherzer 1.50 4.00
TPMMT Mike Trout 8.00 20.00
TPMNA Nolan Arenado 2.00 5.00
TPMPA Pete Alonso 4.00 10.00
TPMPG Paul Goldschmidt 1.50 4.00
TPMRA Ronald Acuna Jr. 5.00 12.00
TPMRD Rafael Devers 2.00 5.00
TPMRH Rhys Hoskins 2.00 5.00
TPMSO Shohei Ohtani 2.00 5.00
TPMTM Trey Mancini 1.50 4.00
TPMVG Vladimir Guerrero Jr. 3.00 8.00
TPMWM Whit Merrifield 1.50 4.00
TPMYA Yordan Alvarez 5.00 12.00
TPMYM Yadier Molina 1.50 4.00

2020 Topps Player of the Decade Mike Trout

STATED ODDS 1:32 HOBBY
*BLUE: 1X TO 2.5X BASIC
*BLACK/299: 1.2X TO 3X BASIC
*GOLD/50: 4X TO 10X BASIC
*RED/10: 6X TO 15X BASIC
MT1 Mike Trout 1.50 4.00
MT2 Mike Trout 1.50 4.00
MT3 Mike Trout 1.50 4.00
MT4 Mike Trout 1.50 4.00
MT5 Mike Trout 1.50 4.00
MT6 Mike Trout 1.50 4.00
MT7 Mike Trout 1.50 4.00
MT8 Mike Trout 1.50 4.00
MT9 Mike Trout 1.50 4.00
MT10 Mike Trout 1.50 4.00
MT11 Mike Trout 1.50 4.00
MT12 Mike Trout 1.50 4.00
MT13 Mike Trout 1.50 4.00
MT14 Mike Trout 1.50 4.00
MT15 Mike Trout 1.50 4.00
MT16 Mike Trout 1.50 4.00
MT17 Mike Trout 1.50 4.00
MT18 Mike Trout 1.50 4.00
MT19 Mike Trout 1.50 4.00
MT20 Mike Trout 1.50 4.00
MT21 Mike Trout 1.50 4.00
MT22 Mike Trout 1.50 4.00
MT23 Mike Trout 1.50 4.00
MT24 Mike Trout 1.50 4.00
MT25 Mike Trout 1.50 4.00

2020 Topps Postseason Performance Autograph Relics

STATED ODDS 1:57,238 HOBBY
PRINT RUNS B/WN 30-50 COPIES PER
EXCHANGE DEADLINE 12/31/2021
PPARDS Dansby Swanson/25 20.00 50.00
PPARGC Gerrit Cole/50 20.00 50.00
PPARGS George Springer/35 15.00 40.00
PPARJA Jose Altuve/35 20.00 50.00
PPARJF Jack Flaherty/50 15.00 40.00
PPARJP Joc Pederson/25 12.00 30.00
PPARMSO Mike Soroka/50 20.00 50.00
PPARPG Paul Goldschmidt/50 20.00 50.00
PPARRA Ronald Acuna Jr./25 75.00 200.00
PPARSD Sean Doolittle/50 12.00 30.00

2020 Topps Postseason Performance Autograph Relics Red

*RED/25: .5X TO 1.2X BASIC
STATED ODDS 1:57,238 HOBBY
PRINT RUNS B/WN 10-25 COPIES PER
NO PRICING ON QTY 10
EXCHANGE DEADLINE 12/31/2021
PPARBS Blake Snell/25 10.00 25.00
PPARMM Max Muncy/25 10.00 25.00

2020 Topps Postseason Performance Autographs

STATED ODDS 1:28,035 HOBBY
PRINT RUNS B/WN 25-50 COPIES PER
EXCHANGE DEADLINE 12/31/2021
*RED/25: .5X TO 1.2X BASIC
PPAAJ Aaron Judge
PPABS Blake Snell/50 8.00 20.00
PPADS Dansby Swanson/25 15.00 40.00
PPAGL Gavin Lux/25 40.00 100.00
PPAGS George Springer/25 15.00 40.00
PPAGT Gleyber Torres/25 40.00 100.00
PPAJA Jose Altuve/25 15.00 40.00
PPAJF Jack Flaherty/50 20.00 50.00
PPAJP Joc Pederson/25 10.00 25.00
PPAJS Juan Soto/25 50.00 120.00
PPAMM Max Muncy/50 8.00 20.00
PPAMS Max Scherzer/25 20.00 50.00
PPAMSO Mike Soroka/50 15.00 40.00
PPAOA Ozzie Albies
PPAPC Patrick Corbin/25 20.00 50.00
PPAPG Paul Goldschmidt/25 20.00 50.00
PPARA Ronald Acuna Jr./25 60.00 150.00
PPASD Sean Doolittle/50 12.00 30.00

2020 Topps Postseason Performance Relics

STATED ODDS 1:3606 HOBBY
STATED PRINT RUN 99 SER.#'d SETS
*RED/25: .75X TO 2X BASIC
PPRAB Alex Bregman 4.00 10.00
PPRAJ Aaron Judge 20.00 50.00
PPRAR Anthony Rendon 8.00 20.00
PPRCB Cody Bellinger 8.00 20.00
PPRCC Carlos Correa 4.00 10.00
PPRDS Dansby Swanson 5.00 12.00
PPRFF Freddie Freeman 8.00 20.00
PPRGC Gerrit Cole 6.00 15.00
PPRGS Giancarlo Stanton 4.00 10.00
PPRGSP George Springer 3.00 8.00
PPRJA Jose Altuve 3.00 8.00
PPRJF Jack Flaherty 3.00 8.00
PPRJP Joc Pederson 3.00 8.00
PPRJS Juan Soto 12.00 30.00
PPRJV Justin Verlander 4.00 10.00
PPRMS Max Scherzer 4.00 10.00
PPRMSO Mike Soroka 4.00 10.00
PPROA Ozzie Albies 4.00 10.00
PPRPC Patrick Corbin 3.00 8.00
PPRPG Paul Goldschmidt 4.00 10.00
PPRRA Ronald Acuna Jr. 10.00 25.00
PPRRZ Ryan Zimmerman 10.00 25.00
PPRSD Sean Doolittle 6.00 15.00
PPRSS Stephen Strasburg 6.00 15.00
PPRTG Tyler Glasnow 2.50 6.00
PPRTT Trea Turner 6.00 15.00
PPRWB Walker Buehler 5.00 12.00
PPRYM Yadier Molina 10.00 25.00

2020 Topps Rhys Hoskins Highlights

COMPLETE SET (30) 8.00 20.00
RANDOM INSERTS IN PACKS
*BLUE: 1.2X TO 3X BASIC
*BLACK/299: 1.5X TO 4X BASIC
*GOLD/50: 4X TO 10X BASIC
*RED/10: 8X TO 20X BASIC
RH1 Rhys Hoskins .40 1.00
RH2 Rhys Hoskins .40 1.00
RH3 Rhys Hoskins .40 1.00
RH4 Rhys Hoskins .40 1.00
RH5 Rhys Hoskins .40 1.00
RH6 Rhys Hoskins .40 1.00
RH7 Rhys Hoskins .40 1.00
RH8 Rhys Hoskins .40 1.00
RH9 Rhys Hoskins .40 1.00
RH10 Rhys Hoskins .40 1.00
RH11 Rhys Hoskins .40 1.00
RH12 Rhys Hoskins .40 1.00
RH13 Rhys Hoskins .40 1.00
RH14 Rhys Hoskins .40 1.00
RH15 Rhys Hoskins .40 1.00
RH16 Rhys Hoskins .40 1.00
RH17 Rhys Hoskins .40 1.00
RH18 Rhys Hoskins .40 1.00
RH19 Rhys Hoskins .40 1.00
RH20 Rhys Hoskins .40 1.00
RH21 Rhys Hoskins .40 1.00
RH22 Rhys Hoskins .40 1.00
RH23 Rhys Hoskins .40 1.00
RH24 Rhys Hoskins .40 1.00
RH25 Rhys Hoskins .40 1.00
RH26 Rhys Hoskins .40 1.00
RH27 Rhys Hoskins .40 1.00
RH28 Rhys Hoskins .40 1.00
RH29 Rhys Hoskins .40 1.00
RH30 Rhys Hoskins .40 1.00

2020 Topps Rhys Hoskins Highlights Autographs

RANDOM INSERTS IN PACKS
STATED PRINT RUN 10 SER.#'d SETS
EXCHANGE DEADLINE 12/31/2021
RHA1 Rhys Hoskins 40.00 100.00
RHA2 Rhys Hoskins 40.00 100.00
RHA3 Rhys Hoskins 40.00 100.00
RHA4 Rhys Hoskins 40.00 100.00
RHA5 Rhys Hoskins 40.00 100.00
RHA6 Rhys Hoskins 40.00 100.00
RHA7 Rhys Hoskins 40.00 100.00
RHA8 Rhys Hoskins 40.00 100.00
RHA9 Rhys Hoskins 40.00 100.00
RHA10 Rhys Hoskins 40.00 100.00
RHA11 Rhys Hoskins 40.00 100.00
RHA12 Rhys Hoskins 40.00 100.00
RHA13 Rhys Hoskins 40.00 100.00
RHA14 Rhys Hoskins 40.00 100.00
RHA15 Rhys Hoskins 40.00 100.00
RHA16 Rhys Hoskins 40.00 100.00
RHA17 Rhys Hoskins 40.00 100.00
RHA18 Rhys Hoskins 40.00 100.00
RHA19 Rhys Hoskins 40.00 100.00
RHA20 Rhys Hoskins 40.00 100.00
RHA21 Rhys Hoskins 40.00 100.00
RHA22 Rhys Hoskins 40.00 100.00
RHA23 Rhys Hoskins 40.00 100.00
RHA24 Rhys Hoskins 40.00 100.00
RHA25 Rhys Hoskins 40.00 100.00
RHA26 Rhys Hoskins 40.00 100.00
RHA27 Rhys Hoskins 40.00 100.00
RHA28 Rhys Hoskins 40.00 100.00
RHA29 Rhys Hoskins 40.00 100.00
RHA30 Rhys Hoskins 40.00 100.00

2020 Topps Rookie Card Retrospective RC Logo Medallions

ONE PER BLASTER BOX
*BLACK/199: 1X TO 2.5X BASIC
*GOLD/50: 1.5X TO 4X BASIC
RCRAJ Aaron Judge 5.00 12.00
RCRAK Al Kaline 2.00 5.00
RCRAP Albert Pujols 3.00 8.00
RCRBG Bob Gibson 1.50 4.00
RCRBH Bryce Harper 3.00 8.00
RCRBJ Bo Jackson 4.00 10.00
RCRBP Buster Posey 4.00 10.00
RCRBR Brooks Robinson 1.50 4.00
RCRCA Jose Canseco 1.50 4.00
RCRCB Cody Bellinger 4.00 10.00
RCRCC Carlos Correa 2.00 5.00
RCRCJ Chipper Jones 3.00 8.00
RCRCK Clayton Kershaw 4.00 10.00
RCRCR Cal Ripken Jr. 6.00 15.00
RCRCY Christian Yelich 2.50 6.00
RCRDG Dwight Gooden
RCRDM Don Mattingly 5.00 12.00
RCRDS Darryl Strawberry 1.25 3.00
RCRDY Dennis Eckersley 1.50 4.00
RCREB Ernie Banks 2.00 5.00
RCREM Eddie Murray 1.50 4.00
RCRFA Frank Thomas 4.00 10.00
RCRFR Frank Robinson 1.50 4.00
RCRFT Fernando Tatis Jr. 8.00 20.00
RCRHA Hank Aaron 5.00 12.00
RCRIS Ichiro 4.00 10.00
RCRJA Jose Altuve 1.50 4.00
RCRJB Jeff Bagwell 1.50 4.00
RCRJS John Smoltz 2.00 5.00
RCRKB Kris Bryant 4.00 10.00
RCRKG Ken Griffey Jr. 6.00 15.00
RCRMC Miguel Cabrera 2.00 5.00
RCRMS Giancarlo Stanton 2.00 5.00
RCRMT Mike Trout 12.00 30.00
RCROS Ozzie Smith 2.50 6.00
RCRPA Pete Alonso 5.00 12.00
RCRRC Roger Clemens 2.50 6.00
RCRRH Rickey Henderson 5.00 12.00
RCRRJ Reggie Jackson 4.00 10.00
RCRRO Roberto Clemente 5.00 12.00
RCRRS Ryne Sandberg 4.00 10.00
RCRRY Rhys Hoskins 2.50 6.00
RCRSA Sandy Alomar Jr. 1.25 3.00
RCRSK Sandy Koufax 4.00 10.00
RCRSO Shohei Ohtani 2.50 6.00
RCRSS Sammy Sosa 2.00 5.00
RCRST Stephen Strasburg 2.00 5.00
RCRTG Tony Gwynn 2.00 5.00
RCRTR Tim Raines 1.50 4.00
RCRVG Vladimir Guerrero Jr. 4.00 10.00

2020 Topps Significant Statistics

STATED ODDS 1:32 HOBBY
*GOLD/50: 1.5X TO 4X BASIC
SS1 Vladimir Guerrero Jr. .60 1.50
SS2 Aaron Judge .75 2.00
SS3 Mike Trout 1.50 4.00
SS4 Mike Trout 1.50 4.00
SS5 Mike Trout 1.50 4.00
SS6 Miguel Sano .25 .60
SS7 Jorge Soler .30 .75
SS8 Nelson Cruz .30 .75
SS9 Joey Gallo .30 .75
SS10 Rafael Devers .40 1.00
SS11 Cody Bellinger .60 1.50
SS12 Mike Trout 1.50 4.00
SS13 Nomar Mazara .20 .50
SS14 Christian Yelich .40 1.00
SS15 Mike Trout 1.50 4.00
SS16 Josh Hader .20 .50
SS17 Jordan Hicks .25 .60
SS18 Jacob deGrom .30 .75
SS19 Victor Robles .40 1.00
SS20 Harrison Bader .25 .60
SS21 Byron Buxton .25 .60
SS22 Lorenzo Cain .20 .50
SS23 J.T. Realmuto .30 .75
SS24 Trea Turner .25 .60
SS25 Austin Hedges .20 .50

2020 Topps Significant Statistics Autographs

STATED ODDS 1:11,458 HOBBY
PRINT RUNS B/WN 10-50 COPIES PER
NO PRICING ON QTY 10
EXCHANGE DEADLINE 4/30/2022
*RED/25: .5X TO 1.2X BASIC
SSAAMU Andres Munoz/50 4.00 10.00
SSABB Byron Buxton/25 15.00 40.00
SSACY Christian Yelich/25 30.00 80.00
SSAJd Jacob deGrom/25 30.00 80.00
SSAJH Josh Hader/50 6.00 15.00
SSAJR J.T. Realmuto/50 15.00 40.00
SSAJS Jorge Soler/50 5.00 12.00
SSARD Rafael Devers/25 20.00 50.00
SSAVG Vladimir Guerrero Jr. EXCH 40.00 100.00
SSAVR Victor Robles/50 12.00 30.00

2020 Topps Significant Statistics Relic Autographs

STATED ODDS 1:11,458 HOBBY
PRINT RUNS B/WN 10-50 COPIES PER
NO PRICING ON QTY 10 OR LESS
EXCHANGE DEADLINE 4/30/2022
*RED/25: .5X TO 1.2X BASIC
SSARAM Andres Munoz/50 5.00 12.00
SSARJH Josh Hader/50 8.00 20.00
SSARJR J.T. Realmuto/50 20.00 50.00
SSARJR2 J.T. Realmuto/50 20.00 50.00
SSARJS Jorge Soler/50 6.00 15.00
SSARVG Vladimir Guerrero Jr. EXCH 50.00 120.00
SSARVR Victor Robles/50 15.00 40.00

2020 Topps Significant Statistics Relics

STATED ODDS 1:5729 HOBBY
STATED PRINT RUN 99 SER.#'d SETS
*RED/25: .6X TO 1.5X BASIC
SSRAJ Aaron Judge 8.00 20.00
SSRCB Cody Bellinger 6.00 15.00
SSRCY Christian Yelich 4.00 10.00
SSRHB Harrison Bader 2.50 6.00
SSRJd Jacob deGrom 3.00 8.00
SSRJG Joey Gallo 3.00 8.00
SSRJR J.T. Realmuto 3.00 8.00
SSRJS Jorge Soler 3.00 8.00
SSRLC Lorenzo Cain 2.00 5.00
SSRMS Miguel Sano 2.50 6.00
SSRMT Mike Trout 15.00 40.00
SSRNC Nelson Cruz 3.00 8.00
SSRRD Rafael Devers 4.00 10.00
SSRTT Trea Turner 2.50 6.00
SSRVG Vladimir Guerrero Jr. 6.00 15.00
SSRVR Victor Robles 4.00 10.00
SSRMT2 Mike Trout 15.00 40.00
SSRMT3 Mike Trout 15.00 40.00
SSRMT4 Mike Trout 15.00 40.00
SSRMT5 Mike Trout 15.00 40.00

2020 Topps Topps Choice

STATED ODDS 1:28 HOBBY
*BLUE: 1.2X TO 3X BASIC
*BLACK/299: 1.5X TO 4X BASIC
*GOLD/50: 4X TO 10X BASIC
TC1 Vladimir Guerrero Jr. .60 1.50
TC2 Yordan Alvarez 1.00 2.50
TC3 Gavin Lux 1.25 3.00
TC4 Babe Ruth .75 2.00
TC5 Pete Alonso .75 2.00
TC6 Ronald Acuna Jr. 1.25 3.00
TC7 Mike Trout 1.50 4.00
TC8 Clayton Kershaw .60 1.50
TC9 Ichiro .40 1.00
TC10 Don Mattingly .60 1.50
TC11 Randy Johnson .30 .75
TC12 Ty Cobb .50 1.25
TC13 Fernando Tatis Jr. 1.25 3.00
TC14 Mookie Betts .60 1.50
TC15 Yadier Molina .30 .75
TC16 Kris Bryant .40 1.00
TC17 Christian Yelich .40 1.00
TC18 Aaron Judge .75 2.00
TC19 Cody Bellinger .60 1.50
TC20 Bryce Harper .50 1.25
TC21 Jose Altuve .25 .60
TC22 Cal Ripken Jr. 1.00 2.50
TC23 Ken Griffey Jr. .60 1.50
TC24 Shohei Ohtani .40 1.00
TC25 Ryne Sandberg .60 1.50

2020 Topps Topps Choice Autographs

STATED ODDS 1:57,238 HOBBY
PRINT RUNS B/WN 5-25 COPIES PER
NO PRICING ON QTY 15 OR LESS
EXCHANGE DEADLINE 12/31/2021
TC1 Vladimir Guerrero Jr./25 100.00 250.00
TC2 Yordan Alvarez/25 150.00 400.00
TC3 Gavin Lux/25 125.00 300.00
TC5 Pete Alonso/25 100.00 250.00
TC6 Ronald Acuna Jr./25 100.00 250.00
TC10 Don Mattingly/25 75.00 200.00
TC13 Fernando Tatis Jr./25 150.00 400.00

2020 Topps Turkey Red '20

STATED ODDS ONE PER BLASTER PACK
*BLUE/50: 4X TO 10X BASIC
TR1 Bryce Harper .50 1.25
TR2 Ronald Acuna Jr. 1.25 3.00
TR3 Ketel Marte .25 .60
TR4 Adam Jones .25 .60
TR5 Zack Greinke .25 .60
TR6 Freddie Freeman .40 1.00
TR7 Nick Markakis .25 .60
TR8 Ozzie Albies .30 .75
TR9 Trey Mancini .30 .75
TR10 Sean Murphy .30 .75
TR11 Dustin May .75 2.00
TR12 John Means .20 .50
TR13 Mookie Betts .60 1.50
TR14 J.D. Martinez .30 .75
TR15 Chris Sale .30 .75
TR16 Tim Anderson .30 .75
TR17 Yoan Moncada .30 .75
TR18 Eloy Jimenez .60 1.50
TR19 Willson Contreras .30 .75
TR20 Javier Baez .40 1.00
TR21 Kris Bryant .40 1.00
TR22 Kyle Schwarber .30 .75
TR23 Nick Senzel .30 .75
TR24 Yasiel Puig .30 .75
TR25 Luis Castillo .25 .60
TR26 Francisco Lindor .30 .75
TR27 Rafael Devers .40 1.00
TR28 Jose Ramirez .25 .60
TR29 Nolan Arenado .40 1.00
TR30 Charlie Blackmon .30 .75
TR31 Brendan Rodgers .30 .75
TR32 Brendan McKay .30 .75
TR33 Matthew Boyd .20 .50
TR34 Miguel Cabrera .30 .75
TR35 Jose Altuve .25 .60
TR36 Alex Bregman .30 .75
TR37 Yordan Alvarez 1.00 2.50
TR38 Justin Verlander .30 .75
TR39 A.J. Puk .40 1.00
TR40 Whit Merrifield .30 .75
TR41 Nico Hoerner .75 2.00
TR42 Cody Bellinger .60 1.50
TR43 Clayton Kershaw .60 1.50
TR44 Walker Buehler .40 1.00
TR45 Albert Pujols .40 1.00
TR46 Mike Trout 1.50 4.00
TR47 Shohei Ohtani .40 1.00
TR48 Brian Anderson .20 .50
TR49 Jesus Luzardo .40 1.00
TR50 Zac Gallen .50 1.25
TR51 Christian Yelich .40 1.00
TR52 Lorenzo Cain .20 .50
TR53 Josh Hader .20 .50
TR54 Eddie Rosario .25 .60
TR55 Nelson Cruz .30 .75
TR56 Xander Bogaerts .30 .75
TR57 Max Kepler .25 .60
TR58 Gary Sanchez .30 .75

TR59 Gleyber Torres .60 1.50
TR60 Aaron Judge .75 2.00
TR61 Giancarlo Stanton .30 .75
TR62 Masahiro Tanaka .30 .75
TR63 Pete Alonso .75 2.00
TR64 Jeff McNeil .25 .60
TR65 Jacob deGrom .30 .75
TR66 Matt Chapman .30 .75
TR67 Khris Davis .30 .75
TR68 Matt Olson .20 .50
TR69 Rhys Hoskins .40 1.00
TR70 Aaron Nola .30 .75
TR71 Gerrit Cole .50 1.25
TR72 Josh Bell .25 .60
TR73 Gavin Lux 1.25 3.00
TR74 Chris Archer .20 .50
TR75 Manny Machado .30 .75
TR76 Fernando Tatis Jr. 1.25 3.00
TR77 Buster Posey .40 1.00
TR78 Brandon Crawford .25 .60
TR79 Yusei Kikuchi .25 .60
TR80 Keston Hiura .40 1.00
TR81 Yadier Molina .30 .75
TR82 Marcell Ozuna .30 .75
TR83 Paul Goldschmidt .30 .75
TR84 Austin Meadows .25 .60
TR85 Blake Snell .25 .60
TR86 Charlie Morton .30 .75
TR87 Joey Gallo .30 .75
TR88 Shin-Soo Choo .25 .60
TR89 Kyle Lewis 1.50 4.00
TR90 Cavan Biggio .40 1.00
TR91 Vladimir Guerrero Jr. .60 1.50
TR92 Marcus Stroman .25 .60
TR93 Aristides Aquino .40 1.00
TR94 Bo Bichette 1.50 4.00
TR95 Juan Soto 1.00 2.50
TR96 Max Scherzer .30 .75
TR97 Anthony Rendon .30 .75
TR98 Sean Doolittle .20 .50
TR99 Gio Urshela .30 .75
TR100 George Springer .25 .60

2020 Topps Turkey Red '20 Series 2

STATED ODDS ONE PER BLASTER PACK
*BLUE/50: 4X TO 10X BASIC
TR1 Ken Griffey Jr. .60 1.50
TR2 Stephen Strasburg .30 .75
TR3 Joey Votto .30 .75
TR4 Noah Syndergaard .25 .60
TR5 Chris Paddack .30 .75
TR6 Jack Flaherty .25 .60
TR7 Don Mattingly .60 1.50
TR8 Frank Thomas .30 .75
TR9 Cal Ripken Jr. 1.00 2.50
TR10 Matt Thaiss .25 .60
TR11 Randy Johnson .30 .75
TR12 Alex Young .20 .50
TR13 Josh Rojas .20 .50
TR14 Chipper Jones .30 .75
TR15 Hank Aaron .60 1.50
TR16 Hunter Harvey .30 .75
TR17 Andrew Benintendi .30 .75
TR18 Roger Clemens .40 1.00
TR19 Ted Williams .60 1.50
TR20 Jackie Robinson .30 .75
TR21 Rod Carew .25 .60
TR22 Nolan Ryan 1.00 2.50
TR23 Robel Garcia .20 .50
TR24 Adbert Alzolay .25 .60
TR25 Anthony Rizzo .50 1.25
TR26 Ryne Sandberg .60 1.50
TR27 Ernie Banks .30 .75
TR28 Dylan Cease .40 1.00
TR29 Zack Collins .25 .60
TR30 Lucas Giolito .25 .60
TR31 Barry Larkin .25 .60
TR32 Sonny Gray .25 .60
TR33 Eugenio Suarez .25 .60
TR34 Shane Bieber .30 .75
TR35 Jim Thome .25 .60
TR36 Trevor Story .30 .75
TR37 Sam Hilliard .30 .75
TR38 David Dahl .20 .50
TR39 Jake Rogers .20 .50
TR40 Nolan Ryan 1.00 2.50
TR41 Jeff Bagwell .25 .60
TR42 George Brett .60 1.50
TR43 Jorge Soler .30 .75
TR44 Hyun-Jin Ryu .25 .60
TR45 Corey Seager .30 .75
TR46 Joc Pederson .25 .60
TR47 Sandy Koufax .60 1.50
TR48 Isan Diaz .30 .75
TR49 Jordan Yamamoto .25 .60
TR50 Trent Grisham .75 2.00
TR51 Robin Yount .30 .75
TR52 Brusdar Graterol .30 .75
TR53 Jose Berrios .25 .60
TR54 Vladimir Guerrero .60 1.50
TR55 Michael Conforto .25 .60
TR56 Darryl Strawberry .20 .50
TR57 Luis Severino .25 .60
TR58 Babe Ruth .75 2.00
TR59 Reggie Jackson .25 .60
TR60 Lou Gehrig .60 1.50
TR61 Rickey Henderson .30 .75
TR62 Mark McGwire .50 1.25
TR63 Seth Brown .20 .50
TR64 Sheldon Neuse .25 .60
TR65 Mike Schmidt .50 1.25
TR66 J.T. Realmuto .30 .75
TR67 Steve Carlton .25 .60
TR68 Bryan Reynolds .25 .60
TR69 Roberto Clemente .75 2.00
TR70 Tony Gwynn .30 .75
TR71 Mauricio Dubon .25 .60
TR72 Jaylin Davis .30 .75
TR73 Ty Cobb .50 1.25
TR74 Honus Wagner .30 .75
TR75 Max Muncy .25 .60
TR76 Will Clark .25 .60
TR77 Willie Mays .60 1.50
TR78 Ichiro .40 1.00
TR79 Edgar Martinez .25 .60
TR80 Justin Dunn .25 .60
TR81 Jake Fraley .25 .60
TR82 Junior Fernandez .20 .50
TR83 Randy Arozarena 1.50 4.00
TR84 Ozzie Smith .40 1.00
TR85 Tommy Edman .30 .75
TR86 Tyler Glasnow .20 .50
TR87 Nick Solak .30 .75
TR88 Brock Burke .20 .50
TR89 Elvis Andrus .25 .60
TR90 Roberto Alomar .25 .60
TR91 Anthony Kay .20 .50
TR92 T.J. Zeuch .20 .50
TR93 Lourdes Gurriel Jr. .25 .60
TR94 Victor Robles .40 1.00
TR95 Patrick Corbin .25 .60
TR96 Ryan Zimmerman .25 .60
TR97 Stan Musial .50 1.25
TR98 Mariano Rivera .40 1.00
TR99 Joe Mauer .25 .60
TR100 Andres Munoz .25 .60

2020 Topps Turkey Red '20 Chrome

STATED ODDS 1:10 BLASTER PACKS
*BLUE REF/50: 3X TO 8X BASIC
TRC1 Bryce Harper 1.50 4.00
TRC2 Ronald Acuna Jr. 4.00 10.00
TRC3 Ketel Marte .75 2.00
TRC4 Adam Jones .75 2.00
TRC5 Zack Greinke .75 2.00
TRC6 Freddie Freeman 1.25 3.00
TRC7 Nick Markakis .75 2.00
TRC8 Ozzie Albies 1.00 2.50
TRC9 Trey Mancini 1.00 2.50
TRC10 Sean Murphy 1.00 2.50
TRC11 Dustin May 2.50 6.00
TRC12 John Means .60 1.50
TRC13 Mookie Betts 2.00 5.00
TRC14 J.D. Martinez 1.00 2.50
TRC15 Chris Sale 1.00 2.50
TRC16 Tim Anderson 1.00 2.50
TRC17 Yoan Moncada 1.00 2.50
TRC18 Eloy Jimenez 2.00 5.00
TRC19 Willson Contreras 1.00 2.50
TRC20 Javier Baez 1.25 3.00
TRC21 Kris Bryant 1.25 3.00
TRC22 Kyle Schwarber 1.00 2.50
TRC23 Nick Senzel 1.00 2.50
TRC24 Yasiel Puig 1.00 2.50
TRC25 Luis Castillo .75 2.00
TRC26 Francisco Lindor 1.00 2.50
TRC27 Rafael Devers 1.25 3.00
TRC28 Jose Ramirez .75 2.00
TRC29 Nolan Arenado 1.25 3.00
TRC30 Charlie Blackmon 1.00 2.50
TRC31 Brendan Rodgers 1.00 2.50
TRC32 Brendan McKay 1.00 2.50
TRC33 Matthew Boyd .60 1.50
TRC34 Miguel Cabrera 1.00 2.50
TRC35 Jose Altuve .75 2.00
TRC36 Alex Bregman 1.00 2.50
TRC37 Yordan Alvarez 3.00 8.00
TRC38 Justin Verlander 1.00 2.50
TRC39 A.J. Puk 1.25 3.00
TRC40 Whit Merrifield 1.00 2.50
TRC41 Nico Hoerner 2.50 6.00
TRC42 Cody Bellinger 2.00 5.00
TRC43 Clayton Kershaw 2.00 5.00
TRC44 Walker Buehler 1.25 3.00
TRC45 Albert Pujols 1.25 3.00
TRC46 Mike Trout 5.00 12.00
TRC47 Shohei Ohtani 1.25 3.00
TRC48 Brian Anderson .60 1.50
TRC49 Jesus Luzardo 1.25 3.00
TRC50 Zac Gallen 1.50 4.00
TRC51 Christian Yelich 1.25 3.00
TRC52 Lorenzo Cain .60 1.50
TRC53 Josh Hader .60 1.50
TRC54 Eddie Rosario .75 2.00
TRC55 Nelson Cruz 1.00 2.50
TRC56 Xander Bogaerts 1.00 2.50
TRC57 Max Kepler .75 2.00
TRC58 Gary Sanchez 1.00 2.50
TRC59 Gleyber Torres 2.00 5.00
TRC60 Aaron Judge 2.50 6.00
TRC61 Giancarlo Stanton 1.00 2.50
TRC62 Masahiro Tanaka 1.00 2.50
TRC63 Pete Alonso 2.50 6.00
TRC64 Jeff McNeil .75 2.00
TRC65 Jacob deGrom 1.00 2.50
TRC66 Matt Chapman 1.00 2.50
TRC67 Khris Davis 1.00 2.50
TRC68 Matt Olson .60 1.50
TRC69 Rhys Hoskins 1.25 3.00
TRC70 Aaron Nola 1.00 2.50
TRC71 Gerrit Cole 1.50 4.00
TRC72 Josh Bell .75 2.00
TRC73 Gavin Lux 4.00 10.00
TRC74 Chris Archer .60 1.50
TRC75 Manny Machado 1.00 2.50
TRC76 Fernando Tatis Jr. 4.00 10.00
TRC77 Buster Posey 1.25 3.00
TRC78 Brandon Crawford .75 2.00
TRC79 Yusei Kikuchi .75 2.00
TRC80 Keston Hiura 1.25 3.00
TRC81 Yadier Molina 1.00 2.50
TRC82 Marcell Ozuna 1.00 2.50
TRC83 Paul Goldschmidt 1.00 2.50
TRC84 Austin Meadows .75 2.00
TRC85 Blake Snell .75 2.00
TRC86 Charlie Morton 1.00 2.50
TRC87 Joey Gallo 1.00 2.50
TRC88 Shin-Soo Choo .75 2.00
TRC89 Kyle Lewis 5.00 12.00
TRC90 Cavan Biggio 1.25 3.00
TRC91 Vladimir Guerrero Jr. 2.00 5.00
TRC92 Marcus Stroman .75 2.00
TRC93 Aristides Aquino 1.25 3.00
TRC94 Bo Bichette 5.00 12.00
TRC95 Juan Soto 3.00 8.00
TRC96 Max Scherzer 1.00 2.50
TRC97 Anthony Rendon 1.00 2.50
TRC98 Sean Doolittle .60 1.50
TRC99 Gio Urshela 1.00 2.50
TRC100 George Springer .75 2.00

2020 Topps Turkey Red '20 Chrome Series 2

STATED ODDS 1:10 BLASTER PACKS
*BLUE REF/50: 3X TO 8X BASIC
TRC1 Ken Griffey Jr. 2.00 5.00
TRC2 Stephen Strasburg 1.00 2.50
TRC3 Joey Votto 1.00 2.50
TRC4 Noah Syndergaard .75 2.00
TRC5 Chris Paddack 1.00 2.50
TRC6 Jack Flaherty .75 2.00
TRC7 Don Mattingly 2.00 5.00
TRC8 Frank Thomas 1.00 2.50
TRC9 Cal Ripken Jr. 3.00 8.00
TRC10 Matt Thaiss .75 2.00
TRC11 Randy Johnson 1.00 2.50
TRC12 Alex Young .60 1.50
TRC13 Josh Rojas .60 1.50
TRC14 Chipper Jones 1.00 2.50
TRC15 Hank Aaron 2.00 5.00
TRC16 Hunter Harvey 1.00 2.50
TRC17 Andrew Benintendi 1.00 2.50
TRC18 Roger Clemens 1.25 3.00
TRC19 Ted Williams 2.00 5.00
TRC20 Jackie Robinson 1.00 2.50
TRC21 Rod Carew .75 2.00
TRC22 Nolan Ryan 3.00 8.00
TRC23 Robel Garcia .60 1.50
TRC24 Adbert Alzolay .75 2.00
TRC25 Anthony Rizzo 1.50 4.00
TRC26 Ryne Sandberg 2.00 5.00
TRC27 Ernie Banks 1.00 2.50
TRC28 Dylan Cease 1.25 3.00
TRC29 Zack Collins .75 2.00
TRC30 Lucas Giolito .75 2.00
TRC31 Barry Larkin .75 2.00
TRC32 Sonny Gray .75 2.00
TRC33 Eugenio Suarez .75 2.00
TRC34 Shane Bieber 1.00 2.50
TRC35 Jim Thome .75 2.00
TRC36 Trevor Story 1.00 2.50
TRC37 Sam Hilliard 1.00 2.50
TRC38 David Dahl .60 1.50
TRC39 Jake Rogers .60 1.50
TRC40 Nolan Ryan 3.00 8.00
TRC41 Jeff Bagwell .75 2.00
TRC42 George Brett 2.00 5.00
TRC43 Jorge Soler 1.00 2.50
TRC44 Hyun-Jin Ryu .75 2.00
TRC45 Corey Seager 1.00 2.50
TRC46 Joc Pederson .75 2.00
TRC47 Sandy Koufax 2.00 5.00
TRC48 Isan Diaz 1.00 2.50
TRC49 Jordan Yamamoto .75 2.00
TRC50 Trent Grisham 2.50 6.00
TRC51 Robin Yount 1.00 2.50
TRC52 Brusdar Graterol 1.00 2.50
TRC53 Jose Berrios .75 2.00
TRC54 Vladimir Guerrero 2.00 5.00
TRC55 Michael Conforto .75 2.00
TRC56 Darryl Strawberry .60 1.50
TRC57 Luis Severino .75 2.00
TRC58 Babe Ruth 2.50 6.00
TRC59 Reggie Jackson .75 2.00
TRC60 Lou Gehrig 2.00 5.00
TRC61 Rickey Henderson 1.00 2.50
TRC62 Mark McGwire 1.50 4.00
TRC63 Seth Brown .60 1.50
TRC64 Sheldon Neuse .75 2.00
TRC65 Mike Schmidt 1.50 4.00
TRC66 J.T. Realmuto 1.00 2.50
TRC67 Steve Carlton .75 2.00
TRC68 Bryan Reynolds .75 2.00
TRC69 Roberto Clemente 2.50 6.00
TRC70 Tony Gwynn 1.00 2.50
TRC71 Ty Cobb 1.50 4.00
TRC72 Honus Wagner 1.00 2.50
TRC73 Mauricio Dubon .75 2.00
TRC74 Jaylin Davis 1.00 2.50
TRC75 Max Muncy .75 2.00
TRC76 Will Clark .75 2.00
TRC77 Willie Mays 2.00 5.00
TRC78 Ichiro 1.25 3.00
TRC79 Edgar Martinez .75 2.00
TRC80 Justin Dunn .75 2.00
TRC81 Jake Fraley .75 2.00
TRC82 Junior Fernandez .60 1.50
TRC83 Randy Arozarena 5.00 12.00
TRC84 Ozzie Smith 1.25 3.00
TRC85 Tommy Edman 1.00 2.50
TRC86 Tyler Glasnow .60 1.50
TRC87 Nick Solak 1.00 2.50
TRC88 Brock Burke .60 1.50
TRC89 Elvis Andrus .75 2.00
TRC90 Roberto Alomar .75 2.00
TRC91 Anthony Kay .60 1.50
TRC92 T.J. Zeuch .60 1.50
TRC93 Lourdes Gurriel Jr. .75 2.00
TRC94 Victor Robles 1.25 3.00
TRC95 Patrick Corbin .75 2.00
TRC96 Ryan Zimmerman .75 2.00
TRC97 Stan Musial 1.50 4.00
TRC98 Mariano Rivera 1.25 3.00
TRC99 Joe Mauer .75 2.00
TRC100 Andres Munoz .75 2.00

2020 Topps Turkey Red '20 Box Toppers

RANDOM INSERTS IN BOXES
OTR1 Mike Trout 3.00 8.00
OTR2 Shohei Ohtani .75 2.00
OTR3 Ketel Marte .50 1.25
OTR4 Ronald Acuna Jr. 2.50 6.00
OTR5 Freddie Freeman .75 2.00
OTR6 Trey Mancini .60 1.50
OTR7 Mookie Betts 1.25 3.00
OTR8 Rafael Devers .75 2.00
OTR9 Javier Baez .75 2.00
OTR10 Kris Bryant .75 2.00
OTR11 Nico Hoerner 1.50 4.00
OTR12 Eloy Jimenez 1.25 3.00
OTR13 Aristides Aquino .75 2.00
OTR14 Francisco Lindor .60 1.50
OTR15 Nolan Arenado .75 2.00
OTR16 Miguel Cabrera .60 1.50
OTR17 Jose Altuve .50 1.25
OTR18 Alex Bregman .60 1.50
OTR19 Yordan Alvarez 2.00 5.00
OTR20 Justin Verlander .60 1.50
OTR21 Whit Merrifield .60 1.50
OTR22 Cody Bellinger 1.25 3.00
OTR23 Clayton Kershaw 1.25 3.00
OTR24 Gavin Lux 2.50 6.00
OTR25 Christian Yelich .75 2.00
OTR26 Keston Hiura .75 2.00
OTR27 Max Kepler .50 1.25
OTR28 Pete Alonso 1.50 4.00
OTR29 Jacob deGrom .60 1.50
OTR30 Gleyber Torres 1.25 3.00
OTR31 Aaron Judge 1.50 4.00
OTR32 Giancarlo Stanton .60 1.50
OTR33 Matt Chapman .60 1.50
OTR34 Jesus Luzardo .75 2.00
OTR35 Bryce Harper 1.00 2.50
OTR36 Rhys Hoskins .75 2.00
OTR37 Josh Bell .50 1.25
OTR38 Manny Machado .60 1.50
OTR39 Fernando Tatis Jr. 2.50 6.00
OTR40 Buster Posey .75 2.00
OTR41 Kyle Lewis 3.00 8.00
OTR42 Yadier Molina .60 1.50
OTR43 Paul Goldschmidt .60 1.50
OTR44 Brendan McKay .60 1.50
OTR45 Joey Gallo .60 1.50
OTR46 Vladimir Guerrero Jr. 1.25 3.00
OTR47 Bo Bichette 3.00 8.00
OTR48 Juan Soto 2.00 5.00
OTR49 Max Scherzer .60 1.50
OTR50 Anthony Rendon .60 1.50

2020 Topps Warriors of the Diamond

STATED ODDS 1:16 HOBBY
*BLUE: 1.2X TO 3X BASIC
*BLACK/299: 2X TO 5X BASIC
*GOLD/50: 5X TO 12X BASIC
WOD1 Babe Ruth .75 2.00
WOD2 Joe Morgan .25 .60
WOD3 Hank Aaron .60 1.50
WOD4 Willie Mays .60 1.50
WOD5 Roger Clemens .40 1.00
WOD6 Tom Seaver .25 .60
WOD7 Rickey Henderson .30 .75
WOD8 Lou Gehrig .60 1.50
WOD9 Alex Rodriguez .40 1.00
WOD10 Honus Wagner .30 .75
WOD11 Stan Musial .50 1.25
WOD12 Ted Williams .60 1.50
WOD13 Ty Cobb .50 1.25
WOD14 Mike Schmidt .50 1.25
WOD15 Randy Johnson .30 .75
WOD16 Albert Pujols .40 1.00
WOD17 Carl Yastrzemski .50 1.25
WOD18 Warren Spahn .25 .60
WOD19 Mike Trout 1.50 4.00
WOD20 Dwight Gooden .20 .50
WOD21 Steve Carlton .25 .60
WOD22 Bob Gibson .25 .60
WOD23 Pedro Martinez .25 .60
WOD24 Sandy Koufax .60 1.50
WOD25 Jacob deGrom .30 .75
WOD26 Justin Verlander .30 .75
WOD27 Max Scherzer .30 .75
WOD28 Nolan Ryan 1.00 2.50
WOD29 Clayton Kershaw .60 1.50
WOD30 Tom Glavine .25 .60
WOD31 Cal Ripken Jr. 1.00 2.50
WOD32 Mookie Betts .60 1.50
WOD33 Chipper Jones .30 .75
WOD34 Ernie Banks .30 .75
WOD35 Cody Bellinger .60 1.50
WOD36 Christian Yelich .40 1.00
WOD37 Alex Bregman .30 .75
WOD38 Bryce Harper .50 1.25
WOD39 Ken Griffey Jr. .60 1.50
WOD40 George Brett .60 1.50
WOD41 Jackie Robinson .30 .75
WOD42 Roberto Clemente .75 2.00
WOD43 Frank Robinson .25 .60
WOD44 Frank Thomas .30 .75
WOD45 Johnny Bench .30 .75
WOD46 Eddie Mathews .30 .75
WOD47 Rod Carew .25 .60
WOD48 Robin Yount .30 .75
WOD49 Al Kaline .30 .75
WOD50 Wade Boggs .25 .60

2020 Topps Vladimir Guerrero Jr. Highlights

COMPLETE SET (30) 20.00 50.00
RANDOM INSERTS IN PACKS
*BLUE: 1.2X TO 3X BASIC
*BLACK/299: 1.5X TO 4X BASIC
*GOLD/50: 4X TO 10X BASIC
*RED/10: 8X TO 20X BASIC
VGJ1 Vladimir Guerrero Jr. .60 1.50
VGJ2 Vladimir Guerrero Jr. .60 1.50
VGJ3 Vladimir Guerrero Jr. .60 1.50
VGJ4 Vladimir Guerrero Jr. .60 1.50
VGJ5 Vladimir Guerrero Jr. .60 1.50
VGJ6 Vladimir Guerrero Jr. .60 1.50
VGJ7 Vladimir Guerrero Jr. .60 1.50
VGJ8 Vladimir Guerrero Jr. .60 1.50
VGJ9 Vladimir Guerrero Jr. .60 1.50
VGJ10 Vladimir Guerrero Jr. .60 1.50
VGJ11 Vladimir Guerrero Jr. .60 1.50
VGJ12 Vladimir Guerrero Jr. .60 1.50
VGJ13 Vladimir Guerrero Jr. .60 1.50
VGJ14 Vladimir Guerrero Jr. .60 1.50
VGJ15 Vladimir Guerrero Jr. .60 1.50
VGJ16 Vladimir Guerrero Jr. .60 1.50
VGJ17 Vladimir Guerrero Jr. .60 1.50
VGJ18 Vladimir Guerrero Jr. .60 1.50
VGJ19 Vladimir Guerrero Jr. .60 1.50
VGJ20 Vladimir Guerrero Jr. .60 1.50
VGJ21 Vladimir Guerrero Jr. .60 1.50
VGJ22 Vladimir Guerrero Jr. .60 1.50
VGJ23 Vladimir Guerrero Jr. .60 1.50
VGJ24 Vladimir Guerrero Jr. .60 1.50
VGJ25 Vladimir Guerrero Jr. .60 1.50
VGJ26 Vladimir Guerrero Jr. .60 1.50
VGJ27 Vladimir Guerrero Jr. .60 1.50
VGJ28 Vladimir Guerrero Jr. .60 1.50
VGJ29 Vladimir Guerrero Jr. .60 1.50
VGJ30 Vladimir Guerrero Jr. .60 1.50

2020 Topps Vladimir Guerrero Jr. Highlights Autographs

RANDOM INSERTS IN PACKS
STATED PRINT RUN 10 SER.#'d SETS
EXCHANGE DEADLINE 12/31/2021
VGJA1 Vladimir Guerrero Jr. 40.00 100.00
VGJA2 Vladimir Guerrero Jr. 40.00 100.00
VGJA3 Vladimir Guerrero Jr. 40.00 100.00
VGJA4 Vladimir Guerrero Jr. 40.00 100.00
VGJA5 Vladimir Guerrero Jr. 40.00 100.00
VGJA6 Vladimir Guerrero Jr. 40.00 100.00
VGJA7 Vladimir Guerrero Jr. 40.00 100.00
VGJA8 Vladimir Guerrero Jr. 40.00 100.00
VGJA9 Vladimir Guerrero Jr. 40.00 100.00
VGJA10 Vladimir Guerrero Jr. 40.00 100.00
VGJA11 Vladimir Guerrero Jr. 40.00 100.00
VGJA12 Vladimir Guerrero Jr. 40.00 100.00
VGJA13 Vladimir Guerrero Jr. 40.00 100.00
VGJA14 Vladimir Guerrero Jr. 40.00 100.00
VGJA15 Vladimir Guerrero Jr. 40.00 100.00
VGJA16 Vladimir Guerrero Jr. 40.00 100.00
VGJA17 Vladimir Guerrero Jr. 40.00 100.00
VGJA18 Vladimir Guerrero Jr. 40.00 100.00
VGJA19 Vladimir Guerrero Jr. 40.00 100.00
VGJA20 Vladimir Guerrero Jr. 40.00 100.00
VGJA21 Vladimir Guerrero Jr. 40.00 100.00
VGJA22 Vladimir Guerrero Jr. 40.00 100.00
VGJA23 Vladimir Guerrero Jr. 40.00 100.00
VGJA24 Vladimir Guerrero Jr. 40.00 100.00
VGJA25 Vladimir Guerrero Jr. 40.00 100.00
VGJA26 Vladimir Guerrero Jr. 40.00 100.00
VGJA27 Vladimir Guerrero Jr. 40.00 100.00
VGJA28 Vladimir Guerrero Jr. 40.00 100.00
VGJA29 Vladimir Guerrero Jr. 40.00 100.00
VGJA30 Vladimir Guerrero Jr. 40.00 100.00

2020 Topps World Series Champion Autograph Relics

STATED ODDS 1:28,035 HOBBY
PRINT RUNS B/WN 35-50 COPIES PER
EXCHANGE DEADLINE 12/31/2021
WCARJS Juan Soto EXCH 100.00 250.00
WCARKS Kurt Suzuki/35 30.00 80.00
WCARMS Max Scherzer
WCARPC Patrick Corbin EXCH 25.00 60.00
WCARRZ Ryan Zimmerman/35 60.00 150.00
WCARSD Sean Doolittle/50 15.00 40.00
WCARVR Victor Robles/50 25.00 60.00
WCARYG Yan Gomes

2020 Topps World Series Champion Autograph Relics Red

*RED: .5X TO 1.2X BASIC
STATED ODDS 1:57,238 HOBBY
STATED PRINT RUN 25 SER.#'d SETS
EXCHANGE DEADLINE 12/31/2021
WCARMS Max Scherzer 125.00 300.00
WCARYG Yan Gomes 30.00 80.00

2020 Topps World Series Champion Autographs

STATED ODDS 1:28,035 HOBBY
STATED PRINT RUN 50 SER.#'d SETS
EXCHANGE DEADLINE 12/31/2021
*RED/25: .5X TO 1.2X BASIC
WCAFR Fernando Rodney 25.00 60.00
WCAHK Howie Kendrick 50.00 120.00
WCAJR Joe Ross 25.00 60.00
WCAJS Juan Soto EXCH 125.00 300.00
WCAMS Max Scherzer 25.00 60.00
WCAPC Patrick Corbin 40.00 100.00
WCASD Sean Doolittle 20.00 50.00
WCAVR Victor Robles 40.00 100.00

2020 Topps World Series Champion Relics

STATED ODDS 1:3606 HOBBY
STATED PRINT RUN 99 SER.#'d SETS
*RED/25: .75X TO 2X BASIC
WCRAC Asdrubal Cabrera 8.00 20.00
WCRAR Anthony Rendon 20.00 50.00
WCRAS Anibal Sanchez 10.00 25.00
WCRBD Brian Dozier 10.00 25.00
WCRJS Juan Soto 30.00 80.00
WCRKS Kurt Suzuki 10.00 25.00
WCRMS Max Scherzer
WCRMT Michael Taylor 8.00 20.00
WCRPC Patrick Corbin 10.00 25.00
WCRRZ Ryan Zimmerman 15.00 40.00
WCRSD Sean Doolittle 8.00 20.00
WCRSS Stephen Strasburg 15.00 40.00
WCRTT Trea Turner 12.00 30.00
WCRVR Victor Robles 12.00 30.00
WCRYG Yan Gomes 10.00 25.00

2020 Topps Update

PRINTING PLATE ODDS 1:7828 HOBBY
PLATE PRINT RUN 1 SET PER COLOR
BLACK-CYAN-MAGENTA-YELLOW ISSUED
NO PLATE PRICING DUE TO SCARCITY
U1 Bo Bichette 3.00 8.00
U2 Adam Engel .15 .40
U3 Trea Turner .20 .50
Wilmer Difo
U4 Mike Trout AS 1.25 3.00
U5 Starlin Castro .15 .40
U6 Mike Moustakas .20 .50
U7 Alex Bregman .60 1.50
Yordan Alvarez
U8 Buster Posey AS .30 .75
U9 Ken Griffey Jr. HRD .50 1.25
U10 Anthony Alford .15 .40
U11 Chris Owings .15 .40
U12 Aaron Bummer .15 .40
U13 Jose Martinez .15 .40
U14 Giancarlo Stanton HRD .25 .60
U15 Aaron Judge AS .60 1.50
U16 Phillip Diehl RC .30 .75
U17 Josh Fuentes .15 .40
U18 Felix Pena .15 .40
U19 Yasmani Grandal .15 .40
U20 Francisco Cervelli .15 .40
U21 Kyle Lewis 3.00 8.00
U22 Cody Stashak RC .25 .60
U23 Cheslor Cuthbert .15 .40
U24 Buck Farmer .15 .40
U25 Josh Taylor RC .40 1.00
U26 Kyle Gibson .15 .40
U27 Kyle Ryan .15 .40
U28 Eduardo Nunez .15 .40
U29 Aristides Aquino .30 .75
U30 Yasmany Tomas .15 .40
U31 Curt Casali .15 .40
U32 Drew Pomeranz .15 .40
U33 Alex Verdugo .20 .50
U34 Justin Verlander .25 .60
U35 Kyle Farmer .15 .40
U36 Robinson Cano HRD .20 .50
U37 Yoenis Cespedes HRD .25 .60
U38 Albert Pujols .30 .75
U39 Kevin Plawecki .15 .40
U40 Antonio Senzatela .15 .40
U41 Josh Lindblom .15 .40
U42 Kris Bryant AS .30 .75
U43 Alex Blandino .15 .40
U44 Jorge Alcala RC .25 .60
U45 Zack Wheeler .20 .50
U46 Jose Suarez .15 .40
U47 Jose Peraza .20 .50
U48 Sandy Leon .15 .40
U49 Jared Walsh .15 .40
U50 Nolan Arenado AS .30 .75
U51 Matt Davidson .20 .50
U52 Kyle Higashioka .15 .40
U53 Brad Miller .15 .40
U54 Alex Avila .15 .40
U55 Miguel Cabrera AS .25 .60
U56 Lane Thomas .15 .40
U57 Yoan Lopez .15 .40
U58 Erick Mejia RC .40 1.00
U59 Ryan Howard HRD .20 .50
U60 Brendan McKay .25 .60
U61 Jedd Gyorko .15 .40
U62 David Ortiz HRD .25 .60
U63 Terrance Gore .15 .40
U64 Alex Bregman AS .25 .60
U65 Yoshi Tsutsugo RC .30 .75
U66 Max Scherzer .25 .60
U67 Michael Fulmer .15 .40
U68 Greg Garcia .15 .40
U69 Derek Holland .15 .40
U70 Skye Bolt .15 .40
U71 Jesus Aguilar .15 .40
U72 Drew Butera .15 .40
U73 Todd Frazier .20 .50
U74 Bryce Harper .40 1.00
Jean Segura
U75 Pedro Martinez AS .20 .50
U76 Edwin Encarnacion .25 .60
U77 Jalen Beeks .15 .40
U78 Joe Jimenez .15 .40
U79 Sean Poppen RC .40 1.00
U80 Cody Bellinger AS .50 1.25
U81 Junior Guerra .15 .40
U82 Kenley Jansen .20 .50
U83 Trent Grisham RC 1.50 4.00
U84 Yusmeiro Petit .15 .40
U85 Felix Hernandez AS .20 .50
U86 Josh Harrison .15 .40
U87 Zack Greinke .20 .50
U88 Craig Kimbrel .20 .50
U89 Brian Johnson .15 .40
U90 Clayton Kershaw .50 1.25
U91 Julio Teheran .20 .50
U92 Jacob deGrom .25 .60
U93 Tyler White .15 .40
U94 Jesus Luzardo .30 .75
U95 Domingo Santana .20 .50
U96 Logan Morrison .15 .40
U97 Donovan Solano .25 .60
U98 Jose Iglesias .20 .50
U99 Cesar Hernandez .15 .40
U100 David Price .20 .50
U101 Nick Dini RC .30 .75
U102 Kevin Ginkel RC .25 .60
U103 Michael Hermosillo .15 .40
U104 Grayson Greiner .15 .40
U105 Jake Newberry RC .25 .60
U106 Meibrys Viloria .15 .40
U107 Eric Thames .15 .40
U108 Taylor Ward .25 .60
U109 Pedro Strop .15 .40
U110 Mark McGwire HRD .40 1.00
U111 Rich Hill .15 .40
U112 Nik Turley RC .25 .60
U113 Devin Williams RC 1.50 4.00
U114 Josh Phegley .15 .40
U115 Brad Peacock .15 .40
U116 Robinson Chirinos .15 .40
U117 Cameron Maybin .15 .40
U118 Frank Schwindel RC .40 1.00
U119 Mike Trout 1.25 3.00
U120 Stevie Wilkerson .25 .60
U121 Ichiro AS .30 .75
U122 Tino Martinez HRD .20 .50
U123 Neil Walker .20 .50
U124 David Ortiz AS .25 .60
U125 Chris Martin .15 .40
U126 Jhoulys Chacin .15 .40
U127 Ryan Weber .15 .40
U128 Jonathan Davis .20 .50
U129 Hunter Pence .20 .50
U130 Richie Martin .15 .40
U131 Alex Reyes .20 .50
U132 Daniel Descalso .15 .40
U133 Chris Iannetta .15 .40
U134 Gleyber Torres AS .50 1.25
U135 Brandon Dixon .15 .40
U136 David McKay .15 .40
U137 Touki Toussaint .20 .50
U138 Tommy Pham .15 .40
U139 Greg Allen .20 .50
U140 Clayton Kershaw .50 1.25
U141 Jonathan Villar .15 .40
U142 Albert Pujols .30 .75
U143 Francisco Lindor AS .25 .60
U144 Mookie Betts .50 1.25
Gleyber Torres
U145 Ronald Acuna Jr. AS 1.00 2.50
U146 Andrew Knizner .15 .40
U147 Robinson Cano .20 .50
U148 Pete Alonso HRD .60 1.50
U149 Nick Solak .25 .60
U150 Ken Griffey Jr. HRD .50 1.25
U151 Jairo Diaz .15 .40
U152 Sam Haggerty RC .40 1.00
U153 Robert Stephenson .15 .40
U154 Mariano Rivera AS .30 .75
U155 Zach Davies .15 .40
U156 Wilmer Flores .20 .50
U157 Deivy Grullon RC .25 .60
U158 Jason Kipnis .20 .50
U159 Steven Souza Jr. .15 .40
U160 Richard Bleier .15 .40
U161 Jake Marisnick .15 .40

62 Giovanny Gallegos .15 .40
63 JT Riddle .15 .40
64 Sam Travis .15 .40
65 Kyle Wright .25 .60
66 Adolis Garcia .15 .40
67 Yoshi Hirano .15 .40
68 Keynan Middleton .15 .40
69 Yadier Molina AS .25 .60
70 Travis Shaw .15 .40
71 Bryse Wilson .20 .50
72 Tyler Wade .15 .40
73 Edwin Encarnacion .25 .60
74 Logan Forsythe .15 .40
75 Diego Castillo .15 .40
76 Brock Holt .15 .40
77 Andy Burns RC .25 .60
78 Jarrod Dyson .15 .40
79 Jeff Hoffman .15 .40
80 C.J. Cron .15 .40
81 Mitch Moreland .15 .40
82 Josh Tomlin .15 .40
83 Steve Cishek .15 .40
84 Miguel Cabrera .25 .60
85 Max Scherzer AS .25 .60
86 Rowdy Tellez .20 .50
87 Pete Alonso AS .60 1.50
88 Luis Severino .20 .50
89 Johnny Davis RC .25 .60
90 Ken Griffey Jr. AS .50 1.25
91 Zack Greinke .20 .50
92 Ian Miller RC .25 .60
93 Miguel Cabrera .25 .60
94 Justin Verlander AS .25 .60
95 Daniel Hudson .15 .40
96 Nestor Cortes RC .25 .60
97 Zach Green RC .25 .60
98 Hunter Renfroe .15 .40
99 Adeiny Hechavarria .15 .40
200 Anthony Rendon .25 .60
201 Anthony Rizzo AS .40 1.00
202 Asdrubal Cabrera .20 .50
203 Austin Pruitt .15 .40
204 Eric Davis HRD .15 .40
205 Kenta Maeda .20 .50
206 Asher Wojciechowski .15 .40
207 Jorge Lopez .15 .40
208 Randy Arozarena RC 5.00 12.00
209 Cal Ripken Jr. AS .75 2.00
210 Gabe Speier RC .25 .60
211 Drew Smyly .15 .40
212 Jordan Lyles .15 .40
213 Keury Mella .15 .40
214 Kendall Graveman .15 .40
215 Joey Votto .25 .60
216 Sean Murphy .25 .60
217 Andrew Suarez .15 .40
218 Matt Chapman .25 .60
Matt Olson
219 Zack Greinke .20 .50
220 Alec Mills RC .25 .60
221 Joe Panik .15 .40
222 Scott Barlow .15 .40
223 Chris Devenski .15 .40
224 Cy Sneed RC .25 .60
225 Jharel Cotton .15 .40
226 Franchy Cordero .15 .40
227 Garrett Richards .20 .50
228 Starling Marte .20 .50
229 Giancarlo Stanton AS .25 .60
230 Cal Ripken Jr. HRD .75 2.00
231 Jordy Mercer .15 .40
232 Jason Castro .15 .40
233 Mike Montgomery .15 .40
234 Gavin Lux 1.00 2.50
235 Javier Baez AS .30 .75
236 Bartolo Colon .15 .40
237 Clayton Kershaw AS .50 1.25
238 Tim Locastro .15 .40
239 Jefry Rodriguez .15 .40
240 Justin Verlander .25 .60
241 Tyler Heineman RC .25 .60
242 Ty France .25 .60
243 Mike Trout 1.25 3.00
244 Wade LeBlanc .15 .40
245 Justin Verlander .25 .60
246 Greg Holland .15 .40
247 Kole Calhoun .15 .40
248 Miguel Cabrera .25 .60
249 Aroldis Chapman .25 .60
250 Omar Narvaez .15 .40
251 Nico Hoerner .60 1.50
252 Alex Wood .15 .40
253 Peter Lambert .20 .50
254 Taijuan Walker .15 .40
255 Bryce Harper HRD .40 1.00
256 Jose Ramirez .25 .60
Francisco Lindor
257 Derek Jeter AS .60 1.50
258 Todd Frazier HRD .20 .50
259 Albert Pujols .30 .75
260 Kyle Crick .15 .40
261 Mike Trout .75 2.00
Justin Upton
262 Ty Buttrey .15 .40
263 Miguel Cabrera .25 .60
264 Aaron Judge HRD .60 1.50
265 Dario Agrazal RC .30 .75
266 Andrew McCutchen AS .25 .60
267 Albert Pujols AS .30 .75
U268 Mookie Betts AS .50 1.25
U269 Christian Yelich AS .30 .75
U270 Dustin Garneau .15 .40
U271 Kevin Pillar .15 .40
U272 Joey Votto AS .25 .60
U273 Rafael Devers .30 .75
Xander Bogaerts
U274 Jordan Montgomery .25 .60
U275 Brett Anderson .15 .40
U276 Joe Kelly .15 .40
U277 Jose Altuve AS .20 .50
U278 Austin Allen .20 .50
U279 Bryce Harper AS .40 1.00
U280 Albert Pujols .30 .75
U281 Joel Kuhnel RC .25 .60
U282 Christian Arroyo .15 .40
U283 Tomas Nido .15 .40
U284 Walker Buehler .30 .75
Russell Martin
U285 Billy Hamilton .20 .50
U286 Chase Anderson .15 .40
U287 Chris Sale AS .25 .60
U288 Giancarlo Stanton .25 .60
U289 Myles Straw .25 .60
U290 Pete Alonso .40 1.00
Jeff McNeil
U291 Trayce Thompson .15 .40
U292 Mike Trout 1.25 3.00
U293 Mike King RC .40 1.00
U294 Adam Plutko .15 .40
U295 Chris Sale .25 .60
U296 Mark McGwire HRD .40 1.00
U297 Jesus Tinoco RC .25 .60
U298 Magneuris Sierra .15 .40
U299 Jacob deGrom AS .25 .60
U300 Yordan Alvarez 2.00 5.00

2020 Topps Update Advanced Stats

*ADVANCED: 3X TO 8X BASIC
*ADVANCED RC: 2X TO 5X BASIC RC
STATED ODDS 1:157 HOBBY
STATED PRINT RUN 300 SER. #'d SETS
U9 Ken Griffey Jr. HRD 12.00 30.00
U83 Trent Grisham 15.00 40.00
U113 Devin Williams 15.00 40.00
U145 Ronald Acuna Jr. AS 15.00 40.00
U150 Ken Griffey Jr. HRD 12.00 30.00
U190 Ken Griffey Jr. AS 12.00 30.00
U208 Randy Arozarena 40.00 100.00

2020 Topps Update Black

*BLACK: 8X TO 20X BASIC
*BLACK RC: 5X TO 12X BASIC RC
STATED ODDS 1:113 HOBBY
STATED PRINT RUN 69 SER. #'d SETS
U4 Mike Trout AS 40.00 100.00
U9 Ken Griffey Jr. HRD 40.00 100.00
U15 Aaron Judge AS 20.00 50.00
U83 Trent Grisham 30.00 80.00
U113 Devin Williams 40.00 100.00
U119 Mike Trout 40.00 100.00
U121 Ichiro AS 20.00 50.00
U145 Ronald Acuna Jr. AS 40.00 100.00
U148 Pete Alonso HRD 15.00 40.00
U150 Ken Griffey Jr. HRD 40.00 100.00
U187 Pete Alonso AS 15.00 40.00
U190 Ken Griffey Jr. AS 40.00 100.00
U208 Randy Arozarena 100.00 250.00
U243 Mike Trout 40.00 100.00
U251 Nico Hoerner 25.00 60.00
U257 Derek Jeter AS 25.00 60.00
U261 Mike Trout 25.00 60.00
Justin Upton
U264 Aaron Judge HRD 20.00 50.00
U292 Mike Trout 40.00 100.00

2020 Topps Update Father's Day Blue

*FD BLUE: 8X TO 20X BASIC
*FD BLUE RC: 5X TO 12X BASIC RC
STATED ODDS 1:626 HOBBY
STATED PRINT RUN 50 SER. #'d SETS
U1 Bo Bichette 60.00 150.00
U4 Mike Trout AS 40.00 100.00
U9 Ken Griffey Jr. HRD 40.00 100.00
U15 Aaron Judge AS 20.00 50.00
U83 Trent Grisham 30.00 80.00
U113 Devin Williams 40.00 100.00
U119 Mike Trout 40.00 100.00
U121 Ichiro AS 20.00 50.00
U145 Ronald Acuna Jr. AS 40.00 100.00
U148 Pete Alonso HRD 15.00 40.00
U150 Ken Griffey Jr. HRD 40.00 100.00
U187 Pete Alonso AS 15.00 40.00
U190 Ken Griffey Jr. AS 40.00 100.00
U208 Randy Arozarena 100.00 250.00
U234 Gavin Lux 40.00 100.00
U243 Mike Trout 40.00 100.00
U251 Nico Hoerner 25.00 60.00
U257 Derek Jeter AS 25.00 60.00
U261 Mike Trout 25.00 60.00
Justin Upton
U264 Aaron Judge HRD 20.00 50.00
U292 Mike Trout 40.00 100.00

2020 Topps Update Gold

*GOLD: 1.5X TO 4X BASIC
*GOLD RC: 1X TO 2.5X BASIC RC
STATED ODDS 1:16 HOBBY
STATED PRINT RUN 2020 SER. #'d SETS
U9 Ken Griffey Jr. HRD 6.00 15.00
U83 Trent Grisham 10.00 25.00
U113 Devin Williams 8.00 20.00
U145 Ronald Acuna Jr. AS 8.00 20.00
U150 Ken Griffey Jr. HRD 6.00 15.00
U190 Ken Griffey Jr. AS 6.00 15.00
U208 Randy Arozarena 20.00 50.00

2020 Topps Update Gold Foil

*GOLD FOIL: 1.2X TO 3X BASIC
*GOLD FOIL RC: .8X TO 2X BASIC RC
STATED ODDS 1:2 JUMBO
U83 Trent Grisham 8.00 20.00
U113 Devin Williams 6.00 15.00
U208 Randy Arozarena 15.00 40.00

2020 Topps Update Independence Day

*INDPNDNCE: 8X TO 20X BASIC
*INDPNDNCE RC: 5X TO 12X BASIC RC
STATED ODDS 1:412 HOBBY
STATED PRINT RUN 76 SER. #'d SETS
U4 Mike Trout AS 40.00 100.00
U9 Ken Griffey Jr. HRD 40.00 100.00
U15 Aaron Judge AS 15.00 40.00
U83 Trent Grisham 30.00 80.00
U113 Devin Williams 40.00 100.00
U119 Mike Trout 40.00 100.00
U121 Ichiro AS 20.00 50.00
U145 Ronald Acuna Jr. AS 40.00 100.00
U148 Pete Alonso HRD 15.00 40.00
U150 Ken Griffey Jr. HRD 40.00 100.00
U187 Pete Alonso AS 15.00 40.00
U190 Ken Griffey Jr. AS 40.00 100.00
U208 Randy Arozarena 100.00 250.00
U243 Mike Trout 40.00 100.00
U257 Derek Jeter AS 25.00 60.00
U264 Aaron Judge HRD 15.00 40.00
U292 Mike Trout 40.00 100.00

2020 Topps Update Memorial Day Camo

*MD CAMO: 12X TO 30X BASIC
*MD CAMO RC: 8X TO 20X BASIC RC
STATED ODDS 1:1252 HOBBY
STATED PRINT RUN 25 SER. #'d SETS
U1 Bo Bichette 100.00 250.00
U4 Mike Trout AS 60.00 150.00
U9 Ken Griffey Jr. HRD 60.00 150.00
U15 Aaron Judge AS 40.00 100.00
U83 Trent Grisham 50.00 120.00
U110 Mark McGwire HRD 20.00 50.00
U113 Devin Williams 60.00 150.00
U119 Mike Trout 60.00 150.00
U121 Ichiro AS 30.00 80.00
U145 Ronald Acuna Jr. AS 60.00 150.00
U148 Pete Alonso HRD 25.00 60.00
U150 Ken Griffey Jr. HRD 60.00 150.00
U187 Pete Alonso AS 25.00 60.00
U190 Ken Griffey Jr. AS 60.00 150.00
U208 Randy Arozarena 150.00 400.00
U234 Gavin Lux 60.00 150.00
U243 Mike Trout 60.00 150.00
U251 Nico Hoerner 40.00 100.00
U257 Derek Jeter AS 40.00 100.00
U261 Mike Trout 40.00 100.00
Justin Upton
U264 Aaron Judge HRD 40.00 100.00
U292 Mike Trout 60.00 150.00
U296 Mark McGwire HRD 20.00 50.00

2020 Topps Update Mother's Day Pink

*MD PINK: 8X TO 20X BASIC
*MD PINK RC: 5X TO 12X BASIC RC
STATED ODDS 1:626 HOBBY
STATED PRINT RUN 50 SER. #'d SETS
U1 Bo Bichette 60.00 150.00
U4 Mike Trout AS 40.00 100.00
U9 Ken Griffey Jr. HRD 40.00 100.00
U15 Aaron Judge AS 20.00 50.00
U83 Trent Grisham 30.00 80.00
U113 Devin Williams 40.00 100.00
U119 Mike Trout 40.00 100.00
U121 Ichiro AS 20.00 50.00
U145 Ronald Acuna Jr. AS 40.00 100.00
U148 Pete Alonso HRD 15.00 40.00
U150 Ken Griffey Jr. HRD 40.00 100.00
U187 Pete Alonso AS 15.00 40.00
U190 Ken Griffey Jr. AS 40.00 100.00
U208 Randy Arozarena 100.00 250.00
U234 Gavin Lux 40.00 100.00
U243 Mike Trout 40.00 100.00
U251 Nico Hoerner 25.00 60.00
U257 Derek Jeter AS 25.00 60.00
U261 Mike Trout 25.00 60.00
Justin Upton
U264 Aaron Judge HRD 20.00 50.00
U292 Mike Trout 40.00 100.00

2020 Topps Update Rainbow Foil

*RNBW FOIL: 1.2X TO 3X BASIC
*RNBW FOIL RC: .8X TO 2X BASIC RC
STATED ODDS 1:10 HOBBY
U83 Trent Grisham 8.00 20.00
U113 Devin Williams 6.00 15.00
U208 Randy Arozarena 15.00 40.00

2020 Topps Update Vintage Stock

*VINTAGE: 6X TO 15X BASIC
*VINTAGE RC: 4X TO 10X BASIC RC
STATED ODDS 1:317 HOBBY
STATED PRINT RUN 99 SER. #'d SETS
U9 Ken Griffey Jr. HRD 30.00 80.00
U15 Aaron Judge AS 12.00 30.00
U83 Trent Grisham 30.00 80.00
U113 Devin Williams 30.00 80.00
U145 Ronald Acuna Jr. AS 30.00 80.00
U150 Ken Griffey Jr. HRD 30.00 80.00
U190 Ken Griffey Jr. AS 30.00 80.00
U208 Randy Arozarena 75.00 200.00
U264 Aaron Judge HRD 12.00 30.00

2020 Topps Update Walgreens Yellow

*YELLOW: 1.2X TO 3X BASIC
*YELLOW RC: .8X TO 2X BASIC RC
EXCLUSIVE TO WALGREENS PACKS
U83 Trent Grisham 8.00 20.00
U113 Devin Williams 6.00 15.00
U208 Randy Arozarena 15.00 40.00

2020 Topps Update Walmart Royal Blue

*ROYAL BLUE: 1.2X TO 3X BASIC
*ROYL BLUE RC: .8X TO 2X BASIC RC
EXCLUSIVE TO WALMART PACKS
U83 Trent Grisham 8.00 20.00
U113 Devin Williams 6.00 15.00
U208 Randy Arozarena 15.00 40.00

2020 Topps Update Photo Variations

STATED ODDS 1:63 HOBBY
STATED SSP ODDS 1:1252 HOBBY
STATED SSSP ODDS 1:XX HOBBY
NO PRICING SSSP DUE TO SCARCITY
U1A Bo Bichette 25.00 60.00
long-sleeved shirt
U1B Bo Bichette SSP 150.00 400.00
back of jsy
U4A Mike Trout 20.00 50.00
interview
U4B Mike Trout SSP 150.00 400.00
back of jsy
U8 Buster Posey 4.00 10.00
waving
U15A Aaron Judge 12.00 30.00
locker room
U15B Aaron Judge SSP 125.00 300.00
Back of jsy
U21 Kyle Lewis 15.00 40.00
in dugout
U29 Aristides Aquino 8.00 20.00
all white jsy
U33 Alex Verdugo 4.00 10.00
interview
U42 Kris Bryant 5.00 12.00
red carpet
U50 Nolan Arenado 2.50 6.00
red carpet
U52 Babe Ruth SSP 100.00 250.00
U55 Miguel Cabrera 4.00 10.00
in dugout
U60 Brendan McKay 2.00 5.00
holding bat
U63 Jackie Robinson SSP 30.00 80.00
U64 Alex Bregman 4.00 10.00
interview
U65 Yoshi Tsutsugo 4.00 10.00
interview
U68 Fernando Tatis Jr. SSP 100.00 250.00
camo jsy
U80A Cody Bellinger 4.00 10.00
at podium
U80B Cody Bellinger SSP 30.00 80.00
in dugout
U83 Trent Grisham 8.00 20.00
interview
U90 Sandy Koufax SSP 50.00 120.00
U94 Jesus Luzardo 6.00 15.00
signing autograph
U100 David Price 3.00 8.00
hard hat
U121A Ichiro 8.00 20.00
interview
U121B Ichiro SSP 75.00 200.00
tipping helmet
U122 Lou Gehrig SSP 100.00 250.00
U124A David Ortiz 5.00 12.00
interview
U129 Willie Mays SSP 100.00 250.00
U134 Gleyber Torres 5.00 12.00
interview
U143 Francisco Lindor 2.00 5.00
interview
U145A Ronald Acuna Jr. 20.00 50.00
portrait
U145B Ronald Acuna Jr. SSP 50.00 120.00
back of jsy
U149 Nick Solak 6.00 15.00
high-fiving
U154A Mariano Rivera 6.00 15.00
smiling
U154B Mariano Rivera SSP 125.00 300.00
back of jsy
U158 Ernie Banks SSP 60.00 150.00
U169 Yadier Molina 4.00 10.00
interview
U173A Luis Robert 60.00 150.00
in suit
U173B Luis Robert SSP 300.00 800.00
signing autograph
U178 Roberto Clemente SSP 60.00 150.00
U185 Max Scherzer 5.00 12.00
holding WS trophy
U187 Pete Alonso 8.00 20.00
at podium
U190A Ken Griffey Jr. 10.00 25.00
interview
U190B Ken Griffey Jr. SSP 75.00 200.00
jsy back
U194 Justin Verlander 4.00 10.00
interview
U199 Hank Aaron SSP 75.00 200.00
U200 Anthony Rendon 2.00 5.00
holding jsy
U201 Anthony Rizzo 6.00 15.00
smiling
U209A Cal Ripken Jr. 8.00 20.00
interview
U209B Cal Ripken Jr. SSP 60.00 150.00
signing autographs
U216 Sean Murphy 5.00 12.00
shaving cream
U229 Giancarlo Stanton 4.00 10.00
ski goggles
U234A Gavin Lux 12.00 30.00
in dugout
U234B Gavin Lux SSP 50.00 120.00
back of jsy
U235 Javier Baez 6.00 15.00
interview
U237 Clayton Kershaw 4.00 10.00
at podium
U251 Nico Hoerner 5.00 12.00
signing autographs
U255 Juan Soto SSP 100.00 250.00
WS celebration
U257A Derek Jeter 10.00 25.00
interview
U257B Derek Jeter SSP 100.00 250.00
back of jsy
U266 Andrew McCutchen 2.00 5.00
press conference
U267 Albert Pujols 2.50 6.00
interview
U268 Mookie Betts 15.00 40.00
hard hat
U269 Christian Yelich 2.50 6.00
red carpet
U269A Christian Yelich SSP 20.00 50.00
back of jsy
U271 Ted Williams SSP 100.00 250.00
U272 Joey Votto 2.00 5.00
interview
U277 Jose Altuve 1.50 4.00
in t-shirt
U279A Bryce Harper 8.00 20.00
interview
U279B Bryce Harper SSP 100.00 250.00
jsy back
U287 Chris Sale 2.00 5.00
in t-shirt
U299 Jacob deGrom 6.00 15.00
interview
U300 Yordan Alvarez 20.00 50.00
at podium

2020 Topps Update '85 Topps

STATED ODDS 1:XX HOBBY
85TB1 Derek Jeter 1.00 2.50
85TB2 Josh Donaldson .30 .75
85TB3 Yoshi Tsutsugo .30 .75
85TB4 Shogo Akiyama .40 1.00
85TB5 Mike Trout 2.00 5.00
85TB6 Starling Marte .30 .75
85TB7 Ronald Acuna Jr. 1.50 4.00
85TB8 Fred McGriff .30 .75
85TB9 Eddie Murray .30 .75
85TB10 Jackie Robinson .40 1.00
85TB11 Ernie Banks .40 1.00
85TB12 Andre Dawson .30 .75
85TB13 Javier Baez .50 1.25
85TB14 Luis Robert 2.50 6.00
85TB15 Yoan Moncada .40 1.00
85TB16 Frank Robinson .30 .75
85TB17 Joe Morgan .30 .75
85TB18 Yordan Alvarez 1.25 3.00
85TB19 Gavin Lux 1.50 4.00
85TB20 Cody Bellinger .75 2.00
85TB21 David Price .30 .75
85TB22 Mookie Betts .75 2.00
85TB23 Christian Yelich .50 1.25
85TB24 Tim Raines .30 .75
85TB25 Willie Mays .75 2.00
85TB26 Dwight Gooden .25 .60
85TB27 David Wright .30 .75
85TB28 Pete Alonso 1.00 2.50
85TB29 Aaron Judge 1.00 2.50
85TB30 Thurman Munson .40 1.00
85TB31 Jesus Luzardo .50 1.25
85TB32 A.J. Puk .50 1.25
85TB33 Bryce Harper .60 1.50
85TB34 Ryan Howard .30 .75
85TB35 Mike Schmidt .60 1.50
85TB36 Willie Stargell .30 .75
85TB37 Fernando Tatis Jr. 1.50 4.00
85TB38 Dave Winfield .30 .75
85TB39 Willie McCovey .30 .75
85TB40 Tim Lincecum .30 .75
85TB41 Ken Griffey Jr. .75 2.00
85TB42 Bob Gibson .30 .75
85TB43 Lou Brock .30 .75
85TB44 Nolan Ryan 1.25 3.00
85TB45 Bo Bichette 2.00 5.00
85TB46 Juan Soto 1.25 3.00
85TB47 Shohei Ohtani .50 1.25
85TB48 Austin Meadows .30 .75
85TB49 Roberto Clemente 1.00 2.50
85TB50 Lewis Brinson .25 .60

2020 Topps Update '85 Topps Black

*BLACK: 1X TO 2.5X
STATED ODDS 1:XX HOBBY
STATED PRINT RUN 299 SER. #'d SETS
85TB1 Derek Jeter 6.00 15.00
85TB10 Jackie Robinson 3.00 8.00
85TB22 Mookie Betts 4.00 10.00
85TB29 Aaron Judge 8.00 20.00
85TB37 Fernando Tatis Jr. 6.00 15.00
85TB41 Ken Griffey Jr. 5.00 12.00
85TB45 Bo Bichette 8.00 20.00

2020 Topps Update '85 Topps Blue

*BLUE: .6X TO 1.5X
STATED ODDS 1:XX HOBBY
85TB41 Ken Griffey Jr. 3.00 8.00
85TB45 Bo Bichette 5.00 12.00

2020 Topps Update '85 Topps Gold

*GOLD: 2.5X TO 6X
STATED ODDS 1:XX HOBBY
STATED PRINT RUN 50 SER. #'d SETS
85TB1 Derek Jeter 15.00 40.00
85TB10 Jackie Robinson 8.00 20.00
85TB22 Mookie Betts 10.00 25.00
85TB29 Aaron Judge 20.00 50.00
85TB37 Fernando Tatis Jr. 15.00 40.00
85TB41 Ken Griffey Jr. 12.00 30.00
85TB45 Bo Bichette 20.00 50.00

2020 Topps Update '85 Topps Autographs

STATED ODDS 1:XX HOBBY
EXCHANGE DEADLINE 8/31/2022
85ABR Bryan Reynolds 8.00 20.00
85ADJ Derek Jeter
85AGS George Springer 25.00 60.00
85AJC Jose Canseco 12.00 30.00
85AJH Josh Hader 2.50 6.00
85AJJ Josh James 4.00 10.00
85AJM Joe Mauer EXCH 40.00 100.00
85AKS Kyle Schwarber 8.00 20.00
85ALR Luis Robert EXCH 75.00 200.00
85AMA Max Kepler 5.00 12.00
85AMK Mitch Keller 4.00 10.00
85AMO Matt Olson 6.00 15.00
85AMS Max Scherzer 25.00 60.00
85AMT Mike Trout EXCH
85AOM Oscar Mercado 3.00 8.00
85APA Pete Alonso EXCH 25.00 60.00
85APC Patrick Corbin 5.00 12.00
85ARD Rafael Devers 20.00 50.00
85ARM Ryan McBroom 8.00 20.00
85ASC Shin-Soo Choo 6.00 15.00
85ASG Sonny Gray EXCH 8.00 20.00
85ATA Tyler Alexander EXCH 4.00 10.00
85ATL Tim Lincecum EXCH 40.00 100.00
85AYD Yonathan Daza 3.00 8.00
85AYT Yoshi Tsutsugo EXCH 10.00 25.00
85AZG Zac Gallen 6.00 15.00
85AAKA Anthony Kay 2.50 6.00
85AARE Anthony Rendon 4.00 10.00
85ADGO Dwight Gooden 12.00 30.00
85AJMA James Marvel 2.50 6.00
85AJRO Josh Rojas 2.50 6.00
85AMCA Miguel Cabrera
85ARDO Randy Dobnak EXCH 10.00 25.00
85ARHE Rickey Henderson
85ARLA Ramon Laureano 4.00 10.00
85BAAO Adam Ottavino 5.00 12.00
85BADL Domingo Leyba 3.00 8.00
85BADV Dan Vogelbach 2.50 6.00
85BAGU Gio Urshela 10.00 25.00
85BAHD Hunter Dozier 6.00 15.00
85BAJA Jim Abbott 10.00 25.00
85BAJD Justin Dunn 3.00 8.00
85BAJS Jorge Soler 6.00 15.00
85BAMB Mike Brosseau 5.00 12.00
85BASL Shed Long 3.00 8.00
85BASN Sheldon Neuse 3.00 8.00
85BAYC Yu Chang 5.00 12.00
85BAJBU Jay Buhner 10.00 25.00
85BATLS Tommy La Stella 2.50 6.00

2020 Topps Update '85 Topps Autographs Black

*BLACK: .5X TO 1.2X
STATED ODDS 1:XX HOBBY
STATED PRINT RUN 199 SER. #'d SETS
EXCHANGE DEADLINE 8/31/2022
85AMA Max Kepler 8.00 20.00
85ASC Shin-Soo Choo 12.00 30.00
85AYT Yoshi Tsutsugo EXCH 15.00 40.00

2020 Topps Update '85 Topps Autographs Gold

*GOLD: .6X TO 1.5X
STATED ODDS 1:XX HOBBY
STATED PRINT RUN 50 SER. #'d SETS
EXCHANGE DEADLINE 8/31/2022
85ABR Bryan Reynolds 15.00 40.00
85AMA Max Kepler 15.00 40.00
85ASC Shin-Soo Choo 20.00 50.00
85AYT Yoshi Tsutsugo EXCH 20.00 50.00
85AZG Zac Gallen 20.00 50.00
85ARHE Rickey Henderson 40.00 100.00
85BAYC Yu Chang 12.00 30.00

2020 Topps Update '85 Topps Autographs Red

*RED: .8X TO 2X
STATED ODDS 1:XX HOBBY
STATED PRINT RUN 25 SER. #'d SETS
EXCHANGE DEADLINE 8/31/2022
85ABR Bryan Reynolds 20.00 50.00
85ALR Luis Robert EXCH 400.00 1000.00
85AMA Max Kepler 25.00 60.00
85ASC Shin-Soo Choo 30.00 80.00
85AYD Yonathan Daza 10.00 25.00
85AYT Yoshi Tsutsugo EXCH 25.00 60.00
85AZG Zac Gallen 40.00 100.00
85AMCA Miguel Cabrera 125.00 300.00
85ARHE Rickey Henderson 50.00 120.00
85BAJA Jim Abbott 25.00 60.00
85BAJD Justin Dunn 12.00 30.00
85BAYC Yu Chang 15.00 40.00

2020 Topps Update '85 Topps Silver Pack Chrome

STATED ODDS 1:XX HOBBY
CPC1 Yordan Alvarez 3.00 8.00
CPC2 Derek Jeter 4.00 10.00
CPC3 Mariano Rivera 2.00 5.00
CPC4 Rhys Hoskins 1.25 3.00
CPC5 Travis Demeritte .75 2.00
CPC6 Walker Buehler 1.25 3.00
CPC7 Shohei Ohtani 1.25 3.00
CPC8 Michael Brosseau 1.25 3.00
CPC9 Luis Robert 10.00 25.00
CPC10 Sonny Gray .75 2.00
CPC11 Cody Bellinger 2.00 5.00
CPC12 Nick Castellanos 1.00 2.50
CPC13 Willson Contreras 1.00 2.50
CPC14 Bo Bichette 6.00 15.00
CPC15 Hyun-Jin Ryu .75 2.00
CPC16 Jesus Luzardo 1.25 3.00
CPC17 Josh Staumont .60 1.50
CPC18 Yoshi Tsutsugo .75 2.00
CPC19 Mookie Betts 4.00 10.00
CPC20 Shogo Akiyama 1.00 2.50
CPC21 A.J. Puk 1.25 3.00
CPC22 Gerrit Cole 1.50 4.00
CPC23 Gavin Lux 4.00 10.00
CPC24 Willi Castro 1.00 2.50
CPC25 Roger Clemens 1.25 3.00
CPC26 Andrew Benintendi 1.00 2.50
CPC27 Brusdar Graterol 1.00 2.50
CPC28 Zac Gallen 1.50 4.00
CPC29 Rangel Ravelo .75 2.00
CPC30 Ronald Acuna Jr. 5.00 12.00
CPC31 Stephen Strasburg 1.00 2.50
CPC32 Cavan Biggio 1.25 3.00
CPC33 Shane Bieber 1.00 2.50
CPC34 Josh Donaldson .75 2.00
CPC35 Fernando Tatis Jr. 5.00 12.00
CPC36 Brock Burke .60 1.50
CPC37 Tommy Edman 1.00 2.50
CPC38 Tony Gonsolin 2.50 6.00
CPC39 Genesis Cabrera 1.00 2.50
CPC40 Bobby Bradley .75 2.00
CPC41 George Springer .75 2.00
CPC42 Mike Yastrzemski 1.50 4.00
CPC43 Trent Grisham 2.50 6.00
CPC44 Dale Murphy 1.00 2.50
CPC45 Mike Trout 5.00 12.00
CPC46 Anthony Rendon 1.00 2.50
CPC47 Yonathan Daza .75 2.00
CPC48 Seth Brown .60 1.50
CPC49 Juan Soto 3.00 8.00
CPC50 Christian Yelich 1.25 3.00

2020 Topps Update '85 Topps Silver Pack Chrome Black Refractors

*BLACK: .8X TO 2X
STATED ODDS 1:XX HOBBY
STATED PRINT RUN 199 SER. #'d SETS
CPC2 Derek Jeter 12.00 30.00
CPC9 Luis Robert 30.00 80.00
CPC14 Bo Bichette 15.00 40.00
CPC45 Mike Trout 15.00 60.00

2020 Topps Update '85 Topps Silver Pack Chrome Blue Refractors

*BLUE: 1X TO 2.5X
STATED ODDS 1:XX HOBBY
STATED PRINT RUN 150 SER. #'d SETS
CPC2 Derek Jeter 15.00 40.00
CPC9 Luis Robert 40.00 100.00
CPC14 Bo Bichette 25.00 60.00
CPC30 Ronald Acuna Jr. 15.00 40.00
CPC35 Fernando Tatis Jr. 15.00 40.00
CPC45 Mike Trout 20.00 50.00

2020 Topps Update '85 Topps Silver Pack Chrome Gold Refractors

*GOLD: 2.5X TO 6X
STATED ODDS 1:XX HOBBY
STATED PRINT RUN 50 SER. #'d SETS
CPC2 Derek Jeter 40.00 100.00
CPC3 Mariano Rivera 15.00 40.00
CPC9 Luis Robert 100.00 250.00
CPC14 Bo Bichette 60.00 150.00

CPC30 Ronald Acuna Jr. 40.00 100.00
CPC35 Fernando Tatis Jr. 75.00 200.00
CPC45 Mike Trout 50.00 120.00
CPC49 Juan Soto 25.00 60.00

2020 Topps Update '85 Topps Silver Pack Chrome Green Refractors

*GREEN: 1.2X TO 3X
STATED ODDS 1:XX HOBBY
STATED PRINT RUN 99 SER.#'d SETS
CPC2 Derek Jeter 20.00 50.00
CPC9 Luis Robert 50.00 120.00
CPC14 Bo Bichette 30.00 80.00
CPC30 Ronald Acuna Jr. 20.00 50.00
CPC35 Fernando Tatis Jr. 20.00 50.00
CPC45 Mike Trout 25.00 60.00

2020 Topps Update '85 Topps Silver Pack Chrome Orange Refractors

*ORANGE: 4X TO 10X
STATED ODDS 1:XX HOBBY
STATED PRINT RUN 25 SER.#'d SETS
CPC2 Derek Jeter 60.00 150.00
CPC3 Mariano Rivera 25.00 60.00
CPC9 Luis Robert 150.00 400.00
CPC14 Bo Bichette 100.00 250.00
CPC30 Ronald Acuna Jr. 100.00 250.00
CPC35 Fernando Tatis Jr. 125.00 300.00
CPC45 Mike Trout 75.00 200.00
CPC49 Juan Soto 40.00 100.00

2020 Topps Update '85 Topps Silver Pack Chrome Purple Refractors

*PURPLE: 1.2X TO 3X
STATED ODDS 1:XX HOBBY
STATED PRINT RUN 75 SER.#'d SETS
CPC2 Derek Jeter 20.00 50.00
CPC9 Luis Robert 50.00 120.00
CPC14 Bo Bichette 30.00 80.00
CPC30 Ronald Acuna Jr. 20.00 50.00
CPC35 Fernando Tatis Jr. 30.00 80.00
CPC45 Mike Trout 25.00 60.00

2020 Topps Update 20 Years of The Captain

STATED ODDS 1:XX HOBBY
*BLUE: .6X TO 1.5X
*BLACK/299: 1X TO 2.5X
*GOLD/50: 2.5X TO 6X
*RED/10: 12X TO 30X
YOC00 Derek Jeter 1.00 2.50
YOC01 Derek Jeter 1.00 2.50
YOC02 Derek Jeter 1.00 2.50
YOC03 Derek Jeter 1.00 2.50
YOC04 Derek Jeter 1.00 2.50
YOC05 Derek Jeter 1.00 2.50
YOC06 Derek Jeter 1.00 2.50
YOC07 Derek Jeter 1.00 2.50
YOC08 Derek Jeter 1.00 2.50
YOC09 Derek Jeter 1.00 2.50
YOC10 Derek Jeter 1.00 2.50
YOC11 Derek Jeter 1.00 2.50
YOC12 Derek Jeter 1.00 2.50
YOC13 Derek Jeter 1.00 2.50
YOC14 Derek Jeter 1.00 2.50
YOC95 Derek Jeter 1.00 2.50
YOC96 Derek Jeter 1.00 2.50
YOC97 Derek Jeter 1.00 2.50
YOC98 Derek Jeter 1.00 2.50
YOC99 Derek Jeter 1.00 2.50

2020 Topps Update 20 Years of The Captain Commemorative Patches

STATED ODDS 1:XX HOBBY
*BLACK/50: 1X TO 2.5X
*GOLD/25: 1.5X TO 4X
*RED/10 5X TO 12X
20YCC00 Derek Jeter 3.00 8.00
20YCC01 Derek Jeter 3.00 8.00
20YCC02 Derek Jeter 3.00 8.00
20YCC03 Derek Jeter 3.00 8.00
20YCC04 Derek Jeter 3.00 8.00
20YCC05 Derek Jeter 3.00 8.00
20YCC06 Derek Jeter 3.00 8.00
20YCC07 Derek Jeter 3.00 8.00
20YCC08 Derek Jeter 3.00 8.00
20YCC09 Derek Jeter 3.00 8.00
20YCC10 Derek Jeter 3.00 8.00
20YCC11 Derek Jeter 3.00 8.00
20YCC12 Derek Jeter 3.00 8.00
20YCC13 Derek Jeter 3.00 8.00
20YCC14 Derek Jeter 3.00 8.00
20YCC95 Derek Jeter 3.00 8.00
20YCC96 Derek Jeter 3.00 8.00
20YCC97 Derek Jeter 3.00 8.00
20YCC98 Derek Jeter 3.00 8.00
20YCC99 Derek Jeter 3.00 8.00

2020 Topps Update A Numbers Game

STATED ODDS 1:XX HOBBY
NG1 Roberto Alomar .30 .75
NG2 Ryne Sandberg .75 2.00
NG3 Roberto Clemente 1.00 2.50
NG4 Randy Johnson .40 1.00
NG5 Rickey Henderson .40 1.00
NG6 Nolan Ryan 1.25 3.00
NG7 Jackie Robinson .40 1.00
NG8 Jeff Bagwell .30 .75
NG9 Chipper Jones .60 1.50
NG10 Ken Griffey Jr. .75 2.00
NG11 Stan Musial .60 1.50
NG12 Robin Yount .40 1.00
NG13 Mariano Rivera .50 1.25
NG14 Ted Williams .75 2.00
NG15 Tony Gwynn .40 1.00
NG16 Cal Ripken Jr. 1.25 3.00
NG17 Mike Piazza .40 1.00
NG18 Willie Mays .75 2.00
NG19 Ernie Banks .40 1.00
NG20 Sandy Koufax .75 2.00
NG21 Ozzie Smith .50 1.25
NG22 Derek Jeter 1.00 2.50
NG23 Mike Schmidt .60 1.50
NG24 Johnny Bench .40 1.00
NG25 Hank Aaron .75 2.00

2020 Topps Update A Numbers Game Black

*BLACK: 1X TO 2.5X
STATED ODDS 1:XX HOBBY
STATED PRINT RUN 299 SER.#'d SETS
NG6 Nolan Ryan 4.00 10.00
NG7 Jackie Robinson 3.00 8.00
NG10 Ken Griffey Jr. 5.00 12.00
NG22 Derek Jeter 6.00 15.00

2020 Topps Update A Numbers Game Blue

*BLUE: .6X TO 1.5X
STATED ODDS 1:XX HOBBY
NG10 Ken Griffey Jr. 3.00 8.00

2020 Topps Update A Numbers Game Gold

*GOLD: 2.5X TO 6X
STATED ODDS 1:XX HOBBY
STATED PRINT RUN 50 SER.#'d SETS
NG6 Nolan Ryan 10.00 25.00
NG7 Jackie Robinson 8.00 20.00
NG10 Ken Griffey Jr. 12.00 30.00
NG16 Cal Ripken Jr. 12.00 30.00
NG22 Derek Jeter 15.00 40.00

2020 Topps Update All Star Stitches

STATED ODDS 1:XX HOBBY
ASSCAJ Aaron Judge 8.00 20.00
ASSCAP Albert Pujols 4.00 10.00
ASSCAR Anthony Rizzo 5.00 12.00
ASSCBC Bartolo Colon 4.00 10.00
ASSCBG Brett Gardner 6.00 15.00
ASSCBH Bryce Harper 5.00 12.00
ASSCBL Brandon Lowe 3.00 8.00
ASSCBP Buster Posey 4.00 10.00
ASSCCB Charlie Blackmon 3.00 8.00
ASSCCC Carlos Correa 3.00 8.00
ASSCCK Clayton Kershaw 6.00 15.00
ASSCCS Corey Seager 3.00 8.00
ASSCDG Dee Gordon 2.00 5.00
ASSCDO David Ortiz 3.00 8.00
ASSCFL Francisco Lindor 5.00 12.00
ASSCGC Gerrit Cole 5.00 12.00
ASSCGS Giancarlo Stanton 3.00 8.00
ASSCJA Jose Altuve 4.00 10.00
ASSCJB Jose Berrios 2.50 6.00
ASSCJC Johnny Cueto 4.00 10.00
ASSCJD Josh Donaldson 2.50 6.00
ASSCJP Joc Pederson 2.50 6.00
ASSCJR Jose Ramirez 2.50 6.00
ASSCJT Justin Turner 4.00 10.00
ASSCJV Joey Votto 3.00 8.00
ASSCKB Kris Bryant 4.00 10.00
ASSCLC Lorenzo Cain 2.00 5.00
ASSCLM Lance McCullers Jr. 2.00 5.00
ASSCLS Luis Severino 2.50 6.00
ASSCMB Mookie Betts 8.00 20.00
ASSCMC Miguel Cabrera 3.00 8.00
ASSCMM Manny Machado 3.00 8.00
ASSCMS Max Scherzer 3.00 8.00
ASSCMT Mike Trout 15.00 40.00
ASSCNA Nolan Arenado 4.00 10.00
ASSCNC Nelson Cruz 3.00 8.00
ASSCPG Paul Goldschmidt 3.00 8.00
ASSCRC Robinson Cano 2.50 6.00
ASSCRZ Ryan Zimmerman 4.00 10.00
ASSCSG Sonny Gray 2.50 6.00
ASSCSP Salvador Perez 5.00 12.00
ASSCSS Stephen Strasburg 3.00 8.00
ASSCTS Trevor Story 3.00 8.00
ASSCXB Xander Bogaerts 5.00 12.00
ASSCYD Yu Darvish 3.00 8.00
ASSCYM Yadier Molina 4.00 10.00
ASSCZG Zack Greinke 4.00 10.00
ASSCAJU Aaron Judge 8.00 20.00
ASSCARI Anthony Rizzo 5.00 12.00
ASSCBHA Bryce Harper 5.00 12.00
ASSCBPO Buster Posey 4.00 10.00
ASSCCCS CC Sabathia 2.50 6.00
ASSCCHS Chris Sale 5.00 12.00
ASSCCKE Clayton Kershaw 6.00 15.00
ASSCCLK Clayton Kershaw 6.00 15.00
ASSCCSA Chris Sale 5.00 12.00
ASSCCSE Corey Seager 3.00 8.00
ASSCDJE Jacob deGrom 8.00 20.00
ASSCGSA Gary Sanchez 3.00 8.00
ASSCGSP George Springer 2.50 6.00
ASSCJAL Jose Altuve 4.00 10.00
ASSCJOA Jose Altuve 4.00 10.00
ASSCJUV Justin Verlander 3.00 8.00
ASSCJVE Justin Verlander 3.00 8.00
ASSCJVO Joey Votto 3.00 8.00
ASSCMBE Mookie Betts 8.00 20.00
ASSCMCO Michael Conforto 2.50 6.00
ASSCMIT Mike Trout 15.00 40.00
ASSCMMA Manny Machado 3.00 8.00
ASSCMSA Miguel Sano 2.50 6.00
ASSCMSC Max Scherzer 3.00 8.00
ASSCMTA Masahiro Tanaka 3.00 8.00
ASSCMTR Mike Trout 15.00 40.00
ASSCNAR Nolan Arenado 4.00 10.00
ASSCNOA Nolan Arenado 4.00 10.00
ASSCPGO Paul Goldschmidt 3.00 8.00
ASSCSAL Chris Sale 5.00 12.00
ASSCTRO Mike Trout 15.00 40.00
ASSCXBO Xander Bogaerts 5.00 12.00
ASSCYMO Yadier Molina 4.00 10.00

2020 Topps Update All Star Stitches Red

*RED: .8X TO 2X
STATED ODDS 1:XX HOBBY
STATED PRINT RUN 25 SER.#'d SETS
ASSCAP Albert Pujols 20.00 50.00
ASSCAR Anthony Rizzo 20.00 50.00
ASSCCK Clayton Kershaw 25.00 60.00
ASSCJR Jose Ramirez 10.00 25.00
ASSCJT Justin Turner 15.00 40.00
ASSCJV Joey Votto 12.00 30.00
ASSCMC Miguel Cabrera 15.00 40.00
ASSCMT Mike Trout 40.00 100.00
ASSCPG Paul Goldschmidt 12.00 30.00
ASSCSG Sonny Gray 10.00 25.00
ASSCXB Xander Bogaerts 12.00 30.00
ASSCYM Yadier Molina 12.00 30.00
ASSCARI Anthony Rizzo 20.00 50.00
ASSCCKE Clayton Kershaw 25.00 60.00
ASSCCLK Clayton Kershaw 25.00 60.00
ASSCJUV Justin Verlander 12.00 30.00
ASSCJVE Justin Verlander 12.00 30.00
ASSCJVO Joey Votto 12.00 30.00
ASSCMIT Mike Trout 40.00 100.00
ASSCMTR Mike Trout 40.00 100.00
ASSCPGO Paul Goldschmidt 12.00 30.00
ASSCTRO Mike Trout 40.00 100.00
ASSCXBO Xander Bogaerts 12.00 30.00
ASSCYMO Yadier Molina 12.00 30.00

2020 Topps Update All Star Stitches Silver

*SILVER: .6X TO 1.5X
STATED ODDS 1:XX HOBBY
STATED PRINT RUN 50 SER.#'d SETS
ASSCAR Anthony Rizzo 10.00 25.00
ASSCJT Justin Turner 12.00 30.00
ASSCJV Joey Votto 10.00 25.00
ASSCMC Miguel Cabrera 12.00 30.00
ASSCSG Sonny Gray 8.00 20.00
ASSCARI Anthony Rizzo 10.00 25.00
ASSCJUV Justin Verlander 10.00 25.00
ASSCJVE Justin Verlander 10.00 25.00
ASSCJVO Joey Votto 10.00 25.00

2020 Topps Update All Star Stitches Autographs

STATED ODDS 1:XX HOBBY
PRINT RUNS B/WN 10-25 COPIES PER
NO PRICING ON QTY 15 OR LESS
EXCHANGE DEADLINE 8/31/2022
ASSAAB Alex Bregman 15.00 40.00
ASSAAM Andrew McCutchen 40.00 100.00
ASSACS Chris Sale
ASSAGC Gerrit Cole 20.00 50.00
ASSAGS George Springer 10.00 25.00
ASSAGT Gleyber Torres
ASSAJA Jose Altuve 10.00 25.00
ASSAJD Jacob deGrom 40.00 100.00
ASSAMC Miguel Cabrera
ASSAMT Mike Trout
ASSANA Nolan Arenado 20.00 50.00
ASSARA Ronald Acuna Jr. 60.00 150.00
ASSASS Stephen Strasburg 20.00 50.00
ASSAWC Willson Contreras 12.00 30.00
ASSAXB Xander Bogaerts 12.00 30.00
ASSAYM Yadier Molina
ASSACSA CC Sabathia 15.00 40.00
ASSAJBE Jose Berrios 10.00 25.00

2020 Topps Update All Star Stitches Dual Autographs

STATED ODDS 1:XX HOBBY
PRINT RUNS B/WN 10-25 COPIES PER
NO PRICING ON QTY 15 OR LESS
EXCHANGE DEADLINE 8/31/2022
ASDAAS Springer/Altuve/25 20.00 50.00
ASDAAT Acuna/Torres/25
ASDABS Springer/Bregman/25 25.00 60.00
ASDAMC McCutchen/Cole
ASDATA Acuna/Trout/25
ASDAYW Molina/Contreras/25 40.00 100.00

2020 Topps Update All Star Stitches Jumbo

STATED ODDS 1:XX HOBBY
PRINT RUNS B/WN 10-25 COPIES PER
NO PRICING ON QTY 15 OR LESS
ASJAC Aroldis Chapman/25 10.00 25.00
ASJAN Aaron Nola/25 15.00 40.00
ASJAR Anthony Rizzo/25 40.00 100.00
ASJBC Bartolo Colon/20 8.00 20.00
ASJBH Bryce Harper/25 40.00 100.00
ASJBP Buster Posey/25 15.00 40.00
ASJBS Blake Snell/25 15.00 40.00
ASJCB Charlie Blackmon/25 15.00 40.00
ASJCC Carlos Correa/25
ASJCK Clayton Kershaw/25 40.00 100.00
ASJCS Chris Sale/25 8.00 20.00
ASJCY Christian Yelich/20 20.00 50.00
ASJDO David Ortiz
ASJES Eugenio Suarez
ASJFF Freddie Freeman
ASJFL Francisco Lindor/25 12.00 30.00
ASJGC Gerrit Cole/25 12.00 30.00
ASJGS Giancarlo Stanton
ASJGT Gleyber Torres
ASJHR Hyun-Jin Ryu/20 8.00 20.00
ASJJA Jose Abreu/25 25.00 60.00
ASJJB Jose Berrios
ASJJD Josh Donaldson/20 6.00 15.00
ASJJM J.D. Martinez
ASJJT Justin Turner/25 25.00 60.00
ASJJV Joey Votto/25 30.00 80.00
ASJKS Kyle Schwarber/25 20.00 50.00
ASJLS Luis Severino/25 15.00 40.00
ASJMB Mookie Betts/25 25.00 60.00
ASJMC Matt Chapman
ASJMM Max Muncy/25 15.00 40.00
ASJMS Max Scherzer/25 15.00 40.00
ASJNA Nolan Arenado
ASJNS Noah Syndergaard
ASJPG Paul Goldschmidt/25
ASJRZ Ryan Zimmerman
ASJSG Sonny Gray/25 20.00 50.00
ASJSP Salvador Perez
ASJTB Trevor Bauer/25 20.00 50.00
ASJTS Trevor Story
ASJWC Willson Contreras/25 30.00 80.00
ASJXB Xander Bogaerts/25 20.00 50.00
ASJYD Yu Darvish
ASJZG Zack Greinke/25 15.00 40.00
ASJALT Jose Altuve/25 15.00 40.00
ASJBPO Buster Posey/25 15.00 40.00
ASJCBL Charlie Blackmon/25 15.00 40.00
ASJCCS CC Sabathia
ASJCHS Chris Sale
ASJCLK Clayton Kershaw
ASJCSA Chris Sale
ASJCSE Corey Seager/25 20.00 50.00
ASJGCO Gerrit Cole/25 12.00 30.00
ASJGSA Gary Sanchez/25 8.00 20.00
ASJGSP George Springer/25 6.00 15.00
ASJGTO Gleyber Torres
ASJJAL Jose Altuve/25 15.00 40.00
ASJJOA Jose Altuve
ASJJRA Jose Ramirez
ASJJUV Justin Verlander/25 15.00 40.00
ASJJVE Justin Verlander
ASJLSE Luis Severino/25 15.00 40.00
ASJMAM Manny Machado/20 12.00 30.00
ASJMAX Max Scherzer/25 15.00 40.00
ASJMBE Mookie Betts/25 25.00 60.00
ASJMMA Manny Machado/25 12.00 30.00
ASJMOB Mookie Betts/25 25.00 60.00
ASJMSA Miguel Sano/25 6.00 15.00
ASJMSO Mike Soroka
ASJMTA Masahiro Tanaka
ASJMTR Mike Trout/25 40.00 100.00
ASJNAR Nolan Arenado
ASJPGO Paul Goldschmidt/25
ASJSST Stephen Strasburg/25
ASJTRO Mike Trout
ASJYAM Yadier Molina
ASJYMO Yadier Molina

2020 Topps Update Baseball Stars Autographs

STATED ODDS 1:XX HOBBY
EXCHANGE DEADLINE 8/31/2022
BSAAK Andrew Knapp 2.50 6.00
BSAAR Anthony Rendon 10.00 25.00
BSABO Brian O'Grady 2.50 6.00
BSACD Corey Dickerson 3.00 8.00
BSACM Charlie Morton 4.00 10.00
BSADA Dario Agrazal 3.00 8.00
BSADB David Bote 3.00 8.00
BSADJ Danny Jansen 2.50 6.00
BSADP David Price 10.00 25.00
BSAER Eduardo Rodriguez 4.00 10.00
BSAET Eric Thames 2.50 6.00
BSAGC Gerrit Cole 20.00 50.00
BSAHR Hyun-Jin Ryu 20.00 50.00
BSAJB Jon Berti 2.50 6.00
BSAJG Joey Gallo 10.00 25.00
BSAJH J.D. Hammer 4.00 10.00
BSAJM Jack Mayfield 2.50 6.00
BSAJS Juan Soto 40.00 100.00
BSAKK Kwang-Hyun Kim 12.00 30.00
BSAKM Ketel Marte 3.00 8.00
BSAKN Kevin Newman 5.00 12.00
BSAKW Kolten Wong 3.00 8.00
BSALB Lewis Brinson 2.50 6.00
BSALR Luis Robert 100.00 250.00
BSALW LaMonte Wade Jr. 4.00 10.00
BSAMM Mike Moustakas
BSAMS Marcus Stroman 20.00 50.00
BSANC Nick Castellanos 8.00 20.00
BSAPS Patrick Sandoval 4.00 10.00
BSARG Robel Garcia 2.50 6.00
BSARM Ryan McMahon 2.50 6.00
BSARV Daniel Vogelbach 2.50 6.00
BSASA Shogo Akiyama 8.00 20.00
BSASH Scott Heineman 2.50 6.00
BSATE Tom Eshelman 3.00 8.00
BSATP Tommy Pham 2.50 6.00
BSAYD Yonathan Daza 3.00 8.00
BSAYG Yasmani Grandal 2.50 6.00
BSAZG Zac Gallen 6.00 15.00
BSAKMA Kenta Maeda
BSAMSE Marcus Semien 2.50 6.00
BSAMST Myles Straw 4.00 10.00
BSASMA Sean Manaea 2.50 6.00

2020 Topps Update Baseball Stars Autographs Black

*BLACK: .5X TO 1.2X
STATED ODDS 1:XX HOBBY
STATED PRINT RUN 199 SER.#'d SETS
EXCHANGE DEADLINE 8/31/2022
BSAKW Kolten Wong 6.00 15.00
BSASA Shogo Akiyama 12.00 30.00
BSAMSE Marcus Semien 5.00 12.00

2020 Topps Update Baseball Stars Autographs Gold

*GOLD: .6X TO 1.5X
STATED ODDS 1:XX HOBBY
STATED PRINT RUN 50 SER.#'d SETS
EXCHANGE DEADLINE 8/31/2022
BSAET Eric Thames 10.00 25.00
BSAKK Kwang-Hyun Kim 30.00 80.00
BSAKW Kolten Wong 12.00 30.00
BSAMM Mike Moustakas 10.00 25.00
BSASA Shogo Akiyama 15.00 40.00
BSAKMA Kenta Maeda 20.00 50.00
BSAMSE Marcus Semien 6.00 15.00

2020 Topps Update Baseball Stars Autographs Red

*RED: .8X TO 2X
STATED ODDS 1:XX HOBBY
STATED PRINT RUN 25 SER.#'d SETS
EXCHANGE DEADLINE 8/31/2022
BSAAR Anthony Rendon 40.00 100.00
BSAET Eric Thames 12.00 30.00
BSAKK Kwang-Hyun Kim 40.00 100.00
BSAKW Kolten Wong 15.00 40.00
BSAMM Mike Moustakas 12.00 30.00
BSASA Shogo Akiyama 20.00 50.00
BSAKMA Kenta Maeda 25.00 60.00
BSAMSE Marcus Semien 8.00 20.00

2020 Topps Update Boxloader Patches

STATED ODDS 1 PER HOBBY
BPAA Aristides Aquino 3.00 8.00
BPAB Alex Bregman 2.50 6.00
BPAJ Aaron Judge 10.00 25.00
BPAM Andrew McCutchen 2.50 6.00
BPAR Anthony Rizzo 4.00 10.00
BPBB Bo Bichette 25.00 60.00
BPBH Bryce Harper 8.00 20.00
BPBM Brendan McKay 2.50 6.00
BPBP Buster Posey 3.00 8.00
BPCB Cody Bellinger 6.00 15.00
BPCK Clayton Kershaw 6.00 15.00
BPCY Christian Yelich 6.00 15.00
BPEJ Eloy Jimenez 5.00 12.00
BPFF Freddie Freeman 8.00 20.00
BPFL Francisco Lindor 2.50 6.00
BPFT Fernando Tatis Jr. 15.00 40.00
BPGL Gavin Lux 10.00 25.00
BPGS Giancarlo Stanton 2.50 6.00
BPGT Gleyber Torres 5.00 12.00
BPJB Javier Baez 3.00 8.00
BPJD Jacob deGrom 2.50 6.00
BPJL Jesus Luzardo 3.00 8.00
BPJS Juan Soto 8.00 20.00
BPJV Joey Votto 2.50 6.00
BPKA Jose Altuve 2.00 5.00
BPKB Kris Bryant 6.00 15.00
BPKL Kyle Lewis 12.00 30.00
BPLR Luis Robert 40.00 100.00
BPMB Mookie Betts 10.00 25.00
BPMC Matt Chapman 2.50 6.00
BPMK Max Kepler 2.00 5.00
BPMS Max Scherzer 2.50 6.00
BPMT Mike Trout 15.00 40.00
BPNA Nolan Arenado 3.00 8.00
BPNH Nico Hoerner 6.00 15.00
BPNS Nick Solak 2.50 6.00
BPPA Pete Alonso 6.00 15.00
BPPG Paul Goldschmidt 2.50 6.00
BPRA Ronald Acuna Jr. 10.00 25.00
BPRD Rafael Devers 3.00 8.00
BPRH Rhys Hoskins 8.00 20.00
BPSM Sean Murphy 2.50 6.00
BPSO Shohei Ohtani 5.00 12.00
BPTS Trevor Story 2.50 6.00
BPVG Vladimir Guerrero Jr. 10.00 25.00
BPWM Whit Merrifield 2.50 6.00
BPYA Yordan Alvarez 10.00 25.00
BPYM Yadier Molina 2.50 6.00
BPJBE Josh Bell 2.00 5.00
BPJVE Justin Verlander 2.50 6.00

2020 Topps Update Coin Cards

STATED ODDS 1:XX HOBBY
TBCAA Aristides Aquino 1.50 4.00
TBCAB Alex Bregman 1.25 3.00
TBCAJ Aaron Judge 3.00 8.00
TBCAR Anthony Rendon 1.25 3.00
TBCBB Bo Bichette 6.00 15.00
TBCBH Bryce Harper 4.00 10.00
TBCBM Brendan McKay 4.00 10.00
TBCBP Buster Posey 1.50 4.00
TBCCB Cody Bellinger 2.50 6.00
TBCCK Clayton Kershaw 2.50 6.00
TBCCY Christian Yelich 1.50 4.00
TBCEJ Eloy Jimenez 2.50 6.00
TBCFF Freddie Freeman 1.50 4.00
TBCFL Francisco Lindor 1.25 3.00
TBCFT Fernando Tatis Jr. 5.00 12.00
TBCGC Gerrit Cole 2.00 5.00
TBCGL Gavin Lux 5.00 12.00
TBCGT Gleyber Torres 2.50 6.00
TBCJB Javier Baez 1.50 4.00
TBCJD Jacob deGrom 4.00 10.00
TBCJG Joey Gallo 1.25 3.00
TBCJL Jesus Luzardo 1.50 4.00
TBCJS Juan Soto 4.00 10.00
TBCJV Justin Verlander 1.25 3.00
TBCKB Kris Bryant 1.50 4.00
TBCKH Keston Hiura 1.50 4.00
TBCKL Kyle Lewis 6.00 15.00
TBCKM Ketel Marte 1.00 2.50
TBCLR Luis Robert 8.00 20.00
TBCMB Mookie Betts 5.00 12.00
TBCMC Matt Chapman 1.25 3.00
TBCMM Manny Machado 1.25 3.00
TBCMS Max Scherzer 1.25 3.00
TBCMT Mike Trout 6.00 15.00
TBCNA Nolan Arenado 2.50 6.00
TBCNH Nico Hoerner 3.00 8.00
TBCPA Pete Alonso 3.00 8.00
TBCPG Paul Goldschmidt 1.25 3.00
TBCRA Ronald Acuna Jr. 5.00 12.00
TBCRD Rafael Devers 1.50 4.00
TBCRH Rhys Hoskins 1.50 4.00
TBCSO Shohei Ohtani 2.50 6.00
TBCVG Vladimir Guerrero Jr. 4.00 10.00
TBCWB Walker Buehler 1.50 4.00
TBCWM Whit Merrifield 1.25 3.00
TBCYA Yordan Alvarez 4.00 10.00
TBCYM Yadier Molina 3.00 8.00
TBCANR Anthony Rizzo 3.00 8.00
TBCJOD Josh Donaldson 1.00 2.50
TBCJOV Joey Votto 1.25 3.00

2020 Topps Update Coin Cards Black

*BLACK: .6X TO 1.5X
STATED ODDS 1:XX HOBBY
STATED PRINT RUN 199 SER.#'d SETS
TBCCY Christian Yelich 8.00 20.00
TBCFF Freddie Freeman 5.00 12.00
TBCLR Luis Robert 15.00 40.00
TBCNA Nolan Arenado 8.00 20.00
TBCRA Ronald Acuna Jr. 10.00 25.00

2020 Topps Update Coin Cards Gold

*GOLD: 1X TO 2.5X
STATED ODDS 1:XX HOBBY
STATED PRINT RUN 50 SER.#'d SETS
TBCCY Christian Yelich 12.00 30.00
TBCFF Freddie Freeman 8.00 20.00
TBCJD Jacob deGrom 10.00 25.00
TBCLR Luis Robert 60.00 150.00
TBCNA Nolan Arenado 12.00 30.00
TBCRA Ronald Acuna Jr. 15.00 40.00
TBCSO Shohei Ohtani 8.00 20.00
TBCVG Vladimir Guerrero Jr. 12.00 30.00

2020 Topps Update Decades' Best

STATED ODDS 1:XX HOBBY
DB1 Whitey Ford .30 .75
DB2 Bob Lemon .30 .75
DB3 Early Wynn .30 .75
DB4 Robin Roberts .30 .75
DB5 Warren Spahn .30 .75
DB6 Hoyt Wilhelm .30 .75
DB7 Bob Feller .30 .75
DB8 Jim Bunning .30 .75
DB9 Sandy Koufax .75 2.00
DB10 Hal Newhouser .30 .75
DB11 Rod Carew .30 .75
DB12 Tom Seaver .30 .75
DB13 Frank Robinson .30 .75
DB14 Carl Yastrzemski .60 1.50
DB15 Brooks Robinson .30 .75
DB16 Sandy Koufax .75 2.00
DB17 Bob Gibson .30 .75
DB18 Roberto Clemente 1.00 2.50
DB19 Willie Mays .75 2.00
DB20 Sandy Koufax .75 2.00
DB21 Cincinnati Reds .25 .60
DB22 Baltimore Orioles .25 .60
DB23 Pittsburgh Pirates .25 .60
DB24 Los Angeles Dodgers .25 .60
DB25 Boston Red Sox .25 .60
DB26 New York Yankees .25 .60
DB27 Oakland Athletics .25 .60
DB28 Philadelphia Phillies .25 .60
DB29 Kansas City Royals .25 .60
DB30 New York Mets .25 .60
DB31 Mike Schmidt .60 1.50
DB32 Ryne Sandberg .75 2.00
DB33 Cal Ripken Jr. 1.25 3.00
DB34 Dale Murphy .40 1.00
DB35 Dwight Gooden .25 .60
DB36 Jose Canseco .30 .75
DB37 Roger Clemens .50 1.25
DB38 Don Mattingly .75 2.00
DB39 Steve Carlton .30 .75
DB40 Mark McGwire .60 1.50
DB41 Roger Clemens .50 1.25
DB42 Randy Johnson .40 1.00
DB43 Tom Glavine .30 .75
DB44 Pedro Martinez .30 .75
DB45 Mike Mussina .30 .75
DB46 John Smoltz .40 1.00
DB47 David Cone .25 .60
DB48 Dennis Eckersley .30 .75
DB49 Andy Pettitte .30 .75
DB50 Mariano Rivera .50 1.25
DB51 Boston Red Sox .25 .60
DB52 New York Yankees .25 .60
DB53 St. Louis Cardinals .25
DB54 Los Angeles Angels .25
DB55 Philadelphia Phillies .25
DB56 Arizona Diamondbacks .25
DB57 Chicago White Sox .25
DB58 Atlanta Braves .25
DB59 Oakland Athletics .25
DB60 Houston Astros .25
DB61 Albert Pujols .50 1.
DB62 Ichiro .50 1.
DB63 Miguel Cabrera .40 1.
DB64 Ryan Howard .30
DB65 Alex Rodriguez .50 1.
DB66 Vladimir Guerrero .30
DB67 Jim Thome .30
DB68 David Ortiz .40 1.
DB69 Todd Helton .30
DB70 Chipper Jones .60 1.
DB71 Mike Trout 2.00 5.
DB72 Andrew McCutchen .40 1.
DB73 Joey Votto .40 1.
DB74 Paul Goldschmidt .40 1.
DB75 Mookie Betts .75 2.
DB76 Miguel Cabrera .40 1.
DB77 Christian Yelich .50 1.
DB78 Nolan Arenado .50 1.
DB79 Freddie Freeman .50 1.
DB80 Jose Altuve .30

2020 Topps Update Decades' Best Black

*BLACK: 1X TO 2.5X
STATED ODDS 1:XX HOBBY
STATED PRINT RUN 299 SER.#'d SETS
DB7 Bob Feller 4.00 10.
DB14 Carl Yastrzemski 5.00 12.
DB34 Dale Murphy 4.00 10.
DB36 Jose Canseco 4.00 10.
DB38 Don Mattingly 5.00 12.
DB62 Ichiro 2.50 6.
DB75 Mookie Betts 4.00 10.

2020 Topps Update Decades' Best Blue

*BLUE: .6X TO 1.5X
STATED ODDS 1:XX HOBBY
DB7 Bob Feller 2.50 6.
DB14 Carl Yastrzemski 3.00 8.
DB36 Jose Canseco 2.50 6.

2020 Topps Update Decades' Best Gold

*GOLD: 2.5X TO 6X
STATED ODDS 1:XX HOBBY
STATED PRINT RUN 50 SER.#'d SETS
DB7 Bob Feller 10.00 25.
DB14 Carl Yastrzemski 12.00 30.
DB33 Cal Ripken Jr. 12.00 30.
DB34 Dale Murphy 10.00 25.
DB36 Jose Canseco 10.00 25.
DB38 Don Mattingly 12.00 30.
DB62 Ichiro 6.00 15.
DB75 Mookie Betts 10.00 25.

2020 Topps Update Dual All St[illegible] Stitches

STATED ODDS 1:XX HOBBY
STATED PRINT RUN 50 SER.#'d SETS
ASSDAC Correa/Altuve 6.00 15.
ASSDDA Alonso/deGrom
ASSDDC deGrom/Colon 10.00 25.
ASSDJJ Jeter/Judge 15.00 40.
ASSDJS Stanton/Judge 12.00 30.
ASSDKT Kershaw/Trout 30.00 80.
ASSDPT Trout/Pujols 20.00 50.
ASSDTA Trout/Acuna 30.00 80.
ASSDTH Trout/Harper 30.00 80.

2020 Topps Update Jeter's Fin[illegible] Season Commemorative Patc[illegible] Autographs

STATED ODDS 1:XX HOBBY
PRINT RUNS B/WN 5-25 COPIES PER
NO PRICING ON QTY 15 OR LESS
EXCHANGE DEADLINE 8/31/2022
JFPAAS Alfonso Soriano/25 40.00 100.
JFPACS CC Sabathia/25
JFPAMT Mark Teixeira/25 50.00 120.
JFPAMTA Masahiro Tanaka/25 50.00 120.

2020 Topps Update Jeter's Fin[illegible] Season Commemorative Patches

STATED ODDS 1:XX HOBBY
*BLACK: 1X TO 2.5X
*GOLD: 1.5X TO 4X
JFPI Ichiro 4.00 10.
JFPAS Alfonso Soriano 1.00 2.
JFPCS CC Sabathia 1.00 2.
JFPJG Joe Girardi 1.00 2.
JFPMT Mark Teixeira 1.00 2.
JFPDJ1 Derek Jeter 3.00 8.
JFPDJ2 Derek Jeter 3.00 8.
JFPDJ3 Derek Jeter 3.00 8.
JFPDJ4 Derek Jeter 3.00 8.
JFPMTA Masahiro Tanaka 1.25 3.

2020 Topps Update Major League Material Autographs

STATED ODDS 1:XX HOBBY
PRINT RUNS B/WN 25-50 COPIES PER
EXCHANGE DEADLINE 8/31/2022

LAAB Alex Bregman 12.00 30.00
LAAJ Aaron Judge
LAAR Anthony Rendon 8.00 20.00
LABB Bo Bichette
LABM Brendan McKay
LACB Cody Bellinger
LADJ David Justice 30.00 80.00
LAEA Elvis Andrus 6.00 15.00
LAEH Eric Hosmer 10.00 25.00
LAFT Fernando Tatis Jr. 60.00 150.00
LAGT Gleyber Torres 25.00 60.00
LAJG Joey Gallo 10.00 25.00
LAJR J.T. Realmuto 15.00 40.00
LAKH Keston Hiura
LALG Lucas Giolito 12.00 30.00
LALR Luis Robert 100.00 250.00
LAMC Matt Chapman 12.00 30.00
LAMG Mark Grace 30.00 80.00
LAMT Mike Trout
LANC Nick Castellanos 15.00 40.00
LANS Noah Syndergaard 30.00 80.00
LAPA Pete Alonso 25.00 60.00
LARA Ronald Acuna Jr. 50.00 120.00
LARD Rafael Devers 10.00 25.00
LARH Rhys Hoskins 25.00 60.00
LASG Sonny Gray 10.00 25.00
LATE Tommy Edman 15.00 40.00
LAVG Vladimir Guerrero Jr. 20.00 50.00
LAWB Walker Buehler 25.00 60.00
LAWC Willson Contreras 8.00 20.00
LAXB Xander Bogaerts
LAYA Yordan Alvarez
LAZG Zac Gallen 12.00 30.00
LAAJO Andruw Jones 20.00 50.00
LAJSO Jorge Soler 8.00 20.00

2020 Topps Update Major League Materials

STATED ODDS 1:XX HOBBY
MLMAA Aristides Aquino 4.00 10.00
MLMAB Alex Bregman 3.00 8.00
MLMAP Albert Pujols 4.00 10.00
MLMAR Anthony Rizzo 5.00 12.00
MLMBH Bryce Harper 5.00 12.00
MLMCK Clayton Kershaw 6.00 15.00
MLMCS CC Sabathia 2.50 6.00
MLMCY Christian Yelich 4.00 10.00
MLMDO David Ortiz 3.00 8.00
MLMEA Elvis Andrus 2.50 6.00
MLMGT Gleyber Torres 6.00 15.00
MLMJB Javier Baez 4.00 10.00
MLMJS Jorge Soler 3.00 8.00
MLMKH Keston Hiura 4.00 10.00
MLMLG Lucas Giolito 2.50 6.00
MLMMC Miguel Cabrera 3.00 8.00
MLMMK Max Kepler 4.00 10.00
MLMMO Matt Olson 2.00 5.00
MLMMS Max Scherzer 3.00 8.00
MLMNA Nolan Arenado 4.00 10.00
MLMPG Paul Goldschmidt 3.00 8.00
MLMRD Rafael Devers 4.00 10.00
MLMRH Rhys Hoskins 4.00 10.00
MLMSG Sonny Gray 2.50 6.00
MLMVG Vladimir Guerrero Jr. 6.00 15.00
MLMVR Victor Robles 4.00 10.00
MLMYM Yadier Molina 4.00 10.00
MLMAMC Andrew McCutchen 3.00 8.00
MLMDJL DJ LeMahieu 3.00 8.00
MLMFTJ Fernando Tatis Jr. 8.00 20.00
MLMGSP George Springer 2.50 6.00
MLMJTR J.T. Realmuto 3.00 8.00
MLMJVO Joey Votto 3.00 8.00
MLMKBR Kris Bryant 4.00 10.00
MLMLCA Lorenzo Cain 2.00 5.00
MLMMCH Matt Chapman 4.00 10.00
MLMMCO Michael Conforto 2.50 6.00
MLMMTR Mike Trout 12.00 30.00
MLMOHT Shohei Ohtani 4.00 10.00

2020 Topps Update Major League Materials Black

*BLACK: .5X TO 1.2X
STATED ODDS 1:XX HOBBY
STATED PRINT RUN 199 SER.#'d SETS
MLMMC Miguel Cabrera 10.00 25.00

2020 Topps Update Major League Materials Gold

*GOLD: .6X TO 1.5X
STATED ODDS 1:XX HOBBY
STATED PRINT RUN 50 SER.#'d SETS
MLMAR Anthony Rizzo 10.00 25.00
MLMMC Miguel Cabrera 12.00 30.00
MLMSG Sonny Gray 8.00 20.00

2020 Topps Update Major League Materials Red

*RED: .8X TO 2X
STATED ODDS 1:XX HOBBY
STATED PRINT RUN 25 SER.#'d SETS
MLMAA Aristides Aquino 12.00 30.00
MLMAP Albert Pujols 20.00 50.00
MLMAR Anthony Rizzo 20.00 50.00
MLMCK Clayton Kershaw 15.00 40.00
MLMMC Miguel Cabrera 15.00 40.00
MLMMK Max Kepler 10.00 25.00
MLMPG Paul Goldschmidt 12.00 30.00
MLMSG Sonny Gray 10.00 25.00
MLMYM Yadier Molina 12.00 30.00
MLMFTJ Fernando Tatis Jr. 20.00 50.00

2020 Topps Update Prospects

STATED ODDS 1:XX HOBBY
P1 Evan White .25 .60
P2 Nate Pearson .50 1.25
P3 Wander Franco 4.00 10.00
P4 Jo Adell 1.00 2.50
P5 Tyler Stephenson .25 .60
P6 MacKenzie Gore .50 1.25
P7 Cristian Pache .75 2.00
P8 Josh Jung .60 1.50
P9 Ke'Bryan Hayes .25 .60
P10 Bobby Dalbec .60 1.50
P11 Colton Welker .25 .60
P12 Alec Bohm 1.50 4.00
P13 Nick Allen .25 .60
P14 Ethan Small .30 .75
P15 Ryan Mountcastle .40 1.00
P16 Andres Gimenez .30 .75
P17 Brady Singer .30 .75
P18 Casey Mize .75 2.00
P19 Alex Kirilloff .50 1.25
P20 Forrest Whitley .25 .60
P21 Keibert Ruiz .60 1.50
P22 Brennen Davis .50 1.25
P23 Sixto Sanchez .40 1.00
P24 Nick Madrigal .75 2.00
P25 Joey Bart .75 2.00
P26 Daulton Varsho .25 .60
P27 Dylan Carlson 1.00 2.50
P28 Nolan Jones .40 1.00
P29 Luis Garcia .40 1.00
P30 Clarke Schmidt .40 1.00

2020 Topps Update Prospects Black

*BLACK: 1X TO 2.5X
STATED ODDS 1:XX HOBBY
STATED PRINT RUN 299 SER.#'d SETS
P3 Wander Franco 30.00 80.00
P4 Jo Adell 5.00 12.00
P6 MacKenzie Gore 3.00 8.00
P7 Cristian Pache 5.00 12.00
P8 Josh Jung 6.00 15.00
P10 Bobby Dalbec 8.00 20.00
P12 Alec Bohm 12.00 30.00
P19 Alex Kirilloff 6.00 15.00
P21 Keibert Ruiz 5.00 12.00
P22 Brennen Davis 5.00 12.00
P24 Nick Madrigal 8.00 20.00
P25 Joey Bart 8.00 20.00
P27 Dylan Carlson 8.00 20.00

2020 Topps Update Prospects Blue

*BLUE: .6X TO 1.5X
STATED ODDS 1:XX HOBBY
P3 Wander Franco 15.00 40.00
P7 Cristian Pache 3.00 8.00
P8 Josh Jung 4.00 10.00
P10 Bobby Dalbec 5.00 12.00
P19 Alex Kirilloff 3.00 8.00
P21 Keibert Ruiz 2.50 6.00
P22 Brennen Davis 3.00 8.00
P24 Nick Madrigal 4.00 10.00
P25 Joey Bart 3.00 8.00
P27 Dylan Carlson 5.00 12.00

2020 Topps Update Prospects Gold

*GOLD: 2.5X TO 6X
STATED ODDS 1:XX HOBBY
STATED PRINT RUN 50 SER.#'d SETS
P3 Wander Franco 75.00 200.00
P4 Jo Adell 12.00 30.00
P6 MacKenzie Gore 12.00 30.00
P7 Cristian Pache 12.00 30.00
P8 Josh Jung 30.00 80.00
P10 Bobby Dalbec 20.00 50.00
P12 Alec Bohm 30.00 80.00
P19 Alex Kirilloff 15.00 40.00
P21 Keibert Ruiz 12.00 30.00
P22 Brennen Davis 12.00 30.00
P24 Nick Madrigal 20.00 50.00
P25 Joey Bart 20.00 50.00
P27 Dylan Carlson 20.00 50.00

2020 Topps Update Prospects Autographs

STATED ODDS 1:XX HOBBY
STATED PRINT RUN 25 SER.#'d SETS
EXCHANGE DEADLINE 8/31/2022
PAAB Alec Bohm 150.00 400.00
PABD Bobby Dalbec
PABS Brady Singer 60.00 150.00
PACM Casey Mize 50.00 120.00
PACP Cristian Pache
PACS Clarke Schmidt 25.00 60.00
PACW Colton Welker 25.00 60.00
PAES Ethan Small
PAEW Evan White 30.00 80.00
PAJA Jo Adell 100.00 250.00
PAJB Joey Bart 100.00 250.00
PAJJ Josh Jung 40.00 100.00
PAKR Keibert Ruiz 15.00 40.00
PALG Luis Garcia 60.00 150.00
PAMG MacKenzie Gore
PANM Nick Madrigal 50.00 120.00
PANP Nate Pearson
PARM Ryan Mountcastle 100.00 250.00
PAWF Wander Franco 200.00 500.00
PABDA Brennen Davis 60.00 150.00

2020 Topps Update Ronald Acuna Jr. Highlights

*BLACK: 1X TO 2.5X BASIC
*GOLD: 2.5X TO 6X BASIC
TRA1 Ronald Acuna Jr. 1.50 4.00
TRA2 Ronald Acuna Jr. 1.50 4.00
TRA3 Ronald Acuna Jr. 1.50 4.00
TRA4 Ronald Acuna Jr. 1.50 4.00
TRA5 Ronald Acuna Jr. 1.50 4.00
TRA6 Ronald Acuna Jr. 1.50 4.00
TRA7 Ronald Acuna Jr. 1.50 4.00
TRA8 Ronald Acuna Jr. 1.50 4.00
TRA9 Ronald Acuna Jr. 1.50 4.00
TRA10 Ronald Acuna Jr. 1.50 4.00
TRA11 Ronald Acuna Jr. 1.50 4.00
TRA12 Ronald Acuna Jr. 1.50 4.00
TRA13 Ronald Acuna Jr. 1.50 4.00
TRA14 Ronald Acuna Jr. 1.50 4.00
TRA15 Ronald Acuna Jr. 1.50 4.00
TRA16 Ronald Acuna Jr. 1.50 4.00
TRA17 Ronald Acuna Jr. 1.50 4.00
TRA18 Ronald Acuna Jr. 1.50 4.00
TRA19 Ronald Acuna Jr. 1.50 4.00
TRA20 Ronald Acuna Jr. 1.50 4.00

2020 Topps Update Triple All Star Stitches

STATED ODDS 1:XX HOBBY
STATED PRINT RUN 50 SER.#'d SETS
ASSTASA Springer/Altuve/Correa
ASSTKDS DeGrom/Kershaw/Strasburg 25.00 60.00
ASSTPCO Cabrera/Pujols/Ortiz 25.00 60.00
ASSTPMC Posey/Contreras/Molina 20.00 50.00
ASSTJA Acuna/Judge/Trout
ASSTZSS Strasburg
Scherzer/Zimmerman 20.00 50.00

2020 Topps Update Turkey Red '20

STATED ODDS 1:XX HOBBY
TR1 CC Sabathia .30 .75
TR2 Willie McCovey .30 .75
TR3 Ozzie Albies .40 1.00
TR4 Hunter Pence .30 .75
TR5 Mookie Betts .75 2.00
TR6 Yordan Alvarez 1.25 3.00
TR7 David Price .30 .75
TR8 Gavin Lux 1.50 4.00
TR9 Craig Biggio .30 .75
TR10 Dave Winfield .30 .75
TR11 Bo Bichette 2.00 5.00
TR12 Carlton Fisk .30 .75
TR13 Andrew McCutchen .40 1.00
TR14 Shogo Akiyama .40 1.00
TR15 Ken Griffey Jr. .75 2.00
TR16 Thurman Munson .40 1.00
TR17 Shun Yamaguchi .30 .75
TR18 Gary Carter .30 .75
TR19 Lewis Brinson .25 .60
TR20 Kwang-Hyun Kim .75 2.00
TR21 Tom Seaver .30 .75
TR22 Gerrit Cole .60 1.50
TR23 Trea Turner .30 .75
TR24 Yoshi Tsutsugo .30 .75
TR25 Marcus Semien .25 .60
TR26 Nick Castellanos .40 1.00
TR27 Luis Robert 2.50 6.00
TR28 Andy Pettitte .30 .75
TR29 Anthony Rendon .40 1.00
TR30 Ron Santo .30 .75
TR31 Johnny Bench .40 1.00
TR32 Mike Piazza .40 1.00
TR33 Yasmani Grandal .25 .60
TR34 Eddie Murray .30 .75
TR35 Dale Murphy .40 1.00
TR36 Mark Grace .30 .75
TR37 Mike Clevinger .30 .75
TR38 Mike Mussina .30 .75
TR39 Trevor Bauer .40 1.00
TR40 Kerry Wood .25 .60
TR41 Corey Kluber .30 .75
TR42 Brooks Robinson .30 .75
TR43 John Smoltz .40 1.00
TR44 Byron Buxton .30 .75
TR45 Carter Kieboom .30 .75
TR46 Wade Boggs .30 .75
TR47 Larry Walker .30 .75
TR48 Willie Stargell .30 .75
TR49 Derek Jeter 1.00 2.50
TR50 Nolan Ryan 1.25 3.00

2020 Topps Update Turkey Red '20 Blue

*BLUE: 4X TO 10X
STATED ODDS 1:XX HOBBY
STATED PRINT RUN 50 SER.#'d SETS
TR11 Bo Bichette 25.00 60.00
TR15 Ken Griffey Jr. 15.00 40.00
TR49 Derek Jeter 40.00 100.00
TR50 Nolan Ryan 20.00 50.00

2020 Topps Update Turkey Red '20 Chrome

STATED ODDS 1:XX HOBBY
TRC1 CC Sabathia .75 2.00
TRC2 Willie McCovey .75 2.00
TRC3 Ozzie Albies 1.00 2.50
TRC4 Hunter Pence .75 2.00
TRC5 Mookie Betts 2.00 5.00
TRC6 Yordan Alvarez 3.00 8.00
TRC7 David Price .75 2.00
TRC8 Gavin Lux 4.00 10.00
TRC9 Craig Biggio .75 2.00
TRC10 Dave Winfield .75 2.00
TRC11 Bo Bichette 5.00 12.00
TRC12 Carlton Fisk .75 2.00
TRC13 Andrew McCutchen 1.00 2.50
TRC14 Shogo Akiyama 1.00 2.50
TRC15 Ken Griffey Jr. 2.00 5.00
TRC16 Thurman Munson 2.00 5.00
TRC17 Shun Yamaguchi .75 2.00
TRC18 Gary Carter .75 2.00
TRC19 Lewis Brinson .60 1.50
TRC20 Kwang-Hyun Kim 2.00 5.00
TRC21 Tom Seaver .75 2.00
TRC22 Gerrit Cole 1.50 4.00
TRC23 Trea Turner .75 2.00
TRC24 Yoshi Tsutsugo .75 2.00
TRC25 Marcus Semien .60 1.50
TRC26 Nick Castellanos 1.00 2.50
TRC27 Luis Robert 6.00 15.00
TRC28 Andy Pettitte .75 2.00
TRC29 Anthony Rendon 1.00 2.50
TRC30 Ron Santo .75 2.00
TRC31 Johnny Bench 1.00 2.50
TRC32 Mike Piazza 1.00 2.50
TRC33 Yasmani Grandal .60 1.50
TRC34 Eddie Murray .75 2.00
TRC35 Dale Murphy 1.00 2.50
TRC36 Mark Grace .75 2.00
TRC37 Mike Clevinger .75 2.00
TRC38 Mike Mussina .75 2.00
TRC39 Trevor Bauer 1.00 2.50
TRC40 Kerry Wood .60 1.50
TRC41 Corey Kluber .75 2.00
TRC42 Brooks Robinson .75 2.00
TRC43 John Smoltz 1.00 2.50
TRC44 Byron Buxton .75 2.00
TRC45 Carter Kieboom .75 2.00
TRC46 Wade Boggs .75 2.00
TRC47 Larry Walker .75 2.00
TRC48 Willie Stargell .75 2.00
TRC49 Derek Jeter 4.00 10.00
TRC50 Nolan Ryan 3.00 8.00

2020 Topps Update Turkey Red '20 Chrome Blue Refractors

*BLUE: 3X TO 8X
STATED ODDS 1:XX HOBBY
STATED PRINT RUN 50 SER.#'d SETS
TRC5 Mookie Betts 100.00 250.00
TRC8 Gavin Lux 50.00 120.00
TRC11 Bo Bichette 60.00 150.00
TRC15 Ken Griffey Jr. 30.00 80.00
TRC18 Gary Carter 10.00 25.00
TRC49 Derek Jeter 100.00 250.00

2020 Topps 206 Wave 1

RANDOM INSERTS IN PACKS
1 Gerrit Cole 1.00 2.50
2 Charlie Morton .60 1.50
3 Patrick Corbin .50 1.25
4 Noah Syndergaard .50 1.25
5 Mike Trout 3.00 8.00
6 Gleyber Torres 1.25 3.00
7 Freddie Freeman .75 2.00
8 Pete Alonso 1.50 4.00
9 D.J. LeMahieu .60 1.50
10 Xander Bogaerts .60 1.50
11 Max Kepler .50 1.25
12 Manny Machado .60 1.50
13 Andrew Benintendi .60 1.50
14 Brandon Lowe .60 1.50
15 George Springer .50 1.25
16 Buster Posey .75 2.00
17 Carlos Correa .60 1.50
18 Hunter Dozier .40 1.00
19 Tyler Glasnow .40 1.00
20 Scott Kingery .50 1.25
21 Randal Grichuk .40 1.00
22 J.T. Realmuto .60 1.50
23 Carlos Santana .50 1.25
24 Blake Snell .50 1.25
25 Jorge Alfaro .40 1.00
26 David Dahl .40 1.00
27 Robbie Ray .40 1.00
28 Amed Rosario .50 1.25
29 Corey Seager .60 1.50
30 Jon Lester .50 1.25
31 Kevin Kiermaier .50 1.25
32 J.D. Martinez .60 1.50
33 Babe Ruth 1.50 4.00
34 Mariano Rivera .75 2.00
35 Reggie Jackson .50 1.25
36 Tony Gwynn 1.50 4.00
37 Carl Yastrzemski 1.00 2.50
38 Mike Schmidt 1.00 2.50
39 Roberto Clemente 1.50 4.00
40 Johnny Bench .60 1.50
41 Vladimir Guerrero .50 1.25
42 Larry Doby .50 1.25
43 Justin Dunn .50 1.25
44 Sean Murphy .60 1.50
45 Gavin Lux 2.50 6.00
46 Logan Webb .50 1.25
47 Randy Dobnak .75 2.00
48 Dillon Tate .40 1.00
49 Bobby Bradley .50 1.25
50 Zack Collins .50 1.25

2020 Topps 206 Wave 1 Cycle Back

*CYCLE/25: 4X TO 10X BASIC
RANDOM INSERTS IN PACKS
STATED PRINT RUN 25 SER.#'d SETS
1 Gerrit Cole 30.00 80.00
5 Mike Trout 200.00 500.00
6 Gleyber Torres 60.00 150.00
8 Pete Alonso 40.00 100.00
33 Babe Ruth 60.00 150.00
35 Reggie Jackson 30.00 80.00
36 Tony Gwynn 25.00 60.00
37 Carl Yastrzemski 30.00 80.00
38 Mike Schmidt 30.00 80.00
39 Roberto Clemente 60.00 150.00
41 Vladimir Guerrero 25.00 60.00
42 Larry Doby 30.00 80.00
45 Gavin Lux 125.00 300.00

2020 Topps 206 Wave 1 Old Mill Back

*OLD MILL: 2.5X TO 6X BASIC
STATED ODDS 1:30 PACKS
1 Gerrit Cole 12.00 30.00
5 Mike Trout 75.00 200.00
6 Gleyber Torres 20.00 50.00
8 Pete Alonso 25.00 60.00
33 Babe Ruth 25.00 60.00
35 Reggie Jackson 12.00 30.00
36 Tony Gwynn 12.00 30.00
37 Carl Yastrzemski 20.00 50.00
38 Mike Schmidt 25.00 60.00
39 Roberto Clemente 25.00 60.00
41 Vladimir Guerrero 10.00 25.00
42 Larry Doby 15.00 40.00
45 Gavin Lux 60.00 150.00

2020 Topps 206 Wave 1 Piedmont Back

*PIEDMONT: .5X TO 1.2X BASIC
INSERTED 2 PER PACK
5 Mike Trout 8.00 20.00

2020 Topps 206 Wave 1 Polar Bear Back

*POLAR BEAR: 2.5X TO 6X BASIC
STATED ODDS 1:18 PACKS
1 Gerrit Cole 12.00 30.00
5 Mike Trout 75.00 200.00
6 Gleyber Torres 20.00 50.00
8 Pete Alonso 25.00 60.00
33 Babe Ruth 20.00 50.00
35 Reggie Jackson 12.00 30.00
36 Tony Gwynn 12.00 30.00
37 Carl Yastrzemski 12.00 30.00
38 Mike Schmidt 12.00 30.00
39 Roberto Clemente 25.00 60.00
41 Vladimir Guerrero 6.00 15.00
42 Larry Doby 12.00 30.00
45 Gavin Lux 30.00 80.00

2020 Topps 206 Wave 1 Sovereign Back

*SOVEREIGN: 1X TO 2.5X BASIC
STATED ODDS 1:6 PACKS
5 Mike Trout 30.00 80.00
6 Gleyber Torres 8.00 20.00
33 Babe Ruth 6.00 15.00
38 Mike Schmidt 5.00 12.00
39 Roberto Clemente 10.00 25.00

2020 Topps 206 Wave 1 Sweet Caporal Back

*S.CAPORAL: .75X TO 2X BASIC
STATED ODDS 1:3 PACKS
5 Mike Trout 15.00 40.00
6 Gleyber Torres 5.00 12.00
33 Babe Ruth 5.00 12.00

2020 Topps 206 Wave 1 Autographs

RANDOM INSERTS IN PACKS
1 Brandon Lowe 20.00 50.00
2 Johnny Bench
3 Mike Trout
4 Patrick Corbin
5 Reggie Jackson 125.00 300.00
6 Zack Collins 20.00 50.00

2020 Topps 206 Wave 2

RANDOM INSERTS IN PACKS
1 Anthony Rendon .60 1.50
2 Ketel Marte .50 1.25
3 Zac Gallen 1.00 2.50
4 Chipper Jones .60 1.50
5 Mike Soroka .60 1.50
6 Cal Ripken Jr. 2.00 5.00
7 John Means .40 1.00
8 Pedro Martinez .50 1.25
9 Kyle Schwarber .60 1.50
10 Yoan Moncada .60 1.50
11 Joey Votto .60 1.50
12 Aristides Aquino .75 2.00
13 Shane Bieber .60 1.50
14 Nolan Arenado .75 2.00
15 Jorge Soler .60 1.50
16 Sandy Koufax 1.25 3.00
17 Cody Bellinger 1.25 3.00
18 Max Muncy .50 1.25
19 Brusdar Graterol .60 1.50
20 Isan Diaz .60 1.50
21 Jorge Polanco .50 1.25
22 David Wright .50 1.25
23 Aaron Judge 1.50 4.00
24 Rickey Henderson .60 1.50
25 Jesus Luzardo .75 2.00
26 Chris Paddack .60 1.50
27 Tommy Pham .40 1.00
28 Brandon Belt .50 1.25
29 Ken Griffey Jr. 1.25 3.00
30 Ozzie Smith .75 2.00
31 Ivan Rodriguez .50 1.25
32 Nick Solak .60 1.50
33 Hyun-Jin Ryu .50 1.25
34 Max Scherzer .60 1.50
35 Albert Pujols .75 2.00
36 Ted Williams 1.25 3.00
37 Jackie Robinson .60 1.50
38 Jose Abreu .60 1.50
39 Charlie Blackmon .60 1.50
40 Al Kaline .60 1.50
41 Keston Hiura .75 2.00
42 Jose Berrios .50 1.25
43 Giancarlo Stanton .60 1.50
44 Didi Gregorius .50 1.25
45 Honus Wagner .60 1.50
46 Chris Archer .40 1.00
47 Eric Hosmer .50 1.25
48 Stan Musial 1.00 2.50
49 Trea Turner .50 1.25
50 Eric Thames .40 1.00

2020 Topps 206 Wave 2 Cycle Back

*CYCLE/25: 4X TO 10X BASIC
RANDOM INSERTS IN PACKS
STATED PRINT RUN 25 SER.#'d SETS
16 Sandy Koufax 60.00 150.00
29 Ken Griffey Jr. 125.00 300.00
36 Ted Williams 40.00 100.00
37 Jackie Robinson 60.00 150.00
45 Honus Wagner 60.00 150.00
48 Stan Musial 40.00 100.00

2020 Topps 206 Wave 2 Polar Bear Back

*POLAR BEAR: 2.5X TO 6X BASIC
STATED ODDS 1:18 PACKS
16 Sandy Koufax 40.00 100.00
29 Ken Griffey Jr. 40.00 100.00
36 Ted Williams 30.00 80.00
37 Jackie Robinson 25.00 60.00
45 Honus Wagner 40.00 100.00
48 Stan Musial 15.00 40.00

2020 Topps 206 Wave 2 Sovereign Back

*SOVEREIGN: 1X TO 2.5X BASIC
STATED ODDS 1:6 PACKS
16 Sandy Koufax 20.00 50.00
29 Ken Griffey Jr. 15.00 40.00
36 Ted Williams 12.00 30.00
37 Jackie Robinson 8.00 20.00
45 Honus Wagner 12.00 30.00

2020 Topps 206 Wave 2 Sweet Caporal Back

*S.CAPORAL: .75X TO 2X BASIC
STATED ODDS 1:3 PACKS
29 Ken Griffey Jr. 8.00 20.00
36 Ted Williams 8.00 20.00
37 Jackie Robinson 6.00 15.00
45 Honus Wagner 6.00 15.00

2020 Topps 206 Wave 2 Autographs

1 Chipper Jones
2 David Wright 150.00 400.00
3 Max Muncy 50.00 120.00
4 Nick Solak 30.00 80.00

2020 Topps 206 Wave 3

RANDOM INSERTS IN PACKS
1 Adley Rutschman 2.50 6.00
2 Wander Franco 4.00 10.00
3 Alex Kirilloff .75 2.00
4 Cristian Pache 1.25 3.00
5 Jarred Kelenic 2.50 6.00
6 Grayson Rodriguez .60 1.50
7 Braden Shewmake .60 1.50
8 Brett Baty 1.25 3.00
9 Alec Bohm 2.50 6.00
10 JJ Bleday 1.25 3.00
11 Riley Greene 1.50 4.00
12 Marco Luciano 1.50 4.00
13 MacKenzie Gore .75 2.00
14 Nolan Jones .60 1.50
15 Andrew Vaughn 1.50 4.00
16 Vidal Brujan 1.25 3.00
17 Sam Huff .75 2.00
18 Matt Manning .50 1.25
19 Nick Madrigal 1.25 3.00
20 CJ Abrams 1.50 4.00
21 Nolan Gorman .75 2.00
22 Ronny Mauricio 1.00 2.50
23 Nate Pearson .75 2.00
24 Kristian Robinson 1.25 3.00
25 Luis Patino .60 1.50
26 Josh Jung 1.00 2.50
27 Jo Adell 1.50 4.00
28 Spencer Howard 1.50 4.00
29 Ryan Mountcastle .60 1.50
30 Julio Rodriguez 2.50 6.00
31 Ian Anderson 1.00 2.50
32 Andy Pages .50 1.25
33 Ke'Bryan Hayes .40 1.00
34 Tarik Skubal 2.00 5.00
35 Royce Lewis 1.00 2.50
36 Brady Singer .50 1.25
37 Jarren Duran 1.50 4.00
38 Keibert Ruiz 1.00 2.50
39 Sixto Sanchez .60 1.50
40 Trevor Larnach .75 2.00
41 Joey Bart 1.25 3.00
42 Deivi Garcia 1.50 4.00
43 Triston Casas 1.00 2.50
44 Bobby Witt Jr. 3.00 8.00
45 Nick Lodolo .60 1.50
46 Daniel Lynch .40 1.00
47 Casey Mize 1.25 3.00
48 Miguel Amaya .50 1.25
49 Drew Waters 1.00 2.50
50 Hunter Greene .60 1.50

2020 Topps 206 Wave 3 Carolina Brights Back

*CAR.BRIGHTS: 2.5X TO 6X BASIC
STATED ODDS 1:20 PACKS
1 Adley Rutschman 25.00 60.00
2 Wander Franco 50.00 120.00
4 Cristian Pache 15.00 40.00
9 Alec Bohm 25.00 60.00
10 JJ Bleday 15.00 40.00
15 Andrew Vaughn 20.00 50.00
16 Vidal Brujan 25.00 60.00
19 Nick Madrigal 15.00 40.00
26 Josh Jung 20.00 50.00
27 Jo Adell 25.00 60.00
41 Joey Bart 15.00 40.00
42 Deivi Garcia 15.00 40.00
43 Triston Casas 12.00 30.00
44 Bobby Witt Jr. 40.00 100.00

2020 Topps 206 Wave 3 Cycle Back

*CYCLE/25: 4X TO 10X BASIC
RANDOM INSERTS IN PACKS
STATED PRINT RUN 25 SER.#'d SETS
1 Adley Rutschman 40.00 100.00
2 Wander Franco 100.00 250.00
4 Cristian Pache 25.00 60.00
9 Alec Bohm 40.00 100.00
10 JJ Bleday 25.00 60.00
11 Riley Greene 25.00 60.00
15 Andrew Vaughn 30.00 80.00
16 Vidal Brujan 40.00 100.00
19 Nick Madrigal 25.00 60.00
20 CJ Abrams 25.00 60.00
21 Nolan Gorman 20.00 50.00
26 Josh Jung 30.00 80.00
27 Jo Adell 40.00 100.00
30 Julio Rodriguez 30.00 80.00
35 Royce Lewis 30.00 80.00
41 Joey Bart 25.00 60.00
42 Deivi Garcia 25.00 60.00
43 Triston Casas 20.00 50.00
44 Bobby Witt Jr. 60.00 150.00

2020 Topps 206 Wave 3 Old Mill Back

*OLD MILL: 2.5X TO 6X BASIC
STATED ODDS 1:30 PACKS
1 Adley Rutschman 25.00 60.00
2 Wander Franco 50.00 120.00
4 Cristian Pache 15.00 40.00
9 Alec Bohm 25.00 60.00
10 JJ Bleday 15.00 40.00
15 Andrew Vaughn 20.00 50.00
16 Vidal Brujan 25.00 60.00
19 Nick Madrigal 15.00 40.00
21 Nolan Gorman 12.00 30.00
26 Josh Jung 20.00 50.00
27 Jo Adell 25.00 60.00
41 Joey Bart 15.00 40.00
42 Deivi Garcia 15.00 40.00
43 Triston Casas 12.00 30.00
44 Bobby Witt Jr. 40.00 100.00

2020 Topps 206 Wave 3 Sovereign Back

*SOVEREIGN: 1X TO 2.5X BASIC
STATED ODDS 1:6 PACKS
9 Alec Bohm 10.00 25.00
44 Bobby Witt Jr. 12.00 30.00

2020 Topps 206 Wave 3 Autographs

RANDOM INSERTS IN PACKS
1 Adley Rutschman 125.00 300.00
2 Andy Pages 75.00 200.00
3 Bobby Witt Jr. 125.00 300.00
4 Brett Baty 50.00 120.00
5 Jarren Duran 40.00 100.00
6 Sam Huff 150.00 400.00

2020 Topps 206 Wave 4

RANDOM INSERTS IN PACKS
1 Christian Yelich .75 2.00
2 Fernando Tatis Jr. 4.00 10.00
3 Bryce Harper 1.00 2.50
4 Josh Donaldson .50 1.25
5 Sonny Gray .50 1.25
6 George Brett 1.25 3.00
7 Mike Piazza 1.50 4.00
8 Lou Brock 1.00 2.50

9 Hank Aaron	1.25	3.00
10 Tim Anderson	.80	2.00
11 Shin Soo Choo	.50	1.25
12 Trevor Story	.60	1.50
13 Willson Contreras	.60	1.50
14 Gary Sanchez	.60	1.50
15 Ty Cobb	1.00	2.50
16 Yordan Alvarez	2.00	5.00
17 Javier Baez	.75	2.00
18 Frank Thomas	1.50	4.00
19 Josh Hader	.40	1.00
20 Clayton Kershaw	1.25	3.00
21 Josh Bell	.50	1.25
22 Eloy Jimenez	1.25	3.00
23 Tom Glavine	.50	1.25
24 Luke Voit	.75	2.00
25 Kyle Lewis	3.00	8.00
26 Randy Johnson	1.50	4.00
27 Matt Olson	.40	1.00
28 Jeff McNeil	.50	1.25
29 Eddie Rosario	.50	1.25
30 Miguel Cabrera	.60	1.50
31 Francisco Lindor	.60	1.50
32 Evan Longoria	.50	1.25
33 Michael Conforto	.50	1.25
34 David Ortiz	1.00	2.50
35 Alex Bregman	.60	1.50
36 Howie Kendrick	.40	1.00
37 Nick Senzel	.60	1.50
38 Nelson Cruz	.60	1.50
39 Kris Bryant	.75	2.00
40 Cavan Biggio	.75	2.00
41 Nico Hoerner	1.50	4.00
42 Nolan Ryan	2.00	5.00
43 Michael Chavis	.50	1.25
44 Justin Turner	.50	1.25
45 Ryne Sandberg	1.25	3.00
46 Paul Goldschmidt	.60	1.50
47 Max Fried	.60	1.50
48 James Karinchak	.60	1.50
49 Brendan McKay	.60	1.50
50 Ozzie Albies	.60	1.50

2020 Topps 206 Wave 4 Background Variation

*BKGRND VAR./25: 4X TO 10X BASIC
RANDOM INSERTS IN PACKS
STATED PRINT RUN 25 SER.#'d SETS

2 Fernando Tatis Jr.	75.00	200.00
6 George Brett	60.00	150.00
7 Mike Piazza	30.00	80.00
8 Lou Brock	40.00	100.00
9 Hank Aaron	40.00	100.00
10 Tim Anderson	25.00	60.00
14 Gary Sanchez	20.00	50.00
15 Ty Cobb	40.00	100.00
16 Yordan Alvarez	30.00	80.00
18 Frank Thomas	30.00	80.00
20 Clayton Kershaw	30.00	80.00
24 Luke Voit	30.00	80.00
25 Kyle Lewis	60.00	150.00
26 Randy Johnson	40.00	100.00
30 Miguel Cabrera	40.00	100.00
34 David Ortiz	25.00	60.00
39 Kris Bryant	100.00	250.00
40 Cavan Biggio	30.00	80.00
42 Nolan Ryan	60.00	150.00
45 Ryne Sandberg	40.00	100.00
46 Paul Goldschmidt	15.00	40.00
50 Ozzie Albies	20.00	50.00

2020 Topps 206 Wave 4 Old Mill Back

*OLD MILL: 2.5X TO 6X BASIC
STATED ODDS 1:30 PACKS

2 Fernando Tatis Jr.	50.00	120.00
6 George Brett	40.00	100.00
7 Mike Piazza	20.00	50.00
8 Lou Brock	25.00	60.00
9 Hank Aaron	25.00	60.00
10 Tim Anderson	15.00	40.00
14 Gary Sanchez	12.00	30.00
15 Ty Cobb	25.00	60.00
16 Yordan Alvarez	20.00	50.00
18 Frank Thomas	20.00	50.00
20 Clayton Kershaw	20.00	50.00
24 Luke Voit	15.00	40.00
25 Kyle Lewis	40.00	100.00
26 Randy Johnson	25.00	60.00
30 Miguel Cabrera	25.00	60.00
34 David Ortiz	15.00	40.00
39 Kris Bryant	25.00	60.00
40 Cavan Biggio	20.00	50.00
42 Nolan Ryan	30.00	80.00
45 Ryne Sandberg	25.00	60.00
46 Paul Goldschmidt	10.00	25.00
50 Ozzie Albies	10.00	25.00

2020 Topps 206 Wave 4 Polar Bear Back

*POLAR BEAR: 2.5X TO 6X BASIC
STATED ODDS 1:18 PACKS

2 Fernando Tatis Jr.	50.00	120.00
6 George Brett	40.00	100.00
7 Mike Piazza	20.00	50.00
8 Lou Brock	25.00	60.00
9 Hank Aaron	25.00	60.00
10 Tim Anderson	15.00	40.00
14 Gary Sanchez	12.00	30.00
15 Ty Cobb	25.00	60.00
16 Yordan Alvarez	20.00	50.00
18 Frank Thomas	20.00	50.00
20 Clayton Kershaw	20.00	50.00
24 Luke Voit	15.00	40.00
25 Kyle Lewis	40.00	100.00
26 Randy Johnson	25.00	60.00
30 Miguel Cabrera	25.00	60.00
34 David Ortiz	15.00	40.00
39 Kris Bryant	25.00	60.00
40 Cavan Biggio	20.00	50.00
42 Nolan Ryan	30.00	80.00
45 Ryne Sandberg	25.00	60.00
46 Paul Goldschmidt	10.00	25.00
50 Ozzie Albies	10.00	25.00

2020 Topps 206 Wave 4 Sovereign Back

*SOVEREIGN: 1X TO 2.5X BASIC
STATED ODDS 1:6 PACKS

2 Fernando Tatis Jr.	15.00	40.00
6 George Brett	12.00	30.00
8 Lou Brock	5.00	12.00
9 Hank Aaron	8.00	20.00
18 Frank Thomas	8.00	20.00
26 Randy Johnson	8.00	20.00
34 David Ortiz	5.00	12.00
42 Nolan Ryan	15.00	40.00

2020 Topps 206 Wave 4 Sweet Caporal Back

*S.CAPORAL: .75X TO 2X BASIC
STATED ODDS 1:3 PACKS

6 George Brett	10.00	25.00
8 Lou Brock	4.00	10.00
9 Hank Aaron	6.00	15.00
34 David Ortiz	4.00	10.00
42 Nolan Ryan	10.00	25.00

2020 Topps 206 Wave 4 Autographs

RANDOM INSERTS IN PACKS

1 Bryce Harper	150.00	400.00
2 David Ortiz	150.00	400.00
3 Nico Hoerner	75.00	200.00
4 Nolan Ryan		
5 Tom Glavine	125.00	300.00
6 Trevor Story	50.00	120.00

2020 Topps 206 Wave 5

RANDOM INSERTS IN PACKS

1 Dansby Swanson	.60	1.50
2 Derek Jeter	1.50	4.00
3 Yu Darvish	.60	1.50
4 Will Smith	.75	2.00
5 John Smoltz	.60	1.50
6 Rafael Devers	.75	2.00
7 Jack Flaherty	.50	1.25
8 Luis Robert	5.00	12.00
9 Matt Chapman	.60	1.50
10 Kwang-Hyun Kim	1.25	3.00
11 Jacob deGrom	.60	1.50
12 Ernie Banks	1.50	4.00
13 Aaron Nola	.60	1.50
14 Juan Soto	2.00	5.00
15 Lou Gehrig	2.00	5.00
16 Roger Clemens	.75	2.00
17 Harmon Killebrew	.60	1.50
18 Bo Bichette	3.00	8.00
19 Jose Canseco	.50	1.25
20 Anthony Rizzo	1.00	2.50
21 Andrew McCutchen	.60	1.50
22 Tom Seaver	.50	1.25
23 Jim Thome	.50	1.25
24 Ronald Acuna Jr.	2.50	6.00
25 Zack Greinke	.50	1.25
26 Willie McCovey	.50	1.25
27 Yadier Molina	.60	1.50
28 Mookie Betts	1.25	3.00
29 Willie Stargell	.50	1.25
30 Dominic Smith	.40	1.00
31 Greg Maddux	.75	2.00
32 Don Mattingly	1.25	3.00
33 Barry Zito	.50	1.25
34 Kirby Puckett	1.50	4.00
35 Dave Winfield	.50	1.25
36 Eddie Murray	.50	1.25
37 Justin Verlander	.60	1.50
38 Lucas Giolito	.50	1.25
39 Brooks Robinson	.50	1.25
40 Mark McGwire	1.00	2.50
41 Andres Galarraga	.50	1.25
42 CC Sabathia	.50	1.25
43 Gary Carter	.50	1.25
44 Wade Boggs	.50	1.25
45 Joe Mauer	.50	1.25
46 Dustin May	1.50	4.00
47 Dennis Eckersley	.50	1.25
48 Andre Dawson	.50	1.25
49 Trevor Bauer	.60	1.50
50 Willie Mays	1.25	3.00

2020 Topps 206 Wave 5 Cycle Back

*CYCLE/25: 4X TO 10X BASIC
RANDOM INSERTS IN PACKS
STATED PRINT RUN 25 SER.#'d SETS

2 Derek Jeter	40.00	100.00
5 John Smoltz	25.00	60.00
8 Luis Robert	125.00	300.00
14 Juan Soto	30.00	80.00
15 Lou Gehrig	40.00	100.00
16 Roger Clemens	20.00	50.00
17 Harmon Killebrew	20.00	50.00
18 Bo Bichette	50.00	120.00
19 Jose Canseco	20.00	50.00
20 Anthony Rizzo	50.00	120.00
23 Jim Thome	15.00	40.00
24 Ronald Acuna Jr.	40.00	100.00
26 Willie McCovey	20.00	50.00
28 Mookie Betts	40.00	100.00
29 Willie Stargell	20.00	50.00
31 Greg Maddux	50.00	120.00
32 Don Mattingly	50.00	120.00
33 Barry Zito	10.00	25.00
34 Kirby Puckett	60.00	150.00
35 Dave Winfield	30.00	80.00
36 Eddie Murray	15.00	40.00
39 Brooks Robinson	15.00	40.00
40 Mark McGwire	20.00	50.00
43 Gary Carter	25.00	60.00
44 Wade Boggs	30.00	80.00
45 Joe Mauer	10.00	25.00
48 Andre Dawson	30.00	80.00
50 Willie Mays	30.00	80.00

2020 Topps 206 Wave 5 Old Mill Back

*OLD MILL: 2.5X TO 6X BASIC
STATED ODDS 1:30 PACKS

2 Derek Jeter	25.00	60.00
8 Luis Robert	75.00	200.00
14 Juan Soto	20.00	50.00
15 Lou Gehrig	25.00	60.00
16 Roger Clemens	12.00	30.00
17 Harmon Killebrew	12.00	30.00
18 Bo Bichette	30.00	80.00
19 Jose Canseco	12.00	30.00
20 Anthony Rizzo	30.00	80.00
24 Ronald Acuna Jr.	25.00	60.00
26 Willie McCovey	12.00	30.00
28 Mookie Betts	15.00	40.00
29 Willie Stargell	12.00	30.00
31 Greg Maddux	30.00	80.00
32 Don Mattingly	30.00	80.00
33 Barry Zito	5.00	12.00
34 Kirby Puckett	40.00	100.00
35 Dave Winfield	20.00	50.00
36 Eddie Murray	6.00	15.00
39 Brooks Robinson	10.00	25.00
40 Mark McGwire	12.00	30.00
43 Gary Carter	15.00	40.00
44 Wade Boggs	20.00	50.00
48 Andre Dawson	12.00	30.00
50 Willie Mays	20.00	50.00

2020 Topps 206 Wave 5 Piedmont Back

*PIEDMONT: .5X TO 1.2X BASIC
INSERTED 2 PER PACK

34 Kirby Puckett	2.50	6.00

2020 Topps 206 Wave 5 Polar Bear Back

*POLAR BEAR: 2.5X TO 6X BASIC
STATED ODDS 1:18 PACKS

2 Derek Jeter	25.00	60.00
8 Luis Robert	75.00	200.00
14 Juan Soto	20.00	50.00
15 Lou Gehrig	25.00	60.00
16 Roger Clemens	12.00	30.00
17 Harmon Killebrew	12.00	30.00
18 Bo Bichette	30.00	80.00
19 Jose Canseco	12.00	30.00
20 Anthony Rizzo	30.00	80.00
24 Ronald Acuna Jr.	25.00	60.00
26 Willie McCovey	12.00	30.00
28 Mookie Betts	15.00	40.00
29 Willie Stargell	12.00	30.00
31 Greg Maddux	15.00	40.00
32 Don Mattingly	30.00	80.00
33 Barry Zito	5.00	12.00
34 Kirby Puckett	40.00	100.00
35 Dave Winfield	12.00	30.00
36 Eddie Murray	6.00	15.00
39 Brooks Robinson	10.00	25.00
43 Gary Carter	15.00	40.00
44 Wade Boggs	20.00	50.00
48 Andre Dawson	12.00	30.00
50 Willie Mays	20.00	50.00

2020 Topps 206 Wave 5 Sovereign Back

*SOVEREIGN: 1X TO 2.5X BASIC
STATED ODDS 1:6 PACKS

15 Lou Gehrig	8.00	20.00
17 Harmon Killebrew	4.00	10.00
32 Don Mattingly	6.00	15.00
34 Kirby Puckett	12.00	30.00
50 Willie Mays	8.00	20.00

2020 Topps 206 Wave 5 Sweet Caporal Back

*S.CAPORAL: .75X TO 2X BASIC
STATED ODDS 1:3 PACKS

15 Lou Gehrig	6.00	15.00
32 Don Mattingly	5.00	12.00
34 Kirby Puckett	5.00	12.00
50 Willie Mays	4.00	10.00

2020 Topps 206 Wave 5 Autographs

RANDOM INSERTS IN PACKS

1 Andres Galarraga	75.00	200.00
2 Barry Zito	30.00	80.00
3 Juan Soto	125.00	300.00
4 Ronald Acuna Jr.	200.00	500.00
5 Will Smith	25.00	60.00

2006 Topps Allen and Ginter

This 350-card set was release in August, 2006. The set was issued in seven-card hobby packs with an $4 SRP. Those packs came 24 to a box and there were 12 boxes in a case. In addition, there were also six-card retail packs issued and those packs came 24 packs to a box and 20 boxes to a case. There were some subsets included in this set including Rookies (251-265); Retired Greats (266-290); Managers (291-300); Modern Personalities (301-314); Reprinted Allen and Ginters (316-319); Famous People of the Past (326-349).

COMPLETE SET (350)	60.00	120.00
COMP.SET w/o SP's (300)	15.00	40.00

SP STATED ODDS 1:2 HOBBY, 1:2 RETAIL
SP CL: 5/15/25/35/45/50-59/65/85/105/115
SP CL: 125/135/145/150-159/165/175/185
SP CL: 205/215/235/245/251/255-256/265
SP CL: 285/295/305/315/325/335/345
FRAMED ORIGINALS ODDS 1:3227 H, 1:3227 R

1 Albert Pujols	.50	1.25
2 Aubrey Huff	.15	.40
3 Mark Teixeira	.25	.60
4 Vernon Wells	.15	.40
5 Ken Griffey Jr. SP	2.50	6.00
6 Nick Swisher	.25	.60
7 Jose Reyes	.25	.60
8 David Wright	.30	.75
9 Vladimir Guerrero	.25	.60
10 Andruw Jones	.15	.40
11 Ramon Hernandez	.15	.40
12 Miguel Tejada	.25	.60
13 Juan Pierre	.15	.40
14 Jim Thome	.25	.60
15 Austin Kearns SP	1.25	3.00
16 Jhonny Peralta	.15	.40
17 Clint Barmes	.15	.40
18 Angel Berroa	.15	.40
19 Nomar Garciaparra	.25	.60
20 Joe Nathan	.15	.40
21 Brandon Webb	.25	.60
22 Chad Tracy	.15	.40
23 Derek Jeter	1.00	2.50
24 Conor Jackson (RC)	.25	.60
25 Jason Giambi SP	1.25	3.00
26 Johnny Estrada	.15	.40
27 Luis Gonzalez	.15	.40
28 Javier Vazquez	.15	.40
29 Orlando Hudson	.15	.40
30 Shawn Green	.15	.40
31 Mark Buehrle	.25	.60
32 Wily Mo Pena	.15	.40
33 C.C. Sabathia	.25	.60
34 Ronnie Belliard	.15	.40
35 Travis Hafner SP	1.25	3.00
36 Mike Jacobs (RC)	.15	.40
37 Roy Oswalt	.25	.60
38 Zack Greinke	.25	.60
39 J.D. Drew	.15	.40
40 Jeff Kent	.15	.40
41 Ben Sheets	.15	.40
42 Luis Castillo	.15	.40
43 Carlos Delgado	.15	.40
44 Cliff Floyd	.15	.40
45 Danny Haren SP	1.25	3.00
46 Bobby Abreu	.15	.40
47 Jeromy Burnitz	.15	.40
48 Khalil Greene	.15	.40
49 Moises Alou	.15	.40
50 Alex Rodriguez SP	2.00	5.00
51 Ervin Santana SP	1.25	3.00
52 Bartolo Colon SP	1.25	3.00
53 John Smoltz SP	1.25	3.00
54 David Ortiz SP	1.25	3.00
55 Hideki Matsui SP	1.25	3.00
56 Jermaine Dye SP	1.25	3.00
57 Victor Martinez SP	1.25	3.00
58 Willy Taveras SP	1.25	3.00
59 Brady Clark SP	1.25	3.00
60 Justin Morneau	.25	.60
61 Xavier Nady	.15	.40
62 Rich Harden	.15	.40
63 Jack Wilson	.15	.40
64 Brian Giles	.15	.40
65 Jon Lieber SP	1.25	3.00
66 Dan Johnson	.15	.40
67 Billy Wagner	.15	.40
68 Rickie Weeks	.15	.40
69 Chris Ray (RC)	.15	.40
70 Chris Shelton	.15	.40
71 Dmitri Young	.15	.40
72 Ivan Rodriguez	.25	.60
73 Jeremy Bonderman	.15	.40
74 Justin Verlander (RC)	1.25	3.00
75 Randy Johnson	.40	1.00
76 Magglio Ordonez	.25	.60
77 Brandon Inge	.15	.40
78 Placido Polanco	.15	.40
79 Ryan Howard	.30	.75
80 Jason Bay	.15	.40
81 Sean Casey	.15	.40
82 Jeremy Hermida (RC)	.15	.40
83 Mike Cameron	.15	.40
84 Trevor Hoffman	.25	.60
85 Mike Matheny SP	1.25	3.00
86 Steve Finley	.15	.40
87 Adam Everett	.15	.40
88 Jason Isringhausen	.15	.40
89 Jonny Gomes	.15	.40
90 Barry Zito	.25	.60
91 Bobby Crosby	.15	.40
92 Eric Chavez	.15	.40
93 Frank Thomas	.40	1.00
94 Huston Street	.15	.40
95 Jorge Posada	.25	.60
96 Casey Kotchman	.15	.40
97 Darin Erstad	.15	.40
98 Chipper Jones	.40	1.00
99 Jeff Francoeur	.40	1.00
100 Barry Bonds	.60	1.50
101 Alfonso Soriano	.25	.60
102 Brandon Claussen	.15	.40
103 Aaron Boone	.15	.40
104 Roger Clemens	.50	1.25
105 Andy Pettitte SP	1.25	3.00
106 Nick Johnson	.15	.40
107 Tom Gordon	.15	.40
108 Orlando Hernandez	.15	.40
109 Francisco Rodriguez	.25	.60
110 Orlando Cabrera	.15	.40
111 Edgar Renteria	.15	.40
112 Tim Hudson	.25	.60
113 Coco Crisp	.15	.40
114 Matt Clement	.15	.40
115 Greg Maddux SP	2.00	5.00
116 Paul Konerko	.25	.60
117 Felipe Lopez	.15	.40
118 Garrett Atkins	.15	.40
119 Akinori Otsuka	.15	.40
120 Craig Biggio	.25	.60
121 Danys Baez	.15	.40
122 Brad Penny	.15	.40
123 Eric Gagne	.15	.40
124 Lew Ford	.15	.40
125 Mariano Rivera SP	1.25	3.00
126 Carlos Beltran	.25	.60
127 Pedro Martinez	.25	.60
128 Todd Helton	.25	.60
129 Aaron Rowand	.15	.40
130 Mike Lieberthal	.15	.40
131 Oliver Perez	.15	.40
132 Ryan Klesko	.15	.40
133 Randy Winn	.15	.40
134 Yuniesky Betancourt	.15	.40
135 David Eckstein SP	1.25	3.00
136 Chad Orvella	.15	.40
137 Toby Hall	.15	.40
138 Hank Blalock	.15	.40
139 B.J. Ryan	.15	.40
140 Roy Halladay	.25	.60
141 Livan Hernandez	.15	.40
142 John Patterson	.15	.40
143 Bengie Molina	.15	.40
144 Brad Wilkerson	.15	.40
145 Jorge Cantu SP	1.25	3.00
146 Mark Mulder	.15	.40
147 Felix Hernandez	.25	.60
148 Paul Lo Duca	.15	.40
149 Prince Fielder (RC)	.75	2.00
150 Johnny Damon SP	1.25	3.00
151 Ryan Langerhans SP	1.25	3.00
152 Kris Benson SP	1.25	3.00
153 Curt Schilling SP	1.25	3.00
154 Manny Ramirez SP	1.25	3.00
155 Robinson Cano SP	1.25	3.00
156 Derrek Lee SP	1.25	3.00
157 A.J. Pierzynski SP	1.25	3.00
158 Adam Dunn SP	1.25	3.00
159 Cliff Lee SP	1.25	3.00
160 Grady Sizemore	.25	.60
161 Jeff Francis	.15	.40
162 Dontrelle Willis	.15	.40
163 Brad Ausmus	.15	.40
164 Preston Wilson	.15	.40
165 Derek Lowe SP	1.25	3.00
166 Chris Capuano	.15	.40
167 Joe Mauer	.25	.60
168 Torii Hunter	.15	.40
169 Chase Utley	.25	.60
170 Zach Duke	.15	.40
171 Jason Schmidt	.15	.40
172 Adrian Beltre	.40	1.00
173 Eddie Guardado	.15	.40
174 Richie Sexson	.15	.40
175 Miguel Cabrera SP	1.25	3.00
176 Julio Lugo	.15	.40
177 Francisco Cordero	.15	.40
178 Kevin Millwood	.15	.40
179 A.J. Burnett	.15	.40
180 Jose Guillen	.15	.40
181 Larry Bigbie	.15	.40
182 Raul Ibanez	.25	.60
183 Jake Peavy	.15	.40
184 Pat Burrell	.15	.40
185 Tom Glavine SP	1.25	3.00
186 J.J. Hardy	.15	.40
187 Emil Brown	.15	.40
188 Lance Berkman	.25	.60
189 Marcus Giles	.15	.40
190 Scott Podsednik	.15	.40
191 Chone Figgins	.15	.40
192 Melvin Mora	.15	.40
193 Mark Loretta	.15	.40
194 Carlos Zambrano	.25	.60
195 Chien-Ming Wang	.25	.60
196 Mark Prior	.25	.60
197 Bobby Jenks	.15	.40
198 Brian Fuentes	.15	.40
199 Garret Anderson	.15	.40
200 Ichiro Suzuki	.50	1.25
201 Brian Roberts	.15	.40
202 Jason Kendall	.15	.40
203 Milton Bradley	.15	.40
204 Jimmy Rollins	.25	.60
205 Brett Myers SP	1.25	3.00
206 Joe Randa	.15	.40
207 Mike Piazza	.40	1.00
208 Matt Morris	.15	.40
209 Omar Vizquel	.25	.60
210 Jeremy Reed	.15	.40
211 Chris Carpenter	.25	.60
212 Jim Edmonds	.25	.60
213 Scott Kazmir	.25	.60
214 Travis Lee	.15	.40
215 Michael Young SP	1.25	3.00
216 Rod Barajas	.15	.40
217 Gustavo Chacin	.15	.40
218 Lyle Overbay	.15	.40
219 Troy Glaus	.15	.40
220 Chad Cordero	.15	.40
221 Jose Vidro	.15	.40
222 Scott Rolen	.25	.60
223 Carl Crawford	.25	.60
224 Rocco Baldelli	.15	.40
225 Mike Mussina	.25	.60
226 Kelvim Escobar	.15	.40
227 Corey Patterson	.15	.40
228 Javy Lopez	.15	.40
229 Jonathan Papelbon (RC)	.75	2.00
230 Aramis Ramirez	.15	.40
231 Tadahito Iguchi	.15	.40
232 Morgan Ensberg	.15	.40
233 Mark Grudzielanek	.15	.40
234 Mike Sweeney	.15	.40
235 Shawn Chacon SP	1.25	3.00
236 Nick Punto	.15	.40
237 Geoff Jenkins	.15	.40
238 Carlos Lee	.15	.40
239 David DeJesus	.15	.40
240 Brad Lidge	.15	.40
241 Bob Wickman	.15	.40
242 Jon Garland	.15	.40
243 Kerry Wood	.15	.40
244 Bronson Arroyo	.15	.40
245 Matt Holliday SP	1.50	4.00
246 Josh Beckett	.15	.40
247 Johan Santana	.25	.60
248 Rafael Furcal	.15	.40
249 Shannon Stewart	.15	.40
250 Gary Sheffield	.15	.40
251 Josh Barfield SP (RC)	1.25	3.00
252 Kenji Johjima RC	.40	1.00
253 Ian Kinsler (RC)	.50	1.25
254 Brian Anderson (RC)	.15	.40
255 Matt Cain SP (RC)	1.25	3.00
256 Josh Willingham SP (RC)	1.25	3.00
257 John Koronka (RC)	.15	.40
258 Chris Duffy (RC)	.15	.40
259 Brian McCann (RC)	.15	.40
260 Hanley Ramirez (RC)	.25	.60
261 Hong-Chih Kuo (RC)	.40	1.00
262 Francisco Liriano (RC)	.40	1.00
263 Anderson Hernandez (RC)	.15	.40
264 Ryan Zimmerman (RC)	.50	1.25
265 Brian Bannister SP (RC)	1.25	3.00
266 Nolan Ryan	1.25	3.00
267 Frank Robinson	.25	.60
268 Roberto Clemente	1.00	2.50
269 Hank Greenberg	.40	1.00
270 Napolean Lajoie	.40	1.00
271 Lloyd Waner	.25	.60
272 Paul Waner	.25	.60
273 Frankie Frisch	.25	.60
274 Moose Skowron	.15	.40
275 Mickey Mantle	1.25	3.00
276 Brooks Robinson	.25	.60
277 Carl Yastrzemski	.60	1.50
278 Johnny Pesky	.15	.40
279 Stan Musial	.60	1.50
280 Bill Mazeroski	.25	.6
281 Harmon Killebrew	.40	1.0
282 Monte Irvin	.15	.4
283 Bob Gibson	.25	.6
284 Ted Williams	.75	2.0
285 Yogi Berra SP	1.25	3.0
286 Ernie Banks	.40	1.0
287 Bobby Doerr	.15	.4
288 Josh Gibson	.40	1.0
289 Bob Feller	.25	.6
290 Cal Ripken	1.25	3.0
291 Bobby Cox MG	.15	.4
292 Terry Francona MG	.15	.4
293 Dusty Baker MG	.15	.4
294 Ozzie Guillen MG	.15	.4
295 Jim Leyland MG SP	1.25	3.0
296 Willie Randolph MG	.15	.4
297 Joe Torre MG	.25	.6
298 Felipe Alou MG	.15	.4
299 Tony La Russa MG	.25	.6
300 Frank Robinson MG	.25	.6
301 Mike Tyson	.60	1.5
302 Duke Paoa Kahanamoku	.15	.4
303 Jennie Finch	1.00	2.5
304 Brandi Chastain	.15	.4
305 Danica Patrick SP	8.00	20.0
306 Wendy Guey	.15	.4
307 Hulk Hogan	.50	1.2
308 Carl Lewis	.15	.4
309 John Wooden	.25	.6
310 Randy Couture	.75	2.0
311 Andy Irons	.15	.4
312 Takeru Kobayashi	.50	1.2
313 Leon Spinks	.15	.4
314 Jim Thorpe	.25	.6
315 Jerry Bailey SP	1.25	3.0
316 Adrian C. Anson REP	.25	.6
317 John M. Ward REP	.25	.6
318 Mike Kelly REP	.15	.4
319 Capt. Jack Glasscock REP	.15	.4
320 Aaron Hill	.15	.4
321 Derrick Turnbow	.15	.4
322 Nick Markakis (RC)	.30	.7
323 Brad Hawpe	.15	.4
324 Kevin Mench	.15	.4
325 John Lackey SP	1.25	3.0
326 Chester A. Arthur	.15	.4
327 Ulysses S. Grant	.15	.4
328 Abraham Lincoln	.15	.4
329 Grover Cleveland	.15	.4
330 Benjamin Harrison	.15	.4
331 Theodore Roosevelt	.15	.4
332 Rutherford B. Hayes	.15	.4
333 Chancellor Otto Von Bismarck	.15	.4
334 Kaiser Wilhelm II	.15	.4
335 Queen Victoria SP	1.25	3.0
336 Pope Leo XIII	.15	.4
337 Thomas Edison	.15	.4
338 Orville Wright	.15	.4
339 Wilbur Wright	.15	.4
340 Nathaniel Hawthorne	.15	.4
341 Herman Melville	.15	.4
342 Stonewall Jackson	.15	.4
343 Robert E. Lee	.15	.4
344 Andrew Carnegie	.15	.4
345 John Rockefeller SP	1.25	3.0
346 Bob Fitzsimmons	.15	.4
347 Billy The Kid	.15	.4
348 Buffalo Bill	.15	.4
349 Jesse James		
350 Statue Of Liberty	.15	.4
NNO Framed Originals	60.00	120.0

2006 Topps Allen and Ginter Mini

*MINI 1-350: 1X TO 2.5X BASIC
*MINI 1-350: 1X TO 2.5X BASIC RC's
APPX.15 MINIS PER 24-CT SEALED BOX
*MINI SP 1-350: .6X TO 1.5X BASIC SP
*MINI SP 1-350: .6X TO 1.5X BASIC SP RC's
MINI SP ODDS 1:13 H, 1:13 R

COMMON CARD (351-375)	20.00	50.0
SEMISTARS 351-375	30.00	60.0
UNLISTED STARS 351-375	30.00	60.0

351-375 RANDOM WITHIN RIP CARDS
OVERALL PLATE ODDS 1:865 H, 1:865 R
PLATE PRINT RUN 1 SET PER COLOR
BLACK-CYAN-MAGENTA-YELLOW ISSUED
NO PLATE PRICING DUE TO SCARCITY

351 Albert Pujols EXT	75.00	150.0
352 Alex Rodriguez EXT	30.00	60.0
353 Andruw Jones EXT	20.00	50.0
354 Barry Bonds EXT	20.00	50.0
355 Cal Ripken EXT	75.00	150.0
356 David Ortiz EXT	40.00	80.0
357 David Wright EXT	20.00	50.0

58 Derek Jeter EXT 75.00 150.00
59 Derrek Lee EXT 20.00 50.00
60 Hideki Matsui EXT 30.00 60.00
61 Ichiro Suzuki EXT 40.00 80.00
62 Johan Santana EXT 30.00 60.00
63 Josh Gibson EXT 20.00 50.00
64 Ken Griffey Jr. EXT 30.00 80.00
65 Manny Ramirez EXT 20.00 50.00
66 Mickey Mantle EXT 75.00 150.00
67 Miguel Cabrera EXT 20.00 50.00
68 Miguel Tejada EXT 20.00 50.00
69 Mike Piazza EXT 30.00 60.00
70 Nolan Ryan EXT 75.00 150.00
71 Roberto Clemente EXT 125.00 200.00
72 Roger Clemens EXT 40.00 80.00
73 Scott Rolen EXT 20.00 50.00
74 Ted Williams EXT 50.00 100.00
75 Vladimir Guerrero EXT 30.00 60.00

2006 Topps Allen and Ginter Mini A and G Back

A & G BACK: 2X TO 5X BASIC
A & G BACK: 1.5X TO 4X BASIC RC's
STATED ODDS 1:5 H, 1:5 R
A & G BACK SP: 1X TO 2.5X BASIC SP
A & G BACK SP: 1X TO 2.5X BASIC SP RC's
SP STATED ODDS 1:65 H, 1:65 R

2006 Topps Allen and Ginter Mini Black

BLACK: 4X TO 10X BASIC
BLACK: 2.5X TO 6X BASIC RC's
STATED ODDS 1:10 H, 1:10 R
BLACK SP: 1.5X TO 4X BASIC SP
BLACK SP: 1.5X TO 4X BASIC SP RC's
SP STATED ODDS 1:130 H, 1:130 R

2006 Topps Allen and Ginter Mini No Card Number

NO NBR: 6X TO 15X BASIC
NO NBR: 4X TO 10X BASIC RC's
NO NBR: 2X TO 5X BASIC SP
NO NBR: 2X TO 5X BASIC SP RC's
STATED ODDS 1:60 H, 1:168 R
STATED PRINT RUN 50 SETS
CARDS ARE NOT SERIAL-NUMBERED
PRINT RUN INFO PROVIDED BY TOPPS

2006 Topps Allen and Ginter Autographs

GROUP A ODDS 1:2467 H, 1:3850 R
GROUP B ODDS 1:14,500 H, 1:32,000 R
GROUP C ODDS 1:2200 H, 1:4300 R
GROUP D ODDS 1:548 H, 1:1090 R
GROUP E ODDS 1:473 H, 1:1000 R
GROUP F ODDS 1:250 H, 1:520 R
GROUP G ODDS 1:158 H, 1:299 R
GROUP A PRINT RUN 50 CARDS PER
GROUP A BONDS PRINT RUN 25 CARDS
GROUP B PRINT RUN 75 CARDS PER
GROUP C PRINT RUN 100 CARDS PER
GROUP D PRINT RUN 200 CARDS PER
GROUP A-D ARE NOT SERIAL-NUMBERED
A-D PRINT RUNS PROVIDED BY TOPPS
NO BONDS PRICING DUE TO SCARCITY
AI Andy Irons D/200 * 100.00 175.00
AR Alex Rodriguez A/50 * 400.00 500.00
BC Brandi Chastain D/200 * 40.00 80.00
BF Bob Feller E 30.00 80.00
BJR B.J. Ryan E 8.00 20.00
BW Billy Wagner F 5.00 12.00
CB Clint Barmes F 5.00 12.00
CL Carl Lewis D/200 * 60.00 120.00
CMW C.Wang C/100 * 500.00 600.00
CR Cal Ripken A/50 * 350.00 400.00
CU Chase Utley E 20.00 50.00
CY Carl Yastrzemski A/50 * 300.00 500.00
DL Derrek Lee E 6.00 15.00
DP Danica Patrick C/100 * 400.00 600.00
DW David Wright E 50.00 100.00
DWI Dontrelle Willis C/100 * 15.00 40.00
EC Eric Chavez G 5.00 12.00
ES Ervin Santana F 5.00 12.00
FL Francisco Liriano G 6.00 15.00
GS Gary Sheffield A/50 * 60.00 120.00
HH Hulk Hogan D/200 * 125.00 250.00
HS Huston Street E 10.00 25.00
JB Jerry Bailey D/200 * 30.00 60.00
JB1 Josh Barfield G 6.00 15.00
JF Jennie Finch D/200 * 50.00 100.00
JG Jonny Gomes G 6.00 15.00
JS Johan Santana C/100 * 75.00 150.00
JW John Wooden D/200 * 125.00 250.00
KJ Kenji Johjima A/50 * 50.00 100.00
LF Lew Ford G 5.00 12.00
LS Leon Spinks D/200 * 30.00 80.00
MC Miguel Cabrera C/100 * 75.00 150.00
MT Mike Tyson D/200 * 250.00 350.00
MY Michael Young E 5.00 12.00
NR Nolan Ryan A/50 * 350.00 450.00
OS Ozzie Smith B/75 * 125.00 250.00
PF Prince Fielder F 5.00 12.00
RA Randy Couture E 50.00 100.00
RC Robinson Cano G 15.00 40.00
RH Ryan Howard F 6.00 15.00
RZ Ryan Zimmerman F 15.00 40.00
SK Scott Kazmir F 5.00 12.00
SM Stan Musial A/50 * 300.00 500.00
TG Tony Gwynn A/50 * 200.00 300.00
TH Travis Hafner F 5.00 12.00
TK Takeru Kobayashi D/200 * 60.00 150.00
VG Vladimir Guerrero A/50 * 30.00 60.00
VM Victor Martinez E 5.00 12.00
WG Wendy Guey F 8.00 20.00
WMP Wily Mo Pena G 5.00 12.00

2006 Topps Allen and Ginter Autographs Red Ink

RANDOM INSERTS WITHIN RIP CARDS
STATED PRINT RUN 10 SETS
CARDS ARE NOT SERIAL-NUMBERED
PRINT RUN INFO PROVIDED BY TOPPS
NO PRICING DUE TO SCARCITY

2006 Topps Allen and Ginter N43

COMPLETE SET (15) 50.00 100.00
STATED ODDS 1:2 SEALED HOBBY BOXES
1 Alex Rodriguez 2.50 6.00
2 Barry Bonds 3.00 8.00
3 Albert Pujols 2.50 6.00
4 Josh Gibson 2.00 5.00
5 Nolan Ryan 6.00 15.00
6 Ichiro Suzuki 2.50 6.00
7 Mickey Mantle 6.00 15.00
8 Ted Williams 4.00 10.00
9 David Wright 1.50 4.00
10 Ken Griffey Jr. 4.00 10.00
11 Mark Teixeira 1.25 3.00
12 Adrian C. Anson 1.25 3.00
13 Mike Tyson 3.00 8.00
14 Kenji Johjima 2.00 5.00
15 Ryan Zimmerman 2.50 6.00

2006 Topps Allen and Ginter N43 Autographs

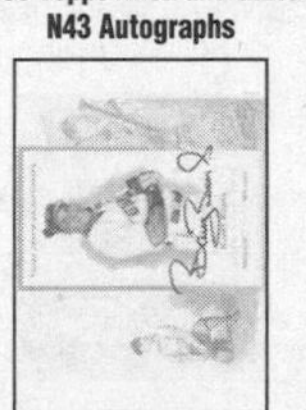

STATED ODDS 1:1970 HOBBY BOXES
STATED PRINT RUN 10 SERIAL #'d SETS
NO PRICING DUE TO SCARCITY

2006 Topps Allen and Ginter N43 Relics

STATED ODDS 1:379 HOBBY BOXES
STATED PRINT RUN 50 SERIAL #'d SETS
AP Albert Pujols Uni 40.00 80.00
JG Josh Gibson Model Bat 200.00 300.00

2006 Topps Allen and Ginter Dick Perez

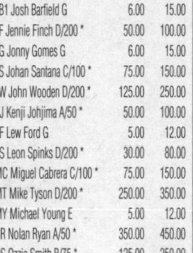

COMPLETE SET (30) 10.00 25.00
ONE PEREZ OR DECOY PER PACK
ORIGINALS RANDOM WITHIN RIP CARDS
ORIGINALS PRINT RUN 1 SERIAL #'d SET
NO ORIG. PRICING DUE TO SCARCITY
1 Shawn Green .25 .60
2 Andruw Jones .25 .60
3 Miguel Tejada .40 1.00
4 David Ortiz .60 1.50
5 Derrek Lee .25 .60
6 Paul Konerko .40 1.00
7 Ken Griffey Jr. 1.25 3.00
8 Travis Hafner .25 .60
9 Todd Helton .40 1.00
10 Ivan Rodriguez .40 1.00
11 Miguel Cabrera .60 1.50
12 Lance Berkman .40 1.00
13 Mike Sweeney .25 .60
14 Vladimir Guerrero .40 1.00
15 Rafael Furcal .25 .60
16 Carlos Lee .25 .60
17 Johan Santana .40 1.00
18 David Wright .50 1.25
19 Alex Rodriguez .75 2.00
20 Huston Street .25 .60
21 Bobby Abreu .25 .60
22 Jason Bay .25 .60
23 Jake Peavy .25 .60
24 Ichiro Suzuki .75 2.00
25 Barry Bonds 1.00 2.50
26 Albert Pujols .75 2.00
27 Aubrey Huff .25 .60
28 Mark Teixeira .40 1.00
29 Vernon Wells .25 .60
30 Alfonso Soriano .40 1.00

2006 Topps Allen and Ginter Postcards

COMPLETE SET (15) 20.00 50.00
STATED ODDS 1:2 HOBBY BOXES
PERSONALIZED ODDS 1:3000 HOB.BOXES
PERSONALIZED PRINT RUN 1 #'d SET
NO PERSONALIZED PRICING AVAILABLE
AP Albert Pujols 2.00 5.00
AR Alex Rodriguez 2.00 5.00
BB Barry Bonds 2.50 6.00
CR Cal Ripken 5.00 12.00
DJ Derek Jeter 4.00 10.00
DO David Ortiz 1.50 4.00
DW David Wright 1.25 3.00
IS Ichiro Suzuki 2.00 5.00
JG Josh Gibson 1.50 4.00
KG Ken Griffey Jr. 3.00 8.00
MM Mickey Mantle 5.00 12.00
MR Manny Ramirez 1.50 4.00
MT Miguel Tejada 1.00 2.50
TW Ted Williams 3.00 8.00
VG Vladimir Guerrero 1.00 2.50

2006 Topps Allen and Ginter Relics

GROUP A ODDS 1:2800 H, 1:4950 R
GROUP B ODDS 1:2000 H, 1:3900 R
GROUP C ODDS 1:140 H, 1:248 R
GROUP D ODDS 1:178 H, 1:413 R
GROUP E ODDS 1:128 H, 1:275 R
GROUP F ODDS 1:60 H, 1:118 R
GROUP G ODDS 1:66 H, 1:152 R
GROUP H ODDS 1:111 H, 1:174 R
GROUP I ODDS 1:178 H, 1:413 R
GROUP A ARE NOT SERIAL-NUMBERED
GROUP A QTY PROVIDED BY TOPPS
AP Albert Pujols Uni F 8.00 20.00
APE Andy Pettitte Jsy F 4.00 10.00
AR Alex Rodriguez Jsy C 4.00 10.00
BB Barry Bonds Uni G 10.00 25.00
BC Bobby Crosby Uni E 3.00 8.00
BM Brandon McCarthy Jsy E 3.00 8.00
CB Carlos Beltran Jsy H 3.00 8.00
CBA Clint Barmes Jsy G 3.00 8.00
CD Carlos Delgado Jsy F 3.00 8.00
CMW Chien-Ming Wang Jsy F 20.00 50.00
CS Curt Schilling Jsy F 4.00 10.00
CU Chase Utley Jsy G 6.00 15.00
DO David Ortiz Jsy G 4.00 10.00
DW David Wright Jsy H 6.00 15.00
DWI Dontrelle Willis Jsy I 3.00 8.00
EC Eric Chavez Uni E 3.00 8.00
FH Felix Hernandez Jsy C 4.00 10.00
FT Frank Thomas Bat F 6.00 15.00
GB G.W. Bush Tie A/150 * 200.00 300.00
GS Gary Sheffield Bat E 3.00 8.00
HCK Hong-Chih Kuo Jsy D 3.00 8.00
HM Hideki Matsui Uni G 6.00 15.00
HS Huston Street Jsy D 3.00 8.00
JC Jorge Cantu Jsy E 3.00 8.00
JD Johnny Damon Jsy C 4.00 10.00
JDY Jermaine Dye Uni G 3.00 8.00
JF Jeff Francouer Bat C 3.00 8.00
JG Jonny Gomes Jsy F 3.00 8.00
JK J.F.K. Sweater A/250 * 200.00 300.00
JP Jake Peavy Jsy C 3.00 8.00
JS Johan Santana Jsy G 4.00 10.00
JT Jim Thome Uni C 4.00 10.00
MB Mark Buehrle Uni F 3.00 8.00
MC Miguel Cabrera Uni B 6.00 15.00
MH Matt Holliday Jsy F 4.00 10.00
MM Mickey Mantle Uni D 30.00 80.00
MP Mark Prior Jsy G 3.00 8.00
MPZ Mike Piazza Bat C 4.00 10.00
MR Manny Ramirez Jsy H 4.00 10.00
MT Miguel Tejada Uni E 3.00 8.00
NS Nick Swisher Jsy E 3.00 8.00
PK Paul Konerko Uni D 3.00 8.00
PM Pedro Martinez Jsy I 4.00 10.00
RC Robinson Cano Uni F 4.00 10.00
RH Ryan Howard Bat C 12.00 30.00
RL Ryan Langerhans Bat C 3.00 8.00
RO Roy Oswalt Jsy G 3.00 8.00
TH Travis Hafner Jsy D 3.00 8.00
VG Vladimir Guerrero Bat F 4.00 10.00
VM Victor Martinez Jsy D 3.00 8.00
WT Willy Taveras Jsy H 3.00 8.00
ZD Zach Duke Jsy C 3.00 8.00

2006 Topps Allen and Ginter Rip Cards

1-50 STATED ODDS 1:265 HOBBY
1-4 PRINT RUN 10 SERIAL #'d SETS
5-9 PRINT RUN 15 SERIAL #'d SETS
10-19 PRINT RUN 25 SERIAL #'d SETS
20-50 PRINT RUN 99 SERIAL #'d SETS
1-19 NO PRICING DUE TO SCARCITY
ALL LISTED PRICES ARE FOR RIPPED
UNRIPPED HAVE ADD'L CARDS WITHIN
COMMON UNRIPPED (20-50) 75.00 150.00
UNRIPPED (30/35/43) 100.00 200.00
UNRIPPED (45/47/49) 100.00 200.00
RIP1 Mickey Mantle Back/10
RIP2 Dontrelle Willis/10
RIP3 Ivan Rodriguez/10
RIP4 Johan Santana/10
RIP5 Mike Piazza/15
RIP6 Randy Johnson/15
RIP7 Robinson Cano/15
RIP8 Scott Rolen/15
RIP9 Todd Helton/15
RIP10 Alex Rodriguez Back/25
RIP11 Alfonso Soriano/25
RIP12 D.Ortiz/A.Rodriguez/25
RIP13 Barry Bonds Back/25
RIP14 C.Beltran/C.Delgado/25
RIP15 David Wright/25
RIP16 Derrek Lee/25
RIP17 Huston Street/25
RIP18 Mariano Rivera/25
RIP19 Nolan Ryan/25
RIP20 Kenji Johjima/99 15.00 40.00
RIP21 Cap Anson/99 15.00 40.00
RIP22 Ryan Zimmerman/99 20.00 50.00
RIP23 Andruw Jones/99 10.00 25.00
RIP24 Barry Bonds at Wall/99 15.00 40.00
RIP25 Cal Ripken/99 30.00 60.00
RIP26 David Ortiz/99 10.00 25.00
RIP27 Hideki Matsui/99 10.00 25.00
RIP28 Ken Griffey Jr./99 20.00 50.00
RIP29 Manny Ramirez/99 10.00 25.00
RIP30 M.Mantle w/Bat/99 50.00 100.00
RIP31 A.Rod Bat Out/99 15.00 40.00
RIP32 Miguel Cabrera/99 6.00 15.00
RIP33 Miguel Tejada/99 6.00 15.00
RIP34 Pedro Martinez/99 10.00 25.00
RIP35 Albert Pujols w/Bat/99 30.00 60.00
RIP36 A.Rod Hands Out/99 15.00 40.00
RIP37 A.Rodriguez/D.Jeter/99 15.00 40.00
RIP38 Barry Bonds 700/99 15.00 40.00
RIP39 Derek Jeter/99 20.00 50.00
RIP40 Ichiro Suzuki/99 15.00 40.00
RIP41 I.Suzuki/H.Matsui/99 15.00 40.00
RIP42 Josh Gibson/99 15.00 40.00
RIP43 M.Mantle Swing/99 50.00 100.00
RIP44 Jonathan Papelbon/99 20.00 50.00
RIP45 M.Mantle/T.Williams/99 50.00 100.00
RIP46 Albert Pujols Back/99 30.00 60.00
RIP47 Roberto Clemente/99 30.00 60.00
RIP48 Roger Clemens/99 15.00 40.00
RIP49 Ted Williams/99 30.00 60.00
RIP50 Vladimir Guerrero/99 10.00 25.00

2007 Topps Allen and Ginter

This 350-card set was released in August, 2007. The set was issued in both hobby and retail versions. The hobby packs, which had an $4 SRP, consisted of eight-cards which came 24 packs to a box and 12 boxes to a case. Similar to the 2006 set, many non-baseball players were interspersed throughout this set. There were also a group of short-printed cards, which were inserted at a stated rate of one in two hobby or retail packs. In addition, some original 19th century Allen and Ginter cards were repurchased for this product and those original cards (featuring both sports and non-sport subjects) were inserted at a stated rate of one in 17, 072 hobby and one in 34, 654 retail packs.

COMPLETE SET (350) 60.00 120.00
COMP.SET w/o SP's (300) 20.00 50.00
SP STATED ODDS 1:2 HOBBY, 1:2 RETAIL
SP CL: 5/43/48/58/63/107/110/119/130/137
SP CL: 152/159/178/193/194/203/219/222
SP CL: 224/243/263/301/302/303/306/307
SP CL: 308/309/310/316/317/318/319/320
SP CL: 321/322/325/326/327/330/331/334
SP CL: 335/336/339/340/345/348/349/350
FRAMED ORIGINALS ODDS 1:17,072 HOBBY
FRAMED ORIGINALS ODDS 1:34,654 RETAIL
1 Ryan Howard .25 .60
2 Mike Gonzalez .12 .30
3 Austin Kearns .12 .30
4 Josh Hamilton .60 1.50
5 Stephen Drew SP 1.25 3.00
6 Matt Murton .12 .30
7 Mickey Mantle 1.00 2.50
8 Howie Kendrick .12 .30
9 Alexander Graham Bell .12 .30
10 Jason Bay .20 .50
11 Hank Blalock .12 .30
12 Johan Santana .20 .50
13 Eleanor Roosevelt .12 .30
14 Kei Igawa RC .50 1.25
15 Jeff Francoeur .30 .75
16 Carl Crawford .20 .50
17 Jhonny Peralta .12 .30
18 Mariano Rivera .40 1.00
19 Mario Andretti .30 .75
20 Vladimir Guerrero .20 .50
21 Adam Wainwright .20 .50
22 Huston Street .12 .30
23 Cael Sanderson .12 .30
24 Susan B. Anthony .12 .30
25 Jay Payton .12 .30
26 P.T. Barnum .12 .30
27 Scott Podsednik .12 .30
28 Willie Randolph .12 .30
29 Sean Casey .12 .30
30 Eiffel Tower .12 .30
31 Kenji Johjima .30 .75
32 Felix Hernandez .20 .50
33 Elijah Dukes RC .30 .75
34 Mark Grudzielanek .12 .30
35 J.D. Drew .12 .30
36 Kevin Kouzmanoff .12 .30
37 Jonathan Papelbon .30 .75
38 Bobby Crosby .12 .30
39 Brooklyn Bridge .12 .30
40 Adam Dunn .20 .50
41 Lyle Overbay .12 .30
42 Brian Fuentes .12 .30
43 Scott Rolen SP 1.25 3.00
44 Matt Lindstrom (RC) .20 .50
45 Carlos Zambrano .20 .50
46 Cole Hamels .25 .60
47 Matt Kemp .25 .60
48 Gary Matthews SP 1.25 3.00
49 J.J. Putz .12 .30
50 Albert Pujols .40 1.00
51 Dan Haren .12 .30
52 Aaron Harang .12 .30
53 Ferris Wheel .12 .30
54 Juan Rivera .12 .30
55 Ken Griffey Jr. .60 1.50
56 Chien-Ming Wang .20 .50
57 Sean Henn (RC) .20 .50
58 Mike Mussina SP 1.25 3.00
59 Ian Snell .12 .30
60 Josh Barfield .12 .30
61 Justin Morneau .20 .50
62 Dwight D. Eisenhower .12 .30
63 Bengie Molina SP 1.25 3.00
64 Brett Myers .12 .30
65 Andy Marte .12 .30
66 Bill Hall .12 .30
67 Ryan Shealy .12 .30
68 Joe B. Scott .12 .30
69 Mike Rabelo RC .20 .50
70 Jermaine Dye .12 .30
71 Andre Ethier .20 .50
72 Bruce Lee .12 .30
73 Nick Punto .12 .30
74 Ervin Santana .12 .30
75 Troy Tulowitzki (RC) .60 1.50
76 Garret Anderson .12 .30
77 Ryan Freel .12 .30
78 Carlos Guillen .12 .30
79 John Smoltz .30 .75
80 Chase Utley .20 .50
81 Mike Sweeney .12 .30
82 Joe Frazier .30 .75
83 Brad Lidge .12 .30
84 Casey Blake .12 .30
85 Ivan Rodriguez .20 .50
86 Roy Oswalt .20 .50
87 Akinori Iwamura RC .50 1.25
88 Francisco Rodriguez .20 .50
89 John Lackey .20 .50
90 Miguel Cabrera .30 .75
91 Kevin Mench .12 .30
92 Victor Martinez .20 .50
93 Chad Tracy .12 .30
94 Charlie Manuel .12 .30
95 Hanley Ramirez .20 .50
96 Dontrelle Willis .12 .30
97 Doug Slaten RC .20 .50
98 Noah Lowry .12 .30
99 Shawn Green .12 .30
100 David Ortiz .30 .75
101 Mark Reynolds RC .60 1.50
102 Preston Wilson .12 .30
103 Mohandas Gandhi .12 .30
104 Jeff Kent .12 .30
105 Lance Berkman .20 .50
106 C.C. Sabathia .20 .50
107 Jason Varitek SP 1.25 3.00
108 Mark Twain .12 .30
109 Melvin Mora .12 .30
110 Michael Young SP 1.25 3.00
111 Scott Hatteberg .12 .30
112 Erik Bedard .12 .30
113 Sitting Bull .12 .30
114 Homer Bailey (RC) .30 .75
115 Mark Teahen .12 .30
116 Ryan Braun (RC) 1.00 2.50
117 John Miles .12 .30
118 Coco Crisp .12 .30
119 Hunter Pence SP (RC) 2.00 5.00
120 Delmon Young (RC) .30 .75
121 Aramis Ramirez .12 .30
122 Magglio Ordonez .20 .50
123 Tadahito Iguchi .12 .30
124 Mark Selby .12 .30
125 Gil Meche .12 .30
126 Curt Schilling .20 .50
127 Brandon Phillips .12 .30
128 Milton Bradley .12 .30
129 Craig Monroe .12 .30
130 Jason Schmidt SP 1.25 3.00
131 Nick Markakis .25 .60
132 Paul Konerko .20 .50
133 Carlos Gomez RC .40 1.00
134 Garrett Atkins .12 .30
135 Jered Weaver .20 .50
136 Edgar Renteria .12 .30
137 Jason Isringhausen SP 1.25 3.00
138 Ray Durham .12 .30
139 Bob Baffert .12 .30
140 Nick Swisher .20 .50
141 Brian McCann .20 .50
142 Orlando Hudson .12 .30
143 Brian Bannister .12 .30
144 Manny Acta .12 .30
145 Jose Vidro .12 .30
146 Carlos Quentin .12 .30
147 Billy Butler (RC) .30 .75
148 Kenny Rogers .12 .30
149 Tom Gordon .12 .30
150 Derek Jeter .75 2.00
151 Bob Wickman .12 .30
152 Carlos Lee SP 1.25 3.00
153 Willy Taveras .12 .30
154 Paul LoDuca .12 .30
155 Ben Sheets .12 .30
156 Brian Roberts .12 .30
157 Freddy Adu .12 .30
158 Jason Kendall .12 .30
159 Michael Barrett SP 1.25 3.00
160 Frank Thomas .30 .75
161 Manny Ramirez .30 .75
162 Stanley Glenn .12 .30
163 Robinson Cano .20 .50
164 Phil Hughes (RC) .50 1.25
165 Joe Mauer .25 .60
166 Derrek Lee .12 .30
167 Jeff Weaver .12 .30
168 Joe Smith RC .12 .30
169 Louis Pasteur .12 .30
170 Gary Sheffield .12 .30
171 Luis Castillo .12 .30
172 Joe Torre .20 .50
173 Andy LaRoche (RC) .20 .50
174 Jamie Fischer .12 .30
175 Carlos Beltran .20 .50
176 Bronson Arroyo .12 .30
177 Rafael Furcal .12 .30
178 Juan Pierre SP 1.25 3.00
179 Matt Cain .20 .50
180 Alfonso Soriano .20 .50
181 Joe Borowski .12 .30
182 Conor Jackson .12 .30
183 Groundhog Day .12 .30
184 Pat Burrell .12 .30
185 Troy Glaus .12 .30
186 Joel Zumaya .12 .30
187 Russell Martin .12 .30
188 Josh Willingham .20 .50
189 Jarrod Saltalamacchia (RC) .30 .75
190 Scott Kazmir .20 .50
191 Jeremy Hermida .12 .30
192 Tower Bridge .12 .30
193 Rich Hill SP 1.25 3.00
194 Francisco Cordero SP 1.25 3.00
195 Mike Piazza .30 .75
196 Brad Ausmus .12 .30
197 Greg Louganis .12 .30
198 Frank Catalanotto .12 .30
199 Alejandro De Aza RC .30 .75
200 David Wright .25 .60
201 Freddy Sanchez .12 .30
202 Shea Hillenbrand .12 .30
203 Justin Verlander SP 1.25 3.00
204 Alex Gordon RC .60 1.50
205 Jimmy Rollins .20 .50
206 Mike Napoli .12 .30
207 Chris Burke .12 .30
208 Chipper Jones .30 .75
209 Randy Johnson .30 .75
210 Daisuke Matsuzaka RC .75 2.00
211 Orlando Cabrera .12 .30
212 B.J. Upton .12 .30
213 Lou Piniella MG .12 .30
214 Mike Cameron .12 .30
215 Luis Gonzalez .12 .30
216 Rickie Weeks .12 .30
217 Hideki Okajima RC 1.00 2.50
218 Johnny Estrada .12 .30
219 Dan Uggla SP 1.25 3.00
220 Ryan Zimmerman .20 .50
221 Tony Gwynn Jr. .12 .30
222 Rocco Baldelli SP 1.25 3.00
223 Xavier Nady .12 .30
224 Josh Bard SP 1.25 3.00
225 Raul Ibanez .20 .50
226 Chris Carpenter .20 .50
227 Matt DeSalvo (RC) .20 .50
228 Jack the Ripper .12 .30
229 Eric Chavez .12 .30
230 Jose Reyes .20 .50
231 Glen Perkins (RC) .20 .50
232 Gregg Zaun .12 .30
233 Jim Thome .20 .50
234 Joe Crede .12 .30
235 Barry Zito .20 .50
236 Yoel Hernandez RC .20 .50
237 Kelly Johnson .12 .30
238 Chris Young .12 .30
239 Fyodor Dostoevsky .12 .30
240 Miguel Tejada .20 .50
241 Doug Mientkiewicz .12 .30
242 Bobby Jenks .12 .30
243 Brad Hawpe SP 1.25 3.00
244 Jay Marshall RC .20 .50
245 Brad Penny .12 .30
246 Johnny Damon .20 .50
247 Dave Roberts .20 .50
248 Ron Washington .12 .30
249 Mike Aponte .12 .30
250 Brandon Webb .20 .50
251 Andy Pettitte .20 .50
252 Bud Black .12 .30
253 Michael Cuddyer .12 .30
254 Chris Stewart RC .20 .50
255 Mark Teixeira .20 .50
256 Hideki Matsui .30 .75
257 Curtis Granderson .25 .60
258 A.J. Pierzynski .12 .30
259 Tony La Russa .20 .50
260 Andruw Jones .12 .30
261 Torii Hunter .12 .30
262 Mark Loretta .12 .30
263 Jim Edmonds SP 1.25 3.00
264 Aaron Rowand .12 .30
265 Roy Halladay .20 .50
266 Freddy Garcia .12 .30
267 Reggie Sanders .12 .30
268 Washington Monument .12 .30
269 Franklin D. Roosevelt .12 .30
270 Alex Rodriguez .40 1.00
271 Wes Helms .12 .30
272 Mia Hamm .12 .30

273 Jorge Posada .20 .50
274 Tim Lincecum RC 1.00 2.50
275 Bobby Abreu .12 .30
276 Zach Duke .12 .30
277 Carlos Delgado .12 .30
278 Julio Juarez .12 .30
279 Brandon Inge .12 .30
280 Todd Helton .20 .50
281 Marcus Giles .12 .30
282 Josh Johnson .30 .75
283 Chris Capuano .12 .30
284 B.J. Ryan .12 .30
285 Nick Johnson .12 .30
286 Khalil Greene .12 .30
287 Travis Hafner .12 .30
288 Ted Lilly .12 .30
289 Jim Leyland .12 .30
290 Prince Fielder .20 .50
291 Trevor Hoffman .20 .50
292 Brian Giles .12 .30
293 Omar Vizquel .20 .50
294 Julio Lugo .12 .30
295 Jake Peavy .12 .30
296 Adrian Beltre .30 .75
297 Josh Beckett .12 .30
298 Harry S. Truman .12 .30
299 Mark Buehrle .20 .50
300 Ichiro Suzuki .40 1.00
301 Chris Duncan SP 1.25 3.00
302 Augie Garrido SP CO 1.25 3.00
303 Tyler Clippard SP (RC) 1.25 3.00
304 Ramon Hernandez .12 .30
305 Jeremy Bonderman .12 .30
306 Morgan Ensberg SP 1.25 3.00
307 J.J. Hardy SP 1.25 3.00
308 Mark Zupan SP 1.25 3.00
309 Laila Ali SP 1.25 3.00
310 Greg Maddux SP 1.50 4.00
311 David Ross .12 .30
312 Chris Duffy .12 .30
313 Moises Alou .12 .30
314 Yadier Molina .30 .75
315 Corey Patterson .12 .30
316 Dan O'Brien SP 1.25 3.00
317 Michael Bourn SP (RC) 1.25 3.00
318 Jonny Gomes SP 1.25 3.00
319 Ken Jennings SP 1.25 3.00
320 Barry Bonds SP 1.50 4.00
321 Gary Hall Jr. SP 1.25 3.00
322 Kerri Walsh SP 1.25 3.00
323 Craig Biggio .20 .50
324 Ian Kinsler .20 .50
325 Grady Sizemore SP 1.25 3.00
326 Alex Rios SP 1.25 3.00
327 Ted Toles SP 1.25 3.00
328 Jason Jennings .12 .30
329 Vernon Wells .12 .30
330 Bob Geren SP MG 1.25 3.00
331 Dennis Rodman SP 1.25 3.00
332 Tom Glavine .20 .50
333 Pedro Martinez .20 .50
334 Gustavo Molina SP RC 1.25 3.00
335 Bartolo Colon SP 1.25 3.00
336 Misty May-Treanor SP 1.25 3.00
337 Randy Winn .12 .30
338 Eric Byrnes .12 .30
339 Jason McElwain SP 1.25 3.00
340 Placido Polanco SP 1.25 3.00
341 Adrian Gonzalez .25 .60
342 Chad Cordero .12 .30
343 Jeff Francis .12 .30
344 Lastings Milledge .20 .50
345 Sammy Sosa SP 1.25 3.00
346 Jacque Jones .12 .30
347 Anibal Sanchez .12 .30
348 Roger Clemens SP 1.50 4.00
349 Jesse Litsch SP RC 1.25 3.00
350 Adam LaRoche SP 1.25 3.00
NNO Framed Originals 50.00 100.00

2007 Topps Allen and Ginter Mini

*MINI 1-350: 1X TO 2.5X BASIC
*MINI 1-350: .6X TO 1.5X BASIC RC's
APPX. ONE MINI PER PACK
*MINI SP 1-350: .6X TO 1.5X BASIC SP
*MINI SP 1-350: .6X TO 1.5X BASIC SP RC's
MINI SP ODDS 1:13 H, 1:13 R
COMMON CARD (351-390) 15.00 40.00
351-390 RANDOM WITHIN RIP CARDS
OVERALL PLATE ODDS 1:788 HOBBY
PLATE PRINT RUN 1 SET PER COLOR
BLACK-CYAN-MAGENTA-YELLOW ISSUED
NO PLATE PRICING DUE TO SCARCITY
351 Alex Rodriguez EXT 20.00 50.00
352 Ryan Zimmerman EXT 20.00 50.00
353 Prince Fielder EXT 40.00 80.00
354 Gary Sheffield EXT 15.00 40.00
355 Jermaine Dye EXT 15.00 40.00
356 Hanley Ramirez EXT 15.00 40.00
357 Jose Reyes EXT 30.00 60.00
358 Miguel Tejada EXT 20.00 50.00
359 Elijah Dukes EXT 15.00 40.00
360 Ryan Howard EXT 15.00 40.00
361 Vladimir Guerrero EXT 15.00 40.00
362 Ichiro Suzuki EXT 30.00 60.00
363 Jason Bay EXT 15.00 40.00
364 Justin Morneau EXT 15.00 40.00
365 Michael Young EXT 15.00 40.00
366 Adam Dunn EXT 15.00 40.00
367 Alfonso Soriano EXT 20.00 50.00
368 Jake Peavy EXT 20.00 50.00
369 Nick Swisher EXT 20.00 50.00
370 David Wright EXT 30.00 60.00
371 Brandon Webb EXT 20.00 50.00
372 Brian McCann EXT 20.00 50.00
373 Frank Thomas EXT 20.00 50.00
374 Albert Pujols EXT 30.00 60.00
375 Russell Martin EXT 20.00 50.00
376 Felix Hernandez EXT 15.00 40.00
377 Barry Bonds EXT 40.00 80.00
378 Lance Berkman EXT 15.00 40.00
379 Joe Mauer EXT 30.00 60.00
380 B.J. Upton EXT 15.00 40.00
381 Todd Helton EXT 15.00 40.00
382 Paul Konerko EXT 15.00 40.00
383 Grady Sizemore EXT 20.00 50.00
384 Magglio Ordonez EXT 15.00 40.00
385 Dan Uggla EXT 20.00 50.00
386 J.D. Drew EXT 15.00 40.00
387 Adam LaRoche EXT 15.00 40.00
388 Carlos Beltran EXT 15.00 40.00
389 Derek Jeter EXT 40.00 80.00
390 Daisuke Matsuzaka EXT 30.00 60.00

2007 Topps Allen and Ginter Mini A and G Back

*A & G BACK: 1.25X TO 3X BASIC
*A & G BACK: .75X TO 2X BASIC RC's
STATED ODDS 1:5 H, 1:5 R
*A & G BACK SP: .75X TO 2X BASIC SP
*A & G BACK SP: .75X TO 2X BASIC SP RC's
SP STATED ODDS 1:65 H, 1:65 R

2007 Topps Allen and Ginter Mini Black

*BLACK: 2X TO 5X BASIC
*BLACK: 1.5X TO 4X BASIC RC's
STATED ODDS 1:10 H, 1:10 R
*BLACK SP: 1.5X TO 4X BASIC SP
*BLACK SP: 1.5X TO 4X BASIC SP RC's
SP STATED ODDS 1:130 H, 1:130 R

2007 Topps Allen and Ginter Mini Black No Number

*BLK NO NBR: 2.5X TO 6X BASIC
*BLK NO NBR: 2X TO 5X BASIC RC's
*BLK NO NBR: 1.5X TO 4X BASIC SP
*BLK NO NBR: 1.5X TO 4X BASIC SP RC's
RANDOM INSERTS IN PACKS
210 Daisuke Matsuzaka 6.00 15.00

2007 Topps Allen and Ginter Mini No Card Number

*NO NBR: 10X TO 25X BASIC
*NO NBR: 6X TO 15X BASIC RC's
*NO NBR: 2.5X TO 6X BASIC SP
*NO NBR: 2.5X TO 6X BASIC SP RC's
STATED ODDS 1:106 H, 1:108 R
STATED PRINT RUN 50 SETS
CARDS ARE NOT SERIAL-NUMBERED
PRINT RUN INFO PROVIDED BY TOPPS
7 Mickey Mantle 40.00 80.00
50 Albert Pujols 30.00 60.00
55 Ken Griffey Jr. 40.00 100.00
56 Chien-Ming Wang 30.00 60.00
150 Derek Jeter 40.00 80.00
270 Alex Rodriguez 30.00 60.00
300 Ichiro Suzuki 40.00 80.00
320 Barry Bonds SP 40.00 80.00

2007 Topps Allen and Ginter Autographs

GROUP A ODDS 1:64,496 H, 1:122200 R
GROUP B ODDS 1:3261 H, 1:6522 R
GROUP C ODDS 1:13,987 H, 1:27,642 R
GROUP D ODDS 1:288 H, 1:578 R
GROUP E ODDS 1:6789 H, 1:13,578 R
GROUP F ODDS 1:162 H, 1:324 R
GROUP G ODDS 1:680 H, 1:1362 R
GROUP A PRINT RUN 25 CARDS PER
GROUP B PRINT RUN 100 CARDS PER
GROUP C PRINT RUN 120 CARDS PER
GROUP D PRINT RUN 200 CARDS PER
GROUP A-D ARE NOT SERIAL-NUMBERED
A-D PRINT RUNS PROVIDED BY TOPPS
NO PUJOLS PRICING DUE TO SCARCITY
EXCH DEADLINE 7/31/2009
AE Andre Ethier F 5.00 12.00
AG Augie Garrido D/200 * 10.00 25.00
AG2 Adrian Gonzalez F 6.00 15.00
AI Akinori Iwamura F 5.00 12.00
AR Alex Rodriguez E/225 * 60.00 120.00
BB Bob Baffert D/200 * 30.00 60.00
BC Brian Cashman B/100 * 40.00 80.00
BH Bill Hall G 6.00 15.00
BPB Brian Bannister F 10.00 25.00
CG Curtis Granderson F 8.00 20.00
CH Cole Hamels F 10.00 25.00
CMW Chien-Ming Wang D/200 * 60.00 120.00
CS Cael Sanderson D/200 * 30.00 60.00
DO Dan O'Brien D/200 * 12.50 30.00
DR Dennis Rodman D/200 * 30.00 60.00
DW David Wright/200 * 20.00 50.00
ES Ervin Santana F 6.00 15.00
FA Freddy Adu D/200 * 10.00 25.00
GH Gary Hall Jr. D/200 * 10.00 25.00
GL Greg Louganis D/200 * 15.00 40.00
HK Howie Kendrick F 6.00 15.00
HR Hanley Ramirez F 8.00 20.00
JBS Joe B. Scott D/200 * 20.00 50.00
JF Jamie Fischer D/200 * 8.00 20.00
JH Jeremy Hermida G 5.00 12.00
JJ Julio Juarez D/200 * 8.00 20.00
JM Justin Morneau F 12.50 30.00
JMC Jason McElwain D/200 * 12.00 30.00
JMM John Miles D/200 * 15.00 40.00
JP Jonathan Papelbon F 15.00 40.00
JS Johan Santana B/100 * 20.00 50.00
JT Jim Thome B/100 * 50.00 100.00
KJ Ken Jennings D/200 * 50.00 120.00
KW Kerri Walsh D/200 * 40.00 80.00
LA Laila Ali D/200 * 50.00 120.00
MA Mike Aponte D/200 * 10.00 25.00
MEI Maicer Izturis F 6.00 15.00
MGA Mario Andretti D/200 * 40.00 80.00
MH Mia Hamm D/200 * 50.00 100.00
MMT Misty May-Treanor D/200 * 50.00 100.00
MN Mike Napoli F 6.00 15.00
MS Mark Selby D/200 * 15.00 40.00
MZ Mark Zupan D/200 * 5.00 12.00
NL Nook Logan G 5.00 12.00
NM Nick Markakis F 5.00 12.00
RH Ryan Howard B/100 * 10.00 25.00
RM Russell Martin F 5.00 12.00
RZ Ryan Zimmerman F 6.00 15.00
SG Stanley Glenn D/200 * 20.00 50.00
SJF Joe Frazier C/120 * 150.00 250.00
TH Torii Hunter F 8.00 20.00
TS Tommie Smith D/200 * 20.00 50.00
TT Ted Toles D/200 * 20.00 50.00
TTT Troy Tulowitzki F 6.00 15.00

2007 Topps Allen and Ginter Dick Perez

COMPLETE SET (30) 6.00 15.00
APPX. ONE PEREZ PER PACK
ORIGINALS RANDOM WITHIN RIP CARDS
ORIGINALS PRINT RUN 1 SERIAL #'d SET
NO ORIG. PRICING DUE TO SCARCITY
1 Brandon Webb .30 .75
2 Chipper Jones .50 1.25
3 Nick Markakis .40 1.00
4 Daisuke Matsuzaka .75 2.00
5 Alfonso Soriano .30 .75
6 Jermaine Dye .20 .50
7 Adam Dunn .30 .75
8 Grady Sizemore .30 .75
9 Troy Tulowitzki .60 1.50
10 Gary Sheffield .20 .50
11 Hanley Ramirez .30 .75
12 Carlos Lee .20 .50
13 Mark Teahen .20 .50
14 Gary Matthews .20 .50
15 Andre Ethier .30 .75
16 Prince Fielder .30 .75
17 Joe Mauer .40 1.00
18 Jose Reyes .30 .75
19 Derek Jeter 1.25 3.00
20 Nick Swisher .30 .75
21 Ryan Howard .40 1.00
22 Freddy Sanchez .20 .50
23 Greg Maddux .60 1.50
24 Raul Ibanez .30 .75
25 Barry Zito .30 .75
26 Jim Edmonds .30 .75
27 Delmon Young .30 .75
28 Michael Young .20 .50
29 Roy Halladay .30 .75
30 Ryan Zimmerman .30 .75

2007 Topps Allen and Ginter Mini Emperors

STATED ODDS 1:72 H, 1:72 R
1 Julius Caesar 2.00 5.00
2 Caesar Augustus 2.00 5.00
3 Tiberius 2.00 5.00
4 Caligula 2.00 5.00
5 Claudius 2.00 5.00
6 Nero 2.00 5.00
7 Titus 2.00 5.00
8 Hadrian 2.00 5.00
9 Marcus Aurelius 2.00 5.00
10 Septimus Severus 2.00 5.00

2007 Topps Allen and Ginter Mini Flags

COMPLETE SET (50) 100.00 175.00
STATED ODDS 1:12 H, 1:12 R
1 Algeria 1.50 4.00
2 Argentina 1.50 4.00
3 Australia 1.50 4.00
4 Austria 1.50 4.00
5 Belgium 1.50 4.00
6 Brazil 1.50 4.00
7 Bulgaria 1.50 4.00
8 Canada 1.50 4.00
9 Chile 1.50 4.00
10 China 1.50 4.00
11 Colombia 1.50 4.00
12 Costa Rica 1.50 4.00
13 Denmark 1.50 4.00
14 Dominican Republic 1.50 4.00
15 Ecuador 1.50 4.00
16 Egypt 1.50 4.00
17 France 1.50 4.00
18 Germany 1.50 4.00
19 Greece 1.50 4.00
20 Greenland 1.50 4.00
21 Honduras 1.50 4.00
22 Iceland 1.50 4.00
23 India 1.50 4.00
24 Indonesia 1.50 4.00
25 Ireland 1.50 4.00
26 Israel 1.50 4.00
27 Italy 1.50 4.00
28 Ivory Coast 1.50 4.00
29 Jamaica 1.50 4.00
30 Japan 1.50 4.00
31 Kenya 1.50 4.00
32 Mexico 1.50 4.00
33 Morocco 1.50 4.00
34 Netherlands 1.50 4.00
35 Nigeria 1.50 4.00
36 Norway 1.50 4.00
37 Panama 1.50 4.00
38 Peru 1.50 4.00
39 Philippines 1.50 4.00
40 Portugal 1.50 4.00
41 Puerto Rico 1.50 4.00
42 Russian Federation 1.50 4.00
43 Spain 1.50 4.00
44 Switzerland 1.50 4.00
45 Taiwan 1.50 4.00
46 Thailand 1.50 4.00
47 Turkey 1.50 4.00
48 United Arab Emirates 1.50 4.00
49 United Kingdom 1.50 4.00
50 United States of America 1.50 4.00

2007 Topps Allen and Ginter Mini Snakes

STATED ODDS 1:144 H, 1:144 R
1 Arizona Coral Snake 8.00 20.00
2 Copperhead 8.00 20.00
3 Black Mamba 8.00 20.00
4 King Cobra 8.00 20.00
5 Cottonmouth 8.00 20.00

2007 Topps Allen and Ginter N43

STATED ODDS 1:3 HOBBY BOX LOADER
AP Albert Pujols 1.25 3.00
AR Alex Rodriguez 1.25 3.00
BB Barry Bonds 1.50 4.00
BL Bruce Lee .40 1.00
DJ Ch Felicity's Diamond Jim 4.00 10.00
DM Daisuke Matsuzaka 1.50 4.00
DW David Wright .75 2.00
GL Greg Louganis .40 1.00
IS Ichiro Suzuki 1.25 3.00
JF Joe Frazier 1.00 2.50
MA Mario Andretti 1.00 2.50
PF Prince Fielder .60 1.50
RH Ryan Howard .75 2.00
RZ Ryan Zimmerman .60 1.50
VG Vladimir Guerrero .60 1.50

2007 Topps Allen and Ginter N43 Autographs

GROUP A ODDS 1:1747 HOBBY BOX LOADER
GROUP B ODDS 1:1034 HOBBY BOX LOADER
GROUP A PRINT RUN 10 SER.#'d SETS
GROUP B PRINT RUN 50 SER.#'d SETS
NO GROUP A PRICING AVAILABLE
DJ Ch Felicity's Diamond Jim B/50 30.00 60.00

2007 Topps Allen and Ginter National Pride

STATED ODDS 1:2 HOBBY BOX LOADER
1 Igawa/Matsuzaka/Matsui/Ichiro 2.00 5.00
2 Okajima/Iwamura/Johjima/Iguchi 2.50 6.00
3 Abreu/Cabrera/King Felix/Johan 1.25 3.00
4 Choo/Park/Kim/Ryu .75 2.00
5 Bay/Russ.Martin/Morneau/Harden .75 2.00
6 Hanley/Manny/Aramis/Vlad 1.25 3.00
7 J.Reyes/Pedro/Papi/Pujols 1.50 4.00
8 Beltran/Delgado/Pudge/Posada .75 2.00
9 Prince/ARod/Howard/Wright 1.50 4.00
10 Webb/Verlander/Maddux/Smoltz 1.50 4.00

2007 Topps Allen and Ginter Relics

GROUP A ODDS 1:1,160,000 H
GROUP A ODDS 1:243,648 R
GROUP B ODDS 1:31,376 H, 1:62,750 R
GROUP C ODDS 1:15,275 H, 1:30,550 R
GROUP D ODDS 1:383 H, 1:766 R
GROUP E ODDS 1:1530 H, 1:3068 R
GROUP F ODDS 1:510 H, 1:1022 R
GROUP G ODDS 1:109 H, 1:218 R
GROUP H ODDS 1:69 H, 1:140 R
GROUP I ODDS 1:340 H, 1:680 R
GROUP J ODDS 1:25 H, 1:48 R
GROUP B PRINT RUN 50 COPIES PER
GROUP C PRINT RUN 100 COPIES PER
GROUP D PRINT RUN 250 COPIES PER
GROUP B-D ARE NOT SERIAL-NUMBERED
GROUP B-D QTY PROVIDED BY TOPPS
NO WASHINGTON PRICING AVAILABLE
AER Alex Rodriguez Bat D/250 * 15.00 40.00
AL Adam LaRoche J 3.00 8.00
AP Albert Pujols Bat E 8.00 20.00
AR Aramis Ramirez J 3.00 8.00
AS Arthur Shorin B/50 * 150.00 300.00
BB Barry Bonds Pants D/250 * 6.00 15.00
BC Brian Cashman D/250 * 15.00 40.00
BL Bruce Lee D/250 * 200.00 400.00
BR Brian Roberts J 3.00 8.00
BZ Barry Zito Pants J 3.00 8.00
CB Carlos Beltran Bat I 3.00 8.00
CC Carl Crawford Bat H 3.00 8.00
CK Casey Kotchman J 3.00 8.00
CLC Coco Crisp Bat D 3.00 8.00
CMS Curt Schilling J 4.00 10.00
CP Corey Patterson Bat F 3.00 8.00
CT Chad Tracy Bat G 3.00 8.00
DAO David Ortiz Bat D/250 * 6.00 15.00
DL Derrek Lee Bat H 3.00 8.00
DO Dan O'Brien D/250 * 10.00 25.00
DW Dontrelle Willis J 3.00 8.00
EC Eric Chavez Pants J 3.00 8.00
EG Eric Gagne J 3.00 8.00
GH Gary Hall Jr. D/250 * 10.00 25.00
HB Hank Blalock J 3.00 8.00
HR Hanley Ramirez Bat G 4.00 10.00
IR Ivan Rodriguez J 4.00 10.00
JB Jason Bay Bat H 3.00 8.00
JF Jamie Fischer D/250 * 10.00 25.00
JG Jason Giambi Bat H 3.00 8.00
JJ Julio Juarez D/250 * 8.00 20.00
KJ Ken Jennings D/250 * 12.00 30.00
KO Keith Olbermann C/100 * 75.00 200.00
KW Kerri Walsh D/250 * 10.00 25.00
LA Laila Ali D/250 * 10.00 25.00
MC1 Miguel Cabrera G 4.00 10.00
MC2 Miguel Cabrera Bat G 4.00 10.00
MCM Mike Mussina Pants J 4.00 10.00
MG Marcus Giles J 3.00 8.00
MH Mia Hamm D/250 * 12.00 30.00
MM Mickey Mantle Bat D/250 * 40.00 80.00
MMU Mark Mulder Pants J 3.00 8.00
MP Mike Piazza Bat H 4.00 10.00
MR Manny Ramirez Bat H 4.00 10.00
MT Miguel Tejada J 3.00 8.00
NS Nick Swisher Bat H 3.00 8.00
PF Prince Fielder Bat G 6.00 15.00
PK Paul Konerko Bat H 3.00 8.00
PL Paul LoDuca J 3.00 8.00
RA Rich Aurilia Bat G 3.00 8.00
RC Robinson Cano Bat F 4.00 10.00
RH Rich Harden Pants J 3.00 8.00
RW Randy Winn J 3.00 8.00
SD Stephen Drew J 3.00 8.00
SJF Joe Frazier D/250 * 20.00 50.00
SP Scott Podsednik Bat G 3.00 8.00
SR1 Scott Rolen G 4.00 10.00
SR2 Scott Rolen Bat G 4.00 10.00
SS Sammy Sosa Bat I 4.00 10.00
TG Troy Glaus Bat H 3.00 8.00
TN Trot Nixon Bat G 3.00 8.00
TS Tommie Smith D/250 * 12.50 30.00
VG Vladimir Guerrero Bat H 4.00 10.00

2007 Topps Allen and Ginter Rip Card

STATED ODDS 1:285 HOBBY
PRINT RUNS B/WN 10-99 COPIES PER
NO PRICING ON QTY 10 OR LESS
ALL LISTED PRICED ARE FOR RIPPED
UNRIPPED HAVE ADD'L CARDS WITHIN
1 Grady Sizemore/90 10.00 25.00
2 Miguel Cabrera/75 10.00 25.00
3 Adam Dunn/95 6.00 15.00
4 Jose Reyes/99 10.00 25.00
5 Alfonso Soriano/90 6.00 15.00
6 Chase Utley/99 10.00 25.00
7 Frank Thomas/95 10.00 25.00
8 Andruw Jones/95 10.00 25.00
9 Nick Markakis/75 10.00 25.00
10 Felix Hernandez/99 10.00 25.00
11 Jered Weaver/99 10.00 25.00
12 Ivan Rodriguez/99 10.00 25.00
13 Joe Mauer/99 10.00 25.00
14 Derek Jeter/99 20.00 50.00
15 Delmon Young/
16 Brandon Webb/10
17 Miguel Tejada/95 6.00 15.00
18 Vladimir Guerrero/75 10.00 25.00
19 Greg Maddux/99 15.00 40.00
20 Michael Young/99 6.00 15.00
21 Barry Zito/99 6.00 15.00
22 Russell Martin/95 6.00 15.00
23 Daisuke Matsuzaka/99 90.00 150.00
24 Stephen Drew/95 10.00 25.00
25 Alex Rodriguez/99 15.00 40.00
26 J.D. Drew/99 6.00 15.00
27 Paul Konerko/99 6.00 15.00
28 Josh Hamilton /90 20.00 50.00
29 Mike Piazza /99 10.00 25.00
30 Ryan Howard/10
31 Carl Crawford/99 6.00 15.00
32 Adam LaRoche/99 6.00 15.00
33 Bill Hall/95 6.00 15.00
34 Scott Kazmir/95 10.00 25.00
35 Gary Matthews/99 6.00 15.00
36 Gary Sheffield/99 6.00 15.00
37 Francisco Rodriguez/95 6.00 15.00
38 Todd Helton/99 10.00 25.00
39 Dontrelle Willis/10
40 David Wright/99 15.00 40.00
41 David Ortiz/10
42 Barry Bonds/99 20.00 50.00
43 Johan Santana/75 10.00 25.00
44 Albert Pujols/90 20.00 50.00
45 Carlos Lee/99 6.00 15.00
46 Cole Hamels/95 10.00 25.00
47 Prince Fielder/99 10.00 25.00
48 Hanley Ramirez/99 10.00 25.00
49 Ryan Zimmerman/90 10.00 25.00
50 Kei Igawa/75 10.00 25.00

2007 Topps Allen and Ginter National Mini Promos

NCC4 Grady Sizemore .75 2.00
NCC5 C.C. Sabathia .60 1.50
NCC6 Victor Martinez .60 1.50

2007 Topps Allen and Ginter National Promos

NCC4 Grady Sizemore .75 2.00
NCC5 C.C. Sabathia .60 1.50
NCC6 Victor Martinez .60 1.50

2008 Topps Allen and Ginter

COMP.SET w/o FUKU.(350) 30.00 60.00
COMP.SET w/o SPs (300) 15.00 40.00
COMMON CARD (1-300) .15 .40
COMMON RC (1-300) .40 1.00
COMMON SP (301-350) 1.25 3.00
SP STATED ODDS 1:2 HOBBY
FRAMED ORIG.ODDS 1:26,500 HOBBY
1 Alex Rodriguez .50 1.25
2 Juan Pierre .15 .40
3 Benjamin Franklin .25 .60
4 Roy Halladay .25 .60
5 C.C. Sabathia .25 .60
6 Brian Barton RC .60 1.50
7 Mickey Mantle 1.25 3.00
8 Brian Bass (RC) .40 1.00
9 Ian Kinsler .25 .60
10 Manny Ramirez .40 1.00
11 Michael Cuddyer .15 .40
12 Ian Snell .15 .40
13 Mike Lowell .15 .40
14 Adrian Gonzalez .25 .60
15 B.J. Upton .25 .60
16 Hiroki Kuroda RC 1.00 2.50
17 Kenji Johjima .15 .40
18 James Loney .15 .40
19 Albert Einstein .25 .60
20 Vladimir Guerrero .25 .60
21 Miguel Tejada .25 .60
22 Chin-Lung Hu (RC) .40 1.00
23 A.J. Burnett .15 .40
24 Bobby Jenks .15 .40
25 Aramis Ramirez .15 .40
26 Corey Hart .15 .40
27 Brad Hawpe .15 .40
28 Adam LaRoche .15 .40
29 Empire State Building .25 .60
30 Miguel Cabrera .40 1.00
31 Ryan Zimmerman .25 .60
32 Mark Ellis .15 .40
33 Nick Swisher .25 .60
34 Bill Hall .15 .40
35 Eric Byrnes .15 .40
36 Michael Young .15 .40
37 Pedro Martinez .25 .60
38 Andruw Jones .15 .40
39 J.R. Towles RC .60 1.50
40 Justin Upton .25 .60
41 Paul Konerko .25 .60
42 Luke Scott .15 .40
43 Rickie Weeks .15 .40
44 Adam Wainwright .25 .60
45 Justin Morneau .25 .60
46 Chris Young .15 .40
47 Chad Billingsley .25 .60
48 Kazuo Matsui .15 .40
49 Shane Victorino .15 .40
50 Albert Pujols .50 1.25
51 Brian McCann .25 .60
52 Carlos Delgado .15 .40
53 Chien-Ming Wang .25 .60
54 Takashi Saito .15 .40
55 Josh Beckett .15 .40
56 Nick Johnson .15 .40
57 Ben Sheets .15 .40
58 Johnny Damon .25 .60
59 Nicky Hayden .25 .60
60 Prince Fielder .25 .60
61 Adam Dunn .25 .60
62 Dustin Pedroia .25 .60
63 Jacoby Ellsbury .30 .75
64 Brad Penny .15 .40
65 Victor Martinez .25 .60
66 Joe Mauer .30 .75
67 Kevin Kouzmanoff .15 .40
68 Frank Thomas .40 1.00
69 Stevie Williams .25 .60
70 Matt Holliday .40 1.00
71 Fausto Carmona .15 .40
72 Clayton Kershaw RC 5.00 12.00
73 Tadahito Iguchi .15 .40
74 Khalil Greene .15 .40
75 Travis Hafner .15 .40
76 Jim Thome .25 .60
77 Joba Chamberlain .15 .40
78 Ivan Rodriguez .25 .60
79 Jose Guillen .15 .40
80 Hanley Ramirez .25 .60
81 Vernon Wells .15 .40
82 Jayson Nix (RC) .40 1.00
83 Masahide Kobayashi RC .60 1.50
84 Bonnie Blair .25 .60
85 Curtis Granderson .25 .60
86 Kelvim Escobar .25 .60
87 Aaron Rowand .15 .40
88 Troy Glaus .25 .60
89 Billy Wagner .15 .40
90 Jose Reyes .25 .60
91 Scott Rolen .25 .60
92 Dan Jansen .25 .60
93 David Eckstein .15 .40
94 Tom Gorzelanny .15 .40
95 Garrett Atkins .15 .40
96 Carlos Zambrano .25 .60
97 Jeff Francis .15 .40
98 Kazuo Fukumori RC .60 1.50
99 John Bowker (RC) .40 1.00
100 David Wright .25 .60
101 Adrian Beltre .40 1.00
102 Ray Durham .15 .40
103 Kerri Strug .25 .60
104 Orlando Hudson .15 .40
105 Jonathan Papelbon .25 .60
106 Brian Schneider .15 .40
107 Matt Biondi .25 .60
108 Alex Romero (RC) .60 1.50
109 Joey Chestnut .25 .60
110 Chase Utley .25 .60
111 Dan Uggla .15 .40
112 Akinori Iwamura .15 .40
113 Curt Schilling .25 .60
114 Trevor Hoffman .25 .60
115 Alex Rios .15 .40
116 Mariano Rivera .50 1.25
117 Jeff Niemann (RC) .40 1.00
118 Geovany Soto .40 1.00
119 Billy Mitchell .25 .60
120 Derek Jeter 1.00 2.50
121 Yovani Gallardo .15 .40
122 The Gateway Arch .25 .60
123 Josh Willingham .25 .60
124 Greg Maddux .50 1.25
125 John Lackey .25 .60
126 Chris Young .15 .40
127 Billy Butler .15 .40

Golden Gate Bridge .25 .60
Joey Votto (RC) 1.50 4.00
Tim Wakefield .25 .60
Todd Helton .25 .60
Gary Matthews .15 .40
Wild Bill Hickok .25 .60
Jason Varitek .40 1.00
Robinson Cano .25 .60
Javier Vazquez .15 .40
Annie Oakley .25 .60
Andy Pettitte .25 .60
Greg Reynolds RC .60 1.50
Jimmy Rollins .25 .60
Jermaine Dye .15 .40
Eugenio Velez RC .40 1.00
J.J. Hardy .15 .40
Grand Canyon .25 .60
Bobby Abreu .15 .40
Scott Kazmir .25 .60
James Fenimore Cooper .25 .60
Mark Buehrle .25 .60
Freddy Sanchez .15 .40
Johan Santana .25 .60
Orlando Cabrera .25 .60
Lyle Overbay .15 .40
Clay Buchholz (RC) .60 1.50
Jesse Carlson RC .60 1.50
Troy Tulowitzki .40 1.00
Delmon Young .25 .60
Ross Ohlendorf RC .60 1.50
Mary Shelley .25 .60
James Shields .15 .40
Alfonso Soriano .25 .60
Randy Winn .15 .40
Austin Kearns .15 .40
Jeremy Hermida .15 .40
Jorge Posada .25 .60
Justin Verlander .40 1.00
Bram Stoker .25 .60
Marie Curie .25 .60
Melky Cabrera .15 .40
Howie Kendrick .15 .40
Jake Peavy .15 .40
J.D. Drew .15 .40
2 Pablo Picasso .25 .60
3 Rick Ankiel .15 .40
4 Jose Valverde .15 .40
5 Chipper Jones .40 1.00
6 Claude Monet .25 .60
7 Evan Longoria RC 2.00 5.00
8 Jose Vidro .15 .40
9 Hideki Matsui .40 1.00
0 Ryan Braun .25 .60
1 Moises Alou .15 .40
2 Nate McLouth .15 .40
3 Harriet Tubman .25 .60
4 Felix Hernandez .25 .60
5 Carlos Pena .25 .60
6 Jarrod Saltalamacchia .15 .40
7 Les Miles .25 .60
8 Kelly Johnson .15 .40
9 Rampage Jackson .40 1.00
0 Grady Sizemore .25 .60
1 Francisco Cordero .15 .40
2 Yunel Escobar .15 .40
3 Edwin Encarnacion .40 1.00
4 Melvin Mora .15 .40
5 Russ Martin .15 .40
6 Edgar Renteria .15 .40
7 Bigfoot .40 1.00
8 Steve Holm RC .40 1.00
9 Daric Barton (RC) .40 1.00
0 David Ortiz .40 1.00
1 Tim Lincecum .25 .60
2 Jeff King .25 .60
3 Jhonny Peralta .15 .40
4 Julio Lugo .15 .40
5 J.J. Putz .15 .40
6 Jeff Francoeur .25 .60
7 Yuniesky Betancourt .15 .40
8 Bruce Jenner .25 .60
9 Clete Thomas RC .60 1.50
0 Carlos Lee .15 .40
1 Josh Hamilton .25 .60
2 Pyotr Ilyich Tchaikovsky .25 .60
3 Brendan Harris .15 .40
4 Dustin McGowan .15 .40
5 Aaron Harang .15 .40
6 Brett Myers .15 .40
7 Friedrich Nietzsche .25 .60
8 John Maine .15 .40
9 Charles Dickens .25 .60
0 Erik Bedard .15 .40
1 Tim Hudson .25 .60
2 Jeremy Bonderman .15 .40
3 Nyjer Morgan (RC) .40 1.00
4 Johnny Cueto RC 1.00 2.50
5 Roy Oswalt .25 .60
6 Rich Hill .15 .40
7 Frederick Douglass .25 .60
8 Derek Lowe .15 .40
9 Joe Blanton .15 .40
0 Carlos Beltran .25 .60
1 Huston Street .25 .60
2 Davy Crockett .25 .60
3 Pluto .25 .60
234 Jered Weaver .25 .60
235 Dan Haren .15 .40
236 Alex Gordon .25 .60
237 Zack Greinke .25 .60
238 Todd Clever .25 .60
239 Brian Bannister .15 .40
240 Magglio Ordonez .25 .60
241 Ryan Garko .15 .40
242 Takudzwa Ngwenya .25 .60
243 Gil Meche .15 .40
244 Mark Teahen .15 .40
245 Carlos Guillen .15 .40
246 Jeff Kent .15 .40
247 Lisa Leslie .40 1.00
248 Lastings Milledge .15 .40
249 Serena Williams .50 1.25
250 Ichiro Suzuki .50 1.25
251 Matt Cain .25 .60
252 Callix Crabbe (RC) .40 1.00
253 Nick Blackburn RC .60 1.50
254 Hunter Pence .25 .60
255 Cole Hamels .30 .75
256 Garret Anderson .15 .40
257 Luis Gonzalez .15 .40
258 Eric Chavez .15 .40
259 Francisco Rodriguez .25 .60
260 Mark Teixeira .25 .60
261 Bob Motley .25 .60
262 Mark Spitz .25 .60
263 Yadier Molina .40 1.00
264 Adam Jones .25 .60
265 Brian Roberts .15 .40
266 Matt Kemp .30 .75
267 Andrew Miller .25 .60
268 Dean Karnazes .25 .60
269 Gary Sheffield .15 .40
270 Lance Berkman .25 .60
271 Paul Lo Duca .15 .40
272 Matt Tolbert RC .60 1.50
273 Jay Bruce (RC) 1.25 3.00
274 John Smoltz .40 1.00
275 Nick Markakis .30 .75
276 Oscar Wilde .25 .60
277 Dontrelle Willis .15 .40
278 Kevin Van Dam .25 .60
279 Jim Edmonds .25 .60
280 Brandon Webb .25 .60
281 Joe Nathan .15 .40
282 Jeanette Lee .25 .60
283 Andrew Litz .25 .60
284 Daisuke Matsuzaka .25 .60
285 Brandon Phillips .15 .40
286 Pat Burrell .15 .40
287 Chris Carpenter .25 .60
288 Pete Weber .25 .60
289 Derrek Lee .15 .40
290 Ken Griffey Jr. .75 2.00
291 Rich Thompson RC .60 1.50
292 Elijah Dukes .15 .40
293 Pedro Feliz .15 .40
294 Torii Hunter .15 .40
295 Chone Figgins .15 .40
296 Hideki Okajima .15 .40
297 Max Scherzer RC 5.00 12.00
298 Greg Smith RC .60 1.50
299 Rafael Furcal .15 .40
300 Ryan Howard .25 .60
301 Felix Pie SP 1.25 3.00
302 Brad Lidge SP 1.25 3.00
303 Jason Bay SP 1.25 3.00
304 Victor Hugo SP 1.25 3.00
305 Randy Johnson SP 1.25 3.00
306 Carlos Gomez SP 1.25 3.00
307 Pat Neshek SP 1.25 3.00
308 Jed Lowrie SP (RC) 1.25 3.00
309 Ryan Church SP 1.25 3.00
310 Michael Bourn SP 1.25 3.00
311 B.J. Ryan SP 1.25 3.00
312 Brandon Wood SP 1.25 3.00
313 Harriet Beecher Stowe SP 1.25 3.00
314 Mike Cameron SP 1.25 3.00
315 Tom Glavine SP 1.25 3.00
316 Ervin Santana SP 1.25 3.00
317 Geoff Jenkins SP 1.25 3.00
318 Andre Ethier SP 1.25 3.00
319 Jason Giambi SP 1.25 3.00
320 Dmitri Young SP 1.25 3.00
321 Wily Mo Pena SP 1.25 3.00
322 Hank Blalock SP 1.25 3.00
323 James Bowie SP 1.25 3.00
324 Casey Kotchman SP 1.25 3.00
325 Stephen Drew SP 1.25 3.00
326 Adam Kennedy SP 1.25 3.00
327 A.J. Pierzynski SP 1.25 3.00
328 Richie Sexson SP 1.25 3.00
329 Jeff Clement SP (RC) 1.25 3.00
330 Luke Hochevar SP RC 1.25 3.00
331 Luis Castillo SP 1.25 3.00
332 Dave Roberts SP 1.25 3.00
333 Coco Crisp SP 1.25 3.00
334 Jo-Jo Reyes SP 1.25 3.00
335 Phil Hughes SP 1.25 3.00
336 Allen Fisher SP 1.25 3.00
337 Jason Schmidt SP 1.25 3.00
338 Placido Polanco SP 1.25 3.00
339 Jack Cust SP 1.25 3.00
340 Carl Crawford SP 1.25 3.00
341 Ty Wigginton SP 1.25 3.00
342 Aubrey Huff SP 1.25 3.00
343 Bengie Molina SP 1.25 3.00
344 Matt Diaz SP 1.25 3.00
345 Francisco Liriano SP 1.25 3.00
346 Brandon Boggs SP (RC) 1.25 3.00
347 David DeJesus SP 1.25 3.00
348 Justin Masterson SP RC 1.50 4.00
349 Frank Morris SP 1.25 3.00
350 Kevin Youkilis SP 1.25 3.00
NNO Kosuke Fukudome 10.00 25.00
NNO Framed Original 50.00 100.00

2008 Topps Allen and Ginter Mini

*MINI 1-300: .75X TO 2X BASIC
*MINI 1-300 RC: .5X TO 1.2X BASIC RC's
APPX. ONE MINI PER PACK
*MINI SP 300-350: .75X TO 2X BASIC SP
MINI SP ODDS 1:13 HOBBY
351-390 RANDOM WITHIN RIP CARDS
OVERALL PLATE ODDS 1:961 HOBBY
PLATE PRINT RUN 1 SET PER COLOR
BLACK-CYAN-MAGENTA-YELLOW ISSUED
NO PLATE PRICING DUE TO SCARCITY
351 Prince Fielder EXT 20.00 50.00
352 Justin Upton EXT 20.00 50.00
353 Russell Martin EXT 30.00 60.00
354 Cy Young EXT 15.00 40.00
355 Hanley Ramirez EXT 20.00 50.00
356 Grady Sizemore EXT 10.00 25.00
357 David Ortiz EXT 10.00 25.00
358 Dan Haren EXT 15.00 40.00
359 Honus Wagner EXT 30.00 60.00
360 Albert Pujols EXT 30.00 60.00
361 Hiroki Kuroda EXT 15.00 40.00
362 Evan Longoria EXT 30.00 60.00
363 Tris Speaker EXT 20.00 50.00
364 Josh Hamilton EXT 10.00 25.00
365 Johan Santana EXT 10.00 25.00
366 Derek Jeter EXT 50.00 100.00
367 Jake Peavy EXT 10.00 25.00
368 Troy Glaus EXT 15.00 40.00
369 Nick Swisher EXT 10.00 25.00
370 George Sisler EXT 20.00 50.00
371 Ichiro Suzuki EXT 40.00 80.00
372 Mark Teixeira EXT 20.00 50.00
373 Justin Verlander EXT 15.00 40.00
374 Jackie Robinson EXT 12.00 30.00
375 Vladimir Guerrero EXT 30.00 60.00
376 Delmon Young EXT 10.00 25.00
377 Lou Gehrig EXT 15.00 40.00
378 Tim Lincecum EXT 20.00 50.00
379 Ryan Zimmerman EXT 15.00 40.00
380 David Wright EXT 15.00 40.00
381 Matt Holliday EXT 10.00 25.00
382 Jose Reyes EXT 30.00 60.00
383 Christy Mathewson EXT 30.00 60.00
384 Hunter Pence EXT 20.00 50.00
385 Chase Utley EXT 20.00 50.00
386 Daisuke Matsuzaka EXT 10.00 25.00
387 Miguel Cabrera EXT 15.00 40.00
388 Torii Hunter EXT 15.00 40.00
389 Carlos Zambrano EXT 20.00 50.00
390 Alex Rodriguez EXT 15.00 40.00
391 Victor Martinez EXT 10.00 25.00
392 Justin Morneau EXT 10.00 25.00
393 Carlos Beltran EXT 10.00 25.00
394 Ryan Braun EXT 20.00 50.00
395 Alfonso Soriano EXT 10.00 25.00
396 Joba Chamberlain EXT 12.50 30.00
397 Nick Markakis EXT 20.00 50.00
398 Ty Cobb EXT 15.00 40.00
399 B.J. Upton EXT 10.00 25.00
400 Ryan Howard EXT 20.00 50.00

2008 Topps Allen and Ginter Mini A and G Back

*A & G BACK: 1X TO 2.5X BASIC
*A & G BACK RCs: .6X TO 1.5X BASIC RCs
STATED ODDS 1:5 HOBBY
*A & G BACK SP: 1X TO 2.5X BASIC SP
SP STATED ODDS 1:65 HOBBY

2008 Topps Allen and Ginter Mini Black

*BLACK: 1.5X TO 4X BASIC
*BLACK RCs: .75X TO 2X BASIC RCs
STATED ODDS 1:10 HOBBY
*BLACK SP: 1.2X TO 3X BASIC SP
SP STATED ODDS 1:130 HOBBY

2008 Topps Allen and Ginter Mini No Card Number

*NO NBR: 10X TO 25X BASIC
*NO NBR RCs: 4X TO 10X BASIC RCs
*NO NBR: 1.5X TO 4X BASIC SP
STATED ODDS 1:151 HOBBY
STATED PRINT RUN 50 SETS
CARDS ARE NOT SERIAL-NUMBERED
PRINT RUN INFO PROVIDED BY TOPPS
7 Mickey Mantle 30.00 60.00
16 Hiroki Kuroda 6.00 15.00
22 Chin-Lung Hu 6.00 15.00
39 J.R. Towles 6.00 15.00
72 Clayton Kershaw 8.00 20.00
153 Clay Buchholz 10.00 25.00
177 Evan Longoria 15.00 40.00
224 Johnny Cueto 10.00 25.00
253 Nick Blackburn 6.00 15.00
273 Jay Bruce 10.00 25.00
297 Max Scherzer 6.00 15.00

2008 Topps Allen and Ginter Autographs

GROUP A ODDS 1:277 HOBBY
GROUP B ODDS 1:256 HOBBY
GROUP C ODDS 1:135 HOBBY
GRP A PRINT RUNS B/W 90-240 COPIES PER
CARDS ARE NOT SERIAL-NUMBERED
PRINT RUNS PROVIDED BY TOPPS
EXCHANGE DEADLINE 7/31/2010
AE Andre Ethier C 6.00 15.00
AF Andrea Farina A/190 * 15.00 40.00
AFI Allen Fisher A/190 * 6.00 15.00
AIR Alex Rios B 6.00 15.00
AL Andrew Litz A/190 * 15.00 40.00
AM Adriano Moraes A/190 * EXCH 15.00 40.00
BB Bonnie Blair A/190 * 10.00 25.00
BJ Bruce Jenner A/190 * 15.00 40.00
BM Bob Motley A/190 * 30.00 60.00
BP Brad Penny A/240 * 12.50 30.00
BPB Brian Bannister C 5.00 12.00
BPM Billy Mitchell A/190 * 20.00 50.00
CB Clay Buchholz B 6.00 25.00
CC Carl Crawford A/240 * 6.00 15.00
CG Curtis Granderson B 6.00 15.00
DB Murray Campbell A/190 * 50.00 100.00
DJ Dan Jansen A/190 * 12.50 30.00
DK Dean Karnazes A/190 * 20.00 50.00
DO David Ortiz A/90 * 30.00 60.00
DW David Wright A/240 * 20.00 50.00
ES Ervin Santana C 5.00 12.00
FC Francisco Cordero C EXCH 5.00 12.00
FCC Fausto Carmona C 5.00 12.00
FM Frank Morris A/190 * 10.00 25.00
GJ Geoff Jenkins B 5.00 12.00
HP Hunter Pence A/90 * 30.00 60.00
HR Hanley Ramirez A/240 * 12.50 30.00
IK Ian Kinsler C 6.00 15.00
JBF Jeff Francoeur C 6.00 15.00
JC Joba Chamberlain B 6.00 25.00
JF Jeff Francis B 5.00 12.00
JJC Joey Chestnut A/190 * 20.00 50.00
JK Jeff King A/190 * EXCH 12.50 30.00
JL Jeanette Lee A/190 * 40.00 80.00
JR Jose Reyes A/90 * 25.00 60.00
JS Jarrod Saltalamacchia C 5.00 12.00
KS Kerri Strug A/190 * 30.00 60.00
KVD Kevin Van Dam A/190 * 20.00 50.00
LL Lisa Leslie A/190 * 12.50 30.00
LM Les Miles A/190 * 15.00 40.00
MB Matt Biondi A/190 * 20.00 50.00
MK Matt Kemp B 8.00 20.00
MR Manny Ramirez A/90 * 50.00 100.00
MS Mark Spitz A/190 * 10.00 25.00
MTH Matt Holliday A/90 * 30.00 60.00
NH Nicky Hayden A/240 * 20.00 50.00
NM Nick Markakis B 5.00 12.00
OH Orlando Hudson B 5.00 12.00
PF Prince Fielder A/90 * 40.00 100.00
PW Pete Weber A/190 * 12.50 30.00
RH Ryan Howard A/90 * 40.00 80.00
RJ Rampage Jackson A/190 * 60.00 120.00
SJW Serena Williams A/190 * 75.00 150.00
SW Stevie Williams A/240 * 10.00 25.00
TC Todd Clever A/190 * 4.00 10.00
TH Torii Hunter A/240 * 8.00 20.00
TLH Travis Hafner A/240 * 10.00 25.00
TN Takudzwa Ngwenya A/190 * 12.50 30.00

2008 Topps Allen and Ginter Cabinet Boxloader

STATED ODDS 1:3 HOBBY BOXES
BH1 Matt Holliday/Jamey Carroll/Michael Barrett/Brian Giles 3.00 8.00
BH2 Lowell/Manny/Papel/Beckett 4.00 10.00
BH3 Howard /Rollins/Utley/Hamels 4.00 10.00
BH4 ARod/Big Hurt/Thome 5.00 12.00
BH5 Verlan/Buehrle/Buchholz 4.00 10.00
HB1 General George Washington/General Nathanael Greene 3.00 8.00
HB2 General Horatio Gates General John Burgoyne 3.00 8.00
HB3 General George Meade General Robert E. Lee 3.00 8.00
HB4 Lt. Col. William B. Travis/Colonel James Bowie/Colonel Davy Crockett/Genera 3.00 8.00
HB5 General Dwight Eisenhower/Field Marshal Bernard Montgomery 3.00 8.00

2008 Topps Allen and Ginter Cabinet Boxloader Autograph

STATED ODDS 1:322 HOBBY BOXES
STATED PRINT RUN 200 SER.#'d SETS
BF Bigfoot 30.00 60.00

2008 Topps Allen and Ginter Mini Ancient Icons

COMPLETE SET (20) 60.00 120.00
STATED ODDS 1:48 HOBBY
A1 Gilgamesh 3.00 8.00
A2 Marduk 3.00 8.00
A3 Beowulf 3.00 8.00
A4 Poseidon 3.00 8.00
A5 The Sphinx 3.00 8.00
A6 Tutankhamen 3.00 8.00
A7 Alexander the Great 3.00 8.00
A8 Cleopatra 3.00 8.00
A9 Sun Tzu 3.00 8.00
A10 Quetzalcoatl 3.00 8.00
A11 Isis 3.00 8.00
A12 Hercules 3.00 8.00
A13 King Arthur 3.00 8.00
A14 Miyamoto Musashi 3.00 8.00
A15 Genghis Khan 3.00 8.00
A16 Zeus 3.00 8.00
A17 Achilles 3.00 8.00
A18 Confucius 3.00 8.00
A19 Attila the Hun 3.00 8.00
A20 Romulus and Remus 3.00 8.00

2008 Topps Allen and Ginter Mini Baseball Icons

COMPLETE SET (17) 20.00 50.00
STATED ODDS 1:48 HOBBY
BI1 Cy Young 4.00 10.00
BI2 Walter Johnson 4.00 10.00
BI3 Jackie Robinson 5.00 12.00
BI4 Thurman Munson 4.00 10.00
BI5 Mel Ott 3.00 8.00
BI6 Honus Wagner 4.00 10.00
BI7 Pee Wee Reese 3.00 8.00
BI8 Tris Speaker 3.00 8.00
BI9 Christy Mathewson 4.00 10.00
BI10 Ty Cobb 4.00 10.00
BI11 Johnny Mize 3.00 8.00
BI12 Jimmie Foxx 4.00 10.00
BI13 Lou Gehrig 5.00 12.00
BI14 Roy Campanella 3.00 8.00
BI15 George Sisler 3.00 8.00
BI16 Rogers Hornsby 3.00 8.00
BI17 Babe Ruth 8.00 20.00

2008 Topps Allen and Ginter Mini Pioneers of Aviation

COMPLETE SET (5) 15.00 40.00
STATED ODDS 1:XX
PA1 Ornithopter 4.00 10.00
PA2 Linen Balloon 4.00 10.00
PA3 Piloted Glider 4.00 10.00
PA4 Aerial Steam Carriage 4.00 10.00
PA5 Aerodrome 4.00 10.00

2008 Topps Allen and Ginter Mini Team Orange

COMPLETE SET (10) 50.00 100.00
STATED ODDS 1:144 HOBBY
TQ1 Cornelius Franks 4.00 10.00
TO2 Mittens McCluskey 4.00 10.00
TO3 Capt. W.P. Mantooth 4.00 10.00
TO4 Wheelbarrow Walker 4.00 10.00
TO5 Archibald Clinker 4.00 10.00
TO6 Minty Beans 4.00 10.00
TO7 Francisco Fiasco 4.00 10.00
TO8 Thurgood Cartwright IV 4.00 10.00
TO9 Enzo DiStubbs 4.00 10.00
TO10 Sir Wagonwheel Stevens 4.00 10.00

2008 Topps Allen and Ginter Mini World's Deadliest Sharks

COMPLETE SET (5) 20.00 50.00
STATED ODDS 1:XX
WDS1 Great White Shark 5.00 12.00
WDS2 Tiger Shark 5.00 12.00
WDS3 Bull Shark 5.00 12.00
WDS4 Oceanic Whitetip Shark 5.00 12.00
WDS5 Mako Shark 5.00 12.00

2008 Topps Allen and Ginter Mini World Leaders

COMPLETE SET (50) 30.00 60.00
STATED ODDS 1:12 HOBBY
WL1 Cristina Fernandez de Kirchner 1.50 4.00
WL2 Kevin Rudd 1.50 4.00
WL3 Guy Verhofstadt 1.50 4.00
WL4 Luiz Inacio Lula da Silva 1.50 4.00
WL5 Stephen Harper 1.50 4.00
WL6 Michelle Bachelet Jeria 1.50 4.00
WL7 Oscar Arias Sanchez 1.50 4.00
WL8 Mirek Topolanek 1.50 4.00
WL9 Anders Fogh Rasmussen 1.50 4.00
WL10 Leonel Fernandez Reyna 1.50 4.00
WL11 Mohamed Hosni Mubarak 1.50 4.00
WL12 Tarja Halonen 1.50 4.00
WL13 Nicolas Sarkozy 1.50 4.00
WL14 Yahya A.J.J. Jammeh 1.50 4.00
WL15 Angela Merkel 1.50 4.00
WL16 Konstandinos Karamanlis 1.50 4.00
WL17 Benedict XVI 2.00 5.00
WL18 Geir H. Haarde 1.50 4.00
WL19 Manmohan Singh 1.50 4.00
WL20 Susilo Bambang Yudhoyono 1.50 4.00
WL21 Bertie Ahern 1.50 4.00
WL22 Ehud Olmert 1.50 4.00
WL23 Bruce Golding 1.50 4.00
WL24 Yasuo Fukuda 1.50 4.00
WL25 Mwai Kibaki 1.50 4.00
WL26 Felipe de Jesus Calderon Hinojosa 1.50 4.00
WL27 Sanjaa Bayar 1.50 4.00
WL28 Armando Guebuza 1.50 4.00
WL29 Girija Prasad Koirala 1.50 4.00
WL30 Jan Peter Balkenende 1.50 4.00
WL31 Helen Clark 1.50 4.00
WL32 Jens Stoltenberg 1.50 4.00
WL33 Qaboos bin Said al-Said 1.50 4.00
WL34 Alan Garcia Perez 1.50 4.00
WL35 Gloria Macapagal-Arroyo 1.50 4.00
WL36 Donald Tusk 1.50 4.00
WL37 Vladimir Vladimirovich Putin 2.50 6.00
WL38 Robert Fico 1.50 4.00
WL39 Thabo Mbeki 1.50 4.00
WL40 Lee Myung-bak 1.50 4.00
WL41 Jose Luis Rodriguez Zapatero 1.50 4.00
WL42 Fredrik Reinfeldt 1.50 4.00
WL43 Pascal Couchepin 1.50 4.00
WL44 Jakaya Kikwete 1.50 4.00
WL45 Samak Sundaravej 1.50 4.00
WL46 Tenzin Gyatso 1.50 4.00
WL47 Patrick Manning 1.50 4.00
WL48 Gordon Brown 2.50 6.00
WL49 George W. Bush 3.00 8.00
WL50 Nguyen Tan Dung 1.50 4.00

2008 Topps Allen and Ginter N43

STATED ODDS 1:3 HOBBY BOXES
CG Curtis Granderson 2.00 5.00
CU Chase Utley 2.00 5.00
DO David Ortiz 3.00 8.00
DW David Wright 2.00 5.00
HR Hanley Ramirez 2.00 5.00
IS Ichiro Suzuki 4.00 10.00
JC Joba Chamberlain 1.25 3.00
JR Jose Reyes 2.00 5.00
MH Matt Holliday 3.00 8.00
MR Manny Ramirez 3.00 8.00
PF Prince Fielder 2.00 5.00
RB Ryan Braun 2.00 5.00
RH Ryan Howard 2.00 5.00
RZ Ryan Zimmerman 2.00 5.00
VG Vladimir Guerrero 2.00 5.00

2008 Topps Allen and Ginter N43 Autographs

STATED PRINT RUN 15 SER.#'d SETS
STATED ODDS 1:428 HOBBY BOXES
NO PRICING DUE TO SCARCITY
EXCHANGE DEADLINE 7/31/2010

2008 Topps Allen and Ginter National Convention

COMPLETE SET (7) 8.00 20.00
1 Babe Ruth 3.00 8.00
2 Lou Gerhig 2.50 6.00
3 Jackie Robinson 1.25 3.00
4 Don Larsen .50 1.25
5 Johnny Unitas 2.50 6.00
6 Roger Maris 1.25 3.00
7 Mickey Mantle 4.00 10.00

2008 Topps Allen and Ginter Relics

GROUP A ODDS 1:280 HOBBY
GROUP B ODDS 1:71 HOBBY
GROUP C ODDS 1:20 HOBBY
RELIC AU ODDS 1:26,431 HOBBY
GROUP A B/W 100-250 COPIES PER
CARDS ARE NOT SERIAL NUMBERED
PRINT RUN INFO PROVIDED BY TOPPS
AD1 Adam Dunn Jsy 3.00 8.00
AD2 Adam Dunn Bat 3.00 8.00
AER Alex Rodriguez Bat A 10.00 25.00
AF Andrea Farina A/250 * 5.00 12.00
AFI Allen Fisher A/250 * 8.00 20.00
AIR Alex Rios Bat B 3.00 8.00
AJP A.J. Pierzynski Jsy C 3.00 8.00
AK Austin Kearns Bat B 3.00 8.00
AL Andrew Litz A/250 * 8.00 20.00
AM Archie Moore A/100 * 15.00 40.00
AP1 Albert Pujols Jsy 6.00 15.00
AP2 Albert Pujols Bat 10.00 25.00
APB Aaron Pryor A/100 * 30.00 60.00
AR Aramis Ramirez Jsy B 3.00 8.00
ASM Adriano Moraes A/250 * 5.00 12.00
ATK Adam Kennedy Jsy C 3.00 8.00
AW Andre Ward A/100 * 15.00 40.00
BA Bobby Abreu Bat B 3.00 8.00
BB Bonnie Blair A/250 * 10.00 25.00
BC Bobby Crosby Jsy C 3.00 8.00
BF Bigfoot A/250 * 30.00 60.00
BH Brad Hawpe Jsy C 3.00 8.00
BJ Bruce Jenner A/250 * 6.00 15.00
BM Billy Mitchell A/250 * 12.00 30.00
BMM Brian McCann Jsy C 3.00 8.00
BR1 Brian Roberts Jsy 3.00 8.00
BR2 Brian Roberts Bat 3.00 8.00
CAM Carlos Marmol Jsy C 3.00 8.00
CC1 Carl Crawford Jsy 3.00 8.00
CC2 Carl Crawford Bat 3.00 8.00
CG Curtis Granderson Jsy C 3.00 8.00
CJ Chipper Jones Jsy C 4.00 10.00
CK Casey Kotchman Jsy B 3.00 8.00
CS Curt Schilling Jsy B 3.00 8.00
CU Chase Utley Jsy C 4.00 10.00
CZ Carlos Zambrano Jsy C 3.00 8.00
DG Danny Green A/100 * 30.00 60.00
DJ Dan Jansen A/250 * 8.00 20.00
DK Dean Karnazes A/250 * 12.50 30.00
DM Daisuke Matsuzaka Jsy A 6.00 15.00
DO1 David Ortiz Jsy 4.00 10.00
DO2 David Ortiz Bat 4.00 10.00
DRY Delwyn Young Jsy C 3.00 8.00

DW David Wright Jsy C 6.00 15.00
DY Dmitri Young Bat B 3.00 8.00
EC Eric Chavez Jsy A 3.00 8.00
EM Edison Miranda A/100 * 15.00 40.00
ER Edgar Renteria Bat B 3.00 8.00
FM Frank Morris A/250 * 6.00 15.00
GA Garret Anderson Jsy C 3.00 8.00
HB Hank Blalock Jsy B 3.00 8.00
IR1 Ivan Rodriguez Jsy B 3.00 8.00
IR2 Ivan Rodriguez Bat B 3.00 8.00
IS Ichiro Suzuki Jsy C 6.00 15.00
JB Jason Bay Jsy C 4.00 10.00
JC Joey Chestnut A/250 * 3.00 8.00
JCJ Joel Casamayor A/100 * 30.00 60.00
JD J.D. Drew Bat B 3.00 8.00
JDD Johnny Damon Bat C 3.00 8.00
JF Jeff Francoeur Jsy C 3.00 8.00
JFB Jeff Fenech A/100 * 15.00 40.00
JG Jay Gibbons Bat B 3.00 8.00
JJH J.J. Hardy Jsy C 3.00 8.00
JK Jeff Kent Bat B 3.00 8.00
JKI Jeff King A/250 * 10.00 25.00
JL Jeanette Lee A/250 * 30.00 60.00
JM Joe Mauer Jsy C 4.00 10.00
JS John Smoltz Jsy C 3.00 8.00
JT Jim Thome Jsy C 4.00 10.00
JTD Jermaine Dye Jsy C 3.00 8.00
JV1 Jason Varitek Bat 4.00 10.00
JV2 Jason Varitek Jsy 4.00 10.00
KP Kelly Pavlik A/100 * 40.00 80.00
KS Kerri Strug A/250 * 15.00 40.00
KVD Kevin Van Dam A/250 * 10.00 25.00
LB Lance Berkman Jsy C 3.00 8.00
LL Lisa Leslie A/250 * 12.50 30.00
LM Les Miles A/250 * 10.00 25.00
MB Matt Biondi A/250 * 8.00 20.00
MC Melky Cabrera Jsy C 3.00 8.00
MDC Matt Capps Jsy C 3.00 8.00
MH Mike Hampton Jsy C 3.00 8.00
MH Marcus Henderson AU/100 * 60.00 120.00
MK Matt Kemp Jsy C 3.00 8.00
MR Manny Ramirez Jsy C 4.00 10.00
MS Mark Spitz A/250 * 12.50 30.00
MT Mark Teixeira Jsy C 3.00 8.00
MY Michael Young Jsy C 3.00 8.00
NH Nicky Hayden A/250 * 10.00 25.00
PF Prince Fielder Bat B 3.00 8.00
PK Paul Konerko Jsy C 3.00 8.00
PL Paul Lo Duca Bat B 3.00 8.00
PW Pete Weber A/250 * 8.00 20.00
RF Rafael Furcal Bat B 3.00 8.00
RH Ryan Howard Jsy C 3.00 8.00
RJ Rampage Jackson A/250 * 15.00 40.00
RM Ray Mancini A/100 * 40.00 80.00
RO Roy Oswalt Jsy C 3.00 8.00
RS Richie Sexson Jsy C 3.00 8.00
SD Stephen Drew Jsy B 3.00 8.00
SJW Serena Williams A/250 * 12.50 30.00
SP Samuel Peter A/100 * 20.00 50.00
SW Stevie Williams A/250 * 8.00 20.00
TC Todd Clever A/250 * 10.00 25.00
TG Tom Glavine Jsy C 3.00 8.00
TH Tim Hudson Jsy C 3.00 8.00
TLH Todd Helton Jsy C 3.00 8.00
TN Takudzwa Ngwenya A/250 * 8.00 20.00
TPH Travis Hafner Jsy C 3.00 8.00
TSG Tom Gorzelanny Jsy C 3.00 8.00
TT Troy Tulowitzki Jsy C 3.00 8.00
VG Vladimir Guerrero Bat B 3.00 8.00
VM Victor Martinez Jsy C 3.00 8.00
WMP Wily Mo Pena Bat B 3.00 8.00

2008 Topps Allen and Ginter Rip Cards

STATED ODDS 1:189 HOBBY
PRINT RUNS B/WN 10-99 COPIES PER
NO PRICING ON QTY 10 OR LESS
ALL LISTED PRICED ARE FOR RIPPED
UNRIPPED HAVE ADD'L CARDS WITHIN
COMMON UNRIPPED p/r 99 50.00 120.00
COMMON UNRIPPED p/r 75 60.00 150.00
COMMON UNRIPPED p/r 50 75.00 200.00
COMMON UNRIPPED p/r 28 100.00 250.00
RC1 Erik Bedard/99 6.00 15.00
RC2 Jacoby Ellsbury/75 10.00 25.00
RC3 Chris Carpenter/99 6.00 15.00
RC4 Brandon Phillips/99 6.00 15.00
RC5 Daric Barton/99 6.00 15.00
RC6 Brian McCann/99 6.00 15.00
RC7 Mickey Mantle/10
RC8 Dan Uggla/75 6.00 15.00
RC9 James Loney/99 10.00 25.00
RC10 James Shields/99 6.00 15.00
RC11 Curtis Granderson/75 10.00 25.00
RC12 Jason Bay/99 6.00 15.00
RC13 Alex Gordon/75 10.00 25.00
RC14 Travis Hafner/99 6.00 15.00
RC15 Derek Jeter/28
RC16 Pedro Feliz/99 6.00 15.00
RC17 Thurman Munson/50 10.00 25.00
RC18 Grady Sizemore/75 10.00 25.00
RC19 Alex Rios/99 6.00 15.00
RC20 David Ortiz/50 10.00 25.00
RC21 Walter Johnson/28
RC22 Scott Rolen/99 10.00 25.00
RC23 John Smoltz/99 10.00 25.00
RC24 Mel Ott/28
RC25 Ryan Howard/50 10.00 25.00
RC26 Hiroki Kuroda/99 10.00 25.00
RC27 Johnny Damon/99 6.00 15.00
RC28 Jose Reyes/75 10.00 25.00
RC29 Felix Hernandez/99 10.00 25.00
RC30 John Lackey/99 6.00 15.00
RC31 Albert Pujols/10
RC32 Mark Teixeira/99 10.00 25.00
RC33 Jim Edmonds/99 6.00 15.00
RC34 Prince Fielder/50 10.00 25.00
RC35 Brian Bannister/99 6.00 15.00
RC36 Chipper Jones/50 10.00 25.00
RC37 Edgar Renteria/99 6.00 15.00
RC38 Roy Campanella/50 10.00 25.00
RC39 Troy Tulowitzki/99 10.00 25.00
RC40 Adam LaRoche/99 6.00 15.00
RC41 Phil Hughes/99 10.00 25.00
RC42 Pee Wee Reese/50 10.00 25.00
RC43 Adam Jones/99 6.00 15.00
RC44 Huston Street/99 6.00 15.00
RC45 Cliff Lee/99 6.00 15.00
RC46 Delmon Young/99 10.00 25.00
RC47 Joe Mauer/99 10.00 25.00
RC48 Johan Santana/28
RC49 Dmitri Young/99 6.00 15.00
RC50 Todd Helton/99 10.00 25.00
RC51 Carlos Beltran/75 10.00 25.00
RC52 J.J. Putz/99 6.00 15.00
RC53 Carlos Lee/99 6.00 15.00
RC54 Billy Butler/99 6.00 15.00
RC55 Miguel Cabrera/99 10.00 25.00
RC56 Derrek Lee/99 6.00 15.00
RC57 Alfonso Soriano/75 10.00 25.00
RC58 Cole Hamels/99 10.00 25.00
RC59 Hanley Ramirez/75 10.00 25.00
RC60 Adrian Gonzalez/99 6.00 15.00
RC61 B.J. Upton/99 6.00 15.00
RC62 Tim Lincecum/75 10.00 25.00
RC63 Gary Matthews/99 6.00 15.00
RC64 Justin Upton/75 10.00 25.00
RC65 Zack Greinke/99 6.00 15.00
RC66 Roy Oswalt/75 6.00 15.00
RC67 Jimmy Rollins/28
RC68 Miguel Tejada/99 6.00 15.00
RC69 Clay Buchholz/99 10.00 25.00
RC70 Andruw Jones/99 6.00 15.00
RC71 Chase Utley/75 10.00 25.00
RC72 Aaron Rowand/99 6.00 15.00
RC73 Johnny Mize/50 10.00 25.00
RC74 Jonathan Papelbon/75 10.00 25.00
RC75 Jarrod Saltalamacchia/99 6.00 15.00
RC76 Lance Berkman/50 6.00 15.00
RC77 Vernon Wells/99 6.00 15.00
RC78 Dontrelle Willis/99 6.00 15.00
RC79 Jim Thome/99 10.00 25.00
RC80 Torii Hunter/99 6.00 15.00
RC81 Russ Martin/75 6.00 15.00
RC82 Jake Peavy/99 10.00 25.00
RC83 Carlos Zambrano/99 6.00 15.00
RC84 Troy Glaus/99 6.00 15.00
RC85 Ryan Zimmerman/75 10.00 25.00
RC86 Evan Longoria/75 10.00 25.00
RC87 Yovani Gallardo/99 6.00 15.00
RC88 Jimmie Foxx/10
RC89 Josh Hamilton/75 10.00 25.00
RC90 Matt Holliday/50 10.00 25.00
RC91 Matt Cain/99 6.00 15.00
RC92 Francisco Cordero/99 6.00 15.00
RC93 Derek Lowe/99 6.00 15.00
RC94 Brandon Webb/75 6.00 15.00
RC95 Carlos Pena/99 6.00 15.00
RC96 Ichiro Suzuki/10
RC97 Khalil Greene/99 10.00 25.00
RC98 Rogers Hornsby/10
RC99 C.C. Sabathia/75 6.00 15.00
RC100 Victor Martinez/99 6.00 15.00

2008 Topps Allen and Ginter United States

COMPLETE SET (50) 10.00 25.00
STATED ODDS 1:XX
US1 Alex Rios .25 .60
US2 Curt Schilling .40 1.00
US3 Brian Bannister .25 .60
US4 Torii Hunter .25 .60
US5 Chase Utley .40 1.00
US6 Roy Halladay .40 1.00
US7 Brad Ausmus .25 .60
US8 Ian Snell .25 .60
US9 Lastings Milledge .25 .60
US10 Nick Markakis .50 1.25
US11 Shane Victorino .25 .60
US12 Jason Schmidt .25 .60
US13 Curtis Granderson .40 1.00
US14 Scott Rolen .40 1.00
US15 Casey Blake .25 .60
US16 Nate Robertson .25 .60
US17 Brandon Webb .40 1.00
US18 Jonathan Papelbon .40 1.00
US19 Tim Stauffer .25 .60
US20 Mark Teixeira .40 1.00
US21 Chris Capuano .25 .60
US22 Jason Varitek .60 1.50
US23 Joe Mauer .50 1.25
US24 Dmitri Young .25 .60
US25 Ryan Howard .40 1.00
US26 Taylor Tankersley .25 .60
US27 Alex Gordon .40 1.00
US28 Barry Zito .40 1.00
US29 Chris Carpenter .40 1.00
US30 Derek Jeter 1.50 4.00
US31 Cody Ross .25 .60
US32 Alex Rodriguez .75 2.00
US33 Ryan Zimmerman .40 1.00
US34 Travis Hafner .25 .60
US35 Nick Swisher .40 1.00
US36 Matt Holliday .60 1.50
US37 Jacoby Ellsbury .50 1.25
US38 Ken Griffey Jr. 1.25 3.00
US39 Paul Konerko .40 1.00
US40 Orlando Hudson .25 .60
US41 Mark Ellis .25 .60
US42 Todd Helton .40 1.00
US43 Adam Dunn .40 1.00
US44 Brandon Lyon .25 .60
US45 Daric Barton .25 .60
US46 David Wright .40 1.00
US47 Grady Sizemore .40 1.00
US48 Seth McClung .25 .60
US49 Pat Neshek .40 1.00
US50 John Buck .25 .60

2008 Topps Allen and Ginter World's Greatest Victories

COMPLETE SET (20) 30.00 60.00
STATED ODDS 1:24 HOBBY
WGV1 Kerri Strug 2.50 6.00
WGV2 Mark Spitz 2.50 6.00
WGV3 Jonas Salk 2.00 5.00
WGV4 Man Walks on the Moon 2.00 5.00
WGV5 Jon Lester 3.00 8.00
WGV6 The Fall of the Berlin Wall 2.00 5.00
WGV7 David and Goliath 2.00 5.00
WGV8 Gary Carter and the '86 Mets 2.50 6.00
WGV9 The Battle of Gettysburg 2.00 5.00
WGV10 Deep Blue 2.00 5.00
WGV11 The Allied Forces 2.00 5.00
WGV12 Don Larsen 2.50 6.00
WGV13 Truman Defeats Dewey 2.00 5.00
WGV14 The American Revolution 2.00 5.00
WGV15 2004 ALCS 3.00 8.00
WGV16 The Battle of Thermopylae 2.00 5.00
WGV17 Brown v. Board of Education 2.00 5.00
WGV18 Team Orange 2.50 6.00
WGV19 Bill Mazeroski 2.50 6.00
WGV20 Cinderella 2.00 5.00

2009 Topps Allen and Ginter

COMPLETE SET (350) 30.00 60.00
COMP.SET w/o SP's (300) 12.50 30.00
COMMON CARD (1-300) .15 .40
COMMON RC (1-300) .40 1.00
COMMON SP (301-350) 1.25 3.00
SP STATED ODDS 1:2 HOBBY
1 Jay Bruce .25 .60
2 Zack Greinke .25 .60
3 Manny Parra .15 .40
4 Jorge Posada .25 .60
5 Luke Hochevar .15 .40
6 Adam Eaton .15 .40
7 John Smoltz .40 1.00
8 Matt Cain .25 .60
9 Ryan Theriot .15 .40
10 Chone Figgins .15 .40
11 Jacoby Ellsbury .30 .75
12 Jermaine Dye .15 .40
13 Travis Hafner .15 .40
14 Troy Tulowitzki .40 1.00
15 Alfred Nobel .15 .40
16 Josh Johnson .25 .60
17 Manny Ramirez .40 1.00
18 Clyde Parris .40 1.00
19 Mike Pelfrey .15 .40
20 Adam Jones .25 .60
21 Robinson Cano .25 .60
22 Mariano Rivera .50 1.25
23 Kristin Armstrong .15 .40
24 Steve Wiebe .15 .40
25 Evan Longoria .25 .60
26 Charles Goodyear .15 .40
27 Chien-Ming Wang .25 .60
28 Ervin Santana .15 .40
29 Jonathan Papelbon .25 .60
30 Ryan Howard .30 .75
31 Nick Markakis .30 .75
32 Jeremy Bonderman .15 .40
33 Florence Nightingale .15 .40
34 Ryan Dempster .15 .40
35 Geovany Soto .25 .60
36 Joba Chamberlain .15 .40
37 Andre Ethier .25 .60
38 Troy Glaus .15 .40
39 Hanley Ramirez .25 .60
40 Jeremy Hermida .15 .40
41 Victor Martinez .25 .60
42 Mark Buehrle .25 .60
43 Koji Uehara RC 1.00 2.50
44 Freddy Sanchez .15 .40
45 Derrek Lee .15 .40
46 Brian Roberts .15 .40
47 J.J. Hardy .15 .40
48 Brigham Young .15 .40
49 Ubaldo Jimenez .15 .40
50 Pat Neshek .25 .60
51 Ryan Perry RC 1.00 2.50
52 Aaron Hill .15 .40
53 Clayton Kershaw .75 2.00
54 Carlos Guillen .15 .40
55 Alex Rios .15 .40
56 Daniel Murphy RC 1.50 4.00
57 Frank Evans .25 .60
58 Brad Hawpe .15 .40
59 Mark Reynolds .15 .40
60 Matt Holliday .40 1.00
61 Burke Kenny .15 .40
62 Dan Uggla .15 .40
63 Andrew Miller .25 .60
64 Jordan Zimmermann RC 1.00 2.50
65 Dexter Fowler (RC) .60 1.50
66 Alex Rodriguez .50 1.25
67 Ian Kinsler .25 .60
68 Jamie Moyer .15 .40
69 James Loney .15 .40
70 Rick Ankiel .15 .40
71 Albert Pujols .50 1.25
72 Carlos Lee .15 .40
73 Vernon Wells .15 .40
74 Matt Tuiasosopo (RC) .40 1.00
75 David Wright .30 .75
76 Brandon Phillips .15 .40
77 Francisco Liriano .15 .40
78 Eric Byrnes .15 .40
79 Electron .15 .40
80 Joe Martinez RC .60 1.50
81 Willie Williams .40 1.00
82 Justin Verlander .40 1.00
83 Ludwig van Beethoven .15 .40
84 Justin Upton .25 .60
85 Jason Jaramillo (RC) .40 1.00
86 Michael Cuddyer .15 .40
87 Aaron Cook .15 .40
88 Brad Penny .15 .40
89 Elvis Andrus RC 1.00 2.50
90 Bobby Crosby .15 .40
91 Alex Gordon .25 .60
92 Joe Mauer .30 .75
93 David DeJesus .15 .40
94 Paul Maholm .15 .40
95 David Patton RC .60 1.50
96 Geronimo .15 .40
97 Art Pennington .40 1.00
98 Josh Whitesell RC .60 1.50
99 Chris Duncan .15 .40
100 Ichiro Suzuki .50 1.25
101 Andrew Bailey RC 1.00 2.50
102 Edinson Volquez .15 .40
103 Aaron Harang .15 .40
104 Jeff Francoeur .25 .60
105 Kurt Suzuki .15 .40
106 Mike Jacobs .15 .40
107 Bryan Berg .15 .40
108 Alamo .15 .40
109 Samuel Morse .15 .40
110 Kevin Youkilis .15 .40
111 Jason Giambi .15 .40
112 Millito Navarro .40 1.00
113 Rafael Furcal .15 .40
114 Hideki Matsui .40 1.00
115 Ryan Doumit .15 .40
116 Charles Darwin .15 .40
117 Blake DeWitt .15 .40
118 Scott Olsen .15 .40
119 Scott Lewis (RC) .40 1.00
120 Edwin Moreno (RC) .40 1.00
121 Ryan Church .15 .40
122 Dontrelle Willis .15 .40
123 Barry Zito .25 .60
124 Donald Veal RC .60 1.50
125 Randy Johnson .40 1.00
126 Trevor Crowe RC .40 1.00
127 J.D. Drew .15 .40
128 Red Moore .40 1.00
129 Brian Giles .15 .40
130 Johnny Damon .25 .60
131 Rickie Weeks .15 .40
132 Anna Tunnicliffe .15 .40
133 Roy Halladay .25 .60
134 Jered Weaver .25 .60
135 Jeff Suppan .15 .40
136 Mickey Mantle 1.25 3.00
137 Mark Teixeira .25 .60
138 Garrett Atkins .15 .40
139 Daisuke Matsuzaka .25 .60
140 Loren Opstedahl .40 1.00
141 Carlos Zambrano .25 .60
142 LaShawn Merritt .15 .40
143 Robbie Maddison .15 .40
144 Joakim Soria .15 .40
145 Todd Wellemeyer .15 .40
146 Rich Harden .15 .40
147 Coco Crisp .15 .40
148 Brad Lidge .15 .40
149 Chipper Jones .40 1.00
150 Prince Fielder .25 .60
151 Cole Hamels .30 .75
152 Phil Coke RC .60 1.50
153 CC Sabathia .25 .60
154 Corey Hart .15 .40
155 Yadier Molina .40 1.00
156 Jayson Werth .25 .60
157 Jason Motte (RC) .60 1.50
158 Sigmund Freud .15 .40
159 Denard Span .15 .40
160 Max Scherzer .40 1.00
161 Justin Morneau .25 .60
162 Shane Victorino .15 .40
163 Matt Garza .15 .40
164 Erik Bedard .15 .40
165 Chase Utley .25 .60
166 Gil Meche .15 .40
167 Jim Thome .25 .60
168 Adrian Gonzalez .30 .75
169 Kazuo Matsui .15 .40
170 Lance Berkman .25 .60
171 Brett Anderson RC .60 1.50
172 Jarrod Saltalamacchia .15 .40
173 Francisco Rodriguez .25 .60
174 John Lannan .15 .40
175 Alfonso Soriano .25 .60
176 Ramiro Pena RC .60 1.50
177 David Freese RC 1.25 3.00
178 Adam LaRoche .15 .40
179 Trevor Hoffman .25 .60
180 Russell Martin .15 .40
181 Aaron Rowand .15 .40
182 Jose Reyes .25 .60
183 Pedro Feliz .15 .40
184 Chris Young .15 .40
185 Dustin Pedroia .30 .75
186 Adrian Beltre .40 1.00
187 Brett Myers .15 .40
188 Chris Davis .25 .60
189 Casey Kotchman .15 .40
190 B.J. Upton .25 .60
191 Hiroki Kuroda .15 .40
192 Ryan Zimmerman .25 .60
193 Khalil Greene .15 .40
194 Brandon Morrow .15 .40
195 Kevin Kouzmanoff .15 .40
196 Joey Votto .40 1.00
197 Jhonny Peralta .15 .40
198 Raul Ibanez .25 .60
199 James McDonald RC 1.00 2.50
200 Carlos Quentin .15 .40
201 Travis Snider RC .60 1.50
202 Conor Jackson .15 .40
203 Scott Kazmir .15 .40
204 Casey Blake .15 .40
205 Ryan Braun .25 .60
206 Miguel Tejada .25 .60
207 Jack Cust .15 .40
208 Michael Young .15 .40
209 St. Patrick's Cathedral .15 .40
210 Johan Santana .25 .60
211 Kevin Millwood .15 .40
212 Mariel Zagunis .15 .40
213 Stephanie Brown Trafton .15 .40
214 Adam Dunn .25 .60
215 Jed Lowrie .15 .40
216 Derek Lowe .15 .40
217 Jorge Cantu .15 .40
218 Bobby Parnell RC .60 1.50
219 Nate McLouth .15 .40
220 Suez Canal .15 .40
221 Brandon Webb .25 .60
222 Akinori Iwamura .15 .40
223 Scott Rolen .25 .60
224 Tim Lincecum .25 .60
225 David Price RC .75 2.00
226 Ricky Romero (RC) .60 1.50
227 Nelson Cruz .40 1.00
228 Will Simpson .15 .40
Archie Bunker
229 Mark Ellis .15 .40
230 Torii Hunter .15 .40
231 David Murphy .15 .40
232 Everth Cabrera RC .60 1.50
233 John Lackey .25 .60
234 Wyatt Earp .15 .40
235 Roy Oswalt .25 .60
236 Edgar Renteria .15 .40
237 Walton Glenn Eller .25 .60
238 Vincent Van Gogh .25 .60
239 Chris Carpenter .25 .60
240 Hank Blalock .15 .40
241 Trevor Cahill RC 1.00 2.50
242 Mark Teahen .15 .40
243 Alexander Cartwright .25 .60
244 Carlos Beltran .25 .60
245 Todd Helton .25 .60
246 General Custer .15 .40
247 Jeff Clement .15 .40
248 Colby Rasmus (RC) .60 1.50
249 John Higby .15 .40
250 Grady Sizemore .25 .60
251 Carl Crawford .25 .60
252 Lastings Milledge .15 .40
253 Miguel Cabrera .40 1.00
254 John Maine .15 .40
255 Aramis Ramirez .15 .40
256 Jose Lopez .15 .40
257 Heinrich Hertz .15 .40
258 Felix Hernandez .25 .60
259 Napoleon Bonaparte .15 .40
260 Louis Braille .15 .40
261 John Danks .15 .40
262 Magglio Ordonez .25 .60
263 Brian Duensing RC .60 1.50
264 Carlos Pena .25 .60
265 Paul Konerko .25 .60
266 Johnny Cueto .25 .60
267 Melvin Mora .15 .40
268 Andy Pettitte .25 .60
269 Brian McCann .25 .60
270 Josh Outman RC .60 1.50
271 Jair Jurrjens .15 .40
272 Brad Nelson (RC) .40 1.00
273 Jason Bay .25 .60
274 Josh Hamilton .25 .60
275 Vladimir Guerrero .25 .60
276 Michael Phelps .75 2.00
277 Kerry Wood .15 .40
278 Herb Simpson .40 1.00
279 Jon Lester .25 .60
280 Shin-Soo Choo .25 .60
281 Jake Peavy .15 .40
282 Eric Chavez .15 .40
283 Mike Aviles .15 .40
284 Kenshin Kawakami RC .60 1.50
285 George Kottaras (RC) .40 1.00
286 Matt Kemp .30 .75
287 James Shields .15 .40
288 Joe Saunders .15 .40
289 Milky Way .15 .40
290 Cat Osterman .50 1.25
291 Josh Beckett .15 .40
292 Oliver Perez .15 .40
293 Ian Snell .15 .40
294 Tim Hudson .25 .60
295 Brett Gardner .25 .60
296 Bobby Abreu .15 .40
297 Kolan McConiughey .15 .40
298 Dan Haren .15 .40
299 Shairon Martis RC .60 1.50
300 David Ortiz .40 1.00
301 Jonathan Sanchez SP 1.25 3.00
302 Stephen Drew SP 1.25 3.00
303 Rocco Baldelli SP 1.25 3.00
304 Yunel Escobar SP 1.25 3.00
305 Javier Vazquez SP 1.25 3.00
306 Cliff Lee SP 1.25 3.00
307 Hunter Pence SP 1.25 3.00
308 Fausto Carmona SP 1.25 3.00
309 Kosuke Fukudome SP 1.25 3.00
310 Old Faithful SP 1.25 3.00
311 Gavin Floyd SP 1.25 3.00
312 A.J. Burnett SP 1.25 3.00
313 Jeff Francis SP 1.25 3.00
314 Chad Billingsley SP 1.25 3.00
315 Andy LaRoche SP 1.25 3.00
316 Rick Porcello SP RC 2.50 6.00
317 John Baker SP 1.25 3.00
318 Delmon Young SP 1.25 3.00
319 Gary Sheffield SP 1.25 3.00
320 B.J. Ryan SP 1.25 3.00
321 Kelly Shoppach SP 1.25 3.00
322 Chris Volstad SP 1.25 3.00
323 Derek Jeter SP 3.00 8.00
324 Wladimir Balentien SP 1.25 3.00
325 Dioner Navarro SP 1.25 3.00
326 Cameron Maybin SP 1.25 3.00
327 Kenji Johjima SP 1.25 3.00
328 Matt LaPorta SP RC 2.00 5.00
329 Carlos Gomez SP 1.25 3.00
330 Cristian Guzman SP 1.25 3.00
331 Jeff Samardzija SP 1.25 3.00
332 Curtis Granderson SP 1.25 3.00
333 Nick Swisher SP 1.25 3.00
334 Pat Burrell SP 1.25 3.00
335 Justin Duchscherer SP 1.25 3.00
336 Ryan Ludwick SP 1.25 3.00
337 Billy Butler SP 1.25 3
338 Jason Wong SP 1.25 3
339 Jordan Schafer SP (RC) 1.25 3
340 Richard Gatling SP 1.25 3
341 Edgar Gonzalez SP 1.25 3
342 Sitting Bull SP 1.25 3
343 Doc Holliday SP 1.25 3
344 Chris Young SP 1.25 3
345 Carlos Delgado SP 1.25 3
346 Dominique Wilkins SP 1.25 3
347 Yovani Gallardo SP 1.25 3
348 Justin Masterson SP 1.25 3
349 Aubrey Huff SP 1.25 3
350 Jimmy Rollins SP 1.25 3

2009 Topps Allen and Ginter Code

*CODE: 2X TO 5X BASIC
STATED ODDS 1:12 HOBBY

2009 Topps Allen and Ginter Mini

COMP.SET w/o EXT (350) 125.00 250
*MINI 1-300: .75X TO 2X BASIC
*MINI 1-300 RC: .5X TO 1.2X BASIC RC's
APPX. ONE MINI PER PACK
*MINI SP 301-350: .5X TO 1.2X BASIC SP
MINI SP ODDS 1:13 HOBBY
351-390 RANDOM WITHIN RIP CARDS
OVERALL PLATE ODDS 1:608 HOBBY
PLATE PRINT RUN 1 SET PER COLOR
BLACK-CYAN-MAGENTA-YELLOW ISSUED
NO PLATE PRICING DUE TO SCARCITY
351 Manny Ramirez EXT 20.00 50
352 Travis Snider EXT 12.00 30
353 CC Sabathia EXT 12.00 30
354 Nick Markakis EXT 15.00 40
355 Jon Lester EXT 12.00 30
356 Cole Hamels EXT 15.00 40
357 Edinson Volquez EXT 8.00 20
358 Hanley Ramirez EXT 12.00 30
359 Alex Rodriguez EXT 25.00 60
360 Francisco Rodriguez EXT 12.00 30
361 Albert Pujols EXT 25.00 60
362 Matt Holliday EXT 20.00 50
363 Max Scherzer EXT 20.00 50
364 Adam Dunn EXT 12.00 30
365 Randy Johnson EXT 20.00 50
366 Roy Halladay EXT 12.00 30
367 Joe Mauer EXT 15.00 40.
368 Roy Oswalt EXT 12.00 30
369 Grady Sizemore EXT 12.00 30
370 Jacoby Ellsbury EXT 15.00 40
371 Nate McLouth EXT 8.00 20
372 Josh Johnson EXT 12.00 30
373 Geovany Soto EXT 12.00 30.
374 Josh Beckett EXT 8.00 20
375 Brian McCann EXT 12.00 30.
376 David Wright EXT 15.00 40
377 Adrian Gonzalez EXT 15.00 40
378 Tim Lincecum EXT 12.00 30.
379 Dan Haren EXT 8.00 20.
380 Alex Rios EXT 8.00 20.
381 Rich Harden EXT 8.00 20
382 Victor Martinez EXT 12.00 30
383 Carlos Lee EXT 8.00 20.
384 Chipper Jones EXT 20.00 50.
385 Clayton Kershaw EXT 40.00 100
386 Daisuke Matsuzaka EXT 12.00 30
387 Carlos Beltran EXT 12.00 30
388 Scott Kazmir EXT 8.00 20.
389 Mark Teixeira EXT 12.00 30.
390 Justin Upton EXT 12.00 30.
391 David Price EXT 15.00 40
392 Felix Hernandez EXT 12.00 30.
393 Mariano Rivera EXT 25.00 60.
394 Joba Chamberlain EXT 8.00 20.
395 Justin Morneau EXT 12.00 30.
396 Ryan Howard EXT 15.00 40
397 Evan Longoria EXT 12.00 30.
398 Ryan Zimmerman EXT 12.00 30.
399 Jason Bay EXT 12.00 30.
400 Miguel Cabrera EXT 20.00 50.

2009 Topps Allen and Ginter Mini A and G Back

*A & G BACK: 1X TO 2.5X BASIC
*A & G BACK RCs: .6X TO 1.5X BASIC RCs
STATED ODDS 1:5 HOBBY
*A & G BACK SP: .6X TO 1.5X BASIC SP
SP STATED ODDS 1:65 HOBBY

2009 Topps Allen and Ginter Mini Black

*BLACK: 2X TO 5X BASIC
*BLACK RCs: .75X TO 2X BASIC RCs
STATED ODDS 1:10 HOBBY
*BLACK SP: .75X TO 2X BASIC SP
SP STATED ODDS 1:130 HOBBY

2009 Topps Allen and Ginter Mini No Card Number

*NO NBR: 8X TO 20X BASIC
*NO NBR RCs: 3X TO 8X BASIC RCs
*NO NBR SP: 1.2X TO 3X BASIC SP
STATED ODDS 1:95 HOBBY
STATED PRINT RUN 50 SETS
11 Jacoby Ellsbury 20.00 50.
22 Mariano Rivera 12.50 30.
66 Alex Rodriguez 20.00 50.
136 Mickey Mantle 40.00 80.
149 Chipper Jones 20.00 50.

6 General Custer 12.50 30.00
6 Rick Porcello 10.00 25.00
3 Derek Jeter 30.00 60.00
8 Matt LaPorta 6.00 15.00
2 Curtis Granderson 10.00 25.00
3 Jason Wong 10.00 25.00
8 Justin Masterson 10.00 25.00

2009 Topps Allen and Ginter Autographs

OUP A ODDS 1:2730 HOBBY
OUP B ODDS 1:51 HOBBY
RDS ARE NOT SERIAL-NUMBERED
INT RUNS PROVIDED BY TOPPS
PHELPS PRICING DUE TO SCARCITY
CHANGE DEADLINE 6/30/2012
Alexi Casilla B 4.00 10.00
Pennington/239 * B 10.00 25.00
Alex Rios B 6.00 15.00
A.Tunnicliffe/239 * B 8.00 20.00
E Bryan Berg/239 * B 5.00 12.00
B.Crowley/239 * B 6.00 15.00
A Cappelletto/239 * B 8.00 20.00
B.Kenny/239 * B 10.00 25.00
The Marlin/239 * B 15.00 40.00
Blake DeWitt B 4.00 10.00
B.Yates/239 * B 5.00 12.00
Carlos Gomez B 4.00 10.00
Conor Jackson B 4.00 10.00
Clayton Kershaw B 50.00 120.00
C.Maybin B 5.00 12.00
C.Osterman/239 * B 12.00 30.00
C.Parris/239 * B 10.00 25.00
D.Ortiz/49 * A 100.00 200.00
W D.Wilkins/239 * B 15.00 40.00
Denard Span B 4.00 10.00
D.Wright/49 * A 15.00 40.00
Evan Longoria B 4.00 10.00
Ervin Santana B 4.00 10.00
F.Evans/230 * B 15.00 40.00
Hanley Ramirez B 5.00 12.00
H.Simpson/239 * B 15.00 40.00
H.Teter/239 * B 5.00 12.00
I.Kyle SP/239 * B 8.00 20.00
Jay Bruce B 8.00 20.00
Chamberlain/49 * A 30.00 60.00
U Jack Cust B 4.00 10.00
Jeff Francoeur B 4.00 10.00
J.Higby/239 * B 8.00 20.00
Josh Johnson B 8.00 20.00
J.Masterson B 4.00 10.00
C Johnny Cueto B 4.00 10.00
J.Papelbon B 4.00 10.00
Jose Reyes/49 * A 8.00 20.00
I Juan Rivera B 4.00 10.00
J.Werth/49 * A 90.00 150.00
K.Armstrong/239 * B 10.00 25.00
M McConiughey/239 * B 8.00 20.00
L.Cox/239 * B 12.50 30.00
L.Merritt/239 * B 8.00 20.00
L.Opstedahl/239 * B 5.00 12.00
C M.Cabrera/49 * A 60.00 150.00
H M.Holliday/49 * A 30.00 60.00
K Matt Kemp B 5.00 12.00
LO Mike Lowell B 8.00 20.00
M M.Metzger/239 * B 6.00 15.00
N M.Navarro/239 * B 20.00 50.00
S Max Scherzer B 30.00 80.00
Z M. Zagunis/239 * B 6.00 15.00
H Phil Hughes B 8.00 20.00
B Ryan Braun B 12.50 30.00
C Ryan Church B 4.00 10.00
F R.Fosbury/239 * B 12.50 30.00
H Ryan Howard/49 * A 15.00 40.00
JH Rich Hill B 4.00 10.00
M R.Moore/239 * B 12.50 30.00
MA R.Maddison/239 * B 10.00 25.00
B S.Trafton/239 * B 8.00 20.00
D S.Davis/239 * B 8.00 20.00
O Scott Olsen B 4.00 10.00
W S.Wiebe/239 * B 15.00 40.00
T Troy Tulowitzki B 5.00 12.00
E W.Eller/239 * B 10.00 25.00
S W.Simpson/239 * B 12.50 30.00
W W.Williams/239 * B 15.00 40.00
M Y.Miyazawa/239 * B 10.00 25.00

2009 Topps Allen and Ginter Cabinet Boxloaders

OMPLETE SET (10) 20.00 50.00
NE CABINET/N43 PER HOBBY BOX
B1 Yurendell de Caster/Gene Kingsale 2.50 6.00
B2 Frederich Cepeda/Yulieski Gourriel 3.00 8.00
B3 D.Wright/B.Roberts 4.00 10.00
B4 N.Aoki/D.Matsuzaka 4.00 10.00
B5 H.Iwakuma/I.Suzuki 4.00 10.00
B6 Thomas Jefferson/John Hancock 2.50 6.00
B7 George Washington
Alexander Hamilton 3.00 8.00
B8 Harry S Truman/Lester B. Pearson 3.00 8.00
B9 Abraham Lincoln/Ulysses S. Grant 3.00 8.00
B10 John F. Kennedy
Nikita Khrushchev 3.00 8.00

2009 Topps Allen and Ginter Baseball Highlights

OMPLETE SET (25) 10.00 25.00
TATED ODDS 1:6 HOBBY
GHS1 Aaron Boone .40 1.00
GHS2 Ken Griffey Jr. 2.00 5.00
AGHS3 Randy Johnson 1.00 2.50
AGHS4 Carlos Zambrano .60 1.50
AGHS5 Josh Hamilton .60 1.50
AGHS6 Josh Beckett .40 1.00
AGHS7 Manny Ramirez 1.00 2.50
AGHS8 Derek Jeter 2.50 6.00
AGHS9 Frank Thomas 1.00 2.50
AGHS10 Jim Thome .60 1.50
AGHS11 Francisco Rodriguez .60 1.50
AGHS12 New York Yankees 1.00 2.50
AGHS13 David Wright .75 2.00
AGHS14 Ichiro Suzuki 1.25 3.00
AGHS15 Jon Lester .60 1.50
AGHS16 Alex Rodriguez 1.25 3.00
AGHS17 Chipper Jones 1.00 2.50
AGHS18 Derek Jeter 2.50 6.00
AGHS19 Albert Pujols 1.25 3.00
AGHS20 CC Sabathia .60 1.50
AGHS21 David Price .75 2.00
AGHS22 Ken Griffey Jr. 2.00 5.00
AGHS23 Brad Lidge .40 1.00
AGHS24 Mariano Rivera 1.25 3.00
AGHS25 Evan Longoria .60 1.50

2009 Topps Allen and Ginter Mini Creatures

COMPLETE SET (20) 75.00 150.00
STATED ODDS 1:48 HOBBY
LMT1 Bigfoot 3.00 8.00
LMT2 The Loch Ness Monster 3.00 8.00
LMT3 Grendel 3.00 8.00
LMT4 Unicorn 3.00 8.00
LMT5 The Invisible Man 3.00 8.00
LMT6 Kraken 3.00 8.00
LMT7 Medusa 3.00 8.00
LMT8 Sphinx 3.00 8.00
LMT9 Minotaur 3.00 8.00
LMT10 Dragon 3.00 8.00
LMT11 Leviathan 3.00 8.00
LMT12 Cyclops 3.00 8.00
LMT13 Vampire 3.00 8.00
LMT14 Griffin 3.00 8.00
LMT15 Chupacabra 3.00 8.00
LMT16 Cerberus 3.00 8.00
LMT17 Hydra 3.00 8.00
LMT18 Werewolf 3.00 8.00
LMT19 Fairy 3.00 8.00
LMT20 Yeti 3.00 8.00

2009 Topps Allen and Ginter Mini Extinct Creatures

RANDOM INSERTS IN PACKS
EA1 Velociraptor 12.50 30.00
EA2 Dodo 12.50 30.00
EA3 Xerces Blue 12.50 30.00
EA4 Labrador Duck 12.50 30.00
EA5 Eastern Elk 12.50 30.00

2009 Topps Allen and Ginter Mini Inventions of the Future

RANDOM INSERTS IN PACKS
FI1 Aeromobile 10.00 25.00
FI2 Clock Defier 10.00 25.00
FI3 Protecto-Bubble 10.00 25.00
FI4 Here-To-There-O-Matic 10.00 25.00
FI5 Mental Movies 10.00 25.00

2009 Topps Allen and Ginter Mini National Heroes

COMPLETE SET (40) 30.00 60.00
STATED ODDS 1:12 HOBBY
NH1 George Washington 2.00 5.00
NH2 Haile Selassie I 1.25 3.00
NH3 Toussaint L'Ouverture 1.25 3.00
NH4 Rigas Feraios 1.25 3.00
NH5 Yi Sun-sin 1.25 3.00
NH6 Giuseppe Garibaldi 1.25 3.00
NH7 Juan Santamaria 1.25 3.00
NH8 Tecun Uman 1.25 3.00
NH9 Jon Sigurosson 1.25 3.00
NH10 Mohandas Gandhi 2.00 5.00
NH11 Simon Bolivar 1.25 3.00
NH12 Alexander Nevsky 1.25 3.00
NH13 Lim Bo Seng 1.25 3.00
NH14 Sun Yat-sen 1.25 3.00
NH15 Tiradentes 1.25 3.00
NH16 Chiang Kai-Shek 1.25 3.00
NH17 William I 1.25 3.00
NH18 Severyn Nalyvaiko 1.25 3.00
NH19 Vasil Levski 1.25 3.00
NH20 Tadeusz Kosciuszko 1.25 3.00
NH21 Andranik Toros Ozanian 1.25 3.00
NH22 William Wallace 1.25 3.00
NH23 Oda Nobunaga 1.25 3.00
NH24 Milos Obilic 1.25 3.00
NH25 Niels Ebbeson 1.25 3.00
NH26 Jose Rizal 1.25 3.00
NH27 Alfonso Ugarte 1.25 3.00
NH28 Mustafa Ataturk 1.25 3.00
NH29 Nelson Mandela 1.25 3.00
NH30 El Cid 1.25 3.00
NH31 William Tell 1.25 3.00
NH32 Winston Churchill 1.25 3.00
NH33 Skanderbeg 1.25 3.00
NH34 General Jose de San Martin 1.25 3.00
NH35 Janos Damjanich 1.25 3.00
NH36 Joan of Arc 1.25 3.00
NH37 Abd al-Qadir 1.25 3.00
NH38 David Ben-Gurion 1.25 3.00
NH39 Benito Juarez 1.25 3.00
NH40 Marcus Garvey 1.25 3.00

2009 Topps Allen and Ginter Mini World's Biggest Hoaxes

COMPLETE SET (20) 12.50 30.00
STATED ODDS 1:12 HOBBY
HHB1 Charles Ponzi 1.25 3.00
HHB2 Alabama Changes Value of Pi 1.25 3.00
HHB3 The Runaway Bride 1.25 3.00
HHB4 Idaho 1.25 3.00
HHB5 The Turk 1.25 3.00
HHB6 Enron 1.25 3.00
HHB7 Anna Anderson 1.25 3.00
HHB8 Ferdinand Waldo Demara 1.25 3.00
HHB9 Sam Serriffe 1.25 3.00
HHB10 D.B. Cooper 1.25 3.00
HHB11 Wisconsin State
Capitol Collapses 1.25 3.00
HHB12 Victor Lustig 1.25 3.00
HHB13 The War of the Worlds 1.25 3.00
HHB14 George Parker 1.25 3.00
HHB15 The Bathtub Hoax 1.25 3.00
HHB16 The Cottingley Fairies 1.25 3.00
HHB17 James Reavis 1.25 3.00
HHB18 The Piltdown Man 1.25 3.00
HHB19 The Cardiff Giant 1.25 3.00
HHB20 Cold Fusion 1.25 3.00

2009 Topps Allen and Ginter N43

COMPLETE SET (15) 20.00 50.00
ONE CABINET/N43 PER HOBBY BOX
AP Albert Pujols 3.00 8.00
AR Alex Rodriguez 3.00 8.00
CJ Chipper Jones 2.50 6.00
DM Daisuke Matsuzaka 1.50 4.00
DW David Wright 2.00 5.00
EL Evan Longoria 1.50 4.00
GS Grady Sizemore 1.50 4.00
JB Jay Bruce 1.50 4.00
JH Josh Hamilton 1.50 4.00
JU Justin Upton 1.50 4.00
MC Miguel Cabrera 2.50 6.00
MR Manny Ramirez 2.50 6.00
RH Ryan Howard 2.00 5.00
TL Tim Lincecum 1.50 4.00
RHA Roy Halladay 1.50 4.00

2009 Topps Allen and Ginter National Pride

COMPLETE SET (75) 10.00 25.00
APPX.ODDS ONE PER HOBBY PACK
NP1 Ervin Santana .30 .75
NP2 Justin Upton .50 1.25
NP3 Jason Bay .50 1.25
NP4 Geovany Soto .50 1.25
NP5 Ryan Dempster .30 .75
NP6 Johnny Cueto .50 1.25
NP7 Chipper Jones .75 2.00
NP8 Fausto Carmona .30 .75
NP9 Carlos Guillen .30 .75
NP10 Jose Reyes .50 1.25
NP11 Hiroki Kuroda .30 .75
NP12 Prince Fielder .50 1.25
NP13 Justin Morneau .50 1.25
NP14 Fransisco Rodriguez .50 1.25
NP15 Jorge Posada .50 1.25
NP16 Jake Peavy .30 .75
NP17 Felix Hernandez .50 1.25
NP18 Robinson Cano .50 1.25
NP19 Erik Bedard .30 .75
NP20 Akinori Iwamura .30 .75
NP21 Scott Hairston .30 .75
NP22 David Wright .60 1.50
NP23 Chien-Ming Wang .50 1.25
NP24 Chase Utley .50 1.25
NP25 Jonathan Sanchez .30 .75
NP26 Yunel Escobar .30 .75
NP27 John Lackey .50 1.25
NP28 Melvin Mora .30 .75
NP29 Alfonso Soriano .50 1.25
NP30 Jose Contreras .30 .75
NP31 Grady Sizemore .50 1.25
NP32 Rich Harden .30 .75
NP33 Hanley Ramirez .50 1.25
NP34 Nick Markakis .60 1.50
NP35 Manny Ramirez .75 2.00
NP36 Yovani Gallardo .30 .75
NP37 Johan Santana .50 1.25
NP38 Mariano Rivera 1.00 2.50
NP39 Shin-Soo Choo .50 1.25
NP40 Hideki Matsui .75 2.00
NP41 Raul Ibanez .50 1.25
NP42 Edgar Renteria .30 .75
NP43 Jose Lopez .30 .75
NP44 Yuniesky Betancourt .30 .75
NP45 Evan Longoria .50 1.25
NP46 Carlos Ruiz .30 .75
NP47 Ryan Howard .60 1.50
NP48 Jorge Cantu .30 .75
NP49 Max Scherzer .75 2.00
NP50 Jair Jurrjens .30 .75
NP51 Albert Pujols 1.00 2.50
NP52 Daisuke Matsuzaka .50 1.25
NP53 Vladimir Guerrero .50 1.25
NP54 Carlos Zambrano .50 1.25
NP55 Kosuke Fukudome .50 1.25
NP56 Edinson Volquez .30 .75
NP57 Victor Martinez .50 1.25
NP58 Derek Jeter 2.00 5.00
NP59 Miguel Cabrera .75 2.00
NP60 Stephen Drew .30 .75
NP61 Mark Teahen .30 .75
NP62 Ryan Braun .50 1.25
NP63 Carlos Beltran .50 1.25
NP64 Francisco Liriano .30 .75
NP65 Carlos Delgado .30 .75
NP66 Joba Chamberlain .30 .75
NP67 Adrian Gonzalez .60 1.50
NP68 Ichiro Suzuki 1.00 2.50
NP69 Ryan Rowland-Smith .30 .75
NP70 Carlos Pena .50 1.25
NP71 Josh Hamilton .50 1.25
NP72 Edgar Gonzalez .30 .75
NP73 Carlos Lee .30 .75
NP74 Yadier Molina .75 2.00
NP75 Alex Rodriguez 1.00 2.50

2009 Topps Allen and Ginter Relics

GROUP A ODDS 1:100 HOBBY
GROUP B ODDS 1:215 HOBBY
GROUP D ODDS 1:17 HOBBY
GROUP C ODDS 1:39 HOBBY
CARDS ARE NOT SERIAL-NUMBERED
PRINT RUNS PROVIDED BY TOPPS
AER Alex Rodriguez Pants 12.50 30.00
AL Adam LaRoche Jsy C 3.00 8.00
AP Albert Pujols Bat 15.00 40.00
AP2 A.Pujols Hat/190 * 20.00 50.00
AP3 A.Pujols Jsy/255 * 15.00 40.00
AR Alex Rios Bat/90 * A 30.00 60.00
AS Alfonso Soriano Bat/191 * A 4.00 10.00
AT A.Rashguard/250 * A 10.00 25.00
BBE B.Berg Card/250 * A 15.00 40.00
BC Bob Crowley A 10.00 25.00
BCA Cappelletto Shirt/250 * A 8.00 20.00
BD Blake DeWitt Bat C 4.00 10.00
BK B.Kenny Hair/250 * A 30.00 60.00
BTM Marlin Jsy/250 * A 10.00 25.00
BU B.J. Upton Jsy D 3.00 8.00
BY Brock Yates/250 * A 8.00 20.00
BZ Barry Zito Pants A 3.00 8.00
CB Carlos Beltran Jsy C 3.00 8.00
CC Coco Crisp Bat A 5.00 12.00
CJ Chipper Jones Jsy C 4.00 10.00
CK Casey Kotchman Jsy A 3.00 8.00
CM Cameron Maybin Bat C 3.00 8.00
CO Osterman/250 * A 15.00 40.00
CP Corey Patterson Bat C 3.00 8.00
CQ Carlos Quentin Jsy D 3.00 8.00
CS CC Sabathia Jsy 3.00 8.00
CU Chase Utley Jsy D 3.00 8.00
CW Chien-Ming Wang Jsy A 4.00 10.00
DAW D.Wright Btg Glv 12.50 30.00
DAW2 David Wright Jsy 3.00 8.00
DM Matsuzaka Jsy/110 * A 20.00 50.00
DO David Ortiz Jsy A 4.00 10.00
DOW D.Wilkins/250 * A 10.00 25.00
DW Dontrelle Willis Pants D 3.00 8.00
EC Chavez Pants/210 * A 12.50 30.00
EG Eric Gagne Jsy B 3.00 8.00
EL Evan Longoria Jsy D 5.00 12.00
FL Fred Lewis Bat C 3.00 8.00
GS Gary Sheffield Bat A 3.00 8.00
GSI Grady Sizemore Jsy D 3.00 8.00
HB Hank Blalock Bat A 3.00 8.00
HM Hideki Matsui Jsy B 10.00 25.00
HR Ramirez Bat/199 * A 12.50 30.00
HT H.Teter/250 * A 12.50 30.00
IK Iris Kyle Suit/250 * A 12.50 30.00
IS Ichiro Suzuki Jsy 6.00 15.00
IS2 Ichiro Suzuki Bat 6.00 15.00
JB Jay Bruce Jsy D 3.00 8.00
JD Jermaine Dye Bat C 3.00 8.00
JHI J.Higby/250 * A 10.00 25.00
JM Joe Mauer Jsy D 3.00 8.00
JR Jimmy Rollins Jsy D 3.00 8.00
JRH Rich Harden Pants A 3.00 8.00
JT Jim Thome Bat B 3.00 8.00
JU Justin Upton Jsy D 3.00 8.00
JW Jered Weaver Jsy D 3.00 8.00
KA Armstrong Jsy/250 * A 6.00 15.00
KF Kosuke Fukudome Jsy D 3.00 8.00
KM McConiughey/250 * A 8.00 20.00
LC Lynne Cox/250 * A 10.00 25.00
LM L.Merritt/250 * A 8.00 20.00
LO Opstedahl/250 * A 12.50 30.00
MC Mike Cameron Bat C 3.00 8.00
MCA Miguel Cabrera Jsy C 3.00 8.00
MH Matt Holliday Jsy D 3.00 8.00
MM Mantle Pants/250 * A 60.00 150.00
MME M.Metzger/250 * A 10.00 25.00
MMO Melvin Mora Bat C 3.00 8.00
MMU Mark Mulder Pants C 3.00 8.00
MO Maggio Ordonez Jsy D 3.00 8.00
MP M.Phelps/250 * A 20.00 50.00
MR Manny Ramirez Jsy A 4.00 10.00
MR2 M.Ramirez Bat/190 * C 8.00 20.00
MT Mark Teixeira Jsy 4.00 10.00
MTE Miguel Tejada Jsy B 3.00 8.00
MZ M.Lame/250 * A 12.50 30.00
NM Nate McLouth Jsy D 3.00 8.00
NS Swisher Bat/164 * A 15.00 40.00
PF Prince Fielder Bat C 3.00 8.00
RB Rocco Baldelli Bat 3.00 8.00
RB2 Rocco Baldelli Jsy 3.00 8.00
RC Robinson Cano Bat/195 * A 10.00 25.00
RD Ryan Doumit Jsy D 3.00 8.00
RF Richard Fosbury A 8.00 20.00
RH Ryan Howard Jsy 4.00 10.00
RH2 Ryan Howard Bat 5.00 12.00
RJB Ryan Braun Jsy D 4.00 10.00
RL Ryan Ludwick Jsy D 3.00 8.00
RMA R.Maddison/250 * A 8.00 20.00
RO Roy Oswalt Jsy A 8.00 20.00
RZ Ryan Zimmerman Bat C 3.00 8.00
SB S.Trafton/250 * A 8.00 20.00
SD S.Davis/250 * A 8.00 20.00
SR Scott Rolen Jsy C 3.00 8.00
SW S.Wiebe/250 * A 8.00 20.00
TH Travis Hafner Jsy C 3.00 8.00
THU Tim Hudson Jsy A 3.00 8.00
TL Tim Lincecum Jsy D 4.00 10.00
TLH Todd Helton Jsy C 3.00 8.00
VG Vladimir Guerrero Bat C 3.00 8.00
VW Vernon Wells Jsy A 3.00 8.00
WE W.Eller/250 * A 12.50 30.00
WS Simpson/250 * A 30.00 60.00
YE Yunel Escobar Jsy D 3.00 8.00
YG Yovani Gallardo Jsy D 3.00 8.00

2009 Topps Allen and Ginter Rip Cards

STATED ODDS 1:257 HOBBY
PRINT RUNS B/WN 5-99 COPIES PER
NO PRICING ON QTY 25 OR LESS
ALL LISTED PRICED ARE FOR RIPPED
UNRIPPED HAVE ADD'L CARDS WITHIN
COMMON UNRIPPED p/r 99 40.00 80.00
COMMON UNRIPPED p/r 50 50.00 100.00
RC4 Paul Konerko/99 6.00 15.00
RC9 Pat Neshek/99 6.00 15.00
RC10 Brian Giles/99 6.00 15.00
RC11 Jeff Francis/99 6.00 15.00
RC12 Jermaine Dye/50 6.00 15.00
RC13 Dan Uggla/50 6.00 15.00
RC14 Tim Hudson/50 6.00 15.00
RC15 Chris Young/50 6.00 15.00
RC19 John Lackey/99 6.00 15.00
RC23 Rafael Furcal/50 6.00 15.00
RC26 Derrek Lee/50 6.00 15.00
RC27 Cameron Maybin/99 6.00 15.00
RC28 Ryan Dempster/50 6.00 15.00
RC31 Yunel Escobar/99 6.00 15.00
RC34 Joakim Soria/50 6.00 15.00
RC38 Miguel Tejada/50 6.00 15.00
RC40 Shane Victorino/99 6.00 15.00
RC43 Garrett Atkins/50 6.00 15.00
RC44 Fausto Carmona/99 6.00 15.00
RC45 Mike Jacobs/99 6.00 15.00
RC47 Oliver Perez/99 6.00 15.00
RC49 James Loney/50 6.00 15.00
RC52 Rickie Weeks/99 6.00 15.00
RC56 Aubrey Huff/99 6.00 15.00
RC57 Chad Billingsley/50 6.00 15.00
RC58 Carlos Gomez/99 6.00 15.00
RC60 Mike Aviles/99 6.00 15.00
RC62 Joe Saunders/99 6.00 15.00
RC63 Derek Lowe/50 6.00 15.00
RC64 Travis Hafner/99 6.00 15.00
RC69 Kevin Kouzmanoff/50 6.00 15.00
RC71 Ryan Ludwick/50 6.00 15.00
RC74 Melvin Mora/99 6.00 15.00
RC76 Yadier Molina/99 6.00 15.00
RC77 Carlos Pena/50 6.00 15.00
RC80 Aramis Ramirez/50 6.00 15.00
RC81 Rocco Baldelli/50 6.00 15.00
RC85 Brandon Phillips/50 6.00 15.00
RC93 Eric Chavez/99 6.00 15.00
RC99 Mark Buehrle/50 6.00 15.00

2010 Topps Allen and Ginter

COMPLETE SET (350) 60.00 120.00
COMP.SET w/o SPs (300) 15.00 40.00
COMMON CARD (1-300) .15 .40
COMMON RC (1-300) .40 1.00
COMMON SP (301-350) 1.25 3.00
SP STATED ODDS 1:2 HOBBY
1 Adam Lind .25 .60
2 Everth Cabrera .15 .40
3 Ryan Braun .25 .60
4 Prince Fielder .25 .60
5 Edwin Jackson .15 .40
6 Madison Bumgarner RC 3.00 8.00
7 Ryan Howard .30 .75
8 Miguel Tejada .25 .60
9 Kelly Kulick .15 .40
10 Gary Stewart .15 .40
11 Wade Davis (RC) .60 1.50
12 Jesus Flores .15 .40
13 B.J. Upton .25 .60
14 Shane Victorino .25 .60
15 Carlos Quentin .15 .40
16 Carl Pavano .15 .40
17 Johan Santana .25 .60
18 Jose Lopez .15 .40
19 Tommy Hanson .15 .40
20 Sacagawea .15 .40
21 Ryan Kennelly .15 .40
22 Lucy .15 .40
23 Joe Mauer .30 .75
24 Brandon Webb .25 .60
25 Max Scherzer .40 1.00
26 Andy Pettitte .25 .60
27 Brad Hawpe .15 .40
28 Felipe Lopez .15 .40
29 Cole Hamels .30 .75
30 Rafael Furcal .15 .40
31 Miguel Montero .15 .40
32 Joba Chamberlain .15 .40
33 Bengie Molina .15 .40
34 Delmon Young .25 .60
35 John Lackey .25 .60
36 Victor Martinez .25 .60
37 Daniel McCutchen RC .60 1.50
38 Tiago Della Vega .15 .40
39 Josh Johnson .25 .60
40 Carlos Beltran .25 .60
41 Daniel Hudson RC .60 1.50
42 Mark DeRosa .15 .40
43 Yovani Gallardo .15 .40
44 Chris Coghlan .15 .40
45 Justin Verlander .40 1.00
46 Chad Billingsley .25 .60
47 Drew Stubbs RC 1.00 2.50
48 Alan Francis .15 .40
49 Jenrry Mejia RC .60 1.50
50 Jason Bay .25 .60
51 Matt Holliday .40 1.00
52 Gavin Floyd .15 .40
53 Jason Heyward RC 1.50 4.00
54 Tony Hawk .40 1.00
55 Esmil Rogers RC .40 1.00
56 Shin-Soo Choo .25 .60
57 Jacoby Ellsbury .30 .75
58 Colby Rasmus .25 .60
59 Ivory Crockett .15 .40
60 Chris Davis .25 .60
61 Michael Cuddyer .15 .40
62 Matt Kemp .30 .75
63 Matt Carson (RC) .40 1.00
64 Josh Beckett .15 .40
65 Andre Ethier .25 .60
66 Orlando Hudson .15 .40
67 Carl Crawford .25 .60
68 Betelgeuse .15 .40
69 Clay Buchholz .15 .40
70 Joey Votto .40 1.00
71 Hunter Pence .25 .60
72 Erick Aybar .15 .40
73 Avery Jenkins .15 .40
74 Ryan Ludwick .15 .40
75 Jayson Werth .25 .60
76 Joakim Soria .15 .40
77 Ricky Romero .15 .40
78 Leonardo da Vinci .15 .40
79 James Loney .15 .40
80 Will Venable .15 .40
81 Cliff Lee .25 .60
82 Justin Upton .25 .60
83 David Wright .30 .75
84 Elvis Andrus .25 .60
85 Yunel Escobar .15 .40
86 Andrew Bailey .15 .40
87 Alexei Ramirez .25 .60
88 Kosuke Fukudome .25 .60
89 Joel Pineiro .15 .40
90 Kevin Kouzmanoff .15 .40
91 Carlos Zambrano .25 .60
92 Randy Oitker .15 .40
93 Brandon Inge .15 .40
94 Luke Hochevar .15 .40
95 Judson Laipply .15 .40
96 Roy Halladay .25 .60
97 Zach Duke .15 .40
98 Johnny Cueto .15 .40
99 Anthony Gatto .15 .40
100 Matt LaPorta .15 .40
101 Mark Buehrle .25 .60
102 Torii Hunter .15 .40
103 Niccolo Machiavelli .15 .40
104 Mahlon Duckett .15 .40
105 Nicolaus Copernicus .15 .40
106 Dustin Pedroia .30 .75
107 Adam Dunn .25 .60
108 Paul Konerko .25 .60
109 Ian Kinsler .25 .60
110 Sherlock Holmes .15 .40
111 Josh Willingham .25 .60
112 Tyler Bradt .15 .40
113 Billy Butler .15 .40
114 Milton Bradley .15 .40
115 Trevor Hoffman .25 .60
116 Galileo Galilei .15 .40
117 Neil Walker (RC) .60 1.50
118 Eric Young Jr. (RC) .40 1.00
119 Dan Uggla .15 .40
120 Nick Swisher .25 .60
121 Francisco Rodriguez .25 .60
122 Yadier Molina .40 1.00
123 Mariano Rivera .50 1.25
124 Andrew McCutchen .40 1.00
125 Hideki Matsui .40 1.00
126 Chipper Jones .40 1.00
127 Albert Pujols .50 1.25
128 Hans Florine .15 .40
129 Johannes Gutenberg .15 .40
130 Area 51 .15 .40
131 Tyler Flowers RC .60 1.50
132 David Price .30 .75
133 Nelson Cruz .40 1.00
134 Vladimir Guerrero .25 .60
135 Ken Blackburn .15 .40
136 Garrett Jones .15 .40
137 Ryan Zimmerman .25 .60
138 Javier Vazquez .15 .40
139 Miguel Cabrera .40 1.00
140 Brandon Allen (RC) .40 1.00
141 Matt Cain .25 .60
142 Ubaldo Jimenez .15 .40
143 Jorge Posada .25 .60
144 Stuart Scott .40 1.00
145 Jim Thome .25 .60
146 Carlos Lee .15 .40
147 Cristian Guzman .15 .40
148 Anne Donovan .15 .40
149 Ichiro Suzuki .50 1.25
150 Grady Sizemore .25 .60
151 Kanekoa Texeira RC .40 1.00
152 The Parthenon .15 .40
153 Jay Bruce .25 .60
154 Juan Francisco RC .60 1.50
155 Carlos Carrasco (RC) 1.00 2.50
156 Cameron Maybin .15 .40
157 Kevin Youkilis .15 .40
158 Mark Teixeira .25 .60
159 Denard Span .15 .40
160 Derrek Lee .15 .40
161 Luis Durango RC .40 1.00
162 Juan Pierre .15 .40
163 Raul Ibanez .25 .60
164 Kyle Blanks .15 .40
165 Nick Jacoby .15 .40
166 Chris Tillman .15 .40
167 Dan Haren .15 .40
168 Rickie Weeks .15 .40
169 Felix Hernandez .25 .60
170 Adrian Gonzalez .30 .75
171 Michael Young .15 .40
172 Ian Desmond (RC) .60 1.50
173 Jimmy Rollins .25 .60
174 Eric Byrnes .15 .40
175 Tim Lincecum .25 .60
176 Preston Pittman .15 .40
177 Pedro Feliz .15 .40
178 Josh Hamilton .25 .60
179 Ben Zobrist .25 .60
180 Gordon Beckham .15 .40
181 Tyler Colvin RC .60 1.50
182 Chris Carpenter .25 .60
183 Tommy Manzella (RC) .40 1.00
184 Jake Peavy .15 .40
185 X-Rays .15 .40
186 Jose Reyes .25 .60
187 Jair Jurrjens .15 .40
188 Jason Bartlett .15 .40
189 Howie Kendrick .15 .40
190 Randy Wolf .15 .40
191 Justin Morneau .25 .60
192 Tom Knapp .15 .40
193 Tony Hoard/Rory .15 .40
194 Nyjer Morgan .15 .40
195 Sergio Santos (RC) .40 1.00
196 Scott Baker .15 .40
197 Johnny Damon .25 .60
198 A.J. Pierzynski .15 .40
199 Summer Sanders .15 .40
200 Lance Berkman .25 .60
201 Pablo Sandoval .25 .60
202 Aramis Ramirez .15 .40
203 Sig Hansen .15 .40
204 Russell Martin .15 .40
205 Meb Keflezighi .15 .40
206 J.D. Drew .15 .40
207 Wandy Rodriguez .15 .40
208 Evan Longoria .25 .60
209 Alex Gordon .25 .60
210 Chris Johnson RC .60 1.50
211 Johnny Strange .15 .40
212 Ken Griffey Jr. .75 2.00
213 Mark Reynolds .15 .40
214 CC Sabathia .25 .60
215 Daniel Murphy .30 .75
216 Jordin Sparks .15 .40
217 James Shields .15 .40
218 Todd Helton .25 .60
219 Adam Wainwright .25 .60
220 Manny Ramirez .40 1.00
221 Mike Leake RC 1.25 3.00
222 Craig Gentry RC .40 1.00
223 Jason Kubel .15 .40
224 Ian Stewart .15 .40
225 Mark Teahen .15 .40
226 Brian McCann .25 .60
227 Henry Rodriguez RC .40 1.00
228 Chase Utley .25 .60
229 Franklin Gutierrez .15 .40

2010 Topps Allen and Ginter Mini

230 Brian Roberts .15 .40
231 Travis Snider .15 .40
232 Hubertus Wawra .15 .40
233 Rick Ankiel .15 .40
234 Nick Johnson .15 .40
235 Carlos Guillen .15 .40
236 Shawn Johnson .40 1.00
237 Kevin Millwood .15 .40
238 Michael Brantley RC .60 1.50
239 Mike Cameron .15 .40
240 Aaron Hill .15 .40
241 Derek Lowe .15 .40
242 Jules Verne .15 .40
243 Jim Zapp .15 .40
244 Aaron Cook .15 .40
245 Michael Dunn RC .40 1.00
246 Geovany Soto .25 .60
247 Rajai Davis .15 .40
248 Jason Marquis .15 .40
249 Alfonso Soriano .25 .60
250 Magglio Ordonez .25 .60
251 Chase Headley .15 .40
252 Matt Garza .15 .40
253 Adam Moore RC .40 1.00
254 Rich Harden .15 .40
255 Robert Scott .15 .40
256 Rick Porcello .25 .60
257 Ervin Santana .15 .40
258 Ryan Dempster .15 .40
259 Scott Feldman .15 .40
260 Chris Young .15 .40
261 Adam Jones .25 .60
262 Zack Greinke .25 .60
263 Ruben Tejada RC .60 1.50
264 Captain Nemo .15 .40
265 Kendry Morales .15 .40
266 Adam LaRoche .15 .40
267 Martin Prado .15 .40
268 Brad Kilby RC .40 1.00
269 A.J. Burnett .15 .40
270 Max Poser .15 .40
271 King Tut .15 .40
272 David Blaine .15 .40
273 David DeJesus .15 .40
274 Nick Markakis .30 .75
275 Clayton Kershaw .75 2.00
276 Daniel Runzler RC .60 1.50
277 Regis Philbin .15 .40
278 Jeff Francoeur .25 .60
279 Curtis Granderson .30 .75
280 Koji Uehara .15 .40
281 Kurt Suzuki .15 .40
282 Tyson Ross RC .40 1.00
283 Hank Presswood .15 .40
284 Dustin Richardson RC .40 1.00
285 Alex Rodriguez .50 1.25
286 Revolving Door .15 .40
287 Drew Brees .40 1.00
288 Bobby Jenks .15 .40
289 Hanley Ramirez .25 .60
290 Jon Lester .25 .60
291 Ron Teasley .15 .40
292 Chris Pettit RC .40 1.00
293 Troy Tulowitzki .40 1.00
294 Buster Posey RC 3.00 8.00
295 Josh Thole RC .60 1.50
296 Barry Zito .25 .60
297 Isaac Newton .15 .40
298 Jorge Cantu .15 .40
299 Robinson Cano .25 .60
300 Nolan Reimold .15 .40
301 Gaby Sanchez SP 1.25 3.00
302 Daric Barton SP 1.25 3.00
303 Trevor Cahill SP 1.25 3.00
304 Carlos Pena SP 1.25 3.00
305 Kelly Johnson SP 1.25 3.00
306 Brandon Phillips SP 1.25 3.00
307 Akinori Iwamura SP 1.25 3.00
308 Adrian Beltre SP 3.00 8.00
309 Casey McGehee SP 1.25 3.00
310 Placido Polanco SP 1.25 3.00
311 Chone Figgins SP 1.25 3.00
312 Carlos Ruiz SP 1.25 3.00
313 Ryan Doumit SP 1.25 3.00
314 Ivan Rodriguez SP 1.25 3.00
315 Bobby Abreu SP 1.25 3.00
316 Nate McLouth SP 1.25 3.00
317 Alex Rios SP .75 2.00
318 Carlos Gonzalez SP 2.00 5.00
319 Austin Jackson SP RC 1.25 3.00
320 Scott Sizemore SP RC 1.25 3.00
321 Carlos Gomez SP 1.25 3.00
322 Gary Matthews SP 1.25 3.00
323 Angel Pagan SP 1.25 3.00
324 Randy Winn SP 1.25 3.00
325 Brett Gardner SP 2.00 5.00
326 Aaron Rowand SP 1.25 3.00
327 Vernon Wells SP 1.25 3.00
328 Jered Weaver SP 2.00 5.00
329 Troy Glaus SP 1.25 3.00
330 Jonathan Papelbon SP 1.25 3.00
331 Huston Street SP 1.25 3.00
332 Ricky Nolasco SP 1.25 3.00
333 Roy Oswalt SP 1.25 3.00
334 Brett Myers SP 1.25 3.00
335 Jonathan Broxton SP 1.25 3.00
336 Hiroki Kuroda SP 1.25 3.00
337 Joe Nathan SP 1.25 3.00
338 Francisco Liriano SP 1.25 3.00
339 Ben Sheets SP 1.25 3.00
340 Brad Lidge SP 1.25 3.00
341 Jon Garland SP 1.25 3.00
342 Erik Bedard SP 1.25 3.00
343 Brad Penny SP 1.25 3.00
344 Derek Holland SP 1.25 3.00
345 Stephen Drew SP 1.25 3.00
346 Ryan Theriot SP 1.25 3.00
347 Orlando Cabrera SP 1.25 3.00
348 Asdrubal Cabrera SP 2.00 5.00
349 Yuniesky Betancourt SP 1.25 3.00
350 Alcides Escobar SP 1.25 3.00

2010 Topps Allen and Ginter Mini

*MINI 1-300: .75X TO 2X BASIC
*MINI 1-300 RC: .5X TO 1.2X BASIC RC's
APPX. ONE MINI PER PACK
*MINI SP 301-350: .5X TO 1.2X BASIC SP
MINI SP ODDS 1:13 HOBBY
COMMON CARD (351-400) 6.00 15.00
351-400 RANDOM WITHIN RIP CARDS
STRASBURG 401 ISSUED IN PACKS
OVERALL PLATE ODDS 1:799 HOBBY
351 Cole Hamels EXT 12.00 30.00
352 Billy Butler EXT 20.00 50.00
353 Daisuke Matsuzaka EXT 30.00 60.00
354 Stephen Drew EXT 30.00 60.00
355 Ryan Braun EXT 20.00 50.00
356 Mark Teixeira EXT 20.00 50.00
357 Chipper Jones EXT 40.00 80.00
358 Justin Morneau EXT 20.00 50.00
359 Adrian Gonzalez EXT 6.00 15.00
360 Dustin Pedroia EXT 30.00 60.00
361 Miguel Cabrera EXT 30.00 60.00
362 Carlos Beltran EXT 10.00 25.00
363 Lance Berkman EXT 30.00 60.00
364 Kevin Kouzmanoff EXT 10.00 25.00
365 A.J. Burnett EXT 20.00 50.00
366 Tim Lincecum EXT 12.50 30.00
367 Francisco Rodriguez EXT 6.00 15.00
368 Zack Greinke EXT 20.00 50.00
369 Andre Ethier EXT 6.00 15.00
370 Hideki Matsui EXT 6.00 15.00
371 Alexei Ramirez EXT 6.00 15.00
372 Grady Sizemore EXT 20.00 50.00
373 Joe Mauer EXT 20.00 50.00
374 Adam Lind EXT 12.00 30.00
375 Kurt Suzuki EXT 10.00 25.00
376 Rick Porcello EXT 20.00 50.00
377 Felix Hernandez EXT 6.00 15.00
378 Albert Pujols EXT 20.00 50.00
379 Adam Dunn EXT 10.00 25.00
380 Brandon Webb EXT 20.00 50.00
381 Pablo Sandoval EXT 12.50 30.00
382 Chris Young EXT 20.00 50.00
383 Tommy Hanson EXT 30.00 60.00
384 Adam Jones EXT 20.00 50.00
385 Joe Nathan EXT 20.00 50.00
386 Andy Pettitte EXT 15.00 40.00
387 Gordon Beckham EXT 20.00 50.00
388 Alfonso Soriano EXT 6.00 15.00
389 Hanley Ramirez EXT 30.00 60.00
390 Torii Hunter EXT 20.00 50.00
391 Matt Garza EXT 6.00 15.00
392 Johnny Cueto EXT 20.00 50.00
393 Prince Fielder EXT 30.00 60.00
394 Andrew McCutchen EXT 30.00 60.00
395 Ken Griffey Jr. EXT 50.00 120.00
396 Ryan Howard EXT 10.00 25.00
397 Todd Helton EXT 6.00 15.00
398 Kosuke Fukudome EXT 30.00 60.00
399 Roy Halladay EXT 20.00 50.00
400 Matt Kemp EXT 40.00 80.00
401 Stephen Strasburg 12.00 30.00

2010 Topps Allen and Ginter Mini A and G Back

*A & G BACK: 1X TO 2.5X BASIC
*A & G BACK RCs: .6X TO 1.5X BASIC RCs
STATED ODDS 1:5 HOBBY
*A & G BACK SP: .6X TO 1.5X BASIC SP
SP STATED ODDS 1:65 HOBBY

2010 Topps Allen and Ginter Mini Black

*BLACK: 2X TO 5X BASIC
*BLACK RCs: .75X TO 2X BASIC RCs
STATED ODDS 1:10 HOBBY
*BLACK SP: .75X TO 2X BASIC SP
SP STATED ODDS 1:130 HOBBY

2010 Topps Allen and Ginter Mini No Card Number

*NO NBR: 8X TO 20X BASIC
*NO NBR RCs: 3X TO 8X BASIC RCs
*NO NBR SP: 1.2X TO 3X BASIC SP
STATED ODDS 1:140 HOBBY

2010 Topps Allen and Ginter Autographs

STATED ODDS 1:HOBBY
ASTERISK EQUALS PARTIAL EXCHANGE
AD Anne Donovan 6.00 15.00
AE Alcides Escobar 4.00 10.00
AEI Andre Ethier EXCH * 4.00 10.00
AF Alan Francis 6.00 15.00
AG Alex Gordon 40.00 80.00
AGA Anthony Gatto 6.00 15.00
AGO Adrian Gonzalez 8.00 20.00
AJ Adam Jones 6.00 15.00
AJE Avery Jenkins 30.00 60.00
AL Adam Lind 5.00 12.00
AM Andrew McCutchen 25.00 60.00
AR Alexei Ramirez 8.00 20.00
BD Brian Duensing 5.00 12.00
BJU B.J. Upton 10.00 25.00
CC Chris Coghlan 6.00 15.00
CK Clayton Kershaw 40.00 100.00
CM Cameron Maybin 4.00 10.00
CP Cliff Pennington 6.00 15.00
CR Colby Rasmus 4.00 10.00
CV Chris Volstad 4.00 10.00
CY Chris Young 4.00 10.00
DB David Blaine 40.00 80.00
DBR Drew Brees 75.00 200.00
DD Dale Davis 8.00 20.00
DM Daniel McCutchen 4.00 10.00
DP Dustin Pedroia 20.00 50.00
DS Drew Stubbs 4.00 10.00
DT Darren Taylor 4.00 10.00
EC Everth Cabrera 4.00 10.00
GS Gary Stewart 10.00 25.00
GSI Glenn Singleman 8.00 20.00
HF Hans Florine 8.00 20.00
HP Hank Presswood 10.00 25.00
HW Hubertus Wawra 5.00 12.00
IC Ivory Crockett 12.50 30.00
IK Ian Kinsler 5.00 12.00
JC Johnny Cueto 6.00 15.00
JCL Jeff Clement 5.00 12.00
JF Jeff Francis 4.00 10.00
JH Jason Heyward 10.00 25.00
JK Jason Kubel 6.00 15.00
JL Judson Laipply 6.00 15.00
JM Jason Motte 5.00 12.00
JO Josh Outman 4.00 10.00
JP Jonathan Papelbon 12.00 30.00
JR Juan Rivera 5.00 12.00
JRT J.R. Towles 4.00 10.00
JS Jordin Sparks 30.00 60.00
JST Johnny Strange 6.00 15.00
JU Justin Upton 8.00 20.00
JW Josh Willingham 5.00 12.00
JZ Jim Zapp 12.00 30.00
KB Ken Blackburn 10.00 25.00
KK Kelly Kulick 10.00 25.00
KU Koji Uehara 8.00 20.00
MB Michael Bourn 5.00 12.00
MC Miguel Cabrera 75.00 150.00
MD Mahlon Duckett 20.00 50.00
MH Matt Holliday 50.00 100.00
MK Matt Kemp 12.50 30.00
MKE Meb Keflezighi 10.00 25.00
MM Marvin Miller 40.00 80.00
MP Mike Parsons 8.00 20.00
MPO Max Poser 4.00 10.00
MS Max Scherzer 25.00 60.00
MTB Mitchell Boggs 5.00 12.00
NF Neftali Feliz 4.00 10.00
PP Placido Polanco 5.00 12.00
PPI Preston Pittman 8.00 20.00
PS Pablo Sandoval 12.00 30.00
RB Ryan Braun 15.00 40.00
RH Ryan Howard 12.00 30.00
RHI Rich Hill 5.00 12.00
RK Ryan Kennelly 10.00 25.00
RN Ricky Nolasco 4.00 10.00
RO Ross Ohlendorf 4.00 10.00
ROI Randy Oitker 5.00 12.00
RP Rick Porcello 6.00 15.00
RPE Ryan Perry 4.00 10.00
RPH Regis Philbin 12.00 50.00
RS Robert Scott 15.00 40.00
RT Ron Teasley 10.00 25.00
RTH Tony Hoard/Rory 8.00 20.00
RZ Ryan Zimmerman 8.00 20.00
SH Sig Hansen 30.00 60.00
SJ Shawn Johnson 50.00 100.00
SK Scott Kazmir 50.00 100.00
SS Stuart Scott 50.00 120.00
SS Stephen Strasburg 400.00 600.00
SSA Summer Sanders 15.00 40.00
SV Shane Victorino 10.00 25.00
TB Tyler Bradt 4.00 10.00
TC Trevor Crowe 4.00 10.00
TDV Tiago Della Vega 4.00 10.00
TH Tommy Hanson 5.00 12.00
THA Tony Hawk 75.00 150.00
TK Tom Knapp 12.50 30.00
TT Troy Tulowitzki 12.50 30.00
VW Vernon Wells 40.00 80.00
YE Yunel Escobar 5.00 12.00
YG Yovani Gallardo 4.00 10.00
ZS Zac Sunderland 4.00 10.00

2010 Topps Allen and Ginter Baseball Highlights

COMPLETE SET (15) 8.00 20.00
STATED ODDS 1:10 HOBBY
AGHS1 Chase Utley .60 1.50
AGHS2 Mark Buehrle .60 1.50
AGHS3 Derek Jeter 2.50 6.00
AGHS4 Mariano Rivera 1.25 3.00
AGHS5 Ichiro Suzuki 1.25 3.00
AGHS6 Johnny Damon .60 1.50
AGHS7 Carl Crawford .60 1.50
AGHS8 Dewayne Wise .40 1.00
AGHS9 Jimmy Rollins .60 1.50
AGHS10 Hideki Matsui 1.00 2.50
AGHS11 Andre Ethier .60 1.50
AGHS12 Troy Tulowitzki 1.00 2.50
AGHS13 Jonathan Sanchez .40 1.00
AGHS14 Mark Teixeira .60 1.50
AGHS15 Daniel Murphy .75 2.00

2010 Topps Allen and Ginter Cabinets

NCCB1 President Chester A. Arthur/Washington Roebling/John A. Roebling/Emily Roeb 2.00 5.00
NCCB2 Andrew McCutchen 2.50 6.00
NCCB3 President Herbert Hoover/Elwood Mead 2.00 5.00
NCCB4 Lance Berkman/Ivan Rodriguez/Carlos Lee 2.00 5.00
NCCB5 President Theodore Roosevelt/John Frank Stevens/George Washington Goethals/ 2.00 5.00
NCCB6 CC/Rivera/Hideki/Jeter 4.00 10.00
NCCB7 Joe Mauer 3.00 8.00
NCCB8 George Washington/Thomas Jefferson/Theodore Roosevelt Abraham Lincoln 2.00 5.00
NCCB9 Ellsbury/Pettitte/Posada 2.50 6.00
NCCB10 Gerald R. Ford Richard M. Nixon/Wally Hickel 2.00 5.00

2010 Topps Allen and Ginter Mini Celestial Stars

RANDOM INSERTS IN PACKS
CS1 Mark Teixeira 1.50 4.00
CS2 Prince Fielder 1.50 4.00
CS3 Tim Lincecum 1.50 4.00
CS4 Derek Jeter 6.00 15.00
CS5 Dustin Pedroia 2.00 5.00
CS6 Cliff Lee 1.50 4.00
CS7 Evan Longoria 1.50 4.00
CS8 Ryan Howard 2.00 5.00
CS9 David Wright 2.00 5.00
CS10 Albert Pujols 3.00 8.00
CS11 Vladimir Guerrero 1.50 4.00
CS12 Johan Santana 1.50 4.00

2010 Topps Allen and Ginter Mini Creatures of Legend, Myth and Joy

STATED ODDS 1:288 HOBBY
CLMJ1 Santa Claus 10.00 25.00
CLMJ2 The Easter Bunny 10.00 25.00
CLMJ3 The Tooth Fairy 10.00 25.00
CLMJ4 Goldilocks 10.00 25.00
CLMJ5 Little Red Riding Hood 10.00 25.00
CLMJ6 Paul Bunyan 10.00 25.00
CLMJ7 Jack and the Beanstalk 10.00 25.00
CLMJ8 Peter Pan 10.00 25.00
CLMJ9 Three Little Pigs 10.00 25.00
CLMJ10 The Little Engine That Could 10.00 25.00

2010 Topps Allen and Ginter Mini Lords of Olympus

COMPLETE SET (25) 12.50 30.00
STATED ODDS 1:12 HOBBY
LO1 Zeus 1.25 3.00
LO2 Poseidon 1.25 3.00
LO3 Hades 1.25 3.00
LO4 Hera 1.25 3.00
LO5 Athena 1.25 3.00
LO6 Apollo 1.25 3.00
LO7 Aphrodite 1.25 3.00
LO8 Hermes 1.25 3.00
LO9 Artemis 1.25 3.00
LO10 Gaea 1.25 3.00
LO11 Uranus 1.25 3.00
LO12 Cronos 1.25 3.00
LO13 Prometheus 1.25 3.00
LO14 Phoebe 1.25 3.00
LO15 Demeter 1.25 3.00
LO16 Persephone 1.25 3.00
LO17 Dionysus 1.25 3.00
LO18 Eros 1.25 3.00
LO19 Helios 1.25 3.00
LO20 Thanatos 1.25 3.00
LO21 Pan 1.25 3.00
LO22 Nemesis 1.25 3.00
LO23 The Fates 1.25 3.00
LO24 The Muses 1.25 3.00
LO25 Atlas 1.25 3.00

2010 Topps Allen and Ginter Mini Monsters of the Mesozoic

COMPLETE SET (25) 12.50 30.00
STATED ODDS 1:12 HOBBY
MM1 Tyrannosaurus Rex 1.25 3.00
MM2 Triceratops 1.25 3.00
MM3 Stegosaurus 1.25 3.00
MM4 Velociraptor 1.25 3.00
MM5 Allosaurus 1.25 3.00
MM6 Megalosaurus 1.25 3.00
MM7 Spinosaurus 1.25 3.00
MM8 Ankylosaurus 1.25 3.00
MM9 Apatosaurus 1.25 3.00
MM10 Brachiosaurus 1.25 3.00
MM11 Diplodocus 1.25 3.00
MM12 Iguanodon 1.25 3.00
MM13 Pachycephalosaurus 1.25 3.00
MM14 Pentaceratops 1.25 3.00
MM15 Protoceratops 1.25 3.00
MM16 Ultrasaurus 1.25 3.00
MM17 Dilophosaurus 1.25 3.00
MM18 Supersaurus 1.25 3.00
MM19 Nomingia 1.25 3.00
MM20 Oviraptor 1.25 3.00
MM21 Bambiraptor 1.25 3.00
MM22 Protarchaeopteryx 1.25 3.00
MM23 Carcharodontosaurus 1.25 3.00
MM24 Carnotaurus 1.25 3.00
MM25 Giganotosaurus 1.25 3.00

2010 Topps Allen and Ginter Mini National Animals

COMPLETE SET (50) 12.50 30.00
STATED ODDS 1:8 HOBBY
NA1 Cougar 1.25 3.00
NA2 Cuban Crocodile 1.25 3.00
NA3 Falcon 1.25 3.00
NA4 Cheetah 1.25 3.00
NA5 Cow 1.25 3.00
NA6 Kangaroo 1.25 3.00
NA7 Ostrich 1.25 3.00
NA8 Chihuahua 1.25 3.00
NA9 Jaguar 1.25 3.00
NA10 Bull 1.25 3.00
NA11 Harpy Eagle 1.25 3.00
NA12 Markhor 1.25 3.00
NA13 African Elephant 1.25 3.00
NA14 Barbary Macaque 1.25 3.00
NA15 Giant Panda 1.25 3.00
NA16 Leopard 1.25 3.00
NA17 Camel 1.25 3.00
NA18 Beaver 1.25 3.00
NA19 Alpaca 1.25 3.00
NA20 Lion 1.25 3.00
NA21 Lynx 1.25 3.00
NA22 Stag 1.25 3.00
NA23 Elk 1.25 3.00
NA24 Condor 1.25 3.00
NA25 Wisent 1.25 3.00
NA26 Gray Wolf 1.25 3.00
NA27 Gallic Rooster 1.25 3.00
NA28 Sable Antelope 1.25 3.00
NA29 Flamingo 1.25 3.00
NA30 Koi 1.25 3.00
NA31 Ashy-faced Owl 1.25 3.00
NA32 Bulldog 1.25 3.00
NA33 Brown Bear 1.25 3.00
NA34 White-tailed Deer 1.25 3.00
NA35 Russian Bear 1.25 3.00
NA36 Dolphin 1.25 3.00
NA37 Komodo Dragon 1.25 3.00
NA38 Llama 1.25 3.00
NA39 Sheep 1.25 3.00
NA40 King Cobra 1.25 3.00
NA41 Green-and-black Streamertail 1.25 3.00
NA42 Carabao 1.25 3.00
NA43 Water Buffalo 1.25 3.00
NA44 Israeli Gazelle 1.25 3.00
NA45 Italian Wolf 1.25 3.00
NA46 Ring Tailed Lemur 1.25 3.00
NA47 Tiger 1.25 3.00
NA48 Dalmatian 1.25 3.00
NA49 Zebra 1.25 3.00
NA50 Bald Eagle 1.50 4.00

2010 Topps Allen and Ginter Mini Saltiest Sailors

RANDOM INSERTS IN PACKS
WSS1 Blackbeard 20.00 50.00
WSS2 Ned Low 20.00 50.00
WSS3 Jack Rackham 20.00 50.00
WSS4 Stede Bonnet 20.00 50.00
WSS5 Black Bart 20.00 50.00
WSS6 Captain Kidd 20.00 50.00
WSS7 Henry Morgan 20.00 50.00
WSS8 Edward England 20.00 50.00
WSS9 Thomas Tew 20.00 50.00
WSS10 Charles Vane 20.00 50.00

2010 Topps Allen and Ginter Mini Sailors of the Seven Sea

COMPLETE SET (10) 10.00 25.00
STATED ODDS 1:24 HOBBY
SSS1 Christopher Columbus 1.50 4.00
SSS2 Sir Francis Drake 1.50 4.00
SSS3 Sir Walter Raleigh 1.50 4.00
SSS4 Vasco Nunez de Balboa 1.50 4.00
SSS5 Francisco Vasquez de Coronado 1.50 4.00
SSS6 Hernando de Cortes 1.50 4.00
SSS7 Hernando de Soto 1.50 4.00
SSS8 Henry Hudson 1.50 4.00
SSS9 Francisco Pizarro 1.50 4.00
SSS10 Juan Ponce de Leon 1.50 4.00

2010 Topps Allen and Ginter Mini World's Biggest

RANDOM INSERTS IN RETAIL PACKS
WB1 Blue Whale 2.00 5.00
WB2 Burj Khalifa 2.00 5.00
WB3 Prague Castle 2.00 5.00
WB4 General Sherman Sequoia 2.00 5.00
WB5 Mount Everest 2.00 5.00
WB6 Antarctica 6.00 15.00
WB7 Sahara 6.00 15.00
WB8 Angel Falls 6.00 15.00
WB9 The Amazon 6.00 15.00
WB10 Steamboat Geyser 6.00 15.00
WB11 Lake Pontchartrain Causeway 6.00 15.00
WB12 The Nile 6.00 15.00
WB13 Russia 6.00 15.00
WB14 Three Gorges Dam 6.00 15.00
WB15 Golden Jubilee 6.00 15.00
WB16 Polar Bear 6.00 15.00
WB17 African Elephant 6.00 15.00
WB18 Eastern Lowland Gorilla 6.00 15.00
WB19 Goliath Birdeater 6.00 15.00
WB20 World's Largest Collection of World's Smallest Versions of World's Largest 6.00 15.00
WB21 Large Hadron Collider 6.00 15.00
WB22 1966 Leonid Meteor Shower 6.00 15.00
WB23 Sedan Crater 6.00 15.00
WB24 Kuthodaw Pagoda 6.00 15.00
WB25 Spring Temple Buddha 6.00 15.00

2010 Topps Allen and Ginter Mini World's Greatest Word Smiths

COMPLETE SET (15) 12.50 30.00
STATED ODDS 1:24 HOBBY
WGWS1 Homer 1.50 4.00
WGWS2 William Shakespeare 1.50 4.00
WGWS3 Washington Irving 1.50 4.00
WGWS4 Miguel de Cervantes 1.50 4.00
WGWS5 Fyodor Dostoevsky 1.50 4.00
WGWS6 Victor Hugo 1.50 4.00
WGWS7 Shen Kuo 1.50 4.00
WGWS8 John Milton 1.50 4.00
WGWS9 Dante Alighieri 1.50 4.00
WGWS10 Edgar Allan Poe 1.50 4.00
WGWS11 Marcus Aurelius 1.50 4.00
WGWS12 Virgil 1.50 4.00
WGWS13 John Bunyan 1.50 4.00
WGWS14 Plato 1.50 4.00
WGWS15 Confucius 1.50 4.00

2010 Topps Allen and Ginter N43

AE Andre Ethier 1.25 3.00
AM Andrew McCutchen 2.00 5.00
AP Albert Pujols 2.50 6.00
AR Alex Rodriguez 2.50 6.00
BU B.J. Upton 1.25 3.00
EL Evan Longoria 1.25 3.00
HP Hunter Pence 1.25 3.00
HR Hanley Ramirez 1.25 3.00
JM Joe Mauer 1.50 4.00
JU Justin Upton 1.25 3.00
MT Mark Teixeira 1.25 3.00
NM Nick Markakis 1.50 4.00
PF Prince Fielder 1.25 3.00
RB Ryan Braun 1.25 3.00
RH Ryan Howard 1.50 4.00

2010 Topps Allen and Ginter Relics

STATED ODDS 1:11 HOBBY
AD Adam Dunn 3.00 8.00
AD Anne Donovan 5.00 12.00
AE Andre Ethier 3.00 8.00
AF Alan Francis 6.00 15.00
AG Adrian Gonzalez Bat 3.00 8.00
AGA Anthony Gatto 5.00 12.00
AH Aaron Hill 3.00 8.00
AJ Adam Jones 3.00 8.00
AJ Avery Jenkins 20.00 50.00
AL Adam Lind 3.00 8.00
ARA Aramis Ramirez 3.00 8.00
AS Alfonso Soriano 3.00 8.00
BA Brett Anderson 3.00 8.00
BB Billy Butler 3.00 8.00
BM Brian McCann 3.00 8.00
BP Buster Posey 10.00 25.00
BR Brian Roberts 3.00 8.00
BU B.J. Upton 3.00 8.00
CC Chris Coghlan 3.00 8.00
CL Carlos Lee 3.00 8.00
CM Carlos Marmol 3.00 8.00
CQ Carlos Quentin 3.00 8.00
CR Colby Rasmus Bat 3.00 8.00
DB David Blaine 15.00 40.00
DBR Drew Brees 10.00 25.00
DD Dale Davis 4.00 10.00
DH Dan Haren 3.00 8.00
DT Darren Taylor 5.00 12.00
DU Dan Uggla 3.00 8.00
DW David Wright 5.00 12.00
DWR David Wright 3.00 8.00
EL Evan Longoria 3.00 8.00
GB Gordon Beckham 3.00 8.00
GS Grady Sizemore 3.00 8.00
GS Gary Stewart 5.00 12.00
GSI Glenn Singleman 4.00 10.00
HF Hans Florine 10.00 25.00
HR Hanley Ramirez 3.00 8.00
HW Hubertus Wawra 6.00 15.00
IC Ivory Crockett 5.00 12.00
IK Ian Kinsler 3.00 8.00
IR Ivan Rodriguez 3.00 8.00
IS Ichiro Suzuki 4.00 10.00
JB Jay Bruce 3.00 8.00
JD John Danks 3.00 8.00
JH Josh Hamilton 3.00 8.00
JJ Josh Johnson 3.00 8.00
JL Judson Laipply 5.00 12.00
JS Jordin Sparks 8.00 20..
JS Johnny Strange 3.00 8.
JSA Jeff Samardzija 3.00 8.
JV Joey Votto 3.00 8.
KB Kyle Blanks 3.00 8.
KB Ken Blackburn 4.00 10.
KF Kosuke Fukudome 3.00 8.
KK Kelly Kulick 8.00 20.
KM Kendry Morales 3.00 8.
LB Lance Berkman 6.00 15.
MC Matt Cain 3.00 8.
MCA Miguel Cabrera 6.00 15.
MCAB Melky Cabrera 3.00 8.
MK Matt Kemp 3.00 8.
MK Meb Keflezighi 5.00 12.
ML Mat Latos 3.00 8.
MM Marvin Miller 5.00 12.
MP Mike Parsons 4.00 10.
MPO Max Poser 6.00 15.
MR Mark Reynolds 3.00 8.
NC Nelson Cruz 3.00 8.
NF Neftali Feliz 30.00 60.
NM Nick Markakis 3.00 8.
PF Prince Fielder 3.00 8.
PP Preston Pittman 6.00 15.
RB Ryan Braun 3.00 8.
RC Robinson Cano 3.00 8.
RH Ryan Howard 4.00 10.
RK Ryan Kennelly 4.00 10.
RN Ricky Nolasco 3.00 8.
RO Randy Oitker 6.00 15.
RP Regis Philbin 12.50 30.
RTH Tony Hoard/Rory 12.50 30.
RZ Ryan Zimmerman 3.00 8.
SD Stephen Drew 3.00 8.
SH Sig Hansen 30.00 60.
SJ Shawn Johnson 15.00 40.
SS Stuart Scott 15.00 40.
SSA Summer Sanders 6.00 15.
SV Shane Victorino 3.00 8.
TB Tyler Bradt 6.00 15.
TDV Tiago Della Vega 5.00 12.
TH Tony Hawk 20.00 50.
THE Todd Helton 3.00 8.
THU Torii Hunter 3.00 8.
TK Tom Knapp 12.50 30.
TT Troy Tulowitzki 3.00 8.
UJ Ubaldo Jimenez 3.00 8.
YE Yunel Escobar 3.00 8.
YG Yovani Gallardo 15.00 40.
ZS Zac Sunderland 4.00 10.

2010 Topps Allen and Ginter Ri Cards

STATED ODDS 1:285 HOBBY
PRINT RUNS B/WN 5-99 COPIES PER
ALL LISTED PRICED ARE FOR RIPPED
UNRIPPED HAVE ADD'L CARDS WITHIN
COMMON UNRIPPED p/r 99 40.00 80.0
COMMON UNRIPPED p/r 50 50.00 100.0
RC1 Rick Ankiel/99 6.00 15.0
RC4 Elijah Dukes/99 6.00 15.0
RC5 Carlos Gomez/99 6.00 15.0
RC7 Erik Bedard/50 6.00 15.0
RC11 Troy Glaus/50 6.00 15.0
RC14 Aramis Ramirez/50 6.00 15.0
RC15 Colby Rasmus/99 6.00 15.0
RC19 Mike Cameron/99 6.00 15.0
RC20 Corey Hart/99 6.00 15.0
RC24 Yunel Escobar/99 6.00 15.0
RC25 Nick Swisher/50 10.00 25.0
RC28 Nate McLouth/99 6.00 15.0
RC31 Jay Bruce/50 10.00 25.0
RC33 Hunter Pence/50 10.00 25.0
RC34 Kendry Morales/50 6.00 15.0
RC35 James Loney/99 6.00 15.0
RC36 Brandon Phillips/50 6.00 15.0
RC38 Carlos Lee/50 6.00 15.0
RC43 Russ Martin/99 6.00 15.0
RC44 Derrek Lee/50 6.00 15.0
RC45 Orlando Hudson/99 6.00 15.0
RC48 Lastings Milledge/99 6.00 15.0
RC50 Denard Span/99 6.00 15.0
RC52 Tim Hudson/50 10.00 25.0
RC53 Joakim Soria/50 6.00 15.0
RC54 Chad Billingsley/99 10.00 25.0
RC58 Tyler Flowers/99 10.00 25.0
RC60 Kyle Blanks/99 6.00 15.0
RC62 Carlos Pena/50 10.00 25.0
RC63 Magglio Ordonez/50 10.00 25.0
RC64 Elvis Andrus/99 10.00 25.0
RC66 Joey Votto/50 10.00 25.0
RC67 Yovani Gallardo/50 6.00 15.0
RC69 Delmon Young/99 10.00 25.0
RC71 Scott Kazmir/99 6.00 15.0
RC74 Tommy Manzella/99 6.00 15.0
RC76 Jim Thome/50 10.00 25.0
RC80 Michael Brantley/99 10.00 25.0
RC81 Franklin Gutierrez/50 6.00 15.0
RC82 Jered Weaver/50 10.00 25.0
RC85 Chris Coghlan/99 6.00 15.0
RC86 Nelson Cruz/50 15.00 40.0
RC87 Aaron Rowand/99 6.00 15.0
RC88 Ben Sheets/50 6.00 15.0
RC89 James Shields/50 6.00 15.0

RC91 Travis Snider/99 6.00 15.00
RC92 Jonathan Broxton/50 6.00 15.00
RC93 Carlos Zambrano/99 10.00 25.00
RC94 Rich Harden/50 6.00 15.00
RC98 Vernon Wells/50 6.00 15.00

2010 Topps Allen and Ginter This Day in History

COMPLETE SET (75) 10.00 25.00
TDH1 Chase Utley .40 1.00
TDH2 Stephen Drew .25 .60
TDH3 Aramis Ramirez .25 .60
TDH4 Lance Berkman .40 1.00
TDH5 Chipper Jones .60 1.50
TDH6 Brian Roberts .25 .60
TDH7 Jason Heyward 1.00 2.50
TDH8 Yunel Escobar .25 .60
TDH9 Pablo Sandoval .40 1.00
TDH10 David Ortiz .60 1.50
TDH11 Jason Bay .40 1.00
TDH12 Andre Ethier .40 1.00
TDH13 Adam Dunn .40 1.00
TDH14 Justin Verlander .60 1.50
TDH15 Manny Ramirez .60 1.50
TDH16 Carlos Gonzalez .40 1.00
TDH17 Joe Mauer .50 1.25
TDH18 Felix Hernandez .40 1.00
TDH19 Robinson Cano .40 1.00
TDH20 CC Sabathia .40 1.00
TDH21 Magglio Ordonez .40 1.00
TDH22 Grady Sizemore .40 1.00
TDH23 Dan Haren .25 .60
TDH24 Joey Votto .60 1.50
TDH25 Ryan Zimmerman .40 1.00
TDH26 Francisco Rodriguez .40 1.00
TDH27 Ken Griffey Jr. 1.25 3.00
TDH28 Jose Reyes .40 1.00
TDH29 Adam Jones .40 1.00
TDH30 Hideki Matsui .60 1.50
TDH31 Mark Teixeira .40 1.00
TDH32 Adrian Gonzalez .50 1.25
TDH33 Kosuke Fukudome .40 1.00
TDH34 Troy Tulowitzki .60 1.50
TDH35 Josh Johnson .40 1.00
TDH36 Hanley Ramirez .40 1.00
TDH37 Ichiro Suzuki .75 2.00
TDH38 Jim Thome .40 1.00
TDH39 Torii Hunter .25 .60
TDH40 Jake Peavy .25 .60
TDH41 Aaron Hill .25 .60
TDH42 Jorge Posada .40 1.00
TDH43 Jonathan Broxton .25 .60
TDH44 B.J. Upton .40 1.00
TDH45 Miguel Cabrera .60 1.50
TDH46 Yovani Gallardo .25 .60
TDH47 Brandon Phillips .25 .60
TDH48 Matt Holliday .60 1.50
TDH49 Justin Morneau .40 1.00
TDH50 Alex Rodriguez .75 2.00
TDH51 Gordon Beckham .25 .60
TDH52 Justin Upton .40 1.00
TDH53 Nick Markakis .50 1.25
TDH54 Derrek Lee .25 .60
TDH55 Ryan Braun .40 1.00
TDH56 Jimmy Rollins .40 1.00
TDH57 Miguel Tejada .40 1.00
TDH58 Dan Uggla .25 .60
TDH59 Hunter Pence .40 1.00
TDH60 Roy Halladay .40 1.00
TDH61 James Shields .25 .60
TDH62 Kevin Youkilis .25 .60
TDH63 Alfonso Soriano .40 1.00
TDH64 Josh Hamilton .40 1.00
TDH65 Zack Greinke .40 1.00
TDH66 Curtis Granderson .50 1.25
TDH67 Josh Beckett .25 .60
TDH68 Brian McCann .40 1.00
TDH69 Alexei Ramirez .40 1.00
TDH70 Andrew McCutchen .60 1.50
TDH71 Billy Butler .25 .60
TDH72 Jay Bruce .40 1.00
TDH73 Ian Kinsler .40 1.00
TDH74 Carlos Lee .25 .60
TDH75 Mariano Rivera .75 2.00

2011 Topps Allen and Ginter

COMPLETE SET (350) 50.00 100.00
COMP.SET w/o SP's (300) 12.50 30.00
COMMON CARD (1-300) .15 .40
COMMON RC (1-300) .40 1.00
COMMON SP (301-350) 1.25 3.00
SP ODDS 1:2 HOBBY
1 Carlos Gonzalez .25 .60
2 Ty Wigginton .15 .40
3 Lou Holtz .15 .40
4 Jhoulys Chacin .15 .40
5 Aroldis Chapman RC 1.25 3.00
6 Micky Ward .15 .40
7 Mickey Mantle 1.25 3.00
8 Alexei Ramirez .25 .60
9 Joe Saunders .15 .40
10 Miguel Cabrera .40 1.00
11 Marc Forgione .15 .40
12 Hope Solo .60 1.50
13 Brett Anderson .15 .40
14 Adrian Beltre .40 1.00
15 Diana Taurasi .15 .40
16 Gordon Beckham .15 .40
17 Jonathan Papelbon .25 .60
18 Daniel Hudson .15 .40
19 Daniel Bard .15 .40
20 Jeremy Hellickson RC 1.00 2.50
21 Logan Morrison .15 .40
22 Michael Bourn .15 .40
23 Aubrey Huff .15 .40
24 Kristi Yamaguchi .15 .40
25 Nelson Cruz .40 1.00
26 Edwin Jackson .15 .40
27 Dillon Gee RC .60 1.50
28 John Lindsey RC .40 1.00
29 Johnny Cueto .25 .60
30 Hanley Ramirez .25 .60
31 Jimmy Rollins .25 .60
32 Dirk Hayhurst .15 .40
33 Curtis Granderson .30 .75
34 Pedro Ciriaco RC .60 1.50
35 Adam Dunn .25 .60
36 Eric Sogard RC .40 1.00
37 Fausto Carmona .15 .40
38 Angel Pagan .15 .40
39 Stephen Drew .15 .40
40 John McEnroe .15 .40
41 Carlos Santana .40 1.00
42 Heath Bell .15 .40
43 Jake LaMotta .15 .40
44 Ozzie Martinez RC .40 1.00
45 Annika Sorenstam .15 .40
46 Edinson Volquez .15 .40
47 Phil Hughes .15 .40
48 Francisco Liriano .15 .40
49 Javier Vazquez .15 .40
50 Carl Crawford .25 .60
51 Tim Collins RC .40 1.00
52 Francisco Cordero .15 .40
53 Chipper Jones .40 1.00
54 Austin Jackson .15 .40
55 Dustin Pedroia .30 .75
56 Scott Kazmir .15 .40
57 Derek Jeter 1.00 2.50
58 Alcides Escobar .25 .60
59 Jeremy Jeffress RC .40 1.00
60 Brandon Belt RC 1.00 2.50
61 Brian Roberts .15 .40
62 Alfonso Soriano .25 .60
63 Neil Walker .25 .60
64 Ricky Romero .15 .40
65 Ryan Howard .30 .75
66 Starlin Castro .25 .60
67 Delmon Young .25 .60
68 Max Scherzer .40 1.00
69 Neftali Feliz .25 .60
70 Evan Longoria .25 .60
71 Chris Perez .15 .40
72 Maxim Shmyrev .15 .40
73 Brandon Morrow .15 .40
74 Torii Hunter .15 .40
75 Jose Reyes .25 .60
76 Chase Headley .15 .40
77 Rafael Furcal .15 .40
78 Luke Scott .15 .40
79 Aimee Mullins .15 .40
80 Joey Votto .40 1.00
81 Yonder Alonso RC .60 1.50
82 Scott Rolen .25 .60
83 Mat Hoffman .15 .40
84 Gregory Infante RC .40 1.00
85 Chris Sale RC 2.50 6.00
86 Greg Halman RC .60 1.50
87 Colby Lewis .15 .40
88 David Ortiz .40 1.00
89 John Axford .15 .40
90 Roy Halladay .25 .60
91 Joel Pineiro .15 .40
92 Michael Pineda RC 1.00 2.50
93 Evan Lysacek .15 .40
94 Josh Rodriguez RC .40 1.00
95 Dan Uggla .15 .40
96 Daniel Boulud .15 .40
97 Zach Britton RC 1.00 2.50
98 Jason Bay .25 .60
99 Placido Polanco .15 .40
100 Albert Pujols .50 1.25
101 Peter Bourjos .25 .60
102 Wandy Rodriguez .15 .40
103 Andres Torres .15 .40
104 Huston Street .15 .40
105 Ubaldo Jimenez .15 .40
106 Jonathan Broxton .15 .40
107 L.L. Zamenhof .15 .40
108 Roy Oswalt .25 .60
109 Martin Prado .15 .40
110 Jake McGee (RC) .40 1.00
111 Pablo Sandoval .25 .60
112 Timothy Shieff .15 .40
113 Miguel Montero .15 .40
114 Brandon Phillips .15 .40
115 Shin-Soo Choo .25 .60
116 Josh Beckett .15 .40
117 Jonathan Sanchez .15 .40
118 Rafael Soriano .15 .40
119 Nancy Lopez .15 .40
120 Adrian Gonzalez .30 .75
121 J.D. Drew .15 .40
122 Ryan Dempster .15 .40
123 Rajai Davis .15 .40
124 Chad Billingsley .25 .60
125 Clayton Kershaw .75 2.00
126 Jair Jurrjens .15 .40
127 James Loney .15 .40
128 Michael Cuddyer .15 .40
129 Kelly Johnson .15 .40
130 Robinson Cano .25 .60
131 Chris Iannetta .15 .40
132 Colby Rasmus .25 .60
133 Geno Auriemma .25 .60
134 Matt Cain .25 .60
135 Kyle Petty .15 .40
136 Dick Vitale .15 .40
137 Carlos Beltran .25 .60
138 Matt Garza .15 .40
139 Tim Howard .15 .40
140 Felix Hernandez .25 .60
141 Vernon Wells .15 .40
142 Michael Young .15 .40
143 Carlos Zambrano .25 .60
144 Jorge Posada .25 .60
145 Victor Martinez .25 .60
146 John Danks .15 .40
147 George Bush .25 .60
148 Sanya Richards .15 .40
149 Lars Anderson RC .60 1.50
150 Troy Tulowitzki .40 1.00
151 Brandon Beachy RC 1.00 2.50
152 Jordan Zimmermann .25 .60
153 Scott Cousins RC .40 1.00
154 Todd Helton .25 .60
155 Josh Johnson .25 .60
156 Marlon Byrd .15 .40
157 Corey Hart .15 .40
158 Billy Butler .15 .40
159 Shawn Michaels .15 .40
160 David Wright .30 .75
161 Casey McGehee .15 .40
162 Mat Latos .25 .60
163 Ian Kennedy .15 .40
164 Heather Mitts .25 .60
165 Jo Frost .15 .40
166 Geovany Soto .25 .60
167 Adam LaRoche .15 .40
168 Carlos Marmol .25 .60
169 Dan Haren .15 .40
170 Tim Lincecum .25 .60
171 John Lackey .25 .60
172 Yunesky Maya RC .40 1.00
173 Mariano Rivera .50 1.25
174 Joakim Soria .15 .40
175 Jose Bautista .25 .60
176 Brian Bogusevic (RC) .40 1.00
177 Aaron Crow RC .60 1.50
178 Ben Revere RC .60 1.50
179 Shane Victorino .25 .60
180 Kyle Drabek RC .60 1.50
181 Mark Buehrle .25 .60
182 Clay Buchholz .15 .40
183 Mike Napoli .15 .40
184 Pedro Alvarez RC .30 .75
185 Justin Upton .25 .60
186 Yunel Escobar .15 .40
187 Jim Nantz .15 .40
188 Daniel Descalso RC .40 1.00
189 Dexter Fowler .15 .40
190 Sue Bird .15 .40
191 Matt Guy .15 .40
192 Carl Pavano .15 .40
193 Jorge De La Rosa .15 .40
194 Rick Porcello .25 .60
195 Tommy Hanson .25 .60
196 Jered Weaver .25 .60
197 Jay Bruce .25 .60
198 Freddie Freeman RC 6.00 15.00
199 Jake Peavy .15 .40
200 Josh Hamilton .25 .60
201 Andrew Romine RC .40 1.00
202 Nick Swisher .25 .60
203 Aaron Hill .15 .40
204 Jim Thome .25 .60
205 Kendrys Morales .15 .40
206 Tsuyoshi Nishioka RC 1.25 3.00
207 Kosuke Fukudome .25 .60
208 Marco Scutaro .25 .60
209 Guy Fieri .15 .40
210 Chase Utley .25 .60
211 Francisco Rodriguez .25 .60
212 Aramis Ramirez .15 .40
213 Xavier Nady .15 .40
214 Elvis Andrus .25 .60
215 Andrew McCutchen .40 1.00
216 Jose Tabata .15 .40
217 Shaun Marcum .15 .40
218 Bobby Abreu .15 .40
219 Johan Santana .25 .60
220 Prince Fielder .25 .60
221 Mark Rogers (RC) .40 1.00
222 James Shields .15 .40
223 Chuck Woolery .15 .40
224 Jason Kubel .15 .40
225 Jack LaLanne .15 .40
226 Andre Ethier .25 .60
227 Lucas Duda RC 1.00 2.50
228 Brandon Snyder (RC) .40 1.00
229 Juan Pierre .15 .40
230 Mark Teixeira .25 .60
231 C.J. Wilson .15 .40
232 Picabo Street .15 .40
233 Ben Zobrist .25 .60
234 Chrissie Wellington .15 .40
235 Cole Hamels .30 .75
236 B.J. Upton .25 .60
237 Carlos Quentin .15 .40
238 Rudy Ruettiger .15 .40
239 Brett Myers .15 .40
240 Matt Holliday .40 1.00
241 Ike Davis .15 .40
242 Cheryl Burke .15 .40
243 Mike Nickeas (RC) .40 1.00
244 Chone Figgins .15 .40
245 Brian McCann .25 .60
246 Ian Kinsler .25 .60
247 Yadier Molina .40 1.00
248 Ervin Santana .15 .40
249 Carlos Ruiz .15 .40
250 Ichiro Suzuki .50 1.25
251 Ian Desmond .15 .40
252 Omar Infante .15 .40
253 Mike Minor .15 .40
254 Denard Span .15 .40
255 David Price .30 .75
256 Hunter Pence .25 .60
257 Andrew Bailey .15 .40
258 Howie Kendrick .15 .40
259 Tim Hudson .25 .60
260 Alex Rodriguez .50 1.25
261 Carlos Pena .25 .60
262 Manny Pacquiao 2.50 6.00
263 Mark Trumbo (RC) 1.00 2.50
264 Adam Jones .25 .60
265 Buster Posey .50 1.25
266 Chris Coghlan .15 .40
267 Brett Sinkbeil RC .40 1.00
268 Dallas Braden .15 .40
269 Derrek Lee .15 .40
270 Kevin Youkilis .15 .40
271 Chris Young .15 .40
272 Wee Man .15 .40
273 Brent Morel RC .40 1.00
274 Stan Lee .15 .40
275 Justin Verlander .40 1.00
276 Desmond Jennings RC .60 1.50
277 Hank Conger RC .60 1.50
278 Travis Snider .15 .40
279 Brian Wilson .40 1.00
280 Adam Wainwright .25 .60
281 Adam Lind .25 .60
282 Reid Brignac .15 .40
283 Daric Barton .15 .40
284 Eric Jackson .15 .40
285 Alex Rios .15 .40
286 Cory Luebke RC .40 1.00
287 Yovani Gallardo .25 .60
288 Rickie Weeks .15 .40
289 Paul Konerko .25 .60
290 Cliff Lee .25 .60
291 Grady Sizemore .25 .60
292 Wade Davis .15 .40
293 William/K.Middleton .40 1.00
294 Jacoby Ellsbury .30 .75
295 Chris Carpenter .25 .60
296 Derek Lowe .15 .40
297 Travis Hafner .15 .40
298 Peter Gammons .15 .40
299 Ana Julaton .15 .40
300 Ryan Braun .25 .60
301 Gio Gonzalez SP 1.25 3.00
302 John Buck SP 1.25 3.00
303 Jaime Garcia SP 1.25 3.00
304 Madison Bumgarner SP 1.25 3.00
305 Justin Morneau SP 1.25 3.00
306 Josh Willingham SP 1.25 3.00
307 Ryan Ludwick SP 1.25 3.00
308 Jhonny Peralta SP 1.25 3.00
309 Kurt Suzuki SP 1.25 3.00
310 Matt Kemp SP 1.25 3.00
311 Ian Stewart SP 1.25 3.00
312 Cody Ross SP 1.25 3.00
313 Leo Nunez SP 1.25 3.00
314 Nick Markakis SP 1.25 3.00
315 Jayson Werth SP 1.25 3.00
316 Manny Ramirez SP 1.25 3.00
317 Brian Matusz SP 1.25 3.00
318 Brett Wallace SP 1.25 3.00
319 Jon Niese SP 1.25 3.00
320 Jon Lester SP 1.25 3.00
321 Mark Reynolds SP 1.25 3.00
322 Trevor Cahill SP 1.25 3.00
323 Orlando Hudson SP 1.25 3.00
324 Domonic Brown SP 1.25 3.00
325 Mike Stanton SP 1.25 3.00
326 Jason Castro SP 1.25 3.00
327 David DeJesus SP 1.25 3.00
328 Chris Johnson SP 1.25 3.00
329 Alex Gordon SP 1.25 3.00
330 CC Sabathia SP 1.25 3.00
331 Carlos Gomez SP 1.25 3.00
332 Luke Hochevar SP 1.25 3.00
333 Carlos Lee SP 1.25 3.00
334 Gaby Sanchez SP 1.25 3.00
335 Jason Heyward SP 1.50 4.00
336 Kevin Kouzmanoff SP 1.25 3.00
337 Drew Storen SP 1.25 3.00
338 Lance Berkman SP 1.25 3.00
339 Miguel Tejada SP 1.25 3.00
340 Ryan Zimmerman SP 1.25 3.00
341 Ricky Nolasco SP 1.25 3.00
342 Mike Pelfrey SP 1.25 3.00
343 Drew Stubbs SP 1.25 3.00
344 Danny Valencia SP 1.25 3.00
345 Zack Greinke SP 1.25 3.00
346 Brett Gardner SP 1.25 3.00
347 Josh Thole SP 1.25 3.00
348 Russell Martin SP 1.25 3.00
349 Yuniesky Betancourt SP 1.25 3.00
350 Joe Mauer SP 1.25 3.00

2011 Topps Allen and Ginter Code Cards

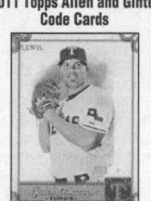

*MINI 1-300: 1.5X TO 4X BASIC
*MINI 1-300 RC: .75X TO 2X BASIC RC's
OVERALL CODE ODDS 1:8 HOBBY
301 Gio Gonzalez 1.25 3.00
302 John Buck .75 2.00
303 Jaime Garcia .75 2.00
304 Madison Bumgarner 1.50 4.00
305 Justin Morneau 1.25 3.00
306 Josh Willingham 1.25 3.00
307 Ryan Ludwick .75 2.00
308 Jhonny Peralta .75 2.00
309 Kurt Suzuki .75 2.00
310 Matt Kemp 1.50 4.00
311 Ian Stewart .75 2.00
312 Cody Ross .75 2.00
313 Leo Nunez .75 2.00
314 Nick Markakis 1.50 4.00
315 Jayson Werth 1.25 3.00
316 Manny Ramirez 2.00 5.00
317 Brian Matusz .75 2.00
318 Brett Wallace .75 2.00
319 Jon Niese .75 2.00
320 Jon Lester 1.25 3.00
321 Mark Reynolds .75 2.00
322 Trevor Cahill .75 2.00
323 Orlando Hudson .75 2.00
324 Domonic Brown 1.50 4.00
325 Mike Stanton 2.00 5.00
326 Jason Castro .75 2.00
327 David DeJesus .75 2.00
328 Chris Johnson .75 2.00
329 Alex Gordon 1.25 3.00
330 CC Sabathia 1.25 3.00
331 Carlos Gomez .75 2.00
332 Luke Hochevar .75 2.00
333 Carlos Lee .75 2.00
334 Gaby Sanchez .75 2.00
335 Jason Heyward 1.50 4.00
336 Kevin Kouzmanoff .75 2.00
337 Drew Storen .75 2.00
338 Lance Berkman 1.25 3.00
339 Miguel Tejada 1.25 3.00
340 Ryan Zimmerman 1.25 3.00
341 Ricky Nolasco .75 2.00
342 Mike Pelfrey .75 2.00
343 Drew Stubbs .75 2.00
344 Danny Valencia 1.25 3.00
345 Zack Greinke 1.25 3.00
346 Brett Gardner 1.25 3.00
347 Josh Thole .75 2.00
348 Russell Martin .75 2.00
349 Yuniesky Betancourt .75 2.00
350 Joe Mauer 1.50 4.00

2011 Topps Allen and Ginter Mini

*MINI 1-300: .75X TO 2X BASIC
*MINI 1-300 RC: .5X TO 1.2X BASIC RC's
*MINI SP 301-350: .5X TO 1.2X BASIC SP
MINI SP ODDS 1:13 HOBBY
COMMON CARD (351-400) 10.00 25.00
351-400 RANDOM WITHIN RIP CARDS
STATED PLATE ODDS 1:751 HOBBY
PLATE PRINT RUN 1 SET PER COLOR
BLACK-CYAN-MAGENTA-YELLOW ISSUED
NO PLATE PRICING DUE TO SCARCITY
352 Jason Heyward EXT 10.00 25.00
353 Ichiro Suzuki EXCH 10.00 25.00
354 Kevin Youkilis EXT 10.00 25.00
355 Roy Halladay EXT 10.00 25.00
356 Starlin Castro EXT 10.00 25.00
357 Mickey Mantle EXT 40.00 80.00
358 Robinson Cano EXT 40.00 80.00
359 Dan Uggla EXT 10.00 25.00
360 Carl Crawford EXT 10.00 25.00
361 Hunter Pence EXT 10.00 25.00
362 Chase Utley EXT 10.00 25.00
363 Justin Upton EXT 10.00 25.00
364 Pedro Alvarez EXT 10.00 25.00
365 Dustin Pedroia EXT 10.00 25.00
366 Albert Pujols EXT 10.00 25.00
367 Mike Stanton EXT 10.00 25.00
368 Joe Mauer EXT 10.00 25.00
369 Evan Longoria EXT 10.00 25.00
370 Carlos Gonzalez EXT 10.00 25.00
371 Adam Dunn EXT 30.00 60.00
372 Derek Jeter EXT 100.00 175.00
373 Jose Bautista EXT 10.00 25.00
374 Ryan Zimmerman EXT 30.00 60.00
375 Troy Tulowitzki EXT 10.00 25.00
376 Mat Latos EXT 10.00 25.00
377 Clayton Kershaw EXT 10.00 25.00
378 Shin-Soo Choo EXT 10.00 25.00
379 Cliff Lee EXT 10.00 25.00
380 Adrian Gonzalez EXT 10.00 25.00
381 Tim Lincecum EXT 10.00 25.00
382 Zack Greinke EXT 10.00 25.00
383 Torii Hunter EXT 10.00 25.00
384 Felix Hernandez EXT 10.00 25.00
385 Aroldis Chapman EXT 10.00 25.00
386 Josh Hamilton EXT 30.00 60.00
387 Hanley Ramirez EXT 10.00 25.00
388 Jon Lester EXT 10.00 25.00
389 Billy Butler EXT 10.00 25.00
390 Miguel Cabrera EXT 12.50 30.00
391 Justin Morneau EXT 30.00 60.00
392 Ubaldo Jimenez EXT 10.00 25.00
393 Alex Rodriguez EXT 10.00 25.00
394 CC Sabathia EXT 10.00 25.00
395 Buster Posey EXT 10.00 25.00
396 Ryan Howard EXT 10.00 25.00
397 Mark Teixeira EXT 40.00 80.00
398 Brett Anderson EXT 10.00 25.00
399 David Wright EXT 10.00 25.00
400 Joey Votto EXT 10.00 25.00

2011 Topps Allen and Ginter Mini A and G Back

*A & G BACK: 1X TO 2.5X BASIC
*A & G BACK RCs: .6X TO 1.5X BASIC RCs
A & G BACK ODDS 1:5 HOBBY
*A & G BACK SP: .6X TO 1.5X BASIC SP
A & G BACK SP ODDS 1:65 HOBBY

2011 Topps Allen and Ginter Mini Black

*BLACK: 2X TO 5X BASIC
*BLACK RCs: .75X TO 2X BASIC RCs
BLACK ODDS 1:10 HOBBY
BLACK SP ODDS 1:130 HOBBY
*BLACK SP: .75X TO 2X BASIC SP

2011 Topps Allen and Ginter Mini No Card Number

*NO NBR: 8X TO 20X BASIC
*NO NBR RCs: 3X TO 8X BASIC RCs
*NO NBR SP: 1.2X TO 3X BASIC SP
STATED ODDS 1:142 HOBBY

2011 Topps Allen and Ginter Glossy

ISSUED VIA TOPPS ONLINE STORE
STATED PRINT RUN 999 SER.#'d SETS
1 Carlos Gonzalez 1.25 3.00
2 Ty Wigginton .75 2.00
3 Lou Holtz .75 2.00
4 Jhoulys Chacin .75 2.00
5 Aroldis Chapman 2.50 6.00
6 Micky Ward .75 2.00
7 Mickey Mantle 6.00 15.00
8 Alexei Ramirez 1.25 3.00
9 Joe Saunders .75 2.00
10 Miguel Cabrera 2.00 5.00
11 Marc Forgione .75 2.00
12 Hope Solo .75 2.00
13 Brett Anderson .75 2.00
14 Adrian Beltre 2.00 5.00
15 Diana Taurasi .75 2.00
16 Gordon Beckham .75 2.00
17 Jonathan Papelbon 1.25 3.00
18 Daniel Hudson .75 2.00
19 Daniel Bard .75 2.00
20 Jeremy Hellickson 2.00 5.00
21 Logan Morrison .75 2.00
22 Michael Bourn .75 2.00
23 Aubrey Huff .75 2.00
24 Kristi Yamaguchi .75 2.00
25 Nelson Cruz 2.00 5.00
26 Edwin Jackson .75 2.00
27 Dillon Gee 1.25 3.00
28 John Lindsey .75 2.00
29 Johnny Cueto 1.25 3.00
30 Hanley Ramirez 1.25 3.00
31 Jimmy Rollins 1.25 3.00
32 Dirk Hayhurst .75 2.00
33 Curtis Granderson 1.50 4.00
34 Pedro Ciriaco 1.25 3.00
35 Adam Dunn 1.25 3.00
36 Eric Sogard .75 2.00
37 Fausto Carmona .75 2.00
38 Angel Pagan .75 2.00
39 Stephen Drew .75 2.00
40 John McEnroe .75 2.00
41 Carlos Santana 2.00 5.00
42 Heath Bell .75 2.00
43 Jake LaMotta .75 2.00
44 Ozzie Martinez .75 2.00
45 Annika Sorenstam .75 2.00
46 Edinson Volquez .75 2.00
47 Phil Hughes .75 2.00
48 Francisco Liriano .75 2.00
49 Javier Vazquez .75 2.00
50 Carl Crawford 1.25 3.00
51 Tim Collins .75 2.00
52 Francisco Cordero .75 2.00
53 Chipper Jones 2.00 5.00
54 Austin Jackson .75 2.00
55 Dustin Pedroia 1.50 4.00
56 Scott Kazmir .75 2.00
57 Derek Jeter 5.00 12.00
58 Alcides Escobar 1.25 3.00
59 Jeremy Jeffress .75 2.00
60 Brandon Belt 2.00 5.00
61 Brian Roberts .75 2.00
62 Alfonso Soriano 1.25 3.00
63 Neil Walker 1.25 3.00
64 Ricky Romero .75 2.00
65 Ryan Howard 1.50 4.00
66 Starlin Castro 1.25 3.00
67 Delmon Young 1.25 3.00
68 Max Scherzer 2.00 5.00
69 Neftali Feliz .75 2.00
70 Evan Longoria 1.25 3.00
71 Chris Perez .75 2.00
72 Maxim Shmyrev .75 2.00
73 Brandon Morrow .75 2.00
74 Torii Hunter .75 2.00
75 Jose Reyes 1.25 3.00
76 Chase Headley .75 2.00
77 Rafael Furcal .75 2.00
78 Luke Scott .75 2.00
79 Aimee Mullins .75 2.00
80 Joey Votto 2.00 5.00
81 Yonder Alonso 1.25 3.00
82 Scott Rolen 1.25 3.00
83 Mat Hoffman .75 2.00
84 Gregory Infante .75 2.00
85 Chris Sale 5.00 12.00
86 Greg Halman 1.25 3.00
87 Colby Lewis .75 2.00
88 David Ortiz 2.00 5.00
89 John Axford .75 2.00
90 Roy Halladay 1.25 3.00
91 Joel Pineiro .75 2.00
92 Michael Pineda 2.00 5.00
93 Evan Lysacek .75 2.00
94 Josh Rodriguez .75 2.00
95 Dan Uggla .75 2.00
96 Daniel Boulud .75 2.00
97 Zach Britton 2.00 5.00
98 Jason Bay 1.25 3.00
99 Placido Polanco .75 2.00
100 Albert Pujols 2.50 6.00
101 Peter Bourjos 1.25 3.00
102 Wandy Rodriguez .75 2.00
103 Andres Torres .75 2.00
104 Huston Street .75 2.00
105 Ubaldo Jimenez .75 2.00
106 Jonathan Broxton .75 2.00
107 L.L. Zamenhof .75 2.00
108 Roy Oswalt 1.25 3.00
109 Martin Prado .75 2.00
110 Jake McGee (RC) .75 2.00
111 Pablo Sandoval 1.25 3.00
112 Timothy Shieff .75 2.00
113 Miguel Montero .75 2.00
114 Brandon Phillips .75 2.00
115 Shin-Soo Choo 1.25 3.00
116 Josh Beckett .75 2.00
117 Jonathan Sanchez .75 2.00
118 Rafael Soriano .75 2.00
119 Nancy Lopez .75 2.00
120 Adrian Gonzalez 1.50 4.00
121 J.D. Drew .75 2.00
122 Ryan Dempster .75 2.00
123 Rajai Davis .75 2.00
124 Chad Billingsley 1.25 3.00
125 Clayton Kershaw 4.00 10.00
126 Jair Jurrjens .75 2.00
127 James Loney .75 2.00
128 Michael Cuddyer .75 2.00
129 Kelly Johnson .75 2.00
130 Robinson Cano 1.25 3.00
131 Chris Iannetta .75 2.00
132 Colby Rasmus 1.25 3.00
133 Geno Auriemma 1.25 3.00
134 Matt Cain 1.25 3.00
135 Kyle Petty .75 2.00
136 Dick Vitale .75 2.00
137 Carlos Beltran 1.25 3.00
138 Matt Garza .75 2.00
139 Tim Howard .75 2.00
140 Felix Hernandez 1.25 3.00

141 Vernon Wells .75 2.00
142 Michael Young .75 2.00
143 Carlos Zambrano 1.25 3.00
144 Jorge Posada 1.25 3.00
145 Victor Martinez 1.25 3.00
146 John Danks .75 2.00
147 George Bush 1.25 3.00
148 Sanya Richards .75 2.00
149 Lars Anderson 1.25 3.00
150 Troy Tulowitzki 2.00 5.00
151 Brandon Beachy 2.00 5.00
152 Jordan Zimmermann 1.25 3.00
153 Scott Cousins .75 2.00
154 Todd Helton 1.25 3.00
155 Josh Johnson 1.25 3.00
156 Marlon Byrd .75 2.00
157 Corey Hart .75 2.00
158 Billy Butler .75 2.00
159 Shawn Michaels .75 2.00
160 David Wright 1.50 4.00
161 Casey McGehee .75 2.00
162 Mat Latos 1.25 3.00
163 Ian Kennedy .75 2.00
164 Heather Mitts 1.25 3.00
165 Jo Frost .75 2.00
166 Geovany Soto 1.25 3.00
167 Adam LaRoche .75 2.00
168 Carlos Marmol 1.25 3.00
169 Dan Haren .75 2.00
170 Tim Lincecum 1.25 3.00
171 John Lackey 1.25 3.00
172 Yunesky Maya .75 2.00
173 Mariano Rivera 2.50 6.00
174 Joakim Soria .75 2.00
175 Jose Bautista 1.25 3.00
176 Brian Bogusevic (RC) .75 2.00
177 Aaron Crow 1.25 3.00
178 Ben Revere 1.25 3.00
179 Shane Victorino 1.25 3.00
180 Kyle Drabek 1.25 3.00
181 Mark Buehrle 1.25 3.00
182 Clay Buchholz .75 2.00
183 Mike Napoli .75 2.00
184 Pedro Alvarez 1.50 4.00
185 Justin Upton 1.25 3.00
186 Yunel Escobar .75 2.00
187 Jim Nantz .75 2.00
188 Daniel Descalso .75 2.00
189 Dexter Fowler 1.25 3.00
190 Sue Bird .75 2.00
191 Matt Guy .75 2.00
192 Carl Pavano .75 2.00
193 Jorge De La Rosa .75 2.00
194 Rick Porcello 1.25 3.00
195 Tommy Hanson 1.25 3.00
196 Jered Weaver 1.25 3.00
197 Jay Bruce 1.25 3.00
198 Freddie Freeman 12.00 30.00
199 Jake Peavy .75 2.00
200 Josh Hamilton 1.25 3.00
201 Andrew Romine .75 2.00
202 Nick Swisher 1.25 3.00
203 Aaron Hill .75 2.00
204 Jim Thome 1.25 3.00
205 Kendrys Morales .75 2.00
206 Tsuyoshi Nishioka 2.50 6.00
207 Kosuke Fukudome 1.25 3.00
208 Marco Scutaro 1.25 3.00
209 Guy Fieri .75 2.00
210 Chase Utley 1.25 3.00
211 Francisco Rodriguez 1.25 3.00
212 Aramis Ramirez .75 2.00
213 Xavier Nady .75 2.00
214 Elvis Andrus 1.25 3.00
215 Andrew McCutchen 2.00 5.00
216 Jose Tabata .75 2.00
217 Shaun Marcum .75 2.00
218 Bobby Abreu .75 2.00
219 Johan Santana 1.25 3.00
220 Prince Fielder 1.25 3.00
221 Mark Rogers (RC) .75 2.00
222 James Shields .75 2.00
223 Chuck Woolery .75 2.00
224 Jason Kubel .75 2.00
225 Jack LaLanne .75 2.00
226 Andre Ethier 1.25 3.00
227 Lucas Duda 2.00 5.00
228 Brandon Snyder (RC) .75 2.00
229 Juan Pierre .75 2.00
230 Mark Teixeira 1.25 3.00
231 C.J. Wilson .75 2.00
232 Picabo Street .75 2.00
233 Ben Zobrist 1.25 3.00
234 Chrissie Wellington .75 2.00
235 Cole Hamels 1.50 4.00
236 B.J. Upton .75 2.00
237 Carlos Quentin .75 2.00
238 Rudy Ruettiger .75 2.00
239 Brett Myers .75 2.00
240 Matt Holliday 2.00 5.00
241 Ike Davis .75 2.00
242 Cheryl Burke .75 2.00
243 Mike Nickeas (RC) .75 2.00
244 Chone Figgins .75 2.00
245 Brian McCann 1.25 3.00
246 Ian Kinsler 1.25 3.00
247 Yadier Molina 2.00 5.00
248 Ervin Santana .75 2.00
249 Carlos Ruiz .75 2.00
250 Ichiro Suzuki 2.50 6.00
251 Ian Desmond .75 2.00
252 Omar Infante .75 2.00
253 Mike Minor .75 2.00
254 Denard Span .75 2.00
255 David Price 1.50 4.00
256 Hunter Pence 1.25 3.00
257 Andrew Bailey .75 2.00
258 Howie Kendrick .75 2.00
259 Tim Hudson 1.25 3.00
260 Alex Rodriguez 2.50 6.00
261 Carlos Pena 1.25 3.00
262 Manny Pacquiao 15.00 40.00
263 Mark Trumbo (RC) 2.00 5.00
264 Adam Jones 1.25 3.00
265 Buster Posey 2.50 6.00
266 Chris Coghlan .75 2.00
267 Brett Sinkbeil .75 2.00
268 Dallas Braden .75 2.00
269 Derrek Lee .75 2.00
270 Kevin Youkilis .75 2.00
271 Chris Young .75 2.00
272 Wee Man .75 2.00
273 Brent Morel .75 2.00
274 Stan Lee .75 2.00
275 Justin Verlander 2.00 5.00
276 Desmond Jennings 1.25 3.00
277 Hank Conger 1.25 3.00
278 Travis Snider .75 2.00
279 Brian Wilson 2.00 5.00
280 Adam Wainwright 1.25 3.00
281 Adam Lind 1.25 3.00
282 Reid Brignac .75 2.00
283 Daric Barton .75 2.00
284 Eric Jackson .75 2.00
285 Alex Rios .75 2.00
286 Cory Luebke .75 2.00
287 Yovani Gallardo .75 2.00
288 Rickie Weeks .75 2.00
289 Paul Konerko 1.25 3.00
290 Cliff Lee 1.25 3.00
291 Grady Sizemore 1.25 3.00
292 Wade Davis .75 2.00
293 Prince William/Kate Middleton 2.00 5.00
294 Jacoby Ellsbury 1.50 4.00
295 Chris Carpenter 1.25 3.00
296 Derek Lowe .75 2.00
297 Travis Hafner .75 2.00
298 Peter Gammons .75 2.00
299 Ana Julaton .75 2.00
300 Ryan Braun 1.25 3.00
301 Gio Gonzalez 1.25 3.00
302 John Buck .75 2.00
303 Jaime Garcia 1.25 3.00
304 Madison Bumgarner 1.50 4.00
305 Justin Morneau 1.25 3.00
306 Josh Willingham 1.25 3.00
307 Ryan Ludwick .75 2.00
308 Jhonny Peralta .75 2.00
309 Kurt Suzuki .75 2.00
310 Matt Kemp 1.50 4.00
311 Ian Stewart .75 2.00
312 Cody Ross .75 2.00
313 Leo Nunez .75 2.00
314 Nick Markakis 1.50 4.00
315 Jayson Werth 1.25 3.00
316 Manny Ramirez 2.00 5.00
317 Brian Matusz 1.25 3.00
318 Brett Wallace .75 2.00
319 Jon Niese .75 2.00
320 Jon Lester 1.25 3.00
321 Mark Reynolds .75 2.00
322 Trevor Cahill .75 2.00
323 Orlando Hudson .75 2.00
324 Domonic Brown 1.50 4.00
325 Mike Stanton 2.00 5.00
326 Jason Castro .75 2.00
327 David DeJesus .75 2.00
328 Chris Johnson .75 2.00
329 Alex Gordon 1.25 3.00
330 CC Sabathia 1.25 3.00
331 Carlos Gomez .75 2.00
332 Luke Hochevar .75 2.00
333 Carlos Lee .75 2.00
334 Gaby Sanchez .75 2.00
335 Jason Heyward 1.50 4.00
336 Kevin Kouzmanoff .75 2.00
337 Drew Storen .75 2.00
338 Lance Berkman 1.25 3.00
339 Miguel Tejada 1.25 3.00
340 Ryan Zimmerman 1.25 3.00
341 Ricky Nolasco .75 2.00
342 Mike Pelfrey .75 2.00
343 Drew Stubbs .75 2.00
344 Danny Valencia 1.25 3.00
345 Zack Greinke 1.25 3.00
346 Brett Gardner 1.25 3.00
347 Josh Thole .75 2.00
348 Russell Martin .75 2.00
349 Yuniesky Betancourt .75 2.00
350 Joe Mauer 1.50 4.00

2011 Topps Allen and Ginter Glossy Rookie Exclusive

STATED PRINT RUN 999 SER.#'d SETS
AGS1 Eric Hosmer 8.00 20.00
AGS2 Dustin Ackley 2.00 5.00
AGS3 Mike Moustakas 3.00 8.00
AGS4 Dee Gordon 2.00 5.00
AGS5 Anthony Rizzo 12.00 30.00
AGS6 Charlie Blackmon 25.00 60.00
AGS7 Brandon Crawford 2.00 5.00
AGS8 Juan Nicasio 1.25 3.00
AGS9 Prince William/Kate Middleton 5.00 12.00
AGS10 U.S. Navy SEALs 2.00 5.00

2011 Topps Allen and Ginter Ascent of Man

COMPLETE SET (26) 10.00 25.00
STATED ODDS 1:6 HOBBY
AOM1 Prokaryotes .60 1.50
AOM2 Eukaryotes .60 1.50
AOM3 Choanoflagellates .60 1.50
AOM4 Porifera .60 1.50
AOM5 Cnidarians .60 1.50
AOM6 Platyhelminthes .60 1.50
AOM7 Chordates .60 1.50
AOM8 Ostracoderms .60 1.50
AOM9 Placoderms .60 1.50
AOM10 Sarcopterygii .60 1.50
AOM11 Amphibians .60 1.50
AOM12 Reptiles .60 1.50
AOM13 Eutherians .60 1.50
AOM14 Haplorrhini .60 1.50
AOM15 Catarrhini .60 1.50
AOM16 Hominoidea .60 1.50
AOM17 Hominidae .60 1.50
AOM18 Homininae .60 1.50
AOM19 Hominini .60 1.50
AOM20 Hominina .60 1.50
AOM21 Australopithecus .60 1.50
AOM22 Homo habilis .60 1.50
AOM23 Homo erectus .60 1.50
AOM24 Homo sapiens .60 1.50
AOM25 Cro-Magnon Man .60 1.50
AOM26 Modern Man .60 1.50

2011 Topps Allen and Ginter Autographs

STATED ODDS 1:68 HOBBY
DUAL AUTO ODDS 1:56,000 HOBBY
EXCHANGE DEADLINE 6/30/2014
AC Aroldis Chapman 10.00 25.00
ADU Angelo Dundee 20.00 50.00
AG Adrian Gonzalez 6.00 15.00
AJU Ana Julaton 6.00 15.00
AMU Aimee Mullins 10.00 25.00
APA Angel Pagan 6.00 15.00
ASO Annika Sorenstam 10.00 25.00
AT Andres Torres 6.00 15.00
BMO Brent Morel 4.00 10.00
BW Brett Wallace 4.00 10.00
CBU Cheryl Burke 20.00 50.00
CCS CC Sabathia 40.00 100.00
CF Chone Figgins 4.00 10.00
CS Chris Sale 12.00 30.00
CU Chase Utley 75.00 200.00
CWE Chrissie Wellington 10.00 25.00
CWO Chuck Woolery 12.50 30.00
DBO Daniel Boulud 12.50 30.00
DD David DeJesus 4.00 10.00
DH Daniel Hudson 6.00 15.00
DHA Dirk Hayhurst 20.00 50.00
DTU Diana Taurasi 12.50 30.00
DVI Dick Vitale 10.00 25.00
EJA Eric Jackson 12.50 30.00
ELY Evan Lysacek 6.00 15.00
FS Freddy Sanchez 5.00 12.00
GAU Geno Auriemma 12.50 30.00
GFI Guy Fieri 20.00 50.00
GG Gio Gonzalez 8.00 20.00
GO A.Gore/K.Olbermann 300.00 400.00
GWB George W. Bush 300.00 600.00
HMI Heather Mitts 10.00 25.00
HSO Hope Solo 30.00 80.00
JB Jose Bautista 12.50 30.00
JH Jason Heyward 10.00 25.00
JHA Josh Hamilton 6.00 15.00
JJ Josh Johnson 6.00 15.00
JLA Jake LaMotta 20.00 50.00
JM Joe Mauer 50.00 200.00
JMC John McEnroe 50.00 120.00
JNA Jim Nantz 10.00 25.00
JOF Jo Frost 12.50 30.00
JT Jose Tabata 6.00 15.00
KPE Kyle Petty 10.00 25.00
KYA Kristi Yamaguchi 40.00 100.00
LH Lou Holtz 25.00 60.00
LHO Larry Holmes 12.50 30.00
MC Miguel Cabrera 60.00 200.00
MFA Marc Forgione 6.00 15.00
MGU Matt Guy 10.00 25.00
MHO Mat Hoffman 8.00 20.00
MMO Mike Morse 4.00 10.00
MPA Manny Pacquiao 350.00 700.00
MSH Maxim Shmyrev 8.00 20.00
MWA Micky Ward 10.00 25.00
NC Nelson Cruz 6.00 15.00
NJA Nick Jacoby 8.00 20.00
NLO Nancy Lopez 10.00 25.00
PGA Peter Gammons 20.00 50.00
PST Picabo Street 12.00 30.00
RH Roy Halladay 200.00 350.00
RJO Rafer Johnson 12.50 30.00
RRU Rudy Ruettiger 10.00 25.00
RTU Ron Turcotte 20.00 50.00
RW Randy Wells 4.00 10.00
SBI Sue Bird 20.00 50.00
SC Starlin Castro 6.00 15.00
SLE Stan Lee 100.00 250.00
SM Sergio Mitre 6.00 15.00
SMI Shawn Michaels 40.00 100.00
SRI Sanya Richards 10.00 25.00
THO Tim Howard 12.00 30.00
TSC Timothy Shieff 10.00 25.00
UJ Ubaldo Jimenez 5.00 12.00
WEE Wee Man 12.00 30.00

2011 Topps Allen and Ginter Baseball Highlight Sketches

COMPLETE SET (25) 6.00 15.00
STATED ODDS 1:6 HOBBY
BHS1 Minnesota Twins .30 .75
BHS2 Jay Bruce .50 1.25
BHS3 Starlin Castro .50 1.25
BHS4 Roy Halladay .50 1.25
BHS5 Albert Pujols 1.00 2.50
BHS6 Jose Bautista .50 1.25
BHS7 CC Sabathia .50 1.25
BHS8 Cody Ross .30 .75
BHS9 Edwin Jackson .30 .75
BHS10 Ryan Howard .60 1.50
BHS11 Trevor Hoffman .50 1.25
BHS12 Armando Galarraga .30 .75
BHS13 San Francisco Giants .30 .75
BHS14 Mariano Rivera 1.00 2.50
BHS15 Aroldis Chapman 1.00 2.50
BHS16 Dallas Braden .30 .75
BHS17 Texas Rangers .30 .75
BHS18 Stephen Strasburg .75 2.00
BHS19 Matt Garza .30 .75
BHS20 Alex Rodriguez 1.00 2.50
BHS21 David Wright .60 1.50
BHS22 Ubaldo Jimenez .30 .75
BHS23 Mark Teixeira .50 1.25
BHS24 Jason Heyward .60 1.50
BHS25 Ichiro Suzuki 1.00 2.50

2011 Topps Allen and Ginter Cabinet Baseball Highlights

STATED ODDS 1:2 HOBBY BOXES
CB1 Galarraga/Miggy/Donald 2.50 6.00
CB2 Halladay/Ruiz/Howard 1.50 4.00
CB3 Dallas Braden/Landon Powell
Daric Barton 2.00 5.00
CB4 Ichiro/Bautista/King Felix 2.00 5.00
CB5 ARod/Jeter/Marcum 4.00 10.00
CB6 Pujols/La Russa/Dempster 2.00 5.00
CB7 Grand Canyon/Woodrow Wilson/Benjamin
Harrison/Theodore Roosevelt 2.00 5.00
CB8 Yosemite National Park
Abraham Lincoln/John Conness 2.00 5.00
CB9 Yellowstone National Park
Ulysses S. Grant/Old Faithful 2.00 5.00
CB10 Redwood National Park/Lyndon B.
Johnson/John E. Raker 2.00 5.00

2011 Topps Allen and Ginter Floating Fortresses

COMPLETE SET (20) 8.00 20.00
STATED ODDS 1:8 HOBBY
FF1 HMS Victory .60 1.50
FF2 Mary Rose .60 1.50
FF3 Henri Grace a Dieu .60 1.50
FF4 Michael .60 1.50
FF5 Sovereign of the Seas .60 1.50
FF6 HMS Indefatigable .60 1.50
FF7 Mahmudiye .60 1.50
FF8 Le Napoleon .60 1.50
FF9 USS Merrimack .60 1.50
FF10 USS Monitor .60 1.50
FF11 Lave .60 1.50
FF12 La Gloire .60 1.50
FF13 HMS Warrior .60 1.50
FF14 Solferino .60 1.50
FF15 USS Cairo .60 1.50
FF16 HMS Dreadnought .60 1.50
FF17 USS Texas .60 1.50
FF18 HMS Devastation .60 1.50
FF19 HMS Revenge .60 1.50
FF20 USS Pennsylvania .60 1.50

2011 Topps Allen and Ginter Hometown Heroes

COMPLETE SET (100) 10.00 25.00
HH1 Buster Posey .60 1.50
HH2 Colby Rasmus .30 .75
HH3 Brian Wilson .50 1.25
HH4 Jason Kubel .20 .50
HH5 Chase Utley .30 .75
HH6 Dan Haren .20 .50
HH7 CC Sabathia .30 .75
HH8 Stephen Drew .20 .50
HH9 Adam Wainwright .30 .75
HH10 Ryan Braun .30 .75
HH11 Jason Heyward .40 1.00
HH12 Andrew McCutchen .50 1.25
HH13 Shane Victorino .30 .75
HH14 Carl Pavano .20 .50
HH15 Matt Holliday .50 1.25
HH16 Dan Uggla .20 .50
HH17 Scott Rolen .30 .75
HH18 Zack Greinke .30 .75
HH19 Nick Swisher .30 .75
HH20 David Price .40 1.00
HH21 Jon Lester .30 .75
HH22 John Danks .20 .50
HH23 Dustin Pedroia .40 1.00
HH24 Ryan Zimmerman .30 .75
HH25 Adam Dunn .30 .75
HH26 Torii Hunter .20 .50
HH27 Brandon Phillips .20 .50
HH28 Grady Sizemore .30 .75
HH29 Rick Porcello .30 .75
HH30 Dexter Fowler .30 .75
HH31 Jake Peavy .20 .50
HH32 Roy Halladay .30 .75
HH33 Austin Jackson .20 .50
HH34 Chipper Jones .50 1.25
HH35 Alex Gordon .30 .75
HH36 Gordon Beckham .20 .50
HH37 Clayton Kershaw 1.00 2.50
HH38 Andre Ethier .30 .75
HH39 Tim Lincecum .30 .75
HH40 Prince Fielder .30 .75
HH41 David DeJesus .20 .50
HH42 David Wright .40 1.00
HH43 Joba Chamberlain .20 .50
HH44 Delmon Young .30 .75
HH45 Ike Davis .20 .50
HH46 Jacoby Ellsbury .40 1.00
HH47 Phil Hughes .20 .50
HH48 Evan Longoria .30 .75
HH49 Danny Valencia .30 .75
HH50 Josh Hamilton .30 .75
HH51 Josh Beckett .20 .50
HH52 Ian Kinsler .30 .75
HH53 Justin Verlander .50 1.25
HH54 Joe Mauer .40 1.00
HH55 Justin Upton .30 .75
HH56 Brett Anderson .20 .50
HH57 Jordan Zimmermann .30 .75
HH58 Jimmy Rollins .30 .75
HH59 Brett Gardner .30 .75
HH60 Alex Rodriguez .60 1.50
HH61 Corey Hart .20 .50
HH62 Pedro Alvarez .40 1.00
HH63 Cody Ross .20 .50
HH64 Matt Cain .30 .75
HH65 Adrian Gonzalez .40 1.00
HH66 Derek Lowe .20 .50
HH67 Jon Jay .20 .50
HH68 Johnny Damon .30 .75
HH69 Yovani Gallardo .20 .50
HH70 Troy Tulowitzki .50 1.25
HH71 Chris Carpenter .30 .75
HH72 Billy Butler .20 .50
HH73 Mark Teixeira .30 .75
HH74 Jayson Werth .30 .75
HH75 Carl Crawford .30 .75
HH76 Adam Lind .30 .75
HH77 Mark Buehrle .30 .75
HH78 Manny Ramirez .50 1.25
HH79 Derek Jeter 1.25 3.00
HH80 Cliff Lee .30 .75
HH81 Neil Walker .30 .75
HH82 Jim Thome .30 .75
HH83 Travis Hafner .20 .50
HH84 Matt Kemp .40 1.00
HH85 Michael Young .20 .50
HH86 Kevin Youkilis .20 .50
HH87 Jeremy Hellickson .50 1.25
HH88 Roy Oswalt .30 .75
HH89 Todd Helton .30 .75
HH90 Ryan Howard .40 1.00
HH91 Madison Bumgarner .40 1.00
HH92 Mike Napoli .20 .50
HH93 Lance Berkman .30 .75
HH94 C.J. Wilson .20 .50
HH95 Kyle Drabek .30 .75
HH96 Brian McCann .30 .75
HH97 Brandon Morrow .20 .50
HH98 Clay Buchholz .20 .50
HH99 Andrew Bailey .20 .50
HH100 Travis Snider .20 .50

2011 Topps Allen and Ginter Minds that Made the Future

COMPLETE SET (40) 20.00 50.00
STATED ODDS 1:8 HOBBY
MMF1 Leonardo da Vinci .60 1.50
MMF2 Alexander Graham Bell .60 1.50
MMF3 Eli Whitney .60 1.50
MMF4 Nicolaus Copernicus .60 1.50
MMF5 Johannes Gutenberg .60 1.50
MMF6 George Washington Carver .60 1.50
MMF7 Samuel Morse .60 1.50
MMF8 Granville Woods .60 1.50
MMF9 Elisha Otis .60 1.50
MMF10 Alessandro Volta .60 1.50
MMF11 Tycho Brahe .60 1.50
MMF12 Gregor Mendel .60 1.50
MMF13 Carl Linnaeus .60 1.50
MMF14 Johannes Kepler .60 1.50
MMF15 Isaac Newton .60 1.50
MMF16 Marie Curie .60 1.50
MMF17 Carl Friedrich Gauss .60 1.50
MMF18 Sigmund Freud .60 1.50
MMF19 Bernhard Riemann .60 1.50
MMF20 Leonhard Euler .60 1.50
MMF21 Robert Fulton .60 1.50
MMF22 Ada Lovelace .60 1.50
MMF23 Florence Nightingale .60 1.50
MMF24 Nikola Tesla .60 1.50
MMF25 Galileo Galilei .60 1.50
MMF26 Charles Darwin .60 1.50
MMF27 Louis Pasteur .60 1.50
MMF28 Guglielmo Marconi .60 1.50
MMF29 Antoine Lavoisier .60 1.50
MMF30 Michael Faraday .60 1.50
MMF31 Dmitri Mendeleev .60 1.50
MMF32 Robert Koch .60 1.50
MMF33 Euclid .60 1.50
MMF34 Archimedes .60 1.50
MMF35 Jagadish Chandra Bose .60 1.50
MMF36 Aristotle .60 1.50
MMF37 John Deere .60 1.50
MMF38 George Eastman .60 1.50
MMF39 Samuel Colt .60 1.50
MMF40 Benjamin Franklin .60 1.50

2011 Topps Allen and Ginter Mini Animals in Peril

COMPLETE SET (30) 10.00 25.00
STATED ODDS 1:12 HOBBY
AP1 Siberian Tiger .75 2.00
AP2 Mountain Gorilla .75 2.00
AP3 Arakan Forest Turtle .75 2.00
AP4 Darwin's Fox .75 2.00
AP5 Gharial .75 2.00
AP6 Vaquita .75 2.00
AP7 Dhole .75 2.00
AP8 Blue Whale .75 2.00
AP9 Bonobo .75 2.00
AP10 Ethiopian Wolf .75 2.00
AP11 Giant Panda .75 2.00
AP12 Snow Leopard .75 2.00
AP13 African Wild Dog .75 2.00
AP14 Indian Rhinoceros .75 2.00
AP15 Philippine Eagle .75 2.00
AP16 Markhor .75 2.00
AP17 Orangutan .75 2.00
AP18 Grevy's Zebra .75 2.00
AP19 Tasmanian Devil .75 2.00
AP20 Bengal Tiger .75 2.00
AP21 Whooping Crane .75 2.00
AP22 Sea Otter .75 2.00
AP23 Red Wolf .75 2.00
AP24 Key Deer .75 2.00
AP25 Black-Footed Ferret .75 2.00
AP26 Amur Leopard .75 2.00
AP27 Anderson's Salamander .75 2.00
AP28 Greater Bamboo Lemur .75 2.00
AP29 Hawaiian Monk Seal .75 2.00
AP30 Kakapo .75 2.00

2011 Topps Allen and Ginter Mini Fabulous Face Flocculence

FFF1 A.Lincoln/The Lincoln 10.00 25.00
FFF2 The Ironing Board 8.00 20.00
FFF3 The Conscientious Objector 8.00 20.00
FFF4 The Bib 8.00 20.00
FFF5 Charles Darwin/The Darwin 8.00 20.00
FFF6 The Neckbeard 8.00 20.00
FFF7 The Goat Patch 8.00 20.00
FFF8 Ambrose Burnside
Burnside's Sidebums 8.00 20.00
FFF9 Thunderchops 8.00 20.00
FFF10 B.Wilson/The Closer 10.00 25.00

2011 Topps Allen and Ginter Mini Flora of the World

COMPLETE SET (5) 20.00 50.00
STATED ODDS 1:144 HOBBY
FOW1 Black-Eyed Susan 6.00 15.00
FOW2 Spurred Snapdragon 6.00 15.00
FOW3 Shirley Poppy 6.00 15.00
FOW4 Mexican Hat 6.00 15.00
FOW5 Sweet Alyssum 6.00 15.00

2011 Topps Allen and Ginter Mini Fortunes for the Taking

FFT1 The Oak Island Money Pit 6.00 15.00
FFT2 Captain Kidd's Treasure 6.00 15.00
FFT3 The Beale Ciphers 6.00 15.00
FFT4 The Amber Room 6.00 15.00
FFT5 The Devonshire
Treasure of Cocos Island 6.00 15.00
FFT6 Blackbeard's Treasure 6.00 15.00
FFT7 The Treasure of Lima 6.00 15.00
FFT8 Montezuma's Treasure 6.00 15.00
FFT9 Butch Cassidy's Loot 6.00 15.00
FFT10 The Lost French Gold of Ohio 6.00 15.00

2011 Topps Allen and Ginter Mini Portraits of Penultimacy

COMPLETE SET (10) 5.00 12.00
STATED ODDS 1:12 HOBBY
PP1 Antonio Meucci .60 1.50
PP2 Mike Gellner .60 1.50
PP3 Dr. Watson .60 1.50
PP4 Igor .60 1.50
PP5 The Hare .60 1.50
PP6 Tonto .60 1.50
PP7 Antonio Salieri .60 1.50
PP8 Sancho Panza .60 1.50
PP9 Thomas E. Dewey .60 1.50
PP10 Toto .60 1.50

2011 Topps Allen and Ginter Mini Step Right Up

COMPLETE SET (10) 5.00 12.00
STATED ODDS 1:15 HOBBY
SRU1 The Bed of Nails .60 1.50
SRU2 Fire Breathing .60 1.50
SRU3 Fire Eating .60 1.50
SRU4 The Flea Circus .60 1.50
SRU5 The Human Cannonball .60 1.50
SRU6 The Human Blockhead .60 1.50
SRU7 Snake Charming .60 1.50
SRU8 The Strongman .60 1.50
SRU9 Knife Throwing .60 1.50
SRU10 Tightrope Walking .60 1.50

2011 Topps Allen and Ginter Mini Uninvited Guests

COMPLETE SET (10) 5.00 12.00
STATED ODDS 1:12 HOBBY
UG1 Bachelor's Grove Cemetery .60 1.50
UG2 The White House .60 1.50
UG3 Waverly Hills Sanatorium .60 1.50
UG4 The Villisca Axe Murder House .60 1.50
UG5 The Amityville Haunting .60 1.50
UG6 The Lemp Mansion .60 1.50
UG7 Alcatraz .60 1.50
UG8 The Winchester Mystery House .60 1.50
UG9 RMS Queen Mary .60 1.50
UG10 The Lizzie Borden House .60 1.50

2011 Topps Allen and Ginter Mini World's Most Mysterious Figures

COMPLETE SET (10) 5.00 12.00
STATED ODDS 1:15 HOBBY
WMF1 Rasputin .60 1.50
WMF2 The Poe Toaster .60 1.50
WMF3 Kasper Hauser .60 1.50
WMF4 Fulcanelli .60 1.50
WMF5 D.B. Cooper .60 1.50
WMF6 The Count of St. Germain .60 1.50
WMF7 The Man in the Iron Mask .60 1.50
WMF8 Nostradamus .60 1.50
WMF9 The Babushka Lady .60 1.50
WMF10 Captain Charles Johnson .60 1.50

2011 Topps Allen and Ginter N43

STATED ODDS 1:2 HOBBY BOXES
AC Aroldis Chapman 2.00 5.00
AP Albert Pujols 4.00 10.00
AW Adam Wainwright 1.25 3.00
CC Carl Crawford 1.25 3.00
CG Carlos Gonzalez 1.25 3.00
DP David Price 1.50 4.00
DW David Wright 1.50 4.00
HR Hanley Ramirez 1.25 3.00
JJ Josh Johnson 1.25 3.00
JV Joey Votto 2.00 5.00
MT Mark Teixeira 1.25 3.00
RC Robinson Cano 1.25 3.00
RH Roy Halladay 1.25 3.00
TL Tim Lincecum 1.25 3.00
UJ Ubaldo Jimenez .75 2.00

2011 Topps Allen and Ginter Relics

STATED ODDS 1:10 HOBBY
EXCHANGE DEADLINE 6/30/2014
AB1 Adrian Beltre Bat 10.00 25.00
AB2 Adrian Beltre Jsy 3.00 8.00
AD1 Adam Dunn Bat 3.00 8.00

AD2 Adam Dunn Jsy 3.00 8.00
ADU Angelo Dundee 4.00 10.00
AE Andre Ethier 3.00 8.00
AES Alcides Escobar 4.00 10.00
AG Adrian Gonzalez 4.00 10.00
AH Aaron Hill 3.00 8.00
AJ Adam Jones 3.00 8.00
AJA1 Austin Jackson Bat 3.00 8.00
AJA2 Austin Jackson Jsy 3.00 8.00
AJB A.J. Burnett 3.00 8.00
AJP A.J. Pierzynski 12.00 30.00
AJU Ana Julaton 10.00 25.00
AL1 Adam Lind Bat 3.00 8.00
AL2 Adam Lind Jsy 3.00 8.00
AM1 Andrew McCutchen Bat 6.00 15.00
AM2 Andrew McCutchen Jsy 12.00 30.00
AMU Aimee Mullins 4.00 10.00
AP1 Albert Pujols Bat 10.00 25.00
AP2 Albert Pujols Jsy 30.00 60.00
AR Alex Rodriguez 5.00 12.00
ARA1 Alexei Ramirez Bat 3.00 8.00
ARA2 Alexei Ramirez Jsy 3.00 8.00
ARM2 Aramis Ramirez Jsy 3.00 8.00
ARM1 Aramis Ramirez Bat 15.00 40.00
AS Alfonso Soriano 4.00 10.00
ASA Anibal Sanchez 3.00 8.00
ASO Annika Sorenstam 12.00 30.00
BB Billy Butler 3.00 8.00
BBO Brennan Boesch 3.00 8.00
BD Blake DeWitt 3.00 8.00
BG Brett Gardner 3.00 8.00
BJU B.J. Upton 3.00 8.00
BM Brian McCann 3.00 8.00
CB Carlos Beltran 10.00 25.00
CBU Cheryl Burke 10.00 25.00
CG Carlos Gomez 3.00 8.00
CJ Chipper Jones 5.00 12.00
CJO Chris Johnson 3.00 8.00
CM Casey McGehee 3.00 8.00
CP Carlos Pena 3.00 8.00
CQ Carlos Quentin 3.00 8.00
CR Cody Ross 5.00 12.00
CRA Colby Rasmus 5.00 12.00
CU Chase Utley 4.00 10.00
CWE Chrissie Wellington 6.00 15.00
CWO Chuck Woolery 5.00 12.00
DBO Daniel Boulud 6.00 15.00
DH Daniel Hudson 3.00 8.00
DJ Derek Jeter 10.00 25.00
DL Derrek Lee 3.00 8.00
DO David Ortiz 3.00 8.00
DP Dustin Pedroia 5.00 12.00
DS1 Drew Stubbs Bat 4.00 10.00
DS2 Drew Stubbs Jsy 3.00 8.00
DTU Diana Taurasi 6.00 15.00
DU1 Dan Uggla Bat 3.00 8.00
DU2 Dan Uggla Jsy 10.00 25.00
DVA Dick Vitale 6.00 15.00
EA Elvis Andrus 3.00 8.00
EJA Eric Jackson 6.00 15.00
EL1 Evan Longoria Bat 3.00 8.00
EL2 Evan Longoria Jsy 5.00 12.00
ELY Evan Lysacek 5.00 12.00
EV Edinson Volquez 3.00 8.00
FC Francisco Cervelli 3.00 8.00
FH Felix Hernandez 3.00 8.00
GAU Geno Auriemma 8.00 20.00
GB Gordon Beckham 3.00 8.00
GFI Guy Fieri 10.00 25.00
GS Grady Sizemore 8.00 20.00
GSO Geovany Soto 3.00 8.00
HK Howie Kendrick 3.00 8.00
HMI Heather Mitts 10.00 25.00
HP Hunter Pence 3.00 8.00
HR1 Hanley Ramirez Bat 3.00 8.00
HR2 Hanley Ramirez Jsy 3.00 8.00
HSO Hope Solo 20.00 50.00
ID1 Ike Davis Bat 3.00 8.00
ID2 Ike Davis Jsy 3.00 8.00
IDE Ian Desmond 3.00 8.00
IR Ivan Rodriguez 3.00 8.00
IS Ichiro Suzuki 6.00 15.00
JB Jason Bay 5.00 12.00
JBA Jose Bautista 4.00 10.00
JBE Josh Beckett 3.00 8.00
JBR Jay Bruce 5.00 12.00
JC Joba Chamberlain 3.00 8.00
JD Johnny Damon 3.00 8.00
JDD J.D. Drew 3.00 8.00
JE1 Jacoby Ellsbury Bat 5.00 12.00
JE2 Jacoby Ellsbury Jsy 3.00 8.00
JH Josh Hamilton 6.00 15.00
JJ Josh Johnson 3.00 8.00
JJA Jon Jay 3.00 8.00
JL James Loney 3.00 8.00
JLA John Lackey 3.00 8.00
JLA Jake LaMotta 15.00 40.00
JLL Jack LaLanne 6.00 15.00
JLO Jed Lowrie 3.00 8.00
JM Joe Maddon 3.00 8.00
JMC John McEnroe 20.00 50.00
JMO Justin Morneau 3.00 8.00
JNA Jim Nantz 6.00 15.00
JOF Jo Frost 6.00 15.00
JP1 Jorge Posada Bat 4.00 10.00
JP2 Jorge Posada Jsy 4.00 10.00
JPA Jonathan Papelbon 3.00 8.00
JR Jimmy Rollins 5.00 12.00
JRE Jose Reyes 6.00 15.00
JS Jarrod Saltalamacchia 3.00 8.00
JSA Jeff Samardzija 4.00 10.00
JT Jose Tabata 4.00 10.00
JU Justin Upton 3.00 8.00
JV1 Joey Votto Bat 4.00 10.00
JV2 Joey Votto Jsy 8.00 20.00
JVE Justin Verlander 4.00 10.00
JW Jayson Werth 3.00 8.00
KB Kyle Blanks 3.00 8.00
KF Kosuke Fukudome 4.00 10.00
KM Kendrys Morales 3.00 8.00
KPE Kyle Petty 10.00 25.00
KS Kurt Suzuki 3.00 8.00
KY Kevin Youkilis 4.00 10.00
KYA Kristi Yamaguchi 10.00 25.00
LHO Lou Holtz 20.00 50.00
LHO Larry Holmes 10.00 25.00
MB Mark Buehrle 3.00 8.00
MBY Marlon Byrd 3.00 8.00
MC Matt Cain 4.00 10.00
MCA1 Melky Cabrera Bat 6.00 15.00
MCA2 Melky Cabrera Jsy 6.00 15.00
MCB Miguel Cabrera 4.00 10.00
MFA Marc Forgione 6.00 15.00
MGU Matt Guy 5.00 12.00
MHO Mat Hoffman 8.00 20.00
MPA Manny Pacquiao 25.00 60.00
MR Mark Reynolds 3.00 8.00
MSH Maxim Shmyrev 8.00 20.00
MT Mark Teixeira 3.00 8.00
MWA Micky Ward 5.00 12.00
MY1 Michael Young Bat 3.00 8.00
MY2 Michael Young Jsy 3.00 8.00
NC Nelson Cruz 4.00 10.00
NF Neftali Feliz 3.00 8.00
NLO Nancy Lopez 12.00 30.00
NM Nick Markakis 5.00 12.00
NS Nick Swisher 3.00 8.00
PF Prince Fielder 3.00 8.00
PGA Peter Gammons 10.00 25.00
PH Phil Hughes 3.00 8.00
PK Paul Konerko 6.00 15.00
PS1 Pablo Sandoval Bat 4.00 10.00
PS2 Pablo Sandoval Jsy 4.00 10.00
PST Picabo Street 10.00 25.00
RB1 Ryan Braun Bat 6.00 15.00
RB2 Ryan Braun Jsy 4.00 10.00
RC Robinson Cano 3.00 8.00
RD Ryan Dempster 3.00 8.00
RDO Ryan Doumit 3.00 8.00
RH Ryan Howard 3.00 8.00
RJO Rafer Johnson 6.00 15.00
RM1 Russell Martin Bat 3.00 8.00
RM2 Russell Martin Jsy 3.00 8.00
RN Ricky Nolasco 3.00 8.00
RP Ryan Perry 3.00 8.00
RRU Rudy Ruettiger 12.00 30.00
RTU Ron Turcotte 8.00 20.00
RW1 Rickie Weeks Bat 3.00 8.00
RW2 Rickie Weeks Jsy 3.00 8.00
RZ Ryan Zimmerman 3.00 8.00
SBI Sue Bird 6.00 15.00
SC1 Starlin Castro Bat 5.00 12.00
SC2 Starlin Castro Jsy 5.00 12.00
SD Stephen Drew 3.00 8.00
SLE Stan Lee 20.00 50.00
SMI Shawn Michaels 10.00 25.00
SR Scott Rolen 3.00 8.00
SRI Sanya Richards 8.00 20.00
SV1 Shane Victorino Bat 4.00 10.00
SV2 Shane Victorino Jsy 3.00 8.00
TC Tyler Colvin 3.00 8.00
TG Tony Gwynn Jr. 10.00 25.00
TH Tim Hudson 3.00 8.00
THA Tommy Hanson 3.00 8.00
THE Todd Helton 3.00 8.00
THO Tim Howard 8.00 20.00
TSC Timothy Shieff 6.00 15.00
TT Troy Tulowitzki 3.00 8.00
TW Tim Wakefield 3.00 8.00
WEE Wee Man 5.00 12.00
WV Will Venable 3.00 8.00
XN Xavier Nady 3.00 8.00
YE Yunel Escobar 4.00 10.00

2011 Topps Allen and Ginter Rip Cards

OVERALL RIP ODDS 1:276 HOBBY
PRINT RUNS B/WN 10-99 COPIES PER
NO PRICING ON QTY 25 OR LESS
ALL LISTED PRICED ARE FOR RIPPED
UNRIPPED HAVE ADD'L CARDS WITHIN
COMMON UNRIPPED p/r 99 60.00 120.00
COMMON UNRIPPED p/r 75 60.00 120.00
COMMON UNRIPPED p/r 50 60.00 120.00
COMMON UNRIPPED p/r 25 100.00 250.00
COMMON UNRIPPED p/r 10 350.00 700.00
RC54 Jayson Werth/50 6.00 15.00
RC55 Jered Weaver/50 6.00 15.00
RC56 Francisco Liriano/50 4.00 10.00
RC57 Zack Greinke/50 6.00 15.00
RC58 Roy Oswalt/50 6.00 15.00
RC59 Hunter Pence/50 6.00 15.00
RC60 Adrian Beltre/50 10.00 25.00
RC61 Martin Prado/50 4.00 10.00
RC62 Jay Bruce/50 6.00 15.00
RC63 Jimmy Rollins/50 6.00 15.00
RC64 Paul Konerko/50 6.00 15.00
RC65 Brandon Phillips/50 4.00 10.00
RC66 Dan Haren/50 4.00 10.00
RC67 Andre Ethier/50 6.00 15.00
RC68 Matt Cain/50 6.00 15.00
RC69 Elvis Andrus/75 6.00 15.00
RC70 Jason Heyward/75 5.00 12.00
RC71 Ian Kinsler/75 6.00 15.00
RC72 Joakim Soria/75 4.00 10.00
RC73 Michael Young/75 4.00 10.00
RC74 Delmon Young/75 6.00 15.00
RC75 Mariano Rivera/75 10.00 25.00
RC76 Mat Latos/75 6.00 15.00
RC77 Colby Rasmus/75 5.00 12.00
RC78 Heath Bell/75 4.00 10.00
RC79 Shane Victorino/75 6.00 15.00
RC80 Derek Jeter/75 15.00 40.00
RC81 Billy Butler/75 4.00 10.00
RC82 Neftali Feliz/75 4.00 10.00
RC83 Carlos Santana/75 8.00 20.00
RC84 Gordon Beckham/99 4.00 10.00
RC85 Mike Stanton/99 10.00 25.00
RC86 Yovani Gallardo/99 4.00 10.00
RC87 Clay Buchholz/99 4.00 10.00
RC88 Pedro Alvarez/99 8.00 20.00
RC89 Matt Garza/99 4.00 10.00
RC90 Aroldis Chapman/99 8.00 20.00
RC91 David Ortiz/99 10.00 25.00
RC92 Jeremy Hellickson/99 6.00 15.00
RC93 Jacoby Ellsbury/99 6.00 15.00
RC94 Stephen Drew/99 4.00 10.00
RC95 Starlin Castro/99 5.00 12.00
RC96 Torii Hunter/99 4.00 10.00
RC97 Madison Bumgarner/99 8.00 20.00
RC99 Vernon Wells/99 4.00 10.00

2011 Topps Allen and Ginter State Map Relics

STATED PRINT RUN 50 SER.#'d SETS
1 New England 90.00 150.00
2 New York 90.00 150.00
3 Penn/N.Jersey 60.00 120.00
4 VA/WV/MD/DE 100.00 200.00
5 N.Carolina/S.Carolina 60.00 120.00
6 Kentucky/Tenn. 50.00 100.00
7 Michigan 50.00 100.00
8 Ohio 50.00 100.00
9 Indiana 60.00 120.00
10 Georgia 40.00 80.00
11 Florida 90.00 150.00
12 Alabama 50.00 100.00
13 Mississippi 50.00 100.00
14 Wisconsin 50.00 100.00
15 Illinois 50.00 100.00
16 Minnesota 60.00 120.00
17 Iowa 60.00 120.00
18 Arkansas 60.00 120.00
19 Missouri 50.00 100.00
20 Louisiana 60.00 120.00
21 North Dakota 40.00 80.00
22 South Dakota 50.00 100.00
23 Nebraska 60.00 120.00
24 Kansas 50.00 100.00
25 Oklahoma 50.00 100.00
26 Texas 90.00 150.00
27 Montana 40.00 80.00
28 Wyoming 30.00 60.00
29 Colorado 50.00 100.00
30 New Mexico 40.00 80.00
31 Idaho 50.00 100.00
32 Utah 75.00 150.00
33 Arizona 40.00 60.00
34 Washington 50.00 100.00
35 Oregon 25.00 60.00
36 Nevada 40.00 80.00
37 California 60.00 120.00
38 Alaska 50.00 100.00
39 Hawaii 75.00 150.00

2012 Topps Allen and Ginter

COMPLETE SET (350) 30.00 60.00
COMP.SET w/o SP's (300) 15.00 40.00
SP ODDS 1:2 HOBBY
1 Albert Pujols .50 1.25
2 Juan Pierre .25 .60
3 Miguel Cabrera .40 1.00
4 Yu Darvish RC 1.50 4.00
5 David Price .30 .75
6 Johnny Bench .40 1.00
7 Mickey Mantle 1.25 3.00
8 Mitch Moreland .25 .60
9 Yonder Alonso .25 .60
10 Dustin Pedroia .30 .75
11 Eric Hosmer .30 .75
12 Bryce Harper RC 8.00 20.00
13 Drew Stubbs .25 .60
14 Nick Markakis .30 .75
15 Joel Hanrahan .25 .60
16 Rulon Gardner .15 .40
17 Lonnie Chisenhall .25 .60
18 Kevin Youkilis .40 1.00
19 Bob Knight .50 1.25
20 Miguel Montero .25 .60
21 Matt Moore RC 1.00 2.50
22 Jair Jurrjens .25 .60
23 Yogi Berra .40 1.00
24 Paul Goldschmidt .40 1.00
25 Shin-Soo Choo .30 .75
26 Hunter Pence .30 .75
27 Ricky Nolasco .25 .60
28 Dustin Ackley .25 .60
29 Hanley Ramirez .30 .75
30 Carlos Zambrano .30 .75
31 Jackie Robinson .40 1.00
32 Ben Zobrist .30 .75
33 Chipper Jones .40 1.00
34 Alex Gordon .30 .75
35 David Ortiz .40 1.00
36 Kirk Herbstreit .15 .40
37 James McDonald .25 .60
38 Pablo Sandoval .30 .75
39 Brad Peacock RC .60 1.50
40 Jimmy Rollins .30 .75
41 Clayton Kershaw .75 2.00
42 Justin Upton .30 .75
43 Josh Johnson .30 .75
44 Brandon League .25 .60
45 Ewa Mataya .15 .40
46 Jarrod Saltalamacchia .25 .60
47 Buster Posey .50 1.25
48 Jordan Walden .25 .60
49 Jeremy Hellickson .25 .60
50 Clay Buchholz .25 .60
51 Don Denkinger .15 .40
52 Cameron Maybin .25 .60
53 Hisashi Iwakuma RC 1.25 3.00
54 Al Kaline .40 1.00
55 Colin Montgomerie .40 1.00
56 Jordan Pacheco RC .60 1.50
57 Michael Pineda .25 .60
58 Ryan Braun .25 .60
59 Johnny Damon .30 .75
60 Reggie Jackson .25 .60
61 Richard Petty .50 1.25
62 Michael Cuddyer .25 .60
63 Zach Britton .30 .75
64 Mat Latos .30 .75
65 Alex Rios .30 .75
66 Yadier Molina .40 1.00
67 Desmond Jennings .30 .75
68 Rickie Weeks .25 .60
69 Kurt Suzuki .25 .60
70 Aroldis Chapman .40 1.00
71 Curtis Granderson .30 .75
72 Joakim Soria .25 .60
73 Jordan Zimmermann .30 .75
74 Johnny Cueto .30 .75
75 Erin Andrews .75 2.00
76 Michael Bourn .25 .60
77 Chris Young .25 .60
78 Joe Mauer .30 .75
79 Yoenis Cespedes RC 1.50 4.00
80 Brooks Robinson .25 .60
81 Jerry Bailey .15 .40
82 Giancarlo Stanton .40 1.00
83 Matt Joyce .25 .60
84 Andre Ethier .30 .75
85 Curly Neal .40 1.00
86 Nyjer Morgan .25 .60
87 Annie Duke .15 .40
88 Stan Musial .60 1.50
89 Edwin Jackson .25 .60
90 Roy Halladay .30 .75
91 Grady Sizemore .30 .75
92 Craig Kimbrel .30 .75
93 Jose Bautista .30 .75
94 Geovany Soto .30 .75
95 Felix Hernandez .30 .75
96 Gavin Floyd .25 .60
97 Max Scherzer .40 1.00
98 Nelson Cruz .40 1.00
99 Sandy Koufax .75 2.00
100 Troy Tulowitzki .40 1.00
101 James Loney .25 .60
102 Huston Street .25 .60
103 Alexi Ogando .25 .60
104 Ian Desmond .25 .60
105 Arnold Palmer .60 1.50
106 Bud Norris .25 .60
107 C.J. Wilson .25 .60
108 J.P. Arencibia .25 .60
109 Tim Lincecum .30 .75
110 Heath Bell .25 .60
111 Wandy Rodriguez .25 .60
112 Chris Carpenter .30 .75
113 Meadowlark Lemon .40 1.00
114 Johan Santana .30 .75
115 Carlos Santana .30 .75
116 Brandon Beachy .25 .60
117 Nick Swisher .30 .75
118 Carl Yastrzemski .60 1.50
119 Asdrubal Cabrera .30 .75
120 Mariano Rivera .50 1.25
121 David Wright .30 .75
122 Brett Lawrie RC .75 2.00
123 Adam Lind .30 .75
124 Jered Weaver .30 .75
125 Ben Revere .30 .75
126 Justin Masterson .25 .60
127 Erick Aybar .25 .60
128 Andrew McCutchen .40 1.00
129 Michael Phelps .50 1.25
130 Madison Bumgarner .30 .75
131 Jim Palmer .25 .60
132 Daniel Hudson .25 .60
133 Carlos Beltran .30 .75
134 David Freese .25 .60
135 Michael Morse .25 .60
136 Jacoby Ellsbury .30 .75
137 George Brett .75 2.00
138 Josh Willingham .30 .75
139 Tim Hudson .30 .75
140 Mike Trout 12.00 30.00
141 Vance Worley .30 .75
142 Jose Reyes .25 .60
143 Nick Hagadone .25 .60
144 Joe Benson RC .60 1.50
145 Drew Storen .25 .60
146 Josh Beckett .25 .60
147 Tsuyoshi Nishioka .30 .75
148 Carlos Gonzalez .30 .75
149 Wilson Ramos .25 .60
150 Norichika Aoki RC .75 2.00
151 Jose Valverde .30 .75
152 Ryan Vogelsong .25 .60
153 Robinson Cano .30 .75
154 Bob Hurley Sr. .15 .40
155 Edinson Volquez .25 .60
156 Trevor Cahill .25 .60
157 Roger Federer .75 2.00
158 Melky Cabrera .25 .60
159 Devin Mesoraco RC .60 1.50
160 Shane Victorino .30 .75
161 Freddie Freeman .50 1.25
162 Jeff Francoeur .30 .75
163 Tom Seaver .25 .60
164 Ike Davis .25 .60
165 Alex Avila .25 .60
166 Ervin Santana .25 .60
167 J.J. Putz .25 .60
168 Jason Kipnis .30 .75
169 Mark Teixeira .30 .75
170 Don Mattingly .75 2.00
171 Stephen Strasburg .40 1.00
172 Chris Perez .25 .60
173 Jay Bruce .30 .75
174 Ubaldo Jimenez .25 .60
175 Luke Hochevar .25 .60
176 Babe Ruth 1.00 2.50
177 Stephen Drew .25 .60
178 Wei-Yin Chen RC 1.50 4.00
179 Cole Hamels .30 .75
180 Tim Federowicz RC .60 1.50
181 Joe DiMaggio .75 2.00
182 Colby Rasmus .30 .75
183 Darwin Barney .25 .60
184 Ara Parseghian .25 .60
185 Starlin Castro .30 .75
186 Jemile Weeks RC .25 .60
187 John Axford .25 .60
188 Tom Milone RC .60 1.50
189 Lance Berkman .30 .75
190 Addison Reed RC .60 1.50
191 Jason Bay .30 .75
192 Brett Pill RC 1.00 2.50
193 Jackie Joyner-Kersee .25 .60
194 J.J. Hardy .25 .60
195 Jhoulys Chacin .25 .60
196 Lou Gehrig .75 2.00
197 Ty Cobb .60 1.50
198 Phil Pfister .15 .40
199 Ricky Romero .25 .60
200 Matt Kemp .30 .75
201 Tommy Hanson .25 .60
202 Jaime Garcia .30 .75
203 Ian Kinsler .30 .75
204 Adam Dunn .30 .75
205 Tony Gwynn .40 1.00
206 Joey Votto .40 1.00
207 Coy Luebke .25 .60
208 Martin Prado .25 .60
209 Coco Crisp .25 .60
210 Willie Mays .75 2.00
211 Keegan Bradley .15 .40
212 Ken Griffey Jr. .75 2.00
213 Joe Nathan .25 .60
214 Yunel Escobar .25 .60
215 Dan Haren .25 .60
216 Corey Hart .25 .60
217 Brian Wilson .40 1.00
218 John Danks .25 .60
219 Ian Kennedy .25 .60
220 James Brown .15 .40
221 Carlos Marmol .25 .60
222 Yovani Gallardo .30 .75
223 CC Sabathia .30 .75
224 Adam Jones .30 .75
225 Roger Maris .40 1.00
226 Jim Thome .30 .75
227 Michael Young .25 .60
228 Dexter Fowler .30 .75
229 Ichiro Suzuki .50 1.25
230 Evan Longoria .30 .75
231 Todd Helton .30 .75
232 Kate Upton .50 1.25
233 Shaun Marcum .25 .60
234 Carlos Lee .25 .60
235 Victor Martinez .30 .75
236 Scott Rolen .30 .75
237 Al Unser Sr. .25 .60
238 Austin Jackson .25 .60
239 Liam Hendriks RC .60 1.50
240 Steve Lombardozzi RC .60 1.50
241 Andrew Bailey .25 .60
242 Alfonso Soriano .30 .75
243 Aramis Ramirez .25 .60
244 Brett Anderson .25 .60
245 Hank Haney .25 .60
246 Torii Hunter .30 .75
247 Hank Aaron .75 2.00
248 Jed Lowrie .25 .60
249 Phil Hughes .25 .60
250 Brennan Boesch .25 .60
251 B.J. Upton .30 .75
252 Tsuyoshi Wada RC .60 1.50
253 Jorge De La Rosa .25 .60
254 Rickey Henderson .40 1.00
255 Dayan Viciedo .25 .60
256 Brandon Morrow .25 .60
257 Dan Uggla .30 .75
258 Doug Fister .25 .60
259 Wade Davis .30 .75
260 Alex Liddi RC .60 1.50
261 Michael Taylor RC .60 1.50
262 Justin Verlander .40 1.00
263 Jason Motte .25 .60
264 Brian McCann .30 .75
265 Chris Parmelee RC .60 1.50
266 Carlos Ruiz .25 .60
267 Neftali Feliz .25 .60
268 Angel Pagan .25 .60
269 Mike Schmidt .60 1.50
270 Anthony Rizzo .60 1.50
271 Mark Reynolds .25 .60
272 Jose Tabata .25 .60
273 Gaby Sanchez .30 .75
274 Derek Jeter 1.00 2.50
275 Kerry Wood .25 .60
276 James Shields .25 .60
277 Jesus Montero RC .60 1.50
278 Fatal1ty .15 .40
279 Brett Gardner .30 .75
280 Brandon Belt .30 .75
281 Matt Cain .30 .75
282 Carlos Quentin .25 .60
283 Dale Webster .15 .40
284 Pedro Alvarez .25 .60
285 Ryan Zimmerman .30 .75
286 Neil Walker .30 .75
287 Hiroki Kuroda .25 .60
288 Alex Rodriguez .50 1.25
289 Brandon Phillips .25 .60
290 Derek Holland .25 .60
291 Chase Utley .30 .75
292 Greg Gumbel .15 .40
293 Cliff Lee .30 .75
294 Elvis Andrus .30 .75
295 Drew Pomeranz RC .60 1.50
296 Mark Trumbo .25 .60
297 Justin Morneau .30 .75
298 Dee Gordon .25 .60
299 Jeff Niemann .25 .60
300 Roberto Clemente 1.00 2.50
301 Adron Chambers SP RC 1.25 3.00
302 Jayson Werth SP 1.50 4.00
303 Ivan Nova SP 1.50 4.00
304 Kyle Farnsworth SP 2.50 6.00
305 Wilin Rosario SP RC 2.00 5.00
306 Ryan Howard SP 1.00 2.50
307 Jhonny Peralta SP 2.00 5.00
308 Paul Konerko SP 1.25 3.00
309 Bela Karolyi SP 1.25 3.00
310 Russell Martin SP 2.00 5.00
311 Bob Gibson SP 1.25 3.00
312 Anibal Sanchez SP 2.00 5.00
313 Carlos Pena SP 1.50 4.00
314 Michael Buffer SP 1.25 3.00
315 Dellin Betances SP RC 1.25 3.00
316 Adrian Gonzalez SP 1.50 4.00
317 Jason Heyward SP 1.00 2.50
318 Mike Moustakas SP 1.50 4.00
319 Adam Wainwright SP 1.50 4.00
320 Jonathan Papelbon SP 1.50 4.00
321 Chad Billingsley SP 2.00 5.00
322 Sergio Santos SP 2.00 5.00
323 Ryan Roberts SP 2.00 5.00
324 Cal Ripken Jr. SP 2.00 5.00
325 Frank Robinson SP 1.25 3.00
326 Logan Morrison SP 2.00 5.00
327 Jon Lester SP 1.25 3.00
328 Josh Hamilton SP 1.00 2.50
329 Billy Butler SP 2.00 5.00
330 Mike Napoli SP 1.25 3.00
331 Carl Crawford SP 1.50 4.00
332 Guy Bluford SP 1.25 3.00
333 Kelly Johnson SP 2.00 5.00
334 Adrian Beltre SP 3.00 8.00
335 Alexei Ramirez SP 2.50 6.00
336 Gio Gonzalez SP 2.50 6.00
337 Matt Holliday SP 1.25 3.00
338 Prince Fielder SP 1.50 4.00
339 Swin Cash SP 3.00 8.00
340 Marty Hogan SP 1.25 3.00
341 Colby Lewis SP 2.00 5.00
342 Ryan Dempster SP 2.00 5.00
343 Zack Greinke SP 1.50 4.00
344 Matt Dominguez SP RC 2.50 6.00
345 Nolan Ryan SP 2.00 5.00
346 Lefty Kreh SP 1.25 3.00
347 Matt Garza SP 2.00 5.00
348 Chase Headley SP 2.00 5.00
349 Danny Espinosa SP 2.00 5.00
350 Howie Kendrick SP 2.00 5.00

2012 Topps Allen and Ginter Mini

*MINI 1-300: .75X TO 2X BASIC
*MINI 1-300 RC: .5X TO 1.2X BASIC RC's
*MINI SP 301-350: .5X TO 1.2X BASIC SP
MINI SP ODDS 1:13 HOBBY
351-400 RANDOM WITHIN RIP CARDS
STATED PLATE ODDS 1:564 HOBBY
PLATE PRINT RUN 1 SET PER COLOR
NO PLATE PRICING DUE TO SCARCITY
12 Bryce Harper 12.00 30.00
352 Matt Kemp EXT 20.00 50.00
353 Ryan Zimmerman EXT 15.00 40.00
354 Derek Jeter EXT 100.00 175.00
355 Carlos Gonzalez EXT 15.00 40.00
356 Mark Teixeira EXT 15.00 40.00
357 Justin Upton EXT 30.00 60.00
358 Ian Kinsler EXT 15.00 40.00
359 Cole Hamels EXT 15.00 40.00
360 Cliff Lee EXT 40.00 80.00
361 James Shields EXT 30.00 60.00
362 Roy Halladay EXT 20.00 50.00
363 Miguel Cabrera EXT 20.00 50.00
364 Josh Hamilton EXT 20.00 50.00
365 Giancarlo Stanton EXT 20.00 50.00
366 Jacoby Ellsbury EXT 30.00 60.00
367 Starlin Castro EXT 20.00 50.00
368 Adrian Gonzalez EXT 15.00 40.00
369 Evan Longoria EXT 40.00 80.00
370 Felix Hernandez EXT 30.00 60.00
371 Ken Griffey Jr. EXT 60.00 150.00
372 Andrew McCutchen EXT 30.00 60.00
373 Ryan Howard EXT 30.00 60.00
374 Tim Lincecum EXT 40.00 80.00
375 Robinson Cano EXT 20.00 50.00
376 Justin Verlander EXT 20.00 50.00
377 Nolan Ryan EXT 125.00 250.00
378 Sandy Koufax EXT 30.00 60.00
379 CC Sabathia EXT 50.00 100.00
380 Dustin Pedroia EXT 30.00 60.00
381 Willie Mays EXT 30.00 60.00
382 Hanley Ramirez EXT 15.00 40.00
383 Ryan Braun EXT 30.00 60.00
384 Alex Rodriguez EXT 30.00 60.00
385 Jered Weaver EXT 20.00 50.00
386 Buster Posey EXT 20.00 50.00
387 Jose Bautista EXT 15.00 40.00
388 Stephen Strasburg EXT 40.00 80.00
389 Ichiro Suzuki EXT 20.00 50.00
390 Reggie Jackson EXT 20.00 50.00
392 Curtis Granderson EXT 50.00 100.00
393 Eric Hosmer EXT 15.00 40.00
394 David Wright EXT 30.00 60.00
395 Jose Reyes EXT 30.00 60.00
396 Troy Tulowitzki EXT 15.00 40.00
397 Clayton Kershaw EXT 20.00 50.00
398 Jose Valverde EXT 30.00 60.00
399 Albert Pujols EXT 40.00 80.00
400 Jay Bruce EXT 20.00 50.00

2012 Topps Allen and Ginter Mini A and G Back

*A & G BACK: 1X TO 2.5X BASIC
*A & G BACK RCs: .6X TO 1.5X BASIC RCs
A & G BACK ODDS 1:5 HOBBY
*A & G BACK SP: .6X TO 1.5X BASIC SP
A & G BACK SP ODDS 1:65 HOBBY
12 Bryce Harper 15.00 40.00

2012 Topps Allen and Ginter Mini Black

*BLACK: 1.5X TO 4X BASIC
*BLACK RCs: .6X TO 1.5X BASIC RCs
BLACK ODDS 1:10 HOBBY

*BLACK SP: 1X TO 2.5X BASIC SP
BLACK SP ODDS 1:130 HOBBY
12 Bryce Harper 15.00 40.00
140 Mike Trout 10.00 25.00

2012 Topps Allen and Ginter Mini Gold Border

*GOLD: .5X TO 1.2X BASIC
*GOLD RCs: .5X TO 1.2X BASIC RCs
COMMON SP (301-350) .40 1.00
SP SEMIS .60 1.50
SP UNLISTED 1.00 2.50
12 Bryce Harper 15.00 40.00
301 Adron Chambers 1.00 2.50
302 Jayson Werth .75 2.00
303 Ivan Nova .75 2.00
304 Kyle Farnsworth .75 2.00
305 Wilin Rosario .60 1.50
306 Ryan Howard .75 2.00
307 Jhonny Peralta .60 1.50
308 Paul Konerko .60 1.50
309 Bela Karolyi .40 1.00
310 Russell Martin .60 1.50
311 Bob Gibson .60 1.50
312 Anibal Sanchez .60 1.50
313 Carlos Pena .75 2.00
314 Michael Buffer .40 1.00
315 Dellin Betances 1.00 2.50
316 Adrian Gonzalez .75 2.00
317 Jason Heyward .75 2.00
318 Mike Moustakas .75 2.00
319 Adam Wainwright .75 2.00
320 Jonathan Papelbon .75 2.00
321 Chad Billingsley .60 1.50
322 Sergio Santos .60 1.50
323 Ryan Roberts .60 1.50
324 Cal Ripken Jr. 3.00 8.00
325 Frank Robinson .60 1.50
326 Logan Morrison .60 1.50
327 Jon Lester .60 1.50
328 Josh Hamilton .75 2.00
329 Billy Butler .60 1.50
330 Mike Napoli .60 1.50
331 Carl Crawford .75 2.00
332 Guy Bluford .40 1.00
333 Kelly Johnson .60 1.50
334 Adrian Beltre 1.00 2.50
335 Alexei Ramirez .75 2.00
336 Gio Gonzalez .75 2.00
337 Matt Holliday 1.00 2.50
338 Prince Fielder .75 2.00
339 Swin Cash 1.00 2.50
340 Marty Hogan .40 1.00
341 Colby Lewis .60 1.50
342 Ryan Dempster .60 1.50
343 Zack Greinke .75 2.00
344 Matt Dominguez .75 2.00
345 Nolan Ryan 3.00 8.00
346 Lefty Kreh .40 1.00
347 Matt Garza .60 1.50
348 Chase Headley .60 1.50
349 Danny Espinosa .60 1.50
350 Howie Kendrick .60 1.50

2012 Topps Allen and Ginter Mini No Card Number

*NO NBR: 5X TO 12X BASIC
*NO NBR RCs: 2X TO 5X BASIC RCs
*NO NBR SP: 1.2X TO 3X BASIC SP
STATED ODDS 1:111 HOBBY
ANNC'D PRINT RUN OF 50 SETS
12 Bryce Harper 50.00 125.00
274 Derek Jeter 40.00 80.00
324 Cal Ripken Jr. 40.00 80.00
345 Nolan Ryan 15.00 40.00

2012 Topps Allen and Ginter Autographs

STATED ODDS 1:51 HOBBY
EXCHANGE DEADLINE 06/30/2015
AC Allen Craig 8.00 20.00
AC Aroldis Chapman 12.00 30.00
ADK Annie Duke 12.00 30.00
AG Adrian Gonzalez 10.00 25.00
AJ Adam Jones 10.00 25.00
AK Al Kaline 100.00 250.00
AMC Andrew McCutchen 30.00 60.00
AO Alexi Ogando 4.00 10.00
APA Ara Parseghian 15.00 40.00
APL Arnold Palmer 100.00 200.00
AR Anthony Rizzo 15.00 40.00
AUS Al Unser Sr. 6.00 15.00
BA Brett Anderson 4.00 10.00
BB Brandon Belt 4.00 10.00
BG Bob Gibson 100.00 200.00
BHS Bob Hurley Sr. 8.00 20.00
BK Bela Karolyi 10.00 25.00
BKN Bob Knight 40.00 80.00
BL Brett Lawrie 6.00 15.00
BM Brian McCann 40.00 80.00
BP Buster Posey 100.00 200.00
BP Brad Peacock 4.00 10.00
BY Bryce Harper 125.00 300.00
CC Carl Crawford 10.00 25.00
CG Craig Gentry 4.00 10.00
CG Carlos Gonzalez 30.00 60.00
CK Clayton Kershaw 40.00 100.00
CMO Colin Montgomerie 8.00 20.00
CNE Curly Neal 20.00 50.00
CRJ Cal Ripken Jr. 300.00 400.00
DB Daniel Bard 4.00 10.00
DDK Don Denkinger 6.00 15.00
DF Dexter Fowler 4.00 10.00
DG Dee Gordon 8.00 20.00
DG Dillon Gee 4.00 10.00
DM Don Mattingly 200.00 300.00
DP David Price 10.00 25.00
DP Dustin Pedroia 20.00 50.00
DU Dan Uggla 8.00 20.00
DW Dale Webster 5.00 12.00
EA Elvis Andrus 6.00 15.00
EAN Erin Andrews 50.00 100.00
EB Ernie Banks 200.00 300.00
EH Eric Hosmer 30.00 60.00
EL Evan Longoria 90.00 150.00
EMA Ewa Mataya 10.00 25.00
FH Felix Hernandez 30.00 60.00
FR Frank Robinson 100.00 200.00
FT1 Fatal1ty 6.00 15.00
GB Gordon Beckham 5.00 12.00
GBL Guy Bluford 10.00 25.00
GGU Greg Gumbel 10.00 25.00
HA Hank Aaron 500.00 700.00
HH Hank Haney 8.00 20.00
JB Johnny Bench 100.00 200.00
JBA Jose Bautista 15.00 40.00
JBA Jerry Bailey 10.00 25.00
JBR Jay Bruce 12.50 30.00
JBR James Brown 10.00 25.00
JC Johnny Cueto 6.00 15.00
JDM J.D. Martinez 15.00 40.00
JE John McEnroe 30.00 80.00
JH Joel Hanrahan 6.00 15.00
JHE Jeremy Hellickson 6.00 15.00
JKJ Jackie Joyner-Kersee 12.50 30.00
JM Joe Mauer 50.00 120.00
JPA J.P. Arencibia 5.00 12.00
JPA Jimmy Paredes 4.00 10.00
JS Jordan Schafer 5.00 12.00
JT Julio Teheran 6.00 15.00
JT Jose Tabata 4.00 10.00
JV Jose Valverde 4.00 10.00
JW Jered Weaver 12.50 30.00
JZ Jordan Zimmermann 6.00 15.00
KBR Keegan Bradley 10.00 25.00
KGJ Ken Griffey Jr. EXCH 125.00 300.00
KH Kirk Herbstreit 10.00 25.00
KUP Kate Upton 250.00 500.00
LKR Lefty Kreh 6.00 15.00
MBF Michael Buffer 12.00 30.00
MC Miguel Cabrera 75.00 150.00
MH Mark Hamburger 4.00 10.00
MHO Marty Hogan 4.00 10.00
MK Matt Kemp 10.00 25.00
MLE Meadowlark Lemon 20.00 50.00
MM Matt Moore 5.00 12.00
MMO Mitch Moreland 4.00 10.00
MMR Mike Morse 5.00 12.00
MP Michael Pineda 4.00 10.00
MPH Michael Phelps 200.00 300.00
MS Max Scherzer 20.00 50.00
MSC Mike Schmidt 100.00 200.00
MST Giancarlo Stanton 75.00 200.00
MT Mark Trumbo 8.00 20.00
MTR Mike Trout 250.00 400.00
NE Nathan Eovaldi 4.00 10.00
NR Nolan Ryan 400.00 600.00
PF Prince Fielder 12.00 30.00
PG Paul Goldschmidt 15.00 40.00
PPF Phil Pfister 5.00 12.00
RB Ryan Braun 20.00 50.00
RC Robinson Cano 20.00 50.00
RFD Roger Federer 175.00 350.00
RG Rulon Gardner 8.00 20.00
RH Roy Halladay EXCH 100.00 200.00
RJ Reggie Jackson 150.00 300.00
RPT Richard Petty 15.00 40.00
RS Ryne Sandberg 150.00 300.00
RZ Ryan Zimmerman 15.00 40.00
SC Starlin Castro 10.00 25.00
SCA Swin Cash 8.00 20.00
SK Sandy Koufax EXCH 350.00 700.00
SM Stan Musial 75.00 200.00
TG Tony Gwynn 75.00 150.00
TH Torii Hunter 10.00 25.00
VW Vernon Wells 40.00 80.00
VW Vance Worley 6.00 15.00
WM Willie Mays EXCH 300.00 500.00
YC Yoenis Cespedes 60.00 120.00
YD Yu Darvish 75.00 150.00
YG Yovani Gallardo 10.00 25.00
ZB Zach Britton 6.00 15.00

2012 Topps Allen and Ginter Baseball Highlights Cabinets

COMPLETE SET (5) 12.50 30.00
STATED ODDS 1:5 HOBBY BOX TOPPER
BH1 D.Jeter/D.Price 2.50 6.00
BH2 David Freese 1.00 2.50
Jaime Garcia
Lance Berkman
Matt Holliday
BH3 C.Ripken Jr./L.Gehrig 3.00 8.00
BH4 Riv/Plou/Cud/Parm 1.25 3.00
BH5 Jeremy Hellickson .75 2.00
Craig Kimbrel

2012 Topps Allen and Ginter Baseball Highlights Sketches

COMPLETE SET (24) 8.00 20.00
STATED ODDS 1:8 HOBBY
BH1 Roger Maris .60 1.50
BH2 Tom Seaver .40 1.00
BH3 Ichiro Suzuki .75 2.00
BH4 Ryne Sandberg 1.25 3.00
BH5 Brooks Robinson .40 1.00
BH6 Frank Thomas .60 1.50
BH7 John Smoltz .75 2.00
BH8 Derek Jeter 1.50 4.00
BH9 Ryan Braun .40 1.00
BH10 Albert Pujols .75 2.00
BH11 Nolan Ryan 2.00 5.00
BH12 Justin Verlander .60 1.50
BH13 Matt Moore .60 1.50
BH14 Mickey Mantle 2.00 5.00
BH15 Ken Griffey Jr. 1.25 3.00
BH16 David Freese .40 1.00
BH17 Cal Ripken Jr. 2.00 5.00
BH18 Ozzie Smith .75 2.00
BH19 Carlton Fisk .40 1.00
BH20 Jose Bautista .50 1.25
BH21 Willie Mays 1.25 3.00
BH22 Joe DiMaggio 1.25 3.00
BH23 Jackie Robinson .60 1.50
BH24 Roberto Clemente 1.50 4.00

2012 Topps Allen and Ginter Colony In A Card

STATED ODDS 1:288 HOBBY
AS Artemia Salina 6.00 15.00

2012 Topps Allen and Ginter Currency of the World Cabinet Relics

STATED ODDS 1:25 HOBBY BOX TOPPER
STATED PRINT RUN 50 SER.#'d SETS
CW1 Austria 20.00 50.00
CW2 Argentina 15.00 40.00
CW3 Belgium 15.00 40.00
CW4 Brazil 20.00 50.00
CW5 Colombia 20.00 50.00
CW6 Ecuador 15.00 40.00
CW7 East Caribbean 15.00 40.00
CW8 Germany 40.00 80.00
CW9 Great Britain 20.00 50.00
CW10 Guatemala 15.00 40.00
CW11 Greece 15.00 40.00
CW12 Falkland Islands 15.00 40.00
CW13 France 20.00 50.00
CW14 Ireland 15.00 40.00
CW15 Israel 20.00 50.00
CW16 Isle of Man 15.00 40.00
CW17 Italy 20.00 50.00
CW18 Jamaica 15.00 40.00
CW19 Mexico 15.00 40.00
CW20 Nicaragua 15.00 40.00
CW21 New Zealand 15.00 40.00
CW22 Pakistan 15.00 40.00
CW23 Poland 20.00 50.00
CW24 Russia 20.00 50.00
CW25 Romania 15.00 40.00
CW26 Turkey 15.00 40.00
CW27 Spain 20.00 50.00
CW28 St. Helena 20.00 50.00
CW29 Venezuela 15.00 40.00
CW30 El Salvador 30.00 60.00

2012 Topps Allen and Ginter Historical Turning Points

COMPLETE SET (20) 4.00 10.00
STATED ODDS 1:8 HOBBY
HTP1 Signing of
Declaration of Independence .25 .60
HTP2 The Battle Waterloo .25 .60
HTP3 The Fall the Roman Empire .25 .60
HTP4 The Reformation .25 .60
HTP5 The Fall the Berlin Wall .25 .60
HTP6 The Treaty Versailles .25 .60
HTP7 Invention of Printing Press .25 .60
HTP8 Allied Victory World War II .25 .60
HTP9 Discovery of New World .25 .60
HTP10 Discovery of Electricity .25 .60
HTP11 Signing of Magna Carta .25 .60
HTP12 The Renaissance .25 .60
HTP13 The Industrial Revolution .25 .60
HTP14 The Emancipation Proclamation.25 .60
HTP15 The First at Kitty Hawk .25 .60
HTP16 The French Revolution .25 .60
HTP17 The Great Depression .25 .60
HTP18 On the Origin of Species .25 .60
HTP19 Sputnik I .25 .60
HTP20 The Agricultural Revolution .25 .60

2012 Topps Allen and Ginter Mini Culinary Curiosities

COMPLETE SET (10) 10.00 25.00
STATED ODDS 1:5 HOBBY
CC1 Nutria 1.00 2.50
CC2 Haggis 1.00 2.50
CC3 Kopi Luwak 1.00 2.50
CC4 Casu Marzu 1.00 2.50
CC5 Rocky Moutain Oysters 1.00 2.50
CC6 Hakarl 1.00 2.50
CC7 Fugu 1.00 2.50
CC8 Sannakji 1.00 2.50
CC9 Balut 1.00 2.50
CC10 Muktuk 1.00 2.50

2012 Topps Allen and Ginter Mini Fashionable Ladies

COMPLETE SET (10) 75.00 150.00
FL1 The First Lady 6.00 15.00
FL2 The Flapper 6.00 15.00
FL3 The Queen 6.00 15.00
FL4 The Victorian 6.00 15.00
FL5 The Bustle 6.00 15.00
FL6 The Weekender 6.00 15.00
FL7 The Bride 6.00 15.00
FL8 The Sportswoman 6.00 15.00
FL9 The Ingenue 6.00 15.00
FL10 The Icon 6.00 15.00

2012 Topps Allen and Ginter Mini Giants of the Deep

COMPLETE SET (15) 12.50 30.00
STATED ODDS 1:5 HOBBY
GD1 Humpback Whale .75 2.00
GD2 Sperm Whale .75 2.00
GD3 Blue Whale .75 2.00
GD4 Narwhal .75 2.00
GD5 Beluga Whale .75 2.00
GD6 Bowhead Whale .75 2.00
GD7 Right Whale .75 2.00
GD8 Fin Whale .75 2.00
GD9 Orca .75 2.00
GD10 Pilot Whale .75 2.00
GD11 Pygmy Sperm Whale .75 2.00
GD12 Minke Whale .75 2.00
GD13 Gray Whale .75 2.00
GD14 Bottlenose Whale .75 2.00
GD15 Bryde's Whale .75 2.00

2012 Topps Allen and Ginter Mini Guys in Hats

COMPLETE SET (10) 75.00 150.00
GH1 The Bowler 6.00 15.00
GH2 The Boater 6.00 15.00
GH3 The Fedora 6.00 15.00
GH4 The Fez 6.00 15.00
GH5 The Pith Helmet 6.00 15.00
GH6 The Top Hat 6.00 15.00
GH7 The Mortarboard 6.00 15.00
GH8 The Flat Cap 6.00 15.00
GH9 The Garrison Cap 6.00 15.00
GH10 The Bicorne 6.00 15.00

2012 Topps Allen and Ginter Mini Man's Best Friend

COMPLETE SET (20) 15.00 40.00
STATED ODDS 1:5 HOBBY
MBF1 Siberian Husky .75 2.00
MBF2 Dalmatian .75 2.00
MBF3 Golden Retriever .75 2.00
MBF4 German Shepherd .75 2.00
MBF5 Beagle .75 2.00
MBF6 Dachshund .75 2.00
MBF7 Yorkshire Terrier .75 2.00
MBF8 Labrador Retriever .75 2.00
MBF9 Boxer .75 2.00
MBF10 Poodle .75 2.00
MBF11 Chihuahua .75 2.00
MBF12 Shih Tzu .75 2.00
MBF13 Collie .75 2.00
MBF14 Pug .75 2.00
MBF15 Cocker Spaniel .75 2.00
MBF16 Saint Bernard .75 2.00
MBF17 Bulldog .75 2.00
MBF18 Boston Terrier .75 2.00
MBF19 Basset Hound .75 2.00
MBF20 Shetland Sheepdog .75 2.00

2012 Topps Allen and Ginter Mini Musical Masters

COMPLETE SET (16) 12.50 30.00
STATED ODDS 1:5 HOBBY
MM1 Johann Sebastian Bach .75 2.00
MM2 Wolfgang Amadeus Mozart .75 2.00
MM3 Ludwig van Beethoven .75 2.00
MM4 Richard Wagner .75 2.00
MM5 Joseph Haydn .75 2.00
MM6 Johannes Brahms .75 2.00
MM7 Franz Schubert .75 2.00
MM8 George Frideric Handel .75 2.00
MM9 Pyotr Ilyich Tchaikovsky .75 2.00
MM10 Sergei Prokofiev .75 2.00
MM11 Antonin Dvorak .75 2.00
MM12 Franz Liszt .75 2.00
MM13 Frederic Chopin .75 2.00
MM14 Igor Stravinsky .75 2.00
MM15 Giuseppe Verdi .75 2.00
MM16 Gustav Mahler .75 2.00

2012 Topps Allen and Ginter Mini People of the Bible

COMPLETE SET (15) 12.50 30.00
STATED ODDS 1:5 HOBBY
PB1 David 1.25 3.00
PB2 Moses 1.25 3.00
PB3 Abraham 1.25 3.00
PB4 Job 1.25 3.00
PB5 Jonah 1.25 3.00
PB6 Daniel 1.25 3.00
PB7 Mary Magdalene 1.25 3.00
PB8 Peter 1.25 3.00
PB9 Jesus 1.25 3.00
PB10 Luke 1.25 3.00
PB11 Adam and Eve 1.25 3.00
PB12 Isaiah 1.25 3.00
PB13 Joseph 1.25 3.00
PB14 Mary 1.25 3.00
PB15 John the Baptist 1.25 3.00

2012 Topps Allen and Ginter Mini World's Greatest Military Leaders

COMPLETE SET (20) 12.50 30.00
STATED ODDS 1:5 HOBBY
ML1 Alexander the Great .60 1.50
ML2 Simon Bolivar .60 1.50
ML3 Oliver Cromwell .60 1.50
ML4 Julius Caesar .60 1.50
ML5 Cyrus the Great .60 1.50
ML6 Hannibal Barca .60 1.50
ML7 Napoleon Bonaparte .60 1.50
ML8 George Washington .60 1.50
ML9 Ulysses S. Grant .60 1.50
ML10 Dwight D. Eisenhower .60 1.50
ML11 Leonidas .60 1.50
ML12 Charlemagne .60 1.50
ML13 Saladin .60 1.50
ML14 Duke of Wellington .60 1.50
ML15 Horatio Nelson .60 1.50
ML16 Frederick the Great .60 1.50
ML17 Duke of Marlborough .60 1.50
ML18 William Wallace .60 1.50
ML19 Darius the Great .60 1.50
ML20 Sun Tzu .60 1.50

2012 Topps Allen and Ginter N43

COMPLETE SET (15) 20.00 50.00
STATED ODDS 1:3 HOBBY BOX TOPPER
1 Albert Pujols 1.25 3.00
2 Brian Wilson 1.00 2.50
3 Don Mattingly 2.00 5.00
4 Eric Hosmer .75 2.00
5 Ernie Banks 1.00 2.50
6 Evan Longoria .75 2.00
7 Hanley Ramirez .75 2.00
8 Joe Mauer .75 2.00
9 Johnny Bench 1.00 2.50
10 Josh Hamilton .75 2.00
11 Ken Griffey Jr. 2.00 5.00
12 Matt Moore 1.00 2.50
13 Miguel Cabrera 1.00 2.50
14 Mike Schmidt 1.50 4.00
15 Tony Gwynn 1.00 2.50

2012 Topps Allen and Ginter Relics

STATED ODDS 1:10 HOBBY
EXCHANGE DEADLINE 06/30/2015
AA Alex Avila 3.00 8.00
AB A.J. Burnett 3.00 8.00
ABA Andrew Bailey 3.00 8.00
ABE Adrian Beltre 3.00 8.00
AD Annie Duke 3.00 8.00
AG Adrian Gonzalez 3.00 8.00
AH Aubrey Huff 3.00 8.00
AL Adam Lind 3.00 8.00
AM Andrew McCutchen 4.00 10.00
AP Albert Pujols 6.00 15.00
AP Arnold Palmer 8.00 20.00
APG Angel Pagan 3.00 8.00
AUS Al Unser Sr. 4.00 10.00
BA Bobby Abreu 3.00 8.00
BB Balloon Boy 5.00 12.00
BBU Billy Butler 3.00 8.00
BH Bob Hurley Sr. 3.00 8.00
BK Bob Knight 5.00 12.00
BL Barry Larkin 5.00 12.00
BM Brian McCann 3.00 8.00
BP Brandon Phillips 3.00 8.00
BU B.J. Upton 3.00 8.00
BW Brian Wilson 5.00 12.00
CB Clay Buchholz 3.00 8.00
CBI Chad Billingsley 3.00 8.00
CH Corey Hart 3.00 8.00
CI Chris Iannetta 3.00 8.00
CJ Chipper Jones 5.00 12.00
CL Carlos Lee 3.00 8.00
CM Casey McGehee 3.00 8.00
CMO Colin Montgomerie 6.00 15.00
CMR Carlos Marmol 3.00 8.00
CN Curly Neal EXCH 6.00 15.00
CP Carlos Pena 3.00 8.00
CQ Carlos Quentin 3.00 8.00
CY Chris Young 3.00 8.00
CZ Carlos Zambrano 3.00 8.00
CZA Carlos Zambrano 3.00 8.00
DD David DeJesus 3.00 8.00
DDE Don Denkinger 3.00 8.00
DG Dillon Gee 3.00 8.00
DJ Derek Jeter 10.00 25.00
DM Don Mattingly 10.00 25.00
DO David Ortiz 3.00 8.00
DP Dustin Pedroia 4.00 10.00
DS Drew Stubbs 3.00 8.00
DU Dan Uggla 3.00 8.00
DW David Wright 4.00 10.00
DWE Dale Webster 4.00 10.00
EA Elvis Andrus 3.00 8.00
EAN Erin Andrews 60.00 120.00
EH1 Eric Hosmer Bat 5.00 12.00
EH2 Eric Hosmer Jsy 20.00 50.00
EL Evan Longoria 3.00 8.00
ELO Evan Longoria 3.00 8.00
EM Evan Meek 3.00 8.00
EMA Ewa Mataya 5.00 12.00
EV Edinson Volquez 3.00 8.00
FF Freddie Freeman 3.00 8.00
FT1 Fatal1ty 4.00 10.00
GB Gordon Beckham 3.00 8.00
GBL Guy Bluford 5.00 12.00
GG Greg Gumbel 3.00 8.00
GS Geovany Soto 3.00 8.00
HA Hank Aaron 150.00 250.00
HB Heath Bell 3.00 8.00
HC Hank Conger 3.00 8.00
HCO Hank Conger 3.00 8.00
HH Hank Haney 3.00 8.00
HR Hanley Ramirez 3.00 8.00
I Ichiro Suzuki 5.00 12.00
ID Ike Davis 3.00 8.00
IK Ian Kinsler 3.00 8.00
JA J.P. Arencibia 3.00 8.00
JB Jose Bautista 4.00 10.00
JBA Jerry Bailey 4.00 10.00
JBE Johnny Bench 30.00 60.00
JBR James Brown 6.00 15.00
JC Johnny Cueto 3.00 8.00
JD Joe DiMaggio 40.00 80.00
JDA Johnny Damon 3.00 8.00
JG Jaime Garcia 3.00 8.00
JH Josh Hamilton 4.00 10.00
JHE Jeremy Hellickson 3.00 8.00
JJ Jon Jay 3.00 8.00
JJK Jackie Joyner-Kersee 3.00 8.00
JL James Loney 3.00 8.00
JLO Jed Lowrie 3.00 8.00
JM John McEnroe 4.00 10.00
JP Jhonny Peralta 3.00 8.00
JPA Jonathan Papelbon 3.00 8.00
JPE Jake Peavy 3.00 8.00
JPO Jorge Posada 3.00 8.00
JR Jackie Robinson 40.00 80.00
JU Justin Upton 3.00 8.00
JW Jayson Werth 3.00 8.00
JWA Jordan Walden 3.00 8.00
JZ Jordan Zimmermann 3.00 8.00
KB Keegan Bradley EXCH 6.00 15.00
KF Kosuke Fukudome 3.00 8.00
KG Ken Griffey Jr. 50.00 100.00
KH Kirk Herbstreit 4.00 10.00
KU Kate Upton 40.00 100.00
LG Lou Gehrig 75.00 150.00
LK Lefty Kreh EXCH 5.00 12.00
MB Marlon Byrd 3.00 8.00
MBO Michael Bourn 3.00 8.00
MBU Michael Buffer 8.00 20.00
MC Melky Cabrera 3.00 8.00
MCA Melky Cabrera 3.00 8.00
MCB Miguel Cabrera 6.00 15.00
MCN Matt Cain 3.00 8.00
MH Marty Hogan 3.00 8.00
MK Matt Kemp 5.00 12.00
ML Mike Leake 3.00 8.00
MLA Mat Latos 3.00 8.00
MLE Meadowlark Lemon 6.00 15.00
MM Mike Moore 3.00 8.00
MMA Mickey Mantle 125.00 250.00
MMO Mitch Moreland 3.00 8.00
MP Michael Pineda 3.00 8.00
MPH Michael Phelps 12.00 30.00
MPR Martin Prado 3.00 8.00
MR Mark Reynolds 3.00 8.00
MS Max Scherzer 3.00 8.00
MY Michael Young 3.00 8.00
NM Nick Markakis 3.00 8.00
NR Nolan Ryan 50.00 100.00
PF Prince Fielder 4.00 10.00
PO Paul O'Neill 3.00 8.00
PP Phil Pfister 3.00 8.00
RA Roberto Alomar 4.00 10.00
RB Ryan Braun 5.00 12.00
RC Roberto Clemente 40.00 80.00
RD Ryan Dempster 3.00 8.00
RDA Rajai Davis 3.00 8.00
RF Roger Federer 6.00 15.00
RG Rulon Gardner 4.00 10.00
RJ Reggie Jackson 12.50 30.00
RM Roger Maris 60.00 120.00
RMA Russell Martin 3.00 8.00
RP Rick Porcello 3.00 8.00
RPE Richard Petty 4.00 10.00
RR Ricky Romero 3.00 8.00
RS Ryne Sandberg 15.00 40.00
RT Ryan Theriot 3.00 8.00
RZ Ryan Zimmerman 3.00 8.00
SC Starlin Castro 6.00 15.00
SCA Swin Cash 3.00 8.00
SCH Shin-Soo Choo 3.00 8.00
SK Sandy Koufax 40.00 80.00
SS Stephen Strasburg 3.00 8.00
TC Ty Cobb 100.00 200.00
TH Torii Hunter 3.00 8.00
UJ Ubaldo Jimenez 3.00 8.00
VM Victor Martinez 3.00 8.00
VW Vernon Wells 3.00 8.00
VWE Vernon Wells 3.00 8.00
WM Willie Mays 75.00 150.00
ZG Zack Greinke 3.00 8.00

2012 Topps Allen and Ginter Rip Cards

OVERALL RIP ODDS 1:287 HOBBY
PRINT RUNS B/WN 10-99 COPIES PER
NO PRICING ON QTY 25 OR LESS
ALL LISTED PRICED ARE FOR RIPPED
UNRIPPED HAVE ADD'L CARDS WITHIN
RC3 Brandon Phillips 6.00 15.00
RC4 Brett Lawrie 6.00 15.00
RC5 Ian Kinsler 6.00 15.00
RC6 Michael Pineda 6.00 15.00
RC12 Jacoby Ellsbury 6.00 15.00
RC22 Ryan Zimmerman 6.00 15.00
RC23 Carlos Gonzalez 6.00 15.00
RC26 Kevin Youkilis 6.00 15.00
RC31 Hunter Pence 6.00 15.00
RC34 Mike Trout 20.00 50.00
RC36 Josh Johnson 6.00 15.00
RC38 Carl Crawford 6.00 15.00
RC41 Starlin Castro 6.00 15.00
RC42 Josh Beckett 6.00 15.00
RC45 David Freese 6.00 15.00
RC46 Jason Heyward 6.00 15.00
RC50 Craig Kimbrel 6.00 15.00
RC51 Carlos Santana 6.00 15.00
RC56 Nelson Cruz 6.00 15.00
RC58 Madison Bumgarner 6.00 15.00
RC59 Adam Jones 6.00 15.00
RC60 Shin-Soo Choo 6.00 15.00
RC62 Giancarlo Stanton 6.00 15.00
RC65 Jesus Montero 6.00 15.00
RC66 Andrew McCutchen 6.00 15.00
RC69 Freddie Freeman 6.00 15.00
RC75 Brian McCann 6.00 15.00
RC78 Tommy Hanson 6.00 15.00
RC79 Jon Lester 6.00 15.00
RC98 David Price 6.00 15.00

2012 Topps Allen and Ginter Rollercoaster Cabinets

COMPLETE SET (5) 10.00 25.00
STATED ODDS 1:4 HOBBY BOX TOPPER
RC1 Leap-the-Dips 2.00 5.00
RC2 Scenic Railway 2.00 5.00
RC3 Rutschebanen 2.00 5.00
RC4 The Wild One 2.00 5.00
RC5 Jack Rabbit 2.00 5.00

2012 Topps Allen and Ginter What's in a Name

COMPLETE SET (100) 12.50 30.00
STATED ODDS 1:2 HOBBY
WIN1 Joe DiMaggio 1.25 3.00
WIN2 Carlos Eduardo Gonzalez .50 1.25
WIN3 Ryan Howard .50 1.25
WIN4 Paul Henry Konerko .40 1.00
WIN5 Troy Trevor Tulowitzki .60 1.50
WIN6 Ryan Braun .40 1.00
WIN7 Chase Cameron Utley .50 1.25
WIN8 Clifton Phifer Lee .50 1.25
WIN10 Lawrence Peter Berra .60 1.50
WIN11 Torii Kedar Hunter .50 1.25
WIN12 Saturnino Orestes Armas Minoso.25 .60
WIN13 Carl Demonte Crawford .50 1.25
WIN14 Larry Wayne Jones .60 1.50
WIN15 Michael Francisco Pineda .40 1.00
WIN16 Jose Miguel Cabrera .60 1.50
WIN17 Dustin Pedroia .50 1.25
WIN18 Stan Musial 1.00 2.50
WIN19 David Allen Wright .50 1.25
WIN20 Don Richard Ashburn .40 1.00
WIN21 Jack Roosevelt Robinson .60 1.50
WIN22 Matthew Ryan Kemp .50 1.25
WIN23 Giancarlo Cruz Michael Stanton.60 1.50
WIN24 Ian Michael Kinsler .50 1.25

N25 Daniel Cooley Uggla .50 1.25
N26 Orlando Manuel Pennes Cepeda .40 1.00
N27 Starlin DeJesus Castro .50 1.25
N28 Elvis Augusto Andrus .50 1.25
N29 Nolan Ryan 2.00 5.00
N30 Hunter Andrew Pence .50 1.25
N31 Andrew Stefan McCutchen .60 1.50
N32 Frederick Charles Freeman .75 2.00
N33 Atanasio Perez Rigal .40 1.00
N34 Clayton Kershaw 1.25 3.00
N35 Brooks Calbert Robinson .40 1.00
N36 Jose Antonio Bautista .50 1.25
N37 Jason Alias Heyward .50 1.25
N38 Harry Leroy Halladay .50 1.25
N39 Montford Merrill Irvin .40 1.00
IN40 Jemile Nykiwa Weeks .40 1.00
IN41 Timothy LeRoy Lincecum .50 1.25
IN42 Cal Ripken Jr. 2.00 5.00
IN43 Justin Verlander .60 1.50
IN44 James Calvin Rollins .50 1.25
IN45 Don Mattingly 1.25 3.00
IN46 James Augustus Hunter .40 1.00
IN47 Jacoby McCabe Ellsbury .50 1.25
IN48 Anthony Keith Gwynn Sr. .60 1.50
IN49 Edwin Donald Snider .40 1.00
IN50 Mike Schmidt 1.00 2.50
IN51 Joshua Holt Hamilton .50 1.25
IN52 Derek Jeter 1.50 4.00
IN53 Justin Ernest George Morneau .50 1.25
IN54 Juan D'Vaughn Pierre .40 1.00
IN55 Robinson Jose Cano .50 1.25
IN56 Albertin Aroldis de la Cruz Chapman .60 1.50
IN57 Joshua Patrick Beckett .40 1.00
WIN58 Rickey Nelson Henley Henderson .60 1.50
WIN59 Buster Posey .75 2.00
WIN60 Jay Allen Bruce .50 1.25
WIN61 James Howard Thome .50 1.25
WIN62 Jered David Weaver .50 1.25
WIN63 Rodney Cline Carew .40 1.00
WIN64 David Americo Ortiz .60 1.50
WIN65 Nicholas Thompson Swisher .50 1.25
WIN66 George Lee Anderson .40 1.00
WIN67 Wilver Dornel Stargell .40 1.00
WIN68 Prince Semien Fielder .50 1.25
WIN69 Felix Abraham Hernandez .50 1.25
WIN70 Jonathan Tyler Lester .40 1.00
WIN71 Joseph Patrick Mauer .50 1.25
WIN72 Carsten Charles Sabathia .50 1.25
WIN73 Ryan Wallace Zimmerman .50 1.25
WIN74 George Thomas Seaver .25 .60
WIN75 Colbert Michael Hamels .50 1.25
WIN76 Melvin Emanuel Upton .50 1.25
WIN77 David Taylor Price .50 1.25
WIN78 Jose Bernabe Reyes .40 1.00
WIN79 Mickey Mantle 2.00 5.00
WIN80 Matthew Thomas Holliday .60 1.50
WIN81 Covelli Loyce Crisp .40 1.00
WIN82 Ty Cobb 1.00 2.50
WIN83 Mark Charles Teixeira .50 1.25
WIN84 Albert Pujols .75 2.00
WIN85 Michael Anthony Napoli .40 1.00
WIN86 Daniel John Haren .40 1.00
WIN87 Joseph Daniel Votto .60 1.50
WIN88 Alex Jonathan Gordon .50 1.25
WIN89 Stephen Strasburg .60 1.50
WIN90 Evan Longoria .50 1.25
WIN91 Alex Rodriguez .75 2.00
WIN92 Paul Edward Goldschmidt .60 1.50
WIN93 Billy Ray Butler .40 1.00
WIN94 Reginald Martinez Jackson .40 1.00
WIN95 Ken Griffey Jr. 1.25 3.00
WIN96 Ozzie Smith .75 2.00
WIN97 Justin Irvin Upton .50 1.25
WIN98 Edward Charles Ford .40 1.00
WIN99 Babe Ruth 1.50 4.00
WIN100 Donald Zackary Greinke .50 1.25

2012 Topps Allen and Ginter World's Tallest Buildings

COMPLETE SET (10) 4.00 10.00
COMMON CARD .40 1.00
STATED ODDS 1:8 HOBBY
WTB1 Burj Khalifa .40 1.00
WTB2 Taipei 101 .40 1.00
WTB3 Petronas Towers .40 1.00
WTB4 Willis Tower .40 1.00
WTB5 1 World Trade Center .40 1.00
WTB6 Empire State Building .40 1.00
WTB7 Chrysler Building .40 1.00
WTB8 40 Wall Street .40 1.00
WTB9 Woolworth Building .40 1.00
WTB10 MetLife Building .40 1.00

2013 Topps Allen and Ginter

COMPLETE SET (350) 20.00 50.00
COMP.SET w/o SP's (300) 12.00 30.00
SP ODDS 1:2 HOBBY
1 Miguel Cabrera .25 .60
2 Derek Jeter .60 1.50
3 Babe Ruth .60 1.50
4 Ty Cobb .40 1.00
5 Albert Pujols .30 .75
6 Chanel Iman .15 .40
7 Mike Trout 2.00 5.00
8 Gary Carter .20 .50
9 Giancarlo Stanton .25 .60
10 Sandy Koufax .50 1.25
11 Robin van Persie .75 2.00
12 Dan Haren .15 .40
13 Adrian Gonzalez .20 .50
14 Ben Revere .15 .40
15 Julia Mancuso .15 .40
16 Amelia Boone .15 .40
17 Roy Jones Jr. .75 2.00
18 Matt Harrison .15 .40
19 Bobby Doerr .20 .50
20 John Smoltz .25 .60
21 Byamba .40 1.00
22 Bob Feller .20 .50
23 Adrian Beltre .25 .60
24 Anthony Gose .15 .40
25 Ernie Banks .25 .60
26 Elvis Andrus .20 .50
27 Shelby Miller RC .60 1.50
28 Paul O'Neill .20 .50
29 Jordan Zimmermann .20 .50
30 Bert Blyleven .20 .50
31 Ian Kennedy .15 .40
32 Aaron Hill .15 .40
33 Nana Meriwether .15 .40
34 Robin Roberts .20 .50
35 Kevin Harvick .60 1.50
36 Early Wynn .20 .50
37 Nelson Cruz .25 .60
38 Johnny Bench .25 .60
39 Desmond Jennings .20 .50
40 Will Middlebrooks .15 .40
41 Hisashi Iwakuma .20 .50
42 Jackie Robinson .25 .60
43 Hunter Pence .20 .50
44 Yasiel Puig RC 1.00 2.50
45 Shawn Nadelen .15 .40
46 Colby Rasmus .20 .50
47 Robin Ventura .15 .40
48 Starling Marte .20 .50
49 Kris Medlen .20 .50
50 Willie Mays .50 1.25
51 Jason Kipnis .20 .50
52 Scott Diamond .15 .40
53 Mark Teixeira .20 .50
54 B.J. Upton .20 .50
55 Fergie Jenkins .20 .50
56 Whitey Ford .20 .50
57 Mike Olt RC .30 .75
58 Shin-Soo Choo .20 .50
59 Joey Votto .25 .60
60 Yoenis Cespedes .25 .60
61 Alex Gordon .20 .50
62 McKayla Maroney .25 .60
63 Jose Bautista .20 .50
64 Neil Walker .20 .50
65 Jose Reyes .20 .50
66 Howie Kendrick .15 .40
67 Hank Aaron .50 1.25
68 Chrissy Teigen .25 .60
69 Jake Peavy .15 .40
70 CC Sabathia .20 .50
71 Ben Zobrist .20 .50
72 Matt Moore .20 .50
73 Tim Hudson .20 .50
74 Yu Darvish .25 .60
75 Lou Gehrig .50 1.25
76 Jim Abbott .15 .40
77 Frank Robinson .30 .75
78 Carlos Santana .20 .50
79 Dylan Bundy RC .60 1.50
80 Willie McCovey .20 .50
81 Al Kaline .40 1.00
82 Roberto Clemente .60 1.50
83 Ted Williams .50 1.25
84 Jason Vargas .25 .60
85 Phil Heath .25 .60
86 Warren Spahn .25 .60
87 Ken Griffey Jr. .75 2.00
88 Clayton Kershaw .50 1.25
89 Michael Brantley .15 .40
90 Jon Lester .30 .75
91 Carlos Ruiz .25 .60
92 Paco Rodriguez RC .40 1.00
93 A.J. Pierzynski .15 .40
94 Billy Butler .15 .40
95 Curtis Granderson .30 .75
96 Jason Heyward .30 .75
97 Tony Gwynn .40 1.00
98 Darryl Strawberry .15 .40
99 Barry Zito .20 .50
100 Bill Walton .40 1.00
101 Yonder Alonso .15 .40
102 Ian Kinsler .30 .75
103 Bronson Arroyo .15 .40
104 Mike Richter .40 1.00
105 Tyler Skaggs .25 .60
106 Mike Minor .25 .60
107 Trevor Bauer .25 .60
108 Bob Gibson .30 .75
109 Asdrubal Cabrera .20 .50
110 Daniel Murphy .30 .75
111 Corey Hart .15 .40
112 Ziggy Marley .25 .60
113 Brandon Beachy .15 .40
114 Yasmani Grandal .25 .60
115 Stan Musial .40 1.00
116 Lindsey Vonn .25 .60
117 Penny Marshall .25 .60
118 Cal Ripken Jr .75 2.00
119 Adam Richman .25 .60
120 Manny Machado RC 1.50 4.00
121 Hiroki Kuroda .15 .40
122 Jay Bruce .20 .50
123 Matt Garza .15 .40
124 Olivia Culpo .25 .60
125 Matt Holliday .25 .60
126 Jon Niese .15 .40
127 Doug Fister .15 .40
128 Joe Mauer .20 .50
129 Miguel Montero .15 .40
130A Pele .75 2.00
130B Pele UER 2.00 5.00
131 Brian Kelly .40 1.00
132 Ryne Sandberg .50 1.25
133 David Ortiz .25 .60
134 Roy Halladay .20 .50
135 Vance Worley .20 .50
136 Panama Canal .25 .60
137 Pedro Alvarez .15 .40
138 Anibal Sanchez .15 .40
139 Red Schoendienst .20 .50
140 Tommy Lee .25 .60
141 Trevor Cahill .15 .40
142 Garrett Jones .15 .40
143 Mike Schmidt .40 1.00
144 Torii Hunter .15 .40
145 Harmon Killebrew .25 .60
146 Vida Blue .15 .40
147 Ian Desmond .15 .40
148 Justin Upton .30 .75
149 Ed O'Neill .25 .60
150 Reggie Jackson .30 .75
151 R.A. Dickey .20 .50
152 Anthony Rendon RC 1.25 3.00
153 Alex Cobb .15 .40
154 Mike Morse .15 .40
155 Austin Jackson .15 .40
156 Jurickson Profar RC .30 .75
157 Adam Jones .20 .50
158 Brooks Robinson .20 .50
159 Jose Altuve .20 .50
160 Brian McCann .20 .50
161 Enos Slaughter .20 .50
162 Ivan Nova .20 .50
163 Don Mattingly .50 1.25
164 Chris Mortensen .25 .60
165 Felix Hernandez .20 .50
166 Jim Johnson .15 .40
167 Rod Carew .20 .50
168 Jesus Montero .15 .40
169 Todd Frazier .20 .50
170 Hanley Ramirez .20 .50
171 Chad Billingsley .20 .50
172 Jon Jay .15 .40
173 Coco Crisp .15 .40
174 Nathan Eovaldi .20 .50
175 Monty Hall .25 .60
176 Abe Vigoda .25 .60
177 Joe Morgan .20 .50
178 Carlos Gonzalez .20 .50
179 Bonnie Bernstein .25 .60
180 Nik Wallenda .25 .60
181 Wade Boggs .20 .50
182 Cody Ross .15 .40
183 Ryan Ludwick .15 .40
184 Mike Joy .25 .60
185 Guillaume Robert-Demolaize .20 .50
186 Andy Pettitte .30 .75
187 Scott Hamilton .25 .60
188 Bill Buckner .15 .40
189 David Freese .15 .40
190 David Murphy .25 .60
191 Bryce Harper .40 1.00
192 Anthony Rizzo .40 1.00
193 Josh Hamilton .30 .75
194 Juan Marichal .20 .50
195 Derek Norris .25 .60
196 Josh Willingham .20 .50
197 Dexter Fowler .30 .75
198 Jayson Werth .20 .50
199 A.J. Burnett .15 .40
200 Dustin Pedroia .30 .75
201 Mike Moustakas .30 .75
202 Angel Pagan .15 .40
203 Adam Eaton .20 .50
204 Phil Niekro .30 .75
205 Justin Verlander .25 .60
206 Tony Perez .20 .50
207 Troy Tulowitzki .40 1.00
208 Allen Craig .20 .50
209 Ike Davis .15 .40
210 Madison Bumgarner .20 .50
211 Jacoby Ellsbury .20 .50
212 Barry Melrose .40 1.00
213 Jim Bunning .20 .50
214 Alexei Ramirez .30 .75
215 Aroldis Chapman .25 .60
216 Jered Weaver .20 .50
217 Pope Francis I .25 .60
218 Zack Cozart .15 .40
219 Freddie Roach .40 1.00
220 Jim Rice .20 .50
221 Salvador Perez .20 .50
222 Andre Ethier .20 .50
223 Matthew Berry .25 .60
224 Brett Lawrie .30 .75
225 David Wright .20 .50
226 Willie Stargell .20 .50
227 Fernando Rodney .25 .60
228 Cecil Fielder .15 .40
229 C.J. Wilson .15 .40
230 Derek Holland .15 .40
231 Artie Lange .25 .60
232 Andre Dawson .20 .50
233 Starlin Castro .15 .40
234 Death Valley .25 .60
235 Carlos Beltran .20 .50
236 Brandon Morrow .25 .60
237 Chris Sale .25 .60
238 Ryan Braun .20 .50
239 Craig Kimbrel .30 .75
240 Mike Leake .15 .40
241 Matt Cain .20 .50
242 Robinson Cano .20 .50
243 Jason Dufner .25 .60
244 Nick Saban .40 1.00
245 Mark Buehrle .20 .50
246 Hyun-Jin Ryu RC 1.00 2.50
247 Ryan Howard .30 .75
248 Mariano Rivera .50 1.25
249 Nick Swisher .30 .75
250 John Calipari .40 1.00
251 Frank Thomas .25 .60
252 Catfish Hunter .20 .50
253 Mark Trumbo .25 .60
254 Lou Brock .20 .50
255 Bobby Bowden .40 1.00
256 Rickie Weeks .25 .60
257 Michael Young .15 .40
258 Billy Williams .20 .50
259 Matthias Blonski .25 .60
260 Duke Snider .20 .50
261 Dwight Gooden .25 .60
262 Jean Segura .20 .50
263 Ralph Kiner .15 .40
264 Adam Dunn .20 .50
265 A.J. Ellis .25 .60
266 Henry Rollins .25 .60
267 Grand Central Terminal .15 .40
268 Denard Span .15 .40
269 Tom Seaver .30 .75
270 James Shields .25 .60
271 Prince Fielder .30 .75
272 Josh Reddick .15 .40
273 Alcides Escobar .30 .75
274 Raul Ibanez .30 .75
275 Josh Beckett .15 .40
276 Lance Lynn .15 .40
277 Paul Goldschmidt .25 .60
278 Mike McCarthy .40 1.00
279 Gio Gonzalez .20 .50
280 Kondrys Morales .15 .40
281 Cliff Lee .20 .50
282 Tim Lincecum .20 .50
283 Jason Motte .15 .40
284 Will Clark .20 .50
285 Jose Fernandez RC .60 1.50
286 Alfonso Soriano .20 .50
287 Bill Mazeroski .20 .50
288 Chris Davis .20 .50
289 Edinson Volquez .15 .40
290 Eddie Murray .20 .50
291 Edwin Encarnacion .25 .60
292 Yovani Gallardo .15 .40
293 Jim Palmer .20 .50
294 Johnny Cueto .20 .50
295 Dan Uggla .15 .40
296 Ekolu Kalama .25 .60
297 Jeff Samardzija .15 .40
298 Evan Longoria .20 .50
299 Ryan Zimmerman .20 .50
300 Bud Selig .15 .40
301 Tommy Hanson SP .75 2.00
302 Brandon McCarthy SP .75 2.00
303 Wade Miley SP .75 2.00
304 Freddie Freeman SP 1.50 4.00
305 Wei-Yin Chen SP .75 2.00
306 Carlton Fisk SP 1.00 2.50
307 Darwin Barney SP .75 2.00
308 Alex Rios SP 1.00 2.50
309 Mat Latos SP 1.00 2.50
310 Brandon Phillips SP .75 2.00
311 Bob Lemon SP 1.00 2.50
312 Wilin Rosario SP .75 2.00
313 Josh Rutledge SP .75 2.00
314 Avisail Garcia SP 1.00 2.50
315 Omar Infante SP .75 2.00
316 Hal Newhouser SP 1.00 2.50
317 George Brett SP 2.50 6.00
318 Eric Hosmer SP 1.00 2.50
319 Matt Kemp SP 1.00 2.50
320 Shaun Marcum SP .75 2.00
321 Wily Peralta SP .75 2.00
322 Robin Yount SP 1.25 3.00
323 Paul Molitor SP 1.25 3.00
324 Justin Morneau SP 1.00 2.50
325 Johan Santana SP 1.00 2.50
326 Ruben Tejada SP .75 2.00
327 Yogi Berra SP 1.25 3.00
328 Alex Rodriguez SP 1.50 4.00
329 Kevin Youkilis SP .75 2.00
330 Rickey Henderson SP 1.25 3.00
331 Tommy Milone SP .75 2.00
332 Cole Hamels SP 1.00 2.50
333 John Kruk SP .75 2.00
334 Russell Martin SP .75 2.00
335 Andrew McCutchen SP 1.25 3.00
336 Chase Headley SP .75 2.00
337 Buster Posey SP 1.50 4.00
338 Marco Scutaro SP 1.00 2.50
339 Kyle Seager SP .75 2.00
340 Yadier Molina SP 1.25 3.00
341 Ozzie Smith SP 1.50 4.00
342 Adam Wainwright SP 1.00 2.50
343 David Price SP 1.00 2.50
344 Nolan Ryan SP 4.00 10.00
345 Melky Cabrera SP .75 2.00
346 Josh Johnson SP 1.00 2.50
347 Stephen Strasburg SP 1.25 3.00
348 Henry Rollins SP .75 2.00
349 Jason Dufner SP .75 2.00
350 Bill Walton SP 1.25 3.00

2013 Topps Allen and Ginter Mini

*MINI 1-300: .75X TO 2X BASIC
*MINI 1-300 RC: .5X TO 1.2X BASIC RCs
*MINI SP 301-350: .5X TO 1.2X BASIC SP
MINI SP ODDS 1:13 HOBBY
351-400 RANDOM WITHIN RIP CARDS
STATED PLATE ODDS 1:594 HOBBY
PLATE PRINT RUN 1 SET PER COLOR
BLACK-CYAN-MAGENTA-YELLOW ISSUED
NO PLATE PRICING DUE TO SCARCITY
351 Mariano Rivera EXT 10.00 25.00
352 Ted Williams EXT 20.00 50.00
353 CC Sabathia EXT 20.00 50.00
354 Ty Cobb EXT 12.50 30.00
355 Justin Verlander EXT 20.00 50.00
356 Prince Fielder EXT 10.00 25.00
357 Cal Ripken Jr. EXT 20.00 50.00
358 Adrian Gonzalez EXT 10.00 25.00
359 Ernie Banks EXT 20.00 50.00
360 Joe Morgan EXT 10.00 25.00
361 Bryce Harper EXT 30.00 80.00
362 Jurickson Profar EXT 20.00 50.00
363 Matt Cain EXT 20.00 50.00
364 Don Mattingly EXT 25.00 60.00
365 Roberto Clemente EXT 30.00 60.00
366 Josh Hamilton EXT 10.00 25.00
367 Jackie Robinson EXT 25.00 60.00
368 David Ortiz EXT 20.00 50.00
369 Cliff Lee EXT 10.00 25.00
370 Jered Weaver EXT 10.00 25.00
371 Mike Trout EXT 25.00 60.00
372 Felix Hernandez EXT 10.00 25.00
373 Joey Votto EXT 20.00 50.00
374 R.A. Dickey EXT 10.00 25.00
375 Dylan Bundy EXT 10.00 25.00
376 Evan Longoria EXT 20.00 50.00
377 Clayton Kershaw EXT 15.00 40.00
378 Manny Machado EXT 15.00 40.00
379 Miguel Cabrera EXT 20.00 50.00
380 Willie Mays EXT 15.00 40.00
381 David Wright EXT 20.00 50.00
382 Babe Ruth EXT 50.00 120.00
383 Troy Tulowitzki EXT 20.00 50.00
384 Ryan Braun EXT 20.00 50.00
385 Frank Thomas EXT 30.00 80.00
386 Stan Musial EXT 25.00 60.00
387 Robinson Cano EXT 15.00 40.00
388 Johnny Bench EXT 20.00 50.00
389 Joe Mauer EXT 20.00 50.00
390 Giancarlo Stanton EXT 12.50 30.00
391 Ken Griffey Jr. EXT 40.00 100.00
392 Yu Darvish EXT 20.00 50.00
393 Mike Schmidt EXT 20.00 50.00
394 Sandy Koufax EXT 15.00 40.00
395 Tom Seaver EXT 15.00 40.00
396 Derek Jeter EXT 30.00 60.00
397 Bob Gibson EXT 10.00 25.00
398 Harmon Killebrew EXT 20.00 50.00
399 Craig Kimbrel EXT 15.00 40.00
400 Jose Reyes EXT 20.00 50.00

2013 Topps Allen and Ginter Mini A and G Back

*A & G BACK: 1X TO 2.5X BASIC
*A & G BACK RCs: .6X TO 1.5X BASIC RCs
A & G BACK ODDS 1:5 HOBBY
*A & G BACK SP: .6X TO 1.5X BASIC SP
A & G BACK SP ODDS 1:65 HOBBY

2013 Topps Allen and Ginter Mini Black

*BLACK: 1.5X TO 4X BASIC
*BLACK RCs: 1X TO 2.5X BASIC RCs
BLACK ODDS 1:10 HOBBY
*BLACK SP: 1X TO 2.5X BASIC SP
BLACK SP ODDS 1:130 HOBBY

2013 Topps Allen and Ginter Across the Years

COMPLETE SET (100) 10.00 25.00
AB Adrian Beltre .50 1.25
AC Aroldis Chapman .50 1.25
AE Andre Ethier .40 1.00
AG Adrian Gonzalez .40 1.00
AJ Adam Jones .40 1.00
AP Andy Pettitte .40 1.00
AR Anthony Rizzo .75 2.00
BG Bob Gibson .40 1.00
BH Bryce Harper .75 2.00
BJU B.J. Upton .40 1.00
BR Brooks Robinson .40 1.00
BRT Babe Ruth 1.25 3.00
CB Carlos Beltran .40 1.00
CCS CC Sabathia .40 1.00
CG Carlos Gonzalez .40 1.00
CGR Curtis Granderson .40 1.00
CJW C.J. Wilson .30 .75
CK Craig Kimbrel .40 1.00
CKW Clayton Kershaw 1.00 2.50
CL Cliff Lee .40 1.00
CRJ Cal Ripken Jr. 1.50 4.00
CS Chris Sale .50 1.25
DB Dylan Bundy .75 2.00
DJ Derek Jeter 1.25 3.00
DM Don Mattingly 1.00 2.50
DO David Ortiz .50 1.25
DP Dustin Pedroia .40 1.00
DW David Wright .40 1.00
EB Ernie Banks .50 1.25
EL Evan Longoria .40 1.00
FH Felix Hernandez .40 1.00
FT Frank Thomas .50 1.25
GG Gio Gonzalez .40 1.00
GS Giancarlo Stanton .50 1.25
HK Harmon Killebrew .50 1.25
IK Ian Kinsler .40 1.00
JA Jose Altuve .40 1.00
JB Johnny Bench .50 1.25
JBR Jay Bruce .40 1.00
JBT Jose Bautista .40 1.00
JC Johnny Cueto .40 1.00
JE Jacoby Ellsbury .40 1.00
JH Josh Hamilton .40 1.00
JHY Jason Heyward .40 1.00
JK Jason Kipnis .40 1.00
JM Joe Morgan .40 1.00
JMR Joe Mauer .40 1.00
JMT Jesus Montero .30 .75
JP Jurickson Profar .40 1.00
JR Jim Rice .40 1.00
JRB Jackie Robinson .50 1.25
JRD Josh Reddick .30 .75
JRY Jose Reyes .40 1.00
JS James Shields .30 .75
JU Justin Upton .40 1.00
JV Joey Votto .50 1.25
JVL Justin Verlander .50 1.25
JW Jered Weaver .40 1.00
JWR Jayson Werth .40 1.00
KGR Ken Griffey Jr. 1.00 2.50
KM Kris Medlen .40 1.00
LG Lou Gehrig 1.00 2.50
MC Miguel Cabrera .50 1.25
MCN Matt Cain .40 1.00
MM Manny Machado 2.00 5.00
MR Mariano Rivera .60 1.50
MS Mike Schmidt .75 2.00
MT Mike Trout 4.00 10.00
MTR Mark Trumbo .30 .75
NS Nick Swisher .40 1.00
PF Prince Fielder .40 1.00
PG Paul Goldschmidt .50 1.25
RAD R.A. Dickey .40 1.00
RB Ryan Braun .40 1.00
RC Robinson Cano .40 1.00
RCL Roberto Clemente 1.25 3.00
RH Roy Halladay .40 1.00
RHO Ryan Howard .40 1.00
RJ Reggie Jackson .40 1.00
RS Ryne Sandberg 1.00 2.50
RZ Ryan Zimmerman .40 1.00
SC Starlin Castro .30 .75
SKX Sandy Koufax 1.00 2.50
SM Shelby Miller .75 2.00
SMU Stan Musial .75 2.00
SP Salvador Perez .40 1.00
TB Trevor Bauer .50 1.25
TC Ty Cobb .75 2.00
TG Tony Gwynn .50 1.25
TL Tim Lincecum .40 1.00
TS Tyler Skaggs .50 1.25
TSV Tom Seaver .40 1.00
TT Troy Tulowitzki .50 1.25
TW Ted Williams 1.00 2.50
WB Wade Boggs .40 1.00
WM Will Middlebrooks .30 .75
WMY Willie Mays 1.00 2.50
WS Willie Stargell .40 1.00
YC Yoenis Cespedes .50 1.25
YD Yu Darvish .50 1.25

2013 Topps Allen and Ginter Autographs

STATED ODDS 1:49 HOBBY
EXCHANGE DEADLINE 07/31/2016
AB Amelia Boone 4.00 10.00
AC Alex Cobb 4.00 10.00
AE Adam Eaton 4.00 10.00
AG Avisail Garcia 4.00 10.00
AGO Anthony Gose 4.00 10.00
AGZ Adrian Gonzalez 15.00 40.00
AJ Adam Jones 12.00 30.00
ALA Artie Lange 15.00 40.00
AR Adam Richman 12.00 30.00
ARO Axl Rose 200.00 400.00
ARZ Anthony Rizzo 20.00 50.00
AV Abe Vigoda 4.00 10.00
B Byamba 5.00 12.00
BB Bobby Bowden 15.00 40.00
BBE Bonnie Bernstein 8.00 20.00
BBU Bill Buckner 8.00 20.00
BJ Brett Jackson 4.00 10.00
BK Brian Kelly 6.00 15.00
BL Brett Lawrie EXCH 12.00 30.00
BM Barry Melrose 8.00 20.00
BP Brandon Phillips 10.00 25.00
BS Bud Selig 12.00 30.00
BSU Bruce Sutter EXCH 20.00 50.00
BW Bill Walton 12.00 30.00
CA Chris Archer 6.00 15.00
CF Cecil Fielder 15.00 40.00
CG Carlos Gonzalez 10.00 25.00
CH Chase Headley 30.00 60.00
CI Chanel Iman 6.00 15.00
CK Casey Kelly 4.00 10.00
CKM Craig Kimbrel 40.00 80.00
CM Chris Mortensen 4.00 10.00
CR Cal Ripken Jr. 75.00 200.00
CT Chrissy Teigen 15.00 40.00
DB Dylan Bundy 10.00 25.00
DM Dale Murphy 60.00 120.00
DMT Don Mattingly 50.00 120.00
DP Dustin Pedroia 30.00 60.00
DS Don Sutton 50.00 100.00
EK Ekolu Kalama 5.00 12.00
EO Ed O'Neill 40.00 80.00
FD Felix Doubront 4.00 10.00
FR Freddie Roach 15.00 40.00
GRD Guillaume Robert-Demolaize 10.00 25.00
HA Hank Aaron EXCH 175.00 350.00
HR Henry Rollins 25.00 60.00
JC John Calipari 20.00 50.00
JCU Johnny Cueto 10.00 25.00
JD Jason Dufner 12.00 30.00
JH Josh Hamilton EXCH 40.00 80.00
JK Jason Kipnis 10.00 25.00
JM Julia Mancuso 10.00 25.00
JML Juan Marichal 40.00 80.00
JP Jurickson Profar 8.00 20.00
JPA Jarrod Parker 4.00 10.00
JR Josh Reddick 4.00 10.00
JRC Jim Rice 12.00 30.00
JS Jean Segura 4.00 10.00
JSD James Shields 10.00 25.00
JZ Jordan Zimmermann 4.00 10.00
KH Kevin Harvick 10.00 25.00
LA Luis Aparicio 60.00 120.00
LL Lance Lynn 4.00 10.00
LV Lindsey Vonn 30.00 80.00
MB Matthias Blonski 5.00 12.00
MBU Madison Bumgarner 25.00 60.00
MBY Matthew Berry 10.00 25.00
MC Mark Cuban 30.00 80.00
MCN Matt Cain
MH Mike Richter 6.00 15.00
MHL Monty Hall 8.00 20.00
MJO Mike Joy 6.00 15.00
MM McKayla Maroney 60.00 120.00
MMC Mike McCarthy 30.00 80.00
MMD Manny Machado EXCH 60.00 120.00
MO Mike Olt 6.00 15.00
MS Mike Schmidt 75.00 150.00
MT Mark Trumbo 12.00 30.00
MTT Mike Trout EXCH
MW Maury Wills 4.00 10.00
NM Nana Meriwether 6.00 15.00
NS Nick Saban 100.00 250.00
NW Nik Wallenda 5.00 12.00
OC Olivia Culpo 10.00 25.00
P Pele 250.00 400.00
PF Prince Fielder EXCH 50.00 100.00
PG Paul Goldschmidt 10.00 25.00
PH Phil Heath 12.00 30.00
PM Penny Marshall 25.00 60.00
PO Paul O'Neill EXCH 25.00 60.00
RD R.A. Dickey
RJR Roy Jones Jr. 20.00 50.00
RVP Robin van Persie 50.00 100.00
RZ Ryan Zimmerman 12.00 30.00
SD Scott Diamond 4.00 10.00
SH Scott Hamilton 8.00 20.00
SK Sandy Koufax 300.00 500.00
SM Starling Marte 4.00 20.00
SMI Shelby Miller 4.00 10.00
SN Shawn Nadelen 5.00 12.00
SP Salvador Perez 15.00 40.00
TB Trevor Bauer EXCH 8.00 20.00
TCG Tony Cingrani 5.00 12.00
TL Tommy Lee EXCH 25.00 60.00

Card	Low	High
TM Tommy Milone	4.00	10.00
TS Tyler Skaggs	4.00	10.00
VB Vida Blue	4.00	10.00
WC Will Clark	20.00	50.00
WJ Wally Joyner	8.00	20.00
WM Wil Myers	4.00	10.00
WMB Will Middlebrooks EXCH	12.00	30.00
WP Wily Peralta	4.00	10.00
WR Wilin Rosario	4.00	10.00
YC Yoenis Cespedes	40.00	80.00
YD Yu Darvish EXCH	75.00	150.00
YG Yasmani Grandal	4.00	10.00
YP Yasiel Puig	125.00	300.00
ZC Zack Cozart	4.00	10.00
ZM Ziggy Marley	20.00	50.00

2013 Topps Allen and Ginter Autographs Red Ink

STATED ODDS 1:931 HOBBY
PRINT RUNS B/WN 10-409 SER.#'d SETS
NO PRICING ON MOST DUE TO SCARCITY
EXCHANGE DEADLINE 07/31/2013

Card	Low	High
DS Don Sutton/66	20.00	50.00
MO Mike Olt/373	4.00	10.00
MTT Mike Trout/31	250.00	500.00
WR Wilin Rosario/409	4.00	10.00

2013 Topps Allen and Ginter Civilizations of Ages Past

Card	Low	High
COMPLETE SET (20)	5.00	12.00
STATED ODDS 1:8 HOBBY		
ASY Assyrians	.60	1.50
AZ Aztecs	.60	1.50
BAY Babylonians	.60	1.50
BYZ Byzantine	.60	1.50
EG Egyptians	.60	1.50
GRK Greeks	.60	1.50
HT Hittites	.60	1.50
IN Inca	.60	1.50
IRV Indus River Valley	.60	1.50
MES Mesopotamians	.60	1.50
MY Mayans	.60	1.50
OL Olmecs	.60	1.50
OTT Ottoman	.60	1.50
PER Persians	.60	1.50
PH Phoenicians	.60	1.50
ROM Romans	.60	1.50
SD Shang Dynasty	.60	1.50
SU Sumerians	.60	1.50
SWA Swahili	.60	1.50
VK Vikings	.60	1.50

2013 Topps Allen and Ginter Curious Cases

Card	Low	High
COMPLETE SET (10)	15.00	40.00
H HAARP	3.00	8.00
A51 Roswell Area 51	3.00	8.00
CH Chemtrails	3.00	8.00
DA Denver Airport	3.00	8.00
FM Faked moon landings	3.00	8.00
JFK Assassination of JFK	3.00	8.00
MK MKULTRA	3.00	8.00
NOW The Illuminati New World Order	3.00	8.00
PE The Philadelphia Experiment	3.00	8.00
UVB UVB-76	3.00	8.00

2013 Topps Allen and Ginter Framed Mini Relics

VERSION A ODDS 1:29 HOBBY
VERSION B ODDS 1:27 HOBBY

Card	Low	High
B Byamba	3.00	8.00
P Pele	10.00	25.00
AA Alex Avila	3.00	8.00
AB Albert Belle	3.00	8.00
ABB Amelia Boone	3.00	8.00
ABT Adrian Beltre	3.00	8.00
AC Asdrubal Cabrera	3.00	8.00
AG Alex Gordon	3.00	8.00
AGZ Adrian Gonzalez	3.00	8.00
AL Artie Lange	6.00	15.00
AR Aramis Ramirez	3.00	8.00
AR Adam Richman	10.00	25.00
AV Abe Vigoda	3.00	8.00
AW Adam Wainwright	4.00	10.00
BB Brandon Belt	3.00	8.00
BBR Bonnie Bernstein	6.00	15.00
BBW Bobby Bowden	4.00	10.00
BG Brett Gardner	3.00	8.00
BK Brian Kelly	4.00	10.00
BM Barry Melrose	6.00	15.00
BMC Brian McCann	3.00	8.00
BP Buster Posey	4.00	10.00
BR Babe Ruth	150.00	300.00
BW Bill Walton	3.00	8.00
CB Clay Buchholz	3.00	8.00
CBL Chad Billingsley	3.00	8.00
CF Cecil Fielder	3.00	8.00
CI Chanel Iman	4.00	10.00
CKM Craig Kimbrel	3.00	8.00
CL Cory Luebke	3.00	8.00
CM Cameron Maybin	3.00	8.00
CMO Chris Mortensen	3.00	8.00
CMR Carlos Marmol	3.00	8.00
CP Carlos Pena	3.00	8.00
CR Cody Ross	3.00	8.00
CT Chrissy Teigen	50.00	100.00
DA Dustin Ackley	3.00	8.00
DF Dexter Fowler	3.00	8.00
DJ Desmond Jennings	3.00	8.00
DP David Price	3.00	8.00
DS Drew Stubbs	3.00	8.00
DW David Wright	50.00	100.00
EA Elvis Andrus	3.00	8.00
EH Eric Hosmer	3.00	8.00
EON Ed O'Neill	6.00	15.00
FH Felix Hernandez	3.00	8.00
FL Fred Lynn	3.00	8.00
FR Frank Robinson	40.00	80.00
FR Freddie Roach	4.00	10.00
GB Gordon Beckham	3.00	8.00
GBR George Brett	60.00	120.00
GC Gary Carter	20.00	50.00
GS Gary Sheffield	3.00	8.00
HA Henderson Alvarez	3.00	8.00
HI Hisashi Iwakuma	3.00	8.00
HK Harmon Killebrew	15.00	40.00
HP Hunter Pence	3.00	8.00
HR Hanley Ramirez	3.00	8.00
ID Ike Davis	3.00	8.00
IDS Ian Desmond	3.00	8.00
IK Ian Kennedy	3.00	8.00
JA Jose Altuve	3.00	8.00
JAX John Axford	3.00	8.00
JBR Jay Bruce	3.00	8.00
JC Johnny Cueto	3.00	8.00
JCA John Calipari	4.00	10.00
JCH Jhoulys Chacin	3.00	8.00
JD Jason Dufner	4.00	10.00
JDM J.D. Martinez	3.00	8.00
JH Josh Hamilton	3.00	8.00
JHK Jeremy Hellickson	3.00	8.00
JHY Jason Heyward	3.00	8.00
JJ Jon Jay	3.00	8.00
JJY Jon Jay	3.00	8.00
JL Jon Lester	3.00	8.00
JM Justin Morneau	3.00	8.00
JMA Julia Mancuso	3.00	8.00
JMD James McDonald	3.00	8.00
JR Jimmy Rollins	3.00	8.00
JT Jose Tabata	3.00	8.00
JV Joey Votto	4.00	10.00
JVR Justin Verlander	4.00	10.00
JW Jered Weaver	3.00	8.00
JZ Jordan Zimmermann	3.00	8.00
KH Kevin Harvick	5.00	12.00
KM Kendrys Morales	3.00	8.00
LB Lou Brock	8.00	20.00
LG Lou Gehrig	50.00	100.00
LLN Lance Lynn	3.00	8.00
LM Logan Morrison	3.00	8.00
LV Lindsey Vonn	6.00	15.00
MB Michael Bourn	3.00	8.00
MBL Matthias Blonski	3.00	8.00
MBU Madison Bumgarner	3.00	8.00
MBY Matthew Berry	6.00	15.00
MC Matt Cain	3.00	8.00
MCU Mark Cuban	4.00	10.00
MH Matt Holliday	3.00	8.00
MHA Monty Hall	3.00	8.00
MJ Mike Joy	3.00	8.00
MKP Matt Kemp	3.00	8.00
ML Mat Latos	3.00	8.00
MM Matt Moore	3.00	8.00
MMA McKayla Maroney	10.00	25.00
MMC Mike McCarthy	6.00	15.00
MSZ Max Scherzer	3.00	8.00
NC Nelson Cruz	3.00	8.00
NM Nana Meriwether	4.00	10.00
NS Nick Saban	12.00	30.00
NW Neil Walker	3.00	8.00
NWA Nik Wallenda	4.00	10.00
OC Olivia Culpo	3.00	8.00
PF Prince Fielder	3.00	8.00
PH Phil Heath	4.00	10.00
PM Paul Molitor	20.00	50.00
PMA Penny Marshall	4.00	10.00
PON Paul O'Neill	4.00	10.00
PS Pablo Sandoval	3.00	8.00
RF Rafael Furcal	3.00	8.00
RH Roy Halladay	3.00	8.00
RHD Ryan Howard	3.00	8.00
RJ Roy Jones Jr.	3.00	8.00
RN Ricky Nolasco	3.00	8.00
RR Ricky Romero	3.00	8.00
SC Starlin Castro	3.00	8.00
SG Steve Garvey	15.00	40.00
SH Scott Hamilton	3.00	8.00
SM Stan Musial	60.00	120.00
SN Shawn Nadelen	3.00	8.00
TH Tim Hudson	3.00	8.00
TL Tim Lincecum	3.00	8.00
TW Ted Williams	60.00	120.00
WM Willie Mays	30.00	60.00
WR Wilin Rosario	3.00	8.00
YD Yu Darvish	4.00	10.00
YG Yovani Gallardo	3.00	8.00
ZG Zack Greinke	3.00	8.00
ZM Ziggy Marley	3.00	8.00

2013 Topps Allen and Ginter Martial Mastery

Card	Low	High
COMPLETE SET (10)	4.00	10.00
STATED ODDS 1:8 HOBBY		
AMZ Amazons	.60	1.50
AP Apache	.60	1.50
AZ Aztecs	.60	1.50
GD Gladiators	.60	1.50
KN Knights	.60	1.50
RM Romans	.60	1.50
SM Samurai	.60	1.50
SP Spartans	.60	1.50
VK Vikings	.60	1.50
ZU Zulu	.60	1.50

2013 Topps Allen and Ginter Mini All in a Days Work

Card	Low	High
B Butcher	6.00	15.00
C Clergy	6.00	15.00
F Firefighter	6.00	15.00
N Nurse	6.00	15.00
P Pilot	6.00	15.00
S Soldier	6.00	15.00
CW Construction Worker	6.00	15.00
PB Paperboy	6.00	15.00
PO Police Officer	6.00	15.00
ST Schoolteacher	6.00	15.00

2013 Topps Allen and Ginter Mini Famous Finds

Card	Low	High
COMPLETE SET (10)	8.00	20.00
STATED ODDS 1:5 HOBBY		
L Olduvai Gorge Lucy	1.00	2.50
P Pompeii	1.00	2.50
CA The Cave of Altamira	1.00	2.50
CG Cairo Geniza	1.00	2.50
DSS Dead Sea Scrolls	1.00	2.50
KTT King Tut's Tomb	1.00	2.50
NHL Nag Hammadi Library	1.00	2.50
PS The Pilate Stone	1.00	2.50
QSH The Tomb of the Qin Shi Huang	1.00	2.50
RS Rosetta Stone	1.00	2.50

2013 Topps Allen and Ginter Mini Heavy Hangs the Head

Card	Low	High
COMPLETE SET (30)	12.50	30.00
STATED ODDS 1:5 HOBBY		
ALX Alexander I	1.25	3.00
ATG Alexander the Great	1.25	3.00
AUG Augustus	1.25	3.00
CHR Charlemagne	1.25	3.00
CLE Cleopatra	1.25	3.00
CON Constantine	1.25	3.00
CTG Cyrus the Great	1.25	3.00
DK King David	1.25	3.00
EM Emperor Meiji	1.25	3.00
FA Ferdinand & Isabella	1.25	3.00
FRD Frederick II	1.25	3.00
GA Gustavus Adolphus	1.25	3.00
ITT Ivan the Terrible	1.25	3.00
JC Julius Caesar	1.25	3.00
KH King Henry VIII	1.25	3.00
KHN King Henry V	1.25	3.00
KJ King James I	1.25	3.00
KL King Louis XIV	1.25	3.00
KR King Richard I	1.25	3.00
KW Krishnaraja Wadiyar III	1.25	3.00
NP Napoleon	1.25	3.00
PW Prince William	1.25	3.00
QB Queen Beatrix	1.25	3.00
QE Queen Elizabeth II	1.25	3.00
QSH Qin Shi Huang	1.25	3.00
QV Queen Victoria	1.25	3.00
RAM Ramses II	1.25	3.00
SLM Solomon	1.25	3.00
STM Suleiman the Magnificent	1.25	3.00
TUT Tutankhamun	1.25	3.00

2013 Topps Allen and Ginter Mini Inquiring Minds

Card	Low	High
COMPLETE SET (21)	10.00	25.00
AR Aristotle	1.00	2.50
AS Arthur Schopenhauer	1.00	2.50
AUG St. Augustine	1.00	2.50
BS Baruch Spinoza	1.00	2.50
EP Epicurus	1.00	2.50
FB Francis Bacon	1.00	2.50
FN Friedrich Nietzsche	1.00	2.50
GH Georg Wilhelm Friedrich Hegel	1.00	2.50
HA Hannah Arendt	1.00	2.50
IK Immanuel Kant	1.00	2.50
JL John Locke	1.00	2.50
JPS Jean-Paul Sartre	1.00	2.50
KM Karl Marx	1.00	2.50
NM Niccolo Machiavelli	1.00	2.50
PTO Plato	1.00	2.50
RD Rene Descartes	1.00	2.50
SCR Socrates	1.00	2.50
SDB Simone de Beauvoir	1.00	2.50
ST Sun Tzu	1.00	2.50
TA Thomas Aquinas	1.00	2.50
TH Thomas Hobbes	1.00	2.50

2013 Topps Allen and Ginter Mini No Card Number

*NO NBR: 4X TO 10X BASIC
*NO NBR RCs: 2.5X TO 6X BASIC RCs
*NO NBR SP: 1.2X TO 3X BASIC SP
STATED ODDS 1:102 HOBBY
ANNC'D PRINT RUN OF 50 SETS

Card	Low	High
2 Derek Jeter	30.00	60.00
344 Nolan Ryan	12.50	30.00

2013 Topps Allen and Ginter Mini Peacemakers

Card	Low	High
COMPLETE SET (10)	10.00	25.00
STATED ODDS 1:5 HOBBY		
AL Abraham Lincoln	1.25	3.00
BC Bill Clinton	1.25	3.00
DL Dalai Lama	1.25	3.00
GND Gandhi	1.25	3.00
GW George Washington	1.25	3.00
HT Harriet Tubman	1.25	3.00
JA Jane Addams	1.25	3.00
JC Jimmy Carter	1.25	3.00
MT Mother Teresa	1.25	3.00
NM Nelson Mandela	1.25	3.00

2013 Topps Allen and Ginter Mini People on Bicycles

Card	Low	High
A Amphibious	6.00	15.00
M Messenger	6.00	15.00
T Tricycle	6.00	15.00
BR Brief Respite	6.00	15.00
NH No Hands	6.00	15.00
PF Penny-Farthing	6.00	15.00
QT Quadracycle for Two	6.00	15.00
TT Tricycle for Two	6.00	15.00
WE Woodland Excursion	6.00	15.00
TRI Triathlete	6.00	15.00

2013 Topps Allen and Ginter Mini The First Americans

Card	Low	High
COMPLETE SET (15)	10.00	25.00
STATED ODDS 1:5 HOBBY		
WCT Wichita	1.00	2.50
ALG Algonquian	1.00	2.50
AP Apache	1.00	2.50
BNK Bannock	1.00	2.50
CHK Cherokee	1.00	2.50
CHY Cheyenne	1.00	2.50
CM Comanche	1.00	2.50
HPI Hopi	1.00	2.50
IRQ Iroquois	1.00	2.50
LK Lakota	1.00	2.50
NV Navajo	1.00	2.50
PUB Pueblo	1.00	2.50
PWN Pawnee	1.00	2.50
SX Sioux	1.00	2.50
ZN Zuni	1.00	2.50

2013 Topps Allen and Ginter N43 Autographs

STATED PRINT RUN 40 SER.#'d SETS

Card	Low	High
N43AP Pele	300.00	500.00

2013 Topps Allen and Ginter Box Toppers

Card	Low	High
AP Albert Pujols	2.00	5.00
BH Bryce Harper	2.50	6.00
DW David Wright	1.25	3.00
GS Giancarlo Stanton	1.50	4.00
JH Josh Hamilton	1.25	3.00
JV Joey Votto	1.50	4.00
MC Miguel Cabrera	1.50	4.00
MK Matt Kemp	1.25	3.00
MT Mike Trout	12.00	30.00
PF Prince Fielder	1.25	3.00
RAD R.A. Dickey	1.25	3.00
RB Ryan Braun	1.25	3.00
RC Robinson Cano	1.25	3.00
SS Stephen Strasburg	1.50	4.00
TT Troy Tulowitzki	1.50	4.00

2013 Topps Allen and Ginter Box Topper Relics

STATED PRINT RUN 25 SER.#'d SETS

Card	Low	High
AR Alex Rodriguez	30.00	60.00
BP Brandon Phillips	15.00	40.00
DJ Derek Jeter	100.00	200.00
HC Hank Conger	6.00	15.00
JB Jay Bruce	15.00	40.00
JV Justin Verlander	20.00	50.00
MC Matt Cain	20.00	50.00
SC Starlin Castro	20.00	50.00

2013 Topps Allen and Ginter Oddity Relics

STATED ODDS 1:7,150 HOBBY
PRINT RUNS B/WN 25-125 COPIES PER

Card	Low	High
BK Grassy Knoll/25	300.00	400.00
WF Wrigley Field/125	40.00	80.00
KHW Kim and Kris/50	60.00	120.00
OIT President Obama/50	125.00	250.00

2013 Topps Allen and Ginter One Little Corner

Card	Low	High
COMPLETE SET (20)	5.00	12.00
STATED ODDS 1:8 HOBBY		
NPT Neptune	.60	1.50
PTO Pluto	.60	1.50
SDN Sedna	.60	1.50
STN Saturn	.60	1.50
SUN Sun	.60	1.50
URN Uranus	.60	1.50
AB Asteroid Belt	.60	1.50
CM Comet	.60	1.50
CR Ceres	.60	1.50
CT Centaur	.60	1.50
ER Eris	.60	1.50
ERT Earth	.60	1.50
HAU Haumea	.60	1.50
JPT Jupiter	.60	1.50
MK Makemake	.60	1.50
MN Moon	.60	1.50
MS Mars	.60	1.50
MY Mercury	.60	1.50
SD Scattered Disc	.60	1.50
VN Venus	.60	1.50

2013 Topps Allen and Ginter Palaces and Strongholds

Card	Low	High
COMPLETE SET (20)	5.00	12.00
STATED ODDS 1:8 HOBBY		
ALH Alhambra	.60	1.50
BP Buckingham Palace	.60	1.50
CC Chateau de Chambord	.60	1.50
FC Forbidden City	.60	1.50
FK Fort Knox	.60	1.50
GY Gyeongbokgung	.60	1.50
HP Hohenschwangau Castle	.60	1.50
LC Leeds Castle	.60	1.50
MP Mysore Palace	.60	1.50
NC Neuschwanstein Castle	.60	1.50
PNP Pena National Palace	.60	1.50
PP Peterhof Palace	.60	1.50
PPC Potala Palace	.60	1.50
SB Schonbrunn Palace	.60	1.50
SP Summer Palace	.60	1.50
TA The Alamo	.60	1.50
TB The Bastille	.60	1.50
TM Taj Mahal	.60	1.50
TP Topkapi Palace	.60	1.50
VSL Palace of Versailles	.60	1.50

2013 Topps Allen and Ginter Relics

STATED ODDS 1:37 HOBBY

Card	Low	High
AC Aroldis Chapman	3.00	8.00
AD Adam Dunn	3.00	8.00
AE Andre Ethier	3.00	8.00
AG Adrian Gonzalez	3.00	8.00
AJ Austin Jackson	3.00	8.00
AL Adam Lind	3.00	8.00
BB Brandon Beachy	3.00	8.00
BBT Billy Butler	3.00	8.00
BD Bobby Doerr	10.00	25.00
BP Brandon Phillips	3.00	8.00
BS Bruce Sutter	20.00	50.00
CCS CC Sabathia	3.00	8.00
CG Carlos Gonzalez	3.00	8.00
CH Chris Heisey	3.00	8.00
CK Craig Kimbrel	3.00	8.00
CL Cliff Lee	3.00	8.00
DB Darwin Barney	3.00	8.00
DDJ David DeJesus	3.00	8.00
DM Don Mattingly	20.00	50.00
DW David Wright	12.50	30.00
GG Goose Gossage	20.00	50.00
HA Hank Aaron	50.00	100.00
HN Hal Newhouser	8.00	20.00
IK Ian Kinsler	3.00	8.00
JG Johnny Giavotella	3.00	8.00
JH Jason Heyward	3.00	8.00
JJH J.J. Hardy	3.00	8.00
JM Justin Masterson	3.00	8.00
JMA Joe Mauer	3.00	8.00
JP Jake Peavy	3.00	8.00
JPA J.P. Arencibia	3.00	8.00
JU Justin Upton	3.00	8.00
JZ Jordan Zimmermann	3.00	8.00
LD Lucas Duda	3.00	8.00
MM Miguel Montero	3.00	8.00
MR Mariano Rivera	6.00	15.00
RB Ryan Braun	3.00	8.00
RC Rod Carew	12.50	30.00
RJ Reggie Jackson	20.00	50.00
RK Ralph Kiner	10.00	25.00
RW Rickie Weeks	3.00	8.00
RY Robin Yount	20.00	50.00
RZ Ryan Zimmerman	3.00	8.00
SC Steve Carlton	30.00	60.00
SMC Shaun Marcum	3.00	8.00
SR Scott Rolen	3.00	8.00
SS Stephen Strasburg	3.00	8.00
TG Tony Gwynn	3.00	8.00
TH Todd Helton	3.00	8.00
UJ Ubaldo Jimenez	3.00	8.00

2013 Topps Allen and Ginter Rip Cards

OVERALL RIP ODDS 1:287 HOBBY
PRINT RUNS B/WN 10-99 COPIES PER
NO PRICING ON QTY 25 OR LESS
ALL LISTED PRICED ARE FOR RIPPED
UNRIPPED HAVE ADD'L CARDS WITHIN

Card	Low	High
RC1 Duke Snider/50	6.00	15.00
RC2 Cliff Lee/25	6.00	15.00
RC4 Ralph Kiner/25	6.00	15.00
RC6 Jason Heyward/50	6.00	15.00
RC7 Mike Olt/50	6.00	15.00
RC8 Yoenis Cespedes/25	10.00	25.00
RC12 Darryl Strawberry/25	6.00	15.00
RC13 Carlos Gonzalez/50	6.00	15.00
RC19 Tim Lincecum/50	6.00	15.00
RC21 David Wright/25	10.00	25.00
RC23 C.J. Wilson/50	6.00	15.00
RC24 David Freese/50	6.00	15.00
RC26 R.A. Dickey/25	6.00	15.00
RC27 Clayton Kershaw/25	10.00	25.00
RC28 Dwight Gooden/50	10.00	25.00
RC29 Giancarlo Stanton/50	6.00	15.00
RC30 Paul O'Neill/50	6.00	15.00
RC33 Jered Weaver/50	6.00	15.00
RC34 Anthony Rizzo/25	10.00	25.00
RC38 Nick Swisher/50	6.00	15.00
RC40 Evan Longoria/25	6.00	15.00
RC41 Torii Hunter/50	6.00	15.00
RC42 Dustin Pedroia/25	10.00	25.00
RC43 Paul Goldschmidt/50	10.00	25.00
RC45 James Shields/50	6.00	15.00
RC46 Matt Cain/50	6.00	15.00
RC47 Gio Gonzalez/50	6.00	15.00
RC50 Lou Gehrig		
RC51 Allen Craig/25	6.00	15.00
RC52 Chris Sale/25	6.00	15.00
RC54 Mark Trumbo/50	6.00	15.00
RC55 Harmon Killebrew/25	10.00	25.00
RC56 Tony Gwynn/25	10.00	25.00
RC57 Justin Upton/25	6.00	15.00
RC58 Gary Carter/25	10.00	25.00
RC59 Warren Spahn/25	10.00	25.00
RC60 Wade Boggs/25	10.00	25.00
RC63 Matt Holliday/25	6.00	15.00
RC64 Ian Kinsler/50	6.00	15.00
RC66 Joey Votto/25	10.00	25.00
RC67 Hanley Ramirez/50	6.00	15.00
RC68 Jose Reyes/50	6.00	15.00
RC70 B.J. Upton/50	6.00	15.00
RC71 Joe Mauer/25	10.00	25.00
RC73 Troy Tulowitzki/50	6.00	15.00
RC74 Bob Gibson/25	6.00	15.00
RC75 Madison Bumgarner/50	6.00	15.00
RC77 Al Kaline/25	10.00	25.00
RC80 Will Middlebrooks/25	6.00	15.00
RC81 Tyler Skaggs/50	6.00	15.00
RC84 Adrian Gonzalez/25	6.00	15.00
RC85 Trevor Bauer/50	6.00	15.00
RC86 Carlos Beltran/50	6.00	15.00
RC88 Roy Halladay/50	6.00	15.00
RC90 Andy Pettitte/25	6.00	15.00
RC91 John Smoltz/25	6.00	15.00
RC93 Adam Eaton/50	6.00	15.00
RC95 Prince Fielder/25	6.00	15.00
RC96 Josh Hamilton/25	6.00	15.00
RC97 Willie Stargell/25	6.00	15.00
RC98 Josh Beckett/50	6.00	15.00
RC99 Starlin Castro/50	6.00	15.00

2013 Topps Allen and Ginter Wonders of the World Cabinets

Card	Low	High
1 Great Pyramid of Giza	3.00	8.00
2 Hanging Gardens of Babylon	3.00	8.00
3 Statue of Zeus at Olympia	3.00	8.00
4 Temple of Artemis at Ephesus	3.00	8.00
5 Mausoleum at Halicarnassus	3.00	8.00
6 Colossus of Rhodes	3.00	8.00
7 Lighthouse of Alexandria	3.00	8.00
8 Channel Tunnel	3.00	8.00
9 CN Tower	3.00	8.00
10 Empire State Building	3.00	8.00
11 Golden Gate Bridge	3.00	8.00
12 Itaipu Dam	3.00	8.00
13 Delta Works	3.00	8.00
14 Panama Canal	3.00	8.00
15 Grand Canyon	3.00	8.00
16 Great Barrier Reef	3.00	8.00
17 Harbor of Rio de Janeiro	3.00	8.00
18 Mount Everest	3.00	8.00
19 Aurora	3.00	8.00
20 Paricutin Volcano	3.00	8.00
21 Victoria Falls	3.00	8.00

2014 Topps Allen and Ginter

Card	Low	High
COMPLETE SET (350)	25.00	60.00
COMP.SET w/o SP's (300)	12.00	30.00
SP ODDS 1:2 HOBBY		
1 Roger Maris	.25	.60
2 Don Mattingly	.50	1.25
3 Matt Davidson RC	.30	.75
4 Edwin Encarnacion	.25	.60
5 Jurickson Profar	.20	.50
6 Laura Phelps Sweatt	.15	.40
7 Hector Santiago	.15	.40
8 Bob Feller	.20	.50
9 Koji Uehara	.15	.40
10 Andrew McCutchen	.25	.60
11 Nick Franklin	.15	.40
12 Jedd Gyorko	.15	.40
13 Gary Sheffield	.15	.40
14 Michael Cuddyer	.15	.40
15 Matt Williams	.15	.40
16 Bartolo Colon	.15	.40
17 Travis d'Arnaud RC	.30	.75
18 Ryne Sandberg	.50	1.25
19 Pablo Sandoval	.20	.50
20 Babe Ruth	.60	1.50
21 Rafael Palmeiro	.20	.50
22 Michael Eisner	.15	.40
23 Snoop Lion	.15	.40
24 Jorge Posada	.20	.50
25 Joe DiMaggio	.50	1.25
26 Fergie Jenkins	.20	.50
27 David Ortiz	.25	.60
28 Mark Trumbo	.15	.40
29 Shelby Miller	.20	.50
30 Judah Friedlander	.15	.40
31 Michael Choice RC	.25	.60
32 Tim Lincecum	.20	.50
33 Alex Avila	.20	.50
34 Felix Hernandez	.20	.50
35 Brooks Robinson	.20	.50
36 Yadier Molina	.25	.60
37 Wil Myers	.15	.40
38 Don Sutton	.20	.50
39 Chris Sale	.25	.60
40 Steve Delabar	.15	.40
41 Lou Gehrig	.50	1.25
42 Junior Lake	.15	.40
43 Craig Kimbrel	.20	.50
44 Ty Cobb	.40	1.00
45 Nomar Garciaparra	.20	.50
46 John L. Sullivan	.15	.40
47 Wilmer Flores RC	.30	.75
48 Alex Rodriguez	.30	.75
49 Felix Doubront	.15	.40
50 Orlando Hernandez	.15	.40
51 Oswaldo Arcia	.15	.40
52 Kevin Smith	.15	.40
53 Sandy Koufax	.50	1.25
54 Yordano Ventura RC	.30	.75
55 Andrew Lambo RC	.15	.40
56 Jason Heyward	.20	.50
57 Carlos Beltran	.20	.50
58 Tyler Skaggs	.15	.40
59 Hal Newhouser	.20	.50
60 Ryan Zimmerman	.20	.50
61 Bo Jackson	.25	.60
62 Diana Nyad	.15	.40
63 Bill Buckner	.15	.40
64 Taijuan Walker RC	.25	.60
65 Fred McGriff	.20	.50
66 Roger Clemens	.30	.75
67 Omar Vizquel	.20	.50
68 Gio Gonzalez	.20	.50
69 Johnny Cueto	.20	.50
70 Dr. James Andrews	.15	.40
71 Wade Boggs	.20	.50
72 Ralph Kiner	.20	.50
73 Joe Morgan	.20	.50
74 Adrian Gonzalez	.20	.50
75 Rod Carew	.20	.50
76 Cal Ripken Jr.	.75	2.00
77 Stan Musial	.40	1.00
78 Zack Greinke	.20	.50
79 Matt Adams	.15	.40
80 Justin Verlander	.25	.60
81 Larry King	.15	.40
82 Jackie Robinson	.25	.60
83 Giancarlo Stanton	.25	.60
84 Francisco Liriano	.15	.40
85 Carlos Santana	.20	.50
86 Randy Johnson	.25	.60
87 Alex Gordon	.20	.50
88 Buffalo Bill Cody	.15	.40
89 Chuck Todd	.15	.40
90 Roy Halladay	.20	.50
91 Clay Buchholz	.15	.40
92 Ernie Banks	.25	.60
93 Willie Mays	.50	1.25
94 Lou Brock	.20	.50
95 Austin Wierschke	.15	.40
96 Madison Bumgarner	.20	.50
97 Sparky Anderson	.20	.50
98 David Wright	.20	.50
99 Wilin Rosario	.15	.40
100 Queen Victoria	.15	.40
101 Mike Trout	1.25	3.00
102 Todd Frazier	.20	.50
103 Jon Lester	.20	.50
104 Troy Tulowitzki	.25	.60
105 Cole Hamels	.20	.50
106 Patrick Corbin	.20	.50
107 Will Middlebrooks	.15	.40
108 Nolan Ryan	.75	2.00
109 Jhoulys Chacin	.15	.40
110 Jeremy Hellickson	.15	.40
111 Frank Robinson	.20	.50
112 Erin Brady	.15	.40
113 Shin-Soo Choo	.20	.50
114 Desmond Jennings	.20	.50
115 Dustin Pedroia	.25	.60
116 Brett Gardner	.20	.50
117 Yu Darvish	.25	.60
118 Adam Schefter	.15	.40
119 Felicia Day	.15	.40
120 Tom Seaver	.20	.50
121 Freddie Freeman	.30	.75
122 Craig Biggio	.20	.50
123 Matt Carpenter	.25	.60
124 Jonathan Schoop	.15	.40
125 Glen Waggoner	.15	.40
126 Willie Stargell	.20	.50
127 Greg Maddux	.30	.75
128 Bill Rancic	.15	.40
129 Hank Aaron	.50	1.25
130 Mike Zunino	.15	.40
131 Buster Posey	.30	.75
132 Ted Williams	.50	1.25
133 Xander Bogaerts RC	.75	2.00
134 Jordan Zimmermann	.20	.50
135 Grant Balfour	.15	.40
136 Carlos Gonzalez	.20	.50
137 Reggie Jackson	.20	.50
138 Mariano Rivera	.30	.75
139 Jacoby Ellsbury	.20	.50
140 Matt Moore	.20	.50
141 Starlin Castro	.15	.40
142 Hiroki Kuroda	.15	.40
143 Eddie Mathews	.25	.60
144 Brett Oberholtzer	.15	.40
145 Derek Jeter	.60	1.50
146 Max Scherzer	.25	.60
147 Mark McGwire	.50	1.25
148 Bryce Harper	.40	1.00
149 Jose Canseco	.20	.50
150 Mike Schmidt	.40	1.00
151 James Paxton RC	.40	1.00
152 Vince Gilligan	.15	.40
153 The Iron Sheik	.15	.40
154 Eric Hosmer	.20	.50
155 Yogi Berra	.25	.60
156 Jean Segura	.20	.50
157 Hisashi Iwakuma	.20	.50
158 Carlton Fisk	.20	.50
159 George Brett	.50	1.25
160 Daniel Okrent	.15	.40
161 Tommy Lasorda	.20	.50
162 George Kell	.20	.50
163 Paul Molitor	.25	.60
164 Jenny Dell	.15	.40
165 Brad Miller	.20	.50
166 Mike Napoli	.15	.40
167 Nick Castellanos RC	.75	2.00
168 Miguel Cabrera	.25	.60
169 Dale Murphy	.25	.60
170 Matt Holliday	.25	.60
171 Dusty Baker	.15	.40
172 Andrelton Simmons	.15	.40
173 Jose Fernandez	.25	.60
174 Ben Zobrist	.20	.50
175 Chase Utley	.20	.50
176 Anthony Robles	.15	.40
177 Anthony Rizzo	.40	1.00
178 Domonic Brown	.20	.50
179 Chris Archer	.15	.40
180 Ryan Riess	.15	.40

Jose Reyes .20 .50
Starling Marte .20 .50
Jim Palmer .20 .50
Gerrit Cole .25 .60
Jose Bautista .20 .50
Billy Hamilton RC .30 .75
David Price .20 .50
Jordan Oliver .15 .40
Clayton Kershaw .50 1.25
Kolten Wong RC .30 .75
Jordan Burroughs .15 .40
2 Daniel Nava .15 .40
3 Tom Glavine .20 .50
4 Avisail Garcia .20 .50
5 Chris Carpenter .20 .50
6 Eddie Murray .20 .50
7 Wade Miley .15 .40
8 Jeff Locke .15 .40
9 Joe Mauer .20 .50
0 Zack Wheeler .20 .50
1 Paul O'Neill .20 .50
2 Jim Rice .20 .50
3 Jered Weaver .20 .50
4 Albert Pujols .30 .75
5 Robin Yount .25 .60
6 Willie McCovey .20 .50
7 Justin Upton .20 .50
8 Al Kaline .25 .60
9 Vladimir Guerrero .20 .50
0 Anthony Bourdain .15 .40
1 Mark Roth .15 .40
2 Doug Fister .15 .40
3 Allyson Felix .15 .40
4 Carli Lloyd .15 .40
5 Johnny Bench .25 .60
6 Matt Besser .15 .40
7 Jose Iglesias .15 .40
8 Casey Kelly .20 .50
9 Evan Gattis .15 .40
20 Josh Hamilton .20 .50
21 Adam Eaton .15 .40
22 Danny Salazar .20 .50
23 Tony Gwynn .25 .60
24 Tanner Foust .15 .40
25 Pedro Martinez .20 .50
26 Bob Gibson .20 .50
27 Jimmy Rollins .20 .50
28 Orlando Cepeda .20 .50
29 Julio Teheran .20 .50
30 Ivan Rodriguez .20 .50
31 Carlos Gomez .15 .40
32 Ozzie Smith .30 .75
33 Dan Straily .15 .40
34 Roberto Clemente .60 1.50
35 Masahiro Tanaka RC .75 2.00
36 J.D. Martinez .25 .60
37 James Shields .15 .40
38 Bert Kreischer .15 .40
39 Jose Altuve .20 .50
240 Tony Cingrani .20 .50
241 Dave Portnoy .15 .40
242 Warren Spahn .20 .50
243 Hellen Keller .15 .40
244 Jake Marisnick RC .25 .60
245 Matt Harvey .20 .50
246 Dwight Gooden .15 .40
247 Billy Williams .20 .50
248 Mark Teixeira .20 .50
249 Aroldis Chapman .25 .60
250 Steve Cishek .15 .40
251 Jason Castro .15 .40
252 Didi Gregorius .20 .50
253 Rickey Henderson .25 .60
254 Maria Gabriela Isler .15 .40
255 Andre Rienzo RC .25 .60
256 Juan Marichal .20 .50
257 Adrian Beltre .25 .60
258 Ricky Nolasco .15 .40
259 Jim Calhoun .15 .40
260 Jay Bruce .20 .50
261 Duke Snider .20 .50
262 Mike Pereira .15 .40
263 Alfonso Soriano .20 .50
264 Mike Piazza .25 .60
265 Sam Calagione .15 .40
266 Prince Fielder .20 .50
267 Kevin Clancy .15 .40
268 Jarrod Parker .15 .40
269 Jose Abreu RC 2.00 5.00
270 Ryan Howard .20 .50
271 Chuck Klosterman .15 .40
272 Tim Raines .20 .50
273 Danielle Kang .15 .40
274 Justin Masterson .15 .40
275 Robinson Cano .20 .50
276 Samantha Briggs .15 .40
277 Trevor Rosenthal .20 .50
278 CC Sabathia .20 .50
279 Steve Carlton .20 .50
280 Whitey Ford .20 .50
281 Yoenis Cespedes .25 .60
282 Salvador Perez .20 .50
283 Gar Ryness .15 .40
284 Will Clark .20 .50
285 Carl Crawford .20 .50
286 Kris Medlen .20 .50
287 Chuck Zito .15 .40
288 Evan Longoria .20 .50
289 Kyle Seager .15 .40
290 Hanley Ramirez .20 .50
291 Aramis Ramirez .15 .40
292 Andre Dawson .20 .50
293 Manny Ramirez .25 .60
294 David Freese .15 .40
295 Ryan Braun .20 .50
296 Joey Votto .25 .60
297 Brian McCann .20 .50
298 Deion Sanders .20 .50
299 Enny Romero RC .25 .60
300 R.A. Dickey .20 .50
301 Matt Kemp SP .75 2.00
302 Polar Vortex SP .60 1.50
303 Ian Kinsler SP .75 2.00
304 Matt Cain SP .75 2.00
305 Jayson Werth SP .75 2.00
306 Hyun-Jin Ryu SP .75 2.00
307 Cliff Lee SP .75 2.00
308 Pedro Alvarez SP .60 1.50
309 Hunter Pence SP .75 2.00
310 Yonder Alonso SP .60 1.50
311 Anibal Sanchez SP .60 1.50
312 Mike Mussina SP .75 2.00
313 Juan Gonzalez SP .60 1.50
314 Nolan Arenado SP 1.25 3.00
315 Brandon Phillips SP .60 1.50
316 Ken Griffey Jr. SP 2.00 5.00
317 Paul Goldschmidt SP 1.00 2.50
318 Jason Kipnis SP .75 2.00
319 Sonny Gray SP .75 2.00
320 Christian Yelich SP 1.25 3.00
321 Adam Jones SP .75 2.00
322 Paul Konerko SP .75 2.00
323 Harmon Killebrew SP 1.00 2.50
324 Adam Wainwright SP .75 2.00
325 Darryl Strawberry SP .60 1.50
326 Mike Olt SP .60 1.50
327 Brett Lawrie SP .75 2.00
328 C.J. Wilson SP .60 1.50
329 Michael Wacha SP .75 2.00
330 Joe Kelly SP .60 1.50
331 Curtis Granderson SP .75 2.00
332 Victor Martinez SP .75 2.00
333 Stephen Strasburg SP 1.00 2.50
334 Erik Johnson SP RC .60 1.50
335 Elvis Andrus SP .75 2.00
336 Wily Peralta SP .60 1.50
337 Josh Donaldson SP .75 2.00
338 Andy Pettitte SP .75 2.00
339 Jeff Samardzija SP .60 1.50
340 Dennis Eckersley SP .75 2.00
341 Barbed Wire SP .60 1.50
342 Chris Davis SP .60 1.50
343 Phil Niekro SP .75 2.00
344 Jason Grilli SP .60 1.50
345 Yasiel Puig SP 1.00 2.50
346 Ivan Nova SP .75 2.00
347 Allen Craig SP .75 2.00
348 Billy Butler SP .60 1.50
349 John Smoltz SP 1.00 2.50
350 Manny Machado SP 1.00 2.50

2014 Topps Allen and Ginter Mini

*MINI 1-300: 1X TO 2.5X BASIC
*MINI 1-300 RC: .6X TO 1.5X BASIC RCs
*MINI SP 301-350: .6X TO 1.5X BASIC SP
MINI SP ODDS 1:13 HOBBY
351-400 RANDOM WITHIN RIP CARDS
STATED PLATE ODDS 1:412 HOBBY
PLATE PRINT RUN 1 SET PER COLOR
BLACK-CYAN-MAGENTA-YELLOW ISSUED
NO PLATE PRICING DUE TO SCARCITY
351 Mark McGwire EXT 50.00 100.00
352 Bob Gibson EXT 10.00 25.00
353 Jose Fernandez EXT 12.00 30.00
354 Nolan Ryan EXT 50.00 100.00
355 Mike Trout EXT 30.00 80.00
356 Adam Jones EXT 10.00 25.00
357 Bryce Harper EXT 20.00 50.00
358 Andrew McCutchen EXT 12.00 30.00
359 Jayson Werth EXT 10.00 25.00
360 Evan Longoria EXT 10.00 25.00
361 Tony Gwynn EXT 12.00 30.00
362 Robinson Cano EXT 10.00 25.00
363 Brooks Robinson EXT 10.00 25.00
364 Pedro Martinez EXT 10.00 25.00
365 Derek Jeter EXT 30.00 80.00
366 Jacoby Ellsbury EXT 10.00 25.00
367 Bo Jackson EXT 12.00 30.00
368 Clayton Kershaw EXT 25.00 60.00
369 Joey Votto EXT 12.00 30.00
370 Cliff Lee EXT 10.00 25.00
371 Buster Posey EXT 15.00 40.00
372 Cal Ripken Jr. EXT 50.00 100.00
373 Matt Carpenter EXT 12.00 30.00
374 David Ortiz EXT 12.00 30.00
375 Justin Verlander EXT 12.00 30.00
376 Miguel Cabrera EXT 20.00 50.00
377 Johnny Bench EXT 12.00 30.00
378 Roberto Clemente EXT 40.00 100.00
379 Max Scherzer EXT 12.00 30.00
380 Giancarlo Stanton EXT 12.00 30.00
381 Stephen Strasburg EXT 12.00 30.00
382 Chris Davis EXT 8.00 20.00
383 Hyun-Jin Ryu EXT 10.00 25.00
384 Paul Goldschmidt EXT 12.00 30.00
385 Jason Kipnis EXT 10.00 25.00
386 Jackie Robinson EXT 12.00 30.00
387 Carlos Gomez EXT 8.00 20.00
388 Dustin Pedroia EXT 12.00 30.00
389 Paul O'Neill EXT 10.00 25.00
390 Tom Seaver EXT 10.00 25.00
391 Yasiel Puig EXT 30.00 60.00
392 Ozzie Smith EXT 15.00 40.00
393 George Brett EXT 25.00 60.00
394 Yu Darvish EXT 12.00 30.00
395 Ken Griffey Jr. EXT 25.00 60.00
396 Troy Tulowitzki EXT 12.00 30.00
397 Darryl Strawberry EXT 8.00 20.00
398 Prince Fielder EXT 10.00 25.00
399 Matt Harvey EXT 10.00 25.00
400 Wil Myers EXT 8.00 20.00

2014 Topps Allen and Ginter Mini A and G Back

*A & G BACK: 1.2X TO 3X BASIC
*A & G BACK RCs: .75X TO 2X BASIC RCs
A & G BACK ODDS 1:5 HOBBY
*A & G BACK SP: .75X TO 2X BASIC SP
A & G BACK SP ODDS 1:65 HOBBY

2014 Topps Allen and Ginter Mini Black

*BLACK: 2X TO 5X BASIC
*BLACK RCs: 1.2X TO 3X BASIC RCs
BLACK ODDS 1:10 HOBBY
*BLACK SP: 1.2X TO 3X BASIC SP
BLACK SP ODDS 1:130 HOBBY

2014 Topps Allen and Ginter Mini Gold

*GOLD: 1.5X TO 4X BASIC
*GOLD RCs: 1X TO 2.5X BASIC RCs
*GOLD SP: 1X TO 2.5X BASIC SP
RANDOM INSERTS IN BACKS

2014 Topps Allen and Ginter Mini No Card Number

*NO NBR: 5X TO 12X BASIC
*NO NBR RCs: 3X TO 8X BASIC RCs
*NO NBR SP: 1.2X TO 3X BASIC SP
STATED ODDS 1:64 HOBBY
ANNC'D PRINT RUN OF 50 SETS
20 Babe Ruth 20.00 50.00
36 Yadier Molina 6.00 15.00
61 Bo Jackson 10.00 25.00
93 Willie Mays 15.00 40.00
127 Greg Maddux 10.00 25.00
129 Hank Aaron 10.00 25.00
145 Derek Jeter 20.00 50.00
147 Mark McGwire 10.00 25.00
159 George Brett 10.00 25.00
168 Miguel Cabrera 8.00 20.00
189 Clayton Kershaw 8.00 20.00
264 Mike Piazza 8.00 20.00
269 Jose Abreu 12.00 30.00
316 Ken Griffey Jr. 12.00 30.00

2014 Topps Allen and Ginter Mini Red

*RED: 12X TO 30X BASIC
*RED RCs: 8X TO 20X BASIC RCs
*RED SP: 5X TO 12X BASIC SP
STATED PRINT RUN 33 SER.#'d SETS
1 Roger Maris 12.00 30.00
20 Babe Ruth 40.00 100.00
36 Yadier Molina 12.00 30.00
53 Sandy Koufax 20.00 50.00
61 Bo Jackson 20.00 50.00
82 Jackie Robinson 15.00 40.00
93 Willie Mays 30.00 80.00
104 Troy Tulowitzki 10.00 25.00
121 Freddie Freeman 10.00 25.00
127 Greg Maddux 20.00 50.00
129 Hank Aaron 20.00 50.00
145 Derek Jeter 60.00 120.00
147 Mark McGwire 20.00 50.00
159 George Brett 20.00 50.00
168 Miguel Cabrera 15.00 40.00
186 Billy Hamilton 12.00 30.00
189 Clayton Kershaw 15.00 40.00
204 Albert Pujols 20.00 50.00
234 Roberto Clemente 20.00 50.00
264 Mike Piazza 15.00 40.00
313 Juan Gonzalez 10.00 25.00
316 Ken Griffey Jr. 60.00 150.00
345 Yasiel Puig 20.00 50.00

2014 Topps Allen and Ginter Air Supremacy

COMPLETE SET (20) 8.00 20.00
STATED ODDS 1:2 HOBBY
AS01 B-17 Bomber .60 1.50
AS02 F-22 Raptor .60 1.50
AS03 Supermarine Spitfire .60 1.50
AS04 P-51 Mustang .60 1.50
AS05 B-52 Stratofortress .60 1.50
AS06 AC-47 Spooky .60 1.50
AS07 F-16 Fighting Falcon .60 1.50
AS08 F/A-18 Hornet .60 1.50
AS09 Republic P-47 Thunderbolt .60 1.50
AS10 Sea Harrier FA2 .60 1.50
AS11 Sopwith Camel .60 1.50
AS12 F-86 Sabre .60 1.50
AS13 F-15C Eagle .60 1.50
AS14 EA-18G Growler .60 1.50
AS15 V-22 Osprey .60 1.50
AS16 Curtiss P-40 Warhawk .60 1.50
AS17 B-25 Mitchell Launch .60 1.50
AS18 MiG-15 .60 1.50
AS19 Hawker Hurricane .60 1.50
AS20 F-15 Eagle .60 1.50

2014 Topps Allen and Ginter Autographs

RANDOM INSERTS IN PACKS
AGFADM Doug McDermott 15.00 40.00

2014 Topps Allen and Ginter Box Topper Relics

STATED ODDS 1:110 HOBBY BOXES
STATED PRINT RUN 25 SER.#'d SETS
BLRAG Adrian Gonzalez 8.00 20.00
BLRAJ Adam Jones 15.00 40.00
BLRDW David Wright 15.00 40.00
BLRJG Juan Gonzalez 12.00 30.00
BLRMM Manny Machado 50.00 100.00
BLRMR Mariano Rivera 20.00 50.00
BLRMT Mike Trout 60.00 120.00
BLRPG Paul Goldschmidt 10.00 25.00
BLRSC Steve Carlton 15.00 40.00
BLRYP Yasiel Puig 10.00 25.00

2014 Topps Allen and Ginter Box Toppers

OVERALL ONE PER HOBBY BOX
BL01 Bo Jackson 2.50 6.00
BL02 Pedro Martinez 2.00 5.00
BL03 Wil Myers 1.50 4.00
BL04 Willie Mays 5.00 12.00
BL05 Mike Trout 6.00 15.00
BL06 Clayton Kershaw 5.00 12.00
BL07 Jose Canseco 2.00 5.00
BL08 Mark McGwire 5.00 12.00
BL09 Jose Abreu 6.00 15.00
BL10 Chris Davis 1.50 4.00
BL11 Bryce Harper 4.00 10.00
BL12 Albert Pujols 3.00 8.00
BL13 Andrew McCutchen 2.50 6.00
BL14 Miguel Cabrera 2.50 6.00
BL15 Jacoby Ellsbury 2.00 5.00

2014 Topps Allen and Ginter Coincidence

RANDOM INSERTS IN RETAIL PACKS
AGC01 Kennedy and Lincoln 4.00 10.00
AGC02 King Umberto and The Waiter from Monza 2.00 5.00
AGC03 1895 Car Crash in Ohio 2.00 5.00
AGC04 Hendrix and Handel were neighbors 2.00 5.00
AGC05 Hugh Williams: Sole Survivor 2.00 5.00
AGC06 RMS Carmania and SMS Cap Trafalgar 2.00 5.00
AGC07 Wilmer McLean and The Civil War 2.00 5.00
AGC08 Mark Twain and Halley's Comet 2.00 5.00
AGC09 Oregon newspaper predicts future lottery numbers 2.00 5.00
AGC10 Morgan Robertson: Novels predict future disasters 2.00 5.00
AGC11 4th of July: Jefferson, Adams, and Monroe 2.00 5.00

2014 Topps Allen and Ginter Double Rip Cards

STATED ODDS 1:714 HOBBY
PRINT RUNS B/WN 5-25 COPIES PER
NO PRICING ON QTY 10 OR LESS
PRICED WITH CLEANLY RIPPED BACKS
DRIP03 W.Myers/M.Trout/25 30.00 80.00
DRIP04 P.Corbin/W.Miley/25 5.00 12.00
DRIP06 T.Tulowitzki/C.Gonzalez/25 6.00 15.00
DRIP08 M.Trout/J.Fernandez/20 30.00 80.00
DRIP10 J.Segura/R.Braun/20 5.00 12.00
DRIP14 B.Hamilton/J.Morgan/20 5.00 12.00
DRIP15 Z.Wheeler/M.Harvey/25 5.00 12.00
DRIP20 McCutchen/Cole/20 6.00 15.00
DRIP23 Posey/Bumgarner/25 8.00 20.00
DRIP25 H.Iwakuma/H.Ryu/25 5.00 12.00
DRIP26 F.Hernandez/T.Walker/20 5.00 12.00
DRIP27 M.Wacha/S.Miller/20 5.00 12.00
DRIP28 Y.Molina/A.Wainwright/20 6.00 15.00
DRIP29 M.Moore/D.Price/20 5.00 12.00
DRIP30 E.Longoria/D.Wright/25 5.00 12.00
DRIP32 F.Freeman/J.Teheran/15 8.00 20.00
DRIP33 J.Reyes/J.Bautista/25 5.00 12.00
DRIP35 G.Gonzalez/J.Zimmermann/15 5.00 12.00
DRIP38 H.Iwakuma/Y.Darvish/15 6.00 15.00
DRIP40 C.Davis/A.Jones/15 5.00 12.00
DRIP44 J.Upton/J.Heyward/15 5.00 12.00
DRIP56 J.Teheran/K.Medlen/15 5.00 12.00
DRIP60 J.Lake/S.Castro/15 4.00 10.00
DRIP66 T.Cingrani/J.Cueto/15 5.00 12.00

2014 Topps Allen and Ginter Festivals and Fairs

COMPLETE SET (10) 3.00 8.00
STATED ODDS 1:2 HOBBY
FAF01 La Tomatina .40 1.00
FAF02 Carnivale .40 1.00
FAF03 Mardi Gras .40 1.00
FAF04 Holi Festival .40 1.00
FAF05 Pingxi Lantern Festival .40 1.00
FAF06 Songkran Water Festival .40 1.00
FAF07 San Fermin Festival .40 1.00
FAF08 Dia de los Muertos .40 1.00
FAF09 Diwali Festival of Lights .40 1.00
FAF10 Junkanoo .40 1.00

2014 Topps Allen and Ginter Fields of Yore

COMPLETE SET (10) 6.00 15.00
STATED ODDS 1:2 HOBBY
FOY01 Ebbets Field .75 2.00
FOY02 Cleveland Municipal Stadium .75 2.00
FOY03 Griffith Stadium .75 2.00
FOY04 Metropolitan Stadium .75 2.00
FOY05 Wrigley Field .75 2.00
FOY06 Yankee Stadium .75 2.00
FOY07 Tiger Stadium .75 2.00
FOY08 Sportsman's Park .75 2.00
FOY09 Astrodome .75 2.00
FOY10 Shea Stadium .75 2.00

2014 Topps Allen and Ginter Fields of Yore Relics

STATED ODDS 1:900 HOBBY
STATED PRINT RUN 250 SER.#'d SETS
FOYRCS Cleveland Municipal Stadium 10.00 25.00
FOYRGS Griffith Stadium 10.00 25.00
FOYRMS Metropolitan Stadium 10.00 25.00
FOYRSP Sportsman's Park 10.00 25.00
FOYRWS Wrigley Field 15.00 40.00

2014 Topps Allen and Ginter Framed Mini Autographs

STATED ODDS 1:52 HOBBY
EXCHANGE DEADLINE 6/30/2017
AGAABO Anthony Bourdain 30.00 80.00
AGAAC Allen Craig 5.00 12.00
AGAAE Adam Eaton 6.00 15.00
AGAAF Allyson Felix 25.00 60.00
AGAAL Andrew Lambo 4.00 10.00
AGAARI Andre Rienzo 4.00 10.00
AGAARO Anthony Robles 6.00 15.00
AGAAS Adam Schefter 6.00 15.00
AGAAWI Austin Wierschke 5.00 12.00
AGABBU Bill Buckner 8.00 20.00
AGABJ Bo Jackson 90.00 150.00
AGABK Bert Kreischer 5.00 12.00
AGABR Bill Rancic 4.00 10.00
AGACA Chris Archer 4.00 10.00
AGACB Craig Biggio 50.00 120.00
AGACKE Casey Kelly 5.00 12.00
AGACKL Chuck Klosterman 12.00 30.00
AGACKR Clayton Kershaw 90.00 150.00
AGACL Carli Lloyd 25.00 60.00
AGACT Chuck Todd 10.00 25.00
AGACY Christian Yelich 20.00 50.00
AGACZ Chuck Zito 10.00 25.00
AGADG Didi Gregorius 5.00 12.00
AGADK Danielle Kang 8.00 20.00
AGADME Devin Mesoraco 10.00 25.00
AGADN Diana Nyad 8.00 20.00
AGADO Daniel Okrent 8.00 20.00
AGADPO David Portnoy 10.00 25.00
AGADR Darin Ruf 5.00 12.00
AGADST Dan Straily 4.00 10.00
AGADW David Wright 90.00 150.00
AGAEB Erin Brady 10.00 25.00
AGAFD Felix Doubront 4.00 10.00
AGAFDA Felicia Day 12.00 30.00
AGAGI Maria Gabriela Isler 15.00 40.00
AGAGR Gar Ryness 6.00 15.00
AGAGSP George Springer 15.00 40.00
AGAGW Glen Waggoner 6.00 15.00
AGAHS Hector Santiago 4.00 10.00
AGAJA Jose Abreu 200.00 300.00
AGAJAN Dr. James Andrews 15.00 40.00
AGAJB Jordan Burroughs 15.00 40.00
AGAJCA Jose Canseco 60.00 120.00
AGAJCL Jim Calhoun 8.00 20.00
AGAJD Jenny Dell 15.00 40.00
AGAJFR Judah Friedlander 5.00 12.00
AGAJGO Juan Gonzalez 20.00 50.00
AGAJGR Jason Grilli 6.00 15.00
AGAJGY Jedd Gyorko 4.00 10.00
AGAJKE Joe Kelly 4.00 10.00
AGAJKI Jason Kipnis 8.00 20.00
AGAJMA Jake Marisnick 4.00 10.00
AGAJO Jordan Oliver 12.00 30.00
AGAJSC Jonathan Schoop 4.00 10.00
AGAJSE Jean Segura 5.00 12.00
AGAKC Kevin Clancy 10.00 25.00
AGAKSM Kevin Smith 30.00 80.00
AGAKW Kolten Wong 10.00 25.00
AGALB Lou Brock 100.00 175.00
AGALK Larry King 15.00 40.00
AGALP Laura Phelps Sweatt 4.00 10.00
AGAMA Matt Adams 8.00 20.00
AGAMB Matt Besser 6.00 15.00
AGAMD Matt Davidson 5.00 12.00
AGAME Michael Elsner 8.00 20.00
AGAMMC Mark McGwire 150.00 300.00
AGAMO Mike Olt 4.00 10.00
AGAMPE Mike Pereira 8.00 20.00
AGAMRO Mark Roth 8.00 20.00
AGAMTR Mike Trout 250.00 350.00
AGAMW Michael Wacha 12.00 30.00
AGAMZ Mike Zunino 8.00 20.00
AGANC Nick Castellanos 15.00 40.00
AGANG Nomar Garciaparra 90.00 150.00
AGAOH Orlando Hernandez 15.00 40.00
AGAPG Paul Goldschmidt 20.00 50.00
AGARR Ryan Riess 6.00 15.00
AGASB Samantha Briggs 6.00 15.00
AGASCA Steve Carlton 60.00 120.00
AGASCI Steve Cishek 4.00 10.00
AGASCL Sam Calagione 10.00 25.00
AGASD Steve Delabar 4.00 10.00
AGASDO Snoop Lion 75.00 200.00
AGASG Sonny Gray 10.00 25.00
AGASMI Shelby Miller 5.00 12.00
AGASN Shabazz Napier 10.00 25.00
AGATC Tony Cingrani 5.00 12.00
AGATD Travis d'Arnaud 12.00 30.00
AGATFO Tanner Foust 4.00 10.00
AGATSH The Iron Sheik 20.00 50.00
AGATW Taijuan Walker 10.00 25.00
AGAVG Vince Gilligan 40.00 80.00
AGAWF Wilmer Flores 5.00 12.00
AGAWMD Will Middlebrooks 10.00 25.00
AGAWMY Wil Myers 12.00 30.00
AGAWP Wily Peralta 4.00 10.00
AGAXB Xander Bogaerts 12.00 30.00

2014 Topps Allen and Ginter Framed Mini Topps Employee Autographs

STATED ODDS 1:7800 HOBBY
EEAAC Arvin Catriz 40.00 100.00
EEAAK Ann Marie Klebon 40.00 100.00
EEAAS Ari Simer 40.00 100.00
EEAET Evan Tanelli 40.00 100.00
EEAJB Jason Berger 40.00 100.00
EEAJS Jon Sprance 40.00 100.00
EEALL Lance Lubin 40.00 100.00
EEASR Sam Roberts 40.00 100.00
EEAVC Vincent Carbellano 40.00 100.00
EEAMSM Michelle Smith 40.00 100.00

2014 Topps Allen and Ginter Jumbo Relics

FSJRVG V.Gilligan Storyboard 75.00 150.00

2014 Topps Allen and Ginter Landmarks and Monuments Cabinet Box Toppers

ONE TOPPER PER HOBBY BOX
LMC01 Jefferson Memorial 2.00 5.00
LMC02 Mount Rushmore 2.00 5.00
LMC03 Washington Monument 2.00 5.00
LMC04 Lincoln Memorial 2.00 5.00
LMC05 Yosemite Falls 2.00 5.00
LMC06 Statue of Liberty 2.00 5.00
LMC07 One World Trade Center 2.00 5.00
LMC08 The U.S. Capitol 2.00 5.00
LMC09 The Liberty Bell 2.00 5.00
LMC10 World War II Memorial 2.00 5.00

2014 Topps Allen and Ginter Mini Athletic Endeavors

STATED ODDS 1:288 HOBBY
AE01 Shovel Racing 6.00 15.00
AE02 Wife Carrying Championship 6.00 15.00
AE03 Rock Paper Scissors 6.00 15.00
AE04 Royal Shrovetide Football 6.00 15.00
AE05 Cheese Rolling 6.00 15.00
AE06 Poohsticks 6.00 15.00
AE07 Chess Boxing 6.00 15.00
AE08 Caber Toss 6.00 15.00
AE09 Sack Races 6.00 15.00
AE10 Roller Derby 6.00 15.00

2014 Topps Allen and Ginter Mini Framed Relics

GROUP A ODDS 1:174 HOBBY
GROUP B ODDS 1:175 HOBBY
RAABC Adrian Beltre A 4.00 10.00
RAAJ Adam Jones A 3.00 8.00
RAAP Andy Pettitte A 5.00 12.00
RAARI Anthony Rizzo A 8.00 20.00
RABH Billy Hamilton A 3.00 8.00
RABPO Buster Posey A 5.00 12.00
RABR Brooks Robinson A 30.00 80.00
RACK Clayton Kershaw A 4.00 10.00
RACKI Craig Kimbrel A 3.00 8.00
RACL Cliff Lee A 3.00 8.00
RADM Don Mattingly A 20.00 50.00
RAEA Elvis Andrus A 3.00 8.00
RAGG Gio Gonzalez A 3.00 8.00
RAHA Hank Aaron A 150.00 250.00
RAHI Hisashi Iwakuma A 3.00 8.00
RAHK Harmon Killebrew A 20.00 50.00
RAHR Hanley Ramirez A 3.00 8.00
RAID Ian Desmond A 2.50 6.00
RAJDI Joe DiMaggio A 90.00 150.00
RAJH Josh Hamilton A 3.00 8.00
RAJR Jackie Robinson A 50.00 120.00
RAJSE Jean Segura A 3.00 8.00
RAMMO Matt Moore A 3.00 8.00
RAMS Max Scherzer A 4.00 10.00
RAPO Paul O'Neill A 6.00 15.00
RARZ Ryan Zimmerman A 3.00 8.00
RASK Sandy Koufax A 60.00 150.00
RASS Stephen Strasburg A 4.00 10.00
RAWB Wade Boggs A 40.00 80.00
RBAR Alex Rodriguez B 15.00 40.00
RBBH Bryce Harper B 15.00 40.00
RBCGN Carlos Gonzalez B 3.00 8.00
RBDJ Derek Jeter B 30.00 60.00
RBDO David Ortiz B 4.00 10.00
RBDPR David Price B 3.00 8.00
RBEE Edwin Encarnacion B 4.00 10.00
RBEL Evan Longoria B 3.00 8.00
RBFF Freddie Freeman B 5.00 12.00
RBFH Felix Hernandez B 3.00 8.00
RBJBR Jay Bruce B 3.00 8.00
RBJH Jason Heyward B 3.00 8.00
RBJRI Jim Rice B 10.00 25.00
RBJVO Joey Votto B 4.00 10.00
RBJZ Jordan Zimmermann B 3.00 8.00
RBKS Kyle Seager B 2.50 6.00
RBMCI Matt Cain B 3.00 8.00
RBMTR Mike Trout B 15.00 40.00
RBMTU Mark Trumbo B 2.50 6.00
RBPF Prince Fielder B 3.00 8.00
RBRB Ryan Braun B 3.00 8.00
RBRCE Roberto Clemente B 75.00 150.00
RBRCR Rod Carew B 10.00 25.00
RBTG Tony Gwynn B 15.00 40.00
RBTT Troy Tulowitzki B 4.00 10.00
RBYD Yu Darvish B 4.00 10.00
RBYM Yadier Molina B 8.00 20.00
RBYP Yasiel Puig B 10.00 25.00
RBZWH Zack Wheeler B 3.00 8.00

2014 Topps Allen and Ginter Mini Into the Unknown

COMPLETE SET (16) 8.00 20.00
STATED ODDS 1:5 HOBBY
ITU01 Christopher Columbus 1.00 2.50
ITU02 Ferdinand Magellan 1.00 2.50
ITU03 Vasco da Gama 1.00 2.50
ITU04 Leif Ericson 1.00 2.50
ITU05 John C. Fremont 1.00 2.50
ITU06 Vitus Bering 1.00 2.50
ITU07 Louis Hennepin 1.00 2.50
ITU08 Henry Hudson 1.00 2.50
ITU09 Pedro Teixeira 1.00 2.50
ITU10 Marco Polo 1.00 2.50
ITU11 Francisco Pizarro 1.00 2.50
ITU12 Lewis and Clark 1.00 2.50
ITU13 Amerigo Vespucci 1.00 2.50
ITU14 John Cabot 1.00 2.50
ITU15 Jacques Marquette 1.00 2.50
ITU16 Hernan Cortes 1.00 2.50

2014 Topps Allen and Ginter Mini Larger Than Life

COMPLETE SET (11) 8.00 20.00
STATED ODDS 1:5 HOBBY
LTL01 Paul Bunyan 1.00 2.50
LTL03 Casey Jones 1.00 2.50
LTL04 John Henry 1.00 2.50
LTL05 Rip Van Winkle 1.00 2.50
LTL06 Johnny Appleseed 1.00 2.50
LTL07 Davy Crockett 1.00 2.50
LTL08 Giacomo Casanova 1.00 2.50
LTL09 William Tell 1.00 2.50
LTL10 Hiawatha 1.00 2.50
LTL11 Sasquatch 1.00 2.50
LTL12 Pocahontas 1.00 2.50

2014 Topps Allen and Ginter Mini Little Lions

COMPLETE SET (16) 15.00 40.00
STATED ODDS 1:5 HOBBY
LL01 Persian Cat 1.25 3.00
LL02 Japanese Bobtail 1.25 3.00
LL03 American Shorthair 1.25 3.00
LL04 Siamese 1.25 3.00
LL05 Cornish Rex 1.25 3.00
LL06 Maine Coon 1.25 3.00
LL07 Oriental Bicolor 1.25 3.00
LL08 Russian Blue 1.25 3.00
LL09 Sphynx 1.25 3.00
LL10 Savannah 1.25 3.00
LL11 Scottish Fold 1.25 3.00
LL12 Norwegian Forest Cat 1.25 3.00
LL13 Exotic 1.25 3.00
LL14 Birman 1.25 3.00
LL15 Abyssinian 1.25 3.00
LL16 Turkish Van 1.25 3.00

2014 Topps Allen and Ginter Mini Urban Fauna

STATED ODDS 1:288 HOBBY
UF01 Sciurus Carolinensis 5.00 12.00
UF02 Periplaneta Americana 5.00 12.00
UF03 Procyon Lotor 5.00 12.00
UF04 Didelphis Virginiana 5.00 12.00
UF05 Anolis Equestris 5.00 12.00
UF06 Tadarida brasiliensis 5.00 12.00
UF07 Mephitis Mephitis 5.00 12.00
UF08 Lymantria Dispar Dispar 5.00 12.00
UF09 Rattus Norvegicus 5.00 12.00
UF10 Columba Livia 5.00 12.00

2014 Topps Allen and Ginter Mini Where Nature Ends

STATED ODDS 1:5 MINI
WNE01 Leonardo da Vinci 1.00 2.50
WNE02 Michelangelo 1.00 2.50
WNE03 Donatello 1.00 2.50
WNE04 Raphael 1.00 2.50
WNE05 Rembrandt van Rijn 1.00 2.50
WNE06 Masaccio 1.00 2.50
WNE07 Vincent van Gogh 1.00 2.50
WNE08 Edgar Degas 1.00 2.50
WNE09 Sandro Botticelli 1.00 2.50
WNE10 John Trumbull 1.00 2.50
WNE11 Gilbert Stuart 1.00 2.50
WNE12 Francisco de Goya 1.00 2.50
WNE13 Martin Johnson Heade 1.00 2.50
WNE14 Winslow Homer 1.00 2.50
WNE15 James Whistler 1.00 2.50
WNE16 Pieter Bruegel 1.00 2.50
WNE17 Diego Velazquez 1.00 2.50
WNE18 Albrecht Durer 1.00 2.50
WNE19 Edouard Manet 1.00 2.50
WNE20 Paul Cezanne 1.00 2.50
WNE21 Giotto di Bondone 1.00 2.50
WNE22 Claude Monet 1.00 2.50
WNE23 J.M.W. Turner 1.00 2.50
WNE24 Paul Gauguin 1.00 2.50
WNE25 William Blake 1.00 2.50
WNE26 Jan Vermeer 1.00 2.50

2014 Topps Allen and Ginter Mini World's Deadliest Predators

COMPLETE SET (22) 15.00 40.00
STATED ODDS 1:5 HOBBY
WDP01 Polar Bear 1.00 2.50
WDP02 Hippopotamus 1.00 2.50
WDP03 Blue-Ringed Octopus 1.00 2.50
WDP04 Lonomia 1.00 2.50
WDP05 Great White Shark 1.00 2.50
WDP06 African Lion 1.00 2.50
WDP07 Black Mamba 1.00 2.50
WDP08 Cape Buffalo 1.00 2.50
WDP09 Poison Dart Frog 1.00 2.50
WDP10 Hyena 1.00 2.50
WDP11 Komodo Dragon 1.00 2.50
WDP12 Clouded Leopard 1.00 2.50
WDP13 Brazilian Wandering Spider 1.00 2.50
WDP14 Saltwater Crocodile 1.00 2.50
WDP15 American Alligator 1.00 2.50
WDP16 Piranha 1.00 2.50
WDP17 Black Eagle 1.00 2.50
WDP18 Gray Wolf 1.00 2.50
WDP19 Wolverine 1.00 2.50
WDP20 Honey Badger 1.00 2.50
WDP21 Australian Box Jellyfish 1.00 2.50
WDP22 Cone Snail 1.00 2.50

2014 Topps Allen and Ginter National Convention Mini

NCCSAB Albert Belle 2.50 6.00
NCCSBF Bob Feller 3.00 8.00
NCCSDJ Derek Jeter 6.00 15.00
NCCSJA Jose Abreu 8.00 20.00
NCCSMT Masahiro Tanaka 6.00 15.00
NCCSMT Mike Trout 4.00 10.00

2014 Topps Allen and Ginter Natural Wonders

COMPLETE SET (20) 6.00 15.00
STATED ODDS 1:2 HOBBY
NW01 The Blue Hole .40 1.00
NW02 The Shilin Stone Forest .40 1.00
NW03 Cave of Crystals .40 1.00
NW04 Iguazu Falls .40 1.00
NW05 Door to Hell .40 1.00
NW06 Puerto Princesa Subterranean River .40 1.00
NW07 Table Mountain .40 1.00
NW08 Ha Long Bay .40 1.00
NW09 Marble Caves .40 1.00
NW10 Lake Retba .40 1.00
NW11 Travertine Pools .40 1.00
NW12 Sailing Stones of Racetrack Playa .40 1.00
NW13 Moeraki Boulders .40 1.00
NW14 Half Dome .40 1.00
NW15 Giant's Causeway .40 1.00
NW16 The Wave at Coyote Buttes .40 1.00
NW17 Luray Caverns .40 1.00
NW18 Socotra Archipelago .40 1.00
NW19 McWay Falls .40 1.00
NW20 Punalu'u Beach .40 1.00

2014 Topps Allen and Ginter Oddity Relics

STATED ODDS 1:51,250 HOBBY
STATED PRINT RUN 25 SER.#'d SETS
AGOR01 Daniel Nava 125.00 250.00

2014 Topps Allen and Ginter Mini Outlaws, Bandits and All-Around Neer Do Wells

COMPLETE SET (11) 10.00 25.00
STATED ODDS 1:5 HOBBY
OBA01 Robin Hood 1.25 3.00
OBA02 Jesse James 1.25 3.00
OBA03 Billy the Kid 1.25 3.00
OBA04 Butch Cassidy 1.25 3.00
OBA05 Juro Janosik 1.25 3.00
OBA06 Bonnie and Clyde 1.25 3.00
OBA07 William Kidd 1.25 3.00
OBA08 Edward Blackbeard Teach 1.25 3.00
OBA09 Jean Lafitte 1.25 3.00
OBA10 Ishikawa Goemon 1.25 3.00
OBA11 Ned Kelly 1.25 3.00

2014 Topps Allen and Ginter Oversized Reprint Cabinet Box Toppers

OVERALL ONE PER HOBBY BOX
ORCBLBH Bryce Harper 3.00 8.00
ORCBLJR Jackie Robinson 2.00 5.00
ORCBLMC Miguel Cabrera 2.00 5.00
ORCBLMT Mike Trout 5.00 12.00
ORCBLNR Nolan Ryan 5.00 12.00
ORCBLRC Roberto Clemente 5.00 12.00
ORCBLSK Sandy Koufax 4.00 10.00
ORCBLSS Stephen Strasburg 2.00 5.00
ORCBLWM Wil Myers 1.25 3.00
ORCBLYP Yasiel Puig 2.00 5.00

2014 Topps Allen and Ginter Pop Star Relics

STATED ODDS 1:4475 HOBBY
STATED PRINT RUN 25 SER.#'d SETS
PSRAP Albert Pujols 15.00 40.00
PSRBH Bryce Harper 20.00 50.00
PSRCK Clayton Kershaw 60.00 150.00
PSRDO David Ortiz 10.00 25.00
PSRDW David Wright 25.00 60.00
PSRMT Mike Trout 90.00 150.00
PSRPF Prince Fielder 10.00 25.00
PSRRC Robinson Cano 10.00 25.00
PSRYD Yu Darvish 25.00 60.00
PSRYP Yasiel Puig 12.00 30.00

2014 Topps Allen and Ginter Relics

GROUP A ODDS 1:24 HOBBY
GROUP B ODDS 1:24 HOBBY
FRBAA Alex Avila B 3.00 8.00
FRBAC Allen Craig B 3.00 8.00
FRBAF Allyson Felix B 5.00 12.00
FRBAJ Adam Jones B 3.00 8.00
FRBAR Anthony Rizzo B 6.00 15.00
FRBARO Anthony Robles B 2.50 6.00
FRBAS Adam Schefter B 2.50 6.00
FRBCB Carlos Beltran B 3.00 8.00
FRBCBU Clay Buchholz B 2.50 6.00
FRBCG Carlos Gonzalez B 3.00 8.00
FRBCGO Carlos Gomez B 2.50 6.00
FRBCK Clayton Kershaw B 8.00 20.00
FRBCKL Chuck Klosterman B 2.50 6.00
FRBCL Cliff Lee B 3.00 8.00
FRBCS Chris Sale B 4.00 10.00
FRBCT Chuck Todd B 4.00 10.00
FRBDB Domonic Brown B 3.00 8.00
FRBDP David Price B 3.00 8.00
FRBDPE Dustin Pedroia B 5.00 12.00
FRBDPO Dave Portnoy B 4.00 10.00
FRBEA Elvis Andrus B 3.00 8.00
FRBEE Edwin Encarnacion B 4.00 10.00
FRBFH Felix Hernandez B 3.00 8.00
FRBGB Grant Balfour B 2.50 6.00
FRBGW Glen Waggoner B 2.50 6.00
FRBID Ian Desmond B 2.50 6.00
FRBJB Jay Bruce B 3.00 8.00
FRBJF Jose Fernandez B 4.00 10.00
FRBJFR Judah Friedlander B 2.50 6.00
FRBJV Joey Votto B 4.00 10.00
FRBKS Kevin Smith B 5.00 12.00
FRBLK Larry King B 10.00 25.00
FRBME Michael Eisner B 5.00 12.00
FRBMM Matt Moore B 3.00 8.00
FRBMR Mark Roth B 2.50 6.00
FRBPA Pedro Alvarez B 2.50 6.00
FRBRB Ryan Braun B 3.00 8.00
FRBRR Ryan Riess B 2.50 6.00
FRBSC Sam Calagione B 2.50 6.00
FRBSL Snoop Lion B 5.00 12.00
FRBSM Starling Marte B 3.00 8.00
FRBTG Tony Gwynn B 8.00 20.00
FRBTT Troy Tulowitzki B 4.00 10.00
FRBYD Yu Darvish B 4.00 10.00
FRBYM Yadier Molina B 4.00 10.00
FRBZG Zack Greinke B 3.00 8.00
FRBZW Zack Wheeler B 3.00 8.00
FSRAB Adrian Beltre A 4.00 10.00
FSRABO Anthony Bourdain A 5.00 12.00
FSRAC Aroldis Chapman A 4.00 10.00
FSRAD Andre Dawson A 6.00 15.00
FSRAG Adrian Gonzalez A 3.00 8.00
FSRAM Andrew McCutchen A 4.00 10.00
FSRAP Andy Pettitte A 3.00 8.00
FSRARO Alex Rodriguez A 4.00 10.00
FSRAW Austin Wierschke A 2.50 6.00
FSRBH Bryce Harper A 8.00 20.00
FSRBK Bert Kreischer A 2.50 6.00
FSRBM Brian McCann A 3.00 8.00
FSRBP Buster Posey A 5.00 12.00
FSRCH Cole Hamels A 3.00 8.00
FSRCKI Craig Kimbrel A 3.00 8.00
FSRCS CC Sabathia A 3.00 8.00
FSRCZ Chuck Zito A 2.50 6.00
FSRDA Dr. James Andrews A 5.00 12.00
FSRDJ Derek Jeter A 10.00 25.00
FSRDK Danielle Kang A 3.00 8.00
FSRDO David Ortiz A 4.00 10.00
FSRDOK Daniel Okrent A 4.00 10.00
FSREB Erin Brady A 4.00 10.00
FSREL Evan Longoria A 3.00 8.00
FSRFD Felicia Day A 5.00 12.00
FSRFF Freddie Freeman A 5.00 12.00
FSRGC Gerrit Cole A 4.00 10.00
FSRGI Maria Gabriela Isler A 4.00 10.00
FSRIS The Iron Sheik A 5.00 12.00
FSRJB Jose Bautista A 3.00 8.00
FSRJH Jason Heyward A 3.00 8.00
FSRJS Jean Segura A 3.00 8.00
FSRJZ Jordan Zimmermann A 3.00 8.00
FSRKC Kevin Clancy A 2.50 6.00
FSRKS Kyle Seager A 2.50 6.00
FSRLP Laura Phelps Sweatt A 2.50 6.00
FSRMA Matt Adams A 2.50 6.00
FSRMB Madison Bumgarner A 6.00 15.00
FSRMBE Matt Besser A 2.50 6.00
FSRMC Miguel Cabrera A 6.00 15.00
FSRMCA Matt Cain A 3.00 8.00
FSRMCR Matt Carpenter A 4.00 10.00
FSRMH Matt Harvey A 3.00 8.00
FSRMK Matt Kemp A 3.00 8.00
FSRMP Mike Pereira A 2.50 6.00
FSRMT Mike Trout A 10.00 25.00
FSRMTA Masahiro Tanaka A 15.00 40.00
FSRPF Prince Fielder A 3.00 8.00
FSRRC Robinson Cano A 3.00 8.00
FSRRZ Ryan Zimmerman A 3.00 8.00
FSRTF Tanner Foust A 2.50 6.00
FSRYP Yasiel Puig A 4.00 10.00

2014 Topps Allen and Ginter Rip Cards Ripped

STATED ODDS 1:178 HOBBY
PRINT RUNS B/WN 5-75 COPIES PER
NO PRICING ON QTY 10 OR LESS
PRICED WITH CLEANLY RIPPED BACKS
RIP01 Mike Trout/25 30.00 80.00
RIP02 Jered Weaver/75 5.00 12.00
RIP03 Paul Goldschmidt/50 6.00 15.00
RIP04 Freddie Freeman/75 8.00 20.00
RIP05 Julio Teheran/75 5.00 12.00
RIP06 Craig Kimbrel/50 5.00 12.00
RIP07 Chris Davis/50 4.00 10.00
RIP08 Manny Machado/50 6.00 15.00
RIP09 Xander Bogaerts/50 12.00 30.00
RIP10 Dustin Pedroia/50 6.00 15.00
RIP11 David Ortiz/25 6.00 15.00
RIP12 Starlin Castro/75 4.00 10.00
RIP13 Anthony Rizzo/75 10.00 25.00
RIP14 Chris Sale/75 6.00 15.00
RIP15 Shin-Soo Choo/75 5.00 12.00
RIP16 Brandon Phillips/75 4.00 10.00
RIP17 Joey Votto/50 6.00 15.00
RIP18 Justin Masterson/75 4.00 10.00
RIP19 Carlos Santana/50 5.00 12.00
RIP20 Carlos Gonzalez/50 5.00 12.00
RIP21 Troy Tulowitzki/50 6.00 15.00
RIP22 Billy Hamilton/50 5.00 12.00
RIP23 Miguel Cabrera/25 6.00 15.00
RIP24 Prince Fielder/50 5.00 12.00
RIP25 Justin Verlander/25 6.00 15.00
RIP26 Jose Altuve/75 5.00 12.00
RIP27 James Shields/75 4.00 10.00
RIP29 Yasiel Puig/50 6.00 15.00
RIP30 Clayton Kershaw/25 12.00 30.00
RIP31 Hyun-Jin Ryu/75 5.00 12.00
RIP32 Giancarlo Stanton/50 6.00 15.00
RIP33 Jose Fernandez/50 6.00 15.00
RIP34 Jean Segura/75 5.00 12.00
RIP35 Ryan Braun/50 5.00 12.00
RIP36 Joe Mauer/75 5.00 12.00
RIP37 David Wright/25 5.00 12.00
RIP38 Matt Harvey/50 5.00 12.00
RIP39 Robinson Cano/50 5.00 12.00
RIP40 Derek Jeter/25 15.00 40.00
RIP41 CC Sabathia/25 5.00 12.00
RIP42 Alex Rodriguez/25 8.00 20.00
RIP43 Yoenis Cespedes/50 6.00 15.00
RIP44 Chase Utley/50 5.00 12.00
RIP45 Cliff Lee/75 5.00 12.00
RIP46 Jedd Gyorko/75 4.00 10.00
RIP47 Pablo Sandoval/50 5.00 12.00
RIP48 Buster Posey/25 8.00 20.00
RIP49 Madison Bumgarner/75 5.00 12.00
RIP50 Felix Hernandez/50 5.00 12.00
RIP51 Hisashi Iwakuma/50 5.00 12.00
RIP52 Allen Craig/75 5.00 12.00
RIP53 Shelby Miller/75 5.00 12.00
RIP54 Wil Myers/50 4.00 10.00
RIP55 Evan Longoria/25 5.00 12.00
RIP56 David Price/50 5.00 12.00
RIP57 Adrian Beltre/50 6.00 15.00
RIP58 Yu Darvish/25 6.00 15.00
RIP59 Jose Reyes/25 5.00 12.00
RIP60 Jose Bautista/25 5.00 12.00
RIP62 Stephen Strasburg/25 6.00 15.00
RIP63 Gio Gonzalez/75 5.00 12.00
RIP65 Gerrit Cole/50 6.00 15.00
RIP66 Taijuan Walker/50 4.00 10.00
RIP67 Travis d'Arnaud/50 5.00 12.00
RIP68 Nick Castellanos/50 12.00 30.00
RIP71 George Brett/25 12.00 30.00
RIP80 Mike Schmidt/25 10.00 25.00
RIP92 Darryl Strawberry/25 4.00 10.00
RIP95 John Smoltz/25 6.00 15.00
RIP96 Dwight Gooden/25 4.00 10.00

2014 Topps Allen and Ginter The Amateur Osteologist

STATED ODDS 1:6600 HOBBY
EXCHANGE DEADLINE 7/31/2015
01 Amateur Osteologist EXCH 75.00 150.00

2014 Topps Allen and Ginter The Pastime's Pastime

COMPLETE SET (100) 20.00 50.00
STATED ODDS 1:2 HOBBY
PPAB Adrian Beltre .40 1.00
PPAC Allen Craig .30 .75
PPAJ Adam Jones .30 .75
PPAK Al Kaline .40 1.00
PPAM Andrew McCutchen .40 1.00
PPAP Albert Pujols .50 1.25
PPAR Anthony Rizzo .60 1.50
PPAW Adam Wainwright .30 .75
PPBG Bob Gibson .30 .75
PPBH Bryce Harper .60 1.50
PPBR Babe Ruth 1.00 2.50
PPCB Clay Buchholz .25 .60
PPCC CC Sabathia .30 .75
PPCD Chris Davis .25 .60
PPCG Carlos Gonzalez .30 .75
PPCH Cole Hamels .30 .75
PPCK Clayton Kershaw .75 2.00
PPCR Cal Ripken Jr. 1.25 3.00
PPCS Chris Sale .40 1.00
PPCU Chase Utley .30 .75
PPDB Domonic Brown .30 .75
PPDG Dwight Gooden .25 .60
PPDJ Derek Jeter 1.00 2.50
PPDM Don Mattingly .75 2.00
PPDO David Ortiz .40 1.00
PPDP Dustin Pedroia .40 1.00
PPDW David Wright .30 .75
PPEB Ernie Banks .40 1.00
PPEL Evan Longoria .30 .75
PPFF Freddie Freeman .50 1.25
PPFH Felix Hernandez .30 .75
PPGC Gerrit Cole .40 1.00
PPGG Gio Gonzalez .30 .75
PPGS Giancarlo Stanton .40 1.00
PPHA Hank Aaron .75 2.00
PPHI Hisashi Iwakuma .30 .75
PPHK Harmon Killebrew .40 1.00
PPHR Hyun-Jin Ryu .30 .75
PPJA Jose Altuve .30 .75
PPJB Jose Bautista .30 .75
PPJE Jacoby Ellsbury .30 .75
PPJF Jose Fernandez .40 1.00
PPJG Jedd Gyorko .25 .60
PPJK Jason Kipnis .30 .75
PPJM Justin Masterson .25 .60
PPJR Jose Reyes .30 .75
PPJS James Shields .25 .60
PPJT Julio Teheran .30 .75
PPJU Justin Upton .30 .75
PPJV Joey Votto .40 1.00
PPJW Jered Weaver .30 .75
PPJZ Jordan Zimmermann .30 .75
PPKG Ken Griffey Jr. .75 2.00
PPLB Lou Brock .30 .75
PPLG Lou Gehrig .75 2.00
PPMB Madison Bumgarner .30 .75
PPMC Miguel Cabrera .40 1.00
PPMH Matt Harvey .30 .75
PPMM Manny Machado .40 1.00
PPMS Max Scherzer .40 1.00
PPMT Mike Trout 2.00 5.00
PPNR Nolan Ryan 1.25 3.00
PPOS Ozzie Smith .50 1.25
PPPF Prince Fielder .30 .75
PPPG Paul Goldschmidt .40 1.00
PPPS Pablo Sandoval .30 .75
PPRB Ryan Braun .30 .75
PPRC Robinson Cano .30 .75
PPRD R.A. Dickey .30 .75
PPRH Ryan Howard .30 .75
PPRJ Reggie Jackson .30 .75
PPRM Roger Maris .40 1.00
PPSC Starlin Castro .25 .60
PPSK Sandy Koufax .75 2.00
PPSM Shelby Miller .30 .75
PPSS Stephen Strasburg .40 1.00
PPTC Ty Cobb .60 1.50
PPTG Tom Glavine .30 .75
PPTL Tim Lincecum .30 .75
PPTT Troy Tulowitzki .40 1.00
PPWM Wil Myers .25 .60
PPYC Yoenis Cespedes .40 1.00
PPYD Yu Darvish .40 1.00
PPYP Yasiel Puig .40 1.00
PPZW Zack Wheeler .30 .75
PPARO Alex Rodriguez .50 1.25
PPCBE Carlos Beltran .30 .75
PPDPR David Price .30 .75
PPHRA Hanley Ramirez .30 .75
PPJMA Joe Mauer .30 .75
PPJMO Joe Morgan .30 .75
PPJRO Jackie Robinson .40 1.00
PPJSE Jean Segura .30 .75
PPJSM John Smoltz .40 1.00
PPJVE Justin Verlander .40 1.00
PPMMA Mark McGwire .75 2.00
PPRHE Rickey Henderson .40 1.00
PPRJO Randy Johnson .40 1.00
PPTWI Ted Williams .75 2.00
PPWMA Willie Mays .75 2.00

2014 Topps Allen and Ginter The World's Capitals

COMPLETE SET (20) 5.00 12.00
STATED ODDS 1:2 HOBBY
WC01 Jerusalem Israel .40 1.00
WC02 New Delhi India .40 1.00
WC03 Moscow Russia .40 1.00
WC04 Beijing China .40 1.00
WC05 Cairo Egypt .40 1.00
WC06 Brasilia Brazil .40 1.00
WC07 Washington D.C. USA .40 1.00
WC08 London UK .40 1.00
WC09 Paris France .40 1.00
WC10 Berlin Germany .40 1.00
WC11 Buenos Aires Argentina .40 1.00
WC12 Brussels Belgium .40 1.00
WC13 Rome Italy .40 1.00
WC14 Tokyo Japan .40 1.00
WC15 Ottawa Canada .40 1.00
WC16 Mexico City Mexico .40 1.00
WC17 Taipei Taiwan .40 1.00
WC18 Bangkok Thailand .40 1.00
WC19 Johannesburg South Africa .40 1.00
WC20 Athens Greece .40 1.00

2015 Topps Allen and Ginter

COMPLETE SET (350) 30.00 80.00
ORIGINAL BUYBACK ODDS 1:7958 HOBBY
ORIG.BUYBACK PRINT RUN 1 SER.#'d SET
1 Madison Bumgarner .20 .50
2 Nick Markakis .20 .50
3 Adrian Gonzalez .20 .50
4 Wilmer Flores .20 .50
5 Craig Kimbrel .20 .50
6 Lucas Duda .20 .50
7 Eric Hosmer .20 .50
8 Garrett Richards .20 .50
9 Jeff Samardzija .15 .40
10 Curtis Granderson .20 .50
11 Carlos Santana .20 .50
12 Nelson Cruz .25 .60
13 Koji Uehara .15 .40
14 LaTroy Hawkins .15 .40
15 Justin Verlander .25 .60
16 Felix Hernandez .20 .50
17 Yadier Molina .25 .60
18 Adam Eaton .15 .40
19 Charlie Blackmon .25 .60
20 Leonys Martin .15 .40
21 Kolten Wong .20 .50
22 Trevor Rosenthal .20 .50
23 Johnny Cueto .20 .50
24 Appomattox Court House .15 .40
25 Mark Trumbo .15 .40
26 Steven Souza Jr. .20 .50
27 Maikel Franco RC .40 1.00
28 Jayson Werth .20 .50
29 Nick Swisher .20 .50
30 Megan Kalmoe .15 .40
31 Frank Caliendo .15 .40
32 James Murray .15 .40
33 Michael Wacha .20 .50
34 Buster Olney .15 .40
35 Paul Goldschmidt .25 .60
36 Anthony Ranaudo RC .30 .75
37 Mike Mills .15 .40
38 Evan Longoria .20 .50
39 Jon Singleton .20 .50
40 J.J. Hardy .15 .40
41 Brandon Finnegan RC .30 .75
42 Max Scherzer .25 .60
43 Adam Jones .20 .50
44 Sal Vulcano .15 .40
45 Chris Owings .15 .40
46 Andrew McCutchen .25 .60
47 Lance Lynn .15 .40
48 Coco Crisp .15 .40
49 Hisashi Iwakuma .20 .50
50 Francisco Rodriguez .20 .50
51 Matt Garza .15 .40
52 Jake Marisnick .15 .40
53 Brandon Crawford .20 .50
54 Javier Baez RC 2.50 6.00
55 Jonah Keri .15 .40
56 Apollo Creed .25 .60
57 David Cross .15 .40
58 Jacob deGrom .25 .60
59 Hector Rondon .15 .40
60 Marcus Semien .15 .40
61 Domonic Brown .20 .50
62 Andrelton Simmons .15 .40
63 Edwin Escobar RC .30 .75
64 Austin Jackson .15 .40
65 David Ortiz .25 .60
66 Billy Butler .15 .40
67 Malcolm Gladwell .15 .40
68 Matt Barnes RC .30 .75
69 Christian Bethancourt .15 .40
70 Kyle Seager .15 .40
71 J.D. Martinez .25 .60
72 Joe Panik .20 .50
73 Daniel Murphy .20 .50
74 Casey McGehee .15 .40
75 Brandon Phillips .15 .40
76 Jake Arrieta .20 .50
77 Jason Hammel .20 .50
78 Carlos Gonzalez .20 .50
79 Grant Miller .15 .40
80 Joe Gatto .15 .40
81 Buck Farmer RC .30 .75
82 Dalton Pompey RC .40 1.00
83 Matt Harvey .20 .50
84 Josh Harrison .15 .40
85 Kris Bryant RC 2.00 5.00
86 Rick Porcello .20 .50
87 Francisco Liriano .15 .40
88 Carl Crawford .20 .50
89 Jonathan Papelbon .20 .50
90 Darren Rovell .15 .40
91 Howie Kendrick .15 .40
92 Michelle Beadle .15 .40
93 Kelia Moniz .15 .40
94 Xander Bogaerts .25 .60
95 Kole Calhoun .15 .40
96 Tim Hudson .20 .50
97 Kendall Graveman RC .30 .75
98 Yimi Garcia RC .30 .75
99 Yan Gomes .15 .40
100 Greg Holland .15 .40
101 Stephen Strasburg .25 .60
102 James Clubber Lang .25 .60
103 Salvador Perez .20 .50
104 Didi Gregorius .20 .50
105 Daniel Norris RC .30 .75
106 Yunel Escobar .15 .40
107 Giancarlo Stanton .25 .60
108 Prince Fielder .20 .50
109 Troy Tulowitzki .25 .60
110 Victor Martinez .20 .50
111 Dellin Betances .20 .50
112 Buck 65 .15 .40
113 Ryan Braun .20 .50
114 Brian McCann .20 .50
115 Dustin Pedroia .25 .60
116 Freddie Freeman .30 .75
117 Corey Kluber .20 .50
118 Adam Lind .20 .50
119 Paul Scheer .15 .40
120 Matt Adams .15 .40
121 Wei-Yin Chen .15 .40
122 Jesse Hahn .15 .40
123 Micah Johnson RC .30 .75
124 Lakey Peterson .15 .40
125 Nori Aoki .15 .40
126 Alexei Ramirez .20 .50
127 Nick Castellanos .25 .60
128 R.A. Dickey .20 .50
129 Yovani Gallardo .15 .40
130 Juan Lagares .15 .40
131 Josh Reddick .15 .40
132 Dilson Herrera RC .40 1.00
133 Addison Russell RC 1.00 2.50
134 Joc Pederson RC .60 1.50
135 Mark Teixeira .20 .50
136 Tyson Ross .15 .40
137 Marlon Byrd .15 .40
138 Michael Pineda .15 .40
139 Chris Sale .25 .60
140 Jose Altuve .20 .50
141 Justin Upton .20 .50
142 Yasiel Puig .25 .60
143 Mike Zunino .15 .40
144 Brandon Belt .20 .50
145 Santiago Casilla .15 .40
146 Michael Morse .15 .40
147 Yoenis Cespedes .20 .50
148 Yasmany Tomas RC .40 1.00
149 Andrew Heaney .15 .40
150 Brody Stevens .15 .40
151 Jorge Soler RC .50 1.25
152 Jacoby Ellsbury .20 .50
153 Brandon Moss .15 .40
154 Rusney Castillo RC .40 1.00
155 Mike Moustakas .20 .50
156 Brian Dozier .20 .50
157 Jose Reyes .20 .50
158 Kurt Suzuki .15 .40
159 Devin Mesoraco .15 .40
160 Danny Santana .15 .40
161 Bartolo Colon .15 .40
162 Anthony Rizzo .40 1.00
163 Zach Lowe .15 .40
164 Adrian Beltre .25 .60
165 Jonathan Lucroy .20 .50
166 Carlos Gomez .15 .40
167 Julie Foudy .15 .40
168 Clay Buchholz .15 .40
169 Yordano Ventura .20 .50
170 Chris Davis .15 .40
171 Anthony Rendon .25 .60
172 Matt Carpenter .25 .60
173 Buster Posey .30 .75
174 Joe Mauer .20 .50
175 DJ LeMahieu .25 .60
176 Jon Niese .15 .40
177 Bernie Williams .20 .50
178 Travis d'Arnaud .20 .50
179 Manny Machado .25 .60
180 Scott Kazmir .15 .40
181 Drew Hutchison .15 .40
182 Todd Frazier .20 .50
183 Edwin Encarnacion .25 .60
184 Marcell Ozuna .25 .60
185 Gus Malzahn .15 .40
186 Desmond Jennings .20 .50
187 Miguel Cabrera .25 .60
188 Shelby Miller .20 .50
189 Kennys Vargas .15 .40
190 Michael Bourn .15 .40
191 John Lackey .20 .50
192 Fernando Rodney .15 .40
193 Aramis Ramirez .15 .40
194 Zack Cozart .15 .40
195 Torii Hunter .15 .40
196 Ian Kinsler .20 .50
197 Melky Cabrera .15 .40
198 Albert Pujols .30 .75
199 Zack Greinke .20 .50
200 Jose Abreu .25 .60
201 Joe Buck .15 .40
202 Travis Ishikawa .15 .40
203 David Wright .20 .50
204 Chase Headley .15 .40
205 Dustin Ackley .15 .40
206 Erick Aybar .15 .40
207 Derek Norris .15 .40
208 Jose Fernandez .25 .60
209 Hanley Ramirez .20 .50
210 Starling Marte .20 .50
211 Kyle Lohse .15 .40
212 Chris Tillman .15 .40
213 Elvis Andrus .20 .50
214 Corey Dickerson .15 .40
215 Joey Votto .25 .60
216 Jake Lamb RC .50 1.25
217 Wade Miley .15 .40
218 Carlos Rodon RC .50 1.25
219 Huston Street .15 .40
220 Yasmani Grandal .15 .40
221 Doug Fister .15 .40
222 Gregory Polanco .20 .50
223 Incredibeard .15 .40
224 Edinson Volquez .15 .40
225 Thunderlips .25 .60
226 Nolan Arenado .30 .75
227 Christian Yelich .30 .75
228 Robb Wolf .15 .40
229 Ivan Drago .25 .60
230 Keith Law .15 .40
231 Henderson Alvarez .15 .40
232 Matt Holliday .25 .60
233 Ike Davis .15 .40
234 Michael Cuddyer .15 .40
235 Michael Taylor RC .30 .75
236 Julio Teheran .20 .50
237 Hyun-Jin Ryu .20 .50
238 Dee Gordon .15 .40
239 Zach Britton .20 .50
240 Trevor May RC .30 .75
241 CC Sabathia .20 .50
242 James McCann RC .50 1.25
243 Jean Segura .20 .50
244 Jason Kipnis .20 .50
245 Ryan Howard .20 .50
246 Andrew Cashner .15 .40
247 George Springer .20 .50
248 Jose Bautista .20 .50
249 Bryce Harper .40 1.00
250 Jimmy Rollins .20 .50
251 Adam LaRoche .15 .40
252 Mike Trout 1.25 3.00
253 Carlos Beltran .20 .50
254 Alex Gordon .20 .50
255 Steven Moya RC .40 1.00
256 Sonny Gray .20 .50
257 Pablo Sandoval .20 .50
258 Rocky Balboa .25 .60
259 Jonathan Schoop .15 .40
260 Hunter Pence .20 .50
261 Yu Darvish .25 .60
262 Alex Cobb .15 .40
263 Pedro Alvarez .15 .40
264 Matt Kemp .20 .50
265 Jung Ho Kang RC .30 .75
266 Drew Storen .15 .40
267 Jered Weaver .20 .50
268 Jimbo Fisher .15 .40
269 Jeremy Roenick .25 .60
270 Mike Foltynewicz RC .30 .75
271 Dexter Fowler .20 .50
272 Glen Perkins .15 .40
273 Cole Hamels .20 .50
274 Mookie Betts .40 1.00
275 Billy Hamilton .20 .50
276 Alex Rodriguez .30
277 Starlin Castro .15
278 Cliff Lee .20
279 Jon Jay .15
280 Jenrry Mejia .15
281 Cory Spangenberg RC .30
282 Adeiny Hechavarria .15
283 Aaron Hill .15
284 Jay Bruce .20
285 Ichiro .30
286 Addison Reed .15
287 Jon Lester .20
288 Robinson Cano .20
289 Wil Myers .15
290 Ryan Zimmerman .20
291 James Shields .15
292 Grant Balfour .15
293 Philae Probe .15
294 Adam Wainwright .20
295 Joe Nathan .15
296 Kenley Jansen .20
297 Magna Carta .15
298 Rubby De La Rosa .15
299 Brian Quinn .15
300 Bryce Brentz RC .30
301 Justin Morneau .20
302 Fall of the Berlin Wall .15
303 Denard Span .15
304 Gary Brown RC .15
305 Chris Carter .15
306 Stephen Drew .15
307 Jorge De La Rosa .15
308 David Freese .15
309 Gabe Kapler .15
310 Chris Coghlan .15
311 Michael Brantley .20
312 Gerrit Cole .25
313 Jhonny Peralta .15
314 Ian Desmond .15
315 Steve Cishek .15
316 Evan Gattis .15
317 Hunter Strickland RC .15
318 David Price .20
319 Brian Windhorst .15
320 Dallas Keuchel .20
321 Ben Zobrist .20
322 Mark Melancon .15
323 Joaquin Benoit .15
324 Will Middlebrooks .15
325 Aroldis Chapman .25
326 Mitch Moreland .15
327 Jeff Mauro .15 .40
328 Val Kilmer .15 .40
329 Brett Gardner .20 .50
330 Jason Heyward .20 .50
331 Alcides Escobar .20 .50
332 Matt Cain .20 .50
333 Chase Utley .20 .50
334 Nick Tropeano .15 .40
335 Collin Cowgill .15 .40
336 Shane Victorino .20 .50
337 Mike Olt .15 .40
338 Mike Napoli .15 .40
339 Clayton Kershaw .50 1.25
340 Neftali Feliz .15 .40
341 Malala Yousafzai .15 .40
342 Josh Donaldson .20 .50
343 Angel Pagan .15 .40
344 Jordan Zimmermann .20 .50
345 Lonnie Chisenhall .15 .40
346 Shin-Soo Choo .20 .50
347 Aaron Paul .15 .40
348 Aaron Sanchez .20 .50
349 Sam Tuivailala RC .15 .40
350 Masahiro Tanaka .20 .50

2015 Topps Allen and Ginter Mini

*MINI 1-300: 1X TO 2.5X BASIC
*MINI 1-300 RC: .5X TO 1.2X BASIC RCs
*MINI SP 301-350: .6X TO 1.5X BASIC
MINI SP ODDS 1:13 HOBBY
351-400 RANDOM WITHIN RIP CARDS
STATED PLATE ODDS 1:495 HOBBY
PLATE PRINT RUN 1 SET PER COLOR
BLACK-CYAN-MAGENTA-YELLOW ISSUED
NO PLATE PRICING DUE TO SCARCITY
351 Joey Votto EXT 25.00 60.00
352 Mike Moustakas EXT 20.00 50.00
353 Javier Baez EXT 125.00 300.00
354 Yasiel Puig EXT 30.00 80.00
355 Prince Fielder EXT 20.00 50.00
356 Stephen Strasburg EXT 25.00 60.00
357 Yoenis Cespedes EXT 25.00 60.00
359 Miguel Cabrera EXT 30.00 80.00
360 Adam Jones EXT 20.00 50.00
361 Jacoby Ellsbury EXT 20.00 50.00
363 Hunter Pence EXT 20.00 50.00
364 Jon Lester EXT 20.00 50.00
365 Jacob deGrom EXT 25.00 60.00
366 Troy Tulowitzki EXT 25.00 60.00
367 Clayton Kershaw EXT 50.00 125.00
368 Matt Harvey EXT 20.00 50.00
369 Rusney Castillo EXT 20.00 50.00
370 Madison Bumgarner EXT 20.00 50.00
371 David Wright EXT 20.00 50.00
372 Corey Kluber EXT 20.00 50.00
373 Joc Pederson EXT 40.00 100.00
374 Joe Mauer EXT 20.00 50.00
375 Edwin Encarnacion EXT 25.00 60.00
376 Eric Hosmer EXT 20.00 50.00
377 Giancarlo Stanton EXT 25.00 60.00
378 Pablo Sandoval EXT 20.00 50.00

379 Yu Darvish EXT 25.00 60.00
381 Matt Kemp EXT 20.00 50.00
382 Bryce Harper EXT 40.00 100.00
383 Andrew McCutchen EXT 25.00 60.00
384 Evan Longoria EXT 20.00 50.00
385 Paul Goldschmidt EXT 25.00 60.00
386 Jose Abreu EXT 30.00 80.00
388 Adam Wainwright EXT 20.00 50.00
389 Victor Martinez EXT 20.00 50.00
390 Mike Trout EXT 40.00 100.00
391 Anthony Rendon EXT 25.00 60.00
392 Robinson Cano EXT 20.00 50.00
393 Nelson Cruz EXT 25.00 60.00
394 Buster Posey EXT 30.00 80.00
395 Jose Bautista EXT 20.00 50.00
396 Brandon Belt EXT 25.00 60.00
397 Jason Heyward EXT 20.00 50.00
398 Alex Gordon EXT 20.00 50.00
399 Hanley Ramirez EXT 20.00 50.00
400 David Ortiz EXT 25.00 60.00

2015 Topps Allen and Ginter Mini A and G Back

*MINI AG 1-300: 1.2X TO 3X BASIC
*MINI AG 1-300 RC: .6X TO 1.5X BASIC RCs
*MINI AG SP 301-350: .75X TO 2X BASIC
MINI AG ODDS 1:5 HOBBY
MINI AG SP ODDS 1:65 HOBBY

2015 Topps Allen and Ginter Mini Black

*MINI BLK 1-300: 2X TO 5X BASIC
*MINI BLK 1-300 RC: 1X TO 2.5X BASIC RCs
*MINI BLK SP 301-350: 1.2X TO 3X BASIC
MINI BLK ODDS 1:10 HOBBY
MINI BLK SP ODDS 1:130 HOBBY

2015 Topps Allen and Ginter Mini Flag Back

*MINI FLAG: 5X TO 12X BASIC
*MINI FLAG RC: 2.5X TO 6X BASIC RCs
MINI FLAG ODDS 1:157 HOBBY
STATED PRINT RUN 25 SER.#'d SETS
1 Madison Bumgarner 10.00 25.00
3 Adrian Gonzalez 8.00 20.00
6 Lucas Duda 6.00 15.00
15 Justin Verlander 6.00 15.00
16 Felix Hernandez 10.00 25.00
17 Yadier Molina 10.00 25.00
27 Maikel Franco 10.00 25.00
35 Paul Goldschmidt 15.00 40.00
56 Apollo Creed 10.00 25.00
72 Joe Panik 12.00 30.00
85 Kris Bryant 100.00 200.00
104 Didi Gregorius 6.00 15.00
111 Dellin Betances 6.00 15.00
113 Ryan Braun 6.00 15.00
116 Freddie Freeman 10.00 25.00
134 Joc Pederson 20.00 50.00
151 Jorge Soler 12.00 30.00
173 Buster Posey 30.00 80.00
187 Miguel Cabrera 10.00 25.00
199 Zack Greinke 6.00 15.00
215 Joey Votto 6.00 15.00
225 Thunderlips 10.00 25.00
237 Hyun-Jin Ryu 6.00 15.00
241 CC Sabathia 6.00 15.00
249 Bryce Harper 15.00 40.00
252 Mike Trout 25.00 60.00
258 Rocky Balboa 15.00 40.00
339 Clayton Kershaw 20.00 50.00

2015 Topps Allen and Ginter Mini No Card Number

*MINI NNO: 6X TO 15X BASIC
*MINI NNO RC: 3X TO 8X BASIC RCs
MINI NNO ODDS 1:79 HOBBY
ANNCD PRINT RUN OF 50 COPIES EACH

2015 Topps Allen and Ginter Mini Red

*MINI RED: 5X TO 12X BASIC
*MINI RED RC: 2.5X TO 6X BASIC RCs
MINI RED ODDS 1:12 HOBBY BOXES
STATED PRINT RUN 40 SER.#'d SETS
1 Madison Bumgarner 10.00 25.00
3 Adrian Gonzalez 8.00 20.00
6 Lucas Duda 6.00 15.00
15 Justin Verlander 6.00 15.00
16 Felix Hernandez 10.00 25.00
17 Yadier Molina 10.00 25.00
27 Maikel Franco 10.00 25.00
35 Paul Goldschmidt 15.00 40.00
56 Apollo Creed 10.00 25.00
72 Joe Panik 12.00 30.00
85 Kris Bryant 100.00 200.00
104 Didi Gregorius 6.00 15.00
111 Dellin Betances 6.00 15.00
113 Ryan Braun 6.00 15.00
116 Freddie Freeman 10.00 25.00
134 Joc Pederson 20.00 50.00
151 Jorge Soler 12.00 30.00
173 Buster Posey 30.00 80.00
187 Miguel Cabrera 10.00 25.00
199 Zack Greinke 6.00 15.00
215 Joey Votto 6.00 15.00
225 Thunderlips 10.00 25.00
237 Hyun-Jin Ryu 6.00 15.00
241 CC Sabathia 6.00 15.00
249 Bryce Harper 15.00 40.00
252 Mike Trout 25.00 60.00
258 Rocky Balboa 15.00 40.00
339 Clayton Kershaw 20.00 50.00

2015 Topps Allen and Ginter Ancient Armory

COMPLETE SET (20) 3.00 8.00
OVERALL INSERT ODDS 1:2 HOBBY
AA1 Catapult .30 .75
AA2 Katana .30 .75
AA3 Quarterstaff .30 .75
AA4 Gauntlet .30 .75
AA5 Chu Ko Nu .30 .75
AA6 Katar .30 .75
AA7 Dane Axe .30 .75
AA8 War Hammer .30 .75
AA9 Flail .30 .75
AA10 Flanged Mace .30 .75
AA11 Claymore .30 .75
AA12 Shuriken .30 .75
AA13 Taiaha .30 .75
AA14 Atlatl .30 .75
AA15 Sling .30 .75
AA16 Tomahawk .30 .75
AA17 Trident .30 .75
AA18 Dory Spear .30 .75
AA19 Cutlass .30 .75
AA20 Shamshir .30 .75

2015 Topps Allen and Ginter Box Topper Autographs

STATED ODDS 1:220 HOBBY BOXES
STATED PRINT RUN 15 SER.#'d SETS
EXCHANGE DEADLINE 6/30/2018
BLADW David Wright 100.00 250.00
BLAFF Freddie Freeman 50.00 120.00
BLAJB Javier Baez 100.00 250.00
BLAJS Jorge Soler 25.00 60.00
BLARC Rusney Castillo EXCH 15.00 40.00
BLACKE Clayton Kershaw EXCH 125.00 300.00
BLACKL Corey Kluber 15.00 40.00

2015 Topps Allen and Ginter Box Topper Relics

STATED ODDS 1:132 HOBBY BOXES
STATED PRINT RUN 25 SER.#'d SETS
BRDW David Wright 15.00 40.00
BRJA Jose Abreu 30.00 80.00
BRJS Jorge Soler 12.00 30.00
BRMB Madison Bumgarner 15.00 40.00
BRRB Ryan Braun 12.00 30.00
BRRC Rusney Castillo 6.00 15.00
BRCKE Clayton Kershaw 20.00 50.00
BRJBU Jose Bautista 6.00 15.00
BRMTA Masahiro Tanaka 15.00 40.00
BRMTR Mike Trout 40.00 100.00

2015 Topps Allen and Ginter Box Toppers

STATED ODDS 1:3 HOBBY BOXES
B1 Mike Trout 8.00 20.00
B2 Jose Abreu 1.50 4.00
B3 Rusney Castillo 1.25 3.00
B4 Jorge Soler 1.50 4.00
B5 Corey Kluber 1.25 3.00
B6 Clayton Kershaw 3.00 8.00
B7 David Wright 1.25 3.00
B8 Yasiel Puig 1.50 4.00
B9 Freddie Freeman 2.00 5.00
B10 Javier Baez 8.00 20.00
B11 Buster Posey 2.00 5.00
B12 Evan Longoria 1.25 3.00
B13 Troy Tulowitzki 1.50 4.00
B14 Joey Votto 1.50 4.00
B15 Giancarlo Stanton 1.50 4.00

2015 Topps Allen and Ginter Framed Mini Autographs

STATED ODDS 1:54 HOBBY
EXCHANGE DEADLINE 6/30/2018
AGAAB Archie Bradley 3.00 8.00
AGAAP Aaron Paul 20.00 50.00
AGAARA Anthony Ranaudo 3.00 8.00
AGAB6 Buck 65 12.00 30.00
AGABBR Bryce Brentz 3.00 8.00
AGABC Brandon Crawford 6.00 15.00
AGABEW Bernie Williams 20.00 50.00
AGABF Brandon Finnegan 3.00 8.00
AGABFA Buck Farmer 3.00 8.00
AGABH Bryce Harper 150.00 300.00
AGABM Brian McCann 30.00 80.00
AGABO Buster Olney 10.00 25.00
AGABQ Brian Quinn 15.00 40.00
AGABS Brody Stevens 6.00 15.00
AGABW Brian Windhorst 4.00 10.00
AGACB Charlie Blackmon 10.00 25.00
AGACKL Corey Kluber 12.00 30.00
AGACR Carlos Rodon 15.00 40.00
AGACSP Cory Spangenberg 3.00 8.00
AGACW Christian Walker 6.00 15.00
AGADB Dellin Betances 4.00 10.00
AGADC David Cross 25.00 60.00
AGADG Didi Gregorius 4.00 10.00
AGADH Dilson Herrera 4.00 10.00
AGADN Daniel Norris 3.00 8.00
AGADPE Dustin Pedroia 40.00 100.00
AGADPO Dalton Pompey 4.00 10.00
AGADR Darren Rovell 3.00 8.00
AGADW David Wright 60.00 150.00
AGAEE Edwin Encarnacion 6.00 15.00
AGAFC Frank Caliendo 8.00 20.00
AGAFF Freddie Freeman 15.00 40.00
AGAGB Gary Brown 3.00 8.00
AGAGK Gabe Kapler 3.00 8.00
AGAGM Gus Malzahn 12.00 30.00
AGAID Ivan Drago 100.00 200.00
AGAIMM Ichiro 300.00 600.00
AGAINY Ichiro 300.00. 600.00
AGAISM Ichiro 300.00 600.00
AGAIW Incredibeard 6.00 15.00
AGAJBU Joe Buck 15.00 40.00
AGAJDE Jacob deGrom 20.00 50.00
AGAJF Jimbo Fisher 8.00 20.00
AGAJFO Julie Foudy 12.00 30.00
AGAJGA Joe Gatto 15.00 40.00
AGAJH Jason Heyward 30.00 80.00
AGAJK Jung-Ho Kang 60.00 150.00
AGAJKE Jonah Keri 4.00 10.00
AGAJMA Jeff Mauro 6.00 15.00
AGAJMU James Murray 20.00 50.00
AGAJPA Joe Panik 10.00 25.00
AGAJPE Joc Pederson 10.00 25.00
AGAJR Jeremy Roenick 12.00 30.00
AGAJSO Jorge Soler 10.00 25.00
AGAJW Justise Winslow 10.00 25.00
AGAKB Kris Bryant 100.00 250.00
AGAKG Kendall Graveman 3.00 8.00
AGAKL Keith Law 4.00 10.00
AGAKM Kelia Moniz 12.00 30.00
AGAKOU Kelly Oubre 10.00 25.00
AGALP Lakey Peterson 6.00 15.00
AGAMA Matt Adams 3.00 8.00
AGAMBA Matt Barnes 3.00 8.00
AGAMBE Michelle Beadle 15.00 40.00
AGAMFR Maikel Franco 6.00 15.00
AGAMG Malcolm Gladwell 8.00 20.00
AGAMK Megan Kalmoe 4.00 10.00
AGAMM Mike Mills 15.00 40.00
AGAMTA Michael Taylor 3.00 8.00
AGANS Noah Syndergaard 30.00 80.00
AGAPSC Paul Scheer 6.00 15.00
AGARB Ryan Braun 30.00 80.00
AGARCN Robinson Cano 12.00 30.00
AGARJH R.J. Hunter 12.00 30.00
AGARW Robb Wolf 4.00 10.00
AGASD Sam Dekker 12.00 30.00
AGASJ Stanley Johnson 25.00 60.00
AGAST Sam Tuivailala 3.00 8.00
AGASV Sal Vulcano 20.00 50.00
AGATH Thunderlips 200.00 300.00
AGATM Trevor May 3.00 8.00
AGAVK Val Kilmer 30.00 80.00
AGAWCS Willie Cauley-Stein 25.00 60.00
AGAWM Wil Myers 10.00 25.00
AGAYGA Yimi Garcia 3.00 8.00
AGAYT Yasmany Tomas 6.00 15.00
AGAZL Zach Lowe 6.00 15.00

2015 Topps Allen and Ginter Framed Mini Relics

STATED ODDS 1:61 HOBBY
FMRAB Adrian Beltre 4.00 10.00
FMRAG Alex Gordon 3.00 8.00
FMRAJ Adam Jones 3.00 8.00
FMRAM Andrew McCutchen 6.00 15.00
FMRAP Angel Pagan 2.50 6.00
FMRAS Aaron Sanchez 3.00 8.00
FMRAW Alex Wood 2.50 6.00
FMRBB Brandon Belt 3.00 8.00
FMRBM Brian McCann 3.00 8.00
FMRCB Charlie Blackmon 4.00 10.00
FMRCG Carlos Gonzalez 3.00 8.00
FMRCH Cole Hamels 3.00 8.00
FMRCK Clayton Kershaw 6.00 15.00
FMRCS CC Sabathia 3.00 8.00
FMRCT Chris Tillman 2.50 6.00
FMRCU Chase Utley 3.00 8.00
FMRDB Domonic Brown 3.00 8.00
FMRDMU Daniel Murphy 3.00 8.00
FMRDO David Ortiz 4.00 10.00
FMRDS Drew Storen 2.50 6.00
FMRDW David Wright 3.00 8.00
FMREH Eric Hosmer 3.00 8.00
FMRFF Freddie Freeman 5.00 12.00
FMRFH Felix Hernandez 3.00 8.00
FMRGC Gerrit Cole 4.00 10.00
FMRGP Gregory Polanco 3.00 8.00
FMRGS Giancarlo Stanton 4.00 10.00
FMRHA Henderson Alvarez 2.50 6.00
FMRHP Hunter Pence 3.00 8.00
FMRJB Jose Bautista 3.00 8.00
FMRJME Jenrry Mejia 2.50 6.00
FMRJMO Justin Morneau 3.00 8.00
FMRJPE Joc Pederson 10.00 25.00
FMRJT Julio Teheran 3.00 8.00
FMRJV Justin Verlander 6.00 15.00
FMRLM Leonys Martin 2.50 6.00
FMRMCA Matt Carpenter 4.00 10.00
FMRMCB Miguel Cabrera 4.00 10.00
FMRMH Matt Holliday 4.00 10.00
FMRMMO Matt Moore 3.00 8.00
FMRMMR Michael Morse 2.50 6.00
FMRMMU Mike Moustakas 3.00 8.00
FMRMTE Mark Teixeira 3.00 8.00
FMRMTR Mike Trout 12.00 30.00
FMRMZ Mike Zunino 2.50 6.00
FMRPA Pedro Alvarez 2.50 6.00
FMRRB Ryan Braun 3.00 8.00
FMRRH Ryan Howard 3.00 8.00
FMRRO Rougned Odor 3.00 8.00
FMRRZ Ryan Zimmerman 3.00 8.00
FMRSCA Starlin Castro 2.50 6.00
FMRSCH Shin-Soo Choo 3.00 8.00
FMRSM Starling Marte 3.00 8.00
FMRSP Salvador Perez 3.00 8.00
FMRTR Tyson Ross 2.50 6.00
FMRTW Taijuan Walker 2.50 6.00
FMRWC Wei-Yin Chen 2.50 6.00
FMRWF Wilmer Flores 3.00 8.00
FMRWM Wil Myers 2.50 6.00
FMRYM Yadier Molina 4.00 10.00
FMRYP Yasiel Puig 4.00 10.00
FMRZC Zack Cozart 2.50 6.00
FMRZW Zack Wheeler 3.00 8.00

2015 Topps Allen and Ginter Great Scott

COMPLETE SET (20) 3.00 8.00
OVERALL INSERT ODDS 1:2 HOBBY
GS1 X-Ray Diffraction .30 .75
GS2 Big Bang .30 .75
GS3 Polio Vaccine .30 .75
GS4 Large Hadron Collider .30 .75
GS5 Artificial Heart .30 .75
GS6 Deoxyribonucleic Acid .30 .75
GS7 Continental Drift .30 .75
GS8 Search Engine .30 .75
GS9 Fingerprints .30 .75
GS10 Dolly the Sheep .30 .75

2015 Topps Allen and Ginter Keys to the City

COMPLETE SET (10) 12.00 30.00
RANDOM INSERTS IN RETAIL PACKS
KTC1 Statue of Liberty 1.25 3.00
KTC2 Gateway Arch 1.25 3.00
KTC3 Liberty Bell 1.25 3.00
KTC4 Willis Tower 1.25 3.00
KTC5 Portland Light Head 1.25 3.00
KTC6 The Alamo 1.25 3.00
KTC7 Golden Gate Bridge 1.25 3.00
KTC8 The Space Needle 1.25 3.00
KTC9 Welcome Sign 1.25 3.00
KTC10 Empire State Building 1.25 3.00

2015 Topps Allen and Ginter Menagerie of the Mind

COMPLETE SET (20) 3.00 8.00
OVERALL INSERT ODDS 1:2 HOBBY
MM1 Troll .30 .75
MM2 Elf .30 .75
MM3 Dragon .30 .75
MM4 Phoenix .30 .75
MM5 Griffin .30 .75
MM6 Pegasus .30 .75
MM7 Unicorn .30 .75
MM8 Werewolf .30 .75
MM9 Hydra .30 .75
MM10 Cerberus .30 .75
MM11 Zombie .30 .75
MM12 Bunyip .30 .75
MM13 Cyclops .30 .75
MM14 Djinn .30 .75
MM15 Banshee .30 .75
MM16 Leprechaun .30 .75
MM17 Chimera .30 .75
MM18 Mermaid .30 .75
MM19 Sphinx .30 .75
MM20 Centaur .30 .75

2015 Topps Allen and Ginter Mini 10th Anniversary '06 Autographs

STATED ODDS 1:1375 HOBBY PACKS
STATED PRINT RUN 10 SER.#'d SETS
*07-15 AUTOS: .4X TO 1X '06 AUTOS
AGA06BB Bonnie Blair 20.00 50.00
AGA06DP Danica Patrick 150.00 250.00
AGA06GL Greg Louganis 20.00 50.00
AGA06HH Hulk Hogan 150.00 250.00
AGA06JC Joey Chestnut 25.00 60.00
AGA06JF Jennie Finch 60.00 120.00
AGA06JL Jeanette Lee 30.00 80.00
AGA06KS Korri Strug 25.00 60.00
AGA06MA Mario Andretti 25.00 60.00
AGA06MH Mia Hamm 40.00 100.00
AGA06MS Mark Spitz 20.00 50.00
AGA06WG Wendy Guey 12.00 30.00

2015 Topps Allen and Ginter Mini A Healthy Mind

STATED ODDS 1:288 HOBBY
MIND1 Rowing a Boat 3.00 8.00
MIND2 Flying a Kite 3.00 8.00
MIND3 Riding a Bicycle 3.00 8.00
MIND4 Reading a Book 3.00 8.00
MIND5 Picnicking 3.00 8.00
MIND6 Bird Watching 3.00 8.00
MIND7 Shuffle Board 3.00 8.00
MIND8 Skipping Rocks 3.00 8.00
MIND9 Bocce 3.00 8.00
MIND10 Chess 3.00 8.00

2015 Topps Allen and Ginter Mini A Healthy Body

STATED ODDS 1:288 HOBBY
BODY1 Vibrating Belt Machine 3.00 8.00
BODY2 Persian Clubs 3.00 8.00
BODY3 Nauheim Baths 3.00 8.00
BODY4 Gymnasticon 3.00 8.00
BODY5 The Turnplatz 3.00 8.00
BODY6 Herbert's Natural Method 3.00 8.00
BODY7 Rope Climbing 3.00 8.00
BODY8 Barbell Lifts 3.00 8.00
BODY9 Caber Tossing 3.00 8.00
BODY10 Grappling 3.00 8.00

2015 Topps Allen and Ginter Mini A World Beneath Our Feet

COMPLETE SET (15) 8.00 20.00
OVERALL MINI INSERT ODDS 1:5 HOBBY
BUG1 Borneo Walking Stick 1.00 2.50
BUG2 Goliath Beetle 1.00 2.50
BUG3 Assassin Bug 1.00 2.50
BUG4 Devil's Flower Mantis 1.00 2.50
BUG5 Seven-Spotted Ladybug 1.00 2.50
BUG6 Monarch Butterfly 1.00 2.50
BUG7 European Honeybee 1.00 2.50
BUG8 Death's Head Hawkmoth 1.00 2.50
BUG9 Deer Tick 1.00 2.50
BUG10 Pennsylvania Firefly 1.00 2.50
BUG11 White-Legged Snake Millipede 1.00 2.50
BUG12 Green-Striped Darner 1.00 2.50
BUG13 Calleta Silkmoth Caterpillar 1.00 2.50
BUG14 Madagascar Hissing Cockroach 1.00 2.50
BUG15 Tsetse Fly 1.00 2.50

2015 Topps Allen and Ginter Mini Birds of Prey

COMPLETE SET (10) 10.00 25.00
OVERALL MINI INSERT ODDS 1:5 HOBBY
BP1 Red-tailed Hawk 1.50 4.00
BP2 Bald Eagle 1.50 4.00
BP3 Great Horned Owl 1.50 4.00
BP4 Burrowing Owl 1.50 4.00
BP5 Black Vulture 1.50 4.00
BP6 Crested Caracara 1.50 4.00
BP7 California Condor 1.50 4.00
BP8 Peregrine Falcon 1.50 4.00
BP9 Osprey 1.50 4.00
BP10 Barn Owl 1.50 4.00

2015 Topps Allen and Ginter Mini First Ladies

COMPLETE SET (41) 30.00 80.00
OVERALL MINI INSERT ODDS 1:5 HOBBY
FIRST1 Eleanor Roosevelt 1.25 3.00
FIRST2 Martha Washington 1.25 3.00
FIRST3 Abigail Adams 1.25 3.00
FIRST4 Dolley Madison 1.25 3.00
FIRST5 Elizabeth Monroe 1.25 3.00
FIRST6 Louisa Adams 1.25 3.00
FIRST7 Anna Harrison 1.25 3.00
FIRST8 Letitia Tyler 1.25 3.00
FIRST9 Julia Tyler 1.25 3.00
FIRST10 Sarah Polk 1.25 3.00
FIRST11 Margaret Taylor 1.25 3.00
FIRST12 Abigail Fillmore 1.25 3.00
FIRST13 Jane Pierce 1.25 3.00
FIRST14 Harriet Lane 1.25 3.00
FIRST15 Mary Lincoln 1.25 3.00
FIRST16 Eliza Johnson 1.25 3.00
FIRST17 Julia Grant 1.25 3.00
FIRST18 Lucy Hayes 1.25 3.00
FIRST19 Lucretia Garfield 1.25 3.00
FIRST20 Frances Cleveland 1.25 3.00
FIRST21 Caroline Harrison 1.25 3.00
FIRST22 Ida McKinley 1.25 3.00
FIRST23 Edith Roosevelt 1.25 3.00
FIRST24 Helen Taft 1.25 3.00
FIRST25 Ellen Wilson 1.25 3.00
FIRST26 Edith Wilson 1.25 3.00
FIRST27 Florence Harding 1.25 3.00
FIRST28 Grace Coolidge 1.25 3.00
FIRST29 Lou Hoover 1.25 3.00
FIRST30 Bess Truman 1.25 3.00
FIRST31 Mamie Eisenhower 1.25 3.00
FIRST32 Jacqueline Kennedy 1.25 3.00
FIRST33 Lady Bird Johnson 1.25 3.00
FIRST34 Pat Nixon 1.25 3.00
FIRST35 Betty Ford 1.25 3.00
FIRST36 Rosalynn Carter 1.25 3.00
FIRST37 Nancy Reagan 1.25 3.00
FIRST38 Barbara Bush 1.25 3.00
FIRST39 Hillary Clinton 1.25 3.00
FIRST40 Laura Bush 1.25 3.00
FIRST41 Michelle Obama 1.25 3.00

2015 Topps Allen and Ginter Mini Hoist the Black Flag

COMPLETE SET (10) 12.00 30.00
OVERALL MINI INSERT ODDS 1:5 HOBBY
HBF1 Blackbeard 1.50 4.00
HBF2 Anne Bonny 1.50 4.00
HBF3 Charles Vane 1.50 4.00
HBF4 Calico Jack Rackham 1.50 4.00
HBF5 Captain William Kidd 1.50 4.00
HBF6 Benjamin Hornigold 1.50 4.00
HBF7 Mary Read 1.50 4.00
HBF8 Stede Bonnet 1.50 4.00
HBF9 Black Bart 1.50 4.00
HBF10 Henry Every 1.50 4.00

2015 Topps Allen and Ginter Mini Magnates Barons and Tycoons

COMPLETE SET (10) 6.00 15.00
OVERALL MINI INSERT ODDS 1:5 HOBBY
MBT1 John D. Rockefeller 1.00 2.50
MBT2 Cornelius Vanderbilt 1.00 2.50
MBT3 James J. Hill 1.00 2.50
MBT4 Andrew Carnegie 1.00 2.50
MBT5 J.P. Morgan 1.00 2.50
MBT6 John Jacob Astor 1.00 2.50
MBT7 James Buchanan Duke 1.00 2.50
MBT8 Henry Flagler 1.00 2.50
MBT9 John W. Gates 1.00 2.50
MBT10 Andrew W. Mellon 1.00 2.50

2015 Topps Allen and Ginter Mini Mythological Menaces

COMPLETE SET (10) 6.00 15.00
OVERALL MINI INSERT ODDS 1:5 HOBBY
MM1 Loki 1.00 2.50
MM2 Pan 1.00 2.50
MM3 The Monkey King 1.00 2.50
MM4 Puck 1.00 2.50
MM5 Prometheus 1.00 2.50
MM6 Wisakedjak 1.00 2.50
MM7 Hermes 1.00 2.50
MM8 Eris 1.00 2.50
MM9 Coyote 1.00 2.50
MM10 Nanabozho 1.00 2.50

2015 Topps Allen and Ginter Oversized Reprint Cabinet Box Toppers

STATED ODDS 1:4 HOBBY BOXES
1 Madison Bumgarner 1.25 3.00
46 Andrew McCutchen 1.50 4.00
85 Kris Bryant 6.00 15.00
151 Jorge Soler 1.50 4.00
154 Rusney Castillo 1.25 3.00
173 Buster Posey 2.00 5.00
187 Miguel Cabrera 1.50 4.00
252 Mike Trout 8.00 20.00
288 Robinson Cano 1.25 3.00
339 Clayton Kershaw 3.00 8.00

2015 Topps Allen and Ginter Pride of the People Cabinet Box Toppers

STATED ODDS 1:4 HOBBY BOXES
PCB1 Christ the Redeemer 2.00 5.00
PCB2 The Great Wall 2.00 5.00
PCB3 Mount Rushmore 2.00 5.00
PCB4 St. Basil's Cathedral 2.00 5.00
PCB5 Eiffel Tower 2.00 5.00
PCB6 Mount Fuji 2.00 5.00
PCB7 Big Ben 2.00 5.00
PCB8 Angkor Wat 2.00 5.00
PCB9 Colosseum 2.00 5.00
PCB10 Great Pyramid of Giza 2.00 5.00

2015 Topps Allen and Ginter Relics

GROUP A ODDS 1:24 HOBBY
GROUP B ODDS 1:24 HOBBY
FSRAAB Adrian Beltre A 3.00 8.00
FSRAAG Adrian Gonzalez A 2.50 6.00
FSRAAJ Adam Jones A 2.50 6.00
FSRAAPA Aaron Paul A 2.50 6.00
FSRAAPU Albert Pujols A 5.00 12.00
FSRAAR Anthony Rizzo A 5.00 12.00
FSRAAS Aaron Sanchez A 2.50 6.00
FSRAAW Adam Wainwright A 2.50 6.00
FSRABHA Bryce Harper A 5.00 12.00
FSRABHM Billy Hamilton A 2.50 6.00
FSRABO Buster Olney A 2.50 6.00
FSRABP Brandon Phillips A 2.00 5.00
FSRABS Brody Stevens A 2.50 6.00
FSRABW Brian Windhorst A 2.50 6.00
FSRACD Chris Davis A 2.00 5.00
FSRACS CC Sabathia A 2.50 6.00
FSRACU Chase Utley A 2.50 6.00
FSRADB Domonic Brown A 2.50 6.00
FSRADP Dustin Pedroia A 3.00 8.00
FSRAEA Elvis Andrus A 2.50 6.00
FSRAEG Evan Gattis A 2.00 5.00
FSRAFC Frank Caliendo A 2.50 6.00
FSRAFH Felix Hernandez A 2.50 6.00
FSRAJBA Jose Bautista A 2.50 6.00
FSRAJBR Jay Bruce A 2.50 6.00
FSRAJBU Joe Buck A 2.50 6.00
FSRAJD Jacob deGrom A 3.00 8.00
FSRAJF Jose Fernandez A 3.00 8.00
FSRAJG Joe Gatto A 2.50 6.00
FSRAJK Jonah Keri A 2.50 6.00
FSRAJMA Jeff Mauro A 2.50 6.00
FSRAJR Jeremy Roenick A 2.50 6.00
FSRAJT Julio Teheran A 2.50 6.00
FSRAMCA Miguel Cabrera A 5.00 12.00
FSRAMCP Matt Carpenter A 3.00 8.00
FSRAMG Malcom Gladwell A 2.50 6.00
FSRAMMI Mike Minor A 2.00 5.00
FSRAMTA Masahiro Tanaka A 2.50 6.00
FSRAMTE Mark Teixeira A 2.50 6.00
FSRAPF Prince Fielder A 2.50 6.00
FSRAPS Paul Scheer A 2.50 6.00
FSRARC Rusney Castillo A 2.50 6.00
FSRARW Robb Wolf A 2.50 6.00
FSRASCA Starlin Castro A 2.00 5.00
FSRASCI Steve Cishek A 2.00 5.00
FSRASM Starling Marte A 2.50 6.00
FSRATR Tyson Ross A 2.00 5.00
FSRATT Troy Tulowitzki A 3.00 8.00
FSRATW Taijuan Walker A 2.00 5.00
FSRAVK Val Kilmer A 2.50 6.00
FSRAVM Victor Martinez A 2.50 6.00
FSRAWF Wilmer Flores A 2.50 6.00
FSRAYC Yoenis Cespedes A 2.50 6.00
FSRAYD Yu Darvish A 3.00 8.00
FSRAYP Yasiel Puig A 4.00 10.00
FSRAYV Yordano Ventura A 2.50 6.00
FSRBAC Aroldis Chapman B 3.00 8.00
FSRBAM Andrew McCutchen B 3.00 8.00
FSRBAS Andrelton Simmons B 2.00 5.00
FSRBBB Brandon Belt B 2.50 6.00
FSRBBM Brian McCann B 2.50 6.00
FSRBBP Buster Posey B 4.00 10.00
FSRBBQ Brian Quinn B 2.50 6.00
FSRBCBE Carlos Beltran B 2.50 6.00
FSRBCBL Charlie Blackmon B 3.00 8.00
FSRBCK Craig Kimbrel B 2.50 6.00
FSRBCT Chris Tillman B 2.00 5.00
FSRBCY Christian Yelich B 4.00 10.00
FSRBDO David Ortiz B 3.00 8.00
FSRBDR Darren Rovell B 2.50 6.00
FSRBDS Drew Storen B 2.00 5.00
FSRBDW David Wright B 2.50 6.00
FSRBEL Evan Longoria B 2.50 6.00
FSRBFF Freddie Freeman B 4.00 10.00
FSRBGK Gabe Kapler B 2.00 5.00
FSRBGS Giancarlo Stanton B 3.00 8.00
FSRBHRA Hanley Ramirez B 2.50 6.00
FSRBHRY Hyun-Jin Ryu B 2.50 6.00
FSRBJA Jose Abreu B 3.00 8.00
FSRBJE Jacoby Ellsbury B 2.50 6.00
FSRBJFO Julie Foudy B 2.50 6.00
FSRBJHA Josh Hamilton B 2.50 6.00
FSRBJHE Jason Heyward B 2.50 6.00
FSRBJMU James Murray B 5.00 12.00
FSRBJSC Jonathan Schoop B 2.00 5.00
FSRBJSO Jorge Soler B 3.00 8.00
FSRBJVE Justin Verlander B 3.00 8.00
FSRBJVO Joey Votto B 3.00 8.00
FSRBKL Keith Law B 2.50 6.00
FSRBKM Kelia Moniz B 4.00 10.00
FSRBLM Leonys Martin B 2.00 5.00
FSRBLP Lakey Peterson B 2.50 6.00
FSRBMBE Michelle Beadle B 2.50 6.00
FSRBMBU Madison Bumgarner B 4.00 10.00
FSRBMH Matt Holliday B 3.00 8.00
FSRBMKA Megan Kalmoe B 2.50 6.00
FSRBMKE Matt Kemp B 2.50 6.00
FSRBMT Mike Trout B 15.00 40.00
FSRBMZ Mike Zunino B 2.00 5.00
FSRBNA Nolan Arenado B 4.00 10.00
FSRBNC Nick Castellanos B 3.00 8.00
FSRBPA Pedro Alvarez B 2.00 5.00
FSRBPS Pablo Sandoval B 2.50 6.00
FSRBRB Ryan Braun B 2.50 6.00
FSRBSP Salvador Perez B 2.50 6.00
FSRBSS Stephen Strasburg B 3.00 8.00
FSRBSV Sal Vulcano B 2.50 6.00
FSRBTD Travis d'Arnaud B 2.50 6.00
FSRBWM Wil Myers B 2.00 5.00
FSRBXB Xander Bogaerts B 3.00 8.00
FSRBYM Yadier Molina B 3.00 8.00
FSRBZL Zach Lowe B 2.50 6.00

2015 Topps Allen and Ginter Starting Points

COMPLETE SET (100) 10.00 25.00
STATED ODDS 1:2 HOBBY
SP1 Felix Hernandez .40 1.00
SP2 Albert Pujols .60 1.50
SP3 Mike Trout 2.50 6.00
SP4 Paul Goldschmidt .50 1.25
SP5 Freddie Freeman .60 1.50
SP6 Craig Kimbrel .40 1.00
SP7 Chris Davis .30 .75
SP8 Adam Jones .40 1.00
SP9 Clay Buchholz .30 .75
SP10 Rusney Castillo .40 1.00
SP11 David Ortiz .50 1.25
SP12 Dustin Pedroia .50 1.25
SP13 Hanley Ramirez .40 1.00
SP14 Pablo Sandoval .40 1.00
SP15 Jon Lester .40 1.00
SP16 Anthony Rizzo .75 2.00
SP17 Jorge Soler .50 1.25
SP18 Jose Abreu .50 1.25
SP19 Chris Sale .50 1.25
SP20 Jeff Samardzija .30 .75
SP21 Aroldis Chapman .50 1.25
SP22 Johnny Cueto .40 1.00
SP23 Joey Votto .50 1.25
SP24 Corey Kluber .40 1.00
SP25 Carlos Gonzalez .40 1.00
SP26 Troy Tulowitzki .50 1.25
SP27 Miguel Cabrera .50 1.25
SP28 Yoenis Cespedes .40 1.00
SP29 Victor Martinez .40 1.00
SP30 David Price .40 1.00
SP31 Justin Verlander .50 1.25
SP32 Jose Altuve .40 1.00
SP33 George Springer .40 1.00
SP34 Alex Gordon .40 1.00
SP35 Eric Hosmer .40 1.00
SP36 Mike Moustakas .40 1.00
SP37 Salvador Perez .40 1.00
SP38 Adrian Gonzalez .40 1.00
SP39 Clayton Kershaw 1.00 2.50
SP40 Yasiel Puig .50 1.25
SP41 Jimmy Rollins .40 1.00
SP42 Hyun-Jin Ryu .40 1.00
SP43 Jose Fernandez .50 1.25
SP44 Dee Gordon .30 .75
SP45 Giancarlo Stanton .50 1.25
SP46 Ryan Braun .40 1.00
SP47 Carlos Gomez .30 .75
SP48 Torii Hunter .30 .75
SP49 Joe Mauer .40 1.00
SP50 Kennys Vargas .30 .75
SP51 Michael Cuddyer .30 .75
SP52 Jacob deGrom .50 1.25
SP53 Lucas Duda .40 1.00
SP54 Matt Harvey .40 1.00
SP55 David Wright .40 1.00
SP56 Carlos Beltran .40 1.00
SP57 Jacoby Ellsbury .40 1.00
SP58 Brian McCann .40 1.00
SP59 Alex Rodriguez .60 1.50
SP60 CC Sabathia .40 1.00
SP61 Billy Butler .30 .75
SP62 Coco Crisp .30 .75
SP63 Sonny Gray .40 1.00
SP64 Josh Reddick .30 .75
SP65 Maikel Franco .40 1.00
SP66 Cole Hamels .40 1.00
SP67 Ryan Howard .40 1.00
SP68 Cliff Lee .40 1.00
SP69 Chase Utley .40 1.00
SP70 Starling Marte .40 1.00
SP71 Andrew McCutchen .50 1.25
SP72 Matt Kemp .40 1.00
SP73 Brandon Belt .40 1.00
SP74 Madison Bumgarner .40 1.00
SP75 Hunter Pence .40 1.00
SP76 Buster Posey .60 1.50
SP77 Robinson Cano .40 1.00
SP78 Nelson Cruz .50 1.25
SP79 Hisashi Iwakuma .40 1.00
SP80 Fernando Rodney .30 .75
SP81 Matt Adams .30 .75

SP82 Jason Heyward .40 1.00
SP83 Matt Holliday .50 1.25
SP84 Yadier Molina .50 1.25
SP85 Adam Wainwright .40 1.00
SP86 Evan Longoria .40 1.00
SP87 Adrian Beltre .50 1.25
SP88 Shin-Soo Choo .40 1.00
SP89 Yu Darvish .50 1.25
SP90 Prince Fielder .40 1.00
SP91 Jose Bautista .40 1.00
SP92 Josh Donaldson .40 1.00
SP93 Edwin Encarnacion .50 1.25
SP94 Jose Reyes .40 1.00
SP95 Ian Desmond .30 .75
SP96 Doug Fister .30 .75
SP97 Bryce Harper .75 2.00
SP98 Max Scherzer .50 1.25
SP99 Stephen Strasburg .50 1.25
SP100 Jayson Werth .40 1.00

2015 Topps Allen and Ginter What Once Was Believed

COMPLETE SET (10) 3.00 8.00
OVERALL INSERT ODDS 1:2 HOBBY
WAS1 Flat Earth .30 .75
WAS2 Open Polar Sea .30 .75
WAS3 Ether .30 .75
WAS4 The Four Classical Elements .30 .75
WAS5 Alchemy .30 .75
WAS6 Brontosaurus .30 .75
WAS7 Rain follows the plow .30 .75
WAS8 Phrenology .30 .75
WAS9 California Island .30 .75
WAS10 Geocentric Solar System .30 .75

2015 Topps Allen and Ginter What Once Would Be

COMPLETE SET (10) 3.00 8.00
OVERALL INSERT ODDS 1:2 HOBBY
WOULD1 Flying Car .30 .75
WOULD2 Jetpacks .30 .75
WOULD3 Robot Housekeepers .30 .75
WOULD4 Automated Kitchen .30 .75
WOULD5 Food in pill form .30 .75
WOULD6 Giant Airliners .30 .75
WOULD7 Easy-clean furniture .30 .75
WOULD8 Mail Via Parachute .30 .75
WOULD9 Vacuum Tube trains .30 .75
WOULD10 Lunar Colonization .30 .75

2015 Topps Allen and Ginter X 10th Anniversary

COMPLETE SET (350)
COMMON CARD (1-350) .25 .60
SEMISTARS .30 .75
UNLISTED STARS .40 1.00
COMMON RC (1-300) .40 1.00
RC SEMIS .50 1.25
RC UNLISTED .60 1.50
COMMON SP (301-350) .50 1.25
SP SEMIS .60 1.50
SP UNLISTED .75 2.00
1 Madison Bumgarner .30 .75
2 Nick Markakis .30 .75
3 Adrian Gonzalez .30 .75
4 Wilmer Flores .30 .75
5 Craig Kimbrel .30 .75
6 Lucas Duda .30 .75
7 Eric Hosmer .30 .75
8 Garrett Richards .30 .75
9 Jeff Samardzija .25 .60
10 Curtis Granderson .30 .75
11 Carlos Santana .30 .75
12 Nelson Cruz .40 1.00
13 Koji Uehara .25 .60
14 LaTroy Hawkins .25 .60
15 Justin Verlander .40 1.00
16 Felix Hernandez .30 .75
17 Yadier Molina .40 1.00
18 Adam Eaton .25 .60
19 Charlie Blackmon .40 1.00
20 Leonys Martin .25 .60
21 Kolten Wong .30 .75
22 Trevor Rosenthal .30 .75
23 Johnny Cueto .30 .75
24 Appomattox Court House .25 .60
25 Mark Trumbo .25 .60
26 Steven Souza Jr. .30 .75
27 Maikel Franco RC .50 1.25
28 Jayson Werth .30 .75
29 Nick Swisher .30 .75
30 Megan Kalmoe .25 .60
31 Frank Caliendo .25 .60
32 James Murray .25 .60
33 Michael Wacha .30 .75
34 Buster Olney .25 .60
35 Paul Goldschmidt .40 1.00
36 Anthony Ranaudo RC .40 1.00
37 Mike Mills .25 .60
38 Evan Longoria .30 .75
39 Jon Singleton .30 .75
40 J.J. Hardy .25 .60
41 Brandon Finnegan RC .40 1.00
42 Max Scherzer .40 1.00
43 Adam Jones .30 .75
44 Sal Vulcano .25 .60
45 Chris Owings .25 .60
46 Andrew McCutchen .40 1.00
47 Lance Lynn .25 .60
48 Coco Crisp .25 .60
49 Hisashi Iwakuma .30 .75
50 Francisco Rodriguez .30 .75
51 Matt Garza .25 .60
52 Jake Marisnick .25 .60
53 Brandon Crawford .30 .75
54 Javier Baez RC 4.00 10.00
55 Jonah Keri .25 .60
56 Apollo Creed .25 .60
57 David Cross .25 .60
58 Jacob deGrom .40 1.00
59 Hector Rondon .25 .60
60 Marcus Semien .25 .60
61 Domonic Brown .30 .75
62 Andrelton Simmons .25 .60
63 Edwin Escobar RC .40 1.00
64 Austin Jackson .25 .60
65 David Ortiz .40 1.00
66 Billy Butler .25 .60
67 Malcolm Gladwell .25 .60
68 Matt Barnes RC .40 1.00
69 Christian Bethancourt .25 .60
70 Kyle Seager .25 .60
71 J.D. Martinez .40 1.00
72 Joe Panik .30 .75
73 Daniel Murphy .30 .75
74 Casey McGehee .25 .60
75 Brandon Phillips .25 .60
76 Jake Arrieta .30 .75
77 Jason Hammel .25 .60
78 Carlos Gonzalez .30 .75
79 Grant Miller .25 .60
80 Joe Gatto .25 .60
81 Buck Farmer RC .40 1.00
82 Dalton Pompey RC .50 1.25
83 Matt Harvey .30 .75
84 Josh Harrison .25 .60
85 Kris Bryant RC 6.00 15.00
86 Rick Porcello .30 .75
87 Francisco Liriano .25 .60
88 Carl Crawford .30 .75
89 Jonathan Papelbon .30 .75
90 Darren Rovell .25 .60
91 Howie Kendrick .25 .60
92 Michelle Beadle .25 .60
93 Kelia Moniz .25 .60
94 Xander Bogaerts .40 1.00
95 Kole Calhoun .25 .60
96 Tim Hudson .30 .75
97 Kendall Graveman RC .40 1.00
98 Yimi Garcia RC .40 1.00
99 Yan Gomes .30 .75
100 Greg Holland .25 .60
101 Stephen Strasburg .40 1.00
102 James Clubber Lang .25 .60
103 Salvador Perez .30 .75
104 Didi Gregorius .30 .75
105 Daniel Norris RC .40 1.00
106 Yunel Escobar .25 .60
107 Giancarlo Stanton .40 1.00
108 Prince Fielder .30 .75
109 Troy Tulowitzki .40 1.00
110 Victor Martinez .30 .75
111 Dellin Betances .30 .75
112 Buck 65 .25 .60
113 Ryan Braun .30 .75
114 Brian McCann .30 .75
115 Dustin Pedroia .40 1.00
116 Freddie Freeman .50 1.25
117 Corey Kluber .30 .75
118 Adam Lind .30 .75
119 Paul Scheer .25 .60
120 Matt Adams .25 .60
121 Wei-Yin Chen .25 .60
122 Jesse Hahn .25 .60
123 Micah Johnson RC .40 1.00
124 Lakey Peterson .25 .60
125 Nori Aoki .25 .60
126 Alexei Ramirez .30 .75
127 Nick Castellanos .40 1.00
128 R.A. Dickey .30 .75
129 Yovani Gallardo .25 .60
130 Juan Lagares .25 .60
131 Josh Reddick .25 .60
132 Dilson Herrera RC .50 1.25
133 Addison Russell RC 1.25 3.00
134 Joc Pederson RC .75 2.00
135 Mark Teixeira .30 .75
136 Tyson Ross .25 .60
137 Marlon Byrd .25 .60
138 Michael Pineda .25 .60
139 Chris Sale .40 1.00
140 Jose Altuve .30 .75
141 Justin Upton .30 .75
142 Yasiel Puig .40 1.00
143 Mike Zunino .25 .60
144 Brandon Belt .30 .75
145 Santiago Casilla .25 .60
146 Michael Morse .30 .75
147 Yoenis Cespedes .25 .60
148 Yasmany Tomas RC .50 1.25
149 Andrew Heaney .25 .60
150 Brody Stevens .25 .60
151 Jorge Soler RC .60 1.50
152 Jacoby Ellsbury .30 .75
153 Brandon Moss .25 .60
154 Rusney Castillo RC .50 1.25
155 Mike Moustakas .30 .75
156 Brian Dozier .30 .75
157 Jose Reyes .30 .75
158 Kurt Suzuki .25 .60
159 Devin Mesoraco .25 .60
160 Danny Santana .25 .60
161 Bartolo Colon .25 .60
162 Anthony Rizzo .60 1.50
163 Zach Lowe .30 .75
164 Adrian Beltre .40 1.00
165 Jonathan Lucroy .30 .75
166 Carlos Gomez .25 .60
167 Julie Foudy .25 .60
168 Clay Buchholz .25 .60
169 Yordano Ventura .30 .75
170 Chris Davis .25 .60
171 Anthony Rendon .40 1.00
172 Matt Carpenter .40 1.00
173 Buster Posey .50 1.25
174 Joe Mauer .30 .75
175 DJ LeMahieu .40 1.00
176 Jon Niese .25 .60
177 Bernie Williams .30 .75
178 Travis d'Arnaud .30 .75
179 Manny Machado .40 1.00
180 Scott Kazmir .25 .60
181 Drew Hutchison .25 .60
182 Todd Frazier .30 .75
183 Edwin Encarnacion .40 1.00
184 Marcell Ozuna .40 1.00
185 Gus Malzahn .25 .60
186 Desmond Jennings .30 .75
187 Miguel Cabrera .40 1.00
188 Shelby Miller .30 .75
189 Kennys Vargas .25 .60
190 Michael Bourn .25 .60
191 John Lackey .30 .75
192 Fernando Rodney .25 .60
193 Aramis Ramirez .25 .60
194 Zack Cozart .25 .60
195 Torii Hunter .25 .60
196 Ian Kinsler .30 .75
197 Melky Cabrera .25 .60
198 Albert Pujols .50 1.25
199 Zack Greinke .30 .75
200 Jose Abreu .40 1.00
201 Joe Buck .25 .60
202 Travis Ishikawa .25 .60
203 David Wright .30 .75
204 Chase Headley .25 .60
205 Dustin Ackley .25 .60
206 Erick Aybar .25 .60
207 Derek Norris .25 .60
208 Jose Fernandez .40 1.00
209 Hanley Ramirez .30 .75
210 Starling Marte .30 .75
211 Kyle Lohse .25 .60
212 Chris Tillman .25 .60
213 Elvis Andrus .30 .75
214 Corey Dickerson .25 .60
215 Joey Votto .40 1.00
216 Jake Lamb RC .60 1.50
217 Wade Miley .25 .60
218 Carlos Rodon RC .60 1.50
219 Huston Street .25 .60
220 Yasmani Grandal .25 .60
221 Doug Fister .25 .60
222 Gregory Polanco .30 .75
223 Incredibeard .25 .60
224 Edinson Volquez .25 .60
225 Thunderlips .25 .60
226 Nolan Arenado .50 1.25
227 Christian Yelich .50 1.25
228 Robb Wolf .25 .60
229 Ivan Drago .25 .60
230 Keith Law .25 .60
231 Henderson Alvarez .25 .60
232 Matt Holliday .40 1.00
233 Ike Davis .25 .60
234 Michael Cuddyer .25 .60
235 Michael Taylor RC .40 1.00
236 Julio Teheran .30 .75
237 Hyun-Jin Ryu .30 .75
238 Dee Gordon .25 .60
239 Zach Britton .30 .75
240 Trevor May RC .40 1.00
241 CC Sabathia .30 .75
242 James McCann RC .60 1.50
243 Jean Segura .25 .60
244 Jason Kipnis .30 .75
245 Ryan Howard .30 .75
246 Andrew Cashner .25 .60
247 George Springer .30 .75
248 Jose Bautista .30 .75
249 Bryce Harper .60 1.50
250 Jimmy Rollins .30 .75
251 Adam LaRoche .25 .60
252 Mike Trout 2.00 5.00
253 Carlos Beltran .30 .75
254 Alex Gordon .30 .75
255 Steven Moya RC .50 1.25
256 Sonny Gray .30 .75
257 Pablo Sandoval .30 .75
258 Rocky Balboa .25 .60
259 Jonathan Schoop .25 .60
260 Hunter Pence .30 .75
261 Yu Darvish .40 1.00
262 Alex Cobb .25 .60
263 Pedro Alvarez .25 .60
264 Matt Kemp .30 .75
265 Jung Ho Kang RC .40 1.00
266 Drew Storen .25 .60
267 Jered Weaver .30 .75
268 Jimbo Fisher .25 .60
269 Jeremy Roenick .25 .60
270 Mike Foltynewicz RC .40 1.00
271 Dexter Fowler .30 .75
272 Glen Perkins .25 .60
273 Cole Hamels .30 .75
274 Mookie Betts .60 1.50
275 Billy Hamilton .30 .75
276 Alex Rodriguez .50 1.25
277 Starlin Castro .25 .60
278 Cliff Lee .30 .75
279 Jon Jay .25 .60
280 Jenrry Mejia .25 .60
281 Cory Spangenberg RC .40 1.00
282 Adeiny Hechavarria .25 .60
283 Aaron Hill .25 .60
284 Jay Bruce .30 .75
285 Ichiro .50 1.25
286 Addison Reed .25 .60
287 Jon Lester .30 .75
288 Robinson Cano .30 .75
289 Wil Myers .25 .60
290 Ryan Zimmerman .30 .75
291 James Shields .25 .60
292 Grant Balfour .25 .60
293 Philae Probe .25 .60
294 Adam Wainwright .30 .75
295 Joe Nathan .25 .60
296 Kenley Jansen .30 .75
297 Magna Carta .25 .60
298 Rubby De La Rosa .25 .60
299 Brian Quinn .25 .60
300 Bryce Brentz RC .40 1.00
301 Justin Morneau .60 1.50
302 Fall of the Berlin Wall .50 1.25
303 Denard Span .50 1.25
304 Gary Brown RC .50 1.25
305 Chris Carter .50 1.25
306 Stephen Drew .50 1.25
307 Jorge De La Rosa .50 1.25
308 David Freese .50 1.25
309 Gabe Kapler .50 1.25
310 Chris Coghlan .50 1.25
311 Michael Brantley .60 1.50
312 Gerrit Cole .75 2.00
313 Jhonny Peralta .50 1.25
314 Ian Desmond .50 1.25
315 Steve Cishek .50 1.25
316 Evan Gattis .50 1.25
317 Hunter Strickland RC .50 1.25
318 David Price .60 1.50
319 Brian Windhorst .50 1.25
320 Dallas Keuchel .60 1.50
321 Ben Zobrist .60 1.50
322 Mark Melancon .50 1.25
323 Joaquin Benoit .50 1.25
324 Will Middlebrooks .50 1.25
325 Aroldis Chapman .75 2.00
326 Mitch Moreland .50 1.25
327 Jeff Mauro .50 1.25
328 Val Kilmer .50 1.25
329 Brett Gardner .60 1.50
330 Jason Heyward .60 1.50
331 Alcides Escobar .60 1.50
332 Matt Cain .60 1.50
333 Chase Utley .60 1.50
334 Nick Tropeano .50 1.25
335 Collin Cowgill .50 1.25
336 Shane Victorino .60 1.50
337 Mike Olt .50 1.25
338 Mike Napoli .50 1.25
339 Clayton Kershaw 1.50 4.00
340 Neftali Feliz .50 1.25
341 Malala Yousafzai .50 1.25
342 Josh Donaldson .60 1.50
343 Angel Pagan .50 1.25
344 Jordan Zimmermann .60 1.50
345 Lonnie Chisenhall .50 1.25
346 Shin-Soo Choo .60 1.50
347 Aaron Paul .60 1.50
348 Aaron Sanchez .60 1.50
349 Sam Tuivailala RC .50 1.25
350 Masahiro Tanaka .60 1.50

2015 Topps Allen and Ginter X 10th Anniversary Mini

*MINI 1-300: 1X TO 2.5X BASIC
*MINI RC 1-300: .6X TO 1.5X BASIC RCs
*MINI SP 301-350: 1X TO 2.5X BASIC
252 Mike Trout 10.00 25.00

2015 Topps Allen and Ginter X 10th Anniversary Mini A and G Back

*MINI AG BACK 1-300: 1.2X TO 3X BASIC
*MINI AG BACK RC 1-300: .75X TO 2X BASIC RCs
*MINI AG BACK SP 301-350: 1.2X TO 3X BASIC
252 Mike Trout 12.00 30.00

2015 Topps Allen and Ginter X 10th Anniversary Mini Silver

*MINI SLVR 1-300: 2X TO 5X BASIC
*MINI SLVR RC 1-300: 1.2X TO 3X BASIC RCs
*MINI SLVR SP 301-350: 2X TO 5X BASIC
54 Javier Baez 40.00 100.00
85 Kris Bryant 60.00 150.00
252 Mike Trout 20.00 50.00

2016 Topps Allen and Ginter

COMPLETE SET (350) 20.00 50.00
COMP.SET w/o SP's (300) 12.00 30.00
SP ODDS 1:2 HOBBY
ORIGINAL BUYBACK ODDS 1:6679 HOBBY
ORIG.BUYBACK PRINT RUN 1 SER.#'d SET
1 Jorge Soler .25 .60
2 Ryan Braun .25 .60
3 Joey Gallo .20 .50
4 Justin Verlander .25 .60
5 Kyle Waldrop RC .30 .75
6 Luke Maile RC .25 .60
7 John Lamb RC .25 .60
8 Denise Austin .20 .50
9 Tom Glavine .20 .50
10 Jason Sklar .20 .50
11 Howie Kendrick .15 .40
12 Trevor Story RC 1.00 2.50
13 Kevin Gausman .15 .40
14 Kendrys Morales .15 .40
15 Mark Trumbo .15 .40
16 Trayce Thompson RC .40 1.00
17 Ian Desmond .15 .40
18 Kolten Wong .20 .50
19 Rollie Fingers .20 .50
20 Michael Pineda .15 .40
21 Ben Zobrist .20 .50
22 Francisco Rodriguez .20 .50
23 Addison Russell .25 .60
24 Max Kepler RC .40 1.00
25 Charlie Blackmon .25 .60
26 John Lackey .20 .50
27 Matt Duffy .15 .40
28 Elvis Andrus .20 .50
29 Jay Bruce .20 .50
30 Curtis Granderson .20 .50
31 Brad Ziegler .15 .40
32 Falcon 9 Rocket .20 .50
33 Ender Inciarte .15 .40
34 Rick Klein .20 .50
35 Jayson Werth .20 .50
36 Alex Rodriguez .30 .75
37 Dawn Spacecraft .20 .50
38 David Peralta .15 .40
39 Paul Goldschmidt .25 .60
40 Jordan Zimmermann .20 .50
41 Drew Smyly .15 .40
42 Cuban Embassy .20 .50
43 Jake Odorizzi .15 .40
44 Miguel Castro RC .25 .60
45 Laurence Leavy .20 .50
46 Ben Revere .15 .40
47 Corey Dickerson .15 .40
48 J.T. Realmuto .25 .60
49 Ketel Marte RC .50 1.25
50 Daniel Murphy .20 .50
51 A.J. Ramos .15 .40
52 Adam Eaton .15 .40
53 Logan Forsythe .15 .40
54 Jose Abreu .25 .60
55 Hector Rondon .15 .40
56 Carlos Correa .25 .60
57 Jim Rice .20 .50
58 Freddie Freeman .30 .75
59 Billy Hamilton .20 .50
60 Devin Mesoraco .15 .40
61 Miguel Cabrera .25 .60
62 Dellin Betances .20 .50
63 Monica Abbott .20 .50
64 Steve Schirripa .20 .50
65 Hisashi Iwakuma .20 .50
66 Miguel Sano RC .40 1.00
67 Melky Cabrera .15 .40
68 Dexter Fowler .20 .50
69 Roberto Alomar .20 .50
70 Chase Headley .15 .40
71 Matt Reynolds RC .25 .60
72 Jake McGee .15 .40
73 James Shields .15 .40
74 Brian Dozier .20 .50
75 Mike Moustakas .20 .50
76 Collin McHugh .15 .40
77 Kevin Pillar .15 .40
78 Jose Berrios RC .30 .75
79 Dustin Garneau RC .25 .60
80 Edwin Encarnacion .25 .60
81 Brian Johnson RC .25 .60
82 Gerardo Parra .15 .40
83 David Wright .20 .50
84 Robinson Cano .20 .50
85 Prince Fielder .20 .50
86 Adam Jones .20 .50
87 Craig Kimbrel .20 .50
88 Jose Fernandez .25 .60
89 Dallas Keuchel .20 .50
90 George Lopez .20 .50
91 Nick Hundley .15 .40
92 Steven Matz .20 .50
93 Mike Piazza .25 .60
94 Todd Frazier .20 .50
95 Jimmy Nelson .15 .40
96 Jason Kipnis .20 .50
97 Kyle Schwarber RC .75 2.00
98 Michael Conforto RC .30 .75
99 Luis Severino RC .30 .75
100 Rob Refsnyder RC .30 .75
101 Roger Clemens .20 .50
102 Aaron Nola RC .50 1.25
103 Carlos Martinez .20 .50
104 Byron Buxton .20 .50
105 Alex Dickerson RC .25 .60
106 Steve Spurrier .20 .50
107 Matt Stonie .20 .50
108 Justin Turner .20 .50
109 Eduardo Rodriguez .15 .40
110 Michele Steele .20 .50
111 Lorenzo Cain .15 .40
112 Kris Bryant .30 .75
113 Alcides Escobar .20 .50
114 Randy Sklar .20 .50
115 Brad Miller .20 .50
116 Jose Reyes .20 .50
117 Robin Yount .20 .50
118 Evan Gattis .15 .40
119 Gennady Golovkin 4.00 10.00
120 K.Maeda RC/J.Urias RC .50 1.25
121 Corey Seager RC 2.00 5.00
122 Andrew Heaney .15 .40
123 Alex Cobb .15 .40
124 Jonathan Lucroy .20 .50
125 Carl Edwards Jr. RC .30 .75
126 Greg Bird RC .30 .75
127 Lucas Duda .20 .50
128 Aroldis Chapman .25 .60
129 Zack Greinke .20 .50
130 Gregory Polanco .20 .50
131 Brooks Robinson .20 .50
132 Leigh Steinberg .20 .50
133 Joc Pederson .20 .50
134 Henry Owens .20 .50
135 Luis Gonzalez .20 .50
136 Matt Kemp .20 .50
137 Marcus Semien .15 .40
138 Cord McCoy .20 .50
139 Gio Gonzalez .20 .50
140 Caleb Cotham RC .30 .75
141 Colin Rea RC .25 .60
142 Jake Arrieta .20 .50
143 Adrian Gonzalez .20 .50
144 Matt Holliday .25 .60
145 Mike Greenberg .20 .50
146 Evan Longoria .20 .50
147 Martin Prado .15 .40
148 Kole Calhoun .15 .40
149 Michael Brantley .15 .40
150 Eric Hosmer .20 .50
151 David Ortiz .25 .60
152 Gary Sanchez RC .75 2.00
153 Jung Ho Kang .15 .40
154 Ervin Santana .15 .40
155 Brandon Phillips .15 .40
156 Jason Heyward .20 .50
157 Gerrit Cole .25 .60
158 Joe McKeehen .20 .50
159 Brett Gardner .20 .50
160 Steve Kerr .20 .50
161 Vinny G .20 .50
162 Josh Harrison .15 .40
163 Zach Lee RC .25 .60
164 Steven Souza Jr. .20 .50
165 Nelson Cruz .25 .60
166 Morgan Spurlock .20 .50
167 Jeff Samardzija .15 .40
168 Don Mattingly .50 1.25
169 Adrian Beltre .25 .60
170 Max Scherzer .25 .60
171 Brandon Crawford .20 .50
172 Joe Morgan .20 .50
173 Billy Burns .15 .40
174 Frankie Montas RC .30 .75
175 Jonathan Schoop .15 .40
176 Neil Walker .20 .50
177 Mark Teixeira .20 .50
178 David Robertson .15 .40
179 Jen Welter .20 .50
180 Ryne Sandberg .50 1.25
181 Alex Wood .15 .40
182 Nolan Arenado .30 .75
183 Andrew McCutchen .25 .60
184 Mookie Betts .40 1.00
185 J.D. Martinez .25 .60
186 Alex Gordon .20 .50
187 Carl Yastrzemski .40 1.00
188 Edgar Martinez .20 .50
189 Buster Posey .30 .75
190 Jon Gray RC .25 .60
191 Anthony Anderson .20 .50
192 Dennis Eckersley .20 .50
193 Huston Street .15 .40
194 Mike Trout 1.25 3.00
195 Joey Votto .25 .60
196 Josh Reddick .15 .40
197 George Springer .20 .50
198 Ari Shaffir .20 .50
199 Carlton Fisk .20 .50
200 Carlos Gomez .15 .40
201 Byung Ho Park RC .30 .75
202 Missy Franklin .20 .50
203 Ernie Johnson .20 .50
204 Drew Storen .15 .40
205 Carlos Santana .20 .50
206 Bob Gibson .20 .50
207 Brandon Belt .20 .50
208 Joe Panik .20 .50
209 Andrew Miller .20 .50
210 Michael Breed .20 .50
211 Albert Pujols .30 .75
212 Maria Sharapova .20 .50
213 Heidi Watney .20 .50
214 Justin Bour .20 .50
215 Khris Davis .25 .60
216 Hannah Storm .20 .50
217 Julio Teheran .20 .50
218 Masahiro Tanaka .20 .50
219 Delino DeShields .15 .40
220 Matt Duffy .15 .40
221 Brian McCann .20 .50
222 Nomar Mazara RC .40 1.00
223 Erick Aybar .15 .40
224 Gary Carter .20 .50
225 Brandon Drury RC .40 1.00
226 Luke Jackson RC .25 .60
227 Timothy Busfield .20 .50
228 Colin Cowherd .20 .50
229 Mitch Moreland .15 .40
230 Jessica Mendoza .20 .50
231 Kaleb Cowart RC .25 .60
232 Hector Olivera RC .30 .75
233 Adam Lind .20 .50
234 Glen Perkins .15 .40
235 Cheyenne Woods .20 .50
236 Brad Boxberger .15 .40
237 Dustin Pedroia .25 .60
238 Tyler White RC .25 .60
239 Brandon Moss .15 .40
240 Robert Raiola .20 .50
241 Orlando Jones .20 .50
242 DJ LeMahieu .25 .60
243 Jay Oakerson .20 .50
244 Gravitational Waves .20 .50
245 Dwier Brown .20 .50
246 Mike Francesa .20 .50
247 Papal Visit .20 .50
248 Jill Martin .20 .50
249 Paul McBeth 1.25 3.00
250 Jose Canseco .20 .50
251 Stephen Piscotty RC .40 1.00
252 Cole Hamels .20 .50
253 Ozzie Smith .30 .75
254 Bryce Harper .40 1.00
255 Nomar Garciaparra .20 .50
256 Starling Marte .20 .50
257 Chris Archer .15 .40
258 Kenley Jansen .20 .50
259 Jose Peraza RC .30 .75
260 Anthony Rizzo .40 1.00
261 Carlos Carrasco .15 .40
262 Giancarlo Stanton .25 .60
263 Hanley Ramirez .20 .50
264 Xander Bogaerts .25 .60
265 Felix Hernandez .20 .50
266 Anthony Rendon .25 .60
267 Sonny Gray .20 .50
268 Frank Thomas .25 .60
269 Maikel Franco .20 .50
270 David Price .20 .50
271 A.J. Pollock .15 .40
272 Troy Tulowitzki .25 .60
273 Dee Gordon .15 .40
274 Chris Sale .25 .60
275 Jacob deGrom .25 .60
276 Matt Harvey .20 .50
277 Manny Machado .25 .60
278 Madison Bumgarner .20 .50
279 Paul Molitor .25 .60
280 Paul O'Neill .20 .50
281 Jose Bautista .20 .50
282 Stephen Strasburg .25 .60
283 Michael Wacha .20 .50
284 Orlando Cepeda .20 .50
285 Josh Donaldson .20 .50
286 Guido Knudson RC .25 .60
287 Andre Dawson .20 .50
288 Lance McCullers .15 .40
289 Jose Quintana .15 .40
290 Andrew Faulkner RC .30 .75
291 Kevin Kiermaier .20 .50
292 Marcell Ozuna .25 .60
293 Jonathan Papelbon .20 .50
294 Carlos Rodon .25 .60
295 Jose Altuve .25 .60
296 Rickey Henderson .25 .60
297 Corey Kluber .20 .50
298 Jacoby Ellsbury .20 .50
299 Clayton Kershaw .50 1.25
300 Trea Turner RC .75 2.00
301 Tyson Ross SP .40 1.00
302 Trevor Brown SP RC .50 1.25
303 Wei-Yin Chen SP .40 1.00
304 Yasmani Grandal SP .40 1.00
305 Tyler Duffey SP RC .40 1.00
306 Yu Darvish SP .60 1.50
307 Russell Martin SP .40 1.00
308 Andy Pettitte SP .50 1.25
309 Yasmany Tomas SP .40 1.00
310 Patrick Corbin SP .50 1.25
311 Wellington Castillo SP .40 1.00
312 Carlos Beltran SP .50 1.25
313 Stephen Vogt SP .50 1.25
314 Starlin Castro SP .40 1.00
315 Santiago Casilla SP .40 1.00
316 Ryan Weber SP RC .40 1.00
317 Yordano Ventura SP .50 1.25
318 Pedro Severino SP RC .40 1.00
319 Yasiel Puig SP .60 1.50
320 Roberto Clemente SP 1.50 4.00
321 Nick Castellanos SP .60 1.50
322 Ryan LaMarre SP RC .40 1.00
323 Victor Martinez SP .50 1.25
324 Rob Refsnyder SP .50 1.25
325 Raisel Iglesias SP .50 1.25
326 Peter O'Brien SP RC .40 1.00
327 Raul Mondesi SP RC .50 1.25
328 Randal Grichuk SP .40 1.00
329 Andre Ethier SP .50 1.25
330 Zack Godley SP RC .40 1.00
331 Taijuan Walker SP .40 1.00
332 Yan Gomes SP .40 1.00
333 Shin-Soo Choo SP .50 1.25
334 Scott Kazmir SP .40 1.00
335 Shawn Tolleson SP .40 1.00
336 Tom Murphy SP RC .40 1.00
337 Steve Cishek SP .40 1.00
338 Stephen Piscotty SP .60 1.50
339 Salvador Perez SP .50 1.25
340 Roberto Osuna SP .40 1.00
341 Richie Shaffer SP RC .40 1.00
342 Trea Turner SP 1.25 3.00
343 Shelby Miller SP .50 1.25
344 Ryan Zimmerman SP .50 1.25
345 Wil Myers SP .40 1.00
346 Pablo Sandoval SP .50 1.25
347 Sean Doolittle SP .40 1.00
348 Trevor Plouffe SP .40 1.00
349 Travis d'Arnaud SP .50 1.25
350 Steve Carlton SP .50 1.25
NNO Julio Urias 4.00 10.00

2016 Topps Allen and Ginter Mini
COMP.SET w/o EXT (350) 100.00 250.00
*MINI 1-300: 1X TO 2.5X BASIC
*MINI 1-300 RC: .6X TO 1.5X BASIC RCs
*MINI SP 301-350: .6X TO 1.5X BASIC
MINI SP ODDS 1:13 HOBBY
351-400 RANDOM WITHIN RIP CARDS
STATED PLATE ODDS 1:415 HOBBY
PLATE PRINT RUN 1 SET PER COLOR
BLACK-CYAN-MAGENTA-YELLOW ISSUED
NO PLATE PRICING DUE TO SCARCITY
351 Stephen Piscotty EXT 20.00 50.00
352 Rickey Henderson EXT 25.00 60.00
353 Carlos Correa EXT 25.00 60.00
354 Andrew McCutchen EXT 20.00 50.00
355 Mike Piazza EXT 20.00 50.00
356 Jason Kipnis EXT 25.00 60.00
357 Adrian Gonzalez EXT 15.00 40.00
358 Clayton Kershaw EXT 40.00 100.00
359 Matt Harvey EXT 20.00 50.00
360 Ryne Sandberg EXT 25.00 60.00
361 Ryan Braun EXT 15.00 40.00
362 Corey Seager EXT 50.00 120.00
363 Adrian Beltre EXT 20.00 50.00
364 Kyle Schwarber EXT 25.00 60.00
365 Dallas Keuchel EXT 15.00 40.00
366 David Price EXT 15.00 40.00
367 Joey Votto EXT 20.00 50.00
368 Jacoby Ellsbury EXT 15.00 40.00
369 Mike Trout EXT 100.00 250.00
370 Jason Heyward EXT 15.00 40.00
371 Todd Frazier EXT 15.00 40.00
372 Nolan Arenado EXT 25.00 60.00
373 Bryce Harper EXT 30.00 80.00
374 Manny Machado EXT 20.00 50.00
375 Felix Hernandez EXT 20.00 50.00
376 Matt Kemp EXT 20.00 50.00
377 Lorenzo Cain EXT 12.00 30.00
378 Luis Severino EXT 15.00 40.00
379 Trea Turner EXT 40.00 100.00
380 Maikel Franco EXT 15.00 40.00
381 Freddie Freeman EXT 25.00 60.00
382 Madison Bumgarner EXT 15.00 40.00
383 Sonny Gray EXT 15.00 40.00
384 Edwin Encarnacion EXT 20.00 50.00
385 J.D. Martinez EXT 20.00 50.00
386 Tom Glavine EXT 20.00 50.00
387 Jake Arrieta EXT 15.00 40.00
388 Zack Greinke EXT 15.00 40.00
389 Brian Dozier EXT 15.00 40.00
390 Michael Conforto EXT 25.00 60.00
391 Corey Dickerson EXT 20.00 50.00
392 Xander Bogaerts EXT 20.00 50.00
393 Robinson Cano EXT 20.00 50.00
394 Paul Molitor EXT 20.00 50.00
395 Joe Morgan EXT 30.00 80.00
396 Max Scherzer EXT 20.00 50.00
397 Dee Gordon EXT 12.00 30.00
398 Joey Gallo EXT 15.00 40.00
399 Chris Archer EXT 12.00 30.00
400 Jose Bautista EXT 15.00 40.00

2016 Topps Allen and Ginter Mini A and G Back
*MINI AG 1-300: 1.2X TO 3X BASIC
*MINI AG 1-300 RC: .75X TO 2X BASIC RCs
*MINI AG SP 301-350: .75X TO 2X BASIC
MINI AG ODDS 1:5 HOBBY
MINI AG SP ODDS 1:65 HOBBY

2016 Topps Allen and Ginter Mini Black
*MINI BLK 1-300: 1.5X TO 4X BASIC
*MINI BLK 1-300 RC: 1X TO 2.5X BASIC RCs
*MINI BLK SP 301-350: 1X TO 2.5X BASIC
MINI BLK ODDS 1:10 HOBBY
MINI BLK SP ODDS 1:130 HOBBY

2016 Topps Allen and Ginter Mini Brooklyn Back
*MINI BRK 1-300: 12X TO 30X BASIC
*MINI BRK 1-300 RC: 8X TO 20X BASIC RCs
*MINI BRK SP 301-350: 5X TO 12X BASIC
MINI BRK ODDS 1:146 HOBBY
STATED PRINT RUN 25 SER.#'d SETS

2016 Topps Allen and Ginter Mini No Card Number
*MINI NNO 1-300: 5X TO 12X BASIC
*MINI NNO 1-300 RC: 3X TO 8X BASIC RCs
*MINI NNO SP 301-350: 2X TO 5X BASIC
MINI NNO ODDS 1:73 HOBBY

2016 Topps Allen and Ginter Ancient Rome Coin Relics
STATED ODDS 1:1110 HOBBY
ARR1 The Colosseum 75.00 200.00
ARR2 Arch of Septimius Severus 50.00 100.00
ARR3 Verona Arena 50.00 100.00
ARR4 Pont du Gard Aqueduct 50.00 100.00
ARR5 Aqueduct of Segovia 50.00 100.00
ARR6 Roman Baths 50.00 100.00
ARR7 Palmyra 50.00 100.00
ARR8 The Pantheon 60.00 150.00
ARR9 Tower of Hercules 50.00 100.00
ARR10 Hadrian's Wall 50.00 100.00
ARR11 Castel Sant'Angelo 50.00 100.00
ARR12 Porta Nigra 50.00 100.00
ARR13 Arch of Constantine 50.00 100.00
ARR14 Arch of Titus 50.00 100.00
ARR15 Baths of Caracalla 50.00 100.00
ARR16 Pompeii 75.00 200.00
ARR17 Arena in Arles 50.00 100.00
ARR18 Pula Arena 50.00 100.00
ARR19 Library of Celsus 50.00 100.00
ARR20 Theatre of Bosra 50.00 100.00
ARR21 Maison Carree 50.00 100.00
ARR22 Curia Julia 50.00 100.00
ARR23 Alcantara Bridge 50.00 120.00
ARR24 Baalbek 50.00 120.00

2016 Topps Allen and Ginter Baseball Legends
COMPLETE SET (25) 6.00 15.00
STATED ODDS 1:5 HOBBY
BL1 Al Kaline .40 1.00
BL2 Carl Yastrzemski .60 1.50
BL3 Babe Ruth 1.00 2.50
BL4 Jackie Robinson .40 1.00
BL5 Ty Cobb .60 1.50
BL6 Duke Snider .30 .75
BL7 Johnny Bench .40 1.00
BL8 George Brett .75 2.00
BL9 Roberto Clemente 1.00 2.50
BL10 Hank Aaron .75 2.00
BL11 Ted Williams .75 2.00
BL12 Reggie Jackson .30 .75
BL13 Jim Palmer .30 .75
BL14 Larry Doby .30 .75
BL15 Whitey Ford .30 .75
BL16 Bob Feller .30 .75
BL17 Honus Wagner .40 1.00
BL18 Willie Mays .75 2.00
BL19 Ken Griffey Jr. .75 2.00
BL20 Willie Stargell .30 .75
BL21 Cal Ripken Jr. 1.25 3.00
BL22 Rod Carew .30 .75
BL23 Nolan Ryan 1.25 3.00
BL24 Sandy Koufax .75 2.00
BL25 Eddie Mathews .40 1.00

2016 Topps Allen and Ginter Box Topper Relics
STATED ODDS 1:111 HOBBY BOXES
STATED PRINT RUN 25 SER.#'d SETS
BLRAM Andrew McCutchen 30.00 80.00
BLRAP Albert Pujols 12.00 30.00
BLRDO David Ortiz 30.00 80.00
BLRDW David Wright 30.00 80.00
BLRGS Giancarlo Stanton 12.00 30.00
BLRJD Jacob deGrom 10.00 25.00
BLRMC Miguel Cabrera 25.00 60.00
BLRMH Matt Harvey 8.00 20.00
BLRMTA Masahiro Tanaka 8.00 20.00
BLRMTR Mike Trout 60.00 150.00

2016 Topps Allen and Ginter Box Toppers
BLAM Andrew McCutchen 1.50 4.00
BLAP Albert Pujols 2.00 5.00
BLAR Anthony Rizzo 2.50 6.00
BLBH Bryce Harper 2.50 6.00
BLBP Buster Posey 2.00 5.00
BLCK Clayton Kershaw 3.00 8.00
BLDO David Ortiz 1.50 4.00
BLDW David Wright 1.25 3.00
BLFH Felix Hernandez 1.25 3.00
BLGS Giancarlo Stanton 1.50 4.00
BLJD Jacob deGrom 1.50 4.00
BLMH Matt Harvey 1.25 3.00
BLMT Mike Trout 8.00 20.00
BLPG Paul Goldschmidt 1.50 4.00
BLTT Troy Tulowitzki 1.50 4.00

2016 Topps Allen and Ginter Double Rip Cards
STATED ODDS 1:720 HOBBY
PRINT RUNS B/WN 25-50 COPIES PER
PRICING FOR UNRIPPED
UNRIPPED HAVE ADD'L CARDS WITHIN
DRIP1 M.Bumgarner/B.Posey 75.00 200.00
DRIP2 K.Schwarber/K.Bryant 75.00 200.00
DRIP3 C.Correa/K.Bryant 75.00 200.00
DRIP4 M.Harvey/J.deGrom 75.00 200.00
DRIP5 B.Harper/M.Trout 75.00 200.00
DRIP6 J.Bautista/J.Donaldson 75.00 200.00
DRIP7 H.Aaron/B.Ruth 175.00 350.00
DRIP8 M.Piazza/K.Griffey Jr. 75.00 200.00
DRIP9 D.Ortiz/H.Owens 75.00 200.00
DRIP10 M.Machado/C.Ripken Jr. 75.00 200.00
DRIP11 S.Perez/A.Gordon 75.00 200.00
DRIP12 J.Arrieta/D.Keuchel 75.00 200.00
DRIP13 J.Verlander/M.Cabrera 75.00 200.00
DRIP14 O.Smith/Y.Molina 75.00 200.00
DRIP15 A.McCutchen/W.Stargell 75.00 200.00
DRIP16 A.Nola/C.Schilling 75.00 200.00
DRIP17 L.Severino/M.Tanaka 75.00 200.00
DRIP18 K.Maeda/C.Kershaw 75.00 200.00
DRIP19 Z.Greinke/R.Johnson 75.00 200.00
DRIP20 I.Suzuki/G.Stanton 75.00 200.00

2016 Topps Allen and Ginter Double Rip Cards Ripped
UNRIPPED ODDS 1:720 HOBBY
PRINT RUNS B/WN 25-50 COPIES PER
PRICING FOR CLEANLY RIPPED CARDS
DRIP1 Bumgarner/Posey/50 4.00 10.00
DRIP2 Schwarber/Bryant/50 6.00 15.00
DRIP3 Correa/Bryant/50 4.00 10.00
DRIP4 Harvey/deGrom/50 3.00 8.00
DRIP5 Harper/Trout/50 15.00 40.00
DRIP6 J.Bautista/J.Donaldson/50 2.50 6.00
DRIP7 Aaron/Ruth/50 8.00 20.00
DRIP8 Piazza/Griffey Jr./50 6.00 15.00
DRIP9 D.Ortiz/H.Owens/50 3.00 8.00
DRIP10 Machado/Ripken/50 10.00 25.00
DRIP11 S.Perez/A.Gordon/25 2.50 6.00
DRIP12 J.Arrieta/D.Keuchel/25 2.50 6.00
DRIP13 Verlander/Cabrera/50 3.00 8.00
DRIP14 Smith/Molina/50 4.00 10.00
DRIP15 A.McCutchen/W.Stargell/50 3.00 8.00
DRIP16 A.Nola/C.Schilling/50 4.00 10.00
DRIP17 L.Severino/M.Tanaka/50 2.50 6.00
DRIP18 Maeda/Kershaw/50 6.00 15.00
DRIP19 Z.Greinke/R.Johnson/50 3.00 8.00
DRIP20 Suzuki/Stanton/50 4.00 10.00

2016 Topps Allen and Ginter Framed Mini Autographs
STATED ODDS 1:48 HOBBY
EXCHANGE DEADLINE 6/30/2018
AGAAA Anthony Anderson 8.00 20.00
AGAAG Andres Galarraga 5.00 12.00
AGAAN Aaron Nola 20.00 50.00
AGAAS Ari Shaffir 4.00 10.00
AGABD Brandon Drury 6.00 15.00
AGABH Bryce Harper 125.00 300.00
AGABHP Byung-Ho Park 5.00 12.00
AGABJ Brian Johnson 4.00 10.00
AGABM Brandon Moss 4.00 10.00
AGABP Buster Posey 40.00 100.00
AGABS Blake Snell 10.00 25.00
AGACA Canelo Alvarez 60.00 150.00
AGACC Colin Cowherd 10.00 25.00
AGACC Carlos Correa 40.00 100.00
AGACE Carl Edwards Jr. 5.00 12.00
AGACM Cord McCoy 4.00 10.00
AGACR Colin Rea 4.00 10.00
AGACSA Chris Sale 10.00 25.00
AGACSE Corey Seager 30.00 80.00
AGACW Cheyenne Woods 8.00 20.00
AGADA Denise Austin 6.00 15.00
AGADB Dwier Brown 4.00 10.00
AGADK Dallas Keuchel 12.00 30.00
AGADL DJ LeMahieu 10.00 25.00
AGAEJ Ernie Johnson 25.00 60.00
AGAES Errol Spence Jr. 25.00 60.00
AGAFH Felix Hernandez 12.00 30.00
AGAFM Frankie Montas 5.00 12.00
AGAFV Fernando Valenzuela 20.00 50.00
AGAFW Frank Whaley 8.00 20.00
AGAGB Greg Bird 5.00 12.00
AGAGG Gennady Golovkin 150.00 400.00
AGAGL George Lopez 12.00 30.00
AGAHA Hank Aaron 120.00 300.00
AGAHOL Hector Olivera 5.00 12.00
AGAHS Hannah Storm 8.00 20.00
AGAHW Heidi Watney 15.00 40.00
AGAJBA Javier Baez 25.00 60.00
AGAJBE Jose Berrios 5.00 12.00
AGAJC Jose Canseco 12.00 30.00
AGAJD Jacob deGrom 20.00 50.00
AGAJM Jill Martin 4.00 10.00
AGAJME Jessica Mendoza 6.00 15.00
AGAJMK Joe McKeehen 6.00 15.00
AGAJO Jay Oakerson 6.00 15.00
AGAJP Jose Peraza 5.00 12.00
AGAJS Jorge Soler 6.00 15.00
AGAJS Jason Sklar 8.00 20.00
AGAJW Jen Welter 4.00 10.00
AGAKB Kris Bryant 75.00 200.00
AGAKG Ken Griffey Jr. 125.00 300.00
AGAKMA Kenta Maeda 20.00 50.00
AGAKMR Ketel Marte 8.00 20.00
AGAKS Kyle Schwarber 20.00 50.00
AGAKW Kyle Waldrop 5.00 12.00
AGALG Luis Gonzalez 5.00 12.00
AGALJ Luke Jackson 4.00 10.00
AGALL Laurence Leavy 4.00 10.00
AGALS Leigh Steinberg 6.00 15.00
AGALS Luis Severino 20.00 50.00
AGAMAB Monica Abbott 6.00 15.00
AGAMB Mike Breed 4.00 10.00
AGAMCA Miguel Castro 4.00 10.00
AGAMCO Michael Conforto 12.00 30.00
AGAMFA Mike Francesa 10.00 25.00
AGAMFR Missy Franklin 10.00 25.00
AGAMG Mike Greenberg 10.00 25.00
AGAMIS Michele Steele 8.00 20.00
AGAMP Mike Piazza 40.00 100.00
AGAMPH Michael Phelps 125.00 300.00
AGAMRE Michael Reed 4.00 10.00
AGAMRY Matt Reynolds 4.00 10.00
AGAMS Miguel Sano 6.00 15.00
AGAMSH Maria Sharapova 60.00 150.00
AGAMSP Morgan Spurlock 6.00 15.00
AGAMST Matt Stonie 12.00 30.00
AGAMST Marcus Stroman 5.00 12.00
AGAMT Mike Trout 150.00 400.00
AGANG Nomar Garciaparra 15.00 40.00
AGANL Nancy Lieberman 10.00 25.00
AGANM Nomar Mazara 12.00 30.00
AGAOJO Orlando Jones 8.00 20.00
AGAPM Paul Molitor 20.00 50.00
AGAPMB Paul McBeth 30.00 80.00
AGARC Ricky Craven 4.00 10.00
AGARC Robinson Cano 8.00 20.00
AGARKI Kevin Costner 175.00 350.00
AGARK Rick Klein 4.00 10.00
AGARR Rob Refsnyder 5.00 12.00
AGARRO Robert Raiola 4.00 10.00
AGARS Richie Shaffer 4.00 10.00
AGARSK Randy Sklar 10.00 25.00
AGASK Steve Kerr 12.00 30.00
AGASP Stephen Piscotty 8.00 20.00
AGASS Steve Spurrier 15.00 40.00
AGASSA Susan Sarandon 50.00 120.00
AGASSC Steve Schirripa 4.00 10.00
AGATB Timothy Busfield 10.00 25.00
AGATM Tom Murphy 4.00 10.00
AGATS Trevor Story 15.00 40.00
AGATT Trea Turner 12.00 30.00
AGATW Tyler White 4.00 10.00
AGAVGU Vinny G 10.00 25.00
AGAZL Zach Lee 4.00 10.00
AGAZW Zack Wheeler 5.00 12.00

2016 Topps Allen and Ginter Framed Mini Autographs Black
*BLACK: .75X TO 2X BASIC
STATED ODDS 1:382 HOBBY
STATED PRINT RUN 25 SER.#'d SETS
EXCHANGE DEADLINE 6/30/2018

2016 Topps Allen and Ginter Framed Mini Relics
STATED ODDS 1:122 HOBBY
AGRI Ichiro Suzuki 6.00 15.00
AGRAG Adrian Gonzalez 4.00 10.00
AGRAJ Adam Jones 4.00 10.00
AGRAM Andrew McCutchen
AGRAPU Albert Pujols 6.00 15.00
AGRARI Anthony Rizzo 5.00 15.00
AGRARU Addison Russell 5.00 12.00
AGRAW Adam Wainwright 4.00 10.00
AGRBH Bryce Harper 6.00 15.00
AGRBL Barry Larkin 8.00 20.00
AGRBP Buster Posey 6.00 15.00
AGRBR Babe Ruth 150.00 300.00
AGRCBE Carlos Beltran 4.00 10.00
AGRCBI Craig Biggio 4.00 10.00
AGRCKE Clayton Kershaw 6.00 15.00
AGRCKL Corey Kluber 4.00 10.00
AGRCR Cal Ripken Jr. 10.00 25.00
AGRCY Carl Yastrzemski 8.00 20.00
AGRDO David Ortiz 5.00 12.00
AGRDPE Dustin Pedroia 5.00 12.00
AGRDW David Wright 4.00 10.00
AGREL Evan Longoria 4.00 10.00
AGRFH Felix Hernandez 4.00 10.00
AGRGB George Brett 8.00 20.00
AGRGST Giancarlo Stanton 5.00 12.00
AGRJAB Jose Abreu 5.00 12.00
AGRJD Josh Donaldson 4.00 10.00
AGRJDG Jacob deGrom 5.00 12.00
AGRJE Jacoby Ellsbury 4.00 10.00
AGRJF Jose Fernandez 5.00 12.00
AGRJL Jon Lester 4.00 10.00
AGRJV Joey Votto 5.00 12.00
AGRKB Kris Bryant 8.00 20.00
AGRMC Miguel Cabrera 5.00 12.00
AGRMH Matt Harvey 4.00 10.00
AGRMMA Manny Machado 5.00 12.00
AGRMMG Mark McGwire 6.00 15.00
AGRMP Mike Piazza 8.00 20.00
AGRMTA Masahiro Tanaka 4.00 10.00
AGRMTR Mike Trout 12.00 30.00
AGRPS Pablo Sandoval 4.00 10.00
AGRRC Rod Carew 4.00 10.00
AGRTC Ty Cobb 125.00 250.00
AGRTL Tim Lincecum 4.00 10.00
AGRTR Tyson Ross 3.00 8.00
AGRTW Ted Williams
AGRVM Victor Martinez 4.00 10.00
AGRYM Yadier Molina 5.00 12.00
AGRYP Yasiel Puig 5.00 12.00
AGRYV Yordano Ventura 4.00 10.00

2016 Topps Allen and Ginter Mascots in the Wild
INSERTED IN RETAIL PACKS
MIW1 Bobcat 1.00 2.50
MIW2 Tiger 1.00 2.50
MIW3 Eagle 1.00 2.50
MIW4 Cardinal 1.00 2.50
MIW5 Bear 1.00 2.50
MIW6 Horse 1.00 2.50
MIW7 Moose 1.00 2.50
MIW8 Elephant 1.00 2.50
MIW9 Parrot 1.00 2.50

2016 Topps Allen and Ginter Mini Ferocious Felines
COMPLETE SET (15) 8.00 20.00
STATED ODDS 1:25 HOBBY
FF1 Bengal Tiger .75 2.00
FF2 Clouded Leopard .75 2.00
FF3 Canadian Lynx .75 2.00
FF4 Jaguar .75 2.00
FF5 African Lion .75 2.00
FF6 North American Cougar .75 2.00
FF7 South African Cheetah .75 2.00
FF8 Cheetah .75 2.00
FF9 Classic Tabby .75 2.00
FF10 Sand Cat .75 2.00
FF11 Manx Cat .75 2.00
FF12 Serval .75 2.00
FF13 Ocelot .75 2.00
FF14 Caracal .75 2.00
FF15 Siberian Tiger .75 2.00

2016 Topps Allen and Ginter Mini Greenland Explorer
STATED ODDS 1:26,436 HOBBY
GE Greenland Explorer 300.00 500.00

2016 Topps Allen and Ginter Mini Laureates of Peace
COMPLETE SET (10) 6.00 15.00
STATED ODDS 1:38 HOBBY
LP1 Martin Luther King, Jr. 1.00 2.50
LP2 Nelson Mandela 1.00 2.50
LP3 Baron Philip Noel-Baker 1.00 2.50
LP4 Ralph Bunche 1.00 2.50
LP5 Henry Dunant 1.00 2.50
LP6 Malala Yousafzai 1.00 2.50
LP7 Shirin Ebadi 1.00 2.50
LP8 Jane Addams 1.00 2.50
LP9 Frank B. Kellogg 1.00 2.50
LP10 Jimmy Carter 1.00 2.50

2016 Topps Allen and Ginter Rip Cards Ripped
UNRIPPED ODDS 1:180 HOBBY
PRINT RUNS B/WN 10-50 COPIES PER
PRICING FOR CLEANLY RIPPED CARDS
NO PRICING ON QTY 10
RIP1 Warren Spahn/50 2.50 6.00
RIP2 Zack Greinke/50 2.50 6.00
RIP3 Reggie Jackson/50 2.50 6.00
RIP4 Matt Kemp/50 2.50 6.00
RIP6 Buster Posey/25 4.00 10.00
RIP7 Rod Carew/50 2.50 6.00
RIP8 Justin Upton/50 2.50 6.00
RIP9 Miguel Cabrera/50 3.00 8.00
RIP11 Adam Jones/20 2.50 6.00
RIP12 Yoenis Cespedes/50 3.00 8.00
RIP13 Albert Pujols/25 4.00 10.00
RIP14 Anthony Rizzo/50 5.00 12.00
RIP15 Troy Tulowitzki/50 3.00 8.00
RIP16 Adam Wainwright/50 2.50 6.00
RIP17 David Price/25 2.50 6.00
RIP18 Jason Kipnis/25 2.50 6.00
RIP19 Sonny Gray/25 2.50 6.00
RIP21 Michael Wacha/25 2.50 6.00
RIP22 Freddie Freeman/25 4.00 10.00
RIP23 Willie Mays/50 6.00 15.00
RIP24 Clayton Kershaw/50 6.00 15.00
RIP25 Hank Aaron/50 6.00 15.00
RIP26 Kris Bryant/50 4.00 10.00
RIP27 Corey Seager/50 15.00 40.00
RIP28 Dee Gordon/25 2.00 5.00
RIP29 Giancarlo Stanton/50 3.00 8.00
RIP30 Yasiel Puig/50 3.00 8.00
RIP31 Joe Morgan
RIP32 Lorenzo Cain/25 2.00 5.00
RIP34 Roberto Clemente/50 8.00 20.00
RIP35 Cole Hamels/50 2.50 6.00
RIP36 Paul Goldschmidt/50 3.00 8.00
RIP37 Wade Boggs/50 2.50 6.00
RIP38 Rickey Henderson/50 3.00 8.00
RIP39 Brian Dozier/25 2.50 6.00
RIP40 Tyson Ross/25 2.00 5.00
RIP41 Adrian Gonzalez
RIP42 David Ortiz/50 3.00 8.00
RIP43 Mookie Betts/25 5.00 12.00
RIP44 J.D. Martinez/25 3.00 8.00
RIP45 Joey Votto/50 3.00 8.00
RIP46 Jackie Robinson/50 3.00 8.00
RIP47 Jeff Bagwell/50 2.50 6.00
RIP48 Tom Seaver/50 2.50 6.00
RIP49 Nolan Arenado/50 4.00 10.00
RIP50 Jose Abreu/50 3.00 8.00
RIP51 Bryce Harper/50 5.00 12.00
RIP52 Mike Trout/25 15.00 40.00
RIP53 Johnny Bench/25 3.00 8.00
RIP54 Carlos Correa/25 3.00 8.00
RIP55 Corey Kluber/25 2.50 6.00
RIP56 Robin Yount/25 3.00 8.00
RIP57 George Springer/50 2.50 6.00
RIP58 Jackie Bradley Jr./25 3.00 8.00
RIP60 Ozzie Smith/50 4.00 10.00
RIP61 Dallas Keuchel/50 2.50 6.00
RIP62 Manny Machado
RIP63 Roger Clemens/50 4.00 10.00
RIP64 Edwin Encarnacion/25 3.00 8.00
RIP65 Masahiro Tanaka/50 2.50 6.00
RIP66 Jacob deGrom/50 3.00 8.00
RIP67 Max Scherzer/50 3.00 8.00
RIP68 Eric Hosmer/50 2.50 6.00
RIP69 Cal Ripken Jr./50 8.00 20.00
RIP70 A.J. Pollock
RIP71 Josh Donaldson/50 2.50 6.00
RIP72 Ken Griffey Jr./50 6.00 15.00
RIP73 Johnny Cueto/25 2.50 6.00
RIP74 Evan Longoria/25 2.50 6.00
RIP76 Felix Hernandez/50 2.50 6.00
RIP77 Chipper Jones/25 3.00 8.00
RIP79 James Shields/25 2.00 5.00
RIP80 Jose Bautista/50 2.50 6.00
RIP81 Matt Harvey/50 2.50 6.00
RIP82 Jose Fernandez/50 3.00 8.00
RIP83 Madison Bumgarner/50 3.00 8.00
RIP85 Ty Cobb/50 5.00 12.00
RIP86 Adrian Beltre/50 3.00 8.00
RIP87 Robinson Cano/50 2.50 6.00
RIP88 Gerrit Cole/50 3.00 8.00
RIP90 Jose Reyes/50 2.50 6.00
RIP91 Andrew McCutchen/50 3.00 8.00
RIP93 Chris Sale/50 3.00 8.00
RIP94 Harmon Killebrew/50 3.00 8.00
RIP95 Prince Fielder/25 2.50 6.00
RIP96 Francisco Lindor/25 3.00 8.00
RIP97 Ryan Braun/25 2.50 6.00
RIP98 Chris Davis/25 2.00 5.00
RIP99 Alex Rodriguez/25 4.00 10.00
RIP100 Frank Robinson/50 2.50 6.00

2016 Topps Allen and Ginter Mini Skippers
STATED ODDS 1:288 HOBBY
S1 Pete Mackanin 6.00 15.00
S2 Bryan Price 6.00 15.00
S3 Dave Roberts 10.00 25.00
S4 Robin Ventura 6.00 15.00
S5 Terry Collins 8.00 20.00
S6 Craig Counsell 6.00 15.00
S7 Mike Matheny 6.00 15.00
S8 Joe Maddon 20.00 50.00
S9 Jeff Banister 6.00 15.00
S10 Dusty Baker 10.00 25.00
S11 Buck Showalter 10.00 25.00
S12 Mike Scioscia 6.00 15.00
S13 Andy Green 6.00 15.00
S14 Brad Ausmus 8.00 20.00
S15 A.J. Hinch 6.00 15.00
S16 Walt Weiss 10.00 25.00
S17 Bruce Bochy 8.00 20.00
S18 John Gibbons 6.00 15.00
S19 Paul Molitor 10.00 25.00
S20 Fredi Gonzalez 6.00 15.00
S21 Scott Servais 6.00 15.00
S22 Terry Francona 8.00 20.00
S23 Chip Hale 10.00 25.00
S24 John Farrell 6.00 15.00
S25 Kevin Cash 8.00 20.00
S26 Clint Hurdle 8.00 20.00
S27 Bob Melvin 6.00 15.00
S28 Don Mattingly 12.00 30.00
S29 Joe Girardi 12.00 30.00
S30 Ned Yost 8.00 20.00

2016 Topps Allen and Ginter Mini Subways and Streetcars
COMPLETE SET (12) 5.00 12.00
STATED ODDS 1:25 HOBBY
SS1 7 Train .60 1.50
SS2 Red Line .60 1.50
SS3 Metromover .60 1.50
SS4 Duquesne Incline .60 1.50
SS5 Market St. Cable Car .60 1.50
SS6 Duck Boat .60 1.50
SS7 Passenger Train .60 1.50
SS8 Aerial Tram .60 1.50
SS9 Motorcycle .60 1.50
SS10 City Bus .60 1.50
SS11 R.V. .60 1.50
SS12 Bikeshare .60 1.50

2016 Topps Allen and Ginter Mini US Mayors
COMPLETE SET (35) 20.00 50.00
STATED ODDS 1:11 HOBBY
USM1 Mick Cornett .75 2.00
USM2 Sylvester Turner .75 2.00
USM3 Sam Liccardo .75 2.00
USM4 Greg Stanton .75 2.00
USM5 Betsy Hodges .75 2.00
USM6 Muriel Bowser .75 2.00
USM7 Kasim Reed .75 2.00
USM8 Frank G. Jackson .75 2.00
USM9 Edwin M. Lee .75 2.00
USM10 Charlie Hales .75 2.00
USM11 Marty Walsh .75 2.00
USM12 Tom Barrett .75 2.00
USM13 Tom Tait .75 2.00
USM14 Mike Duggan .75 2.00
USM15 Tomas Regalado .75 2.00
USM16 Bob Buckhorn .75 2.00
USM17 Jim Kenney .75 2.00
USM18 Stephanie Rawlings-Blake .75 2.00
USM19 Andrew Ginther .75 2.00
USM20 Bill de Blasio .75 2.00
USM21 Ed Murray .75 2.00
USM22 Steven Fulop .75 2.00
USM23 Carolyn Goodman .75 2.00
USM24 Rahm Emanuel .75 2.00
USM25 Mitch Landrieu .75 2.00
USM26 Libby Schaaf .75 2.00
USM27 Kevin Faulconer .75 2.00
USM28 Bill Peduto .75 2.00
USM29 Eric Garcetti .75 2.00
USM30 Francis G. Slay .75 2.00
USM31 Michael Hancock .75 2.00
USM32 Greg Fischer .75 2.00
USM33 Sly James .75 2.00
USM34 Oscar Leeser .75 2.00
USM35 Mike Rawlings .75 2.00

2016 Topps Allen and Ginter Natural Wonders
COMPLETE SET (20) 3.00 8.00
STATED ODDS 1:5 HOBBY
NW1 Grand Canyon .25 .60
NW2 Great Barrier Reef .25 .60
NW3 Mount Everest .25 .60
NW4 Victoria Falls .25 .60
NW5 Amazon Rainforest .25 .60
NW6 Old Faithful .25 .60
NW7 Natural Bridge .25 .60
NW8 Aurora Borealis .25 .60
NW9 Eye of the Sahara .25 .60
NW10 Marble Caves .25 .60
NW11 Baobab Forest .25 .60
NW12 Dead Sea .25 .60
NW13 Komodo Island .25 .60
NW14 Punalu'u Beach .25 .60
NW15 Devils Tower .25 .60
NW16 Pulpit Rock .25 .60
NW17 Cliffs of Moher .25 .60
NW18 Cave of the Crystals .25 .60
NW19 Ngorongoro Crater .25 .60
NW20 Harbor of Rio de Janeiro .25 .60

2016 Topps Allen and Ginter Relics
VERSION A ODDS 1:24 HOBBY
VERSION B ODDS 1:24 HOBBY
FSRAAA Anthony Anderson A 2.50 6.00
FSRAAMI Andrew Miller A 2.50 6.00
FSRAAR Addison Russell A 3.00 8.00
FSRAAW Adam Wainwright A 2.50 6.00
FSRABB Brandon Belt A 2.50 6.00
FSRABC Brandon Crawford A 2.50 6.00
FSRABG Brett Gardner A 2.50 6.00
FSRACB Carlos Beltran A 2.50 6.00
FSRACGO Carlos Gonzalez A 2.50 6.00
FSRACGR Curtis Granderson A 2.50 6.00
FSRACK Corey Kluber A 2.50 6.00
FSRACMA Carlos Martinez A 2.50 6.00
FSRACMC Cord McCoy A 2.00 5.00
FSRACSA Carlos Santana A 2.50 6.00
FSRACSL Chris Sale A 3.00 8.00
FSRADBE Dellin Betances A 2.50 6.00
FSRADBR Dwier Brown A 2.00 5.00
FSRADPE Dustin Pedroia A 3.00 8.00
FSRAEH Eric Hosmer A 2.50 6.00
FSRAFH Felix Hernandez A 2.50 6.00
FSRAGL George Lopez A 2.50 6.00
FSRAGS Giancarlo Stanton A 3.00 8.00
FSRAHS Hannah Storm A 3.00 8.00
FSRAJA Jose Abreu A 3.00 8.00
FSRAJD Jacob deGrom A 3.00 8.00
FSRAJE Jacoby Ellsbury A 2.50 6.00
FSRAJF Jose Fernandez A 3.00 8.00
FSRAJHA Josh Harrison A 2.00 5.00
FSRAJM Joe McKeehen A 2.50 6.00
FSRAJSK Jason Sklar A 2.50 6.00
FSRAJSO Jorge Soler A 3.00 8.00
FSRAJV Joey Votto A 3.00 8.00
FSRAJW Jen Welter A 2.50 6.00
FSRAKC Kole Calhoun A 2.00 5.00
FSRAKSE Kyle Seager A 2.00 5.00
FSRAKW Kolten Wong A 2.50 6.00
FSRALC Lorenzo Cain A 2.00 5.00
FSRAMB Mookie Betts A 5.00 12.00
FSRAMC Miguel Cabrera A 3.00 8.00
FSRAMF Missy Franklin A 2.50 6.00
FSRAMP Michael Phelps A 5.00 12.00
FSRAMS Matt Stonie A 2.50 6.00
FSRANS Noah Syndergaard A 2.50 6.00
FSRAPF Prince Fielder A 2.50 6.00
FSRARCA Rusney Castillo A 2.00 5.00
FSRARCR Ricky Craven A 2.00 5.00
FSRARR Robert Raiola A 3.00 8.00
FSRARS Randy Sklar A 2.50 6.00
FSRASK Steve Kerr A 4.00 10.00
FSRATB Timothy Busfield A 2.50 6.00
FSRATD Travis d'Arnaud A 2.50 6.00
FSRAYM Yadier Molina A 3.00 8.00
FSRBAG Adrian Gonzalez B 2.50 6.00
FSRBAP Albert Pujols B 4.00 10.00
FSRBARI Anthony Rizzo B 5.00 12.00
FSRBAS Ari Shaffir B 2.50 6.00
FSRBBH Bryce Harper B 5.00 12.00
FSRBBM Brian McCann B 2.50 6.00
FSRBBP Buster Posey B 4.00 10.00
FSRBCK Clayton Kershaw B 4.00 10.00
FSRBCW Cheyenne Woods B 2.50 6.00
FSRBDA Denise Austin B 2.00 5.00
FSRBDG Dee Gordon B 2.00 5.00
FSRBDW David Wright B 2.50 6.00
FSRBEL Evan Longoria B 2.50 6.00
FSRBGC Gerrit Cole B 3.00 8.00
FSRBGG Gennady Golovkin B 10.00 25.00
FSRBHO Hector Olivera B 2.50 6.00
FSRBHR Hanley Ramirez B 2.50 6.00
FSRBI Ichiro Suzuki B 4.00 10.00
FSRBJAB Jose Abreu B 3.00 8.00
FSRBJAR Jake Arrieta B 2.50 6.00
FSRBJK Jung Ho Kang B 2.00 5.00
FSRBJL Jon Lester B 2.50 6.00
FSRBJMA Jill Martin B 2.50 6.00
FSRBJME Jessica Mendoza B 2.00 5.00
FSRBJO Jay Oakerson B 2.50 6.00
FSRBJP Joc Pederson B 2.50 6.00
FSRBJSH James Shields B 2.00 5.00
FSRBJV Justin Verlander B 3.00 8.00
FSRBJW Jayson Werth B 2.50 6.00
FSRBLD Lucas Duda B 2.50 6.00
FSRBLL Laurence Leavy B 3.00 8.00
FSRBLS Leigh Steinberg B 2.50 6.00
FSRBMBR Mike Breed B 2.00 5.00
FSRBMF Mike Francesa B 2.50 6.00
FSRBMG Mike Greenberg B 2.50 6.00
FSRBMH Matt Harvey B 2.50 6.00
FSRBMP Michael Pineda B 2.00 5.00
FSRBMSC Max Scherzer B 3.00 8.00
FSRBMSH Maria Sharapova B 5.00 12.00
FSRBMSP Morgan Spurlock B 2.00 5.00
FSRBMST Michele Steele B 2.00 5.00
FSRBMTA Masahiro Tanaka B 2.50 6.00
FSRBMTR Mike Trout B 6.00 15.00
FSRBMW Michael Wacha B 2.50 6.00
FSRBPM Paul McBeth B 8.00 20.00
FSRBPS Pablo Sandoval B 2.50 6.00
FSRBRB Ryan Braun B 2.50 6.00
FSRBRC Robinson Cano B 2.50 6.00
FSRBRK Rick Klein B 3.00 8.00
FSRBSP Salvador Perez B 2.50 6.00
FSRBVM Victor Martinez B 2.50 6.00
FSRBWM Wil Myers B 2.00 5.00
FSRBXB Xander Bogaerts B 3.00 8.00
FSRBYC Yoenis Cespedes B 3.00 8.00
FSRBYP Yasiel Puig B 3.00 8.00

2016 Topps Allen and Ginter The Numbers Game
COMPLETE SET (100) 20.00 50.00
STATED ODDS 1:2 HOBBY
NG1 Noah Syndergaard .25 .60
NG2 Mark McGwire .50 1.25
NG3 Buster Posey .40 1.00
NG4 Hank Aaron .60 1.50
NG5 Carl Yastrzemski .50 1.25
NG6 Corey Seager 1.50 4.00
NG7 Jason Heyward .25 .60
NG8 Mark Teixeira .25 .60
NG9 Nolan Ryan 1.00 2.50
NG10 Andrew McCutchen .30 .75
NG11 Stephen Piscotty .30 .75
NG12 Willie Stargell .25 .60
NG13 Max Scherzer .30 .75

NG14 David Price .25 .60
NG15 David Ortiz .30 .75
NG16 Frank Thomas .30 .75
NG17 Yasiel Puig .30 .75
NG18 Dennis Eckersley .25 .60
NG19 Felix Hernandez .25 .60
NG20 George Springer .25 .60
NG21 Mookie Betts .50 1.25
NG22 Giancarlo Stanton .30 .75
NG23 Manny Machado .30 .75
NG24 Madison Bumgarner .25 .60
NG25 Evan Longoria .25 .60
NG26 Randy Johnson .30 .75
NG27 Jon Lester .25 .60
NG28 Rollie Fingers .25 .60
NG29 Cal Ripken Jr. 1.00 2.50
NG30 Chipper Jones .30 .75
NG31 Mike Trout 1.50 4.00
NG32 Troy Tulowitzki .30 .75
NG33 Yoenis Cespedes .30 .75
NG34 Eric Hosmer .25 .60
NG35 Joe Morgan .25 .60
NG36 Steve Carlton .25 .60
NG37 Matt Harvey .25 .60
NG38 Anthony Rizzo .50 1.25
NG39 Ken Griffey Jr. .60 1.50
NG40 Paul Goldschmidt .30 .75
NG41 Jackie Robinson .30 .75
NG42 Roberto Alomar .25 .60
NG43 Roger Clemens .40 1.00
NG44 Dustin Pedroia .30 .75
NG45 Curt Schilling .25 .60
NG46 Chris Sale .30 .75
NG47 Kris Bryant .40 1.00
NG48 Ozzie Smith .40 1.00
NG49 Babe Ruth .75 2.00
NG50 Jose Abreu .30 .75
NG51 John Smoltz .30 .75
NG52 Jose Altuve .25 .60
NG53 Zack Greinke .25 .60
NG54 Albert Pujols .40 1.00
NG55 Ryan Braun .25 .60
NG56 Miguel Cabrera .30 .75
NG57 Jose Fernandez .30 .75
NG58 A.J. Pollock .20 .50
NG59 Adam Wainwright .25 .60
NG60 Roberto Clemente .75 2.00
NG61 Mike Piazza .30 .75
NG62 Jose Bautista .25 .60
NG63 Jake Arrieta .25 .60
NG64 Dallas Keuchel .25 .60
NG65 Clayton Kershaw .60 1.50
NG66 Reggie Jackson .25 .60
NG67 Ichiro Suzuki .40 1.00
NG68 Johnny Bench .30 .75
NG69 Jacob deGrom .30 .75
NG70 Willie McCovey .25 .60
NG71 Billy Williams .25 .60
NG72 Don Mattingly .60 1.50
NG73 Nomar Garciaparra .25 .60
NG74 Jim Rice .25 .60
NG75 Kyle Seager .20 .50
NG76 Willie Mays .60 1.50
NG77 Robinson Cano .25 .60
NG78 Bill Mazeroski .25 .60
NG79 Rickey Henderson .30 .75
NG80 Greg Maddux .40 1.00
NG81 Wade Boggs .25 .60
NG82 Kenta Maeda .40 1.00
NG83 Matt Kemp .25 .60
NG84 Joey Votto .30 .75
NG85 Rod Carew .25 .60
NG86 Tom Seaver .25 .60
NG87 Carlton Fisk .25 .60
NG88 Prince Fielder .25 .60
NG89 Josh Donaldson .25 .60
NG90 Tom Glavine .25 .60
NG91 Paul Molitor .30 .75
NG92 Andy Pettitte .25 .60
NG93 Miguel Sano .30 .75
NG94 Bryce Harper .50 1.25
NG95 Carlos Correa .30 .75
NG96 Dee Gordon .25 .60
NG97 Stephen Strasburg .30 .75
NG98 Robin Yount .30 .75
NG99 George Brett .60 1.50
NG100 Ryne Sandberg .60 1.50

2017 Topps Allen and Ginter

COMPLETE SET (350) 30.00 80.00
COMP.SET w/o SP's (300) 20.00 50.00
SP ODDS 1:2 HOBBY
1 Kris Bryant .30 .75
2 Albert Pujols .30 .75
3 Tyler Naquin .15 .40
4 Babe Ruth .60 1.50
5 Adrian Gonzalez .20 .50
6 DJ LeMahieu .25 .60
7 Derek Jeter .60 1.50
8 Kevin Gausman .15 .40
9 Ryan Schimpf .15 .40
10 Mike Trout 1.25 3.00
11 Brandon Finnegan .15 .40
12 Corey Bellemore .15 .40
13 Jake Arrieta .20 .50
14 Robert Gsellman RC .25 .60
15 Gary Sanchez .25 .60
16 Garrett Richards .20 .50
17 Jose De Leon RC .25 .60
18 Marcus Semien .15 .40
19 Giancarlo Stanton .25 .60
20 Brooke Hogan .15 .40
21 Eric Hosmer .20 .50
22 Albert Almora .15 .40
23 John Smoltz .25 .60
24 Ken Griffey Jr. .50 1.25
25 Alexa Datt .15 .40
26 Matt Wieters .25 .60
27 Yulieski Gurriel RC .40 1.00
28 Andrew McCutchen .25 .60
29 Maikel Franco .20 .50
30 Jorge Soler .20 .50
31 Carlos Santana .20 .50
32 Peter Rosenberg .15 .40
33 Byron Buxton .20 .50
34 Billy Hamilton .20 .50
35 Johnny Damon .20 .50
36 Edwin Encarnacion .25 .60
37 Devon Travis .15 .40
38 Craig Kimbrel .20 .50
39 Yu Darvish .25 .60
40 Dansby Swanson RC .60 1.50
41 Chris Sale .25 .60
42 Mark Trumbo .15 .40
43 Tanner Roark .15 .40
44 Anthony Rizzo .40 1.00
45 Harriet Tubman .15 .40
46 Chris Archer .15 .40
47 Omar Vizquel .20 .50
48 Carlos Correa .25 .60
49 David Wright .20 .50
50 Bryce Harper .40 1.00
51 Buster Posey .30 .75
52 Trees in India .15 .40
53 Brandon Belt .20 .50
54 Rickey Henderson .25 .60
55 Andre Dawson .20 .50
56 Rick Porcello .20 .50
57 Jharel Cotton RC .25 .60
58 Efren Reyes .15 .40
59 Gary Stevens .15 .40
60 Nolan Ryan .75 2.00
61 Tommy Joseph .25 .60
62 Joc Pederson .20 .50
63 Barry Larkin .20 .50
64 Luis Severino .20 .50
65 Kyle Freeland RC .30 .75
66 Kenta Maeda .20 .50
67 Allie LaForce .15 .40
68 J.D. Martinez .25 .60
69 Carl Yastrzemski .40 1.00
70 Vashti Cunningham .15 .40
71 Julio Teheran .20 .50
72 Dustin Pedroia .25 .60
73 Starling Marte .20 .50
74 Cal Ripken Jr. .75 2.00
75 Max Scherzer .25 .60
76 David Dahl RC .30 .75
77 Brian Dozier .25 .60
78 Greg Maddux .30 .75
79 Rod Carew .20 .50
80 Mookie Betts .40 1.00
81 Carlos Carrasco .15 .40
82 Bobby Abreu .15 .40
83 Ichiro .30 .75
84 Ian Desmond .15 .40
85 Dave Winfield .20 .50
86 Aledmys Diaz .20 .50
87 Henry Owens .15 .40
88 Tyler Austin RC .40 1.00
89 Ken Rosenthal .15 .40
90 Gavin Cecchini RC .25 .60
91 Nomar Mazara .15 .40
92 Hunter Dozier RC .25 .60
93 Chad Pinder RC .25 .60
94 Justin Upton .20 .50
95 Dee Gordon .15 .40
96 Kendrys Morales .15 .40
97 Aroldis Chapman .25 .60
98 Stephen Piscotty .20 .50
99 Teoscar Hernandez RC .75 2.00
100 Ty Cobb .40 1.00
101 Jay Bruce .20 .50
102 Honus Wagner .25 .60
103 Jose Reyes .20 .50
104 Dexter Fowler .20 .50
105 Brett Gardner .20 .50
106 Sean Manaea .15 .40
107 Pedro Martinez .20 .50
108 Ryon Healy RC .30 .75
109 Cole Hamels .20 .50
110 Ted Williams .50 1.25
111 Alex Gordon .20 .50
112 Jayson Werth .20 .50
113 Adam Jones .20 .50
114 Yasiel Puig .25 .60
115 Carlos Rodon .20 .50
116 Aaron Sanchez .20 .50
117 Joe Musgrove RC .25 .60
118 Cameron Maybin .15 .40
119 Garrett McNamara .15 .40
120 Vince Velasquez .15 .40
121 Randal Grichuk .15 .40
122 Reggie Jackson .20 .50
123 George Springer .20 .50
124 Kyle Schwarber .25 .60
125 Paul Goldschmidt .25 .60
126 Adrian Beltre .20 .50
127 Ollie Schniederjans .15 .40
128 Tyler Glasnow RC .30 .75
129 Ozzie Smith .30 .75
130 Renato Nunez RC .50 1.25
131 Dan Jennings EXEC. .15 .40
132 Corey Seager .25 .60
133 Addison Russell .25 .60
134 Steven Matz .20 .50
135 Josh Donaldson .20 .50
136 Bo Jackson .25 .60
137 Nolan Arenado .30 .75
138 Adam Duvall .25 .60
139 David Price .20 .50
140 Ryan Braun .20 .50
141 Michael Fulmer .15 .40
142 Tom Anderson .15 .40
143 Paris Locks .15 .40
144 Frank Thomas .25 .60
145 A.J. Reed .15 .40
146 Justin Verlander .25 .60
147 Salvador Perez .20 .50
148 Jesse Winker RC .25 .60
149 Mike Piazza .25 .60
150 Sandy Koufax .50 1.25
151 Jacoby Ellsbury .20 .50
152 Jackie Robinson .25 .60
153 Sean Doolittle .15 .40
154 David Ortiz .25 .60
155 Joey Votto .25 .60
156 Daniel Murphy .20 .50
157 Carson Fulmer RC .25 .60
158 Xander Bogaerts .25 .60
159 Yoenis Cespedes .25 .60
160 Michal Kapral .15 .40
161 Ernie Banks .25 .60
162 Sonny Gray .20 .50
163 Wesley Bryan .15 .40
164 Gerrit Cole .25 .60
165 Jayson Stark .15 .40
166 Manny Margot RC .25 .60
167 Andres Galarraga .20 .50
168 Robbie Ray .15 .40
169 Antonio Senzatela RC .25 .60
170 Jackie Bradley Jr. .25 .60
171 Jose Canseco .20 .50
172 Aaron Judge RC 5.00 12.00
173 Odubel Herrera .20 .50
174 Danny Duffy .15 .40
175 Noah Syndergaard .20 .50
176 Marcus Stroman .20 .50
177 Valarie Jenkins .15 .40
178 Clayton Kershaw .50 1.25
179 Kirby Smart CO .15 .40
180 Corey Kluber .20 .50
181 Mark McGwire .40 1.00
182 Kyle Hendricks .25 .60
183 Amir Garrett RC .25 .60
184 Jose Altuve .20 .50
185 Wil Myers .15 .40
186 Josh Bell RC .60 1.50
187 Eric LeGrand .15 .40
188 Gregory Polanco .20 .50
189 Joe Manganiello .15 .40
190 Matt Carpenter .25 .60
191 Jay Glazer .15 .40
192 Willson Contreras .25 .60
193 Todd Frazier .15 .40
194 A.J. Pollock .15 .40
195 Matt Kemp .20 .50
196 Jose Bautista .20 .50
197 Ben Zobrist .20 .50
198 Javier Baez .30 .75
199 Curtis Granderson .20 .50
200 Francisco Lindor .25 .60
201 Orlando Arcia RC .40 1.00
202 Jurickson Profar .20 .50
203 Carlos Gonzalez .20 .50
204 Manny Machado .25 .60
205 Alex Bregman RC 1.00 2.50
206 Aaron Nola .20 .50
207 Edwin Diaz .20 .50
208 Felix Hernandez .25 .60
209 Mitch Haniger RC .40 1.00
210 Didi Gregorius .20 .50
211 Ben Smith .15 .40
212 Don Mattingly .50 1.25
213 Blake Snell .20 .50
214 Nick Jonas .15 .40
215 Yasmany Tomas .15 .40
216 Michael Conforto .20 .50
217 Brooks Robinson .20 .50
218 Tim Anderson .25 .60
219 Johnny Cueto .25 .60
220 Chipper Jones .25 .60
221 Yadier Molina .30 .75
222 Jake Thompson RC .25 .60
223 Lucas Giolito .20 .50
224 U.S. National Park Service .15 .40
225 Ian Kinsler .20 .50
226 Ryne Sandberg .50 1.25
227 Jon Gray .15 .40
228 Ryan Zimmerman .20 .50
229 Rougned Odor .20 .50
230 Kyle Seager .15 .40
231 Hank Aaron .50 1.25
232 Jose Abreu .25 .60
233 Jake Lamb .20 .50
234 Charlie Blackmon .25 .60
235 Roger Clemens .30 .75
236 Jason Kipnis .20 .50
237 Andrew Benintendi RC .75 2.00
238 Andrew Miller .20 .50
239 Jameson Taillon .20 .50
240 Masahiro Tanaka .20 .50
241 Zach Britton .20 .50
242 Luke Weaver RC .30 .75
243 Alex Reyes RC .30 .75
244 Khris Davis .25 .60
245 Roman Quinn RC .25 .60
246 William Shatner .15 .40
247 Victor Martinez .20 .50
248 Wilson Ramos .15 .40
249 Sage Steele .15 .40
250 Lyle Thompson .15 .40
251 Matt Harvey .20 .50
252 George Brett .50 1.25
253 Brandon Phillips .15 .40
254 Hunter Pence .20 .50
255 Trea Turner .20 .50
256 Andy Katz .15 .40
257 Lou Gehrig .50 1.25
258 Jose Peraza .20 .50
259 Roger Maris .25 .60
260 Jonathan Villar .15 .40
261 Mike Moustakas .20 .50
262 JaCoby Jones RC .30 .75
263 Kevin Kelley CO .15 .40
264 Robinson Cano .20 .50
265 Kevin Kiermaier .20 .50
266 Greg Bird .20 .50
267 Dellin Betances .20 .50
268 Matt Olson RC .40 1.00
269 Krazy George MAS .15 .40
270 Jason Heyward .20 .50
271 Stephen Strasburg .25 .60
272 J.T. Realmuto .25 .60
273 Jean Segura .20 .50
274 Laurie Hernandez .15 .40
275 Joe Panik .20 .50
276 Giant Panda .15 .40
277 Miguel Sano .25 .60
278 Trevor Story .25 .60
279 Randy Johnson .25 .60
280 Freddie Freeman .30 .75
281 Yoan Moncada RC .75 2.00
282 Christian Yelich .30 .75
283 Chris Davis .15 .40
284 Miguel Cotto .15 .40
285 Hunter Renfroe RC .30 .75
286 Roberto Clemente .60 1.50
287 Elvis Andrus .20 .50
288 Jorge Alfaro RC .30 .75
289 Julio Urias .25 .60
290 Jacob deGrom .25 .60
291 Ender Inciarte .20 .50
292 Evan Longoria .20 .50
293 Johnny Bench .25 .60
294 Miguel Cabrera .25 .60
295 James Shields .15 .40
296 Zack Greinke .20 .50
297 Troy Tulowitzki .25 .60
298 Nelson Cruz .25 .60
299 Stephen A. Smith .15 .40
300 Max Kepler .20 .50
301 Trey Mancini SP RC .75 2.00
302 Jon Lester SP .50 1.25
303 Tim Raines SP .50 1.25
304 Whitey Ford SP .50 1.25
305 Ty Blach SP RC .40 1.00
306 Marcell Ozuna SP .60 1.50
307 J.J. Hardy SP .40 1.00
308 Jordan Zimmermann SP .50 1.25
309 Fernando Rodney SP .40 1.00
310 Brandon Crawford SP .50 1.25
311 Adam Eaton SP .60 1.50
312 Raimel Tapia SP RC .50 1.25
313 Matt Strahm SP RC .40 1.00
314 Dan Vogelbach SP RC .60 1.50
315 Willie McCovey SP .50 1.25
316 Adam Wainwright SP .50 1.25
317 Martin Prado SP .40 1.00
318 Harmon Killebrew SP .60 1.50
319 Seth Lugo SP RC .40 1.00
320 Jeff Hoffman SP RC .40 1.00
321 Drew Pomeranz SP .50 1.25
322 Justin Turner SP .50 1.25
323 Drew Smyly SP .40 1.00
324 Gary Carter SP .50 1.25
325 Danny Salazar SP .50 1.25
326 German Marquez SP RC .60 1.50
327 Steven Wright SP .40 1.00
328 Carlos Martinez SP .50 1.25
329 Jonathan Lucroy SP .50 1.25
330 Mark Melancon SP .40 1.00
331 Corey Dickerson SP .40 1.00
332 Yangervis Solarte SP .40 1.00
333 Dallas Keuchel SP .50 1.25
334 Joe Mauer SP .50 1.25
335 Lorenzo Cain SP .40 1.00
336 Kenley Jansen SP .50 1.25
337 Seung-Hwan Oh SP .75 2.00
338 Stephen Vogt SP .50 1.25
339 Reynaldo Lopez SP RC .40 1.00
340 Hanley Ramirez SP .50 1.25
341 Matt Moore SP .40 1.00
342 Braden Shipley SP RC .40 1.00
343 Brian McCann SP .50 1.25
344 Bartolo Colon SP .50 1.25
345 Lance McCullers SP .40 1.00
346 Hisashi Iwakuma SP .50 1.25
347 Warren Spahn SP .50 1.25
348 Logan Forsythe SP .40 1.00
349 Willie Stargell SP .50 1.25
350 Jeff Bagwell SP .50 1.25

2017 Topps Allen and Ginter Hot Box Foil

*FOIL 1-300: 2X TO 5X BASIC
*FOIL 1-300 RC: 1.2X TO 3X BASIC RCs
*FOIL SP 301-350: .75X TO 2X BASIC
INSERTED IN HOT HOBBY BOXES

2017 Topps Allen and Ginter Mini

*MINI 1-300: 1X TO 2.5X BASIC
*MINI 1-300 RC: .6X TO 1.5X BASIC RCs
*MINI SP 301-350: .6X TO 1.5X BASIC
MINI SP ODDS 1:13 HOBBY
351-400 RANDOM WITHIN RIP CARDS
STATED PLATE ODDS 1:1058 HOBBY
PLATE PRINT RUN 1 SET PER COLOR
BLACK-CYAN-MAGENTA-YELLOW ISSUED
NO PLATE PRICING DUE TO SCARCITY
351 Max Scherzer EXT 25.00 60.00
352 Cal Ripken Jr. EXT 25.00 60.00
353 Justin Verlander EXT 20.00 50.00
354 Yu Darvish EXT 20.00 50.00
355 Francisco Lindor EXT 20.00 50.00
356 Mookie Betts EXT 30.00 80.00
357 Andrew Benintendi EXT 50.00 120.00
358 Robinson Cano EXT 15.00 40.00
359 Aledmys Diaz EXT 15.00 40.00
360 Ernie Banks EXT 20.00 50.00
361 Aaron Judge EXT 150.00 400.00
362 Roberto Clemente EXT 40.00 100.00
363 Bryce Harper EXT 30.00 80.00
364 Buster Posey EXT 25.00 60.00
365 Joey Votto EXT 20.00 50.00
366 Dansby Swanson EXT 20.00 50.00
367 Alex Bregman EXT 20.00 50.00
368 Nolan Arenado EXT 25.00 60.00
369 Miguel Cabrera EXT 30.00 80.00
370 Yoenis Cespedes EXT 15.00 40.00
371 Giancarlo Stanton EXT 20.00 50.00
372 Masahiro Tanaka EXT 15.00 40.00
373 Ken Griffey Jr. EXT 40.00 100.00
374 Josh Donaldson EXT 15.00 40.00
375 Julio Urias EXT 20.00 50.00
376 Mike Trout EXT 40.00 100.00
377 Babe Ruth EXT 30.00 80.00
378 Noah Syndergaard EXT 15.00 40.00
379 Alex Reyes EXT 15.00 40.00
380 Kyle Schwarber EXT 20.00 50.00
381 Clayton Kershaw EXT 20.00 50.00
382 Ted Williams EXT 25.00 60.00
383 Paul Goldschmidt EXT 20.00 50.00
384 Manny Machado EXT 20.00 50.00
385 Derek Jeter EXT 30.00 80.00
386 Hunter Renfroe EXT 20.00 50.00
387 Tyler Glasnow EXT 15.00 40.00
388 Kris Bryant EXT 30.00 80.00
389 Jose Bautista EXT 15.00 40.00
390 Corey Seager EXT 20.00 50.00
391 Felix Hernandez EXT 20.00 50.00
392 Hank Aaron EXT 30.00 80.00
393 Yoan Moncada EXT 25.00 60.00
394 Ichiro EXT 25.00 60.00
395 Sandy Koufax EXT 30.00 80.00
396 Gary Sanchez EXT 25.00 60.00
397 Jackie Robinson EXT 25.00 60.00
398 Anthony Rizzo EXT 30.00 80.00
399 Eric Hosmer EXT 15.00 40.00
400 Carlos Correa EXT 20.00 50.00

2017 Topps Allen and Ginter Mini A and G Back

*MINI AG 1-300: 1.2X TO 3X BASIC
*MINI AG 1-300 RC: .75X TO 2X BASIC RCs
*MINI AG SP 301-350: .75X TO 2X BASIC
MINI AG ODDS 1:5 HOBBY
MINI AG SP ODDS 1:65 HOBBY

2017 Topps Allen and Ginter Mini Black Border

*MINI BLK 1-300: 2X TO 5X BASIC
*MINI BLK 1-300 RC: 1.2X TO 3X BASIC RCs
*MINI BLK SP 301-350: 1.2X TO 3X BASIC
MINI BLK ODDS 1:10 HOBBY
MINI BLK SP ODDS 1:130 HOBBY

2017 Topps Allen and Ginter Mini Brooklyn Back

*MINI BRK 1-300: 12X TO 30X BASIC
*MINI BRK 1-300 RC: 8X TO 20X BASIC RCs
*MINI BRK SP 301-350: 5X TO 12X BASIC
MINI BRK ODDS 1:170 HOBBY
STATED PRINT RUN 25 SER.#'d SETS
7 Derek Jeter 40.00 100.00
172 Aaron Judge 175.00 350.00

2017 Topps Allen and Ginter Mini Gold Border

*MINI GOLD 1-300: 2.5X TO 6X BASIC
*MINI GOLD 1-300 RC: 1.5X TO 4X BASIC RCs
*MINI GOLD 301-350: 1X TO 2.5X BASIC
RANDOMLY INSERTED IN RETAIL PACKS

2017 Topps Allen and Ginter Mini No Number

*MINI NNO 1-300: 5X TO 12X BASIC
*MINI NNO 1-300 RC: 3X TO 8X BASIC RCs
*MINI NNO SP 301-350: 2X TO 5X BASIC
MINI NNO ODDS 1:85 HOBBY
7 Derek Jeter 15.00 40.00

2017 Topps Allen and Ginter Autographs

STATED ODDS 1:731 HOBBY
EXCHANGE DEADLINE 6/30/2019
AGACA Christian Arroyo EXCH 6.00 15.00
AGACB Cody Bellinger 75.00 200.00
AGAIH Ian Happ 15.00 40.00

2017 Topps Allen and Ginter Box Toppers

BLAB Alex Bregman 3.00 8.00
BLAR Anthony Rizzo 2.00 5.00
BLBH Bryce Harper 2.00 5.00
BLBP Buster Posey 1.50 4.00
BLCK Clayton Kershaw 2.50 6.00
BLCS Corey Seager 1.25 3.00
BLDJ Derek Jeter 3.00 8.00
BLDS Dansby Swanson 2.00 5.00
BLGSA Gary Sanchez 1.25 3.00
BLGST Giancarlo Stanton 1.25 3.00
BLJD Josh Donaldson 1.00 2.50
BLKB Kris Bryant 1.50 4.00
BLMM Manny Machado 1.25 3.00
BLMT Mike Trout 6.00 15.00
BLNS Noah Syndergaard 1.00 2.50

2017 Topps Allen and Ginter Framed Mini Autographs

STATED ODDS 1:65 HOBBY
EXCHANGE DEADLINE 6/30/2019
MAABE Andrew Benintendi 25.00 60.00
MAABR Alex Bregman 25.00 60.00
MAADA Alexa Datt 6.00 15.00
MAADI Aledmys Diaz 5.00 12.00
MAADU Adam Duvall 6.00 15.00
MAAG Andres Galarraga 6.00 15.00
MAAJ Aaron Judge 75.00 200.00
MAAK Andy Katz 4.00 10.00
MAAL Allie LaForce 15.00 40.00
MAAN Aaron Nola 8.00 20.00
MAARE Alex Reyes 8.00 20.00
MAAT Andrew Toles 4.00 10.00
MABH Bryce Harper 100.00 250.00
MABHG Brooke Hogan 15.00 40.00
MABJ Bo Jackson EXCH 75.00 200.00
MABP Buster Posey 40.00 100.00
MABSM Ben Smith 4.00 10.00
MABST Bo Steil 4.00 10.00
MABZ Bradley Zimmer 5.00 12.00
MACB Corey Bellemore 4.00 10.00
MACC Carlos Correa EXCH 40.00 100.00
MACF Chris Fehn 20.00 50.00
MACFU Carson Fulmer 4.00 10.00
MACKE Clayton Kershaw 50.00 120.00
MACKL Corey Kluber 10.00 25.00
MACSA Chris Sale 15.00 40.00
MACSE Corey Seager 20.00 50.00
MADB Dellin Betances 5.00 12.00
MADCK David Castor Keene 4.00 10.00
MADF Dexter Fowler 5.00 12.00
MADJ Derek Jeter
MADJE Dan Jennings 4.00 10.00
MADS Dansby Swanson 20.00 50.00
MADV Dan Vogelbach 6.00 15.00
MAEL Eric LeGrand 5.00 12.00
MAFF Freddie Freeman 15.00 40.00
MAFL Francisco Lindor 20.00 50.00
MAFM Floyd Mayweather 150.00 400.00
MAFPJ Freddie Prinze Jr. 25.00 60.00
MAGC Gavin Cecchini 5.00 12.00
MAGM Garrett McNamara 4.00 10.00
MAGSP George Springer 10.00 25.00
MAGST Gary Stevens 5.00 12.00
MAHA Hank Aaron
MAHD Hunter Dozier 4.00 10.00
MAHO Henry Owens 4.00 10.00
MAI Ichiro
MAJAF Jorge Alfaro 5.00 12.00
MAJAL Jose Altuve 15.00 40.00
MAJBA Javier Baez 12.00 30.00
MAJCO Jharel Cotton 4.00 10.00
MAJDG Jacob deGrom 20.00 50.00
MAJDL Jose De Leon 4.00 10.00
MAJDO Josh Donaldson 8.00 20.00
MAJG Jay Glazer 4.00 10.00
MAJM Joe Musgrove 4.00 10.00
MAJMA Joe Manganiello 6.00 15.00
MAJS Jayson Stark 4.00 10.00
MAJTA Jameson Taillon 5.00 12.00
MAJTH Jake Thompson 4.00 10.00
MAJTS Joe Thomas Sr. 5.00 12.00
MAJU Julio Urias 6.00 15.00
MAKB Kris Bryant EXCH
MAKG Krazy George 5.00 12.00
MAKKL Kevin Kelley CO 5.00 12.00
MAKMA Kenta Maeda 6.00 15.00
MAKR Ken Rosenthal 10.00 25.00
MAKSC Kyle Schwarber EXCH 12.00 30.00
MAKSE Kyle Seager EXCH 12.00 30.00
MALH Laurie Hernandez 15.00 40.00
MALT Lyle Thompson EXCH 8.00 20.00
MALW Luke Weaver 5.00 12.00
MAMC Matt Carpenter EXCH 15.00 40.00
MAMCO Miguel Cotto 20.00 50.00
MAMF Michael Fulmer 4.00 10.00
MAMJA Mike Jaspersen
MAMKA Michal Kapral 4.00 10.00
MAMM Manny Machado 15.00 40.00
MAMTA Masahiro Tanaka 50.00 120.00
MAMTR Mike Trout 200.00 500.00
MAND Gene Hackman 60.00 150.00
MANJ Nick Jonas 15.00 40.00
MANS Noah Syndergaard 15.00 40.00
MAOS Ollie Schniederjans 5.00 12.00
MAOV Omar Vizquel 6.00 15.00
MAPF Paul Finebaum 5.00 12.00
MAPR Peter Rosenberg 5.00 12.00
MARGR Randal Grichuk 4.00 10.00
MARGS Robert Gsellman 4.00 10.00
MARH Ryon Healy 5.00 12.00
MARL Reynaldo Lopez 4.00 10.00
MARQ Roman Quinn 4.00 10.00
MART Raimel Tapia 5.00 12.00
MASK Sandy Koufax 200.00 400.00
MASM Starling Marte 5.00 12.00
MASMG Sarah Michelle Gellar 150.00 300.00
MASR Sierra Romero 5.00 12.00
MASS Stephen A. Smith 12.00 30.00
MAST Sage Steele 5.00 12.00
MASW Steven Wright 6.00 15.00
MATA Tyler Austin 6.00 15.00
MATAN Tom Anderson 12.00 30.00
MATAR Tom Arnold 8.00 20.00
MATB Ty Blach 4.00 10.00
MATM Trey Mancini 8.00 20.00
MATR Tom Rinaldi 4.00 10.00
MATS Trevor Story 6.00 15.00
MAVC Vashti Cunningham 4.00 10.00
MAVJ Valarie Jenkins 10.00 25.00
MAWB Wesley Bryan 4.00 10.00
MAWS William Shatner 60.00 150.00
MAYG Yulieski Gurriel 6.00 15.00
MAYM Yoan Moncada 40.00 100.00

2017 Topps Allen and Ginter Framed Mini Autographs Black Border

*BLACK: .75X TO 2X BASIC
STATED ODDS 1:423 HOBBY
STATED PRINT RUN 25 SER.#'d SETS
EXCHANGE DEADLINE 6/30/2019
MAFM Floyd Mayweather 300.00 600.00
MAKB Kris Bryant EXCH 100.00 250.00
MASMG Sarah Michelle Gellar 250.00 500.00

2017 Topps Allen and Ginter Framed Mini Gems and Ancient Fossil Relics

STATED ODDS 1:3600 HOBBY
PRINT RUNS B/WN 2-25 COPIES PER
NO PRICING ON QTY 16 OR LESS
GAFA Amethyst/25 75.00 200.00
GAFC Crystal/25
GAFG Gold/25
GAFP Peridot/25 75.00 200.00
GAFS Sapphire/25
GAFSTT Shark Tooth/25 150.00 300.00
GAFT Tourmaline/21 100.00 250.00

2017 Topps Allen and Ginter Framed Mini Relics

STATED ODDS 1:105 HOBBY
MRABE Andrew Benintendi 10.00 25.00
MRABR Alex Bregman 10.00 25.00
MRAJ Aaron Judge 30.00 80.00
MRAM Andrew McCutchen 4.00 10.00
MRAP Albert Pujols 5.00 12.00
MRARI Anthony Rizzo 6.00 15.00
MRARU Addison Russell 4.00 10.00
MRBB Byron Buxton 3.00 8.00
MRBH Bryce Harper 6.00 15.00
MRBP Buster Posey 5.00 12.00
MRCC Carlos Correa 4.00 10.00
MRCJ Chipper Jones 15.00 40.00
MRCK Clayton Kershaw 8.00 20.00
MRCR Cal Ripken Jr. 30.00 80.00
MRCS Corey Seager 4.00 10.00
MRDJ Derek Jeter 20.00 50.00
MRDM Don Mattingly 20.00 50.00
MRDO David Ortiz 4.00 10.00
MRDS Dansby Swanson 6.00 15.00
MREB Ernie Banks 60.00 150.00
MRFH Felix Hernandez 3.00 8.00
MRFL Francisco Lindor 4.00 10.00
MRFT Frank Thomas 30.00 80.00
MRGSA Gary Sanchez 4.00 10.00
MRGST Giancarlo Stanton 4.00 10.00
MRIC Ichiro 5.00 12.00
MRJD Josh Donaldson 3.00 8.00
MRJR Jackie Robinson
MRJS John Smoltz 6.00 15.00
MRJU Julio Urias 4.00 10.00
MRJVE Justin Verlander 4.00 10.00
MRJVO Joey Votto 4.00 10.00
MRKB Kris Bryant 10.00 25.00
MRKGF Ken Griffey Jr. 25.00 60.00
MRKGR Ken Griffey Jr. 25.00 60.00
MRMB Mookie Betts 6.00 15.00
MRMC Miguel Cabrera 4.00 10.00
MRMMA Manny Machado 4.00 10.00
MRMMG Mark McGwire 20.00 50.00
MRMP Mike Piazza 15.00 40.00
MRMTA Masahiro Tanaka 3.00 8.00
MRMTR Mike Trout 20.00 50.00
MRNA Nolan Arenado 5.00 12.00
MRNS Noah Syndergaard 3.00 8.00
MRPM Pedro Martinez 8.00 20.00
MRRCA Robinson Cano 3.00 8.00
MRRCL Roberto Clemente 50.00 120.00
MRTT Trea Turner 3.00 8.00
MRTW Ted Williams 75.00 200.00
MRYC Yoenis Cespedes 4.00 10.00

2017 Topps Allen and Ginter Mini Bust a Move

COMPLETE SET (15) 12.00 30.00
STATED ODDS 1:20 HOBBY
BAM1 Ballet Dance 1.00 2.50
BAM2 Bavarian Polka Dance 1.00 2.50
BAM3 Belly Dance 1.00 2.50
BAM4 Break Dance 1.00 2.50
BAM5 Charleston Dance 1.00 2.50
BAM6 Cossack Dance 1.00 2.50
BAM7 Flamenco Dance 1.00 2.50
BAM8 Hula Dance 1.00 2.50
BAM9 Irish Dance 1.00 2.50
BAM10 Jitterbug Dance 1.00 2.50
BAM11 Salsa Dance 1.00 2.50
BAM12 Tango Dance 1.00 2.50
BAM13 Twist Dance 1.00 2.50
BAM14 Waltz Dance 1.00 2.50
BAM15 Whirling Dervish Dance 1.00 2.50

2017 Topps Allen and Ginter Mini Constellations

COMPLETE SET (10) 12.00 30.00
STATED ODDS 1:50 HOBBY
C1 Orion 1.25 3.00

2 Ursa Major 1.25 3.00
3 Ursa Minor 1.25 3.00
4 Scorpius 1.25 3.00
5 Cygnus 1.25 3.00
6 Leo 1.25 3.00
7 Perseus 1.25 3.00
8 Hercules 1.25 3.00
9 Aquarius 1.25 3.00
10 Libra 1.25 3.00

2017 Topps Allen and Ginter Mini Horse in the Race

RANDOM INSERTS IN RETAIL PACKS
R1 Friesian Horse 1.50 4.00
R2 Exmoor Pony 1.50 4.00
R3 Shetland Pony 1.50 4.00
R4 American Quarter Horse 1.50 4.00
R5 Camargue Horse 1.50 4.00
R6 American Miniature Horse 1.50 4.00
R7 Grayson Highland Pony 1.50 4.00
R8 Palomino Horse 1.50 4.00
R9 Belgian Horse 1.50 4.00
R10 Bavarian Warmblood Horse 1.50 4.00
R11 East Bulgarian Horse 1.50 4.00
R12 Clydesdale Horse 1.50 4.00
R13 Arabian Horse 1.50 4.00
R14 Shire Horse 1.50 4.00
R15 Andalusian Horse 1.50 4.00
R16 Barb Horse 1.50 4.00
R17 Marwari Horse 1.50 4.00
R18 Scandinavian Coldblood Trotter 1.50 4.00
R19 Arabian Berber Horse 1.50 4.00
R20 Bosnian Pony 1.50 4.00
R21 Percheron Horse 1.50 4.00
R22 Ardennais Horse 1.50 4.00
R23 Mustang Horse 1.50 4.00
R24 Pinto Horse 1.50 4.00
R25 Norwegian Fjord Horse 1.50 4.00

2017 Topps Allen and Ginter Mini Magicians and Illusionists

COMPLETE SET (15) 15.00 40.00
STATED ODDS 1:34 HOBBY
MI1 Papus 1.25 3.00
MI2 Pamela Colman Smith 1.25 3.00
MI3 Arthur Edward Waite 1.25 3.00
MI4 Jean Eugene Robert-Houdin 1.25 3.00
MI5 P. T. Selbit 1.25 3.00
MI6 William Ellsworth Robinson 1.25 3.00
MI7 Thomas Nelson Downs 1.25 3.00
MI8 Horace Goldin 1.25 3.00
MI9 Alexander Herrmann 1.25 3.00
MI10 John Nevil Maskelyne 1.25 3.00
MI11 John Henry Anderson 1.25 3.00
MI12 Howard Thurston 1.25 3.00
MI13 Harry Kellar 1.25 3.00
MI14 Robert Heller 1.25 3.00
MI15 Georges Melies 1.25 3.00

2017 Topps Allen and Ginter Mini Required Reading

COMPLETE SET (15) 15.00 40.00
STATED ODDS 1:50 HOBBY
RR1 Walden 1.25 3.00
RR2 On the Origin of Species 1.25 3.00
RR3 Jane Eyre 1.25 3.00
RR4 A Tale of Two Cities 1.25 3.00
RR5 War and Peace 1.25 3.00
RR6 20,000 Leagues Under the Sea 1.25 3.00
RR7 Heart of Darkness 1.25 3.00
RR8 Moby Dick 1.25 3.00
RR9 Wuthering Heights 1.25 3.00
RR10 The Canterbury Tales 1.25 3.00
RR11 The Illiad 1.25 3.00
RR12 The Prince 1.25 3.00
RR13 The Adventures of Tom Sawyer 1.25 3.00
RR14 The Count of Monte Cristo 1.25 3.00
RR15 Dr. Jekyll and Mr. Hyde 1.25 3.00

2017 Topps Allen and Ginter Relics

VERSION A ODDS 1:24 HOBBY
VERSION B ODDS 1:24 HOBBY
FSRAAB Andrew Benintendi A 6.00 15.00
FSRAAG Adrian Gonzalez A 2.50 6.00
FSRAAJ Aaron Judge A 20.00 50.00
FSRAAK Andy Katz A 2.50 6.00
FSRAAM Andrew McCutchen A 3.00 8.00
FSRAAR Anthony Rizzo A 5.00 12.00
FSRABSM Ben Smith A 2.50 6.00
FSRACB Corey Bellemore A 2.50 6.00
FSRACK Craig Kimbrel A 2.50 6.00
FSRADJ Dan Jennings EXEC A 2.50 6.00
FSRADO David Ortiz A 3.00 8.00
FSRADP Dustin Pedroia A 3.00 8.00
FSRADW David Wright A 2.50 6.00
FSRAEL Evan Longoria A 2.50 6.00
FSRAELG Eric LeGrand A 2.50 6.00
FSRAGP Gregory Polanco A 2.50 6.00
FSRAGS Giancarlo Stanton A 3.00 8.00
FSRAGST Gary Stevens A 2.50 6.00
FSRAHP Hunter Pence A 2.50 6.00
FSRAJG Jay Glazer A 2.50 6.00
FSRAJH Jason Heyward A 2.50 6.00
FSRAJL Jon Lester A 2.50 6.00
FSRAJM Joe Manganiello A 2.50 6.00
FSRAJST Jayson Stark A 2.50 6.00
FSRAJT Jameson Taillon A 2.50 6.00
FSRAJU Justin Upton A 2.50 6.00
FSRAJV Justin Verlander A 3.00 8.00
FSRAKB Kris Bryant A 6.00 15.00
FSRAKK Kevin Kelley A 2.50 6.00
FSRAKR Ken Rosenthal A 2.50 6.00
FSRALH Laurie Hernandez A 3.00 8.00
FSRALT Lyle Thompson A 2.50 6.00
FSRAMB Mookie Betts A 5.00 12.00
FSRAMCA Miguel Cabrera A 3.00 8.00
FSRAMCO Miguel Cotto A 2.50 6.00
FSRAMF Michael Fulmer A 2.00 5.00
FSRAMKA Michal Kapral A 2.50 6.00
FSRAMM Manny Machado A 3.00 8.00
FSRAMT Masahiro Tanaka A 2.50 6.00
FSRANJ Nick Jonas A 2.50 6.00
FSRAPG Paul Goldschmidt A 3.00 8.00
FSRAPR Peter Rosenberg A 2.50 6.00
FSRARB Ryan Braun A 2.50 6.00
FSRARO Rougned Odor A 2.50 6.00
FSRASP Salvador Perez A 2.50 6.00
FSRATAN Tom Anderson A 4.00 10.00
FSRATG Tyler Glasnow A 2.50 6.00
FSRAVJ Valarie Jenkins A 8.00 20.00
FSRAVM Victor Martinez A 2.50 6.00
FSRAWS William Shatner A 4.00 10.00
FSRAYC Yoenis Cespedes A 3.00 8.00
FSRBABR Alex Bregman B 8.00 20.00
FSRBAC Aroldis Chapman B 3.00 8.00
FSRBAJO Adam Jones B 2.50 6.00
FSRBAJU Aaron Judge B 20.00 50.00
FSRBAM Andrew McCutchen B 3.00 8.00
FSRBAP Albert Pujols B 4.00 10.00
FSRBARI Anthony Rizzo B 5.00 12.00
FSRBARU Addison Russell B 3.00 8.00
FSRBAW Adam Wainwright B 2.50 6.00
FSRBBH Bryce Harper B 5.00 12.00
FSRBBP Buster Posey B 4.00 10.00
FSRBCC Carlos Correa B 3.00 8.00
FSRBCG Carlos Gonzalez B 2.50 6.00
FSRBCH Cole Hamels B 2.50 6.00
FSRBCKE Clayton Kershaw B 6.00 15.00
FSRBCKL Corey Kluber B 2.50 6.00
FSRBCSA Chris Sale B 3.00 8.00
FSRBCSE Corey Seager B 3.00 8.00
FSRBCY Christian Yelich B 4.00 10.00
FSRBDPR David Price B 2.50 6.00
FSRBDS Dansby Swanson B 5.00 12.00
FSRBEH Eric Hosmer B 2.50 6.00
FSRBFF Freddie Freeman B 4.00 10.00
FSRBFH Felix Hernandez B 2.50 6.00
FSRBFL Francisco Lindor B 3.00 8.00
FSRBGSA Gary Sanchez B 3.00 8.00
FSRBGSP George Springer B 2.50 6.00
FSRBHR Hanley Ramirez B 2.50 6.00
FSRBIC Ichiro B 4.00 10.00
FSRBIH Ichiro B 4.00 10.00
FSRBJAL Jose Altuve B 2.50 6.00
FSRBJAR Jake Arrieta B 2.50 6.00
FSRBJBA Javier Baez B 4.00 10.00
FSRBJBR Jackie Bradley Jr B 3.00 8.00
FSRBJBU Jose Bautista B 2.50 6.00
FSRBJD Josh Donaldson B 2.50 6.00
FSRBJDG Jacob deGrom B 3.00 8.00
FSRBJU Julio Urias B 3.00 8.00
FSRBJVE Justin Verlander B 3.00 8.00
FSRBJVO Joey Votto B 3.00 8.00
FSRBKM Kenta Maeda B 2.50 6.00
FSRBKS Kyle Seager B 2.00 5.00
FSRBMCA Matt Carpenter B 3.00 8.00
FSRBMCB Miguel Cabrera B 3.00 8.00
FSRBMH Matt Harvey B 2.50 6.00
FSRBMM Manny Machado B 3.00 8.00
FSRBMSA Miguel Sano B 2.50 6.00
FSRBMST Marcus Stroman B 2.50 6.00
FSRBMTA Masahiro Tanaka B 2.50 6.00
FSRBMTR Mike Trout B 8.00 20.00
FSRBNA Nolan Arenado B 4.00 10.00
FSRBNC Nelson Cruz B 3.00 8.00
FSRBNS Noah Syndergaard B 2.50 6.00
FSRBRC Robinson Cano B 2.50 6.00
FSRBSM Starling Marte B 2.50 6.00
FSRBSP Stephen Piscotty B 2.50 6.00
FSRBTS Trevor Story B 3.00 8.00
FSRBWM Wil Myers B 2.00 5.00
FSRBXB Xander Bogaerts B 3.00 8.00
FSRBYM Yadier Molina B 3.00 8.00

2017 Topps Allen and Ginter Revolutionary Battles

COMPLETE SET (10) 4.00 10.00
STATED ODDS 1:10 HOBBY
RB1 Battle of Lexington .75 2.00
RB2 Battle of Bunker Hill .75 2.00
RB3 Battle of Quebec .75 2.00
RB4 Battle of Long Island .75 2.00
RB5 Battle of Trenton .75 2.00
RB6 Battle of Princeton .75 2.00
RB7 Surrender of General Burgoyne .75 2.00
RB8 Battle of Cowpens .75 2.00
RB9 Battle of Guilford Court House .75 2.00
RB10 Battle of the Chesapeake .75 2.00

2017 Topps Allen and Ginter Rip Cards

OVERALL RIP ODDS 1:160 HOBBY
PRINT RUNS B/WN 30-99 COPIES PER
UNRIPPED HAVE ADD'L CARDS WITHIN
RIP1 Gary Sanchez/60 50.00 120.00
RIP2 Jackie Robinson/60 60.00 150.00
RIP3 Ty Cobb/60 50.00 120.00
RIP4 Johnny Bench/60 50.00 120.00
RIP5 Ernie Banks/60
RIP6 Reggie Jackson/60 50.00 120.00
RIP7 Nolan Arenado/60 40.00 100.00
RIP8 Sandy Koufax/60 60.00 150.00
RIP9 Stephen Strasburg/60 50.00 120.00
RIP10 Don Mattingly/60 50.00 120.00
RIP11 Roger Maris/60 50.00 120.00
RIP12 Cal Ripken Jr./60 50.00 120.00
RIP13 Ichiro/60 50.00 120.00
RIP14 Andrew McCutchen/60 40.00 100.00
RIP15 Felix Hernandez/60 40.00 100.00
RIP16 Robinson Cano/60 40.00 100.00
RIP17 Roberto Clemente/60 75.00 200.00
RIP18 Ryan Braun/60 40.00 100.00
RIP19 Adrian Beltre/30 60.00 150.00
RIP20 George Brett/60 50.00 120.00
RIP21 David Ortiz/60 50.00 120.00
RIP22 Corey Seager/60 50.00 120.00
RIP23 Albert Pujols/30 100.00 250.00
RIP24 Nolan Ryan/60 60.00 150.00
RIP25 Mookie Betts/60 75.00 200.00
RIP26 Aaron Judge/60 300.00 600.00
RIP27 Ken Griffey Jr./60 75.00 200.00
RIP28 Xander Bogaerts/30 60.00 150.00
RIP29 Clayton Kershaw/60 60.00 150.00
RIP30 Honus Wagner/60 60.00 150.00
RIP31 Yoenis Cespedes/60 40.00 100.00
RIP32 Buster Posey/60 60.00 150.00
RIP33 Mike Trout/60 75.00 200.00
RIP34 Kenta Maeda/60 40.00 100.00
RIP35 Corey Kluber/60 40.00 100.00
RIP36 Kyle Schwarber/60 50.00 120.00
RIP37 Joey Votto/60 40.00 100.00
RIP38 Manny Machado/60 60.00 150.00
RIP39 Barry Larkin/60 50.00 120.00
RIP40 Adam Jones/30 40.00 100.00
RIP41 Trea Turner/60 40.00 100.00
RIP42 Jacob deGrom/60 40.00 100.00
RIP43 Bryce Harper/60 75.00 200.00
RIP44 Ozzie Smith/60 60.00 150.00
RIP45 Jake Arrieta/30
RIP46 Dave Winfield/60 50.00 120.00
RIP47 Mark McGwire/60
RIP48 Noah Syndergaard/60 50.00 120.00
RIP49 Paul Goldschmidt/30 100.00 250.00
RIP50 Anthony Rizzo/60 50.00 120.00
RIP51 Aledmys Diaz/60 50.00 120.00
RIP52 Alex Bregman/60 50.00 120.00
RIP53 Ted Williams/60 60.00 150.00
RIP54 Andrew Benintendi/60 50.00 120.00
RIP55 Randy Johnson/60
RIP56 Max Scherzer/60 50.00 120.00
RIP57 Jose Canseco/60 50.00 120.00
RIP58 Kris Bryant/60 75.00 200.00
RIP59 Yu Darvish/60 40.00 100.00
RIP60 Hank Aaron/60 75.00 200.00
RIP61 Mike Piazza/60 50.00 120.00
RIP62 Giancarlo Stanton/60 40.00 100.00
RIP63 Matt Kemp/30 60.00 150.00
RIP64 Yoan Moncada/60 50.00 120.00
RIP65 Hunter Pence/30 50.00 120.00
RIP66 Dansby Swanson/60 40.00 100.00
RIP67 Miguel Cabrera/60 60.00 150.00
RIP68 Wil Myers/40 40.00 100.00
RIP69 Chris Sale/60 40.00 100.00
RIP70 Francisco Lindor/60 50.00 120.00
RIP71 Derek Jeter/60 75.00 200.00
RIP72 Greg Maddux/60 60.00 150.00
RIP73 Justin Verlander/60 50.00 120.00
RIP74 Brooks Robinson/60 50.00 120.00
RIP75 Dustin Pedroia/60 40.00 100.00
RIP76 Babe Ruth/60 75.00 200.00
RIP77 Roger Clemens/60 50.00 120.00
RIP78 John Smoltz/60 60.00 150.00
RIP79 Addison Russell/60 40.00 100.00
RIP80 Jose Altuve/60 40.00 100.00
RIP81 Carlos Correa/60 50.00 120.00
RIP83 Freddie Freeman/30 60.00 150.00
RIP84 Chipper Jones/60 60.00 150.00
RIP85 Lou Gehrig/60 60.00 150.00
RIP86 Frank Thomas/60 50.00 120.00
RIP87 Eric Hosmer/30
RIP88 Masahiro Tanaka/60
RIP89 Bo Jackson/60 50.00 120.00
RIP90 Josh Donaldson/60 40.00 100.00
RIP96 Julio Urias/60 50.00 120.00

2017 Topps Allen and Ginter Rip Cards Ripped

UNRIPPED ODDS 1:160 HOBBY
PRINT RUNS B/WN 30-50 COPIES PER
PRICING FOR CLEANLY RIPPED CARDS
RIP1 Gary Sanchez/60 3.00 8.00
RIP2 Jackie Robinson/60 3.00 8.00
RIP3 Ty Cobb/60 5.00 12.00
RIP4 Johnny Bench/60 3.00 8.00
RIP5 Ernie Banks/60 3.00 8.00
RIP6 Reggie Jackson/60 2.50 6.00
RIP7 Nolan Arenado/60 4.00 10.00
RIP8 Sandy Koufax/60 6.00 15.00
RIP9 Stephen Strasburg/60 3.00 8.00
RIP10 Don Mattingly/60 6.00 15.00
RIP11 Roger Maris/60 3.00 8.00
RIP12 Cal Ripken Jr./60 10.00 25.00
RIP13 Ichiro/60 4.00 10.00
RIP14 Andrew McCutchen/60 3.00 8.00
RIP15 Felix Hernandez/60 2.50 6.00
RIP16 Robinson Cano/60 2.50 6.00
RIP17 Roberto Clemente/60 8.00 20.00
RIP18 Ryan Braun/60 2.50 6.00
RIP19 Adrian Beltre/30 3.00 8.00
RIP20 George Brett/60 6.00 15.00
RIP21 David Ortiz/60 3.00 8.00
RIP22 Corey Seager/60 3.00 8.00
RIP23 Albert Pujols/30 4.00 10.00
RIP24 Nolan Ryan/60 10.00 25.00
RIP25 Mookie Betts/60 5.00 12.00
RIP26 Aaron Judge/60 25.00 60.00
RIP27 Ken Griffey Jr./60 6.00 15.00
RIP28 Xander Bogaerts/30 3.00 8.00
RIP29 Clayton Kershaw/60 6.00 15.00
RIP30 Honus Wagner/60 3.00 8.00
RIP31 Yoenis Cespedes/60 3.00 8.00
RIP32 Buster Posey/60 4.00 10.00
RIP33 Mike Trout/60 15.00 40.00
RIP34 Kenta Maeda/60 2.50 6.00
RIP35 Corey Kluber/60 2.50 6.00
RIP36 Kyle Schwarber/60 3.00 8.00
RIP37 Joey Votto/60 3.00 8.00
RIP38 Manny Machado/60 3.00 8.00
RIP39 Barry Larkin/60 2.50 6.00
RIP40 Adam Jones/30 2.50 6.00
RIP41 Trea Turner/60 2.50 6.00
RIP42 Jacob deGrom/60 3.00 8.00
RIP43 Bryce Harper/60 5.00 12.00
RIP44 Ozzie Smith/60 4.00 10.00
RIP45 Jake Arrieta/30 2.50 6.00
RIP46 Dave Winfield/60 2.50 6.00
RIP47 Mark McGwire/60 5.00 12.00
RIP48 Noah Syndergaard/60 2.50 6.00
RIP49 Paul Goldschmidt/30 3.00 8.00
RIP50 Anthony Rizzo/60 5.00 12.00
RIP51 Aledmys Diaz/60 2.50 6.00
RIP52 Alex Bregman/60 8.00 20.00
RIP53 Ted Williams/60 6.00 15.00
RIP54 Andrew Benintendi/60 6.00 15.00
RIP55 Randy Johnson/60 3.00 8.00
RIP56 Max Scherzer/60 3.00 8.00
RIP57 Jose Canseco/60 2.50 6.00
RIP58 Kris Bryant/60 4.00 10.00
RIP59 Yu Darvish/60 3.00 8.00
RIP60 Hank Aaron/60 6.00 15.00
RIP61 Mike Piazza/60 3.00 8.00
RIP62 Giancarlo Stanton/60 3.00 8.00
RIP63 Matt Kemp/30 2.50 6.00
RIP64 Yoan Moncada/60 6.00 15.00
RIP65 Hunter Pence/30 2.50 6.00
RIP66 Dansby Swanson/60 5.00 12.00
RIP67 Miguel Cabrera/60 3.00 8.00
RIP68 Wil Myers/40 2.00 5.00
RIP69 Chris Sale/60 3.00 8.00
RIP70 Francisco Lindor/60 3.00 8.00
RIP71 Derek Jeter/60 8.00 20.00
RIP72 Greg Maddux/60 4.00 10.00
RIP73 Justin Verlander/60 3.00 8.00
RIP74 Brooks Robinson/60 2.50 6.00
RIP75 Dustin Pedroia/60 3.00 8.00
RIP76 Babe Ruth/60 8.00 20.00
RIP77 Roger Clemens/60 4.00 10.00
RIP78 John Smoltz/60 3.00 8.00
RIP79 Addison Russell/60 3.00 8.00
RIP80 Jose Altuve/60 2.50 6.00
RIP81 Carlos Correa/60 3.00 8.00
RIP83 Freddie Freeman/30 4.00 10.00
RIP84 Chipper Jones/60 3.00 8.00
RIP85 Lou Gehrig/60 6.00 15.00
RIP86 Frank Thomas/60 3.00 8.00
RIP87 Eric Hosmer/30 2.50 6.00
RIP88 Masahiro Tanaka/60 2.50 6.00
RIP89 Bo Jackson/60 3.00 8.00
RIP90 Josh Donaldson/60 2.50 6.00
RIP96 Julio Urias/60 3.00 8.00

2017 Topps Allen and Ginter Sport Fish and Fishing Lures

COMPLETE SET (20) 6.00 15.00
STATED ODDS 1:5 HOBBY
SFL1 Northern Pike .60 1.50
SFL2 Walleye .60 1.50
SFL3 Bluegill .60 1.50
SFL4 Bass .60 1.50
SFL5 Salmon .60 1.50
SFL6 Largemouth Bass .60 1.50
SFL7 Trout .60 1.50
SFL8 Rainbow Trout .60 1.50
SFL9 Tarpon .60 1.50
SFL10 Redfish .60 1.50
SFL11 Spotted Sea Trout .60 1.50
SFL12 Grouper .60 1.50
SFL13 Sailfish .60 1.50
SFL14 Giant Trevally .60 1.50
SFL15 Bluefin Tuna .60 1.50
SFL16 Yellowfin Tuna .60 1.50
SFL17 Dorado (Mahi Mahi) .60 1.50
SFL18 Wahoo .60 1.50
SFL19 Barracuda .60 1.50
SFL20 Smallmouth Bass .60 1.50

2017 Topps Allen and Ginter What a Day

COMPLETE SET (100) 25.00 60.00
STATED ODDS 1:2 HOBBY
WAD1 Kris Bryant .50 1.25
WAD2 Buster Posey .50 1.25
WAD3 Hank Aaron .75 2.00
WAD4 Chris Sale .40 1.00
WAD5 Anthony Rizzo .60 1.50
WAD6 Nolan Ryan 1.25 3.00
WAD7 Dansby Swanson .60 1.50
WAD8 Aledmys Diaz .30 .75
WAD9 David Price .30 .75
WAD10 Dustin Pedroia .40 1.00
WAD11 Ryan Braun .30 .75
WAD12 Roger Maris .40 1.00
WAD13 Jose Canseco .30 .75
WAD14 Mike Piazza .40 1.00
WAD15 Brooks Robinson .30 .75
WAD16 Xander Bogaerts .40 1.00
WAD17 Carlos Correa .40 1.00
WAD18 Masahiro Tanaka .30 .75
WAD19 Kyle Schwarber .40 1.00
WAD20 George Brett .75 2.00
WAD21 Stephen Strasburg .40 1.00
WAD22 Honus Wagner .30 .75
WAD23 Kenta Maeda .30 .75
WAD24 Carl Yastrzemski .60 1.50
WAD25 Andrew McCutchen .40 1.00
WAD26 Frank Thomas .40 1.00
WAD27 Mike Trout 2.00 5.00
WAD28 Daniel Murphy .30 .75
WAD29 Sandy Koufax .75 2.00
WAD30 Carlos Gonzalez .30 .75
WAD31 Matt Kemp .30 .75
WAD32 Lou Gehrig .75 2.00
WAD33 Nolan Arenado .50 1.25
WAD34 Yu Darvish .40 1.00
WAD35 Jose Bautista .30 .75
WAD36 George Springer .30 .75
WAD37 Bo Jackson .40 1.00
WAD38 Chris Davis .25 .60
WAD39 John Smoltz .40 1.00
WAD40 Gary Sanchez .40 1.00
WAD41 Eric Hosmer .30 .75
WAD42 Francisco Lindor .40 1.00
WAD43 Adrian Beltre .40 1.00
WAD44 Pedro Martinez .30 .75
WAD45 Clayton Kershaw .75 2.00
WAD46 Chipper Jones .40 1.00
WAD47 Ted Williams .75 2.00
WAD48 Albert Pujols .50 1.25
WAD49 Wil Myers .25 .60
WAD50 Trea Turner .30 .75
WAD51 Joey Votto .40 1.00
WAD52 David Dahl .30 .75
WAD53 Robinson Cano .30 .75
WAD54 Ozzie Smith .50 1.25
WAD55 David Wright .30 .75
WAD56 Don Mattingly .75 2.00
WAD57 Noah Syndergaard .30 .75
WAD58 Corey Seager .40 1.00
WAD59 Andrew Benintendi .75 2.00
WAD60 Ty Cobb .60 1.50
WAD61 Greg Maddux .50 1.25
WAD62 David Ortiz .40 1.00
WAD63 Reggie Jackson .30 .75
WAD64 Adam Jones .30 .75
WAD65 Yoenis Cespedes .40 1.00
WAD66 Justin Verlander .40 1.00
WAD67 Mookie Betts .60 1.50
WAD68 Max Scherzer .40 1.00
WAD69 Johnny Bench .40 1.00
WAD70 Troy Tulowitzki .40 1.00
WAD71 Matt Carpenter .40 1.00
WAD72 Edwin Encarnacion .40 1.00
WAD73 Ken Griffey Jr. .75 2.00
WAD74 Miguel Cabrera .40 1.00
WAD75 Randy Johnson .40 1.00
WAD76 Jake Arrieta .30 .75
WAD77 Felix Hernandez .30 .75
WAD78 Manny Machado .40 1.00
WAD79 Freddie Freeman .50 1.25
WAD80 Derek Jeter 1.00 2.50
WAD81 Addison Russell .40 1.00
WAD82 Ernie Banks .40 1.00
WAD83 Bryce Harper .60 1.50
WAD84 Cal Ripken Jr. 1.25 3.00
WAD85 Corey Kluber .30 .75
WAD86 Roberto Clemente 1.00 2.50
WAD87 Ichiro .50 1.25
WAD88 Babe Ruth 1.00 2.50
WAD89 Roger Clemens .50 1.25
WAD90 Jackie Robinson .40 1.00
WAD91 Jose Altuve .30 .75
WAD92 Javier Baez .50 1.25
WAD93 Josh Donaldson .30 .75
WAD94 Alex Bregman 1.00 2.50
WAD95 Byron Buxton .30 .75
WAD96 Julio Urias .40 1.00
WAD97 Jacob deGrom .40 1.00
WAD98 Giancarlo Stanton .40 1.00
WAD99 Mark McGwire .60 1.50
WAD100 Paul Goldschmidt .40 1.00

2017 Topps Allen and Ginter World Baseball Classic Relics

STATED ODDS 1:274 HOBBY
STATED PRINT RUN 99 SER.#'d SETS
WBCRABE Adrian Beltre 6.00 15.00
WBCRABR Alex Bregman 8.00 20.00
WBCRAG Adrian Gonzalez 5.00 12.00
WBCRAJ Adam Jones 5.00 12.00
WBCRAM Andrew McCutchen 8.00 20.00
WBCRAV Alex Verdugo 8.00 20.00
WBCRBP Buster Posey 8.00 20.00
WBCRCC Carlos Correa 15.00 40.00
WBCRCG Carlos Gonzalez 5.00 12.00
WBCREH Eric Hosmer 10.00 25.00
WBCRFH Felix Hernandez 5.00 12.00
WBCRFL Francisco Lindor 12.00 30.00
WBCRGC Gavin Cecchini 4.00 10.00
WBCRGS Giancarlo Stanton 8.00 20.00
WBCRJA Jose Altuve 6.00 15.00
WBCRJBA Javier Baez 8.00 20.00
WBCRJBU Jose Bautista 5.00 12.00
WBCRMCB Miguel Cabrera 6.00 15.00
WBCRMM Manny Machado 6.00 15.00
WBCRNA Nolan Arenado 8.00 20.00
WBCRPG Paul Goldschmidt 6.00 15.00
WBCRRC Robinson Cano 5.00 12.00
WBCRSF Shintaro Fujinami 5.00 12.00
WBCRSP Salvador Perez 5.00 12.00
WBCRTN Takahiro Norimoto 4.00 10.00
WBCRTS Tomoyuki Sugano 6.00 15.00
WBCRTY Tetsuto Yamada 8.00 20.00
WBCRXB Xander Bogaerts 8.00 20.00
WBCRYM Yadier Molina 12.00 30.00
WBCRYT Yoshitomo Tsutsugoh 6.00 15.00

2017 Topps Allen and Ginter Mini World's Dudes

COMPLETE SET (45) 40.00 100.00
STATED ODDS 1:13 HOBBY
WD1 Surgeon Dude 1.00 2.50
WD2 Conductor Dude 1.00 2.50
WD3 Pilot Dude 1.00 2.50
WD4 Polo Dude 1.00 2.50
WD5 Traffic Cop Dude 1.00 2.50
WD6 Hunting Guide Dude 1.00 2.50
WD7 Deep Sea Dude 1.00 2.50
WD8 Scholar Dude 1.00 2.50
WD9 Japanese Sumo Dude 1.00 2.50
WD10 Algerian Lawyer Dude 1.00 2.50
WD11 Tennis Dude 1.00 2.50
WD12 New York Ferreter Dude 1.00 2.50
WD13 Tunisian Editor Dude 1.00 2.50
WD14 Packer Dude 1.00 2.50
WD15 Barber Dude 1.00 2.50
WD16 Chef Dude 1.00 2.50
WD17 Newsboy Dude 1.00 2.50
WD18 Egyptian Sultan Dude 1.00 2.50
WD19 German Snow Patrol Dude 1.00 2.50
WD20 English Chimney Sweep Dude 1.00 2.50
WD21 Chilean Sailor Dude 1.00 2.50
WD22 University Track Dude 1.00 2.50
WD23 Lumberjack Dude 1.00 2.50
WD24 Violin Dude 1.00 2.50
WD25 American Football Dude 1.00 2.50
WD26 Farmhand Dude 1.00 2.50
WD27 Steel Worker Dude 1.00 2.50
WD28 Irish Golfer Dude 1.00 2.50
WD29 Boxing Dude 1.00 2.50
WD30 Machinist Dude 1.00 2.50
WD31 German Cyclist Dude 1.00 2.50
WD32 Concession Dude 1.00 2.50
WD33 Zookeeper Dude 1.00 2.50
WD34 Ornithology Dude 1.00 2.50
WD35 Camping Dude 1.00 2.50
WD36 Circus Clown Dude 1.00 2.50
WD37 Artist Dude 1.00 2.50
WD38 Polish Prince Dude 1.00 2.50
WD39 Scottish Dude 1.00 2.50
WD40 Park Avenue Dude 1.00 2.50
WD41 Russian Peddler Dude 1.00 2.50
WD42 Scout Dude 1.00 2.50
WD43 Fisherman Dude 1.00 2.50
WD44 Gardener Dude 1.00 2.50
WD45 Secretary to the Sultan Dude 1.00 2.50

2017 Topps Allen and Ginter World's Fair

COMPLETE SET (20) 3.00 8.00
STATED ODDS 1:5 HOBBY
WF1 Life Savers Parachute Jump .30 .75
New York World's Fair
WF2 X-Ray Machine .30 .75
Pan-American Exposition
WF3 The Atomium .30 .75
Expo '58
WF4 The Great Wharf .30 .75
World's Columbian Exposition
WF5 Westinghouse Tower .30 .75
New York World's Fair
WF6 Eiffel Tower .30 .75
Exposition Universelle
WF7 Diesel Engine .30 .75
Exposition Universelle
WF8 Facsimile Machine .30 .75
The Great Exhibition
WF9 Sunsphere .30 .75
82 World's Fair
WF10 Conical Pendulum Clock .30 .75
Exposition Universelle
WF11 Space Needle .30 .75
Century 21 Exposition
WF12 Unisphere .30 .75
64-'65 World's Fair
WF13 Solar Generator .30 .75
Exposition Universelle
WF14 Monorail .30 .75
Centennial Exposition
WF15 Ferris Wheel .30 .75
World's Columbian Exposition
WF16 Biosphere .30 .75
Expo 67
WF17 Statue of Liberty .30 .75
Exposition Universelle
WF18 Statue of the Republic .30 .75
World's Columbian Exposition
WF19 Habitat 67 .30 .75
Expo 67
WF20 Telephone .30 .75
Centennial Exposition

2016 Topps Allen and Ginter X

COMPLETE SET (350)
1 Jorge Soler .40 1.00
2 Ryan Braun .30 .75
3 Joey Gallo .30 .75
4 Justin Verlander .40 1.00
5 Kyle Waldrop RC .50 1.25
6 Luke Maile RC .40 1.00
7 John Lamb RC .40 1.00
8 Denise Austin .25 .60
9 Tom Glavine .30 .75
10 Jason Sklar .25 .60
11 Howie Kendrick .25 .60
12 Trevor Story RC 1.50 4.00
13 Kevin Gausman .25 .60
14 Kendrys Morales .25 .60
15 Mark Trumbo .25 .60
16 Trayce Thompson RC .60 1.50
17 Ian Desmond .25 .60
18 Kolten Wong .30 .75
19 Rollie Fingers .30 .75
20 Michael Pineda .25 .60
21 Ben Zobrist .30 .75
22 Francisco Rodriguez .30 .75
23 Addison Russell .40 1.00
24 Max Kepler RC .60 1.50
25 Charlie Blackmon .40 1.00
26 John Lackey .30 .75
27 Matt Duffy .25 .60
28 Elvis Andrus .30 .75
29 Jay Bruce .30 .75
30 Curtis Granderson .30 .75
31 Brad Ziegler .25 .60
32 Falcon 9 Rocket .25 .60
33 Ender Inciarte .25 .60
34 Rick Klein .25 .60
35 Jayson Werth .30 .75
36 Alex Rodriguez .50 1.25
37 Dawn Spacecraft .25 .60
38 David Peralta .25 .60
39 Paul Goldschmidt .40 1.00
40 Jordan Zimmermann .30 .75
41 Drew Smyly .25 .60
42 Cuban Embassy .25 .60
43 Jake Odorizzi .25 .60
44 Miguel Castro RC .40 1.00
45 Laurence Leavy .25 .60
46 Ben Revere .25 .60
47 Corey Dickerson .25 .60
48 J.T. Realmuto .40 1.00
49 Ketel Marte RC .75 2.00
50 Daniel Murphy .30 .75
51 A.J. Ramos .25 .60
52 Adam Eaton .25 .60
53 Logan Forsythe .25 .60
54 Jose Abreu .40 1.00
55 Hector Rondon .25 .60
56 Carlos Correa .40 1.00
57 Jim Rice .30 .75
58 Freddie Freeman .50 1.25
59 Billy Hamilton .30 .75
60 Devin Mesoraco .25 .60
61 Miguel Cabrera .40 1.00
62 Dellin Betances .30 .75
63 Monica Abbott .25 .60
64 Steve Schirripa .25 .60
65 Hisashi Iwakuma .30 .75
66 Miguel Sano RC .60 1.50
67 Melky Cabrera .25 .60
68 Dexter Fowler .30 .75
69 Roberto Alomar .30 .75
70 Chase Headley .25 .60
71 Matt Reynolds RC .40 1.00
72 Jake McGee .25 .60
73 James Shields .25 .60
74 Brian Dozier .30 .75
75 Mike Moustakas .30 .75
76 Collin McHugh .25 .60
77 Kevin Pillar .25 .60
78 Jose Berrios RC .50 1.25
79 Dustin Garneau RC .40 1.00
80 Edwin Encarnacion .40 1.00
81 Brian Johnson RC .40 1.00
82 Gerardo Parra .25 .60
83 David Wright .30 .75
84 Robinson Cano .30 .75
85 Prince Fielder .30 .75
86 Adam Jones .30 .75
87 Craig Kimbrel .30 .75
88 Jose Fernandez .40 1.00
89 Dallas Keuchel .30 .75
90 George Lopez .25 .60
91 Nick Hundley .25 .60
92 Steven Matz .30 .75
93 Mike Piazza .40 1.00
94 Todd Frazier .30 .75
95 Jimmy Nelson .25 .60
96 Jason Kipnis .30 .75
97 Kyle Schwarber RC 1.25 3.00
98 Michael Conforto RC .50 1.25
99 Luis Severino RC .50 1.25
100 Rob Refsnyder RC .50 1.25
101 Roger Clemens .50 1.25
102 Aaron Nola RC .75 2.00
103 Carlos Martinez .30 .75
104 Byron Buxton .30 .75
105 Alex Dickerson RC .40 1.00
106 Steve Spurrier .25 .60
107 Matt Stonie .25 .60
108 Justin Turner .30 .75
109 Eduardo Rodriguez .25 .60
110 Michele Steele .25 .60
111 Lorenzo Cain .25 .60
112 Kris Bryant .50 1.25
113 Alcides Escobar .30 .75
114 Randy Sklar .25 .60
115 Brad Miller .30 .75
116 Jose Reyes .30 .75
117 Robin Yount .40 1.00
118 Evan Gattis .25 .60
119 Gennady Golovkin 6.00 15.00
120 Kenta Maeda .50 1.25
121 Corey Seager RC 3.00 8.00
122 Andrew Heaney .25 .60
123 Alex Cobb .25 .60
124 Jonathan Lucroy .30 .75
125 Carl Edwards Jr. RC .50 1.25
126 Greg Bird RC .50 1.25
127 Lucas Duda .30 .75
128 Aroldis Chapman .40 1.00
129 Zack Greinke .30 .75
130 Gregory Polanco .30 .75
131 Brooks Robinson .30 .75
132 Leigh Steinberg .25 .60
133 Joc Pederson .30 .75
134 Henry Owens .30 .75

135 Luis Gonzalez .30 .75
136 Matt Kemp .30 .75
137 Marcus Semien .25 .60
138 Cord McCoy .25 .60
139 Gio Gonzalez .30 .75
140 Caleb Cotham RC .50 1.25
141 Colin Rea RC .40 1.00
142 Jake Arrieta .30 .75
143 Adrian Gonzalez .30 .75
144 Matt Holliday .40 1.00
145 Mike Greenberg .25 .60
146 Evan Longoria .30 .75
147 Martin Prado .25 .60
148 Kole Calhoun .25 .60
149 Michael Brantley .30 .75
150 Eric Hosmer .30 .75
151 David Ortiz .40 1.00
152 Gary Sanchez RC 1.25 3.00
153 Jung Ho Kang .25 .60
154 Ervin Santana .25 .60
155 Brandon Phillips .25 .60
156 Jason Heyward .30 .75
157 Gerrit Cole .40 1.00
158 Joe McKeehen .25 .60
159 Brett Gardner .30 .75
160 Steve Kerr .25 .60
161 Vinny G .25 .60
162 Josh Harrison .25 .60
163 Zach Lee RC .40 1.00
164 Steven Souza Jr. .30 .75
165 Nelson Cruz .40 1.00
166 Morgan Spurlock .25 .60
167 Jeff Samardzija .25 .60
168 Don Mattingly .75 2.00
169 Adrian Beltre .40 1.00
170 Max Scherzer .40 1.00
171 Brandon Crawford .30 .75
172 Joe Morgan .30 .75
173 Billy Burns .25 .60
174 Frankie Montas RC .50 1.25
175 Jonathan Schoop .25 .60
176 Neil Walker .25 .60
177 Mark Teixeira .30 .75
178 David Robertson .25 .60
179 Jen Welter .25 .60
180 Ryne Sandberg .75 2.00
181 Alex Wood .25 .60
182 Nolan Arenado .50 1.25
183 Andrew McCutchen .40 1.00
184 Mookie Betts .60 1.50
185 J.D. Martinez .40 1.00
186 Alex Gordon .30 .75
187 Carl Yastrzemski .60 1.50
188 Edgar Martinez .30 .75
189 Buster Posey .50 1.25
190 Jon Gray RC .40 1.00
191 Anthony Anderson .25 .60
192 Dennis Eckersley .30 .75
193 Huston Street .25 .60
194 Mike Trout 5.00 12.00
195 Joey Votto .40 1.00
196 Josh Reddick .25 .60
197 George Springer .30 .75
198 Ari Shaffir .25 .60
199 Carlton Fisk .30 .75
200 Carlos Gomez .25 .60
201 Byung Ho Park RC .50 1.25
202 Missy Franklin .25 .60
203 Ernie Johnson .25 .60
204 Drew Storen .25 .60
205 Carlos Santana .30 .75
206 Bob Gibson .30 .75
207 Brandon Belt .30 .75
208 Joe Panik .30 .75
209 Andrew Miller .30 .75
210 Michael Breed .25 .60
211 Albert Pujols .50 1.25
212 Maria Sharapova .25 .60
213 Heidi Watney .25 .60
214 Justin Bour .30 .75
215 Khris Davis .40 1.00
216 Hannah Storm .25 .60
217 Julio Teheran .30 .75
218 Masahiro Tanaka .30 .75
219 Delino DeShields .25 .60
220 Matt Duffy .25 .60
221 Brian McCann .30 .75
222 Nomar Mazara RC .60 1.50
223 Erick Aybar .25 .60
224 Gary Carter .25 .60
225 Brandon Drury RC .60 1.50
226 Luke Jackson RC .40 1.00
227 Timothy Busfield .25 .60
228 Colin Cowherd .25 .60
229 Mitch Moreland .25 .60
230 Jessica Mendoza .25 .60
231 Kaleb Cowart RC .40 1.00
232 Hector Olivera RC .50 1.25
233 Adam Lind .30 .75
234 Glen Perkins .25 .60
235 Cheyenne Woods .25 .60
236 Brad Boxberger .25 .60
237 Dustin Pedroia .40 1.00
238 Tyler White RC .40 1.00
239 Brandon Moss .25 .60
240 Robert Raiola .25 .60
241 Orlando Jones .25 .60
242 DJ LeMahieu .40 1.00
243 Jay Oakerson .25 .60
244 Gravitational Waves .25 .60
245 Dwier Brown .25 .60
246 Mike Francesa .25 .60
247 Papal Visit .25 .60
248 Jill Martin .25 .60
249 Paul McBeth 1.50 4.00
250 Jose Canseco .30 .75
251 Stephen Piscotty RC .60 1.50
252 Cole Hamels .30 .75
253 Ozzie Smith .50 1.25
254 Bryce Harper .60 1.50
255 Nomar Garciaparra .30 .75
256 Starling Marte .30 .75
257 Chris Archer .25 .60
258 Kenley Jansen .30 .75
259 Jose Peraza RC .50 1.25
260 Anthony Rizzo .60 1.50
261 Carlos Carrasco .25 .60
262 Giancarlo Stanton .40 1.00
263 Hanley Ramirez .30 .75
264 Xander Bogaerts .40 1.00
265 Felix Hernandez .30 .75
266 Anthony Rendon .40 1.00
267 Sonny Gray .30 .75
268 Frank Thomas .40 1.00
269 Maikel Franco .30 .75
270 David Price .30 .75
271 A.J. Pollock .25 .60
272 Troy Tulowitzki .40 1.00
273 Dee Gordon .25 .60
274 Chris Sale .40 1.00
275 Jacob deGrom .40 1.00
276 Matt Harvey .30 .75
277 Manny Machado .40 1.00
278 Madison Bumgarner .30 .75
279 Paul Molitor .40 1.00
280 Paul O'Neill .30 .75
281 Jose Bautista .30 .75
282 Stephen Strasburg .40 1.00
283 Michael Wacha .30 .75
284 Orlando Cepeda .30 .75
285 Josh Donaldson .30 .75
286 Guido Knudson RC .40 1.00
287 Andre Dawson .30 .75
288 Lance McCullers .25 .60
289 Jose Quintana .25 .60
290 Andrew Faulkner RC .50 1.25
291 Kevin Kiermaier .30 .75
292 Marcell Ozuna .40 1.00
293 Jonathan Papelbon .30 .75
294 Carlos Rodon .40 1.00
295 Jose Altuve .30 .75
296 Rickey Henderson .40 1.00
297 Corey Kluber .30 .75
298 Jacoby Ellsbury .30 .75
299 Clayton Kershaw .75 2.00
300 Trea Turner RC 1.25 3.00
301 Tyson Ross SP .50 1.25
302 Trevor Brown SP RC .60 1.50
303 Wei-Yin Chen SP .50 1.25
304 Yasmani Grandal SP .50 1.25
305 Tyler Duffey SP RC .50 1.25
306 Yu Darvish SP .75 2.00
307 Russell Martin SP .50 1.25
308 Andy Pettitte SP .60 1.50
309 Yasmany Tomas SP .50 1.25
310 Patrick Corbin SP .60 1.50
311 Wellington Castillo SP .50 1.25
312 Carlos Beltran SP .60 1.50
313 Stephen Vogt SP .60 1.50
314 Starlin Castro SP .50 1.25
315 Santiago Casilla SP .50 1.25
316 Ryan Weber SP RC .50 1.25
317 Yordano Ventura SP .60 1.50
318 Pedro Severino SP RC .50 1.25
319 Yasiel Puig SP .75 2.00
320 Roberto Clemente SP 2.00 5.00
321 Nick Castellanos SP .75 2.00
322 Ryan LaMarre SP RC .50 1.25
323 Victor Martinez SP .60 1.50
324 Rob Refsnyder SP .60 1.50
325 Raisel Iglesias SP .60 1.50
326 Peter O'Brien SP RC .50 1.25
327 Raul Mondesi SP RC
328 Randal Grichuk SP .50 1.25
329 Andre Ethier SP .60 1.50
330 Zack Godley SP RC .50 1.25
331 Taijuan Walker SP .50 1.25
332 Yan Gomes SP .50 1.25
333 Shin-Soo Choo SP .60 1.50
334 Scott Kazmir SP .50 1.25
335 Shawn Tolleson SP .50 1.25
336 Tom Murphy SP RC .50 1.25
337 Steve Cishek SP .50 1.25
338 Stephen Piscotty SP .75 2.00
339 Salvador Perez SP .60 1.50
340 Roberto Osuna SP .50 1.25
341 Richie Shaffer SP RC .50 1.25
342 Trea Turner SP 1.50 4.00
343 Shelby Miller SP .60 1.50
344 Ryan Zimmerman SP .60 1.50
345 Wil Myers SP .50 1.25
346 Pablo Sandoval SP .60 1.50
347 Sean Doolittle SP .50 1.25
348 Trevor Plouffe SP .50 1.25
349 Travis d'Arnaud SP .60 1.50
350 Steve Carlton SP .60 1.50

2016 Topps Allen and Ginter X Silver Framed Mini Autographs

EXCHANGE DEADLINE 6/30/2018
AGAAA Anthony Anderson 8.00 20.00
AGAAN Aaron Nola 20.00 50.00
AGABH Bryce Harper 125.00 300.00
AGABP Buster Posey 40.00 100.00
AGABS Blake Snell 10.00 25.00
AGACA Canelo Alvarez 60.00 150.00
AGACC Colin Cowherd 10.00 25.00
AGACC Carlos Correa 40.00 100.00
AGACM Cord McCoy 8.00 20.00
AGACSA Chris Sale 10.00 25.00
AGACSE Corey Seager 30.00 80.00
AGADK Dallas Keuchel 12.00 30.00
AGAEJ Ernie Johnson 25.00 60.00
AGAES Errol Spence Jr. 25.00 60.00
AGAFH Felix Hernandez 12.00 30.00
AGAFV Fernando Valenzuela 20.00 50.00
AGAFW Frank Whaley 8.00 20.00
AGAGG Gennady Golovkin 150.00 400.00
AGAGL George Lopez 12.00 30.00
AGAHA Hank Aaron 150.00 300.00
AGAHS Hannah Storm 8.00 20.00
AGAHW Heidi Watney 12.00 30.00
AGAJBA Javier Baez 25.00 60.00
AGAJBE Jose Berrios 10.00 25.00
AGAJC Jose Canseco 12.00 30.00
AGAJD Jacob deGrom 20.00 50.00
AGAJS Jason Sklar 15.00 40.00
AGAKB Kris Bryant 75.00 200.00
AGAKG Ken Griffey Jr. 125.00 300.00
AGAKMA Kenta Maeda 20.00 50.00
AGAKS Kyle Schwarber 20.00 50.00
AGALS Luis Severino 20.00 50.00
AGAMCO Michael Conforto 12.00 30.00
AGAMFA Mike Francesa 10.00 25.00
AGAMFR Missy Franklin 10.00 25.00
AGAMG Mike Greenberg 10.00 25.00
AGAMIS Michele Steele 8.00 20.00
AGAMP Mike Piazza 40.00 100.00
AGAMPH Michael Phelps 125.00 300.00
AGAMSH Maria Sharapova 60.00 150.00
AGAMST Matt Stonie 12.00 30.00
AGAMT Mike Trout 150.00 400.00
AGANG Nomar Garciaparra 15.00 40.00
AGANL Nancy Lieberman 10.00 25.00
AGANM Nomar Mazara 12.00 30.00
AGAOJO Orlando Jones 8.00 20.00
AGAPM Paul Molitor 20.00 50.00
AGAPMB Paul McBeth 30.00 80.00
AGARC Robinson Cano 8.00 20.00
AGARSK Randy Sklar 10.00 25.00
AGASK Steve Kerr 12.00 30.00
AGASP Stephen Piscotty 8.00 20.00
AGASS Steve Spurrier 15.00 40.00
AGASSA Susan Sarandon 50.00 120.00
AGATB Timothy Busfield 10.00 25.00
AGATS Trevor Story 10.00 25.00
AGATT Trea Turner 12.00 30.00
AGAVGU Vinny G 10.00 25.00

2018 Topps Allen and Ginter

COMPLETE SET (350) 25.00 60.00
COMP.SET w/o SP's (300) 15.00 40.00
SP ODDS 1:2 HOBBY
1 Mike Trout 1.25 3.00
2 Derek Jeter .60 1.50
3 Babe Ruth .60 1.50
4 Cameron Maybin .15 .40
5 Kris Bryant .30 .75
6 Chris Taylor .20 .50
7 Aaron Judge .60 1.50
8 Ryan Sickler .15 .40
9 Francisco Mejia RC .30 .75
10 Jose Altuve .20 .50
11 Jose Abreu .25 .60
12 Eddie Rosario .25 .60
13 Sonny Fredrickson .15 .40
14 Craig Kimbrel .20 .50
15 Giancarlo Stanton .25 .60
16 Austin Hays RC .40 1.00
17 Kyle Seager .15 .40
18 Bullpen Car .15 .40
19 Yoan Moncada .25 .60
20 Joey Votto .25 .60
21 Noah Syndergaard .20 .50
22 Michael Conforto .20 .50
23 Jordan Montgomery .20 .50
24 Trey Mancini .20 .50
25 Andre Dawson .20 .50
26 Marwin Gonzalez .15 .40
27 Sean Manaea .15 .40
28 Jack Flaherty RC .40 1.00
29 H. Jon Benjamin .15 .40
30 Carlos Correa .25 .60
31 Joc Pederson .20 .50
32 Anthony Rizzo .40 1.00
33 Nicky Delmonico RC .25 .60
34 Scott Blumstein .15 .40
35 Robinson Cano .20 .50
36 Trevor Story .25 .60
37 Yu Darvish .25 .60
38 Jonathan Lucroy .20 .50
39 Trea Turner .20 .50
40 Max Scherzer .25 .60
41 Didi Gregorius .20 .50
42 Jackie Robinson .25 .60
43 Champ Pederson .15 .40
44 Aaron Hicks .20 .50
45 Dexter Fowler .20 .50
46 Kole Calhoun .15 .40
47 Dansby Swanson .25 .60
48 Manny Margot .15 .40
49 Luke Weaver .20 .50
50 Hank Aaron .50 1.25
51 J.D. Martinez .25 .60
52 Robbie Ray .15 .40
53 Mike Zunino .15 .40
54 Carlos Gonzalez .20 .50
55 Biz Markie .15 .40
56 Justin Bour .15 .40
57 Lindsey Vonn .25 .60
58 Andrelton Simmons .15 .40
59 J.D. Davis RC .30 .75
60 Cal Ripken Jr. .75 2.00
61 Randal Grichuk .15 .40
62 Justin Upton .20 .50
63 Luiz Gohara RC .25 .60
64 Daniel Murphy .20 .50
65 Clint Frazier RC .50 1.25
66 Paul Goldschmidt .25 .60
67 Ozzie Smith .30 .75
68 Yasiel Puig .25 .60
69 Anthony Banda RC .25 .60
70 Jason Heyward .20 .50
71 Matt Carpenter .25 .60
72 Nelson Cruz .25 .60
73 Adrian Beltre .25 .60
74 Eric Hosmer .20 .50
75 Christian Yelich .30 .75
76 Ryan Zimmerman .20 .50
77 Adam Duvall .25 .60
78 Jason Kipnis .20 .50
79 Jonathan Schoop .15 .40
80 Ryan Braun .20 .50
81 Yuli Gurriel .20 .50
82 Method Man .15 .40
83 Cryptocurrency 1.25 3.00
84 Marine National Monument .15 .40
85 Mariano Rivera .30 .75
86 Nicholas Castellanos .25 .60
87 Alex Wood .15 .40
88 Kenta Maeda .20 .50
89 Mike Moustakas .20 .50
90 Avisail Garcia .20 .50
91 Victor Caratini RC .30 .75
92 Barry Larkin .20 .50
93 Stephen Strasburg .25 .60
94 George Brett .50 1.25
95 Victor Robles RC .60 1.50
96 Wil Myers .15 .40
97 Mike Piazza .25 .60
98 A.J. Pollock .15 .40
99 Pedro Martinez .20 .50
100 Shohei Ohtani RC 1.50 4.00
101 Matt Kemp .20 .50
102 Josh Bell .20 .50
103 Lucas Sims RC .25 .60
104 Michael Fulmer .15 .40
105 Jacob deGrom .25 .60
106 David Ortiz .25 .60
107 Roberto Clemente .60 1.50
108 Tommy Pham .15 .40
109 Sonny Gray .20 .50
110 Honus Wagner .20 .50
111 Brian Dozier .20 .50
112 Yadier Molina .25 .60
113 Randy Johnson .25 .60
114 Jim Thome .20 .50
115 Ian Happ .20 .50
116 Ozzie Albies RC .75 2.00
117 Corey Kluber .20 .50
118 Sean Doolittle .15 .40
119 Javier Baez .30 .75
120 Cody Bellinger .50 1.25
121 Dustin Pedroia .25 .60
122 Jimmy Nelson .15 .40
123 John Smoltz .25 .60
124 Nolan Ryan .75 2.00
125 Brian McCann .20 .50
126 Jon Lester .20 .50
127 J.P. Crawford RC .25 .60
128 Dellin Betances .20 .50
129 Stephen Piscotty .15 .40
130 Gary Sanchez .25 .60
131 Greg Maddux .30 .75
132 Masahiro Tanaka .20 .50
133 Johnny Bench .25 .60
134 Trevor Bauer .25 .60
135 Chris Sale .25 .60
136 Maikel Franco .20 .50
137 Josh Donaldson .20 .50
138 Ernie Banks .25 .60
139 Michael Rapaport .15 .40
140 Alex Bregman .25 .60
141 Archie Bradley .15 .40
142 Kevin Pillar .15 .40
143 Hunter Pence .20 .50
144 CC Sabathia .20 .50
145 Genie Bouchard .15 .40
146 Billy Hamilton .20 .50
147 Walker Buehler RC 1.25 3.00
148 Luis Severino .20 .50
149 Steve Simeone .15 .40
150 Zack Greinke .25 .60
151 Don Mattingly .50 1.25
152 Ben Lecomte .15 .40
153 Sloane Stephens .15 .40
154 Raisel Iglesias .20 .50
155 Hunter Renfroe .15 .40
156 Edwin Encarnacion .25 .60
157 Bill James .15 .40
158 Yonder Alonso .15 .40
159 Bob Gibson .20 .50
160 Matt Olson .15 .40
161 Austin Rogers .15 .40
162 Chipper Jones .25 .60
163 Byron Buxton .20 .50
164 Manny Machado .25 .60
165 Ben Zobrist .20 .50
166 Johnny Cueto .20 .50
167 Scott Kingery RC .40 1.00
168 Andrew Benintendi .25 .60
169 Mike Clevinger .20 .50
170 Bradley Zimmer .15 .40
171 Rougned Odor .20 .50
172 Buster Posey .30 .75
173 Nolan Arenado .30 .75
174 Corey Seager .25 .60
175 Lincoln Riley .15 .40
176 Claire Smith .15 .40
177 Dallas Keuchel .20 .50
178 Jon Gray .15 .40
179 Tyronn Lue .15 .40
180 Willson Contreras .25 .60
181 Khris Davis .25 .60
182 Greg Bird .20 .50
183 Dee Gordon .15 .40
184 Andrew McCutchen .25 .60
185 Joe Panik .20 .50
186 George Springer .20 .50
187 Albert Pujols .30 .75
188 Zack Cozart .15 .40
189 Ichiro .30 .75
190 Ted Williams .50 1.25
191 Freddie Freeman .30 .75
192 Chris Archer .15 .40
193 Zack Granite RC .25 .60
194 Justin Smoak .15 .40
195 Tim Anderson .25 .60
196 Tyler Mahle RC .30 .75
197 Kenley Jansen .20 .50
198 Tom Segura .15 .40
199 Garrett Cooper RC .25 .60
200 Sandy Koufax .50 1.25
201 Miguel Andujar RC 1.00 2.50
202 Stugotz .15 .40
203 Amed Rosario RC .30 .75
204 Samesong Park .15 .40
205 Scott Rogowsky .15 .40
206 Paul Blackburn RC .25 .60
207 Ronald Acuna Jr. RC 5.00 12.00
208 Kelsey Plum .15 .40
209 Fernando Rodney .15 .40
210 Francisco Lindor .25 .60
211 Rhys Hoskins RC 1.00 2.50
212 Mark McGwire .40 1.00
213 Ryne Sandberg .50 1.25
214 Josh Reddick .15 .40
215 Brandon Crawford .20 .50
216 Rafael Devers RC .75 2.00
217 Dominic Smith RC .25 .60
218 Christopher McDonald .15 .40
219 Gerrit Cole .25 .60
220 Theo Epstein .25 .60
221 Jeff Bagwell .20 .50
222 Total Solar Eclipse .15 .40
223 Dave Winfield .20 .50
224 Starling Marte .25 .60
225 Lou Gehrig .50 1.25
226 Lucas Giolito .25 .60
227 Aaron Altherr .15 .40
228 Tommy Wiseau .15 .40
229 Roger Maris .25 .60
230 Tim Beckham .20 .50
231 Michael Brantley .20 .50
232 Chance Sisco RC .30 .75
233 Roger Clemens .30 .75
234 Adam Wainwright .20 .50
235 Marcell Ozuna .25 .60
236 Luis Castillo .20 .50
237 Brian Anderson RC .30 .75
238 Pat Neshek .15 .40
239 Evan Longoria .20 .50
240 Gleyber Torres RC 2.50 6.00
241 Jesse Winker .15 .40
242 Yoenis Cespedes .25 .60
243 Yuli Gurriel .20 .50
244 Orlando Arcia .20 .50
245 Mookie Betts .40 1.00
246 Travis Shaw .15 .40
247 Lance McCullers .15 .40
248 Aaron Nola .20 .50
249 Kyle Schwarber .25 .60
250 Bryce Harper .40 1.00
251 Charlie Blackmon .25 .60
252 Gio Gonzalez .20 .50
253 Hanley Ramirez .20 .50
254 Jackie Bradley Jr. .25 .60
255 Willie Calhoun RC .30 .75
256 Jake Arrieta .20 .50
257 Andrew Stevenson RC .25 .60
258 Parker Bridwell RC .25 .60
259 Bomb Cyclone .15 .40
260 Sean Evans .15 .40
261 Brooks Robinson .20 .50
262 Felix Hernandez .20 .50
263 Jose Ramirez .20 .50
264 Reggie Jackson .20 .50
265 Carlos Rodon .20 .50
266 Franklin Barreto .15 .40
267 Garrett Richards .20 .50
268 Jose Berrios .20 .50
269 Phil Coyne USHER .15 .40
270 Eric Thames .20 .50
271 Jose Canseco .20 .50
272 Ryan McMahon RC .30 .75
273 Jake Lamb .20 .50
274 Domingo Santana .20 .50
275 Justin Verlander .25 .60
276 Chris Davis .15 .40
277 Willie McCovey .25 .60
278 Paul DeJong .25 .60
279 Miguel Sano .20 .50
280 Clayton Kershaw .50 1.25
281 Salvador Perez .25 .60
282 Joey Gallo .20 .50
283 Addison Russell .20 .50
284 Ian Kinsler .20 .50
285 Jackson Stephens RC .25 .60
286 Frank Thomas .25 .60
287 Paige Spiranac .15 .40
288 Mike Leake .15 .40
289 Wade Boggs .20 .50
290 Ty Cobb .40 1.00
291 Albert Almora .20 .50
292 Marcus Stroman .20 .50
293 Alex Verdugo RC .40 1.00
294 Steven Matz .20 .50
295 Xander Bogaerts .25 .60
296 Taijuan Walker .15 .40
297 Miguel Cabrera .25 .60
298 Jameson Taillon .20 .50
299 Adam Jones .20 .50
300 Bo Jackson .25 .60
301 Whit Merrifield SP .60 1.50
302 Justin Turner SP .50 1.25
303 Hyun-Jin Ryu SP .50 1.25
304 Brandon Woodruff SP RC .50 1.25
305 Lewis Brinson SP .50 1.25
306 Joe Mauer SP .50 1.25
307 Hideki Matsui SP .60 1.50
308 Brett Gardner SP .50 1.25
309 Aroldis Chapman SP .60 1.50
310 Matt Chapman SP .60 1.50
311 Dustin Fowler SP RC .40 1.00
312 Carlos Santana SP .50 1.25
313 Nick Williams SP RC .50 1.25
314 Gregory Polanco SP .50 1.25
315 Christian Villanueva SP RC .40 1.00
316 Will Clark SP .50 1.25
317 Mitch Haniger SP .50 1.25
318 Carlos Martinez SP .50 1.25
319 Harrison Bader SP RC .60 1.50
320 Corey Dickerson SP .40 1.00
321 Nomar Mazara SP .40 1.00
322 Richard Urena SP RC .40 1.00
323 Erick Fedde SP RC .40 1.00
324 Anthony Rendon SP .60 1.50
325 Cole Hamels SP .50 1.25
326 Elvis Andrus SP .50 1.25
327 Kevin Kiermaier SP .50 1.25
328 Edwin Diaz SP .50 1.25
329 Josh Harrison SP .40 1.00
330 Ryder Jones SP RC .40 1.00
331 Todd Frazier SP .50 1.25
332 Max Kepler SP .50 1.25
333 Zach Davies SP .40 1.00
334 Sandy Alcantara SP RC .40 1.00
335 Julio Urias SP .60 1.50
336 Lorenzo Cain SP .40 1.00
337 Dennis Eckersley SP .50 1.25
338 Darryl Strawberry SP .40 1.00
339 Starlin Castro SP .40 1.00
340 Andy Pettitte SP .50 1.25
341 Rickey Henderson SP .60 1.50
342 Carlos Carrasco SP .40 1.00
343 Sean Newcomb SP .50 1.25
344 Ender Inciarte SP .40 1.00
345 Tyler Glasnow SP .40 1.00
346 Dwight Gooden SP .40 1.00
347 Jay Bruce SP .50 1.25
348 Josh Hader SP .40 1.00
349 German Marquez SP .40 1.00
350 Jen-Ho Tseng SP RC .40 1.00

2018 Topps Allen and Ginter Glossy Silver

*GLS SLVR 1-300: 2X TO 5X BASIC
*GLS SLVR 1-300 RC: 1.2X TO 3X BASIC RCs
*GLS SLVR 301-350: .75X TO 2X BASIC
FOUND ONLY IN HOBBY HOT BOXES

2018 Topps Allen and Ginter Mini

*MINI 1-300: 1X TO 2.5X BASIC
*MINI 1-300 RC: .6X TO 1.5X BASIC RCs
*MINI SP 301-350: .6X TO 1.5X BASIC
MINI SP ODDS 1:13 HOBBY
351-400 RANDOM WITHIN RIP CARDS
STATED PLATE ODDS 1:1328 HOBBY
PLATE PRINT RUN 1 SET PER COLOR
BLACK-CYAN-MAGENTA-YELLOW ISSUED
NO PLATE PRICING DUE TO SCARCITY
351 Mike Trout EXT 30.00 80.00
352 Shohei Ohtani EXT 125.00 300.00
353 Paul Goldschmidt EXT 12.00 30.00
354 Hank Aaron EXT 20.00 50.00
355 Ozzie Albies EXT 20.00 50.00
356 Manny Machado EXT 15.00 40.00
357 Cal Ripken Jr. EXT 30.00 80.00
358 Mookie Betts EXT 20.00 50.00
359 Andrew Benintendi EXT 25.00 60.00
360 Rafael Devers EXT 15.00 40.00
361 Jackie Robinson EXT 15.00 40.00
362 Sandy Koufax EXT 15.00 40.00
363 Anthony Rizzo EXT 15.00 40.00
364 Kris Bryant EXT 15.00 40.00
365 Joey Votto EXT 15.00 4.00
366 Francisco Lindor EXT 12.00 30.00
367 Nolan Arenado EXT 15.00 40.00
368 Miguel Cabrera EXT 12.00 30.00
369 Justin Verlander EXT 12.00 30.00
370 Carlos Correa EXT 12.00 30.00
371 Jose Altuve EXT 25.00 60.00
372 Nolan Ryan EXT 25.00 60.00
373 Bo Jackson EXT 25.00 60.00
374 Cody Bellinger EXT 25.00 60.00
375 Clayton Kershaw EXT 25.00 60.00
376 Corey Seager EXT 12.00 30.00
377 Yu Darvish EXT 12.00 30.00
378 Ichiro EXT 20.00 50.00
379 Byron Buxton EXT 15.00 40.00
380 Noah Syndergaard EXT 10.00 25.00
381 Amed Rosario EXT 10.00 25.00
382 Giancarlo Stanton EXT 12.00 30.00
383 Aaron Judge EXT 40.00 100.00
384 Clint Frazier EXT 15.00 40.00
385 Babe Ruth EXT 20.00 50.00
386 Derek Jeter EXT 20.00 50.00
387 Mariano Rivera EXT 20.00 50.00
388 Mark McGwire EXT 15.00 40.00
389 Rhys Hoskins EXT 20.00 50.00
390 Andrew McCutchen EXT 15.00 40.00
391 Roberto Clemente EXT 30.00 80.00
392 Buster Posey EXT 20.00 50.00
393 Robinson Cano EXT 10.00 25.00
394 Josh Donaldson EXT 10.00 25.00
395 Bryce Harper EXT 15.00 40.00
396 Max Scherzer EXT 15.00 40.00
397 Victor Robles EXT 15.00 40.00
398 Honus Wagner EXT 20.00 50.00
399 George Brett EXT 25.00 60.00
400 Frank Thomas EXT 20.00 50.00

2018 Topps Allen and Ginter Mini A and G Back

*MINI AG 1-300: 1.2X TO 3X BASIC
*MINI AG 1-300 RC: .75X TO 2X BASIC RCs
*MINI AG SP 301-350: .75X TO 2X BASIC
STATED ODDS 1:5 HOBBY
83 Cryptocurrency 10.00 25.00

2018 Topps Allen and Ginter Mini Black Border

*MINI BLK 1-300: 2X TO 5X BASIC
*MINI BLK 1-300 RC: 1.2X TO 3X BASIC RCs
*MINI BLK SP 301-350: 1.2X TO 3X BASIC
MINI BLK ODDS 1:10 HOBBY
83 Cryptocurrency 25.00 60.00

2018 Topps Allen and Ginter Mini Brooklyn Back

*MINI BRKLN 1-300: 12X TO 30X BASIC
*MINI BRKLN 1-300 RC: 8X TO 20X BASIC RCs
*MINI BRKLN 301-350: 5X TO 12X BASIC
STATED ODDS 1:248 HOBBY
STATED PRINT RUN 25 SER.#'d SETS
83 Cryptocurrency 200.00 500.00

2018 Topps Allen and Ginter Mini Glow in the Dark

*MINI GLOW 1-300: 12X TO 30X BASIC
*MINI GLOW 1-300 RC: 8X TO 20X BASIC RCs
*MINI GLOW 301-350: 5X TO 12X BASIC
RANDOM INSERTS IN PACKS
83 Cryptocurrency 500.00 1000.00

2018 Topps Allen and Ginter Mini Gold

*MINI GOLD 1-300: 2.5X TO 6X BASIC
*MINI GOLD 1-300 RC: 1.5X TO 4X BASIC RCs
*MINI GOLD 301-350: 1X TO 2.5X BASIC
RANDOMLY INSERTED IN RETAIL PACKS
83 Cryptocurrency 30.00 80.00

2018 Topps Allen and Ginter Mini No Number

*MINI NNO 1-300: 5X TO 12X BASIC
*MINI NNO 1-300 RC: 3X TO 8X BASIC RCs
*MINI NNO 301-350: 2X TO 5X BASIC
MINI NNO ODDS 1:124 HOBBY
ANNCD PRINT RUN 50 COPIES PER
83 Cryptocurrency 150.00 400.00

2018 Topps Allen and Ginter Autographs

STATED ODDS 1:4163 HOBBY
EXCHANGE DEADLINE 6/30/2020
FSACE Chris Evans 300.00 600.00
FSACH Chris Hemsworth 300.00 600.00
FSAMB Mikal Bridges 12.00 30.00

2018 Topps Allen and Ginter Baseball Equipment of the Ages

COMPLETE SET (30) 12.00 30.00
STATED ODDS 1:6 HOBBY
BEA1 Vintage Glove .40 1.00
BEA2 The Catch Glove .40 1.00
BEA3 Modern Glove .40 1.00
BEA4 Vintage Bat .40 1.00
BEA5 Modern Bat .40 1.00
BEA6 Early Catcher's Mask .40 1.00
BEA7 Modern Catcher's Mask .40 1.00
BEA8 Batting Gloves .40 1.00
BEA9 Vintage Catcher's Mitt .40 1.00
BEA10 Modern Catcher's Mitt .40 1.00
BEA11 Vintage Baseball .40 1.00
BEA12 Modern Baseball .40 1.00
BEA13 Catcher's Chest Protector .40 1.00
BEA14 Flip-Up Sunglasses .40 1.00
BEA15 Vintage Cleats .40 1.00
BEA16 Modern Cleats .40 1.00
BEA17 Baseball Donut .40 1.00
BEA18 Fungo Bat .40 1.00
BEA19 Pitch Counter .40 1.00
BEA20 Rosin Bag .40 1.00
BEA21 Batting Shin Guards .40 1.00
BEA22 Catching Shin Guards .40 1.00
BEA23 Modern Baseball Sunglasses .40 1.00
BEA24 Baseball Hat .40 1.00
BEA25 Batting Helmet .40 1.00
BEA26 Radar Gun .40 1.00
BEA27 Bases .40 1.00
BEA28 Eye Black .40 1.00
BEA29 Baseball Sweater .40 1.00
BEA30 Vintage Uniform .40 1.00

2018 Topps Allen and Ginter Box Toppers

INSERTED IN HOBBY BOXES

BL1 Kris Bryant 2.50 6.00
BL2 Mike Trout 3.00 8.00
BL3 Jose Altuve 1.25 3.00
BL4 Aaron Judge 4.00 10.00
BL5 Clayton Kershaw 3.00 8.00
BL6 Bryce Harper 2.50 6.00
BL7 Shohei Ohtani 5.00 12.00
BL8 Ronald Acuna Jr. 5.00 12.00
BL9 Gleyber Torres 5.00 12.00
BL10 Cal Ripken Jr. 2.50 6.00
BL11 Don Mattingly 2.50 6.00
BL12 Mark McGwire 2.50 6.00
BL13 Chipper Jones 1.50 4.00
BL14 Babe Ruth 2.50 6.00
BL15 Honus Wagner 1.50 4.00

2018 Topps Allen and Ginter Fabled Relics

RANDOM INSERTS IN PACKS
STATED PRINT RUN 25 SER.#'d SETS
MFARC Cupid 75.00 200.00
MFARE El Dorado 75.00 200.00
MFARP Phoenix 75.00 200.00
MFARS Shangri-La 75.00 200.00
MFARKA King Arthur 150.00 300.00
MFARPE Pegasus 75.00 200.00

2018 Topps Allen and Ginter Fantasy Goldmine

COMPLETE SET (50) 15.00 40.00
STATED ODDS 1:4 HOBBY
FG1 Hank Aaron .75 2.00
FG2 Cal Ripken Jr. 1.25 3.00
FG3 Jackie Robinson .40 1.00
FG4 Sandy Koufax .75 2.00
FG5 Nolan Ryan 1.25 3.00
FG6 Bo Jackson .40 1.00
FG7 Babe Ruth 1.00 2.50
FG8 Derek Jeter 1.00 2.50
FG9 Mariano Rivera .50 1.25
FG10 Mark McGwire .60 1.50
FG11 Roberto Clemente 1.00 2.50
FG12 Honus Wagner .40 1.00
FG13 George Brett .75 2.00
FG14 Frank Thomas .40 1.00
FG15 Greg Maddux .50 1.25
FG16 Randy Johnson .40 1.00
FG17 Pedro Martinez .30 .75
FG18 Reggie Jackson .30 .75
FG19 Ted Williams .75 2.00
FG20 Jimmie Foxx .40 1.00
FG21 Ernie Banks .40 1.00
FG22 Ryne Sandberg .75 2.00
FG23 Chipper Jones .40 1.00
FG24 Wade Boggs .30 .75
FG25 Don Mattingly .75 2.00
FG26 Barry Larkin .30 .75
FG27 Nomar Garciaparra .30 .75
FG28 Ozzie Smith .50 1.25
FG29 John Smoltz .40 1.00
FG30 Andy Pettitte .30 .75
FG31 Roberto Alomar .30 .75
FG32 Ty Cobb .60 1.50
FG33 Lou Gehrig .75 2.00
FG34 Johnny Bench .40 1.00
FG35 Rickey Henderson .40 1.00
FG36 Hideki Matsui .40 1.00
FG37 Tom Seaver .30 .75
FG38 Jim Palmer .30 .75
FG39 Willie McCovey .30 .75
FG40 Jim Thome .30 .75
FG41 Brooks Robinson .30 .75
FG42 Al Kaline .40 1.00
FG43 Lou Brock .30 .75
FG44 Mike Piazza .40 1.00
FG45 Roger Clemens .50 1.25
FG46 Rod Carew .30 .75
FG47 Steve Carlton .30 .75
FG48 Ivan Rodriguez .30 .75
FG49 Ichiro .50 1.25
FG50 Bob Gibson .30 .75

2018 Topps Allen and Ginter Framed Mini Autographs

STATED ODDS 1:58 HOBBY
EXCHANGE DEADLINE 6/30/2020
MAAA Aaron Altherr 4.00 10.00
MAAE Austin Meadows 15.00 40.00
MAAH Austin Hays 10.00 25.00
MAAJ Aaron Judge 75.00 200.00
MAAL Alison Lee 10.00 25.00
MAAM A.J. Minter 5.00 12.00
MAAN Anthony Banda 4.00 10.00
MAAO Austin Rogers 6.00 15.00
MAAR Amed Rosario 5.00 12.00
MAAS Andrew Stevenson 4.00 10.00
MABD Brian Dozier 10.00 25.00
MABH Bryce Harper 100.00 250.00
MABI Bill James 10.00 25.00
MABJ Bo Jackson
MABL Ben Lecomte 4.00 10.00
MABM Biz Markie 20.00 50.00
MABW Brandon Woodruff 5.00 12.00
MACM Claire Smith 5.00 12.00
MACO Christopher McDonald 5.00 12.00
MACP Champ Pederson 6.00 15.00
MACS Chance Sisco 5.00 12.00
MADC Dominic Smith 4.00 10.00
MADF Dustin Fowler 4.00 10.00
MADM Don Mattingly 40.00 100.00
MADP Dillon Peters 4.00 10.00
MADS Darryl Strawberry 6.00 15.00
MADU Doris Burke 20.00 50.00
MAFJ Felix Jorge 4.00 10.00
MAFM Francisco Mejia
MAFT Frank Thomas 40.00 100.00
MAGC Garrett Cooper 4.00 10.00
MAGT Gleyber Torres 60.00 150.00
MAGU Genie Bouchard 15.00 40.00
MAHB Harrison Bader 6.00 15.00
MAHJ H. Jon Benjamin 20.00 50.00
MAIH Ian Happ 5.00 12.00
MAJA Jose Altuve 20.00 50.00
MAJB Justin Bour 4.00 10.00
MAJB John Boyega 20.00 50.00
'17 Card in '18 Frame
MAJC J.P. Crawford 4.00 10.00
MAJCK Jack Sock 6.00 15.00
MAJD J.D. Davis 5.00 12.00
MAJH Jordan Hicks 10.00 25.00
MAJI Jose Berrios 5.00 12.00
MAJJ Jaren Jackson Jr. 30.00 80.00
MAJM J.D. Martinez EXCH 20.00 50.00
MAJO Jose Canseco 12.00 30.00
MAJR Jose Ramirez 12.00 30.00
MAJS Jackson Stephens 4.00 10.00
MAJV Joey Votto 25.00 60.00
MAJZ Jon Lovitz 40.00 100.00
MAKB Keon Broxton 4.00 10.00
MAKD Khris Davis 6.00 15.00
MAKP Kelsey Plum 5.00 12.00
MAKR Kris Bryant 60.00 150.00
MALC Luis Castillo 5.00 12.00
MALR Lincoln Riley 25.00 60.00
MALV Lindsey Vonn 25.00 60.00
MAMF Max Fried 25.00 60.00
MAMG Miguel Gomez 4.00 10.00
MAMH Molly McGrath 12.00 30.00
MAMIII Marvin Bagley III 40.00 100.00
MAMM Manny Machado 30.00 80.00
MAMMI Miles Mikolas 5.00 12.00
MAMN Method Man EXCH 30.00 80.00
MAMO Matt Olson 4.00 10.00
MAMR Michael Rapaport 12.00 30.00
MAMT Mike Trout 300.00 500.00
MAMW Mark McGwire
MAMY Madison Keys 8.00 20.00
MANY Noah Syndergaard 12.00 30.00
MAOA Ozzie Albies 25.00 60.00
MAPB Parker Bridwell 4.00 10.00
MAPD Paul DeJong 6.00 15.00
MAPG Paul Goldschmidt 15.00 40.00
MAPL Paul Blackburn 4.00 10.00
MAPSP Paige Spiranac 15.00 40.00
MARA Ronald Acuna 75.00 200.00
MARD Rafael Devers 20.00 50.00
MARI Ryan Sickler 12.00 30.00
MARK Rhys Hoskins 20.00 50.00
MARR Raudy Read 4.00 10.00
MARU Richard Urena 4.00 10.00
MAS Stugotz 20.00 50.00
MASA Sandy Alcantara 4.00 10.00
MASB Scott Blumstein 4.00 10.00
MASF Sean Evans 12.00 30.00
MASF Sonny Fredrickson 5.00 12.00
MASG Sonny Gray
MASKI Scott Kingery 8.00 20.00
MASN Sean Newcomb 5.00 12.00
MASO Shohei Ohtani 150.00 400.00
MASR Scott Rogowsky 10.00 25.00
MASS Steve Simeone 4.00 10.00
MASST Sloane Stephens 6.00 15.00
MASX Collin Sexton 30.00 80.00
MATE Theo Epstein 50.00 120.00
MATG Tom Segura 12.00 30.00
MATH Tony Hawk 50.00 120.00
MATI Tommy Wiseau 20.00 50.00
MATL Tzu-Wei Lin 5.00 12.00
MATLU Tyronn Lue 4.00 10.00
MATM Tyler Mahle 5.00 12.00
MATN Tomas Nido 4.00 10.00
MATS Troy Scribner 4.00 10.00
MATV Travis Shaw 4.00 10.00
MAVC Victor Carafini 6.00 15.00
MAVR Victor Robles 20.00 50.00
MAWB Walker Buehler 25.00 60.00
MAWM Whit Merrifield 8.00 20.00
MAWO Willson Contreras 10.00 25.00

2018 Topps Allen and Ginter Framed Mini Autographs Black Frame

*BLACK: .75X TO 2X BASIC
STATED ODDS 1:527 HOBBY
PRINT RUN B/WN 10-25 SETS PER
NO PRICING QTY 15 OR LESS
EXCHANGE DEADLINE 6/30/2020
MABJ Bo Jackson 60.00 150.00

2018 Topps Allen and Ginter Magnificent Moons

COMPLETE SET (10) 4.00 10.00
STATED ODDS 1:6 HOBBY
MM1 Moon - Earth .40 1.00
MM2 Europa - Jupiter .40 1.00
MM3 Io - Jupiter .40 1.00
MM4 Mimas - Saturn .40 1.00
MM5 Enceladus - Saturn .40 1.00
MM6 Triton - Neptune .40 1.00
MM7 Phobos - Mars .40 1.00
MM8 Titan - Saturn .40 1.00
MM9 Miranda - Uranus .40 1.00
MM10 Ganymede - Jupiter .40 1.00

2018 Topps Allen and Ginter Mini Baseball Superstitions

COMPLETE SET (15) 15.00 40.00
STATED ODDS 1:50 HOBBY
MBS1 No talking about a No-hitter 1.25 3.00
MBS2 Batting Gloves 1.25 3.00
MBS3 Wearing the same Helmet 1.25 3.00
MBS4 Postseason Beards 1.25 3.00
MBS5 Leaping over the Foul line 1.25 3.00
MBS6 Pre-Game Meal 1.25 3.00
MBS7 Rally Caps 1.25 3.00
MBS8 Wearing The Same Hat 1.25 3.00
MBS9 Drawing in the Batter's Box Dirt 1.25 3.00
MBS10 Between-Inning Routine 1.25 3.00
MBS11 Curse of the Bambino 1.25 3.00
MBS12 Not changing seats 1.25 3.00
MBS13 Lucky Jersey Numbers 1.25 3.00
MBS14 Mismatched Socks 1.25 3.00
MBS15 Baseball cards 1.25 3.00

2018 Topps Allen and Ginter Mini DNA Relics

STATED ODDS 1:9666 HOBBY
PRINT RUNS B/WN 2-25 COPIES PER
NO PRICING ON QTY 17 OR LESS
DNARMO Mosasaur Tooth/25 250.00 500.00
DNARMT Megalodon Tooth/25 250.00 500.00

2018 Topps Allen and Ginter Mini Exotic Sports

COMPLETE SET (25) 25.00 60.00
INSERTED IN RETAIL PACKS
MES1 Tug-O-War 1.25 3.00
MES2 Ostrich Racing 1.25 3.00
MES3 Chess Boxing 1.25 3.00
MES4 Underwater Hockey 1.25 3.00
MES5 Zorbing 1.25 3.00
MES6 Sumo Wrestling 1.25 3.00
MES7 Sepak Takraw 1.25 3.00
MES8 Cheese Rolling 1.25 3.00
MES9 Dog Surfing 1.25 3.00
MES10 Cornhole 1.25 3.00
MES11 Downhill Boxcar Racing 1.25 3.00
MES12 Hot Dog Eating Contest 1.25 3.00
MES13 Drone Racing 1.25 3.00
MES14 Elephant Polo 1.25 3.00
MES15 Armwrestling 1.25 3.00
MES16 Disc Golf 1.25 3.00
MES17 Roller Derby 1.25 3.00
MES18 Ultimate 1.25 3.00
MES19 Quidditch 1.25 3.00
MES20 Beer Pong 1.25 3.00
MES21 Belly Flopping 1.25 3.00
MES22 Watercross 1.25 3.00
MES23 Speed Stacking 1.25 3.00
MES24 Redbull Flugtag 1.25 3.00
MES25 Bo-taoshi 1.25 3.00

2018 Topps Allen and Ginter Mini Flags of Lost Nations

COMPLETE SET (25) 25.00 60.00
STATED ODDS 1:50 HOBBY
FLN1 USSR 1.25 3.00
FLN2 Yugoslavia 1.25 3.00
FLN3 Tibet 1.25 3.00
FLN4 Sikkim 1.25 3.00
FLN5 United Arab Republic 1.25 3.00
FLN6 Ceylon 1.25 3.00
FLN7 Republic of Salo 1.25 3.00
FLN8 West Germany 1.25 3.00
FLN9 East Germany 1.25 3.00
FLN10 Czechoslovakia 1.25 3.00
FLN11 Zanzibar 1.25 3.00
FLN12 Zaire 1.25 3.00
FLN13 Tanganyika 1.25 3.00
FLN14 Abyssinia 1.25 3.00
FLN15 Siam 1.25 3.00
FLN16 Rhodesia 1.25 3.00
FLN17 Prussia 1.25 3.00
FLN18 Persia 1.25 3.00
FLN19 Newfoundland 1.25 3.00
FLN20 New Granada 1.25 3.00
FLN21 Hawaii 1.25 3.00
FLN22 Texas 1.25 3.00
FLN23 Vermont 1.25 3.00
FLN24 Ottoman Empire 1.25 3.00
FLN25 Corsica 1.25 3.00

2018 Topps Allen and Ginter Mini Folio of Fears

COMPLETE SET (10) 12.00 30.00
STATED ODDS 1:50 HOBBY
MFF1 Arachnophobia 1.25 3.00
MFF2 Acrophobia 1.25 3.00
MFF3 Entomophobia 1.25 3.00
MFF4 Aviophobia 1.25 3.00
MFF5 Ophidiophobia 1.25 3.00
MFF6 Astraphobia 1.25 3.00
MFF7 Coulrophobia 1.25 3.00
MFF8 Claustrophobia 1.25 3.00
MFF9 Phasmophobia 1.25 3.00
MFF10 Scotophobia 1.25 3.00

2018 Topps Allen and Ginter Mini Framed Relics

STATED ODDS 1:56 HOBBY
MFRAB Andrew Benintendi 5.00 12.00
MFRAE Adrian Beltre 4.00 10.00
MFRAI Anthony Rizzo 6.00 15.00
MFRAJ Adam Jones 3.00 8.00
MFRAO Alex Rodriguez 5.00 12.00
MFRAP Albert Pujols 5.00 12.00
MFRAS Amed Rosario 3.00 8.00
MFRAU Aaron Judge 15.00 40.00
MFRBB Byron Buxton 3.00 8.00
MFRBH Bryce Harper 6.00 15.00
MFRBJ Bo Jackson 12.00 30.00
MFRBL Barry Larkin 3.00 8.00
MFRBP Buster Posey 5.00 12.00
MFRCA Corey Seager 4.00 10.00
MFRCC Carlos Correa 4.00 10.00
MFRCF Clint Frazier 5.00 12.00
MFRCJ Chipper Jones 4.00 10.00
MFRCK Clayton Kershaw 8.00 20.00
MFRCR Cal Ripken Jr. 12.00 30.00
MFRCS Chris Sale 4.00 10.00
MFRDJ Derek Jeter 12.00 30.00
MFRDM Don Mattingly 10.00 25.00
MFRDO David Ortiz 4.00 10.00
MFRDP Dustin Pedroia 4.00 10.00
MFREL Evan Longoria 3.00 8.00
MFRFF Freddie Freeman 5.00 12.00
MFRFT Frank Thomas 8.00 20.00
MFRGA Gary Sanchez 4.00 10.00
MFRGB George Brett 8.00 20.00
MFRGM Greg Maddux 5.00 12.00
MFRI Ichiro 5.00 12.00
MFRJA Jose Altuve 3.00 8.00
MFRJB Javier Baez 5.00 12.00
MFRJC Jose Canseco 3.00 8.00
MFRJD Jacob deGrom 4.00 10.00
MFRJL Justin Verlander 4.00 10.00
MFRJR Jackie Robinson 100.00 250.00
MFRJS John Smoltz 4.00 10.00
MFRJT Jim Thome 3.00 8.00
MFRJU Justin Upton 3.00 8.00
MFRJV Joey Votto 4.00 10.00
MFRKB Kris Bryant 5.00 12.00
MFRMB Mookie Betts 5.00 12.00
MFRMC Mark McGwire 15.00 40.00
MFRMG Mark McGwire 10.00 25.00
MFRMM Manny Machado 4.00 10.00
MFRMP Mike Piazza 4.00 10.00
MFRMR Mariano Rivera 5.00 12.00
MFRMS Miguel Sano 3.00 8.00
MFRMT Mike Trout 20.00 50.00
MFRNR Nolan Ryan 12.00 30.00
MFROA Ozzie Albies 6.00 15.00
MFRPG Paul Goldschmidt 4.00 10.00
MFRPM Pedro Martinez 6.00 15.00
MFRRA Robinson Cano 3.00 8.00
MFRRC Roberto Clemente 125.00 300.00
MFRRD Rafael Devers 5.00 12.00
MFRRH Rickey Henderson 10.00 25.00
MFRYD Yu Darvish 4.00 10.00
MFRYM Yadier Molina 4.00 10.00

2018 Topps Allen and Ginter Mini Indigenous Heroes

COMPLETE SET (25) 20.00 50.00
STATED ODDS 1:10 HOBBY
MIH1 Mangas Coloradas .75 2.00
MIH2 Sitting Bull .75 2.00
MIH3 Cochise .75 2.00
MIH4 Chief Seattle .75 2.00
MIH5 Crazy Horse .75 2.00
MIH6 Geronimo .75 2.00
MIH7 Tecumseh .75 2.00
MIH8 Black Hawk .75 2.00
MIH9 Chief Cornstalk .75 2.00
MIH10 Victorio .75 2.00
MIH11 Red Cloud .75 2.00
MIH12 Squanto .75 2.00
MIH13 Sacajawea .75 2.00
MIH14 Chief Pontiac .75 2.00
MIH15 Will Rogers .75 2.00
MIH16 Sequoyah "George Guess" .75 2.00
MIH17 Pocahontas .75 2.00
MIH18 Hiawatha .75 2.00
MIH19 John Ross .75 2.00
MIH20 Joseph the Younger .75 2.00
MIH21 Jim Thorpe .75 2.00
MIH22 Powhatan .75 2.00
MIH23 Ben Nighthorse Campbell .75 2.00
MIH24 Charles Eastman .75 2.00
MIH25 Maria Tallchief .75 2.00

2018 Topps Allen and Ginter Mini Postage Required

COMPLETE SET (15) 15.00 40.00
STATED ODDS 1:50 HOBBY
MPR1 Hawaiian Missionaries Stamp 1.25 3.00
MPR2 Benjamin Franklin 1.25 3.00
MPR3 Landing of Columbus 1.25 3.00
MPR4 George Washington 1.25 3.00
MPR5 Two Penny Blue 1.25 3.00
MPR6 The Declaration of Independence 1.25 3.00
MPR7 Abraham Lincoln 1.25 3.00
MPR8 Inverted Jenny 1.25 3.00
MPR9 Benjamin Franklin 1.25 3.00
MPR10 Swedish Three Skilling Banco Yellow 1.25 3.00
MPR11 Benjamin Franklin 1.25 3.00
MPR12 British Guiana Magenta 1.25 3.00
MPR13 Baden 9 Kreuzer Error 1.25 3.00
MPR14 Penny Black 1.25 3.00
MPR15 Post Office Mauritius 1.25 3.00

2018 Topps Allen and Ginter Mini Surprise

RANDOM INSERTS IN PACKS
MS1 Cuddy Calabrese 2.00 5.00
MS2 Benjamin Geaux-Homme 2.00 5.00
MS3 Dennis the Rash 2.00 5.00

2018 Topps Allen and Ginter Mini World Hottest Peppers

COMPLETE SET (15) 15.00 40.00
STATED ODDS 1:50 HOBBY
WHP1 Pepper X 1.25 3.00
WHP2 Carolina Reaper 1.25 3.00
WHP3 Trinidad Moruga Scorpion 1.25 3.00
WHP4 7 Pot Douglah 1.25 3.00
WHP5 Primo 1.25 3.00
WHP6 Butch T Trinidad Scorpion 1.25 3.00
WHP7 Naga Viper 1.25 3.00
WHP8 Ghost Pepper 1.25 3.00
WHP9 Komodo Dragon 1.25 3.00
WHP10 Trinidad 7 Pot 1.25 3.00
WHP11 Infinity Pepper 1.25 3.00
WHP12 7 Pot Barrackpore 1.25 3.00
WHP13 Red Savina Habanero 1.25 3.00
WHP14 Naga Morich 1.25 3.00
WHP15 Dorset Naga 1.25 3.00

2018 Topps Allen and Ginter N43 Box Toppers

STATED ODDS 1:6 HOBBY BOXES
ANNCD PRINT RUN 500 SER.#'d SETS
N431 Mike Trout 8.00 20.00
N432 Jose Altuve 1.25 3.00
N433 Carlos Correa 1.50 4.00
N434 Aaron Judge 4.00 10.00
N435 Francisco Lindor 1.50 4.00
N436 Clayton Kershaw 3.00 8.00
N437 Bryce Harper 2.50 6.00
N438 Cody Bellinger 3.00 8.00
N439 Joey Votto 1.50 4.00
N4310 Andrew Benintendi 1.50 4.00
N4311 Kris Bryant 2.00 5.00
N4312 Manny Machado 1.50 4.00
N4313 Rafael Devers 3.00 8.00
N4314 Amed Rosario 1.25 3.00
N4315 Victor Robles 2.50 6.00
N4316 Ozzie Albies 3.00 8.00
N4317 Noah Syndergaard 1.25 3.00
N4318 Paul Goldschmidt 1.50 4.00
N4319 Gary Sanchez 1.50 4.00
N4320 Shohei Ohtani 6.00 15.00

2018 Topps Allen and Ginter Natural Wonders Box Toppers

STATED ODDS 1:8 HOBBY BOXES
ANNCD PRINT RUN 500 COPIES PER
NWB1 Big Sur 3.00 8.00
NWB2 Mount Kilimanjaro 3.00 8.00
NWB3 Zion National Park 3.00 8.00
NWB4 Vatnajokull Glacier Cave 3.00 8.00
NWB5 Amazon Rainforest 3.00 8.00
NWB6 Na Pali Coast 3.00 8.00
NWB7 Phang Nga Bay 3.00 8.00
NWB8 The Antarctic 3.00 8.00
NWB9 Banff National Park 3.00 8.00
NWB10 Seljalandsfoss Waterfall 3.00 8.00

2018 Topps Allen and Ginter Relics

VERSION A ODDS 1:37 HOBBY
VERSION B ODDS 1:20 HOBBY
FSRAAE Anthony Rendon A 3.00 8.00
FSRAAN Aaron Nola A 2.50 6.00
FSRAAR Austin Rogers A 3.00 8.00
FSRAAW Alex Wood A 2.00 5.00
FSRABC Brandon Crawford A 2.50 6.00
FSRABD Brian Dozier A 2.50 6.00
FSRABH Billy Hamilton A 2.50 6.00
FSRABJ Bill James A 3.00 8.00
FSRABL Ben Lecomte A 3.00 8.00
FSRACA Chris Archer A 2.00 5.00
FSRACSM Claire Smith A 3.00 8.00
FSRADF Dexter Fowler A 2.50 6.00
FSRADG Dee Gordon A 2.00 5.00
FSRADR Didi Gregorius A 2.50 6.00
FSRADS Domingo Santana A 2.50 6.00
FSRAEA Elvis Andrus A 2.50 6.00
FSRAET Eric Thames A 2.50 6.00
FSRAGB Greg Bird A 2.50 6.00
FSRAHB H. Jon Benjamin A 3.00 8.00
FSRAIH Ian Happ A 2.50 6.00
FSRAJA Jose Abreu A 3.00 8.00
FSRAJB Jose Berrios A 2.50 6.00
FSRAJC Jonathan Schoop A 2.00 5.00
FSRAJE Jason Heyward A 2.50 6.00
FSRAJH Josh Harrison A 2.00 5.00
FSRAJM Justin Smoak A 2.00 5.00
FSRAKJ Kenley Jansen A 2.50 6.00
FSRAKM Kenta Maeda A 2.50 6.00
FSRALB Lewis Brinson A 2.00 5.00
FSRALS Luis Severino A 2.50 6.00
FSRAMR Michael Rapaport A 5.00 12.00
FSRAPS Paige Spiranac A 4.00 10.00
FSRARH Rhys Hoskins A 6.00 15.00
FSRARO Rougned Odor A 2.50 6.00
FSRARS Ryan Sickler A 3.00 8.00
FSRARZ Ryan Zimmerman A 2.50 6.00
FSRASB Scott Blumstein A 3.00 8.00
FSRASE Sean Evans A 3.00 8.00
FSRASF Sonny Fredrickson A 3.00 8.00
FSRASG Sonny Gray A 2.50 6.00
FSRASM Starling Marte A 2.50 6.00
FSRASP Salvador Perez A 2.50 6.00
FSRAST Scott Rogowsky A 5.00 12.00
FSRASSI Steve Simeone A 3.00 8.00
FSRATA Travis Shaw A 2.00 5.00
FSRATE Theo Epstein A 3.00 8.00
FSRATF Todd Frazier A 2.50 6.00
FSRATS Tom Segura A 5.00 12.00
FSRATW Tommy Wiseau A 5.00 12.00
FSRAWC Willson Contreras A 3.00 8.00
FSRAWM Whit Merrifield A 3.00 8.00
FSRAYM Yoan Moncada A 3.00 8.00
FSRBAB Andrew Benintendi B 3.00 8.00
FSRBAC Aroldis Chapman B 3.00 8.00
FSRBAE Adrian Beltre B 3.00 8.00
FSRBAJ Aaron Judge B 12.00 30.00
FSRBAM Andrew McCutchen B 3.00 8.00
FSRBAP Albert Pujols B 4.00 10.00
FSRBAR Anthony Rizzo B 5.00 12.00
FSRBAU Addison Russell B 2.50 6.00
FSRBBB Byron Buxton B 2.50 6.00
FSRBBH Bryce Harper B 5.00 12.00
FSRBBP Buster Posey B 4.00 10.00
FSRBCA Corey Seager B 3.00 8.00
FSRBCB Charlie Blackmon B 3.00 8.00
FSRBCC Carlos Correa B 3.00 8.00
FSRBCG Carlos Gonzalez B 2.50 6.00
FSRBCR Clayton Kershaw B 6.00 15.00
FSRBCS Chris Sale B 3.00 8.00
FSRBCY Christian Yelich B 4.00 10.00
FSRBDE Dustin Pedroia B 3.00 8.00
FSRBDM Daniel Murphy B 2.50 6.00
FSRBDO David Ortiz B 3.00 8.00
FSRBDP David Price B 2.50 6.00
FSRBEE Edwin Encarnacion B 3.00 8.00
FSRBEL Evan Longoria B 2.50 6.00
FSRBFF Freddie Freeman B 4.00 10.00
FSRBFH Felix Hernandez B 2.50 6.00
FSRBGA Gary Sanchez B 3.00 8.00
FSRBGS George Springer B 2.50 6.00
FSRBGT Giancarlo Stanton B 3.00 8.00
FSRBIK Ian Kinsler B 2.50 6.00
FSRBI Ichiro B 4.00 10.00
FSRBJB Javier Baez B 4.00 10.00
FSRBJd Jacob deGrom B 3.00 8.00
FSRBJE Josh Bell B 2.50 6.00
FSRBJG Joey Gallo B 2.50 6.00
FSRBJL Jake Lamb B 2.50 6.00
FSRBJM J.D. Martinez B 3.00 8.00
FSRBJN Justin Verlander B 3.00 8.00
FSRBJO Josh Donaldson B 2.50 6.00
FSRBJT Jose Altuve B 2.50 6.00
FSRBJU Justin Upton B 2.50 6.00
FSRBJV Joey Votto B 3.00 8.00
FSRBKB Kris Bryant B 4.00 10.00
FSRBKD Khris Davis B 3.00 8.00
FSRBKE Kyle Seager B 2.00 5.00
FSRBKS Kyle Schwarber B 3.00 8.00
FSRBMA Matt Carpenter B 3.00 8.00
FSRBMB Mookie Betts B 4.00 10.00
FSRBMC Miguel Cabrera B 3.00 8.00
FSRBMH Max Scherzer B 3.00 8.00
FSRBMK Masahiro Tanaka B 2.50 6.00
FSRBMM Manny Machado B 3.00 8.00
FSRBMN Michael Conforto B 2.50 6.00
FSRBMS Miguel Sano B 2.50 6.00
FSRBMT Mike Trout B 10.00 25.00
FSRBMZ Marcell Ozuna B 3.00 8.00
FSRBNA Nolan Arenado B 4.00 10.00
FSRBNC Nelson Cruz B 3.00 8.00
FSRBNS Noah Syndergaard B 2.50 6.00
FSRBPG Paul Goldschmidt B 3.00 8.00
FSRBRB Ryan Braun B 2.50 6.00
FSRBRC Robinson Cano B 2.50 6.00
FSRBSS Stephen Strasburg B 3.00 8.00
FSRBTM Trey Mancini B 2.50 6.00
FSRBTP Tommy Pham B 2.00 5.00
FSRBTT Trea Turner B 2.50 6.00
FSRBWM Wil Myers B 2.50 6.00
FSRBXB Xander Bogaerts B 3.00 8.00
FSRBYC Yoenis Cespedes B 3.00 8.00
FSRBYD Yu Darvish B 3.00 8.00
FSRBYM Yadier Molina B 3.00 8.00
FSRBYP Yasiel Puig B 3.00 8.00

2018 Topps Allen and Ginter Rip Cards

STATED UNRIPPED ODDS 1:161 HOBBY
PRINT RUNS B/WN 50-75 COPIES PER
RIP1 Derek Jeter/75 60.00 150.00
RIP2 Mariano Rivera/50 40.00 100.00
RIP3 Brooks Robinson/50 40.00 100.00
RIP4 Byron Buxton/50 40.00 100.00
RIP5 Corey Kluber/50 40.00 100.00
RIP6 Yoan Moncada/50 40.00 100.00
RIP7 Chris Archer/50 40.00 100.00
RIP8 Eric Hosmer/50 40.00 100.00
RIP9 J.D. Martinez/50 40.00 100.00
RIP10 Evan Longoria/50 40.00 100.00
RIP11 Khris Davis/50 40.00 100.00
RIP12 Michael Conforto/50 40.00 100.00
RIP13 Nelson Cruz/50 40.00 100.00
RIP14 Adrian Beltre/50 40.00 100.00
RIP15 Albert Pujols/50 50.00 120.00
RIP16 Alex Bregman/50 40.00 100.00
RIP17 Andrew McCutchen/50 40.00 100.00
RIP18 Barry Larkin/50 40.00 100.00
RIP19 Dustin Pedroia/50 40.00 100.00
RIP20 Felix Hernandez/50 40.00 100.00
RIP21 Freddie Freeman/50 40.00 100.00
RIP22 George Springer/50 40.00 100.00
RIP23 Jacob deGrom/50 40.00 100.00
RIP24 Javier Baez/50 40.00 100.00
RIP25 Johnny Bench/50 40.00 100.00
RIP26 John Smoltz/50 40.00 100.00
RIP27 Jose Canseco/50 60.00 150.00
RIP28 Kyle Schwarber/50 40.00 100.00
RIP29 Marcell Ozuna/50 40.00 100.00
RIP30 Miguel Cabrera/50 40.00 100.00
RIP31 Robinson Cano/50 40.00 100.00
RIP32 Salvador Perez/50 40.00 100.00
RIP33 Starling Marte/50 40.00 100.00
RIP34 Stephen Strasburg/50 40.00 100.00
RIP35 Will Clark/50 50.00 120.00
RIP36 Wil Myers/50 40.00 100.00
RIP37 Yadier Molina/50 40.00 100.00
RIP38 Ozzie Albies/50 50.00 120.00
RIP39 Ty Cobb/50 40.00 100.00
RIP40 Honus Wagner/50 40.00 100.00
RIP41 Chris Sale/50 50.00 120.00
RIP42 Clint Frazier/50 50.00 120.00
RIP43 Cody Bellinger/50 50.00 120.00
RIP44 Corey Seager/50 40.00 100.00
RIP45 Don Mattingly/50 50.00 120.00
RIP46 Francisco Lindor/50 40.00 100.00
RIP47 Frank Thomas/50 50.00 120.00
RIP48 Gary Sanchez/50 40.00 100.00
RIP49 Josh Donaldson/50 40.00 100.00
RIP50 Justin Upton/50 40.00 100.00
RIP51 Nolan Arenado/50 40.00 100.00
RIP52 Ozzie Smith/50 50.00 120.00
RIP53 Paul Goldschmidt/50 40.00 100.00
RIP54 Roger Clemens/50 40.00 100.00
RIP55 Trea Turner/50 40.00 100.00
RIP56 Ernie Banks/60 40.00 100.00
RIP57 Bo Jackson/75 50.00 120.00
RIP58 David Ortiz/75 40.00 100.00
RIP59 Adam Jones/50 40.00 100.00
RIP60 Aaron Judge/75 40.00 100.00
RIP61 Andrew Benintendi/75 40.00 100.00
RIP62 Anthony Rizzo/75 40.00 100.00
RIP63 Babe Ruth/75 50.00 120.00
RIP64 Bryce Harper/75 40.00 100.00
RIP65 Buster Posey/75 40.00 100.00
RIP66 Cal Ripken Jr./75 40.00 100.00
RIP67 Carlos Correa/75 40.00 100.00
RIP68 Chipper Jones/75 40.00 100.00
RIP69 Clayton Kershaw/75 40.00 100.00
RIP70 George Brett/75 50.00 120.00
RIP71 Giancarlo Stanton/75 50.00 120.00
RIP72 Greg Maddux/75 50.00 120.00
RIP73 Hank Aaron/75 50.00 120.00
RIP74 Ichiro/75 50.00 120.00
RIP75 Joey Votto/75 60.00 150.00
RIP76 Jose Altuve/75 40.00 100.00
RIP77 Justin Verlander/75 40.00 100.00
RIP78 Kris Bryant/75 50.00 120.00
RIP79 Lou Gehrig/75 50.00 120.00
RIP80 Manny Machado/75 40.00 100.00
RIP81 Mark McGwire/75 50.00 120.00
RIP82 Masahiro Tanaka/75 40.00 100.00
RIP83 Max Scherzer/75 40.00 100.00
RIP84 Mike Piazza/75 40.00 100.00
RIP85 Mike Trout/75 75.00 200.00
RIP86 Mookie Betts/75 50.00 120.00
RIP87 Noah Syndergaard/75 40.00 100.00
RIP88 Nolan Ryan/75 50.00 120.00
RIP89 Rafael Devers/75 50.00 120.00
RIP90 Randy Johnson/75 40.00 100.00
RIP91 Reggie Jackson/75 40.00 100.00
RIP92 Rhys Hoskins/75 50.00 120.00
RIP93 Roberto Clemente 75.00 200.00
RIP94 Sandy Koufax/75 40.00 100.00
RIP95 Shohei Ohtani/75 60.00 150.00
RIP96 Ted Williams/75 50.00 120.00
RIP97 Victor Robles/75 40.00 100.00
RIP98 Yu Darvish/75 40.00 100.00
RIP99 Amed Rosario/75 40.00 100.00
RIP100 Jackie Robinson/75 50.00 120.00

2018 Topps Allen and Ginter Rip Cards Ripped

STATED UNRIPPED ODDS 1:161 HOBBY
PRINT RUNS B/WN 50-75 COPIES PER
PRICED WITH CLEANLY RIPPED BACKS
RIP1 Derek Jeter/75 6.00 15.00
RIP2 Mariano Rivera/50 3.00 8.00
RIP3 Brooks Robinson/50 2.00 5.00
RIP4 Byron Buxton/50 2.00 5.00
RIP5 Corey Kluber/50 2.00 5.00
RIP6 Yoan Moncada/50 2.50 6.00
RIP7 Chris Archer/50 1.50 4.00
RIP8 Eric Hosmer/50 2.00 5.00
RIP9 J.D. Martinez/50 2.50 6.00
RIP10 Evan Longoria/50 2.00 5.00
RIP11 Khris Davis/50 2.50 6.00
RIP12 Michael Conforto/50 2.00 5.00
RIP13 Nelson Cruz/50 2.50 6.00
RIP14 Adrian Beltre/50 2.50 6.00
RIP15 Albert Pujols/50 3.00 8.00
RIP16 Alex Bregman/50 2.50 6.00
RIP17 Andrew McCutchen/50 2.50 6.00
RIP18 Barry Larkin/50 2.00 5.00
RIP19 Dustin Pedroia/50 2.50 6.00
RIP20 Felix Hernandez/50 2.00 5.00
RIP21 Freddie Freeman/50 3.00 8.00
RIP22 George Springer/50 2.00 5.00
RIP23 Jacob deGrom/50 2.50 6.00
RIP24 Javier Baez/50 3.00 8.00
RIP25 Johnny Bench/50 2.50 6.00
RIP26 John Smoltz/50 2.50 6.00
RIP27 Jose Canseco/50 2.00 5.00
RIP28 Kyle Schwarber/50 2.50 6.00
RIP29 Marcell Ozuna/50 2.50 6.00
RIP30 Miguel Cabrera/50 2.50 6.00
RIP31 Robinson Cano/50 2.00 5.00
RIP32 Salvador Perez/50 2.00 5.00
RIP33 Starling Marte/50 2.00 5.00
RIP34 Stephen Strasburg/50 2.50 6.00
RIP35 Will Clark/50 2.50 6.00
RIP36 Wil Myers/50 1.50 4.00
RIP37 Yadier Molina/50 2.50 6.00
RIP38 Ozzie Albies/50 5.00 12.00
RIP39 Ty Cobb/50 4.00 10.00
RIP40 Honus Wagner/50 2.50 6.00
RIP41 Chris Sale/50 2.50 6.00
RIP42 Clint Frazier/50 3.00 8.00
RIP43 Cody Bellinger/50 5.00 12.00
RIP44 Corey Seager/50 2.50 6.00
RIP45 Don Mattingly/50 5.00 12.00
RIP46 Francisco Lindor/50 2.50 6.00
RIP47 Frank Thomas/50 2.50 6.00
RIP48 Gary Sanchez/50 2.50 6.00
RIP49 Josh Donaldson/50 2.00 5.00
RIP50 Justin Upton/50 2.00 5.00
RIP51 Nolan Arenado/50 3.00 8.00
RIP52 Ozzie Smith/50 3.00 8.00
RIP53 Paul Goldschmidt/50 2.50 6.00
RIP54 Roger Clemens/50 3.00 8.00
RIP55 Trea Turner/50 2.00 5.00
RIP56 Ernie Banks/60 2.50 6.00

RIP57 Bo Jackson/75 2.50 6.00
RIP58 David Ortiz/75 2.50 6.00
RIP59 Adam Jones/50 2.00 5.00
RIP60 Aaron Judge/75 6.00 15.00
RIP61 Andrew Benintendi/75 2.50 6.00
RIP62 Anthony Rizzo/75 4.00 10.00
RIP63 Babe Ruth/75 6.00 15.00
RIP64 Bryce Harper/75 4.00 10.00
RIP65 Buster Posey/75 3.00 8.00
RIP66 Cal Ripken Jr./75 8.00 20.00
RIP67 Carlos Correa/75 2.50 6.00
RIP68 Chipper Jones/75 2.50 6.00
RIP69 Clayton Kershaw/75 5.00 12.00
RIP70 George Brett/75 5.00 12.00
RIP71 Giancarlo Stanton/75 2.50 6.00
RIP72 Greg Maddux/75 3.00 8.00
RIP73 Hank Aaron/75 5.00 12.00
RIP74 Ichiro/75 3.00 8.00
RIP75 Joey Votto/75 2.50 6.00
RIP76 Jose Altuve/75 2.00 5.00
RIP77 Justin Verlander/75 2.50 6.00
RIP78 Kris Bryant/75 3.00 8.00
RIP79 Lou Gehrig/75 5.00 12.00
RIP80 Manny Machado/75 2.50 6.00
RIP81 Mark McGwire/75 4.00 10.00
RIP82 Masahiro Tanaka/75 2.00 5.00
RIP83 Max Scherzer/75 2.50 6.00
RIP84 Mike Piazza/75 2.50 6.00
RIP85 Mike Trout/75 12.00 30.00
RIP86 Mookie Betts/75 4.00 10.00
RIP87 Noah Syndergaard/75 2.00 5.00
RIP88 Nolan Ryan/75 8.00 20.00
RIP89 Rafael Devers/75 5.00 12.00
RIP90 Randy Johnson/75 2.50 6.00
RIP91 Reggie Jackson/75 2.00 5.00
RIP92 Rhys Hoskins/75 6.00 15.00
RIP93 Roberto Clemente/75 6.00 15.00
RIP94 Sandy Koufax/75 5.00 12.00
RIP95 Shohei Ohtani/75 10.00 25.00
RIP96 Ted Williams/75 5.00 12.00
RIP97 Victor Robles/75 4.00 10.00
RIP98 Yu Darvish/75 2.50 6.00
RIP99 Amed Rosario/75 2.00 5.00
RIP100 Jackie Robinson/75 2.50 6.00

2018 Topps Allen and Ginter World Talent

COMPLETE SET (50) 15.00 40.00
STATED ODDS 1:4 HOBBY
WT1 Gleyber Torres 2.50 6.00
WT2 Ronald Acuna Jr. 5.00 12.00
WT3 Xander Bogaerts .40 1.00
WT4 Luiz Gohara .25 .60
WT5 Freddie Freeman .50 1.25
WT6 Joey Votto .40 1.00
WT7 Jose Quintana .25 .60
WT8 Aroldis Chapman .40 1.00
WT9 Jose Abreu .40 1.00
WT10 Yasiel Puig .40 1.00
WT11 Yoan Moncada .40 1.00
WT12 Yoenis Cespedes .40 1.00
WT13 Andruw Jones .25 .60
WT14 Jonathan Schoop .25 .60
WT15 Adrian Beltre .40 1.00
WT16 Albert Pujols .50 1.25
WT17 David Ortiz .40 1.00
WT18 Gary Sanchez .40 1.00
WT19 Manny Machado .40 1.00
WT20 Pedro Martinez .30 .75
WT21 Max Kepler .30 .75
WT22 Brandon Nimmo .30 .75
WT23 Masahiro Tanaka .30 .75
WT24 Shohei Ohtani 1.50 4.00
WT25 Yu Darvish .40 1.00
WT26 Ichiro .50 1.25
WT27 Dovydas Neverauskas .25 .60
WT28 Julio Urias .40 1.00
WT29 Khris Davis .40 1.00
WT30 Didi Gregorius .30 .75
WT31 Erasmo Ramirez .25 .60
WT32 Mariano Rivera .50 1.25
WT33 Rod Carew .30 .75
WT34 Carlos Correa .40 1.00
WT35 Francisco Lindor .40 1.00
WT36 Javier Baez .50 1.25
WT37 Yadier Molina .40 1.00
WT38 Jharel Cotton .25 .60
WT39 Gift Ngoepe .25 .60
WT40 Hyun-Jin Ryu .30 .75
WT41 Shin-Soo Choo .30 .75
WT42 Tzu-Wei Lin .30 .75
WT43 Jose Altuve .30 .75
WT44 Felix Hernandez .30 .75
WT45 Salvador Perez .30 .75
WT46 Aaron Judge 1.00 2.50
WT47 Bryce Harper .60 1.50
WT48 Clayton Kershaw .75 2.00
WT49 Kris Bryant .50 1.25
WT50 Mike Trout 2.00 5.00

2018 Topps Allen and Ginter Worlds Greatest Beaches

COMPLETE SET (10) 4.00 10.00
STATED ODDS 1:6 HOBBY
WGB1 Paradise Island .40 1.00
WGB2 Bora Bora .40 1.00
WGB3 Trunk Bay .40 1.00
WGB4 Roatan .40 1.00
WGB5 South Beach .40 1.00
WGB6 Bondi Beach .40 1.00
WGB7 Venice Beach .40 1.00
WGB8 Bay of Angels .40 1.00
WGB9 Cozumel .40 1.00
WGB10 Harbour Island .40 1.00

2018 Topps Allen and Ginter Worlds Greatest Beaches Relics

STATED ODDS 1:8088 HOBBY
PRINT RUNS B/WN 10-25 COPIES PER
NO PRICING ON QTY 10 OR LESS
WGBR1 Paradise Island/20 60.00 150.00
WGBR2 Bora Bora/25 50.00 120.00
WGBR5 South Beach/25 50.00 120.00
WGBR7 Venice Beach
WGBR10 Harbour Island/20 60.00 150.00

2019 Topps Allen and Ginter

COMPLETE SET (350) 25.00 60.00
COMP.SET w/o SP's (300) 15.00 40.00
SP ODDS 1:2 HOBBY
1 Mookie Betts .40 1.00
2 Christian Yelich .30 .75
3 Babe Ruth .60 1.50
4 Lou Gehrig .50 1.25
5 Shohei Ohtani .30 .75
6 Luis Gonzalez .15 .40
7 Albert Pujols .30 .75
8 Reggie Jackson .20 .50
9 Zack Greinke .20 .50
10 Mike Trout 1.25 3.00
11 Nolan Ryan .75 2.00
12 Blake Treinen .15 .40
13 Ozzie Albies .25 .60
14 Chipper Jones .25 .60
15 Freddie Freeman .30 .75
16 Kris Bryant .30 .75
17 Anthony Rizzo .40 1.00
18 Ryne Sandberg .50 1.25
19 Javier Baez .30 .75
20 Ernie Banks .25 .60
21 Francisco Lindor .25 .60
22 Jose Ramirez .20 .50
23 Bob Feller .20 .50
24 A.J. Burnett .15 .40
25 Ronald Acuna Jr. 1.25 3.00
26 Justin Verlander .25 .60
27 Gerrit Cole .25 .60
28 Jose Altuve .20 .50
29 Alex Bregman .25 .60
30 George Springer .20 .50
31 Jeff Bagwell .20 .50
32 Sandy Koufax .50 1.25
33 Walker Buehler .30 .75
34 Cody Bellinger .50 1.25
35 Mike Piazza .25 .60
36 Starlin Castro .15 .40
37 Josh Hader .15 .40
38 Lorenzo Cain .15 .40
39 Jesus Aguilar .15 .40
40 Ryan Braun .20 .50
41 Robinson Cano .20 .50
42 Jacob deGrom .20 .50
43 Edwin Diaz .20 .50
44 Noah Syndergaard .20 .50
45 Amed Rosario .20 .50
46 Rickey Henderson .25 .60
47 Matt Chapman .25 .60
48 Dennis Eckersley .20 .50
49 Khris Davis .20 .50
50 Hank Aaron .50 1.25
51 Paul Molitor .25 .60
52 Buster Posey .25 .60
53 Willie McCovey .20 .50
54 Juan Marichal .20 .50
55 Evan Longoria .20 .50
56 J.D. Martinez .25 .60
57 Felix Hernandez .20 .50
58 Edgar Martinez .20 .50
59 Justus Sheffield RC .40 1.00
60 Ichiro .30 .75
61 Mark McGwire .40 1.00
62 Paul Goldschmidt .25 .60
63 Yadier Molina .25 .60
64 Stan Musial .40 1.00
65 Ozzie Smith .30 .75
66 Roger Clemens .30 .75
67 Roberto Alomar .20 .50
68 Justin Smoak .15 .40
69 Danny Jansen RC .25 .60
70 Max Scherzer .25 .60
71 Patrick Corbin .20 .50
72 Stephen Strasburg .25 .60
73 Trea Turner .20 .50
74 Cal Ripken Jr. .75 2.00
75 Brooks Robinson .20 .50
76 Jim Palmer .20 .50
77 Tony Gwynn .25 .60
78 Trevor Hoffman .20 .50
79 Luis Urias RC .40 1.00
80 Eric Hosmer .20 .50
81 Andrew McCutchen .25 .60
82 Rhys Hoskins .30 .75
83 Aaron Nola .20 .50
84 Roberto Clemente .60 1.50
85 Chris Archer .15 .40
86 Felipe Vazquez .15 .40
87 Willie Stargell .20 .50
88 Ralph Kiner .20 .50
89 Adrian Beltre .25 .60
90 Ivan Rodriguez .20 .50
91 Elvis Andrus .20 .50
92 Joey Gallo .20 .50
93 Blake Snell .20 .50
94 Willy Adames .15 .40
95 Jose Canseco .20 .50
96 Andrew Benintendi .25 .60
97 Rafael Devers .30 .75
98 Ted Williams .50 1.25
99 Chris Sale .25 .60
100 Ken Griffey Jr. .50 1.25
101 David Price .20 .50
102 Joey Votto .25 .60
103 Johnny Bench .25 .60
104 Tony Perez .20 .50
105 Todd Helton .20 .50
106 Trevor Story .25 .60
107 Nolan Arenado .30 .75
108 Charlie Blackmon .25 .60
109 George Brett .50 1.25
110 Salvador Perez .20 .50
111 Bo Jackson .25 .60
112 Miguel Cabrera .25 .60
113 Al Kaline .25 .60
114 Jose Berrios .20 .50
115 Rod Carew .20 .50
116 Tony Oliva .15 .40
117 Harmon Killebrew .25 .60
118 Frank Thomas .25 .60
119 Michael Kopech RC .50 1.25
120 Yoan Moncada .25 .60
121 Jose Abreu .25 .60
122 Isiah Kiner-Falefa .15 .40
123 Gleyber Torres .50 1.25
124 Miguel Andujar .25 .60
125 Giancarlo Stanton .25 .60
126 Clayton Kershaw .50 1.25
127 Juan Soto .75 2.00
128 Roger Maris .25 .60
129 Jackie Robinson .25 .60
130 Torii Hunter .15 .40
131 Juan Gonzalez .15 .40
132 David Ortiz .25 .60
133 Don Mattingly .50 1.25
134 Derek Jeter .60 1.50
135 Dale Murphy .25 .60
136 Mariano Rivera .30 .75
137 Vladimir Guerrero .20 .50
138 Gary Carter .20 .50
139 Harold Baines .20 .50
140 Luis Severino .20 .50
141 Miles Mikolas .25 .60
142 Mitch Haniger .20 .50
143 Max Muncy .20 .50
144 Whit Merrifield .25 .60
145 Xander Bogaerts .25 .60
146 Josh Donaldson .20 .50
147 J.T. Realmuto .25 .60
148 Corey Kluber .20 .50
149 Manny Machado .25 .60
150 Steve Carlton .20 .50
151 Marc Summers .25 .60
152 Augie Carton .15 .40
153 Jay Larson .20 .50
154 Hailey Dawson .25 .60
155 Gary Vaynerchuk .25 .60
156 Vincent Stio .25 .60
157 Mike Oz .20 .50
158 Kyle Snyder .25 .60
159 Rodney Mullen .25 .60
160 Matthew Mercer .25 .60
161 Sister Mary Jo Sobieck .25 .60
162 Mason Cox .25 .60
163 Loretta Claiborne .20 .50
164 Justin Bonomo .25 .60
165 John Cynn .20 .50
166 1st Tiger Mask .25 .60
Satoru Sayama
167 Mayumi Seto .25 .60
168 Rhea Butcher .20 .50
169 Drew Drechsel .25 .60
170 Lawrence Rocks .15 .40
171 Charles Martinet .25 .60
172 Tyler Kepner .15 .40
173 Ben Schwartz .25 .60
174 Dan Rather .25 .60
175 Danielle Colby .25 .60
176 Post Malone .25 .60
177 Robert Oberst .25 .60
178 Brian Fallon .25 .60
179 Burton Rocks .15 .40
180 Quinn XCII .25 .60
181 Emily Jaenson .25 .60
182 Pete Alonso RC 3.00 8.00
183 Fernando Tatis Jr. RC 6.00 15.00
184 Travis Pastrana .25 .60
185 Hilary Knight .25 .60
186 Wade Boggs .20 .50
187 Jason Varitek .25 .60
188 Didi Gregorius .20 .50
189 Tyler O'Neill .20 .50
190 Eddie Rosario .20 .50
191 Brandon Nimmo .20 .50
192 Lourdes Gurriel Jr. .20 .50
193 Jack Flaherty .20 .50
194 Kevin Newman RC .40 1.00
195 Dakota Hudson RC .30 .75
196 Cedric Mullins RC .40 1.00
197 Brad Keller RC .25 .60
198 David Bote .20 .50
199 Dereck Rodriguez .15 .40
200 Aaron Judge .60 1.50
201 Sean Reid-Foley RC .25 .60
202 Luke Voit .40 1.00
203 Jeff McNeil RC .60 1.50
204 Cionel Perez RC .25 .60
205 Chance Adams RC .25 .60
206 Corbin Burnes RC .40 1.00
207 Ramon Laureano RC .50 1.25
208 Dawel Lugo RC .40 1.00
209 Ryan O'Hearn RC .25 .60
210 Framber Valdez RC .25 .60
211 Patrick Wisdom RC .25 .60
212 Dylan Cozens .15 .40
213 Egg .25 .60
214 Jonathan Lucroy .20 .50
215 Cody Allen .15 .40
216 Justin Bour .15 .40
217 Andrelton Simmons .15 .40
218 Michael Brantley .20 .50
219 Yuli Gurriel .20 .50
220 Josh James RC .40 1.00
221 Stephen Piscotty .15 .40
222 Matt Olson .25 .60
223 Jurickson Profar .20 .50
224 Matt Shoemaker .20 .50
225 Brandon Drury .15 .40
226 Dansby Swanson .25 .60
227 Touki Toussaint RC .30 .75
228 Yasmani Grandal .15 .40
229 Orlando Arcia .15 .40
230 Matt Carpenter .25 .60
231 Paul DeJong .25 .60
232 Willson Contreras .25 .60
233 Cole Hamels .20 .50
234 A.J. Pollock .15 .40
235 Corey Seager .25 .60
236 Brandon Crawford .20 .50
237 Carlos Santana .20 .50
238 Trevor Bauer .25 .60
239 Starling Marte .25 .60
240 Dee Gordon .15 .40
241 Kyle Seager .15 .40
242 Brian Anderson .15 .40
243 Michael Conforto .20 .50
244 Brian Dozier .20 .50
245 Wil Myers .15 .40
246 Odubel Herrera .20 .50
247 Maikel Franco .20 .50
248 David Robertson .15 .40
249 Jake Arrieta .20 .50
250 Yusei Kikuchi RC .40 1.00
251 Gregory Polanco .20 .50
252 Nomar Mazara .15 .40
253 Kevin Kiermaier .20 .50
254 Charlie Morton .25 .60
255 Matt Kemp .20 .50
256 Yasiel Puig .25 .60
257 Sonny Gray .20 .50
258 Daniel Murphy .20 .50
259 David Dahl .15 .40
260 Billy Hamilton .20 .50
261 Nicholas Castellanos .25 .60
262 Willians Astudillo RC .25 .60
263 Byron Buxton .20 .50
264 Yonder Alonso .15 .40
265 Troy Tulowitzki .25 .60
266 DJ LeMahieu .25 .60
267 James Paxton .20 .50
268 Adam Ottavino .15 .40
269 Scooter Gennett .20 .50
270 Ben Zobrist .20 .50
271 Carl Yastrzemski .40 1.00
272 Carlton Fisk .20 .50
273 Fred McGriff .20 .50
274 Dwight Gooden .15 .40
275 Deion Sanders .20 .50
276 Hideki Matsui .25 .60
277 Frank Robinson .25 .60
278 Vladimir Guerrero Jr. RC 1.50 4.00
279 Kolby Allard RC .40 1.00
280 Bryce Harper .40 1.00
281 Bob Gibson .20 .50
282 A.J. Andrews .25 .60
283 Andy Pettitte .20 .50
284 Roy Halladay .20 .50
285 Jorge Alfaro .15 .40
286 Harrison Bader .20 .50
287 Catfish Hunter .20 .50
288 Ryan Yarbrough .15 .40
289 Whitey Ford .20 .50
290 Pee Wee Reese .20 .50
291 Cespedes Family BBQ .25 .60
Jake Mintz
Jordan Shusterman
292 Eddie Murray .20 .50
293 Jon Lester .20 .50
294 German Marquez .15 .40
295 Franmil Reyes .15 .40
296 Cincinnati Red Stockings .25 .60
297 Boston Red Sox .25 .60
298 Ian Happ .20 .50
299 J.A. Happ .20 .50
300 Tino Martinez .20 .50
351 Carlos Correa SP .60 1.50
352 Robin Yount SP .60 1.50
353 Shane Bieber SP .60 1.50
354 Rowdy Tellez SP RC .60 1.50
355 Jordan Hicks SP .50 1.25
356 Kyle Schwarber SP .60 1.50
357 Kenley Jansen SP .50 1.25
358 John Smoltz SP .50 1.25
359 Larry Doby SP .50 1.25
360 Jorge Posada SP .50 1.25
361 Victor Robles SP .75 2.00
362 Fergie Jenkins SP .50 1.25
363 Austin Meadows SP .50 1.25
364 Dustin Pedroia SP .60 1.50
365 Ty Cobb SP 1.00 2.50
366 Daniel Palka SP .40 1.00
367 Masahiro Tanaka SP .50 1.25
368 Eddie Murray SP .50 1.25
369 Rick Porcello SP .50 1.25
370 Marcell Ozuna SP .50 1.25
371 Yu Darvish SP .60 1.50
372 Justin Turner SP .50 1.25
373 Edwin Encarnacion SP .60 1.50
374 Yoenis Cespedes SP .60 1.50
375 Pat Neshek SP .40 1.00
376 Wade Davis SP .40 1.00
377 Christin Stewart SP RC .50 1.25
378 Aroldis Chapman SP .60 1.50
379 Darryl Strawberry SP .40 1.00
380 Nomar Garciaparra SP .50 1.25
381 Scott Kingery SP .50 1.25
382 Dave Winfield SP .50 1.25
383 Sean Doolittle SP .40 1.00
384 Rogers Hornsby SP .50 1.25
385 Gil Hodges SP .50 1.25
386 Eddie Mathews SP .60 1.50
387 Warren Spahn SP .50 1.25
388 Casey Stengel SP .50 1.25
389 Lou Brock SP .50 1.25
390 Phil Rizzuto SP .50 1.25
391 Phil Niekro SP .50 1.25
392 Sammy Sosa SP .60 1.50
393 Alex Rodriguez SP .75 2.00
394 Tom Seaver SP .50 1.25
395 Barry Larkin SP .50 1.25
396 Tommy Lasorda SP .50 1.25
397 Orlando Cepeda SP .50 1.25
398 Eloy Jimenez SP RC 1.50 4.00
399 Tim Raines SP .50 1.25
400 Randy Johnson SP .60 1.50

2019 Topps Allen and Ginter Gold Border

*GLS SLVR 1-300: 1.5X TO 4X BASIC
*GLS SLVR 1-300 RC: 1X TO 2.5X BASIC RCs
*GLS SLVR 351-400: .6X TO 1.5X BASIC
FOUND ONLY IN HOBBY HOT BOXES

2019 Topps Allen and Ginter Autographs

STATED ODDS 1:555 HOBBY
EXCHANGE DEADLINE 6/30/2021
FSA1TM 1st Tiger Mask 30.00 80.00
FSAJH James Holzhauer 20.00 50.00
FSAKB Ken Burns 15.00 40.00
FSANB Nathan Burns 100.00 250.00
FSAPM Post Malone 200.00 400.00
FSATP Travis Pastrana 40.00 100.00
FSAVG Vladimir Guerrero Jr. 60.00 150.00
FSAYK Yusei Kikuchi EXCH 15.00 40.00

2019 Topps Allen and Ginter Baseball Star Signs

COMPLETE SET (50) 12.00 30.00
STATED ODDS 1:4 HOBBY
BSS1 Ronald Acuna Jr. 2.00 5.00
BSS2 Hank Aaron .75 2.00
BSS3 Cal Ripken Jr. 1.25 3.00
BSS4 Mookie Betts .60 1.50
BSS5 Ted Williams .75 2.00
BSS6 David Ortiz .40 1.00
BSS7 Frank Thomas .40 1.00
BSS8 Francisco Lindor .40 1.00
BSS9 Miguel Cabrera .40 1.00
BSS10 Al Kaline .40 1.00
BSS11 Jose Altuve .30 .75
BSS12 Carlos Correa .40 1.00
BSS13 Alex Bregman .40 1.00
BSS14 George Brett .75 2.00
BSS15 Mike Trout 2.00 5.00
BSS16 Shohei Ohtani .50 1.25
BSS17 Rod Carew .30 .75
BSS18 Babe Ruth 1.00 2.50
BSS19 Derek Jeter 1.00 2.50
BSS20 Aaron Judge 1.00 2.50
BSS21 Mariano Rivera .50 1.25
BSS22 Reggie Jackson .30 .75
BSS23 Rickey Henderson .40 1.00
BSS24 Ken Griffey Jr. .75 2.00
BSS25 Ichiro .50 1.25
BSS26 Randy Johnson .40 1.00
BSS27 Blake Snell .30 .75
BSS28 Nolan Ryan 1.25 3.00
BSS29 Kris Bryant .50 1.25
BSS30 Anthony Rizzo .60 1.50
BSS31 Joey Votto .40 1.00
BSS32 Johnny Bench .40 1.00
BSS33 Nolan Arenado .50 1.25
BSS34 Clayton Kershaw .75 2.00
BSS35 Sandy Koufax .75 2.00
BSS36 Jackie Robinson .40 1.00
BSS37 Christian Yelich .50 1.25
BSS38 Jacob deGrom .40 1.00
BSS39 Noah Syndergaard .30 .75
BSS40 Rhys Hoskins .50 1.25
BSS41 Roberto Clemente 1.00 2.50
BSS42 Tony Gwynn .40 1.00
BSS43 Buster Posey .50 1.25
BSS44 Yadier Molina .40 1.00
BSS45 Ozzie Smith .50 1.25
BSS46 Paul Goldschmidt .40 1.00
BSS47 Juan Soto 1.25 3.00
BSS48 Max Scherzer .40 1.00
BSS49 Bryce Harper .60 1.50
BSS50 Manny Machado .40 1.00

2019 Topps Allen and Ginter Box Topper Rip Cards

STATED UNRIPPED ODDS 1:24 HOBBY BOXES
PRINT RUNS B/WN 47-65 COPIES PER
UNRIPPED HAVE ADD'L CARDS WITHIN
BRIP1 Mike Trout/65 150.00 400.00
BRIP2 Shohei Ohtani/65 150.00 400.00
BRIP3 Ichiro/65 100.00 250.00
BRIP4 Ken Griffey Jr./60 125.00 300.00
BRIP5 Clayton Kershaw/65 100.00 250.00
BRIP6 Kris Bryant/65
BRIP7 Derek Jeter/60 150.00 400.00
BRIP8 Aaron Judge/65 150.00 400.00
BRIP9 Hank Aaron/65 100.00 250.00
BRIP10 Ronald Acuna Jr./65 125.00 300.00
BRIP11 Jose Altuve/65 100.00 250.00
BRIP12 Nolan Ryan/60 125.00 300.00
BRIP13 Babe Ruth/50 125.00 300.00
BRIP14 Ted Williams/47 125.00 300.00
BRIP15 Sandy Koufax/55 100.00 250.00
BRIP16 Jackie Robinson/55 100.00 250.00
BRIP17 Cal Ripken Jr./60 125.00 300.00
BRIP18 Roberto Clemente/55 125.00 300.00
BRIP19 Juan Soto/65 100.00 250.00
BRIP20 Mookie Betts/65 100.00 250.00
BRIP21 Tony Gwynn/60 100.00 250.00
BRIP22 Reggie Jackson/60 100.00 250.00
BRIP23 Ozzie Smith/60 100.00 250.00
BRIP24 Frank Thomas/60 100.00 250.00
BRIP25 George Brett/60 125.00 300.00
BRIP26 Randy Johnson/60 100.00 250.00
BRIP27 Bryce Harper/65 100.00 250.00
BRIP28 Francisco Lindor/65 100.00 250.00
BRIP29 Carlos Correa/65 125.00 300.00
BRIP30 Manny Machado/65 100.00 250.00

2019 Topps Allen and Ginter Box Topper Rip Cards Ripped

UNRIPPED STATED ODDS 1:24 HOBBY BOXES
PRINT RUNS B/WN 47-65 COPIES PER
PRICED WITH CLEANLY RIPPED BACKS
BRIP1 Mike Trout/65 15.00 40.00
BRIP2 Shohei Ohtani/65 4.00 10.00
BRIP3 Ichiro/65 4.00 10.00
BRIP4 Ken Griffey Jr./60 6.00 15.00
BRIP5 Clayton Kershaw/65 6.00 15.00
BRIP6 Kris Bryant/65 4.00 10.00
BRIP7 Derek Jeter/60 8.00 20.00
BRIP8 Aaron Judge/65 8.00 20.00
BRIP9 Hank Aaron/55 6.00 15.00
BRIP10 Ronald Acuna Jr./65 15.00 40.00
BRIP11 Jose Altuve/65 2.50 6.00
BRIP12 Nolan Ryan/60 10.00 25.00
BRIP13 Babe Ruth/50 8.00 20.00
BRIP14 Ted Williams/47 6.00 15.00
BRIP15 Sandy Koufax/55 6.00 15.00
BRIP16 Jackie Robinson/55 3.00 8.00
BRIP17 Cal Ripken Jr./60 10.00 25.00
BRIP18 Roberto Clemente/55 8.00 20.00
BRIP19 Juan Soto/65 10.00 25.00
BRIP20 Mookie Betts/65 5.00 12.00
BRIP21 Tony Gwynn/60 3.00 8.00
BRIP22 Reggie Jackson/60 2.50 6.00
BRIP23 Ozzie Smith/60 4.00 10.00
BRIP24 Frank Thomas/60 3.00 8.00
BRIP25 George Brett/60 6.00 15.00
BRIP26 Randy Johnson/60 3.00 8.00
BRIP27 Bryce Harper/65 5.00 12.00
BRIP28 Francisco Lindor/65 3.00 8.00
BRIP29 Carlos Correa/65 3.00 8.00
BRIP30 Manny Machado/65 3.00 8.00

2019 Topps Allen and Ginter Box Toppers

INSERTED IN HOBBY BOXES
BL1 Kris Bryant .75 2.00
BL2 Shohei Ohtani .75 2.00
BL3 Gleyber Torres 1.25 3.00
BL4 Mike Trout 3.00 8.00
BL5 Juan Soto 2.00 5.00
BL6 Ronald Acuna Jr. 3.00 8.00
BL7 Christian Yelich .75 2.00
BL8 Jose Altuve .50 1.25
BL9 Jacob deGrom .60 1.50
BL10 Aaron Judge 1.50 4.00
BL11 Francisco Lindor .60 1.50
BL12 Mookie Betts 1.00 2.50
BL13 Javier Baez .75 2.00
BL14 Bryce Harper 1.00 2.50
BL15 Clayton Kershaw 1.25 3.00

2019 Topps Allen and Ginter Dual Autographs

STATED ODDS 1:5550 HOBBY
EXCHANGE DEADLINE 6/30/2021
DABBH B.Hull/B.Hull 100.00 250.00
DACFB H.Mintz/J.Shusterman 25.00 60.00

2019 Topps Allen and Ginter Framed Mini Autographs

STATED ODDS 1:63 HOBBY
EXCHANGE DEADLINE 6/30/2021
*BLACK/25: .75X TO 2X BASIC
MAAA A.J. Andrews 6.00 15.00
MAAC Augie Carton 4.00 10.00
MAAD Austin Dean 4.00 10.00
MAAG Jeff Bagwell 20.00 50.00
MAAJ Aaron Judge 75.00 200.00
MABB Bert Blyleven 8.00 20.00
MABF Brian Fallon 25.00 60.00
MABK Brad Keller 4.00 10.00
MABN Brandon Nimmo 5.00 12.00
MABRO Burton Rocks 4.00 10.00
MABS Ben Schwartz 15.00 40.00
MABSN Blake Snell 6.00 15.00
MABT Blake Treinen 4.00 10.00
MACA Chance Adams 4.00 10.00
MACBU Corbin Burnes 6.00 15.00
MACM Charles Martinet 12.00 30.00
MACMU Cedric Mullins 6.00 15.00
MACP Cionel Perez 4.00 10.00
MACY Christian Yelich 30.00 80.00
MADB David Bote 5.00 12.00
MADC Danielle Colby 30.00 80.00
MADCO Dylan Cozens 4.00 10.00
MADD Drew Drechsel 8.00 20.00
MADG Didi Gregorius 5.00 12.00
MADH Dakota Hudson 5.00 12.00
MADL Dawel Lugo 6.00 15.00
MADR Dan Rather 40.00 100.00
MADRO Dereck Rodriguez 4.00 10.00
MAEJ Eloy Jimenez 25.00 60.00
MAEJA Emily Jaenson 12.00 30.00
MAER Eddie Rosario 5.00 12.00
MAFM Fred McGriff 20.00 50.00
MAFR Franmil Reyes 4.00 10.00
MAFT Fernando Tatis Jr. 150.00 400.00
MAFV Framber Valdez 4.00 10.00
MAGE Graham Elliot 6.00 15.00
MAGV Gary Vaynerchuk 50.00 120.00
MAHD Hailey Dawson 15.00 40.00
MAHF Harrison Ford 800.00 1500.00
MAHK Hilary Knight 8.00 20.00
MAIK Isiah Kiner-Falefa 4.00 10.00
MAJA Jesus Aguilar 4.00 10.00
MAJAL Jose Altuve 15.00 40.00
MAJB Justin Bonomo 6.00 15.00
MAJC John Cynn 5.00 12.00
MAJD Jacob deGrom 12.00 30.00
MAJFL Jack Flaherty 12.00 30.00
MAJH Josh Hader 4.00 10.00
MAJL Jay Larson 5.00 12.00
MAJP Jorge Posada 20.00 50.00
MAJS Justus Sheffield 6.00 15.00
MAJSO Juan Soto 50.00 120.00
MAJV Jason Varitek 25.00 60.00
MAKB Kris Bryant 50.00 120.00
MAKGJ Ken Griffey Jr. 125.00 300.00
MAKN Kevin Newman 6.00 15.00
MAKS Kyle Snyder 30.00 80.00
MALC Loretta Claiborne 5.00 12.00
MALG Lourdes Gurriel Jr. 6.00 15.00
MALR Lawrence Rocks 4.00 10.00
MALS Luis Severino 8.00 20.00
MALU Luis Urias 12.00 30.00
MALV Luke Voit 15.00 40.00
MAMA Miguel Andujar 12.00 30.00
MAMCO Mason Cox 6.00 15.00
MAMK Michael Kopech 12.00 30.00
MAMM Matthew Mercer 30.00 80.00
MAMMI Miles Mikolas 6.00 15.00
MAMMU Max Muncy 6.00 15.00
MAMO Mike Oz 6.00 15.00
MAMS Mayumi Seto 10.00 25.00
MAMSU Marc Summers 12.00 30.00
MAMT Mike Trout 300.00 600.00
MANR Nolan Ryan 75.00 200.00
MAOA Ozzie Albies 12.00 30.00
MAPA Peter Alonso 75.00 200.00
MAPW Patrick Wisdom 4.00 10.00
MAQX Quinn XCII 6.00 15.00
MARA Ronald Acuna Jr. 75.00 200.00
MARAN Rick Ankiel 5.00 12.00
MARB Rhea Butcher 5.00 12.00
MARL Ramon Laureano 12.00 30.00
MARM Rodney Mullen 10.00 25.00
MARO Robert Oberst 10.00 25.00
MAROH Ryan O'Hearn 4.00 10.00
MASB Shane Bieber 15.00 40.00
MASMJ Sister Mary Jo Sobieck 25.00 60.00
MASO Shohei Ohtani 100.00 250.00
MASR Sean Reid-Foley 4.00 10.00
MATF Thomas Fish
MATH Todd Helton 10.00 25.00
MATHO Trevor Hoffman 8.00 20.00
MATK Tyler Kepner 4.00 10.00
MATO Tyler O'Neill 5.00 12.00
MAVG Vladimir Guerrero 20.00 50.00
MAVS Vincent Stio 4.00 10.00
MAWA Willy Adames 6.00 15.00
MAWB Wade Boggs 30.00 80.00

2019 Topps Allen and Ginter Ginter Greats

COMPLETE SET (50) 12.00 30.00
STATED ODDS 1:4 HOBBY
GG1 Hank Aaron .75 2.00
GG2 Ernie Banks .40 1.00
GG3 Johnny Bench .40 1.00
GG4 George Brett .75 2.00
GG5 Rod Carew .30 .75
GG6 Roger Clemens .50 1.25
GG7 Roberto Clemente 1.00 2.50
GG8 Ty Cobb .60 1.50
GG9 Bob Feller .30 .75
GG10 Lou Gehrig .75 2.00
GG11 Bob Gibson .30 .75
GG12 Ken Griffey Jr .75 2.00
GG13 Tony Gwynn .40 1.00
GG14 Rickey Henderson .40 1.00
GG15 Rogers Hornsby .30 .75
GG16 Reggie Jackson .30 .75
GG17 Derek Jeter 1.00 2.50
GG18 Randy Johnson .40 1.00
GG19 Chipper Jones .40 1.00
GG20 Al Kaline .40 1.00
GG21 Clayton Kershaw .75 2.00
GG22 Harmon Killebrew .40 1.00
GG23 Sandy Koufax .75 2.00
GG24 Pedro Martinez .30 .75
GG25 Willie McCovey .30 .75
GG26 Joe Morgan .30 .75
GG27 Stan Musial .60 1.50
GG28 David Ortiz .40 1.00
GG29 Mel Ott .40 1.00
GG30 Jim Palmer .30 .75
GG31 Mike Piazza .40 1.00
GG32 Albert Pujols .50 1.25
GG33 Cal Ripken Jr. 1.25 3.00
GG34 Mariano Rivera .50 1.25

GG35 Brooks Robinson .30 .75
GG36 Frank Robinson .30 .75
GG37 Jackie Robinson .40 1.00
GG38 Babe Ruth 1.00 2.50
GG39 Nolan Ryan 1.25 3.00
GG40 Ryne Sandberg .75 2.00
GG41 Tom Seaver .30 .75
GG42 Ozzie Smith .50 1.25
GG43 Tris Speaker .30 .75
GG44 Ichiro .50 1.25
GG45 Frank Thomas .40 1.00
GG46 Mike Trout 2.00 5.00
GG47 Honus Wagner .40 1.00
GG48 Ted Williams .75 2.00
GG49 Carl Yastrzemski .60 1.50
GG50 Robin Yount .40 1.00

2019 Topps Allen and Ginter History of Flight

COMPLETE SET (15) 6.00 15.00
STATED ODDS 1:6 HOBBY
HOF1 Wright Flyer .75 2.00
HOF2 A Vlaicu III .75 2.00
HOF3 Demoiselle Monoplane .75 2.00
HOF4 Supermarine S.6B .75 2.00
HOF5 Me 262 .75 2.00
HOF6 Sikorsky R-4 .75 2.00
HOF7 B-17 Flying Fortress .75 2.00
HOF8 DH 106 Comet .75 2.00
HOF9 Boeing 707 .75 2.00
HOF10 Bell X-1 .75 2.00
HOF11 Harrier Jet .75 2.00
HOF12 SR-71 .75 2.00
HOF13 Concorde Jet .75 2.00
HOF14 Shuttle Discovery .75 2.00
HOF15 Shuttle Endeavour .75 2.00

2019 Topps Allen and Ginter Incredible Equipment

COMPLETE SET (20) 6.00 15.00
STATED ODDS 1:6 HOBBY
IE1 Thor's Hammer .75 2.00
IE2 Robin Hood's Bow .75 2.00
IE3 Pecos Bill's Lasso .75 2.00
IE4 Paul Bunyan's Axe .75 2.00
IE5 Old Stormalong's Harpoon .75 2.00
IE6 David's Slingshot .75 2.00
IE7 Rosie the Riveter's Work Gloves .75 2.00
IE8 Don Quixote's Lance .75 2.00
IE9 William Tell's Crossbow .75 2.00
IE10 Achilles's Armor .75 2.00
IE11 Hermes's Sandals .75 2.00
IE12 King Arthur's Sword .75 2.00
IE13 Heracles's Club .75 2.00
IE14 Merlin's Staff .75 2.00
IE15 Poseidon's Trident .75 2.00
IE16 Cupid's Bow .75 2.00
IE17 Santa's Sleigh .75 2.00
IE18 Pied Piper's Pipe .75 2.00
IE19 Odin's Throne .75 2.00
IE20 Johnny Kaw's Scythe .75 2.00

2019 Topps Allen and Ginter Incredible Equipment Relics

STATED ODDS 1:1560 HOBBY
IERDS David's Slingshot 15.00 40.00
IERTH Thor's Hammer 15.00 40.00
IERDQL Don Quixote's Lance 15.00 40.00
IEROSH Old Stormalong's Harpoon 15.00 40.00
IERPBA Paul Bunyan's Axe 15.00 40.00
IERPBL Pecos Bill's Lasso 15.00 40.00
IERRHB Robin Hood's Bow 15.00 40.00
IERRWG Rosie the Riveter's Work Gloves 15.00 40.00
IERWTCB William Tell's Crossbow 15.00 40.00

2019 Topps Allen and Ginter Look Out Below Box Toppers

STATED ODDS 1:8 HOBBY BOXES
LOBB1 Niagara Falls 2.00 5.00
LOBB2 Victoria Falls 2.00 5.00
LOBB3 Angel Falls 2.00 5.00
LOBB4 Iguazu Falls 2.00 5.00
LOBB5 Yosemite Falls 2.00 5.00
LOBB6 Ruby Falls 2.00 5.00
LOBB7 Horseshoe Falls 2.00 5.00
LOBB8 Ban Gioc-Detian Falls 2.00 5.00
LOBB9 Havasu Falls 2.00 5.00
LOBB10 Palouse Falls 2.00 5.00

2019 Topps Allen and Ginter Mares and Stallions

COMPLETE SET (15) 6.00 15.00
STATED ODDS 1:6 HOBBY
MS1 Arabian Horse .75 2.00
MS2 Quarter Horse .75 2.00
MS3 Thoroughbred Horse .75 2.00
MS4 Tennessee Walking Horse .75 2.00
MS5 Morgan Horse .75 2.00
MS6 American Paint Horse .75 2.00
MS7 Appaloosa .75 2.00
MS8 Miniature Horse .75 2.00
MS9 Andalusian Horse .75 2.00
MS10 Kentucky Mountain Horse .75 2.00
MS11 Clydesdale .75 2.00
MS12 Cleveland Bay Horse .75 2.00
MS13 Irish Cob Horse .75 2.00
MS14 Mustang Horse .75 2.00
MS15 Holsteiner Horse .75 2.00

2019 Topps Allen and Ginter Mini

*MINI 1-300: 1X TO 2.5X BASIC
*MINI 1-300 RC: .6X TO 1.5X BASIC RCs
*MINI SP 350-351: .6X TO 1.5X BASIC
MINI SP ODDS 1:13 HOBBY
STATED PLATE ODDS 1:1347 HOBBY
PLATE PRINT RUN 1 SET PER COLOR
BLACK-CYAN-MAGENTA-YELLOW ISSUED
NO PLATE PRICING DUE TO SCARCITY
MS1 Thomas Fish SP 10.00 25.00

2019 Topps Allen and Ginter Mini A and G Back

*MINI AG 1-300: 1.2X TO 3X BASIC
*MINI AG 1-300 RC: .75X TO 2X BASIC RCs
*MINI AG SP 351-400: .75X TO 2X BASIC
STATED ODDS 1:5 HOBBY

2019 Topps Allen and Ginter Mini Black Border

*MINI BLK 1-300: 1.5X TO 4X BASIC
*MINI BLK 1-300 RC: 1X TO 2.5X BASIC RCs
*MINI BLK SP 351-400: 1X TO 2.5X BASIC
MINI BLK ODDS 1:10 HOBBY

2019 Topps Allen and Ginter Mini Brooklyn Back

*MINI BRKLN 1-300: 10X TO 25X BASIC
*MINI BRKLN 1-300 RC: 6X TO 15X BASIC RCs
*MINI BRKLN 351-400: 4X TO 10X BASIC
STATED ODDS 1:264 HOBBY
STATED PRINT RUN 25 SER.#'d SETS

2019 Topps Allen and Ginter Mini Gold Border

*MINI GOLD 1-300: 1.2X TO 3X BASIC
*MINI GOLD 1-300 RC: .75X TO 2X BASIC RCs
*MINI GOLD 351-400: .5X TO 1.2X BASIC
RANDOMLY INSERTED IN RETAIL PACKS

2019 Topps Allen and Ginter Mini No Number

*MINI NNO 1-300: 5X TO 12X BASIC
*MINI NNO 1-300 RC: 3X TO 8X BASIC RCs
*MINI NNO 351-400: 2X TO 5X BASIC
MINI NNO ODDS 1:132 HOBBY
ANNCD PRINT RUN 50 COPIES PER

2019 Topps Allen and Ginter Mini Stained Glass

*MINI STND GLSS: 50X TO 120X BASIC
*MINI STND GLSS RC: 25X TO 60X BASIC RCs
STATED ODDS 1:527 HOBBY
ANNCD PRINT RUN 25 SER.#'d SETS

2019 Topps Allen and Ginter Mini Chugging Along

COMPLETE SET (15) 15.00 40.00
STATED ODDS 1:50 HOBBY
CA1 Monorail Train 1.25 3.00
CA2 Steam Train 1.25 3.00
CA3 Bullet Train 1.25 3.00
CA4 Cable Car 1.25 3.00
CA5 Electric Train 1.25 3.00
CA6 Commuter Train 1.25 3.00
CA7 Subway Train 1.25 3.00
CA8 Trolley 1.25 3.00
CA9 Combined Train 1.25 3.00
CA10 Freight Train 1.25 3.00
CA11 Mine Train 1.25 3.00
CA12 Yard Goat Train 1.25 3.00
CA13 Long-Distance Train 1.25 3.00
CA14 Heritage Train 1.25 3.00
CA15 Overland Train 1.25 3.00

2019 Topps Allen and Ginter Mini Collectible Canines

COMPLETE SET (25) 10.00 25.00
STATED ODDS 1:10 HOBBY
CC1 Beagle .75 2.00
CC2 Boxer .75 2.00
CC3 Vizsla .75 2.00
CC4 German Shepherd .75 2.00
CC5 Siberian Husky .75 2.00
CC6 Golden Retriever .75 2.00
CC7 Great Dane .75 2.00
CC8 Borzoi .75 2.00
CC9 Dachshund .75 2.00
CC10 Black Labrador .75 2.00
CC11 English Bulldog .75 2.00
CC12 English Springer Spaniel .75 2.00
CC13 Rhodesian Ridgeback .75 2.00
CC14 Papillon .75 2.00
CC15 Yellow Labrador .75 2.00
CC16 Chihuahua .75 2.00
CC17 French Bulldog .75 2.00
CC18 Bernese Mountain Dog .75 2.00
CC19 Corgi .75 2.00
CC20 Bullmastiff .75 2.00
CC21 Weimaraner .75 2.00
CC22 Shih Tzu .75 2.00
CC23 West Highland Terrier .75 2.00
CC24 Boston Terrier .75 2.00
CC25 Maltese .75 2.00

2019 Topps Allen and Ginter Mini DNA Relics

STATED ODDS 1:8451 HOBBY
PRINT RUNS BW/N 6-25 COPIES PER
NO PRICING ON QTY 6
DNARFA Fossilized Ammonite/17
DNARFN Fossilized Nautiloid/25 200.00 400.00
DNARFT Fossilized Trilobite/22 200.00 400.00
DNARFDB Fossilized Dinosaur Bone/25 200.00 400.00
DNARFWB Fossilized Whale Bone/25 200.00 400.00

2019 Topps Allen and Ginter Mini Dreams of Blue Ribbons

STATED ODDS 1:50 HOBBY
DBR1 Partner Carrying Contest 1.25 3.00
DBR2 Chili Pepper Eating Contest 1.25 3.00
DBR3 Pie Eating Contest 1.25 3.00
DBR4 Marshmallow-Stuffing Contest 1.25 3.00
DBR5 Toe Wrestling Contest 1.25 3.00
DBR6 Sand Castle Building Contest 1.25 3.00
DBR7 Potato Sack Racing Contest 1.25 3.00
DBR8 Dizzy Bat Contest 1.25 3.00
DBR9 Stocking Challenge Contest 1.25 3.00
DBR10 Pig Racing Contest 1.25 3.00
DBR11 Frog Jumping Contest 1.25 3.00
DBR12 Wheelbarrow Racing Contest 1.25 3.00
DBR13 Giant Pumpkin Contest 1.25 3.00
DBR14 Hot Dog Eating Contest 1.25 3.00
DBR15 Three-legged Race Contest 1.25 3.00

2019 Topps Allen and Ginter Mini Framed Presidential Pieces Relics

STATED ODDS 1:10,837 HOBBY
PRINT RUNS B/WN 5-25 COPIES PER
NO PRICING ON QTY 5
PPRGC Grover Cleveland/25 100.00 250.00
PPRFDR Franklin D. Roosevelt/25 75.00 200.00
PPRJFK John F. Kennedy/25 300.00 600.00
PPRJQA John Quincy Adams

2019 Topps Allen and Ginter Mini Framed Relics

STATED ODDS 1:55 HOBBY
MFRAB Adrian Beltre 4.00 10.00
MFRABE Andrew Benintendi 4.00 10.00
MFRAD Andre Dawson 3.00 8.00
MFRAP Andy Pettitte 3.00 8.00
MFRBJ Bo Jackson 8.00 20.00
MFRBP Buster Posey 5.00 12.00
MFRCC Carlos Correa 4.00 10.00
MFRCF Carlton Fisk 3.00 8.00
MFRCJ Chipper Jones 6.00 15.00
MFRCK Clayton Kershaw 8.00 20.00
MFRCR Cal Ripken Jr. 5.00 12.00
MFRCY Carl Yastrzemski 6.00 15.00
MFRDJ Derek Jeter 12.00 30.00
MFRDM Don Mattingly 8.00 20.00
MFRDO David Ortiz 4.00 10.00
MFRGB George Brett 6.00 15.00
MFRGH Gil Hodges 10.00 25.00
MFRIR Ivan Rodriguez 3.00 8.00
MFRI Ichiro 5.00 12.00
MFRJA Jose Altuve 3.00 8.00
MFRJB Jeff Bagwell 3.00 8.00
MFRJC Jose Canseco 3.00 8.00
MFRJS John Smoltz 4.00 10.00
MFRJV Justin Verlander 4.00 10.00
MFRKB Kris Bryant 5.00 12.00
MFRKG Ken Griffey Jr. 8.00 20.00
MFRMB Mookie Betts 5.00 12.00
MFRMM Mark McGwire 6.00 15.00
MFRMP Mike Piazza 4.00 10.00
MFRMR Mariano Rivera 6.00 15.00
MFRMT Mike Trout 12.00 30.00
MFRNG Nomar Garciaparra 3.00 8.00
MFROA Ozzie Albies 4.00 10.00
MFROS Ozzie Smith 5.00 12.00
MFRPM Pedro Martinez 3.00 8.00
MFRRA Roberto Alomar 3.00 8.00
MFRRC Roberto Clemente 150.00 400.00
MFRRCL Roger Clemens 5.00 12.00
MFRRD Rafael Devers 5.00 12.00
MFRRH Rickey Henderson 6.00 15.00
MFRRHH Rhys Hoskins 5.00 12.00
MFRRHO Rogers Hornsby 10.00 25.00
MFRRJ Reggie Jackson 3.00 8.00
MFRRY Robin Yount 4.00 10.00
MFRSC Steve Carlton 3.00 8.00
MFRSO Shohei Ohtani 10.00 25.00
MFRTG Tony Gwynn 4.00 10.00
MFRTH Todd Helton 3.00 8.00
MFRTM Thurman Munson 30.00 80.00
MFRVG Vladimir Guerrero 3.00 8.00
MFRWB Wade Boggs 3.00 8.00

2019 Topps Allen and Ginter Mini In Bloom

STATED ODDS 1:50 HOBBY
IB1 Black-Eyed Susan 1.50 4.00
IB2 Spurred Snapdragon 1.50 4.00
IB3 Shirley Poppy 1.50 4.00
IB4 Mexican Hat 1.50 4.00
IB5 Sweet Alyssum 1.50 4.00
IB6 Lily of the Valley 1.50 4.00
IB7 Begonia 1.50 4.00
IB8 Moth Orchid 1.50 4.00
IB9 Skaapbos 1.50 4.00
IB10 Flowering Crassula 1.50 4.00
IB11 Crown of Thorns 1.50 4.00
IB12 White Candles 1.50 4.00
IB13 Golden Shrimp 1.50 4.00
IB14 Brazilian Plume 1.50 4.00
IB15 Butterfly Bush 1.50 4.00
IB16 Camellia 1.50 4.00
IB17 Chinese Rain Bell 1.50 4.00
IB18 Natal Lily 1.50 4.00
IB19 Bird of Paradise 1.50 4.00
IB20 Caricature Plant 1.50 4.00
IB21 Tulip 1.50 4.00
IB22 Rose 1.50 4.00
IB23 Johnny Jump Up 1.50 4.00
IB24 Marigold 1.50 4.00
IB25 Oriental Poppy 1.50 4.00

2019 Topps Allen and Ginter Mini In Bloom Plant Me

STATED ODDS 1:2327 HOBBY
IBPMMH Mexican Hat 20.00 50.00
IBPMOP Oriental Poppy 20.00 50.00
IBPMSA Sweet Alyssum 20.00 50.00
IBPMSP Shirley Poppy 20.00 50.00
IBPMSS Spurred Snapdragon 20.00 50.00
IBPMBES Black-Eyed Susan 20.00 50.00

2019 Topps Allen and Ginter Mini Look Out Below

COMPLETE SET (15) 15.00 40.00
STATED ODDS 1:50 HOBBY
LOB1 Niagara Falls 1.25 3.00
LOB2 Victoria Falls 1.25 3.00
LOB3 Iguazu Falls 1.25 3.00
LOB4 Kaieteur Falls 1.25 3.00
LOB5 Gullfoss 1.25 3.00
LOB6 Angel Falls 1.25 3.00
LOB7 Yosemite Falls 1.25 3.00
LOB8 Ban Gioc-Detian Falls 1.25 3.00
LOB9 Horseshoe Falls 1.25 3.00
LOB10 Devil's Throat 1.25 3.00
LOB11 Huangguoshu Waterfall 1.25 3.00
LOB12 Cuquenan Falls 1.25 3.00
LOB13 Havasu Falls 1.25 3.00
LOB14 Palouse Falls 1.25 3.00
LOB15 Ruby Falls 1.25 3.00

2019 Topps Allen and Ginter Mini Lost Languages

COMPLETE SET (10) 15.00 40.00
STATED ODDS 1:50 HOBBY
LL1 Narragansett Language 1.25 3.00
LL2 Tasmanian Language 1.25 3.00
LL3 Martha's Vineyard Sign Language 1.25 3.00
LL4 Upper Chinook Language 1.25 3.00
LL5 Plains Apache Language 1.25 3.00
LL6 Klallam Language 1.25 3.00
LL7 Chiwere Language 1.25 3.00
LL8 Shasta Language 1.25 3.00
LL9 Jersey Dutch Language 1.25 3.00
LL10 Carolina Algonquian Language 1.25 3.00

2019 Topps Allen and Ginter Mini New to the Zoo

COMPLETE SET (15) 15.00 40.00
STATED ODDS 1:8 RETAIL
NTTZ1 Elephant Calf 1.25 3.00
NTTZ2 Hippo Calf 1.25 3.00
NTTZ3 Giraffe Calf 1.25 3.00
NTTZ4 Rhino Calf 1.25 3.00
NTTZ5 Lion Cub 1.25 3.00
NTTZ6 Panda Cub 1.25 3.00
NTTZ7 Fox Pup 1.25 3.00
NTTZ8 Penguin Chick 1.25 3.00
NTTZ9 Orangutan Baby 1.25 3.00
NTTZ10 Baby Shark 1.25 3.00
NTTZ11 Seal Pup 1.25 3.00
NTTZ12 Gorilla Infant 1.25 3.00
NTTZ13 Kangaroo Joey 1.25 3.00
NTTZ14 Tiger Cub 1.25 3.00
NTTZ15 Zebra Foal 1.25 3.00
NTTZ16 Otter Pup 1.25 3.00
NTTZ17 Polar Bear Cub 1.25 3.00
NTTZ18 Koala Joey 1.25 3.00
NTTZ19 Goat Kid 1.25 3.00
NTTZ20 Monkey Infant 1.25 3.00

2019 Topps Allen and Ginter N43 Box Toppers

STATED ODDS 1:5 HOBBY BOXES
N431 Mike Trout 3.00 8.00
N432 Aaron Judge 1.50 4.00
N433 Kris Bryant .75 2.00
N434 Rhys Hoskins .75 2.00
N435 Juan Soto 2.00 5.00
N436 Mookie Betts 1.00 2.50
N437 Shohei Ohtani .75 2.00
N438 Bryce Harper 1.00 2.50
N439 Anthony Rizzo 1.00 2.50
N4310 Jacob deGrom .60 1.50
N4311 J.D. Martinez .60 1.50
N4312 Jose Altuve .50 1.25
N4313 Ronald Acuna Jr. 3.00 8.00
N4314 Max Scherzer .60 1.50
N4315 Manny Machado .60 1.50
N4316 Buster Posey .75 2.00
N4317 Alex Bregman .60 1.50
N4318 Clayton Kershaw 1.25 3.00
N4319 Miguel Cabrera .60 1.50
N4320 Justin Verlander .60 1.50

2019 Topps Allen and Ginter Relics

VERSION A ODDS 1:26 HOBBY
VERSION B ODDS 1:26 HOBBY
FSRAAA A.J. Andrews A 3.00 8.00
FSRAAC Augie Carton A 2.00 5.00
FSRAACH Aroldis Chapman A 3.00 8.00
FSRAAJ Aaron Judge A 8.00 20.00
FSRABB Brandon Belt A 2.50 6.00
FSRABC Brandon Crawford A 2.50 6.00
FSRABF Brian Fallon A 6.00 15.00
FSRABR Burton Rocks A 2.00 5.00
FSRABS Ben Schwartz A 3.00 8.00
FSRACA Chris Archer A 2.00 5.00
FSRACB Cody Bellinger A 6.00 15.00
FSRACM Charles Martinet A 3.00 8.00
FSRADC Danielle Colby A 6.00 15.00
FSRADD David Dahl A 2.00 5.00
FSRADDR Drew Drechsel A 3.00 8.00
FSRADG Dee Gordon A 2.00 5.00
FSRADR Dan Rather A 6.00 15.00
FSRAEA Elvis Andrus A 2.50 6.00
FSRAEJ Emily Jaenson A 3.00 8.00
FSRAGE Graham Elliot A 3.00 8.00
FSRAGV Gary Vaynerchuk A 60.00 150.00
FSRAHD Hailey Dawson A 3.00 8.00
FSRAHK Hilary Knight A 3.00 8.00
FSRAIH Ian Happ A 2.50 6.00
FSRAJB Javier Baez A 4.00 10.00
FSRAJBE Josh Bell A 2.50 6.00
FSRAJBO Justin Bonomo A 3.00 8.00
FSRAJBR Jackie Bradley Jr. A 3.00 8.00
FSRAJC Johnny Cueto A 2.50 6.00
FSRAJCY John Cynn A 2.50 6.00
FSRAJF Jeurys Familia A 2.50 6.00
FSRAJH Jason Heyward A 2.50 6.00
FSRAJL Jay Larson A 2.50 6.00
FSRAJM Jake Mintz A 3.00 8.00
FSRAJS Jordan Shusterman A 3.00 8.00
FSRAKD Khris Davis A 3.00 8.00
FSRAKS Kyle Snyder A 3.00 8.00
FSRALC Lorenzo Cain A 2.00 5.00
FSRALCL Loretta Claiborne A 2.50 6.00
FSRALR Lawrence Rocks A 2.00 5.00
FSRAMC Michael Conforto A 2.50 6.00
FSRAMCO Mason Cox A 3.00 8.00
FSRAMF Maikel Franco A 2.50 6.00
FSRAMM Matthew Mercer A 3.00 8.00
FSRAMO Mike Oz A 3.00 8.00
FSRAMS Mayumi Seto A 3.00 8.00
FSRAMSU Marc Summers A 3.00 8.00
FSRANC Nicholas Castellanos A 3.00 8.00
FSRAOA Orlando Arcia A 2.00 5.00
FSRAOH Odubel Herrera A 2.50 6.00
FSRAQX Quinn XCII A 3.00 8.00
FSRARB Ryan Braun A 2.50 6.00
FSRARBU Rhea Butcher A 2.50 6.00
FSRARH Ryon Healy A 2.00 5.00
FSRARM Rodney Mullen A 6.00 15.00
FSRARO Robert Oberst A 3.00 8.00
FSRASD Sean Doolittle A 2.00 5.00
FSRASS Sister Mary Jo Sobieck A 6.00 15.00
FSRATG Tyler Glasnow A 2.00 5.00
FSRATK Tyler Kepner A 2.00 5.00
FSRATM 1st Tiger Mask A 20.00 50.00
Satoru Sayama
FSRATP Travis Pastrana A 3.00 8.00
FSRAVS Vincent Stio A 3.00 8.00
FSRAWC Willson Contreras A 2.50 6.00
FSRBAA Albert Almora B 2.50 6.00
FSRBAB Andrew Benintendi B 3.00 8.00
FSRBABR Alex Bregman B 3.00 8.00
FSRBAN Aaron Nola B 2.50 6.00
FSRBAP Albert Pujols B 4.00 10.00
FSRBAR Anthony Rizzo B 5.00 12.00
FSRBARO Amed Rosario B 2.50 6.00
FSRBBP Buster Posey B 4.00 10.00
FSRBBZ Ben Zobrist B 2.50 6.00
FSRBCC Carlos Correa B 3.00 8.00
FSRBCK Clayton Kershaw B 6.00 15.00
FSRBCS Chris Sale B 3.00 8.00
FSRBCT Chris Taylor B 2.50 6.00
FSRBDB Dellin Betances B 2.50 6.00
FSRBDG Didi Gregorius B 2.50 6.00
FSRBDP Dustin Pedroia B 3.00 8.00
FSRBDPR David Price B 2.50 6.00
FSRBDS Dansby Swanson B 3.00 8.00
FSRBEL Evan Longoria B 2.50 6.00
FSRBFF Freddie Freeman B 4.00 10.00
FSRBFL Francisco Lindor B 3.00 8.00
FSRBJA Jose Altuve B 2.50 6.00
FSRBJB Jose Berrios B 2.50 6.00
FSRBJG Joey Gallo B 2.50 6.00
FSRBJL Jake Lamb B 2.50 6.00
FSRBJLE Jon Lester B 2.50 6.00
FSRBJM J.D. Martinez B 3.00 8.00
FSRBJMO Jordan Montgomery B 2.50 6.00
FSRBJR Jose Ramirez B 2.50 6.00
FSRBJS Justin Smoak B 2.00 5.00
FSRBJV Justin Verlander B 3.00 8.00
FSRBKB Kris Bryant B 4.00 10.00
FSRBKF Kyle Freeland B 2.50 6.00
FSRBKS Kyle Schwarber B 3.00 8.00
FSRBLS Luis Severino B 2.50 6.00
FSRBMA Miguel Andujar B 3.00 8.00
FSRBMB Mookie Betts B 5.00 12.00
FSRBMC Miguel Cabrera B 3.00 8.00
FSRBMCA Matt Carpenter B 3.00 8.00
FSRBMM Miles Mikolas B 3.00 8.00
FSRBNA Nolan Arenado B 4.00 10.00
FSRBNM Nomar Mazara B 2.00 5.00
FSRBNS Noah Syndergaard B 2.50 6.00
FSRBOA Ozzie Albies B 3.00 8.00
FSRBRD Rafael Devers B 4.00 10.00
FSRBRH Rhys Hoskins B 4.00 10.00
FSRBRO Rougned Odor B 2.50 6.00
FSRBRP Rick Porcello B 2.50 6.00
FSRBSK Scott Kingery B 2.50 6.00
FSRBSN Sean Newcomb B 2.00 5.00
FSRBSP Salvador Perez B 2.50 6.00
FSRBTS Trevor Story B 3.00 8.00
FSRBTT Trea Turner B 2.50 6.00
FSRBVR Victor Robles B 4.00 10.00
FSRBXB Xander Bogaerts B 3.00 8.00
FSRBYM Yadier Molina B 3.00 8.00

2019 Topps Allen and Ginter Rip Cards

STATED UNRIPPED ODDS 1:160 HOBBY
PRINT RUNS B/WN 25-90 COPIES PER
UNRIPPED HAVE ADD'L CARDS WITHIN
RIP1 Hank Aaron/50 60.00 150.00
RIP2 Ronald Acuna Jr/75 60.00 150.00
RIP3 Jose Altuve/75 40.00 100.00
RIP4 Nolan Arenado/75 40.00 100.00
RIP5 Jeff Bagwell/75 40.00 100.00
RIP6 Ernie Banks/50 40.00 100.00
RIP7 Adrian Beltre/75 40.00 100.00
RIP8 Johnny Bench/50 40.00 100.00
RIP9 Andrew Benintendi/75 40.00 100.00
RIP10 Mookie Betts/75 50.00 120.00
RIP11 Alex Bregman/75 50.00 120.00
RIP12 George Brett/75 50.00 120.00
RIP13 Lou Brock/50 40.00 100.00
RIP14 Kris Bryant/75 50.00 120.00
RIP15 Miguel Cabrera/75 40.00 100.00
RIP16 Rod Carew/50 40.00 100.00
RIP17 Steve Carlton/50 40.00 100.00
RIP18 Roberto Clemente/50 60.00 150.00
RIP19 Ty Cobb/25 60.00 150.00
RIP20 Carlos Correa/75
RIP21 Jacob deGrom/75
RIP22 Rafael Devers/75 40.00 100.00
RIP23 Larry Doby/50 40.00 100.00
RIP24 Bob Feller/50
RIP25 Carlton Fisk/75 40.00 100.00
RIP26 Whitey Ford/50 40.00 100.00
RIP27 Lou Gehrig/25 60.00 150.00
RIP28 Bob Gibson/50 40.00 100.00
RIP29 Paul Goldschmidt/75 40.00 100.00
RIP30 Zack Greinke/75 40.00 100.00
RIP31 Ken Griffey Jr/75 60.00 150.00
RIP32 Vladimir Guerrero/75 40.00 100.00
RIP33 Tony Gwynn/75 60.00 150.00
RIP34 Roy Halladay/75
RIP35 Todd Helton/75 40.00 100.00
RIP36 Rickey Henderson/75 50.00 120.00
RIP37 Trevor Hoffman/75 40.00 100.00
RIP38 Rhys Hoskins/75 40.00 100.00
RIP39 Reggie Jackson/50 50.00 120.00
RIP40 Derek Jeter/75 60.00 150.00
RIP41 Randy Johnson/75 50.00 120.00
RIP42 Chipper Jones/75 50.00 120.00
RIP43 Aaron Judge/75 60.00 150.00
RIP44 Al Kaline/50 75.00 200.00
RIP45 Clayton Kershaw/75 40.00 100.00
RIP46 Harmon Killebrew/50 60.00 150.00
RIP47 Sandy Koufax/50 50.00 120.00
RIP48 Barry Larkin/75 40.00 100.00
RIP49 Francisco Lindor/75 40.00 100.00
RIP50 Edgar Martinez/75 50.00 120.00
RIP51 Pedro Martinez/75 50.00 120.00
RIP52 Don Mattingly/75 60.00 150.00
RIP53 Willie McCovey/50
RIP54 Mark McGwire/75 40.00 100.00
RIP55 Yadier Molina/75 60.00 150.00
RIP56 Paul Molitor/75
RIP57 Thurman Munson/50 50.00 120.00
RIP58 Stan Musial/45 60.00 150.00
RIP59 Shohei Ohtani/75 60.00 150.00
RIP60 David Ortiz/75 40.00 100.00
RIP61 Jim Palmer/50
RIP62 Salvador Perez/75
RIP63 Andy Pettitte/75 40.00 100.00
RIP64 Mike Piazza/75
RIP65 Buster Posey/75 50.00 120.00
RIP66 David Price/75
RIP67 Albert Pujols/75 50.00 120.00
RIP68 Jose Ramirez/75 40.00 100.00
RIP69 Cal Ripken Jr/75 50.00 120.00
RIP70 Mariano Rivera/75 50.00 120.00
RIP71 Anthony Rizzo/75 40.00 100.00
RIP72 Jackie Robinson/45 60.00 150.00
RIP73 Brooks Robinson/50 40.00 100.00
RIP74 Frank Robinson/50 40.00 100.00
RIP75 Alex Rodriguez/75 40.00 100.00
RIP76 Ivan Rodriguez/75 40.00 100.00
RIP77 Babe Ruth/25 60.00 150.00
RIP78 Nolan Ryan/75 50.00 120.00
RIP79 Chris Sale/75 40.00 100.00
RIP80 Ryne Sandberg/75 40.00 100.00
RIP81 Max Scherzer/75 40.00 100.00
RIP82 Tom Seaver/75 40.00 100.00
RIP83 Ozzie Smith/75 40.00 100.00
RIP84 Blake Snell/75 40.00 100.00
RIP85 Duke Snider/45 50.00 120.00
RIP86 Sammy Sosa/75 40.00 100.00
RIP87 Juan Soto/75 40.00 100.00
RIP88 Willie Stargell/50 40.00 100.00
RIP89 Trevor Story/75 40.00 100.00
RIP90 Noah Syndergaard/75 40.00 100.00
RIP91 Frank Thomas/75 40.00 100.00
RIP92 Mike Trout/90 75.00 200.00
RIP93 Justin Verlander/75
RIP94 Joey Votto/75
RIP95 Honus Wagner/25 60.00 150.00
RIP96 Ted Williams/45
RIP97 Carl Yastrzemski/75 40.00 100.00
RIP98 Christian Yelich/75 50.00 120.00
RIP99 Robin Yount/75 40.00 100.00
RIP100 Ichiro/75 40.00 100.00

2019 Topps Allen and Ginter Rip Cards Mini

RANDOMLY INSERTED IN RIP PACKS
*RIP STND GLSS: 1.5X TO 4X RIP MINI
351 Aaron Judge 20.00 50.00
352 Al Kaline 10.00 25.00
353 Albert Pujols 12.00 30.00
354 Babe Ruth 20.00 50.00
355 Brooks Robinson 8.00 20.00
356 Javier Baez 12.00 30.00
357 Buster Posey 12.00 30.00
358 Cal Ripken Jr. 15.00 40.00
359 Carl Yastrzemski 15.00 40.00
360 Carlos Correa 15.00 40.00
361 Chipper Jones 10.00 25.00
362 Clayton Kershaw 20.00 50.00
363 David Ortiz 10.00 25.00
364 Derek Jeter 25.00 60.00
365 Francisco Lindor 10.00 25.00
366 Frank Thomas 10.00 25.00
367 George Brett 12.00 30.00
368 Hank Aaron 12.00 30.00
369 Ichiro 12.00 30.00
370 Jackie Robinson 10.00 25.00
371 Johnny Bench 10.00 25.00
372 Jose Altuve 12.00 30.00
373 Juan Soto 15.00 40.00
374 Justin Verlander 20.00 50.00
375 Ken Griffey Jr. 20.00 50.00
376 Kris Bryant 12.00 30.00
377 Lou Gehrig 15.00 40.00
378 Manny Machado 10.00 25.00
379 Mariano Rivera 20.00 50.00
380 Mark McGwire 12.00 30.00
381 Max Scherzer 10.00 25.00
382 Miguel Cabrera 10.00 25.00
383 Mike Trout 40.00 100.00
384 Mike Piazza 10.00 25.00
385 Mookie Betts 12.00 30.00
386 Nolan Ryan 15.00 40.00
387 Pedro Martinez 8.00 20.00
388 Reggie Jackson 12.00 30.00
389 Rickey Henderson 20.00 50.00
390 Roberto Clemente 20.00 50.00
391 Roger Clemens 12.00 30.00
392 Ronald Acuna Jr. 25.00 60.00
393 Ryne Sandberg 15.00 40.00
394 Sandy Koufax 20.00 50.00
395 Shohei Ohtani 20.00 50.00
396 Stan Musial 15.00 40.00
397 Steve Carlton 10.00 25.00
398 Ted Williams 15.00 40.00
399 Tony Gwynn 15.00 40.00
400 Paul Molitor 15.00 40.00

2019 Topps Allen and Ginter Rip Cards Ripped

UNRIPPED STATED ODDS 1:160 HOBBY
PRINT RUNS B/WN 25-90 COPIES PER
PRICED WITH CLEANLY RIPPED BACKS
RIP1 Hank Aaron/50 6.00 15.00
RIP2 Ronald Acuna Jr/75 15.00 40.00
RIP3 Jose Altuve/75 2.50 6.00
RIP4 Nolan Arenado/75 4.00 10.00
RIP5 Jeff Bagwell/75 2.50 6.00
RIP6 Ernie Banks/50 3.00 8.00
RIP7 Adrian Beltre/75 3.00 8.00
RIP8 Johnny Bench/50 3.00 8.00
RIP9 Andrew Benintendi/75 3.00 8.00
RIP10 Mookie Betts/75 5.00 12.00
RIP11 Alex Bregman/75 3.00 8.00
RIP12 George Brett/75 6.00 15.00
RIP13 Lou Brock/50 2.50 6.00
RIP14 Kris Bryant/75 4.00 10.00
RIP15 Miguel Cabrera/75 3.00 8.00
RIP16 Rod Carew/50 2.50 6.00
RIP17 Steve Carlton/50 2.50 6.00
RIP18 Roberto Clemente/50 8.00 20.00
RIP19 Ty Cobb/25 5.00 12.00
RIP20 Carlos Correa/75 3.00 8.00
RIP21 Jacob deGrom/75 3.00 8.00
RIP22 Rafael Devers/75 4.00 10.00
RIP23 Larry Doby/50 2.50 6.00
RIP24 Bob Feller/50 2.50 6.00
RIP25 Carlton Fisk/75 2.50 6.00
RIP26 Whitey Ford/50 2.50 6.00
RIP27 Lou Gehrig/25 6.00 15.00
RIP28 Bob Gibson/50 2.50 6.00
RIP29 Paul Goldschmidt/75 3.00 8.00
RIP30 Zack Greinke/75 2.50 6.00
RIP31 Ken Griffey Jr/75 6.00 15.00
RIP32 Vladimir Guerrero/75 2.50 6.00
RIP33 Tony Gwynn/75 3.00 8.00
RIP34 Roy Halladay/75 2.50 6.00
RIP35 Todd Helton/75 2.50 6.00
RIP36 Rickey Henderson/75 3.00 8.00
RIP37 Trevor Hoffman/75 2.50 6.00
RIP38 Rhys Hoskins/75 4.00 10.00
RIP39 Reggie Jackson/50 2.50 6.00
RIP40 Derek Jeter/75 8.00 20.00
RIP41 Randy Johnson/75 3.00 8.00
RIP42 Chipper Jones/75 3.00 8.00
RIP43 Aaron Judge/75 8.00 20.00
RIP44 Al Kaline/50 3.00 8.00
RIP45 Clayton Kershaw/75 6.00 15.00
RIP46 Harmon Killebrew/50 3.00 8.00
RIP47 Sandy Koufax/50 6.00 15.00
RIP48 Barry Larkin/75 2.50 6.00
RIP49 Francisco Lindor/75 3.00 8.00
RIP50 Edgar Martinez/75 2.50 6.00
RIP51 Pedro Martinez/75 2.50 6.00
RIP52 Don Mattingly/75 6.00 15.00
RIP53 Willie McCovey/50 2.50 6.00
RIP54 Mark McGwire/75 5.00 12.00
RIP55 Yadier Molina/75 3.00 8.00
RIP56 Paul Molitor/75 3.00 8.00
RIP57 Thurman Munson/50 3.00 8.00
RIP58 Stan Musial/45 5.00 12.00
RIP59 Shohei Ohtani/75 4.00 10.00
RIP60 David Ortiz/75 3.00 8.00
RIP61 Jim Palmer/50 2.50 6.00
RIP62 Salvador Perez/75 2.50 6.00
RIP63 Andy Pettitte/75 2.50 6.00
RIP64 Mike Piazza/75 3.00 8.00
RIP65 Buster Posey/75 4.00 10.00
RIP66 David Price/75 2.50 6.00
RIP67 Albert Pujols/75 4.00 10.00
RIP68 Jose Ramirez/75 2.50 6.00
RIP69 Cal Ripken Jr/75 10.00 25.00
RIP70 Mariano Rivera/75 4.00 10.00
RIP71 Anthony Rizzo/75 5.00 12.00
RIP72 Jackie Robinson/45 3.00 8.00
RIP73 Brooks Robinson/50 2.50 6.00
RIP74 Frank Robinson/50 2.50 6.00
RIP75 Alex Rodriguez/75 4.00 10.00
RIP76 Ivan Rodriguez/75 2.50 6.00
RIP77 Babe Ruth/25 8.00 20.00
RIP78 Nolan Ryan/75 10.00 25.00
RIP79 Chris Sale/75 3.00 8.00
RIP80 Ryne Sandberg/75 6.00 15.00
RIP81 Max Scherzer/75 3.00 8.00
RIP82 Tom Seaver/75 2.50 6.00
RIP83 Ozzie Smith/75 4.00 10.00

RIP84 Blake Snell/75 2.50 6.00
RIP85 Duke Snider/45 2.50 6.00
RIP86 Sammy Sosa/75 3.00 8.00
RIP87 Juan Soto/75 10.00 25.00
RIP88 Willie Stargell/50 2.50 6.00
RIP89 Trevor Story/75 3.00 8.00
RIP90 Noah Syndergaard/75 2.50 6.00
RIP91 Frank Thomas/75 3.00 8.00
RIP92 Mike Trout/90 15.00 40.00
RIP93 Justin Verlander/75 3.00 8.00
RIP94 Joey Votto/75 3.00 8.00
RIP95 Honus Wagner/25 3.00 8.00
RIP96 Ted Williams/45 6.00 15.00
RIP97 Carl Yastrzemski/75 5.00 12.00
RIP98 Christian Yelich/75 4.00 10.00
RIP99 Robin Yount/75 3.00 8.00
RIP100 Ichiro/75 4.00 10.00

2020 Topps Allen and Ginter

COMPLETE SET (350) 25.00 60.00
COMP.SET w/o SP's (300) 15.00 40.00
SP ODDS 1:2 HOBBY
1 Tom Glavine .20 .50
2 Randy Johnson .25 .60
3 Paul Goldschmidt .25 .60
4 Larry Doby .20 .50
5 Walker Buehler .30 .75
6 John Smoltz .25 .60
7 Tim Lincecum .20 .50
8 Jeff Bagwell .20 .50
9 Rhys Hoskins .30 .75
10 Rod Carew .20 .50
11 Lou Gehrig .50 1.25
12 George Springer .20 .50
13 Aaron Judge .60 1.50
14 Aaron Nola .25 .60
15 Kris Bryant .30 .75
16 Bryce Harper .40 1.00
17 Ken Griffey Jr. .50 1.25
18 George Brett .50 1.25
19 Keston Hiura .30 .75
20 Joe Mauer .20 .50
21 Ted Williams .50 1.25
22 Eddie Mathews .25 .60
23 Jorge Soler .25 .60
24 Shohei Ohtani .30 .75
25 Carl Yastrzemski .40 1.00
26 Willie McCovey .20 .50
27 Joe Morgan .20 .50
28 Juan Soto .75 2.00
29 Willie Mays .50 1.25
30 Eloy Jimenez .50 1.25
31 Babe Ruth .60 1.50
32 Ichiro .30 .75
33 Edgar Martinez .20 .50
34 Pete Alonso .60 1.50
35 Rickey Henderson .25 .60
36 Alex Bregman .25 .60
37 Mike Mussina .20 .50
38 Miguel Cabrera .25 .60
39 Andy Pettitte .20 .50
40 Mariano Rivera .30 .75
41 David Ortiz .25 .60
42 Jackie Robinson .25 .60
43 Matt Chapman .25 .60
44 Rafael Devers .30 .75
45 Yoan Moncada .25 .60
46 Pedro Martinez .20 .50
47 Freddie Freeman .30 .75
48 Ketel Marte .20 .50
49 Roger Clemens .30 .75
50 Vladimir Guerrero Jr. .50 1.25
51 Roberto Clemente .60 1.50
52 Ivan Rodriguez .20 .50
53 Mike Soroka .25 .60
54 Victor Robles .30 .75
55 Nick Senzel .25 .60
56 Ozzie Albies .25 .60
57 Eddie Murray .20 .50
58 Christian Yelich .30 .75
59 Duke Snider .20 .50
60 Steve Carlton .20 .50
61 Jim Thome .20 .50
62 Whitey Ford .20 .50
63 Marcus Semien .15 .40
64 Andre Dawson .20 .50
65 Cody Bellinger .50 1.25
66 Darryl Strawberry .15 .40
67 Mookie Betts .50 1.25
68 Nomar Garciaparra .20 .50
69 Al Kaline .25 .60
70 Don Mattingly .50 1.25
71 Vladimir Guerrero .20 .50
72 Johnny Bench .25 .60
73 Mark McGwire .40 1.00
74 Ty Cobb .40 1.00
75 Joey Votto .25 .60
76 Chipper Jones .25 .60
77 Javier Baez .30 .75
78 Xander Bogaerts .25 .60
79 Sandy Koufax .50 1.25
80 DJ LeMahieu .25 .60
81 Barry Zito .20 .50
82 Andrew Benintendi .25 .60
83 J.D. Martinez .25 .60
84 Clayton Kershaw .50 1.25
85 Mike Trout 1.25 3.00
86 Anthony Rizzo .40 1.00
87 Trevor Story .25 .60
88 Ronald Acuna Jr. 1.00 2.50
89 Paul Molitor .25 .60
90 Jack Flaherty .25 .60
91 Dave Winfield .20 .50
92 Barry Larkin .20 .50
93 Francisco Lindor .25 .60
94 Max Fried .25 .60
95 Manny Machado .25 .60
96 Frank Thomas .25 .60
97 Aristides Aquino RC .50 1.25
98 Cal Ripken Jr. .75 2.00
99 Gavin Lux RC 1.50 4.00
100 Max Scherzer .25 .60
101 Brooks Robinson .20 .50
102 Robin Yount .25 .60
103 Tim Anderson .25 .60
104 Hank Aaron .50 1.25
105 Todd Helton .20 .50
106 Willie Stargell .20 .50
107 Roger Maris .25 .60
108 Gary Carter .20 .50
109 Reggie Jackson .20 .50
110 Albert Pujols .30 .75
111 Buster Posey .30 .75
112 Bo Bichette RC 2.00 5.00
113 Luis Gonzalez .15 .40
114 Gleyber Torres .50 1.25
115 Fernando Tatis Jr. 1.00 2.50
116 Honus Wagner .25 .60
117 Ernie Banks .25 .60
118 Yordan Alvarez RC 1.25 3.00
119 Giancarlo Stanton .25 .60
120 Bob Gibson .20 .50
121 Zack Greinke .20 .50
122 Trea Turner .20 .50
123 Mike Piazza .25 .60
124 Juan Marichal .20 .50
125 Craig Biggio .20 .50
126 Wade Boggs .20 .50
127 Jose Altuve .20 .50
128 Tony Gwynn .25 .60
129 Josh Bell .20 .50
130 Nolan Arenado .30 .75
131 Stan Musial .40 1.00
132 Jim Palmer .20 .50
133 Justin Verlander .25 .60
134 Roberto Alomar .20 .50
135 Harmon Killebrew .25 .60
136 Carlos Correa .25 .60
137 Yadier Molina .25 .60
138 Tom Seaver .20 .50
139 Nolan Ryan .75 2.00
140 Joe Torre .20 .50
141 Mike Schmidt .40 1.00
142 Patrick Corbin .20 .50
143 Carlton Fisk .20 .50
144 Warren Spahn .20 .50
145 Alex Rodriguez .30 .75
146 Jacob deGrom .25 .60
147 Jose Berrios .20 .50
148 David Wright .25 .60
149 Ryne Sandberg .50 1.25
150 Ozzie Smith .30 .75
151 Kenley Jansen .20 .50
152 J.K. Dobbins .40 1.00
153 Starling Marte .20 .50
154 Tommy La Stella .15 .40
155 Chip Gaines .25 .60
156 Lourdes Gurriel Jr. .20 .50
157 Jeff McNeil .20 .50
158 Kwang-Hyun Kim RC .75 2.00
159 Kyle Lewis RC 2.00 5.00
160 Lorenzo Cain .15 .40
161 Jackie Bradley Jr. .25 .60
162 Kyle Tucker .20 .50
163 Cole Hamels .20 .50
164 Kollen Wong .20 .50
165 Hugo Juice Tandron .25 .60
166 Briana Scurry .25 .60
167 Ken Jeong .25 .60
168 Willson Contreras .25 .60
169 Carter Kieboom .25 .60
170 Nick Thune .25 .60
171 Hunter Pence .20 .50
172 Baseball Brit .25 .60
Joey Mellows
173 Evan Longoria .20 .50
174 Anthony Kay RC .25 .60
175 Kirby Yates .15 .40
176 Justin Dunn RC .30 .75
177 Hunter Harvey RC .40 1.00
178 Marcell Ozuna .25 .60
179 Dallas Keuchel .20 .50
180 Khris Davis .25 .60
181 Adbert Alzolay RC .30 .75
182 Kelsey Cook .25 .60
183 Lucas Giolito .20 .50
184 Joc Pederson .25 .60
185 Austin Meadows .20 .50
186 Bryan Reynolds .20 .50
187 Masahiro Tanaka .25 .60
188 Eugenio Suarez .20 .50
189 Brandon Lowe .20 .50
190 Yuli Gurriel .25 .60
191 Nelson Cruz .25 .60
192 Jose Abreu .25 .60
193 Nyjah Huston .20 .50
194 Mike Doc Emrick .20 .50
195 Rick Porcello .20 .50
196 Noah Syndergaard .20 .50
197 Matt Thaiss RC .30 .75
198 Will Smith .30 .75
199 Nico Hoerner RC 1.00 2.50
200 Jim Abbott .15 .40
201 Sakura Kokumai .25 .60
202 Tino Martinez .25 .60
203 Tony Dunst .25 .60
204 Jared Carrabis .25 .60
205 Salvador Perez .20 .50
206 C.J. Cron .15 .40
207 Brendan McKay RC .40 1.00
208 Mike Moustakas .20 .50
209 Johnny Bananas .25 .60
210 Jose Ramirez .20 .50
211 Ryan Braun .20 .50
212 Chris Paddack .25 .60
213 Oscar Mercado .20 .50
214 Ryan McMahon .15 .40
215 Paul DeJong .25 .60
216 Shun Yamaguchi RC .30 .75
217 Aaron Wheelz Fotheringham .25 .60
218 Andrelton Simmons .15 .40
219 Josh Hader .15 .40
220 Eric Hosmer .20 .50
221 Mike Foltynewicz .15 .40
222 Isan Diaz RC .40 1.00
223 Shane Bieber .25 .60
224 Kole Calhoun .15 .40
225 Austin Riley .40 1.00
226 A.J. Puk RC .50 1.25
227 Max Muncy .20 .50
228 Justine Siegal .20 .50
229 Jordan Yamamoto RC .30 .75
230 Matt Olson .15 .40
231 Bucky Lasek .25 .60
232 Dakota Hudson .20 .50
233 Howie Kendrick .15 .40
234 Jorge Alfaro .15 .40
235 Jesus Luzardo RC .50 1.25
236 Alex Verdugo .20 .50
237 Nick Ahmed .15 .40
238 Gerrit Cole .40 1.00
239 Kyle Schwarber .25 .60
240 Luis Arraez .30 .75
241 Michael Brantley .20 .50
242 Andy Cohen .25 .60
243 Max Kepler .20 .50
244 Brandon Woodruff .15 .40
245 Josh Donaldson .20 .50
246 Mike Clevinger .20 .50
247 Yusei Kikuchi .20 .50
248 Rob Friedman .25 .60
249 Stephen Strasburg .25 .60
250 Charlie Blackmon .25 .60
251 Corey Kluber .20 .50
252 Steve Byrne .25 .60
253 David Price .20 .50
254 Ryan Nyquist .20 .50
255 David Dahl .15 .40
256 Luis Robert RC 2.50 6.00
257 Corey Seager .25 .60
258 Cavan Biggio .30 .75
259 Whit Merrifield .25 .60
260 J.T. Realmuto .25 .60
261 Joey Gallo .25 .60
262 Zac Gallen RC .60 1.50
263 Dansby Swanson .25 .60
264 Abraham Toro RC .30 .75
265 Tommy Edman .25 .60
266 Didi Gregorius .25 .60
267 Elvis Andrus .20 .50
268 Eduardo Escobar .15 .40
269 Miguel Sano .20 .50
270 Luis Castillo .20 .50
271 Michael Conforto .20 .50
272 Jon Lester .20 .50
273 Gregory Polanco .20 .50
274 Steven Tefft .25 .60
275 Jeff Dye .25 .60
276 Jose Urquidy RC .30 .75
277 John Means .15 .40
278 Nick Castellanos .25 .60
279 Maikel Franco .25 .60
280 Jean Segura .20 .50
281 Derrick Goold .25 .60
282 Matthew Boyd .15 .40
283 Nomar Mazara .15 .40
284 Julian Edwards .25 .60
285 Orlando Arcia .15 .40
286 Trey Mancini .25 .60
287 Aroldis Chapman .25 .60
288 Courtney Hansen .25 .60
289 Anthony Rendon .25 .60
290 Ramon Laureano .20 .50
291 Sonny Gray .20 .50
292 Hyun-Jin Ryu .20 .50
293 Daniel Vogelbach .15 .40
294 Mauricio Dubon RC .30 .75
295 Zack Wheeler .20 .50
296 Trevor Bauer .20 .50
297 R.L. Stine .25 .60
298 Adalberto Mondesi .25 .60
299 Blake Snell .20 .50
300 Andres Munoz RC .25 .60
301 Tim Raines SP .50 1.25
302 Thurman Munson SP .60 1.50
303 Earl Weaver SP .50 1.25
304 Darin Erstad SP .40 1.00
305 Bill Mazeroski SP .50 1.25
306 Moises Alou SP .40 1.00
307 Miguel Tejada SP .40 1.00
308 Phil Rizzuto SP .50 1.25
309 Alan Trammell SP .50 1.25
310 Sean Casey SP .40 1.00
311 Bert Blyleven SP .50 1.25
312 Dennis Eckersley SP .50 1.25
313 Fred McGriff SP .50 1.25
314 Dwight Gooden SP .40 1.00
315 Juan Gonzalez SP .40 1.00
316 Billy Williams SP .50 1.25
317 Cecil Fielder SP .40 1.00
318 Andruw Jones SP .40 1.00
319 Tony LaRussa SP .50 1.25
320 Orlando Cepeda SP .50 1.25
321 Trevor Hoffman SP .50 1.25
322 Catfish Hunter SP .50 1.25
323 Bernie Williams SP .50 1.25
324 Lou Brock SP .50 1.25
325 Mark Grace SP .50 1.25
326 Monte Irvin SP .50 1.25
327 Jose Canseco SP .50 1.25
328 Bobby Doerr SP .50 1.25
329 Ryan Howard SP .50 1.25
330 Bob Feller SP .50 1.25
331 Gary Sheffield SP .40 1.00
332 Shawn Green SP .40 1.00
333 Kenny Lofton SP .40 1.00
334 Rollie Fingers SP .50 1.25
335 Tony Perez SP .50 1.25
336 Jermaine Dye SP .40 1.00
337 Ralph Kiner SP .50 1.25
338 Fergie Jenkins SP .50 1.25
339 Kerry Wood SP .40 1.00
340 Magglio Ordonez SP .40 1.00
341 Jim Bunning SP .50 1.25
342 Mo Vaughn SP .40 1.00
343 Jack Morris SP .50 1.25
344 Phil Niekro SP .50 1.25
345 Larry Walker SP .50 1.25
346 Sparky Anderson SP .50 1.25
347 Tommy Lasorda SP .50 1.25
348 Luis Aparicio SP .50 1.25
349 Jay Buhner SP .40 1.00
350 Goose Gossage SP .50 1.25

2020 Topps Allen and Ginter Silver

*GLS SLVR 1-300: 1.5X TO 4X BASIC
*GLS SLVR 1-300 RC: 1X TO 2.5X BASIC RCs
*GLS SLVR 301-350: .6X TO 1.5X BASIC
FOUND ONLY IN HOBBY HOT BOXES

2020 Topps Allen and Ginter A Debut to Remember

COMPLETE SET (30) 10.00 25.00
STATED ODDS 1:XX
DTR1 Yordan Alvarez 1.25 3.00
DTR2 Miguel Cabrera .40 1.00
DTR3 Starlin Castro .25 .60
DTR4 Will Clark .30 .75
DTR5 Brandon Crawford .30 .75
DTR6 Johnny Cueto .30 .75
DTR7 Kyle Farmer .25 .60
DTR8 Joey Gallo .40 1.00
DTR9 Dwight Gooden .25 .60
DTR10 Ken Griffey Jr. .75 2.00
DTR11 Vladimir Guerrero Jr. .75 2.00
DTR12 Jason Heyward .30 .75
DTR13 Nico Hoerner 1.00 2.50
DTR14 Aaron Judge 1.00 2.50
DTR15 Ramon Laureano .40 1.00
DTR16 Juan Marichal .30 .75
DTR17 Steven Matz .30 .75
DTR18 Willie McCovey .30 .75
DTR19 Brendan McKay .40 1.00
DTR20 Shohei Ohtani .50 1.25
DTR21 Chris Paddack .40 1.00
DTR22 Freddy Peralta .25 .60
DTR23 Daniel Ponce de Leon .25 .60
DTR24 Nick Solak .40 1.00
DTR25 Trevor Story .40 1.00
DTR26 Stephen Strasburg .40 1.00
DTR27 Ross Stripling .25 .60
DTR28 Fernando Tatis Jr. 1.50 4.00
DTR29 Luis Tiant .25 .60
DTR30 Ichiro .50 1.25

2020 Topps Allen and Ginter Autographs

STATED ODDS 1:XXX HOBBY
EXCHANGE DEADLINE 7/31/2020
FSAALM Alex Morgan 75.00 200.00
FSACD Charlie Day 60.00 150.00
FSACG Chip Gaines 50.00 120.00
FSACLB Ludacris 75.00 200.00
FSADMC Danny McBride 75.00 200.00
FSAMR Megan Rapinoe 40.00 100.00
FSAMSM Simone Manuel 8.00 20.00
FSAPR Paul Rudd 100.00 250.00
FSASL Spike Lee 75.00 200.00

2020 Topps Allen and Ginter Box Topper Rip Cards

STATED UNRIPPED ODDS 1:XX HOBBY BOXES
UNRIPPED HAVE ADD'L CARDS WITHIN
BRIP1 Hank Aaron 125.00 300.00
BRIP2 Ronald Acuna Jr. 100.00 250.00
BRIP3 Pete Alonso 100.00 250.00
BRIP4 Yordan Alvarez 125.00 300.00
BRIP5 Cody Bellinger 100.00 250.00
BRIP6 Johnny Bench 125.00 300.00
BRIP7 Bo Bichette 125.00 300.00
BRIP8 George Brett 100.00 250.00
BRIP9 Roberto Clemente 125.00 300.00
BRIP10 Ken Griffey Jr. 125.00 300.00
BRIP11 Vladimir Guerrero Jr. 100.00 250.00
BRIP12 Tony Gwynn 100.00 250.00
BRIP13 Bryce Harper 100.00 250.00
BRIP14 Reggie Jackson 100.00 250.00
BRIP15 Aaron Judge 125.00 300.00
BRIP16 Clayton Kershaw 125.00 300.00
BRIP17 Sandy Koufax 125.00 300.00
BRIP18 Willie Mays 125.00 300.00
BRIP19 Shohei Ohtani 125.00 300.00
BRIP20 Mike Piazza 125.00 300.00
BRIP21 Cal Ripken Jr. 125.00 300.00
BRIP22 Mariano Rivera 100.00 250.00
BRIP23 Brooks Robinson 100.00 250.00
BRIP24 Jackie Robinson 125.00 300.00
BRIP25 Babe Ruth 125.00 300.00
BRIP26 Juan Soto 100.00 250.00
BRIP27 Fernando Tatis Jr. 125.00 300.00
BRIP28 Mike Trout 150.00 400.00
BRIP29 Ted Williams 100.00 250.00
BRIP30 Ichiro 100.00 250.00

2020 Topps Allen and Ginter Box Topper Rip Cards Ripped

UNRIPPED STATED ODDS 1:XXX HOBBY
PRICED WITH CLEANLY RIPPED BACKS
BRIP1 Hank Aaron 6.00 15.00
BRIP2 Ronald Acuna Jr. 12.00 30.00
BRIP3 Pete Alonso 8.00 20.00
BRIP4 Yordan Alvarez 10.00 25.00
BRIP5 Cody Bellinger 6.00 15.00
BRIP6 Johnny Bench 3.00 8.00
BRIP7 Bo Bichette 15.00 40.00
BRIP8 George Brett 6.00 15.00
BRIP9 Roberto Clemente 8.00 20.00
BRIP10 Ken Griffey Jr. 6.00 15.00
BRIP11 Vladimir Guerrero Jr. 6.00 15.00
BRIP12 Tony Gwynn 3.00 8.00
BRIP13 Bryce Harper 5.00 12.00
BRIP14 Reggie Jackson 2.50 6.00
BRIP15 Aaron Judge 8.00 20.00
BRIP16 Clayton Kershaw 6.00 15.00
BRIP17 Sandy Koufax 6.00 15.00
BRIP18 Willie Mays 6.00 15.00
BRIP19 Shohei Ohtani 4.00 10.00
BRIP20 Mike Piazza 3.00 8.00
BRIP21 Cal Ripken Jr. 10.00 25.00
BRIP22 Mariano Rivera 4.00 10.00
BRIP23 Brooks Robinson 2.50 6.00
BRIP24 Jackie Robinson 3.00 8.00
BRIP25 Babe Ruth 8.00 20.00
BRIP26 Juan Soto 10.00 25.00
BRIP27 Fernando Tatis Jr. 12.00 30.00
BRIP28 Mike Trout 15.00 40.00
BRIP29 Ted Williams 6.00 15.00
BRIP30 Ichiro 4.00 10.00

2020 Topps Allen and Ginter Box Toppers

INSERTED IN HOBBY BOXES
BLAJ Aaron Judge 1.50 4.00
BLBB Bo Bichette 3.00 8.00
BLBH Bryce Harper 1.00 2.50
BLCB Cody Bellinger 1.25 3.00
BLCK Clayton Kershaw 1.25 3.00
BLCY Christian Yelich .75 2.00
BLFF Freddie Freeman .75 2.00
BLJB Javier Baez .75 2.00
BLJd Jacob deGrom .60 1.50
BLLR Luis Robert 4.00 10.00
BLMT Mike Trout 3.00 8.00
BLPA Pete Alonso 1.50 4.00
BLRA Ronald Acuna Jr. 2.50 6.00
BLYA Yordan Alvarez 2.00 5.00
BLYM Yadier Molina .60 1.50

2020 Topps Allen and Ginter Digging Deep

COMPLETE SET (20) 4.00 10.00
STATED ODDS 1:XX HOBBY
DD1 Red Beryl .40 1.00
DD2 Blue Apatite .40 1.00
DD3 Painite .40 1.00
DD4 Diamond .40 1.00
DD5 Ruby .40 1.00
DD6 Labradorite .40 1.00
DD7 Platinum .40 1.00
DD8 Pyrite .40 1.00
DD9 Chrysoberyl .40 1.00
DD10 Garnet .40 1.00
DD11 Sapphire .40 1.00
DD12 Gold .40 1.00
DD13 Jade .40 1.00
DD14 Pink Opal .40 1.00
DD15 Turquoise .40 1.00
DD16 Silver .40 1.00
DD17 Quartz .40 1.00
DD18 Lapis .40 1.00
DD19 Tanzanite .40 1.00
DD20 Copper .40 1.00

2020 Topps Allen and Ginter Down on the Farm

COMPLETE SET (15) 4.00 10.00
COMMON CARD .40 1.00
STATED ODDS 1:XX HOBBY
DFB Bale of Hay .40 1.00
DFBA Barn .40 1.00
DFC Cow .40 1.00
DFCH Chicken .40 1.00
DFCO Combine .40 1.00
DFCS Corn Stalks .40 1.00
DFD Dog .40 1.00
DFF Farmer .40 1.00
DFG Garden .40 1.00
DFH Horse .40 1.00
DFI Irrigator .40 1.00
DFP Pig .40 1.00
DFR Rooster .40 1.00
DFS Silo .40 1.00
DFT Tractor .40 1.00

2020 Topps Allen and Ginter Dual Autographs

STATED ODDS 1:XX HOBBY
EXCHANGE DEADLINE 7/31/2020
DACJ J.Gaines/C.Gaines 300.00 800.00
DADM Kid/Desus 150.00 400.00

2020 Topps Allen and Ginter Field Generals

COMPLETE SET (20) 5.00 12.00
STATED ODDS 1:XX
FG1 Sandy Alomar Jr. .25 .60
FG2 Johnny Bench .40 1.00
FG3 Gary Carter .30 .75
FG4 Willson Contreras .40 1.00
FG5 Carlton Fisk .30 .75
FG6 Joe Girardi .30 .75
FG7 Yasmani Grandal .25 .60
FG8 Joe Mauer .30 .75
FG9 Yadier Molina .40 1.00
FG10 Thurman Munson .40 1.00
FG11 Salvador Perez .30 .75
FG12 Mike Piazza .40 1.00
FG13 Jorge Posada .30 .75
FG14 Buster Posey .50 1.25
FG15 J.T. Realmuto .40 1.00
FG16 Ivan Rodriguez .30 .75
FG17 Gary Sanchez .40 1.00
FG18 Benito Santiago .25 .60
FG19 Joe Torre .30 .75
FG20 Jason Varitek .40 1.00

2020 Topps Allen and Ginter Framed Mini Autographs

STATED ODDS 1:XX HOBBY
EXCHANGE DEADLINE 7/31/2020
*BLACK/25: .6X TO 1.5X BASIC
MAAA Aristides Aquino 15.00 40.00
MAACO Andy Cohen 30.00 80.00
MAAJ Aaron Judge 100.00 250.00
MAAK Anthony Kay 4.00 10.00
MAAN Austin Nola 6.00 15.00
MAAO Adam Ottavino 4.00 10.00
MAAR Austin Riley 10.00 25.00
MAAWF Aaron Fotheringham 8.00 20.00
MABABR Baseball Britt 8.00 20.00
MABB Bo Bichette 60.00 150.00
MABBR Bobby Bradley 5.00 12.00
MABH Bryce Harper 100.00 250.00
MABL Brandon Lowe 8.00 20.00
MABM Brendan McKay
MABR Bryan Reynolds 5.00 12.00
MABS Blake Snell 6.00 15.00
MABSC Briana Scurry 12.00 30.00
MABUL Bucky Lasek 30.00 80.00
MABZ Barry Zito 8.00 20.00
MACB Cavan Biggio 12.00 30.00
MACF Cecil Fielder 15.00 40.00
MACH Courtney Hansen 20.00 50.00
MACK Carter Kieboom 10.00 25.00
MACM Charlie Morton 6.00 15.00
MACP Chris Paddack 8.00 20.00
MACR Cal Ripken Jr. 100.00 250.00
MACY Christian Yelich 30.00 80.00
MADC David Cone 15.00 40.00
MADE Doc Emrick 25.00 60.00
MADG Derrick Goold 10.00 25.00
MADL DJ LeMahieu 30.00 80.00
MADN Desus Nice 30.00 80.00
MADSW Dansby Swanson 15.00 40.00
MADV Daniel Vogelbach 4.00 10.00
MAEJ Eloy Jimenez 20.00 50.00
MAFT Fernando Tatis Jr. 75.00 200.00
MAFTH Frank Thomas 50.00 120.00
MAGL Gavin Lux 40.00 100.00
MAHJT Juice Tandron EXCH 10.00 25.00
MAJA Jim Abbott 10.00 25.00
MAJBA Johnny Bananas 50.00 120.00
MAJBU Joe Burrow 200.00 500.00
MAJC Jose Canseco 10.00 25.00
MAJCA Jared Carrabis 20.00 50.00
MAJDUN Justin Dunn 5.00 12.00
MAJDY Jeff Dye 4.00 10.00
MAJE Julian Edwards 4.00 10.00
MAJF Junior Fernandez 4.00 10.00
MAJKD J.K. Dobbins 25.00 60.00
MAJL Jesus Luzardo 8.00 20.00
MAJM John Means 4.00 10.00
MAJP Jeff Passan 12.00 30.00
MAJS Juan Soto 50.00 120.00
MAJSI Justine Siegal 10.00 25.00
MAJU Jose Urquidy 5.00 12.00
MAJY Jordan Yamamoto 5.00 12.00
MAKC Kelsey Cook 15.00 40.00
MAKH Keston Hiura 12.00 30.00
MAKJ Ken Jeong 60.00 150.00
MAKL Kyle Lewis 40.00 100.00
MAKW Kerry Wood 10.00 25.00
MALA Luis Arraez 8.00 20.00
MALGU Lourdes Gurriel Jr. 5.00 12.00
MALR Luis Robert 100.00 250.00
MALT Lane Thomas 4.00 10.00
MAMB Matt Beaty 5.00 12.00
MAMC Michael Chavis 5.00 12.00
MAMG Mitch Garver 8.00 20.00
MAMM Max Muncy 8.00 20.00
MAMP Maria Pepe 10.00 25.00
MAMT Mike Trout
MAMTA Mike Tauchman 6.00 15.00
MAMY Mike Yastrzemski 15.00 40.00
MANH Nico Hoerner 20.00 50.00
MANHO Nyjah Huston 25.00 60.00
MANK Najiah Knight 10.00 25.00
MANS Nick Senzel 6.00 15.00
MANSO Nick Solak 6.00 15.00
MANT Nick Thune 10.00 25.00
MAPA Pete Alonso 30.00 80.00
MAPC Patrick Corbin 5.00 12.00
MAPD Paul DeJong 6.00 15.00
MAPN Rob Friedman 10.00 25.00
MARA Ronald Acuna Jr. 75.00 200.00
MARNY Ryan Nyquist 12.00 30.00
MARS R.L. Stine 50.00 120.00
MASB Seth Brown 4.00 10.00
MASBR Sky Brown 40.00 100.00
MASH Sam Hilliard 6.00 15.00
MASK Sakura Kokumai 12.00 30.00
MASO Shohei Ohtani 60.00 150.00
MAST Steven Tefft 8.00 20.00
MASTB Steve Byrne 8.00 20.00
MATA Tim Anderson 10.00 25.00
MATD Tony Dunst 12.00 30.00
MATE Thairo Estrada 5.00 12.00
MATKM The Kid Mero 50.00 120.00
MAVR Victor Robles 8.00 20.00
MAWA Willians Astudillo 4.00 10.00
MAWB Walker Buehler 25.00 60.00
MAWS Will Smith 10.00 25.00
MAYA Yordan Alvarez 40.00 100.00
MAZP Zach Plesac 6.00 15.00

2020 Topps Allen and Ginter Longball Lore

COMPLETE SET (50) 20.00 50.00
STATED ODDS 1:XX
LL1 Hank Aaron .75 2.00
LL2 Ronald Acuna Jr. 1.50 4.00
LL3 Pete Alonso 1.00 2.50
LL4 Nolan Arenado .50 1.25
LL5 Jeff Bagwell .30 .75
LL6 Ernie Banks .40 1.00
LL7 Cody Bellinger .75 2.00
LL8 Kris Bryant .50 1.25
LL9 Miguel Cabrera .40 1.00
LL10 Robinson Cano .30 .75
LL11 Andre Dawson .30 .75
LL12 Cecil Fielder .25 .60
LL13 Lou Gehrig .75 2.00
LL14 Juan Gonzalez .25 .60
LL15 Ken Griffey Jr. .75 2.00
LL16 Vladimir Guerrero .30 .75
LL17 Vladimir Guerrero Jr. .75 2.00
LL18 Bryce Harper .60 1.50
LL19 Ryan Howard .30 .75
LL20 Reggie Jackson .30 .75
LL21 Chipper Jones .40 1.00
LL22 Aaron Judge 1.00 2.50
LL23 Harmon Killebrew .40 1.00
LL24 J.D. Martinez .40 1.00
LL25 Eddie Mathews .40 1.00
LL26 Hideki Matsui .40 1.00
LL27 Willie Mays .75 2.00
LL28 Willie McCovey .30 .75
LL29 Mark McGwire .60 1.50
LL30 Stan Musial .60 1.50
LL31 David Ortiz .40 1.00
LL32 Mike Piazza .40 1.00
LL33 Albert Pujols .50 1.25
LL34 Anthony Rizzo .60 1.50
LL35 Alex Rodriguez .50 1.25
LL36 Babe Ruth 1.00 2.50
LL37 Mike Schmidt .60 1.50
LL38 Gary Sheffield .25 .60
LL39 Giancarlo Stanton .40 1.00
LL40 Willie Stargell .30 .75
LL41 Darryl Strawberry .25 .60
LL42 Frank Thomas .40 1.00
LL43 Jim Thome .30 .75
LL44 Mike Trout 2.00 5.00
LL45 Mo Vaughn .25 .60
LL46 Larry Walker .30 .75
LL47 Ted Williams .75 2.00
LL48 Dave Winfield .30 .75
LL49 Carl Yastrzemski .60 1.50
LL50 Christian Yelich .50 1.25

2020 Topps Allen and Ginter Mini

*MINI 1-300: 1X TO 2.5X BASIC
*MINI 1-300 RC: .6X TO 1.5X BASIC RCs
*MINI SP 301-350: .6X TO 1.5X BASIC
MINI ODDS 1:XX HOBBY
MINI SP ODDS 1:XX HOBBY
EXT CARDS FOUND IN RIP PACKS
STATED PLATE ODDS 1:XXXX HOBBY
PLATE PRINT RUN 1 SET PER COLOR
BLACK-CYAN-MAGENTA-YELLOW ISSUED
NO PLATE PRICING DUE TO SCARCITY
351 Albert Pujols EXT 10.00 25.00
352 Mike Trout EXT 40.00 100.00
353 Shohei Ohtani EXT 10.00 25.00
354 Chipper Jones EXT 8.00 20.00
355 John Smoltz EXT 8.00 20.00
356 Ronald Acuna Jr. EXT 15.00 40.00
357 Brooks Robinson EXT 20.00 50.00
358 Cal Ripken Jr. EXT 20.00 50.00
359 Carl Yastrzemski EXT 12.00 30.00
360 Ted Williams EXT 15.00 40.00
361 David Ortiz EXT 8.00 20.00
362 Roger Clemens EXT 10.00 25.00
363 Jackie Robinson EXT 12.00 30.00
364 Sandy Koufax EXT 15.00 40.00
365 Kris Bryant EXT 10.00 25.00
366 Ryne Sandberg EXT 10.00 25.00
367 Frank Thomas EXT 12.00 30.00
368 Johnny Bench EXT 8.00 20.00
369 Francisco Lindor EXT 8.00 20.00
370 Carlos Correa EXT 8.00 20.00
371 Jose Altuve EXT 6.00 15.00
372 Justin Verlander EXT 8.00 20.00
373 George Brett EXT 15.00 40.00
374 Clayton Kershaw EXT 15.00 40.00
375 Cody Bellinger EXT 12.00 30.00
376 Mike Piazza EXT 12.00 30.00

377 Hank Aaron EXT 15.00 40.00
378 Christian Yelich EXT 15.00 40.00
379 Pedro Martinez EXT 8.00 20.00
380 Jacob deGrom EXT 8.00 20.00
381 Pete Alonso EXT 15.00 40.00
382 Aaron Judge EXT 20.00 50.00
383 Babe Ruth EXT 20.00 50.00
384 Mariano Rivera EXT 15.00 40.00
385 Reggie Jackson EXT 10.00 25.00
386 Rickey Henderson EXT 15.00 40.00
387 Bryce Harper EXT 12.00 30.00
388 Roberto Clemente EXT 20.00 50.00
389 Fernando Tatis Jr. EXT 15.00 40.00
390 Buster Posey EXT 10.00 25.00
391 Willie Mays EXT 15.00 40.00
392 Alex Rodriguez EXT 10.00 25.00
393 Ichiro EXT 12.00 30.00
394 Ken Griffey Jr. EXT 15.00 40.00
395 Randy Johnson EXT 8.00 20.00
396 Mark McGwire EXT 12.00 30.00
397 Nolan Ryan EXT 25.00 60.00
398 Vladimir Guerrero Jr. EXT 15.00 40.00
399 Juan Soto EXT 25.00 60.00
400 Max Scherzer EXT 8.00 20.00

2020 Topps Allen and Ginter Mini Black Border

*MINI BLK 1-300: 1.5X TO 4X BASIC
*MINI BLK 1-300 RC: 1X TO 2.5X BASIC RCs
*MINI BLK SP 301-350: 1X TO 2.5X BASIC
MINI BLK ODDS 1:XXX HOBBY

2020 Topps Allen and Ginter Mini Brooklyn Back

*MINI BRKLN 1-300: 12X TO 30X BASIC
*MINI BRKLN 1-300 RC: 8X TO 20X BASIC RCs
*MINI BRKLN 301-350: 5X TO 12X BASIC
STATED ODDS 1:XXX HOBBY
STATED PRINT RUN 25 SER.#'d SETS
17 Ken Griffey Jr. 40.00 100.00
18 George Brett 25.00 60.00
29 Willie Mays 25.00 60.00
32 Ichiro 30.00 80.00
35 Rickey Henderson 20.00 50.00
40 Mariano Rivera 15.00 40.00
51 Roberto Clemente 30.00 80.00
80 DJ LeMahieu 20.00 50.00

2020 Topps Allen and Ginter Mini Gold Border

*MINI GOLD 1-300: 1.2X TO 3X BASIC
*MINI GOLD 1-300 RC: .75X TO 2X BASIC RCs
*MINI GOLD 301-350: .75X TO 2X BASIC
RANDOMLY INSERTED IN RETAIL PACKS

2020 Topps Allen and Ginter Mini No Number

*MINI NNO 1-300: 5X TO 12X BASIC
*MINI NNO 1-300 RC: 3X TO 8X BASIC RCs
*MINI NNO 301-350: 2X TO 5X BASIC

2020 Topps Allen and Ginter Mini Stained Glass

*MINI STND GLS 1-150: 30X TO 80X BASIC
*MINI STND GLS 1-150 RC: 25X TO 60X BASIC RCs
*MINI STND GLS 351-400: 1.5X TO 4X BASIC
STATED ODDS 1:XXX HOBBY
ANNCD PRINT RUN OF 25 SETS
17 Ken Griffey Jr. 75.00 200.00
18 George Brett 60.00 150.00
29 Willie Mays 50.00 120.00
32 Ichiro 60.00 150.00
35 Rickey Henderson 40.00 100.00
40 Mariano Rivera 30.00 80.00
51 Roberto Clemente 60.00 150.00
79 Sandy Koufax 60.00 150.00
80 DJ LeMahieu 100.00 250.00
85 Mike Trout 125.00 300.00
110 Albert Pujols 60.00 150.00

2020 Topps Allen and Ginter Mini 9 Ways to First Base

COMPLETE SET (9) 8.00 20.00
STATED ODDS 1:XXX HOBBY
M9WF1 Dropped Third Strike 1.25 3.00
M9WF2 Single 1.25 3.00
M9WF3 Base On Balls 1.25 3.00
M9WF4 Hit By Pitch 1.25 3.00
M9WF5 Fielder Interference 1.25 3.00
M9WF6 Fielder's Choice 1.25 3.00
M9WF7 Fielding Error 1.25 3.00
M9WF8 Catcher's Interference 1.25 3.00
M9WF9 Batted Ball hits another runner before a fielder touches it 1.25 3.00

2020 Topps Allen and Ginter Mini Behemoths Beneath

2019 Topps Allen and Ginter Mini Chugging Along 15.00 40.00
2019 Topps Allen and Ginter Mini Chugging Along
MGB1 Colossal Squid 1.25 3.00
MGB2 Blue Whale 1.25 3.00
MGB3 Fin Whale 1.25 3.00
MGB4 Whale Shark 1.25 3.00
MGB5 Sperm Whale 1.25 3.00
MGB6 Giant Manta Ray 1.25 3.00
MGB7 Lion's Mane Jelly 1.25 3.00
MGB8 Orca Whale 1.25 3.00
MGB9 Great White Shark 1.25 3.00
MGB10 Giant Oarfish 1.25 3.00
MGB11 Japanese Spider Crab 1.25 3.00
MGB12 Ocean Sunfish 1.25 3.00
MGB13 Giant Pacific Octopus 1.25 3.00
MGB14 Basking Shark 1.25 3.00
MGB15 Portuguese Man-of-War 1.25 3.00
MGB16 Giant Sea Star 1.25 3.00
MGB17 Giant Clam 1.25 3.00
MGB18 Anglerfish 1.25 3.00
MGB19 Sea Anemone 1.25 3.00
MGB20 Beluga Whale 1.25 3.00

2020 Topps Allen and Ginter Mini Booming Cities

COMPLETE SET (15) 12.00 30.00
STATED ODDS 1:XXX HOBBY
BC1 Dubai United Arab Emirates 1.25 3.00
BC2 Shanghai China 1.25 3.00
BC3 Lagos Nigeria 1.25 3.00
BC4 Dar es Salaam Tanzania 1.25 3.00
BC5 Kampala Uganda 1.25 3.00
BC6 Karachi Pakistan 1.25 3.00
BC7 Dhaka Bangladesh 1.25 3.00
BC8 Istanbul Turkey 1.25 3.00
BC9 Sao Paulo Brazil 1.25 3.00
BC10 Jakarta Indonesia 1.25 3.00
BC11 Singapore 1.25 3.00
BC12 Riyadh Saudi Arabia 1.25 3.00
BC13 Tokyo Japan 1.25 3.00
BC14 Shenzhen China 1.25 3.00
BC15 Seattle Washington, USA 1.25 3.00

2020 Topps Allen and Ginter Mini Buggin Out

COMPLETE SET (20) 15.00 40.00
STATED ODDS 1:XXX HOBBY
MBO1 Ladybird Beetle 1.25 3.00
MBO2 Monarch Butterfly 1.25 3.00
MBO3 Praying Mantis 1.25 3.00
MBO4 Hercules Beetle 1.25 3.00
MBO5 Thorn Bug 1.25 3.00
MBO6 Australian Walking Stick 1.25 3.00
MBO7 Atlas Moth 1.25 3.00
MBO8 Calleta Silkmoth 1.25 3.00
MBO9 Scorpion Fly 1.25 3.00
MBO10 Peacock Spider 1.25 3.00
MBO11 Spiny Orb Weaver 1.25 3.00
MBO12 Leafcutter Ant 1.25 3.00
MBO13 Red Postman Butterfly 1.25 3.00
MBO14 Giraffe Weevil 1.25 3.00
MBO15 Bumblebee 1.25 3.00
MBO16 Fire Ant 1.25 3.00
MBO17 Old World Swallowtail 1.25 3.00
MBO18 Caterpillar 1.25 3.00
MBO19 Dragonfly 1.25 3.00
MBO20 Treehopper 1.25 3.00

2020 Topps Allen and Ginter Mini Citadels and Safeholds

COMPLETE SET (20) 15.00 40.00
STATED ODDS 1:XXX HOBBY
MCS1 Moorish Castle 1.25 3.00
MCS2 Rumeli Castle 1.25 3.00
MCS3 Dover Castle 1.25 3.00
MCS4 Murud-Janjira 1.25 3.00
MCS5 Prague Castle 1.25 3.00
MCS6 The Tower of London 1.25 3.00
MCS7 Citadel of Aleppo 1.25 3.00
MCS8 Bourtange Fort 1.25 3.00
MCS9 Caerphilly Castle 1.25 3.00
MCS10 Ankara Castle 1.25 3.00
MCS11 Spis Castle 1.25 3.00
MCS12 Mehrangarh Fort 1.25 3.00
MCS13 Krak Des Chevaliers 1.25 3.00
MCS14 Conwy Castle 1.25 3.00
MCS15 Fort de Douaumont 1.25 3.00
MCS16 Alcazar of Toledo 1.25 3.00
MCS17 Edinburgh Castle 1.25 3.00
MCS18 Malbork Castle 1.25 3.00
MCS19 Konigstein Fortress 1.25 3.00
MCS20 Balmoral Castle 1.25 3.00

2020 Topps Allen and Ginter Mini DNA Relics

STATED ODDS 1:XXX HOBBY
PRINT RUNS BW/N 17-25 COPIES PER
MDNARFB Fossilized Bison/25 100.00 250.00
MDNARFC Fossilized Crocodile/25 100.00 250.00
MDNARFM Fossilized Mammoth/25 125.00 300.00
MDNARFP Fossilized Pterosaur
MDNARFS Fossilized Spinosaurus/17 200.00 500.00
MDNARFSF Fossilized Sawfish
MDNARFSH Fossilized Shark/25 100.00 250.00
MDNARFT Fossilized Turtle/20 100.00 250.00
MDNARFW Fossilized Whale/25 100.00 250.00

2020 Topps Allen and Ginter Mini Framed Relics

STATED ODDS 1:XXX HOBBY
MFRAA Aristides Aquino 5.00 12.00
MFRAB Andrew Benintendi 4.00 10.00
MFRABR Alex Bregman 4.00 10.00
MFRAJ Aaron Judge 10.00 25.00
MFRAP Andy Pettitte 3.00 8.00
MFRAPU Albert Pujols 5.00 12.00
MFRAR Anthony Rizzo 5.00 12.00
MFRARO Alex Rodriguez 5.00 12.00
MFRBB Bo Bichette 10.00 25.00
MFRBF Bob Feller 25.00 60.00
MFRBH Bryce Harper 10.00 25.00
MFRBL Barry Larkin 3.00 8.00
MFRBP Buster Posey 5.00 12.00
MFRCB Cody Bellinger 5.00 12.00
MFRCBI Craig Biggio 3.00 8.00
MFRCC Carlos Correa 4.00 10.00
MFRCJ Chipper Jones 6.00 15.00
MFRCK Clayton Kershaw 6.00 15.00
MFRCR Cal Ripken Jr. 10.00 25.00
MFRCS CC Sabathia 3.00 8.00
MFRDL DJ LeMahieu 6.00 15.00
MFRDO David Ortiz 4.00 10.00
MFRDP David Price 3.00 8.00
MFREJ Eloy Jimenez 5.00 12.00
MFRFL Francisco Lindor 4.00 10.00
MFRFT Fernando Tatis Jr. 10.00 25.00
MFRGB George Brett 12.00 30.00
MFRGT Gleyber Torres 8.00 20.00
MFRHA Hank Aaron 25.00 60.00
MFRIR Ivan Rodriguez 3.00 8.00
MFRI Ichiro 8.00 20.00
MFRJA Jose Altuve 3.00 8.00
MFRJB Javier Baez 5.00 12.00
MFRJBA Jeff Bagwell 3.00 8.00
MFRJBE Johnny Bench 20.00 50.00
MFRJM J.D. Martinez 4.00 10.00
MFRJV Justin Verlander 4.00 10.00
MFRKB Kris Bryant 5.00 12.00
MFRKG Ken Griffey Jr. 12.00 30.00
MFRKH Keston Hiura 5.00 12.00
MFRLR Luis Robert 20.00 50.00
MFRMB Mookie Betts 8.00 20.00
MFRMC Miguel Cabrera 4.00 10.00
MFRMM Manny Machado 4.00 10.00
MFRMMC Mark McGwire 8.00 20.00
MFRMP Mike Piazza 4.00 10.00
MFRMR Mariano Rivera 6.00 15.00
MFRMT Mike Trout 15.00 40.00
MFRNG Nomar Garciaparra 3.00 8.00
MFRNS Nick Senzel 4.00 10.00
MFRPA Pete Alonso 8.00 20.00
MFRPG Paul Goldschmidt 4.00 10.00
MFRPM Pedro Martinez 3.00 8.00
MFRRA Ronald Acuna Jr. 15.00 40.00
MFRRAL Roberto Alomar 5.00 12.00
MFRRC Roger Clemens 6.00 15.00
MFRRD Rafael Devers 5.00 12.00
MFRRH Rickey Henderson 4.00 10.00
MFRRHO Rhys Hoskins 5.00 12.00
MFRRJ Reggie Jackson 10.00 25.00
MFRRJO Randy Johnson 6.00 15.00
MFRSO Shohei Ohtani 10.00 25.00
MFRTG Tom Glavine 3.00 8.00
MFRTGW Tony Gwynn 6.00 15.00
MFRTW Ted Williams 200.00 500.00
MFRVG Vladimir Guerrero Jr. 6.00 15.00
MFRWB Wade Boggs 3.00 8.00
MFRWM Willie Mays 300.00 800.00
MFRYA Yordan Alvarez 10.00 25.00
MFRYM Yadier Molina 5.00 12.00

2020 Topps Allen and Ginter Mini Safari Sights

COMPLETE SET (15) 12.00 30.00
STATED ODDS 1:XXX HOBBY
SS1 Elephant 1.25 3.00
SS2 Cheetah 1.25 3.00
SS3 Crocodile 1.25 3.00
SS4 Gazelle 1.25 3.00
SS5 Gray Crowned Crane 1.25 3.00
SS6 Hyena 1.25 3.00
SS7 Lion 1.25 3.00
SS8 Warthog 1.25 3.00
SS9 Vervet Monkey 1.25 3.00
SS10 Giraffe 1.25 3.00
SS11 Zebra 1.25 3.00
SS12 Leopard 1.25 3.00
SS13 Hippo 1.25 3.00
SS14 Lion Cub 1.25 3.00
SS15 Safari Truck 1.25 3.00

2020 Topps Allen and Ginter Mini Where Monsters Live

COMPLETE SET (10) 8.00 20.00
STATED ODDS 1:XXX HOBBY
MWML1 The Attic 1.25 3.00
MWML2 A Cave 1.25 3.00
MWML3 The Closet 1.25 3.00
MWML4 The Ocean 1.25 3.00
MWML5 An Old Trunk 1.25 3.00
MWML6 A Sewer Drain 1.25 3.00
MWML7 The Swamp 1.25 3.00
MWML8 A Dark Tunnel 1.25 3.00
MWML9 Under the Bed 1.25 3.00
MWML10 Under the Stairs 1.25 3.00

2020 Topps Allen and Ginter N43 Box Toppers

STATED ODDS 1:XX HOBBY BOXES
BLNAB Alex Bregman .60 1.50
BLNBB Bo Bichette 3.00 8.00
BLNBH Bryce Harper 1.00 2.50
BLNCY Christian Yelich .75 2.00
BLNFL Francisco Lindor .60 1.50
BLNFT Fernando Tatis Jr. 2.50 6.00
BLNGC Gerrit Cole 1.00 2.50
BLNGT Gleyber Torres 1.25 3.00
BLNJB Javier Baez .75 2.00
BLNJBE Jose Berrios .50 1.25
BLNJV Joey Votto .60 1.50
BLNKB Kris Bryant .75 2.00
BLNLR Luis Robert 4.00 10.00
BLNMB Mookie Betts 1.25 3.00
BLNMT Mike Trout 3.00 8.00
BLNNA Nolan Arenado .75 2.00
BLNPA Pete Alonso 1.50 4.00
BLNRA Ronald Acuna Jr. 2.50 6.00
BLNWB Walker Buehler .75 2.00
BLNYA Yordan Alvarez 2.00 5.00

2020 Topps Allen and Ginter Presidential Pin Relics

STATED ODDS 1:XXX HOBBY
PRINT RUNS BW/N 15-25 COPIES PER
FPRBC Bill Clinton/25 100.00 250.00
FPRBO Barack Obama/24 200.00 500.00
FPRDE Dwight D. Eisenhower/25 100.00 250.00
FPRGF Gerald Ford/25 100.00 250.00
FPRGHWB George H.W. Bush/24 100.00 250.00
FPRGWB George W. Bush/15 100.00 250.00
FPRJC Jimmy Carter/20 100.00 250.00
FPRJFK John F. Kennedy/25 200.00 500.00
FPRLBJ Lyndon B. Johnson/25 100.00 250.00
FPRRN Richard Nixon/25 100.00 250.00
FPRRR Ronald Reagan/20 125.00 300.00

2020 Topps Allen and Ginter Reach for the Sky

COMPLETE SET (15) 3.00 8.00
STATED ODDS 1:XX
RFTS1 John Hancock Center .30 .75
RFTS2 Chrysler Building .30 .75
RFTS3 Wilshire Grand Center .30 .75
RFTS4 Comcast Tech Tower .30 .75
RFTS5 Empire State Building .30 .75
RFTS6 432 Park Avenue .30 .75
RFTS7 Steinway Tower .30 .75
RFTS8 Willis Tower .30 .75
RFTS9 Petronas Towers .30 .75
RFTS10 Lakhta Center .30 .75
RFTS11 Taipei 101 .30 .75
RFTS12 One World Trade Center .30 .75
RFTS13 Abraj Al-Bait Clock Tower .30 .75
RFTS14 Shanghai Tower .30 .75
RFTS15 Burj Khalifa .30 .75

2020 Topps Allen and Ginter Relics

VERSION A ODDS 1:XX HOBBY
VERSION B ODDS 1:XX HOBBY
FSRAAA Albert Almora Jr. A 2.50 6.00
FSRAAC Andy Cohen A 3.00 8.00
FSRAAF Aaron Wheelz Fotheringham A 3.00 8.00
FSRAAG Alex Gordon A 2.50 6.00
FSRAAO Adam Ottavino A 2.00 5.00
FSRAAR Austin Riley A 4.00 10.00
FSRABB Baseball Brit Joey Mellows A 2.50 6.00
FSRABL Bucky Lasek A 3.00 8.00
FSRABS Briana Scurry A 2.50 6.00
FSRACF Clint Frazier A 2.50 6.00
FSRACH Courtney Hansen A 2.50 6.00
FSRACS Chris Sale A 3.00 8.00
FSRACV Christian Vazquez A 2.00 5.00
FSRADG Derrick Goold A 2.50 6.00
FSRADGR Didi Gregorius A 2.50 6.00
FSRADP Dustin Pedroia A 3.00 8.00
FSRAEL Evan Longoria A 2.50 6.00
FSRAGU Gio Urshela A 3.00 8.00
FSRAJB Johnny Bananas A 10.00 25.00
FSRAJBJ Jackie Bradley Jr. A 3.00 8.00
FSRAJC Jared Carrabis A 8.00 20.00
FSRAJCU Johnny Cueto A 2.50 6.00
FSRAJD Jeff Dye A 2.50 6.00
FSRAJH J.A. Happ A 2.50 6.00
FSRAJJ Josh James A 3.00 8.00
FSRAJLU Joey Lucchesi A 2.00 5.00
FSRAJM John Means A 2.00 5.00
FSRAJP Jeff Passan A 2.50 6.00
FSRAJS Justine Siegal A 3.00 8.00
FSRAJSE Jean Segura A 2.50 6.00
FSRAKC Kelsey Cook A 3.00 8.00
FSRAKD Khris Davis A 3.00 8.00
FSRAKW Kolten Wong A 2.50 6.00
FSRALG Lourdes Gurriel Jr. A 2.50 6.00
FSRALV Luke Voit A 4.00 10.00
FSRAMC Michael Conforto A 2.50 6.00
FSRAMCA Matt Carpenter A 3.00 8.00
FSRAMDE Mike Doc Emrick A 3.00 8.00
FSRAMG Mitch Garver A 2.00 5.00
FSRAMO Marcell Ozuna A 3.00 8.00
FSRAMP Maria Pepe A 3.00 8.00
FSRANH Nyjah Huston A 2.50 6.00
FSRANT Nick Thune A 2.50 6.00
FSRAOA Orlando Arcia A 2.00 5.00
FSRARF Rob Friedman A 2.50 6.00
FSRARL Ramon Laureano A 3.00 8.00
FSRARS R.L. Stine A 5.00 12.00
FSRASB Steve Byrne A 2.50 6.00
FSRASK Sakura Kokumai A 3.00 8.00
FSRASKI Scott Kingery A 2.50 6.00
FSRAST Steven Tefft A 2.50 6.00
FSRATD Tony Dunst A 2.50 6.00
FSRAWB Walker Buehler A 4.00 10.00
FSRAYK Yusei Kikuchi A 2.50 6.00
FSRBAB Andrew Benintendi B 3.00 8.00
FSRBAC Aroldis Chapman B 3.00 8.00
FSRBAM Andrew McCutchen B 3.00 8.00
FSRBAME Austin Meadows B 2.50 6.00
FSRBAN Aaron Nola B 3.00 8.00
FSRBBG Brett Gardner B 3.00 8.00
FSRBBL Brandon Lowe B 3.00 8.00
FSRBBR Brendan Rodgers B 3.00 8.00
FSRBCBL Charlie Blackmon B 3.00 8.00
FSRBCC Carlos Carrasco B 2.00 5.00
FSRBCY Christian Yelich B 4.00 10.00
FSRBDD David Dahl B 2.00 5.00
FSRBDH Dakota Hudson B 2.50 6.00
FSRBDS Dansby Swanson B 3.00 8.00
FSRBEA Elvis Andrus B 2.50 6.00
FSRBER Eduardo Rodriguez B 2.00 5.00
FSRBES Eugenio Suarez B 2.50 6.00
FSRBGP Gregory Polanco B 2.50 6.00
FSRBGS Gary Sanchez B 3.00 8.00
FSRBGSP George Springer B 2.50 6.00
FSRBGST Giancarlo Stanton B 3.00 8.00
FSRBJB Jose Berrios B 2.50 6.00
FSRBJF Jack Flaherty B 2.50 6.00
FSRBJG Joey Gallo B 3.00 8.00
FSRBJH Josh Hader B 2.00 5.00
FSRBJHE Jason Heyward B 2.50 6.00
FSRBJL Jon Lester B 2.50 6.00
FSRBJM Jeff McNeil B 2.50 6.00
FSRBJP James Paxton B 2.50 6.00
FSRBJPE Joc Pederson B 2.50 6.00
FSRBJPO Jorge Polanco B 2.50 6.00
FSRBJR J.T. Realmuto B 3.00 8.00
FSRBJS Jorge Soler B 3.00 8.00
FSRBJV Joey Votto B 3.00 8.00
FSRBKJ Kenley Jansen B 2.50 6.00
FSRBKS Kyle Schwarber B 3.00 8.00
FSRBLC Lorenzo Cain B 2.00 5.00
FSRBLCA Luis Castillo B 2.50 6.00
FSRBLS Luis Severino B 2.50 6.00
FSRBMA Miguel Andujar B 3.00 8.00
FSRBMC Michael Chavis B 2.50 6.00
FSRBMM Max Muncy B 2.50 6.00
FSRBMO Matt Olson B 2.00 5.00
FSRBMS Miguel Sano B 2.50 6.00
FSRBMSO Mike Soroka B 3.00 8.00
FSRBMST Marcus Stroman B 2.50 6.00
FSRBMT Masahiro Tanaka B 3.00 8.00
FSRBOA Ozzie Albies B 3.00 8.00
FSRBPD Paul DeJong B 3.00 8.00
FSRBRB Ryan Braun B 2.50 6.00
FSRBSC Shin-Soo Choo B 2.50 6.00
FSRBSG Sonny Gray B 2.50 6.00
FSRBTA Tim Anderson B 3.00 8.00
FSRBTS Trevor Story B 3.00 8.00
FSRBWA Willians Astudillo B 2.00 5.00
FSRBWC Willson Contreras B 3.00 8.00
FSRBXB Xander Bogaerts B 3.00 8.00
FSRBYG Yuli Gurriel B 2.50 6.00

2020 Topps Allen and Ginter Rip Cards Ripped

UNRIPPED STATED ODDS 1:XXX HOBBY
PRINT RUNS B/WN XX-XX COPIES PER
PRICED WITH CLEANLY RIPPED BACKS
RIP1 Hank Aaron 6.00 15.00
RIP2 Ronald Acuna Jr. 12.00 30.00
RIP3 Roberto Alomar 2.50 6.00
RIP4 Pete Alonso 8.00 20.00
RIP5 Jose Altuve 2.50 6.00
RIP6 Yordan Alvarez 10.00 25.00
RIP7 Nolan Arenado 4.00 10.00
RIP8 Javier Baez 4.00 10.00
RIP9 Jeff Bagwell 2.50 6.00
RIP10 Ernie Banks 3.00 8.00
RIP11 Cody Bellinger 6.00 15.00
RIP12 Johnny Bench 3.00 8.00
RIP13 Bo Bichette 15.00 40.00
RIP14 Craig Biggio 2.50 6.00
RIP15 Wade Boggs 2.50 6.00
RIP16 Alex Bregman 3.00 8.00
RIP17 George Brett 6.00 15.00
RIP18 Kris Bryant 4.00 10.00
RIP19 Walker Buehler 4.00 10.00
RIP20 Miguel Cabrera 3.00 8.00
RIP21 Rod Carew 2.50 6.00
RIP22 Steve Carlton 2.50 6.00
RIP23 Roger Clemens 4.00 10.00
RIP24 Roberto Clemente 8.00 20.00
RIP25 Ty Cobb 5.00 12.00
RIP26 Gerrit Cole 5.00 12.00
RIP27 Jacob deGrom 3.00 8.00
RIP28 Rafael Devers 4.00 10.00
RIP29 Whitey Ford 2.50 6.00
RIP30 Lou Gehrig 6.00 15.00
RIP31 Bob Gibson 2.50 6.00
RIP32 Paul Goldschmidt 3.00 8.00
RIP33 Gavin Lux 12.00 30.00
RIP34 Ken Griffey Jr. 6.00 15.00
RIP35 Vladimir Guerrero 2.50 6.00
RIP36 Vladimir Guerrero Jr. 6.00 15.00
RIP37 Tony Gwynn 3.00 8.00
RIP38 Bryce Harper 5.00 12.00
RIP39 Rickey Henderson 3.00 8.00
RIP40 Keston Hiura 4.00 10.00
RIP41 Rhys Hoskins 4.00 10.00
RIP42 Reggie Jackson 2.50 6.00
RIP43 Eloy Jimenez 6.00 15.00
RIP44 Randy Johnson 3.00 8.00
RIP45 Chipper Jones 3.00 8.00
RIP46 Aaron Judge 8.00 20.00
RIP47 Al Kaline 3.00 8.00
RIP48 Clayton Kershaw 6.00 15.00
RIP49 Harmon Killebrew 3.00 8.00
RIP50 Sandy Koufax 6.00 15.00
RIP51 Barry Larkin 2.50 6.00
RIP52 Manny Machado 3.00 8.00
RIP53 Pedro Martinez 2.50 6.00
RIP54 Don Mattingly 6.00 15.00
RIP55 Willie Mays 6.00 15.00
RIP56 Willie McCovey 2.50 6.00
RIP57 Mark McGwire 5.00 12.00
RIP58 Yadier Molina 3.00 8.00
RIP59 Joe Morgan 2.50 6.00
RIP60 Thurman Munson 3.00 8.00
RIP61 Eddie Murray 2.50 6.00
RIP62 Stan Musial 5.00 12.00
RIP63 Shohei Ohtani 4.00 10.00
RIP64 David Ortiz 3.00 8.00
RIP65 Jim Palmer 2.50 6.00
RIP66 Andy Pettitte 2.50 6.00
RIP67 Mike Piazza 3.00 8.00
RIP68 Buster Posey 4.00 10.00
RIP69 Albert Pujols 4.00 10.00
RIP70 Cal Ripken Jr. 10.00 25.00
RIP71 Mariano Rivera 4.00 10.00
RIP72 Anthony Rizzo 5.00 12.00
RIP73 Jackie Robinson 3.00 8.00
RIP74 Brooks Robinson 2.50 6.00
RIP75 Frank Robinson 2.50 6.00
RIP76 Alex Rodriguez 4.00 10.00
RIP77 Ivan Rodriguez 2.50 6.00
RIP78 Babe Ruth 8.00 20.00
RIP79 Nolan Ryan 10.00 25.00
RIP80 Ryne Sandberg 6.00 15.00
RIP81 Max Scherzer 3.00 8.00
RIP82 Mike Schmidt 5.00 12.00
RIP83 Tom Seaver 2.50 6.00
RIP84 Ozzie Smith 4.00 10.00
RIP85 John Smoltz 3.00 8.00
RIP86 Duke Snider 2.50 6.00
RIP87 Juan Soto 10.00 25.00
RIP88 Willie Stargell 2.50 6.00
RIP89 Stephen Strasburg 3.00 8.00
RIP90 Ichiro 4.00 10.00
RIP91 Fernando Tatis Jr. 12.00 30.00
RIP92 Frank Thomas 3.00 8.00
RIP93 Jim Thome 2.50 6.00
RIP94 Gleyber Torres 6.00 15.00
RIP95 Mike Trout 15.00 40.00
RIP96 Justin Verlander 3.00 8.00
RIP97 Ted Williams 6.00 15.00
RIP98 Carl Yastrzemski 5.00 12.00
RIP99 Christian Yelich 4.00 10.00
RIP100 Robin Yount 3.00 8.00

2020 Topps Allen and Ginter Chrome

1 Tom Glavine .30 .75
2 Randy Johnson .40 1.00
3 Paul Goldschmidt .40 1.00
4 Larry Doby .30 .75
5 Walker Buehler .50 1.25
6 John Smoltz .40 1.00
7 Tim Lincecum .30 .75
8 Jeff Bagwell .30 .75
9 Rhys Hoskins .50 1.25
10 Rod Carew .30 .75
11 Lou Gehrig .75 2.00
12 George Springer .30 .75
13 Aaron Judge 1.00 2.50
14 Aaron Nola .40 1.00
15 Kris Bryant .50 1.25
16 Bryce Harper .60 1.50
17 Ken Griffey Jr. .75 2.00
18 George Brett .75 2.00
19 Keston Hiura .50 1.25
20 Joe Mauer .30 .75
21 Ted Williams .75 2.00
22 Eddie Mathews .40 1.00
23 Jorge Soler .40 1.00
24 Shohei Ohtani .50 1.25
25 Carl Yastrzemski .60 1.50
26 Willie McCovey .30 .75
27 Joe Morgan .30 .75
28 Juan Soto 1.25 3.00
29 Willie Mays .75 2.00
30 Eloy Jimenez .75 2.00
31 Babe Ruth 1.00 2.50
32 Ichiro .50 1.25
33 Edgar Martinez .30 .75
34 Pete Alonso 1.00 2.50
35 Rickey Henderson .40 1.00
36 Alex Bregman .40 1.00
37 Mike Mussina .30 .75
38 Miguel Cabrera .40 1.00
39 Andy Pettitte .30 .75
40 Mariano Rivera .50 1.25
41 David Ortiz .40 1.00
42 Jackie Robinson .40 1.00
43 Matt Chapman .40 1.00
44 Rafael Devers .50 1.25
45 Yoan Moncada .40 1.00
46 Pedro Martinez .30 .75
47 Freddie Freeman .50 1.25
48 Ketel Marte .30 .75
49 Roger Clemens .50 1.25
50 Vladimir Guerrero Jr. .75 2.00
51 Roberto Clemente 1.00 2.50
52 Ivan Rodriguez .30 .75
53 Mike Soroka .40 1.00
54 Victor Robles .50 1.25
55 Nick Senzel .40 1.00
56 Ozzie Albies .40 1.00
57 Eddie Murray .30 .75
58 Christian Yelich .50 1.25
59 Duke Snider .30 .75
60 Steve Carlton .30 .75
61 Jim Thome .30 .75
62 Whitey Ford .30 .75
63 Marcus Semien .25 .60
64 Andre Dawson .30 .75
65 Cody Bellinger .75 2.00
66 Darryl Strawberry .25 .60
67 Mookie Betts .75 2.00
68 Nomar Garciaparra .30 .75
69 Al Kaline .40 1.00
70 Don Mattingly .75 2.00
71 Vladimir Guerrero .30 .75
72 Johnny Bench .40 1.00
73 Mark McGwire .60 1.50
74 Ty Cobb .60 1.50
75 Joey Votto .40 1.00
76 Chipper Jones .40 1.00
77 Javier Baez .50 1.25
78 Xander Bogaerts .40 1.00
79 Sandy Koufax .75 2.00
80 DJ LeMahieu .40 1.00
81 Barry Zito .30 .75
82 Andrew Benintendi .40 1.00
83 J.D. Martinez .40 1.00
84 Clayton Kershaw .75 2.00
85 Mike Trout 2.00 5.00
86 Anthony Rizzo .60 1.50
87 Trevor Story .40 1.00
88 Ronald Acuna Jr. 1.50 4.00
89 Paul Molitor .40 1.00
90 Jack Flaherty .30 .75
91 Dave Winfield .30 .75
92 Barry Larkin .30 .75
93 Francisco Lindor .40 1.00
94 Max Fried .40 1.00
95 Manny Machado .40 1.00
96 Frank Thomas .40 1.00
97 Aristides Aquino RC 1.25 3.00
98 Cal Ripken Jr. 1.25 3.00
99 Gavin Lux RC 4.00 10.00
100 Max Scherzer .40 1.00
101 Brooks Robinson .30 .75
102 Robin Yount .40 1.00
103 Tim Anderson .40 1.00
104 Hank Aaron .75 2.00
105 Todd Helton .30 .75
106 Willie Stargell .30 .75
107 Roger Maris .40 1.00
108 Gary Carter .30 .75
109 Reggie Jackson .30 .75
110 Albert Pujols .50 1.25
111 Buster Posey .50 1.25
112 Bo Bichette RC 6.00 15.00
113 Luis Gonzalez .25 .60
114 Gleyber Torres .75 2.00
115 Fernando Tatis Jr. 1.50 4.00
116 Honus Wagner .40 1.00
117 Ernie Banks .40 1.00
118 Yordan Alvarez RC 3.00 8.00
119 Giancarlo Stanton .40 1.00
120 Bob Gibson .30 .75
121 Zack Greinke .30 .75
122 Trea Turner .30 .75
123 Mike Piazza .40 1.00
124 Juan Marichal .30 .75
125 Craig Biggio .30 .75
126 Wade Boggs .30 .75
127 Jose Altuve .30 .75
128 Tony Gwynn .40 1.00
129 Josh Bell .30 .75
130 Nolan Arenado .50 1.25
131 Stan Musial .60 1.50
132 Jim Palmer .30 .75
133 Justin Verlander .40 1.00
134 Roberto Alomar .30 .75
135 Harmon Killebrew .40 1.00
136 Carlos Correa .40 1.00
137 Yadier Molina .40 1.00
138 Tom Seaver .30 .75
139 Nolan Ryan 1.25 3.00
140 Joe Torre .30 .75
141 Mike Schmidt .60 1.50
142 Patrick Corbin .30 .75
143 Carlton Fisk .30 .75
144 Warren Spahn .30 .75
145 Alex Rodriguez .50 1.25
146 Jacob deGrom .40 1.00
147 Jose Berrios .30 .75
148 David Wright .30 .75
149 Ryne Sandberg .75 2.00
150 Ozzie Smith .50 1.25
151 Kenley Jansen .30 .75
152 J.K. Dobbins .60 1.50
153 Starling Marte .30 .75
154 Tommy La Stella .25 .60
155 Chip Gaines .40 1.00
156 Lourdes Gurriel Jr. .30 .75
157 Jeff McNeil .30 .75
158 Kwang-Hyun Kim RC 2.00 5.00
159 Kyle Lewis RC 5.00 12.00
160 Lorenzo Cain .25 .60
161 Jackie Bradley Jr. .40 1.00
162 Kyle Tucker .30 .75
163 Cole Hamels .30 .75
164 Kolten Wong .30 .75
165 Hugo Juice Tandron .30 .75
166 Briana Scurry .30 .75
167 Ken Jeong .30 .75
168 Willson Contreras .40 1.00
169 Carter Kieboom .30 .75
170 Nick Thune .30 .75
171 Hunter Pence .30 .75
172 Baseball Brit Joey Mellows .30 .75
173 Evan Longoria .30 .75
174 Anthony Kay RC .60 1.50
175 Kirby Yates .25 .60
176 Justin Dunn RC .75 2.00
177 Hunter Harvey RC 1.00 2.50
178 Marcell Ozuna .40 1.00
179 Dallas Keuchel .30 .75
180 Khris Davis .40 1.00
181 Adbert Alzolay RC .75 2.00
182 Kelsey Cook .40 1.00
183 Lucas Giolito .30 .75
184 Joc Pederson .30 .75
185 Austin Meadows .30 .75
186 Bryan Reynolds .30 .75
187 Masahiro Tanaka .40 1.00
188 Eugenio Suarez .30 .75
189 Brandon Lowe .40 1.00
190 Yuli Gurriel .30 .75
191 Nelson Cruz .40 1.00
192 Jose Abreu .40 1.00
193 Nyjah Huston .30 .75
194 Mike Doc Emrick .40 1.00
195 Robinson Cano .30 .75
196 Noah Syndergaard .30 .75
197 Matt Thaiss RC .75 2.00
198 Will Smith .50 1.25
199 Nico Hoerner RC 2.50 6.00
200 Jim Abbott .25 .60
201 Sakura Kokumai .25 .60
202 Tino Martinez .30 .75

203 Tony Dunst .30 .75
204 Jared Carrabis .40 1.00
205 Salvador Perez .30 .75
206 C.J. Cron .25 .60
207 Brendan McKay RC 1.00 2.50
208 Mike Moustakas .30 .75
209 Johnny Bananas .40 1.00
210 Jose Ramirez .30 .75
211 Ryan Braun .30 .75
212 Chris Paddack .40 1.00
213 Oscar Mercado .30 .75
214 Derek Jeter 2.00 5.00
215 Paul DeJong .40 1.00
216 Shun Yamaguchi RC .75 2.00
217 Aaron Wheelz Fotheringham .40 1.00
218 Andrelton Simmons .25 .60
219 Josh Hader .25 .60
220 Eric Hosmer .30 .75
221 Mike Foltynewicz .25 .60
222 Isan Diaz RC 1.00 2.50
223 Shane Bieber .40 1.00
224 Kole Calhoun .25 .60
225 Austin Riley .60 1.50
226 A.J. Puk RC 1.25 3.00
227 Max Muncy .30 .75
228 Justine Siegal .40 1.00
229 Jordan Yamamoto RC .75 2.00
230 Matt Olson .25 .60
231 Bucky Lasek .40 1.00
232 Dakota Hudson .30 .75
233 Howie Kendrick .25 .60
234 Jorge Alfaro .25 .60
235 Jesus Luzardo RC 1.25 3.00
236 Alex Verdugo .30 .75
237 Nick Ahmed .25 .60
238 Gerrit Cole .60 1.50
239 Kyle Schwarber .40 1.00
240 Luis Arraez .50 1.25
241 Michael Brantley .30 .75
242 Andy Cohen .30 .75
243 Max Kepler .30 .75
244 Brandon Woodruff .25 .60
245 Josh Donaldson .30 .75
246 Mike Clevinger .30 .75
247 Yusei Kikuchi .30 .75
248 Rob Friedman .30 .75
249 Stephen Strasburg .40 1.00
250 Charlie Blackmon .40 1.00
251 Corey Kluber .30 .75
252 Steve Byrne .30 .75
253 David Price .30 .75
254 Ryan Nyquist .30 .75
255 David Dahl .25 .60
256 Luis Robert RC 6.00 15.00
257 Corey Seager .40 1.00
258 Cavan Biggio .50 1.25
259 Whit Merrifield .40 1.00
260 J.T. Realmuto .40 1.00
261 Joey Gallo .40 1.00
262 Zac Gallen RC 1.50 4.00
263 Dansby Swanson .40 1.00
264 Abraham Toro RC .75 2.00
265 Tommy Edman .40 1.00
266 Didi Gregorius .30 .75
267 Elvis Andrus .30 .75
268 Eduardo Escobar .25 .60
269 Miguel Sano .30 .75
270 Luis Castillo .30 .75
271 Michael Conforto .30 .75
272 Jon Lester .30 .75
273 Gregory Polanco .30 .75
274 Steven Tefft .30 .75
275 Jeff Dye .30 .75
276 Jose Urquidy RC .75 2.00
277 John Means .25 .60
278 Nick Castellanos .40 1.00
279 Maikel Franco .30 .75
280 Jean Segura .30 .75
281 Derrick Goold .30 .75
282 Matthew Boyd .25 .60
283 Nomar Mazara .25 .60
284 Julian Edwards .30 .75
285 Orlando Arcia .25 .60
286 Trey Mancini .40 1.00
287 Aroldis Chapman .40 1.00
288 Courtney Hansen .30 .75
289 Anthony Rendon .40 1.00
290 Ramon Laureano .40 1.00
291 Sonny Gray .30 .75
292 Hyun-Jin Ryu .30 .75
293 Daniel Vogelbach .25 .60
294 Mauricio Dubon RC .75 2.00
295 Zack Wheeler .30 .75
296 Trevor Bauer .40 1.00
297 R.L. Stine .40 1.00
298 Adalberto Mondesi .40 1.00
299 Blake Snell .30 .75
300 Andres Munoz RC .75 2.00

2020 Topps Allen and Ginter Chrome Gold Refractors

*GOLD REF.: 4X TO 10X BASIC
*GOLD REF. RC: 1.5X TO 4X BASIC
RANDOM INSERTS IN PACKS
STATED PRINT RUN 50 SER.#'d SETS
13 Aaron Judge 25.00 60.00
14 Aaron Nola 6.00 15.00
15 Kris Bryant 10.00 25.00
16 Bryce Harper 20.00 50.00
17 Ken Griffey Jr. 40.00 100.00
29 Willie Mays 25.00 60.00
31 Babe Ruth 20.00 50.00
32 Ichiro 20.00 50.00
35 Rickey Henderson 15.00 40.00
41 David Ortiz 10.00 25.00
42 Jackie Robinson 12.00 30.00
51 Roberto Clemente 30.00 80.00
67 Mookie Betts 30.00 80.00
70 Don Mattingly 25.00 60.00
74 Ty Cobb 10.00 25.00
76 Chipper Jones 12.00 30.00
85 Mike Trout 75.00 200.00
86 Anthony Rizzo 10.00 25.00
88 Ronald Acuna Jr. 40.00 100.00
98 Cal Ripken Jr. 30.00 80.00
99 Gavin Lux 20.00 50.00
104 Hank Aaron 25.00 60.00
110 Albert Pujols 20.00 501.00
112 Bo Bichette 75.00 200.00
114 Gleyber Torres 15.00 40.00
115 Fernando Tatis Jr. 25.00 60.00
118 Yordan Alvarez 40.00 100.00
128 Tony Gwynn 15.00 40.00
137 Yadier Molina 12.00 30.00
139 Nolan Ryan 25.00 60.00
141 Mike Schmidt 20.00 50.00
145 Alex Rodriguez 15.00 40.00
159 Kyle Lewis 30.00 80.00
167 Ken Jeong 6.00 15.00
193 Nyjah Huston 10.00 25.00
214 Derek Jeter 40.00 100.00
222 Isan Diaz 6.00 15.00
223 Shane Bieber 8.00 20.00
256 Luis Robert 100.00 250.00
294 Mauricio Dubon 10.00 25.00

2020 Topps Allen and Ginter Chrome Green Refractors

*GRN REF.: 3X TO 8X BASIC
*GRN REF. RC: 1.2X TO 3X BASIC
RANDOM INSERTS IN PACKS
STATED PRINT RUN 99 SER.#'d SETS
13 Aaron Judge 10.00 25.00
16 Bryce Harper 8.00 20.00
17 Ken Griffey Jr. 25.00 60.00
29 Willie Mays 20.00 50.00
32 Ichiro 15.00 40.00
35 Rickey Henderson 8.00 20.00
42 Jackie Robinson 5.00 12.00
51 Roberto Clemente 15.00 40.00
67 Mookie Betts 10.00 25.00
70 Don Mattingly 20.00 50.00
74 Ty Cobb 8.00 20.00
85 Mike Trout 30.00 80.00
98 Cal Ripken Jr. 15.00 40.00
104 Hank Aaron 12.00 30.00
110 Albert Pujols 8.00 20.00
112 Bo Bichette 40.00 100.00
114 Gleyber Torres 8.00 20.00
115 Fernando Tatis Jr. 20.00 501.00
118 Yordan Alvarez 20.00 50.00
128 Tony Gwynn 8.00 20.00
139 Nolan Ryan 12.00 30.00
141 Mike Schmidt 8.00 20.00
145 Alex Rodriguez 5.00 12.00
159 Kyle Lewis 25.00 60.00
256 Luis Robert 60.00 150.00

2020 Topps Allen and Ginter Chrome Orange Refractors

*ORNG REF.: 5X TO 12X BASIC
*ORNG REF. RC: 2X TO 5X BASIC
RANDOM INSERTS IN PACKS
STATED PRINT RUN 25 SER.#'d SETS
13 Aaron Judge 60.00 150.00
14 Aaron Nola 10.00 25.00
15 Kris Bryant 12.00 30.00
16 Bryce Harper 25.00 60.00
17 Ken Griffey Jr. 60.00 150.00
29 Willie Mays 30.00 80.00
31 Babe Ruth 100.00 250.00
32 Ichiro 25.00 60.00
35 Rickey Henderson 20.00 50.00
41 David Ortiz 12.00 30.00
42 Jackie Robinson 25.00 60.00
51 Roberto Clemente 50.00 120.00
67 Mookie Betts 40.00 100.00
70 Don Mattingly 30.00 80.00
74 Ty Cobb 12.00 30.00
76 Chipper Jones 15.00 40.00
85 Mike Trout 125.00 300.00
86 Anthony Rizzo 20.00 50.00
88 Ronald Acuna Jr. 50.00 120.00
98 Cal Ripken Jr. 60.00 150.00
99 Gavin Lux 50.00 120.00
104 Hank Aaron 30.00 80.00
110 Albert Pujols 25.00 60.00
112 Bo Bichette 100.00 250.00
114 Gleyber Torres 25.00 60.00
115 Fernando Tatis Jr. 40.00 100.00
118 Yordan Alvarez 50.00 120.00
128 Tony Gwynn 40.00 100.00
137 Yadier Molina 20.00 50.00
139 Nolan Ryan 40.00 100.00
141 Mike Schmidt 25.00 60.00
143 Carlton Fisk 20.00 50.00
145 Alex Rodriguez 20.00 50.00
159 Kyle Lewis 50.00 120.00
167 Ken Jeong 15.00 40.00
193 Nyjah Huston 12.00 30.00
214 Derek Jeter 60.00 150.00
222 Isan Diaz 12.00 30.00
223 Shane Bieber 10.00 25.00
256 Luis Robert 200.00 500.00
294 Mauricio Dubon 12.00 30.00

2020 Topps Allen and Ginter Chrome Refractors

*REF.: 1.5X TO 4X BASIC
*REF. RC: .6X TO 1.5X BASIC
RANDOM INSERTS IN PACKS
17 Ken Griffey Jr. 8.00 20.00
85 Mike Trout 15.00 40.00
112 Bo Bichette 15.00 40.00
118 Yordan Alvarez 8.00 20.00
159 Kyle Lewis 12.00 30.00
256 Luis Robert 25.00 60.00

2020 Topps Allen and Ginter Chrome Autographs

STATED ODDS 1:XX HOBBY
EXCHANGE DEADLINE 10/31/22
ACGI Ichiro 200.00 500.00
ACGAA Aristides Aquino 20.00 50.00
ACGAJ Aaron Judge 75.00 200.00
ACGAP Albert Pujols 200.00 500.00
ACGBB Bo Bichette 150.00 400.00
ACGCB Cody Bellinger 60.00 150.00
ACGCJ Chipper Jones 75.00 200.00
ACGCR Cal Ripken Jr. 100.00 250.00
ACGDJ Derek Jeter 300.00 600.00
ACGDO David Ortiz 60.00 150.00
ACGHA Hank Aaron 200.00 500.00
ACGJB Johnny Bench 60.00 150.00
ACGJS Juan Soto 100.00 250.00
ACGJV Joey Votto 50.00 120.00
ACGKG Ken Griffey Jr. 300.00 600.00
ACGLR Luis Robert EXCH
ACGMM Mark McGwire 60.00 150.00
ACGMR Mariano Rivera 100.00 250.00
ACGMT Mike Trout 600.00 1200.00
ACGNH Nico Hoerner 40.00 100.00
ACGNR Nolan Ryan 125.00 300.00
ACGOS Ozzie Smith 60.00 150.00
ACGPA Pete Alonso 40.00 100.00
ACGPC Patrick Corbin 12.00 30.00
ACGRA Ronald Acuna Jr. 100.00 250.00
ACGRJ Randy Johnson 40.00 100.00
ACGSK Sandy Koufax 200.00 500.00
ACGYA Yordan Alvarez 125.00 300.00
ACGVGU Vladimir Guerrero 40.00 100.00

2020 Topps Allen and Ginter Chrome Mini

*MINI: 1.2X TO 3X BASIC
*MINI RC: .5X TO 1.2X BASIC
RANDOM INSERTS IN PACKS
17 Ken Griffey Jr. 2.50 6.00
256 Luis Robert 12.00 30.00

2020 Topps Allen and Ginter Chrome Mini Booming Cities

COMPLETE SET (15)
STATED ODDS 1:9 HOBBY
BCC1 Dubai United Arab Emirates 1.50 4.00
BCC2 Shanghai China 1.50 4.00
BCC3 Lagos Nigeria 1.50 4.00
BCC4 Dar es Salaam Tanzania 1.50 4.00
BCC5 Kampala Uganda 1.50 4.00
BCC6 Karachi Pakistan 1.50 4.00
BCC7 Dhaka Bangladesh 1.50 4.00
BCC8 Istanbul Turkey 1.50 4.00
BCC9 Sao Paulo Brazil 1.50 4.00
BCC10 Jakarta Indonesia 1.50 4.00
BCC11 Singapore Singapore 1.50 4.00
BCC12 Riyadh Saudi Arabia 1.50 4.00
BCC13 Tokyo Japan 1.50 4.00
BCC14 Shenzhen China 1.50 4.00
BCC15 Seattle Washington USA 1.50 4.00

2020 Topps Allen and Ginter Chrome Mini Buggin Out

COMPLETE SET (20)
STATED ODDS 1:6 HOBBY
MBOC1 Ladybird Beetle 1.50 4.00
MBOC2 Monarch Butterfly 1.50 4.00
MBOC3 Praying Mantis 1.50 4.00
MBOC4 Hercules Beetle 1.50 4.00
MBOC5 Thorn Bug 1.50 4.00
MBOC6 Australian Walking Stick 1.50 4.00
MBOC7 Atlas Moth 1.50 4.00
MBOC8 Calleta Silkmoth 1.50 4.00
MBOC9 Scorpion Fly 1.50 4.00
MBOC10 Peacock Spider 1.50 4.00
MBOC11 Leafcutter Ant 1.50 4.00
MBOC12 Spiny Orb Weaver 1.50 4.00
MBOC13 Red Postman Butterfly 1.50 4.00
MBOC14 Giraffe Weevil 1.50 4.00
MBOC15 Bumblebee 1.50 4.00
MBOC16 Fire Ant 1.50 4.00
MBOC17 Old World Swallowtail 1.50 4.00
MBOC18 Caterpillar 1.50 4.00
MBOC19 Dragonfly 1.50 4.00
MBOC20 Treehopper 1.50 4.00

2020 Topps Allen and Ginter Chrome Mini Safari Sights

COMPLETE SET (15)
STATED ODDS 1:9 HOBBY
SSC1 Elephant 1.50 4.00
SSC2 Cheetah 1.50 4.00
SSC3 Crocodile 1.50 4.00
SSC4 Gazelle 1.50 4.00
SSC5 Gray Crowned Crane 1.50 4.00
SSC6 Hyena 1.50 4.00
SSC7 Lion 1.50 4.00
SSC8 Warthog 1.50 4.00
SSC9 Vervet Monkey 1.50 4.00
SSC10 Giraffe 1.50 4.00
SSC11 Zebra 1.50 4.00
SSC12 Leopard 1.50 4.00
SSC13 Hippo 1.50 4.00
SSC14 Lion Cub 1.50 4.00
SSC15 Safari Truck 1.50 4.00

2018 Topps Allen and Ginter X Mini Framed Autographs

PRINT RUN B/WN 5-25 SETS PER
NO PRICING QTY 15 OR LESS
EXCHANGE DEADLINE 6/30/2020
MAAA Aaron Altherr 8.00 20.00
MAAE Austin Meadows 20.00 50.00
MAAH Austin Hays
MAAL Alison Lee 20.00 50.00
MAAM A.J. Minter 10.00 25.00
MAAN Anthony Banda 8.00 20.00
MAAO Austin Rogers 12.00 30.00
MAAR Amed Rosario 10.00 25.00
MAAS Andrew Stevenson 8.00 20.00
MABD Brian Dozier 10.00 25.00
MABH Bryce Harper
MABI Bill James 20.00 50.00
MABJ Bo Jackson 60.00 150.00
MABL Ben Lecomte 8.00 20.00
MABW Brandon Woodruff 10.00 25.00
MACM Claire Smith 10.00 25.00
MACO Christopher McDonald 10.00 25.00
MACP Champ Pederson 12.00 30.00
MACS Chance Sisco 10.00 25.00
MADC Dominic Smith 8.00 20.00
MADF Dustin Fowler 8.00 20.00
MADM Don Mattingly 75.00 200.00
MADP Dillon Peters 8.00 20.00
MADS Darryl Strawberry
MADU Doris Burke
MAFJ Felix Jorge 8.00 20.00
MAFM Francisco Mejia
MAFT Frank Thomas 75.00 200.00
MAGC Garrett Cooper 8.00 20.00
MAGT Gleyber Torres 75.00 200.00
MAGU Genie Bouchard
MAHB Harrison Bader 12.00 30.00
MAHJ H. Jon Benjamin 40.00 100.00
MAIH Ian Happ 10.00 25.00
MAJA Jose Altuve 40.00 100.00
MAJB Justin Bour 8.00 20.00
MAJC J.P. Crawford 8.00 20.00
MAJCK Jack Sock 12.00 30.00
MAJD J.D. Davis 10.00 25.00
MAJH Jordan Hicks 15.00 40.00
MAJI Jose Berrios 10.00 25.00
MAJM J.D. Martinez EXCH 40.00 100.00
MAJO Jose Canseco 25.00 60.00
MAJR Jose Ramirez 25.00 60.00
MAJS Jackson Stephens 8.00 20.00
MAJV Joey Votto 75.00 200.00
MAJZ Jon Lovitz
MAKB Keon Broxton 8.00 20.00
MAKD Khris Davis
MAKP Kelsey Plum 10.00 25.00
MAKR Kris Bryant 125.00 300.00
MALC Luis Castillo 10.00 25.00
MALR Lincoln Riley
MALV Lindsey Vonn 50.00 120.00
MAMF Max Fried 30.00 80.00
MAMG Miguel Gomez 8.00 20.00
MAMH Molly McGrath 25.00 60.00
MAMM Manny Machado 60.00 150.00
MAMMI Miles Mikolas 15.00 40.00
MAMN Method Man EXCH 60.00 150.00
MAMO Matt Olson 8.00 20.00
MAMR Michael Rapaport 25.00 60.00
MAMT Mike Trout
MAMW Mark McGwire 50.00 120.00
MAMY Madison Keys 15.00 40.00
MANY Noah Syndergaard 25.00 60.00
MAOA Ozzie Albies 50.00 120.00
MAPB Parker Bridwell
MAPD Paul DeJong 12.00 30.00
MAPG Paul Goldschmidt 30.00 80.00
MAPL Paul Blackburn 8.00 20.00
MAPSP Paige Spiranac 30.00 80.00
MARA Ronald Acuna 150.00 400.00
MARD Rafael Devers 30.00 80.00
MARI Ryan Sickler
MARK Rhys Hoskins 60.00 150.00
MARR Raudy Read 8.00 20.00
MARU Richard Urena 8.00 20.00
MAS Stugotz
MASA Sandy Alcantara 8.00 20.00
MASB Scott Blumstein 8.00 20.00
MASE Sean Evans
MASF Sonny Fredrickson 10.00 25.00
MASG Sonny Gray
MASKI Scott Kingery 15.00 40.00
MASN Sean Newcomb 10.00 25.00
MASO Shohei Ohtani 300.00 800.00
MASR Scott Rogowsky 20.00 50.00
MASS Steve Simeone
MASST Sloane Stephens
MATG Tom Segura
MATH Tony Hawk
MATI Tommy Wiseau
MATL Tzu-Wei Lin 10.00 25.00
MATLU Tyronn Lue 8.00 20.00
MATM Tyler Mahle 10.00 25.00
MATN Tomas Nido 8.00 20.00
MATS Troy Scribner 8.00 20.00
MATV Travis Shaw 8.00 20.00
MAVC Victor Caratini 12.00 30.00
MAVR Victor Robles 40.00 100.00
MAWB Walker Buehler 50.00 120.00
MAWM Whit Merrifield 15.00 40.00
MAWO Willson Contreras 20.00 50.00

2019 Topps Allen and Ginter X

1 Mookie Betts .60 1.50
2 Christian Yelich .50 1.25
3 Babe Ruth 1.00 2.50
4 Lou Gehrig .75 2.00
5 Shohei Ohtani .50 1.25
6 Luis Gonzalez .25 .60
7 Albert Pujols .50 1.25
8 Reggie Jackson .30 .75
9 Zack Greinke .30 .75
10 Mike Trout 2.00 5.00
11 Nolan Ryan 1.25 3.00
12 Blake Treinen .25 .60
13 Ozzie Albies .40 1.00
14 Chipper Jones .40 1.00
15 Freddie Freeman .50 1.25
16 Kris Bryant .50 1.25
17 Anthony Rizzo .60 1.50
18 Ryne Sandberg .75 2.00
19 Javier Baez .50 1.25
20 Ernie Banks .40 1.00
21 Francisco Lindor .40 1.00
22 Jose Ramirez .30 .75
23 Bob Feller .30 .75
24 A.J. Burnett .25 .60
25 Ronald Acuna Jr. 2.00 5.00
26 Justin Verlander .40 1.00
27 Gerrit Cole .40 1.00
28 Jose Altuve .30 .75
29 Alex Bregman .40 1.00
30 George Springer .30 .75
31 Jeff Bagwell .30 .75
32 Sandy Koufax .75 2.00
33 Walker Buehler .50 1.25
34 Cody Bellinger .75 2.00
35 Mike Piazza .40 1.00
36 Starlin Castro .25 .60
37 Josh Hader .25 .60
38 Lorenzo Cain .25 .60
39 Jesus Aguilar .25 .60
40 Ryan Braun .30 .75
41 Robinson Cano .30 .75
42 Jacob deGrom .40 1.00
43 Edwin Diaz .30 .75
44 Noah Syndergaard .30 .75
45 Amed Rosario .30 .75
46 Rickey Henderson .40 1.00
47 Matt Chapman .40 1.00
48 Dennis Eckersley .30 .75
49 Khris Davis .40 1.00
50 Hank Aaron .75 2.00
51 Paul Molitor .40 1.00
52 Buster Posey .50 1.25
53 Willie McCovey .30 .75
54 Juan Marichal .30 .75
55 Evan Longoria .30 .75
56 J.D. Martinez .40 1.00
57 Felix Hernandez .30 .75
58 Edgar Martinez .30 .75
59 Justus Sheffield RC .60 1.50
60 Ichiro .50 1.25
61 Mark McGwire .60 1.50
62 Paul Goldschmidt .40 1.00
63 Yadier Molina .40 1.00
64 Stan Musial .60 1.50
65 Ozzie Smith .50 1.25
66 Roger Clemens .50 1.25
67 Roberto Alomar .30 .75
68 Justin Smoak .25 .60
69 Danny Jansen RC .40 1.00
70 Max Scherzer .40 1.00
71 Patrick Corbin .30 .75
72 Stephen Strasburg .40 1.00
73 Trea Turner .30 .75
74 Cal Ripken Jr. 1.25 3.00
75 Brooks Robinson .30 .75
76 Jim Palmer .30 .75
77 Tony Gwynn .40 1.00
78 Trevor Hoffman .30 .75
79 Luis Urias RC .60 1.50
80 Eric Hosmer .30 .75
81 Andrew McCutchen .40 1.00
82 Rhys Hoskins .50 1.25
83 Aaron Nola .30 .75
84 Roberto Clemente 1.00 2.50
85 Chris Archer .25 .60
86 Felipe Vazquez .25 .60
87 Willie Stargell .30 .75
88 Ralph Kiner .30 .75
89 Adrian Beltre .40 1.00
90 Ivan Rodriguez .30 .75
91 Elvis Andrus .30 .75
92 Joey Gallo .30 .75
93 Blake Snell .30 .75
94 Willy Adames .25 .60
95 Jose Canseco .30 .75
96 Andrew Benintendi .40 1.00
97 Rafael Devers .50 1.25
98 Ted Williams .75 2.00
99 Chris Sale .40 1.00
100 Ken Griffey Jr. .75 2.00
101 David Price .30 .75
102 Joey Votto .40 1.00
103 Johnny Bench .40 1.00
104 Tony Perez .30 .75
105 Todd Helton .30 .75
106 Trevor Story .40 1.00
107 Nolan Arenado .50 1.25
108 Charlie Blackmon .40 1.00
109 George Brett .75 2.00
110 Salvador Perez .30 .75
111 Bo Jackson .40 1.00
112 Miguel Cabrera .40 1.00
113 Al Kaline .40 1.00
114 Jose Berrios .30 .75
115 Rod Carew .30 .75
116 Tony Oliva .25 .60
117 Harmon Killebrew .40 1.00
118 Frank Thomas .40 1.00
119 Michael Kopech RC .75 2.00
120 Yoan Moncada .40 1.00
121 Jose Abreu .40 1.00
122 Isiah Kiner-Falefa .25 .60
123 Gleyber Torres .75 2.00
124 Miguel Andujar .40 1.00
125 Giancarlo Stanton .40 1.00
126 Clayton Kershaw .75 2.00
127 Juan Soto 1.25 3.00
128 Roger Maris .40 1.00
129 Jackie Robinson .40 1.00
130 Torii Hunter .25 .60
131 Juan Gonzalez .25 .60
132 David Ortiz .40 1.00
133 Don Mattingly .75 2.00
134 Derek Jeter 1.00 2.50
135 Dale Murphy .40 1.00
136 Mariano Rivera .50 1.25
137 Vladimir Guerrero .30 .75
138 Gary Carter .30 .75
139 Harold Baines .30 .75
140 Luis Severino .30 .75
141 Miles Mikolas .40 1.00
142 Mitch Haniger .30 .75
143 Max Muncy .30 .75
144 Whit Merrifield .40 1.00
145 Xander Bogaerts .40 1.00
146 Josh Donaldson .30 .75
147 J.T. Realmuto .40 1.00
148 Corey Kluber .30 .75
149 Manny Machado .40 1.00
150 Steve Carlton .30 .75
151 Marc Summers .40 1.00
152 Augie Carton .25 .60
153 Jay Larson .30 .75
154 Hailey Dawson .40 1.00
155 Gary Vaynerchuk .40 1.00
156 Vincent Stio .40 1.00
157 Mike Oz .40 1.00
158 Kyle Snyder .40 1.00
159 Rodney Mullen .40 1.00
160 Matthew Mercer .40 1.00
161 Sister Mary Jo Sobieck .40 1.00
162 Mason Cox .40 1.00
163 Loretta Claiborne .30 .75
164 Justin Bonomo .40 1.00
165 John Cynn .30 .75
166 1st Tiger Mask .40 1.00
Satoru Sayama
167 Mayumi Seto .40 1.00
168 Rhea Butcher .30 .75
169 Drew Drechsel .40 1.00
170 Lawrence Rocks .25 .60
171 Charles Martinet .40 1.00
172 Tyler Kepner .25 .60
173 Ben Schwartz .40 1.00
174 Dan Rather .40 1.00
175 Danielle Colby .40 1.00
176 Post Malone .40 1.00
177 Robert Oberst .40 1.00
178 Brian Fallon .40 1.00
179 Burton Rocks .25 .60
180 Quinn XCII .40 1.00
181 Emily Jaenson .40 1.00
182 Pete Alonso RC 6.00 15.00
183 Fernando Tatis Jr. RC 6.00 15.00
184 Travis Pastrana .40 1.00
185 Hilary Knight .40 1.00
186 Wade Boggs .30 .75
187 Jason Varitek .40 1.00
188 Didi Gregorius .30 .75
189 Tyler O'Neill .30 .75
190 Eddie Rosario .30 .75
191 Brandon Nimmo .30 .75
192 Lourdes Gurriel Jr. .30 .75
193 Jack Flaherty .30 .75
194 Kevin Newman RC .60 1.50
195 Dakota Hudson RC
196 Cedric Mullins RC .60 1.50
197 Brad Keller RC .40 1.00
198 David Bote .30 .75
199 Dereck Rodriguez .25 .60
200 Aaron Judge 1.00 2.50
201 Sean Reid-Foley RC .40 1.00
202 Luke Voit .60 1.50
203 Jeff McNeil RC 1.00 2.50
204 Cionel Perez RC .40 1.00
205 Chance Adams RC
206 Corbin Burnes RC .60 1.50
207 Ramon Laureano RC .75 2.00
208 Dawel Lugo RC .60 1.50
209 Ryan O'Hearn RC .40 1.00
210 Framber Valdez RC .40 1.00
211 Patrick Wisdom RC .40 1.00
212 Dylan Cozens .25 .60
213 Egg .25 .60
214 Jonathan Lucroy .30 .75
215 Cody Allen .25 .60
216 Justin Bour .25 .60
217 Andrelton Simmons .25 .60
218 Michael Brantley .30 .75
219 Yuli Gurriel .30 .75
220 Josh James RC
221 Stephen Piscotty .25 .60
222 Matt Olson .25 .60
223 Jurickson Profar .30 .75
224 Matt Shoemaker .30 .75
225 Brandon Drury .25 .60
226 Dansby Swanson .40 1.00
227 Touki Toussaint RC .50 1.25
228 Yasmani Grandal .25 .60
229 Orlando Arcia .25 .60
230 Matt Carpenter .40 1.00
231 Paul DeJong .40 1.00
232 Willson Contreras .30 .75
233 Cole Hamels .30 .75
234 A.J. Pollock .25 .60
235 Corey Seager .40 1.00
236 Brandon Crawford .30 .75
237 Carlos Santana .30 .75
238 Trevor Bauer .40 1.00
239 Starling Marte .30 .75
240 Dee Gordon .25 .60
241 Kyle Seager .25 .60
242 Brian Anderson .25 .60
243 Michael Conforto .30 .75
244 Brian Dozier .30 .75
245 Wil Myers .25 .60
246 Odubel Herrera .30 .75
247 Maikel Franco .30 .75
248 David Robertson .25 .60
249 Jake Arrieta .30 .75
250 Yusei Kikuchi RC .60 1.50
251 Gregory Polanco .30 .75
252 Nomar Mazara .25 .60
253 Kevin Kiermaier .30 .75
254 Charlie Morton .40 1.00
255 Matt Kemp .30 .75
256 Yasiel Puig .40 1.00
257 Sonny Gray .30 .75
258 Daniel Murphy .30 .75
259 David Dahl .25 .60
260 Billy Hamilton .30 .75
261 Nicholas Castellanos .40 1.00
262 Willians Astudillo RC .40 1.00
263 Byron Buxton .30 .75
264 Yonder Alonso .25 .60
265 Troy Tulowitzki .40 1.00
266 DJ LeMahieu .40 1.00
267 James Paxton .30 .75
268 Adam Ottavino .25 .60
269 Scooter Gennett .30 .75
270 Ben Zobrist .30 .75
271 Carl Yastrzemski .60 1.50
272 Carlton Fisk .30 .75
273 Fred McGriff .30 .75
274 Dwight Gooden .25 .60
275 Deion Sanders .30 .75
276 Hideki Matsui .40 1.00
277 Frank Robinson .30 .75
278 Vladimir Guerrero Jr. RC 8.00 20.00
279 Kolby Allard RC .60 1.50
280 Bryce Harper .60 1.50
281 Bob Gibson .30 .75
282 A.J. Andrews .40 1.00
283 Andy Pettitte .30 .75
284 Roy Halladay .30 .75
285 Jorge Alfaro .25 .60
286 Harrison Bader .30 .75
287 Catfish Hunter .30 .75
288 Ryan Yarbrough .25 .60
289 Whitey Ford .30 .75
290 Pee Wee Reese .30 .75
291 Cespedes Family BBQ .40 1.00
Jake Mintz
Jordan Shusterman
292 Eddie Murray .30 .75
293 Jon Lester .30 .75
294 German Marquez .25 .60
295 Franmil Reyes .25 .60
296 Cincinnati Red Stockings .25
297 Boston Red Sox .25
298 Ian Happ .30 .75
299 J.A. Happ .30 .75
300 Tino Martinez .30 .75
351 Carlos Correa SP .75 2.00
352 Robin Yount SP .75 2.00
353 Shane Bieber SP .75 2.00
354 Rowdy Tellez SP RC .75 2.00
355 Jordan Hicks SP .60 1.50
356 Kyle Schwarber SP .75 2.00
357 Kenley Jansen SP .60 1.50
358 John Smoltz SP .75 2.00
359 Larry Doby SP .60 1.50
360 Jorge Posada SP .60 1.50
361 Victor Robles SP 1.00 2.50
362 Fergie Jenkins SP .60 1.50
363 Austin Meadows SP .60 1.50
364 Dustin Pedroia SP .75 2.00
365 Ty Cobb SP 1.25 3.00
366 Daniel Palka SP .50 1.25
367 Masahiro Tanaka SP .60 1.50
368 Eddie Murray SP .60 1.50
369 Rick Porcello SP .60 1.50
370 Marcell Ozuna SP .75 2.00
371 Yu Darvish SP .75 2.00
372 Justin Turner SP .60 1.50
373 Edwin Encarnacion SP .75 2.00
374 Yoenis Cespedes SP .75 2.00
375 Pat Neshek SP .50 1.25
376 Wade Davis SP .50 1.25
377 Christin Stewart SP RC .60 1.50
378 Aroldis Chapman SP .75 2.00
379 Darryl Strawberry SP .50 1.25
380 Nomar Garciaparra SP .60 1.50
381 Scott Kingery SP .60 1.50
382 Dave Winfield SP .60 1.50
383 Sean Doolittle SP .50 1.25
384 Rogers Hornsby SP .60 1.50

385 Gil Hodges SP .60 1.50
386 Eddie Mathews SP .75 2.00
387 Warren Spahn SP .60 1.50
388 Casey Stengel SP .60 1.50
389 Lou Brock SP .60 1.50
390 Phil Rizzuto SP .60 1.50
391 Phil Niekro SP .60 1.50
392 Sammy Sosa SP .75 2.00
393 Alex Rodriguez SP 1.00 2.50
394 Tom Seaver SP .60 1.50
395 Barry Larkin SP .60 1.50
396 Tommy Lasorda SP .60 1.50
397 Orlando Cepeda SP .60 1.50
398 Eloy Jimenez SP RC 4.00 10.00
399 Tim Raines SP .60 1.50
400 Randy Johnson SP .75 2.00

2001 Topps Archives

Issued in two series of 225 cards, this 450 card set features some of the first and last cards of retired superstars and other retired star players. The cards were issued in eight card packs with an SRP of $4. These packs were issued 20 packs to a box and eight boxes to a case. A very annoying feature of this set was the checklist numbers were so small that it was very difficult to tell what the number of the card was if a collector was trying to build a set.

COMPLETE SET (450) 75.00 150.00
COMPLETE SERIES 1 (225) 40.00 80.00
COMPLETE SERIES 2 (225) 40.00 80.00
1 Johnny Antonelli 52 .40 1.00
2 Yogi Berra 52 1.00 2.50
3 Dom DiMaggio 52 .40 1.00
4 Carl Erskine 52 .40 1.00
5 Larry Doby 52 .40 1.00
6 Monte Irvin 52 .40 1.00
7 Vernon Law 52 .40 1.00
8 Eddie Mathews 52 1.00 2.50
9 Willie Mays 52 2.00 5.00
10 Gil McDougald 52 .40 1.00
11 Andy Pafko 52 .60 1.50
12 Phil Rizzuto 52 1.00 2.50
13 Preacher Roe 52 .40 1.00
14 Hank Sauer 52 .40 1.00
15 Bobby Shantz 52 .40 1.00
16 Enos Slaughter 52 .40 1.00
17 Warren Spahn 52 .60 1.50
18 Mickey Vernon 52 .40 1.00
19 Early Wynn 52 .40 1.00
20 Gaylord Perry 62 .40 1.00
21 Johnny Podres 53 .40 1.00
22 Ernie Banks 54 1.00 2.50
23 Moose Skowron 54 .40 1.00
24 Harmon Killebrew 55 1.00 2.50
25 Ted Williams 54 2.00 5.00
26 Jimmy Piersall 56 .40 1.00
27 Frank Thomas 56 .40 1.00
28 Bill Mazeroski 57 1.00 2.50
29 Bobby Richardson 57 .40 1.00
30 Frank Robinson 57 .60 1.50
31 Stan Musial 58 1.50 4.00
32 Johnny Callison 59 .40 1.00
33 Bob Gibson 59 .60 1.50
34 Frank Howard 60 .40 1.00
35 Willie McCovey 60 .40 1.00
36 Carl Yastrzemski 60 1.50 4.00
37 Jim Maloney 61 .40 1.00
38 Ron Santo 61 .60 1.50
39 Lou Brock 62 .60 1.50
40 Tim McCarver 62 .40 1.00
41 Joe Pepitone 62 .20 .50
42 Boog Powell 62 .60 1.50
43 Bill Freehan 63 .40 1.00
44 Dick Allen 64 .40 1.00
45 Willie Horton 64 .20 .50
46 Mickey Lolich 64 .40 1.00
47 Wilbur Wood 64 .20 .50
48 Bert Campaneris 65 .40 1.00
49 Rod Carew 67 .60 1.50
50 Luis Aparicio 56 .40 1.00
51 Joe Morgan 65 .40 1.00
52 Luis Tiant 65 .40 1.00
53 Bobby Murcer 66 .40 1.00
54 Don Sutton 66 .40 1.00
55 Ken Holtzman 67 .20 .50
56 Reggie Smith 67 .40 1.00
57 Hal McRae 68 .40 1.00
58 Roy White 68 .40 1.00
59 Reggie Jackson 69 .60 1.50
60 Graig Nettles 69 .40 1.00
61 Joe Rudi 69 .40 1.00
62 Vida Blue 70 .40 1.00
63 Darrell Evans 70 .40 1.00
64 David Concepcion 71 .40 1.00
65 Bobby Grich 71 .40 1.00
66 Greg Luzinski 71 .40 1.00
67 Ron Cey 72 .40 1.00
68 George Hendrick 72 .20 .50
69 Dwight Evans 73 .60 1.50
70 Gary Matthews 73 .20 .50
71 Mike Schmidt 73 3.00 8.00
72 Jim Kaat 60 .40 1.00
73 Dave Winfield 74 .40 1.00
74 Gary Carter 75 .60 1.50
75 Dennis Eckersley 76 .40 1.00
76 Kent Tekulve 76 .40 1.00
77 Andre Dawson 77 .60 1.50
78 Denny Martinez 77 .40 1.00
79 Bruce Sutter 77 .40 1.00
80 Jack Morris 78 .40 1.00
81 Ozzie Smith 80 2.00 5.00
82 Lee Smith 82 .40 1.00
83 Don Mattingly 84 3.00 8.00
84 Joe Carter 85 .40 1.00
85 Kirby Puckett 85 1.00 2.50
86 Joe Adcock 52 .40 1.00
87 Gus Bell 52 .20 .50
88 Roy Campanella 52 1.00 2.50
89 Jackie Jensen 52 .40 1.00
90 Johnny Mize 52 .60 1.50
91 Allie Reynolds 52 .40 1.00
92 Al Rosen 52 .40 1.00
93 Hal Newhouser 53 .40 1.00
94 Harvey Kuenn 54 .40 1.00
95 Nellie Fox 56 1.00 2.50
96 Elston Howard 56 .60 1.50
97 Sal Maglie 57 .40 1.00
98 Roger Maris 58 1.00 2.50
99 Norm Cash 60 .40 1.00
100 Thurman Munson 70 1.00 2.50
101 Roy Campanella 57 1.00 2.50
102 Larry Doby 59 .40 1.00
103 Dom Dimaggio 53 .40 1.00
104 Johnny Mize 53 .40 1.00
105 Allie Reynolds 53 .40 1.00
106 Preacher Roe 54 .40 1.00
107 Hal Newhouser 55 .20 .50
108 Monte Irvin 56 .40 1.00
109 Carl Erskine 59 .40 1.00
110 Enos Slaughter 59 .40 1.00
111 Gil McDougald 60 .40 1.00
112 Andy Pafko 59 .20 .50
113 Sal Maglie 59 .20 .50
114 Johnny Antonelli 61 .20 .50
115 Phil Rizzuto 61 .60 1.50
116 Yogi Berra 62 1.00 2.50
117 Jim Wynn 77 .20 .50
118 Mickey Vernon 63 .20 .50
119 Gus Bell 64 .20 .50
120 Ted Williams 58 1.25 3.00
121 Frank Thomas 65 .20 .50
122 Bobby Richardson 66 .40 1.00
123 Gaylord Perry 83 .40 1.00
124 Vernon Law 67 .20 .50
125 Jimmy Piersall 67 .20 .50
126 Moose Skowron 67 .40 1.00
127 Joe Adcock 63 .20 .50
128 Johnny Podres 69 .40 1.00
129 Ernie Banks 71 1.00 2.50
130 Jim Maloney 72 .20 .50
131 Johnny Callison 73 .20 .50
132 Eddie Mathews 68 .60 1.50
133 Joe Pepitone 72 .20 .50
134 Warren Spahn 65 .60 1.50
135 Bill Mazeroski 72 .60 1.50
136 Norm Cash 74 .20 .50
137 Bob Gibson 75 .60 1.50
138 Harmon Killebrew 75 1.00 2.50
139 Frank Robinson 75 .60 1.50
140 Ron Santo 75 .40 1.00
141 Hank Sauer 59 .20 .50
142 Bobby Shantz 64 .20 .50
143 Nellie Fox 65 .60 1.50
144 Elston Howard 68 .60 1.50
145 Jackie Jensen 61 .40 1.00
146 Al Rosen 56 .40 1.00
147 Dick Allen 76 .20 .50
148 Bill Freehan 77 .40 1.00
149 Boog Powell 77 .40 1.00
150 Lou Brock 79 .60 1.50
151 Rod Carew 86 .60 1.50
152 Wilbur Wood 79 .20 .50
153 Thurman Munson 79 1.00 2.50
154 Ken Holtzman 80 .20 .50
155 Willie Horton 80 .20 .50
156 Mickey Lolich 80 .20 .50
157 Tim McCarver 80 .20 .50
158 Willie McCovey 80 .40 1.00
159 Roy White 80 .20 .50
160 Bobby Murcer 83 .40 1.00
161 Joe Rudi 83 .20 .50
162 Reggie Smith 83 .20 .50
163 Luis Tiant 83 .20 .50
164 Bert Campaneris 84 .20 .50
165 Frank Howard 73 .20 .50
166 Harvey Kuenn 66 .20 .50
167 Greg Luzinski 85 .20 .50
168 Luis Aparicio 74 .40 1.00
169 Willie Mays 73 1.25 3.00
170 Roger Maris 68 1.00 2.50
171 Vida Blue 87 .20 .50
172 Bobby Grich 87 .20 .50
173 Reggie Jackson 87 .60 1.50
174 Hal McRae 87 .20 .50
175 Carl Yastrzemski 83 1.00 2.50
176 David Concepcion 88 .20 .50
177 Ron Cey 87 .20 .50
178 George Hendrick 88 .20 .50
179 Gary Matthews 88 .20 .50
180 Stan Musial 63 1.00 2.50
181 Graig Nettles 88 .20 .50
182 Don Sutton 88 .40 1.00
183 Kent Tekulve 88 .20 .50
184 Bruce Sutter 89 .40 1.00
185 Darrell Evans 90 .20 .50
186 Mike Schmidt 89 1.50 4.00
187 Jim Kaat 83 .20 .50
188 Dwight Evans 92 .60 1.50
189 Gary Carter 93 .40 1.00
190 Jack Morris 94 .20 .50
191 Joe Morgan 85 .40 1.00
192 Dave Winfield 95 .40 1.00
193 Andre Dawson 96 .40 1.00
194 Lee Smith 96 .20 .50
195 Ozzie Smith 96 1.50 4.00
196 Denny Martinez 97 .20 .50
197 Don Mattingly 96 1.50 4.00
198 Joe Carter 98 .40 1.00
199 Dennis Eckersley 98 .40 1.00
200 Kirby Puckett 96 1.00 2.50
201 Walter Alston MG 56 .40 1.00
202 Casey Stengel MG 60 .40 1.00
203 Sparky Anderson MG 71 .40 1.00
204 Tommy Lasorda MG 88 .40 1.00
205 Whitey Herzog MG 88 .20 .50
206 AL HR Leaders 70 .40 1.00
207 NL HR Leaders 68 .40 1.00
208 AL HR Leaders 67 1.00 2.50
209 AL Batting Leaders 65 .40 1.00
210 NL HR Leaders 64 .40 1.00
211 NL HR Leaders 63 .40 1.00
212 AL HR Leaders 68 1.00 2.50
213 Ernie Banks 59 Thrill 1.00 2.50
214 Hank Aaron 59 Thrill 1.25 3.00
215 Willie Mays 59 Thrill 1.25 3.00
216 Al Kaline 59 Thrill 1.00 2.50
217 Stan Musial 59 Thrill 1.00 2.50
218 Duke Snider 59 Thrill .60 1.50
219 The Champs 67 .60 1.50
220 Pride of the NL 63 1.00 2.50
221 Whitey Ford WS 63 .60 1.50
222 Jerry Koosman WS 70 .20 .50
223 Bob Gibson WS 65 .60 1.50
224 Gil Hodges WS 60 .60 1.50
225 Reggie Jackson WS 78 .60 1.50
226 Hank Bauer 52 .40 1.00
227 Ralph Branca 52 .40 1.00
228 Joe Garagiola 52 .40 1.00
229 Bob Feller 52 .60 1.50
230 Dick Groat 52 .40 1.00
231 George Kell 52 .40 1.00
232 Bob Boone 73 .40 1.00
233 Minnie Minoso 52 .60 1.50
234 Billy Pierce 52 .40 1.00
235 Robin Roberts 52 .40 1.00
236 Johnny Sain 52 .40 1.00
237 Red Schoendienst 52 .40 1.00
238 Curt Simmons 52 .40 1.00
239 Duke Snider 52 .60 1.50
240 Bobby Thomson 52 .60 1.50
241 Hoyt Wilhelm 52 .60 1.50
242 Roy Face 53 .40 1.00
243 Ralph Kiner 53 .40 1.00
244 Hank Aaron 54 2.50 6.00
245 Al Kaline 54 1.00 2.50
246 Don Larsen 56 .40 1.00
247 Tug McGraw 65 .40 1.00
248 Don Newcombe 56 .60 1.50
249 Herb Score 56 .40 1.00
250 Clete Boyer 57 .40 1.00
251 Lindy McDaniel 57 .20 .50
252 Brooks Robinson 57 .60 1.50
253 Orlando Cepeda 58 .40 1.00
254 Larry Bowa 70 .40 1.00
255 Mike Cuellar 59 .40 1.00
256 Jim Perry 59 .40 1.00
257 Dave Parker 74 .40 1.00
258 Maury Wills 60 .40 1.00
259 Willie Davis 61 .20 .50
260 Juan Marichal 61 .40 1.00
261 Jim Bouton 62 .40 1.00
262 Dean Chance 62 .40 1.00
263 Sam McDowell 62 .40 1.00
264 Whitey Ford 53 .60 1.50
265 Bob Uecker 62 .60 1.50
266 Willie Stargell 63 .60 1.50
267 Rico Carty 64 .40 1.00
268 Tommy John 64 .40 1.00
269 Phil Niekro 64 .40 1.00
270 Paul Blair 65 .40 1.00
271 Steve Carlton 65 1.25 3.00
272 Jim Lonborg 65 .40 1.00
273 Tony Perez 65 .40 1.00
274 Ron Swoboda 65 .40 1.00
275 Fergie Jenkins 66 .40 1.00
276 Jim Palmer 66 .40 1.00
277 Sal Bando 67 .40 1.00
278 Tom Seaver 67 1.50 4.00
279 Johnny Bench 68 1.50 4.00
280 Nolan Ryan 68 2.50 6.00
281 Rollie Fingers 69 .40 1.00
282 Sparky Lyle 69 .40 1.00
283 Al Oliver 69 .40 1.00
284 Bob Watson 69 .40 1.00
285 Bill Buckner 70 .40 1.00
286 Bert Blyleven 71 .60 1.50
287 George Foster 71 .40 1.00
288 Al Hrabosky 71 .20 .50
289 Cecil Cooper 72 .40 1.00
290 Carlton Fisk 72 .60 1.50
291 Mickey Rivers 72 .40 1.00
292 Goose Gossage 73 .40 1.00
293 Rick Reuschel 73 .40 1.00
294 Bucky Dent 74 .40 1.00
295 Frank Tanana 74 .40 1.00
296 George Brett 75 3.00 8.00
297 Keith Hernandez 75 .40 1.00
298 Fred Lynn 75 .40 1.00
299 Robin Yount 75 1.00 2.50
300 Ron Guidry 76 .40 1.00
301 Jack Clark 77 .40 1.00
302 Mark Fidrych 77 .40 1.00
303 Dale Murphy 77 .60 1.50
304 Willie Hernandez 78 .20 .50
305 Lou Whitaker 78 .40 1.00
306 Kirk Gibson 81 .40 1.00
307 Wade Boggs 83 .40 1.00
308 Ryne Sandberg 83 2.50 6.00
309 Orel Hershiser 85 .40 1.00
310 Jimmy Key 85 .40 1.00
311 Richie Ashburn 52 .60 1.50
312 Smoky Burgess 52 .40 1.00
313 Gil Hodges 52 1.00 2.50
314 Ted Kluszewski 52 .60 1.50
315 Pee Wee Reese 52 1.00 2.50
316 Jackie Robinson 52 1.00 2.50
317 Jim Wynn 64 .20 .50
318 Satchel Paige 53 1.00 2.50
319 Roberto Clemente 55 2.50 6.00
320 Carl Furillo 56 .40 1.00
321 Don Drysdale 57 .60 1.50
322 Curt Flood 58 .40 1.00
323 Bob Allison 59 .40 1.00
324 Tony Conigliaro 64 .40 1.00
325 Dan Quisenberry 80 .40 1.00
326 Ralph Branca 52 .20 .50
327 Bob Feller 53 .40 1.00
328 Satchel Paige 53 1.00 2.50
329 George Kell 58 .40 1.00
330 Pee Wee Reese 58 .60 1.50
331 Bobby Thomson 60 .40 1.00
332 Carl Furillo 60 .20 .50
333 Hank Bauer 61 .20 .50
334 Herb Score 62 .40 1.00
335 Richie Ashburn 63 .60 1.50
336 Billy Pierce 64 .20 .50
337 Duke Snider 64 .60 1.50
338 Early Wynn 62 .20 .50
339 Robin Roberts 66 .40 1.00
340 Dick Groat 67 .40 1.00
341 Curt Simmons 67 .20 .50
342 Bob Uecker 67 .60 1.50
343 Smoky Burgess 67 .20 .50
344 Jim Bouton 68 .20 .50
345 Roy Face 69 .20 .50
346 Don Drysdale 69 .60 1.50
347 Bob Allison 70 .20 .50
348 Clete Boyer 71 .20 .50
349 Dean Chance 71 .20 .50
350 Tony Conigliaro 71 .20 .50
351 Curt Flood 71 .20 .50
352 Hoyt Wilhelm 72 .40 1.00
353 Ron Swoboda 73 .20 .50
354 Roberto Clemente 73 1.50 4.00
355 Tug McGraw 85 .20 .50
356 Orlando Cepeda 74 .40 1.00
357 Joe Garagiola 52 .20 .50
358 Juan Marichal 74 .40 1.00
359 Sam McDowell 74 .20 .50
360 Johnny Sain 55 .20 .50
361 Ted Kluszewski 61 .40 1.00
362 Al Kaline 74 1.00 2.50
363 Lindy McDaniel 75 .20 .50
364 Don Newcombe 60 .40 1.00
365 Jim Perry 75 .20 .50
366 Hank Aaron 76 1.50 4.00
367 Don Larsen 65 .20 .50
368 Mike Cuellar 77 .20 .50
369 Willie Davis 77 .20 .50
370 Ralph Kiner 53 .40 1.00
371 Minnie Minoso 64 .40 1.00
372 Larry Bowa 85 .20 .50
373 Brooks Robinson 77 .60 1.50
374 Bob Boone 90 .20 .50
375 Jim Lonborg 79 .20 .50
376 Paul Blair 80 .20 .50
377 Rico Carty 80 .20 .50
378 Sal Bando 81 .20 .50
379 Mark Fidrych 81 .20 .50
380 Al Hrabosky 81 .20 .50
381 Willie Stargell 82 .60 1.50
382 Johnny Bench 83 1.00 2.50
383 Dave Parker 91 .20 .50
384 Sparky Lyle 83 .20 .50
385 Fergie Jenkins 84 .40 1.00
386 Jim Palmer 84 .40 1.00
387 Whitey Ford 67 .60 1.50
388 Tony Perez 86 .40 1.00
389 Mickey Rivers 85 .20 .50
390 Bob Watson 85 .20 .50
391 Rollie Fingers 86 .40 1.00
392 George Foster 86 .20 .50
393 Al Oliver 86 .20 .50
394 Tom Seaver 87 .60 1.50
395 Maury Wills 72 .20 .50
396 Steve Carlton 87T .40 1.00
397 Cecil Cooper 88 .20 .50
398 Bill Buckner 88 .20 .50
399 Phil Niekro 87 .40 1.00
400 Red Schoendienst 62 .40 1.00
401 Ron Guidry 89 .20 .50
402 Willie Hernandez 89 .20 .50
403 Tommy John 89 .20 .50
404 Gil Hodges 63 1.00 2.50
405 Bucky Dent 84 .20 .50
406 Keith Hernandez 90 .40 1.00
407 Dan Quisenberry 90 .20 .50
408 Fred Lynn 91 .20 .50
409 Rick Reuschel 91 .20 .50
410 Jackie Robinson 56 1.00 2.50
411 Goose Gossage 92 .20 .50
412 Bert Blyleven 93 .40 1.00
413 Jack Clark 93 .20 .50
414 Carlton Fisk 93 .60 1.50
415 Dale Murphy 93 .60 1.50
416 Frank Tanana 93 .20 .50
417 George Brett 94 1.50 4.00
418 Robin Yount 94 1.00 2.50
419 Kirk Gibson 95 .40 1.00
420 Lou Whitaker 95 .40 1.00
421 Ryne Sandberg 97 2.00 5.00
422 Jimmy Key 98 .40 1.00
423 Nolan Ryan 94 1.50 4.00
424 Wade Boggs 00 .40 1.00
425 Orel Hershiser 00 .20 .50
426 Billy Martin MG 84 .60 1.50
427 Ralph Houk MG 62 .40 1.00
428 Chuck Tanner MG 72 .20 .50
429 Earl Weaver MG 71 .40 1.00
430 Leo Durocher MG 52 .40 1.00
431 AL HR Leaders 66 .40 1.00
432 NL HR Leaders 60 1.00 2.50
433 AL Batting Leaders 62 .40 1.00
434 Leading Firemen 79 .20 .50
435 Strikeout Leaders 77 .60 1.50
436 HR Leaders 74 .40 1.00
437 RBI Leaders 73 .60 1.50
438 Roger Maris Blasts 62 1.00 2.50
439 Carl Yastrzemski WS2 68 1.00 2.50
440 Nolan Ryan RB 78 1.50 4.00
441 Baltimore Orioles 70 .40 1.00
442 Tony Perez RB 86 .20 .50
443 Steve Carlton RB 84 .20 .50
444 Wade Boggs RB 89 .40 1.00
445 Andre Dawson RB 89 .40 1.00
446 Whitey Ford WS 62 .60 1.50
447 Hank Aaron WS 59 1.50 4.00
448 Bob Gibson WS 69 .60 1.50
449 Roberto Clemente WS 72 1.50 4.00
450 Orioles .40 1.00
B Robinson WS 71

2001 Topps Archives Autographs

Inserted at overall odds of one in 20, these 159 cards feature the players signing their reprint cards. The set is checklisted TAA1-TAA170 but 11 cards do not exist as follows: 9, 15, 47, 72, 82, 84, 95, 105, 109, 159 and 161. The only first series exchange card was Keith Hernandez but unfortunately, Topps was unable to fulfill the card and sent collectors an array of other signed cards. The series two exchange card subjects were Juan Marichal, Jack Morris, Billy Pierce, Boog Powell, Ron Santo, Enos Slaughter, Ozzie Smith, Reggie Smith, Don Sutton, Bob Uecker, Jim Wynn and Robin Yount. Of these players, Juan Marichal, Ozzie Smith and Reggie Smith did not return any cards. The series one exchange date was April 30th, 2002 . The series two exchange deadline was exactly one year later - April 30th, 2003.

SER.1 GROUP A ODDS 1:3049
SER.2 GROUP A ODDS 1:2904
SER.1 GROUP B ODDS 1:872
SER.2 GROUP B ODDS 1:480
SER.1 GROUP C ODDS 1:697
SER.2 GROUP C ODDS 1:4782
SER.1 GROUP D ODDS 1:122
SER.2 GROUP D ODDS 1:662
SER.1 GROUP E ODDS 1:26
SER.2 GROUP E ODDS 1:209
SER.1 GROUP F ODDS 1:6097
SER.2 GROUP F ODDS 1:1455
SER.2 GROUP G ODDS 1:320
SER.2 GROUP H ODDS 1:412
SER.2 GROUP I ODDS 1:192
SER.2 GROUP J ODDS 1:38
SER.2 GROUP K ODDS 1:329
SER.1 OVERALL ODDS 1:20
SER.2 OVERALL ODDS 1:20
A1-A2 STATED PRINT RUN 50 SETS
A1-A2/B2 ARE NOT SERIAL-NUMBERED
A1-A2/B2 PRINT RUNS PROVIDED BY TOPPS
SER.1 EXCH.DEADLINE 4/30/02
SER.2 EXCH.DEADLINE 4/30/03
TAA1 Johnny Antonelli E1 6.00 15.00
TAA2 Hank Bauer E1 8.00 20.00
TAA3 Yogi Berra A2 SP/50 *
TAA4 Ralph Branca E1 6.00 15.00
TAA5 Dom DiMaggio E1 25.00 60.00
TAA6 Joe Garagiola E1 25.00 60.00
TAA7 Carl Erskine D1 12.00 30.00
TAA8 Bob Feller E1 12.00 30.00
TAA10 Dick Groat D1 8.00 20.00
TAA11 Monte Irvin E1 6.00 15.00
TAA12 George Kell E1 6.00 15.00
TAA13 Vernon Law E1 8.00 20.00
TAA14 Bob Boone E1 8.00 20.00
TAA16 Willie Mays A2 SP/50 *
TAA17 Gil McDougald E1 6.00 15.00
TAA18 Minnie Minoso E1 12.00 30.00
TAA19 Andy Pafko D2 6.00 15.00
TAA20 Billy Pierce E2 6.00 15.00
TAA21 Phil Rizzuto B2 SP/200 * 50.00 120.00
TAA22 Robin Roberts C1 12.00 30.00
TAA23 Preacher Roe E1 12.50 30.00
TAA24 Johnny Sain E1 6.00 15.00
TAA25 Hank Sauer E1 12.50 30.00
TAA26 Red Schoendienst E1 15.00 40.00
TAA27 Bobby Shantz E1 8.00 20.00
TAA28 Curt Simmons E1 8.00 20.00
TAA29 Enos Slaughter E2 10.00 25.00
TAA30 Duke Snider B1 20.00 50.00
TAA31 Warren Spahn C2 25.00 60.00
TAA32 Bobby Thomson E1 6.00 15.00
TAA33 Mickey Vernon B2 6.00 15.00
TAA34 Hoyt Wilhelm D1 20.00 50.00
TAA35 Jim Wynn E2 6.00 15.00
TAA36 Roy Face E1 6.00 15.00
TAA37 Gaylord Perry C2 6.00 15.00
TAA38 Ralph Kiner B1 25.00 60.00
TAA39 Johnny Podres E2 10.00 25.00
TAA40 Hank Aaron A2 SP/50 *
TAA41 Ernie Banks A2 SP/50 *
TAA42 Al Kaline B1 50.00 120.00
TAA43 Moose Skowron E1 6.00 15.00
TAA44 Don Larsen A1 SP/50 * 200.00 300.00
TAA45 Harmon Killebrew B1 75.00 150.00
TAA46 Tug McGraw E1 12.50 30.00
TAA48 Don Newcombe E1 15.00 40.00
TAA49 Jim Piersall E2 6.00 15.00
TAA50 Herb Score E1 6.00 15.00
TAA51 Frank Thomas E1 8.00 20.00
TAA52 Clete Boyer D1 6.00 15.00
TAA53 Bill Mazeroski C2 30.00 80.00
TAA54 Lindy McDaniel E1 10.00 25.00
TAA55 Bobby Richardson E2 6.00 15.00
TAA56 B.Robinson A1 SP/50 * 250.00 500.00
TAA57 Frank Robinson B1 40.00 80.00
TAA58 Orlando Cepeda B1 30.00 80.00
TAA59 Stan Musial A1 SP/50 * 400.00 600.00
TAA60 Larry Bowa D1 6.00 15.00
TAA61 Johnny Callison E2 6.00 15.00
TAA62 Mike Cuellar D1 10.00 25.00
TAA63 Bob Gibson A1 SP/50 * 200.00 300.00
TAA64 Jim Perry E2 6.00 15.00
TAA65 Frank Howard E1 6.00 15.00
TAA66 Dave Parker E1 10.00 25.00
TAA67 Willie McCovey D2 50.00 120.00
TAA68 Maury Wills E1 8.00 20.00
TAA69 Carl Yastrzemski F1 50.00 100.00
TAA70 Willie Davis E1 6.00 15.00
TAA71 Jim Maloney E2 10.00 25.00
TAA73 Ron Santo E1 25.00 60.00
TAA74 Jim Bouton D1 8.00 20.00
TAA75 Lou Brock A2 SP/50 *
TAA76 Dean Chance E1 6.00 15.00
TAA77 T.McCarver B2 SP/200 * 40.00 80.00
TAA78 Sam McDowell D1 12.00 30.00
TAA79 Joe Pepitone E1 10.00 25.00
TAA80 Whitey Ford F1 20.00 50.00
TAA81 Boog Powell E2 6.00 15.00
TAA83 Bill Freehan D2 6.00 15.00
TAA85 Dick Allen B2 30.00 60.00
TAA86 Rico Carty E1 6.00 15.00
TAA87 Willie Horton E2 12.00 30.00
TAA88 Tommy John E1 6.00 15.00
TAA89 Mickey Lolich E2 8.00 20.00
TAA90 Phil Niekro D1 15.00 40.00
TAA91 Wilbur Wood E1 8.00 20.00
TAA92 Paul Blair E1 6.00 15.00
TAA93 Bert Campaneris E2 6.00 15.00
TAA94 Steve Carlton D1 30.00 80.00
TAA96 Jim Lonborg E1 6.00 15.00
TAA97 Luis Aparicio B1 12.00 30.00
TAA98 Tony Perez D1 30.00 80.00
TAA99 Joe Morgan B2 SP/200 * 20.00 50.00
TAA100 Ron Swoboda D1 8.00 20.00
TAA101 Luis Tiant E2 6.00 15.00
TAA102 Fergie Jenkins D1 15.00 40.00
TAA103 Bobby Murcer D2 12.00 30.00
TAA104 Jim Palmer B1 50.00 100.00
TAA106 Sal Bando E2 6.00 15.00
TAA107 Ken Holtzman B1 30.00 80.00
TAA108 T.Seaver A2 SP/50 *
TAA110 J.Bench A1 SP/50 *
TAA111 Hal McRae E2 6.00 15.00
TAA112 Nolan Ryan A2 SP/50 *
TAA113 Roy White D2 6.00 15.00
TAA114 Rollie Fingers C1 10.00 25.00
TAA115 R.Jackson A2 SP/50 *
TAA116 Sparky Lyle E1 12.00 30.00
TAA117 Graig Nettles D2 6.00 15.00
TAA118 Al Oliver E1 6.00 15.00
TAA119 Joe Rudi B2 6.00 15.00
TAA120 Bob Watson E1 8.00 20.00
TAA121 Vida Blue E2 6.00 15.00
TAA122 Bill Buckner E1 20.00 50.00
TAA123 Darrell Evans E1 6.00 15.00
TAA124 Bert Blyleven D1 20.00 50.00
TAA125 Dave Concepcion D2 30.00 60.00
TAA126 George Foster E1 8.00 20.00
TAA127 Bobby Grich E1 6.00 15.00
TAA128 Al Hrabosky E1 6.00 15.00
TAA129 Greg Luzinski D1 6.00 15.00
TAA130 Cecil Cooper E1 8.00 20.00
TAA131 Ron Cey E2 6.00 15.00
TAA132 Carlton Fisk B1 60.00 120.00
TAA133 George Hendrick E2 6.00 15.00
TAA134 Mickey Rivers E1 6.00 15.00
TAA135 Dwight Evans D2 20.00 50.00
TAA136 Rich Gossage E1 6.00 15.00
TAA137 Gary Matthews B2 6.00 15.00
TAA138 Rick Reuschel E1 6.00 15.00
TAA139 M.Schmidt A1 SP/50 * 300.00 800.00
TAA140 Bucky Dent D1 10.00 25.00
TAA141 Jim Kaat B2 8.00 20.00
TAA142 Frank Tanana E1 6.00 15.00
TAA143 D.Winfield B2 SP/200 * 60.00 120.00
TAA144 G.Brett A1 SP/50 * 400.00 800.00
TAA145 G.Carter B2 SP/200 * 30.00 60.00
TAA147 Fred Lynn C1 20.00 50.00
TAA148 R.Yount B2 SP/200 * 100.00 175.00
TAA149 D.Eckersley B2 SP/200 * 40.00 80.00
TAA150 Ron Guidry E2 10.00 25.00
TAA151 Kent Tekulve D1 6.00 15.00
TAA152 Jack Clark E1 6.00 15.00
TAA153 A.Dawson B2 SP/200 * 50.00 100.00
TAA154 Mark Fidrych E1 20.00 50.00
TAA155 D.Martinez B2 SP/200 * 30.00 60.00
TAA156 Dale Murphy C1 30.00 60.00
TAA157 Bruce Sutter D2 8.00 20.00
TAA158 Willie Hernandez D2 6.00 15.00
TAA160 Lou Whitaker D2 20.00 50.00
TAA162 Kirk Gibson E1 25.00 60.00
TAA163 Lee Smith D2 8.00 20.00
TAA164 Wade Boggs B1 100.00 200.00
TAA165 R.Sandberg B2 SP/200 * 150.00 300.00
TAA166 Don Mattingly D1 40.00 80.00
TAA167 Joe Carter B2 SP/200 * 60.00 120.00
TAA168 Orel Hershiser D2 20.00 50.00
TAA169 Kirby Puckett A2 SP/50 *
TAA170 Jimmy Key C1 20.00 50.00

2001 Topps Archives AutoProofs

Inserted at a rate of one in 2,444 in series one and one in 2,391 in series two these 10 cards feature players signing their actual cards. Each of these cards are serial numbered to 100. Willie McCovey and Willie Mays were both first series exchange cards with a redemption deadline of April 30th, 2002. Carlton Fisk, Robin Roberts and Hoyt Wilhelm were series two exchange cards with a redemption deadline of April 30th, 2003.

SER.1 STATED ODDS 1:2444
SER.2 STATED ODDS 1:2391
STATED PRINT RUN 100 SERIAL #'d SETS
SER.1 EXCH.DEADLINE 04/30/02
SER.2 EXCH.DEADLINE 04/30/03
1 Wade Boggs 99 S1 40.00 80.00
2 Carlton Fisk 93 S2 50.00 100.00
3 Willie Mays 73 S1 100.00 200.00
4 Willie McCovey 80 S1 40.00 80.00
5 Jim Palmer 82/84 S1 30.00 60.00
6 Robin Roberts 66 S2 40.00 80.00
7 Duke Snider 64 S2 40.00 80.00
8 Warren Spahn 65 S2 40.00 80.00
9 Hoyt Wilhelm 63 S2 15.00 40.00
10 Carl Yastrzemski 83 S1 75.00 150.00

2001 Topps Archives Bucks

Randomly inserted in packs, these three cards issued in the style of the old Baseball Bucks were good for money toward Topps 50th anniversary merchandise.

ONE DOLLAR SER.1 ODDS 1:83
ONE DOLLAR SER.2 ODDS 1:80
FIVE DOLLAR SER.1 ODDS 1:1242
FIVE DOLLAR SER.2 ODDS 1:1203
TEN DOLLAR SER.1 ODDS 1:2483
TEN DOLLAR SER.2 ODDS 1:2406
TB1 Willie Mays $1 4.00 10.00
TB2 Roberto Clemente $5 10.00 25.00
TB3 Jackie Robinson $10 10.00 25.00

2001 Topps Archives Future Rookie Reprints

Issued five per sealed Topps factory and HTA sets, these 20 cards feature Rookie Card reprints of today's leading players.

COMPLETE SET (20) 25.00 50.00
FIVE PER SEALED TOPPS FACT.SET
FIVE PER SEALED TOPPS HTA FACT.SET
1 Barry Bonds 87 3.00 8.00
2 Chipper Jones 91 1.25 3.00
3 Cal Ripken 82 4.00 10.00
4 Shawn Green 92 .50 1.25
5 Frank Thomas 90 1.25 3.00
6 Derek Jeter 93 3.00 8.00
7 Geoff Jenkins 96 .50 1.25
8 Jim Edmonds 93 .50 1.25
9 Bernie Williams 90 .75 2.00
10 Sammy Sosa 90 1.25 3.00
11 Rickey Henderson 80 1.25 3.00
12 Tony Gwynn 83 .50 1.25
13 Randy Johnson 89 1.25 3.00
14 Juan Gonzalez 90 .50 1.25
15 Gary Sheffield 89 .50 1.25
16 Manny Ramirez 92 .75 2.00
17 Pokey Reese 92 .50 1.25
18 Preston Wilson 93 .50 1.25
19 Jay Payton 95 .50 1.25
20 Rafael Palmeiro 87 .75 2.00

2001 Topps Archives Rookie Reprint Bat Relics

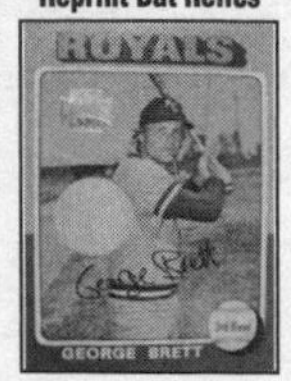

Inserted in series one packs at a rate of one in 1,356 and second series packs at a rate of one in 1,1307 these six cards feature not only the rookie reprint but also a game used bat slice.

SER.1 STATED ODDS 1:1356

SER.2 STATED ODDS 1:1307
TARR1 Johnny Bench 12.00 30.00
TARR2 George Brett 8.00 20.00
TARR3 Fred Lynn 6.00 15.00
TARR4 Reggie Jackson 8.00 20.00
TARR5 Mike Schmidt 8.00 20.00
TARR6 Willie Stargell 8.00 20.00

2002 Topps Archives

This 200 card set was released in early April, 2002. These cards were issued in eight card packs which were issued in 20 pack boxes and were packed eight boxes to a case. The packs had an SRP of $4 per pack. This set was subtitled "Best Years" and it featured a reprint of the player's Topps card from their best year in the majors. Interestingly, Topps changed the backs of most of the cards to include the stats from that selected year. Also, in many of the cards, the text was changed to reflect the best year rather than using the original verbiage.

COMPLETE SET (200) 20.00 50.00
1 Willie Mays 62 2.00 5.00
2 Dale Murphy 83 .60 1.50
3 Dave Winfield 79 .40 1.00
4 Roger Maris 61 1.00 2.50
5 Ron Cey 77 .40 1.00
6 Lee Smith 91 .40 1.00
7 Len Dykstra 93 .40 1.00
8 Ray Fosse 70 .40 1.00
9 Warren Spahn 57 .60 1.50
10 Herb Score 56 .40 1.00
11 Jim Wynn 74 .40 1.00
12 Sam McDowell 70 .40 1.00
13 Fred Lynn 79 .40 1.00
14 Yogi Berra 54 1.00 2.50
15 Ron Santo 64 .60 1.50
16 Alvin Dark 53 .40 1.00
17 Bill Buckner 85 .40 1.00
18 Rollie Fingers 81 .40 1.00
19 Tony Gwynn 97 1.25 3.00
20 Red Schoendienst 53 .40 1.00
21 Gaylord Perry 72 .40 1.00
22 Jose Cruz 83 .40 1.00
23 Dennis Martinez 91 .40 1.00
24 Dave McNally 68 .40 1.00
25 Norm Cash 61 .40 1.00
26 Ted Kluszewski 54 .60 1.50
27 Rick Reuschel 77 .40 1.00
28 Bruce Sutter 77 .40 1.00
29 Don Larsen 56 .40 1.00
30 Claudell Washington 82 .40 1.00
31 Luis Aparicio 60 .40 1.00
32 Clete Boyer 62 .40 1.00
33 Goose Gossage 77 .40 1.00
34 Ray Knight 79 .40 1.00
35 Roy Campanella 53 1.00 2.50
36 Tug McGraw 71 .40 1.00
37 Bob Lemon 52 .40 1.00
38 Willie Stargell 71 .60 1.50
39 Roberto Clemente 66 2.00 5.00
40 Jim Fregosi 70 .40 1.00
41 Reggie Smith 77 .40 1.00
42 Dave Parker 78 .40 1.00
43 Darrell Evans 73 .40 1.00
44 Ryne Sandberg 90 1.50 4.00
45 Manny Mota 72 .40 1.00
46 Dennis Eckersley 92 .40 1.00
47 Nellie Fox 59 .60 1.50
48 Gil Hodges 54 1.00 2.50
49 Reggie Jackson 69 .60 1.50
50 Bobby Shantz 52 .40 1.00
51 Cecil Cooper 80 .40 1.00
52 Jim Kaat 66 .40 1.00
53 George Hendrick 80 .40 1.00
54 Johnny Podres 61 .40 1.00
55 Bob Gibson 68 .60 1.50
56 Vern Law 60 .40 1.00
57 Joe Adcock 56 .40 1.00
58 Jack Clark 87 .40 1.00
59 Bill Mazeroski 60 .60 1.50
60 Carl Yastrzemski 67 1.50 4.00
61 Bobby Murcer 71 .40 1.00
62 Davey Johnson 73 .40 1.00
63 Jim Palmer 75 .40 1.00
64 Roy Face 59 .40 1.00
65 Dean Chance 64 .40 1.00
66 Moose Skowron 60 .60 1.50
67 Dwight Evans 87 .60 1.50
68 Kirk Gibson 88 .40 1.00
69 Sal Bando 69 .40 1.00
70 Mike Schmidt 80 2.00 5.00
71 Bo Jackson 89 1.00 2.50
72 Chris Chambliss 76 .40 1.00
73 Fergie Jenkins 71 .40 1.00
74 Brooks Robinson 64 .60 1.50
75 Bobby Richardson 62 .40 1.00
76 Duke Snider 54 .60 1.50
77 Allie Reynolds 52 .60 1.50
78 Harmon Killebrew 66 1.00 2.50
79 Steve Carlton 72 .40 1.00
80 Bert Blyleven 73 .40 1.00
81 Phil Niekro 69 .40 1.00
82 Lew Burdette 56 .40 1.00
83 Hoyt Wilhelm 64 .40 1.00
84 Curt Flood 65 .40 1.00
85 Willie Hernandez 84 .40 1.00
86 Robin Yount 82 1.00 2.50
87 Robin Roberts 52- .40 1.00
88 Whitey Ford 61 .60 1.50
89 Tony Oliva 64 .40 1.00
90 Don Newcombe 56 .40 1.00
91 Al Oliver 82 .40 1.00
92 Mike Cuellar 69 .40 1.00
93 Mike Scott 86 .40 1.00
94 Dick Allen 66 .40 1.00
95 Jimmy Piersall 56 .40 1.00
96 Bill Freehan 68 .40 1.00
97 Willie Horton 65 .40 1.00
98 Bob Friend 60 .40 1.00
99 Ken Holtzman 73 .40 1.00
100 Rico Carty 70 .40 1.00
101 Gil McDougald 56 .40 1.00
102 Lee May 69 .40 1.00
103 Joe Pepitone 64 .40 1.00
104 Gene Tenace 75 .40 1.00
105 Gary Carter 85 .40 1.00
106 Tim McCarver 67 .40 1.00
107 Ernie Banks 58 1.00 2.50
108 George Foster 77 .40 1.00
109 Lou Brock 74 .60 1.50
110 Dick Groat 60 .40 1.00
111 Graig Nettles 77 .40 1.00
112 Boog Powell 69 .60 1.50
113 Joe Carter 86 .40 1.00
114 Juan Marichal 66 .40 1.00
115 Larry Doby 54 .40 1.00
116 Fernando Valenzuela 86 .40 1.00
117 Luis Tiant 68 .40 1.00
118 Early Wynn 59 .40 1.00
119 Bill Madlock 75 .40 1.00
120 Eddie Mathews 53 1.00 2.50
121 George Brett 80 2.00 5.00
122 Al Kaline 55 1.00 2.50
123 Frank Howard 69 .40 1.00
124 Mickey Lolich 71 .40 1.00
125 Kirby Puckett 88 1.00 2.50
126 Bob Cerv 58 .40 1.00
127 Will Clark 89 .60 1.50
128 Vida Blue 71 .40 1.00
129 Kevin Mitchell 89 .40 1.00
130 Bucky Dent 80 .40 1.00
131 Tom Seaver 69 .60 1.50
132 Jerry Koosman 76 .40 1.00
133 Orlando Cepeda 61 .40 1.00
134 Nolan Ryan 73 2.50 6.00
135 Tony Kubek 60 .60 1.50
136 Don Drysdale 62 .60 1.50
137 Paul Blair 69 .40 1.00
138 Elston Howard 63 .40 1.00
139 Joe Rudi 74 .40 1.00
140 Tommie Agee 70 .40 1.00
141 Richie Ashburn 58 .60 1.50
142 Jim Bunning 65 .40 1.00
143 Hank Sauer 52 .40 1.00
144 Greg Luzinski 77 .40 1.00
145 Ron Guidry 78 .40 1.00
146 Rod Carew 77 .60 1.50
147 Andre Dawson 87 .40 1.00
148 Keith Hernandez 79 .40 1.00
149 Carlton Fisk 77 .60 1.50
150 Cleon Jones 69 .40 1.00
151 Don Mattingly 85 2.00 5.00
152 Vada Pinson 63 .40 1.00
153 Ozzie Smith 87 1.50 4.00
154 Dave Concepcion 79 .40 1.00
155 Al Rosen 53 .40 1.00
156 Tommy John 68 .40 1.00
157 Bob Ojeda 86 .40 1.00
158 Frank Robinson 66 .60 1.50
159 Darryl Strawberry 87 .40 1.00
160 Bobby Bonds 73 .40 1.00
161 Bert Campaneris 70 .40 1.00
162 Catfish Hunter 74 .60 1.50
163 Bud Harrelson 70 .40 1.00
164 Dwight Gooden 85 .40 1.00
165 Wade Boggs 87 .60 1.50
166 Joe Morgan 76 .40 1.00
167 Ron Swoboda 67 .40 1.00
168 Hank Aaron 57 2.00 5.00
169 Steve Garvey 77 .40 1.00
170 Mickey Rivers 77 .40 1.00
171 Johnny Bench 70 1.00 2.50
172 Ralph Terry 62 .40 1.00
173 Billy Pierce 56 .40 1.00
174 Thurman Munson 76 1.00 2.50
175 Don Sutton 72 .40 1.00
176 Sparky Anderson 84 MG .40 1.00
177 Gil Hodges 69 MG 1.00 2.50
178 Davey Johnson 86 MG .40 1.00
179 Frank Robinson 89 MG .60 1.50
180 Red Schoendienst 67 MG .60 1.50
181 Roger Maris 61 AS 1.00 2.50
182 Willie Mays 62 AS 2.00 5.00
183 Luis Aparicio 60 AS .40 1.00
184 Nellie Fox 59 AS .60 1.50
185 Ernie Banks 58 AS 1.00 2.50
186 Orlando Cepeda 62 AS .40 1.00
187 Whitey Ford 61 AS .60 1.50
188 Bob Gibson 69 AS .60 1.50
189 Bill Mazeroski 59 AS .60 1.50
190 Hank Aaron 58 AS 2.00 5.00
191 1971 AL Home Run Ldrs .40 1.00
192 1962 NL Home Run Ldrs .60 1.50
193 1967 NL RBI Ldrs 1.00 2.50
194 1970 NL Win Ldrs .40 1.00
195 1976 AL ERA Ldrs .40 1.00
196 Hank Aaron 76 HL 2.00 5.00
197 Brooks Robinson 78 HL .60 1.50
198 Tom Seaver 70 HL .40 1.00
199 Jim Palmer 71 HL .40 1.00
200 Lou Brock 75 HL .60 1.50

2002 Topps Archives Autographs

Issued at overall stated odds of one in 22 hobby packs and 1:22 retail packs, these 59 cards feature many of the players featured in the 2002 Topps Archives set. Since there were so many groups that the different players belong to 12 different groups. We have notated the group that these players belong to next to their name in our checklist.

GROUP A ODDS 1:19,803 HOB, 1:20,040 RET
GROUP B ODDS 1:12,872 HOB, 1:13,360 RET
GROUP C ODDS 1:11,193 HOB, 1:11,451 RET
GROUP D ODDS 1:8045 HOB, 1:8016 RET
GROUP E ODDS 1:753 HOB, 1:756 RET
GROUP F ODDS 1:3387 HOB, 1:3340 RET
GROUP G ODDS 1:1355 HOB, 1:1359 RET
GROUP H ODDS 1:1129 HOB, 1:1129 RET
GROUP I ODDS 1:847 HOB, 1:844 RET
GROUP J ODDS 1:59 HOB, 1:59 RET
GROUP K ODDS 1:748 HOB, 1:749 RET
GROUP L ODDS 1:45 HOB, 1:45 RET
OVERALL STATED ODDS 1:22 HOB/RET
TAAAD Alvin Dark 53 J 6.00 15.00
TAAAK Al Kaline 55 E 25.00 50.00
TAABB Bobby Bonds 73 J 8.00 20.00
TAABC Bert Campaneris 70 L 6.00 15.00
TAABD Bucky Dent 80 J 6.00 15.00
TAABH Bud Harrelson 70 L 6.00 15.00
TAABJ Bo Jackson 89 F 30.00 80.00
TAABP Billy Pierce 56 J 6.00 15.00
TAABPO Boog Powell 69 J 10.00 25.00
TAABRO B.Robinson 64 E 20.00 50.00
TAABS Bruce Sutter 77 J 15.00 40.00
TAACC Chris Chambliss 76 J 10.00 25.00
TAADA Dick Allen 66 J 10.00 25.00
TAADEV Darrell Evans 73 J 6.00 15.00
TAADG Dwight Gooden 85 G 30.00 80.00
TAADGR Dick Groat 60 L 6.00 15.00
TAADM Dave McNally 68 L 20.00 50.00
TAADN Don Newcombe 56 I 15.00 40.00
TAADP Dave Parker 78 H 15.00 40.00
TAADS Duke Snider 56 E 25.00 60.00
TAADW Dave Winfield 79 D 30.00 80.00
TAAEB Ernie Banks 58 E 60.00 150.00
TAAFJ Fergie Jenkins 71 J 6.00 15.00
TAAFL Fred Lynn 79 J 15.00 40.00
TAAGB George Brett 80 E 100.00 250.00
TAAGC Gary Carter 85 E 20.00 50.00
TAAGF George Foster 77 L 12.00 30.00
TAAGL Greg Luzinski 77 J 6.00 15.00
TAAGP Gaylord Perry 72 J 10.00 25.00
TAAHA Hank Aaron 57 E 200.00 400.00
TAAHK Harmon Killebrew 69 E 25.00 60.00
TAAHW Hoyt Wilhelm 64 L 6.00 15.00
TAAJBU Jim Bunning 65 L 6.00 15.00
TAAJCR Jose Cruz 83 K 6.00 15.00
TAAJF Jim Fregosi 70 I 6.00 15.00
TAAJK Jim Kaat 66 J 6.00 15.00
TAAJKO Jerry Koosman 76 G 20.00 50.00
TAAJP Jim Palmer 75 E 10.00 25.00
TAAJPI Jimmy Piersall 56 J 6.00 15.00
TAAJPO Johnny Podres 61 J 6.00 15.00
TAAJR Joe Rudi 74 J 6.00 15.00
TAAKH Keith Hernandez 79 J 10.00 28.00
TAAKM Kevin Mitchell 89 J 8.00 20.00
TAAKP Kirby Puckett 88 A 150.00 400.00
TAALB Lew Burdette 56 L 10.00 25.00
TAALD Len Dykstra 94 J 6.00 15.00
TAALS Lee Smith 91 H 6.00 15.00
TAAMR Mickey Rivers 77 L 6.00 15.00
TAAMS Mike Schmidt 80 B 25.00 60.00
TAARCE Ron Cey 77 L 6.00 15.00
TAARS Ron Santo 64 L 20.00 50.00
TAARSM Reggie Smith 77 L 10.00 25.00
TAART Ralph Terry 62 J 6.00 15.00
TAARY Robin Yount 82 C 30.00 80.00
TAASB Sal Bando 69 L 6.00 15.00
TAASG Steve Garvey 77 J 10.00 25.00
TAATJ Tommy John 68 L 6.00 15.00
TAATO Tony Oliva 64 J 12.00 30.00
TAAWH Willie Hernandez 84 L 6.00 15.00

2002 Topps Archives Bat Relics

Randomly inserted into hobby and retail packs, these 19 cards feature players from the Archives set along a game-used bat piece. Players in group A were inserted at stated odds of one in 106 while players in group B were inserted at stated odds of one in 282. We have notated what group each player is part of in our checklist.

GROUP A ODDS 1:106 HOB/RET
GROUP B ODDS 1:282 HOB/RET
TBRAD Andre Dawson 87 A 6.00 15.00
TBRBF Bill Freehan 68 A 4.00 10.00
TBRBR Brooks Robinson 64 A 6.00 15.00
TBRCY Carl Yastrzemski 67 B 10.00 25.00
TBRDE Dwight Evans 87 A 4.00 10.00
TBRDM Don Mattingly 85 A 10.00 25.00
TBRDP Dave Parker 78 A 4.00 10.00
TBRGB George Brett 80 A 10.00 25.00
TBRGC Gary Carter 85 A 6.00 15.00
TBRJB Johnny Bench 70 A 10.00 25.00
TBRJC Joe Carter 86 A 4.00 10.00
TBRJM Joe Morgan 76 B 6.00 15.00
TBRNC Norm Cash 61 A 4.00 10.00
TBRRJ Reggie Jackson 69 A 6.00 15.00
TBRRM Roger Maris 61 A 10.00 25.00
TBRRS Ron Santo 64 A 6.00 15.00
TBRRY Robin Yount 82 B 10.00 25.00
TBRWH Willie Horton 65 A 4.00 10.00
TBRWS Willie Stargell 71 A 6.00 15.00

2002 Topps Archives Reprints

Issued at a stated rate of five per sealed 2002 Topps Factory set, these 10 cards feature reprints of first Topps cards of some of the leading superstars in baseball.

COMPLETE SET (10) 10.00 25.00
FIVE PER SEALED TOPPS FACTORY SET
1 Alex Rodriguez 98 1.00 2.50
2 Jason Giambi 94 .75 2.00
3 Pedro Martinez 93 .75 2.00
4 Ichiro Suzuki 01 1.50 4.00
5 Jeff Bagwell 91 .75 2.00
6 Ivan Rodriguez 91 .75 2.00
7 Mike Piazza 93 1.25 3.00
8 Nomar Garciaparra 95 1.25 3.00
9 Ken Griffey Jr. 89 1.50 4.00
10 Albert Pujols 01 1.50 4.00

2002 Topps Archives Seat Relics

Randomly inserted into hobby and retail packs, these 19 cards feature a player from the Archives set along with a piece of a seat from a ballpark they played in. There were three different groups of players and they were inserted at odds ranging from one in 80 packs to one in 1636 packs.

GROUP A ODDS 1:1629 HOB, 1:1636 RET
GROUP B ODDS 1:80 HOB, 1:80 RET
GROUP C ODDS 1:1160 HOB, 1:1162 RET
TSRBL Bob Lemon 52 B 6.00 15.00
TSRDP Dave Parker 78 B 6.00 15.00
TSRDS Duke Snider 54 B 8.00 20.00
TSREB Ernie Banks 58 B 10.00 25.00
TSREM Eddie Mathews 53 B 10.00 25.00
TSRHS Herb Score 56 B 6.00 15.00
TSRJB Jim Bunning 65 B 6.00 15.00
TSRJC Joe Carter 86 B 6.00 15.00
TSRJP Jim Palmer 75 B 6.00 15.00
TSRML Mickey Lolich 71 B 6.00 15.00
TSRNF Nellie Fox 59 B 8.00 20.00
TSRRA Richie Ashburn 58 B 8.00 20.00
TSRRC Rod Carew 77 B 8.00 20.00
TSRRG Ron Guidry 78 C 6.00 15.00
TSRSA Sparky Anderson 84 B 6.00 15.00
TSRSM Sam McDowell 70 B 6.00 15.00
TSRTK Ted Kluszewski 54 B 8.00 20.00
TSRWS Warren Spahn 57 B 10.00 25.00
TSRYB Yogi Berra 54 A 10.00 25.00

2002 Topps Archives Uniform Relics

Inserted into hobby and retail packs at stated odds of one in 28, these 20 cards feature players from the Archives set along with a game-worn uniform swatch of that player.

STATED ODDS 1:28 HOB/RET
TURBB Bobby Bonds 73 2.00 5.00
TURDC Dave Concepcion 79 2.00 5.00
TURDE Dennis Eckersley 92 3.00 8.00
TURDM Dale Murphy 83 5.00 12.00
TURDS Don Sutton 72 3.00 8.00
TURDW Dave Winfield 79 3.00 8.00
TURFL Fred Lynn 79 2.00 5.00
TURFR Frank Robinson 66 3.00 8.00
TURGB George Brett 80 10.00 25.00
TURGP Gaylord Perry 72 3.00 8.00
TURKP Kirby Puckett 88 5.00 12.00
TURNR Nolan Ryan 73 15.00 40.00
TUROC Orlando Cepeda 61 3.00 8.00
TUROS Ozzie Smith 87 3.00 8.00
TURPN Phil Niekro 69 3.00 8.00
TURRS Ryne Sandberg 90 10.00 25.00
TURSA Sparky Anderson 84 3.00 8.00
TURSG Steve Garvey 77 2.00 5.00
TURWB Wade Boggs 87 3.00 8.00
TURWC Will Clark 89 3.00 8.00

2001 Topps Archives Reserve

This 100 card set was issued in five card packs. These five card packs were issued in special display boxes which included one signed baseball per sealed box. These sealed boxes were issued six boxes to a case. The boxes (ball plus packs) had an SPR of $100 per box. All cards have a chrome-like finish to them.

COMPLETE SET (100) 30.00 60.00
1 Joe Adcock 52 .60 1.50
2 Brooks Robinson 57 1.00 2.50
3 Luis Aparicio 74 .60 1.50
4 Richie Ashburn 52 1.00 2.50
5 Hank Bauer 52 .60 1.50
6 Johnny Bench 68 2.50 6.00
7 Wade Boggs 83 1.00 2.50
8 Moose Skowron 54 .60 1.50
9 George Brett 75 4.00 10.00
10 Lou Brock 62 .60 1.50
11 Roy Campanella 52 1.50 4.00
12 Willie Hernandez 78 .60 1.50
13 Steve Carlton 65 2.00 5.00
14 Gary Carter 75 1.00 2.50
15 Hoyt Wilhelm 52 1.00 2.50
16 Orlando Cepeda 58 .60 1.50
17 Roberto Clemente 55 4.00 8.00
18 Dale Murphy 77 1.00 2.50
19 Dave Concepcion 71 .60 1.50
20 Dom DiMaggio 52 .60 1.50
21 Larry Doby 52 .60 1.50
22 Don Drysdale 57 1.00 2.50
23 Dennis Eckersley 76 .60 1.50
24 Bob Feller 52 .60 1.50
25 Rollie Fingers 69 .60 1.50
26 Carlton Fisk 72 1.00 2.50
27 Nellie Fox 56 1.00 2.50
28 Mickey Rivers 72 .60 1.50
29 Tommy John 64 .60 1.50
30 Johnny Sain 52 .60 1.50
31 Keith Hernandez 75 .60 1.50
32 Gil Hodges 52 1.50 4.00
33 Elston Howard 56 1.00 2.50
34 Frank Howard 60 .60 1.50
35 Bob Gibson 59 1.00 2.50
36 Fergie Jenkins 66 .60 1.50
37 Jackie Jensen 52 .60 1.50
38 Al Kaline 54 1.50 4.00
39 Harmon Killebrew 55 1.50 4.00
40 Ralph Kiner 53 .60 1.50
41 Dick Groat 52 .60 1.50
42 Don Larsen 56 .60 1.50
43 Ralph Branca 52 .60 1.50
44 Mickey Lolich 64 .60 1.50
45 Juan Marichal 61 .60 1.50
46 Roger Maris 58 1.50 4.00
47 Bobby Thomson 52 1.00 2.50
48 Eddie Mathews 52 1.50 4.00
49 Don Mattingly 84 4.00 10.00
50 Willie McCovey 60 .60 1.50
51 Gil McDougald 52 .60 1.50
52 Tug McGraw 65 .60 1.50
53 Billy Pierce 52 .60 1.50
54 Minnie Minoso 52 .60 1.50
55 Johnny Mize 52 1.00 2.50
56 Roy Face 53 .60 1.50
57 Joe Morgan 65 .60 1.50
58 Thurman Munson 70 1.50 4.00
59 Stan Musial 58 2.00 5.00
60 Phil Niekro 64 .60 1.50
61 Paul Blair 65 .60 1.50
62 Andy Pafko 52 1.00 2.50
63 Satchel Paige 53 1.50 4.00
64 Tony Perez 65 .60 1.50
65 Sal Bando 67 .60 1.50
66 Jimmy Piersall 56 .60 1.50
67 Kirby Puckett 85 1.50 4.00
68 Phil Rizzuto 52 1.50 4.00
69 Robin Roberts 52 .60 1.50
70 Jackie Robinson 52 1.50 4.00
71 Ryne Sandberg 83 6.00 12.00
72 Mike Schmidt 73 4.00 10.00
73 Red Schoendienst 52 .60 1.50
74 Herb Score 56 .60 1.50
75 Enos Slaughter 52 .60 1.50
76 Ozzie Smith 80 3.00 8.00
77 Warren Spahn 52 1.00 2.50
78 Don Sutton 66 .60 1.50
79 Luis Tiant 65 .60 1.50
80 Ted Kluszewski 52 1.00 2.50
81 Whitey Ford 53 1.00 2.50
82 Maury Wills 60 .60 1.50
83 Dave Winfield 74 .60 1.50
84 Early Wynn 52 .60 1.50
85 Carl Yastrzemski 60 2.00 5.00
86 Robin Yount 75 1.50 4.00
87 Bob Allison 59 .60 1.50
88 Clete Boyer 57 .60 1.50
89 Reggie Jackson 69 1.00 2.50
90 Yogi Berra 52 1.50 4.00
91 Willie Mays 52 4.00 8.00
92 Jim Palmer 66 .60 1.50
93 Pee Wee Reese 52 1.50 4.00
94 Frank Robinson 57 1.00 2.50
95 Boog Powell 62 1.00 2.50
96 Willie Stargell 63 1.00 2.50
97 Nolan Ryan 68 4.00 10.00
98 Tom Seaver 67 2.50 6.00
99 Duke Snider 52 1.00 2.50
100 Bill Mazeroski 57 1.50 4.00

2001 Topps Archives Reserve Autographed Baseballs

Issued one per sealed box, these 30 players signed baseballs for inclusion in this product. Each player signed an amount of ball between 100 and 1000 and we have included that information next to the player's name.

STATED ODDS ONE PER BOX
STATED PRINT RUNS LISTED BELOW
1 Johnny Bench/100 * 50.00 100.00
2 Paul Blair/1000 * 10.00 25.00
3 Clete Boyer/1000 * 10.00 25.00
4 Ralph Branca/400 * 15.00 40.00
5 Roy Face/1000 * 10.00 25.00
6 Bob Feller/1000 * 15.00 40.00
7 Whitey Ford/100 * 20.00 50.00
8 Bob Gibson/1000 * 20.00 50.00
9 Dick Groat/1000 * 10.00 25.00
10 Frank Howard/1000 * 10.00 25.00
11 Reggie Jackson/100 * 50.00 100.00
12 Don Larsen/100 * 15.00 40.00
13 Mickey Lolich/500 * 10.00 25.00
14 Willie Mays/100 * 100.00 250.00
15 Gil McDougald/500 * 15.00 40.00
16 Tug McGraw/1000 * 10.00 25.00
17 Minnie Minoso/1000 * 15.00 40.00
18 Andy Pafko/500 * 15.00 40.00
19 Joe Pepitone/1000 * 10.00 25.00
20 Robin Roberts/1000 * 10.00 25.00
21 Frank Robinson/100 * 30.00 60.00
22 Nolan Ryan/100 * 75.00 150.00
23 Herb Score/500 * 10.00 25.00
24 Tom Seaver/100 * 25.00 60.00
25 Moose Skowron/1000 * 15.00 40.00
26 Warren Spahn/100 * 50.00 100.00
27 Bobby Thomson/400 * 15.00 40.00
28 Luis Tiant/500 * 10.00 25.00
29 Carl Yastrzemski/100 * 75.00 150.00
30 Maury Wills/1000 * 10.00 25.00

2001 Topps Archives Reserve Future Rookie Reprints

Issued five per Topps Limited factory set, these 20 cards are reprints of the featured players rookie card.

COMPLETE SET (20) 60.00 120.00
FIVE PER TOPPS LTD. FACTORY SET
1 Barry Bonds 87 6.00 15.00
2 Chipper Jones 91 2.50 6.00
3 Cal Ripken 82 10.00 25.00
4 Shawn Green 92 1.00 2.50
5 Frank Thomas 90 2.50 6.00
6 Derek Jeter 93 8.00 20.00
7 Geoff Jenkins 96 1.00 2.50
8 Jim Edmonds 93 1.00 2.50
9 Bernie Williams 90 1.50 4.00
10 Sammy Sosa 90 2.50 6.00
11 Rickey Henderson 80 2.50 6.00
12 Tony Gwynn 83 3.00 8.00
13 Randy Johnson 89 2.50 6.00
14 Juan Gonzalez 90 1.00 2.50
15 Gary Sheffield 89 1.00 2.50
16 Manny Ramirez 92 1.50 4.00
17 Pokey Reese 92 1.00 2.50
18 Preston Wilson 93 1.00 2.50
19 Jay Payton 95 1.00 2.50
20 Rafael Palmeiro 87 1.50 4.00

2001 Topps Archives Reserve Rookie Reprint Autographs

Inserted one per 10 packs, these 27 cards feature autographs of the players rookie reprint card. Each player signed a different amount of cards and those are notated by groups A, B or C in our checklist. Cards 15, 20, 22, 24, 28, 30, 31, and 35 do not exist. Willie Mays did not return his cards in time for inclusion in the package. Those cards could be redeemed until July 31, 2003.

STATED OVERALL ODDS 1:10
SKIP-NUMBERED SET
ARA1 Willie Mays C 150.00 400.00
ARA2 Whitey Ford B 20.00 50.00
ARA3 Nolan Ryan A 60.00 120.00
ARA4 Carl Yastrzemski B 50.00 100.00
ARA5 Frank Robinson B 20.00 50.00
ARA6 Tom Seaver A 30.00 80.00
ARA7 Warren Spahn A 20.00 50.00
ARA8 Johnny Bench A 60.00 120.00
ARA9 Reggie Jackson A 60.00 120.00
ARA10 Bob Gibson B 25.00 60.00
ARA11 Bob Feller D 12.00 30.00
ARA12 Gil McDougald A 10.00 25.00
ARA13 Luis Tiant A 6.00 15.00
ARA14 Minnie Minoso D 12.00 30.00
ARA16 Herb Score B 6.00 15.00
ARA17 Moose Skowron C 6.00 15.00
ARA18 Maury Wills D 6.00 15.00
ARA19 Clete Boyer A 8.00 20.00
ARA21 Don Larsen A 6.00 15.00
ARA23 Tug McGraw C 12.00 30.00
ARA25 Robin Roberts C 12.00 30.00
ARA26 Frank Howard A 12.00 30.00
ARA27 Mickey Lolich D 6.00 15.00
ARA29 Tommy John C 6.00 15.00
ARA32 Dick Groat D 6.00 15.00
ARA33 Roy Face D 8.00 20.00
ARA34 Paul Blair D 6.00 15.00

2001 Topps Archives Reserve Rookie Reprint Relics

Issued at a rate of one in 10 packs, these 51 cards feature not only a rookie reprint of the featured player but also a memorabilia piece relating to their career.

STATED ODDS 1:10
ARR1 Brooks Robinson Jsy 8.00 20.00
ARR2 Tony Conigliaro Jsy 10.00 25.00
ARR3 Frank Howard Jsy 2.50 6.00
ARR4 Don Sutton Jsy 4.00 10.00
ARR5 Ferguson Jenkins Jsy 4.00 10.00
ARR6 Frank Robinson Jsy 10.00 25.00
ARR7 Don Mattingly Jsy 12.00 30.00
ARR8 Willie Stargell Jsy 6.00 15.00
ARR9 Moose Skowron Jsy 8.00 20.00
ARR10 Fred Lynn Jsy 2.50 6.00
ARR11 George Brett Jsy 10.00 25.00
ARR12 Nolan Ryan Jsy 20.00 50.00
ARR13 Orlando Cepeda Jsy 6.00 15.00
ARR14 Reggie Jackson Jsy 5.00 12.00
ARR15 Steve Carlton Jsy 4.00 10.00
ARR16 Tom Seaver Jsy 4.00 10.00
ARR17 Thurman Munson Jsy 12.00 30.00
ARR18 Yogi Berra Jsy 6.00 15.00
ARR19 Willie McCovey Jsy 8.00 20.00
ARR20 Robin Yount Jsy 10.00 25.00
ARR21 Al Kaline Bat 8.00 20.00
ARR22 Carl Yastrzemski Bat 10.00 25.00
ARR23 Carlton Fisk Bat 6.00 15.00
ARR24 Dale Murphy Bat 10.00 25.00
ARR25 Dave Winfield Bat 4.00 10.00
ARR26 Dick Groat Bat 2.50 6.00
ARR27 Dom DiMaggio Bat 10.00 25.00
ARR28 Don Mattingly Bat 12.00 30.00
ARR29 Gary Carter Bat 6.00 15.00
ARR30 George Kell Bat 8.00 20.00
ARR31 Harmon Killebrew Bat 12.00 30.00
ARR32 Jackie Jensen Bat 15.00 40.00
ARR33 Jackie Robinson Bat 25.00 60.00
ARR34 Jim Piersall Bat 2.50 6.00
ARR35 Joe Adcock Bat 2.50 6.00
ARR36 Joe Carter Bat 4.00 10.00
ARR37 Johnny Mize Bat 8.00 20.00
ARR38 Kirk Gibson Bat 2.50 6.00
ARR39 Mickey Vernon Bat 6.00 15.00
ARR40 Mike Schmidt Bat 10.00 25.00
ARR41 Ryne Sandberg Bat 12.00 30.00
ARR42 Ozzie Smith Bat 12.00 30.00
ARR43 Ted Kluszewski Bat 8.00 20.00
ARR44 Wade Boggs Bat 6.00 15.00
ARR45 Willie Mays Bat 25.00 60.00
ARR46 Duke Snider Bat 4.00 10.00
ARR47 Harvey Kuenn Bat 6.00 15.00
ARR48 Robin Yount Bat 6.00 15.00
ARR49 Red Schoendienst Bat 4.00 10.00
ARR50 Elston Howard Bat 8.00 20.00
ARR51 Bob Allison Bat 10.00 25.00

2002 Topps Archives Reserve

This 100 card set was released in June, 2002. This 100 card set was issued in four card packs which came 10 packs to a box and four boxes to a case. Each box also contained an autographed baseball.

COMPLETE SET (100) 40.00 80.00
1 Lee Smith 91 .60 1.50
2 Gaylord Perry 72 .60 1.50
3 Al Oliver 82 .60 1.50
4 Goose Gossage 77 .60 1.50
5 Bill Madlock 75 .60 1.50
6 Rod Carew 77 1.00 2.50
7 Fred Lynn 79 .60 1.50
8 Frank Robinson 66 1.00 2.50
9 Al Kaline 55 1.50 4.00
10 Len Dykstra 93 .60 1.50
11 Carlton Fisk 77 1.00 2.50
12 Nellie Fox 59 1.00 2.50
13 Reggie Jackson 69 1.00 2.50
14 Bob Gibson 68 1.00 2.50
15 Bill Buckner 85 .60 1.50
16 Harmon Killebrew 69 1.50 4.00
17 Gary Carter 85 .60 1.50
18 Dave Winfield 79 .60 1.50
19 Ozzie Smith 87 2.50 6.00
20 Dwight Evans 87 1.00 2.50
21 Dave Concepcion 79 .60 1.50
22 Joe Morgan 76 .60 1.50
23 Clete Boyer 62 .60 1.50
24 Will Clark 89 1.00 2.50
25 Lee May 69 .60 1.50
26 Kevin Mitchell 89 .60 1.50
27 Roger Maris 61 1.50 4.00
28 Mickey Lolich 71 .60 1.50
29 Luis Aparicio 60 .60 1.50
30 George Foster 77 .60 1.50
31 Don Mattingly 85 3.00 8.00
32 Fernando Valenzuela 86 .60 1.50
33 Bobby Bonds 73 .60 1.50
34 Jim Palmer 75 .60 1.50
35 Dennis Eckersley 92 .60 1.50
36 Kirby Puckett 88 1.50 4.00
37 Jose Cruz 83 .60 1.50
38 Richie Ashburn 58 1.00 2.50
39 Whitey Ford 61 1.00 2.50
40 Robin Roberts 52 .60 1.50
41 Don Newcombe 56 .60 1.50
42 Roy Campanella 53 1.50 4.00
43 Dennis Martinez 91 .60 1.50
44 Larry Doby 54 .60 1.50
45 Steve Garvey 77 .60 1.50
46 Thurman Munson 76 1.50 4.00
47 Dale Murphy 83 1.00 2.50
48 Moose Skowron 60 1.00 2.50
49 Tom Seaver 69 1.00 2.50
50 Orlando Cepeda 61 .60 1.50
51 Graig Nettles 77 .60 1.50
52 Willie Stargell 71 1.00 2.50
53 Yogi Berra 54 1.50 4.00
54 Steve Carlton 72 .60 1.50
55 Don Sutton 72 .60 1.50
56 Brooks Robinson 64 1.00 2.50
57 Vida Blue 71 .60 1.50
58 Rollie Fingers 81 .60 1.50
59 Jim Bunning 65 .60 1.50
60 Nolan Ryan 73 4.00 10.00
61 Hank Aaron 57 3.00 8.00

62 Fergie Jenkins 71 .60 1.50
63 Andre Dawson 87 .60 1.50
64 Ernie Banks 58 1.50 4.00
65 Early Wynn 59 .60 1.50
66 Duke Snider 54 1.00 2.50
67 Red Schoendienst 53 .60 1.50
68 Don Drysdale 62 1.00 2.50
69 Catfish Hunter 74 1.00 2.50
70 George Brett 80 3.00 8.00
71 Elston Howard 63 1.00 2.50
72 Wade Boggs 87 1.00 2.50
73 Keith Hernandez 79 .60 1.50
74 Billy Pierce 56 .60 1.50
75 Ted Kluszewski 54 1.00 2.50
76 Carl Yastrzemski 67 2.50 6.00
77 Bert Blyleven 73 .60 1.50
78 Tony Oliva 64 .60 1.50
79 Joe Carter 86 .60 1.50
80 Johnny Bench 70 1.50 4.00
81 Tony Gwynn 97 2.00 5.00
82 Mike Schmidt 80 3.00 8.00
83 Phil Niekro 69 .60 1.50
84 Juan Marichal 66 .60 1.50
85 Eddie Mathews 53 1.50 4.00
86 Boog Powell 69 1.00 2.50
87 Dwight Gooden 85 .60 1.50
88 Darryl Strawberry 87 .60 1.50
89 Roberto Clemente 66 4.00 10.00
90 Ryne Sandberg 90 3.00 8.00
91 Jack Clark 87 .60 1.50
92 Willie Mays 62 3.00 8.00
93 Ron Guidry 78 .60 1.50
94 Kirk Gibson 88 .60 1.50
95 Lou Brock 74 1.00 2.50
96 Robin Yount 82 1.50 4.00
97 Bill Mazeroski 60 1.00 2.50
98 Dave Parker 78 .60 1.50
99 Hoyt Wilhelm 64 .60 1.50
100 Warren Spahn 57 1.00 2.50

2002 Topps Archives Reserve Autographed Baseballs

Inserted one per Archives Reserve box, these 21 autographed baseballs feature authentic signatures from some of baseball's best all-time players. Since the players signed a different amount of cards, we have notated that information next to their name in our checklist.

ONE AUTO BALL PER BOX
STATED PRINT RUNS LISTED BELOW
EXCHANGE CARD ODDS 1:219 RETAIL
EXCHANGE DEADLINE 05/27/04
1 Luis Aparicio/1600 10.00 25.00
3 Yogi Berra/100 60.00 150.00
4 Lou Brock/400 20.00 50.00
5 Jim Bunning/500 30.00 60.00
6 Gary Carter/500 12.50 30.00
7 Goose Gossage/500 12.50 30.00
8 Fergie Jenkins/1000 10.00 25.00
9 Al Kaline/250 50.00 120.00
10 Harmon Killebrew/250 30.00 60.00
12 Joe Morgan/250 20.00 50.00
13 Graig Nettles/1600 10.00 25.00
14 Jim Palmer/400 12.50 30.00
15 Gaylord Perry/500 12.50 30.00
16 Brooks Robinson/500 20.00 50.00
17 Mike Schmidt/250 60.00 120.00
18 Duke Snider/100 50.00 100.00
19 Dave Winfield/1650 15.00 40.00
20 Robin Yount/250 50.00 100.00

2002 Topps Archives Reserve Autographs

Inserted at overall stated odds of one in 15 hobby and one in 203 retail, these 17 cards feature the players signed the Archives reserve "reprint" of their key year card. Since the players all signed at a different rate based on their "group", we have listed their group affiliation next to their name in our checklist.

COMMON CARD D-E 6.00 15.00
COMMON CARD B-C 6.00 15.00
GROUP A ODDS 1:1077 RET
GROUP B ODDS 1:1421 RET
GROUP C ODDS 1:947 RET
GROUP D ODDS 1:1421 RET
GROUP E ODDS 1:718 RET
OVERALL STATED ODDS 1:15 HOBBY, 1:203 RETAIL
TRAAK Al Kaline 55 C 30.00 80.00
TRABR Brooks Robinson 64 B 15.00 40.00
TRADS Duke Snider 54 A 15.00 40.00
TRAEB Ernie Banks 58 A 50.00 100.00
TRAFJ Fergie Jenkins 71 E 6.00 15.00
TRAGC Gary Carter 85 B 25.00 60.00
TRAGN Graig Nettles 77 D 6.00 15.00
TRAGP Gaylord Perry 72 C 6.00 15.00
TRAHK H.Killebrew 69 C 30.00 60.00
TRAJM Joe Morgan 76 B 20.00 50.00
TRALA Luis Aparicio 60 D 10.00 25.00
TRALB Lou Brock 74 B 20.00 50.00
TRALS Lee Smith 91 E 6.00 15.00
TRAMS Mike Schmidt 80 A 50.00 100.00
TRARY Robin Yount 82 A 30.00 80.00
TRAWM Willie Mays 62 A 75.00 150.00
TRAYB Yogi Berra 54 A 60.00 150.00

2002 Topps Archives Reserve Bat Relics

Inserted at stated odds of one in 22 hobby packs, these 10 cards feature not only the player's "best card" but also a game-used bat piece from each player. The players belonged to different groups in terms of scarcity and we have put that information next to their name in our checklist.

OVERALL STATED ODDS 1:22 HOBBY
TRRCF Carlton Fisk 77 B 6.00 15.00
TRRDW Dave Winfield 79 C 6.00 15.00
TRROC Orlando Cepeda 61 B 6.00 15.00
TRRRM Roger Maris 61 A 15.00 40.00
TRRTM Thurman Munson 76 B 20.00 50.00
TRRCYB Carl Yastrzemski 67 B 15.00 40.00
TRRDMB Don Mattingly 85 B 10.00 25.00
TRREMB Eddie Mathews 53 B 8.00 20.00
TRRGBB George Brett 80 B 10.00 25.00
TRRHAB Hank Aaron 57 B 12.00 30.00

2002 Topps Archives Reserve Uniform Relics

Inserted at stated odds of one in seven hobby packs, these 15 cards feature not only the player's "best card" but also a game-used bat piece from each player. The players belonged to different groups in terms of scarcity and we have put that information next to their name in our checklist.

OVERALL STATED ODDS 1:7 HOBBY
BR Brooks Robinson 64 Uni D 6.00 15.00
EB Ernie Banks 58 Uni C 10.00 25.00
GC Gary Carter 85 Jsy C 8.00 20.00
JB Johnny Bench 70 Uni D 8.00 20.00
JM Juan Marichal 66 Jsy A 8.00 20.00
KP Kirby Puckett 88 Jsy D 6.00 15.00
NF Nellie Fox 59 Uni C 8.00 20.00
NR Nolan Ryan 73 Jsy D 12.50 30.00
RS Red Schoendienst 53 Jsy B 6.00 15.00
RY Robin Yount 82 Uni D 6.00 15.00
TG Tony Gwynn 97 Jsy D 6.00 15.00
WB Wade Boggs 87 Jsy D 6.00 15.00
WC Will Clark 89 Jsy C 8.00 20.00
WM Willie Mays 62 Uni C 12.50 30.00
WS Willie Stargell 71 Uni D 6.00 15.00

2012 Topps Archives

COMP.SET W/O HARPER (240) 60.00 120.00
COMP.SET W/O SP's (200) 12.50 30.00
COMMON CARD (1-200) .15 .40
COMMON RC (1-200) .25 .60
COMMON SP (201-240) .75 2.00
SP 201-240 ODDS 1:4 HOBBY
PRINTING PLATE ODDS 1:777 HOBBY
PLATE PRINT RUN 1 SET PER COLOR
BLACK-CYAN-MAGENTA-YELLOW ISSUED
NO PLATE PRICING DUE TO SCARCITY
1 Matt Kemp .30 .75
2 Nick Swisher .30 .75
3 Jered Weaver .30 .75
4 Matt Garza .25 .60
5 Freddie Freeman .50 1.25
6 Paul Goldschmidt .40 1.00
7 Cole Hamels .30 .75
8 Matt Moore RC .60 1.50
9 Brett Gardner .30 .75
10 Ryan Braun .25 .60
11 Curtis Granderson .30 .75
12 Pablo Sandoval .30 .75
13 Mark Teixeira .30 .75
14 Yadier Molina .40 1.00
15 Madison Bumgarner .30 .75
16 Yunel Escobar .25 .60
17 Mat Latos .30 .75
18 Tom Seaver .30 .75
19 Brandon Beachy .25 .60
20 Robinson Cano .30 .75
21 Jeremy Hellickson .25 .60
22 Mickey Mantle 1.25 3.00
23 Chris Young .25 .60
24 Lance Berkman .30 .75
25 Dan Haren .25 .60
26 Paul Konerko .25 .60
27 Carl Crawford .30 .75
28 Melky Cabrera .25 .60
29 B.J. Upton .30 .75
30 Jacoby Ellsbury .30 .75
31 Joe Morgan .30 .75
32 Adam Jones .30 .75
33 Jon Lester .25 .60
34 Jaime Garcia .30 .75
35 Zack Greinke .30 .75
36 Martin Prado .25 .60
37 Jose Valverde .25 .60
38 Billy Butler .25 .60
39 Jackie Robinson .40 1.00
40 Nelson Cruz .40 1.00
41 Corey Hart .25 .60
42 Aroldis Chapman .40 1.00
43 Wade Boggs .25 .60
44 Cal Ripken Jr. 1.25 3.00
45 Carlos Ruiz .25 .60
46 John Danks .25 .60
47 Drew Pomeranz RC .40 1.00
48 Grady Sizemore .30 .75
49 Mike Moustakas .30 .75
50 Albert Pujols .50 1.25
51 Roy Halladay .30 .75
52 Geovany Soto .30 .75
53 Adam Wainwright .30 .75
54 Jemile Weeks RC .40 1.00
55 Jesus Montero RC .40 1.00
56 Alex Rodriguez .50 1.25
57 Josh Beckett .25 .60
58 Tommy Hanson .25 .60
59 Hunter Pence .30 .75
60 Mariano Rivera .50 1.25
61 Brian McCann .30 .75
62 Hanley Ramirez .30 .75
63 Tim Hudson .30 .75
64 Derek Holland .25 .60
65 Jordan Zimmermann .30 .75
66 Andrew McCutchen .40 1.00
67 Justin Verlander .40 1.00
68 Drew Storen .25 .60
69 Ryan Zimmerman .30 .75
70 Joey Votto .40 1.00
71 Jimmy Rollins .30 .75
72 Ian Kinsler .30 .75
73 Shaun Marcum .25 .60
74 Ty Cobb .60 1.50
75 Reggie Jackson .25 .60
76 Victor Martinez .30 .75
77 Chipper Jones .40 1.00
78 Miguel Montero .25 .60
79 Ervin Santana .25 .60
80 Troy Tulowitzki .40 1.00
81 Adrian Beltre .40 1.00
82 Jose Reyes .25 .60
83 Craig Kimbrel .25 .60
84 Nyjer Morgan .25 .60
85 Matt Holliday .40 1.00
86 Trevor Cahill .25 .60
87 Clay Buchholz .25 .60
88 Mike Schmidt .60 1.50
89 Lou Gehrig .75 2.00
90 Joe Mauer .30 .75
91 Ted Lilly .25 .60
92 Jordan Walden .25 .60
93 Matt Harrison .25 .60
94 Anibal Sanchez .25 .60
95 Yoenis Cespedes RC 1.00 2.50
96 Phil Rizzuto .25 .60
97 Brett Lawrie RC .50 1.25
98 Johan Santana .30 .75
99 Brandon Belt .30 .75
100 Miguel Cabrera .40 1.00
101 Adrian Gonzalez .30 .75
102 Dee Gordon .25 .60
103 Ricky Romero .25 .60
104 Yovani Gallardo .25 .60
105 Torii Hunter .30 .75
106 Alex Gordon .30 .75
107 Josh Johnson .30 .75
108 Cliff Lee .30 .75
109 Catfish Hunter .25 .60
110 Jose Bautista .30 .75
111 John Axford .25 .60
112 Todd Helton .30 .75
113 Ryan Howard .30 .75
114 Jason Motte .25 .60
115 Gio Gonzalez .30 .75
116 Alex Avila .25 .60
117 George Brett .75 2.00
118 Desmond Jennings .30 .75
119 Yu Darvish RC 1.00 2.50
120 Tim Lincecum .30 .75
121 Heath Bell .25 .60
122 Dustin Pedroia .30 .75
123 Ryan Vogelsong .25 .60
124 Brandon Phillips .25 .60
125 David Freese .25 .60
126 Rickie Weeks .25 .60
127 Evan Longoria .30 .75
128 Shin-Soo Choo .25 .60
129 Darryl Strawberry .15 .40
130 Mike Stanton .40 1.00
131 Elvis Andrus .30 .75
132 Ben Zobrist .25 .60
133 Mark Trumbo .25 .60
134 Chris Carpenter .30 .75
135 Mike Napoli .25 .60
136 David Ortiz .40 1.00
137 Jason Heyward .30 .75
138 Joe DiMaggio .75 2.00
139 Ivan Nova .30 .75
140 Buster Posey .50 1.25
141 J.P. Arencibia .25 .60
142 Ozzie Smith .50 1.25
143 Marco Scutaro .30 .75
144 Ike Davis .25 .60
145 Howie Kendrick .25 .60
146 Jarrod Parker RC .50 1.25
147 Justin Masterson .25 .60
148 R.A. Dickey .30 .75
149 Dustin Ackley .25 .60
150 Clayton Kershaw .75 2.00
151 Stephen Strasburg .40 1.00
152 Johnny Cueto .30 .75
153 Felix Hernandez .30 .75
154 Starlin Castro .30 .75
155 Ichiro Suzuki .50 1.25
156 Ubaldo Jimenez .25 .60
157 Carlos Gonzalez .30 .75
158 Michael Young .25 .60
159 David Price .30 .75
160 Prince Fielder .30 .75
161 Chase Utley .30 .75
162 Jayson Werth .30 .75
163 Aramis Ramirez .25 .60
164 Kevin Youkilis .40 1.00
165 Jay Bruce .30 .75
166 CC Sabathia .30 .75
167 Michael Pineda .25 .60
168 Carlos Santana .25 .60
169 Michael Morse .25 .60
170 Justin Upton .30 .75
171 Lucas Duda .30 .75
172 James Shields .25 .60
173 Daniel Hudson .25 .60
174 Asdrubal Cabrera .30 .75
175 Justin Morneau .30 .75
176 Eric Hosmer .30 .75
177 Shane Victorino .30 .75
178 Adam Lind .30 .75
179 Michael Bourn .25 .60
180 David Wright .30 .75
181 Matt Cain .30 .75
182 Ian Kennedy .25 .60
183 Dan Uggla .30 .75
184 Jim Rice .25 .60
185 Roberto Clemente 1.00 2.50
186 Brian Wilson .40 1.00
187 Nolan Ryan 1.25 3.00
188 Vance Worley .30 .75
189 Babe Ruth 1.00 2.50
190 Josh Hamilton .30 .75
191 Yogi Berra .40 1.00
192 Brad Peacock RC .40 1.00
193 Lonnie Chisenhall .25 .60
194 Gary Carter .25 .60
195 Brandon Morrow .25 .60
196 Andrew Bailey .25 .60
197 Allen Craig .30 .75
198 Casey Kotchman .25 .60
199 Mark Reynolds .25 .60
200 Derek Jeter 1.00 2.50
201 Don Mattingly SP 2.00 5.00
202 Mike Scott SP .75 2.00
203 Willie Mays SP 2.00 5.00
204 Ken Singleton SP .75 2.00
205 Bill Buckner SP .75 2.00
206 Dave Kingman SP .75 2.00
207 Vida Blue SP .75 2.00
208 Frank Howard SP .75 2.00
209 Will Clark SP 1.25 3.00
210 Sandy Koufax SP 2.00 5.00
211 Wally Joyner SP .75 2.00
212 Andy Van Slyke SP .75 2.00
213 Bill Madlock SP .75 2.00
214 Mitch Williams SP .75 2.00
215 Brett Butler SP .75 2.00
216 Bake McBride SP .75 2.00
217 Luis Tiant SP .75 2.00
218 Dave Righetti SP .75 2.00
219 Cecil Cooper SP .75 2.00
220 Ken Griffey Jr. SP 2.00 5.00
221 Jim Abbott SP .75 2.00
222 John Kruk SP .75 2.00
223 Cecil Fielder SP .75 2.00
224 Terry Pendleton SP .75 2.00
225 Ken Griffey SP .75 2.00
226 Jay Buhner SP .75 2.00
227 John Olerud SP .75 2.00
228 Ron Gant SP .75 2.00
229 Roger McDowell SP .75 2.00
230 Lance Parrish SP .75 2.00
231 Jack Clark SP .75 2.00
232 George Bell SP .75 2.00
233 Oscar Gamble SP .75 2.00
234 Shawon Dunston SP .75 2.00
235 Ed Kranepool SP .75 2.00
236 Chili Davis SP .75 2.00
237 Robin Ventura SP .75 2.00
238 Jose Oquendo SP .75 2.00
239 Von Hayes SP .75 2.00
240 Sid Bream SP .75 2.00
241 Bryce Harper SP RC 300.00 600.00

2012 Topps Archives Gold Foil

*GOLD 1-200 VET: 2.5X TO 6X BASIC
*GOLD 1-200 RC: 1.5X TO 4X BASIC RC
STATED ODDS 1:12 HOBBY

2012 Topps Archives 3-D

COMPLETE SET (15) 15.00 40.00
STATED ODDS 1:8 HOBBY
PRINTING PLATE ODDS 1:1196 HOBBY
PLATE PRINT RUN 1 SET PER COLOR
BLACK-CYAN-MAGENTA-YELLOW ISSUED
NO PLATE PRICING DUE TO SCARCITY
AK Al Kaline 1.00 2.50
BR Babe Ruth 2.50 6.00
CS CC Sabathia .75 2.00
CU Chase Utley .75 2.00
DP Dustin Pedroia .75 2.00
FH Felix Hernandez .75 2.00
JU Justin Upton .75 2.00
JV Joey Votto 1.00 2.50
MC Miguel Cabrera 1.00 2.50
MK Matt Kemp .75 2.00
MM Mickey Mantle 3.00 8.00
NC Nelson Cruz 1.00 2.50
RC Robinson Cano .75 2.00
WM Willie Mays 2.00 5.00
RCL Roberto Clemente 2.50 6.00

2012 Topps Archives Autographs

GROUP A ODDS 1:368 HOBBY
GROUP B ODDS 1:21 HOBBY
GROUP C ODDS 1:32 HOBBY
G.CARTER ODDS 1:12,440 HOBBY
Y.DARVISH ODDS 1:1685 HOBBY
EXCHANGE DEADLINE 04/30/2015
AO Al Oliver 6.00 15.00
AOT Amos Otis 5.00 12.00
AVS Andy Van Slyke 6.00 15.00
BB Bob Boone 5.00 12.00
BBE Buddy Bell 5.00 12.00
BBU Bill Buckner 8.00 20.00
BG Bobby Grich 6.00 15.00
BH Bud Harrelson 5.00 12.00
BHA Bryce Harper 150.00 400.00
BL Bill Lee 5.00 12.00
BM Bake McBride 6.00 15.00
BMA Bill Madlock 6.00 15.00
BOG Ben Oglivie 5.00 12.00
BP Boog Powell 8.00 20.00
BR Bobby Richardson 5.00 12.00
BRB Brett Butler 5.00 12.00
BT Bobby Thigpen 5.00 12.00
CC Cecil Cooper 5.00 12.00
CD Chili Davis 6.00 15.00
CF Cecil Fielder 8.00 20.00
CJ Cleon Jones 6.00 15.00
CL Carney Lansford 5.00 12.00
DD Doug DeCinces 5.00 12.00
DDR Doug Drabek 6.00 15.00
DG Dick Groat 6.00 15.00
DK Dave Kingman 6.00 15.00
DM Don Mattingly 40.00 80.00
DMA Dennis Martinez 6.00 15.00
DR Dave Righetti 6.00 15.00
EK Ed Kranepool 5.00 12.00
FH Frank Howard 6.00 15.00
GB George Bell 5.00 12.00
GC Gary Carter 50.00 120.00
GF George Foster 6.00 15.00
GL Greg Luzinski 6.00 15.00
HA Hank Aaron 250.00 500.00
JA Jim Abbott 6.00 15.00
JB Jay Buhner 6.00 15.00
JC Joe Charboneau 6.00 15.00
JCL Jack Clark 5.00 12.00
JKE Jimmy Key 5.00 12.00
JKR John Kruk 8.00 20.00
JMC Jack McDowell 5.00 12.00
JO John Olerud 5.00 12.00
JOQ Jose Oquendo 12.50 30.00
JW Jim Wynn 5.00 12.00
KG Ken Griffey Sr. 10.00 25.00
KGJ Ken Griffey Jr. 200.00 600.00
KS Ken Singleton 6.00 15.00
LP Lance Parrish 5.00 12.00
LT Luis Tiant 5.00 12.00
ML Mickey Lolich 6.00 15.00
MSC Mike Scott 5.00 12.00
MW Maury Wills 6.00 15.00
MWI Mitch Williams 10.00 25.00
OG Oscar Gamble 5.00 12.00
RG Ron Gant 6.00 15.00
RK Ron Kittle 5.00 12.00
RL Ray Lankford 5.00 12.00
RM Roger McDowell 6.00 15.00
RV Robin Ventura 5.00 12.00
SB Steve Balboni 5.00 12.00
SBR Sid Bream 6.00 15.00
SD Shawon Dunston 5.00 12.00
SK Sandy Koufax EXCH 300.00 600.00
SR Steve Rogers 5.00 12.00
TH Tom Herr 5.00 12.00
TP Terry Pendleton 8.00 20.00
VB Vida Blue 5.00 12.00
VH Von Hayes 5.00 12.00
WB Wally Backman 5.00 12.00
WC Will Clark 15.00 40.00
WJ Wally Joyner 6.00 15.00
WM Willie Mays 500.00 800.00
WW Willie Wilson 5.00 12.00
YD Yu Darvish 40.00 100.00
128 Hank Aaron/25

2012 Topps Archives Box Topper Autographs

KK1 Martin Kove 6.00 15.00
KK2 Billy Zabka 10.00 25.00

2012 Topps Archives Cloth Stickers

COMPLETE SET (25) 15.00 40.00
STATED ODDS 1:6 HOBBY
PRINTING PLATE ODDS 1:1196 HOBBY
PLATE PRINT RUN 1 SET PER COLOR
BLACK-CYAN-MAGENTA-YELLOW ISSUED
NO PLATE PRICING DUE TO SCARCITY
AM Andrew McCutchen 1.00 2.50
CC Chris Carpenter .75 2.00
CG Curtis Granderson .75 2.00
CH Catfish Hunter .60 1.50
CL Cliff Lee .75 2.00
DJ Derek Jeter 2.50 6.00
EH Eric Hosmer .75 2.00
GB George Brett 2.00 5.00
GC Gary Carter .60 1.50
JB Johnny Bench 1.00 2.50
JE Jacoby Ellsbury .75 2.00
JH Josh Hamilton .75 2.00
JM Joe Morgan .60 1.50
JR Jim Rice .60 1.50
JV Justin Verlander 1.00 2.50
KY Kevin Youkilis 1.00 2.50
MS Giancarlo Stanton 1.00 2.50
RB Ryan Braun .60 1.50
RC Rod Carew .60 1.50
RH Roy Halladay .75 2.00
RJ Reggie Jackson .60 1.50
RY Robin Yount 1.00 2.50
SC Steve Carlton .60 1.50
WS Willie Stargell .60 1.50
SCA Starlin Castro .75 2.00

2012 Topps Archives Combos

STATED ODDS 1:32 RETAIL
BH G.Brett/E.Hosmer 5.00 12.00
CK M.Cabrera/A.Kaline 2.50 6.00
KK C.Kershaw/S.Koufax 5.00 12.00
KR Matt Kemp 2.50 6.00
Jackie Robinson
LM T.Lincecum/W.Mays 5.00 12.00
SC R.Sandberg/S.Castro 5.00 12.00
SF CC Sabathia 2.00 5.00
Whitey Ford
SH M.Schmidt/R.Halladay 4.00 10.00
VB Joey Votto 2.50 6.00
Johnny Bench
YE Yastrzemski/J.Ellsbury 4.00 10.00

2012 Topps Archives Deckle Edge

COMPLETE SET (15) 12.50 30.00
STATED ODDS 1:12 HOBBY
PRINTING PLATE ODDS 1:1196 HOBBY
PLATE PRINT RUN 1 SET PER COLOR
BLACK-CYAN-MAGENTA-YELLOW ISSUED
NO PLATE PRICING DUE TO SCARCITY
1 Roy Halladay .75 2.00
2 Evan Longoria .75 2.00
3 Jose Bautista .75 2.00
4 Mike Napoli .60 1.50
5 David Freese .60 1.50
6 Ichiro Suzuki 1.25 3.00
7 Joe Mauer .75 2.00
8 Bob Gibson .60 1.50
9 Juan Marichal .60 1.50
10 Orlando Cepeda .60 1.50
11 Carl Yastrzemski 1.50 4.00
12 Roberto Clemente 2.50 6.00
13 Willie Mays 2.00 5.00
14 Harmon Killebrew 1.00 2.50
15 Joe Morgan .60 1.50

2012 Topps Archives In Action

STATED ODDS 1:32 RETAIL
I Ichiro Suzuki 2.00 5.00
CR Cal Ripken Jr. 5.00 12.00
JE Jacoby Ellsbury 1.25 3.00
JH Josh Hamilton 1.25 3.00
JK John Kruk .60 1.50
KG Ken Griffey Jr. 3.00 8.00
MN Mike Napoli 1.00 2.50
RC Roberto Clemente 6.00 15.00
TG Tony Gwynn 1.50 4.00
TT Troy Tulowitzki 1.50 4.00

2012 Topps Archives Relics

STATED ODDS 1:120 HOBBY
I Ichiro Suzuki 8.00 20.00
AA Alex Avila 5.00 12.00
AE Andre Ethier 5.00 12.00
AJ Adam Jones 5.00 12.00
AP Andy Pettitte 6.00 15.00
BB Billy Butler 3.00 8.00
BP Brandon Phillips 4.00 10.00
BU B.J. Upton 3.00 8.00
BW Brian Wilson 6.00 15.00
CB Clay Buchholz 3.00 8.00
CC Cecil Cooper 4.00 10.00
CG Carlos Gonzalez 3.00 8.00
DH Dan Haren 3.00 8.00
DM Don Mattingly 12.50 30.00
DO David Ortiz 4.00 10.00
DP Dustin Pedroia 5.00 12.00
DPR David Price 3.00 8.00
DU Dan Uggla 5.00 12.00
DW David Wright 5.00 12.00
EL Evan Longoria 3.00 8.00
FT Frank Thomas 10.00 25.00
GB George Bell 4.00 10.00
JC Johnny Cueto 3.00 8.00
JG Jaime Garcia 5.00 12.00
JH Jeremy Hellickson 4.00 10.00
JHY Jason Heyward 4.00 10.00
JM Jason Motte 5.00 12.00
JR Jimmy Rollins 4.00 10.00
JS James Shields 3.00 8.00
LB Lance Berkman 6.00 15.00
MB Madison Bumgarner 8.00 20.00
MC Miguel Cabrera 6.00 15.00
MM Mike Morse 4.00 10.00
MMO Matt Moore 4.00 10.00
MR Mariano Rivera 6.00 15.00
MT Mark Trumbo 4.00 10.00
MY Michael Young 3.00 8.00
NC Nelson Cruz 3.00 8.00
NS Nick Swisher 5.00 12.00
OC Orlando Cepeda 5.00 12.00
PN Phil Niekro 5.00 12.00
PS Pablo Sandoval 4.00 10.00
RC Roberto Clemente 75.00 150.00
RC Rod Carew 4.00 10.00
RR Ricky Romero 3.00 8.00
RZ Ryan Zimmerman 4.00 10.00
SC Starlin Castro 8.00 20.00
SCA Steve Carlton 10.00 25.00
TH Tommy Hanson 3.00 8.00
THD Tim Hudson 3.00 8.00
THE Todd Helton 3.00 8.00
THU Torii Hunter 3.00 8.00
TL Tim Lincecum 6.00 15.00
WS Willie Stargell 10.00 25.00
YG Yovani Gallardo 3.00 8.00
ZG Zack Greinke 4.00 10.00

2012 Topps Archives Reprints

COMPLETE SET (50) 40.00 80.00
STATED ODDS 1:4 HOBBY
PRINTING PLATE ODDS 1:1196 HOBBY
PLATE PRINT RUN 1 SET PER COLOR
BLACK-CYAN-MAGENTA-YELLOW ISSUED
NO PLATE PRICING DUE TO SCARCITY
8 Don Mattingly 1.50 4.00
19 George Brett 1.50 4.00
28 Brooks Robinson .50 1.25
62 Monte Irvin .50 1.25
70 Harmon Killebrew .75 2.00
80 Darryl Strawberry .30 .75
80 Rod Carew .50 1.25
81 Jim Palmer .50 1.25
88 Bob Feller .50 1.25
95 Johnny Bench .75 2.00
110 Yogi Berra .75 2.00
116 Ozzie Smith 1.00 2.50
130 Reggie Jackson .50 1.25
150 Duke Snider .50 1.25
160 Whitey Ford .50 1.25
160 Eddie Murray .50 1.25
164 Roberto Clemente 2.00 5.00
164 Harmon Killebrew .75 2.00
176 Willie McCovey .50 1.25
191 Yogi Berra .75 2.00
191 Ralph Kiner .50 1.25
220 Tom Seaver .50 1.25
223 Robin Yount .75 2.00
228 George Brett 1.50 4.00
230 Joe Morgan .50 1.25
243 Larry Doby .50 1.25
244 Willie Mays 1.50 4.00
260 Reggie Jackson .50 1.25
287 Carl Yastrzemski 1.25 3.00
295 Gary Carter .50 1.25
300 Tom Seaver .50 1.25
325 Juan Marichal .50 1.25
333 Fergie Jenkins .50 1.25
337 Joe Morgan .50 1.25
338 Sparky Anderson .50 1.25
380 Willie Stargell .50 1.25
385 Jim Hunter .50 1.25
420 Juan Marichal .50 1.25
440 Willie McCovey .50 1.25
440 Roberto Clemente 2.00 5.00
490 Cal Ripken Jr. 2.50 6.00
490 Wade Boggs .50 1.25
500 Duke Snider .50 1.25
530 Dave Winfield .50 1.25
550 Brooks Robinson .50 1.25
575 Jim Palmer .50 1.25
635 Robin Yount .75 2.00
640 Eddie Murray .50 1.25
660 Tony Gwynn .75 2.00
712 Nolan Ryan 2.50 6.00

2012 Topps Archives Stickers

COMPLETE SET (25) 12.50 30.00
STATED ODDS 1:8 HOBBY
PRINTING PLATE ODDS 1:1196 HOBBY
PLATE PRINT RUN 1 SET PER COLOR
BLACK-CYAN-MAGENTA-YELLOW ISSUED
NO PLATE PRICING DUE TO SCARCITY
I Ichiro Suzuki 1.25 3.00
AG Adrian Gonzalez .75 2.00
CG Carlos Gonzalez .75 2.00
CK Clayton Kershaw 2.00 5.00
CY Carl Yastrzemski 1.50 4.00
DJ Derek Jeter 2.50 6.00
IK Ian Kennedy .60 1.50
JB Jose Bautista .75 2.00
JH Josh Hamilton .75 2.00
JM Joe Mauer .75 2.00
JP Jim Palmer .60 1.50
JV Justin Verlander 1.00 2.50
MC Miguel Cabrera 1.00 2.50
MM Mickey Mantle 3.00 8.00
MR Mariano Rivera 1.25 3.00
MT Mark Teixeira .75 2.00
PS Pablo Sandoval .75 2.00
RB Ryan Braun .60 1.50
RH Ryan Howard .75 2.00
RM Roger Maris 1.00 2.50
TL Tim Lincecum .75 2.00
TS Tom Seaver .60 1.50
TT Troy Tulowitzki 1.00 2.50
WM Willie Mays 2.00 5.00
RHA Roy Halladay .75 2.00

2013 Topps Archives

COMP.SET W/O ERRORS (245) 60.00 120.00
COMP.SET W/O SP's (200) 12.50 30.00
SP 201-245 ODDS 1:4 HOBBY
ERROR VARIATION ODDS 1:1717 HOBBY
PRINTING PLATE ODDS 1:536 HOBBY
1 Babe Ruth .60 1.50
2 Gary Carter .20 .50
3 Carlos Beltran .20 .50
4 Marco Scutaro .20 .50
5 Allen Craig .20 .50
6 Adrian Gonzalez .20 .50
7 Jon Jay .15 .40
8 Roy Halladay .20 .50
9 Ryan Braun .20 .50
10 Matt Kemp .20 .50
11 Joe Nathan .15 .40
12 Jarrod Parker .15 .40
13 Ryan Zimmerman .20 .50
14 Yoenis Cespedes .25 .60
15 Mike Morse .15 .40
16 Cal Ripken Jr. .75 2.00
17 Hanley Ramirez .20 .50
18 Jon Lester .20 .50
19 Tyler Skaggs RC .40 1.00
20A Albert Pujols .30 .75
20B Jason Heyward SP 40.00 80.00
21 Adrian Beltre .25 .60
22 Alex Rios .20 .50
23 Jordan Zimmermann .20 .50
24 Ben Zobrist .20 .50

25 Dexter Fowler .20 .50
26 Jayson Werth .20 .50
27 Manny Machado RC 1.50 4.00
28 Mike Schmidt .40 1.00
29 Angel Pagan .15 .40
30 Yu Darvish .25 .60
31 Brock Holt RC .30 .75
32 Wade Boggs .20 .50
33 Corey Hart .15 .40
34 Dwight Gooden .15 .40
35 Adam Dunn .20 .50
36 Wade Miley .15 .40
37 Elvis Andrus .20 .50
38 Derek Jeter .60 1.50
39 Lance Lynn .15 .40
40 Prince Fielder .20 .50
41 Doug Fister .15 .40
42 Mariano Rivera .30 .75
43 Starling Marte .20 .50
44 Chris Davis .20 .50
45 Chase Headley .15 .40
46 Justin Morneau .20 .50
47 Ryan Howard .20 .50
48 Ryne Sandberg .50 1.25
49 Alcides Escobar .20 .50
50 Miguel Cabrera .25 .60
51 Carlos Gonzalez .20 .50
52 Desmond Jennings .20 .50
53 Brandon Phillips .15 .40
54 Cliff Lee .20 .50
55 CC Sabathia .20 .50
56 Josh Reddick .15 .40
57 Todd Frazier .20 .50
58 Cole Hamels .20 .50
59 Joe Morgan .20 .50
60 Robinson Cano .20 .50
61 Shelby Miller RC .60 1.50
62 Jacoby Ellsbury .20 .50
63 David Freese .15 .40
64 Asdrubal Cabrera .20 .50
65 Paul Konerko .20 .50
66 Tim Hudson .20 .50
67 Rickie Weeks .15 .40
68 Matt Harrison .15 .40
69 Eddie Mathews .25 .60
70 Ozzie Smith .30 .75
71 Darwin Barney .15 .40
72 Harmon Killebrew .25 .60
73 Aroldis Chapman .25 .60
74 Miguel Montero .15 .40
75 C.J. Wilson .15 .40
76 Fernando Rodney .15 .40
77 Tony Cingrani RC .50 1.25
78 Johan Santana .20 .50
79 Josh Willingham .20 .50
80 Jered Weaver .20 .50
81 Will Middlebrooks .15 .40
82 Tom Seaver .20 .50
83 Jim Johnson .15 .40
84 Coco Crisp .15 .40
85 Tony Perez .20 .50
86 Jackie Robinson .25 .60
87 A.J. Burnett .15 .40
88 Derek Holland .15 .40
89 Barry Zito .20 .50
90 Matt Cain .20 .50
91 Brandon Beachy .15 .40
92 Ken Griffey Jr. .50 1.25
93 Ian Desmond .15 .40
94 Curtis Granderson .20 .50
95 Reggie Jackson .20 .50
96 Edwin Encarnacion .25 .60
97 David Wright .20 .50
98 Jesus Montero .15 .40
99 Joey Votto .25 .60
100 Bryce Harper .40 1.00
101 Andrew McCutchen .25 .60
102 Matt Moore .20 .50
103 Mike Minor .15 .40
104 Gio Gonzalez .20 .50
105 Mike Moustakas .20 .50
106 Tim Lincecum .20 .50
107 Kendrys Morales .15 .40
108 Austin Jackson .15 .40
109 Sergio Romo .15 .40
110 Josh Hamilton .20 .50
111 Brandon Morrow .15 .40
112 Kris Medlen .20 .50
113 Jake Peavy .15 .40
114 Robin Yount .25 .60
115 Paul Goldschmidt .25 .60
116 Billy Butler .15 .40
117 Carlos Santana .20 .50
118 Brandon Belt .20 .50
119 Ian Kinsler .20 .50
120 Ted Williams .50 1.25
121 Ian Kennedy .15 .40
122 R.A. Dickey .20 .50
123 Jean Segura .20 .50
124 George Brett .50 1.25
125 Kyle Lohse .15 .40
126 Aaron Hill .15 .40
127 David Price .20 .50
128 Mark Trumbo .15 .40
129 Madison Bumgarner .20 .50
130 Clayton Kershaw .50 1.25
131 Salvador Perez .20 .50
132 Bronson Arroyo .15 .40
133 Jurickson Profar RC .30 .75
134 Wei-Yin Chen .15 .40
135 Adam Wainwright .20 .50
136 Nelson Cruz .25 .60
137 Brian McCann .20 .50
138 David Murphy .15 .40
139 Matt Holliday .25 .60
140 Dylan Bundy RC .60 1.50
141 Adam Jones .20 .50
142 Willie Stargell .20 .50
143 Jake Odorizzi RC .30 .75
144 Paul Molitor .25 .60
145 Alfonso Soriano .20 .50
146 Eddie Murray .20 .50
147 Hiroki Kuroda .15 .40
148 Dustin Pedroia .20 .50
149 Hisashi Iwakuma .20 .50
150 Jose Bautista .20 .50
151 Jason Motte .15 .40
152 Craig Kimbrel .20 .50
153 David Ortiz .25 .60
154 Yovani Gallardo .15 .40
155 Wilin Rosario .15 .40
156 Goose Gossage .20 .50
157 Evan Longoria .20 .50
158 Mike Olt RC .30 .75
159 Troy Tulowitzki .25 .60
160 Felix Hernandez .20 .50
161 Anthony Rizzo .40 1.00
162 Carlos Ruiz .15 .40
163 Hyun-Jin Ryu RC .60 1.50
164 Dan Uggla .15 .40
165 Stephen Strasburg .25 .60
166 Ryan Vogelsong .15 .40
167 Rod Carew .20 .50
168 Pablo Sandoval .20 .50
169 Pedro Alvarez .15 .40
170 Joe Mauer .20 .50
171 Jay Bruce .20 .50
172 Freddie Freeman .30 .75
173 Jason Kipnis .20 .50
174 Ike Davis .15 .40
175 Yogi Berra .25 .60
176 Jose Altuve .20 .50
177 Starlin Castro .15 .40
178 Giancarlo Stanton .25 .60
179 Tommy Milone .15 .40
180 Buster Posey .30 .75
181 Avisail Garcia RC .30 .75
182 Andre Ethier .20 .50
183 Scott Diamond .15 .40
184 Kyle Seager .15 .40
185 Stan Musial .40 1.00
186 Brett Lawrie .20 .50
187 Alex Gordon .20 .50
188 Mat Latos .20 .50
189 Homer Bailey .15 .40
190 Tony Gwynn .25 .60
191 Mark Teixeira .20 .50
192 Adam Eaton RC .40 1.00
193 Jim Palmer .20 .50
194 Yadier Molina .25 .60
195 Dave Winfield .20 .50
196 Johnny Cueto .20 .50
197 Chris Sale .25 .60
198 Jason Heyward .20 .50
199 Eric Hosmer .20 .50
200 Mike Trout 2.00 5.00
201 John Mayberry SP 1.25 3.00
202 Mike Greenwell SP 1.25 3.00
203 Denny McLain SP 1.25 3.00
204 Charlie Hough SP 1.25 3.00
205 Ruben Sierra SP 1.25 3.00
206 Tim Salmon SP 1.25 3.00
207 Lee May SP 1.25 3.00
208 Keith Miller SP 1.25 3.00
209 Dwight Evans SP 1.25 3.00
210 Bob Tewksbury SP 1.25 3.00
211 Tom Brunansky SP 1.25 3.00
212 Otis Nixon SP 1.25 3.00
213 Juan Samuel SP 1.25 3.00
214 Fred McGriff SP 1.50 4.00
215 Bob Welch SP 1.25 3.00
216 Jesse Barfield SP 1.25 3.00
217 Mookie Wilson SP 1.25 3.00
218 Darrell Evans SP 1.25 3.00
219 Dave Lopes SP 1.25 3.00
220 Ellis Burks SP 1.25 3.00
221 Hal Morris SP 1.25 3.00
222 Howard Johnson SP 1.25 3.00
223 Matt Williams SP 1.25 3.00
224 Paul Blair SP 1.25 3.00
225 Kent Hrbek SP 1.25 3.00
226 Larry Bowa SP 1.25 3.00
227 Mickey Rivers SP 1.25 3.00
228 Delino DeShields SP 1.25 3.00
229 Hubie Brooks SP 1.25 3.00
230 Ray Knight SP 1.25 3.00
231 Kevin McReynolds SP 1.25 3.00
232 Travis Fryman SP 1.25 3.00
233 Vince Coleman SP 1.25 3.00
234 Don Baylor SP 1.25 3.00
235 Gregg Jefferies SP 1.25 3.00
236 Jesse Orosco SP 1.25 3.00
237 Sid Fernandez SP 1.25 3.00
238 Frank White SP 1.25 3.00
239 Dave Parker SP 1.25 3.00
240 Darren Daulton SP 1.25 3.00
241 Fred Lynn SP 1.25 3.00
242 Kevin Mitchell SP 1.25 3.00
243 Lloyd Moseby SP 1.25 3.00
244 Eric Davis SP 1.25 3.00
245 Leon Durham SP 1.25 3.00
400 Joey Votto SP 20.00 50.00
414 Chris Sale SP 30.00 60.00
497 Dylan Bundy SP 50.00 100.00
USA1 George W. Bush

2013 Topps Archives Day Glow

*DAY GLOW: 1.5X TO 4X BASIC
*DAY GLOW RC: 1X TO 2.5X BASIC RC
38 Derek Jeter 8.00 20.00

2013 Topps Archives Gold

*GOLD: 2.5X TO 6X BASIC
*GOLD RC: 1.5X TO 4X BASIC RC
STATED ODDS 1:13 HOBBY
STATED PRINT RUN 199 SER.#'d SETS
38 Derek Jeter 20.00 50.00
100 Bryce Harper 15.00 40.00

2013 Topps Archives '72 Basketball Design

COMPLETE SET (20) 50.00 100.00
STATED ODDS 1:24 HOBBY
PRINTING PLATE ODDS 1:1020 HOBBY
PLATE PRINT RUN 1 SET PER COLOR
BLACK-CYAN-MAGENTA-YELLOW ISSUED
NO PLATE PRICING DUE TO SCARCITY
AM Andrew McCutchen 2.00 5.00
CC CC Sabathia 1.50 4.00
DW Dave Winfield 1.50 4.00
GS Giancarlo Stanton 2.00 5.00
JB Johnny Bench 2.00 5.00
JH Jason Heyward 1.50 4.00
JM Joe Morgan
KG Ken Griffey Jr. 4.00 10.00
LB Lou Brock 1.50 4.00
MK Matt Kemp 1.50 4.00
OS Ozzie Smith 2.50 6.00
PF Prince Fielder 1.50 4.00
RC Rod Carew 1.50 4.00
RJ Reggie Jackson 1.50 4.00
TG Tony Gwynn 2.00 5.00
TS Tom Seaver 1.50 4.00
TW Ted Williams 4.00 10.00
WM Willie McCovey 1.50 4.00
WS Willie Stargell 1.50 4.00
YD Yu Darvish 2.00 5.00

2013 Topps Archives '83 All-Stars

COMPLETE SET (30) 12.50 30.00
STATED ODDS 1:4 HOBBY
PRINTING PLATE ODDS 1:1020 HOBBY
PLATE PRINT RUN 1 SET PER COLOR
BLACK-CYAN-MAGENTA-YELLOW ISSUED
NO PLATE PRICING DUE TO SCARCITY
AD Andre Dawson .50 1.25
AM Andrew McCutchen .60 1.50
AP Albert Pujols .75 2.00
BH Bryce Harper 1.00 2.50
BP Buster Posey .75 2.00
CF Carlton Fisk .50 1.25
CR Cal Ripken Jr. 2.00 5.00
DE Darrell Evans .40 1.00
DJ Derek Jeter 1.50 4.00
DS Darryl Strawberry .40 1.00
DW Dave Winfield .50 1.25
FL Fred Lynn .40 1.00
GB George Brett 1.25 3.00
GC Gary Carter .50 1.25
GS Giancarlo Stanton .60 1.50
JB Johnny Bench .60 1.50
JR Jim Rice .50 1.25
JV Justin Verlander .60 1.50
LD Leon Durham .40 1.00
MC Miguel Cabrera .60 1.50
MS Mike Schmidt 1.00 2.50
MT Mike Trout 5.00 12.00
NR Nolan Ryan 2.00 5.00
PG Pedro Guerrero .25 .60
PM Paul Molitor .60 1.50
RC Robinson Cano .50 1.25
RH Rickey Henderson .60 1.50
RS Ryne Sandberg 1.25 3.00
SS Stephen Strasburg .60 1.50
TG Tony Gwynn .60 1.50

2013 Topps Archives '89 All-Stars Retail

AP Albert Pujols 20.00 50.00
AR Anthony Rizzo 10.00 25.00
BH Bryce Harper 50.00 100.00
CK Clayton Kershaw 20.00 50.00
CS Chris Sale 10.00 25.00
DF David Freese 8.00 20.00
DJ Derek Jeter 20.00 50.00
GG Gio Gonzalez 10.00 25.00
JP Jurickson Profar 10.00 25.00
JV Justin Verlander 20.00 50.00
MC Matt Cain 10.00 25.00
MCA Miguel Cabrera 15.00 40.00
MM Manny Machado 60.00 120.00
MT Mike Trout 50.00 100.00
RA R.A. Dickey 8.00 20.00
RB Ryan Braun 8.00 20.00
RC Robinson Cano 12.50 30.00
WM Will Middlebrooks 8.00 20.00
YC Yoenis Cespedes 15.00 40.00
YD Yu Darvish 10.00 25.00

2013 Topps Archives Dual Fan Favorites

BG Dante Bichette .75 2.00
Carlos Gonzalez
DC Rob Dibble 1.00 2.50
Aroldis Chapman
DP Eric Davis .60 1.50
Brandon Phillips
DR Darren Daulton .60 1.50
Carlos Ruiz
EP Dwight Evans .75 2.00
Dustin Pedroia
FW Chuck Finley .75 2.00
Jered Weaver
GJ Kirk Gibson .60 1.50
Austin Jackson
LE Fred Lynn .75 2.00
Jacoby Ellsbury
MB John Mayberry .60 1.50
Billy Butler
MS Kevin Mitchell .75 2.00
Pablo Sandoval
NU Otis Nixon .75 2.00
B.J. Upton
PM D.Parker/A.McCutchen 1.00 2.50
SC Ruben Sierra 1.00 2.50
Nelson Cruz
SR Juan Samuel .75 2.00
Jimmy Rollins
WP M.Williams/B.Posey 1.25 3.00

2013 Topps Archives Fan Favorites Autographs

STATED ODDS 1:153 HOBBY
PELE ODDS 1:41,000 HOBBY
EXCHANGE DEADLINE 5/31/2016
AH Al Hrabosky 6.00 15.00
BS Bret Saberhagen 8.00 20.00
BSA Benito Santiago 5.00 12.00
BT Bob Tewksbury 5.00 12.00
BW Bob Welch 10.00 25.00
CF Chuck Finley 5.00 12.00
CH Charlie Hough 5.00 12.00
DB Don Baylor 6.00 15.00
DBO Dennis Boyd 5.00 12.00
DC Dave Concepcion EXCH 12.00 30.00
DD Delino DeShields 5.00 12.00
DDA Darren Daulton 8.00 20.00
DE Darrell Evans 5.00 12.00
DG Dan Gladden 6.00 15.00
DL Dave Lopes 6.00 15.00
DM Denny McLain 8.00 20.00
DP Dave Parker 10.00 25.00
EB Ellis Burks 5.00 12.00
ED Eric Davis 6.00 15.00
FL Fred Lynn 10.00 25.00
FM Fred McGriff 8.00 20.00
FW Frank White 5.00 12.00
GG Gary Gaetti 5.00 12.00
GJ Gregg Jefferies 6.00 15.00
GN Graig Nettles 6.00 15.00
HB Hubie Brooks 5.00 12.00
HJ Howard Johnson 8.00 20.00
HM Hal Morris 5.00 12.00
JB Jesse Barfield 5.00 12.00
JD Jody Davis 5.00 12.00
JM John Mayberry 6.00 15.00
JO Jesse Orosco 5.00 12.00
JS Juan Samuel 5.00 12.00
KH Kent Hrbek 5.00 12.00
KM Kevin McReynolds 6.00 15.00
KMI Keith Miller 5.00 12.00
KML Kevin Mitchell 6.00 15.00
LB Larry Bowa 6.00 15.00
LD Leon Durham 5.00 12.00
LM Lee May 6.00 15.00
LMO Lloyd Moseby 5.00 12.00
LS Lee Smith 6.00 15.00
MG Mike Greenwell 8.00 20.00
MR Mickey Rivers 6.00 15.00
MT Mickey Tettleton 5.00 12.00
MW Mookie Wilson 8.00 20.00
MWI Matt Williams 5.00 12.00
ON Otis Nixon 6.00 15.00
PB Paul Blair 5.00 12.00
RD Ron Darling 8.00 20.00
RK Ray Knight 5.00 12.00
RR Rick Reuschel 5.00 12.00
RSI Ruben Sierra 5.00 12.00
SF Sid Fernandez 5.00 12.00
TB Tom Brunansky 5.00 12.00
TF Travis Fryman 6.00 15.00
TS Tim Salmon 5.00 12.00
VC Vince Coleman 8.00 20.00
75-P Pele

2013 Topps Archives Four-In-One

COMPLETE SET (15) 12.50 30.00
STATED ODDS 1:8 HOBBY
BBMP Berra/Bench/Mauer/Posey .75 2.00
BPDS Don Baylor/Dave Parker
Eric Davis/Darryl Strawberry .40 1.00
CHNL Vince Coleman/Rickey Henderson/Otis
Nixon/Kenny Lofton .60 1.50
CMGT Cobb/Mays/Griffey/Trout 5.00 12.00
FSRV Fel/Seav/Ryan/Verland 2.00 5.00
GBRS Gwynn/Boggs/Ripken/Sand 2.00 5.00
MCWP McCov/Clark/Will/Posey .75 2.00
OPJR O'Neill/Pett/Jeter/Rivera 1.50 4.00
PDCP Posey/Dickey/Cab/Price .75 2.00
RGBJ Ruth/Gehrig/Berra/Reggie 1.50 4.00
RJMJ Ruth/Reg/Matting/Jeter 1.50 4.00
SKCK Spahn/Koufax/Carlton/Kersh 1.25 3.00
SWGJ Darryl Strawberry/Mookie Wilson/Dwight
Gooden/Howard Johnson .40 1.00
THBK Trout/Harper/Braun/Kemp 5.00 12.00
WRYC Will/Robin/Yaz/Cab 1.25 3.00

2013 Topps Archives Gallery Of Heroes

STATED ODDS 1:31 HOBBY
AP Albert Pujols 2.50 6.00
BP Buster Posey 2.50 6.00
BR Babe Ruth 5.00 12.00
CR Cal Ripken Jr. 6.00 15.00
DJ Derek Jeter 5.00 12.00
JR Jackie Robinson 2.00 5.00
LG Lou Gehrig 4.00 10.00
MC Miguel Cabrera 4.00 10.00
MR Mariano Rivera 2.50 6.00
MT Mike Trout 8.00 20.00
RC Roberto Clemente 5.00 12.00
SK Sandy Koufax 4.00 10.00
TW Ted Williams 4.00 10.00
WM Willie Mays 4.00 10.00
YB Yogi Berra 2.00 5.00

2013 Topps Archives Greatest Moments Box Toppers

STATED ODDS 1:8 HOBBY BOXES
STATED PRINT RUN 99 SER.#'d SETS
1 Jim Rice 12.50 30.00
2 Ryan Braun 6.00 15.00
3 Juan Marichal 12.50 30.00
4 Bob Gibson 10.00 25.00
5 David Freese 8.00 20.00
6 Jim Palmer 8.00 20.00
7 Mike Schmidt 15.00 40.00
8 R.A. Dickey 10.00 25.00
9 Dave Concepcion 12.50 30.00
10 Kirk Gibson 10.00 25.00
11 Manny Machado 30.00 60.00
12 Ken Griffey Jr. 20.00 50.00
13 Will Clark 12.50 30.00
14 Miguel Cabrera 15.00 40.00
15 Bryce Harper 40.00 80.00
16 Mike Trout 40.00 80.00
17 Yu Darvish 6.00 15.00
18 Yoenis Cespedes 12.50 30.00
19 Robinson Cano 15.00 40.00
20 Tom Seaver 15.00 40.00
21 Lou Brock 12.50 30.00
22 Harmon Killebrew 12.50 30.00
23 Vida Blue 6.00 15.00
24 Fergie Jenkins 6.00 15.00
25 Willie Stargell 10.00 25.00

2013 Topps Archives Heavy Metal Autographs

STATED ODDS 1:153 HOBBY
EXCHANGE DEADLINE 5/31/2016
AR Axl Rose 300.00 500.00
BB Bobbie Brown 12.50 30.00
DS Dee Snider 10.00 25.00
KW Kip Winger 6.00 15.00
LF Lita Ford 12.50 30.00
RB Reb Beach 8.00 20.00
SB Sebastian Bach 10.00 25.00
SI Scott Ian 15.00 40.00
SP Stephen Pearcy 10.00 25.00
TL Tommy Lee 20.00 50.00

2013 Topps Archives Mini Tall Boys

COMPLETE SET (40) 20.00 50.00
STATED ODDS 1:5 HOBBY
PRINTING PLATE ODDS 1:1020 HOBBY
PLATE PRINT RUN 1 SET PER COLOR
BLACK-CYAN-MAGENTA-YELLOW ISSUED
NO PLATE PRICING DUE TO SCARCITY
AB Albert Pujols .75 2.00
AK Al Kaline .60 1.50
AR Anthony Rizzo 1.00 2.50
BH Bryce Harper 1.00 2.50
BP Buster Posey .75 2.00
CK Clayton Kershaw 1.25 3.00
CR Cal Ripken Jr. 2.00 5.00
CS Chris Sale .60 1.50
DB Dante Bichette .40 1.00
DBU Dylan Bundy 1.00 2.50
DC Dave Concepcion .40 1.00
DE Dwight Evans .40 1.00
DF David Freese .40 1.00
DJ Derek Jeter 1.50 4.00
DM Denny McLain .40 1.00
DP Dave Parker .40 1.00
DS Dave Stewart .40 1.00
DW David Wright .50 1.25
EB Ellis Burks .40 1.00
ED Eric Davis .40 1.00
FL Fred Lynn .40 1.00
FM Fred McGriff .50 1.25
FW Frank White .40 1.00
GG Gio Gonzalez .50 1.25
KG Kirk Gibson .25 .60
KM Kevin Mitchell .40 1.00
MC Miguel Cabrera .60 1.50
MG Mike Greenwell .40 1.00
MS Mike Schmidt 1.00 2.50
MT Mike Trout 5.00 12.00
MW Matt Williams .40 1.00
ON Otis Nixon .40 1.00
RB Ryan Braun .50 1.25
RC Robinson Cano .50 1.25
RCL Roberto Clemente 1.50 4.00
RD Rob Dibble .40 1.00
SS Stephen Strasburg .60 1.50
WC Will Clark .60 1.50
WM Will Middlebrooks .40 1.00
YC Yoenis Cespedes .60 1.50

2013 Topps Archives Relics

STATED ODDS 1:216 HOBBY
AB Adrian Beltre 4.00 10.00
AD Adam Dunn 4.00 10.00
AE Andre Ethier 3.00 8.00
AJ Austin Jackson 5.00 12.00
AM Andrew McCutchen 5.00 12.00
AW Adam Wainwright 4.00 10.00
BB Billy Butler 3.00 8.00
BG Brett Gardner 4.00 10.00
BH Bryce Harper 12.50 30.00
BM Brandon Morrow 3.00 8.00
BP Brandon Phillips 4.00 10.00
BR Ben Revere 3.00 8.00
CF Cecil Fielder 10.00 25.00
CS Carlos Santana 3.00 8.00
DB Domonic Brown 5.00 12.00
DG Dwight Gooden 6.00 15.00
EA Elvis Andrus 3.00 8.00
EL Evan Longoria 4.00 10.00
GS Gary Sheffield 4.00 10.00
HR Hanley Ramirez 3.00 8.00
ID Ike Davis 4.00 10.00
IDE Ian Desmond 3.00 8.00
IK Ian Kinsler 4.00 10.00
JB Johnny Bench 12.50 30.00
JBR Jay Bruce 6.00 15.00
JK Jason Kubel 3.00 8.00
JM Jesus Montero 3.00 8.00
JV Justin Verlander 6.00 15.00
JZ Jordan Zimmermann 3.00 8.00
KG Ken Griffey Sr. 6.00 15.00
LT Luis Tiant 8.00 20.00
MB Madison Bumgarner 6.00 15.00
MC Matt Cain 5.00 12.00
MH Matt Harvey 8.00 20.00
MM Matt Moore 3.00 8.00
MMO Miguel Montero 3.00 8.00
MMS Mike Moustakas 3.00 8.00
MT Mike Trout 20.00 50.00
NC Nelson Cruz 3.00 8.00
NM1 Nick Markakis Jsy 5.00 12.00
NM2 Nick Markakis Bat 10.00 25.00
PA Pedro Alvarez 4.00 10.00
PF Prince Fielder 6.00 15.00
PG Paul Goldschmidt 4.00 10.00
PK Paul Konerko 3.00 8.00
PO Paul O'Neill 10.00 25.00
RH Ryan Howard 5.00 12.00
RZ Ryan Zimmerman 4.00 10.00
SC Starlin Castro 4.00 10.00
SSC Shin-Soo Choo 5.00 12.00
TC Trevor Cahill 3.00 8.00
VM Victor Martinez 5.00 12.00
WB Wade Boggs 12.50 30.00
YA Yonder Alonso 3.00 8.00

2013 Topps Archives Triumvirate

STATED ODDS 1:24 HOBBY
1A Mike Trout 12.00 30.00
1B Albert Pujols 2.00 5.00
1C Josh Hamilton 1.25 3.00
2A Albert Belle 1.00 2.50
2B Robin Ventura 1.00 2.50
2C Frank Thomas 1.50 4.00
3A Cole Hamels 1.25 3.00
3B Cliff Lee 1.25 3.00
3C Roy Halladay 1.25 3.00
4A Edgar Martinez 1.00 2.50
4B Ken Griffey Jr. 3.00 8.00
4C Alex Rodriguez 2.00 5.00
5A Mariano Rivera 2.00 5.00
5B Derek Jeter 4.00 10.00
5C Andy Pettitte 1.25 3.00
6A Dylan Bundy 2.50 6.00
6B Adam Jones 1.25 3.00
6C Manny Machado 6.00 15.00
7A Miguel Cabrera 1.50 4.00
7B Justin Verlander 1.50 4.00
7C Prince Fielder 1.25 3.00

2014 Topps Archives

COMP.SET w/o SP's (200) 12.00 30.00
SP ODDS 1:4 HOBBY
PRINTING PLATE ODDS 1:151 HOBBY
PLATE PRINT RUN 1 SET PER COLOR
BLACK-CYAN-MAGENTA-YELLOW ISSUED
NO PLATE PRICING DUE TO SCARCITY
1 Yu Darvish .25 .60
2 Bruce Sutter .15 .40
3 Freddie Freeman .30 .75
4 Andrew Lambo RC .25 .60
5 Carl Crawford .20 .50
6 Marcus Semien RC .25 .60
7 Dustin Pedroia .25 .60
8 Zack Greinke .20 .50
9 Josh Donaldson .20 .50
10 Juan Gonzalez .15 .40
11 Adam Wainwright .20 .50
12 James Shields .15 .40
13 Jarred Cosart .15 .40
14 Dennis Eckersley .20 .50
15 Ralph Kiner .20 .50
16 Matt Harvey .25 .60
17 Joey Votto .25 .60
18 Rickey Henderson .25 .60
19 Nolan Arenado .30 .75
20 Will Middlebrooks .15 .40
21 Ty Cobb .40 1.00
22 Jake Marisnick RC .25 .60
23 Chris Carter .15 .40
24 Michael Cuddyer .15 .40
25 Jim Palmer .20 .50
26 Juan Marichal .20 .50
27 Tom Seaver .20 .50
28 Joe Kelly .15 .40
29 Carlos Gomez .15 .40
30 Alex Gordon .20 .50
31 Steve Carlton .20 .50
32 Frank Robinson .20 .50
33 Kyuji Fujikawa .20 .50
34 Enny Romero RC .25 .60
35 Patrick Corbin .20 .50
36 Carlos Beltran .20 .50
37 Wilmer Flores RC .30 .75
38 Jason Grilli .15 .40
39 Chris Sale .25 .60
40 Christian Yelich .30 .75
41 Catfish Hunter .20 .50
42 Junior Lake .15 .40
43 Josmil Pinto RC .25 .60
44 Ernie Banks .25 .60
45 Lou Brock .20 .50
46 Cole Hamels .20 .50
47 Tim Lincecum .20 .50
48 CC Sabathia .20 .50
49 Jonny Gomes .15 .40
50 Derek Jeter .60 1.50
51 Lou Gehrig .50 1.25
52 Michael Wacha .20 .50
53 James Paxton RC .40 1.00
54 Marco Scutaro .20 .50
55 Jay Bruce .20 .50
56 Jon Jay .15 .40
57 Tom Glavine .20 .50
58 Brett Lawrie .20 .50
59 Nick Swisher .20 .50
60 Ozzie Smith .30 .75
61 Matt Davidson RC .30 .75
62 Matt Moore .20 .50
63 Austin Jackson .15 .40
64 Hisashi Iwakuma .20 .50
65 Starling Marte .20 .50
66 Craig Biggio .20 .50
67 Jonathan Villar .15 .40
68 Eddie Mathews .25 .60
69 Mark McGwire .50 1.25
70 Giancarlo Stanton .25 .60
71 Nick Franklin .15 .40
72 Evan Longoria .20 .50
73 Erik Johnson RC .25 .60
74 Jon Lester .20 .50
75 Ken Griffey Jr. .50 1.25
76 Josh Hamilton .20 .50
77 Joe Morgan .20 .50
78 Dylan Bundy .20 .50
79 Duke Snider .20 .50
80 Hiroki Kuroda .15 .40
81 Todd Frazier .20 .50
82 Matt Cain .20 .50
83 Billy Butler .15 .40
84 Tony Perez .20 .50
85 Kevin Pillar RC .25 .60
86 Shelby Miller .20 .50
87 Eric Davis .15 .40
88 Evan Gattis .15 .40
89 R.A. Dickey .20 .50
90 George Brett .50 1.25
91 Roberto Clemente .60 1.50
92 Aroldis Chapman .25 .60
93 Xander Bogaerts RC .75 2.00
94 Mike Napoli .15 .40
95 Matt Carpenter .25 .60
96 Robin Yount .25 .60
97 Ivan Rodriguez .20 .50
98 Chris Owings RC .25 .60
99 Salvador Perez .20 .50
100 Bryce Harper .40 1.00
101 Ted Williams .50 1.25
102 Goose Gossage .20 .50
103 Orlando Hernandez .15 .40
104 Jordan Zimmermann .20 .50
105 Tony Gwynn .25 .60
106 Cliff Lee .20 .50
107 Michael Choice RC .25 .60
108 Carlos Santana .20 .50
109 Jose Reyes .20 .50
110 Yoenis Cespedes .25 .60
111 Jason Heyward .20 .50
112 Ethan Martin RC .25 .60
113 Cal Ripken Jr. .75 2.00
114 Brian McCann .20 .50
115 Manny Machado .25 .60
116 Alex Guerrero RC .30 .75
117 Mike Mussina .20 .50
118 Eddie Murray .20 .50
119 Andrelton Simmons .15 .40
120 Yadier Molina .25 .60
121 Kevin Siegrist (RC) .25 .60
122 Larry Doby .20 .50
123 Jarrod Parker .15 .40
124 Trevor Rosenthal .20 .50
125 Jose Fernandez .25 .60
126 Yordano Ventura RC .30 .75
127 Christian Bethancourt RC .25 .60
128 Avisail Garcia .20 .50
129 Phil Niekro .20 .50
130 Matt Holliday .25 .60
131 Ian Kinsler .20 .50
132 Felix Hernandez .20 .50
133 Yovani Gallardo .15 .40
134 Gio Gonzalez .20 .50
135 Jimmy Nelson RC .25 .60
136 Whitey Ford .20 .50
137 Pedro Alvarez .15 .40
138 Warren Spahn .20 .50
139 Bob Feller .20 .50
140 Tony Cingrani .20 .50
141 Pablo Sandoval .20 .50
142 Joe Mauer .20 .50
143 Mike Schmidt .40 1.00
144 Adrian Beltre .25 .60
146 Starlin Castro .15 .40
147 Jose Bautista .20 .50
148 Anthony Rendon .25 .60
149 Madison Bumgarner .20 .50
150 Miguel Cabrera .25 .60

151 Joe DiMaggio .50 1.25
152 Anthony Rizzo .40 1.00
153 Fergie Jenkins .20 .50
154 Harmon Killebrew .25 .60
155 Lou Boudreau .20 .50
156 Phil Rizzuto .20 .50
157 Rod Carew .20 .50
158 Willie Stargell .20 .50
159 Bob Gibson .20 .50
160 Don Mattingly .50 1.25
161 Johnny Bench .25 .60
162 Paul O'Neill .20 .50
163 Randy Johnson .25 .60
164 Stan Musial .40 1.00
165 Willie McCovey .20 .50
166 David Holmberg RC .25 .60
167 John Ryan Murphy RC .25 .60
168 Jonathan Schoop RC .25 .60
169 Kolten Wong RC .30 .75
170 Travis d'Arnaud RC .30 .75
171 Adam Eaton .15 .40
172 Albert Pujols .30 .75
173 Allen Craig .20 .50
174 Andre Rienzo RC .25 .60
175 Yogi Berra .25 .60
176 Adrian Gonzalez .20 .50
177 Carlos Gonzalez .20 .50
178 Carlos Martinez .20 .50
179 Chris Davis .15 .40
180 Chris Archer .15 .40
181 Craig Kimbrel .20 .50
182 Curtis Granderson .20 .50
183 David Wright .20 .50
184 Domonic Brown .20 .50
185 Doug Fister .15 .40
186 Gerrit Cole .25 .60
187 Hanley Ramirez .20 .50
188 Jered Weaver .20 .50
189 Jose Altuve .20 .50
190 Julio Teheran .20 .50
191 Justin Upton .20 .50
192 Khris Davis .25 .60
193 Matt Kemp .20 .50
194 Max Scherzer .25 .60
195 Mike Zunino .15 .40
196 Prince Fielder .20 .50
197 Ryan Zimmerman .20 .50
198 Shin-Soo Choo .20 .50
199 Sonny Gray .20 .50
200 Buster Posey .30 .75
201 Babe Ruth SP 3.00 8.00
202 Luis Gonzalez SP .75 2.00
203 Zack Wheeler SP 1.00 2.50
204 Manny Ramirez SP 1.25 3.00
205 Mike Trout SP 6.00 15.00
206 David Freese SP .75 2.00
207 Jorge Posada SP 1.00 2.50
208 Andrew McCutchen SP 1.25 3.00
209 Greg Maddux SP 1.50 4.00
210 Clayton Kershaw SP 2.50 6.00
211 Bo Jackson SP 1.25 3.00
212 Jose Canseco SP 1.00 2.50
213 Mookie Wilson SP .75 2.00
214 Fernando Valenzuela SP .75 2.00
215 Reggie Jackson SP 1.00 2.50
216 Robinson Cano SP 1.00 2.50
217 Jose Abreu SP RC 8.00 20.00
218 Nomar Garciaparra SP 1.00 2.50
219 John Smoltz SP 1.25 3.00
220 Sandy Koufax SP 2.50 6.00
221 Hyun-Jin Ryu SP 1.00 2.50
222 Edgar Martinez SP 1.00 2.50
223 Andy Van Slyke SP .75 2.00
224 Troy Tulowitzki SP 1.25 3.00
225 Wil Myers SP .75 2.00
226 Adam Jones SP 1.00 2.50
227 Nick Castellanos SP RC 3.00 8.00
228 Brandon Phillips SP .75 2.00
229 Wade Boggs SP 1.00 2.50
230 Billy Hamilton SP RC 1.25 3.00
231 Paul Goldschmidt SP 1.25 3.00
232 Nolan Ryan SP 4.00 10.00
233 Graig Nettles SP .75 2.00
234 Don Zimmer SP .75 2.00
235 Darren Daulton SP .75 2.00
236 David Price SP 1.00 2.50
237 Dusty Baker SP .75 2.00
238 David Ortiz SP 1.25 3.00
239 Taijuan Walker SP RC 1.00 2.50
240 Mariano Rivera SP 1.50 4.00
241 Masahiro Tanaka SP RC 3.00 8.00
242 Deion Sanders SP 1.00 2.50
243 Willie Mays SP 2.50 6.00
244 Jacoby Ellsbury SP 1.00 2.50
245 John Olerud SP .75 2.00
246 Justin Verlander SP 1.25 3.00
247 Stephen Strasburg SP 1.25 3.00
248 Jurickson Profar SP 1.00 2.50
249 Pedro Martinez SP 1.00 2.50
250 Yasiel Puig SP 1.25 3.00

2014 Topps Archives Gold

*GOLD: 3X TO 8X BASIC
*GOLD RC: 2X TO 5X BASIC RC
STATED ODDS 1:7 HOBBY
STATED PRINT RUN 199 SER.#'d SETS
50 Derek Jeter 10.00 25.00
93 Xander Bogaerts 8.00 20.00

2014 Topps Archives Silver

*SILVER: 4X TO 10X BASIC
*SILVER RC: 2.5X TO 6X BASIC RC
STATED ODDS 1:14 HOBBY
STATED PRINT RUN 99 SER.#'d SETS
50 Derek Jeter 20.00 50.00
75 Ken Griffey Jr. 10.00 25.00
93 Xander Bogaerts 15.00 40.00

2014 Topps Archives '69 Deckle Minis

COMPLETE SET (40) 30.00 80.00
STATED ODDS 1:5 HOBBY
AM Andrew McCutchen 1.25 3.00
AVS Andy Van Slyke .75 2.00
BH Bryce Harper 2.00 5.00
BP Buster Posey 1.50 4.00
CB Carlos Baerga .75 2.00
CK Clayton Kershaw 2.50 6.00
CR Cal Ripken Jr. 4.00 10.00
DD Darren Daulton .75 2.00
DE David Eckstein .75 2.00
DJ Derek Jeter 3.00 8.00
DP Dave Parker .75 2.00
DW David Wright 1.00 2.50
GN Graig Nettles .75 2.00
HJ Howard Johnson .75 2.00
HJR Hyun-Jin Ryu 1.00 2.50
IR Ivan Rodriguez 1.00 2.50
JAB Jose Abreu 4.00 10.00
JC Jose Canseco 1.00 2.50
JF Jose Fernandez 1.25 3.00
JK Joe Kelly .75 2.00
JO John Olerud .75 2.00
JV Justin Verlander 1.25 3.00
JVO Joey Votto 1.25 3.00
MC Miguel Cabrera 1.25 3.00
ML Mark Lemke .75 2.00
MM Mike Matheny .75 2.00
MMA Manny Machado 1.25 3.00
MS Mel Stottlemyre .75 2.00
MSC Max Scherzer 1.25 3.00
MT Mike Trout 6.00 15.00
MTK Masahiro Tanaka 4.00 10.00
MW Michael Wacha 1.00 2.50
OH Orlando Hernandez .75 2.00
RG Ron Gant .75 2.00
RW Rondell White .75 2.00
TT Troy Tulowitzki 1.25 3.00
WM Wil Myers .75 2.00
YD Yu Darvish 1.25 3.00
YM Yadier Molina 1.25 3.00
YP Yasiel Puig 1.25 3.00

2014 Topps Archives '69 Deckle Minis Autographs

STATED ODDS 1:570 HOBBY
STATED PRINT RUN 25 SER.#'d SETS
EXCHANGE DEADLINE 5/31/2017
AVSA Andy Van Slyke 15.00 40.00
CBA Carlos Baerga 20.00 50.00
DPA Dave Parker 20.00 50.00
GNA Graig Nettles 15.00 40.00
IRA Ivan Rodriguez 12.00 30.00
JCA Jose Canseco 10.00 25.00
JKA Joe Kelly 20.00 50.00
MLA Mark Lemke 15.00 40.00
OHA Orlando Hernandez 50.00 120.00
RGA Ron Gant 15.00 25.00
RWA Rondell White 20.00 50.00
WMA Wil Myers 30.00 80.00

2014 Topps Archives '71-72 Hockey

STATED ODDS 1:24 HOBBY
PRINTING PLATE ODDS 1:151 HOBBY
PLATE PRINT RUN 1 SET PER COLOR
BLACK-CYAN-MAGENTA-YELLOW ISSUED
NO PLATE PRICING DUE TO SCARCITY
71HBH Bryce Harper 3.00 8.00
71HBP Brandon Phillips 1.25 3.00
71HCS Chris Sabo 1.25 3.00
71HED Eric Davis 1.25 3.00
71HFF Freddie Freeman 2.50 6.00
71HGN Graig Nettles 1.25 3.00
71HJA Jose Abreu 8.00 20.00
71HJK Joe Kelly 1.25 3.00
71HJV Joey Votto 2.00 5.00
71HMC Miguel Cabrera 2.00 5.00
71HMT Mike Trout 10.00 25.00
71HMTA Masahiro Tanaka 8.00 20.00
71HPG Paul Goldschmidt 2.00 5.00
71HRC Roberto Clemente 5.00 12.00
71HSM Shelby Miller 1.50 4.00
71HTS Tom Seaver 1.50 4.00
71HWM Wil Myers 1.25 3.00
71HWS Willie Stargell 1.50 4.00
71HYP Yasiel Puig 2.00 5.00

2014 Topps Archives '71-72 Hockey Autographs

STATED ODDS 1:1710 HOBBY
STATED PRINT RUN 25 SER.#'d SETS
EXCHANGE DEADLINE 5/31/2017
71HABP Brandon Phillips 15.00 40.00
71HAED Eric Davis 30.00 80.00
71HAPG Paul Goldschmidt 40.00 100.00
71HASM Shelby Miller 15.00 40.00
71HAWM Wil Myers 40.00 100.00

2014 Topps Archives '81 Mini Autographs

STATED ODDS 1:296 HOBBY
STATED PRINT RUN 25 SER.#'d SETS
EXCHANGE DEADLINE 5/31/2017
81MABP Brandon Phillips 15.00 40.00
81MACB Carlos Baerga 20.00 50.00
81MADP Dave Parker 20.00 50.00
81MADW David Wright 40.00 80.00
81MAED Eric Davis 30.00 80.00
81MAFF Freddie Freeman 25.00 60.00
81MAGN Graig Nettles 15.00 40.00
81MAJC Jose Canseco 30.00 80.00
81MAJK Joe Kelly 20.00 50.00
81MAMW Mookie Wilson 20.00 50.00
81MAOH Orlando Hernandez 30.00 80.00
81MAPG Paul Goldschmidt 40.00 100.00
81MAPN Phil Niekro 20.00 50.00
81MARG Ron Gant 20.00 50.00
81MARW Rondell White 20.00 50.00
81MASC Sean Casey 15.00 40.00
81MATT Troy Tulowitzki EXCH 40.00 100.00
81MAWM Wil Myers 30.00 80.00
81MADEC David Eckstein 15.00 40.00

2014 Topps Archives '87 All-Stars

STATED ODDS 1:4 HOBBY
PRINTING PLATE ODDS 1:151 HOBBY
PLATE PRINT RUN 1 SET PER COLOR
BLACK-CYAN-MAGENTA-YELLOW ISSUED
NO PLATE PRICING DUE TO SCARCITY
87BB Billy Butler .60 1.50
87BH Bryce Harper 1.50 4.00
87CD Chris Davis .60 1.50
87CK Clayton Kershaw 2.00 5.00
87DG Dwight Gooden .60 1.50
87DO David Ortiz 1.00 2.50
87FF Freddie Freeman 1.25 3.00
87FH Felix Hernandez .75 2.00
87FJ Fergie Jenkins .75 2.00
87GC Gary Carter .75 2.00
87GG Goose Gossage .75 2.00
87GN Graig Nettles .60 1.50
87HJ Howard Johnson .60 1.50
87JB Jose Bautista .75 2.00
87JF Jose Fernandez 1.00 2.50
87JG Jason Grilli .60 1.50
87JV Justin Verlander 1.00 2.50
87MC Miguel Cabrera 1.00 2.50
87MH Matt Harvey .75 2.00
87MM Manny Machado 1.00 2.50
87MR Mariano Rivera 1.25 3.00
87MT Mike Trout 5.00 12.00
87OS Ozzie Smith 1.25 3.00
87PG Paul Goldschmidt 1.00 2.50
87RZ Ryan Zimmerman .75 2.00
87SK Sandy Koufax 2.00 5.00
87TF Travis Fryman .60 1.50
87VC Vince Coleman .60 1.50
87WB Wade Boggs .75 2.00
87YD Yu Darvish 1.00 2.50

2014 Topps Archives Fan Favorites Autographs

STATED ODDS 1:17 HOBBY
EXCHANGE DEADLINE 5/31/2017
PRINTING PLATE ODDS 1:1400 HOBBY
PLATE PRINT RUN 1 SET PER COLOR
BLACK-CYAN-MAGENTA-YELLOW ISSUED
NO PLATE PRICING DUE TO SCARCITY
FFAAVS Andy Van Slyke 5.00 12.00
FFABH Bob Horner 4.00 10.00
FFABR Bill Russell 5.00 12.00
FFABRO Bip Roberts 4.00 10.00
FFACB Carlos Baerga 4.00 10.00
FFACS Chris Sabo 6.00 15.00
FFADBA Dusty Baker 6.00 15.00
FFADD Darren Daulton 8.00 20.00
FFADEC David Eckstein 4.00 10.00
FFADPA Dave Parker 8.00 20.00
FFADZ Don Zimmer 10.00 25.00
FFAED Eric Davis 6.00 15.00
FFAGN Graig Nettles 6.00 15.00
FFAGV Greg Vaughn 4.00 10.00
FFAHJ Howard Johnson 4.00 10.00
FFAIR Ivan Rodriguez 15.00 40.00
FFAJA Jose Abreu 200.00 300.00
FFAJB Jeromy Burnitz 4.00 10.00
FFAJC Jose Canseco 30.00 60.00
FFAJO John Olerud 4.00 10.00
FFALD Lenny Dykstra 4.00 10.00
FFALH Lenny Harris 4.00 10.00
FFAMG Mike Greenwell 10.00 25.00
FFAML Mark Lemke 4.00 10.00
FFAMMC Mark McGwire 200.00 300.00
FFAMS Mel Stottlemyre 6.00 15.00
FFAMT Mickey Tettleton 4.00 10.00
FFAMW Mookie Wilson 5.00 12.00
FFAOH Orlando Hernandez 15.00 40.00
FFAPGO Paul Goldschmidt 15.00 40.00
FFAPN Phil Niekro 8.00 20.00
FFARD Rob Dibble 8.00 20.00
FFARG Ron Gant 5.00 12.00
FFARH Rickey Henderson 200.00 300.00
FFARW Rondell White 4.00 10.00
FFASC Sean Casey 4.00 10.00
FFATP Terry Pendleton 5.00 12.00

2014 Topps Archives Fan Favorites Autographs Gold

*GOLD: .75X TO 2X BASIC
STATED PRINT RUN 50 SER.#'d SETS
EXCHANGE DEADLINE 5/31/2017

2014 Topps Archives Fan Favorites Autographs Silver

*SILVER: .75X TO 2X BASIC
STATED ODDS 1:211 HOBBY
STATED PRINT RUN 25 SER.#'d SETS
EXCHANGE DEADLINE 5/31/2017
FFAJC Jose Canseco 50.00 100.00

2014 Topps Archives Future Stars

87FED Eric Davis 2.50 6.00
87FHJ Howard Johnson 2.50 6.00
87FHJR Hyun-Jin Ryu 3.00 8.00
87FJA Jose Abreu 10.00 25.00
87FJF Jose Fernandez 4.00 10.00
87FJK Joe Kelly 2.50 6.00
87FMM Manny Machado 4.00 10.00
87FMT Masahiro Tanaka 12.00 30.00
87FPG Paul Goldschmidt 4.00 10.00
87FRG Ron Gant 2.50 6.00
87FRH Rickey Henderson 4.00 10.00
87FSM Shelby Miller 3.00 8.00
87FWM Wil Myers 2.50 6.00
87FYP Yasiel Puig 4.00 10.00

2014 Topps Archives Future Stars Autographs

STATED PRINT RUN 25 SER.#'d SETS
EXCHANGE DEADLINE 5/31/2017
87FASM Shelby Miller 30.00 80.00
87FAWM Wil Myers 20.00 50.00

2014 Topps Archives Major League

COMPLETE SET (4) 8.00 20.00
STATED ODDS 1:12 HOBBY
PRINTING PLATE ODDS 1:151 HOBBY
PLATE PRINT RUN 1 SET PER COLOR
BLACK-CYAN-MAGENTA-YELLOW ISSUED
NO PLATE PRICING DUE TO SCARCITY
MLCEH Eddie Harris 2.00 5.00
MLCJT Jake Taylor 2.00 5.00
MLCRD Roger Dorn 2.00 5.00
MLCRV Ricky Vaughn 3.00 8.00

2014 Topps Archives Major League Gold

*GOLD: 2.5X TO 6X BASIC
STATED ODDS 1:2700 HOBBY
STATED PRINT RUN 25 SER.#'d SETS

2014 Topps Archives Major League Orange

*ORANGE: 2X TO 5X BASIC
STATED PRINT RUN 50 SER.#'d SETS
MLCRV Ricky Vaughn 30.00 60.00

2014 Topps Archives Major League Autographs

STATED ODDS 1:213 HOBBY
EXCHANGE DEADLINE 5/31/2017
MLAEH Ross/Harris 20.00 50.00
MLAJT Berenger/Taylor 40.00 100.00
MLARD Bernsen/Dorn 25.00 60.00
MLARP Whitton/Phelps 25.00 60.00
MLARV Sheen/Vaughn 500.00 700.00

2014 Topps Archives Relics

STATED ODDS 1:215 HOBBY
68TRAB Adrian Beltre 4.00 10.00
68TRAC Asdrubal Cabrera 3.00 8.00
68TRACH Aroldis Chapman 4.00 10.00
68TRAG Alex Gordon 3.00 8.00
68TRBL Brett Lawrie 3.00 8.00
68TRCA Chris Archer 2.50 6.00
68TRDJ Desmond Jennings 3.00 8.00
68TRDM Devin Mesoraco 2.50 6.00
68TRJB Jose Bautista 3.00 8.00
68TRJBR Jay Bruce 3.00 8.00
68TRJM Joe Mauer 3.00 8.00
68TRMM Mike Minor 2.50 6.00
68TRPC Patrick Corbin 3.00 8.00
68TRPG Paul Goldschmidt 4.00 10.00
68TRPS Pablo Sandoval 3.00 8.00
68TRSC Starlin Castro 2.50 6.00
68TRSM Starling Marte 3.00 8.00
68TRSP Salvador Perez 3.00 8.00
68TRTL Tim Lincecum 6.00 15.00
68TRWM Wade Miley 2.50 6.00

2014 Topps Archives Retail

RCBH Bryce Harper 10.00 25.00
RCDW David Wright 12.00 30.00
RCJB Jose Bautista 5.00 12.00
RCJV Justin Verlander 6.00 15.00
RCMC Miguel Cabrera 6.00 15.00
RCMT Mike Trout 30.00 80.00
RCPG Paul Goldschmidt 10.00 25.00
RCRZ Ryan Zimmerman 5.00 12.00
RCTT Troy Tulowitzki 6.00 15.00
RCYD Yu Darvish 6.00 15.00

2014 Topps Archives Stadium Club Firebrand

COMPLETE SET (10) 12.00 30.00
STATED ODDS 1:24 HOBBY
FBCB Carlos Baerga 1.25 3.00
FBED Eric Davis 1.25 3.00
FBGN Graig Nettles 1.25 3.00
FBIR Ivan Rodriguez 1.50 4.00
FBJC Jose Canseco 1.50 4.00
FBPG Pedro Guerrero 1.25 3.00
FBRG Ron Gant 1.25 3.00
FBRW Rondell White 1.25 3.00
FBWM Wil Myers 1.25 3.00
FBYP Yasiel Puig 2.00 5.00

2014 Topps Archives Stadium Club Firebrand Autographs

STATED ODDS 1:822 HOBBY
STATED PRINT RUN 25 SER.#'d SETS
EXCHANGE DEADLINE 5/31/2017
FBAED Eric Davis 20.00 50.00
FBAGN Graig Nettles 15.00 40.00
FBCB Carlos Baerga 20.00 50.00
FBIR Ivan Rodriguez 30.00 60.00
FBJC Jose Canseco 30.00 80.00
FBRG Ron Gant 20.00 50.00
FBRW Rondell White 15.00 40.00
FBWM Wil Myers 40.00 100.00

2014 Topps Archives The Winners Celebrate Box Topper

67WCAJ Adam Jones 4.00 10.00
67WCAW Adam Wainwright 4.00 10.00
67WCBH Bryce Harper 8.00 20.00
67WCBM Bill Mazeroski 4.00 10.00
67WCBP Brandon Phillips 3.00 8.00
67WCBPO Buster Posey 6.00 15.00
67WCCB Craig Biggio 4.00 10.00
67WCCD Chris Davis 3.00 8.00
67WCCF Carlton Fisk 4.00 10.00
67WCDJ Derek Jeter 12.00 30.00
67WCDO David Ortiz 5.00 12.00
67WCDS Darryl Strawberry 3.00 8.00
67WCJB Jose Bautista 4.00 10.00
67WCJBR Jay Bruce 4.00 10.00
67WCJU Justin Upton 4.00 10.00
67WCMA Matt Adams 3.00 8.00
67WCMC Miguel Cabrera 5.00 12.00
67WCMT Mike Trout 25.00 60.00
67WCPG Paul Goldschmidt 5.00 12.00
67WCSK Sandy Koufax 10.00 25.00
67WCSP Salvador Perez 4.00 10.00
67WCWM Wil Myers 3.00 8.00
67WCYC Yoenis Cespedes 5.00 12.00
67WCYP Yasiel Puig 5.00 12.00

2014 Topps Archives Triple Autographs

STATED ODDS 1:2137 HOBBY
EXCHANGE DEADLINE 5/31/2017
ATACMA Adms/Crg/Mrtnz 60.00 120.00
ATACMJ Jns/Cspds/Mrs 75.00 150.00
ATADMR Mth/d'Arn/IRD EXCH 50.00 100.00
ATAGHA Gssge/Hrnn/Abbtt 75.00 150.00
ATAGPS Plmr/Sttn/Gbsn 75.00 150.00
ATAMWW Mrsnck/Wng/Wlkr 75.00 150.00
ATAWJS Strwbrry/HoJo/Wlsn 75.00 150.00

2015 Topps Archives

COMP.SET w/o SP's (300) 20.00 50.00
SP ODDS 1:70 HOBBY
PRINTING PLATE ODDS 1:865 HOBBY
PLATE PRINT RUN 1 SET PER COLOR
BLACK-CYAN-MAGENTA-YELLOW ISSUED
NO PLATE PRICING DUE TO SCARCITY
1 Clayton Kershaw .50 1.25
2 Chris Sale .25 .60
3 Jon Singleton .20 .50
4 Julio Teheran .20 .50
5 Craig Kimbrel .20 .50
6 Alexei Ramirez .20 .50
7 Michael Pineda .15 .40
8 Jayson Werth .20 .50
9 Chris Carter .15 .40
10 Alex Wood .15 .40
11 Bo Jackson .25 .60
12 Brock Holt .15 .40
13 Joe Mauer .20 .50
14 Wade Boggs .20 .50
15 Jason Rogers RC .40 1.00
16 Javier Baez RC 3.00 8.00
17 Buck Farmer RC .40 1.00
18 Homer Bailey .15 .40
19 Hisashi Iwakuma .20 .50
20 Josh Hamilton .20 .50
21 Billy Hamilton .20 .50
22 Josh Donaldson .20 .50
23 Madison Bumgarner .20 .50
24 Cal Ripken Jr. .75 2.00
25 Yasiel Puig .25 .60
26 Curtis Granderson .20 .50
27 Lorenzo Cain .15 .40
28 Elvis Andrus .20 .50
29 Freddie Freeman .30 .75
30 Carlton Fisk .20 .50
31 Christian Yelich .30 .75
32 Robin Yount .25 .60
33 Oswaldo Arcia .15 .40
34 Jeff Samardzija .15 .40
35 Eddie Murray .20 .50
36 Dylan Bundy .20 .50
37 Jhonny Peralta .15 .40
38 Carlos Gonzalez .20 .50
39 Goose Gossage .20 .50
40 Fernando Rodney .15 .40
41 Matt Adams .15 .40
42 Juan Lagares .15 .40
43 Alcides Escobar .20 .50
44 Jonathan Lucroy .20 .50
45 Ryan Howard .20 .50
46 Tyson Ross .15 .40
47 Henderson Alvarez .15 .40
48 Victor Martinez .20 .50
49 Willie Stargell .20 .50
50 Ken Griffey Jr. .50 1.25
51 Yan Gomes .15 .40
52 Dilson Herrera RC .50 1.25
53 Roberto Alomar .20 .50
54 Ozzie Smith .30 .75
55 Trevor May RC .40 1.00
56 Sonny Gray .20 .50
57 Jorge Posada .20 .50
58 Bruce Sutter .20 .50
59 Yadier Molina .25 .60
60 Anthony Ranaudo RC .40 1.00
61 Tanner Roark .20 .50
62 Robin Roberts .20 .50
63 Rod Carew .20 .50
64 Shin-Soo Choo .20 .50
65 Carlos Martinez .20 .50
66 Dalton Pompey RC .50 1.25
67 Jose Altuve .20 .50
68 Aaron Sanchez .20 .50
69 Nomar Garciaparra .20 .50
70 Jake Arrieta .20 .50
71 Matt Holliday .25 .60
72 Chipper Jones .25 .60
73 Anthony Rendon .25 .60
74 Devin Mesoraco .15 .40
75 George Brett .50 1.25
76 R.A. Dickey .20 .50
77 David Eckstein .15 .40
78 Gary Carter .20 .50
79 Albert Pujols .30 .75
80 J.J. Hardy .15 .40
81 Kevin Gausman .15 .40
82 Buster Posey .30 .75
83 Don Sutton .20 .50
84 Vladimir Guerrero .20 .50
85 Maikel Franco RC .50 1.25
86 Mookie Betts .40 1.00
87 Kennys Vargas .15 .40
88 Lenny Dykstra .15 .40
89 C.J. Wilson .15 .40
90 Ian Kinsler .20 .50
91 Kevin Kiermaier .20 .50
92 Mookie Wilson .15 .40
93 Todd Frazier .20 .50
94 Dellin Betances .20 .50
95 Pablo Sandoval .20 .50
96 Matt Cain .20 .50
97 Juan Gonzalez .15 .40
98 Brett Gardner .20 .50
99 Robinson Cano .20 .50
100 Miguel Cabrera .25 .60
101 Mariano Rivera .30 .75
102 Ken Giles .15 .40
103 Adam LaRoche .15 .40
104 Kolten Wong .20 .50
105 Joe DiMaggio .50 1.25
106 Brandon Finnegan RC .40 1.00
107 Willie McCovey .20 .50
108 Matt Carpenter .25 .60
109 Steven Moya RC .50 1.25
110 Jacob deGrom .25 .60
111 Starling Marte .20 .50
112 Jesse Hahn .15 .40
113 Salvador Perez .20 .50
114 Doug Fister .15 .40
115 Barry Larkin .20 .50
116 Carlos Carrasco .15 .40
117 Jose Fernandez .25 .60
118 Ryan Braun .20 .50
119 Lonnie Chisenhall .15 .40
120 Felix Hernandez .20 .50
121 Ian Kennedy .15 .40
122 Lance Lynn .15 .40
123 Anibal Sanchez .15 .40
124 Phil Rizzuto .20 .50
125 Babe Ruth .60 1.50
126 Matt Moore .20 .50
127 Adam Eaton .15 .40
128 Ralph Kiner .20 .50
129 Drew Smyly .15 .40
130 Aramis Ramirez .15 .40
131 Charlie Blackmon .25 .60
132 Stephen Strasburg .25 .60
133 Dennis Eckersley .20 .50
134 Duke Snider .20 .50
135 Michael Taylor RC .40 1.00
136 Luis Gonzalez .15 .40
137 Brian McCann .20 .50
138 Paul Goldschmidt .25 .60
139 Michael Wacha .20 .50
140 Austin Jackson .15 .40
141 Jose Quintana .15 .40
142 Khris Davis UER .25 .60
Carlos Gomez pictured
143 Dee Gordon .15 .40
144 Yordano Ventura .20 .50
145 Daniel Murphy .20 .50
146 Danny Salazar .20 .50
147 Evan Longoria .20 .50
148 Hyun-Jin Ryu .20 .50
149 Hunter Pence .20 .50
150 Sandy Koufax .50 1.25
151 David Wright .20 .50
152 Eddie Mathews .25 .60
153 Frank Thomas .25 .60
154 Bob Feller .20 .50
155 Brian Dozier .20 .50
156 Travis d'Arnaud .15 .40
157 Nick Tropeano RC .40 1.00
158 Kole Calhoun .15 .40
159 Johnny Cueto .20 .50
160 Gerrit Cole .25 .60
161 Xander Bogaerts .25 .60
162 Nolan Arenado .30 .75
163 Deion Sanders .20 .50
164 Aroldis Chapman .25 .60
165 Ty Cobb .40 1.00
166 Max Scherzer .25 .60
167 George Springer .25 .60
168 Mark McGwire .40 1.00
169 Jon Lester .20 .50
170 Warren Spahn .20 .50
171 Ian Desmond .15 .40
172 Corey Dickerson .15 .40
173 Ryan Zimmerman .20 .50
174 Trevor Bauer .25 .60
175 Masahiro Tanaka .25 .60
176 Zack Wheeler .20 .50
177 Rickey Henderson .25 .60
178 Lou Boudreau .20 .50
179 Frank Robinson .20 .50
180 Chase Headley .15 .40
181 Harmon Killebrew .25 .60
182 Christian Walker RC .75 2.00
183 Matt Shoemaker .20 .50
184 Al Kaline .25 .60
185 Zack Greinke .20 .50
186 Brad Ziegler .15 .40
187 Matt Harvey .20 .50
188 Yoenis Cespedes .20 .50
189 Roberto Clemente .60 1.50
190 Daniel Norris RC .40 1.00
191 Prince Fielder .20 .50
192 Matt Barnes RC .40 1.00
193 Billy Williams .20 .50
194 Yusmeiro Petit .15 .40
195 Adrian Beltre .25 .60
196 Corey Kluber .20 .50
197 Bob Lemon .20 .50
198 Michael Brantley .20 .50
199 Joey Votto .25 .60
200 Jose Abreu .25 .60
201 Tony Gwynn .25 .60
202 Johnny Bench .25 .60
203 Yu Darvish .25 .60
204 Wily Peralta .15 .40
205 Chris Davis .15 .40
206 Alex Gordon .20 .50
207 Fergie Jenkins .20 .50
208 Cory Spangenberg RC .40 1.00
209 Tom Seaver .20 .50
210 Carlos Santana .20 .50
211 Kenley Jansen .20 .50
212 Bryce Brentz RC .40 1.00
213 Brooks Robinson .20 .50
214 Orlando Cepeda .20 .50
215 Mark Teixeira .20 .50
216 Wil Myers .15 .40
217 Lou Gehrig .50 1.25
218 Jim Bunning .20 .50
219 Kurt Suzuki .15 .40
220 Jay Bruce .20 .50
221 Marcell Ozuna .25 .60
222 Roenis Elias .15 .40
223 Justin Upton .20 .50
224 Paul Molitor .25 .60
225 Bryce Harper .40 1.00
226 Carlos Beltran .20 .50
227 Reggie Jackson .20 .50
228 Jered Weaver .20 .50
229 Justin Verlander .25 .60
230 Shelby Miller .20 .50
231 Taijuan Walker .15 .40
232 Carlos Gomez .15 .40
233 Greg Holland .20 .50
234 Jacoby Ellsbury .20 .50
235 Giancarlo Stanton .25 .60
236 James Shields .15 .40
237 Jim Rice .20 .50
238 Troy Tulowitzki .25 .60
239 Brandon Belt .20 .50
240 Matt Kemp .20 .50
241 Mike Napoli .15 .40
242 Manny Machado .25 .60
243 Phil Hughes .15 .40
244 Cole Hamels .20 .50
245 Garrett Richards .20 .50
246 Dustin Pedroia .25 .60
247 Eric Hosmer .20 .50
248 Catfish Hunter .20 .50
249 Jake Odorizzi .15 .40
250 Mike Trout 1.25 3.00
251 Omar Vizquel .20 .50
252 Luis Aparicio .20 .50
253 Whitey Ford .20 .50
254 Sean Doolittle .15 .40
255 David Price .20 .50
256 Jason Heyward .20 .50
257 Andrew McCutchen .25 .60
258 Jake Lamb RC .60 1.50
259 J.D. Martinez .25 .60
260 Andrelton Simmons .15 .40
261 Gary Brown RC .40 1.00
262 Chase Utley .20 .50
263 Adam Wainwright .20 .50
264 Joe Morgan .20 .50
265 Starlin Castro .15 .40
266 Gio Gonzalez .20 .50
267 Nick Castellanos .25 .60
268 Kyle Seager .15 .40
269 Jordan Zimmermann .20 .50
270 Nelson Cruz .25 .60
271 Lou Brock .20 .50
272 Adrian Gonzalez .20 .50
273 Orlando Hernandez .15 .40
274 Jose Reyes .20 .50
275 Ted Williams .50 1.25
276 Don Mattingly .50 1.25
277 Edwin Encarnacion .25 .60
278 Alex Cobb .15 .40
279 Joc Pederson RC .75 2.00
280 Brandon Phillips .15 .40
281 Hanley Ramirez .20 .50
282 Mike Zunino .15 .40
283 Mike Schmidt .40 1.00
284 Jim Palmer .20 .50
285 Tony Perez .20 .50
286 Danny Santana .15 .40
287 Justin Morneau .20 .50
288 Gregory Polanco .20 .50
289 Bill Mazeroski .20 .50
290 Jason Kipnis .20 .50
291 Jose Bautista .20 .50
292 David Ortiz .25 .60
293 Josh Harrison .15 .40

294 Chris Archer .15 .40
295 Cliff Lee .20 .50
296 Mike Foltynewicz RC .40 1.00
297 Juan Marichal .20 .50
298 Trevor Rosenthal .20 .50
299 Mark Trumbo .15 .40
300 Willie Mays .50 1.25
301 Nolan Ryan SP 12.00 30.00
302 Rick Ferrell SP 6.00 15.00
303 John Smoltz SP 10.00 25.00
304 John Olerud SP 6.00 15.00
305 Andre Dawson SP 8.00 20.00
306 Ryne Sandberg SP 10.00 25.00
307 Jorge Soler SP RC 10.00 25.00
308 Gary Sheffield SP 6.00 15.00
309 Rob Dibble SP 6.00 15.00
310 Adam Jones SP 8.00 20.00
311 Honus Wagner SP 10.00 25.00
312 Rusney Castillo SP RC 8.00 20.00
313 Devon White SP 6.00 15.00
314 Kris Bryant SP RC 300.00 600.00
315 Anthony Rizzo SP 15.00 40.00
316 Larry Doby SP 8.00 20.00
317 Jose Cruz SP 6.00 15.00
318 Vinny Castilla SP 6.00 15.00
319 Sparky Lyle SP 6.00 15.00
320 Satchel Paige SP 10.00 25.00
321 Jose Vidro SP 6.00 15.00
322 Monte Irvin SP 8.00 20.00
323 Hal Newhouser SP 8.00 20.00
324 Red Schoendienst SP 8.00 20.00
325 Enos Slaughter SP 8.00 20.00
326 George Kell SP 8.00 20.00
327 Early Wynn SP 8.00 20.00
328 Hoyt Wilhelm SP 8.00 20.00
329 Bobby Doerr SP 8.00 20.00
330 Jackie Robinson SP 15.00 40.00

2015 Topps Archives Gold

*GOLD: 8X TO 20X BASIC
*GOLD RC: 3X TO 8X BASIC RC
STATED ODDS 1:70 HOBBY
STATED PRINT RUN 50 SER.#'d SETS
201 Tony Gwynn 12.00 30.00
225 Bryce Harper 12.00 30.00
250 Mike Trout 30.00 80.00
279 Joc Pederson 25.00 60.00

2015 Topps Archives Silver

*SILVER: 4X TO 10X BASIC
*SILVER RC: 1.5X TO 4X BASIC RC
STATED ODDS 1:18 HOBBY
STATED PRINT RUN 199 SER.#'d SETS
279 Joc Pederson 12.00 30.00

2015 Topps Archives '68 Topps Game Inserts

COMPLETE SET (33) 25.00 60.00
STATED ODDS 1:6 HOBBY
1 Yasiel Puig 1.25 3.00
2 Mike Trout 6.00 15.00
3 Jose Abreu 1.25 3.00
4 Ian Kinsler 1.00 2.50
5 Joe Mauer 1.00 2.50
6 Adam Jones 1.00 2.50
7 Robinson Cano 1.00 2.50
8 Buster Posey 1.50 4.00
9 Javier Baez 6.00 15.00
10 David Wright 1.00 2.50
11 Justin Upton 1.00 2.50
12 Edwin Encarnacion 1.25 3.00
13 Manny Machado 1.25 3.00
14 Dustin Pedroia 1.25 3.00
15 Ryan Braun 1.00 2.50
16 David Ortiz 1.25 3.00
17 Anthony Rendon 1.25 3.00
18 Freddie Freeman 1.50 4.00
19 Miguel Cabrera 1.25 3.00
20 Paul Goldschmidt 1.25 3.00
21 Jose Bautista 1.00 2.50
22 Jonathan Lucroy 1.00 2.50
23 Bryce Harper 2.00 5.00
24 Christian Yelich 1.50 4.00
25 Andrew McCutchen 1.25 3.00
26 Jacoby Ellsbury 1.00 2.50
27 Yadier Molina 1.25 3.00
28 Evan Longoria 1.00 2.50
29 Carlos Gomez .75 2.00
30 Jose Altuve 1.00 2.50
31 Billy Hamilton 1.00 2.50
32 Anthony Rizzo 2.00 5.00
33 Giancarlo Stanton 1.25 3.00

2015 Topps Archives '90 Topps #1 Draft Picks

COMPLETE SET (15) 10.00 25.00
STATED ODDS 1:8 HOBBY
*GOLD/50: 2.5X TO 6X BASIC
*NNOF: 10X TO 25X BASIC
90DPIAG Adrian Gonzalez .75 2.00
90DPIBH Bryce Harper 1.50 4.00
90DPIBP Buster Posey 1.25 3.00
90DPICK Clayton Kershaw 2.00 5.00
90DPICS Chris Sale 1.00 2.50
90DPIJB Jay Bruce .75 2.00
90DPIJF Jose Fernandez 1.00 2.50
90DPIJM Joe Mauer .75 2.00
90DPIKW Kolten Wong .75 2.00
90DPIMB Madison Bumgarner .75 2.00
90DPIMS Max Scherzer 1.00 2.50
90DPIMT Mike Trout 5.00 12.00
90DPIRB Ryan Braun .75 2.00
90DPISG Sonny Gray .75 2.00
90DPIMAT Mark Teixeira .75 2.00

2015 Topps Archives '90 Topps #1 Draft Picks No Name On Front

*NNOF: 10X TO 25X BASIC
STATED ODDS 1:1008 HOBBY
90DPIMT Mike Trout 150.00 300.00

2015 Topps Archives '90 Topps #1 Draft Picks Autographs

STATED ODDS 1:619 HOBBY
STATED PRINT RUN 199 SER.#'d SETS
EXCHANGE DEADLINE 5/31/2018
PRINTING PLATE ODDS 1:9247 HOBBY
PLATE PRINT RUN 1 SET PER COLOR
NO PLATE PRICING DUE TO SCARCITY
90DPKW Kolten Wong 12.00 30.00
90DPRB Ryan Braun 12.00 30.00
90DPSG Sonny Gray 10.00 25.00

2015 Topps Archives '90 Topps #1 Draft Picks Autographs Gold

*GOLD: .6X TO 1.5X BASIC
STATED ODDS 1:739 HOBBY
STATED PRINT RUN 50 SER.#'d SETS
EXCHANGE DEADLINE 5/31/2018
90DPAG Adrian Gonzalez 25.00 60.00
90DPCK Clayton Kershaw EXCH 100.00 200.00
90DPCS Chris Sale 40.00 100.00
90DPJF Jose Fernandez 25.00 60.00
90DPMT Mike Trout 250.00 350.00

2015 Topps Archives '90 Topps All Star Rookies

COMPLETE SET (20) 15.00 40.00
STATED ODDS 1:12 HOBBY
PRINTING PLATE ODDS 1:8196 HOBBY
PLATE PRINT RUN 1 SET PER COLOR
NO PLATE PRICING DUE TO SCARCITY
*GOLD/50: 2.5X TO 6X BASIC
90ASIAR Anthony Ranaudo .60 1.50
90ASIBF Brandon Finnegan .60 1.50
90ASIBUF Buck Farmer .60 1.50
90ASICS Cory Spangenberg .60 1.50
90ASICW Christian Walker 1.25 3.00
90ASIDH Dilson Herrera .75 2.00
90ASIDN Daniel Norris .60 1.50
90ASIDP Dalton Pompey .75 2.00
90ASIGB Gary Brown .60 1.50
90ASIJB Javier Baez 5.00 12.00
90ASIJL Jake Lamb 1.00 2.50
90ASIJP Joc Pederson 1.25 3.00
90ASIJS Jorge Soler 1.00 2.50
90ASIMB Matt Barnes .60 1.50
90ASIMF Maikel Franco .75 2.00
90ASIMIF Mike Foltynewicz .60 1.50
90ASIMT Michael Taylor .60 1.50
90ASIRC Rusney Castillo .75 2.00
90ASIRL Rymer Liriano .60 1.50
90ASITM Trevor May .60 1.50

2015 Topps Archives '90 Topps All Star Rookies Autographs

STATED ODDS 1:243 HOBBY
STATED PRINT RUN 199 SER.#'d SETS
EXCHANGE DEADLINE 5/31/2018
PRINTING PLATE ODDS 1:13,870 HOBBY
PLATE PRINT RUN 1 SET PER COLOR
NO PLATE PRICING DUE TO SCARCITY
90ASBF Brandon Finnegan 6.00 15.00
90ASDH Dilson Herrera 8.00 20.00
90ASDN Daniel Norris 6.00 15.00
90ASDP Dalton Pompey 8.00 20.00
90ASJP Joc Pederson 50.00 120.00
90ASJS Jorge Soler 15.00 40.00
90ASMF Maikel Franco 20.00 50.00
90ASMT Michael Taylor 6.00 15.00
90ASYT Yasmany Tomas 8.00 20.00

2015 Topps Archives '90 Topps All Star Rookies Autographs Gold

*GOLD: .75X TO 2X BASIC
STATED ODDS 1:927 HOBBY
STATED PRINT RUN 50 SER.#'d SETS
EXCHANGE DEADLINE 5/31/2018
90ASJP Joc Pederson 75.00 200.00

2015 Topps Archives Fan Favorites Autographs

STATED ODDS 1:18 HOBBY
EXCHANGE DEADLINE 5/31/2018
FFAAJ Andruw Jones 8.00 20.00
FFAAL Al Leiter 10.00 25.00
FFAARU Addison Russell EXCH 200.00 300.00
FFABA Brady Anderson 6.00 15.00
FFABB Bret Boone 4.00 10.00
FFABD Bucky Dent 4.00 10.00
FFABW Bernie Williams 40.00 100.00
FFADOW Dontrelle Willis 4.00 10.00
FFADW Devon White 4.00 10.00
FFAEA Edgardo Alfonzo 4.00 10.00
FFAEK Eric Karros 4.00 10.00
FFAFV Frank Viola 6.00 15.00
FFAFVI Fernando Vina 4.00 10.00
FFAGP Gaylord Perry 10.00 25.00
FFAGS Giancarlo Stanton EXCH 100.00 250.00
FFAHB Harold Baines 5.00 12.00
FFAJC Jose Cruz 4.00 10.00
FFAJCJ Jose Cruz Jr. 4.00 10.00
FFAJCO Jeff Conine 4.00 10.00
FFAJD Jacob deGrom 25.00 60.00
FFAJF John Franco 4.00 10.00
FFAJKE Jason Kendall 4.00 10.00
FFAJO Joe Oliver 4.00 10.00
FFAJR Jose Rijo 4.00 10.00
FFAJS J.T. Snow 4.00 10.00
FFAJV Jose Vidro 4.00 10.00
FFAKB Kris Bryant 250.00 400.00
FFAKT Kent Tekulve 6.00 15.00
FFAMB Mike Bordick 4.00 10.00
FFAMG Marquis Grissom 4.00 10.00
FFAMGR Mark Grace 12.00 30.00
FFAMP Mark Prior 5.00 12.00
FFANR Nolan Ryan 300.00 500.00
FFAOG Oscar Gamble 4.00 10.00
FFAPI Pete Incaviglia 4.00 10.00
FFARJ Reggie Jackson 300.00 500.00
FFARK Ryan Klesko 4.00 10.00
FFASB Sid Bream 4.00 10.00
FFASG Shawn Green 4.00 10.00
FFASH Scott Hatteberg 4.00 10.00
FFASL Sparky Lyle 4.00 10.00
FFATF Tony Fernandez 4.00 10.00
FFAVC Vinny Castilla 4.00 10.00

2015 Topps Archives Fan Favorites Autographs Gold

*GOLD: 1X TO 2.5X BASIC
STATED ODDS 1:190 HOBBY
STATED PRINT RUN 50 SER.#'d SETS
EXCHANGE DEADLINE 5/31/2018
FFAJD Jacob deGrom 40.00 100.00
FFARCU Rusney Castillo 30.00 80.00

2015 Topps Archives Fan Favorites Autographs Silver

*SILVER: .6X TO 1.5X BASIC
STATED ODDS 1:83 HOBBY
STATED PRINT RUN 199 SER.#'d SETS
EXCHANGE DEADLINE 5/31/2018
FFAJD Jacob deGrom 25.00 60.00

2015 Topps Archives Presidential Chronicles

COMPLETE SET (10) 4.00 10.00
STATED ODDS 1:12 HOBBY
PCAL Abraham Lincoln .60 1.50
PCBO Barack Obama .60 1.50
PCGF Gerald Ford .60 1.50
PCHH Herbert Hoover .60 1.50
PCJC Jimmy Carter .60 1.50
PCRN Richard Nixon .60 1.50
PCGHW George H. W. Bush .60 1.50
PCGWB George W. Bush .60 1.50
PCHST Harry S. Truman .60 1.50
PCJFK John F. Kennedy .60 1.50

2015 Topps Archives Will Ferrell

COMPLETE SET (10) 30.00 80.00
STATED ODDS 1:24 HOBBY
WF1 Will Ferrell 4.00 10.00
WF2 Will Ferrell 4.00 10.00
WF3 Will Ferrell 4.00 10.00
WF4 Will Ferrell 4.00 10.00
WF5 Will Ferrell 4.00 10.00
WF6 Will Ferrell 4.00 10.00
WF7 Will Ferrell 4.00 10.00
WF8 Will Ferrell 4.00 10.00
WF9 Will Ferrell 4.00 10.00
WF10 Will Ferrell 4.00 10.00

2016 Topps Archives

COMP.SET w/o SP's (300) 20.00 50.00
SP ODDS 1:41 HOBBY
PRINTING PLATE ODDS 1:682 HOBBY
PLATE PRINT RUN 1 SET PER COLOR
BLACK-CYAN-MAGENTA-YELLOW ISSUED
NO PLATE PRICING DUE TO SCARCITY
1 Albert Pujols .30 .75
2 Carlos Carrasco .15 .40
3 Doc Gooden .15 .40
4 Bret Boone .15 .40
5 Richie Shaffer RC .25 .60
6 Kendrys Morales .15 .40
7 Ketel Marte RC .50 1.25
8 Justin Morneau .20 .50
9 Prince Fielder .20 .50
10 Billy Hamilton .20 .50
11 Matt Reynolds RC .25 .60
12 Robin Yount .25 .60
13 Jason Heyward .20 .50
14 Monte Irvin .20 .50
15 George Springer .20 .50
16 Tony Fernandez .15 .40
17 Elvis Andrus .20 .50
18 Chris Sale .25 .60
19 Don Sutton .20 .50
20 Juan Marichal .20 .50
21 Travis d'Arnaud .20 .50
22 Michael Wacha .20 .50
23 Bernie Williams .20 .50
24 Bert Blyleven .20 .50
25 Kyle Schwarber RC .75 2.00
26 Rafael Palmeiro .20 .50
27 Jim Abbott .15 .40
28 Miguel Almonte RC .25 .60
29 Russell Martin .15 .40
30 Manny Machado .25 .60
31 Henry Owens RC .30 .75
32 Kevin Pillar .15 .40
33 Bucky Dent .15 .40
34 Shin-Soo Choo .20 .50
35 Jim Rice .20 .50
36 Hal Newhouser .20 .50
37 Mac Williamson RC .25 .60
38 Danny Salazar .20 .50
39 David Price .20 .50
40 Jacoby Ellsbury .20 .50
41 Ryne Sandberg .50 1.25
42 J.D. Martinez .25 .60
43 David Wright .20 .50
44 Marcus Stroman .20 .50
45 John Smoltz .25 .60
46 Gio Gonzalez .20 .50
47 Jorge Lopez RC .25 .60
48 Brooks Robinson .20 .50
49 Paul O'Neill .20 .50
50 Max Scherzer .25 .60
51 Tony Perez .20 .50
52 Mark McGwire .40 1.00
53 Greg Bird RC .30 .75
54 Phil Niekro .20 .50
55 Fergie Jenkins .20 .50
56 Brian Johnson RC .25 .60
57 Charlie Blackmon .25 .60
58 Glen Perkins .15 .40
59 Robinson Cano .20 .50
60 Stephen Strasburg .25 .60
61 Kolten Wong .20 .50
62 George Brett .50 1.25
63 Nelson Cruz .25 .60
64 Brad Ziegler .15 .40
65 Justin Upton .20 .50
66 Shelby Miller .20 .50
67 Lorenzo Cain .15 .40
68 Trea Turner RC .75 2.00
69 Collin McHugh .15 .40
70 David Robertson .15 .40
71 Byron Buxton .20 .50
72 Dennis Eckersley .20 .50
73 Kyle Seager .15 .40
74 Dustin Pedroia .25 .60
75 Jon Lester .20 .50
76 Stephen Piscotty RC .40 1.00
77 Jason Kipnis .20 .50
78 Eddie Murray .20 .50
79 John Olerud .15 .40
80 Jose Altuve .20 .50
81 Ralph Kiner .20 .50
82 Justin Bour .20 .50
83 Satchel Paige .25 .60
84 Gregory Polanco .20 .50
85 Joe Mauer .20 .50
86 Alex Rodriguez .30 .75
87 Noah Syndergaard .20 .50
88 A.J. Pollock .15 .40
89 Hanley Ramirez .20 .50
90 Carl Yastrzemski .40 1.00
91 Josh Harrison .15 .40
92 Bartolo Colon .15 .40
93 Zach Lee RC .25 .60
94 Darin Ruf .15 .40
95 Jim Bunning .20 .50
96 Duke Snider .20 .50
97 Randal Grichuk .15 .40
98 Jose Quintana .15 .40
99 Masahiro Tanaka .20 .50
100 Buster Posey .30 .75
101 Babe Ruth .60 1.50
102 Jonathan Lucroy .20 .50
103 Randy Johnson .25 .60
104 Evan Longoria .20 .50
105 Max Kepler RC .40 1.00
106 Oscar Gamble .15 .40
107 Corey Kluber .20 .50
108 Socrates Brito RC .25 .60
109 Eric Hosmer .20 .50
110 Jose Canseco .20 .50
111 Sonny Gray .20 .50
112 Roberto Alomar .20 .50
113 Frankie Montas RC .30 .75
114 Jose Reyes .20 .50
115 Early Wynn .20 .50
116 Stephen Vogt .20 .50
117 Craig Biggio .20 .50
118 Bill Mazeroski .20 .50
119 Madison Bumgarner .25 .60
120 Juan Gonzalez .15 .40
121 Jay Bruce .20 .50
122 Carlton Fisk .20 .50
123 Luis Severino RC .30 .75
124 Chris Archer .15 .40
125 David Ortiz .25 .60
126 Yu Darvish .25 .60
127 Paul Molitor .25 .60
128 Ken Griffey Jr. .50 1.25
129 Mike Trout 1.25 3.00
130 Tom Seaver .20 .50
131 Jim Palmer .20 .50
132 Carlos Santana .20 .50
133 Yordano Ventura .20 .50
134 Carlos Rodon .25 .60
135 Ryan Howard .20 .50
136 Troy Tulowitzki .25 .60
137 Zach Britton .20 .50
138 Curtis Granderson .20 .50
139 Carlos Beltran .20 .50
140 Jung Ho Kang .15 .40
141 Stan Musial .40 1.00
142 Dellin Betances .20 .50
143 DJ LeMahieu .25 .60
144 Tyson Ross .15 .40
145 Felix Hernandez .20 .50
146 Mookie Betts .40 1.00
147 Travis Jankowski RC .25 .60
148 Zack Greinke .25 .60
149 Brian Dozier .20 .50
150 Kris Bryant .30 .75
151 Frank Thomas .25 .60
152 Ian Kinsler .20 .50
153 Honus Wagner .20 .50
154 Jon Gray RC .25 .60
155 Jeurys Familia .20 .50
156 Yasiel Puig .25 .60
157 Jose Abreu .25 .60
158 Gary Sheffield .15 .40
159 Raul Mondesi RC .30 .75
160 Joc Pederson .20 .50
161 Jose Fernandez .25 .60
162 Gary Sanchez RC .75 2.00
163 Bob Feller .20 .50
164 Jacob deGrom .25 .60
165 Yasmany Tomas .15 .40
166 Hank Aaron .50 1.25
167 Ryan Klesko .15 .40
168 Matt Carpenter .25 .60
169 Jorge Soler .25 .60
170 Brandon Belt .20 .50
171 George Kell .20 .50
172 Joey Votto .25 .60
173 Billy Williams .20 .50
174 Tom Murphy RC .25 .60
175 Andrelton Simmons .15 .40
176 Willie McCovey .20 .50
177 Bruce Sutter .20 .50
178 Richie Ashburn .20 .50
179 Brandon Drury RC .40 1.00
180 Ozzie Smith .30 .75
181 Evan Gattis .15 .40
182 Joe Morgan .20 .50
183 Salvador Perez .20 .50
184 Carlos Martinez .20 .50
185 Wade Boggs .20 .50
186 Peter O'Brien RC .25 .60
187 Kole Calhoun .15 .40
188 Brandon Crawford .20 .50
189 Whitey Ford .20 .50
190 Lou Gehrig .50 1.25
191 Andres Galarraga .20 .50
192 Vladimir Guerrero .20 .50
193 Aaron Nola RC .50 1.25
194 Garrett Richards .20 .50
195 Mark Melancon .15 .40
196 Trevor Plouffe .15 .40
197 Reggie Jackson .20 .50
198 Adam Wainwright .20 .50
199 Enos Slaughter .20 .50
200 Bryce Harper .40 1.00
201 Jackie Robinson .25 .60
202 Yadier Molina .25 .60
203 Johnny Bench .25 .60
204 Miguel Cabrera .25 .60
205 Jose Peraza RC .30 .75
206 Hoyt Wilhelm .20 .50
207 Chris Davis .15 .40
208 Matt Harvey .20 .50
209 Phil Rizzuto .20 .50
210 Orlando Cepeda .20 .50
211 Kevin Kiermaier .20 .50
212 Gaylord Perry .20 .50
213 Aroldis Chapman .25 .60
214 Adam Jones .20 .50
215 Yoenis Cespedes .25 .60
216 Rougned Odor .25 .60
217 Hector Olivera RC .30 .75
218 John Franco .15 .40
219 Kelby Tomlinson RC .25 .60
220 Larry Doby .20 .50
221 Cole Hamels .20 .50
222 Matt Kemp .20 .50
223 Goose Gossage .20 .50
224 Hunter Pence .20 .50
225 Clayton Kershaw .50 1.25
226 Ryan Braun .20 .50
227 Freddie Freeman .30 .75
228 Roberto Clemente .60 1.50
229 Billy Butler .15 .40
230 James Shields .15 .40
231 Paul Goldschmidt .25 .60
232 David Peralta .15 .40
233 Edwin Encarnacion .25 .60
234 Jake Arrieta .25 .60
235 Lou Boudreau .20 .50
236 Roger Maris .25 .60
237 Miguel Sano RC .40 1.00
238 Rod Carew .20 .50
239 Xander Bogaerts .25 .60
240 John Kruk .15 .40
241 Rob Refsnyder RC .30 .75
242 Harmon Killebrew .25 .60
243 Cal Ripken Jr. .75 2.00
244 Trevor Rosenthal .20 .50
245 Adam Eaton .15 .40
246 Gary Carter .20 .50
247 Zack Godley RC .25 .60
248 Anthony Rizzo .40 1.00
249 Jose Bautista .20 .50
250 Carlos Correa .25 .60
251 Bobby Doerr .20 .50
252 Trayce Thompson RC .40 1.00
253 Robin Roberts .20 .50
254 Colin Rea RC .25 .60
255 Brandon Phillips .15 .40
256 Chipper Jones .25 .60
257 Giancarlo Stanton .25 .60
258 Odubel Herrera .20 .50
259 Willie Stargell .20 .50
260 Dallas Keuchel .20 .50
261 Joe Mauer .20 .50
262 Andre Dawson .20 .50
263 Eddie Mathews .25 .60
264 Luke Jackson RC .25 .60
265 Warren Spahn .20 .50
266 Hisashi Iwakuma .20 .50
267 Carlos Gonzalez .20 .50
268 Carl Edwards Jr. RC .30 .75
269 Adrian Gonzalez .20 .50
270 Brian McCann .20 .50
271 Ted Williams .50 1.25
272 Taijuan Walker .15 .40
273 Nolan Ryan .75 2.00
274 Michael Brantley .20 .50
275 Corey Seager RC 2.00 5.00
276 Nolan Arenado .30 .75
277 Ichiro Suzuki .30 .75
278 Lucas Duda .20 .50
279 Josh Donaldson .20 .50
280 Josh Reddick .15 .40
281 Francisco Lindor .25 .60
282 Lou Brock .20 .50
283 Michael Conforto RC .30 .75
284 Catfish Hunter .20 .50
285 Maikel Franco .20 .50
286 Willie Mays .50 1.25
287 Adrian Beltre .25 .60
288 Nomar Garciaparra .20 .50
289 Wade Davis .15 .40
290 Anthony Rendon .25 .60
291 Kaleb Cowart RC .25 .60
292 Andrew Miller .20 .50
293 Craig Kimbrel .20 .50
294 Andrew McCutchen .25 .60
295 Todd Frazier .20 .50
296 Edgar Martinez .20 .50
297 Justin Verlander .25 .60
298 Kyle Waldrop RC .30 .75
299 Hector Rondon .15 .40
300 Sandy Koufax .50 1.25
301 Kenta Maeda SP RC 6.00 15.00
302 Randy Jones SP 3.00 8.00
303 Tom Gordon SP 3.00 8.00
304 Al Kaline SP 6.00 15.00
305 Steve Garvey SP 4.00 10.00
306 Tito Francona SP 3.00 8.00
307 Phil Nevin SP 3.00 8.00
308 Charlie Hayes SP 3.00 8.00
309 Kris Benson SP 3.00 8.00
310 Sandy Koufax SP 12.00 30.00

2016 Topps Archives Blue

*BLUE: 3X TO 8X BASIC
*BLUE RC: 2 TO 5X BASIC RC
STATED ODDS 1:14 HOBBY
STATED PRINT RUN 199 SER.#'d SETS
275 Corey Seager 10.00 25.00

2016 Topps Archives Red

*RED: 8X TO 20X BASIC
*RED RC: 5X TO 12X BASIC RC
STATED ODDS 1:55 HOBBY
STATED PRINT RUN 50 SER.#'d SETS
275 Corey Seager 30.00 80.00

2016 Topps Archives '69 Topps Super

COMPLETE SET (30) 30.00 80.00
STATED ODDS 1:6 HOBBY
PRINTING PLATE ODDS 1:6808 HOBBY
PLATE PRINT RUN 1 SET PER COLOR
NO PLATE PRICING DUE TO SCARCITY
*RED/50: 3X TO 8X BASIC
69TSAG Alex Gordon .60 1.50
69TSAM Andrew Miller .60 1.50
69TSAMU Andrew McCutchen .75 2.00
69TSAN Aaron Nola 1.00 2.50
69TSAP A.J. Pollock .50 1.25
69TSBC Brandon Crawford .60 1.50
69TSBH Bryce Harper 1.25 3.00
69TSBP Buster Posey 1.00 2.50
69TSCH Cole Hamels .60 1.50
69TSCS Chris Sale .75 2.00
69TSDG Dee Gordon .50 1.25
69TSDO David Ortiz .75 2.00
69TSEE Edwin Encarnacion .75 2.00
69TSFF Freddie Freeman 1.00 2.50
69TSFL Francisco Lindor .75 2.00
69TSJA Jose Altuve .60 1.50
69TSJAR Jake Arrieta .60 1.50
69TSJD Josh Donaldson .60 1.50
69TSJP Joc Pederson .60 1.50
69TSKB Kris Bryant 1.00 2.50
69TSKS Kyle Schwarber 1.50 4.00
69TSLS Luis Severino .60 1.50
69TSMH Matt Harvey .60 1.50
69TSMM Manny Machado .75 2.00
69TSMS Miguel Sano .75 2.00
69TSMT Mike Trout 4.00 10.00
69TSPG Paul Goldschmidt .75 2.00
69TSSG Sonny Gray .60 1.50
69TSSP Stephen Piscotty .60 1.50
69TSTR Tyson Ross .50 1.25

2016 Topps Archives '69 Topps Super Autographs

STATED ODDS 1:314 HOBBY
PRINT RUNS B/WN 20-99 COPIES PER
EXCHANGE DEADLINE 5/31/2018
69TSAAG Alex Gordon/75 12.00 30.00
69TSAAN Aaron Nola/99 20.00 50.00
69TSAAP A.J. Pollock/99 8.00 20.00
69TSABH Bryce Harper/99 250.00 500.00
69TSACS Chris Sale/75 15.00 40.00
69TSADG Dee Gordon/99 8.00 20.00
69TSADO David Ortiz/25 125.00 250.00
69TSAEE Edwin Encarnacion/75 12.00 30.00
69TSAFL Francisco Lindor/99 12.00 30.00
69TSAJA Jose Altuve/75 25.00 60.00
69TSAJP Joc Pederson/99 10.00 25.00
69TSAKB Kris Bryant/75 125.00 250.00
69TSAKS Kyle Schwarber/99 25.00 60.00
69TSALS Luis Severino/75 20.00 50.00
69TSAMM Manny Machado/50 50.00 120.00
69TSAMS Miguel Sano/99 12.00 30.00
69TSAMT Mike Trout/20 200.00 300.00
69TSASG Sonny Gray/99 10.00 25.00
69TSASP Stephen Piscotty/99 12.00 30.00

2016 Topps Archives '69 Topps Super Autographs Red

*RED: .5X TO 1.2X BASIC
STATED ODDS 1:622 HOBBY
STATED PRINT RUN 50 SER.#'d SETS
EXCHANGE DEADLINE 5/31/2018

2016 Topps Archives '85 Father Son

COMPLETE SET (7) 3.00 8.00
STATED ODDS 1:12 HOBBY
FSAAL S.Alomar Sr./R.Alomar .75 2.00
FSAL S.Alomar Jr./S.Alomar Sr. .60 1.50
FSBB B.Boone/B.Boone .60 1.50
FSFF T.Francona/T.Francona .75 2.00
FSGG K.Griffey Jr./K.Griffey Sr. 2.00 5.00
FSGGO T.Gordon/D.Gordon .60 1.50
FSPP E.Perez/T.Perez .75 2.00

2016 Topps Archives '85 Topps #1 Draft Pick

COMPLETE SET (18) 6.00 15.00
STATED ODDS 1:8 HOBBY
PRINTING PLATE ODDS 1:10,294 HOBBY
PLATE PRINT RUN 1 SET PER COLOR
NO PLATE PRICING DUE TO SCARCITY
*RED/50: 3X TO 8X BASIC
85DPAB Andy Benes .50 1.25
85DPAG Adrian Gonzalez .60 1.50
85DPAR Alex Rodriguez 1.00 2.50
85DPBH Bryce Harper 1.25 3.00
85DPBS B.J. Surhoff .50 1.25
85DPCC Carlos Correa .75 2.00
85DPCJ Chipper Jones .75 2.00
85DPDP David Price .60 1.50
85DPDS Darryl Strawberry .50 1.25
85DPGC Gerrit Cole .75 2.00
85DPHB Harold Baines .60 1.50
85DPJB Jeff Burroughs .50 1.25
85DPJH Josh Hamilton .60 1.50
85DPJM Joe Mauer .60 1.50
85DPKG Ken Griffey Jr. 1.50 4.00
85DPRB Ron Blomberg .50 1.25
85DPRM Rick Monday .50 1.25
85DPSS Stephen Strasburg .75 2.00

2016 Topps Archives '85 Topps #1 Draft Pick Autographs

STATED ODDS 1:1446 HOBBY
PRINT RUNS B/WN 10-50 COPIES PER
NO PRICING ON QTY 10 OR LESS
EXCHANGE DEADLINE 5/31/2018
85DPAG Adrian Gonzalez/25 60.00 150.00
85DPBS B.J. Surhoff/50 10.00 25.00
85DPCC Carlos Correa/25 200.00 400.00
85DPCJ Chipper Jones/20 300.00 500.00
85DPDS Darryl Strawberry/50 40.00 100.00
85DPHB Harold Baines/50 20.00 50.00
85DPJB Jeff Burroughs/50 10.00 25.00
85DPKB Kris Benson/50 10.00 25.00
85DPKG Ken Griffey Jr./15 1000.00 1500.00
85DPRM Rick Monday/50 10.00 25.00

2016 Topps Archives Bull Durham

COMPLETE SET (7) 4.00 10.00
STATED ODDS 1:12 HOBBY
PRINTING PLATE ODDS 1:28,136 HOBBY
PLATE PRINT RUN 1 SET PER COLOR
NO PLATE PRICING DUE TO SCARCITY
*RED/50: 2X TO 5X BASIC
BDB Bobby 1.00 2.50
BDJ Jimmy 1.00 2.50
BDM Millie 1.00 2.50
BDT Tony 1.00 2.50
BDLH Larry 1.00 2.50
BDNL Nuke LaLoosh 1.00 2.50
BDRS Ron Shelton 1.00 2.50

2016 Topps Archives Bull Durham Autographs

STATED ODDS 1:498 HOBBY
PRINT RUNS B/WN 145-695 COPIES PER
ANNIE,CRASH,NUKE NOT NUMBERED
EXCHANGE DEADLINE 5/31/2018
BDAB Bobby/595 6.00 15.00
BDAJ Jimmy/595 6.00 15.00
BDAM Millie/695 6.00 15.00
BDAT Tony/595 6.00 15.00
BDAAS Annie Savoy 175.00 350.00
BDACD Crash Davis 150.00 300.00
BDALH Larry Hockett/145 25.00 60.00
BDANL Nuke LaLoosh/295 40.00 100.00
BDARS Ron Shelton/345 6.00 15.00

2016 Topps Archives Bull Durham Autographs Red

*RED: 1X TO 2.5X BASIC
STATED ODDS 1:2001 HOBBY
STATED PRINT RUN 50 SER.#'d SETS
EXCHANGE DEADLINE 5/31/2018
BDALH Larry Hockett 40.00 100.00
Robert Wuhl

2016 Topps Archives Fan Favorites Autographs

STATED ODDS 1:19 HOBBY
EXCHANGE DEADLINE 5/31/2018
FFAAB Andy Benes 3.00 8.00
FFAAK Al Kaline 20.00 50.00
FFAAN Aaron Nola 10.00 25.00
FFABB Bob Boone 3.00 8.00
FFABC Bert Campaneris 4.00 10.00
FFABH Bryce Harper 200.00 400.00
FFABS B.J. Surhoff 3.00 8.00
FFABW Billy Wagner 4.00 10.00

FACC Carlos Correa 75.00 200.00
FACE Carl Everett 4.00 10.00
FACH Charlie Hayes 3.00 8.00
FADG Doc Gooden 8.00 20.00
FADS Darryl Strawberry 10.00 25.00
FAEP Eduardo Perez 3.00 8.00
FAFH Frank Howard 6.00 15.00
FAFT Fernando Tatis 3.00 8.00
FAI Ichiro Suzuki 500.00 700.00
FAJB Jeff Burroughs 3.00 8.00
FAJK Jim Kaat 5.00 12.00
FAJL Javy Lopez 5.00 12.00
FAJN Jeff Nelson 3.00 8.00
FAJR J.R. Richard 4.00 10.00
FAJV Jose Vizcaino 3.00 8.00
FAKBE Kris Benson 3.00 8.00
FAKM Kenta Maeda 30.00 80.00
FAKS Kyle Schwarber 15.00 40.00
FAMA Moises Alou 4.00 10.00
FAMS Miguel Sano 8.00 20.00
FAMT Mike Trout 250.00 500.00
FAPH Pat Hentgen 3.00 8.00
FAPN Phil Nevin 3.00 8.00
FARB Ron Blomberg 3.00 8.00
FARF Rollie Fingers 12.00 30.00
FARJ Randy Jones 3.00 8.00
FARM Rick Monday 3.00 8.00
FASA Sandy Alomar Jr. 5.00 12.00
FASAJ Sandy Alomar Sr. 5.00 12.00
FASG Steve Garvey 12.00 30.00
FASK Sandy Koufax
FATF Terry Francona 4.00 10.00
FATG Tom Gordon 6.00 15.00
FATH Teddy Higuera 3.00 8.00
FATIF Tito Francona 3.00 8.00
FAVL Vern Law 3.00 8.00

2016 Topps Archives Fan Favorites Autographs Blue

*BLUE: .5X TO 1.2X BASIC
STATED ODDS 1:63 HOBBY
STATED PRINT RUN 199 SER.#'d SETS
EXCHANGE DEADLINE 5/31/2018
FFADEC Dennis Eckersley 12.00 30.00

2016 Topps Archives Fan Favorites Autographs Red

*RED: .6X TO 1.5X BASIC
STATED ODDS 1:237 HOBBY
STATED PRINT RUN 50 SER.#'d SETS
EXCHANGE DEADLINE 5/31/2018
FFADEC Dennis Eckersley 15.00 40.00

2017 Topps Archives

COMP.SET w/o SP's (300) 20.00 50.00
SP ODDS 1:55 HOBBY
1A Mike Trout 1.25 3.00
1B Trt SP Dat on shldr 8.00 20.00
2A Buster Posey .30 .75
2B Posey SP Wht Jrsy 4.00 10.00
3 Earl Weaver .20 .50
4 Goose Gossage .20 .50
5 Tony Perez .20 .50
6 Ryan Braun .20 .50
7 Billy Hamilton .20 .50
8 DJ LeMahieu .25 .60
9 Mark Trumbo .15 .40
10 Rio Ruiz RC .25 .60
11 Nolan Ryan .75 2.00
12 Andres Galarraga .20 .50
13 Jorge Alfaro RC .30 .75
14 Marcell Ozuna .25 .60
15 Brandon Belt .20 .50
16 Jay Bruce .20 .50
17 Melky Cabrera .15 .40
18 Sean Manaea .15 .40
19 Russell Martin .15 .40
20 Jonathan Lucroy .20 .50
21 Jose Ramirez .20 .50
22 Raimel Tapia RC .30 .75
23 Honus Wagner .25 .60
24 Willie McCovey .25 .60
25A David Dahl RC .30 .75
25B Dahl SP Helmet 2.50 6.00
26 Yoenis Cespedes .25 .60
27 Jonathan Schoop .15 .40
28 Evan Longoria .20 .50
29 Josh Donaldson .20 .50
30 Khris Davis .25 .60
31 David Price .20 .50
32 Juan Gonzalez .25 .60
33 Miguel Sano .20 .50
34 Carl Yastrzemski .40 1.00
35 Brooks Robinson .20 .50
36 Yu Darvish .25 .60
37 Jon Gray .15 .40
38 Luis Aparicio .20 .50
39 Rob Segedin RC .25 .60
40 Joc Pederson .25 .60
41 Justin Bour .20 .50
42 David Cone .15 .40
43 Duke Snider .20 .50
44 Julio Teheran .20 .50
45 Javier Baez .30 .75
46 Aaron Sanchez .20 .50
47 Jeff Hoffman RC .25 .60
48 Jim Palmer .20 .50
49 Brian Dozier .25 .60
50A Hank Aaron .50 1.25
50B Aaron SP Bttng stnce 5.00 12.00
51 Robert Gsellman RC .25 .60
52 Bo Jackson .25 .60
53 Freddie Freeman .30 .75
54 Chris Archer .15 .40
55 Fernando Valenzuela .15 .40
56 Eric Hosmer .20 .50
57 Albert Pujols .30 .75
58 Odubel Herrera .20 .50
59 Rollie Fingers .20 .50
60 Catfish Hunter .20 .50
61 Gary Carter .20 .50
62 Aaron Judge RC 10.00 25.00
63 Ryon Healy RC .30 .75
64 Noah Syndergaard .20 .50
65 Stephen Strasburg .25 .60
66 Adrian Beltre .25 .60
67 Edwin Diaz .20 .50
68 Lorenzo Cain .15 .40
69 Jason Heyward .20 .50
70 Ichiro .30 .75
71 German Marquez RC .40 1.00
72 Edgar Martinez .20 .50
73 Bobby Doerr .20 .50
74 Corey Kluber .20 .50
75A Ty Cobb .40 1.00
75B Cobb SP w/Bat 5.00 12.00
76 Curtis Granderson .20 .50
77 Nomar Mazara .15 .40
78 Nolan Arenado .30 .75
79 Brandon Crawford .20 .50
80 Max Scherzer .25 .60
81 Tyler Glasnow RC .30 .75
82A Mike Piazza .25 .60
82B Piazza SP Swinging 3.00 8.00
83 Joe Morgan .20 .50
84 Carson Fulmer RC .25 .60
85 Jon Lester .20 .50
86 Drew Smyly .15 .40
87 Dellin Betances .20 .50
88 Salvador Perez .20 .50
89 Adam Duvall .25 .60
90 Kenley Jansen .20 .50
91 Adam Jones .20 .50
92 Masahiro Tanaka .20 .50
93 Matt Kemp .20 .50
94 Manny Margot RC .25 .60
95 Don Mattingly .50 1.25
96 Bruce Sutter .20 .50
97 Johnny Damon .20 .50
98 Jake Lamb .20 .50
99 Lou Gehrig .50 1.25
100A Corey Seager .25 .60
100B Seager SP Swinging 3.00 8.00
101A Dansby Swanson RC .60 1.50
101B Swnsn SP Blue jrsy 6.00 15.00
102A Carlos Correa .25 .60
102B Correa SP Glove 3.00 8.00
103 Alex Reyes RC .30 .75
104 Bert Blyleven .20 .50
105 Jake Odorizzi .15 .40
106 Fergie Jenkins .20 .50
107 Carlos Gonzalez .20 .50
108 Steven Matz .20 .50
109 Gavin Cecchini RC .25 .60
110 Billy Williams .20 .50
111 Danny Salazar .20 .50
112 Francisco Lindor .25 .60
113 Elvis Andrus .20 .50
114 Jose De Leon RC .25 .60
115 Andy Pettitte .20 .50
116 Curt Schilling .20 .50
117 Dee Gordon .15 .40
118 Drew Pomeranz .20 .50
119 Yulieski Gurriel RC .40 1.00
120 Dexter Fowler .20 .50
121 Marcus Stroman .20 .50
122 Willie Stargell .20 .50
123 Gary Sanchez .25 .60
124 Randal Grichuk .15 .40
125A Jackie Robinson .25 .60
125B Rbnsn SP Kneeling 3.00 8.00
126 Jacoby Ellsbury .20 .50
127 Troy Tulowitzki .25 .60
128 Roberto Alomar .20 .50
129 Yasiel Puig .25 .60
130 Robinson Cano .20 .50
131 Jackie Bradley Jr. .25 .60
132 Andrew Benintendi RC .75 2.00
133 Jake Thompson RC .25 .60
134A Whitey Ford .25 .60
134B Ford SP Pitching 2.50 6.00
135 Sonny Gray .20 .50
136 Rob Manfred .15 .40
137 Kyle Hendricks .25 .60
138A Clayton Kershaw .50 1.25
138B Krshw SP Back of jrsy 6.00 15.00
139 Phil Rizzuto .20 .50
140 Lou Brock .20 .50
141 Dallas Keuchel .20 .50
142 Carlos Asuaje RC .25 .60
143 Willson Contreras .25 .60
144 Ken Giles .15 .40
145 Hisashi Iwakuma .20 .50
146 Michael Fulmer .15 .40
147 Jose Bautista .20 .50
148 Harmon Killebrew .25 .60
149 J.D. Martinez .25 .60
150 Jose Quintana .15 .40
151 Jharel Cotton RC .25 .60
152 Victor Martinez .20 .50
153 Frank Thomas .25 .60
154 Roman Quinn RC .25 .60
155 Cole Hamels .20 .50
156 Maikel Franco .20 .50
157 Aledmys Diaz .20 .50
158 Hunter Renfroe RC .30 .75
159 Pedro Martinez .20 .50
160 Roy Oswalt .20 .50
161 Anthony Rizzo .40 1.00
162 Roger Maris .25 .60
163 John Smoltz .25 .60
164 Larry Doby .20 .50
165 Wade Davis .15 .40
166 Zach Britton .20 .50
167 Dennis Eckersley .20 .50
168 Orlando Arcia RC .40 1.00
169 Starlin Castro .15 .40
170 Nelson Cruz .25 .60
171 Kevin Pillar .15 .40
172 Rich Hill .15 .40
173 Carlos Martinez .20 .50
174 Jonathan Villar .15 .40
175A Sandy Koufax .50 1.25
175B Koufax SP Pitching 6.00 15.00
176 Stephen Piscotty .20 .50
177 Nomar Garciaparra .20 .50
178 Edwin Encarnacion .25 .60
179 Early Wynn .20 .50
180 Danny Duffy .15 .40
181 Eddie Murray .20 .50
182 Justin Turner .20 .50
183 Anthony Rendon .25 .60
184 Teoscar Hernandez RC .75 2.00
185 Ivan Rodriguez .20 .50
186 Monte Irvin .20 .50
187 Jason Kipnis .25 .60
188 Ozzie Smith .30 .75
189 Jeurys Familia .20 .50
190 Zack Greinke .25 .60
191 Sparky Anderson .20 .50
192 Ryne Sandberg .50 1.25
193 Tony Clark .15 .40
194 Xander Bogaerts .25 .60
195 Craig Kimbrel .20 .50
196 Chris Davis .15 .40
197 Jimmie Foxx .25 .60
198 Ben Zobrist .20 .50
199 Carlos Santana .20 .50
200A Kris Bryant .30 .75
200B Brnt SP Gray jrsy 6.00 15.00
201A Roberto Clemente .60 1.50
201B Clmnte SP w/Bat 6.00 15.00
202 Felix Hernandez .20 .50
203 Yasmani Grandal .15 .40
204 Warren Spahn .20 .50
205 Trea Turner .20 .50
206 John Lackey .20 .50
207 Juan Marichal .20 .50
208 Todd Frazier .20 .50
209 George Springer .20 .50
210 Mookie Betts .40 1.00
211 Starling Marte .20 .50
212 Jacob deGrom .25 .60
213 Paul Konerko .20 .50
214 Seung-Hwan Oh .30 .75
215 Tyler Austin RC .40 1.00
216 Christian Yelich .30 .75
217 Kole Calhoun .15 .40
218 Aaron Boone .15 .40
219 Jim Bunning .20 .50
220 Kenta Maeda .20 .50
221 JaCoby Jones RC .30 .75
222 Matt Carpenter .25 .60
223 Jose Abreu .25 .60
224 Bobby Abreu .15 .40
225A Babe Ruth .60 1.50
225B Ruth SP Jacket 6.00 15.00
226 Hanley Ramirez .20 .50
227A Manny Machado .25 .60
227B Mchdo SP Ornge Jrsy 3.00 8.00
228 Bob Lemon .20 .50
229 Gerrit Cole .25 .60
230 Omar Vizquel .20 .50
231 Mark McGwire .40 1.00
232 Lou Boudreau .20 .50
233 A.J. Pollock .15 .40
234 Ian Kinsler .15 .40
235 Chris Sale .25 .60
236 Braden Shipley RC .25 .60
237 Joe Musgrove RC .25 .60
238 Gregory Polanco .20 .50
239 Kelvin Herrera .15 .40
240 Rick Porcello .20 .50
241 Justin Verlander .25 .60
242 Matt Olson RC .40 1.00
243 David Ortiz .25 .60
244 Trevor Story .20 .50
245 Johnny Cueto .20 .50
246 Wil Myers .15 .40
247 Matt Harvey .20 .50
248 Andre Dawson .20 .50
249 Tom Glavine .20 .50
250A Bryce Harper .40 1.00
250B Harper SP Red slve 8.00 20.00
251 Jeff Samardzija .15 .40
252 Evan Gattis .15 .40
253 Jean Segura .20 .50
254 George Brett .50 1.25
255 Reggie Jackson .20 .50
256 Ian Desmond .15 .40
257 T.J. Rivera RC .40 1.00
258 Dustin Pedroia .25 .60
259 Tony La Russa .20 .50
260 Bob Feller .20 .50
261 Rob Zastryzny RC .25 .60
262 Eddie Mathews .25 .60
263 Roberto Osuna .15 .40
264 Kyle Schwarber .20 .50
265 Randy Johnson .20 .50
266 Daniel Murphy .20 .50
267 Seth Lugo RC .25 .60
268 Andrew McCutchen .25 .60
269 Reynaldo Lopez RC .25 .60
270 Mark Melancon .15 .40
271 Justin Upton .20 .50
272 Jose Canseco .20 .50
273 Ted Williams .50 1.25
274 Andrew Miller .20 .50
275A Alex Bregman RC 1.00 2.50
275B Brgmn SP Running 5.00 12.00
276 Giancarlo Stanton .25 .60
277 Yoan Moncada RC .75 2.00
278 Tom Seaver .20 .50
279 Kyle Seager .15 .40
280 Robin Roberts .20 .50
281 Charlie Blackmon .25 .60
282 David Robertson .15 .40
283 Adam Eaton .25 .60
284 Jake Arrieta .20 .50
285 Michael Brantley .20 .50
286 Rougned Odor .20 .50
287 Paul Goldschmidt .25 .60
288 Matt Strahm RC .25 .60
289 Aroldis Chapman .25 .60
290 Kevin Gausman .15 .40
291 Hunter Dozier RC .25 .60
292 Adam Wainwright .20 .50
293 Jose Altuve .20 .50
294 Joey Votto .25 .60
295 Whitey Herzog .15 .40
296 Carlos Carrasco .15 .40
297 Miguel Cabrera .25 .60
298 Addison Russell .25 .60
299 Luis Gonzalez .15 .40
300A Derek Jeter .25 .60
300B Jeter SP Fldng 6.00 15.00

2017 Topps Archives Blackless No Signature

*BLACKLESS: 6X TO 15X BASIC
*BLACKLESS RC: 4X TO 10X BASIC RC
STATED ODDS 1:110 HOBBY

2017 Topps Archives Blue

*BLUE: 5X TO 12X BASIC
*BLUE RC: 3X TO 8X BASIC RC
STATED ODDS 1:37 HOBBY
STATED PRINT RUN 75 SER.#'d SETS
300 Derek Jeter 8.00 20.00

2017 Topps Archives Gold Winner

*GOLD WINNER: 6X TO 15X BASIC
*GOLD WINNER RC: 4X TO 10X BASIC RC
STATED ODDS 1:110 HOBBY
210 Mookie Betts 10.00 25.00
254 George Brett 20.00 50.00
255 Reggie Jackson 12.00 30.00
258 Dustin Pedroia 8.00 20.00
277 Yoan Moncada 20.00 50.00
297 Miguel Cabrera 10.00 25.00
300 Derek Jeter 10.00 25.00

2017 Topps Archives Gray Back

*GRAY BACK: 6X TO 15X BASIC
*GRAY BACK RC: 4X TO 10X BASIC RC
STATED ODDS 1:110 HOBBY
1 Mike Trout 15.00 40.00
95 Don Mattingly 12.00 30.00

2017 Topps Archives Peach

*PEACH: 4X TO 10X BASIC
*PEACH RC: 2.5X TO 6X BASIC RC
STATED ODDS 1:14 HOBBY
STATED PRINT RUN 199 SER.#'d SETS
300 Derek Jeter 6.00 15.00

2017 Topps Archives Red

*RED: 12X TO 30X BASIC
*RED RC: 8X TO 20X BASIC RC
STATED ODDS 1:110 HOBBY
STATED PRINT RUN 25 SER.#'d SETS
300 Derek Jeter 20.00 50.00

2017 Topps Archives '16 Retro Original

COMPLETE SET (20) 15.00 40.00
STATED ODDS 1:12 HOBBY
RO1 Kris Bryant .75 2.00
RO2 Bryce Harper 1.00 2.50
RO3 Yoenis Cespedes .60 1.50
RO4 Anthony Rizzo 1.00 2.50
RO5 Gary Sanchez .60 1.50
RO6 Buster Posey .75 2.00
RO7 Jake Arrieta .50 1.25
RO8 Justin Verlander .60 1.50
RO9 Giancarlo Stanton .60 1.50
RO10 Carlos Correa .60 1.50
RO11 Manny Machado .60 1.50
RO12 Clayton Kershaw 1.25 3.00
RO13 Francisco Lindor .60 1.50
RO14 Mike Trout 3.00 8.00
RO15 Mookie Betts 1.00 2.50
RO16 Josh Donaldson .50 1.25
RO17 Max Scherzer .60 1.50
RO18 Miguel Cabrera .60 1.50
RO19 Nolan Arenado .75 2.00
RO20 Noah Syndergaard .50 1.25

2017 Topps Archives '59 Bazooka

COMPLETE SET (20) 15.00 40.00
STATED ODDS 1:6 HOBBY
*BLUE/75: 2X TO 5X BASIC
*RED/25: 4X TO 10X BASIC
59B1 Carlos Correa .60 1.50
59B2 Ivan Rodriguez .50 1.25
59B3 Stephen Piscotty .50 1.25
59B4 Yulieski Gurriel .60 1.50
59B5 Bryce Harper 1.00 2.50
59B6 Ozzie Smith .75 2.00
59B7 Aaron Judge 8.00 20.00
59B8 Tom Glavine .50 1.25
59B9 Francisco Lindor .60 1.50
59B10 Alex Bregman 1.50 4.00
59B11 Nolan Ryan 2.00 5.00
59B12 Paul Konerko .50 1.25
59B13 Al Kaline .60 1.50
59B14 Corey Seager .60 1.50
59B15 Kris Bryant .75 2.00
59B16 Omar Vizquel .50 1.25
59B17 Sandy Koufax 1.25 3.00
59B18 Yoan Moncada 1.25 3.00
59B19 Dustin Pedroia .60 1.50
59B20 Mike Trout 3.00 8.00

2017 Topps Archives '59 Bazooka Autographs

STATED ODDS 1:309 HOBBY
PRINT RUNS B/WN 35-99 COPIES PER
EXCHANGE DEADLINE 5/31/2019
59BAAB Alex Bregman/99 20.00 50.00
59BAAJ Aaron Judge/99 60.00 150.00
59BAAK Al Kaline/99 25.00 50.00
59BABH Bryce Harper
59BACC Carlos Correa/99 30.00 80.00
59BACS Corey Seager/99 30.00 80.00
59BADP Dustin Pedroia/99 15.00 40.00
59BAFL Francisco Lindor/99 20.00 50.00
59BAKB Kris Bryant/99 100.00 250.00
59BAMT Mike Trout
59BANR Nolan Ryan/35 150.00 300.00
59BAOS Ozzie Smith/99 20.00 50.00
59BAOV Omar Vizquel/99 5.00 12.00
59BAPK Paul Konerko/99 8.00 20.00
59BASP Stephen Piscotty/99 5.00 12.00
59BATG Tom Glavine/99 15.00 40.00
59BAYG Yulieski Gurriel/99 10.00 25.00
59BAYM Yoan Moncada/99 30.00 80.00

2017 Topps Archives '59 Bazooka Autographs Red

*RED: .6X TO 1.5X BASIC
STATED ODDS 1:961 HOBBY
STATED PRINT RUN 25 SER.#'d SETS
EXCHANGE DEADLINE 5/31/2019
59BAMT Mike Trout 400.00 600.00
59BANR Nolan Ryan 200.00 400.00

2017 Topps Archives '60 Rookie Stars

COMPLETE SET (10) 12.00 30.00
STATED ODDS 1:12 HOBBY
*BLUE/75: .75X TO 2X BASIC
*RED/25: 3X TO 8X BASIC
RS1 Yoan Moncada 1.25 3.00
RS2 Orlando Arcia .60 1.50
RS3 Andrew Benintendi 1.25 3.00
RS4 Dansby Swanson 1.00 2.50
RS5 David Dahl .50 1.25
RS6 Alex Reyes .50 1.25
RS7 Yulieski Gurriel .60 1.50
RS8 Tyler Glasnow .50 1.25
RS9 Aaron Judge 8.00 20.00
RS10 Alex Bregman 1.50 4.00

2017 Topps Archives '60 Rookie Stars Autographs

STATED ODDS 1:700 HOBBY
STATED PRINT RUN 150 SER.#'d SETS
EXCHANGE DEADLINE 5/31/2019
RSAAB Alex Bregman 20.00 50.00
RSAABE Andrew Benintendi 60.00 150.00
RSAAJ Aaron Judge 200.00 400.00
RSADD David Dahl 8.00 20.00
RSADS Dansby Swanson
RSAYG Yulieski Gurriel
RSAYM Yoan Moncada

2017 Topps Archives '60 Rookie Stars Autographs Blue

*BLUE: .5X TO 1.2X BASIC
STATED ODDS 1:1401 HOBBY
STATED PRINT RUN 75 SER.#'d SETS
EXCHANGE DEADLINE 5/31/2019
RSADS Dansby Swanson 30.00 80.00
RSAYG Yulieski Gurriel 12.00 30.00
RSAYM Yoan Moncada 50.00 120.00

2017 Topps Archives '60 Rookie Stars Autographs Red

*RED: .6X TO 1.5X BASIC
STATED ODDS 1:4188 HOBBY
STATED PRINT RUN 25 SER.#'d SETS
EXCHANGE DEADLINE 5/31/2019
RSADS Dansby Swanson 40.00 100.00
RSAYG Yulieski Gurriel 15.00 40.00
RSAYM Yoan Moncada 60.00 150.00

2017 Topps Archives Coins

INSERTED IN RETAIL PACKS
*BLUE: 1X TO 2.5X BASIC
C1 Kris Bryant 1.25 3.00
C2 Carlos Correa 1.00 2.50
C3 Gary Sanchez 1.00 2.50
C4 Mookie Betts 1.50 4.00
C5 Yoenis Cespedes 1.00 2.50
C6 Orlando Arcia 1.00 2.50
C7 Noah Syndergaard .75 2.00
C8 Anthony Rizzo 1.50 4.00
C9 David Dahl .75 2.00
C10 Justin Verlander 1.00 2.50
C11 Francisco Lindor 1.00 2.50
C12 Dansby Swanson 1.50 4.00
C13 Nolan Arenado 1.25 3.00
C14 Josh Donaldson .75 2.00
C15 Aaron Judge 8.00 20.00
C16 Yoan Moncada 2.00 5.00
C17 Andrew Benintendi 2.00 5.00
C18 Yulieski Gurriel 1.00 2.50
C19 Mike Trout 5.00 12.00
C20 Bryce Harper 1.50 4.00
C21 Manny Machado 1.00 2.50
C22 Clayton Kershaw 2.00 5.00
C23 Giancarlo Stanton 1.00 2.50
C24 Max Scherzer 1.00 2.50
C25 Alex Bregman 2.50 6.00

2017 Topps Archives Derek Jeter Retrospective

COMP.SET w/o SP's (20) 25.00 60.00
STATED ODDS 1:12 HOBBY
STATED SP ODDS 1:240 HOBBY
*BLUE/150: 1X TO 2.5X BASIC
GREEN/99: 1.2X TO 3X BASIC
GREEN SP/99: .6X TO 1.5X BASIC
*GOLD/50: 3X TO 8X BASIC
*GOLD SP/50: 1.5X TO 4X BASIC
DJ1 Jeter SP '93 Topps 12.00 30.00
DJ2 Derek Jeter 1.50 4.00
'94 Topps
DJ3 Derek Jeter 1.50 4.00
'95 Topps
DJ4 Derek Jeter 1.50 4.00
'96 Topps
DJ5 Derek Jeter 1.50 4.00
'97 Topps
DJ6 Derek Jeter 1.50 4.00
'98 Topps
DJ7 Derek Jeter 1.50 4.00
'99 Topps
DJ8 Derek Jeter 1.50 4.00
'00 Topps
DJ9 Derek Jeter 1.50 4.00
'01 Topps
DJ10 Derek Jeter 1.50 4.00
'02 Topps
DJ11 Derek Jeter 1.50 4.00
'03 Topps
DJ12 Derek Jeter 1.50 4.00
'04 Topps
DJ13 Derek Jeter 1.50 4.00
'05 Topps
DJ14 Derek Jeter 1.50 4.00
'06 Topps
DJ16 Derek Jeter 1.50 4.00
'08 Topps
DJ17 Derek Jeter 1.50 4.00
'09 Topps
DJ18 Derek Jeter 1.50 4.00
'10 Topps
DJ19 Derek Jeter 1.50 4.00
'11 Topps
DJ20 Derek Jeter 1.50 4.00
'12 Topps
DJ21 Derek Jeter 1.50 4.00
'13 Topps
DJ22 Derek Jeter 1.50 4.00
'14 Topps
DJ23 Jeter SP '15 Topps 12.00 30.00

2017 Topps Archives Fan Favorites Autographs

STATED ODDS 1:19 HOBBY
EXCHANGE DEADLINE 5/31/2019
FFAAB Aaron Boone 10.00 25.00
FFAABE Andrew Benintendi 60.00 150.00
FFAABR Alex Bregman 40.00 100.00
FFAAJ Aaron Judge 100.00 250.00
FFAAR Anthony Rizzo 25.00 60.00
FFABB Billy Bean 3.00 8.00
FFABJ Brian Jordan 3.00 8.00
FFABL Bill "Spaceman" Lee 6.00 15.00
FFABT Bobby Thigpen 3.00 8.00
FFABV Bald Vinny 8.00 20.00
FFACC Carlos Correa 40.00 100.00
FFACJ Cleon Jones 6.00 15.00
FFACK Clayton Kershaw 100.00 250.00
FFADD David Dahl 6.00 15.00
FFADJ Derek Jeter 300.00 600.00
FFADMA Dave Magadan 4.00 10.00
FFADS Dave Stieb 6.00 12.00
FFAER Edgar Renteria 3.00 8.00
FFAGB George Bell EXCH 4.00 10.00
FFAGC Gary Cohen 12.00 30.00
FFAHA Hank Aaron
FFAJC Joe Castiglione 20.00 50.00
FFAJE Jim Edmonds 15.00 40.00
FFAJH John Hirschbeck
FFAJJ Jim Joyce 8.00 20.00
FFAJMC Joe McEwing 3.00 8.00
FFAJS John Smiley 4.00 10.00
FFAJST John Sterling 15.00 40.00
FFAKB Kris Bryant 75.00 200.00
FFAKM Kevin Maas 4.00 10.00
FFAKR Ken Rosenthal 8.00 20.00
FFAKS Kevin Seitzer 4.00 10.00
FFALG Lourdes Gourriel Sr. 3.00 8.00
FFALR Lenny Randle 4.00 10.00
FFAMB Marty Brennaman 15.00 40.00
FFAML Mark Langston 3.00 8.00
FFAMM Manny Mota 4.00 10.00
FFAMMU Mark Mulder 3.00 8.00
FFAMS Mike Scott 3.00 8.00
FFAMT Masahiro Tanaka 150.00 300.00
FFAMTT Mike Trout 500.00 800.00
FFAOA Orlando Arcia 4.00 10.00
FFAPG Peter Gammons 15.00 40.00
FFARA Rick Ankiel EXCH 15.00 40.00
FFARCE Ron Cey 6.00 15.00
FFARK Rusty Kuntz 4.00 10.00
FFARM Rob Manfred EXCH 30.00 80.00
FFARO Roy Oswalt 6.00 15.00
FFASA Steve Avery 5.00 12.00
FFASBA Skip Bayless
FFASK Sandy Koufax 1200.00 1600.00
FFATE Theo Epstein
FFATL Tommy Lasorda 40.00 100.00
FFATM Terry Mulholland 3.00 8.00
FFATOC Tony Clark 3.00 8.00
FFATP Tony Pena 5.00 12.00
FFATT Tim Teufel 4.00 10.00
FFATW Tim Wakefield 15.00 40.00
FFATWA Tim Wallach 3.00 8.00
FFATWE Turk Wendell 3.00 8.00
FFATWO Tony Womack 3.00 8.00
FFAWM Wally Moon 5.00 12.00
FFAZH Zack Hample 6.00 15.00

2017 Topps Archives Fan Favorites Autographs Blue

*BLUE: .6X TO 1.5X BASIC
STATED ODDS 1:146 HOBBY
STATED PRINT RUN 75 SER.#'d SETS
EXCHANGE DEADLINE 5/31/2019
FFAAR Anthony Rizzo 30.00 80.00
FFAJC Joe Castiglione 25.00 60.00
FFAJH John Hirschbeck 10.00 25.00
FFAKR Ken Rosenthal 12.00 30.00
FFAPG Peter Gammons 20.00 50.00
FFARA Rick Ankiel EXCH 25.00 60.00
FFASBA Skip Bayless 10.00 25.00
FFATE Theo Epstein 150.00 300.00
FFATW Tim Wakefield 20.00 50.00

2017 Topps Archives Fan Favorites Autographs Peach

*PEACH: .5X TO 1.2X BASIC
STATED ODDS 1:73 HOBBY
STATED PRINT RUN 150 SER.#'d SETS
EXCHANGE DEADLINE 5/31/2019
FFAJH John Hirschbeck 8.00 20.00
FFASBA Skip Bayless 8.00 20.00

2017 Topps Archives Fan Favorites Autographs Red

*RED: .75X TO 2X BASIC
STATED ODDS 1:437 HOBBY
STATED PRINT RUN 25 SER.#'d SETS
EXCHANGE DEADLINE 5/31/2019
FFAAR Anthony Rizzo 40.00 100.00
FFACK Clayton Kershaw 125.00 300.00
FFAJC Joe Castiglione 30.00 80.00
FFAJH John Hirschbeck 12.00 30.00
FFAKR Ken Rosenthal 15.00 40.00
FFAPG Peter Gammons 25.00 60.00
FFARA Rick Ankiel EXCH 30.00 80.00
FFASBA Skip Bayless 12.00 30.00
FFATE Theo Epstein 175.00 350.00
FFATL Tommy Lasorda 75.00 200.00
FFATW Tim Wakefield 25.00 60.00

2017 Topps Archives Originals Autographs

STATED ODDS 1:1753 HOBBY
PRINT RUNS B/WN 5-20 COPIES PER
NO PRICING ON QTY 5
EXCHANGE DEADLINE 5/31/2019
30 Jim Rice 40.00 100.00
97 Curt Schilling 40.00 100.00
JC Jose Canseco
148 Edgar Martinez 20.00 50.00
378 Andy Pettitte 25.00 60.00
382 John Smoltz 60.00 150.00
400 Cal Ripken Jr. 60.00 150.00
414 Frank Thomas 75.00 200.00
500 Chipper Jones 75.00 200.00
551 Carl Yastrzemski 60.00 150.00
586 Rollie Fingers 60.00 150.00
630 Fernando Valenzuela 40.00 100.00
FFAK Al Kaline

2018 Topps Archives

COMP.SET w/o SP's (300) 30.00 80.00
301-320 ODDS 1:8 HOBBY
1 Hank Aaron .50 1.25
2 Noah Syndergaard .20 .50
3 Tom Seaver .20 .50
4 Jack Flaherty RC .40 1.00
5 Andrew McCutchen .25 .60
6 Yasiel Puig .25 .60
7 Orlando Cepeda .20 .50
8 Nomar Garciaparra .20 .50
9 Nicky Delmonico RC .25 .60
10 Lucas Giolito .20 .50
11 Scott Kingery RC .40 1.00
12 Corey Seager .25 .60
13 Larry Doby .20 .50
14 Andrew Benintendi .25 .60
15 Ryne Sandberg .50 1.25
16 Harrison Bader RC .40 1.00
17 Sean Manaea .15 .40
18 Ozzie Albies RC .75 2.00
19 Austin Meadows RC .40 1.00
20 Cal Ripken Jr. .75 2.00
21 Dallas Keuchel .20 .50
22 Jordan Hicks RC .50 1.25
23 Don Mattingly .50 1.25
24 Josh Donaldson .20 .50
25 Sandy Koufax .50 1.25
26 Jorge Polanco .15 .40
27 Max Fried RC 1.00 2.50
28 Jackie Bradley Jr. .25 .60
29 Dansby Swanson .25 .60
30 Honus Wagner .25 .60
31 Aaron Judge .60 1.50
32 Miguel Cabrera .25 .60
33 Justin Upton .20 .50

34 Anthony Rendon .25 .60
35 Greg Maddux .30 .75
36 Adam Jones .20 .50
37 Hoyt Wilhelm .20 .50
38 Marcus Stroman .20 .50
39 Adrian Beltre .25 .60
40 Rafael Devers RC .75 2.00
41 Paul Goldschmidt .25 .60
42 Brian Dozier .20 .50
43 Luke Weaver .20 .50
44 Luis Severino .20 .50
45 Joey Gallo .20 .50
46 Warren Spahn .20 .50
47 Carlton Fisk .20 .50
48 Jose Urena .15 .40
49 Bobby Doerr .20 .50
50 Shohei Ohtani RC 3.00 8.00
51 Mike Piazza .25 .60
52 Avisail Garcia .20 .50
53 Edwin Encarnacion .25 .60
54 Odubel Herrera .20 .50
55 Duke Snider .20 .50
56 Aaron Nola .20 .50
57 Mike Zunino .15 .40
58 Whit Merrifield .25 .60
59 Adam Duvall .25 .60
60 Jim Thome .20 .50
61 Manny Machado .25 .60
62 Addison Russell .20 .50
63 Blake Snell .20 .50
64 Evan Longoria .20 .50
65 Brian Anderson RC .30 .75
66 Wade Davis .15 .40
67 Charlie Blackmon .25 .60
68 Will Clark .20 .50
69 Gary Carter .20 .50
70 Tyler Wade RC .30 .75
71 Jake Odorizzi .15 .40
72 Tyler Glasnow .15 .40
73 Juan Soto RC 8.00 20.00
74 Anthony Banda RC .25 .60
75 Giancarlo Stanton .25 .60
76 Michael Conforto .20 .50
77 Jameson Taillon .20 .50
78 Red Schoendienst .20 .50
79 Luis Castillo .20 .50
80 Danny Duffy .15 .40
81 Goose Gossage .20 .50
82 A.J. Pollock .15 .40
83 Jordan Zimmermann .20 .50
84 Bernie Williams .20 .50
85 Bert Blyleven .20 .50
86 Christian Yelich .30 .75
87 Manny Margot .15 .40
88 Paul DeJong .25 .60
89 Julio Teheran .20 .50
90 Andrew Miller .20 .50
91 Garrett Cooper RC .25 .60
92 Albert Pujols .30 .75
93 Justin Verlander .25 .60
94 Lorenzo Cain .15 .40
95 Willy Adames RC .30 .75
96 Eddie Murray .20 .50
97 Dee Gordon .15 .40
98 Ryan Zimmerman .20 .50
99 Khris Davis .25 .60
100 Kris Bryant .30 .75
101 Francisco Lindor .25 .60
102 Daniel Murphy .20 .50
103 Mike Moustakas .20 .50
104 Chris Davis .15 .40
105 Mookie Betts .40 1.00
106 Francisco Mejia RC .30 .75
107 Richie Ashburn .20 .50
108 Amed Rosario RC .30 .75
109 Justin Turner .20 .50
110 Matt Olson .15 .40
111 Kyle Schwarber .25 .60
112 Early Wynn .20 .50
113 Robin Yount .25 .60
114 Didi Gregorius .20 .50
115 Orlando Arcia .15 .40
116 Raisel Iglesias .20 .50
117 Bob Feller .20 .50
118 Jacob deGrom .25 .60
119 Jim Bunning .20 .50
120 Johnny Bench .25 .60
121 Bruce Sutter .20 .50
122 Nick Markakis .20 .50
123 Joey Lucchesi RC .25 .60
124 Nolan Arenado .30 .75
125 Justin Bour .15 .40
126 Don Sutton .20 .50
127 Yasmany Tomas .15 .40
128 Rickey Henderson .25 .60
129 DJ LeMahieu .25 .60
130 Brandon Belt .20 .50
131 Byron Buxton .20 .50
132 Chris Archer .15 .40
133 Nomar Mazara .15 .40
134 Stephen Strasburg .25 .60
135 Nelson Cruz .25 .60
136 Marcell Ozuna .25 .60
137 Alex Verdugo RC .40 1.00
138 Brooks Robinson .20 .50
139 Jose Berrios .20 .50
140 Pedro Martinez .20 .50
141 George Springer .20 .50
142 Josh Bell .20 .50
143 Carson Fulmer .15 .40
144 Clint Frazier RC .50 1.25
145 Willie McCovey .20 .50
146 Nick Williams RC .30 .75
147 Enos Slaughter .20 .50
148 Phil Rizzuto .20 .50
149 Zack Cozart .15 .40
150 Clayton Kershaw .50 1.25
151 Carlos Santana .20 .50
152 Billy Hamilton .20 .50
153 Roger Clemens .30 .75
154 Andrew Stevenson RC .25 .60
155 Hunter Pence .20 .50
156 Jimmie Foxx .25 .60
157 Alcides Escobar .20 .50
158 Travis d'Arnaud .20 .50
159 Tim Beckham .20 .50
160 Chris Sale .25 .60
161 Justin Smoak .15 .40
162 Felix Hernandez .20 .50
163 Tommy Pham .15 .40
164 Gleyber Torres RC 2.50 6.00
165 Whitey Ford .20 .50
166 Nicholas Castellanos .25 .60
167 Cole Hamels .20 .50
168 Tommy Lasorda .20 .50
169 George Brett .50 1.25
170 Austin Hedges .15 .40
171 Ozzie Smith .30 .75
172 James McCann .20 .50
173 Carlos Correa .25 .60
174 Anthony Rizzo .40 1.00
175 Ryan McMahon RC .30 .75
176 David Ortiz .25 .60
177 Tim Anderson .25 .60
178 Satchel Paige .25 .60
179 Wil Myers .15 .40
180 Dave Winfield .20 .50
181 Masahiro Tanaka .20 .50
182 Lou Boudreau .20 .50
183 Jake Lamb .20 .50
184 Teoscar Hernandez .25 .60
185 Brad Ziegler .15 .40
186 Austin Hays RC .40 1.00
187 Kevin Kiermaier .20 .50
188 Tyler O'Neill RC .40 1.00
189 Hal Newhouser .20 .50
190 Carlos Carrasco .15 .40
191 Andrelton Simmons .15 .40
192 Barry Larkin .20 .50
193 Tyler Mahle RC .30 .75
194 Jack Morris .20 .50
195 Stephen Piscotty .15 .40
196 Felipe Vazquez .20 .50
197 Ender Inciarte .15 .40
198 Walker Buehler RC 1.25 3.00
199 Corey Knebel .15 .40
200 Derek Jeter .60 1.50
201 Roberto Clemente .60 1.50
202 Ernie Banks .25 .60
203 Yoan Moncada .25 .60
204 Bob Gibson .20 .50
205 Buster Posey .30 .75
206 Robinson Cano .20 .50
207 Luiz Gohara RC .25 .60
208 Starling Marte .20 .50
209 Starlin Castro .15 .40
210 Jonathan Schoop .15 .40
211 Chance Sisco RC .30 .75
212 Ronald Acuna Jr. RC 10.00 25.00
213 Trevor Story .25 .60
214 Kenley Jansen .20 .50
215 Jon Gray .15 .40
216 Michael Fulmer .15 .40
217 Rhys Hoskins RC 1.00 2.50
218 Zack Greinke .20 .50
219 Freddie Freeman .30 .75
220 Yoenis Cespedes .25 .60
221 Tom Glavine .20 .50
222 Jose Ramirez .20 .50
223 Jon Lester .20 .50
224 John Smoltz .25 .60
225 Kyle Seager .15 .40
226 George Kell .20 .50
227 Harmon Killebrew .25 .60
228 Johnny Cueto .20 .50
229 Chipper Jones .25 .60
230 Alex Gordon .20 .50
231 Ichiro .30 .75
232 Joe Morgan .20 .50
233 Trea Turner .20 .50
234 Yadier Molina .25 .60
235 Maikel Franco .20 .50
236 Dustin Pedroia .25 .60
237 Ryan Braun .20 .50
238 Daniel Mengden .15 .40
239 Tony Perez .20 .50
240 Eric Thames .15 .40
241 Edgar Martinez .20 .50
242 Alex Bregman .25 .60
243 Matt Duffy .15 .40
244 Rougned Odor .20 .50
245 Monte Irvin .20 .50
246 Scott Schebler .15 .40
247 Lucas Sims RC .25 .60
248 Wade Boggs .20 .50
249 Alex Rodriguez .30 .75
250 Cody Bellinger .50 1.25
251 Catfish Hunter .20 .50
252 Ervin Santana .15 .40
253 Russell Martin .15 .40
254 Rod Carew .20 .50
255 Randy Johnson .25 .60
256 Jesse Biddle RC .30 .75
257 Hunter Renfroe .15 .40
258 Eddie Mathews .25 .60
259 Patrick Corbin .20 .50
260 Elvis Andrus .20 .50
261 Matt Chapman .25 .60
262 Ralph Kiner .20 .50
263 Fergie Jenkins .20 .50
264 Frank Thomas .25 .60
265 Victor Robles RC .60 1.50
266 Ian Kinsler .20 .50
267 Max Kepler .20 .50
268 Nolan Ryan .75 2.00
269 Dustin Fowler RC .25 .60
270 Reggie Jackson .20 .50
271 Trey Mancini .20 .50
272 Jose Altuve .20 .50
273 Yangervis Solarte .15 .40
274 Tomas Nido RC .25 .60
275 Mark McGwire .40 1.00
276 Aaron Altherr .15 .40
277 Max Scherzer .25 .60
278 Sean Newcomb .20 .50
279 Yu Darvish .25 .60
280 J.P. Crawford RC .25 .60
281 Xander Bogaerts .25 .60
282 Miguel Andujar RC 1.00 2.50
283 Salvador Perez .20 .50
284 Corey Kluber .20 .50
285 Brandon Woodruff RC .30 .75
286 Dominic Smith RC .25 .60
287 Mike Soroka RC .75 2.00
288 Joey Votto .25 .60
289 Gary Sanchez .25 .60
290 Kevin Pillar .15 .40
291 Matt Carpenter .25 .60
292 Robin Roberts .20 .50
293 Steven Matz .20 .50
294 Adeiny Hechavarria .15 .40
295 Bob Lemon .20 .50
296 Gregory Polanco .20 .50
297 Willie Stargell .20 .50
298 Jose Abreu .25 .60
299 Mike Trout 1.25 3.00
300 Bryce Harper .40 1.00
301 Benintendi/Betts 1.00 2.50
302 Bryant/Rizzo 1.00 2.50
303 Ohtani/Trout 3.00 8.00
304 Judge/Stanton 1.50 4.00
305 Abreu/Moncada .60 1.50
306 Rosario/Berrios .60 1.50
307 McCutchen/Posey .75 2.00
308 Ichiro/Gordon .75 2.00
309 Pederson/Kemp/Puig .60 1.50
310 Bregman/Altuve/Correa .60 1.50
311 Ichiro TBTC .75 2.00
312 Randy Johnson TBTC .60 1.50
313 Albert Pujols TBTC .75 2.00
314 Mark McGwire TBTC 1.00 2.50
315 Mike Piazza TBTC .60 1.50
316 Jose Canseco TBTC .50 1.25
317 Nolan Ryan TBTC 2.00 5.00
318 Willie McCovey TBTC .50 1.25
319 Hank Aaron TBTC 1.25 3.00
320 Bob Gibson TBTC .50 1.25

2018 Topps Archives Blackless No Signature

*BLACKLESS: 6X TO 15X BASIC
*BLACKLESS RC: 4X TO 10X BASIC RC
STATED ODDS 1:108 HOBBY
73 Juan Soto 125.00 300.00

2018 Topps Archives Blue

*BLUE: 6X TO 15X BASIC
*BLUE RC: 4X TO 10X BASIC RC
STATED ODDS 1:76 HOBBY
STATED PRINT RUN 25 SER.#'d SETS
23 Don Mattingly 40.00 100.00
31 Aaron Judge 30.00 80.00
169 George Brett 20.00 50.00
198 Walker Buehler 25.00 60.00
200 Derek Jeter 30.00 80.00
268 Nolan Ryan 25.00 60.00

2018 Topps Archives Logo Swap

*LOGO SWAP: 8X TO 20X BASIC
*LOGO SWAP RC: 5X TO 12X BASIC RC
STATED ODDS 1:215 HOBBY

2018 Topps Archives Purple

*PURPLE: 4X TO 10X BASIC
*PURPLE RC: 2.5X TO 6X BASIC RC
STATED ODDS 1:31 HOBBY
STATED PRINT RUN 175 SER.#'d SETS

2018 Topps Archives Silver

*SILVER: 4X TO 10X BASIC
*SILVER RC: 2.5X TO 6X BASIC RC
STATED ODDS 1:55 HOBBY
STATED PRINT RUN 99 SER.#'d SETS

2018 Topps Archives Venezuelan Gray Back

*GRAY BACK: 6X TO 15X BASIC
*GRAY BACK RC: 4X TO 10X BASIC RC
STATED ODDS 1:108 HOBBY

2018 Topps Archives '59 Photo Variations

STATED ODDS 1:239 HOBBY
31 Judge Swing 10.00 25.00
50 Ohtani Swing 15.00 40.00
100 Bryant Fldng 4.00 10.00

2018 Topps Archives '77 Photo Variations

STATED ODDS 1:239 HOBBY
108 Rosario At bat 5.00 12.00
150 Kershaw Ptchng 6.00 15.00
200 Jeter Pnstrp Jrsy 10.00 25.00

2018 Topps Archives '81 Future Stars

COMPLETE SET (10) 6.00 15.00
STATED ODDS 1:8 HOBBY
FSBAL Sisco/Hays/Scott .40 1.00
FSBRA Albies/Acuna/Gohara 5.00 12.00
FSLAA Bridwell/Scribner/Ohtani 1.50 4.00
FSLAD Farmer/Verdugo/Buehler 1.25 3.00
FSMIA Alcantara/Anderson/Cooper .30 .75
FSNYM Smith/Nido/Rosario .30 .75
FSPHI Hoskins/Williams/Crawford 1.00 2.50
FSSTL Mejia/Flaherty/Bader .40 1.00
FSWAS Robles/Stevenson/Fedde .60 1.50
FSYAN Frazier/Torres/Andujar 2.50 6.00

2018 Topps Archives '81 Photo Variations

STATED ODDS 1:239 HOBBY
201 Clemente Running 8.00 20.00
202 Banks Pnstp Jrsy 3.00 8.00
300 Harper Wht Jrsy 5.00 12.00

2018 Topps Archives '93 All Stars Dual Autographs

STATED ODDS 1:2149 HOBBY
STATED PRINT RUN 25 SER.#'d SETS
EXCHANGE DEADLINE 7/31/2020
DAAS Altuve/Springer 50.00 120.00
DABT Trout/Bryant EXCH 400.00 800.00
DAHW Hoskins/Williams EXCH 40.00 100.00
DAPK Percival/Kimbrel EXCH 20.00 50.00
DARP Palmer/Robinson EXCH 60.00 150.00
DARS Smith/Rosario 25.00 60.00
DASG Glavine/Smoltz 60.00 150.00
DAWJ Winfield/Judge EXCH 150.00 400.00

2018 Topps Archives Coins

COMPLETE SET (25) 15.00 40.00
INSERTED IN RETAIL PACKS
*SKY BLUE: 3X TO 8X BASIC
C1 Aaron Judge 1.25 3.00
C2 Benny Rodriguez 1.25 3.00
C3 Kris Bryant .60 1.50
C4 Scotty Smalls 1.25 3.00
C5 Squints 1.25 3.00
C6 Carlos Correa .50 1.25
C7 Amed Rosario .40 1.00
C8 Hercules 1.25 3.00
C9 Manny Machado .50 1.25
C10 Rafael Devers 1.00 2.50
C11 Andrew McCutchen .50 1.25
C12 Ozzie Albies 1.00 2.50
C13 Max Scherzer .50 1.25
C14 Victor Robles .75 2.00
C15 Noah Syndergaard .40 1.00
C16 Josh Donaldson .40 1.00
C17 Mike Trout 2.50 6.00
C18 Clint Frazier .60 1.50
C19 Francisco Lindor .50 1.25
C20 Ham 1.25 3.00
C21 Buster Posey .60 1.50
C22 Rhys Hoskins 1.25 3.00
C23 Cody Bellinger 1.00 2.50
C24 Andrew Benintendi .50 1.25
C25 Shohei Ohtani 2.00 5.00

2018 Topps Archives Coming Attraction

COMPLETE SET (20) 10.00 25.00
STATED ODDS 1:6 HOBBY
CA1 Shohei Ohtani 1.50 4.00
CA2 Walker Buehler 1.25 3.00
CA3 Clint Frazier .50 1.25
CA4 Ozzie Albies .75 2.00
CA5 Miguel Andujar .60 1.50
CA6 Alex Verdugo .40 1.00
CA7 Victor Robles .60 1.50
CA8 Austin Hays .40 1.00
CA9 J.P. Crawford .25 .60
CA10 Amed Rosario .30 .75
CA11 Gleyber Torres 2.50 6.00
CA12 Ronald Acuna Jr. 5.00 12.00
CA13 Dustin Fowler .25 .60
CA14 Nick Williams .30 .75
CA15 Francisco Mejia .30 .75
CA16 Rhys Hoskins 1.00 2.50
CA17 Dominic Smith .25 .60
CA18 Harrison Bader .40 1.00
CA19 Jack Flaherty .40 1.00
CA20 Rafael Devers .75 2.00

2018 Topps Archives Coming Attraction Autographs

STATED ODDS 1:536 HOBBY
PRINT RUNS B/WN 40-99 COPIES PER
EXCHANGE DEADLINE 7/31/2020
*BLUE/25: .6X TO 1.5X BASIC
CAAH Austin Hays/99 10.00 25.00
CAAR Amed Rosario
CAAV Alex Verdugo/99 12.00 30.00
CACF Clint Frazier/50 12.00 30.00
CADF Dustin Fowler/99 6.00 15.00
CADS Dominic Smith
CAFM Francisco Mejia EXCH 8.00 20.00
CAGT Gleyber Torres/99 30.00 80.00
CAHB Harrison Bader/99 10.00 25.00
CAJC J.P. Crawford EXCH 6.00 15.00
CAJF Jack Flaherty/99 10.00 25.00
CAND Nicky Delmonico EXCH 6.00 15.00
CANW Nick Williams/70 8.00 20.00
CAOA Ozzie Albies/80 20.00 50.00
CARA Ronald Acuna/99 150.00 400.00
CARD Rafael Devers/40 20.00 50.00
CARH Rhys Hoskins/50 25.00 60.00
CASO Shohei Ohtani
CAVR Victor Robles/50 25.00 60.00
CAWB Walker Buehler EXCH 25.00 60.00

2018 Topps Archives Fan Favorites Autographs

STATED ODDS 1:20 HOBBY
EXCHANGE DEADLINE 7/31/2020
*PURPLE/150: .5X TO 1.2X BASE
*SILVER/99: .6X TO 1.5X BASE
*BLUE/25: .75X TO 2X BASE
FFAAH A.J. Hinch 12.00 30.00
FFAAJ Aaron Judge 150.00 400.00
FFAAK Adam Kennedy 4.00 10.00
FFAAR Amed Rosario 8.00 20.00
FFABA Jeff Bagwell EXCH 25.00 60.00
FFABB Brad Ausmus 4.00 10.00
FFABEB Bert Blyleven 12.00 30.00
FFABF Bob Friend 6.00 15.00
FFABH Bryce Harper
FFABJ Bill James 8.00 20.00
FFABM Bill Madlock 4.00 10.00
FFABR Brad Radke 4.00 10.00
FFABV Bobby Valentine 8.00 20.00
FFACC Chris Chambliss 8.00 20.00
FFACJ Charles Johnson 5.00 12.00
FFACN Charles Nagy 4.00 10.00
FFADJ David Justice 10.00 25.00
FFADJ Derek Jeter 500.00 800.00
FFADK Don Kessinger 4.00 10.00
FFADL Derek Lowe 10.00 25.00
FFADR Dave Roberts 15.00 40.00
FFADW Dave Winfield 75.00 200.00
FFAFL Francisco Lindor 20.00 50.00
FFAFM Felix Millan 5.00 12.00
FFAGM Gary Matthews 3.00 8.00
FFAGP Gary Pettis 3.00 8.00
FFAHA Hank Aaron 300.00 500.00
FFAHB Homer Bush 3.00 8.00
FFAHL Hector Lopez 5.00 12.00
FFAJA Jose Altuve 30.00 80.00
FFAJB Jim Bouton 8.00 20.00
FFAJCO Joey Cora 8.00 20.00
FFAJLE Jim Leyland 12.00 30.00
FFAJM Jose Mesa 5.00 12.00
FFAJP Jim Perry 8.00 20.00
FFAJT John Thorn 3.00 8.00
FFAJTO Joe Torre 25.00 60.00
FFAKA Kevin Appier 3.00 8.00
FFAKB Kris Bryant 40.00 100.00
FFAKF Keith Foulke 6.00 15.00
FFALC Luis Castillo 3.00 8.00
FFAMB Marty Barrett 3.00 8.00
FFAMK Michael Kay 12.00 30.00
FFAML Michael Lewis 4.00 10.00
FFAMS Matt Stairs 4.00 10.00
FFAMST Mike Stanton 6.00 15.00
FFAMT Mike Trout 500.00 800.00
FFAMTI Mike Timlin 4.00 10.00
FFAOM Orlando Merced 3.00 8.00
FFAPG Phil Garner 6.00 15.00
FFAPN Pat Neshek 3.00 8.00
FFARA Rich Aurilia 3.00 8.00
FFARD Rafael Devers 25.00 60.00
FFARF Roy Face EXCH 6.00 15.00
FFARH Rhys Hoskins 15.00 40.00
FFARN Robb Nen 3.00 8.00
FFARP Rico Petrocelli 5.00 12.00
FFASK Sandy Koufax 300.00 600.00
FFASO Shohei Ohtani 150.00 400.00
FFASS Shannon Stewart 3.00 8.00
FFATB Tom Browning 3.00 8.00
FFATL Tony La Russa 12.00 30.00
FFATP Troy Percival 5.00 12.00
FFATS Ted Simmons 40.00 100.00
FFATS Terry Steinbach 3.00 8.00
FFAVR Victor Robles 25.00 60.00
FFAWB Wally Backman 10.00 25.00
FFAWW Willie Wilson 6.00 15.00

2018 Topps Archives Rookie History

STATED ODDS 1:12 HOBBY
SP STATED ODDS 1:240 HOBBY
*PURPLE/150: 1.2X TO 3X BASE
*PURPLE SP/150: .4X TO 1X BASE SP
*GREEN/99: 1.5X TO 4X BASE
*GREEN SP/99: .4X TO 1X BASE SP
*BLUE/50: 5X TO 12X BASE
*BLUE SP/50: .5X TO 1.2X BASE SP
8 Don Mattingly 1.00 2.50
4T Jeff Bagwell .40 1.00
98 Derek Jeter SP 20.00 50.00
116 Ozzie Smith .60 1.50
123 Sandy Koufax SP 10.00 25.00
126 Jim Palmer .40 1.00
128 Hank Aaron SP 10.00 25.00
164 Roberto Clemente SP 12.00 30.00
170 Bo Jackson .50 1.25
201 Al Kaline .50 1.25
223 Robin Yount .50 1.25
247 Mike Piazza .50 1.25
260 Reggie Jackson .40 1.00
316 Willie McCovey .40 1.00
333 Chipper Jones .50 1.25
382 John Smoltz .50 1.25
414 Frank Thomas .50 1.25
456 Dave Winfield .40 1.00
557 Pedro Martinez .40 1.00
661 Bryce Harper .75 2.00
726 Ichiro SP 8.00 20.00
779 Tom Glavine .40 1.00
98T Cal Ripken Jr. 1.50 4.00
UH240 Clayton Kershaw 1.00 2.50
US175 Mike Trout 2.50 6.00

2018 Topps Archives Rookie History Autographs

STATED ODDS 1:268 HOBBY
PRINT RUNS B/WN 20-150 COPIES PER
EXCHANGE DEADLINE 7/31/2020
RHAAK Al Kaline/125 50.00 120.00
RHABJ Bo Jackson/99 50.00 120.00
RHABR Brooks Robinson
RHACB Craig Biggio/99 25.00 60.00
RHACJ Chipper Jones/25 125.00 300.00
RHACRJ Cal Ripken Jr./30 75.00 200.00
RHADE Dennis Eckersley/99 10.00 25.00
RHADG Dwight Gooden/150 20.00 50.00
RHADJ Derek Jeter
RHADM Don Mattingly/150 40.00 100.00
RHADW Dave Winfield/99 25.00 60.00
RHAFT Frank Thomas/99 40.00 100.00
RHAGS Gary Sheffield/150 10.00 25.00
RHAHA Hank Aaron
RHAI Ichiro/20 200.00 500.00
RHAJB Jeff Bagwell/99 30.00 80.00
RHAJD Johnny Damon/150 10.00 25.00
RHAJP Jim Palmer EXCH 20.00 50.00
RHAJS John Smoltz/150 10.00 25.00
RHAMP Mike Piazza/20 60.00 150.00
RHAMT Mike Trout
RHAOS Ozzie Smith/99 25.00 60.00
RHAPM Pedro Martinez
RHARA Roberto Alomar/99 25.00 60.00
RHARJ Reggie Jackson/30 75.00 200.00
RHARY Robin Yount/99 40.00 100.00
RHASK Sandy Koufax
RHATG Tom Glavine/150 12.00 30.00
RHATR Tim Raines/125 20.00 50.00

2018 Topps Archives The Sandlot

COMPLETE SET (11) 10.00 25.00
STATED ODDS 1:8 HOBBY
*GREEN/99: .75X TO 2X BASIC
*BLUE/25: 1.5X TO 4X BASIC
SLH Hercules 1.25 3.00
SLAM Yeah-Yeah McClennan 1.25 3.00
SLBJR Benny Rodriguez 1.25 3.00
SLBW Grover Weeks 1.25 3.00
SLHP Ham Porter 1.25 3.00
SLKD Kenny DeNunez 1.25 3.00
SLMP Squints Palledorous 1.25 3.00
SLSS Scotty Smalls 1.25 3.00
SLTIM Timmy Timmons 1.25 3.00
SLTOM Tommy Timmons 1.25 3.00
SLWP Wendy Peffercorn 1.25 3.00

2018 Topps Archives The Sandlot Autographs

STATED ODDS 1:152 HOBBY
EXCHANGE DEADLINE 7/31/2020
*SILVER/99: .5X TO 1.2X BASIC
*BLUE/25: .75X TO 2X BASIC
SLABW Grant Gelt 12.00 30.00
Bertram Grover Weeks
SLAKD Brandon Adams 15.00 40.00
Kenny DeNunez
SLAMS Mrs. Smalls 60.00 150.00
SLASS Scotty Smalls 30.00 80.00
SLAWP Wendy Peffercorn 40.00 100.00
SLAYYM Marty York 15.00 40.00
Alan Yeah-Yeah McClennan
SLADME David Mickey Evans 20.00 50.00
SLAHHP Ham Porter 50.00 120.00
SLAMSP Squints Palledorous 25.00 60.00
SLATIM Victor DiMattia 12.00 30.00
Timmy Timmons
SLATOM Shane Obedzinski 12.00 30.00
Tommy Timmons

2019 Topps Archives

COMP.SET w/o SP's (300) 30.00 80.00
1 Derek Jeter .60 1.50
2 Patrick Corbin .20 .50
3 Max Scherzer .25 .60
4 Michael Chavis RC .40 1.00
5 Anthony Rizzo .40 1.00
6 Rhys Hoskins .30 .75
7 Roberto Alomar .20 .50
8 Elvis Andrus .20 .50
9 Chance Adams RC .25 .60
10 Matt Duffy .15 .40
11 Nicholas Castellanos .25 .60
12 Hunter Renfroe .15 .40
13 Austin Riley RC 1.25 3.00
14 Vladimir Guerrero Jr. RC 1.50 4.00
15 Carlton Fisk .20 .50
16 Taijuan Walker .15 .40
17 Ozzie Albies .25 .60
18 Freddie Freeman .30 .75
19 Corey Kluber .20 .50
20 Duke Snider .20 .50
21 Kevin Kramer RC .30 .75
22 Starling Marte .20 .50
23 Bob Lemon .20 .50
24 Ted Williams .50 1.25
25 Yusei Kikuchi RC .40 1.00
26 Justin Verlander .25 .60
27 Cavan Biggio RC 1.25 3.00
28 Reggie Jackson .20 .50
29 Vladimir Guerrero .20 .50
30 Robinson Cano .20 .50
31 Ramon Laureano RC .50 1.25
32 Jose Urena .15 .40
33 Max Muncy .20 .50
34 Rowdy Tellez RC .40 1.00
35 Bo Jackson .25 .60
36 Justin Smoak .15 .40
37 Bruce Sutter .20 .50
38 Gregory Polanco .20 .5
39 Pee Wee Reese .20 .5
40 Raisel Iglesias .15 .4
41 Trey Mancini .20 .5
42 Ian Desmond .15 .4
43 Gary Carter .20 .5
44 Jackie Robinson .25 .6
45 Orlando Cepeda .20 .5
46 Jose Berrios .20 .5
47 Carlos Correa .25 .6
48 Kyle Schwarber .25 .6
49 Hunter Dozier .15 .4
50 Mookie Betts .40 1.0
51 Clayton Kershaw .50 1.2
52 Red Schoendienst .20 .5
53 Keston Hiura RC .75 2.0
54 Kyle Seager .15 .4
55 Buster Posey .30 .7
56 Luis Urias RC .40 1.0
57 Trevor Bauer .25 .6
58 Ryan Borucki RC .25 .6
59 Albert Pujols .30 .7
60 Eddie Murray .20 .5
61 Jim Thome .20 .5
62 Lefty Grove .20 .5
63 Eugenio Suarez .20 .5
64 Don Larsen .15 .4
65 Wil Myers .15 .4
66 Rod Carew .20 .5
67 Goose Gossage .20 .5
68 Edwin Diaz .20 .5
69 Yadier Molina .25 .6
70 Jeimer Candelario .15 .4
71 Harrison Bader .20 .5
72 Alex Avila .20 .5
73 Andrew McCutchen .25 .6
74 Byron Buxton .20 .5
75 Fernando Tatis Jr. RC 6.00 15.0
76 Larry Doby .20 .5
77 Josh Hader .15 .4
78 Hank Aaron .50 1.2
79 Starlin Castro .15 .4
80 Ronald Guzman .15 .4
81 Dylan Bundy .20 .5
82 Dee Gordon .15 .4
83 Mike Trout 1.25 3.0
84 Gleyber Torres .50 1.2
85 Jorge Posada .20 .5
86 Sean Manaea .15 .4
87 Randy Johnson .25 .6
88 Chipper Jones .25 .6
89 Whitey Ford .20 .5
90 Alex Rodriguez .30 .7
91 Kyle Wright RC .40 1.0
92 Blake Treinen .15 .4
93 Cole Tucker RC .40 1.0
94 Johnny Bench .25 .6
95 Hoyt Wilhelm .20 .5
96 Lucas Giolito .20 .5
97 Bob Gibson .20 .5
98 Jake Bauers RC .40 1.0
99 Jake Cave RC .30 .7
100 Ronald Acuna Jr. 1.25 3.0
101 Shohei Ohtani .30 .7
102 Mel Ott .25 .6
103 Scooter Gennett .20 .5
104 Paul Goldschmidt .25 .6
105 Matt Olson .15 .4
106 Lou Boudreau .20 .5
107 Bernie Williams .20 .5
108 Catfish Hunter .20 .5
109 Andy Pettitte .20 .5
110 Jon Duplantier RC .25 .6
111 Brandon Lowe RC .40 1.0
112 Maikel Franco .20 .5
113 Max Kepler .20 .5
114 Early Wynn .20 .5
115 Lorenzo Cain .15 .4
116 Matt Boyd .15 .4
117 Francisco Arcia RC .40 1.0
118 Roger Maris .25 .6
119 Juan Soto .75 2.0
120 David Peralta .15 .4
121 Tony Gwynn .25 .6
122 Sandy Koufax .50 1.2
123 Evan Longoria .20 .5
124 Eddie Rosario .20 .5
125 Mariano Rivera .30 .7
126 Chris Shaw RC .40 1.0
127 Jim Bunning .20 .5
128 Ken Griffey Jr. .50 1.2
129 Joey Gallo .20 .5
130 Nolan Ryan .75 2.0
131 Adalberto Mondesi .20 .5
132 Jesse Winker .15 .4
133 Nick Senzel RC .75 2.0
134 Brandon Belt .20 .5
135 Kevin Pillar .15 .4
136 Ty Cobb .40 1.0
137 Marcus Stroman .20 .5
138 Lewis Brinson .15 .4
139 Joey Rickard .15 .4
140 Carter Kieboom RC .40 1.0
141 Touki Toussaint RC .30 .7
142 Deion Sanders .20 .5
143 Rougned Odor .20 .5
144 Gil Hodges .20 .5
145 Hideki Matsui .25 .6
146 Kyle Hendricks .25 .6
147 Rafael Devers .30 .7
148 Chris Sale .25 .6
149 Frank Thomas .25 .6
150 Ichiro .30 .7

151 Al Kaline .25 .60
152 Walker Buehler .30 .75
153 Jeff Bagwell .20 .50
154 Stephen Piscotty .15 .40
155 Michael Kopech RC .50 1.25
156 Blake Snell .20 .50
157 Charlie Blackmon .25 .60
158 Richie Ashburn .20 .50
159 Brad Keller RC .25 .60
160 Josh James RC .40 1.00
161 Andrelton Simmons .15 .40
162 Mitch Haniger .20 .50
163 Shane Greene .15 .40
164 Ivan Rodriguez .20 .50
165 Christy Mathewson .25 .60
166 Willie Stargell .20 .50
167 Tommy Pham .15 .40
168 Luis Severino .20 .50
169 Zack Greinke .20 .50
170 Edwin Encarnacion .25 .60
171 Eloy Jimenez RC 1.00 2.50
172 Steven Duggar RC .30 .75
173 Ryne Sandberg .50 1.25
174 George Springer .20 .50
175 Todd Helton .20 .50
176 Bob Feller .20 .50
177 Josh Donaldson .20 .50
178 Thurman Munson .25 .60
179 Nolan Arenado .30 .75
180 Manny Margot .15 .40
181 Aaron Judge .60 1.50
182 Enos Slaughter .20 .50
183 Tim Anderson .25 .60
184 Danny Jansen RC .25 .60
185 Jameson Taillon .20 .50
186 George Kell .20 .50
187 Enyel De Los Santos RC .25 .60
188 Cody Bellinger .50 1.25
189 Phil Rizzuto .20 .50
190 Hal Newhouser .20 .50
191 Eric Hosmer .20 .50
192 DJ Stewart RC .30 .75
193 Javier Baez .30 .75
194 Christian Yelich .30 .75
195 Tony Perez .20 .50
196 Salvador Perez .20 .50
197 Andrew Benintendi .25 .60
198 Colin Moran .15 .40
199 Jacob deGrom .25 .60
200 Bryce Harper .40 1.00
201 Babe Ruth .60 1.50
202 Kolby Allard RC .40 1.00
203 Ryan O'Hearn RC .25 .60
204 Jeff McNeil RC .60 1.50
205 Yonder Alonso .15 .40
206 Carl Yastrzemski .40 1.00
207 Trea Turner .20 .50
208 Aaron Sanchez .20 .50
209 Manny Machado .25 .60
210 George Brett .50 1.25
211 J.D. Martinez .25 .60
212 Robin Roberts .20 .50
213 Cal Quantrill RC .25 .60
214 Whit Merrifield .25 .60
215 Tris Speaker .20 .50
216 Nate Lowe RC .30 .75
217 Xander Bogaerts .25 .60
218 Ernie Banks .25 .60
219 Don Sutton .20 .50
220 Tim Raines .20 .50
221 Justus Sheffield RC .40 1.00
222 Pete Alonso RC 2.00 5.00
223 Jesus Aguilar .15 .40
224 Gary Sanchez .25 .60
225 Kris Bryant .30 .75
226 Steve Carlton .20 .50
227 Rickey Henderson .25 .60
228 Trevor Story .25 .60
229 Brian Anderson .15 .40
230 J.P. Crawford .15 .40
231 Ralph Kiner .20 .50
232 Victor Robles .30 .75
233 Dizzy Dean .20 .50
234 Monte Irvin .20 .50
235 Rogers Hornsby .20 .50
236 Miguel Cabrera .25 .60
237 Fergie Jenkins .20 .50
238 Joey Votto .25 .60
239 Willie McCovey .20 .50
240 Christin Stewart RC .30 .75
241 Dansby Swanson .25 .60
242 Zack Cozart .15 .40
243 Juan Marichal .20 .50
244 Dakota Hudson RC .30 .75
245 Miguel Andujar .25 .60
246 Franmil Reyes .15 .40
247 Bobby Doerr .20 .50
248 Jose Altuve .20 .50
249 Johnny Mize .20 .50
250 Roberto Clemente .60 1.50
251 Willians Astudillo RC .25 .60
252 Carlos Santana .20 .50
253 Aaron Nola .20 .50
254 Kevin Kiermaier .20 .50
255 Eddie Mathews .25 .60
256 Lourdes Gurriel Jr. .20 .50
257 Carlos Martinez .20 .50
258 John Smoltz .25 .60
259 David Dahl .15 .40
260 Josh Bell .20 .50
261 Chris Davis .15 .40
262 Honus Wagner .25 .60
263 Willy Adames .15 .40
264 Don Mattingly .50 1.25
265 Sandy Alcantara .15 .40
266 Harmon Killebrew .25 .60
267 Corey Seager .25 .60
268 Jorge Polanco .15 .40
269 Bryse Wilson RC .30 .75
270 Brandon Nimmo .20 .50
271 Jose Abreu .25 .60
272 Mike Piazza .25 .60
273 Corbin Burnes RC .40 1.00
274 Ozzie Smith .30 .75
275 Joe Morgan .20 .50
276 Alex Bregman .25 .60
277 Warren Spahn .20 .50
278 Jake Lamb .20 .50
279 Orlando Arcia .15 .40
280 Nick Markakis .20 .50
281 Lou Gehrig .50 1.25
282 Kyle Tucker RC .50 1.25
283 Brandon Crawford .20 .50
284 Nomar Mazara .15 .40
285 David Ortiz .25 .60
286 Matt Chapman .25 .60
287 Paul DeJong .25 .60
288 Justin Upton .20 .50
289 Sammy Sosa .25 .60
290 Cedric Mullins RC .40 1.00
291 Nomar Garciaparra .20 .50
292 Griffin Canning RC .40 1.00
293 Noah Syndergaard .20 .50
294 Billy Hamilton .20 .50
295 Robin Yount .25 .60
296 Joe Panik .20 .50
297 Roger Clemens .30 .75
298 Jose Ramirez .20 .50
299 Mychal Givens .15 .40
300 Francisco Lindor .25 .60
301 Aaron Judge AS 1.50 4.00
302 Francisco Lindor AS .60 1.50
303 Javier Baez AS .75 2.00
304 Jacob deGrom AS .60 1.50
305 Chris Sale AS .60 1.50
306 Christian Yelich AS .75 2.00
307 Nolan Arenado AS .75 2.00
308 Mookie Betts AS 1.00 2.50
309 Freddie Freeman AS .75 2.00
310 Mike Trout AS 3.00 8.00
311 Derek Jeter HL 1.50 4.00
312 Miguel Cabrera HL .60 1.50
313 Josh Hader HL .40 1.00
314 Juan Soto HL 2.00 5.00
315 Ichiro HL .75 2.00
316 Shohei Ohtani HL .75 2.00
317 Mariano Rivera HL .75 2.00
318 Kris Bryant HL .75 2.00
319 Francisco Lindor HL .60 1.50
320 Ronald Acuna Jr. HL 3.00 8.00
321 Eloy Jimenez 1.50 4.00
322 Michael Kopech .75 2.00
323 Rowdy Tellez .60 1.50
324 Vladimir Guerrero Jr. 2.50 6.00
325 Luis Urias .60 1.50
326 Justus Sheffield .60 1.50
327 Jake Bauers .60 1.50
328 Yusei Kikuchi .60 1.50
329 Kyle Wright .60 1.50
330 Pete Alonso 3.00 8.00

2019 Topps Archives Blue

*BLUE: 6X TO 15X BASIC
*BLUE RC: 4X TO 10X BASIC RC
STATED ODDS 1:78 HOBBY
STATED PRINT RUN 25 SER.#'d SETS

2019 Topps Archives Purple

*PURPLE: 4X TO 10X BASIC
*PURPLE RC: 2.5X TO 6X BASIC RC
STATED ODDS 1:30 HOBBY
STATED PRINT RUN 175 SER.#'d SETS

2019 Topps Archives Silver

*SILVER: 5X TO 12X BASIC
*SILVER RC: 3X TO 8X BASIC RC
STATED ODDS 1:53 HOBBY
STATED PRINT RUN 99 SER.#'d SETS

2019 Topps Archives '58 Photo Variations

STATED ODDS 1:207 HOBBY
1 Derek Jeter 12.00 30.00
14 Vladimir Guerrero Jr. 12.00 30.00
50 Mookie Betts 5.00 12.00
100 Ronald Acuna Jr. 15.00 40.00

2019 Topps Archives '75 Photo Variations

STATED ODDS 1:207 HOBBY
101 Shohei Ohtani 10.00 25.00
119 Juan Soto 12.00 30.00
200 Bryce Harper 10.00 25.00

2019 Topps Archives '93 Photo Variations

STATED ODDS 1:207 HOBBY
201 Babe Ruth 8.00 20.00
225 Kris Bryant 10.00 25.00
300 Francisco Lindor 8.00 20.00

2019 Topps Archives '75 Minis

STATED ODDS 1:78 HOBBY
75M1 Shohei Ohtani 4.00 10.00
75M2 Ichiro 4.00 10.00
75M3 Nolan Arenado 4.00 10.00
75M4 Enyel De Los Santos 2.00 5.00
75M5 Javier Baez 4.00 10.00
75M6 Jim Bunning 2.50 6.00
75M7 Chris Shaw 3.00 8.00
75M8 Matt Olson 2.00 5.00
75M9 George Kell 2.50 6.00
75M10 Caffish Hunter 2.50 6.00
75M11 Max Kepler 2.50 6.00
75M12 Mel Ott 3.00 8.00
75M13 David Peralta 2.00 5.00
75M14 Lorenzo Cain 2.00 5.00
75M15 Sandy Koufax 6.00 15.00
75M16 Deion Sanders 2.50 6.00
75M17 Eddie Rosario 2.50 6.00
75M18 Walker Buehler 4.00 10.00
75M19 Maikel Franco 2.50 6.00
75M20 Eric Hosmer 2.50 6.00
75M21 Jesse Winker 2.00 5.00
75M22 Matt Boyd 2.00 5.00
75M23 Brandon Lowe 3.00 8.00
75M24 Tommy Pham 2.00 5.00
75M25 Jacob deGrom 3.00 8.00
75M26 Kyle Hendricks 3.00 8.00
75M27 Christian Yelich 4.00 10.00
75M28 Richie Ashburn 2.50 6.00
75M29 Eloy Jimenez 8.00 20.00
75M30 Hal Newhouser 2.50 6.00
75M31 Willie Stargell 2.50 6.00
75M32 Charlie Blackmon 2.50 6.00
75M33 Bernie Williams 2.50 6.00
75M34 Zack Greinke 2.50 6.00
75M35 Aaron Judge 8.00 20.00
75M36 Tony Gwynn 3.00 8.00
75M37 Roger Maris 3.00 8.00
75M38 Tony Perez 2.50 6.00
75M39 Christy Mathewson 3.00 8.00
75M40 Salvador Perez 2.50 6.00
75M41 Cody Bellinger 6.00 15.00
75M42 Joey Gallo 2.50 6.00
75M43 Early Wynn 2.50 6.00
75M44 Danny Jansen 2.00 5.00
75M45 Lewis Brinson 2.00 5.00
75M46 Scooter Gennett 2.50 6.00
75M47 Adalberto Mondesi 2.50 6.00
75M48 George Springer 2.50 6.00
75M49 Ty Cobb 5.00 12.00
75M50 Bryce Harper 5.00 12.00
75M51 Thurman Munson 3.00 8.00
75M52 Edwin Encarnacion 3.00 8.00
75M53 Nolan Ryan 10.00 25.00
75M54 Rougned Odor 2.50 6.00
75M55 Brandon Belt 2.50 6.00
75M56 Nick Senzel 6.00 15.00
75M57 Brad Keller 2.00 5.00
75M58 Steven Duggar 2.50 6.00
75M59 Paul Goldschmidt 3.00 8.00
75M60 Colin Moran 2.00 5.00
75M61 Stephen Piscotty 2.00 5.00
75M62 Francisco Arcia 3.00 8.00
75M63 DJ Stewart 2.50 6.00
75M64 Kevin Pillar 2.00 5.00
75M65 Enos Slaughter 2.50 6.00
75M66 Shane Greene 2.00 5.00
75M67 Al Kaline 3.00 8.00
75M68 Ivan Rodriguez 2.50 6.00
75M69 Manny Margot 2.00 5.00
75M70 Todd Helton 2.50 6.00
75M71 Gil Hodges 2.50 6.00
75M72 Ryne Sandberg 6.00 15.00
75M73 Rafael Devers 4.00 10.00
75M74 Phil Rizzuto 2.50 6.00
75M75 Jameson Taillon 2.50 6.00
75M76 Chris Sale 3.00 8.00
75M77 Frank Thomas 3.00 8.00
75M78 Blake Snell 2.50 6.00
75M79 Josh Donaldson 2.50 6.00
75M80 Marcus Stroman 2.50 6.00
75M81 Andy Pettitte 2.50 6.00
75M82 Michael Kopech 4.00 10.00
75M83 Hideki Matsui 3.00 8.00
75M84 Carter Kieboom 3.00 8.00
75M85 Touki Toussaint 2.50 6.00
75M86 Luis Severino 2.50 6.00
75M87 Jeff Bagwell 2.50 6.00
75M88 Mitch Haniger 2.50 6.00
75M89 Josh James 3.00 8.00
75M90 Ken Griffey Jr. 6.00 15.00
75M91 Lou Boudreau 2.50 6.00
75M92 Evan Longoria 2.50 6.00
75M93 Tim Anderson 3.00 8.00
75M94 Mariano Rivera 4.00 10.00
75M95 Andrew Benintendi 3.00 8.00
75M96 Andrelton Simmons 2.00 5.00
75M97 Bob Feller 2.50 6.00
75M98 Jon Duplantier 2.00 5.00
75M99 Joey Rickard 2.00 5.00
75M100 Juan Soto 10.00 25.00

2019 Topps Archives '75 Topps Signature Omission

*NO SIG: 8X TO 20X BASIC
*NO SIG RC: 5X TO 12X BASIC RC
STATED ODDS 1:207 HOBBY

2019 Topps Archives '78 Record Breakers Autographs

STATED ODDS 1:10,729 HOBBY
STATED PRINT RUN 25 SER.#'d SETS
EXCHANGE DEADLINE 7/31/2021
RBAFL Francisco Lindor 20.00 50.00
RBAJS Juan Soto 100.00 250.00
RBARAJ Ronald Acuna Jr. 125.00 300.00

2019 Topps Archives '93 Topps Gold

*NO SIG: 8X TO 20X BASIC
*NO SIG RC: 5X TO 12X BASIC RC
STATED ODDS 1:207 HOBBY

2019 Topps Archives '94 Future Stars

COMPLETE SET (25) 20.00 50.00
STATED ODDS 1:12 HOBBY
94FS1 Derek Jeter 1.50 4.00
94FS2 Juan Soto 2.00 5.00
94FS3 Vladimir Guerrero Jr. 2.50 6.00
94FS4 Justus Sheffield .60 1.50
94FS5 Miles Mikolas .60 1.50
94FS6 Pete Alonso 3.00 8.00
94FS7 Alex Rodriguez .75 2.00
94FS8 Shohei Ohtani .75 2.00
94FS9 Mike Piazza .60 1.50
94FS10 Yusei Kikuchi .60 1.50
94FS11 Carter Kieboom .60 1.50
94FS12 Lourdes Gurriel Jr. .50 1.25
94FS13 Willy Adames .40 1.00
94FS14 Christin Stewart .50 1.25
94FS15 Ronald Acuna Jr. 3.00 8.00
94FS16 Austin Meadows .50 1.25
94FS17 Luis Urias .60 1.50
94FS18 Kyle Tucker .75 2.00
94FS19 Scott Kingery .50 1.25
94FS20 Kyle Wright .60 1.50
94FS21 Rowdy Tellez .60 1.50
94FS22 Amed Rosario .50 1.25
94FS23 Michael Kopech .75 2.00
94FS24 Nick Senzel 1.25 3.00
94FS25 Eloy Jimenez 1.50 4.00

2019 Topps Archives '94 Future Stars Autographs

STATED ODDS 1:539 HOBBY
PRINT RUNS B/WN 50-99 COPIES PER
EXCHANGE DEADLINE 7/31/2021
*BLUE/25: .5X TO 1.2X BASIC
94FSAAM Austin Meadows/99 10.00 25.00
94FSAAR Alex Rodriguez
94FSADR Dereck Rodriguez/99 6.00 15.00
94FSAJS Juan Soto/50 40.00 100.00
94FSAJSH Justus Sheffield/99 8.00 20.00
94FSAKW Kyle Wright/99 8.00 20.00
94FSALGJ Lourdes Gurriel Jr./99 10.00 25.00
94FSALU Luis Urias/99 8.00 20.00
94FSAMK Michael Kopech/99 10.00 25.00
94FSAMM Miles Mikolas/99 8.00 20.00
94FSANS Nick Senzel/99 20.00 50.00
94FSARAJ Ronald Acuna Jr./50 100.00 250.00
94FSART Rowdy Tellez/99 8.00 20.00
94FSASK Scott Kingery/99 6.00 15.00
94FSASO Shohei Ohtani
94FSAWA Willy Adames/99 5.00 12.00

2019 Topps Archives 50th Anniversary of the Montreal Expos

STATED ODDS 1:24 HOBBY
*BLUE/150: .5X TO 1.2X BASIC
*GREEN/99: .5X TO 1.2X BASIC
*GOLD/50: 1.2X TO 3X BASIC
MTLAD Andre Dawson 1.25 3.00
MTLAG Andres Galarraga 1.25 3.00
MTLBC Bartolo Colon 1.00 2.50
MTLBG Bill Gullickson 1.00 2.50
MTLCF Cliff Floyd 1.00 2.50
MTLCL Coco Laboy 1.00 2.50
MTLDM Dennis Martinez 1.00 2.50
MTLJF Jeff Fassero 1.00 2.50
MTLJR Jeff Reardon 1.00 2.50
MTLJV Javier Vazquez 1.00 2.50
MTLJVI Jose Vidro 1.00 2.50
MTLKH Ken Hill 1.00 2.50
MTLMA Moises Alou 1.00 2.50
MTLMG Marquis Grissom 1.00 2.50
MTLMW Maury Wills 1.00 2.50
MTLPM Pedro Martinez 1.25 3.00
MTLRJ Randy Johnson 1.50 4.00
MTLRW Rondell White 1.00 2.50
MTLSR Steve Rogers 1.00 2.50
MTLTB Tim Burke 1.00 2.50
MTLTR Tim Raines 1.25 3.00
MTLTW Tim Wallach 1.00 2.50
MTLVG Vladimir Guerrero 6.00 15.00

2019 Topps Archives 50th Anniversary of the Montreal Expos Autographs

STATED ODDS 1:54 HOBBY
EXCHANGE DEADLINE 7/31/2021
*GREEN/99: .5X TO 1.2X BASIC
*GOLD/50: .6X TO 1.5X BASIC
MTLAAD Andre Dawson 20.00 50.00
MTLAAG Andres Galarraga 8.00 20.00
MTLABC Bartolo Colon 8.00 20.00
MTLABG Bill Gullickson 5.00 12.00
MTLACF Cliff Floyd 5.00 12.00
MTLACL Coco Laboy 6.00 15.00
MTLADM Dennis Martinez 8.00 20.00
MTLAJF Jeff Fassero 3.00 8.00
MTLAJR Jeff Reardon 3.00 8.00
MTLAJVI Jose Vidro 3.00 8.00
MTLAKH Ken Hill 3.00 8.00
MTLAMG Marquis Grissom 4.00 10.00
MTLAMW Maury Wills 10.00 25.00
MTLAPM Pedro Martinez 60.00 150.00
MTLARJ Randy Johnson 300.00 500.00
MTLARW Rondell White 4.00 10.00
MTLASR Steve Rogers 3.00 8.00
MTLATB Tim Burke 3.00 8.00
MTLATR Tim Raines 20.00 50.00
MTLATW Tim Wallach 5.00 12.00
MTLAVG Vladimir Guerrero 25.00 60.00

2019 Topps Archives Coins

INSERTED IN RETAIL PACKS
*SKY BLUE: 4X TO 10X BASIC
C1 Shohei Ohtani .60 1.50
C2 Francisco Lindor .50 1.25
C3 Kolby Allard .50 1.25
C4 Juan Soto 1.50 4.00
C5 Luis Urias .50 1.25
C6 George Springer .40 1.00
C7 Aaron Judge 1.25 3.00
C8 Rowdy Tellez .50 1.25
C9 Jose Ramirez .40 1.00
C10 Mike Trout 2.50 6.00
C11 Clayton Kershaw 1.00 2.50
C12 Mookie Betts .75 2.00
C13 Justus Sheffield .50 1.25
C14 J.D. Martinez .50 1.25
C15 Christian Yelich .60 1.50
C16 Kris Bryant .60 1.50
C17 Kyle Tucker .60 1.50
C18 Max Scherzer .50 1.25
C19 Ozzie Albies .50 1.25
C20 Rhys Hoskins .60 1.50
C21 Carlos Correa .50 1.25
C22 Michael Kopech .60 1.50
C23 Gleyber Torres 1.00 2.50
C24 Jacob deGrom .50 1.25
C25 Ronald Acuna Jr. 2.50 6.00

2019 Topps Archives Fan Favorites Autographs

STATED ODDS 1:25 HOBBY
EXCHANGE DEADLINE 7/31/2021
*PURPLE/150: .5X TO 1.2X BASE
*SILVER/99: .6X TO 1.5X BASE
*BLUE/25: .75X TO 2X BASE
FFAAC Alex Cora 15.00 40.00
FFABS Bud Selig 30.00 80.00
FFABVW Brodie Van Wagenen GM 10.00 25.00
FFACK Carter Kieboom 5.00 12.00
FFACR Cookie Rojas 4.00 10.00
FFADJA Dr. James Andrews 12.00 30.00
FFADO David Ortiz 30.00 80.00
FFAFG Eric Gagne 8.00 20.00
FFAEJ Eloy Jimenez 25.00 60.00
FFAFF Freddie Freeman 15.00 40.00
FFAFL Francisco Lindor 12.00 30.00
FFAFS Fred Stanley 4.00 10.00
FFAGT Gorman Thomas 4.00 10.00
FFAHA Hank Aaron 300.00 500.00
FFAJD Jermaine Dye 6.00 15.00
FFAJDA Jody Davis 4.00 10.00
FFAJG Jonny Gomes 8.00 20.00
FFAJI Jeff Idelson 4.00 10.00
FFAJL Jerry Layne 3.00 8.00
FFAJM Jessica Mendoza 12.00 30.00
FFAJMC Jack McKeon 8.00 20.00
FFAJP Joe Pepitone 6.00 15.00
FFAJPO Jorge Posada EXCH 25.00 60.00
FFAJR Jerry Remy 10.00 25.00
FFAJRE Jeff Reardon 3.00 8.00
FFAJS Juan Soto 40.00 100.00
FFAKB Ken Burns 15.00 40.00
FFAKG Kelly Gruber 5.00 12.00
FFAKGJ Ken Griffey Jr. 300.00 600.00
FFAKT Kevin Tapani 3.00 8.00
FFALD Laz Diaz 3.00 8.00
FFALDI Larry Dierker 3.00 8.00
FFAML Mike Lieberthal 4.00 10.00
FFAMM Mario Mendoza 5.00 12.00
FFAMS Mike Sweeney 3.00 8.00
FFAMT Mike Trout 400.00 800.00
FFANS Nick Senzel 15.00 40.00
FFAPH Pat Hughes ANNC 8.00 20.00
FFARAJ Ronald Acuna Jr. 100.00 250.00
FFARH Rick Honeycutt 3.00 8.00
FFARO Rey Ordonez 3.00 8.00
FFASK Sandy Koufax
FFASS Steve Stone 6.00 15.00
FFASSA Steve Sax 8.00 20.00
FFATM Tino Martinez 12.00 30.00
FFATO Tony Oliva 20.00 50.00
FFATP Tony Perez 20.00 50.00
FFAVGJ Vladimir Guerrero Jr. 30.00 80.00
FFAVGS Vladimir Guerrero 30.00 80.00
FFAVW Vernon Wells 3.00 8.00
FFAWM Whit Merrifield 8.00 20.00

2019 Topps Archives Ichiro Retrospective

STATED ODDS 1:12 HOBBY
SP STATED ODDS 1:240 HOBBY
*BLUE/150: 1.5X TO 4X BASE
*GREEN/99: 2X TO 5X BASE
*GREEN SP/99: .5X TO 1.2X BASE SP
*GOLD/50: 5X TO 12X BASE
*GOLD SP/50: .5X TO 1.2X BASE SP
I1 Ichiro Suzuki SP 4.00 10.00
I2 Ichiro SP 4.00 10.00
I3 Ichiro .40 1.00
I4 Ichiro .40 1.00
I5 Ichiro .40 1.00
I6 Ichiro .40 1.00
I7 Ichiro .40 1.00
I8 Ichiro .40 1.00
I9 Ichiro .40 1.00
I10 Ichiro .40 1.00
I11 Ichiro .40 1.00
I12 Ichiro .40 1.00
I13 Ichiro .40 1.00
I14 Ichiro .40 1.00
I15 Ichiro .40 1.00
I16 Ichiro SP 4.00 10.00

2019 Topps Archives Ichiro Retrospective Autographs

COMMON ICHIRO 500.00 1000.00
STATED ODDS 1:9963 HOBBY
STATED PRINT RUN 5 SER.#'d SETS
EXCHANGE DEADLINE 7/31/2021

2019 Topps Archives Topps Magazine

COMPLETE SET (20) 10.00 25.00
STATED ODDS 1:6 HOBBY
TM1 Mike Trout 2.00 5.00
TM2 Jacob deGrom .40 1.00
TM3 Kris Bryant .50 1.25
TM4 Ozzie Smith .50 1.25
TM5 Ken Griffey Jr. .75 2.00
TM6 Ronald Acuna Jr. 2.00 5.00
TM7 Francisco Lindor .40 1.00
TM8 Cal Ripken Jr. 1.25 3.00
TM9 Juan Soto 1.25 3.00
TM10 Shohei Ohtani .50 1.25
TM11 Jose Ramirez .30 .75
TM12 Anthony Rizzo .60 1.50
TM13 Pedro Martinez .30 .75
TM14 Derek Jeter 1.00 2.50
TM15 Rhys Hoskins .50 1.25
TM16 George Springer .30 .75
TM17 Barry Larkin .30 .75
TM18 Bryce Harper .60 1.50
TM19 Jose Altuve .30 .75
TM20 Aaron Judge 1.00 2.50

2019 Topps Archives Topps Magazine Autographs

STATED ODDS 1:255 HOBBY
PRINT RUNS B/WN 20-150 COPIES PER
EXCHANGE DEADLINE 7/31/2021
*BLUE/25: .5X TO 1.2X BASIC
TMAAJ Aaron Judge/30 100.00 250.00
TMAAR Anthony Rizzo/60 30.00 80.00
TMABL Barry Larkin/70 20.00 50.00
TMACF Carlton Fisk/85 15.00 40.00
TMACK Corey Kluber/150 6.00 15.00
TMACRJ Cal Ripken Jr./50 75.00 200.00
TMACS Chris Sale/85 12.00 30.00
TMADJ Derek Jeter EXCH
TMAFL Francisco Lindor/150 12.00 30.00
TMAGS George Springer/85 15.00 40.00
TMAJA Jose Altuve/70 20.00 50.00
TMAJD Jacob deGrom/150 15.00 40.00
TMAJR Jose Ramirez/150 6.00 15.00
TMAJS Juan Soto/150 40.00 100.00
TMAKB Kris Bryant/60 25.00 60.00
TMAKGJ Ken Griffey Jr./35 200.00 400.00
TMALS Luis Severino/150 6.00 15.00
TMAMM Mark McGwire/50 30.00 80.00
TMAMT Mike Trout/20 500.00 1000.00
TMANS Noah Syndergaard/150 10.00 25.00
TMAOA Ozzie Albies/150 15.00 40.00
TMAOS Ozzie Smith/85 20.00 50.00
TMAPM Pedro Martinez/40 30.00 80.00
TMARA Roberto Alomar/85 10.00 25.00
TMARAJ Ronald Acuna Jr./85 75.00 200.00
TMARH Rhys Hoskins/150 15.00 40.00
TMASO Shohei Ohtani/20 125.00 300.00

2020 Topps Archives

301-325 ODDS 1:8 HOBBY
1 Babe Ruth .60 1.50
2 Paul Goldschmidt .25 .60
3 Charlie Blackmon .25 .60
4 Nick Senzel .25 .60
5 Steve Carlton .20 .50
6 Aristides Aquino RC .50 1.25
7 Shohei Ohtani .30 .75
8 Kyle Schwarber .25 .60
9 Joey Gallo .25 .60
10 Mariano Rivera .30 .75
11 Rickey Henderson .25 .60
12 Marcus Stroman .20 .50
13 Seth Brown RC .25 .60
14 Harmon Killebrew .25 .60
15 Albert Pujols .30 .75
16 Willi Castro RC .40 1.00
17 Jorge Soler .25 .60
18 Dylan Cease RC .50 1.25
19 Pete Alonso .60 1.50
20 Whit Merrifield .25 .60
21 Gary Sanchez .25 .60
22 Marcus Semien .15 .40
23 Francisco Lindor .25 .60
24 Xander Bogaerts .25 .60
25 Jackie Robinson .25 .60
26 Keston Hiura .30 .75
27 Mookie Betts .50 1.25
28 Aaron Hicks .20 .50
29 Robin Yount .25 .60
30 George Brett .50 1.25
31 Alex Bregman .25 .60
32 Al Kaline .25 .60
33 Will Smith .30 .75
34 Brusdar Graterol RC .40 1.00
35 Tim Lincecum .20 .50
36 Shane Bieber .25 .60
37 Kyle Lewis RC 2.00 5.00
38 Jose Altuve .20 .50
39 Michael Brantley .20 .50
40 Sam Hilliard RC .40 1.00
41 Deion Sanders .20 .50
42 Jeff McNeil .20 .50
43 Aaron Civale RC .40 1.00
44 Lucas Giolito .20 .50
45 Bo Bichette RC 2.00 5.00
46 Gary Carter .20 .50
47 Goose Gossage .20 .50
48 J.D. Martinez .25 .60
49 George Kell .20 .50
50 Mike Trout 1.25 3.00
51 Brock Burke RC .25 .60
52 Catfish Hunter .20 .50
53 Lou Boudreau .20 .50
54 Max Muncy .20 .50
55 Jose Berrios .20 .50
56 Vladimir Guerrero Jr. .50 1.25
57 Ozzie Albies .25 .60
58 Tim Anderson .25 .60
59 Will Clark .20 .50
60 Carl Yastrzemski .40 1.00
61 Alex Young RC .25 .60
62 Nomar Garciaparra .20 .50
63 Bryan Reynolds .20 .50
64 Joey Votto .25 .60
65 Sean Murphy RC .40 1.00
66 J.T. Realmuto .25 .60
67 Kenta Maeda .20 .50
68 Jack Flaherty .20 .50
69 Trevor Bauer .25 .60
70 Jim Thome .20 .50
71 Zack Greinke .25 .60
72 Isan Diaz RC .40 1.00
73 Ryne Sandberg .50 1.25
74 Ralph Kiner .20 .50
75 Mike Mussina .20 .50
76 Larry Doby .20 .50
77 Paul DeJong .25 .60
78 Gavin Lux RC 1.50 4.00
79 Matt Chapman .25 .60
80 Ramon Laureano .25 .60
81 Corey Seager .25 .60
82 Luis Aparicio .20 .50
83 Tom Glavine .20 .50
84 Amed Rosario .20 .50
85 Jake Fraley RC .30 .75
86 Raisel Iglesias .15 .40
87 Juan Soto .75 2.00
88 Derek Jeter .60 1.50
89 Nolan Arenado .30 .75
90 Nolan Ryan .75 2.00
91 Jordan Yamamoto RC .30 .75
92 Matt Carpenter .25 .60
93 Mallex Smith .15 .40
94 Charlie Morton .25 .60
95 A.J. Puk RC
96 DJ LeMahieu .25 .60
97 Monte Irvin .20 .50
98 Wade Boggs .20 .50
99 Shin-Soo Choo .20 .50
100 Hank Aaron .50 1.25
101 Ted Williams .50 1.25
102 Bob Gibson .20 .50
103 Mike Clevinger .20 .50
104 Christian Walker .20 .50
105 Chris Paddack .25 .60
106 Tony Gwynn .25 .60
107 Kerry Wood .15 .40
108 Mike Piazza .25 .60
109 Randy Johnson .25 .60
110 Abraham Toro RC .30 .75
111 Nick Solak RC .40 1.00
112 Stephen Piscotty .15 .40
113 Hunter Dozier .15 .40
114 Bob Feller .20 .50
115 Mike Moustakas .20 .50
116 Jacob deGrom .25 .60
117 Shogo Akiyama RC .40 1.00
118 Ernie Banks .25 .60
119 Eloy Jimenez .50 1.25
120 Carlos Correa .25 .60
121 Frank Robinson .20 .50
122 Sandy Koufax .50 1.25
123 Jason Heyward .20 .50
124 Trevor Story .25 .60
125 Mike Schmidt .40 1.00
126 Bobby Bradley RC .30 .75
127 Roberto Alomar .20 .50
128 Fred McGriff .20 .50
129 DJ LeMahieu .25 .60
130 Larry Walker .20 .50
131 Eric Hosmer .20 .50
132 Buster Posey .30 .75
133 Tony Gonsolin RC 1.00 2.50
134 Jon Lester .20 .50
135 Yoshi Tsutsugo RC .30 .75
136 Ty Cobb .40 1.00
137 Eduardo Escobar .15 .40
138 Blake Snell .20 .50
139 Mike Soroka .25 .60
140 Zack Collins RC .30 .75
141 Dustin May RC 1.00 2.50
142 Cal Ripken Jr. .75 2.00
143 Brandon Crawford .20 .50
144 Bo Jackson .25 .60
145 Paul Molitor .25 .60
146 Ketel Marte .20 .50
147 Jesus Luzardo RC .50 1.25
148 Josh Hader .15 .40
149 Roberto Clemente .60 1.50
150 Mo Vaughn .15 .40
151 Jeff Bagwell .20 .50
152 Corey Kluber .20 .50
153 Ken Griffey Jr. .50 1.25
154 George Springer .20 .50
155 Justin Dunn RC .30 .75
156 Clayton Kershaw .50 1.25
157 Daniel Vogelbach .15 .40
158 Brooks Robinson .20 .50
159 Luis Robert RC 5.00 12.00
160 Mauricio Dubon RC .30 .75
161 Justin Upton .20 .50
162 Javier Baez .30 .75
163 Max Scherzer .25 .60
164 David Ortiz .25 .60

165 John Smoltz .25 .60
166 Dave Winfield .20 .50
167 Justin Turner .20 .50
168 Nelson Cruz .25 .60
169 Khris Davis .25 .60
170 Rowdy Tellez .20 .50
171 Adbert Alzolay RC .30 .75
172 Zac Gallen RC .60 1.50
173 Lou Brock .20 .50
174 Trey Mancini .25 .60
175 Sammy Sosa .25 .60
176 Duke Snider .20 .50
177 Hyun-Jin Ryu .20 .50
178 Thurman Munson .25 .60
179 Sandy Alcantara .15 .40
180 Gleyber Torres .50 1.25
181 Matthew Boyd .15 .40
182 Willie Stargell .20 .50
183 Walker Buehler .30 .75
184 Trent Grisham RC 1.00 2.50
185 Fernando Tatis Jr. 1.00 2.50
186 Willie McCovey .20 .50
187 Sheldon Neuse RC .30 .75
188 Josh Bell .20 .50
189 Ivan Rodriguez .20 .50
190 Billy Williams .20 .50
191 Andrew Benintendi .25 .60
192 Shun Yamaguchi RC .30 .75
193 Anthony Rizzo .40 1.00
194 Victor Robles .30 .75
195 Tom Seaver .20 .50
196 Rhys Hoskins .30 .75
197 Danny Jansen .15 .40
198 Dansby Swanson .25 .60
199 Giancarlo Stanton .25 .60
200 Marco Gonzales .15 .40
201 Manny Machado .25 .60
202 Anthony Kay RC .25 .60
203 Anthony Rendon .25 .60
204 Michel Baez RC .25 .60
205 Kyle Seager .15 .40
206 Juan Gonzalez .15 .40
207 Carter Kieboom .25 .60
208 Chris Sale .25 .60
209 Kenley Jansen .20 .50
210 Ralph Kiner .20 .50
211 Starling Marte .20 .50
212 Orlando Cepeda .20 .50
213 Randy Arozarena RC 2.00 5.00
214 Austin Meadows .20 .50
215 Frank Thomas .25 .60
216 Robel Garcia RC .25 .60
217 Cody Bellinger .50 1.25
218 Reggie Jackson .20 .50
219 Rollie Fingers .20 .50
220 Chipper Jones .25 .60
221 John Means .15 .40
222 Yordan Alvarez RC 1.25 3.00
223 Brad Keller .15 .40
224 Andrelton Simmons .15 .40
225 Evan Longoria .20 .50
226 David Wright .20 .50
227 Ryan Howard .20 .50
228 Gerrit Cole .40 1.00
229 Eugenio Suarez .20 .50
230 Michael Chavis .20 .50
231 Whitey Ford .20 .50
232 Willson Contreras .25 .60
233 Rod Carew .20 .50
234 Yadier Molina .25 .60
235 Ichiro .30 .75
236 Bryce Harper .40 1.00
237 Trevor Hoffman .20 .50
238 Jorge Alfaro .15 .40
239 Alan Trammell .20 .50
240 Nico Hoerner RC 1.00 2.50
241 Ronald Acuna Jr. 1.00 2.50
242 Matt Olson .15 .40
243 Edgar Martinez .20 .50
244 Brendan McKay RC .40 1.00
245 Yuli Gurriel .20 .50
246 Kole Calhoun .15 .40
247 Craig Biggio .20 .50
248 Christian Yelich .30 .75
249 Vladimir Guerrero .20 .50
250 Carlton Fisk .20 .50
251 Logan Allen RC .25 .60
252 Noah Syndergaard .25 .60
253 Aaron Nola .25 .60
254 Rougned Odor .20 .50
255 Dennis Eckersley .20 .50
256 Jorge Polanco .20 .50
257 Aroldis Chapman .25 .60
258 Roger Clemens .30 .75
259 Anthony Santander .15 .40
260 Yu Darvish .25 .60
261 Harrison Bader .20 .50
262 Honus Wagner .25 .60
263 Michael Conforto .20 .50
264 Alex Rodriguez .30 .75
265 Ryan McMahon .15 .40
266 Barry Larkin .20 .50
267 Rafael Devers .30 .75
268 Eddie Rosario .20 .50
269 Andres Munoz RC .30 .75
270 Jose Abreu .25 .60
271 Jose Ramirez .20 .50
272 Tim Hudson .20 .50
273 Adrian Morejon RC .25 .60
274 Johnny Bench .25 .60
275 Juan Marichal .20 .50
276 Kevin Newman .20 .50
277 Joe Morgan .20 .50
278 Lourdes Gurriel Jr. .20 .50
279 Miguel Cabrera .25 .60
280 Ryan Braun .20 .50
281 Lou Gehrig .50 1.25
282 Brandon Woodruff .15 .40
283 Johnny Cueto .20 .50
284 Wil Myers .15 .40
285 Andruw Jones .15 .40
286 Cavan Biggio .30 .75
287 Jonathan Villar .15 .40
288 Justin Verlander .25 .60
289 Pedro Martinez .20 .50
290 Jose Urquidy RC .30 .75
291 Andy Pettitte .20 .50
292 Yu Chang RC .40 1.00
293 Aaron Judge .60 1.50
294 Elvis Andrus .20 .50
295 Andre Dawson .20 .50
296 Carlos Santana .20 .50
297 Willie Mays .50 1.25
298 Stephen Strasburg .25 .60
299 Kris Bryant .30 .75
300 Freddie Freeman .30 .75
301 Pete Alonso SP 1.25 3.00
302 Aaron Judge SP 1.25 3.00
303 Mike Trout SP 2.50 6.00
304 Francisco Lindor SP .50 1.25
305 Yordan Alvarez SP 1.50 4.00
306 Shohei Ohtani SP .60 1.50
307 Chris Sale SP .50 1.25
308 David Ortiz SP .50 1.25
309 Noah Syndergaard SP .40 1.00
310 Ernie Banks SP .50 1.25
311 Hank Aaron SP 1.00 2.50
312 Mariano Rivera SP .60 1.50
313 Javier Baez SP .60 1.50
315 Duke Snider SP .40 1.00
316 Randy Johnson SP .50 1.25
317 Pedro Martinez SP .40 1.00
318 Miguel Cabrera SP .50 1.25
319 Ryne Sandberg SP 1.00 2.50
320 CC Sabathia SP .40 1.00
321 Jeff Bagwell SP .40 1.00
322 Roberto Alomar SP .40 1.00
323 John Smoltz SP .50 1.25
324 Steve Carlton SP .40 1.00
325 Mark Teixeira SP .40 1.00

2020 Topps Archives Blue

*BLUE: 6X TO 15X BASIC
*BLUE RC: 4X TO 10X BASIC RC
STATED ODDS 1:83 HOBBY
STATED PRINT RUN 25 SER.#'d SETS
27 Mookie Betts 15.00 40.00
88 Derek Jeter 20.00 50.00
149 Roberto Clemente 15.00 40.00
153 Ken Griffey Jr. 30.00 80.00
159 Luis Robert 100.00 250.00
185 Fernando Tatis Jr. 40.00 100.00

2020 Topps Archives Orange Foil

*ORNGE FOIL: 4X TO 10X BASIC
*ORNGE FOIL RC: 2.5X TO 6X BASIC RC
STATED ODDS 1:265 HOBBY
STATED PRINT RUN 75 SER.#'d SETS

2020 Topps Archives Purple

*PURPLE: 3X TO 8X BASIC
*PURPLE RC: 2X TO 5X BASIC RC
STATED ODDS 1:39 HOBBY
STATED PRINT RUN 175 SER.#'d SETS
27 Mookie Betts 8.00 20.00
153 Ken Griffey Jr. 6.00 15.00
185 Fernando Tatis Jr. 12.00 30.00

2020 Topps Archives Red

*RED: 4X TO 10X BASIC
*RED RC: 2.5X TO 6X BASIC RC
STATED ODDS 1:89 HOBBY
STATED PRINT RUN 75 SER.#'d SETS
27 Mookie Betts 10.00 25.00
149 Roberto Clemente 10.00 25.00
153 Ken Griffey Jr. 8.00 20.00
185 Fernando Tatis Jr. 25.00 60.00

2020 Topps Archives Silver

*SILVER: 4X TO 10X BASIC
*SILVER RC: 2.5X TO 6X BASIC RC
STATED ODDS 1:67 HOBBY
STATED PRINT RUN 99 SER.#'d SETS
27 Mookie Betts 10.00 25.00
149 Roberto Clemente 10.00 25.00
153 Ken Griffey Jr. 8.00 20.00
185 Fernando Tatis Jr. 25.00 60.00

2020 Topps Archives Mega Box Foil

*MEGA FOIL: 5X TO 12X BASIC
*MEGA FOIL RC: 3X TO 8X BASIC RC
INSERTED IN MEGA BOXES
27 Mookie Betts 12.00 30.00
149 Roberto Clemente 12.00 30.00
153 Ken Griffey Jr. 25.00 60.00
159 Luis Robert 75.00 200.00
185 Fernando Tatis Jr. 30.00 80.00

2020 Topps Archives '02 Topps Variations

STATED ODDS 1:265 HOBBY
234 Yadier Molina 5.00 12.00

2020 Topps Archives '55 Topps Black and White Variations

STATED ODDS 1:265 HOBBY
6 Aristides Aquino 3.00 8.00
7 Shohei Ohtani 3.00 8.00
56 Vladimir Guerrero Jr. 5.00 12.00
78 Gavin Lux 6.00 15.00
100 Hank Aaron 5.00 12.00

2020 Topps Archives '55 Topps Image Variations

STATED ODDS 1:100 HOBBY
1 Babe Ruth 8.00 20.00
2 Paul Goldschmidt 3.00 8.00
3 Charlie Blackmon 3.00 8.00
4 Nick Senzel 3.00 8.00
5 Steve Carlton 2.50 6.00
6 Aristides Aquino 4.00 10.00
7 Shohei Ohtani 4.00 10.00
8 Kyle Schwarber 3.00 8.00
9 Joey Gallo 3.00 8.00
10 Mariano Rivera 4.00 10.00
11 Rickey Henderson 3.00 8.00
12 Marcus Stroman 2.50 6.00
13 Seth Brown 2.00 5.00
14 Harmon Killebrew 3.00 8.00
15 Albert Pujols 4.00 10.00
16 Willi Castro 3.00 8.00
17 Jorge Soler 3.00 8.00
18 Dylan Cease 4.00 10.00
19 Pete Alonso 8.00 20.00
20 Whit Merrifield 3.00 8.00
21 Gary Sanchez 3.00 8.00
22 Marcus Semien 2.00 5.00
23 Francisco Lindor 3.00 8.00
24 Xander Bogaerts 3.00 8.00
25 Jackie Robinson 3.00 8.00
26 Keston Hiura 4.00 10.00
27 Mookie Betts 6.00 15.00
28 Aaron Hicks 2.50 6.00
29 Robin Yount 3.00 8.00
30 George Brett 6.00 15.00
31 Alex Bregman 3.00 8.00
32 Al Kaline 3.00 8.00
33 Will Smith 4.00 10.00
34 Brusdar Graterol 3.00 8.00
35 Tim Lincecum 2.50 6.00
36 Shane Bieber 3.00 8.00
37 Kyle Lewis 15.00 40.00
38 Jose Altuve 2.50 6.00
39 Michael Brantley 2.50 6.00
40 Sam Hilliard 3.00 8.00
41 Deion Sanders 2.50 6.00
42 Jeff McNeil 2.50 6.00
43 Aaron Civale 3.00 8.00
44 Lucas Giolito 2.50 6.00
45 Bo Bichette 15.00 40.00
46 Gary Carter 2.50 6.00
47 Goose Gossage 2.50 6.00
48 J.D. Martinez 3.00 8.00
49 George Kell 2.50 6.00
50 Mike Trout 30.00 80.00
51 Brock Burke 2.00 5.00
52 Catfish Hunter 2.50 6.00
53 Lou Boudreau 2.50 6.00
54 Max Muncy 2.50 6.00
55 Jose Berrios 2.50 6.00
56 Vladimir Guerrero Jr. 6.00 15.00
57 Ozzie Albies 3.00 8.00
58 Tim Anderson 3.00 8.00
59 Will Clark 2.50 6.00
60 Carl Yastrzemski 5.00 12.00
61 Alex Young 2.00 5.00
62 Nomar Garciaparra 2.50 6.00
63 Bryan Reynolds 2.50 6.00
64 Joey Votto 3.00 8.00
65 Sean Murphy 3.00 8.00
66 J.T. Realmuto 3.00 8.00
67 Kenta Maeda 2.50 6.00
68 Jack Flaherty 2.50 6.00
69 Trevor Bauer 3.00 8.00
70 Jim Thome 2.50 6.00
71 Zack Greinke 2.50 6.00
72 Isan Diaz 3.00 8.00
73 Ryne Sandberg 6.00 15.00
74 Ralph Kiner 2.50 6.00
75 Mike Mussina 2.50 6.00
76 Larry Doby 2.50 6.00
77 Paul DeJong 3.00 8.00
78 Gavin Lux 12.00 30.00
79 Matt Chapman 3.00 8.00
80 Ramon Laureano 3.00 8.00
81 Corey Seager 3.00 8.00
82 Luis Aparicio 2.50 6.00
83 Tom Glavine 2.50 6.00
84 Amed Rosario 2.50 6.00
85 Jake Fraley 2.50 6.00
86 Raisel Iglesias 2.00 5.00
87 Juan Soto 10.00 25.00
88 Derek Jeter 25.00 60.00
89 Nolan Arenado 4.00 10.00
90 Nolan Ryan 10.00 25.00
91 Jordan Yamamoto 2.50 6.00
92 Matt Carpenter 3.00 8.00
93 Mallex Smith 2.00 5.00
94 Charlie Morton 3.00 8.00
95 A.J. Puk 4.00 10.00
96 DJ LeMahieu 3.00 8.00
97 Monte Irvin 2.50 6.00
98 Wade Boggs 2.50 6.00
99 Shin-Soo Choo 2.50 6.00
100 Hank Aaron 6.00 15.00

2020 Topps Archives '74 Topps Variations

STATED ODDS 1:265 HOBBY
105 Chris Paddack 5.00 12.00
163 Max Scherzer 5.00 12.00
185 Fernando Tatis Jr. 20.00 50.00
194 Victor Robles 6.00 15.00

2020 Topps Archives '55 Bowman Archives

STATED ODDS 1:8 HOBBY
B551 Gavin Lux 1.50 4.00
B552 Tony Gonsolin 1.00 2.50
B553 Jesus Luzardo .50 1.25
B554 Jordan Yamamoto .30 .75
B555 Dylan Cease .50 1.25
B556 Adbert Alzolay .30 .75
B557 Justin Dunn .30 .75
B558 A.J. Puk .50 1.25
B559 Bo Bichette 2.00 5.00
B5510 Brusdar Graterol .40 1.00
B5511 Aristides Aquino .50 1.25
B5512 Kyle Lewis 2.00 5.00
B5513 Isan Diaz .40 1.00
B5514 Sean Murphy .40 1.00
B5515 Dustin May 1.00 2.50
B5516 Bobby Bradley .30 .75
B5517 Shun Yamaguchi .30 .75
B5518 Shogo Akiyama .40 1.00
B5519 Zac Gallen .60 1.50
B5520 Luis Robert 6.00 15.00
B5521 Trent Grisham 1.00 2.50
B5522 Nico Hoerner 1.00 2.50
B5523 Logan Allen .25 .60
B5524 Yoshi Tsutsugo .30 .75
B5525 Adrian Morejon .25 .60
B5526 Brendan McKay .40 1.00
B5527 Zack Collins .30 .75
B5528 Nick Solak .40 1.00
B5529 Mauricio Dubon .30 .75
B5530 Yordan Alvarez 1.25 3.00

2020 Topps Archives '55 Bowman Archives Black

*BLACK: 1.5X TO 4X BASIC
STATED ODDS 1:668 HOBBY
STATED PRINT RUN 99 SER.#'d SETS
B5520 Luis Robert 40.00 100.00

2020 Topps Archives '55 Bowman Archives Red

*RED: 6X TO 15X BASIC
STATED ODDS 1:2645 HOBBY
STATED PRINT RUN 25 SER.#'d SETS
B5520 Luis Robert 150.00 400.00

2020 Topps Archives '55 Topps Mini

STATED ODDS 1:100 HOBBY
55M1 Babe Ruth 5.00 12.00
55M2 Paul Goldschmidt 2.00 5.00
55M3 Charlie Blackmon 2.00 5.00
55M4 Nick Senzel 2.00 5.00
55M5 Steve Carlton 1.50 4.00
55M6 Aristides Aquino 2.50 6.00
55M7 Shohei Ohtani 2.50 6.00
55M8 Kyle Schwarber 2.00 5.00
55M9 Joey Gallo 2.00 5.00
55M10 Mariano Rivera 2.50 6.00
55M11 Rickey Henderson 2.00 5.00
55M12 Marcus Stroman 1.50 4.00
55M13 Seth Brown 1.25 3.00
55M14 Harmon Killebrew 2.00 5.00
55M15 Albert Pujols 2.50 6.00
55M16 Willi Castro 2.00 5.00
55M17 Jorge Soler 2.00 5.00
55M18 Dylan Cease 2.50 6.00
55M19 Pete Alonso 5.00 12.00
55M20 Whit Merrifield 2.00 5.00
55M21 Gary Sanchez 2.00 5.00
55M22 Marcus Semien 1.25 3.00
55M23 Francisco Lindor 2.00 5.00
55M24 Xander Bogaerts 2.00 5.00
55M25 Jackie Robinson 2.00 5.00
55M26 Keston Hiura 2.50 6.00
55M27 Mookie Betts 4.00 10.00
55M28 Aaron Hicks 1.50 4.00
55M29 Robin Yount 2.00 5.00
55M30 George Brett 4.00 10.00
55M31 Alex Bregman 2.00 5.00
55M32 Al Kaline 2.00 5.00
55M33 Will Smith 2.50 6.00
55M34 Brusdar Graterol 2.00 5.00
55M35 Tim Lincecum 1.50 4.00
55M36 Shane Bieber 2.00 5.00
55M37 Kyle Lewis 10.00 25.00
55M38 Jose Altuve 1.50 4.00
55M39 Michael Brantley 1.50 4.00
55M40 Sam Hilliard 2.00 5.00
55M41 Deion Sanders 1.50 4.00
55M42 Jeff McNeil 1.50 4.00
55M43 Aaron Civale 2.00 5.00
55M44 Lucas Giolito 1.50 4.00
55M45 Bo Bichette 10.00 25.00
55M46 Gary Carter 1.50 4.00
55M47 Goose Gossage 1.50 4.00
55M48 J.D. Martinez 2.00 5.00
55M49 George Kell 1.50 4.00
55M50 Mike Trout 20.00 50.00
55M51 Brock Burke 1.25 3.00
55M52 Catfish Hunter 1.50 4.00
55M53 Lou Boudreau 1.50 4.00
55M54 Max Muncy 1.50 4.00
55M55 Jose Berrios 1.50 4.00
55M56 Vladimir Guerrero Jr. 4.00 10.00
55M57 Ozzie Albies 2.00 5.00
55M58 Tim Anderson 2.00 5.00
55M59 Will Clark 1.50 4.00
55M60 Carl Yastrzemski 3.00 8.00
55M61 Alex Young 1.25 3.00
55M62 Nomar Garciaparra 1.50 4.00
55M63 Bryan Reynolds 1.50 4.00
55M64 Joey Votto 2.00 5.00
55M65 Sean Murphy 2.00 5.00
55M66 J.T. Realmuto 2.00 5.00
55M67 Kenta Maeda 1.50 4.00
55M68 Jack Flaherty 1.50 4.00
55M69 Trevor Bauer 2.00 5.00
55M70 Jim Thome 1.50 4.00
55M71 Zack Greinke 1.50 4.00
55M72 Isan Diaz 2.00 5.00
55M73 Ryne Sandberg 4.00 10.00
55M74 Ralph Kiner 1.50 4.00
55M75 Mike Mussina 1.50 4.00
55M76 Larry Doby 1.50 4.00
55M77 Paul DeJong 2.00 5.00
55M78 Gavin Lux 8.00 20.00
55M79 Matt Chapman 2.00 5.00
55M80 Ramon Laureano 2.00 5.00
55M81 Corey Seager 2.00 5.00
55M82 Luis Aparicio 1.50 4.00
55M83 Tom Glavine 1.50 4.00
55M84 Amed Rosario 1.50 4.00
55M85 Jake Fraley 1.50 4.00
55M86 Raisel Iglesias 1.25 3.00
55M87 Juan Soto 6.00 15.00
55M88 Derek Jeter 5.00 12.00
55M89 Nolan Arenado 2.50 6.00
55M90 Nolan Ryan 6.00 15.00
55M91 Jordan Yamamoto 1.50 4.00
55M92 Matt Carpenter 2.00 5.00
55M93 Mallex Smith 1.25 3.00
55M94 Charlie Morton 2.00 5.00
55M95 A.J. Puk 2.50 6.00
55M96 DJ LeMahieu 2.00 5.00
55M97 Monte Irvin 1.50 4.00
55M98 Wade Boggs 1.50 4.00
55M99 Shin-Soo Choo 1.50 4.00
55M100 Hank Aaron 4.00 10.00

2020 Topps Archives '55 Topps Mini Autographs

STATED ODDS 1:941 HOBBY
STATED PRINT RUN 20 SER.#'d SETS
EXCHANGE DEADLINE 7/31/2022
55M2 Paul Goldschmidt 25.00 60.00
55M5 Steve Carlton 40.00 100.00
55M6 Aristides Aquino 75.00 200.00
55M7 Shohei Ohtani
55M10 Mariano Rivera 100.00 250.00
55M11 Rickey Henderson 125.00 300.00
55M13 Seth Brown 100.00 250.00
55M16 W.Castro Not #'d 10.00 25.00
55M17 Jorge Soler
55M18 Dylan Cease 40.00 100.00
55M19 Pete Alonso
55M24 Xander Bogaerts 40.00 100.00
55M26 Keston Hiura 40.00 100.00
55M29 Robin Yount 75.00 200.00
55M35 Tim Lincecum 75.00 200.00
55M37 Kyle Lewis 100.00 250.00
55M38 Jose Altuve 40.00 100.00
55M42 Jeff McNeil 25.00 60.00
55M43 Aaron Civale
55M44 Lucas Giolito 30.00 80.00
55M50 Mike Trout
55M51 Brock Burke 20.00 50.00
55M59 Will Clark 60.00 150.00
55M60 Carl Yastrzemski 250.00 600.00
55M61 Alex Young 50.00 120.00
55M62 Nomar Garciaparra 100.00 250.00
55M65 Sean Murphy 40.00 100.00
55M70 Jim Thome 150.00 400.00
55M73 Ryne Sandberg 75.00 200.00
55M75 Mike Mussina
55M77 Paul DeJong 30.00 80.00
55M80 Ramon Laureano 30.00 80.00
55M81 Corey Seager EXCH 60.00 150.00
55M83 Tom Glavine 25.00 60.00
55M85 Jake Fraley 40.00 100.00
55M87 Juan Soto 150.00 400.00
55M88 Don Mattingly 75.00 200.00
55M90 Nolan Ryan 125.00 300.00
55M91 Jordan Yamamoto

2020 Topps Archives '60 Topps All-Star Rookie Autographs

STATED ODDS 1:550 HOBBY
PRINT RUNS B/WN 50-150 COPIES PER
EXCHANGE DEADLINE 7/31/2022
*SILVER/99: .5X TO 1.2X BASIC
*BLUE/25: .6X TO 1.5X BASIC
60ARABR Bryan Reynolds/150 6.00 15.00
60ARAEJ Eloy Jimenez EXCH 20.00 50.00
60ARAFTJ Fernando Tatis Jr. EXCH 125.00 300.00
60ARAJM John Means EXCH 8.00 20.00
60ARAKH Keston Hiura/150 12.00 30.00
60ARAPA Pete Alonso/50 50.00 120.00
60ARAVGJ Vladimir Guerrero Jr. EXCH 20.00 50.00
60ARAVR Victor Robles EXCH 12.00 30.00
60ARAWS Will Smith/150 10.00 25.00

2020 Topps Archives '60 Topps All-Star Rookies

STATED ODDS 1:6 HOBBY
60AREJ Eloy Jimenez .75 2.00
60ARFTJ Fernando Tatis Jr. 2.50 6.00
60ARGT Gleyber Torres .75 2.00
60ARJA Jorge Alfaro .25 .60
60ARJM John Means .25 .60
60ARJS Juan Soto 1.25 3.00
60ARKH Keston Hiura .50 1.25
60ARMA Miguel Andujar .40 1.00
60ARPA Pete Alonso 1.00 2.50
60ARRA Ronald Acuna Jr. 1.50 4.00
60ARRO Ryan O'Hearn .25 .60
60ARSO Shohei Ohtani .50 1.25
60ARVGJ Vladimir Guerrero Jr. .75 2.00
60ARVR Victor Robles .50 1.25
60ARWA Willy Adames .25 .60
60ARWB Walker Buehler .50 1.25
60ARWS Will Smith .50 1.25
60ARYA Yordan Alvarez 1.25 3.00

2020 Topps Archives '60 Topps All-Star Rookies Black

*BLACK: 1.5X TO 4X BASIC
STATED ODDS 1:2849 HOBBY
STATED PRINT RUN 99 SER.#'d SETS

2020 Topps Archives '60 Topps All-Star Rookies Red Foil

*RED: 4X TO 10X BASIC
STATED ODDS 1:4389 HOBBY
STATED PRINT RUN 25 SER.#'d SETS
60ARFTJ Fernando Tatis Jr. 40.00 100.00
60ARGT Gleyber Torres 20.00 50.00

2020 Topps Archives '60 Topps All-Star Rookies Silver Foil

*SILVER: 2X TO 5X BASIC
STATED ODDS 1:2203 HOBBY
STATED PRINT RUN 50 SER.#'d SETS
60ARFTJ Fernando Tatis Jr. 20.00 50.00
60ARGT Gleyber Torres 10.00 25.00

2020 Topps Archives '60 Topps Combo Cards

STATED ODDS 1:6 HOBBY
*BLACK/99: 1.5X TO 4X BASIC
*SILVER/50: 2X TO 5X BASIC
*RED/25: 4X TO 10X BASIC
60CCAA Alvarez/Altuve 1.00 2.50
60CCGB Guerrero Jr./Bichette 1.50 4.00
60CCHH Hoskins/Harper .50 1.25
60CCJT Judge/Torres .75 2.00
60CCSM Smith/Muncy .40 1.00
60CCTO Trout/Ohtani 1.50 4.00
60CCYH Hiura/Yelich .40 1.00

2020 Topps Archives '60 Topps Combo Cards Dual Autographs

STATED ODDS 1:1560 HOBBY
EXCHANGE DEADLINE 7/31/2022
60CCAAA Altuve/Alvarez EXCH 40.00 100.00
60CCAHH Harper/Hoskins EXCH 125.00 300.00
60CCAJT Judge/Torres EXCH
60CCASM Muncy/Smith/150 15.00 40.00
60CCATO Trout/Ohtani EXCH
60CCAYH Hiura/Yelich EXCH 75.00 200.00

2020 Topps Archives '60 Topps Combo Cards Dual Autographs Blue

*BLUE: .75X TO 2X BASIC
STATED ODDS 1:6173 HOBBY
STATED PRINT RUN 25 SER.#'d SETS
EXCHANGE DEADLINE 7/31/2022
60CCAJT Judge/Torres EXCH 200.00 500.00
60CCATO Trout/Ohtani EXCH 500.00 1200.00

2020 Topps Archives '64 Topps Giants

ONE PER BLASTER
*BLUE: X TO X BASIC
640AA Aristides Aquino 1.25 3.00
640AJ Aaron Judge 2.50 6.00
640BB Bo Bichette 5.00 12.00
640BH Bryce Harper 1.50 4.00
640BM Brendan McKay 1.00 2.50
640CJ Chipper Jones 1.00 2.50
640CK Clayton Kershaw 2.00 5.00
640CRJ Cal Ripken Jr. 3.00 8.00
640CY Christian Yelich 1.25 3.00
640DS Deion Sanders .75 2.00
640EJ Eloy Jimenez 2.00 5.00
640FL Francisco Lindor 1.00 2.50
640FTJ Fernando Tatis Jr. 4.00 10.00
640GB George Brett 2.00 5.00
640GL Gavin Lux 4.00 10.00
640JA Jose Altuve .75 2.00
640JR Jackie Robinson 1.00 2.50
640JS Juan Soto 3.00 8.00
640KH Keston Hiura 1.25 3.00
640MB Mookie Betts 2.00 5.00
640MT Mike Trout 5.00 12.00
640NA Nolan Arenado 1.25 3.00
640NH Nico Hoerner 2.50 6.00
640NR Nolan Ryan 3.00 8.00
640PA Pete Alonso 2.50 6.00
640RH Rhys Hoskins 1.25 3.00
640RJ Reggie Jackson .75 2.00
640TM Thurman Munson 1.00 2.50
640VGJ Vladimir Guerrero Jr. 2.00 5.00
640YA Yordan Alvarez 3.00 8.00

2020 Topps Archives '64 Topps Giants Autographs

STATED ODDS 1:1001 BLASTERS
EXCHANGE DEADLINE 7/31/2022
640AA Aristides Aquino 12.00 30.00
640BM Brendan McKay EXCH 10.00 25.00
640CJ Chipper Jones 50.00 120.00
640CRJ Cal Ripken Jr. 100.00 250.00
640JA Jose Altuve 25.00 60.00
640JS Juan Soto 100.00 250.00
640KH Keston Hiura 12.00 30.00
640MT Mike Trout 300.00 800.00
640NH Nico Hoerner 25.00 60.00
640NR Nolan Ryan 100.00 250.00
640PA Pete Alonso 40.00 100.00
640RH Rhys Hoskins 25.00 60.00
640RJ Reggie Jackson 50.00 120.00

2020 Topps Archives '76 Topps Traded Autographs

STATED ODDS 1:3238 HOBBY
EXCHANGE DEADLINE 7/31/2022
*SILVER/99: .5X TO 1.2X BASIC
*BLUE/50: .6X TO 1.5X BASIC
76TACCS CC Sabathia EXCH 20.00 50.00
76TAJB Jeff Bagwell 25.00 60.00
76TAJS John Smoltz 25.00 60.00
76TAMC Miguel Cabrera 75.00 200.00
76TAMT Mark Teixeira 20.00 50.00
76TAPM Pedro Martinez 20.00 50.00
76TARS Ryne Sandberg 50.00 120.00
76TASC Steve Carlton 25.00 60.00

2020 Topps Archives '89 Topps Corn Field Autographs

STATED ODDS 1:334 HOBBY
EXCHANGE DEADLINE 7/31/2022
*PINSTRIPE/27: .75X TO 2X BASIC
89CFAAJ Aaron Judge EXCH 100.00 250.00
89CFADC Dylan Cease 12.00 30.00
89CFADJ DJ LeMahieu 20.00 50.00
89CFAGT Gleyber Torres 40.00 100.00
89CFAGU Gio Urshela 12.00 30.00
89CFALG Lucas Giolito 20.00 50.00
89CFALR Luis Robert EXCH 300.00 800.00
89CFALV Luke Voit 30.00 80.00
89CFAMA Miguel Andujar 6.00 15.00
89CFATA Tim Anderson 20.00 50.00
89CFAYM Yoan Moncada 25.00 60.00

2020 Topps Archives '90 Topps Rookies

STATED ODDS 1:24 HOBBY
90RAA Aristides Aquino 1.00 2.50
90RAJ A.J. Puk 1.00 2.50
90RBB Bo Bichette 4.00 10.00
90RBG Brusdar Graterol .75 2.00
90RBM Brendan McKay .75 2.00
90RDC Dylan Cease 1.00 2.50
90RDM Dustin May 2.00 5.00
90RGL Gavin Lux 3.00 8.00
90RJL Jesus Luzardo 1.00 2.50
90RKL Kyle Lewis 4.00 10.00
90RNH Nico Hoerner 2.00 5.00
90RSB Seth Brown .40 1.00
90RSM Sean Murphy .75 2.00
90RSN Sheldon Neuse .60 1.50
90RYA Yordan Alvarez 2.50 6.00

2020 Topps Archives '90 Topps Rookies Autographs

STATED ODDS 1:742 HOBBY
EXCHANGE DEADLINE 7/31/2022
*BLUE/25: .75X TO 2X BASIC
90RAAA Aristides Aquino 15.00 40.00
90RABM Brendan McKay 6.00 15.00
90RADC Dylan Cease 8.00 20.00
90RADM Dustin May 25.00 60.00
90RAJL Jesus Luzardo 8.00 20.00
90RAKL Kyle Lewis 60.00 150.00
90RASB Seth Brown 4.00 10.00
90RASM Sean Murphy 15.00 40.00

2020 Topps Archives Fan Favorites Autographs

STATED ODDS 1:19 HOBBY
EXCHANGE DEADLINE 7/31/2022
*PURPLE/150: .5X TO 1.2X BASE
*SILVER/99: .6X TO 1.5X BASE
*BLUE/25: .75X TO 2X BASE
FFAAA Andy Ashby 3.00 8.00
FFAAQ Aristides Aquino 12.00 30.00
FFABB Bruce Bochy 15.00 40.00
FFABC Bernie Carbo 3.00 8.00
FFABL Brad Lidge 3.00 8.00
FFABMO Blue Moon Odom 5.00 12.00
FFABS Buck Showalter 5.00 12.00
FFABSA Benito Santiago 6.00 15.00
FFABW Bob Wickman 3.00 8.00
FFABWA Bob Walk 4.00 10.00
FFACM Charlie Manuel 8.00 20.00
FFADB Dante Bichette 10.00 25.00
FFADE Darin Erstad 5.00 12.00
FFADM Dave Martinez 6.00 15.00
FFADT Danny Tartabull 4.00 10.00
FFAFJ Felix Jose 3.00 8.00
FFAGA Garret Anderson 3.00 8.00
FFAGS Gary Sheffield 8.00 20.00
FFAJG Jerry Grote 6.00 15.00
FFAJGI Joe Girardi 10.00 25.00
FFAJO Jose Offerman 4.00 10.00
FFAJS John Stearns 5.00 12.00
FFAKB Kevin Bass 3.00 8.00
FFAKM Kevin Millar 5.00 12.00
FFALM Lloyd McClendon 3.00 8.00
FFALMA Lee Mazzilli 5.00 12.00
FFALS Lonnie Smith 4.00 10.00
FFAMB Mark Buehrle 12.00 30.00
FFAMG Mark Grudzielanek 4.00 10.00
FFAMP Mike Pagliarulo 5.00 12.00
FFAMS Manny Sanguillen 6.00 15.00
FFAMW Mark Wohlers 4.00 10.00
FFAPH Phil Hughes 8.00 20.00
FFAPHA Pete Harnisch 4.00 10.00
FFAPP Placido Polanco 4.00 10.00
FFAPW Preston Wilson 3.00 8.00
FFARD Ray Durham 3.00 8.00
FFARF Rafael Furcal 5.00 12.00
FFARG Ralph Garr 5.00 12.00
FFARGE Rich Gedman 4.00 10.00
FFARK Roberto Kelly 4.00 10.00
FFARS Reggie Sanders 5.00 12.00
FFASF Steve Finley 4.00 10.00
FFASG Shawn Green 8.00 20.00
FFASS Shane Spencer 5.00 12.00
FFATHE Tom Henke 4.00 10.00

FFATP Tom Pagnozzi 3.00 8.00
FFATW Todd Worrell 4.00 10.00
FFAVL Vern Law 6.00 15.00

2020 Topps Archives Fan Favorites Autographs Premium

STATED ODDS 1:1753 HOBBY
PRINT RUNS B/WN 25-50 COPIES PER
EXCHANGE DEADLINE 7/31/2022
FFPAJ Aaron Judge EXCH 200.00 500.00
FFPBH Bryce Harper/25 250.00 600.00
FFPCJ Chipper Jones/50 125.00 300.00
FFPCRJ Cal Ripken Jr./50 150.00 400.00
FFPDJ Derek Jeter
FFPFTJ Fernando Tatis Jr. EXCH 300.00 800.00
FFPHA Hank Aaron/25 250.00 600.00
FFPMR Mariano Rivera/25 200.00 500.00
FFPMS Mike Schmidt/50 200.00 500.00
FFPMT Mike Trout/25 600.00 1500.00
FFPRAJ Ronald Acuna Jr./50 200.00 500.00
FFPVGJ Vladimir Guerrero Jr./50 60.00 150.00

2020 Topps Archives Hobby Nickname Poster Autographs

INSERTED IN HOBBY BOXES
EXCHANGE DEADLINE 7/31/2022
HNPAJ Aaron Judge
HNPBS Blake Snell
HNPHA Hank Aaron
HNPMT Mike Trout
HNPPA Pete Alonso 75.00 200.00

2020 Topps Archives Hobby Nickname Posters

ONE PER HOBBY BOX
HNPAJ Aaron Judge 2.50 6.00
HNPBS Blake Snell .75 2.00
HNPCS Chris Sale 1.00 2.50
HNPDF Duke Snider .75 2.00
HNPDO David Ortiz 1.00 2.50
HNPEB Ernie Banks 1.00 2.50
HNPFL Francisco Lindor 1.00 2.50
HNPHA Hank Aaron 2.00 5.00
HNPJB Javier Baez 1.25 3.00
HNPMR Mariano Rivera 1.25 3.00
HNPMT Mike Trout 5.00 12.00
HNPNS Noah Syndergaard .75 2.00
HNPPA Pete Alonso 2.50 6.00
HNPSO Shohei Ohtani 1.25 3.00
HNPYA Yordan Alvarez 3.00 8.00

2020 Topps Archives Originals Autographs

STATED ODDS 1:6238 HOBBY
PRINT RUNS B/WN 11-20 COPIES PER
NO PRICING ON QTY 17 OR LESS
EXCHANGE DEADLINE 7/31/2022
214 Shawn Green/20 15.00 40.00

2016 Topps Archives 65th Anniversary

COMP.SET w/o SP's (65) 20.00 50.00
SP ODDS 1:21 PACKS
A65I Ichiro .50 1.25
A65AB Andy Benes .25 .60
A65AG Andres Galarraga .30 .75
A65AP A.J. Pollock .25 .60
A65BD Bucky Dent .25 .60
A65BH Bryce Harper .60 1.50
A65BM Bill Mazeroski .30 .75
A65BP Buster Posey .50 1.25
A65BW Billy Williams .30 .75
A65CH Charlie Hayes .25 .60
A65CJ Chipper Jones .40 1.00
A65CK Clayton Kershaw .75 2.00
A65CR Cal Ripken Jr. 1.25 3.00
A65CS Curt Simmons .25 .60
A65CSE Corey Seager 2.00 5.00
A65CY Carl Yastrzemski .60 1.50
A65DM Don Mattingly .75 2.00
A65DW Dontrelle Willis .25 .60
A65DWR David Wright .30 .75
A65EM Eddie Mathews .40 1.00
A65FH Frank Howard .25 .60
A65FT Frank Thomas .40 1.00
A65FTA Fernando Tatis .25 .60
A65FV Fernando Valenzuela .25 .60
A65FVI Fernando Vina .25 .60
A65HA Hank Aaron .75 2.00
A65HB Harold Baines .30 .75
A65JB Johnny Bench .40 1.00
A65JBU Jeff Burroughs .25 .60
A65JC Jose Cruz .25 .60
A65JCA Jose Canseco .30 .75
A65JCO Jeff Conine .25 .60
A65JCR Jose Cruz Jr. .25 .60
A65JM Joe Morgan .30 .75
A65JR Jackie Robinson .40 1.00
A65JRI Jose Rijo .25 .60
A65JV Jose Vidro .25 .60
A65KB Kris Bryant .50 1.25
A65KG Ken Griffey Jr. .75 2.00
A65KT Kent Tekulve .25 .60
A65MB Mike Bordick .25 .60
A65MT Mike Trout 2.00 5.00
A65MTA Masahiro Tanaka .30 .75
A65NR Nolan Ryan 1.25 3.00
A65OS Ozzie Smith .50 1.25
A65OV Omar Vizquel .30 .75
A65RC Roberto Clemente 1.00 2.50
A65RCA Rod Carew .30 .75
A65RCL Roger Clemens .30 .75
A65RF Rollie Fingers .30 .75
A65RJ Randy Jones .25 .60
A65RK Ryan Klesko .25 .60
A65RM Roger Maris .40 1.00
A65SAJ Sandy Alomar Jr. .25 .60
A65SAS Sandy Alomar Sr. .25 .60
A65SC Steve Carlton .30 .75
A65SH Scott Hatteberg .25 .60
A65SK Sandy Koufax .75 2.00
A65SL Sparky Lyle .25 .60
A65TF Tito Francona .30 .75
A65TFE Tony Fernandez .25 .60
A65TH Teddy Higuera .25 .60
A65TW Ted Williams .75 2.00
A65VL Vern Law .25 .60
A65WM Willie Mays .75 2.00
A65SCY Carl Yastrzemski SP 10.00 25.00
A65SHA Hank Aaron SP 15.00 40.00
A65SJB Johnny Bench SP 10.00 25.00
A65SJR Jackie Robinson SP 10.00 25.00
A65SRC Roger Clemens SP 10.00 25.00
A65SSK Sandy Koufax SP 12.00 30.00
A65STW Ted Williams SP 12.00 30.00
A65SWM Willie Mays SP 12.00 30.00
A65SKGJ Ken Griffey Jr. SP 12.00 30.00
A65SRCL Roberto Clemente SP 15.00 40.00

2016 Topps Archives 65th Anniversary Green Back

*GREEN BACK: 2.5X TO 6X BASIC
STATED ODDS 1:5 PACKS
STATED PRINT RUN 150 SER.#'d SETS

2016 Topps Archives 65th Anniversary Autographs

OVERALL ONE AUTO PER BOX
PRINTING PLATE ODDS 1:352 PACKS
PLATE PRINT RUN 1 SET PER COLOR
NO PLATE PRICING DUE TO SCARCITY
*GREEN BACK/99: .5X TO 1.2X BASIC
*RED BACK/25: .75X TO 2X BASIC
A65AG Andres Galarraga
A65BD Bucky Dent 4.00 10.00
A65BP Buster Posey
A65CH Charlie Hayes 2.50 6.00
A65CR Cal Ripken Jr.
A65CS Curt Simmons 3.00 8.00
A65DW Dontrelle Willis 5.00 12.00
A65FTA Fernando Tatis 2.50 6.00
A65HB Harold Baines 4.00 10.00
A65JB Johnny Bench
A65JC Jose Cruz 2.50 6.00
A65JCA Jose Canseco 3.00 8.00
A65JCO Jeff Conine 2.50 6.00
A65JCR Jose Cruz Jr. 2.50 6.00
A65JRI Jose Rijo 3.00 8.00
A65JV Jose Vidro 2.50 6.00
A65KG Ken Griffey Jr.
A65KT Kent Tekulve 3.00 8.00
A65MT Mike Trout
A65MTA Masahiro Tanaka 300.00 500.00
A65OV Omar Vizquel
A65RF Rollie Fingers
A65RK Ryan Klesko 2.50 6.00
A65SAJ Sandy Alomar Jr. 2.50 6.00
A65SAS Sandy Alomar Sr. 2.50 6.00
A65SH Scott Hatteberg 2.50 6.00
A65SL Sparky Lyle 3.00 8.00
A65TFE Tony Fernandez 2.50 6.00
A65VL Vern Law 3.00 8.00

2016 Topps Archives 65th Anniversary Red Back

*RED BACK: 6X TO 15X BASIC
STATED ODDS 1:13 PACKS
STATED PRINT RUN 50 SER.#'d SETS

2016 Topps Archives 65th Anniversary Rookie Autographs

STATED ODDS 1:36 PACKS
A65RAAN Aaron Nola 8.00 20.00
A65RABS Blake Snell 15.00 40.00
A65RAKM Kenta Maeda 25.00 60.00
A65RAKS Kyle Schwarber 75.00 200.00
A65RALS Luis Severino 20.00 50.00
A65RAMS Miguel Sano 12.00 30.00

2016 Topps Archives 65th Anniversary Rookie Variations

STATED ODDS 1:42 PACKS
A65RAN Aaron Nola 8.00 20.00
A65RBS Blake Snell 15.00 40.00
A65RCS Corey Seager 150.00 400.00
A65RKM Kenta Maeda 10.00 25.00
A65RKS Kyle Schwarber 75.00 200.00
A65RLS Luis Severino 12.00 30.00
A65RMC Michael Conforto 25.00 60.00
A65RMS Miguel Sano 30.00 80.00
A65RSP Stephen Piscotty 25.00 60.00
A65RBHP Byung Ho Park 12.00 30.00

2017 Topps Archives Snapshots

ASAB Alex Bregman RC 3.00 8.00
ASABE Andrew Benintendi RC 2.50 6.00
ASAG Andres Galarraga 1.00 2.50
ASAJ Aaron Judge RC 6.00 15.00
ASARI Anthony Rizzo 2.00 5.00
ASBA Bobby Abreu .75 2.00
ASBH Bryce Harper 2.00 5.00
ASCB Carlos Baerga .75 2.00
ASCC Carlos Correa 1.25 3.00
ASCJ Cleon Jones .75 2.00
ASCS Corey Seager 1.25 3.00
ASDD Danny Duffy .75 2.00
ASDJ Derek Jeter 4.00 10.00
ASDS Dansby Swanson RC 2.00 5.00
ASER Edgar Renteria .75 2.00
ASFL Francisco Lindor 1.25 3.00
ASHA Hank Aaron 2.50 6.00
ASHK Harmon Killebrew 1.25 3.00
ASHR Hunter Renfroe RC 1.00 2.50
ASJA Jose Altuve 1.00 2.50
ASJC Jose Canseco 1.00 2.50
ASJCO Jharel Cotton RC .75 2.00
ASJE Jim Edmonds .75 2.00
ASKB Kris Bryant 1.50 4.00
ASKS Kyle Schwarber 1.25 3.00
ASLT Luis Tiant .75 2.00
ASMB Mookie Betts 2.00 5.00
ASML Mark Langston .75 2.00
ASMM Mark Mulder .75 2.00
ASMMA Manny Machado 1.25 3.00
ASMS Matt Strahm RC .75 2.00
ASMT Mike Trout 6.00 15.00
ASNG Nomar Garciaparra 1.00 2.50
ASNS Noah Syndergaard 1.00 2.50
ASOA Orlando Arcia RC 1.25 3.00
ASOG Ozzie Guillen .75 2.00
ASPK Paul Konerko 1.00 2.50
ASPM Pedro Martinez 1.00 2.50
ASRC Ron Cey .75 2.00
ASRG Robert Gsellman RC .75 2.00
ASRH Ryon Healy RC 1.00 2.50
ASRJ Randy Johnson 1.25 3.00
ASSK Sandy Koufax 2.50 6.00
ASTA Tyler Austin RC 1.25 3.00
ASTG Tyler Glasnow RC 1.00 2.50
ASTT Trea Turner 1.00 2.50
ASTW Tim Wakefield 1.00 2.50
ASWM Wally Moon .75 2.00
ASYG Yulieski Gurriel RC 1.25 3.00
ASYM Yoan Moncada RC 2.50 6.00

2017 Topps Archives Snapshots Black and White

*B/W: .6X TO 1.5X BASIC
*B/W RC: .6X TO 1.5X BASIC RC
OVERALL ODDS ONE PARALLEL PER BOX

2017 Topps Archives Snapshots Autographs

OVERALL ODDS ONE AUTO PER BOX
PRINT RUNS B/WN 4-350 COPIES PER
NO PRICING ON QTY 14 OR LESS
EXCHANGE DEADLINE 10/31/2019
ASAB Alex Bregman/20 40.00 100.00
ASABE Andrew Benintendi/60 60.00 150.00
ASAG Andres Galarraga/60 5.00 12.00
ASAJ Aaron Judge/80
ASARI Anthony Rizzo
ASCB Carlos Baerga/350 3.00 8.00
ASCJ Cleon Jones/350 3.00 8.00
ASER Edgar Renteria/60 6.00 15.00
ASFL Francisco Lindor/20 60.00 150.00
ASHR Hunter Renfroe/350 4.00 10.00
ASJA Jose Altuve/20
ASJC Jose Canseco/350 6.00 15.00
ASJCO Jharel Cotton/349 3.00 8.00
ASJE Jim Edmonds/60 10.00 25.00
ASKS Kyle Schwarber/20 15.00 40.00
ASLT Luis Tiant/60 8.00 20.00
ASML Mark Langston/346 4.00 10.00
ASMM Mark Mulder/265 3.00 8.00
ASNS Noah Syndergaard/20 25.00 60.00
ASOG Ozzie Guillen/80 4.00 10.00
ASPK Paul Konerko/20 12.00 30.00
ASRC Ron Cey/263 5.00 12.00
ASRG Robert Gsellman/344 3.00 8.00
ASRH Ryon Healy/350 4.00 10.00
ASTA Tyler Austin/348 5.00 12.00
ASTW Tim Wakefield/60 20.00 50.00
ASWM Wally Moon/350 3.00 8.00
ASYG Yulieski Gurriel/350 5.00 12.00

2017 Topps Archives Snapshots Autographs Black and White

*B/W: .5X TO 1.2X BASIC
OVERALL ODDS ONE AUTO PER BOX
STATED PRINT RUN 25 SER.#'d SETS
EXCHANGE DEADLINE 10/31/2019
ASAJ Aaron Judge 300.00 600.00
ASARI Anthony Rizzo 25.00 60.00

2018 Topps Archives Snapshots

ASAJ Andruw Jones .40 1.00
ASAJU Aaron Judge 1.50 4.00
ASAR Amed Rosario RC .50 1.25
ASAS Andrew Stevenson RC .40 1.00
ASAV Alex Verdugo RC .60 1.50
ASBD Brian Dozier .50 1.25
ASBP Buster Posey .75 2.00
ASCB Charlie Blackmon .60 1.50
ASCC Carlos Correa .60 1.50
ASCH Charlie Hough .40 1.00
ASCJ Chipper Jones .60 1.50
ASCK Clayton Kershaw 1.25 3.00
ASCR Cal Ripken Jr. 2.00 5.00
ASCS Chance Sisco RC .40 1.00
ASDE David Eckstein .40 1.00
ASDG Didi Gregorius .50 1.25
ASEM Edgar Martinez .50 1.25
ASFL Francisco Lindor .60 1.50
ASFM Francisco Mejia RC .50 1.25
ASFV Frank Viola .40 1.00
ASGA Greg Allen RC .40 1.00
ASGS Giancarlo Stanton .60 1.50
ASGT Gleyber Torres RC 4.00 10.00
ASJA Jose Altuve .50 1.25
ASJB Jim Bouton .40 1.00
ASJC Jose Canseco .50 1.25
ASJO John Olerud .40 1.00
ASJT Jim Thome .50 1.25
ASJTO Joe Torre .50 1.25
ASKB Kris Bryant .75 2.00
ASKD Khris Davis .60 1.50
ASMF Max Fried RC 1.50 4.00
ASMO Matt Olson .40 1.00
ASMP Mike Piazza .60 1.50
ASMT Mike Trout 3.00 8.00
ASNR Nolan Ryan 2.00 5.00
ASOA Ozzie Albies RC 1.25 3.00
ASPD Paul DeJong .60 1.50
ASRA Rick Ankiel .40 1.00
ASRAC Ronald Acuna Jr. RC 8.00 20.00
ASRD Rafael Devers RC 1.25 3.00
ASRM Ryan McMahon RC .50 1.25
ASRR Raudy Read RC .40 1.00
ASSA Sandy Alcantara RC .40 1.00
ASSO Shohei Ohtani RC 2.50 6.00
ASTL Tzu-Wei Lin .50 1.25
ASTM Tyler Mahle RC .50 1.25
ASTP Tommy Pham .40 1.00
ASWB Walker Buehler RC 2.00 5.00
ASYM Yadier Molina .60 1.50

2018 Topps Archives Snapshots Black and White

*B/W: .6X TO 1.5X BASIC
*B/W RC: .6X TO 1.5X BASIC RC
OVERALL ODDS ONE PARALLEL PER BOX

2018 Topps Archives Snapshots Blue

*BLUE 2X TO 5X BASIC
*BLUE RC: 2X TO 5X BASIC RC
OVERALL ODDS ONE PARALLEL PER BOX
STATED PRINT RUN 50 SER.#'d SETS

2018 Topps Archives Snapshots Autographs

OVERALL ODDS ONE AUTO PER BOX
EXCHANGE DEADLINE 9/30/2020
ASAJ Andruw Jones 5.00 12.00
ASAJU Aaron Judge
ASAR Amed Rosario 6.00 15.00
ASAS Andrew Stevenson 3.00 8.00
ASAV Alex Verdugo 6.00 15.00
ASCB Charlie Blackmon 5.00 12.00
ASCH Charlie Hough 3.00 8.00
ASCJ Chipper Jones
ASCS Chance Sisco 4.00 10.00
ASDE David Eckstein 3.00 8.00
ASDG Didi Gregorius EXCH 10.00 25.00
ASFL Francisco Lindor 20.00 50.00
ASFV Frank Viola 3.00 8.00
ASGT Gleyber Torres 25.00 60.00
ASJA Jose Altuve 12.00 30.00
ASJB Jim Bouton 6.00 15.00
ASJC Jose Canseco 10.00 25.00
ASJO John Olerud 8.00 20.00
ASJT Joe Torre 20.00 50.00
ASKB Kris Bryant
ASKD Khris Davis 8.00 20.00
ASMO Matt Olson 6.00 15.00
ASMT Mike Trout 300.00 500.00
ASOA Ozzie Albies 10.00 25.00
ASPD Paul DeJong 5.00 12.00
ASRA Rick Ankiel 3.00 8.00
ASRAC Ronald Acuna Jr. 75.00 200.00
ASRD Rafael Devers 20.00 50.00
ASRM Ryan McMahon 4.00 10.00
ASRR Raudy Read 3.00 8.00
ASSA Sandy Alcantara 3.00 8.00
ASSO Shohei Ohtani 200.00 400.00
ASTL Tzu-Wei Lin 4.00 10.00
ASTM Tyler Mahle 4.00 10.00
ASTP Tommy Pham 3.00 8.00
ASWB Walker Buehler EXCH

2018 Topps Archives Snapshots Autographs Black and White

*B/W: .6X TO 1.5X BASIC
OVERALL ODDS ONE AUTO PER BOX
STATED PRINT RUN 25 SER.#'d SETS
EXCHANGE DEADLINE 9/30/2020
ASTL Tzu-Wei Lin 12.00 30.00
ASWB Walker Buehler EXCH 50.00 120.00

2018 Topps Archives Snapshots Autographs Blue

*BLUE: .5X TO 1.2X BASIC
OVERALL ODDS ONE AUTO PER BOX
STATED PRINT RUN 50 SER.#'d SETS
EXCHANGE DEADLINE 9/30/2020
ASTL Tzu-Wei Lin 10.00 25.00
ASWB Walker Buehler EXCH 40.00 100.00

2019 Topps Archives Snapshots

ASAB Alex Bregman .50 1.25
ASBK Brad Keller RC .50 1.25
ASBN Brandon Nimmo .40 1.00
ASBT Blake Treinen .30 .75
ASCY Christian Yelich .60 1.50
ASDB David Bote .40 1.00
ASDC Dylan Cozens RC .40 1.00
ASDH Dakota Hudson RC .60 1.50
ASDS DJ Stewart RC .60 1.50
ASEG Eric Gagne .30 .75
ASEJ Eloy Jimenez RC 2.00 5.00
ASFL Francisco Lindor .50 1.25
ASFV Framber Valdez RC .50 1.25
ASGT Gleyber Torres 1.00 2.50
ASHB Harold Baines .40 1.00
ASI Ichiro .60 1.50
ASJB Javier Baez .60 1.50
ASJD Jacob deGrom .60 1.50
ASJH Josh Hader .30 .75
ASJJ Josh James RC .75 2.00
ASJR Jose Ramirez .40 1.00
ASJS Juan Soto 1.50 4.00
ASKB Kris Bryant .60 1.50
ASKG Ken Griffey Jr. 1.00 2.50
ASKS Kohl Stewart RC .60 1.50
ASKT Kyle Tucker RC 1.00 2.50
ASLU Luis Urias RC .75 2.00
ASMA Miguel Andujar .50 1.25
ASMB Mookie Betts .75 2.00
ASMC Matt Chapman .50 1.25
ASMG Mark Grace .40 1.00
ASMM Manny Machado .50 1.25
ASMMU Max Muncy .40 1.00
ASMT Mike Trout 2.50 6.00
ASOA Ozzie Albies .50 1.25
ASPA Pete Alonso RC 3.00 8.00
ASPC Patrick Corbin .40 1.00
ASPG Paul Goldschmidt .50 1.25
ASRA Ronald Acuna Jr. 2.50 6.00
ASRH Rhys Hoskins .60 1.50
ASRL Ramon Laureano RC 1.00 2.50
ASSO Shohei Ohtani .60 1.50
ASSS Steve Sax .30 .75
ASSSO Sammy Sosa .50 1.25
ASST Stephen Tarpley RC .60 1.50
ASTM Tino Martinez .40 1.00
ASTT Touki Toussaint RC .60 1.50
ASVG Vladimir Guerrero Jr. RC 3.00 8.00
ASVW Vernon Wells .30 .75
ASYK Yusei Kikuchi RC .75 2.00

2019 Topps Archives Snapshots Black and White

*BLK WHT: .75X TO 2X BASIC
*BLK WHT RC: .5X TO 1.2X BASIC RC
RANDOM INSERTS IN PACKS

2019 Topps Archives Snapshots Blue

*BLUE: 3X TO 8X BASIC
*BLUE RC: 2X TO 5X BASIC RC
RANDOM INSERTS IN PACKS
STATED PRINT RUN 50 SER.#'d SETS

2019 Topps Archives Snapshots Autographs

OVERALL AUTO ODDS ONE PER BOX
EXCHANGE DEADLINE 8/31/2021
*BLUE/50: .5X TO 1.2X BASIC
*BLK WHT/25: .6X TO 1.5X BASIC
ASBK Brad Keller 2.50 6.00
ASBN Brandon Nimmo 3.00 8.00
ASBT Blake Treinen 2.50 6.00
ASDB David Bote 3.00 8.00
ASDC Dylan Cozens 2.50 6.00
ASDH Dakota Hudson 3.00 8.00
ASDP Enyel de los Santos 2.50 6.00
ASEG Eric Gagne 2.50 6.00
ASEJ Eloy Jimenez 20.00 50.00
ASFL Francisco Lindor 12.00 30.00
ASFV Framber Valdez 2.50 6.00
ASHB Harold Baines 6.00 15.00
ASJD Jacob deGrom
ASJH Josh Hader 4.00 10.00
ASJJ Josh James 4.00 10.00
ASJR Jose Ramirez 3.00 8.00
ASJS Juan Soto 30.00 80.00
ASKB Kris Bryant
ASKG Ken Griffey Jr.
ASKS Kohl Stewart 3.00 8.00
ASKT Kyle Tucker 10.00 25.00
ASMC Matt Chapman 8.00 20.00
ASMG Mark Grace 8.00 20.00
ASMMU Max Muncy 5.00 12.00
ASMT Mike Trout
ASOA Ozzie Albies 10.00 25.00
ASPA Pete Alonso 60.00 150.00
ASPC Patrick Corbin 3.00 8.00
ASRH Rhys Hoskins 15.00 40.00
ASRL Ramon Laureano 6.00 15.00
ASSS Steve Sax 2.50 6.00
ASSSO Sammy Sosa EXCH
ASTM Tino Martinez 8.00 20.00
ASTW Taylor Ward 2.50 6.00
ASVG Vladimir Guerrero Jr. 50.00 120.00
ASVW Vernon Wells 2.50 6.00

2019 Topps Archives Snapshots Captured in the Moment

RANDOM INSERTS IN PACKS
*BLK WHT/25: 2.5X TO 6X BASIC
CITMAJ Andruw Jones .75 2.00
CITMAJU Aaron Judge 3.00 8.00
CITMBG Bob Gibson 1.00 2.50
CITMCF Carlton Fisk 1.00 2.50
CITMCR Cal Ripken Jr. 4.00 10.00
CITMCY Christian Yelich 1.50 4.00
CITMDB David Bote 1.00 2.50
CITMDG Dwight Gooden .75 2.00
CITMDJ Derek Jeter 3.00 8.00
CITMEG Eric Gagne .75 2.00
CITMHA Hank Aaron 2.50 6.00
CITMI Ichiro 1.50 4.00
CITMJC Jose Canseco 1.00 2.50
CITMJV Jason Varitek 1.00 2.50
CITMLG Luis Gonzalez .75 2.00
CITMMC Miguel Cabrera 1.25 3.00
CITMMM Max Muncy 1.00 2.50
CITMNR Nolan Ryan 4.00 10.00
CITMRH Rickey Henderson 1.25 3.00
CITMRJ Reggie Jackson 1.00 2.50
CITMRJO Randy Johnson 1.25 3.00
CITMSA Sandy Alomar Jr. .75 2.00
CITMSG Scooter Gennett 1.00 2.50
CITMSM Sean Manaea .75 2.00
CITMSP Steve Pearce 1.25 3.00

2019 Topps Archives Snapshots Captured in the Moment Autographs

OVERALL AUTO ODDS ONE PER BOX
PRINT RUNS B/WN 5-40 COPIES PER
NO PRICING ON QTY 15 OR LESS
EXCHANGE DEADLINE 8/31/2021
*BLK WHT/25: .5X TO 1.2X BASIC
CITMAJ Andruw Jones/40 5.00 12.00
CITMBG Bob Gibson EXCH
CITMDB David Bote/40 6.00 15.00
CITMEG Eric Gagne/40 5.00 12.00
CITMJC Jose Canseco/40 10.00 25.00
CITMMM Max Muncy/40 6.00 15.00
CITMSA Sandy Alomar Jr./40 10.00 25.00
CITMSM Sean Manaea

2020 Topps Archives Snapshots

ASAA Adbert Alzolay RC .60 1.50
ASAJ Aaron Judge 1.25 3.00
ASAO Al Oliver .30 .75
ASBA Bryan Abreu RC .50 1.25
ASBB Bo Bichette RC 4.00 10.00
ASBH Bryce Harper .75 2.00
ASBZ Barry Zito .40 1.00
ASCR Cal Ripken Jr. 1.50 4.00
ASDM Dustin May RC 2.00 5.00
ASEK Ed Kranepool .30 .75
ASFT Fernando Tatis Jr. 2.00 5.00
ASGL Gavin Lux RC 3.00 8.00
ASGT Gleyber Torres 1.00 2.50
ASHH Hunter Harvey RC .75 2.00
ASID Isan Diaz RC .75 2.00
ASJA Jim Abbott .30 .75
ASJB Jay Buhner 1.00 2.50
ASJK James Karinchak RC .75 2.00
ASJL Jesus Luzardo RC 1.00 2.50
ASJM Jeff McNeil .40 1.00
ASJS Juan Soto 1.50 4.00
ASJU Jose Urquidy RC .60 1.50
ASKL Kyle Lewis RC 4.00 10.00
ASLA Luis Arraez RC 1.00 2.50
ASLR Luis Robert RC 5.00 12.00
ASMB Mookie Betts 1.00 2.50
ASMD Mauricio Dubon RC .60 1.50
ASMS Mike Schmidt .75 2.00
ASMT Mike Trout 2.50 6.00
ASNH Nico Hoerner RC 2.00 5.00
ASNR Nolan Ryan 2.00 5.00
ASOM Oscar Mercado .40 1.00
ASPA Pete Alonso 1.25 3.00
ASRA Ronald Acuna Jr. 2.00 5.00
ASRJ Randy Johnson 1.00 2.50
ASRS Ruben Sierra .80 2.00
ASSN Sheldon Neuse RC .60 1.50
ASSO Shohei Ohtani .60 1.50
ASSR Steve Rogers .30 .75
ASTE Tommy Edman .50 1.25
ASTG Tony Gonsolin RC 2.00 5.00
ASTL Tim Lincecum 1.00 2.50
ASTZ T.J. Zeuch RC .50 1.25
ASVG Vladimir Guerrero Jr. 1.00 2.50
ASWM Willie Mays 1.00 2.50
ASYA Yordan Alvarez RC 2.50 6.00
ASAAQ Aristides Aquino RC 1.00 2.50
ASBBR Bobby Bradley RC .60 1.50
ASMBE Matt Beaty .40 1.00
ASTGR Trent Grisham RC 2.00 5.00

2020 Topps Archives Snapshots Black and White

*BLK WHT: .75X TO 2X BASIC
*BLK WHT RC: .5X TO 1.2X BASIC RC
STATED ODDS 1 PER HOBBY
ASCR Cal Ripken Jr. 5.00 12.00
ASWM Willie Mays 3.00 8.00

2020 Topps Archives Snapshots Blue

*BLUE: 3X TO 8X BASIC
*BLUE RC: 2X TO 5X BASIC RC
STATED ODDS 1:5 HOBBY
STATED PRINT RUN 50 SER.#'d SETS
ASAJ Aaron Judge 8.00 20.00
ASCR Cal Ripken Jr. 12.00 30.00
ASJB Jay Buhner 6.00 15.00
ASMB Mookie Betts 6.00 15.00
ASMT Mike Trout 15.00 40.00
ASWM Willie Mays 8.00 20.00

2020 Topps Archives Snapshots Autographs

OVERALL AUTO ODDS ONE PER BOX
EXCHANGE DEADLINE 8/31/2022
ASAA Adbert Alzolay 5.00 12.00
ASAO Al Oliver 2.50 6.00
ASBA Bryan Abreu 2.50 6.00
ASBB Bo Bichette EXCH 60.00 150.00
ASBZ Barry Zito 3.00 8.00
ASDM Dustin May 12.00 30.00
ASEK Ed Kranepool 5.00 12.00
ASGT Gleyber Torres 25.00 60.00
ASHH Hunter Harvey 4.00 10.00
ASJA Jim Abbott 8.00 20.00
ASJB Jay Buhner 6.00 15.00
ASJK James Karinchak 6.00 15.00
ASJL Jesus Luzardo 8.00 20.00
ASJM Jeff McNeil 10.00 25.00
ASJS Juan Soto 50.00 120.00
ASJU Jose Urquidy 3.00 8.00
ASKL Kyle Lewis 25.00 60.00
ASLA Luis Arraez 5.00 12.00
ASLR Luis Robert EXCH 100.00 250.00
ASMD Mauricio Dubon 3.00 8.00
ASMT Mike Trout EXCH 400.00 800.00
ASNH Nico Hoerner 10.00 25.00
ASNR Nolan Ryan 75.00 200.00
ASOM Oscar Mercado 3.00 8.00
ASPA Pete Alonso 30.00 80.00
ASRA Ronald Acuna Jr. 60.00 150.00
ASRS Ruben Sierra 5.00 12.00
ASSO Shohei Ohtani
ASSR Steve Rogers 2.50 6.00
ASTE Tommy Edman 6.00 15.00
ASTG Tony Gonsolin 10.00 25.00
ASTL Tim Lincecum 20.00 50.00
ASTZ T.J. Zeuch 2.50 6.00
ASYA Yordan Alvarez 20.00 50.00
ASAAQ Aristides Aquino 6.00 15.00
ASBBR Bobby Bradley 3.00 8.00
ASMBE Matt Beaty 3.00 8.00
ASTGR Trent Grisham EXCH 15.00 40.00

2020 Topps Archives Snapshots Autographs Black and White Image

*BLK WHT/25: .8X TO 2X BASIC
STATED ODDS 1:15 HOBBY
STATED PRINT RUN 25 SER.#'d SETS
EXCHANGE DEADLINE 8/31/2022
ASAA Adbert Alzolay 15.00 40.00
ASBZ Barry Zito 8.00 20.00
ASDM Dustin May 30.00 80.00
ASEK Ed Kranepool 20.00 50.00
ASJA Jim Abbott 20.00 50.00
ASJB Jay Buhner 15.00 40.00
ASJK James Karinchak 20.00 50.00
ASJL Jesus Luzardo 20.00 50.00
ASRS Ruben Sierra 25.00 60.00

2020 Topps Archives Snapshots Autographs Blue

*BLUE/50: .5X TO 1.2X BASIC
STATED ODDS 1:8 HOBBY
STATED PRINT RUN 50 SER.#'d SETS
EXCHANGE DEADLINE 8/31/2022
ASDM Dustin May 20.00 50.00
ASJA Jim Abbott 12.00 30.00
ASJB Jay Buhner 10.00 25.00
ASJK James Karinchak 10.00 25.00
ASJL Jesus Luzardo 12.00 30.00
ASRS Ruben Sierra 15.00 40.00

2020 Topps Archives Snapshots Walk-Off Wires

STATED ODDS 1:2 HOBBY
WWI Ichiro 1.00 2.50
WWBB Bo Bichette 4.00 10.00
WWBH Bryce Harper 1.25 3.00
WWBP Buster Posey 2.00 5.00
WWBW Bernie Williams .60 1.50
WWDL DJ LeMahieu .75 2.00
WWDO David Ortiz .75 2.00
WWDW David Wright 1.50 4.00
WWGB George Brett 6.00 15.00
WWHA Hank Aaron 3.00 8.00
WWJB Johnny Bench 2.50 6.00
WWJC Jose Canseco .60 1.50
WWKH Keston Hiura 1.00 2.50
WWKS Kurt Suzuki 2.00 5.00
WWMK Max Kepler .60 1.50
WWMM Mark McGwire 2.00 5.00
WWMT Mark Teixeira .60 1.50
WWMV Mo Vaughn .50 1.25
WWMY Mike Yastrzemski 1.25 3.00
WWPA Pete Alonso 2.00 5.00
WWRA Ronald Acuna Jr. 3.00 8.00
WWRO Ryan O'Hearn .50 1.25
WWWM Willie Mays 3.00 8.00
WWWS Will Smith 1.50 4.00
WWMTE Miguel Tejada .50 1.25

2020 Topps Archives Snapshots Walk-Off Wires Color Image

*COLOR/25: 3X TO 8X BASIC
STATED ODDS 1:17 HOBBY
STATED PRINT RUN 25 SER.#'d SETS
WWBH Bryce Harper 10.00 25.00
WWBP Buster Posey 6.00 15.00
WWDW David Wright 10.00 25.00
WWGB George Brett 25.00 60.00
WWHA Hank Aaron 20.00 50.00
WWKH Keston Hiura 10.00 25.00
WWKS Kurt Suzuki 10.00 25.00
WWMM Mark McGwire 12.00 30.00
WWPA Pete Alonso 8.00 20.00
WWWM Willie Mays 15.00 40.00

2020 Topps Archives Snapshots Walk-Off Wires Autographs

STATED ODDS 1:17 HOBBY
PRINT RUNS B/WN 5-50 COPIES PER
NO PRICING ON QTY 15 OR LESS
EXCHANGE DEADLINE 8/31/2022
*COLOR/25: .5X TO 1.2X p/r 50
WWBW Bernie Williams 20.00 50.00
WWDL DJ LeMahieu 25.00 60.00
WWDW David Wright 20.00 50.00
WWKH Keston Hiura 15.00 40.00
WWMK Max Kepler 8.00 20.00
WWMV Mo Vaughn 40.00 100.00
WWRA Ronald Acuna Jr. 60.00 150.00
WWWS Will Smith 20.00 50.00
WWMTE Miguel Tejada 6.00 15.00

2018 Topps Big League

COMP.SET w/o EXCH (400) 25.00 60.00
NOW EXCH ODDS 1:10,093 HOBBY
NOW EXCH DEADLINE 11/5/2019
1 Aaron Judge .50 1.25
2 Luis Severino .15 .40
3 J.P. Crawford RC .25 .60
4 Jon Lester .15 .40
5 Jeurys Familia .15 .40
6 Zach Davies .12 .30
7 C.J. Cron .12 .30
8 Felix Hernandez .15 .40
9 Ender Inciarte .12 .30
10 Odubel Herrera .15 .40
11 Corey Dickerson .12 .30

12 Whit Merrifield .20 .50
13 Chris Archer .12 .30
14 Dinelson Lamet .12 .30
15 Cody Bellinger .40 1.00
16 Blake Snell .15 .40
17 Eric Thames .15 .40
18 Manny Margot .12 .30
19 Matt Olson .12 .30
20 Alex Gordon .15 .40
21 Rick Porcello .15 .40
22 Mark Reynolds .12 .30
23 Brian Dozier .15 .40
24 Daniel Mengden .12 .30
25 Bryce Harper .30 .75
26 Max Kepler .15 .40
27 Patrick Corbin .15 .40
28 Joey Votto .20 .50
29 Christian Yelich .25 .60
30 Andrew Miller .15 .40
31 Hunter Renfroe .12 .30
32 Marcus Semien .12 .30
33 Scooter Gennett .15 .40
34 Dominic Smith RC .25 .60
35 Gregory Polanco .15 .40
36 Yasiel Puig .20 .50
37 J.D. Martinez .20 .50
38 Byron Buxton .15 .40
39 Dansby Swanson .20 .50
40 Yoan Moncada .20 .50
41 Jason Vargas .12 .30
42 Hector Neris .12 .30
43 Jordy Mercer .12 .30
44 Trey Mancini .15 .40
45 Travis d'Arnaud .15 .40
46 Trevor Story .20 .50
47 Jeff Samardzija .12 .30
48 Ozzie Albies RC .75 2.00
49 Sean Newcomb .15 .40
50 Clayton Kershaw .40 1.00
51 Ian Kinsler .15 .40
52 Jason Heyward .15 .40
53 Brandon Drury .12 .30
54 Mitch Haniger .15 .40
55 Kevin Pillar .12 .30
56 Wil Myers .12 .30
57 Carlos Martinez .15 .40
58 Khris Davis .20 .50
59 Jameson Taillon .15 .40
60 Gerrit Cole .20 .50
61 Scott Schebler .15 .40
62 Robinson Cano .15 .40
63 Amed Rosario RC .30 .75
64 Alex Colome .12 .30
65 Matt Harvey .15 .40
66 Jose Urena .12 .30
67 Andrew Stevenson RC .25 .60
68 Edwin Encarnacion .20 .50
69 Nolan Arenado .25 .60
70 Francisco Lindor .20 .50
71 Tim Anderson .20 .50
72 Raisel Iglesias .15 .40
73 Jose Quintana .12 .30
74 Jake Lamb .15 .40
75 Garrett Richards .15 .40
76 Aroldis Chapman .20 .50
77 Austin Hays RC .40 1.00
78 Brad Ziegler .12 .30
79 Jonathan Villar .12 .30
80 Corey Seager .20 .50
81 Jonathan Schoop .12 .30
82 Ryan Braun .15 .40
83 Chris Sale .20 .50
84 Rio Ruiz .12 .30
85 Jose Ramirez .15 .40
86 Ken Giles .12 .30
87 Avisail Garcia .15 .40
88 Russell Martin .12 .30
89 Evan Longoria .15 .40
90 Didi Gregorius .15 .40
91 Anthony Rizzo .30 .75
92 Eric Hosmer .15 .40
93 Andrew Cashner .12 .30
94 Jean Segura .12 .30
95 Trevor Bauer .20 .50
96 Salvador Perez .15 .40
97 Zack Granite RC .25 .60
98 Nicky Delmonico RC .25 .60
99 Jose Abreu .20 .50
100 Eddie Rosario .20 .50
101 Aaron Nola .20 .50
102 Felix Jorge RC .25 .60
103 Paul Blackburn RC .25 .60
104 Jose Altuve .20 .50
105 Manny Machado .20 .50
106 Jake Arrieta .15 .40
107 Tommy Pham .12 .30
108 Jed Lowrie .12 .30
109 Yoenis Cespedes .20 .50
110 Richard Urena RC .25 .60
111 Paul Goldschmidt .20 .50
112 Clint Frazier RC .50 1.25
113 Rhys Hoskins RC 1.00 2.50
114 Marcell Ozuna .20 .50
115 Dexter Fowler .15 .40
116 Walker Buehler RC 1.25 3.00
117 Charlie Blackmon .20 .50
118 Lance McCullers Jr. .12 .30
119 Julio Teheran .15 .40
120 Justin Upton .15 .40
121 DJ LeMahieu .20 .50
122 Martin Perez .15 .40
123 Jorge Polanco .12 .30
124 Brandon Nimmo .15 .40
125 Alex Wood .12 .30
126 Roberto Osuna .12 .30
127 Willson Contreras .20 .50
128 Danny Duffy .12 .30
129 Starlin Castro .12 .30
130 Craig Kimbrel .15 .40
131 Josh Donaldson .15 .40
132 Kevin Kiermaier .15 .40
133 Nick Markakis .15 .40
134 Xander Bogaerts .20 .50
135 Freddie Freeman .25 .60
136 Brandon Woodruff RC .30 .75
137 James Paxton .15 .40
138 Johnny Cueto .15 .40
139 Ryan Zimmerman .15 .40
140 Joey Gallo .15 .40
141 Shohei Ohtani RC 1.50 4.00
142 Hunter Pence .15 .40
143 Josh Bell .15 .40
144 Nelson Cruz .20 .50
145 Carlos Carrasco .12 .30
146 Corey Knebel .12 .30
147 Ty Blach .12 .30
148 Dustin Pedroia .20 .50
149 David Peralta .12 .30
150 Mike Trout 1.00 2.50
151 Brandon Belt .15 .40
152 Anibal Sanchez .12 .30
153 Andrew McCutchen .20 .50
154 Matt Chapman .20 .50
155 Steven Souza Jr. .15 .40
156 Mike Leake .12 .30
157 Jake Odorizzi .12 .30
158 Chris Davis .12 .30
159 Mookie Betts .30 .75
160 Juan Lagares .12 .30
161 Tzu-Wei Lin .15 .40
162 Gary Sanchez .20 .50
163 Logan Morrison .12 .30
164 Carson Fulmer .12 .30
165 Chance Sisco RC .30 .75
166 Miguel Andujar RC 1.00 2.50
167 Jack Flaherty RC .40 1.00
168 Nomar Mazara .12 .30
169 Anthony Rendon .20 .50
170 Daniel Murphy .15 .40
171 Giancarlo Stanton .20 .50
172 Dee Gordon .12 .30
173 Tucker Barnhart .12 .30
174 Michael Fulmer .12 .30
175 Ervin Santana .12 .30
176 Lucas Duda .15 .40
177 Luke Weaver .15 .40
178 Albert Pujols .25 .60
179 Reynaldo Lopez .15 .40
180 Francisco Mejia RC .30 .75
181 Travis Shaw .12 .30
182 Trea Turner .15 .40
183 Carlos Santana .15 .40
184 Lorenzo Cain .12 .30
185 Shin-Soo Choo .15 .40
186 Josh Reddick .12 .30
187 Matt Kemp .15 .40
188 Orlando Arcia .12 .30
189 Tyler Saladino .12 .30
190 Sandy Alcantara RC .25 .60
191 Erick Fedde RC .25 .60
192 Javier Baez .25 .60
193 Maikel Franco .15 .40
194 Brandon Crawford .15 .40
195 Yolmer Sanchez .12 .30
196 Dallas Keuchel .15 .40
197 Kyle Schwarber .20 .50
198 Miguel Sano .15 .40
199 Paul DeJong .20 .50
200 Carlos Correa .20 .50
201 Cole Hamels .15 .40
202 Addison Russell .15 .40
203 Buster Posey .25 .60
204 A.J. Pollock .12 .30
205 Chris Taylor .15 .40
206 Kole Calhoun .12 .30
207 Tyler Glasnow .12 .30
208 Yangervis Solarte .12 .30
209 Andrelton Simmons .12 .30
210 Billy Hamilton .12 .30
211 Kendrys Morales .12 .30
212 Elvis Andrus .15 .40
213 Victor Robles RC .60 1.50
214 Dillon Peters RC .25 .60
215 Adam Jones .15 .40
216 Sean Manaea .12 .30
217 Zach Britton .12 .30
218 Gerardo Parra .12 .30
219 Jacob deGrom .20 .50
220 Adam Duvall .12 .30
221 Travis Jankowski .12 .30
222 Joe Panik .15 .40
223 Mike Zunino .12 .30
224 Jordan Zimmermann .15 .40
225 Miguel Gomez RC .25 .60
226 Ichiro .25 .60
227 Vince Velasquez .12 .30
228 Masahiro Tanaka .15 .40
229 Ricky Nolasco .12 .30
230 Adrian Beltre .20 .50
231 Marcus Stroman .15 .40
232 Marco Estrada .12 .30
233 Matt Boyd .12 .30
234 Ivan Nova .15 .40
235 Bartolo Colon .12 .30
236 Luis Castillo .15 .40
237 Ben Gamel .15 .40
238 Miguel Cabrera .20 .50
239 Jon Gray .12 .30
240 Max Scherzer .20 .50
241 Justin Turner .15 .40
242 Nicholas Castellanos .20 .50
243 Keon Broxton .12 .30
244 J.A. Happ .15 .40
245 Luis Perdomo .12 .30
246 Alcides Escobar .15 .40
247 Parker Bridwell RC .25 .60
248 Brad Miller .15 .40
249 Austin Hedges .12 .30
250 Rafael Devers RC .75 2.00
251 Stephen Strasburg .20 .50
252 George Springer .15 .40
253 Chad Bettis .12 .30
254 Yadier Molina .20 .50
255 Justin Smoak .12 .30
256 Kenley Jansen .15 .40
257 Clayton Richard .12 .30
258 Felipe Vazquez .15 .40
259 Tim Beckham .15 .40
260 Luiz Gohara RC .25 .60
261 Domingo Santana .15 .40
262 Jharel Cotton .12 .30
263 Sonny Gray .15 .40
264 Justin Bour .12 .30
265 Stephen Piscotty .12 .30
266 Ryon Healy .12 .30
267 Kevin Gausman .12 .30
268 Mikie Mahtook .12 .30
269 Justin Verlander .20 .50
270 Jose Iglesias .15 .40
271 James McCann .15 .40
272 Brad Hand .12 .30
273 Starling Marte .15 .40
274 Aaron Altherr .12 .30
275 Mike Moustakas .15 .40
276 Andrew Benintendi .20 .50
277 Kyle Seager .12 .30
278 Matt Carpenter .20 .50
279 Greg Allen RC .25 .60
280 Jackie Bradley Jr. .20 .50
281 Ketel Marte .15 .40
282 Noah Syndergaard .15 .40
283 Yasmany Tomas .12 .30
284 Lucas Giolito .15 .40
285 Jorge Alfaro .12 .30
286 Yuli Gurriel .15 .40
287 Alex Bregman .20 .50
288 Logan Forsythe .12 .30
289 Rougned Odor .15 .40
290 Corey Kluber .15 .40
291 Brian Anderson RC .30 .75
292 Jose Berrios .15 .40
293 Carlos Gonzalez .15 .40
294 Matt Moore .15 .40
295 Zack Cozart .12 .30
296 German Marquez .12 .30
297 Nick Williams RC .30 .75
298 Homer Bailey .12 .30
299 Zack Greinke .15 .40
300 Kris Bryant .25 .60
301 Arndo/Bllngr/Gllo .40 1.00
302 Gllo/Dvs/Jdge .50 1.25
303 Gldschmdt/Stntn/Blckmn .25 .60
304 Sprngr/Altve/Jdge .50 1.25
305 Inciarte/Gordon/Blackmon .20 .50
306 Andrs/Hsmr/Altve .15 .40
307 Herrera/Murphy/Arenado .25 .60
308 Btts/Rmrz/Lwre .30 .75
309 Arndo/Ozna/Stntn .25 .60
310 Dvs/Jdge/Cruz .50 1.25
311 Crpntr/Brnt/Vtto .25 .60
312 Trt/Encrncn/Jdge 1.00 2.50
313 Turner/Hamilton/Gordon .15 .40
314 Altve/Mybn/Mrrfeld .20 .50
315 Murphy/Turner/Blackmon .20 .50
316 Hsmr/Grca/Altve .15 .40
317 Frmn/Blckmn/Stntn .25 .60
318 Rmrz/Jdge/Trt 1.00 2.50
319 Strsbrg/Schrzr/Krshw .40 1.00
320 Severino/Sale/Kluber .20 .50
321 Grnke/Dvs/Krshw .40 1.00
322 Vargas/Kluber/Carrasco .15 .40
323 Ray/Scherzer/deGrom .20 .50
324 Archer/Kluber/Sale .20 .50
325 Knebel/Jansen/Holland .15 .40
326 Kimbrel/Osuna/Colome .15 .40
327 Cole/Samardzija/Peters .20 .50
328 Verlander/Santana/Sale .20 .50
329 Strsbrg/Schrzr/Krshw .40 1.00
330 Severino/Kluber/Sale .20 .50
331 Hank Aaron .40 1.00
332 Roger Clemens .25 .60
333 Whitey Ford .15 .40
334 Ernie Banks .20 .50
335 John Smoltz .20 .50
336 Cal Ripken Jr. .60 1.50
337 George Brett .40 1.00
338 Ted Williams .40 1.00
339 Bo Jackson .20 .50
340 Jim Palmer .15 .40
341 Honus Wagner .20 .50
342 Pedro Martinez .15 .40
343 Alex Rodriguez .25 .60
344 Frank Thomas .20 .50
345 Jeff Bagwell .15 .40
346 Rickey Henderson .20 .50
347 Johnny Bench .20 .50
348 Nolan Ryan .60 1.50
349 Mariano Rivera .25 .60
350 Sandy Koufax .40 1.00
351 Bricks Ivy .12 .30
352 Fountains .12 .30
353 Frank Thomas Statue .20 .50
354 Home Run Apple .12 .30
355 Minnie and Paul .12 .30
356 Swimming Pool .12 .30
357 Ernie Banks Statue .20 .50
358 Green Monster .12 .30
359 Touch Tank .12 .30
360 McCovey Cove .12 .30
361 Honus Wagner Statue .20 .50
362 Stan Musial Statue .30 .75
363 Bernie's Dugout .12 .30
364 B&O Warehouse .12 .30
365 Monument Park .12 .30
366 Jordan Hicks RC .50 1.25
367 Tyler O'Neill RC .40 1.00
368 Gleyber Torres RC 2.50 6.00
369 Ronald Acuna Jr. RC 5.00 12.00
370 Lourdes Gurriel Jr. RC .50 1.25
371 Christian Villanueva RC .25 .60
372 Scott Kingery RC .40 1.00
373 Harrison Bader RC .40 1.00
374 Ronald Guzman RC .25 .60
375 Franchy Cordero RC .25 .60
376 Edwin Diaz .15 .40
377 Keynan Middleton .12 .30
378 Jose Martinez .12 .30
379 Todd Frazier .15 .40
380 Dylan Bundy .15 .40
381 Dixon Machado .12 .30
382 Adeiny Hechavarria .12 .30
383 Tyler Austin .20 .50
384 Brett Gardner .15 .40
385 Pedro Alvarez .12 .30
386 Cesar Hernandez .12 .30
387 J.T. Realmuto .20 .50
388 Ben Zobrist .15 .40
389 Yan Gomes .20 .50
390 Jedd Gyorko .12 .30
391 Jason Kipnis .15 .40
392 Chase Utley .15 .40
393 Albert Almora Jr. .15 .40
394 Michael Taylor .12 .30
395 Mitch Moreland .12 .30
396 Jurickson Profar .15 .40
397 Robert Gsellman .12 .30
398 Andrew Triggs .12 .30
399 Chad Kuhl .12 .30
400 Eduardo Rodriguez .12 .30
NNO Topps Now Instant Win 25.00 60.00

2018 Topps Big League Black and White

*BLCK WHTE: 5X TO 12X BASIC
*BLCK WHTE RC: 2.5X TO 6X BASIC RC
STATED ODDS 1:60 HOBBY
STATED PRINT RUN 50 SER.#'d SETS

2018 Topps Big League Blue

*BLUE: 1.5X TO 4X BASIC
*BLUE RC: .75X TO 2X BASIC RC
INSERTED IN RETAIL PACKS

2018 Topps Big League Error Variations

STATED ODDS 1:507 HOBBY
1 Judge Reverse 15.00 40.00
15 Bellinger Reverse 20.00 50.00
25 Harper Blue band 10.00 25.00
50 Kershaw Reverse 12.00 30.00
63 Rosario Flipped 20.00 50.00
70 Lindor Flipped 15.00 40.00
104 Altuve Flipped 12.00 30.00
150 Trout Flipped 30.00 80.00
171 Stanton Grey jsy 20.00 50.00
300 Bryant Reverse 20.00 50.00

2018 Topps Big League Gold

*GOLD: 1.2X TO 3X BASIC
*GOLD RC: .6X TO 1.5X BASIC RC
STATED ODDS 1:1 HOBBY

2018 Topps Big League Players Weekend Photo Variations

STATED ODDS 1:3 HOBBY
1 Aaron Judge 1.50 4.00
19 Matt Olson .40 1.00
28 Joey Votto .60 1.50
38 Byron Buxton .50 1.25
48 Ozzie Albies 1.25 3.00
62 Robinson Cano .50 1.25
63 Amed Rosario .50 1.25
70 Francisco Lindor .60 1.50
80 Corey Seager .60 1.50
91 Anthony Rizzo 1.00 2.50
96 Salvador Perez .50 1.25
99 Jose Abreu .60 1.50
104 Jose Altuve .60 1.50
105 Manny Machado .60 1.50
111 Paul Goldschmidt .60 1.50
113 Rhys Hoskins 1.50 4.00
117 Charlie Blackmon .60 1.50
131 Josh Donaldson .50 1.25
150 Mike Trout 3.00 8.00
159 Mookie Betts 1.00 2.50
162 Gary Sanchez .60 1.50
203 Buster Posey .75 2.00
219 Jacob deGrom .60 1.50
230 Adrian Beltre .60 1.50
250 Rafael Devers 1.25 3.00
254 Yadier Molina .60 1.50
256 Kenley Jansen .50 1.25
276 Andrew Benintendi .60 1.50
287 Alex Bregman .60 1.50
300 Kris Bryant .75 2.00

2018 Topps Big League Rainbow Foil

*RAINBOW: 4X TO 10X BASIC
*RAINBOW RC: 2X TO 5X BASIC RC
STATED ODDS 1:30 HOBBY
STATED PRINT RUN 100 SER.#'d SETS

2018 Topps Big League Autographs

STATED ODDS 1:114 HOBBY
EXCHANGE DEADLINE 6/30/2020
*GOLD/99: .5X TO 1.2X BASIC
*BLCK/WHTE/25: .75X TO 2X BASIC
BLAAA Aaron Altherr 5.00 12.00
BLAAD Adam Duvall 5.00 12.00
BLAAG Avisail Garcia 3.00 8.00
BLABG Ben Gamel 4.00 10.00
BLABP Brandon Belt
BLACSP Cory Spangenberg 2.50 6.00
BLADJ Derek Jeter
BLADS Darryl Strawberry 10.00 25.00
BLAFT Frank Thomas 30.00 80.00
BLAGS Gary Sanchez 12.00 30.00
BLAGW Washington Mascot 12.00 30.00
BLAJA Jose Altuve 20.00 50.00
BLAJB Justin Bour 2.50 6.00
BLAJG Joey Gallo 6.00 15.00
BLAJH Josh Harrison 2.50 6.00
BLAJL Jake Lamb 3.00 8.00
BLAJR Jose Ramirez 12.00 30.00
BLAJS Justin Smoak 6.00 15.00
BLAJT Justin Turner
BLAKB Kris Bryant EXCH 30.00 80.00
BLAKBR Keon Broxton 2.50 6.00
BLAMC Matt Chapman 4.00 10.00
BLAMK Max Kepler 3.00 8.00
BLAMM Mikie Mahtook 2.50 6.00
BLAMO Matt Olson 2.50 6.00
BLAMT Mike Trout 200.00 400.00
BLANS Noah Syndergaard
BLAPP Phillie Phanatic 15.00 40.00
BLART Ronald Torreyes 6.00 15.00
BLASD Sean Doolittle 6.00 15.00
BLASS Steven Souza Jr. 3.00 8.00
BLATB Tim Beckham 8.00 20.00
BLATR Roosevelt Mascot
BLAWM Whit Merrifield 6.00 15.00

2018 Topps Big League Blaster Box Bottoms

HAND CUT FROM BLASTER BOXES
B1 Mike Trout 2.00 5.00
B2 Bryce Harper .60 1.50
B3 Shohei Ohtani 1.50 4.00
B4 Aaron Judge 1.00 2.50

2018 Topps Big League Ministers of Mash

STATED ODDS 1:12 HOBBY
MI1 Aaron Judge 1.25 3.00
MI2 Khris Davis .50 1.25
MI3 Cody Bellinger 1.00 2.50
MI4 Miguel Sano .40 1.00
MI5 Rhys Hoskins 1.25 3.00
MI6 Bryce Harper .75 2.00
MI7 Nelson Cruz .50 1.25
MI8 Giancarlo Stanton .50 1.25
MI9 Kris Bryant .60 1.50
MI10 Mike Trout 2.50 6.00

2018 Topps Big League Rookie Republic Autographs

STATED ODDS 1:102 HOBBY
EXCHANGE DEADLINE 6/30/2020
RRAM A.J. Minter 5.00 12.00
RRAR Amed Rosario 8.00 20.00
RRBA Brian Anderson 4.00 10.00
RRBW Brandon Woodruff 3.00 8.00
RRCF Clint Frazier 12.00 30.00
RRFM Francisco Mejia 4.00 10.00
RRGT Gleyber Torres 50.00 120.00
RRJC J.P. Crawford
RRJD J.D. Davis 4.00 10.00
RRJF Jack Flaherty 4.00 10.00
RRMA Miguel Andujar 15.00 40.00
RRND Nicky Delmonico 2.50 6.00
RROA Ozzie Albies 20.00 50.00
RRRA Ronald Acuna Jr. 60.00 150.00
RRRD Rafael Devers
RRRH Rhys Hoskins 20.00 50.00
RRRU Richard Urena 2.50 6.00
RRSA Sandy Alcantara 2.50 6.00
RRSO Shohei Ohtani 150.00 400.00
RRTN Tomas Nido 5.00 12.00
RRTW Tyler Wade 3.00 8.00
RRVR Victor Robles 15.00 40.00
RRWB Walker Buehler 10.00 25.00

2018 Topps Big League Rookie Republic Autographs Black and White

STATED ODDS 1:1988 HOBBY
STATED PRINT RUN 25 SER.#'d SETS
EXCHANGE DEADLINE 6/30/2020
RRJC J.P. Crawford 8.00 20.00

2018 Topps Big League Rookie Republic Autographs Gold

STATED ODDS 1:716 HOBBY
STATED PRINT RUN 99 SER.#'d SETS
EXCHANGE DEADLINE 6/30/2020
RRJC J.P. Crawford 5.00 12.00

2018 Topps Big League Star Caricature Reproductions

STATED ODDS 1:8 HOBBY
SCRAB Adrian Beltre .50 1.25
SCRAJ Aaron Judge 1.25 3.00
SCRAM Andrew McCutchen .50 1.25
SCRBB Byron Buxton .40 1.00
SCRBH Bryce Harper .75 2.00
SCRBP Buster Posey .60 1.50
SCRCC Carlos Correa .50 1.25
SCRCK Clayton Kershaw 1.00 2.50
SCREL Evan Longoria .40 1.00
SCRFF Freddie Freeman .60 1.50
SCRFL Francisco Lindor .50 1.25
SCRGS Giancarlo Stanton .50 1.25
SCRJA Jose Abreu .50 1.25
SCRJV Joey Votto .50 1.25
SCRKB Kris Bryant .60 1.50
SCRKD Khris Davis .50 1.25
SCRMB Mookie Betts .75 2.00
SCRMC Miguel Cabrera .50 1.25
SCRMM Manny Machado .50 1.25
SCRMS Marcus Stroman .40 1.00
SCRMT Mike Trout 2.50 6.00
SCRNA Nolan Arenado .60 1.50
SCRNS Noah Syndergaard .40 1.00
SCRPG Paul Goldschmidt .50 1.25
SCRRB Ryan Braun .40 1.00
SCRRC Robinson Cano .40 1.00
SCRRH Rhys Hoskins 1.25 3.00
SCRSP Salvador Perez .40 1.00
SCRWM Wil Myers .30 .75
SCRYM Yadier Molina .50 1.25

2019 Topps Big League

COMP.SET w/o EXCH (400) 20.00 50.00
1 Brad Keller RC .25 .60
2 Max Muncy .15 .40
3 Austin Hedges .12 .30
4 Yasiel Puig .20 .50
5 Josh Bell .15 .40
6A Kevin Gausman .12 .30
6B Fernando Tatis Jr. SP 3.00 8.00
7 Anthony Rizzo .30 .75
8 Adam Eaton .20 .50
9 Jake Cave RC .30 .75
10 David Fletcher .40 1.00
11 C.J. Cron .12 .30
12 Adam Engel .12 .30
13 Rougned Odor .15 .40
14 Jason Kipnis .15 .40
15 Ryon Healy .12 .30
16 Todd Frazier .15 .40
17 Shohei Ohtani .25 .60
18 Andrew Benintendi .20 .50
19 DJ LeMahieu .20 .50
20A Matt Carpenter .20 .50
20B Pete Alonso SP 6.00 15.00
21 Tyler Glasnow .12 .30
22 Ryan McMahon .12 .30
23 Austin Meadows .15 .40
24 Stephen Piscotty .12 .30
25 Chris Archer .12 .30
26 Kenley Jansen .15 .40
27 Zack Godley .12 .30
28 Marcus Stroman .15 .40
29 Eduardo Escobar .12 .30
30 Steven Souza Jr. .15 .40
31 Miguel Sano .15 .40
32 Aaron Judge .50 1.25
33 Jon Lester .15 .40
34 Justin Upton .15 .40
35 Corey Seager .20 .50
36 Marcus Semien .12 .30
37 Derek Dietrich .15 .40
38 Kyle Gibson .15 .40
39 Justin Bour .12 .30
40 Blake Snell .15 .40
41 Kevin Kiermaier .15 .40
42 Joey Gallo .15 .40
43 Ryan Braun .15 .40
44 Albert Almora Jr. .15 .40
45 Xander Bogaerts .20 .50
46 Didi Gregorius .15 .40
47 Danny Duffy .12 .30
48 Raisel Iglesias .12 .30
49 Billy Hamilton .15 .40
50 Ronald Acuna Jr. 1.00 2.50
51 Ronald Guzman .12 .30
52 Justin Smoak .12 .30
53 Josh Reddick .12 .30
54 Sean Manaea .12 .30
55 Steven Duggar RC .30 .75
56 Mark Trumbo .12 .30
57 DJ Stewart RC .30 .75
58 Alex Gordon .15 .40
59 Lucas Giolito .15 .40
60 Jhoulys Chacin .12 .30
61 Kyle Seager .12 .30
62 Wade Davis .12 .30
63 Ben Zobrist .15 .40
64 Stephen Strasburg .20 .50
65 Matt Kemp .15 .40
66 David Bote .15 .40
67 Touki Toussaint RC .30 .75
68 Shane Greene .12 .30
69 Brad Boxberger .12 .30
70 Jose Briceno RC .25 .60
71 Gorkys Hernandez .12 .30
72 Adalberto Mondesi .15 .40
73 Andrelton Simmons .12 .30
74A Buster Posey .25 .60
74B Eloy Jimenez SP 3.00 8.00
75 Trevor Bauer .20 .50
76 Nick Williams .12 .30
77 Paul Goldschmidt .20 .50
78 Lourdes Gurriel Jr. .15 .40
79 Eric Thames .12 .30
80 Magneuris Sierra .20 .50
81 Andrew Heaney .12 .30
82 Justus Sheffield .20 .50
83 Niko Goodrum .15 .40
84 Patrick Corbin .15 .40
85 Mike Zunino .12 .30
86 German Marquez .12 .30
87 Jose Ramirez .15 .40
88 Jake Arrieta .15 .40
89 Brandon Nimmo .15 .40
90 Brandon Belt .15 .40
91 Carlos Correa .20 .50
92 Colin Moran .12 .30
93 Salvador Perez .15 .40
94 Leonys Martin .12 .30
95 Kevin Newman RC .40 1.00
96 J.T. Realmuto .20 .50
97 Aaron Hicks .15 .40
98 Michael Fulmer .12 .30
99 Nicky Delmonico .12 .30
100 Jose Altuve .15 .40
101 Travis Jankowski .12 .30
102 Christin Stewart RC .30 .75
103 Jorge Alfaro .12 .30
104 Jose Abreu .20 .50
105 Felix Hernandez .15 .40
106 Orlando Arcia .12 .30
107 Ender Inciarte .12 .30
108 Corey Kluber .15 .40
109 Jameson Taillon .15 .40
110 Ehire Adrianza .12 .30
111 Joey Lucchesi .12 .30
112 Marcell Ozuna .20 .50
113 James McCann .15 .40
114 Yolmer Sanchez .12 .30
115 Mitch Garver .12 .30
116 Jeff McNeil RC .60 1.50
117 Scott Kingery .15 .40
118 Felipe Vazquez .12 .30
119 Mallex Smith .12 .30
120 Hunter Dozier .12 .30
121 Nicholas Castellanos .20 .50
122 Amed Rosario .15 .40
123 Gregory Polanco .15 .40
124 Dawel Lugo RC .40 1.00
125 Juan Soto .60 1.50
126 Jaime Barria .12 .30
127 Delino DeShields .12 .30
128 Yoan Moncada .20 .50
129 Max Scherzer .20 .50
130 Jorge Bonifacio .12 .30
131 Jonathan Schoop .12 .30
132 Yairo Munoz .12 .30
133 J.D. Martinez .20 .50
134 Trea Turner .15 .40
135 Trevor Richards .12 .30
136 Joey Votto .20 .50
137 Nick Ahmed .12 .30
138 Brett Phillips .12 .30
139 Welington Castillo .12 .30
140 Starling Marte .15 .40
141 Joc Pederson .15 .40
142 Chris Iannetta .12 .30
143 David Dahl .12 .30
144 Jose Peraza .15 .40
145 Ryan O'Hearn RC .25 .60
146 Trey Mancini .15 .40
147 Willy Adames .15 .40
148 Kyle Schwarber .20 .50
149 Dee Gordon .12 .30
150 Albert Pujols .25 .60
151 Rick Porcello .15 .40
152 Charlie Blackmon .20 .50
153 Dylan Bundy .15 .40
154 Jose Berrios .15 .40
155 Jean Segura .20 .50
156 Daniel Palka .12 .30
157 Masahiro Tanaka .15 .40
158 Dominic Smith .12 .30
159 Justin Verlander .20 .50
160 Kris Bryant .25 .60
161 Yoenis Cespedes .20 .50
162 Zack Greinke .15 .40
163 Danny Jansen RC .25 .60
164 Luis Severino .15 .40
165 JaCoby Jones .15 .40
166 Matt Chapman .20 .50
167 Adam Duvall .15 .40
168 Manny Machado .20 .50
169 Adam Frazier .12 .30
170 Mike Trout 1.00 2.50
171 Mitch Haniger .15 .40
172 Travis Shaw .12 .30
173 Miguel Rojas .12 .30
174 George Springer .15 .40
175 Greg Allen .12 .30
176 Hunter Renfroe .12 .30
177 Wilmer Difo .12 .30
178 Tim Beckham .15 .40
179 Chris Taylor .15 .40
180 Jonathan Villar .12 .30
181 Michael Conforto .15 .40
182 Miguel Andujar .20 .50
183 Victor Robles .25 .60
184 Alex Bregman .20 .50
185 Eduardo Nunez .12 .30
186 Jon Gray .12 .30
187 Jake Lamb .15 .40
188 Ben Gamel .15 .40
189 Miles Mikolas .20 .50
190 Edwin Encarnacion .20 .50
191 Robbie Ray .12 .30
192 Nolan Arenado .25 .60

193 Kole Calhoun .12 .30
194 Franmil Reyes .12 .30
195 Freddie Freeman .25 .60
196 Jose Martinez .12 .30
197 Mike Foltynewicz .20 .50
198 Clayton Kershaw .40 1.00
199 Joe Panik .15 .40
200 Mookie Betts .30 .75
201 Isiah Kiner-Faleta .12 .30
202 Paul DeJong .20 .50
203 Tommy Pham .12 .30
204 Cedric Mullins RC .40 1.00
205 Matt Boyd .12 .30
206 Johnny Cueto .15 .40
207 Jackie Bradley Jr. .20 .50
208 Ozzie Albies .20 .50
209 Ian Desmond .12 .30
210 Mitch Moreland .12 .30
211 Miguel Cabrera .20 .50
212 Carlos Martinez .15 .40
213 Andrew Cashner .12 .30
214 David Price .15 .40
215 Javier Baez .25 .60
216 Pablo Sandoval .15 .40
217 Wil Myers .12 .30
218 Francisco Cervelli .12 .30
219 Chance Sisco .12 .30
220 Josh James RC .40 1.00
221 Avisail Garcia .15 .40
222 Rowdy Tellez RC .40 1.00
223 Nomar Mazara .12 .30
224 Gary Sanchez .20 .50
225 Jay Bruce .15 .40
226 Dereck Rodriguez .12 .30
227 Jorge Soler .20 .50
228 Rhys Hoskins .25 .60
229 Maikel Franco .15 .40
230 Ketel Marte .15 .40
231 Scooter Gennett .15 .40
232 Cesar Hernandez .12 .30
233 Evan Longoria .15 .40
234 Teoscar Hernandez .20 .50
235 James Paxton .15 .40
236 Giancarlo Stanton .20 .50
237 Ken Giles .12 .30
238 Ramon Laureano RC .50 1.25
239 Aaron Nola .15 .40
240 Trevor Story .20 .50
241 Anthony Rendon .20 .50
242 Whit Merrifield .20 .50
243 Pat Neshek .12 .30
244 Lorenzo Cain .12 .30
245 Taylor Ward RC .25 .60
246 Starlin Castro .12 .30
247 Willians Astudillo RC .25 .60
248 Robinson Cano .15 .40
249 Franklin Barreto .12 .30
250 Jacob deGrom .20 .50
251 Tyler O'Neill .15 .40
252 Dansby Swanson .20 .50
253 Josh Donaldson .15 .40
254 Yu Darvish .20 .50
255 Tim Anderson .20 .50
256 Brandon Crawford .15 .40
257 Matt Duffy .12 .30
258 Johan Camargo .12 .30
259 Sean Newcomb .12 .30
260 Kevin Pillar .12 .30
261 Lewis Brinson .12 .30
262 Eugenio Suarez .15 .40
263 Joey Rickard .12 .30
264 Sandy Alcantara .12 .30
265 Andrew McCutchen .20 .50
266 Michael Kopech RC .50 1.25
267 Francisco Lindor .20 .50
268 Ryan Zimmerman .15 .40
269 Caleb Joseph .12 .30
270 Luke Voit .30 .75
271 Willson Contreras .15 .40
272 Tanner Roark .12 .30
273 Eddie Rosario .15 .40
274 Yonder Alonso .12 .30
275 David Peralta .12 .30
276 Jeimer Candelario .12 .30
277 Sean Doolittle .12 .30
278 Odubel Herrera .15 .40
279 Edwin Diaz .15 .40
280 Corey Dickerson .12 .30
281 Nick Martini RC .25 .60
282 Justin Turner .15 .40
283 Shane Bieber .20 .50
284 Luis Urias RC .40 1.00
285 Cole Hamels .15 .40
286 Zack Wheeler .15 .40
287 Jesus Aguilar .12 .30
288 Yan Gomes .20 .50
289 Austin Dean RC .25 .60
290 Collin McHugh .12 .30
291 Jurickson Profar .15 .40
292 Corbin Burnes RC .40 1.00
293 Josh Hader .12 .30
294 Kyle Tucker RC .50 1.25
295 Jack Flaherty .15 .40
296 Tyler Naquin .12 .30
297 Luis Castillo .15 .40
298 Walker Buehler .25 .60
299 Roberto Osuna .12 .30
300 Christian Yelich .25 .60
301 Harrison Bader .15 .40
302 Kyle Freeland .15 .40
303 Shin-Soo Choo .15 .40
304 Alen Hanson .15 .40
305 Scott Schebler .15 .40
306 Mike Minor .12 .30
307 Carlos Santana .15 .40
308 Tucker Barnhart .12 .30
309 Joey Wendle .12 .30
310 Rafael Devers .25 .60
311 Aledmys Diaz .12 .30
312 Khris Davis .20 .50
313 Jesse Winker .12 .30
314 Kendrys Morales .12 .30
315 Jorge Polanco .12 .30
316 Dustin Pedroia .20 .50
317 Brian Anderson .12 .30
318 Yuli Gurriel .15 .40
319 Gleyber Torres .40 1.00
320 Bryce Harper .30 .75
321 Eric Hosmer .15 .40
322 Manny Margot .12 .30
323 Max Kepler .15 .40
324 Howie Kendrick .12 .30
325 Gerrit Cole .20 .50
326 Ian Happ .15 .40
327 Cody Bellinger .40 1.00
328 Brandon Lowe RC .40 1.00
329 Blake Treinen .12 .30
330 Mike Fiers .12 .30
331 Brock Holt .12 .30
332 Ian Kinsler .15 .40
333 Kirby Yates .15 .40
334 Matt Olson .12 .30
335 Jose Leclerc .12 .30
336 Tyler Austin .20 .50
337 Chris Sale .20 .50
338 Yadier Molina .20 .50
339 Tyler Mahle .12 .30
340 Randal Grichuk .12 .30
341 Jose Urena .12 .30
342 Noah Syndergaard .15 .40
343 Elvis Andrus .15 .40
344 Nolan Arenado .25 .60
Matt Carpenter
Trevor Story
345 Gallo/Martinez/Davis .20 .50
346 Carpenter/Yelich/Blackmon .25 .60
347 Martinez/Lindor/Betts .30 .75
348 Markakis/Yelich/Freeman .25 .60
349 Castellanos/Martinez/Merrifield .20 .50
350 Markakis/Bregman/Freeman .25 .60
351 Betts/Bregman/Anduar .30 .75
352 Arenado/Yelich/Baez .25 .60
353 Encarnacion/Davis/Martinez .20 .50
354 Santana/Votto/Harper .30 .75
355 Bregman/Ramirez/Trout 1.00 2.50
356 Starling Marte .15 .40
Billy Hamilton
Trea Turner
357 Jose Ramirez .20 .50
Mallex Smith
Whit Merrifield
358 Gennett/Freeman/Yelich .25 .60
359 Altuve/Martinez/Betts .30 .75
360 Arenado/Story/Yelich .25 .60
361 Trout/Martinez/Betts 1.00 2.50
362 Max Scherzer .20 .50
Aaron Nola
Jacob deGrom
363 Justin Verlander .20 .50
Trevor Bauer
Blake Snell
364 Max Scherzer .20 .50
Miles Mikolas
Jon Lester
365 Luis Severino .15 .40
Corey Kluber
Blake Snell
366 Patrick Corbin .20 .50
Max Scherzer
Jacob deGrom
367 Sale/Cole/Verlander .20 .50
368 Felipe Vazquez .15 .40
Kenley Jansen
Wade Davis
369 Blake Treinen .15 .40
Craig Kimbrel
Edwin Diaz
370 Aaron Nola .20 .50
Max Scherzer
Jacob deGrom
371 Dallas Keuchel .20 .50
Justin Verlander
Corey Kluber
372 Aaron Nola .20 .50
Max Scherzer
Jacob deGrom
373 Corey Kluber .20 .50
Justin Verlander
Blake Snell
374 J.D. Martinez .20 .50
375 Christian Yelich .25 .60
376 Yadier Molina .20 .50
377 Edwin Diaz .15 .40
378 Josh Hader .12 .30
379 Blake Snell .15 .40
380 Shohei Ohtani .25 .60
381 Ronald Acuna Jr. 1.00 2.50
382 Blake Snell .15 .40
383 Jacob deGrom .20 .50
384 Mookie Betts .30 .75
385 Christian Yelich .25 .60
386 George Springer .15 .40
387 Adrian Beltre .20 .50
388 Sean Manaea .12 .30
389 Mookie Betts .30 .75
390 Albert Pujols .25 .60
391 Walker Buehler .25 .60
392 James Paxton .15 .40
393 Gleyber Torres .40 1.00
394 Edwin Diaz .15 .40
395 Rowdy Tellez .20 .50
396 Shohei Ohtani .25 .60
397 Juan Soto .60 1.50
398 Christian Yelich .25 .60
399 Max Scherzer .20 .50
400 Brock Holt .12 .30

2019 Topps Big League Artist Rendition Black and White

*BLCK WHTE: 5X TO 12X BASIC
*BLCK WHTE RC: 2.5X TO 6X BASIC RC
STATED ODDS 1:XXX
STATED PRINT RUN 50 SER.#'d SETS

2019 Topps Big League Blue

*BLUE: 1.5X TO 4X BASIC
*BLUE RC: .75X TO 2X BASIC RC
STATED ODDS 1:XXX

2019 Topps Big League Gold

*GOLD: 1.2X TO 3X BASIC
*GOLD RC: .6X TO 1.5X BASIC RC
STATED ODDS 1:XXX

2019 Topps Big League Rainbow Foil

*RAINBOW: 4X TO 10X BASIC
*RAINBOW RC: 2X TO 5X BASIC RC
STATED ODDS 1:XXX
STATED PRINT RUN 100 SER.#'d SETS

2019 Topps Big League Autographs

STATED ODDS 1:XXX HOBBY
EXCHANGE DEADLINE 4/31/2021
*GOLD/99: .5X TO 1.2X BASIC
*BLCK/WHTE/25: .75X TO 2X BASIC
BLAO Orbit
BLAAB Alex Bregman EXCH 15.00 40.00
BLAAJ Aaron Judge EXCH 60.00 150.00
BLABN Brandon Nimmo 3.00 8.00
BLABS Blake Snell 3.00 8.00
BLACR Cal Ripken Jr. 50.00 120.00
BLACT Chris Taylor 3.00 8.00
BLADR Dereck Rodriguez 8.00 20.00
BLAER Eddie Rosario 8.00 20.00
BLAFR Franmil Reyes 2.50 6.00
BLAHB Harrison Bader 3.00 8.00
BLAJB Jose Berrios 6.00 15.00
BLAJD Jacob deGrom 20.00 50.00
BLAJH Josh Hader 2.50 6.00
BLAJM Jose Martinez 3.00 8.00
BLAJS Jean Segura 6.00 15.00
BLAJSO Juan Soto 40.00 100.00
BLAKB Kris Bryant 50.00 120.00
BLAKF Kyle Freeland 3.00 8.00
BLALV Luke Voit 25.00 60.00
BLAMC Matt Chapman 6.00 15.00
BLAMH Mitch Haniger 6.00 15.00
BLAMMU Max Muncy 3.00 8.00
BLAMT Mike Trout 200.00 500.00
BLANR Nolan Ryan 60.00 150.00
BLAPN Pat Neshek 5.00 12.00
BLARA Ronald Acuna Jr. 40.00 100.00
BLARY Ryan Yarbrough 2.50 6.00
BLASB Shane Bieber 4.00 10.00
BLASM Sean Manaea 2.50 6.00
BLASO Shohei Ohtani
BLASP Steve Pearce 5.00 12.00
BLATS Trevor Story 6.00 15.00
BLAWA Willy Adames 2.50 6.00
BLAWC Willson Contreras 10.00 25.00

2019 Topps Big League Ballpark Oddities

STATED ODDS 1:XXX
BPO1 Christian Yelich 12.00 30.00
BPO2 Jose Reyes 8.00 20.00
BPO3 Shohei Ohtani 12.00 30.00
BPO4 Francisco Arcia 10.00 25.00
BPO5 Joe Panik 8.00 20.00
BPO6 Edwin Jackson 6.00 15.00
BPO7 Ryan Yarbrough 6.00 15.00
BPO8 Jordan Hicks 8.00 20.00
BPO9 Michael Lorenzen 6.00 15.00
BPO10 Russell Martin 6.00 15.00

2019 Topps Big League Blast Off

STATED ODDS 1:XXX
BO1 Mike Trout 2.50 6.00
BO2 Shohei Ohtani .60 1.50
BO3 J.D. Martinez .50 1.25
BO4 Javier Baez .60 1.50
BO5 Avisail Garcia .40 1.00
BO6 Trevor Story .50 1.25
BO7 Christian Yelich .60 1.50
BO8 Aaron Judge 1.25 3.00
BO9 Gary Sanchez .50 1.25
BO10 Giancarlo Stanton .50 1.25
BO11 Matt Olson .30 .75
BO12 Khris Davis .50 1.25
BO13 Marcell Ozuna .50 1.25
BO14 Joey Gallo .40 1.00
BO15 Bryce Harper .75 2.00

2019 Topps Big League Players Weekend Nicknames

STATED ODDS 1:XXX
PW1 Shohei Ohtani .60 1.50
PW2 Jose Altuve .40 1.00
PW3 Matt Chapman .50 1.25
PW4 Ronald Acuna Jr. 2.50 6.00
PW5 Christian Yelich .60 1.50
PW6 Matt Carpenter .50 1.25
PW7 Javier Baez .60 1.50
PW8 Eduardo Escobar .30 .75
PW9 Walker Buehler .60 1.50
PW10 Brandon Crawford .40 1.00
PW11 Francisco Lindor .50 1.25
PW12 Mitch Haniger .40 1.00
PW13 Todd Frazier .40 1.00
PW14 Juan Soto 1.50 4.00
PW15 Jonathan Villar .30 .75
PW16 Eric Hosmer .40 1.00
PW17 Maikel Franco .40 1.00
PW18 Starling Marte .40 1.00
PW19 Nomar Mazara .30 .75
PW20 Blake Snell .40 1.00
PW21 Mookie Betts .75 2.00
PW22 Mitch Moreland .30 .75
PW23 Nolan Arenado .60 1.50
PW24 Salvador Perez .40 1.00
PW25 Nicholas Castellanos .50 1.25
PW26 Jose Berrios .40 1.00
PW27 Tim Anderson .50 1.25
PW28 Miguel Andujar .50 1.25
PW29 Jason Heyward .40 1.00
PW30 Brian Anderson .30 .75

2019 Topps Big League Rookie Republic Autographs

STATED ODDS 1:XXX HOBBY
EXCHANGE DEADLINE 4/31/2021
*GOLD/99: .5X TO 1.2X BASIC
*BLCK/WHTE/25: .75X TO 2X BASIC
RRABK Brad Keller 4.00 10.00
RRACA Chance Adams 2.50 6.00
RRADL Dawel Lugo 6.00 15.00
RRAEJ Eloy Jimenez 20.00 50.00
RRAFT Fernando Tatis Jr. 50.00 120.00
RRAJM Jeff McNeil 12.00 30.00
RRAJS Justus Sheffield 6.00 15.00
RRAKA Kolby Allard 4.00 10.00
RRAKN Kevin Newman 4.00 10.00
RRAKT Kyle Tucker 10.00 25.00
RRALU Luis Urias 4.00 10.00
RRAMK Michael Kopech 5.00 12.00
RRARO Ryan O'Hearn 5.00 12.00
RRART Rowdy Tellez 4.00 10.00
RRASR Sean Reid-Foley 2.50 6.00
RRATW Taylor Ward 5.00 12.00
RRAVG Vladimir Guerrero Jr.
RRAWA Willians Astudillo 10.00 25.00

2019 Topps Big League Star Caricature Reproductions

STATED ODDS 1:XXX
SCRAB Andrew Benintendi .50 1.25
SCRAG Alex Gordon .40 1.00
SCRAN Aaron Nola .40 1.00
SCRAR Anthony Rizzo .75 2.00
SCRBC Brandon Crawford .40 1.00
SCRBH Billy Hamilton .40 1.00
SCRBS Blake Snell .40 1.00
SCRCA Chris Archer .30 .75
SCRCB Charlie Blackmon .50 1.25
SCRCD Chris Davis .30 .75
SCRCK Corey Kluber .40 1.00
SCRCS Corey Seager .40 1.00
SCRCY Christian Yelich .60 1.50
SCRDG Dee Gordon .30 .75
SCREH Eric Hosmer .40 1.00
SCRGT Gleyber Torres 1.00 2.50
SCRJA Jose Altuve .40 1.00
SCRJB Jose Berrios .40 1.00
SCRLG Lourdes Gurriel Jr. .40 1.00
SCRMC Matt Carpenter .50 1.25
SCRMS Max Scherzer .50 1.25
SCRNC Nicholas Castellanos .50 1.25
SCRNM Nomar Mazara .30 .75
SCRRA Ronald Acuna Jr. 2.50 6.00
SCRSC Starlin Castro .30 .75
SCRSO Shohei Ohtani .60 1.50
SCRSP Stephen Piscotty .30 .75
SCRYM Yoan Moncada .50 1.25
SCRZG Zack Greinke .40 1.00
SCRARO Amed Rosario .40 1.00

2019 Topps Big League Wall Climbers

STATED ODDS 1:XXX
WC1 Kevin Pillar .30 .75
WC2 Ronald Acuna Jr. 2.50 6.00
WC3 Max Kepler .40 1.00
WC4 Christian Yelich .60 1.50
WC5 Odubel Herrera .40 1.00
WC6 Billy Hamilton .40 1.00
WC7 Adam Engel .30 .75
WC8 Corey Dickerson .30 .75
WC9 Mookie Betts .75 2.00
WC10 Mike Trout 2.50 6.00

2020 Topps Big League

COMPLETE SET (300) 15.00 40.00
1 Salvador Perez .15 .40
2 Elvis Andrus .15 .40
3 Patrick Corbin .15 .40
4 Nelson Cruz .20 .50
5 George Springer .15 .40
6 Eric Hosmer .15 .40
7 Jonathan Schoop .12 .30
8 Jose Urquidy RC .15 .40
9 Willson Contreras .20 .50
10 DJ LeMahieu .20 .50
11 Mike Moustakas .15 .40
12 Tommy La Stella .12 .30
13 Dee Gordon .12 .30
14 Joey Votto .20 .50
15 Miguel Sano .15 .40
16 Yusei Kikuchi .15 .40
17 Roberto Perez .12 .30
18 Niko Goodrum .15 .40
19 Lorenzo Cain .12 .30
20 Griffin Canning .20 .50
21 Cole Hamels .15 .40
22 Eduardo Escobar .12 .30
23 Walker Buehler .25 .60
24 Alex Young RC .12 .30
25 Brian Anderson .12 .30
26 Matthew Boyd .12 .30
27 Bryan Reynolds .15 .40
28 Shohei Ohtani .25 .60
29 Pete Alonso .50 1.25
30 Kole Calhoun .12 .30
31 Bryce Harper .30 .75
32 Jorge Soler .20 .50
33 Tommy Edman .20 .50
34 Zack Collins RC .15 .40
35 Joey Lucchesi .12 .30
36 Noah Syndergaard .15 .40
37 Jesus Aguilar .12 .30
38 Ryan McMahon .12 .30
39 Nolan Arenado .25 .60
40 Nomar Mazara .12 .30
41 Michael Chavis .15 .40
42 Jeff McNeil .15 .40
43 Cody Bellinger .40 1.00
44 C.J. Cron .12 .30
45 Whit Merrifield .20 .50
46 Nick Senzel .20 .50
47 Aaron Nola .20 .50
48 Keston Hiura .25 .60
49 David Price .15 .40
50 Austin Riley .30 .75
51 Ramon Laureano .20 .50
52 J.T. Realmuto .20 .50
53 Marcus Stroman .15 .40
54 Ozzie Albies .20 .50
55 Sonny Gray .15 .40
56 Sean Murphy RC .20 .50
57 Christian Yelich .25 .60
58 A.J. Puk RC .25 .60
59 Kolten Wong .15 .40
60 Dustin May RC .50 1.25
61 Jesus Luzardo RC .25 .60
62 Hunter Harvey RC .20 .50
63 Max Kepler .15 .40
64 Evan Longoria .15 .40
65 Blake Snell .15 .40
66 Luis Castillo .15 .40
67 Aaron Civale RC .20 .50
68 Mike Trout 1.00 2.50
69 Eloy Jimenez .40 1.00
70 Adalberto Mondesi .20 .50
71 Aroldis Chapman .20 .50
72 Anthony Rizzo .30 .75
73 Charlie Morton .20 .50
74 Amed Rosario .15 .40
75 Jon Lester .15 .40
76 Mike Minor .12 .30
77 Charlie Blackmon .20 .50
78 Alex Bregman .20 .50
79 Jordan Yamamoto RC .15 .40
80 Ian Desmond .12 .30
81 Yasmani Grandal .12 .30
82 Ronald Acuna Jr. .75 2.00
83 Trent Grisham RC .50 1.25
84 Gerrit Cole .30 .75
85 Rafael Devers .25 .60
86 Trea Turner .15 .40
87 Willy Adames .15 .40
88 Dallas Keuchel .15 .40
89 Paul Goldschmidt .20 .50
90 Xander Bogaerts .20 .50
91 Shin-Soo Choo .15 .40
92 Gleyber Torres .40 1.00
93 Javier Baez .25 .60
94 Stephen Strasburg .20 .50
95 Robinson Cano .15 .40
96 Hunter Dozier .12 .30
97 Trevor Story .20 .50
98 Max Fried .20 .50
99 Nicky Lopez .12 .30
100 Michael Conforto .15 .40
101 Joe Musgrove .12 .30
102 Fernando Tatis Jr. .75 2.00
103 Eugenio Suarez .15 .40
104 Mitch Keller .20 .50
105 Miguel Cabrera .20 .50
106 Starling Marte .15 .40
107 Aristides Aquino RC .25 .60
108 Bo Bichette RC 1.00 2.50
109 Matt Olson .12 .30
110 Andres Munoz RC .15 .40
111 Juan Soto .60 1.50
112 Buster Posey .25 .60
113 Albert Pujols .25 .60
114 Jorge Polanco .15 .40
115 Ryan Braun .15 .40
116 Freddie Freeman .25 .60
117 Austin Meadows .15 .40
118 Jorge Alfaro .12 .30
119 Andrew Benintendi .20 .50
120 Jean Segura .12 .30
121 Jacob deGrom .20 .50
122 Brendan McKay RC .20 .50
123 Yordan Alvarez RC .60 1.50
124 Wil Myers .15 .40
125 Luis Arraez .25 .60
126 Jack Flaherty .15 .40
127 Yadier Molina .20 .50
128 Lourdes Gurriel Jr. .15 .40
129 Dansby Swanson .20 .50
130 Andrelton Simmons .12 .30
131 German Marquez .20 .50
132 Jeff Samardzija .12 .30
133 Trey Mancini .20 .50
134 Max Scherzer .20 .50
135 Jordan Montgomery .20 .50
136 David Peralta .12 .30
137 Chris Archer .12 .30
138 Brandon Crawford .15 .40
139 Nico Hoerner RC .50 1.25
140 Kevin Newman .15 .40
141 Vladimir Guerrero Jr. .40 1.00
142 Eddie Rosario .15 .40
143 Harold Ramirez .12 .30
144 Will Smith .25 .60
145 Marcus Semien .12 .30
146 Danny Santana .12 .30
147 John Means .12 .30
148 Maikel Franco .15 .40
149 Chris Sale .20 .50
150 Hyun-Jin Ryu .15 .40
151 Michel Baez RC .12 .30
152 Christian Walker .15 .40
153 Gary Sanchez .20 .50
154 Shane Bieber .20 .50
155 Mitch Garver .12 .30
156 Nick Solak RC .20 .50
157 Brandon Lowe .20 .50
158 Gavin Lux RC .75 2.00
159 Paul DeJong .20 .50
160 Kris Bryant .25 .60
161 Jose Berrios .15 .40
162 Carter Kieboom .15 .40
163 Mitch Haniger .15 .40
164 Orlando Arcia .12 .30
165 Daniel Murphy .15 .40
166 Giancarlo Stanton .20 .50
167 Josh Donaldson .15 .40
168 Brendan Rodgers .20 .50
169 Isan Diaz RC .20 .50
170 Eduardo Rodriguez .12 .30
171 Corey Kluber .15 .40
172 Chris Paddack .20 .50
173 Hanser Alberto .12 .30
174 Victor Robles .25 .60
175 Dawel Lugo .12 .30
176 Mallex Smith .12 .30
177 Mike Clevinger .15 .40
178 Lucas Giolito .15 .40
179 Jose Abreu .20 .50
180 Kyle Lewis RC 1.00 2.50
181 Chance Sisco .12 .30
182 Jose Ramirez .15 .40
183 Zack Wheeler .15 .40
184 Manny Machado .20 .50
185 Randal Grichuk .12 .30
186 Mike Yastrzemski .30 .75
187 Howie Kendrick .12 .30
188 Rhys Hoskins .25 .60
189 Carlos Correa .20 .50
190 Brandon Woodruff .12 .30
191 Gio Urshela .20 .50
192 Jonathan Villar .12 .30
193 Cavan Biggio .25 .60
194 Josh Hader .12 .30
195 Andrew McCutchen .20 .50
196 J.D. Martinez .20 .50
197 Kyle Seager .12 .30
198 Corey Seager .20 .50
199 Jake Rogers RC .12 .30
200 Renato Nunez .15 .40
201 Trevor Bauer .20 .50
202 Carlos Santana .15 .40
203 Aaron Judge .50 1.25
204 Josh Bell .15 .40
205 Matt Chapman .20 .50
206 Khris Davis .20 .50
207 Mike Soroka .20 .50
208 Robbie Ray .15 .40
209 Daniel Vogelbach .12 .30
210 Ketel Marte .15 .40
211 Tim Anderson .20 .50
212 Kyle Schwarber .20 .50
213 Rowdy Tellez .15 .40
214 Anthony Rendon .20 .50
215 Francisco Lindor .20 .50
216 Joey Gallo .15 .40
217 Zack Greinke .20 .50
218 Max Muncy .15 .40
219 Oscar Mercado .15 .40
220 Jose Altuve .15 .40
221 Didi Gregorius .15 .40
222 Joc Pederson .12 .30
223 Hunter Renfroe .12 .30
224 Gregory Polanco .15 .40
225 Yoan Moncada .20 .50
226 Brandon Belt .15 .40
227 Dakota Hudson .15 .40
228 Kevin Kiermaier .15 .40
229 Zac Gallen RC .30 .75
230 Clayton Kershaw .40 1.00
231 Freddy Galvis .12 .30
232 Luis Robert RC 1.25 3.00
233 Mookie Betts .40 1.00
234 Scott Kingery .20 .50
235 Justin Verlander .20 .50
236 Alnso/Bllngr/Srz LL .50 1.25
237 Brgmn/Trt/Slr LL 1.00 2.50
238 Rndn/Bllngr/Acna Jr. LL .75 2.00
239 Semien/Devers/Betts LL .40 1.00
240 Arenado/Marte/Albies LL .25 .60
241 LeMahieu/Devers/Merrifield LL .25 .60
242 Albies/Seager/Rendon LL .20 .50
243 Semien/Devers/Bogaerts LL .25 .60
244 Frmn/Alnso/Rndn LL .50 1.25
245 Soler/Bogaerts/Abreu LL .20 .50
246 Grndl/Soto/Hskns LL .60 1.50
247 Sntna/Trt/Brgmn LL 1.00 2.50
248 Ylch/Trnr/Acna Jr. LL .75 2.00
249 Villar/Mondesi/Smith LL .20 .50
250 Marte/Rendon/Yelich LL .25 .60
251 Moncada/LeMahieu/Anderson LL .20 .50
252 Rndn/Bllngr/Ylch LL .40 1.00
253 Brgmn/Cruz/Trt LL 1.00 2.50
254 Soroka/deGrom/Ryu LL .20 .50
255 Morton/Verlander/Cole LL .30 .75
256 Kershaw/Fried/Strasburg LL .40 1.00
257 Rodriguez/Cole/Verlander LL .30 .75
258 Scherzer/deGrom/Strasburg LL .20 .50
259 Bieber/Verlander/Cole LL .30 .75
260 Smith/Hader/Yates LL .12 .30
261 Hand/Chapman/Osuna LL .20 .50
262 Nola/Strasburg/deGrom LL .20 .50
263 Cole/Bieber/Verlander LL .30 .75
264 Ryu/Flaherty/deGrom LL .20 .50
265 Bieber/Verlander/Cole LL .30 .75
266 Mike Trout AW 1.00 2.50
267 Cody Bellinger AW .40 1.00
268 Justin Verlander AW .20 .50
269 Jacob deGrom AW .20 .50
270 Yordan Alvarez AW .60 1.50
271 Pete Alonso AW .50 1.25
272 Stephen Strasburg AW .20 .50
273 Shane Bieber AW .20 .50
274 Mike Trout AW 1.00 2.50
275 Christian Yelich AW .25 .60
276 Carlos Carrasco AW .12 .30
277 Josh Donaldson AW .15 .40
278 Aroldis Chapman AW .20 .50
279 Josh Hader AW .12 .30
280 Nelson Cruz AW .20 .50
281 Carlos Carrasco AW .12 .30
282 Curtis Granderson AW .15 .40
283 Mike Trout AW 1.00 2.50
284 Anthony Rendon AW .20 .50
285 Mike Trout AW 1.00 2.50
286 Ichiro HL .25 .60
287 Pete Alonso HL .50 1.25
288 CC Sabathia HL .15 .40
289 Albert Pujols HL .25 .60
290 Bryce Harper HL .30 .75
291 Justin Verlander HL .20 .50
292 Bo Bichette HL 1.00 2.50
293 Mike Trout HL 1.00 2.50
294 Shohei Ohtani HL .25 .60
295 Vladimir Guerrero Jr. HL .40 1.00
296 Yordan Alvarez HL .60 1.50
297 Mike Fiers HL .12 .30
298 Aristides Aquino HL .25 .60
299 Los Angeles Angels HL .12 .30
300 Ronald Acuna Jr. HL .75 2.00

2020 Topps Big League Black and White

*BLACK WHITE: 5X TO 12X BASIC
*BLACK WHITE RC: 2.5X TO 6X BASIC RC
STATED ODDS 1:75 HOBBY
STATED PRINT RUN 50 SER.#'d SETS

2020 Topps Big League Blue

*BLUE: 1.2X TO 3X BASIC
*BLUE RC: .6X TO 1.5X BASIC RC
FIVE PER BLASTER

2020 Topps Big League Orange

*ORANGE: 1.2X TO 3X BASIC
*ORANGE RC: .6X TO 1.5X BASIC RC
THREE PER FAT PACK

2020 Topps Big League Purple Blaster Box Cut Out

CUT FROM RETAIL BLASTER BOXES
B1 Mike Trout 3.00 8.00
B2 Bryce Harper 1.00 2.50
B3 Miguel Cabrera .60 1.50
B4 Aristides Aquino .75 2.00

2020 Topps Big League Rainbow Foil

*RAINBOW: 4X TO 10X BASIC
*RAINBOW RC: 2X TO 5X BASIC RC
STATED ODDS 1:38 HOBBY
STATED PRINT RUN 100 SER.#'d SETS

2020 Topps Big League Autographs

STATED ODDS 1:78 HOBBY
*ORANGE/99: .5X TO 1.2X BASIC
BLAAJ Andrew Jones 8.00 20.00
BLAAO Adam Ottavino 8.00 20.00
BLABL Brandon Lowe 6.00 15.00
BLABR Bryan Reynolds 8.00 20.00
BLABW Brandon Woodruff 2.50 6.00
BLACB Cavan Biggio 8.00 20.00
BLACK Carter Kieboom 6.00 15.00
BLACP Chris Paddack 8.00 20.00
BLADL DJ LeMahieu 15.00 40.00
BLADV Daniel Vogelbach 2.50 6.00
BLAJA Jim Abbott 20.00 50.00
BLAJC Jose Canseco 10.00 25.00
BLAJF Jack Flaherty 8.00 20.00
BLAJM John Means 2.50 6.00
BLAJP Jorge Polanco 3.00 8.00
BLAKH Keston Hiura 10.00 25.00
BLAKM Ketel Marte 3.00 8.00
BLAKT Kyle Tucker 3.00 8.00
BLAKY Kirby Yates 2.50 6.00
BLALG Lourdes Gurriel Jr. 3.00 8.00
BLAMB Matt Beaty 3.00 8.00
BLAMC Matt Chapman 6.00 15.00

BLAMCH Michael Chavis 6.00 15.00
BLAMG Mitch Garver 2.50 6.00
BLAMK Max Kepler 6.00 15.00
BLAMS Mike Soroka 6.00 15.00
BLAMT Mike Trout 150.00 400.00
BLAMY Mike Yastrzemski 8.00 20.00
BLAOM Oscar Mercado 3.00 8.00
BLARN Renato Nunez 3.00 8.00
BLASA Sandy Alomar Jr. 8.00 20.00
BLASN Sheldon Neuse 3.00 8.00
BLATL Tommy La Stella 2.50 6.00
BLAWA Willians Astudillo 2.50 6.00
BLAWS Will Smith 5.00 12.00

2020 Topps Big League Ballpark Oddities

STATED ODDS 1:554 HOBBY
BPO1 Jon Duplantier 5.00 12.00
BPO2 Joey Gallo 8.00 20.00
BPO3 Edwin Jackson 5.00 12.00
BPO4 Stevie Wilkerson 8.00 20.00
BPO5 Vince Velasquez 5.00 12.00
BPO6 Minnesota Twins 8.00 20.00
BPO7 Mookie Betts 15.00 40.00
BPO8 Michael Lorenzen 12.00 30.00
BPO9 Colin Moran 5.00 12.00
BPO10 Jonathan Schoop 5.00 12.00

2020 Topps Big League Defensive Wizards

COMPLETE SET (15) 5.00 12.00
STATED ODDS 1:4 HOBBY
DW1 Javier Baez .40 1.00
DW2 Didi Gregorius .25 .60
DW3 Matt Chapman .30 .75
DW4 Scott Kingery .25 .60
DW5 DJ LeMahieu .30 .75
DW6 Fernando Tatis Jr. 1.25 3.00
DW7 George Springer .25 .60
DW8 David Peralta .20 .50
DW9 Gio Urshela .30 .75
DW10 Charlie Blackmon .30 .75
DW11 Paul DeJong .30 .75
DW12 Bryce Harper .50 1.25
DW13 Carlos Correa .30 .75
DW14 Mike Trout 1.50 4.00
DW15 Nolan Arenado .40 1.00

2020 Topps Big League Defensive Wizards Autographs

STATED ODDS 1:2818 HOBBY
STATED PRINT RUN 25 SER.#'d SETS
DWACB Charlie Blackmon
DWADG Didi Gregorius
DWADL DJ LeMahieu 20.00 50.00
DWADP David Peralta 8.00 20.00
DWAFT Fernando Tatis Jr. 60.00 150.00
DWAGS George Springer
DWAGU Gio Urshela 15.00 40.00
DWAMC Matt Chapman 12.00 30.00
DWAPD Paul DeJong 12.00 30.00
DWASK Scott Kingery

2020 Topps Big League Flipping Out

COMPLETE SET (15) 5.00 12.00
STATED ODDS 1:4 HOBBY
FO1 Tim Anderson .30 .75
FO2 Ronald Acuna Jr. 1.25 3.00
FO3 Eugenio Suarez .25 .60
FO4 Aaron Hicks .25 .60
FO5 Aristides Aquino .40 1.00
FO6 Pete Alonso .75 2.00
FO7 Jorge Soler .30 .75
FO8 Max Kepler .25 .60
FO9 Fernando Tatis Jr. 1.25 3.00
FO10 Max Muncy .25 .60
FO11 Aaron Judge .75 2.00
FO12 Rafael Devers .40 1.00
FO13 Bryce Harper .50 1.25
FO14 Vladimir Guerrero Jr. .60 1.50
FO15 Willson Contreras .30 .75

2020 Topps Big League Flipping Out Autographs

STATED ODDS 1:3862 HOBBY
STATED PRINT RUN 25 SER.#'d SETS
FOAA Aristides Aquino 25.00 60.00
FOFT Fernando Tatis Jr. 60.00 150.00
FOJS Jorge Soler 12.00 30.00
FOMK Max Kepler 25.00 60.00
FOMM Max Muncy 15.00 40.00
FORA Ronald Acuna Jr. 60.00 150.00

2020 Topps Big League Opening Act Autographs

STATED ODDS 1:181 HOBBY
*ORANGE/99: .5X TO 1.2X BASIC
OAAAA Adbert Alzolay 3.00 8.00
OAAAQ Aristides Aquino 5.00 12.00
OAAAK Anthony Kay 2.50 6.00
OAAAP A.J. Puk 5.00 12.00
OAABB Bo Bichette
OAABBR Bobby Bradley 3.00 8.00
OAADM Dustin May 10.00 25.00
OAAHH Hunter Harvey 4.00 10.00
OAAID Isan Diaz 4.00 10.00
OAAJD Justin Dunn 3.00 8.00
OAAJK James Karinchak 12.00 30.00
OAAJU Jose Urquidy 3.00 8.00
OAAKL Kyle Lewis 8.00 20.00
OAAMD Mauricio Dubon 6.00 15.00
OAANH Nico Hoerner 10.00 25.00
OAANS Nick Solak 4.00 10.00
OAASB Seth Brown 2.50 6.00
OAASH Sam Hilliard 4.00 10.00
OAASM Sean Murphy 4.00 10.00
OAATG Trent Grisham 10.00 25.00
OAAYA Yordan Alvarez 25.00 60.00

2020 Topps Big League Roll Call

COMPLETE SET (30) 10.00 25.00
STATED ODDS 1:4 HOBBY
RC1 Ronald Acuna Jr. 1.25 3.00
RC2 Aristides Aquino .40 1.00
RC3 Gavin Lux 1.25 3.00
RC4 Yordan Alvarez 1.00 2.50
RC5 Pete Alonso .75 2.00
RC6 Victor Robles .40 1.00
RC7 Andrew Benintendi .30 .75
RC8 Christian Yelich .40 1.00
RC9 Keston Hiura .40 1.00
RC10 Vladimir Guerrero Jr. .60 1.50
RC11 Max Kepler .25 .60
RC12 Nick Senzel .30 .75
RC13 Matt Chapman .30 .75
RC14 Max Muncy .25 .60
RC15 Tim Anderson .30 .75
RC16 Jacob deGrom .30 .75
RC17 Bryce Harper .50 1.25
RC18 Manny Machado .30 .75
RC19 Mike Trout 1.50 4.00
RC20 Mookie Betts .60 1.50
RC21 Eloy Jimenez .60 1.50
RC22 Juan Soto 1.00 2.50
RC23 Gerrit Cole .50 1.25
RC24 Max Scherzer .30 .75
RC25 Shohei Ohtani .40 1.00
RC26 Cody Bellinger .60 1.50
RC27 Gleyber Torres .60 1.50
RC28 Bo Bichette 1.50 4.00
RC29 Aaron Judge .75 2.00
RC30 Nolan Arenado .40 1.00

2020 Topps Big League Roll Call Autographs

STATED ODDS 1:1938 HOBBY
STATED PRINT RUN 25 SER.#'d SETS
RCAA Aristides Aquino 25.00 60.00
RCAB Andrew Benintendi
RCAJ Aaron Judge 75.00 200.00
RCGC Gerrit Cole 40.00 100.00
RCGL Gavin Lux 50.00 125.00
RCKH Keston Hiura 15.00 40.00
RCMC Matt Chapman 12.00 30.00
RCMK Max Kepler 25.00 60.00
RCMMU Max Muncy 15.00 40.00
RCMS Max Scherzer 25.00 60.00
RCNS Nick Senzel 12.00 30.00
RCRA Ronald Acuna Jr. 60.00 150.00
RCTA Tim Anderson 15.00 40.00
RCVR Victor Robles 25.00 60.00
RCYA Yordan Alvarez 75.00 200.00

2020 Topps Big League Star Caricature Reproductions

STATED ODDS 1:4 HOBBY
SCOAA Aristides Aquino .40 1.00
SCOAM Austin Meadows .25 .60
SCOBA Brian Anderson .20 .50
SCOBH Bryce Harper .50 1.25
SCOCB Cody Bellinger .60 1.50
SCOCY Christian Yelich .40 1.00
SCODL DJ LeMahieu .30 .75
SCODV Daniel Vogelbach .20 .50
SCOEJ Eloy Jimenez .60 1.50
SCOEL Evan Longoria .25 .60
SCOFL Francisco Lindor .30 .75
SCOFT Fernando Tatis Jr. 1.25 3.00
SCOJB Javier Baez .40 1.00
SCOJBE Josh Bell .25 .60
SCOJG Joey Gallo .30 .75
SCOJS Juan Soto 1.00 2.50
SCOKM Ketel Marte .25 .60
SCOMC Miguel Cabrera .30 .75
SCOMCH Matt Chapman .30 .75
SCOMK Max Kepler .25 .60
SCOMT Mike Trout 1.50 4.00
SCOPA Pete Alonso .75 2.00
SCOPG Paul Goldschmidt .30 .75
SCORA Ronald Acuna Jr. 1.25 3.00
SCORD Rafael Devers .40 1.00
SCOTM Trey Mancini .30 .75
SCOTS Trevor Story .30 .75
SCOVG Vladimir Guerrero Jr. .60 1.50
SCOWM Whit Merrifield .30 .75
SCOYA Yordan Alvarez 1.00 2.50

2020 Topps Big League Veteran and Rookie Autographs

INSERTED IN RETAIL PACKS
12 Tommy LaStella 3.00 8.00
20 Griffin Canning 5.00 12.00
22 Eduardo Escobar 3.00 8.00
24 Alex Young 3.00 8.00
28 Shohei Ohtani 75.00 200.00
31 Bryce Harper
33 Tommy Edman 12.00 30.00
38 Ryan McMahon 3.00 8.00
41 Michael Chavis 8.00 20.00
42 Jeff McNeil 8.00 20.00
45 Whit Merrifield 10.00 25.00
46 Nick Senzel
51 Ramon Laureano 10.00 25.00
56 Sean Murphy 5.00 12.00
58 A.J. Puk 6.00 15.00
61 Jesus Luzardo
62 Hunter Harvey 5.00 12.00
73 Charlie Morton
79 Jordan Yamamoto 4.00 10.00
107 Aristides Aquino 6.00 15.00
110 Andres Munoz 4.00 10.00
118 Jorge Alfaro 3.00 8.00
121 Jacob deGrom
123 Yordan Alvarez 25.00 60.00
126 Jack Flaherty 10.00 25.00
134 Max Scherzer
139 Nico Hoerner 12.00 30.00
140 Kevin Newman 4.00 10.00
147 John Means 3.00 8.00
151 Michel Baez 3.00 8.00
158 Gavin Lux
169 Isan Diaz 5.00 12.00
170 Eduardo Rodriguez 6.00 15.00
172 Chris Paddack 10.00 25.00
177 Mike Clevinger
180 Kyle Lewis 10.00 25.00
186 Mike Yastrzemski 10.00 25.00
190 Brandon Woodruff 3.00 8.00
193 Cavan Biggio 10.00 25.00
200 Renato Nunez 4.00 10.00
203 Aaron Judge
210 Ketel Marte 4.00 10.00
218 Max Muncy 6.00 15.00
219 Oscar Mercado 4.00 10.00
227 Dakota Hudson 8.00 20.00

1996 Topps Chrome

The 1996 Topps Chrome set was issued in one series totalling 165 cards and features a selection of players from the 1996 Topps regular set. The four-card packs retailed for $3.00 each. Each chromium card is a replica of its regular version with the exception of the Topps Chrome logo replacing the traditional logo. Included in the set is a Mickey Mantle number 7 Commemorative card and a Cal Ripken Tribute card.

COMPLETE SET (165) 20.00 50.00
1 Tony Gwynn STP .50 1.25
2 Mike Piazza STP .75 2.00
3 Greg Maddux STP .75 2.00
4 Jeff Bagwell STP .30 .75
5 Larry Walker STP .30 .75
6 Barry Larkin STP .30 .75
7 Mickey Mantle COMM 4.00 10.00
8 Tom Glavine STP .30 .75
9 Craig Biggio STP .30 .75
10 Barry Bonds STP 1.00 2.50
11 Heathcliff Slocumb STP .30 .75
12 Matt Williams STP .30 .75
13 Todd Helton 1.50 4.00
14 Paul Molitor .30 .75
15 Glenallen Hill .30 .75
16 Troy Percival .30 .75
17 Albert Belle .30 .75
18 Mark Wohlers .30 .75
19 Kirby Puckett .75 2.00
20 Mark Grace .50 1.25
21 J.T. Snow .30 .75
22 David Justice .30 .75
23 Mike Mussina .50 1.25
24 Bernie Williams .50 1.25
25 Ron Gant .30 .75
26 Carlos Baerga .30 .75
27 Gary Sheffield .30 .75
28 Cal Ripken 2131 2.50 6.00
29 Frank Thomas .75 2.00
30 Kevin Seitzer .30 .75
31 Joe Carter .30 .75
32 Jeff King .30 .75
33 David Cone .30 .75
34 Eddie Murray .75 2.00
35 Brian Jordan .30 .75
36 Garret Anderson .30 .75
37 Hideo Nomo .75 2.00
38 Steve Finley .30 .75
39 Ivan Rodriguez .50 1.25
40 Quilvio Veras .30 .75
41 Mark McGwire 2.00 5.00
42 Greg Vaughn .30 .75
43 Randy Johnson .75 2.00
44 David Segui .30 .75
45 Derek Bell .30 .75
46 John Valentin .30 .75
47 Steve Avery .30 .75
48 Tino Martinez .50 1.25
49 Shane Reynolds .30 .75
50 Jim Edmonds .30 .75
51 Raul Mondesi .30 .75
52 Chipper Jones .75 2.00
53 Gregg Jefferies .30 .75
54 Ken Caminiti .30 .75
55 Brian McRae .30 .75
56 Don Mattingly 2.00 5.00
57 Marty Cordova .30 .75
58 Vinny Castilla .30 .75
59 John Smoltz .50 1.25
60 Travis Fryman .30 .75
61 Ryan Klesko .30 .75
62 Alex Fernandez .30 .75
63 Dante Bichette .30 .75
64 Eric Karros .30 .75
65 Roger Clemens 1.50 4.00
66 Randy Myers .30 .75
67 Cal Ripken 2.50 6.00
68 Rod Beck .30 .75
69 Jack McDowell .30 .75
70 Ken Griffey Jr. 1.50 4.00
71 Ramon Martinez .30 .75
72 Jason Giambi .30 .75
73 Nomar Garciaparra 1.25 3.00
74 Billy Wagner .30 .75
75 Todd Greene .30 .75
76 Paul Wilson .30 .75
77 Johnny Damon .50 1.25
78 Alan Benes .30 .75
79 Karim Garcia .30 .75
80 Derek Jeter 2.00 5.00
81 Kirby Puckett STP .50 1.25
82 Cal Ripken STP 1.25 3.00
83 Albert Belle STP .30 .75
84 Randy Johnson STP .50 1.25
85 Wade Boggs STP .30 .75
86 Carlos Baerga STP .30 .75
87 Ivan Rodriguez STP .30 .75
88 Mike Mussina STP .30 .75
89 Frank Thomas STP .50 1.25
90 Ken Griffey Jr. STP 1.00 2.50
91 Jose Mesa STP .30 .75
92 Matt Morris RC 2.00 5.00
93 Mike Piazza 1.25 3.00
94 Edgar Martinez .50 1.25
95 Chuck Knoblauch .30 .75
96 Andres Galarraga .30 .75
97 Tony Gwynn 1.00 2.50
98 Lee Smith .30 .75
99 Sammy Sosa .75 2.00
100 Jim Thome .50 1.25
101 Bernard Gilkey .30 .75
102 Brady Anderson .30 .75
103 Rico Brogna .30 .75
104 Len Dykstra .30 .75
105 Tom Glavine .50 1.25
106 John Olerud .30 .75
107 Terry Steinbach .30 .75
108 Brian Hunter .30 .75
109 Jay Buhner .30 .75
110 Mo Vaughn .30 .75
111 Jose Mesa .30 .75
112 Brett Butler .30 .75
113 Chili Davis .30 .75
114 Paul O'Neill .50 1.25
115 Roberto Alomar .50 1.25
116 Barry Larkin .50 1.25
117 Marquis Grissom .30 .75
118 Will Clark .50 1.25
119 Barry Bonds 2.00 5.00
120 Ozzie Smith 1.25 3.00
121 Pedro Martinez .50 1.25
122 Craig Biggio .50 1.25
123 Moises Alou .30 .75
124 Robin Ventura .30 .75
125 Greg Maddux 1.25 3.00
126 Tim Salmon .50 1.25
127 Wade Boggs .50 1.25
128 Ismael Valdes .30 .75
129 Juan Gonzalez .30 .75
130 Ray Lankford .30 .75
131 Bobby Bonilla .30 .75
132 Reggie Sanders .30 .75
133 Alex Ochoa .30 .75
134 Mark Loretta .30 .75
135 Jason Kendall .30 .75
136 Brooks Kieschnick .30 .75
137 Chris Snopek .30 .75
138 Ruben Rivera .30 .75
139 Jeff Suppan .30 .75
140 John Wasdin .30 .75
141 Jay Payton .30 .75
142 Rick Krivda .30 .75
143 Jimmy Haynes .30 .75
144 Ryne Sandberg 1.25 3.00
145 Matt Williams .30 .75
146 Jose Canseco .50 1.25
147 Larry Walker .30 .75
148 Kevin Appier .30 .75
149 Javy Lopez .30 .75
150 Dennis Eckersley .30 .75
151 Jason Isringhausen .30 .75
152 Dean Palmer .30 .75
153 Jeff Bagwell .50 1.25
154 Rondell White .30 .75
155 Wally Joyner .30 .75
156 Fred McGriff .50 1.25
157 Cecil Fielder .30 .75
158 Rafael Palmeiro .50 1.25
159 Rickey Henderson .75 2.00
160 Shawon Dunston .30 .75
161 Manny Ramirez .50 1.25
162 Alex Gonzalez .30 .75
163 Shawn Green .30 .75
164 Kenny Lofton .30 .75
165 Jeff Conine .30 .75

1996 Topps Chrome Refractors

COMPLETE SET (165) 1000.00 2000.00
*STARS: 2.5X TO 6X BASIC CARDS
*ROOKIES: 1.5X TO 4X BASIC CARDS
STATED ODDS 1:12 HOBBY
CARDS 111-165 CONDITION SENSITIVE

1996 Topps Chrome Masters of the Game

Randomly inserted in packs at a rate of one in 12, this 20-card set honors players who are masters of their playing positions. The fronts feature color action photography with brilliant color metallization.

COMPLETE SET (20) 15.00 40.00
STATED ODDS 1:12 HOBBY
*REF: 1X TO 2.5X BASIC
REF.STATED ODDS 1:36 HOBBY
1 Dennis Eckersley .75 2.00
2 Denny Martinez .50 1.25
3 Eddie Murray .75 2.00
4 Paul Molitor 1.25 3.00
5 Ozzie Smith 1.50 4.00
6 Rickey Henderson 1.25 3.00
7 Tim Raines .75 2.00
8 Lee Smith .50 1.25
9 Cal Ripken 4.00 10.00
10 Chili Davis .50 1.25
11 Wade Boggs .75 2.00
12 Tony Gwynn 1.25 3.00
13 Don Mattingly 2.50 6.00
14 Bret Saberhagen .50 1.25
15 Kirby Puckett 1.25 3.00
16 Joe Carter .50 1.25
17 Roger Clemens 1.50 4.00
18 Barry Bonds 2.00 5.00
19 Greg Maddux 2.00 5.00
20 Frank Thomas 1.25 3.00

1996 Topps Chrome Wrecking Crew

Randomly inserted in packs at a rate of one in 24, this 15-card set features baseball's top hitters and is printed in color action photography with brilliant color metallization.

COMPLETE SET (15) 12.50 30.00
STATED ODDS 1:24 HOBBY
*REF: 1.5X TO 4X BASIC CHR.WRECKING
REF.STATED ODDS 1:72 HOBBY
WC1 Jeff Bagwell 1.00 2.50
WC2 Albert Belle .60 1.50
WC3 Barry Bonds 2.50 6.00
WC4 Jose Canseco 1.00 2.50
WC5 Joe Carter .60 1.50
WC6 Cecil Fielder .60 1.50
WC7 Ron Gant .60 1.50
WC8 Juan Gonzalez .60 1.50
WC9 Ken Griffey Jr. 3.00 8.00
WC10 Fred McGriff 1.00 2.50
WC11 Mark McGwire 2.50 6.00
WC12 Mike Piazza 1.50 4.00
WC13 Frank Thomas 1.50 4.00
WC14 Mo Vaughn .60 1.50
WC15 Matt Williams .60 1.50

1997 Topps Chrome

The 1997 Topps Chrome set was issued in one series totalling 165 cards and was distributed in four-card packs with a suggested retail price of $3.00. Using Chromium technology to highlight the cards, this set features a metalized version of the cards of some of the best players from the 1997 regular Topps Series one and two. An attractive 8 1/2" by 11" chrome promo sheet was sent to dealers advertising this set.

COMPLETE SET (165) 20.00 50.00
1 Barry Bonds 2.00 5.00
2 Jose Valentin .30 .75
3 Brady Anderson .30 .75
4 Wade Boggs .50 1.25
5 Andres Galarraga .30 .75
6 Rusty Greer .30 .75
7 Derek Jeter 2.00 5.00
8 Ricky Bottalico .30 .75
9 Mike Piazza 1.25 3.00
10 Garret Anderson .30 .75
11 Jeff King .30 .75
12 Kevin Appier .30 .75
13 Mark Grace .50 1.25
14 Jeff D'Amico .30 .75
15 Jay Buhner .30 .75
16 Hal Morris .30 .75
17 Harold Baines .30 .75
18 Jeff Cirillo .30 .75
19 Tom Glavine .50 1.25
20 Andy Pettitte .50 1.25
21 Mark McGwire 2.00 5.00
22 Chuck Knoblauch .30 .75
23 Raul Mondesi .30 .75
24 Albert Belle .30 .75
25 Trevor Hoffman .30 .75
26 Eric Young .30 .75
27 Brian McRae .30 .75
28 Jim Edmonds .30 .75
29 Robb Nen .30 .75
30 Reggie Sanders .30 .75
31 Mike Lansing .30 .75
32 Craig Biggio .50 1.25
33 Ray Lankford .30 .75
34 Charles Nagy .30 .75
35 Paul Wilson .30 .75
36 John Wetteland .30 .75
37 Derek Bell .30 .75
38 Edgar Martinez .50 1.25
39 Rickey Henderson .75 2.00
40 Jim Thome .50 1.25
41 Frank Thomas .75 2.00
42 Jackie Robinson .75 2.00
43 Terry Steinbach .30 .75
44 Kevin Brown .30 .75
45 Joey Hamilton .30 .75
46 Travis Fryman .30 .75
47 Juan Gonzalez .30 .75
48 Ron Gant .30 .75
49 Greg Maddux 1.25 3.00
50 Wally Joyner .30 .75
51 John Valentin .30 .75
52 Bret Boone .30 .75
53 Paul Molitor .30 .75
54 Rafael Palmeiro .50 1.25
55 Todd Hundley .30 .75
56 Ellis Burks .30 .75
57 Bernie Williams .50 1.25
58 Roberto Alomar .50 1.25
59 Jose Mesa .30 .75
60 Troy Percival .30 .75
61 John Smoltz .50 1.25
62 Jeff Conine .30 .75
63 Bernard Gilkey .30 .75
64 Mickey Tettleton .30 .75
65 Justin Thompson .30 .75
66 Tony Phillips .30 .75
67 Ryne Sandberg 1.25 3.00
68 Geronimo Berroa .30 .75
69 Todd Hollandsworth .30 .75
70 Rey Ordonez .30 .75
71 Marquis Grissom .30 .75
72 Tino Martinez .50 1.25
73 Steve Finley .30 .75
74 Andy Benes .30 .75
75 Jason Kendall .30 .75
76 Johnny Damon .50 1.25
77 Jason Giambi .30 .75
78 Henry Rodriguez .30 .75
79 Edgar Renteria .30 .75
80 Ray Durham .30 .75
81 Gregg Jefferies .30 .75
82 Roberto Hernandez .30 .75
83 Joe Carter .30 .75
84 Jermaine Dye .30 .75
85 Julio Franco .30 .75
86 David Justice .30 .75
87 Jose Canseco .50 1.25
88 Paul O'Neill .50 1.25
89 Mariano Rivera .75 2.00
90 Bobby Higginson .30 .75
91 Mark Grudzielanek .30 .75
92 Lance Johnson .30 .75
93 Ken Caminiti .30 .75
94 Gary Sheffield .30 .75
95 Luis Castillo .30 .75
96 Scott Rolen .50 1.25
97 Chipper Jones .75 2.00
98 Darryl Strawberry .30 .75
99 Nomar Garciaparra 1.25 3.00
100 Jeff Bagwell .50 1.25
101 Ken Griffey Jr. 1.50 4.00
102 Sammy Sosa .75 2.00
103 Jack McDowell .30 .75
104 James Baldwin .30 .75
105 Rocky Coppinger .30 .75
106 Manny Ramirez .50 1.25
107 Tim Salmon .50 1.25
108 Eric Karros .30 .75
109 Brett Butler .30 .75
110 Randy Johnson .75 2.00
111 Pat Hentgen .30 .75
112 Rondell White .30 .75
113 Eddie Murray .75 2.00
114 Ivan Rodriguez .50 1.25
115 Jermaine Allensworth .30 .75
116 Ed Sprague .30 .75
117 Kenny Lofton .30 .75
118 Alan Benes .30 .75
119 Fred McGriff .50 1.25
120 Alex Fernandez .30 .75
121 Al Martin .30 .75
122 Devon White .30 .75
123 David Cone .30 .75
124 Karim Garcia .30 .75
125 Chili Davis .30 .75
126 Roger Clemens 1.50 4.00
127 Bobby Bonilla .30 .75
128 Mike Mussina .50 1.25
129 Todd Walker .30 .75
130 Dante Bichette .30 .75
131 Carlos Baerga .30 .75
132 Matt Williams .30 .75
133 Will Clark .50 1.25
134 Dennis Eckersley .30 .75
135 Ryan Klesko .30 .75
136 Dean Palmer .30 .75
137 Javy Lopez .30 .75
138 Greg Vaughn .30 .75
139 Vinny Castilla .30 .75
140 Cal Ripken 2.50 6.00
141 Ruben Rivera .30 .75
142 Mark Wohlers .30 .75
143 Tony Clark .30 .75
144 Jose Rosado .30 .75
145 Tony Gwynn 1.00 2.50
146 Cecil Fielder .30 .75
147 Brian Jordan .30 .75
148 Bob Abreu .50 1.25
149 Barry Larkin .50 1.25
150 Robin Ventura .30 .75
151 John Olerud .30 .75
152 Rod Beck .30 .75
153 Vladimir Guerrero .75 2.00
154 Marty Cordova .30 .75
155 Todd Stottlemyre .30 .75
156 Hideo Nomo .75 2.00
157 Denny Neagle .30 .75
158 John Jaha .30 .75
159 Mo Vaughn .30 .75
160 Andruw Jones .50 1.25
161 Moises Alou .30 .75
162 Larry Walker .30 .75
163 Eddie Murray SH .50 1.25
164 Paul Molitor SH .30 .75
165 Checklist .30 .75

1997 Topps Chrome Refractors

*STARS: 2.5X TO 6X BASIC CARDS
STATED ODDS 1:12
CONDITION SENSITIVE SET

1997 Topps Chrome All-Stars

Randomly inserted in packs at a rate of one in 24, this 22-card set features color player photos printed on rainbow foilboard. The set showcases the top three players from each position from both the American and National leagues as voted on by the Topps Sports Department.

COMPLETE SET (22) 40.00 100.00
STATED ODDS 1:24
*REF: 1X TO 2.5X BASIC CHROME AS
REFRACTOR STATED ODDS 1:72
AS1 Ivan Rodriguez 1.50 4.00
AS2 Todd Hundley 1.00 2.50
AS3 Frank Thomas 2.50 6.00
AS4 Andres Galarraga 1.00 2.50
AS5 Chuck Knoblauch 1.00 2.50
AS6 Eric Young 1.00 2.50
AS7 Jim Thome 1.50 4.00
AS8 Chipper Jones 2.50 6.00
AS9 Cal Ripken 8.00 20.00
AS10 Barry Larkin 1.50 4.00
AS11 Albert Belle 1.00 2.50
AS12 Barry Bonds 6.00 15.00
AS13 Ken Griffey Jr. 5.00 12.00
AS14 Ellis Burks 1.00 2.50
AS15 Juan Gonzalez 1.00 2.50
AS16 Gary Sheffield 1.00 2.50
AS17 Andy Pettitte 1.50 4.00
AS18 Tom Glavine 1.50 4.00
AS19 Pat Hentgen 1.00 2.50
AS20 John Smoltz 1.50 4.00
AS21 Roberto Hernandez 1.00 2.50
AS22 Mark Wohlers 1.00 2.50

1997 Topps Chrome Diamond Duos

Randomly inserted in packs at a rate of one in 36, this 10-card set features color player photos of two superstar teammates on double sided chromium cards.

COMPLETE SET (10) 12.50 30.00
STATED ODDS 1:36
*REF.: 1X TO 2.5X BASIC DIAM.DUOS
REFRACTOR STATED ODDS 1:108
DD1 C.Jones 1.50 4.00
A.Jones
DD2 D.Jeter/B.Williams 4.00 10.00
DD3 K.Griffey Jr./J.Buhner 3.00 8.00
DD4 K.Lofton/M.Ramirez 1.00 2.50
DD5 J.Bagwell/C.Biggio 1.00 2.50
DD6 J.Gonzalez/I.Rodriguez 1.00 2.50
DD7 C.Ripken/B.Anderson 5.00 12.00
DD8 M.Piazza/H.Nomo 1.50 4.00
DD9 A.Galarraga/D.Bichette 1.00 2.50
DD10 F.Thomas/A.Belle 1.50 4.00

1997 Topps Chrome Season's Best

Randomly inserted in packs at a rate of one in 18, this 25-card set features color player photos of the five top players from five statistical categories: most steals (Leading Looters), most home runs (Bleacher Reachers), most wins (Hill Toppers), most RBIs (Number Crunchers), and best slugging percentage (Kings of Swing).

COMPLETE SET (25) 25.00 60.00
STATED ODDS 1:18
*REF: 1X TO 2.5X BASIC SEAS.BEST
REFRACTOR STATED ODDS 1:54
1 Tony Gwynn 2.50 6.00
2 Frank Thomas 2.00 5.00
3 Ellis Burks .75 2.00
4 Paul Molitor .75 2.00
5 Chuck Knoblauch .75 2.00
6 Mark McGwire 5.00 12.00
7 Brady Anderson .75 2.00
8 Ken Griffey Jr. 4.00 10.00
9 Albert Belle .75 2.00
10 Andres Galarraga .75 2.00
11 Andres Galarraga .75 2.00
12 Albert Belle .75 2.00
13 Juan Gonzalez .75 2.00
14 Mo Vaughn .75 2.00
15 Rafael Palmeiro 1.25 3.00
16 John Smoltz 1.25 3.00
17 Andy Pettitte 1.25 3.00
18 Pat Hentgen .75 2.00

19 Mike Mussina 1.25 3.00
20 Andy Benes .75 2.00
21 Kenny Lofton .75 2.00
22 Tom Goodwin .75 2.00
23 Otis Nixon .75 2.00
24 Eric Young .75 2.00
25 Lance Johnson .75 2.00

1997 Topps Chrome Jumbos

This six-card set contains jumbo versions of the six featured players' regular Topps Chrome cards and measures approximately 3 3/4" by 5 1/4". One of these cards was found in a special box with five Topps Chrome packs issued through Wal-Mart. The cards are numbered according to their corresponding number in the regular set.

COMPLETE SET (6) 6.00 15.00
9 Mike Piazza 1.25 3.00
94 Gary Sheffield .50 1.25
97 Chipper Jones 1.00 2.50
101 Ken Griffey Jr. 1.25 3.00
102 Sammy Sosa .60 1.50
140 Cal Ripken Jr. 2.00 5.00

1998 Topps Chrome

The 1998 Topps Chrome set was issued in two separate series of 282 and 221 cards respectively with design and content paralleling the base 1998 Topps set. Four-card packs carried a suggested retail price of $3 each. Card fronts feature color action player photos printed with Chromium technology on metalized cards. The backs carry player information. As is tradition with Topps sets since 1996, card number seven was excluded from the set in honor of Mickey Mantle. Subsets are as follows: Prospects/Draft Picks (245-264/484-501), Season Highlights (265-269/474-478), Inter-League (270-274/479-483), Checklists (275-276/502-503) and World Series (277-283). After four years of being excluded from Topps products, superstar Alex Rodriguez finally made his Topps debut as card number 504. Notable Rookie Cards include Ryan Anderson, Michael Cuddyer, Jack Cust and Troy Glaus.

COMPLETE SET (503) 75.00 150.00
COMPLETE SERIES 1 (282) 30.00 80.00
COMPLETE SERIES 2 (221) 30.00 80.00
REF.STATED ODDS 1:12
CARD NUMBER 7 DOES NOT EXIST
1 Tony Gwynn 1.00 2.50
2 Larry Walker .30 .75
3 Billy Wagner .30 .75
4 Denny Neagle .30 .75
5 Vladimir Guerrero .75 2.00
6 Kevin Brown .50 1.25
8 Mariano Rivera .75 2.00
9 Tony Clark .30 .75
10 Deion Sanders .50 1.25
11 Francisco Cordova .30 .75
12 Matt Williams .30 .75
13 Carlos Baerga .30 .75
14 Mo Vaughn .30 .75
15 Bobby Witt .30 .75
16 Matt Stairs .30 .75
17 Chan Ho Park .30 .75
18 Mike Bordick .30 .75
19 Michael Tucker .30 .75
20 Frank Thomas .75 2.00
21 Roberto Clemente 2.00 5.00
22 Dmitri Young .30 .75
23 Steve Trachsel .30 .75
24 Jeff Kent .30 .75
25 Scott Rolen .50 1.25
26 John Thomson .30 .75
27 Joe Vitiello .30 .75
28 Eddie Guardado .30 .75
29 Charlie Hayes .30 .75
30 Juan Gonzalez .30 .75
31 Garret Anderson .30 .75
32 John Jaha .30 .75
33 Omar Vizquel .50 1.25
34 Brian Hunter .30 .75
35 Jeff Bagwell .50 1.25
36 Mark Lemke .30 .75
37 Doug Glanville .30 .75
38 Dan Wilson .30 .75
39 Steve Cooke .30 .75
40 Chili Davis .30 .75
41 Mike Cameron .30 .75
42 F.P. Santangelo .30 .75
43 Brad Ausmus .30 .75
44 Gary DiSarcina .30 .75
45 Pat Hentgen .30 .75
46 Wilton Guerrero .30 .75
47 Devon White .30 .75
48 Danny Patterson .30 .75
49 Pat Meares .30 .75
50 Rafael Palmeiro .50 1.25
51 Mark Gardner .30 .75
52 Jeff Blauser .30 .75
53 Dave Hollins .30 .75
54 Carlos Garcia .30 .75
55 Ben McDonald .30 .75
56 John Mabry .30 .75
57 Trevor Hoffman .30 .75
58 Tony Fernandez .30 .75
59 Rich Loiselle RC .30 .75
60 Mark Leiter .30 .75
61 Pat Kelly .30 .75
62 John Flaherty .30 .75
63 Roger Bailey .30 .75
64 Tom Gordon .30 .75
65 Ryan Klesko .30 .75
66 Darryl Hamilton .30 .75
67 Jim Eisenreich .30 .75
68 Butch Huskey .30 .75
69 Mark Grudzielanek .30 .75
70 Marquis Grissom .30 .75
71 Mark McLemore .30 .75
72 Gary Gaetti .30 .75
73 Greg Gagne .30 .75
74 Lyle Mouton .30 .75
75 Jim Edmonds .30 .75
76 Shawn Green .30 .75
77 Greg Vaughn .30 .75
78 Terry Adams .30 .75
79 Kevin Polcovich .30 .75
80 Troy O'Leary .30 .75
81 Jeff Shaw .30 .75
82 Rich Becker .30 .75
83 David Wells .30 .75
84 Steve Karsay .30 .75
85 Charles Nagy .30 .75
86 B.J. Surhoff .30 .75
87 Jamey Wright .30 .75
88 James Baldwin .30 .75
89 Edgardo Alfonzo .30 .75
90 Jay Buhner .30 .75
91 Brady Anderson .30 .75
92 Scott Servais .30 .75
93 Edgar Renteria .30 .75
94 Mike Lieberthal .30 .75
95 Rick Aguilera .30 .75
96 Walt Weiss .30 .75
97 Deivi Cruz .30 .75
98 Kurt Abbott .30 .75
99 Henry Rodriguez .30 .75
100 Mike Piazza 1.25 3.00
101 Billy Taylor .30 .75
102 Todd Zeile .30 .75
103 Rey Ordonez .30 .75
104 Willie Greene .30 .75
105 Tony Womack .30 .75
106 Mike Sweeney .30 .75
107 Jeffrey Hammonds .30 .75
108 Kevin Orie .30 .75
109 Alex Gonzalez .30 .75
110 Jose Canseco .50 1.25
111 Paul Sorrento .30 .75
112 Joey Hamilton .30 .75
113 Brad Radke .30 .75
114 Steve Avery .30 .75
115 Esteban Loaiza .30 .75
116 Stan Javier .30 .75
117 Chris Gomez .30 .75
118 Royce Clayton .30 .75
119 Orlando Merced .30 .75
120 Kevin Appier .30 .75
121 Mel Nieves .30 .75
122 Joe Girardi .30 .75
123 Rico Brogna .30 .75
124 Kent Mercker .30 .75
125 Manny Ramirez .50 1.25
126 Jeromy Burnitz .30 .75
127 Kevin Foster .30 .75
128 Matt Morris .30 .75
129 Jason Dickson .30 .75
130 Tom Glavine .50 1.25
131 Wally Joyner .30 .75
132 Rick Reed .30 .75
133 Todd Jones .30 .75
134 Dave Martinez .30 .75
135 Sandy Alomar Jr. .30 .75
136 Mike Lansing .30 .75
137 Sean Berry .30 .75
138 Doug Jones .30 .75
139 Todd Stottlemyre .30 .75
140 Jay Bell .30 .75
141 Jaime Navarro .30 .75
142 Chris Hoiles .30 .75
143 Joey Cora .30 .75
144 Scott Spiezio .30 .75
145 Joe Carter .30 .75
146 Jose Guillen .30 .75
147 Damion Easley .30 .75
148 Lee Stevens .30 .75
149 Alex Fernandez .30 .75
150 Randy Johnson .75 2.00
151 J.T. Snow .30 .75
152 Chuck Finley .30 .75
153 Bernard Gilkey .30 .75
154 David Segui .30 .75
155 Dante Bichette .30 .75
156 Kevin Stocker .30 .75
157 Carl Everett .30 .75
158 Jose Valentin .30 .75
159 Pokey Reese .30 .75
160 Derek Jeter 2.00 5.00
161 Roger Pavlik .30 .75
162 Mark Wohlers .30 .75
163 Ricky Bottalico .30 .75
164 Ozzie Guillen .30 .75
165 Mike Mussina .50 1.25
166 Gary Sheffield .30 .75
167 Hideo Nomo .75 2.00
168 Mark Grace .50 1.25
169 Aaron Sele .30 .75
170 Darryl Kile .30 .75
171 Shawn Estes .30 .75
172 Vinny Castilla .30 .75
173 Ron Coomer .30 .75
174 Jose Rosado .30 .75
175 Kenny Lofton .30 .75
176 Jason Giambi .30 .75
177 Hal Morris .30 .75
178 Darren Bragg .30 .75
179 Orel Hershiser .30 .75
180 Ray Lankford .30 .75
181 Hideki Irabu .30 .75
182 Kevin Young .30 .75
183 Javy Lopez .30 .75
184 Jeff Montgomery .30 .75
185 Mike Holtz .30 .75
186 George Williams .30 .75
187 Cal Eldred .30 .75
188 Tom Candiotti .30 .75
189 Glenallen Hill .30 .75
190 Brian Giles .30 .75
191 Dave Mlicki .30 .75
192 Garrett Stephenson .30 .75
193 Jeff Frye .30 .75
194 Joe Oliver .30 .75
195 Bob Hamelin .30 .75
196 Luis Sojo .30 .75
197 LaTroy Hawkins .30 .75
198 Kevin Elster .30 .75
199 Jeff Reed .30 .75
200 Dennis Eckersley .30 .75
201 Bill Mueller .30 .75
202 Russ Davis .30 .75
203 Armando Benitez .30 .75
204 Quilvio Veras .30 .75
205 Tim Naehring .30 .75
206 Quinton McCracken .30 .75
207 Raul Casanova .30 .75
208 Matt Lawton .30 .75
209 Luis Alicea .30 .75
210 Luis Gonzalez .30 .75
211 Allen Watson .30 .75
212 Gerald Williams .30 .75
213 David Bell .30 .75
214 Todd Hollandsworth .30 .75
215 Wade Boggs .50 1.25
216 Jose Mesa .30 .75
217 Jamie Moyer .30 .75
218 Darren Daulton .30 .75
219 Mickey Morandini .30 .75
220 Rusty Greer .30 .75
221 Jim Bullinger .30 .75
222 Jose Offerman .30 .75
223 Matt Karchner .30 .75
224 Woody Williams .30 .75
225 Mark Loretta .30 .75
226 Mike Hampton .30 .75
227 Willie Adams .30 .75
228 Scott Hatteberg .30 .75
229 Rich Amaral .30 .75
230 Terry Steinbach .30 .75
231 Glendon Rusch .30 .75
232 Bret Boone .30 .75
233 Robert Person .30 .75
234 Jose Hernandez .30 .75
235 Doug Drabek .30 .75
236 Jason McDonald .30 .75
237 Chris Widger .30 .75
238 Tom Martin .30 .75
239 Dave Burba .30 .75
240 Pete Rose Jr. RC .30 .75
241 Bobby Ayala .30 .75
242 Tim Wakefield .30 .75
243 Dennis Springer .30 .75
244 Tim Belcher .30 .75
245 J.Garland .40 1.00
G.Goetz
246 L.Berkman .40 1.00
G.Davis
247 V.Wells .40 1.00
A.Akin
248 A.Kennelly .40 1.00
J.Romano
249 J.Dellaero .40 1.00
T.Cameron
250 J.Sandberg .40 1.00
A.Sanchez
251 P.Ortega .40 1.00
J.Manias
252 Mike Stoner RC .40 1.00
253 J.Patterson .40 1.00
L.Rodriguez
254 R.Minor RC .40 1.00
A.Beltre
255 B.Grieve .40 1.00
D.Brown
256 Wood .40 1.00
Pavano
Meche
257 D.Ortiz 2.00 5.00
Sexson
Ward
258 J.Encarnacion .40 1.00
Winn
Vess
259 Bens .40 1.00
T.Smith RC
C.Dunc RC
260 Warren Morris RC .40 1.00
261 B.Davis .40 1.00
Marrero
R.Hern.
262 E.Chavez .40 1.00
R.Branyan
263 Ryan Jackson RC .40 1.00
264 B.Fuentes RC 2.00 5.00
Clement
Halladay
265 Randy Johnson SH .50 1.25
266 Kevin Brown SH .30 .75
267 Ricardo Rincon SH .30 .75
268 Nomar Garciaparra SH .75 2.00
269 Tino Martinez SH .30 .75
270 Chuck Knoblauch IL .30 .75
271 Pedro Martinez IL .50 1.25
272 Denny Neagle IL .30 .75
273 Juan Gonzalez IL .30 .75
274 Andres Galarraga IL .30 .75
275 Checklist .30 .75
276 Checklist .30 .75
277 Moises Alou WS .30 .75
278 Sandy Alomar Jr. WS .30 .75
279 Gary Sheffield WS .30 .75
280 Matt Williams WS .30 .75
281 Livan Hernandez WS .30 .75
282 Chad Ogea WS .30 .75
283 Marlins Champs .30 .75
284 Tino Martinez .50 1.25
285 Roberto Alomar .50 1.25
286 Jeff King .30 .75
287 Brian Jordan .30 .75
288 Darin Erstad .30 .75
289 Ken Caminiti .30 .75
290 Jim Thome .50 1.25
291 Paul Molitor .30 .75
292 Ivan Rodriguez .50 1.25
293 Bernie Williams .50 1.25
294 Todd Hundley .30 .75
295 Andres Galarraga .30 .75
296 Greg Maddux 1.25 3.00
297 Edgar Martinez .50 1.25
298 Ron Gant .30 .75
299 Derek Bell .30 .75
300 Roger Clemens 1.50 4.00
301 Rondell White .30 .75
302 Barry Larkin .50 1.25
303 Robin Ventura .30 .75
304 Jason Kendall .30 .75
305 Chipper Jones .75 2.00
306 John Franco .30 .75
307 Sammy Sosa .75 2.00
308 Troy Percival .30 .75
309 Chuck Knoblauch .30 .75
310 Ellis Burks .30 .75
311 Al Martin .30 .75
312 Tim Salmon .50 1.25
313 Moises Alou .30 .75
314 Lance Johnson .30 .75
315 Justin Thompson .30 .75
316 Will Clark .50 1.25
317 Barry Bonds 2.00 5.00
318 Craig Biggio .50 1.25
319 John Smoltz .50 1.25
320 Cal Ripken 2.50 6.00
321 Ken Griffey Jr. 1.50 4.00
322 Paul O'Neill .50 1.25
323 Todd Helton .50 1.25
324 John Olerud .30 .75
325 Mark McGwire 2.00 5.00
326 Jose Cruz Jr. .30 .75
327 Jeff Cirillo .30 .75
328 Dean Palmer .30 .75
329 John Wetteland .30 .75
330 Steve Finley .30 .75
331 Albert Belle .30 .75
332 Curt Schilling .30 .75
333 Raul Mondesi .30 .75
334 Andruw Jones .50 1.25
335 Nomar Garciaparra 1.25 3.00
336 David Justice .30 .75
337 Andy Pettitte .50 1.25
338 Pedro Martinez .50 1.25
339 Travis Miller .30 .75
340 Chris Stynes .30 .75
341 Gregg Jefferies .30 .75
342 Jeff Fassero .30 .75
343 Craig Counsell .30 .75
344 Wilson Alvarez .30 .75
345 Bip Roberts .30 .75
346 Kelvim Escobar .30 .75
347 Mark Bellhorn .30 .75
348 Cory Lidle RC 3.00 8.00
349 Fred McGriff .50 1.25
350 Chuck Carr .30 .75
351 Bob Abreu .30 .75
352 Juan Guzman .30 .75
353 Fernando Vina .30 .75
354 Andy Benes .30 .75
355 Dave Nilsson .30 .75
356 Bobby Bonilla .30 .75
357 Ismael Valdes .30 .75
358 Carlos Perez .30 .75
359 Kirk Rueter .30 .75
360 Bartolo Colon .30 .75
361 Mel Rojas .30 .75
362 Johnny Damon .50 1.25
363 Geronimo Berroa .30 .75
364 Reggie Sanders .30 .75
365 Jermaine Allensworth .30 .75
366 Orlando Cabrera .30 .75
367 Jorge Fabregas .30 .75
368 Scott Stahoviak .30 .75
369 Ken Cloude .30 .75
370 Donovan Osborne .30 .75
371 Roger Cedeno .30 .75
372 Neifi Perez .30 .75
373 Chris Holt .30 .75
374 Cecil Fielder .30 .75
375 Marty Cordova .30 .75
376 Tom Goodwin .30 .75
377 Jeff Suppan .30 .75
378 Jeff Brantley .30 .75
379 Mark Langston .30 .75
380 Shane Reynolds .30 .75
381 Mike Fetters .30 .75
382 Todd Greene .30 .75
383 Ray Durham .30 .75
384 Carlos Delgado .30 .75
385 Jeff D'Amico .30 .75
386 Brian McRae .30 .75
387 Alan Benes .30 .75
388 Heathcliff Slocumb .30 .75
389 Eric Young .30 .75
390 Travis Fryman .30 .75
391 David Cone .30 .75
392 Otis Nixon .30 .75
393 Jeremi Gonzalez .30 .75
394 Jeff Juden .30 .75
395 Jose Vizcaino .30 .75
396 Ugueth Urbina .30 .75
397 Ramon Martinez .30 .75
398 Robb Nen .30 .75
399 Harold Baines .30 .75
400 Delino DeShields .30 .75
401 John Burkett .30 .75
402 Sterling Hitchcock .30 .75
403 Mark Clark .30 .75
404 Terrell Wade .30 .75
405 Scott Brosius .30 .75
406 Chad Curtis .30 .75
407 Brian Johnson .30 .75
408 Roberto Kelly .30 .75
409 Dave Dellucci RC .50 1.25
410 Michael Tucker .30 .75
411 Mark Kotsay .30 .75
412 Mark Lewis .30 .75
413 Ryan McGuire .30 .75
414 Shawon Dunston .30 .75
415 Brad Rigby .30 .75
416 Scott Erickson .30 .75
417 Bobby Jones .30 .75
418 Darren Oliver .30 .75
419 John Smiley .30 .75
420 T.J. Mathews .30 .75
421 Dustin Hermanson .30 .75
422 Mike Timlin .30 .75
423 Willie Blair .30 .75
424 Manny Alexander .30 .75
425 Bob Tewksbury .30 .75
426 Pete Schourek .30 .75
427 Reggie Jefferson .30 .75
428 Ed Sprague .30 .75
429 Jeff Conine .30 .75
430 Roberto Hernandez .30 .75
431 Tom Pagnozzi .30 .75
432 Jaret Wright .30 .75
433 Livan Hernandez .30 .75
434 Andy Ashby .30 .75
435 Todd Dunn .30 .75
436 Bobby Higginson .30 .75
437 Rod Beck .30 .75
438 Jim Leyritz .30 .75
439 Matt Williams .30 .75
440 Brett Tomko .30 .75
441 Joe Randa .30 .75
442 Chris Carpenter .30 .75
443 Dennis Reyes .30 .75
444 Al Leiter .30 .75
445 Jason Schmidt .30 .75
446 Ken Hill .30 .75
447 Shannon Stewart .30 .75
448 Enrique Wilson .30 .75
449 Fernando Tatis .30 .75
450 Jimmy Key .30 .75
451 Darrin Fletcher .30 .75
452 John Valentin .30 .75
453 Kevin Tapani .30 .75
454 Eric Karros .30 .75
455 Jay Bell .30 .75
456 Walt Weiss .30 .75
457 Devon White .30 .75
458 Carl Pavano .30 .75
459 Mike Lansing .30 .75
460 John Flaherty .30 .75
461 Richard Hidalgo .30 .75
462 Quinton McCracken .30 .75
463 Karim Garcia .30 .75
464 Miguel Cairo .30 .75
465 Edwin Diaz .30 .75
466 Bobby Smith .30 .75
467 Yamil Benitez .30 .75
468 Rich Butler RC .30 .75
469 Ben Ford RC .30 .75
470 Bubba Trammell .30 .75
471 Brent Brede .30 .75
472 Brooks Kieschnick .30 .75
473 Carlos Castillo .30 .75
474 Brad Radke SH .30 .75
475 Roger Clemens SH .75 2.00
476 Curt Schilling SH .30 .75
477 John Olerud SH .30 .75
478 Mark McGwire SH 1.00 2.50
479 M.Piazza 1.00 2.50
K.Griffey Jr. IL
480 J.Bagwell .50 1.25
F.Thomas IL
481 C.Jones .50 1.25
N.Garciaparra IL
482 L.Walker .30 .75
J.Gonzalez IL
483 G.Sheffield .30 .75
T.Martinez IL
484 D.Gib .40 1.00
M.Colem
Hutchins
485 B.Rose .40 1.00
Looper
Politte
486 E.Milton .40 1.00
Marquis
C.Lee
487 Rob Fick RC .40 1.00
488 A.Ramirez .40 1.00
A.Gonz
Casey
489 D.Bridges .40 1.00
T.Drew RC
490 D.McDonald .40 1.00
N.Ndungidi RC
491 Ryan Anderson RC .40 1.00
492 Troy Glaus RC 2.00 5.00
493 Dan Reichert RC .40 1.00
494 Michael Cuddyer RC 1.00 2.50
495 Jack Cust RC .75 2.00
496 Brian Anderson .40 1.00
497 Tony Saunders .40 1.00
498 J.Sandoval .40 1.00
V.Nunez
499 B.Penny .40 1.00
N.Bierbrodt
500 D.Carr .40 1.00
L.Cruz RC
501 C.Bowers .40 1.00
M.McCain
502 Checklist .30 .75
503 Checklist .30 .75
504 Alex Rodriguez 1.50 4.00

1998 Topps Chrome Refractors

*STARS: 2.5X TO 6X BASIC CARDS
*ROOKIES: 1.25X TO 3X BASIC
STATED ODDS 1:12
CARD NUMBER 7 DOES NOT EXIST

1998 Topps Chrome Baby Boomers

Randomly inserted in first series packs at the rate of one in 24, this 15 card set features color action photos printed on metalized cards with Chromium technology of young players who have already made their mark in the game with less than three years in the majors.

COMPLETE SET (15) 10.00 25.00
SER.1 STATED ODDS 1:24
*REF: .75X TO 2X BASIC CHR.BOOMERS
REFRACTOR SER.1 STATED ODDS 1:72
BB1 Derek Jeter 4.00 10.00
BB2 Scott Rolen 1.00 2.50
BB3 Nomar Garciaparra 1.00 2.50
BB4 Jose Cruz Jr. .60 1.50
BB5 Darin Erstad .60 1.50
BB6 Todd Helton 1.00 2.50
BB7 Tony Clark .60 1.50
BB8 Jose Guillen .60 1.50
BB9 Andruw Jones .60 1.50
BB10 Vladimir Guerrero 1.00 2.50
BB11 Mark Kotsay .60 1.50
BB12 Todd Greene .60 1.50
BB13 Andy Pettitte 1.00 2.50
BB14 Justin Thompson .60 1.50
BB15 Alan Benes .60 1.50

1998 Topps Chrome Clout Nine

Randomly seeded at a rate of one in 24 second series packs, cards from this nine-card set feature a selection of the league's top sluggers. The cards are a straight parallel of the previously released 1998 Topps Clout 9 set, except of course for the Chromium stock fronts.

COMPLETE SET (9) 25.00 60.00
SER.2 STATED ODDS 1:24
*REF: .75X TO 2X BASIC CHR.CLOUT
REFRACTOR SER.2 STATED ODDS 1:72
C1 Edgar Martinez 1.50 4.00
C2 Mike Piazza 4.00 10.00
C3 Frank Thomas 2.50 6.00
C4 Craig Biggio 1.50 4.00
C5 Vinny Castilla 1.00 2.50
C6 Jeff Blauser 1.00 2.50
C7 Barry Bonds 6.00 15.00
C8 Ken Griffey Jr. 5.00 12.00
C9 Larry Walker 1.00 2.50

1998 Topps Chrome Flashback

Randomly inserted in first series packs at the rate of one in 24, this 10-card set features two-sided cards with color action photos of top players printed on metalized cards with Chromium technology. One side displays how they looked "then" as rookies, while the other side shows how they look "now" as stars.

COMPLETE SET (10) 30.00 80.00
SER.1 STATED ODDS 1:24
*REF: .75X TO 2X BASIC CHR.FLASHBACK
REFRACTOR SER.1 STATED ODDS 1:72
FB1 Barry Bonds 6.00 15.00
FB2 Ken Griffey Jr. 5.00 12.00
FB3 Paul Molitor 1.00 2.50
FB4 Randy Johnson 2.50 6.00
FB5 Cal Ripken 8.00 20.00
FB6 Tony Gwynn 3.00 8.00
FB7 Kenny Lofton 1.00 2.50
FB8 Gary Sheffield 1.00 2.50
FB9 Deion Sanders 1.50 4.00
FB10 Brady Anderson 1.00 2.50

1998 Topps Chrome HallBound

Randomly inserted in first series packs at the rate of one in 24, this 15-card set features color photos printed on metalized cards with Chromium technology of top stars who are bound for the Hall of Fame in Cooperstown, New York.

COMPLETE SET (15) 75.00 150.00
SER.1 STATED ODDS 1:24
*REF: .75X TO 2X BASIC HALLBOUND
REFRACTOR SER.1 STATED ODDS 1:72
HB1 Paul Molitor 1.25 3.00
HB2 Tony Gwynn 4.00 10.00
HB3 Wade Boggs 2.00 5.00
HB4 Roger Clemens 6.00 15.00
HB5 Dennis Eckersley 1.25 3.00
HB6 Cal Ripken 10.00 25.00
HB7 Greg Maddux 5.00 12.00
HB8 Rickey Henderson 2.00 5.00
HB9 Ken Griffey Jr. 6.00 15.00
HB10 Frank Thomas 3.00 8.00
HB11 Mark McGwire 8.00 20.00
HB12 Barry Bonds 8.00 20.00
HB13 Mike Piazza 5.00 12.00
HB14 Juan Gonzalez 1.25 3.00
HB15 Randy Johnson 3.00 8.00

1998 Topps Chrome Milestones

Randomly seeded at a rate of one in every 24 second series packs, these 10 cards feature a selection of veteran stars that achieved specific career milestones in 1997. The cards are a straight parallel from the previously released 1998 Topps Milestones inserts except, of course, for the Chromium finish on the fronts.

COMPLETE SET (10) 60.00 120.00
SER.2 STATED ODDS 1:24
*REF: .75X TO 2X BASIC CHR.MILE
REFRACTOR SER.2 STATED ODDS 1:72
MS1 Barry Bonds 5.00 12.00
MS2 Roger Clemens 4.00 10.00
MS3 Dennis Eckersley .75 2.00
MS4 Juan Gonzalez .75 2.00
MS5 Ken Griffey Jr. 4.00 10.00
MS6 Tony Gwynn 2.50 6.00
MS7 Greg Maddux 3.00 8.00
MS8 Mark McGwire 5.00 12.00
MS9 Cal Ripken 6.00 15.00
MS10 Frank Thomas 2.00 5.00

1998 Topps Chrome Rookie Class

Randomly seeded at a rate of one in 12 second series packs, cards from this 10-card set feature a selection of the league's top rookies for 1998. The cards are a straight parallel of the previously released 1998 Topps Rookie Class set, except of course for the Chromium stock fronts.

COMPLETE SET (10) 8.00 20.00
SER.2 STATED ODDS 1:12
*REF: .75X TO 2X BASIC CHR.RK.CLASS
REFRACTOR SER.2 STATED ODDS 1:24
R1 Travis Lee .75 2.00
R2 Richard Hidalgo .75 2.00
R3 Todd Helton 1.25 3.00
R4 Paul Konerko .75 2.00
R5 Mark Kotsay .75 2.00
R6 Derrek Lee .75 2.00
R7 Eli Marrero .75 2.00
R8 Fernando Tatis .75 2.00
R9 Juan Encarnacion .75 2.00
R10 Ben Grieve .75 2.00

1999 Topps Chrome

The 1999 Topps Chrome set totaled 462 cards (though is numbered 1-463 - card number 7 was never issued in honor of Mickey Mantle). The product was distributed in first and second series four-card packs each carrying a suggested retail price of $3. The first series cards were 1-6/8-242, second series cards 243-463. The card fronts feature action color player photos. The backs carry player information. The set contains the following subsets: Season Highlights (200-204), Prospects (205-212/425-437), Draft Picks (213-219/438-444), League Leaders (221-232), World Series (233-240), Strikeout Kings (445-449), All-Topps (450-460) and four Checklist Cards (241-242/462-463). The Mark McGwire Home Run Record Breaker card (220) was released in 70 different variations highlighting every home run that he hit in 1998. The Sammy Sosa Home Run Parade card (461) was issued in 66 different variations. A 462 card set of 1999 Topps Chrome is considered complete with any version of the McGwire 220 and Sosa 461. Rookie Cards of note include Pat Burrell and Alex Escobar

COMPLETE SET (462) 60.00 120.00
COMPLETE SERIES 1 (241) 25.00 60.00
COMPLETE SERIES 2 (221) 25.00 60.00
COMMON CARD (1-6/8-463) .20 .50
COMMON (205-212/425-437) .40 1.00
CARD NUMBER 7 DOES NOT EXIST

SER.1 SET INCLUDES 1 CARD 220 VARIATION
SER.2 SET INCLUDES 1 CARD 461 VARIATION
1 Roger Clemens 1.50 4.00
2 Andres Galarraga .30 .75
3 Scott Brosius .30 .75
4 John Flaherty .20 .50
5 Jim Leyritz .20 .50
6 Ray Durham .30 .75
8 Jose Vizcaino .20 .50
9 Will Clark .50 1.25
10 David Wells .30 .75
11 Jose Guillen .30 .75
12 Scott Hatteberg .20 .50
13 Edgardo Alfonzo .20 .50
14 Mike Bordick .20 .50
15 Manny Ramirez .50 1.25
16 Greg Maddux 1.25 3.00
17 David Segui .20 .50
18 Darryl Strawberry .30 .75
19 Brad Radke .30 .75
20 Kerry Wood .30 .75
21 Matt Anderson .20 .50
22 Derrek Lee .50 1.25
23 Mickey Morandini .20 .50
24 Paul Konerko .30 .75
25 Travis Lee .20 .50
26 Ken Hill .20 .50
27 Kenny Rogers .30 .75
28 Paul Sorrento .20 .50
29 Quilvio Veras .20 .50
30 Todd Walker .20 .50
31 Ryan Jackson .20 .50
32 John Olerud .30 .75
33 Doug Glanville .20 .50
34 Nolan Ryan 2.50 6.00
35 Ray Lankford .30 .75
36 Mark Loretta .20 .50
37 Jason Dickson .20 .50
38 Sean Bergman .20 .50
39 Quinton McCracken .20 .50
40 Bartolo Colon .30 .75
41 Brady Anderson .30 .75
42 Chris Stynes .20 .50
43 Jorge Posada .50 1.25
44 Justin Thompson .20 .50
45 Johnny Damon .50 1.25
46 Armando Benitez .20 .50
47 Brant Brown .20 .50
48 Charlie Hayes .20 .50
49 Darren Dreifort .20 .50
50 Juan Gonzalez .30 .75
51 Chuck Knoblauch .30 .75
52 Todd Helton .50 1.25
53 Rick Reed .20 .50
54 Chris Gomez .20 .50
55 Gary Sheffield .30 .75
56 Rod Beck .20 .50
57 Rey Sanchez .20 .50
58 Garret Anderson .30 .75
59 Jimmy Haynes .20 .50
60 Steve Woodard .20 .50
61 Rondell White .30 .75
62 Vladimir Guerrero .75 2.00
63 Eric Karros .30 .75
64 Russ Davis .20 .50
65 Mo Vaughn .30 .75
66 Sammy Sosa .75 2.00
67 Troy Percival .30 .75
68 Kenny Lofton .30 .75
69 Bill Taylor .20 .50
70 Mark McGwire 2.00 5.00
71 Roger Cedeno .20 .50
72 Javy Lopez .30 .75
73 Damion Easley .20 .50
74 Andy Pettitte .50 1.25
75 Tony Gwynn 1.00 2.50
76 Ricardo Rincon .20 .50
77 F.P. Santangelo .20 .50
78 Jay Bell .30 .75
79 Scott Servais .20 .50
80 Jose Canseco .50 1.25
81 Roberto Hernandez .20 .50
82 Todd Dunwoody .20 .50
83 John Wetteland .30 .75
84 Mike Caruso .20 .50
85 Derek Jeter 2.00 5.00
86 Aaron Sele .20 .50
87 Jose Lima .20 .50
88 Ryan Christenson .20 .50
89 Jeff Cirillo .20 .50
90 Jose Hernandez .20 .50
91 Mark Kotsay .30 .75
92 Darren Bragg .20 .50
93 Albert Belle .30 .75
94 Matt Lawton .20 .50
95 Pedro Martinez .50 1.25
96 Greg Vaughn .20 .50
97 Neifi Perez .20 .50
98 Gerald Williams .20 .50
99 Derek Bell .20 .50
100 Ken Griffey Jr. 1.50 4.00
101 David Cone .30 .75
102 Brian Johnson .20 .50
103 Dean Palmer .30 .75
104 Javier Valentin .20 .50
105 Trevor Hoffman .30 .75
106 Butch Huskey .20 .50
107 Dave Martinez .20 .50
108 Billy Wagner .30 .75
109 Shawn Green .30 .75
110 Ben Grieve .20 .50
111 Tom Goodwin .20 .50
112 Jaret Wright .20 .50
113 Aramis Ramirez .30 .75
114 Dmitri Young .30 .75
115 Hideki Irabu .20 .50
116 Roberto Kelly .20 .50
117 Jeff Fassero .20 .50
118 Mark Clark .20 .50
119 Jason McDonald .20 .50
120 Matt Williams .30 .75
121 Dave Burba .20 .50
122 Bret Saberhagen .30 .75
123 Deivi Cruz .20 .50
124 Chad Curtis .20 .50
125 Scott Rolen .50 1.25
126 Lee Stevens .20 .50
127 J.T. Snow .30 .75
128 Rusty Greer .30 .75
129 Brian Meadows .20 .50
130 Jim Edmonds .30 .75
131 Ron Gant .30 .75
132 A.J. Hinch .30 .75
133 Shannon Stewart .30 .75
134 Brad Fullmer .20 .50
135 Cal Eldred .20 .50
136 Matt Walbeck .20 .50
137 Carl Everett .30 .75
138 Walt Weiss .20 .50
139 Fred McGriff .50 1.25
140 Darin Erstad .30 .75
141 Dave Nilsson .20 .50
142 Eric Young .20 .50
143 Dan Wilson .20 .50
144 Jeff Reed .20 .50
145 Brett Tomko .20 .50
146 Terry Steinbach .20 .50
147 Seth Greisinger .20 .50
148 Pat Meares .20 .50
149 Livan Hernandez .30 .75
150 Jeff Bagwell .50 1.25
151 Bob Wickman .20 .50
152 Omar Vizquel .50 1.25
153 Eric Davis .30 .75
154 Larry Sutton .20 .50
155 Magglio Ordonez .30 .75
156 Eric Milton .20 .50
157 Darren Lewis .20 .50
158 Rick Aguilera .20 .50
159 Mike Lieberthal .20 .50
160 Robb Nen .30 .75
161 Brian Giles .30 .75
162 Jeff Brantley .20 .50
163 Gary DiSarcina .20 .50
164 John Valentin .20 .50
165 Dave Dellucci .20 .50
166 Chan Ho Park .30 .75
167 Masato Yoshii .20 .50
168 Jason Schmidt .30 .75
169 LaTroy Hawkins .20 .50
170 Bret Boone .30 .75
171 Jerry DiPoto .20 .50
172 Mariano Rivera .75 2.00
173 Mike Cameron .20 .50
174 Scott Erickson .30 .75
175 Charles Johnson .30 .75
176 Bobby Jones .20 .50
177 Francisco Cordova .20 .50
178 Todd Jones .20 .50
179 Jeff Montgomery .20 .50
180 Mike Mussina .50 1.25
181 Bob Abreu .30 .75
182 Ismael Valdes .20 .50
183 Andy Fox .20 .50
184 Woody Williams .20 .50
185 Denny Neagle .20 .50
186 Jose Valentin .20 .50
187 Darrin Fletcher .20 .50
188 Gabe Alvarez .20 .50
189 Eddie Taubensee .20 .50
190 Edgar Martinez .50 1.25
191 Jason Kendall .30 .75
192 Darryl Kile .30 .75
193 Jeff King .20 .50
194 Rey Ordonez .20 .50
195 Andruw Jones .50 1.25
196 Tony Fernandez .20 .50
197 Jamey Wright .20 .50
198 B.J. Surhoff .30 .75
199 Vinny Castilla .30 .75
200 David Wells HL .20 .50
201 Mark McGwire HL 1.00 2.50
202 Sammy Sosa HL .50 1.25
203 Roger Clemens HL .75 2.00
204 Kerry Wood HL .20 .50
205 L.Berkman .40 1.00
G.Kapler
206 Alex Escobar RC .40 1.00
207 Peter Bergeron RC .40 1.00
208 M.Barrett .40 1.00
B.Davis
R.Fick
209 J.Werth .40 1.00
Hernandez
Cline
210 R.Anderson .40 1.00
Chen
Enochs
211 B.Penny .40 1.00
Dotel
Lincoln
212 Chuck Abbott RC .40 1.00
213 C.Jones .40 1.00
J.Urban RC
214 T.Torcato .40 1.00
A.McDowell RC
215 J.Tyner .40 1.00
J.McKinley RC
216 M.Burch .40 1.00
S.Etherton RC
217 R.Elder .40 1.00
M.Tucker RC
218 J.M.Gold .40 1.00
R.Mills RC
219 A.Brown .40 1.00
C.Freeman RC
220A Mark McGwire HR 1 20.00 50.00
220B Mark McGwire HR 2 12.50 30.00
220C Mark McGwire HR 3 12.50 30.00
220D Mark McGwire HR 4 12.50 30.00
220E Mark McGwire HR 5 12.50 30.00
220F Mark McGwire HR 6 12.50 30.00
220G Mark McGwire HR 7 12.50 30.00
220H Mark McGwire HR 8 12.50 30.00
220I Mark McGwire HR 9 12.50 30.00
220J Mark McGwire HR 10 12.50 30.00
220K Mark McGwire HR 11 12.50 30.00
220L Mark McGwire HR 12 12.50 30.00
220M Mark McGwire HR 13 12.50 30.00
220N Mark McGwire HR 14 12.50 30.00
220O Mark McGwire HR 15 12.50 30.00
220P Mark McGwire HR 16 12.50 30.00
220Q Mark McGwire HR 17 12.50 30.00
220R Mark McGwire HR 18 12.50 30.00
220S Mark McGwire HR 19 12.50 30.00
220T Mark McGwire HR 20 12.50 30.00
220U Mark McGwire HR 21 12.50 30.00
220V Mark McGwire HR 22 12.50 30.00
220W Mark McGwire HR 23 12.50 30.00
220X Mark McGwire HR 24 12.50 30.00
220Y Mark McGwire HR 25 12.50 30.00
220Z Mark McGwire HR 26 12.50 30.00
220AA Mark McGwire HR 27 12.50 30.00
220AB Mark McGwire HR 28 12.50 30.00
220AC Mark McGwire HR 29 12.50 30.00
220AD Mark McGwire HR 30 12.50 30.00
220AE Mark McGwire HR 31 12.50 30.00
220AF Mark McGwire HR 32 12.50 30.00
220AG Mark McGwire HR 33 12.50 30.00
220AH Mark McGwire HR 34 12.50 30.00
220AI Mark McGwire HR 35 12.50 30.00
220AJ Mark McGwire HR 36 12.50 30.00
220AK Mark McGwire HR 37 12.50 30.00
220AL Mark McGwire HR 38 12.50 30.00
220AM Mark McGwire HR 39 12.50 30.00
220AN Mark McGwire HR 40 12.50 30.00
220AO Mark McGwire HR 41 12.50 30.00
220AP Mark McGwire HR 42 12.50 30.00
220AQ Mark McGwire HR 43 12.50 30.00
220AR Mark McGwire HR 44 12.50 30.00
220AS Mark McGwire HR 45 12.50 30.00
220AT Mark McGwire HR 46 12.50 30.00
220AU Mark McGwire HR 47 12.50 30.00
220AV Mark McGwire HR 48 12.50 30.00
220AW Mark McGwire HR 49 12.50 30.00
220AX Mark McGwire HR 50 12.50 30.00
220AY Mark McGwire HR 51 12.50 30.00
220AZ Mark McGwire HR 52 12.50 30.00
220BB Mark McGwire HR 53 12.50 30.00
220CC Mark McGwire HR 54 12.50 30.00
220DD Mark McGwire HR 55 12.50 30.00
220EE Mark McGwire HR 56 12.50 30.00
220FF Mark McGwire HR 57 12.50 30.00
220GG Mark McGwire HR 58 12.50 30.00
220HH Mark McGwire HR 59 12.50 30.00
220II Mark McGwire HR 60 12.50 30.00
220JJ Mark McGwire HR 61 20.00 50.00
220KK Mark McGwire HR 62 40.00 80.00
220LL Mark McGwire HR 63 20.00 50.00
220MM Mark McGwire HR 64 20.00 50.00
220NN Mark McGwire HR 65 20.00 50.00
220OO Mark McGwire HR 66 20.00 50.00
220PP Mark McGwire HR 67 20.00 50.00
220QQ Mark McGwire HR 68 20.00 50.00
220RR Mark McGwire HR 69 20.00 50.00
220SS Mark McGwire HR 70 60.00 120.00
221 Larry Walker LL .20 .50
222 Bernie Williams LL .30 .75
223 Mark McGwire LL 1.00 2.50
224 Ken Griffey Jr. LL 1.00 2.50
225 Sammy Sosa LL .50 1.25
226 Juan Gonzalez LL .20 .50
227 Dante Bichette LL .20 .50
228 Alex Rodriguez LL .75 2.00
229 Sammy Sosa LL .50 1.25
230 Derek Jeter LL 1.00 2.50
231 Greg Maddux LL .75 2.00
232 Roger Clemens LL .75 2.00
233 Ricky Ledee WS .20 .50
234 Chuck Knoblauch WS .20 .50
235 Bernie Williams WS .30 .75
236 Tino Martinez WS .30 .75
237 Orlando Hernandez WS .30 .75
238 Scott Brosius WS .20 .50
239 Andy Pettitte WS .30 .75
240 Mariano Rivera WS .50 1.25
241 Checklist .20 .50
242 Checklist .20 .50
243 Tom Glavine .50 1.25
244 Andy Benes .20 .50
245 Sandy Alomar Jr. .20 .50
246 Wilton Guerrero .20 .50
247 Alex Gonzalez .20 .50
248 Roberto Alomar .50 1.25
249 Ruben Rivera .20 .50
250 Eric Chavez .30 .75
251 Ellis Burks .30 .75
252 Richie Sexson .30 .75
253 Steve Finley .30 .75
254 Dwight Gooden .30 .75
255 Dustin Hermanson .20 .50
256 Kirk Rueter .20 .50
257 Steve Trachsel .20 .50
258 Gregg Jefferies .20 .50
259 Matt Stairs .20 .50
260 Shane Reynolds .20 .50
261 Gregg Olson .20 .50
262 Kevin Tapani .20 .50
263 Matt Morris .30 .75
264 Carl Pavano .30 .75
265 Nomar Garciaparra 1.25 3.00
266 Kevin Young .30 .75
267 Rick Helling .20 .50
268 Matt Franco .20 .50
269 Brian McRae .20 .50
270 Cal Ripken 2.50 6.00
271 Jeff Abbott .20 .50
272 Tony Batista .20 .50
273 Bill Simas .20 .50
274 Brian Hunter .20 .50
275 John Franco .30 .75
276 Devon White .30 .75
277 Rickey Henderson .75 2.00
278 Chuck Finley .30 .75
279 Mike Blowers .20 .50
280 Mark Grace .50 1.25
281 Randy Winn .20 .50
282 Bobby Bonilla .30 .75
283 David Justice .30 .75
284 Shane Monahan .20 .50
285 Kevin Brown .50 1.25
286 Todd Zeile .30 .75
287 Al Martin .20 .50
288 Troy O'Leary .20 .50
289 Darryl Hamilton .20 .50
290 Tino Martinez .50 1.25
291 David Ortiz .75 2.00
292 Tony Clark .20 .50
293 Ryan Minor .20 .50
294 Mark Leiter .20 .50
295 Wally Joyner .30 .75
296 Cliff Floyd .30 .75
297 Shawn Estes .20 .50
298 Pat Hentgen .20 .50
299 Scott Elarton .20 .50
300 Alex Rodriguez 1.25 3.00
301 Ozzie Guillen .30 .75
302 Hideo Nomo .75 2.00
303 Ryan McGuire .20 .50
304 Brad Ausmus .30 .75
305 Alex Gonzalez .20 .50
306 Brian Jordan .30 .75
307 John Jaha .20 .50
308 Mark Grudzielanek .20 .50
309 Juan Guzman .20 .50
310 Tony Womack .20 .50
311 Dennis Reyes .20 .50
312 Marty Cordova .20 .50
313 Ramiro Mendoza .20 .50
314 Robin Ventura .30 .75
315 Rafael Palmeiro .50 1.25
316 Ramon Martinez .20 .50
317 Pedro Astacio .20 .50
318 Dave Hollins .20 .50
319 Tom Candiotti .20 .50
320 Al Leiter .30 .75
321 Rico Brogna .20 .50
322 Reggie Jefferson .20 .50
323 Bernard Gilkey .20 .50
324 Jason Giambi .30 .75
325 Craig Biggio .50 1.25
326 Troy Glaus .50 1.25
327 Delino DeShields .20 .50
328 Fernando Vina .20 .50
329 John Smoltz .50 1.25
330 Jeff Kent .30 .75
331 Roy Halladay .75 2.00
332 Andy Ashby .20 .50
333 Tim Wakefield .30 .75
334 Roger Clemens 1.50 4.00
335 Bernie Williams .50 1.25
336 Desi Relaford .20 .50
337 John Burkett .20 .50
338 Mike Hampton .30 .75
339 Royce Clayton .20 .50
340 Mike Piazza 1.25 3.00
341 Jeremi Gonzalez .20 .50
342 Mike Lansing .20 .50
343 Jamie Moyer .30 .75
344 Ron Coomer .20 .50
345 Barry Larkin .50 1.25
346 Fernando Tatis .20 .50
347 Chili Davis .30 .75
348 Bobby Higginson .30 .75
349 Hal Morris .20 .50
350 Larry Walker .30 .75
351 Carlos Guillen .30 .75
352 Miguel Tejada .30 .75
353 Travis Fryman .30 .75
354 Jarrod Washburn .20 .50
355 Chipper Jones .75 2.00
356 Todd Stottlemyre .20 .50
357 Henry Rodriguez .20 .50
358 Eli Marrero .20 .50
359 Alan Benes .20 .50
360 Tim Salmon .50 1.25
361 Luis Gonzalez .30 .75
362 Scott Spiezio .20 .50
363 Chris Carpenter .30 .75
364 Bobby Howry .20 .50
365 Raul Mondesi .30 .75
366 Ugueth Urbina .20 .50
367 Tom Evans .20 .50
368 Kerry Ligtenberg RC .30 .75
369 Adrian Beltre .30 .75
370 Ryan Klesko .30 .75
371 Wilson Alvarez .20 .50
372 John Thomson .20 .50
373 Tony Saunders .20 .50
374 Dave Mlicki .20 .50
375 Ken Caminiti .30 .75
376 Jay Buhner .30 .75
377 Bill Mueller .30 .75
378 Jeff Blauser .20 .50
379 Edgar Renteria .30 .75
380 Jim Thome .50 1.25
381 Joey Hamilton .20 .50
382 Calvin Pickering .20 .50
383 Marquis Grissom .30 .75
384 Omar Daal .20 .50
385 Curt Schilling .30 .75
386 Jose Cruz Jr. .20 .50
387 Chris Widger .20 .50
388 Pete Harnisch .20 .50
389 Charles Nagy .20 .50
390 Tom Gordon .20 .50
391 Bobby Smith .20 .50
392 Derrick Gibson .20 .50
393 Jeff Conine .30 .75
394 Carlos Perez .20 .50
395 Barry Bonds 2.00 5.00
396 Mark McLemore .20 .50
397 Juan Encarnacion .20 .50
398 Wade Boggs .50 1.25
399 Ivan Rodriguez .50 1.25
400 Moises Alou .30 .75
401 Jeromy Burnitz .30 .75
402 Sean Casey .30 .75
403 Jose Offerman .20 .50
404 Joe Fontenot .20 .50
405 Kevin Millwood .30 .75
406 Lance Johnson .20 .50
407 Richard Hidalgo .20 .50
408 Mike Jackson .20 .50
409 Brian Anderson .20 .50
410 Jeff Shaw .20 .50
411 Preston Wilson .30 .75
412 Todd Hundley .20 .50
413 Jim Parque .20 .50
414 Justin Baughman .20 .50
415 Dante Bichette .30 .75
416 Paul O'Neill .50 1.25
417 Miguel Cairo .20 .50
418 Randy Johnson .75 2.00
419 Jesus Sanchez .20 .50
420 Carlos Delgado .30 .75
421 Ricky Ledee .20 .50
422 Orlando Hernandez .30 .75
423 Frank Thomas .75 2.00
424 Pokey Reese .20 .50
425 C.Lee .40 1.00
M.Lowell
426 M.Cuddyer .40 1.00
DeRosa
Hairston
427 M.Anderson .40 1.00
Belliard
Cabrera
428 M.Bowie .40 1.00
P.Norton RC
Wolf
429 J.Cressend RC .40 1.00
Rocker
430 R.Mateo .40 1.00
M.Zywica RC
431 J.LaRue .40 1.00
LeCroy
Meluskey
432 Gabe Kapler .40 1.00
433 A.Kennedy .40 1.00
M.Lopez RC
434 Jose Fernandez RC .40 1.00
C.Truby
435 Doug Mientkiewicz RC .60 1.50
436 R.Brown RC .40 1.00
V.Wells
437 A.J. Burnett RC .75 2.00
438 M.Belisle .40 1.00
M.Roney RC
439 A.Kearns 1.50 4.00
C.George RC
440 N.Cornejo .40 1.00
N.Bump RC
441 B.Lidge 1.50 4.00
M.Nannini RC
442 M.Holliday 3.00 8.00
J.Winchester RC
443 A.Everett .60 1.50
C.Ambres RC
444 P.Burrell 1.50 4.00
E.Valent RC
445 Roger Clemens SK .75 2.00
446 Kerry Wood SK .20 .50
447 Curt Schilling SK .20 .50
448 Randy Johnson SK .50 1.25
449 Pedro Martinez SK .50 1.25
450 Bagwell .75 2.00
Galar
McGwire AT
451 Olerud .30 .75
Thome
Martinez AT
452 ARod 1.00 2.50
Nomar
Jeter AT
453 Castilla .50 1.25
Jones
Rolen AT
454 Sosa 1.00 2.50
Griffey
Gonzalez AT
455 Bonds 1.00 2.50
Ramirez
Walker AT
456 Thomas .75 2.00
Salmon
Justice AT
457 Lee .30 .75
Helton
Grieve AT
458 Guerrero .30 .75
Vaughn
B.Will AT
459 Piazza .75 2.00
IRod
Kendall AT
460 Clemens .75 2.00
Wood
Maddux AT
461A Sammy Sosa HR 1 8.00 20.00
461B Sammy Sosa HR 2 5.00 12.00
461C Sammy Sosa HR 3 5.00 12.00
461D Sammy Sosa HR 4 5.00 12.00
461E Sammy Sosa HR 5 5.00 12.00
461F Sammy Sosa HR 6 5.00 12.00
461G Sammy Sosa HR 7 5.00 12.00
461H Sammy Sosa HR 8 5.00 12.00
461I Sammy Sosa HR 9 5.00 12.00
461J Sammy Sosa HR 10 5.00 12.00
461K Sammy Sosa HR 11 5.00 12.00
461L Sammy Sosa HR 12 5.00 12.00
461M Sammy Sosa HR 13 5.00 12.00
461N Sammy Sosa HR 14 5.00 12.00
461O Sammy Sosa HR 15 5.00 12.00
461P Sammy Sosa HR 16 5.00 12.00
461Q Sammy Sosa HR 17 5.00 12.00
461R Sammy Sosa HR 18 5.00 12.00
461S Sammy Sosa HR 19 5.00 12.00
461T Sammy Sosa HR 20 5.00 12.00
461U Sammy Sosa HR 21 5.00 12.00
461V Sammy Sosa HR 22 5.00 12.00
461W Sammy Sosa HR 23 5.00 12.00
461X Sammy Sosa HR 24 5.00 12.00
461Y Sammy Sosa HR 25 5.00 12.00
461Z Sammy Sosa HR 26 5.00 12.00
461AA Sammy Sosa HR 27 5.00 12.00
461AB Sammy Sosa HR 28 5.00 12.00
461AC Sammy Sosa HR 29 5.00 12.00
461AD Sammy Sosa HR 30 5.00 12.00
461AE Sammy Sosa HR 31 5.00 12.00
461AF Sammy Sosa HR 32 5.00 12.00
461AG Sammy Sosa HR 33 5.00 12.00
461AH Sammy Sosa HR 34 5.00 12.00
461AI Sammy Sosa HR 35 5.00 12.00
461AJ Sammy Sosa HR 36 5.00 12.00
461AK Sammy Sosa HR 37 5.00 12.00
461AL Sammy Sosa HR 38 5.00 12.00
461AM Sammy Sosa HR 39 5.00 12.00
461AN Sammy Sosa HR 40 5.00 12.00
461AO Sammy Sosa HR 41 5.00 12.00
461AP Sammy Sosa HR 42 5.00 12.00
461AR Sammy Sosa HR 43 5.00 12.00
461AS Sammy Sosa HR 44 5.00 12.00
461AT Sammy Sosa HR 45 5.00 12.00
461AU Sammy Sosa HR 46 5.00 12.00
461AV Sammy Sosa HR 47 5.00 12.00
461AW Sammy Sosa HR 48 5.00 12.00
461AX Sammy Sosa HR 49 5.00 12.00
461AY Sammy Sosa HR 50 5.00 12.00
461AZ Sammy Sosa HR 51 5.00 12.00
461BB Sammy Sosa HR 52 5.00 12.00
461CC Sammy Sosa HR 53 5.00 12.00
461DD Sammy Sosa HR 54 5.00 12.00
461EE Sammy Sosa HR 55 5.00 12.00
461FF Sammy Sosa HR 56 5.00 12.00
461GG Sammy Sosa HR 57 5.00 12.00
461HH Sammy Sosa HR 58 5.00 12.00
461II Sammy Sosa HR 59 5.00 12.00
461JJ Sammy Sosa HR 60 5.00 12.00
461KK Sammy Sosa HR 61 8.00 20.00
461LL Sammy Sosa HR 62 12.50 30.00
461MM Sammy Sosa HR 63 8.00 20.00
461NN Sammy Sosa HR 64 8.00 20.00
461OO Sammy Sosa HR 65 8.00 20.00
461PP Sammy Sosa HR 66 30.00 60.00
462 Checklist .20 .50
463 Checklist .20 .50

1999 Topps Chrome Refractors

*STARS: 2.5X TO 6X BASIC CARDS
*ROOKIES: 1.25X TO 3X BASIC CARDS
MCGWIRE 220 HR 1 125.00 250.00
MCGWIRE 220 HR 2-60 60.00 120.00
MCGWIRE 220 HR 61 100.00 200.00
MCGWIRE 220 HR 62 150.00 300.00
MCGWIRE 220 HR 63-69 60.00 120.00
MCGWIRE 220 HR 70 200.00 400.00
SOSA 461 HR 1 30.00 60.00
SOSA 461 HR 2-60 10.00 25.00
SOSA 461 HR 61 20.00 50.00
SOSA 461 HR 62 40.00 80.00
SOSA 461 HR 63-65 10.00 25.00
SOSA 461 HR 66 60.00 120.00
REFRACTOR STATED ODDS 1:12
CARD NUMBER 7 DOES NOT EXIST
442 M.Holliday 15.00 40.00
J.Winchester

1999 Topps Chrome All-Etch

Randomly inserted in Series two packs at the rate of one in six, this 30-card set features color player photos printed on All-Etch technology. A refractive parallel version of this set was also produced with an insertion rate of 1:24 packs.

COMPLETE SET (30) 40.00 100.00
SER.2 STATED ODDS 1:6
*REFRACTORS: .75X TO 2X BASIC ALL-ETCH
SER.2 REFRACTOR ODDS 1:24
AE1 Mark McGwire 5.00 12.00
AE2 Sammy Sosa 2.00 5.00
AE3 Ken Griffey Jr. 4.00 10.00
AE4 Greg Vaughn .50 1.25
AE5 Albert Belle .75 2.00
AE6 Vinny Castilla .75 2.00
AE7 Jose Canseco 1.25 3.00
AE8 Juan Gonzalez .75 2.00
AE9 Manny Ramirez 1.25 3.00
AE10 Andres Galarraga .75 2.00
AE11 Rafael Palmeiro 1.25 3.00
AE12 Alex Rodriguez 3.00 8.00
AE13 Mo Vaughn .75 2.00
AE14 Eric Chavez .75 2.00
AE15 Gabe Kapler 1.00 2.50
AE16 Calvin Pickering .50 1.25
AE17 Ruben Mateo 1.00 2.50
AE18 Roy Halladay 2.00 5.00
AE19 Jeremy Giambi .50 1.25
AE20 Alex Gonzalez .50 1.25
AE21 Ron Belliard 1.00 2.50
AE22 Marlon Anderson 1.00 2.50
AE23 Carlos Lee 1.00 2.50
AE24 Kerry Wood .75 2.00
AE25 Roger Clemens 4.00 10.00
AE26 Curt Schilling .75 2.00
AE27 Kevin Brown 1.25 3.00
AE28 Randy Johnson 2.00 5.00
AE29 Pedro Martinez 1.25 3.00
AE30 Orlando Hernandez .75 2.00

1999 Topps Chrome Early Road to the Hall

Randomly inserted in Series one packs at the rate of one in 12, this 10-card set features color photos of ten players with less than 10 years in the Majors but are already headed towards the Hall of Fame in Cooperstown, New York.

COMPLETE SET (10) 10.00 25.00
SER.1 STATED ODDS 1:12
*REFRACTORS: 3X TO 8X BASIC ROAD
SER.1 REFRACTOR ODDS 1:944 HOBBY
REF.PRINT RUN 100 SERIAL #'d SETS
ER1 Nomar Garciaparra .75 2.00
ER2 Derek Jeter 3.00 8.00
ER3 Alex Rodriguez 1.50 4.00
ER4 Juan Gonzalez .50 1.25
ER5 Ken Griffey Jr. 2.50 6.00
ER6 Chipper Jones 1.25 3.00
ER7 Vladimir Guerrero .75 2.00
ER8 Jeff Bagwell .75 2.00
ER9 Ivan Rodriguez .75 2.00
ER10 Frank Thomas 1.25 3.00

1999 Topps Chrome Fortune 15

Randomly inserted into Series two packs at the rate of one in 12, this 15-card set features color photos of the League's most elite veteran and rookie players. A refractor parallel version of this set was also produced with an insertion rate of 1:627 packs and sequentially numbered to 100.

COMPLETE SET (15) 40.00 100.00
SER.2 STATED ODDS 1:12
*REFRACTORS: 4X TO 8X BASIC FORT.15
SER.2 REFRACTOR ODDS 1:627
REF.PRINT RUN 100 SERIAL #'d SETS
FF1 Alex Rodriguez 3.00 8.00
FF2 Nomar Garciaparra 3.00 8.00
FF3 Derek Jeter 5.00 12.00
FF4 Troy Glaus 1.25 3.00
FF5 Ken Griffey Jr. 4.00 10.00
FF6 Vladimir Guerrero 2.00 5.00
FF7 Kerry Wood .75 2.00
FF8 Eric Chavez .75 2.00
FF9 Greg Maddux 3.00 8.00
FF10 Mike Piazza 3.00 8.00
FF11 Sammy Sosa 2.00 5.00
FF12 Mark McGwire 5.00 12.00
FF13 Ben Grieve .50 1.25
FF14 Chipper Jones 2.00 5.00
FF15 Manny Ramirez 1.25 3.00

1999 Topps Chrome Lords of the Diamond

Randomly inserted in Series one packs at the rate of one in eight, this 15-card set features color photos of some of the true masters of the ballfield. A refractive parallel version of this set was also produced with an insertion rate of 1:24.

COMPLETE SET (15) 20.00 50.00
SER.1 STATED ODDS 1:8
*REFRACTORS: .6X TO 1.5X BASIC LORDS
SER.1 REFRACTOR ODDS 1:24
LD1 Ken Griffey Jr. 2.00 5.00
LD2 Chipper Jones 1.00 2.50
LD3 Sammy Sosa 1.00 2.50
LD4 Frank Thomas 1.00 2.50
LD5 Mark McGwire 2.50 6.00
LD6 Jeff Bagwell .60 1.50
LD7 Alex Rodriguez 1.50 4.00
LD8 Juan Gonzalez .40 1.00
LD9 Barry Bonds 2.50 6.00
LD10 Nomar Garciaparra 1.50 4.00
LD11 Darin Erstad .40 1.00
LD12 Tony Gwynn 1.25 3.00
LD13 Andres Galarraga .40 1.00
LD14 Mike Piazza 1.50 4.00
LD15 Greg Maddux 1.50 4.00

1999 Topps Chrome New Breed

Randomly inserted in Series one packs at the rate of one in 24, this 15-card set features color photos of some of today's young stars in Major League Baseball. A refractive parallel version of this set was also produced with an insertion rate of 1:72.

COMPLETE SET (15) 40.00 100.00
SER.1 STATED ODDS 1:24
*REFRACTORS: .6X TO 1.5X BASIC BREED
SER.1 REFRACTOR ODDS 1:72
NB1 Darin Erstad 1.25 3.00
NB2 Brad Fullmer .75 2.00
NB3 Kerry Wood 1.25 3.00
NB4 Nomar Garciaparra 5.00 12.00
NB5 Travis Lee .75 2.00
NB6 Scott Rolen 2.00 5.00
NB7 Todd Helton 2.00 5.00
NB8 Vladimir Guerrero 3.00 8.00
NB9 Derek Jeter 8.00 20.00
NB10 Alex Rodriguez 5.00 12.00
NB11 Ben Grieve .75 2.00
NB12 Andruw Jones 2.00 5.00
NB13 Paul Konerko 1.25 3.00
NB14 Aramis Ramirez 1.25 3.00
NB15 Adrian Beltre 1.25 3.00

1999 Topps Chrome Record Numbers

Randomly inserted in Series two packs at the rate of one in 36, this 10-card set features color photos of top Major League record-setters. A refractive parallel version of this set was also produced with an insertion rate of 1:144.

COMPLETE SET (10) 15.00 40.00
SER.2 STATED ODDS 1:36
*REFRACTORS: .75X TO 2X BASIC REC.NUM.
SER.2 REFRACTOR ODDS 1:144
RN1 Mark McGwire 2.50 6.00
RN2 Mike Piazza 1.50 4.00
RN3 Curt Schilling .60 1.50
RN4 Ken Griffey Jr. 3.00 8.00
RN5 Sammy Sosa 1.50 4.00
RN6 Nomar Garciaparra 1.00 2.50
RN7 Kerry Wood .60 1.50
RN8 Roger Clemens 2.00 5.00
RN9 Cal Ripken 5.00 12.00
RN10 Mark McGwire 2.50 6.00

1999 Topps Chrome Traded

This 121-card set features color photos on Chromium cards of 46 of the most notable transactions of the 1999 season and 75 newcomers accented with the Topps "Rookie Card" logo. The set was distributed only in factory boxes. Due to a very late ship date (January, 2000) this set caused some commotion in the hobby as to its status as a 1999 or 2000 product. Notable Rookie Cards include Carl Crawford, Adam Dunn, Josh Hamilton, Corey Patterson and Alfonso Soriano.

COMP.FACT SET (121) 30.00 60.00
DISTRIBUTED ONLY IN FACTORY SET FORM
CONDITION SENSITIVE SET
T1 Seth Etherton .15 .40
T2 Mark Harriger RC .20 .50
T3 Matt Wise RC .20 .50
T4 Carlos Eduardo Hernandez RC .30 .75
T5 Julio Lugo RC .50 1.25
T6 Mike Nannini .15 .40
T7 Justin Bowles RC .20 .50
T8 Mark Mulder RC 1.25 3.00
T9 Roberto Vaz RC .20 .50
T10 Felipe Lopez RC 1.25 3.00
T11 Matt Belisle .15 .40
T12 Micah Bowie .15 .40
T13 Ruben Quevedo RC .20 .50
T14 Jose Garcia RC .20 .50
T15 David Kelton RC .20 .50
T16 Phil Norton .15 .40
T17 Corey Patterson RC .75 2.00
T18 Ron Walker RC .20 .50
T19 Paul Hoover RC .20 .50
T20 Ryan Rupe RC .20 .50
T21 J.D. Closser RC .30 .75
T22 Rob Ryan RC .20 .50
T23 Steve Colyer RC .20 .50
T24 Bubba Crosby RC .50 1.25
T25 Luke Prokopec RC .20 .50
T26 Matt Blank RC .20 .50
T27 Josh McKinley .15 .40
T28 Nate Bump .20 .50
T29 Giuseppe Chiaramonte RC .20 .50
T30 Arturo McDowell .15 .40
T31 Tony Torcato .15 .40
T32 Dave Roberts RC .50 1.25
T33 C.C. Sabathia RC 4.00 10.00
T34 Sean Spencer RC .20 .50
T35 Chip Ambres .15 .40
T36 A.J. Burnett .75 2.00
T37 Mo Bruce RC .20 .50
T38 Jason Tyner .15 .40
T39 Mamon Tucker .15 .40
T40 Sean Burroughs RC .50 1.25
T41 Kevin Eberwein RC .20 .50
T42 Junior Herndon RC .20 .50
T43 Bryan Wolff RC .20 .50
T44 Pat Burrell 1.25 3.00
T45 Eric Valent .30 .75
T46 Carlos Pena RC .40 1.00
T47 Mike Zywica .15 .40
T48 Adam Everett .40 1.00
T49 Juan Pena RC .20 .50
T50 Adam Dunn RC 3.00 8.00
T51 Austin Kearns 1.25 3.00
T52 Jacobo Sequea RC .20 .50
T53 Choo Freeman .25 .60
T54 Jeff Winchester .15 .40
T55 Matt Burch .20 .50
T56 Chris George .15 .40
T57 Scott Mullen RC .20 .50
T58 Kit Pellow .20 .50
T59 Mark Quinn RC .20 .50
T60 Nate Cornejo .20 .50
T61 Ryan Mills .15 .40
T62 Kevin Beirne RC .20 .50
T63 Kip Wells RC .30 .75
T64 Juan Rivera RC .75 2.00
T65 Alfonso Soriano RC 4.00 10.00
T66 Josh Hamilton RC 5.00 12.00
T67 Josh Girdley RC .20 .50
T68 Kyle Snyder RC .20 .50
T69 Mike Paradis RC .20 .50
T70 Jason Jennings RC .50 1.25
T71 David Walling RC .20 .50
T72 Omar Ortiz RC .20 .50
T73 Jay Gehrke RC .20 .50
T74 Casey Burns RC .20 .50
T75 Carl Crawford RC 3.00 8.00
T76 Reggie Sanders .25 .60
T77 Will Clark .40 1.00
T78 David Wells .25 .60
T79 Paul Konerko .25 .60
T80 Armando Benitez .15 .40
T81 Brant Brown .15 .40
T82 Mo Vaughn .25 .60
T83 Jose Canseco .40 1.00
T84 Albert Belle .25 .60
T85 Dean Palmer .25 .60
T86 Greg Vaughn .15 .40
T87 Mark Clark .15 .40
T88 Pat Meares .15 .40
T89 Eric Davis .25 .60
T90 Brian Giles .25 .60
T91 Jeff Brantley .15 .40
T92 Bret Boone .25 .60
T93 Ron Gant .25 .60
T94 Mike Cameron .15 .40
T95 Charles Johnson .25 .60
T96 Denny Neagle .15 .40
T97 Brian Hunter .15 .40
T98 Jose Hernandez .15 .40
T99 Rick Aguilera .15 .40
T100 Tony Batista .15 .40
T101 Roger Cedeno .15 .40
T102 Creighton Gubanich RC .20 .50
T103 Tim Belcher .15 .40
T104 Bruce Aven .15 .40
T105 Brian Daubach RC .30 .75
T106 Ed Sprague .15 .40
T107 Michael Tucker .15 .40
T108 Homer Bush .15 .40
T109 Armando Reynoso .15 .40
T110 Brook Fordyce .15 .40
T111 Matt Mantei .15 .40
T112 Dave Mlicki .15 .40
T113 Kenny Rogers .25 .60
T114 Livan Hernandez .25 .60
T115 Butch Huskey .15 .40
T116 David Segui .15 .40
T117 Darryl Hamilton .15 .40
T118 Terry Mulholland .15 .40
T119 Randy Velarde .15 .40
T120 Bill Taylor .15 .40
T121 Kevin Appier .25 .60

2000 Topps Chrome

These cards parallel the regular Topps set and are issued using Topps' Chromium technology and color metallization. The first series product was released in February, 2000 and second series in May, 2000. Four card packs for each series carried an SRP of $3.00. Similar to the regular set, no card number 7 was issued and a Mark McGwire rookie reprint card was also inserted into packs. Also, like the base Topps set all of the Magic Moments subset cards (235-239 and 475-479) are available in five variations - each detailing a different highlight in the featured player's career. The base Chrome set is considered complete with any of the Magic Moments variations (for each player). Notable Rookie Cards include Rick Asadoorian, Ben Sheets and Barry Zito.

COMPLETE SET (478) 30.00 60.00
COMPLETE SERIES 1 (239) 12.50 30.00
COMPLETE SERIES 2 (240) 12.50 30.00
COMMON CARD (1-6/8-479) .30 .75
COMMON RC .40 1.00
MCGWIRE MM SET (5) 12.50 30.00
MCGWIRE MM (236A-236E) 4.00 10.00
AARON MM SET (5) 12.50 30.00
AARON MM (237A-237E) 4.00 10.00
RIPKEN MM SET (5) 25.00 60.00
RIPKEN MM (238A-238E) 8.00 20.00
BOGGS MM SET (5) 4.00 10.00
BOGGS MM (239A-239E) 1.25 3.00
GWYNN MM SET (5) 6.00 15.00
GWYNN MM (240A-240E) 2.00 5.00
GRIFFEY MM SET (5) 10.00 25.00
GRIFFEY MM (475A-475E) 3.00 8.00
BONDS MM SET (5) 12.50 30.00
BONDS MM (476A-476E) 4.00 10.00
SOSA MM SET (5) 6.00 15.00
SOSA MM (477A-477E) 2.00 5.00
JETER MM SET (5) 15.00 40.00
JETER MM (478A-478E) 5.00 12.00
A.ROD MM SET (5) 10.00 25.00
A.ROD MM (479A-479E) 3.00 8.00
CARD NUMBER 7 DOES NOT EXIST
SER.1 HAS ONLY 1 VERSION OF 236-240
SER.2 HAS ONLY 1 VERSION OF 475-479
MCGWIRE '85 ODDS 1:32
1 Mark McGwire 1.25 3.00
2 Tony Gwynn .75 2.00
3 Wade Boggs .50 1.25
4 Cal Ripken 2.50 6.00
5 Matt Williams .30 .75
6 Jay Buhner .30 .75
8 Jeff Conine .30 .75
9 Todd Greene .30 .75
10 Mike Lieberthal .30 .75
11 Steve Avery .30 .75
12 Bret Saberhagen .30 .75
13 Magglio Ordonez .50 1.25
14 Brad Radke .30 .75
15 Derek Jeter 2.00 5.00
16 Javy Lopez .30 .75
17 Russ Davis .30 .75
18 Armando Benitez .30 .75
19 B.J. Surhoff .30 .75
20 Darryl Kile .30 .75
21 Mark Lewis .30 .75
22 Mike Williams .30 .75
23 Mark McLemore .30 .75
24 Sterling Hitchcock .30 .75
25 Darin Erstad .30 .75
26 Ricky Gutierrez .30 .75
27 John Jaha .30 .75
28 Homer Bush .30 .75
29 Darrin Fletcher .30 .75
30 Mark Grace .50 1.25
31 Fred McGriff .50 1.25
32 Omar Daal .30 .75
33 Eric Karros .30 .75
34 Orlando Cabrera .30 .75
35 J.T. Snow .30 .75
36 Luis Castillo .30 .75
37 Rey Ordonez .30 .75
38 Bob Abreu .30 .75
39 Warren Morris .30 .75
40 Juan Gonzalez .30 .75
41 Mike Lansing .30 .75
42 Chili Davis .30 .75
43 Dean Palmer .30 .75
44 Hank Aaron 1.50 4.00
45 Jeff Bagwell .50 1.25
46 Jose Valentin .30 .75
47 Shannon Stewart .30 .75
48 Kent Bottenfield .30 .75
49 Jeff Shaw .30 .75
50 Sammy Sosa .75 2.00
51 Randy Johnson .75 2.00
52 Benny Agbayani .30 .75
53 Dante Bichette .30 .75
54 Pete Harnisch .30 .75
55 Frank Thomas .75 2.00
56 Jorge Posada .50 1.25
57 Todd Walker .30 .75
58 Juan Encarnacion .30 .75
59 Mike Sweeney .30 .75
60 Pedro Martinez .50 1.25
61 Lee Stevens .30 .75
62 Brian Giles .30 .75
63 Chad Ogea .30 .75
64 Ivan Rodriguez .50 1.25
65 Roger Cedeno .30 .75
66 David Justice .30 .75
67 Steve Trachsel .30 .75
68 Eli Marrero .30 .75
69 Dave Nilsson .30 .75
70 Ken Caminiti .30 .75
71 Tim Raines .50 1.25
72 Brian Jordan .30 .75
73 Jeff Blauser .30 .75
74 Bernard Gilkey .30 .75
75 John Flaherty .30 .75
76 Brent Mayne .30 .75
77 Jose Vidro .30 .75
78 David Bell .30 .75
79 Bruce Aven .30 .75
80 John Olerud .30 .75
81 Pokey Reese .30 .75
82 Woody Williams .30 .75
83 Ed Sprague .30 .75
84 Joe Girardi .50 1.25
85 Barry Larkin .50 1.25
86 Mike Caruso .30 .75
87 Bobby Higginson .30 .75
88 Roberto Kelly .30 .75
89 Edgar Martinez .50 1.25
90 Mark Kotsay .30 .75
91 Paul Sorrento .30 .75
92 Eric Young .30 .75
93 Carlos Delgado .30 .75
94 Troy Glaus .30 .75
95 Ben Grieve .30 .75
96 Jose Lima .30 .75
97 Garret Anderson .30 .75
98 Luis Gonzalez .30 .75
99 Carl Pavano .30 .75
100 Alex Rodriguez 1.00 2.50
101 Preston Wilson .30 .75
102 Ron Gant .30 .75
103 Brady Anderson .30 .75
104 Rickey Henderson .75 2.00
105 Gary Sheffield .30 .75
106 Mickey Morandini .30 .75
107 Jim Edmonds .30 .75
108 Kris Benson .30 .75
109 Adrian Beltre .75 2.00
110 Alex Fernandez .30 .75
111 Dan Wilson .30 .75
112 Mark Clark .30 .75
113 Greg Vaughn .30 .75
114 Neifi Perez .30 .75
115 Paul O'Neill .50 1.25
116 Jermaine Dye .30 .75
117 Todd Jones .30 .75
118 Terry Steinbach .30 .75
119 Greg Norton .30 .75
120 Curt Schilling .50 1.25
121 Todd Zeile .30 .75
122 Edgardo Alfonzo .30 .75
123 Ryan McGuire .30 .75
124 Rich Aurilia .30 .75
125 John Smoltz .75 2.00
126 Bob Wickman .30 .75
127 Richard Hidalgo .30 .75
128 Chuck Finley .30 .75
129 Billy Wagner .30 .75
130 Todd Hundley .30 .75
131 Dwight Gooden .30 .75
132 Russ Ortiz .30 .75
133 Mike Lowell .30 .75
134 Reggie Sanders .30 .75
135 John Valentin .30 .75
136 Brad Ausmus .30 .75
137 Chad Kreuter .30 .75
138 David Cone .30 .75
139 Brook Fordyce .30 .75
140 Roberto Alomar .50 1.25
141 Charles Nagy .30 .75
142 Brian Hunter .30 .75
143 Mike Mussina .50 1.25
144 Robin Ventura .30 .75
145 Kevin Brown .30 .75
146 Pat Hentgen .30 .75
147 Ryan Klesko .30 .75
148 Derek Bell .30 .75
149 Andy Sheets .30 .75
150 Larry Walker .50 1.25
151 Scott Williamson .30 .75
152 Jose Offerman .30 .75
153 Doug Mientkiewicz .30 .75
154 John Snyder RC .40 1.00
155 Sandy Alomar Jr. .30 .75
156 Joe Nathan .30 .75
157 Lance Johnson .30 .75
158 Odalis Perez .30 .75
159 Hideo Nomo .75 2.00
160 Steve Finley .30 .75
161 Dave Martinez .30 .75
162 Matt Walbeck .30 .75
163 Bill Spiers .30 .75
164 Fernando Tatis .30 .75
165 Kenny Lofton .30 .75
166 Paul Byrd .30 .75
167 Aaron Sele .30 .75
168 Eddie Taubensee .30 .75
169 Reggie Jefferson .30 .75
170 Roger Clemens 1.00 2.50
171 Francisco Cordova .30 .75
172 Mike Bordick .30 .75
173 Wally Joyner .30 .75
174 Marvin Benard .30 .75
175 Jason Kendall .30 .75
176 Mike Stanley .30 .75
177 Chad Allen .30 .75
178 Carlos Beltran .50 1.25
179 Deivi Cruz .30 .75
180 Chipper Jones .75 2.00
181 Vladimir Guerrero .50 1.25
182 Dave Burba .30 .75
183 Tom Goodwin .30 .75
184 Brian Daubach .30 .75
185 Jay Bell .30 .75
186 Roy Halladay .50 1.25
187 Miguel Tejada .50 1.25
188 Armando Rios .30 .75
189 Fernando Vina .30 .75
190 Eric Davis .30 .75
191 Henry Rodriguez .30 .75
192 Joe McEwing .30 .75
193 Jeff Kent .30 .75
194 Mike Jackson .30 .75
195 Mike Morgan .30 .75
196 Jeff Montgomery .30 .75
197 Jeff Zimmerman .30 .75
198 Tony Fernandez .30 .75
199 Jason Giambi .30 .75
200 Jose Canseco .50 1.25
201 Alex Gonzalez .30 .75
202 J.Cust .30 .75
M.Colangelo
D.Brown
203 A.Soriano .75 2.00
F.Lopez
204 Durazo .30 .75
Burrell
Johnson
205 John Sneed RC .40 1.00
K.Wells
206 J.Kalinowski .40 1.00
M.Tejera
C.Mears
207 L.Berkman .50 1.25
C.Patterson
R.Brown
208 K.Pellow .30 .75
K.Barker
R.Branyan
209 B.Garbe .40 1.00
L.Bigbie
210 B.Bradley .40 1.00
E.Munson
211 J.Girdley .30 .75
K.Snyder
212 C.Caple .40 1.00
J.Jennings
213 B.Myers 1.25 3.00
R.Christianson
214 J.Stumm .40 1.00
R.Purvis RC
215 D.Walling .30 .75
M.Paradis
216 O.Ortiz .30 .75
J.Gehrke
217 David Cone HL .30 .75
218 Jose Jimenez HL .30 .75
219 Chris Singleton HL .30 .75
220 Fernando Tatis HL .30 .75
221 Todd Helton HL .50 1.25
222 Kevin Millwood DIV .30 .75
223 Todd Pratt DIV .30 .75
224 Orlando Hernandez DIV .30 .75
225 Pedro Martinez DIV .50 1.25
226 Tom Glavine LCS .50 1.25
227 Bernie Williams LCS .50 1.25
228 Mariano Rivera WS 1.00 2.50
229 Tony Gwynn 20CB .75 2.00
230 Wade Boggs 20CB .50 1.25
231 Lance Johnson CB .30 .75
232 Mark McGwire 20CB 1.25 3.00
233 Rickey Henderson 20CB .75 2.00
234 Rickey Henderson 20CB .75 2.00
235 Roger Clemens 20CB 1.00 2.50
236A M.McGwire MM 1st HR 3.00 8.00
236B M.McGwire MM 1987 ROY 3.00 8.00
236C M.McGwire MM 62nd HR 3.00 8.00
236D M.McGwire MM 70th HR 3.00 8.00
236E M.McGwire MM 500th HR 3.00 8.00
237A H.Aaron MM 1st Career HR 4.00 10.00
237B H.Aaron MM 1957 MVP 4.00 10.00
237C H.Aaron MM 3000th Hit 4.00 10.00
237D H.Aaron MM 715th HR 4.00 10.00
237E H.Aaron MM 755th HR 4.00 10.00
238A C.Ripken MM 1982 ROY 6.00 15.00
238B C.Ripken MM 1991 MVP 6.00 15.00
238C C.Ripken MM 2131 Game 6.00 15.00
238D C.Ripken MM Streak Ends 6.00 15.00
238E C.Ripken MM 400th HR 6.00 15.00
239A W.Boggs MM 1983 Batting 1.25 3.00
239B W.Boggs MM 1988 Batting 1.25 3.00
239C W.Boggs MM 2000th Hit 1.25 3.00
239D W.Boggs MM 1996 Champs 1.25 3.00
239E W.Boggs MM 3000th Hit 1.25 3.00
240A T.Gwynn MM 1984 Batting 2.00 5.00
240B T.Gwynn MM 1984 NLCS 2.00 5.00
240C T.Gwynn MM 1995 Batting 2.00 5.00
240D T.Gwynn MM 1998 NLCS 2.00 5.00
240E T.Gwynn MM 3000th Hit 2.00 5.00
241 Tom Glavine .50 1.25
242 David Wells .30 .75
243 Kevin Appier .30 .75
244 Troy Percival .30 .75
245 Ray Lankford .30 .75
246 Marquis Grissom .30 .75
247 Randy Winn .30 .75
248 Miguel Batista .30 .75
249 Darren Dreifort .30 .75
250 Barry Bonds 1.25 3.00
251 Harold Baines .50 1.25
252 Cliff Floyd .30 .75
253 Freddy Garcia .30 .75
254 Kenny Rogers .30 .75
255 Ben Davis .30 .75
256 Charles Johnson .30 .75
257 Bubba Trammell .30 .75
258 Desi Relaford .30 .75
259 Al Martin .30 .75
260 Andy Pettitte .50 1.25
261 Carlos Lee .30 .75
262 Matt Lawton .30 .75
263 Andy Fox .30 .75
264 Chan Ho Park .50 1.25
265 Billy Koch .30 .75
266 Dave Roberts .50 1.25
267 Carl Everett .30 .75
268 Orel Hershiser .30 .75
269 Trot Nixon .30 .75
270 Rusty Greer .30 .75
271 Will Clark .50 1.25
272 Quilvio Veras .30 .75
273 Rico Brogna .30 .75
274 Devon White .30 .75
275 Tim Hudson .50 1.25
276 Mike Hampton .30 .75
277 Miguel Cairo .30 .75
278 Darren Oliver .30 .75
279 Jeff Cirillo .30 .75
280 Al Leiter .30 .75
281 Shane Andrews .30 .75
282 Carlos Febles .30 .75
283 Pedro Astacio .30 .75
284 Juan Guzman .30 .75
285 Orlando Hernandez .30 .75
286 Paul Konerko .30 .75
287 Tony Clark .30 .75
288 Aaron Boone .30 .75
289 Ismael Valdes .30 .75
290 Moises Alou .30 .75
291 Kevin Tapani .30 .75
292 John Franco .30 .75
293 Todd Zeile .30 .75
294 Jason Schmidt .30 .75
295 Johnny Damon .50 1.25
296 Scott Brosius .30 .75
297 Travis Fryman .30 .75
298 Jose Vizcaino .30 .75
299 Eric Chavez .30 .75
300 Mike Piazza .75 2.00
301 Matt Clement .30 .75
302 Cristian Guzman .30 .75
303 C.J. Nitkowski .30 .75
304 Michael Tucker .30 .75
305 Brett Tomko .30 .75
306 Mike Lansing .30 .75
307 Eric Owens .30 .75
308 Livan Hernandez .30 .75
309 Rondell White .30 .75
310 Todd Stottlemyre .30 .75
311 Chris Carpenter .50 1.25
312 Ken Hill .30 .75
313 Mark Loretta .30 .75
314 John Rocker .30 .75
315 Richie Sexson .30 .75
316 Ruben Mateo .30 .75
317 Joe Randa .30 .75
318 Mike Sirotka .30 .75
319 Jose Rosado .30 .75
320 Matt Mantei .30 .75
321 Kevin Millwood .30 .75
322 Gary Disarcina .30 .75
323 Dustin Hermanson .30 .75
324 Mike Stanton .30 .75
325 Kirk Rueter .30 .75
326 Damian Miller RC .40 1.00
327 Doug Glanville .30 .75
328 Scott Rolen .50 1.25
329 Ray Durham .30 .75
330 Butch Huskey .30 .75
331 Mariano Rivera 1.00 2.50
332 Darren Lewis .30 .75
333 Mike Timlin .30 .75
334 Mark Grudzielanek .30 .75
335 Mike Cameron .30 .75
336 Kelvim Escobar .30 .75
337 Bret Boone .30 .75
338 Mo Vaughn .30 .75
339 Craig Biggio .50 1.25
340 Michael Barrett .30 .75
341 Marlon Anderson .30 .75
342 Bobby Jones .30 .75
343 John Halama .30 .75
344 Todd Ritchie .30 .75
345 Chuck Knoblauch .30 .75
346 Rick Reed .30 .75
347 Kelly Stinnett .30 .75
348 Tim Salmon .30 .75
349 A.J. Hinch .30 .75
350 Jose Cruz Jr. .30 .75
351 Roberto Hernandez .30 .75
352 Edgar Renteria .30 .75
353 Jose Hernandez .30 .75
354 Brad Fullmer .30 .75
355 Trevor Hoffman .50 1.25
356 Troy O'Leary .30 .75
357 Justin Thompson .30 .75
358 Kevin Young .30 .75
359 Hideki Irabu .30 .75
360 Jim Thome .50 1.25
361 Steve Karsay .30 .75
362 Octavio Dotel .30 .75
363 Omar Vizquel .50 1.25
364 Raul Mondesi .30 .75
365 Shane Reynolds .30 .75
366 Bartolo Colon .30 .75
367 Chris Widger .30 .75
368 Gabe Kapler .30 .75
369 Bill Simas .30 .75
370 Tino Martinez .30 .75
371 John Thomson .30 .75
372 Delino Deshields .30 .75
373 Carlos Perez .30 .75
374 Eddie Perez .30 .75
375 Jeromy Burnitz .30 .75
376 Jimmy Haynes .30 .75
377 Travis Lee .30 .75
378 Darryl Hamilton .30 .75
379 Jamie Moyer .30 .75
380 Alex Gonzalez .30 .75
381 John Wetteland .30 .75
382 Vinny Castilla .30 .75
383 Jeff Suppan .30 .75
384 Jim Leyritz .30 .75
385 Robb Nen .30 .75
386 Wilson Alvarez .30 .75
387 Andres Galarraga .50 1.25
388 Mike Remlinger .30 .75
389 Geoff Jenkins .30 .75
390 Matt Stairs .30 .75
391 Bill Mueller .30 .75
392 Mike Lowell .30 .75
393 Andy Ashby .30 .75
394 Ruben Rivera .30 .75
395 Todd Helton .50 1.25
396 Bernie Williams .50 1.25
397 Royce Clayton .30 .75
398 Manny Ramirez .75 2.00
399 Kerry Wood .30 .75
400 Ken Griffey Jr. 1.50 4.00
401 Enrique Wilson .30 .75
402 Joey Hamilton .30 .75
403 Shawn Estes .30 .75
404 Ugueth Urbina .30 .75
405 Albert Belle .30 .75
406 Rick Helling .30 .75
407 Steve Parris .30 .75
408 Eric Milton .30 .75
409 Dave Mlicki .30 .75
410 Shawn Green .30 .75
411 Jaret Wright .30 .75
412 Tony Womack .30 .75
413 Vernon Wells .30 .75
414 Ron Belliard .30 .75
415 Ellis Burks .30 .75
416 Scott Erickson .30 .75
417 Rafael Palmeiro .50 1.25
418 Damion Easley .30 .75
419 Jamey Wright .30 .75
420 Corey Koskie .30 .75
421 Bobby Howry .30 .75
422 Ricky Ledee .30 .75
423 Dmitri Young .30 .75
424 Sidney Ponson .30 .75
425 Greg Maddux 1.00 2.50
426 Jose Guillen .30 .75
427 Jon Lieber .30 .75
428 Andy Benes .30 .75
429 Randy Velarde .30 .75
430 Sean Casey .30 .75
431 Torii Hunter .30 .75
432 Ryan Rupe .30 .75
433 David Segui .30 .75
434 Todd Pratt .30 .75
435 Nomar Garciaparra .50 1.25
436 Denny Neagle .30 .75
437 Ron Coomer .30 .75
438 Chris Singleton .30 .75
439 Tony Batista .30 .75
440 Andruw Jones .30 .75
441 A.Huff .30 .75
S.Burroughs
A.Piatt
442 Furcal .50 1.25
Dawkins
Dellaero
443 M.Lamb RC .40 1.00
J.Crede
W.Veras
444 J.Zuleta .40 1.00
J.Toca
D.Stenson
445 G.Maddox Jr. .40 1.00
G.Matthews Jr.
T.Raines Jr.
446 M.Mulder .50 1.25
C.Sabathia
M.Riley
447 S.Downs .40 1.00
C.George
M.Belisle
448 D.Mirabelli .50 1.25
B.Petrick
J.Werth
449 J.Hamilton 1.25 3.00
C.Meyers
450 B.Christensen .40 1.00
R.Stahl
451 B.Zito 3.00 8.00

B.Sheets RC
452 K.Ainsworth .40 1.00
T.Howington
453 R.Asadoorian .40 1.00
V.Faison
454 K.Reed .40 1.00
J.Heaverlo
455 M.MacDougal .60 1.50
B.Baker
456 Mark McGwire SH 1.25 3.00
457 Cal Ripken SH 2.50 6.00
458 Wade Boggs SH .50 1.25
459 Tony Gwynn SH .75 2.00
460 Jesse Orosco SH .30 .75
461 L.Walker .50 1.25
N.Garciaparra LL
462 K.Griffey Jr. 1.50 4.00
M.McGwire LL
463 M.Ramirez 1.25 3.00
M.McGwire LL
464 P.Martinez .75 2.00
R.Johnson LL
465 P.Martinez .75 2.00
R.Johnson LL
466 D.Jeter 2.00 5.00
L.Gonzalez LL
467 L.Walker .75 2.00
M.Ramirez LL
468 Tony Gwynn 20CB .75 2.00
469 Mark McGwire 20CB 1.25 3.00
470 Frank Thomas 20CB .75 2.00
471 Harold Baines 20CB .50 1.25
472 Roger Clemens 20CB 1.00 2.50
473 John Franco 20CB .30 .75
474 John Franco 20CB .30 .75
475A K.Griffey Jr. MM 350th HR 4.00 10.00
475B K.Griffey Jr. MM 1997 MVP 4.00 10.00
475C K.Griffey Jr. MM HR Dad 4.00 10.00
475D K.Griffey Jr. MM 1992 AS MVP 4.00 10.00
475E K.Griffey Jr. MM 50 HR 1997 4.00 10.00
476A B.Bonds MM 400HR/400SB 3.00 8.00
476B B.Bonds MM 40HR/40SB 3.00 8.00
476C B.Bonds MM 1993 MVP 3.00 8.00
476D B.Bonds MM 1990 MVP 3.00 8.00
476E B.Bonds MM 1992 MVP 3.00 8.00
477A S.Sosa MM 20 HR June 2.00 5.00
477B S.Sosa MM 66 HR 1998 2.00 5.00
477C S.Sosa MM 60 HR 1999 2.00 5.00
477D S.Sosa MM 1998 MVP 2.00 5.00
477E S.Sosa MM HR's 61/62 2.00 5.00
478A D.Jeter MM 1996 ROY 5.00 12.00
478B D.Jeter MM Wins 1999 WS 5.00 12.00
478C D.Jeter MM Wins 1998 WS 5.00 12.00
478D D.Jeter MM Wins 1996 WS 5.00 12.00
478E D.Jeter MM 17 GM Hit Streak 5.00 12.00
479A A.Rodriguez MM 40HR/40SB 2.50 6.00
479B A.Rodriguez MM 100th HR 2.50 6.00
479C A.Rodriguez MM 1996 POY 2.50 6.00
479D A.Rodriguez MM Wins 1 Million 2.50 6.00
479E A.Rodriguez MM
1996 Batting Leader 2.50 6.00
NNO M.McGwire 85 Reprint 3.00 8.00

2000 Topps Chrome Refractors

*REF: 2.5X TO 6X BASIC
*REF MM: 4X TO 10X BASIC
*REF RC 1-474: 2X TO 5X BASIC
CARD NUMBER 7 DOES NOT EXIST
SER.1 HAS ONLY 1 VERSION OF 236-240
SER.2 HAS ONLY 1 VERSION OF 475-479
STATED ODDS 1:12
MCGWIRE '85 ODDS 1:12,116
MCGWIRE '85 PR.RUN 70 SERIAL #'d CARDS
MM McGwire 85 Reprint/70 50.00 125.00

2000 Topps Chrome 21st Century

Inserted at a rate of one in 16, this 10 cards feature players who are expected to be the best in the first part of the 21st century. Card backs carry a "C" prefix.

COMPLETE SET (10) 6.00 15.00
SER.1 STATED ODDS 1:16
*REF: 1X TO 2.5X BASIC 21ST CENT.
SER.1 REFRACTOR ODDS 1:80
C1 Ben Grieve .40 1.00
C2 Alex Gonzalez .40 1.00
C3 Derek Jeter 2.50 6.00
C4 Sean Casey .40 1.00
C5 Nomar Garciaparra .60 1.50
C6 Alex Rodriguez 1.25 3.00
C7 Scott Rolen .60 1.50
C8 Andruw Jones .40 1.00
C9 Vladimir Guerrero .60 1.50
C10 Todd Helton .60 1.50

2000 Topps Chrome All-Star Rookie Team

Randomly inserted into packs at one in 16, this 10-card insert set features players that made the All-Star game their rookie season. Card backs carry a "RT" prefix.

COMPLETE SET (10) 8.00 20.00
SER.2 STATED ODDS 1:16
*REF: 1X TO 2.5X BASIC ASR TEAM
REFRACTOR STATED ODDS 1:80
RT1 Mark McGwire 1.50 4.00
RT2 Chuck Knoblauch .40 1.00
RT3 Chipper Jones 1.00 2.50
RT4 Cal Ripken 3.00 8.00
RT5 Manny Ramirez 1.00 2.50
RT6 Jose Canseco .60 1.50
RT7 Ken Griffey Jr. 2.00 5.00
RT8 Mike Piazza 1.00 2.50
RT9 Dwight Gooden .40 1.00
RT10 Billy Wagner .40 1.00

2000 Topps Chrome All-Topps

Inserted at a rate of one in 32 first and second series packs, these 10 cards feature the best players in the American and National Leagues. National League cards 91-10) were distributed in series one and American league (11-20) in series two. Card backs carry an "AT" prefix.

COMPLETE SET (20) 15.00 40.00
COMPLETE N.L.TEAM (10) 8.00 20.00
COMPLETE A.L.TEAM (10) 8.00 20.00
STATED ODDS 1:32
*REF: 1X TO 2.5X BASIC ALL TOPPS
REFRACTOR ODDS 1:160
N.L. CARDS DISTRIBUTED IN SERIES 1
A.L. CARDS DISTRIBUTED IN SERIES 2
AT1 Greg Maddux 1.25 3.00
AT2 Mike Piazza 1.00 2.50
AT3 Mark McGwire 1.50 4.00
AT4 Craig Biggio .60 1.50
AT5 Chipper Jones 1.00 2.50
AT6 Barry Larkin .60 1.50
AT7 Barry Bonds 1.50 4.00
AT8 Andruw Jones .40 1.00
AT9 Sammy Sosa 1.00 2.50
AT10 Larry Walker .60 1.50
AT11 Pedro Martinez .60 1.50
AT12 Ivan Rodriguez .60 1.50
AT13 Rafael Palmeiro .60 1.50
AT14 Roberto Alomar .60 1.50
AT15 Cal Ripken 3.00 8.00
AT16 Derek Jeter 2.50 6.00
AT17 Albert Belle .40 1.00
AT18 Ken Griffey Jr. 2.00 5.00
AT19 Manny Ramirez 1.00 2.50
AT20 Jose Canseco .60 1.50

2000 Topps Chrome Allegiance

This Topps Chrome exclusive set features 20 players who have spent their entire career with just one team. The Allegiance cards were issued at a rate of one in 16 and have a "TA" prefix.

COMPLETE SET (20) 15.00 40.00
SER.1 STATED ODDS 1:16
*REF: 4X TO 10X BASIC ALLEGIANCE
SER.1 REFRACTOR ODDS 1:424 HOBBY
REFRACTOR PRINT RUN 100 SERIAL #'d SETS
TA1 Derek Jeter 2.50 6.00
TA2 Ivan Rodriguez .60 1.50
TA3 Alex Rodriguez 1.25 3.00
TA4 Cal Ripken 3.00 8.00
TA5 Mark Grace .60 1.50
TA6 Tony Gwynn 1.00 2.50
TA7 Tom Glavine .60 1.50
TA8 Frank Thomas 1.00 2.50
TA9 Manny Ramirez 1.00 2.50
TA10 Barry Larkin .60 1.50
TA11 Bernie Williams .60 1.50
TA12 Eric Karros .40 1.00
TA13 Vladimir Guerrero .60 1.50
TA14 Craig Biggio .60 1.50
TA15 Nomar Garciaparra .60 1.50
TA16 Andruw Jones .40 1.00
TA17 Jim Thome .60 1.50
TA18 Scott Rolen .60 1.50
TA19 Chipper Jones 1.00 2.50
TA20 Ken Griffey Jr. 2.00 5.00

2000 Topps Chrome Combos

Randomly inserted into series two packs at one in 16, this 10-card insert features a variety of player combinations, such as the 1999 MVP's. Card backs carry a "TC" prefix.

COMPLETE SET (10) 12.50 30.00
SER.2 STATED ODDS 1:16
*REFRACTORS: 1X TO 2.5X BASIC COMBO
REFRACTOR ODDS 1:80
TC1 Tribe-unal 1.00 2.50
TC2 Batter Baffler's 1.25 3.00
TC3 Torre's Terrors 2.50 6.00
TC4 All-Star Backstops 1.00 2.50
TC5 Three of a Kind 2.50 6.00
TC6 Home Run Kings 1.50 4.00
TC7 Strikeout Kings 1.00 2.50
TC8 Executive Producers 2.00 5.00
TC9 MVP's 1.00 2.50
TC10 3000 Hit Brigade 3.00 8.00

2000 Topps Chrome Kings

Randomly inserted into series two packs at one in 32, this 10-card insert features some of the greatest players in major league baseball. Card backs carry a "CK" prefix.

COMPLETE SET (10) 8.00 20.00
SER.2 STATED ODDS 1:32
CK1 Mark McGwire 1.50 4.00
CK2 Sammy Sosa 1.00 2.50
CK3 Ken Griffey Jr. 2.00 5.00
CK4 Mike Piazza 1.00 2.50
CK5 Alex Rodriguez 1.25 3.00
CK6 Manny Ramirez 1.00 2.50
CK7 Barry Bonds 1.50 4.00
CK8 Nomar Garciaparra .60 1.50
CK9 Chipper Jones 1.00 2.50
CK10 Vladimir Guerrero .60 1.50

2000 Topps Chrome Kings Refractors

Randomly inserted into series two packs at one in 514, this 10-card insert is a complete parallel of the Chrome Kings insert. Each card was produced using Topps' "refractor" technology. Please note that each card was serial numbered to the amount of homeruns that the individual players had after the 1999 season. Production runs are listed below. Card backs carry a "CK" pefix.

COMPLETE SET (10) 50.00 100.00
SER.2 STATED ODDS 1:514
PRINT RUNS B/WN 92-522 COPIES PER
CK1 Mark McGwire/522 8.00 20.00
CK2 Sammy Sosa/366 5.00 12.00
CK3 Ken Griffey Jr./398 10.00 25.00
CK4 Mike Piazza/240 5.00 12.00
CK5 Alex Rodriguez/148 6.00 15.00
CK6 Manny Ramirez/198 5.00 12.00
CK7 Barry Bonds/445 8.00 20.00
CK8 Nomar Garciaparra/96 3.00 8.00
CK9 Chipper Jones/153 5.00 12.00
CK10 Vladimir Guerrero/92 3.00 8.00

2000 Topps Chrome New Millennium Stars

Randomly inserted into series two packs at one in 32, this 10-card insert features 10 of the major league's hottest young talent. Card backs carry a "NMS" prefix.

COMPLETE SET (10) 6.00 15.00
SER.2 STATED ODDS 1:32
*REFRACTORS: 1X TO 2.5X BASIC MILL.
SER.2 REFRACTOR ODDS 1:160
NMS1 Nomar Garciaparra 1.00 2.50
NMS2 Vladimir Guerrero 1.00 2.50
NMS3 Sean Casey .60 1.50
NMS4 Richie Sexson .60 1.50
NMS5 Todd Helton 1.00 2.50
NMS6 Carlos Beltran 1.00 2.50
NMS7 Kevin Millwood .60 1.50
NMS8 Ruben Mateo .60 1.50
NMS9 Pat Burrell .60 1.50
NMS10 Alfonso Soriano 1.50 4.00

2000 Topps Chrome Own the Game

Randomly inserted into series two packs at one in 11, this 30-card insert features players that are amoung the major league's statistical leaders year after year. Card backs carry an "OTG" prefix.

COMPLETE SET (30) 20.00 50.00
SER.2 STATED ODDS 1:11
*REFRACTORS: 1X TO 2.5X BASIC OWN
SER.2 REFRACTOR ODDS 1:55
OTG1 Derek Jeter 2.50 6.00
OTG2 B.J. Surhoff .40 1.00
OTG3 Luis Gonzalez .40 1.00
OTG4 Manny Ramirez 1.00 2.50
OTG5 Rafael Palmeiro .60 1.50
OTG6 Mark McGwire 1.50 4.00
OTG7 Mark McGwire 1.50 4.00
OTG8 Sammy Sosa 1.00 2.50
OTG9 Ken Griffey Jr. 2.00 5.00
OTG10 Larry Walker .60 1.50
OTG11 Nomar Garciaparra .60 1.50
OTG12 Derek Jeter 2.50 6.00
OTG13 Larry Walker .60 1.50
OTG14 Mark McGwire 1.50 4.00
OTG15 Manny Ramirez 1.00 2.50
OTG16 Pedro Martinez .60 1.50
OTG17 Randy Johnson 1.00 2.50
OTG18 Kevin Millwood .40 1.00
OTG19 Randy Johnson 1.00 2.50
OTG20 Pedro Martinez .60 1.50
OTG21 Kevin Brown .40 1.00
OTG22 Chipper Jones 1.00 2.50
OTG23 Ivan Rodriguez .60 1.50
OTG24 Mariano Rivera 1.25 3.00
OTG25 Scott Williamson .40 1.00
OTG26 Carlos Beltran .60 1.50
OTG27 Randy Johnson 1.00 2.50
OTG28 Pedro Martinez .60 1.50
OTG29 Sammy Sosa 1.00 2.50
OTG30 Manny Ramirez 1.00 2.50

2000 Topps Chrome Power Players

This 20 card set, issued at a rate of one in eight packs, features players who are the leading power hitters in the majors. Card backs carry a "P" prefix.

COMPLETE SET (20) 12.50 30.00
SER.1 STATED ODDS 1:8
*REFRACTORS: 1X TO 2.5X BASIC POWER
SER.1 REFRACTOR ODDS 1:40
P1 Juan Gonzalez .40 1.00
P2 Ken Griffey Jr. 2.00 5.00
P3 Mark McGwire 1.50 4.00
P4 Nomar Garciaparra .60 1.50
P5 Barry Bonds 1.50 4.00
P6 Mo Vaughn .40 1.00
P7 Larry Walker .60 1.50
P8 Alex Rodriguez 1.25 3.00
P9 Jose Canseco .60 1.50
P10 Jeff Bagwell .60 1.50
P11 Manny Ramirez 1.00 2.50
P12 Albert Belle .40 1.00
P13 Frank Thomas 1.00 2.50
P14 Mike Piazza 1.00 2.50
P15 Chipper Jones 1.00 2.50
P16 Sammy Sosa 1.00 2.50
P17 Vladimir Guerrero .60 1.50
P18 Scott Rolen .60 1.50
P19 Raul Mondesi .40 1.00
P20 Derek Jeter 2.50 6.00

2000 Topps Chrome Traded

The 2000 Topps Chrome Traded set was released in late November, 2000 and features a 135-card base set. The set is an exact parallel of the Topps Traded set.This set was produced using Topps' chrome technology. Please note that card backs carry a "T" prefix. Each set came with 135 cards and carried a $99.99 suggested retail price. Notable Rookie Cards include Miguel Cabrera.

COMP.FACT.SET (135) 90.00 150.00
COMMON CARD (T1-T135) .15 .40
COMMON RC .30 .75
T1 Mike MacDougal .25 .60
T2 Andy Tracy RC .30 .75
T3 Brandon Phillips RC 1.25 3.00
T4 Brandon Inge RC 2.00 5.00
T5 Robbie Morrison RC .30 .75
T6 Josh Pressley RC .30 .75
T7 Todd Moser RC .30 .75
T8 Rob Purvis .15 .40
T9 Chance Caple .15 .40
T10 Ben Sheets .40 1.00
T11 Russ Jacobson RC .30 .75
T12 Brian Cole RC .30 .75
T13 Brad Baker .15 .40
T14 Alex Cintron RC .30 .75
T15 Lyle Overbay RC .50 1.25
T16 Mike Edwards RC .30 .75
T17 Sean McGowan RC .30 .75
T18 Jose Molina .15 .40
T19 Marcos Castillo RC .30 .75
T20 Josue Espada RC .30 .75
T21 Alex Gordon RC .30 .75
T22 Rob Pugmire RC .30 .75
T23 Jason Stumm .15 .40
T24 Ty Howington .15 .40
T25 Brett Myers .50 1.25
T26 Maicer Izturis RC .50 1.25
T27 John McDonald .15 .40
T28 Wilfredo Rodriguez RC .30 .75
T29 Carlos Zambrano RC 2.00 5.00
T30 Alejandro Diaz RC .30 .75
T31 Geraldo Guzman RC .30 .75
T32 J.R. House RC .30 .75
T33 Elvin Nina RC .30 .75
T34 Juan Pierre RC 1.50 4.00
T35 Ben Johnson RC .30 .75
T36 Jeff Bailey RC .30 .75
T37 Miguel Olivo RC .50 1.25
T38 Francisco Rodriguez RC 2.00 5.00
T39 Tony Pena Jr. RC .30 .75
T40 Miguel Cabrera RC 40.00 100.00
T41 Asdrubal Oropeza RC .30 .75
T42 Junior Zamora RC .30 .75
T43 Jovanny Cedeno RC .30 .75
T44 John Sneed .15 .40
T45 Josh Kalinowski .15 .40
T46 Mike Young RC 3.00 8.00
T47 Rico Washington RC .30 .75
T48 Chad Durbin RC .30 .75
T49 Junior Brignac RC .30 .75
T50 Carlos Hernandez RC .30 .75
T51 Cesar Izturis RC .30 .75
T52 Oscar Salazar RC .30 .75
T53 Pat Strange RC .30 .75
T54 Rick Asadoorian .15 .40
T55 Keith Reed .15 .40
T56 Leo Estrella RC .30 .75
T57 Wascar Serrano RC .30 .75
T58 Richard Gomez RC .30 .75
T59 Ramon Santiago RC .30 .75
T60 Jovanny Sosa RC .30 .75
T61 Aaron Rowand RC 1.50 4.00
T62 Junior Guerrero RC .30 .75
T63 Luis Terrero RC .30 .75
T64 Brian Sanches RC .30 .75
T65 Scott Sobkowiak RC .30 .75
T66 Gary Majewski RC .30 .75
T67 Barry Zito 1.25 3.00
T68 Ryan Christianson .15 .40
T69 Cristian Guerrero RC .30 .75
T70 Tomas De La Rosa RC .30 .75
T71 Andrew Beinbrink RC .30 .75
T72 Ryan Knox RC .30 .75
T73 Alex Graman RC .30 .75
T74 Juan Guzman RC .30 .75
T75 Ruben Salazar RC .30 .75
T76 Luis Matos RC .30 .75
T77 Tony Mota RC .30 .75
T78 Doug Davis .15 .40
T79 Ben Christensen .15 .40
T80 Mike Lamb .15 .40
T81 Adrian Gonzalez RC 4.00 10.00
T82 Mike Stodolka RC .30 .75
T83 Adam Johnson RC .30 .75
T84 Matt Wheatland RC .30 .75
T85 Corey Smith RC .30 .75
T86 Rocco Baldelli RC .75 2.00
T87 Keith Bucktrot RC .30 .75
T88 Adam Wainwright RC 3.00 8.00
T89 Scott Thorman RC .50 1.25
T90 Tripper Johnson RC .30 .75
T91 Jim Edmonds Cards .15 .40
T92 Masato Yoshii .15 .40
T93 Adam Kennedy .15 .40
T94 Darryl Kile .15 .40
T95 Mark McLemore .15 .40
T96 Ricky Gutierrez .15 .40
T97 Juan Gonzalez .15 .40
T98 Melvin Mora .15 .40
T99 Dante Bichette .15 .40
T100 Lee Stevens .15 .40
T101 Roger Cedeno .15 .40
T102 John Olerud .15 .40
T103 Eric Young .15 .40
T104 Mickey Morandini .15 .40
T105 Travis Lee .15 .40
T106 Greg Vaughn .15 .40
T107 Todd Zeile .15 .40
T108 Chuck Finley .15 .40
T109 Ismael Valdes .15 .40
T110 Reggie Sanders .15 .40
T111 Pat Hentgen .15 .40
T112 Ryan Klesko .15 .40
T113 Derek Bell .15 .40
T114 Hideo Nomo .40 1.00
T115 Aaron Sele .15 .40
T116 Fernando Vina .15 .40
T117 Wally Joyner .15 .40
T118 Brian Hunter .15 .40
T119 Joe Girardi .25 .60
T120 Omar Daal .15 .40
T121 Brook Fordyce .15 .40
T122 Jose Valentin .15 .40
T123 Curt Schilling .25 .60
T124 B.J. Surhoff .15 .40
T125 Henry Rodriguez .15 .40
T126 Mike Bordick .15 .40
T127 David Justice .15 .40
T128 Charles Johnson .15 .40
T129 Will Clark .25 .60
T130 Dwight Gooden .15 .40
T131 David Segui .15 .40
T132 Denny Neagle .15 .40
T133 Jose Canseco .25 .60
T134 Bruce Chen .15 .40
T135 Jason Bere .15 .40

2001 Topps Chrome

The 2001 Topps Chrome product was released in two separate series. The first series shipped in February 2001, and features a 331-card base set produced with Topps' special chrome technology. This set parallels the regular 2001 Topps base set in card design and photography but card numbering differs due to the fact that the manufacturer decided to select only the best 331 cards of the 405 card basic Topps set to be featured in this upgraded Chrome product. Each Topps Chrome pack contains four cards, and carried a suggested retail price of $2.99. Please note, card number 7 does not exist. The number was retired in Topps and Topps Chrome brands back in 1996 in honor of Yankees legend Mickey Mantle. Notable Rookie Cards include Jake Peavy and Albert Pujols.

COMPLETE SET (661) 150.00 300.00
COMPLETE SERIES 1 (331) 75.00 150.00
COMPLETE SERIES 2 (330) 75.00 150.00
CARDS NO.7 AND 465 DO NOT EXIST
1 Cal Ripken 2.50 6.00
2 Chipper Jones .75 2.00
3 Roger Cedeno .20 .50
4 Garret Anderson .30 .75
5 Robin Ventura .30 .75
6 Daryle Ward .20 .50
8 Phil Nevin .30 .75
9 Jermaine Dye .30 .75
10 Chris Singleton .20 .50
11 Mike Redmond .20 .50
12 Jim Thome .50 1.25
13 Brian Jordan .30 .75
14 Dustin Hermanson .20 .50
15 Shawn Green .30 .75
16 Todd Stottlemyre .20 .50
17 Dan Wilson .20 .50
18 Derek Lowe .30 .75
19 Juan Gonzalez .30 .75
20 Pat Meares .20 .50
21 Paul O'Neill .50 1.25
22 Jeffrey Hammonds .20 .50
23 Pokey Reese .20 .50
24 Mike Mussina .50 1.25
25 Rico Brogna .20 .50
26 Jay Buhner .30 .75
27 Steve Cox .20 .50
28 Quilvio Veras .20 .50
29 Marquis Grissom .30 .75
30 Shigetoshi Hasegawa .30 .75
31 Shane Reynolds .20 .50
32 Adam Piatt .20 .50
33 Preston Wilson .30 .75
34 Ellis Burks .30 .75
35 Armando Rios .20 .50
36 Chuck Finley .30 .75
37 Shannon Stewart .30 .75
38 Mark McGwire 2.00 5.00
39 Gerald Williams .20 .50
40 Eric Young .20 .50
41 Peter Bergeron .20 .50
42 Arthur Rhodes .20 .50
43 Bobby Jones .20 .50
44 Matt Clement .30 .75
45 Pedro Martinez .50 1.25
46 Jose Canseco .50 1.25
47 Matt Anderson .20 .50
48 Torii Hunter .30 .75
49 Carlos Lee .30 .75
50 Eric Chavez .30 .75
51 Rick Helling .20 .50
52 John Franco .30 .75
53 Mike Bordick .30 .75
54 Andres Galarraga .30 .75
55 Jose Cruz Jr. .20 .50
56 Mike Matheny .20 .50
57 Randy Johnson .75 2.00
58 Richie Sexson .30 .75
59 Vladimir Nunez .20 .50
60 Aaron Boone .30 .75
61 Darin Erstad .30 .75
62 Alex Gonzalez .20 .50
63 Gil Heredia .20 .50
64 Shane Andrews .20 .50
65 Todd Hundley .20 .50
66 Bill Mueller .30 .75
67 Mark McLemore .20 .50
68 Scott Spiezio .20 .50
69 Kevin McGlinchy .20 .50
70 Manny Ramirez .50 1.25
71 Mike Lamb .20 .50
72 Brian Buchanan .20 .50
73 Mike Sweeney .30 .75
74 John Wetteland .30 .75
75 Rob Bell .20 .50
76 John Burkett .20 .50
77 Derek Jeter 2.00 5.00
78 J.D. Drew .30 .75
79 Jose Offerman .20 .50
80 Rick Reed .20 .50
81 Will Clark .50 1.25
82 Rickey Henderson .75 2.00
83 Kirk Rueter .20 .50
84 Lee Stevens .20 .50
85 Jay Bell .30 .75
86 Fred McGriff .50 1.25
87 Julio Zuleta .20 .50
88 Brian Anderson .20 .50
89 Orlando Cabrera .30 .75
90 Alex Fernandez .20 .50
91 Derek Bell .20 .50
92 Eric Owens .20 .50
93 Dennys Reyes .20 .50
94 Mike Stanley .20 .50
95 Jorge Posada .50 1.25
96 Paul Konerko .30 .75
97 Mike Remlinger .20 .50
98 Travis Lee .20 .50
99 Ken Caminiti .30 .75
100 Kevin Barker .20 .50
101 Ozzie Guillen .30 .75
102 Randy Wolf .30 .75
103 Michael Tucker .20 .50
104 Darren Lewis .20 .50
105 Joe Randa .30 .75
106 Jeff Cirillo .20 .50
107 David Ortiz .75 2.00
108 Herb Perry .20 .50
109 Jeff Nelson .20 .50
110 Chris Stynes .20 .50
111 Johnny Damon .50 1.25
112 Jason Schmidt .30 .75
113 Charles Johnson .30 .75
114 Pat Burrell .30 .75
115 Gary Sheffield .30 .75
116 Tom Glavine .50 1.25
117 Jason Isringhausen .30 .75
118 Chris Carpenter .30 .75
119 Jeff Suppan .20 .50
120 Ivan Rodriguez .50 1.25
121 Luis Sojo .20 .50
122 Ron Villone .20 .50
123 Mike Sirotka .20 .50
124 Chuck Knoblauch .30 .75
125 Jason Kendall .30 .75
126 Bobby Estalella .20 .50
127 Jose Guillen .30 .75
128 Carlos Delgado .20 .50
129 Benji Gil .20 .50
130 Einar Diaz .20 .50
131 Andy Benes .20 .50
132 Adrian Beltre .30 .75
133 Roger Clemens 1.50 4.00
134 Scott Williamson .20 .50
135 Brad Penny .20 .50
136 Troy Glaus .30 .75
137 Kevin Appier .30 .75
138 Walt Weiss .20 .50
139 Michael Barrett .20 .50
140 Mike Hampton .30 .75
141 Francisco Cordova .20 .50
142 David Segui .20 .50
143 Carlos Febles .20 .50
144 Roy Halladay .30 .75
145 Seth Etherton .20 .50
146 Fernando Tatis .20 .50
147 Livan Hernandez .30 .75
148 B.J. Surhoff .30 .75
149 Barry Larkin .50 1.25
150 Bobby Howry .20 .50
151 Dmitri Young .30 .75
152 Brian Hunter .20 .50
153 Alex Rodriguez 1.00 2.50
154 Hideo Nomo .75 2.00
155 Warren Morris .20 .50
156 Antonio Alfonseca .20 .50
157 Edgardo Alfonzo .20 .50
158 Mark Grudzielanek .20 .50
159 Fernando Vina .20 .50
160 Homer Bush .20 .50
161 Jason Giambi .30 .75
162 Steve Karsay .20 .50
163 Matt Lawton .20 .50
164 Rusty Greer .30 .75
165 Billy Koch .20 .50
166 Todd Hollandsworth .20 .50
167 Raul Ibanez .20 .50
168 Tony Gwynn 1.00 2.50
169 Carl Everett .30 .75
170 Hector Carrasco .20 .50
171 Jose Valentin .20 .50
172 Deivi Cruz .20 .50
173 Bret Boone .30 .75
174 Melvin Mora .30 .75
175 Danny Graves .20 .50
176 Jose Jimenez .20 .50
177 James Baldwin .20 .50
178 C.J. Nitkowski .20 .50
179 Jeff Zimmerman .20 .50
180 Mike Lowell .30 .75
181 Hideki Irabu .20 .50
182 Greg Vaughn .20 .50
183 Omar Daal .20 .50
184 Darren Dreifort .20 .50
185 Gil Meche .20 .50
186 Damian Jackson .20 .50
187 Frank Thomas .75 2.00
188 Luis Castillo .20 .50
189 Bartolo Colon .20 .50
190 Craig Biggio .50 1.25
191 Scott Schoeneweis .20 .50
192 Dave Veres .20 .50
193 Ramon Martinez .20 .50
194 Jose Vidro .20 .50
195 Todd Helton .50 1.25
196 Greg Norton .20 .50
197 Jacque Jones .30 .75
198 Jason Grimsley .20 .50
199 Dan Reichert .20 .50
200 Robb Nen .30 .75
201 Scott Hatteberg .20 .50
202 Terry Shumpert .20 .50
203 Kevin Millar .30 .75
204 Ismael Valdes .20 .50
205 Richard Hidalgo .20 .50
206 Randy Velarde .20 .50
207 Bengie Molina .20 .50
208 Tony Womack .20 .50
209 Enrique Wilson .20 .50
210 Jeff Brantley .20 .50
211 Rick Ankiel .20 .50
212 Terry Mulholland .20 .50
213 Ron Belliard .20 .50
214 Terrence Long .20 .50
215 Alberto Castillo .20 .50
216 Royce Clayton .20 .50
217 Joe McEwing .20 .50
218 Jason McDonald .20 .50
219 Ricky Bottalico .20 .50
220 Keith Foulke .30 .75
221 Brad Radke .20 .50
222 Gabe Kapler .30 .75
223 Pedro Astacio .20 .50
224 Armando Reynoso .20 .50
225 Darryl Kile .30 .75
226 Reggie Sanders .30 .75
227 Esteban Yan .20 .50
228 Joe Nathan .30 .75
229 Jay Payton .20 .50
230 Francisco Cordero .20 .50
231 Gregg Jefferies .20 .50
232 LaTroy Hawkins .20 .50
233 Jacob Cruz .20 .50
234 Chris Holt .20 .50
235 Vladimir Guerrero .75 2.00
236 Marvin Benard .20 .50
237 Alex Ramirez .20 .50
238 Mike Williams .20 .50
239 Sean Bergman .20 .50
240 Juan Encarnacion .20 .50
241 Russ Davis .20 .50
242 Ramon Hernandez .20 .50
243 Sandy Alomar Jr. .20 .50
244 Eddie Guardado .20 .50
245 Shane Halter .20 .50
246 Geoff Jenkins .20 .50
247 Brian Meadows .20 .50
248 Damian Miller .20 .50
249 Darrin Fletcher .20 .50
250 Rafael Furcal .30 .75
251 Mark Grace .50 1.25
252 Mark Mulder .30 .75
253 Joe Torre MG .50 1.25
254 Bobby Cox MG .20 .50
255 Mike Scioscia MG .20 .50
256 Mike Hargrove MG .20 .50
257 Jimy Williams MG .20 .50
258 Jerry Manuel MG .20 .50
259 Charlie Manuel MG .20 .50

0 Don Baylor MG .30 .75
1 Phil Garner MG .30 .75
2 Tony Muser MG .20 .50
3 Buddy Bell MG .30 .75
4 Tom Kelly MG .20 .50
5 John Boles MG .20 .50
6 Art Howe MG .20 .50
7 Larry Dierker MG .20 .50
3 Lou Piniella MG .30 .75
9 Larry Rothschild MG .20 .50
0 Davey Lopes MG .30 .75
1 Johnny Oates MG .20 .50
2 Felipe Alou MG .20 .50
3 Bobby Valentine MG .20 .50
4 Tony LaRussa MG .20 .50
5 Bruce Bochy MG .20 .50
6 Dusty Baker MG .30 .75
7 A.Gonzalez 2.50 6.00
A.Johnson
8 M.Wheatland .40 1.00
B.Digby
9 T.Johnson .40 1.00
S.Thorman
0 P.Dumatrait .75 2.00
A.Wainwright
1 David Parrish RC .40 1.00
2 M.Folsom RC .60 1.50
R.Baldelli
3 Dominic Rich RC .40 1.00
4 M.Stodolka .40 1.00
S.Burnett
5 D.Thompson .40 1.00
C.Smith
6 D.Borrell RC .40 1.00
J.Bourgeois RC
7 Josh Hamilton .75 2.00
8 B.Zito .75 2.00
C.Sabathia
9 Ben Sheets .75 2.00
0 Howington .40 1.00
Kalinowski
Girdley
1 Hee Seop Choi RC .75 2.00
2 Bradley .60 1.50
Ainsworth
Tsao
3 Glendenning .40 1.00
Kelly
Silvestre
4 J.R. House .40 1.00
5 Rafael Soriano RC .60 1.50
6 T.Hafner RC 4.00 10.00
B.Jacobsen
7 Conti .40 1.00
Wakeland
Cole
8 Seabol/Huff/Crede 1.00 2.50
9 Everett .40 1.00
Ortiz
Ginter
0 Hernandez .40 1.00
Guzman
Eaton
1 Kielty .60 1.50
Bradley
J.Rivera
02 Mark McGwire GM 1.00 2.50
03 Don Larsen GM .30 .75
04 Bobby Thomson GM .30 .75
05 Bill Mazeroski GM .30 .75
06 Reggie Jackson GM .50 1.25
07 Kirk Gibson GM .30 .75
08 Roger Maris GM .50 1.25
09 Cal Ripken GM 1.25 3.00
10 Hank Aaron GM .75 2.00
11 Joe Carter GM .30 .75
12 Cal Ripken SH 1.25 3.00
13 Randy Johnson SH .50 1.25
14 Ken Griffey Jr. SH 1.00 2.50
15 Troy Glaus SH .30 .75
16 Kazuhiro Sasaki SH .30 .75
17 S.Sosa .50 1.25
T.Glaus LL
18 T.Helton .30 .75
E.Martinez LL
19 T.Helton .75 2.00
N.Garicaparra LL
320 B.Bonds .75 2.00
J.Giambi LL
321 T.Helton .30 .75
M.Ramirez LL
322 T.Helton .30 .75
D.Erstad LL
323 K.Brown .50 1.25
P.Martinez LL
324 R.Johnson .50 1.25
P.Martinez LL
325 Will Clark HL .50 1.25
326 New York Mets HL .75 2.00
327 New York Yankees HL 1.25 3.00
328 Seattle Mariners HL .30 .75
329 Mike Hampton HL .30 .75
330 New York Yankees HL 1.50 4.00
331 New York Yankees Champs 3.00 8.00
332 Jeff Bagwell .50 1.25
333 Andy Pettitte .50 1.25
334 Tony Armas Jr. .20 .50
335 Jeromy Burnitz .30 .75
336 Javier Vazquez .30 .75
337 Eric Karros .30 .75
338 Brian Giles .30 .75
339 Scott Rolen .50 1.25
340 David Justice .30 .75
341 Ray Durham .30 .75
342 Todd Zeile .30 .75
343 Cliff Floyd .30 .75
344 Barry Bonds 2.00 5.00
345 Matt Williams .30 .75
346 Steve Finley .30 .75
347 Scott Elarton .20 .50
348 Bernie Williams .50 1.25
349 David Wells .30 .75
350 J.T. Snow .30 .75
351 Al Leiter .30 .75
352 Magglio Ordonez .30 .75
353 Raul Mondesi .30 .75
354 Tim Salmon .50 1.25
355 Jeff Kent .30 .75
356 Mariano Rivera .75 2.00
357 John Olerud .30 .75
358 Javy Lopez .30 .75
359 Ben Grieve .20 .50
360 Ray Lankford .30 .75
361 Ken Griffey Jr. 1.50 4.00
362 Rich Aurilia .20 .50
363 Andruw Jones .50 1.25
364 Ryan Klesko .30 .75
365 Roberto Alomar .50 1.25
366 Miguel Tejada .30 .75
367 Mo Vaughn .30 .75
368 Albert Belle .30 .75
369 Jose Canseco .50 1.25
370 Kevin Brown .30 .75
371 Rafael Palmeiro .50 1.25
372 Mark Redman .20 .50
373 Larry Walker .30 .75
374 Greg Maddux 1.25 3.00
375 Nomar Garciaparra 1.25 3.00
376 Kevin Millwood .30 .75
377 Edgar Martinez .50 1.25
378 Sammy Sosa .75 2.00
379 Tim Hudson .30 .75
380 Jim Edmonds .30 .75
381 Mike Piazza 1.25 3.00
382 Brant Brown .20 .50
383 Brad Fullmer .20 .50
384 Alan Benes .20 .50
385 Mickey Morandini .20 .50
386 Troy Percival .30 .75
387 Eddie Perez .20 .50
388 Vernon Wells .30 .75
389 Ricky Gutierrez .20 .50
390 Rondell White .30 .75
391 Kelvim Escobar .20 .50
392 Tony Batista .20 .50
393 Jimmy Haynes .20 .50
394 Billy Wagner .30 .75
395 A.J. Hinch .20 .50
396 Matt Morris .30 .75
397 Lance Berkman .30 .75
398 Jeff D'Amico .20 .50
399 Octavio Dotel .20 .50
400 Olmedo Saenz .20 .50
401 Esteban Loaiza .20 .50
402 Adam Kennedy .20 .50
403 Moises Alou .30 .75
404 Orlando Palmeiro .20 .50
405 Kevin Young .20 .50
406 Tom Goodwin .20 .50
407 Mac Suzuki .20 .50
408 Pat Hentgen .20 .50
409 Kevin Stocker .20 .50
410 Mark Sweeney .20 .50
411 Tony Eusebio .20 .50
412 Edgar Renteria .30 .75
413 John Rocker .20 .50
414 Jose Lima .20 .50
415 Kerry Wood .30 .75
416 Mike Timlin .20 .50
417 Jose Hernandez .20 .50
418 Jeremy Giambi .20 .50
419 Luis Lopez .20 .50
420 Mitch Meluskey .20 .50
421 Garrett Stephenson .20 .50
422 Jamey Wright .20 .50
423 John Jaha .20 .50
424 Placido Polanco .20 .50
425 Marty Cordova .20 .50
426 Joey Hamilton .20 .50
427 Travis Fryman .30 .75
428 Mike Cameron .20 .50
429 Matt Mantei .20 .50
430 Chan Ho Park .30 .75
431 Shawn Estes .20 .50
432 Danny Bautista .20 .50
433 Wilson Alvarez .20 .50
434 Kenny Lofton .30 .75
435 Russ Ortiz .20 .50
436 Dave Burba .20 .50
437 Felix Martinez .20 .50
438 Jeff Shaw .20 .50
439 Mike DiFelice .20 .50
440 Roberto Hernandez .20 .50
441 Bryan Rekar .20 .50
442 Ugueth Urbina .20 .50
443 Vinny Castilla .30 .75
444 Carlos Perez .20 .50
445 Juan Guzman .20 .50
446 Ryan Rupe .20 .50
447 Mike Mordecai .20 .50
448 Ricardo Rincon .20 .50
449 Curt Schilling .30 .75
450 Alex Cora .20 .50
451 Turner Ward .20 .50
452 Omar Vizquel .50 1.25
453 Russ Branyan .20 .50
454 Russ Johnson .20 .50
455 Greg Colbrunn .20 .50
456 Charles Nagy .20 .50
457 Wil Cordero .20 .50
458 Jason Tyner .20 .50
459 Devon White .30 .75
460 Kelly Stinnett .20 .50
461 Wilton Guerrero .20 .50
462 Jason Bere .20 .50
463 Calvin Murray .20 .50
464 Miguel Batista .20 .50
466 Luis Gonzalez .30 .75
467 Jaret Wright .20 .50
468 Chad Kreuter .20 .50
469 Armando Benitez .20 .50
470 Erubiel Durazo .20 .50
470 Sidney Ponson .20 .50
471 Adrian Brown .20 .50
472 Sterling Hitchcock .20 .50
473 Timo Perez .20 .50
474 Jamie Moyer .30 .75
475 Delino DeShields .20 .50
476 Glendon Rusch .20 .50
477 Chris Gomez .20 .50
478 Adam Eaton .20 .50
479 Pablo Ozuna .20 .50
480 Bob Abreu .30 .75
481 Kris Benson .20 .50
482 Keith Osik .20 .50
483 Darryl Hamilton .20 .50
484 Marlon Anderson .20 .50
485 Jimmy Anderson .20 .50
486 John Halama .20 .50
487 Nelson Figueroa .20 .50
488 Alex Gonzalez .20 .50
489 Benny Agbayani .20 .50
490 Ed Sprague .20 .50
491 Scott Erickson .20 .50
492 Doug Glanville .20 .50
493 Jesus Sanchez .20 .50
494 Mike Lieberthal .30 .75
495 Aaron Sele .20 .50
496 Pat Mahomes .20 .50
497 Ruben Rivera .20 .50
498 Wayne Gomes .20 .50
499 Freddy Garcia .30 .75
500 Al Martin .20 .50
501 Woody Williams .20 .50
502 Paul Byrd .20 .50
503 Rick White .20 .50
504 Trevor Hoffman .30 .75
505 Brady Anderson .30 .75
506 Robert Person .20 .50
507 Jeff Conine .30 .75
508 Chris Truby .20 .50
509 Emil Brown .20 .50
510 Ryan Dempster .20 .50
511 Ruben Mateo .20 .50
512 Alex Ochoa .20 .50
513 Jose Rosado .20 .50
514 Masato Yoshii .20 .50
515 Brian Daubach .20 .50
516 Jeff D'Amico .20 .50
517 Brent Mayne .20 .50
518 John Thomson .20 .50
519 Todd Ritchie .20 .50
520 John VanderWal .20 .50
521 Neifi Perez .20 .50
522 Chad Curtis .20 .50
523 Kenny Rogers .30 .75
524 Trot Nixon .30 .75
525 Sean Casey .30 .75
526 Wilton Veras .20 .50
527 Troy O'Leary .20 .50
528 Dante Bichette .30 .75
529 Jose Silva .20 .50
530 Darren Oliver .20 .50
531 Steve Parris .20 .50
532 David McCarty .20 .50
533 Todd Walker .20 .50
534 Brian Rose .20 .50
535 Pete Schourek .20 .50
536 Ricky Ledee .20 .50
537 Justin Thompson .20 .50
538 Benito Santiago .30 .75
539 Carlos Beltran .30 .75
540 Gabe White .20 .50
541 Bret Saberhagen .30 .75
542 Ramon Martinez .20 .50
543 John Valentin .20 .50
544 Frank Catalanotto .20 .50
545 Tim Wakefield .30 .75
546 Michael Tucker .20 .50
547 Juan Pierre .30 .75
548 Rich Garces .20 .50
549 Luis Ordaz .20 .50
550 Jerry Spradlin .20 .50
551 Corey Koskie .20 .50
552 Cal Eldred .20 .50
553 Alfonso Soriano .50 1.25
554 Kip Wells .20 .50
555 Orlando Hernandez .30 .75
556 Bill Simas .20 .50
557 Jim Parque .20 .50
558 Joe Mays .20 .50
559 Tim Belcher .20 .50
560 Shane Spencer .20 .50
561 Glenallen Hill .20 .50
562 Matt LeCroy .20 .50
563 Tino Martinez .50 1.25
564 Eric Milton .20 .50
565 Ron Coomer .20 .50
566 Cristian Guzman .20 .50
567 Kazuhiro Sasaki .30 .75
568 Mark Quinn .20 .50
569 Eric Gagne .30 .75
570 Kerry Ligtenberg .20 .50
571 Rolando Arrojo .20 .50
572 Jon Lieber .20 .50
573 Jose Vizcaino .20 .50
574 Jeff Abbott .20 .50
575 Carlos Hernandez .20 .50
576 Scott Sullivan .20 .50
577 Matt Stairs .20 .50
578 Tom Lampkin .20 .50
579 Donnie Sadler .20 .50
580 Desi Relaford .20 .50
581 Scott Downs .20 .50
582 Mike Mussina .50 1.25
583 Ramon Ortiz .20 .50
584 Mike Myers .20 .50
585 Frank Castillo .20 .50
586 Manny Ramirez Sox .50 1.25
587 Alex Rodriguez 1.00 2.50
588 Andy Ashby .20 .50
589 Felipe Crespo .20 .50
590 Bobby Bonilla .30 .75
591 Denny Neagle .20 .50
592 Dave Martinez .20 .50
593 Mike Hampton .30 .75
594 Gary DiSarcina .20 .50
595 Tsuyoshi Shinjo RC .75 2.00
596 Albert Pujols RC 20.00 50.00
597 Oswalt 1.00 2.50
Strange
Rauch
598 Jake Peavy RC 2.00 5.00
599 S.Smyth RC .40 1.00
Bynum
Haynes
600 Cuddyer .40 1.00
Lawrence
Freeman
601 C.Pena .40 1.00
Barnes
Wise
602 E.Almonte RC .40 1.00
F.Lopez
603 Escobar .40 1.00
Valent
Wilkerson
604 Hall .40 1.00
Barajas
Goldbach
605 Romano .60 1.50
Giles
Ozuna
606 D.Brown .40 1.00
Cust
V.Wells
607 L.Montanez RC .40 1.00
D.Espinosa
608 J.Wayne RC .40 1.00
A.Pluta RC
609 J.Axelson RC .40 1.00
C.Cali RC
610 S.Boyd RC .40 1.00
C.Morris RC
611 T.Arko RC .40 1.00
D.Moylan RC
612 L.Cotto RC .40 1.00
L.Escobar
613 B.Mims RC .40 1.00
B.Williams RC
614 C.Russ RC .40 1.00
B.Edwards
615 J.Torres .40 1.00
B.Diggins
616 Edwin Encarnacion RC 3.00 8.00
617 B.Bass RC .40 1.00
O.Ayala RC
618 M.Matthews RC .40 1.00
J.Kanooi
619 S.McFarland RC .40 1.00
A.Sterrett RC
620 D.Krynzel 2.00 5.00
G.Sizemore
621 K.Bucktrot .40 1.00
J.Sardinha
622 Anaheim Angels TC .30 .75
623 Arizona Diamondbacks TC .30 .75
624 Atlanta Braves TC .30 .75
625 Baltimore Orioles TC .30 .75
626 Boston Red Sox TC .30 .75
627 Chicago Cubs TC .30 .75
628 Chicago White Sox TC .30 .75
629 Cincinnati Reds TC .30 .75
630 Cleveland Indians TC .30 .75
631 Colorado Rockies TC .30 .75
632 Detroit Tigers TC .30 .75
633 Florida Marlins TC .30 .75
634 Houston Astros TC .30 .75
635 Kansas City Royals TC .30 .75
636 Los Angeles Dodgers TC .30 .75
637 Milwaukee Brewers TC .30 .75
638 Minnesota Twins TC .30 .75
639 Montreal Expos TC .30 .75
640 New York Mets TC .30 .75
641 New York Yankees TC 1.50 4.00
642 Oakland Athletics TC .30 .75
643 Philadelphia Phillies TC .30 .75
644 Pittsburgh Pirates TC .30 .75
645 San Diego Padres TC .30 .75
646 San Francisco Giants TC .30 .75
647 Seattle Mariners TC .30 .75
648 St. Louis Cardinals TC .30 .75
649 Tampa Bay Devil Rays TC .30 .75
650 Texas Rangers TC .30 .75
651 Toronto Blue Jays TC .30 .75
652 Bucky Dent GM .20 .50
653 Jackie Robinson GM .75 2.00
654 Roberto Clemente GM 1.00 2.50
655 Nolan Ryan GM 1.25 3.00
656 Kerry Wood GM .30 .75
657 Rickey Henderson GM .75 2.00
658 Lou Brock GM .50 1.25
659 David Wells GM .20 .50
660 Andruw Jones GM .30 .75
661 Carlton Fisk GM .30 .75

2001 Topps Chrome Retrofractors

*STARS: 2.5X TO 6X BASIC CARDS
*PROSPECTS 277-301/595-621: 2X TO 5X
*ROOKIES 277-301/595-621: 2X TO 5X
STATED ODDS 1:12
CARD NO.7 DOES NOT EXIST
596 Albert Pujols 400.00 800.00
598 Jake Peavy 12.00 30.00
616 Edwin Encarnacion 20.00 50.00

2001 Topps Chrome Before There Was Topps

This set parallels the regular Before There Was Topps insert cards. These cards were inserted at a rate of one in 20 2001 Topps Chrome series two hobby/retail packs.

COMPLETE SET (10) 30.00 80.00
SER.2 STATED ODDS 1:20 HOBBY/RETAIL
*REFRACTORS: 1.25X TO 3X BASIC BEFORE
SER.2 REFRACTOR ODDS 1:200 HOB/RET
BT1 Lou Gehrig 5.00 12.00
BT2 Babe Ruth 8.00 20.00
BT3 Cy Young 2.50 6.00
BT4 Walter Johnson 2.50 6.00
BT5 Ty Cobb 4.00 10.00
BT6 Rogers Hornsby 2.50 6.00
BT7 Honus Wagner 2.50 6.00
BT8 Christy Mathewson 2.50 6.00
BT9 Grover Alexander 2.50 6.00
BT10 Joe DiMaggio 5.00 12.00

2001 Topps Chrome Combos

Randomly insert into packs at 1:12 Hobby/Retail and 1:4 HTA, this 10-card insert pairs up players that have put up similar statistics throughout their careers. Card backs carry a "TC" prefix. Please note that these cards feature Topps' special chrome technology.

COMPLETE SET (20) 20.00 50.00
COMPLETE SERIES 1 (10) 10.00 25.00
COMPLETE SERIES 2 (10) 10.00 25.00
STATED ODDS 1:12 HOBBY/RETAIL, 1:4 HTA
*REFRACTORS: 1.5X TO 4X BASIC COMBO
REFRACTOR ODDS 1:120 H/R
TC1 Decades of Excellence 2.50 6.00
TC2 Power Corner 1.50 4.00
TC3 Glove Birds 3.00 8.00
TC4 Mound Marksmen .60 1.50
TC5 Tools of Success 1.00 2.50
TC6 Shortstop Supremacy 1.25 3.00
TC7 Big Red Machine 2.00 5.00
TC8 Latin Heat 2.50 6.00
TC9 Home Run Royalty 2.00 5.00
TC10 New York State of Mind .60 1.50
TC11 Dodger Blue 2.00 5.00
TC12 60 Home Run Club 2.50 6.00
TC13 Heroes of Fenway 2.00 5.00
TC14 Mound Masters 1.50 4.00
TC15 Sweetness 2.00 5.00
TC16 Ironmen 3.00 8.00
TC17 Southpaw Greatness 2.00 5.00
TC18 Best There Is 1.00 2.50
Was
TC19 All in the Family 2.00 5.00
TC20 Barrier Breakers 1.00 2.50

2001 Topps Chrome Golden Anniversary

Randomly inserted into packs at 1:10 Hobby/Retail, this 50-card insert celebrates Topp's 50th Anniversary by taking a look at some of the all-time greats. Card backs carry a "GA" prefix. Please note that these cards feature Topps' special chrome technology.

COMPLETE SET (50) 150.00 300.00
SER.1 STATED ODDS 1:10
*REFRACTORS: 1.5X TO 4X BASIC ANNV.
SER.1 REFRACTOR ODDS 1:100
GA1 Hank Aaron 4.00 10.00
GA2 Ernie Banks 2.00 5.00
GA3 Mike Schmidt 4.00 10.00
GA4 Willie Mays 4.00 10.00
GA5 Johnny Bench 2.00 5.00
GA6 Tom Seaver 1.25 3.00
GA7 Frank Robinson 1.25 3.00
GA8 Sandy Koufax 6.00 15.00
GA9 Bob Gibson 1.25 3.00
GA10 Ted Williams 4.00 10.00
GA11 Cal Ripken 6.00 15.00
GA12 Tony Gwynn 2.50 6.00
GA13 Mark McGwire 5.00 12.00
GA14 Ken Griffey Jr. 4.00 10.00
GA15 Greg Maddux 3.00 8.00
GA16 Roger Clemens 4.00 10.00
GA17 Barry Bonds 5.00 12.00
GA18 Rickey Henderson 2.00 5.00
GA19 Mike Piazza 3.00 8.00
GA20 Jose Canseco 1.25 3.00
GA21 Derek Jeter 5.00 12.00
GA22 Nomar Garciaparra 3.00 8.00
GA23 Alex Rodriguez 2.50 6.00
GA24 Sammy Sosa 2.00 5.00
GA25 Ivan Rodriguez 1.25 3.00
GA26 Vladimir Guerrero 2.00 5.00
GA27 Chipper Jones 2.00 5.00
GA28 Jeff Bagwell 1.25 3.00
GA29 Pedro Martinez 1.25 3.00
GA30 Randy Johnson 2.00 5.00
GA31 Pat Burrell .75 2.00
GA32 Josh Hamilton 1.50 4.00
GA33 Ryan Anderson .75 2.00
GA34 Corey Patterson .75 2.00
GA35 Eric Munson .75 2.00
GA36 Sean Burroughs .75 2.00
GA37 C.C. Sabathia .75 2.00
GA38 Chin-Feng Chen .75 2.00
GA39 Barry Zito 1.25 3.00
GA40 Adrian Gonzalez 5.00 12.00
GA41 Mark McGwire 5.00 12.00
GA42 Nomar Garciaparra 3.00 8.00
GA43 Todd Helton 1.25 3.00
GA44 Matt Williams .75 2.00
GA45 Troy Glaus .75 2.00
GA46 Geoff Jenkins .75 2.00
GA47 Frank Thomas 2.00 5.00
GA48 Mo Vaughn .75 2.00
GA49 Barry Larkin 1.25 3.00
GA50 J.D. Drew .75 2.00

2001 Topps Chrome King Of Kings

Randomly inserted into packs at 1:5,157 series one hobby and 1:5,209 series one retail and 1:6383 series two hobby and 1:6,520 series two retail, this seven-card insert features game-used memorabilia from major superstars. Please note that a special fourth card containing game-used memorabilia of all three were inserted into Hobby packs at 1:59,220. Card backs carry a "KKR" prefix.

SER.1 ODDS 1:5175 HOB., 1:5209 RET.
SER.2 GROUP A ODDS 1:11,347 H, 1:11,520 R
SER.2 GROUP B ODDS 1:15,348 H, 1:15,648 R
SER.2 OVERALL ODDS 1:6383 H, 1:6520 R
KKGE SER.1 ODDS 1:59,220 HOBBY
KKR1 Hank Aaron 60.00 120.00
KKR2 Nolan Ryan Rangers 50.00 100.00
KKR3 Rickey Henderson 15.00 40.00
KKR5 Bob Gibson 15.00 40.00
KKR6 Nolan Ryan Angels 50.00 100.00

2001 Topps Chrome King Of Kings Refractors

KKR1-3 SER.1 ODDS 1:16,920 HOBBY
KKR5-6 SER.2 ODDS 1:23,022 HOBBY
KKGE SER.1 ODDS 1:212,160 HOBBY
KKR1-KKR6 PRINT RUN 10 SERIAL #'d SETS
KKGE PRINT RUN 5 SERIAL #'d CARDS
CARD NUMBER 4 DOES NOT EXIST
NO PRICING DUE TO SCARCITY

2001 Topps Chrome Originals

Randomly inserted into Hobby packs at 1:1783 and Retail packs at 1:1788, this ten-card insert features game-used jersey cards of players like Roberto Clemente and Carl Yastrzemski produced with Topps patented chrome technology.

SER.1 ODDS 1:1783 HOBBY, 1:1788 RETAIL
SER.2 GROUP A ODDS 1:4863 H, 1:4943 R
SER.2 GROUP B ODDS 1:7855 H, 1:8229 R
SER.2 GROUP C ODDS 1:6588 H, 1:6803 R
SER.2 GROUP D ODDS 1:46,044 H, 1:57,600 R
SER.2 GROUP E ODDS 1:6588 H, 1:6797 R
SER.2 OVERALL ODDS 1:1513 H, 1:1545 R
REFRACT.1-5 SER.1 ODDS 1:9644 HOBBY
REFRACT.6-10 SER.2 ODDS 1:8372 HOBBY
REFRACTOR PRINT RUN 10 #'d SETS
NO REFRACTOR PRICE DUE TO SCARCITY
1 Roberto Clemente 175.00 300.00
2 Carl Yastrzemski 125.00 200.00
3 Mike Schmidt 20.00 50.00
4 Wade Boggs 30.00 60.00
5 Chipper Jones 30.00 60.00
6 Willie Mays 175.00 300.00
7 Lou Brock 15.00 40.00
8 Dave Parker 15.00 40.00
9 Barry Bonds 75.00 150.00
10 Alex Rodriguez 30.00 60.00

2001 Topps Chrome Past to Present

Randomly insert into packs at 1:18 Hobby/Retail, this 10-card insert pairs up players that have put up similar statistics throughout their careers. Card backs carry a "PTP" prefix. Please note that these cards feature Topps' special chrome technology.

COMPLETE SET (10) 30.00 60.00
SER.1 STATED ODDS 1:18
*REFRACTORS: 1.5X TO 4X BASIC PAST
SER.1 REFRACTOR ODDS 1:180
PTP1 P.Rizzuto 5.00 12.00
D.Jeter
PTP2 W.Spahn 3.00 8.00
G.Maddux
PTP3 Y.Berra 4.00 10.00
J.Posada
PTP4 W.Mays 8.00 20.00
B.Bonds
PTP5 R.Schoendienst 1.50 4.00
F.Vina
PTP6 D.Snider 1.50 4.00
S.Green
PTP7 B.Feller 1.50 4.00
B.Colon
PTP8 J.Mize 1.50 4.00
T.Martinez
PTP9 L.Doby 1.50 4.00
M.Ramirez
PTP10 E.Mathews 2.00 5.00
C.Jones

2001 Topps Chrome Through the Years Reprints

Randomly inserted into packs at 1:10 Hobby/Retail, this 50-card set takes a look at some of the best players to every make it onto a Topps trading card. Please note that these cards were produced with Topps chrome technology.

COMPLETE SET (50) 150.00 300.00
SER.1 STATED ODDS 1:10
*REFRACTORS: 1.5X TO 4X BASIC THROUGH
SER.1 REFRACTOR ODDS 1:100
1 Yogi Berra 57 2.50 6.00
2 Roy Campanella 56 2.50 6.00
3 Willie Mays 53 4.00 10.00
4 Andy Pafko 52 2.50 6.00
5 Jackie Robinson 52 2.50 6.00
6 Stan Musial 59 3.00 8.00
7 Duke Snider 56 2.00 5.00
8 Warren Spahn 56 2.00 5.00
9 Ted Williams 54 6.00 15.00
10 Eddie Mathews 55 2.50 6.00
11 Willie McCovey 60 2.00 5.00
12 Frank Robinson 69 2.00 5.00
13 Ernie Banks 66 2.50 6.00
14 Hank Aaron 65 4.00 10.00
15 Sandy Koufax 61 5.00 12.00
16 Bob Gibson 68 2.00 5.00
17 Harmon Killebrew 67 2.50 6.00
18 Whitey Ford 64 2.00 5.00
19 Roberto Clemente 63 6.00 15.00
20 Juan Marichal 61 2.00 5.00
21 Johnny Bench 70 2.50 6.00
22 Willie Stargell 73 2.00 5.00
23 Joe Morgan 74 2.00 5.00
24 Carl Yastrzemski 71 3.00 8.00
25 Reggie Jackson 76 2.00 5.00
26 Tom Seaver 78 2.00 5.00
27 Steve Carlton 77 2.00 5.00
28 Jim Palmer 79 2.00 5.00
29 Rod Carew 72 2.00 5.00
30 George Brett 75 6.00 15.00
31 Roger Clemens 85 5.00 12.00
32 Don Mattingly 84 6.00 15.00
33 Ryne Sandberg 89 4.00 10.00
34 Mike Schmidt 81 4.00 10.00
35 Cal Ripken 82 8.00 20.00
36 Tony Gwynn 83 3.00 8.00
37 Ozzie Smith 87 4.00 10.00
38 Wade Boggs 88 2.00 5.00
39 Nolan Ryan 80 6.00 15.00
40 Robin Yount 86 2.50 6.00
41 Mark McGwire 85 5.00 12.00
42 Ken Griffey Jr. 92 4.00 10.00
43 Sammy Sosa 90 2.50 6.00
44 Alex Rodriguez 98 2.50 6.00
45 Barry Bonds 94 5.00 12.00
46 Mike Piazza 95 3.00 8.00
47 Chipper Jones 91 2.50 6.00
48 Greg Maddux 96 3.00 8.00
49 Nomar Garciaparra 97 3.00 8.00
50 Derek Jeter 93 6.00 15.00

2001 Topps Chrome What Could Have Been

Inserted a rate of one in 30 hobby/retail packs, these 10 cards parallel the regular What Could Have Been retail set.

COMPLETE SET (10) 15.00 40.00
SER.2 STATED ODDS 1:30 HOBBY/RETAIL
*REFRACTORS: 1.5X TO 4X BASIC WHAT
SER.2 REFRACTOR ODDS 1:300 HOB/RET
WCB1 Josh Gibson 4.00 10.00
WCB2 Satchel Paige 1.50 4.00
WCB3 Buck Leonard 1.50 4.00
WCB4 James Bell 1.50 4.00
WCB5 Rube Foster 1.50 4.00
WCB6 Martin DiHigo 1.50 4.00
WCB7 William Johnson 1.50 4.00
WCB8 Mule Suttles 1.50 4.00
WCB9 Ray Dandridge 1.50 4.00
WCB10 John Lloyd 1.50 4.00

2001 Topps Chrome Traded

This set is a parallel to the 2001 Topps Traded set. Inserted into the 2001 Topps Traded at a rate of two per pack, these cards feature the patented "Chrome" technology which Topps uses.

COMPLETE SET (266) 75.00 150.00
COMMON CARD (1-99/145-266) .30 .75
COMMON REPRINT (100-144) .50 1.25

T1 Sandy Alomar Jr. .30 .75
T2 Kevin Appier .50 1.25
T3 Brad Ausmus .50 1.25
T4 Derek Bell .30 .75
T5 Bret Boone .50 1.25
T6 Rico Brogna .30 .75
T7 Ellis Burks .50 1.25
T8 Ken Caminiti .50 1.25
T9 Roger Cedeno .30 .75
T10 Royce Clayton .30 .75
T11 Enrique Wilson .30 .75
T12 Rheal Cormier .30 .75
T13 Eric Davis .50 1.25
T14 Shawon Dunston .30 .75
T15 Andres Galarraga .50 1.25
T16 Tom Gordon .30 .75
T17 Mark Grace .75 2.00
T18 Jeffrey Hammonds .30 .75
T19 Dustin Hermanson .30 .75
T20 Quinton McCracken .30 .75
T21 Todd Hundley .30 .75
T22 Charles Johnson .50 1.25
T23 Marquis Grissom .50 1.25
T24 Jose Mesa .30 .75
T25 Brian Boehringer .30 .75
T26 John Rocker .50 1.25
T27 Jeff Frye .30 .75
T28 Reggie Sanders .50 1.25
T29 David Segui .30 .75
T30 Mike Sirotka .30 .75
T31 Fernando Tatis .30 .75
T32 Steve Trachsel .30 .75
T33 Ismael Valdes .30 .75
T34 Randy Velarde .30 .75
T35 Ryan Kohlmeier .30 .75
T36 Mike Bordick .50 1.25
T37 Kent Bottenfield .30 .75
T38 Pat Rapp .30 .75
T39 Jeff Nelson .30 .75
T40 Ricky Bottalico .30 .75
T41 Luke Prokopec .30 .75
T42 Hideo Nomo 1.25 3.00
T43 Bill Mueller .50 1.25
T44 Roberto Kelly .30 .75
T45 Chris Holt .30 .75
T46 Mike Jackson .30 .75
T47 Devon White .50 1.25
T48 Gerald Williams .30 .75
T49 Eddie Taubensee .30 .75
T50 Brian Hunter .30 .75
T51 Nelson Cruz .30 .75
T52 Jeff Fassero .30 .75
T53 Bubba Trammell .30 .75
T54 Bo Porter .30 .75
T55 Greg Norton .30 .75
T56 Benito Santiago .50 1.25
T57 Ruben Rivera .30 .75
T58 Dee Brown .30 .75
T59 Jose Canseco .75 2.00
T60 Chris Michalak .30 .75
T61 Tim Worrell .30 .75
T62 Matt Clement .50 1.25
T63 Bill Pulsipher .30 .75
T64 Troy Brohawn RC .40 1.00
T65 Mark Kotsay .50 1.25
T66 Jimmy Rollins .50 1.25
T67 Shea Hillenbrand .50 1.25
T68 Ted Lilly .30 .75
T69 Jermaine Dye .50 1.25
T70 Jerry Hairston Jr. .30 .75
T71 John Mabry .30 .75
T72 Kurt Abbott .30 .75
T73 Eric Owens .30 .75
T74 Jeff Brantley .30 .75
T75 Roy Oswalt 1.25 3.00
T76 Doug Mientkiewicz .50 1.25
T77 Rickey Henderson 1.25 3.00
T78 Jason Grimsley .30 .75
T79 Christian Parker RC .40 1.00
T80 Donne Wall .30 .75
T81 Alex Arias .30 .75
T82 Willis Roberts .30 .75
T83 Ryan Minor .30 .75
T84 Jason LaRue .30 .75
T85 Ruben Sierra .50 1.25
T86 Johnny Damon .75 2.00
T87 Juan Gonzalez .50 1.25
T88 C.C. Sabathia .50 1.25
T89 Tony Batista .30 .75
T90 Jay Witasick .30 .75
T91 Brent Abernathy .30 .75
T92 Paul LoDuca .50 1.25
T93 Wes Helms .30 .75
T94 Mark Wohlers .30 .75
T95 Rob Bell .30 .75
T96 Tim Redding .30 .75
T97 Bud Smith RC .40 1.00
T98 Adam Dunn .75 2.00
T99 I.Suzuki 75.00 200.00
A.Pujols ROY
T100 Carlton Fisk 81 .75 2.00
T101 Tim Raines 81 .50 1.25
T102 Juan Marichal 74 .50 1.25
T103 Dave Winfield 81 .50 1.25
T104 Reggie Jackson 82 .75 2.00
T105 Cal Ripken 82 4.00 10.00
T106 Ozzie Smith 82 2.00 5.00
T107 Tom Seaver 83 .75 2.00
T108 Lou Piniella 74 .50 1.25
T109 Dwight Gooden 84 .50 1.25
T110 Bret Saberhagen 84 .50 1.25
T111 Gary Carter 85 .50 1.25
T112 Jack Clark 85 .50 1.25
T113 Rickey Henderson 85 1.25 3.00
T114 Barry Bonds 86 3.00 8.00
T115 Bobby Bonilla 86 .50 1.25
T116 Jose Canseco 86 .75 2.00
T117 Will Clark 86 .75 2.00
T118 Andres Galarraga 86 .50 1.25
T119 Bo Jackson 86 1.25 3.00
T120 Wally Joyner 86 .50 1.25
T121 Ellis Burks 87 .50 1.25
T122 David Cone 87 .50 1.25
T123 Greg Maddux 87 2.00 5.00
T124 Willie Randolph 76 .50 1.25
T125 Dennis Eckersley 87 .50 1.25
T126 Matt Williams 87 .50 1.25
T127 Joe Morgan 81 .50 1.25
T128 Fred McGriff 87 .75 2.00
T129 Roberto Alomar 88 .75 2.00
T130 Lee Smith 88 .50 1.25
T131 David Wells 88 .50 1.25
T132 Ken Griffey Jr. 89 2.50 6.00
T133 Deion Sanders 89 .75 2.00
T134 Nolan Ryan 89 3.00 8.00
T135 David Justice 90 .50 1.25
T136 Joe Carter 91 .50 1.25
T137 Jack Morris 92 .50 1.25
T138 Mike Piazza 93 2.00 5.00
T139 Barry Bonds 93 3.00 8.00
T140 Terrence Long 94 .50 1.25
T141 Ben Grieve 94 .50 1.25
T142 Richie Sexson 95 .50 1.25
T143 Sean Burroughs 99 .50 1.25
T144 Alfonso Soriano 99 .75 2.00
T145 Bob Boone MG .50 1.25
T146 Larry Bowa MG .50 1.25
T147 Bob Brenly MG .30 .75
T148 Buck Martinez MG .30 .75
T149 Lloyd McClendon MG .30 .75
T150 Jim Tracy MG .30 .75
T151 Jared Abruzzo RC .40 1.00
T152 Kurt Ainsworth .30 .75
T153 Willie Bloomquist .50 1.25
T154 Ben Broussard .30 .75
T155 Bobby Bradley .30 .75
T156 Mike Bynum .30 .75
T157 A.J. Hinch .30 .75
T158 Ryan Christianson .30 .75
T159 Carlos Silva .30 .75
T160 Joe Crede 1.25 3.00
T161 Jack Cust .30 .75
T162 Ben Diggins .30 .75
T163 Phil Dumatrait .30 .75
T164 Alex Escobar .30 .75
T165 Miguel Olivo .30 .75
T166 Chris George .30 .75
T167 Marcus Giles .50 1.25
T168 Keith Ginter .30 .75
T169 Josh Girdley .30 .75
T170 Tony Alvarez .30 .75
T171 Scott Seabol .30 .75
T172 Josh Hamilton .60 1.50
T173 Jason Hart .30 .75
T174 Israel Alcantara .30 .75
T175 Jake Peavy 1.50 4.00
T176 Stubby Clapp RC .40 1.00
T177 D'Angelo Jimenez .30 .75
T178 Nick Johnson .50 1.25
T179 Ben Johnson .50 1.25
T180 Larry Bigbie .30 .75
T181 Allen Levrault .30 .75
T182 Felipe Lopez .50 1.25
T183 Sean Burnett .30 .75
T184 Nick Neugebauer .30 .75
T185 Austin Kearns .50 1.25
T186 Corey Patterson .30 .75
T187 Carlos Pena .30 .75
T188 Ricardo Rodriguez RC .40 1.00
T189 Juan Rivera .30 .75
T190 Grant Roberts .30 .75
T191 Adam Pettyjohn RC .40 1.00
T192 Jared Sandberg .30 .75
T193 Xavier Nady .30 .75
T194 Dane Sardinha .30 .75
T195 Shawn Sonnier .30 .75
T196 Rafael Soriano .40 1.00
T197 Brian Specht RC .40 1.00
T198 Aaron Myette .30 .75
T199 Juan Uribe RC .50 1.25
T200 Jayson Werth .30 .75
T201 Brad Wilkerson .30 .75
T202 Horacio Estrada .30 .75
T203 Joel Pineiro .50 1.25
T204 Matt LeCroy .30 .75
T205 Michael Coleman .30 .75
T206 Ben Sheets .75 2.00
T207 Eric Byrnes .30 .75
T208 Sean Burroughs .30 .75
T209 Ken Harvey .30 .75
T210 Travis Hafner 3.00 8.00
T211 Erick Almonte .40 1.00
T212 Jason Belcher RC .40 1.00
T213 Wilson Betemit RC 1.50 4.00
T214 Hank Blalock RC 2.50 6.00
T215 Danny Borrell .40 1.00
T216 John Buck RC .50 1.25
T217 Freddie Bynum RC .40 1.00
T218 Noel Devarez RC .40 1.00
T219 Juan Diaz RC .40 1.00
T220 Felix Diaz RC .40 1.00
T221 Josh Fogg RC .40 1.00
T222 Matt Ford RC .40 1.00
T223 Scott Heard .30 .75
T224 Ben Hendrickson RC .40 1.00
T225 Cody Ross RC 1.50 4.00
T226 Adrian Hernandez RC .40 1.00
T227 Alfredo Amezaga RC .40 1.00
T228 Bob Keppel RC .40 1.00
T229 Ryan Madson RC .75 2.00
T230 Octavio Martinez RC .40 1.00
T231 Hee Seop Choi .50 1.25
T232 Thomas Mitchell .30 .75
T233 Luis Montanez .40 1.00
T234 Andy Morales RC .40 1.00
T235 Justin Morneau RC 4.00 10.00
T236 Toe Nash RC .40 1.00
T237 Valentino Pascucci RC .40 1.00
T238 Roy Smith RC .40 1.00
T239 Antonio Perez RC .50 1.25
T240 Chad Petty RC .40 1.00
T241 Steve Smyth .40 1.00
T242 Jose Reyes RC 3.00 8.00
T243 Eric Reynolds RC .40 1.00
T244 Dominic Rich .40 1.00
T245 Jason Richardson RC .40 1.00
T246 Ed Rogers RC .40 1.00
T247 Albert Pujols 75.00 200.00
T248 Esix Snead RC .40 1.00
T249 Luis Torres RC .40 1.00
T250 Matt White RC .40 1.00
T251 Blake Williams .40 1.00
T252 Chris Russ .40 1.00
T253 Joe Kennedy RC .50 1.25
T254 Jeff Randazzo RC .40 1.00
T255 Beau Hale RC .40 1.00
T256 Brad Hennessey RC .75 2.00
T257 Jake Gautreau RC .40 1.00
T258 Jeff Mathis RC .50 1.25
T259 Aaron Heilman RC .50 1.25
T260 Bronson Sardinha RC .40 1.00
T261 Irvin Guzman RC 3.00 8.00
T262 Gabe Gross RC .50 1.25
T263 J.D. Martin RC .40 1.00
T264 Chris Smith RC .40 1.00
T265 Kenny Baugh RC .40 1.00
T266 Ichiro Suzuki RC 100.00 250.00

2001 Topps Chrome Traded Retrofractors

*STARS: 1.5X TO 4X BASIC CARDS
*REPRINTS: 1X TO 2.5X BASIC
*ROOKIES: 2.5X TO 6X BASIC
STATED ODDS 1:12 TOPPS TRADED
T99 I.Suzuki 500.00 1200.00
A.Pujols ROY
T210 Travis Hafner 20.00 50.00
T235 Justin Morneau 15.00 40.00
T242 Jose Reyes 6.00 15.00
T247 Albert Pujols 500.00 1200.00
T261 Irvin Guzman 50.00 100.00
T266 Ichiro Suzuki 1000.00 2500.00

2002 Topps Chrome

This product's first series, consisting of cards 1-6 and 8-331, was released in late January, 2002. The second series, consisting of cards 366-695, was released in early June, 2002. Both first and second series packs contained four cards and carried an SRP of $3. Sealed boxes contained 24 packs. The set parallels the 2002 Topps set except, of course, for the upgraded chrome card stock. Unlike the 1999 Topps Chrome product, featuring 70 variations of Mark McGwire's Home Run record card, the 2002 first series product did not include different variations of the Barry Bonds Home Run record cards. Please note, that just as in the basic 2002 Topps set there is no card number 7 as it is still retired in honor of Mickey Mantle. In addition, the foil-coated subset cards from the basic Topps set (cards 332-365 and 696-719) were NOT replicated for this Chrome set, thus it's considered complete at 660 cards. Notable Rookie Cards include Kazuhisa Ishii and Joe Mauer.

COMPLETE SET (660) 100.00 250.00
COMPLETE SERIES 1 (330) 50.00 125.00
COMPLETE SERIES 2 (330) 50.00 125.00
COMMON (1-331/366-695) .20 .50
COMMON (307-326/671-690) .60 1.50
COMMON (327-331/691-695) .60 1.50
VINTAGE TOPPS CARD SER.1 ODDS 1:110
VINTAGE TOPPS CARD SER.2 ODDS 1:70
1 Pedro Martinez .60 1.50
2 Mike Stanton .20 .50
3 Brad Penny .20 .50
4 Mike Matheny .20 .50
5 Johnny Damon .60 1.50
6 Bret Boone .40 1.00
8 Chris Truby .20 .50
9 B.J. Surhoff .40 1.00
10 Mike Hampton .40 1.00
11 Juan Pierre .40 1.00
12 Mark Buehrle .40 1.00
13 Bob Abreu .40 1.00
14 David Cone .40 1.00
15 Aaron Sele .20 .50
16 Fernando Tatis .20 .50
17 Bobby Jones .20 .50
18 Rick Helling .20 .50
19 Dmitri Young .40 1.00
20 Mike Mussina .60 1.50
21 Mike Sweeney .40 1.00
22 Cristian Guzman .20 .50
23 Ryan Kohlmeier .20 .50
24 Adam Kennedy .20 .50
25 Larry Walker .40 1.00
26 Eric Davis .40 1.00
27 Jason Tyner .20 .50
28 Eric Young .20 .50
29 Jason Marquis .20 .50
30 Luis Gonzalez .40 1.00
31 Kevin Tapani .20 .50
32 Orlando Cabrera .40 1.00
33 Marty Cordova .20 .50
34 Brad Ausmus .40 1.00
35 Livan Hernandez .40 1.00
36 Alex Gonzalez .20 .50
37 Edgar Renteria .40 1.00
38 Bengie Molina .20 .50
39 Frank Menechino .20 .50
40 Rafael Palmeiro .60 1.50
41 Brad Fullmer .20 .50
42 Julio Zuleta .20 .50
43 Darren Dreifort .20 .50
44 Trot Nixon .40 1.00
45 Trevor Hoffman .40 1.00
46 Vladimir Nunez .20 .50
47 Mark Kotsay .40 1.00
48 Kenny Rogers .40 1.00
49 Ben Petrick .20 .50
50 Jeff Bagwell .60 1.50
51 Juan Encarnacion .20 .50
52 Ramiro Mendoza .20 .50
53 Brian Meadows .20 .50
54 Chad Curtis .20 .50
55 Aramis Ramirez .40 1.00
56 Mark McLemore .20 .50
57 Dante Bichette .40 1.00
58 Scott Schoeneweis .20 .50
59 Jose Cruz Jr. .20 .50
60 Roger Clemens 2.00 5.00
61 Jose Guillen .40 1.00
62 Darren Oliver .20 .50
63 Chris Reitsma .20 .50
64 Jeff Abbott .20 .50
65 Robin Ventura .40 1.00
66 Denny Neagle .20 .50
67 Al Martin .20 .50
68 Benito Santiago .40 1.00
69 Roy Oswalt .40 1.00
70 Juan Gonzalez .40 1.00
71 Garret Anderson .40 1.00
72 Bobby Bonilla .40 1.00
73 Danny Bautista .20 .50
74 J.T. Snow .40 1.00
75 Derek Jeter 2.50 6.00
76 John Olerud .40 1.00
77 Kevin Appier .40 1.00
78 Phil Nevin .40 1.00
79 Sean Casey .40 1.00
80 Troy Glaus .40 1.00
81 Joe Randa .40 1.00
82 Jose Valentin .20 .50
83 Ricky Bottalico .20 .50
84 Todd Zeile .40 1.00
85 Barry Larkin .60 1.50
86 Bob Wickman .20 .50
87 Jeff Shaw .20 .50
88 Greg Vaughn .20 .50
89 Fernando Vina .20 .50
90 Mark Mulder .40 1.00
91 Paul Bako .20 .50
92 Aaron Boone .40 1.00
93 Esteban Loaiza .20 .50
94 Richie Sexson .40 1.00
95 Alfonso Soriano .40 1.00
96 Tony Womack .20 .50
97 Paul Shuey .20 .50
98 Melvin Mora .40 1.00
99 Tony Gwynn 1.25 3.00
100 Vladimir Guerrero 1.00 2.50
101 Keith Osik .20 .50
102 Bud Smith .20 .50
103 Scott Williamson .20 .50
104 Daryle Ward .20 .50
105 Doug Mientkiewicz .40 1.00
106 Stan Javier .20 .50
107 Russ Ortiz .20 .50
108 Wade Miller .20 .50
109 Luke Prokopec .20 .50
110 Andruw Jones .60 1.50
111 Ron Coomer .20 .50
112 Dan Wilson .20 .50
113 Luis Castillo .20 .50
114 Derek Bell .20 .50
115 Gary Sheffield .40 1.00
116 Ruben Rivera .20 .50
117 Paul O'Neill .60 1.50
118 Craig Paquette .20 .50
119 Kelvim Escobar .20 .50
120 Brad Radke .40 1.00
121 Jorge Fabregas .20 .50
122 Randy Winn .20 .50
123 Tom Goodwin .20 .50
124 Jaret Wright .20 .50
125 Barry Bonds HR 73 5.00 12.00
126 Al Leiter .20 .50
127 Ben Davis .20 .50
128 Frank Catalanotto .20 .50
129 Jose Cabrera .20 .50
130 Magglio Ordonez .40 1.00
131 Jose Macias .20 .50
132 Ted Lilly .20 .50
133 Chris Holt .20 .50
134 Eric Milton .20 .50
135 Shannon Stewart .40 1.00
136 Omar Olivares .20 .50
137 David Segui .20 .50
138 Jeff Nelson .20 .50
139 Matt Williams .40 1.00
140 Ellis Burks .40 1.00
141 Jason Bere .20 .50
142 Jimmy Haynes .20 .50
143 Ramon Hernandez .20 .50
144 Craig Counsell .20 .50
145 John Smoltz .60 1.50
146 Homer Bush .20 .50
147 Quilvio Veras .20 .50
148 Esteban Yan .20 .50
149 Ramon Ortiz .20 .50
150 Carlos Delgado .40 1.00
151 Lee Stevens .20 .50
152 Wil Cordero .20 .50
153 Mike Bordick .40 1.00
154 John Flaherty .20 .50
155 Omar Daal .20 .50
156 Todd Ritchie .20 .50
157 Carl Everett .40 1.00
158 Scott Sullivan .20 .50
159 Deivi Cruz .20 .50
160 Albert Pujols 2.00 5.00
161 Royce Clayton .20 .50
162 Jeff Suppan .20 .50
163 C.C. Sabathia .40 1.00
164 Jimmy Rollins .40 1.00
165 Rickey Henderson 1.00 2.50
166 Rey Ordonez .20 .50
167 Shawn Estes .20 .50
168 Reggie Sanders .40 1.00
169 Jon Lieber .20 .50
170 Armando Benitez .20 .50
171 Mike Remlinger .20 .50
172 Billy Wagner .40 1.00
173 Troy Percival .40 1.00
174 Devon White .40 1.00
175 Ivan Rodriguez .60 1.50
176 Dustin Hermanson .20 .50
177 Brian Anderson .20 .50
178 Graeme Lloyd .20 .50
179 Russell Branyan .20 .50
180 Bobby Higginson .40 1.00
181 Alex Gonzalez .20 .50
182 John Franco .40 1.00
183 Sidney Ponson .20 .50
184 Jose Mesa .20 .50
185 Todd Hollandsworth .20 .50
186 Kevin Young .20 .50
187 Tim Wakefield .40 1.00
188 Craig Biggio .60 1.50
189 Jason Isringhausen .40 1.00
190 Mark Quinn .20 .50
191 Glendon Rusch .20 .50
192 Damian Miller .20 .50
193 Sandy Alomar Jr. .20 .50
194 Scott Brosius .40 1.00
195 Dave Martinez .20 .50
196 Danny Graves .20 .50
197 Shea Hillenbrand .40 1.00
198 Jimmy Anderson .20 .50
199 Travis Lee .20 .50
200 Randy Johnson 1.00 2.50
201 Carlos Beltran .40 1.00
202 Jerry Hairston .20 .50
203 Jesus Sanchez .20 .50
204 Eddie Taubensee .20 .50
205 David Wells .40 1.00
206 Russ Davis .20 .50
207 Michael Barrett .20 .50
208 Marquis Grissom .40 1.00
209 Byung-Hyun Kim .40 1.00
210 Hideo Nomo 1.00 2.50
211 Ryan Rupe .20 .50
212 Ricky Gutierrez .20 .50
213 Darryl Kile .40 1.00
214 Rico Brogna .20 .50
215 Terrence Long .20 .50
216 Mike Jackson .20 .50
217 Jamey Wright .20 .50
218 Adrian Beltre .40 1.00
219 Benny Agbayani .20 .50
220 Chuck Knoblauch .40 1.00
221 Randy Wolf .20 .50
222 Andy Ashby .20 .50
223 Corey Koskie .20 .50
224 Roger Cedeno .20 .50
225 Ichiro Suzuki 2.00 5.00
226 Keith Foulke .40 1.00
227 Ryan Minor .20 .50
228 Shawon Dunston .20 .50
229 Alex Cora .20 .50
230 Jeromy Burnitz .40 1.00
231 Mark Grace .60 1.50
232 Aubrey Huff .40 1.00
233 Jeffrey Hammonds .20 .50
234 Olmedo Saenz .20 .50
235 Brian Jordan .40 1.00
236 Jeremy Giambi .20 .50
237 Joe Girardi .20 .50
238 Eric Gagne .40 1.00
239 Masato Yoshii .20 .50
240 Greg Maddux 1.50 4.00
241 Bryan Rekar .20 .50
242 Ray Durham .40 1.00
243 Torii Hunter .40 1.00
244 Derrek Lee .60 1.50
245 Jim Edmonds .40 1.00
246 Einar Diaz .20 .50
247 Brian Bohanon .20 .50
248 Ron Belliard .20 .50
249 Mike Lowell .40 1.00
250 Sammy Sosa 1.00 2.50
251 Richard Hidalgo .20 .50
252 Bartolo Colon .40 1.00
253 Jorge Posada .60 1.50
254 Latroy Hawkins .20 .50
255 Paul LoDuca .40 1.00
256 Carlos Febles .20 .50
257 Nelson Cruz .20 .50
258 Edgardo Alfonzo .20 .50
259 Joey Hamilton .20 .50
260 Cliff Floyd .40 1.00
261 Wes Helms .20 .50
262 Jay Bell .40 1.00
263 Mike Cameron .20 .50
264 Paul Konerko .40 1.00
265 Jeff Kent .40 1.00
266 Robert Fick .20 .50
267 Allen Levrault .20 .50
268 Placido Polanco .20 .50
269 Marlon Anderson .20 .50
270 Mariano Rivera 1.00 2.50
271 Chan Ho Park .40 1.00
272 Jose Vizcaino .20 .50
273 Jeff D'Amico .20 .50
274 Mark Gardner .20 .50
275 Travis Fryman .40 1.00
276 Darren Lewis .20 .50
277 Bruce Bochy MG .20 .50
278 Jerry Manuel MG .20 .50
279 Bob Brenly MG .20 .50
280 Don Baylor MG .40 1.00
281 Davey Lopes MG .20 .50
282 Jerry Narron MG .20 .50
283 Tony Muser MG .20 .50
284 Hal McRae MG .40 1.00
285 Bobby Cox MG .20 .50
286 Larry Dierker MG .20 .50
287 Phil Garner MG .40 1.00
288 Joe Kerrigan MG .20 .50
289 Bobby Valentine MG .20 .50
290 Dusty Baker MG .40 1.00
291 Lloyd McClendon MG .20 .50
292 Mike Scioscia MG .20 .50
293 Buck Martinez MG .20 .50
294 Larry Bowa MG .40 1.00
295 Tony LaRussa MG .40 1.00
296 Jeff Torborg MG .20 .50
297 Tom Kelly MG .20 .50
298 Mike Hargrove MG .20 .50
299 Art Howe MG .20 .50
300 Lou Piniella MG .40 1.00
301 Charlie Manuel MG .20 .50
302 Buddy Bell MG .40 1.00
303 Tony Perez MG .40 1.00
304 Bob Boone MG .40 1.00
305 Joe Torre MG .60 1.50
306 Jim Tracy MG .20 .50
307 Jason Lane PROS .60 1.50
308 Chris George PROS .60 1.50
309 Hank Blalock PROS 1.00 2.50
310 Joe Borchard PROS .60 1.50
311 Marlon Byrd PROS .60 1.50
312 Raymond Cabrera PROS RC .60 1.50
313 Freddy Sanchez PROS RC 2.50 6.00
314 Scott Wiggins PROS RC .60 1.50
315 Jason Maule PROS RC .60 1.50
316 Dionys Cesar PROS RC .60 1.50
317 Boof Bonser PROS .60 1.50
318 Juan Tolentino PROS RC .60 1.50
319 Earl Snyder PROS RC .60 1.50
320 Travis Wade PROS RC .60 1.50
321 Napolean Calzado PROS RC .60 1.50
322 Eric Glaser PROS RC .60 1.50
323 Craig Kuzmic PROS RC .60 1.50
324 Nic Jackson PROS RC .60 1.50
325 Mike Rivera PROS .60 1.50
326 Jason Bay PROS RC 3.00 8.00
327 Chris Smith DP .60 1.50
328 Jake Gautreau DP .60 1.50
329 Gabe Gross DP .60 1.50
330 Kenny Baugh DP .60 1.50
331 J.D. Martin DP .60 1.50
366 Pat Meares .20 .50
367 Mike Lieberthal .40 1.00
368 Larry Bigbie .20 .50
369 Ron Gant .40 1.00
370 Moises Alou .40 1.00
371 Chad Kreuter .20 .50
372 Willis Roberts .20 .50
373 Toby Hall .20 .50
374 Miguel Batista .20 .50
375 John Burkett .20 .50
376 Cory Lidle .20 .50
377 Nick Neugebauer .20 .50
378 Jay Payton .20 .50
379 Steve Karsay .20 .50
380 Eric Chavez .40 1.00
381 Kelly Stinnett .20
382 Jarrod Washburn .20
383 Rick White .20
384 Jeff Conine .40
385 Fred McGriff .60
386 Marvin Benard .20
387 Joe Crede .40
388 Dennis Cook .20
389 Rick Reed .20
390 Tom Glavine .60
391 Rondell White .40
392 Matt Morris .40
393 Pat Rapp .20
394 Robert Person .20
395 Omar Vizquel .60
396 Jeff Cirillo .20
397 Dave Mlicki .20
398 Jose Ortiz .20
399 Ryan Dempster .20
400 Curt Schilling .40
401 Peter Bergeron .20
402 Kyle Lohse .20
403 Craig Wilson .20
404 David Justice .40
405 Darin Erstad .40
406 Jose Mercedes .20
407 Carl Pavano .40
408 Albie Lopez .20
409 Alex Ochoa .20
410 Chipper Jones 1.00
411 Tyler Houston .20
412 Dean Palmer .40
413 Damian Jackson .20
414 Josh Towers .20
415 Rafael Furcal .40
416 Mike Morgan .20
417 Herb Perry .20
418 Mike Sirotka .20
419 Mark Wohlers .20
420 Nomar Garciaparra 1.50
421 Felipe Lopez .20
422 Joe McEwing .20
423 Jacque Jones .40
424 Julio Franco .40
425 Frank Thomas 1.00
426 So Taguchi RC 1.00
427 Kazuhisa Ishii RC 1.00
428 D'Angelo Jimenez .20
429 Chris Stynes .20
430 Kerry Wood .40
431 Chris Singleton .20
432 Erubiel Durazo .20
433 Matt Lawton .20
434 Bill Mueller .40
435 Jose Canseco .60
436 Ben Grieve .20
437 Terry Mulholland .20
438 David Bell .20
439 A.J. Pierzynski .40
440 Adam Dunn .40
441 Jon Garland .40
442 Jeff Fassero .20
443 Julio Lugo .20
444 Carlos Guillen .40
445 Orlando Hernandez .40
446 Mark Loretta .20
447 Scott Spiezio .20
448 Kevin Millwood .40
449 Jamie Moyer .40
450 Todd Helton .60
451 Todd Walker .20
452 Jose Lima .20
453 Brook Fordyce .20
454 Aaron Rowand .40
455 Barry Zito .40
456 Eric Owens .20
457 Charles Nagy .20
458 Raul Ibanez .20
459 Joe Mays .20
460 Jim Thome .60
461 Adam Eaton .20
462 Felix Martinez .20
463 Vernon Wells .40
464 Donnie Sadler .20
465 Tony Clark .20
466 Jose Hernandez .20
467 Ramon Martinez .20
468 Rusty Greer .40
469 Rod Barajas .20
470 Lance Berkman .40
471 Brady Anderson .40
472 Pedro Astacio .20
473 Shane Halter .20
474 Bret Prinz .20
475 Edgar Martinez .60
476 Steve Trachsel .20
477 Gary Matthews Jr. .20
478 Ismael Valdes .20
479 Juan Uribe .20
480 Shawn Green .40
481 Kirk Rueter .20
482 Damion Easley .20
483 Chris Carpenter .40
484 Kris Benson .20
485 Antonio Alfonseca .20
486 Kyle Farnsworth .20
487 Brandon Lyon .20
488 Hideki Irabu .20
489 David Ortiz 1.00
490 Mike Piazza 1.50
491 Derek Lowe .40
492 Chris Gomez .20
493 Mark Johnson .20

4 John Rocker .40 1.00
5 Eric Karros .40 1.00
6 Bill Haselman .20 .50
7 Dave Veres .20 .50
8 Pete Harnisch .20 .50
9 Tomokazu Ohka .20 .50
00 Barry Bonds 2.50 6.00
01 David Dellucci .20 .50
02 Wendell Magee .20 .50
03 Tom Gordon .20 .50
04 Javier Vazquez .40 1.00
05 Ben Sheets .40 1.00
06 Wilton Guerrero .20 .50
07 John Halama .20 .50
08 Mark Redman .20 .50
09 Jack Wilson .20 .50
10 Bernie Williams .60 1.50
11 Miguel Cairo .20 .50
12 Denny Hocking .20 .50
13 Tony Batista .20 .50
14 Mark Grudzielanek .20 .50
15 Jose Vidro .20 .50
16 Sterling Hitchcock .20 .50
17 Billy Koch .20 .50
18 Matt Clement .40 1.00
19 Bruce Chen .20 .50
20 Roberto Alomar .60 1.50
21 Orlando Palmeiro .20 .50
22 Steve Finley .40 1.00
23 Danny Patterson .20 .50
24 Terry Adams .20 .50
25 Tino Martinez .60 1.50
26 Tony Armas Jr. .20 .50
27 Geoff Jenkins .20 .50
28 Kerry Robinson .20 .50
29 Corey Patterson .20 .50
30 Brian Giles .40 1.00
31 Jose Jimenez .20 .50
32 Joe Kennedy .20 .50
33 Armando Rios .20 .50
34 Osvaldo Fernandez .20 .50
35 Rubon Sicrra .40 1.00
36 Octavio Dotel .20 .50
37 Luis Sojo .20 .50
38 Brent Butler .20 .50
39 Pablo Ozuna .20 .50
40 Freddy Garcia .40 1.00
41 Chad Durbin .20 .50
42 Orlando Merced .20 .50
43 Michael Tucker .20 .50
44 Roberto Hernandez .20 .50
45 Pat Burrell .40 1.00
46 A.J. Burnett .40 1.00
47 Bubba Trammell .20 .50
48 Scott Elarton .20 .50
49 Mike Darr .20 .50
50 Ken Griffey Jr. 2.00 5.00
551 Ugueth Urbina .20 .50
552 Todd Jones .20 .50
553 Delino Deshields .20 .50
554 Adam Piatt .20 .50
555 Jason Kendall .40 1.00
556 Hector Ortiz .20 .50
557 Turk Wendell .20 .50
558 Rob Bell .20 .50
559 Sun Woo Kim .20 .50
560 Raul Mondesi .40 1.00
561 Brent Abernathy .20 .50
562 Seth Etherton .20 .50
563 Shawn Woolen .20 .50
564 Jay Buhner .40 1.00
565 Andres Galarraga .40 1.00
566 Shane Reynolds .20 .50
567 Rod Beck .20 .50
568 Dee Brown .20 .50
569 Pedro Feliz .20 .50
570 Ryan Klesko .40 1.00
571 John Vander Wal .20 .50
572 Nick Bierbrodt .20 .50
573 Joe Nathan .40 1.00
574 James Baldwin .20 .50
575 J.D. Drew .40 1.00
576 Greg Colbrunn .20 .50
577 Doug Glanville .20 .50
578 Brandon Duckworth .20 .50
579 Shawn Chacon .20 .50
580 Rich Aurilia .20 .50
581 Chuck Finley .40 1.00
582 Abraham Nunez .20 .50
583 Kenny Lofton .40 1.00
584 Brian Daubach .20 .50
585 Miguel Tejada .40 1.00
586 Nate Cornejo .20 .50
587 Kazuhiro Sasaki .40 1.00
588 Chris Richard .20 .50
589 Armando Reynoso .20 .50
590 Tim Hudson .40 1.00
591 Neifi Perez .20 .50
592 Steve Cox .20 .50
593 Henry Blanco .20 .50
594 Ricky Ledee .20 .50
595 Tim Salmon .60 1.50
596 Luis Rivas .20 .50
597 Jeff Zimmerman .20 .50
598 Matt Stairs .20 .50
599 Preston Wilson .40 1.00
600 Mark McGwire 2.50 6.00
601 Timo Perez .20 .50
602 Matt Anderson .20 .50
603 Todd Hundley .20 .50
604 Rick Ankiel .20 .50
605 Tsuyoshi Shinjo .40 1.00
606 Woody Williams .20 .50
607 Jason LaRue .20 .50
608 Carlos Lee .40 1.00
609 Russ Johnson .20 .50
610 Scott Rolen .60 1.50
611 Brent Mayne .20 .50
612 Darrin Fletcher .20 .50
613 Ray Lankford .40 1.00
614 Troy O'Leary .20 .50
615 Javier Lopez .40 1.00
616 Randy Velarde .20 .50
617 Vinny Castilla .40 1.00
618 Milton Bradley .40 1.00
619 Ruben Mateo .20 .50
620 Jason Giambi Yankees .40 1.00
621 Andy Benes .20 .50
622 Joe Mauer RC 6.00 15.00
623 Andy Pettitte .60 1.50
624 Jose Offerman .20 .50
625 Mo Vaughn .40 1.00
626 Steve Sparks .20 .50
627 Mike Matthews .20 .50
628 Robb Nen .40 1.00
629 Kip Wells .20 .50
630 Kevin Brown .40 1.00
631 Arthur Rhodes .20 .50
632 Gabe Kapler .40 1.00
633 Jermaine Dye .40 1.00
634 Josh Beckett .40 1.00
635 Pokey Reese .20 .50
636 Benji Gil .20 .50
637 Marcus Giles .40 1.00
638 Julian Tavarez .20 .50
639 Jason Schmidt .40 1.00
640 Alex Rodriguez 1.25 3.00
641 Anaheim Angels TC .40 1.00
642 Arizona Diamondbacks TC .60 1.50
643 Atlanta Braves TC .40 1.00
644 Baltimore Orioles TC .40 1.00
645 Boston Red Sox TC .40 1.00
646 Chicago Cubs TC .40 1.00
647 Chicago White Sox TC .40 1.00
648 Cincinnati Reds TC .40 1.00
649 Cleveland Indians TC .40 1.00
650 Colorado Rockies TC .40 1.00
651 Detroit Tigers TC .40 1.00
652 Florida Marlins TC .40 1.00
653 Houston Astros TC .40 1.00
654 Kansas City Royals TC .40 1.00
655 Los Angeles Dodgers TC .40 1.00
656 Milwaukee Brewers TC .40 1.00
657 Minnesota Twins TC .40 1.00
658 Montreal Expos TC .40 1.00
659 New York Mets TC .40 1.00
660 New York Yankees TC 1.00 2.50
661 Oakland Athletics TC .40 1.00
662 Philadelphia Phillies TC .40 1.00
663 Pittsburgh Pirates TC .40 1.00
664 San Diego Padres TC .40 1.00
665 San Francisco Giants TC .40 1.00
666 Seattle Mariners TC .60 1.50
667 St. Louis Cardinals TC .40 1.00
668 Tampa Bay Devil Rays TC .40 1.00
669 Texas Rangers TC .40 1.00
670 Toronto Blue Jays TC .40 1.00
671 Juan Cruz PROS .60 1.50
672 Kevin Cash PROS RC .60 1.50
673 Jimmy Gobble PROS RC .60 1.50
674 Mike Hill PROS RC .60 1.50
675 Taylor Buchholz PROS RC .60 1.50
676 Bill Hall PROS .60 1.50
677 Brett Roneberg PROS RC .60 1.50
678 Royce Huffman PROS RC .60 1.50
679 Chris Tritle PROS RC .60 1.50
680 Nate Espy PROS .60 1.50
681 Nick Alvarez PROS RC .60 1.50
682 Jason Botts PROS RC .60 1.50
683 Ryan Gripp PROS RC .60 1.50
684 Dan Phillips PROS RC .60 1.50
685 Pablo Arias PROS RC .60 1.50
686 John Rodriguez PROS RC 1.00 2.50
687 Rich Harden PROS RC 3.00 8.00
688 Neal Frendling PROS RC .60 1.50
689 Rich Thompson PROS RC .60 1.50
690 Greg Montalbano PROS RC .60 1.50
691 Len Dinardo DP RC .60 1.50
692 Ryan Raburn DP RC 1.25 3.00
693 Josh Barfield DP RC 2.00 5.00
694 David Bacani DP RC .60 1.50
695 Dan Johnson DP RC 1.00 2.50

2002 Topps Chrome Black Refractors

*BLACK: 6X TO 15X BASIC CARDS
*BLACK 307-331/671-695: 5X TO 12X BASIC
SER.2 STATED ODDS 1:21 HOBBY
STATED PRINT RUN 50 SERIAL #'d SETS
125 Barry Bonds HR 73 175.00 300.00

2002 Topps Chrome Gold Refractors

*GOLD: 2X TO 5X BASIC
*GOLD 307-331/671-695: 1.25X TO 3X BASIC
SER.1 AND 2 STATED ODDS 1:4

2002 Topps Chrome '52 Reprints

Issued in packs at stated odds of one in eight, these nineteen reprint cards feature players who participated in the 1952 World Series which was won by the New York Yankees.

COMPLETE SET (19) 20.00 50.00
COMPLETE SERIES 1 (9) 10.00 25.00
COMPLETE SERIES 2 (10) 10.00 25.00
SER.1 AND 2 STATED ODDS 1:8
*REF: .75X TO 2X BASIC 52 REPRINTS
SER.1 AND 2 REFRACTOR ODDS 1:24
52R1 Roy Campanella 2.00 5.00
52R2 Duke Snider 1.50 4.00
52R3 Carl Erskine 1.50 4.00
52R4 Andy Pafko 1.50 4.00
52R5 Johnny Mize 1.50 4.00
52R6 Billy Martin 1.50 4.00
52R7 Phil Rizzuto 2.00 5.00
52R8 Gil McDougald 1.50 4.00
52R9 Allie Reynolds 1.50 4.00
52R10 Jackie Robinson 2.00 5.00
52R11 Preacher Roe 1.50 4.00
52R12 Gil Hodges 2.00 5.00
52R13 Billy Cox 1.50 4.00
52R14 Yogi Berra 2.00 5.00
52R15 Gene Woodling 1.50 4.00
52R16 Johnny Sain 1.50 4.00
52R17 Ralph Houk 1.50 4.00
52R18 Joe Collins 1.50 4.00
52R19 Hank Bauer 1.50 4.00

2002 Topps Chrome 5-Card Stud Aces Relics

Inserted in second series packs at a stated rate of one in 140, these five cards feature leading pitchers along with a game-worn jersey swatch.

SER.2 STATED ODDS 1:140
5AAL Al Leiter Jsy 6.00 15.00
5ABZ Barry Zito Jsy 6.00 15.00
5ACS Curt Schilling Jsy 6.00 15.00
5AKB Kevin Brown Jsy 6.00 15.00
5ATH Tim Hudson Jsy 6.00 15.00

2002 Topps Chrome 5-Card Stud Deuces are Wild Relics

Inserted in second series packs at an overall stated ratc of onc in 428, thcsc threc cards feature teammates as well as a piece of game-used memorabilia from each player.

SER.2 BAT ODDS 1:1098
SER.2 UNIFORM ODDS 1:704
SER.2 OVERALL ODDS 1:428
5DBT Bernie Bat/Tino Bat 15.00 40.00
5DCA Chipper Bat/Andruw Bat 20.00 50.00
5DRC Dempster Uni/Floyd Uni 6.00 15.00

2002 Topps Chrome 5-Card Stud Jack of all Trades Relics

Inserted in second series packs at a stated rate of one in 428, these three cards feature players who have all five tools along with a piece of game-used memorabilia of that player.

SER.2 BAT ODDS 1:1098
SER.2 JERSEY ODDS 1:704
SER.2 OVERALL ODDS 1:428
5JCJ Chipper Jones Jsy 10.00 25.00
5JMO Magglio Ordonez Bat 6.00 15.00

2002 Topps Chrome 5-Card Stud Kings of the Clubhouse Relics

Inserted in second series packs at a stated rate of one in 303, these three cards feature three of the best team leaders along with a piece of game-used memorabilia from the featured player.

SER.2 BAT ODDS 1:2204
SER.2 JERSEY ODDS 1:704
SER.2 UNIFORM ODDS 1:704
SER.2 OVERALL ODDS 1:303
5KJB Jeff Bagwell Uniform 8.00 20.00
5KTG Tony Gwynn Jsy 12.50 30.00

2002 Topps Chrome 5-Card Stud Three of a Kind Relics

Inserted into second series packs at a stated rate of one in 689, these three cards feature a group of three teammates along with a piece of game-used memorabilia from each player.

SER.2 STATED ODDS 1:689
B ='s Bat, J ='s Jsy, U ='s Uniform
5TAIR A.Rod B/I.Rod J/Raffy U 12.00 30.00
5TBEJ Boone B/Edgar B/Olerud B 12.00 30.00
5TJCL Bag U/Biggio B/Berk B 40.00 80.00

2002 Topps Chrome Summer School Like Father Like Son Relics

Issued in packs at stated odds of one in 790, this card features memorabilia from Preston and Mookie Wilson.

SER.1 STATED ODDS 1:790
FSCWI P.Wilson U/M.Wilson J 6.00 15.00

2002 Topps Chrome Summer School Battery Mates Relics

Inserted at overall odds of one in 349, these two cards feature memorabilia from a pitcher and catcher from the same team. The Hampton/Petrick card was seeded at a rate of 1:716 and the Glavine/Lopez at 1:681.

SER.1 GROUP A ODDS 1:716
SER.1 GROUP B ODDS 1:681
SER.1 OVERALL STATED ODDS 1:349
BMCGL T.Glavine J/J.Lopez J B 10.00 25.00
BMCHP M.Hampton J/B.Petrick J A 6.00 15.00

2002 Topps Chrome Summer School Top of the Order Relics

Inserted into packs at an overall rate of one in 106, these 12 cards featured players who lead off for their teams along with a memorabilia piece. Uniforms (a.k.a. pants), jerseys and bats were utilized for this set. Bat cards were seeded into five different groups at the following ratios: Group A 1:1383, Group B 1:1538, Group C 1:3170, Group D 1:2902, Group E 1:2544. Jersey cards were seeded into two groups as follows: Group A 1:790 and Group B 1:659. Uniform cards were seeded into three groups as follows: Group A 1:920, Group B 1:651 and Group C 1:614.

SER.1 BAT GROUP A ODDS 1:1383
SER.1 BAT GROUP B ODDS 1:1538
SER.1 BAT GROUP C ODDS 1:3170
SER.1 BAT GROUP D ODDS 1:2902
SER.1 BAT GROUP E ODDS 1:2544
SER.1 JSY GROUP A ODDS 1:790
SER.1 JSY GROUP B ODDS 1:659
SER.1 UNI GROUP A ODDS 1:920
SER.1 UNI GROUP B ODDS 1:651
SER.1 UNI GROUP C ODDS 1:614
SER.1 OVERALL STATED ODDS 1:106
TOCBA Benny Agbayani Uni C 6.00 15.00
TOCCB Craig Biggio Uni A 10.00 25.00
TOCCK Chuck Knoblauch Bat E 6.00 15.00
TOCJD Johnny Damon Bat B 10.00 25.00
TOCJK Jason Kendall Bat D 6.00 15.00
TOCJP Juan Pierre Bat A 6.00 15.00
TOCKL Kenny Lofton Uni B 6.00 15.00
TOCPB Peter Bergeron Jsy A 6.00 15.00
TOCPL Paul LoDuca Bat A 6.00 15.00
TOCRF Rafael Furcal Bat C 6.00 15.00
TOCRH Rickey Henderson Bat B 10.00 25.00
TOCSS Shannon Stewart Jsy B 6.00 15.00

2002 Topps Chrome Traded

Inserted at a stated rate of two per 2002 Topps Traded Hobby or Retail Pack and sever per 2002 Topps Traded HTA pack, this is a complete parallel of the 2002 Topps Traded set. Unlike the regular Topps Traded set, all cards are printed in equal quantities.

COMPLETE SET (275) 30.00 60.00
2 PER 2002 TOPPS TRADED HOBBY PACK
7 PER 2002 TOPPS TRADED HTA PACK
2 PER 2002 TOPPS TRADED RETAIL PACK
T1 Jeff Weaver .20 .50
T2 Jay Powell .20 .50
T3 Alex Gonzalez .20 .50
T4 Jason Isringhausen .30 .75
T5 Tyler Houston .20 .50
T6 Ben Broussard .20 .50
T7 Chuck Knoblauch .30 .75
T8 Brian L. Hunter .20 .50
T9 Dustan Mohr .20 .50
T10 Eric Hinske .20 .50
T11 Roger Cedeno .20 .50
T12 Eddie Perez .20 .50
T13 Jeromy Burnitz .30 .75
T14 Bartolo Colon .30 .75
T15 Rick Helling .20 .50
T16 Dan Plesac .20 .50
T17 Scott Strickland .20 .50
T18 Antonio Alfonseca .20 .50
T19 Ricky Gutierrez .20 .50
T20 John Valentin .20 .50
T21 Raul Mondesi .30 .75
T22 Ben Davis .20 .50
T23 Nelson Figueroa .20 .50
T24 Earl Snyder .20 .50
T25 Robin Ventura .30 .75
T26 Jimmy Haynes .20 .50
T27 Kenny Kelly .20 .50
T28 Morgan Ensberg .30 .75
T29 Reggie Sanders .30 .75
T30 Shigetoshi Hasegawa .30 .75
T31 Mike Timlin .20 .50
T32 Russell Branyan .20 .50
T33 Alan Embree .20 .50
T34 D'Angelo Jimenez .20 .50
T35 Kent Mercker .20 .50
T36 Jesse Orosco .20 .50
T37 Gregg Zaun .20 .50
T38 Reggie Taylor .20 .50
T39 Andres Galarraga .30 .75
T40 Chris Truby .20 .50
T41 Bruce Chen .20 .50
T42 Darren Lewis .20 .50
T43 Ryan Kohlmeier .20 .50
T44 John McDonald .20 .50
T45 Omar Daal .20 .50
T46 Matt Clement .30 .75
T47 Glendon Rusch .20 .50
T48 Chan Ho Park .30 .75
T49 Benny Agbayani .20 .50
T50 Juan Gonzalez .30 .75
T51 Carlos Baerga .20 .50
T52 Tim Raines .30 .75
T53 Kevin Appier .30 .75
T54 Marty Cordova .20 .50
T55 Jeff D'Amico .20 .50
T56 Dmitri Young .30 .75
T57 Roosevelt Brown .20 .50
T58 Dustin Hermanson .20 .50
T59 Jose Rijo .20 .50
T60 Todd Ritchie .20 .50
T61 Lee Stevens .20 .50
T62 Placido Polanco .20 .50
T63 Eric Young .20 .50
T64 Chuck Finley .30 .75
T65 Dicky Gonzalez .20 .50
T66 Jose Macias .20 .50
T67 Gabe Kapler .30 .75
T68 Sandy Alomar Jr. .20 .50
T69 Henry Blanco .20 .50
T70 Julian Tavarez .20 .50
T71 Paul Bako .20 .50
T72 Scott Rolen .50 1.25
T73 Brian Jordan .30 .75
T74 Rickey Henderson .75 2.00
T75 Kevin Mench .20 .50
T76 Hideo Nomo .75 2.00
T77 Jeremy Giambi .20 .50
T78 Brad Fullmer .20 .50
T79 Carl Everett .30 .75
T80 David Wells .30 .75
T81 Aaron Sele .20 .50
T82 Todd Hollandsworth .20 .50
T83 Vicente Padilla .20 .50
T84 Kenny Lofton .30 .75
T85 Corky Miller .20 .50
T86 Josh Fogg .20 .50
T87 Cliff Floyd .30 .75
T88 Craig Paquette .20 .50
T89 Jay Payton .20 .50
T90 Carlos Pena .20 .50
T91 Juan Encarnacion .20 .50
T92 Rey Sanchez .20 .50
T93 Ryan Dempster .20 .50
T94 Mario Encarnacion .20 .50
T95 Jorge Julio .20 .50
T96 John Mabry .20 .50
T97 Todd Zeile .30 .75
T98 Johnny Damon .50 1.25
T99 Deivi Cruz .20 .50
T100 Gary Sheffield .30 .75
T101 Ted Lilly .20 .50
T102 Todd Van Poppel .20 .50
T103 Shawn Estes .20 .50
T104 Cesar Izturis .20 .50
T105 Ron Coomer .20 .50
T106 Grady Little MG RC .20 .50
T107 Jimy Williams MGR .20 .50
T108 Tony Pena MGR .20 .50
T109 Frank Robinson MGR .50 1.25
T110 Ron Gardenhire MGR .20 .50
T111 Dennis Tankersley .20 .50
T112 Alejandro Cadena RC .40 1.00
T113 Justin Reid RC .40 1.00
T114 Nate Field RC .40 1.00
T115 Rene Reyes RC .40 1.00
T116 Nelson Castro RC .40 1.00
T117 Miguel Olivo .20 .50
T118 David Espinosa .20 .50
T119 Chris Bootcheck RC .40 1.00
T120 Rob Henkel RC .40 1.00
T121 Steve Bechler RC .40 1.00
T122 Mark Outlaw RC .40 1.00
T123 Henry Pichardo RC .40 1.00
T124 Michael Floyd RC .40 1.00
T125 Richard Lane RC .40 1.00
T126 Pete Zamora RC .40 1.00
T127 Javier Colina .20 .50
T128 Greg Sain RC .40 1.00
T129 Ronnie Merrill .20 .50
T130 Gavin Floyd RC 1.00 2.50
T131 Josh Bonifay RC .40 1.00
T132 Tommy Marx RC .40 1.00
T133 Gary Cates Jr. RC .40 1.00
T134 Neal Cotts RC 1.00 2.50
T135 Angel Berroa .20 .50
T136 Elio Serrano RC .40 1.00
T137 J.J. Putz RC .50 1.25
T138 Ruben Gotay RC .50 1.25
T139 Eddie Rogers .20 .50
T140 Wily Mo Pena .30 .75
T141 Tyler Yates RC .40 1.00
T142 Colin Young RC .30 .75
T143 Chance Caple .20 .50
T144 Ben Howard RC .40 1.00
T145 Ryan Bukvich RC .40 1.00
T146 Cliff Bartosh RC .40 1.00
T147 Brandon Claussen .20 .50
T148 Cristian Guerrero .20 .50
T149 Derrick Lewis .20 .50
T150 Eric Miller RC .40 1.00
T151 Justin Huber RC .75 2.00
T152 Adrian Gonzalez .20 .50
T153 Brian West RC .40 1.00
T154 Chris Baker RC .40 1.00
T155 Drew Henson .20 .50
T156 Scott Hairston RC .50 1.25
T157 Jason Simontacchi RC .40 1.00
T158 Jason Arnold RC .40 1.00
T159 Brandon Phillips .20 .50
T160 Adam Roller RC .40 1.00
T161 Scotty Layfield RC .40 1.00
T162 Freddie Money RC .40 1.00
T163 Noochie Varner RC .40 1.00
T164 Terrance Hill RC .40 1.00
T165 Jeremy Hill RC .40 1.00
T166 Carlos Cabrera RC .40 1.00
T167 Jose Morban RC .40 1.00
T168 Kevin Frederick RC .40 1.00
T169 Mark Teixeira 1.50 4.00
T170 Brian Rogers .20 .50
T171 Anastacio Martinez RC .40 1.00
T172 Bobby Jenks RC 1.50 4.00
T173 David Gil RC .40 1.00
T174 Andres Torres .20 .50
T175 James Barrett RC .40 1.00
T176 Jimmy Journell .20 .50
T177 Brett Kay RC .40 1.00
T178 Jason Young RC .40 1.00
T179 Mark Hamilton RC .40 1.00
T180 Jose Bautista RC 2.50 6.00
T181 Blake McGinley RC .40 1.00
T182 Ryan Mottl RC .40 1.00
T183 Jeff Austin RC .40 1.00
T184 Xavier Nady .20 .50
T185 Kyle Kane RC .40 1.00
T186 Travis Foley RC .40 1.00
T187 Nathan Kaup RC .40 1.00
T188 Eric Cyr .20 .50
T189 Josh Cisneros RC .40 1.00
T190 Brad Nelson RC .40 1.00
T191 Clint Weibl RC .40 1.00
T192 Ron Calloway RC .40 1.00
T193 Jung Bong .20 .50
T194 Rolando Viera RC .40 1.00
T195 Jason Bulger RC .40 1.00
T196 Chone Figgins RC 1.50 4.00
T197 Jimmy Alvarez RC .40 1.00
T198 Joel Crump RC .40 1.00
T199 Ryan Doumit RC .60 1.50
T200 Demetrius Heath RC .40 1.00
T201 John Ennis RC .40 1.00
T202 Doug Sessions RC .40 1.00
T203 Clinton Hosford RC .40 1.00
T204 Chris Narveson RC .40 1.00
T205 Ross Peeples RC .40 1.00
T206 Alex Requena RC .40 1.00
T207 Matt Erickson RC .40 1.00
T208 Brian Forystek RC .40 1.00
T209 Dewon Brazelton .20 .50
T210 Nathan Haynes .20 .50
T211 Jack Cust .20 .50
T212 Jesse Foppert RC .50 1.25
T213 Jesus Cota RC .40 1.00
T214 Juan M. Gonzalez RC .40 1.00
T215 Tim Kalita RC .40 1.00
T216 Manny Delcarmen RC .50 1.25
T217 Jim Kavourias RC .40 1.00
T218 C.J. Wilson RC 1.25 3.00
T219 Edwin Yan RC .40 1.00
T220 Andy Van Hekken .20 .50
T221 Michael Cuddyer .20 .50
T222 Jeff Verplancke RC .40 1.00
T223 Mike Wilson RC .40 1.00
T224 Corwin Malone RC .40 1.00
T225 Chris Snelling RC .60 1.50
T226 Joe Rogers RC .40 1.00
T227 Jason Bay 3.00 8.00
T228 Ezequiel Astacio RC .40 1.00
T229 Joey Hammond RC .40 1.00
T230 Chris Duffy RC .40 1.00
T231 Mark Prior .50 1.25
T232 Hansel Izquierdo RC .40 1.00
T233 Franklyn German RC .40 1.00
T234 Alexis Gomez .20 .50
T235 Jorge Padilla RC .40 1.00
T236 Ryan Snare RC .40 1.00
T237 Deivis Santos .20 .50
T238 Taggert Bozied RC .50 1.25
T239 Mike Peeples RC .40 1.00
T240 Ronald Acuna RC .40 1.00
T241 Koyie Hill .20 .50
T242 Garrett Guzman RC .40 1.00
T243 Ryan Church RC 1.00 2.50
T244 Tony Fontana RC .40 1.00
T245 Keto Anderson RC .40 1.00
T246 Brad Bouras RC .40 1.00
T247 Jason Dubois RC .50 1.25
T248 Angel Guzman RC .75 2.00
T249 Joel Hanrahan RC .40 1.00
T250 Joe Jiannetti RC .40 1.00
T251 Sean Pierce RC .40 1.00
T252 Jake Mauer RC .40 1.00
T253 Marshall McDougall RC .40 1.00
T254 Edwin Almonte RC .40 1.00
T255 Shawn Riggans RC .40 1.00
T256 Steven Shell RC .40 1.00
T257 Kevin Hooper RC .40 1.00
T258 Michael Frick RC .40 1.00
T259 Travis Chapman RC .40 1.00
T260 Tim Hummel RC .40 1.00
T261 Adam Morrissey RC .40 1.00
T262 Dontrelle Willis RC 2.50 6.00
T263 Justin Sherrod RC .40 1.00
T264 Gerald Smiley RC .40 1.00
T265 Tony Miller RC .40 1.00
T266 Nolan Ryan WW 2.00 5.00
T267 Reggie Jackson WW .50 1.25
T268 Steve Garvey WW .30 .75
T269 Wade Boggs WW .50 1.25
T270 Sammy Sosa WW .75 2.00
T271 Curt Schilling WW .30 .75
T272 Mark Grace WW .50 1.25
T273 Jason Giambi WW .20 .50
T274 Ken Griffey Jr. WW 1.50 4.00
T275 Roberto Alomar WW .50 1.25

2002 Topps Chrome Traded Black Refractors

*BLACK REF: 4X TO 10X BASIC
*BLACK REF RC'S: 4X TO 10X BASIC RC'S
STATED ODDS 1:56 HOB/RET, 1:16 HTA
STATED PRINT RUN 100 SERIAL #'d SETS

2002 Topps Chrome Traded Refractors

*REF: 2X TO 5X BASIC
*REF RC'S: 1.5X TO 4X BASIC RC'S
STATED ODDS 1:12 HOB/RET, 1:12 HTA

2003 Topps Chrome

The first series of 2003 Topps Chrome was released in January, 2003. These cards were issued in four card packs which came 24 packs to a box and 10 boxes to a case with an SRP of $3 per pack. Cards numbered 201 through 220 feature players in their first year of Topps cards. The second series, which also consisted of 220 cards, was released in May, 2003. Cards number 421 through 430 were draft pick cards while cards 431 through 440 were two player prospect cards.

COMPLETE SET (440) 20.00 50.00
COMPLETE SERIES 1 (220) 10.00 25.00
COMPLETE SERIES 2 (220) 10.00 25.00
COMMON (1-200/221-420) .40 1.00
COMMON (201-220/421-440) .40 1.00
COM.RC (201-220/409/421-440) .40 1.00
1 Alex Rodriguez 1.25 3.00
2 Eddie Guardado .40 1.00
3 Curt Schilling .60 1.50
4 Andruw Jones .40 1.00
5 Magglio Ordonez .60 1.50
6 Todd Helton .60 1.50
7 Odalis Perez .40 1.00
8 Edgardo Alfonzo .40 1.00
9 Eric Hinske .40 1.00
10 Danny Bautista .40 1.00
11 Sammy Sosa 1.00 2.50
12 Roberto Alomar .60 1.50
13 Roger Clemens 1.25 3.00
14 Austin Kearns .40 1.00
15 Luis Gonzalez .40 1.00
16 Mo Vaughn .40 1.00
17 Alfonso Soriano .60 1.50
18 Orlando Cabrera .40 1.00
19 Hideo Nomo 1.00 2.50
20 Omar Vizquel .60 1.50
21 Greg Maddux 1.25 3.00
22 Fred McGriff .60 1.50
23 Frank Thomas 1.00 2.50
24 Shawn Green .40 1.00
25 Jacque Jones .40 1.00
26 Bernie Williams .60 1.50
27 Corey Patterson .40 1.00
28 Cesar Izturis .40 1.00
29 Larry Walker .60 1.50
30 Darren Dreifort .40 1.00
31 Al Leiter .40 1.00
32 Jason Marquis .40 1.00
33 Sean Casey .40 1.00
34 Craig Counsell .40 1.00
35 Albert Pujols 1.25 3.00
36 Kyle Lohse .40 1.00
37 Paul Lo Duca .40 1.00
38 Roy Oswalt .60 1.50
39 Danny Graves .40 1.00
40 Kevin Millwood .40 1.00
41 Lance Berkman .60 1.50
42 Denny Hocking .40 1.00
43 Jose Valentin .40 1.00
44 Josh Beckett .40 1.00
45 Nomar Garciaparra .60 1.50
46 Craig Biggio .60 1.50
47 Omar Daal .40 1.00
48 Jimmy Rollins .60 1.50
49 Jermaine Dye .40 1.00
50 Edgar Renteria .40 1.00
51 Brandon Duckworth .40 1.00
52 Luis Castillo .40 1.00
53 Andy Ashby .40 1.00
54 Mike Williams .40 1.00
55 Benito Santiago .40 1.00
56 Bret Boone .40 1.00
57 Randy Wolf .40 1.00
58 Ivan Rodriguez .60 1.50
59 Shannon Stewart .40 1.00
60 Jose Cruz Jr. .40 1.00
61 Billy Wagner .40 1.00
62 Alex Gonzalez .40 1.00
63 Ichiro Suzuki 1.25 3.00
64 Joe McEwing .40 1.00
65 Mark Mulder .40 1.00
66 Mike Cameron .40 1.00
67 Corey Koskie .40 1.00
68 Marlon Anderson .40 1.00
69 Jason Kendall .40 1.00
70 J.T. Snow .40 1.00
71 Edgar Martinez .60 1.50
72 Vernon Wells .40 1.00
73 Vladimir Guerrero .60 1.50
74 Adam Dunn .60 1.50
75 Barry Zito .60 1.50
76 Jeff Kent .40 1.00
77 Russ Ortiz .40 1.00
78 Phil Nevin .40 1.00
79 Carlos Beltran .60 1.50

Card	Low	High
80 Mike Lowell	.40	1.00
81 Bob Wickman	.40	1.00
82 Junior Spivey	.40	1.00
83 Melvin Mora	.40	1.00
84 Derrek Lee	.40	1.00
85 Chuck Knoblauch	.40	1.00
86 Eric Gagne	.40	1.00
87 Orlando Hernandez	.40	1.00
88 Robert Person	.40	1.00
89 Elmer Dessens	.40	1.00
90 Wade Miller	.40	1.00
91 Adrian Beltre	1.00	2.50
92 Kazuhiro Sasaki	.40	1.00
93 Timo Perez	.40	1.00
94 Jose Vidro	.40	1.00
95 Geronimo Gil	.40	1.00
96 Trot Nixon	.40	1.00
97 Denny Neagle	.40	1.00
98 Roberto Hernandez	.40	1.00
99 David Ortiz	1.00	2.50
100 Robb Nen	.40	1.00
101 Sidney Ponson	.40	1.00
102 Kevin Appier	.40	1.00
103 Javier Lopez	.40	1.00
104 Jeff Conine	.40	1.00
105 Mark Buehrle	.60	1.50
106 Jason Simontacchi	.40	1.00
107 Jose Jimenez	.40	1.00
108 Brian Jordan	.40	1.00
109 Brad Wilkerson	.40	1.00
110 Scott Hatteberg	.40	1.00
111 Matt Morris	.40	1.00
112 Miguel Tejada	.60	1.50
113 Rafael Furcal	.40	1.00
114 Steve Cox	.40	1.00
115 Roy Halladay	.60	1.50
116 David Eckstein	.40	1.00
117 Tomo Ohka	.40	1.00
118 Jack Wilson	.40	1.00
119 Randall Simon	.40	1.00
120 Jamie Moyer	.40	1.00
121 Andy Benes	.40	1.00
122 Tino Martinez	.40	1.00
123 Esteban Yan	.40	1.00
124 Jason Isringhausen	.40	1.00
125 Chris Carpenter	.60	1.50
126 Aaron Rowand	.40	1.00
127 Brandon Inge	.40	1.00
128 Jose Vizcaino	.40	1.00
129 Jose Mesa	.40	1.00
130 Troy Percival	.40	1.00
131 Jon Lieber	.40	1.00
132 Brian Giles	.40	1.00
133 Aaron Boone	.40	1.00
134 Bobby Higginson	.40	1.00
135 Luis Rivas	.40	1.00
136 Troy Glaus	.40	1.00
137 Jim Thome	.60	1.50
138 Ramon Martinez	.40	1.00
139 Jay Gibbons	.40	1.00
140 Mike Lieberthal	.40	1.00
141 Juan Uribe	.40	1.00
142 Gary Sheffield	.40	1.00
143 Ramon Santiago	.40	1.00
144 Ben Sheets	.40	1.00
145 Tony Armas Jr.	.40	1.00
146 Kazuhisa Ishii	.40	1.00
147 Erubiel Durazo	.40	1.00
148 Jerry Hairston Jr.	.40	1.00
149 Byung-Hyun Kim	.40	1.00
150 Marcus Giles	.40	1.00
151 Johnny Damon	.60	1.50
152 Terrence Long	.40	1.00
153 Juan Pierre	.40	1.00
154 Aramis Ramirez	.40	1.00
155 Brent Abernathy	.40	1.00
156 Ismael Valdes	.40	1.00
157 Mike Mussina	.60	1.50
158 Ramon Hernandez	.40	1.00
159 Adam Kennedy	.40	1.00
160 Tony Womack	.40	1.00
161 Tony Batista	.40	1.00
162 Kip Wells	.40	1.00
163 Jeromy Burnitz	.40	1.00
164 Todd Hundley	.40	1.00
165 Tim Wakefield	.60	1.50
166 Derek Lowe	.40	1.00
167 Jorge Posada	.60	1.50
168 Ramon Ortiz	.40	1.00
169 Brent Butler	.40	1.00
170 Shane Halter	.40	1.00
171 Matt Lawton	.40	1.00
172 Alex Sanchez	.40	1.00
173 Eric Milton	.40	1.00
174 Vicente Padilla	.40	1.00
175 Steve Karsay	.40	1.00
176 Mark Prior	.60	1.50
177 Kerry Wood	.40	1.00
178 Jason LaRue	.40	1.00
179 Danys Baez	.40	1.00
180 Nick Neugebauer	.40	1.00
181 Andres Galarraga	.60	1.50
182 Jason Giambi	.40	1.00
183 Aubrey Huff	.40	1.00
184 Juan Gonzalez	.40	1.00
185 Ugueth Urbina	.40	1.00
186 Rickey Henderson	1.00	2.50
187 Brad Fullmer	.40	1.00
188 Todd Zeile	.40	1.00
189 Jason Jennings	.40	1.00
190 Vladimir Nunez	.40	1.00
191 David Justice	.40	1.00
192 Brian Lawrence	.40	1.00
193 Pat Burrell	.40	1.00
194 Pokey Reese	.40	1.00
195 Robert Fick	.40	1.00
196 C.C. Sabathia	.60	1.50
197 Fernando Vina	.40	1.00
198 Sean Burroughs	.40	1.00
199 Ellis Burks	.40	1.00
200 Joe Randa	.40	1.00
201 Chris Duncan FY RC	1.25	3.00
202 Franklin Gutierrez FY RC	1.00	2.50
203 Adam LaRoche FY	.40	1.00
204 Manuel Ramirez FY RC	.40	1.00
205 Il Kim FY RC	.40	1.00
206 Daryl Clark FY RC	.40	1.00
207 Sean Pierce FY	.40	1.00
208 Andy Marte FY RC	.40	1.00
209 Bernie Castro FY RC	.40	1.00
210 Jason Perry FY RC	.40	1.00
211 Jaime Bubela FY RC	.40	1.00
212 Alexis Rios FY	.40	1.00
213 Brendan Harris FY RC	.40	1.00
214 Ramon Nivar-Martinez FY RC	.40	1.00
215 Terry Tiffee FY RC	.40	1.00
216 Kevin Youkilis FY RC	2.50	6.00
217 Derell McCall FY RC	.40	1.00
218 Scott Tyler FY RC	.40	1.00
219 Craig Brazell FY RC	.40	1.00
220 Walter Young FY	.40	1.00
221 Francisco Rodriguez	.60	1.50
222 Chipper Jones	1.00	2.50
223 Chris Singleton	.40	1.00
224 Cliff Floyd	.40	1.00
225 Bobby Hill	.40	1.00
226 Antonio Osuna	.40	1.00
227 Barry Larkin	.60	1.50
228 Dean Palmer	.40	1.00
229 Eric Owens	.40	1.00
230 Randy Johnson	1.00	2.50
231 Jeff Suppan	.40	1.00
232 Eric Karros	.40	1.00
233 Johan Santana	.60	1.50
234 Javier Vazquez	.40	1.00
235 John Thomson	.40	1.00
236 Nick Johnson	.40	1.00
237 Mark Ellis	.40	1.00
238 Doug Glanville	.40	1.00
239 Ken Griffey Jr.	2.00	5.00
240 Bubba Trammell	.40	1.00
241 Livan Hernandez	.40	1.00
242 Desi Relaford	.40	1.00
243 Eli Marrero	.40	1.00
244 Jared Sandberg	.40	1.00
245 Barry Bonds	1.50	4.00
246 Aaron Sele	.40	1.00
247 Derek Jeter	2.50	6.00
248 Eric Byrnes	.40	1.00
249 Rich Aurilia	.40	1.00
250 Joel Pineiro	.40	1.00
251 Chuck Finley	.40	1.00
252 Bengie Molina	.40	1.00
253 Steve Finley	.40	1.00
254 Marty Cordova	.40	1.00
255 Shea Hillenbrand	.40	1.00
256 Milton Bradley	.40	1.00
257 Carlos Pena	.60	1.50
258 Brad Ausmus	.40	1.00
259 Carlos Delgado	.40	1.00
260 Kevin Mench	.40	1.00
261 Joe Kennedy	.40	1.00
262 Mark McLemore	.40	1.00
263 Bill Mueller	.40	1.00
264 Ricky Ledee	.40	1.00
265 Ted Lilly	.40	1.00
266 Sterling Hitchcock	.40	1.00
267 Scott Strickland	.40	1.00
268 Damion Easley	.40	1.00
269 Torii Hunter	.40	1.00
270 Brad Radke	.40	1.00
271 Geoff Jenkins	.40	1.00
272 Paul Byrd	.40	1.00
273 Morgan Ensberg	.40	1.00
274 Mike Maroth	.40	1.00
275 Mike Hampton	.40	1.00
276 Flash Gordon	.40	1.00
277 John Burkett	.40	1.00
278 Rodrigo Lopez	.40	1.00
279 Tim Spooneybarger	.40	1.00
280 Quinton McCracken	.40	1.00
281 Tim Salmon	.40	1.00
282 Jarrod Washburn	.40	1.00
283 Pedro Martinez	.60	1.50
284 Julio Lugo	.40	1.00
285 Armando Benitez	.40	1.00
286 Raul Mondesi	.40	1.00
287 Robin Ventura	.40	1.00
288 Bobby Abreu	.40	1.00
289 Josh Fogg	.40	1.00
290 Ryan Klesko	.40	1.00
291 Tsuyoshi Shinjo	.40	1.00
292 Jim Edmonds	.60	1.50
293 Chan Ho Park	.60	1.50
294 John Mabry	.40	1.00
295 Woody Williams	.40	1.00
296 Scott Schoeneweis	.40	1.00
297 Brian Anderson	.40	1.00
298 Brett Tomko	.40	1.00
299 Scott Erickson	.40	1.00
300 Kevin Millar Sox	.40	1.00
301 Danny Wright	.40	1.00
302 Jason Schmidt	.40	1.00
303 Scott Williamson	.40	1.00
304 Einar Diaz	.40	1.00
305 Jay Payton	.40	1.00
306 Juan Acevedo	.40	1.00
307 Ben Grieve	.40	1.00
308 Raul Ibanez	.60	1.50
309 Richie Sexson	.40	1.00
310 Rick Reed	.40	1.00
311 Pedro Astacio	.40	1.00
312 Bud Smith	.40	1.00
313 Tomas Perez	.40	1.00
314 Rafael Palmeiro	.60	1.50
315 Jason Tyner	.40	1.00
316 Scott Rolen	.60	1.50
317 Randy Winn	.40	1.00
318 Ryan Jensen	.40	1.00
319 Trevor Hoffman	.60	1.50
320 Craig Wilson	.40	1.00
321 Jeremy Giambi	.40	1.00
322 Andy Pettitte	.60	1.50
323 John Franco	.40	1.00
324 Felipe Lopez	.40	1.00
325 Mike Piazza	1.00	2.50
326 Cristian Guzman	.40	1.00
327 Jose Hernandez	.40	1.00
328 Octavio Dotel	.40	1.00
329 Brad Penny	.40	1.00
330 Dave Veres	.40	1.00
331 Ryan Dempster	.40	1.00
332 Joe Crede	.40	1.00
333 Chad Hermansen	.40	1.00
334 Gary Matthews Jr.	.40	1.00
335 Frank Catalanotto	.40	1.00
336 Darin Erstad	.40	1.00
337 Matt Williams	.40	1.00
338 B.J. Surhoff	.40	1.00
339 Kerry Ligtenberg	.40	1.00
340 Mike Bordick	.40	1.00
341 Joe Girardi	.60	1.50
342 D'Angelo Jimenez	.40	1.00
343 Paul Konerko	.60	1.50
344 Joe Mays	.40	1.00
345 Marquis Grissom	.40	1.00
346 Neifi Perez	.40	1.00
347 Preston Wilson	.40	1.00
348 Jeff Weaver	.40	1.00
349 Eric Chavez	.40	1.00
350 Placido Polanco	.40	1.00
351 Matt Mantei	.40	1.00
352 James Baldwin	.40	1.00
353 Toby Hall	.40	1.00
354 Benji Gil	.40	1.00
355 Damian Moss	.40	1.00
356 Jorge Julio	.40	1.00
357 Matt Clement	.40	1.00
358 Lee Stevens	.40	1.00
359 Dave Roberts	.60	1.50
360 J.C. Romero	.40	1.00
361 Bartolo Colon	.40	1.00
362 Roger Cedeno	.40	1.00
363 Mariano Rivera	1.25	3.00
364 Billy Koch	.40	1.00
365 Manny Ramirez	1.00	2.50
366 Travis Lee	.40	1.00
367 Oliver Perez	.40	1.00
368 Tim Worrell	.40	1.00
369 Damian Miller	.40	1.00
370 John Smoltz	1.00	2.50
371 Willis Roberts	.40	1.00
372 Tim Hudson	.60	1.50
373 Moises Alou	.40	1.00
374 Corky Miller	.40	1.00
375 Ben Broussard	.40	1.00
376 Gabe Kapler	.40	1.00
377 Chris Woodward	.40	1.00
378 Todd Hollandsworth	.40	1.00
379 So Taguchi	.40	1.00
380 John Olerud	.40	1.00
381 Reggie Sanders	.40	1.00
382 Jake Peavy	.40	1.00
383 Kris Benson	.40	1.00
384 Ray Durham	.40	1.00
385 Boomer Wells	.40	1.00
386 Tom Glavine	.60	1.50
387 Antonio Alfonseca	.40	1.00
388 Keith Foulke	.40	1.00
389 Shawn Estes	.40	1.00
390 Mark Grace	.60	1.50
391 Dmitri Young	.40	1.00
392 A.J. Burnett	.40	1.00
393 Richard Hidalgo	.40	1.00
394 Mike Sweeney	.40	1.00
395 Doug Mientkiewicz	.40	1.00
396 Cory Lidle	.40	1.00
397 Jeff Bagwell	.60	1.50
398 Steve Sparks	.40	1.00
399 Sandy Alomar Jr.	.40	1.00
400 John Lackey	.60	1.50
401 Rick Helling	.40	1.00
402 Carlos Lee	.40	1.00
403 Garret Anderson	.40	1.00
404 Vinny Castilla	.40	1.00
405 David Bell	.40	1.00
406 Freddy Garcia	.40	1.00
407 Scott Spiezio	.40	1.00
408 Russell Branyan	.40	1.00
409 Jose Contreras RC	1.00	2.50
410 Kevin Brown	.40	1.00
411 Tyler Houston	.40	1.00
412 A.J. Pierzynski	.40	1.00
413 Peter Bergeron	.40	1.00
414 Brett Myers	.40	1.00
415 Kenny Lofton	.40	1.00
416 Ben Davis	.40	1.00
417 J.D. Drew	.40	1.00
418 Ricky Gutierrez	.40	1.00
419 Mark Redman	.40	1.00
420 Juan Encarnacion	.40	1.00
421 Bryan Bullington DP RC	.40	1.00
422 Jeremy Guthrie DP	.40	1.00
423 Joey Gomes DP RC	.40	1.00
424 Evel Bastida-Martinez DP RC	.40	1.00
425 Brian Wright DP RC	.40	1.00
426 B.J. Upton DP	.60	1.50
427 Jeff Francis DP	.40	1.00
428 Jeremy Hermida DP	.60	1.50
429 Khalil Greene DP	.60	1.50
430 Darrell Rasner DP RC	.40	1.00
431 B.Phillips V.Martinez	.60	1.50
432 H.Choi N.Jackson	.40	1.00
433 D.Willis J.Stokes	.40	1.00
434 C.Tracy L.Overbay	.40	1.00
435 J.Borchard C.Malone	.40	1.00
436 J.Mauer J.Morneau	1.00	2.50
437 D.Henson B.Claussen	.40	1.00
438 C.Utley G.Floyd	.60	1.50
439 T.Bozied X.Nady	.40	1.00
440 A.Heilman J.Reyes	1.00	2.50

2003 Topps Chrome Black Refractors

*BLACK 1-200/221-420: 2X TO 5X
*BLACK 201-220/409/421-440: 2X TO 5X
SERIES 1 STATED ODDS 1:20 HOB/RET
SERIES 2 STATED ODDS 1:17 HOB/RET
STATED PRINT RUN 199 SERIAL #'d SETS

2003 Topps Chrome Gold Refractors

*GOLD 1-200/221-420: 2.5X TO 6X
*GOLD 201-220/409/421-440: 2.5X TO 6X
SERIES 1 STATED ODDS 1:8 HOB/RET
SERIES 2 STATED ODDS 2:8 HOB/RET
STATED PRINT RUN 449 SERIAL #'d SETS

2003 Topps Chrome Refractors

*REF 1-200/201-420: 1.2X TO 2.5X
*REF 201-220/409/421-440: 1.2X TO 2.5X
SERIES 1 STATED ODDS 1:5 HOB/RET
SERIES 2 STATED ODDS 1:5 HOB/RET
STATED PRINT RUN 699 SERIAL #'d SETS

2003 Topps Chrome Silver Refractors

*SILVER REF 221-420: 1.25X TO 3X BASIC
*SILVER REF 421-440: 1.25X TO 3X BASIC
ONE PER SER.2 RETAIL EXCH.CARD
CARDS WERE ONLY PRODUCED FOR SER.2

2003 Topps Chrome Uncirculated X-Fractors

*X-FRACT 1-200/221-420: 4X TO 10X
*X-FRACT 201-220/409/421-440: 4X TO 10X
ONE CARD PER SEALED HOBBY BOX
1-220 PRINT RUN 50 SERIAL #'d SETS
221-440 PRINT RUN 57 SERIAL #'d SETS

2003 Topps Chrome Blue Backs Relics

Randomly inserted into packs, these 20 cards are authentic game-used memorabilia attached to a card which was in 1951 Blue Back design. These cards were issued in three different odds and we have notated those odds as well as what group the player belonged to in our checklist.

BAT ODDS 1:236 HOB/RET
UNI GROUP A ODDS 1:69 HOB/RET
UNI GROUP B ODDS 1:662 HOB/RET

Card	Low	High
AD Adam Dunn Uni B	6.00	15.00
AP Albert Pujols Uni A	10.00	25.00
AR Alex Rodriguez Bat	10.00	25.00
AS Alfonso Soriano Bat	6.00	15.00
BW Bernie Williams Bat	6.00	15.00
EC Eric Chavez Uni A	4.00	10.00
FT Frank Thomas Uni A	6.00	15.00
JB Josh Beckett Uni A	4.00	10.00
JBA Jeff Bagwell Uni A	4.00	10.00
JR Jimmy Rollins Uni A	4.00	10.00
KW Kerry Wood Uni A	4.00	10.00
LB Lance Berkman Bat	6.00	15.00
MO Maggio Ordonez Uni A	4.00	10.00
MP Mike Piazza Uni A	8.00	20.00
NG Nomar Garciaparra Jsy	10.00	25.00
NJ Nick Johnson Bat	6.00	15.00
PK Paul Konerko Uni A	4.00	10.00
RA Roberto Alomar Bat	6.00	15.00
SG Shawn Green Uni A	4.00	10.00
TS Tsuyoshi Shinjo Bat	6.00	15.00

2003 Topps Chrome Record Breakers Relics

Randomly inserted into packs, these 40 cards feature a mix of active and retired players along with a game-used memorabilia piece. These cards were issued in a few different group and we have notated that information next to the player's name in our checklist.

BAT 1 ODDS 1:364 HOB/RET
BAT 2 ODDS 1:131 HOB/RET
UNI GROUP A1 ODDS 1:413 HOB/RET
UNI GROUP B1 ODDS 1:50 HOB/RET
UNI GROUP A2 ODDS 1:1707 HOB/RET
UNI GROUP B2 ODDS 1:127 HOB/RET

Card	Low	High
AR1 Alex Rodriguez Uni B1	5.00	12.00
AR2 Alex Rodriguez Bat 2	5.00	12.00
BB Barry Bonds Walks Uni B2	6.00	15.00
BB2 Barry Bonds Slg Uni B2	6.00	15.00
BB3 Barry Bonds Bat 2	6.00	15.00
CB Craig Biggio Uni B1	2.50	6.00
CD Carlos Delgado Uni B1	1.50	4.00
CF Cliff Floyd Bat 1	1.50	4.00
DE Darin Erstad Bat 2	1.50	4.00
DLE Dennis Eckersley Uni A2	2.50	6.00
DM Don Mattingly Bat 2	8.00	20.00
FT Frank Thomas Uni B1	4.00	10.00
HK Harmon Killebrew Uni B1	4.00	10.00
HR Harold Reynolds Bat 2	1.50	4.00
JB1 Jeff Bagwell Slg Uni B1	2.50	6.00
JB2 Jeff Bagwell RBI Uni B2	2.50	6.00
JC Jose Canseco Bat 2	2.50	6.00
JG Juan Gonzalez Uni B1	1.50	4.00
JM Joe Morgan Bat 1	2.50	6.00
JS John Smoltz Uni B2	4.00	10.00
KS Kazuhiro Sasaki Uni B1	1.50	4.00
LB Lou Brock Bat 1	2.50	6.00
LG1 Luis Gonzalez RBI Bat 1	1.50	4.00
LG2 Luis Gonzalez Avg Bat 2	1.50	4.00
LW Larry Walker Bat 1	2.50	6.00
MP Mike Piazza Uni B1	4.00	10.00
MR Manny Ramirez Bat 2	4.00	10.00
MS Mike Schmidt Uni A1	6.00	15.00
PM Paul Molitor Bat 2	4.00	10.00
RC Rod Carew Avg Bat 2	2.50	6.00
RC2 Rod Carew Hits Bat 2	2.50	6.00
RH1 R.Henderson A's Bat 1	4.00	10.00
RH2 R.Henderson Yanks Bat 2	20.00	50.00
RJ1 Randy Johnson ERA Uni B1	4.00	10.00
RJ2 Randy Johnson Wins Uni B2	4.00	10.00
RY Robin Yount Uni B1	4.00	10.00
SM Stan Musial Uni A1	12.00	30.00
SS Sammy Sosa Bat 2	4.00	10.00
TH Todd Helton Bat 1	2.50	6.00
TS Tom Seaver Uni B2	2.50	6.00

2003 Topps Chrome Red Backs Relics

Randomly inserted into packs, these 20 cards are authentic game-used memorabilia attached to a card which was in 1951 Red Back design. These cards were issued in three different odds and we have notated those odds as well as what group the player belonged to in our checklist.

SERIES 2 BAT A ODDS 1:342 HOB/RET
SERIES 2 BAT B ODDS 1:383 HOB/RET
SERIES 2 JERSEY ODDS 1:49 HOB/RET

Card	Low	High
AD Adam Dunn Jsy	2.50	6.00
AJ Andruw Jones Jsy	1.50	4.00
AP Albert Pujols Bat B	5.00	12.00
AR Alex Rodriguez Jsy	5.00	12.00
AS Alfonso Soriano Bat A	2.50	6.00
CJ Chipper Jones Jsy	4.00	10.00
CS Curt Schilling Jsy	2.50	6.00
GA Garrett Anderson Bat A	4.00	10.00
JB Jeff Bagwell Jsy	2.50	6.00
MP Mike Piazza Jsy	4.00	10.00
MR Manny Ramirez Bat B	4.00	10.00
MS Mike Sweeney Jsy	1.50	4.00
NG Nomar Garciaparra Bat A	6.00	15.00
PB Pat Burrell Bat A	4.00	10.00
PM Pedro Martinez Jsy	2.50	6.00
RA Roberto Alomar Jsy	2.50	6.00
RJ Randy Johnson Jsy	4.00	10.00
SR Scott Rolen Bat A	6.00	15.00
TH Todd Helton Jsy	2.50	6.00
TKH Torii Hunter Jsy	1.50	4.00

2003 Topps Chrome Traded

These cards were issued at a stated rate of two per 2003 Topps Traded pack. Cards numbered 1 through 115 feature veterans who were traded while cards 116 through 120 feature managers. Cards numbered 121 through 165 featured prospects and cards 166 through 275 feature Rookie Cards. All of these cards were issued with a "T" prefix.

Card	Low	High
COMPLETE SET (275)	30.00	60.00
COMMON CARD (T1-T120)	.40	1.00
COMMON CARD (121-165)	.40	1.00
COMMON CARD (166-275)	.40	1.00
2 PER 2003 TOPPS TRADED HOBBY PACK		
2 PER 2003 TOPPS TRADED HTA PACK		
2 PER 2003 TOPPS TRADED RETAIL PACK		
T1 Juan Pierre	.40	1.00
T2 Mark Grudzielanek	.40	1.00
T3 Tanyon Sturtze	.40	1.00
T4 Greg Vaughn	.40	1.00
T5 Greg Myers	.40	1.00
T6 Randall Simon	.40	1.00
T7 Todd Hundley	.40	1.00
T8 Marlon Anderson	.40	1.00
T9 Jeff Reboulet	.40	1.00
T10 Alex Sanchez	.40	1.00
T11 Mike Rivera	.40	1.00
T12 Todd Walker	.40	1.00
T13 Ray King	.40	1.00
T14 Shawn Estes	.40	1.00
T15 Gary Matthews Jr.	.40	1.00
T16 Jaret Wright	.40	1.00
T17 Edgardo Alfonzo	.40	1.00
T18 Omar Daal	.40	1.00
T19 Ryan Rupe	.40	1.00
T20 Tony Clark	.40	1.00
T21 Jeff Suppan	.40	1.00
T22 Mike Stanton	.40	1.00
T23 Ramon Martinez	.40	1.00
T24 Armando Rios	.40	1.00
T25 Johnny Estrada	.40	1.00
T26 Joe Girardi	.60	1.50
T27 Ivan Rodriguez	.60	1.50
T28 Robert Fick	.40	1.00
T29 Rick White	.40	1.00
T30 Robert Person	.40	1.00
T31 Alan Benes	.40	1.00
T32 Chris Carpenter	.60	1.50
T33 Chris Widger	.40	1.00
T34 Travis Hafner	.40	1.00
T35 Mike Venafro	.40	1.00
T36 Jon Lieber	.40	1.00
T37 Orlando Hernandez	.40	1.00
T38 Aaron Myette	.40	1.00
T39 Paul Bako	.40	1.00
T40 Erubiel Durazo	.40	1.00
T41 Mark Guthrie	.40	1.00
T42 Steve Avery	.40	1.00
T43 Damian Jackson	.40	1.00
T44 Rey Ordonez	.40	1.00
T45 John Flaherty	.40	1.00
T46 Byung-Hyun Kim	.40	1.00
T47 Tom Goodwin	.40	1.00
T48 Elmer Dessens	.40	1.00
T49 Al Martin	.40	1.00
T50 Gene Kingsale	.40	1.00
T51 Lenny Harris	.40	1.00
T52 David Ortiz Sox	1.00	2.50
T53 Jose Lima	.40	1.00
T54 Mike Difelice	.40	1.00
T55 Jose Hernandez	.40	1.00
T56 Todd Zeile	.40	1.00
T57 Roberto Hernandez	.40	1.00
T58 Albie Lopez	.40	1.00
T59 Roberto Alomar	.60	1.50
T60 Russ Ortiz	.40	1.00
T61 Brian Daubach	.40	1.00
T62 Carl Everett	.40	1.00
T63 Jeromy Burnitz	.40	1.00
T64 Mark Bellhorn	.40	1.00
T65 Ruben Sierra	.40	1.00
T66 Mike Fetters	.40	1.00
T67 Armando Benitez	.40	1.00
T68 Deivi Cruz	.40	1.00
T69 Jose Cruz Jr.	.40	1.00
T70 Jeremy Fikac	.40	1.00
T71 Jeff Kent	.40	1.00
T72 Andres Galarraga	.60	1.50
T73 Rickey Henderson	1.00	2.50
T74 Royce Clayton	.40	1.00
T75 Troy O'Leary	.40	1.00
T76 Ron Coomer	.40	1.00
T77 Greg Colbrunn	.40	1.00
T78 Wes Helms	.40	1.00
T79 Kevin Millwood	.40	1.00
T80 Damion Easley	.40	1.00
T81 Bobby Kielty	.40	1.00
T82 Keith Osik	.40	1.00
T83 Ramiro Mendoza	.40	1.00
T84 Shea Hillenbrand	.40	1.00
T85 Shannon Stewart	.40	1.00
T86 Eddie Perez	.40	1.00
T87 Ugueth Urbina	.40	1.00
T88 Orlando Palmeiro	.40	1.00
T89 Graeme Lloyd	.40	1.00
T90 John Vander Wal	.40	1.00
T91 Gary Bennett	.40	1.00
T92 Shane Reynolds	.40	1.00
T93 Steve Parris	.40	1.00
T94 Julio Lugo	.40	1.00
T95 John Halama	.40	1.00
T96 Carlos Baerga	.40	1.00
T97 Jim Parque	.40	1.00
T98 Mike Williams	.40	1.00
T99 Fred McGriff	.60	1.50
T100 Kenny Rogers	.40	1.00
T101 Matt Herges	.40	1.00
T102 Jay Bell	.40	1.00
T103 Esteban Yan	.40	1.00
T104 Eric Owens	.40	1.00
T105 Aaron Fultz	.40	1.00
T106 Rey Sanchez	.40	1.00
T107 Jim Thome	.60	1.50
T108 Aaron Boone	.40	1.00
T109 Raul Mondesi	.40	1.00
T110 Kenny Lofton	.40	1.00
T111 Jose Guillen	.40	1.00
T112 Aramis Ramirez	.40	1.00
T113 Sidney Ponson	.40	1.00
T114 Scott Williamson	.40	1.00
T115 Robin Ventura	.40	1.00
T116 Dusty Baker MG	.40	1.00
T117 Felipe Alou MG	.40	1.00
T118 Buck Showalter MG	.40	1.00
T119 Jack McKeon MG	.40	1.00
T120 Art Howe MG	.40	1.00
T121 Bobby Crosby PROS	.40	1.00
T122 Adrian Gonzalez PROS	.75	2.00
T123 Kevin Cash PROS	.40	1.00
T124 Shin-Soo Choo PROS	.60	1.50
T125 Chin-Feng Chen PROS	.40	1.00
T126 Miguel Cabrera PROS	5.00	12.00
T127 Jason Young PROS	.40	1.00
T128 Alex Herrera PROS	.40	1.00
T129 Jason Dubois PROS	.40	1.00
T130 Jeff Mathis PROS	.40	1.00
T131 Casey Kotchman PROS	.40	1.00
T132 Ed Rogers PROS	.40	1.00
T133 Wilson Betemit PROS	.40	1.00
T134 Jim Kavourias PROS	.40	1.00
T135 Taylor Buchholz PROS	.40	1.00
T136 Adam LaRoche PROS	.40	1.00
T137 Dallas McPherson PROS	.40	1.00
T138 Jesus Cota PROS	.40	1.00
T139 Clint Nageotte PROS	.40	1.00
T140 Boof Bonser PROS	.40	1.00
T141 Walter Young PROS	.40	1.00
T142 Joe Crede PROS	.40	1.00
T143 Denny Bautista PROS	.40	1.00
T144 Victor Diaz PROS	.40	1.00
T145 Chris Narveson PROS	.40	1.00
T146 Gabe Gross PROS	.40	1.00
T147 Jimmy Journell PROS	.40	1.00
T148 Rafael Soriano PROS	.40	1.00
T149 Jerome Williams PROS	.40	1.00
T150 Aaron Cook PROS	.40	1.00
T151 Anastacio Martinez PROS	.40	1.00
T152 Scott Hairston PROS	.40	1.00
T153 John Buck PROS	.40	1.00
T154 Ryan Ludwick PROS	.40	1.00
T155 Chris Bootcheck PROS	.40	1.00
T156 John Rheinecker PROS	.40	1.00
T157 Jason Lane PROS	.40	1.00
T158 Shelley Duncan PROS	.40	1.00
T159 Adam Wainwright PROS	.60	1.50
T160 Jason Arnold PROS	.40	1.00
T161 Jonny Gomes PROS	.40	1.00
T162 James Loney PROS	.60	1.50
T163 Mike Fontenot PROS	.40	1.00
T164 Khalil Greene PROS	.60	1.50
T165 Sean Burnett PROS	.40	1.00
T166 David Martinez FY RC	.40	1.00
T167 Felix Pie FY RC	.60	1.50
T168 Joe Valentine FY RC	.40	1.00
T169 Brandon Webb FY RC	1.25	3.00
T170 Matt Diaz FY RC	.60	1.50
T171 Lew Ford FY RC	.40	1.00
T172 Jeremy Griffiths FY RC	.40	1.00
T173 Matt Hensley FY RC	.40	1.00
T174 Charlie Manning FY RC	.40	1.00
T175 Elizardo Ramirez FY RC	.40	1.00
T176 Greg Aquino FY RC	.40	1.00
T177 Felix Sanchez FY RC	.40	1.00
T178 Kelly Shoppach FY RC	.60	1.50
T179 Bubba Nelson FY RC	.40	1.00
T180 Mike O'Keefe FY RC	.40	1.00
T181 Hanley Ramirez FY RC	3.00	8.00
T182 Todd Wellemeyer FY RC	.40	1.00
T183 Dustin Moseley FY RC	.40	1.00
T184 Eric Crozier FY RC	.40	1.00
T185 Ryan Shealy FY RC	.40	1.00
T186 Jeremy Bonderman FY RC	1.50	4.00
T187 T.Story-Harden FY RC	.40	1.00
T188 Dusty Brown FY RC	.40	1.00
T189 Rob Hammock FY RC	.40	1.00
T190 Jorge Piedra FY RC	.40	1.00
T191 Chris De La Cruz FY RC	.40	1.00
T192 Eli Whiteside FY RC	.40	1.00
T193 Jason Kubel FY RC	1.25	3.00
T194 Jon Schuerholz FY RC	.40	1.00
T195 Stephen Randolph FY RC	.40	1.00
T196 Andy Sisco FY RC	.40	1.00
T197 Sean Smith FY RC	.40	1.00
T198 Jon-Mark Sprowl FY RC	.40	1.00
T199 Matt Kata FY RC	.40	1.00
T200 Robinson Cano FY RC	6.00	15.00
T201 Nook Logan FY RC	.40	1.00
T202 Ben Francisco FY RC	.40	1.00
T203 Arnie Munoz FY RC	.40	1.00
T204 Ozzie Chavez FY RC	.40	1.00
T205 Eric Riggs FY RC	.40	1.00
T206 Beau Kemp FY RC	.40	1.00
T207 Travis Wong FY RC	.40	1.00
T208 Dustin Yount FY RC	.40	1.00
T209 Brian McCann FY RC	3.00	8.00
T210 Wilton Reynolds FY RC	.40	1.00
T211 Matt Bruback FY RC	.40	1.00
T212 Andrew Brown FY RC	.40	1.00
T213 Edgar Gonzalez FY RC	.40	1.00
T214 Eider Torres FY RC	.40	1.00
T215 Aquilino Lopez FY RC	.40	1.00
T216 Bobby Basham FY RC	.40	1.00
T217 Tim Olson FY RC	.40	1.00
T218 Nathan Panther FY RC	.40	1.00
T219 Bryan Grace FY RC	.40	1.00
T220 Dusty Gomon FY RC	.40	1.00

221 Wil Ledezma FY RC .40 1.00
222 Josh Willingham FY RC 1.25 3.00
223 David Cash FY RC .40 1.00
224 Oscar Villarreal FY RC .40 1.00
225 Jeff Duncan FY RC .40 1.00
226 Kade Johnson FY RC .40 1.00
227 Luke Steidlmayer FY RC .40 1.00
228 Brandon Watson FY RC .40 1.00
229 Jose Morales FY RC .40 1.00
230 Mike Gallo FY RC .40 1.00
231 Tyler Adamczyk FY RC .40 1.00
232 Adam Stern FY RC .40 1.00
233 Brennan King FY RC .40 1.00
234 Dan Haren FY RC 2.00 5.00
235 Michel Hernandez FY RC .40 1.00
236 Ben Fritz FY RC .40 1.00
237 Clay Hensley FY RC .40 1.00
238 Tyler Johnson FY RC .40 1.00
239 Pete LaForest FY RC .40 1.00
240 Tyler Martin FY RC .40 1.00
241 J.D. Durbin FY RC .40 1.00
242 Shane Victorino FY RC 1.25 3.00
243 Rajai Davis FY RC .40 1.00
244 Ismael Castro FY RC .40 1.00
245 Chien-Ming Wang FY RC 1.50 4.00
246 Travis Ishikawa FY RC 1.00 2.50
247 Corey Shafer FY RC .40 1.00
248 Gary Schneidmiller FY RC .40 1.00
249 Dave Pember FY RC .40 1.00
250 Keith Stamler FY RC .40 1.00
251 Tyson Graham FY RC .40 1.00
252 Ryan Cameron FY RC .40 1.00
253 Eric Eckenstahler FY .40 1.00
254 Matthew Peterson FY RC .40 1.00
255 Dustin McGowan FY RC .40 1.00
256 Prentice Redman FY RC .40 1.00
257 Haj Turay FY RC .40 1.00
258 Carlos Guzman FY RC .40 1.00
259 Matt DeMarco FY RC .40 1.00
260 Derek Michaelis FY RC .40 1.00
261 Brian Burgamy FY RC .40 1.00
262 Jay Sitzman FY RC .40 1.00
263 Chris Fallon FY RC .40 1.00
264 Mike Adams FY RC .60 1.50
265 Clint Barmes FY RC 1.00 2.50
266 Eric Reed FY RC .40 1.00
267 Willie Eyre FY RC .40 1.00
268 Carlos Duran FY RC .40 1.00
269 Nick Trzesniak FY RC .40 1.00
270 Ferdin Tejeda FY RC .40 1.00
271 Michael Garciaparra FY RC .40 1.00
272 Michael Hinckley FY RC .40 1.00
273 Branden Florence FY RC .40 1.00
274 Trent Oeltjen FY RC .40 1.00
275 Mike Neu FY RC .40 1.00

2003 Topps Chrome Traded Refractors

*REF 1-120: 2X TO 5X BASIC
*REF 121-165: 1.5X TO 4X BASIC
*REF 166-275: 1.5X TO 4X BASIC
STATED ODDS 1:12 HOB/RET, 1:4 HTA

2004 Topps Chrome

This 233 card first series was released in January, 2004. A matching second series of 233 cards was released in May, 2004. This set was issued in four-card packs with an $3 SRP which came 20 packs to a box and 10 boxes to a case. The first 210 cards of the first series are veterans while the final 23 cards of the set feature first year cards. Please note that cards 221 through 233 were autographed by the featured players and those cards were inserted at a stated rate of one in 21 hobby packs and one in 33 retail packs. In the second series cards numbered 234 through 246 feature autographs of the rookie pictured and those cards were inserted at a stated rate of one in 22 hobby packs and one in 35 retail packs. Bradley Sullivan (#234) was issued with either the correct back or an incorrect back numbered to 345 which consistitued about 20 percent of the total press run.

COMP.SERIES 1 w/o SP's (220) 40.00 80.00
COMP.SERIES 2 w/o SP's (220) 40.00 80.00
COMMON (1-210/257-466) .40 1.00
COMMON (211-220/247-256) .50 1.25
COMMON AU (221-246) 4.00 10.00
221-233 SERIES 1 ODDS 1:21 H, 1:33 R
234-246 SERIES 2 ODDS 1:22 H, 1:35 R
345 SULLIVAN ERR SHOULD BE NO.234
1 IN EVERY 5 SULLIVAN'S ARE ERR 345
4 IN EVERY 5 SULLIVAN'S ARE COR 234
SULLIVAN INFO PROVIDED BY TOPPS
1 Jim Thome .60 1.50
2 Reggie Sanders .40 1.00
3 Mark Kotsay .40 1.00
4 Edgardo Alfonzo .40 1.00
5 Tim Wakefield .60 1.50
6 Moises Alou .40 1.00
7 Jorge Julio .40 1.00
8 Bartolo Colon .40 1.00
9 Chan Ho Park .60 1.50
10 Ichiro Suzuki 1.25 3.00
11 Kevin Millwood .40 1.00
12 Preston Wilson .40 1.00
13 Tom Glavine .60 1.50
14 Junior Spivey .40 1.00
15 Marcus Giles .40 1.00
16 David Segui .40 1.00
17 Kevin Millar .40 1.00
18 Corey Patterson .40 1.00
19 Aaron Rowand .40 1.00
20 Derek Jeter 2.50 6.00
21 Luis Castillo .40 1.00
22 Manny Ramirez 1.00 2.50
23 Jay Payton .40 1.00
24 Bobby Higginson .40 1.00
25 Lance Berkman .60 1.50
26 Juan Pierre .40 1.00
27 Mike Mussina .60 1.50
28 Fred McGriff .40 1.00
29 Richie Sexson .40 1.00
30 Tim Hudson .60 1.50
31 Mike Piazza 1.00 2.50
32 Brad Radke .40 1.00
33 Jeff Weaver .40 1.00
34 Ramon Hernandez .40 1.00
35 David Bell .40 1.00
36 Randy Wolf .40 1.00
37 Jake Peavy .40 1.00
38 Tim Worrell .40 1.00
39 Gil Meche .40 1.00
40 Albert Pujols 1.25 3.00
41 Michael Young .40 1.00
42 Josh Phelps .40 1.00
43 Brendan Donnelly .40 1.00
44 Steve Finley .40 1.00
45 John Smoltz 1.00 2.50
46 Jay Gibbons .40 1.00
47 Trot Nixon .40 1.00
48 Carl Pavano .40 1.00
49 Frank Thomas 1.00 2.50
50 Mark Prior .60 1.50
51 Danny Graves .40 1.00
52 Milton Bradley .40 1.00
53 Kris Benson .40 1.00
54 Ryan Klesko .40 1.00
55 Mike Lowell .40 1.00
56 Geoff Blum .40 1.00
57 Michael Tucker .40 1.00
58 Paul Lo Duca .40 1.00
59 Vicente Padilla .40 1.00
60 Jacque Jones .40 1.00
61 Fernando Tatis .40 1.00
62 Ty Wigginton .40 1.00
63 Rich Aurilia .40 1.00
64 Andy Pettitte .60 1.50
65 Terrence Long .40 1.00
66 Cliff Floyd .40 1.00
67 Mariano Rivera 1.25 3.00
68 Kelvim Escobar .40 1.00
69 Marlon Byrd .40 1.00
70 Mark Mulder .40 1.00
71 Francisco Cordero .40 1.00
72 Carlos Guillen .40 1.00
73 Fernando Vina .40 1.00
74 Lance Carter .40 1.00
75 Hank Blalock .40 1.00
76 Jimmy Rollins .60 1.50
77 Francisco Rodriguez .60 1.50
78 Javy Lopez .40 1.00
79 Jerry Hairston Jr. .40 1.00
80 Andruw Jones .40 1.00
81 Rodrigo Lopez .40 1.00
82 Johnny Damon .60 1.50
83 Hee Seop Choi .40 1.00
84 Kazuhiro Sasaki .40 1.00
85 Danny Bautista .40 1.00
86 Matt Lawton .40 1.00
87 Juan Uribe .40 1.00
88 Rafael Furcal .40 1.00
89 Kyle Farnsworth .40 1.00
90 Jose Vidro .40 1.00
91 Luis Rivas .40 1.00
92 Hideo Nomo 1.00 2.50
93 Javier Vazquez .40 1.00
94 Al Leiter .40 1.00
95 Jose Valentin .40 1.00
96 Alex Cintron .40 1.00
97 Zach Day .40 1.00
98 Jorge Posada .60 1.50
99 C.C. Sabathia .60 1.50
100 Alex Rodriguez 1.25 3.00
101 Brad Penny .40 1.00
102 Brad Ausmus .40 1.00
103 Raul Ibanez .60 1.50
104 Mike Hampton .40 1.00
105 Adrian Beltre 1.00 2.50
106 Ramiro Mendoza .40 1.00
107 Rocco Baldelli .40 1.00
108 Esteban Loaiza .40 1.00
109 Russell Branyan .40 1.00
110 Todd Helton .60 1.50
111 Braden Looper .40 1.00
112 Octavio Dotel .40 1.00
113 Mike MacDougal .40 1.00
114 Cesar Izturis .40 1.00
115 Johan Santana .60 1.50
116 Jose Contreras .40 1.00
117 Placido Polanco .40 1.00
118 Jason Phillips .40 1.00
119 Orlando Hudson .40 1.00
120 Vernon Wells .40 1.00
121 Ben Grieve .40 1.00
122 Dave Roberts .60 1.50
123 Ismael Valdes .40 1.00
124 Eric Owens .40 1.00
125 Curt Schilling .60 1.50
126 Russ Ortiz .40 1.00
127 Mark Buehrle .60 1.50
128 Doug Mientkiewicz .40 1.00
129 Dmitri Young .40 1.00
130 Kazuhisa Ishii .40 1.00
131 A.J. Pierzynski .40 1.00
132 Brad Wilkerson .40 1.00
133 Joe McEwing .40 1.00
134 Alex Cora .60 1.50
135 Jose Cruz Jr. .40 1.00
136 Carlos Zambrano .60 1.50
137 Jeff Kent .40 1.00
138 Shigetoshi Hasegawa .40 1.00
139 Jarrod Washburn .40 1.00
140 Greg Maddux 1.25 3.00
141 Josh Beckett .40 1.00
142 Miguel Batista .40 1.00
143 Omar Vizquel .60 1.50
144 Alex Gonzalez .40 1.00
145 Billy Wagner .40 1.00
146 Brian Jordan .40 1.00
147 Wes Helms .40 1.00
148 Deivi Cruz .40 1.00
149 Alex Gonzalez .40 1.00
150 Jason Giambi .40 1.00
151 Erubiel Durazo .40 1.00
152 Mike Lieberthal .40 1.00
153 Jason Kendall .40 1.00
154 Xavier Nady .40 1.00
155 Kirk Rueter .40 1.00
156 Mike Cameron .40 1.00
157 Miguel Cairo .40 1.00
158 Woody Williams .40 1.00
159 Toby Hall .40 1.00
160 Bernie Williams .60 1.50
161 Darin Erstad .40 1.00
162 Matt Mantei .40 1.00
163 Shawn Chacon .40 1.00
164 Bill Mueller .40 1.00
165 Damian Miller .40 1.00
166 Tony Graffanino .40 1.00
167 Sean Casey .40 1.00
168 Brandon Phillips .40 1.00
169 Runelvys Hernandez .40 1.00
170 Adam Dunn .60 1.50
171 Carlos Lee .40 1.00
172 Juan Encarnacion .40 1.00
173 Angel Berroa .40 1.00
174 Desi Relaford .40 1.00
175 Joe Mays .40 1.00
176 Ben Sheets .40 1.00
177 Eddie Guardado .40 1.00
178 Rocky Biddle .40 1.00
179 Eric Gagne .40 1.00
180 Eric Chavez .40 1.00
181 Jason Michaels .40 1.00
182 Dustan Mohr .40 1.00
183 Kip Wells .40 1.00
184 Brian Lawrence .40 1.00
185 Bret Boone .40 1.00
186 Tino Martinez .60 1.50
187 Aubrey Huff .40 1.00
188 Kevin Mench .40 1.00
189 Tim Salmon .40 1.00
190 Carlos Delgado .60 1.50
191 John Lackey .60 1.50
192 Eric Byrnes .40 1.00
193 Luis Matos .40 1.00
194 Derek Lowe .40 1.00
195 Mark Grudzielanek .40 1.00
196 Tom Gordon .40 1.00
197 Matt Clement .40 1.00
198 Byung-Hyun Kim .40 1.00
199 Brandon Inge .40 1.00
200 Nomar Garciaparra .60 1.50
201 Frank Catalanotto .40 1.00
202 Cristian Guzman .40 1.00
203 Bo Hart .40 1.00
204 Jack Wilson .40 1.00
205 Ray Durham .40 1.00
206 Freddy Garcia .40 1.00
207 J.D. Drew .40 1.00
208 Orlando Cabrera .40 1.00
209 Roy Halladay .60 1.50
210 David Eckstein .40 1.00
211 Omar Falcon FY RC .50 1.25
212 Todd Self FY RC .50 1.25
213 David Murphy FY RC .75 2.00
214 Dioner Navarro FY RC .75 2.00
215 Marcus McBeth FY RC .50 1.25
216 Chris O'Riordan FY RC .50 1.25
217 Rodney Choy Foo FY RC .50 1.25
218 Tim Frend FY RC .50 1.25
219 Yadier Molina FY RC 12.00 30.00
220 Zach Duke FY RC .75 2.00
221 Anthony Lerew FY AU RC 6.00 15.00
222 B.Hawksworth FY AU RC 6.00 15.00
223 Brayan Pena FY AU RC 4.00 10.00
224 Craig Ansman FY AU RC 4.00 10.00
225 Jon Knott FY AU RC 4.00 10.00
226 Josh Labandeira FY AU RC 4.00 10.00
227 Khalid Ballouli FY AU RC 4.00 10.00
228 Kyle Davies FY AU RC 10.00 25.00
229 Matt Creighton FY AU RC 4.00 10.00
230 Mike Gosling FY AU RC 4.00 10.00
231 Nic Ungs FY AU RC 4.00 10.00
232 Zach Miner FY AU RC 10.00 25.00
233 Donald Levinski FY AU RC 4.00 10.00
234A Bradley Sullivan FY AU RC 6.00 15.00
234B B.Sullivan FY AU ERR 345 10.00 25.00
235 Carlos Quentin FY AU RC 6.00 15.00
236 Conor Jackson FY AU RC 6.00 15.00
237 Estee Harris FY AU RC 6.00 15.00
238 Jeffrey Allison FY AU RC 4.00 10.00
239 Kyle Sleeth FY AU RC 6.00 15.00
240 Matthew Moses FY AU RC 6.00 15.00
241 Tim Stauffer FY AU RC 4.00 10.00
242 Brad Snyder FY AU RC 5.00 12.00
243 Jason Hirsh FY AU RC 10.00 25.00
244 L.Milledge FY AU RC 5.00 12.00
245 Logan Kensing FY AU RC 4.00 10.00
246 Kory Casto FY AU RC 6.00 15.00
247 David Aardsma FY RC .50 1.25
248 Omar Quintanilla FY RC .50 1.25
249 Ervin Santana FY RC 1.25 3.00
250 Merkin Valdez FY RC .50 1.25
251 Vito Chiaravalloti FY RC .50 1.25
252 Travis Blackley FY RC .50 1.25
253 Chris Shelton FY RC .50 1.25
254 Rudy Guillen FY RC .50 1.25
255 Bobby Brownlie FY RC .50 1.25
256 Paul Maholm FY RC .75 2.00
257 Roger Clemens 1.25 3.00
258 Laynce Nix .40 1.00
259 Eric Hinske .40 1.00
260 Ivan Rodriguez .60 1.50
261 Brandon Webb .40 1.00
262 Jhonny Peralta .40 1.00
263 Adam Kennedy .40 1.00
264 Tony Batista .40 1.00
265 Jeff Suppan .40 1.00
266 Kenny Lofton .40 1.00
267 Scott Sullivan .40 1.00
268 Ken Griffey Jr. 2.00 5.00
269 Juan Rivera .40 1.00
270 Larry Walker .60 1.50
271 Todd Hollandsworth .40 1.00
272 Carlos Beltran .60 1.50
273 Carl Crawford .60 1.50
274 Karim Garcia .40 1.00
275 Jose Reyes .60 1.50
276 Brandon Duckworth .40 1.00
277 Brian Giles .40 1.00
278 J.T. Snow .40 1.00
279 Jamie Moyer .40 1.00
280 Julio Lugo .40 1.00
281 Mark Teixeira .60 1.50
282 Cory Lidle .40 1.00
283 Lyle Overbay .40 1.00
284 Troy Percival .40 1.00
285 Robby Hammock .40 1.00
286 Jason Johnson .40 1.00
287 Damian Rolls .40 1.00
288 Antonio Alfonseca .40 1.00
289 Tom Goodwin .40 1.00
290 Paul Konerko .60 1.50
291 D'Angelo Jimenez .40 1.00
292 Ben Broussard .40 1.00
293 Magglio Ordonez .60 1.50
294 Carlos Pena .60 1.50
295 Chad Fox .40 1.00
296 Jeriome Robertson .40 1.00
297 Travis Hafner .40 1.00
298 Joe Randa .40 1.00
299 Brady Clark .40 1.00
300 Barry Zito .60 1.50
301 Ruben Sierra .40 1.00
302 Brett Myers .40 1.00
303 Oliver Perez .40 1.00
304 Benito Santiago .40 1.00
305 David Ross .40 1.00
306 Joe Nathan .40 1.00
307 Jim Edmonds .60 1.50
308 Matt Kata .40 1.00
309 Vinny Castilla .40 1.00
310 Marty Cordova .40 1.00
311 Aramis Ramirez .40 1.00
312 Carl Everett .40 1.00
313 Ryan Freel .40 1.00
314 Mark Bellhorn Sox .40 1.00
315 Joe Mauer .75 2.00
316 Tim Redding .40 1.00
317 Jeromy Burnitz .40 1.00
318 Miguel Cabrera 1.00 2.50
319 Ramon Nivar .40 1.00
320 Casey Blake .40 1.00
321 Adam LaRoche .40 1.00
322 Jermaine Dye .40 1.00
323 Jerome Williams .40 1.00
324 John Olerud .40 1.00
325 Scott Rolen .60 1.50
326 Bobby Kielty .40 1.00
327 Travis Lee .40 1.00
328 Jeff Cirillo .40 1.00
329 Scott Spiezio .40 1.00
330 Melvin Mora .40 1.00
331 Mike Timlin .40 1.00
332 Kerry Wood .40 1.00
333 Tony Womack .40 1.00
334 Jody Gerut .40 1.00
335 Morgan Ensberg .40 1.00
336 Odalis Perez .40 1.00
337 Michael Cuddyer .40 1.00
338 Jose Hernandez .40 1.00
339 LaTroy Hawkins .40 1.00
340 Marquis Grissom .40 1.00
341 Matt Morris .40 1.00
342 Juan Gonzalez .40 1.00
343 Jose Valverde .40 1.00
344 Joe Borowski .40 1.00
345 Josh Bard .40 1.00
346 Austin Kearns .40 1.00
347 Chin-Hui Tsao .40 1.00
348 Wil Ledezma .40 1.00
349 Aaron Guiel .40 1.00
350 Alfonso Soriano .60 1.50
351 Ted Lilly .40 1.00
352 Sean Burroughs .40 1.00
353 Rafael Palmeiro .60 1.50
354 Quinton McCracken .40 1.00
355 David Ortiz 1.00 2.50
356 Randall Simon .40 1.00
357 Wily Mo Pena .40 1.00
358 Brian Anderson .40 1.00
359 Corey Koskie .40 1.00
360 Keith Foulke Sox .40 1.00
361 Sidney Ponson .40 1.00
362 Gary Matthews Jr. .40 1.00
363 Herbert Perry .40 1.00
364 Shea Hillenbrand .40 1.00
365 Craig Biggio .60 1.50
366 Barry Larkin .60 1.50
367 Arthur Rhodes .40 1.00
368 Sammy Sosa 1.00 2.50
369 Joe Crede .40 1.00
370 Gary Sheffield .40 1.00
371 Coco Crisp .40 1.00
372 Torii Hunter .40 1.00
373 Derrek Lee .60 1.50
374 Adam Everett .40 1.00
375 Miguel Tejada .60 1.50
376 Jeremy Affeldt .40 1.00
377 Robin Ventura .40 1.00
378 Scott Podsednik .40 1.00
379 Matthew LeCroy .40 1.00
380 Vladimir Guerrero .60 1.50
381 Steve Karsay .40 1.00
382 Jeff Nelson .40 1.00
383 Chase Utley .60 1.50
384 Bobby Abreu .40 1.00
385 Josh Fogg .40 1.00
386 Trevor Hoffman .60 1.50
387 Matt Stairs .40 1.00
388 Edgar Martinez .60 1.50
389 Edgar Renteria .40 1.00
390 Chipper Jones 1.00 2.50
391 Eric Munson .40 1.00
392 Dewon Brazelton .40 1.00
393 John Thomson .40 1.00
394 Chris Woodward .40 1.00
395 Joe Kennedy .40 1.00
396 Reed Johnson .40 1.00
397 Johnny Estrada .40 1.00
398 Damian Moss .40 1.00
399 Victor Zambrano .40 1.00
400 Dontrelle Willis .40 1.00
401 Troy Glaus .40 1.00
402 Raul Mondesi .40 1.00
403 Jeff Davanon .40 1.00
404 Kurt Ainsworth .40 1.00
405 Pedro Martinez .60 1.50
406 Eric Karros .40 1.00
407 Billy Koch .40 1.00
408 Luis Gonzalez .40 1.00
409 Jack Cust .40 1.00
410 Mike Sweeney .40 1.00
411 Jason Bay .60 1.50
412 Mark Redman .40 1.00
413 Jason Jennings .40 1.00
414 Rondell White .40 1.00
415 Todd Hundley .40 1.00
416 Shannon Stewart .40 1.00
417 Jae Weong Seo .40 1.00
418 Livan Hernandez .40 1.00
419 Mark Ellis .40 1.00
420 Pat Burrell .40 1.00
421 Mark Loretta .40 1.00
422 Robb Nen .40 1.00
423 Joel Pineiro .40 1.00
424 Todd Walker .40 1.00
425 Jeremy Bonderman .40 1.00
426 A.J. Burnett .40 1.00
427 Greg Myers .40 1.00
428 Roy Oswalt .60 1.50
429 Carlos Baerga .40 1.00
430 Garret Anderson .40 1.00
431 Horacio Ramirez .40 1.00
432 Brian Roberts .40 1.00
433 Kevin Brown .40 1.00
434 Eric Milton .40 1.00
435 Ramon Vazquez .40 1.00
436 Alex Escobar .40 1.00
437 Alex Sanchez .40 1.00
438 Jeff Bagwell .60 1.50
439 Claudio Vargas .40 1.00
440 Shawn Green .40 1.00
441 Geoff Jenkins .40 1.00
442 David Wells .40 1.00
443 Nick Johnson .40 1.00
444 Jose Guillen .40 1.00
445 Scott Hatteberg .40 1.00
446 Phil Nevin .40 1.00
447 Jason Schmidt .40 1.00
448 Ricky Ledee .40 1.00
449 So Taguchi .40 1.00
450 Randy Johnson 1.00 2.50
451 Eric Young .40 1.00
452 Chone Figgins .40 1.00
453 Larry Bigbie .40 1.00
454 Scott Williamson .40 1.00
455 Ramon Martinez .40 1.00
456 Roberto Alomar .60 1.50
457 Ryan Dempster .40 1.00
458 Ryan Ludwick .40 1.00
459 Ramon Santiago .40 1.00
460 Jeff Conine .40 1.00
461 Brad Lidge .40 1.00
462 Ken Harvey .40 1.00
463 Guillermo Mota .40 1.00
464 Rick Reed .40 1.00
465 Armando Benitez .40 1.00
466 Wade Miller .40 1.00

2004 Topps Chrome Black Refractors

*BLACK 1-210/257-466: 1.5X TO 4X BASIC
*BLACK 211-220/247-256: 1.2X TO 3X BASIC
1-220 SERIES 1 ODDS 1:10 H, 1:20 R
247-466 SERIES 2 ODDS 1:9 H, 1:20 R
221-233 SERIES 1 ODDS 1:1527 H, 1:2480 R
234-246 SERIES 2 ODDS 1:1579 H, 1:2549 R
221-246 PRINT RUN 25 SERIAL #'d SETS
221-246 NO PRICING DUE TO SCARCITY

2004 Topps Chrome Gold Refractors

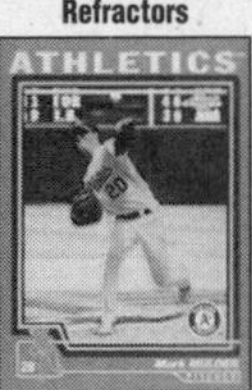

*GOLD 1-210/257-466: 1.25X TO 3X BASIC
*GOLD 211-220/247-256: 1X TO 2.5X BASIC
1-220 SERIES 1 ODDS 1:5 H, 1:10 R
247-466 SERIES 2 ODDS 1:9 H, 1:10 R
*GOLD AU 221-246: 2X TO 4X BASIC AU
221-233 SERIES 1 ODDS 1:759 H, 1:1208 R
234-246 SERIES 2 ODDS 1:790 H, 1:1324 R
221-246 PRINT RUN 50 SERIAL #'d SETS

2004 Topps Chrome Red X-Fractors

*RED XF 1-210/257-466: 3X TO 8X BASIC
*RED XF 211-220/247-256: 3X TO 8X BASIC
1-220 ONE PER SER.1 PARALLEL HOT PACK
247-466 1 PER SER.2 PARALLEL HOT PACK
ONE HOT PACK PER SEALED HOBBY BOX
1-220 STATED PRINT RUN 63 SETS
247-466 STATED PRINT RUN 61 SETS
1-220/247-466 ARE NOT SERIAL #'d
1-220/247-466 PRINT RUN GIVEN BY TOPPS
221-233 SERIES 1 ODDS 1:21,371 HOBBY
234-246 SERIES 2 ODDS 1:20,800 HOBBY
221-246 PRINT RUN 1 SERIAL #'d SET
221-246 NO PRICING DUE TO SCARCITY

2004 Topps Chrome Refractors

*REF 1-210/257-466: 1X TO 2.5X BASIC
*REF 211-220/247-256: .75X TO 2X BASIC
1-220 SERIES 1 ODDS 1:4 H/R
247-466 SERIES 2 ODDS 1:4 H/R
*REF AU 221-246: 1X TO 2.5X BASIC AU
221-233 SERIES 1 ODDS 1:380 H, 1:597 R
234-246 SERIES 2 ODDS 1:375 H, 1:680 R
221-246 PRINT RUN 100 SERIAL #'d SETS
232 Zach Miner FY AU 30.00 60.00

2004 Topps Chrome Fashionably Great Relics

ONE RELIC PER SER.1 GU HOBBY PACK
GROUP A 1:59 SER.1 RETAIL
GROUP B 1:107 SER.1 RETAIL
AD Adam Dunn Jsy A 3.00 8.00
AJ Andruw Jones Uni A 4.00 10.00
AP Albert Pujols Jsy A 10.00 25.00
AR Alex Rodriguez Uni A 6.00 15.00
BM Brett Myers Jsy A 3.00 8.00
BW Billy Wagner Jsy B 3.00 8.00
CB Craig Biggio Uni A 4.00 10.00
CD Carlos Delgado Jsy A 3.00 8.00
CF Cliff Floyd Jsy A 3.00 8.00
CJ Chipper Jones Uni A 4.00 10.00
CS Curt Schilling Jsy A 3.00 8.00
DL Derek Lowe Uni B 3.00 8.00
EC Eric Chavez Uni B 3.00 8.00
FG Freddy Garcia Jsy A 3.00 8.00
FM Fred McGriff Jsy A 4.00 10.00
FT Frank Thomas Uni A 4.00 10.00
HB Hank Blalock Jsy A 3.00 8.00
IR Ivan Rodriguez Uni B 4.00 10.00
JB Jeff Bagwell Uni A 4.00 10.00
JBO Joe Borchard Jsy A 3.00 8.00
JO John Olerud Jsy A 3.00 8.00
JR Juan Rivera Jsy A 3.00 8.00
JS John Smoltz Uni A 4.00 10.00
JV Jose Vidro Jsy A 3.00 8.00
KB Kevin Brown Jsy B 3.00 8.00
MM Mark Mulder Uni A 3.00 8.00
MP Mike Piazza Uni A 6.00 15.00
MR Manny Ramirez Uni A 4.00 10.00
MS Mike Sweeney Uni A 3.00 8.00
NG Nomar Garciaparra Uni B 6.00 15.00
PM Pedro Martinez Jsy A 4.00 10.00
RP Rafael Palmeiro Jsy A 4.00 10.00
SS Sammy Sosa Jsy A 4.00 10.00
TH Tim Hudson Uni B 3.00 8.00
THO Trevor Hoffman Uni A 3.00 8.00
VW Vernon Wells Jsy B 3.00 8.00
WP Wily Mo Pena Jsy A 3.00 8.00

2004 Topps Chrome Presidential First Pitch Seat Relics

SERIES 2 ODDS 1:15 BOX-LOADER HOBBY
SERIES 2 ODDS 1:633 HOBBY
STATED PRINT RUN 100 SETS
CARDS ARE NOT SERIAL-NUMBERED
PRINT RUN INFO PROVIDED BY TOPPS
BC Bill Clinton 20.00 50.00
CC Calvin Coolidge 10.00 25.00
DE Dwight Eisenhower 10.00 25.00
FR Franklin D. Roosevelt 15.00 40.00
GB George W. Bush 20.00 50.00
GF Gerald Ford 15.00 40.00
GHB George H.W. Bush 15.00 40.00
HH Herbert Hoover 10.00 25.00
HT Harry Truman 10.00 25.00
JK John F. Kennedy 20.00 50.00
LJ Lyndon B. Johnson 10.00 25.00
RN Richard Nixon 20.00 50.00
RR Ronald Reagan 30.00 60.00
WH Warren Harding 10.00 25.00
WT William Taft 10.00 25.00
WW Woodrow Wilson 10.00 25.00

2004 Topps Chrome Presidential Pastime Refractors

COMPLETE SET (42) 60.00 120.00
SERIES 2 ODDS 1:9 HOBBY
*X-FRACTOR p/r 26-43: 2X TO 5X BASIC
X-FRACTOR SER.2 ODDS 1:400 H, 1:791 R
X-F PRINT RUNS B/WN 1-43 COPIES PER
NO X-F PRICING ON QTY OF 25 OR LESS
PP1 George Washington 2.50 6.00
PP2 John Adams 1.50 4.00
PP3 Thomas Jefferson 2.50 6.00
PP4 James Madison 1.50 4.00
PP5 James Monroe 1.50 4.00
PP6 John Quincy Adams 1.50 4.00
PP7 Andrew Jackson 1.50 4.00
PP8 Martin Van Buren 1.50 4.00
PP9 William Harrison 1.50 4.00
PP10 John Tyler 1.50 4.00
PP11 James Polk 1.50 4.00
PP12 Zachary Taylor 1.50 4.00
PP13 Millard Fillmore 1.50 4.00
PP14 Franklin Pierce 1.50 4.00
PP15 James Buchanan 1.50 4.00
PP16 Abraham Lincoln 2.50 6.00
PP17 Andrew Johnson 1.50 4.00
PP18 Ulysses S. Grant 2.00 5.00
PP19 Rutherford B. Hayes 1.50 4.00
PP20 James Garfield 1.50 4.00
PP21 Chester Arthur 1.50 4.00
PP22 Grover Cleveland 1.50 4.00
PP23 Benjamin Harrison 1.50 4.00
PP24 William McKinley 1.50 4.00
PP25 Theodore Roosevelt 2.00 5.00
PP26 William Taft 1.50 4.00
PP27 Woodrow Wilson 1.50 4.00
PP28 Warren Harding 1.50 4.00
PP29 Calvin Coolidge 1.50 4.00
PP30 Herbert Hoover 1.50 4.00
PP31 Franklin D. Roosevelt 2.00 5.00
PP32 Harry Truman 1.50 4.00
PP33 Dwight Eisenhower 1.50 4.00
PP34 John F. Kennedy 2.00 5.00
PP35 Lyndon B. Johnson 1.50 4.00
PP36 Richard Nixon 2.00 5.00
PP37 Gerald Ford 2.00 5.00
PP38 Jimmy Carter 1.50 4.00
PP39 Ronald Reagan 5.00 12.00
PP40 George H.W. Bush 2.00 5.00
PP41 Bill Clinton 2.50 6.00
PP42 George W. Bush 2.50 6.00

2004 Topps Chrome Town Heroes Relics

SER.2 ODDS 1 PER HOBBY BOX-LOADER
SER.2 ODDS 1:48 RETAIL
AP Albert Pujols Bat 6.00 15.00
AR Alex Rodriguez Bat 6.00 15.00
BZ Barry Zito Uni 3.00 8.00
CJ Chipper Jones Jsy 4.00 10.00
EC Eric Chavez Uni 3.00 8.00
FT Frank Thomas Jsy 4.00 10.00
HN Hideo Nomo Jsy 4.00 10.00
JG Jason Giambi Uni 3.00 8.00
JR Jose Reyes Bat 3.00 8.00
KW Kerry Wood Jsy 3.00 8.00
LB Lance Berkman Jsy 3.00 8.00
MM Mark Mulder Uni 3.00 8.00
MP Mark Prior Bat 4.00 10.00
MR Manny Ramirez Bat 4.00 10.00
MT Miguel Tejada Bat 3.00 8.00
NG Nomar Garciaparra Bat 4.00 10.00
RH Rich Harden Uni 3.00 8.00
RP Rafael Palmeiro Jsy 4.00 10.00
SS Sammy Sosa Jsy 4.00 10.00
SST Shannon Stewart Jsy 3.00 8.00
TH Tim Hudson Uni 3.00 8.00

2004 Topps Chrome Traded

These cards were issued at a stated rate of two per 2004 Topps Traded pack. Cards numbered 1 through 65 feature veterans who were traded while cards 66 through 70 feature managers. Cards numbered 71 through 90 feature high draft picks, cards numbered 91 through 110 feature prospect and cards 111 through 220 feature Rookie Cards. All of these cards were issued with a "T" prefix.

COMPLETE SET (220) 30.00 60.00
COMMON CARD (1-70) .30 .75

COMMON CARD (71-90) .40 1.00
COMMON CARD (91-110) .40 1.00
COMMON CARD (111-220) .40 1.00
2 PER 2004 TOPPS TRADED HOBBY PACK
2 PER 2004 TOPPS TRADED HTA PACK
2 PER 2004 TOPPS TRADED RETAIL PACK
PLATE ODDS 1:1151 H, 1:1173 R, 1:327 HTA
PLATE PRINT RUN 1 SET PER COLOR
BLACK-CYAN-MAGENTA-YELLOW ISSUED
NO PLATE PRICING DUE TO SCARCITY
T1 Pokey Reese .30 .75
T2 Tony Womack .30 .75
T3 Richard Hidalgo .30 .75
T4 Juan Uribe .30 .75
T5 J.D. Drew .30 .75
T6 Alex Gonzalez .30 .75
T7 Carlos Guillen .30 .75
T8 Doug Mientkiewicz .30 .75
T9 Fernando Vina .30 .75
T10 Milton Bradley .30 .75
T11 Kelvim Escobar .30 .75
T12 Ben Grieve .30 .75
T13 Brian Jordan .30 .75
T14 A.J. Pierzynski .30 .75
T15 Billy Wagner .30 .75
T16 Terrence Long .30 .75
T17 Carlos Beltran .50 1.25
T18 Carl Everett .30 .75
T19 Reggie Sanders .30 .75
T20 Javy Lopez .30 .75
T21 Jay Payton .30 .75
T22 Octavio Dotel .30 .75
T23 Eddie Guardado .30 .75
T24 Andy Pettitte .50 1.25
T25 Richie Sexson .30 .75
T26 Ronnie Belliard .30 .75
T27 Michael Tucker .30 .75
T28 Brad Fullmer .30 .75
T29 Freddy Garcia .30 .75
T30 Bartolo Colon .30 .75
T31 Larry Walker Cards .50 1.25
T32 Mark Kotsay .30 .75
T33 Jason Marquis .30 .75
T34 Dustan Mohr .30 .75
T35 Javier Vazquez .30 .75
T36 Nomar Garciaparra .50 1.25
T37 Tino Martinez .50 1.25
T38 Hee Seop Choi .30 .75
T39 Damian Miller .30 .75
T40 Jose Lima .30 .75
T41 Ty Wigginton .30 .75
T42 Raul Ibanez .50 1.25
T43 Danys Baez .30 .75
T44 Tony Clark .30 .75
T45 Greg Maddux 1.00 2.50
T46 Victor Zambrano .30 .75
T47 Orlando Cabrera Sox .30 .75
T48 Jose Cruz Jr. .30 .75
T49 Kris Benson .30 .75
T50 Alex Rodriguez 1.00 2.50
T51 Steve Finley .30 .75
T52 Ramon Hernandez .30 .75
T53 Esteban Loaiza .30 .75
T54 Ugueth Urbina .30 .75
T55 Jeff Weaver .30 .75
T56 Flash Gordon .30 .75
T57 Jose Contreras .30 .75
T58 Paul Lo Duca .30 .75
T59 Junior Spivey .30 .75
T60 Curt Schilling .50 1.25
T61 Brad Penny .30 .75
T62 Braden Looper .30 .75
T63 Miguel Cairo .30 .75
T64 Juan Encarnacion .30 .75
T65 Miguel Batista .30 .75
T66 Terry Francona MG .30 .75
T67 Lee Mazzilli MG .30 .75
T68 Al Pedrique MG .30 .75
T69 Ozzie Guillen MG .30 .75
T70 Phil Garner MG .30 .75
T71 Matt Bush DP RC .60 1.50
T72 Homer Bailey DP RC .60 1.50
T73 Greg Golson DP RC .40 1.00
T74 Kyle Waldrop DP RC .40 1.00
T75 Richie Robnett DP RC .40 1.00
T76 Jay Rainville DP RC .40 1.00
T77 Bill Bray DP RC .40 1.00
T78 Philip Hughes DP RC 1.00 2.50
T79 Scott Elbert DP RC .40 1.00
T80 Josh Fields DP RC .60 1.50
T81 Justin Orenduff DP RC .60 1.50
T82 Dan Putnam DP RC .40 1.00
T83 Chris Nelson DP RC .40 1.00
T84 Blake DeWitt DP RC .60 1.50
T85 J.P. Howell DP RC .40 1.00
T86 Huston Street DP RC .60 1.50
T87 Kurt Suzuki DP RC .60 1.50
T88 Erick San Pedro DP RC .40 1.00
T89 Matt Tulasosopo DP RC 1.00 2.50
T90 Matt Macri DP RC .60 1.50
T91 Chad Tracy PROS .40 1.00
T92 Scott Hairston PROS .40 1.00
T93 Jonny Gomes PROS .40 1.00
T94 Chin-Feng Chen PROS .40 1.00
T95 Chien-Ming Wang PROS 1.50 4.00
T96 Dustin McGowan PROS .40 1.00
T97 Chris Burke PROS .40 1.00
T98 Denny Bautista PROS .40 1.00
T99 Preston Larrison PROS .40 1.00
T100 Kevin Youkilis PROS .40 1.00
T101 John Maine PROS .40 1.00
T102 Guillermo Quiroz PROS .40 1.00
T103 Dave Krynzel PROS .40 1.00
T104 David Kelton PROS .40 1.00
T105 Edwin Encarnacion PROS 1.00 2.50
T106 Chad Gaudin PROS .40 1.00
T107 Sergio Mitre PROS .40 1.00
T108 Laynce Nix PROS .40 1.00
T109 David Parrish PROS .40 1.00
T110 Brandon Claussen PROS .40 1.00
T111 Frank Francisco FY RC .40 1.00
T112 Brian Dallimore FY RC .40 1.00
T113 Jim Crowell FY RC .40 1.00
T114 Andres Blanco FY RC .40 1.00
T115 Eduardo Villacis FY RC .40 1.00
T116 Kazuhito Tadano FY RC .40 1.00
T117 Aarom Baldiris FY RC .40 1.00
T118 Justin Germano FY RC .40 1.00
T119 Joey Gathright FY RC .40 1.00
T120 Franklyn Gracesqui FY RC .40 1.00
T121 Chin-Lung Hu FY RC .40 1.00
T122 Scott Olsen FY RC .40 1.00
T123 Tyler Davidson FY RC .40 1.00
T124 Fausto Carmona FY RC .60 1.50
T125 Tim Hutting FY RC .40 1.00
T126 Ryan Meaux FY RC .40 1.00
T127 Jon Connolly FY RC .40 1.00
T128 Hector Made FY RC .40 1.00
T129 Jamie Brown FY RC .40 1.00
T130 Paul McAnulty FY RC .40 1.00
T131 Chris Saenz FY RC .40 1.00
T132 Marland Williams FY RC .40 1.00
T133 Mike Huggins FY RC .40 1.00
T134 Jesse Crain FY RC .60 1.50
T135 Chad Bentz FY RC .40 1.00
T136 Kazuo Matsui FY RC .60 1.50
T137 Paul Maholm FY .60 1.50
T138 Brock Jacobsen FY RC .40 1.00
T139 Casey Daigle FY RC .40 1.00
T140 Nyjer Morgan FY RC .40 1.00
T141 Tom Mastny FY RC .40 1.00
T142 Kody Kirkland FY RC .40 1.00
T143 Jose Capellan FY RC .40 1.00
T144 Felix Hernandez FY RC 6.00 15.00
T145 Shawn Hill FY RC .40 1.00
T146 Danny Gonzalez FY RC .40 1.00
T147 Scott Dohmann FY RC .40 1.00
T148 Tommy Murphy FY RC .40 1.00
T149 Akinori Otsuka FY RC .40 1.00
T150 Miguel Perez FY RC .40 1.00
T151 Mike Rouse FY RC .40 1.00
T152 Ramon Ramirez FY RC .40 1.00
T153 Luke Hughes FY RC 1.00 2.50
T154 Howie Kendrick FY RC 2.00 5.00
T155 Ryan Budde FY RC .40 1.00
T156 Charlie Zink FY RC .40 1.00
T157 Warner Madrigal FY RC .40 1.00
T158 Jason Szuminski FY RC .40 1.00
T159 Chad Chop FY RC .40 1.00
T160 Shingo Takatsu FY RC .40 1.00
T161 Matt Lemanczyk FY RC .40 1.00
T162 Wardell Starling FY RC .40 1.00
T163 Nick Gorneault FY RC .40 1.00
T164 Scott Proctor FY RC .40 1.00
T165 Brooks Conrad FY RC .40 1.00
T166 Hector Gimenez FY RC .40 1.00
T167 Kevin Howard FY RC .40 1.00
T168 Vince Perkins FY RC .40 1.00
T169 Brock Peterson FY RC .40 1.00
T170 Chris Shelton FY .40 1.00
T171 Erick Aybar FY RC 1.00 2.50
T172 Paul Bacot FY RC .40 1.00
T173 Matt Capps FY RC .40 1.00
T174 Kory Casto FY .40 1.00
T175 Juan Cedeno FY RC .40 1.00
T176 Vito Chiaravalloti FY .40 1.00
T177 Alec Zumwalt FY RC .40 1.00
T178 J.J. Furmaniak FY RC .40 1.00
T179 Lee Gwaltney FY RC .40 1.00
T180 Donald Kelly FY RC .60 1.50
T181 Benji DeQuin FY RC .40 1.00
T182 Brant Colamarino FY RC .40 1.00
T183 Juan Gutierrez FY RC .40 1.00
T184 Carl Loadenthal FY RC .40 1.00
T185 Ricky Nolasco FY RC .60 1.50
T186 Jeff Salazar FY RC .40 1.00
T187 Rob Tejeda FY RC .40 1.00
T188 Alex Romero FY RC .40 1.00
T189 Yoann Torrealba FY RC .40 1.00
T190 Carlos Sosa FY RC .40 1.00
T191 Tim Bittner FY RC .40 1.00
T192 Chris Aguila FY RC .40 1.00
T193 Jason Frasor FY RC .40 1.00
T194 Reid Gorecki FY RC .40 1.00
T195 Dustin Nippert FY RC .40 1.00
T196 Javier Guzman FY RC .40 1.00
T197 Harvey Garcia FY RC .40 1.00
T198 Ivan Ochoa FY RC .40 1.00
T199 David Wallace FY RC .40 1.00
T200 Joel Zumaya FY RC 1.50 4.00
T201 Casey Kopitzke FY RC .40 1.00
T202 Lincoln Holdzkom FY RC .40 1.00
T203 Chad Santos FY RC .40 1.00
T204 Brian Pilkington FY RC .40 1.00
T205 Terry Jones FY RC .40 1.00
T206 Jerome Gamble FY RC .40 1.00
T207 Brad Eldred FY RC .40 1.00
T208 David Pauley FY RC .60 1.50
T209 Kevin Davidson FY RC .40 1.00
T210 Damaso Espino FY RC .40 1.00
T211 Tom Farmer FY RC .40 1.00
T212 Michael Mooney FY RC .40 1.00
T213 James Tomlin FY RC .40 1.00
T214 Greg Thissen FY RC .40 1.00
T215 Calvin Hayes FY RC .40 1.00
T216 Fernando Cortez FY RC .40 1.00
T217 Sergio Silva FY RC .40 1.00
T218 Jon de Vries FY RC .40 1.00
T219 Don Sutton FY RC .40 1.00
T220 Leo Nunez FY RC .40 1.00

2004 Topps Chrome Traded Refractors

*REF 1-70: 2X TO 5X BASIC
*REF 71-90: 1.5X TO 4X BASIC
*REF 91-110: 1.5X TO 4X BASIC
*REF 111-220: 1.5X TO 4X BASIC
STATED ODDS 1:12 HOB/RET, 1:4 HTA
STATED PRINT RUN 355 SETS
CARDS ARE NOT SERIAL-NUMBERED
PRINT RUN INFO PROVIDED BY TOPPS

2004 Topps Chrome Traded X-Fractors

*XF 1-70: 8X TO 20X BASIC
*XF 91-110: 6X TO 15X BASIC
ONE XF PACK PER SEALED HTA BOX
ONE XF CARD PER XF PACK
STATED PRINT RUN 20 SERIAL #'d SETS
NO PRICING ON 71-90 DUE TO SCARCITY
NO PRICING ON 91-110 DUE TO SCARCITY

2005 Topps Chrome

This 234-card first series was released in January, 2005 while the 238-card second series was released in April, 2005. The cards were issued in four card hobby or retail packs with an $3 SRP which came 20 packs to a box and eight boxes to a case. Cards numbered 1-210 feature veteran players while cards 211-220 feature Rookie Cards and cards numbered 221-234 feature players in their first year with Topps who signed cards for this product. Cards numbered 221-234 were issued to a stated print run of 1771 sets (although these cards were not serial numbered) and were inserted at a stated rate of one in 28 hobby and one in 33 retail packs. In the second series, cards numbered 235 through 252 feature autographs and those cards were issued at a stated rate of one in two mini-boxes and one in 55 retail packs. In addition, these cards were issued to a stated print run of 1770 sets although these cards were not serial numbered.

COMP.SET w/o AU'S (440) 80.00 160.00
COMP.SERIES 1 w/o AU's (220) 40.00 80.00
COMP.SERIES 2 w/o AU's (220) 40.00 80.00
COMMON (1-210/253-467) .40 1.00
COMMON (211-220/468-472) .75 2.00
COMMON AU (221-252) 4.00 10.00
221-234 SER.1 ODDS 1:28 H, 1:33 R
235-252 SER.2 ODDS 1:2 MINI BOX, 1:55 R
221-252 STATED PRINT RUN 1770 SETS
221-252 ARE NOT SERIAL-NUMBERED
221-252 PRINT RUN PROVIDED BY TOPPS
EXCHANGE DEADLINE 05/31/07
1-234 PLATE ODDS 1:310 SER.1 HOBBY
235-252 PLATE ODDS 1:350 SER.2 MINI BOX
253-472 PLATE ODDS 1:29 SER.2 MINI BOX
PLATE PRINT RUN 1 SET PER COLOR
BLACK-CYAN-MAGENTA-YELLOW ISSUED
NO PLATE PRICING DUE TO SCARCITY
1 Alex Rodriguez 1.25 3.00
2 Placido Polanco .40 1.00
3 Torii Hunter .40 1.00
4 Lyle Overbay .40 1.00
5 Johnny Damon .60 1.50
6 Johnny Estrada .40 1.00
7 Rich Harden .40 1.00
8 Francisco Rodriguez .60 1.50
9 Jarrod Washburn .40 1.00
10 Sammy Sosa 1.00 2.50
11 Randy Wolf .40 1.00
12 Jason Bay .40 1.00
13 Tom Glavine .60 1.50
14 Michael Tucker .40 1.00
15 Brian Giles .40 1.00
16 Chad Tracy .40 1.00
17 Jim Edmonds .60 1.50
18 John Smoltz 1.00 2.50
19 Roy Halladay .60 1.50
20 Hank Blalock .40 1.00
21 Darin Erstad .40 1.00
22 Todd Walker .40 1.00
23 Mike Hampton .40 1.00
24 Mark Bellhorn .40 1.00
25 Jim Thome .60 1.50
26 Shingo Takatsu .40 1.00
27 Jody Gerut .40 1.00
28 Vinny Castilla .40 1.00
29 Luis Castillo .40 1.00
30 Ivan Rodriguez .60 1.50
31 Craig Biggio .60 1.50
32 Joe Randa .40 1.00
33 Adrian Beltre 1.00 2.50
34 Scott Podsednik .40 1.00
35 Cliff Floyd .40 1.00
36 Livan Hernandez .40 1.00
37 Eric Byrnes .40 1.00
38 Jose Acevedo .40 1.00
39 Jack Wilson .40 1.00
40 Gary Sheffield .40 1.00
41 Chan Ho Park .60 1.50
42 Carl Crawford .60 1.50
43 Shawn Estes .40 1.00
44 David Bell .40 1.00
45 Jeff DaVanon .40 1.00
46 Brandon Webb .60 1.50
47 Lance Berkman .60 1.50
48 Melvin Mora .40 1.00
49 David Ortiz 1.00 2.50
50 Andruw Jones .40 1.00
51 Chone Figgins .40 1.00
52 Danny Graves .40 1.00
53 Preston Wilson .40 1.00
54 Jeremy Bonderman .40 1.00
55 Carlos Guillen .40 1.00
56 Cesar Izturis .40 1.00
57 Kazuo Matsui .40 1.00
58 Jason Schmidt .40 1.00
59 Jason Marquis .40 1.00
60 Jose Vidro .40 1.00
61 Al Leiter .40 1.00
62 Javier Vazquez .40 1.00
63 Erubiel Durazo .40 1.00
64 Scott Spiezio .40 1.00
65 Scot Shields .40 1.00
66 Edgardo Alfonzo .40 1.00
67 Miguel Tejada .60 1.50
68 Francisco Cordero .40 1.00
69 Brett Myers .40 1.00
70 Curt Schilling .60 1.50
71 Matt Kata .40 1.00
72 Bartolo Colon .40 1.00
73 Rodrigo Lopez .40 1.00
74 Tim Wakefield .60 1.50
75 Frank Thomas 1.00 2.50
76 Jimmy Rollins .60 1.50
77 Barry Zito .60 1.50
78 Hideo Nomo 1.00 2.50
79 Brad Wilkerson .40 1.00
80 Adam Dunn .60 1.50
81 Derrek Lee .40 1.00
82 Joe Crede .40 1.00
83 Nate Robertson .40 1.00
84 John Thomson .40 1.00
85 Mike Sweeney .40 1.00
86 Kip Wells .40 1.00
87 Eric Gagne .40 1.00
88 Zach Day .40 1.00
89 Alex Sanchez .40 1.00
90 Bret Boone .40 1.00
91 Mark Loretta .40 1.00
92 Miguel Cabrera 1.00 2.50
93 Randy Winn .40 1.00
94 Adam Everett .40 1.00
95 Aubrey Huff .40 1.00
96 Kevin Mench .40 1.00
97 Frank Catalanotto .40 1.00
98 Flash Gordon .40 1.00
99 Scott Hatteberg .40 1.00
100 Albert Pujols 1.25 3.00
101 J.Molina .40 1.00
B.Molina
102 Jason Johnson
103 Jay Gibbons .40 1.00
104 Byung-Hyun Kim .40 1.00
105 Joe Borowski .40 1.00
106 Mark Grudzielanek .40 1.00
107 Mark Buehrle .60 1.50
108 Paul Wilson .40 1.00
109 Ronnie Belliard .40 1.00
110 Reggie Sanders .40 1.00
111 Tim Redding .40 1.00
112 Brian Lawrence .40 1.00
113 Travis Hafner .40 1.00
114 Jose Hernandez .40 1.00
115 Ben Sheets .40 1.00
116 Johan Santana .60 1.50
117 Billy Wagner .40 1.00
118 Mariano Rivera 1.25 3.00
119 Steve Trachsel .40 1.00
120 Akinori Otsuka .40 1.00
121 Jose Valentin .40 1.00
122 Orlando Hernandez .40 1.00
123 Raul Ibanez .60 1.50
124 Mike Matheny .40 1.00
125 Vernon Wells .40 1.00
126 Jason Isringhausen .40 1.00
127 Jose Guillen .40 1.00
128 Danny Bautista .40 1.00
129 Marcus Giles .40 1.00
130 Javy Lopez .40 1.00
131 Kevin Millar .40 1.00
132 Kyle Farnsworth .40 1.00
133 Carl Pavano .40 1.00
134 Rafael Furcal .40 1.00
135 Casey Blake .40 1.00
136 Matt Holliday 1.00 2.50
137 Bobby Higginson .40 1.00
138 Adam Kennedy .40 1.00
139 Alex Gonzalez .40 1.00
140 Jeff Kent .40 1.00
141 Aaron Guiel .40 1.00
142 Shawn Green .40 1.00
143 Bill Hall .40 1.00
144 Shannon Stewart .40 1.00
145 Juan Rivera .40 1.00
146 Coco Crisp .40 1.00
147 Mike Mussina .60 1.50
148 Eric Chavez .40 1.00
149 Jon Lieber .40 1.00
150 Vladimir Guerrero .60 1.50
151 Alex Cintron .40 1.00
152 Luis Matos .40 1.00
153 Sidney Ponson .40 1.00
154 Trot Nixon .40 1.00
155 Greg Maddux 1.25 3.00
156 Edgar Renteria .40 1.00
157 Ryan Freel .40 1.00
158 Matt Lawton .40 1.00
159 Mark Prior .60 1.50
160 Josh Beckett .40 1.00
161 Ken Harvey .40 1.00
162 Angel Berroa .40 1.00
163 Juan Encarnacion .40 1.00
164 Wes Helms .40 1.00
165 Brad Radke .40 1.00
166 Phil Nevin .40 1.00
167 Mike Cameron .40 1.00
168 Billy Koch .40 1.00
169 Bobby Crosby .40 1.00
170 Mike Lieberthal .40 1.00
171 Rob Mackowiak .40 1.00
172 Sean Burroughs .40 1.00
173 J.T. Snow .40 1.00
174 Paul Konerko .60 1.50
175 Luis Gonzalez .40 1.00
176 John Lackey .60 1.50
177 Oliver Perez .40 1.00
178 Brian Roberts .40 1.00
179 Bill Mueller .40 1.00
180 Carlos Lee .40 1.00
181 Corey Patterson .40 1.00
182 Sean Casey .40 1.00
183 Cliff Lee .60 1.50
184 Jason Jennings .40 1.00
185 Dmitri Young .40 1.00
186 Juan Uribe .40 1.00
187 Andy Pettitte .60 1.50
188 Juan Gonzalez .40 1.00
189 Orlando Hudson .40 1.00
190 Jason Phillips .40 1.00
191 Braden Looper .40 1.00
192 Lew Ford .40 1.00
193 Mark Mulder .40 1.00
194 Bobby Abreu .40 1.00
195 Jason Kendall .40 1.00
196 Khalil Greene .40 1.00
197 A.J. Pierzynski .40 1.00
198 Tim Worrell .40 1.00
199 So Taguchi .40 1.00
200 Jason Giambi .40 1.00
201 Tony Batista .40 1.00
202 Carlos Zambrano .60 1.50
203 Trevor Hoffman .60 1.50
204 Odalis Perez .40 1.00
205 Jose Cruz Jr. .40 1.00
206 Michael Barrett .40 1.00
207 Chris Carpenter .60 1.50
208 Michael Young UER .40 1.00
209 Toby Hall .40 1.00
210 Woody Williams .40 1.00
211 Chris Denorfia FY RC .40 1.00
212 Darren Fenster FY RC .40 1.00
213 Elvys Quezada FY RC .40 1.00
214 Ian Kinsler FY RC 2.00 5.00
215 Matthew Lindstrom FY RC .40 1.00
216 Ryan Goleski FY RC .40 1.00
217 Ryan Sweeney FY RC .60 1.50
218 Sean Marshall FY RC 1.00 2.50
219 Steve Doetsch FY RC .40 1.00
220 Wade Robinson FY RC .40 1.00
221 Andre Ethier FY AU RC 4.00 10.00
222 Brandon Moss FY AU RC 4.00 10.00
223 Chadd Blasko FY AU RC 4.00 10.00
224 Chris Roberson FY AU RC 4.00 10.00
225 Chris Seddon FY AU RC 4.00 10.00
226 Ian Bladergroen FY AU RC 4.00 10.00
227 Jake Dittler FY AU 4.00 10.00
228 Jose Vaquedano FY AU RC 4.00 10.00
229 Jeremy West FY AU RC 4.00 10.00
230 Kole Strayhorn FY AU RC 4.00 10.00
231 Kevin West FY AU RC 4.00 10.00
232 Luis Ramirez FY AU RC 4.00 10.00
233 Melky Cabrera FY AU RC 4.00 10.00
234 Nate Schierholtz FY AU 4.00 10.00
235 Billy Butler FY AU RC 4.00 10.00
236 Brandon Szymanski FY AU 4.00 10.00
237 Chad Orvella FY AU RC 4.00 10.00
238 Chip Cannon FY AU RC 4.00 10.00
239 Eric Nielsen FY AU RC 4.00 10.00
240 Erik Cordier FY AU RC 4.00 10.00
241 Glen Perkins FY AU RC 4.00 10.00
242 Justin Verlander FY AU RC 150.00 400.00
243 Kevin Melillo FY AU RC 6.00 15.00
244 Landon Powell FY AU RC 4.00 10.00
245 Matt Campbell FY AU RC 4.00 10.00
246 Michael Rogers FY AU RC 4.00 10.00
247 Nate McLouth FY AU RC 4.00 10.00
248 Scott Mathieson FY AU RC 4.00 10.00
249 Shane Costa FY AU RC 4.00 10.00
250 Tony Giarratano FY AU RC 4.00 10.00
251 Tyler Pelland FY AU RC 4.00 10.00
252 Wes Swackhamer FY AU RC 4.00 10.00
253 Garret Anderson .40 1.00
254 Randy Johnson 1.00 2.50
255 Charles Thomas .40 1.00
256 Rafael Palmeiro .60 1.50
257 Kevin Youkilis .40 1.00
258 Freddy Garcia .40 1.00
259 Magglio Ordonez .60 1.50
260 Aaron Harang .40 1.00
261 Grady Sizemore .60 1.50
262 Chin-hui Tsao .40 1.00
263 Eric Munson .40 1.00
264 Juan Pierre .40 1.00
265 Brad Lidge .40 1.00
266 Brian Anderson .40 1.00
267 Todd Helton .60 1.50
268 Chad Cordero .40 1.00
269 Kris Benson .40 1.00
270 Brad Halsey .40 1.00
271 Jermaine Dye .40 1.00
272 Manny Ramirez 1.00 2.50
273 Adam Eaton .40 1.00
274 Brett Tomko .40 1.00
275 Bucky Jacobsen .40 1.00
276 Dontrelle Willis .40 1.00
277 B.J. Upton .60 1.50
278 Rocco Baldelli .40 1.00
279 Ryan Drese .40 1.00
280 Ichiro Suzuki 1.25 3.00
281 Brandon Lyon .40 1.00
282 Nick Green .40 1.00
283 Jerry Hairston Jr. .40 1.00
284 Mike Lowell .40 1.00
285 Kerry Wood .40 1.00
286 Omar Vizquel .60 1.50
287 Carlos Beltran .60 1.50
288 Carlos Pena .60 1.50
289 Jeff Weaver .40 1.00
290 Chad Moeller .40 1.00
291 Joe Mays .40 1.00
292 Termel Sledge .40 1.00
293 Richard Hidalgo .40 1.00
294 Justin Duchscherer .40 1.00
295 Eric Milton .40 1.00
296 Ramon Hernandez .40 1.00
297 Jose Reyes .60 1.50
298 Joel Pineiro .40 1.00
299 Matt Morris .40 1.00
300 John Halama .40 1.00
301 Gary Matthews Jr. .40 1.00
302 Ryan Madson .40 1.00
303 Mark Kotsay .40 1.00
304 Carlos Delgado .40 1.00
305 Casey Kotchman .40 1.00
306 Greg Aquino .40 1.00
307 LaTroy Hawkins .40 1.00
308 Jose Contreras .40 1.00
309 Ken Griffey Jr. 2.00 5.00
310 C.C. Sabathia .60 1.50
311 Brandon Inge .40 1.00
312 John Buck .40 1.00
313 Hee Seop Choi .40 1.00
314 Chris Capuano .40 1.00
315 Jesse Crain .40 1.00
316 Geoff Jenkins .40 1.00
317 Mike Piazza 1.00 2.50
318 Jorge Posada .60 1.50
319 Nick Swisher .60 1.50
320 Kevin Millwood .40 1.00
321 Mike Gonzalez .40 1.00
322 Jake Peavy .40 1.00
323 Dustin Hermanson .40 1.00
324 Jeremy Reed .40 1.00
325 Alfonso Soriano .60 1.50
326 Alexis Rios .40 1.00
327 David Eckstein .40 1.00
328 Shea Hillenbrand .40 1.00
329 Russ Ortiz .40 1.00
330 Kurt Ainsworth .40 1.00
331 Orlando Cabrera .40 1.00
332 Carlos Silva .40 1.00
333 Ross Gload .40 1.00
334 Josh Phelps .40 1.00
335 Mike Maroth .40 1.00
336 Guillermo Mota .40 1.00
337 Chris Burke .40 1.00
338 David DeJesus .40 1.00
339 Jose Lima .40 1.00
340 Cristian Guzman .40 1.00
341 Nick Johnson .40 1.00
342 Victor Zambrano .40 1.00
343 Rod Barajas .40 1.00
344 Damian Miller .40 1.00
345 Chase Utley .60 1.50
346 Sean Burnett .40 1.00
347 David Wells .40 1.00
348 Dustan Mohr .40 1.00
349 Bobby Madritsch .40 1.00
350 Reed Johnson .40 1.00
351 R.A. Dickey .60 1.50
352 Scott Kazmir 1.00 2.50
353 Tony Womack .40 1.00
354 Tomas Perez .40 1.00
355 Esteban Loaiza .40 1.00
356 Tomokazu Ohka .40 1.00
357 Ramon Ortiz .40 1.00
358 Richie Sexson .40 1.00
359 J.D. Drew .40 1.00
360 Barry Bonds 1.50 4.00
361 Aramis Ramirez .40 1.00
362 Wily Mo Pena .40 1.00
363 Jeromy Burnitz .40 1.00
364 Nomar Garciaparra .60 1.50
365 Brandon Backe .40 1.00
366 Derek Lowe .40 1.00
367 Doug Davis .40 1.00
368 Joe Mauer .75 2.00
369 Endy Chavez .40 1.00
370 Bernie Williams .60 1.50
371 Jason Michaels .40 1.00
372 Craig Wilson .40 1.00
373 Ryan Klesko .40 1.00
374 Ray Durham .40 1.00
375 Jose Lopez .40 1.00
376 Jeff Suppan .40 1.00
377 David Bush .40 1.00
378 Marlon Byrd .40 1.00
379 Roy Oswalt .60 1.50
380 Rondell White .40 1.00
381 Troy Glaus .40 1.00
382 Scott Hairston .40 1.00
383 Chipper Jones 1.00 2.50
384 Daniel Cabrera .40 1.00
385 Jon Garland .40 1.00
386 Austin Kearns .40 1.00
387 Jake Westbrook .40 1.00
388 Aaron Miles .40 1.00
389 Omar Infante .40 1.00
390 Paul Lo Duca .40 1.00
391 Morgan Ensberg .40 1.00
392 Tony Graffanino .40 1.00
393 Milton Bradley .40 1.00
394 Keith Ginter .40 1.00
395 Justin Morneau .60 1.50
396 Tony Armas Jr. .40 1.00
397 Kevin Brown .40 1.00
398 Marco Scutaro .60 1.50
399 Tim Hudson .60 1.50
400 Pat Burrell .40 1.00
401 Jeff Cirillo .40 1.00
402 Larry Walker .60 1.50
403 Dewon Brazelton .40 1.00
404 Shigetoshi Hasegawa .40 1.00
405 Octavio Dotel .40 1.00
406 Michael Cuddyer .40 1.00
407 Junior Spivey .40 1.00
408 Zack Greinke 1.00 2.50
409 Roger Clemens 1.25 3.00
410 Chris Shelton .40 1.00
411 Ugueth Urbina .40 1.00
412 Rafael Betancourt .40 1.00
413 Willie Harris .40 1.00
414 Keith Foulke .40 1.00
415 Larry Bigbie .40 1.00
416 Paul Byrd .40 1.00
417 Troy Percival .40 1.00
418 Pedro Martinez .60 1.50
419 Matt Clement .40 1.00
420 Ryan Wagner .40 1.00
421 Jeff Francis .40 1.00
422 Jeff Conine .40 1.00
423 Wade Miller .40 1.00
424 Gavin Floyd .40 1.00
425 Kazuhisa Ishii .40 1.00
426 Victor Santos .40 1.00
427 Jacque Jones .40 1.00
428 Hideki Matsui 1.50 4.00
429 Cory Lidle .40 1.00
430 Jose Castillo .40 1.00
431 Alex Gonzalez .40 1.00
432 Kirk Rueter .40 1.00
433 Jolbert Cabrera .40 1.00
434 Erik Bedard .40 1.00
435 Ricky Ledee .40 1.00
436 Mark Hendrickson .40 1.00
437 Laynce Nix .40 1.00
438 Jason Frasor .40 1.00
439 Kevin Gregg .40 1.00
440 Derek Jeter 2.50 6.00
441 Jaret Wright .40 1.00
442 Edwin Jackson .40 1.00
443 Moises Alou .40 1.00
444 Aaron Rowand .40 1.00
445 Kazuhito Tadano .40 1.00
446 Luis Gonzalez .40 1.00
447 A.J. Burnett .40 1.00
448 Jeff Bagwell .60 1.50
449 Brad Penny .40 1.00
450 Corey Koskie .40 1.00
451 Mark Ellis .40 1.00
452 Hector Luna .40 1.00
453 Miguel Olivo .40 1.00
454 Scott Rolen .60 1.50
455 Ricardo Rodriguez .40 1.00
456 Eric Hinske .40 1.00
457 Tim Salmon .40 1.00
458 Adam LaRoche .40 1.00
459 B.J. Ryan .40 1.00
460 Steve Finley .40 1.00
461 Joe Nathan .40 1.00
462 Vicente Padilla .40 1.00
463 Yadier Molina 1.00 2.50
464 Tino Martinez .60 1.50
465 Mark Teixeira .60 1.50
466 Kelvim Escobar .40 1.00
467 Pedro Feliz .40 1.00
468 Ryan Garko FY RC .40 1.00
469 Bobby Livingston FY RC .40 1.00
470 Yorman Bazardo FY RC .40 1.00
471 Mike Bourn FY RC 1.00 2.50
472 Andy LaRoche FY RC .40 1.00

2005 Topps Chrome Black Refractors

*BLACK 1-210/253-467: 1.5X TO 4X BASIC
*BLACK 211-220/468-472: 1.5X TO 4X BASIC
1-220 SER.1 ODDS 1:10 H, 1:20 R
253-472 SER.2 ODDS 1:1 MINI BOX, 1:36 R
1-220/253-472 PRINT RUN 225 #'d SETS
*BLACK AU 221-252: 1X TO 2.5X BASIC AU
221-234 SER.1 ODDS 1:250 H, 1:291 R
235-252 SER.2 ODDS 1:12 MINI BOX, 1:508 R
221-252 PRINT RUN 200 SERIAL #'d SETS

2005 Topps Chrome Red X-Fractors

*RED XF 1-210/253-467: 6X TO 15X BASIC
1-220 SER.1 ODDS 1:50 HOBBY
221-234 SER.1 AU ODDS 1:779 HOBBY
235-252 SER.2 AU ODDS 1:91 MINI BOX
235-252 SER.2 AU ODDS 1:4042 RETAIL
253-472 SER.2 ODDS 1:3 BOX LOADER
STATED PRINT RUN 25 SERIAL #'d SETS
211-252/468-472 NO PRICING AVAILABLE
360 Barry Bonds 25.00 60.00

2005 Topps Chrome Refractors

*REF 1-210/253-467: 1X TO 2.5X BASIC
*REF 211-220/468-472: 1X TO 2.5X BASIC
1-220 SER.1 ODDS 1:6 H, 1:4 R
253-472 SER.2 ODDS 2 PER MINI BOX, 1:5 R
*REF AU 221-252: .5X TO 1.2X BASIC AU
221-234 SER.1 AU ODDS 1:100 H, 1:118 R

-252 SER.2 AU ODDS 1:5 MINI BOXES
-252 SER.2 AU ODDS 1:199 RETAIL
-252 PRINT RUN 500 SERIAL #'d SETS

2005 Topps Chrome A-Rod Throwbacks

MPLETE SET (4) 3.00 8.00
MMON CARD (1-4) 1.25 3.00
R.2 ODDS 2 PER MINI BOX, 1:5 R
ACK REF: 2X TO 5X BASIC
ACK REF SER.2 ODDS 1:14 BOX LOADER
ACK REF PRINT RUN 225 #'d SETS
LD SUPER SER.2 ODDS 1:2968 BOX LDR
LD SUPER PRINT RUN 1 #'d SET
GOLD SUPER PRICING AVAILABLE
D XF: 6X TO 15X BASIC
D XF SER.2 ODDS 1:124 BOX LOADER
D XF PRINT RUN 25 #'d SETS
EFRACTOR: 1X TO 2.5X BASIC
FRACTOR SER.2 ODDS 1:3 BOX LOADER
lex Rodriguez 1994 1.00 2.50
lex Rodriguez 1995 1.00 2.50
lex Rodriguez 1996 1.00 2.50
lex Rodriguez 1997 1.00 2.50

2005 Topps Chrome Dem Bums Autographs

RIES 1 ODDS 1:1816 H, 1:7270 R
ATED PRINT RUN 50 SETS
RDS ARE NOT SERIAL-NUMBERED
INT RUN INFO PROVIDED BY TOPPS
Carl Erskine 10.00 25.00
Clem Labine 30.00 60.00
Duke Snider 40.00 80.00
Don Zimmer 30.00 60.00
Johnny Podres 10.00 25.00

2005 Topps Chrome the Game Relics

R.1 GROUP A ODDS 1:15 BOX-LOADER
R.1 GROUP B ODDS 1:2 BOX-LOADER
Alex Rodriguez Bat A 6.00 15.00
Alfonso Soriano Uni B 3.00 8.00
Jeff Bagwell Uni B 4.00 10.00
Jorge Posada Uni B 4.00 10.00
John Smoltz Uni B 4.00 10.00
P Mark Prior Jsy B 4.00 10.00
PI Mike Piazza Jsy B 4.00 10.00
Y Michael Young Bat A 3.00 8.00
Sammy Sosa Jsy B 4.00 10.00
Torii Hunter Jsy B 3.00 8.00
B Wade Boggs Uni B 4.00 10.00

2005 Topps Chrome the Game Patch Relics

-COLOR ADD: ADD 20% PREMIUM
R.1 ODDS 1:8 BOX-LOADER
ATED PRINT RUN 70 SETS
RDS ARE NOT SERIAL-NUMBERED
INT RUN INFO PROVIDED BY TOPPS
D1 Adam Dunn Pose 6.00 15.00
D2 Adam Dunn Fielding 6.00 15.00
Albert Pujols 20.00 50.00
Alex Rodriguez 15.00 40.00
B Bret Boone 6.00 15.00
J Chipper Jones 10.00 25.00
S C.C. Sabathia 6.00 15.00
W Dontrelle Willis 6.00 15.00
Frank Thomas 10.00 25.00
N Hideo Nomo 10.00 25.00
B Jeff Bagwell 10.00 25.00
BE Josh Beckett 6.00 15.00
I Kazuhisa Ishii 6.00 15.00
W Kerry Wood 6.00 15.00
D Lance Berkman 6.00 15.00
L Mike Lowell 6.00 15.00
O Magglio Ordonez 6.00 15.00
PI Mike Piazza 10.00 25.00
T Mark Teixeira 10.00 25.00
L Paul Lo Duca 6.00 15.00
M Pedro Martinez 10.00 25.00
S Sammy Sosa 10.00 25.00
G Troy Glaus 6.00 15.00
H Todd Helton 10.00 25.00

2005 Topps Chrome Update

his 237-card set was released in January, 2006. his set was issued in four-card hobby and retail acks with an $3 SRP which came 24 packs per retail ox with 20 retail boxes per case. The hobby boxes re actually two 10-count boxes which come eight ll (or 16 mini) boxes to a case. Cards numbered 1-5 feature players who switched teams from when heir regular Chrome card was printed. Cards umbered 86-105 feature leading prospects while ards numbered 106 through 216 feature players with their first year on Topps cards. Cards numbered 216 through 220 feature players who accomplished mportant feats during the 2005 season. Cards umbered 221 through 237 feature signed Rookie Cards. Those cards were inserted at differing odds depending on whether the player was a group A or a group B autograph.

COMPLETE SET (237) 200.00 300.00
COMP.SET w/o SP's (220) 40.00 80.00
COM (1-85/216-220) .30 .75
COMMON (86-105) .30 .75
COM (14/65/106-215) .30 .75
COMMON (196-215) .75 2.00
SEMIS 196-215 1.25 3.00
UNLISTED 196-215 2.00 5.00
COMMON AU (221-237) 4.00 10.00
221-237 GROUP A ODDS 1:25 H, 1:49 R
221-237 GROUP B ODDS 1:29 H, 1:57 R
1-220 PLATE ODDS 1:347 H
221-237 PLATE AU ODDS 1:4857 H
PLATE PRINT RUN 1 SET PER COLOR
BLACK-CYAN-MAGENTA-YELLOW ISSUED
NO PLATE PRICING DUE TO SCARCITY
1 Sammy Sosa .75 2.00
2 Jeff Francoeur .75 2.00
3 Tony Clark .30 .75
4 Michael Tucker .30 .75
5 Mike Matheny .30 .75
6 Eric Young .30 .75
7 Jose Valentin .30 .75
8 Matt Lawton .30 .75
9 Juan Rivera .30 .75
10 Shawn Green .30 .75
11 Aaron Boone .30 .75
12 Woody Williams .30 .75
13 Brad Wilkerson .30 .75
14 Anthony Reyes RC .50 1.25
15 Gustavo Chacin .30 .75
16 Michael Restovich .30 .75
17 Humberto Quintero .30 .75
18 Matt Ginter .30 .75
19 Scott Podsednik .30 .75
20 Byung-Hyun Kim .30 .75
21 Orlando Hernandez .30 .75
22 Mark Grudzielanek .30 .75
23 Jody Gerut .30 .75
24 Adrian Beltre .75 2.00
25 Scott Schoeneweis .30 .75
26 Marlon Anderson .30 .75
27 Jason Vargas .30 .75
28 Claudio Vargas .30 .75
29 Jason Kendall .30 .75
30 Aaron Small .30 .75
31 Juan Cruz .30 .75
32 Placido Polanco .30 .75
33 Jorge Sosa .30 .75
34 John Olerud .30 .75
35 Ryan Langerhans .30 .75
36 Randy Winn .30 .75
37 Zach Duke .30 .75
38 Garrett Atkins .30 .75
39 Al Leiter .30 .75
40 Shawn Chacon .30 .75
41 Mark DeRosa .30 .75
42 Miguel Ojeda .30 .75
43 A.J. Pierzynski .30 .75
44 Carlos Lee .30 .75
45 LaTroy Hawkins .30 .75
46 Nick Green .30 .75
47 Shawn Estes .30 .75
48 Eli Marrero .30 .75
49 Jeff Kent .30 .75
50 Joe Randa .30 .75
51 Jose Hernandez .30 .75
52 Joe Blanton .30 .75
53 Huston Street .30 .75
54 Marlon Byrd .30 .75
55 Alex Sanchez .30 .75
56 Livan Hernandez .30 .75
57 Chris Young .50 1.25
58 Brad Eldred .30 .75
59 Terrence Long .30 .75
60 Phil Nevin .30 .75
61 Kyle Farnsworth .30 .75
62 Jon Lieber .30 .75
63 Antonio Alfonseca .30 .75
64 Tony Graffanino .30 .75
65 Tadahito Iguchi RC .50 1.25
66 Brad Thompson .30 .75
67 Jose Vidro .30 .75
68 Jason Phillips .30 .75
69 Carl Pavano .30 .75
70 Pokey Reese .30 .75
71 Jerome Williams .30 .75
72 Kazuhisa Ishii .30 .75
73 Felix Hernandez 1.00 2.50
74 Edgar Renteria .30 .75
75 Mike Myers .30 .75
76 Jeff Cirillo .30 .75
77 Endy Chavez .30 .75
78 Jose Guillen .30 .75
79 Ugueth Urbina .30 .75
80 Zach Day .30 .75
81 Javier Vazquez .30 .75
82 Willy Taveras .30 .75
83 Mark Mulder .30 .75
84 Vinny Castilla .30 .75
85 Russ Adams .30 .75
86 Homer Bailey PROS .30 .75
87 Ervin Santana PROS .30 .75
88 Bill Bray PROS .30 .75
89 Thomas Diamond PROS .30 .75
90 Trevor Plouffe PROS .75 2.00
91 James Houser PROS .30 .75
92 Jake Stevens PROS .30 .75
93 Anthony Whittington PROS .30 .75
94 Philip Hughes PROS .75 2.00
95 Greg Golson PROS .30 .75
96 Paul Maholm PROS .30 .75
97 Carlos Quentin PROS .50 1.25
98 Dan Johnson PROS .30 .75
99 Mark Rogers PROS .30 .75
100 Neil Walker PROS .50 1.25
101 Omar Quintanilla PROS .50 1.25
102 Blake DeWitt PROS .50 1.25
103 Taylor Tankersley PROS .50 1.25
104 David Murphy PROS .50 1.25
105 Chris Lambert PROS .50 1.25
106 Drew Anderson FY RC .30 .75
107 Luis Hernandez FY RC .30 .75
108 Jim Burt FY RC .30 .75
109 Mike Morse FY RC 1.00 2.50
110 Elliot Johnson FY RC .30 .75
111 C.J. Smith FY RC .30 .75
112 Casey McGehee FY RC .50 1.25
113 Brian Miller FY RC .30 .75
114 Chris Vines FY RC .30 .75
115 D.J. Houlton FY RC .30 .75
116 Chuck Tiffany FY RC .75 2.00
117 Humberto Sanchez FY RC .50 1.25
118 Baltazar Lopez FY RC .30 .75
119 Russ Martin FY RC 1.00 2.50
120 Dana Eveland FY RC .30 .75
121 Johan Silva FY RC .30 .75
122 Adam Harben FY RC .30 .75
123 Brian Bannister FY RC .50 1.25
124 Adam Boeve FY RC .30 .75
125 Thomas Oldham FY RC .30 .75
126 Cody Haerther FY RC .30 .75
127 Dan Santin FY RC .30 .75
128 Daniel Haigwood FY RC .30 .75
129 Craig Tatum FY RC .30 .75
130 Martin Prado FY RC 2.00 5.00
131 Errol Simonitsch FY RC .30 .75
132 Lorenzo Scott FY RC .30 .75
133 Hayden Penn FY RC .30 .75
134 Heath Totten FY RC .30 .75
135 Nick Masset FY RC .30 .75
136 Pedro Lopez FY RC .30 .75
137 Ben Harrison FY .30 .75
138 Mike Spidale FY RC .30 .75
139 Jeremy Harts FY RC .30 .75
140 Danny Zell FY RC .30 .75
141 Kevin Collins FY RC .30 .75
142 Tony Arnerich FY RC .30 .75
143 Matt Albers FY RC .30 .75
144 Ricky Barrett FY RC .30 .75
145 Hernan Iribarren FY RC .30 .75
146 Sean Tracey FY RC .30 .75
147 Jerry Owens FY RC .30 .75
148 Steve Nelson FY RC .30 .75
149 Brandon McCarthy FY RC .50 1.25
150 David Shepard FY RC .30 .75
151 Steven Bondurant FY RC .30 .75
152 Billy Sadler FY RC .30 .75
153 Ryan Feierabend FY RC .30 .75
154 Stuart Pomeranz FY RC .30 .75
155 Shaun Marcum FY .75 2.00
156 Erik Schindewolf FY RC .30 .75
157 Stefan Bailie FY RC .30 .75
158 Mike Esposito FY RC .30 .75
159 Buck Coats FY RC .30 .75
160 Andy Sides FY RC .30 .75
161 Micah Schnurstein FY RC .30 .75
162 Jesse Gutierrez FY RC .30 .75
163 Jake Postlewait FY RC .30 .75
164 Willy Mota FY RC .30 .75
165 Ryan Speier FY RC .30 .75
166 Frank Mata FY RC .30 .75
167 Jair Jurrjens FY RC 1.50 4.00
168 Nick Touchstone FY RC .30 .75
169 Matthew Kemp FY RC 1.50 4.00
170 Vinny Rottino FY RC .30 .75
171 J.B. Thurmond FY RC .30 .75
172 Kelvin Pichardo FY RC .30 .75
173 Scott Mitchinson FY RC .30 .75
174 Darwinson Salazar FY RC .30 .75
175 George Kottaras FY RC .50 1.25
176 Kenny Durost FY RC .30 .75
177 Jonathan Sanchez FY RC 1.25 3.00
178 Brandon Moorhead FY RC .30 .75
179 Kennard Bibbs FY RC .30 .75
180 David Gassner FY RC .30 .75
181 Micah Furtado FY RC .30 .75
182 Ismael Ramirez FY RC .30 .75
183 Carlos Gonzalez FY RC 2.50 6.00
184 Brandon Sing FY RC .30 .75
185 Jason Motte FY RC .30 .75
186 Chuck James FY RC .75 2.00
187 Andy Santana FY RC .30 .75
188 Manny Parra FY RC .75 2.00
189 Chris B.Young FY RC 1.00 2.50
190 Juan Senreiso FY RC .30 .75
191 Franklin Morales FY RC .50 1.25
192 Jared Gothreaux FY RC .30 .75
193 Jayce Tingler FY RC .30 .75
194 Matt Brown FY RC .30 .75
195 Frank Diaz FY RC .30 .75
196 Stephen Drew FY RC 2.50 6.00
197 Jered Weaver FY RC 4.00 10.00
198 Ryan Braun FY RC 6.00 15.00
199 John Mayberry Jr. FY RC 2.00 5.00
200 Aaron Thompson FY RC 1.25 3.00
201 Ben Copeland FY RC .75 2.00
202 Jacoby Ellsbury FY RC 6.00 15.00
203 Garrett Olson FY RC .75 2.00
204 Cliff Pennington FY RC .75 2.00
205 Colby Rasmus FY RC 2.00 5.00
206 Chris Volstad FY RC 2.00 5.00
207 Ricky Romero FY RC 1.25 3.00
208 Ryan Zimmerman FY RC 4.00 10.00
209 C.J. Henry FY RC 1.25 3.00
210 Nelson Cruz FY RC 6.00 15.00
211 Josh Wall FY RC 1.25 3.00
212 Nick Webber FY RC .75 2.00
213 Paul Kelly FY RC .75 2.00
214 Kyle Winters FY RC .75 2.00
215 Mitch Boggs FY RC .75 2.00
216 Craig Biggio HL .50 1.25
217 Greg Maddux HL 1.00 2.50
218 Bobby Abreu HL .30 .75
219 Alex Rodriguez HL 1.00 2.50
220 Trevor Hoffman HL .50 1.25
221 Trevor Bell FY AU A RC 4.00 10.00
222 Jay Bruce FY AU A RC 10.00 25.00
223 Travis Buck FY AU B RC 4.00 10.00
224 Cesar Carrillo FY AU B RC 4.00 10.00
225 Mike Costanzo FY AU A RC 4.00 10.00
226 Brent Cox FY AU A RC 4.00 10.00
227 Matt Garza FY AU A RC 5.00 12.00
228 Josh Geer FY AU A RC 4.00 10.00
229 Tyler Greene FY AU A RC 4.00 10.00
230 Eli Iorg FY AU A RC 4.00 10.00
231 Craig Italiano FY AU B RC 4.00 10.00
232 Beau Jones FY AU A RC 4.00 10.00
233 M.McCormick FY AU B RC 4.00 10.00
234 A.McCutchen FY AU B RC 30.00 80.00
235 Micah Owings FY AU B RC 5.00 12.00
236 Cesar Ramos FY AU B RC 4.00 10.00
237 Chaz Roe FY AU A RC 4.00 10.00

2005 Topps Chrome Update Refractors

*REF 1-85: 1.25X TO 3X BASIC
*REF 86-105: 1.25X TO 3X BASIC
*REF 14/65/106-215: 1X TO 2.5X BASIC
*REF 216-220: 2X TO 5X BASIC
1-220 ODDS 1:5 HOBBY, 1:5 RETAIL
*REF AU 221-237: .6X TO 1.5X BASIC AU
221-237 AU ODDS 1:53 H, 1:115 R
221-237 AU PRINT RUN 500 #'d SETS

2005 Topps Chrome Update Black Refractors

*BLACK 1-85: 2X TO 5X BASIC
*BLACK 86-105: 2X TO 5X BASIC
*BLACK 14/65/106-215: 1.5X TO 4X BASIC
*BLACK 216-220: 2.5X TO 6X BASIC
1-220 ODDS 1:10 HOBBY, 1:19 RETAIL
1-220 PRINT RUN 250 #'d SETS
*BLACK AU 221-237: 1X TO 2.5X BASIC AU
221-237 AU ODDS 1:140 H, 1:279 R
221-237 AU PRINT RUN 200 #'d SETS
222 Jay Bruce FY AU 50.00 120.00

2005 Topps Chrome Update Red X-Fractors

*RED 1-85: 4X TO 10X BASIC
*RED 86-105: 4X TO 10X BASIC
*RED 14/65/106-215: 5X TO 12X BASIC
*RED 216-220: 5X TO 12X BASIC
1-220 ODDS 1:5 HOBBY
1-220 PRINT RUN 65 #'d SETS
221-237 AU ODDS 1:766 HOBBY
221-237 AU PRINT RUN 25 #'d SETS
221-237 NO PRICING DUE TO SCARCITY
183 Carlos Gonzalez FY 100.00 175.00
198 Ryan Braun FY 40.00 100.00

2005 Topps Chrome Update Barry Bonds Home Run History

COMPLETE SET (29) 20.00 50.00
COMPLETE SERIES 1 (15) 12.50 30.00
COMPLETE SERIES 2 (14) 8.00 20.00
COMMON CARD 1.25 3.00
1-350 ODDS 1:12 HOBBY, 1:23 RETAIL
375-700 ODDS 1:6 HOBBY, 1:23 RETAIL
1-350 PLATE ODDS 1:347 H
375-700 PLATE ODDS 1:300 BOX LDR
PLATE PRINT RUN 1 SET PER COLOR
BLACK-CYAN-MAGENTA-YELLOW ISSUED
*REF: 1.25X TO 3X BASIC
1-350 REF ODDS 1:71 H, 1:141 R
375-700 REF ODDS 1:70 H, 1:350 R
375-700 REF PRINT RUN 500 #'d SETS
*BLACK REF: 2X TO 5X BASIC
1-350 BLACK REF.ODDS 1:178 H, 1:365 R
375-700 BLACK REF.ODDS 1:175 H, 1:950 R
BLACK REF.PRINT RUN 200 #'d SETS
*BLUE: 4X TO 10X BASIC
375-700 BLUE REF ODDS 1:300 RETAIL
BLUE REF.PRINT RUN 100 #'d SETS
1-350 GOLD SUPER ODDS 1:22,548 H
375-700 GOLD SUP.ODDS 1:1234 BOX LDR
GOLD SUPER PRINT RUN 1 #'d SET
NO GOLD SUP.PRICING DUE TO SCARCITY
*RED X-F: 6X TO 15X BASIC
1-350 RED X-F ODDS 1:872 H
375-700 RED X-F ODDS 1:48 BOX LDR
RED X-F PRINT RUN 25 #'d SETS
1-350 ISSUED IN '05 CHROME UPDATE
375-700 ISSUED IN '06 CHROME

2006 Topps Chrome

This 355-card set was released in July, 2006. In a change from previous years, this chrome set was issued all in one series. The set was issued in four-card packs with an $3 SRP and those packs came 24 to a box and 10 boxes to a case. The first 252 cards in this set feature veterans while cards numbered 253-275 feature Award Winners, 276-330 feature rookies and 331-354 feature signed rookies. Card number 285 Kenji Johjima also comes in a signed version. The overall odds of securing a signed rookie card was stated to be one in fifteen hobby packs.

AU 331-354 ODDS 1:15 HOBBY
JOHJIMA AU ODDS 1:1650 HOBBY
1-330 PLATES 1:25 HOBBY BOX LDR
331-354 AU PLATES 1:324 HOBBY BOX LDR
PLATE PRINT RUN 1 SET PER COLOR
BLACK-CYAN-MAGENTA-YELLOW ISSUED
NO PLATE PRICING DUE TO SCARCITY
1 Alex Rodriguez .75 2.00
2 Garrett Atkins .25 .60
3 Carl Crawford .40 1.00
4 Clint Barmes .25 .60
5 Tadahito Iguchi .25 .60
6 Brian Roberts .25 .60
7 Mickey Mantle 2.00 5.00
8 David Wright .50 1.25
9 Jeremy Reed .25 .60
10 Bobby Abreu .25 .60
11 Lance Berkman .40 1.00
12 Jonny Gomes .25 .60
13 Jason Marquis .25 .60
14 Chipper Jones .60 1.50
15 Jon Garland .25 .60
16 Brad Wilkerson .25 .60
17 Rickie Weeks .25 .60
18 Jorge Posada .40 1.00
19 Greg Maddux .75 2.00
20 Jeff Francis .25 .60
21 Felipe Lopez .25 .60
22 Dan Johnson .25 .60
23 Manny Ramirez .60 1.50
24 Joe Mauer .40 1.00
25 Randy Winn .25 .60
26 Pedro Feliz .25 .60
27 Kenny Rogers .25 .60
28 Rocco Baldelli .25 .60
29 Nomar Garciaparra .40 1.00
30 Carlos Lee .25 .60
31 Tom Glavine .40 1.00
32 Craig Biggio .40 1.00
33 Steve Finley .25 .60
34 Eric Gagne .25 .60
35 Dallas McPherson .25 .60
36 Mark Kotsay .25 .60
37 Kerry Wood .25 .60
38 Huston Street .25 .60
39 Hank Blalock .25 .60
40 Brad Radke .25 .60
41 Chien-Ming Wang .40 1.00
42 Mark Buehrle .40 1.00
43 Andy Pettitte .40 1.00
44 Bernie Williams .40 1.00
45 Victor Martinez .40 1.00
46 Darin Erstad .25 .60
47 Gustavo Chacin .25 .60
48 Carlos Guillen .25 .60
49 Lyle Overbay .25 .60
50 Barry Bonds 1.00 2.50
51 Nook Logan .25 .60
52 Mark Teahen .25 .60
53 Mike Lamb .25 .60
54 Jayson Werth .40 1.00
55 Mariano Rivera .75 2.00
56 Julio Lugo .25 .60
57 Adam Dunn .40 1.00
58 Troy Percival .25 .60
59 Chad Tracy .25 .60
60 Edgar Renteria .25 .60
61 Jason Giambi .25 .60
62 Justin Morneau .40 1.00
63 Carlos Delgado .25 .60
64 John Buck .25 .60
65 Shannon Stewart .25 .60
66 Mike Cameron .25 .60
67 Richie Sexson .25 .60
68 Russ Adams .25 .60
69 Josh Beckett .25 .60
70 Ryan Freel .25 .60
71 Victor Zambrano .25 .60
72 Ronnie Belliard .25 .60
73 Brian Giles .25 .60
74 Randy Wolf .25 .60
75 Robinson Cano .40 1.00
76 Joe Blanton .25 .60
77 Esteban Loaiza .25 .60
78 Troy Glaus .25 .60
79 Matt Clement .25 .60
80 Geoff Jenkins .25 .60
81 Roy Oswalt .40 1.00
82 A.J. Pierzynski .25 .60
83 Pedro Martinez .40 1.00
84 Roger Clemens .75 2.00
85 Jack Wilson .25 .60
86 Mike Piazza .60 1.50
87 Paul Lo Duca .25 .60
88 Jeff Bagwell .40 1.00
89 Carlos Zambrano .40 1.00
90 Brandon Claussen .25 .60
91 Travis Hafner .25 .60
92 Chris Shelton .25 .60
93 Rafael Furcal .25 .60
94 Frank Thomas .60 1.50
95 Noah Lowry .25 .60
96 Jhonny Peralta .25 .60
97 Vernon Wells .25 .60
98 Jorge Cantu .25 .60
99 Willy Taveras .25 .60
100 Ivan Rodriguez .40 1.00
101 Jose Reyes .40 1.00
102 Barry Zito .40 1.00
103 Mark Teixeira .40 1.00
104 Chone Figgins .25 .60
105 Todd Helton .40 1.00
106 Tim Wakefield .25 .60
107 Mike Maroth .25 .60
108 Johnny Damon .40 1.00
109 David DeJesus .25 .60
110 Ryan Klesko .25 .60
111 Nick Johnson .25 .60
112 Freddy Garcia .25 .60
113 Torii Hunter .25 .60
114 Mike Sweeney .25 .60
115 Scott Rolen .40 1.00
116 Jim Thome .40 1.00
117 Adam Kennedy .25 .60
118 Albert Pujols .75 2.00
119 Kazuo Matsui .25 .60
120 Zack Greinke .25 .60
121 Jimmy Rollins .40 1.00
122 Edgardo Alfonzo .25 .60
123 Billy Wagner .25 .60
124 B.J. Ryan .25 .60
125 Orlando Hudson .25 .60
126 Preston Wilson .25 .60
127 Melvin Mora .25 .60
128 Alfonso Soriano .40 1.00
129 Javy Lopez .25 .60
130 Wilson Betemit .25 .60
131 Garret Anderson .25 .60
132 Jason Bay .25 .60
133 Adam LaRoche .25 .60
134 C.C. Sabathia .40 1.00
135 Bartolo Colon .25 .60
136 Ichiro Suzuki .75 2.00
137 Jim Edmonds .40 1.00
138 David Eckstein .25 .60
139 Cristian Guzman .25 .60
140 Jeff Kent .25 .60
141 Chris Capuano .25 .60
142 Cliff Floyd .25 .60
143 Zach Duke .25 .60
144 Matt Morris .25 .60
145 Jose Vidro .25 .60
146 David Wells .25 .60
147 John Smoltz .60 1.50
148 Felix Hernandez .40 1.00
149 Orlando Cabrera .25 .60
150 Mark Prior .40 1.00
151 Ted Lilly .25 .60
152 Michael Young .25 .60
153 Livan Hernandez .25 .60
154 Yadier Molina .60 1.50
155 Eric Chavez .25 .60
156 Miguel Batista .25 .60
157 Ben Sheets .25 .60
158 Oliver Perez .25 .60
159 Doug Davis .25 .60
160 Andruw Jones .25 .60
161 Hideki Matsui .60 1.50
162 Reggie Sanders .25 .60
163 Joe Nathan .25 .60
164 John Lackey .40 1.00
165 Matt Murton .25 .60
166 Grady Sizemore .40 1.00
167 Brad Thompson .25 .60
168 Kevin Millwood .25 .60
169 Orlando Hernandez .25 .60
170 Mark Mulder .25 .60
171 Chase Utley .40 1.00
172 Moises Alou .25 .60
173 Wily Mo Pena .25 .60
174 Brian McCann .25 .60
175 Jermaine Dye .25 .60
176 Ryan Madson .25 .60
177 Aramis Ramirez .25 .60
178 Khalil Greene .25 .60
179 Mike Hampton .25 .60
180 Mike Mussina .40 1.00
181 Rich Harden .25 .60
182 Woody Williams .25 .60
183 Chris Carpenter .40 1.00
184 Brady Clark .25 .60
185 Luis Gonzalez .25 .60
186 Raul Ibanez .40 1.00
187 Magglio Ordonez .40 1.00
188 Adrian Beltre .60 1.50
189 Marcus Giles .25 .60
190 Odalis Perez .25 .60
191 Derek Jeter 1.50 4.00
192 Jason Schmidt .25 .60
193 Toby Hall .25 .60
194 Danny Haren .25 .60
195 Tim Hudson .40 1.00
196 Jake Peavy .25 .60
197 Casey Blake .25 .60
198 J.D. Drew .25 .60
199 Ervin Santana .25 .60
200 J.J. Hardy .25 .60
201 Austin Kearns .25 .60
202 Pat Burrell .25 .60
203 Jason Vargas .25 .60
204 Ryan Howard .50 1.25
205 Joe Crede .25 .60
206 Vladimir Guerrero .40 1.00
207 Roy Halladay .40 1.00
208 David Dellucci .25 .60
209 Brandon Webb .40 1.00
210 Ryan Church .25 .60
211 Miguel Tejada .40 1.00
212 Mark Loretta .25 .60
213 Kevin Youkilis .25 .60
214 Jon Lieber .25 .60
215 Miguel Cabrera .60 1.50
216 A.J. Burnett .25 .60
217 David Bell .25 .60
218 Eric Byrnes .25 .60
219 Lance Niekro .25 .60
220 Shawn Green .25 .60
221 Ken Griffey Jr. 1.25 3.00
222 Johnny Estrada .25 .60
223 Omar Vizquel .40 1.00
224 Gary Sheffield .25 .60
225 Brad Halsey .25 .60
226 Aaron Cook .25 .60
227 David Ortiz .60 1.50
228 Scott Kazmir .40 1.00
229 Dustin McGowan .25 .60
230 Gregg Zaun .25 .60
231 Carlos Beltran .40 1.00
232 Bob Wickman .25 .60
233 Brett Myers .25 .60
234 Casey Kotchman .25 .60
235 Jeff Francoeur .60 1.50
236 Paul Konerko .40 1.00
237 Juan Rivera .25 .60
238 Bobby Crosby .25 .60
239 Derrek Lee .25 .60
240 Curt Schilling .40 1.00
241 Jake Westbrook .25 .60
242 Dontrelle Willis .25 .60
243 Brad Lidge .25 .60
244 Randy Johnson .60 1.50
245 Nick Swisher .40 1.00
246 Johan Santana .40 1.00
247 Jeremy Bonderman .25 .60
248 Ramon Hernandez .25 .60
249 Mike Lowell .25 .60
250 Javier Vazquez .25 .60
251 Jose Contreras .25 .60
252 Aubrey Huff .25 .60
253 Kenny Rogers AW .25 .60
254 Mark Teixeira AW .40 1.00
255 Orlando Hudson AW .25 .60
256 Derek Jeter AW 1.50 4.00
257 Eric Chavez AW .25 .60
258 Torii Hunter AW .25 .60
259 Vernon Wells AW .25 .60
260 Ichiro Suzuki AW .75 2.00
261 Greg Maddux AW .75 2.00
262 Mike Matheny AW .25 .60
263 Derrek Lee AW .25 .60
264 Luis Castillo AW .25 .60
265 Omar Vizquel AW .40 1.00
266 Mike Lowell AW .25 .60
267 Andruw Jones AW .25 .60
268 Jim Edmonds AW .40 1.00
269 Bobby Abreu AW .25 .60
270 Bartolo Colon AW .25 .60
271 Chris Carpenter AW .40 1.00
272 Alex Rodriguez AW .75 2.00
273 Albert Pujols AW .75 2.00
274 Huston Street AW .25 .60
275 Ryan Howard AW .50 1.25
276 Chris Denorfia (RC) .40 1.00
277 John Van Benschoten (RC) .40 1.00
278 Russ Martin (RC) .60 1.50
279 Fausto Carmona (RC) .40 1.00
280 Freddie Bynum (RC) .40 1.00
281 Kelly Shoppach (RC) .40 1.00
282 Chris Demaria RC .40 1.00
283 Jordan Tata RC .40 1.00
284 Ryan Zimmerman (RC) 1.25 3.00
285a Kenji Johjima RC 1.00 2.50
285b Kenji Johjima AU 5.00 12.00
286 Ruddy Lugo (RC) .40 1.00
287 Tommy Murphy (RC) .40 1.00
288 Bobby Livingston (RC) .40 1.00
289 Anderson Hernandez (RC) .40 1.00
290 Brian Slocum (RC) .40 1.00
291 Sendy Rleal RC .40 1.00
292 Ryan Spilborghs (RC) .40 1.00
293 Brandon Fahey RC .40 1.00
294 Jason Kubel (RC) .40 1.00
295 James Loney (RC) .60 1.50
296 Jeremy Accardo RC .40 1.00
297 Fabio Castro RC .40 1.00
298 Matt Capps (RC) .40 1.00
299 Casey Janssen RC .40 1.00
300 Martin Prado (RC) .60 1.50
301 Ronny Paulino (RC) .40 1.00
302 Josh Barfield (RC) .40 1.00
303 Joel Zumaya (RC) 1.00 2.50
304 Matt Cain (RC) 2.50 6.00
305 Conor Jackson (RC) .60 1.50
306 Brian Anderson (RC) .40 1.00
307 Prince Fielder (RC) 2.00 5.00
308 Jeremy Hermida (RC) .40 1.00
309 Justin Verlander (RC) 3.00 8.00
310 Brian Bannister (RC) .40 1.00
311 Josh Willingham (RC) .60 1.50
312 John Rheinecker (RC) .40 1.00
313 Nick Markakis (RC) .75 2.00
314 Jonathan Papelbon (RC) 2.00 5.00
315 Mike Jacobs (RC) .40 1.00
316 Jose Capellan (RC) .40 1.00
317 Mike Napoli RC .60 1.50
318 Ricky Nolasco (RC) .40 1.00
319 Ben Johnson (RC) .40 1.00
320 Paul Maholm (RC) .40 1.00
321 Drew Meyer (RC) .40 1.00
322 Jeff Mathis (RC) .40 1.00
323 Fernando Nieve (RC) .40 1.00
324 John Koronka (RC) .40 1.00
325 Wil Nieves (RC) .40 1.00
326 Nate McLouth (RC) .40 1.00
327 Howie Kendrick (RC) .75 2.00
328 Sean Marshall (RC) .40 1.00
329 Brandon Watson (RC) .40 1.00
330 Skip Schumaker (RC) .40 1.00
331 Ryan Garko AU (RC) 4.00 10.00
332 Jason Bergmann AU RC 4.00 10.00
333 Chuck James AU (RC) 6.00 15.00
334 Adam Wainwright AU (RC) 10.00 25.00
335 Dan Ortmeier AU (RC) 4.00 10.00
336 Francisco Liriano AU (RC) 6.00 15.00
337 Craig Breslow AU RC 4.00 10.00
338 Darrell Rasner AU (RC) 4.00 10.00
339 Jason Botts AU (RC) 4.00 10.00
340 Ian Kinsler AU (RC) 8.00 20.00
341 Joey Devine AU RC 4.00 10.00
342 Miguel Perez AU (RC) 4.00 10.00
343 Scott Olsen AU (RC) 4.00 10.00
344 Tyler Johnson AU (RC) 4.00 10.00
345 Anthony Lerew AU (RC) 4.00 10.00
346 Nelson Cruz AU (RC) 25.00 60.00
347 Willie Eyre AU (RC) 4.00 10.00
348 Josh Johnson AU (RC) 6.00 15.00

349 Shaun Marcum AU (RC) 4.00 10.00
350 Dustin Nippert AU (RC) 4.00 10.00
351 Josh Wilson AU (RC) 4.00 10.00
352 Hanley Ramirez AU (RC) 5.00 12.00
353 Reggie Abercrombie AU (RC) 4.00 10.00
354 Dan Uggla AU (RC) 6.00 15.00

2006 Topps Chrome Refractors

*REF 1-275: .6X TO 1.5X BASIC
*REF 276-330: .6X TO 1.5X BASIC RC
1-330 STATED ODDS 1:4 H, 1:4 R
*REF AU 331-354: .5X TO 1.2X BASIC AU
331-354 AU ODDS 1:65 HOBBY
331-354 PRINT RUN 500 SERIAL #'d SETS
354 Dan Uggla AU 10.00 25.00

2006 Topps Chrome Black Refractors

*BLACK REF 1-275: 1.25X TO 3X BASIC
*BLACK REF 276-330: 1.25X TO 3X BASIC RC
1-330 STATED ODDS 1:6 H, 1:19 R
1-330 PRINT RUN 549 SERIAL #'d SETS
*BLK REF AU 331-354: .6X TO 1.5X BASIC AU
331-354 AU ODDS 1:162 HOBBY
331-354 PRINT RUN 200 SERIAL #'d SETS
354 Dan Uggla AU 12.50 30.00

2006 Topps Chrome Blue Refractors

*BLUE REF 1-275: 2X TO 5X BASIC
*BLUE REF 276-330: 2X TO 5X BASIC RC
STATED ODDS 1:8 RETAIL

2006 Topps Chrome Red Refractors

*RED REF 1-275: 4X TO 10X BASIC
*RED REF 276-330: 3X TO 8X BASIC RC
1-330 ODDS 1:2 HOBBY BOX LOADER
1-330 PRINT RUN 90 SERIAL #'d SETS
331-354 AU ODDS 1:52 HOBBY BOX LOADER
331-354 AU PRINT RUN 25 SERIAL #'d SETS
NO AU PRICING DUE TO SCARCITY

2006 Topps Chrome X-Fractors

*X-FRAC 1-275: 1.5X TO 4X BASIC
*X-FRAC 276-330: 1.5X TO 4X BASIC RC
STATED ODDS 1:6 RETAIL

2006 Topps Chrome Declaration of Independence

COMPLETE SET (56) 60.00 120.00
STATED ODDS 1:7 H, 1:7 R
*REF: .5X TO 1.2X BASIC
REF ODDS 1:11 HOBBY, 1:44 RETAIL
AC Abraham Clark 1.25 3.00
AM Arthur Middleton 1.25 3.00
BF Benjamin Franklin 2.00 5.00
BG Button Gwinnett 1.25 3.00
BH Benjamin Harrison 1.25 3.00
BR Benjamin Rush 1.25 3.00
CB Carter Braxton 1.25 3.00
CC Charles Carroll 1.25 3.00
CR Caesar Rodney 1.25 3.00
EG Elbridge Gerry 1.25 3.00
ER Edward Rutledge 1.25 3.00
FH Francis Hopkinson 1.25 3.00
FL Francis Lewis 1.25 3.00
FLL Francis Lightfoot Lee 1.25 3.00
GC George Clymer 1.25 3.00
GR George Ross 1.25 3.00
GRE George Read 1.25 3.00
GT George Taylor 1.25 3.00
GW George Walton 1.25 3.00
GWY George Wythe 1.25 3.00
JA John Adams 1.25 3.00
JB Josiah Bartlett 1.25 3.00
JH John Hancock 1.25 3.00
JHA John Hart 1.25 3.00
JHE Joseph Hewes 1.25 3.00
JM John Morton 1.25 3.00
JP John Penn 1.25 3.00
JS James Smith 1.25 3.00
JW James Wilson 1.25 3.00
JWI John Witherspoon 1.25 3.00
LH Lyman Hall 1.25 3.00
LM Lewis Morris 1.25 3.00
MT Matthew Thornton 1.25 3.00
OW Oliver Wolcott 1.25 3.00
PL Philip Livingston 1.25 3.00
RHL Richard Henry Lee 1.25 3.00
RM Robert Morris 1.25 3.00
RS Roger Sherman 1.25 3.00
RST Richard Stockton 1.25 3.00
RTP Robert Treat Paine 1.25 3.00
SA Samuel Adams 1.25 3.00
SC Samuel Chase 1.25 3.00
SH Stephen Hopkins 1.25 3.00
SHU Samuel Huntington 1.25 3.00
TH Thomas Heyward Jr. 1.25 3.00
TJ Thomas Jefferson 2.00 5.00
TL Thomas Lynch Jr. 1.25 3.00
TM Thomas McKean 1.25 3.00
TN Thomas Nelson Jr. 1.25 3.00
TS Thomas Stone 1.25 3.00
WE William Ellery 1.25 3.00
WF William Floyd 1.25 3.00
WH William Hooper 1.25 3.00
WP William Paca 1.25 3.00
WW William Whipple 1.25 3.00
WWI William Williams 1.25 3.00
HDR1 Header Card 1 1.25 3.00

2006 Topps Chrome Mantle Home Run History

COMPLETE SET (59) 40.00 80.00
COMP.07TCH SET (13) 8.00 20.00
COMP.07TCH SET (29) 15.00 40.00
COMP.08TCH SET (17) 8.00 20.00
COMMON CARD (1-59) 1.00 2.50
STATED 06 ODDS 1:6 HOBBY, 1:23 RETAIL
STATED 07 ODDS 1:8 HOBBY, 1:24 RETAIL
06 PLATE ODDS 1:300 HOBBY BOX LOADER
07 PLATE ODDS 1:116 HOBBY BOX LOADER
08 PLATE ODDS 1:1971 HOBBY
PLATE PRINT RUN 1 SET PER COLOR
BLACK-CYAN-MAGENTA-YELLOW ISSUED
NO PLATE PRICING DUE TO SCARCITY
*REF: .75X TO 2X BASIC
06 REF ODDS 1:70 HOBBY, 1:350 RETAIL
07 REF ODDS 1:27 HOBBY, 1:71 RETAIL
08 REF ODDS 1:31 HOBBY
REF PRINT RUN 500 SERIAL #'d SETS
08 REF PRINT RUN 400 SER.#'d SETS
*BLACK REF: 2.5X TO 6X BASIC
BLACK ODDS 1:175 HOBBY, 1:950 RETAIL
BLACK PRINT RUN 200 SERIAL #'d SETS
*06-07 BLUE REF: 3X TO 8X BASIC
*08 BLUE REF: 2.5X TO 6X BASIC
06 BLUE ODDS 1:300 RETAIL
07 BLUE ODDS 1:72 RETAIL
06-07 BLUE PRINT RUN 100 SERIAL #'d SETS
08 BLUE PRINT RUN 200 SERIAL #'d SETS
*COPPER REF: 3X TO 8X BASIC
COPPER ODDS 1:117 HOBBY
STATED PRINT RUN 100 SERIAL #'d SETS
06 GOLD SF ODDS 1:1234 HOBBY BOX LDR
07 GOLD SF ODDS
08 GOLD SF ODDS 1:7885 HOBBY
GOLD SF PRINT RUN 1 SERIAL #'d SET
NO GOLD SF PRICING DUE TO SCARCITY
*07 RED REF: 3X TO 8X BASIC
*08 RED REF: 12X TO 30X BASIC
07 RED REF ODDS
08 RED REF ODDS 1:315 HOBBY
07 RED REF PRINT RUN 99 SER.#'d SETS
08 RED REF PRINT RUN 25 SER.#'d SETS
*RED XF: 12X TO 30X BASIC
RED XF ODDS 1:48 HOBBY BOX LOADER
RED XF PRINT RUN 25 SERIAL #'d SETS
*WHITE REF: 2.5X TO 6X BASIC
07 WHITE REF ODDS 1:67 HOBBY, 1:185 RETAIL
WHITE REF PRINT RUN 200 SER.#'d SETS

2006 Topps Chrome Rookie Logos

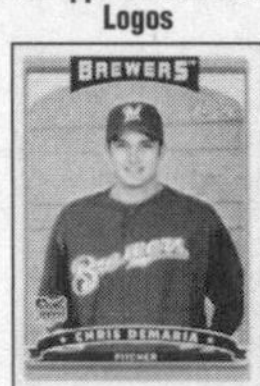

ONE PER UPDATE HOB.BOX LOADER
STATED PRINT RUN 599 SER.#'d SETS
1 Ben Zobrist 6.00 15.00
2 Shane Komine 2.00 5.00
3 Casey Janssen 1.25 3.00
4 Kevin Frandsen 1.25 3.00
5 John Rheinecker 1.25 3.00
6 Matt Kemp 3.00 8.00
7 Scott Mathieson 1.25 3.00
8 Jered Weaver 4.00 10.00
9 Joel Guzman 1.25 3.00
10 Anibal Sanchez 1.25 3.00
11 Melky Cabrera 2.00 5.00
12 Howie Kendrick 2.50 6.00
13 Cole Hamels 4.00 10.00
14 Willy Aybar 1.25 3.00
15 James Shields 4.00 10.00
16 Kevin Thompson 1.25 3.00
17 Jon Lester 5.00 12.00
18 Stephen Drew 2.50 6.00
19 Andre Ethier 4.00 10.00
20 Jordan Tata 1.25 3.00
21 Mike Napoli 2.00 5.00
22 Kason Gabbard 1.25 3.00
23 Lastings Milledge 1.25 3.00
24 Erick Aybar 1.25 3.00
25 Fausto Carmona 1.25 3.00
26 Russ Martin 2.00 5.00
27 David Pauley 1.25 3.00
28 Andy Marte 1.25 3.00
29 Carlos Quentin 2.00 5.00
30 Franklin Gutierrez 1.25 3.00
31 Taylor Buchholz 1.25 3.00
32 Josh Johnson 3.00 8.00
33 Chad Billingsley 2.00 5.00
34 Kendry Morales 3.00 8.00
35 Adam Loewen 1.25 3.00
36 Yusmeiro Petit 1.25 3.00
37 Matt Albers 1.25 3.00
38 John Maine 2.00 5.00
39 Josh Willingham 2.00 5.00
40 Taylor Tankersley 1.25 3.00
41 Pat Neshek 12.00 30.00
42 Francisco Rosario 1.25 3.00
43 Matt Smith 2.00 5.00
44 Jonathan Sanchez 3.00 8.00
45 Chris Demaria 1.25 3.00
46 Manuel Corpas 1.25 3.00
47 Kevin Reese 1.25 3.00
48 Brent Clevlen 2.00 5.00
49 Anderson Hernandez 1.25 3.00
50 Chris Roberson 1.25 3.00

2006 Topps Chrome United States Constitution

COMPLETE SET (42) 30.00 60.00
STATED ODDS 1:15 H, 1:15 R
*REF: .5X TO 1.2X BASIC
REF ODDS 1:9 HOBBY, 1:36 RETAIL
AB Abraham Baldwin .75 2.00
AH Alexander Hamilton .75 2.00
BF Benjamin Franklin 1.25 3.00
CCP Charles Cotesworth Pinckney .75 2.00
CP Charles Pinckney .75 2.00
DB David Brearly .75 2.00
DC Daniel Carroll .75 2.00
DJ Daniel of St. Thomas Jenifer .75 2.00
GB Gunning Bedford Jr. .75 2.00
GC George Clymer .75 2.00
GM Gouverneur Morris .75 2.00
GR George Read .75 2.00
GW George Washington 1.25 3.00
HW Hugh Williamson .75 2.00
JB John Blair .75 2.00
JBR Jacob Broom .75 2.00
JD Jonathan Dayton .75 2.00
JDI John Dickinson .75 2.00
JI Jared Ingersoll .75 2.00
JL John Langdon .75 2.00
JM James Madison .75 2.00
JMC James McHenry .75 2.00
JR John Rutledge .75 2.00
JW James Wilson .75 2.00
NG Nicholas Gilman .75 2.00
NGO Nathaniel Gorham .75 2.00
PB Pierce Butler .75 2.00
RB Richard Bassett .75 2.00
RDS Richard Dobbs Spaight .75 2.00
RK Rufus King .75 2.00
RM Robert Morris .75 2.00
RS Roger Sherman .75 2.00
TF Thomas Fitzsimons .75 2.00
TM Thomas Mifflin .75 2.00
WB William Blount .75 2.00
WF William Few .75 2.00
WJ William Samuel Johnson .75 2.00
WL William Livingston .75 2.00
WP William Paterson .75 2.00
HDR1 Header Card 1 .75 2.00
HDR2 Header Card 2 .75 2.00
HDR3 Header Card 3 .75 2.00

2007 Topps Chrome

This 369-card set was released in July, 2007. The set was issued in both hobby and retail versions. The hobby packs consisted of four-card packs (with an $3 SRP) which came 24 packs to a box and 12 boxes to a case. Cards numbered 1-275 featured veterans while cards 276-330 featured rookies and cards 331-355 (and a featured signed Rookie Cards. The signed cards were inserted into packs at a stated rate of one in 16 hobby and one in 122 retail. In addition, the players in this set who were originally from Japan all were issued in American and Japanese versions and the Japanese cards were issued at a stated rate of one in 82 hobby packs.

COMP.SET w/o AU's (330) 40.00 80.00
COMMON CARD .20 .50
COMMON ROOKIE .40 1.00
JAPANESE VARIATION UNLISTED 2.00 5.00
JAPANESE VARIATION ODDS 1:82 H
COMMON AUTO 3.00 8.00
AUTO ODDS 1:16 HOBBY, 1:122 RETAIL
PRINT.PLATE ODDS 1:36 HOBBY BOX LDR
VAR.PLATES 1:1943 HOBBY BOX LDR
AU PLATES 1:343 HOBBY BOX LDR
PLATE PRINT RUN 1 SET PER COLOR
BLACK-CYAN-MAGENTA-YELLOW ISSUED
NO PLATE PRICING DUE TO SCARCITY
EXCHANGE DEADLINE 07/31/09
1 Nick Swisher .30 .75
2 Bobby Abreu .20 .50
3 Edgar Renteria .20 .50
4 Mickey Mantle 1.50 4.00
5 Preston Wilson .20 .50
6 C.C. Sabathia .30 .75
7 Julio Lugo .20 .50
8 J.D. Drew .20 .50
9 Jason Varitek .50 1.25
10 Orlando Hernandez .20 .50
11 Corey Patterson .20 .50
12 Josh Bard .20 .50
13 Gary Matthews .20 .50
14 Jason Jennings .20 .50
15 Bronson Arroyo .20 .50
16 Andy Pettitte .30 .75
17 Ervin Santana .20 .50
18 Paul Konerko .30 .75
19 Adam LaRoche .20 .50
20 Jim Edmonds .30 .75
21 Derek Jeter 1.25 3.00
22 Aubrey Huff .20 .50
23 Andre Ethier .30 .75
24 Jeremy Sowers .20 .50
25 Miguel Cabrera .50 1.25
26 Carlos Lee .20 .50
27 Mike Piazza .50 1.25
28 Cole Hamels .40 1.00
29 Mark Loretta .20 .50
30 John Smoltz .50 1.25
31 Dan Uggla .20 .50
32 Lyle Overbay .20 .50
33 Michael Barrett .20 .50
34 Ivan Rodriguez .30 .75
35 Jake Westbrook .20 .50
36 Moises Alou .20 .50
37 Jered Weaver .30 .75
38 Lastings Milledge .30 .75
39 Austin Kearns .20 .50
40 Adam Loewen .20 .50
41 Josh Barfield .20 .50
42 Johan Santana .30 .75
43 Ian Kinsler .30 .75
44 Mike Lowell .20 .50
45 Scott Rolen .30 .75
46 Chipper Jones .50 1.25
47 Joe Crede .20 .50
48 Rafael Furcal .20 .50
49 Dave Bush .20 .50
50 Marcus Giles .20 .50
51 Joe Blanton .20 .50
52 Dontrelle Willis .20 .50
53 Scott Kazmir .30 .75
54 Jeff Kent .20 .50
55 Travis Hafner .20 .50
56 Ryan Garko .20 .50
57 Nick Markakis .40 1.00
58 Michael Cuddyer .20 .50
59 Jason Giambi .20 .50
60 Chone Figgins .20 .50
61 Carlos Delgado .20 .50
62 Aramis Ramirez .20 .50
63 Albert Pujols .60 1.50
64 Gary Sheffield .20 .50
65 Adrian Gonzalez .40 1.00
66 Prince Fielder .30 .75
67 Freddy Sanchez .20 .50
68 Jack Wilson .20 .50
69 Jake Peavy .20 .50
70 Javier Vazquez .20 .50
71 Todd Helton .30 .75
72 Bill Hall .20 .50
73 Jeremy Bonderman .20 .50
74 Rocco Baldelli .20 .50
75 Noah Lowry .20 .50
76 Justin Verlander .50 1.25
77 Mark Buehrle .30 .75
78 Hank Blalock .20 .50
79 Mark Teahen .20 .50
80 Chien-Ming Wang .30 .75
81 Roy Halladay .30 .75
82 Melvin Mora .20 .50
83 Grady Sizemore .30 .75
84 Matt Cain .30 .75
85 Carl Crawford .30 .75
86 Johnny Damon .30 .75
87 Freddy Garcia .20 .50
88 Ryan Shealy .20 .50
89 Carlos Beltran .30 .75
90 Chuck James .20 .50
91 Ben Sheets .20 .50
92 Mark Mulder .20 .50
93 Carlos Quentin .20 .50
94 Richie Sexson .20 .50
95 Brian Schneider .20 .50
96a Hideki Matsui .50 1.25
96b H.Matsui Japanese 2.00 5.00
97 Robinson Tejeda .20 .50
98 Scott Hatteberg .20 .50
99 Jeff Francis .20 .50
100 Robinson Cano .30 .75
101 Barry Zito .30 .75
102 Reed Johnson .20 .50
103 Chris Carpenter .30 .75
104 Chad Tracy .20 .50
105 Anibal Sanchez .20 .50
106 Brad Penny .20 .50
107 David Wright .40 1.00
108 Jimmy Rollins .30 .75
109 Alfonso Soriano .30 .75
110 Greg Maddux .60 1.50
111 Curt Schilling .30 .75
112 Stephen Drew .20 .50
113 Matt Holliday .50 1.25
114 Jorge Posada .30 .75
115 Vladimir Guerrero .30 .75
116 Frank Thomas .50 1.25
117 Jonathan Papelbon .50 1.25
118 Manny Ramirez .50 1.25
119 Magglio Ordonez .30 .75
120 Joe Mauer .40 1.00
121 Ryan Howard .40 1.00
122 Chris Young .20 .50
123 A.J. Burnett .20 .50
124 Brian McCann .20 .50
125 Juan Pierre .20 .50
126 Jonny Gomes .20 .50
127 Roger Clemens .60 1.50
128 Chad Billingsley .30 .75
129a Kenji Johjima .50 1.25
129b Kenji Johjima Japanese 2.00 5.00
130 Brian Giles .20 .50
131 Chase Utley .30 .75
132 Carl Pavano .20 .50
133 Curtis Granderson .40 1.00
134 Sean Casey .20 .50
135 Jon Garland .20 .50
136 David Ortiz .50 1.25
137 Bobby Crosby .20 .50
138 Conor Jackson .20 .50
139 Tim Hudson .30 .75
140 Rickie Weeks .20 .50
141 Mark Prior .30 .75
142 Ben Zobrist .30 .75
143 Troy Glaus .20 .50
144 Cliff Lee .30 .75
145 Adrian Beltre .50 1.25
146 Endy Chavez .20 .50
147 Ramon Hernandez .20 .50
148 Chris Young .30 .75
149 Jason Schmidt .20 .50
150 Kevin Millwood .20 .50
151 Placido Polanco .20 .50
152 Torii Hunter .20 .50
153 Roy Oswalt .30 .75
154 Kelvim Escobar .20 .50
155 Milton Bradley .20 .50
156 Chris Capuano .20 .50
157 Juan Encarnacion .20 .50
158a Ichiro Suzuki .60 1.50
158b Ichiro Suzuki Japanese 3.00 8.00
159 Matt Kemp .40 1.00
160 Matt Morris .20 .50
161 Casey Blake .20 .50
162 Josh Willingham .30 .75
163 Nick Johnson .20 .50
164 Khalil Greene .20 .50
165 Tom Glavine .30 .75
166 Jason Bay .30 .75
167 Brandon Phillips .20 .50
168 Jorge Cantu .20 .50
169 Jeff Weaver .20 .50
170 Melky Cabrera .20 .50
171 Dan Haren .20 .50
172 Jeff Francoeur .50 1.25
173 Randy Wolf .20 .50
174 Carlos Zambrano .30 .75
175 Justin Morneau .30 .75
176 Takashi Saito .30 .75
177 Victor Martinez .30 .75
178 Felix Hernandez .30 .75
179 Paul LoDuca .20 .50
180 Miguel Tejada .30 .75
181 Mark Teixeira .30 .75
182 Pat Burrell .20 .50
183 Mike Cameron .20 .50
184 Josh Beckett .20 .50
185 Francisco Liriano .20 .50
186 Ken Griffey Jr. 1.00 2.50
187 Mike Mussina .30 .75
188 Howie Kendrick .20 .50
189 Ted Lilly .20 .50
190 Mike Hampton .20 .50
191 Jeff Suppan .20 .50
192 Jose Reyes .30 .75
193 Russell Martin .30 .75
194 Jhonny Peralta .30 .75
195 Raul Ibanez .30 .75
196 Hanley Ramirez .30 .75
197 Kerry Wood .20 .50
198 Gary Sheffield .20 .50
199 David Dellucci .20 .50
200 Xavier Nady .20 .50
201 Michael Young .20 .50
202 Kevin Youkilis .20 .50
203 Aaron Harang .20 .50
204 Matt Garza .20 .50
205 Jim Thome .30 .75
206 Jose Contreras .20 .50
207 Tadahito Iguchi .20 .50
208 Eric Chavez .20 .50
209 Vernon Wells .20 .50
210 Doug Davis .20 .50
211 Andruw Jones .20 .50
212 David Eckstein .20 .50
213 J.J. Hardy .20 .50
214 Orlando Hudson .20 .50
215 Pedro Martinez .30 .75
216 Brian Roberts .20 .50
217 Brett Myers .20 .50
218 Alex Rodriguez .60 1.50
219 Kenny Rogers .20 .50
220 Jason Kubel .20 .50
221 Jermaine Dye .20 .50
222 Bartolo Colon .20 .50
223 Craig Biggio .30 .75
224 Alex Rios .20 .50
225 Adam Dunn .30 .75
226 Anthony Reyes .20 .50
227 Derrek Lee .20 .50
228 Jeremy Hermida .20 .50
229 Derek Lowe .20 .50
230 Randy Winn .20 .50
231 Brandon Webb .30 .75
232 Jose Vidro .20 .50
233 Erik Bedard .20 .50
234 Jon Lieber .20 .50
235 Wily Mo Pena .20 .50
236 Kelly Johnson .20 .50
237 David DeJesus .20 .50
238 Andy Marte .20 .50
239 Scott Olsen .20 .50
240 Randy Johnson .50 1.25
241 Nelson Cruz .50 1.25
242 Carlos Guillen .20 .50
243 Brandon McCarthy .20 .50
244 Garret Anderson .20 .50
245 Mike Sweeney .20 .50
246 Brian Bannister .20 .50
247 Jose Guillen .20 .50
248 Brad Wilkerson .20 .50
249 Lance Berkman .30 .75
250 Ryan Zimmerman .30 .75
251 Garrett Atkins .20 .50
252 Johan Santana .30 .75
253 Brandon Webb .30 .75
254 Justin Verlander .50 1.25
255 Hanley Ramirez .30 .75
256 Justin Morneau .30 .75
257 Ryan Howard .40 1.00
258 Eric Chavez .20 .50
259 Scott Rolen .30 .75
260 Derek Jeter 1.25 3.00
261 Omar Vizquel .30 .75
262 Mark Grudzielanek .20 .50
263 Orlando Hudson .20 .50
264 Mark Teixeira .30 .75
265 Albert Pujols .60 1.50
266 Ivan Rodriguez .30 .75
267 Brad Ausmus .20 .50
268 Torii Hunter .20 .50
269 Mike Cameron .20 .50
270 Ichiro Suzuki .60 1.50
271 Carlos Beltran .30 .75
272 Vernon Wells .20 .50
273 Andruw Jones .20 .50
274 Kenny Rogers .20 .50
275 Greg Maddux .60 1.50
276 Danny Putnam (RC) .40 1.00
277 Chase Wright RC 1.00 2.50
278 Zach McClellan RC .40 1.00
279 Jamie Vermilyea RC .40 1.00
280 Felix Pie (RC) .40 1.00
281 Phil Hughes (RC) 1.00 2.50
282 Jon Knott (RC) .40 1.00
283 Micah Owings (RC) .40 1.00
284 Devern Hansack RC .40 1.00
285 Andy Cannizaro RC .40 1.00
286 Lee Gardner (RC) .40 1.00
287 Josh Hamilton (RC) 1.25 3.00
288a Angel Sanchez RC .40 1.00
288b Angel Sanchez AU 3.00 8.00
289 J.D. Durbin (RC) .40 1.00
290 Jaime Burke (RC) .40 1.00
291 Joe Bisenius RC .40 1.00
292 Rick Vanden Hurk RC .40 1.00
293 Brian Barden RC .40 1.00
294 Levale Speigner RC .40 1.00
295 Kevin Cameron RC .40 1.00
296 Don Kelly (RC) .40 1.00
297a Hideki Okajima RC 2.00 5.00
297b Hideki Okajima Japanese 3.00 8.00
298 Andrew Miller RC 1.50 4.00
299 Delmon Young (RC) .60 1.50
300 Vinny Rottino (RC) .40 1.00
301 Philip Humber (RC) .40 1.00
302 Drew Anderson RC .40 1.00
303 Jerry Owens (RC) .40 1.00
304 Jose Garcia RC .40 1.00
305 Shane Youman RC .40 1.00
306 Ryan Feierabend (RC) .40 1.00
307 Mike Rabelo RC .40 1.00
308 Josh Fields (RC) .40 1.00
309 Jon Coutlangus (RC) .40 1.00
310 Travis Buck (RC) .40 1.00
311 Doug Slaten RC .40 1.00
312 Ryan Z. Braun RC .40 1.00
313 Juan Salas (RC) .40 1.00
314 Matt Lindstrom (RC) .40 1.00
315 Cesar Jimenez RC .40 1.00
316 Jay Marshall RC .40 1.00
317 Jared Burton RC .40 1.00
318 Juan Perez RC .40 1.00
319 Elijah Dukes RC .60 1.50
320 Juan Lara RC .40 1.00
321 Justin Hampson (RC) .40 1.00
322a Kei Igawa RC 1.00 2.50
322b Kei Igawa Japanese 2.00 5.00
323 Zack Segovia (RC) .40 1.00
324 Alejandro De Aza RC .60 1.50
325 Brandon Morrow RC 2.00 5.00
326 Gustavo Molina RC .40 1.00
327 Joe Smith RC .40 1.00
328 Jesus Flores RC .40 1.00
329 Jeff Baker (RC) .40 1.00
330a Daisuke Matsuzaka RC 4.00 10.00
330b Daisuke Matsuzaka Japanese 4.00 10.00
331 Troy Tulowitzki AU (RC) 6.00 15.00
332 John Danks AU RC 3.00 8.00
333 Kevin Kouzmanoff AU (RC) 3.00 8.00
334 David Murphy AU (RC) 3.00 8.00
335 Ryan Sweeney AU (RC) 3.00 8.00
336 Fred Lewis AU (RC) 3.00 8.00
337 Delwyn Young AU (RC) 3.00 8.00
338 Matt Chico AU (RC) 3.00 8.00
339 Miguel Montero AU (RC) 3.00 8.00
340 Shawn Riggans AU (RC) 3.00 8.00
341 Brian Stokes AU (RC) 3.00 8.00
342 Scott Moore AU (RC) 3.00 8.00
343 Adam Lind AU (RC) 3.00 8.00
344 Chris Narveson AU (RC) 3.00 8.00
345 Alex Gordon AU RC 8.00 20.00
346 Joaquin Arias AU (RC) 3.00 8.00
347 Brian Burres AU (RC) 3.00 8.00
348 Glen Perkins AU (RC) 3.00 8.00
349 Ubaldo Jimenez AU (RC) 3.00 8.00
350 Chris Stewart AU RC 3.00 8.00
351 Beltran Perez AU (RC) 3.00 8.00
352 Dennis Sarfate AU (RC) 3.00 8.00
353 Carlos Maldonado AU (RC) 3.00 8.00
354 Mitch Maier AU RC 3.00 8.00
355 Kory Casto AU (RC) 3.00 8.00
356 Juan Morillo AU (RC) 3.00 8.00
357 Hector Gimenez AU (RC) 3.00 8.00
358 Alexi Casilla AU RC 3.00 8.00
359 Michael Bourn AU (RC) 4.00 10.00
360 Sean Henn AU (RC) 3.00 8.00
361 Tim Gradoville AU RC 3.00 8.
363 Oswaldo Navarro AU RC 3.00 8.

2007 Topps Chrome Refractor

*REF: 1.2X TO 3X BASIC
REF ODDS 1:3 HOB,1:2 RET
*REF RC: .6X TO 1.5X BASIC RC
REF RC ODDS 1:3 HOB, 1:2 RET
*REF VAR: .5X TO 1.2X BASIC VARIATION
REF VAR ODDS 1:73 HOBBY
REF VAR PRINT RUN 500 SER.#'d SETS
*REF AU: .5X TO 1.2X BASIC AUTO
REF AU ODDS 1:71 HOB, 1:570 RET
REF AU PRINT RUN 500 SER.#'d SETS
EXCHANGE DEADLINE 07/31/09

2007 Topps Chrome Blue Refractors

*BLUE: 4X TO 10X BASIC
*BLUE RC: 2.5X TO 6X BASIC RC
STATED ODDS 1:6 RETAIL

2007 Topps Chrome Red Refractors

*RED REF: 4X TO 10X BASIC
*RED REF RC: 2.5X TO 6X BASIC RC
STATED ODDS 1:2 HOB.BOX LDR
STATED PRINT RUN 99 SER.#'d SETS
STATED VAR.ODDS 1:311 HOB.BOX LDR
STATED VAR.PRINT RUN 25 SER.#'d SETS
NO VARIATION PRICING AVAILABLE
STATED AU ODDS 1:55 HOB.BOX LDR
STATED AU PRINT RUN 25 SER.#'d SETS
NO AU PRICING AVAILABLE
EXCHANGE DEADLINE 07/31/09

2007 Topps Chrome White Refractors

*WHITE REF: 1.5X TO 4X BASIC
WHITE REF ODDS 1:6 HOB,1:23 RET
WHITE REF PRINT RUN 660 SER.#'d SETS
*WHITE REF RC: .75X TO 2X BASIC RC
WHITE REF RC ODDS 1:6 HOB, 1:23-RET
WHITE REF RC PRINT RUN 660 SER.#'d SETS
*WHITE REF VAR: .6X TO 1.5X BASIC VAR
WHITE REF VAR ODDS 1:932 HOBBY
WHITE REF VAR PRINT RUN 200 SER.#'d SETS
*WHITE REF AU: .75X TO 2X BASIC AUTO
WHITE REF AU ODDS 1:177 HOB, 1:1475 RET
WHITE REF AU PRINT RUN 200 SER.#'d SETS
EXCHANGE DEADLINE 07/31/09
297b Hideki Okajima Japanese 15.00 40.0
330b Daisuke Matsuzaka Japanese 15.00 40.0

2007 Topps Chrome X-Fractors

*X-F: 1.5X TO 4X BASIC
*X-F RC: 1.5X TO 4X BASIC RC
STATED ODDS 1:3 RETAIL

2007 Topps Chrome Generation Now

COMPLETE SET (41) 10.00 25.0
COMMON A.ETHIER .75 2.0
COMMON R.HOWARD 1.25 3.0
COMMON N.MARKAKIS .50 1.2
COMMON R.MARTIN .30 .7
COMMON J.MORNEAU .50 1.2
COMMON M.NAPOLI .30 .7
COMMON H.RAMIREZ .50 1.2
COMMON N.SWISHER .30 .7
COMMON C.UTLEY .75 2.0
COMMON J.VERLANDER .75 2.0
COMMON C.WANG .75 2.0
COMMON JER.WEAVER .50 1.2
COMMON D.YOUNG .50 1.2
COMMON R.ZIMMERMAN .75 2.0
STATED ODDS 1:5 HOBBY,1:17 RETAIL
PLATE ODDS 1:116 HOB.BOXLOADER
PLATE PRINT RUN 1 SET PER COLOR
BLACK-CYAN-MAGENTA-YELLOW ISSUED
NO PLATE PRICING DUE TO SCARCITY
REF ODDS 1:27 H, 1:71 R
REF PRINT RUN 500 SERIAL #'d SETS
BLUE REF ODDS 1:72 RETAIL
RED REF PRINT RUN 99 SER.#'d SETS
WHITE REF ODDS 1:67 HOBBY,1:185 RETAIL
SUPERFRAC.PRINT RUN 1 SER.#'d SET
NO SUPERFRAC.PRICING DUE TO SCARCITY

2007 Topps Chrome Generation Now Refractors

*REF: 1X TO 2.5X BASIC
STATED ODDS 1:27 H, 1:71 R
STATED PRINT RUN 500 SER.#'d SETS

2007 Topps Chrome Generation Now Blue Refractors

*BLUE REF: 2.5X TO 6X BASIC
STATED ODDS 1:72 RETAIL
STATED PRINT RUN 100 SER.#'d SETS

2007 Topps Chrome Generation Now Red Refractors

*RED REF: 2.5X TO 6X BASIC
STATED ODDS
STATED PRINT RUN 99 SER.#'d SETS

2007 Topps Chrome Generation Now White Refractors

*WHITE REF: 1.25X TO 3X BASIC
STATED ODDS 1:67 HOBBY,1:185 RETAIL
STATED PRINT RUN 200 SER.#'d SETS

2007 Topps Chrome Mickey Mantle Story

COMMON MANTLE (1-40) .75 2.00
1-30 STATED ODDS 1:7 H, :23 R
46-55 STATED ODDS 1:20 HOBBY
1-30 PLATE ODDS 1:116 HOB.BOXLDR
46-55 PLATE ODDS 1:1971 HOBBY
PLATE PRINT RUN 1 SET PER COLOR

ACK-CYAN-MAGENTA-YELLOW ISSUED
PLATE PRICING DUE TO SCARCITY
F: 1X TO 2.5X BASIC
0 REF.ODDS 1:27 H, 1:71 R
55 REF.ODDS 1:31 HOBBY
0 REF PRINT RUN 500 SER.#'d SETS
55 REF PRINT RUN 400 SER.#'d SETS
BLUE REF: 2.5X TO 6X BASIC
BLUE REF: 1.2X TO 3X BASIC
BLUE REF ODDS 1:72 RETAIL
BLUE REF ODDS
BLUE REF PRINT RUN 100 SER.#'d SETS
BLUE REF PRINT RUN 200 SER.#'d SETS
OPPER: 2.5X TO 6X BASIC
ATED ODDS 1:117 HOBBY
ATED PRINT RUN 100 SER.#'d SETS
30 RED REF: 2.5X TO 6X BASIC
-55 RED REF ODDS 1:315 HOBBY
0 RED REF 99 SER.#'d SETS
-55 RED REF 25 SER.#'d SETS
46-55 RED PRICING AVAILABLE
HITE REF: 1.2X TO 3X BASIC
HITE REF.ODDS 1:67 HOBBY,1:185 RETAIL
HITE REF PRINT RUN 200 SER.#'d SETS
-55 SUP.FRAC. ODDS 1:7885
PERFRAC.PRINT RUN 1 SER.#'d SET
SUPERFRAC.PRICING DUE TO SCARCITY
30 ISSUED IN 07 TOPPS CHROME
-55 ISSUED IN 08 TOPPS CHROME

2008 Topps Chrome

MP.SET w/o AU's (220) 30.00 60.00
OMMON CARD .20 .50
OMMON ROOKIE .60 1.50
OMMON AUTO 4.00 10.00
TO ODDS 1:15 HOBBY
INT.PLATE ODDS 1:1896 HOBBY
PLATES 1:10,961 HOBBY
ATE PRINT RUN 1 SET PER COLOR
ACK-CYAN-MAGENTA-YELLOW ISSUED
PLATE PRICING DUE TO SCARCITY
CHANGE DEADLINE 6/30/2010
Alex Rodriguez .60 1.50
Barry Zito .30 .75
Scott Kazmir .30 .75
Stephen Drew .20 .50
Miguel Cabrera .50 1.25
Daisuke Matsuzaka .30 .75
Mickey Mantle 1.50 4.00
Jimmy Rollins .30 .75
Joe Mauer .40 1.00
Cole Hamels .40 1.00
Yovani Gallardo .20 .50
2 Miguel Tejada .30 .75
3 Dontrelle Willis .20 .50
4 Orlando Cabrera .30 .75
5 Jake Peavy .20 .50
6 Erik Bedard .20 .50
7 Victor Martinez .30 .75
8 Chris Young .20 .50
9 Jose Reyes .30 .75
0 Mike Lowell .20 .50
1 Dan Uggla .20 .50
2 Garrett Atkins .20 .50
3 Felix Hernandez .30 .75
4 Ivan Rodriguez .30 .75
5 Alex Rios .20 .50
6 Jason Bay .30 .75
7 Vladimir Guerrero .30 .75
8 John Lackey .30 .75
9 Ryan Howard .30 .75
0 Kevin Youkilis .20 .50
1 Justin Morneau .30 .75
2 Johan Santana .30 .75
3 Jeremy Hermida .20 .50
4 Andruw Jones .20 .50
5 Mike Cameron .20 .50
6 Jason Varitek .50 1.25
7 Tim Hudson .30 .75
8 Justin Upton .30 .75
9 Brad Penny .20 .50
0 Robinson Cano .30 .75
1 Brandon Webb .30 .75
2 Magglio Ordonez .30 .75
3 Aaron Hill .20 .50
4 Alfonso Soriano .30 .75
5 Carlos Zambrano .30 .75
6 Ben Sheets .20 .50
7 Tim Lincecum .30 .75
8 Phil Hughes .20 .50
9 Scott Rolen .30 .75
50 John Maine .20 .50
51 Delmon Young .30 .75
52 Tadahito Iguchi .20 .50
53 Yunel Escobar .20 .50
54 Russell Martin .20 .50
55 Orlando Hudson .20 .50
56 Jim Edmonds .30 .75
57 Todd Helton .30 .75
58 Melky Cabrera .20 .50
59 Adrian Beltre .50 1.25
60 Manny Ramirez .50 1.25
61 Gil Meche .20 .50
62 David DeJesus .20 .50
63 Roy Oswalt .30 .75
64 Mark Buehrle .30 .75
65 Hunter Pence .30 .75
66 Dustin Pedroia .30 .75
67 Roy Halladay .30 .75
68 Rich Harden .20 .50
69 Jim Thome .30 .75
70 Akinori Iwamura .20 .50
71 Dan Haren .20 .50
72 Brandon Phillips .20 .50
73 Brett Myers .20 .50
74 James Loney .20 .50
75 C.C. Sabathia .30 .75
76 Jermaine Dye .20 .50
77 Carlos Ruiz .20 .50
78 Brian McCann .30 .75
79 Paul Konerko .30 .75
80 Jorge Posada .30 .75
81 Chien-Ming Wang .30 .75
82 Carlos Delgado .20 .50
83 Ichiro Suzuki .60 1.50
84 Elijah Dukes .20 .50
85 David Wright .30 .75
86 Carl Crawford .30 .75
87 Mark Teixeira .30 .75
88 Bobby Crosby .20 .50
89 Brian Roberts .20 .50
90 David Ortiz .50 1.25
91 Derrek Lee .20 .50
92 Adam Dunn .30 .75
93 Fausto Carmona .20 .50
94 Grady Sizemore .30 .75
95 Jeff Francoeur .30 .75
96 Jered Weaver .30 .75
97 Troy Tulowitzki .50 1.25
98 Troy Glaus .30 .75
99 Nick Markakis .40 1.00
100 Lance Berkman .30 .75
101 Randy Johnson .50 1.25
102 Kenji Johjima .20 .50
103 Jarrod Saltalamacchia .20 .50
104 Matt Holliday .50 1.25
105 Travis Hafner .20 .50
106 Johnny Damon .30 .75
107 Alex Gordon .30 .75
108 Derek Lowe .20 .50
109 Nick Swisher .30 .75
110 Aaron Harang .20 .50
111 Hanley Ramirez .30 .75
112 Carlos Guillen .20 .50
113 Ryan Braun .30 .75
114 Torii Hunter .20 .50
115 Joe Blanton .20 .50
116 Josh Hamilton .30 .75
117 Pedro Martinez .30 .75
118 Hideki Matsui .50 1.25
119 Cameron Maybin .20 .50
120 Prince Fielder .30 .75
121 Derek Jeter 1.25 3.00
122 Chone Figgins .20 .50
123 Chase Utley .30 .75
124 Jacoby Ellsbury .40 1.00
125 Freddy Sanchez .20 .50
126 Rocco Baldelli .20 .50
127 Tom Gorzelanny .20 .50
128 Adrian Gonzalez .30 .75
129 Geovany Soto .50 1.25
130 Bobby Abreu .20 .50
131 Albert Pujols .60 1.50
132 Chipper Jones .50 1.25
133 Jeremy Bonderman .20 .50
134 B.J. Upton .30 .75
135 Justin Verlander .50 1.25
136 Jeff Francis .20 .50
137 A.J. Burnett .20 .50
138 Travis Buck .30 .75
139 Vernon Wells .20 .50
140 Raul Ibanez .30 .75
141 Ryan Zimmerman .30 .75
142 John Smoltz .50 1.25
143 Carlos Lee .20 .50
144 Chris Young .20 .50
145 Francisco Liriano .20 .50
146 Curt Schilling .30 .75
147 Josh Beckett .20 .50
148 Aramis Ramirez .20 .50
149 Ronnie Belliard .20 .50
150 Homer Bailey .30 .75
151 Curtis Granderson .30 .75
152 Ken Griffey Jr. 1.00 2.50
153 Kazuo Matsui .20 .50
154 Brian Bannister .20 .50
155 Joba Chamberlain .20 .50
156 Tom Glavine .30 .75
157 Carlos Beltran .30 .75
158 Kelly Johnson .20 .50
159 Rich Hill .20 .50
160 Pat Burrell .20 .50
161 Asdrubal Cabrera .30 .75
162 Gary Sheffield .20 .50
163 Greg Maddux .60 1.50
164 Eric Chavez .20 .50
165 Chris Carpenter .30 .75
166 Michael Young .20 .50
167 Carlos Pena .30 .75
168 Frank Thomas .50 1.25
169 Aaron Rowand .20 .50
170 Yadier Molina .50 1.25
171 Luis Castillo .20 .50
172 Ryan Theriot .20 .50
173 Andre Ethier .30 .75
174 Casey Kotchman .20 .50
175 Rickie Weeks .20 .50
176 Milton Bradley .20 .50
177 Daniel Cabrera .20 .50
178 Jo-Jo Reyes .20 .50
179 Livan Hernandez .20 .50
180 Hideki Okajima .20 .50
181 Matt Kemp .40 1.00
182 Jonny Gomes .20 .50
183 Billy Butler .20 .50
184 Adam LaRoche .20 .50
185 Brad Hawpe .20 .50
186 Paul Maholm .20 .50
187 Placido Polanco .20 .50
188 Noah Lowry .20 .50
189 Gregg Zaun .20 .50
190 Nate McLouth .20 .50
191 Edinson Volquez .20 .50
192 Jeff Niemann (RC) .60 1.50
193 Evan Longoria RC 3.00 8.00
194 Adam Jones .30 .75
195 Eugenio Velez RC .60 1.50
196 Joey Votto (RC) 2.50 6.00
197 Nick Blackburn RC 1.00 2.50
198 Harvey Garcia (RC) .60 1.50
199 Hiroki Kuroda RC 1.50 4.00
200 Elliot Johnson (RC) .60 1.50
201 Luis Mendoza (RC) .60 1.50
202 Alex Romero (RC) 1.00 2.50
203 Gregor Blanco (RC) .60 1.50
204 Rico Washington (RC) .60 1.50
205 Brian Bocock RC .60 1.50
206 Evan Meek RC .60 1.50
207 Stephen Holm RC .60 1.50
208 Matt Tupman RC .60 1.50
209 Fernando Hernandez RC .60 1.50
210 Randor Bierd RC .60 1.50
211 Blake DeWitt (RC) 1.00 2.50
212 Randy Wells RC 1.00 2.50
213 Wesley Wright RC .60 1.50
214 Clete Thomas RC 1.00 2.50
215 Kyle McClellan RC .60 1.50
216 Brian Bixler (RC) .60 1.50
217 Kazuo Fukumori RC 1.00 2.50
218 Burke Badenhop RC 1.00 2.50
219 Denard Span (RC) 1.00 2.50
220 Brian Bass (RC) .60 1.50
221 J.R. Towles AU RC 4.00 10.00
222 Felipe Paulino AU RC 4.00 10.00
223 Sam Fuld AU RC 4.00 10.00
224 Kevin Hart AU (RC) 4.00 10.00
225 Nyjer Morgan AU (RC) 4.00 10.00
226 Daric Barton AU (RC) 4.00 10.00
227 Armando Galarraga AU RC 4.00 10.00
228 Chin-Lung Hu AU (RC) 4.00 10.00
229 Buchholz AU (RC) EXCH 4.00 10.00
230 Rich Thompson AU RC 4.00 10.00
231 Brian Barton AU RC 5.00 12.00
232 Ross Ohlendorf AU RC 4.00 10.00
233 Masahide Kobayashi AU RC 4.00 10.00
234 Callix Crabbe AU (RC) 4.00 10.00
235 Matt Tolbert AU RC 4.00 10.00
236 Jayson Nix AU (RC) 4.00 10.00
237 Johnny Cueto AU RC 6.00 15.00
238 Evan Meek AU RC 4.00 10.00
239 Randy Wells AU (RC) 4.00 10.00

2008 Topps Chrome Refractors

*REF: 1.2X TO 3X BASIC
REF ODDS 1:3 HOBBY
*REF RC: .6X TO 1.5X BASIC RC
REF RC ODDS 1:3 HOBBY
*REF AU: .5X TO 1.2X BASIC AUTO
REF AU ODDS 1:95 HOBBY
REF AU PRINT RUN 500 SER.#'d SETS
EXCHANGE DEADLINE 6/30/2010

2008 Topps Chrome Blue Refractors

*BLUE REF: 4X TO 10X BASIC
REF ODDS
*BLUE REF RC: 1.2X TO 3X BASIC RC
REF RC ODDS
*BLUE REF AU: .6X TO 1.5X BASIC AUTO
BLUE REF AU ODDS 1:230 HOBBY
BLUE REF AU PRINT RUN 200 SER.#'d SETS
EXCHANGE DEADLINE 6/30/2010

2008 Topps Chrome Copper Refractors

*COPPER REF: 2X TO 5X BASIC
COPPER.REF ODDS 1:12 HOBBY
*COPPER REF RC: 1X TO 2.5X BASIC RC
REF RC ODDS 1:12 HOBBY
COPPER REF PRINT RUN 599 SER.#'d SETS
*COPPER REF AU: 1X TO 2.5X BASIC AUTO
COPPER REF AU ODDS 1:980 HOBBY
COPPER REF AU PRINT RUN 100 SER.#'d SETS
EXCHANGE DEADLINE 6/30/2010

2008 Topps Chrome Red Refractors

RED 1-220 ODDS 1:143 HOBBY
RED AU 221-239 ODDS 1:2185 HOBBY
STATED PRINT RUN 25 SER.#'d SETS
NO PRICING DUE TO SCARCITY

2008 Topps Chrome National Convention

*NATIONAL 1-200: .5X TO 1.2X BASIC
*NATIONAL 201-220: .5X TO 1.2X BASIC

2008 Topps Chrome 50th Anniversary All Rookie Team

COMPLETE SET (23) 12.50 30.00
STATED ODDS 1:9 HOBBY
PRINTING PLATE ODDS 1:1971 HOBBY
PLATE PRINT RUN 1 SET PER COLOR
BLACK-CYAN-MAGENTA-YELLOW ISSUED
NO PLATE PRICING DUE TO SCARCITY
*REF: .75X TO 2X BASIC
REF ODDS 1:31 HOBBY
REF.PRINT RUN 400 SER.#'d SETS
*BLUE REF: 1.2X TO 3X BASIC
BLUE REF PRINT RUN 200 SER.#'d SETS
*COP.REF: 1X TO 2.5X BASIC
COP.REF ODDS 1:117 HOBBY
COP.REF PRINT RUN 100 SER.#'d SETS
RED.REF ODDS 1:315 HOBBY
RED PRINT RUN 25 SER.#'d SETS
NO RED PRICING DUE TO SCARCITY
SUPFRAC.ODDS 1:7885 HOBBY
SUPFRAC.PRINT RUN 1 SER.#'d SET
NO SUPFRAC.PRICING DUE TO SCARCITY
ARC1 Gary Sheffield .40 1.00
ARC2 Ivan Rodriguez .60 1.50
ARC3 Mike Piazza 1.00 2.50
ARC4 Manny Ramirez 1.00 2.50
ARC5 Chipper Jones 1.00 2.50
ARC6 Derek Jeter 2.50 6.00
ARC7 Andruw Jones .40 1.00
ARC8 Alfonso Soriano .60 1.50
ARC9 Jimmy Rollins .60 1.50
ARC10 Albert Pujols 1.25 3.00
ARC11 Ichiro Suzuki 1.25 3.00
ARC12 Mark Teixeira .60 1.50
ARC13 Matt Holliday 1.00 2.50
ARC14 Joe Mauer .75 2.00
ARC15 Prince Fielder .60 1.50
ARC16 Hideki Okajima .40 1.00
ARC17 Roy Oswalt .60 1.50
ARC18 Hunter Pence .60 1.50
ARC19 Nick Markakis .75 2.00
ARC20 Ryan Zimmerman .60 1.50
ARC21 Ryan Braun .60 1.50
ARC22 C.C. Sabathia .60 1.50
ARC23 Dustin Pedroia .60 1.50

2008 Topps Chrome Dick Perez

EXCLUSIVE TO WALMART PACKS
REF: .5X TO 1.2X
WMDPC1 Manny Ramirez 2.00 5.00
WMDPC2 Cameron Maybin .75 2.00
WMDPC3 Ryan Howard 1.25 3.00
WMDPC4 David Ortiz 2.00 5.00
WMDPC5 Tim Lincecum 1.25 3.00
WMDPC6 David Wright 1.25 3.00
WMDPC7 Mickey Mantle 3.00 8.00
WMDPC8 Joba Chamberlain .75 2.00
WMDPC9 Ichiro Suzuki 2.50 6.00
WMDPC10 Prince Fielder 1.25 3.00
WMDPC11 Jacoby Ellsbury 1.50 4.00
WMDPC12 Jake Peavy .75 2.00
WMDPC13 Miguel Cabrera 2.00 5.00
WMDPC14 Josh Beckett .75 2.00
WMDPC15 Jimmy Rollins 1.25 3.00
WMDPC16 Torii Hunter .75 2.00
WMDPC17 Alfonso Soriano 1.25 3.00
WMDPC18 Jose Reyes 1.25 3.00
WMDPC19 C.C. Sabathia 1.25 3.00
WMDPC20 Alex Rodriguez 2.50 6.00

2008 Topps Chrome T205

EXCLUSIVE TO TARGET PACKS
*REF: .5X TO 1.2X BASIC
TCCP1 Albert Pujols 2.50 6.00
TCCP2 Clay Buchholz 1.25 3.00
TCCP3 Matt Holliday 2.00 5.00
TCCP4 Luke Hochevar 1.25 3.00
TCCP5 Alex Rodriguez 2.50 6.00
TCCP6 Joey Votto 3.00 8.00
TCCP7 Chin-Lung Hu .75 2.00
TCCP8 Ryan Braun 1.25 3.00
TCCP9 Joba Chamberlain .75 2.00
TCCP10 Ryan Howard 1.25 3.00
TCCP11 Ichiro Suzuki 2.50 6.00
TCCP12 Steve Pearce 4.00 10.00
TCCP13 Vladimir Guerrero 1.25 3.00
TCCP14 Wladimir Balentien .75 2.00
TCCP15 David Ortiz 2.00 5.00
TCCP16 Jacoby Ellsbury 1.50 4.00
TCCP17 David Wright 1.25 3.00
TCCP18 Chase Utley 1.25 3.00
TCCP19 Manny Ramirez 2.00 5.00
TCCP20 Dan Haren .75 2.00
TCCP21 Nick Markakis 1.50 4.00
TCCP22 Grady Sizemore 1.25 3.00
TCCP23 Hanley Ramirez 1.25 3.00
TCCP24 Daisuke Matsuzaka 1.25 3.00
TCCP25 Troy Tulowitzki 2.00 5.00
TCCP26 Jose Reyes 1.25 3.00
TCCP27 Tim Lincecum 1.25 3.00
TCCP28 Prince Fielder 1.25 3.00
TCCP29 Alfonso Soriano 1.25 3.00
TCCP30 Andrew Miller 1.25 3.00

2008 Topps Chrome Trading Card History

COMPLETE SET (50) 12.50 30.00
STATED ODDS 1:9 HOBBY
PRINTING PLATE ODDS 1:1971 HOBBY
PLATE PRINT RUN 1 SET PER COLOR
BLACK-CYAN-MAGENTA-YELLOW ISSUED
NO PLATE PRICING DUE TO SCARCITY
*REF: .75X TO 2X BASIC
REF ODDS 1:31 HOBBY
REF.PRINT RUN 400 SER.#'d SETS
BLUE REF PRINT RUN 200 SER.#'d SETS
COP.REF ODDS 1:117 HOBBY
COP.REF PRINT RUN 100 SER.#'d SETS
RED.REF ODDS 1:315 HOBBY
RED PRINT RUN 25 SER.#'d SETS
NO RED PRICING DUE TO SCARCITY
SUPFRAC.ODDS 1:7885 HOBBY
SUPFRAC.PRINT RUN 1 SER.#'d SET
NO SUPFRAC.PRICING DUE TO SCARCITY
TCHC1 Jacoby Ellsbury .75 2.00
TCHC2 Joba Chamberlain .40 1.00
TCHC3 Daisuke Matsuzaka .60 1.50
TCHC4 Prince Fielder .60 1.50
TCHC5 Alex Rodriguez 1.25 3.00
TCHC6 Mickey Mantle 2.50 6.00
TCHC7 Ryan Braun .60 1.50
TCHC8 Albert Pujols 1.25 3.00
TCHC9 Joe Mauer .75 2.00
TCHC10 Jose Reyes .60 1.50
TCHC11 Johan Santana .60 1.50
TCHC12 Hunter Pence .60 1.50
TCHC13 Hideki Okajima .40 1.00
TCHC14 Cameron Maybin .40 1.00
TCHC15 Tim Lincecum .60 1.50
TCHC16 Mark Teixeira/Jeff Francoeur .60 1.50
TCHC17 Justin Upton .60 1.50
TCHC18 Alfonso Soriano .60 1.50
TCHC19 Ichiro Suzuki 1.25 3.00
TCHC20 Grady Sizemore .60 1.50
TCHC21 Ryan Howard .60 1.50
TCHC22 David Wright .60 1.50
TCHC23 Jimmy Rollins .60 1.50
TCHC24 Ken Griffey Jr 2.00 5.00
TCHC25 Chipper Jones 1.00 2.50
TCHC26 Justin Verlander 1.00 2.50
TCHC27 Manny Ramirez 1.00 2.50
TCHC28 Chase Utley .60 1.50
TCHC29 Ivan Rodriguez .60 1.50
TCHC30 Josh Beckett .40 1.00
TCHC31 Vladimir Guerrero .60 1.50
TCHC32 Lance Berkman .60 1.50
TCHC33 Gary Sheffield .40 1.00
TCHC34 David Ortiz 1.00 2.50
TCHC35 Andruw Jones .40 1.00
TCHC36 Hideki Matsui 1.00 2.50
TCHC37 C.C. Sabathia .60 1.50
TCHC38 Magglio Ordonez .60 1.50
TCHC39 Pedro Martinez .60 1.50
TCHC40 Derek Jeter 2.50 6.00
TCHC41 Hanley Ramirez .60 1.50
TCHC42 Jake Peavy .40 1.00
TCHC43 Brandon Webb .60 1.50
TCHC44 Matt Holliday 1.00 2.50
TCHC45 Carlos Beltran .60 1.50
TCHC46 Troy Tulowitzki 1.00 2.50
TCHC47 Justin Morneau .60 1.50
TCHC48 Phil Hughes .40 1.00
TCHC49 Torii Hunter .40 1.00
TCHC50 Brad Hawpe .40 1.00

2008 Topps Chrome Trading Card History Blue Refractors

*BLUE REF: 1.2X TO 3X BASIC
STATED PRINT RUN 200 SER.#'d SETS
TCHC1 Jacoby Ellsbury 30.00 60.00

2008 Topps Chrome Trading Card History Copper Refractors

*COP.REF: 1X TO 2.5X BASIC
STATED ODDS 1:117 HOBBY
STATED PRINT RUN 100 SER.#'d SETS
TCHC1 Jacoby Ellsbury 20.00 50.00

2009 Topps Chrome

COMP SET w/o AU's (220) 30.00 60.00
COMMON CARD .20 .50
COMMON ROOKIE .60 1.50
COMMON AUTO 4.00 10.00
AUTO ODDS 1:20 HOBBY
PRINT.PLATE ODDS 1:303 HOBBY
AU PLATES 1:5330 HOBBY
PLATE PRINT RUN 1 SET PER COLOR
BLACK-CYAN-MAGENTA-YELLOW ISSUED
NO PLATE PRICING DUE TO SCARCITY
1 Alex Rodriguez .60 1.50
2 Kerry Wood .20 .50
3 Dan Uggla .20 .50
4 Nate McLouth .20 .50
5 Brad Lidge .20 .50
6 Jon Lester .30 .75
7 Mickey Mantle 1.50 4.00
8 Jason Giambi .20 .50
9 Mike Lowell .20 .50
10 Ken Griffey Jr. 1.00 2.50
11 Erick Aybar .20 .50
12 Stephen Drew .20 .50
13 Geoff Jenkins .20 .50
14 Aubrey Huff .20 .50
15 Kazuo Matsui .20 .50
16 David Ortiz .50 1.25
17 Mariano Rivera .60 1.50
18 Jermaine Dye .20 .50
19 Rich Harden .20 .50
20 Brian McCann .30 .75
21 Brad Hawpe .20 .50
22 Justin Morneau .30 .75
23 Akinori Iwamura .20 .50
24 David Wright .40 1.00
25 Garrett Atkins .20 .50
26 David DeJesus .20 .50
27 Francisco Liriano .20 .50
28 George Sherrill .20 .50
29 Hideki Matsui .50 1.25
30 Chris Young .20 .50
31 Kevin Youkilis .20 .50
32 Mark Teixeira .30 .75
33 Roy Oswalt .30 .75
34 Orlando Hudson .20 .50
35 Vladimir Guerrero .30 .75
36 Juan Pierre .20 .50
37 Carlos Delgado .20 .50
38 Tim Hudson .30 .75
39 Brandon Webb .30 .75
40 Alex Gordon .30 .75
41 Glen Perkins .20 .50
42 Kosuke Fukudome .30 .75
43 Ian Stewart .20 .50
44a A.J. Pierzynski .20 .50
44b Barack Obama SP 6.00 15.00
45 Roy Halladay .30 .75
46 Carlos Pena .30 .75
47 Evan Longoria .30 .75
48 Matt Kemp .40 1.00
49 CC Sabathia .30 .75
50 Yadier Molina .50 1.25
51 James Shields .20 .50
52 Jeff Samardzija .30 .75
53 Rafael Furcal .20 .50
54 Cliff Lee .30 .75
55 Daniel Murphy RC 2.50 6.00
56 Randy Johnson .50 1.25
57 Jon Garland .20 .50
58 Chien-Ming Wang .30 .75
59 Zack Greinke .30 .75
60 Tim Lincecum .30 .75
61 Conor Jackson .20 .50
62 Chase Utley .30 .75
63 Andy Sonnanstine .20 .50
64 Miguel Tejada .30 .75
65 Geovany Soto .30 .75
66 Jeremy Sowers .20 .50
67 Ian Kinsler .30 .75
68 Jay Bruce .30 .75
69 Max Scherzer .50 1.25
70 Scott Rolen .30 .75
71 Justin Upton .30 .75
72 Xavier Nady .20 .50
73 Erik Bedard .20 .50
74 Chad Billingsley .30 .75
75 Ryan Braun .30 .75
76 Pat Burrell .20 .50
77 Edgar Renteria .20 .50
78 Joe Crede .30 .75
79 Manny Ramirez .50 1.25
80 Carlos Zambrano .30 .75
81 Hunter Pence .30 .75
82 Grady Sizemore .30 .75
83 Brian Roberts .20 .50
84 Alex Rios .20 .50
85 Joe Saunders .20 .50
86 Albert Pujols .60 1.50
87 Derrek Lee .20 .50
88 Ichiro Suzuki .60 1.50
89 Javier Vazquez .20 .50
90 Johan Santana .30 .75
91 Miguel Cabrera .50 1.25
92 Daisuke Matsuzaka .30 .75
93 Chris Young .20 .50
94 Joe Mauer .40 1.00
95 Stephen Drew .20 .50
96 Justin Masterson .20 .50
97 Dustin Pedroia .40 1.00
98 Derek Jeter 1.25 3.00
99 John Smoltz .50 1.25
100 Jason Varitek .50 1.25
101 Jorge Posada .30 .75
102 Mark Buehrle .30 .75
103 Bobby Abreu .20 .50
104 Victor Martinez .30 .75
105 Jeff Francis .20 .50
106 Rickie Weeks .20 .50
107 Carlos Quentin .20 .50
108 Howie Kendrick .20 .50
109 Aramis Ramirez .20 .50
110 Jonathan Papelbon .30 .75
111 Dan Haren .20 .50
112 Barry Zito .30 .75
113 Magglio Ordonez .30 .75
114 Alfonso Soriano .30 .75
115 Todd Helton .30 .75
116 Troy Tulowitzki .50 1.25
117 Josh Beckett .20 .50
118 Andy Pettitte .30 .75
119 Hank Blalock .20 .50
120 Curtis Granderson .40 1.00
121 Francisco Rodriguez .30 .75
122 Carlos Lee .20 .50
123 Gavin Floyd .20 .50
124 Joe Nathan .20 .50
125 Matt Holliday .50 1.25
126 Hanley Ramirez .30 .75
127 Javier Valentin .20 .50
128 John Maine .20 .50
129 Jeremy Bonderman .20 .50
130 Nick Markakis .40 1.00
131 Troy Glaus .20 .50
132 Derek Lowe .20 .50
133 Lance Berkman .30 .75
134 Jered Weaver .30 .75
135 Chipper Jones .50 1.25
136 Prince Fielder .30 .75
137 Travis Hafner .20 .50
138 Joba Chamberlain .20 .50
139 Ryan Howard .40 1.00
140 Paul Konerko .30 .75
141 Kenji Johjima .30 .75
142 Yovani Gallardo .20 .50
143 Adrian Gonzalez .40 1.00
144 Jimmy Rollins .30 .75
145 Nick Swisher .30 .75
146 Felix Hernandez .30 .75
147 Garret Anderson .20 .50
148 Russell Martin .20 .50
149 Jason Bay .30 .75
150 Fausto Carmona .20 .50
151 Matt Garza .20 .50
152 Matt Cain .30 .75
153 Ryan Freel .20 .50
154 Rocco Baldelli .20 .50
155 Scott Kazmir .20 .50
156 Alexei Ramirez .30 .75
157 Adam Dunn .30 .75
158 Johnny Damon .30 .75
159 Jake Peavy .20 .50
160 Jose Reyes .30 .75
161 Rick Ankiel .20 .50
162 Michael Young .20 .50
163 Robinson Cano .30 .75
164 Ryan Zimmerman .30 .75
165 Jim Thome .30 .75
166 A.J. Burnett .20 .50
167 Joakim Soria .20 .50
168 J.D. Drew .20 .50
169 Cole Hamels .40 1.00
170 Jacoby Ellsbury .40 1.00
171 Travis Snider RC 1.00 2.50
172 Josh Outman RC 1.00 2.50
173 Dexter Fowler (RC) 1.00 2.50
174 Matt Tuiasosopo (RC) .60 1.50
175 Bobby Parnell RC 1.00 2.50
176 Jason Motte (RC) 1.00 2.50
177 James McDonald RC 1.50 4.00
178 Scott Lewis (RC) .60 1.50
179 George Kottaras (RC) .60 1.50
180 Phil Coke RC 1.00 2.50
181 Jordan Schafer (RC) 1.00 2.50
182 Joe Martinez RC 1.00 2.50
183 Trevor Crowe RC .60 1.50
184 Shairon Martis RC 1.00 2.50
185 Everth Cabrera RC 1.00 2.50
186 Trevor Cahill RC 1.50 4.00
187 Jesse Chavez RC .60 1.50
188 Josh Whitesell RC 1.00 2.50
189 Brian Duensing RC 1.00 2.50
190 Andrew Bailey RC 1.50 4.00
191 Ryan Perry RC 1.50 4.00
192 Brett Anderson RC 1.00 2.50
193 Ricky Romero (RC) 1.00 2.50
194 Elvis Andrus RC 1.50 4.00
195 Kenshin Kawakami RC 1.00 2.50
196 Colby Rasmus (RC) 1.00 2.50
197 David Patton RC 1.00 2.50
198 David Hernandez RC .60 1.50
199 David Freese RC 2.00 5.00
200 Rick Porcello RC 2.00 5.00
201 Fernando Martinez RC 1.50 4.00
202 Edwin Moreno (RC) .60 1.50
203 Koji Uehara RC 1.50 4.00
204 Jason Jaramillo (RC) .60 1.50
205 Ramiro Pena RC 1.00 2.50
206 Brad Nelson (RC) .60 1.50
207 Michael Hinckley (RC) .60 1.50
208 Ronald Belisario (RC) .60 1.50
209 Chris Jakubauskas RC 1.00 2.50
210 Hunter Jones RC 1.00 2.50
211 Walter Silva RC 1.00 2.50
212 Jordan Zimmermann RC 1.50 4.00
213 Andrew McCutchen (RC) 3.00 8.00
214 Gordon Beckham RC 5.00 12.00
215 Anthony Claggett RC 1.00 2.50
216 Mark Melancon (RC) .60 1.50
217 Brett Cecil RC .60 1.50
218 Derek Holland RC 1.00 2.50
219 Greg Golson (RC) .60 1.50
220 Bobby Scales RC 1.00 2.50
221 Jordan Schafer AU 5.00 12.00
222 Trevor Crowe AU 4.00 10.00
223 Ramiro Pena AU 4.00 10.00
224 Trevor Cahill AU 6.00 15.00
225 Ryan Perry AU 5.00 12.00
226 Brett Anderson AU 4.00 10.00
227 Elvis Andrus AU 15.00 40.00
229 Michael Bowden AU (RC) 4.00 10.00
230 David Freese AU 12.50 30.00
231 Nolan Reimold AU (RC) 4.00 10.00
233 Jason Jaramillo AU 4.00 10.00
234 Ricky Romero AU 5.00 12.00
235 Jordan Zimmermann AU 6.00 15.00
236 Derek Holland AU 5.00 12.00
237 George Kottaras AU 3.00 8.00
239 Sergio Escalona AU RC 3.00 8.00
240 Brian Duensing AU 5.00 12.00
241 Everth Cabrera AU 6.00 15.00
242 Andrew Bailey AU 6.00 15.00
243 Chris Jakubauskas AU 4.00 10.00
CL1 Checklist Card .20 .50
CL2 Checklist Card .20 .50
CL3 Checklist Card .20 .50
NNO1 Tommy Hanson AU RC 6.00 15.00
NNO2 Mark Melancon AU 6.00 15.00
NNO3 Will Venable AU RC 4.00 10.00

2009 Topps Chrome Refractors

*REF: 1X TO 2.5X BASIC
REF ODDS 1:3 HOBBY
*REF RC: .6X TO 1.5X BASIC RC
REF RC ODDS 1:3 HOBBY
*REF AU: .5X TO 1.2X BASIC AUTO
REF AU ODDS 1:47 HOBBY
REF AU PRINT RUN 499 SER.#'d SETS
44b Barack Obama 8.00 20.00

2009 Topps Chrome Blue Refractors

*BLUE REF: 2.5X TO 6X BASIC
BLUE REF ODDS 1:13 HOBBY
*BLUE REF RC: 1.2X TO 3X BASIC RC

BLUE REF RC ODDS 1:13 HOBBY
*BLUE REF AU: .6X TO 1.5X BASIC AU
BLUE REF AU ODDS 1:120 HOBBY
BLUE REF PRINT RUN 199 SER.#'d SETS
44b Barack Obama 12.50 30.00
214 Gordon Beckham 30.00 60.00

2009 Topps Chrome Gold Refractors

*GOLD REF: 4X TO 10X BASIC
GOLD REF ODDS 1:50 HOBBY
*GOLD REF RC: 2X TO 5X BASIC RC
GOLD REF RC ODDS 1:50 HOBBY
GOLD AUTO ODDS 1:473 HOBBY
GOLD REF PRINT RUN 50 SER.#'d SETS
44b Barack Obama 40.00 80.00
214 Gordon Beckham 60.00 120.00
222 Trevor Crowe AU 12.50 30.00
223 Ramiro Pena AU 8.00 20.00
224 Trevor Cahill AU 40.00 80.00
225 Ryan Perry AU 12.50 30.00
226 Brett Anderson AU 12.50 30.00
227 Elvis Andrus AU 40.00 100.00
229 Michael Bowden AU 12.50 30.00
230 David Freese AU 50.00 120.00
231 Nolan Reimold AU 12.50 30.00
233 Jason Jaramillo AU 12.50 30.00
234 Ricky Romero AU 15.00 40.00
235 Jordan Zimmermann AU 15.00 40.00
236 Derek Holland AU 15.00 40.00
237 George Kottaras AU 10.00 25.00
239 Sergio Escalona AU 10.00 25.00
240 Brian Duensing AU 15.00 40.00
241 Everth Cabrera AU 20.00 50.00
242 Andrew Bailey AU 15.00 40.00
243 Chris Jakubauskas AU 12.50 30.00
NNO3 Will Venable AU 12.50 30.00

2009 Topps Chrome Red Refractors

RED 1-220 ODDS 1:100 HOBBY
RED AU ODDS 1:924 HOBBY
STATED PRINT RUN 25 SER.#'d SETS
NO PRICING DUE TO SCARCITY

2009 Topps Chrome X-Fractors

*X-F: 1.5X TO 4X BASIC
*X-F RC: .75X TO 2X BASIC RC
RANDOM INSERTS IN RETAIL PACKS

2009 Topps Chrome World Baseball Classic

STATED ODDS 1:4 HOBBY
PRINT.PLATE ODDS 1:383 HOBBY
PLATE PRINT RUN 1 SET PER COLOR
BLACK-CYAN-MAGENTA-YELLOW ISSUED
NO PLATE PRICING DUE TO SCARCITY
*REF: 1X TO 2.5X BASIC
REF ODDS 1:16 HOBBY
REF PRINT RUN 500 SER.#'d SETS
*BLUE REF: 1.5X TO 4X BASIC
BLUE REF ODDS 1:13 HOBBY
BLUE REF PRINT RUN 199 SER.#'d SETS
*GOLD REF: 2.5X TO 6X BASIC
GOLD REF ODDS 1:50 HOBBY
GOLD REF PRINT RUN 50 SER.#'d SETS
RED REF ODDS 1:100 HOBBY
RED REF PRINT RUN 25 SER.#'d SETS
NO RED REF PRICING AVAILABLE
SUPERFRAC ODDS 1:1532 HOBBY
SUPERFRAC PRINT RUN 1 SER.#'d SET
NO SUPERFRAC PRICING AVAILABLE
W1 Yu Darvish 1.50 4.00
W2 Yulieski Gourriel 1.25 3.00
W3 Yi-Chuan Lin .60 1.50
W4 Ichiro Suzuki 1.25 3.00
W5 Hung-Wen Chen .40 1.00
W6 Yuneski Maya .40 1.00
W7 Chih-Hsien Chiang 1.00 2.50
W8 Kenji Johjima .60 1.50
W9 Hanley Ramirez .60 1.50
W10 Chenhao Li .40 1.00
W11 Yoennis Cespedes 1.50 4.00
W12 Dae Ho Lee .40 1.00
W13 Alex Rodriguez 1.25 3.00
W14 Luis Durango .40 1.00
W15 Chipper Jones 1.00 2.50
W16 Dennis Neuman .40 1.00
W17 Carlos Lee .40 1.00
W18 Tae Kyun Kim .40 1.00
W19 Adrian Gonzalez .75 2.00
W20 Michel Enriquez .40 1.00
W21 Miguel Cabrera 1.00 2.50
W22 Hisashi Iwakuma 1.25 3.00
W23 Aroldis Chapman 2.00 5.00
W24 Daisuke Matsuzaka .60 1.50
W25 Chris Denorfia .40 1.00
W26 David Wright .75 2.00
W27 Alex Rios .40 1.00
W28 Michihiro Ogasawara .60 1.50
W29 Frederich Cepeda .60 1.50
W30 Chen-Chang Lee .60 1.50
W31 Shunsuke Watanabe .60 1.50
W32 Luca Panerati .40 1.00
W33 David Ortiz 1.00 2.50
W34 Tetsuya Yamaguchi .60 1.50
W35 Jin Young Lee .40 1.00
W36 Tom Stuifbergen .40 1.00
W37 Masahiro Tanaka 2.00 5.00
W38 Cheng-Ming Peng .60 1.50
W39 Yoshiyuki Ishihara .60 1.50
W40 Manuel Corpas .40 1.00
W41 Yi-Feng Kuo .40 1.00
W42 Ruben Tejada .40 1.00
W43 Kenley Jansen 1.25 3.00
W44 Shinnosuke Abe .60 1.50
W45 Shuichi Murata .60 1.50
W46 Yolexis Ulacia .40 1.00
W47 Yueh-Ping Lin .60 1.50
W48 James Beresford .40 1.00
W49 Justin Morneau .60 1.50
W50 Brad Harman .40 1.00
W51 Juan Carlos Sulbaran .40 1.00
W52 Ubaldo Jimenez .40 1.00
W53 Joel Naughton .40 1.00
W54 Rafael Diaz .40 1.00
W55 Russell Martin .40 1.00
W56 Concepcion Rodriguez .40 1.00
W57 Po Yu Lin .40 1.00
W58 Chih-Kang Kao .40 1.00
W59 Gregor Blanco .40 1.00
W60 Justin Erasmus .40 1.00
W61 Kosuke Fukudome .60 1.50
W62 Hiroyuki Nakajima .60 1.50
W63 Luke Hughes .40 1.00
W64 Sidney de Jong .40 1.00
W65 Greg Halman .60 1.50
W66 Seiichi Uchikawa .60 1.50
W67 Tao Bu .40 1.00
W68 Pedro Martinez .60 1.50
W69 Jingchao Wang .60 1.50
W70 Arquimedes Nieto .40 1.00
W71 Yang Yang .40 1.00
W72 Alex Liddi .60 1.50
W73 Fei Feng .40 1.00
W74 Pedro Lazo .40 1.00
W75 Magglio Ordonez .60 1.50
W76 Bryan Engelhardt .40 1.00
W77 Yen-Wen Kuo .40 1.00
W78 Norichika Aoki .60 1.50
W79 Jose Reyes .60 1.50
W80 Kangan Xia .40 1.00
W81 Shin-Soo Choo .60 1.50
W82 Frank Catalanotto .40 1.00
W83 Ray Chang .40 1.00
W84 Nelson Cruz 1.00 2.50
W85 Fu-Te Ni .60 1.50
W86 Hein Robb .40 1.00
W87 Hyun-Soo Kim .40 1.00
W88 Tai-Chi Kuo .40 1.00
W89 Akinori Iwamura .40 1.00
W90 Chi-Hung Cheng .40 1.00
W91 Fujia Chu .40 1.00
W92 Gift Ngoepe .40 1.00
W93 Zhenwang Zhang .40 1.00
W94 Bernie Williams .60 1.50
W95 Dustin Pedroia .75 2.00
W96 Dylan Lindsay .60 1.50
W97 Max Ramirez .40 1.00
W98 Yadier Molina 1.00 2.50
W99 Phillippe Aumont .60 1.50
W100 Derek Jeter 2.50 6.00

2010 Topps Chrome

COMPLETE SET (220) 20.00 50.00
COMMON CARD (1-170) .20 .50
COMMON RC (171-220) .40 1.00
PRINTING PLATE ODDS 1:1592 HOBBY
1 Prince Fielder .30 .75
2 Derrek Lee .20 .50
3 Clayton Kershaw 1.00 2.50
4 Bobby Abreu .20 .50
5 Johnny Cueto .30 .75
6 Dexter Fowler .30 .75
7 Mickey Mantle 1.50 4.00
8 Tommy Hanson .20 .50
9 Shane Victorino .30 .75
10 Adam Jones .30 .75
11 Zach Duke .20 .50
12 Victor Martinez .30 .75
13 Rick Porcello .30 .75
14 Josh Johnson .30 .75
15 Marco Scutaro .30 .75
16 Howie Kendrick .20 .50
17 Joey Votto .50 1.25
18 Zack Greinke .30 .75
19 John Lackey .30 .75
20 Manny Ramirez .50 1.25
21 CC Sabathia .30 .75
22 David Wright .40 1.00
23 Nick Swisher .30 .75
24 Cole Hamels .40 1.00
25 Adrian Gonzalez .40 1.00
26 Joe Saunders .20 .50
27 Tim Lincecum .30 .75
28 Ken Griffey Jr. 1.00 2.50
29 J.A. Happ .30 .75
30 Ian Kinsler .30 .75
31 Carl Crawford .30 .75
32 Albert Pujols .60 1.50
33 Daniel Murphy .40 1.00
34 Erick Aybar .20 .50
35 Andrew McCutchen .50 1.25
36 Gordon Beckham .20 .50
37 Jorge Posada .30 .75
38 Ichiro Suzuki .60 1.50
39 Vladimir Guerrero .30 .75
40 Cliff Lee .30 .75
41 Freddy Sanchez .20 .50
42 Ryan Dempster .20 .50
43 Adam Wainwright .30 .75
44 Matt Holliday .50 1.25
45 Chone Figgins .20 .50
46 Tim Hudson .30 .75
47 Rich Harden .20 .50
48 Justin Upton .30 .75
49 Yunel Escobar .20 .50
50 Joe Mauer .40 1.00
51 Vernon Wells .20 .50
52 Miguel Tejada .30 .75
53 Denard Span .20 .50
54 Brandon Phillips .20 .50
55 Jason Bay .30 .75
56 Kendry Morales .20 .50
57 Josh Hamilton .30 .75
58 Yovani Gallardo .20 .50
59 Adam Lind .30 .75
60 Nick Johnson .20 .50
61 Hideki Matsui .50 1.25
62 Pablo Sandoval .30 .75
63 James Shields .20 .50
64 Roy Halladay .30 .75
65 Chris Coghlan .20 .50
66 Alexei Ramirez .30 .75
67 Josh Beckett .20 .50
68 Magglio Ordonez .30 .75
69 Matt Kemp .40 1.00
70 Max Scherzer .50 1.25
71 Curtis Granderson .40 1.00
72 David Price .40 1.00
73 Lance Berkman .30 .75
74 Andre Ethier .30 .75
75 Mark Teixeira .30 .75
76 Edwin Jackson .20 .50
77 Akinori Iwamura .20 .50
78 Placido Polanco .20 .50
79 Jair Jurrjens .20 .50
80 Stephen Drew .20 .50
81 Javier Vazquez .20 .50
82 Lyle Overbay .20 .50
83 Orlando Hudson .20 .50
84 Adam Dunn .30 .75
85 Kevin Youkilis .20 .50
86 Chase Utley .30 .75
87 Elvis Andrus .30 .75
88 Scott Kazmir .20 .50
89 Brian McCann .30 .75
90 Alex Rios .20 .50
91 Wandy Rodriguez .20 .50
92 Felix Hernandez .30 .75
93 Carlos Gonzalez .30 .75
94 Kosuke Fukudome .30 .75
95 A.J. Burnett .20 .50
96 Nelson Cruz .50 1.25
97 Luke Hochevar .20 .50
98 Francisco Liriano .20 .50
99 Chris Carpenter .30 .75
100 Russell Martin .20 .50
101 Carlos Pena .30 .75
102 Jake Peavy .20 .50
103 Jose Lopez .20 .50
104 Todd Helton .30 .75
105 Mike Pelfrey .20 .50
106 Jacoby Ellsbury .40 1.00
107 Edinson Volquez .20 .50
108 Michael Young .20 .50
109 Dustin Pedroia .40 1.00
110 Chipper Jones .50 1.25
111 Brad Hawpe .20 .50
112 Justin Morneau .20 .50
113 Hiroki Kuroda .20 .50
114 Robinson Cano .30 .75
115 Torii Hunter .20 .50
116 Jimmy Rollins .30 .75
117 Delmon Young .30 .75
118 Matt Cain .30 .75
119 Ryan Zimmerman .30 .75
120 Johan Santana .30 .75
121 Roy Oswalt .30 .75
122 Jay Bruce .30 .75
123 Ubaldo Jimenez .20 .50
124 Geovany Soto .20 .50
125 Jon Lester .30 .75
126 Ryan Howard .40 1.00
127 Jayson Werth .30 .75
128 David Ortiz .50 1.25
129 Dan Haren .20 .50
130 Daisuke Matsuzaka .30 .75
131 Michael Bourn .20 .50
132 Michael Cuddyer .20 .50
133 Carlos Quentin .20 .50
134 Justin Verlander .50 1.25
135 Carlos Beltran .30 .75
136 Alfonso Soriano .30 .75
137 Ryan Braun .30 .75
138 Carlos Zambrano .30 .75
139 Jose Reyes .30 .75
140 Koji Uehara .20 .50
141 Evan Longoria .30 .75
142 Mark Buehrle .30 .75
143 Troy Tulowitzki .50 1.25
144 Alex Rodriguez .60 1.50
145 Chad Billingsley .30 .75
146 Shin-Soo Choo .30 .75
147 Mark Reynolds .20 .50
148 Jered Weaver .30 .75
149 Carlos Lee .20 .50
150 B.J. Upton .30 .75
151 Aaron Hill .20 .50
152 Nick Markakis .40 1.00
153 Hanley Ramirez .30 .75
154 Alex Gordon .30 .75
155 Mike Napoli .20 .50
156 Miguel Cabrera .50 1.25
157 Grady Sizemore .30 .75
158 Aramis Ramirez .20 .50
159 Brandon Webb .30 .75
160 Gavin Floyd .20 .50
161 Yadier Molina .50 1.25
162 Nate McLouth .20 .50
163 Dan Uggla .20 .50
164 Hunter Pence .30 .75
165 Derek Jeter 1.25 3.00
166 Brian Roberts .20 .50
167 Franklin Gutierrez .20 .50
168 Glen Perkins .20 .50
169 Matt Garza .20 .50
170 Raul Ibanez .30 .75
171 Eric Young Jr. (RC) .40 1.00
172 Bryan Anderson (RC) .40 1.00
173 Jon Link RC .40 1.00
174 Jason Heyward RC 1.50 4.00
175 Scott Sizemore RC .60 1.50
176 Mike Leake RC 1.25 3.00
177 Austin Jackson RC .60 1.50
178 Jon Jay RC .60 1.50
179 John Ely RC .60 1.50
180 Jason Donald RC .40 1.00
181 Tyler Colvin RC .60 1.50
182 Brennan Boesch RC 1.00 2.50
183 Esmil Rogers RC .40 1.00
184 Ike Davis RC .75 2.00
185 Andrew Cashner RC .40 1.00
186 Cole Gillespie RC .40 1.00
187 Luke Hughes (RC) .40 1.00
188 Alex Burnett RC .40 1.00
189 Wilson Ramos RC 1.00 2.50
190 Mike Stanton RC 8.00 20.00
191 Josh Donaldson RC 2.00 5.00
192 Chris Heisey RC .60 1.50
193 Lance Zawadzki RC .40 1.00
194 Cesar Valdez RC .40 1.00
195 Starlin Castro RC 1.00 2.50
196 Kevin Russo RC .40 1.00
197 Brandon Hicks RC .60 1.50
198 Carlos Santana RC 1.25 3.00
199 Allen Craig RC 1.00 2.50
200 Jenrry Mejia RC .60 1.50
201 Ruben Tejada RC .60 1.50
202 Drew Butera (RC) .40 1.00
203 Jesse English (RC) .40 1.00
204 Tyson Ross RC .40 1.00
205 Ian Desmond (RC) .60 1.50
206 Mike McCoy RC .40 1.00
207 Tommy Manzella (RC) .40 1.00
208 Kanekoa Texeira RC .40 1.00
209 Daniel McCutchen RC .60 1.50
210 Brian Matusz RC 1.00 2.50
211 Sergio Santos (RC) .40 1.00
212 Stephen Strasburg RC 3.00 8.00
213 Jake Arrieta RC 1.00 2.50
214 Ivan Nova RC 2.00 5.00
215 Kila Ka'aihue RC .60 1.50
216 Drew Storen RC .60 1.50
217 Hisanori Takahashi RC .60 1.50
218 Andy Oliver RC .40 1.00
219 Drew Stubbs RC 1.00 2.50
220 Wade Davis (RC) .60 1.50

2010 Topps Chrome Refractors

*REF VET: 1X TO 2.5X BASIC
*REF RC: 1X TO 2.5X BASIC RC
STATED ODDS 1:3 HOBBY

2010 Topps Chrome Blue Refractors

*BLUE VET: 3X TO 8X BASIC
*BLUE RC: 1.5X TO 4X BASIC RC
STATED ODDS 1:58 HOBBY
STATED PRINT RUN 199 SER.#'d SETS

2010 Topps Chrome Gold Refractors

*GOLD VET: 6X TO 15X BASIC
*GOLD RC: 3X TO 8X BASIC RC
STATED ODDS 1:224 HOBBY
STATED PRINT RUN 50 SER.#'d SETS

2010 Topps Chrome Orange Refractors

*ORANGE VET: 1.5X TO 4X BASIC
*ORANGE RC: 1.2X TO 3X BASIC RC
RANDOM INSERTS IN RETAIL PACKS

2010 Topps Chrome Purple Refractors

*PURPLE VET: 2.5X TO 6X BASIC
*PURPLE RC: 1.25X TO 3X BASIC RC
RANDOM INSERTS IN PACKS
STATED PRINT RUN 599 SER.#'d SETS

2010 Topps Chrome X-Fractors

*X-F VET: 1.5X TO 4X BASIC
*X-F RC: 1.2X TO 3X BASIC RC
RANDOM INSERTS IN RETAIL PACKS

2010 Topps Chrome Rookie Autographs

STATED ODDS 1:20 HOBBY
PRINTING PLATE ODDS 1:11,078 HOBBY
171 Eric Young Jr. 3.00 8.00
172 Bryan Anderson 3.00 8.00
173 Jon Link 3.00 8.00
174 Jason Heyward 4.00 10.00
175 Scott Sizemore 3.00 8.00
176 Mike Leake 3.00 8.00
177 Austin Jackson 3.00 8.00
178 Jon Jay 5.00 12.00
179 John Ely 3.00 8.00
181 Tyler Colvin 4.00 10.00
182 Brennan Boesch 5.00 12.00
183 Esmil Rogers 3.00 8.00
184 Ike Davis 4.00 10.00
186 Cole Gillespie 3.00 8.00
187 Luke Hughes 3.00 8.00
188 Alex Burnett 3.00 8.00
189 Wilson Ramos 5.00 12.00
190 Mike Stanton 40.00 100.00
191 Josh Donaldson 10.00 25.00
192 Chris Heisey 3.00 8.00
193 Lance Zawadzki 3.00 8.00
194 Cesar Valdez 3.00 8.00
195 Starlin Castro 6.00 15.00
196 Kevin Russo 3.00 8.00
197 Brandon Hicks 3.00 8.00
198 Carlos Santana 6.00 15.00
199 Allen Craig 3.00 8.00
200 Jenrry Mejia 4.00 10.00
201 Ruben Tejada 3.00 8.00
202 Drew Butera 3.00 8.00
203 Jesse English 3.00 8.00
204 Tyson Ross 3.00 8.00
205 Ian Desmond 5.00 12.00
206 Mike McCoy 3.00 8.00
207 Tommy Manzella 3.00 8.00
208 Kanekoa Texeira 3.00 8.00
209 Daniel McCutchen 3.00 8.00
210 Brian Matusz 3.00 8.00
211 Sergio Santos 3.00 8.00
212 Stephen Strasburg 30.00 80.00
214 Ivan Nova 3.00 8.00
215 Kila Ka'aihue 3.00 8.00
216 Drew Storen 3.00 8.00
217 Hisanori Takahashi 3.00 8.00
219 Drew Stubbs 3.00 8.00
220 Wade Davis 5.00 12.00

2010 Topps Chrome Rookie Autographs Refractors

*REF: .5X TO 1.2X BASIC
STATED ODDS 1:95 HOBBY
STATED PRINT RUN 499 SER.#'d SETS

2010 Topps Chrome Rookie Autographs Blue Refractors

*BLUE: .75X TO 2X BASIC
STATED ODDS 1:238 HOBBY
STATED PRINT RUN 199 SER.#'d SETS

2010 Topps Chrome Rookie Autographs Gold Refractors

*GOLD: 1.25X TO 3X BASIC
STATED ODDS 1:941 HOBBY
STATED PRINT RUN 50 SER.#'d SETS
189 Wilson Ramos 25.00 60.00
200 Jenrry Mejia 20.00 50.00

2010 Topps Chrome 206 Chrome

STATED ODDS 1:25 HOBBY
STATED PRINT RUN 999 SER.#'d SETS
*BLUE: .75X TO 2X BASIC
BLUE ODDS 1:125 HOBBY
BLUE PRINT RUN 199 SER.#'d SETS
*GOLD: 2.5X TO 6X BASIC
GOLD ODDS 1:497 HOBBY
GOLD PRINT RUN 50 SER.#'d SETS
PRINTING PLATE ODDS 1:1595 HOBBY
RED ODDS 1:814 HOBBY
RED PRINT RUN 25 SER.#'d SETS
*REF: .5X TO 1.2X BASIC
REF.ODDS 1:50 HOBBY
REF.PRINT RUN 499 HOBBY
SUPERFRAC.ODDS 1:20,384 HOBBY
SUPERFRAC.PRINT RUN 1 SER.#'d SET
TC1 Matt Holliday 1.50 4.00
TC2 Shane Victorino 1.00 2.50
TC3 Zack Greinke 1.00 2.50
TC4 Mike Leake 2.00 5.00
TC5 Justin Upton 1.00 2.50
TC6 Gordon Beckham .60 1.50
TC7 Yovani Gallardo .60 1.50
TC8 Martin Prado .60 1.50
TC9 Adrian Gonzalez 1.25 3.00
TC10 Justin Verlander 1.50 4.00
TC11 Pablo Sandoval 1.00 2.50
TC12 Josh Beckett .60 1.50
TC13 Matt Kemp 1.25 3.00
TC14 Mickey Mantle 5.00 12.00
TC15 Jorge Posada 1.00 2.50
TC16 Evan Longoria 1.00 2.50
TC17 Howie Kendrick .60 1.50
TC18 Joey Votto 1.50 4.00
TC19 Mark Teixeira 1.00 2.50
TC20 Alex Rodriguez 2.00 5.00
TC21 B.J. Upton 1.00 2.50
TC22 Troy Tulowitzki 1.50 4.00
TC23 Ian Kinsler 1.00 2.50
TC24 Brett Anderson .60 1.50
TC25 Roy Halladay 1.00 2.50
TC26 Cliff Lee 1.00 2.50
TC27 Ryan Braun 1.00 2.50
TC28 Jake Peavy .60 1.50
TC29 Neftali Feliz .60 1.50
TC30 Derek Jeter 4.00 10.00
TC31 Austin Jackson 1.00 2.50
TC32 Stephen Strasburg 5.00 12.00
TC33 Dan Haren .60 1.50
TC34 Hanley Ramirez 1.00 2.50
TC35 Victor Martinez 1.00 2.50
TC36 Stephen Drew .60 1.50
TC37 Adam Jones 1.00 2.50
TC38 Vladimir Guerrero 1.00 2.50
TC39 Jacoby Ellsbury 1.25 3.00
TC40 Joe Mauer 1.25 3.00
TC41 Rick Porcello 1.00 2.50
TC42 Albert Pujols 2.00 5.00
TC43 Francisco Liriano .60 1.50
TC44 Dan Uggla .60 1.50
TC45 Hideki Matsui 1.50 4.00
TC46 Tim Lincecum 1.00 2.50
TC47 Ryan Howard 1.25 3.00
TC48 Carl Crawford 1.00 2.50
TC49 Andrew McCutchen 1.50 4.00
TC50 Alfonso Soriano 1.00 2.50

2010 Topps Chrome National Chicle

STATED ODDS 1:25 HOBBY
STATED PRINT RUN 999 SER.#'d SETS
*BLUE: .75X TO 2X BASIC
BLUE ODDS 1:125 HOBBY
BLUE PRINT RUN 199 SER.#'d SETS
*GOLD: 2.5X TO 6X BASIC
GOLD ODDS 1:497 HOBBY
GOLD PRINT RUN 50 SER.#'d SETS
PRINTING PLATE ODDS 1:1595 HOBBY
RED ODDS 1:814 HOBBY
RED PRINT RUN 25 SER.#'d SETS
*REF: .5X TO 1.2X BASIC
REF.ODDS 1:50 HOBBY
REF.PRINT RUN 499 HOBBY
SUPERFRAC.ODDS 1:20,384 HOBBY
SUPERFRAC.PRINT RUN 1 SER.#'d SET
CC1 Albert Pujols 2.00 5.00
CC2 Grady Sizemore 1.00 2.50
CC3 Ichiro Suzuki 2.00 5.00
CC4 Daisuke Matsuzaka 1.00 2.50
CC5 James Loney .60 1.50
CC6 Tim Wakefield 1.00 2.50
CC7 Shane Victorino 1.00 2.50
CC8 Jacoby Ellsbury 1.25 3.00
CC9 Hunter Pence 1.00 2.50
CC10 Andy Pettitte 1.00 2.50
CC11 David Wright 1.25 3.00
CC12 Derek Jeter 4.00 10.00
CC13 Ryan Howard 1.25 3.00
CC14 Russell Martin .60 1.50
CC15 Michael Young .60 1.50
CC16 Johnny Damon 1.00 2.50
CC17 Robinson Cano 1.00 2.50
CC18 Adrian Gonzalez 1.25 3.00
CC19 Gordon Beckham .60 1.50
CC20 Aramis Ramirez .60 1.50
CC21 Alex Rodriguez 2.00 5.00
CC22 Johan Santana 1.00 2.50
CC23 Vladimir Guerrero 1.00 2.50
CC24 Nick Markakis 1.25 3.00
CC25 Justin Verlander 1.50 4.00
CC26 Adam Jones 1.00 2.50
CC27 Chone Figgins .60 1.50
CC28 Cole Hamels 1.25 3.00
CC29 Roy Oswalt 1.00 2.50
CC30 Ryan Braun 1.00 2.50
CC31 Alexei Ramirez 1.00 2.50
CC32 Adam Dunn 1.00 2.50
CC33 Pablo Sandoval 1.00 2.50
CC34 Todd Helton 1.00 2.50
CC35 Carlos Beltran 1.00 2.50
CC36 Ubaldo Jimenez .60 1.50
CC37 Tommy Hanson .60 1.50
CC38 Zack Greinke 1.00 2.50
CC39 Chris Coghlan .60 1.50
CC40 Chris Young .60 1.50
CC41 Jake Peavy .60 1.50
CC42 Dexter Fowler 1.00 2.50
CC43 Phil Hughes .60 1.50
CC44 Chase Utley 1.00 2.50
CC45 Ian Stewart .60 1.50
CC46 John Danks .60 1.50
CC47 Ichiro Suzuki 2.00 5.00
CC48 Lance Berkman 1.00 2.50
CC49 Ryan Zimmerman 1.00 2.50
CC50 Albert Pujols 2.00 5.00

2010 Topps Chrome Target Exclusive Refractors

COMPLETE SET (5) 6.00 15.00
BC1 Stephen Strasburg 2.50 6.00
BC2 Starlin Castro .75 2.00
BC3 Jason Heyward 1.25 3.00
BC4 Mickey Mantle 2.50 6.00
BC5 Jackie Robinson .75 2.00

2010 Topps Chrome USA Baseball Autographs

STATED ODDS 1:287 HOBBY
USA1 Tyler Anderson 8.00 20.00
USA2 Matt Barnes 5.00 12.00
USA3 Jackie Bradley Jr. 10.00 25.00
USA4 Gerrit Cole 15.00 40.00
USA5 Alex Dickerson 5.00 12.00
USA6 Nolan Fontana 5.00 12.00
USA7 Sean Gilmartin 6.00 15.00
USA8 Sonny Gray 12.00 30.00
USA9 Brian Johnson 8.00 20.00
USA10 Andrew Maggi 8.00 20.00
USA11 Mike Mahtook 10.00 25.00
USA12 Scott McGough 5.00 12.00
USA13 Brad Miller 8.00 20.00
USA14 Brett Mooneyham 8.00 20.00
USA15 Peter O'Brien 8.00 20.00
USA16 Nick Ramirez 8.00 20.00
USA17 Noe Ramirez 8.00 20.00
USA19 Steve Rodriguez 8.00 20.00
USA20 George Springer 25.00 60.00
USA21 Kyle Winkler 8.00 20.00
USA22 Ryan Wright 5.00 12.00

2010 Topps Chrome Wal-Mar Exclusive Refractors

COMPLETE SET (3) 6.00 15.
WME1 Babe Ruth 2.00 5.
WME2 Cal Ripken Jr. 2.50 6.
WME3 Stephen Strasburg 2.50 6.

2010 Topps Chrome Wrapper Redemption Autographs

STATED PRINT RUN 90 SER.#'d SETS
174 Jason Heyward 100.00 200.
221 Buster Posey 300.00 500.

2010 Topps Chrome Wrapper Redemption Refractors

COMPLETE SET (15) 10.00 25.
*GREEN RC: .5X TO 1.2X BASIC
*GREEN VET: .5X TO 1.2X BASIC
GREEN PRINT RUN 599 SER.#'d SETS
174 Jason Heyward 3.00 8.
176 Mike Leake 2.50 6.
177 Austin Jackson 1.25 3.
181 Tyler Colvin 1.25 3.
184 Ike Davis 1.50 4.
190 Mike Stanton 15.00 40.
195 Starlin Castro 2.00 5.
198 Carlos Santana 2.50 6.
212 Stephen Strasburg 6.00 15.
221 Buster Posey 10.00 25.
222 Babe Ruth 5.00 12.
223 Lou Gehrig 4.00 10.
224 Jackie Robinson 2.00 5.
225 Ty Cobb 3.00 8.
226 Mickey Mantle 6.00 15.

2011 Topps Chrome

COMPLETE SET (220) 20.00 50.
COMMON CARD (1-169) .20 .5
COMMON RC (1-220) .40 1.0
PRINTING PLATE ODDS 1:718 HOBBY
PLATE PRINT RUN 1 SET PER COLOR
BLACK-CYAN-MAGENTA-YELLOW ISSUED
NO PLATE PRICING DUE TO SCARCITY
1 Buster Posey .60 1.5
2 Chipper Jones .50 1.2
3 Carl Crawford .30 .7
4 Andre Ethier .30 .7
5 David Wright .40 1.0
6 Zack Greinke .30 .7
7 Mickey Mantle 1.50 4.0
8 Andrew McCutchen .50 1.2
9 Prince Fielder .30 .7
10 Hanley Ramirez .30 .7
11 Ryan Zimmerman .30 .7
12 David Ortiz .50 1.2
13 Evan Longoria .30 .7
14 Adam Dunn .30 .7
15 Tim Lincecum .30 .7
16 Jason Heyward .40 1.0
17 Starlin Castro .30 .7
18 Ian Kinsler .30 .7
19 Joey Votto .50 1.2
20 Derek Jeter 1.25 3.0
21 Carlos Ruiz .20 .5
22 Nick Markakis .40 1.0
23 Russ Martin .20 .5
24 Matt Kemp .40 1.0
25 Adrian Gonzalez .40 1.0
26 Dan Uggla .20 .5
27 Orlando Hudson .20 .5
28 Austin Jackson .20 .5
29 Phil Hughes .20 .5
30 Miguel Cabrera .50 1.25
31 Tommy Hunter .20 .50
32 Yadier Molina .50 1.25
33 Danny Espinosa RC .40 1.00
34 Josh Beckett .20 .50
35 Chase Utley .30 .75
36 Rafael Soriano .20 .50
37 Mike Leake .30 .75
38 Justin Upton .30 .75
39 Travis Wood .20 .50
40 Cliff Lee .30 .75
41 Danny Valencia .30 .75
42 Mariano Rivera .60 1.50
43 Josh Johnson .30 .75
44 David Price .40 1.00
45 Ryan Howard .40 1.00
46 Billy Butler .20 .50
47 James Loney .20 .50
48 Jay Bruce .30 .75
49 Jonathan Papelbon .30 .75
50 Ichiro Suzuki .60 1.50
51 Gordon Beckham .20 .50
52 CC Sabathia .30 .75
53 Carlos Santana .50 1.25
54 Ryan Braun .30 .75
55 Jon Lester .30 .75
56 Gio Gonzalez .30 .75
57 John Jaso .20 .50
58 Jason Bay .30 .75
59 Joe Nathan .20 .50
60 Josh Hamilton .30 .75
61 Yovani Gallardo .20 .50

2 Brian Wilson .50 1.25
3 Neil Walker .30 .75
4 Vernon Wells .20 .50
5 Jason Bartlett .20 .50
6 Neftali Feliz .20 .50
7 Aaron Hill .20 .50
8 Aroldis Chapman RC 1.25 3.00
9 Michael Young .20 .50
0 Robinson Cano .30 .75
1 Colby Rasmus .30 .75
2 Brian McCann .30 .75
3 James Shields .20 .50
4 Nelson Cruz .50 1.25
5 Roy Halladay .30 .75
6 Jose Bautista .30 .75
7 David DeJesus .20 .50
8 Sean Rodriguez .20 .50
9 Jonathan Sanchez .20 .50
0 Joe Mauer .40 1.00
1 Mat Latos .30 .75
2 Franklin Gutierrez .20 .50
3 Adam Jones .30 .75
4 Jorge Posada .30 .75
5 Mike Stanton .50 1.25
6 Drew Stubbs .20 .50
7 Todd Helton .30 .75
8 Joakim Soria .20 .50
9 Gaby Sanchez .20 .50
0 Kevin Youkilis .20 .50
1 Alfonso Soriano .30 .75
2 Jake Peavy .20 .50
3 Pablo Sandoval .30 .75
4 Shane Victorino .30 .75
5 Cameron Maybin .20 .50
6 Hunter Pence .30 .75
7 Ubaldo Jimenez .20 .50
8 Heath Bell .20 .50
9 Kendry Morales .20 .50
100 Alex Rodriguez .60 1.50
101 Tim Hudson .30 .75
102 Jordan Zimmerman .30 .75
103 Shin-Soo Choo .30 .75
104 Matt Garza .20 .50
105 Felix Hernandez .30 .75
106 Ike Davis .20 .50
107 Clayton Kershaw 1.00 2.50
108 Mike Morse .20 .50
109 Ricky Romero .20 .50
110 Carlos Gonzalez .30 .75
111 Marlon Byrd .20 .50
112 Carlos Pena .30 .75
113 Jayson Werth .30 .75
114 Carlos Beltran .30 .75
115 Justin Verlander .50 1.25
116 Clay Buchholz .20 .50
117 Jimmy Rollins .30 .75
118 Francisco Liriano .20 .50
119 Ryan Ludwick .20 .50
120 Stephen Strasburg .50 1.25
121 Chris Carpenter .30 .75
122 Adam Lind .30 .75
123 B.J. Upton .30 .75
124 Jacoby Ellsbury .40 1.00
125 Roy Oswalt .30 .75
126 Johan Santana .30 .75
127 Madison Bumgarner .40 1.00
128 Matt Joyce .20 .50
129 Mark Reynolds .20 .50
130 Matt Holliday .50 1.25
131 Tyler Colvin .20 .50
132 Matt Cain .30 .75
133 Drew Storen .20 .50
134 Grady Sizemore .30 .75
135 Martin Prado .20 .50
136 C.J. Wilson .20 .50
137 Chris Young .20 .50
138 Jose Reyes .30 .75
139 Clayton Richard .20 .50
140 Mark Teixeira .30 .75
141 Lance Berkman .30 .75
142 John Buck .20 .50
143 Brett Anderson .20 .50
144 Johnny Damon .30 .75
145 Rickie Weeks .20 .50
146 Brett Myers .20 .50
147 Chone Figgins .20 .50
148 Derrek Lee .20 .50
149 Ian Desmond .20 .50
150 Albert Pujols .60 1.50
151 Pedro Alvarez .75 2.00
152 Josh Thole .20 .50
153 Jonathan Broxton .20 .50
154 Justin Morneau .30 .75
155 Tommy Hanson .20 .50
156 Cole Hamels .40 1.00
157 Angel Pagan .20 .50
158 Curtis Granderson .40 1.00
159 Paul Konerko .30 .75
160 Troy Tulowitzki .50 1.25
161 Dustin Pedroia .40 1.00
162 Elvis Andrus .30 .75
163 Logan Morrison .20 .50
164 Jered Weaver .30 .75
165 Adrian Beltre .50 1.25
166 Victor Martinez .30 .75
167 Chad Billingsley .30 .75
168 J.A. Happ .30 .75
169 Rafael Furcal .20 .50
170 Eric Hosmer RC 2.50 6.00
171 Tsuyoshi Nishioka RC 1.25 3.00
172 Brandon Belt RC 1.00 2.50
173 Freddie Freeman RC 6.00 15.00
174 Michael Pineda RC 1.00 2.50
175 Ben Revere RC .60 1.50
176 Brandon Beachy RC 1.00 2.50
177 Aneury Rodriguez RC .40 1.00
178 Mark Trumbo (RC) 1.00 2.50
179 Marcos Mateo RC .60 1.50
180 Hank Conger RC .60 1.50
181 Jake McGee (RC) .40 1.00
182 J.P. Arencibia (RC) .40 1.00
183 Jordan Walden RC .40 1.00
184 Eric Sogard RC .40 1.00
185 Matt Young RC .40 1.00
186 Domonic Brown (RC) .75 2.00
187 Scott Cousins RC .40 1.00
188 Alexi Ogando RC 1.00 2.50
189 Mike Nickeas (RC) .40 1.00
190 Ivan DeJesus RC .40 1.00
191 Andrew Cashner (RC) .40 1.00
192 Josh Lueke RC .40 1.00
193 Darwin Barney RC 1.25 3.00
194 Mason Tobin RC .40 1.00
195 Craig Kimbrel RC 1.00 2.50
196 Lance Pendleton RC .40 1.00
197 Julio Teheran RC .60 1.50
198 Eduardo Nunez RC 1.00 2.50
199 Pedro Beato RC .40 1.00
200 Jeremy Hellickson RC 1.00 2.50
201 Vinnie Pestano RC .40 1.00
202 Tom Wilhelmsen RC .40 1.00
203 Brett Wallace (RC) .40 1.00
204 Chris Pettit (RC) .40 1.00
205 Chris Sale RC 2.50 6.00
206 Brandon Kintzler RC .40 1.00
207 Alex Cobb RC .40 1.00
208 Michael Kohn RC .40 1.00
209 Cory Luebke RC .40 1.00
210 Pedro Strop (RC) .40 1.00
211 Jerry Sands RC 1.00 2.50
212 Dee Gordon RC .60 1.50
213 Joe Paterson RC .60 1.50
214 Brent Morel RC .40 1.00
215 Kyle Drabek RC .60 1.50
216 Zach Britton RC 1.00 2.50
217 Mike Minor (RC) .40 1.00
218 Hector Noesi RC .60 1.50
219 Carlos Peguero RC .60 1.50
220 Aaron Crow RC .60 1.50

2011 Topps Chrome Refractors

*REF VET: 1X TO 2.5X BASIC
*REF RC: .6X TO 1.5X BASIC RC
STATED ODDS 1:3 HOBBY

2011 Topps Chrome Atomic Refractors

*ATOMIC VET: 2X TO 5X BASIC
*ATOMIC RC: 1X TO 2.5X BASIC RC
STATED ODDS 1:19 HOBBY
STATED PRINT RUN 225 SER.#'d SETS
170 Eric Hosmer 30.00 60.00

2011 Topps Chrome Black Refractors

*BLACK VET: 4X TO 10X BASIC
*BLACK RC: 2X TO 5X BASIC RC
STATED ODDS 1:84 HOBBY
STATED PRINT RUN 100 SER.#'d SETS

2011 Topps Chrome Blue Refractors

*BLUE VET: 4X TO 10X BASIC
*BLUE RC: 2X TO 5X BASIC RC
STATED ODDS 1:57 HOBBY
STATED PRINT RUN 99 SER.#'d SETS

2011 Topps Chrome Gold Refractors

*GOLD VET: 5X TO 12X BASIC
*GOLD RC: 2.5X TO 6X BASIC RC
STATED ODDS 1:111 HOBBY
STATED PRINT RUN 50 SER.#'d SETS

2011 Topps Chrome Orange Refractors

*ORANGE VET: 1.5X TO 4X BASIC
*ORANGE RC: .75X TO 2X BASIC RC

2011 Topps Chrome Purple Refractors

*PURPLE VET: 2X TO 5X BASIC
*PURPLE RC: 1X TO 2.5X BASIC RC
STATED PRINT RUN 499 SER.#'d SETS
170 Eric Hosmer 12.50 30.00

2011 Topps Chrome Sepia Refractors

*SEPIA VET: 4X TO 10X BASIC
*SEPIA RC: 2X TO 5X BASIC RC
STATED ODDS 1:43 HOBBY
STATED PRINT RUN 99 SER.#'d SETS

2011 Topps Chrome X-Fractors

*X-FRAC.VET: 1.5X TO 4X BASIC
*X-FRAC.RC: .75X TO 2X BASIC RC

2011 Topps Chrome Rookie Autographs

STATED ODDS 1:12 HOBBY
PRINTING PLATE ODDS 1:6217 HOBBY
PLATE PRINT RUN 1 SET PER COLOR
BLACK-CYAN-MAGENTA-YELLOW ISSUED
NO PLATE PRICING DUE TO SCARCITY
EXCHANGE DEADLINE 8/31/2014
33 Danny Espinosa 3.00 8.00
170 Eric Hosmer EXCH 25.00 60.00
171 Tsuyoshi Nishioka EXCH 50.00 100.00
172 Brandon Belt 5.00 12.00
173 Freddie Freeman 60.00 150.00
174 Michael Pineda 5.00 12.00
175 Ben Revere 3.00 8.00
176 Brandon Beachy 3.00 8.00
178 Mark Trumbo 6.00 15.00
181 Jake McGee 3.00 8.00
182 J.P. Arencibia 3.00 8.00
183 Jordan Walden 4.00 10.00
184 Eric Sogard 3.00 8.00
188 Alexi Ogando 3.00 8.00
190 Ivan DeJesus Jr. 3.00 8.00
191 Andrew Cashner 3.00 8.00
193 Darwin Barney 3.00 8.00
195 Craig Kimbrel 15.00 40.00
197 Julio Teheran 4.00 10.00
198 Eduardo Nunez 4.00 10.00
205 Chris Sale 15.00 40.00
207 Alex Cobb 3.00 8.00
214 Brent Morel 3.00 8.00
215 Kyle Drabek 3.00 8.00
216 Zach Britton 5.00 12.00
217 Mike Minor 5.00 12.00
218 Hector Noesi 3.00 8.00
219 Carlos Peguero 3.00 8.00
220 Aaron Crow 3.00 8.00

2011 Topps Chrome Rookie Autographs Refractors

*REF: .5X TO 1.2X BASIC
STATED ODDS 1:72 HOBBY
STATED PRINT RUN 499 SER.#'d SETS
EXCHANGE DEADLINE 8/31/2014

2011 Topps Chrome Rookie Autographs Black Refractors

*BLACK REF: 1X TO 2.5X BASIC
STATED ODDS 1:328 HOBBY
STATED PRINT RUN 100 SER.#'d SETS
EXCHANGE DEADLINE 8/31/2014

2011 Topps Chrome Rookie Autographs Blue Refractors

*BLUE REF: .75X TO 2X BASIC
STATED ODDS 1:181 HOBBY
STATED PRINT RUN 199 SER.#'d SETS
EXCHANGE DEADLINE 8/31/2014

2011 Topps Chrome Rookie Autographs Gold Refractors

*GOLD REF: 1.2X TO 3X BASIC
STATED ODDS 1:694 HOBBY
STATED PRINT RUN 50 SER.#'d SETS
EXCHANGE DEADLINE 8/31/2014
170 Eric Hosmer EXCH 100.00 250.00
171 Tsuyoshi Nishioka EXCH 125.00 300.00

2011 Topps Chrome Rookie Autographs Sepia Refractors

*SEPIA REF: 1X TO 2.5X BASIC
STATED ODDS 1:350 HOBBY
STATED PRINT RUN 99 SER.#'d SETS
EXCHANGE DEADLINE 8/31/2014

2011 Topps Chrome USA Baseball Autographs

EXCHANGE CARD ODDS 1:824 HOBBY
EXCHANGE DEADLINE 9/6/2012
PRINTING PLATE ODDS 1:230,000 HOBBY
PLATE PRINT RUN 1 SET PER COLOR
BLACK-CYAN-MAGENTA-YELLOW ISSUED
NO PLATE PRICING DUE TO SCARCITY
USABB1 Mark Appel 10.00 25.00
USABB2 DJ Baxendale 4.00 10.00
USABB3 Josh Elander 4.00 10.00
USABB4 Chris Elder 4.00 10.00
USABB5 Dominic Ficociello 4.00 10.00
USABB6 Nolan Fontana 4.00 10.00
USABB7 Kevin Gausman 6.00 15.00
USABB8 Brian Johnson 4.00 10.00
USABB9 Branden Kline 4.00 10.00
USABB10 Corey Knebel 5.00 12.00
USABB11 Michael Lorenzen 4.00 10.00
USABB12 David Lyon 4.00 10.00
USABB13 Deven Marrero 4.00 10.00
USABB14 Hoby Milner 4.00 10.00
USABB15 Andrew Mitchell 4.00 10.00
USABB16 Tom Murphy 4.00 10.00
USABB17 Tyler Naquin 12.00 30.00
USABB18 Matt Reynolds 4.00 10.00
USABB19 Brady Rodgers 4.00 10.00
USABB20 Marcus Stroman 8.00 20.00
USABB21 Michael Wacha 25.00 60.00
USABB22 Erich Weiss 4.00 10.00
NNO Exchange Card 30.00 60.00

2011 Topps Chrome USA Baseball Autographs Refractors

*REF: .5X TO 1.2X BASIC
EXCHANGE ODDS 1:1173 HOBBY
STATED PRINT RUN 199 SER.#'d SETS
EXCHANGE DEADLINE 9/6/2012
NNO Exchange Card 40.00 80.00

2011 Topps Chrome USA Baseball Autographs Blue Refractors

*BLUE REF: .75X TO 2X BASIC
EXCHANGE ODDS 1:2397 HOBBY
STATED PRINT RUN 99 SER.#'d SETS
EXCHANGE DEADLINE 9/6/2012
NNO Exchange Card 60.00 120.00

2011 Topps Chrome USA Baseball Autographs Gold Refractors

*GOLD REF: 1.25X TO 3X BASIC
EXCHANGE ODDS 1:4900 HOBBY
STATED PRINT RUN 50 SER.#'d SETS
EXCHANGE DEADLINE 9/6/2012
NNO Exchange Card 100.00 200.00

2011 Topps Chrome USA Baseball Refractors

EXCHANGE CARD ODDS 1:964 HOBBY
STATED PRINT RUN 999 SER.#'d SETS
EXCHANGE DEADLINE 9/6/2012
PRINTING PLATE ODDS 1:230,000 HOBBY
PLATE PRINT RUN 1 SET PER COLOR
BLACK-CYAN-MAGENTA-YELLOW ISSUED
NO PLATE PRICING DUE TO SCARCITY
USABB1 Mark Appel 1.50 4.00
USABB2 DJ Baxendale 1.00 2.50
USABB3 Josh Elander .60 1.50
USABB4 Chris Elder .60 1.50
USABB5 Dominic Ficociello .60 1.50
USABB6 Nolan Fontana .60 1.50
USABB7 Kevin Gausman 2.50 6.00
USABB8 Brian Johnson .60 1.50
USABB9 Branden Kline .60 1.50
USABB10 Corey Knebel .60 1.50
USABB11 Michael Lorenzen .60 1.50
USABB12 David Lyon .60 1.50
USABB13 Deven Marrero 1.50 4.00
USABB14 Hoby Milner .60 1.50
USABB15 Andrew Mitchell .60 1.50
USABB16 Tom Murphy .60 1.50
USABB17 Tyler Naquin 1.25 3.00
USABB18 Matt Reynolds 1.00 2.50
USABB19 Brady Rodgers .60 1.50
USABB20 Marcus Stroman 1.50 4.00
USABB21 Michael Wacha 2.00 5.00
USABB22 Erich Weiss .60 1.50

2011 Topps Chrome USA Baseball Blue Refractors

*BLUE: .6X TO 1.5X BASIC
EXCHANGE ODDS 1:2025 HOBBY
STATED PRINT RUN 499 SER.#'d SETS
EXCHANGE DEADLINE 9/6/2012

2011 Topps Chrome USA Baseball Gold Refractors

*GOLD: 1.5X TO 4X BASIC
EXCHANGE ODDS 1:18,400 HOBBY
STATED PRINT RUN 50 SER.#'d SETS
EXCHANGE DEADLINE 9/6/2012

2011 Topps Chrome Vintage Chrome

COMPLETE SET (50) 20.00 50.00
STATED ODDS 1:6 HOBBY
VC1 Buster Posey 1.00 2.50
VC2 Chipper Jones .75 2.00
VC3 Carl Crawford .50 1.25
VC4 David Wright .60 1.50
VC5 Prince Fielder .50 1.25
VC6 Hanley Ramirez .50 1.25
VC7 Ryan Zimmerman .50 1.25
VC8 David Ortiz .75 2.00
VC9 Evan Longoria .50 1.25
VC10 Tim Lincecum .50 1.25
VC11 Jason Heyward .60 1.50
VC12 Joey Votto .75 2.00
VC13 Derek Jeter 2.00 5.00
VC14 Matt Kemp .60 1.50
VC15 Adrian Gonzalez .60 1.50
VC16 Dan Uggla .30 .75
VC17 Austin Jackson .30 .75
VC18 Starlin Castro .50 1.25
VC19 Chase Utley .50 1.25
VC20 David Price .60 1.50
VC21 Ryan Howard .60 1.50
VC22 Ichiro Suzuki 1.00 2.50
VC23 CC Sabathia .50 1.25
VC24 Ryan Braun .50 1.25
VC25 Josh Hamilton .50 1.25
VC26 Robinson Cano .50 1.25
VC27 Brian McCann .50 1.25
VC28 Nelson Cruz .75 2.00
VC29 Roy Halladay .50 1.25
VC30 Jose Bautista .50 1.25
VC31 Joe Mauer .60 1.50
VC32 Mike Stanton .75 2.00
VC33 Troy Tulowitzki .75 2.00
VC34 Kevin Youkilis .30 .75
VC35 Miguel Cabrera .75 2.00
VC36 Alex Rodriguez 1.00 2.50
VC37 Felix Hernandez .50 1.25
VC38 Stephen Strasburg .75 2.00
VC39 Mark Teixeira .60 1.50
VC40 Albert Pujols 1.00 2.50
VC41 Carlos Gonzalez .50 1.25
VC42 Dustin Pedroia .60 1.50
VC43 Tsuyoshi Nishioka 1.00 2.50
VC44 Brandon Belt .75 2.00
VC45 Freddie Freeman 5.00 12.00
VC46 J.P. Arencibia .30 .75
VC47 Domonic Brown .60 1.50
VC48 Aroldis Chapman 1.00 2.50
VC49 Jeremy Hellickson .75 2.00
VC50 Kyle Drabek .50 1.25

2012 Topps Chrome

COMP.SET w/o VAR (220) 20.00 50.00
PHOTO VAR ODDS 1:918 HOBBY
VARIATIONS ARE REFRACTORS
NO VARIATION PRICING AVAILABLE
PRINTING PLATE ODDS 1:958 HOBBY
PLATE PRINT RUN 1 SET PER COLOR
NO PLATE PRICING DUE TO SCARCITY
1A Tim Lincecum Follow Through .40 1.00
1B Lincecum Arm Back SP 12.50 30.00
2 Craig Kimbrel .40 1.00
3 Shane Victorino .40 1.00
4 David Ortiz .50 1.25
5 Ryan Lavarnway .30 .75
6 Jon Lester .30 .75
7 Michael Pineda .30 .75
8 C.J. Wilson .30 .75
9 Brian McCann .40 1.00
10A Justin Upton Swinging .40 1.00
10B J.Upton Bubble SP 10.00 25.00
11 Ian Kennedy .30 .75
12 Jason Heyward .40 1.00
13 Ian Kinsler .40 1.00
14 CC Sabathia .40 1.00
15 Jimmy Rollins .40 1.00
16 Jose Valverde .40 1.00
17 Chris Carpenter .40 1.00
18 Cameron Maybin .30 .75
19 Freddie Freeman .60 1.50
20 Adrian Gonzalez .40 1.00
21 Dustin Pedroia .40 1.00
22 Shin-Soo Choo .40 1.00
23 Clay Buchholz .30 .75
24 Buster Posey .60 1.50
25 Chase Utley .40 1.00
26 Prince Fielder .40 1.00
27 Mark Reynolds .30 .75
28A Roy Halladay .40 1.00
29 Carl Crawford .40 1.00
30A Josh Hamilton .40 1.00
30B J.Hamilton SP 30.00 60.00
31 Ben Zobrist .40 1.00
32 Giancarlo Stanton .50 1.25
33 Tommy Hanson .30 .75
34 Aroldis Chapman .50 1.25
35 Paul Goldschmidt .50 1.25
36 Cole Hamels .40 1.00
37 Jeremy Hellickson .30 .75
38 Andrew McCutchen .50 1.25
39 Jacob Turner .40 1.00
40 Joey Votto .50 1.25
41 David Wright .40 1.00
42 Zack Cozart .30 .75
43 Desmond Jennings .40 1.00
44 Jhoulys Chacin .30 .75
45 Alex Gordon .40 1.00
46 Dan Uggla .30 .75
47 Billy Butler .30 .75
48 Matt Cain .40 1.00
49A Alex Rodriguez .60 1.50
49B A.Rod Throwing SP 15.00 40.00
50 Joe Mauer .40 1.00
51 Torii Hunter .40 1.00
52 Jered Weaver .40 1.00
53 Gio Gonzalez .40 1.00
54 Ike Davis .30 .75
55 Paul Konerko .30 .75
56 Mike Napoli .30 .75
57 Nelson Cruz .50 1.25
58 Shaun Marcum .30 .75
59 James Shields .30 .75
60 Curtis Granderson .40 1.00
61 Eric Hosmer .40 1.00
62 Michael Morse .30 .75
63 Josh Johnson .30 .75
64 Lucas Duda .30 .75
65 Ubaldo Jimenez .30 .75
66 Mat Latos .40 1.00
67 Daniel Hudson .30 .75
68 Michael Young .30 .75
69 Lance Berkman .40 1.00
70A Stephen Strasburg Arm Back .50 1.25
70B Strasburg Leg Up SP 50.00 100.00
71 Ryan Howard .40 1.00
72 Anibal Sanchez .30 .75
73 Mark Teixeira .40 1.00
74 Hanley Ramirez .40 1.00
75A Jose Reyes .30 .75
75B J.Reyes No Bat SP 15.00 40.00
76 Zack Greinke .40 1.00
77 Tim Hudson .40 1.00
78 Jayson Werth .40 1.00
79 Brandon Phillips .30 .75
80A Albert Pujols .60 1.50
80B Pujols Facing Right SP 12.50 30.00
81 Kyle Blanks .30 .75
82 Hunter Pence .40 1.00
83 Mark Trumbo .30 .75
84A Derek Jeter Jumping 1.25 3.00
84B Jeter Standing SP 50.00 100.00
85 Carlos Gonzalez .40 1.00
86 Ricky Romero .30 .75
87A Jacoby Ellsbury Sliding .40 1.00
87B Ellsbury Running SP 30.00 60.00
88 Jason Motte .30 .75
89 Mike Moustakas .40 1.00
90 Evan Longoria .40 1.00
91 Allen Craig .40 1.00
92 Derek Holland .30 .75
93A Justin Verlander .50 1.25
93B Verlander Arm Up SP 20.00 50.00
94 Justin Morneau .40 1.00
95 Matt Garza .30 .75
96 Chipper Jones .50 1.25
97 Yadier Molina .50 1.25
98 Brian Wilson .50 1.25
99 Jemile Weeks RC .30 .75
100A Ichiro Suzuki .60 1.50
101 Yonder Alonso .30 .75
102 Madison Bumgarner .40 1.00
103 Cliff Lee .40 1.00
104 David Freese .30 .75
105 Adam Lind .40 1.00
106 Adam Jones .40 1.00
107 Dustin Ackley .30 .75
108 Nick Swisher .40 1.00
109 Kevin Youkilis .50 1.25
110A Troy Tulowitzki .50 1.25
111 Miguel Montero .30 .75
112 Clayton Kershaw 1.00 2.50
113 Michael Bourn .30 .75
114 Carlos Santana .40 1.00
115 Josh Beckett .30 .75
116 Felix Hernandez .40 1.00
117 Ryan Braun .30 .75
118 Ryan Zimmerman .40 1.00
119 Jaime Garcia .40 1.00
120A Matt Kemp .40 1.00
120B Kemp Batting SP 30.00 60.00
121 Nyjer Morgan .30 .75
122 Brandon Beachy .30 .75
123 Brandon Belt .40 1.00
124 Salvador Perez .40 1.00
125 Matt Holliday .50 1.25
126 Dan Haren .30 .75
127 Starlin Castro .40 1.00
128 Asdrubal Cabrera .40 1.00
129 Ivan Nova .40 1.00
130 Miguel Cabrera .50 1.25
131 Alex Avila .30 .75
132 Adrian Beltre .50 1.25
133 David Price .40 1.00
134 Melky Cabrera .30 .75
135 Drew Stubbs .30 .75
136 Dee Gordon .30 .75
137 B.J. Upton .40 1.00
138 Ryan Vogelsong .30 .75
139 Pablo Sandoval .40 1.00
140 Jose Bautista .40 1.00
141 Jay Bruce .40 1.00
142 Yovani Gallardo .40 1.00
143 Robinson Cano .40 1.00
144 Mike Trout 20.00 50.00
145 Chris Young .30 .75
146 Aramis Ramirez .30 .75
147 Rickie Weeks .30 .75
148 Johnny Cueto .40 1.00
149 Elvis Andrus .40 1.00
150 Mariano Rivera .60 1.50
151A Yu Darvish Arm Back RC 1.50 4.00
151B Darvish Arm Down SP 20.00 50.00
152 Alex Liddi RC .60 1.50
153 Adron Chambers RC 1.00 2.50
154 Liam Hendriks RC .60 1.50
155 Drew Pomeranz RC .60 1.50
156 Austin Romine RC .60 1.50
157 Tim Federowicz RC .60 1.50
158 Joe Benson RC .60 1.50
159 Matt Dominguez RC .75 2.00
160A Matt Moore Grey Jsy RC 1.00 2.50
160B Moore Lt.Blue Jsy SP 12.50 30.00
161 Jordan Pacheco RC .60 1.50
162 Chris Parmelee RC .60 1.50
163 Brad Peacock RC .60 1.50
164 Brett Pill RC 1.00 2.50
165 Wilin Rosario RC .60 1.50
166 Addison Reed RC .60 1.50
167 Dellin Betances RC 1.00 2.50
168 Kelvin Herrera RC .60 1.50
169 Tom Milone RC .60 1.50
170A Jesus Montero Teal Jsy RC .60 1.50
170B Montero White Jsy SP 10.00 25.00
171 Michael Taylor RC .60 1.50
172 Devin Mesoraco RC .60 1.50
173A Brett Lawrie RC .60 1.50
173B Lawrie One Hand on Bat SP 30.00 60.00
174 James Darnell RC .60 1.50
175 Leonys Martin RC .60 1.50
176 Jeff Locke RC 1.00 2.50
177 Jarrod Parker RC .75 2.00
178 Collin Cowgill RC .60 1.50
179 Taylor Green RC .60 1.50
180A Cespedes Grn Jsy RC 1.50 4.00
180B Cespedes Wht Jsy SP 20.00 50.00
181 Eric Surkamp RC 1.00 2.50
182 Andrelton Simmons RC 1.00 2.50
183 Tyler Pastornicky RC .60 1.50
184 Norichika Aoki RC .75 2.00
185 Tsuyoshi Wada RC .60 1.50
186 Hisashi Iwakuma RC 1.25 3.00
187 Adrian Cardenas RC .60 1.50
188 Wei-Yin Chen RC 1.50 4.00
189 Xavier Avery RC .60 1.50
190 Matt Hague RC .60 1.50
191 Drew Smyly RC .60 1.50
192 Kirk Nieuwenhuis RC .60 1.50
193 Drew Hutchison RC .75 2.00
194 Wily Peralta RC .60 1.50
195 Jordany Valdespin RC .75 2.00
196A Bryce Harper Hitting RC 10.00 25.00
196B B.Harper Sliding SP 75.00 150.00
197 Will Middlebrooks RC .75 2.00
198 Brian Dozier RC 2.00 5.00
199 Matt Adams RC .75 2.00
200 Irving Falu RC .60 1.50
201 Howie Kendrick .30 .75
202 Chris Davis .30 .75
203 Alcides Escobar .40 1.00
204 A.J. Pierzynski .30 .75
205 Edwin Encarnacion .50 1.25
206 Adam Dunn .40 1.00
207 Mike Aviles .30 .75
208 Jason Kipnis .40 1.00
209 Andre Ethier .40 1.00
210 Carlos Beltran .40 1.00
211 Adam LaRoche .30 .75
212 Carlos Ruiz .30 .75
213 Jake Peavy .30 .75
214 Chris Sale .50 1.25
215 R.A. Dickey .40 1.00
216 Mark Buehrle .40 1.00
217 Derek Lowe .30 .75
218 Jason Vargas .30 .75
219 Kyle Seager .30 .75
220 Omar Infante .30 .75

2012 Topps Chrome Refractors

*REF: 1X TO 2.5X BASIC
*REF RC: .5X TO 1.2X BASIC RC
STATED ODDS 1:3 HOBBY
144 Mike Trout 75.00 200.00

2012 Topps Chrome Black Refractors

*BLACK REF: 4X TO 10X BASIC
*BLACK RC: 2X TO 5X BASIC RC
STATED ODDS 1:41 HOBBY
STATED PRINT RUN 100 SER.#'d SETS
144 Mike Trout 250.00 600.00
196 Bryce Harper 40.00 80.00

2012 Topps Chrome Blue Refractors

*BLUE REF: 1.5X TO 4X BASIC
*BLUE RC: 1X TO 2.5X BASIC RC
STATED ODDS 1:21 HOBBY
STATED PRINT RUN 199 SER.#'d SETS
144 Mike Trout 200.00 500.00
188 Wei-Yin Chen 8.00 20.00
196 Bryce Harper 20.00 50.00

2012 Topps Chrome Gold Refractors

*GOLD REF: 6X TO 15X BASIC
*GOLD RC: 3X TO 8X BASIC RC
STATED ODDS 1:82 HOBBY
STATED PRINT RUN 50 SER.#'d SETS
144 Mike Trout 500.00 1200.00
188 Wei-Yin Chen 50.00 100.00
196 Bryce Harper 50.00 100.00

2012 Topps Chrome Orange Refractors

*ORANGE REF: 1.5X TO 4X BASIC
*ORANGE RC: .75X TO 2X BASIC RC
144 Mike Trout 100.00 250.00
196 Bryce Harper 15.00 40.00

2012 Topps Chrome Purple Refractors

*PURPLE: 1.5X TO 4X BASIC
*PURPLE RC: .75X TO 2X BASIC RC
144 Mike Trout 100.00 250.00
196 Bryce Harper 12.50 30.00

2012 Topps Chrome Sepia Refractors

*SEPIA REF: 5X TO 12X BASIC
*SEPIA RC: 2.5X TO 6X BASIC
STATED ODDS 1:55 HOBBY
STATED PRINT RUN 75 SER.#'d SETS
144 Mike Trout 400.00 1000.00
196 Bryce Harper 40.00 80.00

2012 Topps Chrome X-Fractors

*XFRAC: 1.2X TO 3X BASIC
*XFRAC RC: .6X TO 1.5X BASIC
STATED ODDS 1:6 HOBBY
144 Mike Trout 100.00 250.00
196 Bryce Harper 12.50 30.00

2012 Topps Chrome Dynamic Die Cuts

STATED ODDS 1:24 HOBBY
AC Aroldis Chapman 1.50 4.00
AG Adrian Gonzalez 1.25 3.00
AJ Adam Jones 1.25 3.00
AL Adam Lind 1.25 3.00
AM Andrew McCutchen 1.50 4.00
AP Albert Pujols 2.00 5.00
BG Brett Gardner 1.25 3.00
BL Brett Lawrie 1.25 3.00
BP Buster Posey 2.00 5.00
CG Curtis Granderson 1.25 3.00
CK Clayton Kershaw 3.00 8.00
CL Cliff Lee 1.25 3.00
CS CC Sabathia 1.25 3.00
DA Dustin Ackley 1.00 2.50
DJ Derek Jeter 4.00 10.00
DO David Ortiz 1.50 4.00

DPA Dustin Pedroia 1.25 3.00
EA Elvis Andrus 1.25 3.00
EH Eric Hosmer 1.25 3.00
FH Felix Hernandez 1.25 3.00
GS Giancarlo Stanton 1.50 4.00
IK Ian Kinsler 1.25 3.00
IN Ivan Nova 1.25 3.00
I Ichiro Suzuki 2.00 5.00
JB Jose Bautista 1.25 3.00
JBR Jay Bruce 1.25 3.00
JE Jacoby Ellsbury 1.25 3.00
JH Josh Hamilton 1.25 3.00
JM Jesus Montero 1.00 2.50
JR Jose Reyes 1.00 2.50
JU Justin Upton 1.25 3.00
JV Justin Verlander 1.50 4.00
JVO Joey Votto 1.50 4.00
MK Matt Kemp 1.25 3.00
MM Matt Moore 1.50 4.00
MMO Michael Morse 1.00 2.50
MP Michael Pineda 1.00 2.50
MT Mike Trout 40.00 100.00
NC Nelson Cruz 1.50 4.00
PF Prince Fielder 1.25 3.00
PG Paul Goldschmidt 1.50 4.00
PS Pablo Sandoval 1.25 3.00
RB Ryan Braun 1.00 2.50
RC Robinson Cano 1.25 3.00
RH Roy Halladay 1.25 3.00
SC Starlin Castro 1.25 3.00
SS Stephen Strasburg 1.50 4.00
TL Tim Lincecum 1.25 3.00
TT Troy Tulowitzki 1.50 4.00
YD Yu Darvish 2.50 6.00

2012 Topps Chrome Rookie Autographs

STATED ODDS 1:19 HOBBY
PRINTING PLATE ODDS 1:6587 HOBBY
PLATE PRINT RUN 1 SET PER COLOR
NO PLATE PRICING DUE TO SCARCITY
EXCHANGE DEADLINE 07/31/2015
5 Ryan Lavarnway 3.00 8.00
39 Jacob Turner 4.00 10.00
42 Zack Cozart 4.00 10.00
BH Bryce Harper 250.00 400.00
TB Trevor Bauer 15.00 40.00
WP Wily Peralta 3.00 8.00
101 Yonder Alonso 3.00 8.00
151 Yu Darvish 20.00 50.00
154 Liam Hendriks 3.00 8.00
155 Drew Pomeranz 3.00 8.00
156 Austin Romine 3.00 8.00
159 Matt Dominguez 3.00 8.00
160 Matt Moore 4.00 10.00
161 Jordan Pacheco 3.00 8.00
162 Chris Parmelee 3.00 8.00
163 Brad Peacock 3.00 8.00
166 Addison Reed 6.00 15.00
167 Dellin Betances 6.00 15.00
169 Tom Milone 3.00 8.00
170 Jesus Montero 5.00 12.00
172 Devin Mesoraco 3.00 8.00
173 Brett Lawrie 6.00 15.00
177 Jarrod Parker 3.00 8.00
178 Collin Cowgill 3.00 8.00
180 Yoenis Cespedes 20.00 50.00
181 Eric Surkamp 3.00 8.00
183 Tyler Pastornicky 3.00 8.00
185 Tsuyoshi Wada 5.00 12.00
190 Matt Hague 3.00 8.00
191 Drew Smyly 3.00 8.00
192 Kirk Nieuwenhuis 3.00 8.00
193 Drew Hutchison 3.00 8.00

2012 Topps Chrome Rookie Autographs Refractors

*REF: .5X TO 1.2X BASIC
STATED ODDS 1:73 HOBBY
STATED PRINT RUN 499 SER.#'d SETS
EXCHANGE DEADLINE 07/31/2015

2012 Topps Chrome Rookie Autographs Black Refractors

*BLACK REF: 1X TO 2.5X BASIC
STATED ODDS 1:296 HOBBY
STATED PRINT RUN 100 SER.#'d SETS
EXCHANGE DEADLINE 07/31/2015
BH Bryce Harper 300.00 500.00

2012 Topps Chrome Rookie Autographs Blue Refractors

*BLUE REF: .75X TO 2X BASIC
STATED ODDS 1:149 HOBBY
STATED PRINT RUN 199 SER.#'d SETS
EXCHANGE DEADLINE 07/31/2015
BH Bryce Harper 300.00 500.00

2012 Topps Chrome Rookie Autographs Gold Refractors

*GOLD REF: 1.2X TO 3X BASIC
STATED ODDS 1:588 HOBBY
STATED PRINT RUN 50 SER.#'d SETS
EXCHANGE DEADLINE 07/31/2015
BH Bryce Harper 400.00 600.00
185 Tsuyoshi Wada 20.00 50.00
193 Drew Hutchison 15.00 40.00

2012 Topps Chrome Rookie Autographs Sepia Refractors

*SEPIA REF: 1X TO 2.5X BASIC
STATED ODDS 1:395 HOBBY
STATED PRINT RUN 75 SER.#'d SETS
EXCHANGE DEADLINE 07/31/2015
BH Bryce Harper 300.00 500.00

2013 Topps Chrome

COMP.SET w/o VAR (220) 20.00 50.00
PHOTO VAR ODDS 1:968 HOBBY
PRINTING PLATE ODDS 1:1265 HOBBY
PLATE PRINT RUN 1 SET PER COLOR
BLACK-CYAN-MAGENTA-YELLOW ISSUED
NO PLATE PRICING DUE TO SCARCITY
1A Mike Trout 2.50 6.00
1B Trout Holding Award 40.00 80.00
2 Hunter Pence .25 .60
3 Jesus Montero .20 .50
4 Jon Jay .20 .50
5 Lucas Duda .25 .60
6 Jason Heyward .25 .60
7 Lance Lynn .20 .50
8 Matt Cain .25 .60
9 Trevor Bauer .30 .75
10 Derek Jeter .75 2.00
11 Evan Longoria .25 .60
12 Manny Machado RC 2.50 6.00
13 Yovani Gallardo .20 .50
14 Josh Rutledge .20 .50
15 Melky Cabrera .20 .50
16 Wil Myers RC .50 1.25
17 Fernando Rodney .20 .50
18 Kris Medlen .25 .60
19 Adrian Gonzalez .25 .60
20A Matt Kemp .25 .60
20B Kemp VAR w/glv 20.00 50.00
21 Carlos Santana .25 .60
22 Khristopher Davis RC 1.25 3.00
23 Julio Teheran .25 .60
24 Nick Maronde RC .50 1.25
25A Hyun-Jin Ryu RC 1.00 2.50
25B Ryu VAR w/glasses 10.00 25.00
26 Carlos Ruiz .20 .50
27 Rob Brantly .20 .50
28 Hiroki Kuroda .20 .50
29 Shane Victorino .25 .60
30 Adam Warren RC .40 1.00
31 Chase Headley .20 .50
32 Jose Fernandez RC 1.00 2.50
33 Marcell Ozuna RC 1.00 2.50
34A Felix Hernandez .25 .60
34B Hernan VAR w/glasses 10.00 25.00
35 Jose Altuve .25 .60
36 Jim Johnson .20 .50
37 Madison Bumgarner .25 .60
38A Joe Mauer .25 .60
38B Mauer VAR w/glv 15.00 40.00
39 Mike Zunino RC .60 1.50
40 Max Scherzer .30 .75
41 Jayson Werth .25 .60
42 J.P. Arencibia .20 .50
43 Adam Wainwright .25 .60
44 Billy Butler .20 .50
45 Salvador Perez .25 .60
46 Mike Napoli .20 .50
47 Jake Peavy .20 .50
48 Andre Ethier .25 .60
49A Andrew McCutchen .30 .75
49B McCutchen VAR w/glv 20.00 50.00
50 Stephen Strasburg .30 .75
51 Sergio Romo .20 .50
52 Troy Tulowitzki .30 .75
53 Derek Holland .20 .50
54 Brett Lawrie .25 .60
55 Mike Olt RC .50 1.25
56 Carl Crawford .25 .60
57 Jurickson Profar RC .50 1.25
58 Asdrubal Cabrera .25 .60
59 Jeurys Familia RC .60 1.50
60 Jonathon Niese .20 .50
61 Jonathan Papelbon .20 .50
62 R.A. Dickey .25 .60
63 Alex Colome RC .40 1.00
64 Tim Lincecum .25 .60
65 Didi Gregorius RC 1.50 4.00
66 Avisail Garcia RC .50 1.25
67 Ryan Vogelsong .20 .50
68 Paul Konerko .25 .60
69 Brad Ziegler .20 .50
70 Josh Hamilton .25 .60
71 Ryan Wheeler RC .40 1.00
72 Victor Martinez .25 .60
73 Trevor Rosenthal (RC) .75 2.00
74 Michael Bourn .20 .50
75 Robinson Cano .25 .60
76 Cole Hamels .25 .60
77 Josh Johnson .25 .60
78 Nolan Arenado RC 2.00 5.00
79A David Ortiz .30 .75
79B Ortiz VAR w/flag 30.00 60.00
80 Shelby Miller RC 1.00 2.50
81 Starling Marte .25 .60
82 Robbie Grossman RC .40 1.00
83 Shin-Soo Choo .25 .60
84A Starlin Castro .20 .50
84B Castro VAR Helmet off 20.00 50.00
85 Bruce Rondon RC .40 1.00
86 Angel Pagan .20 .50
87 Kyle Gibson RC .60 1.50
88 Tyler Skaggs RC .60 1.50
89 Russell Martin .20 .50
90A Ben Revere .20 .50
90B Revere VAR Hat/glv 12.50 30.00
91A Josh Reddick .20 .50
91B Reddick VAR w/glasses 12.50 30.00
92 Dustin Pedroia .25 .60
93 Brandon Barnes .20 .50
94 Jose Bautista .25 .60
95 Austin Jackson .20 .50
96A Yoenis Cespedes .30 .75
96B Cesped VAR w/glasses 12.50 30.00
97 Nate Freiman RC .40 1.00
98 Johnny Cueto .25 .60
99 Craig Kimbrel .25 .60
100A Miguel Cabrera .30 .75
100B Cabrera VAR w/glasses 12.00 30.00
101 Eury Perez RC .50 1.25
102 Brandon Maurer RC .50 1.25
103 Chase Utley .25 .60
104 Roy Halladay .25 .60
105 Casey Kelly RC .50 1.25
106 Jered Weaver .25 .60
107 Carlos Martinez RC .60 1.50
108 Rickie Weeks .20 .50
109 Jay Bruce .25 .60
110 Matt Magill RC .40 1.00
111 Jon Lester .25 .60
112 Allen Webster RC .50 1.25
113 Brian McCann .25 .60
114 Mark Trumbo .20 .50
115 Edwin Encarnacion .30 .75
116 Adeiny Hechavarria (RC) .50 1.25
117 Matt Harvey .25 .60
118A Mariano Rivera .40 1.00
118B Rivera VAR Shaking hands 20.00 50.00
119 Michael Wacha RC .50 1.25
120 Jason Kipnis .25 .60
121 Allen Craig .25 .60
122 Adrian Beltre .30 .75
123 Todd Frazier .25 .60
124 Aroldis Chapman .30 .75
125 Dylan Bundy RC 1.00 2.50
126 Jonathan Pettibone RC .60 1.50
127A David Price .25 .60
127B Price VAR w/dog 12.50 30.00
128 Anthony Rendon RC 2.00 5.00
129 Jason Kubel .20 .50
130 Kyuji Fujikawa RC .60 1.50
131 Carlos Gonzalez .25 .60
132 Ricky Nolasco .20 .50
133 Will Middlebrooks .20 .50
134 Kendrys Morales .20 .50
135 David Freese .20 .50
136A Albert Pujols .40 1.00
136B Pujols VAR Horizontal 12.50 30.00
137 Mat Latos .25 .60
138A Yasiel Puig RC 1.50 4.00
138B Puig VAR High five 50.00 100.00
139 Wade Miley .20 .50
140 Alex Gordon .25 .60
141 Neftali Feliz .20 .50
142A David Wright .25 .60
142B Wright VAR w/glv 20.00 50.00
143A Justin Upton .25 .60
143B Upton VAR w/glasses 15.00 40.00
144 Alex Rios .25 .60
145 Jose Reyes .25 .60
146 Yadier Molina .30 .75
147 Sean Doolittle RC .40 1.00
148 Evan Gattis RC .75 2.00
149 Yonder Alonso .20 .50
150 Justin Verlander .30 .75
151 Justin Wilson RC .40 1.00
152 Adam Jones .25 .60
153 Dan Straily .20 .50
154 Nick Franklin RC .50 1.25
155 Adam Eaton RC .60 1.50
156 Mike Kickham RC .40 1.00
157 Melky Mesa RC .40 1.00
158 Anthony Rizzo .50 1.25
159 Chris Johnson .20 .50
160 Ian Kinsler .25 .60
161 Zack Greinke .30 .75
162 Donald Lutz RC .40 1.00
163 Ryan Braun .25 .60
164 Alex Wood RC .50 1.25
165 Ryan Howard .25 .60
166 Jackie Bradley Jr. RC 1.00 2.50
167 Brandon Phillips .20 .50
168 Alex Rodriguez .40 1.00
169 A.J. Pierzynski .20 .50
170 Carter Capps RC .40 1.00
171 Tony Cingrani RC .75 2.00
172 Mark Teixeira .25 .60
173 Paul Goldschmidt .30 .75
174 CC Sabathia .25 .60
175A Clayton Kershaw .60 1.50
175B Kershaw VAR w/helmet 15.00 40.00
176 Wilin Rosario .20 .50
177 Mike Moustakas .25 .60
178 Jedd Gyorko RC .75 2.00
179 Aaron Hicks RC .60 1.50
180 Zack Wheeler RC 1.25 3.00
181 Ian Desmond .20 .50
182 Paco Rodriguez RC .60 1.50
183 Matt Holliday .30 .75
184A Prince Fielder .25 .60
184B Fielder VAR Head of hair 20.00 50.00
185 Kevin Youkilis .20 .50
186 Oswaldo Arcia RC .40 1.00
187 Chris Sale .30 .75
188 Martin Prado .20 .50
189 Alfredo Marte RC .60 1.50
190 Adam LaRoche .20 .50
191 Dexter Fowler .25 .60
192 Jake Odorizzi RC .75 2.00
193 Nelson Cruz .30 .75
194 Kevin Gausman RC 1.00 2.50
195 Curtis Granderson .25 .60
196 Jarrod Parker .20 .50
197 Giancarlo Stanton .30 .75
198 Tommy Milone .20 .50
199A Yu Darvish .30 .75
199B Darvish VAR w/glasses 15.00 40.00
200A Buster Posey .40 1.00
200B Posey VAR Shaking hands 40.00 80.00
201 Adam Dunn .25 .60
202 James Shields .20 .50
203 Desmond Jennings .25 .60
204 Jacoby Ellsbury .25 .60
205 Ben Zobrist .25 .60
206 Joey Votto .30 .75
207 Miguel Montero .20 .50
208 Cliff Lee .25 .60
209 Jeremy Hellickson .20 .50
210A Gerrit Cole RC 2.50 6.00
210B Cole VAR Walk to dugout 20.00 50.00
211 Carlos Beltran .25 .60
212 Ryan Zimmerman .25 .60
213 Gio Gonzalez .25 .60
214 Eric Hosmer .25 .60
215 Domonic Brown .25 .60
216 Pablo Sandoval .25 .60
217 Justin Morneau .25 .60
218 B.J. Upton .25 .60
219A Freddie Freeman .40 1.00
219B Freeman VAR over rail 20.00 50.00
220A Bryce Harper .50 1.25
220B Harper VAR w/award 40.00 80.00

2013 Topps Chrome Black Refractors

*BLACK REF: 3X TO 8X BASIC
*BLACK REF RC: 1.5X TO 4X BASIC RC
STATED ODDS 1:55 HOBBY
STATED PRINT RUN 100 SER.#'d SETS
10 Derek Jeter 15.00 40.00
12 Manny Machado 15.00 40.00

2013 Topps Chrome Blue Refractors

*BLUE REF: 2X TO 5X BASIC
*BLUE REF RC: 1X TO 2.5X BASIC RC
STATED ODDS 1:30 HOBBY
STATED PRINT RUN 199 SER.#'d SETS

2013 Topps Chrome Gold Refractors

*GOLD REF: 6X TO 15X BASIC
*GOLD REF RC: 3X TO 8X BASIC RC
STATED ODDS 1:112 HOBBY
STATED PRINT RUN 50 SER.#'d SETS
10 Derek Jeter 40.00 80.00
12 Manny Machado 40.00 80.00

2013 Topps Chrome Orange Refractors

*ORANGE REF: 1.5X TO 4X BASIC
*ORANGE REF RC: .75X TO 2X BASIC RC

2013 Topps Chrome Purple Refractors

*PURPLE REF: 1.5X TO 4X BASIC
*PURPLE REF RC: .75X TO 2X BASIC RC

2013 Topps Chrome Red Refractors

*RED REF: 8X TO 20X BASIC
*RED REF RC: 4X TO 10X BASIC RC
STATED ODDS 1:223 HOBBY
STATED PRINT RUN 25 SER.#'d SETS
10 Derek Jeter 50.00 120.00
12 Manny Machado 40.00 100.00
118 Mariano Rivera 30.00 60.00
130 Kyuji Fujikawa 20.00 50.00
220 Bryce Harper 30.00 80.00

2013 Topps Chrome Refractors

*REF: 1X TO 2.5X BASIC
*REF RC: .5X TO 1.2X BASIC RC
STATED ODDS 1:3 HOBBY
UNCUT SHEET ODDS 1:55,700 HOBBY
SHEET EXCHANGE 9/30/2016
NNO Uncut Sheet EXCH 75.00 150.00

2013 Topps Chrome Sepia Refractors

*SEPIA REF: 4X TO 10X BASIC
*SEPIA REF RC: 2X TO 5X BASIC RC
STATED ODDS 1:75 HOBBY
STATED PRINT RUN 75 SER.#'d SETS
1 Mike Trout 20.00 50.00
10 Derek Jeter 20.00 50.00
12 Manny Machado 20.00 50.00
138 Yasiel Puig 60.00 120.00
220 Bryce Harper 15.00 40.00

2013 Topps Chrome X-Fractors

*X-F: 1.2X TO 3X BASIC
*X-F RC: .6X TO 1.5X BASIC RC
STATED ODDS 1:6 HOBBY
UNCUT SHEET ODDS 1:74,300 HOBBY
SHEET EXCHANGE 9/30/2016
NNO Uncut Sheet EXCH 150.00 250.00

2013 Topps Chrome '72 Chrome

STATED ODDS 1:12 HOBBY
72CAM Andrew McCutchen 1.00 2.50
72CAP Albert Pujols 1.25 3.00
72CBH Bryce Harper 1.50 4.00
72CCK Clayton Kershaw 2.00 5.00
72CDB Dylan Bundy 1.50 4.00
72CDJ Derek Jeter 2.50 6.00
72CGS Giancarlo Stanton 1.00 2.50
72CJH Josh Hamilton .75 2.00
72CJM Joe Mauer .75 2.00
72CJP Jurickson Profar .75 2.00
72CJU Justin Upton .75 2.00
72CJV Justin Verlander 1.00 2.50
72CMC Miguel Cabrera 1.00 2.50
72CMM Manny Machado 4.00 10.00
72CRB Ryan Braun .75 2.00
72CRC Robinson Cano .75 2.00
72CSS Stephen Strasburg 1.00 2.50
72CTS Tyler Skaggs 1.00 2.50
72CWM Wil Myers .75 2.00
72CYC Yoenis Cespedes 1.00 2.50
72CYD Yu Darvish 1.00 2.50
72CYP Yasiel Puig 6.00 15.00
72CCKR Craig Kimbrel .75 2.00
72CHJR Hyun-Jin Ryu 1.50 4.00
72CJHE Jason Heyward .75 2.00

2013 Topps Chrome '72 Chrome Autographs

STATED ODDS 1:10,000 HOBBY
STATED PRINT RUN 25 SER.#'d SETS
EXCHANGE DEADLINE 9/30/2016
72CAJP Jurickson Profar 60.00 150.00
72CAMM Manny Machado EXCH 125.00 250.00
72CATS Tyler Skaggs 30.00 60.00
72CAWM Wil Myers
72CARHJ Hyun-Jin Ryu

2013 Topps Chrome Chrome Connections Die Cuts

STATED ODDS 1:12 HOBBY
CCAB Adrian Beltre 1.00 2.50
CCAG Adrian Gonzalez .75 2.00
CCBH Bryce Harper 1.50 4.00
CCBP Buster Posey 1.25 3.00
CCBU B.J. Upton .75 2.00
CCCG Carlos Gonzalez .75 2.00
CCDF David Freese .60 1.50
CCDJ Derek Jeter 2.50 6.00
CCDO David Ortiz 1.00 2.50
CCDP David Price .75 2.00
CCDW David Wright .75 2.00
CCEL Evan Longoria .75 2.00
CCJB Jose Bautista .75 2.00
CCJH Josh Hamilton .75 2.00
CCJR Jose Reyes .75 2.00
CCJU Justin Upton .75 2.00
CCJV Justin Verlander 1.00 2.50
CCMC Miguel Cabrera 1.00 2.50
CCMH Matt Harvey .75 2.00
CCMK Matt Kemp .75 2.00
CCMT Mike Trout 8.00 20.00
CCPF Prince Fielder .75 2.00
CCRC Robinson Cano .75 2.00
CCSS Stephen Strasburg 1.00 2.50
CCTL Tim Lincecum .75 2.00
CCTT Troy Tulowitzki 1.00 2.50
CCYD Yu Darvish 1.00 2.50
CCDPE Dustin Pedroia .75 2.00
CCJHE Jason Heyward .75 2.00
CCMHO Matt Holliday 1.00 2.50

2013 Topps Chrome Chrome Connections Die Cuts Autographs

STATED ODDS 1:10,000 HOBBY
STATED PRINT RUN 25 SER.#'d SETS
EXCHANGE DEADLINE 9/30/2016
CCBP Buster Posey 100.00 175.00
CCJH Josh Hamilton 20.00 50.00
CCMC Miguel Cabrera 60.00 120.00
CCMT Mike Trout 175.00 350.00
CCPF Prince Fielder EXCH 30.00 60.00

2013 Topps Chrome Chrome Connections Die Cuts Relics

STATED ODDS 1:10,220 HOBBY
STATED PRINT RUN 25 SER.#'d SETS
EXCHANGE DEADLINE 9/30/2016
CCRBH Bryce Harper 20.00 50.00
CCRDJ Derek Jeter 20.00 50.00
CCRJV Justin Verlander 20.00 50.00
CCRRC Robinson Cano 12.50 30.00
CCRSS Stephen Strasburg 10.00 25.00

2013 Topps Chrome Dynamic Die Cuts

STATED ODDS 1:24 HOBBY
DYAC Aroldis Chapman 1.00 2.50
DYAJ Adam Jones .75 2.00
DYAM Andrew McCutchen 1.00 2.50
DYAP Albert Pujols 1.25 3.00
DYAW Adam Wainwright .75 2.00
DYBH Bryce Harper 1.50 4.00
DYCC CC Sabathia .75 2.00
DYCG Carlos Gonzalez .75 2.00
DYCH Cole Hamels .75 2.00
DYCK Clayton Kershaw 2.00 5.00
DYCM Carlos Martinez .75 2.00
DYCS Carlos Santana .75 2.00
DYDB Domonic Brown .75 2.00
DYDF David Freese .60 1.50
DYDJ Derek Jeter 2.50 6.00
DYDW David Wright .75 2.00
DYEL Evan Longoria .75 2.00
DYFH Felix Hernandez .75 2.00
DYGS Giancarlo Stanton 1.00 2.50
DYHR Hanley Ramirez .75 2.00
DYJB Jay Bruce .75 2.00
DYJC Johnny Cueto .75 2.00
DYJH Josh Hamilton .75 2.00
DYJP Jarrod Parker .60 1.50
DYJR Jose Reyes .75 2.00
DYJT Julio Teheran .75 2.00
DYJV Joey Votto 1.00 2.50
DYJW Jered Weaver .75 2.00
DYMC Miguel Cabrera 1.00 2.50
DYMK Matt Kemp .75 2.00
DYMM Manny Machado 4.00 10.00
DYMN Mike Napoli .60 1.50
DYMT Mike Trout 8.00 20.00
DYPG Paul Goldschmidt 1.00 2.50
DYRB Ryan Braun
DYRC Robinson Cano .75 2.00
DYSP Salvador Perez .75 2.00
DYSS Stephen Strasburg 1.00 2.50
DYTB Trevor Bauer 1.00 2.50
DYWR Wilin Rosario .60 1.50
DYYC Yoenis Cespedes 1.00 2.50
DYYD Yu Darvish 1.00 2.50
DYYP Yasiel Puig 2.50 6.00
DYCKR Craig Kimbrel .75 2.00
DYCSA Chris Sale 1.00 2.50
DYDBU Dylan Bundy 1.50 4.00
DYHJR Hyun-Jin Ryu 1.50 4.00
DYJBA Jose Bautista .75 2.00
DYJPR Jurickson Profar .75 2.00
DYJVE Justin Verlander 1.00 2.50

2013 Topps Chrome Dynamic Die Cuts Autographs

STATED ODDS 1:2450 HOBBY 20.00 50.00
STATED PRINT RUN 25 SER.#'d SETS
EXCHANGE DEADLINE 9/30/2016
DYCM Carlos Martinez 12.00 30.00
DYCS Chris Sale 20.00 50.00
DYDB Domonic Brown 12.50 30.00
DYEL Evan Longoria 20.00 50.00
DYFH Felix Hernandez 20.00 50.00
DYJB Jose Bautista 12.50 30.00
DYJB Jay Bruce 20.00 50.00
DYJT Julio Teheran 20.00 50.00
DYJW Jered Weaver 12.00 30.00
DYMC Miguel Cabrera 90.00 150.00
DYMM Manny Machado 100.00 175.00
DYMN Mike Napoli 12.00 30.00
DYMT Mike Trout 150.00 400.00
DYPG Paul Goldschmidt 30.00 60.00
DYSP Salvador Perez 15.00 40.00
DYTB Trevor Bauer 12.50 30.00
DYYD Yu Darvish EXCH 60.00 120.00
DYCSA Carlos Santana 12.50 30.00
DYHJR Hyun-Jin Ryu EXCH 50.00 100.00
DYJPR Jurickson Profar 90.00 150.00

2013 Topps Chrome Red Hot Rookies Autographs

STATED ODDS 1:4945 HOBBY
STATED PRINT RUN 25 SER.#'d SETS
EXCHANGE DEADLINE 9/30/2016
RHRAE Adam Eaton EXCH 10.00 25.00
RHRDB Dylan Bundy 30.00 60.00
RHRGC Gerrit Cole 60.00 120.00
RHRJP Jurickson Profar
RHRMM Manny Machado 150.00 250.00
RHRMO Mike Olt
RHRTS Tyler Skaggs 40.00 80.00
RHRWM Wil Myers 60.00 120.00
RHRZW Zack Wheeler 40.00 80.00
RHRRHJ Hyun-Jin Ryu 40.00 80.00

2013 Topps Chrome Rookie Autographs

STATED ODDS 1:19 HOBBY
PRINTING PLATE ODDS 1:6965 HOBBY
PLATE PRINT RUN 1 SET PER COLOR
BLACK-CYAN-MAGENTA-YELLOW ISSUED
NO PLATE PRICING DUE TO SCARCITY
EXCHANGE DEADLINE 9/30/2016
CY Christian Yelich 75.00 200.00
GC Gerrit Cole 40.00 100.00
KG Kyle Gibson EXCH 3.00 8.00
MZ Mike Zunino 3.00 8.00
NF Nick Franklin 3.00 8.00
WM Wil Myers 8.00 20.00
PY Yasiel Puig 25.00 60.00
ZW Zack Wheeler 4.00 10.00
12 Manny Machado 60.00 150.00
16 Darin Ruf 3.00 8.00
24 Nick Maronde 3.00 8.00
25 Hyun-Jin Ryu 40.00 100.00
27 Rob Brantly 3.00 8.00
32 Jose Fernandez 12.00 30.00
57 Jurickson Profar 3.00 8.00
59 Jeurys Familia 3.00 8.00
65 Didi Gregorius 6.00 15.00
66 Avisail Garcia 3.00 8.00
78 Nolan Arenado 75.00 200.00
80 Shelby Miller 3.00 8.00
85 Bruce Rondon 3.00 8.00
88 Tyler Skaggs 3.00 8.00
102 Brandon Maurer 3.00 8.00
105 Casey Kelly 3.00 8.00
107 Carlos Martinez 4.00 10.00
112 Allen Webster 3.00 8.00
116 Adeiny Hechavarria 3.00 8.00
125 Dylan Bundy 5.00 12.00
128 Anthony Rendon 30.00 80.00
130 Kyuji Fujikawa 3.00 8.00
148 Evan Gattis 3.00 8.00
154 L.J. Hoes 3.00 8.00
155 Adam Eaton 3.00 8.00
157 Melky Mesa 3.00 8.00
171 Tony Cingrani 3.00 8.00
178 Jedd Gyorko 3.00 8.00
182 Paco Rodriguez 3.00 8.00
186 Oswaldo Arcia EXCH 3.00 8.00
189 Alfredo Marte 3.00 8.00
192 Jake Odorizzi 3.00 8.00

2013 Topps Chrome Rookie Autographs Black Refractors

*BLACK REF: .75X TO 2X BASIC
STATED ODDS 1:301 HOBBY
STATED PRINT RUN 100 SER.#'d SETS
EXCHANGE DEADLINE 9/30/2016

2013 Topps Chrome Rookie Autographs Blue Refractors

*BLUE REF: .6X TO 1.5X BASIC
STATED ODDS 1:152 HOBBY
STATED PRINT RUN 199 SER.#'d SETS
EXCHANGE DEADLINE 9/30/2016

2013 Topps Chrome Rookie Autographs Gold Refractors

*GOLD REF: 1.2X TO 3X BASIC
STATED ODDS 1:605 HOBBY
STATED PRINT RUN 50 SER.#'d SETS
EXCHANGE DEADLINE 9/30/2016

2013 Topps Chrome Rookie Autographs Red Refractors

*RED REF: 1.5X TO 4X BASIC
STATED ODDS 1:1210 HOBBY
STATED PRINT RUN 25 SER.#'d SETS
EXCHANGE DEADLINE 9/30/2016
192 Jake Odorizzi 15.00 40.00

2013 Topps Chrome Rookie Autographs Refractors

*REF: .5X TO 1.2X BASIC
STATED ODDS 1:83 HOBBY
STATED PRINT RUN 499 SER.#'d SETS
EXCHANGE DEADLINE 9/30/2016

2013 Topps Chrome Rookie Autographs Sepia Refractors

*SEPIA REF: .75X TO 2X BASIC
STATED ODDS 1:403 HOBBY
STATED PRINT RUN 75 SER.#'d SETS
EXCHANGE DEADLINE 9/30/2016

2013 Topps Chrome Rookie Autographs Silver Ink Black Refractors

*SILVER INK REF: 1.5X TO 4X BASIC
STATED ODDS 1:1210 HOBBY
STATED PRINT RUN 25 SER.#'d SETS
EXCHANGE DEADLINE 9/30/2016

2013 Topps Chrome Update

COMPLETE SET (55) 60.00 120.00
MB1 Robinson Cano .60 1.50
MB2 Miguel Cabrera .75 2.00
MB3 Matt Harvey .60 1.50
MB4 Jose Fernandez RC 1.25 3.00
MB5 Anthony Rendon RC 2.50 6.00
MB6 Yoenis Cespedes .75 2.00
MB7 Justin Verlander .75 2.00
MB8 Clayton Kershaw 1.50 4.00
MB9 Mike Trout 6.00 15.00
MB10 Chris Archer .50 1.25
MB11 Carlos Martinez RC .75 2.00
MB12 Nick Franklin RC .60 1.50
MB13 Allen Craig .60 1.50
MB14 Joey Votto .75 2.00
MB15 Michael Cuddyer .50 1.25
MB16 Justin Upton .60 1.50
MB17 Kevin Gausman RC .75 2.00
MB18 Bud Norris .50 1.25
MB19 Mike Zunino RC .75 2.00
MB20 Gerrit Cole RC 3.00 8.00
MB21 Yu Darvish .75 2.00
MB22 Ian Kennedy .50 1.25
MB23 Dan Haren .50 1.25
MB24 Pedro Alvarez .50 1.25
MB25 Michael Young .50 1.25
MB26 Jake Peavy .50 1.25
MB27 Bryce Harper 1.25 3.00
MB28 Rafael Soriano .50 1.25
MB29 David Wright .60 1.50
MB30 Bryce Harper 1.25 3.00
MB31 James Shields .50 1.25
MB32 Zach Wheeler RC 1.00 2.50
MB33 Alfonso Soriano .60 1.50
MB34 Brian Wilson .75 2.00
MB35 Marcell Ozuna RC 1.25 3.00
MB36 Prince Fielder .60 1.50
MB37 Jose Fernandez 1.25 3.00
MB38 Kyle Gibson RC .75 2.00
MB39 Nolan Arenado RC 10.00 25.00
MB40 Oswaldo Arcia RC .50 1.25
MB41 Yasiel Puig RC 2.00 5.00
MB42 Wil Myers RC .60 1.50
MB43 Mariano Rivera 1.00 2.50
MB44 Shelby Miller RC 1.25 3.00
MB45 David Wright .60 1.50
MB46 Buster Posey 1.00 2.50
MB47 Christian Yelich RC 60.00 150.00
MB48 Adam Wainwright .60 1.50
MB49 Matt Garza .50 1.25
MB50 Francisco Liriano .50 1.25
MB51 Hyun-Jin Ryu 1.25 3.00
MB52 Evan Gattis RC 1.00 2.50
MB53 Yasiel Puig RC 2.00 5.00
MB54 Chris Davis .60 1.50
MB55 Jurickson Profar RC .60 1.50

2013 Topps Chrome Update Black Refractors

*BLACK: 2.5X TO 6X BASIC
STATED PRINT RUN 99 SER.#'d SETS
MB47 Christian Yelich 250.00 500.00

2013 Topps Chrome Update Gold Refractors

*GOLD: 2X TO 5X BASIC
STATED PRINT RUN 250 SER.#'d SETS
MB47 Christian Yelich 200.00 400.00

2014 Topps Chrome

COMP.SET w/o VAR (220) 15.00 40.00
PHOTO VAR ODDS 1:1400 HOBBY
PRINTING PLATE ODDS 1:1480 HOBBY
PLATE PRINT RUN 1 SET PER COLOR
BLACK-CYAN-MAGENTA-YELLOW ISSUED
NO PLATE PRICING DUE TO SCARCITY
1A Mike Trout 1.50 4.00
1B Trout Hi-Five VAR 30.00 60.00

Alex Gordon .25 .60
Enny Romero RC .40 1.00
Nick Castellanos RC 1.25 3.00
Ryan Braun .25 .60
Matt Carpenter .30 .75
Matt Cain .25 .60
Yoenis Cespedes .30 .75
Curtis Granderson .25 .60
0A Masahiro Tanaka RC 1.25 3.00
0B Tanaka Dugout VAR 40.00 80.00
0C Tanaka Japanese 40.00 100.00
1 Norichika Aoki .20 .50
2 Abraham Almonte RC .40 1.00
3 Jean Segura .25 .60
4 Alex Guerrero RC .50 1.25
5 David Robertson .20 .50
16 Yadier Molina .30 .75
17 Stephen Strasburg .30 .75
18 Corey Kluber .25 .60
19 Oscar Taveras RC .50 1.25
20 Hanley Ramirez .25 .60
21 James Paxton RC .60 1.50
22 Taijuan Walker RC .40 1.00
23 Stefen Romero RC .40 1.00
24 Josmil Pinto RC .40 1.00
25A Xander Bogaerts RC 1.25 3.00
26 Erisbel Arruebarrena RC .40 1.00
27 Hiroki Kuroda .20 .50
28 Joey Votto .30 .75
29 Victor Martinez .25 .60
30 Mike Napoli .20 .50
31A Clay Buchholz .20 .50
31B Buchholz Guitar VAR 12.00 30.00
32 CC Sabathia .25 .60
33 Jonathan Schoop RC .40 1.00
34 Adam Jones .25 .60
35 Edwin Encarnacion .30 .75
36 Josh Hamilton .25 .60
37 Cliff Lee .25 .60
38 Carlos Gomez .20 .50
39 Mike Moustakas .25 .60
40 Wilin Rosario .20 .50
41 Jedd Gyorko .20 .50
42 Shane Victorino .25 .60
43 Marcus Semien RC .40 1.00
44 Adam Wainwright .25 .60
45 Jose Ramirez RC 3.00 8.00
46 Gerrit Cole .30 .75
47 Will Middlebrooks .20 .50
48 Alex Cobb .20 .50
50 Adrian Beltre .30 .75
51 Matt Adams .20 .50
52 Jose Altuve .25 .60
53 Chase Headley .20 .50
54 Carlos Martinez .25 .60
55 Jon Singleton RC .50 1.25
56A Derek Jeter .75 2.00
56B Jeter w/crowd VAR 75.00 200.00
57 Jordan Zimmermann .25 .60
58 Anthony Rizzo .50 1.25
59 Rafael Montero RC .40 1.00
60 Jayson Werth .25 .60
61A Felix Hernandez .25 .60
61B King Felix Pointing VAR 20.00 50.00
62 Zach Walters RC .40 1.00
63 David Price .25 .60
64 Brandon Phillips .20 .50
65 Nick Martinez RC .40 1.00
66 Yordano Ventura RC .50 1.25
67 Wilmer Flores RC .50 1.25
68 Billy Butler .20 .50
69 John Ryan Murphy RC .40 1.00
70 Allen Craig .25 .60
71 Prince Fielder .25 .60
72 Mat Latos .25 .60
73 Jered Weaver .25 .60
74 Dexter Fowler .25 .60
75A Billy Hamilton RC .50 1.25
75B Hamilton Fldng VAR 50.00 120.00
76 Marcus Stroman RC .60 1.50
77 Robbie Erlin RC .40 1.00
78 Kenley Jansen .25 .60
79 Mike Minor .20 .50
80A Wil Myers .20 .50
80B Myers Waving VAR 20.00 50.00
81 Kevin Siegrist (RC) .40 1.00
82 Brad Miller .20 .50
83 Jon Lester .25 .60
84 Chris Colabello .20 .50
85 James Shields .20 .50
86 Brian McCann .25 .60
87 Zack Wheeler .25 .60
88 Michael Choice RC .40 1.00
89 Hisashi Iwakuma .25 .60
90A Yasiel Puig .30 .75
90B Puig w/crowd VAR 60.00 150.00
91 Christian Bethancourt RC .40 1.00
92 Matt den Dekker RC .50 1.25
93A Justin Upton .25 .60
93B Upton Throwback VAR 40.00 100.00
94 Alexei Ramirez .25 .60
95 Cole Hamels .25 .60
96 Tony Cingrani .25 .60
97 Ian Desmond .20 .50
98 Erik Johnson RC .40 1.00
99 Evan Longoria .25 .60
100 Clayton Kershaw .60 1.50
101 Ben Zobrist .20 .50
102 Matt Moore .25 .60
103A Jose Fernandez .30 .75
103B J.Fern w/Phanatic VAR 20.00 50.00
104 R.A. Dickey .25 .60
105A Andrew McCutchen .30 .75
105B MCutch On deck VAR 30.00 60.00
106 Kyle Seager .20 .50
107A Hyun-Jin Ryu .25 .60
107B Ryu w/Puig VAR 40.00 80.00
108 Jake Marisnick RC .40 1.00
109 Pedro Alvarez .20 .50
110 Brandon Belt .25 .60
111 Tim Beckham RC .60 1.50
112 Troy Tulowitzki .30 .75
113 Everth Cabrera .20 .50
114 Sonny Gray .25 .60
115 Francisco Liriano .20 .50
116A Robinson Cano .25 .60
116B Cano Gum VAR 12.00 30.00
117 Aroldis Chapman .30 .75
118 Homer Bailey .20 .50
119 Jacoby Ellsbury .25 .60
120 Jeff Samardzija .20 .50
121 Koji Uehara .20 .50
122 Shin-Soo Choo .25 .60
123 Jose Bautista .25 .60
124 Travis d'Arnaud RC .50 1.25
125A Paul Goldschmidt .30 .75
125B Paul Goldschmidt VAR 20.00 50.00
126 Yangervis Solarte RC .40 1.00
127 Tanner Roark RC .40 1.00
128 Ethan Martin RC .40 1.00
129 Johnny Cueto .25 .60
130 Albert Pujols .40 1.00
131 Desmond Jennings .25 .60
132 Chris Davis .20 .50
133 Onelki Garcia RC .40 1.00
134 David Holmberg RC .40 1.00
135 Martin Prado .20 .50
136 Matt Davidson RC .50 1.25
137 Ivan Nova .25 .60
138 George Springer RC 1.50 4.00
139 Matt Holliday .30 .75
140 Justin Verlander .30 .75
141 Trevor Rosenthal .30 .75
142 Grady Sizemore .25 .60
143 Shelby Miller .25 .60
144 Joe Mauer .25 .60
145 J.J. Hardy .20 .50
146 Freddie Freeman .40 1.00
147 Austin Jackson .20 .50
148 Avisail Garcia .25 .60
149 Jose Reyes .25 .60
150A Bryce Harper .50 1.25
150B Harper Drk helmet VAR 75.00 150.00
151 C.J. Cron RC .40 1.00
152 Buster Posey .40 1.00
153 Domonic Brown .25 .60
154 Salvador Perez .25 .60
155 Craig Kimbrel .25 .60
156 Evan Gattis .20 .50
157 Michael Cuddyer .20 .50
158 Aramis Ramirez .20 .50
159 Eric Hosmer .25 .60
160 Nelson Cruz .30 .75
161 Chris Owings RC .40 1.00
162 Zack Greinke .25 .60
163 Greg Holland .20 .50
164 Jay Bruce .25 .60
165A Starlin Castro .20 .50
166 Hunter Pence .25 .60
167 Pablo Sandoval .25 .60
168 Manny Machado .30 .75
169 Kole Calhoun .20 .50
170A David Wright .25 .60
170B Wright Hi-Five VAR 30.00 80.00
171 Andrelton Simmons .20 .50
172 Starling Marte .25 .60
173 Giancarlo Stanton .30 .75
174 Chase Utley .25 .60
175 Yu Darvish .30 .75
176 Ryan Howard .25 .60
177 Sergio Romo .20 .50
178 Danny Salazar .25 .60
179 Carlos Beltran .25 .60
180 Alex Rios .25 .60
181 Chris Sale .30 .75
182 Mark Trumbo .20 .50
183 Brandon Moss .20 .50
184 Jonathan Lucroy .25 .60
185 Ian Kinsler .25 .60
186 Brett Gardner .25 .60
187 Elvis Andrus .25 .60
188 Kolten Wong RC .50 1.25
189A Madison Bumgarner .25 .60
189B Bumgarn Batting VAR 30.00 60.00
190 Carlos Gonzalez .25 .60
191 Joe Nathan .20 .50
192 Carl Crawford .25 .60
193A Josh Donaldson .25 .60
193B J.Donald Water VAR 20.00 50.00
194 Julio Teheran .25 .60
195 Gio Gonzalez .25 .60
196 Jason Kipnis .25 .60
197 Andrew Cashner .20 .50
198 Tommy Medica RC .40 1.00
199A Jose Abreu RC 3.00 8.00
200 Asdrubal Cabrera .25 .60
201A David Ortiz .30 .75
201B Ortiz w/rings VAR 30.00 80.00
202 Matt Kemp .25 .60
203 Jimmy Nelson RC .40 1.00
204A Dustin Pedroia .30 .75
204B Pedroia Flding VAR 60.00 150.00
205 Ryan Zimmerman .25 .60
206 Andre Rienzo RC .40 1.00
207 Anibal Sanchez .20 .50
208 Jason Grilli .20 .50
209 Andrew Lambo RC .40 1.00
210 Carlos Santana .25 .60
211 Jurickson Profar .25 .60
212 Dean Anna RC .40 1.00
213 Rougned Odor RC .75 2.00
214 Jason Heyward .25 .60
215 Christian Yelich .40 1.00
216 Nolan Arenado .40 1.00
217 Aaron Hill .20 .50
218 Max Scherzer .30 .75
219 Brett Lawrie .25 .60
220A Miguel Cabrera .30 .75
220B Cabrera Hi-Five VAR 30.00 80.00

2014 Topps Chrome Black Refractors

*BLACK REF: 4X TO 10X BASIC
*BLACK REF RC: 2X TO 5X BASIC RC
STATED ODDS 1:80 HOBBY
STATED PRINT RUN 100 SER.#'d SETS
56 Derek Jeter 25.00 60.00

2014 Topps Chrome Blue Refractors

*BLUE REF: 2.5X TO 6X BASIC
*BLUE REF RC: 1.2X TO 3X BASIC RC
STATED ODDS 1:40 HOBBY
STATED PRINT RUN 199 SER.#'d SETS
1 Mike Trout 8.00 20.00
56 Derek Jeter 8.00 20.00

2014 Topps Chrome Gold Refractors

*GOLD REF: 8X TO 20X BASIC
*GOLD REF RC: 4X TO 10X BASIC RC
STATED ODDS 1:160 HOBBY
STATED PRINT RUN 50 SER.#'d SETS
1 Mike Trout 50.00 120.00
19 Oscar Taveras 20.00 50.00
100 Clayton Kershaw 15.00 40.00
138 George Springer 20.00 50.00
150 Bryce Harper 15.00 40.00
199 Jose Abreu 60.00 150.00

2014 Topps Chrome Orange Refractors

*ORANGE REF: 2X TO 5X BASIC
*ORANGE REF RC: 1X TO 2.5X BASIC RC
RANDOM INSERTS IN PACKS
1 Mike Trout 6.00 15.00
56 Derek Jeter 6.00 15.00

2014 Topps Chrome Purple Refractors

*PURPLE REF: 2X TO 5X BASIC
*PURPLE REF RC: 1X TO 2.5X BASIC RC
RANDOM INSERTS IN PACKS
1 Mike Trout 6.00 15.00
56 Derek Jeter 6.00 15.00

2014 Topps Chrome Red Refractors

*RED REF: 10X TO 25X BASIC
*RED REF RC: 5X TO 12X BASIC RC
STATED ODDS 1:320 HOBBY
STATED PRINT RUN 25 SER.#'d SETS
1 Mike Trout 60.00 150.00
19 Oscar Taveras 25.00 60.00
56 Derek Jeter 60.00 150.00
100 Clayton Kershaw 20.00 50.00
138 George Springer 25.00 60.00
150 Bryce Harper 20.00 50.00
199 Jose Abreu 75.00 200.00

2014 Topps Chrome Refractors

*REFRACTOR: 1X TO 2.5X BASIC
*REFRACTOR RC: .5X TO 1.2X BASIC RC
STATED ODDS 1:3 HOBBY

2014 Topps Chrome Sepia Refractors

*SEPIA REF: 5X TO 12X BASIC
*SEPIA REF RC: 2.5X TO 6X BASIC RC
STATED ODDS 1:105 HOBBY
STATED PRINT RUN 75 SER.#'d SETS

2014 Topps Chrome X-Fractors

*X-FRACTOR: 1.5X TO 4X BASIC
*X-FRACTOR RC: .75X TO 2X BASIC RC
STATED ODDS 1:6 HOBBY

2014 Topps Chrome '89 Chrome Refractors

COMPLETE SET (25) 20.00 50.00
STATED ODDS 1:12 HOBBY
89TCAM Andrew McCutchen 1.00 2.50
89TCAP Albert Pujols 1.25 3.00
89TCBH Billy Hamilton .75 2.00
89TCBHA Bryce Harper 1.50 4.00
89TCBP Buster Posey 1.25 3.00
89TCCG Carlos Gonzalez .75 2.00
89TCCK Clayton Kershaw 2.00 5.00
89TCDO David Ortiz 1.00 2.50
89TCDP Dustin Pedroia 1.00 2.50
89TCDW David Wright .75 2.00
89TCJA Jose Abreu 4.00 10.00
89TCJE Jacoby Ellsbury .75 2.00
89TCKGJ Ken Griffey Jr. 2.00 5.00
89TCMC Miguel Cabrera 1.00 2.50
89TCMT Mike Trout 5.00 12.00
89TCMTA Masahiro Tanaka 3.00 8.00
89TCNC Nick Castellanos 2.00 5.00
89TCPF Prince Fielder .75 2.00
89TCPG Paul Goldschmidt 1.00 2.50
89TCRB Ryan Braun .75 2.00
89TCRC Robinson Cano .75 2.00
89TCTT Troy Tulowitzki .75 2.00
89TCTW Taijuan Walker .60 1.50
89TCYD Yu Darvish 1.00 2.50
89TCYP Yasiel Puig 1.00 2.50

2014 Topps Chrome All Time Rookies

STATED ODDS 1:280 HOBBY
2 Buster Posey 12.00 30.00
8 Don Mattingly 10.00 25.00
35 Frank Robinson 6.00 15.00
36 Eddie Murray 6.00 15.00
94 Ernie Banks 8.00 20.00
98 Derek Jeter 20.00 50.00
116 Ozzie Smith 10.00 25.00
123 Sandy Koufax 15.00 40.00
164 Roberto Clemente 8.00 20.00
223 Robin Yount 8.00 20.00
228 George Brett 10.00 25.00
260 Reggie Jackson 6.00 15.00
261 Willie Mays 8.00 20.00
312 Jackie Robinson 8.00 20.00
316 Willie McCovey 6.00 15.00
328 Brooks Robinson 20.00 50.00
417 Ken Griffey Jr. 15.00 40.00
482 Rickey Henderson 12.00 30.00
482 Tony Gwynn 8.00 20.00
498 Wade Boggs 6.00 15.00
514 Bob Gibson 6.00 15.00
661 Bryce Harper 10.00 25.00
98T Cal Ripken Jr. 10.00 25.00
T40 Miguel Cabrera 8.00 20.00
US175 Mike Trout 15.00 40.00

2014 Topps Chrome Chrome Connections Die Cuts

COMPLETE SET (30) 20.00 50.00
STATED ODDS 1:12 HOBBY
CCAB Adrian Beltre 1.00 2.50
CCAJ Adam Jones .75 2.00
CCAM Andrew McCutchen 1.00 2.50
CCAP Albert Pujols 1.25 3.00
CCBH Bryce Harper 1.50 4.00
CCCD Chris Davis .60 1.50
CCCG Carlos Gonzalez .75 2.00
CCCK Clayton Kershaw 2.00 5.00
CCDJ Derek Jeter 2.50 6.00
CCDP Dustin Pedroia 1.00 2.50
CCDW David Wright .75 2.00
CCFH Felix Hernandez .75 2.00
CCHR Hanley Ramirez .75 2.00
CCIK Ian Kinsler .75 2.00
CCJE Jacoby Ellsbury .75 2.00
CCJF Jose Fernandez 1.00 2.50
CCJK Jason Kipnis .75 2.00
CCJV Justin Verlander 1.00 2.50
CCMC Miguel Cabrera 1.00 2.50
CCMK Matt Kemp .75 2.00
CCMT Mike Trout 5.00 12.00
CCMTA Masahiro Tanaka 3.00 8.00
CCPF Prince Fielder .75 2.00
CCPG Paul Goldschmidt 1.00 2.50
CCRB Ryan Braun .75 2.00
CCRC Robinson Cano .75 2.00
CCSS Stephen Strasburg 1.00 2.50
CCTT Troy Tulowitzki 1.00 2.50
CCYD Yu Darvish 1.00 2.50
CCYP Yasiel Puig 1.00 2.50

2014 Topps Chrome Chrome Connections Die Cuts Autographs

STATED ODDS 1:14,200 HOBBY
STATED PRINT RUN 25 SER.#'d SETS
EXCHANGE DEADLINE 8/31/2017
CCAAJ Adam Jones 12.00 30.00
CCAMC Miguel Cabrera 100.00 200.00
CCARB Ryan Braun 15.00 40.00
CCARC Robinson Cano 50.00 100.00

2014 Topps Chrome Chrome Connections Die Cuts Relics

STATED ODDS 1:14,000 HOBBY
STATED PRINT RUN 25 SER.#'d SETS
CCRAM Andrew McCutchen 20.00 50.00
CCRCD Chris Davis 15.00 40.00
CCRDJ Derek Jeter 50.00 120.00

2014 Topps Chrome Rookie Autographs

STATED ODDS 1:15 HOBBY
PRINTING PLATE ODDS 1:12,400 HOBBY
PLATE PRINT RUN 1 SET PER COLOR
BLACK-CYAN-MAGENTA-YELLOW ISSUED
NO PLATE PRICING DUE TO SCARCITY
EXCHANGE DEADLINE 8/31/2017
4 Nick Castellanos 8.00 20.00
12 Abraham Almonte 3.00 8.00
22 Taijuan Walker 3.00 8.00
23 Stefen Romero 3.00 8.00
24 Josmil Pinto 3.00 8.00
33 Jonathan Schoop 3.00 8.00
45 Jose Ramirez 30.00 80.00
59 Tyler Collins 3.00 8.00
62 Zach Walters 3.00 8.00
66 Yordano Ventura 4.00 10.00
67 Wilmer Flores 4.00 10.00
69 J.R. Murphy 3.00 8.00
76 Jeff Kobernus 3.00 8.00
81 Kevin Siegrist 3.00 8.00
98 Erik Johnson 3.00 8.00
108 Jake Marisnick 3.00 8.00
126 Yangervis Solarte 3.00 8.00
128 Ethan Martin 3.00 8.00
133 Onelki Garcia 3.00 8.00
134 David Holmberg 3.00 8.00
136 Matt Davidson 4.00 10.00
161 Chris Owings 3.00 8.00
188 Kolten Wong 4.00 10.00
198 Tommy Medica 3.00 8.00
203 Jimmy Nelson 3.00 8.00
209 Andrew Lambo 3.00 8.00
212 Dean Anna 3.00 8.00
AH Andrew Heaney 3.00 8.00
AS Aaron Sanchez 3.00 8.00
EB Eddie Butler 3.00 8.00
ER Enny Romero 3.00 8.00
GP Gregory Polanco 5.00 12.00
GS George Springer 15.00 40.00
JA Jose Abreu 60.00 150.00
MC Michael Choice 3.00 8.00
MST Marcus Stroman 5.00 12.00
NM Nick Martinez 3.00 8.00
OT Oscar Taveras 4.00 10.00
RE Roenis Elias 3.00 8.00

2014 Topps Chrome Rookie Autographs Black Refractors

*BLACK REF: .75X TO 2X BASIC
STATED ODDS 1:610 HOBBY
STATED PRINT RUN 100 SER.#'d SETS
EXCHANGE DEADLINE 8/31/2017
25 Xander Bogaerts 75.00 200.00
124 Travis d'Arnaud 8.00 20.00
AG Alexander Guerrero 15.00 40.00
EA Erisbel Arruebarrena 6.00 15.00
RO Rougned Odor 15.00 40.00

2014 Topps Chrome Rookie Autographs Blue Refractors

*BLUE REF: .6X TO 1.5X BASIC
STATED ODDS 1:306 HOBBY
STATED PRINT RUN 199 SER.#'d SETS
EXCHANGE DEADLINE 8/31/2017
25 Xander Bogaerts 60.00 150.00
AG Alexander Guerrero 12.00 30.00
EA Erisbel Arruebarrena 5.00 12.00
RO Rougned Odor 12.00 30.00

2014 Topps Chrome Rookie Autographs Gold Refractors

*GOLD REF: 1.2X TO 3X BASIC
STATED ODDS 1:1210 HOBBY
STATED PRINT RUN 50 SER.#'d SETS
EXCHANGE DEADLINE 8/31/2017
25 Xander Bogaerts 125.00 300.00
124 Travis d'Arnaud 12.00 30.00
AG Alexander Guerrero 40.00 100.00
EA Erisbel Arruebarrena 10.00 25.00
RO Rougned Odor 25.00 60.00

2014 Topps Chrome Rookie Autographs Red Refractors

*RED REF: 1.5X TO 4X BASIC
STATED ODDS 1:2450 HOBBY
STATED PRINT RUN 25 SER.#'d SETS
EXCHANGE DEADLINE 8/31/2017
25 Xander Bogaerts 125.00 300.00
124 Travis d'Arnaud 20.00 50.00
GS George Springer 150.00 400.00

2014 Topps Chrome Rookie Autographs Refractors

*REF: .5X TO 1.2X BASIC
STATED ODDS 1:128 HOBBY
STATED PRINT RUN 499 SER.#'d SETS
EXCHANGE DEADLINE 8/31/2017
AG Alexander Guerrero 10.00 25.00
EA Erisbel Arruebarrena 4.00 10.00
RO Rougned Odor 10.00 25.00

2014 Topps Chrome Rookie Autographs Sepia Refractors

*SEPIA REF: .75X TO 2X BASIC
STATED ODDS 1:810 HOBBY
STATED PRINT RUN 75 SER.#'d SETS
EXCHANGE DEADLINE 8/31/2017
25 Xander Bogaerts 75.00 200.00
124 Travis d'Arnaud 8.00 20.00
AG Alexander Guerrero 15.00 40.00
EA Erisbel Arruebarrena 6.00 15.00
RO Rougned Odor 15.00 40.00

2014 Topps Chrome Rookie Autographs Silver Ink Black Refractors

*SLVR/BLACK REF: 1.5X TO 4X BASIC
STATED ODDS 1:2450 HOBBY
STATED PRINT RUN 25 SER.#'d SETS
EXCHANGE DEADLINE 8/31/2017
25 Xander Bogaerts 150.00 400.00
EA Erisbel Arruebarrena 12.00 30.00
RO Rougned Odor 30.00 80.00
124 Travis d'Arnaud 15.00 40.00

2014 Topps Chrome Topps of the Class Autographs

STATED ODDS 1:7100 HOBBY
STATED PRINT RUN 25 SER.#'d SETS
EXCHANGE DEADLINE 8/31/2017
TOCBH Billy Hamilton EXCH 60.00 120.00
TOCJA Jose Abreu EXCH 200.00 300.00
TOCKW Kolten Wong 30.00 60.00
TOCMD Matt Davidson 8.00 20.00
TOCTD Travis d'Arnaud 8.00 20.00
TOCYV Yordano Ventura 20.00 50.00

2014 Topps Chrome Topps Shelf Refractors

STATED ODDS 1:24 HOBBY
TSAG Adrian Gonzalez 1.00 2.50
TSAJ Adam Jones 1.00 2.50
TSAM Andrew McCutchen 1.25 3.00
TSAP Albert Pujols 1.50 4.00
TSAW Adam Wainwright 1.00 2.50
TSBH Bryce Harper 2.00 5.00
TSBP Buster Posey 1.50 4.00
TSCD Chris Davis .75 2.00
TSCG Carlos Gonzalez 1.00 2.50
TSCK Clayton Kershaw 2.50 6.00
TSCKI Craig Kimbrel 1.00 2.50
TSCL Cliff Lee 1.00 2.50
TSDJ Derek Jeter 3.00 8.00
TSDO David Ortiz 1.25 3.00
TSDP Dustin Pedroia 1.25 3.00
TSDPR David Price 1.00 2.50
TSDW David Wright 1.00 2.50
TSEL Evan Longoria 1.00 2.50
TSFF Freddie Freeman 1.50 4.00
TSFH Felix Hernandez 1.00 2.50
TSGS Giancarlo Stanton 1.25 3.00
TSGSP George Springer 3.00 8.00
TSHR Hanley Ramirez 1.00 2.50
TSJA Jose Abreu 5.00 12.00
TSJB Jose Bautista 1.00 2.50
TSJBR Jay Bruce 1.00 2.50
TSJE Jacoby Ellsbury 1.00 2.50
TSJF Jose Fernandez 1.25 3.00
TSJH Josh Hamilton 1.00 2.50
TSJK Jason Kipnis 1.00 2.50
TSJR Jose Reyes 1.00 2.50
TSJU Justin Upton 1.00 2.50
TSJV Joey Votto 1.25 3.00
TSJVE Justin Verlander 1.25 3.00
TSMC Miguel Cabrera 1.25 3.00
TSMS Max Scherzer 1.25 3.00
TSMT Mike Trout 6.00 15.00
TSMTA Masahiro Tanaka 4.00 10.00
TSPF Prince Fielder 1.00 2.50
TSPG Paul Goldschmidt 1.25 3.00
TSRB Ryan Braun 1.00 2.50
TSRC Robinson Cano 1.00 2.50
TSSS Stephen Strasburg 1.25 3.00
TSSSC Shin-Soo Choo 1.00 2.50
TSTT Troy Tulowitzki 1.25 3.00
TSWM Wil Myers .75 2.00
TSYC Yoenis Cespedes 1.25 3.00
TSYD Yu Darvish 1.25 3.00
TSYM Yadier Molina 1.25 3.00
TSYP Yasiel Puig 1.25 3.00

2014 Topps Chrome Topps Shelf Autographs

STATED ODDS 1:3560 HOBBY
STATED PRINT RUN 25 SER.#'d SETS
EXCHANGE DEADLINE 8/31/2017
TSAJ Adam Jones 12.00 30.00
TSBH Bryce Harper 75.00 150.00
TSBP Buster Posey 100.00 200.00
TSDP Dustin Pedroia 75.00 150.00
TSDW David Wright 15.00 40.00
TSEL Evan Longoria 15.00 40.00
TSFF Freddie Freeman 30.00 60.00
TSJB Jose Bautista 15.00 40.00
TSJBR Jay Bruce 15.00 40.00
TSJV Joey Votto 75.00 150.00
TSMT Mike Trout 250.00 350.00
TSPG Paul Goldschmidt 30.00 60.00
TSRB Ryan Braun 15.00 40.00
TSRC Robinson Cano 20.00 50.00
TSWM Wil Myers EXCH 15.00 40.00
TSYC Yoenis Cespedes 30.00 60.00

2014 Topps Chrome Update

COMPLETE SET (55) 50.00 100.00
RANDOM INSERTS IN HOLIDAY MEGA BOXES
*GOLD/250: 1.5X TO 4X BASIC
*BLACK/99: 2X TO 5X BASIC
MB1 Brian McCann .60 1.50
MB2 Shin-Soo Choo .60 1.50
MB3 David Freese .50 1.25
MB4 George Springer RC 2.00 5.00
MB5 Ubaldo Jimenez .50 1.25
MB6 Grady Sizemore .60 1.50
MB7 Justin Morneau .60 1.50
MB8 Chris Young .50 1.25
MB9 Daisuke Matsuzaka .60 1.50
MB10 Yangervis Solarte RC .50 1.25
MB11 Michael Choice RC .50 1.25
MB12 Daniel Webb RC .50 1.25
MB13 Stefen Romero RC .50 1.25
MB14 Tommy La Stella RC .50 1.25
MB15 George Springer RD 2.00 5.00
MB16 Adrian Nieto RC .50 1.25
MB17 Robbie Ray RC .50 1.25
MB18 Rafael Montero RC .50 1.25
MB19 Jacob deGrom RC 10.00 25.00
MB20 Mookie Betts RC 50.00 120.00
MB21 James Jones RC .50 1.25
MB22 Jhonny Peralta .50 1.25
MB23 Rougned Odor RC 1.00 2.50
MB24 Nick Tepesch RC .50 1.25
MB25 Tony Sanchez RC .50 1.25
MB26 Bronson Arroyo .50 1.25
MB27 Mark Trumbo .50 1.25
MB28 Raul Ibanez .60 1.50
MB29 Chase Anderson RC .50 1.25
MB30 Erisbel Arruebarrena RC .50 1.25
MB31 Delmon Young .60 1.50
MB32 Jason Giambi .50 1.25
MB33 Rajai Davis .50 1.25
MB34 C.J. Cron RC .60 1.50
MB35 Drew Pomeranz .60 1.50
MB36 Masahiro Tanaka RC 1.50 4.00
MB37 Miguel Cabrera .75 2.00
MB38 Albert Pujols 1.00 2.50
MB39 Jose Abreu RC 4.00 10.00
MB40 Yu Darvish .75 2.00
MB41 Jose Abreu RD 4.00 10.00
MB42 Oscar Taveras RC .60 1.50
MB43 Masahiro Tanaka RD 1.50 4.00
MB44 Jon Singleton RC .60 1.50
MB45 Gregory Polanco RC .75 2.00
MB46 Mookie Betts RD 30.00 80.00
MB47 Andrew Heaney RC .50 1.25
MB48 Gregory Polanco RD .75 2.00
MB49 Oscar Taveras RD .60 1.50
MB50 Jon Singleton RD .60 1.50
MB51 Andrew Heaney RD .50 1.25
MB52 Cam Bedrosian RC .50 1.25
MB53 Marcus Stroman RC .75 2.00
MB54 Jacob deGrom RD 3.00 8.00
MB55 Brandon McCarthy .50 1.25

2014 Topps Chrome Update All-Star Stitches

RANDOM INSERTS IN HOLIDAY MEGA BOXES
ASCRAJ Adam Jones 2.50 6.00
ASCRAM Andrew McCutchen 3.00 8.00
ASCRAR Anthony Rizzo 5.00 12.00
ASCRAW Adam Wainwright 2.50 6.00
ASCRCB Charlie Blackmon 3.00 8.00
ASCRCKL Clayton Kershaw 6.00 15.00
ASCRCU Chase Utley 2.50 6.00
ASCRDJ Derek Jeter 30.00 60.00
ASCRFF Freddie Freeman 4.00 10.00
ASCRFH Felix Hernandez 2.50 6.00
ASCRGS Giancarlo Stanton 3.00 8.00
ASCRJA Jose Abreu 10.00 25.00
ASCRJB Jose Bautista 2.50 6.00
ASCRJL Jonathan Lucroy 2.50 6.00
ASCRKU Koji Uehara 2.00 5.00
ASCRMT Mike Trout 15.00 40.00
ASCRPG Paul Goldschmidt 3.00 8.00
ASCRRC Robinson Cano 2.50 6.00
ASCRTT Troy Tulowitzki 3.00 8.00
ASCRYC Yoenis Cespedes 3.00 8.00
ASCRYD Yu Darvish 3.00 8.00
ASCRYP Yasiel Puig 3.00 8.00

2014 Topps Chrome Update All-Star Stitches Autographs

RANDOM INSERTS IN HOLIDAY MEGA BOXES
STATED PRINT RUN 25 SER.#'d SETS
ASCARGP Glen Perkins 25.00 60.00
ASCARJH Josh Harrison 50.00 120.00
ASCARNC Nelson Cruz 25.00 60.00

2014 Topps Chrome Update World Series Heroes

RANDOM INSERTS IN HOLIDAY MEGA BOXES
WSC1 David Ortiz 1.00 2.50
WSC2 Albert Pujols 1.25 3.00
WSC3 Pedro Martinez .75 2.00
WSC4 Manny Ramirez 1.00 2.50
WSC5 Josh Beckett .60 1.50
WSC6 Randy Johnson 1.00 2.50
WSC7 Derek Jeter 2.50 6.00
WSC8 Mariano Rivera 1.25 3.00
WSC9 Tom Glavine .75 2.00
WSC10 Greg Maddux 1.25 3.00
WSC11 John Smoltz 1.00 2.50
WSC12 Rickey Henderson 1.00 2.50
WSC13 Mookie Wilson .60 1.50
WSC14 George Brett 2.00 5.00
WSC15 Mike Schmidt 1.50 4.00
WSC16 Reggie Jackson .75 2.00
WSC17 Roberto Clemente 2.50 6.00
WSC18 Sandy Koufax 2.00 5.00
WSC19 Hank Aaron 2.00 5.00
WSC20 Brooks Robinson .75 2.00

2015 Topps Chrome

COMP.SET w/o SPs (200) 15.00 40.00
VAR ODDS 1:1,765 H,1:235 J,1:766 R
PLATE ODDS 1:2388 HOB,1:737 JUM,1:2395 RET
PLATE PRINT RUN 1 SET PER COLOR
BLACK-CYAN-MAGENTA-YELLOW ISSUED
NO PLATE PRICING DUE TO SCARCITY
1 Derek Jeter .75 2.00
2 Ryan Rua RC .40 1.00
3 Scooter Gennett .25 .60
4 Joe Mauer .25 .60
5 Starling Marte .25 .60
6 Brandon Phillips .20 .50
7 Adam Jones .25 .60
8 Denard Span .20 .50
9 Andrelton Simmons .20 .50
10 Matt Adams .20 .50
11 Carlos Gonzalez .25 .60
12 Prince Fielder .25 .60
13 Jonathan Lucroy .25 .60
14 Paul Konerko .25 .60
15 Anthony Ranaudo RC .40 1.00
16 Tommy La Stella .20 .50
17 Mike Foltynewicz RC .40 1.00
18 Dalton Pompey RC .50 1.25
19 Kendall Graveman RC .40 1.00
20 Roenis Elias .20 .50
21 Matt Barnes RC .40 1.00
22 Nick Tropeano RC .40 1.00
23A Stephen Strasburg .30 .75
23B Strsbrg SP Goggles 8.00 20.00
24 Addison Russell RC 1.25 3.00
25 Yadier Molina .30 .75
26 Madison Bumgarner .25 .60
27A Joe Panik .25 .60
27B Panik SP Black shirt 15.00 40.00
28 Adeiny Hechavarria .20 .50
29 Yorman Rodriguez RC .40 1.00
30 Alex Gordon .25 .60
31 Jon Lester .25 .60
32 Jonathan Schoop .20 .50
33 Alex Cobb .20 .50
34 Austin Jackson .20 .50
35 Matt Kemp .25 .60
36 Brad Ziegler .20 .50
37 Chris Owings .20 .50
38 Pablo Sandoval .25 .60
39 Hunter Strickland RC .40 1.00
40 Jon Singleton .25 .60

41 Sean Doolittle .20 .50
42 Manny Machado .30 .75
43 Michael Taylor RC .40 1.00
44 Jason Rogers RC .40 1.00
45 David Peralta .20 .50
46 James McCann RC .60 1.50
47 Brandon Belt .25 .60
48 Christian Yelich .40 1.00
49A Jacoby Ellsbury .25 .60
49B Ellsbury SP Hldng hlmt 12.00 30.00
50 Kolten Wong .25 .60
51A Mike Trout 1.50 4.00
51B Trout SP Celebrate 60.00 150.00
52 Yasiel Puig .30 .75
53 Wil Myers .20 .50
54 George Springer .25 .60
55 Clayton Kershaw .60 1.50
56 Ian Desmond .20 .50
57 Chris Sale .30 .75
58 Justin Morneau .25 .60
59 Kevin Kiermaier .25 .60
60 Eric Hosmer .25 .60
61 Russell Martin .20 .50
62 Anthony Rendon .30 .75
63 Nick Castellanos .30 .75
64 Lisalverto Bonilla RC .40 1.00
65 Giancarlo Stanton .30 .75
66 Nolan Arenado .40 1.00
67 Mookie Betts .50 1.25
68 Masahiro Tanaka .25 .60
69 Bryce Brentz RC .40 1.00
70 Dioner Navarro .20 .50
71 Melvin Mercedes RC .40 1.00
72 Todd Frazier .25 .60
73 Carlos Gomez .20 .50
74 Carlos Martinez .25 .60
75 Matt Shoemaker .25 .60
76 Andrew McCutchen .30 .75
77 Charlie Blackmon .30 .75
78 Corey Kluber .25 .60
79 Jordan Zimmermann .25 .60
80 Dilson Herrera RC .50 1.25
81 Bryce Harper .50 1.25
82 Adam Wainwright .25 .60
83 Hunter Pence .25 .60
84 Aroldis Chapman .30 .75
85 Michael Wacha .25 .60
86 Mitch Moreland .20 .50
87 Daniel Norris RC .40 1.00
88 Brett Gardner .25 .60
89 Javier Baez RC 3.00 8.00
90 Carlos Rodon RC .60 1.50
91 Michael Brantley .25 .60
92 Ken Giles .20 .50
93 Ian Kinsler .25 .60
94 Ryan Howard .25 .60
95 Adam Eaton .20 .50
96 Archie Bradley RC .40 1.00
97 Carlos Santana .25 .60
98 Max Scherzer .30 .75
99 Doug Fister .20 .50
100 Chase Utley .25 .60
101 Maikel Franco RC .50 1.25
102 David Wright .25 .60
103 Billy Hamilton .25 .60
104 Johnny Cueto .25 .60
105 Freddie Freeman .40 1.00
106 Paul Goldschmidt .30 .75
107 Steven Souza Jr. .25 .60
108 Rafael Ynoa RC .40 1.00
109 Torii Hunter .20 .50
110 Nelson Cruz .30 .75
111 Brandon Crawford .25 .60
112 Kris Bryant RC 6.00 15.00
113 Albert Pujols .40 1.00
114 Victor Martinez .25 .60
115 Matt Harvey .25 .60
116 Rymer Liriano RC .40 1.00
117 Zack Wheeler .25 .60
118 Trevor May RC .40 1.00
119 Travis d'Arnaud .25 .60
120 R.J. Alvarez RC .40 1.00
121 Anthony Rizzo .50 1.25
122 Guilder Rodriguez RC .40 1.00
123 Yimi Garcia RC .40 1.00
124A David Ortiz .30 .75
124B Ortiz SP w/Teammate 12.00 30.00
125A Troy Tulowitzki .30 .75
126 Gregory Polanco .25 .60
127 Melky Cabrera .20 .50
128 John Holdzkom RC .40 1.00
129A Joc Pederson RC .75 2.00
129B Pdrsn SP w/Teammate 10.00 25.00
130 Terrance Gore RC .40 1.00
131 Miguel Alfredo Gonzalez RC .40 1.00
132 Cory Spangenberg RC .40 1.00
133 Sonny Gray .25 .60
134 Edwin Encarnacion .30 .75
135 Brandon Moss .20 .50
136 Yordano Ventura .25 .60
137 Jose Bautista .25 .60
138 Adrian Gonzalez .25 .60
139 Starlin Castro .20 .50
140 Josh Harrison .20 .50
141 Jose Fernandez .30 .75
142 David Price .25 .60
143 CC Sabathia .25 .60
144 Dallas Keuchel .25 .60
145 Erik Cordier RC .40 1.00
146 J.J. Hardy .20 .50
147 Jonathan Papelbon .25 .60
148 Jake Lamb RC .60 1.50
149 Evan Gattis .20 .50
150 Mike Napoli .20 .50
151A Jose Altuve .25 .60
151B Altuve SP White jsy 12.00 30.00
152 Chris Archer .20 .50
153 Micah Johnson RC .40 1.00
154A Jorge Soler RC .60 1.50
154B Soler SP w/Teammate 8.00 20.00
155 James Shields .20 .50
156 Kennys Vargas .20 .50
157 Aramis Ramirez .20 .50
158 Nick Swisher .25 .60
159 Kyle Lobstein RC .40 1.00
160 Rusney Castillo RC .50 1.25
161 Jose Pirela RC .40 1.00
162 Miguel Cabrera .30 .75
163 Craig Kimbrel .25 .60
164 Mike Moustakas .25 .60
165 Rougned Odor .25 .60
166 Xavier Scruggs RC .40 1.00
167 Danny Santana .20 .50
168 Edwin Escobar RC .40 1.00
169 Salvador Perez .25 .60
170 Ender Inciarte RC .40 1.00
171 Buck Farmer RC .40 1.00
172 Dustin Pedroia .30 .75
173 Robinson Cano .25 .60
174 Samuel Tuivailala RC .40 1.00
175 Josh Reddick .20 .50
176 Lorenzo Cain .20 .50
177 Steven Moya RC .50 1.25
178 Evan Longoria .25 .60
179 Buster Posey .40 1.00
180 Jose Abreu .30 .75
181 Felix Hernandez .25 .60
182 Marcell Ozuna .30 .75
183 Jacob deGrom .30 .75
184 Devon Travis RC .40 1.00
185 Phil Hughes .20 .50
186 Mark Teixeira .25 .60
187 Yu Darvish .30 .75
188 Kyle Seager .20 .50
189 Yasmany Tomas RC .50 1.25
190 Michael Cuddyer .20 .50
191 Justin Verlander .30 .75
192 Christian Walker RC .75 2.00
193 Adrian Beltre .30 .75
194 Dellin Betances .25 .60
195A Brandon Finnegan RC .40 1.00
195B Finnegan SP Gatorade 10.00 25.00
196 Kevin Gausman .20 .50
197 Mike Minor .20 .50
198 Garrett Richards .25 .60
199 Hanley Ramirez .25 .60
200 Ryan Braun .25 .60
201 Noah Syndergaard SP RC 6.00 15.00
202 Francisco Lindor SP RC 100.00 250.00
203 Byron Buxton SP RC 4.00 10.00
204 Joey Gallo SP RC 5.00 12.00
205 Carlos Correa SP RC 15.00 40.00

2015 Topps Chrome Blue Refractors

*BLUE REF: 4X TO 10X BASIC
*BLUE REF RC: 2X TO 5X BASIC RC
STATED ODDS 1:64 H,1:20 J,1:64 R
STATED PRINT RUN 150 SER.#'d SETS
1 Derek Jeter 20.00 50.00
51 Mike Trout 20.00 50.00

2015 Topps Chrome Gold Refractors

*GOLD REF: 6X TO 15X BASIC
*GOLD REF RC: 3X TO 8X BASIC RC
*GOLD REF 201-205: 1.5X TO 4X BASE
STATED ODDS 1:191 H,1:59 J,1:191 R
STATED PRINT RUN 50 SER.#'d SETS
1 Derek Jeter 60.00 150.00
24 Addison Russell 40.00 100.00
51 Mike Trout 60.00 150.00
55 Clayton Kershaw 12.00 30.00
81 Bryce Harper 20.00 50.00
101 Maikel Franco 15.00 40.00
121 Anthony Rizzo 15.00 40.00
179 Buster Posey 20.00 50.00
180 Jose Abreu 5.00 12.00

2015 Topps Chrome Green Refractors

*GREEN REF: 5X TO 12X BASIC
*GREEN REF RC: 2.5X TO 6X BASIC RC
*GREEN REF 201-205: .75X TO 2X BASIC
STATED ODDS 1:97 H,1:30 J,1:97 R
STATED PRINT RUN 99 SER.#'d SETS
1 Derek Jeter 25.00 60.00
51 Mike Trout 20.00 50.00

2015 Topps Chrome Orange Refractors

*ORANGE REF: 10X TO 25X BASIC
*ORANGE REF RC: 5X TO 12X BASIC RC
STATED ODDS 1:382 H,1:118 J,1:383 R
STATED PRINT RUN 25 SER.#'d SETS
1 Derek Jeter 75.00 200.00
24 Addison Russell 50.00 120.00
26 Madison Bumgarner 20.00 50.00
51 Mike Trout 75.00 200.00
55 Clayton Kershaw 15.00 40.00
81 Bryce Harper 25.00 60.00
101 Maikel Franco 20.00 50.00
121 Anthony Rizzo 20.00 50.00
179 Buster Posey 25.00 60.00

2015 Topps Chrome Pink Refractors

*PINK REF: 3X TO 8X BASIC
*PINK REF RC: 1.5X TO 4X BASIC RC
THREE PER RETAIL VALUE PACK

2015 Topps Chrome Prism Refractors

*PRISM REF: 1.5X TO 4X BASIC
*PRISM REF RC: .75X TO 2X BASIC RC
STATED ODDS 1:6 H,1:2 J,1:6 R

2015 Topps Chrome Purple Refractors

*PURPLE REF: 3X TO 8X BASIC
*PURPLE REF RC: 1.5X TO 4X BASIC RC
STATED ODDS 1:38 H,1:12 J,1:38 R
STATED PRINT RUN 250 SER.#'d SETS
1 Derek Jeter 10.00 25.00
51 Mike Trout 10.00 25.00

2015 Topps Chrome Refractors

*REF: 1X TO 2.5X BASIC
*REF RC: .5X TO 1.2X BASIC RC
STATED ODDS 1:3 H,1:1 J,1:3 R

2015 Topps Chrome Sepia Refractors

*SEPIA REF: 2.5X TO 6X BASIC
*SEPIA REF RC: 1.2X TO 3X BASIC RC
FOUR PER RETAIL BLASTER
1 Derek Jeter 8.00 20.00

2015 Topps Chrome Commencements

STATED ODDS 1:48 H,1:12 J
COM1 Jacob deGrom 1.00 2.50
COM2 Masahiro Tanaka .75 2.00
COM3 Yordano Ventura .75 2.00
COM4 Jose Abreu .60 1.50
COM5 Kolten Wong .75 2.00
COM6 Xander Bogaerts 1.00 2.50
COM7 Matt Shoemaker .75 2.00
COM8 Mookie Betts 1.50 4.00
COM9 Arismendy Alcantara .60 1.50
COM10 Kennys Vargas .60 1.50
COM11 Anthony Rendon 1.00 2.50
COM12 Christian Yelich 1.25 3.00
COM13 Jose Fernandez 1.00 2.50
COM14 Gregory Polanco .75 2.00
COM15 Dellin Betances .75 2.00
COM16 Wil Myers .60 1.50
COM17 Billy Hamilton .75 2.00
COM18 Joe Panik .75 2.00
COM19 Yasiel Puig 1.00 2.50
COM20 Julio Teheran .75 2.00

2015 Topps Chrome Culminations

STATED ODDS 1:288 HOBBY
CULAB Adrian Beltre 8.00 20.00
CULAG Adrian Gonzalez 6.00 15.00
CULAP Albert Pujols 10.00 25.00
CULCB Carlos Beltran 6.00 15.00
CULCK Clayton Kershaw 15.00 40.00
CULCS CC Sabathia 6.00 15.00
CULDJ Derek Jeter 40.00 80.00
CULDO David Ortiz 8.00 20.00
CULDP Dustin Pedroia 8.00 20.00
CULDW David Wright 6.00 15.00
CULHR Hanley Ramirez 6.00 15.00
CULJH Josh Hamilton 6.00 15.00
CULJL Jon Lester 6.00 15.00
CULJM Joe Mauer 10.00 25.00
CULMC Miguel Cabrera 10.00 25.00
CULMT Mark Teixeira 10.00 25.00
CULPS Pablo Sandoval 6.00 15.00
CULRB Ryan Braun 6.00 15.00
CULRC Robinson Cano 6.00 15.00
CULYM Yadier Molina 8.00 20.00

2015 Topps Chrome Culminations Autographs

STATED ODDS 1:3785 H,1:770 J,1:13,174 R
STATED PRINT RUN 50 SER.#'d SETS
EXCHANGE DEADLINE 8/31/2018
CULCK Clayton Kershaw 75.00 150.00
CULDP Dustin Pedroia 25.00 60.00
CULHR Hanley Ramirez 6.00 15.00
CULJL Jon Lester 12.00 30.00
CULJM Joe Mauer 20.00 50.00
CULMT Mark Teixeira 12.00 30.00
CULPS Pablo Sandoval 10.00 25.00
CULRC Robinson Cano 12.00 30.00

2015 Topps Chrome Future Stars

STATED ODDS 1:12 H,1:4 J,1:12 R
*GOLD/50: 4X TO 10X BASIC
*ORANGE: 5X TO 12X BASIC
FSC01 Joc Pederson .75 2.00
FSC02 Rusney Castillo .50 1.25
FSC03 Jorge Soler .60 1.50
FSC04 Javier Baez 3.00 8.00
FSC05 Trevor May .40 1.00
FSC06 Dalton Pompey .50 1.25
FSC07 Michael Taylor .40 1.00
FSC08 Steven Moya .50 1.25
FSC09 Matt Barnes .40 1.00
FSC10 Anthony Ranaudo .40 1.00
FSC11 Maikel Franco .50 1.25
FSC12 Christian Walker .75 2.00
FSC13 Jake Lamb .60 1.50
FSC14 Cory Spangenberg .40 1.00
FSC15 Mike Foltynewicz .40 1.00
FSC16 Dilson Herrera .50 1.25
FSC17 Daniel Norris .40 1.00
FSC18 Brandon Finnegan .40 1.00
FSC19 Rafael Ynoa .40 1.00
FSC20 Samuel Tuivailala .40 1.00

2015 Topps Chrome Gallery of Greats

STATED ODDS 1:24 H,1:8 J,1:24 R
GGR01 Clayton Kershaw 1.50 4.00
GGR02 Derek Jeter 2.00 5.00
GGR03 Miguel Cabrera .75 2.00
GGR04 Yasiel Puig .60 1.50
GGR05 Freddie Freeman 1.00 2.50
GGR06 Albert Pujols 1.00 2.50
GGR07 Bryce Harper 1.25 3.00
GGR08 Mike Trout 4.00 10.00
GGR09 Josh Donaldson .60 1.50
GGR10 Corey Kluber .60 1.50
GGR11 Adrian Beltre .75 2.00
GGR12 Felix Hernandez .60 1.50
GGR13 Yu Darvish .75 2.00
GGR14 Chris Sale .75 2.00
GGR15 Alex Gordon .60 1.50
GGR16 Jose Altuve .60 1.50
GGR17 Troy Tulowitzki .75 2.00
GGR18 Jose Abreu .75 2.00
GGR19 Robinson Cano .60 1.50
GGR20 Andrew McCutchen .75 2.00
GGR21 Buster Posey 1.00 2.50
GGR22 Giancarlo Stanton .75 2.00
GGR23 Jose Bautista .60 1.50
GGR24 David Ortiz .75 2.00
GGR25 Anthony Rizzo 1.25 3.00
GGR26 Evan Longoria .60 1.50
GGR27 Paul Goldschmidt .75 2.00
GGR28 Adam Jones .60 1.50
GGR29 Cole Hamels .60 1.50
GGR30 Johnny Cueto .60 1.50

2015 Topps Chrome Gallery of Greats Gold Refractors

*GOLD: 4X TO 10X BASIC
STATED ODDS 1:525 H,1:1031 J
STATED PRINT RUN 50 SER.#'d SETS
GGR02 Derek Jeter 30.00 80.00

2015 Topps Chrome Gallery of Greats Orange Refractors

*ORANGE: 6X TO 15X BASIC
STATED ODDS 1:1091 H,1:677 J
STATED PRINT RUN 25 SER.#'d SETS
GGR02 Derek Jeter 60.00 150.00

2015 Topps Chrome Illustrious Autographs

STATED ODDS 1:1512 H,1:308 J,1:5270 R
STATED PRINT RUN 50 SER.#'d SETS
EXCHANGE DEADLINE 8/31/2018
PLATE ODDS 1:5646 RETAIL
PLATE PRINT RUN 1 SET PER COLOR
NO PLATE PRICING DUE TO SCARCITY
IAAR Anthony Rizzo 20.00 50.00
IACKR Corey Kluber 12.00 30.00
IACS Chris Sale 15.00 40.00
IACY Christian Yelich 12.00 30.00
IAJA Jose Abreu 20.00 50.00
IAJP Joc Pederson 12.00 30.00
IAPG Paul Goldschmidt 20.00 50.00

2015 Topps Chrome Illustrious Autographs Orange Refractors

*ORANGE: .6X TO 1.5X BASIC
STATED ODDS 1:1082 HOBBY
STATED PRINT RUN 25 SER.#'d SETS
EXCHANGE DEADLINE 8/31/2018
IABP Buster Posey 125.00 250.00
IAMT Mike Trout 250.00 350.00

2015 Topps Chrome Rookie Autographs

STATED ODDS 1:21 H,1:3 J,1:137 R
PRINTING PLATE ODDS 1:2955 RETAIL
PLATE PRINT RUN 1 SET PER COLOR
NO PLATE PRICING DUE TO SCARCITY
EXCHANGE DEADLINE 8/31/2018
ARAB Archie Bradley 4.00 10.00
ARAC A.J. Cole 2.50 6.00
ARARU Addison Russell EXCH 100.00 250.00
ARBB Bryce Brentz 2.50 6.00
ARBBN Byron Buxton 15.00 40.00
ARBFN Brandon Finnegan 3.00 8.00
ARBFR Buck Farmer 2.50 6.00
ARBM Bryan Mitchell 2.50 6.00
ARBST Blake Swihart 3.00 8.00
ARCC Carlos Correa 30.00 80.00
ARCS Cory Spangenberg 2.50 6.00
ARCW Christian Walker 5.00 12.00
ARDC Daniel Corcino 2.50 6.00
ARDH Dilson Herrera 3.00 8.00
ARDN Daniel Norris 2.50 6.00
ARDP Dalton Pompey 3.00 8.00
ARDT Devon Travis 2.50 6.00
AREC Erik Cordier 2.50 6.00
AREE Edwin Escobar 2.50 6.00
ARFL Francisco Lindor 50.00 120.00
ARGB Gary Brown 2.50 6.00
ARHS Hunter Strickland 2.50 6.00
ARJB Javier Baez 25.00 60.00
ARJH John Holdzkom 2.50 6.00
ARJK Jung-ho Kang 15.00 40.00
ARJL Jake Lamb 5.00 12.00
ARJLN Jacob Lindgren 3.00 8.00
ARJPA Jose Pirela 3.00 8.00
ARJPN Joc Pederson 8.00 20.00
ARJR Jason Rogers 2.50 6.00
ARJS Jorge Soler 4.00 10.00
ARKB Kris Bryant 100.00 250.00
ARKG Kendall Graveman 2.50 6.00
ARKL Kyle Lobstein 2.50 6.00
ARKP Kevin Plawecki 2.50 6.00
ARMB Matt Barnes 2.50 6.00
ARMC Matt Clark 2.50 6.00
ARMFO Maikel Franco 8.00 20.00
ARMJ Micah Johnson 2.50 6.00
ARMT Michael Taylor 4.00 10.00
ARNT Nick Tropeano 2.50 6.00
ARRAZ R.J. Alvarez 2.50 6.00
ARRC Rusney Castillo 3.00 8.00
ARRI Raisel Iglesias 3.00 8.00
ARRL Rymer Liriano 2.50 6.00
ARRR Ryan Rua 2.50 6.00
ARSM Steven Moya 3.00 8.00
ARST Samuel Tuivailala 2.50 6.00
ARTG Terrance Gore 2.50 6.00
ARTM Trevor May 2.50 6.00
ARXS Xavier Scruggs 3.00 8.00
ARYG Yimi Garcia 2.50 6.00
ARYR Yorman Rodriguez 2.50 6.00

2015 Topps Chrome Rookie Autographs Blue Refractors

*BLUE REF: .6X TO 1.5X BASIC
STATED ODDS 1:280 H,1:57 J,1:982 R
STATED PRINT RUN 150 SER.#'d SETS
EXCHANGE DEADLINE 8/31/2018
ARNS Noah Syndergaard 25.00 60.00
ARYT Yasmany Tomas 5.00 12.00

2015 Topps Chrome Rookie Autographs Gold Refractors

*GOLD REF: 1.5X TO 4X BASIC
STATED ODDS 1:234 R
STATED PRINT RUN 50 SER.#'d SETS
EXCHANGE DEADLINE 8/31/2018
ARNS Noah Syndergaard 60.00 150.00
ARYT Yasmany Tomas 12.00 30.00

2015 Topps Chrome Rookie Autographs Green Refractors

*GREEN REF: .75X TO 2X BASIC
STATED ODDS 1:424 H,1:86 J,1:1484 R
STATED PRINT RUN 99 SER.#'d SETS
EXCHANGE DEADLINE 8/31/2018
ARNS Noah Syndergaard 30.00 80.00
ARYT Yasmany Tomas 6.00 15.00

2015 Topps Chrome Rookie Autographs Orange Refractors

*ORANGE REF: 2X TO 5X BASIC
STATED ODDS 1:602 H
STATED PRINT RUN 25 SER.#'d SETS
EXCHANGE DEADLINE 8/31/2018
ARAB Archie Bradley 20.00 50.00
ARKB Kris Bryant 400.00 800.00
ARNS Noah Syndergaard 75.00 200.00

2015 Topps Chrome Rookie Autographs Purple Refractors

*PURPLE REF: .6X TO 1.5X BASIC
STATED ODDS 1:168 H,1:34 J,1:589 R
STATED PRINT RUN 250 SER.#'d SETS
EXCHANGE DEADLINE 8/31/2018
ARCR Carlos Rodon 6.00 15.00
ARNS Noah Syndergaard 25.00 60.00
ARYT Yasmany Tomas 5.00 12.00

2015 Topps Chrome Rookie Autographs Refractors

*REF: .5X TO 1.2X BASIC
STATED ODDS 1:54 H,1:29 J,1:211 R
STATED PRINT RUN 499 SER.#'d SETS
EXCHANGE DEADLINE 8/31/2018

2015 Topps Chrome Thrill of the Chase Die Cut Autographs

STATED ODDS 1:3595 H,1:731 J,1:12,647 R
STATED PRINT RUN 35 SER.#'d SETS
EXCHANGE DEADLINE 8/31/2018
PLATE ODDS 1:8783 RETAIL
PLATE PRINT RUN 1 SET PER COLOR
NO PLATE PRICING DUE TO SCARCITY
TCCK Clayton Kershaw 60.00 150.00
TCFF Freddie Freeman 25.00 60.00
TCJH Jason Heyward 30.00 80.00
TCJL Jon Lester 30.00 80.00
TCPG Paul Goldschmidt 20.00 50.00
TCRC Robinson Cano EXCH 15.00 40.00

2016 Topps Chrome

COMP.SET w/o SPs (200) 15.00 40.00
VAR ODDS 1:464 HOBBY
ALL VARIATIONS ARE REFRACTORS
PLATE ODDS 1:2900 HOBBY
PLATE PRINT RUN 1 SET PER COLOR
BLACK-CYAN-MAGENTA-YELLOW ISSUED
NO PLATE PRICING DUE TO SCARCITY
1A Mike Trout 1.50 4.00
1B Trt SP REF w/Fans 40.00 100.00
2 Lorenzo Cain .20 .50
3A Francisco Lindor .30 .75
3B Lndr SP REF Slide 8.00 20.00
4 J.D. Martinez .30 .75
5 Masahiro Tanaka .25 .60
6 Salvador Perez .25 .60
7 Addison Russell .30 .75
8 Jon Gray RC .40 1.00
9 Nolan Arenado .40 1.00
10 Freddie Freeman .40 1.00
11 Gerrit Cole .30 .75
12 Adam Jones .25 .60
13 Byung-Ho Park RC .50 1.25
14 Tyler Naquin RC .50 1.25
15 Charlie Blackmon .30 .75
16 Max Scherzer .30 .75
17 Prince Fielder .25 .60
18 Justin Verlander .30 .75
19 Brandon Drury RC .60 1.50
20 Yu Darvish .30 .75
21 Alex Gordon .25 .60
22 Brian McCann .25 .60
23 Jacoby Ellsbury .25 .60
24 Rob Refsnyder RC .50 1.25
25 Jake Arrieta .25 .60
26 Adrian Gonzalez .25 .60
27 Jose Altuve .25 .60
28 Raul Mondesi RC
29 Richie Shaffer RC .40 1.00
30 Manny Machado .30 .75
31 Curtis Granderson .25 .60
32 Trea Turner RC 1.25 3.00
33A Luis Severino RC .50 1.25
33B Luis Severino SP REF Gray jersey 6.00 15.00
34 Michael Brantley .25 .60
35 George Springer .25 .60
36 Joey Gallo .25 .60
37 DJ LeMahieu .30 .75
38 Zack Greinke .25 .60
39 Madison Bumgarner .25 .60
40 Stephen Strasburg .30 .75
41 Joey Rickard RC .40 1.00
42 Robinson Cano .25 .60
43 Jay Bruce .25 .60
44 Nelson Cruz .30 .75
45 Trevor Story RC 1.50 4.00
46 Albert Pujols .40 1.00
47 Chris Davis .20 .50
48 Adrian Beltre .30 .75
49 Patrick Corbin .25 .60
50A Kris Bryant .40 1.00
50B Brnt SP REF w/Fans 30.00 80.00
51 Carlos Gonzalez .25 .60
52 Michael Conforto RC .50 1.25
53A Giancarlo Stanton .30 .75
53B Giancarlo Stanton SP REF Fist bump 8.00 20.00
54 Dee Gordon .20 .50
55 John Lackey .25 .60
56 Yordano Ventura .25 .60
57 Jeurys Familia .25 .60
58 Joc Pederson .25 .60
59 Tom Murphy RC .40 1.00
60 Carlos Martinez .25 .60
61 Hisashi Iwakuma .25 .60
62 Billy Hamilton .25 .60
63 Jose Abreu .30 .75
64 Maikel Franco .25 .60
65 Jung Ho Kang .20 .50
66 Dallas Keuchel .25 .60
67 Adam Wainwright .25 .60
68 Matt Reynolds .20 .50
69 Eric Hosmer .25 .60
70 Tyler White RC .40 1.00
71 Carlos Ruiz .20 .50
72 Ryan Howard .25 .60
73 Noah Syndergaard .25 .60
74 Matt Kemp .25 .60
75A Carlos Correa .30 .75
75B Crra SP REF w/Fans 8.00 20.00
76 Nick Markakis .25 .60
77 Todd Frazier .25 .60
78 Dustin Pedroia .30 .75
79 Michael Wacha .25 .60
80 Brad Ziegler .20 .50
81 Edwin Encarnacion .30 .75
82 Joe Mauer .25 .60
83 Byron Buxton .25 .60
84 Evan Longoria .25 .60
85 Carl Edwards Jr. RC .50 1.25
86 Rougned Odor .25 .60
87 Anthony Rizzo .50 1.25
88 Mark Melancon .20 .50
89 Hector Olivera RC .50 1.25
90 Josh Reddick .20 .50
91 James Shields .20 .50
92A Kenta Maeda RC .75 2.00
92B Mda SP REF Bttng 10.00 25.00
93 Ross Stripling RC .40 1.00
94 Jorge Lopez RC .40 1.00
95 Tyson Ross .20 .50
96 Jackie Bradley Jr. .30 .75
97 Matt Harvey .25 .60
98 Seung-Hwan Oh RC 1.00 2.50
99 Jose Berrios RC .50 1.25
100 Josh Donaldson .25 .60
101 Andrew Heaney .20 .50
102 Kevin Pillar .20 .50
103 Jason Heyward .25 .60
104 Miguel Sano RC .60 1.50
105 Kevin Kiermaier .25 .60
106 Melky Cabrera .20 .50
107 David Price .25 .60
108 Mallex Smith RC .40 1.00
109 Miguel Cabrera .30 .75
110 Jeremy Hazelbaker RC .50 1.25
111 Marcus Stroman .25 .60
112 Sean Doolittle .20 .50
113 Mark Teixeira .25 .60
114 Aaron Nola RC .75 2.00
115 Starling Marte .25 .60
116 Ichiro .40 1.00
117 Alcides Escobar .25 .60
118 Carlos Gomez .20 .50
119 Craig Kimbrel .25 .60
120 Ben Zobrist .25 .60
121 Ketel Marte RC .75 2.00
122 Jake Odorizzi .20 .50
123 Brett Gardner .25 .60
124 Luke Jackson RC .40 1.00
125 Buster Posey .40 1.00
126 Miguel Almonte RC .40 1.00
127 Rusney Castillo .20 .50
128 Greg Bird RC .50 1.25
129 Odubel Herrera .25 .60
130 Frankie Montas RC .50 1.25
131 Trayce Thompson RC .60 1.50
132 Stephen Piscotty RC .60 1.50
133 Henry Owens RC .50 1.25
134 David Wright .25 .60
135 Russell Martin .20 .50
136 Jeff Samardzija .20 .50
137 Brian Johnson RC .40 1.00
138 Max Kepler RC .60 1.50
139 Chris Sale .30 .75
140 Justin Upton .25 .60
141 Aroldis Chapman .30 .75
142 Cole Hamels .25 .60
143 Gary Sanchez RC 4.00 10.00
144 Jacob deGrom .30 .75
145A Clayton Kershaw .60 1.50
145B Krshw SP REF Run 10.00 25.00
146 Alex Rodriguez .40 1.00
147 Johnny Cueto .25 .60
148 Robert Stephenson RC .40 1.00
149 Yasiel Puig .30 .75
150 Corey Seager RC 3.00 8.00
151 Trevor Rosenthal .25 .60
152 Yadier Molina .30 .75
153 David Ortiz .30 .75
154 Matt Garza .20 .50
155 Zach Britton .25 .60
156 Stephen Vogt .25 .60
157 Matt Carpenter .30 .75
158 Carlos Carrasco .20 .50
159 A.J. Pollock .20 .50
160 Taylor Jungmann .20 .50
161 Mookie Betts .50 1.25
162 Paul Goldschmidt .30 .75
163 Ian Kinsler .25 .60
164 Nomar Mazara RC .60 1.50
165 Ryan Braun .25 .60
166A Kyle Schwarber RC 1.25 3.00
166B Schwrbr SP REF Wave 15.00 40.00
167 Hunter Pence .25 .60
168 Dellin Betances .25 .60
169 Yoenis Cespedes .30 .75
170 Garrett Richards .25 .60
171 Zach Lee RC .40 1.00
172 Kyle Seager .20 .50
173 Wei-Yin Chen .20 .50
174 Ben Paulsen .20 .50
175 Andrew McCutchen .30 .75
176 Andrew Miller .25 .60
177 Jose Peraza RC .50 1.25
178 Francisco Liriano .20 .50
179 Dae-Ho Lee RC .60 1.50
180 Hanley Ramirez .25 .60
181 Blake Snell RC .50 1.25
182 Corey Kluber .25 .60
183 Brian Dozier .25 .60
184 Jason Kipnis .25 .60
185 Joey Votto .30 .75
186 Mike Foltynewicz .20 .50
187 Christian Yelich .40 1.00
188 Sonny Gray .25 .60
189 Wade Davis .20 .50
190 Brandon Phillips .20 .50
191 Jose Bautista .25 .60
192 Felix Hernandez .25 .60
193 Julio Teheran .25 .60
194 Troy Tulowitzki .30 .75
195 Steven Matz .25 .60
196 Aaron Blair RC .40 1.00
197 Jose Fernandez .30 .75
198 Daniel Murphy .25 .60
199 Peter O'Brien RC .40 1.00
200A Bryce Harper .50 1.25
200B Hrpr SP REF w/Fans 12.00 30.00

2016 Topps Chrome Black Refractors

*BLACK REF: 3X TO 8X BASIC
*BLACK REF RC: 1.5X TO 4X BASIC RC
HOBBY HOT BOX EXCLUSIVE
150 Corey Seager 20.00 50.00

2016 Topps Chrome Blue Refractors

*BLUE REF: 4X TO 10X BASIC
*BLUE REF RC: 2X TO 5X BASIC RC
STATED ODDS 1:78 HOBBY
STATED PRINT RUN 150 SER.#'d SETS
150 Corey Seager 25.00 60.00

2016 Topps Chrome Gold Refractors

*GOLD REF: 10X TO 25X BASIC
*GOLD REF RC: 5X TO 12X BASIC RC
STATED ODDS 1:232 HOBBY
STATED PRINT RUN 50 SER.#'d SETS
50 Kris Bryant 20.00 50.00
150 Corey Seager 60.00 150.00

2016 Topps Chrome Green Refractors

*GREEN REF: 8X TO 20X BASIC
*GREEN SP REF: .3X TO .8X BASIC
*GREEN REF RC: 4X TO 10X BASIC RC
STATED ODDS 1:117 HOBBY
STATED SP ODDS 1:2337 HOBBY
STATED PRINT RUN 99 SER.#'d SETS
50A Kris Bryant 20.00 50.00
50B Brnt SP REF w/Fans 20.00 50.00
150 Corey Seager 50.00 120.00

2016 Topps Chrome Orange Refractors

*ORANGE REF: 12X TO 30X BASIC
*ORANGE REF RC: 6X TO 15X BASIC RC
STATED ODDS 1:149 HOBBY
STATED SP ODDS 1:9225 HOBBY
STATED PRINT RUN 25 SER.#'d SETS
50A Kris Bryant 25.00 60.00
50B Brnt SP REF w/Fans 25.00 60.00
150 Corey Seager 75.00 200.00

2016 Topps Chrome Pink Refractors
NK REF: 2X TO 5X BASIC
NK REF RC: 1X TO 2.5X BASIC RC
) Corey Seager 12.00 30.00

2016 Topps Chrome Prism Refractors
RISM REF: 1.5X TO 4X BASIC
RISM REF RC: .75X TO 2X BASIC RC
ATED ODDS 1:6 HOBBY
0 Corey Seager 10.00 25.00

2016 Topps Chrome Purple Refractors
URPLE REF: 4X TO 10X BASIC
URPLE REF RC: 2X TO 5X BASIC RC
ATED ODDS 1:43 HOBBY
ATED PRINT RUN 275 SER.#'d SETS
0 Corey Seager 25.00 60.00

2016 Topps Chrome Refractors
REF: 1.2X TO 3X BASIC
REF RC: .6X TO 1.5X BASIC RC
TATED ODDS 1:3 HOBBY
50 Corey Seager 8.00 20.00

2016 Topps Chrome Sepia Refractors
SEPIA REF: 2.5X TO 6X BASIC
SEPIA REF RC: 1.2X TO 3X BASIC RC
50 Corey Seager 15.00 40.00

2016 Topps Chrome Dual Autographs
TATED ODDS 1:8769 HOBBY
TATED PRINT RUN 25 SER.#'d SETS
RINTING PLATE ODDS 1:54,636 HOBBY
LATE PRINT RUN 1 SET PER COLOR
O PLATE PRICING DUE TO SCARCITY
XCHANGE DEADLINE 7/31/2018
DABS Bryant/Schwarber 200.00 400.00
DACL Correa/Lindor 60.00 150.00
DADM Darvish/Maeda 150.00 300.00
DAGE Gordon/Escobar 25.00 60.00
DAHT Harper/Trout 600.00 900.00
DAIG Ichiro/Gordon 150.00 300.00
DASG Gray/Severino 15.00 40.00
DASR Rendon/Scherzer 60.00 150.00
DAST Seager/Turner 250.00 400.00
DAWC Wright/Conforto 40.00 100.00

2016 Topps Chrome First Pitch
COMPLETE SET (20) 20.00 50.00
STATED ODDS 1:24 HOBBY
FPC1 Don Cherry 1.00 2.50
FPC2 Mo'ne Davis 1.00 2.50
FPC3 Evelyn Jones 1.00 2.50
FPC4 Bree Morse 1.00 2.50
FPC5 Jordan Spieth 2.00 5.00
FPC6 Kristaps Porzingis 1.00 2.50
FPC7 James Taylor 1.00 2.50
FPC8 LeVar Burton 1.00 2.50
FPC9 Tony Hawk 1.00 2.50
FPC10 Johnny Knoxville 1.00 2.50
FPC11 Steve Aoki 1.00 2.50
FPC12 Tim McGraw 1.00 2.50
FPC13 Jimmy Kimmel 1.00 2.50
FPC14 Billy Joe Armstrong 1.00 2.50
FPC15 Nina Agdal 1.00 2.50
FPC16 Jim Harbaugh 1.25 3.00
FPC17 Miguel Cotto 1.00 2.50
FPC18 Tom Watson 1.00 2.50
FPC19 George H. W. Bush 1.00 2.50
FPC20 Kendrick Lamar 1.00 2.50

2016 Topps Chrome First Pitch Green Refractors
*GREEN: 1.2X TO 3X BASIC
RANDOM INSERTS IN PACKS
STATED PRINT RUN 99 SER.#'d SETS
FPC5 Jordan Spieth 40.00 100.00

2016 Topps Chrome First Pitch Orange Refractors
*ORANGE: 1.5X TO 4X BASIC
STATED ODDS 1:4643 HOBBY
STATED PRINT RUN 25 SER.#'d SETS
FPC5 Jordan Spieth 125.00 300.00

2016 Topps Chrome Future Stars
STATED ODDS 1:8 HOBBY
*GREEN/99: 2X TO 5X BASIC
*ORANGE/25: 5X TO 12X BASIC
FS1 Kris Bryant .75 2.00
FS2 Francisco Lindor .60 1.50
FS3 Joc Pederson .50 1.25
FS4 Jose Abreu .60 1.50
FS5 Jacob deGrom .60 1.50
FS6 Dellin Betances .50 1.25
FS7 Addison Russell .60 1.50
FS8 Joe Panik .50 1.25
FS9 Roberto Osuna .40 1.00
FS10 Noah Syndergaard .50 1.25
FS11 Byron Buxton .50 1.25
FS12 Steven Matz .50 1.25
FS13 Blake Swihart .50 1.25
FS14 Mookie Betts 1.00 2.50
FS15 Maikel Franco .50 1.25
FS16 Kevin Kiermaier .50 1.25
FS17 George Springer .50 1.25
FS18 Jorge Soler .60 1.50
FS19 Jung Ho Kang .40 1.00
FS20 Carlos Correa .60 1.50

2016 Topps Chrome MLB Debut Autographs
STATED ODDS 1:4305 HOBBY
STATED PRINT RUN 50 SER.#'d SETS
PRINTING PLATE ODDS 1:32,285 HOBBY
PLATE PRINT RUN 1 SET PER COLOR
NO PLATE PRICING DUE TO SCARCITY
EXCHANGE DEADLINE 7/31/2018
MLBAAGO Adrian Gonzalez 10.00 25.00
MLBAAJ Adam Jones 12.00 30.00
MLBAALG Alex Gordon 12.00 30.00
MLBACK Clayton Kershaw 30.00 80.00
MLBACS Chris Sale 15.00 40.00
MLBADG Dee Gordon 8.00 20.00
MLBADK Dallas Keuchel 6.00 15.00
MLBADP Dustin Pedroia 20.00 50.00
MLBAFF Freddie Freeman 15.00 40.00
MLBAFL Francisco Lindor 30.00 80.00
MLBAJA Jose Altuve 50.00 120.00
MLBAJS James Shields 5.00 12.00
MLBAKB Kris Bryant 100.00 250.00
MLBASM Starling Marte 10.00 25.00
MLBAYG Yasmani Grandal 5.00 12.00

2016 Topps Chrome MLB Debut Autographs Orange Refractors
*ORANGE: .5X TO 1.2X BASIC
STATED ODDS 1:5185 HOBBY
STATED PRINT RUN 25 SER.#'d SETS
EXCHANGE DEADLINE 7/31/2018
MLBABH Bryce Harper 150.00 300.00
MLBACC Carlos Correa 100.00 250.00
MLBADW David Wright 15.00 40.00
MLBAMT Mike Trout

2016 Topps Chrome Perspectives
COMPLETE SET (20) 6.00 15.00
STATED ODDS 1:6 HOBBY
*GREEN/99: 3X TO 8X BASIC
*ORANGE/25: 6X TO 15X BASIC
PC1 Andrew McCutchen .50 1.25
PC2 Adrian Gonzalez .40 1.00
PC3 Robinson Cano .40 1.00
PC4 Bryce Harper .75 2.00
PC5 Yasiel Puig .50 1.25
PC6 Troy Tulowitzki .50 1.25
PC7 Kris Bryant .60 1.50
PC8 David Ortiz .50 1.25
PC9 Ichiro .60 1.50
PC10 Byron Buxton .40 1.00
PC11 Yadier Molina .50 1.25
PC12 Evan Longoria .40 1.00
PC13 Mark Teixeira .40 1.00
PC14 Billy Hamilton .40 1.00
PC15 Ryan Braun .40 1.00
PC16 Mike Trout 2.50 6.00
PC17 Miguel Sano .50 1.25
PC18 Corey Seager 2.50 6.00
PC19 Michael Conforto .40 1.00
PC20 Kyle Schwarber 1.00 2.50

2016 Topps Chrome Rookie Autographs
STATED ODDS 1:19 HOBBY
PRINTING PLATE ODDS 1:8879 HOBBY
PLATE PRINT RUN 1 SET PER COLOR
NO PLATE PRICING DUE TO SCARCITY
EXCHANGE DEADLINE 7/31/2018
RAAB Aaron Blair 2.50 6.00
RAAH Alen Hanson 3.00 8.00
RAAJR A.J. Reed 4.00 10.00
RAALA Albert Almora 15.00 40.00
RAAN Aaron Nola 12.00 30.00
RABD Brandon Drury 4.00 10.00
RARF Brian Ellington 2.50 6.00
RABJ Brian Johnson 2.50 6.00
RABP Byung-Ho Park 3.00 8.00
RABS Blake Snell 15.00 40.00
RACE Carl Edwards Jr. 3.00 8.00
RACR Colin Rea 2.50 6.00
RACS Corey Seager 60.00 150.00
RADA Dariel Alvarez 2.50 6.00
RADL Dae-Ho Lee 10.00 25.00
RADS Darnell Sweeney 2.50 6.00
RAFM Frankie Montas 3.00 8.00
RAGB Greg Bird 3.00 8.00
RAHOL Hector Olivera 3.00 8.00
RAHOW Henry Owens 3.00 8.00
RAJE Jerad Eickhoff 4.00 10.00
RAJG Jon Gray 2.50 6.00
RAJHA Jeremy Hazelbaker 3.00 8.00
RAJOS Jose Berrios 8.00 20.00
RAJPA James Pazos 3.00 8.00
RAJPE Jose Peraza 4.00 10.00
RAJR Joey Rickard 2.50 6.00
RAJTA Jameson Taillon 5.00 12.00
RAJU Julio Urias 10.00 25.00
RAKC Kaleb Cowart 2.50 6.00
RAKM Ketel Marte 8.00 20.00
RAKMA Kenta Maeda 8.00 20.00
RAKSA Keyvius Sampson 2.50 6.00
RAKSC Kyle Schwarber 20.00 50.00
RAKT Kelby Tomlinson 2.50 6.00
RAKW Kyle Waldrop 3.00 8.00
RALG Lucas Giolito 5.00 12.00
RALJ Luke Jackson 2.50 6.00
RALS Luis Severino 12.00 30.00
RAMAL Miguel Almonte 2.50 6.00
RAMAR Matt Reynolds 2.50 6.00
RAMC Michael Conforto 15.00 40.00
RAMD Matt Duffy 2.50 6.00
RAMIR Michael Reed 2.50 6.00
RAMK Max Kepler 12.00 30.00
RAMS Miguel Sano 4.00 10.00
RAMSM Mallex Smith 2.50 6.00
RAMW Mac Williamson 2.50 6.00
RANM Nomar Mazara 6.00 15.00
RAPO Peter O'Brien 2.50 6.00
RARD Ryan Dull 2.50 6.00
RARM Raul Mondesi 10.00 25.00
RAROS Robert Stephenson 2.50 6.00
RARR Rob Refsnyder 3.00 8.00
RARS Ross Stripling 2.50 6.00
RARSH Richie Shaffer 2.50 6.00
RASOB Socrates Brito 2.50 6.00
RASP Stephen Piscotty 4.00 10.00
RATA Tim Anderson 40.00 100.00
RATB Trevor Brown 3.00 8.00
RATD Tyler Duffey 2.50 6.00
RATJ Travis Jankowski 2.50 6.00
RATM Tom Murphy 2.50 6.00
RATN Tyler Naquin 3.00 8.00
RATS Trevor Story 30.00 80.00
RATTH Trayce Thompson 4.00 10.00
RATTU Trea Turner 12.00 30.00
RATW Tyler White 2.50 6.00
RATZ Tony Zych 2.50 6.00
RAZG Zack Godley 2.50 6.00
RAZL Zach Lee 2.50 6.00

2016 Topps Chrome Rookie Autographs Blue Refractors
*BLUE REF: .6X TO 1.5X BASIC
STATED ODDS 1:237 HOBBY
STATED PRINT RUN 150 SER.#'d SETS
EXCHANGE DEADLINE 7/31/2018

2016 Topps Chrome Rookie Autographs Gold Refractors
*GOLD REF: 1.5X TO 4X BASIC
STATED ODDS 1:709 HOBBY
STATED PRINT RUN 50 SER.#'d SETS
EXCHANGE DEADLINE 7/31/2018

2016 Topps Chrome Rookie Autographs Green Refractors
*GREEN REF: .75X TO 2X BASIC
RANDOM INSERTS IN PACKS
STATED PRINT RUN 99 SER.#'d SETS
EXCHANGE DEADLINE 7/31/2018

2016 Topps Chrome Rookie Autographs Purple Refractors
*PURPLE REF: .6X TO 1.5X BASIC
STATED ODDS 1:142 HOBBY
STATED PRINT RUN 250 SER.#'d SETS
EXCHANGE DEADLINE 7/31/2018

2016 Topps Chrome Rookie Autographs Refractors
*REF: .5X TO 1.2X BASIC
STATED ODDS 1:82 HOBBY
STATED PRINT RUN 499 SER.#'d SETS
EXCHANGE DEADLINE 7/31/2018

2016 Topps Chrome ROY Chronicles
STATED ODDS 1:288 HOBBY
*GREEN/99: .6X TO 1.5X BASIC
*ORANGE/25: 1.2X TO 3X BASIC
ROYI Ichiro 3.00 8.00
ROYBH Bryce Harper 4.00 10.00
ROYBP Buster Posey 3.00 8.00
ROYCC Carlos Correa 2.50 6.00
ROYDP Dustin Pedroia 2.50 6.00
ROYEL Evan Longoria 2.00 5.00
ROYHR Hanley Ramirez 2.00 5.00
ROYJA Jose Abreu 2.50 6.00
ROYJD Jacob deGrom 2.50 6.00
ROYJF Jose Fernandez 2.50 6.00
ROYJV Justin Verlander 2.50 6.00
ROYKB Kris Bryant 12.00 30.00
ROYMT Mike Trout 12.00 30.00
ROYRB Ryan Braun 2.00 5.00
ROYWM Wil Myers 1.50 4.00

2016 Topps Chrome ROY Chronicles Autographs
STATED ODDS 1:11,098 HOBBY
STATED PRINT RUN 50 SER.#'d SETS
PRINTING PLATE ODDS 1:59,189 HOBBY
PLATE PRINT RUN 1 SET PER COLOR
NO PLATE PRICING DUE TO SCARCITY
EXCHANGE DEADLINE 7/31/2018
ROYADP Dustin Pedroia 20.00 50.00
ROYAHR Hanley Ramirez 6.00 15.00
ROYAJD Jacob deGrom 20.00 50.00
ROYAKB Kris Bryant 200.00 400.00
ROYARB Ryan Braun 12.00 30.00
ROYAWM Wil Myers 5.00 12.00

2016 Topps Chrome ROY Chronicles Autographs Orange Refractors
*ORANGE: .5X TO 1.2X BASIC
STATED ODDS 1:9865 HOBBY
STATED PRINT RUN 25 SER.#'d SETS
EXCHANGE DEADLINE 7/31/2018
ROYAI Ichiro 300.00 500.00
ROYABH Bryce Harper 150.00 300.00
ROYABP Buster Posey
ROYACC Carlos Correa 100.00 250.00
ROYAEL Evan Longoria
ROYAMT Mike Trout 150.00 400.00

2016 Topps Chrome Team Logo Autographs
STATED ODDS 1:5301 HOBBY
PRINT RUNS B/WN 7-99 COPIES PER
NO PRICING ON QTY 7
PRINTING PLATE ODDS 1:41,780 HOBBY
PLATE PRINT RUN 1 SET PER COLOR
NO PLATE PRICING DUE TO SCARCITY
EXCHANGE DEADLINE 7/31/2018
TLACS Chris Sale/75 6.00 15.00
TLADW David Wright/30 20.00 50.00
TLAFF Freddie Freeman/30 20.00 50.00
TLAFL Francisco Lindor/99 20.00 50.00
TLAJF Jose Fernandez/27 30.00 80.00
TLAKB Kris Bryant/30 200.00 400.00
TLASG Sonny Gray/99 5.00 12.00

2016 Topps Chrome Team Logo Autographs Orange Refractors
*ORANGE: .5X TO 1.2X BASIC
STATED ODDS 1:7981 HOBBY
STATED PRINT RUN 25 SER.#'d SETS
EXCHANGE DEADLINE 7/31/2018
TLABH Bryce Harper 150.00 300.00
TLACC Carlos Correa 100.00 250.00
TLAEL Evan Longoria 20.00 50.00
TLAJB Jose Bautista
TLAMT Mike Trout 150.00 400.00

2016 Topps Chrome Youth Impact
COMPLETE SET (20) 6.00 15.00
STATED ODDS 1:12 HOBBY
*GREEN/99: 2X TO 5X BASIC
*ORANGE/25: 5X TO 12X BASIC
YI1 Corey Seager 3.00 8.00
YI2 Byung-Ho Park .50 1.25
YI3 Luis Severino .50 1.25
YI4 Michael Conforto .50 1.25
YI5 Jon Gray .40 1.00
YI6 Miguel Sano .60 1.50
YI7 Kyle Schwarber 1.25 3.00
YI8 Trea Turner 1.25 3.00
YI9 Henry Owens .50 1.25
YI10 Trevor Story 1.50 4.00
YI11 Robert Stephenson .40 1.00
YI12 Aaron Nola .75 2.00
YI13 Nomar Mazara .60 1.50
YI14 Stephen Piscotty .60 1.50
YI15 Carl Edwards Jr. .50 1.25
YI16 Raul Mondesi .50 1.25
YI17 Blake Snell .50 1.25
YI18 Aaron Blair .40 1.00
YI19 Jose Berrios .50 1.25
YI20 Kenta Maeda .75 2.00

2016 Topps Chrome Youth Impact Autographs
STATED ODDS 1:977 HOBBY
PRINT RUNS B/WN 75-150 COPIES PER
PRINTING PLATE ODDS 1:35,513 HOBBY
PLATE PRINT RUN 1 SET PER COLOR
NO PLATE PRICING DUE TO SCARCITY
EXCHANGE DEADLINE 7/31/2018
YIAAN Aaron Nola/150 6.00 15.00
YIACE Carl Edwards Jr./150 10.00 25.00
YIACS Corey Seager/75
YIAFM Frankie Montas/150 5.00 12.00
YIAGB Greg Bird/150 5.00 12.00
YIAHOL Hector Olivera/150 5.00 12.00
YIAHOW Henry Owens/75 5.00 12.00
YIAJG Jon Gray/75 4.00 10.00
YIAJP Jose Peraza/150 5.00 12.00
YIAKM Ketel Marte/150 8.00 20.00
YIAKS Kyle Schwarber/75 30.00 80.00
YIALS Luis Severino/75 10.00 25.00
YIAMC Michael Conforto/75 15.00 40.00
YIAMS Miguel Sano/75 6.00 15.00
YIARM Raul Mondesi/150 5.00 12.00
YIASP Stephen Piscotty/150 12.00 30.00
YIATTH Trayce Thompson/150 6.00 15.00
YIATTU Trea Turner/75 30.00 80.00

2016 Topps Chrome Youth Impact Autographs Orange Refractors
*ORANGE: .75X TO 2X BASE p/r 150
*ORANGE: .5X TO 1.2X BASE p/r 75
STATED ODDS 1:5870 HOBBY
STATED PRINT RUN 25 SER.#'d SETS
EXCHANGE DEADLINE 7/31/2018

2017 Topps Chrome
COMP.SET w/o SPs (200) 25.00 60.00
SP ODDS 1:143 HOBBY
ALL VARIATIONS ARE REFRACTORS
PRINTING PLATE ODDS 1:3779 HOBBY
PLATE PRINT RUN 1 SET PER COLOR
BLACK-CYAN-MAGENTA-YELLOW ISSUED
NO PLATE PRICING DUE TO SCARCITY
1A Kris Bryant .40 1.00
1B Brynt SP REF No hat 5.00 12.00
2 JaCoby Jones RC .50 1.25
3 Matt Holliday .30 .75
4 Michael Fulmer .20 .50
5 Corey Kluber .25 .60
6 Ben Zobrist .25 .60
7 Jake Thompson RC .40 1.00
8A Dansby Swanson RC 1.00 2.50
8B Swnsn SP REF No hlmt 6.00 15.00
9A Alex Bregman RC 1.50 4.00
9B Brgmn SP REF Bttng cage 10.00 25.00
10 Aroldis Chapman .30 .75
11 Zack Greinke .25 .60
12 Carson Fulmer RC .40 1.00
13 Johnny Cueto .25 .60
14 Kenta Maeda .25 .60
15 Jorge Alfaro RC .50 1.25
16 Matt Carpenter .30 .75
17 Kyle Schwarber .30 .75
18A Hunter Renfroe RC .50 1.25
18B Rnfre SP REF Fist bump 3.00 8.00
19 Kyle Hendricks .30 .75
20 Felix Hernandez .25 .60
21A Yoenis Cespedes .30 .75
21B Cspds SP REF Hrzntl 4.00 10.00
22 Edwin Encarnacion .30 .75
23 Mark Trumbo .20 .50
24 Jordan Montgomery RC .60 1.50
25A Clayton Kershaw .60 1.50
25B Krshw SP REF No hat 8.00 20.00
26 Ryan Braun .25 .60
27 Ian Desmond .20 .50
28 Brett Gardner .25 .60
29 Mitch Haniger RC .60 1.50
30 Jose Quintana .20 .50
31 Ender Inciarte .30 .75
32 Yadier Molina .30 .75
33 Bartolo Colon .20 .50
34 Andrew Toles RC .40 1.00
35 Starling Marte .25 .60
36 Addison Russell .30 .75
37 Jose Altuve .25 .60
38 Brandon Drury .20 .50
39 Marcus Stroman .25 .60
40 Manny Machado .30 .75
41 Dee Gordon .20 .50
42 German Marquez RC .60 1.50
43 Robert Gsellman RC .40 1.00
44 Aaron Sanchez .25 .60
45 Xander Bogaerts .30 .75
46 Carlos Martinez .25 .60
47A Trey Mancini RC .75 2.00
47B Mncni SP REF Wht jrsy 5.00 12.00
48A Bryce Harper .50 1.25
48B Harper SP REF Red jrsy 10.00 25.00
49 Max Kepler .25 .60
50 Corey Seager .30 .75
51 Braden Shipley RC .40 1.00
52 A.J. Pollock .20 .50
53 Jake Arrieta .25 .60
54 Joe Mauer .25 .60
55 Willson Contreras .30 .75
56 Stephen Piscotty .25 .60
57 Andrew McCutchen .30 .75
58 Chris Owings .20 .50
59 Kyle Freeland RC .50 1.25
60 Julio Urias .30 .75
61 Luke Weaver RC .50 1.25
62 Gregory Polanco .25 .60
63 J.D. Martinez .30 .75
64 Jackie Bradley Jr. .30 .75
65 Albert Pujols .40 1.00
66 Alex Reyes RC .50 1.25
67 Ryon Healy RC .50 1.25
68 Nick Castellanos .30 .75
69 Starlin Castro .20 .50
70 Jeff Hoffman RC .40 1.00
71 Anthony Rendon .30 .75
72 Christian Yelich .40 1.00
73A Orlando Arcia RC .60 1.50
73B Arcia SP REF Thrwng 4.00 10.00
74 Jesse Winker RC .40 1.00
75A Yoan Moncada RC 1.25 3.00
75B Mncda SP REF Bag 10.00 25.00
76 Carlos Gonzalez .25 .60
77 Jose De Leon RC .40 1.00
78 Tyler Austin RC .60 1.50
79 Cody Bellinger RC 6.00 15.00
80 Jharel Cotton RC .40 1.00
81 Cole Hamels .25 .60
82 Nomar Mazara .20 .50
83 Amir Garrett RC .40 1.00
84 Rick Porcello .25 .60
85 Todd Frazier .25 .60
86 Dan Vogelbach RC .60 1.50
87 Dustin Pedroia .30 .75
88 Aledmys Diaz .25 .60
89 Rob Zastryzny RC .40 1.00
90 Robinson Cano .25 .60
91 Kenley Jansen .25 .60
92 Trevor Story .30 .75
93A Justin Verlander .30 .75
93B Vrlndr SP REF Running 4.00 10.00
94 Joey Votto .30 .75
95 Jameson Taillon .25 .60
96 Gavin Cecchini RC .40 1.00
97 Matt Strahm RC .40 1.00
98 Matt Olson RC .60 1.50
99 Renato Nunez RC .75 2.00
100A Andrew Benintendi RC 1.25 3.00
100B Bnntndi SP REF Warm up 20.00 50.00
101 Hunter Dozier RC .40 1.00
102A Nolan Arenado .40 1.00
102B Arndo SP REF Prple jrsy 5.00 12.00
103A Noah Syndergaard .25 .60
103B Syndrgrd SP REF ATV 3.00 8.00
104 Lucas Giolito .25 .60
105 Adrian Gonzalez .25 .60
106 Mark Melancon .20 .50
107 Yu Darvish .30 .75
108 Kevin Kiermaier .25 .60
109 Jay Bruce .25 .60
110 Steven Matz .25 .60
111 Brandon Crawford .25 .60
112A Carlos Correa .30 .75
112B Crra SP REF Signing 4.00 10.00
113 Adam Wainwright .25 .60
114 Javier Baez .40 1.00
115 Jason Heyward .25 .60
116 Teoscar Hernandez RC 1.25 3.00
117 Odubel Herrera .25 .60
118 Kyle Seager .20 .50
119 Maikel Franco .25 .60
120 Joe Musgrove RC .40 1.00
121 Carlos Santana .25 .60
122 Gary Sanchez .30 .75
123 Wil Myers .20 .50
124 Yulieski Gurriel RC .60 1.50
125 Ian Kinsler .25 .60
126A Francisco Lindor .30 .75
126B Lndr SP REF w/Trophies 4.00 10.00
127 Matt Kemp .25 .60
128 Hunter Pence .25 .60
129 George Springer .25 .60
130 Adrian Beltre .30 .75
131 Lorenzo Cain .20 .50
132 Miguel Cabrera .30 .75
133 Nelson Cruz .30 .75
134 Paul Goldschmidt .30 .75
135 Roman Quinn RC .40 1.00
136 Gerrit Cole .30 .75
137 Antonio Senzatela RC .40 1.00
138 Tyler Naquin .20 .50
139 Seth Lugo RC .40 1.00
140 Joc Pederson .25 .60
141 Chad Pinder RC .40 1.00
142 Jon Lester .25 .60
143 Dellin Betances .25 .60
144 Billy Hamilton .25 .60
145A Buster Posey .40 1.00
145B Posey SP REF In gear 8.00 20.00
146 Freddie Freeman .40 1.00
147 David Price .25 .60
148 Josh Donaldson .25 .60
149A Khris Davis .30 .75
149B Davis SP REF Yllw jrsy 4.00 10.00
150 David Ortiz .30 .75
151 Rougned Odor .25 .60
152 Zach Britton .25 .60
153 Eric Hosmer .25 .60
154 Justin Upton .25 .60
155A Giancarlo Stanton .30 .75
155B Stntn SP REF Running 4.00 10.00
156 Ivan Nova .25 .60
157 Masahiro Tanaka .25 .60
158 Josh Bell RC 1.00 2.50
159A Max Scherzer .30 .75
159B Schrzr SP REF Dugout 4.00 10.00
160 Chris Sale .30 .75
161 Evan Longoria .25 .60
162 Salvador Perez .25 .60
163 Reynaldo Lopez RC .40 1.00
164 Jason Kipnis .25 .60
165 Michael Brantley .25 .60
166 Melky Cabrera .20 .50
167 Jake Odorizzi .20 .50
168 Jose Abreu .30 .75
169A Aaron Judge RC 8.00 20.00
169B Judge SP REF Running 50.00 120.00
170 Adam Jones .25 .60
171 Jose Bautista .25 .60
172 Yasiel Puig .30 .75
173A Anthony Rizzo .50 1.25
173B Rizzo SP REF No helmey 6.00 15.00
174 Adam Duvall .30 .75
175 Andrew Miller .25 .60
176 Brandon Belt .25 .60
177 Chris Archer .20 .50
178 DJ LeMahieu .30 .75
179 Dexter Fowler .25 .60
180 Christian Arroyo RC .60 1.50
181 Justin Bour .25 .60
182 Chris Davis .20 .50
183 Eugenio Suarez .25 .60
184 Jacob deGrom .30 .75
185 Eduardo Rodriguez .20 .50
186 David Dahl RC .50 1.25
187 Ryan Schimpf .20 .50
188 Craig Kimbrel .25 .60
189 Tyler Glasnow RC .50 1.25
190 Brian Dozier .30 .75
191 J.T. Realmuto .30 .75
192 Joe Jimenez RC .40 1.00
193 Brad Ziegler .20 .50
194A Trea Turner .25 .60
194B Trnr SP REF Spring hat 3.00 8.00
195 Edwin Diaz .25 .60
196 Pat Neshek .20 .50
197 Manny Margot RC .40 1.00
198 Troy Tulowitzki .30 .75
199A Mookie Betts .50 1.25
199B Betts SP REF Pointing 6.00 15.00
200A Mike Trout 1.50 4.00
200B Trout SP REF Podium 20.00 50.00

2017 Topps Chrome Blue Refractors
*BLUE REF: 5X TO 12X BASIC
*BLUE REF RC: 2.5X TO 6X BASIC
STATED ODDS 1:101 HOBBY
STATED PRINT RUN 150 SER.#'d SETS
75 Yoan Moncada 12.00 30.00
100 Andrew Benintendi 30.00 80.00

2017 Topps Chrome Blue Wave Refractors
*BLUE WAVE REF: 6X TO 15X BASIC
*BLUE WAVE REF RC: 3X TO 8X BASIC
STATED ODDS 1:135 HOBBY
STATED PRINT RUN 75 SER.#'d SETS
75 Yoan Moncada 25.00 60.00
100 Andrew Benintendi 40.00 100.00
200 Mike Trout 20.00 50.00

2017 Topps Chrome Gold Refractors
*GOLD REF: 8X TO 20X BASIC
*GOLD REF RC: 4X TO 10X BASIC RC
STATED ODDS 1:303 HOBBY
STATED PRINT RUN 50 SER.#'d SETS
48 Bryce Harper 25.00 60.00
75 Yoan Moncada 30.00 80.00
100 Andrew Benintendi 50.00 120.00
169 Aaron Judge 125.00 300.00
200 Mike Trout 40.00 100.00

2017 Topps Chrome Gold Wave Refractors
*GOLD WAVE REF: 8X TO 20X BASIC
*GOLD WAVE REF RC: 4X TO 10X BASIC RC
STATED ODDS 1:202 HOBBY
STATED PRINT RUN 50 SER.#'d SETS
48 Bryce Harper 25.00 60.00
75 Yoan Moncada 30.00 80.00
100 Andrew Benintendi 50.00 120.00
169 Aaron Judge 125.00 300.00
200 Mike Trout 40.00 100.00

2017 Topps Chrome Green Refractors
*GREEN REF: 6X TO 15X BASIC
*GREEN SP REF: .5X TO 1.2X BASIC
*GREEN REF RC: 3X TO 8X BASIC RC
STATED ODDS 1:153 HOBBY
STATED SP ODDS 1:1221 HOBBY
STATED PRINT RUN 99 SER.#'d SETS
75A Yoan Moncada 25.00 60.00
75B Mncda SP REF Bag 25.00 60.00
100A Andrew Benintendi 40.00 100.00
100B Bnntndi SP REF Warm up 40.00 100.00
169B Judge SP REF Running 60.00 150.00
200A Mike Trout 20.00 50.00
200B Trout SP REF Podium 20.00 50.00

2017 Topps Chrome Negative Refractors
*SEPIA REF: 3X TO 8X BASIC
*SEPIA REF RC: 1.5X TO 4X BASIC RC
STATED ODDS 1:38 HOBBY
75 Yoan Moncada 8.00 20.00
100 Andrew Benintendi 20.00 50.00
200 Mike Trout 10.00 25.00

2017 Topps Chrome Orange Refractors
*ORANGE REF: 10X TO 25X BASIC
*ORANGE SP REF: .75X TO 2X BASIC
*ORANGE REF RC: 5X TO 12X BASIC RC
STATED ODDS 1:190 HOBBY
STATED SP ODDS 1:4825 HOBBY
STATED PRINT RUN 25 SER.#'d SETS
48A Bryce Harper 30.00 80.00
48B Harper SP REF Red jrsy 20.00 50.00
75A Yoan Moncada 40.00 100.00
75B Mncda SP REF Bag 40.00 100.00
100A Andrew Benintendi 60.00 150.00
100B Bnntndi SP REF Warm up 60.00 150.00
169A Aaron Judge 150.00 400.00
169B Judge SP REF Running 100.00 250.00
200A Mike Trout 60.00 150.00
200B Trout SP REF Podium 60.00 150.00

2017 Topps Chrome Pink Refractors
*PINK REF: 1.5X TO 4X BASIC
*PINK REF RC: .75X TO 2X BASIC RC
THREE PER RETAIL VALUE BOX
75 Yoan Moncada 4.00 10.00
100 Andrew Benintendi 10.00 25.00

2017 Topps Chrome Prism Refractors
*PRISM REF:1.5X TO 4X BASIC
*PRISM REF RC:.75X TO 2X BASIC RC
STATED ODDS 1:6 HOBBY
75 Yoan Moncada 4.00 10.00
100 Andrew Benintendi 10.00 25.00

2017 Topps Chrome Purple Refractors
*PURPLE REF: 2.5X TO 6X BASIC
*PURPLE REF RC: 1.2X TO 3X BASIC RC
STATED ODDS 1:51 HOBBY
STATED PRINT RUN 299 SER.#'d SETS
75 Yoan Moncada 6.00 15.00
100 Andrew Benintendi 15.00 40.00
200 Mike Trout 8.00 20.00

2017 Topps Chrome Refractors
*REF:1.2X TO 3X BASIC
*REF RC:.6X TO 1.5X BASIC RC
STATED ODDS 1:3 HOBBY
100 Andrew Benintendi 8.00 20.00

2017 Topps Chrome Sepia Refractors
*SEPIA REF: 1.5X TO 4X BASIC
*SEPIA REF RC: .75X TO 2X BASIC RC
FIVE PER RETAIL BLASTER
75 Yoan Moncada 4.00 10.00
100 Andrew Benintendi 10.00 25.00

2017 Topps Chrome X-Fractors
*XFRACTOR: 1.5X TO 4X BASIC
*XFRACTOR RC: .75X TO 2X BASIC RC
TEN PER WALMART MEGA BOX
75 Yoan Moncada 4.00 10.00
100 Andrew Benintendi 10.00 25.00

2017 Topps Chrome '87 Topps
COMPLETE SET (25) 20.00 50.00
STATED ODDS 1:6 HOBBY
87T1 Kris Bryant .75 2.00
87T2 Dansby Swanson 1.00 2.50
87T3 Orlando Arcia .60 1.50
87T4 Manny Machado .60 1.50
87T5 Alex Bregman 1.50 4.00
87T6 Buster Posey .75 2.00
87T7 Corey Seager .60 1.50
87T8 Aaron Judge 6.00 15.00
87T9 Noah Syndergaard .50 1.25
87T10 Carlos Correa .60 1.50
87T11 Francisco Lindor .60 1.50
87T12 George Springer .50 1.25
87T13 Luke Weaver .50 1.25
87T14 Masahiro Tanaka .50 1.25

87T15 Nolan Arenado .75 2.00
87T16 Stephen Piscotty .50 1.25
87T17 Addison Russell .60 1.50
87T18 Jake Arrieta .50 1.25
87T19 Danny Duffy .40 1.00
87T20 Yoan Moncada 1.25 3.00
87T21 Jacob deGrom .60 1.50
87T22 Anthony Rizzo 1.00 2.50
87T23 Yulieski Gurriel .60 1.50
87T24 David Dahl .50 1.25
87T25 Andrew Benintendi 1.25 3.00

2017 Topps Chrome '87 Topps Orange Refractors

*ORANGE: 6X TO 15X BASIC
STATED ODDS 1:4825 HOBBY
STATED PRINT RUN 25 SER.#'d SETS
87T8 Aaron Judge 50.00 120.00

2017 Topps Chrome '87 Topps Autographs

STATED ODDS 1:2817 HOBBY
STATED PRINT RUN 50 SER.#'d SETS
EXCHANGE DEADLINE 6/30/2019
*ORANGE/25: .6X TO 1.5X BASIC
PRINTING PLATE ODDS 1:34,684 HOBBY
PLATE PRINT RUN 1 SET PER COLOR
BLACK-CYAN-MAGENTA-YELLOW ISSUED
NO PLATE PRICING DUE TO SCARCITY
87TAAB Alex Bregman 50.00 120.00
87TAABE Andrew Benintendi 75.00 200.00
87TAAJ Aaron Judge 250.00 500.00
87TAAR Anthony Rizzo 30.00 80.00
87TAARU Addison Russell 15.00 40.00
87TABP Buster Posey
87TACC Carlos Correa
87TADD David Dahl 12.00 30.00
87TADDU Danny Duffy 10.00 25.00
87TAFL Francisco Lindor EXCH 30.00 80.00
87TAGS George Springer 12.00 30.00
87TAJD Jacob deGrom
87TAKB Kris Bryant
87TAMT Masahiro Tanaka
87TANS Noah Syndergaard 25.00 60.00
87TAOA Orlando Arcia 15.00 40.00
87TASP Stephen Piscotty 8.00 20.00
87TAYG Yulieski Gurriel
87TAYM Yoan Moncada

2017 Topps Chrome Bowman Then and Now

COMPLETE SET (20) 20.00 50.00
STATED ODDS 1:24 HOBBY
*GREEN/99: 1.5X TO 4X BASIC
*ORANGE/25: 3X TO 8X BASIC
BTN1 Kris Bryant 1.00 2.50
BTN3 Nomar Mazara .50 1.25
BTN4 Trevor Story .75 2.00
BTN5 Ryan Braun .60 1.50
BTN6 Jacob deGrom .75 2.00
BTN7 Noah Syndergaard .60 1.50
BTN8 Corey Seager .60 1.50
BTN9 Kyle Seager .50 1.25
BTN10 Bryce Harper 1.25 3.00
BTN11 Manny Machado .75 2.00
BTN12 Francisco Lindor .75 2.00
BTN13 Joe Panik .60 1.50
BTN14 Robinson Cano .60 1.50
BTN15 Jose Altuve .60 1.50
BTN16 Carlos Correa .75 2.00
BTN17 Buster Posey 1.00 2.50
BTN18 Nolan Arenado 1.00 2.50
BTN19 Matt Carpenter .75 2.00
BTN20 Mike Trout 4.00 10.00
BTN20 Addison Russell .75 2.00

2017 Topps Chrome Bowman Then and Now Autographs

STATED ODDS 1:3748 HOBBY
STATED PRINT RUN 50 SER.#'d SETS
EXCHANGE DEADLINE 6/30/2019
PRINTING PLATE ODDS 1:45,348 HOBBY
PLATE PRINT RUN 1 SET PER COLOR
BLACK-CYAN-MAGENTA-YELLOW ISSUED
NO PLATE PRICING DUE TO SCARCITY
BTNAAR Addison Russell 20.00 50.00
BTNABH Bryce Harper
BTNABP Buster Posey 50.00 120.00
BTNACC Carlos Correa 40.00 100.00
BTNACS Corey Seager 40.00 100.00
BTNAFL Francisco Lindor EXCH 30.00 80.00
BTNAJA Jose Altuve 25.00 60.00
BTNAJP Joe Panik 12.00 30.00
BTNAKB Kris Bryant 75.00 200.00
BTNAKS Kyle Seager 12.00 30.00
BTNAMC Matt Carpenter 8.00 20.00
BTNAMT Mike Trout
BTNANM Nomar Mazara 10.00 25.00
BTNANS Noah Syndergaard 20.00 50.00
BTNARB Ryan Braun 12.00 30.00
BTNATS Trevor Story 10.00 25.00

2017 Topps Chrome Bowman Then and Now Autographs Orange Refractors

*ORANGE: .5X TO 1.2X BASIC
STATED ODDS 1:7496 HOBBY
STATED PRINT RUN 25 SER.#'d SETS
EXCHANGE DEADLINE 6/30/2019
BTNAMT Mike Trout 350.00 700.00

2017 Topps Chrome Freshman Flash

COMPLETE SET (20) 15.00 40.00
STATED ODDS 1:12 HOBBY
*GREEN/99: 2X TO 5X BASIC
*ORANGE/25: 4X TO 10X BASIC
FF1 Yoan Moncada 1.25 3.00
FF2 Hunter Renfroe .50 1.25
FF3 Christian Arroyo .60 1.50
FF4 David Dahl .50 1.25
FF5 Cody Bellinger 6.00 15.00
FF6 Orlando Arcia .60 1.50
FF7 Jorge Alfaro .50 1.25
FF8 Tyler Austin .60 1.50
FF9 Jose De Leon .40 1.00
FF10 Alex Bregman 1.50 4.00
FF11 Aaron Judge 5.00 12.00
FF12 Tyler Glasnow .50 1.25
FF13 Jharel Cotton .40 1.00
FF14 Manny Margot .40 1.00
FF15 Carson Fulmer .40 1.00
FF16 Luke Weaver .50 1.25
FF17 Alex Reyes .50 1.25
FF18 Dansby Swanson 1.00 2.50
FF19 Yulieski Gurriel .60 1.50
FF20 Andrew Benintendi 1.25 3.00

2017 Topps Chrome Freshman Flash Autographs

STATED ODDS 1:1894 HOBBY
STATED PRINT RUN 99 SER.#'d SETS
EXCHANGE DEADLINE 6/30/2019
*ORANGE/25: .5X TO 1.2X BASIC
PRINTING PLATE ODDS 1:45,348 HOBBY
PLATE PRINT RUN 1 SET PER COLOR
BLACK-CYAN-MAGENTA-YELLOW ISSUED
NO PLATE PRICING DUE TO SCARCITY
FFAAB Alex Bregman 20.00 50.00
FFAABE Andrew Benintendi 40.00 100.00
FFAAJ Aaron Judge 125.00 300.00
FFAAR Alex Reyes 6.00 15.00
FFADD David Dahl 8.00 20.00
FFAHR Hunter Renfroe 8.00 20.00
FFAJA Jorge Alfaro 5.00 12.00
FFAJC Jharel Cotton 4.00 10.00
FFAJDL Jose De Leon 4.00 10.00
FFALW Luke Weaver 10.00 25.00
FFAMM Manny Margot 6.00 15.00
FFAOA Orlando Arcia 10.00 25.00
FFATA Tyler Austin 8.00 20.00
FFATG Tyler Glasnow 5.00 12.00
FFAYG Yulieski Gurriel 6.00 15.00
FFAYM Yoan Moncada 25.00 60.00

2017 Topps Chrome Future Stars

COMPLETE SET (15) 5.00 12.00
STATED ODDS 1:8 HOBBY
*GREEN/99: 2X TO 5X BASIC
*ORANGE/25: 4X TO 10X BASIC
FS1 Gary Sanchez .60 1.50
FS2 Willson Contreras .60 1.50
FS3 Steven Matz .50 1.25
FS4 Tyler Naquin .40 1.00
FS5 Noah Syndergaard .50 1.25
FS6 Michael Fulmer .40 1.00
FS7 Julio Urias .60 1.50
FS8 Nomar Mazara .40 1.00
FS9 Trea Turner .50 1.25
FS10 Francisco Lindor .60 1.50
FS11 Kenta Maeda .50 1.25
FS12 Addison Russell .60 1.50
FS13 Lucas Giolito .50 1.25
FS14 Trevor Story .60 1.50
FS15 Corey Seager .60 1.50

2017 Topps Chrome MLB Award Winners

STATED ODDS 1:288 HOBBY
*GREEN/99: .75X TO 2X BASIC
*ORANGE/25: 1.2X TO 3X BASIC
MAW1 Sandy Koufax 6.00 15.00
MAW2 Mike Piazza 4.00 10.00
MAW3 Mike Trout 12.00 30.00
MAW4 Carlos Correa 3.00 8.00
MAW5 Ichiro 4.00 10.00
MAW6 Clayton Kershaw 6.00 15.00
MAW7 Josh Donaldson 5.00 12.00
MAW8 Frank Thomas 5.00 12.00
MAW9 Ken Griffey Jr. 10.00 25.00
MAW10 Hank Aaron 10.00 25.00
MAW11 Bryce Harper 5.00 12.00
MAW12 Buster Posey 8.00 20.00
MAW13 Derek Jeter 10.00 25.00
MAW14 David Price 2.50 6.00
MAW15 Kris Bryant 4.00 10.00

2017 Topps Chrome MLB Award Winners Autographs

STATED ODDS 1:6573 HOBBY
PRINT RUNS B/WN 15-50 COPIES PER
NO PRICING ON QTY 15
EXCHANGE DEADLINE 6/30/2019
*ORANGE/25: .5X TO 1.2X BASIC
PRINTING PLATE ODDS 1:50,387 HOBBY
PLATE PRINT RUN 1 SET PER COLOR
BLACK-CYAN-MAGENTA-YELLOW ISSUED
NO PLATE PRICING DUE TO SCARCITY
MAWABH Bryce Harper/30 125.00 300.00
MAWACC Carlos Correa/40 30.00 80.00
MAWADP David Price/50 10.00 25.00
MAWAFT Frank Thomas/50 25.00 60.00
MAWAKB Kris Bryant/30 100.00 250.00
MAWAMT Mike Trout/25 300.00 600.00

2017 Topps Chrome Rookie Autographs

STATED ODDS 1:18 HOBBY
PRINTING PLATE ODDS 1:12,775 HOBBY
PLATE PRINT RUN 1 SET PER COLOR
BLACK-CYAN-MAGENTA-YELLOW ISSUED
NO PLATE PRICING DUE TO SCARCITY
EXCHANGE DEADLINE 6/30/2019
RAAB Alex Bregman 30.00 80.00
RAABE Andrew Benintendi 30.00 80.00
RAAG Amir Garrett 4.00 10.00
RAAJ Aaron Judge 100.00 250.00
RAAR Alex Reyes 4.00 10.00
RAAT Andrew Toles 2.50 6.00
RABM Bruce Maxwell 2.50 6.00
RABP Brett Phillips 3.00 8.00
RABS Braden Shipley 2.50 6.00
RABZ Bradley Zimmer 4.00 10.00
RACA Christian Arroyo 4.00 10.00
RACAS Carlos Asuaje 2.50 6.00
RACB Cody Bellinger 125.00 300.00
RACFU Carson Fulmer 4.00 10.00
RACP Chad Pinder 2.50 6.00
RADD David Dahl 5.00 12.00
RADH Donnie Hart 3.00 8.00
RADP David Paulino 3.00 8.00
RADS Dansby Swanson
RADV Dan Vogelbach 4.00 10.00
RAEG Eddie Gamboa 2.50 6.00
RAFB Franklin Barreto 2.50 6.00
RAGM German Marquez 6.00 15.00
RAHD Hunter Dozier 4.00 10.00
RAHR Hunter Renfroe 5.00 12.00
RAIH Ian Happ 6.00 15.00
RAJA Jorge Alfaro 3.00 8.00
RAJC Jharel Cotton 2.50 6.00
RAJDL Jose De Leon 4.00 10.00
RAJH Jeff Hoffman 2.50 6.00
RAJHA Josh Hader 8.00 20.00
RAJHU Jason Hursh 2.50 6.00
RAJJ Joe Jimenez 2.50 6.00
RAJJO JaCoby Jones 3.00 8.00
RAJM Joe Musgrove 2.50 6.00
RAJS Josh Smoker 2.50 6.00
RAJT Jake Thompson 2.50 6.00
RAJW Jesse Winker 6.00 15.00
RALB Lewis Brinson 4.00 10.00
RALW Luke Weaver 5.00 12.00
RAMH Mitch Haniger 4.00 10.00
RAMM Manny Margot 4.00 10.00
RAMO Matt Olson 8.00 20.00
RAMS Matt Strahm 2.50 6.00
RAPV Pat Valaika 3.00 8.00
RARG Robert Gsellman 2.50 6.00
RARH Ryon Healy 3.00 8.00
RARL Reynaldo Lopez 5.00 12.00
RARN Renato Nunez 5.00 12.00
RARQ Roman Quinn 2.50 6.00
RARS Rob Segedin 2.50 6.00
RART Raimel Tapia 3.00 8.00
RARZ Rob Zastryzny 2.50 6.00
RASL Seth Lugo 2.50 6.00
RASN Sean Newcomb 3.00 8.00
RATA Tyler Austin 5.00 12.00
RATBL Ty Blach 3.00 8.00
RATG Tyler Glasnow 6.00 15.00
RATH Teoscar Hernandez 15.00 40.00
RATM Trey Mancini 3.00 8.00
RATR T.J. Rivera 4.00 10.00
RAYG Yulieski Gurriel 6.00 15.00
RAYM Yoan Moncada 30.00 80.00

2017 Topps Chrome Rookie Autographs Blue Refractors

*BLUE REF: .75X TO 2X BASIC
STATED ODDS 1:341 HOBBY
STATED PRINT RUN 150 SER.#'d SETS
EXCHANGE DEADLINE 6/30/2019
RAAJ Aaron Judge 200.00 400.00

2017 Topps Chrome Rookie Autographs Blue Wave Refractors

*BLUE WAVE REF: 1X TO 2.5X BASIC
STATED ODDS 1:479 HOBBY
STATED PRINT RUN 75 SER.#'d SETS
EXCHANGE DEADLINE 6/30/2019
RAAJ Aaron Judge 250.00 500.00
RADS Dansby Swanson 50.00 120.00

2017 Topps Chrome Rookie Autographs Gold Refractors

*GOLD REF: 1.5X TO 4X BASIC
STATED ODDS 1:1023 HOBBY
STATED PRINT RUN 50 SER.#'d SETS
EXCHANGE DEADLINE 6/30/2019
RAAJ Aaron Judge 500.00 1000.00
RADS Dansby Swanson 75.00 200.00

2017 Topps Chrome Rookie Autographs Green Refractors

*GREEN REF: 1X TO 2.5X BASIC
STATED ODDS 1:182 RETAIL
STATED PRINT RUN 99 SER.#'d SETS
EXCHANGE DEADLINE 6/30/2019
RAAJ Aaron Judge 250.00 500.00
RADS Dansby Swanson 50.00 120.00

2017 Topps Chrome Rookie Autographs Orange Refractors

*ORANGE REF: 3X TO 8X BASIC
STATED ODDS 1:677 HOBBY
STATED PRINT RUN 25 SER.#'d SETS
EXCHANGE DEADLINE 6/30/2019
RAABE Andrew Benintendi 250.00 500.00
RAAJ Aaron Judge 600.00 1200.00
RADS Dansby Swanson 150.00 400.00
RAYM Yoan Moncada 200.00 400.00

2017 Topps Chrome Rookie Autographs Purple Refractors

*PURPLE REF: .6X TO 1.5X BASIC
STATED ODDS 1:205 HOBBY
STATED PRINT RUN 250 SER.#'d SETS
EXCHANGE DEADLINE 6/30/2019
RAAJ Aaron Judge 150.00 300.00

2017 Topps Chrome Rookie Autographs Refractors

*REF: .5X TO 1.2X BASIC
STATED ODDS 1:103 HOBBY
STATED PRINT RUN 499 SER.#'d SETS
EXCHANGE DEADLINE 6/30/2019

2017 Topps Chrome Rookie Autographs X-Fractors

*XFRACTOR: 3X TO 8X BASIC
RANDOM INSERTS IN PACKS
STATED PRINT RUN 20 SER.#'d SETS
EXCHANGE DEADLINE 6/30/2019
RAABE Andrew Benintendi 250.00 500.00
RAAJ Aaron Judge 600.00 1200.00
RADS Dansby Swanson 150.00 400.00
RAYM Yoan Moncada 200.00 400.00

2017 Topps Chrome Sophomore Stat Lines Autographs

COMPLETE SET (13)
STATED ODDS 1:2835 HOBBY
STATED PRINT RUN 99 SER.#'d SETS
EXCHANGE DEADLINE 6/30/2019
*ORANGE/25: .5X TO 1.2X BASIC
PRINTING PLATE ODDS 1:69,767 HOBBY
PLATE PRINT RUN 1 SET PER COLOR
BLACK-CYAN-MAGENTA-YELLOW ISSUED
NO PLATE PRICING DUE TO SCARCITY
SSLAAD Aledmys Diaz 5.00 12.00
SSLABS Blake Snell 5.00 12.00
SSLACS Corey Seager 30.00 80.00
SSLAJT Jameson Taillon 5.00 12.00
SSLAJU Julio Urias 10.00 25.00
SSLAKM Kenta Maeda 10.00 25.00
SSLALG Lucas Giolito 8.00 20.00
SSLAMF Michael Fulmer 4.00 10.00
SSLANM Nomar Mazara
SSLASP Stephen Piscotty 10.00 25.00
SSLATS Trevor Story 10.00 25.00
SSLATT Trea Turner 12.00 30.00
SSLAWC Willson Contreras 15.00 40.00

2017 Topps Chrome Update

COMPLETE SET (100) 15.00 40.00
PRINTING PLATE ODDS 1:1375 PACKS
PLATE PRINT RUN 1 SET PER COLOR
BLACK-CYAN-MAGENTA-YELLOW ISSUED
NO PLATE PRICING DUE TO SCARCITY
HMT1 Bryce Harper AS .50 1.25
HMT2 Luis Severino AS .25 .60
HMT3 Trey Mancini RD .40 1.00
HMT4 Kyle Freeland RC .50 1.25
HMT5 Josh Reddick .20 .50
HMT6 Antonio Senzatela RC .40 1.00
HMT7 Bradley Zimmer RC .50 1.25
HMT8 Salvador Perez AS .25 .60
HMT9 Paul Goldschmidt AS .30 .75
HMT10 Cody Bellinger RC 20.00 50.00
HMT11 Derek Fisher RD .25 .60
HMT12 Nolan Arenado AS .40 1.00
HMT13 Yandy Diaz RC .75 2.00
HMT14 Jose De Leon RC .40 1.00
HMT15 Domingo German RC 1.25 3.00
HMT16 Miguel Sano AS .25 .60
HMT17 Joey Votto AS .30 .75
HMT18 Gary Sanchez AS .30 .75
HMT19 Sam Travis RC .40 1.00
HMT20 Buster Posey AS .40 1.00
HMT21 Wade Davis .20 .50
HMT22 Derek Fisher RC .50 1.25
HMT23 Lewis Brinson RC .60 1.50
HMT24 Jorge Bonifacio RC .40 1.00
HMT25 Clayton Kershaw AS .60 1.50
HMT26 Mookie Betts AS .50 1.25
HMT27 Giancarlo Stanton AS .30 .75
HMT28 Yulieski Gurriel RD .30 .75
HMT29 Tyler Austin RD .30 .75
HMT30 Corey Seager AS .30 .75
HMT31 Jesse Winker RC .40 1.00
HMT32 Christian Arroyo RC .60 1.50
HMT33 Alex Reyes RD .25 .60
HMT34 Reynaldo Lopez RC .40 1.00
HMT35 Andrew Benintendi RD .60 1.50
HMT36 Luke Voit RC 6.00 15.00
HMT37 Dinelson Lamet RC .40 1.00
HMT38 Kendrys Morales .20 .50
HMT39 Carlos Correa AS .30 .75
HMT40 Aaron Judge AS 2.50 6.00
HMT41 Yoan Moncada RD .60 1.50
HMT42 Paul DeJong RC 1.25 3.00
HMT43 Ryan Zimmerman AS .25 .60
HMT44 Michael Conforto AS .25 .60
HMT45 Jose Altuve AS .25 .60
HMT46 Jose Quintana .20 .50
HMT47 Carlos Beltran .25 .60
HMT48 Gift Ngoepe RC .40 1.00
HMT49 Tyler Glasnow RD .25 .60
HMT50 Aaron Judge RD 2.50 6.00
HMT51 Ian Happ RC .40 1.00
HMT52 Orlando Arcia RD .30 .75
HMT53 Matt Chapman RC .60 1.50
HMT54 Josh Hader RC .40 1.00
HMT55 Franklin Barreto RC .40 1.00
HMT56 Brian McCann .25 .60
HMT57 Yadier Molina AS .30 .75
HMT58 Jordan Montgomery RC .60 1.50
HMT59 Jose Ramirez .25 .60
HMT60 Alex Bregman RD .75 2.00
HMT61 Jacob Faria RC .40 1.00
HMT62 Jaycob Brugman RC .40 1.00
HMT63 Luis Castillo RC 1.25 3.00
HMT64 Sean Newcomb RC .50 1.25
HMT65 Max Scherzer AS .30 .75
HMT66 Ian Happ RC .75 2.00
HMT67 Francisco Lindor AS .30 .75
HMT68 Daniel Murphy AS .25 .60
HMT69 Charlie Blackmon AS .30 .75
HMT70 Chris Sale .30 .75
HMT71 Christian Arroyo RD .30 .75
HMT72 Magneuris Sierra RC .60 1.50
HMT73 Michael Fulmer AS .20 .50
HMT74 Dellin Betances AS .25 .60
HMT75 Dansby Swanson RD .50 1.25
HMT76 Jeff Hoffman RD .20 .50
HMT77 Brett Phillips RC .50 1.25
HMT78 Amir Garrett RD .20 .50
HMT79 Daniel Robertson RC .40 1.00
HMT80 Chris Sale AS .30 .75
HMT81 Cody Bellinger AS 3.00 8.00
HMT82 Cameron Maybin .20 .50
HMT83 Robinson Cano AS .25 .60
HMT84 Ryon Healy RD .25 .60
HMT85 George Springer AS .25 .60
HMT86 Yu Darvish AS .30 .75
HMT87 Corey Kluber AS .25 .60
HMT88 Justin Upton AS .25 .60
HMT89 Hunter Renfroe RD .25 .60
HMT90 Jean Segura .25 .60
HMT91 Franklin Barreto RD .20 .50
HMT92 Stephen Strasburg AS .30 .75
HMT93 Anthony Alford RC .40 1.00
HMT94 Matt Adams .20 .50
HMT95 Adam Eaton .30 .75
HMT96 Bradley Zimmer RD .25 .60
HMT97 Craig Kimbrel AS .25 .60
HMT98 Yoan Moncada RC 1.25 3.00
HMT99 Cody Bellinger RD 3.00 8.00
HMT100 David Dahl RD .25 .60

2017 Topps Chrome Update Gold Refractors

*GOLD REFRACTORS: 5X TO 12X BASIC
*GOLD REFRACTORS: 2.5X TO 6X BASIC
STATED ODDS 1:110 PACKS
STATED PRINT RUN 50 SER.#'d SETS
HMT40 Aaron Judge AS 50.00 120.00
HMT50 Aaron Judge RD 50.00 120.00

2017 Topps Chrome Update Red Refractors

*RED REFRACTORS: 6X TO 15X BASIC
*RED REFRACTORS RC: 3X TO 8X BASIC
STATED ODDS 1:220 PACKS
STATED PRINT RUN 25 SER.#'d SETS
HMT40 Aaron Judge AS 150.00 400.00
HMT50 Aaron Judge RD 150.00 400.00

2017 Topps Chrome Update Refractors

*REFRACTORS: 1.2X TO 3X BASIC
*REFRACTORS RC: .6X TO 1.5X BASIC
STATED ODDS 1:22 PACKS
STATED PRINT RUN 250 SER.#'d SETS
HMT40 Aaron Judge AS 20.00 50.00
HMT50 Aaron Judge RD 20.00 50.00

2017 Topps Chrome Update X-Fractors

*X-FRACTORS: 1.5X TO 4X BASIC
*X-FRACTORS RC: .75X TO 2X BASIC
STATED ODDS 1:56 PACKS
STATED PRINT RUN 99 SER.#'d SETS
HMT40 Aaron Judge AS 25.00 60.00
HMT50 Aaron Judge RD 25.00 60.00

2017 Topps Chrome Update All Rookie Cup

COMPLETE SET (20) 12.00 30.00
STATED ODDS 1:2 PACKS
TARC1 Bryce Harper 1.25 3.00
TARC2 Carlton Fisk .60 1.50
TARC3 Rod Carew .60 1.50
TARC4 Mark McGwire 1.25 3.00
TARC5 Ichiro 1.00 2.50
TARC6 Buster Posey 1.00 2.50
TARC7 Mike Trout 4.00 10.00
TARC8 Chipper Jones .75 2.00
TARC9 Johnny Bench .75 2.00
TARC10 Noah Syndergaard .60 1.50
TARC11 Eddie Murray .60 1.50
TARC12 Tom Seaver .60 1.50
TARC13 Joe Morgan .60 1.50
TARC14 Derek Jeter 2.00 5.00
TARC15 Kris Bryant 1.00 2.50
TARC16 Ken Griffey Jr. 1.50 4.00
TARC17 Carlos Correa .75 2.00
TARC18 Cal Ripken Jr. 2.50 6.00
TARC19 Joey Votto .75 2.00
TARC20 Willie McCovey .60 1.50

2017 Topps Chrome Update Autographs

STATED ODDS 1:56 PACKS
PRINTING PLATE ODDS 1:2501 PACKS
PLATE PRINT RUN 1 SET PER COLOR
BLACK-CYAN-MAGENTA-YELLOW ISSUED
NO PLATE PRICING DUE TO SCARCITY
EXCHANGE DEADLINE 10/31/2019
HMT1 Bryce Harper 60.00 150.00
HMT2 Luis Severino 8.00 20.00
HMT3 Trey Mancini 6.00 15.00
HMT4 Kyle Freeland 4.00 10.00
HMT5 Josh Reddick
HMT6 Antonio Senzatela 3.00 8.00
HMT9 Paul Goldschmidt 15.00 40.00
HMT10 Cody Bellinger 75.00 200.00
HMT14 Jose De Leon
HMT15 Domingo German 15.00 40.00
HMT17 Joey Votto 20.00 50.00
HMT19 Sam Travis 3.00 8.00
HMT20 Buster Posey EXCH 40.00 100.00
HMT22 Derek Fisher 6.00 15.00
HMT23 Lewis Brinson 5.00 12.00
HMT25 Clayton Kershaw 60.00 150.00
HMT28 Yulieski Gurriel 6.00 15.00
HMT29 Tyler Austin 5.00 12.00
HMT30 Corey Seager EXCH 25.00 60.00
HMT31 Jesse Winker 4.00 10.00
HMT32 Christian Arroyo 5.00 12.00
HMT33 Alex Reyes 6.00 15.00
HMT34 Reynaldo Lopez 3.00 8.00
HMT35 Andrew Benintendi 25.00 60.00
HMT37 Dinelson Lamet 3.00 8.00
HMT38 Kendrys Morales 3.00 8.00
HMT39 Carlos Correa 30.00 80.00
HMT40 Aaron Judge 75.00 200.00
HMT42 Paul DeJong 20.00 50.00
HMT45 Jose Altuve 15.00 40.00
HMT50 Aaron Judge 75.00 200.00
HMT51 Ian Happ 6.00 15.00
HMT54 Josh Hader 6.00 15.00
HMT55 Franklin Barreto 5.00 12.00
HMT56 Brian McCann
HMT58 Jordan Montgomery 10.00 25.00
HMT60 Alex Bregman 20.00 50.00
HMT61 Jacob Faria 3.00 8.00
HMT63 Luis Castillo 15.00 40.00
HMT64 Sean Newcomb 4.00 10.00
HMT66 Ian Happ 6.00 15.00
HMT69 Charlie Blackmon 5.00 12.00
HMT71 Christian Arroyo 5.00 12.00
HMT72 Magneuris Sierra 8.00 20.00
HMT73 Michael Fulmer 3.00 8.00
HMT75 Dansby Swanson 15.00 40.00
HMT77 Brett Phillips 4.00 10.00
HMT79 Daniel Robertson 3.00 8.00
HMT80 Chris Sale 10.00 25.00
HMT81 Cody Bellinger 75.00 200.00
HMT85 George Springer 12.00 30.00
HMT87 Corey Kluber 30.00 80.00
HMT89 Hunter Renfroe 6.00 15.00
HMT90 Jean Segura 4.00 10.00
HMT93 Anthony Alford 3.00 8.00
HMT94 Matt Adams 3.00 8.00
HMT96 Bradley Zimmer
HMT97 Craig Kimbrel
HMT98 Yoan Moncada 25.00 60.00
HMT99 Cody Bellinger 75.00 200.00
HMT100 David Dahl 5.00 12.00

2017 Topps Chrome Update Autographs Gold Refractors

*GOLD REF: .75X TO 2X BASIC
STATED ODDS 1:240 PACKS
STATED PRINT RUN 50 SER.#'d SETS
EXCHANGE DEADLINE 10/31/2019

2017 Topps Chrome Update Autographs Red Refractors

*RED REF: 1X TO 2.5X BASIC
STATED ODDS 1:449 PACKS
STATED PRINT RUN 25 SER.#'d SETS
EXCHANGE DEADLINE 10/31/2019
HMT5 Josh Reddick 12.00 30.00
HMT96 Bradley Zimmer 30.00 80.00

2017 Topps Chrome Update Autographs X-Fractors

*X-FRACTORS: .5X TO 1.2X BASIC
STATED ODDS 1:165 PACKS
STATED PRINT RUN 99 SER.#'d SETS
EXCHANGE DEADLINE 10/31/2019

2018 Topps Chrome

PRINTING PLATE ODDS 1:5397 HOBBY
PLATE PRINT RUN 1 SET PER COLOR
BLACK-CYAN-MAGENTA-YELLOW ISSUED
NO PLATE PRICING DUE TO SCARCITY
1 Aaron Judge .75 2.00
2 Marcus Stroman .25 .60
3 Tim Beckham .25 .60
4 Jack Flaherty RC .60 1.50
5 Alex Reyes .25 .60
6 Didi Gregorius .25 .60
7 Eric Thames .25 .60
8 Josh Donaldson .25 .60
9 Victor Arano RC .40 1.00
10 Masahiro Tanaka .25 .60
11 Kevin Pillar .20 .50
12 Tyler Mahle RC .50 1.25
13 Miguel Gomez RC .40 1.00
14 Miguel Andujar RC 1.50 4.00
15 Billy Hamilton .25 .60
16 Chris Davis .20 .50
17 George Springer .25 .60
18 Wil Myers .20 .50
19 Taijuan Walker .20 .50
20 Corey Kluber .25 .60
21 Ryan McMahon RC .50 1.25
22 Brian Anderson RC .50 1.25
23 Freddie Freeman .40 1.00
24 Yadier Molina .30 .75
25 Rafael Devers RC 1.25 3.00
26 Miguel Cabrera .30 .75
27 Max Kepler .25 .60
28 Gregory Polanco .25 .60
29 Buster Posey .40 1.00
30 Alex Colome .20 .50
31 Gleyber Torres RC 6.00 15.00
32 Tyler Wade RC .50 1.25
33 Matt Carpenter .30 .75
34 Luis Castillo .25 .60
35 Tyler O'Neill RC .60 1.50
36 Justin Turner .25 .60
37 Paul Goldschmidt .30 .75
38 Marwin Gonzalez .20
39 Alex Wood .20
40 Harrison Bader RC .60 1.
41 Eugenio Suarez .25 .6
42 Lucas Sims RC .40 1.0
43 Richard Urena RC .40 1.0
44 Tim Anderson .30 .7
45 Albert Pujols .40 1.0
46 Odubel Herrera .25 .6
47 Byron Buxton .25 .6
48 Jose Quintana .20 .5
49 Anthony Rizzo .50 1.2
50 Kris Bryant .40 1.0
51 Ian Happ .25 .6
52 Robinson Cano .25 .6
53 Craig Kimbrel .25 .6
54 Anthony Banda RC .40 1.0
55 Trevor Bauer .30 .7
56 Kyle Schwarber .30 .7
57 Jacob Faria .20 .5
58 Ender Inciarte .20 .5
59 Hanley Ramirez .25 .6
60 Amed Rosario RC .50 1.2
61 J.P. Crawford RC .40 1.0
62 Manny Margot .20 .5
63 Lucas Giolito .25 .6
64 Matt Olson .20 .5
65 Luis Severino .25 .6
66 Max Fried RC 1.50 4.0
67 Khris Davis .30 .7
68 Justin Bour .20 .5
69 Chris Sale .30 .7
70 Rhys Hoskins RC 1.50 4.0
71 Walker Buehler RC 2.00 5.0
72 Ozzie Albies RC 1.25 3.0
73 Francisco Lindor .30 .7
74 Andrew McCutchen .30 .7
75 Jameson Taillon .25 .6
76 Erick Fedde RC .40 1.0
77 Parker Bridwell RC .40 1.0
78 Josh Bell .25 .6
79 Paul DeJong .30 .75
80 German Marquez .20 .50
81 Rougned Odor .25 .60
82 Raisel Iglesias .25 .60
83 Chris Taylor .25 .60
84 Greg Allen RC .40 1.00
85 Kendrys Morales .20 .50
86 Addison Russell .25 .60
87 Austin Hays RC .60 1.50
88 Luke Weaver .25 .60
89 Ryan Braun .25 .60
90 Nicky Delmonico RC .40 1.00
91 Kenley Jansen .25 .60
92 Francisco Mejia RC .50 1.25
93 Domingo Santana .25 .60
94 Manny Machado .30 .75
95 Evan Longoria .25 .60
96 Justin Verlander .30 .75
97 Andrelton Simmons .20 .50
98 Jonathan Schoop .20 .50
99 Noah Syndergaard .25 .60
100 Mike Trout 1.50 4.00
101 Jen-Ho Tseng RC .40 1.00
102 Chris Archer .20 .50
103 Carlos Correa .30 .75
104 Nicholas Castellanos .30 .75
105 Travis Shaw .20 .50
106 Jake Lamb .25 .60
107 Salvador Perez .25 .60
108 Joey Gallo .25 .60
109 Brett Gardner .25 .60
110 Jackson Stephens RC .40 1.00
111 Brandon Crawford .25 .60
112 David Robertson .20 .50
113 Willie Calhoun RC .50 1.25
114 Nelson Cruz .30 .75
115 Jackie Bradley Jr. .30 .75
116 Maikel Franco .25 .60
117 Andrew Miller .25 .60
118 Tommy Pham .20 .50
119 Yoenis Cespedes .30 .75
120 Raudy Read RC .40 1.00
121 Clayton Kershaw .60 1.50
122 Dillon Peters RC .40 1.00
123 Joey Votto .30 .75
124 Lewis Brinson .20 .50
125 Luiz Gohara RC .40 1.00
126 Scott Kingery RC .60 1.50
127 Felix Jorge RC .40 1.00
128 Sandy Alcantara RC .40 1.00
129 Robbie Ray .20 .50
130 Elvis Andrus .25 .60
131 Adrian Beltre .30 .75
132 Cody Bellinger .60 1.50
133 Chance Sisco RC .50 1.25
134 Cole Hamels .25 .60
135 Orlando Arcia .20 .50
136 Michael Conforto .25 .60
137 Sean Doolittle .20 .50
138 Adam Jones .25 .60
139 Bryce Harper .50 1.25
140 Brian Dozier .25 .60
141 Starlin Castro .20 .50
142 Trey Mancini .25 .60
143 Jacob deGrom .30 .75
144 Whit Merrifield .30 .75
145 Max Scherzer .30 .75
146 Trea Turner .25 .60
147 Nick Williams RC .50 1.25
148 Clint Frazier RC .75 2.00
149 Marcell Ozuna .30 .75
150 Shohei Ohtani RC 5.00 12.00

151 Andrew Benintendi .30 .75
152 Tomas Nido RC .40 1.00
153 Ervin Santana .20 .50
154 Zack Granite RC .40 1.00
155 Edwin Diaz .25 .60
156 Zack Greinke .25 .60
157 Dustin Fowler RC .40 1.00
158 Paul Blackburn RC .40 1.00
159 Kyle Seager .20 .50
160 Yoan Moncada .30 .75
161 Cody Allen .20 .50
162 Dominic Smith RC .40 1.00
163 Nolan Arenado .40 1.00
164 Troy Scribner RC .40 1.00
165 Anthony Rendon .30 .75
166 Dallas Keuchel .25 .60
167 Alex Verdugo RC .60 1.50
168 Yuli Gurriel .25 .60
169 Jose Abreu .30 .75
170 Aaron Altherr .20 .50
171 Jon Gray .20 .50
172 Jay Bruce .25 .60
173 Carlos Carrasco .20 .50
174 Greg Bird .25 .60
175 Victor Robles RC 1.00 2.50
176 Michael Fulmer .20 .50
177 J.D. Davis RC .50 1.25
178 Nomar Mazara .20 .50
179 Brandon Woodruff RC .50 1.25
180 A.J. Minter RC .50 1.25
181 Kenta Maeda .25 .60
182 Gary Sanchez .30 .75
183 Mookie Betts .50 1.25
184 Hunter Renfroe .20 .50
185 Stephen Strasburg .30 .75
186 Giancarlo Stanton .30 .75
187 Jose Berrios .25 .60
188 Garrett Cooper RC .40 1.00
189 Jose Ramirez .25 .60
190 Matt Chapman .30 .75
191 Jon Lester .25 .60
192 Corey Seager .30 .75
193 Ronald Acuna RC 20.00 50.00
194 Charlie Blackmon .30 .75
195 Alex Bregman .30 .75
196 Daniel Murphy .25 .60
197 Willson Contreras .30 .75
198 Andrew Stevenson RC .40 1.00
199 Edwin Encarnacion .30 .75
200 Jose Altuve .25 .60

2018 Topps Chrome Black and White Negative Refractors

*SEPIA REF: 3X TO 8X BASIC
*SEPIA REF RC: 1.5X TO 4X BASIC RC
STATED ODDS 1:53 HOBBY
14 Miguel Andujar 10.00 25.00
25 Rafael Devers 15.00 40.00
31 Gleyber Torres 30.00 80.00
70 Rhys Hoskins 10.00 25.00
150 Shohei Ohtani 30.00 80.00
193 Ronald Acuna 100.00 250.00

2018 Topps Chrome Blue Refractors

*BLUE REF: 5X TO 12X BASIC
*BLUE REF RC: 2.5X TO 6X BASIC
STATED ODDS 1:141 HOBBY
STATED PRINT RUN 150 SER.#'d SETS
14 Miguel Andujar 15.00 40.00
25 Rafael Devers 25.00 60.00
31 Gleyber Torres 50.00 120.00
70 Rhys Hoskins 15.00 40.00
150 Shohei Ohtani 50.00 120.00

2018 Topps Chrome Blue Wave Refractors

*BLUE WAVE REF: 6X TO 15X BASIC
*BLUE WAVE REF RC: 3X TO 8X BASIC
STATED ODDS 1:164 HOBBY
STATED PRINT RUN 75 SER.#'d SETS
14 Miguel Andujar 20.00 50.00
25 Rafael Devers 30.00 80.00
31 Gleyber Torres 60.00 150.00
70 Rhys Hoskins 20.00 50.00
150 Shohei Ohtani 60.00 150.00

2018 Topps Chrome Gold Refractors

*GOLD REF: 8X TO 20X BASIC
*GOLD REF RC: 4X TO 10X BASIC RC
STATED ODDS 1:422 HOBBY
STATED PRINT RUN 50 SER.#'d SETS
1 Aaron Judge 40.00 100.00
14 Miguel Andujar 25.00 60.00
25 Rafael Devers 30.00 80.00
31 Gleyber Torres 75.00 200.00
70 Rhys Hoskins 25.00 60.00
100 Mike Trout 50.00 120.00
150 Shohei Ohtani 125.00 300.00
175 Victor Robles 15.00 40.00

2018 Topps Chrome Gold Wave Refractors

*GOLD REF: 8X TO 20X BASIC
*GOLD REF RC: 4X TO 10X BASIC RC
STATED ODDS 1:246 HOBBY
STATED PRINT RUN 50 SER.#'d SETS
1 Aaron Judge 40.00 100.00
14 Miguel Andujar 25.00 60.00
25 Rafael Devers 30.00 80.00
31 Gleyber Torres 75.00 200.00
70 Rhys Hoskins 25.00 60.00
100 Mike Trout 50.00 120.00
150 Shohei Ohtani 125.00 300.00
175 Victor Robles 15.00 40.00

2018 Topps Chrome Green Refractors

*GREEN REF: 6X TO 15X BASIC
*GREEN REF RC: 3X TO 8X BASIC RC
STATED ODDS 1:213 HOBBY
STATED PRINT RUN 99 SER.#'d SETS
14 Miguel Andujar 20.00 50.00
25 Rafael Devers 25.00 60.00
31 Gleyber Torres 60.00 150.00
150 Shohei Ohtani 60.00 150.00

2018 Topps Chrome Green Wave Refractors

*GREEN WAVE REF: 6X TO 15X BASIC
*GREEN WAVE REF RC: 3X TO 8X BASIC RC
STATED ODDS 1:124 HOBBY
STATED PRINT RUN 99 SER.#'d SETS
14 Miguel Andujar 20.00 50.00
25 Rafael Devers 25.00 60.00
31 Gleyber Torres 60.00 150.00
70 Rhys Hoskins 20.00 50.00
150 Shohei Ohtani 60.00 150.00

2018 Topps Chrome Orange Refractors

*ORANGE REF: 10X TO 25X BASIC
*ORANGE REF RC: 5X TO 12X BASIC RC
STATED ODDS 1:229 HOBBY
STATED PRINT RUN 25 SER.#'d SETS
1 Aaron Judge 50.00 120.00
14 Miguel Andujar 30.00 80.00
25 Rafael Devers 40.00 100.00
31 Gleyber Torres 100.00 250.00
70 Rhys Hoskins 30.00 80.00
100 Mike Trout 60.00 150.00
150 Shohei Ohtani 150.00 400.00
175 Victor Robles 20.00 50.00

2018 Topps Chrome Pink Refractors

*PINK REF: 1.2X TO 3X BASIC
*PINK REF RC: .6X TO 1.5X BASIC RC
STATED ODDS 1:XXX
14 Miguel Andujar 4.00 10.00
25 Rafael Devers 2.00 5.00
31 Gleyber Torres 12.00 30.00
70 Rhys Hoskins 4.00 10.00
150 Shohei Ohtani 12.00 30.00

2018 Topps Chrome Prism Refractors

*PRISM REF:1.2X TO 3X BASIC
*PRISM REF RC:.6X TO 1.5X BASIC RC
STATED ODDS 1:6 HOBBY
14 Miguel Andujar 4.00 10.00
25 Rafael Devers 5.00 12.00
31 Gleyber Torres 12.00 30.00
70 Rhys Hoskins 4.00 10.00
150 Shohei Ohtani 12.00 30.00

2018 Topps Chrome Purple Refractors

*PURPLE REF: 2.5X TO 6X BASIC
*PURPLE REF RC: 1.2X TO 3X BASIC RC
STATED ODDS 1:71 HOBBY
STATED PRINT RUN 299 SER.#'d SETS
14 Miguel Andujar 8.00 20.00
25 Rafael Devers 10.00 25.00
31 Gleyber Torres 25.00 60.00
70 Rhys Hoskins 8.00 20.00
150 Shohei Ohtani 25.00 60.00

2018 Topps Chrome Refractors

*REF: 1X TO 2.5X BASIC
*REF RC:.5X TO 1.2X BASIC RC
STATED ODDS 1:3 HOBBY
14 Miguel Andujar 3.00 8.00
25 Rafael Devers 4.00 10.00
31 Gleyber Torres 10.00 25.00
70 Rhys Hoskins 3.00 8.00
150 Shohei Ohtani 10.00 25.00

2018 Topps Chrome Sepia Refractors

*SEPIA REF: 1.2X TO 3X BASIC
*SEPIA REF RC: .6X TO 1.5X BASIC RC
STATED ODDS 1:XXX
14 Miguel Andujar 4.00 10.00
25 Rafael Devers 2.00 5.00
31 Gleyber Torres 12.00 30.00
70 Rhys Hoskins 4.00 10.00
150 Shohei Ohtani 12.00 30.00

2018 Topps Chrome X-Fractors

*XFRACTOR: 2X TO 5X BASIC
*XFRACTOR RC: 1X TO 2.5X BASIC RC
STATED ODDS 1:XXX
14 Miguel Andujar 6.00 15.00
25 Rafael Devers 8.00 20.00
31 Gleyber Torres 20.00 50.00
70 Rhys Hoskins 6.00 15.00
150 Shohei Ohtani 20.00 50.00

2018 Topps Chrome Base Set Variation Refractors

STATED ODDS 1:999 HOBBY
*GREEN/99: 1X TO 2.5X BASIC
*ORANGE/25: 2X TO 5X BASIC
1 Judge Hoodie 10.00 25.00
8 Donaldson Spryng bat 3.00 8.00
25 Devers Dugout 8.00 20.00
29 Posey Hat 5.00 12.00
49 Rizzo Pullover 6.00 15.00
50 Bryant Signing 5.00 12.00
52 Cano Blue jrsy 3.00 8.00
60 Rosario Holding pen 3.00 8.00
70 Hoskins Fence 10.00 25.00
72 Albies Headset 8.00 20.00
73 Lindor Dugout 4.00 10.00
94 Machado In cage 4.00 10.00
99 Syndergaard Beanie 3.00 8.00
100 Trout Signing 20.00 50.00
121 Kershaw Bubble 8.00 20.00
139 Harper Dugout 6.00 15.00
147 Williams Red jrsy 3.00 8.00
148 Frazier No hat 5.00 12.00
150 Ohtani Running 15.00 40.00
151 Benintendi No hat 4.00 10.00
162 Smith Orange hat 2.50 6.00
167 Verdugo Fence 4.00 10.00
175 Robles Sliding 6.00 15.00
186 Stanton Looking at bat 4.00 10.00
200 Altuve Holding hat 3.00 8.00

2018 Topps Chrome '83 Topps Autographs

STATED ODDS 1:3601 HOBBY
STATED PRINT RUN 50 SER.#'d SETS
PRINTING PLATE ODDS 1:45,458 HOBBY
PLATE PRINT RUN 1 SET PER COLOR
BLACK-CYAN-MAGENTA-YELLOW ISSUED
NO PLATE PRICING DUE TO SCARCITY
EXCHANGE DEADLINE 6/30/2020
*ORANGE/25: .5X TO 1.2X BASIC
83TAAR Amed Rosario 12.00 30.00
83TACS Chris Sale/50 20.00 50.00
83TADG Didi Gregorius/50 40.00 100.00
83TAGT Gleyber Torres 75.00 200.00
83TAIH Ian Happ/50 12.00 30.00
83TAMO Matt Olson/50 6.00 15.00
83TANS Noah Syndergaard 12.00 30.00
83TAPD Paul DeJong 10.00 25.00
83TAPG Paul Goldschmidt 15.00 40.00
83TARA Ronald Acuna 100.00 250.00
83TARH Rhys Hoskins/50 75.00 200.00

2018 Topps Chrome '83 Topps Refractors

COMPLETE SET (25) 12.00 30.00
STATED ODDS 1:6 HOBBY
*GREEN/99: 4X TO 10X BASIC
*ORANGE/25: 10X TO 25X BASIC
83T1 Aaron Judge 1.00 2.50
83T2 Amed Rosario .30 .75
83T3 Ian Happ .30 .75
83T4 Mookie Betts .60 1.50
83T5 Carlos Correa .40 1.00
83T6 Shohei Ohtani 1.50 4.00
83T7 Didi Gregorius .30 .75
83T8 Victor Robles .60 1.50
83T9 Manny Machado .40 1.00
83T10 Kris Bryant .50 1.25
83T11 Matt Olson .25 .60
83T12 Mike Trout 2.00 5.00
83T13 Jake Lamb .30 .75
83T14 Noah Syndergaard .30 .75
83T15 Justin Turner .30 .75
83T16 Dominic Smith .25 .60
83T17 Clint Frazier .50 1.25
83T18 Rafael Devers .75 2.00
83T19 Paul Goldschmidt .30 .75
83T20 Nick Williams .30 .75
83T21 Rhys Hoskins 1.00 2.50
83T22 Paul DeJong .40 1.00
83T23 Giancarlo Stanton .40 1.00
83T24 Clayton Kershaw .75 2.00
83T25 Bryce Harper .60 1.50

2018 Topps Chrome Dual Rookie Autographs

STATED ODDS 1:28,711 HOBBY
STATED PRINT RUN 25 SER.#'d SETS
EXCHANGE DEADLINE 6/30/2020
DRAAA Albies/Acuna EXCH 400.00 800.00
DRAAS Sims/Albies
DRAHW Williams/Hoskins
DRARS Smith/Rosario

2018 Topps Chrome Freshman Flash Autographs

STATED ODDS 1:1816 HOBBY
STATED PRINT RUN 99 SER.#'d SETS
EXCHANGE DEADLINE 6/30/2020
PRINTING PLATE ODDS 1:45,458 HOBBY
PLATE PRINT RUN 1 SET PER COLOR
BLACK-CYAN-MAGENTA-YELLOW ISSUED
NO PLATE PRICING DUE TO SCARCITY
EXCHANGE DEADLINE 6/30/2020
*ORANGE/25: .5X TO 1.2X BASIC
FFAAH Austin Hays/99 10.00 25.00
FFAAR Amed Rosario/99 8.00 20.00
FFAAV Alex Verdugo/99 10.00 25.00
FFADF Dustin Fowler/99 6.00 15.00
FFADS Dominic Smith/99 10.00 25.00
FFAFM Francisco Mejia/99 8.00 20.00
FFAGT Gleyber Torres/99 75.00 200.00
FFAJC J.P. Crawford/99 6.00 15.00
FFAJF Jack Flaherty/99 10.00 25.00
FFAMA Miguel Andujar/99 25.00 60.00
FFAND Nicky Delmonico/99 6.00 15.00
FFAOA Ozzie Albies/99 60.00 150.00
FFARA Ronald Acuna/99 75.00 200.00
FFARH Rhys Hoskins/99 12.00 30.00
FFASA Sandy Alcantara/99 6.00 15.00
FFASO Shohei Ohtani EXCH
FFAWB Walker Buehler/99 30.00 80.00

2018 Topps Chrome Freshman Flash Refractors

COMPLETE SET (15) 8.00 20.00
STATED ODDS 1:12 HOBBY
*GREEN/99: 4X TO 10X BASIC
*ORANGE/25: 10X TO 25X BASIC
FF1 Shohei Ohtani 1.50 4.00
FF2 Rhys Hoskins 1.00 2.50
FF3 Dominic Smith .25 .60
FF4 J.P. Crawford .25 .60
FF5 Francisco Mejia .30 .75
FF6 Austin Hays .40 1.00
FF7 Clint Frazier .50 1.25
FF8 Ozzie Albies .75 2.00
FF9 Amed Rosario .30 .75
FF10 Alex Verdugo .40 1.00
FF11 Victor Robles .60 1.50
FF12 Nick Williams .30 .75
FF13 Willie Calhoun .30 .75
FF14 Harrison Bader .40 1.00
FF15 Rafael Devers .75 2.00

2018 Topps Chrome Future Stars Autographs

STATED ODDS 1:3421 HOBBY
PRINT RUNS B/WN 15-99 COPIES PER
NO PRICING ON QTY 15
PRINTING PLATE ODDS 1:60,611 HOBBY
PLATE PRINT RUN 1 SET PER COLOR
BLACK-CYAN-MAGENTA-YELLOW ISSUED
NO PLATE PRICING DUE TO SCARCITY
EXCHANGE DEADLINE 6/30/2020
*ORANGE/25: .6X TO 1.5X BASIC
FSAABR Alex Bregman/40 20.00 50.00
FSABZ Bradley Zimmer/99 5.00 12.00
FSAFB Franklin Barreto/99 5.00 12.00
FSAGS Gary Sanchez/40 20.00 50.00
FSAIH Ian Happ/99 6.00 15.00
FSAKB Keon Broxton/99 5.00 12.00
FSALW Luke Weaver EXCH 6.00 15.00
FSAMO Matt Olson/99 5.00 12.00
FSAPD Paul DeJong/99 8.00 20.00
FSATM Trey Mancini/99 10.00 25.00

2018 Topps Chrome Future Stars Refractors

COMPLETE SET (20) 6.00 15.00
STATED ODDS 1:8 HOBBY
*GREEN/99: 2.5X TO 6X BASIC
*ORANGE/25: 6X TO 15X BASIC
FS1 Aaron Judge 1.00 2.50
F2 Matt Olson .25 .60
FS3 Gary Sanchez .40 1.00
FS4 Sean Newcomb .30 .75
FS5 Bradley Zimmer .25 .60
FS6 Lucas Giolito .30 .75
FS7 Jordan Montgomery .40 1.00
FS8 Franklin Barreto .25 .60
FS9 Alex Bregman .40 1.00
FS10 Christian Arroyo .25 .60
FS11 Jacob Faria .25 .60
FS12 Ian Happ .30 .75
FS13 Andrew Benintendi .40 1.00
FS14 Joe Jimenez .25 .60
FS15 Luke Weaver .30 .75
FS16 Trey Mancini .30 .75
FS17 Paul DeJong .40 1.00
FS18 Keon Broxton .25 .60
FS19 Lewis Brinson .25 .60
FS20 Cody Bellinger .75 2.00

2018 Topps Chrome Rookie Autographs

STATED ODDS 1:17 HOBBY
UPD.ODDS 1:1451 PACKS
PRINTING PLATE ODDS 1:16,284 HOBBY
UPD.PLATE ODDS 1:53,562 PACKS
PLATE PRINT RUN 1 SET PER COLOR
BLACK-CYAN-MAGENTA-YELLOW ISSUED
NO PLATE PRICING DUE TO SCARCITY
EXCHANGE DEADLINE 6/30/2020
UPD.EXCH.DEADLINE 9/30/2020
RAAR Anthony Banda 2.50 6.00
RAAH Austin Hays 6.00 15.00
RAAM A.J. Minter 3.00 8.00
RAAME Alex Mejia 2.50 6.00
RAANS Anthony Santander 8.00 20.00
RAAR Amed Rosario 6.00 15.00
RAAS Andrew Stevenson 2.50 6.00
RAASA Adrian Sanchez 2.50 6.00
RAAUM Austin Meadows 12.00 30.00
RAAV Alex Verdugo 15.00 40.00
RABA Brian Anderson 5.00 12.00
RABV Breyvic Valera 2.50 6.00
RABW Brandon Woodruff 8.00 20.00
RACF Clint Frazier 12.00 30.00
RACS Chance Sisco 3.00 8.00
RACST Chris Stratton 2.50 6.00
RADF Dustin Fowler 2.50 6.00
RADP Dillon Peters 2.50 6.00
RADS Dominic Smith 4.00 10.00
RAFJ Felix Jorge 2.50 6.00
RAFM Francisco Mejia 3.00 8.00
RAFR Fernando Romero 2.50 6.00
RAGA Greg Allen 2.50 6.00
RAGC Garrett Cooper 2.50 6.00
RAGG Giovanny Gallegos 2.50 6.00
RAGT Gleyber Torres 100.00 250.00
RAHB Harrison Bader 8.00 20.00
RAHW Hunter Wood 2.50 6.00
RAJBA Jacob Barnes 2.50 6.00
RAJC J.P. Crawford 4.00 10.00
RAJD J.D. Davis 3.00 8.00
RAJF Jack Flaherty 15.00 40.00
RAJL Jordan Luplow 2.50 6.00
RAJM Juan Minaya UPD 2.50 6.00
RAJS Jackson Stephens 2.50 6.00
RAKF Kyle Farmer 2.50 6.00
RAKM Kyle Martin UPD 2.50 6.00
RAKM Keury Mella 2.50 6.00
RALS Lucas Sims 2.50 6.00
RAMA Miguel Andujar 15.00 40.00
RAMF Max Fried 20.00 50.00
RAMG Miguel Gomez 2.50 6.00
RAMS Mike Soroka 25.00 60.00
RAND Nicky Delmonico 2.50 6.00
RANW Nick Williams 3.00 8.00
RAOA Ozzie Albies 25.00 60.00
RAPB Paul Blackburn 2.50 6.00
RAPBR Parker Bridwell 2.50 6.00
RARA Ronald Acuna 200.00 500.00
RARD Rafael Devers 75.00 200.00
RARH Rhys Hoskins 20.00 50.00
RARHE Ronald Herrera 3.00 8.00
RARJ Ryder Jones 2.50 6.00
RARM Ryan McMahon 3.00 8.00
RARMO Reyes Moronta 2.50 6.00
RARR Raudy Read 2.50 6.00
RARU Richard Urena 2.50 6.00
RASA Sandy Alcantara 2.50 6.00
RASK Scott Kingery 4.00 10.00
RASO Shohei Ohtani 250.00 500.00
RATD Tyler Danish UPD 2.50 6.00
RATG Tayron Guerrero 2.50 6.00
RATM Tyler Mahle 3.00 8.00
RATN Tomas Nido 2.50 6.00
RATS Troy Scribner 2.50 6.00
RATSC Tanner Scott 2.50 6.00
RATT Travis Taijeron UPD 3.00 8.00
RATV Thyago Vieira 2.50 6.00
RATW Tyler Wade 3.00 8.00
RATWI Trevor Williams 2.50 6.00
RAVA Victor Arano 2.50 6.00
RAVC Victor Caratini 3.00 8.00
RAVR Victor Robles 20.00 50.00
RAWA Willy Adames 8.00 20.00
RAWB Walker Buehler 50.00 120.00
RAZG Zack Granite 2.50 6.00

2018 Topps Chrome Rookie Autographs Blue Refractors

*BLUE REF: .75X TO 2X BASIC
STATED ODDS 1:434 HOBBY
UPD.ODDS 1:2065 PACKS
STATED PRINT RUN 150 SER.#'d SETS
EXCHANGE DEADLINE 6/30/2020
UPD.EXCH.DEADLINE 9/30/2020
RASO Shohei Ohtani 400.00 800.00

2018 Topps Chrome Rookie Autographs Blue Wave Refractors

*BLUE WAVE REF: .75X TO 2X BASIC
STATED ODDS 1:434 HOBBY
UPD.ODDS 1:1950 PACKS
STATED PRINT RUN 150 SER.#'d SETS
EXCHANGE DEADLINE 6/30/2020
UPD.EXCH.DEADLINE 9/30/2020
RASO Shohei Ohtani 400.00 800.00

2018 Topps Chrome Rookie Autographs Gold Refractors

*GOLD REF: 1.2X TO 3X BASIC
STATED ODDS 1:1307 HOBBY
UPD.ODDS 1:5994 PACKS
STATED PRINT RUN 50 SER.#'d SETS
EXCHANGE DEADLINE 6/30/2020
UPD.EXCH.DEADLINE 9/30/2020
RASK Scott Kingery 40.00 100.00
RASO Shohei Ohtani 600.00 1200.00

2018 Topps Chrome Rookie Autographs Gold Wave Refractors

*GOLD WAVE REF: 1.2X TO 3X BASIC
STATED ODDS 1:874 HOBBY
UPD.ODDS 1:5963 PACKS
STATED PRINT RUN 50 SER.#'d SETS
EXCHANGE DEADLINE 6/30/2020
UPD.EXCH.DEADLINE 9/30/2020
RASK Scott Kingery 40.00 100.00
RASO Shohei Ohtani 600.00 1200.00

2018 Topps Chrome Rookie Autographs Green Refractors

*GREEN REF: 1X TO 2.5X BASIC
STATED ODDS 1:XXX
UPD.ODDS 1:3157 PACKS
STATED PRINT RUN 99 SER.#'d SETS
EXCHANGE DEADLINE 6/30/2020
UPD.EXCH.DEADLINE 9/30/2020
RASO Shohei Ohtani 500.00 1000.00

2018 Topps Chrome Rookie Autographs Orange Refractors

*ORANGE REF: 1.5X TO 4X BASIC
STATED ODDS 1:813 HOBBY
UPD.ODDS 1:13,416 PACKS
STATED PRINT RUN 25 SER.#'d SETS
EXCHANGE DEADLINE 6/30/2020
UPD.EXCH.DEADLINE 9/30/2020
RASK Scott Kingery 50.00 120.00
RASO Shohei Ohtani 800.00 1500.00

2018 Topps Chrome Rookie Autographs Purple Refractors

*PURPLE REF: .6X TO 1.5X BASIC
STATED ODDS 1:260 HOBBY
STATED PRINT RUN 250 SER.#'d SETS
EXCHANGE DEADLINE 6/30/2020
RASO Shohei Ohtani 300.00 600.00

2018 Topps Chrome Rookie Autographs Refractors

*REF: .5X TO 1.2X BASIC
STATED ODDS 1:131 HOBBY
STATED PRINT RUN 499 SER.#'d SETS
EXCHANGE DEADLINE 6/30/2020

2018 Topps Chrome Rookie Debut Medal Autographs

STATED ODDS 1:2668 HOBBY
PRINT RUNS B/WN 10-99 COPIES PER
NO PRICING ON QTY 10
EXCHANGE DEADLINE 6/30/2020
RDMAB Adrian Beltre/40 40.00 100.00
RDMAJ Aaron Judge 40.00 100.00
RDMAR Amed Rosario/99 30.00 80.00
RDMBH Bryce Harper/20 150.00 400.00
RDMJC J.P. Crawford/99 10.00 25.00
RDMKB Kris Bryant EXCH 20.00 50.00
RDMMT Mike Trout
RDMOA Ozzie Albies 50.00 120.00
RDMRD Rafael Devers EXCH 40.00 100.00
RDMRH Rhys Hoskins/99 75.00 200.00
RDMVR Victor Robles/99 25.00 60.00

2018 Topps Chrome Rookie Debut Medal Refractors

STATED ODDS 1:466 HOBBY
*GREEN/99: .5X TO 1.2X BASIC
*ORANGE/25: .75X TO 2X BASIC
RDMAB Adrian Beltre 4.00 10.00
RDMAJ Aaron Judge 15.00 40.00
RDMAR Amed Rosario 3.00 8.00
RDMAV Alex Verdugo 4.00 10.00
RDMBH Bryce Harper 6.00 15.00
RDMCB Cody Bellinger 8.00 20.00
RDMCC Carlos Correa 4.00 10.00
RDMCF Clint Frazier 5.00 12.00
RDMCK Corey Kluber 3.00 8.00
RDMDS Dominic Smith 3.00 8.00
RDMFL Francisco Lindor 4.00 10.00
RDMGS Giancarlo Stanton 4.00 10.00
RDMI Ichiro 8.00 20.00
RDMJA Jose Altuve 3.00 8.00
RDMJC J.P. Crawford 2.50 6.00
RDMKB Kris Bryant 5.00 12.00
RDMMT Mike Trout 20.00 50.00
RDMNA Nolan Arenado 5.00 12.00
RDMNS Noah Syndergaard 3.00 8.00
RDMNW Nick Williams 3.00 8.00
RDMOA Ozzie Albies 10.00 25.00
RDMRC Robinson Cano 3.00 8.00
RDMRD Rafael Devers 8.00 20.00
RDMRH Rhys Hoskins 10.00 25.00
RDMVR Victor Robles 6.00 15.00

2018 Topps Chrome Superstar Sensations Autographs

STATED ODDS 1:4786 HOBBY
PRINT RUNS B/WN 15-99 COPIES PER
NO PRICING ON QTY 15
PRINTING PLATE ODDS 1:60,611 HOBBY
PLATE PRINT RUN 1 SET PER COLOR
BLACK-CYAN-MAGENTA-YELLOW ISSUED
NO PLATE PRICING DUE TO SCARCITY
EXCHANGE DEADLINE 6/30/2020
*ORANGE/25: .5X TO 1.2X BASIC
SSAAB Adrian Beltre/30 40.00 100.00
SSAAR Anthony Rizzo/20 30.00 80.00
SSACK Craig Kimbrel/70 10.00 25.00
SSACSA Chris Sale/60 10.00 25.00
SSAFL Francisco Lindor EXCH 25.00 60.00
SSAGS George Springer/60 12.00 30.00
SSAJB Jose Berrios/99 8.00 20.00
SSAKB Kris Bryant/20 50.00 120.00
SSAKS Kyle Schwarber/70 10.00 25.00
SSALS Luis Severino/70 15.00 40.00
SSAMM Manny Machado/30 20.00 50.00
SSANS Noah Syndergaard/40 12.00 30.00
SSAYC Yoenis Cespedes/30 15.00 40.00

2018 Topps Chrome Superstar Sensations Refractors

STATED ODDS 1:24 HOBBY
*GREEN/99: 1.5X TO 4X BASIC
*ORANGE/25: 4X TO 10X BASIC
SS1 Aaron Judge 1.00 2.50
SS2 Manny Machado .40 1.00
SS3 George Springer .30 .75
SS4 Bryce Harper .60 1.50
SS5 Corey Seager .40 1.00
SS6 Mike Trout 2.00 5.00
SS7 Cody Bellinger .75 2.00
SS8 Francisco Lindor .40 1.00
SS9 Anthony Rizzo .60 1.50
SS10 Kyle Schwarber .40 1.00
SS11 Yoenis Cespedes .40 1.00
SS12 Carlos Correa .40 1.00
SS13 Giancarlo Stanton .40 1.00
SS14 Noah Syndergaard .30 .75
SS15 Kris Bryant .50 1.25

2018 Topps Chrome Update

COMPLETE SET (100)
PRINTING PLATE ODDS 1:2981 HOBBY
PLATE PRINT RUN 1 SET PER COLOR
BLACK-CYAN-MAGENTA-YELLOW ISSUED
NO PLATE PRICING DUE TO SCARCITY
HMT1 Shohei Ohtani RC 2.50 6.00
HMT2 Jordan Hicks RC .75 2.00
HMT3 Joey Lucchesi RC .40 1.00
HMT4 Tyler Beede RC .40 1.00
HMT5 Chris Stratton RC .40 1.00
HMT6 Daniel Mengden RC .40 1.00
HMT7 Miles Mikolas RC .50 1.25
HMT8 Tyler O'Neill RC .60 1.50
HMT9 Gleyber Torres RC 4.00 10.00
HMT10 Jesse Biddle RC .50 1.25
HMT11 Lourdes Gurriel Jr. RC .75 2.00
HMT12 Isiah Kiner-Falefa RC .40 1.00
HMT13 Dustin Fowler RC .40 1.00
HMT14 Nick Kingham RC .40 1.00
HMT15 David Bote RC 1.00 2.50
HMT16 Michael Soroka RC 1.25 3.00
HMT17 Fernando Romero RC .40 1.00
HMT18 Jack Flaherty RC .60 1.50
HMT19 Walker Buehler RC 2.00 5.00
HMT20 Miguel Andujar RC 1.50 4.00
HMT21 Clint Frazier RC .75 2.00
HMT22 Victor Robles RC 1.00 2.50
HMT23 Rafael Devers RC 1.25 3.00
HMT24 Scott Kingery RC .60 1.50
HMT25 Ronald Acuna Jr. RC 6.00 15.00
HMT26 Gleyber Torres RC 4.00 10.00
HMT27 Ozzie Albies RC 1.25 3.00
HMT28 Rhys Hoskins RC 1.50 4.00
HMT29 Amed Rosario RC .50 1.25
HMT30 Scott Kingery RD .30 .75
HMT31 Ronald Acuna Jr. RD 4.00 10.00
HMT32 Shohei Ohtani RD 1.25 3.00
HMT33 Gleyber Torres RD 2.00 5.00
HMT34 Jordan Hicks RD .40 1.00
HMT35 Michael Soroka RD .60 1.50
HMT36 Nick Kingham RD .20 .50
HMT37 Andrew McCutchen .30 .75
HMT38 Giancarlo Stanton .30 .75
HMT39 Eric Hosmer .25 .60
HMT40 J.D. Martinez .30 .75
HMT41 Matt Kemp .25 .60
HMT42 Zack Cozart .20 .50
HMT43 Carlos Santana .25 .60
HMT44 Ian Kinsler .25 .60
HMT45 Ichiro .40 1.00
HMT46 Marcell Ozuna .30 .75
HMT47 Christian Yelich .40 1.00
HMT48 Matt Harvey .25 .60
HMT49 Todd Frazier .25 .60
HMT50 Randal Grichuk .20 .50
HMT51 Jose Bautista .25 .60
HMT52 Stephen Piscotty .20 .50
HMT53 Evan Longoria .25 .60
HMT54 Austin Meadows RC .60 1.50
HMT55 Juan Soto RC 30.00 80.00
HMT56 Willy Adames RC .50 1.25
HMT57 Dylan Cozens RC .40 1.00
HMT58 Felipe Vazquez .25 .60
HMT59 Shane Bieber RC 5.00 12.00
HMT60 Jose Abreu .30 .75
HMT61 Freddie Freeman .40 1.00
HMT62 Jose Altuve .25 .60
HMT63 Javier Baez .40 1.00
HMT64 Jose Ramirez .25 .60
HMT65 Nolan Arenado .40 1.00
HMT66 Manny Machado .30 .75
HMT67 Brandon Crawford .25 .60
HMT68 Mookie Betts .50 1.25
HMT69 Mike Trout 1.50 4.00
HMT70 Aaron Judge .75 2.00
HMT71 Nick Markakis .25 .60
HMT72 Matt Kemp .25 .60
HMT73 Bryce Harper .50 1.25
HMT74 Willson Contreras .30 .75
HMT75 J.D. Martinez .30 .75
HMT76 Ozzie Albies .60 1.50
HMT77 Max Scherzer .30 .75
HMT78 Jacob deGrom .30 .75
HMT79 Josh Hader .25 .60
HMT80 Gleyber Torres 2.00 5.00
HMT81 Francisco Lindor .30 .75
HMT82 Alex Bregman .30 .75
HMT83 Chris Sale .30 .75
HMT84 Luis Severino .25 .60
HMT85 Corey Kluber .25 .60
HMT86 Lorenzo Cain .20 .50
HMT87 Yadier Molina .30 .75
HMT88 Mitch Haniger .25 .60
HMT89 Joey Votto .30 .75
HMT90 Gerrit Cole .30 .75
HMT91 Scooter Gennett .25 .60
HMT92 Kenley Jansen .25 .60
HMT93 Freddy Peralta RC .40 1.00
HMT94 Yairo Munoz RC .40 1.00
HMT95 Trevor Story .30 .75
HMT96 Charlie Blackmon .30 .75
HMT97 Manny Machado .30 .75
HMT98 Juan Soto RD 4.00 10.00
HMT99 Austin Meadows RD .30 .75
HMT100 Willy Adames RD .25 .60

2018 Topps Chrome Update Gold Refractors

*GOLD: 6X TO 15X BASIC
*GOLD RC: 3X TO 8X BASIC RC
STATED ODDS 1:236 PACKS
STATED PRINT RUN 50 SER.#'d SETS
HMT1 Shohei Ohtani 75.00 200.00
HMT20 Miguel Andujar 30.00 80.00
HMT22 Victor Robles 15.00 40.00
HMT23 Rafael Devers 20.00 50.00
HMT25 Ronald Acuna Jr. 100.00 250.00
HMT27 Ozzie Albies 15.00 40.00
HMT31 Ronald Acuna Jr. 50.00 120.00
HMT32 Shohei Ohtani 60.00 150.00
HMT54 Austin Meadows 8.00 20.00
HMT55 Juan Soto 600.00 1500.00
HMT68 Mookie Betts 20.00 50.00
HMT69 Mike Trout 40.00 100.00
HMT98 Juan Soto 75.00 200.00

2018 Topps Chrome Update Pink Refractors

*PINK: 1.2X TO 3X BASIC
*PINK RC: .6X TO 1.5X BASIC RC
RANDOM INSERTS IN PACKS
HMT1 Shohei Ohtani 8.00 20.00
HMT32 Shohei Ohtani 4.00 10.00
HMT55 Juan Soto 100.00 250.00

2018 Topps Chrome Update Red Refractors

*RED: 8X TO 20X BASIC
*RED RC: 4X TO 10X BASIC RC
STATED ODDS 1:472 PACKS
STATED PRINT RUN 25 SER.#'d SETS

HMT1 Shohei Ohtani 100.00 250.00
HMT18 Jack Flaherty 25.00 60.00
HMT20 Miguel Andujar 40.00 100.00
HMT22 Victor Robles 20.00 50.00
HMT23 Rafael Devers 25.00 60.00
HMT25 Ronald Acuna Jr. 125.00 300.00
HMT27 Ozzie Albies 20.00 50.00
HMT28 Rhys Hoskins 30.00 80.00
HMT31 Ronald Acuna Jr. 60.00 150.00
HMT32 Shohei Ohtani 75.00 200.00
HMT38 Giancarlo Stanton 50.00 120.00
HMT47 Christian Yelich 30.00 80.00
HMT54 Austin Meadows 10.00 25.00
HMT55 Juan Soto 750.00 2000.00
HMT68 Mookie Betts 40.00 100.00
HMT69 Mike Trout 50.00 120.00
HMT98 Juan Soto 100.00 250.00

2018 Topps Chrome Update Refractors

*REF: 1.5X TO 4X BASIC
*REF RC: 2.5X TO 6X BASIC RC
STATED ODDS 1:48 PACKS
STATED PRINT RUN 250 SER.#'d SETS
HMT1 Shohei Ohtani 20.00 50.00
HMT20 Miguel Andujar 8.00 20.00
HMT23 Rafael Devers 5.00 12.00
HMT25 Ronald Acuna Jr. 30.00 80.00
HMT27 Ozzie Albies 4.00 10.00
HMT31 Ronald Acuna Jr. 15.00 40.00
HMT32 Shohei Ohtani 15.00 40.00
HMT55 Juan Soto 300.00 800.00
HMT98 Juan Soto 20.00 50.00

2018 Topps Chrome Update X-fractors

*X-FRAC: 3X TO 8X BASIC
*X-FRAC RC: 1.5X TO 4X BASIC RC
STATED ODDS 1:119 PACKS
STATED PRINT RUN 99 SER.#'d SETS
HMT1 Shohei Ohtani 40.00 100.00
HMT20 Miguel Andujar 15.00 40.00
HMT23 Rafael Devers 10.00 25.00
HMT25 Ronald Acuna Jr. 50.00 120.00
HMT27 Ozzie Albies 8.00 20.00
HMT31 Ronald Acuna Jr. 25.00 60.00
HMT32 Shohei Ohtani 30.00 80.00
HMT55 Juan Soto 400.00 1000.00
HMT98 Juan Soto 40.00 100.00

2018 Topps Chrome Update An International Affair

COMPLETE SET (20) 8.00 20.00
STATED ODDS 1:2 PACKS
IAI Ichiro .50 1.25
IAAJ Aaron Judge 1.00 2.50
IACC Carlos Correa .40 1.00
IADG Didi Gregorius .30 .75
IAFF Freddie Freeman .50 1.25
IAFL Francisco Lindor .40 1.00
IAGS Gary Sanchez .50 1.25
IAGT Gleyber Torres 2.50 6.00
IAJA Jose Altuve .30 .75
IAJB Javier Baez .50 1.25
IAJV Joey Votto .40 1.00
IAKD Khris Davis .40 1.00
IAMM Manny Machado .40 1.00
IAMT Mike Trout 2.00 5.00
IAOA Ozzie Albies .75 2.00
IARA Ronald Acuna Jr. 5.00 12.00
IARD Rafael Devers .75 2.00
IASO Shohei Ohtani 1.50 4.00
IAYC Yoenis Cespedes .40 1.00
IAYM Yoan Moncada .40 1.00

2018 Topps Chrome Update Autograph Refractors

STATED ODDS 1:49 PACKS
EXCHANGE DEADLINE 9/30/2020
HMT1 Shohei Ohtani 150.00 400.00
HMT2 Jordan Hicks 8.00 20.00
HMT4 Tyler Beede 3.00 8.00
HMT5 Chris Stratton 3.00 8.00
HMT6 Daniel Mengden 3.00 8.00
HMT7 Miles Mikolas 4.00 10.00
HMT9 Gleyber Torres 125.00 300.00
HMT10 Jesse Biddle 4.00 10.00
HMT11 Lourdes Gurriel Jr. 10.00 25.00
HMT12 Isiah Kiner-Falefa 3.00 8.00
HMT13 Dustin Fowler 3.00 8.00
HMT14 Nick Kingham 3.00 8.00
HMT15 David Bote 8.00 20.00
HMT16 Michael Soroka 25.00 60.00
HMT17 Fernando Romero 3.00 8.00
HMT18 Jack Flaherty 20.00 50.00
HMT19 Walker Buehler 25.00 60.00
HMT21 Clint Frazier 12.00 30.00
HMT22 Victor Robles 15.00 40.00
HMT23 Rafael Devers 15.00 40.00
HMT24 Scott Kingery 10.00 25.00
HMT25 Ronald Acuna Jr. 150.00 400.00
HMT27 Ozzie Albies 15.00 40.00
HMT28 Rhys Hoskins 15.00 40.00
HMT29 Amed Rosario 4.00 10.00
HMT37 Andrew McCutchen 20.00 50.00
HMT42 Zack Cozart 3.00 8.00
HMT43 Carlos Santana 4.00 10.00
HMT44 Ian Kinsler 4.00 10.00
HMT45 Ichiro 100.00 250.00
HMT46 Marcell Ozuna 5.00 12.00
HMT47 Christian Yelich 25.00 60.00
HMT53 Evan Longoria 4.00 10.00
HMT54 Austin Meadows 20.00 50.00
HMT55 Juan Soto 150.00 400.00
HMT56 Willy Adames EXCH 4.00 10.00
HMT57 Dylan Cozens EXCH 3.00 8.00
HMT58 Felipe Vazquez 4.00 10.00
HMT59 Shane Bieber 20.00 50.00
HMT79 Josh Hader EXCH 3.00 8.00
HMT88 Mitch Haniger 5.00 12.00
HMT93 Freddy Peralta 3.00 8.00
ACBUFM Francisco Mejia 8.00 20.00

2018 Topps Chrome Update Autograph Gold Refractors

*GOLD: .75X TO 2X BASIC
STATED ODDS 1:514 PACKS
STATED PRINT RUN 50 SER.#'d SETS
EXCHANGE DEADLINE 9/30/2020
HMT27 Ozzie Albies 50.00 120.00
HMT28 Rhys Hoskins 40.00 100.00
HMT55 Juan Soto 500.00 1000.00
HMT56 Willy Adames EXCH 20.00 50.00
HMT88 Mitch Haniger 20.00 50.00

2018 Topps Chrome Update Autograph Orange Refractors

*ORANGE: 1X TO 2.5X BASIC
STATED ODDS 1:1032 PACKS
STATED PRINT RUN 25 SER.#'d SETS
EXCHANGE DEADLINE 9/30/2020
HMT1 Shohei Ohtani 300.00 600.00
HMT27 Ozzie Albies 60.00 150.00
HMT28 Rhys Hoskins 50.00 120.00
HMT45 Ichiro 150.00 400.00
HMT55 Juan Soto 1000.00 1500.00
HMT56 Willy Adames EXCH 25.00 60.00
HMT88 Mitch Haniger 25.00 60.00

2018 Topps Chrome Update Autograph X-fractors

*XF: .6X TO 1.5X BASIC
STATED ODDS 1:206 PACKS
STATED PRINT RUN 125 SER.#'d SETS
EXCHANGE DEADLINE 9/30/2020

2019 Topps Chrome

PRINTING PLATE ODDS 1:6540 HOBBY
PLATE PRINT RUN 1 SET PER COLOR
BLACK-CYAN-MAGENTA-YELLOW ISSUED
NO PLATE PRICING DUE TO SCARCITY
1 Shohei Ohtani .40 1.00
2 Rowdy Tellez RC .60 1.50
3 Hunter Renfroe .20 .50
4 Andrelton Simmons .20 .50
5 Dylan Bundy .25 .60
6 Reese McGuire RC .60 1.50
7 Maikel Franco .25 .60
8 Brandon Nimmo .25 .60
9 David Peralta .20 .50
10 Jesus Aguilar .20 .50
11 Whit Merrifield .30 .75
12 Brian Anderson .20 .50
13 Harrison Bader .25 .60
14 Joe Panik .25 .60
15 J.P. Crawford .20 .50
16 Christian Yelich .40 1.00
17 Michael Kopech RC .75 2.00
18 Starling Marte .25 .60
19 Alex Bregman .30 .75
20 Jose Altuve .25 .60
21 Shane Greene .20 .50
22 Gary Sanchez .30 .75
23 Zack Greinke .25 .60
24 Josh Hader .20 .50
25 Kris Bryant .40 1.00
26 Nomar Mazara .20 .50
27 Albert Pujols .40 1.00
28 Justin Verlander .30 .75
29 Lorenzo Cain .20 .50
30 Francisco Arcia RC .60 1.50
31 Joey Votto .30 .75
32 Max Muncy .25 .60
33 Victor Robles .40 1.00
34 Alex Avila .25 .60
35 Danny Jansen RC .40 1.00
36 Paul DeJong .30 .75
37 Willians Astudillo RC .40 1.00
38 Joey Gallo .25 .60
39 Kyle Tucker RC .75 2.00
40 Ronald Guzman .20 .50
41 Chris Davis .20 .50
42 George Springer .25 .60
43 Zack Cozart .20 .50
44 Carlos Santana .25 .60
45 Tommy Pham .20 .50
46 Matt Chapman .30 .75
47 Trey Mancini .25 .60
48 Javier Baez .40 1.00
49 Mychal Givens .20 .50
50 Mookie Betts .50 1.25
51 Yadier Molina .30 .75
52 Cedric Mullins RC .60 1.50
53 Ryan O'Hearn RC .40 1.00
54 Brad Keller RC .40 1.00
55 Josh James RC .60 1.50
56 Bryse Wilson RC .50 1.25
57 Ozzie Albies .30 .75
58 Scooter Gennett .25 .60
59 Jacob deGrom .30 .75
60 Joey Rickard .20 .50
61 Jesse Winker .20 .50
62 Cionel Perez RC .40 1.00
63 Jeimer Candelario .20 .50
64 Carlos Correa .30 .75
65 Colin Moran .20 .50
66 Matt Olson .20 .50
67 Max Kepler .25 .60
68 Francisco Lindor .30 .75
69 Christin Stewart RC .50 1.25
70 Lucas Giolito .25 .60
71 Jake Bauers RC .60 1.50
72 Justin Upton .25 .60
73 Yusei Kikuchi RC .60 1.50
74 Edwin Diaz .25 .60
75 Daniel Ponce de Leon RC .60 1.50
76 Blake Snell .25 .60
77 Andrew McCutchen .30 .75
78 Taylor Ward RC .40 1.00
79 Dean Deetz RC .40 1.00
80 Eugenio Suarez .25 .60
81 Jorge Polanco .20 .50
82 Buster Posey .40 1.00
83 Matt Boyd .20 .50
84 Corbin Burnes RC .60 1.50
85 Josh Donaldson .25 .60
86 Gleyber Torres .60 1.50
87 Freddie Freeman .40 1.00
88 Kevin Kramer RC .50 1.25
89 Jose Abreu .30 .75
90 Walker Buehler .40 1.00
91 David Dahl .20 .50
92 Franmil Reyes .20 .50
93 Trevor Richards RC .40 1.00
94 Evan Longoria .25 .60
95 Nicholas Castellanos .30 .75
96 Xander Bogaerts .30 .75
97 Heath Fillmyer RC .40 1.00
98 Luis Severino .25 .60
99 Kolby Allard RC .60 1.50
100 Aaron Judge .75 2.00
101 Edwin Encarnacion .30 .75
102 Yonder Alonso .20 .50
103 Odubel Herrera .25 .60
104 Matt Duffy .20 .50
105 Enyel De Los Santos RC .40 1.00
106 Corey Seager .30 .75
107 Trevor Bauer .30 .75
108 Miguel Andujar .30 .75
109 Chance Adams RC .40 1.00
110 Justus Sheffield RC .60 1.50
111 Kyle Schwarber .30 .75
112 Clayton Kershaw .60 1.50
113 Ian Desmond .20 .50
114 Byron Buxton .25 .60
115 Miguel Cabrera .30 .75
116 Jake Lamb .25 .60
117 Ronald Acuna Jr. 1.50 4.00
118 Lourdes Gurriel Jr. .25 .60
119 Sandy Alcantara .20 .50
120 Kyle Wright RC .60 1.50
121 Josh Rogers RC .40 1.00
122 Lewis Brinson .20 .50
123 Jose Berrios .25 .60
124 Nolan Arenado .40 1.00
125 Brandon Belt .25 .60
126 Nick Burdi RC .40 1.00
127 Jose Ramirez .25 .60
128 Marcus Stroman .25 .60
129 Aramis Garcia RC .40 1.00
130 Anthony Rizzo .50 1.25
131 Noah Syndergaard .25 .60
132 Aaron Sanchez .25 .60
133 J.D. Martinez .30 .75
134 Kevin Newman RC .60 1.50
135 DJ Stewart RC .50 1.25
136 Sean Reid-Foley RC .40 1.00
137 Kevin Pillar .20 .50
138 Mitch Haniger .25 .60
139 Paul Goldschmidt .30 .75
140 Max Scherzer .30 .75
141 Luis Urias RC .60 1.50
142 Billy Hamilton .25 .60
143 Taijuan Walker .20 .50
144 Blake Treinen .20 .50
145 Nick Markakis .25 .60
146 Patrick Wisdom RC .40 1.00
147 Eddie Rosario .25 .60
148 Dakota Hudson RC .50 1.25
149 Carlos Martinez .25 .60
150 Steven Duggar RC .50 1.25
151 Brandon Lowe RC .60 1.50
152 Jeff McNeil RC 1.00 2.50
153 Wil Myers .20 .50
154 Manny Margot .20 .50
155 Juan Soto 1.00 2.50
156 Kyle Seager .20 .50
157 Elvis Andrus .25 .60
158 Cody Bellinger .60 1.50
159 Gregory Polanco .25 .60
160 Charlie Blackmon .30 .75
161 Jake Cave RC .50 1.25
162 Josh Bell .25 .60
163 Patrick Corbin .25 .60
164 Adalberto Mondesi .25 .60
165 Chris Sale .30 .75
166 Hunter Dozier .20 .50
167 Stephen Piscotty .20 .50
168 Jonathan Loaisiga RC .50 1.25
169 Dansby Swanson .30 .75
170 Sean Manaea .20 .50
171 Starlin Castro .20 .50
172 Dawel Lugo RC .60 1.50
173 Chris Shaw RC .60 1.50
174 Eric Hosmer .25 .60
175 Trea Turner .25 .60
176 Aaron Nola .25 .60
177 Justin Smoak .20 .50
178 Ramon Laureano RC .75 2.00
179 Willy Adames .20 .50
180 Kevin Kiermaier .25 .60
181 David Fletcher RC 1.25 3.00
182 Jacob Nix RC .50 1.25
183 Trevor Story .30 .75
184 Rafael Devers .40 1.00
185 Kyle Hendricks .30 .75
186 Tim Anderson .30 .75
187 Ryan Borucki RC .40 1.00
188 Corey Kluber .25 .60
189 Orlando Arcia .20 .50
190 Brandon Crawford .25 .60
191 Rougned Odor .25 .60
192 Raisel Iglesias .20 .50
193 Robinson Cano .25 .60
194 Jameson Taillon .25 .60
195 Rhys Hoskins .40 1.00
196 Dee Gordon .20 .50
197 Touki Toussaint RC .50 1.25
198 Salvador Perez .25 .60
199 Jose Urena .20 .50
200 Mike Trout 1.50 4.00
201 Vladimir Guerrero Jr. RC 8.00 20.00
202 Eloy Jimenez RC 5.00 12.00
203 Fernando Tatis Jr. RC 30.00 80.00
204 Pete Alonso RC 6.00 15.00

2019 Topps Chrome Blue Refractors

*BLUE REF: 5X TO 12X BASIC
*BLUE REF RC: 2.5X TO 6X BASIC
STATED ODDS 1:175 HOBBY
STATED PRINT RUN 150 SER.#'d SETS
201 Vladimir Guerrero Jr. 60.00 150.00
203 Fernando Tatis Jr. 300.00 800.00
204 Pete Alonso 60.00 150.00

2019 Topps Chrome Blue Wave Refractors

*BLUE WAVE REF: 6X TO 15X BASIC
*BLUE WAVE REF RC: 3X TO 8X BASIC
STATED ODDS 1:176 HOBBY
STATED PRINT RUN 75 SER.#'d SETS
200 Mike Trout 30.00 80.00
201 Vladimir Guerrero Jr. 75.00 200.00
203 Fernando Tatis Jr. 400.00 1000.00
204 Pete Alonso 75.00 200.00

2019 Topps Chrome Gold Refractors

*GOLD REF: 8X TO 20X BASIC
*GOLD REF RC: 4X TO 10X BASIC RC
STATED ODDS 1:525 HOBBY
STATED PRINT RUN 50 SER.#'d SETS
39 Kyle Tucker 20.00 50.00
117 Ronald Acuna Jr. 60.00 150.00
200 Mike Trout 75.00 200.00
201 Vladimir Guerrero Jr. 100.00 250.00
203 Fernando Tatis Jr. 500.00 1200.00
204 Pete Alonso 100.00 250.00

2019 Topps Chrome Gold Wave Refractors

*GOLD WAVE REF: 8X TO 20X BASIC
*GOLD WAVE REF RC: 4X TO 10X BASIC RC
STATED ODDS 1:264 HOBBY
STATED PRINT RUN 50 SER.#'d SETS
39 Kyle Tucker 20.00 50.00
117 Ronald Acuna Jr. 60.00 150.00
200 Mike Trout 75.00 200.00
201 Vladimir Guerrero Jr. 100.00 250.00
203 Fernando Tatis Jr. 500.00 1200.00
204 Pete Alonso 100.00 250.00

2019 Topps Chrome Green Refractors

*GREEN REF: 6X TO 15X BASIC
*GREEN REF RC: 3X TO 8X BASIC RC
STATED ODDS 1:265 HOBBY
STATED PRINT RUN 99 SER.#'d SETS
200 Mike Trout 30.00 80.00
201 Vladimir Guerrero Jr. 75.00 200.00
203 Fernando Tatis Jr. 400.00 1000.00
204 Pete Alonso 75.00 200.00

2019 Topps Chrome Green Wave Refractors

*GREEN WAVE REF: 6X TO 15X BASIC
*GREEN WAVE REF RC: 3X TO 8X BASIC RC
STATED ODDS 1:134 HOBBY
STATED PRINT RUN 99 SER.#'d SETS
200 Mike Trout 30.00 80.00
201 Vladimir Guerrero Jr. 75.00 200.00
203 Fernando Tatis Jr. 400.00 1000.00
204 Pete Alonso 75.00 200.00

2019 Topps Chrome Negative Refractors

*SEPIA REF: 3X TO 8X BASIC
*SEPIA REF RC: 1.5X TO 4X BASIC RC
STATED ODDS 1:66 HOBBY
201 Vladimir Guerrero Jr. 40.00 100.00
203 Fernando Tatis Jr. 200.00 500.00
204 Pete Alonso 40.00 100.00

2019 Topps Chrome Orange Refractors

*ORANGE REF: 10X TO 25X BASIC
*ORANGE REF RC: 6X TO 15X BASIC RC
STATED ODDS 1:255 HOBBY
STATED PRINT RUN 25 SER.#'d SETS
39 Kyle Tucker 25.00 60.00
117 Ronald Acuna Jr. 75.00 200.00
200 Mike Trout 100.00 250.00
201 Vladimir Guerrero Jr. 125.00 300.00
203 Fernando Tatis Jr. 600.00 1500.00
204 Pete Alonso 125.00 300.00

2019 Topps Chrome Orange Wave Refractors

*ORNGE WAVE REF: 10X TO 25X BASIC
*ORNGE WAVE REF RC: 5X TO 12X BASIC RC
STATED ODDS 1:528 HOBBY
STATED PRINT RUN 25 SER.#'d SETS
39 Kyle Tucker 25.00 60.00
117 Ronald Acuna Jr. 75.00 200.00
200 Mike Trout 100.00 250.00
201 Vladimir Guerrero Jr. 125.00 300.00
203 Fernando Tatis Jr. 600.00 1500.00
204 Pete Alonso 125.00 300.00

2019 Topps Chrome Pink Refractors

*PINK REF: 1.2X TO 3X BASIC
*PINK REF RC: .6X TO 1.5X BASIC RC
THREE PER VALUE PACK
203 Fernando Tatis Jr. 75.00 200.00

2019 Topps Chrome Prism Refractors

*PRISM REF:1.2X TO 3X BASIC
*PRISM REF RC:.6X TO 1.5X BASIC RC
STATED ODDS 1:6 HOBBY
203 Fernando Tatis Jr. 75.00 200.00

2019 Topps Chrome Purple Refractors

*PURPLE REF: 2.5X TO 6X BASIC
*PURPLE REF RC: 1.2X TO 3X BASIC RC
STATED ODDS 1:88 HOBBY
STATED PRINT RUN 299 SER.#'d SETS
201 Vladimir Guerrero Jr. 30.00 80.00
203 Fernando Tatis Jr. 150.00 400.00
204 Pete Alonso 30.00 80.00

2019 Topps Chrome Refractors

*REF: 1X TO 2.5X BASIC
*REF RC:.5X TO 1.2X BASIC RC
STATED ODDS 1:3 HOBBY
203 Fernando Tatis Jr. 60.00 150.00

2019 Topps Chrome Sepia Refractors

*SEPIA REF: 1.2X TO 3X BASIC
*SEPIA REF RC: .6X TO 1.5X BASIC RC
RANDOM INSERTS IN PACKS
203 Fernando Tatis Jr. 75.00 200.00

2019 Topps Chrome X-Fractors

*XFRACTOR: 2X TO 5X BASIC
*XFRACTOR RC: 1X TO 2.5X BASIC RC
TEN PER MEGA BOX
203 Fernando Tatis Jr. 125.00 300.00

2019 Topps Chrome Photo Variation Refractors

STATED ODDS 1:247 HOBBY
*GREEN/99: .6X TO 1.5X BASIC
*GOLD/50: 1X TO 2.5X BASIC
*ORANGE/25: 1.2X TO 3X BASIC
1 Ohtain w/Ichiro 5.00 12.00
2 Rowdy Tellez Fielding 4.00 10.00
16 Yelich Thrwbck 5.00 12.00
17 Kopech Workout 5.00 12.00
25 Bryant Bttng 5.00 12.00
31 Joey Votto Tossing ball 4.00 10.00
39 Tucker Hldng Hlmt 5.00 12.00
48 Baez Bttng 5.00 12.00
50 Betts Workout 6.00 15:00
57 Ozzie Albies Fielding 4.00 10.00
59 Jacob deGrom Dugout 4.00 10.00
64 Carlos Correa Jacket 4.00 10.00
69 Christin Stewart Kneeling 3.00 8.00
71 Jake Bauers Blue jersey 4.00 10.00
73 Kikuchi w/Ichiro 5.00 12.00
100 Judge Bat Shldr 10.00 25.00
110 Justus Sheffield Blue jersey 4.00 10.00
112 Kershaw Fence 8.00 20.00
117 Acuna Knees 40.00 100.00
124 Nolan Arenado Press conference 5.00 12.00
141 Urias Blue jrsy 4.00 10.00
155 Soto Sldng 30.00 80.00
195 Hoskins At wall 5.00 12.00
197 Touki Toussaint Batting 3.00 8.00
200 Trout Dugout 50.00 120.00

2019 Topps Chrome '84 Topps

STATED ODDS 1:6 HOBBY
*GREEN/99: 4X TO 10X BASIC
*GOLD/50: 6X TO 15X BASIC
*ORANGE/25: 8X TO 20X BASIC
84TC1 Aaron Judge 1.00 2.50
84TC2 Juan Soto 1.25 3.00
84TC3 Michael Kopech .50 1.25
84TC4 Cedric Mullins .40 1.00
84TC5 Gleyber Torres .75 2.00
84TC6 Jacob deGrom .40 1.00
84TC7 Joey Votto .40 1.00
84TC8 Matt Chapman .40 1.00
84TC9 Anthony Rizzo .60 1.50
84TC10 Justin Upton .30 .75
84TC11 Luis Urias .40 1.00
84TC12 Noah Syndergaard .30 .75
84TC13 Giancarlo Stanton .40 1.00
84TC14 Ichiro .50 1.25
84TC15 Whit Merrifield .40 1.00
84TC16 Francisco Lindor .40 1.00
84TC17 Mike Trout 3.00 8.00
84TC18 Kyle Tucker .50 1.25
84TC19 Yusei Kikuchi .40 1.00
84TC20 Mookie Betts .60 1.50
84TC21 Jake Bauers .40 1.00
84TC22 Kolby Allard .40 1.00
84TC23 Justus Sheffield .40 1.00
84TC24 Ronald Acuna Jr. 2.00 5.00
84TC25 Shohei Ohtani .50 1.25

2019 Topps Chrome '84 Topps Autographs

STATED ODDS 1:4360 HOBBY
PRINT RUNS B/WN 20-50 COPIES PER
EXCHANGE DEADLINE 6/30/2021
84TCAAJ Aaron Judge
84TCAAR Anthony Rizzo/30 25.00 60.00
84TCACM Cedric Mullins/50 8.00 20.00
84TCAEJ Eloy Jimenez EXCH 75.00 200.00
84TCAFTJ Fernando Tatis Jr./50 500.00 1000.00
84TCAI Ichiro/20 125.00 300.00
84TCAJB Jake Bauers/50 8.00 20.00
84TCAJD Jacob deGrom/50 20.00 50.00
84TCAJS Justus Sheffield/50 8.00 20.00
84TCAJSO Juan Soto/50 50.00 120.00
84TCAJU Justin Upton/50 8.00 20.00
84TCAKA Kolby Allard/50 8.00 20.00
84TCAKT Kyle Tucker/50 20.00 50.00
84TCAMK Michael Kopech/50 15.00 40.00
84TCAMT Mike Trout/20 400.00 800.00
84TCANS Noah Syndergaard/50 20.00 50.00
84TCARAJ Ronald Acuna Jr./50 125.00 300.00
84TCASO Shohei Ohtani/20 125.00 300.00
84TCAVGJ Vladimir Guerrero Jr./50 200.00 500.00
84TCAWM Whit Merrifield/50 10.00 25.00

2019 Topps Chrome '84 Topps Autographs Orange Refractors

*ORANGE/25: .6X TO 1.5X p/r 50
*ORANGE/25: .5X TO 1.2X p/r 30
STATED ODDS 1:9503 HOBBY
STATED PRINT RUN 25 SER.#'d SETS
84TCAJSO Juan Soto 100.00 250.00

2019 Topps Chrome '99 Chrome Autographs

STATED ODDS 1:4439 HOBBY
PRINT RUNS B/WN 15-99 COPIES PER
NO PRICING ON QTY 15
EXCHANGE DEADLINE 6/30/2021
*ORANGE/25: .6X TO 1.5X p/r 75-99
*ORANGE/25: .5X TO 1.2X p/r 30-55
99TCAAB Adrian Beltre/30 25.00 60.00
99TCABW Bernie Williams/45 25.00 60.00
99TCAFTJ Fernando Tatis Jr./99 150.00 400.00
99TCAJA Jose Altuve/30 25.00 60.00
99TCAJS Justus Sheffield/99 8.00 20.00
99TCAJSO Juan Soto/75 40.00 100.00
99TCAKA Kolby Allard/99 8.00 20.00
99TCAKB Kris Bryant/40 40.00 100.00
99TCAMK Michael Kopech/99 10.00 25.00
99TCAMM Mark McGwire/30 75.00 200.00
99TCAPG Paul Goldschmidt/45 20.00 50.00
99TCAPM Pedro Martinez 50.00 120.00
99TCARAJ Ronald Acuna Jr./75 60.00 150.00
99TCAVGJ Vladimir Guerrero Jr./99 150.00 400.00
99TCAYM Yadier Molina/55 30.00 80.00

2019 Topps Chrome Debut Gear

STATED ODDS 1:554 HOBBY
*GREEN/99: .5X TO 1.2X BASIC
*ORANGE/25: 1X TO 2.5X BASIC
DGAB Adrian Beltre 4.00 10.00
DGAC Aroldis Chapman 4.00 10.00
DGAM Andrew McCutchen 4.00 10.00
DGAP Albert Pujols 5.00 12.00
DGAR Alex Rodriguez 5.00 12.00
DGBD Brian Dozier 3.00 8.00
DGCF Carlton Fisk 6.00 15.00
DGCK Craig Kimbrel 3.00 8.00
DGCS Chris Sale 4.00 10.00
DGDG Didi Gregorius 3.00 8.00
DGDM Daniel Murphy 3.00 8.00
DGEL Mike Piazza 4.00 10.00
DGGM Greg Maddux 5.00 12.00
DGGS Giancarlo Stanton 4.00 10.00
DGIK Ian Kinsler 3.00 8.00
DGIR Ivan Rodriguez 3.00 8.00
DGI Ichiro
DGJD Josh Donaldson 3.00 8.00
DGJH Jason Heyward 3.00 8.00
DGJM J.D. Martinez 4.00 10.00
DGJS Jean Segura 4.00 10.00
DGJSC Jonathan Schoop 2.50 6.00
DGJV Justin Verlander 4.00 10.00
DGMM Manny Machado 4.00 10.00
DGMMC Mark McGwire 6.00 15.00
DGMMO Mike Moustakas 3.00 8.00
DGMO Marcell Ozuna 4.00 10.00
DGMS Max Scherzer 4.00 10.00
DGNC Nelson Cruz 4.00 10.00
DGNG Nomar Garciaparra 3.00 8.00
DGRC Robinson Cano 3.00 8.00
DGRCL Roger Clemens 5.00 12.00
DGRH Rickey Henderson 6.00 15.00
DGVGS Vladimir Guerrero 3.00 8.00
DGWM Wil Myers 2.50 6.00
DGYD Yu Darvish 4.00 10.00
DGYM Yoan Moncada 4.00 10.00

2019 Topps Chrome Debut Gear Autographs

STATED ODDS 1:2349 HOBBY
STATED PRINT RUN 50 SER.#'d SETS
EXCHANGE DEADLINE 6/30/2021
DGAB Adrian Beltre 20.00 50.00
DGAM Andrew McCutchen 40.00 100.00
DGAP Albert Pujols 75.00 200.00
DGAR Alex Rodriguez 60.00 510.00
DGCF Carlton Fisk
DGCS Chris Sale 12.00 30.00
DGDG Didi Gregorius 12.00 30.00
DGEL Mike Piazza 40.00 100.00
DGIK Ian Kinsler
DGIR Ivan Rodriguez 20.00 50.00
DGI Ichiro 125.00 300.00
DGJS Jean Segura 8.00 20.00
DGMMC Mark McGwire 25.00 60.00
DGMO Marcell Ozuna 12.00 30.00
DGRCL Roger Clemens 20.00 50.00
DGRH Rickey Henderson 40.00 100.00
DGTP Tommy Pham 5.00 12.00
DGVGS Vladimir Guerrero Sr. 30.00 80.00
DGWC Will Clark

2019 Topps Chrome Dual Rookie Autographs

STATED ODDS 1:25,339 HOBBY
STATED PRINT RUN 25 SER.#'d SETS
EXCHANGE DEADLINE 6/30/2021
DRAAW Allard/Wright 15.00 40.00
DRAFA Arcia/Fletcher 20.00 50.00
DRAGJ Guerrero Jr./Jimenez 125.00 300.00
DRAJT Tellez/ Jansen 15.00 40.00
DRAKO O'Hearn/Keller 30.00 80.00
DRALB Lowe/Bauers 25.00 60.00
DRAPH Hudson/Ponce de Leon 50.00 120.00
DRATU Urias/Tatis Jr. EXCH 400.00 1000.00

2019 Topps Chrome Freshman Flash

STATED ODDS 1:12 HOBBY
*GREEN/99: 4X TO 10X BASIC
*GOLD/50: 6X TO 15X BASIC
*ORANGE/25: 8X TO 20X BASIC
FF1 Kyle Tucker .50 1.25
FF2 Christin Stewart .30 .75
FF3 Chance Adams .25 .60
FF4 Kyle Wright .40 1.00
FF5 Jake Bauers .40 1.00
FF6 Cedric Mullins .40 1.00
FF7 Rowdy Tellez .40 1.00
FF8 Yusei Kikuchi .40 1.00
FF9 Ramon Laureano .50 1.25
FF10 Kolby Allard .40 1.00
FF11 Chris Shaw .40 1.00
FF12 Justus Sheffield .40 1.00
FF13 Ryan O'Hearn .25 .60
FF14 Michael Kopech .50 1.25
FF15 Luis Urias .40 1.00

2019 Topps Chrome Freshman Flash Autographs

STATED ODDS 1:2883 HOBBY
STATED PRINT RUN 99 SER.#'d SETS
EXCHANGE DEADLINE 6/30/2021
*ORANGE/25: .6X TO 1.5X BASIC
FFABK Brad Keller 6.00 15.00
FFABL Brandon Lowe 12.00 30.00
FFACA Chance Adams 5.00 12.00
FFACM Cedric Mullins 8.00 20.00
FFACS Chris Shaw 8.00 20.00
FFACST Christin Stewart 6.00 15.00
FFADF David Fletcher 15.00 40.00
FFADH Dakota Hudson 6.00 15.00
FFADJ Danny Jansen 5.00 12.00
FFAFA Francisco Arcia 8.00 20.00
FFAFTJ Fernando Tatis Jr. 200.00 500.00
FFAJB Jake Bauers 8.00 20.00
FFAJS Justus Sheffield 8.00 20.00
FFAKA Kolby Allard 8.00 20.00
FFAKT Kyle Tucker 15.00 40.00
FFAKW Kyle Wright 8.00 20.00
FFAMK Michael Kopech 6.00 15.00
FFARL Ramon Laureano 20.00 50.00
FFAROH Ryan O'Hearn 5.00 12.00
FFART Rowdy Tellez 8.00 20.00
FFAVGJ Vladimir Guerrero Jr. 100.00 250.00

2019 Topps Chrome Future Stars

STATED ODDS 1:8 HOBBY
*GREEN/99: 4X TO 10X BASIC
*GOLD/50: 6X TO 15X BASIC
*ORANGE/25: 8X TO 20X BASIC
FS1 Shohei Ohtani .50 1.25
FS2 Willy Adames .25 .60
FS3 Miles Mikolas .40 1.00
FS4 David Bote .30 .75
FS5 Lourdes Gurriel Jr. .30 .75
FS6 Nick Kingham .25 .60
FS7 Freddy Peralta .40 1.00
FS8 Dereck Rodriguez .25 .60
FS9 Austin Meadows .30 .75
FS10 Juan Soto 1.25 3.00
FS11 Sandy Alcantara .25 .60
FS12 Franmil Reyes .25 .60
FS13 Dylan Cozens .25 .60
FS14 Gleyber Torres .75 2.00
FS15 Isiah Kiner-Falefa .25 .60
FS16 Brian Anderson .25 .60
FS17 Scott Kingery .30 .75
FS18 Amed Rosario .30 .75
FS19 Carson Kelly .25 .60
FS20 Ronald Acuna Jr. 2.00 5.00

2019 Topps Chrome Future Stars Autographs

STATED ODDS 1:2883 HOBBY
PRINT RUNS B/WN 30-99
EXCHANGE DEADLINE 6/30/2021
*ORANGE/25: .6X TO 1.5X p/r 99
*ORANGE/25: .5X TO 1.2X p/r 30
FSAAM Austin Meadows 6.00 15.00
FSACK Carson Kelly 5.00 12.00
FSADB David Bote 8.00 20.00
FSADC Dylan Cozens 5.00 12.00
FSADR Dereck Rodriguez
FSAFR Franmil Reyes 8.00 20.00

SAJS Juan Soto 40.00 100.00
SALGJ Lourdes Gurriel Jr. 6.00 15.00
SAMM Miles Mikolas 8.00 20.00
SARAJ Ronald Acuna Jr. 60.00 150.00
SASK Scott Kingery 6.00 15.00
SASO Shohei Ohtani/30 75.00 200.00
SAWA Willy Adames 5.00 12.00

2019 Topps Chrome Greatness Returns

STATED ODDS 1:24 HOBBY
GREEN/99: 4X TO 10X BASIC
GOLD/50: 6X TO 15X BASIC
ORANGE/25: 8X TO 20X BASIC
GRE1 Benintendi/Yaz .60 1.50
GRE2 Ryan/Verlander 1.25 3.00
GRE3 Ryan/Ohtani 1.25 3.00
GRE4 Gibson/Scherzer .40 1.00
GRE5 Alomar/Lindor .40 1.00
GRE6 Judge/ Jeter 1.00 2.50
GRE7 Cobb/Harper .60 1.50
GRE8 Hank/Trout 2.00 5.00
GRE9 Yount/ Yelich .50 1.25
GRE10 Acuna Jr./ Trout 2.00 5.00
GRE11 Torres/Jeter 1.00 2.50
GRE12 Williams/Betts .75 2.00
GRE13 Stanton/ Jackson .40 1.00
GRE14 Baez/Banks .50 1.25
GRE15 Koufax/Kershaw .75 2.00

2019 Topps Chrome Rookie Autographs

STATED ODDS 1:17 HOBBY
PRINTING PLATE ODDS 1:15,594 HOBBY
PLATE PRINT RUN 1 SET PER COLOR
BLACK-CYAN-MAGENTA-YELLOW ISSUED
NO PLATE PRICING DUE TO SCARCITY
EXCHANGE DEADLINE 6/30/2021
RAAC Adam Cimber 2.50 6.00
RAAD Austin Dean 2.50 6.00
RAAG Adolis Garcia 2.50 6.00
RAAGA Aramis Garcia 2.50 6.00
RAAR Austin Riley 15.00 40.00
RABK Brad Keller 2.50 6.00
RABL Brandon Lowe 15.00 40.00
RABR Brendan Rodgers 8.00 20.00
RABW Bryse Wilson 6.00 15.00
RACA Chance Adams 2.50 6.00
RACB Corbin Burnes 8.00 20.00
RACM Cedric Mullins 4.00 10.00
RACP Cionel Perez 2.50 6.00
RACPA Chris Paddack 20.00 50.00
RACS Chris Shaw 4.00 10.00
RACST Christin Stewart 3.00 8.00
RADF David Fletcher 6.00 15.00
RADH Dakota Hudson 6.00 15.00
RADJ Danny Jansen EXCH 10.00 25.00
RADL Dawel Lugo 4.00 10.00
RADP Daniel Poncedeleon 4.00 10.00
RADS DJ Stewart 3.00 8.00
RADSA Dennis Santana EXCH 6.00 15.00
RAEDL Enyel De Los Santos 2.50 6.00
RAEJ Eloy Jimenez 30.00 80.00
RAFA Francisco Arcia 4.00 10.00
RAFT Fernando Tatis Jr. 200.00 500.00
RAFV Framber Valdez 6.00 15.00
RAGC Griffin Canning 5.00 12.00
RAHF Heath Fillmyer 2.50 6.00
RAIG Isaac Galloway 2.50 6.00
RAJB Jake Bauers 4.00 10.00
RAJBF Jalen Beeks 2.50 6.00
RAJC Jake Cave 5.00 12.00
RAJD Jon Duplantier 2.50 6.00
RAJJ Josh James 4.00 10.00
RAJM Jeff McNeil 15.00 40.00
RAJN Jacob Nix 3.00 8.00
RAJR Josh Rogers 2.50 6.00
RAJS Jeffrey Springs 2.50 6.00
RAJSH Justus Sheffield 4.00 10.00
RAKA Kolby Allard 4.00 10.00
RAKH Keston Hiura 30.00 80.00
RAKK Kevin Kramer 3.00 8.00
RAKN Kevin Newman 4.00 10.00
RAKT Kyle Tucker 15.00 40.00
RAKW Kyle Wright 10.00 25.00
RAMK Michael Kopech 10.00 25.00
RAMKE Mitch Keller 3.00 8.00
RAMS Myles Straw 4.00 10.00
RANB Nick Burdi 2.50 6.00
RANC Nicholas Ciuffo 2.50 6.00
RANS Nick Senzel 12.00 30.00
RAPA Peter Alonso 60.00 150.00
RAPL Pablo Lopez 5.00 12.00
RAPW Patrick Wisdom 2.50 6.00
RARB Ray Black 2.50 6.00
RARBO Ryan Borucki 2.50 6.00
RARL Ramon Laureano 8.00 20.00
RARM Reese McGuire 4.00 10.00
RAROH Ryan O'Hearn 2.50 6.00
RART Rowdy Tellez 4.00 10.00
RASD Steven Duggar 3.00 8.00
RASG Stephen Gonsalves 2.50 6.00
RASRF Sean Reid-Foley 2.50 6.00
RATB Ty Buttrey 4.00 10.00
RATP Thomas Pannone 4.00 10.00
RATR Trevor Richards 2.50 6.00
RATT Touki Toussaint EXCH 4.00 10.00
RATW Taylor Ward 2.50 6.00
RAVGJ Vladimir Guerrero Jr. 75.00 200.00
RAWA Willians Astudillo 2.50 6.00
RAWS Will Smith 30.00 80.00
RAYK Yusei Kikuchi 6.00 15.00

2019 Topps Chrome Rookie Autographs Blue Refractors

*BLUE REF: .75X TO 2X BASIC
STATED ODDS 1:409 HOBBY
STATED PRINT RUN 150 SER.#'d SETS
EXCHANGE DEADLINE 6/30/2021
RAFT Fernando Tatis Jr. 500.00 1200.00
RAJL Jonathan Loaisiga 10.00 25.00
RALU Luis Urias 20.00 50.00

2019 Topps Chrome Rookie Autographs Blue Wave Refractors

*BLUE WAVE REF: .75X TO 2X BASIC
STATED ODDS 1:409 HOBBY
STATED PRINT RUN 150 SER.#'d SETS
EXCHANGE DEADLINE 6/30/2021
RAFT Fernando Tatis Jr. 500.00 1200.00
RAJL Jonathan Loaisiga 10.00 25.00
RALU Luis Urias 20.00 50.00

2019 Topps Chrome Rookie Autographs Gold Refractors

*GOLD REF: 1.2X TO 3X BASIC
STATED ODDS 1:1227 HOBBY
STATED PRINT RUN 50 SER.#'d SETS
EXCHANGE DEADLINE 6/30/2021
RAAR Austin Riley 100.00 250.00
RABR Brendan Rodgers 30.00 80.00
RACST Christin Stewart 15.00 40.00
RAFT Fernando Tatis Jr. 750.00 2000.00
RAJL Jonathan Loaisiga 15.00 40.00
RAJM Jeff McNeil 60.00 150.00
RAJSH Justus Sheffield 25.00 60.00
RAKH Keston Hiura 150.00 400.00
RALU Luis Urias 60.00 150.00
RAMKE Mitch Keller 15.00 40.00
RAVGJ Vladimir Guerrero Jr. 500.00 1000.00

2019 Topps Chrome Rookie Autographs Gold Wave Refractors

*GOLD WAVE REF: 1.2X TO 3X BASIC
STATED ODDS 1:834 HOBBY
STATED PRINT RUN 50 SER.#'d SETS
EXCHANGE DEADLINE 6/30/2021
RAAR Austin Riley 100.00 250.00
RABR Brendan Rodgers 30.00 80.00
RACST Christin Stewart 15.00 40.00
RAFT Fernando Tatis Jr. 750.00 2000.00
RAJL Jonathan Loaisiga 15.00 40.00
RAJM Jeff McNeil 60.00 150.00
RAJSH Justus Sheffield 25.00 60.00
RAKH Keston Hiura 150.00 400.00
RALU Luis Urias 60.00 150.00
RAMKE Mitch Keller 15.00 40.00
RAVGJ Vladimir Guerrero Jr. 500.00 1000.00

2019 Topps Chrome Rookie Autographs Green Refractors

*GREEN REF: 1X TO 2.5X BASIC
STATED ODDS 1:416 BLASTER
STATED PRINT RUN 99 SER.#'d SETS
EXCHANGE DEADLINE 6/30/2021
RACST Christin Stewart 12.00 30.00
RAFT Fernando Tatis Jr. 600.00 1500.00
RAJL Jonathan Loaisiga 12.00 30.00
RALU Luis Urias 25.00 60.00

2019 Topps Chrome Rookie Autographs Orange Refractors

*ORANGE REF: 1.5X TO 4X BASIC
STATED ODDS 1:793 HOBBY
STATED PRINT RUN 25 SER.#'d SETS
EXCHANGE DEADLINE 6/30/2021
RAAR Austin Riley 150.00 400.00
RABR Brendan Rodgers 40.00 100.00
RACPA Chris Paddack 200.00 500.00
RACST Christin Stewart 20.00 50.00
RAFT Fernando Tatis Jr. 1000.00 2500.00
RAJL Jonathan Loaisiga 20.00 50.00
RAJM Jeff McNeil 75.00 200.00
RAJSH Justus Sheffield 30.00 80.00
RAKH Keston Hiura 200.00 500.00
RALU Luis Urias 75.00 200.00
RAMKE Mitch Keller 20.00 50.00
RAVGJ Vladimir Guerrero Jr. 600.00 1200.00

2019 Topps Chrome Rookie Autographs Orange Wave Refractors

*ORANGE WAVE REF: 1.5X TO 4X BASIC
STATED ODDS 1:1667 HOBBY
STATED PRINT RUN 25 SER.#'d SETS
EXCHANGE DEADLINE 6/30/2021
RAAR Austin Riley 150.00 400.00
RABR Brendan Rodgers 40.00 100.00
RACPA Chris Paddack 200.00 500.00
RACST Christin Stewart 20.00 50.00
RAFT Fernando Tatis Jr. 1000.00 2500.00
RAJL Jonathan Loaisiga 20.00 50.00
RAJM Jeff McNeil 75.00 200.00
RAJSH Justus Sheffield 30.00 80.00
RAKH Keston Hiura 200.00 500.00
RALU Luis Urias 75.00 200.00
RAMKE Mitch Keller 20.00 50.00
RAVGJ Vladimir Guerrero Jr. 600.00 1200.00

2019 Topps Chrome Rookie Autographs Purple Refractors

*PURPLE REF: .6X TO 1.5X BASIC
STATED ODDS 1:246 HOBBY
STATED PRINT RUN 250 SER.#'d SETS
EXCHANGE DEADLINE 6/30/2021
RAJL Jonathan Loaisiga 5.00 12.00
RALU Luis Urias 15.00 40.00

2019 Topps Chrome Rookie Autographs Refractors

*REF: .5X TO 1.2X BASIC
STATED ODDS 1:123 HOBBY
STATED PRINT RUN 499 SER.#'d SETS
EXCHANGE DEADLINE 6/30/2021
RALU Luis Urias 12.00 30.00

2019 Topps Chrome Update

PRINTING PLATE ODDS 1:4576 PACKS
PLATE PRINT RUN 1 SET PER COLOR
BLACK-CYAN-MAGENTA-YELLOW ISSUED
NO PLATE PRICING DUE TO SCARCITY
1 Paul Goldschmidt .30 .75
2 Josh Donaldson .25 .60
3 Yasiel Puig .30 .75
4 Adam Ottavino .20 .50
5 DJ LeMahieu .30 .75
6 Dallas Keuchel .25 .60
7 Charlie Morton .30 .75
8 Zack Britton .20 .50
9 C.J. Cron .20 .50
10 Jonathan Schoop .20 .50
11 Robinson Cano .25 .60
12 Edwin Encarnacion .30 .75
13 Domingo Santana .25 .60
14 J.T. Realmuto .30 .75
15 Hunter Pence .25 .60
16 Edwin Diaz .25 .60
17 Yasmani Grandal .20 .50
18 Chris Paddack RC .75 2.00
19 Jon Duplantier RC .40 1.00
20 Nick Anderson RC .40 1.00
21 Vladimir Guerrero Jr. RC 2.50 6.00
22 Carter Kieboom RC .60 1.50
23 Nate Lowe RC .50 1.25
24 Pedro Avila RC .40 1.00
25 Ryan Helsley RC .50 1.25
26 Lane Thomas RC .60 1.50
27 Michael Chavis RC .60 1.50
28 Thairo Estrada RC .60 1.50
29 Bryan Reynolds RC 1.25 3.00
30 Darwinzon Hernandez RC .40 1.00
31 Griffin Canning RC .60 1.50
32 Nick Senzel RC 1.25 3.00
33 Cal Quantrill RC .40 1.00
34 Matthew Beaty RC .75 2.00
35 Spencer Turnbull RC .60 1.50
36 Corbin Martin RC .60 1.50
37 Austin Riley RC 2.00 5.00
38 Keston Hiura RC 1.25 3.00
39 Nicky Lopez RC .60 1.50
40 Oscar Mercado RC 1.00 2.50
41 Harold Ramirez RC .60 1.50
42 Cavan Biggio RC 2.00 5.00
43 Kevin Cron RC 1.25 3.00
44 Josh Naylor RC .50 1.25
45 Luis Arraez RC 1.50 4.00
46 Shaun Anderson RC .40 1.00
47 Will Smith RC 1.00 2.50
48 Mitch Keller RC .50 1.25
49 Mike Yastrzemski RC 3.00 8.00
50 Craig Kimbrel .25 .60
51 Yusei Kikuchi RD .30 .75
52 Pete Alonso RD 1.50 4.00
53 Eloy Jimenez RD .75 2.00
54 Fernando Tatis Jr. RD 10.00 25.00
55 Chris Paddack RD .40 1.00
56 Nick Senzel RD .60 1.50
57 Michael Chavis RD .30 .75
58 Vladimir Guerrero Jr. RD 1.25 3.00
59 Carter Kieboom RD .30 .75
60 Corbin Martin RD .30 .75
61 Austin Riley RD 1.00 2.50
62 Keston Hiura RD .60 1.50
63 Brendan Rodgers RD .30 .75
64 Cavan Biggio RD 1.00 2.50
65 Griffin Canning RD .30 .75
66 Gary Sanchez AS .30 .75
67 Willson Contreras AS .25 .60
68 Carlos Santana AS .25 .60
69 Freddie Freeman AS .40 1.00
70 DJ LeMahieu AS .30 .75
71 Ketel Marte AS .25 .60
72 Alex Bregman AS .30 .75
73 Nolan Arenado AS .40 1.00
74 Jorge Polanco AS .20 .50
75 Javier Baez AS .40 1.00
76 Mike Trout AS 1.50 4.00
77 Christian Yelich AS .40 1.00
78 George Springer AS .25 .60
79 Cody Bellinger AS .60 1.50
80 Michael Brantley AS .25 .60
81 Ronald Acuna Jr. AS 1.50 4.00
82 Francisco Lindor AS .30 .75
83 Mookie Betts AS .50 1.25
84 Lucas Giolito AS .25 .60
85 Justin Verlander AS .30 .75
86 Pete Alonso AS 1.50 4.00
87 Josh Bell AS .25 .60
88 Kris Bryant AS .40 1.00
89 Walker Buehler AS .40 1.00
90 Trevor Story AS .30 .75
91 Clayton Kershaw AS .60 1.50
92 Jake Odorizzi AS .20 .50
93 Luis Castillo AS .25 .60
94 Matt Chapman AS .30 .75
95 Joey Gallo AS .25 .60
96 Austin Meadows AS .25 .60
97 Charlie Blackmon AS .30 .75
98 Whit Merrifield AS .30 .75
99 David Dahl AS .20 .50
100 Shane Bieber AS .30 .75

2019 Topps Chrome Update Blue Refractors

*BLUE REF: 3X TO 8X BASIC
*BLUE REF RC: 1.5X TO 4X BASIC RC
STATED ODDS 1:123 PACKS
STATED PRINT RUN 150 SER.#'d SETS
18 Chris Paddack 12.00 30.00
21 Vladimir Guerrero Jr. 50.00 120.00
22 Carter Kieboom 20.00 50.00
23 Nate Lowe 5.00 12.00
27 Michael Chavis 8.00 20.00
28 Thairo Estrada 8.00 20.00
29 Bryan Reynolds 10.00 25.00
32 Nick Senzel 20.00 50.00
38 Keston Hiura 30.00 80.00
40 Oscar Mercado 10.00 25.00
45 Luis Arraez 25.00 60.00
47 Will Smith 15.00 40.00
48 Mitch Keller 5.00 12.00
52 Pete Alonso 30.00 80.00
53 Eloy Jimenez 8.00 20.00
58 Vladimir Guerrero Jr. 25.00 60.00
62 Keston Hiura 12.00 30.00
86 Pete Alonso AS 20.00 50.00

2019 Topps Chrome Update Gold Refractors

*GOLD REF: 6X TO 15X BASIC
*GOLD REF RC: 3X TO 8X BASIC RC
STATED ODDS 1:367 PACKS
STATED PRINT RUN 50 SER.#'d SETS
18 Chris Paddack 25.00 60.00
21 Vladimir Guerrero Jr. 100.00 250.00
22 Carter Kieboom 40.00 100.00
23 Nate Lowe 10.00 25.00
27 Michael Chavis 15.00 40.00
28 Thairo Estrada 15.00 40.00
29 Bryan Reynolds 20.00 50.00
32 Nick Senzel 40.00 100.00
37 Austin Riley 30.00 80.00
38 Keston Hiura 60.00 150.00
40 Oscar Mercado 20.00 50.00
45 Luis Arraez 50.00 120.00
47 Will Smith 30.00 80.00
48 Mitch Keller 10.00 25.00
52 Pete Alonso 60.00 150.00
53 Eloy Jimenez 15.00 40.00
58 Vladimir Guerrero Jr. 50.00 120.00
62 Keston Hiura 25.00 60.00
86 Pete Alonso AS 40.00 100.00

2019 Topps Chrome Update Green Refractors

*GREEN REF: 4X TO 10X BASIC
*GREEN REF RC: 2X TO 5X BASIC RC
STATED ODDS 1:186 PACKS
STATED PRINT RUN 99 SER.#'d SETS
18 Chris Paddack 15.00 40.00
21 Vladimir Guerrero Jr. 60.00 150.00
22 Carter Kieboom 25.00 60.00
23 Nate Lowe 6.00 15.00
27 Michael Chavis 10.00 25.00
28 Thairo Estrada 10.00 25.00
29 Bryan Reynolds 12.00 30.00
32 Nick Senzel 25.00 60.00
38 Keston Hiura 40.00 100.00
40 Oscar Mercado 12.00 30.00
45 Luis Arraez 30.00 80.00
47 Will Smith 20.00 50.00
48 Mitch Keller 6.00 15.00
52 Pete Alonso 40.00 100.00
53 Eloy Jimenez 10.00 25.00
58 Vladimir Guerrero Jr. 30.00 80.00
62 Keston Hiura 15.00 40.00
86 Pete Alonso AS 25.00 60.00

2019 Topps Chrome Update Orange Refractors

*ORANGE REF: 8X TO 20X BASIC
*ORANGE REF RC: 4X TO 10X BASIC RC
STATED ODDS 1:734 PACKS
STATED PRINT RUN 25 SER.#'d SETS
18 Chris Paddack 30.00 80.00
21 Vladimir Guerrero Jr. 125.00 300.00
22 Carter Kieboom 50.00 120.00
23 Nate Lowe 12.00 30.00
27 Michael Chavis 20.00 50.00
28 Thairo Estrada 20.00 50.00
29 Bryan Reynolds 25.00 60.00
32 Nick Senzel 50.00 120.00
37 Austin Riley 40.00 100.00
38 Keston Hiura 75.00 200.00
40 Oscar Mercado 25.00 60.00
45 Luis Arraez 60.00 150.00
47 Will Smith 40.00 100.00
48 Mitch Keller 12.00 30.00
52 Pete Alonso 75.00 200.00
53 Eloy Jimenez 20.00 50.00
58 Vladimir Guerrero Jr. 60.00 150.00
62 Keston Hiura 30.00 80.00
86 Pete Alonso AS 60.00 150.00

2019 Topps Chrome Update Pink Refractors

*PINK REF: 2X TO 5X BASIC
*PINK REF RC: 1X TO 2.5X BASIC RC
TWO PER HANGER PACK

2019 Topps Chrome Update Purple Refractors

*PURPLE REF: 2.5X TO 6X BASIC
*PURPLE REF RC: 1.2X TO 3X BASIC RC
STATED ODDS 1:105 PACKS
STATED PRINT RUN 175 SER.#'d SETS
18 Chris Paddack 10.00 25.00
21 Vladimir Guerrero Jr. 40.00 100.00
22 Carter Kieboom 15.00 40.00
23 Nate Lowe 4.00 10.00
27 Michael Chavis 6.00 15.00
28 Thairo Estrada 6.00 15.00
29 Bryan Reynolds 8.00 20.00
32 Nick Senzel 15.00 40.00
38 Keston Hiura 25.00 60.00
40 Oscar Mercado 8.00 20.00
45 Luis Arraez 20.00 50.00
47 Will Smith 12.00 30.00
48 Mitch Keller 4.00 10.00
52 Pete Alonso 25.00 60.00
53 Eloy Jimenez 6.00 15.00
58 Vladimir Guerrero Jr. 20.00 50.00
62 Keston Hiura 10.00 25.00
86 Pete Alonso AS 15.00 40.00

2019 Topps Chrome Update Refractors

*REF: 1.5X TO 4X BASIC
*REF RC: .75X TO 2X BASIC RC
STATED ODDS 1:74 PACKS
STATED PRINT RUN 250 SER.#'d SETS
18 Chris Paddack 6.00 15.00
21 Vladimir Guerrero Jr. 25.00 60.00
22 Carter Kieboom 10.00 25.00
23 Nate Lowe 2.50 6.00
27 Michael Chavis 4.00 10.00
28 Thairo Estrada 4.00 10.00
29 Bryan Reynolds 5.00 12.00
32 Nick Senzel 10.00 25.00
38 Keston Hiura 15.00 40.00
40 Oscar Mercado 5.00 12.00
45 Luis Arraez 12.00 30.00
47 Will Smith 8.00 20.00
48 Mitch Keller 2.50 6.00
52 Pete Alonso 15.00 40.00
53 Eloy Jimenez 4.00 10.00
58 Vladimir Guerrero Jr. 12.00 30.00
62 Keston Hiura 6.00 15.00
86 Pete Alonso AS 10.00 25.00

2019 Topps Chrome Update X-Fractors

*X-FRAC: 2.5X TO 6X BASIC
*X-FRAC RC: 1.2X TO 3X BASIC RC
STATED ODDS 1:93 PACKS
STATED PRINT RUN 199 SER.#'d SETS
18 Chris Paddack 10.00 25.00
21 Vladimir Guerrero Jr. 40.00 100.00
22 Carter Kieboom 15.00 40.00
23 Nate Lowe 4.00 10.00
27 Michael Chavis 6.00 15.00
28 Thairo Estrada 6.00 15.00
29 Bryan Reynolds 8.00 20.00
32 Nick Senzel 15.00 40.00
38 Keston Hiura 25.00 60.00
40 Oscar Mercado 8.00 20.00
45 Luis Arraez 20.00 50.00
47 Will Smith 12.00 30.00
48 Mitch Keller 4.00 10.00
52 Pete Alonso 25.00 60.00
53 Eloy Jimenez 6.00 15.00
58 Vladimir Guerrero Jr. 20.00 50.00
62 Keston Hiura 10.00 25.00
86 Pete Alonso AS 15.00 40.00

2019 Topps Chrome Update 150 Years of Professional Baseball

STATED ODDS 1:4 PACKS
150C1 Nolan Ryan 1.25 3.00
150C2 David Ortiz .40 1.00
150C3 Ichiro .50 1.25
150C4 Rickey Henderson .40 1.00
150C5 Carl Yastrzemski .60 1.50
150C6 Justin Verlander .40 1.00
150C7 Ozzie Smith .50 1.25
150C8 Steve Carlton .30 .75
150C9 Mark McGwire .60 1.50
150C10 Mike Trout 2.00 5.00
150C11 Babe Ruth 1.00 2.50
150C12 Ted Williams .75 2.00
150C13 Cal Ripken Jr. 1.25 3.00
150C14 Ken Griffey Jr. .75 2.00
150C15 Roberto Clemente 1.00 2.50
150C16 Sandy Koufax .75 2.00
150C17 Jackie Robinson .40 1.00
150C18 Frank Robinson .30 .75
150C19 Johnny Bench .40 1.00
150C20 Frank Thomas .40 1.00
150C21 Clayton Kershaw .75 2.00
150C22 Hank Aaron .75 2.00
150C23 Derek Jeter 1.00 2.50
150C24 Tony Gwynn .40 1.00
150C25 George Brett .75 2.00

2019 Topps Chrome Update Autograph Refractors

STATED ODDS 1:40 PACKS
EXCHANGE DEADLINE 9/30/2021
CUAAB Andrew Benintendi 15.00 40.00
CUAAH Adam Haseley 4.00 10.00
CUAAK Andrew Knizner 4.00 10.00
CUAAN Aaron Nola 6.00 15.00
CUAAR Austin Riley 12.00 30.00
CUABL Brandon Lowe 20.00 50.00
CUABRE Bryan Reynolds 8.00 20.00
CUABW Brandon Woodruff 2.50 6.00
CUACA Chance Adams 2.50 6.00
CUACF Clint Frazier 4.00 10.00
CUACP Chris Paddack 10.00 25.00
CUACT Cole Tucker 4.00 10.00
CUADH Darwinzon Hernandez 2.50 6.00
CUADSW Dansby Swanson 10.00 25.00
CUAEL Elvis Luciano 4.00 10.00
CUAGU Gio Urshela 15.00 40.00
CUAHR Harold Ramirez 4.00 10.00
CUAJA Jorge Alfaro 2.50 6.00
CUAJB Jalen Beeks 2.50 6.00
CUAJD Jon Duplantier 2.50 6.00
CUAJH JD Hammer 3.00 8.00
CUAJMA Jason Martin 3.00 8.00
CUAJN Josh Naylor 10.00 25.00
CUAJS Jean Segura 4.00 10.00
CUALA Luis Arraez 25.00 60.00
CUALT Lane Thomas 8.00 20.00
CUALV Luke Voit 50.00 120.00
CUAMKE Merrill Kelly 2.50 6.00
CUAMM Manny Machado 25.00 60.00
CUAMY Mike Yastrzemski 40.00 100.00
CUANL Nicky Lopez 4.00 10.00
CUANLO Nate Lowe 6.00 15.00
CUAPA Pedro Avila 2.50 6.00
CUAPC Patrick Corbin 3.00 8.00
CUARH Ryan Helsley 3.00 8.00
CUARHO Rhys Hoskins 8.00 20.00
CUARL Richard Lovelady 2.50 6.00
CUASA Shaun Anderson 2.50 6.00
CUASO Shohei Ohtani 75.00 200.00
CUATB Trevor Bauer 15.00 40.00
CUATE Thairo Estrada 10.00 25.00
CUATT Trent Thornton 2.50 6.00
CUAVR Victor Robles 6.00 15.00
CUAWS Will Smith 15.00 40.00
CUAZP Zach Plesac 25.00 60.00

2019 Topps Chrome Update Autograph Gold Refractors

*GOLD REF: 1.2X TO 3X BASIC
STATED ODDS 1:715 PACKS
STATED PRINT RUN 50 SER.#'d STES
EXCHANGE DEADLINE 9/30/2021

2019 Topps Chrome Update Autograph Orange Refractors

*ORANGE REF: 1.5X TO 4X BASIC
STATED ODDS 1:1404 PACKS
STATED PRINT RUN 25 SER.#'d STES
EXCHANGE DEADLINE 9/30/2021
CUASO Shohei Ohtani 125.00 300.00

2019 Topps Chrome Update Autograph X-Fractors

*X-FRAC: .6X TO 1.5X BASIC
STATED ODDS 1:292 PACKS
STATED PRINT RUN 125 SER.#'d STES
EXCHANGE DEADLINE 9/30/2021

2019 Topps Chrome Update Rookie Autograph Refractors

STATED ODDS 1:40 PACKS
EXCHANGE DEADLINE 9/30/2021
*X-FRAC/125: .6X TO 1.5X
*GOLD REF/50: 1.2X TO 3X
*ORANGE REF/25: 1.5X TO 4X
RDACK Carter Kieboom 12.00 30.00
RDAEJ Eloy Jimenez 25.00 60.00
RDAFT Fernando Tatis Jr. 100.00 250.00
RDAKH Keston Hiura 20.00 50.00
RDAMC Michael Chavis 12.00 30.00
RDAPA Pete Alonso 75.00 200.00
RDAVG Vladimir Guerrero Jr. 60.00 150.00

2019 Topps Chrome Update The Family Business

STATED ODDS 1:4 PACKS
FBC1 Ken Griffey Jr. .75 2.00
FBC2 Cal Ripken Jr. 1.25 3.00
FBC3 Roberto Alomar .30 .75
FBC4 Vladimir Guerrero .30 .75
FBC5 Ivan Rodriguez .30 .75
FBC6 Roger Clemens .50 1.25
FBC7 Yadier Molina .40 1.00
FBC8 Ronald Acuna Jr. 2.00 5.00
FBC9 Cecil Fielder .25 .60
FBC10 Mariano Rivera .50 1.25
FBC11 Hank Aaron .75 2.00
FBC12 Tim Raines .30 .75
FBC13 Jose Canseco .30 .75
FBC14 Bryce Harper .60 1.50
FBC15 Fernando Tatis Jr. 2.50 6.00
FBC16 Tony Gwynn .40 1.00
FBC17 Corey Seager .40 1.00
FBC18 Nolan Arenado .50 1.25
FBC19 Vladimir Guerrero Jr. 1.50 4.00
FBC20 Robinson Cano .30 .75
FBC21 Cody Bellinger .75 2.00
FBC22 Pedro Martinez .30 .75
FBC23 Manny Machado .30 .75
FBC24 Dee Gordon .25 .60
FBC25 Reggie Jackson .30 .75

2016 Topps Chrome Holiday Mega Box

HMT1 Trevor Story 2.50 6.00
HMT2 Seung-Hwan Oh 1.50 4.00
HMT3 Ian Kennedy .60 1.50
HMT4 Miguel Sano 1.00 2.50
HMT5 Pedro Alvarez .60 1.50
HMT6 Joey Rickard .60 1.50
HMT7 Kenta Maeda 1.25 3.00
HMT8 Hyun-Soo Kim 1.00 2.50
HMT9 Robert Stephenson .60 1.50
HMT10 Todd Frazier .75 2.00
HMT11 Doug Fister .60 1.50
HMT12 Asdrubal Cabrera .75 2.00
HMT13 Zack Greinke .75 2.00
HMT14 Cameron Maybin .60 1.50
HMT15 Byung-Ho Park .75 2.00
HMT16 Denard Span .60 1.50
HMT17 Yonder Alonso .60 1.50
HMT18 Trayce Thompson 1.00 2.50
HMT19 Nomar Mazara 1.00 2.50
HMT20 Jeremy Hazelbaker .75 2.00
HMT21 Ross Stripling .60 1.50
HMT22 Jameson Taillon .75 2.00
HMT23 Mallex Smith .60 1.50
HMT24 Vince Velasquez .60 1.50
HMT25 Tyler Naquin .75 2.00
HMT26 Blake Snell .75 2.00
HMT27 Julio Urias 2.00 5.00
HMT28 Ian Desmond .60 1.50
HMT29 Neil Walker .75 2.00
HMT30 Jeremy Hellickson .60 1.50
HMT31 Craig Kimbrel .75 2.00
HMT32 Albert Almora .75 2.00
HMT33 Aledmys Diaz 1.00 2.50
HMT34 Shelby Miller .75 2.00
HMT35 Starlin Castro .60 1.50
HMT36 Matt Wieters 1.00 2.50
HMT37 Jose Berrios .75 2.00
HMT38 Dexter Fowler .75 2.00
HMT39 James Shields .60 1.50
HMT40 Jed Lowrie .60 1.50
HMT41 Corey Seager 5.00 12.00
HMT42 Michael Fulmer 1.00 2.50
HMT43 Michael Conforto .75 2.00
HMT44 Luis Severino .75 2.00
HMT45 Francisco Rodriguez .75 2.00
HMT46 Stephen Piscotty 1.00 2.50
HMT47 Matt Joyce .60 1.50
HMT48 Aaron Nola 1.25 3.00
HMT49 Kyle Schwarber 2.00 5.00
HMT50 Ben Revere .60 1.50

2016 Topps Chrome Holiday Mega Box Gold Refractors

*GOLD REF: 3X TO 8X BASIC
STATED PRINT RUN 50 SER.#'d SETS

2016 Topps Chrome Holiday Mega Box Refractors

*REF: .75X TO 2X BASIC
STATED PRINT RUN 250 SER.#'d SETS

2016 Topps Chrome Holiday Mega Box X-Fractors

*X-FRACTOR: 1X TO 2.5X BASIC
STATED PRINT RUN 99 SER.#'d SETS

2016 Topps Chrome Holiday Mega Box 3000 Hits Club

3000C1 Carl Yastrzemski 1.50 4.00
3000C2 Ty Cobb 1.50 4.00
3000C3 Hank Aaron 2.00 5.00
3000C4 Stan Musial 1.50 4.00
3000C5 Honus Wagner 1.00 2.50
3000C6 Paul Molitor 1.00 2.50
3000C7 Willie Mays 2.00 5.00
3000C8 Eddie Murray .75 2.00
3000C9 Cal Ripken Jr. 3.00 8.00
3000C10 George Brett 2.00 5.00
3000C11 Robin Yount 1.00 2.50
3000C12 Tony Gwynn 1.00 2.50
3000C13 Ichiro Suzuki 1.25 3.00
3000C14 Craig Biggio .75 2.00
3000C15 Rickey Henderson 1.00 2.50
3000C16 Rod Carew .75 2.00
3000C17 Lou Brock .75 2.00
3000C18 Wade Boggs .75 2.00
3000C19 Roberto Clemente 2.50 6.00
3000C20 Al Kaline 1.00 2.50

2016 Topps Chrome Holiday Mega Box All Star Stitches

ASRCAR Addison Russell 6.00 15.00
ASRCARI Anthony Rizzo 10.00 25.00
ASRCBH Bryce Harper 10.00 25.00
ASRCBP Buster Posey 8.00 20.00
ASRCCK Clayton Kershaw 12.00 30.00
ASRCCS Corey Seager 30.00 80.00
ASRCDO David Ortiz 6.00 15.00
ASRCEE Edwin Encarnacion 6.00 15.00
ASRCEH Eric Hosmer 5.00 12.00
ASRCFL Francisco Lindor 6.00 15.00
ASRCJA Jake Arrieta 5.00 12.00
ASRCJD Josh Donaldson 5.00 12.00
ASRCKB Kris Bryant 8.00 20.00
ASRCMB Mookie Betts 10.00 25.00
ASRCMBU Madison Bumgarner 5.00 12.00
ASRCMC Miguel Cabrera 6.00 15.00
ASRCMMA Manny Machado 6.00 15.00
ASRCMS Max Scherzer 6.00 15.00
ASRCMT Mike Trout 30.00 80.00
ASRCNS Noah Syndergaard 5.00 12.00
ASRCRC Robinson Cano 5.00 12.00
ASRCSP Salvador Perez 5.00 12.00
ASRCSS Stephen Strasburg 6.00 15.00
ASRCXB Xander Bogaerts 6.00 15.00

2017 Topps Chrome Sapphire Edition

1 Kris Bryant
2 Jason Hammel 1.50 4.00
3 Chris Capuano 1.25 3.00
4 Mark Reynolds 1.25 3.00
5 Corey Seager
6 Kevin Pillar 1.25 3.00
7 Gary Sanchez 2.00 5.00
8 Jose Berrios 1.50 4.00
9 Chris Sale 2.00 5.00
10 Steven Souza Jr. 1.50 4.00
11 Jake Smolinski 1.25 3.00
12 Jerad Eickhoff 1.25 3.00
13 Adeiny Hechavarria 1.25 3.00
14 Travis d'Arnaud 1.50 4.00
15 Braden Shipley 1.25 3.00
16 Lance McCullers 1.25 3.00
17 Daniel Descalso 1.25 3.00
18 Jake Arrieta WS HL 1.50 4.00

19 David Wright 1.50 4.00
20 Mike Trout 100.00 250.00
21 Robert Gsellman 1.25 3.00
22 Keone Kela 1.25 3.00
23 Marcell Ozuna 2.00 5.00
24 Christian Friedrich 1.25 3.00
25 Giancarlo Stanton 2.00 5.00
26 David Peralta 1.25 3.00
27 Kurt Suzuki 1.25 3.00
28 Rick Porcello LL 1.50 4.00
29 Marco Estrada 1.25 3.00
30 Josh Bell 15.00 40.00
31 Carlos Carrasco 1.25 3.00
32 Thor and the Dark Knight 1.50 4.00
Matt Harvey
Noah Syndergaard
33 Carson Fulmer 1.25 3.00
34 Bryce Harper 6.00 15.00
35 Nolan Arenado LL 2.50 6.00
36 B'more Boppers 2.00 5.00
Mark Trumbo
Adam Jones
Manny Machado
Chris Davis
37 Toronto Blue Jays 1.25 3.00
38 Stephen Strasburg 2.00 5.00
39 Aroldis Chapman WS HL 2.00 5.00
40 Jordan Zimmermann 1.50 4.00
41 Paulo Orlando 1.25 3.00
42 Trevor Story 2.00 5.00
43 Tyler Austin 2.00 5.00
44 Paul Goldschmidt 2.00 5.00
45 Joakim Soria 1.25 3.00
46 Will Middlebrooks 1.25 3.00
47 Gregor Blanco 1.25 3.00
48 Brian McCann 1.50 4.00
49 Scooter Gennett 1.50 4.00
50 Clayton Kershaw 4.00 10.00
51 Jake Barrett 1.25 3.00
52 Neftali Feliz 1.25 3.00
53 Ryon Healy 1.50 4.00
54 Dellin Betances 1.50 4.00
55 Mark Trumbo LL 1.25 3.00
56 Danny Salazar 1.50 4.00
57 C.J. Cron 1.25 3.00
58 Starling Marte 1.50 4.00
59 Carlos Rodon 1.50 4.00
60 Jose Bautista 1.50 4.00
61 Xander Bogaerts 2.00 5.00
62 Daniel Murphy 1.50 4.00
63 Mike Moustakas 1.50 4.00
64 Adam Eaton 2.00 5.00
65 Madison Bumgarner 1.50 4.00
66 Aaron Altherr 1.25 3.00
67 Teoscar Hernandez 4.00 10.00
68 Zach Britton 1.50 4.00
69 Henry Owens 1.25 3.00
70 Wily Peralta 1.25 3.00
71 Matt Shoemaker 1.50 4.00
72 Chicago Cubs 1.25 3.00
73 Kyle Schwarber 2.00 5.00
74 Brett Lawrie 1.50 4.00
75 Carlos Correa 2.00 5.00
76 Andre Ethier 1.50 4.00
77 Austin Jackson 1.25 3.00
78 Addison Russell WS HL 2.00 5.00
79 Gabriel Ynoa 1.25 3.00
80 Ivan Nova 1.50 4.00
81 DJ LeMahieu LL 2.00 5.00
82 Aaron Sanchez LL 1.50 4.00
83 Anibal Sanchez 1.25 3.00
84 Daniel Murphy LL 1.50 4.00
85 Brandon Finnegan 1.25 3.00
86 Asdrubal Cabrera 1.50 4.00
87 Dansby Swanson 3.00 8.00
88 Freddy Galvis 1.25 3.00
89 Brandon Moss 1.25 3.00
90 Jason Grilli 1.25 3.00
91 Troy Tulowitzki 2.00 5.00
92 Derek Norris 1.25 3.00
93 Matt Joyce 1.25 3.00
94 Kyle Barraclough 1.25 3.00
95 Chris Davis 1.25 3.00
96 Jose Quintana 1.25 3.00
97 Marcus Semien 1.25 3.00
98 Junior Guerra 1.25 3.00
99 Michael Wacha 1.50 4.00
100 Nate Jones 1.25 3.00
101 Pedro Alvarez 1.25 3.00
102 Cameron Maybin 1.25 3.00
103 Alex Reyes 1.50 4.00
104 Dioner Navarro 1.25 3.00
105 Francisco Rodriguez 1.50 4.00
106 Brandon Crawford 1.50 4.00
107 Howie Kendrick 1.25 3.00
108 Nick Hundley 1.25 3.00
109 Nelson Cruz 2.00 5.00
110 Joey Votto LL 2.00 5.00
111 Edinson Volquez 1.25 3.00
112 Angel Pagan 1.25 3.00
113 Kyle Hendricks LL 2.00 5.00
114 Colin Rea 1.25 3.00
115 Joaquin Benoit 1.25 3.00
116 Archie Bradley 1.25 3.00
117 Adrian Gonzalez 1.50 4.00
118 Billy Butler 1.25 3.00
119 Francisco Lindor 2.00 5.00
120 Reynaldo Lopez 1.25 3.00
121 Carlos Santana 1.50 4.00
122 Cleveland Indians 1.25 3.00
123 Jean Segura 1.50 4.00
124 Travis Jankowski 1.25 3.00
125 Yangervis Solarte 1.25 3.00
126 Miguel Sano 1.50 4.00
127 Michael Bourn 1.25 3.00
128 Adam Duvall 2.00 5.00
129 Adonis Garcia 1.25 3.00
130 Dustin Pedroia 2.00 5.00
131 J.A. Happ LL 1.50 4.00
132 Randal Grichuk 1.25 3.00
133 Jace Peterson 1.25 3.00
134 Chase Utley 1.50 4.00
135 Jered Weaver 1.50 4.00
136 Matt Reynolds 1.25 3.00
137 Yan Gomes 2.00 5.00
138 Tyson Ross 1.25 3.00
139 JaCoby Jones 1.50 4.00
140 Jesse Hahn 1.25 3.00
141 Baltimore Orioles 1.25 3.00
142 Carlos Ruiz 1.25 3.00
143 Nick Noonan 1.25 3.00
144 Jon Lester LL 1.50 4.00
145 Max Scherzer LL 2.00 5.00
146 Chad Pinder 1.25 3.00
147 Marcus Stroman 1.50 4.00
148 Tim Anderson 2.00 5.00
149 Gregory Polanco 1.50 4.00
150 Miguel Cabrera 2.00 5.00
151 Jonathan Villar 1.25 3.00
152 Nolan Arenado LL 2.50 6.00
153 Nori Aoki 1.25 3.00
154 Kevin Kiermaier 1.50 4.00
155 Jacob deGrom 2.00 5.00
156 Alex Colome 1.25 3.00
157 Sean Doolittle 1.25 3.00
158 Tommy Pham 1.25 3.00
159 Justin Verlander LL 2.00 5.00
160 Evan Gattis 1.25 3.00
161 Mookie Betts 3.00 8.00
162 Jon Lester LL 1.50 4.00
163 Adam Conley 1.25 3.00
164 Matt Harvey 1.50 4.00
165 Corey Dickerson 1.25 3.00
166 Jorge Soler 2.00 5.00
167 Lorenzo Cain 1.25 3.00
168 Ryan Zimmerman 1.50 4.00
169 Steve Pearce 2.00 5.00
170 Chris Carter LL 1.25 3.00
171 Seth Smith 1.25 3.00
172 Wilmer Flores 1.50 4.00
173 Chicago White Sox 1.25 3.00
174 Philadelphia Phillies 1.25 3.00
175 Houston Astros 1.25 3.00
176 Jaime Garcia 1.25 3.00
177 Sonny Gray 1.50 4.00
178 Rick Porcello 1.50 4.00
179 Matt Moore 1.50 4.00
180 Jake McGee 1.25 3.00
181 Aaron Hicks 1.50 4.00
182 Keon Broxton 1.25 3.00
183 Wade Miley 1.25 3.00
184 Oswaldo Arcia 1.25 3.00
185 Raisel Iglesias 1.50 4.00
186 Andrew Cashner 1.25 3.00
187 Sean Manaea 1.25 3.00
188 Caleb Cotham 1.25 3.00
189 Los Angeles Angels 1.25 3.00
190 Blake Snell 1.50 4.00
191 Wilson Ramos 1.25 3.00
192 San Diego Padres 1.25 3.00
193 Jimmy Nelson 1.25 3.00
194 A.J. Ramos 1.25 3.00
195 Edwin Encarnacion LL 2.00 5.00
196 Colby Rasmus 1.50 4.00
197 Jacoby Ellsbury 1.50 4.00
198 Francisco Cervelli 1.25 3.00
199 Johnny Cueto 1.50 4.00
200 Homer Bailey 1.25 3.00
201 Eddie Rosario 1.50 4.00
202 Masahiro Tanaka LL 1.50 4.00
203 Tyler Naquin 1.25 3.00
204 Anthony Rizzo LL 3.00 8.00
205 Kendrys Morales 1.25 3.00
206 Chicago Cubs WS HL 1.25 3.00
207 Justin Upton 1.50 4.00
208 Masahiro Tanaka 1.50 4.00
209 Jon Gray 1.25 3.00
210 Yoan Moncada 40.00 100.00
211 Noah Syndergaard LL 1.50 4.00
212 Tanner Roark 1.25 3.00
213 Alex Wood 1.25 3.00
214 Jose Altuve LL 1.50 4.00
215 Johnny Giavotella 1.25 3.00
216 Denard Span 1.25 3.00
217 Miami Marlins 1.25 3.00
218 Michael Saunders 1.50 4.00
219 Joe Musgrove 1.50 4.00
220 Ryan Braun 1.50 4.00
221 Adam Wainwright 1.50 4.00
222 Cesar Hernandez 1.25 3.00
223 Jason Heyward 1.50 4.00
224 Hector Rondon 1.25 3.00
225 Wade Davis 1.25 3.00
226 Logan Morrison 1.25 3.00
227 Byron Buxton 1.50 4.00
228 Mike Foltynewicz 1.25 3.00
229 David Ortiz LL 2.00 5.00
230 Northern (High)lights 2.00 5.00
Josh Donaldson
Troy Tulowitzki
231 Rubby De La Rosa 1.25 3.00
232 Geovany Soto 1.25 3.00
233 Nomar Mazara 1.25 3.00
234 Luke Weaver 1.50 4.00
235 San Francisco Giants 1.25 3.00
236 Lucas Duda UER 1.50 4.00
Eric Campbell pictured
237 Joey Gallo 1.50 4.00
238 Ben Zobrist 1.50 4.00
239 Rajai Davis 1.25 3.00
240 Mike Aviles 1.25 3.00
241 Chris Young 1.25 3.00
242 Mookie Betts LL 3.00 8.00
243 Felix Hernandez 1.50 4.00
244 Freddie Freeman 2.50 6.00
245 Jackie Bradley Jr. 2.00 5.00
246 Hunter Strickland 1.25 3.00
247 Hector Neris 1.25 3.00
248 Yasmany Tomas 1.25 3.00
249 New York Yankees 1.25 3.00
250 Sean Rodriguez 1.25 3.00
251 Justin Turner 1.50 4.00
252 Clint Robinson 1.25 3.00
253 Tucker Barnhart 1.25 3.00
254 Wade LeBlanc 1.25 3.00
255 Orlando Arcia 2.00 5.00
256 Tony Watson 1.25 3.00
257 Corey Kluber LL 1.50 4.00
258 Matt Adams 1.25 3.00
259 Taijuan Walker 1.25 3.00
260 Stephen Piscotty 1.50 4.00
261 Nathan Eovaldi 1.50 4.00
262 Liam Hendriks 1.25 3.00
263 Addison Russell 2.00 5.00
264 Cory Spangenberg 1.25 3.00
265 Charlie Blackmon 2.00 5.00
266 Tampa Bay Rays 1.25 3.00
267 Clay Buchholz 1.25 3.00
268 Anthony Gose 1.25 3.00
269 Jose De Leon 1.25 3.00
270 Jake Arrieta LL 1.50 4.00
271 Nelson Cruz LL 2.00 5.00
272 Pat Neshek 1.25 3.00
273 A.J. Reed 1.25 3.00
274 Matt Strahm 1.25 3.00
275 Dallas Keuchel 1.50 4.00
276 Big Fish 2.50 6.00
Marcell Ozuna
Giancarlo Stanton
Christian Yelich
277 Kris Bryant LL 2.50 6.00
278 Julio Teheran 1.50 4.00
279 Leonys Martin 1.25 3.00
280 Adrian Beltre 2.00 5.00
281 Coco Crisp 1.25 3.00
282 Tyler Flowers 1.25 3.00
283 Andrew Benintendi 20.00 50.00
284 Elvis Andrus 1.50 4.00
285 Tyler White 1.25 3.00
286 Drew Pomeranz 1.25 3.00
287 Aaron Judge 125.00 300.00
288 Joey Votto 2.00 5.00
289 Brian Goodwin 1.25 3.00
290 Shin-Soo Choo 1.50 4.00
291 Khris Davis LL 2.00 5.00
292 Fernando Rodney 1.25 3.00
293 Aledmys Diaz 1.50 4.00
294 Kole Calhoun 1.25 3.00
295 Matt Kemp LL 1.50 4.00
296 Tyler Clippard 1.25 3.00
297 Anthony DeSclafani 1.25 3.00
298 New Blake Street Bombers 2.50 6.00
Trevor Story
Nolan Arenado
299 Yulieski Gurriel 2.00 5.00
300 Arodys Vizcaino 1.25 3.00
301 Jeurys Familia 1.50 4.00
302 David Freese 1.25 3.00
303 Pedro Strop 1.25 3.00
304 Minnesota Twins 1.25 3.00
305 Tyler Duffey 1.25 3.00
306 David Dahl 1.50 4.00
307 Zach Duke 1.25 3.00
308 Yovani Gallardo 1.25 3.00
309 Craig Kimbrel 1.50 4.00
310 Scott Schebler 1.50 4.00
311 Tyler Chatwood 1.25 3.00
312 Brandon Drury 1.25 3.00
313 Robbie Grossman 1.25 3.00
314 Ryan Flaherty 1.25 3.00
315 Carlos Beltran 1.50 4.00
316 Justin Smoak 1.25 3.00
317 Mitch Moreland 1.25 3.00
318 Matt Carasiti 1.25 3.00
319 Seth Lugo 1.25 3.00
320 Arizona Diamondbacks 1.25 3.00
321 Dustin Pedroia LL 2.00 5.00
322 Albert Pujols LL 2.50 6.00
323 Jameson Taillon 1.50 4.00
324 Ben Revere 1.25 3.00
325 Chris Hatcher 1.25 3.00
326 Chris Archer 1.25 3.00
327 Danny Espinosa 1.25 3.00
328 Adam Lind 1.50 4.00
329 Josh Reddick 1.25 3.00
330 Doug Fister 1.25 3.00
331 Jake Lamb 1.50 4.00
332 Huston Street 1.25 3.00
333 Jarred Cosart 1.25 3.00
334 Drew Smyly 1.25 3.00
335 Jeff Hoffman 1.25 3.00
336 Hector Santiago 1.25 3.00
337 Scott Van Slyke 1.25 3.00
338 Alcides Escobar 1.50 4.00
339 Daniel Norris 1.25 3.00
340 Aaron Nola 1.50 4.00
341 Alex Bregman 60.00 150.00
342 Josh Tomlin 1.25 3.00
343 Mike Zunino 1.25 3.00
344 Jake Thompson 1.25 3.00
345 Kevin Gausman 1.25 3.00
346 Jonathan Lucroy 1.50 4.00
347 Brandon Belt 1.50 4.00
348 Jeremy Hellickson 1.25 3.00
349 Tyler Glasnow 1.50 4.00
350 David Ortiz 2.00 5.00
351 German Marquez 2.00 5.00
352 Cameron Rupp 1.25 3.00
353 Felipe Rivero 1.50 4.00
354 Nick Tropeano 1.25 3.00
355 Shelby Miller 1.50 4.00
356 Brad Miller 1.50 4.00
357 Kelvin Herrera 1.25 3.00
358 Brad Boxberger 1.25 3.00
359 Matt Carpenter 2.00 5.00
360 Jon Lester 1.50 4.00
361 Dylan Bundy 1.50 4.00
362 John Lackey 1.50 4.00
363 Yunel Escobar 1.25 3.00
364 Koda Glover 1.25 3.00
365 Jorge De La Rosa 1.25 3.00
366 Jayson Werth 1.50 4.00
367 Jurickson Profar 1.50 4.00
368 Jhonny Peralta 1.25 3.00
369 Mark Canha 1.25 3.00
370 St. Louis Cardinals 1.25 3.00
371 Chad Bettis 1.25 3.00
372 Ryan Schimpf 1.25 3.00
373 Yadier Molina 2.00 5.00
374 Jim Johnson 1.25 3.00
375 Yasiel Puig 2.00 5.00
376 Chase Anderson 1.25 3.00
377 Adam Rosales 1.25 3.00
378 They Got Hops! 2.00 5.00
Francisco Lindor
Tyler Naquin
379 Phil Hughes 1.25 3.00
380 Albert Pujols 2.50 6.00
381 Hunter Renfroe 1.50 4.00
382 Josh Harrison 1.25 3.00
383 Adam Frazier 1.25 3.00
384 Welington Castillo 1.25 3.00
385 DJ LeMahieu 2.00 5.00
386 Michael Lorenzen 1.25 3.00
387 Zack Godley 1.25 3.00
388 Yasmani Grandal 1.25 3.00
389 George Springer 1.50 4.00
390 Evan Longoria 1.50 4.00
391 Jonathan Schoop 1.25 3.00
392 Pablo Sandoval 1.50 4.00
393 Koji Uehara 1.25 3.00
394 Detroit Tigers 1.25 3.00
395 Drew Storen 1.25 3.00
396 J.T. Realmuto 2.00 5.00
397 Stephen Cardullo 1.25 3.00
398 Blake Treinen 2.00 5.00
399 Ender Inciarte 2.00 5.00
400 Nolan Arenado 2.50 6.00
401 Manny Margot 1.25 3.00
402 Logan Forsythe 1.25 3.00
403 John Axford 1.25 3.00
404 Joe Mauer 1.50 4.00
405 Max Kepler 1.50 4.00
406 Stephen Vogt 1.50 4.00
407 Eduardo Escobar 1.25 3.00
408 Michael Conforto 1.50 4.00
409 R.A. Dickey 1.50 4.00
410 Jarrett Parker 1.25 3.00
411 Maikel Franco 1.50 4.00
412 Chris Iannetta 1.25 3.00
413 Rob Segedin 1.25 3.00
414 Zack Cozart 1.25 3.00
415 Pat Valaika 1.50 4.00
416 Neil Walker 1.50 4.00
417 Darren O'Day 1.25 3.00
418 James McCann 1.50 4.00
419 Roberto Perez 1.25 3.00
420 Matt Wisler 1.25 3.00
421 Santiago Casilla 1.25 3.00
422 Andrew Miller 1.50 4.00
423 Sergio Romo 1.25 3.00
424 Derek Dietrich 1.50 4.00
425 Carlos Gonzalez 1.50 4.00
426 New York Mets 1.25 3.00
427 Carlos Gomez 1.25 3.00
428 Jay Bruce 1.50 4.00
429 Mark Melancon 1.25 3.00
430 Texas Rangers 1.25 3.00
431 Tommy Joseph 2.00 5.00
432 Lucas Giolito 1.50 4.00
433 Mitch Haniger 2.00 5.00
434 Tyler Saladino 1.25 3.00
435 Robbie Ray 1.25 3.00
436 Cody Allen 1.25 3.00
437 Trevor Rosenthal 1.50 4.00
438 Chris Carter 1.25 3.00
439 Salvador Perez 1.50 4.00
440 Eduardo Rodriguez 1.25 3.00
441 Jose Iglesias 1.25 3.00
442 Javier Baez 2.50 6.00
443 Dee Gordon 1.25 3.00
444 Andrew Heaney 1.25 3.00
445 Alex Gordon 1.50 4.00
446 Dexter Fowler 1.50 4.00
447 Scott Kazmir 1.25 3.00
448 Jose Martinez 2.00 5.00
449 Ian Kennedy 1.25 3.00
450 Justin Verlander 2.00 5.00
451 Jharel Cotton 1.25 3.00
452 Travis Shaw 1.25 3.00
453 Danny Santana 1.25 3.00
454 Andrew Toles 1.25 3.00
455 Mauricio Cabrera 1.25 3.00
456 Steve Cishek 1.25 3.00
457 Brett Gardner 1.50 4.00
458 Hernan Perez 1.25 3.00
459 Wil Myers 1.25 3.00
460 Alejandro De Aza 1.25 3.00
461 Bruce Maxwell 1.25 3.00
462 Rich Hill 1.25 3.00
463 Jeff Samardzija 1.25 3.00
464 Hisashi Iwakuma 1.50 4.00
465 CC Sabathia 1.50 4.00
466 David Robertson 1.25 3.00
467 Adam Ottavino 1.25 3.00
468 Kyle Hendricks 2.00 5.00
469 Francisco Liriano 1.25 3.00
470 Brandon Drury 1.25 3.00
471 Nick Franklin 1.25 3.00
472 Pittsburgh Pirates 1.25 3.00
473 Eugenio Suarez 1.50 4.00
474 Michael Pineda 1.25 3.00
475 Peter O'Brien 1.25 3.00
476 Matt Olson 2.00 5.00
477 Zach Davies 1.25 3.00
478 Rob Zastryzny 1.25 3.00
479 Ryan Madson 1.25 3.00
480 Jason Kipnis 1.50 4.00
481 Kansas City Royals 1.25 3.00
482 Didi Gregorius 1.50 4.00
483 Anthony Rendon 2.00 5.00
484 Yonder Alonso 1.25 3.00
485 Greg Bird 1.50 4.00
486 Aroldis Chapman 2.00 5.00
487 Jose Ramirez 1.50 4.00
488 Jake Odorizzi 1.25 3.00
489 Jarrod Dyson 1.25 3.00
490 Joc Pederson 1.50 4.00
491 Ryan Vogelsong 1.25 3.00
492 Avisail Garcia 1.50 4.00
493 Hunter Dozier 1.25 3.00
494 Tom Murphy 1.25 3.00
495 Adam Jones 1.50 4.00
496 Mike Fiers 1.25 3.00
497 Boston Red Sox 1.25 3.00
498 Roman Quinn 1.25 3.00
499 Danny Valencia 1.50 4.00
500 Anthony Rizzo 3.00 8.00
501 Ian Kinsler 1.50 4.00
502 Willson Contreras 2.00 5.00
503 Jesus Aguilar 2.00 5.00
504 Austin Hedges 1.25 3.00
505 Seung-Hwan Oh 2.50 6.00
506 Jose Peraza 1.50 4.00
507 Matt Garza 1.25 3.00
508 Hanley Ramirez 1.50 4.00
509 Miguel Rojas 1.25 3.00
510 Kelby Tomlinson 1.25 3.00
511 Devin Mesoraco 1.25 3.00
512 Mallex Smith 1.25 3.00
513 Tony Kemp 1.25 3.00
514 Jeremy Jeffress 1.25 3.00
515 Nick Castellanos 2.00 5.00
516 Tony Wolters 1.25 3.00
517 Kolten Wong 1.50 4.00
518 Christian Yelich 2.50 6.00
519 Dan Vogelbach 2.00 5.00
520 Andrelton Simmons 1.25 3.00
521 Brandon Phillips 1.25 3.00
522 Edwin Diaz 1.50 4.00
523 Carlos Martinez 1.50 4.00
524 James Loney 1.25 3.00
525 Curtis Granderson 1.50 4.00
526 Jake Marisnick 1.25 3.00
527 Gio Gonzalez 1.50 4.00
528 Jake Arrieta 1.50 4.00
529 J.J. Hardy 1.25 3.00
530 Jabari Blash 1.25 3.00
531 Nick Markakis 1.50 4.00
532 Eduardo Nunez 1.25 3.00
533 Trevor Bauer 2.00 5.00
534 Cody Asche 1.25 3.00
535 Lonnie Chisenhall 1.25 3.00
536 Trey Mancini 2.50 6.00
537 Gerardo Parra 1.25 3.00
538 Brad Ziegler 1.25 3.00
539 Amir Garrett 1.25 3.00
540 Billy Hamilton 1.50 4.00
541 Shawn Kelley 1.25 3.00
542 Trevor Plouffe 1.25 3.00
543 Brian Dozier 2.00 5.00
544 Luis Severino 1.50 4.00
545 Martin Perez 1.25 3.00
546 Addison Reed 1.25 3.00
547 Vince Velasquez 1.25 3.00
548 David Price 1.50 4.00
549 Miguel Gonzalez 1.25 3.00
550 Mikie Mahtook 1.25 3.00
551 Matt Duffy 1.25 3.00
552 Tom Koehler 1.25 3.00
553 T.J. Rivera 2.00 5.00
554 Jason Castro 1.25 3.00
555 Noah Syndergaard 1.50 4.00
556 Starlin Castro 1.25 3.00
557 Milwaukee Brewers 1.25 3.00
558 Oakland Athletics 1.25 3.00
559 Jason Motte 1.25 3.00
560 Zack Greinke 1.50 4.00
561 Ricky Nolasco 1.25 3.00
562 Nick Ahmed 1.25 3.00
563 Marwin Gonzalez 1.25 3.00
564 Washington Nationals 1.25 3.00
565 J.D. Martinez 2.00 5.00
566 Heart of Texas 1.50 4.00
Elvis Andrus
Rougned Odor
567 Devon Travis 1.25 3.00
568 Ryan Pressly 1.25 3.00
569 Jorge Alfaro 1.50 4.00
570 Josh Donaldson 1.50 4.00
571 J.C. Ramirez 1.25 3.00
572 Atlanta Braves 1.25 3.00
573 Bartolo Colon 1.25 3.00
574 Trayce Thompson 1.50 4.00
575 Chris Owings 1.25 3.00
576 Russell Martin 1.25 3.00
577 Chris Tillman 1.25 3.00
578 Jed Lowrie 1.25 3.00
579 Taylor Jungmann 1.25 3.00
580 Matt Holliday 2.00 5.00
581 Brock Holt 1.25 3.00
582 Julio Urias 2.00 5.00
583 Colorado Rockies 1.25 3.00
584 Tater Triumph 3.00 8.00
Jayson Werth
Bryce Harper
585 Collin McHugh 1.25 3.00
586 Aaron Sanchez 1.50 4.00
587 Gerrit Cole 2.00 5.00
588 Kirk Nieuwenhuis 1.25 3.00
589 Ian Desmond 1.25 3.00
590 Triplet of Twins 1.50 4.00
Miguel Sano
Byron Buxton
Eduardo Escobar
591 Matt Bush 1.50 4.00
592 Kendall Graveman 1.25 3.00
593 Jose Abreu 2.00 5.00
594 Justin Bour 1.50 4.00
595 Max Scherzer 2.00 5.00
596 Ken Giles 1.25 3.00
597 Kenta Maeda 1.50 4.00
598 Michael Taylor 1.25 3.00
599 Cincinnati Reds 1.25 3.00
600 Yoenis Cespedes 2.00 5.00
601 Khris Davis 2.00 5.00
602 Alex Dickerson 1.25 3.00
603 Eric Thames 1.50 4.00
604 Gavin Cecchini 1.25 3.00
605 Michael Brantley 1.50 4.00
606 Glen Perkins 1.25 3.00
607 Tyler Thornburg 1.25 3.00
608 Los Angeles Dodgers 1.25 3.00
609 Adalberto Mejia 1.25 3.00
610 Ryan Buchter 1.25 3.00
611 Victor Martinez 1.50 4.00
612 Odubel Herrera 1.50 4.00
613 Jonathan Broxton 1.25 3.00
614 Shawn O'Malley 1.25 3.00
615 John Jaso 1.25 3.00
616 Mark Trumbo 1.25 3.00
617 A.J. Pollock 1.25 3.00
618 Kenley Jansen 1.50 4.00
619 Brad Brach 1.25 3.00
620 Sam Dyson 1.25 3.00
621 Chase Headley 1.25 3.00
622 Steven Wright 1.25 3.00
623 Melvin Upton Jr. 1.50 4.00
624 Brandon Maurer 1.25 3.00
625 Ty Blach 1.25 3.00
626 Roberto Osuna 1.25 3.00
627 Zach Putnam 1.25 3.00
628 Domingo Santana 1.50 4.00
629 Jordy Mercer 1.25 3.00
630 Edwin Encarnacion 2.00 5.00
631 Zack Wheeler 1.50 4.00
632 Steven Matz 1.50 4.00
633 Hunter Pence 1.50 4.00
634 Danny Duffy 1.25 3.00
635 Michael Fulmer 1.25 3.00
636 Allegheny Armada 2.00 5.00
Andrew McCutchen
John Jaso
637 Ryan Rua 1.25 3.00
638 Luis Valbuena 1.25 3.00
639 Matt Kemp 1.50 4.00
640 Cole Hamels 1.50 4.00
641 Robinson Cano 1.50 4.00
642 Renato Nunez 2.50 6.00
643 Wei-Yin Chen 1.25 3.00
644 Jose Altuve 1.50 4.00
645 Trea Turner 1.50 4.00
646 Corey Knebel 1.25 3.00
647 Jose Reyes 1.50 4.00
648 Seattle Mariners 1.25 3.00
649 Manny Machado 1.50 4.00
650 Andrew McCutchen 2.00 5.00
651 Jose Lobaton 1.25 3.00
652 Kyle Seager 1.25 3.00
653 Cam Bedrosian 1.25 3.00
654 Chris Young 1.25 3.00
655 Garrett Richards 1.50 4.00
656 Todd Frazier 1.50 4.00
657 Kevin Quackenbush 1.25 3.00
658 James Paxton 1.50 4.00
659 Melky Cabrera 1.25 3.00
660 Jeanmar Gomez 1.25 3.00
661 Peter Bourjos 1.25 3.00
662 J.A. Happ 1.50 4.00
663 Ketel Marte 1.50 4.00
664 Blake Swihart 1.50 4.00
665 Yu Darvish 2.00 5.00
666 Rougned Odor 1.50 4.00
667 Alex Cobb 1.25 3.00
668 Jedd Gyorko 1.25 3.00
669 Corey Kluber 1.50 4.00
670 Martin Maldonado 1.25 3.00
671 Joe Ross 1.25 3.00
672 Luke Maile 1.25 3.00
673 Joe Panik 1.50 4.00
674 Martin Prado 1.25 3.00
675 Buster Posey 2.50 6.00
676 Eric Hosmer 1.50 4.00
677 Cheslor Cuthbert 1.25 3.00
678 Ervin Santana 1.25 3.00
679 Jung Ho Kang 1.25 3.00
680 Mike Pelfrey 1.25 3.00
681 Mike Napoli 1.25 3.00
682 James Shields 1.25 3.00
683 Mac Williamson 1.25 3.00
684 Jorge Polanco 1.25 3.00
685 Enrique Hernandez 1.50 4.00
686 Luis Sardinas 1.25 3.00
687 Tyler Collins 1.25 3.00
688 Mike Clevinger 1.50 4.00
689 Jason Vargas 1.25 3.00
690 Andres Blanco 1.25 3.00
691 Richard Bleier 1.25 3.00
692 Rob Refsnyder 1.25 3.00
693 Matt Cain 1.50 4.00
694 Matt Wieters 2.00 5.00
695 Jon Jay 1.25 3.00
696 Jeff Mathis 1.50 4.00
697 Christian Bethancourt 1.25 3.00
698 Tony Cingrani 1.50 4.00
699 Ichiro 2.50 6.00
700 Ryan Goins 1.25 3.00

2018 Topps Chrome Sapphire Edition

1 Aaron Judge 5.00 12.00
2 Clayton Kershaw LL 4.00 10.00
3 Dylan Bundy 1.50 4.00
4 Kevin Pillar 1.25 3.00
5 Chris Tillman 1.25 3.00
6 Dominic Smith 1.25 3.00
7 Clint Frazier 2.50 6.00
8 Detroit Tigers 1.25 3.00
9 Jon Gray 1.25 3.00
10 Francisco Lindor 2.00 5.00
11 Aaron Nola 1.50 4.00
12 Joey Gallo LL 1.50 4.00
13 Jay Bruce 1.50 4.00
14 Amir Garrett 1.25 3.00
15 Andrelton Simmons 1.25 3.00
16 Daniel Coulombe 2.00 5.00
17 Robbie Ray 1.25 3.00
18 Rafael Devers 125.00 300.00
19 Garrett Richards 1.50 4.00
20 Chris Sale 2.00 5.00
21 Harrison Bader 2.00 5.00
22 Edinson Volquez 1.25 3.00
23 Jordy Mercer 1.25 3.00
24 Martin Maldonado 1.25 3.00
25 Manny Machado 2.00 5.00
26 Cesar Hernandez 1.25 3.00
27 Josh Tomlin 1.25 3.00
28 Jayson Werth 1.50 4.00
29 Hunter Renfroe 1.25 3.00
30 Carlos Correa 2.00 5.00
31 Corey Kluber LL 1.50 4.00
32 Jose Iglesias 1.50 4.00
33 Dexter Fowler 1.50 4.00
34 Luis Severino LL 1.50 4.00
35 Logan Forsythe 1.25 3.00
36 Anthony Rendon 2.00 5.00
37 Corey Kluber LL 1.50 4.00
38 Danny Salazar 1.50 4.00
39 Alex Bregman WS HL 2.00 5.00
40 Carlos Santana 1.50 4.00
41 Daniel Norris 1.25 3.00
42 Cody Bellinger 40.00 100.00
43 Eduardo Rodriguez 1.25 3.00
44 Trea Turner 1.50 4.00
45 Giancarlo Stanton LL 2.00 5.00
46 Cam Bedrosian 1.25 3.00
47 Hunter Pence 1.50 4.00
48 Boston Red Sox 1.25 3.00
49 Ervin Santana 1.25 3.00
50 Anthony Rizzo 3.00 8.00
51 Michael Wacha 1.50 4.00
52 Brad Hand 1.25 3.00
53 Alex Avila 1.50 4.00
54 Chase Anderson 1.25 3.00
55 Raisel Iglesias 1.50 4.00
56 Rougned Odor 1.50 4.00
57 Scott Feldman 1.25 3.00
58 Ryan Zimmerman 1.50 4.00
59 Clayton Kershaw LL 4.00 10.00
60 Starling Marte 1.50 4.00
61 Keon Broxton 1.25 3.00
62 Austin Hays 2.00 5.00
63 Amed Rosario 1.50 4.00
64 Giancarlo Stanton LL 2.00 5.00
65 Alex Wood 1.25 3.00
66 Ian Kennedy 1.25 3.00
67 Aledmys Diaz 1.50 4.00
68 Billy Hamilton 1.50 4.00
69 Jed Lowrie 1.25 3.00
70 Johnny Cueto 1.50 4.00
71 Mike Foltynewicz 1.25 3.00
72 Cheslor Cuthbert 1.25 3.00
73 Miami Marlins 1.25 3.00
74 Roberto Osuna 1.25 3.00
75 Andrew Miller 1.50 4.00
76 Eduardo Nunez 1.50 4.00
77 Martin Prado 1.25 3.00
78 Carlos Carrasco LL 1.25 3.00
79 J.T. Realmuto 2.00 5.00
80 Dellin Betances 1.50 4.00
81 Adam Wainwright 1.50 4.00

82 Justin Smoak 1.25 3.00
83 Howie Kendrick 1.25 3.00
84 Todd Frazier 1.50 4.00
85 Antonio Senzatela 1.25 3.00
86 Eric Hosmer 1.50 4.00
87 Brandon Phillips 1.25 3.00
88 Michael Conforto 1.50 4.00
89 Yasiel Puig 2.00 5.00
90 Miguel Cabrera 2.00 5.00
91 Travis d'Arnaud 1.50 4.00
92 Charlie Blackmon LL 2.00 5.00
93 Jack Flaherty 2.00 5.00
94 Robbie Grossman 1.25 3.00
95 Tyler Mahle 1.50 4.00
96 David Dahl 1.25 3.00
97 Dinelson Lamet 1.25 3.00
98 Chicago White Sox 1.25 3.00
99 Greg Allen 1.25 3.00
100 Giancarlo Stanton 2.00 5.00
101 Avisail Garcia 1.50 4.00
102 Wil Myers 1.25 3.00
103 Christian Vazquez 1.25 3.00
104 Mitch Moreland 1.25 3.00
105 Daniel Murphy 1.50 4.00
106 Jharel Cotton 1.25 3.00
107 Jorge Polanco 1.25 3.00
108 Justin Turner LL 1.50 4.00
109 Starlin Castro 1.25 3.00
110 Carlos Gonzalez 1.50 4.00
111 Aaron Judge LL 5.00 12.00
112 Pat Valaika 1.25 3.00
113 Gio Gonzalez 1.50 4.00
114 Cody Bellinger LL 4.00 10.00
115 Zack Granite 1.25 3.00
116 Ariel Miranda 2.00 5.00
117 Kendrys Morales 1.25 3.00
118 Ian Happ 1.50 4.00
119 Los Angeles Angels 1.25 3.00
120 Carlos Carrasco 1.25 3.00
121 Rich Hill 1.25 3.00
122 Chris Owings 1.25 3.00
123 A.J. Ramos 1.25 3.00
124 Julio Urias 2.00 5.00
125 Yoenis Cespedes 2.00 5.00
126 A.Rizzo/B.Harper 3.00 8.00
127 Byron Buxton 1.50 4.00
128 Jake Marisnick 1.25 3.00
129 Chris Sale LL 2.00 5.00
130 Brian Dozier 1.50 4.00
131 Jonathan Schoop 1.25 3.00
132 Marcell Ozuna 2.00 5.00
133 Nomar Mazara 1.25 3.00
134 Lance Lynn 1.25 3.00
135 Atlanta Braves 1.25 3.00
136 Raudy Read 1.25 3.00
137 Michael Lorenzen 1.25 3.00
138 Luiz Gohara 1.25 3.00
139 Zach Davies LL 1.25 3.00
140 Mookie Betts 3.00 8.00
141 Brandon Drury 1.25 3.00
142 Adam Jones 1.50 4.00
143 James Paxton 1.50 4.00
144 Jean Segura 1.25 3.00
145 Michael Fulmer 1.25 3.00
146 Zack Greinke LL 1.50 4.00
147 Randal Grichuk 1.25 3.00
148 Richard Urena 1.25 3.00
149 John Jaso 1.25 3.00
150 Nolan Arenado 2.50 6.00
151 Ryan McMahon 1.50 4.00
152 Matt Barnes 1.25 3.00
153 Scooter Gennett 1.50 4.00
154 George Springer WS HL 1.50 4.00
155 Matt Joyce 1.25 3.00
156 Milwaukee Brewers 1.25 3.00
157 Ichiro 2.50 6.00
158 Stephen Piscotty 1.25 3.00
159 Joc Pederson 1.50 4.00
160 Masahiro Tanaka 1.50 4.00
161 Matt Moore 1.50 4.00
162 Matt Shoemaker 1.50 4.00
163 Mike Leake 1.25 3.00
164 Adeiny Hechavarria 1.25 3.00
165 Ty Blach 1.25 3.00
166 Victor Robles 3.00 8.00
167 Dansby Swanson 2.00 5.00
168 Ricky Nolasco 1.25 3.00
169 Khris Davis LL 2.00 5.00
170 Christian Yelich 2.50 6.00
171 John Lackey 1.50 4.00
172 Willson Contreras 2.00 5.00
173 Mike Moustakas 1.50 4.00
174 Jimmie Sherfy 1.25 3.00
175 Jose Quintana 1.25 3.00
176 Seattle Mariners 1.25 3.00
177 Walker Buehler 50.00 120.00
178 Matt Adams 1.25 3.00
179 Brandon Woodruff 1.50 4.00
180 Ryan Braun 1.50 4.00
181 Garrett Cooper 1.25 3.00
182 Alex Bregman 2.00 5.00
183 Matt Kemp 1.50 4.00
184 Mike Fiers 1.25 3.00
185 Chance Sisco 1.50 4.00
186 Luis Perdomo 1.25 3.00
187 Chad Kuhl 1.25 3.00
188 Matt Harvey 1.50 4.00
189 Jedd Gyorko 1.25 3.00
190 Justin Upton 1.50 4.00
191 Chris Archer 1.25 3.00
192 Nolan Arenado LL 2.50 6.00
193 Aaron Judge LL 5.00 12.00
194 Lonnie Chisenhall 1.25 3.00
195 Avisail Garcia LL 1.50 4.00
196 Orlando Arcia 1.25 3.00
197 Maikel Franco 1.50 4.00
198 Marcus Semien 1.25 3.00
199 Shin-Soo Choo 1.50 4.00
200 Andrew McCutchen 2.00 5.00
201 Gregory Polanco 1.50 4.00
202 Brett Phillips 1.25 3.00
203 Odubel Herrera 1.50 4.00
204 Brett Gardner 1.50 4.00
205 Seattle Slayers 1.50 4.00
Robinson Cano
Kyle Seager
206 Nick Markakis 1.50 4.00
207 Jackson Stephens 1.25 3.00
208 Andrew Cashner 1.25 3.00
209 Eugenio Suarez 1.50 4.00
210 Brandon Belt 1.50 4.00
211 Betts/Bradley/Benintendi 3.00 8.00
212 Lance McCullers WS HL 1.25 3.00
213 J.A. Happ 1.50 4.00
214 Corey Knebel 1.25 3.00
215 Marwin Gonzalez 1.25 3.00
216 A.J. Pollock 1.50 4.00
217 Erick Fedde 1.25 3.00
218 Khris Davis LL 2.00 5.00
219 J.P. Crawford 1.25 3.00
220 Nelson Cruz 2.00 5.00
221 Steven Matz 1.50 4.00
222 Ivan Nova 1.50 4.00
223 Evan Longoria 1.50 4.00
224 Dillon Peters 1.25 3.00
225 Kyle Schwarber 2.00 5.00
226 Nick Williams 1.50 4.00
227 Corey Dickerson 1.25 3.00
228 Zack Wheeler 1.50 4.00
229 Texas Rangers 1.25 3.00
230 Trevor Story 2.00 5.00
231 Joe Mauer 1.50 4.00
232 Nate Jones 1.25 3.00
233 Stephen Strasburg 2.00 5.00
234 Brian Anderson 1.50 4.00
235 Mark Reynolds 1.25 3.00
236 CC Sabathia 1.50 4.00
237 Mike Clevinger 1.50 4.00
238 Jose Bautista 1.50 4.00
239 Cleveland Indians 1.25 3.00
240 Robinson Cano 1.50 4.00
241 Nick Pivetta 1.25 3.00
242 Craig Kimbrel 1.50 4.00
243 James McCann 1.50 4.00
244 Francisco Mejia 1.50 4.00
245 Willie Calhoun 1.50 4.00
246 Yangervis Solarte 1.25 3.00
247 Anthony Banda 1.25 3.00
248 Jake Lamb 1.50 4.00
249 Christian Arroyo 1.25 3.00
250 Buster Posey 2.50 6.00
251 Aaron Sanchez 1.50 4.00
252 Tim Anderson 2.00 5.00
253 Nelson Cruz LL 2.00 5.00
254 Adrian Beltre 2.00 5.00
255 Zach Davies 1.25 3.00
256 Eric Hosmer LL 1.50 4.00
257 J.D. Martinez 2.00 5.00
258 Tyler Saladino 1.25 3.00
259 Rhys Hoskins 30.00 80.00
260 Rick Porcello 1.50 4.00
261 Andrew Stevenson 1.25 3.00
262 Potent Pair 1.50 4.00
Eric Hosmer
Miguel Sano
263 Chase Utley 1.50 4.00
264 Carlos Rodon 1.50 4.00
265 Javier Baez 2.50 6.00
266 Jon Lester 1.50 4.00
267 Yoan Moncada 2.00 5.00
268 Neil Walker 1.50 4.00
269 Greg Holland 1.25 3.00
270 Jackie Bradley Jr. 2.00 5.00
271 Cam Gallagher 1.25 3.00
272 Paul Blackburn 1.25 3.00
273 Charlie Blackmon LL 2.00 5.00
274 Jeff Samardzija 1.25 3.00
275 George Springer 1.50 4.00
276 Ozzie Albies 40.00 100.00
277 Aaron Slegers 2.00 5.00
278 Lucas Sims 1.25 3.00
279 Jordan Zimmermann 1.50 4.00
280 Jose Abreu 2.00 5.00
281 Alex Verdugo 2.00 5.00
282 Ender Inciarte 1.25 3.00
283 Koji Uehara 1.25 3.00
284 Jose Pirela 1.25 3.00
285 Trey Mancini 1.50 4.00
286 New York Yankees 1.25 3.00
287 Mark Trumbo 1.25 3.00
288 Miguel Sano 1.50 4.00
289 Jonathan Villar 1.25 3.00
290 Salvador Perez 1.50 4.00
291 Marcell Ozuna LL 2.00 5.00
292 Baltimore Orioles 1.25 3.00
293 Felipe Rivero 1.25 3.00
294 Jose Altuve LL 1.50 4.00
295 Zack Godley 1.25 3.00
296 Lewis Brinson 1.25 3.00
297 Kevin Kiermaier 1.50 4.00
298 All Smiles 1.50 4.00
Yulieski Gurriel
Jake Marisnick
299 Luis Santos 2.00 5.00
300 Mike Trout 75.00 200.00
301 Brandon Finnegan 1.25 3.00
302 Troy Tulowitzki 2.00 5.00
303 Luis Severino 1.50 4.00
304 Whit Merrifield 2.00 5.00
305 Miguel Andujar 10.00 25.00
306 Nicky Delmonico 1.25 3.00
307 Daniel Murphy LL 1.50 4.00
308 Cameron Rupp 1.25 3.00
309 Josh Reddick 1.25 3.00
310 Jason Kipnis 1.50 4.00
311 Yulieski Gurriel 1.50 4.00
312 Carlos Asuaje 1.25 3.00
313 Raimel Tapia 1.25 3.00
314 Colorado Rockies 1.25 3.00
315 Chris Rowley 2.00 5.00
316 Max Fried 5.00 12.00
317 Chase Headley 1.25 3.00
318 Danny Duffy 1.25 3.00
319 David Peralta 1.25 3.00
320 Yasmani Grandal 1.25 3.00
321 Edwin Diaz 1.50 4.00
322 Parker Bridwell 1.25 3.00
323 Elvis Andrus 1.50 4.00
324 Jake Odorizzi 1.25 3.00
325 Khris Davis 2.00 5.00
326 Joey Gallo 1.50 4.00
327 Jason Vargas LL 1.25 3.00
328 Tyler Flowers 1.25 3.00
329 George Springer WS HL 1.50 4.00
330 Ian Kinsler 1.50 4.00
331 Zack Cozart 1.50 4.00
332 Alex Colome 1.25 3.00
333 Joe Musgrove 1.25 3.00
334 Eddie Rosario 2.00 5.00
335 Stephen Strasburg LL 2.00 5.00
336 Bruce Maxwell 1.25 3.00
337 Nick Ahmed 1.25 3.00
338 Brandon McCarthy 1.25 3.00
339 Philadelphia Phillies 1.25 3.00
340 Gary Sanchez 2.00 5.00
341 J.D. Davis 1.50 4.00
342 Sean Manaea 1.25 3.00
343 Kevin Gausman 1.25 3.00
344 Wilmer Flores 1.50 4.00
345 Jose Reyes 1.50 4.00
346 Max Scherzer LL 2.00 5.00
347 Kolten Wong 1.50 4.00
348 Hisashi Iwakuma 1.50 4.00
349 Washington Nationals 1.25 3.00
350 Clayton Kershaw 4.00 10.00
351 Bryce Harper 3.00 8.00
352 Cincinnati Reds 1.25 3.00
353 Yan Gomes 2.00 5.00
354 Robert Stephenson 1.25 3.00
355 Joe Ross 1.25 3.00
356 Jeff Hoffman 1.25 3.00
357 Josh Hader 1.25 3.00
358 Brad Brach 1.25 3.00
359 Wade Miley 1.25 3.00
360 Taijuan Walker 1.25 3.00
361 C.Correa/J.Altuve 2.00 5.00
362 Miguel Rojas 1.25 3.00
363 Bryan Shaw 1.25 3.00
364 Y.Puig/C.Bellinger 4.00 10.00
365 Mallex Smith 1.25 3.00
366 Tyler Glasnow FS 1.25 3.00
367 Liam Hendriks 1.25 3.00
368 Matt Strahm 1.25 3.00
369 Chris Taylor 1.50 4.00
370 Steven Wright 1.25 3.00
371 Cole Hamels 1.50 4.00
372 Nick Tropeano 1.25 3.00
373 Jorge Bonifacio 1.25 3.00
374 Bradley Zimmer FS 1.25 3.00
375 Evan Gattis 1.25 3.00
376 Kyle McGrath 1.25 3.00
377 Domingo Santana 1.50 4.00
378 Aaron Wilkerson 1.25 3.00
379 Ryan Zimmerman 1.50 4.00
Jayson Werth
Power Up
380 Kelby Tomlinson 1.25 3.00
381 Kole Calhoun 1.25 3.00
382 Brandon Guyer 1.25 3.00
383 JaCoby Jones 1.50 4.00
384 Addison Russell 1.50 4.00
385 Jason Hammel 1.50 4.00
386 James Shields 1.25 3.00
387 Julio Teheran 1.50 4.00
388 Taylor Motter 1.25 3.00
389 G.Stanton/A.Judge 5.00 12.00
390 Jesse Chavez 1.25 3.00
391 Ben Zobrist 1.50 4.00
392 Marcus Stroman 1.50 4.00
393 Corey Kluber 1.50 4.00
394 Chad Pinder 1.25 3.00
395 Martin Perez 1.50 4.00
396 Matt Olson 1.25 3.00
397 Dallas Keuchel 1.50 4.00
398 Sam Dyson 1.25 3.00
399 Chicago Cubs 1.25 3.00
400 Jose Altuve 1.50 4.00
401 Michael Brantley 1.50 4.00
402 Adam Warren 1.25 3.00
403 Luis Torrens 1.25 3.00
404 Alex Claudio 1.25 3.00
405 T.J. Rivera 1.25 3.00
406 Kelvin Herrera 1.25 3.00
407 Pat Neshek 1.25 3.00
408 Mikie Mahtook 1.25 3.00
409 Scott Kingery 2.00 5.00
410 Felix Jorge 1.25 3.00
411 David Price 1.50 4.00
412 Mike Minor 1.25 3.00
413 Trevor Bauer 2.00 5.00
414 Danny Valencia 1.50 4.00
415 Jace Peterson 1.25 3.00
416 Derek Fisher FS 1.25 3.00
417 Yolmer Sanchez 1.25 3.00
418 Jose Ramirez 1.50 4.00
419 Fernando Rodney 1.25 3.00
420 Alex Cobb 1.25 3.00
421 Lorenzo Cain 1.25 3.00
422 Victor Caratini 1.50 4.00
423 Houston Astros 1.25 3.00
424 Matt Wieters 2.00 5.00
425 Shelby Miller 1.50 4.00
426 Jacob Faria 1.25 3.00
427 Jordan Montgomery 2.00 5.00
428 Jakob Junis 1.25 3.00
429 Victor Martinez 1.50 4.00
430 Manny Margot FS 1.25 3.00
431 Charlie Blackmon 2.00 5.00
432 Albert Almora 1.50 4.00
433 Anthony Santander 1.25 3.00
434 Miguel Montero 1.25 3.00
435 Matt Holliday 2.00 5.00
436 Yu Darvish 2.00 5.00
437 J.J. Hardy 1.25 3.00
438 Stephen Vogt 1.50 4.00
439 Dustin Pedroia 2.00 5.00
440 Troy Scribner 1.25 3.00
441 Danny Santana 1.25 3.00
442 Jesus Aguilar 1.25 3.00
443 Gerrit Cole 2.00 5.00
444 Aaron Altherr 1.25 3.00
445 Trevor Cahill 1.25 3.00
446 Lucas Duda 1.50 4.00
447 Carlos Gomez 1.25 3.00
448 Max Kepler 1.50 4.00
449 DJ LeMahieu 2.00 5.00
450 Joey Votto 2.00 5.00
451 Ubaldo Jimenez 1.25 3.00
452 Tucker Barnhart 1.25 3.00
453 Devon Travis 1.25 3.00
454 Kyle Seager 1.25 3.00
455 Hernan Perez 1.25 3.00
456 Jimmy Nelson 1.25 3.00
457 Hanley Ramirez 1.50 4.00
458 Yovani Gallardo 1.25 3.00
459 Brevyic Valera 1.25 3.00
460 Robert Gsellman 1.25 3.00
461 Michael Taylor 1.25 3.00
462 Paul DeJong FS 2.00 5.00
463 Cory Spangenberg 1.25 3.00
464 Travis Jankowski 1.25 3.00
465 San Diego Padres 1.25 3.00
466 Tim Locastro 1.25 3.00
467 Carlos Ramirez 1.25 3.00
468 Tampa Bay Rays 1.25 3.00
469 Sonny Gray 1.25 3.00
470 Alex Mejia 1.25 3.00
471 Josh Harrison 1.25 3.00
472 Matt Garza 1.25 3.00
473 Wilmer Difo 1.25 3.00
474 Jeff Mathis 1.50 4.00
475 Aroldis Chapman 2.00 5.00
476 Wilson Ramos 1.25 3.00
477 Logan Morrison 1.25 3.00
478 Brad Miller 1.50 4.00
479 Daniel Descalso 1.25 3.00
480 Aaron Hicks 1.50 4.00
481 Ronald Torreyes 1.25 3.00
482 Delino DeShields 1.25 3.00
483 Drew Pomeranz 1.25 3.00
484 Kenta Maeda 1.50 4.00
485 Kyle Farmer 1.25 3.00
486 Tomas Nido 1.25 3.00
487 Carl Edwards Jr. 1.25 3.00
488 Joe Panik 1.50 4.00
489 Blake Snell 1.50 4.00
490 Jarrod Dyson 1.25 3.00
491 Andrew Heaney 1.25 3.00
492 Jon Jay 1.25 3.00
493 Kyle Gibson 1.50 4.00
494 Adalberto Mejia 1.25 3.00
495 Aaron Bummer 1.25 3.00
496 Leury Garcia 1.25 3.00
497 Chasen Shreve 1.25 3.00
498 Jen-Ho Tseng 1.25 3.00
499 Justin Bour 1.25 3.00
500 Kris Bryant 2.50 6.00
501 Clayton Richard 1.25 3.00
502 Xander Bogaerts 2.00 5.00
503 Josh Donaldson 1.50 4.00
504 Scott Schebler 1.50 4.00
505 Taylor Williams 1.25 3.00
506 Jose Berrios 1.50 4.00
507 Zack Greinke 1.50 4.00
508 Ryon Healy 1.25 3.00
509 Santiago Casilla 1.25 3.00
510 Freddie Freeman 2.50 6.00
511 Wade Davis 1.25 3.00
512 Mike Napoli 1.50 4.00
513 Mike Zunino 1.25 3.00
514 A.J. Minter 1.50 4.00
515 Greg Bird 1.50 4.00
516 Ken Giles 1.25 3.00
517 Phillip Evans 1.25 3.00
518 Andrew Toles 1.25 3.00
519 Reyes Moronta 1.25 3.00
520 Jim Johnson 1.25 3.00
521 Jose Osuna 1.25 3.00
522 Guillermo Heredia 1.25 3.00
523 Matt Bush 1.25 3.00
524 Steve Pearce 2.00 5.00
525 Johan Camargo 1.25 3.00
526 Tanner Roark 1.25 3.00
527 Francisco Cervelli 1.25 3.00
528 Marco Estrada 1.25 3.00
529 K.Bryant/K.Schwarber 2.50 6.00
530 Jason Vargas 1.25 3.00
531 Chris O'Grady 1.25 3.00
532 Tim Beckham 1.50 4.00
533 Kennys Vargas 1.25 3.00
534 German Marquez 1.25 3.00
535 Jhoulys Chacin 1.25 3.00
536 San Francisco Giants 1.25 3.00
537 Phil Hughes 1.25 3.00
538 Jason Castro 1.25 3.00
539 Lance McCullers 1.25 3.00
540 Mitch Garver 1.25 3.00
541 Dwight Smith Jr. 1.25 3.00
542 Pittsburgh Pirates 1.25 3.00
543 Luis Castillo 1.50 4.00
544 Yadier Molina 2.00 5.00
545 Nicholas Castellanos 2.00 5.00
546 Jordan Luplow 1.25 3.00
547 Travis Wood 1.25 3.00
548 Alex Meyer 1.25 3.00
549 Alex Gordon 1.50 4.00
550 Corey Seager 2.00 5.00
551 Yacksel Rios 1.25 3.00
552 Kyle Hendricks 2.00 5.00
553 Denard Span 1.25 3.00
554 Yonder Alonso 1.25 3.00
555 Jacob deGrom 2.00 5.00
556 Andrew Benintendi FS 2.00 5.00
557 Jacoby Ellsbury 1.50 4.00
558 Ben Gamel 1.50 4.00
559 Ian Desmond 1.25 3.00
560 Mark Melancon 1.25 3.00
561 Dan Straily 1.25 3.00
562 Brian McCann 1.50 4.00
563 Hector Neris 1.25 3.00
564 Joey Rickard 1.25 3.00
565 New York Mets 1.25 3.00
566 Yasmany Tomas 1.25 3.00
567 Felix Hernandez 1.50 4.00
568 J.C. Ramirez 1.25 3.00
569 Keone Kela 1.25 3.00
570 Trevor Williams 1.25 3.00
571 C.J. Cron 1.25 3.00
572 Dillon Maples 1.25 3.00
573 Mark Leiter Jr. 1.50 4.00
574 Jared Hughes 1.25 3.00
575 Adrian Gonzalez 1.50 4.00
576 Didi Gregorius 1.50 4.00
577 Yunel Escobar 1.25 3.00
578 Melky Cabrera 1.25 3.00
579 Carson Fulmer 1.25 3.00
580 Oakland Athletics 1.25 3.00
581 Jesse Winker 1.25 3.00
582 Albert Pujols 2.50 6.00
583 Tommy Joseph 2.00 5.00
584 Toronto Blue Jays 1.25 3.00
585 Brandon Crawford 1.50 4.00
586 Kyle Freeland 1.50 4.00
587 Chris Davis 1.25 3.00
588 David Wright 1.50 4.00
589 Adam Duvall 2.00 5.00
590 Dee Gordon 1.25 3.00
591 Daniel Nava 1.25 3.00
592 Gorkys Hernandez 1.25 3.00
593 Luke Weaver FS 1.50 4.00
594 Sandy Alcantara 1.25 3.00
595 Addison Reed 1.25 3.00
596 Keury Mella 1.25 3.00
597 Caleb Joseph 1.25 3.00
598 David Robertson 1.25 3.00
599 Justin Turner 1.50 4.00
600 Noah Syndergaard 1.50 4.00
601 Jose Peraza 1.50 4.00
602 Michael Pineda 1.25 3.00
603 Zach Britton 1.25 3.00
604 Gerardo Parra 1.25 3.00
605 Lucas Giolito 1.50 4.00
606 Jake Arrieta 1.50 4.00
607 Sean Newcomb FS 1.50 4.00
608 Kurt Suzuki 1.25 3.00
609 Austin Hedges 1.25 3.00
610 Scott Kazmir 1.25 3.00
611 Josh Bell FS 1.50 4.00
612 Steven Souza Jr. 1.50 4.00
613 Cory Gearrin 1.25 3.00
614 Minnesota Twins 1.25 3.00
615 Eric Thames 1.50 4.00
616 Greg Garcia 1.25 3.00
617 Doug Fister 1.25 3.00
618 Paul Goldschmidt 2.00 5.00
619 Jeremy Hellickson 1.25 3.00
620 Chris Young 1.25 3.00
621 Jerad Eickhoff 1.25 3.00
622 Ryan Rua 1.25 3.00
623 Josh Fields 1.25 3.00
624 Franklin Barreto 1.25 3.00
625 Los Angeles Dodgers 1.25 3.00
626 Brandon Maurer 1.25 3.00
627 Matthew Boyd 1.25 3.00
628 Vince Velasquez 1.25 3.00
629 Max Scherzer 2.00 5.00
630 Alcides Escobar 1.50 4.00
631 David Freese 1.25 3.00
632 Edwin Encarnacion 2.00 5.00
633 Jameson Taillon 1.50 4.00
634 Carlos Martinez 1.50 4.00
635 Cody Allen 1.25 3.00
636 Freddy Galvis 1.25 3.00
637 Manny Pina 1.25 3.00
638 Travis Shaw 1.25 3.00
639 Niko Goodrum 2.00 5.00
640 Seth Lugo 1.25 3.00
641 Cameron Maybin 1.25 3.00
642 Ben Revere 1.25 3.00
643 Justin Wilson 1.25 3.00
644 Carlos Perez 1.25 3.00
645 Welington Castillo 1.25 3.00
646 Jose de Leon 1.25 3.00
647 Jose Urena 1.25 3.00
648 Derek Holland 1.25 3.00
649 Curtis Granderson 1.50 4.00
650 Justin Verlander 2.00 5.00
651 JT Riddle 1.25 3.00
652 Matt Carpenter 2.00 5.00
653 Jorge Soler 2.00 5.00
654 Trayce Thompson 1.50 4.00
655 Andre Ethier 1.50 4.00
656 Brian Goodwin 1.25 3.00
657 Derek Dietrich 1.50 4.00
658 Tom Koehler 1.25 3.00
659 Arizona Diamondbacks 1.25 3.00
660 Mitch Haniger FS 1.50 4.00
661 Christian Villanueva 1.25 3.00
662 Patrick Corbin 1.50 4.00
663 Seth Smith 1.25 3.00
664 Gregor Blanco 1.25 3.00
665 Tommy Pham 1.25 3.00
666 Eric Sogard 1.25 3.00
667 Jonathan Lucroy 1.50 4.00
668 Tyler Anderson 1.25 3.00
669 Matt Chapman 2.00 5.00
670 Asdrubal Cabrera 1.50 4.00
671 Tyler Clippard 1.25 3.00
672 Brandon Nimmo 1.50 4.00
673 Adam Frazier 1.25 3.00
674 Jose Martinez 1.25 3.00
675 Victor Arano 1.25 3.00
676 Chad Green 1.25 3.00
677 Brandon Moss 1.25 3.00
678 Chad Bettis 1.25 3.00
679 Tyson Ross 1.25 3.00
680 Enrique Hernandez 1.50 4.00
681 Ehire Adrianza 1.25 3.00
682 Kansas City Royals 1.25 3.00
683 Adam Eaton 2.00 5.00
684 Hunter Strickland 1.25 3.00
685 Russell Martin 1.25 3.00
686 Bud Norris 1.25 3.00
687 Blake Treinen 1.25 3.00
688 Tony Wolters 1.25 3.00
689 Jeurys Familia 1.50 4.00
690 St. Louis Cardinals 1.25 3.00
691 Jason Heyward 1.50 4.00
692 Tony Watson 1.25 3.00
693 Brandon Kintzler 1.25 3.00
694 Anthony DeSclafani 1.25 3.00
695 Matt Davidson 1.50 4.00
696 Kenley Jansen 1.50 4.00
697 Eduardo Escobar 1.25 3.00
698 Ryan Sherriff 1.25 3.00
699 Drew Smyly 1.25 3.00
700 Shohei Ohtani 40.00 100.00

2018 Topps Chrome Sapphire Edition Photo Variations

698 Ronald Acuna Jr. 1500.00 2500.00
699 Gleyber Torres 20.00 50.00

2018 Topps Chrome Sapphire Edition Autographs

OVERALL AUTO ODDS THREE PER BOX
EXCHANGE DEADLINE 9/30/2020
ACAV Alex Verdugo 10.00 25.00
ACCF Clint Frazier 10.00 25.00
ACDF Dustin Fowler 3.00 8.00
ACFM Francisco Mejia 10.00 25.00
ACGT Gleyber Torres EXCH 250.00 600.00
ACHB Harrison Bader 5.00 12.00
ACJF Jack Flaherty 5.00 12.00
ACMA Miguel Andujar 40.00 100.00
ACND Nicky Delmonico 3.00 8.00
ACOA Ozzie Albies 75.00 200.00
ACRA Ronald Acuna 300.00 600.00
ACRD Rafael Devers 100.00 250.00
ACRM Ryan McMahon 4.00 10.00
ACSA Sandy Alcantara 3.00 8.00
ACSO Shohei Ohtani 300.00 600.00
ACVR Victor Robles 40.00 100.00

2018 Topps Chrome Sapphire Edition Autographs Green

*GREEN: .75X TO 2X BASIC
OVERALL AUTO ODDS THREE PER BOX
STATED PRINT RUN 50 SER.#'d SETS
EXCHANGE DEADLINE 9/30/2020
ACDS Dominic Smith 8.00 20.00
ACJC J.P. Crawford 10.00 25.00
ACRH Rhys Hoskins 50.00 120.00

2018 Topps Chrome Sapphire Edition Autographs Orange

*ORANGE: 1.2X TO 3X BASIC
OVERALL AUTO ODDS THREE PER BOX
STATED PRINT RUN 25 SER.#'d SETS
EXCHANGE DEADLINE 9/30/2020
ACDS Dominic Smith 12.00 30.00
ACJC J.P. Crawford 15.00 40.00
ACRH Rhys Hoskins 75.00 200.00
ACSO Shohei Ohtani 800.00 1200.00

2019 Topps Chrome Sapphire

1 Ronald Acuna Jr. 40.00 100.00
2 Tyler Anderson 1.25 3.00
3 Eduardo Nunez 1.25 3.00
4 Dereck Rodriguez 1.25 3.00
5 Chase Anderson 1.25 3.00
6 Max Scherzer 2.00 5.00
7 Gleyber Torres 8.00 20.00
8 Adam Jones 1.50 4.00
9 Ben Zobrist 1.50 4.00
10 Clayton Kershaw 4.00 10.00
11 Mike Zunino 1.25 3.00
12 Rizzo/Perez 3.00 8.00
13 David Price 1.50 4.00
14 Judge/Gregorius 3.00 8.00
15 J.P. Crawford 1.25 3.00
16 Charlie Blackmon 2.00 5.00
17 Caleb Joseph 1.25 3.00
18 Blake Parker 1.25 3.00
19 Jacob deGrom 2.00 5.00
20 Jose Urena 1.25 3.00
21 Jean Segura 2.00 5.00
22 Adalberto Mondesi 1.50 4.00
23 J.D. Martinez 2.00 5.00
24 Blake Snell 1.50 4.00
25 Chad Green 1.25 3.00
26 Angel Stadium 1.25 3.00
27 Mike Leake 1.25 3.00
28 Betts/Benintendi 3.00 8.00
29 Eugenio Suarez 1.50 4.00
30 Josh Hader 1.25 3.00
31 Busch Stadium 1.25 3.00
32 Carlos Correa 2.00 5.00
33 Jacob Nix RC 1.50 4.00
34 Josh Donaldson 1.50 4.00
35 Joey Rickard 1.25 3.00
36 Paul Blackburn 1.25 3.00
37 Marcus Stroman 1.50 4.00
38 Kolby Allard RC 2.00 5.00
39 Richard Urena 1.25 3.00
40 Jon Lester 1.50 4.00
41 Corey Seager 2.00 5.00
42 Edwin Encarnacion 2.00 5.00
43 Nick Burdi RC 1.25 3.00
44 Jay Bruce 1.50 4.00
45 Nick Pivetta 1.25 3.00
46 Jose Abreu 2.00 5.00
47 Yankee Stadium 1.25 3.00
48 PNC Park 1.25 3.00
49 Michael Kopech RC 20.00 50.00
50 Mookie Betts 3.00 8.00
51 Michael Brantley 1.50 4.00
52 J.T. Realmuto 2.00 5.00
53 Brandon Crawford 1.50 4.00
54 Rick Porcello 1.50 4.00
55 Yuli Gurriel 1.50 4.00
56 Christian Villanueva 1.25 3.00
57 Justin Verlander 2.00 5.00
58 Carlos Martinez 1.50 4.00
59 Zack Godley 1.25 3.00
60 Kyle Tucker RC 25.00 60.00
61 Touki Toussaint RC 1.50 4.00
62 Elvis Andrus 1.50 4.00
63 Jake Odorizzi 1.25 3.00
64 Ramon Laureano RC 15.00 40.00
65 Derek Dietrich 1.50 4.00
66 Stephen Piscotty 1.25 3.00
67 Danny Jansen RC 1.25 3.00
68 Nick Ahmed 1.25 3.00
69 Jorge Polanco 1.25 3.00
70 Nolan Arenado 2.50 6.00
71 SunTrust Park 1.25 3.00
72 Chris Taylor 1.50 4.00
73 Jon Gray 1.25 3.00
74 Chad Bettis 1.25 3.00
75 Safeco Field 1.25 3.00
76 J.D. Martinez 2.00 5.00
77 J.D. Martinez 2.00 5.00
78 Francisco Arcia RC 2.00 5.00
79 Miller Park 1.25 3.00
80 Tim Anderson 2.00 5.00
81 Wade Davis 1.25 3.00
82 Lourdes Gurriel Jr. 1.50 4.00
83 Lou Trivino 1.25 3.00
84 Matt Carpenter 2.00 5.00
85 Garrett Hampson RC 1.25 3.00
86 David Bote 1.50 4.00
87 Danny Duffy 1.25 3.00
88 Jonathan Villar 1.25 3.00
89 Corey Dickerson 1.25 3.00
90 Javier Baez 2.50 6.00
91 Hector Rondon 1.25 3.00
92 Clayton Richard 1.25 3.00
93 Matthew Boyd 1.25 3.00
94 Corbin Burnes RC 2.00 5.00
95 Dennis Santana RC 1.25 3.00
96 Trevor Williams 1.25 3.00
97 Harrison Bader 1.50 4.00
98 Chance Adams RC 1.25 3.00
99 Aroldis Chapman 2.00 5.00
100 Mike Trout 20.00 50.00
101 Michael Taylor 1.25 3.00
102 Shin-Soo Choo 1.50 4.00
103 Sean Manaea 1.25 3.00
104 Joe Musgrove 1.25 3.00
105 Jose Quintana 1.25 3.00
106 Adam Ottavino 1.25 3.00
107 Scooter Gennett 1.50 4.00
108 Ian Kennedy 1.25 3.00
109 Michael Conforto 1.50 4.00
110 Trevor Bauer 2.00 5.00
111 Reynaldo Lopez 1.50 4.00
112 Joey Gallo 1.50 4.00
113 Willie Calhoun 1.50 4.00
114 Brandon Lowe RC 5.00 12.00
115 Tyler Glasnow 1.25 3.00
116 Miguel Sano 1.50 4.00
117 Enrique Hernandez 1.50 4.00
118 Julio Teheran 1.50 4.00

119 Willson Contreras 1.50 4.00
120 Robert Gsellman 1.25 3.00
121 Joey Wendle 1.25 3.00
122 Zach Davies 1.25 3.00
123 Jose Martinez 1.25 3.00
124 Jason Kipnis 1.50 4.00
125 Paul DeJong 2.00 5.00
126 Oakland Coliseum 1.25 3.00
127 Seranthony Dominguez 1.25 3.00
128 Yoenis Cespedes 2.00 5.00
129 Kenley Jansen 1.50 4.00
130 Blake Snell 1.50 4.00
131 Mark Trumbo 1.25 3.00
132 Miguel Andujar 2.00 5.00
133 Ryan Zimmerman 1.50 4.00
134 Sean Reid-Foley RC 1.25 3.00
135 Wade LeBlanc 1.25 3.00
136 Brad Peacock 1.25 3.00
137 Carlos Rodon 1.50 4.00
138 Kyle Barraclough 1.25 3.00
139 Mitch Haniger 1.50 4.00
140 Daniel Ponce de Leon RC 2.00 5.00
141 Ryon Healy 1.25 3.00
142 Pedro Strop 1.25 3.00
143 Yan Gomes 2.00 5.00
144 Jake Arrieta 1.50 4.00
145 Harper/ Gennett 3.00 8.00
146 Jesse Winker 1.25 3.00
147 Blake Treinen 1.25 3.00
148 Brandon Belt 1.50 4.00
149 Khris Davis 2.00 5.00
150 Aaron Judge 5.00 12.00
151 Pablo Lopez RC 1.25 3.00
152 Teoscar Hernandez 2.00 5.00
153 Hunter Strickland 1.25 3.00
154 Johnny Cueto 1.50 4.00
155 James McCann 1.50 4.00
156 Luis Castillo 1.50 4.00
157 Buster Posey 2.50 6.00
158 Byron Buxton 1.50 4.00
159 Minute Maid Park 1.25 3.00
160 Fenway Park 1.25 3.00
161 Eric Hosmer 1.50 4.00
162 Yasiel Puig 2.00 5.00
163 Aaron Nola 1.50 4.00
164 Billy Hamilton 1.50 4.00
165 Robbie Ray 1.25 3.00
166 Matt Chapman 2.00 5.00
167 Xander Bogaerts 2.00 5.00
168 Salvador Perez 1.50 4.00
169 Charlie Morton 2.00 5.00
170 Manny Margot 1.25 3.00
171 Kyle Hendricks 2.00 5.00
172 Brandon Nimmo 1.50 4.00
173 Michael Fulmer 1.25 3.00
174 Jose Leclerc 1.25 3.00
175 Tommy Pham 1.25 3.00
176 Trea Turner 1.50 4.00
177 Kohl Stewart RC 1.50 4.00
178 Jose Altuve 1.50 4.00
179 Jackie Bradley Jr. 2.00 5.00
180 Justin Turner 1.50 4.00
181 Antonio Senzatela 1.25 3.00
182 Archie Bradley 1.25 3.00
183 Freddie Freeman 2.50 6.00
184 Ken Giles 1.25 3.00
185 Matt Duffy 1.25 3.00
186 Franmil Reyes 1.25 3.00
187 Citizens Bank Park 1.25 3.00
188 Matt Davidson 1.50 4.00
189 Khris Davis 2.00 5.00
190 Steven Duggar RC 1.50 4.00
191 Dansby Swanson 2.00 5.00
192 Luis Urias RC 12.00 30.00
193 Addison Reed 1.25 3.00
194 Felipe Vazquez 1.25 3.00
195 Brett Phillips 1.25 3.00
196 Adam Engel 1.25 3.00
197 Wrigley Field 1.25 3.00
198 Gregory Polanco 1.50 4.00
199 Mike Clevinger 1.50 4.00
200 Jacob deGrom 2.00 5.00
201 Marcus Semien 1.25 3.00
202 Muncy/Bellinger 2.00 5.00
203 Will Smith 1.25 3.00
204 Zack Cozart 1.25 3.00
205 Todd Frazier 1.50 4.00
206 Jaime Barria 1.25 3.00
207 Richard Bleier 1.25 3.00
208 Josh Bell 1.50 4.00
209 Nicholas Castellanos 2.00 5.00
210 Kris Bryant 2.50 6.00
211 Jeimer Candelario 1.25 3.00
212 Brian Anderson 1.25 3.00
213 Juan Soto 20.00 50.00
214 Colin Moran 1.25 3.00
215 Didi Gregorius 1.50 4.00
216 Arenado/Baez 2.50 6.00
217 Joe Jimenez 1.25 3.00
218 Scott Schebler 1.50 4.00
219 Martin Perez 1.50 4.00
220 Alex Colome 1.25 3.00
221 Luis Severino 1.50 4.00
222 Zack Greinke 1.50 4.00
223 Jose Ramirez 1.50 4.00
224 Odubel Herrera 1.50 4.00
225 Yadier Molina 2.00 5.00
226 Albert Almora 1.50 4.00
227 Adolis Garcia RC 1.25 3.00
228 Rafael Devers 2.50 6.00
229 Shane Greene 1.25 3.00
230 Miguel Cabrera 2.00 5.00
231 Joc Pederson 1.50 4.00
232 Kyle Seager 1.25 3.00
233 Dylan Bundy 1.50 4.00
234 Austin Hedges 1.25 3.00
235 Luke Weaver 1.25 3.00
236 Sean Doolittle 1.25 3.00
237 Seth Lugo 1.25 3.00
238 Whit Merrifield 2.00 5.00
239 Christian Yelich 4.00 10.00
240 Trey Mancini 1.50 4.00
241 James Paxton 1.50 4.00
242 Anthony Rendon 2.00 5.00
243 Jonathan Loaisiga RC 1.50 4.00
244 Tyler Flowers 1.25 3.00
245 Rogers Centre 1.25 3.00
246 Ryan Borucki RC 1.25 3.00
247 Sam Tuivailala 1.25 3.00
248 Justin Bour 1.25 3.00
249 Jordan Zimmermann 1.50 4.00
250 Shohei Ohtani 2.50 6.00
251 Niko Goodrum 1.50 4.00
252 Jakob Junis 1.25 3.00
253 Starling Marte 1.50 4.00
254 Dodger Stadium 1.25 3.00
255 Andrelton Simmons 1.25 3.00
256 Cody Allen 1.25 3.00
257 Andrew Heaney 1.25 3.00
258 Eddie Rosario 1.50 4.00
259 Jonathan Schoop 1.25 3.00
260 Aaron Hicks 1.50 4.00
261 Jedd Gyorko 1.25 3.00
262 Mitch Moreland 1.25 3.00
263 Gray/Gregorius 1.50 4.00
264 Avisail Garcia 1.50 4.00
265 Joey Lucchesi 1.25 3.00
266 Ohtani/Bregman 2.50 6.00
267 Ross Stripling 1.25 3.00
268 Blake Snell 1.50 4.00
269 Francisco Lindor 2.00 5.00
270 Brad Keller RC 1.25 3.00
271 Shane Bieber 2.00 5.00
272 Orlando Arcia 1.25 3.00
273 Kole Calhoun 1.25 3.00
274 Francisco Cervelli 1.25 3.00
275 Steve Pearce 2.00 5.00
276 Nolan Arenado 2.50 6.00
277 Mitch Garver 1.25 3.00
278 Mike Minor 1.25 3.00
279 Rhys Hoskins 2.50 6.00
280 Miles Mikolas 2.00 5.00
281 Jeff McNeil RC 15.00 40.00
282 Tim Beckham 1.50 4.00
283 Rich Hill 1.25 3.00
284 Joey Votto 2.00 5.00
285 Sonny Gray 1.50 4.00
286 Taijuan Walker 1.25 3.00
287 Jesus Aguilar 1.25 3.00
288 Joe Panik 1.50 4.00
289 Matt Olson 1.50 4.00
290 Steven Souza Jr. 1.50 4.00
291 Enyel De Los Santos RC 1.50 4.00
292 Dee Gordon 1.25 3.00
293 Andrew Miller 1.50 4.00
294 Correa/Altuve 2.00 5.00
295 Pujols/Betts 2.00 5.00
296 Lewis Brinson 1.25 3.00
297 Paul Goldschmidt 2.00 5.00
298 Devon Travis 1.25 3.00
299 Edwin Diaz 1.50 4.00
300 Christian Yelich 4.00 10.00
301 Tanner Roark 1.25 3.00
302 Jose Berrios 1.50 4.00
303 Ranger Suarez RC 1.50 4.00
304 Michael Lorenzen 1.25 3.00
305 Brad Boxberger 1.25 3.00
306 Justus Sheffield RC 2.00 5.00
307 Jorge Soler 2.00 5.00
308 Yolmer Sanchez 1.25 3.00
309 Randal Grichuk 1.25 3.00
310 Javier Baez 2.50 6.00
311 Jake Bauers RC 2.00 5.00
312 Mookie Betts 3.00 8.00
313 Robinson Cano 1.50 4.00
314 David Price 1.50 4.00
315 Duane Underwood Jr. RC 1.25 3.00
316 Adam Eaton 2.00 5.00
317 Kevin Gausman 1.25 3.00
318 Cedric Mullins RC 2.00 5.00
319 Alex Gordon 1.50 4.00
320 Ronald Guzman 1.25 3.00
321 Jack Flaherty 1.50 4.00
322 Brian McCann 1.50 4.00
323 George Springer 1.50 4.00
324 Logan Morrison 1.25 3.00
325 Dan Straily 1.25 3.00
326 Heath Fillmyer RC 1.25 3.00
327 Maikel Franco 1.50 4.00
328 Yonder Alonso 1.25 3.00
329 Jordan Hicks 1.50 4.00
330 Lorenzo Cain 1.25 3.00
331 Cesar Hernandez 1.25 3.00
332 Ryan O'Hearn RC 1.25 3.00
333 Ray Black RC 1.25 3.00
334 Jake Lamb 1.50 4.00
335 Ervin Santana 1.25 3.00
336 Corey Kluber 1.50 4.00
337 Mychal Givens 1.25 3.00
338 Andrew Cashner 1.25 3.00
339 Josh Harrison 1.25 3.00
340 Vladimir Guerrero Jr. RC 150.00 400.00
341 Nationals Park 1.25 3.00
342 Wilmer Difo 1.25 3.00
343 Sal Romano 1.25 3.00
344 Max Scherzer 2.00 5.00
345 Justin Upton 1.50 4.00
346 Chris Iannetta 1.25 3.00
347 Kirby Yates 1.50 4.00
348 Russell Martin 1.25 3.00
349 Kyle Schwarber 2.00 5.00
350 Nick Markakis 1.50 4.00
351 Jarrod Dyson 1.25 3.00
352 David Peralta 1.25 3.00
353 Gary Sanchez 2.00 5.00
354 Nomar Mazara 1.25 3.00
355 Stephen Gonsalves RC 1.25 3.00
356 Stephen Strasburg 2.00 5.00
357 Chris Martin 1.25 3.00
358 Leonys Martin 1.25 3.00
359 Noah Syndergaard 1.50 4.00
360 Mark Melancon 1.25 3.00
361 Taylor Davis 1.25 3.00
362 Jeremy Jeffress 1.25 3.00
363 Max Stassi 1.25 3.00
364 Kenta Maeda 1.50 4.00
365 Ketel Marte 1.50 4.00
366 Isiah Kiner-Falefa 1.25 3.00
367 Ohtani/Trout 6.00 15.00
368 Brad Hand 1.25 3.00
369 Charlie Culberson 1.25 3.00
370 Jacoby Ellsbury 1.50 4.00
371 Zack Wheeler 1.50 4.00
372 Yu Darvish 2.00 5.00
373 Christian Vazquez 1.25 3.00
374 Alex Blandino 1.25 3.00
375 Cody Reed 1.25 3.00
376 Framber Valdez RC 1.25 3.00
377 Yoan Moncada 2.00 5.00
378 Brandon Workman 1.25 3.00
379 Carter Kieboom RC 2.00 5.00
380 Chris Archer 1.25 3.00
381 Juan Lagares 1.25 3.00
382 Daniel Norris 1.25 3.00
383 Adalberto Mejia 1.25 3.00
384 Dominic Leone 1.25 3.00
385 Ender Inciarte 1.25 3.00
386 Ryan Pressly 1.25 3.00
387 Mike Foltynewicz 2.00 5.00
388 Dominic Smith 1.25 3.00
389 Victor Caratini 1.25 3.00
390 Evan Longoria 1.50 4.00
391 Jung Ho Kang 1.25 3.00
392 Cionel Perez RC 1.25 3.00
393 Hunter Renfroe 1.25 3.00
394 Miguel Rojas 1.25 3.00
395 Andrew McCutchen 2.00 5.00
396 Masahiro Tanaka 1.50 4.00
397 Lance McCullers Jr. 1.25 3.00
398 Erick Fedde 1.25 3.00
399 Tyler Mahle 1.25 3.00
400 Bryce Harper 3.00 8.00
401 Tony Kemp 1.25 3.00
402 Victor Robles 2.50 6.00
403 Ivan Nova 1.50 4.00
404 Jace Peterson 1.25 3.00
405 Chaz Roe 1.25 3.00
406 Jason Castro 1.25 3.00
407 Eduardo Nunez 1.25 3.00
408 Sean Newcomb 1.25 3.00
409 Nate Jones 1.25 3.00
410 Fernando Tatis Jr. RC 600.00 1500.00
411 Magneuris Sierra 2.00 5.00
412 Clint Frazier 1.50 4.00
413 Mike Fiers 1.25 3.00
414 Michael Soroka 2.00 5.00
415 Bryan Shaw 1.25 3.00
416 Keon Broxton 1.25 3.00
417 Noel Cuevas RC 1.25 3.00
418 Jason Vargas 1.25 3.00
419 Sandy Leon 1.25 3.00
420 Kevin Kiermaier 1.50 4.00
421 Yoshihisa Hirano 1.25 3.00
422 Matt Barnes 1.25 3.00
423 Ji-Man Choi 1.25 3.00
424 Target Field 1.25 3.00
425 Steel City Slammers 1.25 3.00
Corey Dickerson
426 Austin Romine 1.25 3.00
427 Jorge Bonifacio 1.25 3.00
428 Pablo Sandoval 1.50 4.00
429 Wilmer Font 1.25 3.00
430 Roman Quinn 1.25 3.00
431 Lonnie Chisenhall 1.25 3.00
432 Ryan Yarbrough 1.25 3.00
433 Pedro Baez 1.25 3.00
434 Roberto Osuna 1.25 3.00
435 Steven Brault 1.25 3.00
436 Kendrys Morales 1.25 3.00
437 Albert Pujols 2.50 6.00
438 Max Kepler 1.50 4.00
439 Ryan McMahon 1.25 3.00
440 Dustin Pedroia 2.00 5.00
441 Oriole Park at Camden 1.25 3.00
442 Reese McGuire RC 2.00 5.00
443 Steven Matz 1.50 4.00
444 Powerful Pair 3.00 8.00
Aaron Judge
Giancarlo Stanton
445 Walker Buehler 6.00 15.00
446 Francisco Mejia 1.50 4.00
447 Altuve/Springer 1.50 4.00
448 Willians Astudillo RC 1.25 3.00
449 Matt Moore 1.50 4.00
450 Greg Garcia 1.25 3.00
451 Jorge Alfaro 1.25 3.00
452 Chris Paddack RC 25.00 60.00
453 Taylor Rogers 1.25 3.00
454 Matt Kemp 1.50 4.00
455 Zach Eflin 1.25 3.00
456 Austin Barnes 1.25 3.00
457 Nick Ciuffo RC 1.25 3.00
458 Alex Avila 1.50 4.00
459 Trevor Hildenberger 1.25 3.00
460 Trevor Story 2.00 5.00
461 Eduardo Rodriguez 1.25 3.00
462 Luke Voit 3.00 8.00
463 Wily Peralta 1.25 3.00
464 Alex Wood 1.25 3.00
465 Raisel Iglesias 1.25 3.00
466 Yairo Munoz 1.25 3.00
467 A.J. Minter 1.50 4.00
468 Anthony DeSclafani 1.25 3.00
469 Brandon Morrow 1.25 3.00
470 Peter O'Brien 1.25 3.00
471 Kevin Newman RC 2.00 5.00
472 Scott Kingery 1.50 4.00
473 Kyle Wright RC 2.00 5.00
474 Carson Kelly 1.25 3.00
475 Pete Alonso RC 125.00 300.00
476 Arodys Vizcaino 1.25 3.00
477 Mikie Mahtook 1.25 3.00
478 Alen Hanson 1.50 4.00
479 Wei-Yin Chen 1.25 3.00
480 Vince Velasquez 1.25 3.00
481 J.A. Happ 1.50 4.00
482 Starlin Castro 1.25 3.00
483 Alex Cobb 1.25 3.00
484 Andrew Chafin 1.25 3.00
485 Wil Myers 1.25 3.00
486 CC Sabathia 1.50 4.00
487 Renfroe/Hosmer 1.50 4.00
488 Dexter Fowler 1.50 4.00
489 Joe Ross 1.25 3.00
490 Matt Harvey 1.50 4.00
491 Comerica Park 1.25 3.00
492 Adam Plutko 1.25 3.00
493 JaCoby Jones 1.50 4.00
494 Ian Desmond 1.25 3.00
495 Progressive Field 1.25 3.00
496 Buck Farmer 1.25 3.00
497 Citi Field 1.25 3.00
498 Pablo Reyes RC 1.25 3.00
499 Daniel Murphy 1.50 4.00
500 Manny Machado 2.00 5.00
501 Carlos Carrasco 1.25 3.00
502 Mike Montgomery 1.25 3.00
503 Marcell Ozuna 2.00 5.00
504 Stephen Tarpley RC 1.50 4.00
505 Dellin Betances 1.50 4.00
506 Ben Gamel 1.50 4.00
507 Cody Bellinger 4.00 10.00
508 Albies/Acuna Jr. 10.00 25.00
509 Globe Life Park in Arlington 1.25 3.00
510 Patrick Corbin 1.50 4.00
511 Rougned Odor 1.50 4.00
512 Franklin Barreto 1.25 3.00
513 Brett Gardner 1.50 4.00
514 Greg Allen 1.50 4.00
515 Hyun-Jin Ryu 1.50 4.00
516 Keone Kela 1.25 3.00
517 Shawn Armstrong 1.25 3.00
518 Steven Wright 1.25 3.00
519 Julio Urias 2.00 5.00
520 David Fletcher RC 4.00 10.00
521 Chase Field 1.25 3.00
522 Brian Johnson 1.25 3.00
523 Marco Gonzales 1.25 3.00
524 Chad Pinder 1.25 3.00
525 Ian Kinsler 1.50 4.00
526 Sandy Alcantara 1.25 3.00
527 Guaranteed Rate Field 1.25 3.00
528 Jon Edwards 1.25 3.00
529 Chance Sisco 1.25 3.00
530 Ian Happ 1.50 4.00
531 Josh Reddick 1.25 3.00
532 Lance Lynn 1.25 3.00
533 Matt Shoemaker 1.50 4.00
534 Aaron Altherr 1.25 3.00
535 Tyler Naquin 1.25 3.00
536 Molina/Ozuna 2.00 5.00
537 Ronald Torreyes 1.25 3.00
538 Seung-Hwan Oh 1.50 4.00
539 Franchy Cordero 1.25 3.00
540 Cole Hamels 1.50 4.00
541 Michael Wacha 1.50 4.00
542 Chris Davis 1.25 3.00
543 Nick Williams 1.25 3.00
544 Jake Marisnick 1.25 3.00
545 Tyler White 1.25 3.00
546 Brock Holt 1.25 3.00
547 Trevor Richards RC 1.25 3.00
548 Chris Owings 1.25 3.00
549 Sale/Vazquez 2.00 5.00
550 Adam Cimber RC 1.25 3.00
551 Kolten Wong 1.50 4.00
552 David Hess 1.25 3.00
553 Daniel Mengden 1.25 3.00
554 Corey Knebel 1.25 3.00
555 Marlins Park 1.25 3.00
556 Rowdy Tellez RC 2.00 5.00
557 Adam Duvall 1.50 4.00
558 Phillip Ervin 1.25 3.00
559 Ildemaro Vargas 1.25 3.00
560 Victor Reyes RC 1.25 3.00
561 Ozzie Albies 2.00 5.00
562 Willy Adames 1.25 3.00
563 Keynan Middleton 1.25 3.00
564 Austin Meadows 1.50 4.00
565 Andrew Triggs 1.25 3.00
566 Tropicana Field 1.25 3.00
567 Josh Rogers RC 1.25 3.00
568 Giancarlo Stanton 2.00 5.00
569 Carl Edwards Jr. 1.25 3.00
570 Eduardo Escobar 1.25 3.00
571 Bobby Poyner RC 1.50 4.00
572 Gerrit Cole 2.00 5.00
573 Tucker Barnhart 1.25 3.00
574 Jeff Samardzija 1.25 3.00
575 Jimmy Yacabonis 1.25 3.00
576 Jake Cave RC 1.50 4.00
577 Nicky Delmonico 1.25 3.00
578 Patrick Wisdom RC 1.25 3.00
579 Andrew Benintendi 2.00 5.00
580 DJ Stewart RC 1.50 4.00
581 Travis Jankowski 1.25 3.00
582 Austin Wynns RC 1.25 3.00
583 Nick Senzel RC 20.00 50.00
584 Josh James RC 2.00 5.00
585 Carlos Santana 1.50 4.00
586 Drew VerHagen 1.25 3.00
587 Johan Camargo 1.25 3.00
588 Taylor Ward RC 1.25 3.00
589 Jeurys Familia 1.50 4.00
590 Jose Peraza 1.50 4.00
591 Wilson Ramos 1.25 3.00
592 Eric Lauer 1.25 3.00
593 John Hicks 1.25 3.00
594 Austin Slater 1.25 3.00
595 Yandy Diaz 1.50 4.00
596 Anthony Rizzo 3.00 8.00
597 Kyle Gibson 1.50 4.00
598 Chris Devenski 1.25 3.00
599 Daniel Palka 1.25 3.00
600 Shohei Ohtani 2.50 6.00
601 David Dahl 1.25 3.00
602 German Marquez 1.25 3.00
603 J.D. Davis 1.25 3.00
604 Coors Field 1.25 3.00
605 Jeffrey Springs RC 1.25 3.00
606 Johnny Field RC 1.50 4.00
607 J.T. Riddle 1.25 3.00
608 Ehire Adrianza 1.25 3.00
609 Kauffman Stadium 1.25 3.00
610 Howie Kendrick 1.25 3.00
611 Chris Shaw RC 2.00 5.00
612 Mark Canha 1.25 3.00
613 Wellington Castillo 1.25 3.00
614 Ryan Braun 1.50 4.00
615 Nick Tropeano 1.25 3.00
616 Oracle Park 1.25 3.00
617 Hernan Perez 1.25 3.00
618 Nick Martini RC 1.25 3.00
619 Tommy Hunter 1.25 3.00
620 Jared Hughes 1.25 3.00
621 Pat Valaika 1.25 3.00
622 Troy Tulowitzki 2.00 5.00
623 Kevin Pillar 1.25 3.00
624 Amed Rosario 1.50 4.00
625 Yelich/Arcia 2.50 6.00
626 Robbie Erlin 1.25 3.00
627 Freddy Peralta 2.00 5.00
628 Roenis Elias 1.25 3.00
629 Myles Straw RC 2.00 5.00
630 Dustin Fowler 1.25 3.00
631 Tyler Austin 2.00 5.00
632 Yusei Kikuchi RC 2.00 5.00
633 Addison Russell 1.50 4.00
634 John Gant 1.25 3.00
635 Adam Frazier 1.25 3.00
636 Jace Fry 1.25 3.00
637 Yusmeiro Petit 1.25 3.00
638 Kristopher Negron 1.25 3.00
639 Roberto Perez 1.25 3.00
640 Brian Goodwin 1.25 3.00
641 Bryse Wilson RC 1.50 4.00
642 Jhoulys Chacin 1.25 3.00
643 Chris Sale 2.00 5.00
644 Delino DeShields 1.25 3.00
645 Steve Cishek 1.25 3.00
646 Jason Heyward 1.50 4.00
647 Kyle Freeland 1.50 4.00
648 Kevin Kramer RC 1.50 4.00
649 Carlos Tocci RC 1.25 3.00
650 Austin Riley RC 25.00 60.00
651 Jorge Lopez 1.25 3.00
652 Rosell Herrera RC 1.25 3.00
653 Greg Bird 1.50 4.00
654 Kurt Suzuki 1.25 3.00
655 Tyler O'Neill 1.50 4.00
656 Jacob Faria 1.25 3.00
657 JC Ramirez 1.25 3.00
658 Max Muncy 1.50 4.00
659 Aramis Garcia RC 1.25 3.00
660 Dawel Lugo RC 2.00 5.00
661 Zack Greinke 1.50 4.00
662 Jameson Taillon 1.50 4.00
663 Adam Conley 1.25 3.00
664 Lucas Giolito 1.50 4.00
665 David Freese 1.25 3.00
666 Cam Gallagher 1.25 3.00
667 Ronny Rodriguez RC 1.25 3.00
668 Pat Neshek 1.25 3.00
669 Mallex Smith 1.25 3.00
670 Eloy Jimenez RC 75.00 200.00
671 Alex Verdugo 1.50 4.00
672 Christin Stewart RC 1.50 4.00
673 Danny Salazar 1.50 4.00
674 Collin McHugh 1.25 3.00
675 Nelson Cruz 2.00 5.00
676 Travis Shaw 1.25 3.00
677 Aaron Sanchez 1.50 4.00
678 Brendan Rodgers RC 12.00 30.00
679 Adam Wainwright 1.50 4.00
680 Justin Smoak 1.25 3.00
681 Jeff Mathis 1.50 4.00
682 Petco Park 1.25 3.00
683 Isaac Galloway RC 1.25 3.00
684 Keston Hiura RC 125.00 300.00
685 Billy McKinney 1.25 3.00
686 Brandon Drury 1.25 3.00
687 Brandon Woodruff 1.25 3.00
688 Jalen Beeks RC 1.25 3.00
689 Jose Briceno RC 1.25 3.00
690 Hunter Dozier 1.25 3.00
691 Great American Ball Park 1.25 3.00
692 Fernando Rodney 1.25 3.00
693 Ryan Brasier 1.25 3.00
694 Steve Pearce 2.00 5.00
695 Eric Thames 1.25 3.00
696 Sam Dyson 1.25 3.00
697 Dakota Hudson RC 1.50 4.00
698 Baez/Contreras 2.00 5.00
699 Felix Hernandez 1.50 4.00
700 Alex Bregman 2.00 5.00

2019 Topps Chrome Sapphire Orange

STATED ODDS 1:11 HOBBY
STATED PRINT RUN 25 SER.#'d SETS
EXCHANGE DEADLINE 8/31/2021
*ORANGE: 1X TO 2.5X BASIC
1 Ronald Acuna Jr. 75.00 200.00
7 Gleyber Torres 125.00 300.00
10 Clayton Kershaw 12.00 30.00
28 Boston's Boys 12.00 30.00
Mookie Betts
Andrew Benintendi
64 Ramon Laureano 40.00 100.00
100 Mike Trout 150.00 400.00
150 Aaron Judge 75.00 200.00
157 Buster Posey 15.00 40.00
178 Jose Altuve 12.00 30.00
213 Juan Soto 125.00 300.00
216 Bring It In 12.00 30.00
Nolan Arenado
Javier Baez
250 Shohei Ohtani 60.00 150.00
340 Vladimir Guerrero Jr. 400.00 800.00
367 Ohtani Gets Hot 25.00 60.00
Shohei Ohtani
Mike Trout
475 Pete Alonso 1000.00 1500.00
507 Cody Bellinger 15.00 40.00
561 Ozzie Albies 12.00 30.00
600 Shohei Ohtani 60.00 150.00
650 Austin Riley 100.00 250.00

2019 Topps Chrome Sapphire Rookie Autographs

CSAAR Austin Riley 50.00 120.00
CSABK Brad Keller 8.00 20.00
CSABL Brandon Lowe 40.00 100.00
CSABW Bryse Wilson 8.00 20.00
CSACK Carter Kieboom 40.00 100.00
CSACM Cedric Mullins 5.00 12.00
CSACS Chris Shaw 10.00 25.00
CSADH Dakota Hudson 10.00 25.00
CSADL Dawel Lugo 5.00 12.00
CSADP Daniel Ponce de Leon 5.00 12.00
CSADS DJ Stewart 4.00 10.00
CSAEJ Eloy Jimenez 100.00 250.00
CSAJC Jake Cave 4.00 10.00
CSAJJ Josh James 5.00 12.00
CSAJN Jacob Nix 4.00 10.00
CSAJS Justus Sheffield 15.00 40.00
CSAKA Kolby Allard 5.00 12.00
CSAKK Kevin Kramer 6.00 15.00
CSAKN Kevin Newman 10.00 25.00
CSAKS Kohl Stewart 4.00 10.00
CSAKT Kyle Tucker 75.00 200.00
CSAKW Kyle Wright 6.00 15.00
CSAMS Myles Straw 5.00 12.00
CSANC Nick Ciuffo 8.00 20.00
CSAPA Pete Alonso 600.00 1000.00
CSARB Ray Black 3.00 8.00
CSARM Reese McGuire 10.00 25.00
CSARR Ronny Rodriguez 3.00 8.00
CSART Rowdy Tellez 6.00 15.00
CSASD Steven Duggar 4.00 10.00
CSASG Stephen Gonsalves 3.00 8.00
CSATB Ty Buttrey 5.00 12.00
CSATT Touki Toussaint 8.00 20.00
CSATW Taylor Ward 8.00 20.00
CSAWA Willians Astudillo 3.00 8.00
CSAYK Yusei Kikuchi 15.00 40.00
CSAFTJ Fernando Tatis Jr. EXCH 750.00 2000.00
CSAMKE Mitch Keller 12.00 30.00
CSAVGJ Vladimir Guerrero Jr. 300.00 600.00

2019 Topps Chrome Sapphire Rookie Autographs Green

CSAAR Austin Riley
CSACK Carter Kieboom
CSAEJ Eloy Jimenez
CSAKW Kyle Wright 20.00 50.00
CSAPA Pete Alonso
CSAFTJ Fernando Tatis Jr. EXCH
CSAVGJ Vladimir Guerrero Jr. 600.00 1200.00

2019 Topps Chrome Sapphire Rookie Autographs Orange

CSAAR Austin Riley
CSACK Carter Kieboom
CSAEJ Eloy Jimenez
CSAKW Kyle Wright 30.00 80.00
CSAPA Pete Alonso
CSAFTJ Fernando Tatis Jr. EXCH
CSAVGJ Vladimir Guerrero Jr. 800.00 1500.00

2020 Topps Chrome

PRINTING PLATE ODDS 1:8634 HOBBY
PLATE PRINT RUN 1 SET PER COLOR
BLACK-CYAN-MAGENTA-YELLOW ISSUED
NO PLATE PRICING DUE TO SCARCITY
1 Mike Trout 1.50 4.00
2 Liam Hendriks .20 .50
3 Bobby Bradley RC .50 1.25
4 Rogelio Armenteros RC .50 1.25
5 Jesus Luzardo RC .75 2.00
6 Miguel Cabrera .30 .75
7 Trea Turner .25 .60
8 Brendan McKay RC .60 1.50
9 Joey Votto .30 .75
10 Domingo Leyba RC .50 1.25
11 Austin Nola RC .60 1.50
12 Juan Soto 1.00 2.50
13 Max Muncy .25 .60
14 Archie Bradley .20 .50
15 David Peralta .20 .50
16 Luis Castillo .25 .60
17 Bryan Reynolds .25 .60
18 Michael Fulmer .20 .50
19 Jeimer Candelario .20 .50
20 Jorge Soler .30 .75
21 Shohei Ohtani .40 1.00
22 Cavan Biggio .40 1.00
23 Seth Brown RC .40 1.00
24 Nick Senzel .30 .75
25 Keston Hiura .40 1.00
26 Travis Demeritte RC .50 1.25
27 Christian Walker .25 .60
28 Andrew Heaney .20 .50
29 Carlos Correa .30 .75
30 Dan Vogelbach .20 .50
31 Adalberto Mondesi .30 .75
32 Sean Murphy RC .60 1.50
33 Nick Solak RC .60 1.50
34 Gio Urshela .30 .75
35 Michael Conforto .25 .60
36 Ian Desmond .20 .50
37 Mitch Haniger .25 .60
38 Jean Segura .25 .60
39 Chris Paddack .30 .75
40 Josh Hader .20 .50
41 Corey Kluber .25 .60
42 Jose Altuve .25 .60
43 Dylan Cease RC .75 2.00
44 German Marquez .30 .75
45 Gleyber Torres .60 1.50
46 Lucas Giolito .25 .60
47 Jake Rogers RC .40 1.00
48 Yusei Kikuchi .25 .60
49 Randy Arozarena RC 3.00 8.00
50 Aaron Judge .75 2.00
51 Danny Jansen .20 .50
52 Kyle Seager .20 .50
53 Kris Bryant .40 1.00
54 Chris Archer .20 .50
55 DJ LeMahieu .30 .75
56 Abraham Toro RC .50 1.25
57 Andrew Benintendi .30 .75
58 Noah Syndergaard .25 .60
59 Trevor Story .30 .75
60 Luis Robert RC 25.00 60.00
61 Sheldon Neuse RC .50 1.25
62 Ozzie Albies .30 .75
63 Hunter Dozier .20 .50
64 Scott Kingery .25 .60
65 Dansby Swanson .30 .75
66 Jose Abreu .30 .75
67 Sam Hilliard RC .60 1.50
68 Blake Snell .25 .60
69 Nelson Cruz .30 .75
70 Jeff McNeil .25 .60
71 Anthony Rizzo .50 1.25
72 Andrelton Simmons .20 .50
73 Charlie Blackmon .30 .75
74 Matthew Boyd .20 .50
75 Jonathan Villar .20 .50
76 Manny Machado .30 .75
77 Cody Bellinger .60 1.50
78 Eddie Rosario .25 .60
79 Hanser Alberto .20 .50
80 Pete Alonso .75 2.00
81 Jacob deGrom .30 .75
82 Jordan Yamamoto RC .50 1.25
83 Matt Thaiss RC .50 1.25
84 Fernando Tatis Jr. 1.25 3.00
85 Kyle Schwarber .30 .75
86 Adrian Morejon RC .40 1.00
87 Zack Collins RC .50 1.25
88 Brandon Crawford .25 .60
89 Paul Goldschmidt .30 .75
90 Tim Anderson .30 .75
91 Brusdar Graterol RC .60 1.50
92 Nicky Lopez .20 .50
93 Rafael Devers .40 1.00
94 Tommy Edman .30 .75
95 Edwin Rios RC 1.00 2.50
96 Mike Soroka .30 .75
97 Bryce Harper .50 1.25
98 Kevin Newman .25 .60
99 Colin Moran .20 .50
100 Mookie Betts .60 1.50
101 Trent Grisham RC 1.50 4.00
102 Alex Bregman .30 .75
103 Mike Yastrzemski .50 1.25
104 Walker Buehler .40 1.00
105 Miguel Rojas .20 .50
106 Harold Ramirez .20 .50
107 Dee Gordon .20 .50

08 Eric Hosmer .25 .60
09 Nomar Mazara .20 .50
10 Adbert Alzolay RC .50 1.25
11 Aristides Aquino RC .75 2.00
12 Ronald Acuna Jr. 1.25 3.00
13 Austin Meadows .25 .60
14 Tony Gonsolin RC 1.50 4.00
15 Alex Young RC .40 1.00
16 A.J. Puk RC .75 2.00
17 Logan Webb RC .50 1.25
18 Tyler Glasnow .20 .50
19 Brandon Lowe .30 .75
20 Anthony Kay RC .40 1.00
21 John Means .20 .50
22 Clayton Kershaw .60 1.50
23 Jon Lester .25 .60
24 Max Kepler .25 .60
125 Jose Berrios .25 .60
126 Victor Reyes .20 .50
27 Albert Pujols .40 1.00
128 Eugenio Suarez .25 .60
129 Ronald Guzman .20 .50
130 Anthony Santander .20 .50
131 Freddie Freeman .40 1.00
132 Zac Gallen RC 1.00 2.50
133 Vladimir Guerrero Jr. .60 1.50
134 Eloy Jimenez .60 1.50
135 Jack Flaherty .25 .60
136 Justin Dunn RC .50 1.25
137 Xander Bogaerts .30 .75
138 Christian Yelich .40 1.00
139 Max Scherzer .30 .75
140 Orlando Arcia .20 .50
141 Rowdy Tellez .25 .60
142 Jose Urquidy RC .50 1.25
143 Aaron Civale RC .60 1.50
144 Marcus Semien .20 .50
145 Yoan Moncada .30 .75
146 Brian Anderson .20 .50
147 Brandon Belt .25 .60
148 Gavin Lux RC 2.50 6.00
149 Andres Munoz RC .50 1.25
150 Bo Bichette RC 8.00 20.00
151 Ketel Marte .25 .60
152 Pablo Lopez .20 .50
153 Lorenzo Cain .20 .50
154 Whit Merrifield .30 .75
155 Logan Allen RC .40 1.00
156 Francisco Lindor .30 .75
157 Buster Posey .40 1.00
158 Elvis Andrus .25 .60
159 Brock Burke RC .40 1.00
160 Ramon Laureano .30 .75
161 Nico Hoerner RC 1.50 4.00
162 Junior Fernandez RC .40 1.00
163 Trevor Williams .20 .50
164 Justin Verlander .30 .75
165 Carlos Santana .25 .60
166 Masahiro Tanaka .30 .75
167 Lourdes Gurriel Jr. .25 .60
168 Mauricio Dubon RC .50 1.25
169 Luis Urias .25 .60
170 Isan Diaz RC .60 1.50
171 Carter Kieboom .25 .60
172 Luis Arraez .40 1.00
173 Yu Chang RC .60 1.50
174 Nolan Arenado .40 1.00
175 Raisel Iglesias .20 .50
176 Dustin May RC 2.50 6.00
177 Shin Soo Choo .25 .60
178 Paul DeJong .30 .75
179 Willy Adames .20 .50
180 Miles Mikolas .20 .50
181 Robel Garcia RC .40 1.00
182 Oscar Mercado .25 .60
183 Matt Olson .20 .50
184 Rhys Hoskins .40 1.00
185 Jose Urena .20 .50
186 Kyle Lewis RC 6.00 15.00
187 Michel Baez RC .40 1.00
188 Trey Mancini .30 .75
189 J.D. Martinez .30 .75
190 Jose Ramirez .25 .60
191 Joey Gallo .30 .75
192 Robbie Ray .20 .50
193 Matt Chapman .30 .75
194 George Springer .25 .60
195 Patrick Corbin .25 .60
196 Corey Seager .30 .75
197 Jeff Samardzija .20 .50
198 Javier Baez .40 1.00
199 Aaron Nola .30 .75
200 Yordan Alvarez RC 5.00 12.00

2020 Topps Chrome Blue Refractors

*BLUE REF: 5X TO 12X BASIC
*BLUE REF RC: 2.5X TO 6X BASIC RC
STATED ODDS 1:230 HOBBY
STATED PRINT RUN 150 SER.#'d SETS
1 Mike Trout 50.00 120.00
62 Ozzie Albies 8.00 20.00
84 Fernando Tatis Jr. 40.00 100.00
100 Mookie Betts 30.00 80.00
101 Trent Grisham 25.00 60.00
112 Ronald Acuna Jr. 25.00 60.00
132 Zac Gallen 15.00 40.00
134 Eloy Jimenez 15.00 40.00
148 Gavin Lux 50.00 120.00
150 Bo Bichette 100.00 250.00
160 Ramon Laureano 10.00 25.00
161 Nico Hoerner 25.00 60.00
186 Kyle Lewis 75.00 200.00
200 Yordan Alvarez 50.00 120.00

2020 Topps Chrome Blue Wave Refractors

*BLUE REF: 6X TO 15X BASIC
*BLUE REF RC: 3X TO 8X BASIC RC
STATED ODDS 1:187 HOBBY
STATED PRINT RUN 75 SER.#'d SETS
1 Mike Trout 60.00 150.00
55 DJ LeMahieu 8.00 20.00
62 Ozzie Albies 10.00 25.00
84 Fernando Tatis Jr. 50.00 120.00
100 Mookie Betts 40.00 100.00
101 Trent Grisham 30.00 80.00
112 Ronald Acuna Jr. 30.00 80.00
132 Zac Gallen 20.00 50.00
134 Eloy Jimenez 20.00 50.00
148 Gavin Lux 60.00 150.00
150 Bo Bichette 125.00 300.00
156 Francisco Lindor 15.00 40.00
160 Ramon Laureano 12.00 30.00
161 Nico Hoerner 30.00 80.00
186 Kyle Lewis 100.00 250.00
200 Yordan Alvarez 60.00 150.00

2020 Topps Chrome Gold Refractors

*GOLD REF: 8X TO 20X BASIC
*GOLD REF RC: 4X TO 10X BASIC RC
STATED ODDS 1:690 HOBBY
STATED PRINT RUN 50 SER.#'d SETS
1 Mike Trout 125.00 300.00
5 Jesus Luzardo 30.00 80.00
12 Juan Soto 40.00 100.00
21 Shohei Ohtani 20.00 50.00
45 Gleyber Torres 25.00 60.00
50 Aaron Judge 40.00 100.00
55 DJ LeMahieu 10.00 25.00
57 Andrew Benintendi 12.00 30.00
62 Ozzie Albies 12.00 30.00
77 Cody Bellinger 20.00 50.00
80 Pete Alonso 20.00 50.00
84 Fernando Tatis Jr. 200.00 500.00
90 Tim Anderson 15.00 40.00
91 Brusdar Graterol 15.00 40.00
95 Edwin Rios 20.00 50.00
96 Mike Soroka 15.00 40.00
97 Bryce Harper 30.00 80.00
100 Mookie Betts 75.00 200.00
101 Trent Grisham 75.00 200.00
111 Aristides Aquino 20.00 50.00
112 Ronald Acuna Jr. 40.00 100.00
114 Tony Gonsolin 20.00 50.00
122 Clayton Kershaw 20.00 50.00
131 Freddie Freeman 15.00 40.00
132 Zac Gallen 25.00 60.00
133 Vladimir Guerrero Jr. 25.00 60.00
134 Eloy Jimenez 25.00 60.00
137 Xander Bogaerts 12.00 30.00
143 Aaron Civale 20.00 50.00
148 Gavin Lux 75.00 200.00
150 Bo Bichette 150.00 400.00
156 Francisco Lindor 20.00 50.00
160 Ramon Laureano 15.00 40.00
161 Nico Hoerner 50.00 120.00
170 Isan Diaz 15.00 40.00
173 Yu Chang 10.00 25.00
186 Kyle Lewis 125.00 300.00
191 Joey Gallo 15.00 40.00
198 Javier Baez 20.00 50.00
199 Aaron Nola 10.00 25.00
200 Yordan Alvarez 100.00 250.00

2020 Topps Chrome Gold Wave Refractors

*GOLD WAVE REF: 8X TO 20X BASIC
*GOLD WAVE REF RC: 4X TO 10X BASIC RC
STATED ODDS 1:280 HOBBY
STATED PRINT RUN 50 SER.#'d SETS
1 Mike Trout 125.00 300.00
5 Jesus Luzardo 30.00 80.00
12 Juan Soto 40.00 100.00
21 Shohei Ohtani 20.00 50.00
45 Gleyber Torres 25.00 60.00
50 Aaron Judge 40.00 100.00
55 DJ LeMahieu 10.00 25.00
57 Andrew Benintendi 12.00 30.00
62 Ozzie Albies 12.00 30.00
77 Cody Bellinger 20.00 50.00
80 Pete Alonso 20.00 50.00
84 Fernando Tatis Jr. 200.00 500.00
90 Tim Anderson 15.00 40.00
91 Brusdar Graterol 15.00 40.00
95 Edwin Rios 20.00 50.00
96 Mike Soroka 15.00 40.00
97 Bryce Harper 30.00 80.00
100 Mookie Betts 75.00 200.00
101 Trent Grisham 75.00 200.00
111 Aristides Aquino 20.00 50.00
112 Ronald Acuna Jr. 40.00 100.00
114 Tony Gonsolin 20.00 50.00
122 Clayton Kershaw 20.00 50.00
131 Freddie Freeman 15.00 40.00
132 Zac Gallen 25.00 60.00
133 Vladimir Guerrero Jr. 25.00 60.00
134 Eloy Jimenez 25.00 60.00
137 Xander Bogaerts 12.00 30.00
143 Aaron Civale 20.00 50.00
148 Gavin Lux 75.00 200.00
150 Bo Bichette 150.00 400.00
156 Francisco Lindor 20.00 50.00
160 Ramon Laureano 15.00 40.00
161 Nico Hoerner 50.00 120.00
170 Isan Diaz 15.00 40.00
173 Yu Chang 10.00 25.00
186 Kyle Lewis 125.00 300.00
191 Joey Gallo 15.00 40.00
198 Javier Baez 20.00 50.00
199 Aaron Nola 10.00 25.00
200 Yordan Alvarez 100.00 250.00

2020 Topps Chrome Green Refractors

*GREEN REF: 6X TO 15X BASIC
*GREEN REF RC: 3X TO 8X BASIC RC
STATED ODDS 1:349 HOBBY
STATED PRINT RUN 99 SER.#'d SETS
1 Mike Trout 60.00 150.00
55 DJ LeMahieu 8.00 20.00
62 Ozzie Albies 10.00 25.00
84 Fernando Tatis Jr. 50.00 120.00
100 Mookie Betts 40.00 100.00
101 Trent Grisham 30.00 80.00
112 Ronald Acuna Jr. 30.00 80.00
132 Zac Gallen 20.00 50.00
134 Eloy Jimenez 20.00 50.00
148 Gavin Lux 60.00 150.00
150 Bo Bichette 125.00 300.00
156 Francisco Lindor 15.00 40.00
160 Ramon Laureano 12.00 30.00
161 Nico Hoerner 30.00 80.00
186 Kyle Lewis 100.00 250.00
200 Yordan Alvarez 60.00 150.00

2020 Topps Chrome Green Wave Refractors

*GREEN WAVE REF: 6X TO 15X BASIC
*GREEN WAVE REF RC: 3X TO 8X BASIC RC
STATED ODDS 1:142 HOBBY
STATED PRINT RUN 99 SER.#'d SETS
1 Mike Trout 60.00 150.00
55 DJ LeMahieu 8.00 20.00
62 Ozzie Albies 10.00 25.00
84 Fernando Tatis Jr. 50.00 120.00
100 Mookie Betts 40.00 100.00
101 Trent Grisham 30.00 80.00
112 Ronald Acuna Jr. 30.00 80.00
132 Zac Gallen 20.00 50.00
134 Eloy Jimenez 20.00 50.00
148 Gavin Lux 60.00 150.00
150 Bo Bichette 125.00 300.00
156 Francisco Lindor 15.00 40.00
160 Ramon Laureano 12.00 30.00
161 Nico Hoerner 30.00 80.00
186 Kyle Lewis 100.00 250.00
200 Yordan Alvarez 60.00 150.00

2020 Topps Chrome Negative Refractors

*NEG REF: 4X TO 10X BASIC
*NEG REF RC: 2X TO 5X BASIC RC
STATED ODDS 1:87 HOBBY
1 Mike Trout 40.00 100.00
62 Ozzie Albies 6.00 15.00
84 Fernando Tatis Jr. 30.00 80.00
100 Mookie Betts 25.00 60.00
101 Trent Grisham 20.00 50.00
112 Ronald Acuna Jr. 20.00 50.00
132 Zac Gallen 12.00 30.00
134 Eloy Jimenez 12.00 30.00
148 Gavin Lux 40.00 100.00
150 Bo Bichette 75.00 200.00
161 Nico Hoerner 20.00 50.00
186 Kyle Lewis 60.00 150.00
200 Yordan Alvarez 40.00 100.00

2020 Topps Chrome Orange Refractors

*ORANGE REF: 10X TO 25X BASIC
*ORANGE REF RC: 5X TO 12X BASIC RC
STATED ODDS 1:273 HOBBY
STATED PRINT RUN 25 SER.#'d SETS
1 Mike Trout 150.00 400.00
5 Jesus Luzardo 40.00 100.00
12 Juan Soto 50.00 120.00
21 Shohei Ohtani 25.00 60.00
45 Gleyber Torres 30.00 80.00
50 Aaron Judge 50.00 120.00
55 DJ LeMahieu 12.00 30.00
57 Andrew Benintendi 15.00 40.00
62 Ozzie Albies 15.00 40.00
77 Cody Bellinger 25.00 60.00
80 Pete Alonso 25.00 60.00
84 Fernando Tatis Jr. 250.00 600.00
90 Tim Anderson 20.00 50.00
91 Brusdar Graterol 20.00 50.00
95 Edwin Rios 25.00 60.00
96 Mike Soroka 20.00 50.00
97 Bryce Harper 40.00 100.00
100 Mookie Betts 100.00 250.00
101 Trent Grisham 100.00 250.00
111 Aristides Aquino 25.00 60.00
112 Ronald Acuna Jr. 50.00 120.00
114 Tony Gonsolin 25.00 60.00
122 Clayton Kershaw 25.00 60.00
131 Freddie Freeman 20.00 50.00
132 Zac Gallen 30.00 80.00
133 Vladimir Guerrero Jr. 30.00 80.00
134 Eloy Jimenez 30.00 80.00
137 Xander Bogaerts 15.00 40.00
143 Aaron Civale 25.00 60.00
148 Gavin Lux 100.00 250.00
150 Bo Bichette 200.00 500.00
156 Francisco Lindor 25.00 60.00
160 Ramon Laureano 20.00 50.00
161 Nico Hoerner 60.00 150.00
170 Isan Diaz 20.00 50.00
173 Yu Chang 12.00 30.00
186 Kyle Lewis 150.00 400.00
191 Joey Gallo 20.00 50.00
198 Javier Baez 25.00 60.00
199 Aaron Nola 12.00 30.00
200 Yordan Alvarez 125.00 300.00

2020 Topps Chrome Orange Wave Refractors

*ORANGE WAVE REF: 10X TO 25X BASIC
*ORANGE WAVE REF RC: 5X TO 12X BASIC RC
STATED ODDS 1:560 HOBBY
STATED PRINT RUN 25 SER.#'d SETS
1 Mike Trout 150.00 400.00
5 Jesus Luzardo 40.00 100.00
12 Juan Soto 50.00 120.00
21 Shohei Ohtani 25.00 60.00
45 Gleyber Torres 30.00 80.00
50 Aaron Judge 50.00 60.00
55 DJ LeMahieu 12.00 30.00
57 Andrew Benintendi 15.00 40.00
62 Ozzie Albies 15.00 40.00
77 Cody Bellinger 25.00 60.00
80 Pete Alonso 25.00 60.00
84 Fernando Tatis Jr. 250.00 600.00
90 Tim Anderson 20.00 50.00
91 Brusdar Graterol 20.00 50.00
95 Edwin Rios 25.00 60.00
96 Mike Soroka 20.00 50.00
97 Bryce Harper 40.00 100.00
100 Mookie Betts 100.00 250.00
101 Trent Grisham 100.00 250.00
111 Aristides Aquino 25.00 60.00
112 Ronald Acuna Jr. 50.00 120.00
114 Tony Gonsolin 25.00 60.00
122 Clayton Kershaw 25.00 60.00
131 Freddie Freeman 20.00 50.00
132 Zac Gallen 30.00 80.00
133 Vladimir Guerrero Jr. 30.00 80.00
134 Eloy Jimenez 30.00 80.00
137 Xander Bogaerts 15.00 40.00
143 Aaron Civale 25.00 60.00
148 Gavin Lux 100.00 250.00
150 Bo Bichette 200.00 500.00
156 Francisco Lindor 25.00 60.00
160 Ramon Laureano 20.00 50.00
161 Nico Hoerner 60.00 150.00
170 Isan Diaz 20.00 50.00
173 Yu Chang 12.00 30.00
186 Kyle Lewis 150.00 400.00
191 Joey Gallo 20.00 50.00
198 Javier Baez 25.00 60.00
199 Aaron Nola 12.00 30.00
200 Yordan Alvarez 125.00 300.00

2020 Topps Chrome Pink Refractors

*PINK REF: 1.2X TO 3X BASIC
*PINK REF RC:.6X TO 1.5X BASIC RC
FIVE PER VALUE PACK
84 Fernando Tatis Jr. 6.00 15.00
150 Bo Bichette 25.00 60.00

2020 Topps Chrome Prism Refractors

*PRISM REF: 1.5X TO 4X BASIC
*PRISM REF RC:.75X TO 2X BASIC RC
STATED ODDS 1:6 HOBBY
84 Fernando Tatis Jr. 8.00 20.00
150 Bo Bichette 30.00 80.00

2020 Topps Chrome Purple Refractors

*PURPLE REF: 2.5X TO 6X BASIC
*PURPLE REF RC:1.2X TO 3X BASIC RC
STATED ODDS 1:116 HOBBY
STATED PRINT RUN 250 SER.#'d SETS
1 Mike Trout 25.00 60.00
62 Ozzie Albies 4.00 10.00
84 Fernando Tatis Jr. 20.00 50.00
100 Mookie Betts 15.00 40.00
101 Trent Grisham 12.00 30.00
112 Ronald Acuna Jr. 12.00 30.00
132 Zac Gallen 8.00 20.00
134 Eloy Jimenez 8.00 20.00
148 Gavin Lux 25.00 60.00
150 Bo Bichette 50.00 120.00
161 Nico Hoerner 12.00 30.00
186 Kyle Lewis 40.00 100.00
200 Yordan Alvarez 25.00 60.00

2020 Topps Chrome Refractors

*REF: 1X TO 2.5X BASIC
*REF RC:.5X TO 1.2X BASIC RC
STATED ODDS 1:3 HOBBY
84 Fernando Tatis Jr. 5.00 12.00
150 Bo Bichette 20.00 50.00

2020 Topps Chrome X-Fractors

*XFRACTOR: 2X TO 5X BASIC
*XFRACTOR RC: 1X TO 2.5X BASIC RC
84 Fernando Tatis Jr. 15.00 40.00
132 Zac Gallen 6.00 15.00
150 Bo Bichette 30.00 80.00
200 Yordan Alvarez 20.00 50.00

2020 Topps Chrome Photo Variation Refractors

STATED ODDS 1:406 HOBBY
*GREEN/99: .6X TO 1.5X BASIC
*GOLD/50: 1X TO 2.5X BASIC
*ORANGE/25: 1.2X TO 3X BASIC
1A Trout Horizontal 75.00 200.00
1B Mike Trout Backwards cap
12 Soto Running 30.00 80.00
50A Judge Catching 15.00 40.00
50B Derek Jeter
60A Robert Throwing 100.00 250.00
60B Luis Robert T-Shirt
77A Bellinger Horizontal 10.00 25.00
77B Jackie Robinson
80 Alonso Horizontal 10.00 25.00
81 deGrom Blue jrsy 6.00 15.00
84 Tatis Jr. Horizontal 60.00 150.00
97 Harper Horizontal 8.00 20.00
111 Aquino Horizontal 8.00 20.00
112 Acuna Jr. Horizontal 20.00 50.00
125 Jose Berrios Horizontal 4.00 10.00
138 Yelich Blue jrsy 5.00 12.00
148 Lux Horizontal 30.00 80.00
150 Bichette Blue shirt 100.00 250.00
157 Willie Mays
161 Hoerner Pinstripe jrsy 20.00 50.00
174 Arenado Horizontal 5.00 12.00
186 Lewis Blue jrsy 60.00 150.00
198 Baez Horizontal 10.00 25.00
200 Alvarez Horizontal 40.00 100.00

2020 Topps Chrome Super Short Prints

STATED ODDS 1:13,868 HOBBY
1 Mike Trout 250.00 600.00
50 Derek Jeter 125.00 300.00
60 Luis Robert 1000.00 2000.00
77 Jackie Robinson 40.00 100.00
157 Willie Mays 100.00 250.00

2020 Topps Chrome '85 Topps

STATED ODDS 1:6 HOBBY
*GREEN/99: 4X TO 10X BASIC
85TC1 Mike Trout 2.00 5.00
85TC2 Bo Bichette 2.00 5.00
85TC3 Juan Soto 1.25 3.00
85TC4 Yordan Alvarez 1.25 3.00
85TC5 Gavin Lux 1.50 4.00
85TC6 Vladimir Guerrero Jr. .75 2.00
85TC7 Shohei Ohtani .50 1.25
85TC8 Rafael Devers .50 1.25
85TC9 Kris Bryant .50 1.25
85TC10 Jesus Luzardo .50 1.25
85TC11 Eloy Jimenez .75 2.00
85TC12 Nico Hoerner 1.00 2.50
85TC13 Brendan McKay .40 1.00
85TC14 A.J. Puk .50 1.25
85TC15 Christian Yelich .50 1.25
85TC16 Keston Hiura .50 1.25
85TC17 Luis Robert 8.00 20.00
85TC18 Pete Alonso 1.00 2.50
85TC19 Jose Altuve .30 .75
85TC20 Rhys Hoskins .50 1.25
85TC21 Aristides Aquino .50 1.25
85TC22 Kyle Lewis 3.00 8.00
85TC23 Austin Riley .60 1.50
85TC24 Nolan Arenado .50 1.25
85TC25 Ronald Acuna Jr. 1.50 4.00

2020 Topps Chrome '85 Topps Gold Refractors

*GOLD: 6X TO 15X BASIC
STATED ODDS 1:5524 HOBBY
STATED PRINT RUN 50 SER.#'d SETS
85TC1 Mike Trout 125.00 300.00

2020 Topps Chrome '85 Topps Orange Refractors

*ORANGE: 8X TO 20X BASIC
STATED ODDS 1:11,040 HOBBY
STATED PRINT RUN 25 SER.#'d SETS
85TC1 Mike Trout 150.00 400.00

2020 Topps Chrome '85 Topps Autographs

STATED ODDS 1:5669 HOBBY
STATED PRINT RUN 99 SER.#'d SETS
EXCHANGE DEADLINE 6/30/2022
*ORANGE/25: .5X TO 1.2X p/r 50
*ORANGE/25: .4X TO 1X p/r 20-40
85TCAAA Aristides Aquino/50 30.00 80.00
85TCAAR Austin Riley/40 25.00 60.00
85TCABB Bo Bichette EXCH
85TCAGL Gavin Lux/50 75.00 200.00
85TCAJA Jose Altuve/30 20.00 50.00
85TCAJL Jesus Luzardo/50 40.00 100.00
85TCAJS Juan Soto/40 125.00 300.00
85TCAKB Kris Bryant/25 60.00 150.00
85TCAKH Keston Hiura/50 25.00 60.00
85TCAKL Kyle Lewis/50 125.00 300.00
85TCAMT Mike Trout/20 300.00 800.00
85TCANH Nico Hoerner/50 100.00 250.00
85TCAPA Pete Alonso/40 60.00 150.00
85TCARAJ Ronald Acuna Jr./40 75.00 200.00
85TCARH Rhys Hoskins/40 25.00 60.00
85TCASO Shohei Ohtani/20 100.00 250.00
85TCAYA Yordan Alvarez/50 50.00 120.00

2020 Topps Chrome All Time Rookie Cup Team Autographs

STATED ODDS 1:12,537 HOBBY
PRINT RUNS B/WN 15-40 COPIES PER
EXCHANGE DEADLINE 6/30/2022
*ORANGE/25: .6X TO 1.5X p/r 40
*ORANGE/25: .4X TO 1X p/r 25-30
RCTAAJ Aaron Judge/20 125.00 300.00
RCTAAR Anthony Rizzo/25 40.00 100.00
RCTACJ Chipper Jones/30 75.00 200.00
RCTACRJ Cal Ripken Jr./30 50.00 120.00
RCTAJB Johnny Bench/30 100.00 250.00
RCTAKB Kris Bryant/30 75.00 200.00
RCTAMM Mark McGwire/30 50.00 120.00
RCTAMTE Mark Teixeira/40 15.00 40.00
RCTAOS Ozzie Smith/40 30.00 80.00
RCTARAJ Ronald Acuna Jr./40 100.00 250.00
RCTARS Ryne Sandberg/25 100.00 250.00

2020 Topps Chrome Decade of Dominance Die Cut

STATED ODDS 1:24 HOBBY
*GREEN/99: 4X TO 10X BASIC
*GOLD/50: 6X TO 15X BASIC
*ORANGE/25: 8X TO 20X BASIC
DOD1 Mike Trout 2.00 5.00
DOD2 Mariano Rivera .50 1.25
DOD3 Rickey Henderson .40 1.00
DOD4 Hank Aaron .75 2.00
DOD5 Ted Williams .75 2.00
DOD6 Johnny Bench .40 1.00
DOD7 Willie Mays .75 2.00
DOD8 Sandy Koufax .75 2.00
DOD9 Randy Johnson .40 1.00
DOD10 Nolan Ryan 1.25 3.00
DOD11 Honus Wagner .40 1.00
DOD12 Mark McGwire .60 1.50
DOD13 Alex Rodriguez .50 1.25
DOD14 Ichiro .50 1.25
DOD15 Babe Ruth 1.00 2.50

2020 Topps Chrome Dual Rookie Autographs

STATED ODDS 1:30:321 HOBBY
STATED PRINT RUN 25 SER.#'d SETS
EXCHANGE DEADLINE 6/30/2022
DRAAT Y.Alvarez/A.Toro 125.00 300.00
DRAHG R.Garcia/N.Hoerner 125.00 300.00
DRALD J.Dunn/K.Lewis 75.00 200.00
DRAML D.May/G.Lux 125.00 300.00
DRANM S.Neuse/S.Murphy 60.00 150.00

2020 Topps Chrome Freshman Flash

STATED ODDS 1:12 HOBBY
*GREEN/99: 4X TO 10X BASIC
*GOLD/50: 5X TO 12X BASIC
*ORANGE/25: 6X TO 15X BASIC
FF1 Bo Bichette 2.00 5.00
FF2 Aristides Aquino .50 1.25
FF3 Dylan Cease .50 1.25
FF4 Dustin May 1.00 2.50
FF5 Luis Robert 2.50 6.00
FF6 Brendan McKay .40 1.00
FF7 Sheldon Neuse .30 .75
FF8 Jesus Luzardo .50 1.25
FF9 A.J. Puk .50 1.25
FF10 Nico Hoerner 1.00 2.50
FF11 Sean Murphy .40 1.00
FF12 Gavin Lux 1.50 4.00
FF13 Kyle Lewis 2.00 5.00
FF14 Isan Diaz .40 1.00
FF15 Yordan Alvarez 1.25 3.00

2020 Topps Chrome Freshman Flash Autographs

STATED ODDS 1:2362 HOBBY
STATED PRINT RUN 99 SER.#'d SETS
EXCHANGE DEADLINE 6/30/2022
*ORANGE/25: .6X TO 1.5X BASIC
FFAAA Aristides Aquino 10.00 25.00
FFAAAL Adbert Alzolay 6.00 15.00
FFAAT Abraham Toro 6.00 15.00
FFABB Bo Bichette EXCH 75.00 200.00
FFABM Brendan McKay 8.00 20.00
FFADC Dylan Cease 10.00 25.00
FFADM Dustin May 25.00 60.00
FFAGL Gavin Lux 60.00 150.00
FFAID Isan Diaz 8.00 20.00
FFAJL Jesus Luzardo 10.00 25.00
FFAJY Jordan Yamamoto 6.00 15.00
FFAKL Kyle Lewis 100.00 250.00
FFAMD Mauricio Dubon 6.00 15.00
FFANH Nico Hoerner 20.00 50.00
FFASB Seth Brown 5.00 12.00
FFASM Sean Murphy 8.00 20.00
FFASN Sheldon Neuse 6.00 15.00
FFAYA Yordan Alvarez 50.00 120.00

2020 Topps Chrome Future Stars

STATED ODDS 1:8 HOBBY
*GREEN/99: 4X TO 10X BASIC
*GOLD/50: 6X TO 15X BASIC
*ORANGE/25: 8X TO 20X BASIC
FS1 Pete Alonso 1.00 2.50
FS2 Will Smith .50 1.25
FS3 Eloy Jimenez .75 2.00
FS4 Michael Chavis .30 .75
FS5 Mike Yastrzemski .60 1.50
FS6 Carter Kieboom .30 .75
FS7 Victor Robles .50 1.25
FS8 Chris Paddack .40 1.00
FS9 Bryan Reynolds .30 .75
FS10 Mitch Keller .40 1.00
FS11 Fernando Tatis Jr. 1.50 4.00
FS12 Brendan Rodgers .40 1.00
FS13 Cavan Biggio .50 1.25
FS14 Ramon Laureano .40 1.00
FS15 Keston Hiura .50 1.25
FS16 Austin Riley .60 1.50
FS17 Willians Astudillo .25 .60
FS18 John Means .25 .60
FS19 Mike Tauchman .40 1.00
FS20 Vladimir Guerrero Jr. .75 2.00

2020 Topps Chrome Future Stars Autographs

STATED ODDS 1:3141 HOBBY
STATED PRINT RUN 99 SER.#'d SETS
EXCHANGE DEADLINE 6/30/2022
*ORANGE/25: .6X TO 1.5X BASIC
FSAAR Austin Riley 20.00 50.00
FSABR Bryan Reynolds 6.00 15.00
FSABRE Brendan Rodgers 8.00 20.00
FSACB Cavan Biggio 12.00 30.00
FSACK Carter Kieboom 6.00 15.00
FSACP Chris Paddack 8.00 20.00
FSAEJ Eloy Jimenez 20.00 50.00
FSAFTJ Fernando Tatis Jr. 150.00 400.00
FSAJM John Means 12.00 30.00
FSAKH Keston Hiura 20.00 50.00
FSAMC Michael Chavis 6.00 15.00
FSAMK Mitch Keller 8.00 20.00
FSAMT Mike Tauchman 12.00 30.00
FSAMY Mike Yastrzemski 25.00 60.00
FSAPA Pete Alonso 40.00 100.00
FSARL Ramon Laureano 20.00 50.00
FSAVR Victor Robles 10.00 25.00
FSAWS Will Smith 15.00 40.00

2020 Topps Chrome Retro Rookie Chrome Relic Autographs

STATED ODDS 1:2366 HOBBY
PRINT RUNS B/WN 25-99 COPIES PER
EXCHANGE DEADLINE 6/30/2022
ARRCRAJ Aaron Judge/30 125.00 300.00
ARRCRBH Bryce Harper/25 150.00 400.00
ARRCRCJ Chipper Jones/40 125.00 300.00
ARRCRCRJ Cal Ripken Jr./50 100.00 250.00
ARRCRCY Carl Yastrzemski/50 75.00 200.00
ARRCRDM Don Mattingly/75 60.00 150.00
ARRCRFT Frank Thomas/75 75.00 200.00
ARRCRGT Gleyber Torres/99 100.00 250.00
ARRCRI Ichiro/25 400.00 1000.00
ARRCRJA Jose Altuve/75 30.00 80.00
ARRCRJS Juan Soto/99 200.00 500.00
ARRCRKB Kris Bryant/60 50.00 120.00
ARRCRKGJ Ken Griffey Jr./35 500.00 1200.00
ARRCRMT Mark Teixeira/99 15.00 40.00
ARRCRMTR Mike Trout/25 1250.00 3000.00
ARRCRRAJ Ronald Acuna Jr./99 200.00 500.00
ARRCRRH Rickey Henderson
ARRCRRJ Reggie Jackson/50 100.00 250.00

2020 Topps Chrome Retro Rookie Chrome Relics

STATED ODDS 1:517 HOBBY
*GREEN REF/99: .5X TO 1.2X BASIC
*ORANGE REF/25: .75X TO 2X BASIC
RRCRAB Alex Bregman 5.00 12.00
RRCRAJ Aaron Judge 12.00 30.00
RRCRAP Albert Pujols 20.00 50.00
RRCRAR Anthony Rizzo 10.00 25.00
RRCRBH Bryce Harper 10.00 25.00
RRCRBP Buster Posey 10.00 25.00
RRCRCB Cody Bellinger 10.00 25.00
RRCRCJ Chipper Jones 12.00 30.00
RRCRCK Clayton Kershaw 15.00 40.00
RRCRCRJ Cal Ripken Jr. 15.00 40.00
RRCRCY Carl Yastrzemski 12.00 30.00
RRCRDM Don Mattingly 15.00 40.00
RRCREM Eddie Mathews 10.00 25.00
RRCRFT Frank Thomas 15.00 40.00
RRCRGB George Brett 15.00 40.00
RRCRGT Gleyber Torres 10.00 25.00
RRCRI Ichiro 15.00 40.00
RRCRJA Jose Altuve 6.00 15.00
RRCRJB Johnny Bench 12.00 30.00
RRCRJBA Javier Baez 8.00 20.00
RRCRJV Justin Verlander 12.00 30.00
RRCRJVO Joey Votto 10.00 25.00
RRCRKB Kris Bryant 10.00 25.00
RRCRKGJ Ken Griffey Jr. 30.00 80.00
RRCRMB Mookie Betts 15.00 40.00
RRCRMT Mark Teixeira 4.00 10.00
RRCRMTA Masahiro Tanaka 5.00 12.00
RRCRMTR Mike Trout 60.00 150.00
RRCROS Ozzie Smith 10.00 25.00
RRCRRAJ Ronald Acuna Jr. 30.00 80.00
RRCRRC Roberto Clemente 40.00 100.00
RRCRRH Rickey Henderson 30.00 80.00
RRCRRJ Reggie Jackson 10.00 25.00
RRCRTG Tony Gwynn 12.00 30.00
RRCRTW Ted Williams 25.00 60.00

2020 Topps Chrome Rookie Autographs

STATED ODDS 1:17 HOBBY
PRINTING PLATE ODDS 1:15,900 HOBBY
PLATE PRINT RUN 1 SET PER COLOR
BLACK-CYAN-MAGENTA-YELLOW ISSUED
NO PLATE PRICING DUE TO SCARCITY
EXCHANGE DEADLINE 6/30/2022
RAAA Adbert Alzolay 3.00 8.00
RAAAQ Aristides Aquino 12.00 30.00
RAAC Aaron Civale 4.00 10.00
RAAJP A.J. Puk EXCH 12.00 30.00
RAAK Anthony Kay 2.50 6.00
RAAMU Andres Munoz 3.00 8.00
RAAN Austin Nola 5.00 12.00
RAAT Abraham Toro 3.00 8.00
RAAY Alex Young 2.50 6.00
RABA Bryan Abreu 2.50 6.00
RABB Bobby Bradley 3.00 8.00
RABBI Bo Bichette EXCH 125.00 300.00
RABBU Brock Burke 2.50 6.00
RABG Brusdar Graterol 6.00 15.00
RABM Brendan McKay 5.00 12.00
RACPO Colin Poche 2.50 6.00
RADA Dario Agrazal 3.00 8.00
RADCE Dylan Cease 8.00 20.00
RADL Domingo Leyba 3.00 8.00
RADM Dustin May 20.00 50.00
RADME Danny Mendick 5.00 12.00
RADN Dom Nunez 3.00 8.00
RAEC Emmanuel Clase 3.00 8.00
RAGL Gavin Lux EXCH 40.00 100.00
RAHH Hunter Harvey 4.00 10.00

RAID Isan Diaz 4.00 10.00
RAJD Justin Dunn 3.00 8.00
RAJDA Jaylin Davis 4.00 10.00
RAJF Jake Fraley 3.00 8.00
RAJFE Junior Fernandez 2.50 6.00
RAJH Jonathan Hernandez 2.50 6.00
RAJL Jesus Luzardo 10.00 25.00
RAJMA James Marvel 2.50 6.00
RAJPO Joe Palumbo 2.50 6.00
RAJR Jake Rogers 2.50 6.00
RAJRO Jose Rodriguez 2.50 6.00
RAJS Josh Staumont 8.00 20.00
RAJT Jesus Tinoco 2.50 6.00
RAJU Jose Urquidy 3.00 8.00
RAJW Jacob Waguespack 3.00 8.00
RAJY Jordan Yamamoto 3.00 8.00
RAKG Kyle Garlick 4.00 10.00
RAKL Kyle Lewis 50.00 120.00
RAKW Kean Wong 3.00 8.00
RALA Logan Allen 2.50 6.00
RALR Luis Robert 200.00 500.00
RALT Lewis Thorpe 2.50 6.00
RALW Logan Webb 3.00 8.00
RAMB Michel Baez 2.50 6.00
RAMBR Michael Brosseau 5.00 12.00
RAMD Mauricio Dubon 5.00 12.00
RAMK Mike King 4.00 10.00
RAMT Matt Thaiss 3.00 8.00
RANH Nico Hoerner 20.00 50.00
RANS Nick Solak 6.00 15.00
RARA Rogelio Armenteros 3.00 8.00
RARAR Randy Arozarena 60.00 150.00
RARD Robert Dugger 2.50 6.00
RARG Robel Garcia 2.50 6.00
RARR Rangel Ravelo 3.00 8.00
RASA Shogo Akiyama 12.00 30.00
RASB Seth Brown 2.50 6.00
RASH Sam Hilliard 5.00 12.00
RASM Sean Murphy 8.00 20.00
RASN Sheldon Neuse 3.00 8.00
RATA Tyler Alexander 4.00 10.00
RATD Travis Demeritte 3.00 8.00
RATE Tom Eshelman 3.00 8.00
RATG Tony Gonsolin 8.00 20.00
RATGR Trent Grisham 15.00 40.00
RATL Tim Lopes 3.00 8.00
RATLA Travis Lakins 2.50 6.00
RATZ T.J. Zeuch 2.50 6.00
RAWC Willi Castro 12.00 30.00
RAYA Yordan Alvarez 50.00 120.00
RAZC Zack Collins 3.00 8.00
RAZG Zac Gallen 15.00 40.00

2020 Topps Chrome Rookie Autographs Blue Refractors

*BLUE REF: .75X TO 2X BASIC
STATED ODDS 1:426 HOBBY
STATED PRINT RUN 150 SER.#'d SETS
EXCHANGE DEADLINE 6/30/2022

2020 Topps Chrome Rookie Autographs Blue Wave Refractors

*BLUE WAVE REF: .75X TO 2X BASIC
STATED ODDS 1:426 HOBBY
STATED PRINT RUN 150 SER.#'d SETS
EXCHANGE DEADLINE 6/30/2022

2020 Topps Chrome Rookie Autographs Gold Refractors

*GOLD REF: 1.2X TO 3X BASIC
STATED ODDS 1:1278 HOBBY
STATED PRINT RUN 50 SER.#'d SETS
EXCHANGE DEADLINE 6/30/2022

2020 Topps Chrome Rookie Autographs Gold Wave Refractors

*GOLD WAVE REF: 1.2X TO 3X BASIC
STATED ODDS 1:755 HOBBY
STATED PRINT RUN 50 SER.#'d SETS
EXCHANGE DEADLINE 6/30/2022

2020 Topps Chrome Rookie Autographs Orange Refractors

*ORANGE REF: 2X TO 5X BASIC
STATED ODDS 1:736 HOBBY
STATED PRINT RUN 25 SER.#'d SETS
EXCHANGE DEADLINE 6/30/2022

2020 Topps Chrome Rookie Autographs Orange Wave Refractors

*ORANGE WAVE REF: 2X TO 5X BASIC
STATED ODDS 1:1509 HOBBY
STATED PRINT RUN 25 SER.#'d SETS
EXCHANGE DEADLINE 6/30/2022

2020 Topps Chrome Rookie Autographs Purple Refractors

*PURPLE REF: .6X TO 1.5X BASIC
STATED ODDS 1:256 HOBBY
STATED PRINT RUN 250 SER.#'d SETS
EXCHANGE DEADLINE 6/30/2022

2020 Topps Chrome Rookie Autographs Refractors

*REF: .5X TO 1.2X BASIC
STATED ODDS 1:130 HOBBY
STATED PRINT RUN 499 SER.#'d SETS
EXCHANGE DEADLINE 6/30/2022

2020 Topps Chrome Topps Fire Preview

COMPLETE SET (9) 10.00 25.00
FIVE PER TARGET HANGER
FP1 Aaron Judge 1.25 3.00
FP2 Mike Trout 2.50 6.00
FP3 Ken Griffey Jr. 1.00 2.50
FP4 Luis Robert 3.00 8.00
FP5 Fernando Tatis Jr. 2.00 5.00
FP6 Juan Soto 1.50 4.00
FP7 Bryce Harper .75 2.00
FP8 David Ortiz .50 1.25
FP9 Pete Alonso 1.25 3.00

2020 Topps Chrome Topps Gallery Preview

COMPLETE SET (10) 8.00 20.00
FIVE PER WALMART HANGER
GP1 Mike Trout 2.00 5.00
GP2 Ronald Acuna Jr. 1.50 4.00
GP3 Fernando Tatis Jr. 1.50 4.00
GP4 Aaron Judge 1.00 2.50
GP5 Christian Yelich .50 1.25
GP6 Bryce Harper .60 1.50
GP7 Juan Soto 1.25 3.00
GP8 Pete Alonso 1.00 2.50
GP9 Yordan Alvarez 1.25 3.00
GP10 Cody Bellinger .75 2.00

2020 Topps Chrome Topps Update Preview

COMPLETE SET (8) 8.00 20.00
UP1 Bo Bichette 2.50 6.00
UP2 Brendan McKay .50 1.25
UP3 Yordan Alvarez 1.50 4.00
UP4 Gavin Lux 2.00 5.00
UP5 Kyle Lewis 2.50 6.00
UP6 Nico Hoerner 1.25 3.00
UP7 Jesus Luzardo .60 1.50
UP8 Aristides Aquino .60 1.50

2020 Topps Chrome Black

1 Cody Bellinger 4.00 10.00
2 Jose Urquidy RC .75 2.00
3 Manny Machado .60 1.50
4 Ketel Marte .50 1.25
5 Eloy Jimenez 1.25 3.00
6 Nico Hoerner RC 4.00 10.00
7 Domingo Leyba RC .75 2.00
8 Chris Paddack .60 1.50
9 Brendan McKay RC 1.00 2.50
10 Nolan Arenado 2.50 6.00
11 Jack Flaherty .50 1.25
12 Trent Grisham RC 6.00 15.00
13 Luis Robert RC 50.00 120.00
14 Shohei Ohtani 4.00 10.00
15 Pete Alonso 4.00 10.00
16 Keston Hiura 1.50 4.00
17 Gary Sanchez .60 1.50
18 Michel Baez RC .60 1.50
19 Max Scherzer .60 1.50
20 Mookie Betts 6.00 15.00
21 Tommy Edman .60 1.50
22 A.J. Puk RC 1.25 3.00
23 Xander Bogaerts .60 1.50
24 Yu Chang RC 1.00 2.50
25 Fernando Tatis Jr. 20.00 50.00
26 Alex Bregman .60 1.50
27 Isan Diaz RC 1.00 2.50
28 Nick Castellanos .60 1.50
29 Danny Mendick RC .75 2.00
30 Aaron Judge 5.00 12.00
31 Rhys Hoskins 2.00 5.00
32 Gleyber Torres 4.00 10.00
33 Shogo Akiyama RC 1.00 2.50
34 Paul Goldschmidt .60 1.50
35 Javier Baez 1.50 4.00
36 Travis Demeritte RC .75 2.00
37 Aristides Aquino RC 4.00 10.00
38 Kris Bryant 2.00 5.00
39 Chad Wallach RC .60 1.50
40 Bryce Harper 3.00 8.00
41 Trevor Story .60 1.50
42 Freddie Freeman 2.00 5.00
43 Jake Rogers RC .60 1.50
44 Whit Merrifield .60 1.50
45 Joey Gallo .60 1.50
46 Austin Meadows .50 1.25
47 Bobby Bradley RC .75 2.00
48 Willson Contreras .60 1.50
49 Marcus Semien .40 1.00
50 Vladimir Guerrero Jr. 4.00 10.00
51 Gavin Lux RC 12.00 30.00
52 Luis Castillo .50 1.25
53 Zac Gallen RC 6.00 15.00
54 Jorge Soler .60 1.50
55 Kwang-Hyun Kim RC 1.25 3.00
56 Josh Bell .50 1.25
57 Walker Buehler 1.25 3.00
58 Mitch Garver .40 1.00
59 Jake Fraley RC .75 2.00
60 Juan Soto 12.00 30.00
61 Jaylin Davis RC 1.00 2.50
62 Trevor Bauer .60 1.50
63 Tony Gonsolin RC 2.50 6.00
64 Logan Allen RC .60 1.50
65 Justin Dunn RC .75 2.00
66 Stephen Strasburg .60 1.50
67 Tim Anderson .60 1.50
68 Jesus Luzardo RC 4.00 10.00
69 Luis Arraez .75 2.00
70 Gerrit Cole 1.50 4.00
71 Sean Murphy RC 1.00 2.50
72 Seth Brown RC .60 1.50
73 Zack Collins RC .75 2.00
74 Josh Donaldson .50 1.25
75 Ronald Acuna Jr. 12.00 30.00
76 Carter Kieboom .50 1.25
77 Justin Verlander .60 1.50
78 Nick Solak RC 1.00 2.50
79 John Means .40 1.00
80 Francisco Lindor .60 1.50
81 Bo Bichette RC 40.00 100.00
82 Hyun-Jin Ryu .50 1.25
83 Corey Kluber .50 1.25
84 Trey Mancini .60 1.50
85 Dylan Cease RC 1.25 3.00
86 Jacob deGrom .60 1.50
87 Rafael Devers 2.00 5.00
88 Shun Yamaguchi .50 1.25
89 Dustin May RC 4.00 10.00
90 Anthony Rendon .60 1.50
91 Brusdar Graterol RC 1.00 2.50
92 James Karinchak RC 1.00 2.50
93 Christian Yelich 2.00 5.00
94 Mauricio Dubon RC .75 2.00
95 Matt Chapman .60 1.50
96 Yordan Alvarez RC 20.00 50.00
97 Jeff McNeil .50 1.25
98 Kyle Lewis RC 25.00 60.00
99 Clayton Kershaw 3.00 8.00
100 Mike Trout 40.00 100.00

2020 Topps Chrome Black Blue Refractors

*BLUE REF.: 2X TO 5X BASIC
*BLUE REF. RC: 1.2X TO 3X BASIC
STATED ODDS 1:XX HOBBY
STATED PRINT RUN 75 SER.#'d SETS
13 Luis Robert 200.00 500.00
20 Mookie Betts 40.00 100.00
33 Shogo Akiyama 5.00 12.00
35 Javier Baez 15.00 40.00
37 Aristides Aquino 15.00 40.00
38 Kris Bryant 12.00 30.00
42 Freddie Freeman 12.00 30.00
68 Jesus Luzardo 15.00 40.00
81 Bo Bichette 150.00 400.00
87 Rafael Devers 12.00 30.00
89 Dustin May 15.00 40.00
93 Christian Yelich 15.00 40.00
99 Clayton Kershaw 15.00 40.00

2020 Topps Chrome Black Gold Refractors

*GOLD REF.: 2.5X TO 6X BASIC
*GOLD REF. RC: 1.5X TO 4X BASIC
STATED ODDS 1:XX HOBBY
STATED PRINT RUN 50 SER.#'d SETS
1 Cody Bellinger 30.00 80.00
13 Luis Robert 250.00 600.00
16 Keston Hiura 12.00 30.00
20 Mookie Betts 50.00 120.00
33 Shogo Akiyama 10.00 25.00
35 Javier Baez 20.00 50.00
37 Aristides Aquino 20.00 50.00
38 Kris Bryant 20.00 50.00
40 Bryce Harper 25.00 60.00
42 Freddie Freeman 15.00 40.00
55 Kwang-Hyun Kim 10.00 25.00
57 Walker Buehler 12.00 30.00
68 Jesus Luzardo 20.00 50.00
81 Bo Bichette 200.00 500.00
85 Dylan Cease 8.00 20.00
87 Rafael Devers 15.00 40.00
89 Dustin May 25.00 60.00
93 Christian Yelich 25.00 60.00
99 Clayton Kershaw 25.00 60.00

2020 Topps Chrome Black Green Refractors

*GRN REF.: 1.5X TO 4X BASIC
*GRN REF. RC: 1X TO 2.5X BASIC
STATED ODDS 1:XX HOBBY
STATED PRINT RUN 99 SER.#'d SETS
13 Luis Robert 150.00 400.00
20 Mookie Betts 30.00 80.00
33 Shogo Akiyama 4.00 10.00
35 Javier Baez 12.00 30.00
38 Kris Bryant 10.00 25.00
81 Bo Bichette 125.00 300.00
89 Dustin May 12.00 30.00
93 Christian Yelich 12.00 30.00

2020 Topps Chrome Black Orange Refractors

*ORNG REF.: 3X TO 8X BASIC
*ORNG REF. RC: 2X TO 5X BASIC
STATED ODDS 1:XX HOBBY
STATED PRINT RUN 25 SER.#'d SETS
1 Cody Bellinger 40.00 100.00
13 Luis Robert 300.00 800.00
14 Shohei Ohtani 60.00 150.00
16 Keston Hiura 15.00 40.00
20 Mookie Betts 60.00 150.00
22 A.J. Puk 15.00 40.00
30 Aaron Judge 50.00 120.00
33 Shogo Akiyama 12.00 30.00
35 Javier Baez 25.00 60.00
37 Aristides Aquino 25.00 60.00
38 Kris Bryant 25.00 60.00
40 Bryce Harper 30.00 80.00
42 Freddie Freeman 25.00 60.00
55 Kwang-Hyun Kim 30.00 80.00
57 Walker Buehler 15.00 40.00
68 Jesus Luzardo 25.00 60.00
70 Gerrit Cole 15.00 40.00
81 Bo Bichette 250.00 600.00
85 Dylan Cease 10.00 25.00
87 Rafael Devers 20.00 50.00
89 Dustin May 30.00 80.00
93 Christian Yelich 30.00 80.00
99 Clayton Kershaw 40.00 100.00

2020 Topps Chrome Black Refractors

*REF.: 1X TO 2.5X BASIC
*REF. RC: .6X TO 1.5X BASIC
STATED ODDS 1:XX HOBBY
STATED PRINT RUN 199 SER.#'d SETS
13 Luis Robert 100.00 250.00
20 Mookie Betts 20.00 50.00
81 Bo Bichette 75.00 200.00
89 Dustin May 8.00 20.00

2020 Topps Chrome Black Autographs

STATED ODDS 1:XX HOBBY
EXCHANGE DEADLINE 10/31/22
*REF./150: .5X TO 1.2X BASIC
*GRN REF./99: .6X TO 1.5X BASIC
CBAAR Anthony Rendon 20.00 50.00
CBAAV Alex Verdugo 20.00 50.00
CBABL Adrian Beltre 25.00 60.00
CBABR Bryan Reynolds 8.00 20.00
CBACB Miguel Cabrera 40.00 100.00
CBACF Carlton Fisk 12.00 30.00
CBACJ Chipper Jones 50.00 120.00
CBACR Cal Ripken Jr. 60.00 150.00
CBACS Corey Seager 30.00 80.00
CBADE Dennis Eckersley 10.00 25.00
CBADJ Derek Jeter 200.00 500.00
CBADM Dustin May 25.00 60.00
CBAED Edgar Martinez 20.00 50.00
CBAFT Frank Thomas 40.00 100.00
CBAGC Gerrit Cole 40.00 100.00
CBAGS Gary Sheffield 15.00 40.00
CBAGT Gleyber Torres 40.00 100.00
CBAHA Hank Aaron 150.00 400.00
CBAHR Hyun-Jin Ryu 25.00 60.00
CBAIR Ivan Rodriguez 20.00 50.00
CBAIS Ichiro 150.00 400.00
CBAJD J.D. Martinez 12.00 30.00
CBAJM Jeff McNeil 12.00 30.00
CBAJO Joe Mauer 20.00 50.00
CBAJR J.T. Realmuto 15.00 40.00
CBAJS Juan Soto 100.00 250.00
CBAKM Ketel Marte 6.00 15.00
CBALA Luis Arraez 10.00 25.00
CBALC Luis Castillo 3.00 8.00
CBALG Lucas Giolito 15.00 40.00
CBALR Luis Robert EXCH 300.00 600.00
CBALV Luke Voit 12.00 30.00
CBALW Larry Walker 25.00 60.00
CBAMA Miguel Andujar 10.00 25.00
CBAMB Michael Brantley 3.00 8.00
CBAMC Matt Carpenter 8.00 20.00
CBAMO Matt Olson 12.00 30.00
CBAMR Mariano Rivera 75.00 200.00
CBAMS Mike Schmidt 60.00 150.00
CBAMT Mike Trout 500.00 1000.00
CBAMY Mike Yastrzemski 30.00 80.00
CBANC Nick Castellanos. 10.00 25.00
CBANG Nomar Garciaparra 15.00 40.00
CBANH Nico Hoerner 15.00 40.00
CBANS Nick Solak 10.00 25.00
CBAPA Pete Alonso 30.00 80.00
CBAPC Patrick Corbin 3.00 8.00
CBAPD Paul DeJong 6.00 15.00
CBAPG Paul Goldschmidt 15.00 40.00
CBAPM Pedro Martinez 50.00 120.00
CBARA Ronald Acuna Jr. 75.00 200.00
CBARC Rod Carew 20.00 50.00
CBARD Rafael Devers 20.00 50.00
CBARH Rhys Hoskins 12.00 30.00
CBASA Shogo Akiyama 12.00 30.00
CBASC Shin-Soo Choo 15.00 40.00
CBASK Sandy Koufax 150.00 400.00
CBASY Shun Yamaguchi 3.00 8.00
CBATE Tommy Edman 8.00 20.00
CBATG Tom Glavine 20.00 50.00
CBATP Tony Perez 20.00 50.00
CBAVG Vladimir Guerrero 20.00 50.00
CBAVR Victor Robles 10.00 25.00
CBAWB Walker Buehler 30.00 80.00
CBAWC Willson Contreras 12.00 30.00
CBAWM Whit Merrifield 8.00 20.00
CBAXB Xander Bogaerts 25.00 60.00
CBAYA Yordan Alvarez 60.00 150.00
CBAYG Yuli Gurriel 3.00 8.00
CBAZG Zac Gallen 20.00 50.00
CBAARD Alex Rodriguez 60.00 150.00
CBABRG Alex Bregman 20.00 50.00
CBACDY Cody Bellinger 75.00 200.00
CBACKL Corey Kluber 6.00 15.00
CBACLK Will Clark 25.00 60.00
CBADLY Domingo Leyba 8.00 20.00
CBADMT Don Mattingly 50.00 120.00
CBADST Darryl Strawberry 15.00 40.00
CBADWT David Wright 30.00 80.00
CBADYL Dylan Cease 12.00 30.00
CBAGRY Sonny Gray 10.00 25.00
CBAGSP George Springer 20.00 50.00
CBAJYG Joey Gallo 10.00 25.00
CBALFT Kenny Lofton 15.00 40.00
CBAMAX Max Kepler 10.00 25.00
CBAMMC Mark McGwire 50.00 120.00
CBASOL Jorge Soler 4.00 10.00
CBASOR Mike Soroka 15.00 40.00
CBATEJ Miguel Tejada 10.00 25.00
CBAVGJ Vladimir Guerrero Jr. 40.00 100.00

2020 Topps Chrome Black Autographs Gold Refractors

*GOLD REF.: .8X TO 2X BASIC
STATED ODDS 1:XX HOBBY
STATED PRINT RUN 50 SER.#'d SETS
EXCHANGE DEADLINE 10/31/22
CBACS Corey Seager 75.00 200.00
CBADM Dustin May 60.00 150.00
CBALR Luis Robert EXCH 800.00 1500.00
CBAMT Mike Trout 800.00 1500.00
CBANS Nick Solak 30.00 80.00

2020 Topps Chrome Black Autographs Orange Refractors

*ORNG REF.: 1X TO 2.5X BASIC
STATED ODDS 1:XX HOBBY
STATED PRINT RUN 25 SER.#'d SETS
EXCHANGE DEADLINE 10/31/22
CBACS Corey Seager 100.00 250.00
CBADM Dustin May 75.00 200.00
CBAJS Juan Soto 400.00 1000.00
CBALR Luis Robert EXCH 1500.00 2500.00
CBAMT Mike Trout 1000.00 2000.00
CBANS Nick Solak 50.00 120.00
CBAPG Paul Goldschmidt 50.00 120.00
CBAYA Yordan Alvarez 200.00 500.00
CBASOL Jorge Soler 15.00 40.00

2020 Topps Chrome Black Super Futures Autographs

STATED ODDS 1:XX HOBBY
STATED PRINT RUN 99 SER.#'d SETS
EXCHANGE DEADLINE 10/31/22
SFAAM Austin Meadows 15.00 40.00
SFAJS Juan Soto 100.00 250.00
SFAKM Ketel Marte 10.00 25.00
SFAKN Kevin Newman 8.00 20.00
SFANH Nico Hoerner 20.00 50.00
SFAOM Oscar Mercado 5.00 12.00
SFAPA Pete Alonso 40.00 100.00
SFARA Ronald Acuna Jr. 100.00 250.00
SFARD Rafael Devers 20.00 50.00
SFARH Rhys Hoskins 12.00 30.00
SFATE Tommy Edman 12.00 30.00
SFAVG Vladimir Guerrero Jr. 30.00 80.00
SFAVR Victor Robles 12.00 30.00
SFAWB Walker Buehler 30.00 80.00
SFAYA Yordan Alvarez 60.00 150.00

2020 Topps Chrome Black Super Futures Autographs Gold Refractors

*GOLD REF.: .5X TO 1.2X BASIC
STATED ODDS 1:XX HOBBY
STATED PRINT RUN 50 SER.#'d SETS
EXCHANGE DEADLINE 10/31/22
SFAAM Austin Meadows 25.00 60.00
SFAJS Juan Soto 150.00 400.00
SFAPA Pete Alonso 60.00 150.00
SFAVG Vladimir Guerrero Jr. 50.00 120.00

2020 Topps Chrome Black Super Futures Autographs Orange Refractors

*ORNG REF.: .6X TO 1.5X BASIC
STATED ODDS 1:XX HOBBY
STATED PRINT RUN 25 SER.#'d SETS
EXCHANGE DEADLINE 10/31/22
SFAAM Austin Meadows 30.00 80.00
SFAJS Juan Soto 200.00 500.00
SFAPA Pete Alonso 75.00 200.00
SFARH Rhys Hoskins 40.00 100.00
SFAVG Vladimir Guerrero Jr. 60.00 150.00

2017 Topps Clearly Authentic Autographs

OVERALL AUTO ODDS 1:1 HOBBY
EXCHANGE DEADLINE 6/30/2019
CAAUAB Andrew Benintendi RC 20.00 50.00
CAAUABR Alex Bregman RC 20.00 50.00
CAAUAD Aledmys Diaz 5.00 12.00
CAAUAJ Aaron Judge RC 125.00 300.00
CAAUAJO Adam Jones 10.00 25.00
CAAUAJU Aaron Judge RC 125.00 300.00
CAAUALB Alex Bregman RC 20.00 50.00
CAAUAN Aaron Nola 5.00 12.00
CAAUANB Andrew Benintendi RC 40.00 100.00
CAAUAR Alex Reyes RC 6.00 15.00
CAAUARE Alex Reyes RC 6.00 15.00
CAAUARI Anthony Rizzo 15.00 40.00
CAAUARU Addison Russell 10.00 25.00
CAAUAT Andrew Toles RC 4.00 10.00
CAAUBH Bryce Harper 100.00 250.00
CAAUBP Buster Posey 40.00 100.00
CAAUCF Carson Fulmer RC 4.00 10.00
CAAUCK Clayton Kershaw 50.00 120.00
CAAUCKL Corey Kluber 12.00 30.00
CAAUCS Chris Sale 20.00 50.00
CAAUCSE Corey Seager 25.00 60.00
CAAUDB Dellin Betances 5.00 12.00
CAAUDD David Dahl RC 5.00 12.00
CAAUDDU Danny Duffy 5.00 12.00
CAAUDO David Ortiz 40.00 100.00
CAAUDSW Dansby Swanson RC 25.00 60.00
CAAUDV Dan Vogelbach RC 6.00 15.00
CAAUFF Freddie Freeman 15.00 40.00
CAAUGS George Springer 5.00 12.00
CAAUHD Hunter Dozier RC 5.00 12.00
CAAUHR Hunter Renfroe RC 6.00 15.00
CAAUHRE Hunter Renfroe RC 6.00 15.00
CAAUI Ichiro 150.00 400.00
CAAUJA Jorge Alfaro RC 6.00 15.00
CAAUJAL Jose Altuve 25.00 60.00
CAAUJB Javier Baez 12.00 30.00
CAAUJC Jharel Cotton RC 4.00 10.00
CAAUJD Jose De Leon RC 5.00 12.00
CAAUJDE Jacob deGrom 15.00 40.00
CAAUJH Jeff Hoffman RC 4.00 10.00
CAAUJJ JaCoby Jones RC 6.00 15.00
CAAUJMU Joe Musgrove RC 4.00 10.00
CAAUJP Joe Panik 5.00 12.00
CAAUJT Jake Thompson RC 4.00 10.00
CAAUJTA Jameson Taillon 5.00 12.00
CAAUJU Julio Urias 8.00 20.00
CAAUJV Joey Votto 30.00 80.00
CAAUKB Kris Bryant 100.00 250.00
CAAUKM Kenta Maeda 12.00 30.00
CAAUKSE Kyle Seager 6.00 15.00
CAAULG Lucas Giolito 15.00 40.00
CAAULW Luke Weaver RC 10.00 25.00
CAAULWE Luke Weaver RC 10.00 25.00
CAAUMF Maikel Franco 5.00 12.00
CAAUMFU Michael Fulmer 8.00 20.00
CAAUMM Manny Machado 30.00 80.00
CAAUMMA Manny Margot RC 10.00 25.00
CAAUMO Matt Olson RC 8.00 20.00
CAAUMT Masahiro Tanaka 50.00 120.00
CAAUMTR Mike Trout 175.00 350.00
CAAUNS Noah Syndergaard 10.00 25.00
CAAURB Ryan Braun
CAAURG Randal Grichuk 4.00 10.00
CAAURGS Robert Gsellman RC 5.00 12.00
CAAURH Ryon Healy RC 5.00 12.00
CAAURL Reynaldo Lopez RC 6.00 15.00
CAAURQ Roman Quinn RC 6.00 15.00
CAAURT Raimel Tapia RC 5.00 12.00
CAAUSL Seth Lugo RC 6.00 15.00
CAAUSMA Steven Matz
CAAUTA Tyler Austin RC 6.00 15.00
CAAUTB Ty Blach RC 4.00 10.00
CAAUTG Tyler Glasnow RC 5.00 12.00
CAAUTGL Tyler Glasnow RC 5.00 12.00
CAAUTH Teoscar Hernandez RC 8.00 20.00
CAAUTM Trey Mancini RC 5.00 12.00
CAAUTN Tyler Naquin 4.00 10.00
CAAUTS Trevor Story 8.00 20.00
CAAUWC Willson Contreras 12.00 30.00
CAAUYG Yulieski Gurriel RC 10.00 25.00
CAAUYGU Yulieski Gurriel RC 10.00 25.00
CAAUYM Yoan Moncada RC

2017 Topps Clearly Authentic Autographs Blue

BLUE: .75X TO 2X BASIC
STATED ODDS ODDS 1:17 HOBBY
STATED PRINT RUN 25 SER.#'d SETS
EXCHANGE DEADLINE 6/30/2019
CAAUAJ Aaron Judge 500.00 1000.00
CAAUAJU Aaron Judge 500.00 1000.00
CAAUDSW Dansby Swanson 50.00 120.00
CAAUI Ichiro 250.00 500.00
CAAUKB Kris Bryant 150.00 400.00
CAAUMT Masahiro Tanaka 100.00 250.00
CAAUMTR Mike Trout 250.00 500.00
CAAURB Ryan Braun 12.00 30.00
CAAUSMA Steven Matz 15.00 40.00
CAAUYM Yoan Moncada 60.00 150.00

2017 Topps Clearly Authentic Autographs Green

GREEN: .5X TO 1.2X BASIC
OVERALL AUTO ODDS 1:1 HOBBY
STATED PRINT RUN 99 SER.#'d SETS
EXCHANGE DEADLINE 6/30/2019

2017 Topps Clearly Authentic Autographs Red

RED: .6X TO 1.5X BASIC
STATED ODDS ODDS 1:10 HOBBY
STATED PRINT RUN 50 SER.#'d SETS
EXCHANGE DEADLINE 6/30/2019
CAAUDSW Dansby Swanson 40.00 100.00
CAAUKB Kris Bryant 125.00 300.00
CAAURB Ryan Braun 10.00 25.00
CAAUSMA Steven Matz 12.00 30.00
CAAUYM Yoan Moncada 50.00 120.00

2017 Topps Clearly Authentic Reprint Autographs

STATED ODDS 1:10 HOBBY
PRINT RUNS B/WN 30-135 COPIES PER
EXCHANGE DEADLINE 6/30/2019
CARAUAG Andres Galarraga/135 12.00 30.00
CARAUAKA Al Kaline/110 50.00 120.00
CARAUAR Addison Russell/135 15.00 40.00
CARAUBJ Bo Jackson/40 150.00 400.00
CARAUBJA Bo Jackson/70 150.00 400.00
CARAUBP Buster Posey/45 100.00 250.00
CARAUCJ Chipper Jones/110 75.00 200.00
CARAUCR Cal Ripken Jr./45 150.00 400.00
CARAUCY Carl Yastrzemski/45 60.00 150.00
CARAUDJ Derek Jeter/30 400.00 800.00
CARAUDM Don Mattingly/110 75.00 200.00
CARAUFL Francisco Lindor/135 25.00 60.00
CARAUFR Frank Robinson/110 50.00 120.00
CARAUFT Frank Thomas/135 50.00 120.00
CARAUGM Greg Maddux/40 75.00 200.00
CARAUHA Hank Aaron/30 300.00 600.00
CARAUI Ichiro/30 350.00 700.00
CARAUJB Johnny Bench/45 100.00 250.00
CARAUJC Jose Canseco/135 30.00 80.00
CARAUJD Jacob DeGrom/135 15.00 40.00
CARAUJV Joey Votto/135 50.00 120.00
CARAUKB Kris Bryant/70 150.00 400.00
CARAULB Lou Brock/135 40.00 100.00
CARAUMMC Mark McGwire/70 100.00 250.00
CARAUMT Mike Trout/40 1000.00 1500.00
CARAUNR Nolan Ryan/45 200.00 400.00
CARAUNRY Nolan Ryan/40 200.00 400.00
CARAUNS Noah Syndergaard/135 25.00 60.00
CARAUOC Orlando Cepeda/135 25.00 60.00
CARAUOS Ozzie Smith/135 30.00 80.00
CARAUOV Omar Vizquel/135 20.00 50.00
CARAURC Rod Carew/110 30.00 80.00
CARAURH Rickey Henderson/55 60.00 150.00
CARAURJ Reggie Jackson/45 125.00 300.00
CARAURJO Randy Johnson/40 75.00 200.00
CARAURS Ryne Sandberg/110 60.00 150.00
CARAUSC Steve Carlton/110 30.00 80.00
CARAUSK Sandy Koufax/30 250.00 600.00
CARAUWB Wade Boggs/135 40.00 100.00

2018 Topps Clearly Authentic Autographs

OVERALL AUTO ODDS 1:1 HOBBY
EXCHANGE DEADLINE 6/30/2020
CAAAB Anthony Banda RC 3.00 8.00
CAAAH Austin Hays RC 8.00 20.00
CAAAJ Aaron Judge 150.00 300.00
CAAAME Austin Meadows RC 8.00 20.00
CAAAN Aaron Nola 6.00 15.00
CAAAR Amed Rosario RC 5.00 12.00
CAAAV Alex Verdugo RC 15.00 40.00
CAACF Clint Frazier RC 6.00 15.00
CAACT Chris Taylor 4.00 10.00
CAACV Christian Villanueva RC 6.00 15.00
CAADF Dustin Fowler RC 3.00 8.00
CAADM Dillon Maples RC 3.00 8.00
CAAFM Francisco Mejia RC EXCH 4.00 10.00
CAAGA Greg Allen RC 6.00 15.00
CAAGT Gleyber Torres RC 60.00 150.00
CAAJA Jose Altuve 12.00 30.00
CAAJB Justin Bour 3.00 8.00
CAAJS Jackson Stephens RC 3.00 8.00
CAAJSH Jimmie Sherfy RC 3.00 8.00
CAAJV Joey Votto 25.00 60.00
CAAKB Kris Bryant 75.00 200.00
CAAKS Kyle Schwarber 10.00 25.00
CAALC Luis Castillo 4.00 10.00
CAAMA Miguel Andujar RC 12.00 30.00
CAAMF Max Fried RC 25.00 60.00
CAAMG Miguel Gomez RC 3.00 8.00
CAAMM Manny Machado EXCH 12.00 30.00
CAAMO Matt Olson 5.00 12.00
CAAMT Mike Trout 200.00 400.00
CAANG Niko Goodrum RC 8.00 20.00
CAANSY Noah Syndergaard EXCH 10.00 25.00
CAAOA Ozzie Albies RC 12.00 30.00
CAAPB Paul Blackburn RC 3.00 8.00
CAAPD Paul DeJong 5.00 12.00
CAARA Ronald Acuna RC 100.00 250.00
CAARD Rafael Devers RC 20.00 50.00
CAARH Rhys Hoskins RC 10.00 25.00
CAARR Raudy Read RC 3.00 8.00
CAARU Richard Urena RC 3.00 8.00
CAASA Sandy Alcantara RC 3.00 8.00
CAASO Shohei Ohtani RC EXCH 125.00 300.00
CAATLO Tim Locastro RC 3.00 8.00
CAATN Tomas Nido RC 3.00 8.00
CAATP Tommy Pham 3.00 8.00
CAATS Travis Shaw 3.00 8.00
CAATSC Troy Scribner RC 3.00 8.00
CAAVA Victor Arano RC 3.00 8.00
CAAVR Victor Robles RC 8.00 20.00
CAAWB Walker Buehler RC EXCH 25.00 60.00
CAAWM Whit Merrifield 8.00 20.00

2018 Topps Clearly Authentic Autographs Black

*BLACK: .5X TO 1.2X BASIC
OVERALL AUTO ODDS 1:15 HOBBY
STATED PRINT RUN 75 SER.#'d SETS
EXCHANGE DEADLINE 6/30/2020
CAAAA Aaron Altherr 4.00 10.00
CAADS Dominic Smith 8.00 20.00

2018 Topps Clearly Authentic Autographs Blue

*BLUE: .75X TO 2X BASIC
STATED ODDS ODDS 1:41 HOBBY
STATED PRINT RUN 25 SER.#'d SETS
EXCHANGE DEADLINE 6/30/2020
CAAAA Aaron Altherr 6.00 15.00
CAADS Dominic Smith 12.00 30.00
CAAMT Mike Trout 250.00 500.00

2018 Topps Clearly Authentic Autographs Green

*GREEN: .5X TO 1.2X BASIC
OVERALL AUTO ODDS 1:14 HOBBY
STATED PRINT RUN 99 SER.#'d SETS
EXCHANGE DEADLINE 6/30/2020
CAAAA Aaron Altherr 4.00 10.00
CAADS Dominic Smith 8.00 20.00

2018 Topps Clearly Authentic Autographs Red

*RED: .5X TO 1.2X BASIC
STATED ODDS ODDS 1:22 HOBBY
STATED PRINT RUN 50 SER.#'d SETS
EXCHANGE DEADLINE 6/30/2020
CAAAA Aaron Altherr 4.00 10.00
CAADS Dominic Smith 8.00 20.00

2018 Topps Clearly Authentic '93 Finest Stars Autographs

STATED ODDS 1:14 HOBBY
PRINT RUNS B/WN 10-99 COPIES PER
NO PRICING ON 15 OR LESS
EXCHANGE DEADLINE 6/30/2020
93FSAABR Alex Bregman EXCH 30.00 80.00
93FSAAR Anthony Rizzo/30 75.00 200.00
93FSAARO Amed Rosario/199 10.00 25.00
93FSABJ Bo Jackson/30 75.00 200.00
93FSACF Clint Frazier EXCH 10.00 25.00
93FSACJ Chipper Jones/30 125.00 300.00
93FSACR Cal Ripken Jr. EXCH 100.00 250.00
93FSADM Don Mattingly/50 75.00 200.00
93FSAFL Francisco Lindor/99 20.00 50.00
93FSAFM Francisco Mejia/199 10.00 25.00
93FSAFT Frank Thomas/50 60.00 150.00
93FSAJC Jose Canseco/99 20.00 50.00
93FSAJP Joc Pederson/99 10.00 25.00
93FSAJSM John Smoltz/50 50.00 120.00
93FSAKB Kris Bryant EXCH 100.00 250.00
93FSAKS Kyle Schwarber/99 15.00 40.00
93FSAMM Manny Machado EXCH 30.00 80.00
93FSAMMC Mark McGwire/30 60.00 150.00

93FSANR Nolan Ryan/30 125.00 300.00
93FSANS Noah Syndergaard EXCH
93FSAOA Ozzie Albies EXCH 40.00 100.00
93FSARD Rafael Devers/199 15.00 40.00
93FSASG Sonny Gray/99 10.00 25.00
93FSATG Tom Glavine/50 40.00 100.00
93FSATM Trey Mancini/99 12.00 30.00
93FSAVR Victor Robles/199 20.00 50.00
93FSAWCO Willson Contreras/99 12.00 30.00

2018 Topps Clearly Authentic Legendary Autographs

STATED ODDS 1:227 HOBBY
PRINT RUNS B/WN 10-25 COPIES PER
NO PRICING ON 10 OR LESS
EXCHANGE DEADLINE 6/30/2020
CLAAK Al Kaline/25 30.00 80.00
CLABJ Bo Jackson EXCH
CLACJ Chipper Jones/25 75.00 200.00
CLADJ Derek Jeter
CLADM Don Mattingly/25 60.00 150.00
CLADO David Ortiz/25 40.00 100.00
CLAFT Frank Thomas/25
CLAHA Hank Aaron
CLAMM Mark McGwire
CLANR Nolan Ryan/25 100.00 250.00
CLAOS Ozzie Smith/25 30.00 80.00

2018 Topps Clearly Authentic MLB Awards Autographs

OVERALL AUTO ODDS 1:17 HOBBY
EXCHANGE DEADLINE 6/30/2020
MLBAABB Byron Buxton 5.00 12.00
MLBAACBL Charlie Blackmon 10.00 25.00
MLBAACK Craig Kimbrel 10.00 25.00
MLBAAGSP George Springer 12.00 30.00
MLBAAJA Jose Altuve 20.00 50.00
MLBAAJR Jose Ramirez EXCH 12.00 30.00

2018 Topps Clearly Authentic MLB Awards Autographs Black

*BLACK: .5X TO 1.2X BASIC
OVERALL AUTO ODDS 1:50 HOBBY
STATED PRINT RUN 75 SER.#'d SETS
EXCHANGE DEADLINE 6/30/2020
MLBAACKL Corey Kluber 15.00 40.00
MLBAAFL Francisco Lindor 20.00 50.00
MLBAAGS Gary Sanchez 20.00 50.00
MLBAAPG Paul Goldschmidt 15.00 40.00
MLBAAPGO Paul Goldschmidt 15.00 40.00

2018 Topps Clearly Authentic MLB Awards Autographs Blue

*BLUE: .75X TO 2X BASIC
STATED ODDS ODDS 1:117 HOBBY
STATED PRINT RUN 25 SER.#'d SETS
EXCHANGE DEADLINE 6/30/2020
MLBAAAR Anthony Rizzo 50.00 120.00
MLBAACKL Corey Kluber 25.00 60.00
MLBAAFL Francisco Lindor 30.00 80.00
MLBAAGS Gary Sanchez 30.00 80.00
MLBAAPG Paul Goldschmidt 25.00 60.00
MLBAAPGO Paul Goldschmidt 25.00 60.00

2018 Topps Clearly Authentic MLB Awards Autographs Green

*GREEN: .5X TO 1.2X BASIC
OVERALL AUTO ODDS 1:52 HOBBY
STATED PRINT RUN 99 SER.#'d SETS
EXCHANGE DEADLINE 6/30/2020
MLBAABD Brian Dozier 5.00 12.00
MLBAAPG Paul Goldschmidt 15.00 40.00
MLBAAPGO Paul Goldschmidt 15.00 40.00

2018 Topps Clearly Authentic MLB Awards Autographs Red

*RED: .5X TO 1.2X BASIC
STATED ODDS ODDS 1:59 HOBBY
STATED PRINT RUN 50 SER.#'d SETS
EXCHANGE DEADLINE 6/30/2020
MLBAAAR Anthony Rizzo 30.00 80.00
MLBAAFL Francisco Lindor 20.00 50.00
MLBAAGS Gary Sanchez 20.00 50.00
MLBAAPG Paul Goldschmidt 15.00 40.00
MLBAAPGO Paul Goldschmidt 15.00 40.00

2018 Topps Clearly Authentic Reprint Autographs

STATED ODDS 1:22 HOBBY
PRINT RUNS B/WN 15-199 COPIES PER
NO PRICING ON 15 OR LESS
EXCHANGE DEADLINE 6/30/2020
CARAK Al Kaline/99 50.00 120.00
CARAKA Al Kaline/99 50.00 120.00
CARBH Bryce Harper/15 150.00 400.00
CARBJ Bo Jackson/50 100.00 250.00
CARBL Barry Larkin/99 40.00 100.00
CARCR Cal Ripken Jr./30 100.00 250.00
CARDG Dwight Gooden/99 40.00 100.00
CARDM Don Mattingly/50 75.00 200.00
CARDS Darryl Strawberry/99 25.00 60.00
CARFT Frank Thomas/99 40.00 100.00
CARIR Ivan Rodriguez/99 30.00 80.00
CARJC Jose Canseco/99 40.00 100.00
CARJCA Jose Canseco/199 25.00 60.00
CARJP Jim Palmer/99 20.00 50.00
CARLB Lou Brock/99 25.00 60.00
CARNR Nolan Ryan/30 200.00 400.00
CAROS Ozzie Smith/99 50.00 120.00
CARRA Roberto Alomar/150 15.00 40.00
CARRH Rickey Henderson/30 100.00 250.00
CARRJ Reggie Jackson/30 150.00 400.00
CARRY Robin Yount/99 30.00 80.00
CARWB Wade Boggs/50 40.00 100.00

2018 Topps Clearly Authentic Salute Autographs

OVERALL AUTO ODDS 1:9 HOBBY
EXCHANGE DEADLINE 6/30/2020
CASABG Ben Gamel 4.00 10.00
CASADB Dellin Betances 4.00 10.00
CASADG Didi Gregorius EXCH 10.00 25.00
CASADS Domingo Santana 4.00 10.00
CASAET Eric Thames 4.00 10.00
CASAHR Hunter Renfroe 4.00 10.00
CASAIH Ian Happ 8.00 20.00
CASAJBE Jose Berrios 4.00 10.00
CASAKB Keon Broxton 3.00 8.00
CASAKD Khris Davis 10.00 25.00

2018 Topps Clearly Authentic Salute Autographs Black

*BLACK: .5X TO 1.2X BASIC
OVERALL AUTO ODDS 1:37 HOBBY
STATED PRINT RUN 75 SER.#'d SETS
EXCHANGE DEADLINE 6/30/2020
CASACS Chris Sale EXCH 12.00 30.00
CASAJS Jean Segura 4.00 10.00
CASAPG Paul Goldschmidt 15.00 40.00

2018 Topps Clearly Authentic Salute Autographs Blue

*BLUE: .75X TO 2X BASIC
STATED ODDS ODDS 1:103 HOBBY
STATED PRINT RUN 25 SER.#'d SETS
EXCHANGE DEADLINE 6/30/2020
CASACS Chris Sale EXCH 20.00 50.00
CASAJS Jean Segura 6.00 15.00
CASAPG Paul Goldschmidt 25.00 60.00

2018 Topps Clearly Authentic Salute Autographs Green

*GREEN: .5X TO 1.2X BASIC
OVERALL AUTO ODDS 1:28 HOBBY
STATED PRINT RUN 99 SER.#'d SETS
EXCHANGE DEADLINE 6/30/2020
CASACS Chris Sale EXCH 12.00 30.00
CASAJS Jean Segura 4.00 10.00
CASAPG Paul Goldschmidt 15.00 40.00

2018 Topps Clearly Authentic Salute Autographs Red

*RED: .5X TO 1.2X BASIC
STATED ODDS ODDS 1:37 HOBBY
STATED PRINT RUN 50 SER.#'d SETS
EXCHANGE DEADLINE 6/30/2020
CASACS Chris Sale EXCH 12.00 30.00
CASAJS Jean Segura 4.00 10.00
CASAPG Paul Goldschmidt 15.00 40.00

2019 Topps Clearly Authentic Autographs

RANDOM INSERTS IN PACKS
*GREEN/99: .5X TO 1.2X BASIC
*BLACK/75: .5X TO 1.2X BASIC
*RED/50: .5X TO 1.2X BASIC
*BLUE/25: .75X TO 2X BASIC
CAABL Brandon Lowe RC 15.00 40.00
CAACB Corbin Burnes RC 5.00 12.00
CAACH Christin Stewart RC 4.00 10.00
CAACK Carter Kieboom RC 10.00 25.00
CAACM Cedric Mullins RC 5.00 12.00
CAACS Chris Sale 8.00 20.00
CAACT Cole Tucker RC 10.00 25.00
CAADJ Danny Jansen RC 3.00 8.00
CAADP Daniel Ponce de Leon RC 5.00 12.00
CAADR Dereck Rodriguez 4.00 10.00
CAAEJ Eloy Jimenez RC 30.00 80.00
CAAFF Freddie Freeman 15.00 40.00
CAAFL Francisco Lindor 12.00 30.00
CAAFT Fernando Tatis Jr. RC 150.00 400.00
CAAGS George Springer 12.00 30.00
CAAJA Jesus Aguilar 3.00 8.00
CAAJF Jean Segura 5.00 12.00
CAAJU Jose Martinez 3.00 8.00
CAAJS Justus Sheffield RC 8.00 20.00
CAAJU Juan Soto 50.00 120.00
CAAKB Kris Bryant 30.00 80.00
CAAKK Kevin Kramer RC 4.00 10.00
CAAKT Kyle Tucker RC 15.00 40.00
CAAKW Kyle Wright RC 5.00 12.00
CAALT Lane Thomas RC 6.00 15.00
CAAMC Michael Chavis RC 12.00 30.00
CAAMK Michael Kopech RC 10.00 25.00
CAAMM Max Muncy 8.00 20.00
CAAMT Mike Trout
CAAPA Peter Alonso RC 60.00 150.00
CAAPG Paul Goldschmidt 20.00 50.00
CAARA Ronald Acuna Jr. 50.00 120.00
CAARH Rhys Hoskins 10.00 25.00
CAART Rowdy Tellez RC 5.00 12.00
CAASB Shane Bieber 20.00 50.00
CAASM Sean Manaea 3.00 8.00
CAASO Shohei Ohtani 75.00 200.00
CAASP Salvador Perez 8.00 20.00
CAASR Sean Reid-Foley RC 3.00 8.00
CAATA Tim Anderson 10.00 25.00
CAATE Thairo Estrada RC 10.00 25.00
CAATT Touki Toussaint RC 4.00 10.00
CAAVG Vladimir Guerrero Jr. RC 60.00 150.00
CAAYK Yusei Kikuchi RC 5.00 12.00

2019 Topps Clearly Authentic '52 Reimagining Autographs

STATED ODDS 1:25 HOBBY
PRINT RUNS B/WN 5-50 COPIES PER
NO PRICING ON QTY 15 OR LESS
RAAD Andre Dawson/50 25.00 60.00
RAAM Andrew McCutchen/50 50.00 120.00
RAAP Andy Pettitte/50 25.00 60.00
RAAT Anthony Rizzo/50 40.00 100.00
RABG Bob Gibson/50 40.00 100.00
RABJ Bo Jackson/25 75.00 200.00
RACK Clayton Kershaw/50 40.00 100.00
RACR Cal Ripken Jr./25 75.00 200.00
RACS Chris Sale/50 15.00 40.00
RACY Carl Yastrzemski/25 60.00 150.00
RADJ Derek Jeter
RADM Dale Murphy/50 30.00 80.00
RAFL Francisco Lindor/50 20.00 50.00
RAFT Frank Thomas/50
RAHM Hideki Matsui/25 40.00 100.00
RAJA Jose Altuve/50 40.00 100.00
RAJB Javier Baez/50 20.00 50.00
RAJE Jeff Bagwell/50 30.00 80.00
RAJF Jack Flaherty/50 25.00 60.00
RAJK Jason Varitek/50 20.00 50.00
RAJO Johnny Bench/25 75.00 200.00
RAJP Jorge Posada/50 25.00 60.00
RAJV Joey Votto/50 30.00 80.00
RAKB Kris Bryant/25 75.00 200.00
RAMA Miguel Andujar/50 20.00 50.00
RAMM Mark McGwire/25 50.00 120.00
RANR Nolan Ryan/25 75.00 200.00
RANS Noah Syndergaard/50 20.00 50.00
RAOS Ozzie Smith/50 30.00 80.00
RAPG Paul Goldschmidt/50 25.00 60.00
RARA2 Roberto Alomar/50 20.00 50.00
RARAJ Ronald Acuna Jr./50 75.00 200.00
RARH Rhys Hoskins/50 25.00 60.00
RARJ Reggie Jackson/25 50.00 120.00
RAVG Vladimir Guerrero/50 50.00 120.00
RAWC Willson Contreras/50 30.00 80.00
RAWI Will Clark/50 50.00 120.00

2019 Topps Clearly Authentic '84 Topps Autographs

STATED ODDS 1:8 HOBBY
*GREEN/99: .5X TO 1.2X BASIC
*BLACK/75: .5X TO 1.2X BASIC
*RED/50: .5X TO 1.2X BASIC
*BLUE/25: .75X TO 2X BASIC
TBABM Brandon Nimmo 6.00 15.00
TBABS Blake Snell 6.00 15.00
TBACY Christian Yelich 30.00 80.00
TBADM Don Mattingly 50.00 120.00
TBADS Darryl Strawberry 10.00 25.00
TBAJB Jose Berrios 6.00 15.00
TBAJC Jose Canseco 8.00 20.00
TBAJD Jacob deGrom 20.00 50.00
TBAKS Kyle Schwarber 20.00 50.00
TBAMH Mitch Haniger 6.00 15.00
TBAMM Miles Mikolas 5.00 12.00
TBAMO Matt Olson 6.00 15.00
TBAOA Ozzie Albies 20.00 50.00
TBAPD Paul DeJong 5.00 12.00
TBATM Trey Mancini 6.00 15.00
TBAVR Victor Robles 12.00 30.00
TBAWM Whit Merrifield 6.00 15.00

2019 Topps Clearly Authentic 150 Years of Professional Baseball Autographs

STATED ODDS 1:20 HOBBY
*GREEN/99: .5X TO 1.2X BASIC
*BLACK/75: .5X TO 1.2X BASIC
*RED/50: .5X TO 1.2X BASIC
*BLUE/25: .75X TO 2X BASIC
YBPCF Carlton Fisk 12.00 30.00
YBPAK Al Kaline 20.00 50.00
YBPBB Bert Blyleven 8.00 20.00
YBPDE Dennis Eckersley 10.00 25.00
YBPDG Dwight Gooden 10.00 25.00
YBPDS Don Sutton 6.00 15.00
YBPIR Ivan Rodriguez 15.00 40.00
YBPJE Jim Rice 8.00 20.00
YBPJG Juan Gonzalez 10.00 25.00
YBPJM Juan Marichal 12.00 30.00
YBPJO Johnny Damon 6.00 15.00
YBPRC Rod Carew 15.00 40.00
YBPSC Steve Carlton 10.00 25.00

2019 Topps Clearly Authentic T206 Autographs

STATED ODDS 1:19 HOBBY
PRINT RUNS B/WN 15-99 COPIES PER
NO PRICING ON QTY 15
*BLUE/25: .75X TO 2X p/r 50-99
*BLUE/25: .4X TO 1X p/r 30
TAAB Adrian Beltre/30 30.00 80.00
TAAK Al Kaline/50 40.00 100.00
TAAT Alan Trammell/99 15.00 40.00
TABL Barry Larkin/30 25.00 60.00
TACF Carlton Fisk/30 25.00 60.00
TACJ Chipper Jones/30 50.00 120.00
TACY Christian Yelich/50 50.00 120.00
TADM Don Mattingly/50 50.00 120.00
TADS Darryl Strawberry/99 15.00 40.00
TAEJ Eloy Jimenez/99 25.00 60.00
TAFF Freddie Freeman/99 30.00 80.00
TAFT Fernando Tatis Jr./50 125.00 300.00
TAGS George Springer/50 30.00 80.00
TAJC Jose Canseco/99 15.00 40.00
TAJR Jose Ramirez/99 12.00 30.00
TAJS Juan Soto/99 60.00 150.00
TAJU Justin Smoak/50 4.00 10.00
TAKS Kyle Schwarber/99 10.00 25.00
TAKW Kerry Wood/50 12.00 30.00
TALB Lou Brock/99 25.00 60.00
TANG Nomar Garciaparra/30 20.00 50.00
TAOA Ozzie Albies/99 12.00 30.00
TARA Rick Ankiel/50 8.00 20.00
TARD Rafael Devers/99 20.00 50.00
TARO Rod Carew/50 20.00 50.00
TARS Ryne Sandberg/30 30.00 80.00
TASC Steve Carlton/50 15.00 40.00
TATG Tom Glavine/30 20.00 50.00
TATS Trevor Story/99 12.00 30.00
TAWB Wade Boggs/99 25.00 60.00

2020 Topps Clearly Authentic Autographs

RANDOM INSERTS IN PACKS
EXCHANGE DEADLINE 5/31/2022
CCAAA Adbert Alzolay 8.00 20.00
CCAAC Aaron Civale 8.00 20.00
CCAAK Anthony Kay 6.00 15.00
CCAAT Abraham Toro 4.00 10.00
CCAAY Alex Young 3.00 8.00
CCABB Bobby Bradley 8.00 20.00
CCABM Brendan McKay 5.00 12.00
CCABO Bo Bichette EXCH 50.00 120.00
CCADC Dylan Cease 10.00 25.00
CCAGL Gavin Lux 40.00 100.00
CCAHH Hunter Harvey 5.00 12.00
CCAJD Justin Dunn 8.00 20.00
CCAJF Junior Fernandez 3.00 8.00
CCAJL Jesus Luzardo 12.00 30.00
CCAJR Jake Rogers 3.00 8.00
CCAJY Jordan Yamamoto 8.00 20.00
CCAKL Kyle Lewis 40.00 100.00
CCALA Logan Allen 3.00 8.00
CCALR Luis Robert 150.00 400.00
CCALW Logan Webb 6.00 15.00
CCAMD Mauricio Dubon 10.00 25.00
CCAMT Matt Thaiss 8.00 20.00
CCANH Nico Hoerner 25.00 60.00
CCANS Nick Solak 10.00 25.00
CCARA Randy Arozarena 40.00 100.00
CCASB Seth Brown 3.00 8.00
CCASH Sam Hilliard 8.00 20.00
CCASM Sean Murphy 8.00 20.00
CCATG Trent Grisham 15.00 40.00
CCAYA Yordan Alvarez 40.00 100.00
CCAZC Zack Collins 6.00 15.00
CCAAAQ Aristides Aquino 15.00 40.00
CCAJDA Jaylin Davis 8.00 20.00
CCAJFR Jake Fraley 4.00 10.00
CCAJRO Josh Rojas 3.00 8.00
CCAJUR Jose Urquidy 4.00 10.00

2020 Topps Clearly Authentic Autographs Black

*BLACK: .5X TO 1.2X BASIC
STATED ODDS 1:17 HOBBY
STATED PRINT RUN 75 SER.#'d SETS
EXCHANGE DEADLINE 5/31/2022
CCAGL Gavin Lux 60.00 150.00
CCAJL Jesus Luzardo 20.00 50.00
CCAJY Jordan Yamamoto 15.00 40.00
CCASH Sam Hilliard 15.00 40.00
CCAYA Yordan Alvarez 60.00 150.00

2020 Topps Clearly Authentic Autographs Blue

*BLUE: .8X TO 2X BASIC
STATED ODDS 1:51 HOBBY
STATED PRINT RUN 25 SER.#'d SETS
EXCHANGE DEADLINE 5/31/2022
CCADC Dylan Cease 30.00 80.00
CCAGL Gavin Lux 100.00 250.00
CCAJL Jesus Luzardo 30.00 80.00
CCAJY Jordan Yamamoto 25.00 60.00
CCAMT Matt Thaiss 25.00 60.00
CCASH Sam Hilliard 25.00 60.00
CCASM Sean Murphy 25.00 60.00
CCAYA Yordan Alvarez 125.00 300.00
CCAAAQ Aristides Aquino 50.00 120.00

2020 Topps Clearly Authentic Autographs Green

*GREEN: .5X TO 1.2X BASIC
STATED ODDS 1:13 HOBBY
STATED PRINT RUN 99 SER.#'d SETS
EXCHANGE DEADLINE 5/31/2022
CCAGL Gavin Lux 60.00 150.00
CCAJL Jesus Luzardo 20.00 50.00
CCASH Sam Hilliard 12.00 30.00

2020 Topps Clearly Authentic Autographs Red

*RED: .5X TO 1.2X BASIC
STATED ODDS 1:26 HOBBY
STATED PRINT RUN 50 SER.#'d SETS
EXCHANGE DEADLINE 5/31/2022
CCADC Dylan Cease 20.00 50.00
CCAGL Gavin Lux 60.00 150.00
CCAJL Jesus Luzardo 20.00 50.00
CCAJY Jordan Yamamoto 15.00 40.00
CCAMT Matt Thaiss 15.00 40.00
CCASH Sam Hilliard 15.00 40.00
CCASM Sean Murphy 15.00 40.00
CCAYA Yordan Alvarez 75.00 200.00
CCAAAQ Aristides Aquino 30.00 80.00

2020 Topps Clearly Authentic '51 Red Blue Backs Autographs

STATED ODDS 1:26 HOBBY
PRINT RUNS B/WN 15-99 COPIES PER
NO PRICING ON QTY 15 OR LESS
EXCHANGE DEADLINE 5/31/2022
*BLUE: .6X TO 1.5X p/r 50-99
*BLUE: .4X TO 2X p/r 25-30
51AI Ichiro 125.00 300.00
51AAA Aristides Aquino 20.00 50.00
51ABH Bryce Harper 125.00 300.00
51ABL Barry Larkin 20.00 50.00
51ABP Buster Posey 75.00 200.00
51ACF Carlton Fisk 30.00 80.00
51ACY Christian Yelich 50.00 120.00
51ADM Don Mattingly 60.00 150.00
51ADO David Ortiz 50.00 120.00
51AEJ Eloy Jimenez 25.00 60.00
51AFT Fernando Tatis Jr. 50.00 120.00
51AGS George Springer 20.00 50.00
51AJC Jose Canseco 25.00 60.00
51AJS Juan Soto 50.00 120.00
51AKB Kris Bryant 75.00 200.00
51ALB Rhys Hoskins 20.00 50.00
51AMM Mike Mussina 25.00 60.00
51ARD Rafael Devers 30.00 80.00
51ARO Rod Carew 20.00 50.00
51ARS Ryne Sandberg 40.00 100.00
51ASC Jacob deGrom 40.00 100.00
51ASO Shohei Ohtani 75.00 200.00
51ATG Tom Glavine 25.00 60.00
51ATH Rickey Henderson 75.00 200.00
51AVG Vladimir Guerrero Jr. EXCH 40.00 100.00
51ADMA Dustin May 20.00 50.00
51AJLU Jesus Luzardo 15.00 40.00
51AKWO Kerry Wood 30.00 80.00
51ALWE Kyle Lewis 50.00 120.00
51APAL Pete Alonso 60.00 150.00

2020 Topps Clearly Authentic '53 Topps Reimagining Autographs

STATED ODDS 1:19 HOBBY
PRINT RUNS B/WN 10-99 COPIES PER
NO PRICING ON QTY 15 OR LESS
EXCHANGE DEADLINE 5/31/2022
RAAD Andre Dawson 30.00 80.00
RAAJ Aaron Judge 30.00 80.00
RAAP Andy Pettitte 15.00 40.00
RAAT Anthony Rizzo 40.00 100.00
RABB Bo Bichette EXCH 60.00 150.00
RABG Bob Gibson 50.00 120.00
RACK Clayton Kershaw 75.00 200.00
RACR Cal Ripken Jr. 100.00 250.00
RACS Chris Sale 15.00 40.00
RADJ Derek Jeter EXCH
RADM Dale Murphy 60.00 60.00
RAFM Fred McGriff 20.00 50.00
RAFT Frank Thomas 40.00 100.00
RAGL Gavin Lux 100.00 250.00
RAGT Gleyber Torres 60.00 150.00
RAHM Hideki Matsui 40.00 100.00
RAJA Jose Altuve 20.00 50.00
RAJF Jack Flaherty 30.00 80.00
RAJK Jason Varitek 20.00 50.00
RAJO Johnny Bench 60.00 150.00
RAJS John Smoltz 25.00 60.00
RAJV Joey Votto 30.00 80.00
RAMM Mark McGwire 60.00 150.00
RAMT Mike Trout 400.00 1000.00
RANH Nico Hoerner 40.00 100.00
RANR Nolan Ryan 75.00 200.00
RAOS Ozzie Smith 30.00 80.00
RAPG Paul Goldschmidt 20.00 50.00
RARH Rhys Hoskins 25.00 60.00
RARJ Reggie Jackson 30.00 80.00
RASO Shohei Ohtani 15.00 40.00
RAWC Willson Contreras 15.00 40.00
RAWI Will Clark 100.00 250.00
RAYA Yordan Alvarez 50.00 120.00
RAFTJ Fernando Tatis Jr. 60.00 150.00
RAKGJ Ken Griffey Jr. 250.00 600.00
RARAJ Ronald Acuna Jr. 100.00 250.00

2020 Topps Clearly Authentic '85 Topps Autographs

STATED ODDS 1:7 HOBBY
EXCHANGE DEADLINE 5/31/2022
TBAAJ Aaron Judge 100.00 250.00
TBAAR Austin Riley 15.00 40.00
TBADW David Wright 20.00 50.00
TBAED Eric Davis 25.00 60.00
TBAEJ Eloy Jimenez 25.00 60.00
TBAFT Fernando Tatis Jr. 100.00 250.00
TBAJA Jose Altuve 15.00 40.00
TBAJF Jack Flaherty 15.00 40.00
TBAJS Juan Soto 50.00 120.00
TBAKH Kyle Hendricks 10.00 25.00
TBALV Luke Voit 20.00 50.00
TBAMK Max Kepler 4.00 10.00
TBAMS Mike Soroka 12.00 30.00
TBAMT Mike Trout 400.00 800.00
TBAPA Pete Alonso 60.00 150.00
TBAPC Patrick Corbin 4.00 10.00
TBARH Rhys Hoskins 6.00 15.00
TBATE Tommy Edman 15.00 40.00
TBAVR Victor Robles 12.00 30.00
TBAWC Will Clark 30.00 80.00
TBAECK Dennis Eckersley 15.00 40.00
TBAJCA Jose Canseco 20.00 50.00
TBAJSO Jorge Soler 10.00 25.00
TBAJTR J.T. Realmuto 20.00 50.00
TBAKHI Keston Hiura 12.00 30.00
TBAMMC Mark McGwire 60.00 150.00
TBAMMU Max Muncy 10.00 25.00
TBAOSM Ozzie Smith 25.00 60.00
TBATAN Tim Anderson 15.00 40.00
TBATLI Tim Lincecum 20.00 50.00
TBAWCO Willson Contreras 12.00 30.00
TBAWSM Will Smith 12.00 30.00
TBARYNO Ryne Sandberg 40.00 100.00

2020 Topps Clearly Authentic '85 Topps Autographs Black

*BLACK: .5X TO 1.2X BASIC
STATED ODDS 1:21 HOBBY
STATED PRINT RUN 75 SER.#'d SETS
EXCHANGE DEADLINE 5/31/2022
TBAJF Jack Flaherty 25.00 60.00
TBARH Rhys Hoskins 12.00 30.00
TBATE Tommy Edman 25.00 60.00
TBAJSO Jorge Soler 25.00 60.00

2020 Topps Clearly Authentic '85 Topps Autographs Blue

*BLUE: .8X TO 2X BASIC
STATED ODDS 1:50 HOBBY
STATED PRINT RUN 25 SER.#'d SETS
EXCHANGE DEADLINE 5/31/2022
TBAJF Jack Flaherty 50.00 120.00
TBAJS Juan Soto 125.00 300.00
TBARH Rhys Hoskins 40.00 100.00
TBATE Tommy Edman 40.00 100.00
TBAJSO Jorge Soler 40.00 100.00
TBAJTR J.T. Realmuto 50.00 120.00

2020 Topps Clearly Authentic '85 Topps Autographs Green

*GREEN: .5X TO 1.2X BASIC
STATED ODDS 1:16 HOBBY
STATED PRINT RUN 99 SER.#'d SETS
EXCHANGE DEADLINE 5/31/2022
TBARH Rhys Hoskins 12.00 30.00
TBAJSO Jorge Soler 25.00 60.00

2020 Topps Clearly Authentic '85 Topps Autographs Red

*RED: .5X TO 1.2X BASIC
STATED ODDS 1:29 HOBBY
STATED PRINT RUN 50 SER.#'d SETS
EXCHANGE DEADLINE 5/31/2022
TBAJF Jack Flaherty 30.00 80.00
TBAJS Juan Soto 75.00 200.00
TBARH Rhys Hoskins 25.00 60.00
TBATE Tommy Edman 25.00 60.00
TBAJSO Jorge Soler 25.00 60.00
TBAJTR J.T. Realmuto 30.00 80.00

2020 Topps Clearly Authentic Decades Best Autographs

STATED ODDS 1:35 HOBBY
EXCHANGE DEADLINE 5/31/2022
DBABB Bert Blyleven 8.00 20.00
DBABG Bob Gibson 25.00 60.00
DBABL Barry Larkin 20.00 50.00
DBACJ Chipper Jones 50.00 120.00
DBADM Don Mattingly 40.00 100.00
DBADO David Ortiz 25.00 60.00
DBADS Darryl Strawberry 15.00 40.00
DBAFT Frank Thomas 30.00 80.00
DBAJR Jim Rice 10.00 25.00
DBAMT Mike Trout 300.00 600.00
DBARA Roberto Alomar 15.00 40.00
DBARC Rod Carew 20.00 50.00
DBASC Steve Carlton 15.00 40.00
DBATH Todd Helton 12.00 30.00
DBAVG Vladimir Guerrero 20.00 50.00
DBADMU Dale Murphy 20.00 50.00
DBAJBE Johnny Bench 40.00 100.00
DBAJVO Joey Votto 20.00 50.00
DBAMCA Miguel Cabrera 50.00 120.00

2020 Topps Clearly Authentic Decades Best Autographs Blue

*BLUE: .8X TO 2X BASIC
STATED ODDS 1:84 HOBBY
STATED PRINT RUN 25 SER.#'d SETS
EXCHANGE DEADLINE 5/31/2022
DBABB Bert Blyleven 25.00 60.00
DBAMT Mike Trout 400.00 800.00
DBAMCA Miguel Cabrera 125.00 300.00

2020 Topps Clearly Authentic Decades Best Autographs Red

*RED: .5X TO 1.2X BASIC
STATED ODDS 1:50 HOBBY
STATED PRINT RUN 50 SER.#'d SETS
EXCHANGE DEADLINE 5/31/2022
DBABB Bert Blyleven 15.00 40.00
DBAMCA Miguel Cabrera 75.00 200.00

2017 Topps Definitive Collection Autograph Relics

RANDOM INSERTS IN PACKS
PRINT RUNS B/WN 5-50 COPIES PER
NO PRICING ON QTY 15 OR LESS
EXCHANGE DEADLINE 6/30/2019
ARCAB Andrew Benintendi/50 RC 50.00 120.00
ARCABR Alex Bregman/50 RC 25.00 60.00
ARCAD Aledmys Diaz/50 6.00 15.00
ARCAJ Adam Jones/30 10.00 25.00
ARCAJU Aaron Judge/50 RC 200.00 400.00
ARCAR Alex Reyes/20 RC 10.00 25.00
ARCBH Bryce Harper EXCH
ARCCK Clayton Kershaw/30 60.00 150.00
ARCCKL Corey Kluber/50 12.00 30.00
ARCCSE Corey Seager/50 20.00 50.00
ARCDD David Dahl/50 RC 8.00 20.00
ARCDP Dustin Pedroia/50 20.00 50.00
ARCDPR David Price/50 12.00 30.00
ARCDS Dansby Swanson RC
ARCFF Freddie Freeman/30 15.00 40.00
ARCFL Francisco Lindor EXCH 12.00 30.00
ARCGSP George Springer/50 12.00 30.00
ARCI Ichiro EXCH
ARCJA Jose Altuve EXCH 25.00 60.00
ARCJB Javier Baez/50 25.00 60.00
ARCJD Jacob deGrom/50 20.00 50.00
ARCJP Joe Panik
ARCJPE Joc Pederson
ARCJU Julio Urias EXCH 12.00 30.00
ARCKM Kenta Maeda/50 8.00 20.00
ARCKS Kyle Schwarber EXCH 12.00 30.00
ARCKSE Kyle Seager/35 10.00 25.00
ARCMCA Matt Carpenter/50 10.00 25.00
ARCMF Maikel Franco/50 8.00 20.00
ARCMS Miguel Sano
ARCNM Nomar Mazara/50 6.00 15.00
ARCNS Noah Syndergaard/50 20.00 50.00
ARCRB Ryan Braun/50 12.00 30.00
ARCSM Starling Marte/50 12.00 30.00
ARCSMA Steven Matz/50 8.00 20.00
ARCSP Stephen Piscotty/50 8.00 20.00
ARCTS Trevor Story/50 10.00 25.00
ARCWC Willson Contreras/50 20.00 50.00

2017 Topps Definitive Collection Autograph Relics Green

*GREEN: .75X TO 2X BASIC
RANDOM INSERTS IN PACKS
PRINT RUNS B/WN 10-25 COPIES PER
NO PRICING DUE TO SCARICITY
NO PRICING ON QTY 10
ARCJP Joe Panik/25 20.00 50.00
ARCJPE Joc Pederson/25 12.00 30.00
ARCMS Miguel Sano/25 25.00 60.00

2017 Topps Definitive Collection Autographs

RANDOM INSERTS IN PACKS
PRINT RUNS B/WN 5-50 COPIES PER
NO PRICING ON QTY 15 OR LESS
EXCHANGE DEADLINE 6/30/2019
DCAIAB Andrew Benintendi/35 150.00 400.00
DCAIABR Alex Bregman/35 30.00 80.00
DCAIAG Andres Galarraga/35 12.00 30.00
DCAIAJ Aaron Judge/35 350.00 800.00
DCAIAR Anthony Rizzo/35 40.00 100.00
DCAIBH Bryce Harper/5
DCAICK Clayton Kershaw/25 100.00 250.00
DCAICR Cal Ripken Jr.
DCAICS Corey Seager/35 25.00 60.00
DCAIDM Don Mattingly/25 50.00 120.00
DCAIDS Dansby Swanson/35 15.00 40.00
DCAIFL Francisco Lindor/35 50.00 120.00
DCAIFT Frank Thomas/25 40.00 100.00
DCAIJS John Smoltz/35 25.00 60.00
DCAIJU Julio Urias/35 20.00 50.00
DCAIKM Kenta Maeda/35 20.00 50.00
DCAIMM Manny Machado/35 60.00 150.00
DCAIMMC Mark McGwire/5
DCAINR Nolan Ryan
DCAINS Noah Syndergaard/35 25.00 60.00
DCAIOS Ozzie Smith/35 25.00 60.00
DCAIOV Omar Vizquel/35 12.00 30.00
DCAIPM Pedro Martinez/25 150.00 300.00
DCAIWB Wade Boggs/35 60.00 150.00
DCAIYM Yoan Moncada/35 40.00 100.00

2017 Topps Definitive Collection Definitive Autograph Relics

RANDOM INSERTS IN PACKS
PRINT RUNS B/WN 5-40 COPIES PER
NO PRICING ON QTY 15 OR LESS
EXCHANGE DEADLINE 6/30/2019
DCARAD Andre Dawson/40 20.00 50.00
DCARAG Andres Galarraga/40 8.00 20.00
DCARAP Andy Pettitte/40 20.00 50.00
DCARBH Bryce Harper EXCH
DCARBL Barry Larkin/40 20.00 50.00
DCARCB Craig Biggio/40 12.00 30.00
DCARCC Carlos Correa/20 50.00 120.00
DCARCJ Chipper Jones/25 50.00 120.00
DCARCK Clayton Kershaw/40 60.00 150.00
DCARCR Cal Ripken Jr./25 75.00 200.00
DCARCS Corey Seager/40 30.00 80.00
DCARDM Don Mattingly/40 40.00 100.00
DCARDP Dustin Pedroia/30 25.00 60.00
DCARFF Freddie Freeman/40 20.00 50.00
DCARFL Francisco Lindor EXCH 30.00 80.00
DCARFT Frank Thomas/40 30.00 80.00
DCARHA Hank Aaron/15
DCARIR Ivan Rodriguez/40 20.00 50.00
DCARJC Jose Canseco/40 20.00 50.00
DCARJD Johnny Damon/40 15.00 40.00
DCARJS John Smoltz/40 20.00 50.00
DCARJV Joey Votto/40 40.00 100.00
DCARKB Kris Bryant/40 100.00 250.00
DCARKS Kyle Schwarber EXCH 30.00 80.00
DCARMM Manny Machado/40 40.00 100.00
DCARMMC Mark McGwire/25 60.00 150.00
DCARMP Mike Piazza
DCARMTR Mike Trout
DCARNS Noah Syndergaard/40 25.00 60.00
DCAROS Ozzie Smith/40 25.00 60.00
DCAROSM Ozzie Smith/40 25.00 60.00
DCARRA Roberto Alomar/40 20.00 50.00
DCARRC Rod Carew/40 20.00 50.00
DCARRCL Roger Clemens
DCARRH Rickey Henderson/30 40.00 100.00
DCARRY Robin Yount/25 25.00 60.00
DCARSC Steve Carlton/40 15.00 40.00
DCARTG Tom Glavine/40 15.00 40.00
DCARTS Trevor Story/40 10.00 25.00
DCARWB Wade Boggs/25 25.00 60.00

2017 Topps Definitive Collection Dual Autograph Relics

RANDOM INSERTS IN PACKS
PRINT RUNS B/WN 10-35 COPIES PER
NO PRICING ON QTY 15 OR LESS
EXCHANGE DEADLINE 6/30/2019
DARCBA Biggio/Altuve/35 75.00 200.00
DARCBC Bregman/Correa/35 75.00 200.00
DARCCA Altuve/Correa/25 125.00 250.00
DARCCD Diaz/Carpenter/35 15.00 40.00
DARCCP Piscotty/Carpenter/25 15.00 40.00
DARCFS Swnsn/Frmn EXCH 50.00 120.00
DARCGR Gonzalez/Rodriguez/25 25.00 60.00
DARCKL Klbr/Lindor EXCH 15.00 40.00
DARCKS Seager/Kershaw/25 125.00 300.00
DARCMU Maeda/Urias EXCH 25.00 60.00
DARCOD Ortiz/Damon/25 50.00 120.00
DARCOP Ortiz/Pedroia/25 75.00 200.00
DARCPO Pettitte/O'Neill/35
DARCPP Price/Pedroia/20 30.00 80.00

DARCRC Carew/Ryan/25 100.00 250.00
DARCRUB Baez/Russell/35 50.00 120.00
DARCRYS Syndrgrd/Ryan/25 100.00 250.00
DARCSG Smoltz/Glavine/25 50.00 120.00
DARCSD Syndrgrd/dGrm EXCH 75.00 200.00
DARCSU Urias/Seager/35 30.00 80.00
DARCTK Trout/Kershaw EXCH

2017 Topps Definitive Collection Dual Autographs

RANDOM INSERTS IN PACKS
PRINT RUNS B/WN 10-35 COPIES PER
NO PRICING ON QTY 15 OR LESS
EXCHANGE DEADLINE 6/30/2019
DCDABA Altuve/Biggio EX 40.00 100.00
DCDABC Bregman/Correa/35 50.00 120.00
DCDABR Rizzo/Bryant EX 125.00 300.00
DCDABT Bryant/Trout/10
DCDACA Correa/Altuve/35 75.00 200.00
DCDACD Carpenter/Diaz/35 15.00 40.00
DCDAFS Swanson/Freeman/35 20.00 50.00
DCDAGA Abreu/Galarraga/35 10.00 25.00
DCDAGR Gonzalez/Rodriguez/35 30.00 80.00
DCDAGV Galarraga/Vizquel/35 20.00 50.00
DCDAJS Smoltz/Jones/25 60.00 150.00
DCDAKL Lindor/Kluber EX 60.00 150.00
DCDAKS Seager/Kershaw/35 100.00 250.00
DCDAMU Maeda/Urias/35 15.00 40.00
DCDAOD Ortiz/Damon/25 60.00 150.00
DCDAPO O'Neill/Pettitte/35 30.00 80.00
DCDARC Carew/Ryan/20 100.00 250.00
DCDARYS Syndergaard/Ryan/25
DCDASB Sandberg/Bryant/25 125.00 300.00
DCDASD deGrom/Syndrgrd/35 60.00 150.00
DCDASG Smoltz/Glavine/35 50.00 120.00
DCDASU Seager/Urias/35 30.00 80.00
DCDATH Trout/Harper EX 800.00 1200.00
DCDAVD Damon/Varitek/35 30.00 80.00
DCDAVL Lindor/Vizquel EX 50.00 120.00
DCDAVU Urias/Valenzuela/35 40.00 100.00

2017 Topps Definitive Collection Framed Autograph Patches

RANDOM INSERTS IN PACKS
PRINT RUNS B/WN 5-30 COPIES PER
NO PRICING ON QTY 15 OR LESS
EXCHANGE DEADLINE 6/30/2019
DFAPAB Andrew Benintendi/30 100.00 250.00
DFAPABR Alex Bregman/30 75.00 200.00
DFAPAJ Adam Jones/30 20.00 50.00
DFAPAJU Aaron Judge
DFAPBH Bryce Harper
DFAPBP Buster Posey
DFAPCSE Corey Seager/30 100.00 250.00
DFAPDP Dustin Pedroia/25 40.00 100.00
DFAPFF Freddie Freeman/20 30.00 80.00
DFAPFL Francisco Lindor/20 75.00 200.00
DFAPJA Jose Altuve/30 75.00 200.00
DFAPJB Javier Baez/30 60.00 150.00
DFAPJD Jacob deGrom/30 30.00 80.00
DFAPJU Julio Urias/25 25.00 60.00
DFAPKM Kenta Maeda/20 30.00 80.00
DFAPKSE Kyle Seager/30 20.00 50.00
DFAPMCA Matt Carpenter/30 25.00 60.00
DFAPMM Manny Machado/25 30.00 80.00
DFAPNS Noah Syndergaard/30 40.00 100.00
DFAPSM Starling Marte/20 40.00 100.00
DFAPSP Stephen Piscotty/30 12.00 30.00
DFAPTS Trevor Story/30 25.00 60.00

2017 Topps Definitive Collection Framed Autographs

RANDOM INSERTS IN PACKS
PRINT RUNS B/WN 5-30 COPIES PER
NO PRICING ON QTY 15 OR LESS
EXCHANGE DEADLINE 6/30/2019
DCFAAB Andrew Benintendi/30 75.00 200.00
DCFAABR Alex Bregman/30 40.00 100.00
DCFAAG Andres Galarraga/30 12.00 30.00
DCFAAJ Aaron Judge/30 250.00 500.00
DCFAAR Anthony Rizzo/30 60.00 150.00
DCFABH Bryce Harper/5
DCFABJ Bo Jackson EXCH 100.00 250.00
DCFABL Barry Larkin/25 30.00 80.00
DCFACC Carlos Correa/25 60.00 150.00
DCFACJ Chipper Jones/25 60.00 150.00
DCFACK Clayton Kershaw/25 75.00 200.00
DCFACR Cal Ripken Jr.
DCFACS Corey Seager/30 40.00 100.00
DCFACY Carl Yastrzemski/30 50.00 120.00
DCFADM Don Mattingly/25 40.00 100.00
DCFAFL Francisco Lindor/30 30.00 80.00
DCFAGM Greg Maddux/30 75.00 200.00
DCFAHA Hank Aaron EXCH
DCFAJB Johnny Bench/30 50.00 120.00
DCFAJS John Smoltz/25 25.00 60.00
DCFAJU Julio Urias/30 15.00 40.00
DCFAKB Kris Bryant/25 125.00 300.00
DCFAMM Manny Machado/30 40.00 100.00
DCFANR Nolan Ryan/30 75.00 200.00
DCFANS Noah Syndergaard/30 30.00 80.00
DCFAOS Ozzie Smith/25 30.00 80.00
DCFAOV Omar Vizquel/30 12.00 30.00
DCFAPM Pedro Martinez/30 50.00 120.00
DCFARH Rickey Henderson/30 40.00 100.00
DCFARJO Randy Johnson EXCH 60.00 150.00
DCFARS Ryne Sandberg/30 40.00 100.00
DCFAYM Yoan Moncada/25 40.00 100.00

2017 Topps Definitive Collection Helmets

RANDOM INSERTS IN PACKS
PRINT RUNS B/WN 25-50 COPIES PER
EXCHANGE DEADLINE 6/30/2019
DHCAB Alex Bregman/50 20.00 50.00
DHCAR Anthony Rizzo/50 40.00 100.00
DHCGS George Springer/25 15.00 40.00
DHCJB Javier Baez/50 25.00 60.00
DHCJH Jason Heyward/25 15.00 40.00
DHCJM J.D. Martinez/25 25.00 60.00
DHCJU Justin Upton/25 15.00 40.00
DHCMM Manny Machado/50 40.00 100.00
DHCSP Stephen Piscotty/50 15.00 40.00
DHCVM Victor Martinez/25 30.00 80.00

2017 Topps Definitive Collection Jumbo Relics

RANDOM INSERTS IN PACKS
STATED PRINT RUN 50 SER.#'d SETS
*BLUE/30: .4X TO 1X BASIC
DJRCAM Andrew McCutchen 30.00 80.00
DJRCAMC Andrew McCutchen 30.00 80.00
DJRCAP Albert Pujols 15.00 40.00
DJRCBP Brandon Phillips 4.00 10.00
DJRCCA Chris Archer 4.00 10.00
DJRCCB Carlos Beltran 6.00 15.00
DJRCCC Carlos Correa 6.00 15.00
DJRCCG Carlos Gonzalez 5.00 12.00
DJRCCGO Carlos Gonzalez 5.00 12.00
DJRCCGR Curtis Granderson 5.00 12.00
DJRCCH Cole Hamels 6.00 15.00
DJRCCK Corey Kluber 5.00 12.00
DJRCCS Carlos Santana 8.00 20.00
DJRCCY Christian Yelich 8.00 20.00
DJRCCYE Christian Yelich 8.00 20.00
DJRCDB Dellin Betances 8.00 20.00
DJRCEL Evan Longoria 6.00 15.00
DJRCELON Evan Longoria 6.00 15.00
DJRCFH Felix Hernandez 10.00 25.00
DJRCGP Gregory Polanco 12.00 30.00
DJRCGPO Gregory Polanco 12.00 30.00
DJRCJB Jose Bautista 6.00 15.00
DJRCJD Jacob deGrom 8.00 20.00
DJRCJDO Josh Donaldson 6.00 15.00
DJRCJL Jon Lester 5.00 12.00
DJRCJP Joe Panik 8.00 20.00
DJRCJV Justin Verlander 10.00 25.00
DJRCKS Kyle Seager 10.00 25.00
DJRCMC Michael Conforto 8.00 20.00
DJRCMH Matt Harvey 5.00 12.00
DJRCMS Miguel Sano 8.00 20.00
DJRCMTE Mark Teixeira 6.00 15.00
DJRCNC Nelson Cruz 8.00 20.00
DJRCNM Nomar Mazara 8.00 20.00
DJRCRB Ryan Braun 8.00 20.00
DJRCSM Starling Marte 15.00 40.00
DJRCSMA Steven Matz 5.00 12.00
DJRCTT Troy Tulowitzki 6.00 15.00
DJRCYC Yoenis Cespedes 8.00 20.00
DJRCZG Zack Greinke 8.00 20.00

2017 Topps Definitive Collection Legendary Autographs

RANDOM INSERTS IN PACKS
PRINT RUNS B/WN 5-50 COPIES PER
NO PRICING ON QTY 15 OR LESS
EXCHANGE DEADLINE 6/30/2019
DCLAAD Andre Dawson/35 20.00 50.00
DCLAAG Andres Galarraga/35 12.00 30.00
DCLAAK Al Kaline/35 25.00 50.00
DCLAAR Alex Rodriguez/25 75.00 200.00
DCLABL Barry Larkin/25 30.00 80.00
DCLACB Craig Biggio/50 12.00 30.00
DCLACJ Chipper Jones/25 60.00 150.00
DCLACY Carl Yastrzemski/25 50.00 120.00
DCLADM Don Mattingly/25 40.00 100.00
DCLAHA Hank Aaron EXCH
DCLAIR Ivan Rodriguez/35 20.00 50.00
DCLAJB Johnny Bench/25 50.00 120.00
DCLAJD Johnny Damon/50 20.00 50.00
DCLAJS John Smoltz/35 20.00 50.00
DCLALB Lou Brock/35 25.00 60.00
DCLANR Nolan Ryan/25 75.00 200.00
DCLAOS Ozzie Smith/35 40.00 100.00
DCLAOV Omar Vizquel/35 12.00 30.00
DCLARA Roberto Alomar/35 20.00 50.00
DCLARC Rod Carew/35 20.00 50.00
DCLARH Rickey Henderson/25 40.00 100.00
DCLASC Steve Carlton/35
DCLATG Tom Glavine/50 12.00 30.00
DCLAWB Wade Boggs/25 30.00 80.00

2017 Topps Definitive Collection Rookie Autographs

RANDOM INSERTS IN PACKS
PRINT RUNS B/WN 30-50 COPIES PER
EXCHANGE DEADLINE 6/30/2019
*GREEN/25: .5X TO 1.2X BASIC
DCRAAB Andrew Benintendi/50 50.00 120.00
DCRAABE Andrew Benintendi/50 50.00 120.00
DCRAABR Alex Bregman/50 30.00 80.00
DCRAABRE Alex Bregman/50 30.00 80.00
DCRAAJ Aaron Judge/50 150.00 300.00
DCRAAJU Aaron Judge/50 150.00 300.00
DCRAAR Alex Reyes/50 10.00 25.00
DCRAARE Alex Reyes/50 10.00 25.00
DCRACF Carson Fulmer/50 6.00 15.00
DCRADD David Dahl/50 8.00 20.00
DCRADS Dansby Swanson/50 20.00 50.00
DCRADSW Dansby Swanson/50 20.00 50.00
DCRADV Dan Vogelbach/30 10.00 25.00
DCRAGC Gavin Cecchini/30 8.00 20.00
DCRAHD Hunter Dozier/50 6.00 15.00
DCRAHR Hunter Renfroe/50 10.00 25.00
DCRAHRE Hunter Renfroe/50 10.00 25.00
DCRAJA Jorge Alfaro/50 10.00 25.00
DCRAJC Jharel Cotton/30 6.00 15.00
DCRAJD Jose De Leon/50 6.00 15.00
DCRAJH Jeff Hoffman/30 6.00 15.00
DCRAJJ JaCoby Jones/30 8.00 20.00
DCRAJM Joe Musgrove/30 6.00 15.00
DCRAJTH Jake Thompson/50 6.00 15.00
DCRALW Luke Weaver/50 10.00 25.00
DCRALWE Luke Weaver/50 10.00 25.00
DCRAMM Manny Margot/40 8.00 20.00
DCRARH Ryon Healy/30 8.00 20.00
DCRARL Reynaldo Lopez/30 6.00 15.00
DCRATG Tyler Glasnow/50 8.00 20.00
DCRATGL Tyler Glasnow/50 8.00 20.00
DCRATM Trey Mancini/30 15.00 40.00
DCRAYG Yulieski Gurriel/50 12.00 30.00
DCRAYGU Yulieski Gurriel/50 12.00 30.00
DCRAYMO Yoan Moncada/50 30.00 80.00

2018 Topps Definitive Collection Autograph Relics

RANDOM INSERTS IN PACKS
PRINT RUNS B/WN 5-30 COPIES PER
NO PRICING ON QTY 15 OR LESS
EXCHANGE DEADLINE 6/30/2020
ARCABE Andrew Benintendi EXCH
ARCABR Alex Bregman/30 30.00 80.00
ARCAJ Adam Jones/30 12.00 30.00
ARCARO Amed Rosario/30 RC 12.00 30.00
ARCARU Addison Russell/30 12.00 30.00
ARCAV Alex Verdugo/30 RC 10.00 25.00
ARCCF Clint Frazier/30 RC 12.00 30.00
ARCCS Chris Sale/30 15.00 40.00
ARCCSE Corey Seager/30 20.00 50.00
ARCDG Didi Gregorius/30 15.00 40.00
ARCDP Dustin Pedroia/30 20.00 50.00
ARCDS Dominic Smith/30 RC 8.00 20.00
ARCET Eric Thames/30 8.00 20.00
ARCFF Freddie Freeman
ARCFM Francisco Mejia/30 RC 12.00 30.00
ARCGSP George Springer/30 20.00 50.00
ARCIH Ian Happ/30 15.00 40.00
ARCJA Jose Altuve/30 15.00 40.00
ARCJB Javier Baez/30 40.00 100.00
ARCJC J.P. Crawford/30 RC 20.00 50.00
ARCJD Jacob deGrom
ARCKB Kris Bryant/5
ARCKS Kyle Schwarber/30 15.00 40.00
ARCLS Luis Severino/30 20.00 50.00
ARCMS Miguel Sano/30 8.00 20.00
ARCNS Noah Syndergaard/30 20.00 50.00
ARCPD Paul DeJong/30 10.00 25.00
ARCPG Paul Goldschmidt/30 30.00 80.00
ARCRD Rafael Devers/30 RC 20.00 50.00
ARCRH Rhys Hoskins/30 RC 15.00 40.00
ARCRM Ryan McMahon/30 RC 8.00 20.00
ARCSG Sonny Gray/30 10.00 25.00
ARCTM Trey Mancini/30 12.00 30.00
ARCVR Victor Robles/30 RC 25.00 60.00
ARCWCO Willson Contreras/30 20.00 50.00
ARCYC Yoenis Cespedes/20 8.00 20.00

2018 Topps Definitive Collection Autograph Relics Green

*GREEN/25: .4X TO 1X BASIC
RANDOM INSERTS IN PACKS
PRINT RUNS B/WN 10-25 COPIES PER
NO PRICING ON QTY 15 OR LESS
EXCHANGE DEADLINE 6/30/2020

2018 Topps Definitive Collection Autographs

RANDOM INSERTS IN PACKS
PRINT RUNS B/WN 5-35 COPIES PER
EXCHANGE DEADLINE 6/30/2020
DCAAR Anthony Rizzo/25 40.00 100.00
DCAARO Amed Rosario/35 15.00 40.00
DCABJ Bo Jackson/25 50.00 120.00
DCABL Barry Larkin/35 25.00 60.00
DCABP Buster Posey
DCACF Clint Frazier/35 30.00 80.00
DCACJ Chipper Jones/25 75.00 200.00
DCACK Clayton Kershaw/25 50.00 120.00
DCACSA Chris Sale/35 12.00 30.00
DCADM Don Mattingly/25 75.00 200.00
DCAFL Francisco Lindor/25 25.00 60.00
DCAFT Frank Thomas/35 30.00 80.00
DCAGS Gary Sanchez/25 50.00 120.00
DCAGSP George Springer/35 12.00 30.00
DCAIABR Alex Bregman/35 50.00 120.00
DCAIAP Andy Pettitte/35 15.00 40.00
DCAIBW Bernie Williams/25 40.00 100.00
DCAIEM Edgar Martinez/25 25.00 60.00
DCAIJA Jose Altuve/25 150.00 300.00
DCAIJD Johnny Damon/25 25.00 60.00
DCAING Nomar Garciaparra/35 30.00 80.00
DCAIOC Orlando Cepeda/35 10.00 25.00
DCAITGL Tom Glavine/35 25.00 40.00
DCAJS John Smoltz/35 25.00 60.00
DCAKB Kris Bryant EXCH 125.00 300.00
DCAMM Manny Machado/25 40.00 100.00
DCAMS Miguel Sano/35 10.00 25.00
DCANR Nolan Ryan
DCANS Noah Syndergaard/25 25.00 60.00
DCAOS Ozzie Smith/35 25.00 60.00
DCARA Roberto Alomar/25 30.00 80.00
DCARD Rafael Devers/35 40.00 100.00
DCARHO Rhys Hoskins/35 30.00 80.00
DCARS Ryne Sandberg/25 75.00 200.00
DCARY Robin Yount/25 40.00 100.00
DCAWB Wade Boggs/25

2018 Topps Definitive Collection Definitive Autograph Relics

RANDOM INSERTS IN PACKS
PRINT RUNS B/WN 5-40 COPIES PER
NO PRICING ON QTY 15 OR LESS
EXCHANGE DEADLINE 6/30/2020
DCARAD Andre Dawson/40 20.00 50.00
DCARAK Al Kaline/40 30.00 80.00
DCARAP Andy Pettitte/40 20.00 50.00
DCARAR Anthony Rizzo/35 25.00 60.00
DCARAROS Amed Rosario/40 20.00 50.00
DCARBJ Bo Jackson/35 40.00 100.00
DCARBL Barry Larkin/35 20.00 50.00
DCARCF Clint Frazier/40 12.00 30.00
DCARCJ Chipper Jones/35 40.00 100.00
DCARCK Clayton Kershaw/35 60.00 150.00
DCARCS Corey Seager/40 20.00 50.00
DCARDM Don Mattingly/35 30.00 80.00
DCARDP Dustin Pedroia/40 12.00 30.00
DCARFF Freddie Freeman/35 25.00 60.00
DCARFT Frank Thomas/40 30.00 80.00
DCARGS Gary Sanchez/40 30.00 80.00
DCARHA Hank Aaron
DCARIR Ivan Rodriguez/40 15.00 40.00
DCARJB Johnny Bench
DCARJC Jose Canseco/40 20.00 50.00
DCARJS John Smoltz/40 25.00 60.00
DCARJV Joey Votto/35 30.00 80.00
DCARKB Kris Bryant EXCH
DCARKS Kyle Schwarber/40 15.00 40.00
DCARMM Manny Machado/35 30.00 80.00
DCARMTR Mike Trout
DCARNG Nomar Garciaparra/40 10.00 25.00
DCARNS Noah Syndergaard/40 15.00 40.00
DCAROS Ozzie Smith/40 20.00 50.00
DCARRA Roberto Alomar/40 25.00 60.00
DCARRC Rod Carew/40 15.00 40.00
DCARRD Rafael Devers/40 20.00 50.00
DCARRS Ryne Sandberg/35 30.00 80.00
DCARRY Robin Yount/35 30.00 80.00
DCARSC Steve Carlton/40 15.00 40.00
DCARTG Tom Glavine/40 15.00 40.00
DCARWB Wade Boggs/35 15.00 40.00

2018 Topps Definitive Collection Dual Autograph Relics

RANDOM INSERTS IN PACKS
PRINT RUNS B/WN 10-35 COPIES PER
NO PRICING ON QTY 15 OR LESS
EXCHANGE DEADLINE 6/30/2020
DARCBA Altuve/Biggio EXCH 75.00 200.00
DARCBR Bryant/Rizzo EXCH 100.00 250.00
DARCBRO Beltre/IRod/25 50.00 120.00
DARCBT Thames/Braun/35 20.00 50.00
DARCBTR Bryant/Trout EXCH
DARCCB Contreras/Baez/35 40.00 100.00
DARCGRS Sancez/Gregorius EXCH 40.00 100.00
DARCGS Severino/Gray/35 10.00 25.00
DARCJM Mancini/Jones/35 30.00 80.00
DARCJSM Smoltz/Chipper/35 75.00 200.00
DARCPW Williams/Pettitte/35 40.00 100.00
DARCRS Rizzo/Schwarber EXCH 40.00 100.00
DARCRSM Amed Rosario Dominic Smith/35 12.00 30.00
DARCRUB Russell/Baez EXCH 40.00 100.00
DARCSAL Altuve/Springer/35 60.00 150.00
DARCSB Sandberg/Bryant EXCH
DARCSBU Byron Buxton Miguel Sano/35 12.00 30.00
DARCSD deGrom/Syndergaard/35 40.00 100.00
DARCSG Glavine/Smoltz/35 75.00 200.00
DARCSK Sale/Kimbrel/35 40.00 100.00
DARCSR Rosario/Sybdergaard/35 30.00 80.00
DARCSS Sanchez/Severino EXCH 40.00 100.00

2018 Topps Definitive Collection Dual Autographs

RANDOM INSERTS IN PACKS
PRINT RUNS B/WN 10-35 COPIES PER
NO PRICING ON QTY 15 OR LESS
EXCHANGE DEADLINE 6/30/2020
DACAL Lindor/Alomar/35 40.00 100.00
DACBB Biggio/Bagwell/35 60.00 150.00
DACBD Benintendi/Devers EXCH 25.00 60.00
DACBT Bryant/Trout EXCH
DACCB Buxton/Carew/25 25.00 60.00
DACCBA Baez/Contreras/35 75.00 200.00
DACFE Eckersley/Fingers/35 12.00 30.00
DACGS Severino/Gray/35 20.00 50.00
DACGSA Sanchez/Gregorius/35 15.00 40.00
DACHN Hoskins/Nola/35 60.00 150.00
DACJJ Jeter/Judge
DACJR Rivera/Jeter
DACJS Chipper/Smoltz/25 75.00 200.00
DACJUS Sanchez/Judge/35 200.00 400.00
DACKK Koufax/Kershaw
DACKL Kluber/Lindor/35 40.00 100.00
DACLV Larkin/Votto/30 50.00 120.00
DACPW Williams/Pettitte/35 15.00 40.00
DACRS Rizzo/Schwarber/35 25.00 60.00
DACRYS Ryan/Syndergaard/25 60.00 150.00
DACSA Altuve/Springer/35 30.00 80.00
DACSB Miguel Sano Byron Buxton/35 12.00 30.00
DACSBE Benintendi/Sale EXCH 50.00 120.00
DACSC Strawberry/Cespedes/35 25.00 60.00
DACSG Smoltz/Glavine/35 75.00 200.00
DACSGO Strawberry/Gooden/35 12.00 30.00
DACSR Syndergaard/Rosario/35 30.00 80.00
DACSS Sanchez/Severino EXCH 40.00 100.00
DACTH Harper/Trout
DACTKL Kluber/Thome EXCH 60.00 150.00

2018 Topps Definitive Collection Framed Autograph Patches

RANDOM INSERTS IN PACKS
PRINT RUNS B/WN 10-30 COPIES PER
NO PRICING ON QTY 15 OR LESS
EXCHANGE DEADLINE 6/30/2020
DFAPAJ Adam Jones/30 30.00 80.00
DFAPARO Amed Rosario/30 30.00 80.00
DFAPBB Byron Buxton/30 30.00 80.00
DFAPCF Clint Frazier/30 50.00 125.00
DFAPCS Chris Sale/30 25.00 60.00
DFAPCSE Corey Seager/30 50.00 120.00
DFAPDGR Didi Gregorius/30 30.00 80.00
DFAPFF Freddie Freeman/30 60.00 150.00
DFAPGSP George Springer/30 30.00 80.00
DFAPJA Jose Altuve/30 40.00 100.00
DFAPJB Javier Baez/20 75.00 200.00
DFAPJD Jacob deGrom/30 40.00 100.00
DFAPKB Kris Bryant EXCH
DFAPKS Kyle Schwarber/30 40.00 100.00
DFAPLS Luis Severino/30 30.00 80.00
DFAPMM Manny Machado/30 60.00 150.00
DFAPMS Miguel Sano/30 30.00 80.00
DFAPMT Masahiro Tanaka
DFAPNS Noah Syndergaard/30 30.00 80.00
DFAPPG Paul Goldschmidt/30 30.00 80.00
DFAPRD Rafael Devers/30 50.00 120.00
DFAPTMA Trey Mancini/30 30.00 80.00
DFAPWC Willson Contreras/30 60.00 150.00
DFAPYC Yoenis Cespedes 10.00 25.00

2018 Topps Definitive Collection Framed Autographs

RANDOM INSERTS IN PACKS
PRINT RUNS B/WN 5-30 COPIES PER
EXCHANGE DEADLINE 6/30/2020
DCFAAP Andy Pettitte/30 20.00 50.00
DCFAAR Anthony Rizzo/30 30.00 80.00
DCFAARO Amed Rosario/30 20.00 50.00
DCFABB Byron Buxton/30 12.00 30.00
DCFABJ Bo Jackson/25 50.00 210.00
DCFABL Barry Larkin/30 25.00 60.00
DCFACF Clint Frazier/30 15.00 40.00
DCFACK Clayton Kershaw/25
DCFACKL Corey Kluber/30 15.00 40.00
DCFACS Corey Seager/30 25.00 60.00
DCFADE Dennis Eckersley/30
DCFADM Don Mattingly/30 30.00 80.00
DCFAEM Edgar Martinez/30 20.00 50.00
DCFAFL Francisco Lindor/30 30.00 80.00
DCFAFT Frank Thomas/30 50.00 120.00
DCFAJA Jose Altuve/30 25.00 60.00
DCFAJBA Javier Baez/30 40.00 100.00
DCFAJC Jose Canseco/30 30.00 80.00
DCFAJD Josh Donaldson/25 20.00 50.00
DCFAJDA Johnny Damon/30 10.00 25.00
DCFAJS John Smoltz/30 25.00 60.00
DCFAJT Jim Thome/25 25.00 120.00
DCFAJV Joey Votto/25 20.00 50.00
DCFAMM Manny Machado/25 40.00 100.00
DCFANS Noah Syndergaard/30 20.00 50.00
DCFAOS Ozzie Smith/30 40.00 100.00
DCFAPG Paul Goldschmidt/30 25.00 60.00
DCFARA Roberto Alomar/30 20.00 50.00
DCFARD Rafael Devers/30 25.00 60.00
DCFARHO Rhys Hoskins/30 40.00 100.00
DCFASO Shohei Ohtani/30 150.00 400.00
DCFATG Tom Glavine/30 15.00 40.00
DCFAVR Victor Robles/30 30.00 80.00

2018 Topps Definitive Collection Helmet Collection

RANDOM INSERTS IN PACKS
PRINT RUNS B/WN 45-50 COPIES PER
DHCBB Byron Buxton/50 10.00 25.00
DHCBC Brandon Crawford/50 12.00 30.00
DHCBG Brett Gardner/50 20.00 50.00
DHCJP Joc Pederson/50 20.00 50.00
DHCMM Manny Machado/50 20.00 50.00
DHCNS Noah Syndergaard/50 15.00 40.00
DHCRB Ryan Braun/45 12.00 30.00

2018 Topps Definitive Collection Jumbo Relics

RANDOM INSERTS IN PACKS
PRINT RUNS B/WN 20-50 COPIES PER
*BLUE/20-25: .6X TO 1.5X p/r 40-50
*BLUE/20-25: .5X TO 1.2X p/r 30
*BLUE/20-25: .4X TO 1X p/r 20-25
DJRCAB Andrew Benintendi/40 12.00 30.00
DJRCABE Andrew Benintendi/40 12.00 30.00
DJRCAM Andrew McCutchen/50 12.00 30.00
DJRCAN Aaron Nola/30 15.00 40.00
DJRCAP Albert Pujols/30 10.00 25.00
DJRCAPU Albert Pujols/50 8.00 20.00
DJRCAR Amed Rosario/30 6.00 15.00
DJRCAW Adam Wainwright/30 8.00 20.00
DJRCAWA Adam Wainwright/50 6.00 15.00
DJRCBG Brett Gardner/25 12.00 30.00
DJRCBP Buster Posey/30 12.00 30.00
DJRCCB Charlie Blackmon/45 6.00 15.00
DJRCCC Carlos Correa/30 8.00 20.00
DJRCCK Clayton Kershaw/30 10.00 25.00
DJRCCKI Craig Kimbrel/30 12.00 30.00
DJRCCM Carlos Martinez/40 5.00 12.00
DJRCCS Corey Seager/30 8.00 20.00
DJRCCY Christian Yelich/30 10.00 25.00
DJRCDB Dellin Betances/30 6.00 15.00
DJRCDGR Didi Gregorius/25 8.00 20.00
DJRCDK Dallas Keuchel/25 8.00 20.00
DJRCDP Dustin Pedroia/30 8.00 20.00
DJRCEH Eric Hosmer/50 5.00 12.00
DJRCEI Ender Inciarte/50 4.00 10.00
DJRCET Eric Thames/20 10.00 25.00
DJRCHR Hanley Ramirez/20 8.00 20.00
DJRCHRY Hyun-Jin Ryu/50 5.00 12.00
DJRCJA Jose Altuve/50 5.00 12.00
DJRCJB Josh Bell/50 12.00 30.00
DJRCJBR Jackie Bradley Jr./30 8.00 20.00
DJRCJH Josh Harrison/30 8.00 20.00
DJRCJHA Josh Harrison/50 6.00 15.00
DJRCJHE Jason Heyward/30 12.00 30.00
DJRCJV Joey Votto/50 10.00 25.00
DJRCKD Khris Davis/20 10.00 25.00
DJRCKS Kyle Schwarber/20 15.00 40.00
DJRCMC Miguel Cabrera/50 6.00 15.00
DJRCMCA Miguel Cabrera/50 6.00 15.00
DJRCMCO Michael Conforto/50 5.00 12.00
DJRCMM Manny Machado/50 15.00 40.00
DJRCMT Masahiro Tanaka/20 12.00 30.00
DJRCNC Nelson Cruz/50 6.00 15.00
DJRCNS Noah Syndergaard/50 5.00 12.00
DJRCRB Ryan Braun/20 8.00 20.00
DJRCRC Robinson Cano/50 5.00 12.00
DJRCRZ Ryan Zimmerman/50 5.00 12.00
DJRCSST Stephen Strasburg/30 12.00 30.00
DJRCTS Trevor Story/25 15.00 40.00
DJRCTT Trea Turner/30 8.00 20.00
DJRCYG Yuli Gurriel/50 5.00 12.00
DJRCYM Yadier Molina/40 12.00 30.00

2018 Topps Definitive Collection Legendary Autographs

RANDOM INSERTS IN PACKS
PRINT RUNS B/WN 5-35 COPIES PER
NO PRICING ON QTY 15 OR LESS
EXCHANGE DEADLINE 6/30/2020
DCLAAD Andre Dawson/35 12.00 30.00
DCLAAK Al Kaline/35 25.00 50.00
DCLAAP Andy Pettitte/35 20.00 50.00
DCLAAR Alex Rodriguez
DCLABJ Bo Jackson/25 40.00 100.00
DCLABL Barry Larkin/35 20.00 50.00
DCLABW Bernie Williams/35 40.00 100.00
DCLACJ Chipper Jones/25 40.00 100.00
DCLADE Dennis Eckersley/35 12.00 30.00
DCLADM Don Mattingly/35 30.00 80.00
DCLAEM Edgar Martinez/35 12.00 30.00
DCLAFT Frank Thomas/35 30.00 80.00
DCLAGM Greg Maddux
DCLAI Ichiro
DCLAJD Johnny Damon/35 12.00 30.00
DCLAJP Jim Palmer/35 12.00 30.00
DCLAJS John Smoltz/35 20.00 50.00
DCLALB Lou Brock/35 15.00 40.00
DCLANG Nomar Garciaparra/35 12.00 30.00
DCLAOC Orlando Cepeda/30 12.00 30.00
DCLAOS Ozzie Smith/35 25.00 60.00
DCLARA Roberto Alomar/35 15.00 40.00
DCLARC Rod Carew/35 15.00 40.00
DCLARH Rickey Henderson/25 50.00 120.00
DCLARS Ryne Sandberg/25 50.00 120.00
DCLARY Robin Yount/25 40.00 100.00
DCLASC Steve Carlton/35 20.00 50.00
DCLATG Tom Glavine/35 12.00 30.00
DCLAWB Wade Boggs/25 25.00 60.00

2018 Topps Definitive Collection Rookie Autographs

RANDOM INSERTS IN PACKS
PRINT RUNS B/WN 30-50 COPIES PER
EXCHANGE DEADLINE 6/30/2020
*GREEN/25: .5X TO 1.2X BASIC
DRAAB Anthony Banda/50 4.00 10.00
DRAAH Austin Hays/50 6.00 15.00
DRAAHA Austin Hays/50 6.00 15.00
DRAAR Amed Rosario/50 5.00 12.00
DRAARO Amed Rosario/50 5.00 12.00
DRAAV Alex Verdugo/50 12.00 30.00
DRAAVE Alex Verdugo/50 12.00 30.00
DRABW Brandon Woodruff/50 5.00 12.00
DRACF Clint Frazier/50 12.00 30.00
DRACFR Clint Frazier/50 12.00 30.00
DRACS Chance Sisco/50 5.00 12.00
DRADF Dustin Fowler/50 6.00 15.00
DRADS Dominic Smith/30 4.00 10.00
DRADSM Dominic Smith/30 4.00 10.00
DRAFM Francisco Mejia/50 12.00 30.00
DRAFME Francisco Mejia/50 12.00 30.00
DRAHB Harrison Bader/50 6.00 15.00
DRAHBA Harrison Bader/50 6.00 15.00
DRAJCR J.P. Crawford/50 6.00 15.00
DRAJD J.D. Davis/50 5.00 12.00
DRAJF Jack Flaherty/50 6.00 15.00
DRAJFL Jack Flaherty/50 6.00 15.00
DRAJPC J.P. Crawford/50 6.00 15.00
DRALS Lucas Sims/50 4.00 10.00
DRAMA Miguel Andujar/50 40.00 100.00
DRAND Nicky Delmonico/50 4.00 10.00
DRAOA Ozzie Albies/50 30.00 80.00
DRAOAL Ozzie Albies/50 30.00 80.00
DRARD Rafael Devers/50 20.00 50.00
DRARDE Rafael Devers/50 20.00 50.00
DRARH Rhys Hoskins/50 40.00 100.00
DRARHO Rhys Hoskins/50 40.00 100.00
DRARM Ryan McMahon/50 5.00 12.00
DRARMC Ryan McMahon/50 5.00 12.00
DRASO Shohei Ohtani/50 400.00 800.00
DRATM Tyler Mahle/50 6.00 15.00
DRATMA Tyler Mahle/50 6.00 15.00
DRAVR Victor Robles/50 20.00 50.00
DRAVRO Victor Robles/50 20.00 50.00
DRAWB Walker Buehler/50 25.00 60.00
DRAWBU Walker Buehler/50 25.00 60.00
DRAZG Zack Granite/50 4.00 10.00

2019 Topps Definitive Collection Autograph Relics

RANDOM INSERTS IN PACKS
PRINT RUNS B/WN 5-50 COPIES PER
NO PRICING ON QTY 15 OR LESS
EXCHANGE DEADLINE 5/31/2021
ARCALB Alex Bregman/50 20.00 50.00
ARCAR Anthony Rizzo/35 40.00 100.00
ARCCS Chris Sale/50 20.00 50.00
ARCDG Didi Gregorius/50 15.00 40.00
ARCDP Dustin Pedroia/50 10.00 25.00
ARCFF Freddie Freeman/50 30.00 80.00
ARCFL Francisco Lindor/50 20.00 50.00
ARCGS George Springer/50 15.00 40.00
ARCGSA Gary Sanchez/35 25.00 60.00
ARCGT Gleyber Torres/50 40.00 100.00
ARCJA Jose Altuve/35 30.00 80.00
ARCJBA Javier Baez/50 40.00 100.00
ARCJD Jacob deGrom/50 15.00 40.00
ARCJS Juan Soto/50 30.00 80.00
ARCJU Justin Upton/50 10.00 25.00
ARCJUS Justus Sheffield RC/50 10.00 25.00
ARCJV Joey Votto/35 20.00 50.00
ARCKS Kyle Schwarber/50 15.00 40.00
ARCKT Kyle Tucker RC/50 15.00 40.00
ARCLS Luis Severino/50 12.00 30.00
ARCMAN Miguel Andujar/50 10.00 25.00
ARCMCH Matt Chapman/50 12.00 30.00
ARCMMI Miles Mikolas/35 10.00 25.00
ARCNS Noah Syndergaard/50 12.00 30.00
ARCOA Ozzie Albies/50 15.00 40.00
ARCPG Paul Goldschmidt/50 15.00 40.00
ARCRA Ronald Acuna Jr./50 60.00 150.00
ARCRD Rafael Devers/35 15.00 40.00
ARCRH Rhys Hoskins/50 20.00 50.00
ARCSP Salvador Perez/50 10.00 25.00
ARCWC Willson Contreras/50 8.00 20.00
ARCYM Yadier Molina/50 30.00 80.00

2019 Topps Definitive Collection Autograph Relics Green

*GREEN/25: .5X TO 1.2X BASIC
RANDOM INSERTS IN PACKS
PRINT RUNS B/WN 10-25 COPIES PER
NO PRICING ON QTY 15 OR LESS
EXCHANGE DEADLINE 5/31/2021
ARCBSN Blake Snell/25 20.00 50.00
ARCIH Ian Happ/25 10.00 25.00
ARCKD Khris Davis/25 15.00 40.00
ARCMAT Matt Carpenter/25 12.00 30.00
ARCMH Mitch Haniger/25 20.00 50.00
ARCMO Marcell Ozuna/25 12.00 30.00

2019 Topps Definitive Collection Autographs

RANDOM INSERTS IN PACKS
PRINT RUNS B/WN 5-25 COPIES PER
NO PRICING ON QTY 10 OR LESS
EXCHANGE DEADLINE 5/31/2021
DCAABR Alex Bregman/25 30.00 80.00
DCAAP Andy Pettitte/25 15.00 40.00
DCAAR Anthony Rizzo/25 75.00 200.00
DCABG Bob Gibson/25 25.00 60.00
DCABL Barry Larkin/25 40.00 100.00
DCACR Cal Ripken Jr.
DCADE Dennis Eckersley/25 15.00 40.00
DCADM Don Mattingly/25 30.00 80.00
DCAEJ Eloy Jimenez/25 40.00 100.00
DCAFF Freddie Freeman/25 60.00 150.00
DCAFL Francisco Lindor/25 20.00 50.00
DCAFT Frank Thomas/25 40.00 100.00
DCAJA Jose Altuve/25 25.00 60.00
DCAJR Jose Ramirez/25 12.00 30.00
DCAJS Juan Soto/25 75.00 200.00
DCAJSM John Smoltz/25 30.00 80.00
DCAJV Joey Votto
DCAMMA Manny Machado EXCH
DCANS Noah Syndergaard/25 8.00 20.00
DCAOA Ozzie Albies/25 75.00 200.00
DCAOS Ozzie Smith/25 30.00 80.00
DCAPG Paul Goldschmidt/25 25.00 60.00
DCARA Roberto Alomar/25 25.00 60.00
DCARAJ Ronald Acuna Jr./25 60.00 150.00
DCARH Rhys Hoskins/25 60.00 150.00
DCARJO Randy Johnson
DCAVG Vladimir Guerrero/25 40.00 100.00
DCAVGJ Vladimir Guerrero Jr./25 300.00 600.00
DCAWC Will Clark/25 30.00 80.00
DCAYM Yadier Molina/25 30.00 80.00

2019 Topps Definitive Collection Defining Moments Autographs

RANDOM INSERTS IN PACKS
PRINT RUNS B/WN 5-30 COPIES PER
NO PRICING ON QTY 19 OR LESS
EXCHANGE DEADLINE 5/31/2021
DMACBW Bernie Williams/22 30.00 80.00
DMACDO David Ortiz/20 30.00 80.00
DMACDS Darryl Strawberry/25 20.00 50.00
DMACNG Nomar Garciaparra/30 20.00 50.00
DMACRA Roberto Alomar/30 20.00 50.00
DMACWC Will Clark/29 20.00 50.00

2019 Topps Definitive Collection Definitive Autograph Relics

RANDOM INSERTS IN PACKS
PRINT RUNS B/WN 10-50 COPIES PER
NO PRICING ON QTY 10 OR LESS
EXCHANGE DEADLINE 5/31/2021
DARCAD Andre Dawson/50 20.00 50.00
DARCAK Al Kaline/50 30.00 80.00
DARCAP Andy Pettitte/50 20.00 50.00
DARCBGI Bob Gibson/50 40.00 100.00
DARCBL Barry Larkin/50 25.00 60.00
DARCBO Bo Jackson/25 40.00 100.00
DARCBW Bernie Williams/50 20.00 50.00
DARCCF Carlton Fisk/50 20.00 50.00
DARCCJ Chipper Jones/50 60.00 150.00
DARCCR Cal Ripken Jr./25 40.00 100.00
DARCCY Carl Yastrzemski/25 50.00 120.00
DARCDM Dale Murphy/50 15.00 40.00
DARCDMA Don Mattingly/50 40.00 100.00

DARCDO David Ortiz/25 25.00 60.00
DARCFM Fred McGriff/50 20.00 50.00
DARCFT Frank Thomas/50 25.00 60.00
DARCHM Hideki Matsui/25 75.00 200.00
DARCICH Ichiro
DARCIR Ivan Rodriguez/50 15.00 40.00
DARCJB Johnny Bench/25 50.00 120.00
DARCJC Jose Canseco/50 25.00 60.00
DARCJD Johnny Damon/50 15.00 40.00
DARCJMA Juan Marichal/50 25.00 60.00
DARCJP Jorge Posada/50 25.00 60.00
DARCJS John Smoltz/50 20.00 50.00
DARCKB Kris Bryant/50 40.00 100.00
DARCMM Mark McGwire/25 30.00 80.00
DARCMP Mike Piazza/10 40.00 100.00
DARCNG Nomar Garciaparra/50 20.00 50.00
DARCNR Nolan Ryan/25 75.00 200.00
DARCOS Ozzie Smith/50 30.00 80.00
DARCRA Roberto Alomar/50 15.00 40.00
DARCRCA Rod Carew/50 20.00 50.00
DARCRH Rickey Henderson/25 40.00 100.00
DARCRJ Reggie Jackson/25 40.00 100.00
DARCRS Ryne Sandberg/50 30.00 80.00
DARCRY Robin Yount/50 25.00 60.00
DARCSC Steve Carlton/50 25.00 60.00
DARCTG Tom Glavine/50 15.00 40.00
DARCTR Tim Raines/50 15.00 40.00
DARCWB Wade Boggs/50 20.00 50.00
DARCWC Will Clark/50 25.00 60.00

2019 Topps Definitive Collection Dual Autograph Relics

RANDOM INSERTS IN PACKS
PRINT RUNS B/WN 10-35 COPIES PER
NO PRICING ON QTY 15 OR LESS
EXCHANGE DEADLINE 5/31/2021
DARAA Acuna Jr./Albies/35 125.00 300.00
DARAP Pettitte/Posada/35 40.00 100.00
DARAH Rodriguez/Beltre EXCH 25.00 60.00
DARBA Altuve/Bregman EXCH 60.00 150.00
DARBR Rizzo/Bryant EXCH 100.00 250.00
DARCH Hunter/Carew/35 30.00 80.00
DARGB Springer/Bregman/35 50.00 120.00
DARGS Smith/Gibson/35 75.00 200.00
DARHU Hunter/Upton/35 30.00 80.00
DARIM Rodriguez/Molina/35 60.00 150.00
DARJA Acuna Jr./Jones/35 100.00 250.00
DARLR Lindor/Ramirez/35 25.00 60.00
DARMS Murphy/Smoltz/35 30.00 80.00
DAROM Molina/Smith/35 75.00 200.00
DARPS Pedroia/Sale/35 15.00 40.00
DARRC Hoskins/Carlton/35 40.00 100.00
DARRS Schwarber/Rizzo/35 30.00 80.00
DARSD deGrom/Syndergaard/35 75.00 200.00
DARSM McGriff/Smoltz/35 40.00 100.00
DARSR Soto/Robles/35 60.00 150.00
DARTF Yastrzemski/Fisk/35 75.00 200.00
DARTS Pedroia/Sale/35 40.00 100.00

2019 Topps Definitive Collection Dual Autographs

RANDOM INSERTS IN PACKS
PRINT RUNS B/WN 10-35 COPIES PER
NO PRICING ON QTY 15 OR LESS
EXCHANGE DEADLINE 5/31/2021
DACAA Albies/Acuna Jr./35 100.00 250.00
DACBR Bryant/Rizzo EXCH 75.00 200.00
DACBS Baez/Schwarber/35 40.00 100.00
DACCG Guerrero/Carew/25 40.00 100.00
DACCM McGwire/Clark/35 75.00 200.00
DACDG Guerrero/Dawson/35 40.00 100.00
DACGB Brock/Gibson/35 75.00 200.00
DACGG Guerrero Jr./Guerrero/35 150.00 400.00
DACGR Rodriguez/Molina/35 50.00 120.00
DACHC Henderson/Canseco/35 60.00 150.00
DACJA Jones/Albies/35 50.00 120.00
DACJG Jones/Glavine/25 75.00 200.00
DACJT Torres/Judge/25 125.00 300.00
DACKM Kershaw/Machado EXCH
DACLR Lindor/Ramirez/35 25.00 60.00
DACMJ Jones/Murphy/35 75.00 200.00
DACMS Martinez/Sale/25 40.00 100.00
DACPS Sale/Pedroia/35 30.00 80.00
DACRA Altuve/Ryan/25 60.00 150.00
DACRG Gonzalez/Rodriguez/25 30.00 80.00
DACSB Bregman/Springer/35 40.00 100.00
DACSD Syndergaard/deGrom/35 40.00 100.00
DACSM Smith/Molina EXCH 75.00 200.00
DACSR Soto/Robles/35 50.00 120.00
DACTS Severino/Torres/35 40.00 100.00
DACWP Williams/Posada/35 50.00 120.00
DACYF Fisk/Yastrzemski/25 75.00 200.00

2019 Topps Definitive Collection Framed Autograph Patches

RANDOM INSERTS IN PACKS
PRINT RUNS B/WN 5-30 COPIES PER
NO PRICING ON QTY 15 OR LESS
EXCHANGE DEADLINE 5/31/2021
FACAJ Aaron Judge
FACDP Dustin Pedroia/30 20.00 50.00
FACFF Freddie Freeman/30 50.00 125.00
FACFL Francisco Lindor
FACGSP George Springer/30 25.00 60.00
FACJA Jose Altuve/30 50.00 125.00
FACJD Jacob deGrom/30 30.00 80.00
FACJV Joey Votto/30 40.00 100.00
FACKD Khris Davis/30 15.00 40.00
FACKS Kyle Schwarber/30 25.00 60.00
FACLS Luis Severino/30 12.00 30.00
FACMC Matt Carpenter/30 15.00 40.00
FACNS Noah Syndergaard/30
FACSP Salvador Perez/30 12.00 30.00
FACWC Willson Contreras/30 30.00 80.00

2019 Topps Definitive Collection Framed Autographs

RANDOM INSERTS IN PACKS
PRINT RUNS B/WN 5-30 COPIES PER
NO PRICING ON QTY 15 OR LESS
EXCHANGE DEADLINE 5/31/2021
DCFAABR Alex Bregman/25 30.00 80.00
DCFAAR Anthony Rizzo/25 75.00 200.00
DCFABG Bob Gibson/25 25.00 60.00
DCFABL Barry Larkin/30 20.00 50.00
DCFADE Dennis Eckersley/30 15.00 40.00
DCFADM Don Mattingly/25 40.00 100.00
DCFAEJ Eloy Jimenez/25 40.00 100.00
DCFAFL Francisco Lindor/25 20.00 50.00
DCFAFT Frank Thomas/25 40.00 100.00
DCFAGT Gleyber Torres/30 50.00 120.00
DCFAJA Jose Altuve/25 25.00 60.00
DCFAJBE Johnny Bench/30 40.00 100.00
DCFAJR Jose Ramirez/25 12.00 30.00
DCFAJS Juan Soto/30 60.00 150.00
DCFAJV Joey Votto/25 25.00 60.00
DCFAMM Manny Machado EXCH 30.00 80.00
DCFAOS Ozzie Smith/30 30.00 80.00
DCFAPG Paul Goldschmidt/30 25.00 60.00
DCFARA Roberto Alomar/30 20.00 50.00
DCFARAJ Ronald Acuna Jr./30 60.00 150.00
DCFARH Rhys Hoskins/30 40.00 100.00
DCFARS Ryne Sandberg/30 40.00 100.00
DCFAVG Vladimir Guerrero/25 40.00 100.00
DCFAVGJ Vladimir Guerrero Jr. EXCH 300.00 600.00
DCFAWC Will Clark/30 30.00 80.00
DCFAYK Yusei Kikuchi EXCH 25.00 60.00
DCFAYM Yadier Molina/30 30.00 80.00

2019 Topps Definitive Collection Helmets

RANDOM INSERTS IN PACKS
PRINT RUNS B/WN 25-35 COPIES PER
EXCHANGE DEADLINE 5/31/2021
DHCFL Francisco Lindor/25
DHCGS Gary Sanchez/25 30.00 80.00
DHCJA Jose Altuve/25 25.00 60.00
DHCJD Jacob deGrom/35 15.00 40.00
DHCKD Khris Davis/25
DHCMC Matt Chapman/25 20.00 50.00
DHCMCA Matt Carpenter/25 15.00 40.00
DHCRH Rhys Hoskins/35 25.00 60.00
DHCWC Willson Contreras/35 20.00 50.00
DHCYM Yadier Molina/35 40.00 100.00

2019 Topps Definitive Collection Jumbo Relics

RANDOM INSERTS IN PACKS
PRINT RUNS B/WN 20-50 COPIES PER
*BLUE/20: .6X TO 1.5X p/r 35-50
*BLUE/20: .4X TO 1X p/r 20
DJRCAB Andrew Benintendi/50 6.00 15.00
DJRCAM Andrew McCutchen/35 12.00 30.00
DJRCBP Buster Posey/35 10.00 25.00
DJRCCB Cody Bellinger/50 20.00 50.00
DJRCCBL Charlie Blackmon/35 6.00 15.00
DJRCCC Carlos Correa/50 10.00 25.00
DJRCDB Dellin Betances/35 5.00 12.00
DJRCDG Dee Gordon/35 8.00 20.00
DJRCDK Dallas Keuchel/35 6.00 15.00
DJRCDO David Ortiz/50 10.00 25.00
DJRCDP Dustin Pedroia/35 6.00 15.00
DJRCDPR David Price/35 5.00 12.00
DJRCDS Dansby Swanson/35 20.00 50.00
DJRCEE Edwin Encarnacion/35 6.00 15.00
DJRCEH Eric Hosmer/35 8.00 20.00
DJRCEL Evan Longoria/35 10.00 25.00
DJRCFF Freddie Freeman/50 25.00 60.00
DJRCFFRE Freddie Freeman/35 25.00 60.00
DJRCFL Francisco Lindor/35 10.00 25.00
DJRCGSP George Springer/50 10.00 25.00
DJRCJAB Jose Abreu/20 15.00 40.00
DJRCJH Jason Heyward/35 5.00 12.00
DJRCJM J.D. Martinez/50 6.00 15.00
DJRCJP Joc Pederson/35 10.00 25.00
DJRCJR Jose Ramirez/35 5.00 12.00
DJRCJT Jameson Taillon/35 5.00 12.00
DJRCJV Joey Votto/35 10.00 25.00
DJRCKB Kris Bryant/50 12.00 30.00
DJRCKD Khris Davis/35 6.00 15.00
DJRCKS Kyle Schwarber/35 8.00 20.00
DJRCLS Luis Severino/35 6.00 15.00
DJRCMB Mookie Betts/50 12.00 30.00
DJRCMCA Miguel Cabrera/35 20.00 50.00
DJRCMCH Matt Chapman/35 6.00 15.00
DJRCMCO Michael Conforto/35 5.00 12.00
DJRCMO Marcell Ozuna/50 6.00 15.00
DJRCMS Max Scherzer/35 12.00 30.00
DJRCNA Nolan Arenado/50 12.00 30.00
DJRCNAR Nolan Arenado/35 12.00 30.00
DJRCNC Nicholas Castellanos/35 6.00 15.00
DJRCNM Nomar Mazara/35 4.00 10.00
DJRCPD Paul DeJong/50 6.00 15.00
DJRCPG Paul Goldschmidt/50 10.00 25.00
DJRCRB Ryan Braun/35 10.00 25.00
DJRCRD Rafael Devers/50 10.00 25.00
DJRCRH Rhys Hoskins/50 8.00 20.00
DJRCRZ Ryan Zimmerman/35 5.00 12.00
DJRCSG Scooter Gennett/35 10.00 25.00
DJRCTM Trey Mancini/35 8.00 20.00
DJRCTS Trevor Story/35 8.00 20.00
DJRCTT Trea Turner/35 5.00 12.00
DJRCWC Willson Contreras/35 15.00 40.00
DJRCWM Whit Merrifield/35 15.00 40.00
DJRCXB Xander Bogaerts/35 12.00 30.00
DJRCYM Yoan Moncada/35 6.00 15.00
DJRCYMO Yadier Molina/35 10.00 25.00
DJRCZG Zack Greinke/35 8.00 20.00

2019 Topps Definitive Collection Legendary Autographs

RANDOM INSERTS IN PACKS
PRINT RUNS B/WN 5-25 COPIES PER
NO PRICING ON QTY 10 OR LESS
EXCHANGE DEADLINE 5/31/2021
LACAD Andre Dawson/25 12.00 30.00
LACAK Al Kaline/25 50.00 120.00
LACAP Andy Pettitte/25 15.00 40.00
LACBG Bob Gibson/25 25.00 60.00
LACBJA Bo Jackson/25 40.00 100.00
LACCJ Chipper Jones/25 60.00 150.00
LACCR Cal Ripken Jr./25 50.00 120.00
LACDE Dennis Eckersley/25 15.00 40.00
LACDM Dale Murphy/25 40.00 100.00
LACDMA Don Mattingly/25 40.00 100.00
LACDO David Ortiz/25 40.00 100.00
LACFM Fred McGriff/25 20.00 50.00
LACFT Frank Thomas/25 40.00 100.00
LACHM Hideki Matsui/25 60.00 150.00
LACJB Johnny Bench/25 30.00 80.00
LACJM Juan Marichal/25 20.00 50.00
LACLB Lou Brock/25 20.00 50.00
LACMMC Mark McGwire/25 40.00 100.00
LACNR Nolan Ryan/25 50.00 120.00
LACOS Ozzie Smith/25 25.00 60.00
LACRA Roberto Alomar/25 15.00 40.00
LACRC Rod Carew/25 20.00 50.00
LACRH Rickey Henderson/25 30.00 80.00
LACRJA Reggie Jackson/25 25.00 60.00
LACRS Ryne Sandberg/25 25.00 60.00
LACRY Robin Yount/25 20.00 50.00
LACSC Steve Carlton/25 15.00 40.00
LACWB Wade Boggs/25 25.00 60.00
LACWC Will Clark/25 25.00 60.00

2019 Topps Definitive Collection Rookie Autographs

RANDOM INSERTS IN PACKS
STATED PRINT RUN 50 SER.#'d SETS
EXCHANGE DEADLINE 5/31/2021
*GREEN/25: .5X TO 1.2X BASIC
DRABL Brandon Lowe 10.00 25.00
DRACA Chance Adams 8.00 20.00
DRACAD Chance Adams 8.00 20.00
DRACBU Corbin Burnes 6.00 15.00
DRACM Cedric Mullins 6.00 15.00
DRACMU Cedric Mullins 6.00 15.00
DRACS Christin Stewart 12.00 30.00
DRACST Christin Stewart 12.00 30.00
DRADJ Danny Jansen 8.00 20.00
DRADJA Danny Jansen 8.00 20.00
DRAELJ Eloy Jimenez 30.00 80.00
DRAFTJ Fernando Tatis Jr. EXCH 125.00 300.00
DRAJB Jake Bauers 6.00 15.00
DRAJM Jeff McNeil 12.00 30.00
DRAJMC Jeff McNeil 12.00 30.00
DRAJS Justus Sheffield 8.00 20.00
DRAJUS Justus Sheffield 8.00 20.00
DRAKA Kolby Allard 6.00 15.00
DRAKOA Kolby Allard 6.00 15.00
DRAKT Kyle Tucker 20.00 50.00
DRAKW Kyle Wright 6.00 15.00
DRAKWR Kyle Wright 6.00 15.00
DRAKYT Kyle Tucker 20.00 50.00
DRALU Luis Urias 30.00 80.00
DRALUR Luis Urias 30.00 80.00
DRAMIK Michael Kopech 15.00 40.00
DRAMK Michael Kopech 15.00 40.00
DRAPA Peter Alonso EXCH 75.00 200.00
DRARL Ramón Laureano 20.00 50.00
DRARO Ryan O'Hearn 4.00 10.00
DRASD Steven Duggar 10.00 25.00
DRATT Touki Toussaint 5.00 12.00
DRATTO Touki Toussaint 5.00 12.00
DRAVGJ Vladimir Guerrero Jr. 200.00 400.00
DRAYK Yusei Kikuchi EXCH 30.00 80.00

2020 Topps Definitive Collection Autograph Relics

RANDOM INSERTS IN PACKS
PRINT RUN BTW 15-50 COPIES PER
NO PRICING QTY 15 OR LESS
EXCHANGE DEADLINE 3/31/2022
ARCAN Aaron Nola/30 20.00 50.00
ARCBB Bo Bichette/35 RC 50.00 125.00
ARCBM Brendan McKay/30 RC 15.00 40.00
ARCCS CC Sabathia/30 25.00 60.00
ARCCY Christian Yelich/30 60.00 150.00
ARCDS Dansby Swanson/30 15.00 40.00
ARCGS George Springer/30 20.00 50.00
ARCGT Gleyber Torres/30 75.00 200.00
ARCJA Jose Altuve/30 20.00 50.00
ARCJD Jacob deGrom/30 30.00 80.00
ARCJS Juan Soto/50 50.00 120.00
ARCKH Keston Hiura/30 25.00 60.00
ARCNS Nick Senzel/30 15.00 40.00
ARCPA Pete Alonso/50 50.00 120.00
ARCPC Patrick Corbin/30 12.00 30.00
ARCPG Paul Goldschmidt/30 20.00 50.00
ARCRA Ronald Acuna Jr./30 150.00 400.00
ARCRD Rafael Devers/50 20.00 50.00
ARCRH Rhys Hoskins/30 40.00 100.00
ARCWB Walker Buehler/30 25.00 60.00
ARCWC Willson Contreras/30 20.00 50.00
ARCWM Whit Merrifield/30 12.00 30.00
ARCXB Xander Bogaerts/30 25.00 60.00
ARCYA Yordan Alvarez/50 RC 60.00 150.00
ARCCKI Carter Kieboom/30 15.00 40.00
ARCCSA Chris Sale/30 12.00 30.00
ARCFTJ Fernando Tatis Jr./50 75.00 200.00
ARCJDM J.D. Martinez/30 20.00 50.00
ARCMCA Miguel Cabrera/30 50.00 120.00
ARCMKE Max Kepler/30 25.00 60.00
ARCMTA Masahiro Tanaka EXCH/50 50.00 120.00
ARCMTE Mark Teixeira/30 30.00 80.00

2020 Topps Definitive Collection Autograph Relics Green

*GREEN: .5X TO 1.2X p/r 30-50
RANDOM INSERTS IN PACKS
STATED PRINT RUN 25 SER.#'d SETS
EXCHANGE DEADLINE 3/31/2022
ARCAN Aaron Nola 30.00 80.00
ARCDS Dansby Swanson 25.00 60.00
ARCGC Gerrit Cole 40.00 100.00
ARCPd Paul deJong
ARCRD Rafael Devers 30.00 80.00
ARCMKE Max Kepler 40.00 100.00

2020 Topps Definitive Collection Autograph Ultra Patches

DAUPPG Paul Goldschmidt/12
DAUPCCJ Chipper Jones/14
DAUPCCY Christian Yelich/10
DAUPCDO David Ortiz
DAUPCJS John Smoltz/13
DAUPCKH Keston Hiura/8
DAUPCMT Mike Trout/12
DAUPCRH Rhys Hoskins/12
DAUPCWB Walker Buehler/9
DAUPCXB Xander Bogaerts/14

2020 Topps Definitive Collection Autographs

RANDOM INSERTS IN PACKS
PRINT RUN BTW 5-50 COPIES PER
NO PRICING QTY 15 OR LESS
EXCHANGE DEADLINE 3/31/2022
DCAAP Andy Pettitte/25 40.00 100.00
DCAAR Anthony Rizzo/25 50.00 120.00
DCABB Bo Bichette/35 125.00 300.00
DCABL Barry Larkin/25 30.00 80.00
DCACC CC Sabathia/25 40.00 100.00
DCADE Dennis Eckersley/25 20.00 50.00
DCADM Dale Murphy/50 40.00 100.00
DCAEJ Pete Alonso/35 75.00 200.00
DCAFL Francisco Lindor/25 75.00 200.00
DCAFT Frank Thomas/35 50.00 120.00
DCAGS Fernando Tatis Jr./35 125.00 300.00
DCAJA Jose Altuve/25 40.00 100.00
DCAJS Juan Soto/35 150.00 400.00
DCAJT Jim Thome/50 30.00 80.00
DCALS Luis Severino/50 15.00 40.00
DCAOS Ozzie Smith/25 50.00 120.00
DCARA Roberto Alomar/25 30.00 80.00
DCARD Rafael Devers/35 25.00 60.00
DCARH Rhys Hoskins/25 50.00 120.00
DCARJ Reggie Jackson/25 40.00 100.00
DCASK Sandy Koufax
DCATG Tom Glavine/50 30.00 80.00
DCAVG Vladimir Guerrero/35 40.00 100.00
DCAWC Will Clark/35 30.00 80.00
DCAXB Xander Bogaerts/50 60.00 150.00
DCAABR Yordan Alvarez 75.00 200.00
DCACKL Christian Yelich/25 60.00 150.00
DCADMA Don Mattingly/35 60.00 150.00
DCAICH Ichiro/5
DCAJDE Jacob deGrom/50 125.00 300.00
DCAJSM John Smoltz/50 25.00 60.00
DCAMCA Miguel Cabrera/35 75.00 200.00
DCARAJ Ronald Acuna Jr./35 150.00 400.00

2020 Topps Definitive Collection Definitive Autograph Relics

RANDOM INSERTS IN PACKS
PRINT RUN BTW 5-50 COPIES PER
NO PRICING QTY 15 OR LESS
EXCHANGE DEADLINE 3/31/2022
DARCAN Andy Pettitte/50 30.00 80.00
DARCAP Andy Pettitte/50 30.00 80.00
DARCBL Barry Larkin/50 36.00 60.00
DARCBW Bernie Williams/50 30.00 80.00
DARCCF Carlton Fisk/25 30.00 80.00
DARCCJ Chipper Jones/25 75.00 200.00
DARCCR Cal Ripken Jr./25 50.00 120.00
DARCCY Carl Yastrzemski/25 40.00 100.00
DARCDM Don Mattingly/50 75.00 200.00
DARCDS Darryl Strawberry/50 25.00 60.00
DARCFM Fred McGriff/50 30.00 80.00
DARCFT Frank Thomas/50 40.00 100.00
DARCHM Hideki Matsui/25 40.00 100.00
DARCJB Johnny Bench/25 50.00 120.00
DARCJC Jose Canseco/50 30.00 80.00
DARCJP Jorge Posada/50 25.00 60.00
DARCJS John Smoltz/50 20.00 50.00
DARCJT Jim Thome/50 30.00 80.00
DARCMM Mark McGwire/25 50.00 120.00
DARCNG Nomar Garciaparra/50 25.00 60.00
DARCNR Nolan Ryan/25 100.00 250.00
DARCOS Ozzie Smith/25 30.00 80.00
DARCPM Pedro Martinez/25 50.00 120.00
DARCRA Roberto Alomar/50 20.00 50.00
DARCRH Rickey Henderson/25 50.00 120.00
DARCRJ Randy Johnson/25 50.00 120.00
DARCRS Ryne Sandberg/25 40.00 100.00
DARCRY Robin Yount/50 30.00 80.00
DARCSC Steve Carlton/50 25.00 60.00
DARCTG Tom Glavine/50 25.00 60.00
DARCTR Tim Raines/50 20.00 50.00
DARCVG Vladimir Guerrero/50 30.00 80.00
DARCWB Wade Boggs/25 30.00 80.00
DARCWC Will Clark/50 30.00 80.00
DARCCFI Carlton Fisk/50 25.00 60.00
DARCDMU Dale Murphy/50 25.00 60.00
DARCJBA Jeff Bagwell/50 30.00 80.00
DARCJTH Jim Thome/50 30.00 80.00
DARCNRY Nolan Ryan/25 100.00 250.00
DARCRCA Rod Carew/50 20.00 50.00
DARCRJA Reggie Jackson/25 40.00 100.00
DARCWBO Wade Boggs/25 30.00 80.00
DARCRCAR Rod Carew/50 20.00 50.00
DARCRJAC Reggie Jackson/25 40.00 100.00

2020 Topps Definitive Collection Dual Autograph Relics

RANDOM INSERTS IN PACKS
PRINT RUN BTW 10-35 COPIES PER
NO PRICING QTY 15 OR LESS
EXCHANGE DEADLINE 3/31/2022
DARAC G.Cole/J.Altuve 40.00 100.00
DARAR N.Arenado/B.Rodgers 50.00 120.00
DARAS G.Springer/J.Altuve 40.00 100.00
DARBB X.Bogaerts/A.Benintendi 75.00 200.00
DARDA P.Alonso/J.deGrom 125.00 300.00
DARDB R.Devers/X.Bogaerts 75.00 200.00
DARDF J.Flaherty/P.DeJong 30.00 80.00
DARDR A.Riley/D.Swanson 30.00 80.00
DARGB B.Bichette/V.Guerrero Jr. 300.00 600.00
DARGT K.Griffey Jr./M.Trout
DARHN R.Hoskins/A.Nola 50.00 120.00
DARHY K.Hiura/C.Yelich 100.00 250.00
DARJY Y.Alvarez/J.Altuve 60.00 150.00
DARNA N.Senzel/A.Aquino 60.00 150.00
DAROD R.Devers/D.Ortiz 75.00 200.00
DARSA G.Springer/Y.Alvarez 50.00 120.00
DARSM B.Snell/B.McKay 30.00 80.00
DARTP F.Tatis Jr./C.Paddack 150.00 400.00
DARTS M.Teixeira/C.Sabathia 50.00 120.00
DARVS J.Votto/N.Senzel 60.00 150.00
DARYH R.Yount/K.Hiura 60.00 150.00

2020 Topps Definitive Collection Dual Autographs

RANDOM INSERTS IN PACKS
PRINT RUN BTW 5-50 COPIES PER
NO PRICING QTY 15 OR LESS
EXCHANGE DEADLINE 3/31/2022
DACAL R.Alomar/F.Lindor 75.00 200.00
DACAS J.Soto/R.Acuna Jr. 400.00 800.00
DACBA J.Bagwell/J.Altuve
DACBD R.Devers/X.Bogaerts 60.00 150.00
DACBR A.Rizzo/K.Bryant 75.00 200.00
DACCE D.Eckersley/J.Canseco 40.00 100.00
DACCN A.Nola/S.Carlton 60.00 150.00
DACDA J.deGrom/P.Alonso 125.00 300.00
DACFV J.Varitek/C.Fisk 60.00 150.00
DACGB V.Guerrero Jr./B.Bichette 150.00 400.00
DACJY J.Altuve/Y.Alvarez 75.00 200.00
DACKC M.Cabrera/A.Kaline 150.00 400.00
DACMC M.McGwire/W.Clark 75.00 200.00
DACMJ C.Jones/D.Murphy 125.00 300.00
DACML G.Lux/M.Muncy 60.00 150.00
DACMS C.Sale/J.Martinez 30.00 80.00
DACMT D.Mattingly/G.Torres 200.00 500.00
DACNR N.Ryan/R.Carew 100.00 250.00
DACPC W.Clark/B.Posey 100.00 250.00
DACPM M.Mussina/A.Pettitte 60.00 150.00
DACRC G.Cole/N.Ryan 125.00 300.00
DACSA P.Alonso/D.Strawberry 100.00 250.00
DACSG P.Goldschmidt/O.Smith 60.00 150.00
DACSR R.Sandberg/A.Rizzo 75.00 200.00
DACTJ F.Thomas/E.Jimenez 100.00 250.00
DACVA A.Aquino/J.Votto 60.00 150.00
DACVF V.Guerrero Jr./F.Tatis Jr. 400.00 1000.00
DACYY R.Yount/C.Yelich 100.00 250.00

2020 Topps Definitive Collection Framed Autograph Patches

RANDOM INSERTS IN PACKS
PRINT RUN BTW 10 25 COPIES PER
NO PRICING QTY 15 OR LESS
EXCHANGE DEADLINE 3/31/2022
FACAB Andrew Benintendi/25
FACGC Gerrit Cole/25 40.00 100.00
FACKH Keston Hiura/25 60.00 150.00
FACNA Nolan Arenado EXCH/30 50.00 120.00
FACWB Walker Buehler/25 60.00 150.00

2020 Topps Definitive Collection Framed Autographs

RANDOM INSERTS IN PACKS
PRINT RUN BTW 5-50 COPIES PER
NO PRICING QTY 15 OR LESS
EXCHANGE DEADLINE 3/31/2022
DCFAAA Aristides Aquino/30 40.00 100.00
DCFABB Bo Bichette/30 125.00 300.00
DCFACJ Chipper Jones/30 60.00 150.00
DCFACS Chris Sale/30 25.00 60.00
DCFACY Christian Yelich/30 60.00 150.00
DCFADM Don Mattingly/30 60.00 150.00
DCFAFL Francisco Lindor/30 40.00 100.00
DCFAFT Frank Thomas/30 50.00 120.00
DCFAGL Gavin Lux/30 100.00 250.00
DCFAGT Gleyber Torres/30 100.00 250.00
DCFAHM Hideki Matsui/30 50.00 120.00
DCFAJA Jose Altuve/30 20.00 50.00
DCFAJB Jeff Bagwell/30 40.00 100.00
DCFAJD Jacob deGrom/30 40.00 100.00
DCFAJS Juan Soto/30 75.00 200.00
DCFAMM Mark McGwire/30 50.00 120.00
DCFANR Nolan Ryan/30 75.00 200.00
DCFAOS Ozzie Smith/30 30.00 80.00
DCFAPA Pete Alonso/30 100.00 250.00
DCFAPG Paul Goldschmidt/30 25.00 60.00
DCFARD Rafael Devers/30 25.00 60.00
DCFARH Rickey Henderson/30 40.00 100.00
DCFARS Ryne Sandberg/30 50.00 120.00
DCFAWC Will Clark/30 30.00 80.00
DCFAYA Yordan Alvarez/30 100.00 250.00
DCFAARI Anthony Rizzo/30 40.00 100.00
DCFACRJ Cal Ripken Jr./30 60.00 150.00
DCFACYA Carl Yastrzemski/30 50.00 120.00
DCFAFTJ Fernando Tatis Jr./30 200.00 500.00
DCFARAJ Ronald Acuna Jr./30 125.00 300.00
DCFARHO Rhys Hoskins/30 25.00 60.00
DCFARJA Reggie Jackson/30 40.00 100.00

2020 Topps Definitive Collection Rookie Autographs

RANDOM INSERTS IN PACKS
STATED PRINT RUN 50 SER.#'d SETS
EXCHANGE DEADLINE 3/31/2022
DRAAA Aristides Aquino 40.00 100.00
DRAAP A.J. Puk 10.00 25.00
DRABB Bo Bichette 75.00 200.00
DRABM Brendan McKay 12.00 30.00
DRADC Dylan Cease 15.00 40.00
DRADM Dustin May 25.00 60.00
DRAGL Gavin Lux 75.00 200.00
DRAJL Jesus Luzardo 10.00 25.00
DRAJY Jordan Yamamoto 6.00 15.00
DRAKL Kyle Lewis 15.00 40.00
DRALR Luis Robert EXCH 150.00 400.00
DRANH Nico Hoerner 30.00 80.00
DRASM Sean Murphy 8.00 20.00
DRATG Trent Grisham 20.00 50.00
DRAYA Yordan Alvarez 75.00 200.00
DRAAAQ Aristides Aquino 40.00 100.00
DRAAPU A.J. Puk 10.00 25.00
DRABBI Bo Bichette 75.00 200.00
DRABMC Brendan McKay 12.00 30.00
DRABOB Bo Bichette 75.00 200.00
DRABRM Brendan McKay 12.00 30.00
DRADCE Dylan Cease 15.00 40.00
DRADMA Dustin May 25.00 60.00
DRAGLU Gavin Lux 75.00 200.00
DRAJLU Jesus Luzardo 10.00 25.00
DRAJOY Jordan Yamamoto 6.00 15.00
DRAKLE Kyle Lewis 15.00 40.00
DRALRO Luis Robert EXCH 150.00 400.00
DRALUZ Jesus Luzardo 10.00 25.00
DRANHO Nico Hoerner 30.00 80.00
DRANHR Nico Hoerner 30.00 80.00
DRASMU Sean Murphy 8.00 20.00
DRATGR Trent Grisham 20.00 50.00
DRAYAL Yordan Alvarez 75.00 200.00
DRAYOA Yordan Alvarez 75.00 200.00
DRAAAQU Aristides Aquino 40.00 100.00
DRAGLUX Gavin Lux 75.00 200.00

2020 Topps Definitive Collection Rookie Autographs Green

*GREEN: .5X TO 1.2X BASIC
RANDOM INSERTS IN PACKS
STATED PRINT RUN 25 SER.#'d SETS
EXCHANGE DEADLINE 3/31/2022
DRABB Bo Bichette 150.00 400.00
DRABBI Bo Bichette 150.00 400.00
DRABOB Bo Bichette 150.00 400.00

2020 Topps Definitive Collection Helmets

RANDOM INSERTS IN PACKS
STATED PRINT RUN 35 COPIES PER
DHCAR Anthony Rizzo 30.00 80.00
DHCEJ Eloy Jimenez 20.00 50.00
DHCFF Freddie Freeman 25.00 60.00
DHCFL Francisco Lindor 20.00 50.00
DHCGS George Springer 15.00 40.00
DHCJS Juan Soto 30.00 80.00
DHCKH Keston Hiura 20.00 50.00
DHCOA Ozzie Albies 20.00 50.00
DHCRH Rhys Hoskins 20.00 50.00
DHCTS Trevor Story 15.00 40.00

2020 Topps Definitive Collection Jumbo Relics

RANDOM INSERTS IN PACKS
PRINT RUN BTW 35-50 COPIES PER
DJRCAA Aristides Aquino/50 8.00 20.00
DJRCAB Alex Bregman/50 8.00 20.00
DJRCAE Adam Eaton/35 15.00 40.00
DJRCAM Adalberto Mondesi/35 8.00 20.00
DJRCAR Amed Rosario/35 5.00 12.00
DJRCBC Brandon Crawford/35 5.00 12.00
DJRCCS Chris Sale/50 8.00 20.00
DJRCDD David Dahl/50 4.00 10.00
DJRCDP Dustin Pedroia/35 8.00 20.00
DJRCEA Elvis Andrus/50 5.00 12.00
DJRCEE Eduardo Escobar/35 4.00 10.00
DJRCEL Evan Longoria/35 5.00 12.00
DJRCHD Hunter Dozier/35 4.00 10.00
DJRCHR Hunter Renfroe/35 4.00 10.00
DJRCJA Jose Altuve/50 8.00 20.00
DJRCJG Joey Gallo/45 6.00 15.00
DJRCJH Josh Hader/35 4.00 10.00
DJRCJM Jeff McNeil/35 5.00 12.00
DJRCJP Joc Pederson/50 5.00 12.00
DJRCJR Jose Ramirez/35 5.00 12.00
DJRCJS Jorge Soler/35 6.00 15.00
DJRCJT Julio Teheran/35 5.00 12.00
DJRCJV Joey Votto/50 12.00 30.00
DJRCKD Khris Davis/50 6.00 15.00
DJRCKK Kevin Kiermaier/35 5.00 12.00
DJRCKW Kolten Wong/35 5.00 12.00
DJRCLC Lorenzo Cain/35 4.00 10.00
DJRCLG Lucas Giolito/45 5.00 12.00
DJRCMC Michael Chavis/35 5.00 12.00
DJRCMK Max Kepler/50 5.00 12.00
DJRCMS Marcus Semien/35 4.00 10.00
DJRCMT Mike Trout/50 50.00 120.00
DJRCNS Nick Senzel/50 6.00 15.00
DJRCRB Ryan Braun/35 5.00 12.00
DJRCRC Robinson Cano/35 5.00 12.00
DJRCRD Rafael Devers/50 12.00 30.00
DJRCRZ Ryan Zimmerman/35 5.00 12.00
DJRCSP Stephen Piscotty/35 4.00 10.00
DJRCSS Stephen Strasburg/50 8.00 20.00
DJRCTP Tommy Pham/35 4.00 10.00
DJRCTS Trevor Story/50 6.00 15.00
DJRCTT Trea Turner/50 5.00 12.00
DJRCXB Xander Bogaerts/50 6.00 15.00
DJRCYG Yuli Gurriel/35 5.00 12.00
DJRCAMC Andrew McCutchen/50 15.00 40.00
DJRCDDO David Ortiz/50 12.00 30.00
DJRCJPA James Paxton/35 5.00 12.00
DJRCJTR J.T. Realmuto/50 10.00 25.00
DJRCLGR Lourdes Gurriel Jr./35 5.00 12.00
DJRCMCO Michael Conforto/50 5.00 12.00
DJRCMSA Miguel Sano/50 5.00 12.00
DJRCMTE Mark Teixeira/35 5.00 12.00
DJRCYGR Yasmani Grandal 4.00 10.00

2020 Topps Definitive Collection Jumbo Relics Blue

*BLUE/29-30: .4X TO 1X BASIC
*BLUE/20: .5X TO 1.2X BASIC
RANDOM INSERTS IN PACKS
PRINT RUN BTW 20-30 COPIES PER
EXCHANGE DEADLINE 3/31/2022
DJRCAM Adalberto Mondesi/30 10.00 25.00
DJRCMT Mike Trout/30 125.00 300.00
DJRCAMC Andrew McCutchen/30 25.00 60.00
DJRCDDO David Ortiz/30 20.00 50.00

2020 Topps Definitive Collection Legendary Autographs

RANDOM INSERTS IN PACKS
PRINT RUN BTW 5-50 COPIES PER
NO PRICING QTY 15 OR LESS
EXCHANGE DEADLINE 3/31/2022
LACAD Andre Dawson/35 20.00 50.00
LACAK Al Kaline/35 40.00 100.00
LACAP Andy Pettitte/35 25.00 60.00
LACAR Alex Rodriguez
LACBL Barry Larkin/25 30.00 80.00
LACBW Bernie Williams/50 25.00 60.00
LACCF Carlton Fisk/35 20.00 50.00
LACCJ Chipper Jones/25 75.00 200.00
LACCR Cal Ripken Jr./25 75.00 200.00
LACCY Carl Yastrzemski/25 60.00 150.00
LACDE Dennis Eckersley/35 15.00 40.00
LACDM Dale Murphy/35 40.00 100.00
LACFM Fred McGriff/50 25.00 60.00
LACFT Frank Thomas/35 50.00 120.00
LACJB Johnny Bench/25 50.00 120.00
LACJM Juan Marichal/50 30.00 80.00
LACJS John Smoltz/35 25.00 60.00
LACJT Jim Thome/35 30.00 80.00
LACLB Lou Brock/35 25.00 60.00
LACMM Mike Mussina/35 30.00 80.00
LACNG Nomar Garciaparra/50 25.00 60.00
LACNR Nolan Ryan/25 100.00 250.00
LACOS Ozzie Smith/35 30.00 80.00
LACRA Roberto Alomar/35 25.00 60.00
LACRC Rod Carew/35 30.00 80.00
LACRS Ryne Sandberg/25 50.00 120.00
LACRY Robin Yount/25 40.00 100.00
LACSC Steve Carlton/35 20.00 50.00
LACTG Tom Glavine/50 30.00 80.00
LACWB Wade Boggs/35 30.00 80.00
LACWC Will Clark/35 30.00 80.00
LACDMA Don Mattingly/35 60.00 150.00
LACDST Darryl Strawberry/50 25.00 60.00
LACICH Ichiro
LACJBA Jeff Bagwell/50 40.00 100.00
LACMMC Mark McGwire/25 50.00 120.00
LACRJA Reggie Jackson/25 40.00 100.00

2017 Topps Diamond Icons Autographs

STATED PRINT RUN 25 SER.#'d SETS
EXCHANGE DEADLINE 9/30/2019
AUAB Andrew Benintendi RC 30.00 80.00
AUABE Adrian Beltre 60.00 150.00
AUABR Alex Bregman RC 25.00 60.00
AUAG Andres Galarraga 8.00 20.00
AUAJU Aaron Judge RC 250.00 500.00
AUAK Al Kaline 25.00 50.00
AUAP Andy Pettitte 20.00 50.00
AUAPU Albert Pujols
AUAR Alex Reyes RC 12.00 30.00
AUARI Anthony Rizzo 30.00 80.00
AUARO Alex Rodriguez
AUBA Bobby Abreu 10.00 25.00
AUBB Barry Bonds 75.00 200.00
AUBH Bryce Harper
AUBJ Bo Jackson 40.00 100.00
AUBL Barry Larkin 20.00 50.00
AUBP Buster Posey
AUCB Craig Biggio 12.00 30.00
AUCBE Cody Bellinger RC 60.00 150.00
AUCC Carlos Correa 40.00 100.00
AUCJ Chipper Jones 40.00 100.00
AUCK Clayton Kershaw 60.00 150.00
AUCR Cal Ripken Jr.
AUCS Chris Sale 20.00 50.00
AUCSC Curt Schilling 20.00 50.00
AUCSE Corey Seager 25.00 60.00
AUCY Carl Yastrzemski
AUDD David Dahl RC 10.00 25.00
AUDJ Derek Jeter
AUDM Don Mattingly 40.00 100.00
AUDO David Ortiz 30.00 80.00
AUDP Dustin Pedroia 12.00 30.00
AUDPR David Price 8.00 20.00

AUDSW Dansby Swanson RC 15.00 40.00
AUDW David Wright 15.00 40.00
AUFB Franklin Barreto RC 6.00 15.00
AUFL Francisco Lindor 20.00 50.00
AUFR Frank Robinson 15.00 40.00
AUFT Frank Thomas 30.00 80.00
AUGM Greg Maddux
AUGS George Springer 12.00 30.00
AUHA Hank Aaron
AUHM Hideki Matsui 75.00 200.00
AUIH Ian Happ RC 25.00 60.00
AUIR Ivan Rodriguez 15.00 40.00
AUI Ichiro
AUJAU Jose Altuve 30.00 80.00
AUJB Jeff Bagwell 20.00 50.00
AUJBE Johnny Bench
AUJD Jacob deGrom 15.00 40.00
AUJDO Josh Donaldson 25.00 60.00
AUJH Jason Heyward 25.00 60.00
AUJS John Smoltz 12.00 30.00
AUJT Jim Thome 60.00 150.00
AUJU Julio Urias 10.00 25.00
AUJV Jason Varitek 20.00 50.00
AUKB Kris Bryant 75.00 200.00
AUKM Kenta Maeda 12.00 30.00
AUKS Kyle Schwarber 10.00 25.00
AULG Lucas Giolito 8.00 20.00
AULW Luke Weaver RC 15.00 40.00
AUMF Michael Fulmer 6.00 15.00
AUMM Manny Machado 15.00 40.00
AUMMC Mark McGwire 50.00 120.00
AUMP Mike Piazza
AUMT Masahiro Tanaka
AUMTR Mike Trout 400.00 800.00
AUNM Nomar Mazara 6.00 15.00
AUNR Nolan Ryan 75.00 200.00
AUNS Noah Syndergaard 15.00 40.00
AUOS Ozzie Smith 20.00 50.00
AUOV Omar Vizquel 8.00 20.00
AUPG Paul Goldschmidt 25.00 60.00
AURCL Roger Clemens
AURCR Rod Carew 25.00 60.00
AURH Rickey Henderson
AURJ Reggie Jackson
AURJO Randy Johnson
AURS Ryne Sandberg 20.00 50.00
AUSC Steve Carlton 12.00 30.00
AUSK Sandy Koufax
AUTG Tom Glavine 12.00 30.00
AUTR Tim Raines 12.00 30.00
AUTS Trevor Story 10.00 25.00
AUWB Wade Boggs
AUYG Yulieski Gurriel RC 12.00 30.00
AUYMO Yoan Moncada RC 60.00 150.00

2017 Topps Diamond Icons Authenticated Jumbo Patch Autographs

STATED PRINT RUN 25 SER.#'d SETS
EXCHANGE DEADLINE 9/30/2019
JPAAB Andrew Benintendi
JPAABR Alex Bregman
JPAAJ Adam Jones 25.00 60.00
JPAAP Andy Pettitte
JPAAPU Albert Pujols
JPAARI Anthony Rizzo
JPABH Bryce Harper
JPABP Buster Posey 100.00 250.00
JPACC Carlos Correa 100.00 250.00
JPACJ Chipper Jones 75.00 200.00
JPACK Clayton Kershaw
JPACSE Corey Seager
JPADJ Derek Jeter
JPADO David Ortiz 75.00 200.00
JPADP Dustin Pedroia 30.00 80.00
JPADPR David Price
JPAFL Francisco Lindor
JPAFT Frank Thomas 75.00 200.00
JPAIR Ivan Rodriguez 25.00 60.00
JPAI Ichiro 250.00 400.00
JPAJA Jose Altuve
JPAJB Jeff Bagwell
JPAJD Josh Donaldson
JPAJd Jacob deGrom 30.00 80.00
JPAJS John Smoltz
JPAJT Jim Thome
JPAKB Kris Bryant
JPAKM Kenta Maeda
JPAMP Mike Piazza
JPAMT Masahiro Tanaka 100.00 250.00
JPAMTR Mike Trout
JPANS Noah Syndergaard
JPAPM Pedro Martinez
JPATG Tom Glavine
JPATR Tim Raines
JPATS Trevor Story

2017 Topps Diamond Icons Diamond Autographs

STATED PRINT RUN 25 SER.#'d SETS
EXCHANGE DEADLINE 9/30/2019
DAAB Alex Bregman 40.00 100.00
DAABE Andrew Benintendi 60.00 150.00
DAAG Andres Galarraga 8.00 20.00
DAAJ Aaron Judge 350.00 700.00
DAAP Andy Pettitte 20.00 50.00
DAARE Alex Reyes 12.00 30.00
DAARI Anthony Rizzo 30.00 80.00
DABA Bobby Abreu 10.00 25.00
DACB Craig Biggio
DACC Carlos Correa 30.00 80.00
DACK Clayton Kershaw 60.00 510.00
DACS Chris Sale 20.00 50.00
DACSC Curt Schilling 20.00 50.00
DACSE Corey Seager 60.00 150.00
DADJ Derek Jeter
DADM Don Mattingly 40.00 100.00
DADO David Ortiz 50.00 120.00
DADP David Price 8.00 20.00
DADS Dansby Swanson 25.00 60.00
DAFL Francisco Lindor 40.00 100.00
DAIR Ivan Rodriguez 15.00 40.00
DAJBA Jeff Bagwell 30.00 80.00
DAJD Jacob deGrom 15.00 40.00
DAJS John Smoltz 20.00 50.00
DAJU Julio Urias 10.00 25.00
DAJV Jason Varitek 50.00 120.00
DAKB Kris Bryant
DAKM Kenta Maeda 12.00 30.00
DAKS Kyle Schwarber 20.00 50.00
DAMM Mark McGwire 50.00 120.00
DAMT Mike Trout 250.00 500.00
DANR Nolan Ryan 75.00 200.00
DANS Noah Syndergaard 15.00 40.00
DAOS Ozzie Smith 20.00 50.00
DAOV Omar Vizquel 12.00 30.00
DATG Tom Glavine 20.00 50.00
DATS Trevor Story 10.00 25.00
DAYG Yulieski Gurriel 12.00 30.00
DAYM Yoan Moncada 60.00 150.00

2017 Topps Diamond Icons Red Ink Autographs

STATED PRINT RUN 25 SER.#'d SETS
EXCHANGE DEADLINE 9/30/2019
RAAB Andrew Benintendi 25.00 60.00
RAABE Adrian Beltre 50.00 120.00
RAABR Alex Bregman 40.00 100.00
RAAG Andres Galarraga 8.00 20.00
RAAJU Aaron Judge 350.00 700.00
RAAK Al Kaline 25.00 50.00
RAAP Andy Pettitte 20.00 50.00
RAAPU Albert Pujols
RAAR Alex Reyes 12.00 30.00
RAARI Anthony Rizzo 30.00 80.00
RAARO Alex Rodriguez
RABA Bobby Abreu 10.00 25.00
RABH Bryce Harper
RABJ Bo Jackson 30.00 80.00
RABL Barry Larkin 20.00 50.00
RABP Buster Posey
RACB Craig Biggio 20.00 50.00
RACBE Cody Bellinger
RACC Carlos Correa 30.00 80.00
RACJ Chipper Jones 40.00 100.00
RACK Clayton Kershaw 60.00 150.00
RACR Cal Ripken Jr.
RACS Chris Sale 20.00 50.00
RACSC Curt Schilling 10.00 25.00
RACSE Corey Seager 40.00 100.00
RACY Carl Yastrzemski
RADD David Dahl 10.00 25.00
RADJ Derek Jeter
RADM Don Mattingly 40.00 100.00
RADO David Ortiz 20.00 50.00
RADP Dustin Pedroia 12.00 30.00
RADPO David Price 8.00 20.00
RADSW Dansby Swanson 15.00 40.00
RADW David Wright 8.00 20.00
RAFB Franklin Barreto 6.00 15.00
RAFL Francisco Lindor 40.00 100.00
RAFR Frank Robinson
RAFT Frank Thomas 30.00 80.00
RAGM Greg Maddux
RAGS George Springer 12.00 30.00
RAHA Hank Aaron
RAHM Hideki Matsui 75.00 200.00
RAIR Ivan Rodriguez 15.00 40.00
RAI Ichiro
RAJA Jose Altuve 30.00 80.00
RAJB Jeff Bagwell 15.00 40.00
RAJBE Johnny Bench
RAJD Jacob deGrom 15.00 40.00
RAJDO Josh Donaldson 25.00 60.00
RAJH Jason Heyward
RAJS John Smoltz 20.00 50.00
RAJT Jim Thome 40.00 100.00
RAJU Julio Urias 10.00 25.00
RAJV Jason Varitek 20.00 50.00
RAKB Kris Bryant
RAKM Kenta Maeda 12.00 30.00
RAKS Kyle Schwarber 10.00 25.00
RALG Lucas Giolito 8.00 20.00
RALW Luke Weaver 15.00 40.00
RAMF Michael Fulmer 15.00 40.00
RAMM Manny Machado 15.00 40.00
RAMMC Mark McGwire 50.00 120.00
RAMP Mike Piazza
RAMT Masahiro Tanaka
RAMTR Mike Trout 250.00 500.00
RANM Nomar Mazara
RANR Nolan Ryan 75.00 200.00
RANS Noah Syndergaard 30.00 80.00
RAOS Ozzie Smith 20.00 50.00
RAOV Omar Vizquel 8.00 20.00
RAPG Paul Goldschmidt 25.00 60.00
RARCL Roger Clemens
RARCR Rod Carew 25.00 60.00
RARH Rickey Henderson
RARJ Reggie Jackson
RARJO Randy Johnson
RARS Ryne Sandberg 20.00 50.00
RASC Steve Carlton 12.00 30.00
RASK Sandy Koufax
RATG Tom Glavine 10.00 25.00
RATR Tim Raines 12.00 30.00
RATS Trevor Story 10.00 25.00
RAWB Wade Boggs
RAYG Yulieski Gurriel 12.00 30.00
RAYMN Yoan Moncada 30.00 80.00

2018 Topps Diamond Icons Autographs

RANDOM INSERTS IN PACKS
STATED PRINT RUN 25 SER.#'d SETS
EXCHANGE DEADLINE 7/31/2020
ACAB Alex Bregman 25.00 60.00
ACAD Andre Dawson 20.00 50.00
ACAJU Aaron Judge 125.00 300.00
ACAK Al Kaline 40.00 100.00
ACAP Andy Pettitte 15.00 40.00
ACAR Addison Russell 8.00 20.00
ACARI Anthony Rizzo 30.00 80.00
ACARO Alex Rodriguez 100.00 250.00
ACARS Amed Rosario RC 10.00 25.00
ACBH Bryce Harper
ACBJ Bo Jackson 40.00 100.00
ACBL Barry Larkin 20.00 50.00
ACBP Buster Posey 40.00 100.00
ACBW Bernie Williams 15.00 40.00
ACCBI Craig Biggio 15.00 40.00
ACCF Clint Frazier RC 20.00 50.00
ACCJ Chipper Jones 40.00 100.00
ACCK Corey Kluber 12.00 30.00
ACCKE Clayton Kershaw 50.00 120.00
ACCKI Craig Kimbrel 12.00 30.00
ACCS Chris Sale 20.00 50.00
ACDE Dennis Eckersley 15.00 40.00
ACDMA Don Mattingly 40.00 100.00
ACDO David Ortiz 30.00 80.00
ACDS Dominic Smith RC 6.00 15.00
ACDW Dave Winfield 12.00 30.00
ACEM Edgar Martinez 25.00 60.00
ACFF Freddie Freeman 30.00 80.00
ACFL Francisco Lindor 25.00 60.00
ACFT Frank Thomas 30.00 60.00
ACGM Greg Maddux 50.00 120.00
ACGS Gary Sanchez 15.00 40.00
ACGT Gleyber Torres RC 125.00 300.00
ACHA Hank Aaron 150.00 400.00
ACHM Hideki Matsui 60.00 150.00
ACIH Ian Happ 8.00 20.00
ACI Ichiro 200.00 400.00
ACJA Jose Altuve 25.00 60.00
ACJB Javier Baez 50.00 120.00
ACJBA Jeff Bagwell 20.00 50.00
ACJBE Johnny Bench 40.00 100.00
ACJC Jose Canseco 12.00 30.00
ACJD Jacob deGrom 20.00 50.00
ACJDA Johnny Damon
ACJP Jim Palmer 15.00 40.00
ACJR Jose Ramirez 20.00 50.00
ACJS John Smoltz 25.00 60.00
ACJV Joey Votto 30.00 80.00
ACKS Kyle Schwarber 10.00 25.00
ACLB Lou Brock 15.00 40.00
ACLS Luis Severino 15.00 40.00
ACMM Manny Machado 25.00 60.00
ACMMC Mark McGwire 40.00 100.00
ACMR Mariano Rivera
ACNG Nomar Garciaparra
ACNR Nolan Ryan 75.00 200.00
ACNS Noah Syndergaard 15.00 40.00
ACOA Ozzie Albies RC 30.00 80.00
ACOC Orlando Cepeda 12.00 30.00
ACOS Ozzie Smith 25.00 60.00
ACPG Paul Goldschmidt 20.00 50.00
ACPM Pedro Martinez 50.00 120.00
ACRA Ronald Acuna RC 150.00 400.00
ACRAL Roberto Alomar 12.00 30.00
ACRC Rod Carew 30.00 80.00
ACRD Rafael Devers RC 20.00 50.00
ACRH Rickey Henderson 40.00 100.00
ACRHO Rhys Hoskins RC 40.00 100.00
ACRJ Reggie Jackson 30.00 80.00
ACRJO Randy Johnson
ACRS Ryne Sandberg 25.00 60.00
ACRY Robin Yount 25.00 60.00
ACSC Steve Carlton 15.00 40.00
ACSK Sandy Koufax
ACSO Shohei Ohtani RC 400.00 800.00
ACTG Tom Glavine 15.00 40.00
ACTS Tom Seaver 50.00 120.00
ACVR Victor Robles RC 20.00 50.00
ACWB Wade Boggs 20.00 50.00
ACWC Willson Contreras 10.00 25.00

2018 Topps Diamond Icons Diamond Autographs

RANDOM INSERTS IN PACKS
STATED PRINT RUN 25 SER.#'d SETS
EXCHANGE DEADLINE 7/31/2020
DAAJ Aaron Judge 125.00 300.00
DAAK Al Kaline 40.00 100.00
DAAR Amed Rosario 12.00 30.00
DAARI Anthony Rizzo 30.00 80.00
DABJ Bo Jackson 40.00 100.00
DABL Barry Larkin 20.00 50.00
DACF Clint Frazier 20.00 50.00
DACJ Chipper Jones 50.00 120.00
DACR Cal Ripken Jr. 50.00 120.00
DACS Chris Sale 15.00 40.00
DADJ Derek Jeter
DADM Don Mattingly 50.00 120.00
DADO David Ortiz 30.00 80.00
DAFF Freddie Freeman 30.00 80.00
DAFL Francisco Lindor 25.00 60.00
DAFT Frank Thomas 40.00 100.00
DAGSA Gary Sanchez 25.00 60.00
DAGT Gleyber Torres 125.00 300.00
DAHA Hank Aaron 150.00 400.00
DAI Ichiro 200.00 400.00
DAJA Jose Altuve 25.00 60.00
DAJC Jose Canseco 25.00 60.00
DAJS John Smoltz 25.00 60.00
DAJV Joey Votto 30.00 80.00
DAKB Kris Bryant 75.00 200.00
DAKS Kyle Schwarber 20.00 50.00
DALS Luis Severino 15.00 40.00
DAMG Mark McGwire 40.00 100.00
DAMM Manny Machado 25.00 60.00
DAMT Mike Trout
DANR Nolan Ryan 75.00 200.00
DANS Noah Syndergaard 25.00 60.00
DAOA Ozzie Albies 30.00 80.00
DAOS Ozzie Smith 25.00 60.00
DAPG Paul Goldschmidt 20.00 50.00
DARA Ronald Acuna 150.00 400.00
DARD Rafael Devers 20.00 50.00
DARH Rhys Hoskins 40.00 100.00
DASO Shohei Ohtani 400.00 800.00
DASOH Shohei Ohtani 400.00 800.00
DAVR Victor Robles 20.00 50.00

2018 Topps Diamond Icons Jumbo Patch Autographs

RANDOM INSERTS IN PACKS
STATED PRINT RUN 25 SER.#'d SETS
EXCHANGE DEADLINE 7/31/2020
AJPAAB Alex Bregman 50.00 120.00
AJPAAJ Adam Jones 30.00 80.00
AJPAAP Albert Pujols
AJPAAR Addison Russell 25.00 60.00
AJPAARI Anthony Rizzo 75.00 200.00
AJPAARO Amed Rosario
AJPABB Byron Buxton 30.00 80.00
AJPABH Bryce Harper
AJPABP Buster Posey 50.00 120.00
AJPACK Craig Kimbrel 25.00 60.00
AJPACKE Clayton Kershaw 75.00 200.00
AJPACKL Corey Kluber 40.00 100.00
AJPACS Chris Sale
AJPADG Didi Gregorius 25.00 60.00
AJPAFF Freddie Freeman 40.00 100.00
AJPAGS George Springer 25.00 60.00
AJPAGSA Gary Sanchez 30.00 80.00
AJPAIH Ian Happ 25.00 60.00
AJPAJA Jose Altuve 50.00 120.00
AJPAJB Javier Baez 75.00 200.00
AJPAJD Jacob deGrom 30.00 80.00
AJPAJDO Josh Donaldson 25.00 60.00
AJPAJV Joey Votto 50.00 120.00
AJPAKB Kris Bryant 125.00 300.00
AJPAKS Kyle Schwarber 40.00 100.00
AJPALS Luis Severino 25.00 60.00
AJPAMM Manny Machado 50.00 120.00
AJPAMT Mike Trout
AJPANS Noah Syndergaard 25.00 60.00
AJPAOA Ozzie Albies
AJPAPG Paul Goldschmidt 30.00 80.00
AJPARD Rafael Devers
AJPASM Starling Marte 25.00 60.00
AJPAVR Victor Robles
AJPAWC Willson Contreras
AJPAYMO Yadier Molina

2018 Topps Diamond Icons Red Ink Autographs

RANDOM INSERTS IN PACKS
STATED PRINT RUN 25 SER.#'d SETS
EXCHANGE DEADLINE 7/31/2020
RIAAB Alex Bregman 25.00 60.00
RIAAD Andre Dawson 10.00 25.00
RIAAK Al Kaline 40.00 100.00
RIAAP Andy Pettitte 15.00 40.00
RIAAR Addison Russell 8.00 20.00
RIAARI Anthony Rizzo 25.00 60.00
RIAARO Alex Rodriguez 60.00 150.00
RIAARS Amed Rosario 12.00 30.00
RIABG Bob Gibson 25.00 60.00
RIABH Bryce Harper
RIABJ Bo Jackson 40.00 100.00
RIABL Barry Larkin 20.00 50.00
RIABP Buster Posey 40.00 100.00
RIABR Brooks Robinson
RIABW Bernie Williams 15.00 40.00
RIACBI Craig Biggio 15.00 40.00
RIACF Clint Frazier 20.00 50.00
RIACJ Chipper Jones 50.00 120.00
RIACK Craig Kimbrel 15.00 40.00
RIACKE Clayton Kershaw 50.00 120.00
RIACKL Corey Kluber 12.00 30.00
RIACR Cal Ripken Jr. 50.00 120.00
RIACS Chris Sale 15.00 40.00
RIADE Dennis Eckersley 15.00 40.00
RIADG Didi Gregorius 20.00 50.00
RIADMA Don Mattingly 50.00 120.00
RIADO David Ortiz 30.00 80.00
RIADW Dave Winfield 12.00 30.00
RIAEM Edgar Martinez 25.00 60.00
RIAFF Freddie Freeman 30.00 80.00
RIAFL Francisco Lindor 25.00 60.00
RIAFT Frank Thomas 40.00 100.00
RIAGM Greg Maddux 50.00 120.00
RIAGSA Gary Sanchez 25.00 60.00
RIAGT Gleyber Torres 125.00 300.00
RIAHM Hideki Matsui 60.00 150.00
RIAIH Ian Happ 8.00 20.00
RIAI Ichiro 200.00 400.00
RIAJA Jose Altuve 25.00 60.00
RIAJB Jeff Bagwell 15.00 40.00
RIAJBE Johnny Bench 40.00 100.00
RIAJBU Javier Baez 50.00 120.00
RIAJC Jose Canseco 15.00 40.00
RIAJD Jacob deGrom 20.00 50.00
RIAJP Jim Palmer 15.00 40.00
RIAJS John Smoltz 15.00 40.00
RIAJU Justin Upton 10.00 25.00
RIAJV Joey Votto 30.00 80.00
RIAKB Kris Bryant 50.00 120.00
RIAKS Kyle Schwarber 20.00 50.00
RIALB Lou Brock 25.00 60.00
RIALS Luis Severino 15.00 40.00
RIAMM Manny Machado 25.00 60.00
RIAMMA Mark McGwire 40.00 100.00
RIANG Nomar Garciaparra
RIANR Nolan Ryan 75.00 200.00
RIANS Noah Syndergaard 12.00 30.00
RIAOA Ozzie Albies 30.00 80.00
RIAOC Orlando Cepeda 12.00 30.00
RIAOS Ozzie Smith 10.00 25.00
RIAPG Paul Goldschmidt 20.00 50.00
RIAPM Pedro Martinez 50.00 120.00
RIARA Ronald Acuna 150.00 400.00
RIARAL Roberto Alomar 10.00 25.00
RIARC Rod Carew 15.00 80.00
RIARD Rafael Devers 20.00 50.00
RIARH Rhys Hoskins 40.00 100.00
RIARHE Rickey Henderson 40.00 100.00
RIARJ Reggie Jackson 30.00 80.00
RIARS Ryne Sandberg 25.00 60.00
RIARY Robin Yount 25.00 60.00
RIASC Steve Carlton 15.00 40.00
RIASO Shohei Ohtani 400.00 800.00
RIATG Tom Glavine 12.00 30.00
RIATS Tom Seaver 50.00 120.00
RIAVR Victor Robles 20.00 50.00
RIAWB Wade Boggs 25.00 60.00
RIAWCL Will Clark 40.00 100.00
RIAWCO Willson Contreras 8.00 20.00
RIAYM Yadier Molina 50.00 120.00

2019 Topps Diamond Icons Autographs

RANDOM INSERTS IN PACKS
STATED PRINT RUN 25 SER.#'d SETS
EXCHANGE DEADLINE 6/30/2021
ACAD Andre Dawson 12.00 30.00
ACAJU Aaron Judge 100.00 250.00
ACAK Al Kaline 30.00 80.00
ACAP Andy Pettitte 12.00 30.00
ACARI Anthony Rizzo 30.00 80.00
ACARO Alex Rodriguez 50.00 120.00
ACBG Bob Gibson 15.00 40.00
ACBJ Bo Jackson 40.00 100.00
ACBL Barry Larkin 20.00 50.00
ACCF Carlton Fisk 30.00 80.00
ACCJ Chipper Jones 40.00 100.00
ACCK Corey Kluber 8.00 20.00
ACCKE Clayton Kershaw EXCH 60.00 150.00
ACCR Cal Ripken Jr. 50.00 120.00
ACCS Chris Sale 10.00 25.00
ACDE Dennis Eckersley 12.00 30.00
ACDMA Don Mattingly 40.00 100.00
ACDMU Dale Murphy 60.00 150.00
ACDO David Ortiz 25.00 60.00
ACDP Dustin Pedroia
ACEJ Eloy Jimenez RC 75.00 200.00
ACEM Edgar Martinez 25.00 60.00
ACFF Freddie Freeman 30.00 80.00
ACFL Francisco Lindor 25.00 60.00
ACFM Fred McGriff 15.00 40.00
ACFT Frank Thomas 30.00 80.00
ACFTJ Fernando Tatis Jr. RC 250.00 600.00
ACGSP George Springer 8.00 20.00
ACHA Hank Aaron
ACHM Hideki Matsui 50.00 120.00
ACI Ichiro 150.00 400.00
ACJA Jose Altuve 15.00 40.00
ACJBA Jeff Bagwell 15.00 40.00
ACJBE Johnny Bench 30.00 80.00
ACJC Jose Canseco 25.00 60.00
ACJD Jacob deGrom 15.00 40.00
ACJDA Johnny Damon 8.00 20.00
ACJM Juan Marichal 12.00 30.00
ACJP Jorge Posada 15.00 40.00
ACJS John Smoltz 20.00 50.00
ACJSO Juan Soto 40.00 100.00
ACJV Joey Votto 20.00 50.00
ACJVA Jason Varitek 20.00 50.00
ACKB Kris Bryant 60.00 150.00
ACKS Kyle Schwarber 12.00 30.00
ACKT Kyle Tucker RC 15.00 40.00
ACLB Lou Brock 20.00 50.00
ACLS Luis Severino 8.00 20.00
ACMA Miguel Andujar 50.00 120.00
ACMC Miguel Cabrera 50.00 120.00
ACMCA Matt Carpenter 10.00 25.00
ACMMC Mark McGwire 40.00 100.00
ACMP Mike Piazza 40.00 100.00
ACMT Mike Trout 300.00 500.00
ACMTA Masahiro Tanaka 15.00 40.00
ACNG Nomar Garciaparra 15.00 40.00
ACNR Nolan Ryan 60.00 150.00
ACNS Noah Syndergaard 15.00 40.00
ACOA Ozzie Albies 20.00 50.00
ACOS Ozzie Smith 25.00 60.00
ACPA Peter Alonso RC
ACPG Paul Goldschmidt 25.00 60.00
ACPM Pedro Martinez 30.00 80.00
ACRA Ronald Acuna Jr. 60.00 150.00
ACRAL Roberto Alomar 15.00 40.00
ACRC Rod Carew 20.00 50.00
ACRH Rickey Henderson 40.00 100.00
ACRHO Rhys Hoskins 25.00 60.00
ACRJ Reggie Jackson 25.00 60.00
ACRS Ryne Sandberg 30.00 80.00
ACRY Robin Yount 25.00 60.00
ACSC Steve Carlton 8.00 20.00
ACSK Sandy Koufax
ACSO Shohei Ohtani 150.00 400.00
ACTG Tom Glavine 15.00 40.00
ACVG Vladimir Guerrero 25.00 60.00
ACVGJ Vladimir Guerrero Jr. RC 250.00 500.00
ACVR Victor Robles 12.00 30.00
ACWB Wade Boggs 30.00 80.00
ACWC Willson Contreras 10.00 25.00
ACWCL Will Clark 25.00 60.00

2019 Topps Diamond Icons Diamond Icons Autographs

RANDOM INSERTS IN PACKS
STATED PRINT RUN 25 SER.#'d SETS
EXCHANGE DEADLINE 6/30/2021
DIAAJ Aaron Judge 100.00 250.00
DIAAK Al Kaline 30.00 80.00
DIAAZ Anthony Rizzo 30.00 80.00
DIABG Bob Gibson 30.00 80.00
DIABL Barry Larkin 20.00 50.00
DIABP Buster Posey 40.00 100.00
DIACJ Chipper Jones 40.00 100.00
DIACRJ Cal Ripken Jr. 50.00 120.00
DIACS Chris Sale 10.00 25.00
DIADJ Derek Jeter
DIADM Don Mattingly 40.00 100.00
DIAEJ Eloy Jimenez 75.00 200.00
DIAEM Edgar Martinez 25.00 60.00
DIAFF Freddie Freeman 30.00 80.00
DIAFL Francisco Lindor 25.00 60.00
DIAFT Frank Thomas 40.00 100.00
DIAFTJ Fernando Tatis Jr. 250.00 600.00
DIAHA Hank Aaron
DIAHM Hideki Matsui 50.00 120.00
DIAIS Ichiro 150.00 400.00
DIAJA Jose Altuve 15.00 40.00
DIAJB Johnny Bench 30.00 80.00
DIAJD Jacob deGrom 15.00 40.00
DIAJR Jose Ramirez 8.00 20.00
DIAJS Juan Soto 30.00 80.00
DIAJV Joey Votto 30.00 80.00
DIAKB Kris Bryant 60.00 150.00
DIAKS Kyle Schwarber 12.00 30.00
DIALB Lou Brock 15.00 40.00
DIAMT Mike Trout 300.00 500.00
DIANR Nolan Ryan 60.00 150.00
DIAOS Ozzie Smith 25.00 60.00
DIAPG Paul Goldschmidt 25.00 60.00
DIARAJ Ronald Acuna Jr. 60.00 150.00
DIARC Rod Carew 20.00 50.00
DIARH Rickey Henderson 40.00 100.00
DIARJ Reggie Jackson 25.00 60.00
DIARS Ryne Sandberg 30.00 80.00
DIARY Rhys Hoskins 25.00 60.00
DIASK Sandy Koufax
DIASO Shohei Ohtani 150.00 400.00
DIAVG Vladimir Guerrero Jr. 250.00 500.00
DIAWB Wade Boggs 30.00 80.00
DIAWI Will Clark 25.00 60.00

2019 Topps Diamond Icons Jumbo Patch Autographs

RANDOM INSERTS IN PACKS
STATED PRINT RUN 25 SER.#'d SETS
EXCHANGE DEADLINE 6/30/2021
AJPAD Adrian Beltre 30.00 80.00
AJPAJ Aaron Judge
AJPAN Aaron Nola EXCH 30.00 80.00
AJPAR Anthony Rizzo 40.00 100.00
AJPBP Buster Posey 60.00 150.00
AJPCB Charlie Blackmon 20.00 50.00
AJPCL Clayton Kershaw EXCH 60.00 150.00
AJPCS Chris Sale 20.00 50.00
AJPDP Dustin Pedroia
AJPFF Freddie Freeman 40.00 100.00
AJPFL Francisco Lindor 25.00 60.00
AJPGS George Springer 30.00 80.00
AJPJA Jose Altuve 40.00 100.00
AJPJD Jacob deGrom 25.00 60.00
AJPJR Jose Ramirez 20.00 50.00
AJPJS Juan Soto 75.00 200.00
AJPJU Justin Upton 20.00 50.00
AJPJV Joey Votto 40.00 100.00
AJPKB Kris Bryant 125.00 300.00
AJPKD Khris Davis EXCH 15.00 40.00
AJPKS Kyle Schwarber 30.00 80.00
AJPLS Luis Severino 20.00 50.00
AJPMA Matt Carpenter 25.00 60.00
AJPMC Miguel Cabrera 75.00 200.00
AJPMH Masahiro Tanaka
AJPMJ Miguel Andujar 15.00 40.00
AJPMP Matt Chapman EXCH 30.00 80.00
AJPMT Mike Trout 400.00 800.00
AJPNS Noah Syndergaard 15.00 40.00
AJPOA Ozzie Albies
AJPPG Paul Goldschmidt 40.00 100.00
AJPRY Rhys Hoskins
AJPSO Shohei Ohtani
AJPSP Salvador Perez 20.00 50.00
AJPTM Trey Mancini 20.00 50.00
AJPWC Willson Contreras 40.00 100.00
AJPWM Whit Merrifield 30.00 80.00
AJPYM Yadier Molina 25.00 60.00

2019 Topps Diamond Icons Red Ink Autographs

RANDOM INSERTS IN PACKS
STATED PRINT RUN 25 SER.#'d SETS
EXCHANGE DEADLINE 6/30/2021
RIAJ Aaron Judge 100.00 250.00
RIAK Al Kaline 30.00 80.00
RIAN Anthony Rizzo 30.00 80.00
RIAP Andy Pettitte 12.00 30.00
RIBG Bob Gibson 30.00 80.00
RIBL Barry Larkin 20.00 50.00
RIBP Buster Posey 40.00 100.00
RICF Carlton Fisk 30.00 80.00
RICJ Chipper Jones 40.00 100.00
RICR Cal Ripken Jr. 50.00 120.00
RICS Chris Sale 10.00 25.00
RIDE Dennis Eckersley 12.00 30.00
RIDJ Derek Jeter
RIDM Don Mattingly 40.00 100.00
RIDO David Ortiz 30.00 80.00
RIEM Edgar Martinez 25.00 60.00
RIFF Freddie Freeman 30.00 80.00
RIFL Francisco Lindor 25.00 60.00
RIFT Frank Thomas 40.00 100.00
RIGS George Springer 8.00 20.00
RIHM Hideki Matsui 50.00 120.00
RIIS Ichiro 150.00 400.00
RIJA Jose Altuve 15.00 40.00
RIJB Johnny Bench 30.00 80.00
RIJC Jose Canseco 25.00 60.00
RIJD Jacob deGrom 15.00 40.00
RIJM Juan Marichal 20.00 50.00
RIJO Johnny Damon 8.00 20.00
RIJS Jason Varitek 20.00 50.00
RIJU Juan Soto 30.00 80.00
RIJV Joey Votto 30.00 80.00
RIKB Kris Bryant 60.00 150.00
RIKS Kyle Schwarber 12.00 30.00
RILB Lou Brock 15.00 40.00
RILS Luis Severino 8.00 20.00
RIMM Mark McGwire 40.00 100.00
RIMP Mike Piazza 40.00 100.00
RIMR Mariano Rivera 125.00 300.00
RIMS Masahiro Tanaka 40.00 100.00
RING Nomar Garciaparra 15.00 40.00
RINR Nolan Ryan 60.00 150.00
RINS Noah Syndergaard 15.00 40.00
RIOA Ozzie Albies 20.00 50.00
RIOS Ozzie Smith 25.00 60.00
RIPG Paul Goldschmidt 15.00 40.00
RIPM Pedro Martinez 30.00 80.00
RIRA Ronald Acuna Jr. 60.00 150.00
RIRC Rod Carew 20.00 50.00
RIRH Rickey Henderson 40.00 100.00
RIRJ Reggie Jackson 25.00 60.00
RIRS Ryne Sandberg 30.00 80.00
RIRY Rhys Hoskins 25.00 60.00
RISO Shohei Ohtani 150.00 400.00
RITG Tom Glavine 15.00 40.00
RIWB Wade Boggs 15.00 40.00
RIWC Willson Contreras 20.00 50.00
RIWI Will Clark 25.00 60.00

2019 Topps Diamond Icons Silver Ink Autographs

RANDOM INSERTS IN PACKS
STATED PRINT RUN 25 SER.#'d SETS
EXCHANGE DEADLINE 6/30/2021
SIAK Al Kaline 30.00 80.00
SIAR Anthony Rizzo 30.00 80.00
SIBJ Bo Jackson 40.00 100.00
SIBL Barry Larkin 20.00 50.00
SIDM Don Mattingly 40.00 100.00
SIDO David Ortiz 25.00 60.00
SIEJ Eloy Jimenez 75.00 200.00
SIEM Edgar Martinez 25.00 60.00
SIFT Frank Thomas 40.00 100.00
SIHM Hideki Matsui 50.00 120.00
SIJD Jacob deGrom 15.00 40.00
SIJM Juan Marichal 20.00 50.00
SIJS Juan Soto 30.00 80.00
SIJV Jason Varitek 20.00 50.00
SIKB Kris Bryant 60.00 150.00
SIMA Miguel Andujar 15.00 40.00
SIMC Miguel Cabrera 50.00 120.00
SIMI Mike Trout 400.00 800.00
SIMT Masahiro Tanaka 40.00 100.00
SINR Nolan Ryan 60.00 150.00
SIOS Ozzie Smith 25.00 60.00
SIRA Roberto Alomar 15.00 40.00
SIRAJ Ronald Acuna Jr. 60.00 150.00
SIRC Rod Carew 20.00 50.00
SIRH Rhys Hoskins 25.00 60.00
SIRI Rickey Henderson 40.00 100.00
SIRS Ryne Sandberg 30.00 80.00
SIVG Vladimir Guerrero 25.00 60.00
SIVGJ Vladimir Guerrero Jr. 250.00 500.00

2020 Topps Diamond Icons Autographs

RANDOM INSERTS IN PACKS
PRINT RUN BTW 15-25 COPIES PER
NO PRICING QTY 15 OR LESS
EXCHANGE DEADLINE 5/31/2022
ACI Ichiro
ACAD Andre Dawson 25.00 60.00
ACAK Al Kaline 40.00 100.00
ACAP Andy Pettitte 25.00 60.00
ACBG Bob Gibson 30.00 80.00
ACBL Barry Larkin 25.00 60.00
ACCF Carlton Fisk 20.00 50.00
ACCJ Chipper Jones 50.00 120.00
ACCR Cal Ripken Jr. 60.00 150.00
ACCS Chris Sale 20.00 50.00
ACDE Dennis Eckersley 12.00 30.00
ACDO David Ortiz 50.00 120.00
ACEJ Eloy Jimenez 30.00 80.00
ACEM Edgar Martinez 15.00 40.00
ACFM Fred McGriff 20.00 50.00
ACFT Frank Thomas 40.00 100.00
ACGT Gleyber Torres 60.00 150.00
ACHA Hank Aaron
ACHM Hideki Matsui 40.00 100.00
ACJA Jose Altuve 15.00 40.00

ACJC Jose Canseco 20.00 50.00
ACJD Jacob deGrom 50.00 120.00
ACJM Juan Marichal 25.00 60.00
ACJS John Smoltz 25.00 60.00
ACJV Joey Votto 20.00 50.00
ACKB Kris Bryant 50.00 120.00
ACKH Christian Yelich 40.00 100.00
ACKS Kyle Schwarber 15.00 40.00
ACLB Lou Brock 20.00 50.00
ACLS DJ LeMahieu 30.00 80.00
ACMC Miguel Cabrera 60.00 150.00
ACMT Mike Trout
ACNG Nomar Garciaparra 25.00 60.00
ACNH Nico Hoerner RC 40.00 100.00
ACNR Nolan Ryan 75.00 200.00
ACOS Ozzie Smith 30.00 80.00
ACPA Pete Alonso 60.00 150.00
ACPG Paul Goldschmidt 20.00 50.00
ACRA Ronald Acuna Jr. 75.00 200.00
ACRC Rod Carew 25.00 60.00
ACRH Rickey Henderson 40.00 100.00
ACRJ Reggie Jackson 25.00 60.00
ACRS Ryne Sandberg 30.00 80.00
ACRY Robin Yount 40.00 100.00
ACSC Steve Carlton 25.00 60.00
ACSK Sandy Koufax
ACSO Shohei Ohtani
ACTG Tom Glavine 30.00 80.00
ACVG Vladimir Guerrero 30.00 80.00
ACWB Wade Boggs 30.00 80.00
ACWC Willson Contreras 20.00 50.00
ACYA Yordan Alvarez RC 75.00 200.00
ACAAQ Aristides Aquino RC 40.00 100.00
ACAJU Aaron Judge
ACARI Anthony Rizzo 30.00 80.00
ACARO Alex Rodriguez
ACBIC Bo Bichette RC EXCH 100.00 250.00
ACCKE Clayton Kershaw
ACDMA Don Mattingly 60.00 150.00
ACDMU Dale Murphy 30.00 80.00
ACDWR David Wright 30.00 80.00
ACFTJ Fernando Tatis Jr. 75.00 200.00
ACGCO Gerrit Cole 75.00 200.00
ACGLU Gavin Lux RC 75.00 200.00
ACGSP George Springer 15.00 40.00
ACJBA Jeff Bagwell 30.00 80.00
ACJBE Johnny Bench 30.00 80.00
ACJDA Johnny Damon 8.00 20.00
ACJLU Jesus Luzardo RC 12.00 30.00
ACJSO Juan Soto 60.00 150.00
ACJTH Jim Thome 30.00 80.00
ACJVA Jason Varitek 30.00 80.00
ACKGJ Ken Griffey Jr.
ACLRO Luis Robert RC 150.00 400.00
ACLUX Gavin Lux RC 75.00 200.00
ACMMC Mark McGwire 50.00 120.00
ACMSC Mike Schmidt 100.00 250.00
ACMTA Masahiro Tanaka
ACRAL Roberto Alomar 25.00 60.00
ACRCL Roger Clemens
ACRDE Rafael Devers 25.00 60.00
ACRHO Rhys Hoskins 40.00 100.00
ACRJO Randy Johnson
ACSBI Shane Bieber 20.00 50.00
ACSCH Max Scherzer 50.00 120.00
ACWBU Walker Buehler 30.00 80.00
ACWCL Will Clark 25.00 60.00
ACYAL Yordan Alvarez RC 75.00 200.00

2020 Topps Diamond Icons Diamond Icons Autographs

RANDOM INSERTS IN PACKS
STATED PRINT RUN 25 COPIES PER
EXCHANGE DEADLINE 5/31/2022

DIAAJ Aaron Judge 100.00 250.00
DIAAR Alex Rodriguez
DIABH Bryce Harper 125.00 300.00
DIABL Barry Larkin 25.00 60.00
DIACC CC Sabathia 30.00 80.00
DIACY Christian Yelich 40.00 100.00
DIADM Don Mattingly 60.00 150.00
DIADO David Ortiz 50.00 120.00
DIADS Darryl Strawberry 25.00 60.00
DIADW David Wright 30.00 80.00
DIAEJ Eloy Jimenez 30.00 80.00
DIAFT Frank Thomas 40.00 100.00
DIAGT Gleyber Torres 60.00 150.00
DIAHM Hideki Matsui 40.00 100.00
DIAIS Ichiro
DIAJF Jack Flaherty 25.00 60.00
DIAJS Juan Soto 60.00 150.00
DIAKH Keston Hiura 25.00 60.00
DIALR Luis Robert 150.00 400.00
DIAMM Mark McGwire 50.00 120.00
DIAMS Max Scherzer 50.00 120.00
DIAMT Mike Trout
DIANR Nolan Ryan 75.00 200.00
DIAOS Ozzie Smith 30.00 80.00
DIAPA Pete Alonso 60.00 150.00
DIARC Roger Clemens 30.00 80.00
DIARH Rickey Henderson 40.00 100.00
DIARY Robin Yount 40.00 100.00
DIASK Sandy Koufax
DIASO Shohei Ohtani
DIATL Tim Lincecum 75.00 200.00
DIAWB Walker Buehler 30.00 80.00
DIAAAQ Aristides Aquino 40.00 100.00
DIAANO Aaron Nola 30.00 80.00
DIABBI Bo Bichette EXCH 100.00 250.00
DIACRJ Cal Ripken Jr. 60.00 150.00
DIAFTJ Fernando Tatis Jr. 125.00 300.00
DIAGCO Gerrit Cole 75.00 200.00
DIAGLU Gavin Lux 75.00 200.00
DIAJBA Jeff Bagwell 30.00 80.00
DIAJTH Jim Thome 30.00 80.00
DIAKGJ Ken Griffey Jr. 150.00 400.00
DIAMSC Mike Schmidt 100.00 250.00
DIARAJ Ronald Acuna Jr. 125.00 300.00
DIASCA Steve Carlton 25.00 60.00
DIAYAL Yordan Alvarez 75.00 200.00

2020 Topps Diamond Icons Jumbo Patch Autographs

RANDOM INSERTS IN PACKS
PRINT RUN BTW 15-25 COPIES PER
NO PRICING QTY 15 OR LESS
EXCHANGE DEADLINE 5/31/2022

AJPAJ Aaron Judge
AJPAN Aaron Nola 40.00 100.00
AJPAR Anthony Rizzo 50.00 120.00
AJPBH Bryce Harper
AJPBP Buster Posey 60.00 150.00
AJPCL Clayton Kershaw EXCH 75.00 200.00
AJPCP Chris Paddack 25.00 60.00
AJPCY Christian Yelich
AJPDO David Ortiz 60.00 150.00
AJPGS George Springer 20.00 50.00
AJPGT Gleyber Torres
AJPJA Jose Altuve 20.00 50.00
AJPJR Jose Ramirez 20.00 50.00
AJPJV Joey Votto 40.00 100.00
AJPKS Kyle Schwarber 25.00 60.00
AJPMC Miguel Cabrera 75.00 200.00
AJPMH Masahiro Tanaka
AJPMT Mike Trout
AJPPG Paul Goldschmidt 25.00 60.00
AJPSO Shohei Ohtani
AJPTL Tim Lincecum 100.00 250.00
AJPWB Walker Buehler 75.00 200.00
AJPWC Willson Contreras 25.00 60.00
AJPWM Whit Merrifield 25.00 60.00
AJPXB Xander Bogaerts 30.00 80.00
AJPYA Yordan Alvarez 80.00 200.00
AJPABE Andrew Benintendi 40.00 100.00
AJPEMA Edgar Martinez 40.00 100.00
AJPFTJ Fernando Tatis Jr.
AJPJFL Jack Flaherty 40.00 100.00
AJPKGJ Ken Griffey Jr.
AJPKHI Keston Hiura 60.00 150.00
AJPMAX Max Scherzer 50.00 120.00
AJPMTE Mark Teixeira 20.00 50.00
AJPRAJ Ronald Acuna Jr.
AJPRAL Roberto Alomar
AJPRHE Rickey Henderson
AJPRHO Rhys Hoskins 50.00 120.00
AJPSBI Shane Bieber 25.00 60.00
AJPWBO Wade Boggs 25.00 60.00

2020 Topps Diamond Icons Red Ink Autographs

RANDOM INSERTS IN PACKS
PRINT RUN BTW 15-25 COPIES PER
NO PRICING QTY 15 OR LESS
EXCHANGE DEADLINE 5/31/2022

RIAA Aristides Aquino 40.00 100.00
RIAP Andy Pettitte 25.00 60.00
RIBG Bob Gibson 30.00 80.00
RIBH Bryce Harper
RIBL Barry Larkin 25.00 60.00
RIBP Buster Posey 40.00 100.00
RICF Carlton Fisk 20.00 50.00
RICJ Chipper Jones 50.00 120.00
RICR Cal Ripken Jr.
RICS Chris Sale 20.00 50.00
RIDE Dennis Eckersley 12.00 30.00
RIFE Fernando Tatis Jr. 125.00 300.00
RIGL Gavin Lux 75.00 200.00
RIGS George Springer 15.00 40.00
RIGT Gleyber Torres 60.00 150.00
RIHM Hideki Matsui
RIJA Jose Altuve 15.00 40.00
RIJB Johnny Bench
RIJD Jacob deGrom 50.00 120.00
RIJS Juan Soto 60.00 150.00
RIJV Joey Votto 40.00 100.00
RILB Lou Brock 20.00 50.00
RIMC Miguel Cabrera 60.00 150.00
RIMM Mark McGwire
RIMT Masahiro Tanaka
RING Nomar Garciaparra 25.00 60.00
RIPG Paul Goldschmidt 20.00 50.00
RIRD Rafael Devers 25.00 60.00
RIRH Rhys Hoskins 40.00 100.00
RIRJ Reggie Jackson 25.00 60.00
RISO Shohei Ohtani
RITG Tom Glavine 30.00 80.00
RITL Tim Lincecum 75.00 200.00
RIVG Vladimir Guerrero 30.00 80.00
RIWB Wade Boggs 30.00 80.00
RIWI Will Clark 25.00 60.00
RIYA Yordan Alvarez 75.00 200.00
RIAJU Aaron Judge 100.00 250.00
RIAKA Al Kaline 40.00 100.00
RIARI Anthony Rizzo 30.00 80.00
RIDMA Don Mattingly 60.00 150.00
RIDOR David Ortiz 50.00 120.00
RIEJI Eloy Jimenez 30.00 80.00
RIEMA Edgar Martinez 20.00 50.00
RIFTH Frank Thomas 40.00 100.00
RIICH Ichiro
RIJMA Juan Marichal 25.00 60.00
RIKBR Kris Bryant 50.00 120.00
RIKGJ Ken Griffey Jr.
RILRO Luis Robert 150.00 400.00
RIMMU Mike Mussina 30.00 80.00
RIMTR Mike Trout
RINHO Nico Hoerner 40.00 100.00
RINRY Nolan Ryan 75.00 200.00
RIOZM Ozzie Smith 30.00 80.00
RIRAJ Ronald Acuna Jr. 125.00 300.00
RIRAL Roberto Alomar 25.00 60.00
RIRCA Rod Carew 25.00 60.00
RIRHE Rickey Henderson
RIRJO Randy Johnson
RIRSA Ryne Sandberg 30.00 80.00
RIWBU Walker Buehler 30.00 80.00

2020 Topps Diamond Icons Silver Ink Autographs

RANDOM INSERTS IN PACKS
STATED PRINT RUN 25 COPIES PER
EXCHANGE DEADLINE 5/31/2022

SIAR Anthony Rizzo 30.00 80.00
SIBL Barry Larkin 25.00 60.00
SIBS Blake Snell 15.00 40.00
SIDM Don Mattingly 60.00 150.00
SIDS Darryl Strawberry 25.00 60.00
SIGL Gavin Lux 75.00 200.00
SIGT Gleyber Torres 60.00 150.00
SIHM Hideki Matsui 40.00 100.00
SIJD Jacob deGrom 50.00 120.00
SIJM Juan Marichal 25.00 60.00
SIJS Juan Soto 60.00 150.00
SIKB Kris Bryant 50.00 120.00
SIKG Ken Griffey Jr.
SIKH Keston Hiura 25.00 60.00
SILR Luis Robert 150.00 400.00
SIMS Max Scherzer 50.00 120.00
SIMT Masahiro Tanaka
SINR Nolan Ryan 75.00 200.00
SIOZ Ozzie Smith 30.00 80.00
SIPA Pete Alonso 60.00 150.00
SIRC Rod Carew 25.00 60.00
SIRD Rafael Devers 25.00 60.00
SIRH Rickey Henderson 40.00 100.00
SIRS Ryne Sandberg 30.00 80.00
SIVG Vladimir Guerrero 30.00 80.00
SIXB Xander Bogaerts 30.00 80.00
SIYA Yordan Alvarez 75.00 200.00
SIAJU Aaron Judge
SIAKA Al Kaline 40.00 100.00
SIDOR David Ortiz
SIFTH Frank Thomas 40.00 100.00
SIFTJ Fernando Tatis Jr. 125.00 300.00
SIICH Ichiro
SIRAJ Ronald Acuna Jr. 125.00 300.00
SIRHO Rhys Hoskins 40.00 100.00

2014 Topps Dynasty Autograph Patches

OVERALL AUTO ODDS 1:1
STATED PRINT RUN 10 SER.#'d SETS
ALL VERSION EQUALLY PRICED
EXCHANGE DEADLINE 12/31/2017

APAG1 Adrian Gonzalez 50.00 125.00
APAG2 Adrian Gonzalez 50.00 125.00
APAG3 Adrian Gonzalez 50.00 125.00
APAG4 Adrian Gonzalez 50.00 125.00
APAG5 Adrian Gonzalez 50.00 125.00
APAG6 Adrian Gonzalez 50.00 125.00
APAP1 Albert Pujols 200.00 300.00
APAP2 Albert Pujols 200.00 300.00
APAP3 Albert Pujols 200.00 300.00
APAP4 Albert Pujols 200.00 300.00
APBH1 Bryce Harper 300.00 600.00
APBH2 Bryce Harper 300.00 600.00
APBH3 Bryce Harper 300.00 600.00
APBH4 Bryce Harper 300.00 600.00
APBH5 Bryce Harper 300.00 600.00
APBH6 Bryce Harper 300.00 600.00
APBH7 Bryce Harper 300.00 600.00
APBH8 Bryce Harper 300.00 600.00
APBH9 Bryce Harper 300.00 600.00
APBH10 Bryce Harper 300.00 600.00
APBH11 Bryce Harper 300.00 600.00
APBJ1 Bo Jackson 150.00 300.00
APBJ2 Bo Jackson 150.00 300.00
APBJ3 Bo Jackson 150.00 300.00
APBJ4 Bo Jackson 150.00 300.00
APBJ5 Bo Jackson 150.00 300.00
APBJ6 Bo Jackson 150.00 300.00
APBJ7 Bo Jackson 150.00 300.00
APBJ8 Bo Jackson 150.00 300.00
APBP1 Buster Posey 200.00 300.00
APBP2 Buster Posey 200.00 300.00
APBP3 Buster Posey 200.00 300.00
APBP4 Buster Posey 80.00 200.00
APBP5 Buster Posey 80.00 200.00
APCB1 Craig Biggio 50.00 125.00
APCB2 Craig Biggio 50.00 125.00
APCB3 Craig Biggio 50.00 125.00
APCB4 Craig Biggio 50.00 125.00
APCB5 Craig Biggio 50.00 125.00
APCB6 Craig Biggio 50.00 125.00
APCB7 Craig Biggio 50.00 125.00
APCB8 Craig Biggio 50.00 125.00
APCF1 Carlton Fisk 100.00 200.00
APCF2 Carlton Fisk 100.00 200.00
APCF3 Carlton Fisk 100.00 200.00
APCF4 Carlton Fisk 100.00 200.00
APCF5 Carlton Fisk 100.00 200.00
APCF6 Carlton Fisk 100.00 200.00
APCJ1 Chipper Jones 150.00 300.00
APCJ10 Chipper Jones 60.00 150.00
APCJ11 Chipper Jones 60.00 150.00
APCJ2 Chipper Jones 150.00 300.00
APCJ3 Chipper Jones 150.00 300.00
APCJ4 Chipper Jones 150.00 300.00
APCJ5 Chipper Jones 150.00 300.00
APCJ6 Chipper Jones 150.00 300.00
APCJ7 Chipper Jones 150.00 300.00
APCJ8 Chipper Jones 150.00 300.00
APCJ9 Chipper Jones 150.00 300.00
APCK1 Clayton Kershaw 250.00 400.00
APCK2 Clayton Kershaw 250.00 400.00
APCK3 Clayton Kershaw 250.00 400.00
APCK4 Clayton Kershaw 250.00 400.00
APCK5 Clayton Kershaw 250.00 400.00
APCR1 Cal Ripken Jr. 200.00 300.00
APCR2 Cal Ripken Jr. 200.00 300.00
APCR3 Cal Ripken Jr. 200.00 300.00
APCR4 Cal Ripken Jr. 200.00 300.00
APCR5 Cal Ripken Jr. 200.00 300.00
APCR6 Cal Ripken Jr. 200.00 300.00
APCR7 Cal Ripken Jr. 200.00 300.00
APCR8 Cal Ripken Jr. 200.00 300.00
APDM1 Daisuke Matsuzaka 100.00 200.00
APDM2 Daisuke Matsuzaka 100.00 200.00
APDM3 Daisuke Matsuzaka 100.00 200.00
APDM4 Daisuke Matsuzaka 100.00 200.00
APDM5 Daisuke Matsuzaka 100.00 200.00
APDM6 Daisuke Matsuzaka 100.00 200.00
APDM7 Daisuke Matsuzaka 100.00 200.00
APDM8 Daisuke Matsuzaka 100.00 200.00
APDMT1 Don Mattingly 125.00 300.00
APDMT2 Don Mattingly 125.00 300.00
APDMT3 Don Mattingly 125.00 300.00
APDMT4 Don Mattingly 125.00 300.00
APDMT5 Don Mattingly 125.00 300.00
APDMT6 Don Mattingly 125.00 300.00
APDMT7 Don Mattingly 125.00 300.00
APDMT8 Don Mattingly 125.00 300.00
APDO1 David Ortiz 150.00 300.00
APDO2 David Ortiz 150.00 300.00
APDO3 David Ortiz 150.00 300.00
APDO4 David Ortiz 150.00 300.00
APDO5 David Ortiz 150.00 300.00
APDO6 David Ortiz 150.00 300.00
APDP1 Dustin Pedroia 100.00 250.00
APDP2 Dustin Pedroia 100.00 250.00
APDP3 Dustin Pedroia 100.00 250.00
APDP4 Dustin Pedroia 100.00 250.00
APDP5 Dustin Pedroia 100.00 250.00
APDP6 Dustin Pedroia 100.00 250.00
APDW1 David Wright 100.00 200.00
APDW2 David Wright 100.00 200.00
APDW3 David Wright 100.00 200.00
APDW4 David Wright 100.00 200.00
APDW5 David Wright 100.00 200.00
APDW6 David Wright 100.00 200.00
APEL1 Evan Longoria 50.00 125.00
APEL2 Evan Longoria 50.00 125.00
APEL3 Evan Longoria 50.00 125.00
APEL4 Evan Longoria 50.00 125.00
APEL5 Evan Longoria 50.00 125.00
APEL6 Evan Longoria 50.00 125.00
APEL7 Evan Longoria 50.00 125.00
APEL8 Evan Longoria 50.00 125.00
APEL9 Evan Longoria 50.00 125.00
APEL10 Evan Longoria 50.00 125.00
APEL11 Evan Longoria 50.00 125.00
APFF1 Freddie Freeman 80.00 200.00
APFF2 Freddie Freeman 80.00 200.00
APFF3 Freddie Freeman 80.00 200.00
APFF4 Freddie Freeman 80.00 200.00
APFF5 Freddie Freeman 80.00 200.00
APFF6 Freddie Freeman 80.00 200.00
APFF7 Freddie Freeman 80.00 200.00
APFF8 Freddie Freeman 80.00 200.00
APFF9 Freddie Freeman 80.00 200.00
APFF10 Freddie Freeman 80.00 200.00
APFF11 Freddie Freeman 80.00 200.00
APFT1 Frank Thomas 200.00 300.00
APFT2 Frank Thomas 200.00 300.00
APFT3 Frank Thomas 200.00 300.00
APFT4 Frank Thomas 200.00 300.00
APFT5 Frank Thomas 200.00 300.00
APFT6 Frank Thomas 200.00 300.00
APFT7 Frank Thomas 200.00 300.00
APFT8 Frank Thomas 200.00 300.00
APGM1 Greg Maddux EXCH 200.00 300.00
APGP1 Gregory Polanco RC 60.00 150.00
APGP2 Gregory Polanco RC 60.00 150.00
APGP3 Gregory Polanco RC 60.00 150.00
APGP4 Gregory Polanco RC 60.00 150.00
APGP5 Gregory Polanco RC 60.00 150.00
APGP6 Gregory Polanco RC 60.00 150.00
APGP7 Gregory Polanco RC 60.00 150.00
APGP8 Gregory Polanco RC 60.00 150.00
APGS1 Giancarlo Stanton 150.00 300.00
APGS2 Giancarlo Stanton 150.00 300.00
APGS3 Giancarlo Stanton 150.00 300.00
APGS4 Giancarlo Stanton 150.00 300.00
APGS5 Giancarlo Stanton 150.00 300.00
APGS6 Giancarlo Stanton 150.00 300.00
APGSP1 George Springer RC 150.00 400.00
APGSP2 George Springer RC 150.00 400.00
APGSP3 George Springer RC 150.00 400.00
APHI1 Hisashi Iwakuma 100.00 200.00
APHI2 Hisashi Iwakuma 100.00 200.00
APHI3 Hisashi Iwakuma 100.00 200.00
APHI4 Hisashi Iwakuma 100.00 200.00
APHI5 Hisashi Iwakuma 100.00 200.00
APHI6 Hisashi Iwakuma 100.00 200.00
APHI7 Hisashi Iwakuma 100.00 200.00
APHI8 Hisashi Iwakuma 100.00 200.00
APHR1 Hanley Ramirez 50.00 125.00
APHR2 Hanley Ramirez 50.00 125.00
APHR3 Hanley Ramirez 50.00 125.00
APHR4 Hanley Ramirez 50.00 125.00
APHR5 Hanley Ramirez 50.00 125.00
APHR6 Hanley Ramirez 50.00 125.00
APHR7 Hanley Ramirez 50.00 125.00
APHR8 Hanley Ramirez 50.00 125.00
APJA1 Jose Abreu RC 250.00 400.00
APJA2 Jose Abreu RC 250.00 400.00
APJA3 Jose Abreu RC 250.00 400.00
APJA4 Jose Abreu RC 250.00 400.00
APJA5 Jose Abreu RC 250.00 400.00
APJA6 Jose Abreu RC 250.00 400.00
APJA7 Jose Abreu RC 250.00 400.00
APJA8 Jose Abreu RC 250.00 400.00
APJF1 Jose Fernandez 100.00 200.00
APJF2 Jose Fernandez 100.00 200.00
APJF3 Jose Fernandez 100.00 200.00
APJF4 Jose Fernandez 100.00 200.00
APJF5 Jose Fernandez 100.00 200.00
APJF6 Jose Fernandez 100.00 200.00
APJF7 Jose Fernandez 100.00 200.00
APJF8 Jose Fernandez 100.00 200.00
APJH1 Josh Hamilton 50.00 125.00
APJH2 Josh Hamilton 50.00 125.00
APJH3 Josh Hamilton 50.00 125.00
APJH4 Josh Hamilton 50.00 125.00
APJH5 Josh Hamilton 50.00 125.00
APJH6 Josh Hamilton 50.00 125.00
APJH7 Josh Hamilton 50.00 125.00
APJHE1 Jason Heyward 50.00 125.00
APJHE2 Jason Heyward 50.00 125.00
APJHE3 Jason Heyward 50.00 125.00
APJHE4 Jason Heyward 50.00 125.00
APJHE5 Jason Heyward 50.00 125.00
APJHE6 Jason Heyward 50.00 125.00
APJHE7 Jason Heyward 50.00 125.00
APJM1 Joe Mauer 125.00 250.00
APJM2 Joe Mauer 125.00 250.00
APJM3 Joe Mauer 125.00 250.00
APJM4 Joe Mauer 125.00 250.00
APJM5 Joe Mauer 125.00 250.00
APJM6 Joe Mauer 125.00 250.00
APJS1 John Smoltz 125.00 250.00
APJS2 John Smoltz 125.00 250.00
APJS3 John Smoltz 125.00 250.00
APJS4 John Smoltz 125.00 250.00
APJS5 John Smoltz 125.00 250.00
APJS6 John Smoltz 125.00 250.00
APJS7 John Smoltz 125.00 250.00
APJV1 Joey Votto 60.00 150.00
APJV2 Joey Votto 60.00 150.00
APJV3 Joey Votto 60.00 150.00
APJV4 Joey Votto 60.00 150.00
APJV5 Joey Votto 60.00 150.00
APJV6 Joey Votto 60.00 150.00
APJV7 Joey Votto 60.00 150.00
APJV8 Joey Votto 60.00 150.00
APKG1 Ken Griffey Jr. 200.00 400.00
Cincinnati Reds
APKG2 Ken Griffey Jr. 200.00 400.00
Cincinnati Reds
APKG3 Ken Griffey Jr. 200.00 400.00
Cincinnati Reds
APKG4 Ken Griffey Jr. 200.00 400.00
Cincinnati Reds
APKG5 Ken Griffey Jr. 200.00 400.00
Cincinnati Reds
APKG6 Ken Griffey Jr. 200.00 400.00
Cincinnati Reds
APKG7 Ken Griffey Jr. 200.00 400.00
Cincinnati Reds
APKG8 Ken Griffey Jr. 200.00 400.00
Cincinnati Reds
APKG9 Ken Griffey Jr. 200.00 400.00
Seattle Mariners
APKG10 Ken Griffey Jr. 200.00 400.00
Seattle Mariners
APKG11 Ken Griffey Jr. 200.00 400.00
Seattle Mariners
APKG12 Ken Griffey Jr. 200.00 400.00
Seattle Mariners
APKG13 Ken Griffey Jr. 200.00 400.00
Seattle Mariners
APKG14 Ken Griffey Jr. 200.00 400.00
Seattle Mariners
APKG15 Ken Griffey Jr. 200.00 400.00
Seattle Mariners
APKG16 Ken Griffey Jr. 200.00 400.00
Seattle Mariners
APMC1 Miguel Cabrera 250.00 400.00
APMC2 Miguel Cabrera 250.00 400.00
APMC3 Miguel Cabrera 250.00 400.00
APMC4 Miguel Cabrera 250.00 400.00
APMC5 Miguel Cabrera 250.00 400.00
APMC6 Miguel Cabrera 250.00 400.00
APMC7 Miguel Cabrera 250.00 400.00
APMC8 Miguel Cabrera 250.00 400.00
APMM1 Mark McGwire 125.00 300.00
APMM2 Mark McGwire 125.00 300.00
APMM3 Mark McGwire 125.00 300.00
APMM4 Mark McGwire 125.00 300.00
APMM5 Mark McGwire 125.00 300.00
APMM6 Mark McGwire 125.00 300.00
APMM7 Mark McGwire 125.00 300.00
APMM8 Mark McGwire 125.00 300.00
APMMA1 Manny Machado 100.00 200.00
APMMA2 Manny Machado 100.00 200.00
APMMA3 Manny Machado 100.00 200.00
APMMA4 Manny Machado 100.00 200.00
APMMA5 Manny Machado 100.00 200.00
APMMA6 Manny Machado 100.00 200.00
APMMA7 Manny Machado 100.00 200.00
APMMA8 Manny Machado 100.00 200.00
APMP1 Mike Piazza 125.00 250.00
New York Mets
APMP2 Mike Piazza 125.00 250.00
New York Mets
APMP3 Mike Piazza 125.00 250.00
New York Mets
APMP4 Mike Piazza 125.00 250.00
New York Mets
APMP5 Mike Piazza 125.00 250.00
New York Mets
APMP6 Mike Piazza 125.00 250.00
New York Mets
APMP7 Mike Piazza 125.00 250.00
New York Mets
APMP8 Mike Piazza 125.00 250.00
New York Mets
APMP9 Mike Piazza 125.00 250.00
Los Angeles Dodgers
APMP10 Mike Piazza 125.00 250.00
Los Angeles Dodgers
APMP11 Mike Piazza 125.00 250.00
Los Angeles Dodgers
APMP12 Mike Piazza 125.00 250.00
Los Angeles Dodgers
APMP13 Mike Piazza 125.00 250.00
Los Angeles Dodgers
APMP14 Mike Piazza 125.00 250.00
Los Angeles Dodgers
APMP15 Mike Piazza 125.00 250.00
Los Angeles Dodgers
APMP16 Mike Piazza 125.00 250.00
Los Angeles Dodgers
APMR1 Mariano Rivera 300.00 500.00
APMR2 Mariano Rivera 300.00 500.00
APMR3 Mariano Rivera 300.00 500.00
APMR4 Mariano Rivera 300.00 500.00
APMR5 Mariano Rivera 300.00 500.00
APMR6 Mariano Rivera 300.00 500.00
APMR7 Mariano Rivera 300.00 500.00
APMT1 Mike Trout 400.00 600.00
APMT2 Mike Trout 400.00 600.00
APMT3 Mike Trout 400.00 600.00
APMT4 Mike Trout 400.00 600.00
APMT5 Mike Trout 400.00 600.00
APMT6 Mike Trout 400.00 600.00
APMT7 Mike Trout 400.00 600.00
APMT8 Mike Trout 400.00 600.00
APMW1 Michael Wacha 50.00 125.00
APMW2 Michael Wacha 50.00 125.00
APMW3 Michael Wacha 50.00 125.00
APMW4 Michael Wacha 50.00 125.00
APMW5 Michael Wacha 50.00 125.00
APMW6 Michael Wacha 50.00 125.00
APMW7 Michael Wacha 50.00 125.00
APNC1 Nick Castellanos RC 50.00 120.00
APNC2 Nick Castellanos RC 50.00 120.00
APNC3 Nick Castellanos RC 50.00 120.00
APNC4 Nick Castellanos RC 50.00 120.00
APNC5 Nick Castellanos RC 50.00 120.00
APNC6 Nick Castellanos RC 50.00 120.00
APNR1 Nolan Ryan 150.00 250.00
Houston Astros
APNR2 Nolan Ryan 150.00 250.00
Houston Astros
APNR3 Nolan Ryan 150.00 250.00
Houston Astros
APNR4 Nolan Ryan 150.00 250.00
Houston Astros
APNR5 Nolan Ryan 150.00 250.00
Houston Astros
APNR6 Nolan Ryan 150.00 250.00
Houston Astros
APNR7 Nolan Ryan 150.00 250.00
Houston Astros
APNR8 Nolan Ryan 150.00 250.00
Houston Astros
APNR9 Nolan Ryan 150.00 250.00
Texas Rangers
APNR10 Nolan Ryan 150.00 250.00
Texas Rangers
APNR11 Nolan Ryan 150.00 250.00
Texas Rangers
APNR12 Nolan Ryan 150.00 250.00
Texas Rangers
APNR13 Nolan Ryan 150.00 250.00
Texas Rangers
APNR14 Nolan Ryan 150.00 250.00
Texas Rangers
APNR15 Nolan Ryan 150.00 250.00
Texas Rangers
APNR16 Nolan Ryan 150.00 250.00
Texas Rangers
APOT1 Oscar Taveras RC 50.00 120.00
APOT2 Oscar Taveras RC 50.00 120.00
APOT3 Oscar Taveras RC 50.00 120.00
APOT4 Oscar Taveras RC 50.00 120.00
APOT5 Oscar Taveras RC 50.00 120.00
APOT6 Oscar Taveras RC 50.00 120.00
APOT7 Oscar Taveras RC 50.00 120.00
APPG1 Paul Goldschmidt 60.00 150.00
APPG2 Paul Goldschmidt 60.00 150.00
APPG3 Paul Goldschmidt 60.00 150.00
APPG4 Paul Goldschmidt 60.00 150.00
APPG5 Paul Goldschmidt 60.00 150.00
APPG6 Paul Goldschmidt 60.00 150.00
APPG7 Paul Goldschmidt 60.00 150.00
APPG8 Paul Goldschmidt 60.00 150.00
APPG9 Paul Goldschmidt 60.00 150.00
APPM1 Pedro Martinez 100.00 200.00
APPM2 Pedro Martinez 100.00 200.00
APPM3 Pedro Martinez 100.00 200.00
APPM4 Pedro Martinez 100.00 200.00
APPM5 Pedro Martinez 100.00 200.00
APPM6 Pedro Martinez 100.00 200.00
APPM7 Pedro Martinez 100.00 200.00
APRA1 Roberto Alomar 100.00 200.00
APRA2 Roberto Alomar 100.00 200.00
APRA3 Roberto Alomar 100.00 200.00
APRA4 Roberto Alomar 100.00 200.00
APRA5 Roberto Alomar 100.00 200.00
APRA6 Roberto Alomar 100.00 200.00
APRA7 Roberto Alomar 100.00 200.00
APRB1 Ryan Braun 50.00 125.00
APRB2 Ryan Braun 50.00 125.00
APRB3 Ryan Braun 50.00 125.00
APRB4 Ryan Braun 50.00 125.00
APRB5 Ryan Braun 50.00 125.00
APRB6 Ryan Braun 50.00 125.00
APRB7 Ryan Braun 50.00 125.00
APRB8 Ryan Braun 50.00 125.00
APRB9 Ryan Braun 50.00 125.00
APRB10 Ryan Braun 50.00 125.00
APRB11 Ryan Braun 50.00 125.00
APRCL1 Roger Clemens 125.00 250.00
APRCL2 Roger Clemens 125.00 250.00
APRCL3 Roger Clemens 125.00 250.00
APRCL4 Roger Clemens 125.00 250.00
APRCL5 Roger Clemens 125.00 250.00
APRCL6 Roger Clemens 125.00 250.00
APRCL7 Roger Clemens 125.00 250.00
APRH1 Rickey Henderson EXCH 100.00 200.00
New York Mets
APRH10 Rickey Henderson 100.00 200.00
(Oakland Athletics
APRJ1 Reggie Jackson 60.00 150.00
APRJ2 Reggie Jackson 60.00 150.00
APRJ3 Reggie Jackson 60.00 150.00
APRJ4 Reggie Jackson 60.00 150.00
APRJ5 Reggie Jackson 60.00 150.00
APRJ6 Reggie Jackson 60.00 150.00
APRJ7 Reggie Jackson 60.00 150.00
APRJO1 Randy Johnson 150.00 300.00
APRJO2 Randy Johnson 150.00 300.00
APRJO3 Randy Johnson 150.00 300.00
APRJO4 Randy Johnson 150.00 300.00
APRJO5 Randy Johnson 150.00 300.00
APRJO6 Randy Johnson 150.00 300.00
APRJO7 Randy Johnson 150.00 300.00
APRJO8 Randy Johnson 150.00 300.00
APRS1 Ryne Sandberg 125.00 250.00
APRS2 Ryne Sandberg 125.00 250.00
APRS3 Ryne Sandberg 125.00 250.00
APRS4 Ryne Sandberg 125.00 250.00
APRY1 Robin Yount 60.00 150.00
APRY2 Robin Yount 60.00 150.00
APRY3 Robin Yount 60.00 150.00
APRY4 Robin Yount 60.00 150.00
APRY5 Robin Yount 60.00 150.00
APRY6 Robin Yount 60.00 150.00
APSC1 Steve Carlton 60.00 150.00
APSC2 Steve Carlton 60.00 150.00
APSC3 Steve Carlton 60.00 150.00
APSC4 Steve Carlton 60.00 150.00
APSC5 Steve Carlton 60.00 150.00
APSC6 Steve Carlton 60.00 150.00
APSC7 Steve Carlton 60.00 150.00
APSG1 Sonny Gray 50.00 120.00
APSG2 Sonny Gray 50.00 120.00
APSG3 Sonny Gray 50.00 120.00
APSG4 Sonny Gray 50.00 120.00
APSG5 Sonny Gray 50.00 120.00
APSG6 Sonny Gray 50.00 120.00
APSM1 Shelby Miller 50.00 125.00
APSM2 Shelby Miller 50.00 125.00
APSM3 Shelby Miller 50.00 125.00
APSM4 Shelby Miller 50.00 125.00
APSM5 Shelby Miller 50.00 125.00
APTGL1 Tom Glavine 100.00 200.00
APTGL2 Tom Glavine 100.00 200.00
APTGL3 Tom Glavine 100.00 200.00
APTGL4 Tom Glavine 100.00 200.00
APTGL5 Tom Glavine 100.00 200.00
APTT1 Troy Tulowitzki 60.00 150.00
APTT2 Troy Tulowitzki 60.00 150.00
APTT3 Troy Tulowitzki 60.00 150.00
APTT4 Troy Tulowitzki 60.00 150.00
APTT5 Troy Tulowitzki 60.00 150.00
APTT6 Troy Tulowitzki 60.00 150.00
APTT7 Troy Tulowitzki 60.00 150.00
APTT8 Troy Tulowitzki 60.00 150.00
APTW1 Taijuan Walker RC 40.00 100.00
APTW2 Taijuan Walker RC 40.00 100.00
APTW3 Taijuan Walker RC 40.00 100.00
APTW4 Taijuan Walker RC 40.00 100.00
APTW5 Taijuan Walker RC 40.00 100.00
APTW6 Taijuan Walker RC 40.00 100.00
APTW7 Taijuan Walker RC 40.00 100.00
APVG1 Vladimir Guerrero 60.00 150.00
Los Angeles Angels
APVG2 Vladimir Guerrero 60.00 150.00
Los Angeles Angels
APVG3 Vladimir Guerrero 60.00 150.00
Los Angeles Angels
APVG4 Vladimir Guerrero 60.00 150.00
Los Angeles Angels
APVG5 Vladimir Guerrero 60.00 150.00
Los Angeles Angels
APVG6 Vladimir Guerrero 60.00 150.00
Los Angeles Angels
APVG7 Vladimir Guerrero 60.00 150.00
Los Angeles Angels
APVG8 Vladimir Guerrero 60.00 150.00
Los Angeles Angels
APVGE1 Vladimir Guerrero 60.00 150.00
Montreal Expos
APVGE2 Vladimir Guerrero 60.00 150.00
Montreal Expos
APVGE3 Vladimir Guerrero 60.00 150.00
Montreal Expos
APVGE4 Vladimir Guerrero 60.00 150.00
Montreal Expos
APVGE5 Vladimir Guerrero 60.00 150.00

Montreal Expos
APVGE6 Vladimir Guerrero 60.00 150.00
Montreal Expos
APVGE7 Vladimir Guerrero 60.00 150.00
Montreal Expos
APVGE8 Vladimir Guerrero 60.00 150.00
Montreal Expos
APWB1 Wade Boggs 50.00 125.00
New York Yankees
APWB2 Wade Boggs 50.00 125.00
New York Yankees
APWB3 Wade Boggs 50.00 125.00
New York Yankees
APWB4 Wade Boggs 50.00 125.00
New York Yankees
APWB5 Wade Boggs 50.00 125.00
New York Yankees
APWB6 Wade Boggs 100.00 200.00
New York Yankees
APWB7 Wade Boggs 100.00 200.00
New York Yankees
APWB8 Wade Boggs 100.00 200.00
New York Yankees
APWB9 Wade Boggs 100.00 200.00
Boston Red Sox
APWB10 Wade Boggs 100.00 200.00
Boston Red Sox
APWB11 Wade Boggs 100.00 200.00
Boston Red Sox
APWB12 Wade Boggs 100.00 200.00
Boston Red Sox
APWB13 Wade Boggs 100.00 200.00
Boston Red Sox
APWB14 Wade Boggs 100.00 200.00
Boston Red Sox
APWB15 Wade Boggs 100.00 200.00
Boston Red Sox
APWB16 Wade Boggs 100.00 200.00
Boston Red Sox
APWM1 Wil Myers 40.00 100.00
APWM2 Wil Myers 40.00 100.00
APWM3 Wil Myers 40.00 100.00
APWM4 Wil Myers 40.00 100.00
APWM5 Wil Myers 40.00 100.00
APWM6 Wil Myers 40.00 100.00
APWM7 Wil Myers 40.00 100.00
APWM8 Wil Myers 40.00 100.00
APWMA1 Willie Mays EXCH 400.00 600.00
APYC1 Yoenis Cespedes 60.00 150.00
APYC2 Yoenis Cespedes 60.00 150.00
APYC3 Yoenis Cespedes 60.00 150.00
APYC4 Yoenis Cespedes 60.00 150.00
APYC5 Yoenis Cespedes 60.00 150.00
APYD1 Yu Darvish 125.00 250.00
APYD2 Yu Darvish 125.00 250.00
APYM1 Yadier Molina 150.00 300.00
APYM2 Yadier Molina 150.00 300.00
APYM3 Yadier Molina 150.00 300.00
APYM4 Yadier Molina 150.00 300.00
APYM5 Yadier Molina 150.00 300.00
APYM6 Yadier Molina 150.00 300.00
APYM7 Yadier Molina 150.00 300.00
APYP1 Yasiel Puig 200.00 400.00
APYP2 Yasiel Puig 200.00 400.00
APYP3 Yasiel Puig 200.00 400.00
APYP4 Yasiel Puig 200.00 400.00
APYP5 Yasiel Puig 200.00 400.00
APYP6 Yasiel Puig 200.00 400.00
APYP7 Yasiel Puig 200.00 400.00
APYP8 Yasiel Puig 200.00 400.00

2014 Topps Dynasty Dual Relic Autographs

OVERALL AUTO ODDS 1:1
STATED PRINT RUN 5 SER.#'d SETS
ALL VERSION EQUALLY PRICED
NO MAYS OR KOUFAX PRICING AVAILABLE
EXCHANGE DEADLINE 12/31/2017
DRGDM1 Don Mattingly 100.00 200.00
DRGDM2 Don Mattingly 100.00 200.00
DRGDM3 Don Mattingly 100.00 200.00
DRGDM4 Don Mattingly 100.00 200.00
DRGDM5 Don Mattingly 100.00 200.00
DRGEB1 Ernie Banks 150.00 300.00
DRGEB2 Ernie Banks 150.00 300.00
DRGEB3 Ernie Banks 150.00 300.00
DRGEB4 Ernie Banks 150.00 300.00
DRGEB5 Ernie Banks 150.00 300.00
DRGHA1 Hank Aaron 300.00 500.00
DRGHA2 Hank Aaron 300.00 500.00
DRGHA3 Hank Aaron 300.00 500.00
DRGHA4 Hank Aaron 300.00 500.00
DRGHA5 Hank Aaron 300.00 500.00
DRGJB1 Johnny Bench 100.00 250.00
DRGJB2 Johnny Bench 100.00 250.00
DRGJB3 Johnny Bench 100.00 250.00
DRGJB4 Johnny Bench 100.00 250.00
DRGJB5 Johnny Bench 100.00 250.00
DRGJB6 Johnny Bench 100.00 250.00

2015 Topps Dynasty Autograph Patches

OVERALL AUTO ODDS 1:1
STATED PRINT RUN 10 SER.#'d SETS
ALL VERSIONS EQUALLY PRICED
EXCHANGE DEADLINE 12/31/2017
APAGA1 Andres Galarraga 300.00 600.00
APAGA2 Andres Galarraga 300.00 600.00
APAGA3 Andres Galarraga 300.00 600.00
APAGA4 Andres Galarraga 300.00 600.00
APAGA5 Andres Galarraga 300.00 600.00
APAGA6 Andres Galarraga 300.00 600.00
APAGA7 Andres Galarraga 300.00 600.00
APAGA8 Andres Galarraga 300.00 600.00
APAP1 Albert Pujols 150.00 300.00
APAP2 Albert Pujols 150.00 300.00
APAP3 Albert Pujols 150.00 300.00
APAP4 Albert Pujols 150.00 300.00
APAP5 Albert Pujols 150.00 300.00
APAR1 Anthony Rizzo 125.00 250.00
APAR2 Anthony Rizzo 125.00 250.00
APAR3 Anthony Rizzo 125.00 250.00
APAR4 Anthony Rizzo 125.00 250.00
APAR5 Anthony Rizzo 125.00 250.00
APAR6 Anthony Rizzo 125.00 250.00
APBBU1 Byron Buxton RC 100.00 200.00
APBBU2 Byron Buxton RC 100.00 200.00
APBBU3 Byron Buxton RC 100.00 200.00
APBBU4 Byron Buxton RC 100.00 200.00
APBH1 Bryce Harper 300.00 500.00
APBH2 Bryce Harper 300.00 500.00
APBH3 Bryce Harper 300.00 500.00
APBH4 Bryce Harper 300.00 500.00
APBH5 Bryce Harper 300.00 500.00
APBH6 Bryce Harper 300.00 500.00
APBJA1 Bo Jackson 100.00 200.00
APBJA2 Bo Jackson 100.00 200.00
APBJA3 Bo Jackson 100.00 200.00
APBJA4 Bo Jackson 100.00 200.00
APBJA5 Bo Jackson 100.00 200.00
APBJA6 Bo Jackson 100.00 200.00
APBP1 Buster Posey 150.00 300.00
APBP2 Buster Posey 150.00 300.00
APBP3 Buster Posey 150.00 300.00
APBP4 Buster Posey 150.00 300.00
APBP5 Buster Posey 150.00 300.00
APBP6 Buster Posey 150.00 300.00
APBP7 Buster Posey 150.00 300.00
APBP8 Buster Posey 150.00 300.00
APBP9 Buster Posey 150.00 300.00
APCB1 Craig Biggio 75.00 150.00
APCB2 Craig Biggio 75.00 150.00
APCB3 Craig Biggio 75.00 150.00
APCB4 Craig Biggio 75.00 150.00
APCB5 Craig Biggio 75.00 150.00
APCF1 Carlton Fisk 100.00 200.00
APCF2 Carlton Fisk 100.00 200.00
APCF3 Carlton Fisk 100.00 200.00
APCF4 Carlton Fisk 100.00 200.00
APCH1 Cole Hamels 60.00 120.00
APCH2 Cole Hamels 60.00 120.00
APCH3 Cole Hamels 60.00 120.00
APCH4 Cole Hamels 60.00 120.00
APCH5 Cole Hamels 60.00 120.00
APCJ1 Chipper Jones 125.00 250.00
APCJ2 Chipper Jones 125.00 250.00
APCJ3 Chipper Jones 125.00 250.00
APCJ4 Chipper Jones 125.00 250.00
APCJ5 Chipper Jones 125.00 250.00
APCK1 Clayton Kershaw 150.00 300.00
APCK2 Clayton Kershaw 150.00 300.00
APCK3 Clayton Kershaw 150.00 300.00
APCK4 Clayton Kershaw 150.00 300.00
APCK5 Clayton Kershaw 150.00 300.00
APCKL1 Corey Kluber 50.00 100.00
APCKL2 Corey Kluber 50.00 100.00
APCKL3 Corey Kluber 50.00 100.00
APCKL4 Corey Kluber 50.00 100.00
APCKL5 Corey Kluber 50.00 100.00
APCRJ1 Cal Ripken Jr. 200.00 400.00
APCRJ2 Cal Ripken Jr. 200.00 400.00
APCRJ3 Cal Ripken Jr. 200.00 400.00
APCRJ4 Cal Ripken Jr. 200.00 400.00
APCRJ5 Cal Ripken Jr. 200.00 400.00
APCRJ6 Cal Ripken Jr. 200.00 400.00
APDE1 Dennis Eckersley 50.00 100.00
APDE2 Dennis Eckersley 50.00 100.00
APDE3 Dennis Eckersley 50.00 100.00
APDE4 Dennis Eckersley 50.00 100.00
APDE5 Dennis Eckersley 50.00 100.00
APDM1 Dan Marino 250.00 400.00
APDM2 Dan Marino 250.00 400.00
APDO1 David Ortiz 125.00 250.00
APDO2 David Ortiz 125.00 250.00
APDO3 David Ortiz 125.00 250.00
APDO4 David Ortiz 125.00 250.00
APDO5 David Ortiz 125.00 250.00
APDO6 David Ortiz 125.00 250.00
APDP1 Dustin Pedroia 75.00 150.00
APDP2 Dustin Pedroia 75.00 150.00
APDP3 Dustin Pedroia 75.00 150.00
APDP4 Dustin Pedroia 75.00 150.00
APDP5 Dustin Pedroia 75.00 150.00
APDS1 Deion Sanders 100.00 200.00
APDS2 Deion Sanders 100.00 200.00
APDS3 Deion Sanders 100.00 200.00
APDS4 Deion Sanders 100.00 200.00
APDS5 Deion Sanders 100.00 200.00
APDW1 David Wright 60.00 120.00
APDW2 David Wright 60.00 120.00
APDW3 David Wright 60.00 120.00
APDW4 David Wright 60.00 120.00
APDW5 David Wright 60.00 120.00
APEL1 Evan Longoria 50.00 100.00
APEL2 Evan Longoria 50.00 100.00
APEL3 Evan Longoria 50.00 100.00
APEL4 Evan Longoria 50.00 100.00
APEL5 Evan Longoria 50.00 100.00
APFF1 Freddie Freeman 60.00 120.00
APFF2 Freddie Freeman 60.00 120.00
APFF3 Freddie Freeman 60.00 120.00
APFF4 Freddie Freeman 60.00 120.00
APFF5 Freddie Freeman 60.00 120.00
APFH1 Felix Hernandez 100.00 200.00
APFH2 Felix Hernandez 100.00 200.00
APFH3 Felix Hernandez 100.00 200.00
APFH4 Felix Hernandez 100.00 200.00
APFH5 Felix Hernandez 100.00 200.00
APFL1 Francisco Lindor RC 100.00 200.00
APFL2 Francisco Lindor RC 100.00 200.00
APFL3 Francisco Lindor RC 100.00 200.00
APFL4 Francisco Lindor RC 100.00 200.00
APFL5 Francisco Lindor RC 100.00 200.00
APFM1 Fred McGriff 50.00 100.00
APFM2 Fred McGriff 50.00 100.00
APFM3 Fred McGriff 50.00 100.00
APFM4 Fred McGriff 50.00 100.00
APFM5 Fred McGriff 50.00 100.00
APFT1 Frank Thomas 150.00 300.00
APFT2 Frank Thomas 150.00 300.00
APFT3 Frank Thomas 150.00 300.00
APFT4 Frank Thomas 150.00 300.00
APFT5 Frank Thomas 150.00 300.00
APGM1 Greg Maddux EXCH 150.00 300.00
APGM2 Greg Maddux EXCH 150.00 300.00
APGM3 Greg Maddux EXCH 150.00 300.00
APGM4 Greg Maddux EXCH 150.00 300.00
APGM5 Greg Maddux EXCH 150.00 300.00
APHR1 Hanley Ramirez 50.00 100.00
APHR2 Hanley Ramirez 50.00 100.00
APHR3 Hanley Ramirez 50.00 100.00
APHR4 Hanley Ramirez 50.00 100.00
APHR5 Hanley Ramirez 50.00 100.00
APHR6 Hanley Ramirez 50.00 100.00
API1 Ichiro Suzuki 400.00 600.00
API2 Ichiro Suzuki 400.00 600.00
API3 Ichiro Suzuki 400.00 600.00
API4 Ichiro Suzuki 400.00 600.00
API5 Ichiro Suzuki 400.00 600.00
API6 Ichiro Suzuki 400.00 600.00
API7 Ichiro Suzuki 400.00 600.00
API8 Ichiro Suzuki 400.00 600.00
API9 Ichiro Suzuki 400.00 600.00
API10 Ichiro Suzuki 400.00 600.00
APJA1 Jose Abreu 75.00 150.00
APJA2 Jose Abreu 75.00 150.00
APJA3 Jose Abreu 75.00 150.00
APJA4 Jose Abreu 75.00 150.00
APJA5 Jose Abreu 75.00 150.00
APJA6 Jose Abreu 75.00 150.00
APJB1 Jeff Bagwell 100.00 200.00
APJB2 Jeff Bagwell 100.00 200.00
APJB3 Jeff Bagwell 100.00 200.00
APJB4 Jeff Bagwell 100.00 200.00
APJC1 Jose Canseco 125.00 250.00
APJC2 Jose Canseco 125.00 250.00
APJC3 Jose Canseco 125.00 250.00
APJC4 Jose Canseco 125.00 250.00
APJC5 Jose Canseco 125.00 250.00
APJD1 Jacob deGrom 150.00 300.00
APJD2 Jacob deGrom 150.00 300.00
APJD3 Jacob deGrom 150.00 300.00
APJD4 Jacob deGrom 150.00 300.00
APJD5 Jacob deGrom 150.00 300.00
APJD6 Jacob deGrom 150.00 300.00
APJE1 John Elway 250.00 400.00
APJE2 John Elway 250.00 400.00
APJF1 Jose Fernandez 75.00 150.00
APJF2 Jose Fernandez 75.00 150.00
APJF3 Jose Fernandez 75.00 150.00
APJF4 Jose Fernandez 75.00 150.00
APJF5 Jose Fernandez 75.00 150.00
APJF6 Jose Fernandez 75.00 150.00
APJG1 Joey Gallo RC 100.00 200.00
APJG2 Joey Gallo RC 100.00 200.00
APJG3 Joey Gallo RC 100.00 200.00
APJG4 Joey Gallo RC 100.00 200.00
APJG5 Joey Gallo RC 100.00 200.00
APJH1 Jason Heyward 75.00 150.00
APJH2 Jason Heyward 75.00 150.00
APJH3 Jason Heyward 75.00 150.00
APJH4 Jason Heyward 75.00 150.00
APJH5 Jason Heyward 75.00 150.00
APJHK1 Jung Ho Kang EXCH 200.00 400.00
APJHK2 Jung Ho Kang EXCH 200.00 400.00
APJHK3 Jung Ho Kang EXCH 200.00 400.00
APJHK4 Jung Ho Kang EXCH 200.00 400.00
APJL1 Jon Lester 75.00 150.00
APJL2 Jon Lester 75.00 150.00
APJL3 Jon Lester 75.00 150.00
APJL4 Jon Lester 75.00 150.00
APJL5 Jon Lester 75.00 150.00
APJM1 Joe Mauer 100.00 200.00
APJM2 Joe Mauer 100.00 200.00
APJM3 Joe Mauer 100.00 200.00
APJM4 Joe Mauer 100.00 200.00
APJM5 Joe Mauer 100.00 200.00
APJM6 Joe Mauer 100.00 200.00
APJP1 Joc Pederson RC 100.00 200.00
APJP2 Joc Pederson RC 100.00 200.00
APJP3 Joc Pederson RC 100.00 200.00
APJS1 John Smoltz 75.00 150.00
APJS2 John Smoltz 75.00 150.00
APJS3 John Smoltz 75.00 150.00
APJS4 John Smoltz 75.00 150.00
APJV1 Joey Votto 60.00 120.00
APJV2 Joey Votto 60.00 120.00
APJV3 Joey Votto 60.00 120.00
APJV4 Joey Votto 60.00 120.00
APJV5 Joey Votto 60.00 120.00
APKB1 Kris Bryant RC 600.00 900.00
APKB2 Kris Bryant RC 600.00 900.00
APKB3 Kris Bryant RC 600.00 900.00
APKB4 Kris Bryant RC 600.00 900.00
APKB5 Kris Bryant RC 600.00 900.00
APKG1 Ken Griffey Jr. 250.00 500.00
APKG2 Ken Griffey Jr. 250.00 500.00
APKG3 Ken Griffey Jr. 250.00 500.00
APKG4 Ken Griffey Jr. 250.00 500.00
APKG5 Ken Griffey Jr. 250.00 500.00
APKG6 Ken Griffey Jr. 250.00 500.00
APKG7 Ken Griffey Jr. 250.00 500.00
APKG8 Ken Griffey Jr. 250.00 500.00
APKG9 Ken Griffey Jr. 250.00 500.00
APKS1 Kyle Seager 60.00 120.00
APKS2 Kyle Seager 60.00 120.00
APKS3 Kyle Seager 60.00 120.00
APKS4 Kyle Seager 60.00 120.00
APKS5 Kyle Seager 60.00 120.00
APMC1 Matt Carpenter 60.00 120.00
APMC2 Matt Carpenter 60.00 120.00
APMC3 Matt Carpenter 60.00 120.00
APMC4 Matt Carpenter 60.00 120.00
APMC5 Matt Carpenter 60.00 120.00
APMH1 Matt Harvey EXCH 100.00 200.00
APMH2 Matt Harvey EXCH 100.00 200.00
APMH3 Matt Harvey EXCH 100.00 200.00
APMH4 Matt Harvey EXCH 100.00 200.00
APMH5 Matt Harvey EXCH 100.00 200.00
APMH6 Matt Harvey EXCH 100.00 200.00
APMM1 Manny Machado 150.00 300.00
APMM2 Manny Machado 150.00 300.00
APMM3 Manny Machado 150.00 300.00
APMM4 Manny Machado 150.00 300.00
APMM5 Manny Machado 150.00 300.00
APMMC1 Mark McGwire 150.00 300.00
APMMC2 Mark McGwire 150.00 300.00
APMMC3 Mark McGwire 150.00 300.00
APMMC4 Mark McGwire 150.00 300.00
APMMC5 Mark McGwire 150.00 300.00
APMMC6 Mark McGwire 150.00 300.00
APMMC7 Mark McGwire 150.00 300.00
APMMC8 Mark McGwire 150.00 300.00
APMMC9 Mark McGwire 150.00 300.00
APMP1 Mike Piazza 150.00 300.00
APMP2 Mike Piazza 150.00 300.00
APMP3 Mike Piazza 150.00 300.00
APMP4 Mike Piazza 150.00 300.00
APMP5 Mike Piazza 150.00 300.00
APMR1 Mariano Rivera 200.00 400.00
APMR2 Mariano Rivera 200.00 400.00
APMR3 Mariano Rivera 200.00 400.00
APMR4 Mariano Rivera 200.00 400.00
APMR5 Mariano Rivera 200.00 400.00
APMS1 Max Scherzer 100.00 250.00
APMS2 Max Scherzer 100.00 250.00
APMS3 Max Scherzer 100.00 250.00
APMS4 Max Scherzer 100.00 250.00
APMS5 Max Scherzer 100.00 250.00
APMT1 Mike Trout 300.00 600.00
APMT2 Mike Trout 300.00 600.00
APMT3 Mike Trout 300.00 600.00
APMT4 Mike Trout 300.00 600.00
APMT5 Mike Trout 300.00 600.00
APMT6 Mike Trout 300.00 600.00
APMT7 Mike Trout 300.00 600.00
APMT8 Mike Trout 300.00 600.00
APMT9 Mike Trout 300.00 600.00
APMW1 Michael Wacha 75.00 150.00
APMW2 Michael Wacha 75.00 150.00
APMW3 Michael Wacha 75.00 150.00
APMW4 Michael Wacha 75.00 150.00
APMW5 Michael Wacha 75.00 150.00
APNG1 Nomar Garciaparra 75.00 150.00
APNG2 Nomar Garciaparra 75.00 150.00
APNG3 Nomar Garciaparra 75.00 150.00
APNG4 Nomar Garciaparra 75.00 150.00
APNG5 Nomar Garciaparra 75.00 150.00
APNG6 Nomar Garciaparra 75.00 150.00
APNS1 Noah Syndergaard RC 150.00 300.00
APNS2 Noah Syndergaard RC 150.00 300.00
APNS3 Noah Syndergaard RC 150.00 300.00
APNS4 Noah Syndergaard RC 150.00 300.00
APNS5 Noah Syndergaard RC 150.00 300.00
APNS6 Noah Syndergaard RC 150.00 300.00
APPF1 Prince Fielder 60.00 120.00
APPF2 Prince Fielder 60.00 120.00
APPF3 Prince Fielder 60.00 120.00
APPF4 Prince Fielder 60.00 120.00
APPF5 Prince Fielder 60.00 120.00
APPG1 Paul Goldschmidt 100.00 200.00
APPG2 Paul Goldschmidt 100.00 200.00
APPG3 Paul Goldschmidt 100.00 200.00
APPG4 Paul Goldschmidt 100.00 200.00
APPG5 Paul Goldschmidt 100.00 200.00
APPS1 Pablo Sandoval 50.00 100.00
APPS2 Pablo Sandoval 50.00 100.00
APPS3 Pablo Sandoval 50.00 100.00
APPS4 Pablo Sandoval 50.00 100.00
APPS5 Pablo Sandoval 50.00 100.00
APPS6 Pablo Sandoval 50.00 100.00
APRA1 Roberto Alomar 60.00 120.00
APRA2 Roberto Alomar 60.00 120.00
APRA3 Roberto Alomar 60.00 120.00
APRA4 Roberto Alomar 60.00 120.00
APRA5 Roberto Alomar 60.00 120.00
APRC1 Robinson Cano 75.00 150.00
APRC2 Robinson Cano 75.00 150.00
APRC3 Robinson Cano 75.00 150.00
APRC4 Robinson Cano 75.00 150.00
APRC5 Robinson Cano 75.00 150.00
APRC6 Robinson Cano 75.00 150.00
APRC7 Robinson Cano 75.00 150.00
APRCL1 Roger Clemens 100.00 200.00
APRCL2 Roger Clemens 100.00 200.00
APRCL3 Roger Clemens 100.00 200.00
APRCL4 Roger Clemens 100.00 200.00
APRCL5 Roger Clemens 100.00 200.00
APRCL6 Roger Clemens 100.00 200.00
APRCL7 Roger Clemens 100.00 200.00
APRCL8 Roger Clemens 100.00 200.00
APRCL9 Roger Clemens 100.00 200.00
APRCS1 Rusney Castillo RC 60.00 120.00
APRCS2 Rusney Castillo RC 60.00 120.00
APRCS3 Rusney Castillo RC 60.00 120.00
APRCS4 Rusney Castillo RC 60.00 120.00
APRCS5 Rusney Castillo RC 60.00 120.00
APRH1 Rickey Henderson 100.00 200.00
APRH2 Rickey Henderson 100.00 200.00
APRH3 Rickey Henderson 100.00 200.00
APRH4 Rickey Henderson 100.00 200.00
APRH5 Rickey Henderson 100.00 200.00
APRH6 Rickey Henderson 100.00 200.00
APRH7 Rickey Henderson 100.00 200.00
APRH8 Rickey Henderson 100.00 200.00
APRH9 Rickey Henderson 100.00 200.00
APRJA1 Reggie Jackson 75.00 150.00
APRJA2 Reggie Jackson 75.00 150.00
APRJA3 Reggie Jackson 75.00 150.00
APRJA4 Reggie Jackson 75.00 150.00
APRJA5 Reggie Jackson 75.00 150.00
APRJA6 Reggie Jackson 75.00 150.00
APRJA7 Reggie Jackson 75.00 150.00
APRJN1 Randy Johnson 125.00 250.00
APRJN2 Randy Johnson 125.00 250.00
APRJN3 Randy Johnson 125.00 250.00
APRJN4 Randy Johnson 125.00 250.00
APRJN5 Randy Johnson 125.00 250.00
APRJN6 Randy Johnson 125.00 250.00
APRJN7 Randy Johnson 125.00 250.00
APRJN8 Randy Johnson 125.00 250.00
APRJN9 Randy Johnson 125.00 250.00
APRJO1 Reggie Jackson 75.00 150.00
APRJO2 Reggie Jackson 75.00 150.00
APRJO3 Reggie Jackson 75.00 150.00
APRJO4 Reggie Jackson 75.00 150.00
APRJO5 Reggie Jackson 75.00 150.00
APRJO6 Reggie Jackson 75.00 150.00
APRW1 Russell Wilson 250.00 400.00
APRW2 Russell Wilson 250.00 400.00
APSC1 Steve Carlton 75.00 150.00
APSG1 Sonny Gray 60.00 120.00
APSG2 Sonny Gray 60.00 120.00
APSG3 Sonny Gray 60.00 120.00
APSG4 Sonny Gray 60.00 120.00
APSG5 Sonny Gray 60.00 120.00
APSM1 Steven Matz RC 125.00 250.00
APSM2 Steven Matz RC 125.00 250.00
APSM3 Steven Matz RC 125.00 250.00
APSM4 Steven Matz RC 125.00 250.00
APSM5 Steven Matz RC 125.00 250.00
APTG1 Tom Glavine 75.00 150.00
APTG2 Tom Glavine 75.00 150.00
APTG3 Tom Glavine 75.00 150.00
APTG4 Tom Glavine 75.00 150.00
APTG5 Tom Glavine 75.00 150.00
APTG6 Tom Glavine 75.00 150.00
APTL1 Tim Lincecum 150.00 300.00
APTL2 Tim Lincecum 150.00 300.00
APTL3 Tim Lincecum 150.00 300.00
APTL4 Tim Lincecum 150.00 300.00
APTL5 Tim Lincecum 150.00 300.00
APVG1 Vladimir Guerrero 50.00 100.00
APVG2 Vladimir Guerrero 50.00 100.00
APVG3 Vladimir Guerrero 50.00 100.00
APVG4 Vladimir Guerrero 50.00 100.00
APVG5 Vladimir Guerrero 50.00 100.00
APVG6 Vladimir Guerrero 50.00 100.00
APVG7 Vladimir Guerrero 50.00 100.00
APWFA1 Will Ferrell 300.00 500.00
APWFA2 Will Ferrell 300.00 500.00
APWFA3 Will Ferrell 300.00 500.00
APWFA4 Will Ferrell 300.00 500.00
APWFA5 Will Ferrell 300.00 500.00
APWFD1 Will Ferrell 300.00 500.00
APWFD2 Will Ferrell 300.00 500.00
APWFD3 Will Ferrell 300.00 500.00
APWFD4 Will Ferrell 300.00 500.00
APWFD5 Will Ferrell 300.00 500.00
APYC1 Yoenis Cespedes EXCH 60.00 120.00
APYC2 Yoenis Cespedes EXCH 60.00 120.00
APYC3 Yoenis Cespedes EXCH 60.00 120.00
APYC4 Yoenis Cespedes EXCH 60.00 120.00
APYC5 Yoenis Cespedes EXCH 60.00 120.00
APYC6 Yoenis Cespedes EXCH 60.00 120.00
APYD1 Yu Darvish 60.00 120.00
APYD2 Yu Darvish 60.00 120.00
APYD3 Yu Darvish 60.00 120.00
APYD4 Yu Darvish 60.00 120.00
APYD5 Yu Darvish 60.00 120.00
APYD6 Yu Darvish 60.00 120.00
APYP1 Yasiel Puig 100.00 200.00
APYP2 Yasiel Puig 100.00 200.00
APYP3 Yasiel Puig 100.00 200.00
APYP4 Yasiel Puig 100.00 200.00
APYP5 Yasiel Puig 100.00 200.00
APYT1 Yasmany Tomas RC 50.00 100.00
APYT2 Yasmany Tomas RC 50.00 100.00
APYT3 Yasmany Tomas RC 50.00 100.00
APYT4 Yasmany Tomas RC 50.00 100.00
APYT5 Yasmany Tomas RC 50.00 100.00

2015 Topps Dynasty Autograph Patches Emerald

*EMERALD: .6X TO 1.5X BASIC
RANDOM INSERTS IN PACKS
STATED PRINT RUN 5 SER.#'d SETS
EXCHANGE DEADLINE 12/31/2017

2015 Topps Dynasty Dual Relic Greats Autographs

STATED ODDS 1:38 PACKS
STATED PRINT RUN 5 SER.#'d SETS
ALL VERSIONS EQUALLY PRICED
EXCHANGE DEADLINE 12/31/2017
ADRGDM1 Don Mattingly 100.00 250.00
ADRGDM2 Don Mattingly 100.00 250.00
ADRGDM3 Don Mattingly 100.00 250.00
ADRGDM4 Don Mattingly 100.00 250.00
ADRGDM5 Don Mattingly 100.00 250.00
ADRGFR1 Frank Robinson 75.00 150.00
ADRGFR2 Frank Robinson 75.00 150.00
ADRGFR3 Frank Robinson 75.00 150.00
ADRGFR4 Frank Robinson 75.00 150.00
ADRGFR5 Frank Robinson 75.00 150.00
ADRGHA1 Hank Aaron 250.00 500.00
ADRGHA2 Hank Aaron 250.00 500.00
ADRGHA3 Hank Aaron 250.00 500.00
ADRGHA4 Hank Aaron 250.00 500.00
ADRGHA5 Hank Aaron 250.00 500.00
ADRGJB1 Johnny Bench 150.00 300.00
ADRGJB2 Johnny Bench 150.00 300.00
ADRGJB3 Johnny Bench 150.00 300.00
ADRGJB4 Johnny Bench 150.00 300.00
ADRGJB5 Johnny Bench 150.00 300.00
ADRGOS1 Ozzie Smith 75.00 150.00
ADRGOS2 Ozzie Smith 75.00 150.00
ADRGOS3 Ozzie Smith 75.00 150.00
ADRGOS4 Ozzie Smith 75.00 150.00
ADRGOS5 Ozzie Smith 75.00 150.00
ADRGSC1 Steve Carlton 60.00 120.00
ADRGSC2 Steve Carlton 60.00 120.00
ADRGSC3 Steve Carlton 60.00 120.00
ADRGSC4 Steve Carlton 60.00 120.00
ADRGSC5 Steve Carlton 60.00 120.00
ADRGSK1 Sandy Koufax 600.00 800.00
ADRGSK2 Sandy Koufax 600.00 800.00
ADRGSK3 Sandy Koufax 600.00 800.00
ADRGSK4 Sandy Koufax 600.00 800.00
ADRGSK5 Sandy Koufax 600.00 800.00

2016 Topps Dynasty Autograph Patches

OVERALL AUTO ODDS 1:1
STATED PRINT RUN 10 SER.#'d SETS
ALL VERSIONS EQUALLY PRICED
EXCHANGE DEADLINE 11/30/2018
LOGO/TAG PATCHES MAY SELL FOR PREMIUM
API1 Ichiro Suzuki 300.00 600.00
API2 Ichiro Suzuki 300.00 600.00
API3 Ichiro Suzuki 300.00 600.00
API4 Ichiro Suzuki 300.00 600.00
API5 Ichiro Suzuki 300.00 600.00
API6 Ichiro Suzuki 300.00 600.00
API7 Ichiro Suzuki 300.00 600.00
API8 Ichiro Suzuki 300.00 600.00
API9 Ichiro Suzuki 300.00 600.00
API10 Ichiro Suzuki 300.00 600.00
APP1 Pele 250.00 400.00
APP2 Pele 250.00 400.00
APP3 Pele 250.00 400.00
APP4 Pele 250.00 400.00
APP5 Pele 250.00 400.00
APP6 Pele 250.00 400.00
APAG1 Adrian Gonzalez 40.00 100.00
APAG2 Adrian Gonzalez 40.00 100.00
APAG3 Adrian Gonzalez 40.00 100.00
APAG4 Adrian Gonzalez 40.00 100.00
APAG5 Adrian Gonzalez 40.00 100.00
APAG6 Adrian Gonzalez 40.00 100.00
APAG7 Adrian Gonzalez 40.00 100.00
APAG8 Adrian Gonzalez 40.00 100.00
APAGO1 Alex Gordon 40.00 100.00
APAGO2 Alex Gordon 40.00 100.00
APAGO3 Alex Gordon 40.00 100.00
APAGO4 Alex Gordon 40.00 100.00
APAJ1 Adam Jones 60.00 150.00
APAJ2 Adam Jones 60.00 150.00
APAJ3 Adam Jones 60.00 150.00
APAJ4 Adam Jones 60.00 150.00
APAJ5 Adam Jones 60.00 150.00
APAJ6 Adam Jones 60.00 150.00
APAP1 Andy Pettitte 50.00 120.00
APAP2 Andy Pettitte 50.00 120.00
APAP3 Andy Pettitte 50.00 120.00
APAP4 Andy Pettitte 50.00 120.00
APAP5 Andy Pettitte 50.00 120.00
APAP6 Andy Pettitte 50.00 120.00
APAP7 Andy Pettitte 50.00 120.00
APAPT1 Andy Pettitte 50.00 120.00
APAPT2 Andy Pettitte 50.00 120.00
APAPT3 Andy Pettitte 50.00 120.00
APAPT4 Andy Pettitte 50.00 120.00
APAPT5 Andy Pettitte 50.00 120.00
APAPU1 Albert Pujols 150.00 300.00
APAPU2 Albert Pujols 150.00 300.00
APAPU3 Albert Pujols 150.00 300.00
APAPU4 Albert Pujols 150.00 300.00
APAPU5 Albert Pujols 150.00 300.00
APAPU6 Albert Pujols 150.00 300.00
APAR1 Anthony Rizzo 100.00 250.00
APAR2 Anthony Rizzo 100.00 250.00
APAR3 Anthony Rizzo 100.00 250.00
APAR4 Anthony Rizzo 100.00 250.00
APAR5 Anthony Rizzo 100.00 250.00
APAR6 Anthony Rizzo 100.00 250.00
APAR7 Anthony Rizzo 100.00 250.00
APARD1 Alex Rodriguez 125.00 300.00
APARD2 Alex Rodriguez 125.00 300.00
APARD3 Alex Rodriguez 125.00 300.00
APARD4 Alex Rodriguez 125.00 300.00
APARU1 Addison Russell 75.00 200.00
APARU2 Addison Russell 75.00 200.00
APARU3 Addison Russell 75.00 200.00
APARU4 Addison Russell 75.00 200.00
APARU5 Addison Russell 75.00 200.00
APARU6 Addison Russell 75.00 200.00
APBA8 Bobby Abreu 40.00 100.00
APBA9 Bobby Abreu 40.00 100.00
APBA10 Bobby Abreu 40.00 100.00
APBA11 Bobby Abreu 40.00 100.00
APBA12 Bobby Abreu 40.00 100.00
APBA13 Bobby Abreu 40.00 100.00
APBH1 Bryce Harper 200.00 400.00
APBH2 Bryce Harper 200.00 400.00
APBH3 Bryce Harper 200.00 400.00
APBH4 Bryce Harper 200.00 400.00
APBH5 Bryce Harper 200.00 400.00
APBH6 Bryce Harper 200.00 400.00
APBH7 Bryce Harper 200.00 400.00
APBH8 Bryce Harper 200.00 400.00
APBL1 Barry Larkin 60.00 150.00
APBL2 Barry Larkin 60.00 150.00
APBL3 Barry Larkin 60.00 150.00
APBL4 Barry Larkin 60.00 150.00
APBL5 Barry Larkin 60.00 150.00
APBL6 Barry Larkin 60.00 150.00
APBP1 Buster Posey 100.00 250.00
APBP2 Buster Posey 100.00 250.00
APBP3 Buster Posey 100.00 250.00
APBP4 Buster Posey 100.00 250.00
APBP5 Buster Posey 100.00 250.00
APBP6 Buster Posey 100.00 250.00
APBP7 Buster Posey 100.00 250.00
APCB1 Craig Biggio 40.00 100.00
APCB2 Craig Biggio 40.00 100.00
APCB3 Craig Biggio 40.00 100.00
APCB4 Craig Biggio 40.00 100.00
APCB5 Craig Biggio 40.00 100.00
APCB6 Craig Biggio 40.00 100.00
APCC1 Carlos Correa 125.00 300.00
APCC2 Carlos Correa 125.00 300.00
APCC3 Carlos Correa 125.00 300.00
APCC4 Carlos Correa 125.00 300.00
APCC5 Carlos Correa 125.00 300.00
APCC6 Carlos Correa 125.00 300.00
APCC7 Carlos Correa 125.00 300.00
APCC8 Carlos Correa 125.00 300.00
APCF1 Carlton Fisk 50.00 120.00
APCF2 Carlton Fisk 50.00 120.00
APCF3 Carlton Fisk 50.00 120.00
APCF4 Carlton Fisk 50.00 120.00
APCF5 Carlton Fisk 50.00 120.00
APCH1 Cole Hamels 30.00 80.00
APCH2 Cole Hamels 30.00 80.00
APCH3 Cole Hamels 30.00 80.00
APCH4 Cole Hamels 30.00 80.00
APCH6 Cole Hamels 30.00 80.00
APCJ1 Chipper Jones 125.00 300.00
APCJ2 Chipper Jones 125.00 300.00
APCJ3 Chipper Jones 125.00 300.00
APCJ4 Chipper Jones 125.00 300.00
APCJ5 Chipper Jones 125.00 300.00
APCJ6 Chipper Jones 125.00 300.00
APCJ7 Chipper Jones 125.00 300.00
APCJ8 Chipper Jones 125.00 300.00
APCK1 Clayton Kershaw 125.00 250.00
APCK2 Clayton Kershaw 125.00 250.00
APCK3 Clayton Kershaw 125.00 250.00
APCK4 Clayton Kershaw 125.00 250.00
APCK6 Clayton Kershaw 125.00 250.00
APCK7 Clayton Kershaw 125.00 250.00
APCS1 Corey Seager RC 500.00 700.00
APCS2 Corey Seager RC 500.00 700.00
APCS3 Corey Seager RC 500.00 700.00
APCS4 Corey Seager RC 500.00 700.00
APCS5 Corey Seager RC 500.00 700.00
APCS6 Corey Seager RC 500.00 700.00
APCS7 Corey Seager RC 500.00 700.00
APCSL1 Chris Sale 50.00 120.00
APCSL2 Chris Sale 50.00 120.00
APCSL3 Chris Sale 50.00 120.00
APCSL4 Chris Sale 50.00 120.00
APCSL5 Chris Sale 50.00 120.00
APCSL6 Chris Sale 50.00 120.00
APDJ1 Derek Jeter 800.00 1200.00
APDJ2 Derek Jeter 800.00 1200.00
APDJ3 Derek Jeter 800.00 1200.00
APDJ4 Derek Jeter 800.00 1200.00
APDJ5 Derek Jeter 800.00 1200.00
APDMU1 Dale Murphy 75.00 200.00
APDMU2 Dale Murphy 75.00 200.00
APDMU3 Dale Murphy 75.00 200.00
APDMU4 Dale Murphy 75.00 200.00
APDO1 David Ortiz 150.00 300.00
APDO2 David Ortiz 150.00 300.00
APDO3 David Ortiz 150.00 300.00
APDO4 David Ortiz 150.00 300.00
APDO5 David Ortiz 150.00 300.00
APDO6 David Ortiz 150.00 300.00
APDO7 David Ortiz 150.00 300.00
APDP1 Dustin Pedroia 60.00 150.00
APDP2 Dustin Pedroia 60.00 150.00
APDP3 Dustin Pedroia 60.00 150.00
APDP4 Dustin Pedroia 60.00 150.00
APDP5 Dustin Pedroia 60.00 150.00
APDP6 Dustin Pedroia 60.00 150.00
APDP7 Dustin Pedroia 60.00 150.00
APDP8 Dustin Pedroia 60.00 150.00
APDPR1 David Price 50.00 120.00
APDPR2 David Price 50.00 120.00
APDPR3 David Price 50.00 120.00
APDPR4 David Price 50.00 120.00
APDPR5 David Price 50.00 120.00
APDPR6 David Price 50.00 120.00
APDSA1 Deion Sanders 40.00 100.00
APDSA2 Deion Sanders 40.00 100.00
APDSA3 Deion Sanders 40.00 100.00
APDSA4 Deion Sanders 40.00 100.00
APDSA5 Deion Sanders 40.00 100.00

APDW1 David Wright 60.00 150.00
APDW2 David Wright 60.00 150.00
APDW3 David Wright 60.00 150.00
APDW4 David Wright 60.00 150.00
APDW5 David Wright 60.00 150.00
APDW6 David Wright 60.00 150.00
APDW7 David Wright 60.00 150.00
APDW8 David Wright 60.00 150.00
APFF1 Freddie Freeman 50.00 120.00
APFF2 Freddie Freeman 50.00 120.00
APFF3 Freddie Freeman 50.00 120.00
APFF4 Freddie Freeman 50.00 120.00
APFF5 Freddie Freeman 50.00 120.00
APFF6 Freddie Freeman 50.00 120.00
APFF7 Freddie Freeman 50.00 120.00
APFF8 Freddie Freeman 50.00 120.00
APFH1 Felix Hernandez 40.00 100.00
APFH2 Felix Hernandez 40.00 100.00
APFH3 Felix Hernandez 40.00 100.00
APFH4 Felix Hernandez 40.00 100.00
APFH5 Felix Hernandez 40.00 100.00
APFH6 Felix Hernandez 40.00 100.00
APFL1 Francisco Lindor 75.00 200.00
APFL2 Francisco Lindor 75.00 200.00
APFL3 Francisco Lindor 75.00 200.00
APFL4 Francisco Lindor 75.00 200.00
APFL5 Francisco Lindor 75.00 200.00
APFL6 Francisco Lindor 75.00 200.00
APFT1 Frank Thomas 75.00 200.00
APFT2 Frank Thomas 75.00 200.00
APFT3 Frank Thomas 75.00 200.00
APFT4 Frank Thomas 75.00 200.00
APFT5 Frank Thomas 75.00 200.00
APGS1 George Springer 40.00 100.00
APGS2 George Springer 40.00 100.00
APGS3 George Springer 40.00 100.00
APGS4 George Springer 40.00 100.00
APGS5 George Springer 40.00 100.00
APGS6 George Springer 40.00 100.00
APJA1 Jose Altuve 75.00 200.00
APJA2 Jose Altuve 75.00 200.00
APJA3 Jose Altuve 75.00 200.00
APJA4 Jose Altuve 75.00 200.00
APJA5 Jose Altuve 75.00 200.00
APJA6 Jose Altuve 75.00 200.00
APJA7 Jose Altuve 75.00 200.00
APJAR1 Jake Arrieta EXCH 150.00 300.00
APJAR2 Jake Arrieta EXCH 150.00 300.00
APJAR3 Jake Arrieta EXCH 150.00 300.00
APJAR4 Jake Arrieta EXCH 150.00 300.00
APJAR5 Jake Arrieta EXCH 150.00 300.00
APJAR6 Jake Arrieta EXCH 150.00 300.00
APJD1 Jacob deGrom 60.00 150.00
APJD2 Jacob deGrom 60.00 150.00
APJD3 Jacob deGrom 60.00 150.00
APJD4 Jacob deGrom 60.00 150.00
APJD5 Jacob deGrom 60.00 150.00
APJD6 Jacob deGrom 60.00 150.00
APJD7 Jacob deGrom 60.00 150.00
APJH1 Jason Heyward 50.00 120.00
APJH2 Jason Heyward 50.00 120.00
APJH3 Jason Heyward 50.00 120.00
APJH4 Jason Heyward 50.00 120.00
APJH5 Jason Heyward 50.00 120.00
APJP1 Joc Pederson 50.00 120.00
APJP2 Joc Pederson 50.00 120.00
APJP3 Joc Pederson 50.00 120.00
APJP4 Joc Pederson 50.00 120.00
APJP5 Joc Pederson 50.00 120.00
APJP6 Joc Pederson 50.00 120.00
APJP7 Joc Pederson 50.00 120.00
APJS1 John Smoltz 60.00 150.00
APJS2 John Smoltz 60.00 150.00
APJS3 John Smoltz 60.00 150.00
APJS4 John Smoltz 60.00 150.00
APJS5 John Smoltz 60.00 150.00
APJS6 John Smoltz 60.00 150.00
APJS7 John Smoltz 60.00 150.00
APJS8 John Smoltz 60.00 150.00
APJU1 Julio Urias RC 50.00 120.00
APJU2 Julio Urias RC 50.00 120.00
APJU3 Julio Urias RC 50.00 120.00
APJU4 Julio Urias RC 50.00 120.00
APJU5 Julio Urias RC 50.00 120.00
APJVO1 Joey Votto 40.00 100.00
APJVO2 Joey Votto 40.00 100.00
APJVO3 Joey Votto 40.00 100.00
APJVO4 Joey Votto 40.00 100.00
APJVO5 Joey Votto 40.00 100.00
APJVO6 Joey Votto 40.00 100.00
APJVO7 Joey Votto 40.00 100.00
APJVO8 Joey Votto 40.00 100.00
APKB1 Kris Bryant 500.00 800.00
APKB2 Kris Bryant 500.00 800.00
APKB3 Kris Bryant 500.00 800.00
APKB4 Kris Bryant 500.00 800.00
APKB5 Kris Bryant 500.00 800.00
APKB6 Kris Bryant 500.00 800.00
APKB7 Kris Bryant 500.00 800.00
APKG1 Ken Griffey Jr. 400.00 800.00
APKG5 Ken Griffey Jr. 400.00 800.00
APKG6 Ken Griffey Jr. 400.00 800.00
APKG7 Ken Griffey Jr. 400.00 800.00
APKG8 Ken Griffey Jr. 400.00 800.00
APKG9 Ken Griffey Jr. 400.00 800.00
APKM1 Kenta Maeda RC 50.00 120.00
APKM2 Kenta Maeda RC 50.00 120.00
APKM3 Kenta Maeda RC 50.00 120.00
APKM4 Kenta Maeda RC 50.00 120.00
APKM5 Kenta Maeda RC 50.00 120.00
APKM6 Kenta Maeda RC 50.00 120.00
APKM7 Kenta Maeda RC 50.00 120.00
APKS1 Kyle Schwarber RC 125.00 300.00
APKS2 Kyle Schwarber RC 125.00 300.00
APKS3 Kyle Schwarber RC 125.00 300.00
APKS4 Kyle Schwarber RC 125.00 300.00
APKS5 Kyle Schwarber RC 125.00 300.00
APKS6 Kyle Schwarber RC 125.00 300.00
APKS7 Kyle Schwarber RC 125.00 300.00
APLG1 Lucas Giolito RC 30.00 80.00
APLG2 Lucas Giolito RC 30.00 80.00
APLG3 Lucas Giolito RC 30.00 80.00
APLG4 Lucas Giolito RC 30.00 80.00
APLG5 Lucas Giolito RC 30.00 80.00
APLS1 Luis Severino RC 30.00 80.00
APLS2 Luis Severino RC 30.00 80.00
APLS3 Luis Severino RC 30.00 80.00
APLS4 Luis Severino RC 30.00 80.00
APLS5 Luis Severino RC 30.00 80.00
APLS6 Luis Severino RC 30.00 80.00
APLS7 Luis Severino RC 30.00 80.00
APMM1 Mark McGwire 75.00 200.00
APMM10 Mark McGwire 75.00 200.00
APMM2 Mark McGwire 75.00 200.00
APMM3 Mark McGwire 75.00 200.00
APMM4 Mark McGwire 75.00 200.00
APMM5 Mark McGwire 75.00 200.00
APMM6 Mark McGwire 75.00 200.00
APMM7 Mark McGwire 75.00 200.00
APMM8 Mark McGwire 75.00 200.00
APMM9 Mark McGwire 75.00 200.00
APMMA1 Manny Machado 100.00 250.00
APMMA2 Manny Machado 100.00 250.00
APMMA3 Manny Machado 100.00 250.00
APMMA4 Manny Machado 100.00 250.00
APMMA5 Manny Machado 100.00 250.00
APMMA6 Manny Machado 100.00 250.00
APMMA7 Manny Machado 100.00 250.00
APMMA8 Manny Machado 100.00 250.00
APMP1 Mike Piazza 100.00 250.00
APMP10 Mike Piazza 100.00 250.00
APMP2 Mike Piazza 100.00 250.00
APMP3 Mike Piazza 100.00 250.00
APMP4 Mike Piazza 100.00 250.00
APMP5 Mike Piazza 100.00 250.00
APMP6 Mike Piazza 100.00 250.00
APMP7 Mike Piazza 100.00 250.00
APMP8 Mike Piazza 100.00 250.00
APMP9 Mike Piazza 100.00 250.00
APMS1 Miguel Sano RC 30.00 80.00
APMS2 Miguel Sano RC 30.00 80.00
APMS3 Miguel Sano RC 30.00 80.00
APMS4 Miguel Sano RC 30.00 80.00
APMS5 Miguel Sano RC 30.00 80.00
APMS6 Miguel Sano RC 30.00 80.00
APMS7 Miguel Sano RC 30.00 80.00
APMT1 Mike Trout 300.00 600.00
APMT2 Mike Trout 300.00 600.00
APMT3 Mike Trout 300.00 600.00
APMT4 Mike Trout 300.00 600.00
APMT5 Mike Trout 300.00 600.00
APMT6 Mike Trout 300.00 600.00
APMT7 Mike Trout 300.00 600.00
APMT8 Mike Trout 300.00 600.00
APMW1 Michael Wacha 30.00 80.00
APMW2 Michael Wacha 30.00 80.00
APMW3 Michael Wacha 30.00 80.00
APMW4 Michael Wacha 30.00 80.00
APMW5 Michael Wacha 30.00 80.00
APMW6 Michael Wacha 30.00 80.00
APNA1 Nolan Arenado 60.00 150.00
APNA2 Nolan Arenado 60.00 150.00
APNA3 Nolan Arenado 60.00 150.00
APNA4 Nolan Arenado 60.00 150.00
APNA5 Nolan Arenado 60.00 150.00
APNA6 Nolan Arenado 60.00 150.00
APNR1 Nolan Ryan 150.00 300.00
APNR2 Nolan Ryan 150.00 300.00
APNR3 Nolan Ryan 150.00 300.00
APNR4 Nolan Ryan 150.00 300.00
APNR5 Nolan Ryan 150.00 300.00
APNR6 Nolan Ryan 150.00 300.00
APNR7 Nolan Ryan 150.00 300.00
APNR8 Nolan Ryan 150.00 300.00
APNR9 Nolan Ryan 150.00 300.00
APNS1 Noah Syndergaard 75.00 200.00
APNS2 Noah Syndergaard 75.00 200.00
APNS3 Noah Syndergaard 75.00 200.00
APNS4 Noah Syndergaard 75.00 200.00
APNS5 Noah Syndergaard 75.00 200.00
APNS6 Noah Syndergaard 75.00 200.00
APNS7 Noah Syndergaard 75.00 200.00
APNS8 Noah Syndergaard 75.00 200.00
APPF1 Prince Fielder 30.00 80.00
APPF2 Prince Fielder 30.00 80.00
APPF3 Prince Fielder 30.00 80.00
APPF4 Prince Fielder 30.00 80.00
APPF5 Prince Fielder 30.00 80.00
APPF6 Prince Fielder 30.00 80.00
APPMA1 Pedro Martinez 60.00 150.00
APPMA10 Pedro Martinez 60.00 150.00
APPMA11 Pedro Martinez 60.00 150.00
APPMA12 Pedro Martinez 60.00 150.00
APPMA13 Pedro Martinez 60.00 150.00
APPMA14 Pedro Martinez 60.00 150.00
APPMA15 Pedro Martinez 60.00 150.00
APPMA16 Pedro Martinez 60.00 150.00
APPMA17 Pedro Martinez 60.00 150.00
APPMA2 Pedro Martinez 60.00 150.00
APPMA3 Pedro Martinez 60.00 150.00
APPMA4 Pedro Martinez 60.00 150.00
APPMA5 Pedro Martinez 60.00 150.00
APPMA6 Pedro Martinez 60.00 150.00
APPMA7 Pedro Martinez 60.00 150.00
APPMA8 Pedro Martinez 60.00 150.00
APPMA9 Pedro Martinez 60.00 150.00
APRC1 Roger Clemens 60.00 150.00
APRC2 Roger Clemens 60.00 150.00
APRC3 Roger Clemens 60.00 150.00
APRC4 Roger Clemens 60.00 150.00
APRC5 Roger Clemens 60.00 150.00
APRCA1 Robinson Cano 50.00 120.00
APRCA2 Robinson Cano 50.00 120.00
APRCA3 Robinson Cano 50.00 120.00
APRCA4 Robinson Cano 50.00 120.00
APRCA5 Robinson Cano 50.00 120.00
APRCA6 Robinson Cano 50.00 120.00
APRCR1 Rod Carew 50.00 120.00
APRCR2 Rod Carew 50.00 120.00
APRCR3 Rod Carew 50.00 120.00
APRCR4 Rod Carew 50.00 120.00
APRCR5 Rod Carew 50.00 120.00
APRH1 Rickey Henderson 75.00 200.00
APRH2 Rickey Henderson 75.00 200.00
APRH3 Rickey Henderson 75.00 200.00
APRH4 Rickey Henderson 75.00 200.00
APRH5 Rickey Henderson 75.00 200.00
APRH6 Rickey Henderson 75.00 200.00
APRH7 Rickey Henderson 75.00 200.00
APRJ1 Reggie Jackson 50.00 120.00
APRJ2 Reggie Jackson 50.00 120.00
APRJ3 Reggie Jackson 50.00 120.00
APRJ4 Reggie Jackson 50.00 120.00
APRJ5 Reggie Jackson 50.00 120.00
APRJ6 Reggie Jackson 50.00 120.00
APRY1 Robin Yount 75.00 200.00
APRY2 Robin Yount 75.00 200.00
APRY3 Robin Yount 75.00 200.00
APRY4 Robin Yount 75.00 200.00
APSC1 Steve Carlton 50.00 120.00
APSC2 Steve Carlton 50.00 120.00
APSC2 Steve Carlton 50.00 120.00
APSG1 Sonny Gray 30.00 80.00
APSG2 Sonny Gray 30.00 80.00
APSG3 Sonny Gray 30.00 80.00
APSG4 Sonny Gray 30.00 80.00
APSG5 Sonny Gray 30.00 80.00
APSG6 Sonny Gray 30.00 80.00
APSM2 Steven Matz 50.00 120.00
APSM3 Steven Matz 50.00 120.00
APSM4 Steven Matz 50.00 120.00
APSM5 Steven Matz 50.00 120.00
APSM6 Steven Matz 50.00 120.00
APTGL1 Tom Glavine 50.00 120.00
APTGL2 Tom Glavine 50.00 120.00
APTGL3 Tom Glavine 50.00 120.00
APTGL4 Tom Glavine 50.00 120.00
APTGL5 Tom Glavine 50.00 120.00
APTGL6 Tom Glavine 50.00 120.00
APTS1 Trevor Story RC 60.00 150.00
APTS2 Trevor Story RC 60.00 150.00
APTS3 Trevor Story RC 60.00 150.00
APTS4 Trevor Story RC 60.00 150.00
APTS5 Trevor Story RC 60.00 150.00
APTS6 Trevor Story RC 60.00 150.00
APTT1 Troy Tulowitzki 40.00 100.00
APTT2 Troy Tulowitzki 40.00 100.00
APTT3 Troy Tulowitzki 40.00 100.00
APTT4 Troy Tulowitzki 40.00 100.00
APTT5 Troy Tulowitzki 40.00 100.00
APTT6 Troy Tulowitzki 40.00 100.00
APVG1 Vladimir Guerrero 40.00 100.00
APVG2 Vladimir Guerrero 40.00 100.00
APVG3 Vladimir Guerrero 40.00 100.00
APVG4 Vladimir Guerrero 40.00 100.00
APVG5 Vladimir Guerrero 40.00 100.00
APVG6 Vladimir Guerrero 40.00 100.00
APWB1 Wade Boggs 50.00 120.00
APWB2 Wade Boggs 50.00 120.00
APWB3 Wade Boggs 50.00 120.00
APWB5 Wade Boggs 50.00 120.00
APWBO2 Wade Boggs 50.00 120.00
APWBO3 Wade Boggs 50.00 120.00
APWBO4 Wade Boggs 50.00 120.00
APWBO5 Wade Boggs 50.00 120.00
APWBO1 Wade Boggs 50.00 120.00

2016 Topps Dynasty Autograph Patches 5

*EMERALD: .5X TO 1.2X BASIC
RANDOM INSERTS IN PACKS
STATED PRINT RUN 5 SER.#'d SETS
EXCHANGE DEADLINE 11/30/2018
LOGO/TAG PATCHES MAY SELL FOR PREMIUM

2016 Topps Dynasty Dual Relic Greats Autographs

STATED ODDS 1:28
STATED PRINT RUN 5 SER.#'d SETS
ALL VERSIONS EQUALLY PRICED
EXCHANGE DEADLINE 11/30/2018
ADRGAD1 Andre Dawson 40.00 100.00
ADRGAD2 Andre Dawson 40.00 100.00
ADRGAD3 Andre Dawson 40.00 100.00
ADRGAD4 Andre Dawson 40.00 100.00
ADRGAD5 Andre Dawson 40.00 100.00
ADRGAK1 Al Kaline 75.00 200.00
ADRGAK2 Al Kaline 75.00 200.00
ADRGAK3 Al Kaline 75.00 200.00
ADRGAK4 Al Kaline 75.00 200.00
ADRGAK5 Al Kaline 75.00 200.00
ADRGCY1 Carl Yastrzemski 60.00 150.00
ADRGCY2 Carl Yastrzemski 60.00 150.00
ADRGCY3 Carl Yastrzemski 60.00 150.00
ADRGCY4 Carl Yastrzemski 60.00 150.00
ADRGCY5 Carl Yastrzemski 60.00 150.00
ADRGDM1 Don Mattingly 100.00 250.00
ADRGDM2 Don Mattingly 100.00 250.00
ADRGDM3 Don Mattingly 100.00 250.00
ADRGDM4 Don Mattingly 100.00 250.00
ADRGDM5 Don Mattingly 100.00 250.00
ADRGFR1 Frank Robinson 50.00 120.00
ADRGFR2 Frank Robinson 50.00 120.00
ADRGFR3 Frank Robinson 50.00 120.00
ADRGFR4 Frank Robinson 50.00 120.00
ADRGFR5 Frank Robinson 50.00 120.00
ADRGHA1 Hank Aaron 200.00 400.00
ADRGHA2 Hank Aaron 200.00 400.00
ADRGHA3 Hank Aaron 200.00 400.00
ADRGHA4 Hank Aaron 200.00 400.00
ADRGHA5 Hank Aaron 200.00 400.00
ADRGJB1 Johnny Bench 75.00 200.00
ADRGJB2 Johnny Bench 75.00 200.00
ADRGJB3 Johnny Bench 75.00 200.00
ADRGJB4 Johnny Bench 75.00 200.00
ADRGJB5 Johnny Bench 75.00 200.00
ADRGLB1 Lou Brock 50.00 120.00
ADRGLB2 Lou Brock 50.00 120.00
ADRGLB3 Lou Brock 50.00 120.00
ADRGLB4 Lou Brock 50.00 120.00
ADRGLB5 Lou Brock 50.00 120.00
ADRGOS1 Ozzie Smith 60.00 150.00
ADRGOS2 Ozzie Smith 60.00 150.00
ADRGOS3 Ozzie Smith 60.00 150.00
ADRGOS4 Ozzie Smith 60.00 150.00
ADRGOS5 Ozzie Smith 60.00 150.00
ADRGOV1 Omar Vizquel 75.00 200.00
ADRGOV2 Omar Vizquel 75.00 200.00
ADRGOV3 Omar Vizquel 75.00 200.00
ADRGOV4 Omar Vizquel 75.00 200.00
ADRGRS1 Ryne Sandberg 60.00 150.00
ADRGRS2 Ryne Sandberg 60.00 150.00
ADRGRS3 Ryne Sandberg 60.00 150.00
ADRGRS4 Ryne Sandberg 60.00 150.00
ADRGRS5 Ryne Sandberg 60.00 150.00
ADRGSC1 Steve Carlton 40.00 100.00
ADRGSC2 Steve Carlton 40.00 100.00

2017 Topps Dynasty Autograph Patches

OVERALL AUTO ODDS 1:1
STATED PRINT RUN 10 SER.#'d SETS
ALL VERSIONS EQUALLY PRICED
LOGO/TAG PATCHES MAY SELL FOR PREMIUM
EXCHANGE DEADLINE 10/31/2019
APAA1 Aaron Judge RC 600.00 1000.00
APAA2 Aaron Judge RC 600.00 1000.00
APAA3 Aaron Judge RC 600.00 1000.00
APAB1 Alex Bregman RC 75.00 150.00
APAB2 Alex Bregman RC 75.00 150.00
APAB3 Alex Bregman RC 75.00 150.00
APAB4 Alex Bregman RC 75.00 150.00
APAB5 Alex Bregman RC 75.00 150.00
APAB6 Alex Bregman RC 75.00 150.00
APAB7 Alex Bregman RC 75.00 150.00
APAB8 Alex Bregman RC 75.00 150.00
APADB1 Adrian Beltre 60.00 150.00
APADB2 Adrian Beltre 60.00 150.00
APADB3 Adrian Beltre 60.00 150.00
APADB4 Adrian Beltre 60.00 150.00
APADB5 Adrian Beltre 60.00 150.00
APADB6 Adrian Beltre 60.00 150.00
APADB7 Adrian Beltre 60.00 150.00
APADB8 Adrian Beltre 60.00 150.00
APADR1 Addison Russell 40.00 100.00
APADR2 Addison Russell 40.00 100.00
APADR3 Addison Russell 40.00 100.00
APADR4 Addison Russell 40.00 100.00
APADR5 Addison Russell 40.00 100.00
APADR6 Addison Russell 40.00 100.00
APADR7 Addison Russell 40.00 100.00
APADR8 Addison Russell 40.00 100.00
APAJ1 Adam Jones 30.00 80.00
APAJ2 Adam Jones 30.00 80.00
APAJ3 Adam Jones 30.00 80.00
APAJ4 Adam Jones 30.00 80.00
APAJ5 Adam Jones 30.00 80.00
APAJ6 Adam Jones 30.00 80.00
APAJ7 Adam Jones 30.00 80.00
APAJ8 Adam Jones 30.00 80.00
APALB1 Andrew Benintendi RC 100.00 250.00
APALB2 Andrew Benintendi RC 100.00 250.00
APALB3 Andrew Benintendi RC 100.00 250.00
APALB4 Andrew Benintendi RC 100.00 250.00
APALB5 Andrew Benintendi RC 100.00 250.00
APALB6 Andrew Benintendi RC 100.00 250.00
APALB7 Andrew Benintendi RC 100.00 250.00
APALB8 Andrew Benintendi RC 100.00 250.00
APAO1 Alex Rodriguez 100.00 250.00
APAO2 Alex Rodriguez 100.00 250.00
APAO3 Alex Rodriguez 100.00 250.00
APAO4 Alex Rodriguez 100.00 250.00
APAO5 Alex Rodriguez 100.00 250.00
APAO6 Alex Rodriguez 100.00 250.00
APAP1 Albert Pujols 100.00 250.00
APAP2 Albert Pujols 100.00 250.00
APAP3 Albert Pujols 100.00 250.00
APAP4 Albert Pujols 100.00 250.00
APAP5 Albert Pujols 100.00 250.00
APAP6 Albert Pujols 100.00 250.00
APAPT1 Andy Pettitte 30.00 80.00
APAPT4 Andy Pettitte 30.00 80.00
APAPT5 Andy Pettitte 30.00 80.00
APAPT6 Andy Pettitte 30.00 80.00
APAZ1 Anthony Rizzo 75.00 200.00
APAZ2 Anthony Rizzo 75.00 200.00
APAZ3 Anthony Rizzo 75.00 200.00
APAZ4 Anthony Rizzo 75.00 200.00
APAZ5 Anthony Rizzo 75.00 200.00
APAZ6 Anthony Rizzo 75.00 200.00
APBH3 Bryce Harper 150.00 400.00
APBH4 Bryce Harper 150.00 400.00
APBH5 Bryce Harper 150.00 400.00
APBH6 Bryce Harper 150.00 400.00
APBH7 Bryce Harper 150.00 400.00
APBH8 Bryce Harper 150.00 400.00
APBL1 Barry Larkin 30.00 80.00
APBL2 Barry Larkin 30.00 80.00
APBL3 Barry Larkin 30.00 80.00
APBL4 Barry Larkin 30.00 80.00
APBL5 Barry Larkin 30.00 80.00
APBL6 Barry Larkin 30.00 80.00
APBP1 Buster Posey 75.00 200.00
APBP2 Buster Posey 75.00 200.00
APBP3 Buster Posey 75.00 200.00
APBP4 Buster Posey 75.00 200.00
APBP5 Buster Posey 75.00 200.00
APBP6 Buster Posey 75.00 200.00
APBR1 Bryce Harper 150.00 400.00
APBR2 Bryce Harper 150.00 400.00
APCB1 Cody Bellinger RC 200.00 500.00
APCB2 Cody Bellinger RC 200.00 500.00
APCB3 Cody Bellinger RC 200.00 500.00
APCB4 Cody Bellinger RC 200.00 500.00
APCB5 Cody Bellinger RC 200.00 500.00
APCB6 Cody Bellinger RC 200.00 500.00
APCC1 Carlos Correa 100.00 250.00
APCC10 Carlos Correa 100.00 250.00
APCC11 Carlos Correa 100.00 250.00
APCC12 Carlos Correa 100.00 250.00
APCC13 Carlos Correa 100.00 250.00
APCC2 Carlos Correa 100.00 250.00
APCC3 Carlos Correa 100.00 250.00
APCC4 Carlos Correa 100.00 250.00
APCC5 Carlos Correa 100.00 250.00
APCC6 Carlos Correa 100.00 250.00
APCC7 Carlos Correa 100.00 250.00
APCC8 Carlos Correa 100.00 250.00
APCC9 Carlos Correa 100.00 250.00
APCE1 Clayton Kershaw EXCH 100.00 250.00
APCE2 Clayton Kershaw EXCH 100.00 250.00
APCE3 Clayton Kershaw EXCH 100.00 250.00
APCE4 Clayton Kershaw EXCH 100.00 250.00
APCE5 Clayton Kershaw EXCH 100.00 250.00
APCE6 Clayton Kershaw EXCH 100.00 250.00
APCI1 Craig Biggio 30.00 80.00
APCI2 Craig Biggio 30.00 80.00
APCI3 Craig Biggio 30.00 80.00
APCI4 Craig Biggio 30.00 80.00
APCI5 Craig Biggio 30.00 80.00
APCI6 Craig Biggio 30.00 80.00
APCJ1 Chipper Jones 75.00 200.00
APCJ2 Chipper Jones 75.00 200.00
APCJ3 Chipper Jones 75.00 200.00
APCJ4 Chipper Jones 75.00 200.00
APCJ5 Chipper Jones 75.00 200.00
APCJ6 Chipper Jones 75.00 200.00
APCJ7 Chipper Jones 75.00 200.00
APCJ8 Chipper Jones 75.00 200.00
APCOS1 Corey Seager 75.00 200.00
APCOS2 Corey Seager 75.00 200.00
APCOS3 Corey Seager 75.00 200.00
APCOS4 Corey Seager 75.00 200.00
APCOS5 Corey Seager 75.00 200.00
APCOS6 Corey Seager 75.00 200.00
APCOS7 Corey Seager 75.00 200.00
APCOS8 Corey Seager 75.00 200.00
APCR1 Cal Ripken Jr. 100.00 250.00
APCR2 Cal Ripken Jr. 100.00 250.00
APCR3 Cal Ripken Jr. 100.00 250.00
APCR4 Cal Ripken Jr. 100.00 250.00
APCR5 Cal Ripken Jr. 100.00 250.00
APCS1 Chris Sale 30.00 80.00
APCS2 Chris Sale 30.00 80.00
APCS3 Chris Sale 30.00 80.00
APCS4 Chris Sale 30.00 80.00
APCS5 Chris Sale 30.00 80.00
APCS6 Chris Sale 30.00 80.00
APCS7 Chris Sale 30.00 80.00
APCS8 Chris Sale 30.00 80.00
APDJ1 Derek Jeter 400.00 800.00
APDJ2 Derek Jeter 400.00 800.00
APDJ3 Derek Jeter 400.00 800.00
APDJ4 Derek Jeter 400.00 800.00
APDJ5 Derek Jeter 400.00 800.00
APDJ6 Derek Jeter 400.00 800.00
APDO1 David Ortiz 75.00 200.00
APDO2 David Ortiz 75.00 200.00
APDO3 David Ortiz 75.00 200.00
APDO4 David Ortiz 75.00 200.00
APDO5 David Ortiz 75.00 200.00
APDO6 David Ortiz 75.00 200.00
APDO7 David Ortiz 75.00 200.00
APDO8 David Ortiz 75.00 200.00
APDP1 David Price 25.00 60.00
APDP2 David Price 25.00 60.00
APDP3 David Price 25.00 60.00
APDP4 David Price 25.00 60.00
APDP5 David Price 25.00 60.00
APDP6 David Price 25.00 60.00
APDS2 Dansby Swanson RC 50.00 120.00
APDS3 Dansby Swanson RC 50.00 120.00
APDS4 Dansby Swanson RC 50.00 120.00
APDS5 Dansby Swanson RC 50.00 120.00
APDS6 Dansby Swanson RC 50.00 120.00
APDS7 Dansby Swanson RC 50.00 120.00
APDS8 Dansby Swanson RC 50.00 120.00
APDUP1 Dustin Pedroia 40.00 100.00
APDUP2 Dustin Pedroia 40.00 100.00
APDUP3 Dustin Pedroia 40.00 100.00
APDUP4 Dustin Pedroia 40.00 100.00
APDUP5 Dustin Pedroia 40.00 100.00
APDUP6 Dustin Pedroia 40.00 100.00
APDW1 Dave Winfield 40.00 100.00
APDW2 Dave Winfield 40.00 100.00
APDW3 Dave Winfield 40.00 100.00
APDW4 Dave Winfield 40.00 100.00
APDW5 Dave Winfield 40.00 100.00
APDW6 Dave Winfield 40.00 100.00
APDW7 Dave Winfield 40.00 100.00
APEE1 Edwin Encarnacion EXCH 40.00 100.00
APEE2 Edwin Encarnacion EXCH 40.00 100.00
APEE3 Edwin Encarnacion EXCH 40.00 100.00
APFF1 Freddie Freeman 50.00 120.00
APFF2 Freddie Freeman 50.00 120.00
APFF3 Freddie Freeman 50.00 120.00
APFF4 Freddie Freeman 50.00 120.00
APFF5 Freddie Freeman 50.00 120.00
APFF6 Freddie Freeman 50.00 120.00
APFF7 Freddie Freeman 50.00 120.00
APFF8 Freddie Freeman 50.00 120.00
APFL1 Francisco Lindor 60.00 150.00
APFL2 Francisco Lindor 60.00 150.00
APFL3 Francisco Lindor 60.00 150.00
APFL4 Francisco Lindor 60.00 150.00
APFL5 Francisco Lindor 60.00 150.00
APFL6 Francisco Lindor 60.00 150.00
APFM1 Floyd Mayweather Jr. 200.00 500.00
APFM2 Floyd Mayweather Jr. 200.00 500.00
APFM3 Floyd Mayweather Jr. 200.00 500.00
APFM4 Floyd Mayweather Jr. 200.00 500.00
APFM5 Floyd Mayweather Jr. 200.00 500.00
APFT1 Frank Thomas 75.00 200.00
APFT2 Frank Thomas 75.00 200.00
APFT3 Frank Thomas 75.00 200.00
APFT4 Frank Thomas 75.00 200.00
APFT5 Frank Thomas 75.00 200.00
APFT6 Frank Thomas 75.00 200.00
APGA1 Gary Sheffield
APGA2 Gary Sheffield
APGA3 Gary Sheffield
APGA4 Gary Sheffield
APGA5 Gary Sheffield
APGA6 Gary Sheffield
APGA7 Gary Sheffield
APGM1 Greg Maddux 75.00 200.00
APGM2 Greg Maddux 75.00 200.00
APGM3 Greg Maddux 75.00 200.00
APGM4 Greg Maddux 75.00 200.00
APGM5 Greg Maddux 75.00 200.00
APGS1 George Springer 50.00 120.00
APGS2 George Springer 50.00 120.00
APGS3 George Springer 50.00 120.00
APGS4 George Springer 50.00 120.00
APGS5 George Springer 50.00 120.00
APGS6 George Springer 50.00 120.00
APGS7 George Springer 50.00 120.00
APGS8 George Springer 50.00 120.00
APGY1 Gary Sanchez 60.00 150.00
APGY2 Gary Sanchez 60.00 150.00
APGY3 Gary Sanchez 60.00 150.00
APGY4 Gary Sanchez 60.00 150.00
APGY5 Gary Sanchez 60.00 150.00
APGY6 Gary Sanchez 60.00 150.00
APIR1 Ivan Rodriguez 50.00 120.00
APIR2 Ivan Rodriguez 50.00 120.00
APIR3 Ivan Rodriguez 50.00 120.00
APIR4 Ivan Rodriguez 50.00 120.00
APIR5 Ivan Rodriguez 50.00 120.00
API1 Ichiro 300.00 600.00
API2 Ichiro 300.00 600.00
API5 Ichiro 300.00 600.00
API6 Ichiro 300.00 600.00
API7 Ichiro 300.00 600.00
API8 Ichiro 300.00 600.00
API9 Ichiro 300.00 600.00
API10 Ichiro 300.00 600.00
APJA1 Jose Altuve 75.00 200.00
APJA2 Jose Altuve 75.00 200.00
APJA3 Jose Altuve 75.00 200.00
APJA4 Jose Altuve 75.00 200.00
APJA5 Jose Altuve 75.00 200.00
APJA6 Jose Altuve 75.00 200.00
APJA7 Jose Altuve 75.00 200.00
APJA8 Jose Altuve 75.00 200.00
APJB1 Javier Baez
APJB2 Javier Baez
APJB3 Javier Baez
APJB4 Javier Baez
APJB5 Javier Baez
APJB6 Javier Baez
APJB7 Javier Baez
APJB8 Javier Baez
APJD1 Jacob deGrom 50.00 120.00
APJD2 Jacob deGrom 50.00 120.00
APJD3 Jacob deGrom 50.00 120.00
APJD4 Jacob deGrom 50.00 120.00
APJD5 Jacob deGrom 50.00 120.00
APJD6 Jacob deGrom 50.00 120.00
APJE1 Jeff Bagwell 75.00 200.00
APJE2 Jeff Bagwell 75.00 200.00
APJE3 Jeff Bagwell 75.00 200.00
APJE4 Jeff Bagwell 75.00 200.00
APJE5 Jeff Bagwell 75.00 200.00
APJE6 Jeff Bagwell 75.00 200.00
APJH1 Jason Heyward EXCH 25.00 60.00
APJH2 Jason Heyward EXCH 25.00 60.00
APJH3 Jason Heyward EXCH 25.00 60.00
APJH4 Jason Heyward EXCH 25.00 60.00
APJH5 Jason Heyward EXCH 25.00 60.00
APJH6 Jason Heyward EXCH 25.00 60.00
APJO1 Josh Donaldson 30.00 80.00
APJO2 Josh Donaldson 30.00 80.00
APJO3 Josh Donaldson 30.00 80.00
APJO4 Josh Donaldson 30.00 80.00
APJO5 Josh Donaldson 30.00 80.00
APJO6 Josh Donaldson 30.00 80.00
APJS1 John Smoltz 40.00 100.00
APJS2 John Smoltz 40.00 100.00
APJS3 John Smoltz 40.00 100.00
APJS4 John Smoltz 40.00 100.00
APJS5 John Smoltz 40.00 100.00
APJS6 John Smoltz 40.00 100.00
APJS7 John Smoltz 40.00 100.00
APJS8 John Smoltz 40.00 100.00
APJT1 Jim Thome 60.00 150.00
APJT2 Jim Thome 60.00 150.00
APJT3 Jim Thome 60.00 150.00
APJT4 Jim Thome 60.00 150.00
APJT5 Jim Thome 60.00 150.00
APJT6 Jim Thome 60.00 150.00
APJV1 Joey Votto 60.00 150.00
APJV2 Joey Votto 60.00 150.00
APJV3 Joey Votto 60.00 150.00
APJV4 Joey Votto 60.00 150.00
APJV5 Joey Votto 60.00 150.00
APJV6 Joey Votto 60.00 150.00
APKB1 Kris Bryant 150.00 400.00
APKB2 Kris Bryant 150.00 400.00
APKB3 Kris Bryant 150.00 400.00
APKB4 Kris Bryant 150.00 400.00
APKB5 Kris Bryant 150.00 400.00
APKB6 Kris Bryant 150.00 400.00
APKB7 Kris Bryant 150.00 400.00
APKM1 Kenta Maeda 25.00 60.00
APKM2 Kenta Maeda 25.00 60.00
APKM3 Kenta Maeda 25.00 60.00
APKM4 Kenta Maeda 25.00 60.00
APKM5 Kenta Maeda 25.00 60.00
APKM6 Kenta Maeda 25.00 60.00
APKS1 Kyle Schwarber 40.00 100.00
APKS2 Kyle Schwarber 40.00 100.00
APKS3 Kyle Schwarber 40.00 100.00
APKS4 Kyle Schwarber 40.00 100.00
APKS5 Kyle Schwarber 40.00 100.00
APKS6 Kyle Schwarber 40.00 100.00
APKS7 Kyle Schwarber 40.00 100.00
APKS8 Kyle Schwarber 40.00 100.00
APMF2 Michael Fulmer 25.00 60.00
APMF3 Michael Fulmer 25.00 60.00
APMF4 Michael Fulmer 25.00 60.00
APMF5 Michael Fulmer 25.00 60.00
APMF6 Michael Fulmer 25.00 60.00
APMF7 Michael Fulmer 25.00 60.00
APMF8 Michael Fulmer 25.00 60.00
APMM1 Mark McGwire 60.00 150.00
APMM2 Mark McGwire 60.00 150.00
APMM3 Mark McGwire 60.00 150.00
APMM4 Mark McGwire 60.00 150.00
APMM5 Mark McGwire 60.00 150.00
APMM6 Mark McGwire 60.00 150.00
APMM7 Mark McGwire 60.00 150.00
APMM8 Mark McGwire 60.00 150.00
APMMA1 Manny Machado 60.00 150.00
APMMA2 Manny Machado 60.00 150.00
APMMA3 Manny Machado 60.00 150.00
APMMA4 Manny Machado 60.00 150.00
APMMA5 Manny Machado 60.00 150.00
APMMA6 Manny Machado 60.00 150.00
APMO1 Mike Trout 150.00 400.00
APMO2 Mike Trout 150.00 400.00
APMP1 Mike Piazza 60.00 150.00
APMP2 Mike Piazza 60.00 150.00
APMP3 Mike Piazza 60.00 150.00
APMP4 Mike Piazza 60.00 150.00
APMP5 Mike Piazza 60.00 150.00
APMP6 Mike Piazza 60.00 150.00
APMP7 Mike Piazza 60.00 150.00
APMP8 Mike Piazza 60.00 150.00
APMT3 Mike Trout 150.00 400.00
APMT4 Mike Trout 150.00 400.00
APMT5 Mike Trout 150.00 400.00
APMT6 Mike Trout 150.00 400.00
APMT7 Mike Trout 150.00 400.00
APMT8 Mike Trout 150.00 400.00
APMTA1 Masahiro Tanaka 75.00 200.00
APMTA2 Masahiro Tanaka 75.00 200.00
APMTA3 Masahiro Tanaka 75.00 200.00
APMTA4 Masahiro Tanaka 75.00 200.00
APMTA5 Masahiro Tanaka 75.00 200.00
APMTA6 Masahiro Tanaka 75.00 200.00
APMTA7 Masahiro Tanaka 75.00 200.00
APNR5 Nolan Ryan 125.00 300.00
APNR6 Nolan Ryan 125.00 300.00
APNR7 Nolan Ryan 125.00 300.00
APNR8 Nolan Ryan 125.00 300.00
APNR9 Nolan Ryan 125.00 300.00
APNS1 Noah Syndergaard 40.00 100.00
APNS2 Noah Syndergaard 40.00 100.00
APNS3 Noah Syndergaard 40.00 100.00
APNS4 Noah Syndergaard 40.00 100.00
APNS5 Noah Syndergaard 40.00 100.00
APNS6 Noah Syndergaard 40.00 100.00
APNS7 Noah Syndergaard 40.00 100.00
APNS8 Noah Syndergaard 40.00 100.00
APPG1 Paul Goldschmidt 50.00 120.00
APPG2 Paul Goldschmidt 50.00 120.00
APPG3 Paul Goldschmidt 50.00 120.00
APPG4 Paul Goldschmidt 50.00 120.00
APPG5 Paul Goldschmidt 50.00 120.00
APPG6 Paul Goldschmidt 50.00 120.00
APPM1 Pedro Martinez 50.00 120.00
APPM2 Pedro Martinez 50.00 120.00
APPM3 Pedro Martinez 50.00 120.00
APPM4 Pedro Martinez 50.00 120.00
APPM5 Pedro Martinez 50.00 120.00
APPM6 Pedro Martinez 50.00 120.00
APPM7 Pedro Martinez 50.00 120.00
APPM8 Pedro Martinez 50.00 120.00
APPM9 Pedro Martinez 50.00 120.00
APRB1 Ryan Braun 25.00 60.00
APRB2 Ryan Braun 25.00 60.00
APRB3 Ryan Braun 25.00 60.00

APRB4 Ryan Braun 25.00 60.00
APRB5 Ryan Braun 25.00 60.00
APRB6 Ryan Braun 25.00 60.00
APRB7 Ryan Braun 25.00 60.00
APRB8 Ryan Braun 25.00 60.00
APRC1 Rod Carew 30.00 80.00
APRC2 Rod Carew 30.00 80.00
APRE1 Rickey Henderson 60.00 150.00
APRE2 Rickey Henderson 60.00 150.00
APRE3 Rickey Henderson 60.00 150.00
APRE4 Rickey Henderson 60.00 150.00
APRE5 Rickey Henderson 60.00 150.00
APRH1 Roy Halladay 100.00 250.00
APRH2 Roy Halladay 100.00 250.00
APRH3 Roy Halladay 100.00 250.00
APRH4 Roy Halladay 100.00 250.00
APRH5 Roy Halladay 100.00 250.00
APRH6 Roy Halladay 100.00 250.00
APRJ1 Reggie Jackson 50.00 120.00
APRJ2 Reggie Jackson 50.00 120.00
APRJ3 Reggie Jackson 50.00 120.00
APRJ4 Reggie Jackson 50.00 120.00
APRJ5 Reggie Jackson 50.00 120.00
APRL1 Roger Clemens 75.00 200.00
APRL2 Roger Clemens 75.00 200.00
APRL3 Roger Clemens 75.00 200.00
APRL4 Roger Clemens 75.00 200.00
APRL5 Roger Clemens 75.00 200.00
APRO1 Robinson Cano 40.00 100.00
APRO2 Robinson Cano 40.00 100.00
APRO3 Robinson Cano 40.00 100.00
APRO4 Robinson Cano 40.00 100.00
APRO5 Robinson Cano 40.00 100.00
APRO6 Robinson Cano 40.00 100.00
APRR1 Randy Johnson 60.00 150.00
APRR2 Randy Johnson 60.00 150.00
APRS1 Ryne Sandberg 125.00 300.00
APRS2 Ryne Sandberg 125.00 300.00
APRS3 Ryne Sandberg 125.00 300.00
APSP4 Stephen Piscotty 25.00 60.00
APSP5 Stephen Piscotty 25.00 60.00
APSP6 Stephen Piscotty 25.00 60.00
APSP7 Stephen Piscotty 25.00 60.00
APSP8 Stephen Piscotty 25.00 60.00
APTE1 Theo Epstein 75.00 200.00
APTE2 Theo Epstein 75.00 200.00
APTE3 Theo Epstein 75.00 200.00
APTL1 Tom Glavine 40.00 100.00
APTL2 Tom Glavine 40.00 100.00
APTL3 Tom Glavine 40.00 100.00
APTL4 Tom Glavine 40.00 100.00
APTL5 Tom Glavine 40.00 100.00
APTS1 Trevor Story 25.00 60.00
APTS2 Trevor Story 25.00 60.00
APTS3 Trevor Story 25.00 60.00
APTS4 Trevor Story 25.00 60.00
APTS5 Trevor Story 25.00 60.00
APTS6 Trevor Story 25.00 60.00
APTS7 Trevor Story 25.00 60.00
APTS8 Trevor Story 25.00 60.00
APTT1 Trea Turner
APTT2 Trea Turner
APTT3 Trea Turner
APTT4 Trea Turner
APTT5 Trea Turner
APTT6 Trea Turner
APTT7 Trea Turner
APTT8 Trea Turner
APYC1 Yoenis Cespedes 30.00 80.00
APYC2 Yoenis Cespedes 30.00 80.00
APYC3 Yoenis Cespedes 30.00 80.00
APYC4 Yoenis Cespedes 30.00 80.00
APYC5 Yoenis Cespedes 30.00 80.00
APYC6 Yoenis Cespedes 30.00 80.00
APYG1 Yulieski Gurriel RC 30.00 80.00
APYG2 Yulieski Gurriel RC 30.00 80.00
APYG3 Yulieski Gurriel RC 30.00 80.00
APYG4 Yulieski Gurriel RC 30.00 80.00
APYG5 Yulieski Gurriel RC 30.00 80.00
APYG6 Yulieski Gurriel RC 30.00 80.00
APYG7 Yulieski Gurriel RC 30.00 80.00
APYM1 Yoan Moncada RC 60.00 150.00
APYM2 Yoan Moncada RC 60.00 150.00
APYM3 Yoan Moncada RC 60.00 150.00
APYM4 Yoan Moncada RC 60.00 150.00
APYM5 Yoan Moncada RC 60.00 150.00
APYM6 Yoan Moncada RC 60.00 150.00

2017 Topps Dynasty Autograph Patches Gold

*GOLD: .5X TO 1.2X BASIC
RANDOM INSERTS IN PACKS
STATED PRINT RUN 5 SER.#'d SETS
ALL VERSIONS EQUALLY PRICED
LOGO/TAG PATCHES MAY SELL FOR PREMIUM
EXCHANGE DEADLINE 10/31/2019
APFM1 Floyd Mayweather Jr. 400.00 800.00
APJB1 Javier Baez 125.00 300.00

2017 Topps Dynasty Dual Relic Autographs

STATED ODDS 1:63 BOXES
STATED PRINT RUN 5 SER.#'d SETS
MOST NOT PRICED DUE TO SCARCITY
ALL VERSIONS EQUALLY PRICED
ADRDM1 Don Mattingly 60.00 150.00
ADRDM2 Don Mattingly 60.00 150.00
ADRDM3 Don Mattingly 60.00 150.00
ADRJB1 Johnny Bench 100.00 250.00
ADRJB2 Johnny Bench 100.00 250.00
ADRJB3 Johnny Bench 100.00 250.00

2018 Topps Dynasty Autograph Patches

OVERALL AUTO ODDS 1:1
STATED PRINT RUN 10 SER.#'d SETS
ALL VERSIONS EQUALLY PRICED
LOGO/TAG PATCHES MAY SELL FOR PREMIUM
EXCHANGE DEADLINE 10/31/2020
APAB1 Alex Bregman 60.00 150.00
APAB2 Alex Bregman 60.00 150.00
APAB3 Alex Bregman 60.00 150.00
APAB4 Alex Bregman 60.00 150.00
APAB5 Alex Bregman 60.00 150.00
APAB6 Alex Bregman 60.00 150.00
APAB7 Alex Bregman 60.00 150.00
APAB8 Alex Bregman 60.00 150.00
APABL1 Adrian Beltre 50.00 120.00
APABL2 Adrian Beltre 50.00 120.00
APABL3 Adrian Beltre 50.00 120.00
APABL4 Adrian Beltre 50.00 120.00
APABL5 Adrian Beltre 50.00 120.00
APABL6 Adrian Beltre 50.00 120.00
APABL7 Adrian Beltre 50.00 120.00
APABL8 Adrian Beltre 50.00 120.00
APABN1 Andrew Benintendi 60.00 150.00
APABN2 Andrew Benintendi 60.00 150.00
APABN3 Andrew Benintendi 60.00 150.00
APABN4 Andrew Benintendi 60.00 150.00
APABN5 Andrew Benintendi 60.00 150.00
APABN6 Andrew Benintendi 60.00 150.00
APABN7 Andrew Benintendi 60.00 150.00
APABN8 Andrew Benintendi 60.00 150.00
APAJ1 Adam Jones 30.00 80.00
APAJ2 Adam Jones 30.00 80.00
APAJ3 Adam Jones 30.00 80.00
APAJ4 Adam Jones 30.00 80.00
APAJ5 Adam Jones 30.00 80.00
APALO1 Roberto Alomar 50.00 120.00
APALO2 Roberto Alomar 50.00 120.00
APALO3 Roberto Alomar 50.00 120.00
APAM1 Andrew McCutchen 75.00 200.00
APAM2 Andrew McCutchen 75.00 200.00
APAM3 Andrew McCutchen 75.00 200.00
APAM4 Andrew McCutchen 75.00 200.00
APAM5 Andrew McCutchen 75.00 200.00
APAMR1 Amed Rosario RC 25.00 60.00
APAMR2 Amed Rosario RC 25.00 60.00
APAMR3 Amed Rosario RC 25.00 60.00
APAMR4 Amed Rosario RC 25.00 60.00
APAMR5 Amed Rosario RC 25.00 60.00
APAMR6 Amed Rosario RC 25.00 60.00
APAMR7 Amed Rosario RC 25.00 60.00
APAMR8 Amed Rosario RC 25.00 60.00
APAP1 Albert Pujols 100.00 250.00
APAP2 Albert Pujols 100.00 250.00
APAPT4 Andy Pettitte 40.00 100.00
APAPT5 Andy Pettitte 40.00 100.00
APAPT6 Andy Pettitte 40.00 100.00
APAR1 Alex Rodriguez 100.00 250.00
APAR2 Alex Rodriguez 100.00 250.00
APAR3 Alex Rodriguez 100.00 250.00
APAR4 Alex Rodriguez 100.00 250.00
APAR5 Alex Rodriguez 100.00 250.00
APARJ1 Aaron Judge 250.00 500.00
APARJ2 Aaron Judge 250.00 500.00
APARJ3 Aaron Judge 250.00 500.00
APARJ4 Aaron Judge 250.00 500.00
APAZ1 Anthony Rizzo 50.00 120.00
APAZ2 Anthony Rizzo 50.00 120.00
APAZ3 Anthony Rizzo 50.00 120.00
APAZ4 Anthony Rizzo 50.00 120.00
APAZ5 Anthony Rizzo 50.00 120.00
APAZ6 Anthony Rizzo 50.00 120.00
APBH1 Bryce Harper 125.00 300.00
APBH2 Bryce Harper 125.00 300.00
APBH3 Bryce Harper 125.00 300.00
APBH4 Bryce Harper 125.00 300.00
APBH5 Bryce Harper 125.00 300.00
APBL1 Barry Larkin 40.00 100.00
APBL2 Barry Larkin 40.00 100.00
APBL3 Barry Larkin 40.00 100.00
APBL4 Barry Larkin 40.00 100.00
APBL5 Barry Larkin 40.00 100.00
APBL6 Barry Larkin 40.00 100.00
APBP1 Buster Posey 60.00 150.00
APBP2 Buster Posey 60.00 150.00
APBP3 Buster Posey 60.00 150.00
APBP4 Buster Posey 60.00 150.00
APBP5 Buster Posey 60.00 150.00
APBP6 Buster Posey 60.00 150.00
APCBG1 Craig Biggio 40.00 100.00
APCBG2 Craig Biggio 40.00 100.00
APCBG3 Craig Biggio 40.00 100.00
APCBG4 Craig Biggio 40.00 100.00
APCBL1 Charlie Blackmon 40.00 100.00
APCBL2 Charlie Blackmon 40.00 100.00
APCBL3 Charlie Blackmon 40.00 100.00
APCBL4 Charlie Blackmon 40.00 100.00
APCBL5 Charlie Blackmon 40.00 100.00
APCBL6 Charlie Blackmon 40.00 100.00
APCBL7 Charlie Blackmon 40.00 100.00
APCF1 Clint Frazier RC 30.00 80.00
APCF2 Clint Frazier RC 30.00 80.00
APCF3 Clint Frazier RC 30.00 80.00
APCF4 Clint Frazier RC 30.00 80.00
APCF5 Clint Frazier RC 30.00 80.00
APCF6 Clint Frazier RC 30.00 80.00
APCJ1 Chipper Jones 75.00 200.00
APCJ2 Chipper Jones 75.00 200.00
APCJ3 Chipper Jones 75.00 200.00
APCJ4 Chipper Jones 75.00 200.00
APCJ5 Chipper Jones 75.00 200.00
APCJ6 Chipper Jones 75.00 200.00
APCK1 Clayton Kershaw 75.00 200.00
APCK2 Clayton Kershaw 75.00 200.00
APCK3 Clayton Kershaw 75.00 200.00
APCK4 Clayton Kershaw 75.00 200.00
APCK5 Clayton Kershaw 75.00 200.00
APCK6 Clayton Kershaw 75.00 200.00
APCR1 Cal Ripken Jr. 100.00 250.00
APCR2 Cal Ripken Jr. 100.00 250.00
APCR3 Cal Ripken Jr. 100.00 250.00
APCR4 Cal Ripken Jr. 100.00 250.00
APCR5 Cal Ripken Jr. 100.00 250.00
APCSL1 Chris Sale 40.00 100.00
APCSL2 Chris Sale 40.00 100.00
APCSL3 Chris Sale 40.00 100.00
APCSL4 Chris Sale 40.00 100.00
APCSL5 Chris Sale 40.00 100.00
APCSL6 Chris Sale 40.00 100.00
APCSL7 Chris Sale 40.00 100.00
APCSL8 Chris Sale 40.00 100.00
APCY1 Christian Yelich 50.00 120.00
APCY2 Christian Yelich 50.00 120.00
APCY3 Christian Yelich 50.00 120.00
APDG1 Didi Gregorius 40.00 100.00
APDG2 Didi Gregorius 40.00 100.00
APDG3 Didi Gregorius 40.00 100.00
APDG4 Didi Gregorius 40.00 100.00
APDG5 Didi Gregorius 40.00 100.00
APDJ1 Derek Jeter 400.00 800.00
APDJ2 Derek Jeter 400.00 800.00
APDO1 David Ortiz 60.00 150.00
APDO2 David Ortiz 60.00 150.00
APDO3 David Ortiz 60.00 150.00
APDO4 David Ortiz 60.00 150.00
APDO5 David Ortiz 60.00 150.00
APDO6 David Ortiz 60.00 150.00
APDO7 David Ortiz 60.00 150.00
APDO8 David Ortiz 60.00 150.00
APDP1 Dustin Pedroia 40.00 100.00
APDP2 Dustin Pedroia 40.00 100.00
APDP3 Dustin Pedroia 40.00 100.00
APDP4 Dustin Pedroia 40.00 100.00
APDP5 Dustin Pedroia 40.00 100.00
APDP6 Dustin Pedroia 40.00 100.00
APDP7 Dustin Pedroia 40.00 100.00
APDP8 Dustin Pedroia 40.00 100.00
APFF1 Freddie Freeman 50.00
APFF2 Freddie Freeman 50.00 120.00
APFF3 Freddie Freeman 50.00 120.00
APFF4 Freddie Freeman 50.00 120.00
APFF5 Freddie Freeman 50.00 120.00
APFF6 Freddie Freeman 50.00 120.00
APFF7 Freddie Freeman 50.00 120.00
APFF8 Freddie Freeman 50.00 120.00
APFL1 Francisco Lindor 50.00 120.00
APFL2 Francisco Lindor 50.00 120.00
APFL3 Francisco Lindor 50.00 120.00
APFL4 Francisco Lindor 50.00 120.00
APFL5 Francisco Lindor 50.00 120.00
APFL6 Francisco Lindor 50.00 120.00
APFL7 Francisco Lindor 50.00 120.00
APFL8 Francisco Lindor 50.00 120.00
APFT1 Frank Thomas 60.00 150.00
APFT2 Frank Thomas 60.00 150.00
APFT3 Frank Thomas 60.00 150.00
APFT4 Frank Thomas 60.00 150.00
APFT5 Frank Thomas 60.00 150.00
APFT6 Frank Thomas 60.00 150.00
APGS1 Gary Sanchez 30.00 80.00
APGS2 Gary Sanchez 30.00 80.00
APGS3 Gary Sanchez 30.00 80.00
APGS4 Gary Sanchez 30.00 80.00
APGS5 Gary Sanchez 30.00 80.00
APGS6 Gary Sanchez 30.00 80.00
APGSP1 George Springer 40.00 100.00
APGSP2 George Springer 40.00 100.00
APGSP3 George Springer 40.00 100.00
APGSP4 George Springer 40.00 100.00
APGSP5 George Springer 40.00 100.00
APGSP6 George Springer 40.00 100.00
APGSP7 George Springer 40.00 100.00
APGSP8 George Springer 40.00 100.00
APGT1 Gleyber Torres RC 125.00 300.00
APGT2 Gleyber Torres RC 125.00 300.00
APGT3 Gleyber Torres RC 125.00 300.00
APIR1 Ivan Rodriguez 40.00 100.00
APIR2 Ivan Rodriguez 40.00 100.00
APIR3 Ivan Rodriguez 40.00 100.00
APIR4 Ivan Rodriguez 40.00 100.00
APIR5 Ivan Rodriguez 40.00 100.00
API3 Ichiro 300.00 600.00
API4 Ichiro 300.00 600.00
APJA1 Jose Altuve 50.00 120.00
APJA2 Jose Altuve 50.00 120.00
APJA3 Jose Altuve 50.00 120.00
APJA4 Jose Altuve 50.00 120.00
APJA5 Jose Altuve 50.00 120.00
APJA6 Jose Altuve 50.00 120.00
APJA7 Jose Altuve 50.00 120.00
APJA8 Jose Altuve 50.00 120.00
APJB1 Jeff Bagwell 75.00 200.00
APJB2 Jeff Bagwell 75.00 200.00
APJB3 Jeff Bagwell 75.00 200.00
APJB4 Jeff Bagwell 75.00 200.00
APJBZ1 Javier Baez 75.00 200.00
APJBZ2 Javier Baez 75.00 200.00
APJBZ3 Javier Baez 75.00 200.00
APJBZ4 Javier Baez 75.00 200.00
APJBZ5 Javier Baez 75.00 200.00
APJBZ6 Javier Baez 75.00 200.00
APJBZ7 Javier Baez 75.00 200.00
APJBZ8 Javier Baez 75.00 200.00
APJDG1 Jacob deGrom 40.00 100.00
APJDG2 Jacob deGrom 40.00 100.00
APJDG3 Jacob deGrom 40.00 100.00
APJDG4 Jacob deGrom 40.00 100.00
APJDG5 Jacob deGrom 40.00 100.00
APJDG6 Jacob deGrom 40.00 100.00
APJDG7 Jacob deGrom 40.00 100.00
APJDG8 Jacob deGrom 40.00 100.00
APJRM1 Jose Ramirez 40.00 100.00
APJRM2 Jose Ramirez 40.00 100.00
APJRM3 Jose Ramirez 40.00 100.00
APJRM4 Jose Ramirez 40.00 100.00
APJSM1 John Smoltz 40.00 100.00
APJSM2 John Smoltz 40.00 100.00
APJSM3 John Smoltz 40.00 100.00
APJSM4 John Smoltz 40.00 100.00
APJSM5 John Smoltz 40.00 100.00
APJSM6 John Smoltz 40.00 100.00
APJSO1 Juan Soto RC 500.00 1000.00
APJSO2 Juan Soto RC 500.00 1000.00
APJSO3 Juan Soto RC 500.00 1000.00
APJU1 Justin Upton 25.00 60.00
APJU2 Justin Upton 25.00 60.00
APJU3 Justin Upton 25.00 60.00
APJV1 Joey Votto 50.00 120.00
APJV2 Joey Votto 50.00 120.00
APJV3 Joey Votto 50.00 120.00
APJV4 Joey Votto 50.00 120.00
APJV5 Joey Votto 50.00 120.00
APJV6 Joey Votto 50.00 120.00
APKB1 Kris Bryant EXCH 100.00 250.00
APKB2 Kris Bryant EXCH 100.00 250.00
APKB3 Kris Bryant EXCH 100.00 250.00
APKB4 Kris Bryant EXCH 100.00 250.00
APKB5 Kris Bryant EXCH 100.00 250.00
APKS1 Kyle Schwarber 30.00 80.00
APKS2 Kyle Schwarber 30.00 80.00
APKS3 Kyle Schwarber 30.00 80.00
APKS4 Kyle Schwarber 30.00 80.00
APKS5 Kyle Schwarber 30.00 80.00
APKS6 Kyle Schwarber 30.00 80.00
APKS7 Kyle Schwarber 30.00 80.00
APKS8 Kyle Schwarber 30.00 80.00
APLS1 Luis Severino 40.00 100.00
APLS2 Luis Severino 40.00 100.00
APLS3 Luis Severino 40.00 100.00
APLS4 Luis Severino 40.00 100.00
APLS5 Luis Severino 40.00 100.00
APLS6 Luis Severino 40.00 100.00
APLS7 Luis Severino 40.00 100.00
APLS8 Luis Severino 40.00 100.00
APMCG1 Mark McGwire 60.00 150.00
APMCG2 Mark McGwire 60.00 150.00
APMCG3 Mark McGwire 60.00 150.00
APMCG4 Mark McGwire 60.00 150.00
APMK1 Masahiro Tanaka 60.00 150.00
APMK2 Masahiro Tanaka 60.00 150.00
APMK3 Masahiro Tanaka 60.00 150.00
APMK4 Masahiro Tanaka 60.00 150.00
APMM1 Manny Machado 100.00 250.00
APMM2 Manny Machado 100.00 250.00
APMM3 Manny Machado 100.00 250.00
APMM4 Manny Machado 100.00 250.00
APMM5 Manny Machado 100.00 250.00
APMM6 Manny Machado 100.00 250.00
APMP1 Mike Piazza 60.00 150.00
APMP2 Mike Piazza 60.00 150.00
APMP3 Mike Piazza 60.00 150.00
APMP4 Mike Piazza 60.00 150.00
APMP5 Mike Piazza 60.00 150.00
APMP6 Mike Piazza 60.00 150.00
APMR1 Mariano Rivera 100.00 250.00
APMR2 Mariano Rivera 100.00 250.00
APMR3 Mariano Rivera 100.00 250.00
APMT1 Mike Trout 400.00 800.00
APMT2 Mike Trout 400.00 800.00
APMT3 Mike Trout 400.00 800.00
APMT4 Mike Trout 400.00 800.00
APMT5 Mike Trout 400.00 800.00
APMT6 Mike Trout 400.00 800.00
APNG1 Nomar Garciaparra 40.00 100.00
APNG2 Nomar Garciaparra 40.00 100.00
APNG3 Nomar Garciaparra 40.00 100.00
APNG4 Nomar Garciaparra 40.00 100.00
APNS1 Noah Syndergaard 30.00 80.00
APNS2 Noah Syndergaard 30.00 80.00
APNS3 Noah Syndergaard 30.00 80.00
APNS4 Noah Syndergaard 30.00 80.00
APNS5 Noah Syndergaard 30.00 80.00
APNS6 Noah Syndergaard 30.00 80.00
APOA1 Ozzie Albies RC 50.00 120.00
APOA2 Ozzie Albies RC 50.00 120.00
APOA3 Ozzie Albies RC 50.00 120.00
APOA4 Ozzie Albies RC 50.00 120.00
APOA5 Ozzie Albies RC 50.00 120.00
APOA6 Ozzie Albies RC 50.00 120.00
APOA7 Ozzie Albies RC 50.00 120.00
APOA8 Ozzie Albies RC 50.00 120.00
APPG1 Paul Goldschmidt 40.00 100.00
APPG2 Paul Goldschmidt 40.00 100.00
APPG3 Paul Goldschmidt 40.00 100.00
APPG4 Paul Goldschmidt 40.00 100.00
APPG5 Paul Goldschmidt 40.00 100.00
APPG6 Paul Goldschmidt 40.00 100.00
APPG7 Paul Goldschmidt 40.00 100.00
APPG8 Paul Goldschmidt 40.00 100.00
APPM1 Pedro Martinez 40.00 100.00
APPM2 Pedro Martinez 40.00 100.00
APPM3 Pedro Martinez 40.00 100.00
APPM4 Pedro Martinez 40.00 100.00
APPM6 Pedro Martinez 40.00 100.00
APPM7 Pedro Martinez 40.00 100.00
APPM8 Pedro Martinez 40.00 100.00
APRAC1 Ronald Acuna Jr. RC 300.00 600.00
APRAC2 Ronald Acuna Jr. RC 300.00 600.00
APRAC3 Ronald Acuna Jr. RC 300.00 600.00
APRAC4 Ronald Acuna Jr. RC 300.00 600.00
APRAC5 Ronald Acuna Jr. RC 300.00 600.00
APRAC6 Ronald Acuna Jr. RC 300.00 600.00
APRC1 Roger Clemens 60.00 150.00
APRC2 Roger Clemens 60.00 150.00
APRC3 Roger Clemens 60.00 150.00
APRC4 Roger Clemens 60.00 150.00
APRC5 Roger Clemens 60.00 150.00
APRD1 Rafael Devers RC EXCH 60.00 150.00
APRD2 Rafael Devers RC EXCH 60.00 150.00
APRD3 Rafael Devers RC EXCH 60.00 150.00
APRD4 Rafael Devers RC EXCH 60.00 150.00
APRD5 Rafael Devers RC EXCH 60.00 150.00
APRD6 Rafael Devers RC EXCH 60.00 150.00
APRD7 Rafael Devers RC EXCH 60.00 150.00
APRH1 Rickey Henderson 60.00 150.00
APRH2 Rickey Henderson 60.00 150.00
APRH3 Rickey Henderson 60.00 150.00
APRH4 Rickey Henderson 60.00 150.00
APRH5 Rickey Henderson 60.00 150.00
APRHY1 Rhys Hoskins RC 75.00 200.00
APRHY2 Rhys Hoskins RC 75.00 200.00
APRHY3 Rhys Hoskins RC 75.00 200.00
APRHY4 Rhys Hoskins RC 75.00 200.00
APRHY5 Rhys Hoskins RC 75.00 200.00
APRHY6 Rhys Hoskins RC 75.00 200.00
APRHY7 Rhys Hoskins RC 75.00 200.00
APRJX1 Reggie Jackson 40.00 100.00
APRJX2 Reggie Jackson 40.00 100.00
APRJX3 Reggie Jackson 40.00 100.00
APRJX4 Reggie Jackson 40.00 100.00
APRJX5 Reggie Jackson 40.00 100.00
APRW1 Russell Wilson 125.00 300.00
APRW2 Russell Wilson 125.00 300.00
APRW3 Russell Wilson 125.00 300.00
APRW4 Russell Wilson 125.00 300.00
APRW5 Russell Wilson 125.00 300.00
APRY1 Robin Yount 60.00 150.00
APRY2 Robin Yount 60.00 150.00
APSO1 Shohei Ohtani RC 600.00 1200.00
APSO2 Shohei Ohtani RC 600.00 1200.00
APSO3 Shohei Ohtani RC 600.00 1200.00
APSO4 Shohei Ohtani RC 600.00 1200.00
APSO5 Shohei Ohtani RC 600.00 1200.00
APSO6 Shohei Ohtani RC 600.00 1200.00
APSO7 Shohei Ohtani RC 600.00 1200.00
APTG1 Tom Glavine 30.00 80.00
APTG2 Tom Glavine 30.00 80.00
APTG3 Tom Glavine 30.00 80.00
APVG1 Vladimir Guerrero 50.00 120.00
APVG2 Vladimir Guerrero 50.00 120.00
APVG3 Vladimir Guerrero 50.00 120.00
APVG4 Vladimir Guerrero 50.00 120.00
APWC1 Willson Contreras 40.00 100.00
APWC2 Willson Contreras 40.00 100.00
APWC3 Willson Contreras 40.00 100.00
APWC4 Willson Contreras 40.00 100.00
APWC5 Willson Contreras 40.00 100.00
APWC6 Willson Contreras 40.00 100.00
APWC7 Willson Contreras 40.00 100.00
APWCL1 Will Clark 60.00 150.00
APWCL2 Will Clark 60.00 150.00
APWCL3 Will Clark 60.00 150.00
APWCL4 Will Clark 60.00 150.00
APWCL5 Will Clark 60.00 150.00
APWCL6 Will Clark 60.00 150.00
APYML1 Yadier Molina EXCH 75.00 200.00
APYML2 Yadier Molina EXCH 75.00 200.00
APYML3 Yadier Molina EXCH 75.00 200.00
APYML4 Yadier Molina EXCH 75.00 200.00
APYML5 Yadier Molina EXCH 75.00 200.00
APYML6 Yadier Molina EXCH 75.00 200.00
APYML7 Yadier Molina EXCH 75.00 200.00
APYML8 Yadier Molina EXCH 75.00 200.00

2018 Topps Dynasty Autograph Patches Blue

*GOLD: .5X TO 1.2X BASIC
RANDOM INSERTS IN PACKS
STATED PRINT RUN 5 SER.#'d SETS
ALL VERSIONS EQUALLY PRICED
LOGO/TAG PATCHES MAY SELL FOR PREMIUM
EXCHANGE DEADLINE 10/31/2020

2019 Topps Dynasty Autograph Patches

OVERALL AUTO ODDS 1:1
STATED PRINT RUN 10 SER.#'d SETS
SOME NOT PRICED DUE TO SCARCITY
ALL VERSIONS EQUALLY PRICED
LOGO/TAG PATCHES MAY SELL FOR PREMIUM
EXCHANGE DEADLINE 10/31/2021
DAPAB1 Alex Bregman 40.00 100.00
DAPAB2 Alex Bregman 40.00 100.00
DAPAB3 Alex Bregman 40.00 100.00
DAPAB4 Alex Bregman 40.00 100.00
DAPAB5 Alex Bregman 40.00 100.00
DAPAB6 Alex Bregman 40.00 100.00
DAPAB7 Alex Bregman 40.00 100.00
DAPAB8 Alex Bregman 40.00 100.00
DAPABE1 Adrian Beltre 40.00 100.00
DAPABE2 Adrian Beltre 40.00 100.00
DAPABE4 Adrian Beltre 40.00 100.00
DAPABE5 Adrian Beltre 40.00 100.00
DAPABE6 Adrian Beltre 40.00 100.00
DAPABE7 Adrian Beltre 40.00 100.00
DAPABN1 Andrew Benintendi 50.00 120.00
DAPABN2 Andrew Benintendi 50.00 120.00
DAPABN3 Andrew Benintendi 50.00 120.00
DAPABN4 Andrew Benintendi 50.00 120.00
DAPABN5 Andrew Benintendi 50.00 120.00
DAPABN6 Andrew Benintendi 50.00 120.00
DAPABN7 Andrew Benintendi 50.00 120.00
DAPABN8 Andrew Benintendi 50.00 120.00
DAPAJ1 Aaron Judge 100.00 250.00
DAPAJ2 Aaron Judge 100.00 250.00
DAPAJ3 Aaron Judge 100.00 250.00
DAPAJ4 Aaron Judge 100.00 250.00
DAPAJ5 Aaron Judge 100.00 250.00
DAPAJ6 Aaron Judge 100.00 250.00
DAPAN1 Aaron Nola 50.00 120.00
DAPAN2 Aaron Nola 50.00 120.00
DAPAN3 Aaron Nola 50.00 120.00
DAPAN4 Aaron Nola 50.00 120.00
DAPAN5 Aaron Nola 50.00 120.00
DAPAP1 Andy Pettitte 40.00 100.00
DAPAP2 Andy Pettitte 40.00 100.00
DAPAR1 Alex Rodriguez 75.00 200.00
DAPAR1 Austin Riley RC 60.00 150.00
DAPAR2 Austin Riley RC 60.00 150.00
DAPAR2 Alex Rodriguez 75.00 200.00
DAPAR3 Alex Rodriguez 75.00 200.00
DAPAR3 Austin Riley RC 60.00 150.00
DAPAR4 Alex Rodriguez 75.00 200.00
DAPARZ1 Anthony Rizzo 40.00 100.00
DAPARZ2 Anthony Rizzo 40.00 100.00
DAPARZ3 Anthony Rizzo 40.00 100.00
DAPARZ4 Anthony Rizzo 40.00 100.00
DAPARZ5 Anthony Rizzo 40.00 100.00
DAPARZ6 Anthony Rizzo 40.00 100.00
DAPBH1 Bryce Harper 150.00 400.00
DAPBH2 Bryce Harper 150.00 400.00
DAPBH3 Bryce Harper 150.00 400.00
DAPBL1 Barry Larkin 40.00 100.00
DAPBL2 Barry Larkin 40.00 100.00
DAPBL3 Barry Larkin 40.00 100.00
DAPBL4 Barry Larkin 40.00 100.00
DAPBP1 Buster Posey 40.00 100.00
DAPBP2 Buster Posey 40.00 100.00
DAPBP3 Buster Posey 40.00 100.00
DAPBP4 Buster Posey 40.00 100.00
DAPBP5 Buster Posey 40.00 100.00
DAPBP6 Buster Posey 40.00 100.00
DAPBR1 Brendan Rodgers RC 30.00 80.00
DAPBR2 Brendan Rodgers RC 30.00 80.00
DAPBR3 Brendan Rodgers RC 30.00 80.00
DAPBR4 Brendan Rodgers RC 30.00 80.00
DAPBR5 Brendan Rodgers RC 30.00 80.00
DAPBR6 Brendan Rodgers RC 30.00 80.00
DAPBS1 Blake Snell 25.00 60.00
DAPBS2 Blake Snell 25.00 60.00
DAPBS3 Blake Snell 25.00 60.00
DAPBS4 Blake Snell 25.00 60.00
DAPBS5 Blake Snell 25.00 60.00
DAPCBL1 Charlie Blackmon 40.00 100.00
DAPCBL2 Charlie Blackmon 40.00 100.00
DAPCBL3 Charlie Blackmon 40.00 100.00
DAPCC1 CC Sabathia 50.00 120.00
DAPCC2 CC Sabathia 50.00 120.00
DAPCC3 CC Sabathia 50.00 120.00
DAPCC4 CC Sabathia 50.00 120.00
DAPCC5 CC Sabathia 50.00 120.00
DAPCC6 CC Sabathia 50.00 120.00
DAPCJ1 Chipper Jones 60.00 150.00
DAPCJ2 Chipper Jones 60.00 150.00
DAPCJ3 Chipper Jones 60.00 150.00
DAPCJ4 Chipper Jones 60.00 150.00
DAPCJ5 Chipper Jones 60.00 150.00
DAPCJ6 Chipper Jones 60.00 150.00
DAPCK1 Clayton Kershaw 60.00 150.00
DAPCK2 Clayton Kershaw 60.00 150.00
DAPCP1 Chris Paddack RC 40.00 100.00
DAPCP2 Chris Paddack RC 40.00 100.00
DAPCP3 Chris Paddack RC 40.00 100.00
DAPCP4 Chris Paddack RC 40.00 100.00
DAPCSA1 Chris Sale 40.00 100.00
DAPCSA2 Chris Sale 40.00 100.00
DAPCSA3 Chris Sale 40.00 100.00
DAPCSA4 Chris Sale 40.00 100.00
DAPCSA5 Chris Sale 40.00 100.00
DAPCSA6 Chris Sale 40.00 100.00
DAPCSA7 Chris Sale 40.00 100.00
DAPCSA8 Chris Sale 40.00 100.00
DAPCY1 Christian Yelich 75.00 200.00
DAPCY2 Christian Yelich 75.00 200.00
DAPCY3 Christian Yelich 75.00 200.00
DAPCY4 Christian Yelich 75.00 200.00
DAPDJ1 Derek Jeter 250.00 600.00
DAPDJ2 Derek Jeter 250.00 600.00
DAPDO1 David Ortiz 50.00 120.00
DAPDO2 David Ortiz 50.00 120.00
DAPDO3 David Ortiz 50.00 120.00
DAPDO4 David Ortiz 50.00 120.00
DAPDO5 David Ortiz 50.00 120.00
DAPDO6 David Ortiz 50.00 120.00
DAPDP1 David Price 25.00 60.00
DAPDP1 Dustin Pedroia 30.00 80.00
DAPDP2 Dustin Pedroia 30.00 80.00
DAPDP2 David Price 25.00 60.00
DAPDP3 Dustin Pedroia 30.00 80.00
DAPDP4 Dustin Pedroia 30.00 80.00
DAPDP5 Dustin Pedroia 30.00 80.00
DAPDP6 Dustin Pedroia 30.00 80.00
DAPDPR1 David Price 25.00 60.00
DAPDPR2 David Price 25.00 60.00
DAPFF1 Freddie Freeman 50.00 125.00
DAPFF2 Freddie Freeman 50.00 125.00
DAPFF3 Freddie Freeman 50.00 125.00
DAPFF4 Freddie Freeman 50.00 125.00
DAPFF5 Freddie Freeman 50.00 125.00
DAPFF6 Freddie Freeman 50.00 125.00
DAPFF7 Freddie Freeman 50.00 125.00
DAPFF8 Freddie Freeman 50.00 125.00
DAPFL1 Francisco Lindor 50.00 120.00
DAPFL2 Francisco Lindor 50.00 120.00
DAPFL3 Francisco Lindor 50.00 120.00
DAPFL4 Francisco Lindor 50.00 120.00
DAPFL5 Francisco Lindor 50.00 120.00
DAPFL6 Francisco Lindor 50.00 120.00
DAPFL7 Francisco Lindor 50.00 120.00
DAPFM1 Fred McGriff 50.00 120.00
DAPFM2 Fred McGriff 50.00 120.00
DAPFT1 Frank Thomas 75.00 200.00
DAPFT2 Frank Thomas 75.00 200.00
DAPFT3 Frank Thomas 75.00 200.00
DAPFTJ1 Fernando Tatis Jr. RC 400.00 1000.00
DAPFTJ2 Fernando Tatis Jr. RC 400.00 1000.00
DAPFTJ3 Fernando Tatis Jr. RC 400.00 1000.00
DAPFTJ4 Fernando Tatis Jr. RC 400.00 1000.00
DAPFTJ5 Fernando Tatis Jr. RC 400.00 1000.00
DAPFTJ6 Fernando Tatis Jr. RC 400.00 1000.00
DAPFTJ7 Fernando Tatis Jr. RC 400.00 1000.00
DAPFTJ8 Fernando Tatis Jr. RC 400.00 1000.00
DAPGC1 Gerrit Cole 50.00 120.00
DAPGC2 Gerrit Cole 50.00 120.00
DAPGC3 Gerrit Cole 50.00 120.00
DAPGC4 Gerrit Cole 50.00 120.00
DAPGC5 Gerrit Cole 50.00 120.00
DAPGC6 Gerrit Cole 50.00 120.00
DAPGSP1 George Springer 30.00 80.00
DAPGSP2 George Springer 30.00 80.00
DAPGSP3 George Springer 30.00 80.00
DAPGSP4 George Springer 30.00 80.00
DAPGSP5 George Springer 30.00 80.00
DAPGSP6 George Springer 30.00 80.00
DAPGSP7 George Springer 30.00 80.00
DAPGSP8 George Springer 30.00 80.00
DAPIR1 Ivan Rodriguez 40.00 100.00
DAPIR2 Ivan Rodriguez 40.00 100.00
DAPIR3 Ivan Rodriguez 40.00 100.00
DAPIR4 Ivan Rodriguez 40.00 100.00
DAPI1 Ichiro 150.00 400.00
DAPI2 Ichiro 150.00 400.00
DAPJA1 Jose Altuve 60.00 150.00
DAPJA2 Jose Altuve 60.00 150.00
DAPJA3 Jose Altuve 60.00 150.00
DAPJA4 Jose Altuve 60.00 150.00
DAPJA5 Jose Altuve 60.00 150.00
DAPJA6 Jose Altuve 60.00 150.00
DAPJA7 Jose Altuve 60.00 150.00
DAPJA8 Jose Altuve 60.00 150.00
DAPJB1 Jeff Bagwell 100.00 250.00
DAPJB2 Jeff Bagwell 100.00 250.00
DAPJB3 Jeff Bagwell 100.00 250.00
DAPJB4 Jeff Bagwell 100.00 250.00
DAPJdG1 Jacob deGrom 50.00 120.00
DAPJdG2 Jacob deGrom 50.00 120.00
DAPJdG3 Jacob deGrom 50.00 120.00
DAPJdG4 Jacob deGrom 50.00 120.00
DAPJdG5 Jacob deGrom 50.00 120.00
DAPJdG6 Jacob deGrom 50.00 120.00
DAPJdG7 Jacob deGrom 50.00 120.00
DAPJdG8 Jacob deGrom 50.00 120.00
DAPJDM1 J.D. Martinez 30.00 80.00
DAPJDM2 J.D. Martinez 30.00 80.00
DAPJDM3 J.D. Martinez 30.00 80.00
DAPJDM4 J.D. Martinez 30.00 80.00
DAPJDM5 J.D. Martinez 30.00 80.00
DAPJDM6 J.D. Martinez 30.00 80.00
DAPJDM7 J.D. Martinez 30.00 80.00
DAPJDM8 J.D. Martinez 30.00 80.00
DAPJR1 Jose Ramirez 30.00 80.00
DAPJR2 Jose Ramirez 30.00 80.00
DAPJR3 Jose Ramirez 30.00 80.00
DAPJR4 Jose Ramirez 30.00 80.00
DAPJR5 Jose Ramirez 30.00 80.00
DAPJR6 Jose Ramirez 30.00 80.00
DAPJR7 Jose Ramirez 30.00 80.00
DAPJR8 Jose Ramirez 30.00 80.00
DAPJS1 Juan Soto 100.00 250.00
DAPJS1 John Smoltz 50.00 120.00
DAPJS2 John Smoltz 50.00 120.00
DAPJS2 Juan Soto 100.00 250.00
DAPJS3 Juan Soto 100.00 250.00
DAPJS3 John Smoltz 50.00 120.00
DAPJS4 John Smoltz 50.00 120.00
DAPJS4 Juan Soto 100.00 250.00
DAPJS5 Juan Soto 100.00 250.00
DAPJS6 Juan Soto 100.00 250.00
DAPJS7 Juan Soto 100.00 250.00
DAPJS8 Juan Soto 100.00 250.00
DAPJT1 Jim Thome 40.00 100.00
DAPJT2 Jim Thome 40.00 100.00
DAPJT3 Jim Thome 40.00 100.00
DAPJV1 Joey Votto 40.00 100.00
DAPJV2 Joey Votto 40.00 100.00
DAPJV3 Joey Votto 40.00 100.00
DAPJV4 Joey Votto 40.00 100.00
DAPJV5 Joey Votto 40.00 100.00
DAPJV6 Joey Votto 40.00 100.00
DAPKB1 Kris Bryant 60.00 150.00
DAPKB2 Kris Bryant 60.00 150.00
DAPKB3 Kris Bryant 60.00 150.00
DAPKB4 Kris Bryant 60.00 150.00
DAPKB5 Kris Bryant 60.00 150.00
DAPKB6 Kris Bryant 60.00 150.00
DAPKG1 Ken Griffey Jr. 400.00 1000.00
DAPKG2 Ken Griffey Jr. 400.00 1000.00
DAPKG3 Ken Griffey Jr. 400.00 1000.00
DAPKG4 Ken Griffey Jr. 400.00 1000.00
DAPKG5 Ken Griffey Jr. 400.00 1000.00
DAPKG6 Ken Griffey Jr. 400.00 1000.00
DAPKG7 Ken Griffey Jr. 400.00 1000.00
DAPKH1 Keston Hiura RC 100.00 250.00
DAPKH2 Keston Hiura RC 100.00 250.00
DAPKH3 Keston Hiura RC 100.00 250.00
DAPKH4 Keston Hiura RC 100.00 250.00
DAPKH5 Keston Hiura RC 100.00 250.00
DAPKIE1 Carter Kieboom RC 50.00 120.00
DAPKIE2 Carter Kieboom RC 50.00 120.00
DAPKIE3 Carter Kieboom RC 50.00 120.00
DAPKIE4 Carter Kieboom RC 50.00 120.00
DAPKIE5 Carter Kieboom RC 50.00 120.00

DAPKS1 Kyle Schwarber 40.00 100.00
DAPKS2 Kyle Schwarber 40.00 100.00
DAPKS3 Kyle Schwarber 40.00 100.00
DAPKS4 Kyle Schwarber 40.00 100.00
DAPLS1 Luis Severino 30.00 80.00
DAPLS2 Luis Severino 30.00 80.00
DAPLS3 Luis Severino 30.00 80.00
DAPLS4 Luis Severino 30.00 80.00
DAPLS5 Luis Severino 30.00 80.00
DAPLS6 Luis Severino 30.00 80.00
DAPLS7 Luis Severino 30.00 80.00
DAPMC1 Miguel Cabrera 75.00 200.00
DAPMC2 Miguel Cabrera 75.00 200.00
DAPMC3 Miguel Cabrera 75.00 200.00
DAPMC4 Miguel Cabrera 75.00 200.00
DAPMC5 Miguel Cabrera 75.00 200.00
DAPMC6 Miguel Cabrera 75.00 200.00
DAPMC7 Miguel Cabrera 75.00 200.00
DAPMC8 Miguel Cabrera 75.00 200.00
DAPMCA1 Matt Chapman 50.00 120.00
DAPMCA2 Matt Chapman 50.00 120.00
DAPMCA3 Matt Chapman 50.00 120.00
DAPMCH1 Michael Chavis RC 40.00 100.00
DAPMCH2 Michael Chavis RC 40.00 100.00
DAPMCH3 Michael Chavis RC 40.00 100.00
DAPMCH4 Michael Chavis RC 40.00 100.00
DAPMCH5 Michael Chavis RC 40.00 100.00
DAPMMC1 Mark McGwire 50.00 120.00
DAPMMC2 Mark McGwire 50.00 120.00
DAPMMC3 Mark McGwire 50.00 120.00
DAPMMC4 Mark McGwire 50.00 120.00
DAPMMC5 Mark McGwire 50.00 120.00
DAPMR1 Mariano Rivera 125.00 300.00
DAPMR2 Mariano Rivera 125.00 300.00
DAPMR3 Mariano Rivera 125.00 300.00
DAPMT1 Masahiro Tanaka 50.00 120.00
DAPMT2 Masahiro Tanaka 50.00 120.00
DAPMT3 Masahiro Tanaka 50.00 120.00
DAPMTR1 Mike Trout 250.00 600.00
DAPMTR2 Mike Trout 250.00 600.00
DAPMTR3 Mike Trout 250.00 600.00
DAPMTR4 Mike Trout 250.00 600.00
DAPMTR5 Mike Trout 250.00 600.00
DAPMTR6 Mike Trout 250.00 600.00
DAPNA1 Nolan Arenado 75.00 200.00
DAPNA2 Nolan Arenado 75.00 200.00
DAPNA3 Nolan Arenado 75.00 200.00
DAPNA4 Nolan Arenado 75.00 200.00
DAPNA5 Nolan Arenado 75.00 200.00
DAPNA6 Nolan Arenado 75.00 200.00
DAPNA7 Nolan Arenado 75.00 200.00
DAPNA8 Nolan Arenado 75.00 200.00
DAPNS1 Noah Syndergaard 25.00 60.00
DAPNS2 Noah Syndergaard 25.00 60.00
DAPNS3 Noah Syndergaard 25.00 60.00
DAPNS4 Noah Syndergaard 25.00 60.00
DAPNS5 Noah Syndergaard 25.00 60.00
DAPNS6 Noah Syndergaard 25.00 60.00
DAPNS7 Noah Syndergaard 25.00 60.00
DAPNS8 Noah Syndergaard 25.00 60.00
DAPOA1 Ozzie Albies 40.00 100.00
DAPOA2 Ozzie Albies 40.00 100.00
DAPOA3 Ozzie Albies 40.00 100.00
DAPOA4 Ozzie Albies 40.00 100.00
DAPOA5 Ozzie Albies 40.00 100.00
DAPOA6 Ozzie Albies 40.00 100.00
DAPPA1 Pete Alonso RC 200.00 500.00
DAPPA2 Pete Alonso RC 200.00 500.00
DAPPA3 Pete Alonso RC 200.00 500.00
DAPPA4 Pete Alonso RC 200.00 500.00
DAPPG1 Paul Goldschmidt 50.00 120.00
DAPPG2 Paul Goldschmidt 50.00 120.00
DAPPG3 Paul Goldschmidt 50.00 120.00
DAPPG4 Paul Goldschmidt 50.00 120.00
DAPPG5 Paul Goldschmidt 50.00 120.00
DAPPG6 Paul Goldschmidt 50.00 120.00
DAPPG7 Paul Goldschmidt 50.00 120.00
DAPPG8 Paul Goldschmidt 50.00 120.00
DAPPM3 Pedro Martinez 50.00 120.00
DAPPM4 Pedro Martinez 50.00 120.00
DAPPM5 Pedro Martinez 50.00 120.00
DAPPM7 Pedro Martinez 50.00 120.00
DAPRA1 Roberto Alomar 60.00 150.00
DAPRA1 Ronald Acuna Jr. 150.00 400.00
DAPRA2 Ronald Acuna Jr. 150.00 400.00
DAPRA2 Roberto Alomar 60.00 150.00
DAPRA3 Roberto Alomar 60.00 150.00
DAPRA3 Ronald Acuna Jr. 150.00 400.00
DAPRA4 Ronald Acuna Jr. 150.00 400.00
DAPRA4 Roberto Alomar 60.00 150.00
DAPRA5 Roberto Alomar 60.00 150.00
DAPRA5 Ronald Acuna Jr. 150.00 400.00
DAPRA6 Ronald Acuna Jr. 150.00 400.00
DAPRA6 Roberto Alomar 60.00 150.00
DAPRA7 Ronald Acuna Jr. 150.00 400.00
DAPRD1 Rafael Devers 50.00 125.00
DAPRD2 Rafael Devers 50.00 125.00
DAPRD3 Rafael Devers 50.00 125.00
DAPRD4 Rafael Devers 50.00 125.00
DAPRH1 Rickey Henderson 60.00 150.00
DAPRH2 Rickey Henderson 60.00 150.00
DAPRH3 Rickey Henderson 60.00 150.00
DAPRH5 Rickey Henderson 60.00 150.00
DAPRHO1 Rhys Hoskins 50.00 125.00
DAPRHO2 Rhys Hoskins 50.00 125.00
DAPRHO3 Rhys Hoskins 50.00 125.00
DAPRHO4 Rhys Hoskins 50.00 125.00
DAPRHO5 Rhys Hoskins 50.00 125.00
DAPRHO6 Rhys Hoskins 50.00 125.00
DAPRHO7 Rhys Hoskins 50.00 125.00
DAPRHO8 Rhys Hoskins 50.00 125.00
DAPRJ1 Randy Johnson 75.00 200.00
DAPRJ2 Randy Johnson 75.00 200.00
DAPRJ3 Randy Johnson 75.00 200.00
DAPRJ4 Randy Johnson 75.00 200.00
DAPRY1 Robin Yount 50.00 120.00
DAPRY2 Robin Yount 50.00 120.00
DAPRY3 Robin Yount 50.00 120.00
DAPSO1 Shohei Ohtani 125.00 300.00
DAPSO2 Shohei Ohtani 125.00 300.00
DAPSO3 Shohei Ohtani 125.00 300.00
DAPSO4 Shohei Ohtani 125.00 300.00
DAPTBA1 Trevor Bauer 40.00 100.00
DAPTBA2 Trevor Bauer 40.00 100.00
DAPTBA3 Trevor Bauer 40.00 100.00
DAPTBA4 Trevor Bauer 40.00 100.00
DAPTBA5 Trevor Bauer 40.00 100.00
DAPTBA6 Trevor Bauer 40.00 100.00
DAPTG1 Tom Glavine 40.00 100.00
DAPTG2 Tom Glavine 40.00 100.00
DAPVGJ1 Vladimir Guerrero Jr. RC 250.00 600.00
DAPVGJ2 Vladimir Guerrero Jr. RC 250.00 600.00
DAPVGJ3 Vladimir Guerrero Jr. RC 250.00 600.00
DAPVGJ4 Vladimir Guerrero Jr. RC 250.00 600.00
DAPVGJ5 Vladimir Guerrero Jr. RC 250.00 600.00
DAPVR1 Victor Robles 40.00 100.00
DAPVR2 Victor Robles 40.00 100.00
DAPVR3 Victor Robles 40.00 100.00
DAPVR4 Victor Robles 40.00 100.00
DAPVR5 Victor Robles 40.00 100.00
DAPVR6 Victor Robles 40.00 100.00
DAPWB1 Walker Buehler 75.00 200.00
DAPWB1 Wade Boggs 40.00 100.00
DAPWB2 Wade Boggs 40.00 100.00
DAPWB2 Walker Buehler 75.00 200.00
DAPWB3 Walker Buehler 75.00 200.00
DAPWC1 Willson Contreras 30.00 80.00
DAPWC2 Willson Contreras 30.00 80.00
DAPWC3 Willson Contreras 30.00 80.00
DAPWC4 Willson Contreras 30.00 80.00
DAPWC5 Willson Contreras 30.00 80.00
DAPXB1 Xander Bogaerts 75.00 200.00
DAPXB2 Xander Bogaerts 75.00 200.00
DAPXB3 Xander Bogaerts 75.00 200.00
DAPXB4 Xander Bogaerts 75.00 200.00
DAPXB5 Xander Bogaerts 75.00 200.00
DAPXB6 Xander Bogaerts 75.00 200.00
DAPYK1 Yusei Kikuchi RC 40.00 100.00
DAPYK2 Yusei Kikuchi RC 40.00 100.00
DAPYM1 Yadier Molina 75.00 200.00
DAPYM2 Yadier Molina 75.00 200.00
DAPYM3 Yadier Molina 75.00 200.00
DAPYM4 Yadier Molina 75.00 200.00
DAPYM5 Yadier Molina 75.00 200.00
DAPYM6 Yadier Molina 75.00 200.00
DAPYM7 Yadier Molina 75.00 200.00

2019 Topps Dynasty Autograph Patches Silver

*GOLD: .5X TO 1.2X BASIC
RANDOM INSERTS IN PACKS
STATED PRINT RUN 5 SER.#'d SETS
SOME NOT PRICED DUE TO SCARCITY
ALL VERSIONS EQUALLY PRICED
LOGO/TAG PATCHES MAY SELL FOR PREMIUM
EXCHANGE DEADLINE 10/31/2021

2020 Topps Dynasty Autograph Patches

OVERALL AUTO ODDS 1:1
STATED PRINT RUN 10 SER.#'d SETS
SOME NOT PRICED DUE TO SCARCITY
ALL VERSIONS EQUALLY PRICED
LOGO/TAG PATCHES MAY SELL FOR PREMIUM
EXCHANGE DEADLINE 10/31/2022

DAPAA1 Aristides Aquino RC 50.00 125.00
DAPAA2 Aristides Aquino RC 50.00 125.00
DAPAA3 Aristides Aquino RC 50.00 125.00
DAPAA4 Aristides Aquino RC 50.00 125.00
DAPAA5 Aristides Aquino RC 50.00 125.00
DAPAB1 Alex Bregman 60.00 150.00
DAPAB2 Alex Bregman 60.00 150.00
DAPAB3 Alex Bregman 60.00 150.00
DAPAB4 Alex Bregman 60.00 150.00
DAPAB5 Alex Bregman 60.00 150.00
DAPAB6 Alex Bregman 60.00 150.00
DAPAB7 Alex Bregman 60.00 150.00
DAPAB8 Alex Bregman 60.00 150.00
DAPABE1 Adrian Beltre 60.00 150.00
DAPABE2 Adrian Beltre 60.00 150.00
DAPABE3 Adrian Beltre 60.00 150.00
DAPABE4 Adrian Beltre 60.00 150.00
DAPABN1 Andrew Benintendi 40.00 100.00
DAPABN2 Andrew Benintendi 40.00 100.00
DAPABN3 Andrew Benintendi 40.00 100.00
DAPABN4 Andrew Benintendi 40.00 100.00
DAPABN5 Andrew Benintendi 40.00 100.00
DAPABN6 Andrew Benintendi 40.00 100.00
DAPABN7 Andrew Benintendi 40.00 100.00
DAPABN8 Andrew Benintendi 40.00 100.00
DAPAJ1 Aaron Judge 125.00 300.00
DAPAJ2 Aaron Judge 125.00 300.00
DAPAJ3 Aaron Judge 125.00 300.00
DAPAJ4 Aaron Judge 125.00 300.00
DAPAJP A.J. Puk RC 50.00 125.00
DAPAJP2 A.J. Puk RC 50.00 125.00
DAPAM1 Austin Meadows 50.00 120.00
DAPAM2 Austin Meadows 50.00 120.00
DAPAM3 Austin Meadows 50.00 120.00
DAPAM4 Austin Meadows 50.00 120.00
DAPAM5 Austin Meadows 50.00 120.00
DAPAM6 Austin Meadows 50.00 120.00
DAPAN1 Aaron Nola 50.00 120.00
DAPAN2 Aaron Nola 50.00 120.00
DAPAN3 Aaron Nola 50.00 120.00
DAPAN4 Aaron Nola 50.00 120.00
DAPAN5 Aaron Nola 50.00 120.00
DAPAN6 Aaron Nola 50.00 120.00
DAPAP1 Albert Pujols 250.00 600.00
DAPAP1 Andy Pettitte 40.00 100.00
DAPAP2 Andy Pettitte 40.00 100.00
DAPAP2 Albert Pujols 250.00 600.00
DAPAP3 Andy Pettitte 40.00 100.00
DAPAP4 Andy Pettitte 40.00 100.00
DAPAP5 Andy Pettitte 40.00 100.00
DAPARZ1 Anthony Rizzo 75.00 200.00
DAPARZ2 Anthony Rizzo 75.00 200.00
DAPARZ3 Anthony Rizzo 75.00 200.00
DAPARZ4 Anthony Rizzo 75.00 200.00
DAPARZ5 Anthony Rizzo 75.00 200.00
DAPARZ6 Anthony Rizzo 75.00 200.00
DAPARZ7 Anthony Rizzo 75.00 200.00
DAPARZ8 Anthony Rizzo 75.00 200.00
DAPBB1 Bo Bichette RC EXCH 200.00 500.00
DAPBB2 Bo Bichette RC EXCH 200.00 500.00
DAPBB3 Bo Bichette RC EXCH 200.00 500.00
DAPBH1 Bryce Harper 150.00 400.00
DAPBH2 Bryce Harper 150.00 400.00
DAPBH3 Bryce Harper 150.00 400.00
DAPBH4 Bryce Harper 150.00 400.00
DAPBL1 Barry Larkin 30.00 80.00
DAPBL2 Barry Larkin 30.00 80.00
DAPBL3 Barry Larkin 30.00 80.00
DAPBP1 Buster Posey 75.00 200.00
DAPBP2 Buster Posey 75.00 200.00
DAPBP3 Buster Posey 75.00 200.00
DAPBP4 Buster Posey 75.00 200.00
DAPBP5 Buster Posey 75.00 200.00
DAPBP6 Buster Posey 75.00 200.00
DAPBS1 Blake Snell 50.00 120.00
DAPBS2 Blake Snell 50.00 120.00
DAPBS3 Blake Snell 50.00 120.00
DAPCB1 Cody Bellinger 125.00 300.00
DAPCB2 Cody Bellinger 125.00 300.00
DAPCB3 Cody Bellinger 125.00 300.00
DAPCB4 Cody Bellinger 125.00 300.00
DAPCB5 Cody Bellinger 125.00 300.00
DAPCB6 Cody Bellinger 125.00 300.00
DAPCB7 Cody Bellinger 125.00 300.00
DAPCB8 Cody Bellinger 125.00 300.00
DAPCC1 CC Sabathia 50.00 120.00
DAPCC2 CC Sabathia 50.00 120.00
DAPCC3 CC Sabathia 50.00 120.00
DAPCC4 CC Sabathia 50.00 120.00
DAPCC5 CC Sabathia 50.00 120.00
DAPCC6 CC Sabathia 50.00 120.00
DAPCF1 Carlton Fisk 50.00 120.00
DAPCF2 Carlton Fisk 50.00 120.00
DAPCF3 Carlton Fisk 50.00 120.00
DAPCJ1 Chipper Jones 100.00 250.00
DAPCJ2 Chipper Jones 100.00 250.00
DAPCJ3 Chipper Jones 100.00 250.00
DAPCJ4 Chipper Jones 100.00 250.00
DAPCJ5 Chipper Jones 100.00 250.00
DAPCJ6 Chipper Jones 100.00 250.00
DAPCS1 Corey Seager 75.00 200.00
DAPCS2 Corey Seager 75.00 200.00
DAPCS3 Corey Seager 75.00 200.00
DAPCS4 Corey Seager 75.00 200.00
DAPCS5 Corey Seager 75.00 200.00
DAPCS6 Corey Seager 75.00 200.00
DAPCSA1 Chris Sale 40.00 100.00
DAPCSA2 Chris Sale 40.00 100.00
DAPCSA3 Chris Sale 40.00 100.00
DAPCY1 Christian Yelich 75.00 200.00
DAPCY2 Christian Yelich 75.00 200.00
DAPCY3 Christian Yelich 75.00 200.00
DAPCY4 Christian Yelich 75.00 200.00
DAPCY5 Christian Yelich 75.00 200.00
DAPCY6 Christian Yelich 75.00 200.00
DAPCY7 Christian Yelich 75.00 200.00
DAPCY8 Christian Yelich 75.00 200.00
DAPDJ1 Derek Jeter 300.00 800.00
DAPDJ2 Derek Jeter 300.00 800.00
DAPDJL1 DJ LeMahieu 75.00 200.00
DAPDJL2 DJ LeMahieu 75.00 200.00
DAPDJL3 DJ LeMahieu 75.00 200.00
DAPDJL4 DJ LeMahieu 75.00 200.00
DAPDJL5 DJ LeMahieu 75.00 200.00
DAPDJL6 DJ LeMahieu 75.00 200.00
DAPDO1 David Ortiz 75.00 200.00
DAPDO2 David Ortiz 75.00 200.00
DAPDO3 David Ortiz 75.00 200.00
DAPDO4 David Ortiz 75.00 200.00
DAPDO5 David Ortiz 75.00 200.00
DAPDO6 David Ortiz 75.00 200.00
DAPDO7 David Ortiz 75.00 200.00
DAPDSA1 Deion Sanders 75.00 200.00
DAPDSA2 Deion Sanders 75.00 200.00
DAPDW1 David Wright 60.00 150.00
DAPDW2 David Wright 60.00 150.00
DAPDW3 David Wright 60.00 150.00
DAPEA1 Elvis Andrus 40.00 100.00
DAPEA2 Elvis Andrus 40.00 100.00
DAPEA3 Elvis Andrus 40.00 100.00
DAPFF1 Freddie Freeman 100.00 250.00
DAPFF2 Freddie Freeman 100.00 250.00
DAPFF3 Freddie Freeman 100.00 250.00
DAPFF4 Freddie Freeman 100.00 250.00
DAPFF5 Freddie Freeman 100.00 250.00
DAPFF6 Freddie Freeman 100.00 250.00
DAPFF7 Freddie Freeman 100.00 250.00
DAPFF8 Freddie Freeman 100.00 250.00
DAPFT1 Frank Thomas 75.00 200.00
DAPFT2 Frank Thomas 75.00 200.00
DAPFT3 Frank Thomas 75.00 200.00
DAPFTJ1 Fernando Tatis Jr. EXCH 250.00 600.00
DAPFTJ2 Fernando Tatis Jr. EXCH 250.00 600.00
DAPFTJ3 Fernando Tatis Jr. EXCH 250.00 600.00
DAPFTJ4 Fernando Tatis Jr. EXCH 250.00 600.00
DAPFTJ5 Fernando Tatis Jr. EXCH 250.00 600.00
DAPFTJ6 Fernando Tatis Jr. EXCH 250.00 600.00
DAPFTJ7 Fernando Tatis Jr. EXCH 250.00 600.00
DAPFTJ8 Fernando Tatis Jr. EXCH 250.00 600.00
DAPGM1 Greg Maddux 125.00 300.00
DAPGM2 Greg Maddux 125.00 300.00
DAPGM3 Greg Maddux 125.00 300.00
DAPGSP1 George Springer 50.00 120.00
DAPGSP2 George Springer 50.00 120.00
DAPGSP3 George Springer 50.00 120.00
DAPGSP4 George Springer 50.00 120.00
DAPGSP5 George Springer 50.00 120.00
DAPGSP6 George Springer 50.00 120.00
DAPGSP7 George Springer 50.00 120.00
DAPGSP8 George Springer 50.00 120.00
DAPGT1 Gleyber Torres 80.00 200.00
DAPGT2 Gleyber Torres 80.00 200.00
DAPGT3 Gleyber Torres 80.00 200.00
DAPGT4 Gleyber Torres 80.00 200.00
DAPGT5 Gleyber Torres 80.00 200.00
DAPGT6 Gleyber Torres 80.00 200.00
DAPGT7 Gleyber Torres 80.00 200.00
DAPGT8 Gleyber Torres 80.00 200.00
DAPI1 Ichiro 250.00 600.00
DAPI3 Ichiro 250.00 600.00
DAPJA1 Jose Altuve 40.00 100.00
DAPJA2 Jose Altuve 40.00 100.00
DAPJA3 Jose Altuve 40.00 100.00
DAPJA4 Jose Altuve 40.00 100.00
DAPJA5 Jose Altuve 40.00 100.00
DAPJA6 Jose Altuve 40.00 100.00
DAPJA7 Jose Altuve 40.00 100.00
DAPJA8 Jose Altuve 40.00 100.00
DAPJB1 Jeff Bagwell 125.00 300.00
DAPJB2 Jeff Bagwell 125.00 300.00
DAPJdG1 Jacob deGrom 100.00 250.00
DAPJdG2 Jacob deGrom 100.00 250.00
DAPJdG3 Jacob deGrom 100.00 250.00
DAPJdG4 Jacob deGrom 100.00 250.00
DAPJdG5 Jacob deGrom 100.00 250.00
DAPJdG6 Jacob deGrom 100.00 250.00
DAPJF1 Jack Flaherty 60.00 150.00
DAPJF2 Jack Flaherty 60.00 150.00
DAPJF3 Jack Flaherty 60.00 150.00
DAPJL1 Jesus Luzardo RC 60.00 150.00
DAPJL2 Jesus Luzardo RC 60.00 150.00
DAPJL3 Jesus Luzardo RC 60.00 150.00
DAPJL4 Jesus Luzardo RC 60.00 150.00
DAPJS1 John Smoltz 50.00 120.00
DAPJS1 Juan Soto 150.00 400.00
DAPJS2 John Smoltz 50.00 120.00
DAPJS2 Juan Soto 150.00 400.00
DAPJS3 John Smoltz 50.00 120.00
DAPJS3 Juan Soto 150.00 400.00
DAPJS4 John Smoltz 50.00 120.00
DAPJS5 John Smoltz 50.00 120.00
DAPJS6 John Smoltz 50.00 120.00
DAPJT1 Jim Thome 40.00 100.00
DAPJT2 Jim Thome 40.00 100.00
DAPJTR1 J.T. Realmuto 60.00 150.00
DAPJTR2 J.T. Realmuto 60.00 150.00
DAPJTR3 J.T. Realmuto 60.00 150.00
DAPJV1 Joey Votto 60.00 150.00
DAPJV2 Joey Votto 60.00 150.00
DAPJV3 Joey Votto 60.00 150.00
DAPJV4 Joey Votto 60.00 150.00
DAPJV5 Joey Votto 60.00 150.00
DAPJV6 Joey Votto 60.00 150.00
DAPJV7 Joey Votto 60.00 150.00
DAPJV8 Joey Votto 60.00 150.00
DAPKG1 Ken Griffey Jr. 250.00 600.00
DAPKG2 Ken Griffey Jr. 250.00 600.00
DAPKG5 Ken Griffey Jr. 250.00 600.00
DAPKG6 Ken Griffey Jr. 250.00 600.00
DAPKH1 Keston Hiura 50.00 125.00
DAPKH2 Keston Hiura 50.00 125.00
DAPKH3 Keston Hiura 50.00 125.00
DAPKH4 Keston Hiura 50.00 125.00
DAPKH5 Keston Hiura 50.00 125.00
DAPKH6 Keston Hiura 50.00 125.00
DAPKL1 Kyle Lewis RC 125.00 300.00
DAPKL2 Kyle Lewis RC 125.00 300.00
DAPKL3 Kyle Lewis RC 125.00 300.00
DAPKS1 Kyle Schwarber 40.00 100.00
DAPKS2 Kyle Schwarber 40.00 100.00
DAPKS3 Kyle Schwarber 40.00 100.00
DAPLW1 Larry Walker 60.00 150.00
DAPLW2 Larry Walker 60.00 150.00
DAPLW3 Larry Walker 60.00 150.00
DAPLW4 Larry Walker 60.00 150.00
DAPMC1 Miguel Cabrera 100.00 250.00
DAPMC2 Miguel Cabrera 100.00 250.00
DAPMC3 Miguel Cabrera 100.00 250.00
DAPMC4 Miguel Cabrera 100.00 250.00
DAPMC5 Miguel Cabrera 100.00 250.00
DAPMC6 Miguel Cabrera 100.00 250.00
DAPMC7 Miguel Cabrera 100.00 250.00
DAPMC8 Miguel Cabrera 100.00 250.00
DAPMCA1 Matt Chapman 60.00 150.00
DAPMCA2 Matt Chapman 60.00 150.00
DAPMCA3 Matt Chapman 60.00 150.00
DAPMCA4 Matt Chapman 60.00 150.00
DAPMCA5 Matt Chapman 60.00 150.00
DAPMMC1 Mark McGwire 100.00 250.00
DAPMMC2 Mark McGwire 100.00 250.00
DAPMMC3 Mark McGwire 100.00 250.00
DAPMMU1 Max Muncy 40.00 100.00
DAPMMU2 Max Muncy 40.00 100.00
DAPMMU3 Max Muncy 40.00 100.00
DAPMMU4 Max Muncy 40.00 100.00
DAPMMU5 Max Muncy 40.00 100.00
DAPMR1 Mariano Rivera 150.00 400.00
DAPMR2 Mariano Rivera 150.00 400.00
DAPMR3 Mariano Rivera 150.00 400.00
DAPMS1 Mike Soroka 60.00 150.00
DAPMS2 Mike Soroka 60.00 150.00
DAPMS3 Mike Soroka 60.00 150.00
DAPMS4 Mike Soroka 60.00 150.00
DAPMS5 Mike Soroka 60.00 150.00
DAPMS6 Mike Soroka 60.00 150.00
DAPMT1 Masahiro Tanaka 60.00 150.00
DAPMT2 Masahiro Tanaka 60.00 150.00
DAPMT3 Masahiro Tanaka 60.00 150.00
DAPMT4 Masahiro Tanaka 60.00 150.00
DAPMT5 Masahiro Tanaka 60.00 150.00
DAPMT6 Masahiro Tanaka 60.00 150.00
DAPMTR1 Mike Trout 600.00 1500.00
DAPMTR2 Mike Trout 600.00 1500.00
DAPMTR3 Mike Trout 600.00 1500.00
DAPMTR4 Mike Trout 600.00 1500.00
DAPMTR5 Mike Trout 600.00 1500.00
DAPMTR6 Mike Trout 600.00 1500.00
DAPMTR7 Mike Trout 600.00 1500.00
DAPNA1 Nolan Arenado 50.00 125.00
DAPNA2 Nolan Arenado 50.00 125.00
DAPNA3 Nolan Arenado 50.00 125.00
DAPNA4 Nolan Arenado 50.00 125.00
DAPNA5 Nolan Arenado 50.00 125.00
DAPNA6 Nolan Arenado 50.00 125.00
DAPNA7 Nolan Arenado 50.00 125.00
DAPNA8 Nolan Arenado 50.00 125.00
DAPPA1 Pete Alonso 100.00 250.00
DAPPA2 Pete Alonso 100.00 250.00
DAPPA3 Pete Alonso 100.00 250.00
DAPPM1 Pedro Martinez 75.00 200.00
DAPPM2 Pedro Martinez 75.00 200.00
DAPPM3 Pedro Martinez 75.00 200.00
DAPPM4 Pedro Martinez 75.00 80.00
DAPRA1 Ronald Acuna Jr. 200.00 500.00
DAPRA1 Roberto Alomar 50.00 120.00
DAPRA2 Ronald Acuna Jr. 200.00 500.00
DAPRA2 Roberto Alomar 50.00 120.00
DAPRA3 Ronald Acuna Jr. 200.00 500.00
DAPRA4 Ronald Acuna Jr. 200.00 500.00
DAPRA4 Roberto Alomar 50.00 120.00
DAPRA5 Ronald Acuna Jr. 200.00 500.00
DAPRA6 Ronald Acuna Jr. 200.00 500.00
DAPRA6 Roberto Alomar 50.00 120.00
DAPRA7 Ronald Acuna Jr. 200.00 500.00
DAPRA8 Ronald Acuna Jr. 200.00 500.00
DAPRC1 Rod Carew 40.00 100.00
DAPRC2 Rod Carew 40.00 100.00
DAPRC2 Roger Clemens 75.00 200.00
DAPRC3 Rod Carew 40.00 100.00
DAPRC3 Roger Clemens 75.00 200.00
DAPRC4 Roger Clemens 75.00 200.00
DAPRC5 Roger Clemens 75.00 200.00
DAPRD1 Rafael Devers 50.00 125.00
DAPRD2 Rafael Devers 50.00 125.00
DAPRD3 Rafael Devers 50.00 125.00
DAPRD4 Rafael Devers 50.00 125.00
DAPRD5 Rafael Devers 50.00 125.00
DAPRD6 Rafael Devers 50.00 125.00
DAPRD7 Rafael Devers 50.00 125.00
DAPRD8 Rafael Devers 50.00 125.00
DAPRH1 Rickey Henderson 100.00 250.00
DAPRH2 Rickey Henderson 100.00 250.00
DAPRH3 Rickey Henderson 100.00 250.00
DAPRH5 Rickey Henderson 100.00 250.00
DAPRH6 Rickey Henderson 100.00 250.00
DAPRHO1 Rhys Hoskins 50.00 125.00
DAPRHO2 Rhys Hoskins 50.00 125.00
DAPRHO3 Rhys Hoskins 50.00 125.00
DAPRHO4 Rhys Hoskins 50.00 125.00
DAPRHO5 Rhys Hoskins 50.00 125.00
DAPRHO6 Rhys Hoskins 50.00 125.00
DAPRHO7 Rhys Hoskins 50.00 125.00
DAPRHO8 Rhys Hoskins 50.00 125.00
DAPRJA1 Reggie Jackson 60.00 150.00
DAPRJA2 Reggie Jackson 60.00 150.00
DAPRJA3 Reggie Jackson 60.00 150.00
DAPRJA4 Reggie Jackson 60.00 150.00
DAPRY1 Robin Yount 60.00 150.00
DAPRY2 Robin Yount 60.00 150.00
DAPRY3 Robin Yount 60.00 150.00
DAPRY4 Robin Yount 60.00 150.00
DAPRY5 Robin Yount 60.00 150.00
DAPSC1 Steve Carlton 50.00 120.00
DAPSC2 Steve Carlton 50.00 120.00
DAPSG1 Sonny Gray 40.00 100.00
DAPSG2 Sonny Gray 40.00 100.00
DAPSG3 Sonny Gray 40.00 100.00
DAPSO1 Shohei Ohtani 125.00 300.00
DAPSO2 Shohei Ohtani 125.00 300.00
DAPSO3 Shohei Ohtani 125.00 300.00
DAPSTR1 Stephen Strasburg 75.00 200.00
DAPSTR2 Stephen Strasburg 75.00 200.00
DAPSTR3 Stephen Strasburg 75.00 200.00
DAPSTR4 Stephen Strasburg 75.00 200.00
DAPSTR5 Stephen Strasburg 75.00 200.00
DAPSTR6 Stephen Strasburg 75.00 200.00
DAPTBA1 Trevor Bauer 75.00 200.00
DAPTBA2 Trevor Bauer 75.00 200.00
DAPTBA3 Trevor Bauer 75.00 200.00
DAPTG1 Tom Glavine 50.00 120.00
DAPTG2 Tom Glavine 50.00 120.00
DAPTG3 Tom Glavine 50.00 120.00
DAPTS1 Trevor Story 40.00 100.00
DAPTS2 Trevor Story 40.00 100.00
DAPTS3 Trevor Story 40.00 100.00
DAPTS4 Trevor Story 40.00 100.00
DAPTS5 Trevor Story 40.00 100.00
DAPTS6 Trevor Story 40.00 100.00
DAPVR1 Victor Robles 50.00 125.00
DAPVR2 Victor Robles 50.00 125.00
DAPVR3 Victor Robles 50.00 125.00
DAPVR4 Victor Robles 50.00 125.00
DAPVR5 Victor Robles 50.00 125.00
DAPVR6 Victor Robles 50.00 125.00
DAPWB1 Walker Buehler 75.00 200.00
DAPWB1 Wade Boggs 75.00 200.00
DAPWB2 Walker Buehler 75.00 200.00
DAPWB2 Wade Boggs 75.00 200.00
DAPWB3 Walker Buehler 75.00 200.00
DAPWB3 Wade Boggs 75.00 200.00
DAPWB4 Walker Buehler 75.00 200.00
DAPWB4 Wade Boggs 75.00 200.00
DAPWB5 Walker Buehler 75.00 200.00
DAPWB6 Walker Buehler 75.00 200.00
DAPWB7 Walker Buehler 75.00 200.00
DAPWB8 Walker Buehler 75.00 200.00
DAPWC1 Willson Contreras 50.00 120.00
DAPWC1 Will Clark 60.00 150.00
DAPWC2 Willson Contreras 50.00 120.00
DAPWC2 Will Clark 60.00 150.00
DAPWC3 Willson Contreras 50.00 120.00
DAPWC4 Willson Contreras 50.00 120.00
DAPWC5 Willson Contreras 50.00 120.00
DAPWC6 Willson Contreras 50.00 120.00
DAPWM1 Whit Merrifield 50.00 120.00
DAPWM2 Whit Merrifield 50.00 120.00
DAPWM3 Whit Merrifield 50.00 120.00
DAPXB1 Xander Bogaerts 50.00 120.00
DAPXB2 Xander Bogaerts 50.00 120.00
DAPXB3 Xander Bogaerts 50.00 120.00
DAPXB4 Xander Bogaerts 50.00 120.00
DAPXB5 Xander Bogaerts 50.00 120.00
DAPXB6 Xander Bogaerts 50.00 120.00
DAPXB7 Xander Bogaerts 50.00 120.00
DAPXB8 Xander Bogaerts 50.00 120.00
DAPYA1 Yordan Alvarez RC 125.00 300.00
DAPYA2 Yordan Alvarez RC 125.00 300.00
DAPYA3 Yordan Alvarez RC 125.00 300.00
DAPYA4 Yordan Alvarez RC 125.00 300.00
DAPYA5 Yordan Alvarez RC 125.00 300.00
DAPYA6 Yordan Alvarez RC 125.00 300.00
DAPYA7 Yordan Alvarez RC 125.00 300.00
DAPYA8 Yordan Alvarez RC 125.00 300.00
DAPZG1 Zac Gallen RC 60.00 150.00
DAPZG2 Zac Gallen RC 60.00 150.00

2020 Topps Dynasty Autograph Patches Silver

*GOLD: .5X TO 1.2X BASIC
RANDOM INSERTS IN PACKS
STATED PRINT RUN 5 SER.#'d SETS
SOME NOT PRICED DUE TO SCARCITY
ALL VERSIONS EQUALLY PRICED
LOGO/TAG PATCHES MAY SELL FOR PREMIUM
EXCHANGE DEADLINE 10/31/2022

2017 Topps Fire

COMPLETE SET (200) 30.00 80.00
1 Kris Bryant .40 1.00
2 A.J. Pollock .20 .50
3 Matt Olson RC .50 1.25
4 Randy Johnson .30 .75
5 Evan Longoria .25 .60
6 Freddie Freeman .40 1.00
7 Sean Newcomb RC .40 1.00
8 Aledmys Diaz .25 .60
9 Seth Lugo RC .30 .75
10 Chris Sale .30 .75
11 Gary Carter .25 .60
12 Willie Stargell .25 .60
13 Mark Melancon .20 .50
14 Cal Ripken Jr. 1.00 2.50
15 Adam Jones .25 .60
16 Paul Konerko .25 .60
17 Nomar Garciaparra .25 .60
18 Andy Pettitte .25 .60
19 Justin Verlander .30 .75
20 Andrew Miller .25 .60
21 Phil Niekro .25 .60
22 Mark McGwire .50 1.25
23 Daniel Murphy .25 .60
24 Greg Maddux .40 1.00
25 Sandy Koufax .60 1.50
26 Corey Kluber .25 .60
27 Jon Lester .25 .60
28 Johnny Cueto .25 .60
29 Curt Schilling .25 .60
30 Lorenzo Cain .20 .50
31 Javier Baez .40 1.00
32 Michael Fulmer .20 .50
33 Harmon Killebrew .30 .75
34 Tom Glavine .25 .60
35 David Ortiz .30 .75
36 Ender Inciarte .30 .75
37 Eric Hosmer .25 .60
38 Jonathan Villar .20 .50
39 Paul Goldschmidt .30 .75
40 Rob Zastryzny RC .30 .75
41 Joe Musgrove RC .30 .75
42 George Brett .60 1.50
43 Eddie Mathews .30 .75
44 Frank Thomas .30 .75
45 Pedro Martinez .25 .60
46 Gary Sanchez .30 .75
47 Lou Brock .25 .60
48 Masahiro Tanaka .25 .60
49 Bo Jackson .30 .75
50 Mike Trout 1.50 4.00
51 Billy Hamilton .25 .60
52 Jacob deGrom .30 .75
53 Johnny Damon .25 .60
54 Lou Gehrig .60 1.50
55 Jim Edmonds .20 .50
56 Nelson Cruz .30 .75
57 Warren Spahn .25 .60
58 Jeff Hoffman RC .30 .75
59 Jeurys Familia .25 .60
60 Matt Carpenter .30 .75
61 Mookie Betts .50 1.25
62 Aaron Judge RC 4.00 10.00
63 Reynaldo Lopez RC .30 .75
64 Steven Wright .20 .50
65 Andrew Benintendi RC 1.00 2.50
66 Kyle Hendricks .30 .75
67 Tony Perez .25 .60
68 Ian Kinsler .25 .60
69 Yu Darvish .30 .75
70 Dennis Eckersley .25 .60
71 Aaron Boone .20 .50
72 Roberto Clemente .75 2.00
73 George Springer .25 .60
74 Fergie Jenkins .25 .60
75 Derek Jeter .75 2.00
76 Bryce Harper .50 1.25
77 Kenta Maeda .25 .60
78 David Dahl RC .40 1.00
79 Robinson Cano .25 .60
80 Raimel Tapia RC .40 1.00
81 Jharel Cotton RC .30 .75
82 Dan Vogelbach RC .50 1.25
83 Ken Griffey Jr. .60 1.50
84 Lewis Brinson RC .50 1.25
85 Wade Davis .20 .50
86 Andre Dawson .25 .60
87 Wil Myers .20 .50
88 Rickey Henderson .30 .75
89 Aroldis Chapman .30 .75
90 Dellin Betances .25 .60
91 Ted Williams .60 1.50
92 Edwin Encarnacion .30 .75
93 Stephen Strasburg .30 .75
94 Ryon Healy RC .40 1.00
95 Jose Canseco .25 .60
96 Ian Happ RC .60 1.50
97 Edgar Renteria .20 .50
98 Maikel Franco .25 .60
99 Adrian Beltre .30 .75
100 Yoan Moncada RC 1.00 2.50
101 Jackie Robinson .30 .75
102 Yoenis Cespedes .30 .75
103 Addison Russell .30 .75
104 Stephen Piscotty .25 .60
105 Renato Nunez RC .60 1.50
106 Yulieski Gurriel RC .50 1.25
107 Julio Urias .30 .75
108 Noah Syndergaard .25 .60
109 Christian Yelich .40 1.00
110 Miguel Cabrera .30 .75
111 Tyler Glasnow RC .40 1.00
112 Didi Gregorius .25 .60
113 Chris Davis .20 .50
114 Ryne Sandberg .60 1.50
115 Trea Turner .25 .60
116 Carlos Martinez .25 .60
117 Aaron Sanchez .25 .60
118 Jason Heyward .25 .60
119 Brian Dozier .30 .75
120 Clayton Kershaw .60 1.50
121 Cody Bellinger RC 5.00 12.00
122 Jose De Leon RC .30 .75
123 Jose Altuve .25 .60
124 Anthony Rizzo .50 1.25
125 Steven Matz .25 .60
126 Alex Bregman RC 1.25 3.00
127 Ichiro .40 1.00
128 Carlos Correa .30 .75
129 Ivan Rodriguez .25 .60
130 JaCoby Jones RC .40 1.00
131 Larry Doby .25 .60
132 Andrew McCutchen .30 .75
133 Carl Yastrzemski .50 1.25
134 Manny Machado .30 .75
135 Hunter Renfroe RC .40 1.00
136 Max Scherzer .30 .75
137 Brooks Robinson .25 .60
138 Danny Duffy .20 .50
139 Ernie Banks .30 .75
140 Adam Duvall .30 .75
141 Albert Pujols .40 1.00
142 Gavin Cecchini RC .30 .75
143 Jorge Alfaro RC .40 1.00
144 Hunter Dozier RC .30 .75
145 Chipper Jones .30 .75
146 Seung-Hwan Oh .40 1.00
147 Yasmani Grandal .20 .50
148 Kyle Seager .20 .50
149 Joey Votto .30 .75
150 Corey Seager .30 .75
151 Gregory Polanco .25 .60
152 Kyle Schwarber .30 .75
153 Orlando Arcia RC .50 1.25
154 Luke Weaver RC .40 1.00
155 Trey Mancini RC .60 1.50
156 Dave Winfield .25 .60
157 Drew Pomeranz .25 .60
158 Jose Bautista .25 .60
159 Chris Archer .20 .50
160 Willie McCovey .25 .60
161 Josh Bell RC .75 2.00
162 Dansby Swanson RC .75 2.00
163 Hank Aaron .60 1.50
164 Braden Shipley RC .30 .75
165 Jackie Bradley Jr. .30 .75
166 Steve Carlton .25 .60
167 Willson Contreras .30 .75
168 Giancarlo Stanton .30 .75
169 Dexter Fowler .25 .60

170 Dustin Pedroia .30 .75
171 Xander Bogaerts .30 .75
172 Roberto Osuna .20 .50
173 Zach Britton .25 .60
174 Alex Reyes RC .40 1.00
175 Nolan Arenado .40 1.00
176 Ryan Braun .25 .60
177 Carson Fulmer RC .30 .75
178 Jose Abreu .30 .75
179 Justin Upton .25 .60
180 Nolan Ryan 1.00 2.50
181 David Price .25 .60
182 Reggie Jackson .25 .60
183 Tyler Austin RC .50 1.25
184 Lucas Giolito .25 .60
185 Manny Margot RC .30 .75
186 Odubel Herrera .25 .60
187 Trevor Story .30 .75
188 Robert Gsellman RC .30 .75
189 Luis Severino .25 .60
190 Josh Donaldson .25 .60
191 Omar Vizquel .25 .60
192 Mike Piazza .30 .75
193 Jake Arrieta .25 .60
194 Henry Owens .20 .50
195 Jake Thompson RC .30 .75
196 Francisco Lindor .30 .75
197 Jacoby Ellsbury .25 .60
198 Carlos Gonzalez .25 .60
199 Rougned Odor .25 .60
200 Babe Ruth .75 2.00

2017 Topps Fire Blue Chip

*BLUE CHIP: 1.2X TO 3X BASIC
*BLUE CHIP RC: .75X TO 2X BASIC RC
121 Cody Bellinger 6.00 15.00
180 Nolan Ryan 5.00 12.00

2017 Topps Fire Flame

*FLAME: 1.2X TO 3X BASIC
*FLAME RC: .75X TO 2X BASIC RC
STATED ODDS 1:4 RETAIL
121 Cody Bellinger 6.00 15.00
180 Nolan Ryan 5.00 12.00

2017 Topps Fire Gold Minted

*GOLD MINTED: 1.2X TO 3X BASIC
*GOLD MINTED RC: .75X TO 2X BASIC RC
121 Cody Bellinger 6.00 15.00
180 Nolan Ryan 5.00 12.00

2017 Topps Fire Green

*GREEN: 2X TO 5X BASIC
*GREEN RC: 1.2X TO 3X BASIC RC
STATED ODDS 1:14 RETAIL
STATED PRINT RUN 199 SER.#'d SETS
14 Cal Ripken Jr. 8.00 20.00
42 George Brett 10.00 25.00
62 Aaron Judge 15.00 40.00
72 Roberto Clemente 8.00 20.00
83 Ken Griffey Jr. 5.00 12.00
91 Ted Williams 8.00 20.00
121 Cody Bellinger 10.00 25.00
180 Nolan Ryan 8.00 20.00

2017 Topps Fire Magenta

*MAGENTA: 4X TO 10X BASIC
*MAGENTA RC: 2.5X TO 6X BASIC RC
STATED ODDS 1:108 RETAIL
STATED PRINT RUN 25 SER.#'d SETS
14 Cal Ripken Jr. 15.00 40.00
42 George Brett 20.00 50.00
49 Bo Jackson 12.00 30.00
62 Aaron Judge 30.00 80.00
72 Roberto Clemente 15.00 40.00
75 Derek Jeter 20.00 50.00
83 Ken Griffey Jr. 10.00 25.00
91 Ted Williams 15.00 40.00
121 Cody Bellinger 20.00 50.00
180 Nolan Ryan 15.00 40.00

2017 Topps Fire Orange

*ORANGE: 1.5X TO 4X BASIC
*ORANGE RC: 1X TO 2.5X BASIC RC
STATED ODDS 1:10 RETAIL
STATED PRINT RUN 299 SER.#'d SETS
14 Cal Ripken Jr. 6.00 15.00
42 George Brett 8.00 20.00
83 Ken Griffey Jr. 4.00 10.00
91 Ted Williams 6.00 15.00
121 Cody Bellinger 8.00 20.00
180 Nolan Ryan 6.00 15.00

2017 Topps Fire Purple

*PURPLE: 2.5X TO 6X BASIC
*PURPLE RC: 1.5X TO 4X BASIC RC
STATED ODDS 1:128 RETAIL
STATED PRINT RUN 99 SER.#'d SETS
14 Cal Ripken Jr. 10.00 25.00
42 George Brett 12.00 30.00
49 Bo Jackson 8.00 20.00
62 Aaron Judge 20.00 50.00
72 Roberto Clemente 10.00 25.00
83 Ken Griffey Jr. 6.00 15.00
91 Ted Williams 10.00 25.00
121 Cody Bellinger 12.00 30.00
180 Nolan Ryan 10.00 25.00

2017 Topps Fire Autograph Patches

STATED ODDS 1:303 RETAIL
STATED PRINT RUN 25 SER.#'d SETS
EXCHANGE DEADLINE 8/31/2019
FAPAB Alex Bregman 25.00 60.00
FAPAD Aledmys Diaz
FAPAJ Aaron Judge
FAPAN Aaron Nola 20.00 50.00
FAPARE Alex Reyes 8.00 20.00
FAPBS Blake Snell 8.00 20.00
FAPCC Carlos Correa
FAPCF Carson Fulmer
FAPCS Corey Seager
FAPDD David Dahl
FAPFL Francisco Lindor EXCH 25.00 60.00
FAPHR Hunter Renfroe
FAPJC Jharel Cotton
FAPJT Jameson Taillon
FAPKB Kris Bryant 75.00 200.00
FAPLG Lucas Giolito
FAPLS Luis Severino
FAPLW Luke Weaver
FAPMF Michael Fulmer
FAPMM Manny Machado
FAPMT Mike Trout 125.00 300.00
FAPNS Noah Syndergaard 8.00 20.00
FAPRG Robert Gsellman 6.00 15.00
FAPRH Ryon Healy
FAPRT Raimel Tapia
FAPSM Steven Matz
FAPSP Stephen Piscotty
FAPTA Tim Anderson 10.00 25.00
FAPTAU Tyler Austin 10.00 25.00
FAPTT Trea Turner
FAPWC Willson Contreras 25.00 60.00
FAPYG Yulieski Gurriel 20.00 50.00
FAPYM Yoan Moncada 30.00 80.00

2017 Topps Fire Autographs

STATED ODDS 1:29 RETAIL
PRINT RUNS B/WN 40-500 COPIES PER
EXCHANGE DEADLINE 8/31/2019
FAAJ Aaron Judge/250 75.00 200.00
FAAR Anthony Rizzo/40 10.00 25.00
FAARE Alex Reyes/420 4.00 10.00
FACC Carlos Correa/40 20.00 50.00
FADG Didi Gregorius/490 6.00 15.00
FADV Dan Vogelbach/486 4.00 10.00
FAEI Ender Inciarte/500 4.00 10.00
FAFJ Fergie Jenkins/250 6.00 15.00
FAFT Frank Thomas/40 25.00 60.00
FAHA Hank Aaron
FAHO Henry Owens/466 2.50 6.00
FAHR Hunter Renfroe/500 3.00 8.00
FAIH Ian Happ/200 15.00 40.00
FAJA Jorge Alfaro/500 3.00 8.00
FAJC Jharel Cotton/500 2.50 6.00
FAJJ JaCoby Jones/500 3.00 8.00
FAJT Jake Thompson/120 2.50 6.00
FALS Luis Severino/350 10.00 25.00
FALW Luke Weaver/500 3.00 8.00
FAMF Michael Fulmer/325 2.50 6.00
FAMM Manny Machado/40 25.00 60.00
FAMO Matt Olson/500 6.00 15.00
FARL Reynaldo Lopez/500 2.50 6.00
FARO Roberto Osuna/230 5.00 12.00
FART Raimel Tapia/500 3.00 8.00
FASK Sandy Koufax
FASL Seth Lugo/500 2.50 6.00
FASM Steven Matz/200 4.00 10.00
FATA Tyler Austin/500 4.00 10.00
FATT Trea Turner/65 3.00 8.00
FAWD Wade Davis/490 2.50 6.00
FAYG Yasmani Grandal/490 2.50 6.00
FAYM Yoan Moncada/40 40.00 100.00

2017 Topps Fire Autographs Green

*GREEN: .5X TO 1.2X BASIC
STATED ODDS 1:76 RETAIL
STATED PRINT RUN 75 SER.#'d SETS
EXCHANGE DEADLINE 8/31/2019
FAAB Alex Bregman EXCH 12.00 30.00
FAAP A.J. Pollock 3.00 8.00
FACB Cody Bellinger EXCH 75.00 200.00
FANS Noah Syndergaard 8.00 20.00
FAPN Phil Niekro

2017 Topps Fire Autographs Magenta

*MAGENTA: .75X TO 2X BASIC
STATED ODDS 1:226 RETAIL
STATED PRINT RUN 25 SER.#'d SETS
EXCHANGE DEADLINE 8/31/2019
FAAB Alex Bregman EXCH 20.00 50.00
FAABE Andrew Benintendi 50.00 120.00
FAAP A.J. Pollock 5.00 12.00
FABH Bryce Harper EXCH 75.00 200.00
FACB Cody Bellinger EXCH 125.00 300.00
FACD Chris Davis 20.00 50.00
FACS Corey Seager EXCH 60.00 150.00
FAEB Ernie Banks 30.00 80.00
FAFL Francisco Lindor EXCH 40.00 100.00
FAGM Greg Maddux 40.00 100.00
FAKB Kris Bryant 75.00 200.00
FAKGJ Ken Griffey Jr. 75.00 200.00
FALG Lucas Giolito 8.00 20.00
FAMS Max Scherzer 30.00 80.00
FAMT Mike Trout 125.00 300.00
FANS Noah Syndergaard 12.00 30.00
FAPM Pedro Martinez 40.00 100.00
FAPN Phil Niekro 20.00 50.00
FARH Ryon Healy EXCH 10.00 25.00

2017 Topps Fire Autographs Purple

*PURPLE: .6X TO 1.5X BASIC
STATED ODDS 1:114 RETAIL
STATED PRINT RUN 50 SER.#'d SETS
EXCHANGE DEADLINE 8/31/2019
FAAB Alex Bregman EXCH 15.00 40.00
FAABE Andrew Benintendi 40.00 100.00
FAAP A.J. Pollock 4.00 10.00
FACB Cody Bellinger EXCH 100.00 250.00
FACD Chris Davis 15.00 40.00
FACS Corey Seager EXCH
FAFL Francisco Lindor EXCH 30.00 80.00
FALG Lucas Giolito 6.00 15.00
FAMS Max Scherzer 25.00 60.00
FANS Noah Syndergaard 10.00 25.00
FAPN Phil Niekro

2017 Topps Fire Fired Up

STATED ODDS 1:20 RETAIL
*BLUE: .6X TO 1.5X BASIC
*GOLD: .75X TO 2X BASIC
F1 Kris Bryant .75 2.00
F2 Clayton Kershaw 1.25 3.00
F3 Yasiel Puig .60 1.50
F4 Noah Syndergaard .50 1.25
F5 Mike Trout 3.00 8.00
F6 Jose Bautista .50 1.25
F7 Marcus Stroman .50 1.25
F8 Carlos Correa .60 1.50
F9 Max Scherzer .60 1.50
F10 Bryce Harper 1.00 2.50

2017 Topps Fire Flame Throwers

STATED ODDS 1:14 RETAIL
*BLUE: .6X TO 1.5X BASIC
*GOLD: .75X TO 2X BASIC
FT1 Aroldis Chapman .60 1.50
FT2 Chris Archer .40 1.00
FT3 Carlos Martinez .50 1.25
FT4 Edwin Diaz .50 1.25
FT5 Stephen Strasburg .60 1.50
FT6 Dellin Betances .50 1.25
FT7 Chris Sale .60 1.50
FT8 Noah Syndergaard .50 1.25
FT9 Justin Verlander .60 1.50
FT10 Andrew Miller .50 1.25
FT11 Kelvin Herrera .40 1.00
FT12 Max Scherzer .60 1.50
FT13 Craig Kimbrel .50 1.25
FT14 Felix Hernandez .50 1.25
FT15 Clayton Kershaw 1.25 3.00

2017 Topps Fire Golden Grabs

STATED ODDS 1:10 RETAIL
*BLUE: .6X TO 1.5X BASIC
*GOLD: .75X TO 2X BASIC
GG1 Anthony Rizzo 1.00 2.50
GG2 Manny Machado .60 1.50
GG3 Kole Calhoun .40 1.00
GG4 Mookie Betts 1.00 2.50
GG5 Melky Cabrera .40 1.00
GG6 Ryan Braun .50 1.25
GG7 Kevin Kiermaier .50 1.25
GG8 George Springer .50 1.25
GG9 Kevin Kiermaier .50 1.25
GG10 Andrew Benintendi 1.25 3.00
GG11 Curtis Granderson .50 1.25
GG12 Travis Jankowski .40 1.00
GG13 Xander Bogaerts .60 1.50
GG14 Joey Votto .60 1.50
GG15 Billy Hamilton .50 1.25
GG16 Nolan Arenado .75 2.00
GG17 Byron Buxton .50 1.25
GG18 George Springer .50 1.25
GG19 Kevin Pillar .40 1.00
GG20 Mike Trout 3.00 8.00

2017 Topps Fire Monikers

STATED ODDS 1:5 RETAIL
*BLUE: .5X TO 1.2X BASIC
*GOLD: .6X TO 1.5X BASIC
M1 Babe Ruth 2.50 6.00
M2 Cal Ripken Jr. 3.00 8.00
M3 Felix Hernandez .75 2.00
M4 Rickey Henderson 1.00 2.50
M5 Roger Clemens 1.25 3.00
M6 David Ortiz 1.00 2.50
M7 Brooks Robinson .75 2.00
M8 Nelson Cruz 1.00 2.50
M9 Miguel Cabrera 1.00 2.50
M10 Jose Bautista .75 2.00
M11 Jose Altuve .75 2.00
M12 Frank Thomas 1.00 2.50
M13 Bob Feller .75 2.00
M14 Cecil Fielder .60 1.50
M15 Ryne Sandberg 2.00 5.00
M16 Wade Boggs .75 2.00
M17 Reggie Jackson .75 2.00
M18 Mike Moustakas .75 2.00
M19 Mark McGwire 1.50 4.00
M20 Bill Lee .60 1.50
M21 Bryce Harper 1.50 4.00
M22 Duke Snider .75 2.00
M23 Ozzie Smith 1.25 3.00
M24 Aaron Judge 8.00 20.00
M25 Chris Davis .60 1.50
M26 Noah Syndergaard .75 2.00
M27 Matt Harvey .75 2.00
M28 Brandon Belt .75 2.00
M29 Whitey Ford .75 2.00
M30 Phil Rizzuto .75 2.00
M31 Carl Yastrzemski 1.50 4.00
M32 Randy Johnson 1.00 2.50
M33 Gary Carter .75 2.00
M34 Mike Trout 5.00 12.00
M35 Jacob deGrom 1.00 2.50
M36 Jim Hunter .75 2.00
M37 Rich Gossage .75 2.00
M38 Nolan Ryan 3.00 8.00
M39 Don Mattingly 2.00 5.00
M40 Derek Jeter 2.50 6.00

2017 Topps Fire Relics

STATED ODDS 1:71 RETAIL
STATED PRINT RUN 110 SER.#'d SETS
*GREEN/75: .4X TO 1X BASIC
*PURPLE/50: .5X TO 1.2X BASIC
MAGENTA/25: .6X TO 1.5X BASIC
FRAB Andrew Benintendi 8.00 20.00
FRAD Aledmys Diaz 3.00 8.00
FRAG Alex Bregman 5.00 12.00
FRAJ Aaron Judge 30.00 80.00
FRAR Alex Reyes 3.00 8.00
FRCC Carlos Correa 4.00 10.00
FRCF Carson Fulmer 2.50 6.00
FRCS Corey Seager 4.00 10.00
FRDD David Dahl 3.00 8.00
FRDS Dansby Swanson 6.00 15.00
FRFL Francisco Lindor 4.00 10.00
FRHR Hunter Renfroe 3.00 8.00
FRJC Jharel Cotton 2.50 6.00
FRJT Jameson Taillon 3.00 8.00
FRJU Julio Urias 4.00 10.00
FRKB Kris Bryant 5.00 12.00
FRKS Kyle Schwarber 4.00 10.00
FRLG Lucas Giolito 3.00 8.00
FRLS Luis Severino 3.00 8.00
FRLW Luke Weaver 3.00 8.00
FRMF Michael Fulmer 2.50 6.00
FRMM Manny Machado 4.00 10.00
FRMS Miguel Sano 3.00 8.00
FRMT Mike Trout 20.00 50.00
FRNS Noah Syndergaard 3.00 8.00
FRRH Ryon Healy 3.00 8.00
FRSM Steven Matz 3.00 8.00
FRSP Stephen Piscotty 3.00 8.00
FRTAU Tyler Austin 4.00 10.00
FRTG Tyler Glasnow 3.00 8.00
FRTS Trevor Story 4.00 10.00
FRTT Trea Turner 3.00 8.00
FRWC Willson Contreras 4.00 10.00
FRYG Yulieski Gurriel 4.00 10.00
FRYM Yoan Moncada 5.00 12.00

2017 Topps Fire Walk It Off

STATED ODDS 1:14 RETAIL
*BLUE: .6X TO 1.5X BASIC
*GOLD: .75X TO 2X BASIC
WO1 Kris Bryant .75 2.00
WO2 George Springer .50 1.25
WO3 Edwin Encarnacion .60 1.50
WO4 Khris Davis .60 1.50
WO5 Albert Pujols .75 2.00
WO6 Justin Upton .50 1.25
WO7 Freddie Freeman .75 2.00
WO8 Josh Donaldson .50 1.25
WO9 Adrian Beltre .60 1.50
WO10 Carlos Correa .60 1.50
WO11 Mark Trumbo .40 1.00
WO12 Brian Dozier .60 1.50
WO13 Tyler Naquin .40 1.00
WO14 Joey Votto .60 1.50
WO15 Bryce Harper 1.00 2.50

2018 Topps Fire

COMPLETE SET (200) 30.00 80.00
1 Aaron Judge .75 2.00
2 Derek Jeter .75 2.00
3 Dwight Gooden .20 .50
4 Adam Duvall .30 .75
5 Dustin Fowler RC .30 .75
6 Xander Bogaerts .30 .75
7 Ian Kinsler .25 .60
8 Pedro Martinez .25 .60
9 Eric Hosmer .25 .60
10 Ryne Sandberg .60 1.50
11 Alex Verdugo RC .50 1.25
12 Stephen Piscotty .20 .50
13 Joe Mauer .25 .60
14 Luke Weaver .25 .60
15 Josh Bell .25 .60
16 Goose Gossage .25 .60
17 Justin Smoak .20 .50
18 Bob Feller .25 .60
19 Orlando Arcia .20 .50
20 Satchel Paige .30 .75
21 Jake Lamb .25 .60
22 Scott Kingery RC .50 1.25
23 Justin Verlander .30 .75
24 Corey Knebel .20 .50
25 Victor Robles RC .75 2.00
26 Kevin Kiermaier .25 .60
27 Josh Donaldson .25 .60
28 Max Fried RC 1.25 3.00
29 Ozzie Albies RC 1.00 2.50
30 Greg Bird .25 .60
31 Joey Gallo .25 .60
32 Ryan McMahon RC .40 1.00
33 Khris Davis .30 .75
34 Salvador Perez .25 .60
35 Jonathan Schoop .20 .50
36 Anthony Banda RC .30 .75
37 Rickey Henderson .30 .75
38 Willie McCovey .25 .60
39 Ian Happ .25 .60
40 David Ortiz .30 .75
41 Chance Sisco RC .40 1.00
42 Carson Kelly .20 .50
43 Gary Sanchez .30 .75
44 Hunter Pence .25 .60
45 Paul Goldschmidt
46 Alex Rodriguez .40 1.00
47 Luis Severino .25 .60
48 Byron Buxton .25 .60
49 Duke Snider .25 .60
50 Rhys Hoskins RC 1.25 3.00
51 Andrew Stevenson RC .30 .75
52 Chris Archer .20 .50
53 Bryce Harper .50 1.25
54 Trevor Story .30 .75
55 Maikel Franco .25 .60
56 Zack Greinke .25 .60
57 Wade Boggs .25 .60
58 Billy Hamilton .25 .60
59 Sean Doolittle .20 .50
60 Max Scherzer .30 .75
61 Corey Kluber .25 .60
62 Lucas Giolito .25 .60
63 Amed Rosario RC .40 1.00
64 Marcell Ozuna .30 .75
65 Dansby Swanson .30 .75
66 Don Mattingly .60 1.50
67 Garrett Richards .25 .60
68 Adrian Beltre .30 .75
69 Paul DeJong .30 .75
70 Miguel Gomez RC .30 .75
71 Phil Rizzuto .25 .60
72 Anthony Rizzo .50 1.25
73 Ernie Banks .30 .75
74 Javier Baez .40 1.00
75 Matt Chapman .30 .75
76 Scooter Gennett .30 .75
77 Justin Bour .20 .50
78 Carlos Correa .30 .75
79 Manny Machado .30 .75
80 Clayton Kershaw .60 1.50
81 Jose Abreu .30 .75
82 Trey Mancini .25 .60
83 Eddie Mathews .30 .75
84 Mike Piazza .30 .75
85 Evan Longoria .25 .60
86 J.D. Davis RC .40 1.00
87 Yu Darvish .30 .75
88 George Springer .25 .60
89 Nicholas Castellanos .30 .75
90 Lorenzo Cain .20 .50
91 Chris Sale .30 .75
92 Lewis Brinson .20 .50
93 Austin Hays RC .50 1.25
94 Jacob deGrom .30 .75
95 Michael Fulmer .20 .50
96 Victor Arano RC .30 .75
97 Kris Bryant .40 1.00
98 Hunter Renfroe .20 .50
99 Stephen Strasburg .30 .75
100 Mike Trout 1.50 4.00
101 Whit Merrifield .30 .75
102 Paul Blackburn RC .30 .75
103 Clint Frazier RC .60 1.50
104 Christian Yelich .40 1.00
105 Jose Altuve .25 .60
106 Starlin Castro .20 .50
107 Miguel Andujar RC 1.25 3.00
108 Robinson Cano .25 .60
109 Ronald Acuna Jr. RC 6.00 15.00
110 Tyler Mahle RC .40 1.00
111 A.J. Pollock .20 .50
112 Nolan Ryan 1.00 2.50
113 Francisco Lindor .30 .75
114 Cody Bellinger .60 1.50
115 Aaron Altherr .20 .50
116 Carlos Martinez .25 .60
117 Chris Davis .20 .50
118 Rafael Devers RC 1.00 2.50
119 Gleyber Torres RC 3.00 8.00
120 Josh Harrison .20 .50
121 Gregory Polanco .25 .60
122 Ronald Torreyes .20 .50
123 Franklin Barreto .20 .50
124 Lou Boudreau .25 .60
125 Giancarlo Stanton .30 .75
126 Randy Johnson .30 .75
127 Travis Shaw .20 .50
128 Tyler O'Neill RC .50 1.25
129 Ichiro .40 1.00
130 Tom Seaver .25 .60
131 Justin Upton .25 .60
132 Greg Maddux .40 1.00
133 Sandy Alcantara RC .30 .75
134 Frank Thomas .30 .75
135 Andrelton Simmons .20 .50
136 Cal Ripken Jr. 1.00 2.50
137 Noah Syndergaard .25 .60
138 Jose Ramirez .25 .60
139 Walker Buehler RC 1.50 4.00
140 Tyler Wade RC .40 1.00
141 Zack Granite RC .30 .75
142 Miguel Cabrera .30 .75
143 Nolan Arenado .40 1.00
144 Andrew McCutchen .30 .75
145 Reynaldo Lopez .25 .60
146 Whitey Ford .25 .60
147 Brian Anderson RC .40 1.00
148 Lucas Sims RC .30 .75
149 Max Kepler .25 .60
150 Shohei Ohtani RC 2.00 5.00
151 Freddie Freeman .40 1.00
152 Blake Snell .25 .60
153 Bert Blyleven .25 .60
154 Wil Myers .20 .50
155 Brandon Woodruff RC .40 1.00
156 Jed Lowrie .20 .50
157 Mike Moustakas .25 .60
158 Garrett Cooper RC .30 .75
159 Yoan Moncada .30 .75
160 Raisel Iglesias .25 .60
161 Chris Taylor .25 .60
162 Tomas Nido RC .30 .75
163 Harrison Bader RC .50 1.25
164 Charlie Blackmon .30 .75
165 Kyle Schwarber .30 .75
166 Francisco Mejia RC .40 1.00
167 Jake Arrieta .25 .60
168 Alex Gordon .25 .60
169 Andrew Benintendi .30 .75
170 Joey Votto .30 .75
171 Fernando Romero RC .30 .75
172 Matt Olson .20 .50
173 Martin Maldonado .20 .50
174 Zack Godley .25 .60
175 Jack Flaherty RC .50 1.25
176 George Brett .60 1.50
177 Jose Canseco .25 .60
178 Jose Berrios .25 .60
179 Joe Morgan .25 .60
180 Felix Hernandez .25 .60
181 Juan Soto RC 6.00 15.00
182 Justin Turner .25 .60
183 Reggie Jackson .25 .60
184 Chipper Jones .30 .75
185 Tommy Pham .20 .50
186 Willy Adames RC .40 1.00
187 Zack Cozart .20 .50
188 Johnny Bench .30 .75
189 Ralph Kiner .25 .60
190 Mark McGwire .50 1.25
191 Nicky Delmonico RC .30 .75
192 Yadier Molina .30 .75
193 Dominic Smith RC .30 .75
194 Jordan Hicks RC .60 1.50
195 Yoenis Cespedes .30 .75
196 Dave Winfield .25 .60
197 Willson Contreras .30 .75
198 Roger Clemens .40 1.00
199 Tim Beckham .25 .60
200 Sandy Koufax .60 1.50

2018 Topps Fire Blue

*BLUE: .75X TO 2X BASIC
*BLUE RC: .5X TO 1.2X BASIC RC
RANDOM INSERTS IN PACKS
109 Ronald Acuna Jr. 8.00 20.00
112 Nolan Ryan 4.00 10.00
136 Cal Ripken Jr. 5.00 12.00
150 Shohei Ohtani 6.00 15.00
176 George Brett 4.00 10.00

2018 Topps Fire Flame

*FLAME: .75X TO 2X BASIC
*FLAME RC: .5X TO 1.2X BASIC RC
STATED ODDS 1:4 RETAIL
109 Ronald Acuna Jr. 8.00 20.00
112 Nolan Ryan 4.00 10.00
136 Cal Ripken Jr. 5.00 12.00
150 Shohei Ohtani 6.00 15.00
176 George Brett 4.00 10.00

2018 Topps Fire Gold

*GOLD: .75X TO 2X BASIC
*GOLD RC: .5X TO 1.2X BASIC RC
RANDOM INSERTS IN PACKS
109 Ronald Acuna Jr. 8.00 20.00
112 Nolan Ryan 4.00 10.00
136 Cal Ripken Jr. 5.00 12.00
150 Shohei Ohtani 6.00 15.00
176 George Brett 4.00 10.00

2018 Topps Fire Green

*GREEN: 1.2X TO 3X BASIC
*GREEN RC: .75X TO 2X BASIC RC
STATED ODDS 1:19 RETAIL
STATED PRINT RUN 199 SER.#'d SETS
109 Ronald Acuna Jr. 12.00 30.00
112 Nolan Ryan 6.00 15.00
136 Cal Ripken Jr. 8.00 20.00
150 Shohei Ohtani 10.00 25.00
176 George Brett 6.00 15.00

2018 Topps Fire Magenta

*MAGENTA: 3X TO 8X BASIC
*MAGENTA RC: 2X TO 5X BASIC RC
STATED ODDS 1:152 RETAIL
STATED PRINT RUN 25 SER.#'d SETS
109 Ronald Acuna Jr. 30.00 80.00
112 Nolan Ryan 15.00 40.00
136 Cal Ripken Jr. 20.00 50.00
150 Shohei Ohtani 25.00 60.00
176 George Brett 15.00 40.00

2018 Topps Fire Orange

*ORANGE: 1.2X TO 3X BASIC
*ORANGE RC: .75X TO 2X BASIC RC
STATED ODDS 1:13 RETAIL
STATED PRINT RUN 299 SER.#'d SETS
109 Ronald Acuna Jr. 12.00 30.00
112 Nolan Ryan 6.00 15.00
136 Cal Ripken Jr. 8.00 20.00
150 Shohei Ohtani 10.00 25.00
176 George Brett 6.00 15.00

2018 Topps Fire Purple

*PURPLE: 1.5X TO 4X BASIC
*PURPLE RC: 1X TO 2.5X BASIC RC
STATED ODDS 1:39 RETAIL
STATED PRINT RUN 99 SER.#'d SETS
109 Ronald Acuna Jr. 15.00 40.00
112 Nolan Ryan 8.00 20.00
136 Cal Ripken Jr. 10.00 25.00
150 Shohei Ohtani 12.00 30.00
176 George Brett 8.00 20.00

2018 Topps Fire Autograph Patches

STATED ODDS 1:518 RETAIL
STATED PRINT RUN 25 SER.#'d SETS
EXCHANGE DEADLINE 7/31/2020
FAPAC Alex Colome/25
FAPAJ Aaron Judge/25
FAPAS Andrew Stevenson/25
FAPBA Brian Anderson/25
FAPBD Brian Dozier/25
FAPCF Carson Fulmer/25 8.00 20.00
FAPCK Corey Kluber/25
FAPDF Dustin Fowler/25
FAPDS Dominic Smith/25
FAPDV Dan Vogelbach/25
FAPFL Francisco Lindor/25
FAPFM Francisco Mejia/25
FAPGC Garrett Cooper/25 8.00 20.00
FAPHB Harrison Bader/25
FAPHD Hunter Dozier/25
FAPJA Jorge Alfaro/25
FAPJK Jason Kipnis/25
FAPJM Joe Musgrove/25 8.00 20.00
FAPKB Kris Bryant/25 75.00
FAPKH Kelvin Herrera/25
FAPKS Kyle Schwarber/25
FAPLS Lucas Sims/25 8.00 20.00
FAPLW Luke Weaver/25
FAPMA Miguel Andujar/25 75.00 200.00
FAPMG Miguel Gomez/25 20.00 50.00
FAPMM Manny Machado/25
FAPND Nicky Delmonico/25
FAPNS Noah Syndergaard/25 20.00 50.00
FAPOA Ozzie Albies/25
FAPRG Robert Gsellman/25
FAPRH Rhys Hoskins/25 30.00 80.00
FAPRQ Roman Quinn/25
FAPRS Robert Stephenson/22
FAPRT Raimel Tapia/25 8.00 20.00
FAPSM Steven Matz/25
FAPSO Shohei Ohtani/25
FAPSP Salvador Perez/25 20.00 50.00
FAPTM Trey Mancini/25 20.00 50.00
FAPTMA Tyler Mahle/20
FAPTN Tyler Naquin/25
FAPVR Victor Robles/25
FAPWC Willson Contreras/25 30.00 80.00
FAPYG Yuli Gurriel/25

2018 Topps Fire Autographs

STATED ODDS 1:29 RETAIL
EXCHANGE DEADLINE 7/31/2020
*GREEN/75: .5X TO 1.2X BASE
*PURPLE/50: .6X TO 1.5X BASE
*MAGENTA/25: .75X TO 2X BASE
FAAB Anthony Banda 2.50 6.00
FAAD Adam Duvall 5.00 12.00
FAAH Austin Hays 8.00 20.00
FAAJ Aaron Judge 60.00 150.00
FAAR Anthony Rizzo
FAARO Amed Rosario 8.00 20.00
FAAV Alex Verdugo 4.00 10.00
FABA Brian Anderson 3.00 8.00
FABS Blake Snell 6.00 15.00
FABW Brandon Woodruff 3.00 8.00
FACF Clint Frazier
FACK Carson Kelly 2.50 6.00
FACRJ Cal Ripken Jr. 40.00 100.00
FACT Chris Taylor 5.00 12.00
FACY Christian Yelich 20.00 50.00
FADG Dwight Gooden 12.00 30.00
FADJ Derek Jeter
FADO David Ortiz
FAGB Greg Bird 3.00 8.00
FAGT Gleyber Torres 25.00 60.00
FAHB Harrison Bader 4.00 10.00
FAIH Ian Happ 6.00 15.00
FAJA Jose Altuve 30.00 80.00
FAJB Jose Berrios 3.00 8.00
FAJC Jose Canseco 12.00 30.00
FAJD J.D. Davis 3.00 8.00
FAJL Jake Lamb 3.00 8.00
FAKB Kris Bryant 40.00 100.00
FAKD Khris Davis 6.00 15.00
FALG Lucas Giolito 3.00 8.00
FALW Luke Weaver 3.00 8.00
FAMAM Martin Maldonado 2.50 6.00
FAMC Matt Chapman 8.00 20.00
FAMF Max Fried 4.00 10.00
FAMG Miguel Gomez 2.50 6.00
FAMK Max Kepler 3.00 8.00
FAMM Mark McGwire 30.00 80.00
FAMMA Manny Machado 12.00 30.00
FAMO Matt Olson 5.00 12.00
FAMP Mike Piazza 40.00 100.00
FAMT Mike Trout
FAND Nicky Delmonico 2.50 6.00
FAOA Ozzie Albies 12.00 30.00
FAPB Paul Blackburn 2.50 6.00
FAPD Paul DeJong
FARAJ Ronald Acuna Jr. 75.00 200.00
FARC Roger Clemens 40.00 100.00
FARD Rafael Devers 12.00 30.00
FARH Rhys Hoskins 20.00 50.00
FARHE Rickey Henderson
FARI Raisel Iglesias 3.00 8.00
FARJ Randy Johnson
FARL Reynaldo Lopez 3.00 8.00
FARM Ryan McMahon 3.00 8.00
FARO Ronald Torreyes 5.00 12.00
FASA Sandy Alcantara 2.50 6.00
FASD Sean Doolittle 2.50 6.00
FASO Shohei Ohtani
FASP Salvador Perez 8.00 20.00
FATM Trey Mancini 20.00 50.00
FATN Tomas Nido 2.50 6.00
FAVA Victor Arano 2.50 6.00
FAVR Victor Robles 8.00 20.00
FAWB Walker Buehler 20.00 50.00
FAWC Willson Contreras 10.00 25.00
FAWM Whit Merrifield 4.00 10.00
FAYM Yadier Molina 25.00 60.00

2018 Topps Fire Cannons

STATED ODDS 1:14 RETAIL

BLUE: .6X TO 1.5X BASIC
GOLD: .75X TO 2X BASIC
1 Ichiro .75 2.00
2 Avisail Garcia .50 1.25
3 Alex Gordon .50 1.25
4 Yadier Molina .60 1.50
5 Andrew Benintendi .60 1.50
6 Tucker Barnhart .40 1.00
7 Adam Duvall .60 1.50
8 Nolan Arenado .75 2.00
9 Carlos Correa .60 1.50
10 Brett Gardner .50 1.25
11 Gary Sanchez .60 1.50
12 Billy Hamilton .50 1.25
13 Manny Machado .60 1.50
14 Hunter Renfroe .40 1.00
15 Bryce Harper 1.00 2.50

2018 Topps Fire Dual Autographs
STATED ODDS 1:4559 RETAIL
STATED PRINT RUN 20 SER.#'d SETS
EXCHANGE DEADLINE 7/31/2020
FDAAA Acuna/Albies
FDAAF Albies/Fried 40.00 100.00
FDADC Canseco/Davis 75.00 200.00
FDAGD Delmonico/Giolito
FDAMD Molina/DeJong 50.00 120.00
FDAMH Hays/Mancini 60.00 150.00
FDAOC Chapman/Olson 40.00 100.00
FDAOR Ortiz/Devers
FDAPM Perez/Merrifield
FDAVT Verdugo/Taylor
FDAWK Weaver/Kelly

2018 Topps Fire Fired Up
STATED ODDS 1:14 RETAIL
*BLUE: .6X TO 1.5X BASIC
*GOLD: .75X TO 2X BASIC
F1 Mike Trout 3.00 8.00
F2 Charlie Blackmon .60 1.50
F3 Francisco Lindor .60 1.50
F4 Chris Sale .60 1.50
F5 Cody Bellinger 1.25 3.00
F6 Manny Machado .60 1.50
F7 Carlos Correa .60 1.50
F8 Giancarlo Stanton .60 1.50
F9 Noah Syndergaard .50 1.25
F10 Aaron Judge 1.50 4.00
F11 Jose Altuve .50 1.25
F12 Clayton Kershaw 1.25 3.00
F13 Andrew Benintendi .60 1.50
F14 Max Scherzer .60 1.50
F15 Bryce Harper 1.00 2.50

2018 Topps Fire Flame Throwers
STATED ODDS 1:14 RETAIL
*BLUE: .6X TO 1.5X BASIC
*GOLD: .75X TO 2X BASIC
FT1 Max Scherzer .60 1.50
FT2 Robbie Ray
FT3 Craig Kimbrel .50 1.25
FT4 Zack Greinke .50 1.25
FT5 Noah Syndergaard .50 1.25
FT6 Kenley Jansen .50 1.25
FT7 Luis Severino .50 1.25
FT8 Stephen Strasburg .60 1.50
FT9 Luis Castillo .50 1.25
FT10 Walker Buehler 2.00 5.00
FT11 Justin Verlander .60 1.50
FT12 Carlos Martinez .50 1.25
FT13 Shohei Ohtani 2.50 6.00
FT14 Chris Sale .60 1.50
FT15 Aroldis Chapman .60 1.50

2018 Topps Fire Golden Sledgehammer
STATED ODDS 1:14 RETAIL
*BLUE: .6X TO 1.5X BASIC
*GOLD: .75X TO 2X BASIC
PP1 Joey Gallo .50 1.25
PP2 Giancarlo Stanton .60 1.50
PP3 Kendrys Morales .40 1.00
PP4 Mark Reynolds .40 1.00
PP5 Aaron Judge 1.50 4.00
PP6 J.D. Martinez .60 1.50
PP7 Marcell Ozuna .60 1.50
PP8 Gary Sanchez .60 1.50
PP9 Miguel Sano .50 1.25
PP10 Mike Trout 3.00 8.00
PP11 Charlie Blackmon .60 1.50
PP12 Ryon Healy .40 1.00
PP13 Wil Myers .40 1.00
PP14 Mike Zunino .40 1.00
PP15 Jake Lamb .50 1.25

2018 Topps Fire Hot Starts
STATED ODDS 1:8 RETAIL
*BLUE: .6X TO 1.5X BASIC
*GOLD: .75X TO 2X BASIC
HS1 Shohei Ohtani 2.50 6.00
HS2 Charlie Morton .60 1.50
HS3 Manny Machado .60 1.50
HS4 Khris Davis .60 1.50
HS5 Carlos Correa .60 1.50
HS6 Didi Gregorius .50 1.25
HS7 Patrick Corbin .50 1.25
HS8 Corey Kluber .50 1.25
HS9 Jed Lowrie .40 1.00
HS10 Bryce Harper 1.00 2.50
HS11 Rick Porcello .50 1.25
HS12 Rhys Hoskins 1.50 4.00
HS13 Aaron Judge 1.50 4.00
HS14 Jarlin Garcia .40 1.00
HS15 Javier Baez .75 2.00
HS16 Christian Villanueva .40 1.00
HS17 Mookie Betts 1.00 2.50
HS18 Johnny Cueto .50 1.25
HS19 Charlie Blackmon .60 1.50
HS20 Edwin Diaz .50 1.25
HS21 Gerrit Cole .60 1.50
HS22 Joey Lucchesi .40 1.00
HS23 Mitch Haniger .50 1.25
HS24 A.J. Pollock .40 1.00

2018 Topps Fire Relics
STATED ODDS 1:29 RETAIL
*GREEN/75: .5X TO 1.5X BASIC
*PURPLE/50: .6X TO 1.5X BASIC
MAGENTA/25: .75X TO 2X BASIC
FRAH Austin Hays 3.00 8.00
FRAJ Aaron Judge 8.00 20.00
FRAR Amed Rosario 2.50 6.00
FRAS Andrew Stevenson 2.00 5.00
FRBD Brian Dozier 2.50 6.00
FRCF Clint Frazier 4.00 10.00
FRCK Corey Kluber 2.50 6.00
FRCS Chance Sisco 2.50 6.00
FRDF Dustin Fowler 2.00 5.00
FRDS Dominic Smith 2.00 5.00
FRFL Francisco Lindor 3.00 8.00
FRFM Francisco Mejia 2.50 6.00
FRGC Garrett Cooper 2.00 5.00
FRHB Harrison Bader 3.00 8.00
FRJF Jack Flaherty 3.00 8.00
FRJK Jason Kipnis 2.50 6.00
FRKB Kris Bryant 4.00 10.00
FRKS Kyle Schwarber 3.00 8.00
FRLS Lucas Sims 2.00 5.00
FRLW Luke Weaver 2.50 6.00
FRMA Miguel Andujar 5.00 12.00
FRMG Miguel Gomez 2.00 5.00
FRMM Manny Machado 3.00 8.00
FRND Nicky Delmonico 2.00 5.00
FRNS Noah Syndergaard 2.50 6.00
FROA Ozzie Albies 6.00 15.00
FRRD Rafael Devers 6.00 15.00
FRRH Rhys Hoskins 5.00 12.00
FRRM Ryan McMahon 2.50 6.00
FRSM Steven Matz 2.50 6.00
FRSO Shohei Ohtani 6.00 15.00
FRSP Salvador Perez 2.50 6.00
FRTM Trey Mancini 2.50 6.00
FRTMA Tyler Mahle 2.50 6.00
FRTW Tyler Wade 2.50 6.00
FRVR Victor Robles 4.00 10.00
FRWC Willson Contreras 3.00 8.00
FRYG Yuli Gurriel 2.50 6.00
FRZC Zack Granite 2.00 5.00

2018 Topps Fire Speed Demons
STATED ODDS 1:14 RETAIL
*BLUE: .6X TO 1.5X BASIC
*GOLD: .75X TO 2X BASIC
SD1 Jose Altuve .50 1.25
SD2 Amed Rosario .50 1.25
SD3 Elvis Andrus .50 1.25
SD4 Trea Turner .50 1.25
SD5 Starling Marte .50 1.25
SD6 Brett Gardner .50 1.25
SD7 Mike Trout 3.00 8.00
SD8 Dee Gordon .40 1.00
SD9 Mookie Betts 1.00 2.50
SD10 Whit Merrifield .60 1.50
SD11 A.J. Pollock .40 1.00
SD12 Byron Buxton .50 1.25
SD13 Tommy Pham .40 1.00
SD14 Lorenzo Cain .40 1.00
SD15 Billy Hamilton .50 1.25

2019 Topps Fire
COMPLETE SET (200) 30.00 80.00
1 Shohei Ohtani .40 1.00
2 Chipper Jones .30 .75
3 Heath Fillmyer RC .30 .75
4 Willians Astudillo RC .30 .75
5 Orlando Arcia .20 .50
6 Zack Greinke .25 .60
7 Kolby Allard RC .50 1.25
8 Aramis Garcia RC .30 .75
9 Albert Pujols .40 1.00
10 Willson Contreras .25 .60
11 Steven Duggar RC .40 1.00
12 Nick Markakis .25 .60
13 Kris Bryant .40 1.00
14 Lourdes Gurriel Jr. .25 .60
15 Rowdy Tellez RC .50 1.25
16 Carter Kieboom RC .50 1.25
17 Ozzie Albies .30 .75
18 Christian Yelich .40 1.00
19 Mike Trout 1.50 4.00
20 Jonathan Loaisiga RC .40 1.00
21 Jeff McNeil RC .75 2.00
22 Yadier Molina .30 .75
23 Mike Fiers .20 .50
24 Justin Verlander .30 .75
25 Danny Jansen RC .30 .75
26 Khris Davis .30 .75
27 Ryan O'Hearn RC .30 .75
28 Freddie Freeman .40 1.00
29 Javier Baez .40 1.00
30 Lorenzo Cain .20 .50
31 Marcus Stroman .25 .60
32 Anthony Rizzo .50 1.25
33 Jake Lamb .25 .60
34 Justin Upton .25 .60
35 Griffin Canning RC .50 1.25
36 Chris Shaw RC .50 1.25
37 Ronald Acuna Jr. 1.50 4.00
38 Ken Griffey Jr. .60 1.50
39 Justin Turner .25 .60
40 Christin Stewart RC .40 1.00
41 Mariano Rivera .40 1.00
42 Taylor Ward RC .30 .75
43 Harrison Bader .25 .60
44 Corey Seager .30 .75
45 Mike Foltynewicz .30 .75
46 Jack Flaherty .25 .60
47 Dansby Swanson .30 .75
48 Cal Quantrill RC .30 .75
49 Ryan Borucki RC .30 .75
50 Justus Sheffield RC .50 1.25
51 Dakota Hudson RC .40 1.00
52 Clayton Kershaw .60 1.50
53 Brandon Lowe RC .50 1.25
54 Nick Ahmed .20 .50
55 Ramon Laureano RC .60 1.50
56 Cedric Mullins RC .50 1.25
57 Chance Adams RC .30 .75
58 Michael Kopech RC .60 1.50
59 Cody Bellinger .60 1.50
60 Jurickson Profar .25 .60
61 Luis Urias RC .50 1.25
62 Derek Jeter .75 2.00
63 Trevor Hoffman .25 .60
64 Kyle Schwarber .30 .75
65 Josh James RC .50 1.25
66 Paul Goldschmidt .30 .75
67 Matt Chapman .30 .75
68 Corbin Burnes RC .50 1.25
69 George Springer .25 .60
70 Kyle Tucker RC .60 1.50
71 DJ Stewart RC .40 1.00
72 Alex Bregman .30 .75
73 Sean Reid-Foley RC .30 .75
74 Blake Treinen .20 .50
75 Enyel De Los Santos RC .30 .75
76 Brad Keller RC .30 .75
77 Jhoulys Chacin .20 .50
78 Alex Rodriguez .40 1.00
79 Touki Toussaint RC .40 1.00
80 Jose Altuve .25 .60
81 Freddy Galvis .20 .50
82 Gerrit Cole .30 .75
83 Kevin Pillar .20 .50
84 Ryan Braun .25 .60
85 Robbie Ray .20 .50
86 Jake Bauers RC .50 1.25
87 David Fletcher RC 1.00 2.50
88 Jake Cave RC .40 1.00
89 Walker Buehler .40 1.00
90 Jim Thome .25 .60
91 Jon Duplantier RC .30 .75
92 Todd Helton .25 .60
93 David Ortiz .30 .75
94 Kevin Kramer RC .40 1.00
95 Jon Lester .25 .60
96 Kevin Newman RC .50 1.25
97 Nick Senzel RC 1.00 2.50
98 Andrelton Simmons .20 .50
99 Jordan Hicks .30 .75
100 Cal Ripken Jr. 1.00 2.50
101 Tim Anderson .30 .75
102 David Price .25 .60
103 Trevor Bauer .30 .75
104 Nelson Cruz .30 .75
105 Whit Merrifield .30 .75
106 Charlie Blackmon .30 .75
107 Manny Machado .30 .75
108 Brian Anderson .20 .50
109 Grayson Greiner .20 .50
110 Trey Mancini .25 .60
111 Mitch Haniger .25 .60
112 Jose Urena .20 .50
113 Francisco Lindor .30 .75
114 Noah Syndergaard .25 .60
115 Trea Turner .25 .60
116 Shin-Soo Choo .25 .60
117 Adalberto Mondesi .25 .60
118 Chris Archer .20 .50
119 Jordan Zimmermann .25 .60
120 Willy Adames .20 .50
121 Tucker Barnhart .20 .50
122 Aaron Judge .75 2.00
123 Byron Buxton .25 .60
124 Ryan Zimmerman .25 .60
125 Starlin Castro .20 .50
126 Giancarlo Stanton .30 .75
127 Corey Dickerson .20 .50
128 Pete Alonso RC 4.00 10.00
129 Miguel Cabrera .30 .75
130 Nolan Arenado .40 1.00
131 Aaron Nola .25 .60
132 Vladimir Guerrero Jr. RC 4.00 10.00
133 Xander Bogaerts .30 .75
134 Amed Rosario .25 .60
135 Elvis Andrus .25 .60
136 Joey Lucchesi .20 .50
137 Bryce Harper .50 1.25
138 Blake Snell .25 .60
139 Jose Berrios .25 .60
140 Joey Gallo .25 .60
141 Edwin Encarnacion .30 .75
142 Jonathan Villar .20 .50
143 James Paxton .20 .50
144 Andrew Benintendi .30 .75
145 Trevor May .20 .50
146 Lewis Brinson .20 .50
147 Jose Ramirez .25 .60
148 Yonder Alonso .20 .50
149 Nicholas Castellanos .30 .75
150 Juan Soto 1.00 2.50
151 Jose Abreu .30 .75
152 Wil Myers .20 .50
153 Sean Doolittle .20 .50
154 Rougned Odor .25 .60
155 Alex Gordon .25 .60
156 Kevin Kiermaier .25 .60
157 Fernando Tatis Jr. RC 3.00 8.00
158 Jacob deGrom .30 .75
159 Mike Clevinger .25 .60
160 Corey Kluber .25 .60
161 Sonny Gray .25 .60
162 Scooter Gennett .25 .60
163 Starling Marte .25 .60
164 Chance Sisco .20 .50
165 Brandon Belt .25 .60
166 Alex Cobb .20 .50
167 Josh Bell .25 .60
168 Eloy Jimenez RC 1.25 3.00
169 Eric Hosmer .25 .60
170 Luis Severino .25 .60
171 Kyle Freeland .25 .60
172 Kyle Gibson .25 .60
173 Dee Gordon .20 .50
174 Ryan McMahon .20 .50
175 Yoan Moncada .30 .75
176 Max Scherzer .30 .75
177 Michael Conforto .25 .60
178 Robinson Cano .25 .60
179 Rhys Hoskins .40 1.00
180 Miguel Andujar .30 .75
181 Reynaldo Lopez .25 .60
182 Stephen Strasburg .30 .75
183 Marco Gonzales .20 .50
184 J.D. Martinez .30 .75
185 Ryon Healy .20 .50
186 Mookie Betts .50 1.25
187 Trevor Story .30 .75
188 Brandon Crawford .25 .60
189 Ryan Yarbrough .20 .50
190 J.T. Realmuto .30 .75
191 Buster Posey .40 1.00
192 Chris Sale .30 .75
193 Gleyber Torres .60 1.50
194 Joey Votto .30 .75
195 Austin Hedges .20 .50
196 Evan Longoria .25 .60
197 Jake Arrieta .25 .60
198 Felipe Vazquez .20 .50
199 Hunter Dozier .20 .50
200 Yasiel Puig .30 .75

2019 Topps Fire Blue
*BLUE: 1X TO 2.5X BASIC
*BLUE RC: .6X TO 1.5X BASIC RC
RANDOM INSERTS IN PACKS

2019 Topps Fire Gold Mint
*GOLD: 1X TO 2.5X BASIC
*GOLD RC: .6X TO 1.5X BASIC RC
RANDOM INSERTS IN PACKS

2019 Topps Fire Green
*GREEN: 1.5X TO 4X BASIC
*GREEN RC: 1X TO 2.5X BASIC RC
STATED ODDS 1:17 RETAIL
STATED PRINT RUN 199 SER.#'d SETS

2019 Topps Fire Magenta
*MAGENTA: 6X TO 15X BASIC
*MAGENTA RC: 4X TO 10X BASIC RC
STATED ODDS 1:129 RETAIL
STATED PRINT RUN 25 SER.#'d SETS

2019 Topps Fire Orange
*ORANGE: 1.5X TO 4X BASIC
*ORANGE RC: 1X TO 2.5X BASIC RC
STATED ODDS 1:11 RETAIL
STATED PRINT RUN 299 SER.#'d SETS

2019 Topps Fire Purple
*PURPLE: 2X TO 5X BASIC
*PURPLE RC: 1.2X TO 3X BASIC RC
STATED ODDS 1:33 RETAIL
STATED PRINT RUN 99 SER.#'d SETS

2019 Topps Fire Autograph Patches
STATED ODDS 1:549 RETAIL
STATED PRINT RUN 25 SER.#'d SETS
EXCHANGE DEADLINE 7/31/2021
FAPAJ Aaron Judge
FAPBK Brad Keller
FAPBN Brandon Nimmo 10.00 25.00
FAPBS Blake Snell 10.00 25.00
FAPBT Blake Treinen
FAPCA Chance Adams
FAPCB Corbin Burnes
FAPCM Cedric Mullins
FAPCS Chris Shaw
FAPDH Dakota Hudson
FAPDJ Danny Jansen 8.00 20.00
FAPFL Francisco Lindor 40.00 100.00
FAPJA Jesus Aguilar 8.00 20.00
FAPJC Jake Cave
FAPJH Josh Hader 8.00 20.00
FAPJN Jacob Nix 10.00 25.00
FAPJR Josh Rogers
FAPJS Justus Sheffield 12.00 30.00
FAPKB Kris Bryant
FAPKS Kyle Schwarber 12.00 30.00
FAPKT Kyle Tucker 50.00 120.00
FAPKW Kyle Wright 12.00 30.00
FAPMA Miguel Andujar
FAPMH Mitch Haniger
FAPMT Mike Trout
FAPNC Nick Ciuffo
FAPNS Noah Syndergaard 20.00 50.00
FAPOA Ozzie Albies
FAPRAJ Ronald Acuna Jr. 75.00 200.00
FAPRB Ryan Borucki 8.00 20.00
FAPRH Rhys Hoskins
FAPRL Ramon Laureano 60.00 150.00
FAPRT Rowdy Tellez
FAPSK Scott Kingery
FAPSO Shohei Ohtani
FAPSRF Sean Reid-Foley 8.00 20.00
FAPTW Taylor Ward
FAPVR Victor Robles

2019 Topps Fire Autographs
STATED ODDS 1:29 RETAIL
EXCHANGE DEADLINE 7/31/2021
*GREEN/75: .5X TO 1.2X BASE
*PURPLE/50: .6X TO 1.5X BASE
*MAGENTA/25: .75X TO 2X BASE
FAAR Anthony Rizzo 12.00 30.00
FABK Brad Keller 2.50 6.00
FABP Buster Posey 25.00 60.00
FABS Blake Snell 3.00 8.00
FACG Chad Green 5.00 12.00
FACJ Chipper Jones 20.00 50.00
FACS Christin Stewart
FADO David Ortiz 20.00 50.00
FADP Daniel Ponce de Leon 4.00 10.00
FAEJ Eloy Jimenez 15.00 40.00
FAFL Francisco Lindor 12.00 30.00
FAFT Frank Thomas 20.00 50.00
FAFTJ Fernando Tatis Jr. 60.00 150.00
FAGCA Griffin Canning 4.00 10.00
FAGH Garrett Hampson 2.50 6.00
FAGS George Springer 12.00 30.00
FAHB Harrison Bader 3.00 8.00
FAI Ichiro 100.00 250.00
FAJDU Jon Duplantier
FAJJ Josh James 4.00 10.00
FAJM Jose Martinez 2.50 6.00
FAJN Jacob Nix 3.00 8.00
FAJR Josh Rogers 2.50 6.00
FAJRA Jose Ramirez 15.00 40.00
FAJS Juan Soto 20.00 50.00
FAKB Kris Bryant
FAKK Kevin Kramer 3.00 8.00
FAKN Kevin Newman 4.00 10.00
FALV Luke Voit 10.00 25.00
FAMC Miguel Cabrera
FAMM Max Muncy 6.00 15.00
FAMMA Manny Machado 20.00 50.00
FAMMI Miles Mikolas 4.00 10.00
FAMS Myles Straw 4.00 10.00
FAMT Mike Trout 200.00 400.00
FANC Nick Ciuffo 2.50 6.00
FANSE Nick Senzel
FAPA Pete Alonso 40.00 100.00
FAPC Patrick Corbin 3.00 8.00
FARAJ Ronald Acuna Jr. 50.00 120.00
FARH Rhys Hoskins 12.00 30.00
FARL Ramon Laureano 6.00 15.00
FASO Shohei Ohtani 75.00 200.00
FATB Trevor Bauer 4.00 10.00
FATW Taylor Ward 2.50 6.00
FAVGJ Vladimir Guerrero Jr. 50.00 120.00
FAWA Willians Astudillo 2.50 6.00
FAYK Yusei Kikuchi 10.00 25.00

2019 Topps Fire Dual Autographs
STATED ODDS 1:2005 RETAIL
PRINT RUNS B/WN 10-20 COPIES PER
NO PRICING ON QTY 15 OR LESS
EXCHANGE DEADLINE 7/31/2021
FDABR Bryant/Rizzo/20 75.00 200.00
FDACD Davis/Canseco
FDAHM McCutchen/Hoskins
FDAJA Jones/Acuna/20
FDAMU Urias/Machado
FDANK Newman/Kramer
FDAST Springer/Tucker/20

2019 Topps Fire En Fuego
STATED ODDS 1:8 RETAIL
*BLUE: .6X TO 1.5X BASIC
*GOLD: .75X TO 2X BASIC
EF1 Aaron Judge 1.25 3.00
EF2 Yadier Molina .50 1.25
EF3 Starling Marte .40 1.00
EF4 Max Scherzer .50 1.25
EF5 Corey Kluber .40 1.00
EF6 Yuli Gurriel .40 1.00
EF7 Francisco Lindor .50 1.25
EF8 Ivan Rodriguez .40 1.00
EF9 Shohei Ohtani .60 1.50
EF10 Christian Yelich .60 1.50
EF11 Clayton Kershaw 1.00 2.50
EF12 Whit Merrifield .50 1.25
EF13 Miguel Cabrera .50 1.25
EF14 Adrian Beltre .50 1.25
EF15 Rickey Henderson .50 1.25
EF16 Trevor Story .50 1.25
EF17 Derek Jeter 1.25 3.00
EF18 Freddie Freeman .60 1.50
EF19 Nolan Arenado .60 1.50
EF20 Kris Bryant .60 1.50
EF21 Matt Chapman .50 1.25
EF22 Khris Davis .50 1.25
EF23 Mariano Rivera .60 1.50
EF24 Anthony Rizzo .75 2.00
EF25 Mike Trout 2.50 6.00

2019 Topps Fire Fired Up
STATED ODDS 1:14 RETAIL
*BLUE: .6X TO 1.5X BASIC
*GOLD: .75X TO 2X BASIC
FIU1 Mike Trout 2.50 6.00
FIU2 Francisco Lindor .50 1.25
FIU3 Javier Baez .60 1.50
FIU4 Chris Sale .50 1.25
FIU5 Josh Hader .30 .75
FIU6 Bryce Harper .75 2.00
FIU7 Jacob deGrom .50 1.25
FIU8 Juan Soto 1.50 4.00
FIU9 George Springer .40 1.00
FIU10 Aaron Judge 1.25 3.00
FIU11 Max Scherzer .50 1.25
FIU12 Ronald Acuna Jr. 2.50 6.00
FIU13 Mookie Betts .75 2.00
FIU14 Carlos Correa .50 1.25
FIU15 Shohei Ohtani .60 1.50

2019 Topps Fire Flame
*FLAME: 1X TO 2.5X BASIC
*FLAME RC: .6X TO 1.5X BASIC RC
STATED ODDS 1:4 RETAIL

2019 Topps Fire Flame Throwers
STATED ODDS 1:14 RETAIL
*BLUE: .6X TO 1.5X BASIC
*GOLD: .75X TO 2X BASIC
FT1 Shohei Ohtani .60 1.50
FT2 Aroldis Chapman .50 1.25
FT3 Walker Buehler .60 1.50
FT4 Max Scherzer .50 1.25
FT5 Gerrit Cole .50 1.25
FT6 Trevor Bauer .50 1.25
FT7 Blake Treinen .30 .75
FT8 Luis Severino .40 1.00
FT9 Justin Verlander .50 1.25
FT10 Josh Hader .30 .75
FT11 Nathan Eovaldi .40 1.00
FT12 Chris Sale .50 1.25
FT13 Edwin Diaz .40 1.00
FT14 Noah Syndergaard .40 1.00
FT15 Jacob deGrom .50 1.25

2019 Topps Fire Lasting Legacies
STATED ODDS 1:14 RETAIL
*BLUE: .6X TO 1.5X BASIC
*GOLD: .75X TO 2X BASIC
LL1 Kershaw/Koufax 1.00 2.50
LL2 Ryan/Verlander 1.50 4.00
LL3 Benintendi/Yaz .75 2.00
LL4 Harper/Cobb .75 2.00
LL5 Roberto Alomar .50 1.25
Francisco Lindor
LL6 Acuna/Trout 2.50 6.00
LL7 Betts/Williams 1.00 2.50
LL8 Yount/Yelich .60 1.50
LL9 Bob Gibson .50 1.25
Max Scherzer
LL10 Judge/Jeter 1.25 3.00
LL11 Giancarlo Stanton .50 1.25
Reggie Jackson
LL12 Trout/Aaron 2.50 6.00
LL13 Torres/Jeter 1.25 3.00
LL14 Baez/Banks .60 1.50
LL15 Ohtani/Ryan 1.50 4.00

2019 Topps Fire Maximum Velocity
STATED ODDS 1:14 RETAIL
*BLUE: .6X TO 1.5X BASIC
*GOLD: .75X TO 2X BASIC
MV1 Joey Gallo .40 1.00
MV2 Miguel Cabrera .50 1.25
MV3 David Bote .40 1.00
MV4 Aaron Judge 1.25 3.00
MV5 Nelson Cruz .50 1.25
MV6 Giancarlo Stanton .50 1.25
MV7 Franchy Cordero .30 .75
MV8 Matt Chapman .50 1.25
MV9 Matt Olson .30 .75
MV10 Mark Trumbo .30 .75
MV11 Derek Fisher .30 .75
MV12 Robinson Cano .40 1.00
MV13 Tommy Pham .30 .75
MV14 Luke Voit .75 2.00
MV15 J.D. Martinez .50 1.25

2019 Topps Fire Relics
STATED ODDS 1:32 RETAIL
*GREEN/75: .5X TO 1.2X BASIC
*PURPLE/50: .6X TO 1.5X BASIC
MAGENTA/25: .75X TO 2X BASIC
FRAB Alex Bregman 2.50 6.00
FRABE Andrew Benintendi 2.50 6.00
FRAJ Aaron Judge 12.00 30.00
FRAV Alex Verdugo 2.00 5.00
FRBK Brad Keller 1.50 4.00
FRBT Blake Treinen 1.50 4.00
FRBW Bryse Wilson 2.00 5.00
FRCA Chance Adams 1.50 4.00
FRCC Carlos Correa 2.50 6.00
FRCF Clint Frazier 2.00 5.00
FRCM Cedric Mullins 2.50 6.00
FRCS Corey Seager 2.50 6.00
FRDJ Danny Jansen 1.50 4.00
FRDL Dawel Lugo 2.50 6.00
FRDR Dereck Rodriguez 1.50 4.00
FRFL Francisco Lindor 2.50 6.00
FRGT Gleyber Torres 5.00 12.00
FRHB Harrison Bader 2.00 5.00
FRIH Ian Happ 2.00 5.00
FRJA Jesus Aguilar 1.50 4.00
FRJB Javier Baez 3.00 8.00
FRJF Jack Flaherty 2.00 5.00
FRJH Josh Hader 1.50 4.00
FRJS Justus Sheffield 2.50 6.00
FRKA Kolby Allard 2.50 6.00
FRKB Kris Bryant 3.00 8.00
FRKS Kyle Schwarber 2.50 6.00
FRKT Kyle Tucker 3.00 8.00
FRKW Kyle Wright 2.50 6.00
FRLU Luis Urias 2.50 6.00
FRLV Luke Voit 4.00 10.00
FRMA Miguel Andujar 2.50 6.00
FRMK Michael Kopech 3.00 8.00
FRMM Miles Mikolas 2.50 6.00
FRMO Matt Olson 1.50 4.00
FRMT Mike Trout 15.00 40.00
FRNS Noah Syndergaard 2.00 5.00
FROA Ozzie Albies 2.50 6.00
FRRAJ Ronald Acuna Jr. 12.00 30.00
FRRD Rafael Devers 3.00 8.00
FRRH Rhys Hoskins 3.00 8.00
FRRL Ramon Laureano 3.00 8.00
FRRO Ryan O'Hearn 1.50 4.00
FRRT Rowdy Tellez 2.50 6.00
FRSK Scott Kingery 2.00 5.00
FRSO Shohei Ohtani 6.00 15.00
FRTS Trevor Story 2.50 6.00
FRTT Trea Turner 2.00 5.00
FRVR Victor Robles 3.00 8.00
FRWC Willson Contreras 2.00 5.00

2019 Topps Fire Smoke and Mirrors
STATED ODDS 1:14 RETAIL
*BLUE: .6X TO 1.5X BASIC
*GOLD: .75X TO 2X BASIC
SM1 Clayton Kershaw 1.00 2.50
SM2 Carlos Carrasco .30 .75
SM3 Mike Foltynewicz .50 1.25
SM4 Aaron Nola .40 1.00
SM5 Jameson Taillon .40 1.00
SM6 Trevor Bauer .50 1.25
SM7 German Marquez .30 .75
SM8 Jordan Hicks .40 1.00
SM9 Corey Kluber .40 1.00
SM10 Jose Berrios .40 1.00
SM11 Zack Greinke .40 1.00
SM12 Luis Severino .40 1.00
SM13 Gerrit Cole .50 1.25
SM14 Blake Snell .40 1.00
SM15 Aroldis Chapman .50 1.25

2020 Topps Fire
1 Lorenzo Cain .20 .50
2 Chris Sale .30 .75
3 Nico Hoerner RC 1.25 3.00
4 Luis Severino .25 .60
5 Shun Yamaguchi .25 .60
6 Anthony Rizzo .50 1.25
7 Brandon Crawford .25 .60
8 Pete Alonso .75 2.00
9 Blake Snell .25 .60
10 Willson Contreras .30 .75
11 Tim Lincecum .25 .60
12 Eric Hosmer .25 .60
13 Joe Mauer .25 .60
14 Jameson Taillon .25 .60
15 DJ LeMahieu .30 .75
16 Jorge Alfaro .20 .50
17 Jordan Zimmermann .25 .60
18 Ichiro .40 1.00
19 Kyle Freeland .25 .60
20 Javier Baez .40 1.00
21 Nathan Eovaldi .25 .60
22 Trey Mancini .30 .75
23 Danny Hultzen RC .40 1.00
24 Francisco Lindor .30 .75
25 Evan Longoria .25 .60
26 Michael Kopech .40 1.00
27 Clayton Kershaw .60 1.50
28 Ronald Acuna Jr. 1.25 3.00
29 Cedric Mullins .30 .75
30 Jesus Aguilar .20 .50
31 Albert Pujols .40 1.00
32 Carlos Correa .30 .75
33 Aaron Judge .75 2.00
34 Trevor Story .30 .75
35 Matt Olson .20 .50
36 Bubba Starling RC .60 1.50
37 Rafael Devers .40 1.00
38 Gerrit Cole .50 1.25
39 Ozzie Albies .30 .75
40 Danny Mendick RC .40 1.00
41 Marcus Semien .20 .50
42 Max Scherzer .30 .75
43 Matt Kemp .25 .60
44 Nick Senzel .30 .75
45 Trent Grisham RC 1.25 3.00
46 Jeff Bagwell .25 .60
47 Juan Soto 1.00 2.50
48 Jacob deGrom .30 .75
49 Shohei Ohtani .40 1.00
50 Willy Adames .20 .50
51 Aaron Nola .30 .75
52 Ryan Braun .25 .60
53 Dylan Cease RC .60 1.50
54 John Means .20 .50
55 Jose Berrios .25 .60
56 Mookie Betts .60 1.50
57 Stephen Strasburg .30 .75
58 Joey Gallo .30 .75
59 Eugenio Suarez .25 .60
60 Ronald Guzman .20 .50
61 Cavan Biggio .40 1.00
62 Kolten Wong .25 .60
63 Tim Anderson .30 .75
64 Jose Abreu .30 .75
65 Gleyber Torres .60 1.50
66 Michael Conforto .25 .60
67 Zack Greinke .25 .60
68 Matt Thaiss RC .40 1.00

69 Joey Votto .30 .75
70 Giancarlo Stanton .30 .75
71 Bo Bichette RC 4.00 10.00
72 Josh Bell .25 .60
73 J.T. Realmuto .30 .75
74 Freddie Freeman .40 1.00
75 Gregory Polanco .25 .60
76 Gary Sanchez .30 .75
77 Junior Fernandez RC .30 .75
78 Rhys Hoskins .40 1.00
79 Randy Dobnak RC .60 1.50
80 Cody Bellinger .60 1.50
81 Jake Lamb .25 .60
82 Carlos Carrasco .20 .50
83 Ramon Laureano .30 .75
84 Dallas Keuchel .25 .60
85 Jorge Soler .30 .75
86 Trea Turner .25 .60
87 Trevor Bauer .30 .75
88 Mike Foltynewicz .20 .50
89 Michael Brosseau RC .60 1.50
90 Byron Buxton .25 .60
91 Jesus Luzardo RC .60 1.50
92 Dee Gordon .20 .50
93 Mariano Rivera .40 1.00
94 Jorge Polanco .25 .60
95 Fernando Tatis Jr. 1.25 3.00
96 Kris Bryant .40 1.00
97 David Ortiz .30 .75
98 Aristides Aquino RC .60 1.50
99 Didi Gregorius .25 .60
100 Luis Castillo .25 .60
101 Matthew Boyd .20 .50
102 Mike Clevinger .25 .60
103 Elvis Andrus .25 .60
104 Alex Verdugo .25 .60
105 Willi Castro RC .50 1.25
106 Brusdar Graterol RC .50 1.25
107 Adbert Alzolay RC .40 1.00
108 Corey Kluber .25 .60
109 Jon Lester .25 .60
110 Dustin May RC 1.25 3.00
111 Brendan McKay RC .50 1.25
112 Austin Nola RC .50 1.25
113 A.J. Puk RC .60 1.50
114 Mauricio Dubon RC .40 1.00
115 Max Muncy .25 .60
116 Andrew McCutchen .30 .75
117 Lewis Thorpe RC .30 .75
118 Jake Fraley RC .40 1.00
119 Robinson Cano .25 .60
120 Yusei Kikuchi .25 .60
121 Nolan Arenado .40 1.00
122 Sammy Sosa .30 .75
123 Kyle Schwarber .30 .75
124 Mallex Smith .20 .50
125 Sandy Alcantara .20 .50
126 George Springer .25 .60
127 Austin Meadows .25 .60
128 Dan Vogelbach .20 .50
129 Anthony Rendon .30 .75
130 Kyle Lewis RC 4.00 10.00
131 Cole Tucker .30 .75
132 Manny Machado .30 .75
133 Robbie Ray .20 .50
134 Salvador Perez .25 .60
135 Nick Solak RC .50 1.25
136 Shane Bieber .30 .75
137 Zack Wheeler .25 .60
138 Jose Quintana .20 .50
139 Eloy Jimenez .60 1.50
140 Robel Garcia RC .30 .75
141 Jordan Yamamoto RC .40 1.00
142 Walker Buehler .40 1.00
143 Domingo Leyba RC .40 1.00
144 Alex Cobb .20 .50
145 Noah Syndergaard .25 .60
146 Buster Posey .40 1.00
147 Nelson Cruz .30 .75
148 Vladimir Guerrero Jr. .60 1.50
149 Paul DeJong .30 .75
150 Eddie Rosario .25 .60
151 Brandon Belt .25 .60
152 Justin Dunn RC .40 1.00
153 Hyun-Jin Ryu .25 .60
154 Jeimer Candelario .20 .50
155 Luis Robert RC 5.00 12.00
156 Chris Paddack .30 .75
157 Yoan Moncada .30 .75
158 Bryce Harper .50 1.25
159 Ryan Zimmerman .25 .60
160 Kole Calhoun .20 .50
161 Lourdes Gurriel Jr. .25 .60
162 Alex Bregman .30 .75
163 Austin Hedges .20 .50
164 Sean Manaea .20 .50
165 Jackie Bradley Jr. .30 .75
166 Miguel Cabrera .30 .75
167 Edwin Rios RC .75 2.00
168 Miguel Sano .25 .60
169 Seth Brown RC .30 .75
170 Justin Verlander .30 .75
171 Shogo Akiyama .30 .75
172 Jose Altuve .25 .60
173 Andres Munoz RC .40 1.00
174 Whit Merrifield .30 .75
175 Jack Flaherty .30 .75
176 Ken Griffey Jr. .60 1.50
177 Victor Robles .40 1.00
178 Brendan Rodgers .30 .75
179 Brandon Lowe .30 .75
180 Nick Ahmed .20 .50
181 Tony Gwynn .30 .75
182 Gavin Lux RC 2.00 5.00
183 Josh Hader RC .30 .75
184 Paul Goldschmidt .30 .75
185 Kwang-Hyun Kim .60 1.50
186 Sam Hilliard RC .50 1.25
187 Yoshi Tsutsugo RC .40 1.00
188 Tony Gonsolin RC 1.25 3.00
189 Ketel Marte .25 .60
190 Matt Chapman .30 .75
191 Corey Seager .30 .75
192 Jose Ramirez .25 .60
193 Barry Zito .25 .60
194 Andrew Benintendi .30 .75
195 Yordan Alvarez RC 1.50 4.00
196 Jakob Junis .20 .50
197 Mike Trout 1.50 4.00
198 Christian Yelich .40 1.00
199 Max Kepler .25 .60
200 Patrick Corbin .25 .60

2020 Topps Fire Green

*GREEN: 1.5X TO 4X BASIC
*GREEN RC: 1X TO 2.5X BASIC
STATED ODDS 1:XX HOBBY
STATED PRINT RUN 199 SER.#'d SETS
95 Fernando Tatis Jr. 8.00 20.00
130 Kyle Lewis 20.00 50.00
176 Ken Griffey Jr. 15.00 40.00
182 Gavin Lux 8.00 20.00

2020 Topps Fire Magenta

*MAGENTA: 6X TO 15X BASIC
*MAGENTA RC: 4X TO 10X BASIC
STATED ODDS 1:XX HOBBY
STATED PRINT RUN 25 SER.#'d SETS
65 Gleyber Torres 15.00 40.00
95 Fernando Tatis Jr. 40.00 100.00
130 Kyle Lewis 75.00 200.00
176 Ken Griffey Jr. 75.00 200.00
182 Gavin Lux 30.00 80.00

2020 Topps Fire Orange

*ORANGE: 1.5X TO 4X BASIC
*ORANGE RC: 1X TO 2.5X BASIC
STATED ODDS 1:XX HOBBY
STATED PRINT RUN 299 SER.#'d SETS
95 Fernando Tatis Jr. 8.00 20.00
130 Kyle Lewis 12.00 30.00
176 Ken Griffey Jr. 12.00 30.00
182 Gavin Lux 8.00 20.00

2020 Topps Fire Purple

*PURPLE: 2X TO 5X BASIC
*PURPLE RC: 1.2X TO 3X BASIC
STATED ODDS 1:XX HOBBY
STATED PRINT RUN 99 SER.#'d SETS
95 Fernando Tatis Jr. 12.00 30.00
130 Kyle Lewis 25.00 60.00
176 Ken Griffey Jr. 20.00 50.00
182 Gavin Lux 10.00 25.00

2020 Topps Fire Arms Ablaze

STATED ODDS 1:XX HOBBY
AA1 Aaron Judge 1.25 3.00
AA2 Yasiel Puig .50 1.25
AA3 Trevor Story .50 1.25
AA4 Ronald Acuna Jr. 2.00 5.00
AA5 Andrelton Simmons .30 .75
AA6 Cody Bellinger 1.00 2.50
AA7 Jackie Bradley Jr. .50 1.25
AA8 Nolan Arenado .60 1.50
AA9 Bryce Harper .75 2.00
AA10 Javier Baez .60 1.50
AA11 Mookie Betts 1.00 2.50
AA12 Matt Chapman .50 1.25
AA13 Carlos Correa .50 1.25
AA14 Aaron Hicks .40 1.00
AA15 Trea Turner .40 1.00
AA16 Manny Machado .50 1.25
AA17 Ramon Laureano .50 1.25
AA18 Orlando Arcia .30 .75
AA19 Jason Heyward .40 1.00
AA20 Luis Robert 10.00 25.00

2020 Topps Fire Arms Ablaze Gold Minted

*GOLD: .8X TO 2X BASIC
STATED ODDS 1:XX HOBBY
AA20 Luis Robert 15.00 40.00

2020 Topps Fire Autographs

STATED ODDS 1:XX HOBBY
EXCHANGE DEADLINE 7/31/22
FAAA Adbert Alzolay 3.00 8.00
FAAN Austin Nola 4.00 10.00
FAAP A.J. Puk 5.00 12.00
FABA Bryan Abreu 2.50 6.00
FABM Brendan McKay 4.00 10.00
FABR Brendan Rodgers 4.00 10.00
FACA Chance Adams 2.50 6.00
FACK Carter Kieboom 3.00 8.00
FADC Dylan Cease 5.00 12.00
FADL Domingo Leyba 3.00 8.00
FADN Dom Nunez 3.00 8.00
FAGC Griffin Canning 4.00 10.00
FAGL Gavin Lux 20.00 50.00
FAID Isan Diaz 4.00 10.00
FAJL Jesus Luzardo 5.00 12.00
FAJM Jeff McNeil 3.00 8.00
FAJP Joe Palumbo 2.50 6.00
FAJR Jake Rogers 2.50 6.00
FAJY Jordan Yamamoto 2.50 6.00
FAKH Keston Hiura 6.00 15.00
FAKK Kwang-Hyun Kim 15.00 40.00
FALA Logan Allen 2.50 6.00
FAMB Matt Beaty 3.00 8.00
FAMC Michael Chavis 3.00 8.00
FARG Robel Garcia 2.50 6.00
FARR Rangel Ravelo 3.00 8.00
FASA Shogo Akiyama 4.00 10.00
FASM Sean Murphy 4.00 10.00
FASY Shun Yamaguchi 3.00 8.00
FATG Tony Gonsolin 8.00 20.00
FATL Tim Lopes 3.00 8.00
FAVR Victor Robles 5.00 12.00
FAWM Whit Merrifield 4.00 10.00
FAWS Will Smith 5.00 12.00
FAYA Yordan Alvarez 25.00 60.00
FAYC Yu Chang 4.00 10.00
FAZP Zach Plesac 6.00 15.00
FAAAQ Aristides Aquino 10.00 25.00
FADMA Dustin May 20.00 50.00
FAJBA Jake Bauers 3.00 8.00
FAJLO Jonathan Loaisiga 3.00 8.00
FAJMO Jordan Montgomery 4.00 10.00
FAMBR Michael Brosseau 5.00 12.00
FAMTH Matt Thaiss 3.00 8.00
FANSO Nick Solak 4.00 10.00

2020 Topps Fire Autographs Green

*GREEN/75: .5X TO 1.2X BASIC
STATED ODDS 1:XX HOBBY
STATED PRINT RUN 75 SER.#'d SETS
EXCHANGE DEADLINE 7/31/22
FAGL Gavin Lux 30.00 80.00
FALR Luis Robert 150.00 400.00
FAPA Pete Alonso 40.00 100.00
FAVG Vladimir Guerrero Jr. 25.00 60.00
FAARI Austin Riley 15.00 40.00

2020 Topps Fire Autographs Magenta

*MAGENTA/25: .8X TO 2X BASIC
STATED ODDS 1:XX HOBBY
STATED PRINT RUN 25 SER.#'d SETS
EXCHANGE DEADLINE 7/31/22
FABB Bo Bichette EXCH 100.00 250.00
FACY Christian Yelich 30.00 80.00
FAEJ Eloy Jimenez 50.00 120.00
FAGL Gavin Lux 75.00 200.00
FAGT Gleyber Torres 40.00 100.00
FAJd Jacob deGrom 50.00 120.00
FALR Luis Robert 250.00 600.00
FAMT Mike Trout 200.00 500.00
FAPA Pete Alonso 60.00 150.00
FASO Shohei Ohtani 60.00 150.00
FAVG Vladimir Guerrero Jr. 40.00 100.00
FAARI Austin Riley 25.00 60.00
FAJMA J.D. Martinez 10.00 25.00
FAJSO Juan Soto 60.00 150.00

2020 Topps Fire Autographs Orange

*ORANGE/99: .5X TO 1.2X BASIC
STATED ODDS 1:XX HOBBY
STATED PRINT RUN 99 SER.#'d SETS
EXCHANGE DEADLINE 7/31/22
FAGL Gavin Lux 30.00 80.00
FAPA Pete Alonso 40.00 100.00
FAARI Austin Riley 15.00 40.00

2020 Topps Fire Autographs Purple

*PURPLE/50: .6X TO 1.5X BASIC
STATED ODDS 1:XX HOBBY
STATED PRINT RUN 50 SER.#'d SETS
EXCHANGE DEADLINE 7/31/22
FABB Bo Bichette EXCH 75.00 200.00
FAEJ Eloy Jimenez 40.00 100.00
FAGL Gavin Lux 60.00 150.00
FAJd Jacob deGrom 20.00 50.00
FALR Luis Robert 200.00 500.00
FAPA Pete Alonso 50.00 120.00
FAVG Vladimir Guerrero Jr. 30.00 80.00
FAARI Austin Riley 20.00 50.00
FAJMA J.D. Martinez 8.00 20.00
FAJSO Juan Soto 50.00 120.00

2020 Topps Fire Dual Autographs

STATED ODDS 1:XX HOBBY
STATED PRINT RUN 20 SER.#'d SETS
EXCHANGE DEADLINE 7/31/22
DAAA J.Altuve/Y.Alvarez 50.00 125.00
DAAD J.deGrom/P.Alonso 75.00 200.00
DABM X.Bogaerts/J.Martinez
DAHH R.Hoskins/B.Harper
DALM G.Lux/D.May
DARJ L.Robert/E.Jimenez 250.00 600.00
DASM B.Snell/B.McKay
DAAAL Y.Alvarez/P.Alonso
DAAAQ A.Aquino/N.Senzel
DARAJ A.Riley/R.Acuna Jr. 100.00 250.00

2020 Topps Fire Fired Up

STATED ODDS 1:XX HOBBY
*GOLD: .8X TO 2X BASIC
FIU1 Bryce Harper .75 2.00
FIU2 Bo Bichette 5.00 12.00
FIU3 Aristides Aquino .60 1.50
FIU4 Francisco Lindor .50 1.25
FIU5 Rafael Devers .60 1.50
FIU6 Cody Bellinger 1.00 2.50
FIU7 Javier Baez .60 1.50
FIU8 Justin Verlander .50 1.25
FIU9 Alex Bregman .50 1.25
FIU10 Nolan Arenado .60 1.50
FIU11 Christian Yelich .60 1.50
FIU12 Mookie Betts 1.00 2.50
FIU13 Charlie Blackmon .50 1.25
FIU14 Gleyber Torres 1.00 2.50
FIU15 Manny Machado .50 1.25

2020 Topps Fire Flame Throwers

STATED ODDS 1:XX HOBBY
*GOLD: .8X TO 2X BASIC
FT1 Jacob deGrom .50 1.25
FT2 Raisel Iglesias .30 .75
FT3 Josh Hader .30 .75
FT4 Aroldis Chapman .50 1.25
FT5 Shane Bieber .50 1.25
FT6 Jack Flaherty .40 1.00
FT7 Noah Syndergaard .40 1.00
FT8 Mike Soroka .50 1.25
FT9 Aaron Nola .50 1.25
FT10 Gerrit Cole .75 2.00
FT11 Lucas Giolito .40 1.00
FT12 Brendan McKay .50 1.25
FT13 Stephen Strasburg .50 1.25
FT14 Walker Buehler .60 1.50
FT15 Max Scherzer .50 1.25

2020 Topps Fire Power and Pride

STATED ODDS 1:XX HOBBY
*GOLD: .8X TO 2X BASIC
PP1 Shohei Ohtani .60 1.50
PP2 Ronald Acuna Jr. 2.00 5.00
PP3 Aroldis Chapman .50 1.25
PP4 Francisco Lindor .50 1.25
PP5 Xander Bogaerts .50 1.25
PP6 Eugenio Suarez .40 1.00
PP7 Aristides Aquino .60 1.50
PP8 Juan Soto 1.50 4.00
PP9 Aaron Judge 1.25 3.00
PP10 Jose Berrios .40 1.00
PP11 Cody Bellinger 1.00 2.50
PP12 Javier Baez .60 1.50
PP13 Jose Altuve .40 1.00
PP14 Freddie Freeman .60 1.50
PP15 Raisel Iglesias .30 .75

2020 Topps Fire Shattering Stats

STATED ODDS 1:XX HOBBY
*GOLD: .8X TO 2X BASIC
SS1 Pete Alonso 1.25 3.00
SS2 Ronald Acuna Jr. 2.00 5.00
SS3 Mike Trout 2.50 6.00
SS4 Alex Rodriguez .60 1.50
SS5 Miguel Cabrera .50 1.25
SS6 Rickey Henderson .50 1.25
SS7 Kris Bryant .60 1.50
SS8 Nolan Arenado .60 1.50
SS9 Albert Pujols .60 1.50
SS10 Mariano Rivera .60 1.50
SS11 Jacob deGrom .50 1.25
SS12 Cody Bellinger 1.00 2.50
SS13 Shohei Ohtani .60 1.50
SS14 Nelson Cruz .50 1.25
SS15 Aaron Judge 1.25 3.00

2020 Topps Fire Smoke and Mirrors

STATED ODDS 1:XX HOBBY
*GOLD: .8X TO 2X BASIC
SM1 Blake Snell .40 1.00
SM2 Andrew Miller .40 1.00
SM3 Jose Berrios .40 1.00
SM4 Max Scherzer .50 1.25
SM5 Chris Sale .50 1.25
SM6 Jameson Taillon .40 1.00
SM7 Josh Hader .30 .75
SM8 Clayton Kershaw 1.00 2.50
SM9 Adam Ottavino .30 .75
SM10 Joey Lucchesi .30 .75
SM11 Raisel Iglesias .30 .75
SM12 Jacob deGrom .50 1.25
SM13 Corey Kluber .40 1.00
SM14 Brendan McKay .50 1.25
SM15 Aroldis Chapman .50 1.25
SM16 Shohei Ohtani 2.50 6.00
SM17 Shun Yamaguchi .50 1.25
SM18 Justin Verlander .50 1.25
SM19 Michael Kopech .60 1.50
SM20 Jake Arrieta .40 1.00

2012 Topps Five Star

STATED PRINT RUN 80 SER.#'d SETS
1 Bryce Harper RC 125.00 250.00
2 Eddie Murray 2.50 6.00
3 Johnny Bench 4.00 10.00
4 Buster Posey 5.00 12.00
5 Ichiro Suzuki 5.00 12.00
6 Stephen Strasburg 4.00 10.00
7 Jered Weaver 3.00 8.00
8 Roy Halladay 3.00 8.00
9 CC Sabathia 3.00 8.00
10 Ryan Braun 2.50 6.00
11 Jacoby Ellsbury 3.00 8.00
12 Don Mattingly 8.00 20.00
13 Harmon Killebrew 4.00 10.00
14 Giancarlo Stanton 4.00 10.00
15 Alex Rodriguez 5.00 12.00
16 David Ortiz 4.00 10.00
17 Andre Ethier 3.00 8.00
18 Curtis Granderson 3.00 8.00
19 Derek Jeter 10.00 25.00
20 Joey Votto 4.00 10.00
21 Willie Mays 8.00 20.00
22 Ralph Kiner 2.50 6.00
23 Cole Hamels 3.00 8.00
24 Robinson Cano 3.00 8.00
25 Mariano Rivera 5.00 12.00
26 Felix Hernandez 3.00 8.00
27 Ian Kinsler 3.00 8.00
28 Joe DiMaggio 8.00 20.00
29 Paul Konerko 2.50 6.00
30 Babe Ruth 10.00 25.00
31 Carlos Gonzalez 3.00 8.00
32 Troy Tulowitzki 4.00 10.00
33 Mike Schmidt 6.00 15.00
34 Tom Seaver 2.50 6.00
35 Albert Pujols 5.00 12.00
36 David Price 3.00 8.00
37 Mike Trout 125.00 300.00
38 Andrew McCutchen 4.00 10.00
39 Adam Jones 3.00 8.00
40 Sandy Koufax 8.00 20.00
41 Joe Mauer 3.00 8.00
42 Jackie Robinson 4.00 10.00
43 George Brett 8.00 20.00
44 Dave Winfield 2.50 6.00
45 Jose Bautista 3.00 8.00
46 David Freese 2.50 6.00
47 Tim Lincecum 3.00 8.00
48 Prince Fielder 3.00 8.00
49 Adrian Gonzalez 3.00 8.00
50 Josh Hamilton 3.00 8.00
51 Roberto Clemente 10.00 25.00
52 Dustin Pedroia 3.00 8.00
53 Carl Yastrzemski 6.00 15.00
54 Nolan Ryan 12.00 30.00
55 Joe Morgan 2.50 6.00
56 Cliff Lee 3.00 8.00
57 Evan Longoria 3.00 8.00
58 David Wright 3.00 8.00
59 Yogi Berra 4.00 10.00
60 Ken Griffey Jr. 8.00 20.00
61 Yu Darvish RC 20.00 50.00
62 Mark Trumbo 2.50 6.00
63 Ty Cobb 6.00 15.00
64 Wade Boggs 2.50 6.00
65 Justin Verlander 4.00 10.00
66 Reggie Jackson 2.50 6.00
67 Cal Ripken Jr. 12.00 30.00
68 Johan Santana 3.00 8.00
69 Starlin Castro 3.00 8.00
70 Clayton Kershaw 8.00 20.00
71 Hanley Ramirez 3.00 8.00
72 Jim Palmer 2.50 6.00
73 Rod Carew 2.50 6.00
74 Justin Upton 3.00 8.00
75 Rickey Henderson 4.00 10.00
76 Matt Kemp 3.00 8.00
77 Mickey Mantle 12.00 30.00
78 Bob Gibson 2.50 6.00
79 Lou Gehrig 8.00 20.00
80 Miguel Cabrera 4.00 10.00

2012 Topps Five Star Active Autographs

PRINT RUNS B/WN 40-150 COPIES PER
EXCHANGE DEADLINE 10/31/2015
AE Andre Ethier/50 10.00 25.00
AG Adrian Gonzalez/150 6.00 15.00
AP Albert Pujols/40 100.00 200.00
AR Anthony Rizzo/150 15.00 40.00
BH Bryce Harper/150 125.00 250.00
BL Brett Lawrie/150 6.00 15.00
BP Buster Posey/150 40.00 80.00
CJ Chipper Jones/150 30.00 80.00
CJW C.J. Wilson/150 6.00 15.00
CK Clayton Kershaw/150 40.00 80.00
DF David Freese/150 6.00 15.00
DP Dustin Pedroia/150 15.00 40.00
DU Dan Uggla/150 6.00 15.00
DW David Wright/150 12.00 30.00
EH Eric Hosmer/150 15.00 40.00
EL Evan Longoria/106 30.00 60.00
GS Giancarlo Stanton/150 20.00 50.00
JBA Jose Bautista/150 12.00 30.00
JBR Jay Bruce/150 10.00 25.00
JHA Josh Hamilton/150 12.00 30.00
JHE Jason Heyward/150 12.00 30.00
JM Joe Mauer/150 15.00 40.00
JMO Jesus Montero/150 6.00 15.00
JW Jered Weaver EXCH 8.00 20.00
MB Madison Bumgarner/113 15.00 40.00
MC Miguel Cabrera/106 60.00 120.00
MK Matt Kemp/150 10.00 25.00
MM Matt Moore/150 6.00 15.00
MN Mike Napoli/113 6.00 15.00
MT Mike Trout/150 300.00 800.00
NC Nelson Cruz/150 6.00 15.00
PF Prince Fielder/150 20.00 50.00
PG Paul Goldschmidt/150 15.00 40.00
PS Pablo Sandoval/150 6.00 15.00
RB Ryan Braun/150 10.00 25.00
RC Robinson Cano 15.00 40.00
RHA Roy Halladay EXCH 25.00 60.00
RZ Ryan Zimmerman/150 6.00 15.00
SC Starlin Castro/150 8.00 20.00
TB Trevor Bauer/150 12.00 30.00
WMB Will Middlebrooks/150 12.00 30.00
YC Yoenis Cespedes/150 10.00 25.00
YD Yu Darvish/150 75.00 200.00

2012 Topps Five Star Jumbo Jersey

PRINT RUNS B/WN 54-92 COPIES PER
I Ichiro Suzuki 15.00 40.00
AB Adrian Beltre 5.00 12.00
AE Andre Ethier 6.00 15.00
AG Adrian Gonzalez 8.00 20.00
AM Andrew McCutchen 8.00 20.00
AP Albert Pujols 12.50 30.00
AR Alex Rodriguez 10.00 25.00
BH Bryce Harper 20.00 50.00
BP Buster Posey 12.50 30.00
CCS CC Sabathia 8.00 20.00
CG Carlos Gonzalez 5.00 12.00
CGA Curtis Granderson 10.00 25.00
CH Cole Hamels 10.00 25.00
CJ Chipper Jones 10.00 25.00
CK Clayton Kershaw 8.00 20.00
CL Cliff Lee 10.00 25.00
CW C.J. Wilson 5.00 12.00
DF David Freese 12.50 30.00
DJ Derek Jeter 30.00 60.00
DO David Ortiz 8.00 20.00
DP Dustin Pedroia 6.00 15.00
DPR David Price 6.00 15.00
DW David Wright 6.00 15.00
EL Evan Longoria 8.00 20.00
FH Felix Hernandez 8.00 20.00
GS Giancarlo Stanton 6.00 15.00
HR Hanley Ramirez 5.00 12.00
IK Ian Kinsler 5.00 12.00
JB Jose Bautista 6.00 15.00
JE Jacoby Ellsbury 10.00 25.00
JH Josh Hamilton 10.00 25.00
JM Joe Mauer 8.00 20.00
JS Johan Santana 6.00 15.00
JU Justin Upton 5.00 12.00
JV Justin Verlander 12.50 30.00
JVO Joey Votto 10.00 25.00
JW Jered Weaver 5.00 12.00
MC Miguel Cabrera 12.50 30.00
MK Matt Kemp 8.00 20.00
MM Matt Moore 5.00 12.00
MR Mariano Rivera 15.00 40.00
MT Mike Trout 125.00 300.00
PF Prince Fielder 6.00 15.00
PK Paul Konerko 10.00 25.00
RB Ryan Braun 8.00 20.00
RH Roy Halladay 10.00 25.00
SC Starlin Castro 8.00 20.00
SS Stephen Strasburg/54 12.50 30.00
TL Tim Lincecum 10.00 25.00
TT Troy Tulowitzki 8.00 20.00
YD Yu Darvish 15.00 40.00

2012 Topps Five Star Jumbo Relic Autograph Books

STATED ODDS 1:30 HOBBY
STATED PRINT RUN 49 SER.#'d SETS
EXCHANGE DEADLINE 10/31/2015
BH Bryce Harper 250.00 350.00
JB Jose Bautista 20.00 50.00
JW Jered Weaver EXCH 20.00 50.00
MH Matt Holliday EXCH 40.00 80.00
SK Sandy Koufax 400.00 600.00

2012 Topps Five Star Legends Relics

STATED ODDS 1:12 HOBBY
STATED PRINT RUN 25 SER.#'d SETS
BR Babe Ruth 100.00 200.00
CY Carl Yastrzemski 20.00 50.00
DW Dave Winfield 10.00 25.00
EB Ernie Banks 20.00 50.00
JB Johnny Bench 20.00 50.00
JD Joe DiMaggio 30.00 60.00
JR Jackie Robinson 40.00 80.00
MM Mickey Mantle 200.00 300.00
MS Mike Schmidt 12.50 30.00
RC Roberto Clemente 125.00 250.00
RH Rickey Henderson 30.00 60.00
RK Ralph Kiner 12.50 30.00
RS Ryne Sandberg 15.00 40.00
SC Steve Carlton 10.00 25.00
SK Sandy Koufax 50.00 100.00
SM Stan Musial 20.00 50.00
TC Ty Cobb 30.00 60.00
TG Tony Gwynn 20.00 50.00
TS Tom Seaver 30.00 60.00
WM Willie Mays 50.00 100.00
WMC Willie McCovey 10.00 25.00

2012 Topps Five Star Quad Relic Autograph Books

STATED ODDS 1:31 HOBBY
PRINT RUNS B/WN 23-49 COPIES PER
EXCHANGE DEADLINE 10/31/2015
EL Evan Longoria/49 50.00 100.00
JV Justin Verlander/49 60.00 120.00
MT Mike Trout/49 300.00 800.00
YD Yu Darvish/49 150.00 250.00

2012 Topps Five Star Relic Autographs

PRINT RUNS B/WN 9-97 COPIES PER
NO PRICING ON QTY 25 OR LESS
EXCHANGE DEADLINE 10/31/2015
AB Albert Belle/97 8.00 20.00
AD Andre Dawson/55 12.50 30.00
AE Andre Ethier/97 8.00 20.00
AG Adrian Gonzalez/97 6.00 15.00
AK Al Kaline/97 20.00 50.00
BL Brett Lawrie/97 6.00 15.00
BP Brandon Phillips/73 5.00 12.00
CF Carlton Fisk/43 20.00 50.00
CG Carlos Gonzalez/97 10.00 25.00
CJ Chipper Jones/97 50.00 120.00
CK Clayton Kershaw/97 40.00 80.00
CW C.J. Wilson/97 10.00 25.00
DF David Freese 15.00 40.00
DM Dale Murphy/97 20.00 50.00
DP Dustin Pedroia/97 15.00 40.00
DU Dan Uggla/97 8.00 20.00
EH Eric Hosmer/97 15.00 40.00
FH Felix Hernandez EXCH 20.00 50.00
FT Frank Thomas/97 25.00 60.00
GG Gio Gonzalez/97 6.00 15.00
GS Giancarlo Stanton/97 20.00 50.00
HA Hank Aaron/97 150.00 300.00
JB Jose Bautista/97 15.00 40.00
JH Josh Hamilton/97 12.50 30.00
JM Jesus Montero/97 10.00 25.00
JU Justin Upton/97 10.00 25.00
MC Miguel Cabrera/97 50.00 100.00
MK Matt Kemp/97 10.00 25.00
MM Matt Moore/97 8.00 20.00
MN Mike Napoli/73 6.00 15.00
MS Mike Schmidt/97 25.00 60.00
PF Prince Fielder/97 30.00 60.00
PM Paul Molitor/97 12.00 30.00
PO Paul O'Neill/97 12.50 30.00
PS Pablo Sandoval/97 6.00 15.00
RB Ryan Braun/97 8.00 20.00
RS Ryne Sandberg/97 25.00 60.00
SC Starlin Castro/97 8.00 20.00
TG Tony Gwynn/68 30.00 80.00
WC Will Clark/97 20.00 50.00
YC Yoenis Cespedes/97 20.00 50.00

2012 Topps Five Star Relic Autographs Gold

*GOLD: 4X TO 1X BASIC
STATED ODDS 1:4
PRINT RUNS B/WN 43-55 COPIES PER
EXCHANGE DEADLINE 10/31/2015

2012 Topps Five Star Retired Autographs

PRINT RUNS B/WN 25-208 COPIES PER
EXCHANGE DEADLINE 10/31/2015
AB Albert Belle/208 6.00 15.00
AD Andre Dawson/106 15.00 40.00
AK Al Kaline/208 20.00 50.00
BB Bill Buckner/208 10.00 25.00
BG Bob Gibson/106 20.00 50.00
BW Billy Williams/208 12.50 30.00
CF Carlton Fisk/106 20.00 50.00
CFI Cecil Fielder/208 10.00 25.00
CR Cal Ripken Jr./40 75.00 150.00
CY Carl Yastrzemski/62 40.00 80.00
DE Dennis Eckersley/208 6.00 15.00
DK Dave Kingman/208 6.00 15.00
DM Dale Murphy/208 6.00 15.00
EB Ernie Banks/62 60.00 150.00
EM Edgar Martinez/208 10.00 25.00
FJ Fergie Jenkins/208 6.00 15.00
FR Frank Robinson/62 30.00 60.00
GB George Bell/208 8.00 20.00
HA Hank Aaron/208 125.00 300.00
JB Johnny Bench/62 25.00 60.00
JK John Kruk/208 6.00 15.00
JMA Juan Marichal/208 12.50 30.00
JS John Smoltz/208 15.00 40.00
KG Ken Griffey Jr./62 75.00 150.00
KGS Ken Griffey Sr./208 8.00 20.00
LT Luis Tiant/208 6.00 15.00
MS Mike Schmidt/106 30.00 60.00
MW Maury Wills/208 12.00 30.00
NR Nolan Ryan/62 40.00 100.00
OC Orlando Cepeda/208 12.00 30.00
PM Paul Molitor/208 12.00 30.00
PO Paul O'Neill/106 10.00 25.00
RH Rickey Henderson/62 40.00 100.00
RJ Reggie Jackson/62 30.00 60.00
RS Ryne Sandberg/106 30.00 60.00
RV Robin Ventura/208 6.00 15.00
SK Sandy Koufax/25 200.00 400.00
SM Stan Musial/62 30.00 80.00
VB Vida Blue/208 4.00 10.00
WC Will Clark/208 12.00 30.00
WM Willie Mays/25 200.00 300.00

2012 Topps Five Star Silver Ink Autographs

PRINT RUNS B/WN 69-99 COPIES PER
EXCHANGE DEADLINE 10/31/2015
AB Albert Belle/99 6.00 15.00
AD Andre Dawson/99 10.00 25.00
AE Andre Ethier/99 6.00 15.00
AJ Adam Jones/99 6.00 15.00
AP Andy Pettitte/99 20.00 50.00
BB Bill Buckner/99 8.00 20.00
BL Brett Lawrie/99 10.00 25.00
BW Billy Williams/99 6.00 15.00
CG Carlos Gonzalez/99 10.00 25.00
CK Clayton Kershaw/99 40.00 100.00
CS Chris Sale/99 10.00 25.00
CW C.J. Wilson/99 8.00 20.00
DE Dennis Eckersley/99 10.00 25.00
DF David Freese/99 15.00 40.00
DK Dave Kingman/99 10.00 25.00
DM Dale Murphy/99 12.50 30.00
DW David Wright/99 15.00 40.00
EM Edgar Martinez/99 12.50 30.00
FF Freddie Freeman/99 20.00 50.00
FJ Fergie Jenkins/99 6.00 15.00
GF George Foster/99 10.00 25.00
GS Giancarlo Stanton/99 30.00 60.00
HR Hanley Ramirez/99 12.50 30.00
JB Jay Bruce/99 10.00 25.00
JH Jeremy Hellickson/99 10.00 25.00
JK John Kruk/99 10.00 25.00
JM Juan Marichal/99 10.00 25.00
JMO Jesus Montero/99 8.00 20.00
JP Jim Palmer/99 10.00 25.00
JR Jim Rice/99 10.00 25.00
KG Ken Griffey Jr./99 75.00 150.00
KGS Ken Griffey Sr./99 10.00 25.00
LT Luis Tiant/99 6.00 15.00
MK Matt Kemp/99 12.50 30.00
MM Matt Moore/99 10.00 25.00
MT Mike Trout/99 300.00 800.00
MW Maury Wills/99 10.00 25.00
NC Nelson Cruz/99 6.00 15.00
PO Paul O'Neill/99 10.00 25.00

AD R.A. Dickey/99 10.00 25.00
C Robinson Cano/99 15.00 40.00
V Robin Ventura/75 10.00 25.00
C Starlin Castro/99 10.00 25.00
K Sandy Koufax/69 150.00 250.00
P Terry Pendleton/99 6.00 15.00
B Vida Blue/99 6.00 15.00
C Will Clark/99 15.00 40.00
M Will Middlebrooks/99 3.00 8.00
C Yoenis Cespedes/99 10.00 25.00

2012 Topps Five Star Triple Relic Autograph Books

STATED ODDS 1:30 HOBBY
STATED PRINT RUN 49 SER.#'d SETS
EXCHANGE DEADLINE 10/31/2015
DM Don Mattingly 75.00 150.00
DW David Wright 25.00 60.00
MS Mike Schmidt 60.00 120.00
RB Ryan Braun 30.00 60.00
SM Stan Musial 150.00 300.00

2013 Topps Five Star

STATED PRINT RUN 75 SER.#'d SETS
1 Buster Posey 8.00 20.00
2 Zack Wheeler RC 10.00 25.00
3 Yoenis Cespedes 6.00 15.00
4 Whitey Ford 6.00 15.00
5 Willie Stargell 5.00 12.00
6 Giancarlo Stanton 6.00 15.00
7 Troy Tulowitzki 6.00 15.00
8 Adam Jones 5.00 12.00
9 Adrian Beltre 6.00 15.00
10 Shelby Miller RC 12.00 30.00
11 Ryan Braun 5.00 12.00
12 Lou Gehrig 12.00 30.00
13 Babe Ruth 15.00 40.00
14 Wade Boggs 10.00 25.00
15 Adam Wainwright 5.00 12.00
16 Ozzie Smith 8.00 20.00
17 Don Mattingly 12.00 30.00
18 Jose Bautista 5.00 12.00
19 Mike Schmidt 10.00 25.00
20 Roberto Clemente 25.00 60.00
21 Prince Fielder 5.00 12.00
22 Matt Cain 5.00 12.00
23 Derek Jeter 20.00 50.00
24 Ted Williams 12.00 30.00
25 Bo Jackson 6.00 15.00
26 Robinson Cano 5.00 12.00
27 Willie Mays 12.00 30.00
28 Miguel Cabrera 12.00 30.00
29 Josh Hamilton 5.00 12.00
30 Stan Musial 10.00 25.00
31 Bob Gibson 5.00 12.00
32 Andrew McCutchen 6.00 15.00
33 Joey Votto 10.00 25.00
34 Gerrit Cole RC 12.00 30.00
35 CC Sabathia 5.00 12.00
36 Mike Trout 50.00 125.00
37 Monte Irvin 4.00 10.00
38 Wil Myers RC 6.00 15.00
39 Cliff Lee 5.00 12.00
40 Fergie Jenkins 6.00 15.00
41 Clayton Kershaw 12.50 30.00
42 Matt Harvey 5.00 12.00
43 Robin Yount 6.00 15.00
44 John Smoltz 6.00 15.00
45 Mike Zunino RC 8.00 20.00
46 Ken Griffey Jr. 12.00 30.00
47 Al Kaline 6.00 15.00
48 Aroldis Chapman 6.00 15.00
49 Johnny Bench 6.00 15.00
50 Bryce Harper 15.00 40.00
51 Paul Molitor 6.00 15.00
52 Alex Rodriguez 8.00 20.00
53 George Kell 5.00 12.00
54 Yadier Molina 6.00 15.00
55 Juan Marichal 5.00 12.00
56 Ryan Howard 5.00 12.00
57 R.A. Dickey 5.00 12.00
58 Jurickson Profar RC 6.00 15.00
59 Frank Robinson 5.00 12.00
60 Yasiel Puig RC 75.00 150.00
61 Lou Brock 5.00 12.00
62 Evan Longoria 5.00 12.00
63 Bob Feller 10.00 25.00
64 Gary Carter 5.00 12.00
65 Harmon Killebrew 6.00 15.00
66 Carlos Gonzalez 5.00 12.00
67 Anthony Rendon RC 12.00 30.00
68 Stephen Strasburg 6.00 15.00
69 Carlton Fisk 5.00 12.00
70 Paul Goldschmidt 6.00 15.00
71 Andre Dawson 5.00 12.00
72 Mariano Rivera 8.00 20.00
73 Joe Mauer 5.00 12.00
74 Felix Hernandez 8.00 20.00
75 Dylan Bundy RC 12.00 30.00
76 Reggie Jackson 5.00 12.00
77 Manny Machado RC 50.00 100.00
78 Nolan Ryan 12.00 30.00
79 Ernie Banks 6.00 15.00
80 Adrian Gonzalez 5.00 12.00
81 Cal Ripken Jr. 20.00 50.00
82 Larry Doby 4.00 10.00
83 Dustin Pedroia 6.00 15.00
84 Billy Williams 5.00 12.00
85 Cole Hamels 5.00 12.00
86 Frank Thomas 8.00 20.00
87 Albert Pujols 8.00 20.00
88 Chipper Jones 6.00 15.00
89 Rickey Henderson 6.00 15.00
90 Sandy Koufax 15.00 40.00
91 Justin Verlander 6.00 15.00
92 Chris Davis 5.00 12.00
93 David Price 5.00 12.00
94 Chris Sale 6.00 15.00
95 Jacoby Ellsbury 8.00 20.00
96 Ryne Sandberg 12.50 30.00
97 David Wright 12.50 30.00
98 Matt Kemp 5.00 12.00
99 Ty Cobb 10.00 25.00
100 Yu Darvish 10.00 25.00

2013 Topps Five Star Autographs

PRINT RUNS B/WN 50-386 COPIES PER
EXCHANGE DEADLINE 11/30/2016
AD Andre Dawson/386 10.00 25.00
AG Adrian Gonzalez/333 10.00 25.00
AJ Adam Jones/353 12.00 30.00
AK Al Kaline/353 25.00 50.00
AR Anthony Rizzo/386 20.00 50.00
BB Billy Butler/386 4.00 10.00
BG Bob Gibson/50 30.00 60.00
BH Bryce Harper/30 150.00 250.00
BJ Bo Jackson/50 50.00 100.00
BP Buster Posey/50 60.00 120.00
BW Billy Williams/353 8.00 20.00
CB Craig Biggio/333 15.00 40.00
CH Cole Hamels/386 5.00 12.00
CR Cal Ripken Jr./30 75.00 200.00
CS Chris Sale/353 8.00 20.00
DB Dylan Bundy/386 8.00 20.00
DE Dennis Eckersley/353 10.00 25.00
DF David Freese/353 5.00 12.00
DM Don Mattingly/50 50.00 100.00
DMU Dale Murphy/386 12.00 30.00
DP Dustin Pedroia/333 20.00 50.00
DS Dave Stewart/386 5.00 12.00
DW David Wright/50 25.00 60.00
EB Ernie Banks/50 40.00 100.00
ED Eric Davis/386 15.00 40.00
EL Evan Longoria/50 20.00 50.00
FM Edgar Martinez/386 20.00 50.00
FF Freddie Freeman/386 15.00 40.00
FJ Fergie Jenkins/333 6.00 15.00
FL Fred Lynn/353 6.00 15.00
FM Fred McGriff/333 8.00 20.00
FT Frank Thomas/50 60.00 120.00
GC Gerrit Cole/333 15.00 40.00
GS Giancarlo Stanton 40.00 100.00
HA Hank Aaron/30 150.00 300.00
JB Jose Bautista/333 12.00 30.00
JBE Johnny Bench/50 40.00 80.00
JC Johnny Cueto/386 5.00 12.00
JF Jose Fernandez/386 20.00 50.00
JH Josh Hamilton/333 12.50 30.00
JHE Jason Heyward/333 6.00 15.00
JM Juan Marichal/353 10.00 25.00
JP Jurickson Profar/386 5.00 12.00
JPA Jim Palmer/333 10.00 25.00
JR Jim Rice/386 10.00 25.00
JS John Smoltz/333 15.00 40.00
JSH James Shields/386 4.00 10.00
JU Justin Upton/333 5.00 12.00
KGR Ken Griffey Jr./30 150.00 300.00
KL Kenny Lofton/386 20.00 50.00
LS Lee Smith/386 6.00 15.00
MB Madison Bumgarner/386 15.00 40.00
MC Miguel Cabrera/50 60.00 120.00
MM Matt Moore/386 4.00 10.00
MMA Manny Machado 30.00 80.00
MMU Mike Mussina/333 10.00 25.00
MS Mike Schmidt/50 40.00 80.00
MT Mike Trout/50 125.00 250.00
MTR Mark Trumbo/386 4.00 10.00
MW Matt Williams/386 6.00 15.00
NG Nomar Garciaparra/333 15.00 40.00
NR Nolan Ryan/50 75.00 150.00
OC Orlando Cepeda/333 6.00 15.00
PG Paul Goldschmidt/386 12.00 30.00
PM Pedro Martinez/50 60.00 120.00
PMO Paul Molitor/386 10.00 25.00
PO Paul O'Neill/386 12.00 30.00
RB Ryan Braun/333 10.00 25.00
RD R.A. Dickey/333 6.00 15.00
RH Rickey Henderson/50 60.00 120.00
RJ Reggie Jackson/50 40.00 80.00
RS Ryne Sandberg/50 40.00 80.00
RZ Ryan Zimmerman/386 8.00 20.00
SK Sandy Koufax/30 175.00 350.00
SM Shelby Miller/386 4.00 10.00
SP Salvador Perez/386 15.00 40.00
TG Tom Glavine/333 12.00 30.00
TGW Tony Gwynn/50 30.00 60.00
TS Tom Seaver/50 40.00 100.00
WC Will Clark/353 15.00 40.00
WMA Willie Mays/30 200.00 400.00
WMY Wil Myers/386 6.00 15.00
YC Yoenis Cespedes/353 12.00 30.00
YD Yu Darvish 50.00 120.00

2013 Topps Five Star Autographs Rainbow

*RAINBOW: .6X TO 1.5X BASIC p/r 333-386
*RAINBOW: .5X TO 1.2X BASIC p/r 30-50
STATED PRINT RUN 25 SER.#'d SETS
EXCHANGE DEADLINE 11/30/2016
AR Anthony Rizzo 60.00 150.00
HR Hyun-Jin Ryu 50.00 100.00
YP Yasiel Puig 200.00 400.00

2013 Topps Five Star Jumbo Jersey

STATED PRINT RUN 35 SER.#'d SETS
AC Aroldis Chapman 6.00 15.00
AGZ Adrian Gonzalez 5.00 12.00
AP Andy Pettitte 6.00 15.00
APU Albert Pujols 10.00 25.00
AR Alex Rodriguez 15.00 40.00
ARZ Anthony Rizzo 6.00 15.00
BB Billy Butler 4.00 10.00
BH Bryce Harper 12.50 30.00
BH2 Bryce Harper 12.50 30.00
BP Buster Posey 12.50 30.00
CB Craig Biggio 6.00 15.00
CCS CC Sabathia 12.00 30.00
CD Chris Davis 8.00 20.00
CF Carlton Fisk 6.00 15.00
CG Curtis Granderson 4.00 10.00
CGZ Carlos Gonzalez 6.00 15.00
CS Chris Sale 6.00 15.00
DJ Derek Jeter 20.00 50.00
DM Don Mattingly 20.00 50.00
DP Dustin Pedroia 4.00 10.00
DW David Wright 10.00 25.00
EL Evan Longoria 6.00 15.00
FH Felix Hernandez 6.00 15.00
FM Fred McGriff 4.00 10.00
GG Gio Gonzalez 4.00 10.00
GS Giancarlo Stanton 6.00 15.00
JB Jose Bautista 4.00 10.00
JH Josh Hamilton 6.00 15.00
JP Jurickson Profar 6.00 15.00
JR Jose Reyes 6.00 15.00
JRC Jim Rice 6.00 15.00
JU Justin Upton 6.00 15.00
LT Luis Tiant 5.00 12.00
MC Miguel Cabrera 10.00 25.00
MH Matt Harvey 10.00 25.00
MK Matt Kemp 4.00 10.00
MM Matt Moore 5.00 12.00
MR Mariano Rivera 10.00 25.00
MT Mike Trout 25.00 60.00
PF Prince Fielder 5.00 12.00
PN Phil Niekro 12.50 30.00
RAD R.A. Dickey 6.00 15.00
RB Ryan Braun 5.00 12.00
RH Ryan Howard 10.00 25.00
SC Starlin Castro 6.00 15.00
SS Stephen Strasburg 8.00 20.00
TL Tim Lincecum 10.00 25.00
TT Troy Tulowitzki 10.00 25.00
YC Yoenis Cespedes 5.00 12.00
YD Yu Darvish 10.00 25.00
YP Yasiel Puig 30.00 60.00

2013 Topps Five Star Jumbo Jersey Blue

*BLUE: .4X TO 1X BASIC
STATED PRINT RUN 30 SER.#'d SETS
EXCHANGE DEADLINE 11/30/2016

2013 Topps Five Star Jumbo Jersey Red

*RED: .5X TO 1.2X BASIC
STATED PRINT RUN 25 SER.#'d SETS
EXCHANGE DEADLINE 11/30/2016

2013 Topps Five Star Jumbo Relic Autographs Books

STATED PRINT RUN 49 SER.#'d SETS
EXCHANGE DEADLINE 11/30/2016
JB Johnny Bench 60.00 120.00
KG Ken Griffey Jr. 125.00 300.00
RJ Reggie Jackson 60.00 120.00
TG Tony Gwynn 50.00 100.00
WM Willie Mays 175.00 350.00

2013 Topps Five Star Legends Autographs

PRINT RUNS B/WN 49-75 COPIES PER
EXCHANGE DEADLINE 11/30/2016
P Pele 250.00 350.00
BB Bjorn Borg 30.00 60.00
BR Bill Russell 60.00 120.00

2013 Topps Five Star Legends Relics

STATED PRINT RUN 25 SER.#'d SETS
BF Bob Feller 30.00 60.00
BG Bob Gibson 20.00 50.00
CRJ Cal Ripken Jr. 20.00 50.00
EB Ernie Banks 20.00 50.00
EM Eddie Mathews 12.50 30.00
GB George Brett 20.00 50.00
HK Harmon Killebrew 12.50 30.00
JB Johnny Bench 15.00 40.00
JB2 Johnny Bench 15.00 40.00
JF Jimmie Foxx 30.00 60.00
JR Jackie Robinson 40.00 80.00
KGJ Ken Griffey Jr. 50.00 100.00
MS Mike Schmidt 12.50 30.00
NR Nolan Ryan 30.00 60.00
RC Roberto Clemente 75.00 150.00
RC2 Roberto Clemente 75.00 150.00
RH Rickey Henderson 30.00 60.00
RJ Reggie Jackson 10.00 25.00
SM Stan Musial 20.00 50.00
TC Ty Cobb 40.00 80.00
TC2 Ty Cobb 40.00 80.00
TW Ted Williams 30.00 80.00
WM Willie Mays 50.00 100.00
WMC Willie McCovey 20.00 50.00
YB Yogi Berra 15.00 40.00

2013 Topps Five Star Patch Autographs

STATED PRINT RUN 35 SER.#'d SETS
AJ Adam Jones 50.00 100.00
BP Buster Posey 100.00 200.00
CR Cal Ripken Jr. 100.00 200.00
CS Chris Sale 15.00 40.00
DP Dustin Pedroia 40.00 80.00
DW David Wright 40.00 80.00
JC Johnny Cueto EXCH 10.00 25.00
JH Jason Heyward 20.00 50.00
JS John Smoltz 30.00 60.00
MC Miguel Cabrera 125.00 250.00
MM Mike Mussina 20.00 50.00
MS Mike Schmidt 50.00 120.00
MT Mike Trout 175.00 350.00
PS Pablo Sandoval 15.00 40.00
RC Robinson Cano 20.00 50.00

2013 Topps Five Star Quad Relic Autographs Books

STATED PRINT RUN 49 SER.#'d SETS
EXCHANGE DEADLINE 11/30/2016
BH Bryce Harper 75.00 200.00
CB Craig Biggio 40.00 80.00
DW David Wright 60.00 120.00
MC Miguel Cabrera 100.00 250.00
RB Ryan Braun 30.00 60.00

2013 Topps Five Star Silver Signings

STATED PRINT RUN 65 SER.#'d SETS
EXCHANGE DEADLINE 11/30/2016
AD Andre Dawson 10.00 25.00
AG Adrian Gonzalez 12.50 30.00
AK Al Kaline 25.00 50.00
AR Anthony Rizzo 20.00 50.00
CB Craig Biggio 15.00 40.00
CF Carlton Fisk 15.00 40.00
CH Cole Hamels 10.00 25.00
CK Clayton Kershaw 50.00 100.00
CS Chris Sale 12.50 30.00
DB Dylan Bundy 12.50 30.00
DE Dennis Eckersley 10.00 25.00
DF David Freese 10.00 25.00
DM Dale Murphy 10.00 25.00
DS Dave Stewart 8.00 20.00
DSN Deion Sanders 20.00 50.00
DW David Wright 20.00 50.00
ED Eric Davis 6.00 15.00
FF Freddie Freeman 15.00 40.00
FL Fred Lynn 10.00 25.00
FM Fred McGriff 15.00 40.00
HA Hank Aaron 100.00 250.00
HR Hyun-Jin Ryu
JBA Jose Bautista 10.00 25.00
JC Johnny Cueto 8.00 20.00
JF Jose Fernandez 30.00 60.00
JM Juan Marichal 10.00 25.00
JP Jurickson Profar 10.00 25.00
JR Jim Rice 10.00 25.00
JS John Smoltz 20.00 50.00
JSH James Shields 8.00 20.00
JU Justin Upton 10.00 25.00
LS Lee Smith 5.00 12.00
MB Madison Bumgarner 20.00 50.00
MC Matt Cain 10.00 25.00
MM Matt Moore 10.00 25.00
MMA Manny Machado 30.00 60.00
MMU Mike Mussina 10.00 25.00
MTR Mike Trout 100.00 250.00
MW Matt Williams 10.00 25.00
NG Nomar Garciaparra 20.00 50.00
OC Orlando Cepeda 10.00 25.00
PG Paul Goldschmidt 15.00 40.00
PM Paul Molitor 6.00 15.00
PO Paul O'Neill 15.00 40.00
SM Shelby Miller 10.00 25.00
SP Salvador Perez 10.00 25.00
TG Tom Glavine 20.00 50.00
TR Tim Raines 8.00 20.00
WM Wil Myers 12.00 30.00
YC Yoenis Cespedes 20.00 50.00
ZW Zack Wheeler 20.00 50.00

2013 Topps Five Star Silver Signings Blue

*BLUE: .5X TO 1.2X BASIC
STATED PRINT RUN 25 SER.#'d SETS
EXCHANGE DEADLINE 11/30/2016

2013 Topps Five Star Triple Relic Autographs Books

STATED PRINT RUN 49 SER.#'d SETS
EXCHANGE DEADLINE 11/30/2016
CR Cal Ripken Jr. 100.00 200.00
MS Mike Schmidt 60.00 120.00
MT Mike Trout 150.00 300.00
NG Nomar Garciaparra 20.00 50.00
YD Yu Darvish 100.00 200.00

2014 Topps Five Star Autographs

RANDOM INSERTS IN PACKS
PRINT RUNS B/WN 50-499 COPIES PER
EXCHANGE DEADLINE 11/30/2017
FSAAA Arismendy Alcantara/499 3.00 8.00
FSAAC Allen Craig/399 4.00 10.00
FSAAD Andre Dawson/149 10.00 25.00
FSAAG Alex Guerrero/499 4.00 10.00
FSAAGO Adrian Gonzalez/149 8.00 20.00
FSAAS Andrelton Simmons/499 4.00 10.00
FSAASA Aaron Sanchez/499 3.00 8.00
FSABHA Bryce Harper/50 100.00 200.00
FSABJ Bo Jackson/50 50.00 120.00
FSACB Craig Biggio/149 12.00 30.00
FSACF Carlton Fisk/50 20.00 50.00
FSACG Carlos Gonzalez/138 12.00 30.00
FSACJ Chipper Jones/50 60.00 150.00
FSACK Clayton Kershaw/50 75.00 200.00
FSACO Chris Owings/499 3.00 8.00
FSACR Cal Ripken Jr./50 75.00 200.00
FSACS Chris Sabo/499 6.00 15.00
FSACSA Chris Sale/399 8.00 20.00
FSACW C.J. Wilson/399 3.00 8.00
FSADAI Daisuke Matsuzaka/499 12.00 30.00
FSADC David Cone/399 6.00 15.00
FSADE Dennis Eckersley/299 4.00 10.00
FSADM Dale Murphy/299 10.00 25.00
FSADMA Don Mattingly/50 30.00 80.00
FSADPA Dave Parker/499 3.00 8.00
FSADW David Wright/50 15.00 40.00
FSAEBU Eddie Butler/399 3.00 8.00
FSAEL Evan Longoria/50 8.00 20.00
FSAEM Edgar Martinez/399 8.00 20.00
FSAFF Freddie Freeman/199 10.00 25.00
FSAFT Frank Thomas/50 50.00 120.00
FSAFV Fernando Valenzuela/199 10.00 25.00
FSAGP Gregory Polanco/399 4.00 10.00
FSAGS Giancarlo Stanton/136 15.00 40.00
FSAGSP George Springer/499 12.00 30.00
FSAHR Hanley Ramirez/50 10.00 25.00
FSAIR Ivan Rodriguez/149 12.00 30.00
FSAJA Jose Abreu/199 10.00 25.00
FSAJB Jay Bruce/399 4.00 10.00
FSAJBE Johnny Bench/50 30.00 80.00
FSAJC Jose Canseco/399 8.00 20.00
FSAJD Josh Donaldson/399 10.00 25.00
FSAJF Jose Fernandez/299 10.00 25.00
FSAJG Juan Gonzalez/399 3.00 8.00
FSAJH Jason Heyward/199 4.00 10.00
FSAJM Joe Mauer/50 15.00 40.00
FSAJP Jorge Posada/149 20.00 50.00
FSAJR Jim Rice/399 6.00 15.00
FSAJS John Smoltz/149 15.00 40.00
FSAJSC Jonathan Schoop/499 8.00 20.00
FSAJT Julio Teheran/105 4.00 10.00
FSAJTA Junichi Tazawa/499 3.00 8.00
FSAJV Joey Votto/50 25.00 60.00
FSAKG Ken Griffey Jr./50 100.00 200.00
FSAKU Koji Uehara/499 10.00 25.00
FSAKW Kolten Wong/499 4.00 10.00
FSALB Lou Brock/299 12.00 30.00
FSALH Livan Hernandez/499 3.00 8.00
FSAMA Matt Adams/499 3.00 8.00
FSAMB M.Bumgarner/299 25.00 60.00
FSAMBE Mookie Betts/499 100.00 250.00
FSAMC Miguel Cabrera/50 40.00 100.00
FSAMCA Matt Carpenter/499 6.00 15.00
FSAMM Manny Machado/105 12.00 30.00
FSAMMC Mark McGwire/50 75.00 200.00
FSAMP Mike Piazza/50 50.00 120.00
FSAMS Mike Schmidt/50 20.00 50.00
FSAMSC Max Scherzer/299 30.00 80.00
FSAMT Mike Trout/50 150.00 250.00
FSAMW Michael Wacha/399 4.00 10.00
FSANC Nick Castellanos/499 10.00 25.00
FSANG Nomar Garciaparra/50 10.00 25.00
FSANR Nolan Ryan/50 60.00 150.00
FSAOH Orlando Hernandez/499 3.00 8.00
FSAOS Ozzie Smith/50 20.00 50.00
FSAOTA Oscar Taveras/399 4.00 10.00
FSAOV Omar Vizquel/499 6.00 15.00
FSAPG Paul Goldschmidt/399 12.00 30.00
FSAPMO Paul Molitor/50 15.00 40.00
FSAPN Phil Niekro/299 4.00 10.00
FSAPO Paul O'Neill/399 6.00 15.00
FSARA Roberto Alomar/149 15.00 40.00
FSARB Ryan Braun/50 15.00 40.00
FSARC Robinson Cano/50 15.00 40.00
FSARCA Rod Carew/149 15.00 40.00
FSARJ Reggie Jackson/50 30.00 80.00
FSARP Rafael Palmeiro/299 6.00 15.00
FSARY Robin Yount/50 40.00 100.00
FSARZ Ryan Zimmerman/399 4.00 10.00
FSASC Steve Carlton/149 12.00 30.00
FSASM Shelby Miller/499 4.00 10.00
FSATGL Tom Glavine/50 10.00 25.00
FSATT Troy Tulowitzki/50 5.00 12.00
FSATW Taijuan Walker/499 3.00 8.00
FSAVG Vladimir Guerrero/149 15.00 40.00
FSAWM Wil Myers/399 3.00 8.00
FSAYC Yoenis Cespedes/399 5.00 12.00
FSAYM Yadier Molina/149 40.00 100.00
FSAYS Yangervis Solarte/499 3.00 8.00
FSAZW Zack Wheeler/499 4.00 10.00

2014 Topps Five Star Autographs Rainbow

*RAINBOW: .6X TO 1.5X BASE p/r 149-499
*RAINBOW: .5X TO 1.2X BASE p/r 50
STATED PRINT RUN 25 SER.#'d SETS
EXCHANGE DEADLINE 11/30/2017
FSADMO Dan Marino 100.00 250.00
FSASK Sandy Koufax 200.00 400.00
FSAWMA Willie Mays EXCH 150.00 300.00

2014 Topps Five Star Golden Graphs

RANDOM INSERTS IN PACKS
STATED PRINT RUN 50 SER.#'d SETS
EXCHANGE DEADLINE 11/30/2017
*PURPLE/25: .5X TO 1.2X BASIC
FSGGAA Arismendy Alcantara 6.00 15.00
FSGGAG Adrian Gonzalez 8.00 20.00
FSGGCB Craig Biggio 15.00 40.00
FSGGCS CC Sabathia 25.00 60.00
FSGGDC David Cone 12.00 30.00
FSGGDM Don Mattingly 30.00 80.00
FSGGDMA Daisuke Matsuzaka 15.00 40.00
FSGGEL Evan Longoria 15.00 40.00
FSGGEM Edgar Martinez 5.00 12.00
FSGGFF Freddie Freeman 12.00 30.00
FSGGGS George Springer 20.00 50.00
FSGGJB Johnny Bench 30.00 80.00
FSGGJC Jose Canseco 15.00 40.00
FSGGJV Joey Votto 15.00 40.00
FSGGMB Mookie Betts 75.00 200.00
FSGGMR Mariano Rivera 75.00 200.00
FSGGNC Nick Castellanos 20.00 50.00
FSGGNG Nomar Garciaparra 10.00 25.00
FSGGPG Paul Goldschmidt 15.00 40.00
FSGGPO Paul O'Neill 15.00 40.00
FSGGRA Roberto Alomar 15.00 40.00
FSGGRC Rod Carew 15.00 40.00
FSGGTG Tom Glavine 20.00 50.00
FSGGTT Troy Tulowitzki 20.00 50.00
FSGGYC Yoenis Cespedes 10.00 25.00
FSGGZW Zack Wheeler 8.00 20.00

2014 Topps Five Star Jumbo Patch Autographs

RANDOM INSERTS IN PACKS
STATED PRINT RUN 35 SER.#'d SETS
EXCHANGE DEADLINE 11/30/2017
FAJPAG Adrian Gonzalez 20.00 50.00
FAJPBH Billy Hamilton 20.00 50.00
FAJPBP Buster Posey 150.00 250.00
FAJPCG Carlos Gonzalez 20.00 50.00
FAJPDM Daisuke Matsuzaka 40.00 100.00
FAJPDO David Ortiz 60.00 150.00
FAJPDW David Wright 40.00 100.00
FAJPFF Freddie Freeman 40.00 100.00
FAJPGS Giancarlo Stanton 60.00 150.00
FAJPHR Hanley Ramirez 20.00 50.00
FAJPJM Joe Mauer 40.00 100.00
FAJPJP Jorge Posada 25.00 60.00
FAJPJV Joey Votto 30.00 80.00
FAJPPG Paul Goldschmidt 25.00 60.00
FAJPRA Roberto Alomar 25.00 60.00
FAJPRB Ryan Braun 25.00 60.00
FAJPTW Taijuan Walker 15.00 40.00
FAJPYV Yordano Ventura 20.00 50.00

2014 Topps Five Star Jumbo Relic Autographs Books

RANDOM INSERTS IN PACKS
STATED PRINT RUN 50 SER.#'d SETS
EXCHANGE DEADLINE 11/30/2017
FSABDW David Wright 30.00 80.00
FSABMS Mike Schmidt 50.00 120.00
FSABNG Nomar Garciaparra 30.00 80.00
FSABRCL Roger Clemens 60.00 150.00
FSABRS Ryne Sandberg 50.00 120.00
FSABRY Robin Yount 25.00 60.00

2014 Topps Five Star Legends Relics

RANDOM INSERTS IN PACKS
STATED PRINT RUN 25 SER.#'d SETS
FSLRAK Al Kaline 15.00 40.00
FSLRBF Bob Feller 20.00 50.00
FSLRBR Babe Ruth 60.00 150.00
FSLRDJ Derek Jeter 50.00 120.00
FSLRDS Duke Snider 50.00 120.00
FSLREM Eddie Mathews 25.00 60.00
FSLRES Enos Slaughter 20.00 50.00
FSLREW Early Wynn 20.00 50.00
FSLRHA Hank Aaron 40.00 100.00
FSLRHK Harmon Killebrew 25.00 60.00
FSLRJD Joe DiMaggio 40.00 100.00
FSLRJM Joe Morgan 20.00 50.00
FSLRJR Jackie Robinson 30.00 80.00
FSLRLG Lou Gehrig 60.00 150.00
FSLRMT Masahiro Tanaka 30.00 80.00
FSLRRC Roberto Clemente 60.00 150.00
FSLRRF Rick Ferrell 40.00 100.00
FSLRRM Roger Maris 25.00 60.00
FSLRRS Red Schoendienst 20.00 50.00
FSLRTP Tony Perez 20.00 50.00
FSLRWF Whitey Ford 20.00 50.00
FSLRWS Warren Spahn 25.00 60.00
FSLRWST Willie Stargell 20.00 50.00

2014 Topps Five Star Quad Relic Autographs Books

RANDOM INSERTS IN PACKS
STATED PRINT RUN 50 SER.#'d SETS
EXCHANGE DEADLINE 11/30/2017
FSSBBR Brooks Robinson 50.00 120.00
FSSBCR Cal Ripken Jr. 60.00 150.00
FSSBDM Don Mattingly 40.00 100.00
FSSBMM Mark McGwire 100.00 200.00
FSSBMS Max Scherzer 40.00 100.00
FSSBOZ Ozzie Smith 50.00 120.00
FSSBRB Ryan Braun 20.00 50.00
FSSBTGL Tom Glavine 40.00 100.00

2014 Topps Five Star Silver Signatures

RANDOM INSERTS IN PACKS
STATED PRINT RUN 50 SER.#'d SETS
EXCHANGE DEADLINE 11/30/2017
*PURPLE/25: .5X TO 1.2X BASIC
FSSSAA Arismendy Alcantara 8.00 20.00
FSSSAG Adrian Gonzalez 10.00 25.00
FSSSCB Craig Biggio 20.00 50.00
FSSSCS CC Sabathia 10.00 25.00
FSSSDC David Cone 12.00 30.00
FSSSDM Don Mattingly 25.00 60.00
FSSSDMA Daisuke Matsuzaka 30.00 80.00
FSSSEL Evan Longoria 15.00 40.00
FSSSEM Edgar Martinez 12.00 30.00
FSSSFF Freddie Freeman 12.00 30.00
FSSSGS George Springer 25.00 60.00
FSSSIR Ivan Rodriguez 12.00 30.00
FSSSJB Johnny Bench 30.00 80.00
FSSSJC Jose Canseco 10.00 25.00
FSSSJP Jim Palmer 15.00 40.00
FSSSJV Joey Votto 20.00 50.00
FSSSMB Mookie Betts 40.00 100.00
FSSSNC Nick Castellanos 25.00 60.00
FSSSNG Nomar Garciaparra 15.00 40.00
FSSSPG Paul Goldschmidt 15.00 40.00
FSSSPO Paul O'Neill 15.00 40.00
FSSSRA Roberto Alomar 25.00 60.00
FSSSRC Rod Carew 15.00 40.00
FSSSRJ Randy Johnson 40.00 100.00
FSSSTG Tom Glavine 20.00 50.00
FSSSTT Troy Tulowitzki 12.00 30.00
FSSSTW Taijuan Walker 8.00 20.00
FSSSZW Zack Wheeler 10.00 25.00

2015 Topps Five Star Autographs

OVERALL TWO AUTOS PER BOX
EXCHANGE DEADLINE 9/30/2017
FSAAB Archie Bradley RC 5.00 12.00
FSAACO A.J. Cole RC 3.00 8.00
FSAAG Andres Galarraga 6.00 15.00
FSAAGA Andres Galarraga 6.00 15.00
FSAAJ Andruw Jones 3.00 8.00
FSAAL Al Leiter 4.00 10.00
FSAARU Addison Russell RC 8.00 20.00
FSABB Brandon Belt 4.00 10.00
FSABBR Bryce Brentz RC 4.00 10.00
FSABBU Byron Buxton RC 6.00 15.00
FSABF Brandon Finnegan RC 3.00 8.00
FSABS Blake Swihart RC 4.00 10.00
FSABW Bernie Williams 15.00 40.00
FSACB Craig Biggio 12.00 30.00
FSACD Carlos Delgado 5.00 12.00
FSACK Clayton Kershaw 6.00 15.00
FSACKL Corey Kluber 4.00 10.00
FSACRO Carlos Rodon RC 5.00 12.00
FSADE Dennis Eckersley 6.00 15.00
FSADF Doug Fister 3.00 8.00
FSADG Didi Gregorius 10.00 25.00
FSAEE Edwin Encarnacion 5.00 12.00
FSAEI Ender Inciarte 3.00 8.00
FSAEM Edgar Martinez 12.00 30.00
FSAFF Freddie Freeman 6.00 15.00
FSAFL Francisco Lindor RC 20.00 50.00
FSAFV Fernando Valenzuela 20.00 50.00
FSAHR Hanley Ramirez 4.00 10.00
FSAJA Jose Abreu 8.00 20.00
FSAJAL Jose Altuve 10.00 25.00
FSAJBA Javier Baez RC 40.00 100.00
FSAJD Jacob deGrom 25.00 60.00
FSAJH Josh Harrison 3.00 8.00
FSAJHK Jung-Ho Kang RC 10.00 25.00
FSAJL Jon Lester 15.00 40.00
FSAJLI Jacob Lindgren RC 4.00 10.00
FSAJP Joc Pederson RC 6.00 15.00
FSAJPI Jose Pirela RC 3.00 8.00
FSAJS John Smoltz 10.00 25.00
FSAJSH James Shields 3.00 8.00
FSAJSO Jorge Soler RC 10.00 25.00
FSAJUG Juan Gonzalez 8.00 20.00
FSAKB Kris Bryant RC 75.00 200.00
FSAKC Kole Calhoun 3.00 8.00
FSAKP Kevin Plawecki RC 3.00 8.00
FSAMC Matt Carpenter 5.00 12.00
FSAMFR Maikel Franco RC 6.00 15.00
FSAMG Mark Grace 10.00 25.00
FSAMGR Marquis Grissom 3.00 8.00
FSAMJ Micah Johnson RC 3.00 8.00
FSAMTA Michael Taylor RC 3.00 8.00
FSAMW Matt Wisler RC 5.00 12.00
FSAMWA Michael Wacha 5.00 12.00
FSAMZ Mike Zunino 3.00 8.00
FSANS Noah Syndergaard RC 20.00 50.00
FSAOS Ozzie Smith 15.00 40.00
FSAOV Omar Vizquel 5.00 12.00
FSAPO Paul O'Neill 4.00 10.00
FSAPS Pablo Sandoval 8.00 20.00
FSARB Ryan Braun 4.00 10.00
FSARI Raisel Iglesias RC 4.00 10.00
FSARJA Reggie Jackson 20.00 50.00
FSARO Roberto Osuna 3.00 8.00
FSARP Rick Porcello 4.00 10.00
FSARPA Rafael Palmeiro 5.00 12.00
FSARUC Rusney Castillo RC 8.00 20.00
FSASC Steve Carlton 10.00 25.00
FSASG Shawn Green 3.00 8.00
FSASM Starling Marte 5.00 12.00
FSASMA Steven Matz RC 3.00 8.00
FSASS Steven Souza 4.00 10.00
FSATG Tom Glavine 12.00 30.00
FSAVC Vinny Castilla 3.00 8.00
FSAYGO Yan Gomes 3.00 8.00

2015 Topps Five Star Autographs Gold

*GOLD: .5X TO 1.2X BASIC
RANDOM INSERTS IN PACKS
STATED PRINT RUN 50 SER.#'d SETS
EXCHANGE DEADLINE 9/30/2017
FSABL Barry Larkin 20.00 50.00
FSACK Clayton Kershaw 40.00 100.00
FSADM Don Mattingly 20.00 50.00
FSAFR Frank Robinson 20.00 50.00
FSAI Ichiro Suzuki 250.00 350.00
FSANG Nomar Garciaparra 10.00 25.00
FSAPF Prince Fielder 10.00 25.00

2015 Topps Five Star Autographs Rainbow

*RAINBOW: .6X TO 1.5X BASIC
STATED ODDS 1:6 HOBBY
STATED PRINT RUN 25 SER.#'d SETS
EXCHANGE DEADLINE 9/30/2017
FSAAG Andres Galarraga 30.00 80.00
FSAAGA Andres Galarraga 30.00 80.00
FSABJ Bo Jackson 50.00 120.00
FSABL Barry Larkin 25.00 60.00
FSABP Buster Posey 60.00 150.00
FSACK Clayton Kershaw 50.00 120.00
FSACR Cal Ripken Jr. 100.00 200.00
FSADM Don Mattingly 25.00 60.00
FSADO David Ortiz 40.00 100.00

FSAEL Evan Longoria 10.00 25.00
FSAFR Frank Robinson 25.00 60.00
FSAFT Frank Thomas 50.00 120.00
FSAI Ichiro Suzuki 300.00 400.00
FSAMM Mark McGwire 100.00 200.00
FSAMP Mike Piazza 100.00 200.00
FSAMR Mariano Rivera 150.00 250.00
FSAMT Mike Trout 300.00 400.00
FSANG Nomar Garciaparra 12.00 30.00
FSANR Nolan Ryan 75.00 150.00
FSAPF Prince Fielder 12.00 30.00
FSARC Roger Clemens 40.00 100.00
FSARCA Robinson Cano 15.00 40.00
FSARH Rickey Henderson 30.00 80.00
FSARJ Randy Johnson 75.00 150.00
FSARS Ryne Sandberg 25.00 60.00
FSASK Sandy Koufax 200.00 300.00
FSAWB Wade Boggs 30.00 80.00

2015 Topps Five Star Five Tools Autographs

STATED ODDS 1:27 HOBBY
STATED PRINT RUN 25 SER.#'d SETS
EXCHANGE DEADLINE 9/30/2017
FTAAD Andre Dawson 20.00 50.00
FTAAJ Adam Jones 30.00 80.00
FTABB Byron Buxton 15.00 40.00
FTABH Bryce Harper 125.00 250.00
FTABJ Bo Jackson 40.00 100.00
FTACB Craig Biggio 15.00 40.00
FTACJ Chipper Jones 150.00 250.00
FTADP Dustin Pedroia 15.00 40.00
FTADW David Wright 12.00 30.00
FTAHA Hank Aaron 200.00 300.00
FTAHR Hanley Ramirez 12.00 30.00
FTAKB Kris Bryant 200.00 400.00
FTAKG Ken Griffey Jr. 300.00 400.00
FTAMM Manny Machado 60.00 150.00
FTAMT Mike Trout 300.00 400.00
FTANG Nomar Garciaparra 12.00 30.00
FTAPM Paul Molitor 30.00 80.00
FTARB Ryan Braun 12.00 30.00
FTARH Rickey Henderson 30.00 80.00
FTASM Starling Marte 12.00 30.00

2015 Topps Five Star Golden Graphs

STATED ODDS 1:13 HOBBY
STATED PRINT RUN 50 SER.#'d SETS
EXCHANGE DEADLINE 9/30/2017
*BLUE/20: .5X TO 1.2X
*PURPLE/25: .5X TO 1.2X
GGAL Al Leiter 10.00 25.00
GGBL Barry Larkin 20.00 50.00
GGCB Craig Biggio 12.00 30.00
GGCK Corey Kluber 8.00 20.00
GGDE Dennis Eckersley 12.00 30.00
GGDF Doug Fister 6.00 15.00
GGDG Didi Gregorius 10.00 25.00
GGDM Don Mattingly 25.00 60.00
GGEE Edwin Encarnacion 10.00 25.00
GGFF Freddie Freeman 12.00 30.00
GGFV Fernando Valenzuela 10.00 25.00
GGJB Javier Baez 12.00 30.00
GGJD Jacob deGrom 15.00 40.00
GGJH Josh Harrison 6.00 15.00
GGJHK Jung-Ho Kang 6.00 15.00
GGJP Joc Pederson 20.00 50.00
GGJS James Shields 6.00 15.00
GGJSM John Smoltz 15.00 40.00
GGKW Kolten Wong 12.00 30.00
GGMC Matt Carpenter 12.00 30.00
GGMF Maikel Franco 15.00 40.00
GGMG Mark Grace 12.00 30.00
GGOS Ozzie Smith 20.00 50.00
GGPF Prince Fielder 8.00 20.00
GGRCL Roger Clemens 25.00 60.00
GGSG Sonny Gray 8.00 20.00
GGTG Tom Glavine 20.00 50.00

2015 Topps Five Star Jumbo Patch Autographs

STATED ODDS 1:23 HOBBY
STATED PRINT RUN 35 SER.#'d SETS
EXCHANGE DEADLINE 9/30/2017
FSAJAG Adrian Gonzalez 25.00 60.00
FSAJAJ Adam Jones 25.00 60.00
FSAJBB Brandon Belt 25.00 60.00
FSAJBM Brian McCann 25.00 60.00
FSAJCK Clayton Kershaw 75.00 200.00
FSAJDO David Ortiz 60.00 150.00
FSAJDW David Wright 25.00 60.00
FSAJEL Evan Longoria 30.00 80.00
FSAJJA Jose Altuve 60.00 150.00
FSAJJB Javier Baez 50.00 120.00
FSAJKG Ken Griffey Jr. 200.00 300.00
FSAJLD Lucas Duda 50.00 120.00
FSAJMA Matt Adams 20.00 50.00
FSAJMC Matt Carpenter 30.00 80.00
FSAJPG Paul Goldschmidt 30.00 80.00
FSAJRC Rusney Castillo 25.00 60.00
FSAJRCA Robinson Cano 60.00 150.00

2015 Topps Five Star Silver Signatures

STATED ODDS 1:13 HOBBY
STATED PRINT RUN 50 SER.#'d SETS
EXCHANGE DEADLINE 9/30/2017
*BLUE/20: .5X TO 1.2X
*PURPLE/25: .5X TO 1.2X
SSAG Andres Galarraga 15.00 40.00
SSBB Brandon Belt 8.00 20.00
SSBL Barry Larkin 25.00 60.00
SSCB Craig Biggio 12.00 30.00
SSCK Corey Kluber 8.00 20.00
SSCKE Clayton Kershaw 40.00 100.00
SSDF Doug Fister 6.00 15.00
SSDG Didi Gregorius 10.00 25.00
SSDM Don Mattingly 25.00 60.00
SSEE Edwin Encarnacion 10.00 25.00
SSEM Edgar Martinez 8.00 20.00
SSFV Fernando Valenzuela 10.00 25.00
SSGS George Springer 12.00 30.00
SSJA Jose Altuve 25.00 60.00
SSJAB Jose Abreu 10.00 25.00
SSJB Javier Baez 12.00 30.00
SSJHK Jung-Ho Kang 30.00 80.00
SSJP Joc Pederson 20.00 50.00
SSJS Jorge Soler 10.00 25.00
SSMF Maikel Franco 15.00 40.00
SSMG Mark Grace 8.00 20.00
SSOS Ozzie Smith 20.00 50.00
SSOV Omar Vizquel 15.00 40.00
SSPF Prince Fielder 12.00 30.00
SSPO Paul O'Neill 8.00 20.00
SSRC Rusney Castillo 8.00 20.00
SSRCL Roger Clemens 25.00 60.00
SSSM Starling Marte 10.00 25.00
SSTG Tom Glavine 15.00 40.00

2016 Topps Five Star Autographs

EXCHANGE DEADLINE 8/31/2018
FSAADZ Aledmys Diaz RC 4.00 10.00
FSAAGA Andres Galarraga 4.00 10.00
FSAAK Al Kaline 12.00 30.00
FSAAN Aaron Nola RC 5.00 12.00
FSAAP Andy Pettitte 15.00 40.00
FSAARE A.J. Reed RC 3.00 8.00
FSAARI Anthony Rizzo 25.00 60.00
FSAARU Addison Russell 10.00 25.00
FSABBO Barry Bonds
FSABH Bryce Harper
FSABJA Bo Jackson
FSABPO Buster Posey
FSABSN Blake Snell RC 10.00 25.00
FSACB Craig Biggio
FSACC Carlos Correa 12.00 30.00
FSACJ Chipper Jones
FSACRI Cal Ripken Jr.
FSACRO Carlos Rodon 8.00 20.00
FSACSA Chris Sale
FSACSC Curt Schilling
FSACSE Corey Seager RC 30.00 80.00
FSACY Carl Yastrzemski
FSADM Don Mattingly
FSADO David Ortiz 40.00 120.00
FSADW David Wright
FSAFH Felix Hernandez
FSAFL Franciso Lindor
FSAFT Frank Thomas
FSAGM Greg Maddux
FSAGS George Springer 8.00 20.00
FSAHA Hank Aaron
FSAHOL Hector Olivera RC 4.00 10.00
FSAHOW Henry Owens RC 4.00 10.00
FSAI Ichiro Suzuki
FSAIR Ivan Rodriguez
FSAJA Jose Altuve 30.00 80.00
FSAJBE Jose Berrios RC 4.00 10.00
FSAJDA Johnny Damon
FSAJDG Jacob deGrom 6.00 15.00
FSAJGR Jon Gray 3.00 8.00
FSAJPD Joc Pederson 8.00 20.00
FSAJPE Jose Peraza RC 5.00 12.00
FSAJR Jim Rice 8.00 20.00
FSAJSM John Smoltz
FSAJSO Jorge Soler 5.00 12.00
FSAJU Julio Urias RC
FSAJVA Jason Varitek 15.00 40.00
FSAKB Kris Bryant 75.00 200.00
FSAKG Ken Griffey Jr.
FSAKMA Kenta Maeda RC 8.00 20.00
FSAKS Kyle Schwarber RC 10.00 25.00
FSALGI Lucas Giolito RC 5.00 12.00
FSALGO Luis Gonzalez 4.00 10.00
FSALS Luis Severino RC 8.00 20.00
FSAMK Max Kepler RC 5.00 12.00
FSAMMA Manny Machado
FSAMMG Mark McGwire
FSAMP Mike Piazza
FSAMS Mallex Smith RC 3.00 8.00
FSAMSA Miguel Sano RC 5.00 12.00
FSAMTE Mark Teixeira
FSAMTR Mike Trout
FSANA Nolan Arenado 30.00 80.00
FSANM Nomar Mazara RC 10.00 25.00
FSANR Nolan Ryan
FSANS Noah Syndergaard 15.00 40.00
FSAOG Ozzie Guillen 3.00 8.00
FSAOS Ozzie Smith
FSAOV Omar Vizquel 5.00 12.00
FSAP Pele
FSAPOB Peter O'Brien RC 3.00 8.00
FSARCL Roger Clemens
FSARH Rickey Henderson
FSARJA Reggie Jackson
FSARJO Randy Johnson
FSARM Raul Mondesi 5.00 12.00
FSARP Rafael Palmeiro 6.00 15.00
FSARS Ross Stripling 3.00 8.00
FSARSA Ryne Sandberg
FSARST Robert Stephenson RC 3.00 8.00
FSASG Sonny Gray 5.00 12.00
FSASK Sandy Koufax
FSASMA Steven Matz 4.00 10.00
FSASP Stephen Piscotty RC 3.00 8.00
FSATGL Tom Glavine
FSATN Tyler Naquin RC 4.00 10.00
FSATS Trevor Story RC 10.00 25.00
FSATTR Trea Turner RC 10.00 25.00
FSATTU Troy Tulowitzki
FSATW Tyler White RC 5.00 12.00
FSAVS Vin Scully
FSAWC Willson Contreras RC 15.00 40.00

2016 Topps Five Star Autographs Gold

*GOLD: .5X TO 1.2X BASIC
STATED PRINT RUN 50 SER.#'d SETS
EXCHANGE DEADLINE 8/31/2018
FSAAP Andy Pettitte 20.00 50.00
FSACB Craig Biggio 15.00 40.00
FSACJ Chipper Jones 60.00 150.00
FSACRI Cal Ripken Jr. 60.00 150.00
FSACSC Curt Schilling 8.00 20.00
FSACSE Corey Seager 40.00 100.00
FSACY Carl Yastrzemski 50.00 120.00
FSADO David Ortiz 60.00 150.00
FSADW David Wright
FSAFH Felix Hernandez 20.00 50.00
FSAGM Greg Maddux
FSAJDA Johnny Damon 12.00 30.00
FSAJU Julio Urias 25.00 60.00
FSAJVA Jason Varitek 20.00 50.00
FSAMMA Manny Machado 50.00 120.00
FSAMMG Mark McGwire 60.00 150.00
FSAMP Mike Piazza
FSAMTE Mark Teixeira 10.00 25.00
FSANR Nolan Ryan 50.00 120.00
FSARCL Roger Clemens
FSARH Rickey Henderson
FSATGL Tom Glavine 15.00 40.00
FSAVS Vin Scully 300.00 600.00

2016 Topps Five Star Autographs Rainbow

*RAINBOW: .6X TO 1.5X BASIC
STATED ODDS 1:8 HOBBY
STATED PRINT RUN 25 SER.#'d SETS
EXCHANGE DEADLINE 8/31/2018
FSAAP Andy Pettitte 25.00 60.00
FSABBO Barry Bonds 100.00 250.00
FSABH Bryce Harper 100.00 250.00
FSABPO Buster Posey 60.00 150.00
FSACB Craig Biggio 20.00 50.00
FSACJ Chipper Jones 75.00 200.00
FSACRI Cal Ripken Jr. 75.00 200.00
FSACSA Chris Sale 20.00 50.00
FSACSC Curt Schilling 12.00 30.00
FSACSE Corey Seager 50.00 120.00
FSACY Carl Yastrzemski 60.00 150.00
FSADO David Ortiz 75.00 200.00
FSADW David Wright 20.00 50.00
FSAFH Felix Hernandez 25.00 60.00
FSAGM Greg Maddux 75.00 200.00
FSAI Ichiro Suzuki 400.00 600.00
FSAJDA Johnny Damon 15.00 40.00
FSAJU Julio Urias 30.00 80.00
FSAJVA Jason Varitek 25.00 60.00
FSAMMA Manny Machado 60.00 150.00
FSAMMG Mark McGwire 75.00 200.00
FSAMP Mike Piazza 75.00 200.00
FSAMTE Mark Teixeira 12.00 30.00
FSANR Nolan Ryan 60.00 150.00
FSARCL Roger Clemens 60.00 150.00
FSARH Rickey Henderson 60.00 150.00
FSATGL Tom Glavine 20.00 50.00
FSAVS Vin Scully 400.00 800.00

2016 Topps Five Star Golden Graphs

STATED ODDS 1:13 HOBBY
STATED PRINT RUN 50 SER.#'d SETS
EXCHANGE DEADLINE 8/31/2018
*BLUE/20: .5X TO 1.2X
*PURPLE/25: .5X TO 1.2X
FSGCAG Alex Gordon
FSGCAN Aaron Nola 6.00 15.00
FSGCAP Andy Pettitte
FSGCBJ Bo Jackson 30.00 80.00
FSGCBL Barry Larkin 20.00 50.00
FSGCBP Buster Posey 40.00 100.00
FSGCBW Bernie Williams 15.00 40.00
FSGCCB Craig Biggio 10.00 25.00
FSGCCC Carlos Correa 30.00 80.00
FSGCDO David Ortiz 50.00 120.00
FSGCEM Edgar Martinez 12.00 30.00
FSGCFL Francisco Lindor 40.00 100.00
FSGCFV Fernando Valenzuela 10.00 25.00
FSGCHOW Henry Owens
FSGCJA Jose Altuve 30.00 80.00
FSGCJC Jose Canseco 20.00 50.00
FSGCJS Jorge Soler
FSGCJV Jason Varitek 20.00 50.00
FSGCKB Kris Bryant 125.00 250.00
FSGCKM Kenta Maeda 15.00 40.00
FSGCKS Kyle Schwarber 30.00 80.00
FSGCLS Luis Severino 10.00 25.00
FSGCMS Miguel Sano 12.00 30.00
FSGCNG Nomar Garciaparra 15.00 40.00
FSGCNS Noah Syndergaard 12.00 30.00
FSGCOG Ozzie Guillen
FSGCOS Ozzie Smith 20.00 50.00
FSGCPM Paul Molitor 10.00 25.00
FSGCRF Rollie Fingers 8.00 20.00
FSGCRY Robin Yount 20.00 50.00
FSGCSP Stephen Piscotty
FSGCYC Yoenis Cespedes 12.00 30.00

2016 Topps Five Star Heart of a Champion Autographs

STATED PRINT RUN 25 SER.#'d SETS
EXCHANGE DEADLINE 8/31/2018
FSHCAP Andy Pettitte
FSHCBW Bernie Williams 15.00 40.00
FSHCCF Carlton Fisk
FSHCCS Curt Schilling 25.00 60.00
FSHCDE Dennis Eckersley 12.00 30.00
FSHCDO David Ortiz
FSHCEM Edgar Martinez 15.00 40.00
FSHCIR Ivan Rodriguez 20.00 50.00
FSHCJB Johnny Bench 25.00 60.00
FSHCJD Jacob deGrom
FSHCJS John Smoltz
FSHCLG Luis Gonzalez
FSHCLH Livan Hernandez
FSHCMW Michael Wacha
FSHCOS Ozzie Smith
FSHCPM Paul Molitor 15.00 40.00
FSHCRA Roberto Alomar
FSHCRC Roger Clemens 20.00 50.00
FSHCRF Rollie Fingers
FSHCRH Rickey Henderson 30.00 80.00
FSHCRJA Reggie Jackson 20.00 50.00
FSHCRJO Randy Johnson
FSHCSK Sandy Koufax
FSHCTG Tom Glavine 30.00 80.00
FSHCWD Wade Davis

2016 Topps Five Star Jumbo Patch Autographs

STATED ODDS 1:51 HOBBY
STATED PRINT RUN 25 SER.#'d SETS
EXCHANGE DEADLINE 8/31/2018
FAJPAP Andy Pettitte
FAJPBH Bryce Harper 150.00 300.00
FAJPCB Craig Biggio 60.00 150.00
FAJPCR Cal Ripken Jr.
FAJPDW David Wright 40.00 100.00
FAJPFF Freddie Freeman
FAJPFH Felix Hernandez
FAJPJD Jacob deGrom 40.00 100.00
FAJPMM Manny Machado 100.00 250.00
FAJPPM Paul Molitor 60.00 150.00
FAJPSM Steven Matz 100.00 250.00
FAJPVG Vladimir Guerrero

2016 Topps Five Star Silver Signatures

STATED ODDS 1:13 HOBBY
STATED PRINT RUN 50 SER.#'d SETS
EXCHANGE DEADLINE 8/31/2018
*BLUE/20: .5X TO 1.2X
*PURPLE/25: .5X TO 1.2X
FSSSAG Alex Gordon 6.00 15.00
FSSSAN Aaron Nola 12.00 30.00
FSSSAP Andy Pettitte 20.00 50.00
FSSSBJ Bo Jackson 30.00 80.00
FSSSBL Barry Larkin 20.00 50.00
FSSSBP Buster Posey 40.00 100.00
FSSSCB Craig Biggio 6.00 15.00
FSSSCK Clayton Kershaw 40.00 100.00
FSSSCS Chris Sale
FSSSDO David Ortiz 40.00 100.00
FSSSEM Edgar Martinez 12.00 30.00
FSSSFL Francisco Lindor 12.00 30.00
FSSSHOW Henry Owens
FSSSJA Jose Altuve 20.00 50.00
FSSSJC Jose Canseco 15.00 40.00
FSSSJH Jason Heyward 6.00 15.00
FSSSJV Jason Varitek 12.00 30.00
FSSSKB Kris Bryant 100.00 250.00
FSSSKM Kenta Maeda 10.00 25.00
FSSSKS Kyle Schwarber
FSSSLG Luis Gonzalez 8.00 20.00
FSSSLS Luis Severino 10.00 25.00
FSSSMS Miguel Sano 10.00 25.00
FSSSMT Mark Teixeira 20.00 50.00
FSSSNG Nomar Garciaparra 15.00 40.00
FSSSNS Noah Syndergaard 25.00 60.00
FSSSOG Ozzie Guillen 6.00 15.00
FSSSOS Ozzie Smith 10.00 25.00
FSSSRC Rod Carew 10.00 25.00
FSSSSP Stephen Piscotty
FSSSYC Yoenis Cespedes

2017 Topps Five Star Autographs

EXCHANGE DEADLINE 9/30/2019
FSAABE Andrew Benintendi RC 20.00 50.00
FSAABR Alex Bregman RC 25.00 60.00
FSAADI Aledmys Diaz 4.00 10.00
FSAAG Andres Galarraga 4.00 10.00
FSAAJ Aaron Judge RC 60.00 150.00
FSAAK Al Kaline 15.00 40.00
FSAARE Alex Reyes RC 4.00 10.00
FSAARI Anthony Rizzo 15.00 40.00
FSAARU Addison Russell 8.00 20.00
FSAAT Andrew Toles RC 3.00 8.00
FSABH Bryce Harper 75.00 200.00
FSABL Barry Larkin
FSACB Cody Bellinger RC 50.00 120.00
FSACC Carlos Correa
FSACFU Carson Fulmer RC 3.00 8.00
FSACJ Chipper Jones
FSACKE Clayton Kershaw
FSACKL Corey Kluber 6.00 15.00
FSACR Cal Ripken Jr.
FSACSA Chris Sale 10.00 25.00
FSACSE Corey Seager 15.00 40.00
FSADB Dellin Betances 4.00 10.00
FSADJ Derek Jeter
FSADM Don Mattingly
FSADS Dansby Swanson RC 12.00 30.00
FSADV Dan Vogelbach RC 5.00 12.00
FSADW Dave Winfield
FSAEM Edgar Martinez 6.00 15.00
FSAFF Freddie Freeman 10.00 25.00
FSAFL Francisco Lindor 12.00 30.00
FSAGC Gavin Cecchini RC 3.00 8.00
FSAGSP George Springer 8.00 20.00
FSAHA Hank Aaron
FSAHR Hunter Renfroe RC 4.00 10.00
FSAIR Ivan Rodriguez 6.00 15.00
FSAI Ichiro
FSAJAT Jose Altuve 20.00 50.00
FSAJBA Jeff Bagwell 20.00 50.00
FSAJBE Javier Baez 20.00 50.00
FSAJCA Jose Canseco 8.00 20.00
FSAJCO Jharel Cotton RC 3.00 8.00
FSAJDA Johnny Damon 6.00 15.00
FSAJDG Jacob deGrom 8.00 20.00
FSAJDL Jose De Leon RC 3.00 8.00
FSAJDO Josh Donaldson
FSAJG Juan Gonzalez 5.00 12.00
FSAJM Joe Musgrove RC 3.00 8.00
FSAJS John Smoltz
FSAJTH Jake Thompson RC 3.00 8.00
FSAJU Julio Urias 5.00 12.00
FSAKB Kris Bryant
FSAKM Kenta Maeda 6.00 15.00
FSAKSC Kyle Schwarber 5.00 12.00
FSAKSE Kyle Seager 3.00 8.00
FSALG Lucas Giolito 4.00 10.00
FSALW Luke Weaver RC 4.00 10.00
FSAMC Matt Carpenter 5.00 12.00
FSAMMA Manny Machado
FSAMMG Mark McGwire
FSAMMR Manny Margot RC 3.00 8.00
FSAMTA Masahiro Tanaka
FSAMTR Mike Trout
FSANR Nolan Ryan
FSANS Noah Syndergaard 8.00 20.00
FSAOS Ozzie Smith
FSAOV Omar Vizquel 4.00 10.00
FSARGR Randal Grichuk 3.00 8.00
FSARGS Robert Gsellman RC 3.00 8.00
FSARH Ryon Healy RC 4.00 10.00
FSARL Reynaldo Lopez RC 3.00 8.00
FSARO Roy Oswalt 4.00 10.00
FSART Raimel Tapia RC 4.00 10.00
FSASK Sandy Koufax
FSASMR Starling Marte 4.00 10.00
FSASMZ Steven Matz 4.00 10.00
FSATA Tyler Austin RC 5.00 12.00
FSATE Theo Epstein 50.00 120.00
FSATGS Tyler Glasnow RC 4.00 10.00
FSATGV Tom Glavine
FSATM Trey Mancini RC 4.00 10.00
FSATR Tim Raines 5.00 12.00
FSATS Trevor Story 5.00 12.00
FSAYG Yulieski Gurriel RC 8.00 20.00

2017 Topps Five Star Autographs Blue

*BLUE: .6X TO 1.5X BASIC
STATED PRINT RUN 25 SER.#'d SETS
EXCHANGE DEADLINE 9/30/2019
FSABL Barry Larkin 20.00 50.00
FSACC Carlos Correa 40.00 100.00
FSACJ Chipper Jones 50.00 120.00
FSACKE Clayton Kershaw 50.00 120.00
FSACR Cal Ripken Jr. 60.00 150.00
FSADM Don Mattingly 30.00 80.00
FSADW Dave Winfield 20.00 50.00
FSAJDO Josh Donaldson 10.00 25.00
FSAJS John Smoltz 12.00 30.00
FSAKB Kris Bryant 60.00 150.00
FSAMMA Manny Machado 30.00 80.00
FSAMMG Mark McGwire 40.00 100.00
FSANR Nolan Ryan 100.00 250.00
FSAOS Ozzie Smith 20.00 50.00
FSATGV Tom Glavine 12.00 30.00

2017 Topps Five Star Autographs Purple

*PURPLE: .5X TO 1.2X BASIC
STATED PRINT RUN 50 SER.#'d SETS
EXCHANGE DEADLINE 9/30/2019
FSABL Barry Larkin 15.00 40.00
FSACC Carlos Correa 30.00 80.00
FSACKE Clayton Kershaw 40.00 100.00
FSADM Don Mattingly 25.00 60.00
FSADW Dave Winfield 15.00 40.00
FSAJDO Josh Donaldson 8.00 20.00
FSAJS John Smoltz 10.00 25.00
FSAKB Kris Bryant 50.00 120.00
FSAMMA Manny Machado 25.00 60.00
FSAOS Ozzie Smith 15.00 40.00
FSATGV Tom Glavine 10.00 25.00

2017 Topps Five Star Golden Graphs

PRINT RUNS B/WN 30-50 COPIES PER
EXCHANGE DEADLINE 9/30/2019
GGABE Andrew Benintendi/50 25.00 60.00
GGABR Alex Bregman/50 15.00 40.00
GGARE Alex Reyes/50 8.00 20.00
GGCC Carlos Correa
GGCJ Chipper Jones
GGCK Corey Kluber/30 10.00 25.00
GGCSA Chris Sale/30 15.00 40.00
GGDPE Dustin Pedroia
GGDPR David Price
GGDS Dansby Swanson/50 15.00 40.00
GGDW Dave Winfield
GGFF Freddie Freeman/30 12.00 30.00
GGFL Francisco Lindor/50 20.00 50.00
GGGM Greg Maddux
GGJA Jose Altuve EXCH 25.00 60.00
GGJB Jeff Bagwell
GGJD Josh Donaldson
GGJS John Smoltz
GGJV Joey Votto
GGKB Kris Bryant
GGKM Kenta Maeda/30 10.00 25.00
GGKS Kyle Schwarber/50 15.00 40.00
GGMM Manny Machado
GGNS Noah Syndergaard/50 12.00 30.00
GGOV Omar Vizquel/30 6.00 15.00
GGRG Roger Clemens
GGRJ Randy Johnson
GGTG Tyler Glasnow/50 6.00 15.00
GGTR Tim Raines
GGYG Yulieski Gurriel/50 15.00 40.00

2017 Topps Five Star Golden Graphs Blue

*BLUE: .5X TO 1.2X BASIC
STATED PRINT RUN 20 SER.#'d SETS
EXCHANGE DEADLINE 9/30/2019
GGCC Carlos Correa 30.00 80.00
GGDPE Dustin Pedroia 20.00 50.00
GGDPR David Price 8.00 20.00
GGDW Dave Winfield 15.00 40.00
GGJB Jeff Bagwell 15.00 40.00
GGJS John Smoltz 15.00 40.00
GGJV Joey Votto 40.00 100.00
GGKB Kris Bryant 100.00 250.00
GGMM Manny Machado 30.00 80.00
GGTR Tim Raines 15.00 40.00

2017 Topps Five Star Golden Graphs Purple

*PURPLE: .5X TO 1.2X BASIC
STATED PRINT RUN 25 SER.#'d SETS
EXCHANGE DEADLINE 9/30/2019
GGDPE Dustin Pedroia 20.00 50.00
GGDPR David Price 8.00 20.00
GGDW Dave Winfield 15.00 40.00
GGJB Jeff Bagwell 15.00 40.00
GGJS John Smoltz 15.00 40.00
GGJV Joey Votto
GGKB Kris Bryant 100.00 250.00
GGMM Manny Machado 30.00 80.00
GGTR Tim Raines 15.00 40.00

2017 Topps Five Star Heart of a Champion Autographs

PRINT RUNS B/WN 5-35 COPIES PER
NO PRICING ON QTY 15 OR LESS
EXCHANGE DEADLINE 9/30/2019
FSHCAK Al Kaline/35 50.00 120.00
FSHCAP Andy Pettitte/35 15.00 40.00
FSHCARI Anthony Rizzo/35 30.00 80.00
FSHCARO Alex Rodriguez/25 100.00 250.00
FSHCARU Addison Russell/35 20.00 50.00
FSHCBL Barry Larkin/35 25.00 60.00
FSHCBP Buster Posey/25 50.00 120.00
FSHCCJ Chipper Jones/25 60.00 150.00
FSHCCK Corey Kluber/35 15.00 40.00
FSHCDO David Ortiz/25 50.00 120.00
FSHCDP Dustin Pedroia/35 20.00 50.00
FSHCEL Evan Longoria/25 15.00 40.00
FSHCEM Edgar Martinez/35 20.00 50.00
FSHCFR Frank Robinson/35 25.00 60.00
FSHCHA Hank Aaron/5
FSHCJBA Jeff Bagwell/35 20.00 50.00
FSHCJBE Javier Baez/35 30.00 80.00
FSHCJD Johnny Damon/35 12.00 30.00
FSHCJS John Smoltz/35 30.00 80.00
FSHCKB Kris Bryant/25 125.00 300.00
FSHCKS Kyle Schwarber/35 20.00 50.00
FSHCMM Mark McGwire/25 60.00 150.00
FSHCOS Ozzie Smith/35 20.00 50.00
FSHCOV Omar Vizquel/35 12.00 30.00
FSHCPK Paul Konerko/35 25.00 60.00
FSHCPM Pedro Martinez/25 50.00 120.00
FSHCRO Roy Oswalt/35 25.00 60.00
FSHCTG Tom Glavine/35 20.00 50.00

2017 Topps Five Star Jumbo Patch Autographs

PRINT RUNS B/WN 35-50 COPIES PER
EXCHANGE DEADLINE 9/30/2019
FAJPAJ Adam Jones/35 25.00 60.00
FAJPARI Anthony Rizzo
FAJPARU Addison Russell EXCH 15.00 40.00
FAJPBP Buster Posey
FAJPCC Carlos Correa/50 60.00 150.00
FAJPCJ Chipper Jones
FAJPCK Corey Kluber
FAJPDB Dellin Betances/50 12.00 30.00
FAJPDO David Ortiz
FAJPDPE Dustin Pedroia/35 25.00 60.00
FAJPDPR David Price
FAJPEL Evan Longoria/50 20.00 50.00
FAJPFF Freddie Freeman EXCH 20.00 50.00
FAJPGS George Springer/50 30.00 80.00
FAJPI Ichiro
FAJPJA Jose Altuve 40.00 100.00
FAJPJDG Jacob deGrom/50 25.00 60.00
FAJPJS John Smoltz/35 25.00 60.00
FAJPJT Jameson Taillon/35 20.00 50.00
FAJPJV Joey Votto/50 40.00 100.00
FAJPKSE Kyle Seager/35 20.00 50.00
FAJPMC Matt Carpenter/35 15.00 40.00
FAJPMF Michael Fulmer/35 10.00 25.00
FAJPMM Manny Machado
FAJPMS Miguel Sano/35 30.00 80.00
FAJPMT Masahiro Tanaka
FAJPNSY Noah Syndergaard/50 25.00 60.00
FAJPPM Pedro Martinez
FAJPSM Starling Marte/35 12.00 30.00
FAJPSP Stephen Piscotty
FAJPTGS Tyler Glasnow/35 20.00 50.00
FAJPTGV Tom Glavine
FAJPYC Yoenis Cespedes EXCH 25.00 60.00
FAJPYG Yulieski Gurriel

2017 Topps Five Star Jumbo Patch Autographs Gold

*GOLD: .5X TO 1.2X BASIC
STATED PRINT RUN 25 SER.#'d SETS
EXCHANGE DEADLINE 9/30/2019
FAJPCK Corey Kluber 40.00 100.00
FAJPDPR David Price 20.00 50.00
FAJPI Ichiro 400.00 600.00
FAJPMT Masahiro Tanaka 100.00 250.00
FAJPSP Stephen Piscotty 20.00 50.00
FAJPTGV Tom Glavine 40.00 100.00

2017 Topps Five Star Signatures

PRINT RUNS B/WN 5-20 COPIES PER
NO PRICING ON QTY 15 OR LESS
EXCHANGE DEADLINE 9/30/2019
FSIABE Andrew Benintendi/20 75.00 200.00
FSIAG Andres Galarraga/20 5.00 12.00
FSIBH Bryce Harper EXCH
FSICB Craig Biggio
FSICK Clayton Kershaw EXCH
FSICS Corey Seager EXCH
FSIJA Jose Altuve
FSIJC Jose Canseco/20 25.00 60.00
FSIJDO Josh Donaldson EXCH
FSIMMG Mark McGwire
FSIMT Mike Trout
FSIOV Omar Vizquel/20 20.00 50.00
FSIPM Pedro Martinez
FSISK Sandy Koufax

2017 Topps Five Star Silver Signatures

PRINT RUNS B/WN 30-50 COPIES PER
EXCHANGE DEADLINE 9/30/2019
SSABE Andrew Benintendi EXCH 30.00 80.00
SSAD Aledmys Diaz/50 5.00 12.00
SSAG Andres Galarraga/30 5.00 12.00
SSAJ Aaron Judge/50 125.00 300.00
SSAK Al Kaline
SSAP Andy Pettitte
SSARE Alex Reyes/50 6.00 15.00
SSBH Bryce Harper
SSBL Barry Larkin
SSCB Craig Biggio
SSCK Clayton Kershaw
SSCS Corey Seager
SSDM Don Mattingly
SSDS Dansby Swanson
SSEM Edgar Martinez/30 10.00 25.00
SSFT Frank Thomas
SSIR Ivan Rodriguez 10.00 25.00
SSJC Jose Canseco/30 25.00 60.00
SSJD Johnny Damon
SSJDG Jacob deGrom
SSJG Juan Gonzalez/30 12.00 30.00
SSJU Julio Urias/50 6.00 15.00
SSKS Kyle Schwarber/50 12.00 30.00
SSNS Noah Syndergaard/50 20.00 50.00
SSOS Ozzie Smith
SSOV Omar Vizquel/50 6.00 15.00
SSRO Roy Oswalt/30 5.00 12.00
SSYM Yoan Moncada

2017 Topps Five Star Silver Signatures Blue

*BLUE: .5X TO 1.2X BASIC
STATED PRINT RUN 20 SER.#'d SETS
EXCHANGE DEADLINE 9/30/2019
SSAK Al Kaline 25.00 50.00
SSAP Andy Pettitte 15.00 40.00
SSBL Barry Larkin 20.00 50.00
SSCS Corey Seager EXCH 25.00 60.00
SSDM Don Mattingly 30.00 80.00
SSDS Dansby Swanson 15.00 40.00
SSIR Ivan Rodriguez 12.00 30.00
SSJD Johnny Damon 10.00 25.00
SSJDG Jacob deGrom 20.00 50.00
SSOS Ozzie Smith 20.00 50.00

2017 Topps Five Star Silver Signatures Purple

*PURPLE: .5X TO 1.2X BASIC
STATED PRINT RUN 25 SER.#'d SETS
EXCHANGE DEADLINE 9/30/2019
SSAK Al Kaline 25.00 50.00
SSAP Andy Pettitte 15.00 40.00
SSBL Barry Larkin
SSCS Corey Seager EXCH 25.00 60.00
SSDM Don Mattingly 30.00 80.00
SSDS Dansby Swanson 15.00 40.00
SSIR Ivan Rodriguez 12.00 30.00
SSJD Johnny Damon 10.00 25.00
SSJDG Jacob deGrom 20.00 50.00

2018 Topps Five Star Autographs

EXCHANGE DEADLINE 8/31/2020
FSAAB Anthony Banda RC 3.00 8.00
FSAAH Austin Hays RC 5.00 12.00
FSAAI Anthony Rizzo EXCH 15.00 40.00
FSAAJ Aaron Judge 60.00 150.00
FSAAM Austin Meadows RC 10.00 25.00
FSAAN Aaron Nola 6.00 15.00
FSAAR Amed Rosario RC 5.00 12.00
FSAAV Alex Verdugo RC 5.00 12.00
FSAAW Alex Wood 3.00 8.00
FSABA Brian Anderson RC 4.00 10.00
FSABD Brian Dozier 4.00 10.00
FSABH Bryce Harper 75.00 200.00
FSABJ Bo Jackson 50.00 120.00
FSACB Charlie Blackmon 5.00 12.00
FSACF Clint Frazier RC 6.00 15.00
FSACK Corey Kluber 8.00 20.00
FSACR Cal Ripken Jr. 60.00 150.00
FSACS Chance Sisco RC 4.00 10.00

FSACT Chris Taylor EXCH 4.00 10.00
FSADF Dustin Fowler RC 3.00 8.00
FSADJ Derek Jeter 125.00 300.00
FSADM Don Mattingly 25.00 60.00
FSADO Dwight Gooden 10.00 25.00
FSADT Darryl Strawberry 12.00 30.00
FSAFL Francisco Lindor 25.00 60.00
FSAFM Francisco Mejia RC 4.00 10.00
FSAFT Frank Thomas 20.00 50.00
FSAGP George Springer 10.00 25.00
FSAGS Gary Sanchez 10.00 25.00
FSAGT Gleyber Torres RC 40.00 100.00
FSAHA Hank Aaron 175.00 350.00
FSAHB Harrison Bader RC 5.00 12.00
FSAHR Hunter Renfroe 3.00 8.00
FSAIH Ian Happ 4.00 10.00
FSAIK Ian Kinsler 4.00 10.00
FSAJA Jose Altuve 15.00 40.00
FSAJC Jose Canseco 10.00 25.00
FSAJE Jose Berrios 4.00 10.00
FSAJF Jack Flaherty RC 15.00 40.00
FSAJI J.D. Davis RC 4.00 10.00
FSAJL Jake Lamb 4.00 10.00
FSAJR Jose Ramirez 10.00 25.00
FSAJS Justin Smoak 3.00 8.00
FSAJSO Juan Soto RC 75.00 200.00
FSAJU Justin Upton 8.00 20.00
FSAJV Joey Votto EXCH 20.00 50.00
FSAKB Kris Bryant EXCH 50.00 120.00
FSAKD Khris Davis 5.00 12.00
FSAKS Kyle Schwarber 8.00 20.00
FSALS Lucas Sims RC 3.00 8.00
FSAMA Miguel Andujar RC 20.00 50.00
FSAMF Max Fried RC 10.00 25.00
FSAMM Mark McGwire 30.00 80.00
FSAMO Matt Olson 3.00 8.00
FSAMR Manny Margot 3.00 8.00
FSAMT Mike Trout 150.00 400.00
FSANR Nolan Ryan
FSAOA Ozzie Albies RC 12.00 30.00
FSAPD Paul DeJong 5.00 12.00
FSAPG Paul Goldschmidt 10.00 25.00
FSARA Ronald Acuna RC 75.00 200.00
FSARD Rafael Devers RC 12.00 30.00
FSARH Rhys Hoskins RC 20.00 50.00
FSARM Ryan McMahon RC 4.00 10.00
FSASI Scott Kingery RC 12.00 30.00
FSASK Sandy Koufax
FSASM Starling Marte 5.00 12.00
FSASO Shohei Ohtani RC 125.00 300.00
FSATA Tyler Mahle RC 4.00 10.00
FSATM Trey Mancini 4.00 10.00
FSATP Tommy Pham 3.00 8.00
FSATS Travis Shaw 3.00 8.00
FSAVC Victor Caratini RC 4.00 10.00
FSAVR Victor Robles RC 10.00 25.00
FSAWB Walker Buehler RC 40.00 100.00
FSAWC Willson Contreras 8.00 20.00
FSAWM Whit Merrifield 8.00 20.00

2018 Topps Five Star Autographs Blue

*BLUE: .5X TO 1.5X BASIC
STATED ODDS 1:10 HOBBY
STATED PRINT RUN 25 SER.#'d SETS
EXCHANGE DEADLINE 8/31/2020
FSAHA Hank Aaron 200.00 400.00
FSANR Nolan Ryan 50.00 120.00

2018 Topps Five Star Autographs Purple

*PURPLE: .5X TO 1.2X BASIC
RANDOM INSERTS IN PACKS
STATED PRINT RUN 50 SER.#'d SETS
EXCHANGE DEADLINE 8/31/2020

2018 Topps Five Star Career Year Autographs

STATED ODDS 1:18 HOBBY
PRINT RUNS B/WN 5-50 COPIES PER
NO PRICING ON QTY 15 OR LESS
EXCHANGE DEADLINE 8/31/2020
CRAAJ Andruw Jones/50 12.00 30.00
CRAAK Al Kaline/35 25.00 50.00
CRABG Bob Gibson/45 12.00 30.00
CRACJ Chipper Jones/25 60.00 150.00
CRACR Cal Ripken Jr./25 60.00 150.00
CRADE Dennis Eckersley/35 10.00 25.00
CRADM Don Mattingly/45 40.00 100.00
CRADP Dustin Pedroia/45 12.00 30.00
CRADS Darryl Strawberry/45 12.00 30.00
CRAEM Edgar Martinez/35 15.00 40.00
CRAFT Frank Thomas/45 40.00 100.00
CRAJC Jose Canseco/35 15.00 40.00
CRAJP Jim Palmer/35 15.00 40.00
CRAJS John Smoltz/45 20.00 50.00
CRAJV Joey Votto/35 20.00 50.00
CRAKB Kris Bryant/45 50.00 120.00
CRALB Lou Brock/50 12.00 30.00
CRAMM Mark McGwire/25 40.00 100.00
CRAOS Ozzie Smith/45 20.00 50.00
CRARA Roberto Alomar/35 15.00 40.00
CRARS Ryne Sandberg/25 25.00 60.00
CRARY Robin Yount/45 30.00 80.00
CRASC Steve Carlton/45 15.00 40.00
CRATG Tom Glavine/45 12.00 30.00
CRAWB Wade Boggs/25 40.00 100.00
CRAWC Will Clark/45 25.00 60.00

2018 Topps Five Star Golden Graphs

STATED ODDS 1:18 HOBBY
PRINT RUNS B/WN 35-50 COPIES PER
EXCHANGE DEADLINE 8/31/2020
FGGAR Amed Rosario/35 8.00 20.00
FGGAT Alan Trammell/35 25.00 60.00
FGGBG Bob Gibson/35 15.00 40.00
FGGDP Dustin Pedroia/35 12.00 30.00
FGGET Eric Thames/50 5.00 12.00
FGGFF Freddie Freeman/35 20.00 50.00
FGGFL Francisco Lindor/35 25.00 60.00
FGGGS George Springer/35 12.00 30.00
FGGJC Jose Canseco/35 12.00 30.00
FGGJd Jacob deGrom/35 20.00 50.00
FGGJM Jack Morris/35 20.00 50.00
FGGJP Jim Palmer EXCH 12.00 30.00
FGGLB Lou Brock/35 15.00 40.00
FGGNS Noah Syndergaard/35 10.00 25.00
FGGPD Paul DeJong/35 6.00 15.00
FGGPG Paul Goldschmidt/35 12.00 30.00
FGGSM Starling Marte/35 8.00 20.00
FGGTG Tom Glavine/35 12.00 30.00
FGGWC Will Clark/35 30.00 80.00
FGGYM Yadier Molina/35 40.00 100.00

2018 Topps Five Star Golden Graphs Blue

*BLUE: .5X TO 1.2X BASIC
STATED ODDS 1:45 HOBBY
STATED PRINT RUN 20 SER.#'d SETS
EXCHANGE DEADLINE 8/31/2020
FGGAN Aaron Nola 15.00 40.00
FGGCJ Chipper Jones 50.00 120.00
FGGCK Corey Kluber 15.00 40.00
FGGJA Jose Altuve 25.00 60.00
FGGJS John Smoltz 30.00 80.00
FGGKB Kris Bryant EXCH 50.00 120.00
FGGSO Shohei Ohtani 200.00 500.00

2018 Topps Five Star Golden Graphs Purple

*PURPLE: .5X TO 1.2X BASIC
STATED ODDS 1:36 HOBBY
STATED PRINT RUN 25 SER.#'d SETS
EXCHANGE DEADLINE 8/31/2020
FGGCK Corey Kluber 15.00 40.00
FGGSO Shohei Ohtani 200.00 500.00

2018 Topps Five Star Jumbo Patch Autographs

STATED ODDS 1:16 HOBBY
PRINT RUNS B/WN 30-35 COPIES PER
EXCHANGE DEADLINE 8/31/2020
FSJPAB Andrew Benintendi EXCH 50.00 120.00
FSJPCB Charlie Blackmon/30 25.00 60.00
FSJPCI Craig Kimbrel/30 25.00 60.00
FSJPCS Chris Sale/30 30.00 80.00
FSJPDG Didi Gregorius/30 40.00 100.00
FSJPIR Ivan Rodriguez/35 50.00 120.00
FSJPJA Jose Altuve/30 50.00 120.00
FSJPJd Jacob deGrom/30 40.00 100.00
FSJPJH Josh Harrison/30 20.00 50.00
FSJPJM Johnny Damon/30 15.00 40.00
FSJPKD Khris Davis/30 15.00 40.00
FSJPKE Kyle Seager/30 10.00 25.00
FSJPPM Pedro Martinez/35 50.00 120.00
FSJPRA Roberto Alomar/30 40.00 100.00
FSJPRD Rafael Devers/30 40.00 100.00
FSJPRH Rickey Henderson/35 40.00 100.00
FSJPRHE Rickey Henderson/35 40.00 100.00
FSJPTG Tom Glavine/30 20.00 50.00
FSJPWM Whit Merrifield/35 20.00 50.00

2018 Topps Five Star Jumbo Patch Autographs Gold

*GOLD: .5X TO 1.2X BASIC
STATED ODDS 1:28 HOBBY
PRINT RUNS B/WN 5-25 COPIES PER
NO PRICING ON QTY 5
EXCHANGE DEADLINE 8/31/2020
FSJPAG Alex Bregman 50.00 120.00
FSJPAN Aaron Nola 50.00 120.00
FSJPBB Byron Buxton 20.00 50.00
FSJPBP Buster Posey EXCH 60.00 150.00
FSJPCJ Chipper Jones 60.00 150.00
FSJPDO David Ortiz 75.00 200.00
FSJPDP Dustin Pedroia 50.00 120.00
FSJPFF Freddie Freeman 50.00 120.00
FSJPGS Gary Sanchez 30.00 80.00
FSJPI Ichiro 300.00 500.00
FSJPIH Ian Happ 15.00 40.00
FSJPJC J.P. Crawford 12.00 30.00
FSJPJV Joey Votto 40.00 100.00
FSJPKS Kyle Schwarber 15.00 40.00
FSJPOA Ozzie Albies 40.00 100.00
FSJPPG Paul Goldschmidt 30.00 80.00
FSJPSM Starling Marte 40.00 100.00
FSJPTP Tommy Pham 6.00 15.00
FSJPYG Yuli Gurriel 15.00 40.00
FSJPYM Yadier Molina 100.00 250.00

2018 Topps Five Star Signatures

STATED ODDS 1:13 HOBBY
PRINT RUNS B/WN 5-50 COPIES PER
NO PRICING ON QTY 15 OR LESS
EXCHANGE DEADLINE 8/31/2020
FSSAI Anthony Rizzo/35 20.00 50.00
FSSAK Al Kaline/35 25.00 50.00
FSSAP Andy Pettitte/35 25.00 60.00
FSSAR Amed Rosario/45 6.00 15.00
FSSBG Bob Gibson/35 15.00 40.00
FSSBH Bryce Harper EXCH 75.00 200.00
FSSBJ Bo Jackson/25 40.00 100.00
FSSBP Buster Posey EXCH 30.00 80.00
FSSCB Craig Biggio/35 10.00 25.00
FSSCF Clint Frazier/45 10.00 25.00
FSSCJ Chipper Jones/35 50.00 120.00
FSSCR Cal Ripken Jr./25 60.00 150.00
FSSCS Chris Sale/35 15.00 40.00
FSSDM Don Mattingly/35 40.00 100.00
FSSFL Francisco Lindor/35 20.00 50.00
FSSFT Frank Thomas/35 30.00 80.00
FSSGS Gary Sanchez/35 15.00 40.00
FSSGT Gleyber Torres/50 40.00 100.00
FSSJA Jose Altuve/45 20.00 50.00
FSSJB Jeff Bagwell/35 12.00 30.00
FSSJD Johnny Damon/35 8.00 20.00
FSSJN Jose Canseco/35 12.00 30.00
FSSJS John Smoltz/35 20.00 50.00
FSSJU Justin Upton/35 8.00 20.00
FSSJV Joey Votto/35 25.00 60.00
FSSKB Kris Bryant 50.00 120.00
FSSMC Mark McGwire/25 40.00 100.00
FSSMP Mike Piazza/20 40.00 100.00
FSSMR Mariano Rivera/20 125.00 300.00
FSSNR Nolan Ryan/25 75.00 200.00
FSSOA Ozzie Albies/35 15.00 40.00
FSSOS Ozzie Smith/35 20.00 50.00
FSSPM Pedro Martinez/20 50.00 120.00
FSSRA Ronald Acuna/50 75.00 200.00
FSSRC Roger Clemens/20 25.00 60.00
FSSRD Rafael Devers/35 20.00 50.00
FSSRJ Randy Johnson/20 40.00 100.00
FSSSO Shohei Ohtani/25 75.00 200.00
FSSTG Tom Glavine/35 15.00 40.00
FSSTR Tim Raines/35 8.00 20.00
FSSWL Will Clark/45 25.00 60.00
FSSYM Yadier Molina/45 40.00 100.00

2018 Topps Five Star Silver Signatures

STATED ODDS 1:18 HOBBY
PRINT RUNS B/WN 35-50 COPIES PER
EXCHANGE DEADLINE 8/31/2020
FFSSAO Amed Rosario/35 8.00 20.00
FFSSBB Byron Buxton/35 5.00 12.00
FFSSBD Brian Dozier/35 6.00 15.00
FFSSBY Bert Blyleven/35 10.00 25.00
FFSSCA Charlie Blackmon EXCH 6.00 15.00
FFSSCF Clint Frazier/35 10.00 25.00
FFSSCK Craig Kimbrel/35 8.00 20.00
FFSSCS Chris Sale/35 15.00 40.00
FFSSCY Christian Yelich/50 25.00 60.00
FFSSDE Dennis Eckersley/35 10.00 25.00
FFSSJD Johnny Damon/35 8.00 20.00
FFSSOA Ozzie Albies/35 20.00 50.00
FFSSRD Rafael Devers/35 20.00 50.00
FFSSTM Trey Mancini/35 10.00 25.00
FFSSTR Tim Raines/35 8.00 20.00

2018 Topps Five Star Silver Signatures Blue

*BLUE: .5X TO 1.2X BASIC
STATED ODDS 1:45 HOBBY
STATED PRINT RUN 20 SER.#'d SETS
EXCHANGE DEADLINE 8/31/2020
FFSSAB Adrian Beltre 25.00 60.00
FFSSAK Al Kaline 25.00 50.00
FFSSAR Anthony Rizzo EXCH 25.00 60.00
FFSSJU Justin Upton 12.00 30.00
FFSSJV Joey Votto EXCH 20.00 50.00
FFSSLS Luis Severino 15.00 40.00
FFSSRA Roberto Alomar 20.00 50.00
FFSSRC Rod Carew 15.00 40.00
FFSSRS Ryne Sandberg 25.00 60.00
FFSSSO Shohei Ohtani EXCH 200.00 500.00
FFSSVR Victor Robles 20.00 50.00
FFSSWB Wade Boggs 25.00 60.00
FFSSWC Willson Contreras 12.00 30.00

2018 Topps Five Star Silver Signatures Purple

*PURPLE: .5X TO 1.2X BASIC
STATED ODDS 1:36 HOBBY
STATED PRINT RUN 25 SER.#'d SETS
EXCHANGE DEADLINE 8/31/2020
FFSSAK Al Kaline 25.00 50.00
FFSSJU Justin Upton 12.00 30.00
FFSSRA Roberto Alomar 20.00 50.00
FFSSSO Shohei Ohtani EXCH 200.00 500.00
FFSSVR Victor Robles 20.00 50.00
FFSSWC Willson Contreras 12.00 30.00

2019 Topps Five Star Autographs

EXCHANGE DEADLINE 8/31/2021
FSAAA Aaron Judge 75.00 200.00
FSAAN Aaron Nola 6.00 15.00
FSAAR Anthony Rizzo 15.00 40.00
FSABM Brandon Nimmo 4.00 10.00
FSABW Bryse Wilson RC 8.00 20.00
FSACB Corbin Burnes RC 5.00 12.00
FSACM Cedric Mullins RC 5.00 12.00
FSACRJ Cal Ripken Jr. 60.00 150.00
FSADH Dakota Hudson RC 4.00 10.00
FSADJ Danny Jansen RC 3.00 8.00
FSADP Daniel Ponce de Leon RC 5.00 12.00
FSADS Darryl Strawberry 12.00 30.00
FSADST DJ Stewart RC 4.00 10.00
FSAEJ Eloy Jimenez RC 25.00 60.00
FSAFF Freddie Freeman 15.00 40.00
FSAFL Francisco Lindor 30.00 80.00
FSAFT Frank Thomas 20.00 50.00
FSAFTJ Fernando Tatis Jr. RC 125.00 300.00
FSAJA Jose Altuve 15.00 40.00
FSAJB Jake Bauers RC 5.00 12.00
FSAJC Jake Cave RC 4.00 10.00
FSAJCA Jose Canseco 10.00 25.00
FSAJD Jacob deGrom 8.00 20.00
FSAJE Jean Segura 5.00 12.00
FSAJF Jack Flaherty 8.00 20.00
FSAJH Josh Hader 5.00 12.00
FSAJJ Josh James RC 5.00 12.00
FSAJM Jeff McNeil RC 12.00 30.00
FSAJR Jose Ramirez 6.00 15.00
FSAJS Justus Sheffield RC 12.00 30.00
FSAJSM Justin Smoak 3.00 8.00
FSAJSO Juan Soto 40.00 100.00
FSAJV Joey Votto 15.00 40.00
FSAKA Kolby Allard RC 5.00 12.00
FSAKIE Carter Kieboom RC 10.00 25.00
FSAKST Kohl Stewart RC 4.00 10.00
FSAKW Kyle Wright RC 5.00 12.00
FSALS Luis Severino 6.00 15.00
FSALV Luke Voit 30.00 80.00
FSAMA Matt Kemp 4.00 10.00
FSAMCH Matt Chapman 6.00 15.00
FSAMH Mitch Haniger 4.00 10.00
FSAMI Miguel Andujar 5.00 12.00
FSAMK Michael Kopech RC 10.00 25.00
FSAMM Max Muncy 6.00 15.00
FSAMO Matt Olson 3.00 8.00
FSAMR Mark McGwire
FSAMS Myles Straw RC 5.00 12.00
FSAMT Mike Trout
FSANM Nick Martini RC 3.00 8.00
FSANS Nick Senzel RC EXCH 12.00 30.00
FSAPA Pete Alonso RC 50.00 120.00
FSAPC Patrick Corbin 6.00 15.00
FSAPD Paul DeJong 8.00 20.00
FSAPG Paul Goldschmidt 10.00 25.00
FSAPW Patrick Wisdom RC 3.00 8.00
FSARA Ronald Acuna Jr. 60.00 150.00
FSARD Rafael Devers 12.00 30.00
FSARH Rhys Hoskins 10.00 25.00
FSARL Ramon Laureano RC 10.00 25.00
FSARM Reese McGuire RC 5.00 12.00
FSART Rowdy Tellez RC 5.00 12.00
FSASD Steven Duggar RC 4.00 10.00
FSASM Steven Matz 4.00 10.00
FSASO Shohei Ohtani 100.00 250.00
FSATB Trevor Bauer 5.00 12.00
FSATP Tommy Pham 3.00 8.00
FSATRI Trevor Richards RC 3.00 8.00
FSATT Touki Toussaint RC 3.00 8.00
FSAVGJ Vladimir Guerrero Jr. RC 50.00 120.00
FSAVR Victor Robles 8.00 20.00
FSAWA Williams Astudillo RC 3.00 8.00
FSAWM Whit Merrifield 10.00 25.00
FSAYK Yusei Kikuchi RC 6.00 15.00

2019 Topps Five Star Autographs Blue

*BLUE: .6X TO 1.5X BASIC
STATED ODDS 1:11 HOBBY
STATED PRINT RUN 25 SER.#'d SETS
EXCHANGE DEADLINE 8/31/2021
FSABJ Bo Jackson 40.00 100.00
FSAKB Kris Bryant 60.00 150.00
FSAKD Khris Davis 8.00 20.00

2019 Topps Five Star Autographs Purple

*PURPLE: .5X TO 1.2X BASIC
STATED ODDS 1:6 HOBBY
STATED PRINT RUN 50 SER.#'d SETS
EXCHANGE DEADLINE 8/31/2021
FSAKD Khris Davis 6.00 15.00

2019 Topps Five Star Five Tool Phenom Autographs

STATED ODDS 1:24 HOBBY
STATED PRINT RUN 25 SER.#'d SETS
EXCHANGE DEADLINE 8/31/2021
FTPAJ Aaron Judge 100.00 250.00
FTPBB Byron Buxton 6.00 15.00
FTPBM Brandon Nimmo 6.00 15.00
FTPFL Francisco Lindor 15.00 40.00
FTPFTJ Fernando Tatis Jr. 250.00 600.00
FTPJS Juan Soto 75.00 200.00
FTPKB Kris Bryant 60.00 150.00
FTPKS Kyle Schwarber EXCH 12.00 30.00
FTPMA Miguel Andujar 8.00 20.00
FTPMC Matt Chapman 10.00 25.00
FTPMO Matt Olson 10.00 25.00
FTPMT Mike Trout 300.00 500.00
FTPNS Nick Senzel EXCH 50.00 120.00
FTPOA Ozzie Albies EXCH 15.00 40.00
FTPPA Pete Alonso 100.00 250.00
FTPRAC Ronald Acuna Jr. 75.00 200.00
FTPRD Rafael Devers 15.00 40.00
FTPRH Rhys Hoskins 20.00 50.00
FTPSO Shohei Ohtani 100.00 250.00
FTPVGJ Vladimir Guerrero Jr. 100.00 250.00
FTPVR Victor Robles 10.00 25.00
FTPWC Willson Contreras 6.00 15.00

2019 Topps Five Star Golden Graphs

STATED ODDS 1:26 HOBBY
PRINT RUNS B/WN 25-50 COPIES PER
EXCHANGE DEADLINE 8/31/2021
*PURPLE/25: .4X TO 1X p/r 30
*PURPLE/25: .5X TO 1.2X p/r 50
*BLUE/20: .4X TO 1X p/r 25-30
*BLUE/20: .5X TO 1.2X p/r 50
GGTP Tony Perez/30 15.00 40.00
GGAB Adrian Beltre/25 20.00 50.00
GGAK Al Kaline/30 25.00 50.00
GGBB Bert Blyleven/50 8.00 20.00
GGBS Blake Snell/30 6.00 15.00
GGDA Dale Murphy/30 25.00 60.00
GGDAP David Price/30 8.00 20.00
GGDM Don Mattingly/25 40.00 100.00
GGFM Fred McGriff/30 15.00 40.00
GGGS George Springer/25 15.00 40.00
GGJC Jose Canseco/30 12.00 30.00
GGJM Juan Marichal/30 12.00 30.00
GGJV Jason Varitek/30 15.00 40.00
GGKB Kris Bryant/25 50.00 120.00
GGKD Khris Davis/30 10.00 25.00
GGKS Kyle Schwarber/30 12.00 30.00
GGMC Matt Carpenter/30 8.00 20.00
GGMK Matt Kemp/50 6.00 15.00
GGMO Marcell Ozuna/50 6.00 15.00
GGNR Nolan Ryan/25 75.00 200.00
GGPA Peter Alonso/50 40.00 100.00
GGPD Paul DeJong/50 8.00 20.00
GGRC Rod Carew/25 15.00 40.00
GGRH Rhys Hoskins/30 30.00 80.00
GGRS Ryne Sandberg/25 40.00 100.00
GGRY Robin Yount/25 20.00 50.00

2019 Topps Five Star Jumbo Patch Autographs

STATED ODDS 1:45 HOBBY
PRINT RUNS B/WN 15-25 COPIES PER
NO PRICING ON QTY 15
EXCHANGE DEADLINE 8/31/2021
AJPAN Aaron Nola
AJPAP Albert Pujols
AJPAR Anthony Rizzo
AJPBN Brandon Nimmo
AJPBS Blake Snell
AJPCF Carlton Fisk
AJPCK Corey Kluber
AJPCRJ Cal Ripken Jr.
AJPDE Dennis Eckersley
AJPDJ Derek Jeter
AJPDP David Price/25 15.00 40.00
AJPFF Freddie Freeman/25 30.00 80.00
AJPIS Ichiro
AJPJF Jack Flaherty
AJPJUS Justin Smoak
AJPJV Joey Votto/25 50.00 120.00
AJPKB Kris Bryant
AJPKD Khris Davis/25 20.00 50.00
AJPKGJ Ken Griffey Jr.
AJPKS Kyle Schwarber
AJPLS Luis Severino
AJPLU Luis Urias
AJPMA Miguel Andujar
AJPMAC Matt Chapman
AJPMAM Max Muncy
AJPMAO Marcell Ozuna
AJPMC Miguel Cabrera/25 75.00 200.00
AJPMO Matt Olson
AJPMP Mike Piazza
AJPMR Mariano Rivera
AJPMT Mike Trout
AJPNS Noah Syndergaard/25 15.00 40.00
AJPOA Ozzie Albies
AJPPD Paul DeJong
AJPRD Rafael Devers/25 40.00 100.00
AJPRH Rhys Hoskins/25 50.00 12.00
AJPSO Shohei Ohtani
AJPSP Salvador Perez
AJPTHU Torii Hunter
AJPTT Touki Toussaint
AJPVR Victor Robles
AJPWC Willson Contreras
AJPWM Whit Merrifield

2019 Topps Five Star Pentamerous Penmanship Autographs

STATED ODDS 1:27 HOBBY
PRINT RUN B/WN 15-25 COPIESPER
NO PRICING ON QTY 15
EXCHANGE DEADLINE 8/31/2021
PPAK Al Kaline/25 30.00 80.00
PPBL Barry Larkin/25 20.00 50.00
PPCS Chris Sale/25 10.00 25.00
PPDM Don Mattingly/25 60.00 150.00
PPFL Francisco Lindor/25 15.00 40.00
PPFT Frank Thomas/25 40.00 100.00
PPJA Jose Altuve/25 20.00 50.00
PPJDG Jacob deGrom/25 30.00 80.00
PPJO Juan Soto/25 40.00 100.00
PPKGJ Ken Griffey Jr./25
PPMP Mike Piazza
PPMR Mariano Rivera
PPOS Ozzie Smith/25 10.00 25.00
PPPG Paul Goldschmidt/25 20.00 50.00
PPR Ronald Acuna Jr./25 75.00 200.00
PPRH Rhys Hoskins/25 25.00 60.00
PPRY Robin Yount/25 25.00 60.00
PPSK Sandy Koufax
PPVGJ Vladimir Guerrero Jr./25 100.00 250.00

2019 Topps Five Star Signatures

STATED ODDS 1:27 HOBBY
PRINT RUNS B/WN 5-20 COPIES PER
NO PRICING ON QTY 10 OR LESS
EXCHANGE DEADLINE 8/31/2021
FSAK Al Kaline/20 30.00 80.00
FSAR Anthony Rizzo/20 40.00 100.00
FSBG Bob Gibson/20 15.00 40.00
FSBL Barry Larkin/20 20.00 50.00
FSBP Buster Posey
FSCS Chris Sale/20 15.00 40.00
FSDJ Derek Jeter EXCH
FSDM Dale Murphy/20 50.00 120.00
FSDON Don Mattingly/20 40.00 100.00
FSDS Deion Sanders/20 40.00 100.00
FSFL Francisco Lindor/20 25.00 60.00
FSHA Hank Aaron EXCH
FSHM Hideki Matsui/20 50.00 120.00
FSJA Jose Altuve/20 50.00 120.00
FSJAV Jason Varitek/20 40.00 100.00
FSJDG Jacob deGrom/20 50.00 120.00
FSJM Juan Marichal/20 12.00 30.00
FSJUS Juan Soto/20 75.00 200.00
FSKB Kris Bryant/20 75.00 200.00
FSKGJ Ken Griffey Jr./20 125.00 300.00
FSKS Kyle Schwarber/20 20.00 50.00
FSMM Mark McGwire
FSMP Mike Piazza
FSMT Mike Trout
FSOS Ozzie Smith/20 25.00 60.00
FSPG Paul Goldschmidt/20 20.00 50.00
FSRA Ronald Acuna Jr./20 100.00 250.00
FSSO Shohei Ohtani
FSVGJ Vladimir Guerrero Jr./20 100.00 250.00

2019 Topps Five Star Silver Signatures

COMMON p/r 25-30 5.00 12.00
SEMIS p/r 25-30 6.00 15.00
UNLISTED p/r 25-30 8.00 20.00
STATED ODDS 1:25 HOBBY
PRINT RUNS B/WN 25-50 COPIES PER
EXCHANGE DEADLINE 8/31/2021
*PURPLE/25: .4X TO 1X p/r 30
*PURPLE/25: .5X TO 1.2X p/r 50
*BLUE/20: .4X TO 1X p/r 25-30
*BLUE/20: .5X TO 1.2X p/r 50
SSAD Andre Dawson/30 12.00 30.00
SSAM Andrew McCutchen/30 50.00 120.00
SSBG Bob Gibson/30 20.00 50.00
SSCAF Carlton Fisk/30 15.00 40.00
SSCJ Chipper Jones/25 50.00 120.00
SSCS Chris Sale/30 12.00 30.00
SSDE Dennis Eckersley/30 12.00 30.00
SSDS Darryl Strawberry/50 15.00 40.00
SSEJ Eloy Jimenez/30 50.00 120.00
SSEM Edgar Martinez/30 20.00 50.00
SSIR Ivan Rodriguez/30 20.00 50.00
SSJP Jorge Posada/30 20.00 50.00
SSJS Juan Soto/50 75.00 200.00
SSJSM John Smoltz/30 15.00 40.00
SSLB Lou Brock/30 15.00 40.00
SSMC Miguel Cabrera/25 50.00 120.00
SSMK Michael Kopech/50 8.00 20.00
SSMR Mariano Rivera/25 100.00 250.00
SSRA Roberto Alomar/30 20.00 50.00
SSRP Rafael Palmeiro/50 6.00 15.00
SSSC Steve Carlton/30 15.00 40.00
SSTG Tom Glavine/30 12.00 30.00
SSTH Torii Hunter/30 10.00 25.00
SSTR Tim Raines/30 8.00 20.00
SSVG Vladimir Guerrero/30 25.00 60.00
SSVGJ Vladimir Guerrero Jr./30 100.00 250.00
SSVR Victor Robles/50 10.00 25.00
SSYK Yusei Kikuchi/30 10.00 25.00

2020 Topps Five Star Autographs

STATED ODDS 1:8 HOBBY
EXCHANGE DEADLINE 7/31/2022
FSAAA Aaron Judge EXCH 100.00 250.00
FSAAAZ Aristides Aquino RC 8.00 20.00
FSAAN Aaron Nola 10.00 25.00
FSAAT Abraham Toro RC 4.00 10.00
FSABB Bo Bichette RC EXCH 50.00 120.00
FSABM Brendan McKay RC 5.00 12.00
FSABP Buster Posey
FSACRJ Cal Ripken Jr.
FSADC Dylan Cease RC 6.00 15.00
FSADM Dustin May RC 20.00 50.00
FSAEJ Eloy Jimenez 15.00 40.00
FSAFF Dansby Swanson 12.00 30.00
FSAFT Frank Thomas 40.00 100.00
FSAFTJ Fernando Tatis Jr. EXCH 100.00 250.00
FSAGL Gavin Lux RC EXCH 30.00 80.00
FSAGS George Springer 8.00 20.00
FSAGT Gleyber Torres 30.00 80.00
FSAJA Jose Altuve 12.00 30.00
FSAJCA Jose Canseco 12.00 30.00
FSAJD Jacob deGrom 12.00 30.00
FSAJF Jack Flaherty 10.00 25.00
FSAJL Jesus Luzardo RC 6.00 15.00
FSAJM Jeff McNeil 8.00 20.00
FSAJR J.T. Realmuto 15.00 40.00
FSAJRZ Jake Rogers RC 3.00 8.00
FSAJS Jorge Soler 5.00 12.00
FSAJSO Juan Soto 60.00 150.00
FSAJV Jaylin Davis RC 5.00 12.00
FSAJX Justin Dunn RC 4.00 10.00
FSAJY Jordan Yamamoto RC 4.00 10.00
FSAKH Keston Hiura 8.00 20.00
FSAKHK Kwang-Hyun Kim RC 40.00 100.00
FSAKIE Carter Kieboom 5.00 12.00
FSAKL Kyle Lewis RC 40.00 100.00
FSALR Luis Robert RC 150.00 400.00
FSALW Logan Webb RC 4.00 10.00
FSAMD Mauricio Dubon RC 4.00 10.00
FSAMGZ Mitch Garver 3.00 8.00
FSAMO Matt Olson 10.00 25.00
FSAMR Mark McGwire
FSAMSO Mike Soroka 10.00 25.00
FSAMT Mike Trout 250.00 600.00
FSAMW Matt Thaiss RC 4.00 10.00
FSANH Nico Hoerner RC 12.00 30.00
FSANS Nick Senzel 5.00 12.00
FSANX Nick Solak RC 8.00 20.00
FSAPA Pete Alonso 30.00 80.00
FSAPC Patrick Corbin 4.00 10.00
FSAPG Paul Goldschmidt 20.00 50.00
FSARA Ronald Acuna Jr. 75.00 200.00
FSARG Robel Garcia RC 3.00 8.00
FSARH Rhys Hoskins 12.00 30.00
FSARL Ramon Laureano 6.00 15.00
FSARRA Randy Arozarena RC 50.00 120.00
FSASA Shogo Akiyama RC 12.00 30.00
FSASH Sam Hilliard RC 5.00 12.00
FSASM Sean Murphy RC 5.00 12.00
FSASO Shohei Ohtani
FSASY Shun Yamaguchi RC 4.00 10.00
FSATE Tommy Edman 8.00 20.00
FSATG Trent Grisham RC 10.00 25.00
FSAWC Willson Contreras 8.00 20.00
FSAWM Whit Merrifield 5.00 12.00
FSAWS Will Smith 6.00 15.00
FSAYA Yordan Alvarez RC 30.00 80.00
FSAYT Yoshi Tsutsugo RC 40.00 100.00

2020 Topps Five Star Autographs Blue

*BLUE: .6X TO 1.5X BASIC
STATED ODDS 1:14 HOBBY
STATED PRINT RUN 25 SER.#'d SETS
EXCHANGE DEADLINE 7/31/2022

2020 Topps Five Star Autographs Purple

*PURPLE: .5X TO 1.2X BASIC
STATED ODDS 1:8 HOBBY
STATED PRINT RUN 50 SER.#'d SETS
EXCHANGE DEADLINE 7/31/2022

2020 Topps Five Star Five Tool Phenom Autographs

STATED ODDS 1:28 HOBBY
STATED PRINT RUN 25 SER.#'d SETS
EXCHANGE DEADLINE 7/31/2020
FTPAJ Aaron Judge EXCH 125.00 300.00
FTPARI Austin Riley 20.00 50.00
FTPBB Luis Robert
FTPBH Bryce Harper 125.00 300.00
FTPBMC Brendan McKay 10.00 25.00
FTPBR Brendan Rodgers
FTPCKI Carter Kieboom 6.00 15.00
FTPCY Christian Yelich EXCH 40.00 100.00
FTPDSW Dansby Swanson 30.00 80.00
FTPFTJ Fernando Tatis Jr. EXCH 100.00 250.00
FTPGT Gleyber Torres 60.00 150.00
FTPJS Juan Soto 75.00 200.00
FTPKHI Keston Hiura 20.00 50.00
FTPMC Nolan Arenado 50.00 120.00
FTPMT Mike Trout 300.00 800.00
FTPNHO Nico Hoerner 30.00 80.00
FTPNS Aristides Aquino 20.00 50.00
FTPNSE Nick Senzel 8.00 20.00
FTPPA Pete Alonso 50.00 120.00
FTPRAC Ronald Acuna Jr.
FTPRD Rafael Devers 20.00 50.00
FTPRH Rhys Hoskins 25.00 60.00
FTPSO Shohei Ohtani 75.00 200.00
FTPVGJ Vladimir Guerrero Jr.
FTPVR Victor Robles 10.00 25.00
FTPWC Willson Contreras 12.00 30.00
FTPYAL Yordan Alvarez

2020 Topps Five Star Golden Graphs

STATED ODDS 1:24 HOBBY
STATED PRINT RUN 40 SER.#'d SETS
EXCHANGE DEADLINE 7/31/2022
*PURPLE/25: .5X TO 1.2X BASIC
*BLUE/20: .5X TO 1.2X BASIC
GGAAQ Aristides Aquino
GGAD Andre Dawson 15.00 40.00
SSEM Edgar Martinez 20.00 50.00
GGBG Bob Gibson 25.00 60.00
GGBLA Barry Larkin 20.00 50.00
GGBMC Brendan McKay
GGCAF Carlton Fisk 10.00 25.00
GGCCS CC Sabathia EXCH 15.00 40.00
GGCFI Cecil Fielder 15.00 40.00
GGCPA Chris Paddack 10.00 25.00
GGCY Christian Yelich
GGDE Dennis Eckersley 10.00 25.00
GGDJ David Justice 15.00 40.00
GGDST Jesus Luzardo
GGFTJ Fernando Tatis Jr. EXCH
GGJAB Jim Abbott 15.00 40.00
GGJBA Jeff Bagwell 25.00 60.00
GGJDE Johnny Dench
GGJLU Darryl Strawberry 12.00 30.00
GGJMA Joe Mauer 30.00 80.00
GGJSM John Smoltz 25.00 60.00
GGJTH Jim Thome EXCH 30.00 80.00
GGJVO Joey Votto
GGLB Lou Brock 30.00 80.00
GGMC Miguel Cabrera
GGMVA Mo Vaughn
GGNGA Nomar Garciaparra 15.00 40.00
GGNRY Nolan Ryan
GGOZZ Ozzie Smith 25.00 60.00
GGRA Roberto Alomar 15.00 40.00
GGRHE Rickey Henderson
GGSC Steve Carlton 10.00 25.00
GGTGL Tom Glavine 15.00 40.00
GGTL Tim Lincecum 30.00 80.00
GGTR Tim Raines 12.00 30.00
GGVG Vladimir Guerrero 20.00 50.00
GGWBO Wade Boggs 20.00 50.00
GGYAL Yordan Alvarez

2020 Topps Five Star Jumbo Patch Autographs

STATED ODDS 1:26 HOBBY
PRINT RUNS B/WN 15-25 COPIESPER
NO PRICING ON QTY 15 OR LESS
EXCHANGE DEADLINE 7/31/2022
AJPAA Aristides Aquino/25 50.00 120.00
AJPAB Andrew Benintendi/25 30.00 80.00
AJPAN Aaron Nola/25 50.00 120.00
AJPBH Bryce Harper
AJPBMC Brendan McKay/25
AJPBS Blake Snell EXCH
AJPCCS CC Sabathia/25 30.00 80.00
AJPCY Christian Yelich EXCH
AJPDJL DJ LeMahieu/25 60.00 150.00
AJPEJ Eloy Jimenez
AJPFM Fred McGriff
AJPFTJ Fernando Tatis Jr. EXCH
AJPGS George Springer/25 30.00 80.00
AJPGTO Gleyber Torres/25 75.00 200.00

AJPIROD Ivan Rodriguez
AJPJA Jose Altuve/25
AJPJD Jacob deGrom
AJPJDM J.D. Martinez/25 15.00 40.00
AJPJF Jack Flaherty/25 60.00 150.00
AJPJMA Joe Mauer
AJPJMC Jeff McNeil/25 30.00 80.00
AJPJS Juan Soto
AJPJTR J.T. Realmuto/25 75.00 200.00
AJPJVA Jason Varitek
AJPKHI Keston Hiura/25 60.00 150.00
AJPMA Miguel Andujar/25 25.00 60.00
AJPMC Miguel Cabrera/25 60.00 150.00
AJPMKE Max Kepler/25 25.00 60.00
AJPMT Mike Trout/25 500.00 1200.00
AJPMTA Masahiro Tanaka EXCH
AJPMTE Mark Teixeira/25 30.00 80.00
AJPPCO Patrick Corbin
AJPRD Rafael Devers/25 40.00 100.00
AJPRHO Ryan Howard
AJPSO Shohei Ohtani
AJPTL Tim Lincecum
AJPVGJ Vladimir Guerrero Jr.
AJPWBO Wade Boggs
AJPWC Willson Contreras
AJPWM Whit Merrifield/25 30.00 80.00
AJPXBO Xander Bogaerts/25 40.00 100.00

2020 Topps Five Star Pentamerous Penmanship Autographs

STATED ODDS 1:29 HOBBY
PRINT RUNS B/WN 15-25 COPIESPER
NO PRICING ON QTY 15 OR LESS
EXCHANGE DEADLINE 7/31/2022
PPAJ Aaron Judge
PPBHA Bryce Harper
PPCRJ Cal Ripken Jr.
PPDM Don Mattingly/25 50.00 120.00
PPDMU Dale Murphy/25 25.00 60.00
PPFTJ Fernando Tatis Jr. EXCH
PPJB Jeff Bagwell/25 20.00 50.00
PPJSO Juan Soto/25 100.00 250.00
PPKGJ Ken Griffey Jr.
PPMM Darryl Strawberry/25 25.00 60.00
PPMSC Mike Schmidt
PPNAR Nolan Arenado/25 75.00 200.00
PPPA Pete Alonso/25 50.00 120.00
PPPG Paul Goldschmidt/25 25.00 60.00
PPRAJ Ronald Acuna Jr.
PPRD Rafael Devers/25 25.00 60.00
PPVGJ Vladimir Guerrero Jr./25
PPWBO Wade Boggs
PPWBU Walker Buehler/25 30.00 80.00
PPWC Will Clark/25 30.00 80.00

2020 Topps Five Star Signatures

STATED ODDS 1:31 HOBBY
PRINT RUNS B/WN 5-25 COPIES PER
NO PRICING ON QTY 10 OR LESS
EXCHANGE DEADLINE 7/31/2022
FSAJ Aaron Judge EXCH
FSBG Yordan Alvarez/20
FSBL Barry Larkin/20 25.00 60.00
FSCFI Carlton Fisk/20 20.00 50.00
FSCY Christian Yelich EXCH
FSDJ Derek Jeter/25 250.00 600.00
FSDM Dale Murphy/20 15.00 40.00
FSDON Don Mattingly/20 40.00 100.00
FSDWR David Wright/20 25.00 60.00
FSEJ Luis Robert/20 200.00 500.00
FSEM Edgar Martinez
FSFT Frank Thomas/20 40.00 100.00
FSFTJ Fernando Tatis Jr.
FSGT Gleyber Torres/20 40.00 100.00
FSHA Hank Aaron/20 200.00 500.00
FSJA Jose Altuve/20 15.00 40.00
FSJB Jeff Bagwell/20 40.00 100.00
FSJDG Jacob deGrom/20 25.00 60.00
FSJMA Joe Mauer/20 40.00 100.00
FSJUS Juan Soto
FSMR Mariano Rivera
FSMS Mike Schmidt
FSMT Mike Trout
FSNAR Nolan Arenado/20 50.00 120.00
FSOS Ozzie Smith/20 30.00 80.00
FSPA Pete Alonso/20 60.00 150.00
FSPG Paul Goldschmidt/20 20.00 50.00
FSRA Ronald Acuna Jr.
FSRC Roger Clemens
FSRD Rafael Devers/20 20.00 50.00
FSRH Rhys Hoskins/20 15.00 40.00
FSTG Tom Glavine/20 20.00 50.00
FSTL Tim Lincecum/20 30.00 80.00
FSVGJ Vladimir Guerrero Jr./20 50.00 120.00
FSWC Will Clark/20 30.00 80.00
FSWIC Willson Contreras

2020 Topps Five Star Silver Signatures

STATED ODDS 1:24 HOBBY
STATED PRINT RUN 40 SER.#'d SETS
EXCHANGE DEADLINE 7/31/2022
*PURPLE/25: .5X TO 1.2X BASIC
*BLUE/20: .5X TO 1.2X BASIC
SSAPE Andy Pettitte 15.00 40.00
SSBB Bert Blyleven 8.00 20.00
SSDM Don Mattingly 40.00 100.00
SSDMU Dale Murphy 25.00 60.00
SSDWR David Wright 20.00 50.00
SSFM Fred McGriff 20.00 50.00
SSIROD Ivan Rodriguez 15.00 40.00
SSJDM J.D. Martinez 12.00 30.00
SSJGO Juan Gonzalez 12.00 30.00
SSJM Juan Marichal 12.00 30.00
SSJV Jason Varitek 12.00 30.00
SSKLE Kyle Lewis 100.00 250.00
SSKWO Kerry Wood 15.00 40.00
SSLRO Luis Robert
SSLT Luis Tiant 8.00 20.00
SSMBR Michael Brantley 10.00 25.00
SSMGR Mark Grace 20.00 50.00
SSMSC Mike Schmidt
SSNHO Nico Hoerner
SSRHO Ryan Howard 25.00 60.00
SSPA Pete Alonso
SSRC Rod Carew 15.00 40.00
SSRF Rollie Fingers 10.00 25.00
SSRS Ryne Sandberg
SSRY Robin Yount 25.00 60.00
SSTHE Todd Helton 15.00 40.00
SSTMA Tino Martinez 20.00 50.00
SSTPE Tony Perez 15.00 40.00
SSWB Walker Buehler 20.00 50.00
SSWC Will Clark 25.00 60.00
SSYTS Yoshi Tsutsugo 50.00 120.00

2017 Topps Gallery

COMP.SET w/o SP's (150) 20.00 50.00
STATED SP ODDS 1:20 PACKS
PRINTING PLATE ODDS 1:1217 HOBBY
PLATE PRINT RUN 1 SET PER COLOR
BLACK-CYAN-MAGENTA-YELLOW ISSUED
NO PLATE PRICING DUE TO SCARCITY
1 Mike Trout 1.50 4.00
2 Yoenis Cespedes .30 .75
3 Andrew McCutchen .30 .75
4 Jose Berrios .25 .60
5 Carlos Rodon .25 .60
6 Archie Bradley
7 Joey Gallo .25 .60
8 Steven Matz .25 .60
9 Amir Garrett RC .30 .75
10 Jose Altuve .25 .60
11 Adam Jones .25 .60
12 Max Kepler .25 .60
13 Carlos Correa .30 .75
14 Tyler Austin RC .50 1.25
15 Yoan Moncada RC 1.00 2.50
16 Trevor Story .30 .75
17 George Springer .25 .60
18 Addison Russell .30 .75
19 Carson Fulmer RC .30 .75
20 Evan Longoria .25 .60
21 Hunter Pence .25 .60
22 Ryon Healy RC .40 1.00
23 Hunter Dozier RC .30 .75
24 Charlie Blackmon .30 .75
25 Bryce Harper .50 1.25
26 Yu Darvish .30 .75
27 Noah Syndergaard .25 .60
28 Sean Newcomb RC .30 .75
29 Taijuan Walker .20 .50
30 Justin Bour .25 .60
31 Francisco Lindor .30 .75
32 Gregory Polanco .25 .60
33 Dansby Swanson RC .75 2.00
34 Jake Arrieta .25 .60
35 Antonio Senzatela RC .30 .75
36 Tim Anderson .30 .75
37 DJ LeMahieu .30 .75
38 Tyler Glasnow RC .40 1.00
39 Adrian Beltre .30 .75
40 Josh Donaldson .25 .60
41 Brett Phillips RC .40 1.00
42 Alex Bregman RC 1.25 3.00
43 Matt Carpenter .30 .75
44 Eduardo Rodriguez .20 .50
45 Matt Kemp .25 .60
46 Wil Myers .20 .50
47 Jackie Bradley Jr. .30 .75
48 Dustin Pedroia .30 .75
49 Jharel Cotton RC .30 .75
50 Kris Bryant .40 1.00
51 Javier Baez .40 1.00
52 Paul DeJong RC 1.00 2.50
53 Kenta Maeda .25 .60
54 Jose De Leon RC .30 .75
55 Jose Bautista .25 .60
56 Hunter Renfroe RC .40 1.00
57 Jameson Taillon .25 .60
58 Daniel Murphy .25 .60
59 Khris Davis .30 .75
60 Paul Goldschmidt .30 .75
61 Jacob deGrom .30 .75
62 Yasmani Grandal .20 .50
63 Kendall Graveman .20 .50
64 German Marquez RC .50 1.25
65 Aaron Nola .25 .60
66 Maikel Franco .25 .60
67 Kyle Seager .20 .50
68 Orlando Arcia RC .50 1.25
69 Blake Snell .25 .60
70 Giancarlo Stanton .30 .75
71 Alex Reyes RC .40 1.00
72 Luis Severino .25 .60
73 Corey Kluber .25 .60
74 Michael Conforto .25 .60
75 Stephen Strasburg .30 .75
76 Stephen Piscotty .25 .60
77 Miguel Sano .25 .60
78 Edwin Encarnacion .30 .75
79 Jake Thompson RC .30 .75
80 Freddie Freeman .40 1.00
81 Magneuris Sierra RC .50 1.25
82 Anthony Alford RC .30 .75
83 Aledmys Diaz .25 .60
84 Trey Mancini RC .60 1.50
85 Troy Tulowitzki .30 .75
86 Trea Turner .25 .60
87 Kevin Kiermaier .25 .60
88 Yulieski Gurriel RC .50 1.25
89 Hanley Ramirez .25 .60
90 Eric Thames .25 .60
91 Dinelson Lamet RC .30 .75
92 Mark Trumbo .20 .50
93 Ian Happ RC .60 1.50
94 Jesse Winker RC .30 .75
95 Josh Bell RC .75 2.00
96 Manny Margot RC .30 .75
97 Ketel Marte .25 .60
98 Salvador Perez .25 .60
99 Randal Grichuk .20 .50
100 Clayton Kershaw .60 1.50
101 Cole Hamels .25 .60
102 Chris Davis .20 .50
103 Ty Blach RC .30 .75
104 Reynaldo Lopez RC .30 .75
105 Daniel Norris .20 .50
106 Robert Gsellman RC .30 .75
107 Bradley Zimmer RC .40 1.00
108 Joe Musgrove RC .30 .75
109 Mitch Haniger RC .50 1.25
110 Chris Sale .30 .75
111 Ryan Braun .25 .60
112 Keon Broxton .20 .50
113 Andrew Toles .20 .50
114 David Dahl RC .40 1.00
115 Justin Verlander .30 .75
116 Felix Hernandez .25 .60
117 Aaron Judge RC 4.00 10.00
118 Adrian Gonzalez .25 .60
119 Buster Posey .40 1.00
120 Corey Seager .30 .75
121 Christian Yelich .40 1.00
122 Zack Greinke .25 .60
123 Carlos Gonzalez .25 .60
124 Christian Arroyo RC .50 1.25
125 Manny Machado .30 .75
126 Andrew Benintendi RC 1.00 2.50
127 Rick Porcello .25 .60
128 Greg Bird .25 .60
129 Jordan Montgomery RC .50 1.25
130 Nolan Arenado .40 1.00
131 Matt Harvey .25 .60
132 David Price .25 .60
133 Gary Sanchez .30 .75
134 Matt Duffy .20 .50
135 Kyle Schwarber .30 .75
136 Brian Dozier .30 .75
137 Ichiro .40 1.00
138 Luke Weaver RC .40 1.00
139 Jake Lamb .25 .60
140 Anthony Rizzo .50 1.25
141 Julio Urias .30 .75
142 Michael Fulmer .20 .50
143 Cody Bellinger RC 3.00 8.00
144 J.D. Martinez .30 .75
145 Didi Gregorius .25 .60
146 Gerrit Cole .30 .75
147 Brandon Finnegan .20 .50
148 Lucas Giolito .25 .60
149 Lewis Brinson RC .50 1.25
150 Max Scherzer .30 .75
151 Gary Carter SP 3.00 8.00
152 Jose Abreu SP 4.00 10.00
153 Willson Contreras SP 4.00 10.00
154 Johnny Cueto SP 3.00 8.00
155 Lou Gehrig SP 6.00 15.00
156 Nelson Cruz SP 4.00 10.00
157 Andrew Miller SP 3.00 8.00
158 Eric Hosmer SP 3.00 8.00
159 Todd Frazier SP 3.00 8.00
160 Roberto Clemente SP 10.00 25.00
161 Albert Pujols SP 5.00 12.00
162 Frank Thomas SP 4.00 10.00
163 Joey Votto SP 5.00 12.00
164 Tom Glavine SP 3.00 8.00
165 Ted Williams SP 6.00 15.00
166 Bo Jackson SP 4.00 10.00
167 Ian Kinsler SP 3.00 8.00
168 Jonathan Lucroy SP 3.00 8.00
169 Chipper Jones SP 4.00 10.00
170 Ernie Banks SP 4.00 10.00
171 Miguel Cabrera SP 6.00 15.00
172 Ian Desmond SP 2.50 6.00
173 Jason Kipnis SP 3.00 8.00
174 Chris Archer SP 2.50 6.00
175 Jackie Robinson SP 6.00 15.00
176 Starling Marte SP 3.00 8.00
177 Jose Canseco SP 3.00 8.00
178 Fernando Valenzuela SP 5.00 12.00
179 Xander Bogaerts SP 4.00 10.00
180 Derek Jeter SP 10.00 25.00
181 Dee Gordon SP 5.00 12.00
182 Jon Lester SP 3.00 8.00
183 Rickey Henderson SP 6.00 15.00
184 Rougned Odor SP 3.00 8.00
185 Cal Ripken Jr. SP 8.00 20.00
186 Kolie Calhoun SP 2.50 6.00
187 Mark McGwire SP 5.00 12.00
188 John Smoltz SP 6.00 15.00
189 Don Mattingly SP 8.00 20.00
190 Ken Griffey Jr. SP 5.00 12.00
191 Marcell Ozuna SP 4.00 10.00
192 Robinson Cano SP 3.00 8.00
193 Mookie Betts SP 6.00 15.00
194 Ryne Sandberg SP 5.00 12.00
195 Nolan Ryan SP 6.00 15.00
196 Duke Snider SP 3.00 8.00
197 David Ortiz SP 4.00 10.00
198 Masahiro Tanaka SP 3.00 8.00
199 Adam Eaton SP 4.00 10.00
200 Babe Ruth SP 5.00 12.00

2017 Topps Gallery Artist Promo

DB Dan Bergren 1.00 2.50
MS Mayumi Seto 1.00 2.50

2017 Topps Gallery Artist Proof

*ARTIST PROOF: .75X TO 2X BASIC
*ARTIST PROOF RC: .5X TO 1.2X BASIC
FOUR PER VALUE BLASTER

2017 Topps Gallery Blue

*BLUE: 4X TO 10X BASIC
*BLUE RC: 2.5X TO 6X BASIC
STATED ODDS 1:98 PACKS
STATED PRINT RUN 50 SER.#'d SETS

2017 Topps Gallery Canvas

*CANVAS: .1X TO 2.5X BASIC
*CANVAS RC: .6X TO 1.5X BASIC
TWO PER FAT PACK

2017 Topps Gallery Green

*GREEN: 2X TO 5X BASIC
*GREEN RC: 1.2X TO 3X BASIC
STATED ODDS 1:50 PACKS
STATED PRINT RUN 99 SER.#'d SETS

2017 Topps Gallery Orange

*ORANGE: 6X TO 15X BASIC
*ORANGE RC: 4X TO 10X BASIC
STATED ODDS 1:196 PACKS
STATED PRINT RUN 25 SER.#'d SETS

2017 Topps Gallery Private Issue

*PRIVATE: 1.5X TO 4X BASIC
*PRIVATE RC: 1X TO 2.5X BASIC
STATED ODDS 1:8 PACKS
STATED PRINT RUN 250 SER.#'d SETS

2017 Topps Gallery Autographs

STATED ODDS 1:15 PACKS
STATED SP ODDS 1:2115 PACKS
NO SP PRICING DUE TO SCARCITY
EXCHANGE DEADLINE 10/31/2019
1 Mike Trout
5 Carlos Rodon 3.00 8.00
6 Archie Bradley 2.50 6.00
7 Joey Gallo 6.00 15.00
8 Steven Matz 3.00 8.00
9 Amir Garrett 2.50 6.00
10 Jose Altuve 25.00 60.00
11 Adam Jones
13 Carlos Correa
14 Tyler Austin 6.00 15.00
15 Yoan Moncada 25.00 60.00
17 George Springer 8.00 20.00
20 Evan Longoria 6.00 15.00
25 Bryce Harper
27 Noah Syndergaard 10.00 25.00
28 Sean Newcomb 3.00 8.00
29 Taijuan Walker 2.50 6.00
30 Justin Bour
33 Dansby Swanson 10.00 25.00
35 Antonio Senzatela 2.50 6.00
36 Tim Anderson 4.00 10.00
37 DJ LeMahieu
40 Josh Donaldson
41 Brett Phillips 3.00 8.00
42 Alex Bregman 15.00 40.00
44 Eduardo Rodriguez 2.50 6.00
49 Jharel Cotton 2.50 6.00
50 Kris Bryant
52 Paul DeJong 4.00 10.00
56 Hunter Renfroe 4.00 10.00
57 Jameson Taillon
60 Paul Goldschmidt 12.00 30.00
61 Jacob DeGrom 10.00 25.00
63 Kendall Graveman 2.50 6.00
64 German Marquez 4.00 10.00
71 Alex Reyes 5.00 12.00
72 Luis Severino
76 Stephen Piscotty
78 Edwin Encarnacion 10.00 25.00
81 Magneuris Sierra 6.00 15.00
82 Anthony Alford 3.00 8.00
84 Trey Mancini 6.00 15.00
85 Troy Tulowitzki
87 Kevin Kiermaier 3.00 8.00
88 Yulieski Gurriel 5.00 12.00
91 Dinelson Lamet 2.50 6.00
93 Ian Happ 5.00 12.00
94 Jesse Winker 4.00 10.00
96 Manny Margot 2.50 6.00
97 Ketel Marte 3.00 8.00
103 Ty Blach 2.50 6.00
104 Reynaldo Lopez 2.50 6.00
105 Daniel Norris 3.00 8.00
106 Robert Gsellman 2.50 6.00
108 Joe Musgrove 3.00 8.00
109 Mitch Haniger 4.00 10.00
110 Chris Sale
111 Ryan Braun
112 Keon Broxton 3.00 8.00
113 Andrew Toles 2.50 6.00
116 Felix Hernandez
117 Aaron Judge 75.00 200.00
119 Buster Posey
120 Corey Seager
124 Christian Arroyo 4.00 10.00
125 Manny Machado 25.00 60.00
126 Andrew Benintendi 20.00 50.00
128 Greg Bird 3.00 8.00
129 Jordan Montgomery 4.00 10.00
134 Matt Duffy 2.50 6.00
135 Kyle Schwarber 5.00 12.00
137 Ichiro 150.00 400.00
138 Luke Weaver 3.00 8.00
140 Anthony Rizzo
143 Cody Bellinger EXCH 50.00 120.00
147 Brandon Finnegan 2.50 6.00
148 Lucas Giolito 3.00 8.00
149 Lewis Brinson 4.00 10.00

2017 Topps Gallery Autographs Blue

*BLUE: .6X TO 1.5X BASIC
STATED ODDS 1:116 PACKS
PRINT RUNS B/WN 40-50 COPIES PER
EXCHANGE DEADLINE 10/31/2019
10 Jose Altuve/50 40.00 100.00
30 Justin Bour/40 5.00 12.00
57 Jameson Taillon/50 12.00 30.00
72 Luis Severino/50 10.00 25.00
76 Stephen Piscotty/50 10.00 25.00
85 Troy Tulowitzki/50 6.00 15.00

2017 Topps Gallery Autographs Green

*GREEN: .5X TO 1.2X BASIC
STATED ODDS 1:69 PACKS
STATED PRINT RUN 99 SER.#'d SETS
EXCHANGE DEADLINE 10/31/2019
72 Luis Severino 8.00 20.00

2017 Topps Gallery Autographs Orange

*ORANGE: .75X TO 2X BASIC
STATED ODDS 1:195 PACKS
PRINT RUNS B/WN 10-25 COPIES PER
NO PRICING ON QTY 10
EXCHANGE DEADLINE 10/31/2019
10 Jose Altuve/25 50.00 120.00
15 Yoan Moncada/25 30.00 80.00
27 Noah Syndergaard/25 12.00 30.00
30 Justin Bour/25 6.00 15.00
72 Luis Severino/25 12.00 30.00
76 Stephen Piscotty/25 12.00 30.00
110 Chris Sale/25 12.00 30.00
119 Buster Posey/10 40.00 100.00
120 Corey Seager/25 40.00 100.00

2017 Topps Gallery Expressionists

STATED ODDS 1:82 PACKS
E1 Paul Goldschmidt 3.00 8.00
E2 Ichiro 4.00 10.00
E3 Yoenis Cespedes 3.00 8.00
E4 Addison Russell 3.00 8.00
E5 Carlos Santana 2.50 6.00
E6 Jose Altuve 2.50 6.00
E7 Jackie Bradley Jr. 3.00 8.00
E8 Matt Carpenter 3.00 8.00
E9 Mike Trout 12.00 30.00
E10 David Price 2.50 6.00
E11 Kris Bryant 10.00 25.00
E12 Bryce Harper 5.00 12.00
E13 Francisco Lindor 3.00 8.00
E14 Corey Seager 3.00 8.00
E15 Corey Kluber 2.50 6.00
E16 Clayton Kershaw 6.00 15.00
E17 Noah Syndergaard 2.50 6.00
E18 Adrian Beltre 3.00 8.00
E19 Daniel Murphy 2.50 6.00
E20 Justin Verlander 3.00 8.00
E21 Max Scherzer 3.00 8.00
E22 Felix Hernandez 2.50 6.00
E23 Nolan Arenado 4.00 10.00
E24 Giancarlo Stanton 3.00 8.00
E25 Chris Sale 3.00 8.00
E26 Josh Donaldson 2.50 6.00
E27 Carlos Correa 3.00 8.00
E28 Mookie Betts 5.00 12.00
E29 Evan Longoria 2.50 6.00
E30 Buster Posey 4.00 10.00

2017 Topps Gallery Hall of Fame

STATED ODDS 1:5 PACKS
*GREEN/250: 1.2X TO 3X BASIC
*BLUE/99: 2X TO 5X BASIC
*ORAGE/25: 3X TO 8X BASIC
HOF1 Ken Griffey Jr. 1.25 3.00
HOF2 Ted Williams 1.25 3.00
HOF3 Carlton Fisk .50 1.25
HOF4 Bob Feller .50 1.25
HOF5 Craig Biggio .50 1.25
HOF6 Hank Aaron 1.25 3.00
HOF7 Richie Ashburn .50 1.25
HOF8 George Brett 1.50 4.00
HOF9 Tim Raines .50 1.25
HOF10 Roberto Clemente 1.50 4.00
HOF11 Willie McCovey .50 1.25
HOF12 Joe Morgan .50 1.25
HOF13 Harmon Killebrew .60 1.50
HOF14 Dave Winfield .50 1.25
HOF15 Sandy Koufax 1.25 3.00
HOF16 Johnny Bench .60 1.50
HOF17 Lou Gehrig 1.25 3.00
HOF18 Ivan Rodriguez .50 1.25
HOF19 Jim Palmer .50 1.25
HOF20 Randy Johnson .60 1.50
HOF21 Rod Carew .50 1.25
HOF22 Reggie Jackson .50 1.25
HOF23 Wade Boggs .50 1.25
HOF24 Roberto Alomar .50 1.25
HOF25 Cal Ripken Jr. 2.00 5.00
HOF26 Ozzie Smith .75 2.00
HOF27 Ernie Banks .60 1.50
HOF28 Robin Yount .60 1.50
HOF29 Al Kaline .60 1.50
HOF30 Mike Piazza .60 1.50

2017 Topps Gallery Heritage

STATED ODDS 1:10 PACKS
*GREEN/250: 1.2X TO 3X BASIC
*BLUE/99: 2X TO 5X BASIC
*ORAGE/25: 3X TO 8X BASIC
H1 Andrew Benintendi 1.25 3.00
H2 Nolan Arenado .75 2.00
H3 Andrew McCutchen .60 1.50
H4 Johnny Cueto .50 1.25
H5 Cody Bellinger 1.50 4.00
H6 Yu Darvish .60 1.50
H7 Carlos Martinez .50 1.25
H8 Aaron Judge 4.00 10.00
H9 Jacob deGrom .60 1.50
H10 Freddie Freeman .75 2.00
H11 Manny Machado .60 1.50
H12 Chris Sale .60 1.50
H13 Kris Bryant .75 2.00
H14 Francisco Lindor .60 1.50
H15 Anthony Rizzo 1.00 2.50
H16 Dansby Swanson 1.00 2.50
H17 Bryce Harper 1.00 2.50
H18 Miguel Sano .50 1.25
H19 Noah Syndergaard .50 1.25
H20 Alex Bregman 1.50 4.00
H21 Jose Abreu .60 1.50
H22 Corey Seager .60 1.50
H23 Buster Posey .75 2.00
H24 Yadier Molina .60 1.50
H25 Robinson Cano .50 1.25
H26 Kyle Seager .40 1.00
H27 Matt Carpenter .60 1.50
H28 Yoenis Cespedes .60 1.50
H29 Corey Kluber .50 1.25
H30 Trevor Story .60 1.50
H31 Evan Longoria .50 1.25
H32 Christian Yelich .75 2.00
H33 Troy Tulowitzki .60 1.50
H34 Clayton Kershaw 1.25 3.00
H35 Jose Altuve .50 1.25
H36 Trea Turner .50 1.25
H37 Javier Baez .75 2.00
H38 Mike Trout 3.00 8.00
H39 Daniel Murphy .50 1.25
H40 Miguel Cabrera .60 1.50

2017 Topps Gallery Masterpieces

STATED ODDS 1:10 PACKS
*GREEN/250: 1.2X TO 3X BASIC
*BLUE/99: 2X TO 5X BASIC
*ORAGE/25: 3X TO 8X BASIC
MP1 Andres Galarraga .50 1.25
MP2 Rickey Henderson .60 1.50
MP3 Carlos Correa .60 1.50
MP4 Joey Votto .60 1.50
MP5 Max Scherzer .60 1.50
MP6 Adrian Beltre .60 1.50
MP7 Omar Vizquel .50 1.25
MP8 Josh Donaldson .50 1.25
MP9 Justin Verlander .60 1.50
MP10 Ichiro .75 2.00
MP11 Mookie Betts 1.00 2.50
MP12 Adam Jones .50 1.25
MP13 Albert Pujols .75 2.00
MP14 Bryce Harper 1.00 2.50
MP15 Wil Myers .40 1.00
MP16 Brian Dozier .60 1.50
MP17 Felix Hernandez .50 1.25
MP18 Bo Jackson .60 1.50
MP19 Giancarlo Stanton .60 1.50
MP20 Mike Trout 3.00 8.00
MP21 Nolan Ryan 2.00 5.00
MP22 Kris Bryant .75 2.00
MP23 Mark McGwire 1.00 2.50
MP24 Derek Jeter 1.50 4.00
MP25 Frank Thomas .60 1.50
MP26 Ken Griffey Jr. 1.25 3.00
MP27 Greg Maddux .75 2.00
MP28 Paul Goldschmidt .60 1.50
MP29 Eric Hosmer .50 1.25
MP30 Don Mattingly 1.50 4.00

2018 Topps Gallery

COMP.SET w/o SP's (150) 30.00 80.00
151-200 STATED ODDS 1:5 PACKS
1 Aaron Judge .75 2.00
2 George Springer .25 .60
3 Sean Doolittle .20 .50
4 Michael Taylor .20 .50
5 Christian Yelich .40 1.00
6 A.J. Minter RC .40 1.00
7 Scott Kingery RC .50 1.25
8 Chris Stratton RC .30 .75
9 Tim Locastro RC .30 .75
10 Alex Verdugo RC .50 1.25
11 Matt Chapman .30 .75
12 Lewis Brinson .20 .50
13 Jake Odorizzi .20 .50
14 Don Mattingly .60 1.50
15 Luke Weaver .20 .50
16 Franmil Reyes RC .50 1.25
17 Javier Baez .40 1.00
18 Yasiel Puig .30 .75
19 Jose Abreu .30 .75
20 Max Fried RC 1.25 3.00
21 Garrett Cooper RC .30 .75
22 Jackson Stephens RC .30 .75
23 Steven Souza Jr. .25 .60
24 Mike Foltynewicz .20 .50
25 Mike Soroka RC 1.00 2.50
26 Lourdes Gurriel Jr. RC .60 1.50
27 Matt Olson .20 .50
28 Greg Bird .25 .60
29 Dustin Pedroia .30 .75
30 Marcell Ozuna .30 .75
31 Jose Berrios .25 .60
32 Avisail Garcia .25 .60
33 Ryon Healy .20 .50
34 Chris Taylor .25 .60
35 Bryce Harper .50 1.25
36 Whit Merrifield .30 .75
37 Zack Greinke .25 .60
38 Victor Robles RC .75 2.00
39 Carlos Correa .30 .75
40 Miles Mikolas RC .40 1.00
41 Kyle Seager .20 .50
42 Troy Scribner .20 .50
43 Mark McGwire .50 1.25
44 Paul Goldschmidt .30 .75
45 Anthony Rizzo .50 1.25
46 Luis Severino .25 .60
47 Parker Bridwell .20 .50
48 Nolan Ryan 1.00 2.50
49 Daniel Mengden .20 .50
50 Giancarlo Stanton .30 .75
51 Andrew McCutchen .30 .75
52 Aaron Altherr .20 .50
53 Brian Anderson RC .40 1.00
54 Christian Arroyo RC .30 .75
55 Will Clark .25 .60
56 Aaron Nola .25 .60
57 Felix Hernandez .25 .60
58 J.D. Davis RC .40 1.00
59 Paul Blackburn .20 .50
60 Trevor Williams .20 .50
61 Brandon Woodruff .25 .60
62 Buster Posey .40 1.00
63 Justin Verlander .30 .75
64 Christian Villanueva RC .30 .75
65 Justin Upton .25 .60
66 Willy Adames RC .40 1.00
67 Ozzie Albies RC 1.00 2.50
68 Bo Jackson .30 .75
69 Adrian Beltre .30 .75
70 Corey Kluber .25 .60
71 Dominic Smith RC .30 .75
72 Adam Duvall .30 .75
73 Tyler O'Neill RC .50 1.25
74 Nick Pivetta .20 .50
75 Kris Bryant .40 1.00
76 Blake Snell .25 .60
77 Paul DeJong .30 .75
78 Jose Canseco .25 .60
79 J.D. Martinez .30 .75
80 Martin Maldonado .20 .50
81 Ildemaro Vargas RC .30 .75
82 Jose Urena .20 .50
83 Jack Flaherty RC .50 1.25
84 Cal Ripken Jr. 1.00 2.50
85 Clint Frazier RC .60 1.50
86 Anthony Banda RC .30 .75
87 Fernando Romero RC .30 .75
88 Jesse Winker .30 .75
89 Gleyber Torres RC 3.00 8.00
90 Austin Meadows RC .50 1.25
91 David Ortiz .30 .75
92 Joey Votto .30 .75
93 Trea Turner .25 .60
94 Chipper Jones .30 .75
95 Dylan Cozens RC .30 .75
96 Harrison Bader RC .50 1.25
97 Richard Urena RC .30 .75
98 Ian Kinsler .25 .60
99 Austin Hays RC .50 1.25
100 Mike Trout 1.50 4.00
101 Miguel Andujar RC 1.25 3.00
102 Ian Happ .25 .60
103 Ryan McMahon RC .40 1.00
104 Zack Godley .20 .50
105 Amed Rosario RC .40 1.00
106 Tyler Wade RC .40 1.00
107 Nick Williams RC .40 1.00
108 Dillon Peters .20 .50
109 Josh Donaldson .25 .60
110 Evan Longoria .25 .60
111 Kyle Farmer RC .30 .75
112 Frank Thomas .30 .75
113 Adam Jones .25 .60
114 Ryne Sandberg .60 1.50
115 Chad Green .20 .50
116 Shohei Ohtani RC 2.00 5.00
117 Trevor Story .30 .75
118 Freddy Peralta RC .30 .75
119 Albert Pujols .40 1.00
120 Chris Sale .30 .75
121 Trey Mancini .30 .75
122 Raudy Read RC .30 .75
123 Salvador Perez .25 .60
124 Yasmani Grandal .20 .50
125 Jose Altuve .25 .60
126 Juan Soto RC 6.00 15.00
127 Rafael Devers RC 1.00 2.50
128 Freddie Freeman .40 1.00
129 Rickey Henderson .30 .75
130 Drew Smyly .20 .50
131 Nick Kingham RC .30 .75
132 Jacob deGrom .30 .75
133 Rhys Hoskins RC 1.25 3.00
134 Jordan Hicks RC .60 1.50
135 Miguel Gomez RC .30 .75
136 Victor Arano RC .30 .75
137 Victor Caratini RC .40 1.00
138 Zack Cozart .20 .50
139 Clayton Kershaw .60 1.50
140 Ronald Acuna Jr. RC 6.00 15.00
141 Walker Buehler RC 1.50 4.00

142 Willson Contreras .30 .75
143 Didi Gregorius .25 .60
144 Manny Machado .30 .75
145 John Smoltz .30 .75
146 Charlie Blackmon .30 .75
147 Starling Marte .25 .60
148 Ichiro .40 1.00
149 Cam Gallagher RC .30 .75
150 Babe Ruth .75 2.00
151 Roberto Clemente SP 4.00 10.00
152 Kyle Schwarber SP 1.50 4.00
153 Willie Calhoun SP RC 1.25 3.00
154 Justin Smoak SP 1.00 2.50
155 Max Scherzer SP 1.50 4.00
156 Greg Maddux SP 2.00 5.00
157 Stephen Strasburg SP 1.50 4.00
158 Jon Lester SP 1.25 3.00
159 Eric Hosmer SP 1.25 3.00
160 Mookie Betts SP 2.50 6.00
161 Khris Davis SP 1.50 4.00
162 Francisco Lindor SP 1.50 4.00
163 Ted Williams SP 3.00 8.00
164 George Brett SP 3.00 8.00
165 Hideki Matsui SP 1.50 4.00
166 Xander Bogaerts SP 1.50 4.00
167 Ernie Banks SP 1.50 4.00
168 Yu Darvish SP 1.50 4.00
169 Nelson Cruz SP 1.50 4.00
170 Darryl Strawberry SP 1.00 2.50
171 Gary Sanchez SP 1.50 4.00
172 Rick Ankiel SP 1.00 2.50
173 Masahiro Tanaka SP 1.25 3.00
174 Dustin Fowler SP 1.00 2.50
175 Derek Jeter SP 4.00 10.00
176 Dee Gordon SP 1.00 2.50
177 Randy Johnson SP 1.50 4.00
178 Lou Gehrig SP 3.00 8.00
179 Alex Bregman SP 1.50 4.00
180 Pedro Martinez SP 1.25 3.00
181 Corey Seager SP 1.50 4.00
182 Gerrit Cole SP 1.50 4.00
183 Miguel Cabrera SP 1.50 4.00
184 Carlos Rodon SP 1.25 3.00
185 Yadier Molina SP 1.50 4.00
186 Julio Urias SP 1.50 4.00
187 Max Kepler SP 1.25 3.00
188 Hank Aaron SP 3.00 8.00
189 Dallas Keuchel SP 1.25 3.00
190 Matt Kemp SP 1.25 3.00
191 Michael Conforto SP 1.25 3.00
192 Nolan Arenado SP 2.00 5.00
193 Chance Sisco SP RC 1.25 3.00
194 Andrew Benintendi SP 1.50 4.00
195 Noah Syndergaard SP 1.25 3.00
196 Franklin Barreto SP 1.00 2.50
197 Joc Pederson SP 1.25 3.00
198 Sandy Koufax SP 3.00 8.00
199 Robinson Cano SP 1.25 3.00
200 Jackie Robinson SP 1.50 4.00

2018 Topps Gallery Artists Proof

*AP: 1X TO 2.5X BASIC
*AP RC: .6X TO 1.5X BASIC RC
FOUR PER BLASTER BOX

2018 Topps Gallery Blue

*BLUE: 3X TO 8X BASIC
*BLUE RC: 2X TO 5X BASIC RC
STATED ODDS 1:171 PACKS
STATED PRINT RUN 50 SER.#'d SETS

2018 Topps Gallery Canvas

*CANVAS: 1.2X TO 3X BASIC
*CANVAS RC: .75X TO 2X BASIC RC
TWO PER FAT PACK

2018 Topps Gallery Green

*GREEN: 2.5X TO 6X BASIC
*GREEN RC: 1.5X TO 4X BASIC RC
STATED ODDS 1:86 PACKS
STATED PRINT RUN 99 SER.#'d SETS

2018 Topps Gallery Orange

*ORANGE: 5X TO 12X BASIC
*ORANGE RC: 3X TO 8X BASIC RC
STATED ODDS 1:340 PACKS
STATED PRINT RUN 25 SER.#'d SETS

2018 Topps Gallery Private Issue

*PI: 1.5X TO 4X BASIC
*PI RC: 1X TO 2.5X BASIC RC
STATED ODDS 1:13 PACKS
STATED PRINT RUN 250 SER.#'d SETS

2018 Topps Gallery Autographs

STATED ODDS 1:14 PACKS
SP ODDS 1:4074 PACKS
SP PRINT RUN 10 SER.#'d SETS
NO SP PRICING DUE TO SCARCITY
EXCHANGE DEADLINE 10/31/2020
*GREEN/99: .5X TO 1.2X
*BLUE/50: .6X TO 1.5X
*ORANGE/25: .75X TO 2X
1 Aaron Judge
2 George Springer
3 Sean Doolittle 4.00 10.00
4 Michael Taylor 2.50 6.00
5 Christian Yelich 15.00 40.00
6 A.J. Minter 3.00 8.00
7 Scott Kingery 5.00 12.00
8 Chris Stratton 2.50 6.00
9 Tim Locastro 4.00 10.00
10 Alex Verdugo
11 Matt Chapman 6.00 15.00
12 Lewis Brinson 2.50 6.00
13 Jake Odorizzi 2.50 6.00
15 Luke Weaver 3.00 8.00
16 Franmil Reyes
20 Max Fried 10.00 25.00
21 Garrett Cooper 2.50 6.00
22 Jackson Stephens 2.50 6.00
23 Steven Souza Jr. 3.00 8.00
24 Mike Foltynewicz 2.50 6.00
25 Mike Soroka 10.00 25.00
26 Lourdes Gurriel Jr. 5.00 12.00
27 Matthew Olson 5.00 12.00
28 Greg Bird 3.00 8.00
30 Marcell Ozuna
31 Jose Berrios
32 Avisail Garcia 3.00 8.00
33 Ryon Healy 2.50 6.00
34 Chris Taylor 3.00 8.00
35 Bryce Harper
36 Whit Merrifield 10.00 25.00
38 Victor Robles 10.00 25.00
39 Carlos Correa
40 Miles Mikolas 6.00 15.00
41 Kyle Seager
42 Troy Scribner 2.50 6.00
43 Mark McGwire
45 Anthony Rizzo
46 Luis Severino
47 Parker Bridwell 2.50 6.00
49 Daniel Mengden 2.50 6.00
51 Andrew McCutchen
52 Aaron Altherr 2.50 6.00
54 Christian Arroyo 2.50 6.00
55 Will Clark 30.00 80.00
58 J.D. Davis 3.00 8.00
59 Paul Blackburn 2.50 6.00
60 Trevor Williams 2.50 6.00
61 Brandon Woodruff 3.00 8.00
64 Christian Villanueva
65 Justin Upton
66 Willy Adames
67 Ozzie Albies EXCH 12.00 30.00
68 Bo Jackson
69 Adrian Beltre
70 Corey Kluber
71 Dominic Smith
72 Adam Duvall 6.00 15.00
73 Tyler O'Neill 4.00 10.00
74 Nick Pivetta 2.50 6.00
75 Kris Bryant
76 Blake Snell 6.00 15.00
77 Paul DeJong 4.00 10.00
78 Jose Canseco 6.00 15.00
80 Martin Maldonado 2.50 6.00
81 Ildemaro Vargas 2.50 6.00
82 Jose Urena 2.50 6.00
83 Jack Flaherty 4.00 10.00
85 Clint Frazier 6.00 15.00
86 Anthony Banda 2.50 6.00
87 Fernando Romero 2.50 6.00
88 Jesse Winker 2.50 6.00
89 Gleyber Torres EXCH 50.00 120.00
90 Austin Meadows 4.00 10.00
91 David Ortiz
94 Chipper Jones
96 Harrison Bader 4.00 10.00
97 Richard Urena 2.50 6.00
98 Ian Kinsler 3.00 8.00
99 Austin Hays 5.00 12.00
100 Mike Trout 150.00 400.00
101 Miguel Andujar 20.00 50.00
102 Ian Happ 3.00 8.00
103 Ryan Mcmahon 3.00 8.00
104 Zack Godley 2.50 6.00
105 Amed Rosario
106 Tyler Wade
108 Dillon Peters 2.50 6.00
110 Evan Longoria
111 Kyle Farmer 2.50 6.00
115 Chad Green 6.00 15.00
116 Shohei Ohtani 100.00 250.00
118 Freddy Peralta 2.50 6.00
119 Albert Pujols
121 Trey Mancini 6.00 15.00
122 Raudy Read 2.50 6.00
123 Salvador Perez 6.00 15.00
124 Yasmani Grandal 2.50 6.00
125 Jose Altuve 12.00
126 Juan Soto 60.00 150.00
127 Rafael Devers EXCH 10.00 25.00
129 Rickey Henderson
130 Drew Smyly 2.50 6.00
131 Nick Kingham 2.50 6.00
132 Jacob deGrom
133 Rhys Hoskins 15.00 40.00
135 Miguel Gomez 2.50 6.00
136 Victor Arano 2.50 6.00
137 Victor Caratini 3.00 8.00
138 Zack Cozart 2.50 6.00
140 Ronald Acuna Jr. 75.00 200.00
141 Walker Buehler 15.00 40.00
142 Willson Contreras
144 Manny Machado
146 Charlie Blackmon 5.00 12.00
148 Ichiro
149 Cam Gallagher 2.50 6.00

2018 Topps Gallery Boxloader

STATED ODDS 1 PER BOX
OBTAB Adrian Beltre 4.00 10.00
OBTAJ Aaron Judge 10.00 25.00
OBTAM Andrew McCutchen 4.00 10.00
OBTAME Austin Meadows 4.00 10.00
OBTAP Albert Pujols 5.00 12.00
OBTBH Bryce Harper 6.00 15.00
OBTBJ Bo Jackson 4.00 10.00
OBTBP Buster Posey 5.00 12.00
OBTBR Babe Ruth 8.00 20.00
OBTCK Clayton Kershaw 8.00 20.00
OBTCR Cal Ripken Jr. 10.00 25.00
OBTCS Corey Seager 4.00 10.00
OBTDJ Derek Jeter 10.00 25.00
OBTDM Don Mattingly 8.00 20.00
OBTDO David Ortiz 4.00 10.00
OBTDP Dustin Pedroia 4.00 10.00
OBTEB Ernie Banks 4.00 10.00
OBTFL Francisco Lindor 4.00 10.00
OBTFT Frank Thomas 4.00 10.00
OBTGB George Brett 8.00 20.00
OBTGS Giancarlo Stanton 4.00 10.00
OBTGT Gleyber Torres 8.00 20.00
OBTHM Hideki Matsui 4.00 10.00
OBTI Ichiro 5.00 12.00
OBTJA Jose Altuve 3.00 8.00
OBTJB Javier Baez 5.00 12.00
OBTJD Josh Donaldson 3.00 8.00
OBTJR Jackie Robinson 4.00 10.00
OBTJS Juan Soto 12.00 30.00
OBTJV Justin Verlander 4.00 10.00
OBTJVO Joey Votto 4.00 10.00
OBTKB Kris Bryant 5.00 12.00
OBTLG Lou Gehrig 8.00 20.00
OBTMB Mookie Betts 6.00 15.00
OBTMC Michael Conforto 3.00 8.00
OBTMM Manny Machado 4.00 10.00
OBTMS Max Scherzer 4.00 10.00
OBTMT Mike Trout 8.00 20.00
OBTNA Nolan Arenado 5.00 12.00
OBTNR Nolan Ryan 10.00 25.00
OBTNS Noah Syndergaard 3.00 8.00
OBTOA Ozzie Albies 8.00 20.00
OBTRA Ronald Acuna Jr. 10.00 25.00
OBTRC Roberto Clemente 8.00 20.00
OBTRH Rickey Henderson 6.00 15.00
OBTRJ Randy Johnson 4.00 10.00
OBTSK Sandy Koufax 8.00 20.00
OBTSO Shohei Ohtani 10.00 25.00
OBTWC Will Clark 3.00 8.00
OBTYM Yadier Molina 4.00 10.00

2018 Topps Gallery Hall of Fame

STATED ODDS 1:10 PACKS
*GREEN/250: 1.2X TO 3X BASIC
*BLUE/99: 2X TO 5X BASIC
*ORANGE/25: 3X TO 8X BASIC
HOF1 Honus Wagner .60 1.50
HOF2 Ty Cobb 1.00 2.50
HOF3 Jeff Bagwell .50 1.25
HOF4 Bob Gibson .50 1.25
HOF5 Eddie Mathews .60 1.50
HOF6 Reggie Jackson .50 1.25
HOF7 Eddie Murray .50 1.25
HOF8 Jackie Robinson .60 1.50
HOF9 Lou Brock .50 1.25
HOF10 Brooks Robinson .50 1.25
HOF11 Andre Dawson .50 1.25
HOF12 Steve Carlton .50 1.25
HOF13 Ryne Sandberg 1.25 3.00
HOF14 Pedro Martinez .50 1.25
HOF15 Randy Johnson .50 1.25
HOF16 Paul Molitor .60 1.50
HOF17 Trevor Hoffman .50 1.25
HOF18 Frank Thomas .60 1.50
HOF19 Jim Thome .50 1.25
HOF20 Rod Carew .50 1.25
HOF21 Juan Marichal .50 1.25
HOF22 Barry Larkin .50 1.25
HOF23 Tom Seaver .50 1.25
HOF24 Whitey Ford .50 1.25
HOF25 Hank Aaron 1.25 3.00
HOF26 Babe Ruth 1.50 4.00
HOF27 Rickey Henderson .60 1.50
HOF28 Nolan Ryan 2.00 5.00
HOF29 George Brett 1.25 3.00
HOF30 Chipper Jones .60 1.50

2018 Topps Gallery Heritage

STATED ODDS 1:5 PACKS
*GREEN/250: .75X TO 2X BASIC
*BLUE/99: 1.2X TO 3X BASIC
*ORANGE/25: 2X TO 5X BASIC
H1 Max Scherzer .60 1.50
H2 Rafael Devers 1.25 3.00
H3 Miguel Andujar 1.50 4.00
H4 Nolan Arenado .75 2.00
H5 Josh Donaldson .50 1.25
H6 Willie Calhoun .50 1.25
H7 Jose Altuve .50 1.25
H8 Victor Robles 1.00 2.50
H9 Yu Darvish .60 1.50
H10 Ichiro .75 2.00
H11 Joey Votto .60 1.50
H12 Rhys Hoskins 1.50 4.00
H13 Clint Frazier .75 2.00
H14 Andrew Benintendi .60 1.50
H15 Cody Bellinger 1.25 3.00
H16 Yadier Molina .60 1.50
H17 Paul Goldschmidt .60 1.50
H18 Ozzie Albies 1.25 3.00
H19 Bryce Harper 1.00 2.50
H20 Francisco Lindor .60 1.50
H21 Amed Rosario .50 1.25
H22 Manny Machado .60 1.50
H23 Carlos Correa .60 1.50
H24 Gary Sanchez .60 1.50
H25 Buster Posey .75 2.00
H26 Shohei Ohtani 2.50 6.00
H27 Corey Seager .60 1.50
H28 Noah Syndergaard .50 1.25
H29 Mookie Betts 1.00 2.50
H30 Trea Turner .50 1.25
H31 Andrew McCutchen .60 1.50
H32 Francisco Mejia .50 1.25
H33 Clayton Kershaw 1.25 3.00
H34 Gleyber Torres 4.00 10.00
H35 Mike Trout 3.00 8.00
H36 Giancarlo Stanton .60 1.50
H37 Anthony Rizzo 1.00 2.50
H38 Walker Buehler 2.00 5.00
H39 Aaron Judge 1.50 4.00
H40 Ronald Acuna Jr. 8.00 20.00

2018 Topps Gallery Impressionists

STATED ODDS 1:142 PACKS
I1 Clint Frazier 6.00 15.00
I2 Kris Bryant 6.00 15.00
I3 Anthony Rizzo 8.00 20.00
I4 Ichiro 6.00 15.00
I5 Max Scherzer 5.00 12.00
I6 Manny Machado 5.00 12.00
I7 Bryce Harper 8.00 20.00
I8 Ozzie Albies 10.00 25.00
I9 Amed Rosario 4.00 10.00
I10 Shohei Ohtani 25.00 60.00
I11 Carlos Correa 5.00 12.00
I12 Giancarlo Stanton 5.00 12.00
I13 Mookie Betts 8.00 20.00
I14 Paul Goldschmidt 5.00 12.00
I15 Rhys Hoskins 12.00 30.00
I16 Victor Robles 8.00 20.00
I17 Buster Posey 6.00 15.00
I18 Andrew Benintendi 5.00 12.00
I19 Yu Darvish 5.00 12.00
I20 Jose Altuve 4.00 10.00
I21 Andrew McCutchen 5.00 12.00
I22 Rafael Devers 10.00 25.00
I23 Clayton Kershaw 10.00 25.00
I24 Aaron Judge 15.00 40.00
I25 Francisco Lindor 5.00 12.00
I26 Corey Seager 5.00 12.00
I27 Gary Sanchez 5.00 12.00
I28 Yadier Molina 5.00 12.00
I29 Joey Votto 5.00 12.00
I30 Cody Bellinger 10.00 25.00

2018 Topps Gallery Masterpiece

STATED ODDS 1:10 PACKS
*GREEN/250: .75X TO 2X BASIC
*BLUE/99: 1.2X TO 3X BASIC
*ORANGE/25: 2X TO 5X BASIC
M1 Derek Jeter 1.50 4.00
M2 Clint Frazier .75 2.00
M3 Charlie Blackmon .60 1.50
M4 Amed Rosario .50 1.25
M5 Bryce Harper 1.00 2.50
M6 Andrew McCutchen .60 1.50
M7 Andrew Benintendi .60 1.50
M8 Cal Ripken Jr. 2.00 5.00
M9 Rhys Hoskins 1.50 4.00
M10 Mike Trout 3.00 8.00
M11 Cody Bellinger 1.25 3.00
M12 Noah Syndergaard .50 1.25
M13 David Ortiz .60 1.50
M14 Chipper Jones .60 1.50
M15 Aaron Judge 1.50 4.00
M16 Yadier Molina .60 1.50
M17 Rickey Henderson .60 1.50
M18 Victor Robles 1.00 2.50
M19 Randy Johnson .60 1.50
M20 Rafael Devers 1.25 3.00
M21 Roberto Clemente 1.50 4.00
M22 Anthony Rizzo 1.00 2.50
M23 Clayton Kershaw 1.25 3.00
M24 Gleyber Torres 4.00 10.00
M25 Jose Altuve .50 1.25
M26 Hank Aaron 1.25 3.00
M27 Ronald Acuna Jr. 8.00 20.00
M28 Ichiro .75 2.00
M29 Francisco Lindor .60 1.50
M30 Shohei Ohtani 2.50 6.00

2019 Topps Gallery

151-200 STATED ODDS 1:5 PACKS
1 Willians Astudillo RC .30 .75
2 Nate Lowe RC .40 1.00
3 Clayton Kershaw .60 1.50
4 Lance McCullers Jr. .20 .50
5 Austin Riley RC 1.50 4.00
6 Shane Bieber .30 .75
7 Juan Soto 1.00 2.50
8 David Peralta .20 .50
9 George Springer .25 .60
10 Nolan Arenado .40 1.00
11 Ramon Laureano RC .60 1.50
12 Bryan Reynolds RC .60 1.50
13 Brendan Rodgers RC .50 1.25
14 Trevor Story .30 .75
15 Javier Baez .40 1.00
16 Harold Ramirez RC .50 1.25
17 Justin Upton .25 .60
18 Rowdy Tellez RC .50 1.25
19 Myles Straw RC .50 1.25
20 Xander Bogaerts .30 .75
21 Jon Duplantier RC .30 .75
22 Jalen Beeks RC .30 .75
23 Jonathan Villar .20 .50
24 Pete Alonso RC 2.50 6.00
25 Shohei Ohtani .40 1.00
26 Michael Kopech RC .60 1.50
27 Albert Pujols .40 1.00
28 Austin Meadows .25 .60
29 Kris Bryant .40 1.00
30 Bryce Harper .50 1.25
31 Taylor Ward RC .30 .75
32 Aaron Judge .75 2.00
33 Carson Kelly .20 .50
34 Daniel Ponce de Leon RC .50 1.25
35 Mitch Keller RC .40 1.00
36 Brad Keller RC .30 .75
37 Mike Foltynewicz .30 .75
38 Nicky Lopez RC .50 1.25
39 Heath Fillmyer RC .30 .75
40 Josh Naylor RC .40 1.00
41 Jake Bauers RC .50 1.25
42 Yu Darvish .30 .75
43 Jon Lester .25 .60
44 Brandon Lowe RC .50 1.25
45 Jeff McNeil RC .75 2.00
46 Kolby Allard RC .50 1.25
47 Matt Chapman .30 .75
48 Pablo Lopez RC .30 .75
49 Justus Sheffield RC .50 1.25
50 Francisco Lindor .30 .75
51 Khris Davis .30 .75
52 Adam Cimber .20 .50
53 Keston Hiura RC 1.00 2.50
54 Pedro Avila RC .30 .75
55 Kevin Newman RC .50 1.25
56 Fernando Tatis Jr. RC 3.00 8.00
57 Nicholas Castellanos .30 .75
58 Dakota Hudson RC .40 1.00
59 Blake Snell .25 .60
60 Michael Chavis RC .50 1.25
61 Max Scherzer .30 .75
62 Christian Yelich .40 1.00
63 Trevor Bauer .30 .75
64 Zack Greinke .25 .60
65 Jacob Nix RC .40 1.00
66 Chris Paddack RC .60 1.50
67 Joey Votto .30 .75
68 Kohl Stewart RC .40 1.00
69 Corey Kluber .25 .60
70 Lane Thomas RC .50 1.25
71 Jose Berrios .25 .60
72 Gary Sanchez .30 .75
73 Josh James RC .50 1.25
74 Josh Hader .20 .50
75 Touki Toussaint RC .40 1.00
76 Josh Donaldson .25 .60
77 Bryse Wilson RC .40 1.00
78 Ronald Acuna Jr. 1.50 4.00
79 Kyle Freeland .25 .60
80 Christin Stewart RC .40 1.00
81 Justin Verlander .30 .75
82 Dawel Lugo RC .50 1.25
83 Andrew McCutchen .30 .75
84 Whit Merrifield .30 .75
85 Reese McGuire RC .50 1.25
86 Steven Duggar RC .40 1.00
87 Ozzie Albies .30 .75
88 Matt Carpenter .30 .75
89 Sean Reid-Foley RC .30 .75
90 Mike Clevinger .25 .60
91 Alex Bregman .30 .75
92 Willson Contreras .25 .60
93 Noah Syndergaard .25 .60
94 Byron Buxton .25 .60
95 Trey Mancini .25 .60
96 Cedric Mullins RC .50 1.25
97 Kyle Wright RC .50 1.25
98 Vladimir Guerrero Jr. RC 2.00 5.00
99 Jake Cave RC .40 1.00
100 Salvador Perez .25 .60
101 Jacob deGrom .40 1.00
102 Mike Yastrzemski RC 2.00 5.00
103 Will Smith RC .75 2.00
104 Merrill Kelly RC .30 .75
105 Mike Trout 1.50 4.00
106 Rhys Hoskins .40 1.00
107 Max Muncy .25 .60
108 Carter Kieboom RC .50 1.25
109 Shaun Anderson RC .30 .75
110 Anthony Rizzo .50 1.25
111 Chance Adams RC .30 .75
112 Elvis Luciano RC .50 1.25
113 Domingo Santana .25 .60
114 Danny Jansen RC .30 .75
115 Buster Posey .40 1.00
116 Yusei Kikuchi RC .50 1.25
117 Mookie Betts .50 1.25
118 David Fletcher RC 1.00 2.50
119 DJ Stewart RC .40 1.00
120 Dennis Santana RC .30 .75
121 Kyle Tucker RC .60 1.50
122 Ryan Borucki RC .30 .75
123 Luis Severino .25 .60
124 JD Hammer RC .40 1.00
125 Garrett Hampson RC .30 .75
126 Ryan Helsley RC .40 1.00
127 Aaron Nola .25 .60
128 Cole Tucker RC .50 1.25
129 Jose Altuve .25 .60
130 Kyle Schwarber .30 .75
131 Paul Goldschmidt .30 .75
132 Luke Voit .50 1.25
133 Nick Senzel RC 1.00 2.50
134 Trent Thornton RC .30 .75
135 Luis Arraez RC 1.25 3.00
136 Freddie Freeman .40 1.00
137 Jose Ramirez .25 .60
138 Cavan Biggio RC 1.50 4.00
139 Miguel Andujar .30 .75
140 Chris Sale .30 .75
141 Dustin Pedroia .30 .75
142 Patrick Wisdom RC .30 .75
143 Manny Machado .30 .75
144 Framber Valdez RC .30 .75
145 Miguel Cabrera .30 .75
146 Thairo Estrada RC .50 1.25
147 Eloy Jimenez RC 1.25 3.00
148 Rafael Devers .40 1.00
149 Mitch Haniger .25 .60
150 Yadier Molina .30 .75
151 Ichiro 2.00 5.00
152 Rickey Henderson 1.50 4.00
153 Cal Ripken Jr. 5.00 12.00
154 Mark McGwire 2.50 6.00
155 Frank Thomas 1.50 4.00
156 Chipper Jones 1.50 4.00
157 Nolan Ryan 5.00 12.00
158 Babe Ruth 4.00 10.00
159 Derek Jeter 4.00 10.00
160 Jackie Robinson 1.50 4.00
161 Hank Aaron 3.00 8.00
162 Stan Musial 2.50 6.00
163 Ted Williams 3.00 8.00
164 Lou Gehrig 3.00 8.00
165 Ken Griffey Jr. 3.00 8.00
166 Joey Gallo 1.25 3.00
167 Lorenzo Cain 1.00 2.50
168 Charlie Blackmon 1.50 4.00
169 Starling Marte 1.25 3.00
170 Giancarlo Stanton 1.50 4.00
171 Robinson Cano 1.25 3.00
172 Ernie Banks 1.50 4.00
173 Adrian Beltre 1.50 4.00
174 Felix Hernandez 1.25 3.00
175 Stephen Strasburg 1.50 4.00
176 Evan Longoria 1.25 3.00
177 Eric Hosmer 1.25 3.00
178 J.D. Martinez 1.50 4.00
179 Carlos Correa 1.50 4.00
180 Gerrit Cole 1.50 4.00
181 Cody Bellinger 3.00 8.00
182 Andrew Benintendi 1.50 4.00
183 Josh Bell 1.25 3.00
184 Trea Turner 1.25 3.00
185 Marcus Stroman 1.25 3.00
186 Michael Conforto 1.25 3.00
187 Gleyber Torres 3.00 8.00
188 Chris Archer 1.00 2.50
189 Miguel Sano 1.25 3.00
190 Amed Rosario 1.25 3.00
191 Corey Seager 1.50 4.00
192 Walker Buehler 2.00 5.00
193 Victor Robles 2.00 5.00
194 Yoan Moncada 1.50 4.00
195 J.T. Realmuto 1.50 4.00
196 Willie Mays 3.00 8.00
197 Tony Gwynn 1.50 4.00
198 Roberto Clemente 4.00 10.00
199 George Brett 3.00 8.00
200 Johnny Bench 1.50 4.00

2019 Topps Gallery Artist Proof

*AP: 1X TO 2.5X BASIC
*AP RC: .6X TO 1.5X BASIC RC
STATED ODDS 4 PER BLASTER BOX
24 Pete Alonso 6.00 15.00

2019 Topps Gallery Blue

*BLUE: 3X TO 8X BASIC
*BLUE RC: 2X TO 5X BASIC RC
STATED ODDS 1:174 PACKS
STATED PRINT RUN 50 SER.#'d SETS
24 Pete Alonso 20.00 50.00

2019 Topps Gallery Green

*GREEN: 2.5X TO 5X BASIC
*GREEN RC: 1.5X TO 4X BASIC RC
STATED ODDS 1:88 PACKS
STATED PRINT RUN 99 SER.#'d SETS
24 Pete Alonso 15.00 40.00

2019 Topps Gallery Orange

*ORANGE: 5X TO 12X BASIC
*ORANGE RC: 3X TO 8X BASIC RC
STATED ODDS 1:349 PACKS
STATED PRINT RUN 25 SER.#'d SETS
24 Pete Alonso 30.00 80.00

2019 Topps Gallery Private Issue

*PI: 1.5X TO 4X BASIC
*PI RC: 1X TO 2.5X BASIC RC
STATED ODDS 1:14 PACKS
STATED PRINT RUN 250 SER.#'d SETS
24 Pete Alonso 10.00 25.00

2019 Topps Gallery Autographs

STATED ODDS 1:14 PACKS
EXCHANGE DEADLINE XX/XX/XX
*GREEN/99: .5X TO 1.2X
*BLUE/50: .6X TO 1.5X
*ORANGE/25: .75X TO 2X
1 Willians Astudillo 5.00 12.00
2 Nate Lowe 3.00 8.00
3 Clayton Kershaw
5 Austin Riley 12.00 30.00
6 Shane Bieber 4.00 10.00
7 Juan Soto
8 David Peralta 2.50 6.00
9 George Springer 8.00 20.00
10 Nolan Arenado 20.00 50.00
11 Ramon Laureano 10.00 25.00
12 Bryan Reynolds 6.00 15.00
16 Harold Ramirez 4.00 10.00
17 Justin Upton 3.00 8.00
18 Rowdy Tellez 4.00 10.00
19 Myles Straw 4.00 10.00
21 Jon Duplantier 2.50 6.00
22 Jalen Beeks 2.50 6.00
24 Pete Alonso 50.00 120.00
25 Shohei Ohtani
26 Michael Kopech 5.00 12.00
27 Albert Pujols 125.00 300.00
29 Kris Bryant 25.00 60.00
31 Taylor Ward 2.50 6.00
33 Carson Kelly 2.50 6.00
34 Daniel Ponce de Leon 4.00 10.00
35 Mitch Keller 3.00 8.00
36 Brad Keller 2.50 6.00
37 Mike Foltynewicz 4.00 10.00
38 Nicky Lopez 4.00 10.00
39 Heath Fillmyer 2.50 6.00
40 Josh Naylor 3.00 8.00
41 Jake Bauers 4.00 10.00
44 Brandon Lowe 6.00 15.00
45 Jeff McNeil 12.00 30.00
46 Kolby Allard 4.00 10.00
47 Matt Chapman 4.00 10.00
48 Pablo Lopez 2.50 6.00
49 Justus Sheffield 4.00 10.00
52 Adam Cimber 2.50 6.00
53 Keston Hiura 12.00 30.00
54 Pedro Avila 2.50 6.00
55 Kevin Newman 4.00 10.00
56 Fernando Tatis Jr. 75.00 200.00
58 Dakota Hudson 6.00 15.00
59 Blake Snell 6.00 15.00
60 Michael Chavis 8.00 20.00
61 Max Scherzer 12.00 30.00
62 Christian Yelich 30.00 80.00
63 Trevor Bauer 4.00 10.00
65 Jacob Nix 3.00 8.00
66 Chris Paddack 10.00 25.00
67 Joey Votto 15.00 40.00
68 Kohl Stewart 3.00 8.00
69 Corey Kluber 10.00 25.00
70 Lane Thomas 5.00 12.00
71 Jose Berrios 3.00 8.00
72 Gary Sanchez
74 Josh Hader 2.50 6.00
75 Touki Toussaint 3.00 8.00
77 Bryse Wilson 3.00 8.00
78 Ronald Acuna Jr. 40.00 100.00
80 Christin Stewart 3.00 8.00
82 Dawel Lugo 4.00 10.00
83 Andrew McCutchen 20.00 50.00
84 Whit Merrifield 4.00 10.00
85 Reese McGuire 4.00 10.00
87 Ozzie Albies 10.00 25.00
88 Matt Carpenter 4.00 10.00
89 Sean Reid-Foley 2.50 6.00
90 Mike Clevinger
92 Willson Contreras 3.00 8.00
93 Noah Syndergaard
94 Byron Buxton
95 Trey Mancini 6.00 15.00
96 Cedric Mullins 4.00 10.00
97 Kyle Wright
98 Vladimir Guerrero Jr. 60.00 150.00
99 Jake Cave 3.00 8.00
100 Salvador Perez
101 Jacob deGrom 15.00 40.00
102 Mike Yastrzemski 20.00 50.00
103 Will Smith 8.00 20.00
104 Merrill Kelly 2.50 6.00
105 Mike Trout 125.00 300.00
106 Rhys Hoskins 15.00 40.00
107 Max Muncy 3.00 8.00
108 Carter Kieboom 8.00 20.00
109 Shaun Anderson 5.00 12.00
110 Anthony Rizzo
112 Elvis Luciano 4.00 10.00
113 Domingo Santana 3.00 8.00
114 Danny Jansen 2.50 6.00
115 Buster Posey
116 Yusei Kikuchi 4.00 10.00
118 David Fletcher 8.00 20.00
119 DJ Stewart 3.00 8.00
120 Dennis Santana 2.50 6.00
121 Kyle Tucker 4.00 10.00
123 Luis Severino
124 JD Hammer 3.00 8.00
125 Garrett Hampson 2.50 6.00
126 Ryan Helsley 3.00 8.00
127 Aaron Nola
128 Cole Tucker 4.00 10.00
129 Jose Altuve
130 Kyle Schwarber 6.00 15.00
131 Paul Goldschmidt
135 Luis Arraez 10.00 25.00
137 Jose Ramirez 8.00 20.00
139 Miguel Andujar
140 Chris Sale
141 Dustin Pedroia 15.00 40.00
143 Manny Machado 12.00 30.00
145 Miguel Cabrera 20.00 50.00
146 Thairo Estrada 4.00 10.00
147 Eloy Jimenez
148 Rafael Devers 10.00 25.00
149 Mitch Haniger 3.00 8.00

2019 Topps Gallery Box Toppers

STATED ODDS 1 PER BOX
OBTAB Alex Bregman 4.00 10.00
OBTAJ Aaron Judge 10.00 25.00
OBTAR Anthony Rizzo 6.00 15.00
OBTBB Byron Buxton 3.00 8.00
OBTBH Bryce Harper 6.00 15.00
OBTBP Buster Posey 5.00 12.00
OBTBS Blake Snell 3.00 8.00
OBTCB Cody Bellinger 8.00 20.00
OBTCK Clayton Kershaw 8.00 20.00
OBTCS Chris Sale 4.00 10.00
OBTCY Christian Yelich 5.00 12.00

OBTEJ Eloy Jimenez 10.00 25.00
OBTFL Francisco Lindor 4.00 10.00
OBTGS George Springer 3.00 8.00
OBTJA Jose Altuve 3.00 8.00
OBTJB Javier Baez 5.00 12.00
OBTJD Jacob deGrom 4.00 10.00
OBTJR Jose Ramirez 3.00 8.00
OBTJS Juan Soto 12.00 30.00
OBTJV Justin Verlander 4.00 10.00
OBTKB Kris Bryant 5.00 12.00
OBTKD Khris Davis 4.00 10.00
OBTMB Mookie Betts 6.00 15.00
OBTMC Miguel Cabrera 4.00 10.00
OBTMM Manny Machado 4.00 10.00
OBTMS Max Scherzer 4.00 10.00
OBTMT Mike Trout 20.00 50.00
OBTNA Nolan Arenado 5.00 12.00
OBTNS Noah Syndergaard 3.00 8.00
OBTOA Ozzie Albies 4.00 10.00
OBTPA Pete Alonso 20.00 50.00
OBTPG Paul Goldschmidt 4.00 10.00
OBTRA Ronald Acuna Jr. 20.00 50.00
OBTRD Rafael Devers 5.00 12.00
OBTRH Rhys Hoskins 5.00 12.00
OBTSO Shohei Ohtani 5.00 12.00
OBTTM Trey Mancini 3.00 8.00
OBTWM Whit Merrifield 4.00 10.00
OBTYK Yusei Kikuchi 4.00 10.00
OBTYM Yadier Molina 4.00 10.00
OBTZG Zack Greinke 3.00 8.00
OBTCBI Cavan Biggio 12.00 30.00
OBTFTJ Fernando Tatis Jr. 25.00 60.00
OBTGSA Gary Sanchez 4.00 10.00
OBTJBE Jose Berrios 3.00 8.00
OBTJVO Joey Votto 4.00 10.00
OBTMCH Matt Chapman 4.00 10.00
OBTNSE Nick Senzel 8.00 20.00
OBTVGJ Vladimir Guerrero Jr. 15.00 40.00
OBTWCO Willson Contreras 3.00 8.00

2019 Topps Gallery Hall of Fame

STATED ODDS 1:10 PACKS
*GREEN/250: .75X TO 2X BASIC
*BLUE/99: 1.2X TO 3X BASIC
*ORANGE/25: 2X TO 5X BASIC
HOFG1 Tony Gwynn .60 1.50
HOFG2 Stan Musial 1.00 2.50
HOFG3 Edgar Martinez .50 1.25
HOFG4 Mel Ott .60 1.50
HOFG5 Roy Halladay .50 1.25
HOFG6 Pee Wee Reese .50 1.25
HOFG7 Christy Mathewson .60 1.50
HOFG8 Lou Gehrig 1.25 3.00
HOFG9 Roberto Clemente 1.50 4.00
HOFG10 Rogers Hornsby .50 1.25
HOFG11 Ernie Banks .60 1.50
HOFG12 Ted Williams 1.25 3.00
HOFG13 Hank Aaron 1.25 3.00
HOFG14 Sandy Koufax 1.25 3.00
HOFG15 Willie Mays 1.25 3.00
HOFG16 Robin Yount .60 1.50
HOFG17 Johnny Bench .60 1.50
HOFG18 Ozzie Smith .75 2.00
HOFG19 Ken Griffey Jr. 2.00 5.00
HOFG20 Mariano Rivera .75 2.00

2019 Topps Gallery Hall of Fame Blue

*BLUE/99: 1.2X TO 3X BASIC
STATED ODDS 1:628 PACKS
STATED PRINT RUN 99 SER.#'d SETS
HOFG2 Stan Musial 4.00 10.00
HOFG8 Lou Gehrig 6.00 15.00
HOFG12 Ted Williams 8.00 20.00
HOFG15 Willie Mays 10.00 25.00
HOFG19 Ken Griffey Jr. 15.00 40.00

2019 Topps Gallery Hall of Fame Green

*GREEN/250: .75X TO 2X BASIC
STATED ODDS 1:260 PACKS
STATED PRINT RUN 250 SER.#'d SETS
HOFG12 Ted Williams 4.00 10.00
HOFG15 Willie Mays 6.00 15.00
HOFG19 Ken Griffey Jr. 6.00 15.00

2019 Topps Gallery Hall of Fame Orange

*ORANGE/25: 2X TO 5X BASIC
STATED ODDS 1:2601 PACKS
STATED PRINT RUN 25 SER.#'d SETS
HOFG2 Stan Musial 15.00 40.00
HOFG8 Lou Gehrig 10.00 25.00
HOFG9 Roberto Clemente 15.00 40.00
HOFG12 Ted Williams 12.00 30.00
HOFG15 Willie Mays 15.00 40.00
HOFG19 Ken Griffey Jr. 25.00 60.00

2019 Topps Gallery Heritage

STATED ODDS 1:5 PACKS
*GREEN/250: .75X TO 2X BASIC
*BLUE/99: 1.2X TO 3X BASIC
*ORANGE/25: 2X TO 5X BASIC
HT1 Mike Trout 3.00 8.00
HT2 Shohei Ohtani .75 2.00
HT3 Freddie Freeman .75 2.00
HT4 Ronald Acuna Jr. 3.00 8.00
HT5 Mookie Betts 1.00 2.50
HT6 J.D. Martinez .60 1.50
HT7 Javier Baez .75 2.00
HT8 Kris Bryant .75 2.00
HT9 Joey Votto .60 1.50
HT10 Francisco Lindor .60 1.50
HT11 Nolan Arenado .75 2.00
HT12 Jose Altuve .50 1.25
HT13 Alex Bregman .60 1.50
HT14 Kyle Tucker .75 2.00
HT15 Justin Verlander .60 1.50
HT16 Clayton Kershaw 1.25 3.00
HT17 Christian Yelich .75 2.00
HT18 Jacob deGrom .60 1.50
HT19 Noah Syndergaard .50 1.25
HT20 Miguel Andujar .60 1.50
HT21 Gary Sanchez .60 1.50
HT22 Aaron Judge 1.50 4.00
HT23 Giancarlo Stanton .60 1.50
HT24 Khris Davis .60 1.50
HT25 Andrew McCutchen .60 1.50
HT26 Rhys Hoskins .75 2.00
HT27 Manny Machado .60 1.50
HT28 Buster Posey .75 2.00
HT29 Andrew Benintendi .60 1.50
HT30 Ichiro .75 2.00
HT31 Yusei Kikuchi .60 1.50
HT32 Paul Goldschmidt .60 1.50
HT33 Yadier Molina .60 1.50
HT34 Blake Snell .50 1.25
HT35 Bryce Harper 1.00 2.50
HT36 Juan Soto 2.00 5.00
HT37 Trea Turner .50 1.25
HT38 Fernando Tatis Jr. 4.00 10.00
HT39 Vladimir Guerrero Jr. 2.50 6.00
HT40 Eloy Jimenez 1.50 4.00

2019 Topps Gallery Heritage Blue

*BLUE/99: 1.2X TO 3X BASIC
STATED ODDS 1:329 PACKS
STATED PRINT RUN 99 SER.#'d SETS
HT1 Mike Trout 15.00 40.00
HT22 Aaron Judge 15.00 40.00

2019 Topps Gallery Heritage Green

*GREEN/250: .75X TO 2X BASIC
STATED ODDS 1:131 PACKS
STATED PRINT RUN 250 SER.#'d SETS
HT22 Aaron Judge 10.00 25.00

2019 Topps Gallery Heritage Orange

*ORANGE/25: 2X TO 5X BASIC
STATED ODDS 1:1316 PACKS
STATED PRINT RUN 25 SER.#'d SETS
HT1 Mike Trout 25.00 60.00
HT22 Aaron Judge 25.00 60.00
HT35 Bryce Harper 12.00 30.00
HT39 Vladimir Guerrero Jr. 30.00 80.00

2019 Topps Gallery Impressionists

STATED ODDS 1:87 PACKS
IM1 Mike Trout 12.00 30.00
IM2 Shohei Ohtani 3.00 8.00
IM3 Eloy Jimenez 6.00 15.00
IM4 Ronald Acuna Jr. 12.00 30.00
IM5 Mookie Betts 8.00 20.00
IM6 Andrew Benintendi 2.50 6.00
IM7 Javier Baez 3.00 8.00
IM8 Kris Bryant 3.00 8.00
IM9 Joey Votto 2.50 6.00
IM10 Francisco Lindor 2.50 6.00
IM11 Nolan Arenado 3.00 8.00
IM12 Jose Altuve 2.00 5.00
IM13 Alex Bregman 2.50 6.00
IM14 Carlos Correa 2.50 6.00
IM15 Clayton Kershaw 5.00 12.00
IM16 Christian Yelich 3.00 8.00
IM17 Jacob deGrom 2.50 6.00
IM18 Fernando Tatis Jr. 15.00 40.00
IM19 Aaron Judge 6.00 15.00
IM20 Yusei Kikuchi 2.50 6.00
IM21 Khris Davis 2.50 6.00
IM22 Rhys Hoskins 3.00 8.00
IM23 Vladimir Guerrero Jr. 10.00 25.00
IM24 Manny Machado 2.50 6.00
IM25 Buster Posey 3.00 8.00
IM26 Yadier Molina 2.50 6.00
IM27 Paul Goldschmidt 2.50 6.00
IM28 Bryce Harper 8.00 20.00
IM29 Juan Soto 12.00 30.00
IM30 Max Scherzer 2.50 6.00

2019 Topps Gallery Master and Apprentice

STATED ODDS 1:5 PACKS
*GREEN/250: .75X TO 2X BASIC
*BLUE/99: 1.2X TO 3X BASIC
*ORANGE/25: 2X TO 5X BASIC
MAAA Aaron/Acuna Jr. 3.00 8.00
MAGM Tony Gwynn .60 1.50
Manny Machado
MAKK Kershaw/Koufax 1.25 3.00
MAMG Goldschmidt/Musial 1.00 2.50
MARJ Judge/Ruth 1.50 4.00
MATJ Jimenez/Thomas 1.50 4.00
MAWB Williams/Betts 1.25 3.00
MAYY Yelich/Yount .75 2.00
MAGGJ Guerrero/Guerrero Jr. 2.50 6.00
MAMTJ Tatis Jr./Machado 4.00 10.00

2019 Topps Gallery Master and Apprentice Blue

*BLUE/99: 1.2X TO 3X BASIC
STATED ODDS 1:1316 PACKS
STATED PRINT RUN 99 SER.#'d SETS
MARJ Aaron Judge 10.00 25.00
Babe Ruth
MAWB Ted Williams 12.00 30.00
Mookie Betts

2019 Topps Gallery Master and Apprentice Green

*GREEN/250: .75X TO 2X BASIC
STATED ODDS 1:523 PACKS
STATED PRINT RUN 250 SER.#'d SETS
MARJ Aaron Judge 6.00 15.00
Babe Ruth
MAWB Ted Williams 8.00 20.00
Mookie Betts

2019 Topps Gallery Master and Apprentice Orange

*ORANGE/25: 2X TO 5X BASIC
STATED ODDS 1:5201 PACKS
STATED PRINT RUN 25 SER.#'d SETS
MAAA Hank Aaron 25.00 60.00
Ronald Acuna Jr.
MARJ Aaron Judge 15.00 40.00
Babe Ruth
MAWB Ted Williams 20.00 50.00
Mookie Betts

2019 Topps Gallery Masterpiece

STATED ODDS 1:10 PACKS
*GREEN/250: .75X TO 2X BASIC
*BLUE/99: 1.2X TO 3X BASIC
*ORANGE/25: 2X TO 5X BASIC
MP1 Mike Trout 3.00 8.00
MP2 Ronald Acuna Jr. 3.00 8.00
MP3 Randy Johnson .60 1.50
MP4 Cal Ripken Jr. 2.00 5.00
MP5 Mookie Betts 1.00 2.50
MP6 Kris Bryant .75 2.00
MP7 Frank Thomas .60 1.50
MP8 Johnny Bench .60 1.50
MP9 Francisco Lindor .60 1.50
MP10 Nolan Arenado .75 2.00
MP11 Alex Bregman .60 1.50
MP12 George Brett 1.25 3.00
MP13 Clayton Kershaw 1.25 3.00
MP14 Christian Yelich .75 2.00
MP15 Jacob deGrom .60 1.50
MP16 Rod Carew .50 1.25
MP17 Mariano Rivera .75 2.00
MP18 Mark McGwire 1.00 2.50
MP19 Rhys Hoskins .75 2.00
MP20 Roberto Clemente 1.50 4.00
MP21 Tony Gwynn .60 1.50
MP22 Nolan Ryan 2.00 5.00
MP23 Willie Mays 1.25 3.00
MP24 Ken Griffey Jr. 1.25 3.00
MP25 Paul Goldschmidt .60 1.50
MP26 Blake Snell .50 1.25
MP27 Miguel Cabrera .60 1.50
MP28 Javier Baez .75 2.00
MP29 Vladimir Guerrero Jr. 2.50 6.00
MP30 Max Scherzer .60 1.50

2019 Topps Gallery Masterpiece Blue

*BLUE/99: 1.2X TO 3X BASIC
STATED ODDS 1:439 PACKS
STATED PRINT RUN 99 SER.#'d SETS
MP1 Mike Trout 15.00 40.00
MP4 Cal Ripken Jr. 10.00 25.00
MP17 Mariano Rivera 5.00 12.00
MP20 Roberto Clemente 8.00 20.00
MP24 Ken Griffey Jr. 8.00 20.00
MP29 Vladimir Guerrero Jr. 15.00 40.00

2019 Topps Gallery Masterpiece Green

*GREEN/250: .75X TO 2X BASIC
STATED ODDS 1:174 PACKS
STATED PRINT RUN 250 SER.#'d SETS
MP1 Mike Trout 10.00 25.00
MP4 Cal Ripken Jr. 6.00 15.00
MP17 Mariano Rivera 3.00 8.00
MP20 Roberto Clemente 5.00 12.00
MP29 Vladimir Guerrero Jr. 10.00 25.00

2019 Topps Gallery Masterpiece Orange

*ORANGE/25: 2X TO 5X BASIC
STATED ODDS 1:1776 PACKS
STATED PRINT RUN 25 SER.#'d SETS
MP1 Mike Trout 25.00 60.00
MP4 Cal Ripken Jr. 15.00 40.00
MP17 Mariano Rivera 8.00 20.00
MP20 Roberto Clemente 20.00 50.00
MP21 Tony Gwynn 10.00 25.00
MP24 Ken Griffey Jr. 12.00 30.00
MP29 Vladimir Guerrero Jr. 25.00 60.00

2020 Topps Gallery

151-200 STATED ODDS 1:5 PACKS
1 Mike Trout 1.50 4.00
2 Gleyber Torres .60 1.50
3 Aristides Aquino RC .60 1.50
4 Juan Soto 1.00 2.50
5 Matthew Boyd .20 .50
6 Mauricio Dubon RC .40 1.00
7 Marcell Ozuna .30 .75
8 Christian Yelich .40 1.00
9 Kyle Schwarber .30 .75
10 Jose Altuve .25 .60
11 Ryan McMahon .20 .50
12 Mike Clevinger .25 .60
13 Logan Webb RC .40 1.00
14 Andrew McCutchen .30 .75
15 Matt Olson .20 .50
16 Yordan Alvarez RC 1.50 4.00
17 Hyun-Jin Ryu .25 .60
18 Nico Hoerner RC 1.25 3.00
19 Mike Moustakas .25 .60
20 Dereck Rodriguez .20 .50
21 Eloy Jimenez .60 1.50
22 Jesus Tinoco RC .30 .75
23 Paul Goldschmidt .30 .75
24 Xander Bogaerts .30 .75
25 Christian Walker .25 .60
26 Shane Bieber .30 .75
27 Stephen Gonsalves .20 .50
28 DJ Stewart .20 .50
29 Matt Thaiss RC .40 1.00
30 Pablo Lopez .20 .50
31 Nick Solak RC .50 1.25
32 Francisco Lindor .30 .75
33 Jesus Luzardo RC .60 1.50
34 Kyle Lewis RC 2.50 6.00
35 Shogo Akiyama .30 .75
36 Gerrit Cole .50 1.25
37 Ryan Yarbrough .20 .50
38 Adam Haseley .30 .75
39 Nolan Arenado .40 1.00
40 Gary Sanchez .30 .75
41 Shohei Ohtani .40 1.00
42 Dario Agrazal RC .40 1.00
43 Luis Severino .25 .60
44 Colin Moran .20 .50
45 Jeff McNeil .25 .60
46 Josh VanMeter .20 .50
47 Corey Kluber .25 .60
48 Mike King RC .50 1.25
49 Lane Thomas .20 .50
50 Hunter Harvey RC .50 1.25
51 Martin Maldonado .20 .50
52 Lewis Thorpe RC .30 .75
53 Cesar Hernandez .20 .50
54 Tommy Edman .30 .75
55 Rafael Devers .40 1.00
56 Aaron Civale RC .50 1.25
57 Jaylin Davis RC .50 1.25
58 Chris Sale .30 .75
59 Miguel Cabrera .30 .75
60 Carter Kieboom .25 .60
61 A.J. Puk RC .60 1.50
62 George Springer .25 .60
63 Jose Berrios .25 .60
64 Anthony Kay RC .30 .75
65 Brendan McKay RC .50 1.25
66 Junior Fernandez RC .30 .75
67 Andres Munoz RC .40 1.00
68 Jordan Luplow .20 .50
69 Shed Long .25 .60
70 Travis Demeritte RC .40 1.00
71 Eric Hosmer .25 .60
72 Sean Murphy RC .50 1.25
73 Yusei Kikuchi .25 .60
74 Alex Young RC .30 .75
75 Matt Chapman .30 .75
76 Robel Garcia RC .30 .75
77 Noah Syndergaard .25 .60
78 J.T. Realmuto .30 .75
79 Seth Brown RC .30 .75
80 Rhys Hoskins .40 1.00
81 Max Muncy .25 .60
82 Bryce Harper .50 1.25
83 Yoshi Tsutsugo .25 .60
84 Mitch Moreland .20 .50
85 Framber Valdez .20 .50
86 Salvador Perez .25 .60
87 Byron Buxton .25 .60
88 Fernando Tatis Jr. 1.25 3.00
89 Kyle Tucker .25 .60
90 Eric Thames .20 .50
91 Pete Alonso .75 2.00
92 Jake Rogers RC .30 .75
93 Tommy Kahnle .20 .50
94 Whit Merrifield .30 .75
95 Elvis Andrus .25 .60
96 Bryan Abreu RC .30 .75
97 Willson Contreras .30 .75
98 Zac Gallen RC .75 2.00
99 Max Scherzer .30 .75
100 Aaron Judge .75 2.00
101 Albert Pujols .40 1.00
102 Abraham Toro RC .40 1.00
103 Anthony Rizzo .50 1.25
104 Jonathan Villar .20 .50
105 Justin Upton .25 .60
106 Keston Hiura .40 1.00
107 Gavin Lux RC 2.00 5.00
108 Adbert Alzolay RC .40 1.00
109 Lance McCullers Jr. .20 .50
110 James Karinchak RC .50 1.25
111 Marwin Gonzalez .20 .50
112 Jordan Montgomery .30 .75
113 Jorge Soler .30 .75
114 Charlie Blackmon .30 .75
115 Kris Bryant .40 1.00
116 Blake Snell .25 .60
117 Daniel Mengden .20 .50
118 Marcus Stroman .25 .60
119 Dustin May RC 1.25 3.00
120 Patrick Sandoval RC .50 1.25
121 Sheldon Neuse RC .40 1.00
122 Ketel Marte .25 .60
123 Nick Burdi .20 .50
124 Buster Posey .40 1.00
125 Shin-Soo Choo .25 .60
126 Trevor Richards .20 .50
127 Mike Tauchman .30 .75
128 Zack Collins RC .30 .75
129 Matt Kemp .25 .60
130 Bo Bichette RC 2.50 6.00
131 Manny Machado .30 .75
132 Kyle Freeland .25 .60
133 Zack Littell .20 .50
134 Shun Yamaguchi .25 .60
135 Mike Yastrzemski .50 1.25
136 Trevor Bauer .30 .75
137 Ozzie Albies .30 .75
138 Dean Deetz .20 .50
139 Walker Buehler .40 1.00
140 Alex Bregman .30 .75
141 Kwang-Hyun Kim .60 1.50
142 Jack Flaherty .25 .60
143 T.J. Zeuch RC .30 .75
144 Luis Robert RC 3.00 8.00
145 Vladimir Guerrero Jr. .60 1.50
146 Sam Hilliard RC .50 1.25
147 Jacob deGrom .30 .75
148 J.D. Martinez .30 .75
149 Joey Votto .30 .75
150 Ronald Acuna Jr. 1.25 3.00
151 Miguel Andujar SP 1.50 4.00
152 Sandy Koufax SP 3.00 8.00
153 Carlos Correa SP 1.50 4.00
154 Willie Mays SP 3.00 8.00
155 Trea Turner SP 1.25 3.00
156 Jackie Robinson SP 1.50 4.00
157 Cal Ripken Jr. SP 5.00 12.00
158 Mitch Keller SP 1.50 4.00
159 Mookie Betts SP 3.00 8.00
160 Joey Gallo SP 1.50 4.00
161 Anthony Rendon SP 1.50 4.00
162 Yoan Moncada SP 1.50 4.00
163 Clayton Kershaw SP 3.00 8.00
164 Roberto Clemente SP 4.00 10.00
165 Josh Donaldson SP 1.25 3.00
166 Corey Seager SP 1.50 4.00
167 Yadier Molina SP 1.50 4.00
168 Cody Bellinger SP 3.00 8.00
169 Hank Aaron SP 3.00 8.00
170 Rickey Henderson SP 1.50 4.00
171 Frank Thomas SP 1.50 4.00
172 Yu Darvish SP 1.50 4.00
173 Babe Ruth SP 4.00 10.00
174 George Brett SP 3.00 8.00
175 Ichiro SP 2.00 5.00
176 Josh Bell SP 1.25 3.00
177 Tony Gwynn SP 1.50 4.00
178 Javier Baez SP 2.00 5.00
179 Ty Cobb SP 2.50 6.00
180 Mark McGwire SP 2.50 6.00
181 Aaron Nola SP 1.50 4.00
182 Ted Williams SP 3.00 8.00
183 Ken Griffey Jr. SP 5.00 12.00
184 Robinson Cano SP 1.25 3.00
185 Austin Meadows SP 1.25 3.00
186 Trevor Story SP 1.50 4.00
187 Johnny Bench SP 1.50 4.00
188 Ernie Banks SP 1.50 4.00
189 Nolan Ryan SP 5.00 12.00
190 Justin Verlander SP 1.50 4.00
191 Don Mattingly SP 3.00 8.00
192 Andrew Benintendi SP 1.50 4.00
193 Freddie Freeman SP 2.00 5.00
194 Stan Musial SP 2.50 6.00
195 Stephen Strasburg SP 1.50 4.00
196 Nelson Cruz SP 1.50 4.00
197 Michael Conforto SP 1.25 3.00
198 Ramon Laureano SP 1.50 4.00
199 Victor Robles SP 2.00 5.00
200 Derek Jeter SP 4.00 10.00

2020 Topps Gallery Artist Proof

*AP: 1X TO 2.5X BASIC
*AP RC: .6X TO 1.5X BASIC RC
STATED ODDS 4 PER BLASTER BOX
144 Luis Robert 8.00 20.00

2020 Topps Gallery Blue

*BLUE: 3X TO 8X BASIC
*BLUE RC: 2X TO 5X BASIC RC
STATED ODDS 1:175 PACKS
STATED PRINT RUN 50 SER.#'d SETS
16 Yordan Alvarez 10.00 25.00
141 Kwang-Hyun Kim 6.00 15.00
144 Luis Robert 25.00 60.00

2020 Topps Gallery Green

*GREEN: 2.5X TO 5X BASIC
*GREEN RC: 1.5X TO 4X BASIC RC
STATED ODDS 1:89 PACKS
STATED PRINT RUN 99 SER.#'d SETS
16 Yordan Alvarez 8.00 20.00
141 Kwang-Hyun Kim 5.00 12.00
144 Luis Robert 20.00 50.00

2020 Topps Gallery Private Issue

*PI: 1.5X TO 4X BASIC
*PI RC: 1X TO 2.5X BASIC RC
STATED ODDS 1:15 PACKS
STATED PRINT RUN 250 SER.#'d SETS
144 Luis Robert 15.00 40.00

2020 Topps Gallery Rainbow Foil

*RAINBOW: 1X TO 2.5X BASIC
*RAINBOW RC: .6X TO 1.5X BASIC RC
STATED ODDS 1:3 PACKS
144 Luis Robert 8.00 20.00

2020 Topps Gallery Wood

*WOOD: 1.2X TO 3X BASIC
*WOOD RC: .8X TO 2X BASIC RC
STATED ODDS 2 PER HANGER PACK
144 Luis Robert 10.00 25.00

2020 Topps Gallery Autographs

RANDOM INSERTS IN PACKS
1 Mike Trout
2 Gleyber Torres 25.00 60.00
3 Aristides Aquino 5.00 12.00
4 Juan Soto
5 Matthew Boyd 2.50 6.00
6 Mauricio Dubon 3.00 8.00
7 Marcell Ozuna 12.00 30.00
10 Jose Altuve 8.00 20.00
11 Ryan McMahon 2.50 6.00
12 Mike Clevinger 3.00 8.00
13 Logan Webb 3.00 8.00
14 Andrew McCutchen 40.00 100.00
16 Yordan Alvarez
17 Hyun-Jin Ryu 10.00 25.00
18 Nico Hoerner 8.00 20.00
19 Mike Moustakas 8.00 20.00
20 Dereck Rodriguez 5.00 12.00
22 Jesus Tinoco 2.50 6.00
23 Paul Goldschmidt
24 Xander Bogaerts 15.00 40.00
25 Christian Walker 3.00 8.00
26 Shane Bieber 20.00 50.00
27 Stephen Gonsalves 2.50 6.00
28 DJ Stewart 2.50 6.00
29 Matt Thaiss 3.00 8.00
30 Pablo Lopez 2.50 6.00
31 Nick Solak 4.00 10.00
33 Jesus Luzardo 5.00 12.00
34 Kyle Lewis 25.00 60.00
35 Shogo Akiyama 4.00 10.00
36 Gerrit Cole 15.00 40.00
37 Ryan Yarbrough 2.50 6.00
38 Adam Haseley 4.00 10.00
40 Gary Sanchez 10.00 25.00
41 Shohei Ohtani 50.00 120.00
42 Dario Agrazal 3.00 8.00
43 Luis Severino
44 Colin Moran 2.50 6.00
46 Josh VanMeter 2.50 6.00
47 Corey Kluber 3.00 8.00
48 Mike King 4.00 10.00
49 Lane Thomas 2.50 6.00
50 Hunter Harvey 4.00 10.00
51 Martin Maldonado 2.50 6.00
52 Lewis Thorpe 2.50 6.00
53 Cesar Hernandez 2.50 6.00
54 Tommy Edman 4.00 10.00
56 Aaron Civale 4.00 10.00
57 Jaylin Davis 4.00 10.00
58 Chris Sale 6.00 15.00
59 Miguel Cabrera 100.00 250.00
61 A.J. Puk
62 George Springer
63 Jose Berrios 3.00 8.00
64 Anthony Kay 2.50 6.00
65 Brendan McKay 4.00 10.00
66 Junior Fernandez 2.50 6.00
67 Andres Munoz 3.00 8.00
68 Jordan Luplow 2.50 6.00
69 Shed Long 3.00 8.00
70 Travis Demeritte 3.00 8.00
71 Eric Hosmer 8.00 20.00
72 Sean Murphy 4.00 10.00
73 Yusei Kikuchi 3.00 8.00
74 Alex Young 2.50 6.00
76 Robel Garcia 2.50 6.00
77 Noah Syndergaard 8.00 20.00
78 J.T. Realmuto 10.00 25.00
79 Seth Brown 2.50 6.00
80 Rhys Hoskins 15.00 40.00
82 Bryce Harper 60.00 150.00
83 Yoshi Tsutsugo
84 Mitch Moreland 2.50 6.00
85 Framber Valdez 2.50 6.00
86 Salvador Perez
88 Fernando Tatis Jr.
89 Kyle Tucker 8.00 20.00
90 Eric Thames 2.50 6.00
91 Pete Alonso 25.00 60.00
92 Jake Rogers 2.50 6.00
93 Tommy Kahnle 2.50 6.00
95 Elvis Andrus 8.00 20.00
96 Bryan Abreu 2.50 6.00
98 Zac Gallen 15.00 40.00
100 Aaron Judge 30.00 80.00
101 Albert Pujols 40.00 100.00
102 Abraham Toro 3.00 8.00
103 Anthony Rizzo
104 Jonathan Villar 2.50 6.00
105 Justin Upton 3.00 8.00
107 Gavin Lux EXCH 25.00 60.00
108 Adbert Alzolay 3.00 8.00
109 Lance McCullers Jr. 2.50 6.00
110 James Karinchak 4.00 10.00
111 Marwin Gonzalez 2.50 6.00
112 Jordan Montgomery 4.00 10.00
115 Kris Bryant 25.00 60.00
117 Daniel Mengden 2.50 6.00
119 Dustin May
120 Patrick Sandoval 4.00 10.00
121 Sheldon Neuse 3.00 8.00
122 Ketel Marte 5.00 12.00
123 Nick Burdi 2.50 6.00
124 Buster Posey 30.00 80.00
125 Shin-Soo Choo 6.00 15.00
126 Trevor Richards 2.50 6.00
127 Mike Tauchman 4.00 10.00
128 Zack Collins 3.00 8.00
129 Matt Kemp 3.00 8.00
130 Bo Bichette EXCH 30.00 80.00
131 Manny Machado
132 Kyle Freeland 3.00 8.00
133 Zack Littell 2.50 6.00
134 Shun Yamaguchi 3.00 8.00
135 Mike Yastrzemski
136 Trevor Bauer 6.00 15.00
138 Dean Deetz 2.50 6.00
140 Alex Bregman
141 Kwang-Hyun Kim 12.00 30.00
143 T.J. Zeuch 2.50 6.00
144 Luis Robert EXCH 50.00 120.00
145 Vladimir Guerrero Jr.
146 Sam Hilliard 4.00 10.00
147 Jacob deGrom
149 Joey Votto 20.00 50.00
150 Ronald Acuna Jr. 40.00 100.00
152 Sandy Koufax
157 Cal Ripken Jr.
158 Mitch Keller 4.00 10.00
160 Joey Gallo 10.00 25.00
161 Anthony Rendon
163 Clayton Kershaw
166 Corey Seager 20.00 50.00
167 Yadier Molina 40.00 100.00
168 Cody Bellinger 40.00 100.00
170 Rickey Henderson
171 Frank Thomas
175 Ichiro 75.00 200.00
180 Mark McGwire 40.00 100.00
181 Aaron Nola 8.00 20.00
185 Austin Meadows
187 Johnny Bench 25.00 60.00
189 Nolan Ryan
191 Don Mattingly
192 Andrew Benintendi 12.00 30.00
193 Freddie Freeman
195 Stephen Strasburg
198 Ramon Laureano 4.00 10.00
200 Derek Jeter 150.00 400.00

2020 Topps Gallery Autographs Blue

*BLUE/50: .6X TO 1.5X BASIC
STATED ODDS 1:135 HOBBY
STATED PRINT RUN 50 SER.#'d SETS
EXCHANGE DEADLINE 8/31/22
16 Yordan Alvarez 40.00 100.00
34 Kyle Lewis 50.00 120.00
65 Brendan McKay 8.00 20.00
86 Salvador Perez 10.00 25.00
125 Shin-Soo Choo 12.00 30.00
136 Trevor Bauer 12.00 30.00

2020 Topps Gallery Autographs Green

*GREEN/99: .5X TO 1.2X BASIC
STATED ODDS 1:XX HOBBY
STATED PRINT RUN 99 SER.#'d SETS
EXCHANGE DEADLINE 8/31/22
16 Yordan Alvarez 30.00 80.00
34 Kyle Lewis 40.00 100.00
65 Brendan McKay 6.00 15.00
125 Shin-Soo Choo 10.00 25.00
136 Trevor Bauer 10.00 25.00

2020 Topps Gallery Autographs Orange

*ORANGE/25: .8X TO 2X BASIC
STATED ODDS 1:266 HOBBY
STATED PRINT RUN 25 SER.#'d SETS
EXCHANGE DEADLINE 8/31/22
1 Mike Trout 125.00 300.00
16 Yordan Alvarez 50.00 120.00
34 Kyle Lewis 60.00 150.00
43 Luis Severino 8.00 20.00
62 George Springer 20.00 50.00
65 Brendan McKay 10.00 25.00
83 Yoshi Tsutsugo 15.00 40.00
86 Salvador Perez 12.00 30.00
125 Shin-Soo Choo 20.00 50.00
135 Mike Yastrzemski 20.00 50.00
136 Trevor Bauer 15.00 40.00
144 Luis Robert EXCH 200.00 500.00
145 Vladimir Guerrero Jr. 25.00 60.00

2020 Topps Gallery Box Toppers

STATED ODDS 1 PER BOX
OBTI Ichiro 6.00 15.00
OBTAB Alex Bregman 3.00 8.00
OBTAJ Aaron Judge 4.00 10.00
OBTAP Albert Pujols 4.00 10.00
OBTAR Anthony Rizzo 5.00 12.00
OBTBH Bryce Harper 6.00 15.00
OBTBR Babe Ruth 8.00 20.00
OBTCB Cody Bellinger 6.00 15.00
OBTCK Clayton Kershaw 6.00 15.00
OBTCY Christian Yelich 4.00 10.00
OBTDJ Derek Jeter 6.00 15.00
OBTDM Don Mattingly 10.00 25.00
OBTFL Francisco Lindor 3.00 8.00
OBTFT Frank Thomas 8.00 20.00
OBTGB George Brett 6.00 15.00
OBTGC Gerrit Cole 5.00 12.00
OBTGL Gavin Lux 6.00 15.00
OBTHA Hank Aaron 6.00 15.00
OBTJB Javier Baez 4.00 10.00
OBTJD Jacob deGrom 3.00 8.00
OBTJL Jesus Luzardo 4.00 10.00
OBTJR Jackie Robinson 4.00 10.00
OBTJS Juan Soto 6.00 15.00
OBTJV Justin Verlander 3.00 8.00
OBTKB Kris Bryant 4.00 10.00
OBTKL Kyle Lewis 4.00 10.00
OBTLR Luis Robert 8.00 20.00
OBTMB Mookie Betts 6.00 15.00
OBTMS Max Scherzer 3.00 8.00
OBTMT Mike Trout 8.00 20.00
OBTNA Nolan Arenado 4.00 10.00
OBTNC Nelson Cruz 3.00 8.00
OBTNR Nolan Ryan 6.00 15.00
OBTPA Pete Alonso 8.00 20.00
OBTRA Ronald Acuna Jr. 8.00 20.00
OBTRC Roberto Clemente 8.00 20.00

BTRD Rafael Devers 4.00 10.00
BTRH Rickey Henderson 5.00 12.00
BTSK Sandy Koufax 6.00 15.00
BTSO Shohei Ohtani 6.00 15.00
BTTG Tony Gwynn 8.00 20.00
BTWM Willie Mays 6.00 15.00
BTYA Yordan Alvarez 8.00 20.00
BTYM Yadier Molina 3.00 8.00
BTBBI Bo Bichette 8.00 20.00
BTCRJ Cal Ripken Jr. 8.00 20.00
BTFTJ Fernando Tatis Jr. 5.00 12.00
BTJVO Joey Votto 3.00 8.00
BTKGJ Ken Griffey Jr. 10.00 25.00
BTVGJ Vladimir Guerrero Jr. 6.00 15.00

2020 Topps Gallery Hall of Fame

STATED ODDS 1:XX HOBBY
HOFG1 Lou Gehrig 1.25 3.00
HOFG2 Derek Jeter 1.50 4.00
HOFG3 Ted Williams 1.25 3.00
HOFG4 George Brett 1.25 3.00
HOFG5 Sandy Koufax 1.25 3.00
HOFG6 Willie Mays 1.25 3.00
HOFG7 Rickey Henderson .60 1.50
HOFG8 Chipper Jones .60 1.50
HOFG9 Jeff Bagwell .50 1.25
HOFG10 Nolan Ryan 2.00 5.00
HOFG11 Randy Johnson .60 1.50
HOFG12 Barry Larkin .50 1.25
HOFG13 Cal Ripken Jr. 2.00 5.00
HOFG14 Ryne Sandberg 1.25 3.00
HOFG15 Roberto Clemente 1.50 4.00
HOFG16 Roberto Alomar .50 1.25
HOFG17 Jackie Robinson .60 1.50
HOFG18 Mike Schmidt 1.00 2.50
HOFG19 Ken Griffey Jr. 1.25 3.00
HOFG20 Mariano Rivera .75 2.00

2020 Topps Gallery Hall of Fame Blue

*BLUE/99: 1.2X TO 3X BASIC
STATED ODDS 1:XX HOBBY
STATED PRINT RUN 99 SER.#'d SETS
HOFG2 Derek Jeter 6.00 15.00
HOFG3 Ted Williams 10.00 25.00
HOFG6 Willie Mays 8.00 20.00
HOFG19 Ken Griffey Jr. 12.00 30.00

2020 Topps Gallery Hall of Fame Green

HOFG6 Willie Mays 4.00 10.00
HOFG19 Ken Griffey Jr. 8.00 20.00

2020 Topps Gallery Hall of Fame Orange

*ORANGE/25: 2X TO 5X BASIC
STATED ODDS 1:2617 HOBBY
STATED PRINT RUN 25 SER.#'d SETS
HOFG2 Derek Jeter 10.00 25.00
HOFG3 Ted Williams 15.00 40.00
HOFG6 Willie Mays 12.00 30.00
HOFG17 Jackie Robinson 10.00 25.00
HOFG19 Ken Griffey Jr. 20.00 50.00

2020 Topps Gallery Heritage

STATED ODDS 1:XX HOBBY
HT1 Mike Trout 3.00 8.00
HT2 Shohei Ohtani .75 2.00
HT3 Freddie Freeman .75 2.00
HT4 Ronald Acuna Jr. 2.50 6.00
HT5 Mookie Betts 1.25 3.00
HT6 Rafael Devers .75 2.00
HT7 Javier Baez .75 2.00
HT8 Kris Bryant .75 2.00
HT9 Joey Votto .60 1.50
HT10 Francisco Lindor .60 1.50
HT11 Nolan Arenado .75 2.00
HT12 Jose Altuve .50 1.25
HT13 Alex Bregman .60 1.50
HT14 Yordan Alvarez 2.00 5.00
HT15 Justin Verlander .60 1.50
HT16 Clayton Kershaw 1.25 3.00
HT17 Christian Yelich .75 2.00
HT18 Jacob deGrom .60 1.50
HT19 Pete Alonso 1.50 4.00
HT20 Gavin Lux 2.50 6.00
HT21 Gleyber Torres 1.25 3.00
HT22 Aaron Judge 1.50 4.00
HT23 Giancarlo Stanton .60 1.50
HT24 Jesus Luzardo .75 2.00
HT25 Bo Bichette 3.00 8.00
HT26 Aristides Aquino .75 2.00
HT27 Walker Buehler .75 2.00
HT28 Buster Posey .75 2.00
HT29 Luis Robert 4.00 10.00
HT30 Nico Hoerner 1.50 4.00
HT31 Kyle Lewis 3.00 8.00
HT32 Paul Goldschmidt .60 1.50
HT33 Yadier Molina .60 1.50
HT34 Brendan McKay .60 1.50
HT35 Bryce Harper 1.00 2.50
HT36 Juan Soto 2.00 5.00
HT37 Max Scherzer .60 1.50
HT38 Fernando Tatis Jr. 2.50 6.00
HT39 Vladimir Guerrero Jr. 1.50 4.00
HT40 Eloy Jimenez 1.25 3.00

2020 Topps Gallery Heritage Blue

*BLUE/99: 1.2X TO 3X BASIC
STATED ODDS 1:XX HOBBY
STATED PRINT RUN 99 SER.#'d SETS
HT1 Mike Trout 20.00 50.00
HT38 Fernando Tatis Jr. 10.00 25.00

2020 Topps Gallery Heritage Green

*GREEN/250: .8X TO 2X BASIC
STATED ODDS 1:XX HOBBY
STATED PRINT RUN 250 SER.#'d SETS
HT1 Mike Trout 12.00 30.00

2020 Topps Gallery Heritage Orange

*ORANGE/25: 2X TO 5X BASIC
STATED ODDS 1:1309 HOBBY
STATED PRINT RUN 25 SER.#'d SETS
HT1 Mike Trout 30.00 80.00
HT38 Fernando Tatis Jr. 20.00 50.00

2020 Topps Gallery Impressionists

STATED ODDS 1:88 HOBBY
IM1 Mike Trout 15.00 40.00
IM2 Shohei Ohtani 3.00 8.00
IM3 Luis Robert 15.00 40.00
IM4 Ronald Acuna Jr. 8.00 20.00
IM5 Mookie Betts 8.00 20.00
IM6 Cody Bellinger 6.00 15.00
IM7 Javier Baez 3.00 8.00
IM8 Kris Bryant 3.00 8.00
IM9 Joey Votto 2.50 6.00
IM10 Francisco Lindor 2.50 6.00
IM11 Nolan Arenado 3.00 8.00
IM12 Gavin Lux 8.00 20.00
IM13 Alex Bregman 2.50 6.00
IM14 Pete Alonso 12.00 30.00
IM15 Clayton Kershaw 5.00 12.00
IM16 Christian Yelich 3.00 8.00
IM17 Jacob deGrom 2.50 6.00
IM18 Fernando Tatis Jr. 10.00 25.00
IM19 Aaron Judge 8.00 20.00
IM20 Yordan Alvarez 10.00 25.00
IM21 Jesus Luzardo 3.00 8.00
IM22 Bo Bichette 10.00 25.00
IM23 Vladimir Guerrero Jr. 5.00 12.00
IM24 Gerrit Cole 4.00 10.00
IM25 Buster Posey 3.00 8.00
IM26 Yadier Molina 2.50 6.00
IM27 Paul Goldschmidt 2.50 6.00
IM28 Bryce Harper 4.00 10.00
IM29 Juan Soto 6.00 15.00
IM30 Max Scherzer 2.50 6.00

2020 Topps Gallery Master and Apprentice

STATED ODDS 1:XX HOBBY
MA1 Aaron Judge 1.50 4.00
Don Mattingly
MA2 Rafael Devers .75 2.00
David Ortiz
MA3 Yordan Alvarez 2.00 5.00
Jeff Bagwell
MA4 Gavin Lux 2.50 6.00
Cody Bellinger
MA5 Pete Alonso 1.50 4.00
Jacob deGrom
MA6 Luis Robert 4.00 10.00
Frank Thomas
MA7 Fernando Tatis Jr. 2.50 6.00
Tony Gwynn
MA8 Walker Buehler 1.25 3.00
Clayton Kershaw
MA9 Roberto Alomar 3.00 8.00
Bo Bichette
MA10 Kris Bryant .75 2.00
Ron Santo

2020 Topps Gallery Master and Apprentice Blue

*BLUE/99: 1.2X TO 3X BASIC
STATED ODDS 1:XX HOBBY
STATED PRINT RUN 99 SER.#'d SETS
MA1 Aaron Judge 15.00 40.00
Don Mattingly
MA5 Pete Alonso 15.00 40.00
Jacob deGrom
MA7 Fernando Tatis Jr. 20.00 50.00
Tony Gwynn
MA8 Walker Buehler 6.00 15.00
Clayton Kershaw

2020 Topps Gallery Master and Apprentice Green

MA1 Aaron Judge 10.00 25.00
Don Mattingly
MA7 Fernando Tatis Jr. 6.00 15.00
Tony Gwynn
MA8 Walker Buehler 4.00 10.00
Clayton Kershaw

2020 Topps Gallery Master and Apprentice Orange

*ORANGE/25: 2X TO 5X BASIC
MA1 Aaron Judge 25.00 60.00
Don Mattingly
MA3 Yordan Alvarez 25.00 60.00
Jeff Bagwell
MA5 Pete Alonso 25.00 60.00
Jacob deGrom
MA6 Luis Robert 5.00 120.00
Frank Thomas
MA7 Fernando Tatis Jr. 30.00 80.00
Tony Gwynn
MA8 Walker Buehler 10.00 25.00
Clayton Kershaw

2020 Topps Gallery Modern Artists

STATED ODDS 1:XX HOBBY
MP1 Mike Trout 3.00 8.00
MP2 Ronald Acuna Jr. 2.50 6.00
MP3 Vladimir Guerrero Jr. 1.25 3.00
MP4 Juan Soto 2.00 5.00
MP5 Fernando Tatis Jr. 2.50 6.00
MP6 Kris Bryant .75 2.00
MP7 Bo Bichette 3.00 8.00
MP8 Aristides Aquino .75 2.00
MP9 Gavin Lux 2.50 6.00
MP10 Gleyber Torres 1.25 3.00
MP11 Alex Bregman .60 1.50
MP12 Nolan Arenado .75 2.00
MP13 Yordan Alvarez 2.00 5.00
MP14 Pete Alonso 1.50 4.00
MP15 Ozzie Albies .60 1.50
MP16 Rafael Devers .75 2.00
MP17 Shane Bieber .60 1.50
MP18 Jack Flaherty .50 1.25
MP19 Shohei Ohtani .75 2.00
MP20 Walker Buehler .75 2.00
MP21 Francisco Lindor .60 1.50
MP22 Javier Baez .75 2.00
MP23 Eloy Jimenez 1.25 3.00
MP24 Cody Bellinger 1.25 3.00
MP25 Jesus Luzardo .75 2.00
MP26 Mookie Betts 1.25 3.00
MP27 Aaron Judge 1.50 4.00
MP28 Luis Robert 4.00 10.00
MP29 Matt Chapman .60 1.50
MP30 Christian Yelich .75 2.00

2020 Topps Gallery Modern Artists Blue

MP1 Mike Trout 15.00 40.00
MP5 Fernando Tatis Jr. 12.00 30.00
MP28 Luis Robert 15.00 40.00

2020 Topps Gallery Modern Artists Green

*GREEN/250: .8X TO 2X BASIC
STATED ODDS 1:XX HOBBY
STATED PRINT RUN 250 SER.#'d SETS
MP1 Mike Trout 10.00 25.00
MP5 Fernando Tatis Jr. 8.00 20.00
MP28 Luis Robert 10.00 25.00

2020 Topps Gallery Modern Artists Orange

*ORANGE/25: 2X TO 5X BASIC
MP1 Mike Trout 25.00 60.00
MP5 Fernando Tatis Jr. 25.00 60.00
MP28 Luis Robert 25.00 60.00

2016 Topps Gold Label Class 1

COMPLETE SET (100) 25.00 60.00
1 Mike Trout 2.00 5.00
2 Carlos Gonzalez .30 .75
3 George Springer .30 .75
4 Eric Hosmer .30 .75
5 Johnny Bench .40 1.00
6 Chris Archer .25 .60
7 Jose Altuve .30 .75
8 Cal Ripken Jr. 1.25 3.00
9 Reggie Jackson .30 .75
10 Justin Upton .30 .75
11 Yu Darvish .40 1.00
12 Troy Tulowitzki .40 1.00
13 Albert Pujols .50 1.25
14 Nolan Arenado .50 1.25
15 Craig Kimbrel .30 .75
16 Bo Jackson .40 1.00
17 Kris Bryant .50 1.25
18 Kenta Maeda RC .50 1.25
19 Darryl Strawberry .25 .60
20 Giancarlo Stanton .40 1.00
21 Roberto Clemente 1.00 2.50
22 Clayton Kershaw .75 2.00
23 Don Mattingly .75 2.00
24 Ken Griffey Jr. .75 2.00
25 Jose Fernandez .40 1.00
26 Jose Bautista .30 .75
27 David Wright .30 .75
28 Buster Posey .50 1.25
29 Yoenis Cespedes .40 1.00
30 Chipper Jones .40 1.00
31 Sandy Koufax .75 2.00
32 David Ortiz .40 1.00
33 Ryan Braun .30 .75
34 Bryce Harper .60 1.50
35 Frank Thomas .40 1.00
36 Jose Abreu .40 1.00
37 Stephen Strasburg .40 1.00
38 Mookie Betts .60 1.50
39 Hyun-Soo Kim RC .40 1.00
40 Felix Hernandez .30 .75
41 Aroldis Chapman .40 1.00
42 Nolan Ryan 1.25 3.00
43 Byung-Ho Park RC .30 .75
44 Anthony Rizzo .60 1.50
45 Zack Greinke .30 .75
46 Lucas Giolito RC .40 1.00
47 Stan Musial .60 1.50
48 Josh Donaldson .30 .75
49 Jacob deGrom .30 .75
50 Hunter Pence .30 .75
51 Ichiro Suzuki .50 1.25
52 Wade Boggs .30 .75
53 Johnny Cueto .30 .75
54 Sonny Gray .30 .75
55 Jose Berrios RC .30 .75
56 Edwin Encarnacion .40 1.00
57 Roger Clemens .50 1.25
58 Prince Fielder .30 .75
59 Robinson Cano .30 .75
60 Kyle Schwarber RC .75 2.00
61 David Price .30 .75
62 Julio Urias RC .75 2.00
63 Miguel Sano RC .40 1.00
64 Freddie Freeman .50 1.25
65 Mark McGwire .60 1.50
66 Gerrit Cole .40 1.00
67 Jason Heyward .30 .75
68 Michael Conforto RC .30 .75
69 Luis Severino RC .30 .75
70 Stephen Piscotty RC .40 1.00
71 Andre Dawson .30 .75
72 Jake Arrieta .30 .75
73 Manny Machado .40 1.00
74 Trea Turner RC .75 2.00
75 Corey Seager RC 2.00 5.00
76 Carl Yastrzemski .60 1.50
77 Aaron Nola RC .50 1.25
78 Mike Piazza .40 1.00
79 Chris Sale .40 1.00
80 Blake Snell RC .30 .75
81 Miguel Cabrera .40 1.00
82 Matt Harvey .30 .75
83 Andrew McCutchen .40 1.00
84 Hank Aaron .75 2.00
85 Carlos Correa .40 1.00
86 Paul Goldschmidt .40 1.00
87 Ozzie Smith .50 1.25
88 Greg Maddux .50 1.25
89 Randy Johnson .40 1.00
90 Yasiel Puig .40 1.00
91 Joey Votto .40 1.00
92 Justin Verlander .40 1.00
93 Adrian Gonzalez .30 .75
94 Madison Bumgarner .30 .75
95 Adam Jones .30 .75
96 Todd Frazier .30 .75
97 Matt Kemp .30 .75
98 Noah Syndergaard .30 .75
99 Max Scherzer .40 1.00
100 Willie Mays .75 2.00

2016 Topps Gold Label Class 1 Blue

*CLASS 1 BLUE: .5X TO 1.2X CLASS 1
*CLASS 1 BLUE RC: .5X TO 1.2X CLASS 1 RC
STATED ODDS 1:2 HOBBY

2016 Topps Gold Label Class 1 Red

*CLASS 1 RED: 2.5X TO 6X CLASS 1
*CLASS 1 RED RC: 2.5X TO 6X CLASS 1 RC
STATED ODDS 1:13 HOBBY
STATED PRINT RUN 100 SER.#'d SETS

2016 Topps Gold Label Class 2

COMPLETE SET (100) 60.00 150.00
*CLASS 2: 1X TO 2.5X CLASS 1
*CLASS 2 RC: 1X TO 2.5X CLASS 1 RC

2016 Topps Gold Label Class 2 Blue

*CLASS 2 BLUE: 2X TO 5X CLASS 1
*CLASS 2 BLUE RC: 2X TO 5X CLASS 1 RC
STATED ODDS 1:6 HOBBY

2016 Topps Gold Label Class 2 Red

*CLASS 2 RED: 3X TO 8X CLASS 1
*CLASS 2 RED RC: 3X TO 8X CLASS 1 RC
STATED ODDS 1:25 HOBBY
STATED PRINT RUN 50 SER.#'d SETS

2016 Topps Gold Label Class 3

*CLASS 3: 1.5X TO 4X CLASS 1
*CLASS 3 RC: 1.5X TO 4X CLASS 1 RC

2016 Topps Gold Label Class 3 Blue

*CLASS 3 BLUE: 4X TO 10X CLASS 1
*CLASS 3 BLUE RC: 4X TO 10X CLASS 1 RC
STATED ODDS 1:20 HOBBY

2016 Topps Gold Label Class 3 Red

*CLASS 3 RED: 8X TO 20X CLASS 1
*CLASS 3 RED RC: 8X TO 20X CLASS 1 RC
STATED ODDS 1:50 HOBBY
STATED PRINT RUN 25 SER.#'d SETS

2016 Topps Gold Label Framed Autographs Black Frame

*BLACK/50: .5X TO 1.2X BASIC
*BLACK/25: .75X TO 2X BASIC
STATED ODDS 1:49 HOBBY
PRINT RUNS B/WN 3-50 COPIES PER
NO PRICING ON QTY 15 OR LESS
EXCHANGE DEADLINE 9/30/2018
GLFAMM Mark McGwire/25 75.00 200.00

2016 Topps Gold Label Framed Autographs Gold Frame

STATED ODDS 1:9 HOBBY
EXCHANGE DEADLINE 9/30/2018
GLFAAC Alex Cobb 4.00 10.00
GLFAAG Alex Gordon 10.00 25.00
GLFAAGA Andres Galarraga 5.00 12.00
GLFAAJ Andruw Jones 4.00 10.00
GLFAAN Aaron Nola 20.00 50.00
GLFAAP A.J. Pollock 4.00 10.00
GLFAAR Anthony Rizzo 60.00 150.00
GLFABH Bryce Harper
GLFABJ Bo Jackson 60.00 150.00
GLFABP Byung-Ho Park 8.00 20.00
GLFABS Blake Snell 5.00 12.00
GLFACD Corey Dickerson 4.00 10.00
GLFACE Carl Edwards Jr. 5.00 12.00
GLFACJ Chipper Jones 75.00 200.00
GLFACK Clayton Kershaw 60.00 150.00
GLFACKL Corey Kluber 15.00 40.00
GLFACM Carlos Martinez 6.00 15.00
GLFACR Cal Ripken Jr.
GLFACS Corey Seager
GLFADG Didi Gregorius 6.00 15.00
GLFADM Don Mattingly
GLFAFL Francisco Lindor 25.00 60.00
GLFAFM Frankie Montas 5.00 12.00
GLFAFT Frank Thomas
GLFAGB Greg Bird 5.00 12.00
GLFAGS George Springer 5.00 12.00
GLFAHA Hank Aaron 150.00 250.00
GLFAHO Henry Owens 5.00 12.00
GLFAHOL Hector Olivera 5.00 12.00
GLFAI Ichiro Suzuki 300.00 50.00
GLFAJA Jose Altuve EXCH 40.00 100.00
GLFAJAB Jim Abbott 6.00 15.00
GLFAJC Jose Canseco 10.00 25.00
GLFAJd Jacob deGrom 20.00 50.00
GLFAJE Jerad Eickhoff 6.00 15.00
GLFAJG Juan Gonzalez 8.00 20.00
GLFAJH Jason Heyward 12.00 30.00
GLFAJO John Olerud 12.00 30.00
GLFAJPE Jose Peraza 6.00 15.00
GLFAJR Jim Rice 10.00 25.00
GLFAJSO Jorge Soler 8.00 20.00
GLFAJUR Julio Urias EXCH 12.00 30.00
GLFAKB Kris Bryant 50.00 120.00
GLFAKC Kole Calhoun 4.00 10.00
GLFAKG Ken Griffey Jr. EXCH 200.00 300.00
GLFAKM Kenta Maeda 15.00 40.00
GLFAKMA Ketel Marte 8.00 20.00
GLFAKS Kyle Schwarber 15.00 40.00
GLFALG Lucas Giolito 12.00 30.00
GLFALS Luis Severino 15.00 40.00
GLFAMF Maikel Franco 5.00 12.00
GLFAMM Mark McGwire
GLFAMP Mike Piazza
GLFAMS Miguel Sano 6.00 15.00
GLFAMT Mike Trout
GLFANA Nolan Arenado 30.00 80.00
GLFANS Noah Syndergaard 15.00 40.00
GLFAOV Omar Vizquel 8.00 20.00
GLFAPOB Peter O'Brien 4.00 10.00
GLFARM Raul Mondesi
GLFARR Rob Refsnyder 5.00 12.00
GLFASD Sean Doolittle 4.00 10.00
GLFASG Sonny Gray 8.00 20.00
GLFASGR Shawn Green 4.00 10.00
GLFASK Sandy Koufax EXCH 200.00 300.00
GLFASM Starling Marte 5.00 12.00
GLFASMA Steven Matz 5.00 12.00
GLFASP Stephen Piscotty 6.00 15.00
GLFATT Trea Turner 12.00 30.00
GLFATTO Trayce Thompson 4.00 10.00

2017 Topps Gold Label Class 1

COMPLETE SET (100) 30.00 80.00
1 Bryce Harper 1.00 2.50
2 Jose Bautista .50 1.25
3 Trevor Story .60 1.50
4 Felix Hernandez .50 1.25
5 Carl Yastrzemski 1.00 2.50
6 Jake Arrieta .50 1.25
7 Aledmys Diaz .50 1.25
8 Addison Russell .60 1.50
9 Stephen Strasburg .60 1.50
10 Buster Posey .75 2.00
11 Ozzie Smith .75 2.00
12 Giancarlo Stanton .60 1.50
13 Sonny Gray .50 1.25
14 Trea Turner .50 1.25
15 David Dahl RC .50 1.25
16 Robinson Cano .50 1.25
17 Eric Hosmer .50 1.25
18 Evan Longoria .50 1.25
19 Cody Bellinger RC 6.00 15.00
20 Dansby Swanson RC 1.00 2.50
21 Alex Bregman RC 1.50 4.00
22 Yoenis Cespedes .60 1.50
23 Jharel Cotton RC .30 .75
24 Don Mattingly 1.25 3.00
25 Mike Trout 3.00 8.00
26 Roberto Clemente 1.50 4.00
27 Ernie Banks .60 1.50
28 Max Scherzer .60 1.50
29 Matt Kemp .50 1.25
30 Justin Verlander .60 1.50
31 Corey Seager .60 1.50
32 Paul Goldschmidt .60 1.50
33 Julio Urias .60 1.50
34 Mike Piazza .60 1.50
35 Sandy Koufax 1.25 3.00
36 Johnny Bench .60 1.50
37 Freddie Freeman .75 2.00
38 Jake Thompson RC .40 1.00
39 Miguel Sano .50 1.25
40 Anthony Rizzo 1.00 2.50
41 Tyler Glasnow RC .50 1.25
42 Adam Jones .50 1.25
43 Jacob deGrom .60 1.50
44 Ian Happ RC .75 2.00
45 Chipper Jones .60 1.50
46 Javier Baez .75 2.00
47 Manny Machado .60 1.50
48 Andrew Benintendi RC 1.25 3.00
49 Josh Bell RC 1.00 2.50
50 Kris Bryant .75 2.00
51 Hunter Pence .50 1.25
52 Frank Thomas .60 1.50
53 Ryan Braun .50 1.25
54 Yulieski Gurriel RC .60 1.50
55 George Brett 1.25 3.00
56 Yoan Moncada RC 1.25 3.00
57 Adrian Gonzalez .50 1.25
58 Trey Mancini RC .75 2.00
59 Alex Reyes RC .50 1.25
60 Brooks Robinson .50 1.25
61 Randy Johnson .60 1.50
62 Luke Weaver RC .50 1.25
63 Andrew McCutchen .60 1.50
64 Johnny Cueto .50 1.25
65 Albert Pujols .75 2.00
66 Joey Votto .60 1.50
67 Yu Darvish .60 1.50
68 Miguel Cabrera .60 1.50
69 Edwin Encarnacion .60 1.50
70 Josh Donaldson .50 1.25
71 Jose Altuve .50 1.25
72 David Ortiz .60 1.50
73 Wil Myers .40 1.00
74 Troy Tulowitzki .60 1.50
75 Mookie Betts 1.00 2.50
76 Mitch Haniger RC .60 1.50
77 Gary Sanchez .60 1.50
78 Jose Abreu .60 1.50
79 Ken Griffey Jr. 1.25 3.00
80 Chris Sale .60 1.50
81 Masahiro Tanaka .50 1.25
82 Nolan Ryan 2.00 5.00
83 Kenta Maeda .50 1.25
84 Bo Jackson .60 1.50
85 Clayton Kershaw 1.25 3.00
86 Aaron Judge RC 5.00 12.00
87 Francisco Lindor .60 1.50
88 Greg Maddux .75 2.00
89 Christian Arroyo RC .60 1.50
90 Carlos Correa .60 1.50
91 Hank Aaron 1.25 3.00
92 Reggie Jackson .50 1.25
93 Nolan Arenado .75 2.00
94 Kyle Schwarber .60 1.50
95 Ichiro .75 2.00
96 Noah Syndergaard .50 1.25
97 Cal Ripken Jr. 2.00 5.00
98 Carlos Gonzalez .50 1.25
99 Roger Clemens .75 2.00
100 Mark McGwire 1.00 2.50

2017 Topps Gold Label Class 1 Black

*CLASS 1 BLACK: .5X TO 1.2X CLASS 1
*CLASS 1 BLACK RC: .5X TO 1.2X CLASS 1 RC

2017 Topps Gold Label Class 1 Blue

*CLASS 1 BLUE: 1X TO 2.5X CLASS 1
*CLASS 1 BLUE RC: 1X TO 2.5X CLASS 1 RC
STATED PRINT RUN 150 SER.#'d SETS
86 Aaron Judge 20.00 50.00
97 Cal Ripken Jr. 6.00 15.00

2017 Topps Gold Label Class 1 Red

*CLASS 1 BLUE: 1.2X TO 3X CLASS 1
*CLASS 1 BLUE RC: 1.2X TO 3X CLASS 1 RC
STATED PRINT RUN 75 SER.#'d SETS
86 Aaron Judge 25.00 60.00
97 Cal Ripken Jr. 8.00 20.00

2017 Topps Gold Label Class 2

*CLASS 2: .6X TO 1.5X CLASS 1
*CLASS 2 RC: .6X TO 1.5X CLASS 1 RC

2017 Topps Gold Label Class 2 Black

*CLASS 2 BLACK: .75X TO 2X CLASS 1
*CLASS 2 BLACK RC: .75X TO 2X CLASS 1 RC
86 Aaron Judge 12.00 30.00

2017 Topps Gold Label Class 2 Blue

*CLASS 2 BLUE: 1.2X TO 3X CLASS 1
*CLASS 2 BLUE RC: 1.2X TO 3X CLASS 1 RC
STATED PRINT RUN 99 SER.#'d SETS
86 Aaron Judge 25.00 60.00
97 Cal Ripken Jr. 8.00 20.00

2017 Topps Gold Label Class 2 Red

*CLASS 2 RED: 1.5X TO 4X CLASS 1
*CLASS 2 RED RC: 1.5X TO 4X CLASS 1 RC
STATED PRINT RUN 50 SER.#'d SETS
55 George Brett 10.00 25.00
79 Ken Griffey Jr. 8.00 20.00
82 Nolan Ryan 10.00 25.00
86 Aaron Judge 30.00 80.00
97 Cal Ripken Jr. 10.00 25.00

2017 Topps Gold Label Class 3

*CLASS 3: .75X TO 2X CLASS 1
*CLASS 3 RC: .75X TO 2X CLASS 1 RC
86 Aaron Judge 12.00 30.00

2017 Topps Gold Label Class 3 Black

*CLASS 3 BLACK: 1X TO 2.5X CLASS 1
*CLASS 3 BLACK RC: 1X TO 2.5X CLASS 1 RC
55 George Brett 12.00 30.00
79 Ken Griffey Jr. 10.00 25.00
82 Nolan Ryan 12.00 30.00
86 Aaron Judge 40.00 100.00
97 Cal Ripken Jr. 12.00 30.00

2017 Topps Gold Label Class 3 Blue

*CLASS 3 BLUE: 1.5X TO 4X CLASS 1
*CLASS 3 BLUE RC: 1.5X TO 4X CLASS 1 RC
STATED PRINT RUN 50 SER.#'d SETS
55 George Brett 10.00 25.00
79 Ken Griffey Jr. 8.00 20.00
82 Nolan Ryan 10.00 25.00
86 Aaron Judge 30.00 80.00
97 Cal Ripken Jr. 10.00 25.00

2017 Topps Gold Label Class 3 Red

*CLASS 3 RED: 2.5X TO 6X CLASS 1
*CLASS 3 RED RC: 2.5X TO 6X CLASS 1 RC
STATED PRINT RUN 25 SER.#'d SETS
19 Cody Bellinger 60.00 150.00
24 Don Mattingly 15.00 40.00
25 Mike Trout 20.00 50.00
26 Roberto Clemente 30.00 80.00
49 Josh Bell 12.00 30.00
55 George Brett 15.00 40.00
79 Ken Griffey Jr. 12.00 30.00
82 Nolan Ryan 15.00 40.00
86 Aaron Judge 75.00 200.00
91 Hank Aaron 15.00 40.00
92 Reggie Jackson 10.00 25.00
95 Ichiro 15.00 40.00
97 Cal Ripken Jr. 25.00 60.00
100 Mark McGwire 12.00 30.00

2017 Topps Gold Label Framed Autographs

PRINT RUNS B/WN 50-501 COPIES PER
NOT ALL CARDS SERIAL NUMBERED
EXCHANGE DEADLINE 8/31/2019
*BLACK/75: .5X TO 1.2X BASIC
*BLACK/25: .6X TO 1.5X BASIC
*BLUE/50: .5X TO 1.2X BASIC
*RED/25: .6X TO 1.5X BASIC
FAABE Andrew Benintendi 30.00 80.00
FAABR Alex Bregman 20.00 50.00
FAAD Aledmys Diaz 4.00 10.00
FAAG Andres Galarraga 8.00 20.00
FAAJ Aaron Judge 75.00 200.00
FAAP Andy Pettitte 25.00 60.00
FAARE Alex Reyes 4.00 10.00
FAARI Anthony Rizzo 30.00 80.00
FAARU Addison Russell
FAAT Andrew Toles 3.00 8.00
FABH Bryce Harper EXCH
FABL Barry Larkin 20.00 50.00
FABP Buster Posey
FABZ Bradley Zimmer/492 4.00 10.00
FACB Cody Bellinger/100 60.00 150.00
FACC Carlos Correa 40.00 100.00
FACFU Carson Fulmer 3.00 8.00
FACK Clayton Kershaw
FACS Corey Seager 30.00 80.00
FADB Dellin Betances 4.00 10.00
FADJ Derek Jeter
FADS Dansby Swanson EXCH
FADV Dan Vogelbach 5.00 12.00
FAEM Edgar Martinez/50 15.00 40.00
FAFB Franklin Barreto/491 5.00 12.00
FAFL Francisco Lindor EXCH 25.00 60.00
FAGC Gavin Cecchini 3.00 8.00
FAHA Hank Aaron
FAHD Hunter Dozier/501 3.00 8.00
FAHR Hunter Renfroe 4.00 10.00
FAI Ichiro
FAIR Ivan Rodriguez EXCH 20.00 50.00
FAJAF Jorge Alfaro/486 4.00 10.00
FAJBA Jeff Bagwell 20.00 50.00
FAJBZ Javier Baez 25.00 60.00
FAJCA Jose Canseco 12.00 30.00
FAJCO Jharel Cotton 3.00 8.00
FAJDG Jacob deGrom/50 15.00 40.00
FAJDL Jose De Leon 3.00 8.00
FAJDO Josh Donaldson EXCH 20.00 50.00
FAJJO JaCoby Jones 4.00 10.00
FAJM Joe Musgrove 3.00 8.00
FAJS John Smoltz 20.00 50.00
FAJT Jake Thompson 3.00 8.00
FAJU Julio Urias EXCH 6.00 15.00
FAKB Kris Bryant 150.00 300.00
FAKSE Kyle Seager 10.00 25.00
FALB Lewis Brinson/400 10.00 25.00
FALW Luke Weaver 3.00 8.00
FAMMA Manny Machado 15.00 40.00
FAMMG Mark McGwire
FAMMR Manny Margot 5.00 12.00
FAMTA Masahiro Tanaka
FAMTR Mike Trout
FANS Noah Syndergaard 15.00 40.00
FAOV Omar Vizquel
FARG Robert Gsellman 3.00 8.00
FARH Ryon Healy 4.00 10.00
FARL Reynaldo Lopez 3.00 8.00
FARQ Roman Quinn/300 3.00 8.00
FART Raimel Tapia 4.00 10.00
FASK Sandy Koufax
FASMA Steven Matz 4.00 10.00
FASN Sean Newcomb/400 4.00 10.00
FATA Tyler Austin 8.00 20.00
FATB Ty Blach 5.00 12.00
FATGL Tyler Glasnow 5.00 12.00
FATM Trey Mancini 8.00 20.00
FATS Trevor Story 8.00 20.00
FAYG Yulieski Gurriel 10.00 25.00
FAYM Yoan Moncada 25.00 60.00

2017 Topps Gold Label Legend Relics

PRINT RUNS B/WN 10-75 COPIES PER
NO PRICING ON QTY 10 OR LESS
GLRBJ Bo Jackson/75 12.00 30.00
GLRCJ Chipper Jones/75 8.00 20.00
GLRCR Cal Ripken Jr./75 8.00 20.00
GLRCY Carl Yastrzemski/75 8.00 20.00
GLRDM Don Mattingly/75 10.00 25.00
GLREM Eddie Murray/75 12.00 30.00
GLRGM Greg Maddux/75 6.00 15.00
GLRJB Johnny Bench/75 8.00 20.00
GLRJR Jackie Robinson
GLRKG Ken Griffey Jr./75 10.00 25.00
GLRMM Mark McGwire/75 8.00 20.00
GLRMP Mike Piazza/75 5.00 12.00
GLRNR Nolan Ryan/75 20.00 50.00
GLROS Ozzie Smith/75 8.00 20.00
GLRRCA Rod Carew/75 6.00 15.00
GLRRCL Roberto Clemente/50 30.00 80.00
GLRRH Rickey Henderson/75 8.00 20.00

GLRRJ Reggie Jackson/75 6.00 15.00
GLRTW Ted Williams/50 25.00 60.00

2018 Topps Gold Label Class 1

COMPLETE SET (100) 25.00 60.00
1 Rafael Devers RC 1.25 3.00
2 Aaron Judge 1.50 4.00
3 Bryce Harper 1.00 2.50
4 Jose Altuve .50 1.25
5 Hank Aaron 1.25 3.00
6 Mike Trout 3.00 8.00
7 Greg Maddux .75 2.00
8 Chipper Jones .60 1.50
9 Freddie Freeman .75 2.00
10 Ozzie Albies RC 1.25 3.00
11 Manny Machado .60 1.50
12 Adam Jones .50 1.25
13 Cal Ripken Jr. 2.00 5.00
14 Trey Mancini .50 1.25
15 Austin Hays RC .60 1.50
16 Justin Upton .50 1.25
17 Shohei Ohtani RC 2.50 6.00
18 Paul Goldschmidt .60 1.50
19 Zack Greinke .50 1.25
20 Mookie Betts 1.00 2.50
21 Chris Sale .60 1.50
22 Ted Williams 1.25 3.00
23 David Ortiz .60 1.50
24 Andrew Benintendi .60 1.50
25 Jackie Robinson .60 1.50
26 Kris Bryant .75 2.00
27 Anthony Rizzo 1.00 2.50
28 Yu Darvish .60 1.50
29 Ernie Banks .60 1.50
30 Ryne Sandberg 1.25 3.00
31 Javier Baez .75 2.00
32 Ian Happ .50 1.25
33 Frank Thomas .60 1.50
34 Yoan Moncada .60 1.50
35 Joey Votto .60 1.50
36 Johnny Bench .60 1.50
37 Barry Larkin .50 1.25
38 Francisco Lindor .60 1.50
39 Corey Kluber .50 1.25
40 Francisco Mejia RC .50 1.25
41 Nolan Arenado .75 2.00
42 Charlie Blackmon .60 1.50
43 Ryan McMahon RC .50 1.25
44 Miguel Cabrera .60 1.50
45 Justin Verlander .60 1.50
46 Carlos Correa .60 1.50
47 Nolan Ryan 2.00 5.00
48 George Springer .50 1.25
49 Alex Bregman .60 1.50
50 George Brett 1.25 3.00
51 Bo Jackson .60 1.50
52 Clayton Kershaw 1.25 3.00
53 Corey Seager .60 1.50
54 Cody Bellinger 1.25 3.00
55 Sandy Koufax 1.25 3.00
56 Walker Buehler RC 2.00 5.00
57 Alex Verdugo RC .60 1.50
58 Christian Yelich .75 2.00
59 Byron Buxton .50 1.25
60 Miguel Sano .50 1.25
61 Brian Dozier .50 1.25
62 Noah Syndergaard .50 1.25
63 Jacob deGrom .60 1.50
64 Yoenis Cespedes .60 1.50
65 Mike Piazza .60 1.50
66 Michael Conforto .50 1.25
67 Giancarlo Stanton .60 1.50
68 Masahiro Tanaka .50 1.25
69 Gary Sanchez .60 1.50
70 Derek Jeter 1.50 4.00
71 Don Mattingly 1.25 3.00
72 Luis Severino .50 1.25
73 Clint Frazier RC .75 2.00
74 Mariano Rivera .75 2.00
75 Miguel Andujar RC 1.50 4.00
76 Khris Davis .60 1.50
77 Matt Olson .40 1.00
78 Rhys Hoskins RC 1.50 4.00
79 J.P. Crawford RC .40 1.00
80 Roberto Clemente 1.50 4.00
81 Eric Hosmer .50 1.25
82 Wil Myers .40 1.00
83 Buster Posey .75 2.00
84 Andrew McCutchen .60 1.50
85 Ichiro .75 2.00
86 Felix Hernandez .50 1.25
87 Robinson Cano .50 1.25
88 Randy Johnson .60 1.50
89 Mark McGwire 1.00 2.50
90 Ozzie Smith .75 2.00
91 Marcell Ozuna .60 1.50
92 Chris Archer .40 1.00
93 Adrian Beltre .60 1.50
94 Josh Donaldson .50 1.25
95 Max Scherzer .60 1.50
96 Stephen Strasburg .60 1.50
97 Victor Robles RC 1.00 2.50
98 Gleyber Torres RC 4.00 10.00
99 Ronald Acuna Jr. RC 8.00 20.00
100 Scott Kingery RC .60 1.50

2018 Topps Gold Label Class 1 Black

*CLASS 1 BLACK: .5X TO 1.2X CLASS 1
*CLASS 1 BLACK RC: .5X TO 1.2X CLASS 1 RC
STATED ODDS 1:2 HOBBY

2018 Topps Gold Label Class 1 Blue

*CLASS 1 BLUE: 1X TO 2.5X CLASS 1
*CLASS 1 BLUE RC: 1X TO 2.5X CLASS 1 RC
STATED ODDS 1:14 HOBBY
STATED PRINT RUN 150 SER.#'d SETS

2018 Topps Gold Label Class 1 Red

*CLASS 1 BLUE: 1.2X TO 3X CLASS 1
*CLASS 1 BLUE RC: 1.2X TO 3X CLASS 1 RC
STATED ODDS 1:28 HOBBY
STATED PRINT RUN 75 SER.#'d SETS
17 Shohei Ohtani 20.00 50.00

2018 Topps Gold Label Class 2

*CLASS 2: .6X TO 1.5X CLASS 1
*CLASS 2 RC: .6X TO 1.5X CLASS 1 RC

2018 Topps Gold Label Class 2 Black

*CLASS 2 BLACK: .75X TO 2X CLASS 1
*CLASS 2 BLACK RC: .75X TO 2X CLASS 1 RC
STATED ODDS 1:6 HOBBY

2018 Topps Gold Label Class 2 Blue

*CLASS 2 BLUE: 1.2X TO 3X CLASS 1
*CLASS 2 BLUE RC: 1.2X TO 3X CLASS 1 RC
STATED ODDS 1:21 HOBBY
STATED PRINT RUN 99 SER.#'d SETS
17 Shohei Ohtani 20.00 50.00

2018 Topps Gold Label Class 2 Red

*CLASS 2 RED: 1.5X TO 4X CLASS 1
*CLASS 2 RED RC: 1.5X TO 4X CLASS 1 RC
STATED ODDS 1:42 HOBBY
STATED PRINT RUN 50 SER.#'d SETS
17 Shohei Ohtani 25.00 60.00
99 Ronald Acuna Jr. 25.00 60.00

2018 Topps Gold Label Class 3

*CLASS 3: .75X TO 2X CLASS 1
*CLASS 3 RC: .75X TO 2X CLASS 1 RC

2018 Topps Gold Label Class 3 Black

*CLASS 3 BLACK: 1X TO 2.5X CLASS 1
*CLASS 3 BLACK RC: 1X TO 2.5X CLASS 1 RC
STATED ODDS 1:20 HOBBY

2018 Topps Gold Label Class 3 Blue

*CLASS 3 BLUE: 1.5X TO 4X CLASS 1
*CLASS 3 BLUE RC: 1.5X TO 4X CLASS 1 RC
STATED ODDS 1:42 HOBBY
STATED PRINT RUN 50 SER.#'d SETS
17 Shohei Ohtani 25.00 60.00
99 Ronald Acuna Jr. 25.00 60.00

2018 Topps Gold Label Class 3 Red

*CLASS 3 RED: 2.5X TO 6X CLASS 1
*CLASS 3 RED RC: 2.5X TO 6X CLASS 1 RC
STATED ODDS 1:83 HOBBY
STATED PRINT RUN 25 SER.#'d SETS
17 Shohei Ohtani 40.00 100.00
99 Ronald Acuna Jr. 40.00 100.00

2018 Topps Gold Label Framed Autographs

STATED ODDS 1:11 HOBBY
EXCHANGE DEADLINE 9/30/2020
FAAB Anthony Banda 3.00 8.00
FAAH Austin Hays 6.00 15.00
FAAI Anthony Rizzo EXCH 25.00 60.00
FAAJ Aaron Judge
FAAM Austin Meadows 10.00 25.00
FAAN Aaron Nola 8.00 20.00
FAAR Amed Rosario 4.00 10.00
FAAV Alex Verdugo 15.00 40.00
FABD Brian Dozier 6.00 15.00
FABY Bryce Harper EXCH
FACF Clint Frazier 12.00 30.00
FACS Chance Sisco 4.00 10.00
FACST Chris Stratton 3.00 8.00
FACT Chris Taylor 4.00 10.00
FACY Christian Yelich 25.00 60.00
FADF Dustin Fowler 3.00 8.00
FADG Dwight Gooden 6.00 15.00
FADR Didi Gregorius EXCH 8.00 20.00
FADS Darryl Stawberry 12.00 30.00
FAEP George Springer 15.00 40.00
FAFM Francisco Mejia 6.00 15.00
FAGC Garrett Cooper 3.00 8.00
FAGT Gleyber Torres 40.00 100.00
FAHB Harrison Bader 5.00 12.00
FAIH Ian Happ 6.00 15.00
FAIK Ian Kinsler 4.00 10.00
FAJA Jose Altuve 20.00 50.00
FAJB Jose Berrios 4.00 10.00
FAJC Jose Canseco 10.00 25.00
FAJD J.D. Davis 4.00 10.00
FAJE Jacob deGrom 12.00 30.00
FAJF Jack Flaherty 15.00 40.00
FAJL Jake Lamb 4.00 10.00
FAJR Jose Ramirez 15.00 40.00
FAJSO Juan Soto EXCH 100.00 250.00
FAJU Justin Upton 8.00 20.00
FAJV Joey Votto 25.00 60.00
FAJW J.P. Crawford 4.00 10.00
FAKB Kris Bryant EXCH 60.00 150.00
FAKD Khris Davis 10.00 25.00
FALB Lewis Brinson EXCH 3.00 8.00
FALC Luis Castillo 4.00 10.00
FALS Lucas Sims 3.00 8.00
FAMA Miguel Andujar 20.00 50.00
FAMF Max Fried 8.00 20.00
FAMO Matt Olson 3.00 8.00
FAND Nicky Delmonico 3.00 8.00
FANY Noah Syndergaard 10.00 25.00
FAOA Ozzie Albies 25.00 60.00
FAPB Paul Blackburn 3.00 8.00
FAPD Paul DeJong 6.00 15.00
FAPG Paul Goldschmidt 15.00 40.00
FAPT Tommy Pham 3.00 8.00
FARA Ronald Acuna Jr. 100.00 250.00
FARD Rafael Devers 30.00 80.00
FARE Trey Mancini 5.00 12.00
FARH Rhys Hoskins 20.00 50.00
FARM Ryan McMahon 4.00 10.00
FARN Rick Ankiel 3.00 8.00
FASKI Scott Kingery 6.00 15.00
FASM Starling Marte 4.00 10.00
FASN Sean Newcomb 4.00 10.00
FASO Shohei Ohtani 300.00 600.00
FASP Salvador Perez 10.00 25.00
FAST Travis Shaw 3.00 8.00
FATM Tyler Mahle 4.00 10.00
FAVC Victor Caratini 4.00 10.00
FAVR Victor Robles 10.00 25.00
FAWB Walker Buehler 25.00 60.00
FAWC Willson Contreras 15.00 40.00
FAWM Whit Merrifield 8.00 20.00

2018 Topps Gold Label Framed Autographs Black

*BLACK/75: .5X TO 1.2X BASIC
STATED ODDS 1:45 HOBBY
PRINT RUNS B/WN 15-75 COPIES PER
NO PRICING ON QTY 15
EXCHANGE DEADLINE 9/30/2020
FAAJ Aaron Judge 125.00 300.00
FACL Charlie Blackmon 6.00 15.00
FADS Darryl Strawberry 6.00 15.00

2018 Topps Gold Label Framed Autographs Blue

*BLUE/50: .5X TO 1.2X BASIC
STATED ODDS 1:67 HOBBY
PRINT RUNS B/WN 10-50 COPIES PER
NO PRICING ON QTY 10
EXCHANGE DEADLINE 9/30/2020
FAAJ Aaron Judge 125.00 300.00
FACL Charlie Blackmon 6.00 15.00
FADS Darryl Strawberry 6.00 15.00

2018 Topps Gold Label Framed Autographs Red

*RED/25: .6X TO 1.5X BASIC
STATED ODDS 1:134 HOBBY
PRINT RUNS B/WN 5-25 COPIES PER
NO PRICING ON QTY 5
EXCHANGE DEADLINE 9/30/2020
FAAJ Aaron Judge 150.00 400.00
FABA Brian Anderson 15.00 40.00
FACL Charlie Blackmon 8.00 20.00
FADS Darryl Strawberry 8.00 20.00

2018 Topps Gold Label Golden Greats Framed Autograph Relics

STATED ODDS 1:611 HOBBY
PRINT RUNS B/WN 10-25 COPIES PER
NO PRICING ON QTY 10
EXCHANGE DEADLINE 9/30/2020
GGARAK Al Kaline/25 40.00 100.00
GGARAP Andy Pettitte/25 20.00 50.00
GGARBJ Bo Jackson/15 50.00 120.00
GGARBL Barry Larkin EXCH 40.00 100.00
GGARCB Craig Biggio
GGARDE Dennis Eckersley/25 10.00 25.00
GGARDM Don Mattingly/25 50.00 120.00
GGARFT Frank Thomas/25 60.00 150.00
GGARGM Greg Maddux
GGARJS John Smoltz/25
GGARMP Mike Piazza
GGARNG Nomar Garciaparra/25
GGAROS Ozzie Smith/25 60.00 150.00
GGARRL Roger Clemens
GGARRO Randy Johnson
GGARRS Ryne Sandberg

2018 Topps Gold Label Legends Relics

STATED ODDS 1:122 HOBBY
PRINT RUNS B/WN 25-50 COPIES PER
LRBL Barry Larkin/75 5.00 12.00
LRCB Craig Biggio/75 5.00 12.00
LRCR Cal Ripken Jr./75 8.00 20.00
LRDJ Derek Jeter/50 20.00 50.00
LRDM Don Mattingly/75 15.00 40.00
LRFT Frank Thomas/75 6.00 15.00
LRGB George Brett/75 15.00 40.00
LRGM Greg Maddux/75 6.00 15.00
LRHA Hank Aaron/50 15.00 40.00
LRJB Johnny Bench/75 6.00 15.00
LRJS John Smoltz/75 6.00 15.00
LRMM Mark McGwire/75 8.00 20.00
LRMP Mike Piazza/75 6.00 15.00
LRNG Nomar Garciaparra/75 5.00 12.00
LRNR Nolan Ryan/75 15.00 40.00
LROS Ozzie Smith/75 10.00 25.00
LRPM Pedro Martinez/75 5.00 12.00
LRRC Roberto Clemente/25 60.00 150.00
LRRH Rickey Henderson/75 6.00 15.00
LRRJ Reggie Jackson/75 6.00 15.00
LRRL Roger Clemens/75 8.00 20.00
LRTG Tom Glavine/75 6.00 15.00
LRTS Tom Seaver/25 10.00 25.00
LRTW Ted Williams/50 20.00 50.00
LRWB Wade Boggs/75 8.00 20.00

2019 Topps Gold Label Class 1

COMPLETE SET (100) 25.00 60.00
1 Mike Trout 3.00 8.00
2 Albert Pujols .75 2.00
3 Shohei Ohtani .75 2.00
4 Paul Goldschmidt .60 1.50
5 Freddie Freeman .75 2.00
6 Ozzie Albies .60 1.50
7 Ronald Acuna Jr. 3.00 8.00
8 Mookie Betts 1.00 2.50
9 Chris Sale .60 1.50
10 Andrew Benintendi .60 1.50
11 J.D. Martinez .60 1.50
12 Kris Bryant .75 2.00
13 Anthony Rizzo 1.00 2.50
14 Javier Baez .75 2.00
15 Michael Kopech RC .75 2.00
16 Joey Votto .60 1.50
17 Francisco Lindor .60 1.50
18 Yusei Kikuchi RC .60 1.50
19 Trevor Bauer .60 1.50
20 Jose Ramirez .50 1.25
21 Nolan Arenado .75 2.00
22 Charlie Blackmon .60 1.50
23 Trevor Story .60 1.50
24 Miguel Cabrera .60 1.50
25 Justin Verlander .60 1.50
26 Carlos Correa .60 1.50
27 Jose Altuve .50 1.25
28 George Springer .50 1.25
29 Alex Bregman .60 1.50
30 Kyle Tucker RC .75 2.00
31 Pete Alonso RC 3.00 8.00
32 Whit Merrifield .60 1.50
33 Manny Machado .60 1.50
34 Clayton Kershaw 1.25 3.00
35 Corey Seager .60 1.50
36 Cody Bellinger 1.25 3.00
37 Christian Yelich .75 2.00
38 Noah Syndergaard .50 1.25
39 Jacob deGrom .60 1.50
40 Robinson Cano .50 1.25
41 Giancarlo Stanton .60 1.50
42 Masahiro Tanaka .50 1.25
43 Gary Sanchez .60 1.50
44 Aaron Judge 1.50 4.00
45 Luis Severino .50 1.25
46 Gleyber Torres 1.25 3.00
47 Brendan Rodgers RC .60 1.50
48 Khris Davis .60 1.50
49 Matt Chapman .60 1.50
50 Rhys Hoskins .75 2.00
51 Aaron Nola .50 1.25
52 Carter Kieboom RC .60 1.50
53 Keston Hiura RC 1.25 3.00
54 Buster Posey .75 2.00
55 Ichiro Suzuki .75 2.00
56 Ken Griffey Jr. 1.25 3.00
57 Nick Senzel RC 1.25 3.00
58 Yadier Molina .60 1.50
59 Blake Snell .50 1.25
60 Austin Riley RC 2.00 5.00
61 Joey Gallo .50 1.25
62 Bryce Harper 1.00 2.50
63 Max Scherzer .60 1.50
64 Trea Turner .50 1.25
65 Stephen Strasburg .60 1.50
66 Juan Soto 2.00 5.00
67 Josh Donaldson .50 1.25
68 Roberto Alomar .50 1.25
69 J.T. Realmuto .60 1.50
70 Luis Urias RC .60 1.50
71 Hideki Matsui .60 1.50
72 Rickey Henderson .60 1.50
73 Chipper Jones .60 1.50
74 Cal Ripken Jr. 2.00 5.00
75 Ted Williams 1.25 3.00
76 David Ortiz .60 1.50
77 Mariano Rivera .75 2.00
78 Jackie Robinson .60 1.50
79 Ernie Banks .60 1.50
80 Ryne Sandberg 1.25 3.00
81 Frank Thomas .60 1.50
82 Johnny Bench .60 1.50
83 Barry Larkin .50 1.25
84 Nolan Ryan 2.00 5.00
85 Bo Jackson .60 1.50
86 Sandy Koufax 1.25 3.00
87 Walker Buehler .75 2.00
88 Mike Piazza .60 1.50
89 Derek Jeter 1.50 4.00
90 Don Mattingly 1.25 3.00
91 Roberto Clemente 1.50 4.00
92 Tony Gwynn .60 1.50
93 Mark McGwire 1.00 2.50
94 Ozzie Smith .75 2.00
95 Chris Archer .40 1.00
96 Deion Sanders .50 1.25
97 Roger Clemens .75 2.00
98 Eloy Jimenez RC 1.50 4.00
99 Vladimir Guerrero Jr. RC 2.50 6.00
100 Fernando Tatis Jr. RC 4.00 10.00

2019 Topps Gold Label Class 1 Black

2018 Topps Gold Label Class 1 Black
2018 Topps Gold Label Class 1 Black
2018 Topps Gold Label Class 1 Black

2019 Topps Gold Label Class 1 Blue

*CLASS 1 BLUE: 1X TO 2.5X CLASS 1
*CLASS 1 BLUE RC: 1X TO 2.5X CLASS 1 RC
STATED ODDS 1:15 HOBBY
STATED PRINT RUN 150 SER.#'d SETS
56 Ken Griffey Jr. 8.00 20.00
72 Rickey Henderson 4.00 10.00
84 Nolan Ryan 6.00 15.00
89 Derek Jeter 8.00 20.00
90 Don Mattingly 5.00 12.00

2019 Topps Gold Label Class 1 Red

*CLASS 1 BLUE: 1.2X TO 3X CLASS 1
*CLASS 1 BLUE RC: 1.2X TO 3X CLASS 1 RC
STATED ODDS 1:30 HOBBY
STATED PRINT RUN 75 SER.#'d SETS
56 Ken Griffey Jr. 10.00 25.00
72 Rickey Henderson 5.00 12.00
84 Nolan Ryan 8.00 20.00
89 Derek Jeter 10.00 25.00
90 Don Mattingly 6.00 15.00

2019 Topps Gold Label Class 2

*CLASS 2: .6X TO 1.5X CLASS 1
*CLASS 2 RC: .6X TO 1.5X CLASS 1 RC

2019 Topps Gold Label Class 2 Black

*CLASS 2 BLACK: .75X TO 2X CLASS 1
*CLASS 2 BLACK RC: .75X TO 2X CLASS 1 RC
STATED ODDS 1:6 HOBBY

2019 Topps Gold Label Class 2 Blue

*CLASS 2 BLUE: 1.2X TO 3X CLASS 1
*CLASS 2 BLUE RC: 1.2X TO 3X CLASS 1 RC
STATED ODDS 1:23 HOBBY
STATED PRINT RUN 99 SER.#'d SETS
56 Ken Griffey Jr. 1.00 25.00
72 Rickey Henderson 5.00 12.00
84 Nolan Ryan 8.00 20.00
89 Derek Jeter 10.00 25.00
90 Don Mattingly 6.00 15.00

2019 Topps Gold Label Class 2 Red

*CLASS 2 RED: 1.5X TO 4X CLASS 1
*CLASS 2 RED RC: 1.5X TO 4X CLASS 1 RC
STATED ODDS 1:45 HOBBY
STATED PRINT RUN 50 SER.#'d SETS
56 Ken Griffey Jr. 12.00 30.00
72 Rickey Henderson 6.00 15.00
84 Nolan Ryan 10.00 25.00
89 Derek Jeter 12.00 30.00
90 Don Mattingly 8.00 20.00

2019 Topps Gold Label Class 3

*CLASS 3: .75X TO 2X CLASS 1
*CLASS 3 RC: .75X TO 2X CLASS 1 RC

2019 Topps Gold Label Class 3 Black

*CLASS 3 BLACK: 1X TO 2.5X CLASS 1
*CLASS 3 BLACK RC: 1X TO 2.5X CLASS 1 RC
STATED ODDS 1:20 HOBBY
56 Ken Griffey Jr. 8.00 20.00
72 Rickey Henderson 4.00 10.00
84 Nolan Ryan 6.00 15.00
89 Derek Jeter 8.00 20.00
90 Don Mattingly 5.00 12.00

2019 Topps Gold Label Class 3 Blue

*CLASS 3 BLUE: 1.5X TO 4X CLASS 1
*CLASS 3 BLUE RC: 1.5X TO 4X CLASS 1 RC
STATED ODDS 1:45 HOBBY
STATED PRINT RUN 50 SER.#'d SETS
56 Ken Griffey Jr. 12.00 30.00
72 Rickey Henderson 6.00 15.00
84 Nolan Ryan 10.00 25.00
89 Derek Jeter 12.00 30.00
90 Don Mattingly 8.00 20.00

2019 Topps Gold Label Class 3 Red

*CLASS 3 RED: 2.5X TO 6X CLASS 1
*CLASS 3 RED RC: 2.5X TO 6X CLASS 1 RC
STATED ODDS 1:90 HOBBY
STATED PRINT RUN 25 SER.#'d SETS
56 Ken Griffey Jr. 20.00 50.00
72 Rickey Henderson 10.00 25.00
84 Nolan Ryan 15.00 40.00
89 Derek Jeter 20.00 50.00
90 Don Mattingly 12.00 30.00

2019 Topps Gold Label Framed Autographs

STATED ODDS 1:10 HOBBY
EXCHANGE DEADLINE 8/31/2021
GLAAM Andrew McCutchen 25.00 60.00
GLABK Brad Keller 3.00 8.00
GLABL Brandon Lowe 20.00 50.00
GLABW Bryse Wilson 6.00 15.00
GLACB Corbin Burnes 5.00 12.00
GLACM Cedric Mullins 5.00 12.00
GLACSH Chris Shaw 5.00 12.00
GLADH Dakota Hudson 4.00 10.00
GLADJ Danny Jansen 3.00 8.00
GLADMU Dale Murphy 40.00 100.00
GLADP Daniel Ponce de Leon 5.00 12.00
GLADR Dereck Rodriguez 5.00 12.00
GLADS Darryl Strawberry 12.00 30.00
GLADST DJ Stewart 4.00 10.00
GLAEJ Eloy Jimenez 25.00 60.00
GLAEM Edgar Martinez 25.00 60.00
GLAFL Francisco Lindor 20.00 50.00
GLAFTA Fernando Tatis Jr. 100.00 250.00
GLAJA Jose Altuve 25.00 60.00
GLAJC Jose Canseco 10.00 25.00
GLAJd Jacob deGrom 25.00 60.00
GLAJF Jack Flaherty 10.00 25.00
GLAJH Josh Hader 5.00 12.00
GLAJJ Josh James 5.00 12.00
GLAJM Jeff McNeil 10.00 25.00
GLAJS Juan Soto 30.00 80.00
GLAJSH Justus Sheffield 5.00 12.00
GLAJSM Justin Smoak 3.00 8.00
GLAKA Kolby Allard 4.00 10.00
GLAKK Kevin Kramer 4.00 10.00
GLAKN Kevin Newman 5.00 12.00
GLAKS Kyle Schwarber 10.00 25.00
GLAKST Kohl Stewart 4.00 10.00
GLAKT Kyle Tucker 15.00 40.00
GLAKW Kyle Wright 10.00 25.00
GLALU Luis Urias 8.00 20.00
GLALV Luke Voit 15.00 40.00
GLAMA Miguel Andujar 8.00 20.00
GLAMMU Max Muncy 12.00 30.00
GLAMS Myles Straw 5.00 12.00
GLANM Nick Martini 3.00 8.00
GLANSY Noah Syndergaard 12.00 30.00
GLAPA Pete Alonso 60.00 150.00
GLAPG Paul Goldschmidt 15.00 40.00
GLAPW Patrick Wisdom 3.00 8.00
GLARA Ronald Acuna Jr. 50.00 120.00
GLARD Rafael Devers 15.00 40.00
GLARH Rhys Hoskins 15.00 40.00
GLARL Ramon Laureano 12.00 30.00
GLARM Reese McGuire 5.00 12.00
GLARO Ryan O'Hearn 5.00 12.00
GLART Rowdy Tellez 5.00 12.00
GLASD Steven Duggar 4.00 10.00
GLASK Sandy Koufax
GLASR Sean Reid-Foley 3.00 8.00
GLATB Trevor Bauer 5.00 12.00
GLATT Touki Toussaint 4.00 10.00
GLAVG Vladimir Guerrero Jr. 40.00 100.00
GLAWA Willians Astudillo 3.00 8.00
GLAYK Yusei Kikuchi 8.00 20.00

2019 Topps Gold Label Framed Autographs Black

*BLACK/75: .5X TO 1.2X BASIC
STATED ODDS 1:56 HOBBY
PRINT RUNS B/WN 15-75 COPIES PER
NO PRICING ON QTY 15
EXCHANGE DEADLINE 8/31/2021
GLAMH Mitch Haniger/75 8.00 20.00
GLAMK Michael Kopech/75 12.00 30.00

2019 Topps Gold Label Framed Autographs Blue

*BLUE/50: .5X TO 1.2X BASIC
STATED ODDS 1:83 HOBBY
PRINT RUNS B/WN 10-50 COPIES PER
NO PRICING ON QTY 10
EXCHANGE DEADLINE 8/31/2021
GLACK Carter Kieboom/50 15.00 40.00
GLAMH Mitch Haniger/50 8.00 20.00
GLAMK Michael Kopech/50 12.00 30.00
GLANS Nick Senzel/50 40.00 100.00

2019 Topps Gold Label Framed Autographs Red

*RED/25: .75X TO 2X BASIC
STATED ODDS 1:165 HOBBY
PRINT RUNS B/WN 5-25 COPIES PER
NO PRICING ON QTY 5
EXCHANGE DEADLINE 8/31/2021
GLACK Carter Kieboom/25 25.00 60.00
GLAMH Mitch Haniger/25 12.00 30.00
GLAMK Michael Kopech/25 20.00 50.00
GLANS Nick Senzel/25 60.00 150.00

2019 Topps Gold Label Gold Prospect Relics

STATED ODDS 1:866 HOBBY
STATED PRINT RUN 25 SER.#'d SETS
GPREJ Eloy Jimenez 60.00 150.00
GPRFT Fernando Tatis Jr. 100.00 250.00
GPRGT Gleyber Torres
GPRJS Juan Soto
GPRNS Nick Senzel 75.00 200.00
GPRPA Pete Alonso
GPRRA Ronald Acuna Jr.
GPRSO Shohei Ohtani 125.00 300.00
GPRVG Vladimir Guerrero Jr. 150.00 400.00
GPRVR Victor Robles
GPRWB Walker Buehler
GPRYK Yusei Kikuchi 40.00 100.00

2019 Topps Gold Label Golden Greats Framed Autograph Relics

STATED ODDS 1:572 HOBBY
PRINT RUNS B/WN 10-25 COPIES PER
NO PRICING ON QTY 15 OR LESS
EXCHANGE DEADLINE 8/31/2021
GGARAD Andre Dawson/25 25.00 60.00
GGARAK Al Kaline/25
GGARCF Carlton Fisk/25 15.00 40.00
GGARDE Dennis Eckersley/25
GGARDJ Derek Jeter
GGARHA Hank Aaron
GGARMR Mariano Rivera
GGAROS Ozzie Smith
GGARRC Rod Carew/25
GGARRJ Reggie Jackson
GGARRY Robin Yount/25 30.00 80.00
GGARVG Vladimir Guerrero/25
GGARWC Will Clark/25 50.00 120.00

2019 Topps Gold Label Legends Relics

STATED ODDS 1:151 HOBBY
PRINT RUNS B/WN 10-50 COPIES PER
BLRAK Al Kaline
BLRBF Bob Feller
BLRBG Bob Gibson/50
BLRBL Barry Larkin/50 6.00 15.00
BLRCR Cal Ripken Jr./50 20.00 50.00
BLRDJ Derek Jeter/50 25.00 60.00
BLRDM Don Mattingly/50
BLREM Eddie Mathews/50 10.00 25.00
BLRFT Frank Thomas/50
BLRGB George Brett
BLRHA Hank Aaron/25 20.00 50.00
BLRJB Johnny Bench/25 10.00 25.00
BLRJS John Smoltz/50 10.00 25.00
BLRKG Ken Griffey Jr./50 25.00 60.00
BLRMM Mark McGwire/50 6.00 15.00
BLRMP Mike Piazza/50 6.00 15.00
BLRNG Nomar Garciaparra/50 5.00 12.00
BLRNR Nolan Ryan/50 20.00 50.00
BLROS Ozzie Smith/50 8.00 20.00
BLRPM Pedro Martinez/50 5.00 12.00
BLRPR Pee Wee Reese/50 5.00 12.00
BLRRC Roberto Clemente 15.00 40.00
BLRRH Rickey Henderson
BLRRJ Reggie Jackson/25 10.00 25.00
BLRRS Ryne Sandberg/50 12.00 30.00
BLRRY Robin Yount/50 10.00 25.00
BLRTG Tony Gwynn/50 10.00 25.00
BLRTW Ted Williams/25 25.00 60.00
BLRWB Wade Boggs/50 10.00 25.00
BLRWM Willie McCovey/50 12.00 30.00
BLREMU Eddie Murray/50 5.00 12.00
BLRRCL Roger Clemens 8.00 20.00
BLRRHO Rogers Hornsby/50 12.00 30.00
BLRTGL Tom Glavine/50

2020 Topps Gold Label Class 1

1 Mike Trout 3.00 8.00
2 Albert Pujols .75 2.00
3 Shohei Ohtani .75 2.00
4 Anthony Rendon .60 1.50
5 Ketel Marte .50 1.25
6 Freddie Freeman .75 2.00
7 Ozzie Albies .60 1.50
8 Ronald Acuna Jr. 2.50 6.00
9 Chipper Jones .60 1.50
10 Cal Ripken Jr. 2.00 5.00
11 Mookie Betts 1.25 3.00
12 Chris Sale .60 1.50
13 Rafael Devers .75 2.00
14 J.D. Martinez .60 1.50
15 Xander Bogaerts .60 1.50
16 Jackie Robinson .60 1.50
17 Nico Hoerner RC 1.50 4.00
18 Kris Bryant .75 2.00
19 Anthony Rizzo 1.00 2.50
20 Javier Baez .75 2.00
21 Robel Garcia RC .40 1.00
22 Willson Contreras .60 1.50
23 Frank Thomas .60 1.50
24 Eloy Jimenez 1.25 3.00
25 Tim Anderson .60 1.50
26 Yoan Moncada .60 1.50
27 Joey Votto .60 1.50
28 Nick Castellanos .60 1.50
29 Max Kepler .50 1.25
30 Sonny Gray .50 1.25
31 Aristides Aquino RC .75 2.00
32 Francisco Lindor .60 1.50
33 Shane Bieber .60 1.50
34 Mike Clevinger .50 1.25
35 Carlos Santana .50 1.25
36 Nolan Arenado .75 2.00
37 Charlie Blackmon .60 1.50
38 Trevor Story .60 1.50
39 Miguel Cabrera .60 1.50
40 Justin Verlander .60 1.50
41 Carlos Correa .60 1.50
42 Jose Altuve .50 1.25
43 George Springer .50 1.25
44 Alex Bregman .60 1.50
45 Yordan Alvarez RC 2.00 5.00
46 Whit Merrifield .60 1.50
47 Jorge Soler .60 1.50
48 Clayton Kershaw 1.25 3.00
49 Cody Bellinger 1.25 3.00
50 Walker Buehler .75 2.00
51 Gavin Lux RC 2.50 6.00
52 Christian Yelich .75 2.00
53 Keston Hiura .75 2.00
54 Robin Yount .60 1.50
55 Noah Syndergaard .50 1.25
56 Jacob deGrom .60 1.50
57 Robinson Cano .50 1.25
58 Pete Alonso 1.50 4.00
59 Darryl Strawberry .40 1.00
60 Giancarlo Stanton .60 1.50
61 Masahiro Tanaka .60 1.50
62 Aaron Judge 1.50 4.00
63 Gleyber Torres 1.25 3.00
64 Don Mattingly 1.25 3.00
65 Mariano Rivera .75 2.00
66 Gerrit Cole 1.00 2.50
67 A.J. Puk RC .75 2.00
68 Jesus Luzardo RC .75 2.00
69 Matt Chapman .60 1.50
70 Rickey Henderson .60 1.50
71 Mark McGwire 1.00 2.50
72 Rhys Hoskins .75 2.00
73 Andrew McCutchen .60 1.50
74 J.T. Realmuto .60 1.50
75 Bryce Harper 1.00 2.50
76 Mike Schmidt 1.00 2.50
77 Zac Gallen RC 1.00 2.50
78 Josh Bell .50 1.25
79 Luis Robert RC 4.00 10.00
80 Manny Machado .60 1.50
81 Tony Gwynn .60 1.50
82 Fernando Tatis Jr. 2.50 6.00
83 Buster Posey .75 2.00
84 Willie Mays 1.25 3.00
85 Ichiro .75 2.00
86 Ken Griffey Jr. 1.25 3.00
87 Kyle Lewis RC 3.00 8.00
88 Paul Goldschmidt .60 1.50
89 Yadier Molina .60 1.50

0 Yoshi Tsutsugo .50 1.25
Brendan McKay RC .60 1.50
2 Blake Snell .50 1.25
3 Nolan Ryan 2.00 5.00
Joey Gallo .60 1.50
5 Bo Bichette RC 3.00 8.00
5 Vladimir Guerrero Jr. 1.25 3.00
7 Max Scherzer .60 1.50
8 Trea Turner .50 1.25
9 Stephen Strasburg .60 1.50
00 Juan Soto 2.00 5.00

2020 Topps Gold Label Class 1 Black
CLASS 1 BLACK: .5X TO 1.2X CLASS 1
CLASS 1 BLACK RC: .5X TO 1.2X CLASS 1 RC
TATED ODDS 1:2 HOBBY

2020 Topps Gold Label Class 1 Blue
CLASS 1 BLUE: 1X TO 2.5X CLASS 1
CLASS 1 BLUE RC: 1X TO 2.5X CLASS 1 RC
TATED ODDS 1:17 HOBBY
TATED PRINT RUN 150 SER.#'d SETS
1 Mookie Betts 5.00 12.00
8 Clayton Kershaw 5.00 12.00
4 Don Mattingly 5.00 12.00
6 Mike Schmidt 4.00 10.00
5 Ichiro 4.00 10.00
6 Ken Griffey Jr. 10.00 25.00
3 Nolan Ryan 8.00 20.00

2020 Topps Gold Label Class 1 Red
CLASS 1 BLUE: 1.2X TO 3X CLASS 1
CLASS 1 BLUE RC: 1.2X TO 3X CLASS 1 RC
TATED ODDS 1:34 HOBBY
TATED PRINT RUN 75 SER.#'d SETS
0 Cal Ripken Jr. 8.00 20.00
1 Mookie Betts 6.00 15.00
8 Clayton Kershaw 8.00 20.00
4 Don Mattingly 8.00 20.00
1 Mark McGwire 5.00 12.00
6 Mike Schmidt 8.00 20.00
5 Ichiro 5.00 12.00
6 Ken Griffey Jr. 12.00 30.00
3 Nolan Ryan 10.00 25.00

2020 Topps Gold Label Class 2
CLASS 2: .6X TO 1.5X CLASS 1
CLASS 2 RC: .6X TO 1.5X CLASS 1 RC
TATED ODDS 1 PER HOBBY

2020 Topps Gold Label Class 2 Black
*CLASS 2 BLACK: .75X TO 2X CLASS 1
*CLASS 2 BLACK RC: .75X TO 2X CLASS 1 RC
STATED ODDS 1:6 HOBBY

2020 Topps Gold Label Class 2 Blue
*CLASS 2 BLUE: 1.2X TO 3X CLASS 1
*CLASS 2 BLUE RC: 1.2X TO 3X CLASS 1 RC
STATED ODDS 1:26 HOBBY
STATED PRINT RUN 99 SER.#'d SETS
0 Cal Ripken Jr. 8.00 20.00
1 Mookie Betts 6.00 15.00
8 Clayton Kershaw 8.00 20.00
4 Don Mattingly 8.00 20.00
1 Mark McGwire 5.00 12.00
6 Mike Schmidt 8.00 20.00
85 Ichiro 5.00 12.00
86 Ken Griffey Jr. 12.00 30.00
93 Nolan Ryan 10.00 25.00

2020 Topps Gold Label Class 3
*CLASS 3: .75X TO 2X CLASS 1
*CLASS 3 RC: .75X TO 2X CLASS 1 RC
STATED ODDS 1:2 HOBBY

2020 Topps Gold Label Class 3 Black
*CLASS 3 BLACK: 1X TO 2.5X CLASS 1
*CLASS 3 BLACK RC: 1X TO 2.5X CLASS 1 RC
STATED ODDS 1:20 HOBBY
11 Mookie Betts 5.00 12.00
48 Clayton Kershaw 5.00 12.00
64 Don Mattingly 5.00 12.00
76 Mike Schmidt 4.00 10.00
85 Ichiro 4.00 10.00
86 Ken Griffey Jr. 10.00 25.00
93 Nolan Ryan 8.00 20.00

2020 Topps Gold Label Class 3 Blue
*CLASS 3 BLUE: 1.5X TO 4X CLASS 1
*CLASS 3 BLUE RC: 1.5X TO 4X CLASS 1 RC
STATED ODDS 1:50 HOBBY
STATED PRINT RUN 50 SER.#'d SETS
1 Mike Trout 15.00 40.00
10 Cal Ripken Jr. 12.00 30.00
11 Mookie Betts 8.00 20.00
48 Clayton Kershaw 10.00 25.00
64 Don Mattingly 12.00 30.00
65 Mariano Rivera 6.00 15.00
71 Mark McGwire 6.00 15.00
76 Mike Schmidt 12.00 30.00
85 Ichiro 10.00 25.00
86 Ken Griffey Jr. 15.00 40.00
87 Kyle Lewis 15.00 40.00
93 Nolan Ryan 15.00 40.00
95 Bo Bichette 25.00 60.00

2020 Topps Gold Label Class 3 Red
*CLASS 3 RED: 2.5X TO 6X CLASS 1
*CLASS 3 RED RC: 2.5X TO 6X CLASS 1 RC
STATED ODDS 1:100 HOBBY
STATED PRINT RUN 25 SER.#'d SETS
1 Mike Trout 50.00 120.00
10 Cal Ripken Jr. 25.00 60.00
11 Mookie Betts 15.00 40.00
45 Yordan Alvarez 15.00 40.00
48 Clayton Kershaw 15.00 40.00
64 Don Mattingly 25.00 60.00
65 Mariano Rivera 15.00 40.00
71 Mark McGwire 15.00 40.00
76 Mike Schmidt 20.00 50.00
79 Luis Robert 50.00 120.00
85 Ichiro 15.00 40.00
86 Ken Griffey Jr. 25.00 60.00
87 Kyle Lewis 25.00 60.00
93 Nolan Ryan 30.00 80.00
95 Bo Bichette 40.00 100.00

2020 Topps Gold Label Framed Autographs
STATED ODDS 1:10 HOBBY
EXCHANGE DEADLINE 8/31/2022
GLAAA Aristides Aquino 10.00 25.00
GLAAH Aaron Hicks 8.00 20.00
GLAAJ Aaron Judge
GLAAK Anthony Kay 3.00 8.00
GLAAT Abraham Toro 5.00 12.00
GLABA Bryan Abreu 6.00 15.00
GLABB Bo Bichette 75.00 200.00
GLABH Bryce Harper
GLABM Brendan McKay 5.00 12.00
GLACR Cal Ripken Jr.
GLACY Christian Yelich 30.00 80.00
GLADC Dylan Cease 8.00 20.00
GLADJ Derek Jeter
GLADM Dale Murphy 30.00 80.00
GLADS Darryl Strawberry 20.00 50.00
GLADW David Wright 50.00 120.00
GLAEJ Eloy Jimenez
GLAEM Edgar Martinez 20.00 50.00
GLAES Eugenio Suarez 4.00 10.00
GLAGL Gavin Lux EXCH 40.00 100.00
GLAHH Hunter Harvey 5.00 12.00
GLAJC Jose Canseco 10.00 25.00
GLAJR Jake Rogers 3.00 8.00
GLAJS Juan Soto
GLAJU Josh Urquidy 4.00 10.00
GLAJY Jordan Yamamoto 4.00 10.00
GLAKH Keston Hiura 10.00 25.00
GLAKK Kwang-Hyun Kim 20.00 50.00
GLAKM Ketel Marte 8.00 20.00
GLALR Luis Robert EXCH 75.00 200.00
GLALW Logan Webb 4.00 10.00
GLAMB Michael Brosseau 5.00 12.00
GLAMD Mauricio Dubon 6.00 15.00
GLAMK Max Kepler 8.00 20.00
GLAMM Mark McGwire
GLAMT Mike Trout
GLANH Nico Hoerner 15.00 40.00
GLANS Nick Solak 5.00 12.00
GLAPA Pete Alonso
GLAPC Patrick Corbin 6.00 15.00
GLAPG Paul Goldschmidt 30.00 80.00
GLARA Ronald Acuna Jr.
GLARD Rafael Devers 15.00 40.00
GLARG Robel Garcia 3.00 8.00
GLARH Rhys Hoskins
GLASA Shogo Akiyama 12.00 30.00
GLASM Sean Murphy 5.00 12.00
GLASO Shohei Ohtani
GLATL Tim Lincecum 30.00 80.00
GLAVG Vladimir Guerrero Jr.
GLAAAL Adbert Alzolay 6.00 15.00
GLABBR Bobby Bradley 4.00 10.00
GLADMA Dustin May 15.00 40.00
GLADMT Don Mattingly 10.00 25.00
GLAJDA Jaylin Davis 5.00 12.00
GLAJDU Justin Dunn 4.00 10.00
GLAJFE Junior Fernandez 3.00 8.00
GLAJRE J.T. Realmuto 12.00 30.00
GLAMKI Mike King 5.00 12.00
GLAMTH Matt Thaiss 4.00 10.00
GLARAR Randy Arozarena 60.00 150.00
GLARHO Ryan Howard 25.00 10.00
GLARRA Rangel Ravelo 4.00 10.00
GLAWCA Willi Castro 12.00 30.00
GLAWCL Will Clark 25.00 60.00

2020 Topps Gold Label Framed Autographs Black
*BLACK/75: .5X TO 1.2X BASIC
STATED ODDS 1:66 HOBBY
PRINT RUNS B/WN 15-75 COPIES PER
NO PRICING ON QTY 15
EXCHANGE DEADLINE 8/31/2022
GLAJS Juan Soto/75 50.00 120.00
GLAKK Kwang-Hyun Kim/75 30.00 80.00
GLALR Luis Robert EXCH/75 125.00 300.00
GLAPA Pete Alonso/75 50.00 120.00
GLARA Ronald Acuna Jr./75 75.00 200.00
GLARH Rhys Hoskins/75 12.00 30.00
GLAVG Vladimir Guerrero Jr./75 30.00 80.00
GLAWCA Willi Castro/75 20.00 50.00

2020 Topps Gold Label Framed Autographs Blue
*BLUE/50: .5X TO 1.2X BASIC
STATED ODDS 1:97 HOBBY
PRINT RUNS B/WN 10-50 COPIES PER
NO PRICING ON QTY 10
EXCHANGE DEADLINE 8/31/2022
GLAJS Juan Soto/50 50.00 120.00
GLAKH Keston Hiura/50 15.00 40.00
GLAKK Kwang-Hyun Kim/50 30.00 80.00
GLALR Luis Robert EXCH/50 200.00 500.00
GLAMD Mauricio Dubon/50 10.00 25.00
GLAPA Pete Alonso/50 50.00 120.00
GLARA Ronald Acuna Jr./50 75.00 200.00
GLARH Rhys Hoskins/50 12.00 30.00
GLAVG Vladimir Guerrero Jr./50 30.00 80.00
GLARAR Randy Arozarena/50 100.00 250.00
GLAWCA Willi Castro/50 20.00 50.00

2020 Topps Gold Label Framed Autographs Red
*RED/25: .75X TO 2X BASIC
STATED ODDS 1:194 HOBBY
PRINT RUNS B/WN 5-25 COPIES PER
NO PRICING ON QTY 5
EXCHANGE DEADLINE 8/31/2022
GLAEJ Eloy Jimenez/25 40.00 100.00
GLAJS Juan Soto/25 125.00 300.00
GLAKH Keston Hiura/25 25.00 60.00
GLAKK Kwang-Hyun Kim/25 100.00 250.00
GLALR Luis Robert EXCH/25 300.00 800.00
GLAMD Mauricio Dubon/25 15.00 40.00
GLAPA Pete Alonso/25 75.00 200.00
GLARA Ronald Acuna Jr./25 125.00 300.00
GLARH Rhys Hoskins/25 20.00 50.00
GLAVG Vladimir Guerrero Jr./25 50.00 120.00
GLARAR Randy Arozarena/25 150.00 400.00
GLAWCA Willi Castro/25 30.00 80.00

2020 Topps Gold Label Golden Greats Framed Autograph Relics
STATED ODDS 1:482 HOBBY
PRINT RUNS B/WN 10-25 COPIES PER
NO PRICING ON QTY 15 OR LESS
EXCHANGE DEADLINE 8/31/22
GLRAP Andy Pettitte/25 30.00 80.00
GLRCF Carlton Fisk/25 15.00 40.00
GLRDE Dennis Eckersley/25
GLREM Edgar Martinez/25 30.00 80.00
GLRFT Frank Thomas/25 50.00 120.00
GLRMS Mike Schmidt/25 60.00 150.00
GLROS Ozzie Smith/25 40.00 100.00
GLRRC Rod Carew/25 15.00 40.00
GLRRS Ryne Sandberg/25 50.00 120.00
GLRRY Robin Yount/25 30.00 80.00
GLRSC Steve Carlton/25 30.00 80.00
GLRVG Vladimir Guerrero/25 30.00 80.00
GLRWB Wade Boggs/25 40.00 100.00
GLRWC Will Clark/25 40.00 100.00
GLRJBA Jeff Bagwell/25 50.00 120.00
GLRKGJ Ken Griffey Jr.

2020 Topps Gold Label Legends Relics
STATED ODDS 1:145 HOBBY
PRINT RUNS B/WN 10-50 COPIES PER
NO PRICING ON QTY 15 OR LESS
MLRI Ichiro/25 15.00 40.00
MLRAK Al Kaline/50 6.00 15.00
MLRBL Barry Larkin/50 10.00 25.00
MLRBR Brooks Robinson/50 10.00 25.00
MLRCJ Chipper Jones/50 20.00 50.00
MLRCR Cal Ripken Jr./50 25.00 60.00
MLRCY Carl Yastrzemski/50 12.00 30.00
MLRDM Don Mattingly/50 15.00 40.00
MLREM Eddie Mathews/25 20.00 50.00
MLRFR Frank Robinson/25 30.00 80.00
MLRFT Frank Thomas
MLRGB George Brett/50 20.00 50.00
MLRHA Hank Aaron/25 20.00 50.00
MLRJB Johnny Bench/50 10.00 25.00
MLRJM Joe Morgan/50 10.00 25.00
MLRJS John Smoltz/50 8.00 20.00
MLRKG Ken Griffey Jr./50 20.00 50.00
MLRMM Mark McGwire/50 10.00 25.00
MLRMR Mariano Rivera/50 15.00 40.00
MLRMS Mike Schmidt/50 30.00 80.00
MLRNG Nomar Garciaparra/50 5.00 12.00
MLRNR Nolan Ryan/50 20.00 50.00
MLROS Ozzie Smith/50 15.00 40.00
MLRPM Pedro Martinez/50 5.00 12.00
MLRRH Rickey Henderson/50 20.00 50.00
MLRRJ Reggie Jackson/25 15.00 40.00
MLRRS Ryne Sandberg/50 12.00 30.00
MLRRY Robin Yount/50 6.00 15.00
MLRTG Tony Gwynn/50 15.00 40.00
MLRTW Ted Williams/25 50.00 120.00
MLRWB Wade Boggs/50 10.00 25.00
MLRWM Willie McCovey/50 10.00 25.00
MLREMU Eddie Murray/50 15.00 40.00
MLRRCA Rod Carew/50 12.00 30.00
MLRRCL Roger Clemens/50 10.00 25.00
MLRRJO Randy Johnson/25 30.00 80.00
MLRTGL Tom Glavine/50 5.00 12.00
MLRWMA Willie Mays/25 25.00 60.00

2011 Topps Gypsy Queen
COMPLETE SET (350)
COMP.SET w/o SP's (300) 30.00 60.00
COMMON CARD (1-300) .15 .40
COMMON RC (1-300) .40 1.00
COMMON SP (301-350) 1.50 4.00
PLATE PRINT RUN 1 SET PER COLOR
BLACK-CYAN-MAGENTA-YELLOW ISSUED
NO PLATE PRICING DUE TO SCARCITY
1 Ichiro Suzuki .50 1.25
2 Roy Halladay .25 .60
3 Cole Hamels .30 .75
4 Jackie Robinson .40 1.00
5 Tris Speaker .25 .60
6 Frank Robinson .25 .60
7 Jim Palmer .25 .60
8 Troy Tulowitzki .40 1.00
9 Scott Rolen .25 .60
10 Jason Heyward .30 .75
11 Zack Greinke .25 .60
12 Ryan Howard .30 .75
13 Joey Votto .40 1.00
14 Brooks Robinson .25 .60
15 Matt Kemp .30 .75
16 Chris Carpenter .25 .60
17 Mark Teixeira .25 .60
18 Christy Mathewson .40 1.00
19 Jon Lester .25 .60
20 Andre Dawson .25 .60
21 David Wright .30 .75
22 Barry Larkin .25 .60
23 Johnny Cueto .25 .60
24 Chipper Jones .40 1.00
25 Mel Ott .40 1.00
26 Adrian Gonzalez .30 .75
27 Roy Oswalt .25 .60
28 Tony Gwynn .40 1.00
29 Ty Cobb .60 1.50
30 Hanley Ramirez .25 .60
31 Joe Mauer .30 .75
32 Carl Crawford .25 .60
33 Ian Kinsler .25 .60
34 Johan Santana .25 .60
35 Pee Wee Reese .25 .60
36 Vladimir Guerrero .25 .60
37 Ryan Braun .25 .60
38 Walter Johnson .40 1.00
39 Johnny Mize .25 .60
40 George Sisler .25 .60
41 Matt Holliday .40 1.00
42 Jose Reyes .25 .60
43 Matt Cain .25 .60
44 Bob Gibson .25 .60
45 Carlos Gonzalez .25 .60
46 Thurman Munson .40 1.00
47 Jimmy Rollins .25 .60
48 Roger Maris .40 1.00
49 Honus Wagner .40 1.00
50 Al Kaline .40 1.00
51 Alex Rodriguez .50 1.25
52 Carlos Santana .40 1.00
53 Jimmie Foxx .40 1.00
54 Frank Thomas .40 1.00
55 Evan Longoria .25 .60
56 Mat Latos .25 .60
57 David Ortiz .40 1.00
58 Dale Murphy .40 1.00
59 Duke Snider .25 .60
60 Rogers Hornsby .25 .60
61 Robin Yount .40 1.00
62 Red Schoendienst .25 .60
63 Jimmie Foxx .40 1.00
64 Josh Hamilton .25 .60
65 Babe Ruth 1.00 2.50
66 Sandy Koufax .75 2.00
67 Dave Winfield .25 .60
68 Gary Carter .25 .60
69 Kevin Youkilis .15 .40
70 Rogers Hornsby .25 .60
71 CC Sabathia .25 .60
72 Justin Morneau .25 .60
73 Carl Yastrzemski .60 1.50
74 Tom Seaver .25 .60
75 Albert Pujols .50 1.25
76 Felix Hernandez .25 .60
77 Hunter Pence .25 .60
78 Ryne Sandberg .75 2.00
79 Andrew McCutchen .40 1.00
80 Stephen Strasburg .40 1.00
81 Nelson Cruz .40 1.00
82 Starlin Castro .25 .60
83 David Price .30 .75
84 Tim Lincecum .25 .60
85 Frank Robinson .25 .60
86 Prince Fielder .25 .60
87 Clayton Kershaw .75 2.00
88 Robinson Cano .25 .60
89 Mickey Mantle 1.25 3.00
90 Derek Jeter 1.00 2.50
91 Josh Johnson .25 .60
92 Mariano Rivera .50 1.25
93 Victor Martinez .25 .60
94 Buster Posey .50 1.25
95 George Sisler .25 .60
96 Ubaldo Jimenez .15 .40
97 Stan Musial .60 1.50
98 Aroldis Chapman RC 1.25 3.00
99 Ozzie Smith .50 1.25
100 Nolan Ryan 1.25 3.00
101 Ricky Nolasco .15 .40
102 Jorge Posada .25 .60
103 Magglio Ordonez .25 .60
104 Lucas Duda RC 1.00 2.50
105 Chris Carter .15 .40
106 Ben Revere RC .60 1.50
107 Brian Wilson .40 1.00
108 Brett Wallace .15 .40
109 Chris Volstad .15 .40
110 Todd Helton .25 .60
111 Jason Bay .25 .60
112 Carlos Zambrano .25 .60
113 Jose Bautista .25 .60
114 Chris Coghlan .15 .40
115 Jeremy Jeffress RC .40 1.00
116 Jake Peavy .15 .40
117 Dallas Braden .15 .40
118 Mike Pelfrey .15 .40
119 Brian Bogusevic (RC) .40 1.00
120 Gaby Sanchez .15 .40
121 Michael Cuddyer .15 .40
122 Derrek Lee .15 .40
123 Ted Lilly .15 .40
124 J.J. Hardy .15 .40
125 Francisco Liriano .15 .40
126 Billy Butler .15 .40
127 Rickie Weeks .15 .40
128 Dan Haren .15 .40
129 Aaron Hill .15 .40
130 Will Venable .15 .40
131 Cody Ross .15 .40
132 David Murphy .15 .40
133 Pablo Sandoval .25 .60
134 Kelly Johnson .15 .40
135 Ryan Dempster .15 .40
136 Brett Myers .15 .40
137 Ricky Romero .15 .40
138 Yovani Gallardo .15 .40
139 Raul Ibanez .25 .60
140 Shaun Marcum .15 .40
141 Brandon Inge .15 .40
142 Max Scherzer .40 1.00
143 Carl Pavano .15 .40
144 Jon Niese .15 .40
145 Jason Bartlett .15 .40
146 Melky Cabrera .15 .40
147 Kurt Suzuki .15 .40
148 Carlos Quentin .15 .40
149 Adam Jones .25 .60
150 Kosuke Fukudome .25 .60
151 Michael Young .15 .40
152 Paul Maholm .15 .40
153 Delmon Young .25 .60
154 Dan Uggla .15 .40
155 R.A. Dickey .25 .60
156 Brennan Boesch .25 .60
157 Ryan Ludwick .15 .40
158 Madison Bumgarner .30 .75
159 Ervin Santana .15 .40
160 Miguel Montero .15 .40
161 Aramis Ramirez .15 .40
162 Cliff Lee .25 .60
163 Russell Martin .15 .40
164 Cy Young .40 1.00
165 Yadier Molina .40 1.00
166 Gordon Beckham .15 .40
167 Cal Ripken Jr. 1.25 3.00
168 Alex Gordon .25 .60
169 Orlando Hudson .15 .40
170 Nick Swisher .25 .60
171 Manny Ramirez .40 1.00
172 Ryan Zimmerman .25 .60
173 Adam Dunn .25 .60
174 Reggie Jackson .25 .60
175 Edwin Jackson .15 .40
176 Kendry Morales .15 .40
177 Bernie Williams .25 .60
178 Chone Figgins .15 .40
179 Neil Walker .25 .60
180 Alexei Ramirez .25 .60
181 Lars Anderson .25 .60
182 Bobby Abreu .15 .40
183 Rafael Furcal .15 .40
184 Gerardo Parra .15 .40
185 Logan Morrison .15 .40
186 Tommy Hunter .15 .40
187 Lance Berkman .25 .60
188 Chris Sale RC 2.50 6.00
189 Mike Aviles .15 .40
190 Jaime Garcia .25 .60
191 Desmond Jennings RC .60 1.50
192 Jair Jurrjens .15 .40
193 Carlos Beltran .25 .60
194 Lorenzo Cain .15 .40
195 Bronson Arroyo .15 .40
196 Pat Burrell .15 .40
197 Colby Rasmus .25 .60
198 Jayson Werth .25 .60
199 James Shields .15 .40
200 John Lackey .15 .40
201 Travis Snider .15 .40
202 Adam Wainwright .25 .60
203 Brian Matusz .15 .40
204 Neftali Feliz .15 .40
205 Chris Johnson .15 .40
206 Torii Hunter .15 .40
207 Kyle Drabek RC .60 1.50
208 Mike Stanton .40 1.00
209 Tim Hudson .25 .60
210 Aaron Rowand .15 .40
211 Rollie Fingers .25 .60
212 Miguel Tejada .25 .60
213 Rick Porcello .25 .60
214 Pedro Alvarez RC .75 2.00
215 Trevor Cahill .15 .40
216 Angel Pagan .15 .40
217 Adrian Beltre .40 1.00
218 Austin Jackson .15 .40
219 Casey McGehee .15 .40
220 Tyler Colvin .15 .40
221 Martin Prado .15 .40
222 Heath Bell .15 .40
223 Ivan Rodriguez .25 .60
224 Drew Stubbs .15 .40
225 Vernon Wells .15 .40
226 Geovany Soto .15 .40
227 Cameron Maybin .15 .40
228 Ryan Kalish .25 .60
229 Alex Gonzalez .15 .40
230 Ian Desmond .15 .40
231 Mark Reynolds .15 .40
232 Jhonny Peralta .15 .40
233 Yunesky Maya RC .40 1.00
234 Sean Rodriguez .15 .40
235 Johnny Bench .40 1.00
236 Alex Rios .15 .40
237 Roy Campanella .40 1.00
238 Brandon Beachy RC 1.00 2.50
239 Josh Willingham .25 .60
240 Fausto Carmona .15 .40
241 Brian Roberts .15 .40
242 Joba Chamberlain .15 .40
243 Jim Thome .25 .60
244 Scott Kazmir .15 .40
245 Hank Conger RC .60 1.50
246 A.J. Burnett .15 .40
247 Matt Garza .15 .40
248 Dustin Pedroia .30 .75
249 Jacoby Ellsbury .30 .75
250 Joe Saunders .15 .40
251 Mark Buehrle .25 .60
252 David DeJesus .15 .40
253 Carlos Lee .15 .40
254 Brandon Phillips .15 .40
255 Barry Zito .25 .60
256 Wade Davis .15 .40
257 James Loney .15 .40
258 Freddy Sanchez .15 .40
259 Aubrey Huff .15 .40
260 Marlon Byrd .15 .40
261 Daniel Bard .15 .40
262 Marco Scutaro .25 .60
263 Johnny Damon .25 .60
264 Jeremy Hellickson RC 1.00 2.50
265 Stephen Drew .15 .40
266 Daric Barton .15 .40
267 Jake Arrieta .30 .75
268 Wandy Rodriguez .15 .40
269 Curtis Granderson .30 .75
270 Brad Lidge .15 .40
271 John Danks .15 .40
272 Felix Pie .15 .40
273 Chad Billingsley .25 .60
274 Jose Tabata .15 .40
275 Ruben Tejada .15 .40
276 Ian Stewart .15 .40
277 Derek Lowe .15 .40
278 Denard Span .15 .40
279 Josh Thole .15 .40
280 Jonathan Sanchez .15 .40
281 Juan Pierre .15 .40
282 B.J. Upton .25 .60
283 Rick Ankiel .15 .40
284 Jed Lowrie .15 .40
285 Colby Lewis .15 .40
286 Jason Kubel .15 .40
287 Jorge De La Rosa .15 .40
288 C.J. Wilson .15 .40
289 Will Rhymes .15 .40
290 Jake McGee (RC) .40 1.00
291 Chris Young .15 .40
292 Andre Ethier .25 .60
293 Joakim Soria .15 .40
294 Garrett Jones .15 .40
295 Phil Hughes .15 .40
296 Ty Cobb .60 1.50
297 Grady Sizemore .25 .60
298 Tris Speaker .25 .60
299 Andruw Jones .15 .40
300 Franklin Gutierrez .15 .40
301 Alfonso Soriano SP 2.00 5.00
302 Brian McCann SP 2.00 5.00
303 Johnny Mize SP 2.00 5.00
304 Brian Duensing SP 1.50 4.00
305 Mark Ellis SP 1.50 4.00
306 Tommy Hanson SP 2.00 5.00
307 Danny Valencia SP 2.00 5.00
308 Kila Ka'aihue SP 1.50 4.00
309 Clay Buchholz SP 2.00 5.00
310 Jon Garland SP 1.50 4.00
311 Hisanori Takahashi SP 1.50 4.00
312 Justin Verlander SP 2.00 5.00
313 Mike Minor SP 1.50 4.00
314 Yonder Alonso RC SP 2.00 5.00
315 Jered Weaver SP 1.50 4.00
316 Lou Gehrig SP 4.00 10.00
317 Justin Upton SP 1.50 4.00
318 Hank Aaron SP 4.00 10.00
319 Elvis Andrus SP 2.00 5.00
320 Dexter Fowler SP 2.00 5.00
321 Brett Sinkbeil SP 1.50 4.00
322 Ike Davis SP 2.00 5.00
323 Shin-Soo Choo SP 2.50 6.00
324 Jay Bruce SP 2.00 5.00
325 Jason Castro SP 2.00 5.00
326 Chase Utley SP 2.50 6.00
327 Miguel Cabrera SP 2.50 6.00
328 Brett Anderson SP 2.00 5.00
329 Ian Kennedy SP 1.50 4.00
330 Brandon Morrow SP 1.50 4.00
331 Greg Halman RC SP 2.50 6.00
332 Ty Wigginton SP 1.50 4.00
333 Travis Wood SP 1.50 4.00
334 Nick Markakis SP 2.50 6.00
335 Freddie Freeman RC SP 5.00 12.00
336 Domonic Brown SP 2.50 6.00
337 Jason Vargas SP 1.50 4.00
338 Babe Ruth SP 5.00 12.00
339 Omar Infante SP 1.50 4.00
340 Miguel Olivo SP 1.50 4.00
341 Nyjer Morgan SP 1.50 4.00
342 Placido Polanco SP 1.50 4.00
343 Mitch Moreland SP 1.50 4.00
344 Josh Beckett SP 2.00 5.00
345 Erik Bedard SP 1.50 4.00
346 Shane Victorino SP 2.00 5.00
347 Michael Schmidt RC SP 1.50 4.00
348 J.A. Happ SP 2.00 5.00
349 Xavier Nady SP 1.50 4.00
350 Carlos Pena SP 2.00 5.00

2011 Topps Gypsy Queen Framed Green
*GREEN: 1.2X TO 3X BASIC
*GREEN RC: .5X TO 1.2X BASIC RC

2011 Topps Gypsy Queen Framed Paper
*PAPER: 1.5X TO 4X BASIC
*PAPER RC: .6X TO 1.5X BASIC RC
STATED PRINT RUN 999 SER.#'d SETS

2011 Topps Gypsy Queen Mini
*MINI 1-300: 1.2X TO 3X BASIC
*MINI RC 1-300: .5X TO 1.2X BASIC
PLATE PRINT RUN 1 SET PER COLOR
BLACK-CYAN-MAGENTA-YELLOW ISSUED
NO PLATE PRICING DUE TO SCARCITY
1B Suzuki SP Follow Through 5.00 12.00
2B Roy Halladay SP/Facing right 2.50 6.00
3B Cole Hamels SP/Arm back 3.00 8.00
4B Jackie Robinson SP/Glove up 4.00 10.00
5B Tris Speaker SP/Standing 2.50 6.00
6B Frank Robinson SP/Portrait 2.50 6.00
7B Jim Palmer SP/Portrait 2.50 6.00
8B Troy Tulowitzki SP/Swinging 4.00 10.00
9B Scott Rolen SP/Running 2.50 6.00
10B Heyward SP Swing 3.00 8.00
11B Zack Greinke SP/White jersey 2.50 6.00
12B Howard SP Follow Through 3.00 8.00
13B Joey Votto SP/Running 4.00 10.00
14B Brooks Robinson SP/Fielding 2.50 6.00
15B Matt Kemp SP/Front leg up 3.00 8.00
16B Chris Carpenter SP/Pitching 2.50 6.00
17B Mark Teixeira SP/Swinging 2.50 6.00
18B Christy Mathewson SP/With bat 4.00 10.00
19B Jon Lester SP/Front leg up 2.50 6.00
20B Andre Dawson SP/Cubs 2.50 6.00
21B Wright SP Swing 3.00 8.00
22B Barry Larkin SP/Running 2.00 5.00
23B Johnny Cueto SP/Pitching 2.50 6.00
24B Chipper Jones SP/Swinging 4.00 10.00
25B Mel Ott SP/Bat on shoulder 4.00 10.00
26B Adrian Gonzalez SP/Running 3.00 8.00
27B Roy Oswalt SP/Knee up 2.50 6.00
28B Tony Gwynn SP/Pinstripped jersey 4.00 10.00
29B Cobb SP w/Glove 6.00 15.00
30B Hanley Ramirez SP/Swinging 2.50 6.00
31B Joe Mauer SP/Blue jersey 3.00 8.00
32B Carl Crawford SP/Bat on shoulder 2.50 6.00
33B Ian Kinsler SP/Red jersey 2.50 6.00
34B Johan Santana SP/Arm up 2.50 6.00
35B Pee Wee Reese SP/With bat 2.50 6.00
36B Vladimir Guerrero SP/Swinging 2.50 6.00
37B Braun SP Running 2.50 6.00
38B Walter Johnson SP
Pitch follow through 4.00 10.00
39B Johnny Mize SP/Yankees 2.50 6.00
40B George Sisler SP/Bat on shoulder 2.50 6.00
41B Matt Holliday SP/Swinging 4.00 10.00
42B Jose Reyes SP/Swinging 2.50 6.00
43B Matt Cain SP/Portrait 2.50 6.00
44B Bob Gibson SP/Leg up 2.50 6.00
45B Carlos Gonzalez SP/Front leg up 2.50 6.00
46B Thurman Munson SP
Swing follow through 4.00 10.00
47B Jimmy Rollins SP/Facing right 2.50 6.00
48B Roger Maris SP/Cardinals 4.00 10.00
49B Honus Wagner SP/With glove 4.00 10.00
50B Al Kaline SP/With glove 3.00 8.00
51B Rodriguez SP Running 5.00 12.00
52B Carlos Santana SP/With bat 4.00 10.00
53B Jimmie Foxx SP
Bat on left shoulder 4.00 10.00
54B Frank Thomas SP/Facing left 4.00 10.00
55B Longoria SP Running 2.50 6.00
56B Mat Latos SP/Hands together 2.50 6.00
57B David Ortiz SP/Front leg down 4.00 10.00
58B Dale Murphy SP/Red jersey 4.00 10.00
59B Duke Snider SP/Hands together 2.00 5.00
60B Rogers Hornsby SP
Leaning on knee 2.00 5.00
61B Robin Yount SP/Blue jersey 3.00 8.00
62B Red Schoendienst SP/With ball 2.50 6.00
63B Jimmie Foxx SP/Glove up 4.00 10.00
64B Josh Hamilton SP/Blue jersey 2.50 6.00
65B Ruth SP w/Bat 8.00 20.00
66B Koufax SP Hands Together 8.00 20.00
67B Dave Winfield SP
Swing follow through 2.50 6.00
68B Gary Carter SP/Mets 2.50 6.00
69B Kevin Youkilis SP/Facing left 1.50 4.00
70B Rogers Hornsby SP/Giants 2.00 5.00
71B CC Sabathia SP
No crowd in background 2.00 5.00
72B Justin Morneau SP/Blue jersey 2.50 6.00
73B Carl Yastrzemski SP/Bat up 6.00 15.00

74B Tom Seaver SP/Arms up 2.00 5.00
75B Pujols SP w/Bat 5.00 12.00
76B Felix Hernandez SP/White jersey 2.50 6.00
77B Hunter Pence SP/Facing right 2.50 6.00
78B Sandberg SP w/Bat 6.00 15.00
79B McCutchen SP Arms back 4.00 10.00
80B Strasburg SP 37 Showing 4.00 10.00
81B Nelson Cruz SP/Red jersey 4.00 10.00
82B Starlin Castro SP/Blue jersey 2.50 6.00
83B David Price SP/Hands together 3.00 8.00
84B Lincecum SP Blk Jsy 2.50 6.00
85B Frank Robinson SP/Fielding 2.50 6.00
86B Prince Fielder SP/Bat up 2.50 6.00
87B C.Kershaw SP Leg up 8.00 20.00
88B Robinson Cano SP/Swinging 2.50 6.00
89B Mantle SP Bat Up 12.00 30.00
90B Jeter SP w/Bat 40.00 80.00
91B Josh Johnson SP/Leg up 2.00 5.00
92B Mariano Rivera SP 5.00 12.00
93B Victor Martinez SP/Facing right 2.50 6.00
94B Posey SP w/Bat 5.00 12.00
95B George Sisler SP/Both hands on bat 2.50 6.00
96B Ubaldo Jimenez SP/Portrait 1.50 4.00
97B Musial SP Facing Left 5.00 12.00
98B Chapman SP Portrait 5.00 12.00
99B Smith SP w/Bat 5.00 12.00
100B Ryan SP Angels 12.00 30.00
301 Alfonso Soriano 1.00 2.50
302 Brian McCann 1.00 2.50
303 Johnny Mize 1.00 2.50
304 Brian Duensing .60 1.50
305 Mark Ellis .60 1.50
306 Tommy Hanson .60 1.50
307 Danny Valencia 1.00 2.50
308 Kila Ka'aihue .60 1.50
309 Clay Buchholz .60 1.50
310 Jon Garland .60 1.50
311 Hisanori Takahashi .60 1.50
312 Justin Verlander 1.50 4.00
313 Mike Minor .60 1.50
314 Yonder Alonso 1.00 2.50
315 Jered Weaver 1.00 2.50
316 Lou Gehrig 3.00 8.00
317 Justin Upton 1.00 2.50
318 Hank Aaron 3.00 8.00
319 Elvis Andrus 1.00 2.50
320 Dexter Fowler 1.00 2.50
321 Brett Sinkbeil .60 1.50
322 Ike Davis .60 1.50
323 Shin-Soo Choo 1.00 2.50
324 Jay Bruce 1.00 2.50
325 Jason Castro .60 1.50
326 Chase Utley 1.00 2.50
327 Miguel Cabrera 1.50 4.00
328 Brett Anderson .60 1.50
329 Ian Kennedy .60 1.50
330 Brandon Morrow .60 1.50
331 Greg Halman 1.00 2.50
332 Ty Wigginton .60 1.50
333 Travis Wood .60 1.50
334 Nick Markakis 1.25 3.00
335 Freddie Freeman 10.00 25.00
336 Domonic Brown 1.25 3.00
337 Jason Vargas .60 1.50
338 Babe Ruth 4.00 10.00
339 Omar Infante .60 1.50
340 Miguel Olivo .60 1.50
341 Nyjer Morgan .60 1.50
342 Placido Polanco .60 1.50
343 Mitch Moreland .60 1.50
344 Josh Beckett .60 1.50
345 Erik Bedard .60 1.50
346 Shane Victorino 1.00 2.50
347 Konrad Schmidt .60 1.50
348 J.A. Happ 1.00 2.50
349 Xavier Nady .60 1.50
350 Carlos Pena 1.00 2.50

2011 Topps Gypsy Queen Mini Black

*BLACK: 2.5X TO 6X BASIC
*BLACK RC: 1X TO 2.5X BASIC
90 Derek Jeter 20.00 50.00
301 Alfonso Soriano 1.50 4.00
302 Brian McCann 1.50 4.00
303 Johnny Mize 1.50 4.00
304 Brian Duensing 1.00 2.50
305 Mark Ellis 1.00 2.50
306 Tommy Hanson 1.00 2.50
307 Danny Valencia 1.50 4.00
308 Kila Ka'aihue 1.00 2.50
309 Clay Buchholz 1.00 2.50
310 Jon Garland 1.00 2.50
311 Hisanori Takahashi 1.00 2.50
312 Justin Verlander 2.50 6.00
313 Mike Minor 1.00 2.50
314 Yonder Alonso 1.50 4.00
315 Jered Weaver 1.50 4.00
316 Lou Gehrig 5.00 12.00
317 Justin Upton 1.50 4.00
318 Hank Aaron 5.00 12.00
319 Elvis Andrus 1.50 4.00
320 Dexter Fowler 1.50 4.00
321 Brett Sinkbeil 1.00 2.50
322 Ike Davis 1.00 2.50
323 Shin-Soo Choo 1.50 4.00
324 Jay Bruce 1.50 4.00
325 Jason Castro 1.00 2.50
326 Chase Utley 1.50 4.00
327 Miguel Cabrera 2.50 6.00
328 Brett Anderson 1.00 2.50
329 Ian Kennedy 1.00 2.50
330 Brandon Morrow 1.00 2.50
331 Greg Halman 1.50 4.00
332 Ty Wigginton 1.00 2.50
333 Travis Wood 1.00 2.50
334 Nick Markakis 2.00 5.00
335 Freddie Freeman 15.00 40.00
336 Domonic Brown 2.00 5.00
337 Jason Vargas 1.00 2.50
338 Babe Ruth 6.00 15.00
339 Omar Infante 1.00 2.50
340 Miguel Olivo 1.00 2.50
341 Nyjer Morgan 1.00 2.50
342 Placido Polanco 1.00 2.50
343 Mitch Moreland 1.00 2.50
344 Josh Beckett 1.00 2.50
345 Erik Bedard 1.00 2.50
346 Shane Victorino 1.50 4.00
347 Konrad Schmidt 1.00 2.50
348 J.A. Happ 1.50 4.00
349 Xavier Nady 1.00 2.50
350 Carlos Pena 1.50 4.00

2011 Topps Gypsy Queen Mini Red Gypsy Queen Back

*RED: 1.5X TO 4X BASIC
*RED RC: .6X TO 1.5X BASIC
167 Cal Ripken Jr. 15.00 40.00
301 Alfonso Soriano 1.00 2.50
302 Brian McCann 1.00 2.50
303 Johnny Mize 1.00 2.50
304 Brian Duensing .60 1.50
305 Mark Ellis .60 1.50
306 Tommy Hanson .60 1.50
307 Danny Valencia 1.00 2.50
308 Kila Ka'aihue .60 1.50
309 Clay Buchholz .60 1.50
310 Jon Garland .60 1.50
311 Hisanori Takahashi .60 1.50
312 Justin Verlander 1.50 4.00
313 Mike Minor .60 1.50
314 Yonder Alonso 1.00 2.50
315 Jered Weaver 1.00 2.50
316 Lou Gehrig 3.00 8.00
317 Justin Upton 1.00 2.50
318 Hank Aaron 3.00 8.00
319 Elvis Andrus 1.00 2.50
320 Dexter Fowler 1.00 2.50
321 Brett Sinkbeil .60 1.50
322 Ike Davis .60 1.50
323 Shin-Soo Choo 1.00 2.50
324 Jay Bruce 1.00 2.50
325 Jason Castro .60 1.50
326 Chase Utley .60 1.50
327 Miguel Cabrera 1.50 4.00
328 Brett Anderson .60 1.50
329 Ian Kennedy .60 1.50
330 Brandon Morrow .60 1.50
331 Greg Halman 1.00 2.50
332 Ty Wigginton .60 1.50
333 Travis Wood .60 1.50
334 Nick Markakis 1.25 3.00
335 Freddie Freeman 10.00 25.00
336 Domonic Brown 1.25 3.00
337 Jason Vargas .60 1.50
338 Babe Ruth 4.00 10.00
339 Omar Infante .60 1.50
340 Miguel Olivo .60 1.50
341 Nyjer Morgan .60 1.50
342 Placido Polanco .60 1.50
343 Mitch Moreland .60 1.50
344 Josh Beckett .60 1.50
345 Erik Bedard .60 1.50
346 Shane Victorino 1.00 2.50
347 Konrad Schmidt .60 1.50
348 J.A. Happ 1.00 2.50
349 Xavier Nady .60 1.50
350 Carlos Pena 1.00 2.50

2011 Topps Gypsy Queen Mini Sepia

*SEPIA: 3X TO 8X BASIC
*SEPIA RC: 1.2X TO 3X BASIC RC
STATED PRINT RUN 99 SER.#'d SETS
1 Ichiro Suzuki 6.00 15.00
29 Ty Cobb 6.00 15.00
78 Ryne Sandberg 8.00 20.00
80 Stephen Strasburg 12.50 30.00
84 Tim Lincecum 6.00 15.00
90 Derek Jeter 20.00 50.00

2011 Topps Gypsy Queen Autographs

EXCHANGE DEADLINE 4/30/2014
AC Andrew Cashner 4.00 10.00
ACH Aroldis Chapman 60.00 120.00
AK Al Kaline 12.00 30.00
AP Angel Pagan 4.00 10.00
AT Andres Torres 4.00 10.00
BC Brett Cecil 4.00 10.00
BR Brooks Robinson 12.00 30.00
CB Clay Buchholz 5.00 12.00
CR Cal Ripken Jr. 30.00 80.00
CS CC Sabathia 20.00 50.00
CSA Chris Sale 10.00 25.00
DB Domonic Brown 4.00 10.00
DD David DeJesus 5.00 12.00
DH Daniel Hudson 4.00 10.00
DO David Ortiz 30.00 60.00
EL Evan Longoria 15.00 40.00
FF Freddie Freeman 10.00 25.00
FR Frank Robinson 10.00 25.00
GB Gordon Beckham 4.00 10.00
GG Gio Gonzalez 5.00 12.00
HA Hank Aaron 150.00 250.00
JB Jose Bautista 6.00 15.00
JC Jason Castro 6.00 15.00
JH Josh Hamilton 5.00 12.00
JHE Jason Heyward 10.00 25.00
JJA Jon Jay 6.00 15.00
JJ Josh Johnson 4.00 10.00
JT Josh Tomlin 5.00 12.00
MB Marlon Byrd 4.00 10.00
MS Mike Stanton 60.00 150.00
NC Nelson Cruz 4.00 10.00
NF Neftali Feliz 6.00 15.00
NM Nick Markakis 6.00 15.00
PS Pablo Sandoval 10.00 25.00
RH Roy Halladay 75.00 150.00
RHA Ryan Howard 30.00 60.00
RN Ricky Nolasco 8.00 10.00
RS Ryne Sandberg 20.00 50.00
RSH Red Schoendienst 10.00 25.00
SK Sandy Koufax 200.00 500.00
SV Shane Victorino 8.00 20.00
TH Tommy Hunter 4.00 10.00
WV Will Venable 4.00 10.00
YA Yonder Alonso 4.00 10.00

2011 Topps Gypsy Queen Framed Mini Reli

BL Barry Larkin 4.00 10.00
BR Babe Ruth 75.00 150.00
CR Cal Ripken Jr. 6.00 15.00
CU Chase Utley 4.00 10.00
DJ Derek Jeter 10.00 25.00
DO David Ortiz 3.00 8.00
DU Dan Uggla 4.00 10.00
DW David Wright 4.00 10.00
EL Evan Longoria 4.00 10.00
FR Frank Robinson 4.00 10.00
JH Josh Hamilton 5.00 12.00
JR Jackie Robinson 15.00 40.00
LG Lou Gehrig 25.00 60.00
MC Miguel Cabrera 3.00 8.00
MH Matt Holliday 5.00 12.00
MK Matt Kemp 3.00 8.00
NR Nolan Ryan 12.50 30.00
OS Ozzie Smith 5.00 12.00
PF Prince Fielder 3.00 8.00
RC Robinson Cano 6.00 15.00
RH Ryan Howard 3.00 8.00
RHE Rickey Henderson 4.00 10.00
SM Stan Musial 10.00 25.00
TM Thurman Munson 12.50 30.00

2011 Topps Gypsy Queen Future Stars

COMPLETE SET (20) 10.00 25.00
PLATE PRINT RUN 1 SET PER COLOR
BLACK-CYAN-MAGENTA-YELLOW ISSUED
NO PLATE PRICING DUE TO SCARCITY
*MINI: .75X TO 2X BASIC
FS1 Brian Matusz .40 1.00
FS2 Kyle Drabek .60 1.50
FS3 Yonder Alonso .60 1.50
FS4 Freddie Freeman 6.00 15.00
FS5 Desmond Jennings .60 1.50
FS6 Trevor Cahill .40 1.00
FS7 Ike Davis .40 1.00
FS8 Jason Heyward .75 2.00
FS9 Starlin Castro .60 1.50
FS10 Phil Hughes .40 1.00
FS11 Buster Posey 1.25 3.00
FS12 Neftali Feliz .40 1.00
FS13 Stephen Strasburg 1.00 2.50
FS14 Mat Latos .60 1.50
FS15 Jose Tabata .40 1.00
FS16 David Price .75 2.00
FS17 Clay Buchholz .40 1.00
FS18 Aroldis Chapman 1.25 3.00
FS19 Gordon Beckham .40 1.00
FS20 Mike Stanton 1.00 2.50

2011 Topps Gypsy Queen Great Ones

COMPLETE SET (30) 20.00 50.00
PLATE PRINT RUN 1 SET PER COLOR
BLACK-CYAN-MAGENTA-YELLOW ISSUED
NO PLATE PRICING DUE TO SCARCITY
*MINI: .75X TO 2X BASIC
GO1 Andre Dawson .60 1.50
GO2 Babe Ruth 2.50 6.00
GO3 Bob Gibson .60 1.50
GO4 Brooks Robinson .60 1.50
GO5 Christy Mathewson 1.00 2.50
GO6 Frank Robinson .60 1.50
GO7 George Sisler .60 1.50
GO8 Jackie Robinson 1.00 2.50
GO9 Jim Palmer .60 1.50
GO10 Jimmie Foxx 1.00 2.50
GO11 Johnny Mize .60 1.50
GO12 Johnny Bench 1.00 2.50
GO13 Lou Gehrig 2.00 5.00
GO14 Mel Ott 1.00 2.50
GO15 Mickey Mantle 3.00 8.00
GO16 Nolan Ryan 3.00 8.00
GO17 Pee Wee Reese .60 1.50
GO18 Robin Yount 1.00 2.50
GO19 Rogers Hornsby .60 1.50
GO20 Rollie Fingers .60 1.50
GO21 Thurman Munson 1.00 2.50
GO22 Tom Seaver .60 1.50
GO23 Tris Speaker .60 1.50
GO24 Ty Cobb 1.50 4.00
GO25 Walter Johnson 1.00 2.50
GO26 Honus Wagner 1.00 2.50
GO27 Cy Young 1.00 2.50
GO28 Babe Ruth 2.50 6.00
GO29 Frank Robinson .60 1.50
GO30 Nolan Ryan 3.00 8.00

2011 Topps Gypsy Queen Gypsy Queens

COMPLETE SET (19) 30.00 60.00
*RED TAROT: .6X TO 1.5X BASIC
GQ1 Zenda 1.50 4.00
GQ2 Oriana 1.50 4.00
GQ3 Halaveni 1.50 4.00
GQ4 Keyseria 1.50 4.00
GQ5 Sonia 1.50 4.00
GQ6 Sheerah 1.50 4.00
GQ7 Kara 1.50 4.00
GQ8 Dianamara 1.50 4.00
GQ9 Kali 1.50 4.00
GQ10 Levitia 1.50 4.00
GQ11 Mahrya 1.50 4.00
GQ12 Adara 1.50 4.00
GQ13 Mirela 1.50 4.00
GQ14 Angelina 1.50 4.00
GQ15 Lavenia 1.50 4.00
GQ16 Stefumari 1.50 4.00
GQ17 Olga 1.50 4.00
GQ18 Hevalia 1.50 4.00
GQ19 Adamina 1.50 4.00

2011 Topps Gypsy Queen Gypsy Queens Autographs

GQA1 Zenda 8.00 20.00
GQA2 Oriana 8.00 20.00
GQA3 Halaveni 8.00 20.00
GQA4 Keyseria 8.00 20.00
GQA5 Sonia 8.00 20.00
GQA6 Sheerah 8.00 20.00
GQA7 Kara 8.00 20.00
GQA8 Dianamara 8.00 20.00
GQA9 Kali 8.00 20.00
GQA10 Levitia 8.00 20.00
GQA11 Mahrya 8.00 20.00
GQA12 Adara 8.00 20.00
GQA13 Mirela 8.00 20.00
GQA14 Angelina 8.00 20.00
GQA15 Lavenia 8.00 20.00
GQA16 Stefumari 8.00 20.00
GQA17 Olga 8.00 20.00
GQA18 Hevalia 8.00 20.00
GQA19 Adamina 8.00 20.00

2011 Topps Gypsy Queen Gypsy Queens Jewel Relics

GQR1 Zenda 12.50 30.00
GQR2 Oriana 12.50 30.00
GQR3 Halaveni 12.50 30.00
GQR4 Keyseria 12.50 30.00
GQR5 Sonia 12.50 30.00
GQR6 Sheerah 12.50 30.00
GQR7 Kara 12.50 30.00
GQR8 Dianamara 12.50 30.00
GQR9 Kali 12.50 30.00
GQR10 Levitia 12.50 30.00
GQR11 Mahrya 12.50 30.00
GQR12 Adara 12.50 30.00
GQR13 Mirela 12.50 30.00
GQR14 Angelina 12.50 30.00
GQR15 Lavenia 12.50 30.00
GQR16 Stefumari 12.50 30.00
GQR17 Olga 12.50 30.00
GQR18 Hevalia 12.50 30.00
GQR19 Adamina 12.50 30.00

2011 Topps Gypsy Queen Home Run Heroes

COMPLETE SET (25) 10.00 25.00
PLATE PRINT RUN 1 SET PER COLOR
BLACK-CYAN-MAGENTA-YELLOW ISSUED
NO PLATE PRICING DUE TO SCARCITY
*MINI: .75X TO 2X BASIC
HH1 Babe Ruth 2.50 6.00
HH2 Albert Pujols 1.25 3.00
HH3 Jose Bautista .60 1.50
HH4 Mark Teixeira .60 1.50
HH5 Carlos Pena .60 1.50
HH6 Ryan Howard .75 2.00
HH7 Miguel Cabrera 1.00 2.50
HH8 Prince Fielder .60 1.50
HH9 Alex Rodriguez 1.25 3.00
HH10 David Ortiz 1.00 2.50
HH11 Andruw Jones .40 1.00
HH12 Adrian Beltre 1.00 2.50
HH13 Manny Ramirez 1.00 2.50
HH14 Jim Thome .60 1.50
HH15 Troy Glaus .40 1.00
HH16 Andre Dawson .60 1.50
HH17 Frank Robinson .60 1.50
HH18 Jimmie Foxx 1.00 2.50
HH19 Johnny Mize .60 1.50
HH20 Johnny Bench 1.00 2.50
HH21 Lou Gehrig 2.00 5.00
HH22 Mel Ott 1.00 2.50
HH23 Mickey Mantle 3.00 8.00
HH24 Rogers Hornsby .60 1.50
HH25 Tris Speaker .60 1.50

2011 Topps Gypsy Queen Relics

AR Alex Rodriguez 5.00 12.00
BG Brett Gardner 3.00 8.00
CR Cal Ripken Jr. 8.00 20.00
DJ Derek Jeter 8.00 20.00
DO David Ortiz 3.00 8.00
DP Dustin Pedroia 4.00 10.00
HR Hanley Ramirez 3.00 8.00
JE Jacoby Ellsbury 3.00 8.00
JJ Josh Johnson 3.00 8.00
JP Jorge Posada 3.00 8.00
KF Kosuke Fukudome 3.00 8.00
KY Kevin Youkilis 3.00 8.00
PF Prince Fielder 3.00 8.00
RB Ryan Braun 4.00 10.00
RC Robinson Cano 5.00 12.00
RH Ryan Howard 4.00 10.00
SC Scott Rolen 3.00 8.00
TH Tommy Hanson 3.00 8.00
YM Yadier Molina 5.00 12.00
JWE Jayson Werth 3.00 8.00

2011 Topps Gypsy Queen Royal Wedding Jewel Relic

PWR Prince William/K.Middleton 100.00 200.00

2011 Topps Gypsy Queen Sticky Fingers

SF1 Derek Jeter 2.50 6.00
SF2 Chase Utley .60 1.50
SF3 David Eckstein .40 1.00
SF4 Starlin Castro .60 1.50
SF5 Elvis Andrus .60 1.50
SF6 Mark Teixeira .60 1.50
SF7 Jose Reyes .60 1.50
SF8 Ivan Rodriguez .60 1.50
SF9 Brandon Phillips .40 1.00
SF10 David Wright .75 2.00
SF11 Hanley Ramirez .60 1.50
SF12 Orlando Hudson .40 1.00
SF13 Kevin Youkilis .40 1.00
SF14 Alcides Escobar .60 1.50
SF15 Jason Bartlett .40 1.00

2011 Topps Gypsy Queen Wall Climbers

WC1 Torii Hunter .40 1.00
WC2 Mike Stanton 1.00 2.50
WC3 Nick Swisher .60 1.50
WC4 Denard Span .40 1.00
WC5 Rajai Davis .40 1.00
WC6 Ichiro Suzuki 1.25 3.00
WC7 Franklin Gutierrez .40 1.00
WC8 Michael Brantley .40 1.00
WC9 Jason Heyward .75 2.00
WC10 David DeJesus .40 1.00

2012 Topps Gypsy Queen

COMP.SET w/o SP's (300) 20.00 50.00
COMMON CARD (1-350) .15 .40
COMMON RC (1-350) .40 1.00
COMMON VAR SP (1-350) .75 2.00
PRINTING PLATE ODDS 1:1424 HOBBY
PLATE PRINT RUN 1 SET PER COLOR
BLACK-CYAN-MAGENTA-YELLOW ISSUED
NO PLATE PRICING DUE TO SCARCITY
1A Jesus Montero RC .60 1.50
1B Jesus Montero VAR SP 1.25 3.00
2 Hunter Pence .30 .75
3 Billy Butler .25 .60
4 Nyjer Morgan .25 .60
5 Russell Martin .25 .60
6A Matt Moore RC 1.00 2.50
6B M.Moore VAR SP 2.00 5.00
7 Aroldis Chapman .40 1.00
8 Jordan Zimmermann .30 .75
9 Max Scherzer .40 1.00
10A Roy Halladay .30 .75
10B Roy Halladay VAR SP 1.50 4.00
11 Matt Joyce .25 .60
12 Brennan Boesch .25 .60
13 Anibal Sanchez .25 .60
14 Miguel Montero .25 .60
15 Asdrubal Cabrera .30 .75
16A Eric Hosmer .30 .75
16B Eric Hosmer VAR SP 1.50 4.00
17 Trevor Cahill .25 .60
18 Jackie Robinson .40 1.00
19 Seth Smith .25 .60
20 Chipper Jones .40 1.00
21 Mat Latos .30 .75
22A Kevin Youkilis .25 .60
22B Kevin Youkilis VAR SP 2.00 5.00
23 Phil Hughes .25 .60
24 Matt Cain .30 .75
25 Doug Fister .25 .60
26 Brian Wilson .40 1.00
27 Mark Reynolds .25 .60
28 Michael Morse .25 .60
29 Ryan Roberts .25 .60
30 Cole Hamels .30 .75
31 Ted Lilly .25 .60
32 Michael Pineda .25 .60
33 Ben Zobrist .30 .75
34 Mark Trumbo .25 .60
35 Jon Lester .25 .60
36 Adam Lind .30 .75
37 Drew Storen .25 .60
38 James Loney .25 .60
39 Jaime Garcia .30 .75
40A Ichiro Suzuki .50 1.25
40B Ichiro Suzuki VAR SP 2.50 6.00
41 Yadier Molina .40 1.00
42 Tommy Hanson .25 .60
43 Stephen Drew .25 .60
44A Matt Kemp .30 .75
44B Matt Kemp VAR SP 1.50 4.00
45 Madison Bumgarner .30 .75
46 Chad Billingsley .25 .60
47 Derek Holland .25 .60
48 Jay Bruce .30 .75
49 Adrian Beltre .40 1.00
50A Miguel Cabrera .40 1.00
50B Miguel Cabrera VAR SP 2.00 5.00
51 Ian Desmond .25 .60
52 Colby Lewis .25 .60
53 Angel Pagan .25 .60
54A Mariano Rivera .50 1.25
54B Mariano Rivera VAR SP 2.50 6.00
55 Matt Holliday .40 1.00
56 Edwin Jackson .25 .60
57 Michael Young .25 .60
58 Zack Greinke .30 .75
59 Clay Buchholz .25 .60
60A Jacoby Ellsbury .30 .75
60B Jacoby Ellsbury VAR SP 1.50 4.00
61 Yunel Escobar .25 .60
62 Jhonny Peralta .25 .60
63 John Axford .25 .60
64 Jason Kipnis .30 .75
65 Alex Avila .25 .60
66 Brandon Belt .30 .75
67A Josh Hamilton .30 .75
67B Josh Hamilton VAR SP 1.50 4.00
68 Alex Rodriguez .50 1.25
69 Troy Tulowitzki .40 1.00
70 David Price .30 .75
71A Ian Kennedy .25 .60
71B Ian Kennedy VAR SP 1.25 3.00
72 Ryan Dempster .25 .60
73 Ben Revere .30 .75
74 Bobby Abreu .25 .60
75 Ivan Nova .30 .75
76A Mike Napoli .25 .60
76B Mike Napoli VAR SP 1.25 3.00
77 J.P. Arencibia .25 .60
78 Sergio Santos .25 .60
79 Melky Cabrera .25 .60
80A Ryan Braun .25 .60
80B Ryan Braun VAR SP 1.25 3.00
81 Alcides Escobar .30 .75
82 David Wright .30 .75
83A Ryan Howard .30 .75
83B Ryan Howard VAR SP 1.50 4.00
84A Freddie Freeman .50 1.25
84B Freddie Freeman VAR SP 2.50 6.00
85 Adam Jones .30 .75
86 Jhoulys Chacin .25 .60
87 Jayson Werth .30 .75
88 Erick Aybar .25 .60
89 Bud Norris .25 .60
90 Mark Teixeira .30 .75
91 Tim Hudson .30 .75
92 Adrian Gonzalez .30 .75
93 Johnny Cueto .30 .75
94 Matt Garza .25 .60
95 Dexter Fowler .25 .60
96 Alexi Ogando .25 .60
97 Ubaldo Jimenez .25 .60
98 Jason Heyward .30 .75
99 Hanley Ramirez .30 .75
100A Derek Jeter 1.00 2.50
100B D.Jeter VAR SP 5.00 12.00
101 Paul Konerko .25 .60
102 Pedro Alvarez .25 .60
103 Shaun Marcum .25 .60
104 Desmond Jennings .30 .75
105 Pablo Sandoval .30 .75
106 John Danks .25 .60
107 Chris Sale .40 1.00
108 Guillermo Moscoso .25 .60
109 Cory Luebke .25 .60
110A Jose Bautista .30 .75
110B Jose Bautista VAR SP 1.50 4.00
111 Jose Tabata .25 .60
112 Neil Walker .30 .75
113 Carlos Ruiz .25 .60
114 Brad Peacock RC .60 1.50
115 Kurt Suzuki .25 .60
116 Josh Reddick .25 .60
117 Marco Scutaro .30 .75
118 Ike Davis .25 .60
119 Justin Morneau .30 .75
120A Mickey Mantle 1.25 3.00
120B M.Mantle VAR SP 6.00 15.00
121 Scott Baker .25 .60
122 Casey McGehee .25 .60
123 Geovany Soto .25 .60
124 Dee Gordon .25 .60
125 David Robertson .25 .60
126 Brett Myers .25 .60
127 Drew Pomeranz RC .60 1.50
128 Grady Sizemore .30 .75
129 Scott Rolen .30 .75
130 Justin Verlander .40 1.00
131 Domonic Brown .30 .75
132 Brandon McCarthy .25 .60
133 Mike Adams .25 .60
134 Juan Nicasio .25 .60
135A Clayton Kershaw .75 2.00
135B Clayton Kershaw VAR SP 4.00 10.00
136 Martin Prado .25 .60
137 Jose Reyes .25 .60
138 Chris Carpenter .30 .75
139 James Shields .25 .60
140 Joe Mauer .30 .75
141A Roy Oswalt .25 .60
141B Roy Oswalt VAR SP 1.50 4.00
142A Carlos Gonzalez .30 .75
142B Carlos Gonzalez VAR SP 1.50 4.00
143A Dustin Pedroia .30 .75
143B Dustin Pedroia VAR SP 1.50 4.00
144 Andrew McCutchen .40 1.00
145A Ian Kinsler .30 .75
145B Ian Kinsler VAR SP 1.50 4.00
146 Elvis Andrus .30 .75
147A Mike Stanton .40 1.00
147B Mike Stanton VAR SP 2.00 5.00
148 Dan Haren .25 .60
149A Ryan Zimmerman .30 .75
149B Ryan Zimmerman VAR SP 1.50 4.00
150A CC Sabathia .30 .75
150B CC Sabathia VAR SP 1.50 4.00
151 Carl Crawford .30 .75
152 Dan Uggla .30 .75
153 Alex Gordon .30 .75
154 Victor Martinez .30 .75
155 Yovani Gallardo .30 .75
156 Michael Bourn .25 .60
157A Nelson Cruz .40 1.00
157B Nelson Cruz VAR SP 2.00 5.00
158 Rickie Weeks .25 .60
159 Shane Victorino .30 .75
160 Prince Fielder .30 .75
161 Aramis Ramirez .25 .60
162 Shin-Soo Choo .30 .75
163 Brandon Phillips .25 .60
164 Brian McCann .30 .75
165 Drew Stubbs .25 .60
166 Corey Hart .25 .60
167 Brett Gardner .30 .75
168 Ricky Romero .25 .60
169 B.J. Upton .30 .75
170A Cliff Lee .30 .75
170B Cliff Lee VAR SP 1.50 4.00
171 Jimmy Rollins .30 .75
172 Cameron Maybin .25 .60
173 David Ortiz .40 1.00
174 Josh Beckett .25 .60
175 Nick Swisher .30 .75
176 Howie Kendrick .25 .60
177 Nick Markakis .30 .75
178 Jose Valverde .25 .60
179 Paul Goldschmidt .40 1.00
180 Albert Pujols .50 1.25
181 Jeremy Hellickson .25 .60
182 Buster Posey .50 1.25
183 Heath Bell .25 .60
184A Stephen Strasburg .40 1.00
184B S.Strasburg VAR SP 2.00 5.00
185 Lance Berkman .30 .75
186 Josh Johnson .30 .75
187 Brandon Beachy .25 .60
188 J.J. Hardy .25 .60
189 Neftali Feliz .25 .60
190A Robinson Cano .30 .75
190B Robinson Cano VAR SP 1.50 4.00
191 Michael Cuddyer .25 .60
192 Ervin Santana .25 .60
193 Chris Young .25 .60
194 Torii Hunter .25 .60
195 Mike Trout 12.00 30.00
196 Adam Wainwright .30 .75
197A David Freese .25 .60
197B David Freese VAR SP 1.25 3.00
198 Lucas Duda .30 .75
199 Casey Kotchman .25 .60
200A Felix Hernandez .30 .75
200B Felix Hernandez VAR SP 1.50 4.00
201 Allen Craig .30 .75
202 Jason Motte .25 .60
203 Matt Harrison .25 .60
204 Jemile Weeks .60 1.50
205 Devin Mesoraco RC .60 1.50
206 David Murphy .25 .60
207 Matt Dominguez RC .75 2.00
208 Adron Chambers RC 1.00 2.50
209 Dellin Betances RC 1.00 2.50
210A Justin Upton .30 .75
210B Justin Upton VAR SP 1.50 4.00
211 Mike Moustakas .30 .75
212 Salvador Perez .30 .75
213 Ryan Lavarnway .30 .75
214 J.D. Martinez .40 1.00
215 Lonnie Chisenhall .25 .60
216 Jesus Guzman .25 .60
217 Eric Thames .30 .75
218 Colby Rasmus .30 .75
219 Alex Cobb .15 .40
220A Joey Votto .40 1.00
220B Joey Votto VAR SP 2.00 5.00
221 Javier Vazquez .15 .40
222 Ryan Vogelsong .25 .60
223 R.A. Dickey .30 .75
224 Luis Aparicio .25 .60
225 Albert Belle .15 .40
226A Johnny Bench .40 1.00
226B Johnny Bench VAR SP 2.00 5.00
227 Ralph Kiner .25 .60
228 Eddie Mathews .40 1.00

29A Ty Cobb .60 1.50
29B Ty Cobb VAR SP 3.00 8.00
30A Evan Longoria .30 .75
30B Evan Longoria VAR SP 1.50 4.00
31 Andre Dawson .25 .60
32A Joe DiMaggio .75 2.00
32B J.DiMaggio VAR SP 4.00 10.00
33 Duke Snider .25 .60
34 Carlton Fisk .25 .60
35 Orlando Cepeda .25 .60
36A Lou Gehrig .75 2.00
36B L.Gehrig VAR SP 4.00 10.00
37 Bob Gibson .25 .60
38 Rollie Fingers .25 .60
39 Juan Marichal .25 .60
40A Tim Lincecum .30 .75
40B Tim Lincecum VAR SP 1.50 4.00
41 Larry Doby .25 .60
42 Al Kaline .40 1.00
43 Catfish Hunter .25 .60
44 Roger Maris .40 1.00
45 Darryl Strawberry .15 .40
46 Willie McCovey .25 .60
47 Paul Molitor .40 1.00
48A Wade Boggs .25 .60
48B Wade Boggs VAR SP 1.25 3.00
49 Stan Musial .60 1.50
50A Ken Griffey Jr. .75 2.00
50B Ken Griffey Jr. VAR SP 4.00 10.00
51 Gary Carter .25 .60
52A Tony Gwynn .40 1.00
52B Tony Gwynn VAR SP 2.00 5.00
53 Cal Ripken Jr. 1.25 3.00
54 Brooks Robinson .25 .60
55 Frank Robinson .25 .60
56 Nolan Ryan 1.25 3.00
57 Ryne Sandberg .75 2.00
58A Mike Schmidt .60 1.50
58B Mike Schmidt VAR SP 3.00 8.00
59 Dave Winfield .25 .60
60A Curtis Granderson .30 .75
60B Curtis Granderson VAR SP 1.50 4.00
61 John Smoltz .40 1.00
62 Frank Thomas .40 1.00
63 Eddie Murray .25 .60
64 Ernie Banks .40 1.00
65 Warren Spahn .25 .60
66 Carl Yastrzemski .60 1.50
67 Bob Feller .25 .60
68 Rod Carew .25 .60
69 Willie Stargell .25 .60
70A Roberto Clemente 1.00 2.50
70B R.Clemente VAR SP 5.00 12.00
71A Jered Weaver .30 .75
71B Jered Weaver VAR SP 1.50 4.00
72 Craig Kimbrel .30 .75
73 Starlin Castro .30 .75
74 Justin Masterson .25 .60
75 Mark Melancon .25 .60
76 Ricky Nolasco .25 .60
77 Vance Worley .30 .75
78 Dustin Ackley .25 .60
79 Jeff Niemann .25 .60
80 Willie Mays .75 2.00
81 James McDonald .25 .60
82 Jordan Walden .25 .60
83 Mike Leake .25 .60
84 Todd Helton .30 .75
85 Carlos Santana .30 .75
86 Chase Utley .30 .75
87 Daniel Hudson .25 .60
88A C.J. Wilson .25 .60
88B Yu Darvish VAR SP RC 60.00 200.00
89 Gio Gonzalez .30 .75
90 Sandy Koufax .75 2.00
91 Jarrod Parker RC .75 2.00
92 Delmon Young .30 .75
93 Yogi Berra .40 1.00
94A Reggie Jackson .25 .60
94B Reggie Jackson VAR SP 1.25 3.00
95 Doc Gooden .15 .40
96A Tom Seaver .25 .60
96B Tom Seaver VAR SP 1.25 3.00
97 Lou Brock .25 .60
98 Brandon Morrow .25 .60
99 Mike Carp .25 .60
300 Babe Ruth 1.00 2.50

2012 Topps Gypsy Queen Framed Blue

*FRAMED BLUE VET: 1.2X TO 3X BASIC VET
*FRAMED BLUE RC: .5X TO 1.2X BASIC RC
STATED ODDS 1:15 HOBBY
STATED PRINT RUN 599 SER.#'d SETS

2012 Topps Gypsy Queen Autographs

GROUP A ODDS 1:2310 HOBBY
GROUP B ODDS 1:201 HOBBY
GROUP C ODDS 1:80 HOBBY
GROUP D ODDS 1:16 HOBBY
EXCHANGE DEADLINE 3/31/2015
AB Albert Belle 10.00 25.00
AC Aroldis Chapman 10.00 25.00
ACR Allen Craig 6.00 15.00
AE Alcides Escobar 3.00 8.00
AET Andre Ethier 8.00 20.00
AG Adrian Gonzalez 10.00 25.00
AK Al Kaline 20.00 50.00
AL Adam Lind 3.00 8.00
AP Albert Pujols 100.00 200.00
AR Aramis Ramirez 6.00 15.00
BA Brett Anderson 3.00 8.00
BB Brandon Belt 4.00 10.00
BG Bob Gibson 20.00 50.00
BL Brett Lawrie 6.00 15.00
BP Brandon Phillips 4.00 10.00
BPK Brad Peacock 3.00 8.00
CC Carl Crawford 4.00 10.00
CF Carlton Fisk 15.00 40.00
CG Carlos Gonzalez 10.00 25.00
CH Chris Heisey 3.00 8.00
CK Clayton Kershaw 60.00 150.00
CR Cal Ripken Jr. 25.00 60.00
CY Chris Young 3.00 8.00
DB Daniel Bard 3.00 8.00
DE Dennis Eckersley 8.00 20.00
DES Danny Espinosa 3.00 8.00
DH Daniel Hudson 3.00 8.00
DM Don Mattingly 30.00 60.00
DP Dustin Pedroia 15.00 40.00
DS Drew Stubbs 4.00 10.00
DU Dan Uggla 6.00 15.00
EA Elvis Andrus 3.00 8.00
EH Eric Hosmer 10.00 25.00
FH Felix Hernandez 20.00 50.00
FR Frank Robinson 15.00 40.00
FT Frank Thomas 30.00 80.00
GS Gaby Sanchez 3.00 8.00
HA Hank Aaron 200.00 300.00
JA J.P. Arencibia 4.00 10.00
JB Jose Bautista 12.00 30.00
JBE Joe Benson 3.00 8.00
JC Johnny Cueto 3.00 8.00
JJ Jon Jay 3.00 8.00
JM Jesus Montero 3.00 8.00
JMO Jason Motte 6.00 15.00
JN Jon Niese 3.00 8.00
JP Jhonny Peralta 5.00 12.00
JS John Smoltz 15.00 40.00
JW Jered Weaver 12.50 30.00
JWE Jemile Weeks 3.00 8.00
JZ Jordan Zimmermann 5.00 12.00
KG Ken Griffey Jr. 200.00 300.00
KS Kyle Seager 5.00 12.00
MB Marlon Byrd 3.00 8.00
MC Miguel Cabrera 75.00 150.00
MK Matt Kemp 6.00 15.00
MM Mike Morse 5.00 12.00
MMO Mitch Moreland 6.00 15.00
MMR Matt Moore 4.00 10.00
NC Nelson Cruz 4.00 10.00
NE Nathan Eovaldi 5.00 12.00
NW Neil Walker 3.00 10.00
RC Robinson Cano 20.00 50.00
RD Randall Delgado 4.00 10.00
RS Ryne Sandberg 30.00 60.00
RZ Ryan Zimmerman 3.00 8.00
SC Starlin Castro 4.00 10.00
SK Sandy Koufax 150.00 400.00
SP Salvador Perez 12.00 30.00
TC Trevor Cahill 3.00 8.00
TW Travis Wood 3.00 8.00
YD Yu Darvish 200.00 400.00

2012 Topps Gypsy Queen Framed Mini Relics

GROUP A ODDS 1:227 HOBBY
GROUP B ODDS 1:365 HOBBY
GROUP C ODDS 1:27 HOBBY
AA Alex Avila 3.00 8.00
AJ Adam Jones 3.00 8.00
AM Andrew McCutchen 4.00 10.00
APE Andy Pettitte 3.00 8.00
BM Brian McCann 3.00 8.00
BP Brandon Phillips 4.00 10.00
CF Carlton Fisk 4.00 10.00
DF David Freese 8.00 20.00
DH Dan Haren 3.00 8.00
DHO Derek Holland 4.00 10.00
DO David Ortiz 3.00 8.00
DPR David Price 3.00 8.00
DW David Wright 4.00 10.00
EL Evan Longoria 3.00 8.00
EM Eddie Murray 4.00 10.00
FH Felix Hernandez 4.00 10.00
JB Jose Bautista 5.00 12.00
JD Joe DiMaggio 40.00 80.00
JH Jeremy Hellickson 3.00 8.00
JHE Jason Heyward 3.00 8.00
JL Jon Lester 3.00 8.00
JR Jose Reyes 3.00 8.00
JRO Jimmy Rollins 3.00 8.00
JS James Shields 3.00 8.00
JU Justin Upton 5.00 12.00
KY Kevin Youkilis 3.00 8.00
MB Madison Bumgarner 4.00 10.00
MCA Miguel Cabrera 8.00 20.00
MR Mariano Rivera 5.00 12.00
MT Mark Trumbo 3.00 8.00
NC Nelson Cruz 3.00 8.00
OS Ozzie Smith 6.00 15.00
PF Prince Fielder 3.00 8.00
PN Phil Niekro 10.00 25.00
PS Pablo Sandoval 4.00 10.00
RCL Roberto Clemente 40.00 80.00
RK Ralph Kiner 8.00 20.00
RM Roger Maris 12.00 30.00
RR Ricky Romero 3.00 8.00
RY Robin Yount 8.00 20.00
RZ Ryan Zimmerman 3.00 8.00
SC Steve Carlton 6.00 15.00
SG Steve Garvey 4.00 10.00
TH Tim Hudson 3.00 8.00
THA Tommy Hanson 3.00 8.00
TL Tim Lincecum 5.00 12.00
VM Victor Martinez 3.00 8.00
WB Wade Boggs 4.00 10.00
WS Willie Stargell 5.00 12.00
YG Yovani Gallardo 3.00 8.00
ZG Zack Greinke 3.00 8.00

2012 Topps Gypsy Queen Future Stars

COMPLETE SET (15) 10.00 25.00
PRINTING PLATE ODDS 1:1980 HOBBY
PLATE PRINT RUN 1 SET PER COLOR
BLACK-CYAN-MAGENTA-YELLOW ISSUED
NO PLATE PRICING DUE TO SCARCITY
BB Brandon Beachy .60 1.50
CK Craig Kimbrel .75 2.00
DH Derek Holland .60 1.50
DJ Desmond Jennings .75 2.00
EH Eric Hosmer .75 2.00
FF Freddie Freeman 1.25 3.00
JH Jeremy Hellickson .60 1.50
JM Jesus Montero .60 1.50
JU Justin Upton .75 2.00
MM Matt Moore 1.00 2.50
MP Michael Pineda .60 1.50
MS Mike Stanton 1.00 2.50
MT Mark Trumbo .60 1.50
PG Paul Goldschmidt 1.00 2.50
SC Starlin Castro .75 2.00

2012 Topps Gypsy Queen Glove Stories

COMPLETE SET (10) 5.00 12.00
STATED ODDS 1:6 HOBBY
PRINTING PLATE ODDS 1:1980 HOBBY
PLATE PRINT RUN 1 SET PER COLOR
BLACK-CYAN-MAGENTA-YELLOW ISSUED
NO PLATE PRICING DUE TO SCARCITY
BR Ben Revere .75 2.00
CY Chris Young .60 1.50
DJ Derek Jeter 2.50 6.00
DV Endy Chavez .60 1.50
DW Dewayne Wise .40 1.00
JF Jeff Francoeur .75 2.00
JH Josh Hamilton .75 2.00
KG Ken Griffey Jr. 2.00 5.00
TR Trayvon Robinson .60 1.50
WM Willie Mays 2.00 5.00

2012 Topps Gypsy Queen Glove Stories Mini

COMPLETE SET (10) 6.00 15.00
STATED ODDS 1 PER MINI BOX TOPPER
MINI PLATE ODDS 1:14,850 HOBBY
PLATE PRINT RUN 1 SET PER COLOR
BLACK-CYAN-MAGENTA-YELLOW ISSUED
NO PLATE PRICING DUE TO SCARCITY
BR Ben Revere 1.00 2.50
CY Chris Young .75 2.00
DJ Derek Jeter 3.00 8.00
DV Endy Chavez .75 2.00
DW Dewayne Wise .50 1.25
JF Jeff Francoeur 1.00 2.50
JH Josh Hamilton 1.00 2.50
KG Ken Griffey Jr. 2.50 6.00
TR Trayvon Robinson .75 2.00
WM Willie Mays 2.50 6.00

2012 Topps Gypsy Queen Gypsy King Autographs

STATED ODDS 1:495 HOBBY
1 Drago Koval 6.00 15.00
2 Zoran Marko 6.00 15.00
3 Zorislav Dragon 6.00 15.00
4 Prince Wasso 6.00 15.00
5 King Pavlov 6.00 15.00
6 Felek Horvath 6.00 15.00
7 Adamo the Bold 6.00 15.00
8 Aladar the Cruel 6.00 15.00
9 Damian Dolinski 6.00 15.00
10 Kosta Sarov 6.00 15.00
11 Antoni Stojka 6.00 15.00
12 Savo the Savage 6.00 15.00

2012 Topps Gypsy Queen Gypsy King Relics

STATED ODDS 1:1980 HOBBY
STATED PRINT RUN 25 SER.#'d SETS
1 Drago Koval 8.00 20.00
2 Zoran Marko 8.00 20.00
3 Zorislav Dragon 8.00 20.00
4 Prince Wasso 8.00 20.00
5 King Pavlov 8.00 20.00
6 Felek Horvath 8.00 20.00
7 Adamo the Bold 8.00 20.00
8 Aladar the Cruel 8.00 20.00
9 Damian Dolinski 8.00 20.00
10 Kosta Sarov 8.00 20.00
11 Antoni Stojka 8.00 20.00
12 Savo the Savage 8.00 20.00

2012 Topps Gypsy Queen Gypsy Kings

COMPLETE SET 20.00 50.00
STATED ODDS 1:48 HOBBY
1 Drago Koval 2.00 5.00
2 Zoran Marko 2.00 5.00
3 Zorislav Dragon 2.00 5.00
4 Prince Wasso 2.00 5.00
5 King Pavlov 2.00 5.00
6 Felek Horvath 2.00 5.00
7 Adamo the Bold 2.00 5.00
8 Aladar the Cruel 2.00 5.00
9 Damian Dolinski 2.00 5.00
10 Kosta Sarov 2.00 5.00
11 Antoni Stojka 2.00 5.00
12 Savo the Savage 2.00 5.00

2012 Topps Gypsy Queen Hallmark Heroes

COMPLETE SET (15) 12.50 30.00
PRINTING PLATE ODDS 1:1980 HOBBY
PLATE PRINT RUN 1 SET PER COLOR
BLACK-CYAN-MAGENTA-YELLOW ISSUED
NO PLATE PRICING DUE TO SCARCITY
BG Bob Gibson .40 1.00
CR Cal Ripken Jr. 2.00 5.00
EB Ernie Banks .60 1.50
FR Frank Robinson .40 1.00
JB Johnny Bench .60 1.50
JD Joe DiMaggio 1.25 3.00
JR Jackie Robinson .60 1.50
LG Lou Gehrig 1.25 3.00
MM Mickey Mantle 2.00 5.00
NR Nolan Ryan 2.00 5.00
RC Roberto Clemente 1.50 4.00
SK Sandy Koufax 1.25 3.00
SM Stan Musial 1.00 2.50
TC Ty Cobb 1.00 2.50
WM Willie Mays 1.25 3.00

2012 Topps Gypsy Queen Mini

PRINTING PLATE ODDS 1:336 HOBBY
PLATE PRINT RUN 1 SET PER COLOR
BLACK-CYAN-MAGENTA-YELLOW ISSUED
NO PLATE PRICING DUE TO SCARCITY
1A Jesus Montero .60 1.50
1B Jesus Montero VAR .75 2.00
2A Hunter Pence .75 2.00
2B Hunter Pence VAR 1.00 2.50
3 Billy Butler .60 1.50
4 Nyjer Morgan .60 1.50
5 Russell Martin .60 1.50
6A Matt Moore 1.00 2.50
6B Matt Moore VAR 1.25 3.00
7 Aroldis Chapman 1.00 2.50
8 Jordan Zimmermann .75 2.00
9 Max Scherzer 1.00 2.50
10A Roy Halladay .75 2.00
10B Roy Halladay VAR 1.00 2.50
11 Matt Joyce .60 1.50
12 Brennan Boesch .60 1.50
13 Anibal Sanchez .60 1.50
14 Miguel Montero .60 1.50
15 Asdrubal Cabrera .60 1.50
16A Eric Hosmer .75 2.00
16B Eric Hosmer VAR 1.00 2.50
17 Trevor Cahill .60 1.50
18 Jackie Robinson 1.00 2.50
19 Seth Smith .60 1.50
20 Chipper Jones 1.00 2.50
21 Mat Latos .75 2.00
22A Kevin Youkilis 1.00 2.50
22B Kevin Youkilis VAR 1.25 3.00
23 Phil Hughes .60 1.50
24 Matt Cain .75 2.00
25 Doug Fister .60 1.50
26A Brian Wilson 1.00 2.50
26B Brian Wilson VAR 1.25 3.00
27 Mark Reynolds .60 1.50
28 Michael Morse .60 1.50
29 Ryan Roberts .60 1.50
30A Cole Hamels .75 2.00
30B Cole Hamels VAR 1.00 2.50
31 Ted Lilly .60 1.50
32 Michael Pineda .60 1.50
33 Ben Zobrist .75 2.00
34A Mark Trumbo .60 1.50
34B Mark Trumbo VAR .75 2.00
35A Jon Lester .60 1.50
35B Jon Lester VAR .75 2.00
36 Adam Lind .75 2.00
37 Drew Storen .60 1.50
38 James Loney .60 1.50
39A Jaime Garcia .75 2.00
39B Jaime Garcia VAR 1.00 2.50
40A Ichiro Suzuki 1.25 3.00
40B Ichiro Suzuki VAR 1.50 4.00
41A Yadier Molina 1.00 2.50
41B Yadier Molina VAR 1.25 3.00
42A Tommy Hanson .60 1.50
42B Tommy Hanson VAR .75 2.00
43 Stephen Drew .60 1.50
44A Matt Kemp .75 2.00
44B Matt Kemp VAR 1.00 2.50
45A Madison Bumgarner .75 2.00
45B Madison Bumgarner VAR 1.00 2.50
46 Chad Billingsley .60 1.50
47 Derek Holland .60 1.50
48A Jay Bruce .75 2.00
48B Jay Bruce VAR 1.00 2.50
49 Adrian Beltre .75 2.00
50A Miguel Cabrera 1.00 2.50
50B Miguel Cabrera VAR 1.25 3.00
51 Ian Desmond .60 1.50
52 Colby Lewis .60 1.50
53 Angel Pagan .60 1.50
54A Mariano Rivera 1.25 3.00
54B Mariano Rivera VAR 1.50 4.00
55A Matt Holliday 1.00 2.50
55B Matt Holliday VAR 1.25 3.00
56 Edwin Jackson .60 1.50
57 Michael Young .60 1.50
58 Zack Greinke .75 2.00
59 Clay Buchholz .60 1.50
60A Jacoby Ellsbury .75 2.00
60B Jacoby Ellsbury VAR 1.00 2.50
61 Yunel Escobar .60 1.50
62 Jhonny Peralta .60 1.50
63 John Axford .60 1.50
64 Jason Kipnis .75 2.00
65A Alex Avila .60 1.50
65B Alex Avila VAR .75 2.00
66 Brandon Belt .75 2.00
67A Josh Hamilton .75 2.00
67B Josh Hamilton VAR 1.00 2.50
68A Alex Rodriguez 1.25 3.00
68B Alex Rodriguez VAR 1.50 4.00
69 Troy Tulowitzki 1.00 2.50
70 David Price .75 2.00
71A Ian Kennedy .60 1.50
71B Ian Kennedy VAR .75 2.00
72 Ryan Dempster .60 1.50
73 Ben Revere .75 2.00
74 Bobby Abreu .60 1.50
75 Ivan Nova .75 2.00
76A Mike Napoli .60 1.50
76B Mike Napoli VAR .75 2.00
77 J.P. Arencibia .60 1.50
78 Sergio Santos .60 1.50
79 Melky Cabrera .60 1.50
80A Ryan Braun .60 1.50
80B Ryan Braun VAR .75 2.00
81 Alcides Escobar .75 2.00
82A David Wright .75 2.00
82B David Wright VAR 1.00 2.50
83A Ryan Howard .75 2.00
83B Ryan Howard VAR 1.00 2.50
84A Freddie Freeman 1.25 3.00
84B Freddie Freeman VAR 1.50 4.00
85A Adam Jones .75 2.00
85B Adam Jones VAR 1.00 2.50
86 Jhoulys Chacin .60 1.50
87 Jayson Werth .75 2.00
88 Erick Aybar .60 1.50
89 Bud Norris .60 1.50
90A Mark Teixeira .75 2.00
90B Mark Teixeira VAR 1.00 2.50
91 Tim Hudson .75 2.00
92 Adrian Gonzalez .75 2.00
93 Johnny Cueto .75 2.00
94 Matt Garza .60 1.50
95 Dexter Fowler .75 2.00
96 Alexi Ogando .60 1.50
97 Ubaldo Jimenez .60 1.50
98A Jason Heyward .75 2.00
98B Jason Heyward VAR 1.00 2.50
99 Hanley Ramirez .75 2.00
100A Derek Jeter 2.50 6.00
100B Derek Jeter VAR 3.00 8.00
101A Paul Konerko .60 1.50
101B Paul Konerko VAR .75 2.00
102 Pedro Alvarez .60 1.50
103 Shaun Marcum .60 1.50
104 Desmond Jennings .75 2.00
105A Pablo Sandoval .75 2.00
105B Pablo Sandoval VAR 1.00 2.50
106 John Danks .60 1.50
107 Chris Sale 1.00 2.50
108 Guillermo Moscoso .75 2.00
109 Cory Luebke .60 1.50
110A Jose Bautista .75 2.00
110B Jose Bautista VAR 1.00 2.50
111 Jose Tabata .60 1.50
112 Neil Walker .75 2.00
113 Carlos Ruiz .60 1.50
114 Brad Peacock .60 1.50
115 Kurt Suzuki .60 1.50
116 Josh Reddick .60 1.50
117 Marco Scutaro .75 2.00
118 Ike Davis .60 1.50
119 Justin Morneau .75 2.00
120A Mickey Mantle 3.00 8.00
120B Mickey Mantle VAR 4.00 10.00
121 Scott Baker .60 1.50
122 Casey McGehee .60 1.50
123 Geovany Soto .75 2.00
124 Dee Gordon .60 1.50
125 David Robertson .60 1.50
126 Brett Myers .60 1.50
127 Drew Pomeranz .60 1.50
128 Grady Sizemore .60 1.50
129 Scott Rolen .75 2.00
130 Justin Verlander 1.00 2.50
131 Domonic Brown .75 2.00
132 Brandon McCarthy .60 1.50
133 Mike Adams .60 1.50
134 Juan Nicasio .60 1.50
135A Clayton Kershaw 2.00 5.00
135B Clayton Kershaw VAR 2.50 6.00
136 Martin Prado .60 1.50
137 Jose Reyes .60 1.50
138A Chris Carpenter .75 2.00
138B Chris Carpenter VAR 1.00 2.50
139A James Shields .60 1.50
139B James Shields VAR .75 2.00
140A Joe Mauer .75 2.00
140B Joe Mauer VAR 1.00 2.50
141A Roy Oswalt .75 2.00
141B Roy Oswalt VAR 1.00 2.50
142A Carlos Gonzalez .75 2.00
142B Carlos Gonzalez VAR 1.00 2.50
143A Dustin Pedroia .75 2.00
143B Dustin Pedroia VAR 1.00 2.50
144A Andrew McCutchen 1.00 2.50
144B McCutchen VAR 1.25 3.00
145A Ian Kinsler .75 2.00
145B Ian Kinsler VAR 1.00 2.50
146 Elvis Andrus .75 2.00
147A Mike Stanton 1.00 2.50
147B Mike Stanton VAR 1.25 3.00
148 Dan Haren .60 1.50
149A Ryan Zimmerman .75 2.00
149B Ryan Zimmerman VAR 1.00 2.50
150A CC Sabathia .75 2.00
150B CC Sabathia VAR 1.00 2.50
151 Carl Crawford .75 2.00
152A Dan Uggla .75 2.00
152B Dan Uggla VAR 1.00 2.50
153A Alex Gordon .75 2.00
153B Alex Gordon VAR 1.00 2.50
154A Victor Martinez .75 2.00
154B Victor Martinez VAR 1.00 2.50
155A Yovani Gallardo .75 2.00
155B Yovani Gallardo VAR 1.00 2.50
156 Michael Bourn .60 1.50
157A Nelson Cruz 1.00 2.50
157B Nelson Cruz VAR 1.25 3.00
158 Rickie Weeks .60 1.50
159 Shane Victorino .75 2.00
160 Prince Fielder .75 2.00
161 Aramis Ramirez .60 1.50
162 Shin-Soo Choo .75 2.00
163 Brandon Phillips .60 1.50
164 Brian McCann .75 2.00
165 Drew Stubbs .60 1.50
166 Corey Hart .60 1.50
167 Brett Gardner .75 2.00
168 Ricky Romero .60 1.50
169 B.J. Upton .75 2.00
170A Cliff Lee .75 2.00
170B Cliff Lee VAR 1.00 2.50
171A Jimmy Rollins .75 2.00
171B Jimmy Rollins VAR 1.00 2.50
172 Cameron Maybin .60 1.50
173A David Ortiz 1.00 2.50
173B David Ortiz VAR 1.25 3.00
174 Josh Beckett .60 1.50
175 Nick Swisher .75 2.00
176 Howie Kendrick .60 1.50
177 Nick Markakis .75 2.00
178 Jose Valverde .75 2.00
179A Paul Goldschmidt 1.00 2.50
179B Paul Goldschmidt VAR 1.25 3.00
180 Albert Pujols 1.25 3.00
181A Jeremy Hellickson .60 1.50
181B Jeremy Hellickson VAR .75 2.00
182A Buster Posey 1.25 3.00
182B Buster Posey VAR 1.50 4.00
183 Heath Bell .60 1.50
184A Stephen Strasburg 1.00 2.50
184B Stephen Strasburg VAR 1.25 3.00
185A Lance Berkman .75 2.00
185B Lance Berkman VAR 1.00 2.50
186A Josh Johnson .75 2.00
186B Josh Johnson VAR 1.00 2.50
187A Brandon Beachy .60 1.50
187B Brandon Beachy VAR .75 2.00
188 J.J. Hardy .60 1.50
189 Neftali Feliz .60 1.50
190A Robinson Cano .75 2.00
190B Robinson Cano VAR 1.00 2.50
191 Michael Cuddyer .60 1.50
192 Ervin Santana .60 1.50
193 Chris Young .60 1.50
194 Torii Hunter .75 2.00
195 Mike Trout 30.00 80.00
196 Adam Wainwright .75 2.00
197A David Freese .60 1.50
197B David Freese VAR .75 2.00
198 Lucas Duda .75 2.00
199 Casey Kotchman .60 1.50
200A Felix Hernandez .75 2.00
200B Felix Hernandez VAR 1.00 2.50
201 Allen Craig .75 2.00
202 Jason Motte .60 1.50
203 Matt Harrison .60 1.50
204 Jemile Weeks .60 1.50
205 Devin Mesoraco .60 1.50
206 David Murphy .60 1.50
207 Matt Dominguez .75 2.00
208 Adron Chambers 1.00 2.50
209 Dellin Betances 1.00 2.50
210A Justin Upton .75 2.00
210B Justin Upton VAR 1.00 2.50
211 Mike Moustakas .75 2.00
212 Salvador Perez .75 2.00
213 Ryan Lavarnway .60 1.50
214 J.D. Martinez 1.00 2.50
215 Lonnie Chisenhall .60 1.50
216 Jesus Guzman .60 1.50
217 Eric Thames .75 2.00
218 Colby Rasmus .75 2.00
219 Alex Cobb .40 1.00
220A Joey Votto 1.00 2.50
220B Joey Votto VAR 1.25 3.00
221 Javier Vazquez .40 1.00
222 Ryan Vogelsong .60 1.50
223 R.A. Dickey .75 2.00
224 Luis Aparicio .60 1.50
225 Albert Belle .40 1.00
226A Johnny Bench 1.00 2.50
226B Johnny Bench VAR 1.25 3.00
227 Ralph Kiner .60 1.50
228 Eddie Mathews 1.00 2.50
229A Ty Cobb 1.50 4.00
229B Ty Cobb VAR 2.00 5.00
230A Evan Longoria .75 2.00
230B Evan Longoria VAR 1.00 2.50
231 Andre Dawson .60 1.50
232A Joe DiMaggio 2.00 5.00
232B Joe DiMaggio VAR 2.50 6.00
233 Duke Snider .60 1.50
234 Carlton Fisk .60 1.50
235 Orlando Cepeda .60 1.50
236A Lou Gehrig 2.00 5.00
236B Lou Gehrig VAR 2.50 6.00
237 Bob Gibson .60 1.50
238 Rollie Fingers .60 1.50
239 Juan Marichal .60 1.50
240A Tim Lincecum .75 2.00
240B Tim Lincecum VAR 1.00 2.50
241 Larry Doby .60 1.50
242 Al Kaline 1.00 2.50
243 Catfish Hunter .60 1.50
244 Roger Maris 1.00 2.50
245 Darryl Strawberry .40 1.00
246 Willie McCovey .60 1.50
247 Paul Molitor 1.00 2.50
248A Wade Boggs .60 1.50
248B Wade Boggs VAR .75 2.00
249 Stan Musial 1.50 4.00
250A Ken Griffey Jr. 2.00 5.00
250B Ken Griffey Jr. VAR 2.50 6.00
251 Gary Carter .60 1.50
252A Tony Gwynn 1.00 2.50
252B Tony Gwynn VAR 1.25 3.00
253 Cal Ripken Jr. 3.00 8.00
254 Brooks Robinson .60 1.50
255 Frank Robinson .60 1.50
256 Nolan Ryan 3.00 8.00
257 Ryne Sandberg 2.00 5.00
258A Mike Schmidt 1.50 4.00
258B Mike Schmidt VAR 2.00 5.00
259 Dave Winfield .60 1.50
260A Curtis Granderson .75 2.00
260B Curtis Granderson VAR 1.00 2.50
261 John Smoltz 1.00 2.50
262 Frank Thomas 1.00 2.50
263 Eddie Murray .60 1.50
264 Ernie Banks 1.00 2.50
265 Warren Spahn .60 1.50
266 Carl Yastrzemski 1.50 4.00
267 Bob Feller .60 1.50
268 Rod Carew .60 1.50
269 Willie Stargell .60 1.50
270A Roberto Clemente 2.50 6.00
270B Roberto Clemente VAR 3.00 8.00
271A Jered Weaver .75 2.00
271B Jered Weaver VAR 1.00 2.50
272A Craig Kimbrel .75 2.00
272B Craig Kimbrel VAR 1.00 2.50
273A Starlin Castro .75 2.00
273B Starlin Castro VAR 1.00 2.50
274 Justin Masterson .60 1.50
275 Mark Melancon .60 1.50
276 Ricky Nolasco .60 1.50
277 Vance Worley .75 2.00
278 Dustin Ackley .60 1.50
279 Jeff Niemann .60 1.50
280 Willie Mays 2.00 5.00
281 James McDonald .60 1.50
282 Jordan Walden .60 1.50
283 Mike Leake .60 1.50
284 Todd Helton .75 2.00
285A Carlos Santana .75 2.00
285B Carlos Santana VAR 1.00 2.50
286A Chase Utley .75 2.00
286B Chase Utley VAR 1.00 2.50
287A Daniel Hudson .60 1.50
287B Daniel Hudson VAR .75 2.00
288 C.J. Wilson .60 1.50
289A Gio Gonzalez .75 2.00
289B Gio Gonzalez VAR 1.00 2.50
290 Sandy Koufax 2.00 5.00
291 Jarrod Parker .75 2.00
292 Delmon Young .75 2.00
293 Yogi Berra 1.00 2.50
294A Reggie Jackson .60 1.50
294B Reggie Jackson VAR .75 2.00
295 Doc Gooden .40 1.00
296A Tom Seaver .60 1.50
296B Tom Seaver VAR .75 2.00
297 Lou Brock .60 1.50
298 Brandon Morrow .60 1.50
299 Mike Carp .60 1.50
300 Babe Ruth 2.50 6.00
301 Billy Butler .75 2.00
302 Anibal Sanchez .75 2.00
303 Asdrubal Cabrera 1.00 2.50
304 Seth Smith .75 2.00
305 Matt Cain 1.00 2.50
306 Mark Reynolds .75 2.00
307 Michael Morse .75 2.00
308 Adrian Beltre 1.25 3.00
309 Michael Young .75 2.00
310 Zack Greinke 1.00 2.50
311 Brandon Belt 1.00 2.50
312 Troy Tulowitzki 1.25 3.00
313 David Price 1.00 2.50
314 Bobby Abreu .75 2.00
315 J.P. Arencibia .75 2.00
316 Jayson Werth 1.00 2.50
317 Tim Hudson 1.00 2.50
318 Johnny Cueto 1.00 2.50
319 Hanley Ramirez 1.00 2.50
320 Justin Verlander 1.25 3.00
321 Jose Reyes 1.00 2.50
322 Elvis Andrus .75 2.00
323 Michael Bourn .75 2.00
324 Rickie Weeks .75 2.00
325 Shane Victorino .75 2.00
326 Prince Fielder 1.00 2.50
327 Brandon Phillips .75 2.00
328 Drew Stubbs .75 2.00
329 Lou Brock .75 2.00
330 B.J. Upton 1.00 2.50
331 Josh Beckett .75 2.00
332 Nick Swisher 1.00 2.50
333 Albert Pujols 1.50 4.00

334 Heath Bell .75 2.00
335 Chris Young .75 2.00
336 Mike Trout 40.00 100.00
337 Eric Thames 1.00 2.50
338 Ryan Vogelsong .75 2.00
339 Albert Belle .50 1.25
340 Duke Snider .75 2.00
341 Larry Doby .75 2.00
342 Darryl Strawberry .50 1.25
343 Gary Carter .75 2.00
344 Cal Ripken Jr. 4.00 10.00
345 John Smoltz 1.25 3.00
346 Frank Thomas 1.25 3.00
347 Ernie Banks 1.25 3.00
348 Bob Feller .75 2.00
349 Dustin Ackley .75 2.00
350 Delmon Young 1.00 2.50

2012 Topps Gypsy Queen Mini Black

*BLACK 1-300: .6X TO 1.5X BASIC 1-300
*BLACK 301-350: .5X TO 1.2X BASIC 301-350
STATED ODDS 1:12 HOBBY

2012 Topps Gypsy Queen Mini Green

*GREEN 1-300: .6X TO 1.5X BASIC 1-300
*GREEN 301-350: .5X TO 1.2X BASIC 301-350
STATED ODDS 1:24 HOBBY
100 Derek Jeter 12.00 30.00

2012 Topps Gypsy Queen Mini Gypsy Queen Back

*GQ BACK 1-300: .5X TO 1.2X BASIC 1-300
*GQ BACK 301-350: .4X TO 1X BASIC 301-350
STATED ODDS 1:6 HOBBY

2012 Topps Gypsy Queen Mini Sepia

*SEPIA 1-300: 1.2X TO 3X BASIC 1-300
*SEPIA 301-350: 1X TO 2.5X BASIC 301-350
STATED ODDS 1:20 HOBBY
STATED PRINT RUN 99 SER.#'d SETS
100 Derek Jeter 12.50 30.00

2012 Topps Gypsy Queen Mini Straight Cut Back

*STRAIGHT 1-300: .5X TO 1.2X BASIC 1-300
*STRAIGHT 301-350: .4X TO 1X BASIC 301-350
STATED ODDS 1:6 HOBBY

2012 Topps Gypsy Queen Mini Stadium Seat Relics

STATED ODDS 1:2125 HOBBY
STATED PRINT RUN 100 SER.#'d SETS
SP Sportsman's Park 10.00 25.00
TS Tiger Stadium 15.00 40.00
WF Wrigley Field 12.50 30.00
MCS Milwaukee County Stadium 10.00 25.00
SHP Shibe Park 20.00 50.00

2012 Topps Gypsy Queen Moonshots

COMPLETE SET (20) 6.00 15.00
STATED ODDS 1:3 HOBBY
PRINTING PLATE ODDS 1:1980 HOBBY
PLATE PRINT RUN 1 SET PER COLOR
BLACK-CYAN-MAGENTA-YELLOW ISSUED
NO PLATE PRICING DUE TO SCARCITY
AB Albert Belle .40 1.00
AP Albert Pujols 1.25 3.00
BR Babe Ruth 2.50 6.00
CG Curtis Granderson .75 2.00
EL Evan Longoria .75 2.00
FR Frank Robinson .60 1.50
FT Frank Thomas 1.00 2.50
JB Jose Bautista .75 2.00
JH Josh Hamilton .75 2.00
JT Jim Thome .75 2.00
MM Mickey Mantle 3.00 8.00
MS Mike Stanton 1.00 2.50
NC Nelson Cruz 1.00 2.50
PF Prince Fielder .75 2.00
RH Ryan Howard .75 2.00
RJ Reggie Jackson .60 1.50
RK Ralph Kiner .60 1.50
WM Willie Mays 2.00 5.00
MSC Mike Schmidt 1.50 4.00
WMC Willie McCovey .60 1.50

2012 Topps Gypsy Queen Moonshots Mini

COMPLETE SET (20) 8.00 20.00
STATED ODDS 1 PER MINI BOX TOPPER
MINI PLATE ODDS 1:7425 HOBBY
PLATE PRINT RUN 1 SET PER COLOR
BLACK-CYAN-MAGENTA-YELLOW ISSUED
AB Albert Belle .50 1.25
AP Albert Pujols 1.50 4.00
BR Babe Ruth 3.00 8.00
CG Curtis Granderson 1.00 2.50
EL Evan Longoria 1.00 2.50
FR Frank Robinson .75 2.00
FT Frank Thomas 1.25 3.00
JB Jose Bautista 1.00 2.50
JH Josh Hamilton 1.00 2.50
JT Jim Thome 1.00 2.50
MM Mickey Mantle 4.00 10.00
MS Mike Stanton 1.25 3.00
NC Nelson Cruz 1.25 3.00
PF Prince Fielder 1.00 2.50
RH Ryan Howard 1.00 2.50
RJ Reggie Jackson .75 2.00
RK Ralph Kiner .75 2.00
WM Willie Mays 2.50 6.00
MSC Mike Schmidt 2.00 5.00
WMC Willie McCovey .75 2.00

2012 Topps Gypsy Queen Relic Autographs

STATED ODDS 1:1420 HOBBY
PRINT RUNS B/WN 5-25 COPIES PER
NO PRICING ON QTY 10 OR LESS
EXCHANGE DEADLINE 03/31/2015
AJ Adam Jones EXCH 25.00 60.00
AK Al Kaline/25 60.00 150.00
AR Aramis Ramirez/25 10.00 25.00
CF Carlton Fisk/25 30.00 80.00
CG Carlos Gonzalez/25 25.00 60.00
DE Danny Espinosa/25 10.00 25.00
DH Daniel Hudson/25 10.00 25.00
DM Don Mattingly/25 60.00 150.00
DU Dan Uggla/25 12.00 30.00
FT Frank Thomas/25
JB Jay Bruce/25 30.00 80.00
JJ Jon Jay EXCH 15.00 40.00
JV Justin Verlander/25 75.00 200.00
MC Miguel Cabrera/25 60.00 150.00
NC Nelson Cruz/25 15.00 40.00
RB Ryan Braun EXCH 40.00 100.00
RJ Reggie Jackson/25 60.00 150.00
SC Starlin Castro/25 12.00 30.00
TH Tommy Hanson/25 10.00 25.00
JMA Joe Mauer EXCH 40.00 100.00

2012 Topps Gypsy Queen Relics

GROUP A ODDS 1:576 HOBBY
GROUP B ODDS 1:313 HOBBY
GROUP C ODDS 1:28 HOBBY
AA Alex Avila 3.00 8.00
AJ Adam Jones 3.00 8.00
AM Andrew McCutchen 4.00 10.00
AP Andy Pettitte 3.00 8.00
BBU Billy Butler 3.00 8.00
BM Brian McCann 3.00 8.00
BP Brandon Phillips 3.00 8.00
CF Carlton Fisk 4.00 10.00
CW C.J. Wilson 3.00 8.00
DF David Freese 5.00 12.00
DH Dan Haren 3.00 8.00
DHO Derek Holland 3.00 8.00
DO David Ortiz 3.00 8.00
DP Dustin Pedroia 5.00 12.00
DPR David Price 3.00 8.00
DW David Wright 3.00 8.00
EL Evan Longoria 4.00 10.00
EM Eddie Murray 3.00 8.00
EMA Eddie Mathews 6.00 15.00
FR Frank Robinson 8.00 20.00
JD Joe DiMaggio 30.00 60.00
JE Jacoby Ellsbury 4.00 10.00
JH Jeremy Hellickson 3.00 8.00
JHE Jason Heyward 3.00 8.00
JL Jon Lester 3.00 8.00
JR Jose Reyes 3.00 8.00
JRO Jimmy Rollins 3.00 8.00
JS James Shields 3.00 8.00
JU Justin Upton 3.00 8.00
JW Jayson Werth 3.00 8.00
KY Kevin Youkilis 3.00 8.00
MB Madison Bumgarner 4.00 10.00
MC Matt Cain 3.00 8.00
MCA Miguel Cabrera 12.50 30.00
MH Matt Holliday 4.00 10.00
MR Mariano Rivera 5.00 12.00
MS Mike Stanton 3.00 8.00
MT Mark Trumbo 3.00 8.00
NC Nelson Cruz 3.00 8.00
OS Ozzie Smith 4.00 10.00
PF Prince Fielder 3.00 8.00
PN Phil Niekro 3.00 8.00
PS Pablo Sandoval 3.00 8.00
RC Rod Carew 3.00 8.00
RCL Roberto Clemente 30.00 60.00
RJ Reggie Jackson 10.00 25.00
RK Ralph Kiner 6.00 15.00
RM Roger Maris 12.50 30.00
RR Ricky Romero 3.00 8.00
RY Robin Yount 8.00 20.00
RZ Ryan Zimmerman 3.00 8.00
SC Steve Carlton 4.00 10.00
SG Steve Garvey 3.00 8.00
TG Tony Gwynn 6.00 15.00
TH Tim Hudson 3.00 8.00
THA Tommy Hanson 3.00 8.00
TL Tim Lincecum 4.00 10.00
VM Victor Martinez 3.00 8.00
WB Wade Boggs 4.00 10.00
WS Willie Stargell 6.00 15.00
YG Yovani Gallardo 3.00 8.00
ZG Zack Greinke 3.00 8.00

2012 Topps Gypsy Queen Sliding Stars

COMPLETE SET (15) 4.00 10.00
STATED ODDS 1:3 HOBBY
PRINTING PLATE ODDS 1:1980 HOBBY
PLATE PRINT RUN 1 SET PER COLOR
BLACK-CYAN-MAGENTA-YELLOW ISSUED
NO PLATE PRICING DUE TO SCARCITY
AM Andrew McCutchen 1.00 2.50
CG Curtis Granderson .75 2.00
DG Dee Gordon .60 1.50
DJ Derek Jeter 2.50 6.00
DP Dustin Pedroia .75 2.00
EA Elvis Andrus .75 2.00
IK Ian Kinsler .75 2.00
JE Jacoby Ellsbury .75 2.00
JR Jose Reyes .60 1.50
JW Jemile Weeks .60 1.50
MK Matt Kemp .75 2.00
NM Nyjer Morgan .60 1.50
RB Ryan Braun .60 1.50
SC Starlin Castro .75 2.00
JRO Jimmy Rollins .75 2.00

2012 Topps Gypsy Queen Sliding Stars Mini

COMPLETE SET (15) 5.00 12.00
STATED ODDS 1 PER MINI BOX TOPPER
MINI PLATE ODDS 1:9900 HOBBY
PLATE PRINT RUN 1 SET PER COLOR
BLACK-CYAN-MAGENTA-YELLOW ISSUED
AM Andrew McCutchen 1.25 3.00
CG Curtis Granderson 1.00 2.50
DG Dee Gordon .75 2.00
DJ Derek Jeter 3.00 8.00
DP Dustin Pedroia 1.00 2.50
EA Elvis Andrus 1.00 2.50
IK Ian Kinsler 1.00 2.50
JE Jacoby Ellsbury 1.00 2.50
JR Jose Reyes .75 2.00
JW Jemile Weeks .75 2.00
MK Matt Kemp 1.00 2.50
NM Nyjer Morgan .75 2.00
RB Ryan Braun .75 2.00
SC Starlin Castro 1.00 2.50
JRO Jimmy Rollins 1.00 2.50

2013 Topps Gypsy Queen

COMP.SET w/o SP's (300) 15.00 40.00
SP ODDS 1:24 HOBBY
SP VAR ODDS 1:465 HOBBY
PRINTING PLATE ODDS 1:459 HOBBY
1A Adam Jones .30 .75
1B A.Jones SP VAR 50.00 100.00
2 Joe Nathan .25 .60
3A Adrian Beltre .40 1.00
3B A.Beltre SP VAR 10.00 25.00
4 L.J. Hoes RC .50 1.25
5 Adrian Gonzalez .30 .75
6 Alex Rodriguez .50 1.25
7 Mike Schmidt SP 2.50 6.00
8 Andre Dawson .30 .75
9A Andrew McCutchen .40 1.00
9B A.McCutchen SP VAR 30.00 60.00
10 Al Kaline .40 1.00
11 Anthony Rizzo .60 1.50
12 Aroldis Chapman .40 1.00
13 Wei-Yin Chen .25 .60
14A Mike Trout SP 12.00 30.00
14B M.Trout SP VAR 50.00 100.00
15 Tyler Skaggs RC .60 1.50
16 Brandon Beachy .25 .60
17 Brandon Belt .30 .75
18 Brett Jackson .25 .60
19 Nolan Ryan SP 5.00 12.00
20A Albert Pujols .50 1.25
20B A.Pujols SP VAR 20.00 50.00
21 Ivan Nova .30 .75
22 CC Sabathia .30 .75
23 Cecil Fielder .25 .60
24 Chris Carter .25 .60
25 Chris Sale .40 1.00
26A Clayton Kershaw .75 2.00
26B Clayton Kershaw SP VAR 12.50 30.00
In Dugout
27 Chad Billingsley .30 .75
28 R.A. Dickey SP 1.25 3.00
29 Cole Hamels .30 .75
30 Bert Blyleven .30 .75
31 Josh Willingham .30 .75
32 Darin Ruf RC .75 2.00
33 Rob Brantly RC .40 1.00
34A David Freese .30 .75
34B David Freese SP VAR 12.50 30.00
High-fiving
35A David Price .30 .75
35B David Price SP VAR 12.50 30.00
With Jose Molina
36 Avisail Garcia RC .50 1.25
37 David Wright .30 .75
38 Derek Norris .25 .60
39 Dexter Fowler .30 .75
40 Bill Buckner .25 .60
41 Dylan Bundy RC 1.00 2.50
42 Jose Quintana .25 .60
43 Enos Slaughter .30 .75
44 Evan Longoria .30 .75
45A Felix Hernandez .30 .75
45B Felix Hernandez SP VAR 12.50 30.00
Hugging
46 Frank Thomas .40 1.00
47 Freddie Freeman .50 1.25
48 Gary Carter .30 .75
49 George Kell .30 .75
50 Babe Ruth 1.00 2.50
51 Clay Buchholz .25 .60
52 Hanley Ramirez .30 .75
53 Clayton Richard .25 .60
54 Jacoby Ellsbury .30 .75
55 Nathan Eovaldi .30 .75
56 Jason Heyward .30 .75
57 Jayson Werth .30 .75
58 Jean Segura .30 .75
59 Jered Weaver .30 .75
60 Billy Williams .30 .75
61A Joe Mauer .30 .75
61B Joe Mauer SP VAR 12.50 30.00
With Justin Morneau
62A Ryan Braun SP 1.25 3.00
62B R.Braun SP VAR 20.00 50.00
63 Joe Morgan .30 .75
64A Joey Votto .40 1.00
64B J.Votto SP VAR 20.00 50.00
65 Johan Santana .30 .75
66 John Kruk .25 .60
67 John Smoltz .40 1.00
68 Johnny Cueto .30 .75
69 Jon Jay .25 .60
70 Bob Feller .30 .75
71 Jose Bautista .30 .75
72 Josh Hamilton .30 .75
73 Casey Kelly RC .50 1.25
74 Josh Rutledge .25 .60
75 Juan Marichal .30 .75
76 Jurickson Profar RC .50 1.25
77 Justin Upton .30 .75
78 Kyle Seager .25 .60
79 Ken Griffey Jr. .75 2.00
80 Bob Gibson .30 .75
81 Larry Doby .25 .60
82 Lou Brock .30 .75
83 Lou Gehrig .75 2.00
84 Madison Bumgarner .30 .75
85 Manny Machado RC 2.50 6.00
86 Mariano Rivera .50 1.25
87 Stan Musial SP 2.50 6.00
88 Mark Trumbo .25 .60
89 Matt Adams .25 .60
90 Brooks Robinson .25 .60
91 Matt Holliday .40 1.00
92 Tim Lincecum SP 1.25 3.00
93 Matt Moore .30 .75
94 Melky Cabrera .25 .60
95 Michael Bourn .25 .60
96 Michael Fiers .25 .60
97 Troy Tulowitzki SP 1.50 4.00
98 Jake Odorizzi RC .50 1.25
99A Yu Darvish SP 1.50 4.00
99B Y.Darvish SP VAR 15.00 40.00
100A Bryce Harper .60 1.50
100B B.Harper SP VAR 50.00 100.00
101 Mike Olt RC .50 1.25
102 Tyler Colvin .25 .60
103 Trevor Rosenthal (RC) .75 2.00
104 Paco Rodriguez RC .60 1.50
105 Allen Craig .30 .75
106 Monte Irvin .25 .60
107 Alcides Escobar SP 1.25 3.00
108 Nick Maronde RC .50 1.25
109 Andy Pettitte .30 .75
110A Buster Posey .50 1.25
110B B.Posey SP VAR 10.00 25.00
111 Carlos Ruiz SP 1.00 2.50
112 Paul Goldschmidt .40 1.00
113 Paul Molitor .40 1.00
114 Alex Rios SP 1.25 3.00
115 Pedro Alvarez .25 .60
116 Phil Niekro .30 .75
117A Prince Fielder .30 .75
117B P.Fielder SP VAR 20.00 50.00
118 Ruben Tejada .25 .60
119 Torii Hunter .25 .60
120 Cal Ripken Jr. 1.25 3.00
121 Rickey Henderson .40 1.00
122 Early Wynn SP 1.25 3.00
123 Jon Niese .25 .60
124 Elvis Andrus SP 1.25 3.00
125 Robin Yount .40 1.00
126 Edwin Encarnacion SP 1.50 4.00
127 Rod Carew .30 .75
128 Roger Bernadina .15 .40
129 Roy Halladay .30 .75
130 Carlton Fisk .30 .75
131 Hal Newhouser SP 1.25 3.00
132 Ryan Howard .30 .75
133 Adam Dunn SP 1.25 3.00
134 Ryan Zimmerman .30 .75
135 Ryne Sandberg .75 2.00
136 Salvador Perez .25 .60
137 Sandy Koufax .75 2.00
138 Scott Diamond .25 .60
139 Shaun Marcum .25 .60
140 Catfish Hunter .30 .75
141 Alex Gordon .30 .75
142 Starlin Castro .30 .75
143 Starling Marte .30 .75
144 Red Schoendienst SP 1.25 3.00
145 Ryan Ludwick .25 .60
146 Erick Aybar .25 .60
147 David Ortiz .40 1.00
148 Todd Frazier .30 .75
149 Tom Seaver .30 .75
150A Derek Jeter 1.00 2.50
150B D.Jeter SP VAR 30.00 60.00
151 Travis Snider .25 .60
152 Trevor Bauer .40 1.00
153 Raul Ibanez .30 .75
154 Jim Palmer .30 .75
155 Ty Cobb .60 1.50
156 Cody Ross .25 .60
157 Vida Blue .25 .60
158 Wade Boggs .30 .75
159 Wade Miley .30 .75
160 Don Mattingly .75 2.00
161 Whitey Ford .30 .75
162 Bruce Sutter SP 1.25 3.00
163 Will Clark .30 .75
164 Will Middlebrooks .25 .60
165 Russell Martin .25 .60
166 Austin Jackson .25 .60
167 Willie McCovey .30 .75
168 Willie Stargell .30 .75
169 Wily Peralta .25 .60
170 Don Sutton .25 .60
171 Yasmani Grandal .25 .60
172A Yoenis Cespedes .40 1.00
172B Yoenis Cespedes SP VAR 12.50 30.00
High-fiving
173 Yonder Alonso .25 .60
174 Yovani Gallardo .25 .60
175 Brandon Moss .25 .60
176 Tony Perez .30 .75
177 Michael Brantley .25 .60
178 David Murphy .25 .60
179 Carlos Santana .30 .75
180 Duke Snider .30 .75
181 Nick Swisher SP 1.25 3.00
182 Alejandro de Aza .25 .60
183 Al Lopez SP 1.00 2.50
184 Chris Davis .30 .75
185 Ryan Doumit .25 .60
186 Alexei Ramirez .30 .75
187 Curtis Granderson SP 1.25 3.00
188 Jose Altuve .30 .75
189A Cliff Lee SP 1.25 3.00
189B C.Lee SP VAR 15.00 40.00
190 Eddie Murray .30 .75
191 Jordan Pacheco .25 .60
192 James Shields SP 1.00 2.50
193 Chase Headley .25 .60
194 Brandon Phillips .25 .60
195 Chris Johnson .25 .60
196 Omar Infante .25 .60
197 Garrett Jones .25 .60
198 Ian Kinsler SP 1.25 3.00
199 Carlos Beltran .30 .75
200 Ernie Banks .40 1.00
201 Justin Morneau .30 .75
202 Goose Gossage SP 1.25 3.00
203 Dayan Viciedo .25 .60
204 Andre Ethier SP 1.25 3.00
205 Jay Bruce .30 .75
206 Danny Espinosa .25 .60
207 Zack Cozart .25 .60
208 Gio Gonzalez SP 1.25 3.00
209 Mike Moustakas .30 .75
210 Fergie Jenkins .30 .75
211 Dan Uggla .25 .60
212 Kevin Youkilis .25 .60
213 Rick Ferrell SP 1.00 2.50
214 Jemile Weeks .25 .60
215 Kris Medlen SP 1.25 3.00
216 Colby Rasmus .30 .75
217 Neil Walker .30 .75
218 Adam Wainwright SP 1.25 3.00
219 Jake Peavy .25 .60
220 Frank Robinson .30 .75
221 Jason Kipnis .30 .75
222 A.J. Burnett .25 .60
223 Jeff Samardzija .25 .60
224 C.J. Wilson .25 .60
225 Homer Bailey .25 .60
226 Jon Lester .30 .75
227 Francisco Liriano .25 .60
228 Hiroki Kuroda .25 .60
229 Josh Johnson .25 .60
230 George Brett .75 2.00
231 Edinson Volquez .25 .60
232 Felix Doubront .25 .60
233 Ike Davis .25 .60
234 Corey Hart .25 .60
235 Ben Zobrist .30 .75
236 Kendrys Morales .25 .60
237 Coco Crisp .25 .60
238 Angel Pagan .25 .60
239 Josh Reddick SP 1.00 2.50
240 Harmon Killebrew .40 1.00
241 Chris Capuano .25 .60
242 Asdrubal Cabrera .30 .75
243 Brett Lawrie .30 .75
244 Ian Kennedy .25 .60
245 Derek Holland .25 .60
246 Mike Minor .25 .60
247 Jose Reyes .30 .75
248 Matt Harrison SP 1.00 2.50
249 Dan Haren .25 .60
250 Hank Aaron .75 2.00
251 Doug Fister .25 .60
252 Jason Vargas .25 .60
253 Tommy Milone .25 .60
254 Bronson Arroyo .25 .60
255 Mark Buehrle .30 .75
256 Eric Hosmer .30 .75
257 Craig Kimbrel .30 .75
258 Eddie Mathews SP 1.50 4.00
259A Justin Verlander .40 1.00
259B J.Verlander SP VAR 20.00 50.00
260 Jackie Robinson .40 1.00
261 Vance Worley .30 .75
262 Hisashi Iwakuma .30 .75
263 Brandon Morrow .25 .60
264 Jaime Garcia .25 .60
265 Josh Beckett .25 .60
266 Fernando Rodney .25 .60
267 Hoyt Wilhelm SP 1.25 3.00
268 Jim Johnson .25 .60
269 Ben Revere .25 .60
270 Jim Abbott .25 .60
271 Adam Eaton RC .60 1.50
272 Anthony Gose .25 .60
273 Carlos Gonzalez .30 .75
274 Jonny Gomes .25 .60
275 Dustin Pedroia .30 .75
276A Giancarlo Stanton .40 1.00
276B G.Stanton SP VAR 15.00 40.00
277 Orlando Cepeda SP 1.25 3.00
278 Jordan Zimmermann .30 .75
279 Lance Lynn .25 .60
280 Jim Rice .25 .60
281 Matt Cain .30 .75
282 Mike Morse .25 .60
283 Daniel Murphy .30 .75
284 Reggie Jackson .30 .75
285 Matt Garza .25 .60
286 Brandon McCarthy .25 .60
287 Tony Gwynn .40 1.00
288 Jim Bunning SP 1.25 3.00
289 Yadier Molina .40 1.00
290 Dwight Gooden .25 .60
291 Howie Kendrick .25 .60
292 Ian Desmond .25 .60
293 Delmon Young .30 .75
294 Rickie Weeks .25 .60
295 Bobby Doerr SP 1.25 3.00
296 Phil Hughes .25 .60
297 Trevor Cahill .25 .60
298 Michael Young .25 .60
299 Barry Zito .30 .75
300 Johnny Bench .40 1.00
301 Tommy Hanson .25 .60
302 Lou Boudreau SP 1.25 3.00
303 Billy Butler .25 .60
304 Ralph Kiner SP 1.00 2.50
305 Brian McCann .30 .75
306 Mike Leake .25 .60
307 Shelby Miller RC 1.00 2.50
308 Mark Teixeira .30 .75
309 Bob Lemon SP 1.25 3.00
310A Miguel Cabrera SP 1.50 4.00
310B M.Cabrera SP VAR 40.00 80.00
311A Matt Kemp .30 .75
311B M.Kemp SP VAR 15.00 40.00
312 Miguel Gonzalez .25 .60
313 Miguel Montero .25 .60
314 Nelson Cruz .40 1.00
315 Ozzie Smith .50 1.25
316 Paul O'Neill .30 .75
317 Alex Cobb .25 .60
318 Robin Roberts SP 1.25 3.00
319 Robin Ventura .25 .60
320 Roberto Clemente SP 4.00 10.00
321A Robinson Cano .30 .75
321B R.Cano SP VAR 30.00 60.00
322 Jason Motte .25 .60
323 Ryan Vogelsong .25 .60
324A Stephen Strasburg .40 1.00
324B S.Strasburg SP VAR 15.00 40.00
325 Wilin Rosario .25 .60
326 Aaron Hill .25 .60
327 A.J. Pierzynski .25 .60
328 Denard Span .25 .60
329 Shin-Soo Choo .30 .75
330 Ted Williams SP 3.00 8.00
331 Darryl Strawberry SP 1.00 2.50
332 Marco Scutaro .30 .75
333 A.J. Ellis .25 .60
334 Bill Mazeroski SP 1.25 3.00
335 Alfonso Soriano .30 .75
336 Hunter Pence .30 .75
337 Desmond Jennings .30 .75
338 Mark Reynolds .25 .60
339 Anibal Sanchez .25 .60
340 Willie Mays SP 3.00 8.00
341 Darwin Barney .25 .60
342 B.J. Upton .30 .75
343 Kyle Lohse .25 .60
344 Tim Hudson .30 .75
345 Grant Balfour .25 .60
346 Phil Rizzuto SP 1.25 3.00
347 Jesus Montero .25 .60
348 Warren Spahn 1.25 3.00
349 Mat Latos .30 .75
350 Yogi Berra SP 1.50 4.00

2013 Topps Gypsy Queen Framed Blue

STATED ODDS 1:21 HOBBY
STATED PRINT RUN 499 SER.#'d SETS
1 Adam Jones .75 2.00
3 Adrian Beltre 1.00 2.50
9 Andrew McCutchen 1.00 2.50
10 Al Kaline 1.00 2.50
13 Wei-Yin Chen .60 1.50
17 Brandon Belt .75 2.00
23 Cecil Fielder .60 1.50
26 Clayton Kershaw 2.00 5.00
29 Cole Hamels .75 2.00
30 Bert Blyleven .75 2.00
31 Josh Willingham .75 2.00
34 David Freese .60 1.50
37 David Wright .75 2.00
39 Dexter Fowler .75 2.00
42 Jose Quintana .60 1.50
48 Gary Carter .75 2.00
54 Jacoby Ellsbury .75 2.00
57 Jayson Werth .75 2.00
63 Joe Morgan .75 2.00
65 Johan Santana .75 2.00
70 Bob Feller .75 2.00
71 Jose Bautista .75 2.00
74 Josh Rutledge .60 1.50
78 Kyle Seager .60 1.50
80 Bob Gibson .60 1.50
81 Larry Doby .60 1.50
86 Mariano Rivera 1.25 3.00
89 Matt Adams .60 1.50
90 Brooks Robinson .75 2.00
93 Matt Moore .75 2.00
95 Michael Bourn .60 1.50
102 Tyler Colvin .60 1.50
105 Allen Craig .75 2.00
109 Andy Pettitte .75 2.00
112 Paul Goldschmidt 1.00 2.50
117 Prince Fielder .75 2.0
120 Cal Ripken Jr. 3.00 8.0
123 Jon Niese .60 1.5
129 Roy Halladay .75 2.0
130 Carlton Fisk .75 2.0
137 Sandy Koufax 2.00 5.0
141 Alex Gordon .75 2.0
145 Ryan Ludwick .60 1.5
148 Todd Frazier .75 2.0
154 Jim Palmer .75 2.0
158 Wade Boggs .75 2.0
161 Whitey Ford .75 2.0
163 Will Clark .75 2.0
166 Austin Jackson .60 1.5
168 Willie Stargell .75 2.0
173 Yonder Alonso .60 1.5
176 Tony Perez .75 2.0
179 Carlos Santana .75 2.0
180 Duke Snider .75 2.0
182 Alejandro de Aza .60 1.5
184 Chris Davis .75 2.0
193 Chase Headley .60 1.5
196 Omar Infante .60 1.5
199 Carlos Beltran .75 2.0
200 Ernie Banks 1.00 2.5
205 Jay Bruce .75 2.0
207 Zack Cozart .60 1.5
211 Dan Uggla .60 1.5
214 Jemile Weeks .60 1.5
220 Frank Robinson .75 2.0
221 Jason Kipnis .75 2.0
224 C.J. Wilson .60 1.5
229 Josh Johnson .75 2.0
233 Ike Davis .60 1.5
237 Coco Crisp .60 1.5
240 Harmon Killebrew 1.00 2.5
241 Chris Capuano .60 1.5
243 Brett Lawrie .75 2.0
245 Derek Holland .60 1.5
247 Jose Reyes .75 2.0
249 Dan Haren .60 1.5
253 Tommy Milone .60 1.5
255 Mark Buehrle .75 2.0
257 Craig Kimbrel .75 2.0
261 Vance Worley .75 2.0
263 Brandon Morrow .60 1.5
265 Josh Beckett .60 1.5
269 Ben Revere .60 1.5
270 Jim Abbott .60 1.5
276 Giancarlo Stanton 1.00 2.5
284 Reggie Jackson .75 2.0
289 Yadier Molina 1.00 2.5
292 Ian Desmond .60 1.5
296 Phil Hughes .60 1.5
300 Johnny Bench 1.00 2.5
301 Tommy Hanson .60 1.5
303 Billy Butler .60 1.5
313 Miguel Montero .60 1.5
321 Robinson Cano .75 2.0
323 Ryan Vogelsong .60 1.5
328 Denard Span .60 1.5
332 Marco Scutaro .75 2.0
335 Alfonso Soriano .75 2.0
337 Desmond Jennings .75 2.0
341 Darwin Barney .60 1.5

2013 Topps Gypsy Queen Framed White

1 Adam Jones .50 1.25
3 Adrian Beltre .60 1.50
9 Andrew McCutchen .60 1.50
10 Al Kaline .60 1.50
13 Wei-Yin Chen .40 1.00
17 Brandon Belt .50 1.25
23 Cecil Fielder .40 1.00
26 Clayton Kershaw 1.25 3.00
29 Cole Hamels .50 1.25
30 Bert Blyleven .50 1.25
31 Josh Willingham .50 1.25
34 David Freese .40 1.00
37 David Wright .50 1.25
39 Dexter Fowler .50 1.25
42 Jose Quintana .40 1.00
48 Gary Carter .50 1.25
54 Jacoby Ellsbury .50 1.25
57 Jayson Werth .50 1.25
63 Joe Morgan .50 1.25
65 Johan Santana .50 1.25
70 Bob Feller .50 1.25
71 Jose Bautista .50 1.25
74 Josh Rutledge .40 1.00
78 Kyle Seager .40 1.00
80 Bob Gibson .50 1.25
81 Larry Doby .40 1.00
86 Mariano Rivera .75 2.00
89 Matt Adams .40 1.00
90 Brooks Robinson .50 1.25
93 Matt Moore .50 1.25
95 Michael Bourn .40 1.00
102 Tyler Colvin .40 1.00
105 Allen Craig .50 1.25
109 Andy Pettitte .50 1.25
112 Paul Goldschmidt .60 1.50
117 Prince Fielder .50 1.25
120 Cal Ripken Jr. 2.00 5.00
123 Jon Niese .40 1.00
129 Roy Halladay .50 1.25
130 Carlton Fisk .50 1.25
137 Sandy Koufax 1.25 3.00
141 Alex Gordon .50 1.25
145 Ryan Ludwick .40 1.00
148 Todd Frazier .50 1.25
154 Jim Palmer .50 1.25

58 Wade Boggs .50 1.25
61 Whitey Ford .50 1.25
63 Will Clark .50 1.25
66 Austin Jackson .40 1.00
68 Willie Stargell .50 1.25
73 Yonder Alonso .40 1.00
76 Tony Perez .50 1.25
79 Carlos Santana .50 1.25
80 Duke Snider .50 1.25
82 Alejandro de Aza .40 1.00
84 Chris Davis .50 1.25
93 Chase Headley .40 1.00
96 Omar Infante .40 1.00
99 Carlos Beltran .50 1.25
00 Ernie Banks .60 1.50
05 Jay Bruce .50 1.25
07 Zack Cozart .40 1.00
11 Dan Uggla .40 1.00
14 Jemile Weeks .40 1.00
20 Frank Robinson .50 1.25
21 Jason Kipnis .50 1.25
24 C.J. Wilson .40 1.00
29 Josh Johnson .50 1.25
33 Ike Davis .40 1.00
37 Coco Crisp .40 1.00
40 Harmon Killebrew .60 1.50
41 Chris Capuano .40 1.00
43 Brett Lawrie .50 1.25
45 Derek Holland .40 1.00
47 Jose Reyes .50 1.25
49 Dan Haren .40 1.00
53 Tommy Milone .40 1.00
55 Mark Buehrle .50 1.25
57 Craig Kimbrel .50 1.25
61 Vance Worley .50 1.25
63 Brandon Morrow .40 1.00
65 Josh Beckett .40 1.00
69 Ben Revere .40 1.00
70 Jim Abbott .40 1.00
76 Giancarlo Stanton .60 1.50
84 Reggie Jackson .50 1.25
89 Yadier Molina .60 1.50
92 Ian Desmond .40 1.00
96 Phil Hughes .40 1.00
00 Johnny Bench .60 1.50
01 Tommy Hanson .40 1.00
03 Billy Butler .40 1.00
13 Miguel Montero .40 1.00
21 Robinson Cano .50 1.25
23 Ryan Vogelsong .40 1.00
28 Denard Span .40 1.00
32 Marco Scutaro .50 1.25
35 Alfonso Soriano .50 1.25
37 Desmond Jennings .50 1.25
41 Darwin Barney .40 1.00

2013 Topps Gypsy Queen Autographs

TATED ODDS 1:13 HOBBY
XCHANGE DEADLINE 02/28/2016
E Adam Eaton 4.00 10.00
G Anthony Gose 4.00 10.00
R Anthony Rizzo 20.00 50.00
RA A.J. Ramos 4.00 10.00
B Billy Butler 6.00 15.00
H Brock Holt 4.00 10.00
HA Bryce Harper 100.00 200.00
J Brett Jackson 4.00 10.00
W Billy Williams 10.00 25.00
A Chris Archer 4.00 10.00
D Cole De Vries 4.00 10.00
F Cecil Fielder 10.00 25.00
R Carlos Ruiz 4.00 10.00
RJ Cal Ripken Jr. EXCH 50.00 100.00
B Dylan Bundy 12.00 30.00
F David Freese 4.00 10.00
L DJ LeMahieu 6.00 15.00
R Darin Ruf 4.00 10.00
S Dave Stewart 5.00 12.00
F Freddie Freeman 10.00 25.00
R Garrett Richards 4.00 10.00
A Jim Abbott 5.00 12.00
B Jose Bautista 10.00 25.00
F Jeurys Familia 4.00 10.00
J Jon Jay 5.00 12.00
K John Kruk 4.00 10.00
M Jesus Montero 4.00 10.00
P Jurickson Profar 50.00 100.00
R Josh Rutledge 4.00 10.00
S Jean Segura 5.00 12.00
SH James Shields 4.00 10.00
U Justin Upton 5.00 12.00
Z Jordan Zimmermann 6.00 15.00
L Kenny Lofton 6.00 15.00
N Kirk Nieuwenhuis 4.00 10.00
L Lance Lynn 6.00 15.00
MA Matt Adams 4.00 10.00
MC Matt Cain 4.00 10.00
MCA Matt Carpenter 8.00 20.00
MF Michael Fiers 4.00 10.00
MM Mike Morse 5.00 12.00
MMA Manny Machado 30.00 80.00
MMO Matt Moore 4.00 10.00
MT Mark Trumbo 4.00 10.00
MTR Mike Trout 125.00 250.00
NC Nelson Cruz 4.00 10.00
NM Nick Maronde 4.00 10.00
NR Nolan Ryan 25.00 60.00
PG Paul Goldschmidt 10.00 25.00
RD R.A. Dickey 4.00 10.00
SD Scott Diamond 4.00 10.00
SM Starling Marte 6.00 15.00
SMA Shaun Marcum 4.00 10.00
TB Trevor Bauer 6.00 15.00
TF Todd Frazier 6.00 15.00
TG Tony Gwynn 40.00 80.00
VB Vida Blue 6.00 15.00
WJ Wally Joyner 6.00 15.00
WM Wade Miley 4.00 10.00
WMA Willie Mays EXCH 125.00 250.00
WP Wily Peralta 4.00 10.00
WR Wilin Rosario 4.00 10.00
YA Yonder Alonso 4.00 10.00
YC Yoenis Cespedes 8.00 20.00
YG Yovani Gallardo 5.00 12.00
YGR Yasmani Grandal 4.00 10.00
ZC Zack Cozart 4.00 10.00

2013 Topps Gypsy Queen Collisions At The Plate

COMPLETE SET (10) 5.00 12.00
STATED ODDS 1:8 HOBBY
PRINTING PLATE ODDS 1:2131 HOBBY
BM Brian McCann .60 1.50
BP Buster Posey 1.00 2.50
CF Carlton Fisk .60 1.50
CR Carlos Ruiz .50 1.25
GC Gary Carter .60 1.50
JB Johnny Bench .75 2.00
MM Miguel Montero .50 1.25
SP Salvador Perez .60 1.50
WR Wilin Rosario .50 1.25
YM Yadier Molina .75 2.00

2013 Topps Gypsy Queen Dealing Aces

COMPLETE SET (20)
STATED ODDS 1:4 HOBBY
PRINTING PLATE ODDS 1:2131 HOBBY
AW Adam Wainwright .60 1.50
CC CC Sabathia .60 1.50
CK Clayton Kershaw 1.50 4.00
CL Cliff Lee .60 1.50
CS Chris Sale .75 2.00
DB Dylan Bundy 1.25 3.00
DP David Price .60 1.50
FH Felix Hernandez .60 1.50
GG Gio Gonzalez .60 1.50
JC Johnny Cueto .60 1.50
JV Justin Verlander .75 2.00
JW Jered Weaver .60 1.50
MB Madison Bumgarner .60 1.50
MC Matt Cain .60 1.50
MM Matt Moore .60 1.50
RD R.A. Dickey .60 1.50
RH Roy Halladay .60 1.50
SS Stephen Strasburg .75 2.00
TB Trevor Bauer .75 2.00
YD Yu Darvish .75 2.00

2013 Topps Gypsy Queen Framed Mini Relics

STATED ODDS 1:25 HOBBY
AG Alex Gordon 4.00 10.00
AJ Austin Jackson 4.00 10.00
AJO Adam Jones 3.00 8.00
AM Andrew McCutchen 4.00 10.00
AO Alexi Ogando 3.00 8.00
AR Addison Reed 3.00 8.00
BB Brandon Beachy 3.00 8.00
DBE Brandon Belt 4.00 10.00
BBU Billy Butler 3.00 8.00
BM Brian McCann 3.00 8.00
BMO Brandon Morrow 3.00 8.00
BP Brandon Phillips 3.00 8.00
BPO Buster Posey 8.00 20.00
BU B.J. Upton 3.00 8.00
CF Carlton Fisk 4.00 10.00
CH Corey Hart 3.00 8.00
CK Clayton Kershaw 5.00 12.00
CKI Craig Kimbrel 4.00 10.00
CQ Carlos Quentin 3.00 8.00
CS Carlos Santana 3.00 8.00
DH Dan Haren 3.00 8.00
DM Devin Mesoraco 3.00 8.00
DS Drew Stubbs 3.00 8.00
EH Eric Hosmer 3.00 8.00
EL Evan Longoria 4.00 10.00
EM Eddie Murray 5.00 12.00
FF Freddie Freeman 4.00 10.00
FM Fred McGriff 4.00 10.00
IK Ian Kinsler 3.00 8.00
IKE Ian Kennedy 3.00 8.00
JB Jay Bruce 3.00 8.00
JH Jason Heyward 4.00 10.00
JHA Josh Hamilton 4.00 10.00
JHN Joel Hanrahan 3.00 8.00
JJ Jon Jay 3.00 8.00
JM Jason Motte 3.00 8.00
JMO Justin Morneau 3.00 8.00
JP Jordan Pacheco 3.00 8.00
JPE Jake Peavy 3.00 8.00
JPR Jhonny Peralta 3.00 8.00
JR Jimmy Rollins 3.00 8.00
JR Jackie Robinson 40.00 80.00
JV Justin Verlander 6.00 15.00
JZ Jordan Zimmermann 3.00 8.00
KN Kirk Nieuwenhuis 3.00 8.00
MC Melky Cabrera 3.00 8.00
MG Matt Garza 3.00 8.00
MH Matt Harvey 10.00 25.00
MHO Matt Holliday 4.00 10.00
MK Matt Kemp 4.00 10.00
MM Mike Minor 3.00 8.00
MMR Mitch Moreland 3.00 8.00
MN Mike Napoli 3.00 8.00
MR Mark Reynolds 3.00 8.00
NF Neftali Feliz 3.00 8.00
PA Pedro Alvarez 3.00 8.00
PK Paul Konerko 3.00 8.00
PN Phil Niekro 4.00 10.00
RC Rod Carew 4.00 10.00
RH Roy Halladay 4.00 10.00
RHO Ryan Howard 4.00 10.00
RN Ricky Nolasco 3.00 8.00
RR Ricky Romero 3.00 8.00
RY Robin Yount 6.00 15.00
SC Starlin Castro 5.00 12.00
SM Shaun Marcum 3.00 8.00
SR Scott Rolen 3.00 8.00
TC Trevor Cahill 3.00 8.00
TG Tony Gwynn 5.00 12.00
TH Torii Hunter 3.00 8.00
TL Tim Lincecum 6.00 15.00
WR Wilin Rosario 3.00 8.00
YA Yonder Alonso 3.00 8.00
YG Yovani Gallardo 3.00 8.00

2013 Topps Gypsy Queen Glove Stories

COMPLETE SET (10) 6.00 15.00
STATED ODDS 1:6 HOBBY
PRINTING PLATE ODDS 1:2131 HOBBY
BH Bryce Harper 1.25 3.00
CC Coco Crisp .50 1.25
DJ Derek Jeter 2.00 5.00
GB Gregor Blanco .50 1.25
JJ Jon Jay .50 1.25
JW Jayson Werth .60 1.50
MM Manny Machado 3.00 8.00
MT Mike Trout 6.00 15.00
RB Roger Bernadina .30 .75
TS Travis Snider .50 1.25

2013 Topps Gypsy Queen No Hitters

COMPLETE SET (15) 6.00 15.00
STATED ODDS 1:4 HOBBY
PRINTING PLATE ODDS 1:2131 HOBBY
BF Bob Feller .60 1.50
CH Catfish Hunter .60 1.50
FH Felix Hernandez .60 1.50
HB Homer Bailey .50 1.25
JA Jim Abbott .50 1.25
JS Johan Santana .60 1.50
JV Justin Verlander .75 2.00
JW Jered Weaver .60 1.50
KM Kevin Millwood .50 1.25
MC Matt Cain .60 1.50
NR Nolan Ryan 2.50 6.00
PH Philip Humber .50 1.25
RH Roy Halladay .60 1.50
SK Sandy Koufax 1.50 4.00
WS Warren Spahn .60 1.50

2013 Topps Gypsy Queen Relics

STATED ODDS 1:25 HOBBY
AA Alex Avila 3.00 8.00
AB Adrian Beltre 3.00 8.00
AC Asdrubal Cabrera 3.00 8.00
AD Adam Dunn 3.00 8.00
AE Andre Ethier 3.00 8.00
AES Alcides Escobar 3.00 8.00
AG Alex Gordon 4.00 10.00
BB Brandon Beachy 3.00 8.00
BBE Brandon Belt 4.00 10.00
BBU Billy Butler 3.00 8.00
BM Brandon Morrow 3.00 8.00
BP Brandon Phillips 3.00 8.00
BU B.J. Upton 3.00 8.00
CG Carlos Gonzalez 3.00 8.00
CR Colby Rasmus 3.00 8.00
CS Chris Sale 3.00 8.00
CSA Carlos Santana 3.00 8.00
DE Danny Espinosa 3.00 8.00
DG Dee Gordon 3.00 8.00
DH Dan Haren 3.00 8.00
DM Devin Mesoraco 3.00 8.00
DMA Don Mattingly 10.00 25.00
DP David Price 3.00 8.00
DU Dan Uggla 3.00 8.00
EA Elvis Andrus 3.00 8.00
EL Evan Longoria 3.00 8.00
GG Gio Gonzalez 3.00 8.00
HK Harmon Killebrew 10.00 25.00
ID Ian Desmond 3.00 8.00
IK Ian Kinsler 3.00 8.00
JB Jay Bruce 4.00 10.00
JBE Johnny Bench 12.50 30.00
JC Johnny Cueto 3.00 8.00
JG Jaime Garcia 3.00 8.00
JH Jason Heyward 4.00 10.00
JM Jason Motte 3.00 8.00
JP Jake Peavy 3.00 8.00
JPA Jordan Pacheco 3.00 8.00
JPE Jhonny Peralta 3.00 8.00
JR Jim Rice 4.00 10.00
JV Justin Verlander 5.00 12.00
JZ Jordan Zimmermann 3.00 8.00
KN Kirk Nieuwenhuis 3.00 8.00
MB Michael Bourn 3.00 8.00
MBU Madison Bumgarner 6.00 15.00
MC Melky Cabrera 3.00 8.00
MCA Matt Cain 5.00 12.00
MCB Miguel Cabrera 6.00 15.00
MG Matt Garza 3.00 8.00
MM Miguel Montero 3.00 8.00
MMO Mitch Moreland 3.00 8.00
MMR Mike Morse 3.00 8.00
MS Max Scherzer 5.00 12.00
MSC Mike Schmidt 10.00 25.00
NA Norichika Aoki 4.00 10.00
NC Nelson Cruz 3.00 8.00
NG Nomar Garciaparra 5.00 12.00
NM Nick Markakis 3.00 8.00
PA Pedro Alvarez 3.00 8.00
PK Paul Konerko 3.00 8.00
PS Pablo Sandoval 4.00 10.00
SC Shin-Soo Choo 3.00 8.00
SCA Starlin Castro 4.00 10.00
SM Shaun Marcum 3.00 8.00
SR Scott Rolen 3.00 8.00
TC Trevor Cahill 3.00 8.00
TG Tony Gwynn 5.00 12.00
TH Tommy Hanson 3.00 8.00
THU Tim Hudson 3.00 8.00
WB Wade Boggs 4.00 10.00
WR Wilin Rosario 3.00 8.00
YA Yonder Alonso 3.00 8.00
YG Yovani Gallardo 3.00 8.00

2013 Topps Gypsy Queen Sliding Stars

COMPLETE SET (15) 6.00 15.00
STATED ODDS 1:6 HOBBY
PRINTING PLATE ODDS 1:2131 HOBBY
AJ Austin Jackson .50 1.25
AM Andrew McCutchen .75 2.00
BH Bryce Harper 1.25 3.00
CG Carlos Gonzalez .60 1.50
DJ Derek Jeter 2.00 5.00
JH Jason Heyward .60 1.50
JM Joe Morgan .60 1.50
KG Ken Griffey Jr. 1.50 4.00
LB Lou Brock .60 1.50
MT Mike Trout 6.00 15.00
OS Ozzie Smith 1.00 2.50
PF Prince Fielder .60 1.50
RB Ryan Braun .60 1.50
RH Rickey Henderson .75 2.00
AJO Adam Jones .60 1.50

2013 Topps Gypsy Queen Mini

PRINTING PLATE ODDS 1:331 HOBBY
1A Adam Jones .75 2.00
1B Adam Jones SP VAR 1.00 2.50
2 Joe Nathan .60 1.50
3A Adrian Beltre 1.00 2.50
3B Adrian Beltre SP VAR 1.25 3.00
4 L.J. Hoes .75 2.00
5A Adrian Gonzalez .75 2.00
5B Adrian Gonzalez SP VAR 1.00 2.50
6A Alex Rodriguez 1.25 3.00
6B A.Rodriguez SP VAR 1.50 4.00
7A Mike Schmidt 1.50 4.00
7B M.Schmidt SP VAR 2.00 5.00
8 Andre Dawson .75 2.00
9A Andrew McCutchen 1.00 2.50
9B Andrew McCutchen SP VAR 1.25 3.00
10A Al Kaline 1.00 2.50
10B Al Kaline SP VAR 1.25 3.00
11A Anthony Rizzo 1.50 4.00
11B Anthony Rizzo SP VAR 2.00 5.00
12A Aroldis Chapman 1.00 2.50
12B Aroldis Chapman SP VAR 1.25 3.00
13 Wei-Yin Chen .60 1.50
14A Mike Trout 8.00 20.00
14B Mike Trout SP VAR 10.00 25.00
15 Tyler Skaggs 1.00 2.50
16 Brandon Beachy .60 1.50
17 Brandon Belt .75 2.00
18 Brett Jackson .60 1.50
20A Albert Pujols 1.25 3.00
20B Albert Pujols SP VAR 1.50 4.00
21 Ivan Nova .75 2.00
22A CC Sabathia .75 2.00
22B CC Sabathia SP VAR 1.00 2.50
23 Cecil Fielder .60 1.50
24 Chris Carter .60 1.50
25 Chris Sale 1.00 2.50
26A Clayton Kershaw 2.00 5.00
26B Clayton Kershaw SP VAR 2.50 6.00
27 Chad Billingsley .75 2.00
28A R.A. Dickey .75 2.00
28B R.A. Dickey SP VAR 1.00 2.50
29A Cole Hamels .75 2.00
29B Cole Hamels SP VAR 1.00 2.50
30 Bert Blyleven .75 2.00
31 Josh Willingham .75 2.00
32 Darin Ruf 1.25 3.00
33 Rob Brantly .60 1.50
34A David Freese .60 1.50
34B David Freese SP VAR .75 2.00
35A David Price .75 2.00
35B David Price SP VAR 1.00 2.50
36 Avisail Garcia .75 2.00
37A David Wright .75 2.00
37B David Wright SP VAR 1.00 2.50
38 Derek Norris .60 1.50
39 Dexter Fowler .75 2.00
40 Bill Buckner .60 1.50
41A Dylan Bundy 1.50 4.00
41B Dylan Bundy SP VAR 2.00 5.00
42 Jose Quintana .60 1.50
43 Enos Slaughter .75 2.00
44A Evan Longoria .75 2.00
44B Evan Longoria SP VAR 1.00 2.50
45A Felix Hernandez .75 2.00
45B Felix Hernandez SP VAR 1.00 2.50
46A Frank Thomas 1.00 2.50
46B Frank Thomas SP VAR 1.25 3.00
47 Freddie Freeman 1.25 3.00
48 Gary Carter .75 2.00
49A George Kell .75 2.00
49B George Kell SP VAR 1.00 2.50
50A Babe Ruth 2.50 6.00
50B Babe Ruth SP VAR 3.00 8.00
51 Clay Buchholz .60 1.50
52 Hanley Ramirez .75 2.00
53 Clayton Richard .60 1.50
54 Jacoby Ellsbury .75 2.00
55 Nathan Eovaldi .75 2.00
56 Jason Heyward .75 2.00
57 Jayson Werth .75 2.00
58 Jean Segura .75 2.00
59A Jered Weaver .75 2.00
59B Jered Weaver SP VAR 1.00 2.50
60 Billy Williams .75 2.00
61A Joe Mauer .75 2.00
61B Joe Mauer SP VAR 1.00 2.50
62A Ryan Braun .75 2.00
62B Ryan Braun SP VAR 1.00 2.50
63A Joe Morgan .75 2.00
63B Joe Morgan SP VAR 1.00 2.50
64A Joey Votto 1.00 2.50
64B Joey Votto SP VAR 1.25 3.00
65 Johan Santana .75 2.00
66 John Kruk .60 1.50
67A John Smoltz 1.00 2.50
67B John Smoltz SP VAR 1.25 3.00
68A Johnny Cueto .75 2.00
68B Johnny Cueto SP VAR 1.00 2.50
69 Jon Jay .60 1.50
70A Bob Feller .75 2.00
70B Bob Feller SP VAR 1.00 2.50
71A Jose Bautista .75 2.00
71B Jose Bautista SP VAR 1.00 2.50
72A Josh Hamilton .75 2.00
72B Josh Hamilton SP VAR 1.00 2.50
73 Casey Kelly .75 2.00
74 Josh Rutledge .60 1.50
75A Juan Marichal .75 2.00
75B Juan Marichal SP VAR 1.00 2.50
76A Jurickson Profar .75 2.00
76B J.Profar SP VAR 1.00 2.50
77A Justin Upton .75 2.00
77B Justin Upton SP VAR 1.00 2.50
78 Kyle Seager .60 1.50
79A Ken Griffey Jr. 2.00 5.00
79B Ken Griffey Jr. SP VAR 2.50 6.00
80A Bob Gibson .75 2.00
80B Bob Gibson SP VAR 1.00 2.50
81A Larry Doby .60 1.50
81B Larry Doby SP VAR .75 2.00
82A Lou Brock .75 2.00
82B Lou Brock SP VAR 1.00 2.50
83A Lou Gehrig 2.00 5.00
83B Lou Gehrig SP VAR 2.50 6.00
84 Madison Bumgarner .75 2.00
85A Manny Machado 4.00 10.00
85B M.Machado SP VAR 5.00 12.00
86A Mariano Rivera 1.25 3.00
86B Mariano Rivera SP VAR 1.50 4.00
87A Stan Musial 1.50 4.00
87B Stan Musial SP VAR 2.00 5.00
88 Mark Trumbo .60 1.50
89 Matt Adams .60 1.50
90A Brooks Robinson .75 2.00
90B Brooks Robinson SP VAR 1.00 2.50
91 Matt Holliday 1.00 2.50
92 Tim Lincecum .75 2.00
93 Matt Moore .75 2.00
94 Melky Cabrera .60 1.50
95 Michael Bourn .60 1.50
96 Michael Fiers .60 1.50
97A Troy Tulowitzki 1.00 2.50
97B Troy Tulowitzki SP VAR 1.25 3.00
98 Jake Odorizzi .75 2.00
99A Yu Darvish 1.00 2.50
99B Yu Darvish SP VAR 1.25 3.00
100A Bryce Harper 1.50 4.00
100B Bryce Harper SP VAR 2.00 5.00
101 Mike Olt .75 2.00
102 Tyler Colvin .60 1.50
103 Trevor Rosenthal 1.25 3.00
104 Paco Rodriguez 1.00 2.50
105A Allen Craig .75 2.00
105B Allen Craig SP VAR 1.00 2.50
106 Monte Irvin .60 1.50
107 Alcides Escobar .75 2.00
108 Nick Maronde .75 2.00
109 Andy Pettitte .75 2.00
110A Buster Posey 1.25 3.00
110B Buster Posey SP VAR 1.50 4.00
111 Carlos Ruiz .60 1.50
112A Paul Goldschmidt 1.00 2.50
112B Paul Goldschmidt SP VAR 1.25 3.00
113A Paul Molitor 1.00 2.50
113B Paul Molitor SP VAR 1.25 3.00
114 Alex Rios .75 2.00
115 Pedro Alvarez .60 1.50
116 Phil Niekro .75 2.00
117A Prince Fielder .75 2.00
117B Prince Fielder SP VAR 1.00 2.50
118 Ruben Tejada .60 1.50
119 Torii Hunter .60 1.50
120A Cal Ripken Jr. 3.00 8.00
120B C.Ripken Jr. SP VAR 4.00 10.00
121A Rickey Henderson 1.00 2.50
121B Rickey Henderson SP VAR 1.25 3.00
122 Early Wynn .75 2.00
123 Jon Niese .60 1.50
124 Elvis Andrus .75 2.00
125A Robin Yount 1.00 2.50
125B Robin Yount SP VAR 1.25 3.00
126 Edwin Encarnacion 1.00 2.50
127 Rod Carew .75 2.00
128 Roger Bernadina .40 1.00
129A Roy Halladay .75 2.00
129B Roy Halladay SP VAR 1.00 2.50
130 Carlton Fisk .75 2.00
131 Hal Newhouser .75 2.00
132 Ryan Howard .75 2.00
133 Adam Dunn .75 2.00
134 Ryan Zimmerman .75 2.00
135 Ryne Sandberg 2.00 5.00
136 Salvador Perez .75 2.00
137A Sandy Koufax 2.00 5.00
137B Sandy Koufax SP VAR 2.50 6.00
138 Scott Diamond .60 1.50
139 Shaun Marcum .60 1.50
140 Catfish Hunter .75 2.00
141 Alex Gordon .75 2.00
142A Starlin Castro .60 1.50
142B Starlin Castro SP VAR .75 2.00
143 Starling Marte .75 2.00
144 Red Schoendienst .75 2.00
145 Ryan Ludwick .60 1.50
146 Erick Aybar .60 1.50
147 David Ortiz 1.00 2.50
148 Todd Frazier .75 2.00
149A Tom Seaver .75 2.00
149B Tom Seaver SP VAR 1.00 2.50
150A Derek Jeter 2.50 6.00
150B Derek Jeter SP VAR 3.00 8.00
151 Travis Snider .60 1.50
152A Trevor Bauer 1.00 2.50
152B Trevor Bauer SP VAR 1.25 3.00
153 Raul Ibanez .75 2.00
154 Jim Palmer .75 2.00
155A Ty Cobb 1.50 4.00
155B Ty Cobb SP VAR 2.00 5.00
156 Cody Ross .60 1.50
157 Vida Blue .60 1.50
158A Wade Boggs .75 2.00
158B Wade Boggs SP VAR 1.00 2.50
159 Wade Miley .60 1.50
160 Don Mattingly 2.00 5.00
161 Whitey Ford .75 2.00
162 Bruce Sutter .75 2.00
163A Will Clark .75 2.00
163B Will Clark SP VAR 1.00 2.50
164A Will Middlebrooks .60 1.50
164B W.Middlebrooks SP VAR .75 2.00
165 Russell Martin .60 1.50
166 Austin Jackson .60 1.50
167A Willie McCovey .75 2.00
167B Willie McCovey SP VAR 1.00 2.50
168A Willie Stargell .75 2.00
168B Willie Stargell SP VAR 1.00 2.50
169 Wily Peralta .60 1.50
170 Don Sutton .60 1.50
171 Yasmani Grandal .60 1.50
172A Yoenis Cespedes 1.00 2.50
172B Y.Cespedes SP VAR 1.25 3.00
173 Yonder Alonso .60 1.50
174 Yovani Gallardo .60 1.50
175 Brandon Moss .60 1.50
176 Tony Perez .75 2.00
177 Michael Brantley .60 1.50
178 David Murphy .60 1.50
179 Carlos Santana .75 2.00
180A Duke Snider .75 2.00
180B Duke Snider SP VAR 1.00 2.50
181 Nick Swisher .75 2.00
182 Alejandro de Aza .60 1.50
183 Al Lopez .60 1.50
184 Chris Davis .75 2.00
185 Ryan Doumit .60 1.50
186 Alexei Ramirez .75 2.00
187 Curtis Granderson .75 2.00
188 Jose Altuve .75 2.00
189 Cliff Lee .75 2.00
190A Eddie Murray .75 2.00
190B Eddie Murray SP VAR 1.00 2.50
191 Jordan Pacheco .60 1.50
192 James Shields .60 1.50
193 Chase Headley .60 1.50
194 Brandon Phillips .60 1.50
195 Chris Johnson .60 1.50
196 Omar Infante .60 1.50
197 Garrett Jones .60 1.50
198 Ian Kinsler .75 2.00
199 Carlos Beltran .75 2.00
19A Nolan Ryan 3.00 8.00
19B Nolan Ryan SP VAR 4.00 10.00
200A Ernie Banks 1.00 2.50
200B Ernie Banks SP VAR 1.25 3.00
201 Justin Morneau .75 2.00
202 Goose Gossage .75 2.00
203 Dayan Viciedo .60 1.50
204 Andre Ethier .75 2.00
205 Jay Bruce .75 2.00
206 Danny Espinosa .60 1.50
207 Zack Cozart .60 1.50
208A Gio Gonzalez .75 2.00
208B Gio Gonzalez SP VAR 1.00 2.50
209 Mike Moustakas .75 2.00
210 Fergie Jenkins .75 2.00
211 Dan Uggla .60 1.50
212 Kevin Youkilis .60 1.50
213 Rick Ferrell .60 1.50
214 Jemile Weeks .60 1.50
215 Kris Medlen .75 2.00
216 Colby Rasmus .75 2.00
217 Neil Walker .75 2.00
218 Adam Wainwright .75 2.00
219 Jake Peavy .60 1.50
220 Frank Robinson .75 2.00
221 Jason Kipnis .75 2.00
222 A.J. Burnett .60 1.50
223 Jeff Samardzija .60 1.50
224 C.J. Wilson .60 1.50
225 Homer Bailey .60 1.50
226 Jon Lester .75 2.00
227 Francisco Liriano .60 1.50
228 Hiroki Kuroda .60 1.50
229 Josh Johnson .75 2.00
230A George Brett 2.00 5.00
230B George Brett SP VAR 2.50 6.00
231 Edinson Volquez .60 1.50
232 Felix Doubront .60 1.50
233 Ike Davis .60 1.50
234 Corey Hart .60 1.50
235 Ben Zobrist .75 2.00
236 Kendrys Morales .60 1.50
237 Coco Crisp .60 1.50
238 Angel Pagan .60 1.50
239 Josh Reddick .60 1.50
240A Harmon Killebrew 1.00 2.50
240B Harmon Killebrew SP VAR 1.25 3.00
241 Chris Capuano .60 1.50
242 Asdrubal Cabrera .75 2.00
243 Brett Lawrie .75 2.00
244 Ian Kennedy .60 1.50
245 Derek Holland .60 1.50
246 Mike Minor .60 1.50
247 Jose Reyes .75 2.00
248 Matt Harrison .60 1.50
249 Dan Haren .60 1.50
250A Hank Aaron 2.00 5.00
250B Hank Aaron SP VAR 2.50 6.00
251 Doug Fister .60 1.50
252 Jason Vargas .60 1.50
253 Tommy Milone .60 1.50
254 Bronson Arroyo .60 1.50
255 Mark Buehrle .75 2.00
256 Eric Hosmer .75 2.00
257 Craig Kimbrel .75 2.00
258A Eddie Mathews 1.00 2.50
258B Eddie Mathews SP VAR 1.25 3.00
259A Justin Verlander 1.00 2.50
259B Justin Verlander SP VAR 1.25 3.00
260A Jackie Robinson 1.00 2.50
260B Jackie Robinson SP VAR 1.25 3.00
261 Vance Worley .75 2.00
262 Hisashi Iwakuma .75 2.00
263 Brandon Morrow .60 1.50
264 Jaime Garcia .75 2.00
265 Josh Beckett .60 1.50
266 Fernando Rodney .60 1.50
267 Hoyt Wilhelm .75 2.00
268 Jim Johnson .60 1.50
269 Ben Revere .60 1.50
270 Jim Abbott .60 1.50
271 Adam Eaton 1.00 2.50
272 Anthony Gose .60 1.50
273A Carlos Gonzalez .75 2.00
273B Carlos Gonzalez SP VAR 1.00 2.50
274 Jonny Gomes .60 1.50
275A Dustin Pedroia .75 2.00
275B Dustin Pedroia SP VAR 1.00 2.50
276A Giancarlo Stanton 1.00 2.50
276B Giancarlo Stanton SP VAR 1.25 3.00
277A Orlando Cepeda .75 2.00
277B Orlando Cepeda SP VAR 1.00 2.50
278 Jordan Zimmermann .75 2.00
279 Lance Lynn .60 1.50
280 Jim Rice .75 2.00
281A Matt Cain .75 2.00
281B Matt Cain SP VAR 1.00 2.50
282 Mike Morse .60 1.50
283 Daniel Murphy .75 2.00
284A Reggie Jackson .75 2.00
284B Reggie Jackson SP VAR 1.00 2.50
285 Matt Garza .60 1.50
286 Brandon McCarthy .60 1.50
287A Tony Gwynn 1.00 2.50
287B Tony Gwynn SP VAR 1.25 3.00
288 Jim Bunning .75 2.00
289A Yadier Molina 1.00 2.50
289B Yadier Molina SP VAR 1.25 3.00
290 Dwight Gooden .60 1.50
291 Howie Kendrick .60 1.50
292 Ian Desmond .60 1.50
293 Delmon Young .75 2.00
294 Rickie Weeks .60 1.50
295 Bobby Doerr .75 2.00
296 Phil Hughes .60 1.50
297 Trevor Cahill .60 1.50
298 Michael Young .60 1.50
299 Barry Zito .75 2.00
300A Johnny Bench 1.00 2.50
300B Johnny Bench SP VAR 1.25 3.00
301 Tommy Hanson .60 1.50
302 Lou Boudreau .75 2.00
303A Billy Butler .60 1.50
303B Billy Butler SP VAR .75 2.00
304A Ralph Kiner .60 1.50
304B Ralph Kiner SP VAR .75 2.00
305 Brian McCann .75 2.00
306 Mike Leake .60 1.50
307 Shelby Miller 1.50 4.00
308 Mark Teixeira .75 2.00
309 Bob Lemon .75 2.00
310A Miguel Cabrera 1.00 2.50
310B Miguel Cabrera SP VAR 1.25 3.00
311A Matt Kemp .75 2.00
311B Matt Kemp SP VAR 1.00 2.50
312 Miguel Gonzalez .60 1.50
313 Miguel Montero .60 1.50
314 Nelson Cruz 1.00 2.50
315A Ozzie Smith 1.25 3.00
315B Ozzie Smith SP VAR 1.50 4.00
316 Paul O'Neill .75 2.00
317 Alex Cobb .60 1.50

318 Robin Roberts .75 2.00
319 Robin Ventura .60 1.50
320 Roberto Clemente 2.50 6.00
321 Robinson Cano .75 2.00
322 Jason Motte .60 1.50
323A Ryan Vogelsong .60 1.50
323B Ryan Vogelsong SP VAR .75 2.00
324A Stephen Strasburg 1.00 2.50
324B S.Strasburg SP VAR 1.25 3.00
325 Wilin Rosario .60 1.50
326 Aaron Hill .60 1.50
327 A.J. Pierzynski .60 1.50
328 Denard Span .60 1.50
329 Shin-Soo Choo .75 2.00
330A Ted Williams 2.00 5.00
330B Ted Williams SP VAR 2.50 6.00
331 Darryl Strawberry .60 1.50
332 Marco Scutaro .75 2.00
333 A.J. Ellis .60 1.50
334 Bill Mazeroski .75 2.00
335 Alfonso Soriano .75 2.00
336 Hunter Pence .75 2.00
337 Desmond Jennings .75 2.00
338 Mark Reynolds .60 1.50
339 Anibal Sanchez .60 1.50
340A Willie Mays 2.00 5.00
340B Willie Mays SP VAR 2.50 6.00
341 Darwin Barney .60 1.50
342 B.J. Upton .75 2.00
343 Kyle Lohse .60 1.50
344 Tim Hudson .75 2.00
345 Grant Balfour .60 1.50
346 Phil Rizzuto .75 2.00
347 Jesus Montero .60 1.50
348 Warren Spahn .75 2.00
349 Mat Latos .75 2.00
350A Yogi Berra 1.00 2.50
350B Yogi Berra SP VAR 1.25 3.00

2013 Topps Gypsy Queen Mini Black

*BLACK: .6X TO 1.5X BASIC MINI
STATED ODDS 1:15 HOBBY
STATED PRINT RUN 199 SER.#'d SETS

2013 Topps Gypsy Queen Mini Green

*GREEN: .75X TO 2X BASIC MINI
STATED ODDS 1:30 HOBBY
STATED PRINT RUN 99 SER.#'d SETS

2013 Topps Gypsy Queen Mini Sepia

*SEPIA: 1X TO 2.5X BASIC MINI
STATED ODDS 1:59 HOBBY
STATED PRINT RUN 50 SER.#'d SETS
19 Nolan Ryan 20.00 50.00
100 Bryce Harper 20.00 50.00
120 Cal Ripken Jr. 20.00 50.00
150 Derek Jeter 20.00 50.00

2012 Topps Gypsy Queen Mini National Convention

1 Bryce Harper 12.50 30.00
2 Yu Darvish 5.00 12.00
3 Yoenis Cespedes 4.00 10.00

2013 Topps Gypsy Queen National Convention

NCCYP Yasiel Puig 10.00 25.00

2014 Topps Gypsy Queen

COMPLETE SET (400)
COMP.SET w/o SP's (300) 12.00 30.00
SP ODDS 1:4 HOBBY
REV NEG SP ODDS 1:118 HOBBY
PRINTING PLATE ODDS 1:292 HOBBY
PLATE PRINT RUN 1 SET PER COLOR
BLACK-CYAN-MAGENTA-YELLOW ISSUED
NO PLATE PRICING DUE TO SCARCITY
1A Miguel Cabrera .30 .75
1B Cabrera Rev Neg SP 12.00 30.00
2 Frank Robinson .25 .60
3 Robin Yount .30 .75
4 Taijuan Walker RC .30 .75
5A CC Sabathia .25 .60
5B CC Sabathia Rev Neg SP 5.00 12.00
6 Nick Swisher .25 .60
7 Freddie Freeman .40 1.00
8 Alex Gordon .25 .60
9 Nolan Arenado .40 1.00
10A Jim Palmer .25 .60
10B Jim Palmer Rev Neg SP 5.00 12.00
11 Domonic Brown .25 .60
12 Kyuji Fujikawa .25 .60
13A Xander Bogaerts RC 1.00 2.50
13B Xander Rev Neg SP 12.00 30.00
14 Shane Victorino .25 .60
15 Kolten Wong RC .40 1.00
16 Jake Marisnick RC .30 .75
17 Adeiny Hechavarria .20 .50
18 Hiroki Kuroda .20 .50
19 Nelson Cruz .30 .75
20 Derek Holland .20 .50
21 Elvis Andrus .25 .60
22 Starlin Castro .20 .50
23 Billy Butler .20 .50
24 John Smoltz .30 .75
25A Derek Jeter .75 2.00
25B Jeter Rev Neg SP 25.00 60.00
26 Chris Owings RC .30 .75
27 Kevin Gausman .25 .60
28 Lou Boudreau .25 .60
29 Ralph Kiner .25 .60
30 Bronson Arroyo .20 .50
31 Jay Bruce .25 .60
32 Christian Bethancourt RC .30 .75
33 Nick Franklin .20 .50
34 Colby Rasmus .25 .60
35 Anibal Sanchez .20 .50
36 Robin Roberts .25 .60
37 Lou Brock .25 .60
38 Julio Teheran .25 .60
39 Salvador Perez .25 .60
40 Fergie Jenkins .25 .60
41 Jered Weaver .25 .60
42A Mariano Rivera SP 1.50 4.00
42B Rivera Rev Neg SP 10.00 25.00
43A Juan Marichal .25 .60
43B Juan Marichal Rev Neg SP 5.00 12.00
44 Trevor Rosenthal .25 .60
45 Evan Gattis .20 .50
46 Mike Zunino .20 .50
47 Mike Leake .20 .50
48 Kevin Pillar RC .30 .75
49A Wil Myers .20 .50
49B Wil Myers Rev Neg SP 8.00 20.00
50 Roberto Clemente .75 2.00
51 Goose Gossage .25 .60
52 Jayson Werth .25 .60
53A Tony Gwynn .30 .75
53B Tony Gwynn Rev Neg SP 6.00 15.00
54 Tim Lincecum .25 .60
55 Jake Peavy .20 .50
56A Yoenis Cespedes .30 .75
56B Yoenis Cespedes Rev Neg SP 6.00 15.00
57 Brandon Beachy .20 .50
58 Shin-Soo Choo .25 .60
59 Wilmer Flores RC .40 1.00
60 Andrelton Simmons .20 .50
61 Tony Cingrani .25 .60
62 Yadier Molina .30 .75
63 Anthony Rizzo .50 1.25
64 Jarrod Saltalamacchia .20 .50
65 Todd Frazier .25 .60
66 Jonny Gomes .20 .50
67 Hisashi Iwakuma .25 .60
68 Fernando Rodney .20 .50
69 Enny Romero RC .30 .75
70 James Loney .20 .50
71 Nick Markakis .25 .60
72 Marco Estrada .20 .50
73 Ben Zobrist .25 .60
74 Troy Tulowitzki .30 .75
75 Greg Maddux .40 1.00
76 Bruce Sutter .20 .50
77A Reggie Jackson .25 .60
77B Reggie Jackson Rev Neg SP 5.00 12.00
78 Marcus Semien RC .30 .75
79 Yasmani Grandal .20 .50
80 Adam Jones .25 .60
81 Brett Oberholtzer .20 .50
82 Juan Gonzalez .20 .50
83 Ian Desmond .20 .50
84 Joe Kelly .20 .50
85 David Ross .20 .50
86 J.J. Hardy .20 .50
87 Mike Minor .20 .50
88 Jason Grilli .20 .50
89 Craig Biggio .25 .60
90 Juan Uribe .20 .50
91 Marcell Ozuna .30 .75
92 Travis d'Arnaud RC .40 1.00
93 Yordano Ventura RC .40 1.00
94 Matt Cain .25 .60
95 Nick Castellanos RC 1.00 2.50
96 Asdrubal Cabrera .25 .60
97 Khris Davis .30 .75
98 Phil Niekro .25 .60
99 Eric Hosmer .25 .60
100A Bryce Harper .50 1.25
100B Harper Rev Neg SP 15.00 40.00
101 Doug Fister .20 .50
102 A.J. Griffin .20 .50
103 Daniel Murphy .25 .60
104 Andrew Lambo RC .30 .75
105 Hanley Ramirez .25 .60
106 Francisco Liriano .20 .50
107 Edwin Encarnacion .30 .75
108 Lance Lynn .20 .50
109 Adam Lind .25 .60
110 Anthony Rendon .30 .75
111 Ernie Banks .30 .75
112 Matt Holliday .30 .75
113 Michael Choice RC .30 .75
114 Deion Sanders .25 .60
115 Daniel Nava .20 .50
116 Mike Schmidt .50 1.25
117 Matt Garza .20 .50
118 Jose Quintana .20 .50
119 Kyle Lohse .20 .50
120 Jon Jay .20 .50
121 Kevin Siegrist (RC) .30 .75
122 Adrian Gonzalez .25 .60
123 Felix Hernandez .25 .60
124 Jason Kipnis .25 .60
125 Justin Verlander .30 .75
126A Pedro Martinez .25 .60
126B Pedro Martinez Rev Neg SP 5.00 12.00
127 Kyle Gibson .25 .60
128 Ethan Martin RC .30 .75
129 Omar Infante .20 .50
130 Jedd Gyorko .20 .50
131 Jose Iglesias .25 .60
132 Kris Medlen .25 .60
133 Kyle Seager .20 .50
134 Ryan Vogelsong .20 .50
135 Gio Gonzalez .25 .60
136 Willie Stargell .25 .60
137 Jeff Locke .20 .50
138 Curtis Granderson .25 .60
139A Yu Darvish .30 .75
139B Yu Darvish Rev Neg SP 6.00 15.00
140 Craig Kimbrel .25 .60
141 Christian Yelich .40 1.00
142 Gerrit Cole .30 .75
143 Dustin Pedroia .30 .75
144 Eddie Mathews .30 .75
145 Joey Votto .30 .75
146 Kendrys Morales .20 .50
147 A.J. Burnett .20 .50
148 Raul Ibanez .25 .60
149 Russell Martin .20 .50
150 Robinson Cano .25 .60
151A Michael Wacha .25 .60
151B Wacha Rev Neg SP 5.00 12.00
152 J.R. Murphy RC .30 .75
153 Harmon Killebrew .30 .75
154 Jason Castro .20 .50
155 Koji Uehara .20 .50
156A Tom Glavine .25 .60
156B Tom Glavine Rev Neg SP 5.00 12.00
157A Joe Mauer .25 .60
157B Joe Mauer Rev Neg SP 5.00 12.00
158 R.A. Dickey .25 .60
159 Matt Dominguez .20 .50
160 Jonathan Lucroy .25 .60
161 Phil Rizzuto .25 .60
162 Brad Ziegler .20 .50
163 Carlos Gomez .20 .50
164 Ian Kennedy .20 .50
165 Giancarlo Stanton .30 .75
166 A.J. Pierzynski .20 .50
167 Josh Reddick .20 .50
168 Adam Wainwright .25 .60
169 Chase Headley .20 .50
170A Randy Johnson .30 .75
170B Randy Johnson Rev Neg SP 6.00 15.00
171 Mike Moustakas .25 .60
172 Prince Fielder .25 .60
173 Carlos Martinez .25 .60
174 Yovani Gallardo .20 .50
175A Cal Ripken Jr. 1.00 2.50
175B Ripken Rev Neg SP 20.00 50.00
176 Brett Lawrie .25 .60
177 Brad Miller .25 .60
178 Jose Altuve .25 .60
179 Ian Kinsler .25 .60
180 Max Scherzer .30 .75
181 Paul Konerko .25 .60
182 Peter Bourjos .20 .50
183 Jeff Bagwell .25 .60
184 Jeff Samardzija .20 .50
185 George Brett .60 1.50
186 Chris Archer .20 .50
187 Oswaldo Arcia .20 .50
188 Adam Eaton .20 .50
189A Rod Carew .25 .60
189B Rod Carew Rev Neg SP 5.00 12.00
190 Jean Segura .25 .60
191A Mark McGwire .60 1.50
191B McGw Rev Neg SP 12.00 30.00
192 Mark Trumbo .20 .50
193 Miguel Gonzalez .20 .50
194 Aroldis Chapman .30 .75
195 Josmil Pinto RC .30 .75
196 Zack Greinke .25 .60
197 Henderson Alvarez .20 .50
198 Pete Kozma .20 .50
199 Larry Doby .25 .60
200 Rickey Henderson .30 .75
201 Ben Revere .20 .50
202 Ozzie Smith .40 1.00
203 Dan Haren .20 .50
204 Carlos Ruiz .20 .50
205 Joe Nathan .20 .50
206 Carlos Santana .25 .60
207 Carlos Gonzalez .25 .60
208 Adrian Beltre .30 .75
209 Jorge De La Rosa .20 .50
210 Homer Bailey .20 .50
211 Bob Feller .25 .60
212 Allen Craig .25 .60
213 Jordan Zimmermann .25 .60
214 Junior Lake .20 .50
215 Tony Perez .25 .60
216 Andre Rienzo RC .30 .75
217 Willie McCovey .25 .60
218 Jim Bunning .25 .60
219 Brandon Moss .20 .50
220 Brandon Belt .25 .60
221 Matt Davidson RC .40 1.00
222 Desmond Jennings .25 .60
223 Jake Odorizzi .20 .50
224 Wei-Yin Chen .20 .50
225A Nolan Ryan 1.00 2.50
225B Ryan Rev Neg SP 20.00 50.00
226 Neil Walker .25 .60
227A Chris Davis .20 .50
227B Chris Davis Rev Neg SP 4.00 10.00
228 Brandon Phillips .20 .50
229 Jon Lester .25 .60
230 Andrew McCutchen .30 .75
231 Mat Latos .25 .60
232 Pablo Sandoval .25 .60
233 Johnny Cueto .25 .60
234 Jim Johnson .20 .50
235 Ryan Zimmerman .25 .60
236 Miguel Montero .20 .50
237 Pedro Alvarez .20 .50
238 Stan Musial .50 1.25
239 Johnny Bench .30 .75
240 Victor Martinez .25 .60
241 Tommy Milone .20 .50
242 C.J. Wilson .20 .50
243 Matt Kemp .25 .60
244 Carl Crawford .25 .60
245 Wade Miley .20 .50
246 Michael Brantley .25 .60
247 Chris Johnson .20 .50
248 Jarrod Parker .20 .50
249A Bob Gibson .25 .60
249B Bob Gibson Rev Neg SP 5.00 12.00
250A Sandy Koufax .60 1.50
250B Koufax Rev Neg SP 12.00 30.00
251 Erik Johnson RC .30 .75
252 Marco Scutaro .25 .60
253 Andrew Cashner .20 .50
254 Avisail Garcia .25 .60
255 Chase Utley .25 .60
256 Ryan Wheeler .20 .50
257 Coco Crisp .20 .50
258A Steve Carlton .25 .60
258B Steve Carlton Rev Neg SP 5.00 12.00
259 Martin Prado .20 .50
260 Jonathan Schoop RC .30 .75
261 Joe Morgan .25 .60
262 Jhoulys Chacin .20 .50
263 Catfish Hunter .25 .60
264 Jose Reyes .25 .60
265 Tyler Skaggs .20 .50
266A Whitey Ford .25 .60
266B Whitey Ford Rev Neg SP 5.00 12.00
267 Jed Lowrie .20 .50
268 Tim Hudson .25 .60
269 Travis Wood .20 .50
270A Don Mattingly .60 1.50
270B Matting Rev Neg SP 12.00 30.00
271 Ty Cobb .50 1.25
272 Aaron Hill .20 .50
273 Alejandro De Aza .20 .50
274 Alex Cobb .20 .50
275A Buster Posey .40 1.00
275B Posey Rev Neg SP 8.00 20.00
276A Duke Snider .25 .60
276B Duke Snider Rev Neg SP 5.00 12.00
277 Ubaldo Jimenez .20 .50
278 David Freese .20 .50
279 Chris Tillman .20 .50
280A Manny Machado .30 .75
280B Mach Rev Neg SP 6.00 15.00
281 Trevor Bauer .30 .75
282 Alex Rios .25 .60
283 James Shields .20 .50
284 Austin Jackson .20 .50
285 Bartolo Colon .20 .50
286 John Lackey .25 .60
287 Adam Dunn .25 .60
288 Chris Carter .20 .50
289 Andre Ethier .25 .60
290 David Holmberg RC .30 .75
291 Starling Marte .25 .60
292 Neftali Feliz .20 .50
293 Brian McCann .25 .60
294 Jonathan Villar .20 .50
295 Eddie Murray .25 .60
296 Jimmy Nelson RC .30 .75
297 Cole Hamels .25 .60
298 Patrick Corbin .25 .60
299 Jason Heyward .25 .60
300 Clayton Kershaw .60 1.50
301A Babe Ruth SP 3.00 8.00
301B Ruth Rev Neg SP 10.00 25.00
302A Bo Jackson SP 1.25 3.00
302B Bo Jackson Rev Neg SP 6.00 15.00
303 Mike Napoli SP .75 2.00
304A Ted Williams SP 2.50 6.00
304B Williams Rev Neg SP 10.00 25.00
305A Chris Sale SP 1.25 3.00
305B Sale Rev Neg SP 6.00 15.00
306 Carlos Beltran SP 1.00 2.50
307 Josh Hamilton SP 1.00 2.50
308 Evan Longoria SP 1.00 2.50
309A Matt Harvey SP 1.00 2.50
309B Matt Harvey Rev Neg SP 12.00 30.00
310A Albert Pujols SP 1.50 4.00
310B Pujols Rev Neg SP 8.00 20.00
311A Paul Goldschmidt SP 1.25 3.00
311B Paul Goldschmidt Rev Neg SP 6.00 15.00
312 Joe DiMaggio SP 2.50 6.00
313 Josh Donaldson SP 1.00 2.50
314 Hyun-Jin Ryu SP 1.00 2.50
315 Zack Wheeler SP 1.00 2.50
316 Jacoby Ellsbury SP 1.00 2.50
317 Michael Cuddyer SP .75 2.00
318 Luis Gonzalez SP .75 2.00
319A Jose Fernandez SP 1.25 3.00
319B Jose Fernandez Rev Neg SP 6.00 15.00
320A Jose Abreu RC SP 6.00 15.00
320B Abreu Rev Neg SP 25.00 60.00
321A David Price SP 1.00 2.50
321B David Price Rev Neg SP 5.00 12.00
322A David Wright SP 1.00 2.50
322B David Wright Rev Neg SP 5.00 12.00
323 Cliff Lee SP 1.00 2.50
324 James Paxton SP RC 1.25 3.00
325A Warren Spahn 1.00 2.50
325B Warren Spahn Rev Neg SP 5.00 12.00
326 Madison Bumgarner SP 1.00 2.50
327 Wade Boggs SP 1.00 2.50
328A Willie Mays SP 2.50 6.00
328B Mays Rev Neg SP 8.00 20.00
329A David Ortiz SP 1.25 3.00
329B David Ortiz Rev Neg SP 6.00 15.00
330 Ivan Rodriguez SP 1.00 2.50
331 Eric Davis SP .75 2.00
332 Matt Carpenter SP 1.25 3.00
333 Torii Hunter SP .75 2.00
334A Stephen Strasburg SP 1.25 3.00
334B Stephen Strasburg Rev Neg SP 6.00 15.00
335 Hunter Pence SP 1.00 2.50
336 Ivan Nova SP 1.00 2.50
337 Sonny Gray SP 1.00 2.50
338 Alfonso Soriano SP 1.00 2.50
339 Shelby Miller SP 1.00 2.50
340 Justin Upton SP 1.00 2.50
341 Jose Bautista SP 1.00 2.50
342 Jurickson Profar SP 1.00 2.50
343 Matt Moore SP 1.00 2.50
344 Billy Hamilton SP RC 1.00 2.50
345 Will Middlebrooks SP .75 2.00
346A Masahiro Tanaka SP RC 2.50 6.00
346B Tanaka Rev Neg SP 25.00 60.00
347 Jarred Cosart SP .75 2.00
348A Lou Gehrig SP 2.50 6.00
348B Gehrig Rev Neg SP 12.00 30.00
349A Mike Trout SP 6.00 15.00
349B Trout Rev Neg SP 25.00 60.00
350A Yasiel Puig SP 1.25 3.00
350B Puig Rev Neg SP 6.00 15.00

2014 Topps Gypsy Queen Framed Blue

*BLUE: 1.2X TO 3X BASIC
*BLUE RC: .75X TO 2X BASIC RC
STATED ODDS 1:13 HOBBY
STATED PRINT RUN 499 SER.#'d SETS
25 Derek Jeter 4.00 10.00

2014 Topps Gypsy Queen Framed White

*WHITE VET: .75X TO 2X BASIC
*WHITE RC: .5X TO 1.2X BASIC RC

2014 Topps Gypsy Queen Mini

*MINI VET: 1X TO 2.5X BASIC VET
*MINI RC: .6X TO 1.5X BASIC RC
*MINI SP: .4X TO 1X BASIC SP
MINI SP ODDS 1:24 HOBBY
COMMON VAR (1-350) .60 1.50
VAR SEMIS .75 2.00
VAR UNLISTED 1.00 2.50
PRINTING PLATE ODDS 1:227 HOBBY
PLATE PRINT RUN 1 SET PER COLOR
BLACK-CYAN-MAGENTA-YELLOW ISSUED
NO PLATE PRICING DUE TO SCARCITY
1B Cabrera Bat up 1.00 2.50
4B Walker Ball top .60 1.50
5B Sabathia No ball .75 2.00
7B Freeman Stance 1.25 3.00
13B Bogaerts Running 2.00 5.00
25B Jeter Logo showing 2.50 6.00
42B Rivera Grey jsy 1.25 3.00
49B Myers Running .60 1.50
50B Clemente Ylw helmet 2.50 6.00
54B Lincecum Standing .75 2.00
56B Cespedes Ylw jsy 1.00 2.50
62B Molina Mask up 1.00 2.50
67B Iwakuma Blue jsy .75 2.00
74B Tulo Batting 1.00 2.50
75B Maddux No ball 1.25 3.00
77B Reggie White jsy .75 2.00
80B A.Jones White jsy .75 2.00
100B Harper TB jsy 1.50 4.00
105B Hanley Bat up .75 2.00
116B Schmidt Bat down 1.50 4.00
122B A.Gonz Batting .75 2.00
123B F.Hernan White jsy .75 2.00
125B Verlander White jsy 1.00 2.50
126B Pedro Hands together .75 2.00
136B Stargell Swinging .75 2.00
139B Darvish White jsy 1.00 2.50
140B Kimbrel Pitching .75 2.00
141B Yelich Orange jsy 1.25 3.00
142B G.Cole Arm back 1.00 2.50
143B D.Pedr 1 hand on bat 1.00 2.50
145B Votto White jsy 1.00 2.50
150B Cano Swinging .75 2.00
157B Mauer Pinstripes .75 2.00
165B Stanton Orange jsy 1.00 2.50
168B Wainwright Blue hat .75 2.00
170B Johnson Leg up 1.00 2.50
172B Fielder Glasses .75 2.00
175B Ripken Face left 3.00 8.00
180B Scherz Short sleeve 1.00 2.50
196B Greinke Fist .75 2.00
200B R.Henderson Green jsy 1.00 2.50
202B Ozzie Swinging 1.25 3.00
207B C.Gonzalez Batting .75 2.00
208B A.Beltre Blue jsy 1.00 2.50
212B A.Craig Swinging .75 2.00
213B J.Zim Red jsy .75 2.00
225B N.Ryan w/ball 3.00 8.00
227B C.Davis Bat up .60 1.50
228B Phillips Red jsy .60 1.50
230B McCutch Face left 1.00 2.50
232B P.Sandoval Fldng .75 2.00
235B R.Zim Throwback jersey .75 2.00
238B S.Musial w/bat 1.50 4.00
239B Bench Batting 1.00 2.50
249B Gibson Face right .75 2.00
250B Koufax Hand hip 2.00 5.00
255B C.Utley Fielding .75 2.00
266B Ford Throwing .75 2.00
270B Mattingly w/bat 2.00 5.00
271B Cobb D visible 1.50 4.00
275B Posey Batting 1.25 3.00
280B Machado Batting 1.00 2.50
300B Kershaw White jsy 2.00 5.00
301B B.Ruth In jacket 2.50 6.00
302B B.Jackson Fldng 1.00 2.50
303B Napoli Red undershirt .60 1.50
304B Williams Standing 2.00 5.00
305B C.Sale Black hat 1.00 2.50
306B Beltran Running .75 2.00
307B Hamilton Bttng .75 2.00
308B Longoria Running .75 2.00
309B Harvey Pinstripe jsy .75 2.00
310B Pujols Pointing up 1.25 3.00
311B Goldschmidt Fldng 1.00 2.50
312B DiMaggio Bat back 2.00 5.00
313B Donaldson Bttng .75 2.00
314B Ryu Grey jsy .75 2.00
316B Ellsbury Face right .75 2.00
319B Fernandez Orange jsy 1.00 2.50
320B Abreu Facing left 5.00 12.00
321B Price Glasses .75 2.00
322B Wright White jsy .75 2.00
323B C.Lee Red hat .75 2.00
326B Bumgarner Black hat .75 2.00
328B Mays w/bat 2.00 5.00
329B Ortiz White jsy 1.00 2.50
330B I.Rod Batting .75 2.00
332B Carpenter Running 1.00 2.50
333B Hunter Face left .60 1.50
334B Strasburg Brown glv 1.00 2.50
339B Miller Hands together .75 2.00
340B Upton Face right .75 2.00
341B Bautista White jsy .75 2.00
342B Profar Batting .75 2.00
343B M.Moore Arm up .75 2.00
344B Hamilton Running .75 2.00
348B Gehrig Sitting 2.00 5.00
349B Trout Swinging 5.00 12.00
350B Puig Throwing 1.00 2.50

2014 Topps Gypsy Queen Mini Black

*BLK VET: 1.5X TO 4X BASIC VET
*BLK RC: 1X TO 2.5X BASIC RC
*BLK SP: .4X TO 1X BASIC SP
STATED ODDS 1:9 HOBBY
STATED PRINT RUN 199 SER.#'d SETS
25 Derek Jeter 6.00 15.00
42 Mariano Rivera 5.00 12.00
185 George Brett 4.00 10.00
191 Mark McGwire 5.00 12.00
320 Jose Abreu 10.00 25.00
349 Mike Trout 6.00 15.00

2014 Topps Gypsy Queen Mini Red

*RED VET: 5X TO 12X BASIC VET
*RED RC: 3X TO 8X BASIC RC
*RED SP: 1.2X TO 3X BASIC SP
STATED PRINT RUN 99 SER.#'d SETS
25 Derek Jeter 12.00 30.00
42 Mariano Rivera 10.00 25.00
50 Roberto Clemente 8.00 20.00
185 George Brett 10.00 25.00
191 Mark McGwire 8.00 20.00
270 Don Mattingly 6.00 15.00
304 Ted Williams 6.00 15.00
320 Jose Abreu 20.00 50.00
348 Lou Gehrig 6.00 15.00

2014 Topps Gypsy Queen Mini Sepia

*SEPIA VET: 6X TO 15X BASIC VET
*SEPIA RC: 4X TO 10X BASIC RC
*SEPIA SP: 1.5X TO 4X BASIC SP
STATED ODDS 1:32 HOBBY
STATED PRINT RUN 50 SER.#'d SETS
25 Derek Jeter 25.00 60.00
42 Mariano Rivera 12.00 30.00
50 Roberto Clemente 10.00 25.00
185 George Brett 12.00 30.00
191 Mark McGwire 10.00 25.00
270 Don Mattingly 8.00 20.00
304 Ted Williams 8.00 20.00
320 Jose Abreu 20.00 50.00
348 Lou Gehrig 8.00 20.00

2014 Topps Gypsy Queen Around the Horn Autographs

STATED ODDS 1:10,280 HOBBY
STATED PRINT RUN 25 SER.#'d SETS
EXCHANGE DEADLINE 3/31/2017
ATHCB Craig Biggio 25.00 60.00
ATHCS Chris Sale 15.00 40.00
ATHFF Freddie Freeman 40.00 80.0
ATHJB Jose Bautista 40.00 80.0
ATHJU Justin Upton 30.00 60.0
ATHJW Jered Weaver 20.00 50.0
ATHPG Paul Goldschmidt 40.00 80.0
ATHSK Sandy Koufax 150.00 300.0
ATHSM Shelby Miller 75.00 150.0
ATHWM Wil Myers 20.00 50.0

2014 Topps Gypsy Queen Autographs

STATED ODDS 1:15 HOBBY
EXCHANGE DEADLINE 3/31/2017
GQAAE Adam Eaton 2.50 6.0
GQAAH Adeiny Hechavarria 2.50 6.0
GQAAJ Adam Jones 8.00 20.0
GQAAR Anthony Rizzo 12.00 30.0
GQAAW Allen Webster 2.50 6.0
GQAAWO Alex Wood 2.50 6.0
GQABJ Bo Jackson 40.00 80.0
GQABM Brandon Maurer 2.50 6.0
GQABP Brandon Phillips 4.00 10.0
GQABR Ben Revere 5.00 12.0
GQABZ Ben Zobrist 3.00 8.0
GQACM Carlos Martinez 3.00 8.0
GQADG Didi Gregorius 3.00 8.0
GQADH Derek Holland 4.00 10.0
GQADP David Phelps 2.50 6.0
GQADS Dave Stewart 2.50 6.0
GQADW David Wright 20.00 50.0
GQAEB Ernie Banks 25.00 60.0
GQAED Eric Davis 12.00 30.0
GQAEG Evan Gattis 10.00 25.0
GQAFL Fred Lynn 6.00 15.0
GQAFM Fred McGriff 8.00 20.0
GQAGN Graig Nettles 6.00 15.0
GQAHA Hank Aaron 150.00 300.0
GQAJBE Johnny Bench 30.00 60.0
GQAJC Jose Canseco 25.00 60.0
GQAJH Jeremy Hefner 2.50 6.0
GQAJL Jeff Locke 2.50 6.0
GQAJO Jake Odorizzi 2.50 6.0
GQAJP Jonathan Pettibone 2.50 6.0
GQAJPO Jorge Posada 20.00 50.0
GQAJQ Jose Quintana 8.00 20.0
GQAJS Jean Segura 3.00 8.0
GQAJT Julio Teheran 8.00 20.0
GQAKM Kris Medlen 3.00 8.0
GQAKMI Kevin Mitchell 5.00 12.0
GQAKS Kyle Seager 2.50 6.0
GQALM Leonys Martin 2.50 6.0
GQALS Lee Smith 5.00 12.0
GQAMC Miguel Cabrera 75.00 150.0
GQAMK Mike Kickham 2.50 6.0
GQAMM Matt Moore 3.00 8.0
GQAMMA Matt Magill 2.50 6.0
GQAMMC Mark McGwire 100.00 200.0
GQAMMI Mike Minor 5.00 12.0
GQAMW Matt Williams 5.00 12.0
GQAMWA Michael Wacha 10.00 25.0
GQAOCB Oil Can Boyd 6.00 15.0
GQAPC Patrick Corbin 3.00 8.0
GQAPG Paul Goldschmidt 12.00 30.0
GQAPO Paul O'Neill 12.00 30.0
GQARH Rickey Henderson 50.00 100.0
GQARN Ricky Nolasco 2.50 6.0
GQARY Robin Yount 30.00 60.0
GQASD Steve Delabar 2.50 6.0
GQATD Travis d'Arnaud 3.00 8.0
GQATR Tim Raines 8.00 20.0
GQATT Troy Tulowitzki 10.00 25.0
GQAWF Wilmer Flores 3.00 8.0
GQAWM Wil Myers 10.00 25.0
GQAYD Yu Darvish 60.00 120.0
GQAZW Zack Wheeler 8.00 20.0

2014 Topps Gypsy Queen Autographs Gold

*GOLD: .6X TO 1.5X BASIC
STATED PRINT RUN 25 SER.#'d SETS
STATED ODDS 1:266 HOBBY
EXCHANGE DEADLINE 3/31/2017
GQACM Carlos Martinez 15.00 40.0
GQADP David Phelps 6.00 15.0
GQAHA Hank Aaron 150.00 300.0
GQAKS Kyle Seager 8.00 20.0
GQARH Rickey Henderson 60.00 120.0
GQAWF Wilmer Flores 8.00 20.0
GQAYD Yu Darvish 75.00 150.0

2014 Topps Gypsy Queen Autographs Red

*RED: .5X TO 1.2X BASIC
STATED PRINT RUN 49 SER.#'d SETS
STATED ODDS 1:157 HOBBY
EXCHANGE DEADLINE 3/31/2017
GQACM Carlos Martinez 8.00 20.0
GQADP David Phelps 5.00 12.0
GQAKS Kyle Seager 6.00 15.0
GQAWF Wilmer Flores 6.00 15.0

2014 Topps Gypsy Queen Dealing Aces

COMPLETE SET (20) 4.00 10.0
STATED ODDS 1:4 HOBBY
PRINTING PLATE ODDS 1:1460 HOBBY
PLATE PRINT RUN 1 SET PER COLOR
BLACK-CYAN-MAGENTA-YELLOW ISSUED
NO PLATE PRICING DUE TO SCARCITY
DAAW Adam Wainwright .40 1.0
DACC CC Sabathia .40 1.0
DACK Clayton Kershaw 1.00 2.5
DACL Cliff Lee .40 1.0
DACS Chris Sale .50 1.2
DADP David Price .40 1.0
DAFH Felix Hernandez .40 1.0

AGC Gerrit Cole .50 1.25
AGM Greg Maddux .60 1.50
AHR Hyun-Jin Ryu .40 1.00
AJF Jose Fernandez .50 1.25
AJT Julio Teheran .40 1.00
AJV Justin Verlander .50 1.25
AMB Madison Bumgarner .40 1.00
AMS Max Scherzer .50 1.25
AMW Michael Wacha .40 1.00
APM Pedro Martinez .40 1.00
ARJ Randy Johnson .50 1.25
ASS Stephen Strasburg .50 1.25
AYD Yu Darvish .50 1.25

2014 Topps Gypsy Queen Debut All Stars
COMPLETE SET (15) 4.00 10.00
STATED ODDS 1:6 HOBBY
PRINTING PLATE ODDS 1:1460 HOBBY
PLATE PRINT RUN 1 SET PER COLOR
BLACK-CYAN-MAGENTA-YELLOW ISSUED
NO PLATE PRICING DUE TO SCARCITY
SBH Bryce Harper .75 2.00
SCK Clayton Kershaw 1.00 2.50
SDO David Ortiz .50 1.25
SEL Evan Longoria .40 1.00
SFH Felix Hernandez .40 1.00
SJF Jose Fernandez .50 1.25
SJV Justin Verlander .50 1.25
SMC Miguel Cabrera .50 1.25
SMH Matt Harvey .40 1.00
SMM Manny Machado .50 1.25
SMT Mike Trout 2.50 6.00
SPF Prince Fielder .40 1.00
SPG Paul Goldschmidt .50 1.25
SRC Robinson Cano .40 1.00
SYD Yu Darvish .50 1.25

2014 Topps Gypsy Queen Framed Mini Relics
STATED ODDS 1:25 HOBBY
GMRAB Adrian Beltre 3.00 8.00
GMRAC Alex Cobb 2.00 5.00
GMRAG Alex Gordon 2.50 6.00
GMRAJ Adam Jones 2.50 6.00
GMRAL Adam Lind 2.50 6.00
GMRAR Anthony Rizzo 5.00 12.00
GMRAS Andrelton Simmons 2.00 5.00
GMRBL Brett Lawrie 2.50 6.00
GMRBM Brian McCann 2.50 6.00
GMRBR Bruce Rondon 2.00 5.00
GMRCA Chris Archer 2.00 5.00
GMRCH Chase Headley 2.00 5.00
GMRCK Craig Kimbrel 2.50 6.00
GMRCR Carlos Ruiz 2.00 5.00
GMRCS CC Sabathia 2.50 6.00
GMRDB Domonic Brown 2.50 6.00
GMRDD Daniel Descalso 2.00 5.00
GMRDG Dillon Gee 2.00 5.00
GMRDH Derek Holland 2.00 5.00
GMRDJ Desmond Jennings 2.50 6.00
GMREA Elvis Andrus 2.50 6.00
GMREE Edwin Encarnacion 3.00 8.00
GMREG Evan Gattis 2.00 5.00
GMREH Eric Hosmer 2.50 6.00
GMRGG Gio Gonzalez 2.50 6.00
GMRJB Jose Bautista 2.50 6.00
GMRJBR Jay Bruce 2.50 6.00
GMRJC Jhoulys Chacin 2.00 5.00
GMRJH Jeremy Hellickson 2.00 5.00
GMRJP Jhonny Peralta 2.00 5.00
GMRJT Julio Teheran 2.50 6.00
GMRJU Justin Upton 2.50 6.00
GMRJV Joey Votto 3.00 8.00
GMRJZ Jordan Zimmermann 2.50 6.00
GMRKS Kyle Seager 2.00 5.00
GMRMA Matt Adams 2.00 5.00
GMRML Mike Leake 2.00 5.00
GMRMM Mike Minor 2.00 5.00
GMRMMO Matt Moore 2.50 6.00
GMRPB Peter Bourjos 2.00 5.00
GMRPC Patrick Corbin 2.50 6.00
GMRRB Ryan Braun 2.50 6.00
GMRRP Rick Porcello 2.50 6.00
GMRRZ Ryan Zimmerman 2.50 6.00
GMRSM Starling Marte 2.50 6.00
GMRSP Salvador Perez 2.50 6.00
GMRTH Todd Helton 2.50 6.00
GMRTT Troy Tulowitzki 3.00 8.00
GMRWM Wade Miley 2.00 5.00
GMRWR Wilin Rosario 2.00 5.00
GMRYM Yadier Molina 5.00 12.00

2014 Topps Gypsy Queen Glove Stories
COMPLETE SET (10) 3.00 8.00
STATED ODDS 1:6 HOBBY
PRINTING PLATE ODDS 1:1460 HOBBY
PLATE PRINT RUN 1 SET PER COLOR
BLACK-CYAN-MAGENTA-YELLOW ISSUED
NO PLATE PRICING DUE TO SCARCITY
GSAR Anthony Rizzo .75 2.00
GSBH Bryce Harper .75 2.00
GSCC Carl Crawford .40 1.00
GSCG Carlos Gomez .30 .75
GSDJ Derek Jeter 1.25 3.00
GSJD Josh Donaldson .40 1.00
GSJI Jose Iglesias .40 1.00
GSMT Mike Trout 2.50 6.00
GSYP Yasiel Puig .50 1.25
GSYP2 Yasiel Puig .50 1.25

2014 Topps Gypsy Queen Jumbo Relics Black
STATED ODDS 1:27 HOBBY
STATED PRINT RUN 25 SER.#'d SETS
GJRAB Adrian Beltre 8.00 20.00
GJRAC Allen Craig 20.00 50.00
GJRAD Andre Dawson 12.00 30.00
GJRAJ Adam Jones 15.00 40.00
GJRAP Andy Pettitte 6.00 15.00
GJRAPU Albert Pujols 10.00 25.00
GJRBH Bryce Harper 12.00 30.00
GJRBP Buster Posey 10.00 25.00
GJRBW Billy Williams 6.00 15.00
GJRCG Carlos Gonzalez 6.00 15.00
GJRCK Clayton Kershaw 15.00 40.00
GJRCKI Craig Kimbrel 20.00 50.00
GJRCS CC Sabathia 6.00 15.00
GJRCSA Chris Sale 8.00 20.00
GJRDJ Derek Jeter 20.00 50.00
GJRDO David Ortiz 12.00 30.00
GJRDP David Price 6.00 15.00
GJREB Ernie Banks 20.00 50.00
GJREH Eric Hosmer 6.00 15.00
GJREL Evan Longoria 6.00 15.00
GJRFF Freddie Freeman 10.00 25.00
GJRFH Felix Hernandez 6.00 15.00
GJRGS Giancarlo Stanton 8.00 20.00
GJRHJR Hyun-Jin Ryu 6.00 15.00
GJRJF Jose Fernandez 8.00 20.00
GJRJM Joe Morgan 15.00 40.00
GJRJU Justin Upton 6.00 15.00
GJRJV Joey Votto 15.00 40.00
GJRJVE Justin Verlander 8.00 20.00
GJRMC Miguel Cabrera 15.00 40.00
GJRMH Matt Harvey 6.00 15.00
GJRMM Manny Machado 20.00 50.00
GJRMMO Matt Moore 6.00 15.00
GJRMR Mariano Rivera 20.00 50.00
GJRMS Max Scherzer 8.00 20.00
GJRMT Mike Trout 40.00 100.00
GJRPF Prince Fielder 6.00 15.00
GJRPG Paul Goldschmidt 8.00 20.00
GJRPN Phil Niekro 15.00 40.00
GJRSM Shelby Miller 15.00 40.00
GJRSS Stephen Strasburg 8.00 20.00
GJRTG Tom Glavine 15.00 40.00
GJRTGW Tony Gwynn 12.00 30.00
GJRTH Torii Hunter 5.00 12.00
GJRTL Tim Lincecum 6.00 15.00
GJRTT Troy Tulowitzki 8.00 20.00
GJRWB Wade Boggs 15.00 40.00
GJRWM Wil Myers 5.00 12.00
GJRYD Yu Darvish 12.00 30.00
GJRYM Yadier Molina 20.00 50.00
GJRYP Yasiel Puig 8.00 20.00

2014 Topps Gypsy Queen N174 Gypsy Queen
COMPLETE SET (15) 6.00 15.00
STATED ODDS 1:4 HOBBY
PRINTING PLATE ODDS 1:1460 HOBBY
PLATE PRINT RUN 1 SET PER COLOR
BLACK-CYAN-MAGENTA-YELLOW ISSUED
NO PLATE PRICING DUE TO SCARCITY
N174BH Bryce Harper .75 2.00
N174BR Babe Ruth 1.25 3.00
N174CK Clayton Kershaw 1.00 2.50
N174CR Cal Ripken Jr. 1.50 4.00
N174DJ Derek Jeter 1.25 3.00
N174MC Miguel Cabrera .50 1.25
N174MR Mariano Rivera .60 1.50
N174MS Max Scherzer .50 1.25
N174MT Mike Trout 2.50 6.00
N174RH Rickey Henderson .50 1.25
N174RJ Reggie Jackson .40 1.00
N174TS Tom Seaver .40 1.00
N174WB Wade Boggs .40 1.00
N174YB Yogi Berra .50 1.25
N174YP Yasiel Puig .50 1.25

2014 Topps Gypsy Queen Relic Autographs
STATED ODDS 1:892 HOBBY
STATED PRINT RUN 25 SER.#'d SETS
EXCHANGE DEADLINE 3/31/2017
ARAJ Adam Jones 30.00 60.00
ARAR Anthony Rizzo 20.00 50.00
ARBP Brandon Phillips 15.00 40.00
ARBZ Ben Zobrist 15.00 40.00
ARCB Craig Biggio EXCH 20.00 50.00
ARDH Derek Holland 10.00 25.00
ARDW David Wright 20.00 50.00
AREG Evan Gattis 10.00 25.00
ARFF Freddie Freeman 30.00 60.00
ARJG Jedd Gyorko EXCH 10.00 25.00
ARJS Jean Segura 10.00 25.00
ARJT Julio Teheran EXCH 10.00 25.00
ARMM Matt Moore 10.00 25.00
ARMMI Mike Minor 12.00 30.00
ARMT Mike Trout 150.00 250.00
ARPG Paul Goldschmidt 20.00 50.00
ARRH Rickey Henderson EXCH 50.00 100.00
ARTT Troy Tulowitzki 30.00 60.00
ARWM Wil Myers 30.00 60.00
ARZW Zack Wheeler 20.00 50.00

2014 Topps Gypsy Queen Relics
STATED ODDS 1:27 HOBBY
GQRAB Adrian Beltre 3.00 8.00
GQRAC Alex Cobb 2.00 5.00
GQRACR Allen Craig 2.50 6.00
GQRAG Alex Gordon 2.50 6.00
GQRAJ Adam Jones 2.50 6.00
GQRAL Adam Lind 2.50 6.00
GQRAS Andrelton Simmons 2.00 5.00
GQRAW Allen Webster 2.00 5.00
GQRBL Brett Lawrie 2.50 6.00
GQRBM Brian McCann 2.50 6.00
GQRBR Bruce Rondon 2.00 5.00
GQRBZ Ben Zobrist 2.50 6.00
GQRCA Chris Archer 2.00 5.00
GQRCK Craig Kimbrel 2.50 6.00
GQRCT Chris Tillman 2.00 5.00
GQRDB Domonic Brown 2.50 6.00
GQRDJ Desmond Jennings 2.50 6.00
GQRDP David Price 2.50 6.00
GQREE Edwin Encarnacion 3.00 8.00
GQRFF Freddie Freeman 4.00 10.00
GQRFH Felix Hernandez 2.50 6.00
GQRHP Hunter Pence 2.50 6.00
GQRID Ian Desmond 2.00 5.00
GQRJB Jose Bautista 2.50 6.00
GQRJBR Jay Bruce 2.50 6.00
GQRJC Jhoulys Chacin 2.00 5.00
GQRJH Jeremy Hellickson 2.00 5.00
GQRJP Jhonny Peralta 2.00 5.00
GQRJSH James Shields 2.00 5.00
GQRJT Julio Teheran 2.50 6.00
GQRKM Kris Medlen 2.50 6.00
GQRMA Matt Adams 2.00 5.00
GQRMC Matt Cain 2.50 6.00
GQRML Mike Leake 2.00 5.00
GQRMM Mike Minor 2.00 5.00
GQRMP Martin Perez 2.50 6.00
GQRMW Michael Wacha 5.00 12.00
GQRNA Nolan Arenado 4.00 10.00
GQRPA Pedro Alvarez 4.00 10.00
GQRRB Ryan Braun 2.50 6.00
GQRRP Rick Porcello 2.50 6.00
GQRSM Starling Marte 2.50 6.00
GQRSP Salvador Perez 2.50 6.00
GQRTF Todd Frazier 2.50 6.00
GQRTH Torii Hunter 2.00 5.00
GQRTL Tim Lincecum 2.50 6.00
GQRWB Wade Boggs 4.00 10.00
GQRWM Wil Myers 2.00 5.00
GQRWMI Will Middlebrooks 2.00 5.00
GQRZG Zack Greinke 2.50 6.00
GQRZW Zack Wheeler 2.50 6.00

2015 Topps Gypsy Queen
COMP.SET w/o SP's (300) 12.00 30.00
SP ODDS 1:4 HOBBY
SP VAR ODDS 1:165 HOBBY
PRINTING PLATE ODDS 1:281 HOBBY
PLATE PRINT RUN 1 SET PER COLOR
BLACK-CYAN-MAGENTA-YELLOW ISSUED
NO PLATE PRICING DUE TO SCARCITY
1A Mike Trout 1.50 4.00
1B Trout VAR Hands up 60.00 150.00
2 Hank Aaron .60 1.50
3 Joc Pederson RC .60 1.50
4 Maikel Franco RC .40 1.00
5A Derek Jeter .75 2.00
5B Jeter VAR Hands up 40.00 100.00
6 David Wright .25 .60
7 Yordano Ventura .25 .60
8 Jose Canseco .25 .60
9 Bo Jackson .30 .75
10 David Price .25 .60
11 Hanley Ramirez .25 .60
12A Jordan Zimmermann .25 .60
12B Jordan Zimmermann VAR 10.00 25.00
Arm Up
13 Zack Greinke .25 .60
14A Jose Altuve .25 .60
14B Altuve Arm Up 10.00 25.00
15 Todd Frazier .25 .60
16 Paul Goldschmidt .30 .75
17 Ty Cobb .50 1.25
18 Tom Glavine .25 .60
19A Yu Darvish .30 .75
19B Yu Darvish VAR 12.00 30.00
Clapping
20 Frank Thomas .30 .75
21 Robin Yount .30 .75
22 Kevin Gausman .20 .50
23A Adam Jones .25 .60
23B Adam Jones VAR 10.00 25.00
Hugging
24 Joey Votto .30 .75
25A Matt Carpenter .30 .75
25B Matt Carpenter VAR 12.00 30.00
Clapping
26A Freddie Freeman .40 1.00
26B Freeman VAR Hug 20.00 50.00
27 John Lackey .25 .60
28 Wil Myers .20 .50
29 Chris Sale .30 .75
30A Jose Bautista .25 .60
30B Jose Bautista VAR 10.00 25.00
Running
31 Mike Mussina .25 .60
32 Hisashi Iwakuma .25 .60
33 Starlin Castro .20 .50
34A Andrew McCutchen .30 .75
34B McCutchen VAR Gry jsy 12.00 30.00
35 Nolan Ryan 1.00 2.50
36 Don Sutton .25 .60
37 Mark McGwire .50 1.25
38 Matt Kemp .25 .60
39 Lou Gehrig .60 1.50
40 Jorge Soler RC .50 1.25
41A Ivan Rodriguez .25 .60
41B Ivan Rodriguez VAR 10.00 25.00
Making fist
42 Kennys Vargas .20 .50
43 Josh Hamilton .25 .60
44 Steve Carlton .25 .60
45A Bryce Harper .50 1.25
45B Harper VAR Yelll 20.00 50.00
46A Adrian Beltre .30 .75
46B Adrian Beltre VAR 12.00 30.00
Celebrating
47 Ozzie Smith .40 1.00
48 Shelby Miller .25 .60
49 Albert Pujols .40 1.00
50A Salvador Perez .25 .60
50B Salvador Perez VAR 10.00 25.00
Making fist
51A Anthony Rendon .30 .75
51B Anthony Rendon VAR 12.00 30.00
Laughing
52 Nelson Cruz .30 .75
53 Prince Fielder .25 .60
54 Brandon Finnegan RC .30 .75
55A Robinson Cano .25 .60
55B Robinson Cano VAR 10.00 25.00
Pointing up
56 Vladimir Guerrero .25 .60
57 Jason Vargas .20 .50
58 Yovani Gallardo .20 .50
59 Adam Wainwright .25 .60
60A Mookie Betts .50 1.25
60B Betts High five 20.00 50.00
61 Derek Holland .20 .50
62A Kenley Jansen .25 .60
62B Kenley Jansen VAR 10.00 25.00
With bat
63 Huston Street .20 .50
64 Tony Perez .25 .60
65 Devin Mesoraco .20 .50
66 Joe Mauer .25 .60
67A Eric Hosmer .25 .60
67B Eric Hosmer VAR 10.00 25.00
Celebrating
68 Alex Wood .20 .50
69 Nick Markakis .25 .60
70 Adam LaRoche .20 .50
71A Aroldis Chapman .30 .75
71B Aroldis Chapman VAR 12.00 30.00
Red jersey
72 Carlos Martinez .25 .60
73 Ben Zobrist .25 .60
74 Julio Teheran .25 .60
75 Mat Latos .25 .60
76 Gio Gonzalez .25 .60
77 Andrew Cashner .20 .50
78 Charlie Blackmon .30 .75
79 Andre Dawson .25 .60
80 Gerrit Cole .30 .75
81 Josh Donaldson .25 .60
82 Mookie Wilson .20 .50
83A Jacoby Ellsbury .25 .60
83B Jacoby Ellsbury VAR 10.00 25.00
Pointing
84 John Smoltz .30 .75
85 Jon Singleton .25 .60
86 Juan Marichal .25 .60
87 Cal Ripken Jr. 1.00 2.50
88 Justin Upton .25 .60
89 Jon Lester .25 .60
90 Carlos Santana .25 .60
91A Javier Baez RC 2.50 6.00
91B Javier Baez VAR 60.00 150.00
Pointing up
92 Matt Harvey .25 .60
93 Max Scherzer .30 .75
94 Evan Longoria .25 .60
95 Corey Kluber .25 .60
96 Edwin Encarnacion .30 .75
97 Anthony Rizzo .50 1.25
98A Jose Reyes .25 .60
98B Jose Reyes VAR 10.00 25.00
Celebrating
99 Roger Maris .30 .75
100 Willie Mays .60 1.50
101 Lucas Duda .25 .60
102 Johnny Cueto .25 .60
103 Taijuan Walker .20 .50
104 Matt Moore .25 .60
105A Billy Hamilton .25 .60
105B Billy Hamilton VAR 10.00 25.00
Running
106 Alex Cobb .20 .50
107 Dalton Pompey RC .40 1.00
108 Yoenis Cespedes .25 .60
109 David Cone .25 .60
110 Justin Verlander .30 .75
111A Adrian Gonzalez .25 .60
111B Adrian Gonzalez VAR 10.00 25.00
Arms up
112 Evan Gattis .20 .50
113 Craig Biggio .25 .60
114A Jose Abreu .30 .75
114B J.Abreu VAR Laugh 12.00 30.00
115 Chipper Jones .30 .75
116 Nolan Arenado .40 1.00
117A Manny Machado .30 .75
117B Manny Machado VAR 12.00 30.00
Glasses
118 Goose Gossage .25 .60
119A Clayton Kershaw .50 1.25
119B Kershaw VAR Celebrat 25.00 60.00
120 Joe DiMaggio .60 1.50
121A Gregory Polanco .25 .60
121B Gregory Polanco VAR 10.00 25.00
With glove
122 Ken Griffey Jr. .60 1.50
123 Yusmeiro Petit .20 .50
124 Mike Piazza .30 .75
125 Roger Clemens .40 1.00
126 Carlos Gonzalez .25 .60
127 Dee Gordon .20 .50
128 Anthony Ranaudo RC .30 .75
129 Drew Smyly .20 .50
130 Tim Hudson .25 .60
131 Zack Wheeler .25 .60
132 Jose Fernandez .30 .75
133 Ernie Banks .30 .75
134 Ralph Kiner .25 .60
135 Craig Kimbrel .25 .60
136A Jonathan Papelbon .25 .60
136B Jonathan Papelbon VAR 10.00 25.00
Making fist
137 Chris Davis .20 .50
138 Greg Maddux .40 1.00
139 Jason Kipnis .25 .60
140 Mark Teixeira .25 .60
141 Nomar Garciaparra .25 .60
142 Larry Doby .25 .60
143A Masahiro Tanaka .25 .60
143B Tanaka VAR Tipping 10.00 25.00
144 Justin Morneau .25 .60
145 Deion Sanders .25 .60
146 Matt Cain .25 .60
147 Jarrod Parker .20 .50
148 Anibal Sanchez .20 .50
149A Miguel Cabrera .30 .75
149B Cabrera VAR Looki left 12.00 30.00
150A Felix Hernandez .25 .60
150B Hernandez VAR Tip cap 20.00 50.00
151 Ryne Sandberg .60 1.50
152 Rod Carew .25 .60
153 Wade Boggs .25 .60
154 Ryan Howard .25 .60
155 Troy Tulowitzki .30 .75
156 Ted Williams .60 1.50
157 Rusney Castillo RC .40 1.00
158 Rymer Liriano RC .30 .75
159 Roberto Alomar .25 .60
160 Hyun-Jin Ryu .25 .60
161 Lorenzo Cain .20 .50
162 Jonathan Lucroy .25 .60
163 Willie McCovey .25 .60
164 Tony Gwynn .30 .75
165 Michael Brantley .25 .60
166 Jeff Samardzija .20 .50
167 Ian Kinsler .25 .60
168A David Ortiz .30 .75
168B Ortiz VAR Hands up 25.00 60.00
169 Ryan Braun .25 .60
170 Christian Yelich .40 1.00
171A Dilson Herrera RC .40 1.00
171B Dilson Herrera VAR 10.00 25.00
Pointing up
172 Phil Hughes .20 .50
173A Jayson Werth .25 .60
173B Jayson Werth VAR 10.00 25.00
Red jersey
174 Chase Utley .25 .60
175 Cole Hamels .25 .60
176A Yasiel Puig .30 .75
176B Puig VAR Making fist 12.00 30.00
177 Martin Prado .20 .50
178 Ryan Zimmerman .25 .60
179A James Shields .20 .50
179B James Shields VAR 8.00 20.00
Arms down
180 Giancarlo Stanton .30 .75
181 Cliff Lee .25 .60
182 Sonny Gray .25 .60
183 George Springer .25 .60
184 Michael Wacha .25 .60
185 Chris Archer .20 .50
186 Stephen Strasburg .30 .75
187A Xander Bogaerts .30 .75
187B Xander Bogaerts VAR 12.00 30.00
Smiling
188A Carlos Gomez .20 .50
188B Carlos Gomez VAR 8.00 20.00
Finger to mouth
189 Daniel Norris RC .30 .75
190 Rickey Henderson .30 .75
191 Pablo Sandoval .25 .60
192 Garrett Richards .25 .60
193 CC Sabathia .25 .60
194A Alex Gordon .25 .60
194B Alex Gordon VAR 10.00 25.00
Making fists
195 Jacob deGrom .30 .75
196 Travis d'Arnaud .25 .60
197 Matt Adams .20 .50
198 J.J. Hardy .20 .50
199 Mike Zunino .20 .50
200 Mike Napoli .20 .50
201 Marcell Ozuna .30 .75
202 Juan Lagares .20 .50
203 Nick Castellanos .30 .75
204 Jake Odorizzi .20 .50
205 Dylan Bundy .25 .60
206 Roenis Elias .20 .50
207 Jonathon Niese .20 .50
208A Dellin Betances .25 .60
208B Betances VAR Hug 20.00 50.00
209A Sean Doolittle .20 .50
209B Doolittle VAR w/catcher 20.00 50.00
210 David Robertson .25 .60
211 Fernando Rodney .20 .50
212 Mark Melancon .20 .50
213 LaTroy Hawkins .20 .50
214A Daniel Murphy .25 .60
214B Murphy VAR fists 15.00 40.00
215 Kyle Seager .20 .50
216 Scott Kazmir .20 .50
217 Desmond Jennings .25 .60
218 Jake Peavy .20 .50
219 Carlos Carrasco .20 .50
220 Francisco Liriano .20 .50
221 Jean Segura .25 .60
222 Russell Martin .20 .50
223 Ian Desmond .20 .50
224 Patrick Corbin .25 .60
225 Alexei Ramirez .25 .60
226 Melky Cabrera .20 .50
227 Tanner Roark .20 .50
228 Jhonny Peralta .20 .50
229 Coco Crisp .20 .50
230 Howie Kendrick .20 .50
231 Ian Kennedy .20 .50
232 Matt Garza .20 .50
233A Bartolo Colon .20 .50
233B Bartolo Colon VAR 8.00 20.00
Batting
234 Jarred Cosart .20 .50
235 Tyson Ross .20 .50
236 Jake McGee .20 .50
237 Billy Butler .20 .50
238 Carlos Beltran .25 .60
239 Victor Martinez .25 .60
240 Cody Allen .20 .50
241 Curtis Granderson .25 .60
242 Satchel Paige .30 .75
243 Pedro Alvarez .20 .50
244 Nori Aoki .20 .50
245 Andrelton Simmons .20 .50
246 Brian McCann .25 .60
247 Chris Carter .20 .50
248 Jose Quintana .20 .50
249 Brandon Moss .20 .50
250 Aramis Ramirez .20 .50
251 Ervin Santana .20 .50
252 Wily Peralta .20 .50
253 A.J. Burnett .20 .50
254 Andrew Miller .25 .60
255 Zach Britton .25 .60
256 Francisco Rodriguez .25 .60
257 Yan Gomes .20 .50
258A Starling Marte .25 .60
258B Starling Marte VAR 10.00 25.00
Celebrating
259 Mike Foltynewicz RC .30 .75
260 Babe Ruth .75 2.00
261A Hunter Pence .25 .60
261B Pence VAR fists 20.00 50.00
262 Lonnie Chisenhall .20 .50
263 Mark Buehrle .25 .60
264 Alex Rios .25 .60
265 Jason Heyward .25 .60
266 Austin Jackson .20 .50
267 Trevor Bauer .30 .75
268 Elvis Andrus .25 .60
269 Mike Leake .20 .50
270 Mike Minor .20 .50
271 Lance Lynn .20 .50
272 Josh Harrison .20 .50
273 Allen Craig .20 .50
274 Dan Haren .20 .50
275 Khris Davis .30 .75
276 R.A. Dickey .25 .60
277 Henderson Alvarez .20 .50
278 Nathan Eovaldi .25 .60
279 Jered Weaver .25 .60
280 C.J. Wilson .25 .60
281 Wade Davis .25 .60
282 Greg Holland .20 .50
283 Steve Cishek .20 .50
284 Trevor Rosenthal .25 .60
285A Jenrry Mejia .20 .50
285B Jenrry Mejia VAR 8.00 20.00
Orange jersey
286 Ken Giles .20 .50
287 Brian Dozier .25 .60
288 Wilin Rosario .20 .50
289 Mark Trumbo .20 .50
290 Jay Bruce .25 .60
291A Brett Gardner .25 .60
291B Brett Gardner VAR 10.00 25.00
Arm up
292 Aaron Sanchez .25 .60
293 Danny Salazar .25 .60
294 Brandon Phillips .20 .50
295 Shin-Soo Choo .25 .60
296 Brandon Belt .25 .60
297 Homer Bailey .20 .50
298 Ubaldo Jimenez .20 .50
299A Kolten Wong .20 .50
299B Kolten Wong VAR 10.00 25.00
Yelling
300 Jesse Hahn .20 .50
301 Jackie Robinson SP 1.25 3.00
302 Eddie Mathews SP 1.25 3.00
303 Duke Snider SP 1.00 2.50
304 Bill Mazeroski SP 1.00 2.50
305 Whitey Ford SP 1.00 2.50
306 Sandy Koufax SP 2.50 6.00
307 Lou Brock SP 1.00 2.50
308 Brooks Robinson SP 1.00 2.50
309 Orlando Cepeda SP 1.00 2.50
310 Al Kaline SP 1.25 3.00
311 Tom Seaver SP 1.00 2.50
312 Jim Palmer SP 1.00 2.50
313 Willie Stargell SP 1.00 2.50
314 Catfish Hunter SP 1.00 2.50
315 Hoyt Wilhelm SP 1.00 2.50
316 Phil Rizzuto SP 1.00 2.50
317 Johnny Bench SP 1.25 3.00
318 Joe Morgan SP 1.00 2.50
319 Reggie Jackson SP 1.00 2.50
320 Gary Carter SP 1.00 2.50
321 Dave Parker SP .75 2.00
322 Mike Schmidt SP 2.00 5.00
323 Fernando Valenzuela SP .75 2.00
324 Bruce Sutter SP 1.00 2.50
325 Sparky Anderson SP 1.00 2.50
326 George Brett SP 2.50 6.00
327 Dwight Gooden SP .75 2.00
328 Dennis Eckersley SP 1.00 2.50
329 Eric Davis SP .75 2.00
330 David Cone SP .75 2.00
331 John Olerud SP .75 2.00
332 Fred McGriff SP 1.00 2.50
333 Luis Aparicio SP 1.00 2.50
334 Livan Hernandez SP .75 2.00
335 Orlando Hernandez SP .75 2.00
336 Mariano Rivera SP 1.50 4.00
337 Jorge Posada SP 1.00 2.50
338 Luis Gonzalez SP .75 2.00
339 David Eckstein SP .75 2.00
340 Josh Beckett SP .75 2.00
341 Paul Konerko SP 1.00 2.50
342 Matt Holliday SP 1.25 3.00
343 Dustin Pedroia SP 1.25 3.00
344 Jimmy Rollins SP 1.00 2.50
345 Alex Rodriguez SP 1.50 4.00
346 Tim Lincecum SP 1.00 2.50
347 Yadier Molina SP 1.25 3.00
348 Buster Posey SP 1.50 4.00
349 Koji Uehara SP .75 2.00
350 Madison Bumgarner SP 1.00 2.50

2015 Topps Gypsy Queen Framed Bronze
*FRME BRNZ: 1.5X TO 4X BASIC
*FRME BRNZ RC: 1X TO 2.5X BASIC RC
STATED ODDS 1:17 HOBBY
STATED PRINT RUN 499 SER.#'d SETS
5 Derek Jeter 6.00 15.00

2015 Topps Gypsy Queen Framed White
*FRME WHTE: 1.2X TO 3X BASIC
*FRME WHTE RC: .75X TO 2X BASIC RC
RANDOM INSERTS IN PACKS
5 Derek Jeter 5.00 12.00

2015 Topps Gypsy Queen Mini
*MINI 1-300: 1.2X TO 3X BASIC
*MINI 1-300 RC: .75X TO 2X BASIC
*MINI 301-350: .5X TO 1.2X BASIC
MINI SP ODDS 1:24 HOBBY

2015 Topps Gypsy Queen Mini Box Variations
*MINI BOX VAR: 1.2X TO 3X BASIC
*MINI BOX VAR RC: .75X TO 2X BASIC RC
ONE MINI BOX PER HOBBY BOX
TEN CARDS PER MINI BOX

2015 Topps Gypsy Queen Mini Gold
*GOLD 1-300: 4X TO 10X BASIC
*GOLD 1-300 RC: 2.5X TO 6X BASIC
*GOLD 301-350: 1X TO 2.5X BASIC
RANDOM INSERTS IN PACKS
STATED PRINT RUN 99 SER.#'d SETS
1 Mike Trout 12.00 30.00
3 Joc Pederson 10.00 25.00
5 Derek Jeter 15.00 40.00
20 Frank Thomas 8.00 20.00
34 Andrew McCutchen 6.00 15.00
47 Ozzie Smith 6.00 15.00
87 Cal Ripken Jr. 12.00 30.00
119 Clayton Kershaw 8.00 20.00
122 Ken Griffey Jr. 8.00 20.00
176 Yasiel Puig 8.00 20.00
319 Reggie Jackson SP 6.00 15.00
322 Mike Schmidt SP 8.00 20.00
326 George Brett SP 10.00 25.00
347 Yadier Molina SP 8.00 20.00

2015 Topps Gypsy Queen Mini Red
*RED 1-300: 4X TO 10X BASIC
*RED 1-300 RC: 2.5X TO 6X BASIC
*RED 301-350: 1X TO 2.5X BASIC
STATED ODDS 1:48 PACKS
STATED PRINT RUN 50 SER.#'d SETS
1 Mike Trout 15.00 40.00
3 Joc Pederson 12.00 30.00
5 Derek Jeter 20.00 50.00
20 Frank Thomas 10.00 25.00
34 Andrew McCutchen 8.00 20.00
47 Ozzie Smith 8.00 20.00
87 Cal Ripken Jr. 15.00 40.00
119 Clayton Kershaw 10.00 25.00
122 Ken Griffey Jr. 10.00 25.00
176 Yasiel Puig 10.00 25.00
319 Reggie Jackson SP 8.00 20.00
322 Mike Schmidt SP 10.00 25.00
326 George Brett SP 12.00 30.00
347 Yadier Molina SP 10.00 25.00

2015 Topps Gypsy Queen Mini Silver
*SILVER 1-300: 2.5X TO 6X BASIC
*SILVER 1-300 RC: 1.5X TO 4X BASIC
*SILVER 301-350: .75X TO 2X BASIC
STATED ODDS 1:12 HOBBY
STATED PRINT RUN 199 SER.#'d SETS
1 Mike Trout 8.00 20.00
3 Joc Pederson 6.00 15.00
5 Derek Jeter 10.00 25.00
20 Frank Thomas 5.00 12.00
87 Cal Ripken Jr. 8.00 20.00
319 Reggie Jackson SP 5.00 12.00
322 Mike Schmidt SP 6.00 15.00
326 George Brett SP 8.00 20.00
347 Yadier Molina SP 6.00 15.00

2015 Topps Gypsy Queen Autographs
STATED ODDS 1:14 HOBBY
EXCHANGE DEADLINE 3/31/2018
GQAAA Abraham Almonte 2.50 6.00
GQAAR Anthony Ranaudo 2.50 6.00
GQABC Brandon Crawford 5.00 12.00
GQABF Brandon Finnegan 2.50 6.00
GQABHO Brock Holt 2.50 6.00
GQACA Chris Archer 2.50 6.00
GQACJ Chris Johnson 2.50 6.00
GQACS Cory Spangenberg 2.50 6.00
GQACY Christian Yelich 15.00 40.00
GQADC David Cone 4.00 10.00
GQADN Daniel Norris 2.50 6.00
GQADPO Dalton Pompey 3.00 8.00
GQAEG Evan Gattis 2.50 6.00
GQAGS George Springer 12.00 30.00
GQAJB Javier Baez 30.00 80.00
GQAJC Jose Canseco 10.00 25.00
GQAJD Jacob deGrom 15.00 40.00
GQAJG Juan Gonzalez 4.00 10.00
GQAJL Juan Lagares 2.50 6.00
GQAJP Joc Pederson 5.00 12.00
GQAJS Jorge Soler 4.00 10.00
GQAJW Josh Willingham 2.50 6.00
GQAKG Kevin Gausman 2.50 6.00
GQAKV Kennys Vargas 2.50 6.00
GQAKW Kolten Wong 3.00 8.00
GQAMA Matt Adams 3.00 8.00
GQAMF Maikel Franco 3.00 8.00
GQAMJ Matt Joyce 2.50 6.00
GQAMSH Matt Shoemaker 3.00 8.00
GQAMT Michael Taylor 2.50 6.00
GQARC Rusney Castillo 3.00 8.00
GQASS Scott Sizemore 2.50 6.00
GQAYV Yordano Ventura 5.00 12.00

2015 Topps Gypsy Queen Autographs Gold
*GOLD: .6X TO 1.5X BASIC
STATED ODDS 1:403 HOBBY
STATED PRINT RUN 25 SER.#'d SETS
EXCHANGE DEADLINE 3/31/2018
GQAAD Andre Dawson 25.00 60.00
GQAAJ Adam Jones 5.00 12.00
GQABJ Bo Jackson 50.00 100.00
GQACK Clayton Kershaw 75.00 150.00
GQACR Cal Ripken Jr. EXCH 75.00 150.00
GQADP Dustin Pedroia 25.00 60.00
GQAFF Freddie Freeman 25.00 60.00
GQAFT Frank Thomas 50.00 120.00
GQAGP Gregory Polanco 20.00 50.00
GQAHA Hank Aaron 250.00 350.00
GQAJA Jose Abreu 40.00 100.00
GQAJF Jose Fernandez 20.00 50.00
GQAJSM John Smoltz 40.00 80.00
GQAKGR Ken Griffey Jr. EXCH 200.00 300.00
GQAMTR Mike Trout 200.00 300.00
GQANG Nomar Garciaparra 30.00 80.00
GQAOS Ozzie Smith 30.00 80.00
GQAPG Paul Goldschmidt 15.00 40.00
GQAPN Phil Niekro 12.00 30.00
GQARH Rickey Henderson EXCH 30.00 80.00
GQATG Tom Glavine EXCH 25.00 60.00
GQATT Troy Tulowitzki EXCH 25.00 60.00
GQAYP Yasiel Puig 75.00 150.00

2015 Topps Gypsy Queen Autographs Silver
*SILVER: .5X TO 1.2X BASIC
STATED ODDS 1:199 HOBBY
STATED PRINT RUN 50 SER.#'d SETS
EXCHANGE DEADLINE 3/31/2018
GQAAJ Adam Jones 4.00 10.00
GQACK Clayton Kershaw 60.00 120.00
GQAFF Freddie Freeman 20.00 50.00
GQAGP Gregory Polanco 15.00 40.00
GQAJA Jose Abreu 30.00 80.00
GQAJF Jose Fernandez 15.00 40.00
GQAPG Paul Goldschmidt 12.00 30.00
GQAPN Phil Niekro 10.00 25.00

2015 Topps Gypsy Queen Basics of Base Ball Minis
COMPLETE SET (15) 20.00 50.00
STATED ODDS 1:24 HOBBY
BBMR1 Windup 1.50 4.00
BBMR2 Grip the Bat 1.50 4.00
BBMR3 Sacrifice Fly 1.50 4.00
BBMR4 Head-First Slide 1.50 4.00
BBMR5 Cut-Off 1.50 4.00
BBMR6 Take a Lead 1.50 4.00
BBMR7 Tag Up 1.50 4.00
BBMR8 Infield Shift 1.50 4.00
BBMR9 Pitchout 1.50 4.00
BBMR10 Steal 1.50 4.00
BBMR11 Intentional Walk 1.50 4.00
BBMR12 Squeeze Bunt 1.50 4.00
BBMR13 Rundown 1.50 4.00
BBMR14 Crowd the Plate 1.50 4.00
BBMR15 Knuckleball 1.50 4.00

2015 Topps Gypsy Queen Framed Mini Relics
STATED ODDS 1:28 HOBBY
*GOLD/25: .6X TO 1.5X BASIC
GMRAB Adrian Beltre 3.00 8.00
GMRAC Aroldis Chapman 3.00 8.00
GMRAG Adrian Gonzalez 2.50 6.00
GMRAW Adam Wainwright 2.50 6.00
GMRCA Chris Archer 2.00 5.00
GMRCC Carl Crawford 2.50 6.00
GMRCD Chris Davis 2.00 5.00
GMRCH Cole Hamels 2.50 6.00
GMRCK Clayton Kershaw 6.00 15.00
GMRCS Chris Sale 3.00 8.00
GMRCY Christian Yelich 4.00 10.00
GMRDO David Ortiz 3.00 8.00
GMRDP David Price 2.50 6.00
GMRDW David Wright 2.50 6.00
GMREA Elvis Andrus 2.50 6.00
GMREG Evan Gattis 2.00 5.00
GMREH Eric Hosmer 2.50 6.00
GMRFF Freddie Freeman 4.00 10.00
GMRGB Gary Brown 2.00 5.00
GMRGC Gerrit Cole 3.00 8.00
GMRGG Gio Gonzalez 2.50 6.00
GMRGP Gregory Polanco 2.50 6.00
GMRHI Hisashi Iwakuma 2.50 6.00
GMRHR Hyun-Jin Ryu 2.50 6.00
GMRIK Ian Kinsler 2.50 6.00
GMRJH Jason Heyward 2.50 6.00
GMRJS Jon Singleton 2.50 6.00
GMRJU Justin Upton 2.50 6.00
GMRJV Justin Verlander 5.00 12.00
GMRKW Kolten Wong 2.50 6.00
GMRMA Matt Adams 2.00 5.00
GMRMB Madison Bumgarner 2.50 6.00
GMRMC Miguel Cabrera 3.00 8.00
GMRMH Matt Holliday 3.00 8.00
GMRMMI Mike Minor 2.00 5.00
GMRMT Masahiro Tanaka 2.50 6.00
GMRMTR Mike Trout 10.00 25.00
GMRMW Michael Wacha 2.50 6.00
GMRNC Nick Castellanos 3.00 8.00
GMRPS Pablo Sandoval 2.50 6.00
GMRRB Ryan Braun 2.50 6.00
GMRSC Starlin Castro 2.00 5.00
GMRSCI Steve Cishek 2.00 5.00
GMRSM Shelby Miller 2.50 6.00
GMRSP Salvador Perez 2.50 6.00
GMRSS Stephen Strasburg 3.00 8.00
GMRTD Travis d'Arnaud 2.50 6.00
GMRTW Taijuan Walker 2.00 5.00
GMRVM Victor Martinez 2.50 6.00
GMRWM Wil Myers 2.50 6.00
GMRXB Xander Bogaerts 3.00 8.00
GMRYM Yadier Molina 5.00 12.00
GMRYV Yordano Ventura 2.50 6.00
GMRZG Zack Greinke 2.50 6.00

2015 Topps Gypsy Queen Glove Stories
COMPLETE SET (15) 3.00 8.00
STATED ODDS 1:6 HOBBY
PRINTING PLATE ODDS 1:13,441 HOBBY
PLATE PRINT RUN 1 SET PER COLOR
NO PLATE PRICING DUE TO SCARCITY
GS1 Steven Souza Jr. .40 1.00
GS2 Billy Hamilton .40 1.00
GS3 Adam Eaton .30 .75
GS4 Peter Bourjos .30 .75
GS5 Mike Aviles .30 .75
GS6 Dustin Ackley .30 .75
GS7 Ben Revere .30 .75
GS8 Mookie Betts .75 2.00
GS9 Alex Gordon .40 1.00
GS10 Pablo Sandoval .40 1.00
GS11 Norichika Aoki .30 .75
GS12 Hunter Pence .40 1.00
GS13 Carlos Gomez .30 .75
GS14 Aaron Hicks .40 1.00
GS15 Mike Moustakas .40 1.00

2015 Topps Gypsy Queen Jumbo Relics
STATED ODDS 1:651 HOBBY
STATED PRINT RUN 50 SER.#'d SETS
*GOLD/25: .6X TO 1.5X BASIC
GJRAM Andrew McCutchen 15.00 40.00
GJRAR Anthony Rendon 6.00 15.00
GJRAS Andrelton Simmons 12.00 30.00
GJRAW Adam Wainwright 10.00 25.00
GJRBH Billy Hamilton 5.00 12.00
GJRBP Buster Posey 25.00 60.00
GJRCK Clayton Kershaw 12.00 30.00
GJRCS Chris Sale 6.00 15.00
GJRDJ Derek Jeter 50.00 100.00
GJRFH Felix Hernandez 10.00 25.00
GJRGS Giancarlo Stanton 6.00 15.00
GJRHR Hyun-Jin Ryu 5.00 12.00
GJRJB Jose Bautista 12.00 30.00
GJRMC Miguel Cabrera 6.00 15.00
GJRMP Mike Piazza 6.00 15.00
GJRMS Max Scherzer 6.00 15.00
GJRMT Mike Trout 30.00 80.00
GJRMTA Masahiro Tanaka 5.00 12.00
GJRRB Ryan Braun 5.00 12.00
GJRRC Roger Clemens 8.00 20.00
GJRRP Rafael Palmeiro 15.00 40.00
GJRSS Stephen Strasburg 6.00 15.00
GJRVM Victor Martinez 8.00 20.00
GJRYC Yoenis Cespedes 8.00 20.00
GJRYP Yasiel Puig 6.00 15.00

2015 Topps Gypsy Queen Mini Relic Autograph Booklets
STATED ODDS 1:628 MINI BOX
STATED PRINT RUN 25 SER.#'d SETS
EXCHANGE DEADLINE 3/31/2018
MARAD Andre Dawson 40.00 100.00
MARAJ Adam Jones 40.00 100.00
MARBM Brian McCann 50.00 120.00
MARCB Craig Biggio 50.00 120.00
MARCK Clayton Kershaw 100.00 250.00
MARCR Cal Ripken Jr. 150.00 300.00
MARCS Chris Sale 50.00 120.00
MARDP Dustin Pedroia 75.00 200.00
MARFF Freddie Freeman 50.00 120.00
MARGSN Giancarlo Stanton EXCH 50.00 125.00
MARJA Jose Abreu 100.00 250.00
MARJB Javier Baez 250.00 600.00
MARJD Josh Donaldson 40.00 100.00
MARJG Juan Gonzalez 30.00 80.00
MARJM Joe Mauer 50.00 120.00
MARJP Joc Pederson 100.00 250.00
MARKG Ken Griffey Jr. 250.00 400.00
MARMS Max Scherzer 50.00 120.00
MARMT Mike Trout 250.00 400.00
MARRB Ryan Braun 40.00 100.00
MARRC Robinson Cano 60.00 150.00
MARRCA Rusney Castillo 40.00 100.00
MARSG Sonny Gray 40.00 100.00

2015 Topps Gypsy Queen Pillars of the Community
COMPLETE SET (10) 12.00 30.00
STATED ODDS 1:24 HOBBY
PCBH Bryce Harper 2.00 5.00
PCBP Buster Posey 1.50 4.00
PCDO David Ortiz 1.25 3.00
PCDW David Wright 1.00 2.50
PCJA Jose Abreu 1.25 3.00
PCJB Jose Bautista 1.00 2.50
PCMT Masahiro Tanaka 1.00 2.50
PCRC Robinson Cano 1.00 2.50
PCYM Yadier Molina 1.25 3.00
PCYP Yasiel Puig 1.25 3.00

2015 Topps Gypsy Queen Relic Autographs
STATED ODDS 1:815 HOBBY
STATED PRINT RUN 50 SER.#'d SETS
EXCHANGE DEADLINE 3/31/2018
*GOLD/25: .5X TO 1.2X BASIC
ARCG Carlos Gonzalez EXCH 6.00 15.00
ARCK Clayton Kershaw 60.00 150.00
ARCS Chris Sale 10.00 25.00
ARDP Dustin Pedroia 20.00 50.00
ARFF Freddie Freeman 15.00 40.00
ARFT Frank Thomas 20.00 50.00
ARGSN Giancarlo Stanton EXCH 40.00 80.00
ARJA Jose Abreu 30.00 80.00
ARJF Jose Fernandez 30.00 80.00
ARJP Joc Pederson 10.00 25.00
ARJT Julio Teheran 6.00 15.00
ARMA Matt Adams 15.00 40.00
ARMF Maikel Franco 25.00 60.00
ARMS Max Scherzer EXCH 15.00 40.00
ARPG Paul Goldschmidt 20.00 50.00
ARRH Rickey Henderson 25.00 60.00
ARYD Yu Darvish 30.00 80.00
ARYP Yasiel Puig 40.00 100.00
ARYV Yordano Ventura 10.00 25.00

2015 Topps Gypsy Queen Relics
STATED ODDS 1:28 HOBBY
*GOLD/25: .6X TO 1.5X BASIC
GQRAD Andre Dawson 2.50 6.00
GQRAG Adrian Gonzalez 2.50 6.00
GQRAH Adeiny Hechavarria 2.00 5.00
GQRAJ Adam Jones 2.50 6.00
GQRAS Andrelton Simmons 2.00 5.00
GQRAW Adam Wainwright 2.50 6.00
GQRBH Billy Hamilton 2.50 6.00
GQRBP Buster Posey 4.00 10.00
GQRCA Chris Archer 2.00 5.00
GQRCC Carl Crawford 2.50 6.00
GQRCH Cole Hamels 2.50 6.00
GQRCK Clayton Kershaw 6.00 15.00
GQRCKI Craig Kimbrel 2.50 6.00
GQRDJ Derek Jeter 10.00 25.00
GQRDM Don Mattingly 5.00 12.00
GQRDP David Price 2.50 6.00
GQRDW David Wright 2.50 6.00
GQREA Elvis Andrus 2.50 6.00
GQRFF Freddie Freeman 4.00 10.00
GQRFH Felix Hernandez 2.50 6.00
GQRFT Frank Thomas 5.00 12.00
GQRGC Gerrit Cole 3.00 8.00
GQRGG Gio Gonzalez 2.50 6.00
GQRHI Hisashi Iwakuma 2.50 6.00
GQRHR Hyun-Jin Ryu 2.50 6.00
GQRIK Ian Kinsler 2.50 6.00
GQRJB Jose Bautista 2.50 6.00
GQRJH Jason Heyward 2.50 6.00
GQRJM Joe Mauer 2.50 6.00
GQRJS Jon Singleton 2.50 6.00
GQRJV Justin Verlander 3.00 8.00
GQRJVO Joey Votto 3.00 8.00
GQRKW Kolten Wong 2.50 6.00
GQRMA Matt Adams 2.00 5.00
GQRMH Matt Holliday 3.00 8.00
GQRNA Nolan Arenado 4.00 10.00
GQRNC Nick Castellanos 3.00 8.00
GQRPS Pablo Sandoval 2.50 6.00
GQRRC Robinson Cano 2.50 6.00
GQRSC Starlin Castro 2.00 5.00
GQRSM Starling Marte 2.50 6.00
GQRSMI Shelby Miller 2.50 6.00
GQRTD Travis d'Arnaud 2.50 6.00
GQRTW Taijuan Walker 2.00 5.00
GQRVG Vladimir Guerrero 2.50 6.00
GQRVM Victor Martinez 2.50 6.00
GQRXB Xander Bogaerts 3.00 8.00
GQRYC Yoenis Cespedes 2.50 6.00
GQRYM Yadier Molina 5.00 12.00
GQRYP Yasiel Puig 3.00 8.00
GQRYV Yordano Ventura 2.50 6.00
GQRZG Zack Greinke 2.50 6.00

2015 Topps Gypsy Queen Framed Mini Retail Autographs
RANDOM INSERTS IN RETAIL PACKS
RMAAR Anthony Rizzo EXCH 50.00 100.00
RMACK Clayton Kershaw 125.00 250.00
RMACR Cal Ripken Jr. 50.00 120.00
RMADP Dustin Pedroia 75.00 150.00
RMAFF Freddie Freeman 75.00 150.00
RMAFT Frank Thomas 50.00 100.00
RMAGSR George Springer 50.00 100.00
RMAJA Jose Abreu 50.00 120.00
RMAJP Joc Pederson 100.00 200.00
RMAJSR Jorge Soler 150.00 250.00
RMAMF Maikel Franco 75.00 150.00
RMARC Rusney Castillo 30.00 80.00
RMAYV Yordano Ventura 12.00 30.00

2015 Topps Gypsy Queen The Queen's Throwbacks
COMPLETE SET (25) 5.00 12.00
STATED ODDS 1:6 HOBBY
PRINTING PLATE ODDS 1:8182 HOBBY
PLATE PRINT RUN 1 SET PER COLOR
NO PLATE PRICING DUE TO SCARCITY
QT1 Miguel Cabrera .50 1.25
QT2 Andrelton Simmons .30 .75
QT3 Anthony Rizzo .75 2.00
QT4 Michael Morse .30 .75
QT5 Alex Gordon .40 1.00
QT6 James Shields .30 .75
QT7 Nelson Cruz .50 1.25
QT8 Ian Kinsler .40 1.00
QT9 Adrian Beltre .50 1.25
QT10 Rougned Odor .40 1.00
QT11 Jose Altuve .40 1.00
QT12 Miguel Gonzalez .30 .75
QT13 George Springer .40 1.00
QT14 Robinson Cano .40 1.00
QT15 Ryan Braun .40 1.00
QT16 Joe Mauer .40 1.00
QT17 Starlin Castro .30 .75
QT18 Gerrit Cole .50 1.25
QT19 Curtis Granderson .40 1.00
QT20 Manny Machado .50 1.25
QT21 Sonny Gray .40 1.00
QT22 Mike Trout 2.50 6.00
QT23 Jered Weaver .40 1.00
QT24 Julio Teheran .40 1.00
QT25 Jason Kipnis .40 1.00

2015 Topps Gypsy Queen Walk Off Winners
COMPLETE SET (25) 5.00 12.00
STATED ODDS 1:4 HOBBY
PRINTING PLATE ODDS 1:8182 HOBBY
PLATE PRINT RUN 1 SET PER COLOR
NO PLATE PRICING DUE TO SCARCITY
GWO1 Bill Mazeroski .40 1.00
GWO2 Ken Griffey Jr. 1.00 2.50
GWO3 Giancarlo Stanton .50 1.25
GWO4 David Ortiz .50 1.25
GWO5 Derek Jeter 1.25 3.00
GWO6 Derek Jeter 1.25 3.00
GWO7 David Freese .30 .75
GWO8 Carlton Fisk .40 1.00
GWO9 Ozzie Smith .60 1.50
GWO10 Mike Trout 2.50 6.00
GWO11 Raul Ibanez .40 1.00
GWO12 Scott Hatteberg .30 .75
GWO13 Luis Gonzalez .30 .75
GWO14 Salvador Perez .40 1.00
GWO15 Bryce Harper .75 2.00
GWO16 Evan Longoria .40 1.00
GWO17 Lenny Dykstra .30 .75
GWO18 Carlos Gonzalez .40 1.00
GWO19 Travis Ishikawa .30 .75
GWO20 Jason Giambi .30 .75
GWO21 Kolten Wong .40 1.00
GWO22 Jayson Werth .40 1.00
GWO23 Alex Gordon .40 1.00
GWO24 Neil Walker .40 1.00
GWO25 Mookie Wilson .30 .75

2016 Topps Gypsy Queen
COMP.SET w/SP (350) 50.00 120.00
COMP.SET w/o SP's (300) 12.00 30.00
SP ODDS 1:4 HOBBY
SP VAR ODDS 1:58 HOBBY
PRINTING PLATE ODDS 1:512 HOBBY
PLATE PRINT RUN 1 SET PER COLOR
BLACK-CYAN-MAGENTA-YELLOW ISSUED
NO PLATE PRICING DUE TO SCARCITY
1A Giancarlo Stanton .30 .75
Batting
1B Giancarlo Stanton SP 5.00 12.00
Fielding
2A Buster Posey .40 1.00
Batting
2B Posey SP Ctchng 10.00 25.00
3A A.J. Pollock .20 .50
Running
3B A.J. Pollock SP 3.00 8.00
Fielding
4 Adam Jones .25 .60
5 Albert Pujols .40 1.00
6 Carlos Gonzalez .25 .60
7A Corey Seager RC 2.50 6.00
Running
7B Seager SP Fldng 15.00 40.00
8A Freeman Gry Jrsy .40 1.00
8B Freeman SP In rain 10.00 25.00
9 Hector Olivera RC .40 1.00
10A Ichiro Suzuki .40 1.00
Throwing
10B Ichiro SP Rnnng 6.00 15.00
11 Jason Heyward .25 .60
12A Jose Bautista .25 .60
Running
12B Jose Bautista SP 4.00 10.00
w/Glove
13A Luis Severino RC .40 1.00
Gray jersey
13B Luis Severino SP 4.00 10.00
Pinstripes
14A Marcus Stroman .25 .60
Blue jersey
14B Marcus Stroman SP 4.00 10.00
White jersey
15 Michael Brantley .25 .60
16A Miguel Sano RC .50 1.25
Batting
16B Sano SP Fldng 5.00 12.00
17A Nolan Arenado .40 1.00
Gray jersey
17B Nolan Arenado SP 6.00 15.00
Purple jersey
18A Robinson Cano .25 .60
Batting
18B Robinson Cano SP 4.00 10.00
Fielding
19A Stephen Strasburg .30 .75
Pitching
19B Stephen Strasburg SP 5.00 12.00
Batting
20 Todd Frazier .25 .60
21A Adam Wainwright .25 .60
Pitching
21B Adam Wainwright SP 4.00 10.00
Red cap
22 Aroldis Chapman .30 .75
23A Bryce Harper .50 1.25
Batting
23B Harper SP w/Glve 15.00 40.00
24 Charlie Blackmon .30 .75
25A Sale Pitching .30 .75
25B Sale Wht Jrsy 5.00 12.00
26 Cole Hamels .25 .60
27 Craig Kimbrel .25 .60
28 David Price .25 .60
29 Eric Hosmer .25 .60
30A Jake Arrieta .25 .60
Pitching
30B Jake Arrieta SP 4.00 10.00
Batting
31 Jason Kipnis .25 .60
32 Johnny Cueto .25 .60
33A Jose Fernandez .30 .75
Arm back
33B Jose Fernandez SP 5.00 12.00
Brown glove
34 Justin Verlander .30 .75
35 Jacoby Ellsbury .25 .60
36 Joe Mauer .25 .60
37 John Lackey .25 .60
38 Justin Upton .25 .60
39 Randal Grichuk .20 .50
40 Carlos Martinez .25 .60
41 Garrett Richards .25 .60
42 Gio Gonzalez .25 .60
43 Henry Owens RC .40 1.00
44 Hyun-Jin Ryu .25 .60
45 J.D. Martinez .30 .75
46 Jordan Zimmermann .25 .60
47 Jung Ho Kang .20 .50
48 Andre Ethier .25 .60
49 David Peralta .20 .50
50 Dexter Fowler .25 .60
51 Frankie Montas .25 .60
52 Jeff Samardzija .20 .50
53 Jonathan Papelbon .25 .60
54 Matt Kemp .25 .60
55 Andrelton Simmons .20 .50
56 Daniel Murphy .25 .60
57 Kolten Wong .25 .60
58 Eduardo Rodriguez .20 .50
59A Madison Bumgarner .25 .60
Pitching
59B Bumgarner SP Bttng 8.00 20.00
60A Matt Carpenter .30 .75
Red cap
60B Matt Carpenter SP 5.00 12.00
Dark cap
61A Michael Conforto RC .40 1.00
Running
61B Conforto SP Blu jsy 20.00 50.00
62A Sonny Gray .25 .60
Ball in glove
62B Sonny Gray SP 4.00 10.00
Ball visable
63 Steven Matz .25 .60
64A Truner RC No Ball 1.00 2.50
64B Truner SP Ball 10.00 25.00
65 Xander Bogaerts .30 .75
66 Zack Greinke .25 .60
67A Addison Russell .30 .75
Batting
67B Addison Russell SP 5.00 12.00
Fielding
68 Anthony Rendon .30 .75
69 Edwin Encarnacion .30 .75
70 Evan Gattis .20 .50
71A Francisco Lindor .30 .75
Batting
71B Lindor SP Fldng 8.00 20.00
72 Gary Sanchez RC 1.00 2.50
73 Greg Bird RC .40 1.00
74 Hisashi Iwakuma .25 .60
75 Jeurys Familia .25 .60
76 Jon Gray RC .30 .75
77 Jorge Soler .30 .75
78A Josh Donaldson .25 .60
Arm forward
78B Josh Donaldson SP 4.00 10.00
Arm back
79A Kris Bryant .40 1.00
White jersey
79B Bryant SP Blu jsy 6.00 15.00
80 Maikel Franco .25 .60
81A Matt Duffy RC .30 .75
Batting
81B Duffy SP Fldng 15.00 40.00
82 Nelson Cruz .30 .75
83 Salvador Perez .25 .60
84 Starlin Castro .20 .50
85 Yu Darvish .30 .75
86 Adrian Beltre .30 .75
87 Alex Gordon .25 .60
88A Andrew McCutchen .30 .75
Batting
88B McCtchn SP w/Glve 10.00 25.00
89A A.Rizzo Bttng .50 1.25
89B Anthony Rizzo SP 8.00 20.00
Fielding
90A Carlos Correa .30 .75
Orange jersey
90B Correa SP Gray jsy 5.00 12.00
91A Chris Archer .20 .50
Pitching
91B Chris Archer SP 3.00 8.00
In dugout
92 Lance McCullers .20 .50
93 Matt Moore .25 .60
94 Rougned Odor .25 .60
95 Aaron Nola RC .60 1.50
96 Alex Cobb .20 .50
97 Carlos Carrasco .20 .50
98 Carlos Rodon .30 .75
99 Daniel Norris .20 .50
100 Mike Moustakas .25 .60
101 Rusney Castillo .20 .50
102 Yadier Molina .30 .75
103 Zack Wheeler .25 .60
104 Ben Zobrist .25 .60
105 Danny Salazar .25 .60
106 David Wright .25 .60
107A Devin Mesoraco .20 .50
Batting
107B Devin Mesoraco SP 3.00 8.00
Catching
108 Richie Shaffer RC .30 .75
109 Tyson Ross .20 .50
110 Yovani Gallardo .20 .50
111 Brandon Belt .25 .60
112 Brett Gardner .25 .60
113 Joe Ross .20 .50
114 Jose Iglesias .25 .60
115 Michael Pineda .20 .50
116 Brandon Crawford .25 .60
117 Carlos Santana .25 .60
118 Christian Yelich .40 1.00
119 Drew Smyly .20 .50
120 Victor Martinez .25 .60
121 Brian Dozier .25 .60
122 Corey Dickerson .25 .60
123 George Springer .25 .60
124 Jon Lester .25 .60
125 Jose Abreu .30 .75
126A Kyle Schwarber RC 1.00 2.50
Blue jersey
126B Schwrbr SP Gray jsy 10.00 25.00
127 Lorenzo Cain .20 .50
128A Manny Machado .30 .75
Batting
128B Machado SP Blck jsy 8.00 20.00
129 Mark Teixeira .25 .60
130A Matt Harvey .25 .60
Pitching
130B Harvey SP Bttng 8.00 20.00
131A Max Scherzer .30 .75
Pitching
131B Max Scherzer SP 5.00 12.00
Batting
132A Michael Wacha .25 .60
Pitching
132B Michael Wacha SP 4.00 10.00
Batting
133A Mike Trout 1.50 4.00
On base
133B Trout SP w/Glve 25.00 60.00
134A Prince Fielder .25 .60
Batting
134B Prince Fielder SP 4.00 10.00
Throwing
135 Starling Marte .25 .60
136A Wade Davis .20 .50
Blue jersey
136B Wade Davis SP 3.00 8.00
Gray jersey
137A Yasiel Puig .30 .75
White jersey
137B Puig SP Gray jsy 8.00 20.00
138 Adrian Gonzalez .25 .60
139 Alex Rodriguez .40 1.00
140 Andrew Miller .25 .60
141 Byung-Ho Park RC .40 1.00
142 Carlos Gomez .20 .50
143 Chris Davis .20 .50
144A Clayton Kershaw .60 1.50
Pitching
144B Kershaw SP Bttng 8.00 20.00
145 Corey Kluber .25 .60
146A Dallas Keuchel .25 .60
Orange jersey
146B Dallas Keuchel SP 4.00 10.00
Light jersey
147 David Ortiz .30 .75
148 Dee Gordon .20 .50
149 Dustin Pedroia .30 .75
150 Felix Hernandez .25 .60
151A Gerrit Cole .30 .75
Black jersey
151B Gerrit Cole SP 5.00 12.00
White jersey
152 Hanley Ramirez .25 .60
153 Jacob deGrom .30 .75
154 Joey Votto .30 .75
155 Jose Altuve .25 .60
156 Masahiro Tanaka .25 .60
157A Miguel Cabrera .30 .75
Running
157B Cabrera SP Fldng 12.00 30.00
158A Betts Batting .50 1.25
158B Betts SP Fldng 8.00 20.00
159A Noah Syndergaard .25 .60
Pitching
159B Syndrgrd SP Bttng 8.00 20.00
160A Paul Goldschmidt .30 .75
Red jersey
160B Paul Goldschmidt SP 5.00 12.00
w/Glove
161 Ryan Braun .25 .60
162 Shelby Miller .25 .60
163 Stephen Piscotty RC .50 1.25
164A Troy Tulowitzki .30 .75
Running
164B Troy Tulowitzki SP 5.00 12.00
Fielding
165 Yoenis Cespedes .30 .75
166 Evan Longoria .25 .60
167 Francisco Liriano .20 .50
168 Gregory Polanco .25 .60
169 Jay Bruce .25 .60
170 Joey Gallo .25 .60
171 Taijuan Walker .20 .50
172 Travis d'Arnaud .25 .60
173 Kenley Jansen .25 .60
174 Matt Holliday .30 .75
175 Jose Peraza RC .40 1.00
176 Billy Hamilton .25 .60
177 Ian Kinsler .25 .60
178 James Shields .20 .50
179 Jonathan Lucroy .25 .60
180 Jose Quintana .20 .50
181 Josh Harrison .20 .50
182 Kyle Seager .20 .50
183 Yasmany Tomas .20 .50
184 Wil Myers .20 .50
185 Ian Kennedy .20 .50
186 Jhonny Peralta .20 .50
187 Josh Hamilton .25 .60
188 Scott Kazmir .20 .50
189 Trevor Rosenthal .25 .60
190 Devon Travis .20 .50
191 Joc Pederson .25 .60
192 Justin Turner .25 .60
193 Raisel Iglesias .25 .60
194 Roberto Osuna .20 .50
195 Taylor Jungmann .20 .50
196 Anibal Sanchez .20 .50
197 Arodys Vizcaino .20 .50
198 Blake Swihart .25 .60
199 Brandon Finnegan .20 .50
200 Brian McCann .25 .60
201 Carl Edwards Jr. .25 .60
202 CC Sabathia .25 .60
203 Chris Heston .20 .50
204 Cody Anderson .20 .50
205 R.A. Dickey .25 .60
206 Delino DeShields Jr. .20 .50
207 Eddie Rosario .25 .60
208 Enrique Hernandez .25 .60
209 Hunter Pence .25 .60
210 Jose Reyes .25 .60
211 Julio Teheran .25 .60
212 Ketel Marte RC .60 1.50
213 Koji Uehara .20 .50
214 Lance Lynn .20 .50
215 Matt Adams .20 .50
216 Nathan Eovaldi .25 .60
217 Pedro Alvarez .20 .50
218 Ryan Howard .25 .60
219 Shin-Soo Choo .25 .60
220 Trayce Thompson RC .50 1.25
221 Tyler Duffey RC .30 .75
222 Wilmer Flores .25 .60
223 Yordano Ventura .25 .60
224 Zach Lee .20 .50
225 Aaron Altherr .20 .50
226 Alcides Escobar .25 .60
227 Anthony DeSclafani .20 .50
228 Brad Ziegler .20 .50
229 Brandon Phillips .20 .50
230 Carlos Beltran .25 .60
231 Dellin Betances .25 .60
232 Didi Gregorius .25 .60
233 Francisco Cervelli .20 .50
234 Jerad Eickhoff RC .50 1.25
235 Joe Panik .25 .60
236 Kole Calhoun .20 .50
237 Kevin Gausman .20 .50
238 Mark Canha .20 .50
239 Mike Minor .20 .50
240 Nathan Karns .20 .50
241 Odubel Herrera .25 .60
242 Peter O'Brien RC .30 .75
243 Ryan Zimmerman .25 .60
244 Tom Murphy RC .30 .75
245 Andrew Heaney .20 .50
246 Bartolo Colon .20 .50

7 Chi Chi Gonzalez .20 .50
8 Christian Colon .20 .50
9 Collin McHugh .20 .50
0 Curtis Granderson .25 .60
1 David Robertson .20 .50
2 Derek Holland .20 .50
3 Domingo Santana .25 .60
4 Ian Desmond .20 .50
5 J.J. Hardy .20 .50
6 Jake Odorizzi .20 .50
7 Javier Baez .40 1.00
8 Justin Bour .25 .60
9 Ken Giles .20 .50
0 Kevin Kiermaier .25 .60
1 Logan Forsythe .20 .50
2 Mark Melancon .20 .50
3 Max Kepler RC .50 1.25
4 Pablo Sandoval .25 .60
5 Preston Tucker .20 .50
6 Rob Refsnyder RC .40 1.00
7 Steven Souza Jr. .25 .60
8 Tommy Pham .20 .50
9 Trevor Bauer .30 .75
0 Aaron Sanchez .25 .60
1 Miguel Almonte RC .30 .75
2 DJ LeMahieu .30 .75
3 Elvis Andrus .25 .60
4 Homer Bailey .20 .50
5 J.T. Realmuto .30 .75
6 James McCann .25 .60
7 Justin Nicolino .20 .50
8 Kendrys Morales .20 .50
9 Kevin Pillar .20 .50
0 Nick Ahmed .20 .50
1 Patrick Corbin .25 .60
2 Robbie Ray .20 .50
3 Russell Martin .20 .50
4 Zach Britton .25 .60
5 Adam Eaton .20 .50
6 Kyle Waldrop RC .40 1.00
7 Brandon Drury RC .50 1.25
8 Brian Johnson RC .30 .75
9 Carson Smith .20 .50
0 Ender Inciarte .20 .50
1 Francisco Rodriguez .25 .60
2 Howie Kendrick .20 .50
3 Jean Segura .25 .60
4 Kevin Plawecki .20 .50
5 Lucas Duda .25 .60
6 Marco Estrada .20 .50
7 Dilson Herrera .25 .60
8 Zach Davies RC .40 1.00
9 Marcell Ozuna .30 .75
00 Nick Castellanos .30 .75
01 Johnny Bench SP 1.00 2.50
02 Bill Mazeroski SP .75 2.00
03 Al Kaline SP 1.00 2.50
04 Don Sutton SP .75 2.00
05 Ralph Kiner SP .75 2.00
06 Larry Doby SP .75 2.00
07 Willie McCovey SP .75 2.00
08 Eddie Mathews SP 1.00 2.50
09 Duke Snider SP .75 2.00
10 Whitey Ford SP .75 2.00
11 Brooks Robinson SP .75 2.00
12 Jim Palmer SP .75 2.00
13 Willie Stargell SP .75 2.00
14 Catfish Hunter SP .75 2.00
15 Joe Morgan SP .75 2.00
16 Bruce Sutter SP .75 2.00
17 George Brett SP 2.00 5.00
18 Phil Rizzuto SP .75 2.00
19 Sparky Anderson SP .75 2.00
20 Gary Carter SP .75 2.00
21 Tony Perez SP .75 2.00
22 Goose Gossage SP .75 2.00
23 Sandy Koufax SP 2.00 5.00
24 Satchel Paige SP 1.00 2.50
25 John Smoltz SP 1.00 2.50
26 Cal Ripken Jr. SP 3.00 8.00
27 Willie Mays SP 2.00 5.00
28 Rod Carew SP .75 2.00
29 Craig Biggio SP .75 2.00
30 Wade Boggs SP .75 2.00
31 Orlando Cepeda SP .75 2.00
32 Dennis Eckersley SP .75 2.00
33 Bo Jackson SP 1.00 2.50
34 Robin Yount SP 1.00 2.50
35 Luis Aparicio SP .75 2.00
36 Babe Ruth SP 2.50 6.00
37 Lou Brock SP .75 2.00
38 Bob Feller SP .75 2.00
39 Fergie Jenkins SP .75 2.00
40 Harmon Killebrew SP 1.00 2.50
41 Juan Marichal SP .75 2.00
42 Eddie Murray SP .75 2.00
43 Kenta Maeda SP RC 6.00 15.00
44 Ozzie Smith SP 1.25 3.00
45 Warren Spahn SP .75 2.00
46 Roberto Alomar SP .75 2.00
47 Torii Hunter SP .60 1.50
48 Roger Clemens SP 1.25 3.00
49 Hank Aaron SP 2.00 5.00
50 Tom Seaver SP .75 2.00

2016 Topps Gypsy Queen Framed Blue

*FRME BLUE: 1.5X TO 4X BASIC
*FRME BLUE RC: 1X TO 2.5X BASIC RC
RANDOM INSERTS IN RETAIL PACKS

2016 Topps Gypsy Queen Framed Green

*FRME GREEN: 3X TO 8X BASIC
*FRME GREEN RC: 2X TO 5X BASIC RC
STATED ODDS 1:73 HOBBY
STATED PRINT RUN 99 SER.#'d SETS
7 Corey Seager 12.00 30.00

2016 Topps Gypsy Queen Framed Purple

*FRME PURPLE: 2X TO 5X BASIC
*FRME PURPLE RC: 1.2X TO 3X BASIC RC
STATED ODDS 1:29 HOBBY
STATED PRINT RUN 250 SER.#'d SETS

2016 Topps Gypsy Queen Mini

*MINI 1-300: 1.2X TO 3X BASIC
*MINI 1-300 RC: .75X TO 2X BASIC
*MINI 301-350: .5X TO 1.2X BASIC
MINI SP ODDS 1:24 HOBBY
PRINTING PLATE ODDS 1:512 HOBBY
PLATE PRINT RUN 1 SET PER COLOR
NO PLATE PRICING DUE TO SCARCITY
343 Kenta Maeda SP 1.50 4.00

2016 Topps Gypsy Queen Mini Foil

*FOIL: .6X TO 1.5X BASIC
RANDOM INSERTS IN PACKS
343 Kenta Maeda 5.00 12.00

2016 Topps Gypsy Queen Mini Gold

*GOLD 1-300: 5X TO 12X BASIC
*GOLD 1-300 RC: 3X TO 8X BASIC
*GOLD 301-350: 1.5X TO 4X BASIC
STATED ODDS 1:41 HOBBY
STATED PRINT RUN 50 SER.#'d SETS
7 Corey Seager 15.00 40.00
90 Carlos Correa 15.00 40.00

2016 Topps Gypsy Queen Mini Green

*GREEN 1-300: 3X TO 8X BASIC
*GREEN 1-300 RC: 2X TO 5X BASIC
*GREEN 301-350: 1X TO 2.5X BASIC
RANDOM INSERTS IN PACKS
STATED PRINT RUN 99 SER.#'d SETS
343 Kenta Maeda 3.00 8.00

2016 Topps Gypsy Queen Mini Purple

*PURPLE 1-300: 2X TO 5X BASIC
*PURPLE 1-300 RC: 1.2X TO 3X BASIC
*PURPLE 301-350: .6X TO 1.5X BASIC
STATED ODDS 1:9 HOBBY
STATED PRINT RUN 250 SER.#'d SETS

2016 Topps Gypsy Queen Mini Variations

*MINI BOX VAR: 1.2X TO 3X BASIC
*MINI BOX VAR RC: .75X TO 2X BASIC RC
ONE MINI BOX PER HOBBY BOX
TEN CARDS PER MINI BOX
343 Kenta Maeda 1.25 3.00

2016 Topps Gypsy Queen Autographs

STATED ODDS 1:17 HOBBY
GQAAE Alcides Escobar 5.00 12.00
GQAAJ Andruw Jones 6.00 15.00
GQAAM Andrew Miller 6.00 15.00
GQAAN Aaron Nola 5.00 12.00
GQAAP A.J. Pollock 2.50 6.00
GQABJ Brian Johnson 2.50 6.00
GQACD Corey Dickerson 2.50 6.00
GQACDE Carlos Delgado 4.00 10.00
GQACE Carl Edwards Jr. 3.00 8.00
GQACK Corey Kluber 4.00 10.00
GQACS Corey Seager 30.00 80.00
GQADG Dee Gordon 10.00 25.00
GQADL DJ LeMahieu 8.00 20.00
GQAER Eduardo Rodriguez 4.00 10.00
GQAGB Greg Bird 3.00 8.00
GQAGH Greg Holland 6.00 15.00
GQAGS George Springer 6.00 15.00
GQAHO Henry Owens 3.00 8.00
GQAHOL Hector Olivera 6.00 15.00
GQAJFA Jeurys Familia 4.00 10.00
GQAJGR Jon Gray 2.50 6.00
GQAJP Jimmy Paredes 2.50 6.00
GQAKM Ketel Marte 5.00 12.00
GQAKMA Kenta Maeda 75.00 200.00
GQAKS Kyle Schwarber 15.00 40.00
GQALS Luis Severino 10.00 25.00
GQAMA Miguel Almonte 2.50 6.00
GQAMF Maikel Franco 3.00 8.00
GQAMK Max Kepler 6.00 15.00
GQAMSA Miguel Sano 6.00 15.00
GQAPO Peter O'Brien 2.50 6.00
GQARO Roberto Osuna 2.50 6.00
GQARR Rob Refsnyder 3.00 8.00
GQASM Steve Matz
GQASP Stephen Piscotty 4.00 10.00
GQATT Trea Turner 8.00 20.00
GQAVC Vinny Castilla 2.50 6.00
GQAWD Wade Davis 2.50 6.00
GQAYG Yasmani Grandal 5.00 12.00
GQAZL Zach Lee 2.50 6.00

2016 Topps Gypsy Queen Autographs Gold

*GOLD: .6X TO 1.5X BASIC
STATED ODDS 1:183 HOBBY
STATED PRINT RUN 50 SER.#'d SETS
GQABBU Byron Buxton 20.00 50.00
GQAJS Jorge Soler 10.00 25.00
GQAMC Michael Conforto 40.00 100.00
GQANS Noah Syndergaard 30.00 80.00
GQASG Sonny Gray 8.00 20.00

2016 Topps Gypsy Queen Autographs Green

*GREEN: .5X TO 1.2X BASIC
STATED ODDS 1:101 HOBBY
STATED PRINT RUN 99 SER.#'d SETS
GQAJPE Joc Pederson 4.00 10.00
GQAJS Jorge Soler 8.00 20.00
GQAMC Michael Conforto 30.00 80.00
GQANS Noah Syndergaard 25.00 60.00
GQASG Sonny Gray 6.00 15.00
GQASM Steven Matz 4.00 10.00

2016 Topps Gypsy Queen Glove Stories

COMPLETE SET (10) 3.00 8.00
STATED ODDS 1:6 HOBBY
PRINTING PLATE ODDS 1:17,589 HOBBY
PLATE PRINT RUN 1 SET PER COLOR
NO PLATE PRICING DUE TO SCARCITY
GS1 Mike Trout 2.50 6.00
GS2 Nolan Arenado .60 1.50
GS3 Kevin Kiermaier .40 1.00
GS4 Juan Perez .30 .75
GS5 Kevin Pillar .30 .75
GS6 Billy Burns .30 .75
GS7 Mookie Betts .75 2.00
GS8 George Springer .40 1.00
GS9 Freddy Galvis .30 .75
GS10 Joey Votto .50 1.25

2016 Topps Gypsy Queen Mini Autographs

STATED ODDS 1:22 MINI BOX
STATED PRINT RUN 25 SER.#'d SETS
GMAAN Aaron Nola 20.00 50.00
GMABB Byron Buxton 30.00 80.00
GMABJ Brian Johnson 6.00 15.00
GMACK Corey Kluber 10.00 25.00
GMACS Corey Seager 100.00 200.00
GMADE Dennis Eckersley 20.00 50.00
GMAER Eduardo Rodriguez 6.00 15.00
GMAFF Freddie Freeman 30.00 80.00
GMAHO Henry Owens 12.00 30.00
GMAHOL Hector Olivera 15.00 40.00
GMAJD Jacob deGrom 25.00 60.00
GMAJG Jon Gray
GMAJP Joc Pederson 20.00 50.00
GMAJS Jorge Soler 15.00 40.00
GMAKB Kris Bryant 200.00 300.00
GMAKS Kyle Schwarber 50.00 120.00
GMALS Luis Severino 20.00 50.00
GMAMH Matt Harvey 30.00 80.00
GMAMM Manny Machado 125.00 250.00
GMAMS Miguel Sano 40.00 100.00
GMAMSC Max Scherzer 30.00 80.00
GMANS Noah Syndergaard 50.00 120.00
GMARR Rob Refsnyder 15.00 40.00
GMASM Steven Matz 30.00 80.00
GMASP Stephen Piscotty 25.00 60.00
GMATT Trea Turner 15.00 40.00

2016 Topps Gypsy Queen Mini Patch Autograph Booklets

STATED ODDS 1:27 MINI BOX
PRINT RUNS B/WN 20-30 COPIES PER
MAPAJ Andruw Jones/20 40.00 100.00
MAPBH Bryce Harper/20 250.00 400.00
MAPCK Corey Kluber/30 15.00 40.00
MAPCS Chris Sale/30 30.00 00.00
MAPDP Dustin Pedroia/20 60.00 150.00
MAPFF Freddie Freeman/30 60.00 150.00
MAPFT Frank Thomas/20 100.00 200.00
MAPJP Joc Pederson/20 30.00 80.00
MAPMF Maikel Franco/30 40.00 100.00
MAPMM Manny Machado/30 60.00 150.00
MAPMP Mike Piazza/30 75.00 200.00
MAPMT Mike Trout/20 250.00 400.00
MAPNS Noah Syndergaard/20 150.00 250.00
MAPRC Roger Clemens/20 60.00 150.00
MAPSM Starling Marte/30 40.00 100.00
MAPTW Taijuan Walker/30 25.00 60.00

2016 Topps Gypsy Queen Mini Relics

STATED ODDS 1:31 HOBBY
*GOLD/50: .6X TO 1.5X BASIC
GMRAP Albert Pujols 5.00 12.00
GMRAR Anthony Rizzo 6.00 15.00
GMRBP Buster Posey 5.00 12.00
GMRCB Craig Biggio 3.00 8.00
GMRCE Carl Edwards Jr. 3.00 8.00
GMRCJ Chipper Jones 5.00 12.00
GMRCK Corey Kluber 3.00 8.00
GMRCKE Clayton Kershaw 8.00 20.00
GMRCR Cal Ripken Jr. 10.00 25.00
GMRCSA Chris Sale 4.00 10.00
GMRCSE Corey Seager 8.00 20.00
GMRDO David Ortiz 4.00 10.00
GMREL Evan Longoria 3.00 8.00
GMRFM Frankie Montas 3.00 8.00
GMRFT Frank Thomas 5.00 12.00
GMRGC Gerrit Cole 4.00 10.00
GMRGS Gary Sanchez 8.00 20.00
GMRJBA Javier Baez 5.00 12.00
GMRJD Johnny Damon 3.00 8.00
GMRJDG Jacob deGrom 4.00 10.00
GMRJF Jose Fernandez 4.00 10.00
GMRJS John Smoltz 5.00 12.00
GMRJV Joey Votto 4.00 10.00
GMRKG Ken Griffey Jr. 10.00 25.00
GMRKM Ketel Marte 5.00 12.00
GMRMBE Mookie Betts 6.00 15.00
GMRMCA Miguel Cabrera 4.00 10.00
GMRMMA Manny Machado 5.00 12.00
GMRMMG Mark McGwire 10.00 25.00
GMRMP Mike Piazza 5.00 12.00
GMRMTA Masahiro Tanaka 3.00 8.00
GMRMTR Mike Trout 20.00 50.00
GMROS Ozzie Smith 5.00 12.00
GMRPG Paul Goldschmidt 4.00 10.00
GMRPO Peter O'Brien 2.50 6.00
GMRRCA Robinson Cano 3.00 8.00
GMRRCL Roger Clemens 5.00 12.00
GMRRH Rickey Henderson 4.00 10.00
GMRRJA Reggie Jackson 5.00 12.00
GMRRJO Randy Johnson 4.00 10.00
GMRSM Starling Marte 3.00 8.00
GMRSMI Shelby Miller 3.00 8.00
GMRWM Willie Mays 20.00 50.00
GMRXB Xander Bogaerts 4.00 10.00
GMRYM Yadier Molina 6.00 15.00

2016 Topps Gypsy Queen MVP Minis

COMPLETE SET (25) 8.00 20.00
STATED ODDS 1:8 HOBBY
PRINTING PLATE ODDS 1:7196 HOBBY
PLATE PRINT RUN 1 SET PER COLOR
NO PLATE PRICING DUE TO SCARCITY
MVPMBE Johnny Bench .60 1.50
MVPMBH Bryce Harper 1.00 2.50
MVPMBL Barry Larkin .50 1.25
MVPMBP Buster Posey .75 2.00
MVPMBR Babe Ruth 1.50 4.00
MVPMCJ Chipper Jones .60 1.50
MVPMCK Clayton Kershaw 1.25 3.00
MVPMCR Cal Ripken Jr. 2.00 5.00
MVPMCY Carl Yastrzemski 1.00 2.50
MVPMDE Dennis Eckersley .50 1.25
MVPMDP Dustin Pedroia .60 1.50
MVPMFR Frank Robinson .50 1.25
MVPMFT Frank Thomas .60 1.50
MVPMHA Hank Aaron 1.25 3.00
MVPMJB Jeff Bagwell .50 1.25
MVPMJR Jackie Robinson .60 1.50
MVPMLG Lou Gehrig 1.25 3.00
MVPMMT Mike Trout 3.00 8.00
MVPMRC Roger Clemens .75 2.00
MVPMRJ Reggie Jackson .50 1.25
MVPMSK Sandy Koufax 1.25 3.00
MVPMSM Stan Musial 1.00 2.50
MVPMTC Ty Cobb 1.00 2.50
MVPMTW Ted Williams 1.25 3.00
MVPMWM Willie Mays 1.25 3.00

2016 Topps Gypsy Queen MVP Minis Autographs

STATED ODDS 1:2111 HOBBY
PRINT RUNS B/WN 15-25 COPIES PER
MVPABL Barry Larkin/25 25.00 60.00
MVPABP Buster Posey/15
MVPACJ Chipper Jones/15 125.00 250.00
MVPACK Clayton Kershaw/25 150.00 250.00
MVPACR Cal Ripken Jr./15
MVPADE Dennis Eckersley/25 20.00 50.00
MVPAFR Frank Robinson/25 100.00 200.00
MVPAFT Frank Thomas/25 60.00 150.00
MVPAJB Jeff Bagwell/25 40.00 100.00
MVPAJBE Johnny Bench/15 60.00 150.00
MVPAJR Jim Rice/25 20.00 50.00
MVPAMT Mike Trout/15 300.00 500.00
MVPARB Ryan Braun/25 25.00 60.00
MVPARC Roger Clemens/15 30.00 80.00
MVPARJ Reggie Jackson/15
MVPASK Sandy Koufax/15
MVPAVG Vladimir Guerrero/25 15.00 40.00

2016 Topps Gypsy Queen Power Alley

COMPLETE SET (30) 6.00 15.00
STATED ODDS 1:4 HOBBY
PRINTING PLATE ODDS 1:5974 HOBBY
PLATE PRINT RUN 1 SET PER COLOR
NO PLATE PRICING DUE TO SCARCITY
PA1 Willie Mays 1.00 2.50
PA2 Ted Williams 1.00 2.50
PA3 Jose Canseco .40 1.00
PA4 Frank Thomas .50 1.25
PA5 Carlos Delgado .30 .75
PA6 Chipper Jones .50 1.25
PA7 Dave Winfield .40 1.00
PA8 Alex Rodriguez .60 1.50
PA9 Frank Robinson .40 1.00
PA10 Andre Dawson .40 1.00
PA11 Reggie Jackson .40 1.00
PA12 Willie Stargell .40 1.00
PA13 Stan Musial .75 2.00
PA14 Eddie Mathews .50 1.25
PA15 Fred McGriff .40 1.00
PA16 Lou Gehrig 1.00 2.50
PA17 Babe Ruth 1.25 3.00
PA18 Ken Griffey Jr. 1.00 2.50
PA19 David Ortiz .50 1.25
PA20 Vladimir Guerrero .40 1.00
PA21 Mark McGwire .75 2.00
PA22 Harmon Killebrew .50 1.25
PA23 Willie McCovey .40 1.00
PA24 Rafael Palmeiro .40 1.00
PA25 Eddie Murray .40 1.00
PA26 Albert Pujols .60 1.50
PA27 Hank Aaron 1.00 2.50
PA28 Jeff Bagwell .40 1.00
PA29 Carl Yastrzemski .75 2.00
PA30 Andres Galarraga .40 1.00

2016 Topps Gypsy Queen Relic Autographs

STATED ODDS 1:266 HOBBY
STATED PRINT RUN 50 SER.#'d SETS
GQARBB Brandon Belt 20.00 50.00
GQARBM Brandon Moss 15.00 40.00
GQARBS Blake Swihart 10.00 25.00
GQARCB Craig Biggio 15.00 40.00
GQARCS Chris Sale 12.00 30.00
GQARDG Dee Gordon 8.00 20.00
GQARFL Francisco Lindor 20.00 50.00
GQARGH Greg Holland 8.00 20.00
GQARJA Jose Altuve 25.00 60.00
GQARJC Jose Canseco 20.00 50.00
GQARJH Josh Harrison 8.00 20.00
GQARJPE Joc Pederson 10.00 25.00
GQARJS Jorge Soler 12.00 30.00
GQARKB Kris Bryant 125.00 250.00
GQARKW Kolten Wong 10.00 25.00
GQARMC Matt Carpenter 10.00 25.00
GQARMF Maikel Franco 15.00 40.00
GQARMH Matt Harvey 30.00 80.00
GQARNS Noah Syndergaard 30.00 80.00
GQARRO Roberto Osuna 8.00 20.00
GQARSM Starling Marte 20.00 50.00
GQARTW Taijuan Walker 12.00 30.00
GQARYG Yasmani Grandal 8.00 20.00
GQARZW Zack Wheeler 10.00 25.00

2016 Topps Gypsy Queen Relics

STATED ODDS 1:25 HOBBY
GQRAP Albert Pujols 4.00 10.00
GQRBP Buster Posey 4.00 10.00
GQRCB Craig Biggio 2.50 6.00
GQRCJ Chipper Jones 3.00 8.00
GQRCK Clayton Kershaw 6.00 15.00
GQRCR Cal Ripken Jr. 5.00 12.00
GQRDO David Ortiz 3.00 8.00
GQRDW David Wright 2.50 6.00
GQREL Evan Longoria 2.50 6.00
GQRFT Frank Thomas 3.00 8.00
GQRGC Gerrit Cole 3.00 8.00
GQRGS Gary Sanchez 6.00 15.00
GQRJD Jacob deGrom 3.00 8.00
GQRJG Joey Gallo 2.50 6.00
GQRJK Jason Kipnis 2.50 6.00
GQRJM J.D. Martinez 3.00 8.00
GQRKG Ken Griffey Jr. 5.00 12.00
GQRKM Ketel Marte 4.00 10.00
GQRMH Matt Harvey 2.50 6.00
GQRMP Michael Pineda 2.00 5.00
GQROS Ozzie Smith 4.00 10.00
GQRPG Paul Goldschmidt 3.00 8.00
GQRPO Peter O'Brien 2.00 5.00
GQRRH Rickey Henderson 4.00 10.00
GQRRJ Reggie Jackson 3.00 8.00
GQRSM Steven Matz 2.50 6.00
GQRTH Torii Hunter 2.00 5.00
GQRTW Taijuan Walker 2.00 5.00
GQRXB Xander Bogaerts 3.00 8.00
GQRYP Yasiel Puig 3.00 8.00
GQRARE Anthony Rendon 3.00 8.00
GQRARI Anthony Rizzo 5.00 12.00
GQRCSA Chris Sale 3.00 8.00
GQRCSE Corey Seager 5.00 12.00
GQRJFE Jose Fernandez 3.00 8.00
GQRJHK Jung Ho Kang 2.00 5.00
GQRJSM John Smoltz 3.00 8.00
GQRJSO Jorge Soler 3.00 8.00
GQRMBE Mookie Betts 5.00 12.00
GQRMCA Miguel Cabrera 3.00 8.00
GQRMCR Matt Carpenter 3.00 8.00
GQRMMA Manny Machado 3.00 8.00
GQRMMC Mark McGwire 5.00 12.00
GQRMMO Mike Moustakas 2.50 6.00
GQRMPI Mike Piazza 3.00 8.00
GQRMTA Masahiro Tanaka 2.50 6.00
GQRMTR Mike Trout 8.00 20.00
GQRRCA Robinson Cano 2.50 6.00
GQRRCL Roger Clemens 4.00 10.00
GQRRCS Rusney Castillo 2.00 5.00
GQRRJO Randy Johnson 3.00 8.00

2016 Topps Gypsy Queen Relics Gold

*GOLD: .6X TO 1.5X BASIC
STATED ODDS 1:221 HOBBY
STATED PRINT RUN 50 SER.#'d SETS
GQRCR Cal Ripken Jr. 20.00 50.00
GQRFT Frank Thomas 12.00 30.00
GQRKG Ken Griffey Jr. 20.00 50.00
GQROS Ozzie Smith 12.00 30.00
GQRCSE Corey Seager 12.00 30.00
GQRMCA Miguel Cabrera 10.00 25.00
GQRMMC Mark McGwire 12.00 30.00
GQRMTR Mike Trout 20.00 50.00

2016 Topps Gypsy Queen Walk Off Winners

COMPLETE SET (10) 3.00 8.00
STATED ODDS 1:6 HOBBY
PRINTING PLATE ODDS 1:17,589 HOBBY
PLATE PRINT RUN 1 SET PER COLOR
NO PLATE PRICING DUE TO SCARCITY
GWO1 Eric Hosmer .40 1.00
GWO2 Manny Machado .50 1.25
GWO3 Andruw Jones .30 .75
GWO4 Jackie Robinson .50 1.25
GWO5 Josh Donaldson .40 1.00
GWO6 Starling Marte .40 1.00
GWO7 Wilmer Flores .40 1.00
GWO8 Omar Vizquel .40 1.00
GWO9 Mike Trout 2.50 6.00
GWO10 Kris Bryant .60 1.50

2017 Topps Gypsy Queen

COMP.SET w/SP (320) 75.00 200.00
COMP.SET w/o SP's (300) 20.00 50.00
SP ODDS 1:24 HOBBY
CAPLESS ODDS 1:158 HOBBY
THRWBCK ODDS 1:420 HOBBY
GUM BACK ODDS 1:629 HOBBY
1A Kris Bryant .40 1.00
1B Bryant SP No Cap 6.00 15.00
1C Kris Bryant SP TB 8.00 20.00
1D Kris Bryant SP VAR Gum back
2 Edwin Diaz .25 .60
3 Marcus Semien .20 .50
4 Jorge Alfaro RC .40 1.00
5 Adrian Gonzalez .25 .60
6 Bartolo Colon .20 .50
7 Stephen Strasburg .30 .75
8 Carlos Martinez .25 .60
9 Matt Harvey .25 .60
10A Miguel Cabrera .30 .75
10B Cabrera SP No Cap 5.00 12.00
10C Miguel Cabrera SP GB 5.00 12.00
11 Jordan Zimmermann .25 .60
12 Greg Bird .25 .60
13 Taijuan Walker .20 .50
14 Matt Olson RC .50 1.25
15 Danny Valencia .25 .60
16 Trea Turner .25 .60
17 Dexter Fowler .25 .60
18 Kendall Graveman .20 .50
19A David Dahl RC .40 1.00
19B Dahl SP No Cap 4.00 10.00
20 Zack Greinke .25 .60
21 Braden Shipley RC .30 .75
22 Yulieski Gurriel RC .50 1.25
23 Blake Snell .25 .60
24 Adam Ottavino .20 .50
25 Michael Fulmer .20 .50
26 Alex Gordon .25 .60
27 Roberto Osuna .20 .50
28 Odubel Herrera .25 .60
29 JaCoby Jones RC .40 1.00
30 Jonathan Schoop .20 .50
31 Brandon Phillips .20 .50
32 Johnny Cueto .25 .60
33 Tom Murphy .20 .50
34 Rick Porcello .25 .60
35 Jim Johnson .20 .50
36 Hisashi Iwakuma .25 .60
37 Alex Reyes RC .40 1.00
38 David Robertson .20 .50
39 Jacoby Ellsbury .25 .60
40 Nomar Mazara .20 .50
41 A.J. Ramos .20 .50
42 J.D. Martinez .30 .75
43 Manny Margot RC .30 .75
44 Kirk Nieuwenhuis .20 .50
45 Chris Carter .20 .50
46 Brandon Belt .25 .60
47 Yangervis Solarte .20 .50
48 Hunter Renfroe RC .40 1.00
49 Kevin Gausman .20 .50
50A Anthony Rizzo .50 1.25
50B Rizzo SP No Cap 8.00 20.00
51 Kevin Kiermaier .25 .60
52 Jose Bautista .25 .60
53 Jace Peterson .20 .50
54 Starlin Castro .20 .50
55 Corey Dickerson .20 .50
56 Yasmani Grandal .20 .50
57 Jean Segura .25 .60
58 Jung Ho Kang .20 .50
59 Kenley Jansen .25 .60
60 Jameson Taillon .25 .60
61 Kyle Hendricks .30 .75
62 Mark Trumbo .20 .50
63 Madison Bumgarner .25 .60
64 Khris Davis .30 .75
65 Matt Strahm RC .30 .75
66 Justin Upton .25 .60
67 Trevor Story .30 .75
68 Alcides Escobar .25 .60
69 Randal Grichuk .20 .50
70 Leonys Martin .20 .50
71 Huston Street .20 .50
72 Cameron Rupp .20 .50
73 Brett Gardner .25 .60
74A Carlos Correa .30 .75
74B Correa SP No Cap 5.00 12.00
74C Carlos Correa SP GB 5.00 12.00
75A Clayton Kershaw .60 1.50
75B Kershaw SP No Cap 10.00 25.00
75C Clayton Kershaw SP GB 10.00 25.00
76 Scott Kazmir .20 .50
77 Gary Sanchez .30 .75
78 Robert Gsellman RC .30 .75
79 Nelson Cruz .30 .75
80 Scooter Gennett .25 .60
81 Starling Marte .25 .60
82 Brad Ziegler .20 .50
83 Tyler Austin RC .50 1.25
84 Ender Inciarte .30 .75
85 Raimel Tapia RC .40 1.00
86 Chris Archer .20 .50
87 Jake Lamb .25 .60
88 Ian Kennedy .20 .50
89 Yu Darvish .30 .75
90 Justin Turner .25 .60
91A Dansby Swanson RC .75 2.00
91B Swanson SP No Cap 10.00 25.00
92 Vince Velasquez .20 .50
93 Ichiro .40 1.00
94 Ryan Schimpf .20 .50
95 Carlos Rodon .25 .60
96 Daniel Murphy .25 .60
97 Gavin Cecchini RC .30 .75
98 Adam Wainwright .25 .60
99 Brandon Crawford .25 .60
100A Mookie Betts .50 1.25
100B Betts SP No Cap 8.00 20.00
100C Mookie Betts SP TB 10.00 25.00
101 Seth Lugo RC .30 .75
102 Albert Pujols .40 1.00
103 Mitch Moreland .20 .50
104 Jeanmar Gomez .20 .50
105A Andrew McCutchen .30 .75
105B McCutchen SP TB 6.00 15.00
106 Hunter Dozier RC .30 .75
107 Tim Anderson .30 .75
108 Giancarlo Stanton .30 .75
109 Dan Straily .20 .50
110 David Paulino RC .40 1.00
111 Freddie Freeman .40 1.00
112 Paul Goldschmidt .30 .75
113 Edwin Encarnacion .30 .75
114 Carlos Carrasco .20 .50
115 Byron Buxton .25 .60
116 Robbie Ray .20 .50
117 Jonathan Villar .20 .50
118 Wade Davis .20 .50
119 Kendrys Morales .20 .50
120 Jered Weaver .25 .60
121A Jacob deGrom .30 .75
121B deGrom SP No Cap 8.00 20.00
121C Jacob deGrom SP TB 6.00 15.00
122 Dee Gordon .20 .50
123 Jerad Eickhoff .20 .50
124 Buster Posey .40 1.00
125 Francisco Cervelli .20 .50
126 Justin Verlander .30 .75
127 Yoenis Cespedes .30 .75
128 Reynaldo Lopez RC .30 .75
129 Mike Napoli .20 .50
130 Chris Tillman .20 .50
131 Mark Melancon .20 .50
132 Teoscar Hernandez RC 1.00 2.50
133 Seung-hwan Oh .40 1.00
134 Chad Pinder RC .30 .75
135 Jeurys Familia .25 .60
136 Kyle Seager .20 .50
137 David Price .25 .60
138 Matt Moore .25 .60
139 Curtis Granderson .25 .60
140 Craig Kimbrel .25 .60
141 Adonis Garcia .20 .50
142 Todd Frazier .25 .60
143 Jimmy Nelson .20 .50
144A Francisco Lindor .30 .75
144B Lindor SP No Cap 5.00 12.00
144C Francisco Lindor SP TB 6.00 15.00
144D Francisco Lindor SP GB 5.00 12.00
145 Zack Cozart .20 .50
146 Ricky Nolasco .20 .50
147 Jose Berrios .25 .60
148 Aledmys Diaz .25 .60
149 Matt Holliday .30 .75
150A Corey Seager .30 .75
150B Seager SP No Cap 5.00 12.00
150C Corey Seager SP GB 12.00 30.00
151 Danny Duffy .20 .50
152 Wilson Ramos .20 .50
153 Logan Forsythe .20 .50
154A Manny Machado .30 .75
154B Manny Machado SP Thowback
155 Max Kepler .25 .60
156 Marcus Stroman .25 .60
157 Jason Kipnis .25 .60
158 Hanley Ramirez .25 .60
159 Matt Kemp .25 .60
160 Josh Donaldson .25 .60
161A Wil Myers .20 .50
161B Wil Myers SP TB 4.00 10.00
162 A.J. Pollock .20 .50
163 Renato Nunez RC .60 1.50
164 Ryon Healy RC .40 1.00
165 J.A. Happ .25 .60
166 Joe Mauer .25 .60
167 Jackie Bradley Jr. .30 .75
168A Aaron Judge RC 4.00 10.00
168B Judge SP No Cap 30.00 80.00
169 Stephen Vogt .25 .60
170 Stephen Piscotty .25 .60
171A Bryce Harper .50 1.25
171B Harper SP No Cap 8.00 20.00
171C Bryce Harper SP TB 10.00 25.00
171D Bryce Harper SP GB 15.00 40.00
172 Jon Gray .20 .50
173 Zach Britton .25 .60
174 Evan Longoria .25 .60
175 Gregory Polanco .25 .60
176 Carson Fulmer RC .30 .75
177A Xander Bogaerts .30 .75
177B Bogaerts SP No Cap 8.00 20.00
177C Xander Bogaerts SP TB 6.00 15.00
178 Dallas Keuchel .25 .60
179 Martin Prado .20 .50
180 Tanner Roark .20 .50
181 Sean Manaea .20 .50
182 Sam Dyson .20 .50
183 George Springer .25 .60
184 Austin Hedges .20 .50
185 Francisco Rodriguez .25 .60
186 Matt Wieters .30 .75
187 Kenta Maeda .25 .60
188 Anthony DeSclafani .20 .50
189 Felix Hernandez .25 .60
190 Miguel Sano .25 .60
191 Marcell Ozuna .30 .75
192 Christian Yelich .40 1.00
193 Joe Musgrove RC .30 .75
194A Joey Votto .30 .75
194B Joey Votto SP TB 6.00 15.00

195 Sonny Gray .25 .60
196 Russell Martin .20 .50
197 Luis Perdomo .20 .50
198A Noah Syndergaard .25 .60
198B Syndergaard SP No Cap 4.00 10.00
198C Syndergaard SP TB 5.00 12.00
199 Jose Quintana .20 .50
200A Mike Trout 1.50 4.00
200B Trout SP No Cap 25.00 60.00
200C Mike Trout SP TB 30.00 80.00
200D Mike Trout SP GB 25.00 60.00
201 Ben Zobrist .25 .60
202 Welington Castillo .20 .50
203 Jharel Cotton RC .30 .75
204 Carlos Gonzalez .25 .60
205 Alex Dickerson .20 .50
206 Dustin Pedroia .30 .75
207 Jeremy Hellickson .20 .50
208 Billy Hamilton .25 .60
209 Hunter Pence .25 .60
210 Adam Jones .25 .60
211 Travis Jankowski .20 .50
212 Masahiro Tanaka .25 .60
213 Elvis Andrus .25 .60
214 Corey Kluber .25 .60
215 Bruce Maxwell RC .30 .75
216 Aaron Sanchez .25 .60
217 Josh Harrison .20 .50
218 Ken Giles .20 .50
219A Lorenzo Cain .20 .50
219B Lorenzo Cain SP TB 4.00 10.00
220 Maikel Franco .25 .60
221 Rob Segedin RC .30 .75
222 Evan Gattis .20 .50
223 Troy Tulowitzki .30 .75
224 Matt Carpenter .30 .75
225 Jose De Leon RC .30 .75
226 Eric Hosmer .25 .60
227 Jeff Samardzija .20 .50
228 Andrew Miller .25 .60
229 Julio Teheran .25 .60
230 Aroldis Chapman .30 .75
231 Yadier Molina .30 .75
232 Justin Bour .25 .60
233 Adam Duvall .30 .75
234 Andrelton Simmons .20 .50
235A Jake Arrieta .25 .60
235B Jake Arrieta SP GB 4.00 10.00
236 Nick Markakis .25 .60
237 Jon Lester .25 .60
238 Tyler Naquin .20 .50
239 Asdrubal Cabrera .25 .60
240A Alex Bregman RC 1.25 3.00
240B Alex Bregman SP GB 12.00 30.00
241 Josh Bell RC .75 2.00
242 Chris Davis .20 .50
243A Chris Sale .30 .75
243B Sale SP No Cap 5.00 12.00
244 Ian Desmond .20 .50
245 DJ LeMahieu .30 .75
246 Kole Calhoun .20 .50
247 Charlie Blackmon .30 .75
248 Gerrit Cole .30 .75
249 Luke Weaver RC .40 1.00
250A Yoan Moncada RC 1.00 2.50
250B Moncada SP No Cap 10.00 25.00
251 Pat Neshek .20 .50
252A Nolan Arenado .40 1.00
252B Arenado SP No Cap 6.00 15.00
253 C.J. Cron .20 .50
254 Danny Salazar .25 .60
255 Matt Wisler .20 .50
256 Cole Hamels .25 .60
257 Addison Russell .30 .75
258 Ervin Santana .20 .50
259 Rougned Odor .25 .60
260 Trey Mancini RC .60 1.50
261 Jose Iglesias .25 .60
262 Robinson Cano .25 .60
263 Colin Rea .20 .50
264A Adrian Beltre .30 .75
264B Adrian Beltre SP TB 6.00 15.00
265 Eugenio Suarez .25 .60
266 Yunel Escobar .20 .50
267 Zach Davies .20 .50
268 Joe Panik .25 .60
269 Brian Dozier .30 .75
270 Tyler Thornburg .20 .50
271 Colby Rasmus .20 .50
272 Robbie Grossman .20 .50
273 Ian Kinsler .25 .60
274 Jake Odorizzi .20 .50
275 Dellin Betances .25 .60
276 Tyler Glasnow RC .40 1.00
277 Salvador Perez .25 .60
278 Alex Colome .20 .50
279 Ryan Braun .25 .60
280 Joc Pederson .25 .60
281 Steven Matz .25 .60
282 Andrew Benintendi RC 1.00 2.50
283 Lance McCullers .20 .50
284 Tommy Joseph .30 .75
285 Kirby Yates .25 .60
286 Roman Quinn RC .30 .75
287 Tony Watson .20 .50
288 Jeff Hoffman RC .30 .75
289A Max Scherzer .30 .75
289B Scherzer SP No Cap 5.00 12.00
290 Yonder Alonso .20 .50
291 Didi Gregorius .25 .60
292 Ryan Zimmerman .25 .60
293 Carlos Santana .25 .60
294 Melky Cabrera .20 .50
295 Yasmany Tomas .20 .50
296 Jose Abreu .30 .75
297 Adam Lind .25 .60
298 Jose Altuve .25 .60
299A Orlando Arcia RC .50 1.25
299B Orlando Arcia SP TB 6.00 15.00
300 David Ortiz .30 .75
301 Babe Ruth SP 4.00 10.00
302 Ryne Sandberg SP 3.00 8.00
303 Derek Jeter SP 4.00 10.00
304 Mike Piazza SP 1.50 4.00
305 Whitey Ford SP 1.25 3.00
306 Ken Griffey Jr. SP 3.00 8.00
307 Randy Johnson SP 1.50 4.00
308 Jackie Robinson SP 1.50 4.00
309 Andy Pettitte SP 1.25 3.00
310 Lou Gehrig SP 3.00 8.00
311 Ozzie Smith SP 2.00 5.00
312 Mark McGwire SP 2.50 6.00
313 Ty Cobb SP 2.50 6.00
314 Hank Aaron SP 3.00 8.00
315 Rod Carew SP 1.25 3.00
316 Ivan Rodriguez SP 1.25 3.00
317 Jim Palmer SP 1.25 3.00
318 George Brett SP 3.00 8.00
319 Phil Rizzuto SP 1.25 3.00
320 Sandy Koufax SP 3.00 8.00

2017 Topps Gypsy Queen Black and White

*BLACK WHITE: 5X TO 12X BASIC
*BLACK WHITE RC: 3X TO 8X BASIC RC
STATED ODDS 1:31 HOBBY
STATED PRINT RUN 50 SER.#'d SETS
1A Kris Bryant 20.00 50.00
200 Mike Trout 20.00 50.00

2017 Topps Gypsy Queen Green

*GREEN: 1.5X TO 4X BASIC
*GREEN RC: 1X TO 2.5X BASIC RC
*GREEN SP: .75X TO 2X BASIC SP
*GREEN CL: .5X TO 1.2X BASE CL
*GREEN TB: .3X TO .8X BASE TB
INSERTED IN RETAIL PACKS
SP/CL/TB ALL SERIAL #'d/99

2017 Topps Gypsy Queen Green Back

*GREEN BCK: 5X TO 12X BASIC
*GREEN BCK RC: 3X TO 8X BASIC RC
*GREEN BCK SP: X TO X BASIC SP
STATED ODDS 1:63 HOBBY
SP ODDS 1:943 HOBBY
ANNCD PRINT RUN 50 COPIES PER

2017 Topps Gypsy Queen Missing Blackplate

*NO BLACK: 2X TO 5X BASIC
*NO BLACK RC: 1.2X TO 3X BASIC RC
*NO BLACK SP: X TO X BASIC SP
*NO BLACK CL: X TO X BASE CL
*NO BLACK TB: X TO X BASE TB
*NO BLACK GB: X TO X BASE GB
STATED ODDS 1:9 HOBBY
SP ODDS 1:135 HOBBY
CAPLESS ODDS 1:315 HOBBY
THROWBACK ODDS 1:629 HOBBY
GUM BACK ODDS 1:943 HOBBY
282 Andrew Benintendi 10.00 25.00

2017 Topps Gypsy Queen Missing Nameplate

*NO NAME: 3X TO 8X BASIC
*NO NAME RC: 2X TO 5X BASIC RC
*NO NAME SP: X TO X BASIC SP
STATED ODDS 1:21 HOBBY
SP ODDS 1:315 HOBBY
282 Andrew Benintendi 15.00 40.00

2017 Topps Gypsy Queen Purple

*PURPLE: 2.5X TO 6X BASIC
*PURPLE RC: 1.5X TO 4X BASIC RC
STATED ODDS 1:13 HOBBY
STATED PRINT RUN 250 SER.#'d SETS
282 Andrew Benintendi 12.00 30.00

2017 Topps Gypsy Queen Autograph Garments

STATED ODDS 1:486 HOBBY
STATED PRINT RUN 50 SER.#'d SETS
EXCHANGE DEADLINE 2/28/2019
AGAR Anthony Rizzo 50.00 120.00
AGBH Bryce Harper 100.00 250.00
AGCC Carlos Correa 40.00 100.00
AGCS Chris Sale 10.00 25.00
AGDE Dennis Eckersley 12.00 30.00
AGDG Didi Gregorius 20.00 50.00
AGFL Francisco Lindor 60.00 150.00
AGHO Henry Owens 8.00 20.00
AGJA Jose Altuve 25.00 60.00
AGJC Jose Canseco 25.00 60.00
AGJD Jacob deGrom 20.00 50.00
AGJG Juan Gonzalez 15.00 40.00
AGJM J.D. Martinez 12.00 30.00
AGJP Joe Panik 10.00 25.00
AGJS John Smoltz 25.00 60.00
AGKB Kris Bryant 60.00 150.00
AGKK Kevin Kiermaier 10.00 25.00
AGMS Miguel Sano 12.00 30.00
AGNS Noah Syndergaard 30.00 80.00
AGSMA Steven Matz 15.00 40.00
AGWC Willson Contreras 40.00 100.00

2017 Topps Gypsy Queen Autograph Patch Booklet

STATED ODDS 1:1686 HOBBY
STATED PRINT RUN 20 SER.#'d SETS
EXCHANGE DEADLINE 2/28/2019
APBAR Anthony Rizzo 200.00 400.00
APBCC Carlos Correa 150.00 300.00
APBDG Didi Gregorius 60.00 150.00
APBFL Francisco Lindor 200.00 400.00
APBIR Ivan Rodriguez 60.00 150.00
APBJD Jacob deGrom 125.00 250.00
APBJM J.D. Martinez
APBJP Joe Panik 150.00 250.00
APBJS John Smoltz 75.00 200.00
APBKB Kris Bryant
APBKK Kevin Kiermaier 60.00 150.00
APBMS Miguel Sano 60.00 150.00
APBMST Marcus Stroman 75.00 200.00
APBNS Noah Syndergaard
APBSMA Steven Matz 60.00 150.00

2017 Topps Gypsy Queen Autographs

STATED ODDS 1:19 HOBBY
EXCHANGE DEADLINE 2/28/2019
*PURPLE/150: .5X TO 1.2X BASIC
*BW/99: .6X TO 1.5X BASIC
*NO BLACK: .6X TO 1.5X BASIC
*NO NAME: .75X TO 2X BASIC
GQAAB Alex Bregman 15.00 40.00
GQAABE Andrew Benintendi 25.00 60.00
GQAAC Adam Conley 2.50 6.00
GQAAJ Aaron Judge 100.00 250.00
GQAAR Alex Reyes 3.00 8.00
GQABB Barry Bonds
GQABH Bryce Harper 100.00 250.00
GQABS Blake Snell 6.00 15.00
GQABSH Braden Shipley 2.50 6.00
GQACC Carlos Correa 30.00 80.00
GQACJ Chipper Jones 60.00 150.00
GQACP Chad Pinder 2.50 6.00
GQACR Cal Ripken Jr. 60.00 150.00
GQACRE Cody Reed 2.50 6.00
GQACRO Carlos Rodon 3.00 8.00
GQACSE Corey Seager 25.00 60.00
GQADD David Dahl 5.00 12.00
GQADDU Danny Duffy 4.00 10.00
GQADF Dexter Fowler 8.00 20.00
GQADJ Derek Jeter
GQADS Dansby Swanson 12.00 30.00
GQAFL Francisco Lindor 15.00 40.00
GQAHO Henry Owens 2.50 6.00
GQAIR Ivan Rodriguez 15.00 40.00
GQAJDL Jose De Leon 4.00 10.00
GQAJMU Joe Musgrove 4.00 10.00
GQAJPE Jose Peraza 3.00 8.00
GQAJU Julio Urias 6.00 15.00
GQAKB Kris Bryant 50.00 120.00
GQAKG Ken Giles 2.50 6.00
GQALS Luis Severino 5.00 12.00
GQALV Logan Verrett 2.50 6.00
GQALW Luke Weaver 3.00 8.00
GQAMF Michael Fulmer 8.00 20.00
GQAMP Mike Piazza 40.00 100.00
GQAMST Matt Strahm 4.00 10.00
GQAMT Mike Trout 200.00 400.00
GQAMTA Masahiro Tanaka EXCH 125.00 250.00
GQANE Nathan Eovaldi 3.00 8.00
GQANM Nomar Mazara 8.00 20.00
GQANS Noah Syndergaard 10.00 25.00
GQAOV Omar Vizquel 5.00 12.00
GQAPV Pat Venditte 2.50 6.00
GQARG Robert Gsellman 2.50 6.00
GQARH Ryon Healy 3.00 8.00
GQART Raimel Tapia 3.00 8.00
GQASP Stephen Piscotty 5.00 12.00
GQASW Steven Wright 4.00 10.00
GQATA Tyler Austin 6.00 15.00
GQATGL Tyler Glasnow 5.00 12.00
GQATS Trevor Story 4.00 10.00
GQAYG Yulieski Gurriel 4.00 10.00
GQAYM Yoan Moncada 75.00 200.00

2017 Topps Gypsy Queen Chewing Gum Mini Autographs

STATED ODDS 1:771 HOBBY
EXCHANGE DEADLINE 2/28/2019
*NO BLACK: .5X TO 1.2X BASIC
CGMAAB Alex Bregman 30.00 80.00
CGMAAG Andres Galarraga 10.00 25.00
CGMACC Carlos Correa 40.00 100.00
CGMADF Dexter Fowler 10.00 25.00
CGMAHA Hank Aaron
CGMAJU Julio Urias EXCH 15.00 40.00
CGMANM Nomar Mazara 8.00 20.00
CGMANS Noah Syndergaard 20.00 50.00
CGMAOV Omar Vizquel 10.00 25.00
CGMASK Sandy Koufax 250.00 400.00
CGMASMA Steven Matz 10.00 25.00
CGMASP Stephen Piscotty 10.00 25.00
CGMATS Trevor Story 12.00 30.00
CGMAYG Yulieski Gurriel 10.00 25.00
CGMAYM Yoan Moncada 30.00 80.00

2017 Topps Gypsy Queen Fortune Teller Mini

COMPLETE SET (20) 8.00 20.00
STATED ODDS 1:6 HOBBY
*GREEN/99: 2X TO 5X BASIC
*RED: 5X TO 12X BASIC
FTAB Alex Bregman 1.25 3.00
FTABE Adrian Beltre .50 1.25
FTAG Adrian Gonzalez .40 1.00
FTAJ Aaron Judge 4.00 10.00
FTAP Albert Pujols .60 1.50
FTCH Cole Hamels .40 1.00
FTCK Clayton Kershaw 1.00 2.50
FTDS Dansby Swanson .75 2.00
FTGS Gary Sanchez .50 1.25
FTIR Ivan Rodriguez .40 1.00
FTJA Jose Altuve .40 1.00
FTJL Jon Lester .40 1.00
FTKB Kris Bryant .60 1.50
FTMB Madison Bumgarner .40 1.00
FTMS Max Scherzer .50 1.25
FTMT Mike Trout 2.50 6.00
FTRB Ryan Braun .40 1.00
FTRC Robinson Cano .40 1.00
FTYG Yulieski Gurriel .50 1.25
FTYM Yoan Moncada 1.00 2.50

2017 Topps Gypsy Queen GlassWorks Box Topper

*PURPLE/150: .6X TO 1.5X BASIC
*RED/25: 1.2X TO 3X BASIC
GWAM Andrew McCutchen 3.00 8.00
GWAR Anthony Rizzo 5.00 12.00
GWBH Bryce Harper 5.00 12.00
GWBP Buster Posey 4.00 10.00
GWCC Carlos Correa 3.00 8.00
GWCK Clayton Kershaw 6.00 15.00
GWCS Chris Sale
GWDP David Price 2.50 6.00
GWFH Felix Hernandez 2.50 6.00
GWFL Francisco Lindor 3.00 8.00
GWJA Jake Arrieta 2.50 6.00
GWJF Jose Fernandez 3.00 8.00
GWKB Kris Bryant 4.00 10.00
GWMB Madison Bumgarner 2.50 6.00
GWMC Miguel Cabrera 3.00 8.00
GWMS Marcus Stroman 2.50 6.00
GWMT Mike Trout 15.00 40.00
GWNA Nolan Arenado 4.00 10.00
GWNM Nomar Mazara 2.00 5.00
GWRC Robinson Cano 2.50 6.00
GWSM Steven Matz 2.50 6.00
GWSP Stephen Piscotty 2.50 6.00
GWTS Trevor Story 3.00 8.00
GWXB Xander Bogaerts 3.00 8.00
GWZG Zack Greinke 2.50 6.00

2017 Topps Gypsy Queen GlassWorks Box Topper Autographs

STATED ODDS 1:50 HOBBY BOXES
STATED PRINT RUN 25 SER.#'d SETS
EXCHANGE DEADLINE 2/28/2019
GWAR Anthony Rizzo 200.00 400.00
GWBH Bryce Harper 300.00 500.00
GWBP Buster Posey 150.00 300.00
GWCC Carlos Correa 100.00 250.00
GWFL Francisco Lindor 100.00 250.00
GWKB Kris Bryant 300.00 500.00
GWMT Mike Trout 300.00 500.00
GWNM Nomar Mazara 30.00 80.00
GWTS Trevor Story 50.00 125.00

2017 Topps Gypsy Queen Gum Back Autographs

STATED ODDS 1:824 HOBBY
EXCHANGE DEADLINE 2/28/2019
CBCAAB Alex Bregman 75.00 200.00
CBCABH Bryce Harper
CBCACC Carlos Correa 60.00 150.00
CBCADF Dexter Fowler 12.00 30.00
CBCAFL Francisco Lindor 40.00 100.00
CBCAGS George Springer 10.00 25.00
CBCAKA Jose Altuve 30.00 80.00
CBCAKB Kris Bryant
CBCANS Noah Syndergaard
CBCASM Steven Matz 10.00 25.00
CBCASP Stephen Piscotty 10.00 25.00
CBCATS Trevor Story 12.00 30.00

2017 Topps Gypsy Queen Hand Drawn Art Reproductions

COMPLETE SET (38) 25.00 60.00
STATED ODDS 1:8 HOBBY
GQARAJ1 Adam Jones .40 1.00
GQARAJ2 Adam Jones .40 1.00
GQARAR1 Anthony Rizzo .75 2.00
GQARAR2 Anthony Rizzo .75 2.00
GQARBH1 Bryce Harper .75 2.00
GQARBH2 Bryce Harper .75 2.00
GQARBL1 Barry Larkin .40 1.00
GQARBL2 Barry Larkin .40 1.00
GQARCC1 Carlos Correa .50 1.25
GQARCC2 Carlos Correa .50 1.25
GQARCH1 Cole Hamels .40 1.00
GQARCH2 Cole Hamels .40 1.00
GQARCS1 Chris Sale .50 1.25
GQARCS2 Chris Sale .50 1.25
GQARGS1 Giancarlo Stanton .50 1.25
GQARGS2 Giancarlo Stanton .50 1.25
GQARI2 Ichiro .60 1.50
GQARI1 Ichiro .60 1.50
GQARKB1 Kris Bryant .60 1.50
GQARKB2 Kris Bryant .60 1.50
GQARMM1 Manny Machado .50 1.25
GQARMM2 Manny Machado .50 1.25
GQARMMC1 Mark McGwire .75 2.00
GQARMMC2 Mark McGwire .75 2.00
GQARMS1 Max Scherzer .50 1.25
GQARMS2 Max Scherzer .50 1.25
GQARMT1 Mike Trout 2.50 6.00
GQARMT2 Mike Trout 2.50 6.00
GQARNS1 Noah Syndergaard .40 1.00
GQARNS2 Noah Syndergaard .40 1.00
GQARRC1 Robinson Cano .40 1.00
GQARRC2 Robinson Cano .40 1.00
GQARRCL1 Roger Clemens .60 1.50
GQARRCL2 Roger Clemens .60 1.50
GQARXB1 Xander Bogaerts .50 1.25
GQARXB2 Xander Bogaerts .50 1.25
GQARZG1 Zack Greinke .40 1.00
GQARZG2 Zack Greinke .40 1.00

2018 Topps Gypsy Queen

COMP.SET w/o SP's (300) 20.00 50.00
SP ODDS 1:24 HOBBY
1 Mike Trout 1.50 4.00
2 Corey Knebel .20 .50
3 Andrew Stevenson RC .30 .75
4 Lucas Giolito .25 .60
5 Andrew Cashner .20 .50
6 Yadier Molina .30 .75
7 Rick Porcello .25 .60
8 Eric Hosmer .25 .60
9 Kevin Pillar .20 .50
10 Max Kepler .25 .60
11 Zach Davies .20 .50
12 Maikel Franco .25 .60
13 Ivan Nova .25 .60
14 Yoenis Cespedes .30 .75
15 Starling Marte .25 .60
16 Luis Severino .25 .60
17 Jeff Samardzija .20 .50
18 Wil Myers .25 .60
19 Nick Castellanos .30 .75
20 Johnny Cueto .25 .60
21 Juan Lagares .20 .50
22 Amed Rosario RC .40 1.00
23 Francisco Lindor .30 .75
24 Byron Buxton .25 .60
25 Carlos Correa .30 .75
26 Clint Frazier RC .60 1.50
27 Scooter Gennett .25 .60
28 Alex Colome .20 .50
29 Matt Carpenter .30 .75
30 A.J. Jimenez RC .30 .75
31 Felipe Rivero .25 .60
32 Martin Perez UER .25 .60
Nick Martinez Pictured
33 Zack Granite RC .30 .75
34 Matt Boyd .20 .50
35 Ichiro .40 1.00
36 Jack Flaherty RC .50 1.25
37 Stephen Strasburg .30 .75
38 David Peralta .20 .50
39 Kendrys Morales .20 .50
40 Zack Greinke .25 .60
41 Mikie Mahtook .20 .50
42 Adam Jones .25 .60
43 Gerardo Parra .20 .50
44 Brad Miller .25 .60
45 Jason Vargas .20 .50
46 Adam Duvall .30 .75
47 Jose Iglesias .25 .60
48 Parker Bridwell RC .30 .75
49 Yolmer Sanchez .20 .50
50 Bryce Harper .50 1.25
51 Sandy Alcantara RC .30 .75
52 Anibal Sanchez .20 .50
53 Rafael Devers RC 1.00 2.50
54 Aroldis Chapman .30 .75
55 Jonathan Villar .20 .50
56 Josh Reddick .20 .50
57 Gary Sanchez .30 .75
58 Ryan Zimmerman .25 .60
59 Steven Souza Jr. .25 .60
60 Stephen Piscotty .20 .50
61 Eddie Rosario .30 .75
62 J.A. Happ .25 .60
63 Alex Gordon .25 .60
64 Cole Hamels .25 .60
65 Trevor Story .30 .75
66 Tucker Barnhart .20 .50
67 Ketel Marte .25 .60
68 Christian Yelich .40 1.00
69 Paul DeJong .30 .75
70 Jose Quintana .20 .50
71 Ken Giles .20 .50
72 Rio Ruiz .20 .50
73 Lorenzo Cain .20 .50
74 Noah Syndergaard .25 .60
75 Shin-Soo Choo .25 .60
76 Chris Taylor .25 .60
77 Ian Kinsler .25 .60
78 Luiz Gohara RC .30 .75
79 Jose Altuve .25 .60
80 Billy Hamilton .25 .60
81 Buster Posey .40 1.00
82 Paul Goldschmidt .30 .75
83 Mark Reynolds .20 .50
84 Josh Bell .25 .60
85 Brandon Drury .20 .50
86 Ervin Santana .20 .50
87 Anthony Rizzo .50 1.25
88 Jose Berrios .25 .60
89 Shohei Ohtani RC 6.00 15.00
90 Luis Perdomo .20 .50
91 Julio Teheran .25 .60
92 Zack Cozart .20 .50
93 Jon Gray .20 .50
94 Nick Markakis .25 .60
95 Jon Lester .25 .60
96 Aaron Nola .25 .60
97 Jonathan Schoop .20 .50
98 Manny Machado .30 .75
99 Tyler Glasnow .30 .75
100 Chris Sale .30 .75
101 Jed Lowrie .20 .50
102 Miguel Gomez RC .25 .60
103 Trea Turner .25 .60
104 Felix Jorge RC .30 .75
105 Brandon Crawford .25 .60
106 Kevin Kiermaier .25 .60
107 Mike Leake .20 .50
108 Garrett Richards .25 .60
109 Jordan Zimmermann .25 .60
110 Patrick Corbin .25 .60
111 Andrelton Simmons .20 .50
112 Logan Forsythe .20 .50
113 Elvis Andrus .25 .60
114 Dominic Smith RC .30 .75
115 Willson Contreras .30 .75
116 James McCann .25 .60
117 Starlin Castro .20 .50
118 Eric Thames .25 .60
119 Austin Hedges .20 .50
120 Dinelson Lamet .20 .50
121 Austin Hays RC .50 1.25
122 Felix Hernandez .25 .60
123 Alex Bregman .30 .75
124 Matt Harvey .25 .60
125 Corey Seager .30 .75
126 Melky Cabrera .20 .50
127 Scott Schebler .25 .60
128 Matt Chapman .30 .75
129 Ricky Nolasco .20 .50
130 Michael Fulmer .20 .50
131 Gerrit Cole .30 .75
132 Kyle Schwarber .30 .75
133 Lance McCullers Jr. .20 .50
134 Marcell Ozuna .30 .75
135 Addison Russell .25 .60
136 Carlos Santana .25 .60
137 Carlos Gonzalez .25 .60
138 Jose Urena .20 .50
139 Mike Zunino .20 .50
140 Blake Snell .25 .60
141 Russell Martin .20 .50
142 Clayton Richard .20 .50
143 Yoan Moncada .30 .75
144 Odubel Herrera .25 .60
145 Paul Blackburn RC .30 .75
146 Carlos Martinez .25 .60
147 Jason Heyward .25 .60
148 Josh Donaldson .25 .60
149 Anthony Rendon .30 .75
150 Clayton Kershaw .60 1.50
151 Xander Bogaerts .30 .75
152 Chance Sisco RC .40 1.00
153 Justin Upton .25 .60
154 Travis Shaw .20 .50
155 Brandon Nimmo .25 .60
156 Yasiel Puig .30 .75
157 Jharel Cotton .20 .50
158 Gregory Polanco .25 .60
159 Travis Jankowski .20 .50
160 Chad Bettis .20 .50
161 Kenley Jansen .25 .60
162 Francisco Mejia RC .40 1.00
163 Ozzie Albies RC 1.00 2.50
164 Hunter Renfroe .20 .50
165 Justin Turner .25 .60
166 Ben Gamel .25 .60
167 Masahiro Tanaka .25 .60
168 Jorge Polanco .20 .50
169 J.D. Martinez .30 .75
170 Ryon Healy .20 .50
171 Tzu-Wei Lin RC .40 1.00
172 Danny Duffy .20 .50
173 Mike Moustakas .25 .60
174 Dallas Keuchel .25 .60
175 Joe Panik .25 .60
176 Jacob deGrom .30 .75
177 Jeurys Familia .25 .60
178 Brandon Woodruff RC .40 1.00
179 Yasmany Tomas .20 .50
180 Mookie Betts .50 1.25
181 Jarrett Parker .20 .50
182 Brandon Belt .25 .60
183 Zach Britton .25 .60
184 Dansby Swanson .30 .75
185 Jean Segura .25 .60
186 Travis d'Arnaud .25 .60
187 Matt Olson .25 .60
188 Jordy Mercer .20 .50
189 Miguel Cabrera .30 .75
190 Matt Kemp .25 .60
191 Andrew McCutchen .30 .75
192 Joey Gallo .25 .60
193 Erick Fedde RC .30 .75
194 Corey Kluber .25 .60
195 Vince Velasquez .20 .50
196 Nick Williams RC .40 1.00
197 Evan Longoria .25 .60
198 Didi Gregorius .25 .60
199 Rhys Hoskins RC 1.25 3.00
200 Cody Bellinger .60 1.50
201 Chris Archer .20 .50
202 George Springer .25 .60
203 C.J. Cron .20 .50
204 Tommy Pham .20 .50
205 Reynaldo Lopez .20 .50
206 DJ LeMahieu .30 .75
207 Luis Castillo .25 .60
208 Khris Davis .30 .75
209 Kevin Gausman .25 .60
210 Domingo Santana .20 .50
211 Corey Dickerson .20 .50
212 Sonny Gray .25 .60
213 Mitch Haniger .30 .75
214 Manny Margot .20 .50
215 Greg Allen RC .30 .75
216 Marcus Semien .25 .60
217 Joey Votto .30 .75
218 Chris Davis .20 .50
219 Nicky Delmonico RC .30 .75
220 Brian Anderson RC .40 1.00
221 Sean Newcomb .25 .60
222 Walker Buehler RC 1.50 4.00
223 Albert Pujols .40 1.00
224 Giancarlo Stanton .30 .75
225 Kyle Seager .20 .50
226 Yangervis Solarte .20 .50
227 Whit Merrifield .30 .75
228 Brad Ziegler .20 .50
229 Justin Bour .20 .50
230 Logan Morrison .20 .50
231 Miguel Sano .25 .60
232 A.J. Pollock .20 .50
233 Robinson Cano .25 .60
234 Dillon Peters RC .30 .75
235 Avisail Garcia .25 .60
236 J.P. Crawford RC .30 .75
237 Andrew Benintendi .30 .75
238 Marco Estrada .20 .50
239 Carson Fulmer .20 .50
240 Jose Abreu .30 .75
241 Brad Hand .20 .50
242 Daniel Murphy .25 .60
243 Matt Moore .25 .60
244 Jackie Bradley Jr. .30 .75
245 Trevor Bauer .30 .75
246 Ryan Braun .25 .60
247 Richard Urena RC .30 .75
248 Orlando Arcia .20 .50
249 Jameson Taillon .25 .60
250 Max Scherzer .30 .75
251 Hunter Pence .25 .60
252 Ender Inciarte .20 .50
253 Jose Ramirez .25 .60
254 Victor Robles RC .75 2.00
255 Roberto Osuna .20 .50
256 James Paxton .25 .60
257 Adrian Beltre .30 .75
258 Hector Neris .20 .50
259 Edwin Encarnacion .30 .75
260 Kris Bryant .40 1.00
261 Dexter Fowler .25 .60
262 Justin Smoak .20 .50
263 Sean Manaea .20 .50
264 Freddie Freeman .40 1.00
265 Justin Verlander .30 .75
266 Aaron Altherr .20 .50
267 Dustin Pedroia .30 .75
268 Rougned Odor .25 .60
269 Brian Dozier .25 .60
270 Alex Wood .20 .50
271 Kole Calhoun .20 .50
272 Raisel Iglesias .20 .50
273 Alcides Escobar .25 .60
274 Tim Beckham .25 .60
275 Craig Kimbrel .25 .60
276 Homer Bailey .20 .50
277 Miguel Andujar RC 1.25 3.00
278 Javier Baez .40 1.00
279 Keon Broxton .20 .50
280 Yuli Gurriel .25 .60
281 Andrew Miller .25 .60
282 Tim Anderson .30 .75
283 Luke Weaver .25 .60
284 Jake Odorizzi .20 .50
285 Carlos Carrasco .20 .50
286 Jake Lamb .25 .60
287 Charlie Blackmon .30 .75
288 Jorge Alfaro .20 .50
289 Tyler Saladino .20 .50
290 Jake Arrieta .25 .60
291 Trey Mancini .25 .60
292 Nolan Arenado .40 1.00
293 Daniel Mengden RC .30 .75
294 Nomar Mazara .20 .50
295 Marcus Stroman .25 .60
296 German Marquez .20 .50
297 Nelson Cruz .30 .75
298 Salvador Perez .25 .60
299 Dee Gordon .20 .50
300 Aaron Judge .75 2.00
301 Hank Aaron SP 2.50 6.00
302 Jeff Bagwell SP 1.00 2.50
303 Cal Ripken Jr. SP 4.00 10.00
304 George Brett SP 2.50 6.00
305 Alex Rodriguez SP 1.50 4.00
306 Satchel Paige SP 1.25 3.00
307 Nolan Ryan SP 4.00 10.00
308 Carlton Fisk SP 1.00 2.50
309 Jimmie Foxx SP 1.25 3.00
310 Mariano Rivera SP 1.50 4.00
311 Whitey Ford SP 1.00 2.50
312 Johnny Bench SP 1.25 3.00
313 Frank Thomas SP 1.25 3.00
314 Roger Clemens SP 1.50 4.00
315 Ted Williams SP 2.50 6.00
316 Honus Wagner SP 1.25 3.00
317 Rickey Henderson SP 1.25 3.00
318 Bo Jackson SP 1.25 3.00
319 Pedro Martinez SP 1.00 2.50
320 Sandy Koufax SP 2.50 6.00

2018 Topps Gypsy Queen Bazooka Back

*BAZOOKA: 3X TO 8X BASIC
*BAZOOKA RC: 2X TO 5X BASIC RC
*BAZOOKA SP: 2.5X TO 6X BASIC SP
STATED ODDS 1:43 HOBBY
STATED SP ODDS 1:1263 HOBBY
89 Shohei Ohtani 100.00 250.00

2018 Topps Gypsy Queen Black and White

*BLACK WHITE: 5X TO 12X BASIC
*BLACK WHITE RC: 3X TO 8X BASIC RC
STATED ODDS 1:41 HOBBY

ATED PRINT RUN 50 SER.#'d SETS
Shohei Ohtani 150.00 400.00

2018 Topps Gypsy Queen Capless Variations

ATED ODDS 1:121 HOBBY
WAP: .6X TO 1.5X BASIC
Amed Rosario 3.00 8.00
Francisco Lindor 4.00 10.00
Ichiro 5.00 12.00
Bryce Harper 6.00 15.00
Jose Altuve 3.00 8.00
Buster Posey 5.00 12.00
Manny Machado 4.00 10.00
0 Chris Sale 4.00 10.00
8 Josh Donaldson 3.00 8.00
5 Justin Turner 3.00 8.00
5 Ben Gamel 3.00 8.00
6 Jacob deGrom 4.00 10.00
9 Rhys Hoskins 10.00 25.00
0 Cody Bellinger 8.00 20.00
8 Khris Davis 4.00 10.00
0 Scooter Gennett 3.00 8.00
0 Yuli Gurriel 3.00 8.00
7 Charlie Blackmon 4.00 10.00
7 Nelson Cruz 4.00 10.00
0 Aaron Judge 15.00 40.00

2018 Topps Gypsy Queen GQ Logo Swap

WAP: 2.5X TO 6X BASIC
WAP RC: 1.5X TO 4X BASIC RC
WAP SP: 2X TO 5X BASIC SP
ATED ODDS 1:22 HOBBY
ATED SP ODDS 1:843 HOBBY
Shohei Ohtani 40.00 100.00

2018 Topps Gypsy Queen Green

GREEN: 1.5X TO 4X BASIC
GREEN RC: 1X TO 2.5X BASIC RC
ANDOM INSERTS IN RETAIL PACKS
Shohei Ohtani 25.00 60.00

2018 Topps Gypsy Queen Indigo

NDIGO: 3X TO 8X BASIC
NDIGO RC: 2X TO 5X BASIC RC
ATED ODDS 1:17 HOBBY
ATED PRINT RUN 250 SER.#'d SETS
Shohei Ohtani 60.00 150.00

2018 Topps Gypsy Queen Jackie Robinson Day Variations

ATED ODDS 1:106 HOBBY
SWAP: .6X TO 1.5X BASIC
Eric Hosmer 3.00 8.00
Yoenis Cespedes 4.00 10.00
Francisco Lindor 4.00 10.00
Carlos Correa 4.00 10.00
Ichiro 5.00 12.00
Adam Jones 3.00 8.00
Bryce Harper 6.00 15.00
Trevor Story 4.00 10.00
Jose Altuve 3.00 8.00
Ervin Santana 2.50 6.00
Manny Machado 4.00 10.00
0 Chris Sale 4.00 10.00
8 Eric Thames 3.00 8.00
3 Alex Bregman 4.00 10.00
5 Corey Seager 4.00 10.00
3 Lance McCullers Jr. 2.50 6.00
6 Carlos Martinez 3.00 8.00
56 Yasiel Puig 4.00 10.00
76 Jacob deGrom 4.00 10.00
91 Andrew McCutchen 4.00 10.00
32 Corey Kluber 3.00 8.00
32 George Springer 3.00 8.00
38 Khris Davis
17 Joey Votto 4.00 10.00
11 Daniel Murphy 3.00 8.00
56 James Paxton 3.00 8.00
59 Edwin Encarnacion 4.00 10.00
55 Justin Verlander 4.00 10.00
87 Charlie Blackmon 4.00 10.00
32 Nolan Arenado 5.00 12.00

2018 Topps Gypsy Queen Missing Blackplate

NO BLACK: 1.2X TO 3X BASIC
NO BLACK RC: .75X TO 2X BASIC RC
NSERTED IN RETAIL PACKS
9 Shohei Ohtani 20.00 50.00

2018 Topps Gypsy Queen Missing Nameplate

NO NAME: 1.5X TO 4X BASIC
NO NAME RC: 1X TO 2.5X BASIC RC
NO NAME SP: 1.2X TO 3X BASIC SP
TATED ODDS 1:16 HOBBY
TATED SP ODDS 1:422 HOBBY
9 Shohei Ohtani 25.00 60.00

2018 Topps Gypsy Queen Team Swap Variations

TATED ODDS 1:843 HOBBY
Mike Trout 30.00 80.00
Dodgers
5 Carlos Correa 8.00 20.00
Rangers
0 Bryce Harper 20.00 50.00
Orioles
3 Rafael Devers 20.00 50.00
Yankees
4 Noah Syndergaard 20.00 50.00
Phillies
25 Corey Seager 25.00 60.00
Giants
63 Albies Mets 15.00 40.00
64 Hunter Renfroe 5.00 12.00
Diamondbacks

187 Matt Olson 5.00 12.00
Mariners
199 Rhys Hoskins 30.00 80.00
Nationals
233 Robinson Cano 6.00 15.00
Athletics
253 J.Ramirez DET 6.00 15.00
260 Kris Bryant 30.00 80.00
Cardinals
268 Rougned Odor 6.00 15.00
Angels
300 Aaron Judge 40.00 100.00
Red Sox

2018 Topps Gypsy Queen Autograph Garments

STATED ODDS 1:921 HOBBY
PRINT RUNS B/WN 10-50 COPIES PER
AGAB Andrew Benintendi/50 150.00 400.00
AGAJ Aaron Judge EXCH 300.00 600.00
AGBJ Bo Jackson/25
AGBP Brett Phillips/50 12.00 30.00
AGBZ Bradley Zimmer/50 12.00 30.00
AGCA Christian Arroyo/50 12.00 30.00
AGCF Clint Frazier/50 30.00 80.00
AGCK Craig Kimbrel/50 30.00 80.00
AGCSA Chris Sale/50 30.00 80.00
AGDB Dellin Betances/50 12.00 30.00
AGDM Daniel Murphy EXCH 20.00 50.00
AGDP David Price/50 15.00 40.00
AGFB Franklin Barreto/50 12.00 30.00
AGIH Ian Happ/50 15.00 40.00
AGKB Kris Bryant EXCH 150.00 400.00
AGLS Luis Severino/50 25.00 60.00
AGMT Mike Trout/10
AGNS Noah Syndergaard/50 60.00 150.00

2018 Topps Gypsy Queen Autograph Patch Booklets

STATED ODDS 1:2877 HOBBY
STATED PRINT RUN 20 SER.#'d SETS
EXCHANGE DEADLINE 2/28/2020
GQAPAB Andrew Benintendi EXCH 150.00 400.00
GQAPBJ Bo Jackson 100.00 250.00
GQAPBP Brett Phillips 75.00 200.00
GQAPCF Clint Frazier 100.00 250.00
GQAPDB Dellin Betances 50.00 120.00
GQAPIH Ian Happ 100.00 250.00
GQAPKD Khris Davis 50.00 120.00
GQAPLS Luis Severino 60.00 150.00
GQAPMT Mike Trout
GQAPNS Noah Syndergaard EXCH 75.00 200.00
GQAPRH Rickey Henderson 100.00 250.00

2018 Topps Gypsy Queen Autographs

STATED ODDS 1:19 HOBBY
EXCHANGE DEADLINE 2/28/2020
GQAAB Anthony Banda 3.00 8.00
GQAAD Adam Duvall 5.00 12.00
GQAAJ Aaron Judge EXCH 60.00 150.00
GQAAR Amed Rosario 4.00 10.00
GQAAS Andrew Stevenson 3.00 8.00
GQAAT Andrew Toles 3.00 8.00
GQAAV Alex Verdugo 8.00 20.00
GQABJ Bo Jackson 60.00 150.00
GQABP Brett Phillips 3.00 8.00
GQABS Blake Snell 6.00 15.00
GQABW Brandon Woodruff 4.00 10.00
GQACA Christian Arroyo 3.00 8.00
GQACC Carlos Correa 25.00 60.00
GQACCA Carlos Carrasco 3.00 8.00
GQACF Clint Frazier 12.00 30.00
GQACK Craig Kimbrel 4.00 10.00
GQADF Dustin Fowler 3.00 8.00
GQADJ Derek Jeter 400.00 600.00
GQADR Daniel Robertson 3.00 8.00
GQADSM Dominic Smith 6.00 15.00
GQAFB Franklin Barreto 3.00 8.00
GQAFM Francisco Mejia
GQAGC Garrett Cooper 3.00 8.00
GQAGSA Gary Sanchez 30.00 80.00
GQAHB Harrison Bader 5.00 12.00
GQAHM Hideki Matsui EXCH 75.00 200.00
GQAJB Jose Berrios 4.00 10.00
GQAJC J.P. Crawford 4.00 10.00
GQAJF Jacob Faria 3.00 8.00
GQAJM Jordan Montgomery 5.00 12.00
GQAJT Jim Thome EXCH 25.00 60.00
GQAKB Kris Bryant 100.00 250.00
GQAKD Khris Davis 6.00 15.00
GQAKG Koda Glover 3.00 8.00
GQALB Lewis Brinson 3.00 8.00
GQALG Lucas Giolito 5.00 12.00
GQAMA Miguel Andujar 10.00 25.00
GQAMB Matt Bush 3.00 8.00
GQAMM Manny Machado 25.00 60.00
GQAMT Mike Trout 300.00 500.00
GQAOA Ozzie Albies 20.00 50.00
GQAPB Parker Bridwell 3.00 8.00
GQAPD Paul DeJong 6.00 15.00
GQARD Rafael Devers 20.00 50.00
GQARHO Rhys Hoskins 15.00 40.00
GQARM Ryan McMahon 4.00 10.00
GQASK Sandy Koufax 200.00 400.00
GQASN Sean Newcomb 4.00 10.00
GQASO Shohei Ohtani 250.00 600.00
GQATP Tommy Pham 3.00 8.00
GQAZG Zack Granite 3.00 8.00

2018 Topps Gypsy Queen Autographs Bazooka Back

*BAZOOKA: 1X TO 2.5X BASIC
STATED ODDS 1:668 HOBBY
STATED PRINT RUN BTWN 24-25 SER.#'d SETS
EXCHANGE DEADLINE 2/28/2020
GQABJ Bo Jackson/25 60.00 150.00
GQAFM Francisco Mejia/25 30.00 80.00
GQAGSA Gary Sanchez/25 60.00 150.00
GQAJT Jim Thome EXCH 60.00 150.00
GQAMM Manny Machado/25 40.00 100.00
GQASO Shohei Ohtani/25 600.00 1200.00

2018 Topps Gypsy Queen Autographs Black and White

*BW: .75X TO 2X BASIC
STATED ODDS 1:247 HOBBY
PRINT RUNS B/WN 35-50 COPIES PER
EXCHANGE DEADLINE 2/28/2020
GQAFM Francisco Mejia/50 25.00 60.00
GQAGSA Gary Sanchez/50 50.00 120.00
GQAJT Jim Thome EXCH 50.00 120.00
GQAMM Manny Machado/50 30.00 80.00
GQASO Shohei Ohtani/50 500.00 1000.00

2018 Topps Gypsy Queen Autographs GQ Logo Swap

*SWAP: .6X TO 1.5X BASIC
STATED ODDS 1:169 HOBBY
PRINT RUNS B/WN 80-99 COPIES PER
EXCHANGE DEADLINE 2/28/2020
GQAFM Francisco Mejia/99 20.00 50.00
GQAGSA Gary Sanchez/99 40.00 100.00

2018 Topps Gypsy Queen Autographs Indigo

*INDIGO: .5X TO 1.2X BASIC
STATED ODDS 1:112 HOBBY
PRINT RUNS B/WN 92-150 COPIES PER
EXCHANGE DEADLINE 2/28/2020
GQAFM Francisco Mejia/150 15.00 40.00

2018 Topps Gypsy Queen Autographs Jackie Robinson Day Variations

RANDOMLY INSERTED IN PACKS
PRINT RUNS B/WN 30-99 COPIES PER
EXCHANGE DEADLINE 2/28/2020
*BW/42: .5X TO 1.2X BASIC
25 Carlos Correa/30 60.00 150.00
42 Adam Jones/70 20.00 50.00
79 Jose Altuve EXCH 40.00 100.00
98 Manny Machado/40 40.00 100.00
100 Chris Sale/70 25.00 60.00
118 Eric Thames/99 6.00 15.00
123 Alex Bregman/75 20.00 50.00
194 Corey Kluber/45 20.00 50.00
208 Khris Davis/99 6.00 15.00
217 Joey Votto/30 75.00 200.00
242 Daniel Murphy EXCH 15.00 40.00
259 Edwin Encarnacion EXCH 15.00 40.00

2018 Topps Gypsy Queen Bases Around the League Autographs

STATED ODDS 1:4015 HOBBY
STATED PRINT RUN 20 SER.#'d SETS
EXCHANGE DEADLINE 2/28/2020
BALAB Andrew Benintendi/20 150.00 400.00
BALAJ Aaron Judge/20 400.00 800.00
BALAR Anthony Rizzo/20 150.00 400.00
BALCC Carlos Correa/20 150.00 400.00
BALKB Kris Bryant EXCH 300.00 500.00
BALMM Manny Machado/20 300.00 500.00
BALMT Mike Trout/10
BALPG Paul Goldschmidt/20 150.00 400.00

2018 Topps Gypsy Queen Fortune Teller Mini

STATED ODDS 1:6 HOBBY
*INDIGO/250: 1X TO 2.5X BASIC
*GREEN/99: 2.5X TO 6X BASIC
FTM1 Aaron Judge 1.25 3.00
FTM2 Manny Machado .50 1.25
FTM3 Carlos Carrasco .30 .75
FTM4 J.P. Crawford .30 .75
FTM5 Rafael Devers 1.00 2.50
FTM6 Kris Bryant .60 1.50
FTM7 Khris Davis .50 1.25
FTM8 Corey Seager .50 1.25
FTM9 Daniel Murphy .40 1.00
FTM10 Cody Bellinger 1.00 2.50
FTM11 Carlos Correa .50 1.25
FTM12 Gary Sanchez .50 1.25
FTM13 Bryce Harper .75 2.00
FTM14 Bradley Zimmer .30 .75
FTM15 Noah Syndergaard .40 1.00
FTM16 Amed Rosario .40 1.00
FTM17 Dellin Betances .40 1.00
FTM18 Clint Frazier .60 1.50
FTM19 Trey Mancini .40 1.00
FTM20 Mike Trout 2.50 6.00

2018 Topps Gypsy Queen Fortune Teller Mini Autographs

STATED ODDS 1:1526 HOBBY
PRINT RUNS B/WN 20-50 COPIES PER
EXCHANGE DEADLINE 2/28/2020
GFTAAR Amed Rosario/50 20.00 50.00
GFTABZ Bradley Zimmer/50 6.00 15.00
GFTACC Carlos Correa/20 40.00 100.00
GFTACCA Carlos Carrasco/50 10.00 25.00
GFTACF Clint Frazier/50 12.00 30.00
GFTADB Dellin Betances/50 10.00 25.00
GFTADM Daniel Murphy EXCH 12.00 30.00
GFTAGSA Gary Sanchez/30
GFTAJC J.P. Crawford/50 15.00 40.00
GFTAKB Kris Bryant EXCH 150.00 400.00
GFTAKD Khris Davis/50 10.00 25.00
GFTAMM Manny Machado/20 30.00 80.00
GFTAMT Mike Trout
GFTANS Noah Syndergaard/30 60.00 150.00
GFTARD Rafael Devers/50 12.00 30.00
GFTATM Trey Mancini/50 25.00 60.00

2018 Topps Gypsy Queen Glassworks Box Topper

STATED ODDS 1:1 HOBBY BOXES
*INDIGO/150: .75X TO 2X BASIC
*RED/25: 3X TO 8X BASIC
GWAB Andrew Benintendi 2.50 6.00
GWAJ Aaron Judge 6.00 15.00
GWAR Anthony Rizzo 4.00 10.00
GWBH Bryce Harper 4.00 10.00
GWBP Buster Posey 3.00 8.00
GWCB Cody Bellinger 5.00 12.00
GWCC Carlos Correa 2.50 6.00
GWCK Clayton Kershaw 5.00 12.00
GWCS Corey Seager 2.50 6.00
GWCSA Chris Sale 2.50 6.00
GWFF Freddie Freeman 3.00 8.00
GWFL Francisco Lindor 2.50 6.00
GWGS Giancarlo Stanton 2.50 6.00
GWIH Ian Happ 2.00 5.00
GWJA Jose Altuve 2.00 5.00
GWJD Josh Donaldson 2.00 5.00
GWKB Kris Bryant 8.00 20.00
GWMB Mookie Betts 4.00 10.00
GWMM Manny Machado 2.50 6.00
GWMS Max Scherzer 2.50 6.00
GWMT Mike Trout 10.00 25.00
GWNA Nolan Arenado 3.00 8.00
GWNS Noah Syndergaard 2.00 5.00
GWPG Paul Goldschmidt 2.50 6.00
GWTS Trevor Story 2.50 6.00

2018 Topps Gypsy Queen Glassworks Box Topper Autographs

STATED ODDS 1:1584 HOBBY BOXES
STATED PRINT RUN 25 SER.#'d SETS
EXCHANGE DEADLINE 2/28/2020
GWAB Andrew Benintendi EXCH 100.00 250.00
GWAR Anthony Rizzo 100.00 250.00
GWCC Carlos Correa 60.00 150.00
GWFF Freddie Freeman 75.00 200.00
GWIH Ian Happ 75.00 200.00
GWJA Jose Altuve EXCH 60.00 150.00
GWKB Kris Bryant EXCH 150.00 400.00
GWMT Mike Trout 300.00 600.00
GWPG Paul Goldschmidt 60.00 150.00

2018 Topps Gypsy Queen Mini Rookie Autographs

STATED ODDS 1:809 HOBBY
STATED PRINT RUN 99 SER.#'d SETS
EXCHANGE DEADLINE 2/28/2020
*BW/50: .5X TO 1.2X BASIC
GQRAAR Amed Rosario
GQRAAV Alex Verdugo 15.00 40.00
GQRABW Brandon Woodruff 5.00 12.00
GQRACF Clint Frazier 15.00 40.00
GQRADF Dustin Fowler 4.00 10.00
GQRADS Dominic Smith 4.00 10.00
GQRAFM Francisco Mejia 20.00 50.00
GQRAJC J.P. Crawford 10.00 25.00
GQRAOA Ozzie Albies EXCH 25.00 60.00
GQRAPB Parker Bridwell 4.00 10.00
GQRARD Rafael Devers 60.00 150.00
GQRARH Rhys Hoskins 40.00 100.00

2018 Topps Gypsy Queen Tarot of the Diamond

STATED ODDS 1:8 HOBBY
*INDIGO/250: 1X TO 2.5X BASIC
*GREEN/99: 2X TO 5X BASIC
TOD1 Aaron Judge 1.25 3.00
TOD2 Rafael Devers 1.00 2.50
TOD3 Giancarlo Stanton .50 1.25
TOD4 Chris Sale .50 1.25
TOD5 Cody Bellinger 1.00 2.50
TOD6 Kenley Jansen .40 1.00
TOD7 Francisco Lindor .50 1.25
TOD8 Clayton Kershaw 1.00 2.50
TOD9 Marcus Stroman .40 1.00
TOD10 Giancarlo Stanton .50 1.25
TOD11 Khris Davis .50 1.25
TOD12 Carlos Correa .50 1.25
TOD13 Aroldis Chapman .50 1.25
TOD14 Aaron Judge 1.25 3.00
TOD15 Chris Sale .50 1.25
TOD16 Kevin Kiermaier .40 1.00
TOD17 Noah Syndergaard .40 1.00
TOD18 Bryce Harper .75 2.00
TOD19 Yasiel Puig .50 1.25
TOD20 Albert Pujols .60 1.50
TOD21 Ichiro .60 1.50
TOD22 Mike Trout 2.50 6.00

2019 Topps Gypsy Queen

SP ODDS 1:24 HOBBY
1 Mike Trout 1.50 4.00
2 Jesus Aguilar .20 .50
3 Khris Davis .30 .75
4 Kyle Schwarber .30 .75
5 Carlos Carrasco .20 .50
6 Yadier Molina .30 .75
7 JaCoby Jones .25 .60
8 Julio Teheran .25 .60
9 Victor Robles .40 1.00
10 Giancarlo Stanton .30 .75
11 Charlie Blackmon .30 .75
12 Jose Peraza .25 .60
13 Kyle Seager .20 .50
14 Josh Reddick .20 .50
15 Alex Gordon .25 .60
16 Jacob Nix RC .40 1.00
17 Buster Posey .40 1.00
18 Cody Bellinger .60 1.50
19 Mike Fiers .20 .50
20 Aaron Nola .25 .60
21 Matt Davidson .25 .60
22 Ryan Borucki RC .30 .75
23 Xander Bogaerts .30 .75
24 Matt Boyd .20 .50
25 Kolby Allard RC .50 1.25
26 Dee Gordon .20 .50
27 Kevin Kiermaier .25 .60
28 Hunter Renfroe .20 .50
29 Dawel Lugo RC .50 1.25
30 Jean Segura .30 .75
31 Jake Arrieta .25 .60
32 Anthony Rizzo .50 1.25
33 Corey Kluber .25 .60
34 Lewis Brinson .20 .50
35 Starling Marte .25 .60
36 Justin Upton .25 .60
37 Eddie Rosario .25 .60
38 Johan Camargo .20 .50
39 Avisail Garcia .25 .60
40 Mike Zunino .20 .50
41 Mookie Betts .50 1.25
42 Archie Bradley .20 .50
43 Josh Rogers RC .30 .75
44 Jeimer Candelario .20 .50
45 Paul DeJong .30 .75
46 Brandon Belt .25 .60
47 Jalen Beeks RC .30 .75
48 Josh Bell .25 .60
49 Josh Harrison .20 .50
50 Mike Minor .20 .50
51 Kendrys Morales .20 .50
52 Jakob Junis .20 .50
53 Freddie Freeman .40 1.00
54 Michael Brantley .25 .60
55 Shohei Ohtani .40 1.00
56 Elvis Andrus .25 .60
57 Juan Soto 1.00 2.50
58 Addison Reed .20 .50
59 Zack Wheeler .25 .60
60 Mark Trumbo .20 .50
61 Dereck Rodriguez .20 .50
62 Zack Greinke .25 .60
63 Carlos Correa .30 .75
64 Dakota Hudson RC .40 1.00
65 Mike Clevinger .25 .60
66 Miguel Cabrera .30 .75
67 Jake Lamb .25 .60
68 Ian Happ .25 .60
69 Maikel Franco .25 .60
70 Nick Williams .25 .60
71 Miles Mikolas .30 .75
72 Eugenio Suarez .25 .60
73 Carlos Santana .25 .60
74 Max Muncy .25 .60
75 Dustin Pedroia .30 .75
76 Marcus Stroman .25 .60
77 Andrew McCutchen .30 .75
78 Byron Buxton .25 .60
79 Willson Contreras .25 .60
80 Ronald Guzman .20 .50
81 Trevor Bauer .30 .75
82 Whit Merrifield .30 .75
83 Kyle Hendricks .30 .75
84 Marcell Ozuna .30 .75
85 Ryan McMahon .20 .50
86 C.J. Cron .20 .50
87 Taijuan Walker .20 .50
88 Tyler Mahle .20 .50
89 Ian Desmond .20 .50
90 Brett Phillips .20 .50
91 Albert Almora Jr. .25 .60
92 Gleyber Torres .60 1.50
93 Tyler Glasnow .20 .50
94 Francisco Lindor .30 .75
95 J.T. Realmuto .30 .75
96 Seranthony Dominguez .20 .50
97 Austin Meadows .20 .50
98 Enyel De Los Santos .20 .50
99 Christian Yelich .40 1.00
100 Kris Bryant .40 1.00
101 Blake Snell .25 .60
102 Rhys Hoskins .40 1.00
103 Miguel Andujar .30 .75
104 Ozzie Albies .30 .75
105 Bryce Harper .50 1.25
106 Robinson Chirinos .20 .50
107 Max Kepler .25 .60
108 Steven Duggar RC .40 1.00
109 Gerrit Cole .30 .75
110 Salvador Perez .25 .60
111 Justin Verlander .30 .75
112 Kevin Kramer RC .40 1.00
113 Jorge Polanco .20 .50
114 Chris Davis .20 .50
115 Manny Machado .30 .75
116 Manny Margot .20 .50
117 Francisco Arcia RC .50 1.25
118 Starlin Castro .20 .50
119 Luis Guillorme .20 .50
120 Ramon Laureano RC .60 1.50
121 Joey Votto .30 .75
122 J.D. Martinez .30 .75
123 Daniel Palka .20 .50
124 Joey Gallo .25 .60
125 Tim Anderson .30 .75
126 Wil Myers .20 .50
127 Sean Doolittle .20 .50
128 Rick Porcello .25 .60
129 Joe Panik .25 .60
130 Michael Kopech RC .60 1.50
131 JT Riddle .20 .50
132 Blake Treinen .20 .50
133 George Springer .25 .60
134 Yolmer Sanchez .20 .50
135 Wade Davis .20 .50
136 Lorenzo Cain .20 .50
137 Todd Frazier .20 .50
138 Chris Sale .30 .75
139 Taylor Ward RC .30 .75
140 Scott Schebler .25 .60
141 Chance Adams RC .30 .75
142 Dylan Bundy .25 .60
143 Mitch Haniger .25 .60
144 Daniel Poncedeleon RC .50 1.25
145 Ryan O'Hearn RC .30 .75
146 Kyle Freeland .25 .60
147 Rafael Devers .40 1.00
148 Trey Mancini .25 .60
149 Gregory Polanco .25 .60
150 Ronald Acuna Jr. 1.50 4.00
151 Brandon Woodruff .20 .50
152 Willians Astudillo RC .30 .75
153 Trevor Story .30 .75
154 Carlos Rodon .25 .60
155 Javier Baez .40 1.00
156 Jake Cave RC .40 1.00
157 Raisel Iglesias .20 .50
158 Luis Urias RC .50 1.25
159 Dennis Santana RC .30 .75
160 Jackie Bradley Jr. .30 .75
161 Seth Lugo .20 .50
162 Robbie Ray .20 .50
163 Stephen Piscotty .20 .50
164 Jake Odorizzi .20 .50
165 Aramis Garcia RC .30 .75
166 Jose Altuve .25 .60
167 Tim Beckham .25 .60
168 Kevin Pillar .20 .50
169 Travis Shaw .20 .50
170 Lou Trivino .20 .50
171 Clayton Kershaw .60 1.50
172 Ryan Braun .25 .60
173 Scooter Gennett .25 .60
174 Corey Seager .30 .75
175 Jack Flaherty .25 .60
176 Brandon Nimmo .25 .60
177 Zack Godley .20 .50
178 Corey Dickerson .20 .50
179 Adam Eaton .30 .75
180 Tommy Pham .20 .50
181 Niko Goodrum .25 .60
182 Yu Darvish .30 .75
183 Adam Cimber RC .30 .75
184 Yuli Gurriel .25 .60
185 Jose Leclerc .20 .50
186 Brandon Lowe RC .50 1.25
187 Justus Sheffield RC .50 1.25
188 Cory Spangenberg .20 .50
189 Edwin Encarnacion .30 .75
190 Yan Gomes .30 .75
191 Corbin Burnes .30 .75
192 Walker Buehler .40 1.00
193 Johnny Cueto .25 .60
194 Jeremy Jeffress .20 .50
195 Tucker Barnhart .20 .50
196 Yoan Moncada .30 .75
197 Sean Manaea .20 .50
198 Joey Lucchesi .20 .50
199 Austin Dean RC .20 .50
200 Jacob deGrom .30 .75
201 Marcus Semien .20 .50
202 Kyle Wright RC .50 1.25
203 James Paxton .25 .60
204 Josh Hader .20 .50
205 Andrew Benintendi .30 .75
206 Sandy Alcantara .20 .50
207 Andrelton Simmons .20 .50
208 Dansby Swanson .30 .75
209 Scott Kingery .25 .60
210 Paul Goldschmidt .30 .75
211 Stephen Strasburg .30 .75
212 Christin Stewart RC .40 1.00
213 Nolan Arenado .40 1.00
214 David Peralta .20 .50
215 Chris Archer .20 .50
216 Lourdes Gurriel Jr. .25 .60
217 Framber Valdez RC .25 .60
218 Kevin Newman RC .50 1.25
219 Kole Calhoun .20 .50
220 Heath Fillmyer RC .20 .50
221 Justin Turner .25 .60
222 Ryon Healy .20 .50
223 Tyler Austin .20 .50
224 Masahiro Tanaka .25 .60
225 Kyle Tucker RC .60 1.50
226 Billy Hamilton .20 .50
227 Jose Ramirez .20 .50
228 Trevor Richards RC .30 .75
229 Zack Cozart .20 .50
230 Brad Keller RC .50 1.25
231 Tyler Skaggs .20 .50
232 Dylan Bundy .20 .50
233 Harrison Bader .25 .60
234 Anthony Rendon .30 .75
235 Luis Severino .25 .60
236 Justin Smoak .20 .50
237 Luis Castillo .25 .60
238 Jose Berrios .25 .60
239 James McCann .25 .60
240 Jon Gray .20 .50
241 David Dahl .20 .50
242 Felix Hernandez .25 .60
243 Francisco Mejia .25 .60
244 Felipe Vazquez .20 .50
245 Jameson Taillon .25 .60
246 Shane Greene .20 .50
247 Edwin Diaz .25 .60
248 Chris Shaw RC .50 1.25
249 Jake Bauers RC .50 1.25
250 Sean Newcomb .20 .50
251 Didi Gregorius .25 .60
252 Orlando Arcia .20 .50
253 Ender Inciarte .20 .50
254 Hunter Dozier .20 .50
255 Jeffrey Springs RC .30 .75
256 Brian Anderson .20 .50
257 Jeff McNeil RC .75 2.00
258 Shin-Soo Choo .25 .60
259 Amed Rosario .25 .60
260 Matt Chapman .30 .75
261 Billy McKinney .20 .50
262 Tanner Roark .20 .50
263 David Price .25 .60
264 Evan Longoria .25 .60
265 Brandon Crawford .25 .60
266 Jose Martinez .20 .50
267 Alex Bregman .30 .75
268 Willy Adames .20 .50
269 Nomar Mazara .20 .50
270 Alex Cobb .20 .50
271 Trea Turner .25 .60
272 Jason Heyward .25 .60
273 Jose Urena .20 .50
274 Nicholas Castellanos .30 .75
275 Antonio Senzatela .20 .50
276 Rowdy Tellez .30 .75
277 Max Scherzer .30 .75
278 Enrique Hernandez .25 .60
279 Patrick Corbin .25 .60
280 Matt Olson .20 .50
281 Ken Giles .20 .50
282 Rougned Odor .20 .50
283 Danny Jansen RC .30 .75
284 Jonathan Villar .20 .50
285 Robinson Cano .25 .60
286 Kenley Jansen .25 .60
287 Cedric Mullins RC .50 1.25
288 Jose Abreu .30 .75
289 Franmil Reyes .20 .50
290 Pablo Lopez RC .30 .75
291 Noah Syndergaard .25 .60
292 Matt Carpenter .30 .75
293 Eric Hosmer .25 .60
294 Reynaldo Lopez .25 .60
295 Eduardo Escobar .20 .50
296 Adalberto Mondesi .25 .60
297 Michael Conforto .25 .60
298 Albert Pujols .40 1.00
299 Odubel Herrera .25 .60
300 Aaron Judge .75 2.00
301 Jackie Robinson SP 1.25 3.00
302 Roberto Alomar SP 1.00 2.50
303 Tommy Lasorda SP 1.00 2.50
304 Reggie Jackson SP 1.00 2.50
305 Vladimir Guerrero SP 1.00 2.50
306 Mark McGwire SP 2.00 5.00
307 Roberto Clemente SP 3.00 8.00
308 Ivan Rodriguez SP 1.00 2.50
309 Roger Maris SP 1.25 3.00
310 Pedro Martinez SP 1.00 2.50
311 Hank Aaron SP 2.50 6.00
312 Gary Carter SP 1.00 2.50
313 Don Mattingly SP 2.50 6.00
314 Derek Jeter SP 3.00 8.00
315 George Brett SP 2.50 6.00
316 Bo Jackson SP 1.25 3.00
317 Lou Gehrig SP 2.50 6.00
318 Ty Cobb SP 2.00 5.00
319 Sandy Koufax SP 2.50 6.00
320 Babe Ruth SP 3.00 8.00

2019 Topps Gypsy Queen Bazooka Back

*BAZOOKA: 4X TO 10X BASIC
*BAZOOKA RC: 2.5X TO 6X BASIC RC
*BAZOOKA SP: 2X TO 5X BASIC SP
STATED ODDS 1:57 HOBBY
STATED SP ODDS 1:1687 HOBBY

2019 Topps Gypsy Queen Black and White

*BLACK WHITE: 6X TO 15X BASIC
*BLACK WHITE RC: 4X TO 10X BASIC RC
STATED ODDS 1:47 HOBBY
STATED PRINT RUN 50 SER.#'d SETS

2019 Topps Gypsy Queen GQ Logo Swap

*SWAP: 2.5X TO 6X BASIC
*SWAP RC: 1.5X TO 4X BASIC RC
*SWAP SP: 1.2X TO 3X BASIC SP
STATED ODDS 1:29 HOBBY
STATED SP ODDS 1:1125 HOBBY

2019 Topps Gypsy Queen Green

*GREEN: 1X TO 2.5X BASIC
*GREEN RC: .6X TO 1.5X BASIC RC
RANDOM INSERTS IN RETAIL PACKS

2019 Topps Gypsy Queen Indigo

*INDIGO: 3X TO 8X BASIC
*INDIGO RC: 2X TO 5X BASIC RC
STATED ODDS 1:23 HOBBY
STATED PRINT RUN 250 SER.#'d SETS

2019 Topps Gypsy Queen Missing Nameplate

*NO NAME: 1.5X TO 4X BASIC
*NO NAME RC: 1X TO 2.5X BASIC RC
*NO NAME SP: 1.2X TO 3X BASIC SP
STATED ODDS 1:21 HOBBY
STATED SP ODDS 1:563 HOBBY

2019 Topps Gypsy Queen Purple

*PURPLE: 1X TO 2.5X BASIC

*PURPLE RC: .6X TO 1.5X BASIC RC

RANDOM INSERTS IN RETAIL PACKS

2019 Topps Gypsy Queen 4th of July Variations

STATED ODDS 1:1125 HOBBY

55 Shohei Ohtani	50.00	120.00
76 Marcus Stroman	10.00	25.00
81 Trevor Bauer	20.00	50.00
92 Gleyber Torres	30.00	80.00
99 Christian Yelich	30.00	80.00
114 Chris Davis	8.00	20.00
132 Blake Treinen	8.00	20.00
147 Rafael Devers	15.00	40.00
150 Ronald Acuna Jr.	125.00	300.00
155 Javier Baez	15.00	40.00
166 Jose Altuve	10.00	25.00
173 Scooter Gennett	10.00	25.00
196 Yoan Moncada	12.00	30.00
233 Harrison Bader	15.00	40.00
299 Odubel Herrera	10.00	25.00

2019 Topps Gypsy Queen Jackie Robinson Day Variations

STATED ODDS 1:141 HOBBY

*SWAP: .6X TO 1.5X BASIC

1 Mike Trout	20.00	50.00
3 Khris Davis	4.00	10.00
6 Yadier Molina	4.00	10.00
10 Giancarlo Stanton	4.00	10.00
11 Charlie Blackmon	4.00	10.00
26 Dee Gordon	2.50	6.00
32 Anthony Rizzo	6.00	15.00
53 Freddie Freeman	5.00	12.00
63 Carlos Correa	4.00	10.00
77 Andrew McCutchen	4.00	10.00
82 Whit Merrifield	4.00	10.00
92 Gleyber Torres	8.00	20.00
94 Francisco Lindor	6.00	15.00
100 Kris Bryant	6.00	15.00
105 Bryce Harper	6.00	15.00
127 Sean Doolittle	2.50	6.00
138 Chris Sale	6.00	15.00
153 Trevor Story	4.00	10.00
155 Javier Baez	5.00	12.00
166 Jose Altuve	3.00	8.00
171 Clayton Kershaw	8.00	20.00
177 Zack Godley	2.50	6.00
198 Joey Lucchesi	2.50	6.00
199 Brandon Nimmo	3.00	8.00
210 Paul Goldschmidt	4.00	10.00
271 Trea Turner	3.00	8.00
291 Noah Syndergaard	3.00	8.00
300 Aaron Judge	20.00	50.00

2019 Topps Gypsy Queen Players Weekend Variations

STATED ODDS 1:139 HOBBY

*SWAP: .6X TO 1.5X BASIC

1 Mike Trout	20.00	50.00
18 Cody Bellinger	8.00	20.00
31 Jake Arrieta	3.00	8.00
32 Anthony Rizzo	6.00	15.00
35 Starling Marte	3.00	8.00
37 Eddie Rosario	3.00	8.00
41 Mookie Betts	6.00	15.00
59 Zack Wheeler	4.00	10.00
77 Giancarlo Stanton	6.00	15.00
94 Francisco Lindor	6.00	15.00
118 Starlin Castro	2.50	6.00
166 Jose Altuve	3.00	8.00
173 Scooter Gennett	4.00	10.00
201 Marcus Semien	2.50	6.00
238 Jose Berrios	3.00	8.00
247 Edwin Diaz	3.00	8.00
274 Nicholas Castellanos	6.00	15.00
289 Franmil Reyes	2.50	6.00
297 Michael Conforto	3.00	8.00
300 Aaron Judge	10.00	25.00

2019 Topps Gypsy Queen Autograph Garments

STATED ODDS 1:1245 HOBBY

PRINT RUNS B/WN 10-50 COPIES PER

NO PRICING ON QTY 10

EXCHANGE DEADLINE 2/28/2020

AGAR Anthony Rizzo/25	40.00	100.00
AGCF Clint Frazier/50	15.00	40.00
AGCY Christian Yelich/50	60.00	150.00
AGDG Didi Gregorius/50	50.00	120.00
AGJA Jose Altuve/30	50.00	120.00
AGJD Jacob deGrom/50	40.00	100.00
AGKB Kris Bryant EXCH	125.00	300.00
AGKD Khris Davis/50	40.00	100.00
AGKT Kyle Tucker/50	30.00	80.00
AGLS Luis Severino/50	30.00	80.00
AGOA Ozzie Albies/50	20.00	50.00
AGRH Rickey Henderson/25	60.00	150.00
AGRI Raisel Iglesias/50	12.00	30.00
AGSK Scott Kingery/50	60.00	510.00
AGTM Trey Mancini/50	40.00	100.00
AGVGS Vladimir Guerrero/30	75.00	200.00
AGYM Yadier Molina/40	60.00	150.00

2019 Topps Gypsy Queen Autograph Patch Booklets

STATED ODDS 1:5463 HOBBY

STATED PRINT RUN 20 SER.#'d SETS

EXCHANGE DEADLINE 2/28/2020

GQAPFT Frank Thomas	150.00	400.00
GQAPGS George Springer	75.00	200.00
GQAPJB Jose Berrios	75.00	200.00
GQAPJD Jacob deGrom	75.00	200.00
GQAPKT Kyle Tucker	125.00	300.00
GQAPLS Luis Severino	75.00	200.00
GQAPMT Mike Trout	400.00	800.00
GQAPWM Whit Merrifield	75.00	200.00

2019 Topps Gypsy Queen Autographs

STATED ODDS 1:16 HOBBY

EXCHANGE DEADLINE 2/28/2020

*INDIGO/150: .5X TO 1.2X BASIC

*SWAP/99: .5X TO 1.2X BASIC

GQAAJ Aaron Judge	100.00	250.00
GQAAM Andrew McCutchen	20.00	50.00
GQAAME Austin Meadows	4.00	10.00
GQABK Brad Keller	3.00	8.00
GQABN Brandon Nimmo	4.00	10.00
GQABW Bryse Wilson	4.00	10.00
GQACA Chance Adams	3.00	8.00
GQACB Corbin Burnes	5.00	12.00
GQACH Cesar Hernandez	3.00	8.00
GQACK Carson Kelly	3.00	8.00
GQACM Colin Moran	3.00	8.00
GQACMU Cedric Mullins	5.00	12.00
GQACS Carlos Santana	4.00	10.00
GQACST Christin Stewart	4.00	10.00
GQACY Christian Yelich	40.00	100.00
GQADB David Bote	4.00	10.00
GQADC Dylan Cozens	3.00	8.00
GQADJ Danny Jansen	8.00	20.00
GQADM Daniel Mengden	3.00	8.00
GQAER Eddie Rosario	6.00	15.00
GQAFA Francisco Arcia	5.00	12.00
GQAFL Francisco Lindor	15.00	40.00
GQAGS George Springer	10.00	25.00
GQAJA Jose Altuve	20.00	50.00
GQAJB Jake Bauers	5.00	12.00
GQAJD Jacob deGrom	12.00	30.00
GQAJM Jose Martinez	4.00	10.00
GQAJS Juan Soto	50.00	120.00
GQAKA Kolby Allard	5.00	12.00
GQAKB Kris Bryant EXCH	75.00	200.00
GQAKD Khris Davis	5.00	12.00
GQAKT Kyle Tucker	12.00	30.00
GQALU Luis Urias	5.00	12.00
GQAMC Matt Chapman	10.00	25.00
GQAMF Mike Foltynewicz	5.00	12.00
GQAMH Mitch Haniger	4.00	10.00
GQAMK Michael Kopech	8.00	20.00
GQAMM Max Muncy	6.00	15.00
GQAMO Matt Olson	3.00	8.00
GQAMR Mariano Rivera	100.00	250.00
GQAMT Mike Trout	300.00	600.00
GQARB Ryan Borucki	3.00	8.00
GQARI Raisel Iglesias	3.00	8.00
GQASD Steven Duggar	4.00	10.00
GQASK Sandy Koufax	150.00	400.00
GQASO Shohei Ohtani	200.00	400.00
GQATH Torii Hunter	10.00	25.00
GQATS Trevor Story	10.00	25.00
GQAVGS Vladimir Guerrero	25.00	60.00
GQAWA Willy Adames	3.00	8.00
GQAWM Whit Merrifield	6.00	15.00
GQAYK Yusei Kikuchi EXCH	12.00	30.00

2019 Topps Gypsy Queen Autographs Bazooka Back

*BAZOOKA: .75X TO 2X BASIC

STATED ODDS 1:826 HOBBY

STATED PRINT RUN 25 SER.#'d SETS

EXCHANGE DEADLINE 2/28/2020

GQAAJ Aaron Judge	125.00	300.00
GQAKB Kris Bryant EXCH	100.00	250.00

2019 Topps Gypsy Queen Autographs Black and White

*BW: .6X TO 1.5X BASIC

STATED ODDS 1:302 HOBBY

STATED PRINT RUN 50 SER.#'d SETS

EXCHANGE DEADLINE 2/28/2020

2019 Topps Gypsy Queen Autographs Jackie Robinson Day Variations

STATED ODDS 1:1281 HOBBY

PRINT RUNS B/WN 10-99 COPIES PER

NO PRICING ON QTY 10

EXCHANGE DEADLINE 2/28/2020

*BW/42: .5X TO 1.2X BASIC

3 Khris Davis/99	15.00	40.00
6 Yadier Molina/50	60.00	150.00
32 Anthony Rizzo/25	60.00	150.00
53 Freddie Freeman/50	50.00	120.00
77 Andrew McCutchen/40	50.00	120.00
82 Whit Merrifield/99	12.00	30.00
94 Francisco Lindor/50	30.00	80.00
100 Kris Bryant EXCH	100.00	250.00
127 Sean Doolittle/99	10.00	25.00
153 Trevor Story/99	10.00	25.00
155 Javier Baez/45	40.00	100.00
166 Jose Altuve/40	25.00	60.00
291 Noah Syndergaard		
300 Aaron Judge		

2019 Topps Gypsy Queen Bases Around the League Autographs

STATED ODDS 1:6121 HOBBY

STATED PRINT RUN 20 SER.#'d SETS

EXCHANGE DEADLINE 2/28/2020

BALBB Byron Buxton	60.00	150.00
BALCS Carlos Santana	75.00	200.00
BALER Eddie Rosario	75.00	200.00
BALI Ichiro	400.00	800.00
BALJD Jacob deGrom	100.00	250.00

2019 Topps Gypsy Queen Chrome Box Topper Autographs

STATED ODDS 1:75 HOBBY BOXES

STATED PRINT RUN 25 SER.#'d SETS

EXCHANGE DEADLINE 2/28/2020

GQCAAM Andrew McCutchen	50.00	120.00
GQCAAR Anthony Rizzo	50.00	120.00
GQCABH Bryce Harper	150.00	400.00
GQCABN Brandon Nimmo	20.00	50.00
GQCACB Corbin Burnes	25.00	60.00
GQCAFL Francisco Lindor	50.00	120.00
GQCAJA Jose Altuve	50.00	120.00
GQCAJD Jacob deGrom	40.00	100.00
GQCAKB Kris Bryant EXCH	100.00	250.00
GQCAKT Kyle Tucker	75.00	200.00
GQCAMH Mitch Haniger	30.00	80.00
GQCAPD Paul DeJong	25.00	60.00
GQCATH Torii Hunter	30.00	80.00
GQCATS Trevor Story	25.00	60.00
GQCAVGS Vladimir Guerrero	40.00	100.00

2019 Topps Gypsy Queen Chrome Box Toppers

*INDIGO: 1X TO 2.5X BASIC

1 Mike Trout	8.00	20.00
2 Jesus Aguilar	1.00	2.50
3 Khris Davis	1.50	4.00
4 Kyle Schwarber	1.50	4.00
6 Yadier Molina	1.50	4.00
11 Charlie Blackmon	1.50	4.00
18 Cody Bellinger	3.00	8.00
20 Aaron Nola	1.25	3.00
23 Xander Bogaerts	1.50	4.00
29 Dawel Lugo	1.50	4.00
30 Jean Segura	1.50	4.00
32 Anthony Rizzo	2.50	6.00
33 Corey Kluber	1.25	3.00
34 Lewis Brinson	1.00	2.50
36 Justin Upton	1.25	3.00
37 Eddie Rosario	1.25	3.00
41 Mookie Betts	2.50	6.00
45 Paul DeJong	1.50	4.00
48 Josh Bell	1.25	3.00
50 Shohei Ohtani	2.00	5.00
53 Freddie Freeman	2.00	5.00
57 Juan Soto	5.00	12.00
62 Zack Greinke	1.25	3.00
63 Carlos Correa	1.50	4.00
66 Miguel Cabrera	1.50	4.00
69 Maikel Franco	1.25	3.00
72 Eugenio Suarez	1.25	3.00
73 Carlos Santana	1.25	3.00
76 Marcus Stroman	1.25	3.00
80 Ronald Guzman	1.00	2.50
82 Whit Merrifield	1.50	4.00
92 Gleyber Torres	3.00	8.00
94 Francisco Lindor	1.50	4.00
100 Kris Bryant	2.00	5.00
101 Blake Snell	1.25	3.00
102 Rhys Hoskins	2.00	5.00
103 Miguel Andujar	1.50	4.00
104 Ozzie Albies	1.50	4.00
107 Max Kepler	1.25	3.00
110 Salvador Perez	1.25	3.00
111 Justin Verlander	1.50	4.00
118 Starlin Castro	1.00	2.50
120 Ramon Laureano	2.00	5.00
121 Joey Votto	1.50	4.00
122 J.D. Martinez	1.50	4.00
124 Joey Gallo	1.25	3.00
126 Wil Myers	1.00	2.50
130 Michael Kopech	2.00	5.00
133 George Springer	1.25	3.00
136 Lorenzo Cain	1.00	2.50
143 Mitch Haniger	1.25	3.00
145 Ryan O'Hearn	1.00	2.50
147 Rafael Devers	2.00	5.00
148 Trey Mancini	1.25	3.00
149 Gregory Polanco	1.25	3.00
150 Ronald Acuna Jr.	8.00	20.00
155 Javier Baez	2.00	5.00
158 Luis Urias	1.50	4.00
163 Trevor Story	1.50	4.00
166 Jose Altuve	1.25	3.00
168 Kevin Pillar	1.00	2.50
171 Clayton Kershaw	3.00	8.00
176 Brandon Nimmo	1.25	3.00
189 Edwin Encarnacion	1.50	4.00
196 Yoan Moncada	1.50	4.00
200 Jacob deGrom	1.50	4.00
203 James Paxton	1.25	3.00
204 Josh Hader	1.00	2.50
208 Dansby Swanson	1.50	4.00
210 Paul Goldschmidt	1.50	4.00
213 Nolan Arenado	2.00	5.00
214 David Peralta	1.00	2.50
215 Chris Archer	1.00	2.50
221 Justin Turner	1.25	3.00
226 Billy Hamilton	1.25	3.00
227 Jose Ramirez	1.25	3.00
232 Dylan Bundy	1.25	3.00
235 Luis Severino	1.25	3.00
238 Jose Berrios	1.25	3.00
248 Chris Shaw	1.50	4.00
249 Jake Bauers	1.50	4.00
250 Max Scherzer	1.50	4.00
256 Brian Anderson	1.00	2.50
260 Matt Chapman	1.50	4.00
264 Evan Longoria	1.25	3.00
265 Brandon Crawford	1.25	3.00
266 Jose Martinez	1.00	2.50
268 Willy Adames	1.00	2.50
271 Trea Turner	1.25	3.00
274 Nicholas Castellanos	1.50	4.00
280 Matt Olson	1.00	2.50
282 Rougned Odor	1.25	3.00
283 Danny Jansen	1.00	2.50
286 Kenley Jansen	1.25	3.00
287 Cedric Mullins	1.50	4.00
288 Jose Abreu	1.50	4.00
291 Noah Syndergaard	1.25	3.00
292 Matt Carpenter	1.50	4.00
293 Eric Hosmer	1.25	3.00
300 Aaron Judge	4.00	10.00

2019 Topps Gypsy Queen Chrome Box Toppers Gold Refractors

*GOLD: 1.5X TO 4X BASIC

STATED ODDS 1:6 HOBBY BOXES

STATED PRINT RUN 50 SER.#'d SETS

1 Mike Trout	50.00	120.00

2019 Topps Gypsy Queen Fortune Teller Mini

STATED ODDS 1:6 HOBBY

*INDIGO/250: 1X TO 2.5X BASIC

GREEN/99: 2X TO 5X BASIC

FTMAJ Aaron Judge	1.25	3.00
FTMAN Aaron Nola	.40	1.00
FTMBS Blake Snell	.40	1.00
FTMCY Christian Yelich	.60	1.50
FTMED Edwin Diaz	.40	1.00
FTMFF Freddie Freeman	.60	1.50
FTMGT Gleyber Torres	1.00	2.50
FTMJA Jose Altuve	.40	1.00
FTMJB Javier Baez	.60	1.50
FTMJD Jacob deGrom	.50	1.25
FTMJM J.D. Martinez	.50	1.25
FTMJS Juan Soto	1.50	4.00
FTMJV Justin Verlander	.50	1.25
FTMKB Kris Bryant	.60	1.50
FTMKD Khris Davis	.50	1.25
FTMKT Kyle Tucker	.60	1.50
FTMLU Luis Urias	.50	1.25
FTMMS Max Scherzer	.50	1.25
FTMNA Nolan Arenado	.60	1.50
FTMRAJ Ronald Acuna Jr.	2.50	6.00

2019 Topps Gypsy Queen Fortune Teller Mini Autographs

STATED ODDS 1:1691 HOBBY

PRINT RUNS B/WN 10-50 COPIES PER

NO PRICING ON QTY 10

EXCHANGE DEADLINE 2/28/2020

FTMAAM Andrew McCutchen/20	40.00	100.00
FTMAAME Austin Meadows/50	12.00	30.00
FTMABN Brandon Nimmo/50	12.00	30.00
FTMACS Carlos Santana/50	15.00	40.00
FTMAFL Francisco Lindor/40	30.00	80.00
FTMAGS George Springer/40	20.00	50.00
FTMAJB Jake Bauers/50	15.00	40.00
FTMAJS Juan Soto/50	75.00	200.00
FTMAKB Kris Bryant EXCH	75.00	200.00
FTMAMA Miguel Andujar/50	20.00	50.00
FTMAPD Paul DeJong/50	15.00	40.00
FTMATS Trevor Story/50	15.00	40.00
FTMAWA Willy Adames/50	10.00	25.00

2019 Topps Gypsy Queen Mini Rookie Autographs

STATED ODDS 1:999 HOBBY

STATED PRINT RUN 99 SER.#'d SETS

EXCHANGE DEADLINE 2/28/2020

*BW/50: .5X TO 1.2X BASIC

MRABK Brad Keller	12.00	30.00
MRABW Bryse Wilson	15.00	40.00
MRACA Chance Adams	8.00	20.00
MRACB Corbin Burnes	10.00	25.00
MRACM Cedric Mullins	10.00	25.00
MRADJ Danny Jansen	4.00	10.00
MRAKA Kolby Allard	6.00	15.00
MRAKT Kyle Tucker	25.00	60.00
MRALU Luis Urias	15.00	40.00
MRAMK Michael Kopech	10.00	25.00

2019 Topps Gypsy Queen Mystery Redemption Autographs

RANDOM INSERTS IN PACKS

EXCHANGE DEADLINE 2/28/2020

*INDIGO/150: .5X TO 1.2X BASIC

*SWAP/99: .6X TO 1.5X BASIC

*BW/50: .75X TO 2X BASIC

*BAZOOKA/25: 1X TO 2.5X BASIC

NNO1 Mystery EXCH A	75.00	200.00
NNO2 Mystery EXCH B	60.00	150.00

2019 Topps Gypsy Queen Tarot of the Diamond

STATED ODDS 1:8 HOBBY

*INDIGO/250: 1X TO 2.5X BASIC

*GREEN/99: 2X TO 5X BASIC

1 Shohei Ohtani	.60	1.50
2 Edwin Encarnacion	.50	1.25
3 Xander Bogaerts	.50	1.25
4 Craig Kimbrel	.40	1.00
5 Mike Trout	2.50	6.00
6 J.D. Martinez	.50	1.25
7 Nolan Arenado	.60	1.50
8 Giancarlo Stanton	.50	1.25
9 Clayton Kershaw	1.00	2.50
10 Jacob deGrom	.50	1.25
11 Yasiel Puig	.50	1.25
12 Ozzie Albies	.50	1.25
13 Edwin Diaz	.40	1.00
14 Bryce Harper	.75	2.00
15 Mookie Betts	.75	2.00
16 Khris Davis	.50	1.25
17 Shohei Ohtani	.60	1.50
18 Ronald Acuna Jr.	2.50	6.00
19 Jose Altuve	.40	1.00
20 Corey Kluber	.40	1.00
21 Jesus Aguilar	.30	.75
22 Aaron Judge	1.25	3.00

2020 Topps Gypsy Queen

SP ODDS 1:24 HOBBY

1 Mookie Betts	.60	1.50
2 J.T. Realmuto	.30	.75
3 Ramon Laureano	.30	.75
4 Matt Olson	.20	.50
5 Dom Nunez RC	.40	1.00
6 Brandon Woodruff	.20	.50
7 Zack Greinke	.25	.60
8 Garrett Hampson	.20	.50
9 Harold Ramirez	.20	.50
10 Rangel Ravelo RC	.40	1.00
11 Cedric Mullins	.30	.75
12 Max Kepler	.25	.60
13 Howie Kendrick	.20	.50
14 John Means	.20	.50
15 Justin Smoak	.20	.50
16 Michael Brantley	.25	.60
17 Bo Bichette RC	2.50	6.00
18 Asdrubal Cabrera	.25	.60
19 Brock Holt	.20	.50
20 Yusei Kikuchi	.25	.60
21 Clayton Kershaw	.60	1.50
22 Victor Robles	.40	1.00
23 Trent Grisham RC	1.25	3.00
24 Michael Conforto	.25	.60
25 Christian Yelich	.40	1.00
26 Adrian Morejon RC	.30	.75
27 Joey Votto	.30	.75
28 Brock Burke RC	.30	.75
29 Willson Contreras	.30	.75
30 Carter Kieboom	.25	.60
31 Carlos Santana	.25	.60
32 Dawel Lugo	.20	.50
33 Tom Eshelman RC	.40	1.00
34 Adbert Alzolay RC	.40	1.00
35 Aristides Aquino RC	.60	1.50
36 Hanser Alberto	.20	.50
37 Dario Agrazal RC	.40	1.00
38 Kris Bryant	.40	1.00
39 Yolmer Sanchez	.20	.50
40 Danny Jansen	.20	.50
41 Blake Snell	.25	.60
42 Gio Urshela	.30	.75
43 Jacob deGrom	.30	.75
44 Alex Colome	.20	.50
45 Didi Gregorius	.25	.60
46 Willians Astudillo	.20	.50
47 Paul Goldschmidt	.30	.75
48 Vladimir Guerrero Jr.	.60	1.50
49 Brandon Crawford	.25	.60
50 Aaron Judge	.75	2.00
51 Austin Dean	.20	.50
52 Brendan McKay RC	.50	1.25
53 Harrison Bader	.25	.60
54 Jeff McNeil	.25	.60
55 Trea Turner	.25	.60
56 Giancarlo Stanton	.30	.75
57 Jose Altuve	.25	.60
58 Ty France	.30	.75
59 Willie Calhoun	.20	.50
60 Joe Jimenez	.20	.50
61 Josh Bell	.25	.60
62 Dylan Cease RC	.60	1.50
63 Austin Nola RC	.50	1.25
64 Mitch Haniger	.25	.60
65 Pete Alonso	.75	2.00
66 Kirby Yates	.20	.50
67 David Price	.25	.60
68 Randy Arozarena RC	2.50	6.00
69 Max Fried	.30	.75
70 Bobby Bradley RC	.40	1.00
71 Jose Berrios	.25	.60
72 Kyle Hendricks	.30	.75
73 Jorge Alfaro	.20	.50
74 T.J. Zeuch RC	.30	.75
75 David Dahl	.20	.50
76 Bryce Harper	.50	1.25
77 Josh Staumont RC	.30	.75
78 A.J. Minter	.25	.60
79 Jack Flaherty	.25	.60
80 Tim Lopes RC	.40	1.00
81 David Peralta	.20	.50
82 Matt Thaiss RC	.40	1.00
83 Noah Syndergaard	.25	.60
84 Eric Hosmer	.25	.60
85 Eduardo Rodriguez	.20	.50
86 Anthony Rizzo	.50	1.25
87 Junior Fernandez RC	.30	.75
88 Wilson Ramos	.20	.50
89 Jake Arrieta	.25	.60
90 Brandon Belt	.25	.60
91 Seth Brown RC	.30	.75
92 Justin Turner	.25	.60
93 Gerrit Cole	.50	1.25
94 Eloy Jimenez	.60	1.50
95 Jorge Polanco	.25	.60
96 Xander Bogaerts	.30	.75
97 Kyle Seager	.20	.50
98 Nick Solak RC	.50	1.25
99 Matthew Boyd	.20	.50
100 Gleyber Torres	.60	1.50
101 Sean Murphy RC	.50	1.25
102 Mike Soroka	.30	.75
103 Charlie Blackmon	.30	.75
104 Fernando Tatis Jr.	1.25	3.00
105 Eugenio Suarez	.25	.60
106 Meibrys Viloria	.20	.50
107 Nelson Cruz	.30	.75
108 Logan Webb RC	.40	1.00
109 Andrelton Simmons	.20	.50
110 Brian Anderson	.20	.50
111 Trevor Story	.30	.75
112 Jonathan Hernandez RC	.30	.75
113 A.J. Puk RC	.60	1.50
114 David Fletcher	.30	.75
115 Rhys Hoskins	.40	1.00
116 Brendan Rodgers	.30	.75
117 Andrew Benintendi	.30	.75
118 Ender Inciarte	.20	.50
119 Robbie Ray	.20	.50
120 Lourdes Gurriel Jr.	.25	.60
121 Chance Sisco	.20	.50
122 Luis Robert RC	3.00	8.00
123 Logan Allen RC	.30	.75
124 Mark Melancon	.20	.50
125 Tyler Alexander	.30	.75
126 Amed Rosario	.25	.60
127 Jose Rodriguez RC	.30	.75
128 Zac Gallen RC	.75	2.00
129 Tommy Pham	.20	.50
130 Kevin Newman	.25	.60
131 Colin Moran	.20	.50
132 Yoan Moncada	.30	.75
133 Kole Calhoun	.20	.50
134 Tim Anderson	.30	.75
135 Corey Seager	.30	.75
136 Rafael Devers	.40	1.00
137 Yordan Alvarez RC	1.50	4.00
138 Jose Urena	.20	.50
139 Eduardo Escobar	.20	.50
140 Eric Thames	.20	.50
141 Lorenzo Cain	.20	.50
142 Luis Severino	.25	.60
143 Robert Dugger RC	.30	.75
144 Justin Dunn RC	.40	1.00
145 Mitch Garver	.20	.50
146 Anthony Santander	.20	.50
147 Bubba Starling RC	.60	1.50
148 Nomar Mazara	.20	.50
149 Shin-Soo Choo	.25	.60
150 Cody Bellinger	.60	1.50
151 Michael Lorenzen	.20	.50
152 Gary Sanchez	.30	.75
153 Austin Hays	.30	.75
154 Nick Williams	.20	.50
155 Dustin May RC	1.25	3.00
156 Rougned Odor	.25	.60
157 Yuli Gurriel	.25	.60
158 Walker Buehler	.40	1.00
159 Carlos Correa	.30	.75
160 Mike Minor	.20	.50
161 Kean Wong RC	.40	1.00
162 Anthony Kay RC	.30	.75
163 Patrick Corbin	.25	.60
164 Shane Bieber	.30	.75
165 Jose Abreu	.30	.75
166 Max Scherzer	.30	.75
167 Bryan Reynolds	.25	.60
168 Jake Fraley RC	.40	1.00
169 Adam Ottavino	.20	.50
170 Kyle Schwarber	.30	.75
171 Yu Chang RC	.50	1.25
172 Jon Lester	.25	.60
173 Jordan Yamamoto RC	.40	1.00
174 Gavin Lux RC	2.00	5.00
175 Hyun-Jin Ryu	.25	.60
176 Kevin Kiermaier	.25	.60
177 James Paxton	.25	.60
178 Juan Soto	1.00	2.50
179 Nicky Lopez	.20	.50
180 Keston Hiura	.40	1.00
181 Jean Segura	.25	.60
182 Brandon Dixon	.20	.50
183 Yasmani Grandal	.20	.50
184 Miles Mikolas	.20	.50
185 Jose Iglesias	.25	.60
186 Evan Longoria	.25	.60
187 Ronald Acuna Jr.	1.25	3.00
188 Matt Chapman	.30	.75
189 Tyler Glasnow	.20	.50
190 Eddie Rosario	.25	.60
191 Victor Reyes	.20	.50
192 Ryan O'Hearn	.20	.50
193 Trevor Williams	.20	.50
194 Jaylin Davis RC	.50	1.25
195 J.D. Martinez	.30	.75
196 Mitch Keller	.30	.75
197 Hunter Harvey RC	.50	1.25
198 Alex Young RC	.30	.75
199 Adam Haseley	.30	.75
200 Alex Bregman	.30	.75
201 Nico Hoerner RC	1.25	3.00
202 Max Muncy	.25	.60
203 Luis Arraez	.40	1.00
204 Albert Pujols	.40	1.00
205 Austin Meadows	.25	.60
206 Christian Vazquez	.20	.50
207 Paul DeJong	.30	.75
208 Adalberto Mondesi	.30	.75
209 J.D. Davis	.20	.50
210 Khris Davis	.30	.75
211 Austin Riley	.50	1.25
212 Marcus Semien	.20	.50
213 Aroldis Chapman	.30	.75
214 Danny Duffy	.20	.50
215 Anthony Rendon	.30	.75
216 Willy Adames	.20	.50
217 Sheldon Neuse RC	.40	1.00
218 Starling Marte	.25	.60
219 Will Smith	.40	1.00
220 James Marvel RC	.30	.75
221 Dansby Swanson	.30	.75
222 Michael Chavis	.25	.60
223 Cavan Biggio	.40	1.00
224 Trey Mancini	.30	.75
225 Jake Rogers RC	.30	.75
226 Kyle Lewis RC	2.50	6.00
227 Oscar Mercado	.25	.60
228 Francisco Lindor	.30	.75
229 Emmanuel Clase RC	.40	1.00
230 Francisco Mejia	.25	.60
231 Aaron Nola	.30	.75
232 Aaron Civale RC	.50	1.25
233 Javier Baez	.40	1.00
234 Michel Baez RC	.30	.75
235 Ryan McMahon	.20	.50
236 Derek Dietrich	.25	.60
237 Sandy Alcantara	.20	.50
238 Ozzie Albies	.30	.75
239 Nick Senzel	.30	.75
240 Scott Kingery	.25	.60
241 Ryan Braun	.25	.60
242 Hunter Dozier	.20	.50
243 Buster Posey	.40	1.00
244 Shed Long	.25	.60
245 Marcus Stroman	.25	.60
246 Brusdar Graterol RC	.50	1.25
247 Ronald Guzman	.20	.50
248 Steven Matz	.25	.60
249 Luis Castillo	.25	.60
250 Justin Verlander	.30	.75
251 Jose Ramirez	.25	.60
252 Will Smith	.20	.50
253 Rowdy Tellez	.25	.60
254 Chris Archer	.20	.50
255 Luke Weaver	.20	.50
256 Christian Walker	.25	.60
257 Willi Castro RC	.30	.75
258 Mike Yastrzemski	.50	1.25
259 Starlin Castro	.20	.50
260 Zack Collins RC	.40	1.00
261 Shohei Ohtani	.40	1.00
262 Andres Munoz RC	.40	1.00
263 Dwight Smith Jr.	.20	.50
264 Trevor Bauer	.30	.75
265 Sam Hilliard RC	.50	1.25
266 Miguel Cabrera	.30	.75
267 Peter Lambert	.25	.60
268 Mauricio Dubon RC	.40	1.00
269 Jorge Soler	.30	.75
270 Franmil Reyes	.20	.50
271 Michael Brosseau RC	.60	1.50
272 Raisel Iglesias	.20	.50
273 Yadier Molina	.30	.75
274 Andrew Heaney	.20	.50
275 Jeff Samardzija	.20	.50
276 George Springer	.25	.60
277 Lucas Giolito	.25	.60
278 DJ LeMahieu	.30	.75
279 Randal Grichuk	.20	.50
280 Travis d'Arnaud	.25	.60
281 Whit Merrifield	.30	.75
282 Aaron Nola	.30	.75
283 Zach Davies	.20	.50
284 Robel Garcia RC	.30	.75
285 Stephen Strasburg	.30	.75
286 Domingo Leyba RC	.40	1.00
287 Jesus Luzardo RC	.60	1.50
288 Josh Hader	.20	.50
289 Byron Buxton	.25	.60
290 Tommy La Stella	.20	.50
291 Tommy Edman	.30	.75
292 Manny Machado	.30	.75
293 Isan Diaz RC	.50	1.25
294 Nolan Arenado	.40	1.00
295 Ketel Marte	.25	.60
296 Archie Bradley	.20	.50
297 Travis Demeritte RC	.40	1.00
298 Freddie Freeman	.40	1.00
299 Sonny Gray	.25	.60
300 Mike Trout	1.50	4.00
301 Babe Ruth SP	3.00	8.00
302 Mariano Rivera SP	1.50	4.00
303 Deion Sanders SP	1.00	2.50
304 Reggie Jackson SP	1.00	2.50
305 Tony Gwynn SP	1.25	3.00
306 Carl Yastrzemski SP	2.00	5.00
307 Mike Schmidt SP	2.00	5.00
308 Roberto Clemente SP	3.00	8.00
309 Johnny Bench SP	1.25	3.00
310 Vladimir Guerrero SP	1.00	2.50
311 Chipper Jones SP	1.25	3.00
312 Sammy Sosa SP	1.25	3.00
313 Pedro Martinez SP	1.00	2.50
314 Ted Williams SP	2.50	6.00
315 Sandy Koufax SP	2.50	6.00
316 Rickey Henderson SP	1.25	3.00
317 Cal Ripken Jr. SP	4.00	10.00
318 Ken Griffey Jr. SP	2.50	6.00
319 Honus Wagner SP	1.25	3.00
320 Jackie Robinson SP	1.25	3.00

2020 Topps Gypsy Queen Armed Forces Day Variations

STATED ODDS 1:1210 HOBBY

1 Mookie Betts	30.00	80.00
25 Christian Yelich	25.00	60.00
31 Carlos Santana	10.00	25.00
71 Jose Berrios	15.00	40.00
76 Bryce Harper	30.00	80.00
86 Anthony Rizzo	25.00	60.00
132 Yoan Moncada	12.00	30.00
136 Rafael Devers	25.00	60.00
188 Matt Chapman	20.00	50.00

0 Eddie Rosario 20.00 50.00
0 Alex Bregman 15.00 40.00
8 Ozzie Albies 25.00 60.00
78 DJ LeMahieu 25.00 60.00
4 Nolan Arenado 20.00 50.00
8 Freddie Freeman 25.00 60.00

2020 Topps Gypsy Queen Bazooka Back

BAZOOKA: 4X TO 10X BASIC
BAZOOKA RC: 2.5X TO 6X BASIC RC
BAZOOKA SP: 8X TO 20X BASIC SP
STATED ODDS 1:61 HOBBY
STATED SP ODDS 1:1817 HOBBY
22 Luis Robert 75.00 200.00
00 Mike Trout 50.00 120.00

2020 Topps Gypsy Queen Black and White

BLACK WHITE: 6X TO 15X BASIC
BLACK WHITE RC: 4X TO 10X BASIC RC
STATED ODDS 1:50 HOBBY
STATED PRINT RUN 50 SER.#'d SETS
22 Luis Robert 100.00 250.00
00 Mike Trout 60.00 150.00

2020 Topps Gypsy Queen Blue

BLUE: 5X TO 12X BASIC
BLUE RC: 3X TO 8X BASIC RC
BLUE SP: 1.5X TO 4X BASIC RC
STATED ODDS 1:41 HOBBY
STATED PRINT RUN 150 SER.#'d SETS
22 Luis Robert 75.00 200.00

2020 Topps Gypsy Queen GQ Logo Swap

SWAP: 2.5X TO 6X BASIC
SWAP RC: 1.5X TO 4X BASIC RC
SWAP SP: 1.2X TO 3X BASIC SP
STATED ODDS 1:31 HOBBY
STATED SP ODDS 1:1210 HOBBY
22 Luis Robert 50.00 120.00

2020 Topps Gypsy Queen Green

GREEN: 1X TO 2.5X BASIC
GREEN RC: .6X TO 1.5X BASIC RC
VE PER BLASTER BOX

2020 Topps Gypsy Queen Indigo

INDIGO: 2.5X TO 6X BASIC
INDIGO RC: 1.5X TO 4X BASIC RC
STATED ODDS 1:25 HOBBY
STATED PRINT RUN 250 SER.#'d SETS
22 Luis Robert 50.00 120.00

2020 Topps Gypsy Queen Jackie Robinson Day Variations

STATED ODDS 1:152 HOBBY
SWAP: .75X TO 2X BASIC
1 Clayton Kershaw 6.00 15.00
5 Christian Yelich 4.00 10.00
9 Willson Contreras 3.00 8.00
8 Kris Bryant 4.00 10.00
6 Willians Astudillo 2.00 5.00
5 Pete Alonso 8.00 20.00
3 Noah Syndergaard 2.50 6.00
6 Xander Bogaerts 3.00 8.00
04 Fernando Tatis Jr. 12.00 30.00
15 Rhys Hoskins 4.00 10.00
34 Tim Anderson 3.00 8.00
36 Rafael Devers 4.00 10.00
95 J.D. Martinez 3.00 8.00
00 Alex Bregman 3.00 8.00
02 Max Muncy 2.50 6.00
33 Javier Baez 4.00 10.00
63 Dwight Smith Jr. 2.00 5.00
64 Trevor Bauer 3.00 8.00
82 Aaron Nola 3.00 8.00
92 Manny Machado 3.00 8.00

2020 Topps Gypsy Queen Missing Nameplate

NO NAME: 1.5X TO 4X BASIC
NO NAME RC: 1X TO 2.5X BASIC RC
NO NAME SP: 2X TO 5X BASIC SP
STATED ODDS 1:23 HOBBY
STATED SP ODDS 1:605 HOBBY
22 Luis Robert 30.00 80.00

2020 Topps Gypsy Queen Players Weekend Variations

STATED ODDS 1:150 HOBBY
SWAP: .75X TO 2X BASIC
Harold Ramirez 2.00 5.00
4 John Means 2.00 5.00
1 Clayton Kershaw 6.00 15.00
5 Christian Yelich 4.00 10.00
5 Aristides Aquino 4.00 10.00
8 Kris Bryant 4.00 10.00
3 Jacob deGrom 3.00 8.00
8 Vladimir Guerrero Jr. 6.00 15.00
0 Aaron Judge 12.00 30.00
2 Dylan Cease 4.00 10.00
6 Kirby Yates 2.00 5.00
1 Jose Berrios 2.50 6.00
96 Xander Bogaerts 3.00 8.00
97 Kyle Seager 2.00 5.00
98 Nick Solak 3.00 8.00
103 Charlie Blackmon 3.00 8.00
167 Bryan Reynolds 2.50 6.00
176 Kevin Kiermaier 2.50 6.00
178 Juan Soto 10.00 25.00
187 Ronald Acuna Jr. 12.00 30.00
207 Paul DeJong 3.00 8.00
212 Marcus Semien 2.00 5.00
227 Oscar Mercado 2.50 6.00
242 Hunter Dozier 2.00 5.00
258 Mike Yastrzemski 5.00 12.00
266 Miguel Cabrera 3.00 8.00
276 George Springer 2.50 6.00

282 Aaron Nola 3.00 8.00
295 Ketel Marte 2.50 6.00
300 Mike Trout 30.00 80.00

2020 Topps Gypsy Queen Silver

*SILVER: 1X TO 2.5X BASIC
*SILVER RC: .6X TO 1.5X BASIC RC
TWELVE PER MONSTER BOX

2020 Topps Gypsy Queen Autograph Garments

STATED ODDS 1:1930 HOBBY
PRINT RUNS B/WN 10-50 COPIES PER
NO PRICING ON QTY 10
EXCHANGE DEADLINE 2/29/2022
AGAN Aaron Nola/50 20.00 50.00
AGCA Chance Adams/50 12.00 30.00
AGCP Chris Paddack/50 20.00 50.00
AGCY Christian Yelich/40 50.00 120.00
AGFTJ Fernando Tatis Jr./50 125.00 300.00
AGGT Gleyber Torres/40 75.00 200.00
AGGU Gio Urshela/50 20.00 50.00
AGJD Jon Duplantier/50 12.00 30.00
AGKB Kris Bryant/25 75.00 200.00
AGKH Keston Hiura/50 25.00 60.00
AGMC Michael Chavis/50 15.00 40.00
AGMM Max Muncy/50 15.00 40.00
AGMS Max Scherzer/40 60.00 150.00
AGRAJ Ronald Acuna Jr./40 100.00 250.00
AGRH Rhys Hoskins/50 30.00 80.00
AGSO Shohei Ohtani EXCH 100.00 250.00
AGVGJ Vladimir Guerrero Jr./50 50.00 120.00
AGWC Willson Contreras/50 20.00 50.00
AGYA Yordan Alvarez/50 75.00 200.00

2020 Topps Gypsy Queen Autograph Patch Booklets

STATED ODDS 1:8135 HOBBY
PRINT RUNS B/WN 10-20 COPIES PER
NO PRICING ON QTY 10
EXCHANGE DEADLINE 2/29/2022
GQAPAJ Aaron Judge/10
GQAPFTJ Fernando Tatis Jr./20 300.00 800.00
GQAPGH Garrett Hampson/20 40.00 100.00
GQAPJDM J.D. Martinez/20 60.00 150.00
GQAPJF Jack Flaherty/20 125.00 300.00
GQAPNA Nolan Arenado/20 125.00 300.00
GQAPRH Rickey Henderson
GQAPSO Shohei Ohtani EXCH 250.00 600.00
GQAPWA Willians Astudillo/20 40.00 100.00
GQAPWM Whit Merrifield 80.00 200.00
GQAPYA Yordan Alvarez 250.00 600.00

2020 Topps Gypsy Queen Autographs

STATED ODDS 1:15 HOBBY
EXCHANGE DEADLINE 2/29/2020
GQAAA Adbert Alzolay 3.00 8.00
GQAAAQ Aristides Aquino 20.00 50.00
GQAAC Aaron Civale 4.00 10.00
GQAAJ Aaron Judge 100.00 250.00
GQAAM Austin Meadows 8.00 20.00
GQAAP A.J. Puk 5.00 12.00
GQAAR Austin Riley 15.00 40.00
GQAAY Alex Young 2.50 6.00
GQABB Bobby Bradley 4.00 10.00
GQABBI Bo Bichette 50.00 120.00
GQABM Brendan McKay 10.00 25.00
GQACD Corey Dickerson 3.00 8.00
GQACJ Carter Kieboom 3.00 8.00
GQACM Charlie Morton 4.00 10.00
GQACP Chris Paddack 6.00 15.00
GQACY Christian Yelich 30.00 80.00
GQADC Dylan Cease 5.00 12.00
GQADP David Peralta 3.00 8.00
GQADSJ Dwight Smith Jr. 3.00 8.00
GQAGL Gavin Lux 20.00 50.00
GQAGT Gleyber Torres 50.00 120.00
GQAGU Gio Urshela 8.00 20.00
GQAID Isan Diaz 5.00 12.00
GQAJDM J.D. Martinez 12.00 30.00
GQAJF Jack Flaherty 12.00 30.00
GQAJL Jesus Luzardo 12.00 30.00
GQAJY Jordan Yamamoto 3.00 8.00
GQAKA Kolby Allard 2.50 6.00
GQAKH Keston Hiura 12.00 30.00
GQAKN Kevin Newman 3.00 8.00
GQALA Logan Allen 4.00 10.00
GQALGJ Lourdes Gurriel Jr. 3.00 8.00
GQALMJ Lance McCullers Jr. 4.00 10.00
GQALR Luis Robert EXCH 125.00 300.00
GQAMB Michel Baez 2.50 6.00
GQAMBE Matt Beaty 5.00 12.00
GQAMC Miguel Cabrera 30.00 80.00
GQAMCH Michael Chavis 6.00 15.00
GQAMF Mike Foltynewicz 4.00 10.00
GQAMM Mike Mussina 25.00 60.00
GQAMMI Miles Mikolas EXCH 6.00 15.00
GQAMMU Max Muncy 8.00 20.00
GQAMT Mike Trout 400.00 800.00
GQANH Nico Hoerner 10.00 25.00
GQANS Nick Senzel 10.00 25.00
GQAPD Paul DeJong 4.00 10.00
GQARAJ Ronald Acuna Jr. 100.00 250.00
GQARG Robel Garcia 2.50 6.00
GQARH Rickey Henderson 50.00 120.00
GQASL Shed Long 3.00 8.00
GQATE Thairo Estrada 5.00 12.00
GQATG Dustin May 15.00 40.00
GQATW Taylor Ward 4.00 10.00
GQAVGJ Vladimir Guerrero Jr. 40.00 100.00
GQAWA Willians Astudillo 4.00 10.00
GQAWM Whit Merrifield 5.00 12.00
GQAWS Will Smith 6.00 15.00
GQAYA Yordan Alvarez 50.00 120.00
GQAZC Zack Collins 3.00 8.00

2020 Topps Gypsy Queen Autographs Bazooka Back

*BAZOOKA: .75X TO 2X BASIC
STATED ODDS 1:1218 HOBBY
PRINT RUNS B/WN 24-25 COPIES PER
EXCHANGE DEADLINE 2/29/2020
GQAAJ Aaron Judge/25 125.00 300.00
GQABBI Bo Bichette/25 150.00 400.00
GQABR Bryan Reynolds/25 20.00 50.00
GQACA Chance Adams/25 10.00 25.00
GQACY Christian Yelich/25 100.00 250.00
GQAFTJ Fernando Tatis Jr./25 EXCH 150.00 400.00
GQAKH Keston Hiura/25 40.00 100.00
GQAKN Kevin Newman/25 25.00 60.00
GQAMS Max Scherzer/25 EXCH 50.00 120.00
GQAMT Mike Trout/25 500.00 1000.00
GQAPA Pete Alonso/25 75.00 200.00
GQAPD Paul DeJong/25 20.00 50.00
GQARH Rickey Henderson/25 60.00 150.00
GQASO Shohei Ohtani/24 125.00 300.00
GQAWM Whit Merrifield/25 25.00 60.00
GQAWS Will Smith/25 25.00 60.00
GQAYA Yordan Alvarez/25 200.00 500.00

2020 Topps Gypsy Queen Autographs Black and White

*BW: .6X TO 1.5X BASIC
STATED ODDS 1:272 HOBBY
PRINT RUNS B/WN 34-50 COPIES PER
EXCHANGE DEADLINE 2/29/2020
GQABR Bryan Reynolds/50 15.00 40.00
GQACA Chance Adams/50 8.00 20.00
GQAFTJ Fernando Tatis Jr./50 EXCH 125.00 300.00
GQAMS Max Scherzer/50 EXCH 40.00 100.00
GQAPA Pete Alonso/50 60.00 150.00
GQASO Shohei Ohtani/34 100.00 250.00

2020 Topps Gypsy Queen Autographs Blue

*BLUE: .5X TO 1.2X BASIC
STATED ODDS 1:387 HOBBY
STATED PRINT RUN 99 SER.#'d SETS
EXCHANGE DEADLINE 2/29/2020
GQABR Bryan Reynolds 12.00 30.00
GQACA Chance Adams 6.00 15.00
GQAPA Pete Alonso 50.00 120.00

2020 Topps Gypsy Queen Autographs GQ Logo Swap

*GQ LOGO: .5X TO 1.2X BASIC
STATED ODDS 1:343 HOBBY
STATED PRINT RUN 99 SER.#'d SETS
EXCHANGE DEADLINE 2/29/2020
GQABR Bryan Reynolds 12.00 30.00
GQACA Chance Adams 6.00 15.00
GQAFTJ Fernando Tatis Jr. EXCH 100.00 250.00
GQAMS Max Scherzer EXCH 30.00 80.00
GQAPA Pete Alonso 50.00 120.00

2020 Topps Gypsy Queen Autographs Indigo

*INDIGO: .5X TO 1.2X BASIC
STATED ODDS 1:279 HOBBY
STATED PRINT RUN 150 SER.#'d SETS
EXCHANGE DEADLINE 2/29/2020
GQABR Bryan Reynolds 12.00 30.00
GQACA Chance Adams 6.00 15.00
GQAPA Pete Alonso 50.00 210.00

2020 Topps Gypsy Queen Autographs Jackie Robinson Day Variations

STATED ODDS 1:1734 HOBBY
PRINT RUNS B/WN 15-99 COPIES PER
NO PRICING ON QTY 15
EXCHANGE DEADLINE 2/29/2022
*BW/42: .5X TO 1.2X BASIC
25 Christian Yelich/40 60.00 150.00
29 Willson Contreras/40 15.00 40.00
38 Kris Bryant/25 100.00 250.00
46 Willians Astudillo/99 6.00 15.00
115 Rhys Hoskins/70 25.00 60.00
134 Tim Anderson/99 10.00 25.00
136 Rafael Devers/70 25.00 60.00
195 J.D. Martinez/50 20.00 50.00
202 Max Muncy/99 10.00 25.00
263 Dwight Smith Jr./99 10.00 25.00
264 Trevor Bauer/75 12.00 30.00
282 Aaron Nola/75 12.00 30.00

2020 Topps Gypsy Queen Bases Around the League Autographs

STATED ODDS 1:11,185 HOBBY
STATED PRINT RUN 20 SER.#'d SETS
EXCHANGE DEADLINE 2/29/2022
BALBH Bryce Harper 300.00 600.00
BALMY Mike Yastrzemski 100.00 250.00
BALPA Pete Alonso 300.00 600.00
BALPD Paul DeJong 50.00 125.00
BALRH Rhys Hoskins 125.00 300.00
BALRAJ Ronald Acuna Jr. 400.00 800.00

2020 Topps Gypsy Queen Chrome Box Topper Autographs

STATED ODDS 1:87 HOBBY BOXES
STATED PRINT RUN 25 SER.#'d SETS
EXCHANGE DEADLINE 2/29/2022
25 Christian Yelich 125.00 300.00
42 Gio Urshela
48 Vladimir Guerrero Jr. 100.00 250.00
50 Aaron Judge 125.00 300.00
52 Brendan McKay 20.00 50.00
62 Dylan Cease 25.00 60.00
100 Gleyber Torres 125.00 300.00
137 Yordan Alvarez 150.00 400.00
180 Keston Hiura 50.00 120.00
187 Ronald Acuna Jr. 200.00 500.00
202 Max Muncy 30.00 80.00

205 Austin Meadows 30.00 80.00
222 Michael Chavis 15.00 40.00

2020 Topps Gypsy Queen Chrome Box Toppers

INSERTED IN HOBBY BOXES
1 Mookie Betts 2.00 5.00
2 J.T. Realmuto 1.00 2.50
7 Zack Greinke .75 2.00
12 Max Kepler .75 2.00
16 Michael Brantley .75 2.00
17 Bo Bichette 5.00 12.00
21 Clayton Kershaw 2.00 5.00
24 Michael Conforto .75 2.00
25 Christian Yelich 1.25 3.00
30 Carter Kieboom .75 2.00
31 Carlos Santana .75 2.00
35 Aristides Aquino 1.25 3.00
38 Kris Bryant 1.25 3.00
42 Gio Urshela 1.00 2.50
43 Jacob deGrom 1.00 2.50
45 Didi Gregorius .75 2.00
46 Willians Astudillo .60 1.50
47 Paul Goldschmidt 1.00 2.50
48 Vladimir Guerrero Jr. 2.00 5.00
50 Aaron Judge 3.00 8.00
52 Brendan McKay 1.00 2.50
54 Jeff McNeil .75 2.00
55 Trea Turner .75 2.00
57 Jose Altuve .75 2.00
61 Josh Bell .75 2.00
62 Dylan Cease 1.25 3.00
65 Pete Alonso 2.50 6.00
66 Kirby Yates .60 1.50
71 Jose Berrios .75 2.00
72 Kyle Hendricks 1.00 2.50
76 Bryce Harper 1.50 4.00
83 Noah Syndergaard .75 2.00
86 Anthony Rizzo 1.50 4.00
91 Seth Brown .60 1.50
92 Justin Turner .75 2.00
93 Gerrit Cole 1.50 4.00
95 Jorge Polanco .75 2.00
96 Xander Bogaerts 1.00 2.50
100 Gleyber Torres 2.00 5.00
103 Charlie Blackmon 1.00 2.50
104 Fernando Tatis Jr. 4.00 10.00
105 Eugenio Suarez .75 2.00
107 Nelson Cruz 1.00 2.50
111 Trevor Story 1.00 2.50
113 A.J. Puk 1.25 3.00
115 Rhys Hoskins 1.25 3.00
117 Andrew Benintendi 1.00 2.50
123 Logan Allen .60 1.50
129 Tommy Pham .60 1.50
136 Rafael Devers 1.25 3.00
137 Yordan Alvarez 6.00 15.00
139 Eduardo Escobar .60 1.50
150 Cody Bellinger 2.00 5.00
152 Gary Sanchez 1.00 2.50
157 Yuli Gurriel .75 2.00
158 Walker Buehler 1.25 3.00
163 Patrick Corbin .75 2.00
164 Shane Bieber 1.00 2.50
165 Jose Abreu 1.00 2.50
166 Max Scherzer 1.00 2.50
173 Jordan Yamamoto .75 2.00
174 Gavin Lux 4.00 10.00
177 James Paxton .75 2.00
178 Juan Soto 3.00 8.00
180 Keston Hiura 1.25 3.00
187 Ronald Acuna Jr. 4.00 10.00
188 Matt Chapman 1.00 2.50
190 Eddie Rosario .75 2.00
195 J.D. Martinez 1.00 2.50
200 Alex Bregman 1.00 2.50
202 Max Muncy .75 2.00
205 Austin Meadows .75 2.00
207 Paul DeJong .75 2.00
208 Adalberto Mondesi 1.00 2.50
210 Khris Davis .75 2.00
212 Marcus Semien .60 1.50
213 Aroldis Chapman 1.00 2.50
218 Starling Marte .75 2.00
219 Will Smith 1.25 3.00
222 Michael Chavis .75 2.00
224 Trey Mancini 1.00 2.50
228 Francisco Lindor 1.00 2.50
233 Javier Baez 1.25 3.00
238 Ozzie Albies 1.00 2.50
239 Nick Senzel 1.00 2.50
246 Brusdar Graterol 1.00 2.50
250 Justin Verlander 1.00 2.50
261 Shohei Ohtani 1.25 3.00
270 Franmil Reyes .60 1.50
276 George Springer .75 2.00
277 Lucas Giolito .75 2.00
278 DJ LeMahieu 1.00 2.50
281 Whit Merrifield 1.00 2.50
282 Aaron Nola 1.00 2.50
285 Stephen Strasburg 1.00 2.50
292 Manny Machado 1.00 2.50
294 Nolan Arenado 1.25 3.00
295 Ketel Marte 1.00 2.50
298 Freddie Freeman 1.25 3.00
300 Mike Trout 5.00 12.00

2020 Topps Gypsy Queen Chrome Box Toppers Blue Refractors

*BLUE REF: 1.2X TO 3X BASIC
STATED ODDS 1:4 HOBBY BOXES
STATED PRINT RUN 99 SER.#'d SETS

50 Aaron Judge 20.00 50.00
300 Mike Trout 25.00 60.00

2020 Topps Gypsy Queen Chrome Box Toppers Gold Refractors

*GOLD REF: 2.5X TO 6X BASIC
STATED ODDS 1:7 HOBBY BOXES
STATED PRINT RUN 50 SER.#'d SETS
50 Aaron Judge 40.00 100.00
300 Mike Trout 60.00 150.00

2020 Topps Gypsy Queen Chrome Box Toppers Indigo Refractors

*INDIGO: .75X TO 2X BASIC
STATED ODDS 1:3 HOBBY BOXES
STATED PRINT RUN 150 SER.#'d SETS
50 Aaron Judge 12.00 30.00
300 Mike Trout 15.00 40.00

2020 Topps Gypsy Queen Fortune Teller Mini

STATED ODDS 1:6 HOBBY
*INDIGO/250: 1X TO 2.5X BASIC
GREEN/99: 2X TO 5X BASIC
FTM1 Shohei Ohtani .60 1.50
FTM2 Mike Trout 2.50 6.00
FTM3 Luis Robert 3.00 8.00
FTM4 Michael Chavis .40 1.00
FTM5 Yordan Alvarez 1.50 4.00
FTM6 Paul DeJong .50 1.25
FTM7 Brendan McKay .50 1.25
FTM8 Max Scherzer .50 1.25
FTM9 Bo Bichette 2.50 6.00
FTM10 Gleyber Torres 1.00 2.50
FTM11 Vladimir Guerrero Jr. 1.00 2.50
FTM12 Keston Hiura .60 1.50
FTM13 Christian Yelich .60 1.50
FTM14 Nick Senzel .50 1.25
FTM15 Ronald Acuna Jr. 2.00 5.00
FTM16 Fernando Tatis Jr. 2.00 5.00
FTM17 Dylan Cease .60 1.50
FTM18 Austin Meadows .40 1.00
FTM19 Willians Astudillo .30 .75
FTM20 Aaron Judge 1.25 3.00

2020 Topps Gypsy Queen Fortune Teller Mini Autographs

STATED ODDS 1:3314 HOBBY
PRINT RUNS B/WN 20-50 COPIES PER
EXCHANGE DEADLINE 2/29/2022
FTMAAJ Aaron Judge
FTMAAM Austin Meadows/50 12.00 30.00
FTMABB Bo Bichette/50 75.00 200.00
FTMABM Brendan McKay/40 20.00 50.00
FTMACY Christian Yelich/20 60.00 150.00
FTMADC Dylan Cease 20.00 50.00
FTMAGT Gleyber Torres/20 60.00 150.00
FTMAMC Michael Chavis/50 30.00 80.00
FTMAPD Paul DeJong/50 12.00 30.00
FTMARAJ Ronald Acuna Jr./20 150.00 400.00
FTMAVGJ Vladimir Guerrero Jr./40 60.00 150.00
FTMAWA Willians Astudillo/50 10.00 25.00
FTMAYA Yordan Alvarez/40 60.00 150.00

2020 Topps Gypsy Queen Mini Rookie Autographs

STATED ODDS 1:1135 HOBBY
PRINT RUNS B/WN 15-99 COPIES PER
NO PRICING ON QTY 15
*RW/50: .5X TO 1.2X BASIC
MRAAA Adbert Alzolay 4.00 10.00
MRAAC Aaron Civale 8.00 20.00
MRAAP A.J. Puk 6.00 15.00
MRABB Bobby Bradley 8.00 20.00
MRABBI Bo Bichette 60.00 150.00
MRABM Brendan McKay 10.00 25.00
MRADC Dylan Cease 8.00 20.00
MRAJL Jesus Luzardo 6.00 15.00
MRAJY Jordan Yamamoto 10.00 25.00
MRALA Logan Allen 8.00 20.00
MRARG Robel Garcia 8.00 20.00
MRAYA Yordan Alvarez 60.00 150.00
MRAZC Zack Collins 8.00 20.00

2020 Topps Gypsy Queen Tarot of the Diamond

STATED ODDS 1:8 HOBBY
*INDIGO/250: 1X TO 2.5X BASIC
*GREEN/99: 2X TO 5X BASIC
TOD1 Ronald Acuna Jr. 2.00 5.00
TOD2 Noah Syndergaard .40 1.00
TOD3 Bo Bichette 2.50 6.00
TOD4 Starling Marte .40 1.00
TOD5 Yordan Alvarez 1.50 4.00
TOD6 Trevor Story .50 1.25
TOD7 Walker Buehler .60 1.50
TOD8 Mike Trout 2.50 6.00
TOD9 Pete Alonso 1.25 3.00
TOD10 Christian Yelich .60 1.50
TOD11 Aroldis Chapman .50 1.25
TOD12 Kris Bryant .60 1.50
TOD13 George Springer .40 1.00
TOD14 Freddie Freeman .60 1.50
TOD15 Justin Verlander .50 1.25
TOD16 Alex Bregman .50 1.25
TOD17 Bryce Harper .75 2.00
TOD18 Javier Baez .60 1.50
TOD19 Aaron Judge 1.25 3.00
TOD20 Aaron Nola .50 1.25
TOD21 Rafael Devers .60 1.50
TOD22 Cody Bellinger 1.00 2.50

2001 Topps Heritage

The 2001 Topps Heritage product was released in February 2001. Each pack contained eight cards and carried a $1.99 SRP. The base set features 407 cards. Please note that all low series cards 1-80, feature both red and black back variations and are in shorter supply than mid-series cards 81-310. Also, high series cards 311-407 are short-printed with an announced seeding ratio of 1:2 packs. Finally, the following mid-series cards were erroneously printed exclusively in black back format: 103, 159, 171, 176, 179, 188, 201, 212, 224 and 241. All told, a master set of all red and black variations consists of 487-cards (397 red backs and 90 black backs). Most collectors in pursuit of a 407-card complete set typically intermingle red and black back cards.

COMP.MASTER SET (487) 350.00 500.00
COMPLETE SET (407) 200.00 400.00
COMP.BASIC SET (230) 30.00 60.00
COMMON CARD (81-310) .20 .50
FOLLOWING AVAIL.ONLY AS BLACK-BACKS
103/159/171/176/179/188/201/212/224/241
COMMON CARD (1-80) 1.00 2.50
RED-BLACK BACKS: EQUAL QUANTITIES
RED-BLACK BACKS: EQUAL VALUE
COMMON CARD (311-407) 2.00 5.00
311-407 STATED ODDS 1:2
'52 CARD REDEMPTION ODDS 1:3,689
REPLICA HAT-JSY REDEMPTION ODDS 1:9,581
EXCHANGE DEADLINE 2/28/02
RED OR BLACK BACKS OK IN 407-CARD SET
1 Kris Benson 1.00 2.50
1 Kris Benson Black 1.00 2.50
2 Brian Jordan 1.00 2.50
2 Brian Jordan Black 1.00 2.50
3 Fernando Vina 1.00 2.50
3 Fernando Vina Black 1.00 2.50
4 Mike Sweeney 1.00 2.50
4 Mike Sweeney Black 1.00 2.50
5 Rafael Palmeiro 1.00 2.50
5 Rafael Palmeiro Black 1.00 2.50
6 Paul O'Neill 1.00 2.50
6 Paul O'Neill Black 1.00 2.50
7 Todd Helton 1.00 2.50
7 Todd Helton Black 1.00 2.50
8 Ramiro Mendoza 1.00 2.50
8 Ramiro Mendoza Black 1.00 2.50
9 Kevin Millwood 1.00 2.50
9 Kevin Millwood Black 1.00 2.50
10 Chuck Knoblauch 1.00 2.50
10 Chuck Knoblauch Black 1.00 2.50
11 Derek Jeter 4.00 10.00
11 Derek Jeter Black 10.00 25.00
12 Alex Rodriguez Rangers 2.00 5.00
12 A.Rod Black Rangers 2.00 5.00
13 Geoff Jenkins 1.00 2.50
13 Geoff Jenkins Black 1.00 2.50
14 David Justice 1.00 2.50
14 David Justice Black 1.00 2.50
15 David Cone 1.00 2.50
15 David Cone Black 1.00 2.50
16 Andres Galarraga 1.00 2.50
16 Andres Galarraga Black 1.00 2.50
17 Garret Anderson 1.00 2.50
17 Garret Anderson Black 1.00 2.50
18 Roger Cedeno 1.00 2.50
18 Roger Cedeno Black 1.00 2.50
19 Randy Velarde 1.00 2.50
19 Randy Velarde Black 1.00 2.50
20 Carlos Delgado 1.00 2.50
20 Carlos Delgado Black 1.00 2.50
21 Quilvio Veras 1.00 2.50
21 Quilvio Veras Black 1.00 2.50
22 Jose Vidro 1.00 2.50
22 Jose Vidro Black 1.00 2.50
23 Corey Patterson 1.00 2.50
23 Corey Patterson Black 1.00 2.50
24 Jorge Posada 1.00 2.50
24 Jorge Posada Black 1.00 2.50
25 Eddie Perez 1.00 2.50
25 Eddie Perez Black 1.00 2.50
26 Jack Cust 1.00 2.50
26 Jack Cust Black 1.00 2.50
27 Sean Burroughs 1.00 2.50
27 Sean Burroughs Black 1.00 2.50
28 Randy Wolf 1.00 2.50
28 Randy Wolf Black 1.00 2.50
29 Mike Lamb 1.00 2.50
29 Mike Lamb Black 1.00 2.50
30 Rafael Furcal 1.00 2.50
30 Rafael Furcal Black 1.00 2.50
31 Barry Bonds 4.00 10.00
31 Barry Bonds Black 4.00 10.00
32 Tim Hudson 1.00 2.50
32 Tim Hudson Black 1.00 2.50
33 Tom Glavine 1.00 2.50
33 Tom Glavine Black 1.00 2.50
34 Javy Lopez 1.00 2.50
34 Javy Lopez Black 1.00 2.50
35 Aubrey Huff 1.00 2.50
35 Aubrey Huff Black 1.00 2.50
36 Wally Joyner 1.00 2.50
36 Wally Joyner Black 1.00 2.50
37 Magglio Ordonez 1.00 2.50
37 Magglio Ordonez Black 1.00 2.50
38 Matt Lawton 1.00 2.50
38 Matt Lawton Black 1.00 2.50
39 Mariano Rivera 1.50 4.00
39 Mariano Rivera Black 1.50 4.00
40 Andy Ashby 1.00 2.50
40 Andy Ashby Black 1.00 2.50
41 Mark Buehrle 1.00 2.50
41 Mark Buehrle Black 1.00 2.50
42 Esteban Loaiza 1.00 2.50
42 Esteban Loaiza Black 1.00 2.50
43 Mark Redman 1.00 2.50
43 Mark Redman Black 1.00 2.50

44 Mark Quinn 1.00 2.50
44 Mark Quinn Black 1.00 2.50
45 Tino Martinez 1.00 2.50
45 Tino Martinez Black 1.00 2.50
46 Joe Mays 1.00 2.50
46 Joe Mays Black 1.00 2.50
47 Walt Weiss 1.00 2.50
47 Walt Weiss Black 1.00 2.50
48 Roger Clemens 3.00 8.00
48 Roger Clemens Black 3.00 8.00
49 Greg Maddux 2.50 6.00
49 Greg Maddux Black 2.50 6.00
50 Richard Hidalgo 1.00 2.50
50 Richard Hidalgo Black 1.00 2.50
51 Orlando Hernandez 1.00 2.50
51 Orlando Hernandez Black 1.00 2.50
52 Chipper Jones 1.50 4.00
52 Chipper Jones Black 1.50 4.00
53 Ben Grieve 1.00 2.50
53 Ben Grieve Black 1.00 2.50
54 Jimmy Haynes 1.00 2.50
54 Jimmy Haynes Black 1.00 2.50
55 Ken Caminiti 1.00 2.50
55 Ken Caminiti Black 1.00 2.50
56 Tim Salmon 1.00 2.50
56 Tim Salmon Black 1.00 2.50
57 Andy Pettitte 1.00 2.50
57 Andy Pettitte Black 1.00 2.50
58 Darin Erstad 1.00 2.50
58 Darin Erstad Black 1.00 2.50
59 Marquis Grissom 1.00 2.50
59 Marquis Grissom Black 1.00 2.50
60 Raul Mondesi 1.00 2.50
60 Raul Mondesi Black 1.00 2.50
61 Bengie Molina 1.00 2.50
61 Bengie Molina Black 1.00 2.50
62 Miguel Tejada 1.00 2.50
62 Miguel Tejada Black 1.00 2.50
63 Jose Cruz Jr. 1.00 2.50
63 Jose Cruz Jr. Black 1.00 2.50
64 Billy Koch 1.00 2.50
64 Billy Koch Black 1.00 2.50
65 Troy Glaus 1.00 2.50
65 Troy Glaus Black 1.00 2.50
66 Cliff Floyd 1.00 2.50
66 Cliff Floyd Black 1.00 2.50
67 Tony Batista 1.00 2.50
67 Tony Batista Black 1.00 2.50
68 Jeff Bagwell 1.00 2.50
68 Jeff Bagwell Black 1.00 2.50
69 Billy Wagner 1.00 2.50
69 Billy Wagner Black 1.00 2.50
70 Eric Chavez 1.00 2.50
70 Eric Chavez Black 1.00 2.50
71 Troy Percival 1.00 2.50
71 Troy Percival Black 1.00 2.50
72 Andruw Jones 1.00 2.50
72 Andruw Jones Black 1.00 2.50
73 Shane Reynolds 1.00 2.50
73 Shane Reynolds Black 1.00 2.50
74 Barry Zito 1.00 2.50
74 Barry Zito Black 1.00 2.50
75 Roy Halladay 1.00 2.50
75 Roy Halladay Black 1.00 2.50
76 David Wells 1.00 2.50
76 David Wells Black 1.00 2.50
77 Jason Giambi 1.00 2.50
77 Jason Giambi Black 1.00 2.50
78 Scott Elarton 1.00 2.50
78 Scott Elarton Black 1.00 2.50
79 Moises Alou 1.00 2.50
79 Moises Alou Black 1.00 2.50
80 Adam Platt 1.00 2.50
80 Adam Platt Black 1.00 2.50
81 Wilton Veras .20 .50
82 Darryl Kile .25 .60
83 Johnny Damon .40 1.00
84 Tony Armas Jr. .20 .50
85 Ellis Burks .25 .60
86 Jamey Wright .20 .50
87 Jose Vizcaino .20 .50
88 Bartolo Colon .25 .60
89 Carmen Cali RC .20 .50
90 Kevin Brown .25 .60
91 Josh Hamilton .40 1.00
92 Jay Buhner .25 .60
93 Scott Pratt RC .25 .60
94 Alex Cora .20 .50
95 Luis Montanez RC .25 .60
96 Dmitri Young .25 .60
97 J.T. Snow .25 .60
98 Damion Easley .20 .50
99 Greg Norton .20 .50
100 Matt Wheatland .20 .50
101 Chin-Feng Chen .25 .60
102 Tony Womack .20 .50
103 Adam Kennedy Black .20 .50
104 J.D. Drew .25 .60
105 Carlos Febles .20 .50
106 Jim Thome .40 1.00
107 Danny Graves .20 .50
108 Dave Mlicki .20 .50
109 Ron Coomer .20 .50
110 James Baldwin .20 .50
111 Shaun Boyd RC .20 .50
112 Brian Bohanon .20 .50
113 Jacque Jones .25 .60
114 Alfonso Soriano .40 1.00
115 Tony Clark .20 .50
116 Terrence Long .20 .50
117 Todd Hundley .20 .50
118 Kazuhiro Sasaki .25 .60
119 Brian Sellier RC .20 .50

120 John Olerud .25 .60
121 Javier Vazquez .25 .60
122 Sean Burnett .20 .50
123 Matt LeCroy .20 .50
124 Erubiel Durazo .20 .50
125 Juan Encarnacion .20 .50
126 Pablo Ozuna .20 .50
127 Russ Ortiz .20 .50
128 David Segui .20 .50
129 Mark McGwire 1.50 4.00
130 Mark Grace .40 1.00
131 Fred McGriff .40 1.00
132 Carl Pavano .25 .60
133 Derek Thompson .20 .50
134 Shawn Green .25 .60
135 B.J. Surhoff .25 .60
136 Michael Tucker .20 .50
137 Jason Isringhausen .25 .60
138 Eric Milton .20 .50
139 Mike Stodolka .20 .50
140 Milton Bradley .25 .60
141 Curt Schilling .25 .60
142 Sandy Alomar Jr. .20 .50
143 Brent Mayne .20 .50
144 Todd Jones .20 .50
145 Charles Johnson .25 .60
146 Dean Palmer .25 .60
147 Masato Yoshii .20 .50
148 Edgar Renteria .25 .60
149 Joe Randa .25 .60
150 Adam Johnson .20 .50
151 Greg Vaughn .20 .50
152 Adrian Beltre .25 .60
153 Glenallen Hill .20 .50
154 David Parrish RC .20 .50
155 Neifi Perez .20 .50
156 Pete Harnisch .20 .50
157 Paul Konerko .25 .60
158 Dennys Reyes .20 .50
159 Jose Lima Black .20 .50
160 Eddie Taubensee .20 .50
161 Miguel Cairo .20 .50
162 Jeff Kent .25 .60
163 Dustin Hermanson .20 .50
164 Alex Gonzalez .20 .50
165 Hideo Nomo .60 1.50
166 Sammy Sosa .60 1.50
167 C.J. Nitkowski .20 .50
168 Cal Eldred .20 .50
169 Jeff Abbott .20 .50
170 Jim Edmonds .25 .60
171 Mark Mulder Black .25 .60
172 Dominic Rich RC .20 .50
173 Ray Lankford .25 .60
174 Danny Borrell RC .20 .50
175 Rick Aguilera .20 .50
176 Shannon Stewart Black .25 .60
177 Steve Finley .25 .60
178 Jim Parque .20 .50
179 Kevin Appier Black .25 .60
180 Adrian Gonzalez 1.25 3.00
181 Tom Goodwin .20 .50
182 Kevin Tapani .20 .50
183 Fernando Tatis .20 .50
184 Mark Grudzielanek .20 .50
185 Ryan Anderson .20 .50
186 Jeffrey Hammonds .20 .50
187 Corey Koskie .20 .50
188 Brad Fullmer Black .20 .50
189 Rey Sanchez .20 .50
190 Michael Barrett .20 .50
191 Rickey Henderson .60 1.50
192 Jermaine Dye .25 .60
193 Scott Brosius .25 .60
194 Matt Anderson .20 .50
195 Brian Buchanan .20 .50
196 Derrek Lee .40 1.00
197 Larry Walker .25 .60
198 Dan Moylan RC .20 .50
199 Vinny Castilla .25 .60
200 Ken Griffey Jr. 1.25 3.00
201 Matt Stairs Black .20 .50
202 Ty Howington .20 .50
203 Andy Benes .20 .50
204 Luis Gonzalez .25 .60
205 Brian Moehler .20 .50
206 Harold Baines .25 .60
207 Pedro Astacio .20 .50
208 Cristian Guzman .20 .50
209 Kip Wells .20 .50
210 Frank Thomas .60 1.50
211 Jose Rosado .20 .50
212 Vernon Wells Black .25 .60
213 Bobby Higginson .25 .60
214 Juan Gonzalez .25 .60
215 Omar Vizquel .40 1.00
216 Bernie Williams .40 1.00
217 Aaron Sele .20 .50
218 Shawn Estes .20 .50
219 Roberto Alomar .40 1.00
220 Rick Ankiel .20 .50
221 Josh Kalinowski .20 .50
222 David Bell .20 .50
223 Keith Foulke .25 .60
224 Craig Biggio Black .40 1.00
225 Josh Axelson RC .20 .50
226 Scott Williamson .20 .50
227 Ron Belliard .20 .50
228 Chris Singleton .20 .50
229 Alex Serrano RC .20 .50
230 Deivi Cruz .20 .50
231 Eric Munson .20 .50
232 Luis Castillo .20 .50
233 Edgar Martinez .40 1.00
234 Jeff Shaw .20 .50
235 Jeromy Burnitz .25 .60
236 Richie Sexson .25 .60
237 Will Clark .40 1.00
238 Ron Villone .20 .50
239 Kerry Wood .25 .60
240 Rich Aurilia .20 .50
241 Mo Vaughn Black .25 .60
242 Travis Fryman .25 .60
243 Manny Ramirez Sox .40 1.00
244 Chris Stynes .20 .50
245 Ray Durham .25 .60
246 Juan Uribe RC .40 1.00
247 Juan Guzman .20 .50
248 Lee Stevens .20 .50
249 Devon White .25 .60
250 Kyle Lohse RC .40 1.00
251 Bryan Wolff .20 .50
252 Matt Galante RC .25 .60
253 Eric Young .20 .50
254 Freddy Garcia .25 .60
255 Jay Bell .25 .60
256 Steve Cox .20 .50
257 Torii Hunter .25 .60
258 Jose Canseco .40 1.00
259 Brad Ausmus .25 .60
260 Jeff Cirillo .20 .50
261 Brad Penny .20 .50
262 Antonio Alfonseca .20 .50
263 Russ Branyan .20 .50
264 Chris Morris RC .20 .50
265 John Lackey .20 .50
266 Justin Wayne RC .25 .60
267 Brad Radke .25 .60
268 Todd Stottlemyre .20 .50
269 Mark Loretta .20 .50
270 Matt Williams .25 .60
271 Kenny Lofton .25 .60
272 Jeff D'Amico .20 .50
273 Jamie Moyer .25 .60
274 Darren Dreifort .20 .50
275 Denny Neagle .20 .50
276 Orlando Cabrera .25 .60
277 Chuck Finley .25 .60
278 Miguel Batista .25 .60
279 Carlos Beltran .25 .60
280 Eric Karros .25 .60
281 Mark Kotsay .25 .60
282 Ryan Dempster .20 .50
283 Barry Larkin .40 1.00
284 Jeff Suppan .20 .50
285 Gary Sheffield .25 .60
286 Jose Valentin .20 .50
287 Robb Nen .25 .60
288 Chan Ho Park .25 .60
289 John Halama .20 .50
290 Steve Smyth RC .25 .60
291 Gerald Williams .20 .50
292 Preston Wilson .25 .60
293 Victor Hall RC .25 .60
294 Ben Sheets .40 1.00
295 Eric Davis .25 .60
296 Kirk Rueter .20 .50
297 Chad Petty RC .20 .50
298 Kevin Millar .25 .60
299 Marvin Benard .20 .50
300 Vladimir Guerrero .60 1.50
301 Livan Hernandez .25 .60
302 Travis Baptist RC .20 .50
303 Bill Mueller .25 .60
304 Mike Cameron .20 .50
305 Randy Johnson .60 1.50
306 Alan Mahaffey RC .20 .50
307 Timo Perez UER .20 .50
308 Pokey Reese .20 .50
309 Ryan Rupe .20 .50
310 Carlos Lee .25 .60
311 Doug Glanville SP 2.00 5.00
312 Jay Payton SP 2.00 5.00
313 Troy O'Leary SP 2.00 5.00
314 Francisco Cordero SP 2.00 5.00
315 Rusty Greer SP 2.00 5.00
316 Cal Ripken SP 10.00 25.00
317 Ricky Ledee SP 2.00 5.00
318 Brian Daubach SP 2.00 5.00
319 Robin Ventura SP 2.00 5.00
320 Todd Zeile SP 2.00 5.00
321 Francisco Cordova SP 2.00 5.00
322 Henry Rodriguez SP 2.00 5.00
323 Pat Meares SP 2.00 5.00
324 Glendon Rusch SP 2.00 5.00
325 Keith Osik SP 2.00 5.00
326 Robert Keppel SP RC 2.00 5.00
327 Bobby Jones SP 2.00 5.00
328 Alex Ramirez SP 2.00 5.00
329 Robert Person SP 2.00 5.00
330 Ruben Mateo SP 2.00 5.00
331 Rob Bell SP 2.00 5.00
332 Carl Everett SP 2.00 5.00
333 Jason Schmidt SP 2.00 5.00
334 Scott Rolen SP 3.00 8.00
335 Jimmy Anderson SP 2.00 5.00
336 Bret Boone SP 2.00 5.00
337 Delino DeShields SP 2.00 5.00
338 Trevor Hoffman SP 2.00 5.00
339 Bob Abreu SP 2.00 5.00
340 Mike Williams SP 2.00 5.00
341 Mike Hampton SP 2.00 5.00
342 John Wetteland SP 2.00 5.00
343 Scott Erickson SP 2.00 5.00
344 Enrique Wilson SP 2.00 5.00
345 Tim Wakefield SP 2.00 5.00
346 Mike Lowell SP 2.00 5.00
347 Todd Pratt SP 2.00 5.00
348 Brook Fordyce SP 2.00 5.00
349 Benny Agbayani SP 2.00 5.00
350 Gabe Kapler SP 2.00 5.00
351 Sean Casey SP 2.00 5.00
352 Darren Oliver SP 2.00 5.00
353 Todd Ritchie SP 2.00 5.00
354 Kenny Rogers SP 2.00 5.00
355 Jason Kendall SP 2.00 5.00
356 John Vander Wal SP 2.00 5.00
357 Ramon Martinez SP 2.00 5.00
358 Edgardo Alfonzo SP 2.00 5.00
359 Phil Nevin SP 2.00 5.00
360 Albert Belle SP 2.00 5.00
361 Ruben Rivera SP 2.00 5.00
362 Pedro Martinez SP 3.00 8.00
363 Derek Lowe SP 2.00 5.00
364 Pat Burrell SP 2.00 5.00
365 Mike Mussina SP 3.00 8.00
366 Brady Anderson SP 2.00 5.00
367 Darren Lewis SP 2.00 5.00
368 Sidney Ponson SP 2.00 5.00
369 Adam Eaton SP 2.00 5.00
370 Eric Owens SP 2.00 5.00
371 Aaron Boone SP 2.00 5.00
372 Matt Clement SP 2.00 5.00
373 Derek Bell SP 2.00 5.00
374 Trot Nixon SP 2.00 5.00
375 Travis Lee SP 2.00 5.00
376 Mike Benjamin SP 2.00 5.00
377 Jeff Zimmerman SP 2.00 5.00
378 Mike Lieberthal SP 2.00 5.00
379 Rick Reed SP 2.00 5.00
380 Nomar Garciaparra SP 5.00 12.00
381 Omar Daal SP 2.00 5.00
382 Ryan Klesko SP 2.00 5.00
383 Rey Ordonez SP 2.00 5.00
384 Kevin Young SP 2.00 5.00
385 Rick Helling SP 2.00 5.00
386 Brian Giles SP 2.00 5.00
387 Tony Gwynn SP 4.00 10.00
388 Ed Sprague SP 2.00 5.00
389 J.R. House SP 2.00 5.00
390 Scott Hatteberg SP 2.00 5.00
391 John Valentin SP 2.00 5.00
392 Melvin Mora SP 2.00 5.00
393 Royce Clayton SP 2.00 5.00
394 Jeff Fassero SP 2.00 5.00
395 Manny Alexander SP 2.00 5.00
396 John Franco SP 2.00 5.00
397 Luis Alicea SP 2.00 5.00
398 Ivan Rodriguez SP 3.00 8.00
399 Kevin Jordan SP 2.00 5.00
400 Jose Offerman SP 2.00 5.00
401 Jeff Conine SP 2.00 5.00
402 Seth Etherton SP 2.00 5.00
403 Mike Bordick SP 2.00 5.00
404 Al Leiter SP 2.00 5.00
405 Mike Piazza SP 5.00 12.00
406 Armando Benitez SP 2.00 5.00
407 Warren Morris SP 2.00 5.00
CL1 Checklist 1 .10 .25
CL2 Checklist 2 .10 .25

2001 Topps Heritage Chrome

STATED ODDS 1:25 HOB/RET
STATED PRINT RUN 552 SERIAL #'d SETS
CP1 Cal Ripken 50.00 120.00
CP2 Jim Thome 12.00 30.00
CP3 Derek Jeter 60.00 150.00
CP4 Andres Galarraga 5.00 12.00
CP5 Carlos Delgado 3.00 8.00
CP6 Roberto Alomar 5.00 12.00
CP7 Tom Glavine 5.00 12.00
CP8 Gary Sheffield 3.00 8.00
CP9 Mo Vaughn 3.00 8.00
CP10 Preston Wilson 3.00 8.00
CP11 Mike Mussina 5.00 12.00
CP12 Greg Maddux 20.00 50.00
CP13 Ivan Rodriguez 5.00 12.00
CP14 Al Leiter 3.00 8.00
CP15 Seth Etherton 3.00 8.00
CP16 Edgardo Alfonzo 3.00 8.00
CP17 Richie Sexson 3.00 8.00
CP18 Andruw Jones 5.00 12.00
CP19 Bartolo Colon 3.00 8.00
CP20 Darin Erstad 3.00 8.00
CP21 Kevin Brown 3.00 8.00
CP22 Mike Sweeney 3.00 8.00
CP23 Mike Piazza 15.00 40.00
CP24 Rafael Palmeiro 5.00 12.00
CP25 Terrence Long 3.00 8.00
CP26 Kazuhiro Sasaki 3.00 8.00
CP27 John Olerud 3.00 8.00
CP28 Mark McGwire 25.00 60.00
CP29 Fred McGriff 5.00 12.00
CP30 Todd Helton 5.00 12.00
CP31 Curt Schilling 3.00 8.00
CP32 Alex Rodriguez 20.00 50.00
CP33 Jeff Kent 3.00 8.00
CP34 Pat Burrell 3.00 8.00
CP35 Jim Edmonds 5.00 12.00
CP36 Mark Mulder 3.00 8.00
CP37 Troy Glaus 3.00 8.00
CP38 Jay Payton 3.00 8.00
CP39 Jermaine Dye 3.00 8.00
CP40 Larry Walker 5.00 12.00
CP41 Ken Griffey Jr. 30.00 80.00
CP42 Jeff Bagwell 5.00 12.00
CP43 Rick Ankiel 3.00 8.00
CP44 Mark Redman 3.00 8.00
CP45 Edgar Martinez 5.00 12.00
CP46 Mike Hampton 3.00 8.00
CP47 Manny Ramirez Sox 8.00 20.00
CP48 Ray Durham 3.00 8.00
CP49 Rafael Furcal 3.00 8.00
CP50 Sean Casey 3.00 8.00
CP51 Jose Canseco 5.00 12.00
CP52 Barry Bonds 15.00 40.00
CP53 Tim Hudson 3.00 8.00
CP54 Barry Zito 5.00 12.00
CP55 Chuck Finley 3.00 8.00
CP56 Magglio Ordonez 3.00 8.00
CP57 David Wells 3.00 8.00
CP58 Jason Giambi 3.00 8.00
CP59 Tony Gwynn 10.00 25.00
CP60 Vladimir Guerrero 12.00 30.00
CP61 Randy Johnson 10.00 25.00
CP62 Bernie Williams 5.00 12.00
CP63 Craig Biggio 5.00 12.00
CP64 Jason Kendall 3.00 8.00
CP65 Pedro Martinez 5.00 12.00
CP66 Mark Quinn 3.00 8.00
CP67 Frank Thomas 30.00 80.00
CP68 Nomar Garciaparra 15.00 40.00
CP69 Brian Giles 3.00 8.00
CP70 Shawn Green 3.00 8.00
CP71 Roger Clemens 20.00 50.00
CP72 Sammy Sosa 5.00 12.00
CP73 Juan Gonzalez 3.00 8.00
CP74 Orlando Hernandez 3.00 8.00
CP75 Chipper Jones 12.00 30.00
CP76 Josh Hamilton 5.00 12.00
CP77 Adam Johnson 3.00 8.00
CP78 Shaun Boyd 3.00 8.00
CP79 Alfonso Soriano 5.00 12.00
CP80 Derek Thompson 3.00 8.00
CP81 Adrian Gonzalez 10.00 25.00
CP82 Ryan Anderson 3.00 8.00
CP83 Corey Patterson 3.00 8.00
CP84 J.R. House 3.00 8.00
CP85 Sean Burroughs 3.00 8.00
CP86 Bryan Wolff 3.00 8.00
CP87 John Lackey 5.00 12.00
CP88 Ben Sheets 3.00 8.00
CP89 Timo Perez 3.00 8.00
CP90 Robert Keppel 3.00 8.00
CP91 Luis Montanez 3.00 8.00
CP92 Sean Burnett 3.00 8.00
CP93 Justin Wayne 3.00 8.00
CP94 Eric Munson 3.00 8.00
CP95 Steve Smyth 3.00 8.00
CP96 Matt Galante 3.00 8.00
CP97 Carmen Cali 3.00 8.00
CP98 Brian Sellier 3.00 8.00
CP99 David Parrish 3.00 8.00
CP100 Danny Borrell 3.00 8.00
CP101 Chad Petty 3.00 8.00
CP102 Dominic Rich 3.00 8.00
CP103 Josh Axelson 3.00 8.00
CP104 Alex Serrano 3.00 8.00
CP105 Juan Uribe 3.00 8.00
CP106 Travis Baptist 3.00 8.00
CP107 Alan Mahaffey 3.00 8.00
CP108 Kyle Lohse 3.00 8.00
CP109 Victor Hall 3.00 8.00
CP110 Scott Pratt 3.00 8.00

2001 Topps Heritage Autographs

Randomly inserted into packs at one in 142 HOB/RET, this 51-card insert set features authentic autographs from many of the Major League's top players. Please note that a few of the players packed out as exchange cards, and must be redeemed by 1/31/02. Due to the untimely passing of Eddie Mathews, please note the exchange card issued for him went unredeemed. In addition, Larry Doby's card was originally seeded in packs as exchange cards (of which carried a January 31st, 2002 deadline).

STATED ODDS 1:142 HOB/RET
*RED INK: .75X TO 1.5X BASIC AU
RED INK ODDS 1:545 HOB, 1:546 RET
RED INK PRINT RUN 52 SERIAL #'d SETS
THAAH Aubrey Huff 10.00 25.00
THAAP Andy Pafko 50.00 100.00
THAAR Alex Rodriguez 75.00 150.00
THABB Barry Bonds 150.00 400.00
THABS Bobby Shantz 10.00 25.00
THABT Bobby Thomson 15.00 40.00
THACD Carlos Delgado 15.00 40.00
THACF Cliff Floyd 10.00 25.00
THACJ Chipper Jones 100.00 250.00
THACP Corey Patterson 12.50 30.00
THACS Curt Simmons 20.00 50.00
THADD Dom DiMaggio 30.00 80.00
THADG Dick Groat 25.00 60.00
THADS Duke Snider 40.00 100.00
THAES Enos Slaughter 60.00 150.00
THAFV Fernando Vina 10.00 25.00
THAGJ Geoff Jenkins 10.00 25.00
THAGM Gil McDougald 25.00 60.00
THAHB Hank Bauer 20.00 50.00
THAHS Hank Sauer 30.00 60.00
THAHW Hoyt Wilhelm 25.00 60.00
THAJG Joe Garagiola 25.00 60.00
THAJM Joe Mays 10.00 25.00
THAJS Johnny Sain 25.00 60.00
THAJV Jose Vidro 10.00 25.00
THAKB Kris Benson 10.00 25.00
THAMB Mark Buehrle 25.00 60.00
THAMI Monte Irvin 20.00 50.00
THAML Mike Lamb 12.00 30.00
THAML Matt Lawton 10.00 25.00
THAMM Minnie Minoso 25.00 60.00
THAMO Magglio Ordonez 10.00 25.00
THAMQ Mark Quinn 20.00 50.00
THAMR Mark Redman 10.00 25.00
THAMS Mike Sweeney 10.00 25.00
THAMV Mickey Vernon 15.00 40.00
THANG Nomar Garciaparra 60.00 150.00
THAPR Preacher Roe 20.00 50.00
THAPFR Phil Rizzuto 75.00 200.00
THARH Richard Hidalgo 10.00 25.00
THARR Robin Roberts 25.00 60.00
THARS Red Schoendienst 30.00 80.00
THARW Randy Wolf 10.00 25.00
THASPB Sean Burroughs 10.00 25.00
THATG Tom Glavine 40.00 100.00
THATH Todd Helton 15.00 40.00
THATL Terrence Long 10.00 25.00
THAVL Vernon Law 20.00 50.00
THAWM Willie Mays 150.00 400.00
THAWS Warren Spahn 60.00 150.00

2001 Topps Heritage Autographs Red Ink

STATED ODDS 1:545 HOBBY, 1:546 RETAIL
STATED PRINT RUN 52 SERIAL #'d SETS

2001 Topps Heritage AutoProofs

Randomly inserted at approximately 1 in every 5749 boxes, this card is an actual 1952 Topps Willie Mays card that was bought from the Topps Company, then individually autographed by Willie Mays, and distributed into packs. Please note that each card is individually serial numbered to 25.

NO PRICING DUE TO SCARCITY
AUTOPROOF IS A REAL '52 TOPPS CARD

2001 Topps Heritage Classic Renditions

Randomly inserted into packs at one in 5 Hobby, and one in 9 Retail, this 10-card insert set features artist drawn sketches of some of the best modern day ballplayers. Card backs carry a "CR" prefix.

COMPLETE SET (10) 8.00 20.00
STATED ODDS 1:5 HOBBY, 1:9 RETAIL
CR1 Mark McGwire 1.50 4.00
CR2 Nomar Garciaparra 1.00 2.50
CR3 Barry Bonds 1.50 4.00
CR4 Sammy Sosa .60 1.50
CR5 Chipper Jones .60 1.50
CR6 Pat Burrell .40 1.00
CR7 Frank Thomas .60 1.50
CR8 Manny Ramirez .40 1.00
CR9 Derek Jeter 1.50 4.00
CR10 Ken Griffey Jr. 1.25 3.00

2001 Topps Heritage Classic Renditions Autograph

Randomly inserted into packs at one in 19,710 Hobby, and 1:20,926 Retail, this three-card insert set is a partial parallel of the Classic Renditions insert. Each of these cards have been autographed by the given player and are individually serial numbered to 25. Due to market scarcity, no pricing is provided.

2001 Topps Heritage Clubhouse Collection

Randomly inserted into packs, this 22-card insert features game-used memorabilia cards from past and present stars. Included in the set are game-used bat and jersey cards. Please note that a numbered of the players have autographed 25 of each of these cards. Also note that a few of the cards packed out as exchange cards, and must have been redeemed by 01/31/02. Common Bat cards were inserted at a rate of 1:590 and Jersey cards at 1:798 Hobby/1:799 Retail. Dual Bat cards were inserted at 1:5701 Hobby/1:5772 Retail. Dual Jersey cards were inserted into packs at 1:28,744 Hobby/1:29,820 Retail. Autographed Bat cards were inserted at 1:19,710 Hobby/1:20,928 Retail, and Autographed Jerseys at 1:62,714 Hobby/1:83,712 Retail. Exchange cards - with a deadline of Janury 31st, 2002 - were seeded into packs for the following cards: Eddie Mathews Bat, Duke Snider Bat AU and Willie Mays Bat AU.

BAT ODDS 1:590 HOB/RET
JERSEY ODDS 1:798 HOB, 1:799 RET
DUAL BAT ODDS 1:5701 HOB, 1:5772 RET
DUAL JERSEY ODDS 1:28,744 H, 1:29820 R
AU BAT ODDS 1:19,710 HOB, 1:20,928 RET
AU JERSEY ODDS 1:62,714 H, 1:83,712 R
NO PRICING ON QTY OF 25 OR LESS
BB Barry Bonds Bat 40.00 80.00
CJ Chipper Jones Bat 20.00 50.00
DS Duke Snider Bat 12.00 30.00
EM Eddie Mathews Bat 12.00 30.00
FT Frank Thomas Jsy 15.00 40.00
FV Fernando Vina Bat 15.00 40.00
MM Minnie Minoso Jsy 15.00 40.00
RA Richie Ashburn Bat 20.00 50.00
RS Red Schoendienst Bat 15.00 40.00
SG Shawn Green Bat 15.00 40.00
SR Scott Rolen Bat 20.00 50.00
WM Willie Mays Bat 30.00 60.00
DSSG Snider/Green Bat/52 60.00 150.00
EMCJ Mathews/Jones Bat/52 100.00 200.00
MMFT Minoso/Thomas Jsy/52 60.00 150.00
RASR Ashburn/Rolen Bat/52 100.00 250.00
RSFV Schoen/Vina Bat/52 125.00 200.00
WMBB Mays/Bonds Bat/52 200.00 350.00

2001 Topps Heritage Grandstand Glory

Randomly inserted into packs at 1:211 Hobby/Retail, this seven-card insert set features a swatch of original stadium seating. Card backs carry the player's initials as numbering.

STATED ODDS 1:211 HOB/RET
JR Jackie Robinson 10.00 25.00
NF Nellie Fox 10.00 25.00
PR Phil Rizzuto 15.00 40.00
RA Richie Ashburn 10.00 25.00
RR Robin Roberts 10.00 25.00
WM Willie Mays 20.00 50.00
YB Yogi Berra 15.00 40.00

2001 Topps Heritage New Age Performers

Randomly inserted into packs at 1:8 Hobby, 1:15 Retail, this 15-card insert set features players that have become the superstars of the future. Card backs carry a "NAP" prefix.

COMPLETE SET (15) 20.00 50.00
STATED ODDS 1:8 HOBBY, 1:15 RETAIL
NAP1 Mike Piazza 1.50 4.00
NAP2 Sammy Sosa 1.00 2.50
NAP3 Alex Rodriguez 1.25 3.00
NAP4 Barry Bonds 2.50 6.00
NAP5 Ken Griffey Jr. 2.00 5.00
NAP6 Chipper Jones 1.00 2.50
NAP7 Randy Johnson 1.00 2.50
NAP8 Derek Jeter 2.50 6.00
NAP9 Nomar Garciaparra 1.50 4.00
NAP10 Mark McGwire 2.50 6.00
NAP11 Jeff Bagwell 1.00 2.50
NAP12 Pedro Martinez 1.00 2.50
NAP13 Todd Helton 1.00 2.50
NAP14 Vladimir Guerrero 1.00 2.50
NAP15 Greg Maddux 1.50 4.00

2001 Topps Heritage Then and Now

Randomly inserted into Hobby packs at 1:8 and Retail packs at 1:15, this 10-card set pairs up modern day heroes with players from the past that compare statistically. Card backs carry a "TH" prefix.

COMPLETE SET (10) 15.00 30.00
STATED ODDS 1:8 HOBBY, 1:15 RETAIL
TH1 Y.Berra / M.Piazza 1.25 3.00
TH2 D.Snider / S.Sosa .75 2.00
TH3 W.Mays / K.Griffey Jr. 2.00 5.00
TH4 P.Rizzuto / D.Jeter 2.00 5.00
TH5 P.Reese / N.Garciaparra 1.25 3.00
TH6 J.Robinson / A.Rodriguez 1.00 2.50
TH7 J.Mize / M.McGwire 2.00 5.00
TH8 B.Feller / P.Martinez .75 2.00
TH9 R.Roberts / G.Maddux 1.25 3.00
TH10 W.Spahn / R.Johnson .75 2.00

2001 Topps Heritage Time Capsule

This unique set features swatches of fabric taken from actual combat uniforms from the 1952 Korean War. It's important to note that though these cards do indeed feature patches of vintage Korean War uniforms, they were not worn by the athlete featured on the card. Stated odds for the four single-player cards was 1:369. Unlike the other cards in this set, the lone dual-player Willie Mays-Ted Williams card is hand-numbered on back. Only 52 copies of this card were produced, and each is marked by hand on back in black pen "X/52". The stated odds for this dual-player card is 1:28,744 packs.

STATED ODDS 1:369 HOB/RET
COMBO ODDS 1:28744 HOB, 1:29820 RET
DN Don Newcombe 10.00 25.00
TW Ted Williams 40.00 80.00
WF Whitey Ford 10.00 25.00
WM Willie Mays 20.00 50.00
WMTW Mays/Williams/52 125.00 200.00

2002 Topps Heritage

Issued in early February 2002, this set was the second year that Topps used their Heritage brand and achieved success in the secondary market. These cards were issued in eight card packs which were packed 24 to a box and had a SRP of $3 per pack. The set consists of 440 cards with seven short prints among the low numbers as well as all cards from 364 through 446 as short prints. Those cards were all inserted at a rate of one in two packs. In addition, there was an unnannounced variation in which 10 cards were printed in both day and night versions. The night versions were also inserted into packs at rate of one in two.

COMPLETE SET (450) 200.00 400.0
COMP.SET w/o SP's (350) 40.00 80.0
COMMON CARD (1-363) .20 .5
COMMON SP (364-446) 2.00 5.0
SP STATED ODDS 1:2
LOW SERIES SP'S: 1/37/53/82/104/220/244
253/261/267/268/271/275 DO NOT EXIST
1953 REPURCHASED EXCH.ODDS 1:1163
1 Ichiro Suzuki SP 6.00 15.0
2 Darin Erstad .25 .6
3 Rod Beck .25 .6
4 Doug Mientkiewicz .25 .6
5 Mike Sweeney .25 .6
6 Roger Clemens 1.25 3.0
7 Jason Tyner .20 .5
8 Alex Gonzalez .20 .5
9 Eric Young .20 .5
10 Randy Johnson .60 1.5
10N Randy Johnson Night SP 3.00 8.0
11 Aaron Sele .20 .5
12 Tony Clark .20 .5
13 C.C. Sabathia .25 .6
14 Melvin Mora .25 .6
15 Tim Hudson .25 .6
16 Ben Petrick .20 .5
17 Tom Glavine .40 1.0
18 Jason Lane .25 .6
19 Larry Walker .25 .6
20 Mark Mulder .25 .6
21 Steve Finley .25 .6
22 Bengie Molina .20 .5
23 Rob Bell .20 .5
24 Nathan Haynes .20 .5
25 Rafael Furcal .25 .6
25N Rafael Furcal Night SP 2.00 5.0
26 Mike Mussina .40 1.0
27 Paul LoDuca .25 .6
28 Torii Hunter .25 .6
29 Carlos Lee .25 .6
30 Jimmy Rollins .25 .6
31 Arthur Rhodes .20 .5
32 Ivan Rodriguez .40 1.0
33 Wes Helms .20 .5
34 Cliff Floyd .25 .6
35 Julian Tavarez .20 .5
36 Mark McGwire 1.50 4.0
37 Chipper Jones SP 3.00 8.0
38 Denny Neagle .20 .5
39 Odalis Perez .20 .5
40 Antonio Alfonseca .20 .5
41 Edgar Renteria .25 .6
42 Troy Glaus .25 .6
43 Scott Brosius .25 .6
44 Abraham Nunez .20 .5
45 Jamey Wright .20 .5
46 Bobby Bonilla .25 .6
47 Ismael Valdes .20 .5
48 Chris Reitsma .20 .5
49 Neifi Perez .20 .5
50 Juan Cruz .20 .5
51 Kevin Brown .25 .6
52 Ben Grieve .20 .5
53 Alex Rodriguez SP 4.00 10.0
54 Charles Nagy .20 .5
55 Reggie Sanders .25 .6
56 Nelson Figueroa .20 .5
57 Felipe Lopez .20 .5
58 Bill Ortega .20 .5
59 Jeffrey Hammonds .25 .6
60 Johnny Estrada .20 .5
61 Bob Wickman .20 .5
62 Doug Glanville .20 .5
63 Jeff Cirillo .20 .5
63N Jeff Cirillo Night SP 2.00 5.0
64 Corey Patterson .20 .50
65 Aaron Myette .20 .50
66 Magglio Ordonez .25 .6
67 Ellis Burks .25 .60
68 Miguel Tejada .25 .60
69 John Olerud .25 .60
69N John Olerud Night SP 2.00 5.00
70 Greg Vaughn .20 .50
71 Andy Pettitte .40 1.00
72 Mike Matheny .20 .50
73 Brandon Duckworth .20 .50
74 Scott Schoeneweis .20 .50
75 Mike Lowell .25 .60
76 Einar Diaz .20 .50
77 Tino Martinez .40 1.00
78 Matt Williams .25 .60
79 Jason Young RC .40 1.00
80 Nate Cornejo .20 .50
81 Andres Galarraga .25 .60
82 Bernie Williams SP 3.00 8.00
83 Ryan Klesko .25 .60
84 Dan Wilson .20 .50
85 Henry Pichardo RC .40 1.00
86 Ray Durham .25 .60
87 Omar Daal .20 .50
88 Derrek Lee .40 1.00
89 Al Leiter .25 .60
90 Darrin Fletcher .20 .50
91 Josh Beckett .25 .60
92 Johnny Damon .40 1.00
92N Johnny Damon Night SP 3.00 8.00
93 Abraham Nunez .20 .50
94 Ricky Ledee .20 .50
95 Richie Sexson .25 .60
96 Adam Kennedy .20 .50

97 Raul Mondesi .25 .60
98 John Burkett .25 .60
99 Ben Sheets .25 .60
99N Ben Sheets Night SP 2.00 5.00
100 Preston Wilson .25 .60
100N Preston Wilson Night SP 2.00 5.00
101 Boof Bonser .20 .50
102 Shigetoshi Hasegawa .25 .60
103 Carlos Febles .20 .50
104 Jorge Posada SP 3.00 8.00
105 Michael Tucker .20 .50
106 Roberto Hernandez .25 .60
107 John Rodriguez RC .40 1.00
108 Danny Graves .20 .50
109 Rich Aurilia .20 .50
110 Jon Lieber .20 .50
111 Tim Hummel RC .40 1.00
112 J.T. Snow .25 .60
113 Kris Benson .20 .50
114 Derek Jeter 1.50 4.00
115 John Franco .25 .60
116 Matt Stairs .20 .50
117 Ben Davis .20 .50
118 Darryl Kile .25 .60
119 Mike Peeples RC .40 1.00
120 Kevin Tapani .20 .50
121 Armando Benitez .20 .50
122 Damian Miller .20 .50
123 Jose Jimenez .20 .50
124 Pedro Astacio .20 .50
125 Marlyn Tisdale RC .40 1.00
126 Deivi Cruz .20 .50
127 Paul O'Neill .40 1.00
128 Jermaine Dye .25 .60
129 Marcus Giles .25 .60
130 Mark Loretta .20 .50
131 Garret Anderson .25 .60
132 Todd Ritchie .20 .50
133 Joe Crede .25 .60
134 Kevin Millwood .25 .60
135 Shane Reynolds .20 .50
136 Mark Grace .40 1.00
137 Shannon Stewart .25 .60
138 Nick Neugebauer .20 .50
139 Nic Jackson RC .40 1.00
140 Robb Nen UER .25 .60
141 Dmitri Young .25 .60
142 Kevin Appier .25 .60
143 Jack Cust .20 .50
144 Andres Torres .20 .50
145 Frank Thomas .60 1.50
146 Jason Kendall .25 .60
147 Greg Maddux 1.00 2.50
148 David Justice .25 .60
149 Hideo Nomo .60 1.50
150 Bret Boone .25 .60
151 Wade Miller .20 .50
152 Jeff Kent .25 .60
153 Scott Williamson .20 .50
154 Julio Lugo .20 .50
155 Bobby Higginson .25 .60
156 Geoff Jenkins .20 .50
157 Darren Dreifort .20 .50
158 Freddy Sanchez RC 1.25 3.00
159 Bud Smith .20 .50
160 Phil Nevin .25 .60
161 Cesar Izturis .20 .50
162 Sean Casey .25 .60
163 Jose Ortiz .20 .50
164 Brent Abernathy .20 .50
165 Kevin Young .20 .50
166 Daryle Ward .20 .50
167 Trevor Hoffman .25 .60
168 Rondell White .25 .60
169 Kip Wells .20 .50
170 John Vander Wal .20 .50
171 Jose Lima .20 .50
172 Wilton Guerrero .20 .50
173 Aaron Dean RC .40 1.00
174 Rick Helling .20 .50
175 Juan Pierre .25 .60
176 Jay Bell .25 .60
177 Craig House .20 .50
178 David Bell .20 .50
179 Pat Burrell .25 .60
180 Eric Gagne .25 .60
181 Adam Pettyjohn .20 .50
182 Ugueth Urbina .20 .50
183 Peter Bergeron .20 .50
184 Adrian Gonzalez .20 .50
184N Adrian Gonzalez Night SP 2.00 5.00
185 Damion Easley .20 .50
186 Gookie Dawkins .20 .50
187 Matt Lawton .20 .50
188 Frank Catalanotto .20 .50
189 David Wells .25 .60
190 Roger Cedeno .20 .50
191 Brian Giles .25 .60
192 Julio Zuleta .20 .50
193 Timo Perez .20 .50
194 Billy Wagner .25 .60
195 Craig Counsell .20 .50
196 Bart Miadich .20 .50
197 Gary Sheffield .25 .60
198 Richard Hidalgo .20 .50
199 Juan Uribe .20 .50
200 Curt Schilling .25 .60
201 Javy Lopez .25 .60
202 Jimmy Haynes .20 .50
203 Jim Edmonds .25 .60
204 Pokey Reese .20 .50
204N Pokey Reese Night SP 2.00 5.00
205 Matt Clement .25 .60
206 Dean Palmer .25 .60
207 Nick Johnson .25 .60
208 Nate Espy RC .40 1.00
209 Pedro Feliz .20 .50
210 Aaron Rowand .25 .60
211 Masato Yoshii .20 .50
212 Jose Cruz Jr. .20 .50
213 Paul Byrd .20 .50
214 Mark Phillips RC .40 1.00
215 Benny Agbayani .20 .50
216 Frank Menechino .20 .50
217 John Flaherty .20 .50
218 Brian Boehringer .20 .50
219 Todd Hollandsworth .20 .50
220 Sammy Sosa SP 3.00 8.00
221 Steve Sparks .20 .50
222 Homer Bush .20 .50
223 Mike Hampton .25 .60
224 Bobby Abreu .25 .60
225 Barry Larkin .40 1.00
226 Ryan Rupe .20 .50
227 Bubba Trammell .20 .50
228 Todd Zeile .25 .60
229 Jeff Shaw .20 .50
230 Alex Ochoa .20 .50
231 Orlando Cabrera .25 .60
232 Jeremy Giambi .20 .50
233 Tomo Ohka .20 .50
234 Luis Castillo .20 .50
235 Chris Holt .20 .50
236 Shawn Green .25 .60
237 Sidney Ponson .20 .50
238 Lee Stevens .20 .50
239 Hank Blalock .40 1.00
240 Randy Winn .20 .50
241 Pedro Martinez .40 1.00
242 Vinny Castilla .25 .60
243 Steve Karsay .20 .50
244 Barry Bonds SP 8.00 20.00
245 Jason Bere .20 .50
246 Scott Rolen .40 1.00
246N Scott Rolen Night SP 3.00 8.00
247 Ryan Kohlmeier .20 .50
248 Kerry Wood .25 .60
249 Aramis Ramirez .40 1.00
250 Lance Berkman .25 .60
251 Omar Vizquel .40 1.00
252 Juan Encarnacion .25 .60
254 David Segui .20 .50
255 Brian Anderson .20 .50
256 Jay Payton .20 .50
257 Mark Grudzielanek .25 .60
258 Jimmy Anderson .20 .50
259 Eric Valent .20 .50
260 Chad Durbin .20 .50
262 Alex Gonzalez .25 .60
263 Scott Dunn .20 .50
264 Scott Elarton .20 .50
265 Tom Gordon .20 .50
266 Moises Alou .25 .60
269 Mark Buehrle .25 .60
270 Jerry Hairston .20 .50
272 Luke Prokopec .20 .50
273 Graeme Lloyd .20 .50
274 Bret Prinz .20 .50
276 Chris Carpenter .40 1.00
277 Ryan Minor .20 .50
278 Jeff D'Amico .20 .50
279 Raul Ibanez .20 .50
280 Joe Mays .20 .50
281 Livan Hernandez .20 .50
282 Robin Ventura .25 .60
283 Gabe Kapler .25 .60
284 Tony Batista .20 .50
285 Ramon Hernandez .20 .50
286 Craig Paquette .20 .50
287 Mark Kotsay .25 .60
288 Mike Lieberthal .25 .60
289 Joe Borchard .20 .50
290 Cristian Guzman .20 .50
291 Craig Biggio .40 1.00
292 Joaquin Benoit .20 .50
293 Ken Caminiti .25 .60
294 Sean Burroughs .20 .50
295 Eric Karros .25 .60
296 Eric Chavez .25 .60
297 LaTroy Hawkins .20 .50
298 Alfonso Soriano .25 .60
299 John Smoltz .40 1.00
300 Adam Dunn .25 .60
301 Ryan Dempster .20 .50
302 Travis Hafner .25 .60
303 Russell Branyan .20 .50
304 Dustin Hermanson .20 .50
305 Jim Thome .40 1.00
306 Carlos Beltran .25 .60
307 Jason Botts RC .25 .60
308 David Cone .25 .60
309 Ivanon Coffie .20 .50
310 Brian Jordan .25 .60
311 Todd Walker .25 .60
312 Jeromy Burnitz .25 .60
313 Tony Armas Jr. .20 .50
314 Jeff Conine .25 .60
315 Todd Jones .20 .50
316 Roy Oswalt .25 .60
317 Aubrey Huff .25 .60
318 Josh Fogg .20 .50
319 Jose Vidro .20 .50
320 Jace Brewer .20 .50
321 Mike Redmond .20 .50
322 Noochie Varner RC .40 1.00
323 Russ Ortiz .20 .50
324 Edgardo Alfonzo .20 .50
325 Ruben Sierra .25 .60
326 Calvin Murray .20 .50
327 Marlon Anderson .20 .50
328 Albie Lopez .20 .50
329 Chris Gomez .20 .50
330 Fernando Tatis .20 .50
331 Stubby Clapp .20 .50
332 Rickey Henderson .60 1.50
333 Brad Radke .25 .60
334 Brent Mayne .20 .50
335 Cory Lidle .20 .50
336 Edgar Martinez .40 1.00
337 Aaron Boone .25 .60
338 Jay Witasick .20 .50
339 Benito Santiago .25 .60
340 Jose Mercedes .20 .50
341 Fernando Vina .20 .50
342 A.J. Pierzynski .25 .60
343 Jeff Bagwell .40 1.00
344 Brian Bohanon .20 .50
345 Adrian Beltre .25 .60
346 Troy Percival .25 .60
347 Napoleon Calzado RC .40 1.00
348 Ruben Rivera .20 .50
349 Rafael Soriano .20 .50
350 Damian Jackson .20 .50
351 Joe Randa .25 .60
352 Chan Ho Park .25 .60
353 Dante Bichette .25 .60
354 Bartolo Colon .25 .60
355 Jason Bay RC 2.00 5.00
356 Shea Hillenbrand .25 .60
357 Matt Morris .25 .60
358 Brad Penny .20 .50
359 Mark Quinn .20 .50
360 Marquis Grissom .25 .60
361 Henry Blanco .20 .50
362 Billy Koch .20 .50
363 Mike Cameron .20 .50
364 Albert Pujols SP 6.00 15.00
365 Paul Konerko SP 2.00 5.00
366 Eric Milton SP 2.00 5.00
367 Nick Bierbrodt SP 2.00 5.00
368 Rafael Palmeiro SP 3.00 8.00
369 Jorge Padilla SP RC 2.00 5.00
370 Jason Giambi Yankees SP 2.00 5.00
371 Mike Piazza SP 5.00 12.00
372 Alex Cora SP 2.00 5.00
373 Todd Helton SP 3.00 8.00
374 Juan Gonzalez SP 2.00 5.00
375 Mariano Rivera SP 10.00 25.00
376 Jason LaRue SP 2.00 5.00
377 Tony Gwynn SP 4.00 10.00
378 Wilson Betemit SP 2.00 5.00
379 J.J. Trujillo SP RC 2.00 5.00
380 Brad Ausmus SP 2.00 5.00
381 Chris George SP 2.00 5.00
382 Jose Canseco SP 3.00 8.00
383 Ramon Ortiz SP 2.00 5.00
384 John Rocker SP 2.00 5.00
385 Rey Ordonez SP 2.00 5.00
386 Ken Griffey Jr. SP 6.00 15.00
387 Juan Pena SP 2.00 5.00
388 Michael Barrett SP 2.00 5.00
389 J.D. Drew SP 2.00 5.00
390 Corey Koskie SP 2.00 5.00
391 Vernon Wells SP 2.00 5.00
392 Juan Tolentino SP RC 2.00 5.00
393 Luis Gonzalez SP 2.00 5.00
394 Terrence Long SP 2.00 5.00
395 Travis Lee SP 2.00 5.00
396 Earl Snyder SP RC 2.00 5.00
397 Nomar Garciaparra SP 5.00 12.00
398 Jason Schmidt SP 2.00 5.00
399 David Espinosa SP 2.00 5.00
400 Steve Green SP 2.00 5.00
401 Jack Wilson SP 2.00 5.00
402 Chris Tritle SP RC 2.00 5.00
403 Angel Berroa SP 2.00 5.00
404 Josh Towers SP 2.00 5.00
405 Andruw Jones SP 3.00 8.00
406 Brent Butler SP 2.00 5.00
407 Craig Kuzmic SP 2.00 5.00
408 Derek Bell SP 2.00 5.00
409 Eric Glaser SP RC 2.00 5.00
410 Joel Pineiro SP 2.00 5.00
411 Alexis Gomez SP 2.00 5.00
412 Mike Rivera SP 2.00 5.00
413 Shawn Estes SP 2.00 5.00
414 Milton Bradley SP 2.00 5.00
415 Carl Everett SP 2.00 5.00
416 Kazuhiro Sasaki SP 2.00 5.00
417 Tony Fontana SP RC 2.00 5.00
418 Josh Pearce SP 2.00 5.00
419 Gary Matthews Jr. SP 2.00 5.00
420 Raymond Cabrera SP RC 2.00 5.00
421 Joe Kennedy SP 2.00 5.00
422 Jason Maule SP RC 2.00 5.00
423 Casey Fossum SP 2.00 5.00
424 Christian Parker SP 2.00 5.00
425 Laynce Nix SP RC 4.00 10.00
426 Byung-Hyun Kim SP 2.00 5.00
427 Freddy Garcia SP 2.00 5.00
428 Herbert Perry SP 2.00 5.00
429 Jason Marquis SP 2.00 5.00
430 Sandy Alomar Jr. SP 2.00 5.00
431 Roberto Alomar SP 3.00 8.00
432 Tsuyoshi Shinjo SP 2.00 5.00
433 Tim Wakefield SP 2.00 5.00
434 Robert Fick SP 2.00 5.00
435 Vladimir Guerrero SP 3.00 8.00
436 Jose Mesa SP 2.00 5.00
437 Scott Spiezio SP 2.00 5.00
438 Jose Hernandez SP 2.00 5.00
439 Jose Acevedo SP 2.00 5.00
440 Brian West SP RC 2.00 5.00
441 Barry Zito SP 2.00 5.00
442 Luis Maza SP 2.00 5.00
443 Marlon Byrd SP 2.00 5.00
444 A.J. Burnett SP 2.00 5.00
445 Dee Brown SP 2.00 5.00
446 Carlos Delgado SP 2.00 5.00
CL1 Checklist 1 .20 .50
CL2 Checklist 2 .20 .50

2002 Topps Heritage Chrome

STATED ODDS 1:29
STATED PRINT RUN 553 SERIAL #'d SETS
THC1 Darin Erstad 5.00 12.00
THC2 Doug Mientkiewicz 5.00 12.00
THC3 Mike Sweeney 5.00 12.00
THC4 Roger Clemens 15.00 40.00
THC5 C.C. Sabathia 5.00 12.00
THC6 Tim Hudson 5.00 12.00
THC7 Jason Lane 5.00 12.00
THC8 Larry Walker 5.00 12.00
THC9 Mark Mulder 5.00 12.00
THC10 Mike Mussina 5.00 12.00
THC11 Paul LoDuca 5.00 12.00
THC12 Jimmy Rollins 5.00 12.00
THC13 Ivan Rodriguez 5.00 12.00
THC14 Mark McGwire 20.00 50.00
THC15 Edgar Renteria 5.00 12.00
THC16 Scott Brosius 5.00 12.00
THC17 Juan Cruz 5.00 12.00
THC18 Kevin Brown 5.00 12.00
THC19 Charles Nagy 5.00 12.00
THC20 Bill Ortega 5.00 12.00
THC21 Corey Patterson 5.00 12.00
THC22 Magglio Ordonez 5.00 12.00
THC23 Brandon Duckworth 5.00 12.00
THC24 Scott Schoeneweis 5.00 12.00
THC25 Tino Martinez 5.00 12.00
THC26 Jason Young 5.00 12.00
THC27 Nate Cornejo 5.00 12.00
THC28 Ryan Klesko 5.00 12.00
THC29 Omar Daal 5.00 12.00
THC30 Raul Mondesi 5.00 12.00
THC31 Boof Bonser 5.00 12.00
THC32 Rich Aurilia 5.00 12.00
THC33 Jon Lieber 5.00 12.00
THC34 Tim Hummel 5.00 12.00
THC35 J.T. Snow 5.00 12.00
THC36 Derek Jeter 30.00 80.00
THC37 Darryl Kile 5.00 12.00
THC38 Armando Benitez 5.00 12.00
THC39 Marlyn Tisdale 5.00 12.00
THC40 Shannon Stewart 5.00 12.00
THC41 Nic Jackson 5.00 12.00
THC42 Robb Nen UER 5.00 12.00
THC43 Dmitri Young 5.00 12.00
THC44 Greg Maddux 12.50 30.00
THC45 Hideo Nomo 8.00 20.00
THC46 Bret Boone 5.00 12.00
THC47 Wade Miller 5.00 12.00
THC48 Jeff Kent 5.00 12.00
THC49 Freddy Sanchez 8.00 20.00
THC50 Bud Smith 5.00 12.00
THC51 Sean Casey 5.00 12.00
THC52 Brent Abernathy 5.00 12.00
THC53 Trevor Hoffman 5.00 12.00
THC54 Aaron Dean 5.00 12.00
THC55 Juan Pierre 5.00 12.00
THC56 Pat Burrell 5.00 12.00
THC57 Gookie Dawkins 5.00 12.00
THC58 Roger Cedeno 5.00 12.00
THC59 Brian Giles 5.00 12.00
THC60 Jim Edmonds 5.00 12.00
THC61 Dean Palmer 5.00 12.00
THC62 Nick Johnson 5.00 12.00
THC63 Nate Espy 5.00 12.00
THC64 Aaron Rowand 5.00 12.00
THC65 Mark Phillips 5.00 12.00
THC66 Mike Hampton 5.00 12.00
THC67 Bobby Abreu 5.00 12.00
THC68 Alex Ochoa 5.00 12.00
THC69 Shawn Green 5.00 12.00
THC70 Hank Blalock 5.00 12.00
THC71 Pedro Martinez 5.00 12.00
THC72 Ryan Kohlmeier 5.00 12.00
THC73 Kerry Wood 5.00 12.00
THC74 Aramis Ramirez 5.00 12.00
THC75 Lance Berkman 5.00 12.00
THC76 Scott Dunn 5.00 12.00
THC77 Moises Alou 5.00 12.00
THC78 Mark Buehrle 5.00 12.00
THC79 Jerry Hairston 5.00 12.00
THC80 Joe Borchard 5.00 12.00
THC81 Cristian Guzman 5.00 12.00
THC82 Sean Burroughs 5.00 12.00
THC83 Alfonso Soriano 5.00 12.00
THC84 Adam Dunn 5.00 12.00
THC85 Jim Thome 5.00 12.00
THC86 Jason Botts 5.00 12.00
THC87 Jeromy Burnitz 5.00 12.00
THC88 Roy Oswalt 5.00 12.00
THC89 Russ Ortiz 5.00 12.00
THC90 Marlon Anderson 5.00 12.00
THC91 Stubby Clapp 5.00 12.00
THC92 Rickey Henderson 8.00 20.00
THC93 Brad Radke 5.00 12.00
THC94 Jeff Bagwell 5.00 12.00
THC95 Troy Percival 5.00 12.00
THC96 Napoleon Calzado 5.00 12.00
THC97 Joe Randa 5.00 12.00
THC98 Chan Ho Park 5.00 12.00
THC99 Jason Bay 10.00 25.00
THC100 Mark Quinn 5.00 12.00

2002 Topps Heritage Classic Renditions

Inserted into packs at stated odds of one in 12, these 10 cards show how current players might look like if they played in their 1953 team uniforms. These cards are printed on grayback paper stock.

COMPLETE SET (10) 8.00 20.00
STATED ODDS 1:12
CR1 Kerry Wood .75 2.00
CR2 Brian Giles .75 2.00
CR3 Roger Cedeno .75 2.00
CR4 Jason Giambi .75 2.00
CR5 Albert Pujols 2.00 5.00
CR6 Mark Buehrle .75 2.00
CR7 Cristian Guzman .75 2.00
CR8 Jimmy Rollins .75 2.00
CR9 Jim Thome .75 2.00
CR10 Shawn Green .75 2.00

2002 Topps Heritage Clubhouse Collection

Inserted into packs at a rate for jersey cards of one in 332 and bat cards at a rate of one in 498, these 12 cards feature a mix of active and retired players with a memorabilia swatch.

BAT STATED ODDS 1:498
JERSEY STATED ODDS 1:332
CCAD Alvin Dark Bat 10.00 25.00
CCBB Barry Bonds Bat 12.50 30.00
CCCP Corey Patterson Bat 10.00 25.00
CCEM Eddie Mathews Jsy 15.00 40.00
CCGK George Kell Jsy 15.00 40.00
CCGM Greg Maddux Jsy 15.00 40.00
CCHS Hank Sauer Bat 10.00 25.00
CCJP Jorge Posada Bat 10.00 25.00
CCNG Nomar Garciaparra Bat 10.00 25.00
CCRA Rich Aurilia Bat 10.00 25.00
CCWM Willie Mays Bat 15.00 40.00
CCYB Yogi Berra Jsy 10.00 25.00

2002 Topps Heritage Clubhouse Collection Autographs

These four cards parallel the Clubhouse Collection insert set. These cards feature autographs from the noted players are are serial numbered to 25. Due to market scarcity, no pricing is provided for these players.

2002 Topps Heritage Clubhouse Collection Duos

Inserted into packs at stated odds of one in 5016, these six cards feature one current player and one 1953 franchise alum from that same team with a relic from each player. These cards have a stated print run of 53 serial numbered sets. Due to market scarcity, no pricing is provided for these cards.

STATED ODDS 1:5016
STATED PRINT RUN 53 SERIAL #'d SETS
NO PRICING DUE TO SCARCITY
CC2BP Y.Berra/J.Posada 40.00 80.00
CC2DA A.Dark/R.Aurilia 40.00 80.00
CC2KR G.Kell/N.Garciaparra 40.00 80.00
CC2MB W.Mays/B.Bonds 150.00 250.00
CC2SM E.Mathews/G.Maddux 40.00 80.00
CC2SP H.Sauer/C.Patterson 30.00 60.00

2002 Topps Heritage Grandstand Glory

Inserted into packs at different rates depending on which grop the player is from, these 12 cards feature retired 1950's players along with an authentic relic from an historic 1950's stadium.

GROUP A STATED ODDS 1:4115
GROUP B STATED ODDS 1:531
GROUP C STATED ODDS 1:1576
GROUP D STATED ODDS 1:370
GROUP E STATED ODDS 1:483
GGBF Bob Feller E 10.00 25.00
GGBM Billy Martin B 10.00 25.00
GGBP Billy Pierce B 8.00 20.00
GGBS Bobby Shantz D 8.00 20.00
GGEW Early Wynn E 10.00 25.00
GGHN Hal Newhouser B 10.00 25.00
GGHS Hank Sauer C 8.00 20.00
GGRC Roy Campanella D 15.00 40.00
GGSP Satchel Paige A 12.50 30.00
GGTK Ted Kluszewski E 15.00 40.00
GGWF Whitey Ford D 10.00 25.00
GGWS Warren Spahn D 15.00 40.00

2002 Topps Heritage New Age Performers

Inserted into packs at stated odds of one in 15, these 15 cards feature powerhouse players whose accomplishments have cemented their names in major league history.

COMPLETE SET (15) 10.00 25.00
STATED ODDS 1:15
NA1 Luis Gonzalez .40 1.00
NA2 Mark McGwire 1.50 4.00
NA3 Barry Bonds 1.50 4.00
NA4 Ken Griffey Jr. 2.00 5.00
NA5 Ichiro Suzuki 1.25 3.00
NA6 Sammy Sosa 1.00 2.50
NA7 Andruw Jones .40 1.00
NA8 Derek Jeter 2.50 6.00
NA9 Todd Helton .60 1.50
NA10 Alex Rodriguez 1.25 3.00
NA11 Jason Giambi Yankees .40 1.00
NA12 Bret Boone .40 1.00
NA13 Roberto Alomar .60 1.50
NA14 Albert Pujols 2.00 5.00
NA15 Vladimir Guerrero .60 1.50

2002 Topps Heritage Real One Autographs

Inserted into packs at different odds depending on which group the player belongs to, this 28 card set features a mix of authentic autographs between active players and those who were active in the 1953 season. Please note that the group which each player belongs to is listed next to their name in our checklist. The Roger Clemens card has been signed in both blue and black, please let us know if any other players are signed in more than one color.

GROUP 1 STATED ODDS 1:346
GROUP 2 STATED ODDS 1:6363
GROUP 3 STATED ODDS 1:4908
GROUP 4 STATED ODDS 1:3196
GROUP 5 STATED ODDS 1:498
*RED INK: .75X TO 1.5X BASIC AUTO'S
RED INK ODDS 1:306
RED INK PRINT RUN 53 SERIAL #'d SETS
ROAC Andy Carey 1 30.00 60.00
ROAD Alvin Dark 1 10.00 25.00
ROAR Al Rosen 1 20.00 50.00
ROARO Alex Rodriguez 2 30.00 80.00
ROASC Al Schoendienst 1 30.00 60.00
ROBF Bob Feller 1 50.00 100.00
ROBG Brian Giles 5 10.00 25.00
ROBS Bobby Shantz 1 20.00 50.00
ROCG Cristian Guzman 5 6.00 15.00
RODD Dom DiMaggio 1 25.00 60.00
ROES Enos Slaughter 1 30.00 60.00
ROGK George Kell 1 20.00 50.00
ROGM Gil McDougald 1 15.00 40.00
ROHW Hoyt Wilhelm 1 50.00 100.00
ROJB Joe Black 1 30.00 60.00
ROJE Jim Edmonds 4 15.00 40.00
ROJP John Podres 1 15.00 40.00
ROMI Monte Irvin 1 20.00 50.00
ROOM Minnie Minoso 1 30.00 60.00
ROPR Phil Rizzuto 1 50.00 100.00
ROPRO Preacher Roe 1 30.00 60.00
RORB Ray Boone 1 50.00 100.00
RORF Roy Face 1 10.00 25.00
RORCL Roger Clemens 3 30.00 80.00
ROWF Whitey Ford 1 40.00 100.00
ROWM Willie Mays 1 150.00 400.00
ROWS Warren Spahn 1 25.00 60.00
ROYB Yogi Berra 1 40.00 100.00

2002 Topps Heritage Then and Now

Inserted into packs at stated odds of one in 15, these 10 cards feature a 1953 player as well as a current stand-out. These cards offer statistical comparisions in major stat categories and are printed in greyback paper stock.

COMPLETE SET (10) 12.50 30.00
STATED ODDS 1:15
TN1 E.Mathews B.Bonds 2.50 6.00
TN2 A.Rosen A.Rodriguez 1.25 3.00
TN3 C.Furillo L.Walker .75 2.00
TN4 M.Minoso I.Suzuki 2.00 5.00
TN5 R.Ashburn R.Aurilia .75 2.00
TN6 A.Rosen B.Boone .75 2.00
TN7 D.Snider S.Sosa 1.00 2.50
TN8 A.Rosen A.Rodriguez 1.25 3.00
TN9 R.Roberts R.Johnson 1.00 2.50
TN10 B.Pierce H.Nomo 1.00 2.50

2003 Topps Heritage

This 430-card set, which was designed to honor the 1954 Topps set, was released in February, 2003. These cards were issued in five card packs with an $3 SRP. These packs were issued in 24 pack boxes which came eight boxes to a case. In addition, many cards in the set were issued in two varieties. A few cards were issued featuring either a logo used today or a scarcer version in which the logo was used in the 1954 set. In addition, some cards were printed with either the originally designed version or a black background. The black background version is the tougher of the two versions of each card. A few cards between 1 and 363 were produced in less quantities and all cards from 364 on up were short printed as well. In a nod to the 1954 set, Alex Rodriguez had both cards 1 and 250; just as Ted Williams had in the original 1954 Topps set.

COMPLETE SET (453) 125.00 250.00
COMP.SET w/o SP's (353) 30.00 60.00
COMMON CARD .20 .50
COMMON RC .40 1.00
COMMON SP 2.00 5.00
COMMON SP RC 2.00 5.00
SP STATED ODDS 1:2
BASIC SP: 3/25/85/94/128/132/141/170
BASIC SP: 175/200/201/239/250/364-430
BLACK SP: 1/7/18/20/50/80/139/150
BLACK SP: 260/340
OLD LOGO SP: 6/10/11/27/30/100/156/190
OLD LOGO SP: 302/325
1A Alex Rodriguez Red .60 1.50
1B Alex Rodriguez Black SP 5.00 12.00
2 Jose Cruz Jr. .20 .50
3 Ichiro Suzuki SP 6.00 15.00
4 Rich Aurilia .20 .50
5 Trevor Hoffman .30 .75
6A Brian Giles New Logo .20 .50
6B Brian Giles Old Logo SP 2.00 5.00
7A Albert Pujols Orange .60 1.50
7B Albert Pujols Black SP 6.00 15.00
8 Vicente Padilla .20 .50
9 Bobby Crosby .20 .50
10A Derek Jeter New Logo 1.25 3.00
10B Derek Jeter Old Logo SP 6.00 15.00
11A Pat Burrell New Logo .20 .50
11B Pat Burrell Old Logo SP 2.00 5.00
12 Armando Benitez .20 .50
13 Javier Vazquez .20 .50
14 Justin Morneau .30 .75
15 Doug Mientkiewicz .20 .50
16 Kevin Brown .20 .50
17 Alexis Gomez .20 .50
18A Lance Berkman Blue .30 .75
18B Lance Berkman Black SP 3.00 8.00
19 Adrian Gonzalez .40 1.00
20A Todd Helton Green .30 .75
20B Todd Helton Black SP 3.00 8.00
21 Carlos Pena .30 .75
22 Matt Lawton .20 .50
23 Elmer Dessens .20 .50
24 Hee Seop Choi .20 .50
25 Chris Duncan SP RC 5.00 12.00
26 Ugueth Urbina .20 .50
27A Rodrigo Lopez New Logo .20 .50
27B Rodrigo Lopez Old Logo SP 2.00 5.00
28 Damian Moss .20 .50
29 Steve Finley .20 .50
30A Sammy Sosa New Logo .50 1.25
30B Sammy Sosa Old Logo SP 5.00 12.00
31 Kevin Cash .20 .50
32 Kenny Rogers .20 .50
33 Ben Grieve .20 .50
34 Jason Simontacchi .20 .50
35 Shin-Soo Choo .30 .75
36 Freddy Garcia .20 .50
37 Jesse Foppert .20 .50
38 Tony LaRussa MG .30 .75
39 Mark Kotsay .20 .50
40 Barry Zito .30 .75
41 Josh Fogg .20 .50
42 Marlon Byrd .20 .50
43 Marcus Thames .20 .50
44 Al Leiter .20 .50
45 Michael Barrett .20 .50
46 Jake Peavy .20 .50
47 Dustan Mohr .20 .50
48 Alex Sanchez .20 .50
49 Chin-Feng Chen .20 .50
50A Kazuhisa Ishii Blue .20 .50
50B Kazuhisa Ishii Black SP 2.00 5.00
51 Carlos Beltran .30 .75
52 Franklin Gutierrez RC 1.00 2.50
53 Miguel Cabrera 2.50 6.00
54 Roger Clemens .60 1.50
55 Juan Cruz .20 .50
56 Jason Young .20 .50
57 Alex Herrera .20 .50
58 Aaron Boone .20 .50
59 Mark Buehrle .30 .75
60 Larry Walker .30 .75
61 Morgan Ensberg .20 .50
62 Barry Larkin .30 .75
63 Joe Borchard .20 .50
64 Jason Dubois .20 .50
65 Shea Hillenbrand .20 .50
66 Jay Gibbons .20 .50
67 Vinny Castilla .20 .50
68 Jeff Mathis .20 .50
69 Curt Schilling .30 .75
70 Garret Anderson .20 .50
71 Josh Phelps .20 .50
72 Chan Ho Park .30 .75
73 Edgar Renteria .20 .50
74 Kazuhiro Sasaki .20 .50
75 Lloyd McClendon MG .20 .50
76 Jon Lieber .20 .50
77 Rolando Viera .20 .50
78 Jeff Conine .20 .50
79 Kevin Millwood .20 .50
80A Randy Johnson Green .50 1.25
80B Randy Johnson Black SP 5.00 12.00
81 Troy Percival .20 .50
82 Cliff Floyd .20 .50
83 Tony Graffanino .20 .50
84 Austin Kearns .20 .50
85 Manuel Ramirez SP RC 2.00 5.00

86 Jim Tracy MG .20 .50
87 Rondell White .20 .50
88 Trot Nixon .20 .50
89 Carlos Lee .20 .50
90 Mike Lowell .20 .50
91 Raul Ibanez .30 .75
92 Ricardo Rodriguez .20 .50
93 Ben Sheets .20 .50
94 Jason Perry SP RC 2.00 5.00
95 Mark Teixeira .30 .75
96 Brad Fullmer .20 .50
97 Casey Kotchman .20 .50
98 Craig Counsell .20 .50
99 Jason Marquis .20 .50
100A N.Garciaparra New Logo .30 .75
100B N.Garciaparra Old Logo SP 3.00 8.00
101 Ed Rogers .20 .50
102 Wilson Betemit .20 .50
103 Wayne Lydon RC .40 1.00
104 Jack Cust .20 .50
105 Derrek Lee .20 .50
106 Jim Kavourias .20 .50
107 Joe Randa .20 .50
108 Taylor Buchholz .20 .50
109 Gabe Kapler .20 .50
110 Preston Wilson .20 .50
111 Craig Biggio .30 .75
112 Paul Lo Duca .20 .50
113 Eddie Guardado .20 .50
114 Andres Galarraga .30 .75
115 Edgardo Alfonzo .20 .50
116 Robin Ventura .20 .50
117 Jeremy Giambi .20 .50
118 Ray Durham .20 .50
119 Mariano Rivera .60 1.50
120 Jimmy Rollins .30 .75
121 Dennis Tankersley .20 .50
122 Jason Schmidt .20 .50
123 Bret Boone .20 .50
124 Josh Hamilton .30 .75
125 Scott Rolen .30 .75
126 Steve Cox .20 .50
127 Larry Bowa MG .20 .50
128 Adam LaRoche SP 2.00 5.00
129 Ryan Klesko .20 .50
130 Tim Hudson .30 .75
131 Brandon Claussen .20 .50
132 Craig Brazell SP RC 2.00 5.00
133 Grady Little MG .20 .50
134 Jarrod Washburn .20 .50
135 Lyle Overbay .20 .50
136 John Burkett .20 .50
137 Daryl Clark RC .40 1.00
138 Kirk Rueter .20 .50
139A Mauer Brothers Green .50 1.25
139B Mauer Brothers Black SP 5.00 12.00
140 Troy Glaus .20 .50
141 Trey Hodges SP 2.00 5.00
142 Dallas McPherson .20 .50
143 Art Howe MG .20 .50
144 Jesus Cota .20 .50
145 J.R. House .20 .50
146 Reggie Sanders .20 .50
147 Clint Nageotte .20 .50
148 Jim Edmonds .30 .75
149 Carl Crawford .30 .75
150A Mike Piazza Blue .50 1.25
150B Mike Piazza Black SP 5.00 12.00
151 Seung Song .20 .50
152 Roberto Hernandez .20 .50
153 Marquis Grissom .20 .50
154 Billy Wagner .20 .50
155 Josh Beckett .20 .50
156A Randall Simon New Logo .20 .50
156B Randall Simon Old Logo SP 2.00 5.00
157 Ben Broussard .20 .50
158 Russell Branyan .20 .50
159 Frank Thomas .50 1.25
160 Alex Escobar .20 .50
161 Mark Bellhorn .20 .50
162 Melvin Mora .20 .50
163 Andruw Jones .20 .50
164 Danny Bautista .20 .50
165 Ramon Ortiz .20 .50
166 Wily Mo Pena .20 .50
167 Jose Jimenez .20 .50
168 Mark Redman .20 .50
169 Angel Berroa .20 .50
170 Andy Marte SP RC 2.00 5.00
171 Juan Gonzalez .20 .50
172 Fernando Vina .20 .50
173 Joel Pineiro .20 .50
174 Boof Bonser .20 .50
175 Bernie Castro SP RC 2.00 5.00
176 Bobby Cox MG .20 .50
177 Jeff Kent .20 .50
178 Oliver Perez .20 .50
179 Chase Utley .30 .75
180 Mark Mulder .20 .50
181 Bobby Abreu .20 .50
182 Ramiro Mendoza .20 .50
183 Aaron Heilman .20 .50
184 A.J. Pierzynski .20 .50
185 Eric Gagne .20 .50
186 Kirk Saarloos .20 .50
187 Ron Gardenhire MG .20 .50
188 Dmitri Young .20 .50
189 Todd Zeile .20 .50
190A Jim Thome New Logo .30 .75
190B Jim Thome Old Logo SP 3.00 8.00
191 Cliff Lee 1.25 3.00
192 Matt Morris .20 .50
193 Robert Fick .20 .50
194 C.C. Sabathia .30 .75
195 Alexis Rios .20 .50
196 D'Angelo Jimenez .20 .50
197 Edgar Martinez .30 .75
198 Robb Nen .20 .50
199 Taggert Bozied .20 .50
200 Vladimir Guerrero SP 3.00 8.00
201 Walter Young SP 2.00 5.00
202 Brendan Harris RC .40 1.00
203 Mike Hargrove MG .20 .50
204 Vernon Wells .20 .50
205 Hank Blalock .20 .50
206 Mike Cameron .20 .50
207 Tony Batista .20 .50
208 Matt Williams .20 .50
209 Tony Womack .20 .50
210 Ramon Nivar-Martinez RC .40 1.00
211 Aaron Sele .20 .50
212 Mark Grace .30 .75
213 Joe Crede .20 .50
214 Ryan Dempster .20 .50
215 Omar Vizquel .30 .75
216 Juan Pierre .20 .50
217 Denny Bautista .20 .50
218 Chuck Knoblauch .20 .50
219 Eric Karros .20 .50
220 Victor Diaz .20 .50
221 Jacque Jones .20 .50
222 Jose Vidro .20 .50
223 Joe McEwing .20 .50
224 Nick Johnson .20 .50
225 Eric Chavez .20 .50
226 Jose Mesa .20 .50
227 Aramis Ramirez .20 .50
228 John Lackey .30 .75
229 David Bell .20 .50
230 John Olerud .20 .50
231 Tino Martinez .30 .75
232 Randy Winn .20 .50
233 Todd Hollandsworth .20 .50
234 Ruddy Lugo RC .40 1.00
235 Carlos Delgado .20 .50
236 Chris Narveson .20 .50
237 Tim Salmon .20 .50
238 Orlando Palmeiro .20 .50
239 Jeff Clark SP RC 2.00 5.00
240 Byung-Hyun Kim .20 .50
241 Mike Remlinger .20 .50
242 Johnny Damon .30 .75
243 Corey Patterson .20 .50
244 Paul Konerko .30 .75
245 Danny Graves .20 .50
246 Ellis Burks .20 .50
247 Gavin Floyd .20 .50
248 Jaime Bubela RC .40 1.00
249 Sean Burroughs .20 .50
250 Alex Rodriguez SP 5.00 12.00
251 Gabe Gross .20 .50
252 Rafael Palmeiro .30 .75
253 Dewon Brazelton .20 .50
254 Jimmy Journell .20 .50
255 Rafael Soriano .20 .50
256 Jerome Williams .20 .50
257 Xavier Nady .20 .50
258 Mike Williams .20 .50
259 Randy Wolf .20 .50
260A Miguel Tejada Orange .30 .75
260B Miguel Tejada Black SP 3.00 8.00
261 Juan Rivera .20 .50
262 Rey Ordonez .20 .50
263 Bartolo Colon .20 .50
264 Eric Milton .20 .50
265 Jeffrey Hammonds .20 .50
266 Odalis Perez .20 .50
267 Mike Sweeney .20 .50
268 Richard Hidalgo .20 .50
269 Alex Gonzalez .20 .50
270 Aaron Cook .20 .50
271 Earl Snyder .20 .50
272 Todd Walker .20 .50
273 Aaron Rowand .20 .50
274 Matt Clement .20 .50
275 Anastacio Martinez .20 .50
276 Mike Bordick .20 .50
277 John Smoltz .50 1.25
278 Scott Hairston .20 .50
279 David Eckstein .20 .50
280 Shannon Stewart .20 .50
281 Carl Everett .20 .50
282 Aubrey Huff .20 .50
283 Mike Mussina .30 .75
284 Ruben Sierra .20 .50
285 Russ Ortiz .20 .50
286 Brian Lawrence .20 .50
287 Kip Wells .20 .50
288 Placido Polanco .20 .50
289 Ted Lilly .20 .50
290 Andy Pettitte .30 .75
291 John Buck .20 .50
292 Orlando Cabrera .20 .50
293 Cristian Guzman .20 .50
294 Ruben Quevedo .20 .50
295 Cesar Izturis .20 .50
296 Ryan Ludwick .20 .50
297 Roy Oswalt .30 .75
298 Jason Stokes .20 .50
299 Mike Hampton .20 .50
300 Pedro Martinez .30 .75
301 Nic Jackson .20 .50
302A Magglio Ordonez New Logo .30 .75
302B Magglio Ordonez Old Logo SP 3.00 8.00
303 Manny Ramirez .50 1.25
304 Jorge Julio .20 .50
305 Javy Lopez .20 .50
306 Roy Halladay .30 .75
307 Kevin Mench .20 .50
308 Jason Isringhausen .20 .50
309 Carlos Guillen .20 .50
310 Tsuyoshi Shinjo .20 .50
311 Phil Nevin .20 .50
312 Pokey Reese .20 .50
313 Jorge Padilla .20 .50
314 Jermaine Dye .20 .50
315 David Wells .20 .50
316 Mo Vaughn .20 .50
317 Bernie Williams .30 .75
318 Michael Restovich .20 .50
319 Jose Hernandez .20 .50
320 Richie Sexson .20 .50
321 Daryle Ward .20 .50
322 Luis Castillo .20 .50
323 Rene Reyes .20 .50
324 Victor Martinez .30 .75
325A Adam Dunn New Logo .30 .75
325B Adam Dunn Old Logo SP 3.00 8.00
326 Corwin Malone .20 .50
327 Kerry Wood .20 .50
328 Rickey Henderson .50 1.25
329 Marty Cordova .20 .50
330 Greg Maddux .60 1.50
331 Miguel Batista .20 .50
332 Chris Bootcheck .20 .50
333 Carlos Baerga .20 .50
334 Antonio Alfonseca .20 .50
335 Shane Halter .20 .50
336 Juan Encarnacion .20 .50
337 Tom Gordon .20 .50
338 Hideo Nomo .50 1.25
339 Torii Hunter .20 .50
340A Alfonso Soriano Yellow .30 .75
340B Alfonso Soriano Black SP 3.00 8.00
341 Roberto Alomar .30 .75
342 David Justice .20 .50
343 Mike Lieberthal .20 .50
344 Jeff Weaver .20 .50
345 Timo Perez .20 .50
346 Travis Lee .20 .50
347 Sean Casey .20 .50
348 Willie Harris .20 .50
349 Derek Lowe .20 .50
350 Tom Glavine .30 .75
351 Eric Hinske .20 .50
352 Rocco Baldelli .20 .50
353 J.D. Drew .20 .50
354 Jamie Moyer .20 .50
355 Todd Linden .20 .50
356 Benito Santiago .20 .50
357 Brad Baker .20 .50
358 Alex Gonzalez .20 .50
359 Brandon Duckworth .20 .50
360 John Rheinecker .20 .50
361 Orlando Hernandez .20 .50
362 Pedro Astacio .20 .50
363 Brad Wilkerson .20 .50
364 David Ortiz SP 5.00 12.00
365 Geoff Jenkins SP 2.00 5.00
366 Brian Jordan SP 2.00 5.00
367 Paul Byrd SP 2.00 5.00
368 Jason Lane SP 2.00 5.00
369 Jeff Bagwell SP 3.00 8.00
370 Bobby Higginson SP 2.00 5.00
371 Juan Uribe SP 2.00 5.00
372 Lee Stevens SP 2.00 5.00
373 Jimmy Haynes SP 2.00 5.00
374 Jose Valentin SP 2.00 5.00
375 Ken Griffey Jr. SP 6.00 15.00
376 Barry Bonds SP 6.00 15.00
377 Gary Matthews Jr. SP 2.00 5.00
378 Gary Sheffield SP 2.00 5.00
379 Rick Helling SP 2.00 5.00
380 Junior Spivey SP 2.00 5.00
381 Francisco Rodriguez SP 3.00 8.00
382 Chipper Jones SP 5.00 12.00
383 Orlando Hudson SP 2.00 5.00
384 Ivan Rodriguez SP 3.00 8.00
385 Chris Snelling SP 2.00 5.00
386 Kenny Lofton SP 2.00 5.00
387 Eric Cyr SP 2.00 5.00
388 Jason Kendall SP 2.00 5.00
389 Marlon Anderson SP 2.00 5.00
390 Billy Koch SP 2.00 5.00
391 Shelley Duncan SP 2.00 5.00
392 Jose Reyes SP 5.00 12.00
393 Fernando Tatis SP 2.00 5.00
394 Michael Cuddyer SP 2.00 5.00
395 Mark Prior SP 3.00 8.00
396 Dontrelle Willis SP 2.00 5.00
397 Jay Payton SP 2.00 5.00
398 Brandon Phillips SP 2.00 5.00
399 Dustin Moseley SP RC 2.00 5.00
400 Jason Giambi SP 2.00 5.00
401 John Mabry SP 2.00 5.00
402 Ron Gant SP 2.00 5.00
403 J.T. Snow SP 2.00 5.00
404 Jeff Cirillo SP 2.00 5.00
405 Darin Erstad SP 2.00 5.00
406 Luis Gonzalez SP 2.00 5.00
407 Marcus Giles SP 2.00 5.00
408 Brian Daubach SP 2.00 5.00
409 Moises Alou SP 2.00 5.00
410 Raul Mondesi SP 2.00 5.00
411 Adrian Beltre SP 5.00 12.00
412 A.J. Burnett SP 2.00 5.00
413 Jason Jennings SP 2.00 5.00
414 Edwin Almonte SP 2.00 5.00
415 Fred McGriff SP 3.00 8.00
416 Tim Raines Jr. SP 2.00 5.00
417 Rafael Furcal SP 2.00 5.00
418 Erubiel Durazo SP 2.00 5.00
419 Drew Henson SP 2.00 5.00
420 Kevin Appier SP 2.00 5.00
421 Chad Tracy SP 2.00 5.00
422 Adam Wainwright SP 3.00 8.00
423 Choo Freeman SP 2.00 5.00
424 Sandy Alomar Jr. SP 2.00 5.00
425 Corey Koskie SP 2.00 5.00
426 Jeromy Burnitz SP 2.00 5.00
427 Jorge Posada SP 3.00 8.00
428 Jason Arnold SP 2.00 5.00
429 Brett Myers SP 2.00 5.00
430 Shawn Green SP 2.00 5.00
CL1 Checklist 1 .20 .50
CL2 Checklist 2 .20 .50
CL3 Checklist 3 .20 .50

2003 Topps Heritage Chrome

STATED ODDS 1:8
STATED PRINT RUN 1954 SERIAL #'d SETS
THC1 Alex Rodriguez 4.00 10.00
THC2 Ichiro Suzuki 4.00 10.00
THC3 Brian Giles 1.25 3.00
THC4 Albert Pujols 4.00 10.00
THC5 Derek Jeter 8.00 20.00
THC6 Pat Burrell 1.25 3.00
THC7 Lance Berkman 2.00 5.00
THC8 Todd Helton 2.00 5.00
THC9 Chris Duncan 4.00 10.00
THC10 Rodrigo Lopez 1.25 3.00
THC11 Sammy Sosa 3.00 8.00
THC12 Barry Zito 2.00 5.00
THC13 Marlon Byrd 1.25 3.00
THC14 Al Leiter 1.25 3.00
THC15 Kazuhisa Ishii 1.25 3.00
THC16 Franklin Gutierrez 3.00 8.00
THC17 Roger Clemens 4.00 10.00
THC18 Mark Buehrle 2.00 5.00
THC19 Larry Walker 2.00 5.00
THC20 Curt Schilling 2.00 5.00
THC21 Garret Anderson 1.25 3.00
THC22 Randy Johnson 3.00 8.00
THC23 Cliff Floyd 1.25 3.00
THC24 Austin Kearns 1.25 3.00
THC25 Manuel Ramirez 1.25 3.00
THC26 Raul Ibanez 2.00 5.00
THC27 Jason Perry 1.25 3.00
THC28 Mark Teixeira 2.00 5.00
THC29 Nomar Garciaparra 2.00 5.00
THC30 Wayne Lydon 1.25 3.00
THC31 Preston Wilson 1.25 3.00
THC32 Paul Lo Duca 1.25 3.00
THC33 Edgardo Alfonzo 1.25 3.00
THC34 Jeremy Giambi 1.25 3.00
THC35 Mariano Rivera 4.00 10.00
THC36 Jimmy Rollins 2.00 5.00
THC37 Bret Boone 1.25 3.00
THC38 Scott Rolen 2.00 5.00
THC39 Adam LaRoche 1.25 3.00
THC40 Tim Hudson 2.00 5.00
THC41 Craig Brazell 1.25 3.00
THC42 Daryl Clark 1.25 3.00
THC43 Mauer Brothers 3.00 8.00
THC44 Troy Glaus 1.25 3.00
THC45 Trey Hodges 1.25 3.00
THC46 Carl Crawford 2.00 5.00
THC47 Mike Piazza 3.00 8.00
THC48 Josh Beckett 1.25 3.00
THC49 Randall Simon 1.25 3.00
THC50 Frank Thomas 3.00 8.00
THC51 Andruw Jones 1.25 3.00
THC52 Andy Marte 1.25 3.00
THC53 Bernie Castro 1.25 3.00
THC54 Jim Thome 2.00 5.00
THC55 Alexis Rios 1.25 3.00
THC56 Vladimir Guerrero 2.00 5.00
THC57 Walter Young 1.25 3.00
THC58 Hank Blalock 1.25 3.00
THC59 Ramon Nivar-Martinez 1.25 3.00
THC60 Jacque Jones 1.25 3.00
THC61 Nick Johnson 1.25 3.00
THC62 Ruddy Lugo 1.25 3.00
THC63 Carlos Delgado 1.25 3.00
THC64 Jeff Clark 1.25 3.00
THC65 Johnny Damon 2.00 5.00
THC66 Jaime Bubela 1.25 3.00
THC67 Alex Rodriguez 4.00 10.00
THC68 Rafael Palmeiro 2.00 5.00
THC69 Miguel Tejada 2.00 5.00
THC70 Bartolo Colon 1.25 3.00
THC71 Mike Sweeney 1.25 3.00
THC72 John Smoltz 3.00 8.00
THC73 Shannon Stewart 1.25 3.00
THC74 Mike Mussina 2.00 5.00
THC75 Roy Oswalt 2.00 5.00
THC76 Pedro Martinez 2.00 5.00
THC77 Magglio Ordonez 2.00 5.00
THC78 Manny Ramirez 3.00 8.00
THC79 David Wells 1.25 3.00
THC80 Richie Sexson 1.25 3.00
THC81 Adam Dunn 2.00 5.00
THC82 Greg Maddux 4.00 10.00
THC83 Alfonso Soriano 2.00 5.00
THC84 Roberto Alomar 2.00 5.00
THC85 Derek Lowe 1.25 3.00
THC86 Tom Glavine 2.00 5.00
THC87 Jeff Bagwell 2.00 5.00
THC88 Ken Griffey Jr. 6.00 15.00
THC89 Barry Bonds 5.00 12.00
THC90 Gary Sheffield 1.25 3.00
THC91 Chipper Jones 3.00 8.00
THC92 Orlando Hudson 1.25 3.00
THC93 Jose Cruz Jr. 1.25 3.00
THC94 Mark Prior 2.00 5.00
THC95 Jason Giambi 1.25 3.00
THC96 Luis Gonzalez 1.25 3.00
THC97 Drew Henson 1.25 3.00
THC98 Cristian Guzman 1.25 3.00
THC99 Shawn Green 1.25 3.00
THC100 Jose Vidro 1.25 3.00

2003 Topps Heritage Chrome Refractors

RANDOM INSERTS IN PACKS
STATED PRINT RUN 554 SERIAL #'d SETS

2003 Topps Heritage Clubhouse Collection Relics

Inserted at different odds depending on the relic, these 12 cards feature a mix of active and retire players and various game-used relics used during their career.

BAT A STATED ODDS 1:2569
BAT B STATED ODDS 1:2506
BAT C STATED ODDS 1:2464
BAT D STATED ODDS 1:1989
UNI A STATED ODDS 1:4223
UNI B STATED ODDS 1:1207
UNI C STATED ODDS 1:921
UNI D STATED ODDS 1:171
AD Adam Dunn Uni D 6.00 15.00
AK Al Kaline Bat D 6.00 15.00
AP Albert Pujols Uni D 8.00 20.00
AR Alex Rodriguez Uni D 8.00 20.00
CJ Chipper Jones Uni D 6.00 15.00
DS Duke Snider Uni A 15.00 40.00
EB Ernie Banks Bat C 8.00 20.00
EM Eddie Mathews Bat B 6.00 15.00
JG Jim Gilliam Uni B 6.00 15.00
KW Kerry Wood Uni D 6.00 15.00
SG Shawn Green Uni C 6.00 15.00
WM Willie Mays Bat A 15.00 40.00

2003 Topps Heritage Flashbacks

Inserted at a stated rate of one in 12, these 10 cards feature thrilling moments from the 1954 season.

COMPLETE SET (10) 6.00 15.00
STATED ODDS 1:12
F1 Willie Mays 2.00 5.00
F2 Yogi Berra 1.00 2.50
F3 Ted Kluszewski .60 1.50
F4 Stan Musial 1.50 4.00
F5 Hank Aaron 2.00 5.00
F6 Duke Snider .60 1.50
F7 Richie Ashburn .60 1.50
F8 Robin Roberts .60 1.50
F9 Mickey Vernon .40 1.00
F10 Don Larsen .40 1.00

2003 Topps Heritage Grandstand Glory Stadium Relics

Inserted at different odds depending on the group, these 12 cards feature a player photo along with a seat relic from any of nine historic ballparks involved in their career.

GROUP A ODDS 1:2804
GROUP B ODDS 1:514
GROUP C ODDS 1:1446
GROUP D ODDS 1:1356
GROUP E ODDS 1:654
GROUP F ODDS 1:214
AK Al Kaline F 8.00 20.00
AP Andy Pafko F 4.00 10.00
DG Dick Groat D 6.00 15.00
DS Duke Snider A 10.00 25.00
EB Ernie Banks C 10.00 25.00
EM Eddie Mathews F 6.00 15.00
PR Phil Rizzuto E 8.00 20.00
RA Richie Ashburn B 8.00 20.00
TK Ted Kluszewski B 8.00 20.00
WM Willie Mays B 15.00 40.00
WS Warren Spahn F 8.00 20.00
YB Yogi Berra E 10.00 25.00

2003 Topps Heritage New Age Performers

Issued at a stated rate of one in 15, these 15 cards feature prominent active players who have taken the game of baseball to new levels.

COMPLETE SET (15) 10.00 25.00
STATED ODDS 1:15
NA1 Mike Piazza 1.00 2.50
NA2 Ichiro Suzuki 1.25 3.00
NA3 Derek Jeter 2.50 6.00
NA4 Alex Rodriguez 1.25 3.00
NA5 Sammy Sosa 1.00 2.50
NA6 Jason Giambi .40 1.00
NA7 Vladimir Guerrero .60 1.50
NA8 Albert Pujols 1.25 3.00
NA9 Todd Helton .60 1.50
NA10 Nomar Garciaparra .60 1.50
NA11 Randy Johnson 1.00 2.50
NA12 Jim Thome .60 1.50
NA13 Barry Bonds 1.50 4.00
NA14 Miguel Tejada .60 1.50
NA15 Alfonso Soriano .60 1.50

2003 Topps Heritage Real One Autographs

Inserted at various odds depending on what group the player belonged to, these cards feature authentic autographs from the featured player. Topps made an effort to secure autographs from every person who was still living that was in the 1954 Topps set. Hank Aaron, Yogi Berra and Johnny Sain did not return their cards in time for inclusion in this set and a collector could redeem these cards until February 28th, 2005. Sain never did sign his cards before his passing in November, 2006.

RETIRED ODDS 1:188
ACTIVE A ODDS 1:6168
ACTIVE B ODDS 1:1540
ACTIVE C ODDS 1:2802
*RED INK: 1X TO 2X BASIC RETIRED
*RED INK: .75X TO 1.5X BASIC ACTIVE A
*RED INK: .75X TO 1.5X BASIC ACTIVE B
*RED INK: .75X TO 1.5X BASIC ACTIVE C
RED INK STATED ODDS 1:696
RED INK PRINT RUN 54 SERIAL #'d SETS
AK Al Kaline 30.00 80.00
AP Andy Pafko 15.00 40.00
BR Bob Ross 10.00 25.00
BS Bill Skowron 10.00 25.00
BSH Bobby Shantz 10.00 25.00
BT Bob Talbot 10.00 25.00
BWE Bill Werle 10.00 25.00
CH Cal Hogue 10.00 25.00
CK Charlie Kress 15.00 40.00
CS Carl Scheib 12.50 30.00
DG Dick Groat 10.00 25.00
DK Dick Kryhoski 12.00 30.00
DL Don Lenhardt 10.00 25.00
DLU Don Lund 10.00 25.00
DS Duke Snider 25.00 60.00
EB Ernie Banks 75.00 200.00
EM Eddie Mayo 10.00 25.00
GH Gene Hermanski 10.00 25.00
HA Hank Aaron 250.00 500.00
HB Hank Bauer 15.00 40.00
JC Jose Cruz Jr. B 10.00 25.00
JP Joe Presko 12.00 30.00
JPO Johnny Podres 20.00 50.00
JR Jimmy Rollins C 10.00 25.00
JV Jose Vidro B 6.00 15.00
JW Jim Willis 10.00 25.00
LB Lance Berkman A 12.50 30.00
LJ Larry Jansen 15.00 40.00
LW Leroy Wheat 10.00 25.00
MB Matt Batts 12.50 30.00
MBL Mike Blyzka 12.00 30.00
MI Monte Irvin 15.00 40.00
MM Mickey Micelotta 6.00 15.00
MS Mike Sandlock 10.00 25.00
PP Paul Penson 10.00 25.00
PR Phil Rizzuto 30.00 60.00
PRO Preacher Roe 15.00 40.00
RF Roy Face 15.00 40.00
RM Ray Murray 10.00 25.00
TL Tom Lasorda 50.00 100.00
VL Vern Law 10.00 25.00
WF Whitey Ford 50.00 100.00
WM Willie Mays 250.00 500.00
YB Yogi Berra 60.00 150.00

2003 Topps Heritage Then and Now

Issued at a stated rate of one in 15, these 10 cards feature an 1954 star along with a current standout. The backs compare 10 league leaders of 1954 to the league leaders of 2002. Interestingly enough, Ted Kluszewski and Alex Rodriguez are on both the first two cards in this set.

COMPLETE SET (10) 8.00 20.00
STATED ODDS 1:15
TN1 T.Kluszewski / A.Rod HR 1.25 3.00
TN2 T.Kluszewski / A.Rod RBI 1.25 3.00
TN3 W.Mays / B.Bonds BTG 2.00 5.00
TN4 D.Mueller / A.Soriano .60 1.50
TN5 S.Musial / G.Anderson 1.50 4.00
TN6 M.Minoso / J.Damon .60 1.50
TN7 W.Mays / B.Bonds SLG 2.00 5.00
TN8 D.Snider / A.Rodriguez 1.25 3.00
TN9 R.Roberts / R.Johnson 1.00 2.50
TN10 J.Antonelli / P.Martinez .60 1.50

2004 Topps Heritage

This 495 card set was released in February, 2004. As this was the fourth year this set was issued, the cards were designed in the style of the 1955 Topps set. This set was issued in eight card packs which came 24 packs to a box and eight boxes to a case. This set features a mix of cards printed to standard amounts as well as various Short Prints and then even some variation short prints. Any type of short printed card was issued to a stated rate of one in two. We have delineated in our checklist what the various variations are. In addition, all cards from 398 through 475 are SP's.

COMPLETE SET (499) 100.00 250.00
COMP.SET w/o SP's (389) 30.00 60.00
COMMON CARD .20 .50
COMMON RC .30 .75
COMMON SP 1.50 4.00
COMMON SP RC 1.50 4.00
SP STATED ODDS 1:2
BASIC SP: 2/4/28/47/50/92/123/124/164
BASIC SP: 194/198/210/398-475
VARIATION SP: 1/8/10/30/40/49/60/70
VARIATION SP: 85/100/117/120/180/182
VARIATION SP: 200/213/250/311/342/361
SEE BECKETT.COM FOR VAR.DESCRIPTIONS
1A Jim Thome Fielding .30 .75
1B Jim Thome Hitting SP 3.00 8.00
2 Nomar Garciaparra SP 4.00 10.00
3 Aramis Ramirez .20 .50
4 Rafael Palmeiro SP 3.00 8.00
5 Danny Graves .20 .50
6 Casey Blake .20 .50
7 Juan Uribe .20 .50
8A Dmitri Young New Logo .20 .50
8B Dmitri Young Old Logo SP 2.00 5.00
9 Billy Wagner .20 .50
10A Jason Giambi Swinging .20 .50
10B Jason Giambi Btg Stance SP 2.00 5.00
11 Carlos Beltran .30 .75
12 Chad Hermansen .20 .50
13 B.J. Upton .30 .75
14 Dustan Mohr .20 .50
15 Endy Chavez .20 .50
16 Cliff Floyd .20 .50
17 Bernie Williams .30 .75
18 Eric Chavez .20 .50
19 Chase Utley .30 .75
20 Randy Johnson .60 1.50
21 Vernon Wells .20 .50
22 Juan Gonzalez .20 .50
23 Joe Kennedy .20 .50
24 Bengie Molina .20 .50
25 Carlos Lee .20 .50
26 Horacio Ramirez .20 .50
27 Anthony Acevedo RC .30 .75
28 Sammy Sosa SP 3.00 8.00
29 Jon Garland .20 .50
30A Adam Dunn Fielding .30 .75
30B Adam Dunn Hitting SP 2.00 5.00
31 Aaron Rowand .20 .50
32 Jody Gerut .20 .50
33 Chin-Hui Tsao .20 .50
34 Alex Sanchez .20 .50
35 A.J. Burnett .20 .50
36 Brad Ausmus .20 .50
37 Blake Hawksworth RC .30 .75
38 Francisco Rodriguez .30 .75
39 Alex Cintron .20 .50
40A Chipper Jones Pointing .60 1.50
40B Chipper Jones Fielding SP 3.00 8.00
41 Deivi Cruz .20 .50
42 Bill Mueller .20 .50
43 Joe Borowski .20 .50
44 Jimmy Haynes .20 .50
45 Mark Loretta .20 .50
46 Jerome Williams .20 .50
47 Gary Sheffield Yanks SP 3.00 8.00
48 Richard Hidalgo .20 .50
49A Jason Kendall New Logo .20 .50
49B Jason Kendall Old Logo SP 2.00 5.00
50 Ichiro Suzuki SP 5.00 12.00
51 Jim Edmonds .30 .75
52 Frank Catalanotto .20 .50
53 Jose Contreras .20 .50
54 Mo Vaughn .20 .50
55 Brendan Donnelly .20 .50
56 Luis Gonzalez .20 .50
57 Robert Fick .20 .50
58 Laynce Nix .20 .50
59 Johnny Damon .30 .75
60A Magglio Ordonez Running .30 .75
60B Magglio Ordonez Hitting SP 2.00 5.00
61 Matt Clement .20 .50
62 Ryan Ludwick .20 .50
63 Luis Castillo .20 .50
64 Dave Crouthers RC .30 .75
65 Dave Berg .20 .50
66 Kyle Davies RC .30 .75
67 Tim Salmon .20 .50
68 Marcus Giles .20 .50
69 Marty Cordova .20 .50
70A Todd Helton White Jsy .30 .75
70B Todd Helton Purple Jsy SP 3.00 8.00
71 Jeff Kent .20 .50
72 Michael Tucker .20 .50
73 Cesar Izturis .20 .50
74 Paul Quantrill .20 .50
75 Conor Jackson RC 1.00 2.50
76 Placido Polanco .20 .50
77 Adam Eaton .20 .50
78 Ramon Hernandez .20 .50
79 Edgardo Alfonzo .20 .50
80 Dioner Navarro RC .50 1.25
81 Woody Williams .20 .50
82 Rey Ordonez .20 .50

83 Randy Winn .20 .50
84 Casey Myers RC .30 .75
85A R.Choy Foo New Logo RC .30 .75
85B R.Choy Foo Old Logo SP 2.00 5.00
86 Ray Durham .20 .50
87 Sean Burroughs .20 .50
88 Tim Frend RC .30 .75
89 Shigetoshi Hasegawa .20 .50
90 Jeffrey Allison RC .30 .75
91 Orlando Hudson .20 .50
92 Matt Creighton SP RC .30 .75
93 Tim Worrell .20 .50
94 Kris Benson .20 .50
95 Mike Lieberthal .20 .50
96 David Wells .20 .50
97 Jason Phillips .20 .50
98 Bobby Cox MGR .20 .50
99 Johan Santana .60 1.50
100A Alex Rodriguez Hitting 1.00 2.50
100B Alex Rodriguez Throwing SP 4.00 10.00
101 John Vander Wal .20 .50
102 Orlando Cabrera .20 .50
103 Hideo Nomo .60 1.50
104 Todd Walker .20 .50
105 Jason Johnson .20 .50
106 Matt Mantei .20 .50
107 Jarrod Washburn .20 .50
108 Preston Wilson .20 .50
109 Carl Pavano .20 .50
110 Geoff Blum .20 .50
111 Eric Gagne .20 .50
112 Geoff Jenkins .20 .50
113 Joe Torre MG .30 .75
114 Jon Knott RC .30 .75
115 Hank Blalock .20 .50
116 John Olerud .20 .50
117A Pat Burrell New Logo .20 .50
117B Pat Burrell Old Logo SP 2.00 5.00
118 Aaron Boone .20 .50
119 Zach Day .20 .50
120A Frank Thomas New Logo .60 1.50
120B Frank Thomas Old Logo SP 3.00 8.00
121 Kyle Farnsworth .20 .50
122 Derek Lowe .20 .50
123 Zach Miner SP RC 3.00 8.00
124 Matthew Moses SP RC 3.00 8.00
125 Jesse Roman RC .30 .75
126 Josh Phelps .20 .50
127 Nic Ungs RC .30 .75
128 Dan Haren .20 .50
129 Kirk Rueter .20 .50
130 Jack McKeon MGR .20 .50
131 Keith Foulke .20 .50
132 Garrett Stephenson .20 .50
133 Wes Helms .20 .50
134 Raul Ibanez .30 .75
135 Morgan Ensberg .20 .50
136 Jay Payton .20 .50
137 Billy Koch .20 .50
138 Mark Grudzielanek .20 .50
139 Rodrigo Lopez .20 .50
140 Corey Patterson .20 .50
141 Troy Percival .20 .50
142 Shea Hillenbrand .20 .50
143 Brad Fullmer .20 .50
144 Ricky Nolasco RC .50 1.25
145 Mark Teixeira .30 .75
146 Tydus Meadows RC .30 .75
147 Toby Hall .20 .50
148 Orlando Palmeiro .20 .50
149 Khalid Ballouli RC .20 .50
150 Grady Little MGR .20 .50
151 David Eckstein .20 .50
152 Kenny Perez RC .30 .75
153 Ben Grieve .20 .50
154 Ismael Valdes .20 .50
155 Bret Boone .20 .50
156 Jesse Foppert .20 .50
157 Vicente Padilla .20 .50
158 Bobby Abreu .20 .50
159 Scott Hatteberg .20 .50
160 Carlos Quentin RC 1.25 3.00
161 Anthony Lerew RC .30 .75
162 Lance Carter .20 .50
163 Robb Nen .20 .50
164 Zach Duke SP RC 4.00 10.00
165 Xavier Nady .20 .50
166 Kip Wells .20 .50
167 Kevin Millwood .20 .50
168 Jon Lieber .20 .50
169 Jose Reyes .30 .75
170 Eric Byrnes .20 .50
171 Paul Konerko .30 .75
172 Chris Lubanski .20 .50
173 Jae Weong Seo .20 .50
174 Corey Koskie .20 .50
175 Tim Stauffer RC .50 1.25
176 John Lackey .30 .75
177 Danny Bautista .20 .50
178 Shane Reynolds .20 .50
179 Jorge Julio .20 .50
180A Manny Ramirez New Logo .50 1.25
180B Manny Ramirez Old Logo SP 3.00 8.00
181 Alex Gonzalez .20 .50
182A Moises Alou New Logo .20 .50
182B Moises Alou Old Logo SP 2.00 5.00
183 Mark Buehrle .30 .75
184 Carlos Guillen .30 .75
185 Nate Cornejo .20 .50
186 Billy Traber .20 .50
187 Jason Jennings .20 .50
188 Eric Munson .20 .50
189 Braden Looper .20 .50
190 Juan Encarnacion .20 .50
191 Dusty Baker MGR .20 .50
192 Travis Lee .20 .50
193 Miguel Cairo .20 .50
194 Rich Aurilia SP 2.00 5.00
195 Tom Gordon .20 .50
196 Freddy Garcia .20 .50
197 Brian Lawrence .20 .50
198 Jorge Posada SP 3.00 8.00
199 Javier Vazquez .20 .50
200A Albert Pujols New Logo 1.25 3.00
200B Albert Pujols Old Logo SP 5.00 12.00
201 Victor Zambrano .20 .50
202 Eli Marrero .20 .50
203 Joel Pineiro .20 .50
204 Rondell White .20 .50
205 Craig Ansman RC .30 .75
206 Michael Young .20 .50
207 Carlos Baerga .20 .50
208 Andruw Jones .20 .50
209 Jerry Hairston Jr. .20 .50
210 Shawn Green SP 2.00 5.00
211 Ron Gardenhire MGR .20 .50
212 Darin Erstad .20 .50
213A Brandon Webb Glove Chest .20 .50
213B Brandon Webb Glove Out SP 2.00 5.00
214 Greg Maddux 1.00 2.50
215 Reed Johnson .20 .50
216 John Thomson .20 .50
217 Tino Martinez .30 .75
218 Mike Cameron .20 .50
219 Edgar Martinez .30 .75
220 Eric Young .20 .50
221 Reggie Sanders .20 .50
222 Randy Wolf .20 .50
223 Erubiel Durazo .20 .50
224 Mike Mussina .30 .75
225 Tom Glavine .30 .75
226 Troy Glaus .20 .50
227 Oscar Villarreal .20 .50
228 David Segui .20 .50
229 Jeff Suppan .20 .50
230 Kenny Lofton .20 .50
231 Esteban Loaiza .20 .50
232 Felipe Lopez .20 .50
233 Matt Lawton .20 .50
234 Mark Bellhorn .20 .50
235 Wil Ledezma .20 .50
236 Todd Hollandsworth .20 .50
237 Octavio Dotel .20 .50
238 Darren Dreifort .20 .50
239 Paul Lo Duca .20 .50
240 Richie Sexson .20 .50
241 Doug Mientkiewicz .20 .50
242 Luis Rivas .20 .50
243 Claudio Vargas .20 .50
244 Mark Ellis .20 .50
245 Brett Myers .20 .50
246 Jake Peavy .20 .50
247 Marquis Grissom .20 .50
248 Armando Benitez .20 .50
249 Ryan Franklin .20 .50
250A Alfonso Soriano Throwing .30 .75
250B Alfonso Soriano Fielding SP 2.00 5.00
251 Tim Hudson .20 .50
252 Shannon Stewart .20 .50
253 A.J. Pierzynski .20 .50
254 Runelvys Hernandez .20 .50
255 Roy Oswalt .30 .75
256 Shawn Chacon .20 .50
257 Tony Graffanino .20 .50
258 Tim Wakefield .30 .75
259 Damian Miller .20 .50
260 Joe Crede .20 .50
261 Jason LaRue .20 .50
262 Jose Jimenez .20 .50
263 Juan Pierre .20 .50
264 Wade Miller .20 .50
265 Odalis Perez .20 .50
266 Eddie Guardado .20 .50
267 Rocky Biddle .20 .50
268 Jeff Nelson .20 .50
269 Terrence Long .20 .50
270 Ramon Ortiz .20 .50
271 Raul Mondesi .20 .50
272 Ugueth Urbina .20 .50
273 Jeromy Burnitz .20 .50
274 Brad Radke .20 .50
275 Jose Vidro .20 .50
276 Bobby Jenks .20 .50
277 Ty Wigginton .20 .50
278 Jose Guillen .20 .50
279 Delmon Young .30 .75
280 Brian Giles .20 .50
281 Jason Schmidt .20 .50
282 Nick Markakis .40 1.00
283 Felipe Alou MGR .20 .50
284 Carl Crawford .30 .75
285 Neifi Perez .20 .50
286 Miguel Tejada .20 .50
287 Victor Martinez .30 .75
288 Adam Kennedy .20 .50
289 Kerry Ligtenberg .20 .50
290 Scott Williamson .20 .50
291 Tony Womack .20 .50
292 Travis Hafner .20 .50
293 Bobby Crosby .30 .75
294 Chad Billingsley .30 .75
295 Russ Ortiz .20 .50
296 John Burkett .20 .50
297 Carlos Zambrano .30 .75
298 Randall Simon .20 .50
299 Juan Castro .20 .50
300 Mike Lowell .20 .50
301 Fred McGriff .20 .50
302 Glendon Rusch .20 .50
303 Sung Jung RC .30 .75
304 Rocco Baldelli .20 .50
305 Fernando Vina .20 .50
306 Gil Meche .20 .50
307 Jose Cruz Jr. .20 .50
308 Bernie Castro .20 .50
309 Scott Spiezio .20 .50
310 Paul Byrd .20 .50
311A Jay Gibbons New Logo .20 .50
311B Jay Gibbons Old Logo SP 2.00 5.00
312 Trot Nixon .20 .50
313 Chris O'Riordan RC .30 .75
314 Julio Lugo .20 .50
315 Ben Davis .20 .50
316 Mike Williams .20 .50
317 Trevor Hoffman .30 .75
318 Andy Pettitte .30 .75
319 Orlando Hernandez .20 .50
320 Juan Rivera .20 .50
321 Elizardo Ramirez .20 .50
322 Junior Spivey .20 .50
323 Tony Batista .20 .50
324 Mike Remlinger .20 .50
325 Alex Gonzalez .20 .50
326 Aaron Hill .20 .50
327 Steve Finley .20 .50
328 Vinny Castilla .20 .50
329 Eric Duncan .20 .50
330 Mike Gosling RC .30 .75
331 Eric Hinske .20 .50
332 Scott Rolen .30 .75
333 Benito Santiago .20 .50
334 Jimmy Gobble .20 .50
335 Bobby Higginson .20 .50
336 Kelvim Escobar .20 .50
337 Mike DeJean .20 .50
338 Sidney Ponson .20 .50
339 Todd Self RC .30 .75
340 Jeff Cirillo .20 .50
341 Jimmy Rollins .30 .75
342A Barry Zito White Jsy .30 .75
342B Barry Zito Green Jsy SP 2.00 5.00
343 Felix Pie .20 .50
344 Matt Morris .20 .50
345 Kazuhiro Sasaki .20 .50
346 Jack Wilson .20 .50
347 Nick Johnson .20 .50
348 Wil Cordero .20 .50
349 Ryan Madson .20 .50
350 Torii Hunter .20 .50
351 Andy Ashby .20 .50
352 Aubrey Huff .20 .50
353 Brad Lidge .20 .50
354 Derrek Lee .20 .50
355 Yadier Molina RC 12.00 30.00
356 Paul Wilson .20 .50
357 Omar Vizquel .30 .75
358 Rene Reyes .20 .50
359 Marlon Anderson .20 .50
360 Bobby Kielty .20 .50
361A Ryan Wagner New Logo .20 .50
361B Ryan Wagner Old Logo SP 2.00 5.00
362 Justin Morneau .30 .75
363 Shane Spencer .20 .50
364 David Bell .20 .50
365 Matt Stairs .20 .50
366 Joe Borchard .20 .50
367 Mark Redman .20 .50
368 Dave Roberts .30 .75
369 Desi Relaford .20 .50
370 Rich Harden .20 .50
371 Fernando Tatis .20 .50
372 Eric Karros .20 .50
373 Eric Milton .20 .50
374 Mike Sweeney .20 .50
375 Brian Daubach .20 .50
376 Brian Snyder .20 .50
377 Chris Reitsma .20 .50
378 Kyle Lohse .20 .50
379 Livan Hernandez .20 .50
380 Robin Ventura .20 .50
381 Jacque Jones .20 .50
382 Danny Kolb .20 .50
383 Casey Kotchman .20 .50
384 Cristian Guzman .20 .50
385 Josh Beckett .20 .50
386 Khalil Greene .30 .75
387 Greg Myers .20 .50
388 Francisco Cordero .20 .50
389 Donald Levinski RC .30 .75
390 Roy Halladay .20 .50
391 J.D. Drew .20 .50
392 Jamie Moyer .20 .50
393 Ken Macha MGR .20 .50
394 Jeff Davanon .20 .50
395 Matt Kata .20 .50
396 Jack Cust .20 .50
397 Mike Timlin .20 .50
398 Zack Greinke SP 4.00 10.00
399 Byung-Hyun Kim SP 1.50 4.00
400 Kazuhisa Ishii SP 1.50 4.00
401 Brayan Pena SP RC 1.50 4.00
402 Garret Anderson SP 1.50 4.00
403 Kyle Sleeth SP RC 1.50 4.00
404 Javy Lopez SP 1.50 4.00
405 Damian Moss SP 1.50 4.00
406 David Ortiz SP 4.00 10.00
407 Pedro Martinez SP 2.50 6.00
408 Hee Seop Choi SP 1.50 4.00
409 Carl Everett SP 1.50 4.00
410 Dontrelle Willis SP 1.50 4.00
411 Ryan Harvey SP 1.50 4.00
412 Russell Branyan SP 1.50 4.00
413 Milton Bradley SP 1.50 4.00
414 Marcus McBeth SP RC 1.50 4.00
415 Carlos Pena SP 2.50 6.00
416 Ivan Rodriguez SP 2.50 6.00
417 Craig Biggio SP 2.50 6.00
418 Angel Berroa SP 1.50 4.00
419 Brian Jordan SP 1.50 4.00
420 Scott Podsednik SP 1.50 4.00
421 Omar Falcon SP RC 1.50 4.00
422 Joe Mays SP 1.50 4.00
423 Brad Wilkerson SP 1.50 4.00
424 Al Leiter SP 1.50 4.00
425 Derek Jeter SP 40.00 100.00
426 Mark Mulder SP 1.50 4.00
427 Marlon Byrd SP 1.50 4.00
428 David Murphy SP RC 2.50 6.00
429 Phil Nevin SP 1.50 4.00
430 J.T. Snow SP 1.50 4.00
431 Brad Sullivan SP RC 1.50 4.00
432 Bo Hart SP 1.50 4.00
433 Josh Labandeira SP RC 1.50 4.00
434 Chan Ho Park SP 2.50 6.00
435 Carlos Delgado SP 1.50 4.00
436 Curt Schilling Sox SP 2.50 6.00
437 John Smoltz SP 4.00 10.00
438 Luis Matos SP 1.50 4.00
439 Mark Prior SP 2.50 6.00
440 Roberto Alomar SP 2.50 6.00
441 Coco Crisp SP 1.50 4.00
442 Austin Kearns SP 1.50 4.00
443 Larry Walker SP 2.50 6.00
444 Neal Cotts SP 1.50 4.00
445 Jeff Bagwell SP 2.50 6.00
446 Adrian Beltre SP 4.00 10.00
447 Grady Sizemore SP 2.50 6.00
448 Keith Ginter SP 1.50 4.00
449 Vladimir Guerrero SP 2.50 6.00
450 Lyle Overbay SP 1.50 4.00
451 Rafael Furcal SP 1.50 4.00
452 Melvin Mora SP 1.50 4.00
453 Kerry Wood SP 1.50 4.00
454 Jose Valentin SP 1.50 4.00
455 Ken Griffey Jr. SP 8.00 20.00
456 Brandon Phillips SP 1.50 4.00
457 Miguel Cabrera SP 4.00 10.00
458 Edwin Jackson SP 1.50 4.00
459 Eric Owens SP 1.50 4.00
460 Miguel Batista SP 1.50 4.00
461 Mike Hampton SP 1.50 4.00
462 Kevin Millar SP 1.50 4.00
463 Bartolo Colon SP 1.50 4.00
464 Sean Casey SP 1.50 4.00
465 C.C. Sabathia SP 2.50 6.00
466 Rickie Weeks SP 1.50 4.00
467 Brad Penny SP 1.50 4.00
468 Mike MacDougal SP 1.50 4.00
469 Kevin Brown SP 1.50 4.00
470 Lance Berkman SP 2.50 6.00
471 Ben Sheets SP 1.50 4.00
472 Mariano Rivera SP 20.00 50.00
473 Mike Piazza SP 4.00 10.00
474 Ryan Klesko SP 1.50 4.00
475 Edgar Renteria SP 1.50 4.00
CL1 Checklist 1 .20 .50
CL2 Checklist 2 .20 .50
CL3 Checklist 3 .20 .50
CL4 Checklist 4 .20 .50

2004 Topps Heritage Chrome

COMPLETE SET (110) 150.00 250.00
STATED ODDS 1:7
STATED PRINT RUN 1955 SERIAL #'d SETS
THC1 Sammy Sosa 3.00 8.00
THC2 Nomar Garciaparra 2.00 5.00
THC3 Ichiro Suzuki 4.00 10.00
THC4 Rafael Palmeiro 2.00 5.00
THC5 Carlos Delgado 1.25 3.00
THC6 Troy Glaus 1.25 3.00
THC7 Jay Gibbons 1.25 3.00
THC8 Frank Thomas 3.00 8.00
THC9 Pat Burrell 1.25 3.00
THC10 Albert Pujols 4.00 10.00
THC11 Brandon Webb 1.25 3.00
THC12 Chipper Jones 3.00 8.00
THC13 Magglio Ordonez 2.00 5.00
THC14 Adam Dunn 2.00 5.00
THC15 Todd Helton 2.00 5.00
THC16 Jason Giambi 2.00 5.00
THC17 Alfonso Soriano 2.00 5.00
THC18 Barry Zito 2.00 5.00
THC19 Jim Thome 2.00 5.00
THC20 Alex Rodriguez 4.00 10.00
THC21 Hee Seop Choi 1.25 3.00
THC22 Pedro Martinez 2.00 5.00
THC23 Kerry Wood 1.25 3.00
THC24 Bartolo Colon 1.25 3.00
THC25 Austin Kearns 1.25 3.00
THC26 Ken Griffey Jr. 6.00 15.00
THC27 Coco Crisp 1.25 3.00
THC28 Larry Walker 2.00 5.00
THC29 Ivan Rodriguez 2.00 5.00
THC30 Dontrelle Willis 1.25 3.00
THC31 Miguel Cabrera 3.00 8.00
THC32 Jeff Bagwell 2.00 5.00
THC33 Lance Berkman 2.00 5.00
THC34 Shawn Green 1.25 3.00
THC35 Kevin Brown 1.25 3.00
THC36 Vladimir Guerrero 2.00 5.00
THC37 Mike Piazza 3.00 8.00
THC38 Derek Jeter 15.00 40.00
THC39 John Smoltz 3.00 8.00
40 Mark Prior 2.00 5.00
THC41 Gary Sheffield Yanks 1.25 3.00
THC42 Curt Schilling Sox 2.00 5.00
THC43 Randy Johnson 3.00 8.00
THC44 Luis Gonzalez 1.25 3.00
THC45 Andruw Jones 1.25 3.00
THC46 Greg Maddux 4.00 10.00
THC47 Tony Batista 1.25 3.00
THC48 Esteban Loaiza 1.25 3.00
THC49 Chin-Hui Tsao 1.25 3.00
THC50 Mike Lowell 1.25 3.00
THC51 Jeff Kent 1.25 3.00
THC52 Richie Sexson 1.25 3.00
THC53 Torii Hunter 1.25 3.00
THC54 Jose Vidro 1.25 3.00
THC55 Jose Reyes 2.00 5.00
THC56 Jimmy Rollins 2.00 5.00
THC57 Bret Boone 1.25 3.00
THC58 Rocco Baldelli 1.25 3.00
THC59 Hank Blalock 1.25 3.00
THC60 Rickie Weeks 1.25 3.00
THC61 Rodney Choy Foo 1.25 3.00
THC62 Zach Miner 2.00 5.00
THC63 Brayan Pena 1.25 3.00
THC64 David Murphy 2.00 5.00
THC65 Matt Creighton 1.25 3.00
THC66 Kyle Sleeth 1.25 3.00
THC67 Matthew Moses 2.00 5.00
THC68 Josh Labandeira 1.25 3.00
THC69 Grady Sizemore 2.00 5.00
THC70 Edwin Jackson 1.25 3.00
THC71 Marcus McBeth 1.25 3.00
THC72 Brad Sullivan 1.25 3.00
THC73 Zach Duke 2.00 5.00
THC74 Omar Falcon 1.25 3.00
THC75 Conor Jackson 4.00 10.00
THC76 Carlos Quentin 5.00 12.00
THC77 Craig Ansman 1.25 3.00
THC78 Mike Gosling 1.25 3.00
THC79 Kyle Davies 1.25 3.00
THC80 Anthony Lerew 1.25 3.00
THC81 Sung Jung 1.25 3.00
THC82 Dave Crouthers 1.25 3.00
THC83 Kenny Perez 1.25 3.00
THC84 Jeffrey Allison 1.25 3.00
THC85 Nic Ungs 1.25 3.00
THC86 Donald Levinski 1.25 3.00
THC87 Anthony Acevedo 1.25 3.00
THC88 Todd Self 1.25 3.00
THC89 Tim Frend 1.25 3.00
THC90 Tydus Meadows 1.25 3.00
THC91 Khalid Ballouli 1.25 3.00
THC92 Dioner Navarro 2.00 5.00
THC93 Casey Myers 1.25 3.00
THC94 Jon Knott 1.25 3.00
THC95 Tim Stauffer 2.00 5.00
THC96 Ricky Nolasco 2.00 5.00
THC97 Blake Hawksworth 1.25 3.00
THC98 Jesse Roman 1.25 3.00
THC99 Yadier Molina 15.00 40.00
THC100 Chris O'Riordan 1.25 3.00
THC101 Cliff Floyd 1.25 3.00
THC102 Nick Johnson 1.25 3.00
THC103 Edgar Martinez 2.00 5.00
THC104 Brett Myers 1.25 3.00
THC105 Francisco Rodriguez 2.00 5.00
THC106 Scott Rolen 2.00 5.00
THC107 Mark Teixeira 2.00 5.00
THC108 Miguel Tejada 2.00 5.00
THC109 Vernon Wells 1.25 3.00
THC110 Jerome Williams 1.25 3.00

2004 Topps Heritage Chrome Black Refractors

*BLACK REF: 2.5X TO 6X CHROME
*BLACK REF: 2.5X TO 6X CHROME RC YR
STATED ODDS 1:251
STATED PRINT RUN 55 SERIAL #'d SETS

2004 Topps Heritage Chrome Refractors

*REFRACTOR: .6X TO 1.5X CHROME
*REFRACTOR: .6X TO 1.5X CHROME RC YR
STATED ODDS 1:25
STATED PRINT RUN 555 SERIAL #'d SETS

2004 Topps Heritage Clubhouse Collection Relics

GROUP A ODDS 1:3037
GROUP B ODDS 1:4142
GROUP C ODDS 1:138
GROUP D ODDS 1:92
GROUP A STATED PRINT RUN 100 SETS
GROUP A PRINT RUN PROVIDED BY TOPPS
GROUP A ARE NOT SERIAL-NUMBERED
AD Adam Dunn Jsy D 3.00 8.00
AJ Andruw Jones Jsy C 4.00 10.00
AK Al Kaline Bat A 20.00 50.00
AP Albert Pujols Uni C 6.00 15.00
AR Alex Rodriguez Jsy C 4.00 10.00
AS Alfonso Soriano Uni D 3.00 8.00
BA Bobby Abreu Jsy D 3.00 8.00
BB Bret Boone Jsy D 3.00 8.00
BM Brett Myers Jsy D 3.00 8.00
BZ Barry Zito Uni C 3.00 8.00
CJ Chipper Jones Jsy D 4.00 10.00
CS C.C. Sabathia Jsy D 3.00 8.00
DS Duke Snider Bat A 15.00 40.00
EC Eric Chavez Uni D 3.00 8.00
EG Eric Gagne Uni D 3.00 8.00
FM Fred McGriff Bat C 4.00 10.00
GM Greg Maddux Jsy C 6.00 15.00
GS Gary Sheffield Uni D 3.00 8.00
HB Hank Blalock Jsy D 3.00 8.00
HK Harmon Killebrew Jsy C 10.00 25.00
IR Ivan Rodriguez Bat C 4.00 10.00
JD Johnny Damon Uni D 4.00 10.00
JG Jason Giambi Uni D 3.00 8.00
JL Javy Lopez Jsy D 3.00 8.00
JR Jimmy Rollins Jsy D 3.00 8.00
JRE Jose Reyes Jsy D 3.00 8.00
JS John Smoltz Jsy C 4.00 10.00
JT Jim Thome Bat D 4.00 10.00
KB Kevin Brown Uni D 3.00 8.00
KI Kazuhisa Ishii Uni D 3.00 8.00
KW Kerry Wood Jsy D 3.00 8.00
LB Lance Berkman Jsy C 3.00 8.00
LG Luis Gonzalez Jsy D 3.00 8.00
MG Marcus Giles Jsy C 3.00 8.00
MM Mark Mulder Uni D 3.00 8.00
MR Manny Ramirez Jsy C 4.00 10.00
MS Mike Sweeney Jsy D 3.00 8.00
MT Miguel Tejada Uni D 3.00 8.00
MTB Miguel Tejada Bat C 3.00 8.00
MTE Mark Teixeira Jsy D 4.00 10.00
NG Nomar Garciaparra Uni C 6.00 15.00
PL Paul Lo Duca Uni C 3.00 8.00
PM Pedro Martinez Jsy D 4.00 10.00
RB Rocco Baldelli Jsy D 3.00 8.00
RC Roger Clemens Uni D 6.00 15.00
RF Rafael Furcal Jsy D 3.00 8.00
RJ Randy Johnson Jsy C 4.00 10.00
SG Shawn Green Uni C 3.00 8.00
SM Stan Musial Bat A 30.00 60.00
SR Scott Rolen Uni B 4.00 10.00
SRB Scott Rolen Bat C 4.00 10.00
SS Sammy Sosa Jsy C 4.00 10.00
TG Troy Glaus Uni C 3.00 8.00
TH Tim Hudson Uni D 3.00 8.00
THU Torii Hunter Bat C 3.00 8.00
VW Vernon Wells Jsy C 3.00 8.00
WM Willie Mays Uni A 30.00 60.00
YB Yogi Berra Jsy A 20.00 50.00

2004 Topps Heritage Clubhouse Collection Dual Relics

STATED ODDS 1:9244
STATED PRINT RUN 55 SERIAL #'d SETS
BC Y.Berra Uni/R.Clemens Uni 75.00 150.00
GS S.Green Jsy/D.Snider Uni 75.00 150.00
MP A.Pujols Jsy/S.Musial Uni 75.00 150.00

2004 Topps Heritage Doubleheader

ONE PER SEALED HOBBY BOX
VINTAGE D-HEADERS RANDOMLY SEEDED
12 A.Rodriguez 2.00 5.00
N.Garciaparra
34 I.Suzuki 2.00 5.00
A.Pujols
56 S.Sosa 4.00 10.00
D.Jeter
78 J.Thome 1.00 2.50
A.Dunn
910 J.Giambi 1.00 2.50
I.Rodriguez
1112 T.Helton 1.00 2.50
L.Gonzalez
1314 J.Bagwell 1.00 2.50
L.Berkman
1516 A.Soriano 1.00 2.50
D.Willis
1718 M.Prior 1.00 2.50
V.Guerrero
1920 M.Piazza 2.00 5.00
R.Clemens
2122 R.Johnson 1.50 4.00
C.Schilling
2324 G.Sheffield 1.00 2.50
P.Martinez
2526 C.Delgado 1.00 2.50
J.Rollins
2728 A.Jones 1.50 4.00
C.Jones
2930 R.Baldelli .60 1.50
H.Blalock
NNO Vintage Buyback

2004 Topps Heritage Flashbacks

COMPLETE SET (10) 6.00 15.00
STATED ODDS 1:12
F1 Duke Snider .60 1.50
F2 Johnny Podres .40 1.00
F3 Don Newcombe .40 1.00
F4 Al Kaline 1.00 2.50
F5 Willie Mays 2.00 5.00
F6 Stan Musial 1.50 4.00
F7 Harmon Killebrew 1.00 2.50
F8 Herb Score .40 1.00
F9 Whitey Ford .60 1.50
F10 Robin Roberts .60 1.50

2004 Topps Heritage Grandstand Glory Stadium Seat Relics

GROUP A ODDS 1:27,731
GROUP A ODDS 1:606
GROUP A STATED PRINT RUN 55 CARDS
GROUP A PRINT RUN PROVIDED BY TOPPS
GROUP A IS NOT SERIAL-NUMBERED
AK Al Kaline B 10.00 25.00
HK Harmon Killebrew B 10.00 25.00
SM Stan Musial B 10.00 25.00
WM Willie Mays A 90.00 150.00
WS Warren Spahn B 10.00 25.00
YB Yogi Berra B 10.00 25.00

2004 Topps Heritage New Age Performers

COMPLETE SET (15) 10.00 25.00
STATED ODDS 1:15
NA1 Jason Giambi .40 1.00
NA2 Ichiro Suzuki 1.25 3.00
NA3 Alex Rodriguez 1.25 3.00
NA4 Alfonso Soriano .60 1.50
NA5 Albert Pujols 1.25 3.00
NA6 Nomar Garciaparra .60 1.50
NA7 Mark Prior .60 1.50
NA8 Derek Jeter 2.50 6.00
NA9 Sammy Sosa 1.00 2.50
NA10 Carlos Delgado .40 1.00
NA11 Jim Thome .60 1.50
NA12 Todd Helton .60 1.50
NA13 Gary Sheffield .40 1.00
NA14 Vladimir Guerrero .60 1.50
NA15 Josh Beckett .40 1.00

2004 Topps Heritage Real One Autographs

These autograph cards feature a mix of players who are active today; players who had cards in the 1955 Topps set and Stan Musial signing cards as if he were in the 1955 set. Scott Rolen did not return his cards in time for pack out and those exchange cards could be redeemed until February 28th, 2006.

STATED ODDS 1:230
STATED PRINT RUN 200 SETS
PRINT RUN INFO PROVIDED BY TOPPS
BASIC AUTOS ARE NOT SERIAL-NUMBERED
*RED INK: .75X TO 1.5X RETIRED
*RED INK MAYS: 1.25X TO 2X BASIC MAYS
*RED INK: .75X TO 1.5X ACTIVE
RED INK ODDS 1:835
RED INK PRINT RUN 55 #'d SETS
RED INK ALSO CALLED SPECIAL EDITION
AH Aubrey Huff 10.00 25.00
AK Al Kaline 40.00 100.00
BB Bob Borkowski 10.00 25.00
BC Billy Consolo 10.00 25.00
BG Bill Glynn 10.00 25.00
BK Bob Kline 10.00 25.00
BM Bob Milliken 10.00 25.00
BW Bill Wilson 20.00 50.00
CF Cliff Floyd 10.00 25.00
DN Don Newcombe 12.00 30.00
DP Duane Pillette 10.00 25.00
DS Duke Snider 30.00 60.00
DW Dontrelle Willis 10.00 25.00
EB Ernie Banks 40.00 80.00
FS Frank Smith 10.00 25.00
GA Gair Allie 10.00 25.00
HE Harry Elliott 10.00 25.00
HK Harmon Killebrew 40.00 100.00
HP Harry Perkowski 10.00 25.00
HV Corky Valentine 10.00 25.00
JG Johnny Gray 10.00 25.00
JP Jim Pearce 12.00 30.00
JPO Johnny Podres 10.00 25.00
LL Lou Limmer 10.00 25.00
ML Mike Lowell 10.00 25.00
MO Magglio Ordonez 10.00 25.00
SK Steve Kraly 30.00 60.00
SM Stan Musial 100.00 200.00
SR Scott Rolen 15.00 40.00
TK Thornton Kipper 10.00 25.00
TW Tom Wright 10.00 25.00
VT Jake Thies 10.00 25.00
WM Willie Mays 150.00 300.00
YB Yogi Berra 40.00 100.00

2004 Topps Heritage Then and Now

COMPLETE SET (6) 4.00 10.00
STATED ODDS 1:15
TN1 W.Mays 2.00 5.00
J.Thome
TN2 A.Kaline 1.25 3.00
A.Pujols
TN3 D.Snider .60 1.50
C.Delgado
TN4 R.Roberts .60 1.50
R.Halladay
TN5 D.Newcombe .60 1.50
J.Santana
TN6 H.Score .40 1.00
K.Wood

2005 Topps Heritage

This 495-card set was released in February, 2005. This set was issued in eight-card hobby/retail packs with an $3 SRP which came 24 packs to a box and eight boxes to a case. The 2005 version of Heritage honored the 1956 Topps set. Sprinkled throughout the set was a grouping of variation cards and other short printed cards. The Short print cards were issued at a stated rate of one in two hobby/retail packs.

COMPLETE SET (497) 250.00 400.00
COMP.SET w/o SP's (387) 30.00 60.00
COMMON CARD .20 .50
COMMON RC .20 .50
COMMON TEAM CARD .20 .50
COMMON SP 3.00 8.00
COMMON SP RC 3.00 8.00
SP STATED ODDS 1:2 HOBBY/RETAIL
BASIC SP: 5/20/30/31/33/79/101/110/130
BASIC SP: 135/260/292/396-475
VARIATION SP: 3/6/7/31/50/69/78/82/118
VARIATION SP: 125/135/155/261/273/286
VARIATION SP: 296/300/312/353/389
SEE BECKETT.COM FOR VAR.DESCRIPTIONS
1 Will Harridge .20 .50
2 Warren Giles .20 .50
3A Alfonso Soriano Fldg .30 .75
3B Alfonso Soriano Running SP 3.00 8.00
4 Mark Mulder .20 .50
5 Todd Helton SP 3.00 8.00
6A Jason Bay Black Cap .20 .50
6B Jason Bay Yellow Cap SP 3.00 8.00
7A Ichiro Suzuki Running .60 1.50
7B Ichiro Suzuki Crouch SP 4.00 10.00
8 Jim Tracy MG .20 .50
9 Gavin Floyd .20 .50
10 John Smoltz .50 1.25
11 Chicago Cubs TC .30 .75
12 Darin Erstad .20 .50
13 Chad Tracy .20 .50
14 Charles Thomas .20 .50
15 Miguel Tejada .30 .75
16 Andre Ethier RC 1.50 4.00
17 Jeff Francis .20 .50
18 Derrek Lee .20 .50
19 Juan Uribe .20 .50
20 Jim Edmonds SP 3.00 8.00
21 Kenny Lofton .20 .50
22 Brad Ausmus .20 .50
23 Jon Garland .20 .50
24 Edwin Jackson .20 .50
25 Joe Mauer .40 1.00
26 Wes Helms .20 .50
27 Brian Schneider .20 .50
28 Kazuo Matsui .20 .50
29 Flash Gordon .20 .50
30 Hideo Nomo SP 3.00 8.00
31A Albert Pujols Red Hat SP 5.00 12.00
31B Albert Pujols Blue Hat SP 5.00 12.00
32 Carl Crawford .30 .75
33 Vladimir Guerrero SP 3.00 8.00
34 Nick Green .20 .50
35 Jay Gibbons .20 .50
36 Kevin Youkilis .20 .50
37 Billy Wagner .20 .50
38 Terrence Long .20 .50
39 Kevin Mench .20 .50
40 Garret Anderson .20 .50
41 Reed Johnson .20 .50
42 Reggie Sanders .20 .50
43 Kirk Rueter .20 .50
44 Jay Payton .20 .50
45 Tike Redman .20 .50
46 Mike Lieberthal .20 .50
47 Damian Miller .20 .50
48 Zach Day .20 .50
49 Juan Rincon .20 .50
50A Jim Thome At Bat .30 .75
50B Jim Thome Fldg SP 3.00 8.00
51 Jose Guillen .20 .50
52 Richie Sexson .20 .50
53 Juan Cruz .20 .50
54 Byung-Hyun Kim .20 .50
55 Carlos Zambrano .30 .75
56 Carlos Lee .20 .50
57 Adam Dunn .30 .75
58 David Riske .20 .50
59 Carlos Guillen .20 .50
60 Larry Bowa MG .20 .50
61 Barry Bonds .75 2.00
62 Chris Woodward .20 .50
63 Matt DeSalvo RC .20 .50
64 Brian Stavisky RC .20 .50
65 Scot Shields .20 .50
66 J.D. Drew .20 .50
67 Erik Bedard .20 .50
68 Scott Williamson .20 .50
69A M.Prior New C on Cap .30 .75
69B M.Prior Old C on Cap SP 3.00 8.00
70 Ken Griffey Jr. 1.00 2.50
71 Kazuhito Tadano .20 .50
72 Philadelphia Phillies TC .20 .50
73 Jeremy Reed .20 .50
74 Ricardo Rodriguez .20 .50
75 Carlos Delgado .20 .50
76 Eric Milton .20 .50
77 Miguel Olivo .20 .50
78A E.Alfonzo No Socks .20 .50
78B E.Alfonzo Black Socks SP 3.00 8.00
79 Kazuhisa Ishii SP 3.00 8.00
80 Jason Giambi .20 .50
81 Cliff Floyd .20 .50
82A Torii Hunter Twins Cap .20 .50
82B Torii Hunter Wash Cap SP 3.00 8.00
83 Odalis Perez .20 .50
84 Scott Podsednik .20 .50
85 Cleveland Indians TC .20 .50
86 Jeff Suppan .20 .50
87 Ray Durham .20 .50
88 Tyler Clippard RC 1.25 3.00
89 Ryan Howard .40 1.00
90 Cincinnati Reds TC .20 .50
91 Bengie Molina .20 .50
92 Danny Bautista .20 .50
93 Eli Marrero .20 .50
94 Larry Bigbie .20 .50
95 Atlanta Braves TC .30 .75
96 Merkin Valdez .20 .50
97 Rocco Baldelli .20 .50
98 Woody Williams .20 .50
99 Jason Frasor .20 .50
100 Baltimore Orioles TC .20 .50
101 Ivan Rodriguez SP 3.00 8.00
102 Joe Kennedy .20 .50
103 Mike Lowell .20 .50
104 Armando Benitez .20 .50
105 Craig Biggio .30 .75
106 David DeJesus .20 .50
107 Adrian Beltre .50 1.25
108 Phil Nevin .20 .50
109 Cristian Guzman .20 .50
110 Jorge Posada SP 3.00 8.00
111 Boston Red Sox TC .50 1.25
112 Jeff Mathis .30 .75
113 Bartolo Colon .20 .50
114 Alex Cintron .20 .50
115 Russ Ortiz .20 .50
116 Doug Mientkiewicz .20 .50
117 Placido Polanco .20 .50
118A M.Ordonez Black Uni .30 .75
118B M.Ordonez White Uni SP 3.00 8.00
119 Chris Seddon RC .20 .50
120 Bobby Abreu .20 .50
121 Pittsburgh Pirates TC .20 .50
122 Dallas McPherson .20 .50
123 Rodrigo Lopez .20 .50
124 Mark Bellhorn .20 .50
125A N.Garciaparra Red Brim Cap .30 .75
125B N.Garciaparra Blue Brim Cap SP 3.00 8.00
126 Sean Casey .20 .50
127 Ronnie Belliard .20 .50
128 Tom Goodwin .20 .50
129 Preston Wilson .20 .50
130 Andruw Jones SP 3.00 8.00
131 Roberto Alomar .30 .75
132 John Buck .20 .50
133 Jason LaRue .20 .50
134 St. Louis Cardinals TC .30 .75
135A Alex Rodriguez Fldg SP 4.00 10.00
135B Alex Rodriguez At Bat SP 4.00 10.00
136 Nate Robertson .20 .50
137 Juan Pierre .20 .50
138 Morgan Ensberg .20 .50
139 Vinny Castilla .20 .50
140 Jake Dittler .20 .50
141 Chan Ho Park .30 .75
142 Felix Hernandez .60 1.50
143 Jason Isringhausen .20 .50
144 Dustan Mohr .20 .50
145 Khalil Greene .20 .50
146 Minnesota Twins TC .20 .50
147 Vicente Padilla .20 .50
148 Oliver Perez .20 .50
149 Brian Giles .20 .50
150 Shawn Green .20 .50
151 Matt Lawton .20 .50
152 Casey Blake .20 .50
153 Frank Thomas .50 1.25
154 Orlando Hernandez .20 .50
155A Eric Chavez Green Cap .20 .50
155B Eric Chavez Blue Cap SP 3.00 8.00
156 Chase Utley .30 .75
157 John Olerud .20 .50
158 Adam Eaton .20 .50
159 Josh Fogg .20 .50
160 Michael Tucker .20 .50
161 Kevin Brown .20 .50
162 Bobby Crosby .20 .50
163 Jason Schmidt .30 .75
164 Shannon Stewart .20 .50
165 Tony Womack .20 .50
166 Los Angeles Dodgers TC .20 .50
167 Franklin Gutierrez .60 1.50
168 Ted Lilly .20 .50
169 Mark Teixeira .30 .75
170 Matt Morris .20 .50
171 Bucky Jacobsen .20 .50
172 Steve Doetsch RC .20 .50
173 Jeff Weaver .20 .50
174 Tony Graffanino .20 .50
175 Jeff Bagwell .30 .75
176 Carl Pavano .20 .50
177 Junior Spivey .20 .50
178 Carlos Silva .20 .50
179 Tim Redding .20 .50
180 Brett Myers .20 .50
181 Mike Mussina .30 .75
182 Richard Hidalgo .20 .50
183 Nick Johnson .20 .50
184 Lew Ford .20 .50
185 Barry Zito .30 .75
186 Jimmy Rollins .30 .75
187 Jack Wilson .20 .50
188 Chicago White Sox TC .20 .50
189 Guillermo Quiroz .20 .50
190 Mark Hendrickson .20 .50
191 Jeremy Bonderman .20 .50
192 Jason Jennings .20 .50
193 Paul Lo Duca .20 .50
194 A.J. Burnett .20 .50
195 Ken Harvey .20 .50
196 Geoff Jenkins .20 .50
197 Joe Mays .20 .50
198 Jose Vidro .20 .50
199 David Wright .40 1.00
200 Randy Johnson .50 1.25
201 Jeff DaVanon .20 .50
202 Paul Byrd .20 .50
203 David Ortiz .50 1.25
204 Kyle Farnsworth .20 .50
205 Keith Foulke .20 .50
206 Joe Crede .20 .50
207 Austin Kearns .20 .50
208 Jody Gerut .20 .50
209 Shawn Chacon .20 .50
210 Carlos Pena .30 .75
211 Luis Castillo .20 .50
212 Chris Denorfia RC .20 .50
213 Detroit Tigers TC .20 .50
214 Aubrey Huff .20 .50
215 Brad Fullmer .20 .50
216 Frank Catalanotto .20 .50
217 Raul Ibanez .30 .75
218 Ryan Klesko .20 .50
219 Octavio Dotel .20 .50
220 Rob Mackowiak .20 .50
221 Scott Hatteberg .20 .50
222 Pat Burrell .20 .50
223 Bernie Williams .30 .75
224 Kris Benson .20 .50
225 Eric Gagne .20 .50
226 San Francisco Giants TC .20 .50
227 Roy Oswalt .30 .75
228 Josh Beckett .20 .50
229 Lee Mazzilli MG .20 .50
230 Rickie Weeks .20 .50
231 Troy Glaus .20 .50
232 Chone Figgins .20 .50
233 John Thomson .20 .50
234 Trot Nixon .20 .50
235 Brad Penny .20 .50
236 Oakland A's TC .20 .50
237 Miguel Batista .20 .50
238 Ryan Drese .20 .50
239 Aaron Miles .20 .50
240 Randy Wolf .20 .50
241 Brian Lawrence .20 .50
242 A.J. Pierzynski .20 .50
243 Jamie Moyer .20 .50
244 Chris Carpenter .30 .75
245 So Taguchi .20 .50
246 Rob Bell .20 .50
247 Francisco Cordero .20 .50
248 Tom Glavine .30 .75
249 Jermaine Dye .20 .50
250 Cliff Lee .30 .75
251 New York Yankees TC .50 1.25
252 Vernon Wells .20 .50
253 R.A. Dickey .30 .75
254 Larry Walker .30 .75
255 Randy Winn .20 .50
256 Pedro Feliz .20 .50
257 Mark Loretta .20 .50
258 Tim Worrell .20 .50
259 Kip Wells .20 .50
260 Cesar Izturis SP 3.00 8.00
261A Carlos Beltran Fldg .30 .75
261B Carlos Beltran At Bat SP 3.00 8.00
262 Juan Encarnacion .20 .50
263 Luis A. Gonzalez .20 .50
264 Grady Sizemore .30 .75
265 Paul Wilson .20 .50
266 Mark Buehrle .30 .75
267 Todd Hollandsworth .20 .50
268 Orlando Cabrera .20 .50
269 Sidney Ponson .20 .50
270 Mike Hampton .20 .50
271 Luis Gonzalez .20 .50
272 Brendan Donnelly .20 .50
273A Chipper Jones Slide .50 1.25
273B Chipper Jones Fldg SP 3.00 8.00
274 Brandon Webb .30 .75
275 Marty Cordova .20 .50
276 Greg Maddux .60 1.50
277 Jose Contreras .20 .50
278 Aaron Harang .20 .50
279 Coco Crisp .20 .50
280 Bobby Higginson .20 .50
281 Guillermo Mota .20 .50
282 Andy Pettitte .30 .75
283 Jeremy West RC .20 .50
284 Craig Brazell .20 .50
285 Eric Hinske .20 .50
286A Hank Blalock Hitting .20 .50
286B Hank Blalock Fldg SP 3.00 8.00
287 B.J. Upton .30 .75
288 Jason Marquis .20 .50
289 Matt Herges .20 .50
290 Ramon Hernandez .20 .50
291 Marlon Byrd .30 .75
292 Ryan Sweeney SP RC 3.00 8.00
293 Esteban Loaiza .20 .50
294 Al Leiter .20 .50
295 Alex Gonzalez .20 .50
296A J.Santana Twins Cap .30 .75
296B J.Santana Wash Cap SP 3.00 8.00
297 Milton Bradley .20 .50
298 Mike Sweeney .20 .50
299 Wade Miller .20 .50
300A Sammy Sosa Hitting .50 1.25
300B Sammy Sosa Standing SP 3.00 8.00
301 Wily Mo Pena .20 .50
302 Tim Wakefield .30 .75
303 Rafael Palmeiro .30 .75
304 Rafael Furcal .20 .50
305 David Eckstein .20 .50
306 David Segui .20 .50
307 Kevin Millar .20 .50
308 Matt Clement .20 .50
309 Wade Robinson RC .20 .50
310 Brad Radke .20 .50
311 Steve Finley .20 .50
312A Lance Berkman Hitting .30 .75
312B Lance Berkman Fldg SP 3.00 8.00
313 Joe Randa .20 .50
314 Miguel Cabrera .50 1.25
315 Billy Koch .20 .50
316 Alex Sanchez .20 .50
317 Chin-Hui Tsao .20 .50
318 Omar Vizquel .30 .75
319 Ryan Freel .20 .50
320 LaTroy Hawkins .20 .50
321 Aaron Rowand .20 .50
322 Paul Konerko .30 .75
323 Joe Borowski .20 .50
324 Jarrod Washburn .20 .50
325 Jaret Wright .20 .50
326 Johnny Damon .30 .75
327 Corey Patterson .20 .50
328 Travis Hafner .20 .50
329 Shingo Takatsu .20 .50
330 Dmitri Young .30 .75
331 Matt Holliday .50 1.25
332 Jeff Kent .20 .50
333 Desi Relaford .20 .50
334 Jose Hernandez .20 .50
335 Lyle Overbay .20 .50
336 Jacque Jones .20 .50
337 Termel Sledge .20 .50
338 Victor Zambrano .20 .50
339 Gary Sheffield .20 .50
340 Brad Wilkerson .20 .50
341 Ian Kinsler RC 1.00 2.50
342 Jesse Crain .20 .50
343 Orlando Hudson .20 .50
344 Laynce Nix .20 .50
345 Jose Cruz Jr. .20 .50
346 Edgar Renteria .20 .50
347 Eddie Guardado .20 .50
348 Jerome Williams .20 .50
349 Trevor Hoffman .30 .75
350 Mike Piazza .50 1.25
351 Jason Kendall .20 .50
352 Kevin Millwood .20 .50
353A Tim Hudson Atl Cap .30 .75
353B Tim Hudson Milw Cap SP 3.00 8.00
354 Paul Quantrill .20 .50
355 Jon Lieber .20 .50
356 Braden Looper .20 .50
357 Chad Cordero .20 .50
358 Joe Nathan .20 .50
359 Doug Davis .20 .50
360 Ian Bladergroen RC .20 .50
361 Val Majewski .20 .50
362 Francisco Rodriguez .30 .75
363 Kelvim Escobar .20 .50
364 Marcus Giles .20 .50
365 Darren Fenster RC .20 .50
366 David Bell .20 .50
367 Shea Hillenbrand .20 .50
368 Manny Ramirez .50 1.25
369 Ben Broussard .20 .50
370 Luis Ramirez RC .20 .50
371 Dustin Hermanson .20 .50
372 Akinori Otsuka .20 .50
373 Chadd Blasko RC .30 .75
374 Delmon Young .50 1.25
375 Michael Young .20 .50
376 Bret Boone .20 .50
377 Jake Peavy .20 .50
378 Matthew Lindstrom RC .20 .50
379 Sean Burroughs .20 .50
380 Rich Harden .20 .50
381 Chris Roberson RC .20 .50
382 John Lackey .20 .50
383 Johnny Estrada .20 .50
384 Matt Rogelstad RC .20 .50
385 Toby Hall .20 .50
386 Adam LaRoche .20 .50
387 Bill Hall .20 .50
388 Tim Salmon .20 .50
389A Curt Schilling Throw .30 .75
389B Curt Schilling Glove Up SP 3.00 8.00
390 Michael Barrett .20 .50
391 Jose Acevedo .20 .50
392 Nate Schierholtz .20 .50
393 J.T. Snow Jr. .20 .50
394 Mark Redman .20 .50
395 Ryan Madson .20 .50
396 Kevin West RC .20 .50
397 Ramon Ortiz .20 .50
398 Derek Lowe SP 3.00 8.00
399 Kerry Wood SP 3.00 8.00
400 Derek Jeter SP 12.00 30.00
401 Livan Hernandez SP 3.00 8.00
402 Casey Kotchman SP 3.00 8.00
403 Chaz Lytle SP RC 3.00 8.00
404 Alexis Rios SP 3.00 8.00
405 Scott Spiezio SP 3.00 8.00
406 Craig Wilson SP 3.00 8.00
407 Felix Rodriguez SP 3.00 8.00
408 D'Angelo Jimenez SP 3.00 8.00
409 Rondell White SP 3.00 8.00
410 Shawn Estes SP 3.00 8.00
411 Troy Percival SP 3.00 8.00
412 Melvin Mora SP 3.00 8.00
413 Aramis Ramirez SP 3.00 8.00
414 Carl Everett SP 3.00 8.00
415 Elvys Quezada SP RC 3.00 8.00
416 Ben Sheets SP 3.00 8.00
417 Matt Stairs SP 3.00 8.00
418 Adam Everett SP 3.00 8.00
419 Jason Johnson SP 3.00 8.00
420 Billy Butler SP RC 4.00 10.00
421 Justin Morneau SP 3.00 8.00
422 Jose Reyes SP 3.00 8.00
423 Mariano Rivera SP 30.00 80.00
424 Jose Vaquedano SP RC 3.00 8.00
425 Gabe Gross SP 3.00 8.00
426 Scott Rolen SP 3.00 8.00
427 Ty Wigginton SP 3.00 8.00
428 James Jurries SP RC 3.00 8.00
429 Pedro Martinez SP 3.00 8.00
430 Mark Grudzielanek SP 3.00 8.00
431 Josh Phelps SP 3.00 8.00
432 Ryan Goleski SP RC 3.00 8.00
433 Mike Matheny SP 3.00 8.00
434 Bobby Kielty SP 3.00 8.00
435 Tony Batista SP 3.00 8.00
436 Corey Koskie SP 3.00 8.00
437 Brad Lidge SP 3.00 8.00
438 Dontrelle Willis SP 3.00 8.00
439 Angel Berroa SP 3.00 8.00
440 Jason Kubel SP 3.00 8.00
441 Roy Halladay SP 3.00 8.00
442 Brian Roberts SP 3.00 8.00
443 Bill Mueller SP 3.00 8.00
444 Adam Kennedy SP 3.00 8.00
445 Brandon Moss SP RC 3.00 8.00
446 Sean Burnett SP 3.00 8.00
447 Eric Byrnes SP 3.00 8.00
448 Matt Campbell SP RC 3.00 8.00
449 Ryan Webb SP 3.00 8.00
450 Jose Valentin SP 3.00 8.00
451 Jake Westbrook SP 3.00 8.00
452 Glen Perkins SP RC 3.00 8.00
453 Alex Gonzalez SP 3.00 8.00
454 Jeromy Burnitz SP 3.00 8.00
455 Zack Greinke SP 3.00 8.00
456 Sean Marshall SP RC 2.50 6.00
457 Erubiel Durazo SP 3.00 8.00
458 Michael Cuddyer SP 3.00 8.00
459 Hee Seop Choi SP 3.00 8.00
460 Melky Cabrera SP RC 4.00 10.00
461 Jerry Hairston Jr. SP 3.00 8.00
462 Moises Alou SP 3.00 8.00
463 Michael Rogers SP RC 3.00 8.00
464 Javy Lopez SP 3.00 8.00
465 Freddy Garcia SP 3.00 8.00
466 Brett Harper SP RC 3.00 8.00
467 Juan Gonzalez SP 3.00 8.00
468 Kevin Melillo SP RC 3.00 8.00
469 Todd Walker SP 3.00 8.00
470 C.C. Sabathia SP 3.00 8.00
471 Kole Strayhorn SP RC 3.00 8.00
472 Mark Kotsay SP 3.00 8.00
473 Javier Vazquez SP 3.00 8.00
474 Mike Cameron SP 3.00 8.00
475 Wes Swackhamer SP RC 3.00 8.00
CL1 Checklist 1 .20 .50
CL2 Checklist 2 .20 .50

2005 Topps Heritage White Backs

COMPLETE SET (220) 75.00 150.00
*WHITE BACKS: .75X TO 2X BASIC
RANDOM INSERTS IN PACKS
SEE BECKETT.COM FOR FULL CHECKLIST

2005 Topps Heritage Chrome

STATED ODDS 1:7 HOBBY/RETAIL
STATED PRINT RUN 1956 SERIAL #'d SETS
TCH1 Will Harridge 1.50 4.00
THC2 Warren Giles 1.50 4.00
THC3 Alex Rodriguez 5.00 12.00
THC4 Alfonso Soriano 2.50 6.00
THC5 Barry Bonds 6.00 15.00
THC6 Todd Helton 2.50 6.00
THC7 Kazuo Matsui 1.50 4.00
THC8 Garret Anderson 1.50 4.00
THC9 Mark Prior 2.50 6.00
THC10 Jim Thome 2.50 6.00
THC11 Jason Giambi 1.50 4.00
THC12 Ivan Rodriguez 2.50 6.00
THC13 Mike Lowell 1.50 4.00
THC14 Vladimir Guerrero 2.50 6.00
THC15 Adrian Beltre 4.00 10.00
THC16 Andruw Jones 1.50 4.00
THC17 Jose Vidro 1.50 4.00
THC18 Josh Beckett 1.50 4.00
THC19 Mike Sweeney 1.50 4.00
THC20 Sammy Sosa 4.00 10.00
THC21 Scott Rolen 2.50 6.00
THC22 Javy Lopez 1.50 4.00
THC23 Albert Pujols 5.00 12.00
THC24 Adam Dunn 2.50 6.00
THC25 Ken Griffey Jr. 8.00 20.00
THC26 Torii Hunter 1.50 4.00
THC27 Jorge Posada 2.50 6.00
THC28 Magglio Ordonez 2.50 6.00
THC29 Shawn Green 1.50 4.00
THC30 Frank Thomas 4.00 10.00
THC31 Barry Zito 2.50 6.00
THC32 David Ortiz 4.00 10.00
THC33 Pat Burrell 1.50 4.00
THC34 Luis Gonzalez 1.50 4.00
THC35 Chipper Jones 4.00 10.00
THC36 Hank Blalock 1.50 4.00
THC37 Rafael Palmeiro 2.50 6.00
THC38 Lance Berkman 2.50 6.00
THC39 Miguel Cabrera 4.00 10.00
THC40 Paul Konerko 2.50 6.00
THC41 Jeff Kent 1.50 4.00
THC42 Gary Sheffield 1.50 4.00
THC43 Mike Piazza 4.00 10.00
THC44 Bret Boone 1.50 4.00
THC45 Kerry Wood 1.50 4.00
THC46 Derek Jeter 10.00 25.00
THC47 Pedro Martinez 2.50 6.00
THC48 Jason Bay 1.50 4.00
THC49 Ichiro Suzuki 5.00 12.00
THC50 Miguel Tejada 2.50 6.00
THC51 Richie Sexson 1.50 4.00
THC52 Jeff Bagwell 2.50 6.00
THC53 Lew Ford 1.50 4.00
THC54 Randy Johnson 4.00 10.00
THC55 Carlos Beltran 2.50 6.00
THC56 Greg Maddux 5.00 12.00
THC57 Lyle Overbay 1.50 4.00
THC58 Michael Young 1.50 4.00
THC59 Curt Schilling 2.50 6.00
THC60 Jose Reyes 2.50 6.00
THC61 Dontrelle Willis 1.50 4.00
THC62 Nomar Garciaparra 2.50 6.00
THC63 Paul Lo Duca 1.50 4.00
THC64 Larry Walker 2.50 6.00
THC65 Andre Ethier 12.00 30.00
THC66 Matt DeSalvo 1.50 4.00
THC67 Brian Stavisky 1.50 4.00
THC68 Tyler Clippard 10.00 25.00
THC69 Chris Seddon 1.50 4.00
THC70 Steve Doetsch 1.50 4.00
THC71 Chris Denorfia 1.50 4.00
THC72 Jeremy West 1.50 4.00
THC73 Ryan Sweeney 2.50 6.00
THC74 Ian Kinsler 8.00 20.00
THC75 Ian Bladergroen 1.50 4.00
THC76 Darren Fenster 1.50 4.00
THC77 Luis Ramirez 1.50 4.00
THC78 Chadd Blasko 2.50 6.00
THC79 Matthew Lindstrom 1.50 4.00
THC80 Chris Roberson 1.50 4.00
THC81 Matt Rogelstad 1.50 4.00
THC82 Nate Schierholtz 1.50 4.00
THC83 Kevin West 1.50 4.00
THC84 Chaz Lytle 2.50 6.00
THC85 Elvys Quezada 1.50 4.00
THC86 Billy Butler 8.00 20.00
THC87 Jose Vaquedano 1.50 4.00
THC88 James Jurries 1.50 4.00
THC89 Ryan Goleski 1.50 4.00
THC90 Brandon Moss 6.00 15.00
THC91 Matt Campbell 1.50 4.00
THC92 Ryan Webb 1.50 4.00
THC93 Glen Perkins 1.50 4.00
THC94 Sean Marshall 4.00 10.00
THC95 Melky Cabrera 5.00 12.00
THC96 Michael Rogers 1.50 4.00
THC97 Brett Harper 1.50 4.00
THC98 Kevin Melillo 1.50 4.00
THC99 Kole Strayhorn 1.50 4.00
THC100 Wes Swackhamer 1.50 4.00
THC101 Rickie Weeks 1.50 4.00
THC102 Delmon Young 4.00 10.00
THC103 Kazuhito Tadano 1.50 4.00
THC104 Kazuhisa Ishii 1.50 4.00
THC105 David Wright 3.00 8.00
THC106 Eric Gagne 1.50 4.00
THC107 So Taguchi 1.50 4.00
THC108 B.J. Upton 2.50 6.00
THC109 Shingo Takatsu 1.50 4.00
THC110 Akinori Otsuka 1.50 4.00

2005 Topps Heritage Chrome Black Refractors

*BLACK REF: 4X TO 8X CHROME
*BLACK REF: 4X TO 8X CHROME RC YR
STATED ODDS 1:250 HOBBY/RETAIL
STATED PRINT RUN 56 SERIAL #'d SETS

2005 Topps Heritage Chrome Refractors

*REFRACTOR: .6X TO 1.5X CHROME
*REFRACTOR: .6X TO 1.5X CHROME RC YR
STATED ODDS 1:25 HOBBY/RETAIL
STATED PRINT RUN 556 SERIAL #'d SETS

2005 Topps Heritage Clubhouse Collection Relics

GROUP A ODDS 1:291 H, 1:292 R
GROUP B ODDS 1:384 H, 1:387 R
GROUP C ODDS 1:1303 H, 1:1307 R
GROUP D ODDS 1:497 H, 1:499 R
GROUP E ODDS 1:384 H, 1:387 R
AK Al Kaline Bat A 8.00 20.00
AP Albert Pujols Bat B 8.00 20.00
AR Alex Rodriguez Bat D 6.00 15.00
AS Alfonso Soriano Bat C 3.00 8.00
BW Bernie Williams Bat A 4.00 10.00
DW Dontrelle Willis Jsy E 3.00 8.00
EB Ernie Banks Bat A 8.00 20.00
GS Gary Sheffield Bat B 3.00 8.00
HK Harmon Killebrew Bat A 8.00 20.00
LA Luis Aparicio Bat A 4.00 10.00
LB Lance Berkman Bat D 3.00 8.00
MC Miguel Cabrera Bat A 4.00 10.00
MR Manny Ramirez Jsy E 4.00 10.00
MT Miguel Tejada Bat B 3.00 8.00
RS Red Schoendienst Bat B 4.00 10.00

2005 Topps Heritage Clubhouse Collection Dual Relics

STATED ODDS 1:9249 H, 1:9490 R
STATED PRINT RUN 56 SERIAL #'d SETS
BG Banks Bat/Garciaparra Bat 30.00 60.00
KR Kaline Bat/I.Rodriguez Bat 30.00 60.00
MP Musial Jsy/Pujols Jsy 125.00 200.00

2005 Topps Heritage Flashbacks

COMPLETE SET (10) 5.00 12.00
STATED ODDS 1:12 HOBBY/RETAIL
AK Al Kaline 1.00 2.50
BF Bob Feller .60 1.50
DL Don Larsen .40 1.00
DS Duke Snider .60 1.50
EB Ernie Banks 1.00 2.50
FR Frank Robinson .60 1.50
HA Hank Aaron 2.00 5.00
HS Herb Score .40 1.00
LA Luis Aparicio .60 1.50
SM Stan Musial 1.50 4.00

2005 Topps Heritage Flashbacks Seat Relics

STATED ODDS 1:96 HOBBY/RETAIL
AK Al Kaline 6.00 15.00
BF Bob Feller 6.00 15.00
DL Don Larsen 6.00 15.00
DS Duke Snider 6.00 15.00
EB Ernie Banks 6.00 15.00
FR Frank Robinson 4.00 10.00
HA Hank Aaron 8.00 20.00
HS Herb Score 4.00 10.00
LA Luis Aparicio 4.00 10.00
SM Stan Musial 8.00 20.00

2005 Topps Heritage New Age Performers

COMPLETE SET (15) 10.00 25.00
STATED ODDS 1:15 HOBBY/RETAIL
1 Alfonso Soriano .60 1.50
2 Alex Rodriguez 1.25 3.00
3 Ichiro Suzuki 1.25 3.00
4 Albert Pujols 1.25 3.00
5 Vladimir Guerrero .60 1.50
6 Jim Thome .60 1.50
7 Derek Jeter 2.50 6.00
8 Sammy Sosa 1.00 2.50
9 Ivan Rodriguez .60 1.50
10 Manny Ramirez 1.00 2.50
11 Todd Helton .60 1.50
12 David Ortiz 1.00 2.50
13 Gary Sheffield .40 1.00
14 Nomar Garciaparra .60 1.50
15 Randy Johnson 1.00 2.50

2005 Topps Heritage Real One Autographs

STATED ODDS 1:333 H, 1:332 R
STATED PRINT RUN 200 SETS
PRINT RUN INFO PROVIDED BY TOPPS
BASIC AUTOS ARE NOT SERIAL-NUMBERED
*RED INK: .75X TO 1.5X BASIC
RED INK ODDS 1:1195 H, 1:1196 R
RED INK PRINT RUN 56 SERIAL #'d SETS
RED INK ALSO CALLED SPECIAL EDITION
AS Art Swanson 20.00 50.00
BF Bob Feller 40.00 80.00
BN Bob Nelson 15.00 40.00
BT Bill Tremel 10.00 25.00
CD Chuck Diering 10.00 25.00
DS Duke Snider 50.00 100.00
EB Ernie Banks 60.00 150.00
FM Fred Marsh 10.00 25.00
HA Hank Aaron 150.00 250.00
JA Joe Astroth 10.00 25.00
JB Jim Brady 20.00 50.00
JG Jim Greengrass 15.00 40.00
JM Jake Martin 15.00 40.00
JS Johnny Schmitz 20.00 50.00
JSA Jose Santiago 20.00 50.00
LP Laurin Pepper 10.00 25.00
LPO Leroy Powell 10.00 25.00
MI Monte Irvin 20.00 50.00
PM Paul Minner 10.00 25.00
RM Rudy Minarcin 10.00 25.00
SJ Spook Jacobs 10.00 25.00

W Wally Westlake 10.00 25.00
8 Yogi Berra 50.00 120.00

2005 Topps Heritage Then and Now

COMPLETE SET (10) 5.00 12.00
STATED ODDS 1:15 HOBBY/RETAIL
N1 H.Aaron 2.00 5.00
I.Suzuki
N2 D.Newcombe .60 1.50
C.Schilling
N3 R.Roberts .60 1.50
L.Hernandez
N4 B.Friend .40 1.00
L.Hernandez
N5 H.Score 1.00 2.50
R.Johnson
N6 W.Ford .60 1.50
J.Peavy
N7 J.Piersall .40 1.00
L.Overbay
N8 C.Labine 1.25 3.00
M.Rivera
N9 B.Bruton .60 1.50
C.Crawford
N10 E.Yost .40 1.00
B.Abreu

2006 Topps Heritage

This 494-card set was released in February, 2006. This set, using the same design as the 1957 Topps baseball set, was issued in eight-card hobby and retail packs, both with an $3 SRP which came 24 packs to a box and eight boxes to a case. Card number 297, which was intended to be Alex Gordon had to be pulled from production as there was no approval to print that card as he had yet to participate in a major league game. In addition, cards numbered 265-352, with the curious exception of card #329 were short printed similar to the original 1957 Topps set in which those cards were issued in shorter quantities than the rest of the 57 set. A few variation and short prints were scattered around the rest of the set.

COMPLETE SET (494) 250.00 400.00
COMP.SET w/o SP's (384) 15.00 40.00
SP STATED ODDS 1:2 HOBBY/RETAIL
SP CL: 1/2/10/18/20B/23B/25/35/55
SP CL: 70/76/80B/91/95A/95B/99/106
SP CL: 123/127/165B/200B/212B/265-269
SP CL: 271-274/276-316/318-323/325A
SP CL: 325B/326-328/330-349/350A/350B
SP CL: 351 352/400/407/475B
VARIATION CL: 20/23/80/95/165/200
VARIATION CL: 212/325/350/475
TWO VERSIONS OF EACH VARIATION EXIST
SEE BECKETT.COM FOR VAR.DESCRIPTIONS
CARD 255 NOT INTENDED FOR RELEASE
COMP.SET EXCLUDES CARD 255 CUT OUT
1 David Ortiz SP 3.00 8.00
2 Mike Piazza SP 4.00 10.00
3 Daryle Ward .20 .50
4 Rafael Furcal .20 .50
5 Derek Lowe .20 .50
6 Eric Chavez .20 .50
7 Juan Uribe .20 .50
8 C.C. Sabathia .30 .75
9 Sean Casey .20 .50
10 Barry Bonds SP 5.00 12.00
11 Gary Sheffield .20 .50
12 Ted Lilly .20 .50
13 Lew Ford .20 .50
14 Tom Gordon .20 .50
15 Curt Schilling .30 .75
16 Jason Kendall .20 .50
17 Frank Catalanotto .20 .50
18 Pedro Martinez SP 3.00 8.00
19 David Dellucci .20 .50
20A A.Jones w .20 .50
o Seats
20B A.Jones w 3.00 8.00
Seats SP
21 Brad Halsey .20 .50
22 Vernon Wells .20 .50
23A D.Jeter Yellow 1.25 3.00
White Ltr
23B D.Jeter Blue Ltr SP 5.00 12.00
24 Todd Helton .30 .75
25 Randy Johnson SP 4.00 10.00
26 Jay Gibbons .20 .50
27 Joe Mays .20 .50
28 Paul Konerko .30 .75
29 Lyle Overbay .20 .50
30 Jorge Posada .30 .75
31 Brandon Webb .30 .75
32 Marcus Giles .20 .50
33 J.T. Snow .20 .50
34 Todd Walker .20 .50
35 Wily Mo Pena SP 3.00 8.00
36 Carlos Delgado .20 .50
37 David Wright .40 1.00
38 Shea Hillenbrand .20 .50
39 Daniel Cabrera .20 .50
40 Trevor Hoffman .30 .75
41 Matt Morris .20 .50
42 Mariano Rivera .60 1.50
43 Jeff Bagwell .30 .75
44 J.D. Drew .20 .50
45 Carl Pavano .20 .50
46 Placido Polanco .20 .50
47 Adrian Beltre .50 1.25
48 J.D. Closser .20 .50
49 Paul Lo Duca .20 .50
50 Scott Rolen .30 .75
51 Bernie Williams .30 .75
52 Jose Guillen .20 .50
53 Aubrey Huff .20 .50
54 Greg Maddux .60 1.50
55 Derrek Lee SP 3.00 8.00
56 Hideki Matsui .50 1.25
57 Jose Bautista .50 1.25
58 Kyle Farnsworth .20 .50
59 Nate Robertson .20 .50
60 Sammy Sosa .50 1.25
61 Javier Vazquez .20 .50
62 Jeff Mathis .20 .50
63 Mark Buehrle .30 .75
64 Orlando Hernandez .20 .50
65 Brandon Claussen .20 .50
66 Miguel Batista .20 .50
67 Eddie Guardado .20 .50
68 Alex Gonzalez .20 .50
69 Kris Benson .20 .50
70 Bobby Abreu SP 3.00 8.00
71 Vinny Castilla .20 .50
72 Ben Broussard .20 .50
73 Travis Hafner .20 .50
74 Dmitri Young .20 .50
75 Alex S. Gonzalez .20 .50
76 Jason Bay SP 3.00 8.00
77 Charlton Jimerson .20 .50
78 Ryan Garko .20 .50
79 Lance Berkman .30 .75
80A T.Hudson Red .30 .75
Blue Ltr
80B T.Hudson Blue Ltr SP 3.00 8.00
81 Guillermo Mota .20 .50
82 Chris B. Young .50 1.25
83 Brad Lidge .20 .50
84 A.J. Pierzynski .20 .50
85 Maicer Izturis .20 .50
86 Vladimir Guerrero .30 .75
87 J.J. Hardy .20 .50
88 Cesar Izturis .20 .50
89 Mark Ellis .20 .50
90 Chipper Jones .50 1.25
91 Chris Snelling SP 3.00 8.00
92 Jose Reyes .30 .75
93 Mike Lieberthal .20 .50
94 Octavio Dotel .20 .50
95A A.Rodriguez Fielding SP 4.00 10.00
95B A.Rodriguez w 4.00 10.00
Bat SP
96 Brett Myers .20 .50
97 New York Yankees TC .30 .75
98 Ryan Klesko .20 .50
99 Brian Jordan SP 3.00 8.00
100 W.Harridge .20 .50
W.Giles
101 Adam Eaton .20 .50
102 Aaron Boone .20 .50
103 Alex Rios .20 .50
104 Andy Pettitte .30 .75
105 Barry Zito .30 .75
106 Bengie Molina SP 3.00 8.00
107 Austin Kearns .20 .50
108 Adam Everett .20 .50
109 A.J. Burnett .20 .50
110 Mark Prior .30 .75
111 Russ Ortiz .20 .50
112 Adam Dunn .30 .75
113 Byung-Hyun Kim
114 Atlanta Braves TC .20 .50
115 Carlos Silva .20 .50
116 Chad Cordero .20 .50
117 Chone Figgins .20 .50
118 Chris Reitsma .20 .50
119 Coco Crisp .20 .50
120 David DeJesus .20 .50
121 Chris Snyder .20 .50
122 Brad Eldred .20 .50
123 Humberto Cota SP 3.00 8.00
124 Erubiel Durazo .20 .50
125 Josh Beckett .20 .50
126 Kenny Lofton .20 .50
127 Joe Nathan SP 3.00 8.00
128 Bryan Bullington .20 .50
129 Jim Thome .30 .75
130 Shawn Green .20 .50
131 LaTroy Hawkins .20 .50
132 Mark Kotsay .20 .50
133 Matt Lawton .20 .50
134 Luis Castillo .20 .50
135 Michael Barrett .20 .50
136 Preston Wilson .20 .50
137 Orlando Cabrera .20 .50
138 Chuck James .20 .50
139 Raul Ibanez .30 .75
140 Frank Thomas .50 1.25
141 Orlando Hudson .20 .50
142 Scott Kazmir .30 .75
143 Steve Finley .20 .50
144 Danny Sandoval RC .20 .50
145 Javy Lopez .20 .50
146 Tony Giarratano .20 .50
147 Terrence Long .20 .50
148 Victor Martinez .30 .75
149 Toby Hall .20 .50
150 Fausto Carmona .20 .50
151 Tim Wakefield .30 .75
152 Troy Percival .20 .50
153 Chris Denorfia .20 .50
154 Junior Spivey .20 .50
155 Desi Relaford .20 .50
156 Francisco Liriano .50 1.25
157 Corey Koskie .20 .50
158 Chris Carpenter .30 .75
159 Robert Andino RC .20 .50
160 Cliff Floyd .20 .50
161 Pittsburgh Pirates TC .20 .50
162 Anderson Hernandez .20 .50
163 Mike Maroth .20 .50
164 Aaron Rowand .20 .50
165A A.Pujols Grey Shirt .60 1.50
165B A.Pujols Red Shirt SP 5.00 12.00
166 David Bell .20 .50
167 Angel Berroa .20 .50
168 B.J. Ryan .20 .50
169 Bartolo Colon .20 .50
170 Hong-Chih Kuo .50 1.25
171 Cincinnati Reds TC .20 .50
172 Bill Mueller .20 .50
173 John Koronka .20 .50
174 Billy Wagner .20 .50
175 Zack Greinke .30 .75
176 Rick Short .20 .50
177 Yadier Molina .50 1.25
178 Willy Taveras .20 .50
179 Wes Helms .20 .50
180 Wade Miller .20 .50
181 Luis Gonzalez .20 .50
182 Victor Zambrano .20 .50
183 Chicago Cubs TC .20 .50
184 Victor Santos .20 .50
185 Tyler Walker .20 .50
186 Bobby Crosby .20 .50
187 Trot Nixon .20 .50
188 Nick Johnson .20 .50
189 Nick Swisher .30 .75
190 Brian Roberts .20 .50
191 Nomar Garciaparra .30 .75
192 Oliver Perez .20 .50
193 Ramon Hernandez .20 .50
194 Randy Winn .20 .50
195 Ryan Church .20 .50
196 Ryan Wagner .20 .50
197 Todd Hollandsworth .20 .50
198 Detroit Tigers TC .20 .50
199 Tino Martinez .20 .50
200A R.Clemens On Mound .60 1.50
200B R.Clemens Red Shirt SP 4.00 10.00
201 Shawn Estes .20 .50
202 Justin Morneau .30 .75
203 Jeff Francis .20 .50
204 Oakland Athletics TC .20 .50
205 Jeff Francoeur .50 1.25
206 C.J. Wilson .30 .75
207 Francisco Rodriguez .30 .75
208 Edgardo Alfonzo .20 .50
209 David Eckstein .20 .50
210 Cory Lidle .20 .50
211 Chase Utley .30 .75
212A R.Baldelli Yellow .20 .50
White Ltr
212B R.Baldelli Blue Ltr SP 3.00 8.00
213 So Taguchi .20 .50
214 Philadelphia Phillies TC .20 .50
215 Brad Hawpe .20 .50
216 Walter Young .20 .50
217 Tom Gorzelanny .20 .50
218 Shaun Marcum .20 .50
219 Ryan Howard .40 1.00
220 Damian Jackson .20 .50
221 Craig Counsell .20 .50
222 Damian Miller .20 .50
223 Derrick Turnbow .20 .50
224 Hank Blalock .20 .50
225 Brayan Pena .20 .50
226 Grady Sizemore .30 .75
227 Ivan Rodriguez .30 .75
228 Jason Isringhausen .20 .50
229 Brian Fuentes .20 .50
230 Jason Phillips .20 .50
231 Jason Schmidt .20 .50
232 Jose Valentin .20 .50
233 Jeff Kent .20 .50
234 John Buck .20 .50
235 Mike Matheny .20 .50
236 Jorge Cantu .20 .50
237 Jose Castillo .20 .50
238 Kenny Rogers .20 .50
239 Kerry Wood .20 .50
240 Kevin Mench .20 .50
241 Tim Stauffer .20 .50
242 Eric Milton .20 .50
243 St. Louis Cardinals TC .30 .75
244 Shawn Chacon .20 .50
245 Mike Jacobs .20 .50
246 Ryan Dempster .20 .50
247 Todd Jones .20 .50
248 Tom Glavine .30 .75
249 Tony Graffanino .20 .50
250 Ichiro Suzuki .60 1.50
251 Baltimore Orioles TC .20 .50
252 Brad Radke .20 .50
253 Brad Wilkerson .20 .50
254 Carlos Lee .20 .50
255 Alex Gordon Cut Out 125.00 250.00
256 Gustavo Chacin .20 .50
257 Jermaine Dye .20 .50
258 Jose Mesa .20 .50
259 Julio Lugo .20 .50
260 Mark Redman .20 .50
261 Brandon Watson .20 .50
262 Pedro Feliz .20 .50
263 Esteban Loaiza .20 .50
264 Anthony Reyes .20 .50
265 Jose Contreras SP 3.00 8.00
266 Tadahito Iguchi SP 3.00 8.00
267 Mark Loretta SP 3.00 8.00
268 Ray Durham SP 3.00 8.00
269 Neifi Perez SP 3.00 8.00
270 Washington Nationals TC .20 .50
271 Troy Glaus SP 3.00 8.00
272 Matt Holliday SP 4.00 10.00
273 Kevin Millwood SP 3.00 8.00
274 Jon Lieber SP 3.00 8.00
275 Cleveland Indians TC .20 .50
276 Jeremy Reed SP 3.00 8.00
277 Garrett Atkins SP 3.00 8.00
278 Geoff Jenkins SP 3.00 8.00
279 Joey Gathright SP 3.00 8.00
280 Ben Sheets SP 3.00 8.00
281 Melvin Mora SP 3.00 8.00
282 Jonathan Papelbon SP 4.00 10.00
283 John Smoltz SP 3.00 8.00
284 Jake Peavy SP 3.00 8.00
285 Felix Hernandez SP 3.00 8.00
286 Alfonso Soriano SP 3.00 8.00
287 Bronson Arroyo SP 3.00 8.00
288 Adam LaRoche SP 3.00 8.00
289 Aramis Ramirez SP 3.00 8.00
290 Brad Hennessey SP 3.00 8.00
291 Conor Jackson SP 3.00 8.00
292 Rod Barajas SP 3.00 8.00
293 Chris R. Young SP 3.00 8.00
294 Jeremy Bonderman SP 3.00 8.00
295 Jack Wilson SP 3.00 8.00
296 Jay Payton SP 3.00 8.00
297 Danys Baez SP 3.00 8.00
298 Jose Lima SP 3.00 8.00
299 Luis A. Gonzalez SP 3.00 8.00
300 Mike Sweeney SP 3.00 8.00
301 Nelson Cruz SP 3.00 8.00
302 Eric Gagne SP 3.00 8.00
303 Juan Castro SP 3.00 8.00
304 Joe Mauer SP 3.00 8.00
305 Richie Sexson SP 3.00 8.00
306 Roy Oswalt SP 3.00 8.00
307 Rickie Weeks SP 3.00 8.00
308 Pat Borders SP 3.00 8.00
309 Mike Morse SP 3.00 8.00
310 Matt Stairs SP 3.00 8.00
311 Chad Tracy SP 3.00 8.00
312 Matt Cain SP 3.00 8.00
313 Mark Mulder SP 3.00 8.00
314 Mark Grudzielanek SP 3.00 8.00
315 Johnny Damon Yanks SP 4.00 10.00
316 Casey Kotchman SP 3.00 8.00
317 San Francisco Giants TC .20 .50
318 Chris Burke SP 3.00 8.00
319 Carl Crawford SP 3.00 8.00
320 Edgar Renteria SP 3.00 8.00
321 Chan Ho Park SP 3.00 8.00
322 Boston Red Sox TC SP 3.00 8.00
323 Robinson Cano SP 3.00 8.00
324 Los Angeles Dodgers TC .30 .75
325A M.Tejada w/Bat SP 3.00 8.00
325B M.Tejada Hand Up SP 3.00 8.00
326 Jimmy Rollins SP 3.00 8.00
327 Juan Pierre SP 3.00 8.00
328 Dan Johnson SP 3.00 8.00
329 Chicago White Sox TC .20 .50
330 Pat Burrell SP 3.00 8.00
331 Ramon Ortiz SP 3.00 8.00
332 Rondell White SP 3.00 8.00
333 David Wells SP 3.00 8.00
334 Michael Young SP 3.00 8.00
335 Mike Mussina SP 3.00 8.00
336 Moises Alou SP 3.00 8.00
337 Scott Podsednik SP 3.00 8.00
338 Rich Harden SP 3.00 8.00
339 Mark Teahen SP 3.00 8.00
340 Jacque Jones SP 3.00 8.00
341 Jason Giambi SP 3.00 8.00
342 Bill Hall SP 3.00 8.00
343 Jon Garland SP 3.00 8.00
344 Dontrelle Willis SP 3.00 8.00
345 Danny Haren SP 3.00 8.00
346 Brian Giles SP 3.00 8.00
347 Brad Penny SP 3.00 8.00
348 Brandon McCarthy SP 3.00 8.00
349 Chien-Ming Wang SP 4.00 10.00
350A T.Hunter Red 3.00 8.00
Blue Ltr SP
350B T.Hunter Blue Ltr SP 3.00 8.00
351 Yhency Brazoban SP 3.00 8.00
352 Rodrigo Lopez SP 3.00 8.00
353 Paul McAnulty .20 .50
354 Francisco Cordero .20 .50
355 Brandon Inge .20 .50
356 Jason Lane .20 .50
357 Brian Schneider .20 .50
358 Dustin Hermanson .30 .75
359 Eric Hinske .20 .50
360 Jarrod Washburn .20 .50
361 Jayson Werth .30 .75
362 Craig Breslow RC .20 .50
363 Jeff Weaver .20 .50
364 Jeromy Burnitz .20 .50
365 Jhonny Peralta .20 .50
366 Joe Crede .20 .50
367 Johan Santana .30 .75
368 Jose Valentin .20 .50
369 Keith Foulke .20 .50
370 Larry Bigbie .20 .50
371 Manny Ramirez .50 1.25
372 Jim Edmonds .30 .75
373 Horacio Ramirez .20 .50
374 Garret Anderson .20 .50
375 Felipe Lopez .20 .50
376 Eric Byrnes .20 .50
377 Darin Erstad .20 .50
378 Carlos Zambrano .30 .75
379 Craig Biggio .30 .75
380 Darrell Rasner .20 .50
381 Dave Roberts .30 .75
382 Hanley Ramirez .30 .75
383 Geoff Blum .20 .50
384 Joel Pineiro .20 .50
385 Kip Wells .20 .50
386 Kelvim Escobar .20 .50
387 John Patterson .20 .50
388 Jody Gerut .20 .50
389 Marshall McDougall .20 .50
390 Mike MacDougal .20 .50
391 Orlando Palmeiro .20 .50
392 Rich Aurilia .20 .50
393 Ronnie Belliard .20 .50
394 Rich Hill .50 1.25
395 Scott Hatteberg .20 .50
396 Ryan Langerhans .20 .50
397 Richard Hidalgo .20 .50
398 Omar Vizquel .30 .75
399 Mike Lowell .20 .50
400 Astros Aces SP 3.00 8.00
401 Mike Cameron .20 .50
402 Matt Clement .20 .50
403 Miguel Cabrera .50 1.25
404 Milton Bradley .20 .50
405 Laynce Nix .20 .50
406 Rob Mackowiak .20 .50
407 White Sox Power Hitters SP 3.00 8.00
408 Mark Teixeira .30 .75
409 Brady Clark .20 .50
410 Johnny Estrada .20 .50
411 Juan Encarnacion .20 .50
412 Morgan Ensberg .20 .50
413 Nook Logan .20 .50
414 Phil Nevin .20 .50
415 Reggie Sanders .20 .50
416 Roy Halladay .30 .75
417 Livan Hernandez .20 .50
418 Jose Vidro .20 .50
419 Shannon Stewart .20 .50
420 Brian Bruney .20 .50
421 Royce Clayton .20 .50
422 Chris Demaria RC .20 .50
423 Eduardo Perez .20 .50
424 Jeff Suppan .20 .50
425 Jaret Wright .20 .50
426 Joe Randa .20 .50
427 Bobby Kielty .20 .50
428 Jason Ellison .20 .50
429 Gregg Zaun .20 .50
430 Runelvys Hernandez .20 .50
431 Joe McEwing .20 .50
432 Jason LaRue .20 .50
433 Aaron Miles .20 .50
434 Adam Kennedy .20 .50
435 Ambiorix Burgos .20 .50
436 Armando Benitez .20 .50
437 Brad Ausmus .20 .50
438 Brandon Backe .20 .50
439 Brian James Anderson
440 Bruce Chen .20 .50
441 Carlos Guillen .20 .50
442 Casey Blake .20 .50
443 Chris Capuano .20 .50
444 Chris Duffy .20 .50
445 Chris Ray .20 .50
446 Clint Barmes .20 .50
447 Andrew Sisco .20 .50
448 Dallas McPherson .20 .50
449 Tanyon Sturtze .20 .50
450 Carlos Beltran .30 .75
451 Jason Vargas .20 .50
452 Ervin Santana .20 .50
453 Jason Marquis .20 .50
454 Juan Rivera .20 .50
455 Jake Westbrook .20 .50
456 Jason Johnson
457 Joe Blanton .20 .50
458 Kevin Millar .20 .50
459 John Thomson .20 .50
460 J.P. Howell .20 .50
461 Justin Verlander 1.50 4.00
462 Kelly Johnson
463 Kyle Davies .20 .50
464 Lance Niekro .20 .50
465 Magglio Ordonez .30 .75
466 Melky Cabrera .30 .75
467 Nick Punto .20 .50
468 Paul Byrd .20 .50
469 Randy Wolf .20 .50
470 Ruben Gotay .20 .50
471 Ryan Madson .20 .50
472 Victor Diaz .20 .50
473 Xavier Nady .20 .50
474 Zach Duke .30 .75
475A H.Street Yellow .20 .50
White Ltr
475B H.Street Blue Ltr SP 3.00 8.00
476 Brad Thompson .20 .50
477 Jonny Gomes .20 .50
478 B.J. Upton .20 .50
479 Jamey Carroll .20 .50
480 Mike Hampton .20 .50
481 Tony Clark .20 .50
482 Antonio Alfonseca .20 .50
483 Justin Duchscherer .20 .50
484 Mike Timlin .20 .50
485 Joe Saunders .20 .50

2006 Topps Heritage Checklists

COMPLETE SET (5) .75 2.00
COMMON CARD (1-5) .20 .50
RANDOM INSERTS IN PACKS

2006 Topps Heritage Chrome

COMPLETE SET (109) 200.00 300.00
COMMON (1-102/104-110) 1.50 4.00
STATED ODDS 1:9 HOBBY, 1:10 RETAIL
STATED PRINT RUN 1957 SERIAL #'d SETS
CARD 103 DOES NOT EXIST
1 Rafael Furcal 1.25 3.00
2 C.C. Sabathia 2.00 5.00
3 Sean Casey 1.25 3.00
4 Gary Sheffield 1.25 3.00
5 W.Harridge 1.25 3.00
W.Giles
6 Curt Schilling 2.00 5.00
7 Jay Gibbons 1.25 3.00
8 Paul Konerko 2.00 5.00
9 Lyle Overbay 1.25 3.00
10 Jorge Posada 2.00 5.00
11 Todd Walker 1.25 3.00
12 Carlos Delgado 1.25 3.00
13 David Wright 2.50 6.00
14 Matt Morris 1.25 3.00
15 Mariano Rivera 4.00 10.00
16 Jeff Bagwell 2.00 5.00
17 Carl Pavano 1.25 3.00
18 Adrian Beltre 3.00 8.00
19 Scott Rolen 2.00 5.00
20 Aubrey Huff 1.25 3.00
21 Hideki Matsui 3.00 8.00
22 Andruw Jones 1.25 3.00
23 Sammy Sosa 3.00 8.00
24 Mark Buehrle 2.00 5.00
25 Orlando Hernandez 1.25 3.00
26 Travis Hafner 1.25 3.00
27 Vladimir Guerrero 2.00 5.00
28 Chipper Jones 3.00 8.00
29 Jose Reyes 2.00 5.00
30 Roger Clemens 4.00 10.00
31 Aaron Boone 1.25 3.00
32 Andy Pettitte 2.00 5.00
33 David DeJesus 1.25 3.00
34 Shawn Green 1.25 3.00
35 Luis Castillo 1.25 3.00
36 Frank Thomas 3.00 8.00
37 Javy Lopez 1.25 3.00
38 Victor Martinez 2.00 5.00
39 Tim Wakefield 2.00 5.00
40 Cliff Floyd 1.25 3.00
41 Bartolo Colon 1.25 3.00
42 Billy Wagner 1.25 3.00
43 Dmitri Young 1.25 3.00
44 Mark Prior 2.00 5.00
45 Nick Johnson 1.25 3.00
46 Brian Roberts 1.25 3.00
47 Nomar Garciaparra 2.00 5.00
48 Jorge Cantu 1.25 3.00
49 Jeff Francoeur 3.00 8.00
50 Barry Bonds 5.00 12.00
51 Francisco Rodriguez 2.00 5.00
52 Rocco Baldelli 1.25 3.00
53 Ryan Howard 2.50 6.00
54 Hank Blalock 1.25 3.00
55 Ivan Rodriguez 2.00 5.00
56 Jason Schmidt 1.25 3.00
57 Jeff Kent 1.25 3.00
58 Jose Castillo 1.25 3.00
59 Kerry Wood 1.25 3.00
60 Chase Utley 2.00 5.00
61 Shawn Chacon 1.25 3.00
62 Tom Glavine 2.00 5.00
63 Ichiro Suzuki 4.00 10.00
64 Carlos Lee 1.25 3.00
65 Jeff Weaver 1.25 3.00
66 Jeromy Burnitz 1.25 3.00
67 Jhonny Peralta 1.25 3.00
68 Johan Santana 2.00 5.00
69 Keith Foulke 1.25 3.00
70 Manny Ramirez 3.00 8.00
71 Jim Edmonds 2.00 5.00
72 Garret Anderson 1.25 3.00
73 Felipe Lopez 1.25 3.00
74 Craig Biggio 2.00 5.00
75 Ryan Langerhans 1.25 3.00
76 Mike Cameron 1.25 3.00
77 Matt Clement 1.25 3.00
78 Miguel Cabrera 3.00 8.00
79 Mark Teixeira 2.00 5.00
80 Johnny Estrada 1.25 3.00
81 Nook Logan 1.25 3.00
82 Livan Hernandez 1.25 3.00
83 Roy Halladay 2.00 5.00
84 Jose Vidro 1.25 3.00
85 Shannon Stewart 1.25 3.00
86 Brian Bruney 1.25 3.00
87 Jaret Wright 1.25 3.00
88 Gregg Zaun 1.25 3.00
89 Jason LaRue 1.25 3.00
90 Adam Kennedy 1.25 3.00
91 Armando Benitez 1.25 3.00
92 Chris Ray 1.25 3.00
93 Clint Barmes 1.25 3.00
94 Ervin Santana 1.25 3.00
95 Justin Verlander 10.00 25.00
96 Maggio Ordonez 2.00 5.00
97 Todd Helton 2.00 5.00
98 Zach Duke 1.25 3.00
99 Huston Street 1.25 3.00
100 Alex Rodriguez 4.00 10.00
101 Mike Hampton 1.25 3.00
102 Tony Clark 1.25 3.00
104 Barry Zito 2.00 5.00
105 Anderson Hernandez 1.25 3.00
106 B.J. Upton 1.25 3.00
107 Albert Pujols 4.00 10.00
108 Tim Hudson 2.00 5.00
109 Derek Jeter 8.00 20.00
110 Greg Maddux 4.00 10.00

2006 Topps Heritage Chrome Refractors

*CHROME REF: .6X TO 1.5X CHROME
STATED ODDS 1:33 HOBBY, 1:34 RETAIL
STATED PRINT RUN 557 SERIAL #'d SETS
CARD 103 DOES NOT EXIST

2006 Topps Heritage Chrome Black Refractors

*BLACK: 2.5X TO 6X CHROME
STATED ODDS 1:328 HOBBY, 1:328 RETAIL
STATED PRINT RUN 57 SERIAL #'d SETS
CARD 103 DOES NOT EXIST

2006 Topps Heritage Clubhouse Collection Relics

GROUP A ODDS 1:3440 H, 1:3457 R
GROUP B ODDS 1:8164 H, 1:8232 R
GROUP C ODDS 1:1639 H, 1:1650 R
GROUP D ODDS 1:2928 H, 1:2935 R
GROUP E ODDS 1:4082 H, 1:4116 R
GROUP F ODDS 1:3404 H, 1:3426 R
GROUP G ODDS 1:487 H, 1:490 R
GROUP H ODDS 1:2583 H, 1:2600 R
GROUP I ODDS 1:206 H, 1:207 R
GROUP J ODDS 1:257 H, 1:255 R
GROUP K ODDS 1:1370 H, 1:1364 R
GROUP L ODDS 1:421 H, 1:419 R
OVERALL AU-RELIC ODDS 1:36 H, 1:36 R
GROUP A PRINT RUN 99 COPIES PER
GROUP B PRINT RUN 125 COPIES PER
GROUP A-B CARDS ARE NOT SERIAL #'d
A-B PRINT RUN INFO PROVIDED BY TOPPS
AD Adam Dunn Bat G 3.00 8.00
AJ Andruw Jones Uni G 4.00 10.00
AK Al Kaline Bat B/125 * 30.00 60.00
AP Albert Pujols Jsy I 8.00 20.00
AR Alex Rodriguez Bat A/99 * 40.00 80.00
AR2 Alex Rodriguez Jsy D 20.00 50.00
AS Alfonso Soriano Bat I 3.00 8.00
BB Barry Bonds Uni A/99 * 50.00 100.00
BM Bill Mazeroski Jsy A/99 * 50.00 100.00
BR Brian Roberts Bat I 3.00 8.00
BRO Brooks Robinson Bat A/99 * 15.00 40.00
BR2 Brian Roberts Jsy J 3.00 8.00
CB Clint Barmes Jsy J 3.00 8.00
CC Carl Crawford Bat I 3.00 8.00
CJ Conor Jackson Bat I 3.00 8.00
CS Curt Schilling Jsy C 4.00 10.00
DL Derrek Lee Bat I 4.00 10.00
DO David Ortiz Jsy C 20.00 50.00
DW David Wright Jsy L 4.00 10.00
DWI Dontrelle Willis Jsy J 3.00 8.00
EC Eric Chavez Uni L 3.00 8.00
EG Eric Gagne Jsy F 3.00 8.00
FJF Jeff Francis Jsy L 3.00 8.00
FR Frank Robinson Bat B/125 * 30.00 60.00
GS Gary Sheffield Bat I 3.00 8.00
JD Johnny Damon Bat E 4.00 10.00
JD2 Johnny Damon Jsy G 4.00 10.00
JE Jim Edmonds Jsy H 3.00 8.00
JP Jake Peavy Jsy J 3.00 8.00
JS Johan Santana Jsy J 4.00 10.00
KG Khalil Greene Jsy D 4.00 10.00
MC Miguel Cabrera Jsy G 4.00 10.00
ME Morgan Ensberg Bat I 3.00 8.00
MH Matt Holliday Bat I 4.00 10.00
MM Mickey Mantle Bat A/99 * 125.00 200.00
MMU Mark Mulder Uni K 3.00 8.00
MP Mike Piazza Bat C 12.50 30.00
MR Manny Ramirez Jsy C 4.00 10.00
MR2 Manny Ramirez Bat J 4.00 10.00
MT Miguel Tejada Uni I 3.00 8.00
MTE Mark Teixeira Jsy G 4.00 10.00
PM Pedro Martinez Jsy C 4.00 10.00
RC Robinson Cano Bat I 4.00 10.00
RW Rickie Weeks Bat G 3.00 8.00
SC Shin-Soo Choo Bat I 3.00 8.00
SM Stan Musial Bat A/99 * 100.00 200.00
TI Tadahito Iguchi Jsy J 3.00 8.00
VG Vladimir Guerrero Bat J 4.00 10.00

2006 Topps Heritage Clubhouse Collection Autograph Relics

STATED ODDS 1:16,400 H, 1:16,400 R
STATED PRINT RUN 25 SERIAL #'d SETS
EXCHANGE DEADLINE 02/28/08
NO PRICING DUE TO SCARCITY

2006 Topps Heritage Clubhouse Collection Cut Signature Relic

STATED ODDS 1:963,072 HOBBY
STATED PRINT RUN 1 SERIAL #'d CARD
NO PRICING DUE TO SCARCITY

2006 Topps Heritage Clubhouse Collection Dual Relics

STATED ODDS 1:12,067 H, 1:12,067 R
STATED PRINT RUN 57 SERIAL #'d SETS
BR B.Robinson B/B.Roberts J 25.00 60.00
MP S.Musial B/A.Pujols J 125.00 200.00
MR M.Mantle B/A.Rod J 150.00 300.00

2006 Topps Heritage Flashbacks

COMPLETE SET (10) 10.00 25.00
STATED ODDS 1:12 HOBBY, 1:12 RETAIL
AK Al Kaline 1.00 2.50
BM Bill Mazeroski .60 1.50
BR Brooks Robinson .60 1.50
BRI Bobby Richardson .40 1.00
EB Ernie Banks 1.00 2.50
FR Frank Robinson .60 1.50
MM Mickey Mantle 3.00 8.00
SM Stan Musial 1.50 4.00
WF Whitey Ford .60 1.50
YB Yogi Berra 1.00 2.50

2006 Topps Heritage Flashbacks Autographs

STATED ODDS 1:16,400 H, 1:16,400 R
STATED PRINT RUN 25 SERIAL #'d SETS
NO PRICING DUE TO SCARCITY

2006 Topps Heritage Flashbacks Seat Relics

GROUP A ODDS 1:14,607 H, 1:14,607 R
GROUP B ODDS 1:6225 H, 1:6175 R
GROUP C ODDS 1:721 H, 1:719 R
GROUP D ODDS 1:1711 H, 1:1703 R
GROUP E ODDS 1:308 H, 1:306 R
OVERALL AU-RELIC ODDS 1:36 H, 1:36 R
GROUP A PRINT RUN 140 COPIES
GROUP A CARD IS NOT SERIAL #'d
GROUP A PRINT RUN PROVIDED BY TOPPS
AK Al Kaline E 12.50 30.00
BM Bill Mazeroski B 10.00 25.00
BR Brooks Robinson E 6.00 15.00
BR Bobby Richardson C 10.00 25.00
EB Ernie Banks D 10.00 25.00
FR Frank Robinson E 4.00 10.00
MM Mickey Mantle E 10.00 25.00
SM Stan Musial A/140 * 40.00 80.00
WF Whitey Ford C 6.00 15.00
YB Yogi Berra C 10.00 25.00

2006 Topps Heritage New Age Performers

COMPLETE SET (15) 15.00 40.00
STATED ODDS 1:15 HOBBY, 1:15 RETAIL
AP Albert Pujols 1.25 3.00
AR Alex Rodriguez 1.25 3.00
BB Barry Bonds 1.50 4.00
CL Carlos Lee .40 1.00
DL Derrek Lee .40 1.00
DO David Ortiz 1.00 2.50
GM Mark Prior .60 1.50
GS Gary Sheffield .40 1.00
IS Ichiro Suzuki 1.25 3.00
MC Miguel Cabrera 1.00 2.50
MR Manny Ramirez 1.00 2.50
MT Mark Teixeira .60 1.50
PM Pedro Martinez .60 1.50
RC Roger Clemens 1.25 3.00
VG Vladimir Guerrero .60 1.50

2006 Topps Heritage Real One Autographs

Charley Thompson and Red Murff cards were originally seeded into packs as redemption cards with an exchange deadline of February 28th, 2008.

STATED ODDS 1:366 HOBBY, 1:366 RETAIL
STATED PRINT RUN 200 SETS
CARDS ARE NOT SERIAL-NUMBERED
PRINT RUN INFO PROVIDED BY TOPPS
*RED INK: .75X TO 1.5X BASIC
RED INK ODDS 1:1280 H, 1:1288 R
RED INK PRINT RUN 57 SERIAL #'d SETS
RED INK ALSO CALLED SPECIAL EDITION
EXCHANGE DEADLINE 02/28/08
BC Bob Chakales 10.00 25.00
BW Bob Wiesler 10.00 25.00
CT Charley Thompson 10.00 25.00
DK Don Kaiser 10.00 25.00
DR Dusty Rhodes 30.00 60.00
DS Duke Snider 40.00 100.00
EB Ernie Banks 75.00 150.00
EO Ernie Oravetz 10.00 25.00
EOB Eddie O'Brien 10.00 25.00
FR Frank Robinson 50.00 100.00
JAC Jackie Collum 20.00 50.00
JCR Jack Crimian 10.00 25.00
JD Jack Dittmer 10.00 25.00
JM Joe Margoneri 10.00 25.00
JP Jim Pyburn 20.00 50.00
JRM Red Murff 10.00 25.00
JSM Jim Small 10.00 25.00
JSN Jerry Snyder UER 30.00 60.00
KO Karl Olson 10.00 25.00
LK Lou Kretlow 20.00 50.00
MP Mel Parnell 10.00 25.00
NK Nellie King 20.00 50.00
PL Paul LaPalme 10.00 25.00
RN Ron Negray 10.00 25.00
SM Stan Musial 125.00 250.00
TB Tommy Byrne 12.50 30.00
WF Whitey Ford 50.00 100.00
WM Windy McCall 12.00 30.00
YB Yogi Berra 60.00 150.00

2006 Topps Heritage Then and Now

COMPLETE SET (10) 10.00 25.00
STATED ODDS 1:15 HOBBY, 1:15 RETAIL
TN1 M.Mantle 3.00 8.00
A.Rodriguez
TN2 T.Williams 2.00 5.00
M.Young
TN3 M.Mantle 3.00 8.00
J.Giambi
TN4 L.Aparicio .60 1.50
C.Figgins
TN5 T.Williams 2.00 5.00
A.Rodriguez
TN6 S.Musial 1.50 4.00
D.Lee
TN7 S.Musial 1.50 4.00
D.Lee
TN8 R.Schoendienst .60 1.50
D.Lee
TN9 J.Podres 1.25 3.00
R.Clemens
TN10 C.Labine .40 1.00
C.Cordero

2007 Topps Heritage

This 527-card set was released in March, 2007. This set was issued through both hobby and retail channels. The set was issued in eight-card hobby packs (with an $3 SRP) which came 24 packs to a box and 12 boxes to a case. Each pack also included a sealed piece of bubble gum. In the tradition of previous Heritage sets, this product honored the 1958 Topps set. In addition, in homage to the original 1958 set, some cards issued between 1-110 were issued in two varieties (a white and yellow letter version). Those yellow cards were inserted at a stated rate of one in six hobby or retail packs. Also, just like the original 1958 Topps set, there was no card #145 issued. In another long-standing Heritage tradition, many cards throughout the set were short-printed. Those short prints were inserted at a stated rate of one in two. In other tributes to the original 1958 sets, many multi-player cards and team checklist cards were inserted in the same card number as the original set and the set concludes with a 20-card All-Star set (476-495).

COMPLETE SET (527) 250.00 400.00
COMP.SET w/o SP's (384) 30.00 60.00
COMMON CARD .20 .50
COMMON RC .20 .50
COMMON TEAM CARD .20 .50
COMMON SP 2.50 6.00
SP STATED ODDS 1:2 HOBBY/RETAIL
SEE BECKETT.COM FOR SP CHECKLIST
COMMON YELLOW 2.00 5.00
YELLOW STATED ODDS 1:6 HOBBY/RETAIL
SEE BECKETT.COM FOR YELLOW CL
CARD 145 DOES NOT EXIST
1 David Ortiz .50 1.25
2a Roger Clemens .60 1.50
2b Roger Clemens YT 3.00 8.00
3 David Wells .20 .50
4 Ronny Paulino SP 2.50 6.00
5 Derek Jeter SP 12.00 30.00
6 Felix Hernandez .30 .75
7 Todd Helton .30 .75
8a David Eckstein .20 .50
8b David Eckstein YN 2.00 5.00
9 Craig Wilson .20 .50
10 John Smoltz .50 1.25
11a Rob Mackowiak .20 .50
11b Rob Mackowiak YT 2.00 5.00
12 Scott Hatteberg .20 .50
13a Wilfredo Ledezma SP 2.50 6.00
13b Wilfredo Ledezma YT 2.00 5.00
14 Bobby Abreu SP 2.50 6.00
15 Mike Stanton .20 .50
16 Wilson Betemit .20 .50
17 Darren Oliver .20 .50
18 Josh Beckett .20 .50
19 San Francisco Giants TC .20 .50
20a Robinson Cano .20 .50
20b Robinson Cano YT 2.50 6.00
21 Matt Cain .30 .75
22 Jason Kendall SP 2.50 6.00
23a Mark Kotsay SP 2.50 6.00
23b Mark Kotsay YN 2.00 5.00
24a Yadier Molina .50 1.25
24b Yadier Molina YN 2.00 5.00
25 Brad Penny .20 .50
26 Adrian Gonzalez .40 1.00
27 Danny Haren .20 .50
28 Brian Giles .20 .50
29 Jose Lopez .20 .50
30a Ichiro Suzuki .60 1.50
30b Ichiro Suzuki YN 3.00 8.00
31 Beltran Perez SP (RC) 2.50 6.00
32 Brad Hawpe SP 2.50 6.00
33a Jim Thome .30 .75
33b Jim Thome YT 2.50 6.00
34 Mark DeRosa .20 .50
35a Woody Williams .20 .50
35b Woody Williams YT 2.00 5.00
36 Luis Gonzalez .20 .50
37 Billy Sadler (RC) .20 .50
38 Dave Roberts .30 .75
39 Mitch Maier RC .20 .50
40 Francisco Cordero SP 2.50 6.00
41 Anthony Reyes SP 2.50 6.00
42 Russell Martin .20 .50
43 Scott Proctor .20 .50
44 Washington Nationals TC .20 .50
45 Shane Victorino .20 .50
46a Joel Zumaya .20 .50
46b Joel Zumaya YN 2.50 6.00
47 Delmon Young (RC) .30 .75
48 Alex Rios .20 .50
49 Willy Taveras SP 2.50 6.00
50a Mark Buehrle SP 2.50 6.00
50b Mark Buehrle YT 2.00 5.00
51 Livan Hernandez .20 .50
52a Jason Bay .30 .75
52b Jason Bay YT 2.00 5.00
53a Jose Valentin .20 .50
53b Jose Valentin YN 2.00 5.00
54 Kevin Reese .20 .50
55 Felipe Lopez .20 .50
56 Ryan Sweeney (RC) .20 .50
57a Kelvim Escobar .20 .50
57b Kelvim Escobar YN 2.00 5.00
58a N.Swisher Sm.Print SP 2.50 6.00
58b N.Swisher Lg.Print YT 2.00 5.00
59 Kevin Millwood SP 2.50 6.00
60a Preston Wilson .20 .50
60b Preston Wilson YN 2.00 5.00
61a Mariano Rivera .60 1.50
61b Mariano Rivera YN 2.50 6.00
62 Josh Barfield .20 .50
63 Ryan Freel .20 .50
64 Tim Hudson .30 .75
65a Chris Narveson (RC) .20 .50
65b Chris Narveson YN (RC) 2.00 5.00
66 Matt Murton .20 .50
67 Melvin Mora SP 2.50 6.00
68 Jason Jennings SP 2.50 6.00
69 Emil Brown .20 .50
70a Magglio Ordonez .30 .75
70b Magglio Ordonez YN 2.00 5.00
71 Los Angeles Dodgers TC .20 .50
72 Ross Gload .20 .50
73 David Ross .20 .50
74 Juan Uribe .20 .50
75 Scott Podsednik .20 .50
76a Cole Hamels SP 3.00 8.00
76b Cole Hamels YT 2.50 6.00
77a Rafael Furcal SP 2.50 6.00
77b Rafael Furcal YT 2.00 5.00
78a Ryan Theriot .20 .50
78b Ryan Theriot YN 2.00 5.00
79a Corey Patterson .20 .50
79b Corey Patterson YT 2.00 5.00
80 Jered Weaver .30 .75
81a Stephen Drew .20 .50
81b Stephen Drew YT 2.50 6.00
82 Adam Kennedy .20 .50
83 Tony Gwynn Jr. .20 .50
84 Kazuo Matsui .20 .50
85a Omar Vizquel SP 3.00 8.00
85b Omar Vizquel YT 2.50 6.00
86 Fred Lewis SP (RC) 2.50 6.00
87a Shawn Chacon .20 .50
87b Shawn Chacon YN 2.00 5.00
88 Frank Catalanotto .20 .50
89 Orlando Hudson .20 .50
90 Pat Burrell .20 .50
91 David DeJesus .20 .50
92a David Wright .40 1.00
92b David Wright YN 3.00 8.00
93 Conor Jackson .20 .50
94 Xavier Nady SP 2.50 6.00
95 Bill Hall SP 2.50 6.00
96 Kip Wells .20 .50
97a Jeff Suppan .20 .50
97b Jeff Suppan YN 2.00 5.00
98a Ryan Zimmerman .30 .75
98b Ryan Zimmerman YN 2.50 6.00
99 Wes Helms .20 .50
100a Jose Contreras .20 .50
100b Jose Contreras YT 2.00 5.00
101a Miguel Cairo .20 .50
101b Miguel Cairo YN 2.00 5.00
102 Brian Roberts .20 .50
103 Carl Crawford SP 2.50 6.00
104 Mike Lamb SP 2.50 6.00
105 Mark Ellis .20 .50
106 Scott Rolen .30 .75
107 Garrett Atkins .20 .50
108a Hanley Ramirez .30 .75
108b Hanley Ramirez YT 2.50 6.00
109 Trot Nixon .20 .50
110 Edgar Renteria .20 .50
111 Jeff Francis .20 .50
112 Marcus Thames SP 2.50 6.00
113 Brian Burres SP (RC) 2.50 6.00
114 Brian Schneider .20 .50
115 Jeremy Bonderman .20 .50
116 Ryan Madson .20 .50
117 Gerald Laird .20 .50
118 Roy Halladay .30 .75
119 Victor Martinez .30 .75
120 Greg Maddux .60 1.50
121 Jay Payton SP 2.50 6.00
122 Jacque Jones SP 2.50 6.00
123 Juan Lara RC .20 .50
124 Derrick Turnbow .20 .50
125 Adam Everett .20 .50
126 Michael Cuddyer .20 .50
127 Gil Meche .20 .50
128 Willy Aybar .20 .50
129 Jerry Owens (RC) .20 .50
130 Manny Ramirez SP 3.00 8.00
131 Howie Kendrick SP 2.50 6.00
132 Byung-Hyun Kim .20 .50
133 Kevin Kouzmanoff (RC) .20 .50
134 Philadelphia Phillies TC .20 .50
135 Joe Blanton .20 .50
136 Ray Durham .20 .50
137 Luke Hudson .20 .50
138 Eric Byrnes .20 .50
139 Ryan Braun SP RC 2.50 6.00
140 Johnny Damon SP 3.00 8.00
141 Ambiorix Burgos .20 .50
142 Hideki Matsui .50 1.25
143 Josh Johnson .50 1.25
144 Miguel Cabrera .50 1.25
146 Delwyn Young (RC) .20 .50
147 Chuck James .20 .50
148 Morgan Ensberg .20 .50
149 Jose Vidro SP 2.50 6.00
150 Alex Rodriguez SP 5.00 12.00
151 Carlos Maldonado (RC) .20 .50
152 Jason Schmidt .20 .50
153 Alex Escobar .20 .50
154 Chris Gomez .20 .50
155 Endy Chavez .20 .50
156 Kris Benson .20 .50
157 Bronson Arroyo .20 .50
158 Cleveland Indians TC SP 2.50 6.00
159 Chris Ray SP 2.50 6.00
160 Richie Sexson .20 .50
161 Huston Street .20 .50
162 Kevin Youkilis .20 .50
163 Armando Benitez .20 .50
164 Vinny Rottino (RC) .20 .50
165 Garret Anderson .20 .50
166 Todd Greene .20 .50
167 Brian Stokes SP (RC) 2.50 6.00
168 Albert Pujols SP 6.00 15.00
169 Todd Coffey .20 .50
170 Jason Michaels .20 .50
171 David Dellucci .20 .50
172 Eric Milton .20 .50
173 Austin Kearns .20 .50
174 Oakland Athletics TC .20 .50
175 Andy Cannizaro RC .20 .50
176 David Weathers SP 2.50 6.00
177 Jermaine Dye SP 2.50 6.00
178 Wily Mo Pena .20 .50
179 Chris Burke .20 .50
180 Jeff Weaver .20 .50
181 Edwin Encarnacion .50 1.25
182 Jeremy Hermida .20 .50
183 Tim Wakefield .30 .75
184 Rich Hill .20 .50
185 Aaron Hill SP 2.50 6.00
186 Scot Shields SP 2.50 6.00
187 Randy Johnson .50 1.25
188 Dan Johnson .20 .50
189 Sean Marshall .20 .50
190 Marcus Giles .20 .50
191 Jonathan Broxton .20 .50
192 Mike Piazza .50 1.25
193 Carlos Quentin .20 .50
194 Derek Lowe SP 2.50 6.00
195 Russell Branyan SP 2.50 6.00
196 Jason Marquis .20 .50
197 Khalil Greene .20 .50
198 Ryan Dempster .20 .50
199 Ronnie Belliard .20 .50
200 Josh Fogg .20 .50
201 Carlos Lee .20 .50
202 Chris Denorfia .20 .50
203 Kendry Morales SP 3.00 8.00
204 Rafael Soriano SP 2.50 6.00
205 Brandon Phillips .20 .50
206 Andrew Miller RC .75 2.00
207 John Koronka .20 .50
208 Luis Castillo .20 .50
209 Angel Guzman .20 .50
210 Jim Edmonds .30 .75
211 Patrick Misch (RC) .20 .50
212 Ty Wigginton SP 2.50 6.00
213 Brandon Inge SP 2.50 6.00
214 Royce Clayton .20 .50
215 Ben Broussard .20 .50
216 St. Louis Cardinals TC .20 .50
217 Mark Mulder .20 .50
218 Kenji Johjima .50 1.25
219 Joe Crede .20 .50
220 Shea Hillenbrand .20 .50
221 Josh Fields SP (RC) 2.50 6.00
222 Pat Neshek SP 3.00 8.00
223 Reed Johnson .20 .50
224 Mike Mussina .30 .75
225 Randy Winn .20 .50
226 Brian Rogers .20 .50
227 Juan Rivera .20 .50
228 Shawn Green .20 .50
229 Mike Napoli .20 .50
230 Chase Utley SP 3.00 8.00
231 John Nelson SP (RC) 2.50 6.00
232 Casey Blake .20 .50
233 Lyle Overbay .20 .50
234 Adam LaRoche .20 .50
235 Julio Lugo .20 .50
236 Johnny Estrada .20 .50
237 James Shields .20 .50
238 Jose Castillo .20 .50
239 Doug Davis SP 2.50 6.00
240 Jason Giambi SP 2.50 6.00
241 Mike Gonzalez .20 .50
242 Scott Downs .20 .50
243 Joe Inglett .20 .50
244 Matt Kemp .40 1.00
245 Ted Lilly .20 .50
246 New York Yankees TC .50 1.25
247 Jamey Carroll .20 .50
248 Adam Wainwright SP 2.50 6.00
249 Matt Thornton SP 2.50 6.00
250 Alfonso Soriano .30 .75
251 Tom Gordon .20 .50
252 Dennis Sarfate (RC) .20 .50
253 Zach Duke .20 .50
254 Hank Blalock .20 .50
255 Johan Santana .30 .75
256 Chicago White Sox TC .20 .50
257 Aaron Cook SP 2.50 6.00
258 Cliff Lee SP 2.50 6.00
259 Miguel Tejada .30 .75
260 Mike Lowell .20 .50
261 Ian Snell .20 .50
262 Jason Tyner .20 .50
263 Troy Tulowitzki (RC) .60 1.50
264 Ervin Santana .20 .50
265 Jon Lester .30 .75
266 Andy Pettitte SP 3.00 8.00
267 A.J. Pierzynski SP 2.50 6.00
268 Rich Aurilia .20 .50
269 Phil Nevin .20 .50
270 Tom Glavine .30 .75
271 Chris Coste .20 .50
272 Moises Alou .20 .50
273 J.D. Drew .20 .50
274 Abraham Nunez .20 .50
275 Jorge Posada SP 3.00 8.00
276 Jeff Conine SP 2.50 6.00
277 Chad Cordero .20 .50
278 Nick Johnson .20 .50
279 Kevin Millar .20 .50
280 Mark Grudzielanek .20 .50
281 Chris Stewart RC .20 .50
282 Nate Robertson .20 .50
283 Drew Anderson RC .20 .50
284 Doug Mientkiewicz SP 2.50 6.00
285 Ken Griffey Jr. SP 5.00 12.00
286 Cory Sullivan .20 .50
287 Chris Carpenter .30 .75
288 Gary Matthews .20 .50
289 J.Verlander .50 1.25
Jef.Weaver
290 Vicente Padilla .20 .50
291 Chris Roberson .20 .50
292 Chris R. Young .20 .50
293 Ryan Garko SP 2.50 6.00
294 Miguel Batista SP 2.50 6.00
295 B.J. Upton .20 .50
296 Justin Verlander .50 1.25
297 Ben Zobrist .20 .50
298 Ben Sheets .20 .50
299 Eric Chavez .20 .50
300 Scott Schoeneweis .20 .50
301 Placido Polanco .20 .50
302 Angel Sanchez SP RC 2.50 6.00
303 Freddy Sanchez SP 2.50 6.00
304 M.Ordonez .30 .75
C.Monroe
305 A.J. Burnett .20 .50
306 Juan Perez RC .20 .50
307 Chris Britton .20 .50
308 Jon Garland .20 .50
309 Pedro Feliz .20 .50
310 Ryan Howard .40 1.00
311 Aaron Harang SP 2.50 6.00
312 Boston Red Sox TC SP 3.00 8.00
313 Chad Billingsley .30 .75
314 C.Jones .50 1.25
B.Cox MG
315 Bengie Molina .20 .50
316 Juan Pierre .20 .50
317 Luke Scott .20 .50
318 Javier Valentin .20 .50
319 Mark Loretta .20 .50
320 Kenny Lofton SP 2.50 6.00
321 V.Guerrero 3.00 8.00
I.Rodriguez SP
322 Josh Willingham .30 .75
323 Lance Berkman .30 .75
324 Anibal Sanchez .20 .50
325 Maicer Izturis .20 .50
326 Brett Myers .20 .50
327 Chicago Cubs TC .30 .75
328 Francisco Liriano .20 .50
329 Craig Monroe SP 2.50 6.00
330 Paul LoDuca SP 2.50 6.00
331 Steve Trachsel .20 .50
332 Bernie Williams .30 .75
333 Carlos Guillen .20 .50
334 C.Wang .30 .75
M.Mussina
335 Dave Bush .20 .50
336 Carlos Beltran .30 .75
337 Jason Isringhausen .20 .50
338 Todd Walker SP 2.50 6.00
339 Jarrod Washburn SP 2.50 6.00
340 Brandon Webb .30 .75
341 Pittsburgh Pirates TC .20 .50
342 Daryle Ward .20 .50
343 Chad Santos .20 .50
344 Brad Lidge .20 .50
345 Brad Ausmus .20 .50
346 Carlos Delgado .20 .50
347 Boone Logan SP 2.50 6.00
348 Jimmy Rollins SP 2.50 6.00
349 Orlando Hernandez .20 .50
350 Gary Sheffield .20 .50
351 Pujols .60 1.50
Belliard
Eckstein
Rolen
352 Jake Peavy .20 .50
353 Jason Varitek .50 1.25
354 Freddy Garcia .20 .50
355 Matt Diaz .20 .50
356 Bernie Castro SP 2.50 6.00
357 Eric Stults SP RC 2.50 6.00
358 John Lackey .30 .75
359 Bobby Jenks .20 .50
360 Mark Teixeira .30 .75
361 Jonathan Papelbon .50 1.25
362 Paul Konerko .30 .75
363 Erik Bedard .20 .50
364 Eliezer Alfonzo .20 .50
365 Fernando Rodney SP 2.50 6.00
366 Chris Duncan SP 2.50 6.00
367 Jose Diaz (RC) .20 .50
368 Travis Hafner .20 .50
369 Matt Capps .20 .50
370 Ivan Rodriguez .30 .75
371 David Murphy (RC) .20 .50
372 Carlos Zambrano .30 .75
373 Chris Iannetta .20 .50
374 Jose Mesa SP 2.50 6.00
375 Michael Young SP 2.50 6.00
376 Bill Bray .20 .50
377 Atlanta Braves TC .30 .75
378 Jeff Cirillo .20 .50
379 Barry Zito .30 .75
380 Clay Hensley .20 .50
381 J.J. Putz .20 .50
382 C.C. Sabathia .30 .75
383 Eduardo Perez SP 2.50 6.00
384 Scott Moore SP (RC) 2.50 6.00
385 Scott Olsen .20 .50
386 R.Howard .40 1.00
C.Utley
387 Aaron Rowand .20 .50
388 Mike Rouse .20 .50
389 Alexis Gomez .20 .50
390 Brian McCann .20 .50
391 Ryan Shealy .20 .50
392 Shane Youman SP RC 2.50 6.00
393 Melky Cabrera SP 2.50 6.00
394 Jeremy Sowers .20 .50
395 Casey Janssen .20 .50
396 Travis Chick (RC) .20 .50
397 Detroit Tigers TC .20 .50
398 Reggie Abercrombie .20 .50
399 Ricky Nolasco .20 .50
400 Tadahito Iguchi .20 .50
401 Jose Reyes SP 2.50 6.00
402 Juan Encarnacion SP 2.50 6.00
403 Brandon Harper .20 .50
404 Torii Hunter .20 .50
405 Dan Uggla .20 .50
406 Orlando Cabrera .20 .50
407 Jose Capellan .20 .50
408 Baltimore Orioles TC .20 .50
409 Frank Thomas .50 1.25
410 Francisco Rodriguez SP 2.50 6.00
411 Ian Kinsler SP 3.00 8.00
412 Billy Wagner .20 .50
413 Andy Marte .20 .50
414 Mike Jacobs .20 .50
415 Raul Ibanez .30 .75
416 Jhonny Peralta .20 .50
417 Chris B. Young .20 .50
418 A.Pujols .60 1.50
M.Ordonez
419 Scott Kazmir SP 3.00 8.00
420 Norris Hopper SP 2.50 6.00
421 Chris Capuano .20 .50
422 Troy Glaus .20 .50
423 Roy Oswalt .30 .75
424 Grady Sizemore .30 .75
425 Chone Figgins .20 .50
426 Chad Tracy .20 .50
427 Brian Fuentes .20 .50
428 Cincinnati Reds TC SP 2.50 6.00
429 Ramon Hernandez SP 2.50 6.0
430 Mike Cameron .20 .5
431 Dontrelle Willis .20 .5
432 Josh Sharpless .20 .5
433 Adrian Beltre .50 1.2
434 Curtis Granderson .40 1.0
435 B.J. Ryan .20 .5
436 D.Wright .40 1.0
R.Howard
437 Vernon Wells SP 2.50 6.0
438 Vladimir Guerrero SP 3.00 8.0
439 Jake Westbrook .20 .5
440 Chipper Jones .50 1.2
441 James Loney .20 .5
442 Nook Logan .20 .5
443 Oswaldo Navarro RC .20 .5
444 Joe Mauer .40 1.0
445 Miguel Montero (RC) .20 .50
446 Franklin Gutierrez SP 2.50 6.00
447 Mark Redman SP 2.50 6.00
448 Mike Rabelo RC .20 .50
449 Philip Humber (RC) .20 .50
450 Justin Morneau .30 .75
451 Hector Gimenez (RC) .20 .50
452 Matt Holliday .50 1.25
453 Akinori Otsuka .20 .50
454 Prince Fielder .30 .75
455 Chien-Ming Wang SP 4.00 10.00
456 Shawn Riggans SP 2.50 6.00
457 John Maine .20 .50
458 Adam Lind (RC) .20 .50
459 Ubaldo Jimenez (RC) .60 1.50
460 Jaret Wright .20 .50
461 Cla Meredith .20 .50
462 Joaquin Arias (RC) .20 .50
463 Kenny Rogers .20 .50
464 Jose Garcia SP RC 2.50 6.00
465 Pedro Martinez SP 3.00 8.00
466 Jeff Salazar (RC) .20 .50
467 Glen Perkins .20 .50
468 Travis Ishikawa .20 .50
469 Joe Borowski .20 .50
470 Jeremy Brown .20 .50
471 Andre Ethier .30 .75
472 Taylor Tankersley .20 .50
473 Lastings Milledge SP 3.00 8.00
474 Brian Sanches SP 2.50 6.00
475 O.Guillen AS MG .20 .50
P.Garner AS MG
476 Albert Pujols AS .60 1.50
477 David Ortiz AS .50 1.25
478 Chase Utley AS .30 .75
479 Mark Loretta AS .20 .50
480 David Wright AS .40 1.00
481 Alex Rodriguez AS .60 1.50
482 Edgar Renteria AS SP 2.50 6.00
483 Derek Jeter AS SP 10.00 25.00
484 Alfonso Soriano AS .30 .75
485 Vladimir Guerrero AS .30 .75
486 Carlos Beltran AS .30 .75
487 Vernon Wells AS .20 .50
488 Jason Bay AS .30 .75
489 Ichiro Suzuki AS .60 1.50
490 Paul LoDuca AS .20 .50
491 Ivan Rodriguez AS SP 3.00 8.00
492 Brad Penny AS SP 2.50 6.00
493 Roy Halladay AS .30 .75
494 Brian Fuentes AS .20 .50
495 Kenny Rogers AS .20 .50

2007 Topps Heritage Chrome

STATED ODDS 1:11 HOBBY, 1:12 RETAIL
STATED PRINT RUN 1958 SERIAL #'d SETS
THC1 David Ortiz 2.50 6.00
THC2 John Smoltz 2.50 6.00
THC3 San Francisco Giants TC 1.00 2.50
THC4 Brian Giles 1.00 2.50
THC5 Billy Sadler 1.00 2.50
THC6 Joel Zumaya 1.00 2.50
THC7 Felipe Lopez 1.00 2.50
THC8 Tim Hudson 1.50 4.00
THC9 David Ross 1.00 2.50
THC10 Adam Kennedy 1.00 2.50
THC11 David DeJesus 1.00 2.50
THC12 Jose Contreras 1.00 2.50
THC13 Trot Nixon 1.00 2.50
THC14 Roy Halladay 1.50 4.00
THC15 Gil Meche 1.00 2.50
THC16 Ray Durham 1.00 2.50
THC17 Delwyn Young 1.00 2.50
THC18 Endy Chavez 1.00 2.50
THC19 Vinny Rottino 1.00 2.50
THC20 Austin Kearns 1.00 2.50
THC21 Jeremy Hermida 1.00 2.50
THC22 Jonathan Broxton 1.00 2.50
THC23 Josh Fogg 1.00 2.50
THC24 Angel Guzman 1.00 2.50
THC25 Kenji Johjima 2.50 6.00
THC26 Juan Rivera 1.00 2.50
THC27 Johnny Estrada 1.00 2.50
THC28 Ted Lilly 1.00 2.50
THC29 Hank Blalock 1.00 2.50

THC30 Troy Tulowitzki 3.00 8.00
THC31 Moises Alou 1.00 2.50
THC32 Chris Stewart 1.00 2.50
THC33 Vicente Padilla 1.00 2.50
THC34 Eric Chavez 1.00 2.50
THC35 Jon Garland 1.00 2.50
THC36 Luke Scott 1.00 2.50
THC37 Brett Myers 1.00 2.50
THC38 Dave Bush 1.00 2.50
THC39 Brad Lidge 1.00 2.50
THC40 Jason Varitek 2.50 6.00
THC41 Paul Konerko 1.50 4.00
THC42 David Murphy 1.00 2.50
THC43 Clay Hensley 1.00 2.50
THC44 Alexis Gomez 1.00 2.50
THC45 Reggie Abercrombie 1.00 2.50
THC46 Jose Capellan 1.00 2.50
THC47 Jhonny Peralta 1.00 2.50
THC48 Chone Figgins 1.00 2.50
THC49 Curtis Granderson 2.00 5.00
THC50 Oswaldo Navarro 1.00 2.50
THC51 Matt Holliday 2.50 6.00
THC52 Cla Meredith 1.00 2.50
THC53 Jeremy Brown 1.00 2.50
THC54 Mark Loretta AS 1.00 2.50
THC55 Jason Bay AS 1.50 4.00
THC56 Roger Clemens 3.00 8.00
THC57 Rob Mackowiak 1.00 2.50
THC58 Robinson Cano 1.50 4.00
THC59 Jose Lopez 1.00 2.50
THC60 Dave Roberts 1.50 4.00
THC61 Delmon Young 1.50 4.00
THC62 Ryan Sweeney 1.00 2.50
THC63 Chris Narveson 1.00 2.50
THC64 Juan Uribe 1.00 2.50
THC65 Tony Gwynn Jr. 1.00 2.50
THC66 David Wright 2.00 5.00
THC67 Miguel Cairo 1.00 2.50
THC68 Edgar Renteria 1.00 2.50
THC69 Victor Martinez 1.50 4.00
THC70 Willy Aybar 1.00 2.50
THC71 Luke Hudson 1.00 2.50
THC72 Chuck James 1.00 2.50
THC73 Kris Benson 1.00 2.50
THC74 Garret Anderson 1.00 2.50
THC75 Oakland Athletics TC 1.00 2.50
THC76 Tim Wakefield 1.50 4.00
THC77 Mike Piazza 2.50 6.00
THC78 Carlos Lee 1.00 2.50
THC79 Jim Edmonds 1.50 4.00
THC80 Joe Crede 1.00 2.50
THC81 Shawn Green 1.00 2.50
THC82 James Shields 1.00 2.50
THC83 New York Yankees TC 2.50 6.00
THC84 Johan Santana 1.50 4.00
THC85 Ervin Santana 1.00 2.50
THC86 J.D. Drew 1.00 2.50
THC87 Nate Robertson 1.00 2.50
THC88 Chris Roberson 1.00 2.50
THC89 Scott Schoeneweis 1.00 2.50
THC90 Pedro Feliz 1.00 2.50
THC91 Javier Valentin 1.00 2.50
THC92 Chicago Cubs TC 1.00 2.50
THC93 Carlos Beltran 1.50 4.00
THC94 Brad Ausmus 1.00 2.50
THC95 Freddy Garcia 1.00 2.50
THC96 Erik Bedard 1.00 2.50
THC97 Carlos Zambrano 1.50 4.00
THC98 J.J. Putz 1.00 2.50
THC99 Brian McCann 1.00 2.50
THC100 Ricky Nolasco 1.00 2.50
THC101 Baltimore Orioles TC 1.00 2.50
THC102 Chris B. Young 1.00 2.50
THC103 Chad Tracy 1.00 2.50
THC104 B.J. Ryan 1.00 2.50
THC105 Joe Mauer 2.00 5.00
THC106 Akinori Otsuka 1.00 2.50
THC107 Joaquin Arias 1.00 2.50
THC108 Andre Ethier 1.50 4.00
THC109 David Wright AS 2.00 5.00
THC110 Ichiro Suzuki AS 3.00 8.00

2007 Topps Heritage Chrome Refractors

*CHROME REF: 1X TO 2.5X
STATED ODDS 1:39 HOBBY, 1:40 RETAIL
STATED PRINT RUN 558 SERIAL #'d SETS

2007 Topps Heritage Chrome Black Refractors

STATED ODDS 1:383 HOBBY/RETAIL
STATED PRINT RUN 58 SERIAL #'d SETS
THC1 David Ortiz 30.00 80.00
THC2 John Smoltz 30.00 80.00
THC3 San Francisco Giants TC 12.00 30.00
THC4 Brian Giles 12.00 30.00
THC5 Billy Sadler 12.00 30.00
THC6 Joel Zumaya 12.00 30.00
THC7 Felipe Lopez 12.00 30.00
THC8 Tim Hudson 20.00 50.00
THC9 David Ross 12.00 30.00
THC10 Adam Kennedy 12.00 30.00
THC11 David DeJesus 12.00 30.00
THC12 Jose Contreras 12.00 30.00
THC13 Trot Nixon 12.00 30.00
THC14 Roy Halladay 20.00 50.00
THC15 Gil Meche 12.00 30.00
THC16 Ray Durham 12.00 30.00
THC17 Delwyn Young 12.00 30.00
THC18 Endy Chavez 12.00 30.00
THC19 Vinny Rottino 12.00 30.00
THC20 Austin Kearns 12.00 30.00
THC21 Jeremy Hermida 12.00 30.00
THC22 Jonathan Broxton 12.00 30.00
THC23 Josh Fogg 12.00 30.00
THC24 Angel Guzman 12.00 30.00
THC25 Kenji Johjima 30.00 80.00
THC26 Juan Rivera 12.00 30.00
THC27 Johnny Estrada 12.00 30.00
THC28 Ted Lilly 12.00 30.00
THC29 Hank Blalock 12.00 30.00
THC30 Troy Tulowitzki 40.00 100.00
THC31 Moises Alou 12.00 30.00
THC32 Chris Stewart 12.00 30.00
THC33 Vicente Padilla 12.00 30.00
THC34 Eric Chavez 12.00 30.00
THC35 Jon Garland 12.00 30.00
THC36 Luke Scott 12.00 30.00
THC37 Brett Myers 12.00 30.00
THC38 Dave Bush 12.00 30.00
THC39 Brad Lidge 12.00 30.00
THC40 Jason Varitek 30.00 80.00
THC41 Paul Konerko 20.00 50.00
THC42 David Murphy 12.00 30.00
THC43 Clay Hensley 12.00 30.00
THC44 Alexis Gomez 12.00 30.00
THC45 Reggie Abercrombie 12.00 30.00
THC46 Jose Capellan 12.00 30.00
THC47 Jhonny Peralta 12.00 30.00
THC48 Chone Figgins 12.00 30.00
THC49 Curtis Granderson 25.00 60.00
THC50 Oswaldo Navarro 12.00 30.00
THC51 Matt Holliday 30.00 80.00
THC52 Cla Meredith 12.00 30.00
THC53 Jeremy Brown 12.00 30.00
THC54 Mark Loretta AS 12.00 30.00
THC55 Jason Bay AS 20.00 50.00
THC56 Roger Clemens 40.00 100.00
THC57 Rob Mackowiak 12.00 30.00
THC58 Robinson Cano 20.00 50.00
THC59 Jose Lopez 12.00 30.00
THC60 Dave Roberts 20.00 50.00
THC61 Delmon Young 20.00 50.00
THC62 Ryan Sweeney 12.00 30.00
THC63 Chris Narveson 12.00 30.00
THC64 Juan Uribe 12.00 30.00
THC65 Tony Gwynn Jr. 12.00 30.00
THC66 David Wright 25.00 60.00
THC67 Miguel Cairo 12.00 30.00
THC68 Edgar Renteria 12.00 30.00
THC69 Victor Martinez 20.00 50.00
THC70 Willy Aybar 12.00 30.00
THC71 Luke Hudson 12.00 30.00
THC72 Chuck James 12.00 30.00
THC73 Kris Benson 12.00 30.00
THC74 Garret Anderson 12.00 30.00
THC75 Oakland Athletics TC 12.00 30.00
THC76 Tim Wakefield 20.00 50.00
THC77 Mike Piazza 30.00 80.00
THC78 Carlos Lee 12.00 30.00
THC79 Jim Edmonds 20.00 50.00
THC80 Joe Crede 12.00 30.00
THC81 Shawn Green 12.00 30.00
THC82 James Shields 12.00 30.00
THC83 New York Yankees TC 30.00 80.00
THC84 Johan Santana 20.00 50.00
THC85 Ervin Santana 12.00 30.00
THC86 J.D. Drew 12.00 30.00
THC87 Nate Robertson 12.00 30.00
THC88 Chris Roberson 12.00 30.00
THC89 Scott Schoeneweis 12.00 30.00
THC90 Pedro Feliz 12.00 30.00
THC91 Javier Valentin 12.00 30.00
THC92 Chicago Cubs TC 12.00 30.00
THC93 Carlos Beltran 20.00 50.00
THC94 Brad Ausmus 12.00 30.00
THC95 Freddy Garcia 12.00 30.00
THC96 Erik Bedard 12.00 30.00
THC97 Carlos Zambrano 20.00 50.00
THC98 J.J. Putz 12.00 30.00
THC99 Brian McCann 12.00 30.00
THC100 Ricky Nolasco 12.00 30.00
THC101 Baltimore Orioles TC 12.00 30.00
THC102 Chris B. Young 12.00 30.00
THC103 Chad Tracy 12.00 30.00
THC104 B.J. Ryan 12.00 30.00
THC105 Joe Mauer 25.00 60.00
THC106 Akinori Otsuka 12.00 30.00
THC107 Joaquin Arias 12.00 30.00
THC108 Andre Ethier 20.00 50.00
THC109 David Wright AS 25.00 60.00
THC110 Ichiro Suzuki AS 40.00 100.00

2007 Topps Heritage '58 Home Run Champion

COMPLETE SET (42) 30.00 60.00
COMMON MANTLE .60 1.50
STATED ODDS 1:6 HOBBY, 1:6 RETAIL

2007 Topps Heritage Clubhouse Collection Relics

GROUP A ODDS 1:2425 HOBBY/RETAIL
GROUP B ODDS 1:202 HOBBY/RETAIL
GROUP C ODDS 1:67 HOBBY/RETAIL
GROUP D ODDS 1:808 HOBBY/RETAIL
AJP Albert Pujols Pants C 8.00 20.00
AK Al Kaline Bat C 8.00 20.00
ALR Anthony Reyes Jsy C 3.00 8.00
AR Alex Rodriguez Bat C 8.00 20.00
AW Adam Wainwright Jsy C 4.00 10.00
BR Brian Roberts Jsy B 3.00 8.00
BR Brooks Robinson Pants C 6.00 15.00
BS Ben Sheets Bat B 4.00 10.00
BU B.J. Upton Bat C 3.00 8.00
BW Billy Wagner Jsy C 3.00 8.00
BZ Barry Zito Pants D 3.00 8.00
CC Chris Carpenter Jsy C 3.00 8.00
CD Chris Duncan Jsy C 6.00 15.00
CJ Chipper Jones Jsy C 4.00 10.00
CJ Conor Jackson Bat B 3.00 8.00
CU Chase Utley Jsy B 5.00 12.00
DE David Eckstein Bat B 6.00 15.00
DM Doug Mientkiewicz Bat C 3.00 8.00
DO David Ortiz Jsy C 4.00 10.00
DS Duke Snider Pants C 6.00 15.00
DW David Wright Jsy A 12.50 30.00
DWW Dontrelle Willis Jsy C 3.00 8.00
DY Delmon Young Bat C 3.00 8.00
EC Eric Chavez Pants C 3.00 8.00
ER Edgar Renteria Bat C 3.00 8.00
ES Ervin Santana Jsy C 3.00 8.00
FL Francisco Liriano Jsy C 4.00 10.00
FR Frank Robinson Pants C 3.00 8.00
GS Gary Sheffield Bat C 3.00 8.00
HB Hank Blalock Jsy B 3.00 8.00
IR Ivan Rodriguez Jsy B 10.00 25.00
JBR Jose Reyes Jsy A 8.00 20.00
JD Johnny Damon Bat C 4.00 10.00
JM Justin Morneau Bat A 6.00 15.00
JP Juan Pierre Bat B 3.00 8.00
JR Jimmy Rollins Jsy C 3.00 8.00
JRP Jorge Posada Pants C 4.00 10.00
JS Jeff Suppan Jsy C 3.00 8.00
JSA Johan Santana Jsy C 4.00 10.00
JV Jose Vidro Bat B 3.00 8.00
JW Jeff Weaver Jsy C 3.00 8.00
LB Lance Berkman Jsy B 3.00 8.00
LG Luis Gonzalez Bat C 3.00 8.00
MA Moises Alou Bat C 3.00 8.00
MC Miguel Cabrera Bat B 4.00 10.00
MK Mark Kotsay Bat B 3.00 8.00
MM Melvin Mora Jsy C 3.00 8.00
MO Magglio Ordonez Bat C 3.00 8.00
MOT Miguel Tejada Pants C 3.00 8.00
MP Mike Piazza Bat B 6.00 15.00
MR Manny Ramirez Jsy C 4.00 10.00
MT Mark Teixeira Jsy B 4.00 10.00
NS Nick Swisher Jsy C 3.00 8.00
OV Omar Vizquel Bat C 4.00 10.00
PB Pat Burrell Bat B 3.00 8.00
PP Placido Polanco Bat B 10.00 25.00
RB Ronnie Belliard Bat B 3.00 8.00
RF Rafael Furcal Bat D 3.00 8.00
RH Ryan Howard Bat A 12.50 30.00
RS Richie Sexson Bat B 3.00 8.00
SM Stan Musial Pants B 12.50 30.00
TH Todd Helton Jsy B 4.00 10.00
TKH Torii Hunter Jsy B 3.00 8.00
VM Victor Martinez Jsy B 3.00 8.00
YB Yogi Berra Bat B 12.50 30.00
YM Yadier Molina Jsy B 10.00 25.00

2007 Topps Heritage Clubhouse Collection Relics Autographs

STATED ODDS 1:16,100 HOBBY
STATED ODDS 1:16,275 RETAIL
STATED PRINT RUN 25 SER.#'d SETS
NO PRICING DUE TO SCARCITY

2007 Topps Heritage Clubhouse Collection Relics Dual

STATED ODDS 1:13,900 HOBBY
STATED ODDS 1:14,000 RETAIL
STATED PRINT RUN 58 SER.#'d SETS
BR Y.Berra P/A.Rodriguez P 125.00 250.00
KR A.Kaline B/I.Rodriguez B 75.00 150.00
MP S.Musial P/A.Pujols P 125.00 250.00

2007 Topps Heritage Felt Logos

COMPLETE SET (13) 20.00 50.00
1 PER HOBBY BOX TOPPER
BOS Boston Red Sox 5.00 12.00
CHC Chicago Cubs 2.00 5.00
CHW Chicago White Sox 2.00 5.00
CIN Cincinnati Redlegs 2.00 5.00
KCA Kansas City Athletics 2.00 5.00
LAD Los Angeles Dodgers 2.00 5.00
NYY New York Yankees 5.00 12.00
PHI Philadelphia Phillies 2.00 5.00
PIT Pittsburgh Pirates 2.00 5.00
SFG San Francisco Giants 2.00 5.00
STL St. Louis Cardinals 2.00 5.00
WAS Washington Senators 2.00 5.00
BAL Baltimore Orioles 2.00 5.00

2007 Topps Heritage Flashbacks

COMPLETE SET (10) 5.00 12.00
STATED ODDS 1:12 HOBBY, 1:12 RETAIL
FB1 Al Kaline .75 2.00
FB2 Brooks Robinson .50 1.25
FB3 Red Schoendienst .50 1.25
FB4 Warren Spahn .50 1.25
FB5 Stan Musial 1.25 3.00
FB6 Lew Burdette .30 .75
FB7 Eddie Yost .30 .75
FB8 Jim Bunning .50 1.25
FB9 Richie Ashburn .50 1.25
FB10 Hoyt Wilhelm .50 1.25

2007 Topps Heritage Flashbacks Seat Relics

STATED ODDS 1:484 HOBBY, 1:484 RETAIL
AK Al Kaline 10.00 25.00
BR Brooks Robinson 10.00 25.00
EY Eddie Yost 8.00 20.00
HW Hoyt Wilhelm 8.00 20.00
JB Jim Bunning 10.00 25.00
RA Richie Ashburn 8.00 20.00
LB Lew Burdette 8.00 20.00
RS Red Schoendienst 8.00 20.00
SM Stan Musial 8.00 20.00
WS Warren Spahn 10.00 25.00

2007 Topps Heritage New Age Performers

COMPLETE SET (15) 10.00 25.00
STATED ODDS 1:15 HOBBY, 1:15 RETAIL
NP1 Ryan Howard .75 2.00
NP2 Alex Rodriguez 1.25 3.00
NP3 Alfonso Soriano .60 1.50
NP4 David Ortiz 1.00 2.50
NP5 Trevor Hoffman .60 1.50
NP6 Derek Jeter 2.50 6.00
NP7 Anibal Sanchez .40 1.00
NP8 Roger Clemens 1.25 3.00
NP9 Johan Santana .60 1.50
NP10 Albert Pujols 1.25 3.00
NP11 Chipper Jones 1.00 2.50
NP12 Frank Thomas 1.00 2.50
NP13 Ivan Rodriguez .60 1.50
NP14 Ichiro Suzuki 1.25 3.00
NP15 Craig Biggio .60 1.50

2007 Topps Heritage Real One Autographs

STATED ODDS 1:327 HOBBY, 1:328 RETAIL
STATED PRINT RUN 200 SETS
CARDS ARE NOT SERIAL-NUMBERED
PRINT RUN INFO PROVIDED BY TOPPS
RED INK ODDS 1:1129 HOBBY/RETAIL
RED INK PRINT RUN 58 SERIAL #'d SETS
RED INK ALSO CALLED SPECIAL EDITION
EXCHANGE DEADLINE 02/28/09
AK Al Kaline 30.00 80.00
BH Bob Henrich 10.00 25.00
BM Bobby Morgan 10.00 25.00
BP Buddy Pritchard 10.00 25.00
BR Brooks Robinson 40.00 100.00
BT Bill Taylor 10.00 25.00
BW Bill Wight 10.00 25.00
CH Chuck Harmon 10.00 25.00
CJD Jim Derrington 10.00 25.00
CR Charley Rabe 10.00 25.00
DM Dave Melton 10.00 25.00
DS Duke Snider 30.00 80.00
DW David Wright 30.00 80.00
DWW Dontrelle Willis 10.00 25.00
DY Delmon Young 10.00 25.00
DZ Don Zimmer 25.00 60.00
EN Ed Mayer 12.50 30.00
GK George Kell 12.00 30.00
HP Harding Peterson 12.50 30.00
JB Jim Bunning 25.00 60.00
JC Joe Caffie 10.00 25.00
JD Joe Durham 12.50 30.00
JL Joe Lonnett 12.50 30.00
JM Justin Morneau 20.00 50.00
JP Johnny Podres 10.00 25.00
LA Luis Aparicio 30.00 80.00
LM Lloyd Merritt 10.00 25.00
LS Lou Sleater 10.00 25.00
MB Milt Bolling 10.00 25.00
MEB Mack Burk 10.00 25.00
OH Orlando Hudson 12.50 30.00
PS Paul Smith 10.00 25.00
RC Ray Crone 10.00 25.00
RH Ryan Howard 12.00 30.00
RS Red Schoendienst 25.00 60.00
SP Stan Palys 10.00 25.00
TT Tim Thompson 20.00 50.00

2007 Topps Heritage Real One Autographs Red Ink

*RED INK: .75X TO 2X BASIC
STATED ODDS 1:1129 HOBBY/RETAIL
STATED PRINT RUN 58 SERIAL #'d SETS
RED INK ALSO CALLED SPECIAL EDITION
EXCHANGE DEADLINE 02/28/09

2007 Topps Heritage Then and Now

COMPLETE SET (10) 8.00 20.00
STATED ODDS 1:15 HOBBY, 1:15 RETAIL
TN1 F.Robinson/R.Howard .60 1.50
TN2 M.Mantle/D.Ortiz 2.50 6.00
TN3 T.Williams/J.Mauer 1.50 4.00
TN4 L.Aparicio/J.Reyes .50 1.25
TN5 L.Burdette/J.Santana .50 1.25
TN6 J.Podres/A.Harang .30 .75
TN7 R.Ashburn/I.Suzuki 1.00 2.50
TN8 S.Musial/T.Hafner 1.25 3.00
TN9 J.Bunning/A.Sanchez .50 1.25
TN10 W.Spahn/C.Wang .50 1.25

2007 Topps Heritage National Convention '57

408 Roger Maris 1.50 4.00
409 Roberto Clemente 4.00 10.00
410 Mickey Mantle 5.00 12.00
411 Mickey Mantle/Yogi Berra 5.00 12.00
412 Bob Feller 1.00 2.50

2008 Topps Heritage

COMP.SET w/o SP's (425) 40.00 80.00
COMP.HN SET (220) 125.00 200.00
COMP.HN SET w/o SP's (150) 12.50 30.00
COMMON CARD .15 .40
COMMON RC .40 1.00
COMMON TEAM CARD .15 .40
COMMON GB SP .40 1.00
COMMON SP 2.50 6.00
SP STATED ODDS 1:3 HOBBY/RETAIL
HN SP ODDS 1:3 HOBBY/RETAIL
1 Vladimir Guerrero .25 .60
2 Placido Polanco GB SP .40 1.00
3 Eric Byrnes GB SP .40 1.00
4 Mark Teixeira .25 .60
5 Javier Vazquez GB SP .40 1.00
6 Jacoby Ellsbury .30 .75
7 Joey Gathright GB SP .40 1.00
8 Philadelphia Phillies GB SP .40 1.00
9 Andre Ethier GB SP .60 1.50
10 Alex Rodriguez .50 1.25
11 Luke Scott SP 2.50 6.00
12 Curt Schilling GB SP .60 1.50
13 Billy Wagner GB SP .40 1.00
14 Gary Matthews GB SP .40 1.00
15 Sean Marshall .15 .40
16 I.Suzuki GB SP 1.25 3.00
17 Wilson/Bay/Sanchez .25 .60
18 Dontrelle Willis GB SP .40 1.00
19 Josh Willingham .25 .60
20 Jeff Kent .15 .40
21 Troy Tulowitzki GB SP 1.00 2.50
22 Brian Fuentes GB SP .40 1.00
23 Robinson Cano GB SP .60 1.50
24 Felix Hernandez GB SP .60 1.50
25 Edwin Encarnacion .40 1.00
26 Fausto Carmona .15 .40
27 Greg Maddux .50 1.25
28 Ivan Rodriguez GB SP .60 1.50
29 Joe Nathan .15 .40
30 Paul Konerko .25 .60
31 Nook Logan .15 .40
32 Derek Lowe .15 .40
33 Jose Lopez .15 .40
34 Ordonez/Granderson GB SP .60 1.50
35 Adam LaRoche GB SP .40 1.00
36 Kenny Lofton .15 .40
37 Matt Capps .15 .40
38 Mark Reynolds .15 .40
39 Joe Mauer .30 .75
40 Tim Hudson GB SP .60 1.50
41 Kelvim Escobar GB SP .60 1.50
42 Jason Jennings GB SP .40 1.00
43 Victor Martinez .25 .60
44 Jason Kendall .15 .40
45 Chris Ray GB SP .40 1.00
46 Jason Bergmann .15 .40
47 Jason Marquis .15 .40
48 Baltimore Orioles .15 .40
49 Bill Hall GB SP .40 1.00
50 Ken Griffey Jr. .75 2.00
51 Chad Cordero .15 .40
52 Omar Vizquel GB SP .60 1.50
53 Jim Edmonds .25 .60
54 Justin Upton GB SP .60 1.50
55 Josh Beckett .15 .40
56 Jeff Francis .15 .40
57 Brad Lidge GB SP .40 1.00
58 Paul Lo Duca GB SP .40 1.00
59 John Patterson .15 .40
60 Andy Pettitte GB SP .60 1.50
61 Brendan Harris GB SP .40 1.00
62 Chris Young GB SP .40 1.00
63 Eric Chavez .15 .40
64 Francisco Rodriguez .25 .60
65 Jason Giambi GB SP .40 1.00
66 B.J. Ryan .15 .40
67 Rich Hill GB SP .40 1.00
68 Derek Jeter 1.00 2.50
69 San Francisco Giants GB SP .40 1.00
70 Carlos Guillen .15 .40
71 Trevor Hoffman GB SP .60 1.50
72 Zach Duke .15 .40
73 Dustin Pedroia .25 .60
74 D.Young/R.Zimmerman .25 .60
75 Cole Hamels .30 .75
76 Carlos Delgado .15 .40
77 Jonathan Broxton .15 .40
78 J.Hamilton GB SP .60 1.50
79 Mark Loretta GB SP .60 1.50
80 Grady Sizemore .25 .60
81 Torii Hunter GB SP .40 1.00
82 Carlos Beltran GB SP .60 1.50
83 Jason Isringhausen GB SP .40 1.00
84 Brad Penny GB SP .40 1.00
85 Jayson Werth .25 .60
86 Alex Gordon .25 .60
87 David DeJesus .15 .40
88 Clay Buchholz .25 .60
89 Conor Jackson .15 .40
90 Hideki Matsui GB SP 1.00 2.50
91 Matt Garza GB SP .40 1.00
92 P.Hughes GB SP .40 1.00
93 Mike Piazza .40 1.00
94 Chicago White Sox GB SP .40 1.00
95 Buddy Carlyle .15 .40
96 Mark DeRosa .15 .40
97 Brandon Webb .25 .60
98 Jon Garland GB SP .40 1.00
99 Mariano Rivera .50 1.25
100 Jack Cust .15 .40
101 Carlos Ruiz .15 .40
102 Moises Alou GB SP .40 1.00
103 Bengie Molina .15 .40
104 Adam Jones .25 .60
105 Alfonso Soriano .25 .60
106 Troy Glaus .25 .60
107 John Maine .15 .40
108 Pat Burrell .15 .40
109 David Eckstein .15 .40
110 Homer Bailey .25 .60
111 Cincinnati Reds .15 .40
112 Corey Hart .15 .40
113 Orlando Hernandez .15 .40
114 Orlando Cabrera .25 .60
115 Ryan Garko .15 .40
116 Wladimir Balentien GB SP (RC) .40 1.00
117 Daric Barton GB SP (RC) .40 1.00
118 Emilio Bonifacio RC 1.00 2.50
119 Lance Broadway (RC) .40 1.00
120 Jeff Clement (RC) .60 1.50
121 Dave Davidson RC .60 1.50
122 Ross Detwiler GB SP RC .60 1.50
123 Sam Fuld RC 1.25 3.00
124 Armando Galarraga RC .60 1.50
125 Harvey Garcia (RC) .40 1.00
126 Dan Giese GB SP (RC) .40 1.00
127 Alberto Gonzalez GB SP RC .60 1.50
128 Kevin Hart (RC) .40 1.00
129 Luke Hochevar GB SP RC .60 1.50
130 Chin-Lung Hu GB SP (RC) .40 1.00
131 Brandon Jones RC 1.00 2.50
132 Joe Koshansky (RC) .40 1.00
133 Radhames Liz RC .60 1.50
134 Donny Lucy (RC) .40 1.00
135 Mitch Stetter GB SP RC .60 1.50
136 Nyjer Morgan (RC) .40 1.00
137 Ross Ohlendorf RC .60 1.50
138 Steve Pearce RC 2.00 5.00
139 Jeff Ridgway RC .60 1.50
140 Bronson Sardinha (RC) .40 1.00
141 Seth Smith (RC) .40 1.00
142 Rich Thompson RC .60 1.50
143 Erick Threets (RC) .40 1.00
144 J.R. Towles RC .60 1.50
145 Eugenio Velez RC .40 1.00
146 Joey Votto (RC) 1.50 4.00
147 Soriano/A.Ramirez/D.Lee .25 .60
148 Hunter Pence .25 .60
149 Barry Zito .25 .60
150 Albert Pujols 1.25 3.00
151 Sammy Sosa .40 1.00
152 Brian Bannister .15 .40
153 Reggie Willits .15 .40
154 Bobby Abreu .15 .40
155 Johnny Damon GB SP .60 1.50
156 B.Webb/J.Peavy .25 .60
157 Aramis Ramirez .15 .40
158 Aaron Cook .15 .40
159 David Weathers .15 .40
160 Jack Wilson .15 .40
161 Josh Fogg .15 .40
162 Garrett Atkins .15 .40
163 Brad Ausmus .15 .40
164 Gil Meche .15 .40
165 Jeff Francoeur .25 .60
166 V.Mart/Hafner/Sizemore .25 .60
167 Juan Pierre .15 .40
168 Rafael Furcal .15 .40
169 J.J. Hardy .15 .40
170 Nick Markakis .30 .75
171 Delmon Young .25 .60
172 Oakland Athletics .15 .40
173 Ronny Paulino GB SP .40 1.00
174 Mike Cameron GB SP .40 1.00
175 Jeff Weaver GB SP .40 1.00
176 Preston Wilson GB SP .40 1.00
177 Robinson Tejada GB SP .40 1.00
178 Adam Lind GB SP .40 1.00
179 Austin Kearns GB SP .40 1.00
180 Jorge Posada GB SP .60 1.50
181 Tadahito Iguchi .15 .40
182 Matt Cain .25 .60
183 Yunjesky Betancourt .15 .40
184 Bronson Arroyo .15 .40
185 Brad Hawpe GB SP .40 1.00
186 Rickie Weeks GB SP .40 1.00
187 Carlos Silva GB SP .40 1.00
188 Adrian Gonzalez .25 .60
189 Kenji Johjima .15 .40
190 Chris Duncan .15 .40
191 James Shields .15 .40
192 Akinori Iwamura .15 .40
193 David Murphy .15 .40
194 Alex Rios .15 .40
195 Carlos Quentin GB SP .40 1.00
196 Jose Valverde GB SP .40 1.00
197 Derrek Lee GB SP .40 1.00
198 Jerry Owens GB SP .40 1.00
199 Russell Martin .15 .40
200 Yovani Gallardo .15 .40
201a Johan Santana Twins .25 .60
201b J.Santana Mets 30.00 60.00
202 Nick Swisher .25 .60
203 So Taguchi .15 .40
204 Justin Morneau .25 .60
205 Milton Bradley .15 .40
206 Jake Westbrook .15 .40
207 Dave Roberts .25 .60
208 Billy Butler .15 .40
209 Lance Berkman .25 .60
210 J.J. Putz GB SP .40 1.00
211 Mike Sweeney GB SP .40 1.00
212 A.Jones/C.Jones .40 1.00
213 Ricky Nolasco .15 .40
214 Andy LaRoche .15 .40
215 Ray Durham .15 .40
216 Francisco Cordero .15 .40
217 Jered Weaver .25 .60
218 Rafael Soriano .15 .40
219 Orlando Hudson .15 .40
220 Mike Lowell .15 .40
221 Chris Snyder .15 .40
222 Cesar Izturis .15 .40
223 St. Louis Cardinals .15 .40
224 D.Wright GB SP .60 1.50
225 Pedro Martinez GB SP .60 1.50
226 Rich Harden GB SP .40 1.00
227 Shane Victorino GB SP .40 1.00
228 Andrew Miller GB SP .60 1.50
229 Chris Young .15 .40
230 Andruw Jones .15 .40
231 Kevin Gregg SP 2.50 6.00
232 C.C. Sabathia .25 .60
233 Hanley Ramirez .25 .60
234 Wandy Rodriguez .15 .40
235 Roy Oswalt .25 .60
236 Mark Grudzielanek .15 .40
237 Jeter/Wang/Cano 1.00 2.50
238 Todd Helton .25 .60
239 Zack Greinke .25 .60
240 Carlos Gomez .15 .40
241 Lastings Milledge .15 .40
242 Huston Street .25 .60
243 Dan Haren .15 .40
244 Carlos Pena .25 .60
245 Brad Wilkerson .15 .40
246 Roy Halladay .25 .60
247 Dmitri Young .15 .40
248 Boston Red Sox .60 1.50
249 Jonathan Papelbon .25 .60
250 Felix Pie .15 .40
251 Alex Gonzalez .15 .40
252 Bobby Crosby .15 .40
253 Justin Ruggiano RC .60 1.50
254 Freddy Garcia .15 .40
255 Khalil Greene .15 .40
256 Rich Aurilia .15 .40
257 Jarrod Washburn .15 .40
258 B.J. Upton .25 .60
259 Michael Young .15 .40
260 Carlos Zambrano .25 .60
261 Livan Hernandez .15 .40
262 Billingsley/Lowe/Penny GB SP .60 1.50
263 Melky Cabrera GB SP .40 1.00
264 Shannon Stewart GB SP .40 1.00
265 Aaron Rowand GB SP .40 1.00
266 Matt Morris GB SP .40 1.00
267 Xavier Nady GB SP .40 1.00
268 Jim Thome .25 .60
269 Horacio Ramirez .15 .40
270 Prince Fielder .25 .60
271 Andy Phillips .15 .40
272 Aaron Harang .15 .40
273 Josh Barfield .15 .40
274 Ubaldo Jimenez .15 .40
275 Anibal Sanchez .15 .40
276 Carlos Lee .15 .40
277 Mark Teahen .15 .40
278 Delwyn Young .15 .40
279 Kurt Suzuki .15 .40
280 Nate Schierholtz .15 .40
281 Raul Ibanez .25 .60
282 Jose Vidro .15 .40
283 Miguel Cabrera GB SP 1.00 2.50
284 Luis Gonzalez GB SP .40 1.00
285 Chad Billingsley GB SP .60 1.50
286 Tony Gwynn GB SP .40 1.00
287 Matt Kemp .30 .75
288 James Loney .15 .40
289 Brett Myers .15 .40
290 Nate McLouth .15 .40
291 M.Chico/J.Bergmann GB SP .40 1.00
292 Chad Tracy .15 .40
293 Edgar Renteria .15 .40
294 Jay Payton .15 .40
295 Josh Johnson .25 .60
296 Josh Banks (RC) .40 1.00
297 Bill Murphy (RC) .40 1.00
298 Ben Sheets .15 .40
299 Jose Reyes .25 .60
300 Chase Utley .25 .60
301 Ronnie Belliard GB SP .40 1.00
302 Wily Mo Pena .15 .40
303 Tim Lincecum .25 .60
304 Chicago Cubs .25 .60
305 John Lackey .25 .60
306 Stephen Drew .15 .40
307 Kelly Johnson .15 .40
308 Daisuke Matsuzaka .25 .60
309 Craig Monroe .15 .40
310 Jerry Owens .15 .40
311 Jeff Suppan .15 .40
312 Tom Glavine .25 .60
313 Kei Igawa .15 .40
314 Mark Kotsay .15 .40
315 Jacque Jones SP 2.50 6.00
316 Melvin Mora .15 .40
317 M.Holliday/H.Ramirez .40 1.00
318 Jarrod Saltalamacchia .15 .40
319 A.J. Burnett .15 .40
320 Casey Kotchman .15 .40
321 Randy Winn GB SP .40 1.00
322 Richie Sexson GB SP .40 1.00
323 Juan Encarnacion GB SP .40 1.00
324 Rick Ankiel GB SP .40 1.00
325 Dan Wheeler GB SP .40 1.00
326 Brian Roberts .15 .40
327 David Ortiz .40 1.00
328 Garret Anderson .15 .40
329 Detroit Tigers .15 .40
330 Ty Wigginton GB SP .60 1.50
331 Travis Hafner .15 .40
332 Howie Kendrick GB SP .40 1.00
333 Kevin Kouzmanoff GB SP .40 1.00
334 Matt Holliday GB SP 1.00 2.50

335 Brandon Phillips GB SP .40 1.00
336 Ian Kinsler GB SP .60 1.50
337 Lyle Overbay GB SP .40 1.00
338 Justin Verlander GB SP 1.00 2.50
339 Ian Snell .15 .40
340 Hank Blalock .15 .40
341 Vernon Wells .15 .40
342 Matt Chico .15 .40
343 Tim Wakefield .25 .60
344 Michael Bourn .15 .40
345 Chris Carpenter .25 .60
346 Matsuzaka/Beckett .25 .60
347 Chuck James GB SP .40 1.00
348 Joba Chamberlain .15 .40
349 Erik Bedard .15 .40
350 Jimmy Rollins GB SP .60 1.50
351 Anthony Reyes .15 .40
352 Carl Crawford .25 .60
353 Jeremy Hermida .15 .40
354 Ervin Santana .15 .40
355 Edgar Gonzalez .15 .40
356 Yunel Escobar .15 .40
357 Yorvit Torrealba .15 .40
358 Hideki Okajima .15 .40
359 Paul Byrd .15 .40
360 Magglio Ordonez GB SP .60 1.50
361 Joe Borowski .15 .40
362 Clint Sammons (RC) .40 1.00
363 Chris Duffy .15 .40
364 Fred Lewis .15 .40
365 Adrian Beltre .40 1.00
366 Alex Rodriguez BT .50 1.25
367 Troy Tulowitzki BT .40 1.00
368 Prince Fielder BT .25 .60
369 Clay Buchholz BT .25 .60
370 Justin Verlander BT GB SP 1.00 2.50
371 Pedro Martinez BT GB SP .60 1.50
372 R.Howard BT GB SP .60 1.50
373 Ichiro Suzuki BT .50 1.25
374 Kenny Lofton BT .15 .40
375 Manny Ramirez BT .40 1.00
376 Randy Johnson .40 1.00
377 Chris Capuano .15 .40
378 Johnny Estrada .15 .40
379 Franklin Morales .15 .40
380 Ryan Howard .25 .60
381 Casey Blake SP 2.50 6.00
382 Coco Crisp .15 .40
383 J.Maine/W.Randolph MG .15 .40
384 Jeremy Guthrie .15 .40
385 Geoff Jenkins .15 .40
386 Marlon Byrd .15 .40
387 Jeremy Bonderman .15 .40
388 Jason Varitek .40 1.00
389 Joe Girardi MG .25 .60
390 Ryan Braun .25 .60
391 Ryan Zimmerman .25 .60
392 Lowell/Youkilis/Pedroia .25 .60
393 Pittsburgh Pirates .15 .40
394 Ryan Spilborghs .15 .40
395 Eric Gagne .15 .40
396 Joe Blanton .15 .40
397 Washington Nationals .15 .40
398 Ryan Church .15 .40
399 Ted Lilly .15 .40
400 Manny Ramirez .40 1.00
401 Chad Gaudin .25 .60
402 Dustin McGowan .15 .40
403 Scott Baker .15 .40
404 Franklin Gutierrez .15 .40
405 Dave Bush .15 .40
406 Aubrey Huff .15 .40
407 Jermaine Dye .15 .40
408 C.Utley/J.Rollins .25 .60
409 Jon Lester SP 5.00 12.00
410 Mark Buehrle .25 .60
411 Sergio Mitre .15 .40
412 Jason Bartlett .15 .40
413 Edwin Jackson .15 .40
414 J.D. Drew .15 .40
415 Freddy Sanchez GB SP .40 1.00
416 Asdrubal Cabrera .25 .60
417 Nate Robertson .15 .40
418 Shaun Marcum .15 .40
419 Atlanta Braves .25 .60
420 Noah Lowry .15 .40
421 Jamie Moyer .15 .40
422 Michael Cuddyer .15 .40
423 Randy Wolf .15 .40
424 Juan Uribe .15 .40
425 Brian McCann .25 .60
426 Kyle Lohse SP 2.50 6.00
427 Doug Davis SP 2.50 6.00
428 Snell/Capps/Gorz/Maholm SP 2.50 6.00
429 Miguel Batista SP 2.50 6.00
430 C.Wang SP 4.00 10.00
431 Jeff Salazar SP 2.50 6.00
432 Yadier Molina SP 2.50 6.00
433 Adam Wainwright SP 2.50 6.00
434 Scott Kazmir SP 2.50 6.00
435 Adam Dunn SP 2.50 6.00
436 Ryan Freel SP 2.50 6.00
437 Jhonny Peralta SP 2.50 6.00
438 Kazuo Matsui SP 2.50 6.00
439 Daniel Cabrera .15 .40
440a John Smoltz .40 1.00
440b J.Smoltz Jon Var 50.00 120.00
441 Emil Brown SP 2.50 6.00
442 Gary Sheffield SP 2.50 6.00
443 Jake Peavy SP 3.00 8.00
444 Scott Rolen SP 3.00 8.00
445 Kason Gabbard SP 2.50 6.00
446 Aaron Hill SP 2.50 6.00
447 Felipe Lopez SP 2.50 6.00
448 Dan Uggla SP 2.50 6.00
449 Willy Taveras SP 2.50 6.00
450 Chipper Jones SP 3.00 8.00
451 Josh Anderson SP (RC) 3.00 8.00
452 Young/Upton/Byrnes SP 3.00 8.00
453 Braden Looper SP 2.50 6.00
454 Brandon Inge SP 2.50 6.00
455 Brian Giles SP 2.50 6.00
456 Corey Patterson SP 2.50 6.00
457 Los Angeles Dodgers SP 3.00 8.00
458 Sean Casey SP 2.50 6.00
459 Pedro Feliz SP 2.50 6.00
460 Tom Gorzelanny .15 .40
461 Chone Figgins SP 2.50 6.00
462 Kyle Kendrick SP 2.50 6.00
463 Tony Pena SP 2.50 6.00
464 Marcus Giles SP 2.50 6.00
465 Augie Ojeda SP 2.50 6.00
466 Micah Owings SP 2.50 6.00
467 Ryan Theriot SP 2.50 6.00
468 Shawn Green SP 2.50 6.00
469 Frank Thomas SP 3.00 8.00
470 Lenny DiNardo SP 2.50 6.00
471 Jose Bautista SP 2.50 6.00
472 Manny Corpas SP 2.50 6.00
473 Kevin Millwood SP 2.50 6.00
474 Kevin Youkilis SP 2.50 6.00
475 Jose Contreras SP 2.50 6.00
476 Cleveland Indians .15 .40
477 Julio Lugo SP 2.50 6.00
478 Jason Bay .25 .60
479 Tony LaRussa AS MG SP 2.50 6.00
480 Jim Leyland AS MG SP 2.50 6.00
481 Derrek Lee AS SP 2.50 6.00
482 Justin Morneau AS SP 2.50 6.00
483 Orlando Hudson AS SP 2.50 6.00
484 Brian Roberts AS SP 2.50 6.00
485 Miguel Cabrera AS SP 3.00 8.00
486 Mike Lowell AS SP 2.50 6.00
487 J.J. Hardy AS SP 2.50 6.00
488 Carlos Guillen AS SP 2.50 6.00
489 K.Griffey Jr. AS SP 5.00 12.00
490 Vladimir Guerrero AS SP 3.00 8.00
491 Alfonso Soriano AS SP 3.00 8.00
492 I.Suzuki AS SP 4.00 10.00
493 Matt Holliday AS SP 3.00 8.00
494 Magglio Ordonez AS SP 3.00 8.00
495 Brian McCann AS SP 2.50 6.00
496 Victor Martinez AS SP 2.50 6.00
497 Brad Penny AS SP 2.50 6.00
498 Josh Beckett AS SP 3.00 8.00
499 Cole Hamels AS SP 3.00 8.00
500 Justin Verlander AS SP 4.00 10.00
501 John Danks .15 .40
502 Jamey Wright .15 .40
503 Johnny Cueto RC 1.00 2.50
504 Todd Wellemeyer .15 .40
505 Chase Headley .15 .40
506 Takashi Saito .15 .40
507 Skip Schumaker .15 .40
508 Tampa Bay Rays .15 .40
509 Marcus Thames .15 .40
510 Joe Saunders .15 .40
511 Jair Jurrjens .15 .40
512 Ryan Sweeney .15 .40
513 Darin Erstad .15 .40
514 Brandon Backe GB SP .40 1.00
515 Chris Volstad (RC) .40 1.00
516 Salomon Torres .15 .40
517 Brian Burres .15 .40
518 Brandon Boggs (RC) .60 1.50
519 Max Scherzer RC 5.00 12.00
520 Cliff Lee .25 .60
521 Angel Pagan .15 .40
522 Jason Kubel .15 .40
523 Jose Molina GB SP .40 1.00
524 Hiroki Kuroda RC 1.00 2.50
525 Matt Harrison (RC) .60 1.50
526 C.J. Wilson .15 .40
527 Robb Quinlan .15 .40
528 Darrell Rasner .40 1.00
529 Frank Catalanotto GB SP .40 1.00
530 Mike Mussina .25 .60
531 Ryan Doumit GB SP .40 1.00
532 Willie Bloomquist GB SP .40 1.00
533 Jonny Gomes .15 .40
534 Jesse Litsch .25 .60
535 Curtis Granderson .25 .60
536 A.J. Pierzynski .15 .40
537 Toronto Blue Jays .25 .60
538 Brian Buscher GB SP .40 1.00
539 Kelly Shoppach GB SP .40 1.00
540 Edinson Volquez .15 .40
541 Jon Rauch GB SP .40 1.00
542 Ramon Castro GB SP .40 1.00
543 Greg Smith RC .40 1.00
544 Sean Gallagher .15 .40
545 Justin Masterson GB SP RC 1.00 2.50
546 Milwaukee Brewers .15 .40
547 Jay Bruce (RC) 1.25 3.00
548 Glendon Rusch .15 .40
549 Jeremy Sowers GB SP .40 1.00
550 Ryan Dempster .15 .40
551 Clete Thomas RC .60 1.50
552 Jose Castillo .15 .40
553 Brandon Lyon .15 .40
554 Vicente Padilla .15 .40
555 Jeff Keppinger .15 .40
556 Colorado Rockies .15 .40
557 Dallas Braden GB SP .60 1.50
558 Adam Kennedy .15 .40
559 Luis Mendoza (RC) .40 1.00
560 Justin Duchscherer .15 .40
561 Mike Aviles RC .60 1.50
562 Jed Lowrie (RC) .40 1.00
563 Doug Mientkiewicz GB SP .40 1.00
564 Chris Burke .15 .40
565 Dana Eveland .15 .40
566 Bryan Lahair RC 3.00 8.00
567 Denard Span (RC) .60 1.50
568 Damion Easley .15 .40
569 Josh Fields .15 .40
570 Geovany Soto .40 1.00
571 Gerald Laird UER .15 .40
572 Bobby Jenks .15 .40
573 Andy Marte .15 .40
574 Mike Pelfrey .15 .40
575 Jerry Hairston .15 .40
576 Mike Lamb .15 .40
577 Ben Zobrist .25 .60
578 Carlos Gonzalez (RC) 1.00 2.50
579 Jose Guillen GB SP .40 1.00
580 Kosuke Fukudome RC 1.25 3.00
581 Gabe Kapler GB SP .40 1.00
582 Florida Marlins .15 .40
583 Ramon Vazquez GB SP .40 1.00
584 Wes Helms GB SP .40 1.00
585 Minnesota Twins .15 .40
586 Cody Ross .15 .40
587 Mike Napoli .25 .60
588 Alexi Casilla .15 .40
589 Emmanuel Burriss RC .60 1.50
590 Brian Wilson .40 1.00
591 Rod Barajas .15 .40
592 Mike Hampton GB SP .40 1.00
593 Nick Blackburn RC .60 1.50
594 Joe Mather RC .60 1.50
595 Clayton Kershaw GB SP RC 6.00 15.00
596 Cliff Floyd GB SP .40 1.00
597 Sidney Ponson GB SP .40 1.00
598 Brian Anderson .15 .40
599 Joe Inglett .15 .40
600 Miguel Tejada .25 .60
601 San Diego Padres .15 .40
602 Scott Hairston GB SP .40 1.00
603 Joel Pineiro .15 .40
604 Fernando Tatis .15 .40
605 Greg Reynolds RC .60 1.50
606 Brian Moehler .15 .40
607 Kevin Millar GB SP .40 1.00
608 Ben Francisco .15 .40
609 Troy Percival .15 .40
610 Kerry Wood .15 .40
611 Max Ramirez RC .40 1.00
612 Jeff Baker .15 .40
613 Houston Astros .15 .40
614 Russell Branyan .15 .40
615 Todd Jones .15 .40
616 Brian Schneider .15 .40
617 Gregorio Petit RC .60 1.50
618 Matt Diaz .15 .40
619 Blake DeWitt GB SP (RC) .60 1.50
620 Cristian Guzman .15 .40
621 Jeff Samardzija GB SP RC 1.25 3.00
622 John Baker (RC) .40 1.00
623 Eric Hinske .15 .40
624 Scott Olsen .15 .40
625 Greg Dobbs .15 .40
626 Carlos Marmol GB SP .60 1.50
627 Kansas City Royals .15 .40
628 Esteban German .15 .40
629 Dennis Sarfate .15 .40
630 Ryan Ludwick .15 .40
631 Mike Jacobs .15 .40
632 Tyler Yates .15 .40
633 Joel Hanrahan .25 .60
634 Manny Parra .15 .40
635 Maicer Izturis .15 .40
636 Juan Rivera .15 .40
637 Tim Redding .15 .40
638 Jose Arredondo RC .60 1.50
639 Mike Redmond GB SP .40 1.00
640 Joe Crede .15 .40
641 Omar Infante .15 .40
642 Nick Punto .15 .40
643 Jeff Mathis .15 .40
644 Andy Sonnanstine .15 .40
645 Masahide Kobayashi RC .60 1.50
646 Marco Scutaro .25 .60
647 Matt Macri (RC) .25 .60
648 Ian Stewart SP 2.50 6.00
649 David Dellucci GB SP .40 1.00
650 Evan Longoria RC 2.00 5.00
651 Martin Prado GB SP .40 1.00
652 Glen Perkins .15 .40
653 Alfredo Amezaga GB SP .40 1.00
654 Brett Gardner (RC) 1.00 2.50
655 Angel Berroa GB SP .40 1.00
656 Pablo Sandoval RC 5.00 12.00
657 Jody Gerut .15 .40
658 Arizona Diamondbacks .15 .40
659 Ryan Freel GB SP .40 1.00
660 Dioner Navarro .15 .40
661 Endy Chavez GB SP .40 1.00
662 Jorge Campillo .15 .40
663 Mark Ellis .15 .40
664 John Buck .15 .40
665 Texas Rangers .15 .40
666 Jason Michaels .15 .40
667 Chris Dickerson RC .60 1.50
668 Kevin Mench .15 .40
669 Aaron Miles .15 .40
670 Joakim Soria .15 .40
671 Chris Davis RC .75 2.00
672 Taylor Teagarden GB SP RC .60 1.50
673 Willy Aybar .15 .40
674 Paul Maholm .15 .40
675 Mike Gonzalez .15 .40
676 Seattle Mariners .15 .40
677 Ryan Langerhans SP 2.50 6.00
678 Alex Romero (RC) .60 1.50
679 Erick Aybar .15 .40
680 George Sherrill .15 .40
681 John Bowker (RC) .40 1.00
682 Zach Miner GB SP .40 1.00
683 Jorge Cantu .15 .40
684 Jo-Jo Reyes .15 .40
685 Ryan Raburn .15 .40
686 Gavin Floyd SP 2.50 6.00
687 Kevin Slowey SP 2.50 6.00
688 Gio Gonzalez SP (RC) 2.50 6.00
689 Eric Patterson SP 2.50 6.00
690 Jonathan Sanchez SP 2.50 6.00
691 Oliver Perez SP 2.50 6.00
692 John Lannan SP 2.50 6.00
693 Ramon Hernandez SP 2.50 6.00
694 Mike Fontenot SP 2.50 6.00
695 Ross Gload SP 2.50 6.00
696 Mark Sweeney SP 2.50 6.00
697 Nick Hundley SP (RC) 2.50 6.00
698 Kevin Correia SP 2.50 6.00
699 Jeremy Reed SP 2.50 6.00
700 Eddie Kunz SP RC 2.50 6.00
701 Miguel Montero SP 2.50 6.00
702 Gabe Gross SP 2.50 6.00
703 Matt Stairs SP 2.50 6.00
704 Kenny Rogers SP 2.50 6.00
705 Mark Hendrickson SP 2.50 6.00
706 Heath Bell SP 2.50 6.00
707 Wilson Betemit SP 2.50 6.00
708 Brandon Morrow SP 2.50 6.00
709 Brendan Ryan SP 2.50 6.00
710 Eric Hurley SP (RC) 2.50 6.00
711 Los Angeles Angels SP 2.50 6.00
712 Jack Hannahan SP 2.50 6.00
713 Seth McClung SP 2.50 6.00
714 New York Mets SP 2.50 6.00
715 Chris Perez SP RC 2.50 6.00
716 Clayton Richard SP (RC) 2.50 6.00
717 Jaime Garcia SP RC 2.50 6.00
718 Matt Joyce SP RC 2.50 6.00
719 Brad Ziegler SP RC 2.50 6.00
720 Ivan Ochoa (RC) .60 1.50

2008 Topps Heritage Black Back

*BLK BACK VET: .4X TO 1X BASIC
*BLK BACK RC: .4X TO 1X BASIC RC
RANDOM INSERTS IN PACKS

2008 Topps Heritage Chrome

1-100 ODDS 1:8 HOBBY, 1:18 RETAIL
1-100 INSERTED IN 08 HERITAGE
101-200 ODDS 1:6 HOBBY
101-200 INSERTED IN 08 TOPPS CHROME
201-300 ODDS 1:3 HOBBY
201-300 INSERTED IN 08 HERITAGE HN
STATED PRINT RUN 1959 SERIAL #'d SETS

C1 Hunter Pence 1.50 4.00
C2 Andre Ethier 1.50 4.00
C3 Curt Schilling 1.50 4.00
C4 Gary Matthews 1.00 2.50
C5 Dontrelle Willis 1.00 2.50
C6 Troy Tulowitzki 2.50 6.00
C7 Robinson Cano 1.50 4.00
C8 Felix Hernandez 1.50 4.00
C9 Josh Hamilton 1.50 4.00
C10 Justin Upton 1.50 4.00
C11 Brad Penny 1.00 2.50
C12 Hideki Matsui 2.50 6.00
C13 J.J. Putz 1.00 2.50
C14 Jorge Posada 1.50 4.00
C15 Albert Pujols 3.00 8.00
C16 Aaron Rowand 1.00 2.50
C17 Ronnie Belliard 1.00 2.50
C18 Rick Ankiel 1.00 2.50
C19 Ian Kinsler 1.50 4.00
C20 Justin Verlander 2.50 6.00
C21 Lyle Overbay 1.00 2.50
C22 Tim Hudson 1.50 4.00
C23 Ryan Zimmerman 1.50 4.00
C24 Ryan Braun 1.50 4.00
C25 Jimmy Rollins 1.50 4.00
C26 Kelvim Escobar 1.50 4.00
C27 Adam LaRoche 1.00 2.50
C28 Ivan Rodriguez 1.50 4.00
C29 Billy Wagner 1.00 2.50
C30 Ichiro Suzuki 3.00 8.00
C31 Chris Young 1.00 2.50
C32 Trevor Hoffman 1.50 4.00
C33 Torii Hunter 1.00 2.50
C34 Jason Isringhausen 1.00 2.50
C35 Jose Valverde 1.00 2.50
C36 Derrek Lee 1.00 2.50
C37 Rich Harden 1.00 2.50
C38 Andrew Miller 1.50 4.00
C39 Miguel Cabrera 2.50 6.00
C40 David Wright 1.50 4.00
C41 Brandon Phillips 1.00 2.50
C42 Magglio Ordonez 1.50 4.00
C43 Eric Byrnes 1.00 2.50
C44 John Smoltz 2.50 6.00
C45 Brandon Webb 1.50 4.00
C46 Barry Zito 1.50 4.00
C47 Sammy Sosa 2.50 6.00
C48 James Shields 1.00 2.50
C49 Alex Rios 1.00 2.50
C50 Matt Holliday 2.50 6.00
C51 Chris Young 1.00 2.50
C52 Roy Oswalt 1.50 4.00
C53 Matt Kemp 3.00 8.00
C54 Tim Lincecum 1.50 4.00
C55 Hanley Ramirez 1.50 4.00
C56 Vladimir Guerrero 1.50 4.00
C57 Mark Teixeira 1.50 4.00
C58 Fausto Carmona 1.00 2.50
C59 B.J. Ryan 1.00 2.50
C60 Manny Ramirez 2.50 6.00
C61 Carlos Delgado 1.00 2.50
C62 Matt Cain 1.50 4.00
C63 Brian Bannister 1.00 2.50
C64 Russell Martin 1.00 2.50
C65 Todd Helton 1.50 4.00
C66 Roy Halladay 1.50 4.00
C67 Lance Berkman 1.50 4.00
C68 John Lackey 1.50 4.00
C69 Daisuke Matsuzaka 1.50 4.00
C70 Joe Mauer 2.00 5.00
C71 Francisco Rodriguez 1.50 4.00
C72 Derek Jeter 6.00 15.00
C73 Homer Bailey 1.50 4.00
C74 Jonathan Papelbon 1.50 4.00
C75 Billy Butler 1.00 2.50
C76 B.J. Upton 1.50 4.00
C77 Ubaldo Jimenez 1.00 2.50
C78 Erik Bedard 1.00 2.50
C79 Jeff Kent 1.00 2.50
C80 Ken Griffey Jr. 5.00 12.00
C81 Josh Beckett 1.00 2.50
C82 Jeff Francis 1.00 2.50
C83 Grady Sizemore 1.50 4.00
C84 John Maine 1.00 2.50
C85 Cole Hamels 2.00 5.00
C86 Nick Markakis 2.00 5.00
C87 Ben Sheets 1.00 2.50
C88 Jose Reyes 1.50 4.00
C89 Vernon Wells 1.00 2.50
C90 Justin Morneau 1.50 4.00
C91 Brian McCann 1.50 4.00
C92 Jacoby Ellsbury 2.00 5.00
C93 Clay Buchholz 1.50 4.00
C94 Prince Fielder 1.50 4.00
C95 David Ortiz 2.50 6.00
C96 Joba Chamberlain 1.00 2.50
C97 Chien-Ming Wang 1.50 4.00
C98 Chipper Jones 2.50 6.00
C99 Chase Utley 1.50 4.00
C100 Alex Rodriguez 3.00 8.00
C101 Phil Hughes 1.00 2.50
C102 Hideki Okajima 1.00 2.50
C103 Chone Figgins 1.00 2.50
C104 Jose Vidro 1.00 2.50
C105 Johan Santana 1.50 4.00
C106 Paul Konerko 1.00 2.50
C107 Alfonso Soriano 1.50 4.00
C108 Kei Igawa 1.00 2.50
C109 Lastings Milledge 1.00 2.50
C110 Asdrubal Cabrera 1.50 4.00
C111 Brandon Jones 2.50 6.00
C112 Tom Gorzelanny 1.00 2.50
C113 Delmon Young 1.50 4.00
C114 Daric Barton 1.00 2.50
C115 David DeJesus 1.00 2.50
C116 Ryan Howard 1.50 4.00
C117 Tom Glavine 1.50 4.00
C118 Frank Thomas 2.50 6.00
C119 J.R. Towles 1.50 4.00
C120 Jeremy Bonderman 1.00 2.50
C121 Adrian Beltre 2.50 6.00
C122 Dan Haren 1.00 2.50
C123 Kazuo Matsui 1.00 2.50
C124 Joe Blanton 1.00 2.50
C125 Dan Uggla 1.00 2.50
C126 Stephen Drew 1.00 2.50
C127 Daniel Cabrera 1.00 2.50
C128 Jeff Clement 1.50 4.00
C129 Pedro Martinez 1.50 4.00
C130 Josh Anderson 1.00 2.50
C131 Orlando Hudson 1.00 2.50
C132 Jason Bay 1.50 4.00
C133 Eric Chavez 1.00 2.50
C134 Johnny Damon 1.50 4.00
C135 Lance Broadway 1.00 2.50
C136 Jake Peavy 1.00 2.50
C137 Carl Crawford 1.00 2.50
C138 Kenji Johjima 1.00 2.50
C139 Melky Cabrera 1.50 4.00
C140 Aaron Hill 1.00 2.50
C141 Carlos Lee 1.00 2.50
C142 Mark Buehrle 1.50 4.00
C143 Carlos Beltran 1.50 4.00
C144 Chin-Lung Hu 1.00 2.50
C145 C.C. Sabathia 1.50 4.00
C146 Dustin Pedroia 1.50 4.00
C147 Freddy Sanchez 1.00 2.50
C148 Kevin Youkilis 1.00 2.50
C149 Radhames Liz 1.50 4.00
C150 Jim Thome 1.50 4.00
C151 Greg Maddux 3.00 8.00
C152 Rich Hill 1.00 2.50
C153 Andy LaRoche 1.00 2.50
C154 Gil Meche 1.00 2.50
C155 Victor Martinez 1.50 4.00
C156 Mariano Rivera 3.00 8.00
C157 Kyle Kendrick 1.00 2.50
C158 Jarrod Saltalamacchia 1.00 2.50
C159 Tadahito Iguchi 1.00 2.50
C160 Eric Gagne 1.00 2.50
C161 Garrett Atkins 1.00 2.50
C162 Pat Burrell 1.00 2.50
C163 Akinori Iwamura 1.00 2.50
C164 Melvin Mora 1.00 2.50
C165 Joey Votto 4.00 10.00
C166 Brian Roberts 1.00 2.50
C167 Brett Myers 1.00 2.50
C168 Michael Young 1.00 2.50
C169 Adam Jones 1.50 4.00
C170 Carlos Zambrano 1.50 4.00
C171 Jeff Francoeur 1.50 4.00
C172 Brad Hawpe 1.00 2.50
C173 Andy Pettitte 1.50 4.00
C174 Ryan Garko 1.00 2.50
C175 Adrian Gonzalez 1.50 4.00
C176 Ted Lilly 1.00 2.50
C177 J.J. Hardy 1.00 2.50
C178 Jon Lester 1.50 4.00
C179 Carlos Pena 1.50 4.00
C180 Ross Detwiler 1.50 4.00
C181 Andruw Jones 1.00 2.50
C182 Gary Sheffield 1.00 2.50
C183 Dmitri Young 1.00 2.50
C184 Carlos Guillen 1.00 2.50
C185 Yovani Gallardo 1.00 2.50
C186 Alex Gordon 1.50 4.00
C187 Aaron Harang 1.00 2.50
C188 Travis Hafner 1.00 2.50
C189 Orlando Cabrera 1.50 4.00
C190 Bobby Abreu 1.00 2.50
C191 Randy Johnson 2.50 6.00
C192 Scott Kazmir 1.50 4.00
C193 Jason Varitek 2.50 6.00
C194 Mike Lowell 1.00 2.50
C195 A.J. Burnett 1.00 2.50
C196 Garret Anderson 1.00 2.50
C197 Chris Carpenter 1.50 4.00
C198 Jermaine Dye 1.00 2.50
C199 Luke Hochevar 1.50 4.00
C200 Steve Pearce 5.00 12.00
C201 Joe Saunders 1.00 2.50
C202 Cliff Lee 1.50 4.00
C203 Mike Mussina 1.50 4.00
C204 Ryan Dempster 1.00 2.50
C205 Edinson Volquez 1.00 2.50
C206 Justin Duchscherer 1.00 2.50
C207 Geovany Soto 2.50 6.00
C208 Brian Wilson 2.50 6.00
C209 Kerry Wood 1.00 2.50
C210 Kosuke Fukudome 3.00 8.00
C211 Cristian Guzman 1.00 2.50
C212 Ryan Ludwick 1.50 4.00
C213 Joe Crede 1.00 2.50
C214 Dioner Navarro 1.00 2.50
C215 Miguel Tejada 1.50 4.00
C216 Joakim Soria 1.00 2.50
C217 George Sherrill 1.00 2.50
C218 John Danks 1.00 2.50
C219 Jair Jurrjens 1.00 2.50
C220 Evan Longoria 5.00 12.00
C221 Hiroki Kuroda 2.50 6.00
C222 Greg Smith 1.00 2.50
C223 Dana Eveland 1.00 2.50
C224 Ryan Sweeney 1.00 2.50
C225 Mike Pelfrey 1.00 2.50
C226 Nick Blackburn 1.50 4.00
C227 Scott Olsen 1.00 2.50
C228 Manny Parra 1.00 2.50
C229 Tim Redding 1.00 2.50
C230 Paul Maholm 1.00 2.50
C231 Todd Wellemeyer 1.00 2.50
C232 Jesse Litsch 1.50 4.00
C233 Andy Sonnanstine 1.00 2.50
C234 Johnny Cueto 2.50 6.00
C235 Vicente Padilla 1.00 2.50
C236 Glen Perkins 1.00 2.50
C237 Brian Burres 1.00 2.50
C238 Jamey Wright 1.00 2.50
C239 Chase Headley 1.00 2.50
C240 Takashi Saito 1.00 2.50
C241 Skip Schumaker 1.00 2.50
C242 Curtis Granderson 1.50 4.00
C243 A.J. Pierzynski 1.00 2.50
C244 Jorge Cantu 1.00 2.50
C245 Maicer Izturis 1.00 2.50
C246 Kevin Mench 1.00 2.50
C247 Jason Kubel 1.00 2.50
C248 Rod Barajas 1.00 2.50
C249 Jed Lowrie 1.00 2.50
C250 Bobby Jenks 1.00 2.50
C251 Jonny Gomes 1.00 2.50
C252 Clete Thomas 1.50 4.00
C253 Eric Hinske 1.00 2.50
C254 Brett Gardner 2.50 6.00
C255 Denard Span 1.50 4.00
C256 Brian Anderson 1.00 2.50
C257 Troy Percival 1.00 2.50
C258 Darrell Rasner 1.00 2.50
C259 Willy Aybar 1.00 2.50
C260 John Bowker 1.00 2.50
C261 Marco Scutaro 1.50 4.00
C262 Adam Kennedy 1.00 2.50
C263 Nick Punto 1.00 2.50
C264 Mike Napoli 1.50 4.00
C265 Carlos Gonzalez 2.50 6.00
C266 Matt Macri 1.00 2.50
C267 Marcus Thames 1.00 2.5
C268 Ben Zobrist 1.50 4.0
C269 Mark Ellis 1.00 2.5
C270 Mike Aviles 1.50 4.0
C271 Angel Pagan 1.00 2.5
C272 Erick Aybar 1.00 2.50
C273 Todd Jones 1.00 2.50
C274 Brandon Boggs 1.50 4.00
C275 Mike Jacobs 1.00 2.50
C276 Mike Gonzalez 1.00 2.50
C277 Mike Lamb 1.00 2.50
C278 Robb Quinlan 1.00 2.50
C279 Salomon Torres 1.00 2.50
C280 Jose Castillo 1.00 2.50
C281 Damion Easley 1.00 2.50
C282 Jo-Jo Reyes 1.00 2.50
C283 Cody Ross 1.00 2.50
C284 Alexi Casilla 1.00 2.50
C286 Brandon Lyon 1.00 2.50
C287 Greg Dobbs 1.00 2.50
C288 Joel Pineiro 1.00 2.50
C289 Chris Davis 2.00 5.00
C290 Masahide Kobayashi 1.50 4.00
C291 Darin Erstad 1.00 2.50
C292 Matt Diaz 1.00 2.50
C293 Brian Schneider 1.00 2.50
C294 Gerald Laird 1.00 2.50
C295 Ben Francisco 1.00 2.50
C296 Brian Moehler 1.00 2.50
C297 Aaron Miles 1.00 2.50
C298 Max Scherzer 6.00 15.00
C299 C.J. Wilson 1.00 2.50
C300 Jay Bruce 3.00 8.00

2008 Topps Heritage Chrome Refractors

*CHROME REF: .6X TO 1.5X
1-100 ODDS 1:29 HOBBY, 1:59 RETAIL
1-100 INSERTED IN 08 TOPPS HERITAGE
101-200 ODDS 1:21 HOBBY
101-200 INSERTED IN 08 TOPPS CHROME
201-300 ODDS 1:11 HOBBY
201-300 INSERTED IN 08 HERITAGE HN
STATED PRINT RUN 559 SERIAL #'d SETS

C72 Derek Jeter 12.50 30.00
C100 Alex Rodriguez 12.50 30.00
C220 Evan Longoria 8.00 20.00

2008 Topps Heritage Chrome Refractors Black

1-100 ODDS 1:315 HOB,1:450 RET
1-100 INSERTED IN 08 TOPPS HERITAGE
101-200 ODDS 1:196 HOBBY
201-300 INSERTED IN 08 HERITAGE HN
201-300 ODDS 1:99 HOBBY
101-200 INSERTED IN 08 TOPPS CHROME
STATED PRINT RUN 59 SERIAL #'d SETS

C1 Hunter Pence 12.00 30.00
C2 Andre Ethier 12.00 30.00
C3 Curt Schilling 12.00 30.00
C4 Gary Matthews 8.00 20.00
C5 Dontrelle Willis 8.00 20.00
C6 Troy Tulowitzki 20.00 50.00
C7 Robinson Cano 12.00 30.00
C8 Felix Hernandez 12.00 30.00
C9 Josh Hamilton 12.00 30.00
C10 Justin Upton 12.00 30.00
C11 Brad Penny 8.00 20.00
C12 Hideki Matsui 20.00 50.00
C13 J.J. Putz 8.00 20.00
C14 Jorge Posada 12.00 30.00
C15 Albert Pujols 25.00 60.00
C16 Aaron Rowand 8.00 20.00
C17 Ronnie Belliard 8.00 20.00
C18 Rick Ankiel 8.00 20.00
C19 Ian Kinsler 12.00 30.00
C20 Justin Verlander 20.00 50.00
C21 Lyle Overbay 8.00 20.00
C22 Tim Hudson 12.00 30.00
C23 Ryan Zimmerman 12.00 30.00
C24 Ryan Braun 12.00 30.00
C25 Jimmy Rollins 12.00 30.00
C26 Kelvim Escobar 12.00 30.00
C27 Adam LaRoche 8.00 20.00
C28 Ivan Rodriguez 12.00 30.00
C29 Billy Wagner 8.00 20.00
C30 Ichiro Suzuki 25.00 60.00
C31 Chris Young 8.00 20.00
C32 Trevor Hoffman 12.00 30.00
C33 Torii Hunter 8.00 20.00
C34 Jason Isringhausen 8.00 20.00
C35 Jose Valverde 8.00 20.00
C36 Derrek Lee 8.00 20.00
C37 Rich Harden 8.00 20.00
C38 Andrew Miller 12.00 30.00
C39 Miguel Cabrera 20.00 50.00
C40 David Wright 12.00 30.00
C41 Brandon Phillips 8.00 20.00
C42 Magglio Ordonez 12.00 30.00
C43 Eric Byrnes 8.00 20.00
C44 John Smoltz 20.00 50.00
C45 Brandon Webb 12.00 30.00
C46 Barry Zito 12.00 30.00

Card	Low	High
C47 Sammy Sosa	20.00	50.00
C48 James Shields	8.00	20.00
C49 Alex Rios	8.00	20.00
C50 Matt Holliday	20.00	50.00
C51 Chris Young	8.00	20.00
C52 Roy Oswalt	12.00	30.00
C53 Matt Kemp	15.00	40.00
C54 Tim Lincecum	12.00	30.00
C55 Hanley Ramirez	12.00	30.00
C56 Vladimir Guerrero	12.00	30.00
C57 Mark Teixeira	12.00	30.00
C58 Fausto Carmona	8.00	20.00
C59 B.J. Ryan	8.00	20.00
C60 Manny Ramirez	20.00	50.00
C61 Carlos Delgado	8.00	20.00
C62 Matt Cain	12.00	30.00
C63 Brian Bannister	8.00	20.00
C64 Russell Martin	8.00	20.00
C65 Todd Helton	12.00	30.00
C66 Roy Halladay	12.00	30.00
C67 Lance Berkman	12.00	30.00
C68 John Lackey	12.00	30.00
C69 Daisuke Matsuzaka	12.00	30.00
C70 Joe Mauer	15.00	40.00
C71 Francisco Rodriguez	12.00	30.00
C72 Derek Jeter	50.00	125.00
C73 Homer Bailey	12.00	30.00
C74 Jonathan Papelbon	12.00	30.00
C75 Billy Butler	8.00	20.00
C76 B.J. Upton	12.00	30.00
C77 Ubaldo Jimenez	8.00	20.00
C78 Erik Bedard	8.00	20.00
C79 Jeff Kent	8.00	20.00
C80 Ken Griffey Jr.	40.00	100.00
C81 Josh Beckett	8.00	20.00
C82 Jeff Francis	8.00	20.00
C83 Grady Sizemore	12.00	30.00
C84 John Maine	8.00	20.00
C85 Cole Hamels	15.00	40.00
C86 Nick Markakis	15.00	40.00
C87 Ben Sheets	8.00	20.00
C88 Jose Reyes	12.00	30.00
C89 Vernon Wells	8.00	20.00
C90 Justin Morneau	12.00	30.00
C91 Brian McCann	12.00	30.00
C92 Jacoby Ellsbury	15.00	40.00
C93 Clay Buchholz	12.00	30.00
C94 Prince Fielder	12.00	30.00
C95 David Ortiz	20.00	50.00
C96 Joba Chamberlain	8.00	20.00
C97 Chien-Ming Wang	12.00	30.00
C98 Chipper Jones	20.00	50.00
C99 Chase Utley	12.00	30.00
C100 Alex Rodriguez	25.00	60.00
C101 Phil Hughes	8.00	20.00
C102 Hideki Okajima	8.00	20.00
C103 Chone Figgins	8.00	20.00
C104 Jose Vidro	8.00	20.00
C105 Johan Santana	12.00	30.00
C106 Paul Konerko	12.00	30.00
C107 Alfonso Soriano	12.00	30.00
C108 Kei Igawa	8.00	20.00
C109 Lastings Milledge	8.00	20.00
C110 Asdrubal Cabrera	12.00	30.00
C111 Brandon Jones	20.00	50.00
C112 Tom Gorzelanny	8.00	20.00
C113 Delmon Young	12.00	30.00
C114 Daric Barton	8.00	20.00
C115 David DeJesus	8.00	20.00
C116 Ryan Howard	12.00	30.00
C117 Tom Glavine	12.00	30.00
C118 Frank Thomas	20.00	50.00
C119 J.R. Towles	12.00	30.00
C120 Jeremy Bonderman	8.00	20.00
C121 Adrian Beltre	20.00	50.00
C122 Dan Haren	8.00	20.00
C123 Kazuo Matsui	8.00	20.00
C124 Joe Blanton	8.00	20.00
C125 Dan Uggla	8.00	20.00
C126 Stephen Drew	8.00	20.00
C127 Daniel Cabrera	8.00	20.00
C128 Jeff Clement	12.00	30.00
C129 Pedro Martinez	12.00	30.00
C130 Josh Anderson	8.00	20.00
C131 Orlando Hudson	8.00	20.00
C132 Jason Bay	12.00	30.00
C133 Eric Chavez	8.00	20.00
C134 Johnny Damon	12.00	30.00
C135 Lance Broadway	8.00	20.00
C136 Jake Peavy	8.00	20.00
C137 Carl Crawford	12.00	30.00
C138 Kenji Johjima	8.00	20.00
C139 Melky Cabrera	8.00	20.00
C140 Aaron Hill	8.00	20.00
C141 Carlos Lee	8.00	20.00
C142 Mark Buehrle	12.00	30.00
C143 Carlos Beltran	12.00	30.00
C144 Chin-Lung Hu	8.00	20.00
C145 C.C. Sabathia	12.00	30.00
C146 Dustin Pedroia	12.00	30.00
C147 Freddy Sanchez	8.00	20.00
C148 Kevin Youkilis	8.00	20.00
C149 Radhames Liz	12.00	30.00
C150 Jim Thome	12.00	30.00
C151 Greg Maddux	25.00	60.00
C152 Rich Hill	8.00	20.00
C153 Andy LaRoche	8.00	20.00
C154 Gil Meche	8.00	20.00
C155 Victor Martinez	12.00	30.00
C156 Mariano Rivera	25.00	60.00
C157 Kyle Kendrick	8.00	20.00
C158 Jarrod Saltalamacchia	8.00	20.00
C159 Tadahito Iguchi	8.00	20.00
C160 Eric Gagne	8.00	20.00
C161 Garrett Atkins	8.00	20.00
C162 Pat Burrell	8.00	20.00
C163 Akinori Iwamura	8.00	20.00
C164 Melvin Mora	8.00	20.00
C165 Joey Votto	30.00	80.00
C166 Brian Roberts	8.00	20.00
C167 Brett Myers	8.00	20.00
C168 Michael Young	8.00	20.00
C169 Adam Jones	12.00	30.00
C170 Carlos Zambrano	12.00	30.00
C171 Jeff Francoeur	12.00	30.00
C172 Brad Hawpe	8.00	20.00
C173 Andy Pettitte	12.00	30.00
C174 Ryan Garko	8.00	20.00
C175 Adrian Gonzalez	12.00	30.00
C176 Ted Lilly	8.00	20.00
C177 J.J. Hardy	8.00	20.00
C178 Jon Lester	12.00	30.00
C179 Carlos Pena	12.00	30.00
C180 Ross Detwiler	12.00	30.00
C181 Andruw Jones	8.00	20.00
C182 Gary Sheffield	8.00	20.00
C183 Dmitri Young	8.00	20.00
C184 Carlos Guillen	8.00	20.00
C185 Yovani Gallardo	8.00	20.00
C186 Alex Gordon	12.00	30.00
C187 Aaron Harang	8.00	20.00
C188 Travis Hafner	8.00	20.00
C189 Orlando Cabrera	12.00	30.00
C190 Bobby Abreu	8.00	20.00
C191 Randy Johnson	20.00	50.00
C192 Scott Kazmir	12.00	30.00
C193 Jason Varitek	20.00	50.00
C194 Mike Lowell	8.00	20.00
C195 A.J. Burnett	8.00	20.00
C196 Garret Anderson	12.00	30.00
C197 Chris Carpenter	12.00	30.00
C198 Jermaine Dye	8.00	20.00
C199 Luke Hochevar	12.00	30.00
C200 Steve Pearce	40.00	100.00
C201 Joe Saunders	8.00	20.00
C202 Cliff Lee	12.00	30.00
C203 Mike Mussina	12.00	30.00
C204 Ryan Dempster	8.00	20.00
C205 Edinson Volquez	8.00	20.00
C206 Justin Duchscherer	8.00	20.00
C207 Geovany Soto	20.00	50.00
C208 Brian Wilson	20.00	50.00
C209 Kerry Wood	8.00	20.00
C210 Kosuke Fukudome	25.00	60.00
C211 Cristian Guzman	8.00	20.00
C212 Ryan Ludwick	8.00	20.00
C213 Joe Crede	8.00	20.00
C214 Dioner Navarro	8.00	20.00
C215 Miguel Tejada	12.00	30.00
C216 Joakim Soria	8.00	20.00
C217 George Sherrill	8.00	20.00
C218 John Danks	8.00	20.00
C219 Jair Jurrjens	8.00	20.00
C220 Evan Longoria	40.00	100.00
C221 Hiroki Kuroda	20.00	50.00
C222 Greg Smith	8.00	20.00
C223 Dana Eveland	8.00	20.00
C224 Ryan Sweeney	8.00	20.00
C225 Mike Pelfrey	8.00	20.00
C226 Nick Blackburn	12.00	30.00
C227 Scott Olsen	8.00	20.00
C228 Manny Parra	8.00	20.00
C229 Tim Redding	8.00	20.00
C230 Paul Maholm	8.00	20.00
C231 Todd Wellemeyer	8.00	20.00
C232 Jesse Litsch	12.00	30.00
C233 Andy Sonnanstine	8.00	20.00
C234 Johnny Cueto	20.00	50.00
C235 Vicente Padilla	8.00	20.00
C236 Glen Perkins	8.00	20.00
C237 Brian Burres	8.00	20.00
C238 Jamey Wright	8.00	20.00
C239 Chase Headley	8.00	20.00
C240 Takashi Saito	8.00	20.00
C241 Skip Schumaker	8.00	20.00
C242 Curtis Granderson	12.00	30.00
C243 A.J. Pierzynski	8.00	20.00
C244 Jorge Cantu	8.00	20.00
C245 Maicer Izturis	8.00	20.00
C246 Kevin Mench	8.00	20.00
C247 Jason Kubel	8.00	20.00
C248 Rod Barajas	8.00	20.00
C249 Jed Lowrie	8.00	20.00
C250 Bobby Jenks	8.00	20.00
C251 Jonny Gomes	8.00	20.00
C252 Clete Thomas	12.00	30.00
C253 Eric Hinske	8.00	20.00
C254 Brett Gardner	20.00	50.00
C255 Denard Span	12.00	30.00
C256 Brian Anderson	8.00	20.00
C257 Troy Percival	8.00	20.00
C258 Darrell Rasner	8.00	20.00
C259 Willy Aybar	8.00	20.00
C260 John Bowker	8.00	20.00
C261 Marco Scutaro	12.00	30.00
C262 Adam Kennedy	8.00	20.00
C263 Nick Punto	8.00	20.00
C264 Mike Napoli	12.00	30.00
C265 Carlos Gonzalez	20.00	50.00
C266 Matt Macri	8.00	20.00
C267 Marcus Thames	8.00	20.00
C268 Ben Zobrist	12.00	30.00
C269 Mark Ellis	8.00	20.00
C270 Mike Aviles	12.00	30.00
C271 Angel Pagan	8.00	20.00
C272 Erick Aybar	8.00	20.00
C273 Todd Jones	8.00	20.00
C274 Brandon Boggs	12.00	30.00
C275 Mike Jacobs	8.00	20.00
C276 Mike Gonzalez	8.00	20.00
C277 Mike Lamb	8.00	20.00
C278 Robb Quinlan	8.00	20.00
C279 Salomon Torres	8.00	20.00
C280 Jose Castillo	8.00	20.00
C281 Damion Easley	8.00	20.00
C282 Jo-Jo Reyes	8.00	20.00
C283 Cody Ross	8.00	20.00
C284 Alexi Casilla	8.00	20.00
C285 Jerry Hairston	8.00	20.00
C286 Brandon Lyon	8.00	20.00
C287 Greg Dobbs	8.00	20.00
C288 Joel Pineiro	8.00	20.00
C289 Chris Davis	15.00	40.00
C290 Masahide Kobayashi	12.00	30.00
C291 Darin Erstad	8.00	20.00
C292 Matt Diaz	8.00	20.00
C293 Brian Schneider	8.00	20.00
C294 Gerald Laird	8.00	20.00
C295 Ben Francisco	8.00	20.00
C296 Brian Moehler	8.00	20.00
C297 Aaron Miles	8.00	20.00
C298 Max Scherzer	100.00	250.00
C299 C.J. Wilson	8.00	20.00
C300 Jay Bruce	25.00	60.00

2008 Topps Heritage Flashbacks

Card	Low	High
COMPLETE SET (10)	6.00	15.00
STATED ODDS 1:12 HOBBY		
FB1 Mark Teixeira	.75	2.00
FB2 Tim Lincecum	.75	2.00
FB3 Jon Lester	.75	2.00
FB4 Ken Griffey Jr.	2.50	6.00
FB5 Kosuke Fukudome	1.50	4.00
FB6 Albert Pujols	1.50	4.00
FB7 Ichiro Suzuki	1.50	4.00
FB8 Felix Hernandez	.75	2.00
FB9 Carlos Delgado	.50	1.25
FB10 Josh Hamilton	.75	2.00

2008 Topps Heritage Advertising Panels

Cards are un-numbered. Cards are listed alphabetically by the last name of the first player listed.

ISSUED AS A BOX TOPPER

Card	Low	High
1 Bronson Arroyo	.60	1.50
J.R. Towles		
B.J. Ryan		
2 Willy Aybar	.40	1.00
Darrell Rasner		
Troy Percival HN		
3 Lance Berkman	.60	1.50
Jeff Francoeur		
Hanley Ramirez		
4 Yuniesky Betancourt	.60	1.50
Tim Lincecum		
Jason Kendall		
5 Brandon Boggs	.60	1.50
Todd Jones		
Erick Aybar HN		
6 Lance Broadway	.60	1.50
Russ Ohlendorf		
Matt Capps		
7 Jay Bruce	5.00	12.00
C.J. Wilson		
Max Scherzer HN		
8 Emmanuel Burriss	.60	1.50
Tyler Yates		
Clayton Richard HN		
9 Alexi Casilla	.40	1.00
Jerry Hairston		
Brandon Lyon HN		
10 Jose Castillo	.40	1.00
Salomon Torres		
Robb Quinlan HN		
11 Eric Chavez	.60	1.50
Zack Greinke		
Josh Willingham		
12 Chad Cordero	.60	1.50
Kenji Johjima		
Alfonso Soriano		
13 Joe Crede	.40	1.00
Ryan Ludwick		
Cristian Guzman HN		
14 Chicago Cubs	1.25	3.00
Tadahito Iguchi		
Mariano Rivera		
15 Johnny Cueto	1.00	2.50
Andy Sonnanstine		
Jesse Litsch HN		
16 Jack Cust	.60	1.50
Aaron Harang		
Vladimir Guerrero		
17 Carlos Delgado	.60	1.50
Lance Broadway		
Russ Ohlendorf		
18 Ryan Dempster	.40	1.00
Edinson Volquez		
Justin Duchscherer HN		
19 Greg Dobbs	.75	2.00
Joel Pineiro		
Chris Davis HN		
20 Stephen Drew	.40	1.00
Joe Nathan		
Bronson Arroyo		
21 Damion Easley	.40	1.00
JoJo Reyes		
Cody Ross HN		
22 Jim Edmonds	.60	1.50
Horatio Ramirez		
Brian Bannister		
23 Dana Eveland	.40	1.00
Ryan Sweeney		
Mike Pelfrey HN		
24 Josh Fields	.60	1.50
Emmanuel Burriss		
Tyler Yates HN		
25 Jeff Francoeur	.60	1.50
Hanley Ramirez		
Josh Barfield		
26 Armando Galarraga	.60	1.50
Wandy Rodriguez		
Wily Mo Pena		
27 Brett Gardner	1.00	2.50
Eric Hinske		
Clete Thomas HN		
28 Carlos Gomez	1.00	2.50
Sammy Sosa		
Russ Martin		
29 Mike Gonzalez	.60	1.50
Mike Jacobs		
Brandon Boggs HN		
30 Zack Greinke	.60	1.50
Josh Willingham		
Armando Galarraga		
31 Mark Grudzielanek	.60	1.50
Jim Thome		
Joe Koshansky		
32 J.J. Hardy	.60	1.50
Alex Rios		
Johan Santana		
33 Kevin Hart	.60	1.50
Radhames Liz		
Jack Wilson		
34 Todd Helton	1.25	3.00
Kelly Johnson		
Alex Rodriguez		
35 Eric Hinske	.60	1.50
Clete Thomas		
Jonny Gomes HN		
36 Tadahito Iguchi	1.25	3.00
Mariano Rivera		
Brandon Webb		
37 Akinori Iwamuri	.60	1.50
Yuniesky Betancourt		
Tim Lincecum		
38 Randy Johnson	1.00	2.50
Brett Myers		
Kenny Lofton BT		
39 Andruw Jones	.40	1.00
Stephen Drew		
Joe Nathan		
40 Todd Jones	.40	1.00
Erick Aybar		
Angel Pagan HN		
41 Jair Jurrjens	.40	1.00
John Danks		
George Sherrill HN		
42 Matt Kemp	.75	2.00
Carlos Pena		
Fausto Carmona		
43 Adam Kennedy	.60	1.50
Nick Punto		
Mike Napoli HN		
44 Gerald Laird UER	.40	1.00
Brian Schneider		
Matt Diaz HN		
45 Cliff Lee	.60	1.50
Mike Mussina		
Ryan Dempster HN		
46 Rhadhames Liz	.40	1.00
Jack Wilson		
Carlos Gomez		
47 Greg Maddux	1.25	3.00
Carlos Ruiz		
Nick Swisher		
48 Sean Marshall	.40	1.00
Craig Monroe		
Aramis Ramirez		
49 Victor Martinez	.60	1.50
C.C. Sabathia		
Carlos Delgado		
50 Aaron Miles	.40	1.00
Brian Moehler		
Ben Francisco HN		
51 Lastings Milledge	.60	1.50
Dmitri Young		
Ryan Zimmerman		
Barry Zito		
52 Bengie Molina	.60	1.50
David Murphy		
John Lackey		
53 David Murphy	.60	1.50
John Lackey		
Buddy Carlyle		
54 Mike Napoli	1.00	2.50
Carlos Gonzalez		
Matt Macri HN		
55 Dioner Navarro	.40	1.00
Joe Crede		
Ryan Ludwick HN		
56 Russ Ohlendorf	.60	1.50
Matt Capps		
Chris Young		
57 Scott Olsen	.40	1.00
Manny Parra		
Tim Redding HN		
58 Manny Parra	.40	1.00
Tim Redding		
Paul Maholm HN		
59 Hunter Pence	.60	1.50
Carlos Guillen		
David Weathers		
60 Troy Percival	.60	1.50
Brian Anderson		
Denard Span HN		
61 Glen Perkins	1.00	2.50
Vicente Padilla		
Johnny Cueto HN		
62 A.J. Pierzynski	.40	1.00
Jorge Cantu		
Matt Diaz HN		
63 Joel Pineiro	.75	2.00
Chris Davis		
Masahide Kobayashi HN		
64 Nick Punto	1.00	2.50
Mike Napoli		
Carlos Gonzalez HN		
65 Robb Quinlan	.40	1.00
Mike Lamb		
Mike Gonzalez HN		
66 Hanley Ramirez	.60	1.50
Josh Barfield		
Chad Cordero		
67 Horatio Ramirez	1.00	2.50
Brian Bannister		
Manny Ramirez		
68 Manny Ramirez	1.00	2.50
Randy Johnson		
Brett Myers		
69 Darrell Rasner	.40	1.00
Troy Percival		
Brian Anderson HN		
70 Alex Rios	.60	1.50
Johan Santana		
Roy Halladay		
71 Alex Rodriguez	1.25	3.00
Huston Street		
Mark Grudzielanek		
72 Carlos Ruiz	.60	1.50
Nick Swisher		
Kevin Hart		
73 C.C. Sabathia	.60	1.50
Carlos Delgado		
Lance Broadway		
74 Pablo Sandoval	1.50	4.00
Alex Romero		
Ivan Ochoa HN		
75 Johan Santana	.60	1.50
Roy Halladay		
Brad Wilkinson		
76 Joe Saunders	.60	1.50
Cliff Lee		
Mike Mussina HN		
77 Brian Schneider	.40	1.00
Matt Diaz		
Darin Erstad HN		
78 Skip Schumaker	.60	1.50
Curtis Granderson		
A.J. Pierzynski HN		
79 Marco Scutaro	.60	1.50
Adam Kennedy		
Nick Punto HN		
80 George Sherrill	.60	1.50
Joakim Soria		
Miguel Tejada HN		
81 James Shields	.60	1.50
Nate McLouth		
Rich Thompson		
82 John Smoltz	1.00	2.50
Andruw Jones		
Chipper Jones		
Andruw Jones		
83 Andy Sonnanstine	.60	1.50
Jesse Litsch		
Todd Wellemeyer HN		
84 Sammy Sosa	1.00	2.50
Russ Martin		
Mark Buehrle		
85 Ryan Sweeney	.60	1.50
Mike Pelfrey		
Nick Blackburn HN		
86 Nick Swisher	.60	1.50
Kevin Hart		
Rhadhames Liz		
87 Mark Teixeira	1.00	2.50
John Smoltz		
Andruw Jones		
Chipper Jones		
88 Marcus Thames	.60	1.50
Ben Zobrist		
Mark Ellis HN		
89 Jim Thome	.60	1.50
Joe Koshansky		
Adrian Gonzalez		
90 Salomon Torres	.40	1.00
Rob Quinlan		
Mike Lamb HN		
91 J.R. Towles	.60	1.50
B.J. Ryan		
Roy Oswalt		
92 Eugenio Velez	.40	1.00
Akinori Iwamura		
Yuniesky Betancourt		
93 Edinson Volquez	1.00	2.50
Justin Duchscherer		
Geovany Soto HN		
94 Brad Wilkerson	.40	1.00
Juan Pierre		
Bengie Molina		
95 Brian Wilson	1.25	3.00
Kerry Wood		
Kosuke Fukudome HN		
96 Jamey Wright	.40	1.00
Brian Burres		
Glen Perkins HN		
97 Dmitri Young	.60	1.50
Ryan Zimmerman		
Barry Zito		
Dmitri Young		
98 Dmitri Young	.40	1.00
Yovanni Gallardo		
Chris Duncan		
99 Barry Zito	.60	1.50
Dmitri Young		
Yovanni Gallardo		
100 Ben Zobrist	.60	1.50
Mark Ellis		
Mike Aviles HN		
101 C.J. Wilson	5.00	12.00
Max Scherzer		
Aaron Miles		
102 Chris Volstad	.60	1.50
Josh Fields		
Emmanuel Burriss		
103 Joakim Soria	.60	1.50
Miguel Tejada		
Dioner Navarro		
104 Greg Smith	.40	1.00
Dana Eveland		
Ryan Sweeney		
105 Juan Pierre	.40	1.00
Bengie Molina		
David Murphy		
106 Hiroki Kuroda	1.00	2.50
Greg Smith		
Dana Eveland		
107 Kelly Johnson	1.25	3.00
Alex Rodriguez		
Huston Street		
108 Carlos Gonzalez	1.00	2.50
Matt Macri		
Marcus Thames		

2008 Topps Heritage Baseball Flashbacks

Card	Low	High
COMPLETE SET (10)	5.00	12.00
STATED ODDS 1:12 HOBBY,1:12 RETAIL		
BF1 Minnie Minoso	.50	1.25
BF2 Luis Aparicio	.75	2.00
BF3 Ernie Banks	1.25	3.00
BF4 Bill Mazeroski	.75	2.00
BF5 Bob Gibson	.75	2.00
BF6 Frank Robinson	.75	2.00
BF7 Brooks Robinson	.75	2.00
BF8 Mickey Mantle	2.00	5.00
BF9 Orlando Cepeda	.75	2.00
BF10 Eddie Mathews	1.25	3.00

2008 Topps Heritage Clubhouse Collection Relics

GROUP A ODDS 1:4100 H,1:7400 R
GROUP B ODDS 1:18,000 H,1:7800 R
GROUP C ODDS 1:90 H,1:182 R
GROUP D ODDS 1:54 H, 1:108 R
HN GROUP A ODDS 1:3600 HOBBY
HN GROUP B ODDS 1:74 HOBBY
HN GROUP C ODDS 1:55 HOBBY
NO HN GRP A PRICING AVAILABLE

Card	Low	High
AD Adam Dunn C	3.00	8.00
AG Alex Gordon HN C	4.00	10.00
AJ Andruw Jones C	3.00	8.00
AJ Andruw Jones HN B	3.00	8.00
AL Al Kaline HN A	50.00	120.00
AP Albert Pujols HN B	6.00	15.00
AR Aramis Ramirez C	3.00	8.00
AR Aramis Ramirez HN B	3.00	8.00
BA Bobby Abreu C	3.00	8.00
BD Blake DeWitt HN B	6.00	15.00
BG Bob Gibson A	50.00	120.00
BG Bob Gibson HN B	10.00	25.00
BM Bill Mazeroski HN B	10.00	25.00
BR Brooks Robinson HN B	10.00	25.00
BS Bill Skowron HN A	50.00	120.00
CAB Craig Biggio C	4.00	10.00
CB Carlos Beltran C	3.00	8.00
CB Carlos Beltran HN B	3.00	8.00
CC Carl Crawford C	3.00	8.00
CD Carlos Delgado C	3.00	8.00
CG Curtis Granderson HN C	3.00	8.00
CL Carlos Lee C	3.00	8.00
CL Carlos Lee HN B	3.00	8.00
DH Dan Haren HN C	3.00	8.00
DL Derrek Lee C	3.00	8.00
DL Derrek Lee HN B	3.00	8.00
DO David Ortiz C	4.00	10.00
DO David Ortiz HN B	4.00	10.00
DS Duke Snider HN A	50.00	120.00
DY Dmitri Young C	3.00	8.00
DY Dmitri Young HN B	3.00	8.00
EB Erik Bedard HN C	3.00	8.00
EC Eric Chavez C	3.00	8.00
FR Frank Robinson HN A	50.00	120.00
FT Frank Thomas C	4.00	10.00
FT Frank Thomas HN B	4.00	10.00
GA Garret Anderson D	3.00	8.00
HB Hank Blalock D	3.00	8.00
IR Ivan Rodriguez C	4.00	10.00
JB Jeremy Bonderman HN C	3.00	8.00
JD Johnny Damon C	3.00	8.00
JD Jermaine Dye HN C	3.00	8.00
JE Jim Edmonds D	3.00	8.00
JE Johnny Estrada HN C	3.00	8.00
JL Julio Lugo HN C	3.00	8.00
JP Jorge Posada C	4.00	10.00
JS John Smoltz D	4.00	10.00
JV Justin Verlander C	4.00	10.00
LA Luis Aparicio A	30.00	60.00
LB Lance Berkman D	3.00	8.00
MC Miguel Cabrera D	4.00	10.00
MIM Minnie Minoso B	8.00	20.00
MM Mike Mussina D	3.00	8.00
MT Miguel Tejada D	3.00	8.00
MT Miguel Tejada HN B	3.00	8.00
NF Nellie Fox HN B	12.50	30.00
PM Pedro Martinez D	4.00	10.00
PM Pedro Martinez HN B	3.00	8.00
RH Ryan Howard D	5.00	12.00
RO Roy Oswalt D	3.00	8.00
RO Roy Oswalt HN B	3.00	8.00
RR Robin Roberts HN B	8.00	20.00
RS Richie Sexson D	3.00	8.00
RS Darrell Rasner HN B	3.00	8.00
RZ Ryan Zimmerman D	4.00	10.00
RZ Ryan Zimmerman HN B	3.00	8.00
SG Shawn Green C	3.00	8.00
ST Steve Pearce HN C	3.00	8.00
TH Todd Helton C	4.00	10.00
TKH Torii Hunter D	3.00	8.00
TLH Travis Hafner D	3.00	8.00
WM Bill Mazeroski A	20.00	50.00
YB Yogi Berra A	25.00	60.00

2008 Topps Heritage Clubhouse Collection Relics Autographs

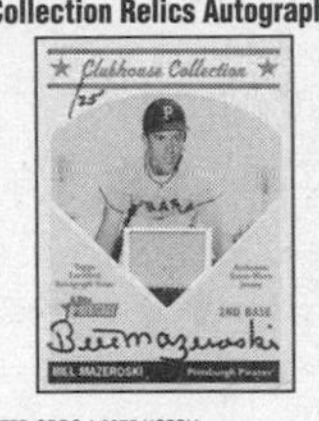

STATED ODDS 1:6875 HOBBY
STATED ODDS 1:14,200 RETAIL
HN ODDS 1:1815 HOBBY
STATED PRINT RUN 25 SER.#'d SETS
NO PRICING DUE TO SCARCITY
EXCHANGE DEADLINE 2/28/2010
HN EXCH DEADLINE 11/30/2010

2008 Topps Heritage Clubhouse Collection Relics Dual

STATED ODDS 1:5582 H,1:11,000 R
HN STATED ODDS 1:1900 HOBBY
HN PRINT RUN 59 SER.#'d SETS

Card	Low	High
AK L.Aparicio/P.Konerko	30.00	60.00
BL E.Banks/D.Lee	30.00	60.00
CL Cepeda/Lewis HN	30.00	60.00
GE B.Gibson/J.Edmonds	30.00	60.00
KG Kaline/Granderson HN	30.00	60.00
MB B.Mazeroski/J.Bay	30.00	60.00
MH M.Minoso/T.Hafner	30.00	60.00
RB F.Robinson/Bruce HN	30.00	60.00
SK Snider/Kershaw HN	30.00	60.00
SR Skowron/Rasner HN	30.00	60.00

2008 Topps Heritage Dick Perez

Card	Low	High
COMPLETE SET (10)	30.00	60.00
THREE PER $9.99 WALMART BOX		
SIX PER $19.99 WALMART BOX		
HDP1 Manny Ramirez	1.25	3.00
HDP2 Cameron Maybin	.50	1.25
HDP3 Ryan Howard	.75	2.00
HDP4 David Ortiz	1.25	3.00
HDP5 Tim Lincecum	.75	2.00
HDP6 David Wright	.75	2.00
HDP7 Mickey Mantle	2.50	6.00
HDP8 Joba Chamberlain	.50	1.25
HDP9 Ichiro Suzuki	1.50	4.00
HDP10 Prince Fielder	.75	2.00

2008 Topps Heritage Flashbacks Autographs

STATED ODDS 1:14,900 HOBBY
STATED ODDS 1:20,000 RETAIL
STATED PRINT RUN 25 SER.#'d SETS
NO PRICING DUE TO SCARCITY
EXCHANGE DEADLINE 2/28/10

2008 Topps Heritage Flashbacks Seat Relics

STATED ODDS 1:162 H,1:327 R
HN ODDS 1:3175 HOBBY
HN PRINT RUN 59 SER.#'d SETS

Card	Low	High
BG Bob Gibson	10.00	25.00
BR Brooks Robinson	10.00	25.00
DE Dwight D. Eisenhower HN	30.00	60.00
EB Ernie Banks	10.00	25.00
EM Eddie Mathews	10.00	25.00

FR Frank Robinson 8.00 20.00
LA Luis Aparicio 8.00 20.00
MIM Minnie Minoso 8.00 20.00
MM Mickey Mantle 12.00 30.00
MO Motown HN 30.00 60.00
NK Nikita Khrushchev HN 30.00 60.00
OC Orlando Cepeda 8.00 20.00
WM Bill Mazeroski 10.00 25.00

2008 Topps Heritage High Numbers Then and Now

COMPLETE SET (10) 6.00 15.00
STATED ODDS 1:12 HOBBY
TN1 Ernie Banks/Jimmy Rollins 1.25 3.00
TN2 N.Fox/A.Rodriguez 1.50 4.00
TN3 Larry Sherry/Mike Lowell .50 1.25
TN4 W.McCovey/R.Braun .75 2.00
TN5 B.Allison/D.Pedroia .75 2.00
TN6 Del Crandall/Russ Martin .50 1.25
TN7 Luis Aparicio/Orlando Cabrera .75 2.00
TN8 E.Wynn/A.Rodriguez 1.50 4.00
TN9 Early Wynn/Jake Peavy .75 2.00
TN10 Sam Jones/CC Sabathia .75 2.00

2008 Topps Heritage National Convention

1 Ted Williams 2.50 6.00
145 Bob Gibson .75 2.00
150 Mickey Mantle 4.00 10.00
310 Ernie Banks 1.25 3.00
496 Mickey Mantle 4.00 10.00

2008 Topps Heritage New Age Performers

COMPLETE SET (15) 10.00 25.00
STATED ODDS 1:15 HOBBY,1:15 RETAIL
NAP1 Magglio Ordonez .60 1.50
NAP2 Ichiro Suzuki 1.25 3.00
NAP3 Matt Holliday 1.00 2.50
NAP4 Prince Fielder .60 1.50
NAP5 David Wright .60 1.50
NAP6 Jake Peavy .40 1.00
NAP7 Alex Rodriguez 1.25 3.00
NAP8 John Lackey .60 1.50
NAP9 Vladimir Guerrero .60 1.50
NAP10 Ryan Howard .60 1.50
NAP11 Brandon Webb .60 1.50
NAP12 Manny Ramirez 1.00 2.50
NAP13 Josh Beckett .40 1.00
NAP14 Jimmy Rollins .60 1.50
NAP15 David Ortiz 1.00 2.50

2008 Topps Heritage News Flashbacks

COMPLETE SET (10) 4.00 10.00
COMMON CARD .60 1.50
STATED ODDS 1:12 HOBBY,1:12 RETAIL

2008 Topps Heritage Real One Autographs

STATED ODDS 1:247 H,1:495 R
HN ODDS 1:110 HOBBY
EXCHANGE DEADLINE 02/28/2010
HN EXCH DEADLINE 11/30/2010
AJ Al Jackson HN 15.00 40.00
AK Al Kaline HN 50.00 120.00
AR Aramis Ramirez 20.00 50.00
BB Bob Blaylock 10.00 25.00
BM Bob Martyn 10.00 25.00
BM Brian McCann HN 10.00 25.00
BMS Bill Skowron HN 10.00 25.00
BR Bill Renna 10.00 25.00
BS Bob Smith 10.00 25.00
BS Barney Schultz HN 15.00 40.00
BSP Bob Speake 10.00 25.00
CE Carl Erskine 15.00 40.00
CE Chuck Essegian HN 10.00 25.00
CG Curtis Granderson HN 15.00 40.00
CK Chick King 10.00 25.00
CK Clayton Kershaw HN 600.00 1000.00
DP Dustin Pedroia HN 40.00 80.00
DR Dusty Rhodes HN 12.50 30.00
DS Duke Snider HN 50.00 100.00
FL Fred Lewis HN 10.00 25.00
FR Frank Robinson HN 20.00 50.00
FS Freddy Sanchez 10.00 25.00
GEZ Gus Zernial 10.00 25.00
GS Geovany Soto HN 10.00 25.00
GZ George Zuverink 10.00 25.00
HL Hector Lopez HN 20.00 50.00
HP Herb Plews 10.00 25.00
JAB Jay Bruce HN 12.50 30.00
JB Jim Bolger 12.50 30.00
JB Jim Brosnan HN 10.00 25.00
JC Joba Chamberlain 10.00 25.00
JF Jack Fisher HN 10.00 25.00
JH Jay Hook HN 10.00 25.00
JK Jim Kaat HN 15.00 40.00
JO Johnny O'Brien 20.00 50.00
JP J.W. Porter 10.00 25.00
KL Ken Lehman 10.00 25.00
LA Luis Aparicio 20.00 50.00
LM Les Moss 15.00 40.00
LT Lee Tate 10.00 25.00
MB Mike Baxes 10.00 25.00
MIM Minnie Minoso 30.00 60.00
MM Morrie Martin 10.00 25.00
MW Maury Wills HN 10.00 25.00
OC Orlando Cepeda HN 25.00 60.00
PC Phil Clark 10.00 25.00
PG Pumpsie Green HN 12.50 30.00
RC Roger Craig HN 10.00 25.00
RH Russ Heman 10.00 25.00
RJ Randy Jackson 10.00 25.00
SP Scott Podsednik 10.00 25.00
TC Tom Carroll 10.00 25.00
TD Tommy Davis HN 15.00 40.00
TK Ted Kazanski 10.00 25.00
TQ Tom Qualters 10.00 25.00
VV Vito Valentinetti 10.00 25.00
WM Bill Mazeroski 30.00 60.00
YB Yogi Berra 60.00 150.00

2008 Topps Heritage Real One Autographs Red Ink

*RED INK: .6X TO 1.5X BASIC
STATED ODDS 1:835 H,1:1650 R
HN ODDS 1:439 HOBBY
STATED PRINT RUN 59 SERIAL #'d SETS
RED INK ALSO CALLED SPECIAL EDITION
EXCHANGE DEADLINE 02/28/2010
HN EXCH DEADLINE 11/30/2010
CK Clayton Kershaw HN 1200.00 1600.00
DS Duke Snider HN 100.00 200.00
GS Geovany Soto HN 15.00 40.00
MIM Minnie Minoso 60.00 120.00
WM Bill Mazeroski 125.00 250.00

2008 Topps Heritage Rookie Performers

COMPLETE SET (15) 12.50 30.00
STATED ODDS 1:12 HOBBY
RP1 Clayton Kershaw 8.00 20.00
RP2 Mike Aviles .75 2.00
RP3 Armando Galarraga .75 2.00
RP4 Joey Votto 2.00 5.00
RP5 Kosuke Fukudome 1.50 4.00
RP6 Chris Davis 1.00 2.50
RP7 Jeff Samardzija 1.50 4.00
RP8 Carlos Gonzalez 1.25 3.00
RP9 Max Scherzer 6.00 15.00
RP10 Evan Longoria 2.50 6.00
RP11 Johnny Cueto 1.25 3.00
RP12 Hiroki Kuroda 1.25 3.00
RP13 John Bowker .50 1.25
RP14 Justin Masterson 1.25 3.00
RP15 Jay Bruce 1.50 4.00

2008 Topps Heritage T205 Mini

THREE PER $9.99 TARGET BOX
SIX PER $19.99 TARGET BOX
HTCP1 Albert Pujols 2.50 6.00
HTCP2 Clay Buchholz 3.00 8.00
HTCP3 Matt Holliday 2.00 5.00
HTCP4 Luke Hochevar 1.25 3.00
HTCP5 Alex Rodriguez 2.50 6.00
HTCP6 Joey Votto 3.00 8.00
HTCP7 Chin-Lung Hu .75 2.00
HTCP8 Ryan Braun 1.25 3.00
HTCP9 Joba Chamberlain .75 2.00
HTCP10 Ryan Howard 1.25 3.00
HTCP11 Ichiro Suzuki 2.50 6.00
HTCP12 Steve Pearce 4.00 10.00
HTCP13 Vladimir Guerrero 1.25 3.00
HTCP14 Wladimir Balentien .75 2.00
HTCP15 David Ortiz 2.00 5.00

2008 Topps Heritage Then and Now

COMPLETE SET (10) 6.00 15.00
STATED ODDS 1:15 HOBBY,1:15 RETAIL
TN1 A.Rodriguez/E.Mathews 1.50 4.00
TN2 A.Rodriguez/E.Banks 1.50 4.00
TN3 M.Ordonez/O.Cepeda .75 2.00
TN4 J.Reyes/L.Aparicio .75 2.00
TN5 D.Ortiz/M.Mantle 2.50 6.00
TN6 E.Bedard/J.Podres .50 1.25
TN7 J.Beckett/E.Wynn .75 2.00
TN8 I.Suzuki/M.Minoso 1.50 4.00
TN9 D.Ortiz/F.Robinson 1.25 3.00
TN10 J.Peavy/D.Drysdale .75 2.00

2009 Topps Heritage

This set was released on February 27, 2009. The base set consists of 500 cards.

COMPLETE SET (733)
COMP.LO.SET w/o VAR (425) 30.00 60.00
COMP.HI.SET w/o VAR (220) 90.00 150.00
COMP.HI.SET w/o SP's (185) 15.00 40.00
COMMON CARD (1-733) .15 .40
COMMON ROOKIE (1-733) .40 1.00
COMMON SP (426-500/586-720) 2.50 6.00
SP ODDS 1:3 HOBBY
1 Mark Buehrle .25 .60
2 Nyjer Morgan .15 .40
3 Casey Kotchman .15 .40
4 Edinson Volquez .15 .40
5 Andre Ethier .25 .60
6 Brandon Inge .15 .40
7 T.Lincecum/B.Bochy .25 .60
8 Gil Meche .15 .40
9 Brad Hawpe .15 .40
10 Hanley Ramirez .25 .60
11 Ross Gload .15 .40
12 Jeremy Guthrie .15 .40
13 Garret Anderson .15 .40
14 Jeremy Sowers .15 .40
15a Dustin Pedroia .30 .75
15b D.Pedroia SP VAR 60.00 120.00
16 Chris Perez .15 .40
17 Adam Lind .15 .40
18 Los Angeles Dodgers TC .15 .40
19 Stephen Drew .15 .40
20 Matt Capps .15 .40
21 Mike Napoli .15 .40
22 Khalil Greene .15 .40
23 Andy Sonnanstine .15 .40
24 Marco Scutaro .25 .60
25 Paul Konerko .25 .60
26 Miguel Tejada .25 .60
27 Nick Blackburn .15 .40
28 Nick Markakis .30 .75
29 Johan Santana .25 .60
30 Grady Sizemore .25 .60
31 Raul Ibanez .25 .60
32 Jay Bruce/Johnny Cueto .25 .60
33 Randy Johnson .40 1.00
34 Ian Kinsler .25 .60
35 Andy Pettitte .25 .60
36 Lyle Overbay .15 .40
37 Jeff Francoeur .25 .60
38 Justin Duchscherer .15 .40
39 Mike Cameron .15 .40
40 Ryan Ludwick .25 .60
41 Dave Bush .15 .40
42 Pablo Sandoval (RC) .75 2.00
43 Washington Nationals TC .15 .40
44 Dana Eveland .15 .40
45 Jeff Keppinger .15 .40
46 Brandon Backe .15 .40
47 Ryan Theriot .15 .40
48 Vernon Wells .15 .40
49 Doug Davis .15 .40
50 Curtis Granderson .30 .75
51 Aaron Laffey .15 .40
52 Chris Young .15 .40
53 Adam Jones .25 .60
54 Jonathan Papelbon .25 .60
55 Nate McLouth .15 .40
56 Hunter Pence .25 .60
57 Scot Shields/Francisco Rodriguez .25 .60
58a Conor Jackson ARI .15 .40
58b C.Jackson TB SP 15.00 40.00
59 John Maine .15 .40
60 Ramon Hernandez .15 .40
61 Jorge De La Rosa .15 .40
62 Greg Maddux .50 1.25
63 Carlos Beltran .25 .60
64 Matt Harrison (RC) .40 1.00
65 Ivan Rodriguez .25 .60
66 Jesse Litsch .15 .40
67 Omar Vizquel .25 .60
68 Edwin Jackson .15 .40
69 Ray Durham .15 .40
70a Tom Glavine .25 .60
70b Tom Glavine UER SP 8.00 20.00
71 Darin Erstad .15 .40
72 Detroit Tigers TC .15 .40
73 David Price RC .75 2.00
74 Marlon Byrd .15 .40
75 Ryan Garko .15 .40
76 Jered Weaver .25 .60
77 Kelly Shoppach .15 .40
78 Joe Saunders .15 .40
79 Carlos Pena .25 .60
80 Brian Wilson .40 1.00
81 Carlos Gonzalez .25 .60
82 Scott Baker .15 .40
83a Derek Jeter 1.00 2.50
83b D.Jeter SP VAR 100.00 200.00
84 Yadier Molina .40 1.00
85 Justin Verlander .40 1.00
86 Jose Lopez .15 .40
87 Jarrod Washburn .15 .40
88 Russell Martin .15 .40
89 Garrett Olson .15 .40
90 Erick Aybar .15 .40
91 Kevin Millwood .15 .40
92 Jose Guillen .15 .40
93 Rickie Weeks .15 .40
94 Yovani Gallardo .15 .40
95 Aramis Ramirez .15 .40
96 Phil Hughes .15- .40
97 Kevin Kouzmanoff .15 .40
98 Shaun Marcum .15 .40
99 Lastings Milledge .15 .40
100 Jair Jurrjens .15 .40
101 Gio Gonzalez .25 .60
102a Adrian Gonzalez .30 .75
102b A.Gonzalez Rgr Logo 20.00 50.00
103 Brad Lidge .15 .40
104 Chris Davis .25 .60
105 Brad Penny .15 .40
106 David Eckstein .15 .40
107 Jo-Jo Reyes .15 .40
108 John Buck .15 .40
109 Delmon Young .25 .60
110 Johnny Cueto .25 .60
111 Kevin Youkilis .15 .40
112 Scott Lewis (RC) .40 1.00
113 Brandon Moss .15 .40
114 Alexi Casilla .15 .40
115 Jonathan Papelbon/Tim Wakefield .25 .60
116 Emil Brown .15 .40
117 Michael Bowden (RC) .40 1.00
118 Chris Lambert (RC) .40 1.00
119 Wilkin Castillo RC .40 1.00
120 Fernando Perez (RC) .40 1.00
121 Angel Salome (RC) .40 1.00
122 Dexter Fowler (RC) .60 1.50
123 Will Venable RC .40 1.00
124 Jason Motte (RC) .60 1.50
125 Jesus Delgado RC .60 1.50
126 Alfredo Simon (RC) .40 1.00
127 Gaby Sanchez RC .60 1.50
128 Scott Elbert (RC) .40 1.00
129 James Parr (RC) .40 1.00
130 Greg Golson (RC) .40 1.00
131 Jonathon Niese RC .60 1.50
132 Mat Gamel RC 1.00 2.50
133 Luis Cruz RC .40 1.00
134 Phil Coke RC .60 1.50
135 Devon Lowery (RC) .40 1.00
136 Matt Tuiasosopo (RC) .40 1.00
137 Kila Ka'aihue (RC) .60 1.50
138 Andrew Carpenter RC .60 1.50
139 Jensen Lewis (RC) .40 1.00
140 Lou Marson (RC) .40 1.00
141 Wade LeBlanc RC .60 1.50
142 Juan Miranda RC .60 1.50
143 Alcides Escobar RC .60 1.50
144 Matt Antonelli RC .60 1.50
145 Jesse Chavez RC .40 1.00
146 Ramon Ramirez (RC) .40 1.00
147 Aaron Cunningham RC .40 1.00
148 Travis Snider RC .60 1.50
149 Adam Dunn .25 .60
150 John Danks .15 .40
151 San Francisco Giants TC .15 .40
152 Jorge Cantu .15 .40
153 Jacoby Ellsbury .30 .75
154 Rich Aurilia .15 .40
155 Jeff Kent .15 .40
156 Salomon Torres .15 .40
157 Juan Uribe .15 .40
158 Gregor Blanco .15 .40
159 Shin-Soo Choo .25 .60
160 D.Wright/A.Rodriguez AS .50 1.25
161 Jose Valverde .15 .40
162 B.J. Upton .25 .60
163 Johnny Damon .25 .60
164 Cincinnati Reds TC .15 .40
165 Tim Lincecum .25 .60
166 Carl Crawford .25 .60
167 Jeff Mathis .15 .40
168 Felipe Lopez .15 .40
169 Joe Nathan .15 .40
170 Brian McCann .25 .60
171 Matt Joyce .15 .40
172 Cameron Maybin .15 .40
173 Brandon Phillips .15 .40
174 Cleveland Indians TC .15 .40
175 Tim Redding .15 .40
176 Corey Patterson .15 .40
177 Joakim Soria .15 .40
178 Jhonny Peralta .15 .40
179 Daniel Murphy RC 1.50 4.00
180 Ryan Church .15 .40
181 Josh Johnson .25 .60
182 Carlos Zambrano .25 .60
183 Pittsburgh Pirates TC .15 .40
184 Boston Red Sox TC .25 .60
185 Kyle Kendrick .15 .40
186 Joel Zumaya .15 .40
187 Bronson Arroyo .15 .40
188 Joey Gathright .15 .40
189 Mike Gonzalez .15 .40
190 Luke Scott .15 .40
191 Jonathan Broxton .15 .40
192 Jeff Baker .15 .40
193 Brian Fuentes .15 .40
194 Pat Burrell .15 .40
195 Ryan Franklin .25 .60
196 Alex Gordon .25 .60
197 Orlando Hudson .15 .40
198 Chris Dickerson .15 .40
199 David Purcey .15 .40
200 Ken Griffey Jr. .75 2.00
201 Chad Tracy .15 .40
202 Troy Percival .15 .40
203 Chris Iannetta .15 .40
204 Baltimore Orioles TC .15 .40
205 Yunel Escobar .15 .40
206 Dan Haren .15 .40
207 Aubrey Huff .15 .40
208 Chicago White Sox TC .15 .40
209 Randy Wolf .15 .40
210 Ryan Zimmerman .25 .60
211 Manny Parra .15 .40
212 Manny Acta MG .15 .40
213 Dusty Baker MG .15 .40
214 Bruce Bochy MG .25 .60
215 Bobby Cox MG .15 .40
216 Terry Francona MG .25 .60
217 Joe Girardi MG .25 .60
218 Ozzie Guillen MG .15 .40
219 Bob Geren MG .15 .40
220 Tony La Russa MG .25 .60
221 Jim Leyland MG .15 .40
222 Charlie Manuel MG .15 .40
223 Lou Piniella MG .15 .40
224 John Russell MG .15 .40
225 Joe Torre MG .25 .60
226 Dave Trembley MG .15 .40
227 Eric Wedge MG .15 .40
228 Jeff Suppan .15 .40
229 Kaz Matsui .15 .40
230 Beckett/Lester/Matsuzaka .25 .60
231 Mark Reynolds .15 .40
232 Jay Payton .15 .40
233 Kerry Wood .15 .40
234 Juan Pierre .15 .40
235 Ryan Freel .15 .40
236 Ryan Feierabend .15 .40
237 Xavier Nady .15 .40
238 Ronny Paulino .15 .40
239 A.J. Burnett .15 .40
240 Orlando Cabrera .15 .40
241 Corey Hart .15 .40
242 St. Louis Cardinals TC .15 .40
243 Andy Marte .15 .40
244 Trevor Hoffman .25 .60
245 Carlos Guillen .15 .40
246 Brandon Jones .15 .40
247 Hideki Matsui .40 1.00
248 Henry Blanco .15 .40
249 Jon Lester .25 .60
250a Albert Pujols .50 1.25
250b A.Pujols SP VAR 100.00 200.00
251 Manny Ramirez .40 1.00
252 Brian Bannister .15 .40
253 Alex Cintron .15 .40
254 Brandon Lyon .15 .40
255 Blake DeWitt .15 .40
256 Luis Castillo .15 .40
257 Mark Teixeira .25 .60
258 Jack Wilson .15 .40
259 Kosuke Fukudome .25 .60
260 Manny Ramirez/Andre Ethier .40 1.00
261 Scott Kazmir .15 .40
262 Mark Teahen .15 .40
263 Dioner Navarro .15 .40
264 Cole Hamels .30 .75
265 Justin Upton .25 .60
266 Ricky Nolasco .15 .40
267 Hank Blalock .15 .40
268 John Lackey .25 .60
269 Jeremy Hermida .15 .40
270 Chien-Ming Wang .25 .60
271 Lance Berkman .25 .60
272 Scott Olsen .15 .40
273 Alex Rios .15 .40
274 Matt Garza .15 .40
275 Skip Schumaker .15 .40
276 Greg Smith .15 .40
277 Bobby Crosby .15 .40
278 Hiroki Kuroda .15 .40
279 Gary Matthews .15 .40
280 Tim Wakefield .25 .60
281 Mike Jacobs .15 .40
282 Chris Volstad .15 .40
283 Jeff Clement .15 .40
284 Max Scherzer .40 1.00
285 Chase Headley .15 .40
286 Francisco Rodriguez .25 .60
287 Moises Alou .15 .40
288 Jeff Francis .15 .40
289 Carlos Delgado .15 .40
290 Jose Reyes .25 .60
291 Ubaldo Jimenez .15 .40
292 Kelly Shoppach/Victor Martinez .25 .60
293 Joe Blanton .15 .40
294 Mark DeRosa .25 .60
295 Casey Blake .15 .40
296 Mike Pelfrey .15 .40
297 Aaron Boone .15 .40
298 Aaron Cook .15 .40
299 Daric Barton .15 .40
300 Ryan Howard .30 .75
301 Ty Wigginton .25 .60
302 Philadelphia Phillies TC .15 .40
303 Barry Zito .25 .60
304 Jake Peavy .15 .40
305 Alfonso Soriano .25 .60
306 Scott Linebrink .15 .40
307 Torii Hunter .15 .40
308 Zack Greinke .25 .60
309 Ryan Sweeney .15 .40
310 Mike Lowell .15 .40
311 Jason Marquis .15 .40
312 Aaron Rowand .15 .40
313 Brandon Morrow .15 .40
314 Edgar Renteria .15 .40
315 Mariano Rivera .50 1.25
316 Wilson Betemit .15 .40
317 Joey Votto .40 1.00
318 Evan Longoria .25 .60
319 Mike Aviles .15 .40
320 Jay Bruce .25 .60
321 Denard Span .15 .40
322 David Murphy .15 .40
323 Geovany Soto .25 .60
324 John Lannan .15 .40
325 Brad Ziegler .15 .40
326 Ichiro Suzuki .50 1.25
327 Kyle Lohse .15 .40
328 Jesus Flores .15 .40
329 Edwin Encarnacion .40 1.00
330 Franklin Gutierrez .15 .40
331 Troy Glaus .15 .40
332 David Ortiz .40 1.00
333 Anibal Sanchez .15 .40
334 Jimmy Rollins .25 .60
335 Kelly Johnson .15 .40
336 Paul Byrd .15 .40
337 Akinori Iwamura .15 .40
338 Milton Bradley .15 .40
339 Miguel Olivo .15 .40
340 Ian Snell .15 .40
341 Vladimir Guerrero .25 .60
342 Asdrubal Cabrera .25 .60
343 Clayton Kershaw .75 2.00
344 Rafael Furcal .15 .40
345 Aaron Harang .15 .40
346a Fred Lewis .15 .40
346b F.Lewis UER Winn SP 15.00 40.00
347 Jack Cust .15 .40
348 Todd Helton .25 .60
349 Steve Pearce .40 1.00
350 Javier Vazquez .15 .40
351 Ben Sheets .15 .40
352 Joey Votto/Edwin Encarnacion/Jay Bruce .40 1.00
353 Luke Hochevar .15 .40
354 Chris Snyder .15 .40
355 Rick Ankiel .15 .40
356 Emmanuel Burriss .15 .40
357 Vicente Padilla .15 .40
358 Yuniesky Betancourt .15 .40
359 Willy Taveras .15 .40
360 Gavin Floyd .15 .40
361 Gerald Laird .15 .40
362 Roy Oswalt .25 .60
363 Coco Crisp .15 .40
364 Felix Hernandez .25 .60
365 Carlos Quentin .15 .40
366 Ervin Santana .15 .40
367 David DeJesus .15 .40
368 Aaron Miles .15 .40
369 B.J. Ryan .15 .40
370 Jason Giambi .15 .40
371 J.J. Putz .15 .40
372 Brian Schneider .15 .40
373 Andy LaRoche .15 .40
374 Tim Hudson .25 .60
375 Garrett Atkins .15 .40
376 James Shields .15 .40
377 Alex Rodriguez .50 1.25
378 J.J. Hardy .15 .40
379 Michael Young .15 .40
380 Prince Fielder .25 .60
381 Atlanta Braves TC .15 .40
382 Chone Figgins .15 .40
383 David Wright .30 .75
384 Brian Giles .15 .40
385 Chase Utley WS .25 .60
386 Eric Bruntlett WS .15 .40
387 Carlos Ruiz WS .15 .40
388 Ryan Howard WS .30 .75
389 Jayson Werth WS .25 .60
390 B.J. Upton WS .25 .60
391 Brad Lidge .15 .40
392 Chad Cordero .15 .40
393 Ryan Doumit .15 .40
394 James Loney .15 .40
395 George Sherrill .15 .40
396 Gary Sheffield .15 .40
397 Chicago Cubs TC .15 .40
398 Rich Harden .15 .40
399 Kazmir/Price/Shields .30 .75
400 Magglio Ordonez .25 .60
401 Dan Uggla .15 .40
402 Adam LaRoche .15 .40
403 Taylor Teagarden .15 .40
404 Chris Young .15 .40
405 Robinson Cano .25 .60
406 Dustin McGowan .15 .40
407a Randy Winn .15 .40
407b Winn UER Lewis SP 15.00 40.00
408 Carlos Lee .15 .40
409 Kurt Suzuki .15 .40
410 Matt Cain .25 .60
411 Paul Bako .15 .40
412 Ted Lilly .15 .40
413 Kansas City Royals TC .15 .40
414 Miguel Cabrera .40 1.00
415 Jayson Werth .25 .60
416 J.C. Romero .15 .40
417 Martin Prado .15 .40
418 Armando Galarraga .15 .40
419 Brian Roberts .15 .40
420 Chipper Jones .40 1.00
421 Bengie Molina .15 .40
422 Matt Kemp .30 .75
423 Brian Buscher .15 .40
424 Erik Bedard .15 .40
425 Chad Billingsley .25 .60
426 Scott Rolen SP 2.00 5.00
427 Ben Francisco SP 2.50 6.00
428 Jermaine Dye SP 2.50 6.00
429 Dustin Pedroia 3.00 8.00
Ichiro Suzuki SP
430 Kevin Slowey SP 3.00 8.00
431 Jason Bartlett SP 2.50 6.00
432 Glen Perkins SP 2.50 6.00
433 Carlos Gomez SP 2.50 6.00
434 Jon Garland SP 2.50 6.00
435 Joe Crede SP 4.00 10.00
436 Billy Butler SP 2.50 6.00
437 Zach Duke SP 2.50 6.00
438 Chris Coste SP 2.50 6.00
439 Daisuke Matsuzaka SP 1.50 4.00
440 Elijah Dukes SP 2.50 6.00
441 Fausto Carmona SP 2.50 6.00
442 Joe Mauer SP 4.00 10.00
443 Marcus Thames SP 2.50 6.00
444 Mike Fontenot SP 2.50 6.00
445a J.Smoltz ATL SP 3.00 8.00
445b J.Smoltz BOS SP 30.00 60.00
446 Pedro Martinez SP 3.00 8.00
447 Adrian Beltre SP 6.00 15.00
448 Kevin Millar SP 2.50 6.00
449 Nick Swisher SP 4.00 10.00
450 Justin Morneau SP 3.00 8.00
451 Shane Victorino SP 2.50 6.00
452 Placido Polanco SP 2.50 6.00
453 Ryan Dempster SP 2.50 6.00
454 Frank Thomas SP 3.00 8.00
455 Dave Jauss/Juan Samuel John Shelby CO SP 2.50 6.00
456 Brad Mills/John Farrell Dave Magadan CO SP 2.50 6.00
457 Alan Trammell/Larry Rothschild Matt Sinatro CO SP 4.00 10.00
458 Joey Cora/Harold Baines Jeff Cox CO SP 4.00 10.00
459 Chris Speier/Billy Hatcher Dick Pole CO SP 2.50 6.00
460 Jeff Datz/Luis Rivera/Carl Willis Joel Skinner CO SP 2.50 6.00
461 Lloyd McClendon/Andy Van Slyke Rafael Belliard CO SP 2.50 6.00
462 Jim Hickey/Steve Henderson Tom Foley CO SP 2.50 6.00
463 Larry Bowa/Rick Honeycutt/Mariano Duncan/Bob Schaefer CO SP 2.50 6.00
464 Roger McDowell/Terry Pendleton/Chino Cadahia/Glenn Hubbard CO SP 2.50 6.00
465 Rob Thomson/Tony Pena/Kevin Long Dave Eiland CO SP 2.50 6.00
466 Milt Thompson/Rich Dubee Davey Lopes CO SP 2.50 6.00
467 Tony Beasley/Joe Kerrigan Don Long CO SP 2.50 6.00
468 Dave Duncan/Hal McRae Jose Oquendo/Dave McKay CO SP 2.50 6.00
469 Sandy Alomar Sr./Howard Johnson Dan Warthen CO SP 2.50 6.00
470 Randy St. Claire/Marquis Grissom/Jim Riggleman CO SP 2.50 6.00
471 Brad Ausmus SP 2.50 6.00
472 Melvin Mora SP 2.50 6.00
473 Austin Kearns SP 2.50 6.00
474 Josh Willingham SP 4.00 10.00
475 Derek Lowe SP 2.50 6.00
476 Nick Punto SP 2.50 6.00
477 A.J. Pierzynski SP 2.50 6.00
478 Troy Tulowitzki SP 5.00 12.00
479 CC Sabathia SP 3.00 8.00
480 Jorge Posada SP 3.00 8.00
481 Kevin Youkilis AS SP 2.00 5.00
482 Lance Berkman AS SP 3.00 8.00
483 Dustin Pedroia AS SP 2.50 6.00
484 Chase Utley AS SP 2.00 5.00
485 Alex Rodriguez AS SP 3.00 8.00
486 Chipper Jones AS SP 3.00 8.00
487 Derek Jeter AS SP 5.00 12.00
488a H.Ramirez AS FLA SP 2.00 5.00
488b H.Ramirez AS BOS SP 10.00 25.00
489 Josh Hamilton AS SP 2.00 5.00
490 Ryan Braun AS SP 2.00 5.00
491 Manny Ramirez AS SP 3.00 8.00
492 Kosuke Fukudome AS SP 2.00 5.00
493 Ichiro Suzuki AS SP 3.00 8.00
494 Matt Holliday AS SP 5.00 12.00
495 Joe Mauer AS SP 4.00 10.00
496 Geovany Soto AS SP 3.00 8.00
497 Roy Halladay AS SP 4.00 10.00
498 Ben Sheets AS SP 2.50 6.00
499 Cliff Lee AS SP 3.00 8.00
500 Billy Wagner AS SP 2.50 6.00
501 Shane Robinson RC .40 1.00
502 Mat Latos RC 1.25 3.00
503 Aaron Poreda RC .40 1.00
504 Takashi Saito .15 .40
505 Adam Everett .15 .40
506 Adam Kennedy .15 .40
507 John Smoltz .40 1.00
508 Alex Cora .25 .60
509 Alfredo Aceves .25 .60
510 Alfredo Figaro RC .40 1.00
511 Andrew Bailey RC 1.00 2.50
512 Jhoulys Chacin RC .60 1.50
513 Andruw Jones .15 .40
514 Anthony Swarzak (RC) .40 1.00
515 Antonio Bastardo RC .40 1.00
516 Bartolo Colon .15 .40
517 Michael Saunders RC 1.00 2.50
518 Blake Hawksworth (RC) .40 1.00
519 Bud Norris RC .40 1.00
520 Bobby Scales RC .60 1.50
521 Nick Evans .15 .40
522 Brad Bergensen (RC) .40 1.00
524 Brad Penny .15 .40
525 Braden Looper .15 .40
526 Brandon Lyon .15 .40
527 Brandon Wood .15 .40
528 Aaron Bates RC .40 1.00
529 Brett Cecil RC .40 1.00
530 Brett Gardner .25 .60
531 Brett Hayes (RC) .40 1.00
532 C.J. Wilson .15 .40
533 Carl Pavano .15 .40
534 Cesar Izturis .15 .40
535 Chad Qualls .15 .40
536 Marc Rzepczynski RC .60 1.50
537 Chris Gimenez RC .40 1.00
538 Chris Jakubauskas RC .60 1.50
539 Chris Perez .15 .40
540 Clay Zavada RC .60 1.50
541 Clayton Mortensen RC .40 1.00
542 Clayton Richard .15 .40
543 Cliff Floyd .15 .40
544 Coco Crisp .15 .40
545a Neftali Feliz RC .60 1.50
545b N.Feliz SP VAR 125.00 250.00
546 Craig Counsell .15 .40
547 Craig Stammen RC .40 1.00
548 Cristian Guzman .15 .40
549 Dallas Braden .25 .60
550 Daniel Bard RC .40 1.00
551 Jack Wilson .15 .40
552 Daniel Schlereth RC .40 1.00
553 David Aardsma .15 .40
554 David Eckstein .15 .40
555 David Freese RC 1.25 3.00
556 David Hernandez RC .40 1.00

557 David Huff RC .40 1.00
558 David Ross .15 .40
559 Delwyn Young .25 .60
560 Derek Holland RC .60 1.50
561 Derek Lowe .15 .40
562 Diory Hernandez RC .40 1.00
563a Pedro Martinez .25 .60
563b P.Martinez SP VAR 40.00 80.00
564 Emilio Bonifacio .15 .40
565 Endy Chavez .15 .40
566 Eric Byrnes .15 .40
567 Eric Hinske .15 .40
568 Everth Cabrera RC .60 1.50
569a Alex Rios .15 .40
569b A.Rios SP VAR 40.00 80.00
570 Fernando Nieve .15 .40
571 Francisco Cervelli RC 1.00 2.50
572 Frank Catalanotto .15 .40
573 Fu-Te Ni RC .60 1.50
574 Gabe Kapler .15 .40
575 Scott Rolen .25 .60
576 Garrett Olson .15 .40
577 Adam LaRoche .15 .40
578 Gerardo Parra RC .60 1.50
579 George Sherrill .15 .40
580 Graham Taylor RC .60 1.50
581 Gregg Zaun .15 .40
582 Homer Bailey .15 .40
583 Garrett Jones .25 .60
584 Julio Lugo .15 .40
585 J.A. Happ .25 .60
586 J.J. Putz .15 .40
587 J.P. Howell .15 .40
588 Jake Fox .25 .60
589 Jamey Carroll .15 .40
590 Jarrett Hoffpauir (RC) .40 1.00
591 Felipe Lopez .15 .40
592 Cliff Lee .25 .60
593 Jason Giambi .15 .40
594 Jason Jaramillo (RC) .40 1.00
595 Jason Kubel .15 .40
596 Jason Marquis .15 .40
597 Jason Vargas .15 .40
598 Jeff Baker .15 .40
599 Jeff Francoeur .25 .60
600 Jeremy Reed .15 .40
601 Jerry Hairston .15 .40
602 Jesus Guzman RC .40 1.00
603 Jody Gerut .15 .40
604 Joe Crede .25 .60
605 Alex Gonzalez .15 .40
606 Joel Hanrahan .25 .60
607 John Mayberry Jr (RC) .60 1.50
608 Jon Garland .15 .40
609 Jonny Gomes .15 .40
610 Jordan Schafer (RC) .60 1.50
611 Victor Martinez .25 .60
612 Jose Contreras .15 .40
613 Josh Bard .15 .40
614 Josh Outman .25 .60
615 Juan Rivera .15 .40
616 Juan Uribe .15 .40
617 Julio Borbon RC .40 1.00
618 Jarrod Washburn .15 .40
619 Justin Masterson .15 .40
620 Kenshin Kawakami RC .60 1.50
621 Kevin Correia .15 .40
622 Kevin Gregg .15 .40
623 Kevin Millar .15 .40
624 Koji Uehara RC 1.00 2.50
625 Kris Medlen RC 1.00 2.50
626 Tim Redding .15 .40
627 Kyle Farnsworth .15 .40
628 Landon Powell (RC) .40 1.00
629 Lastings Milledge .15 .40
630 LaTroy Hawkins .15 .40
631 Laynce Nix .15 .40
632 Billy Wagner .15 .40
633 Tony Gwynn Jr. .15 .40
634 Mark Loretta .15 .40
635 Matt Diaz .15 .40
636 Ben Francisco .15 .40
637 Travis Ishikawa .15 .40
638 Matt Maloney (RC) .40 1.00
639 Scott Kazmir .15 .40
640 Melky Cabrera .15 .40
641 Micah Hoffpauir .15 .40
642 Micah Owings .15 .40
643 Mike Carp (RC) .60 1.50
644 Mike Hampton .15 .40
645 Mike Sweeney .15 .40
646 Milton Bradley .15 .40
647 Mitch Jones (RC) .40 1.00
648 Trevor Crowe RC .40 1.00
649 Ty Wigginton .25 .60
650 Jim Thome .25 .60
651 Nick Green .15 .40
652 Tyler Greene (RC) .40 1.00
653 Nyjer Morgan .15 .40
654 Omar Vizquel .25 .60
655 Omir Santos RC .40 1.00
656 Orlando Cabrera .15 .40
657 Vin Mazzaro RC .40 1.00
658 Pat Burrell .15 .40
659 Rafael Soriano .15 .40
660 Ramiro Pena RC .60 1.50
661 Freddy Sanchez .15 .40
662 Ramon Ramirez .15 .40
663 Wilkin Ramirez RC .40 1.00
664 Randy Wells .15 .40
665 Randy Wolf .15 .40
666 Rich Hill .15 .40
667 Willy Taveras .15 .40
668 Xavier Paul (RC) .40 1.00
669 Rocco Baldelli .15 .40
670 Ross Detwiler .15 .40
671 Ross Gload .15 .40
672 Aubrey Huff .15 .40
673 Yuniesky Betancourt .15 .40
674 Ryan Church .15 .40
675 Ryan Garko .15 .40
676 Ryan Perry RC 1.00 2.50
677 Ryan Sadowski RC .40 1.00
678 Ryan Spilborghs .15 .40
679 Scott Downs .15 .40
680 Scott Hairston .15 .40
681 Scott Olsen .15 .40
682 Scott Podsednik .15 .40
683 Bill Hall .15 .40
684 Sean O'Sullivan RC .40 1.00
685 Sean West (RC) .60 1.50
686 Aaron Hill SP 2.50 6.00
687 Adam Dunn SP 4.00 10.00
688 McCutchen SP (RC) 6.00 15.00
689 Ben Zobrist SP 4.00 10.00
690 Chris Tillman SP RC 4.00 10.00
691 Bobby Abreu SP 2.50 6.00
692 Brett Anderson SP RC 4.00 10.00
693 Chris Coghlan SP RC 3.00 8.00
694 Colby Rasmus SP (RC) 3.00 8.00
695 Elvis Andrus SP RC 5.00 12.00
696 Fernando Martinez SP RC 6.00 15.00
697 Garret Anderson SP 2.50 6.00
698 Gary Sheffield SP 2.50 6.00
699 G.Beckham SP RC 1.50 4.00
700 Huston Street SP 2.50 6.00
701 Ivan Rodriguez SP 3.00 8.00
702 Jason Bay SP 3.00 8.00
703 Jordan Zimmermann SP RC 6.00 15.00
704 Ken Griffey Jr. SP 5.00 12.00
705 Kendry Morales SP 2.50 6.00
706 Kyle Blanks SP RC 4.00 10.00
707 T.Hanson SP RC 2.50 6.00
708 Mark DeRosa SP 4.00 10.00
709 Matt Holliday SP 5.00 12.00
710 Matt LaPorta SP RC 2.00 5.00
711 Trevor Cahill SP RC 5.00 12.00
712 Nate McLouth SP 2.50 6.00
713 Trevor Hoffman SP 4.00 10.00
714 Nelson Cruz SP 6.00 15.00
715 Nolan Reimold SP (RC) 2.50 6.00
716 Orlando Hudson SP 2.50 6.00
717 Randy Johnson SP 5.00 12.00
718 R.Porcello SP RC 2.50 6.00
719 Ricky Romero SP (RC) 3.00 8.00
720 Russell Branyan SP 2.50 6.00

2009 Topps Heritage Chrome

COMP.HIGH SET (100) 100.00 200.00
1-100 STATED ODDS 1:6 HOBBY
101-200 STATED ODDS 1:3 HOBBY
STATED PRINT RUN 1960 SER.#'d SETS
C1 Manny Ramirez 2.50 6.00
C2 Andre Ethier 1.50 4.00
C3 Miguel Tejada 1.50 4.00
C4 Nick Markakis 2.00 5.00
C5 Johan Santana 1.50 4.00
C6 Grady Sizemore 1.50 4.00
C7 Ian Kinsler 1.50 4.00
C8 Ryan Ludwick 1.50 4.00
C9 Jonathan Papelbon 1.50 4.00
C10 Albert Pujols 3.00 8.00
C11 Carlos Beltran 1.50 4.00
C12 David Price 2.00 5.00
C13 Carlos Pena 1.50 4.00
C14 Derek Jeter 6.00 15.00
C15 Mark Teixeira 1.50 4.00
C16 Aramis Ramirez 1.00 2.50
C17 Dexter Fowler 1.50 4.00
C18 Brad Lidge 1.00 2.50
C19 Johnny Cueto 1.50 4.00
C20 David Wright 2.00 5.00
C21 Mat Gamel 2.50 6.00
C22 B.J. Upton 1.50 4.00
C23 Carl Crawford 1.50 4.00
C24 Mariano Rivera 3.00 8.00
C25 Scott Kazmir 1.00 2.50
C26 Vladimir Guerrero 1.50 4.00
C27 Clayton Kershaw 5.00 12.00
C28 Ben Sheets 1.00 2.50
C29 Rick Ankiel 1.00 2.50
C30 Nate McLouth 1.00 2.50
C31 Roy Oswalt 1.50 4.00
C32 Felix Hernandez 1.50 4.00
C33 Ervin Santana 1.00 2.50
C34 Prince Fielder 1.50 4.00
C35 Cole Hamels 2.00 5.00
C36 Jon Lester 1.50 4.00
C37 Kosuke Fukudome 1.50 4.00
C38 Justin Upton 1.50 4.00
C39 John Lackey 1.50 4.00
C40 Lance Berkman 1.50 4.00
C41 Chien-Ming Wang 1.50 4.00
C42 Alex Rios 1.00 2.50
C43 Carlos Delgado 1.00 2.50
C44 Jake Peavy 1.00 2.50
C45 Hanley Ramirez 1.50 4.00
C46 Alfonso Soriano 1.50 4.00
C47 Jimmy Rollins 1.50 4.00
C48 J.J. Hardy 1.00 2.50
C49 James Loney 1.00 2.50
C50 Ryan Howard 2.00 5.00
C51 Rich Harden 1.00 2.50
C52 Dan Uggla 1.00 2.50
C53 Miguel Cabrera 2.50 6.00
C54 Matt Kemp 2.00 5.00
C55 Russell Martin 1.00 2.50
C56 Chipper Jones 2.50 6.00
C57 Stephen Drew 1.00 2.50
C58 Randy Johnson 2.50 6.00
C59 Andy Pettitte 1.50 4.00
C60 Francisco Rodriguez 1.50 4.00
C61 Vernon Wells 1.00 2.50
C62 Ivan Rodriguez 1.50 4.00
C63 Joe Saunders 1.00 2.50
C64 Yadier Molina 2.50 6.00
C65 Ken Griffey Jr. 5.00 12.00
C66 Justin Verlander 2.50 6.00
C67 Edinson Volquez 1.00 2.50
C68 Phil Hughes 1.00 2.50
C69 Yovani Gallardo 1.00 2.50
C70 Jose Reyes 1.50 4.00
C71 Gio Gonzalez 1.50 4.00
C72 Adrian Gonzalez 2.00 5.00
C73 Chris Davis 1.50 4.00
C74 Brad Penny 1.00 2.50
C75 Dustin Pedroia 2.00 5.00
C76 Kevin Youkilis 1.00 2.50
C77 Angel Salome 1.00 2.50
C78 Kila Ka'aihue 1.50 4.00
C79 Lou Marson 1.00 2.50
C80 Ichiro Suzuki 3.00 8.00
C81 Alcides Escobar 1.50 4.00
C82 Travis Snider 1.50 4.00
C83 Adam Dunn 1.50 4.00
C84 Jacoby Ellsbury 2.00 5.00
C85 Jay Bruce 1.50 4.00
C86 Ryan Doumit 1.00 2.50
C87 Tim Lincecum 1.50 4.00
C88 Joe Nathan 1.00 2.50
C89 Brian McCann 1.50 4.00
C90 Evan Longoria 1.50 4.00
C91 Carlos Zambrano 1.50 4.00
C92 Pat Burrell 1.00 2.50
C93 Alex Gordon 1.50 4.00
C94 Ryan Zimmerman 1.50 4.00
C95 Carlos Quentin 1.00 2.50
C96 Xavier Nady 1.00 2.50
C97 Max Scherzer 2.50 6.00
C98 Hiroki Kuroda 1.00 2.50
C99 Carlos Lee 1.00 2.50
C100 Alex Rodriguez 3.00 8.00
CHR101 Chad Qualls 1.00 2.50
CHR102 Daniel Schlereth 1.00 2.50
CHR103 Derek Lowe 1.00 2.50
CHR104 Jason Giambi 1.00 2.50
CHR105 Jason Marquis 1.00 2.50
CHR106 Kevin Correia 1.00 2.50
CHR107 Koji Uehara 2.50 6.00
CHR108 Matt Diaz 1.00 2.50
CHR109 Melky Cabrera 1.00 2.50
CHR110 Milton Bradley 1.00 2.50
CHR111 Rafael Soriano 1.00 2.50
CHR112 Scott Downs 1.00 2.50
CHR113 David Aardsma 1.00 2.50
CHR114 Eric Byrnes 1.00 2.50
CHR115 Gerardo Parra 1.50 4.00
CHR116 Homer Bailey 1.00 2.50
CHR117 J.P. Howell 1.00 2.50
CHR118 Joe Crede 1.50 4.00
CHR119 John Mayberry Jr 1.50 4.00
CHR120 Josh Outman 1.50 4.00
CHR121 Lastings Milledge 1.00 2.50
CHR122 Mike Hampton 1.00 2.50
CHR123 Orlando Cabrera 1.00 2.50
CHR124 Randy Wells 1.00 2.50
CHR125 Michael Saunders 2.50 6.00
CHR126 Tony Gwynn Jr. 1.00 2.50
CHR127 Trevor Crowe 1.00 2.50
CHR128 Vin Mazzaro 1.00 2.50
CHR129 Andruw Jones 1.00 2.50
CHR130 Brad Penny 1.00 2.50
CHR131 Brandon Wood 1.00 2.50
CHR132 Cristian Guzman 1.00 2.50
CHR133 David Huff 1.00 2.50
CHR134 J.A. Happ 1.50 4.00
CHR135 Jason Kubel 1.50 4.00
CHR136 Ryan Garko 1.00 2.50
CHR137 Jose Contreras 1.00 2.50
CHR138 Juan Rivera 1.00 2.50
CHR139 Jhoulys Chacin 1.50 4.00
CHR140 Randy Wolf 1.00 2.50
CHR141 Aaron Hill 1.00 2.50
CHR142 Adam Dunn 1.50 4.00
CHR143 Andrew Bailey 2.50 6.00
CHR144 Andrew McCutchen 5.00 12.00
CHR145 Ben Zobrist 1.50 4.00
CHR146 Bobby Abreu 1.00 2.50
CHR147 Brett Anderson 1.50 4.00
CHR148 Chris Coghlan 2.50 6.00
CHR149 Colby Rasmus 1.50 4.00
CHR150 Elvis Andrus 2.50 6.00
CHR151 Fernando Martinez 2.50 6.00
CHR152 Garret Anderson 1.00 2.50
CHR153 Gary Sheffield 1.00 2.50
CHR154 Gordon Beckham 1.50 4.00
CHR155 Huston Street 1.00 2.50
CHR156 Ivan Rodriguez 1.50 4.00
CHR157 Jason Bay 1.50 4.00
CHR158 Jeff Francoeur 1.50 4.00
CHR159 Jordan Zimmermann 2.50 6.00
CHR160 Ken Griffey Jr. 5.00 12.00
CHR161 Kendry Morales 1.00 2.50
CHR162 Kyle Blanks 1.50 4.00
CHR163 Mark DeRosa 1.50 4.00
CHR164 Matt Holliday 2.50 6.00
CHR165 Matt LaPorta 1.50 4.00
CHR166 Nate McLouth 1.00 2.50
CHR167 Nelson Cruz 2.50 6.00
CHR168 Nolan Reimold 1.00 2.50
CHR169 Orlando Hudson 1.00 2.50
CHR170 Randy Johnson 2.50 6.00
CHR171 Rick Porcello 3.00 8.00
CHR172 Ricky Romero 1.50 4.00
CHR173 Russell Branyan 1.00 2.50
CHR174 Tommy Hanson 2.50 6.00
CHR175 Trevor Cahill 2.50 6.00
CHR176 Trevor Hoffman 1.50 4.00
CHR177 Aaron Poreda 1.00 2.50
CHR178 John Smoltz 2.50 6.00
CHR179 Brad Mills 1.00 2.50
CHR180 Brett Gardner 1.50 4.00
CHR181 Carl Pavano 1.00 2.50
CHR182 Daniel Bard 1.00 2.50
CHR183 David Hernandez 1.00 2.50
CHR184 Fu-Te Ni 1.50 4.00
CHR185 Jerry Hairston 1.00 2.50
CHR186 Jordan Schafer 1.50 4.00
CHR187 Julio Borbon 1.00 2.50
CHR188 Kris Medlen 2.50 6.00
CHR189 Micah Hoffpauir 1.00 2.50
CHR190 Nyjer Morgan 1.00 2.50
CHR191 Derek Holland 1.50 4.00
CHR192 Jack Wilson 1.00 2.50
CHR193 Cliff Lee 1.50 4.00
CHR194 Freddy Sanchez 1.00 2.50
CHR195 Pat Burrell 1.00 2.50
CHR196 Ryan Spilborghs 1.00 2.50
CHR197 Takashi Saito 1.00 2.50
CHR198 Bud Norris 1.00 2.50
CHR199 Chris Tillman 1.50 4.00
CHR200 Everth Cabrera 1.50 4.00

2009 Topps Heritage Chrome Refractors

*REF: .6X TO 1.5X BASIC INSERTS
1-100 STATED ODDS 1:23 HOBBY
101-200 STATED ODDS 1:11 HOBBY
STATED PRINT RUN 560 SER.#'d SETS

2009 Topps Heritage Chrome Refractors Black

1-100 STATED ODDS 1:255 HOBBY
101-200 STATED ODDS 1:102 HOBBY
STATED PRINT RUN 60 SER.#'d SETS
C1 Manny Ramirez 12.00 30.00
C2 Andre Ethier 8.00 20.00
C3 Miguel Tejada 8.00 20.00
C4 Nick Markakis 10.00 25.00
C5 Johan Santana 8.00 20.00
C6 Grady Sizemore 8.00 20.00
C7 Ian Kinsler 8.00 20.00
C8 Ryan Ludwick 8.00 20.00
C9 Jonathan Papelbon 8.00 20.00
C10 Albert Pujols 40.00 100.00
C11 Carlos Beltran 8.00 20.00
C12 David Price 10.00 25.00
C13 Carlos Pena 8.00 20.00
C14 Derek Jeter 125.00 300.00
C15 Mark Teixeira 8.00 20.00
C16 Aramis Ramirez 5.00 12.00
C17 Dexter Fowler 8.00 20.00
C18 Brad Lidge 5.00 12.00
C19 Johnny Cueto 8.00 20.00
C20 David Wright 10.00 25.00
C21 Mat Gamel 12.00 30.00
C22 B.J. Upton 8.00 20.00
C23 Carl Crawford 8.00 20.00
C24 Mariano Rivera 40.00 100.00
C25 Scott Kazmir 5.00 12.00
C26 Vladimir Guerrero 8.00 20.00
C27 Clayton Kershaw 25.00 60.00
C28 Ben Sheets 5.00 12.00
C29 Rick Ankiel 5.00 12.00
C30 Nate McLouth 5.00 12.00
C31 Roy Oswalt 8.00 20.00
C32 Felix Hernandez 8.00 20.00
C33 Ervin Santana 5.00 12.00
C34 Prince Fielder 8.00 20.00
C35 Cole Hamels 10.00 25.00
C36 Jon Lester 8.00 20.00
C37 Kosuke Fukudome 8.00 20.00
C38 Justin Upton 8.00 20.00
C39 John Lackey 8.00 20.00
C40 Lance Berkman 8.00 20.00
C41 Chien-Ming Wang 8.00 20.00
C42 Alex Rios 5.00 12.00
C43 Carlos Delgado 5.00 12.00
C44 Jake Peavy 5.00 12.00
C45 Hanley Ramirez 8.00 20.00
C46 Alfonso Soriano 8.00 20.00
C47 Jimmy Rollins 8.00 20.00
C48 J.J. Hardy 5.00 12.00
C49 James Loney 5.00 12.00
C50 Ryan Howard 10.00 25.00
C51 Rich Harden 5.00 12.00
C52 Dan Uggla 5.00 12.00
C53 Miguel Cabrera 12.00 30.00
C54 Matt Kemp 10.00 25.00
C55 Russell Martin 5.00 12.00
C56 Chipper Jones 12.00 30.00
C57 Stephen Drew 5.00 12.00
C58 Randy Johnson 12.00 30.00
C59 Andy Pettitte 8.00 20.00
C60 Francisco Rodriguez 8.00 20.00
C61 Vernon Wells 5.00 12.00
C62 Ivan Rodriguez 8.00 20.00
C63 Joe Saunders 5.00 12.00
C64 Yadier Molina 12.00 30.00
C65 Ken Griffey Jr. 40.00 100.00
C66 Justin Verlander 12.00 30.00
C67 Edinson Volquez 5.00 12.00
C68 Phil Hughes 5.00 12.00
C69 Yovani Gallardo 5.00 12.00
C70 Jose Reyes 8.00 20.00
C71 Gio Gonzalez 8.00 20.00
C72 Adrian Gonzalez 10.00 25.00
C73 Chris Davis 8.00 20.00
C74 Brad Penny 5.00 12.00
C75 Dustin Pedroia 10.00 25.00
C76 Kevin Youkilis 5.00 12.00
C77 Angel Salome 5.00 12.00
C78 Kila Ka'aihue 8.00 20.00
C79 Lou Marson 5.00 12.00
C80 Ichiro Suzuki 40.00 100.00
C81 Alcides Escobar 8.00 20.00
C82 Travis Snider 8.00 20.00
C83 Adam Dunn 8.00 20.00
C84 Jacoby Ellsbury 10.00 25.00
C85 Jay Bruce 8.00 20.00
C86 Ryan Doumit 5.00 12.00
C87 Tim Lincecum 8.00 20.00
C88 Joe Nathan 5.00 12.00
C89 Brian McCann 8.00 20.00
C90 Evan Longoria 8.00 20.00
C91 Carlos Zambrano 8.00 20.00
C92 Pat Burrell 5.00 12.00
C93 Alex Gordon 8.00 20.00
C94 Ryan Zimmerman 8.00 20.00
C95 Carlos Quentin 5.00 12.00
C96 Xavier Nady 5.00 12.00
C97 Max Scherzer 12.00 30.00
C98 Hiroki Kuroda 5.00 12.00
C99 Carlos Lee 5.00 12.00
C100 Alex Rodriguez 15.00 40.00
CHR101 Chad Qualls 5.00 12.00
CHR102 Daniel Schlereth 5.00 12.00
CHR103 Derek Lowe 5.00 12.00
CHR104 Jason Giambi 5.00 12.00
CHR105 Jason Marquis 5.00 12.00
CHR106 Kevin Correia 5.00 12.00
CHR107 Koji Uehara 12.00 30.00
CHR108 Matt Diaz 5.00 12.00
CHR109 Melky Cabrera 5.00 12.00
CHR110 Milton Bradley 5.00 12.00
CHR111 Rafael Soriano 5.00 12.00
CHR112 Scott Downs 5.00 12.00
CHR113 David Aardsma 5.00 12.00
CHR114 Eric Byrnes 5.00 12.00
CHR115 Gerardo Parra 8.00 20.00
CHR116 Homer Bailey 5.00 12.00
CHR117 J.P. Howell 5.00 12.00
CHR118 Joe Crede 8.00 20.00
CHR119 John Mayberry Jr 8.00 20.00
CHR120 Josh Outman 8.00 20.00
CHR121 Lastings Milledge 5.00 12.00
CHR122 Mike Hampton 5.00 12.00
CHR123 Orlando Cabrera 5.00 12.00
CHR124 Randy Wells 5.00 12.00
CHR125 Michael Saunders 12.00 30.00
CHR126 Tony Gwynn Jr. 5.00 12.00
CHR127 Trevor Crowe 5.00 12.00
CHR128 Vin Mazzaro 5.00 12.00
CHR129 Andruw Jones 5.00 12.00
CHR130 Brad Penny 5.00 12.00
CHR131 Brandon Wood 5.00 12.00
CHR132 Cristian Guzman 5.00 12.00
CHR133 David Huff 5.00 12.00
CHR134 J.A. Happ 8.00 20.00
CHR135 Jason Kubel 8.00 20.00
CHR136 Ryan Garko 5.00 12.00
CHR137 Jose Contreras 5.00 12.00
CHR138 Juan Rivera 5.00 12.00
CHR139 Jhoulys Chacin 8.00 20.00
CHR140 Randy Wolf 5.00 12.00
CHR141 Aaron Hill 5.00 12.00
CHR142 Adam Dunn 8.00 20.00
CHR143 Andrew Bailey 12.00 30.00
CHR144 Andrew McCutchen 25.00 60.00
CHR145 Ben Zobrist 8.00 20.00
CHR146 Bobby Abreu 5.00 12.00
CHR147 Brett Anderson 8.00 20.00
CHR148 Chris Coghlan 12.00 30.00
CHR149 Colby Rasmus 8.00 20.00
CHR150 Elvis Andrus 12.00 30.00
CHR151 Fernando Martinez 12.00 30.00
CHR152 Garret Anderson 5.00 12.00
CHR153 Gary Sheffield 5.00 12.00
CHR154 Gordon Beckham 8.00 20.00
CHR155 Huston Street 5.00 12.00
CHR156 Ivan Rodriguez 8.00 20.00
CHR157 Jason Bay 8.00 20.00
CHR158 Jeff Francoeur 8.00 20.00
CHR159 Jordan Zimmermann 12.00 30.00
CHR160 Ken Griffey Jr. 40.00 100.00
CHR161 Kendry Morales 5.00 12.00
CHR162 Kyle Blanks 8.00 20.00
CHR163 Mark DeRosa 8.00 20.00
CHR164 Matt Holliday 12.00 30.00
CHR165 Matt LaPorta 8.00 20.00
CHR166 Nate McLouth 5.00 12.00
CHR167 Nelson Cruz 12.00 30.00
CHR168 Nolan Reimold 5.00 12.00
CHR169 Orlando Hudson 5.00 12.00
CHR170 Randy Johnson 12.00 30.00
CHR171 Rick Porcello 15.00 40.00
CHR172 Ricky Romero 8.00 20.00
CHR173 Russell Branyan 5.00 12.00
CHR174 Tommy Hanson 12.00 30.00
CHR175 Trevor Cahill 12.00 30.00
CHR176 Trevor Hoffman 8.00 20.00
CHR177 Aaron Poreda 5.00 12.00
CHR178 John Smoltz 12.00 30.00
CHR179 Brad Mills 5.00 12.00
CHR180 Brett Gardner 8.00 20.00
CHR181 Carl Pavano 5.00 12.00
CHR182 Daniel Bard 5.00 12.00
CHR183 David Hernandez 5.00 12.00
CHR184 Fu-Te Ni 8.00 20.00
CHR185 Jerry Hairston 5.00 12.00
CHR186 Jordan Schafer 8.00 20.00
CHR187 Julio Borbon 5.00 12.00
CHR188 Kris Medlen 12.00 30.00
CHR189 Micah Hoffpauir 5.00 12.00
CHR190 Nyjer Morgan 5.00 12.00
CHR191 Derek Holland 8.00 20.00
CHR192 Jack Wilson 5.00 12.00
CHR193 Cliff Lee 8.00 20.00
CHR194 Freddy Sanchez 5.00 12.00
CHR195 Pat Burrell 5.00 12.00
CHR196 Ryan Spilborghs 5.00 12.00
CHR197 Takashi Saito 5.00 12.00
CHR198 Bud Norris 5.00 12.00
CHR199 Chris Tillman 8.00 20.00
CHR200 Everth Cabrera 8.00 20.00

2009 Topps Heritage Advertising Panels

ISSUED AS BOX TOPPER
1 Garret Anderson .60 1.50
Brandon Backe
Shin Soo Choo
2 Matt Antonelli 1.25 3.00
David Wright
Alex Rodriguez
Alfredo Simon
3 Bronson Arroyo .60 1.50
Detroit Tigers TC
Matt Cain
4 Brandon Backe .60 1.50
Shin Soo Choo
Ozzie Guillen
5 Carlos Beltran .60 1.50
Andre Ethier
Kelly Shoppach
Victor Martinez
6 Brad Bergesen .60 1.50
Dallas Braden
Garrett Olson HN
7 Nick Blackburn .40 1.00
Scott Lewis
Ramon Ramirez
8 Aaron Boone .40 1.00
James Loney
Gerald Laird
9 Julio Borbon .40 1.00
Jarrett Hoffpauir
David Hernandez HN
10 Emil Brown .60 1.50
Scott Shields
Francisco Rodriguez
David Murphy
11 Pat Burrell .40 1.00
Brian Bannister
Jesus Flores
12 Mike Cameron .60 1.50
Ted Lilly
John Lackey
13 Mike Carp .60 1.50
Jody Gerut
Daniel Schlereth HN
14 Brett Cecil .40 1.00
Aubrey Huff
Mike Hampton HN
15 Shin-Soo Choo .60 1.50
Ozzie Guillen
Mike Aviles
16 Jeff Clement .40 1.00
Bronson Arroyo
Detroit Tigers TC
17 John Danks .60 1.50
Carlos Beltran
Andre Ethier
18 Jesus Delgado 1.00 2.50
Brian Wilson
Gary Mathews
19 Stephen Drew .60 1.50
Ryan Feirebrand
Andy Pettitte
20 Scott Elbert .40 1.00
Fernando Perez
Jeremy Guthrie
21 Yunel Escobar .60 1.50
Gaby Sanchez
Vernon Wells
22 Andre Ethier .60 1.50
Kelly Shoppach
Victor Martinez
Ronny Paulino
23 Cliff Floyd .40 1.00
Alfredo Figaro
Anthony Swarzak HN
24 Ryan Franklin .60 1.50
Emil Brown
Scott Shields
Francisco Rodriguez
25 David Freese 1.25 3.00
J.J. Putz
Juan Uribe HN
26 Jody Gerut .40 1.00
Daniel Schlereth
Brett Cecil HN
27 Ross Gload .60 1.50
Miguel Tejada
Matt Harrison
28 Khalil Greene .75 2.00
Cole Hamels
Juan Pierre
29 Jeremy Guthrie .40 1.00
Nick Blackburn
Scott Lewis
30 Scott Hairston .40 1.00
Orlando Cabrera
Matt Maloney HN
31 Bill Hall .40 1.00
Randy Wells
Kevin Gregg HN
32 Cole Hamels .75 2.00
Juan Pierre
Yunel Escobar
33 Mike Hampton .40 1.00
Jerry Hairston
Scott Downs HN
34 Dan Haren .60 1.50
John Danks
Carlos Beltran
35 Corey Hart .40 1.00
Aubrey Huff
Rich Aurilia
36 Brad Hawpe .60 1.50
Roy Oswalt
Mike Jacobs
37 David Hernandez 1.00 2.50
Brandon Lyon
Koji Uehara HN
38 Aubrey Huff .40 1.00
Mike Hampton
Jerry Hairston HN
39 Aubrey Huff .40 1.00
Rich Aurilia
Scott Baker
40 Mike Jacobs .75 2.00
Terry Francona
Jacoby Ellsbury
41 Scott Kazmir .40 1.00
Jeff Clement
Bronson Arroyo
42 John Lackey .60 1.50
Lyle Overbay
Chris Lambert
43 Aaron Laffey .60 1.50
Hanley Ramirez
Scott Olsen
44 Gerald Laird .60 1.50
Chien-Ming Wang
Corey Hart
45 Chris Lambert .60 1.50
Carlos Zambrano
Dave Tremblay
46 Ted Lilly .60 1.50
John Lackey
Lyle Overbay
47 James Loney .60 1.50
Gerald Laird
Chien-Ming Wang
48 Los Angeles Dodgers TC 1.00 2.50
Jesus Delgado
Brian Wilson
49 Matt Maloney .40 1.00
Julio Borbon
Jarret Hoffpauir HN
50 Hideki Matsui 1.00 2.50
Ty Wigginton
Vicente Padilla
51 John Mayberry Jr .60 1.50
David Aardsma
Scott Podsednik HN
52 Gil Meche .75 2.00
David Price
Luke Scott
53 Brad Mills .40 1.00
David Ross
Chris Perez HN
54 Daniel Murphy 1.50 4.00
Hideki Matsui
Ty Wigginton
55 Mike Napoli .75 2.00
David Wright
Matt Antonelli
56 Scott Olsen .60 1.50
Ryan Franklin
Emil Brown
57 Roy Oswalt .60 1.50
Mike Jacobs
Terry Francona
58 Josh Outman .60 1.50
Homer Bailey
Daniel Bard HN
59 Lyle Overbay .60 1.50
Chris Lambert
Carlos Zambrano
60 Vicente Padilla .60 1.50
Brad Hawpe
Roy Oswalt
61 Jon Papelbon .60 1.50
Tim Wakefield
Corey Patterson
Pat Burrell
62 Corey Patterson .40 1.00
Pat Burrell
Brian Bannister
63 Xavier Paul .60 1.50
John Mayberry Jr
David Aardsma HN
64 Chris Perez .60 1.50
Ramiro Pena
Rocco Baldelli HN
65 Fernando Perez .40 1.00
Jeremy Guthrie
Nick Blackburn
66 Juan Pierre .60 1.50
Yunel Escobar

Gaby Sanchez
67 Lou Piniella .40 1.00
Scott Kazmir
Jeff Clement
68 Aaron Poreda .40 1.00
Bill Hall
Randy Wells HN
69 David Price .75 2.00
Luke Scott
Jeff Suppan
70 Albert Pujols 1.25 3.00
Dan Haren
John Danks
71 Hanley Ramirez .60 1.50
Scott Olsen
Ryan Franklin
72 Tim Redding .40 1.00
Jamey Carroll
Endy Chavez
73 Jeremy Reed .40 1.00
Laynce Nix
Ryan Sadowski HN
74 Edgar Renteria .40 1.00
Brian Giles
Greg Smith
75 Gaby Sanchez .60 1.50
Vernon Wells
Ross Gload
76 Bobby Scales .60 1.50
Clay Zavada
Jason Jaramillo HN
77 Daniel Schlereth .40 1.00
Brett Cecil
Aubrey Huff HN
78 Kelly Shoppach .60 1.50
Victor Martinez
Ronny Paulino
Mike Gonzalez
79 John Smoltz 1.00 2.50
Mike Carp
Jody Gerut HN
80 Rafael Soriano .40 1.00
Ross Gload
Vin Mazzaro HN
81 Craig Stammen 1.00 2.50
John Smoltz
Mike Carp HN
82 Anthony Swarzak .40 1.00
C.J. Wilson
Derek Lowe HN
83 Miguel Tejada .60 1.50
Matt Harrison
James Parr
84 Detroit Tigers TC .60 1.50
Matt Cain
Jeff Francis
85 Dave Tremblay .40 1.00
Edgar Renteria
Brian Giles
86 Koji Uehara 1.00 2.50
Brad Bergesen
Dallas Braden HN
87 Juan Uribe .40 1.00
Rafael Soriano
Ross Gload HN
88 Jason Vargas .40 1.00
Eric Byrnes
Brad Mills HN
89 Chien-Ming Wang .60 1.50
Corey Hart
Aubrey Huff
90 Randy Wells .40 1.00
Kevin Gregg
J.P. Howell HN
91 Vernon Wells .60 1.50
Ross Gload
Miguel Tejada
92 Sean West .60 1.50
Melky Cabrera
Braden Looper HN
93 Ty Wigginton .60 1.50
Vicente Padilla
Brad Hawpe
94 Brian Wilson 1.00 2.50
Gary Mathews
Ubaldo Jimenez
95 Jack Wilson .40 1.00
Cincinnati Reds TC
Dustin McGowan
96 Kerry Wood .40 1.00
Scott Elbert
Fernando Perez
97 David Wright 1.25 3.00
Matt Antonelli
David Wright
Alex Rodriguez
99 David Aardsma .40 1.00
Scott Podsednik
Milton Bradley
98 Carlos Zambrano .60 1.50
Dave Tremblay
Edgar Renteria
100 Ryan Church .60 1.50
Dexter Fowler
Stephen Drew
101 Mike Gonzalez .60 1.50
Wade LeBlanc
Brandon Inge
102 Ozzie Guillen .40 1.00
Mike Aviles
Gil Meche
103 Jair Jurrjens 1.50 4.00
Daniel Murphy
Hideki Matsui
104 Lastings Milledge .40 1.00
Mitch Jones
Xavier Paul
105 Scot Shields .60 1.50
Francisco Rodriguez
David Murphy
Jack Wilson
106 David Wright 1.25 3.00
Alex Rodriguez
Alfredo Simon
Dodgers TC

2009 Topps Heritage Baseball Flashbacks

COMPLETE SET (10) 5.00 12.00
STATED ODDS 1:12 HOBBY
BF1 Mickey Mantle 1.50 4.00
BF2 Bill Mazeroski .75 2.00
BF3 Juan Marichal .75 2.00
BF4 Paul Richards/Hoyt Wilhelm .75 2.00
BF5 Luis Aparicio .75 2.00
BF6 Frank Robinson .75 2.00
BF7 Brooks Robinson .75 2.00
BF8 Ernie Banks 1.25 3.00
BF9 Mickey Mantle 1.50 4.00
BF10 Bobby Richardson .50 1.25

2009 Topps Heritage Clubhouse Collection Relics

GROUP A ODDS 1:219 HOBBY
GROUP B ODDS 1:52 HOBBY
GROUP C ODDS 1:97 HOBBY
HN ODDDS 1:26 HOBBY
AG Adrian Gonzalez HN 2.50 6.00
AJ Adam Jones HN 2.50 6.00
ALR Alexei Ramirez HN 2.50 6.00
AR Aramis Ramirez HN 2.50 6.00
AR Aramis Ramirez Jsy 2.50 6.00
AS Alfonso Soriano HN 2.50 6.00
BJU B.J. Upton HN 2.50 6.00
BM Brian McCann HN 2.50 6.00
BR Brooks Robinson HN 50.00 100.00
BU B.J. Upton Bat 2.50 6.00
CB Chad Billingsley HN 2.50 6.00
CB Clay Buchholz Jsy 2.50 6.00
CC Carl Crawford Uni 2.50 6.00
CH Cole Hamels HN 4.00 10.00
CJ Chipper Jones HN 4.00 10.00
CM Cameron Maybin Bat 2.50 6.00
CQ Carlos Quentin HN 2.50 6.00
CT Curtis Thigpen Jsy 2.50 6.00
CU Chase Utley HN 5.00 12.00
CU Chase Utley Jsy 5.00 12.00
DJ Dan Johnson Jsy 2.50 6.00
DP Dustin Pedroia Jsy 5.00 12.00
DS Duke Snider HN 20.00 50.00
DU Dan Uggla Jsy 2.50 6.00
DW David Wright HN 4.00 10.00
DW Dontrelle Willis Jsy 2.50 6.00
DWR David Wright Jsy 4.00 10.00
EB Ernie Banks HN 30.00 60.00
EL Evan Longoria HN 5.00 12.00
EVL Evan Longoria HN 5.00 12.00
FH Felix Hernandez HN 4.00 10.00
FR Frank Robinson HN 40.00 80.00
GS Geovany Soto HN 4.00 10.00
HR Hanley Ramirez HN 2.50 6.00
IK Ian Kinsler HN 2.50 6.00
JAB Jay Bruce HN 4.00 10.00
JB Jay Bruce HN 4.00 10.00
JD J.D. Drew Jsy 2.50 6.00
JL Jon Lester Jsy 4.00 10.00
JM Joe Mauer HN 4.00 10.00
JR Jimmy Rollins HN 4.00 10.00
JS Joakim Soria HN 2.50 6.00
JU Justin Upton HN 2.50 6.00
KFM Kevin Mench Jsy 2.50 6.00
KK Kenshin Kawakami HN 4.00 10.00
KM Kevin Millwood Jsy 2.50 6.00
KS Kurt Suzuki Bat 2.50 6.00
KU Koji Uehara HN 4.00 10.00
KY Kevin Youkilis Jsy 4.00 10.00
LM Lastings Milledge Bat 2.50 6.00
MH Matt Holliday HN 4.00 10.00
MIC Miguel Cabrera HN 4.00 10.00
MM Mickey Mantle HN 50.00 100.00
MR Manny Ramirez Jsy 5.00 12.00
MT Miguel Tejada Bat 2.50 6.00
RB Ryan Braun HN 4.00 10.00
RB Rocco Baldelli Jsy 2.50 6.00
RH Ryan Howard HN 4.00 10.00
RM Roger Maris HN 40.00 80.00
SM Stan Musial HN 40.00 80.00
SP Scott Podsednik Jsy 2.50 6.00
TL Tim Lincecum HN 5.00 12.00
VW Vernon Wells Jsy 2.50 6.00
WM Willie McCovey HN 50.00 100.00

2009 Topps Heritage Clubhouse Collection Relics Dual

STATED ODDS 1:4800 HOBBY
HN STATED ODDS 1:2020 HOBBY
STATED PRINT RUN 60 SER.#'d SETS
BR Bruce Bat/Robinson Pants 20.00 50.00
HM M.Holliday/S.Musial HN 40.00 80.00
LM Lincecum/J.Marichal HN 30.00 60.00
MR N.Markakis/Brooks HN 30.00 60.00
PM J.Posada/M.Mantle HN 30.00 60.00
PM Pujols Bat/Musial Pants 40.00 80.00
RM Rodriguez Jsy/Mantle Jsy 40.00 80.00
SB Soriano Bat/Banks Bat 30.00 60.00
SK D.Snider/M.Kemp HN 20.00 50.00
TM Teixeira Bat/Mantle Jsy 60.00 120.00

2009 Topps Heritage Flashback Stadium Relics

STATED ODDS 1:383 HOBBY
HN STATED ODDS 1:925 HOBBY
AK Al Kaline 10.00 25.00
BM Bill Mazeroski 6.00 15.00
BR Brooks Robinson 6.00 15.00
BRI Bobby Richardson 4.00 10.00
EB Ernie Banks 10.00 25.00
FR Frank Robinson 6.00 15.00
LA Luis Aparicio 6.00 15.00
MM Mickey Mantle 15.00 40.00
MM2 Mickey Mantle 15.00 40.00
SM Stan Musial 12.00 30.00

2009 Topps Heritage High Number Flashbacks

COMPLETE SET (10) 5.00 12.00
STATED ODDS 1:12 HOBBY
FB01 Jonathan Sanchez .50 1.25
FB02 Jason Giambi .50 1.25
FB03 Randy Johnson 1.25 3.00
FB04 Ian Kinsler .75 2.00
FB05 Carl Crawford .75 2.00
FB06 Albert Pujols 1.50 4.00
FB07 Todd Helton .75 2.00
FB08 Mariano Rivera 1.50 4.00
FB09 Gary Sheffield .50 1.25
FB10 Ichiro Suzuki 1.50 4.00

2009 Topps Heritage High Number Rookie Performers

COMPLETE SET (15) 12.50 30.00
STATED ODDS 1:12 HOBBY
RP01 Colby Rasmus 1.00 2.50
RP02 Tommy Hanson 1.50 4.00
RP03 Andrew McCutchen 3.00 8.00
RP04 Rick Porcello 2.00 5.00
RP05 Nolan Reimold .60 1.50
RP06 Mat Latos 2.00 5.00
RP07 Gordon Beckham 1.00 2.50
RP08 Brett Anderson 1.00 2.50
RP09 Chris Coghlan 1.50 4.00
RP10 Jordan Zimmermann 1.50 4.00
RP11 Brad Bergesen .60 1.50
RP12 Elvis Andrus 1.50 4.00
RP13 Ricky Romero 1.00 2.50
RP14 Dexter Fowler 1.00 2.50
RP15 David Price 1.25 3.00

2009 Topps Heritage High Number Then and Now

COMPLETE SET (10) 5.00 12.00
STATED ODDS 1:12 HOBBY
TN01 D.Pedroia/R.Maris 1.00 2.50
TN02 Jimmy Rollins/Ernie Banks 1.00 2.50
TN03 Adrian Beltre/Brooks Robinson 1.00 2.50
TN04 Michael Young/Ernie Banks 1.00 2.50
TN05 I.Suzuki/R.Maris 1.25 3.00
TN06 Grady Sizemore/Roger Maris 1.00 2.50
TN07 A.Pujols/R.Maris 1.25 3.00
TN08 D.Wright/B.Robinson .75 2.00
TN09 Cole Hamels/Bobby Richardson .75 2.00
TN10 Torii Hunter/Roger Maris 1.00 2.50

2009 Topps Heritage Mayo

COMPLETE SET (10) 15.00 40.00
RANDOM INSERTS IN PACKS
AP Albert Pujols 2.50 6.00
AR Alex Rodriguez 2.50 6.00
ARI Alex Rios .75 2.00
AS Alfonso Soriano 1.25 3.00
CJ Chipper Jones 2.00 5.00
DM Daisuke Matsuzaka 1.25 3.00
DO David Ortiz 2.00 5.00
DP Dustin Pedroia 1.50 4.00
DW David Wright 1.50 4.00
EL Evan Longoria 1.25 3.00
GS Grady Sizemore 1.25 3.00
HR Hanley Ramirez 1.25 3.00
IS Ichiro Suzuki 2.50 6.00
JH Josh Hamilton 1.25 3.00
JS Johan Santana 1.25 3.00
MR Manny Ramirez 2.00 5.00
RB Ryan Braun 1.25 3.00
RH Ryan Howard 1.50 4.00
TL Tim Lincecum 1.25 3.00
VG Vladimir Guerrero 1.25 3.00

2009 Topps Heritage New Age Performers

COMPLETE SET (15) 12.50 30.00
STATED ODDS 1:15 HOBBY
NAP1 David Wright .75 2.00
NAP2 Manny Ramirez 1.00 2.50
NAP3 Mark Teixeira .60 1.50
NAP4 Josh Hamilton .60 1.50
NAP5 Chase Utley .60 1.50
NAP6 Tim Lincecum .60 1.50
NAP7 Stephen Drew .40 1.00
NAP8 Cliff Lee .60 1.50
NAP9 Carlos Quentin .40 1.00
NAP10 Ryan Braun .60 1.50
NAP11 Cole Hamels .75 2.00
NAP12 Dustin Pedroia .75 2.00
NAP13 Geovany Soto .60 1.50
NAP14 Scott Kazmir .40 1.00
NAP15 Evan Longoria .60 1.50

2009 Topps Heritage News Flashbacks

COMPLETE SET (10) 6.00 15.00
STATED ODDS 1:12 HOBBY
NF1 Aswan High Dam .50 1.25
NF2 Bathyscaphe Trieste .50 1.25
NF3 Weather Satellite - TIROS-1 .50 1.25
NF4 Civil Rights Act of 1960 .50 1.25
NF5 Fifty-Star Flag .50 1.25
NF6 USS Seadragon .50 1.25
NF7 Marshall Space Flight Center .50 1.25
NF8 Presidential Debate 1.00 2.50
NF9 John F. Kennedy 1.25 3.00
NF10 Polaris Missle .50 1.25

2009 Topps Heritage Real One Autographs

STATED ODDS 1:308 HOBBY
HN STATED ODDS 1:372 HOBBY
EXCHANGE DEADLINE 2/28/2012
AC Art Ceccarelli 6.00 15.00
AD Alvin Dark HN 30.00 60.00
AS Art Schult 6.00 15.00
BB Brian Barton HN 6.00 15.00
BG Buddy Gilbert 10.00 25.00
BJ Bob Johnson HN 6.00 15.00
BJ Ben Johnson 6.00 15.00
BR Bob Rush 6.00 15.00
BTH Bill Harris 6.00 15.00
BWI Bobby Wine HN 15.00 40.00
CK Clayton Kershaw HN 100.00 200.00
CK Clayton Kershaw 100.00 200.00
CM Carl Mathias 6.00 15.00
CN Cal Neeman 6.00 15.00
CP Cliff Pennington HN 6.00 15.00
CR Curt Raydon 6.00 15.00
DB Dick Burwell HN 6.00 15.00
DG Dick Gray 6.00 15.00
DW Don Williams EXCH 6.00 15.00
FC Fausto Carmona 6.00 15.00
GB Gordon Beckham HN 60.00 120.00
GC Gio Gonzalez HN 6.00 15.00
GM Gil McDougald 6.00 15.00
IN Irv Noren HN 6.00 20.00
IN Irv Noren 6.00 15.00
JB Jay Bruce HN 12.50 30.00
JB Jay Bruce 12.50 30.00
JG Johnny Groth 10.00 25.00
JH Jack Harshman 6.00 15.00
JM Justin Masterson 6.00 15.00
JP Jim Proctor 6.00 15.00
JR John Romonosky 6.00 15.00
JS Joe Shipley 6.00 15.00
JSS Jake Striker 6.00 15.00
MB Milton Bradley HN 6.00 15.00
MG Mat Gamel 6.00 15.00
ML Mike Lee 6.00 15.00
NC Nelson Chittum 6.00 15.00
RI Raul Ibanez HN 20.00 50.00
RJW Red Wilson 6.00 15.00
RS Ron Samford 6.00 15.00
RW Ray Webster 6.00 15.00
SK Steve Korcheck 6.00 15.00
SL Stan Lopata 6.00 15.00
TP Taylor Phillips 6.00 15.00
TW Ted Wieand EXCH 6.00 15.00
WL Whitey Lockman 6.00 15.00
WT Wayne Terwilliger 6.00 15.00

2009 Topps Heritage Real One Autographs Red Ink

STATED ODDS 1:514 HOBBY
HN STATED ODDS 1:623 HOBBY
STATED PRINT RUN 60 SER.#'d SETS
EXCHANGE DEADLINE 2/28/2012
AC Art Ceccarelli 8.00 20.00
AD Alvin Dark HN 40.00 80.00
AS Art Schult 8.00 20.00
BB Brian Barton HN 8.00 20.00
BG Buddy Gilbert 12.50 30.00
BJ Bob Johnson HN 8.00 20.00
BJ Ben Johnson 8.00 20.00
BR Bob Rush 8.00 20.00
BTH Bill Harris 8.00 20.00
BWI Bobby Wine HN 20.00 50.00
CK Clayton Kershaw HN 200.00 400.00
CK Clayton Kershaw 200.00 400.00
CM Carl Mathias 8.00 20.00
CN Cal Neeman 8.00 20.00
CP Cliff Pennington HN 8.00 20.00
CR Curt Raydon 8.00 20.00
DB Dick Burwell HN 8.00 20.00
DG Dick Gray 8.00 20.00
DW Don Williams EXCH 8.00 20.00
FC Fausto Carmona 8.00 20.00
GB Gordon Beckham HN 100.00 200.00
GC Gio Gonzalez HN 8.00 20.00
GM Gil McDougald 8.00 20.00
IN Irv Noren HN 8.00 20.00
IN Irv Noren 6.00 15.00
JB Jay Bruce HN 15.00 40.00
JB Jay Bruce 15.00 40.00
JG Johnny Groth 12.00 30.00
JH Jack Harshman 8.00 20.00
JM Justin Masterson 8.00 20.00
JP Jim Proctor 8.00 20.00
JR John Romonosky 8.00 20.00
JS Joe Shipley 8.00 20.00
JSS Jake Striker 8.00 20.00
MB Milton Bradley HN 8.00 20.00
MG Mat Gamel 8.00 20.00
ML Mike Lee 8.00 20.00
NC Nelson Chittum 8.00 20.00
RI Raul Ibanez HN 30.00 60.00
RJW Red Wilson 8.00 20.00
RS Ron Samford 8.00 20.00
RW Ray Webster 8.00 20.00
SK Steve Korcheck 8.00 20.00
SL Stan Lopata 8.00 20.00
TP Taylor Phillips 8.00 20.00
TW Ted Wieand 8.00 20.00
WL Whitey Lockman 8.00 20.00
WT Wayne Terwilliger 8.00 20.00

2009 Topps Heritage Then and Now

COMPLETE SET (10) 8.00 20.00
STATED ODDS 1:15 HOBBY
TN1 E.Banks/R.Howard 1.00 2.50
TN2 E.Banks/R.Howard 1.00 2.50
TN3 Minnie Minoso/Chipper Jones 1.00 2.50
TN4 Luis Aparicio/Willy Taveras .60 1.50
TN5 M.Mantle/A.Dunn 1.50 4.00
TN6 Bob Friend/Johan Santana .60 1.50
TN7 J.Podres/T.Lincecum .60 1.50
TN8 Bob Friend/Cliff Lee .60 1.50
TN9 Bob Friend/Roy Halladay .60 1.50
TN10 Whitey Ford/CC Sabathia .60 1.50

2009 Topps Heritage '59 National Convention VIP

COMPLETE SET (5) 8.00 20.00
573A Mickey Mantle Facing Left 4.00 10.00
573B Mickey Mantle Facing Right 4.00 10.00
574 Roy Campanella 1.25 3.00
575 Jackie Robinson 1.25 3.00
576 Roger Maris 1.25 3.00

2010 Topps Heritage

COMP.SET w/o SPs (425) 30.00 60.00
COMMON CARD (1-425) .15 .40
COMMON RC (1-425) .40 1.00
DICE ODDS 1:72 HOBBY
COMMON NAME VAR (1-427) 30.00 60.00
61 CHASE MINORS
61 CHASE SEMIS
61 CHASE UNLISTED
61 CHASE ODDS 1:435 HOBBY
COMMON SP (426-500) 2.50 6.00
SP ODDS 1:3 HOBBY
1a Albert Pujols .50 1.25
1b A.Pujols Dice SP 3.00 8.00
1c A.Pujols Blk Name SP 30.00 60.00
2a Joe Mauer .30 .75
2b Joe Mauer Dice Back SP 2.50 6.00
2c Joe Mauer All Black Nameplate SP 30.00 60.00
3 Joe Blanton .15 .40
4 Delmon Young .25 .60
5 Kelly Shoppach .15 .40
6 Ronald Belisario .15 .40
7 Chicago White Sox .15 .40
8 Rajai Davis .15 .40
9 Aaron Harang .15 .40
10 Brian Roberts .15 .40
11 Adam Wainwright .25 .60
12 Geovany Soto .25 .60
13 Ramon Santiago .15 .40
14 Albert Callaspo .15 .40
15a Grady Sizemore .25 .60
15b Grady Sizemore Dice Back SP 3.00 8.00
15c Grady Sizemore Red Green Nameplate SP 30.00 60.00
16 Clay Buchholz .15 .40
17 Checklist .15 .40
18 David Huff .15 .40
19a Alex Rodriguez .50 1.25
20 Cole Hamels .30 .75
21 Orlando Cabrera .15 .40
22 Ross Ohlendorf .15 .40
23a Matt Kemp .30 .75
23b Matt Kemp Dice Back SP 4.00 10.00
24 Andrew Bailey .15 .40
25 Juan Francisco/Jay Bruce/Joey Votto .40 1.00
26 Chris Tillman .15 .40
27 Mike Fontenot .15 .40
28 Melky Cabrera .15 .40
29 Reid Gorecki (RC) .60 1.50
30 Jayson Nix .15 .40
31 Bengie Molina .15 .40
32 Chris Carpenter .25 .60
33 Jason Bay .25 .60
34 Fausto Carmona .15 .40
35 Gordon Beckham .15 .40
36 Glen Perkins .15 .40
37 Curtis Granderson .30 .75
38 Rafael Furcal .15 .40
39 Matt Carson (RC) .40 1.00
40 A.J. Burnett .15 .40
41 Ram/San/Puj/Hel .50 1.25
42 Mau/Ich/Jet/Cab 1.00 2.50
43 Puj/Fie/How/Rey .50 1.25
44 C.Pena/Teixeira/J.Bay/A.Hill .25 .60
45 Car/Lin/Jur/Wai .25 .60
46 Greinke/F.Hernandez Halladay/Sabathia .25 .60
47 Wainwright/C. Carpenter De La Rosa/B.Arroyo .25 .60
48 Felix/CC/Verland/Beck .40 1.00
49 Lin/J.Vaz/Har/Wai .25 .60
50 Verlan/Grein/Lest/Felix .40 1.00
51 Detroit Tigers .15 .40
52 Ronny Cedeno .15 .40
53 Jason Varitek .40 1.00
54 Daniel McCutchen RC .60 1.50
55a Pablo Sandoval .25 .60
55b Pablo Sandoval Yellow-Green Nameplate SP 30.00 60.00
56a Jake Peavy .15 .40
56b Mickey Mantle SP 15.00 40.00
57 Billy Butler .15 .40
58 Ryan Dempster .15 .40
59 Neil Walker (RC) .60 1.50
60a Asdrubal Cabrera .25 .60
60b Babe Ruth SP 12.00 30.00
61a Ryan Church .15 .40
61b Roger Maris SP 12.00 30.00
62 Nick Markakis .30 .75
63 Nick Blackburn .15 .40
64 Mark DeRosa .15 .40
65 Paul Konerko .25 .60
66 Daniel Ray Herrera .15 .40
67 Brandon Inge .25 .60
68 Josh Thole RC .60 1.50
69 Josh Beckett .15 .40
70 Lastings Milledge .15 .40
71 Robert Andino .15 .40
72 Matt Cain .25 .60
73 Nate McLouth .15 .40
74 Russell Martin .15 .40
75 A.Pujols/D.Wright .50 1.25
76 Jay Bruce .25 .60
77a J.A. Happ .25 .60
77b Happ Org-Blu Name SP 15.00 40.00
78 Jayson Werth .25 .60
79 A.J. Pierzynski .15 .40
80 Michael Cuddyer .15 .40
81 Dustin Richardson RC .40 1.00
82a Justin Upton .25 .60
82b Justin Upton Dice Back SP 3.00 8.00
83 Rick Porcello .25 .60
84 Garret Anderson .15 .40
85 Jeremy Guthrie .15 .40
86 Los Angeles Dodgers .25 .60
87 Juan Uribe .15 .40
88 Alfonso Soriano .25 .60
89 Martin Prado .15 .40
90 Gavin Floyd .15 .40
91 Colby Rasmus .25 .60
92a Mark Teixeira .25 .60
92b Mark Teixeira Dice Back SP 3.00 8.00
93 Raul Ibanez .25 .60
94a Zack Greinke .25 .60
94b Greinke YB Name SP 50.00 100.00
95 Miguel Cabrera .40 1.00
96 Randy Johnson .40 1.00
97 Chris Dickerson .15 .40
98 Checklist .15 .40
99 Jed Lowrie .15 .40
100 Zach Duke .15 .40
101 Jhonny Peralta .15 .40
102 Nolan Reimold .15 .40
103 Jimmy Rollins .25 .60
104 Jorge Posada .25 .60
105 Tim Hudson .25 .60
106 Scott Hairston .15 .40
107 Rich Harden .15 .40
108 Jason Kubel .15 .40
109 Clayton Kershaw .75 2.00
110 Willy Taveras .15 .40
111 Brett Myers .15 .40
112 Adam Everett .15 .40
113 Jonathan Papelbon .25 .60
114 Buster Posey RC 6.00 15.00
115 Kerry Wood .15 .40
116 Jerry Hairston Jr. .15 .40
117 Adam Dunn .25 .60
118 Yadier Molina .40 1.00
119 David DeJesus/Alex Gordon .25 .60
120a Chipper Jones .40 1.00
120b Chipper Jones Dice Back SP 3.00 8.00
121 John Lackey .25 .60
122 Chicago Cubs .25 .60
123 Nick Punto .15 .40
124 Daniel Hudson RC .60 1.50
125 David Hernandez .15 .40
126 Garrett Jones .15 .40
127 Joel Pineiro .15 .40
128 Jacoby Ellsbury .30 .75
129 Ian Desmond (RC) .60 1.50
130 James Loney .15 .40
131 Dave Trembley MG .15 .40
132 Ozzie Guillen MG .15 .40
133 Joe Girardi MG .25 .60
134 Jim Riggleman MG .15 .40
135 Dusty Baker MG .15 .40
136 Joe Torre MG .25 .60
137 Bobby Cox MG .15 .40
138 John Russell MG .15 .40
139 Tony LaRussa MG .25 .60
140 Jarrod Saltalamacchia .15 .40
141 Kosuke Fukudome .25 .60
142 Mariano Rivera .50 1.25
143 David DeJesus .15 .40
144 Jon Niese .15 .40
145 Jair Jurrjens .25 .60
146 Josh Willingham .25 .60
147 Chris Pettit RC .40 1.00
148 Chris Getz .15 .40
149 Ryan Doumit .15 .40
150 Aaron Rowand .15 .40
151 Brad Kilby RC .40 1.00
152 Prince Fielder .25 .60
153 Scott Baker .15 .40
154 Shane Victorino .25 .60
155 Luis Valbuena .15 .40
156 Drew Stubbs RC 1.00 2.50
157 Mark Buehrle .25 .60
158 Josh Bard .15 .40
159 Baltimore Orioles .15 .40
160 Andy Pettitte .25 .60
161 M.Bumgarner RC 3.00 8.00
162 Johnny Cueto .25 .60
163 Jeff Mathis .15 .40
164 Yunel Escobar .15 .40
165 Steve Pearce .40 1.00
166 Ramon Hernandez .15 .40
167 San Francisco Giants .15 .40
168 Chris Coghlan .15 .40
169 Ted Lilly .15 .40
170 Alex Rios .15 .40
171 Justin Verlander .40 1.00
172 Michael Brantley RC .60 1.50
173 D.Pedroia/J.Ellsbury .30 .75
174 Craig Stammen .15 .40
175 Scott Rolen .25 .60
176 Howie Kendrick .15 .40
177 Trevor Cahill .15 .40
178 Matt Holliday .40 1.00
179a Chase Utley .25 .60
179b Chase Utley Dice Back SP 3.00 8.00
180 Robinson Cano .25 .60
181 Paul Maholm .15 .40
182a Adam Jones .25 .60
182b Adam Jones Dice Back SP 3.00 8.00
183 Felipe Lopez .15 .40
184 Kendry Morales .15 .40
185 John Danks .15 .40
186 Denard Span .15 .40
187 Nyjer Morgan .15 .40
188 Adrian Gonzalez .30 .75
189 Checklist .15 .40
190 Chad Billingsley .25 .60
191 Travis Hafner .15 .40
192 Gerald Laird .15 .40
193a Daisuke Matsuzaka .25 .60
193b Matsuzaka Dice SP 1.50 4.00
194 Joey Votto .40 1.00
195 Jered Weaver .25 .60
196 Ryan Theriot .15 .40
197 Gio Gonzalez .25 .60
198 Chris Iannetta .15 .40
199 Mike Jacobs .15 .40
19b A.Rod Dice SP 3.00 8.00
200 Javier Vasquez .15 .40
201 Josh Beckett/Johan Santana .25 .60
202 Torii Hunter .15 .40
203 Juan Rivera .15 .40
204 Brandon Phillips .15 .40
205 Edwin Jackson .15 .40
206 Lance Berkman .25 .60
207 Gil Meche .15 .40
208 Jorge Cantu .15 .40
209 Eric Young Jr (RC) .40 1.00
210 Andre Ethier .25 .60
211 Rickie Weeks .15 .40
212 Omir Santos .15 .40
213 Mat Latos .25 .60
214 Tyler Colvin RC .60 1.50
215a Derek Jeter 1.00 2.50
215b D.Jeter Dice SP 6.00 15.00
215c Jeter Red-Yel Name SP 50.00 100.00
216 Carlos Pena .25 .60
217 Carlos Ruiz .15 .40
218 Jason Marquis .15 .40
219 Charlie Manuel MG .15 .40
220 Bruce Bochy MG .25 .60
221 Terry Francona MG .25 .60
222 Manny Acta MG .15 .40
223 Jim Leyland MG .15 .40
224 Bob Geren MG .15 .40
225 Mike Scioscia MG .15 .40
226 Ron Gardenhire MG .15 .40
227 Luis Castillo .15 .40
228 New York Mets .25 .60
229 Carlos Carrasco (RC) 1.00 2.50
230 Chone Figgins .15 .40
231 Johan Santana .25 .60
232 Max Scherzer .40 1.00
233a Ian Kinsler .25 .60
233b Ian Kinsler Dice Back SP 3.00 8.00
234 Jeff Samardzija .15 .40
235 Will Venable .15 .40
236 Cristian Guzman .15 .40
237 Alexei Ramirez .25 .60
238 B.J. Upton .15 .40
239 Derek Lowe .15 .40
240 Elvis Andrus .25 .60
241 Joakim Soria .15 .40
242 Chase Headley .15 .40
243 Adam Lind .25 .60
244a Ichiro Suzuki .50 1.25
244b Ichiro Dice SP 3.00 8.00
245 Ryan Howard .30 .75
246 Johnny Damon .25 .60
247 Casey Blake .15 .40
248 Kevin Millwood .15 .40
249 Cincinnati Reds .15 .40
250 A.McCutchen/G.Jones .40 1.00
251 Jarrod Washburn .15 .40
252 Dan Uggla .15 .40
253 Cliff Lee .25 .60

54 Chris Davis .25 .60
55 Jordan Zimmermann .25 .60
56 Pedro Feliz .15 .40
57 Carlos Quentin .15 .40
58 Derek Holland .15 .40
59 Jose Reyes .25 .60
60 Manny Ramirez .40 1.00
61 David Ortiz .40 1.00
62 Andrew McCutchen .40 1.00
63 Brian Fuentes .15 .40
64 Nelson Cruz .40 1.00
65 Dexter Fowler .25 .60
66 Carlos Beltran .25 .60
67 Michael Young .15 .40
68 Chris Young .15 .40
269 Edgar Renteria .15 .40
270 Vin Mazzaro .15 .40
271 Gary Sheffield .15 .40
272 Roy Oswalt .25 .60
273 Checklist .15 .40
274 Stephen Drew .15 .40
275 John Lannan .15 .40
276 Tyler Flowers RC .60 1.50
277 Coco Crisp UER
Athletics spelled incorrectly .15 .40
278 Luis Durango RC .40 1.00
279 Erick Aybar .15 .40
280 Tobi Stoner RC .60 1.50
281 Cody Ross .15 .40
282 Koji Uehara .15 .40
283 Cleveland Indians .15 .40
284 Yovani Gallardo .15 .40
285 Wilkin Ramirez .15 .40
286 Roy Halladay .25 .60
287 Juan Francisco RC .60 1.50
288 Carlos Zambrano .25 .60
289 Carl Crawford .25 .60
290 Joba Chamberlain .15 .40
291 Fernando Martinez .15 .40
292 Jhoulys Chacin .15 .40
293 Felix Hernandez .25 .60
294 Josh Hamilton .25 .60
295 Rick Ankiel .15 .40
296 Hiroki Kuroda .15 .40
297 Oakland Athletics .15 .40
298 Wade Davis (RC) .60 1.50
299 Derrek Lee .15 .40
300a Hanley Ramirez .25 .60
300b Hanley Ramirez Dice Back SP 3.00 8.00
301 Ryan Spilborghs .15 .40
302 Adrian Beltre .40 1.00
303 James Shields .15 .40
304 Alex Gordon .25 .60
305 Brad Bergesen .15 .40
306 Lee Dominates .25 .60
307 Burnett Outduels Pedro .25 .60
308 AROD Homer .50 1.25
309 Damon Steals 2 Bags on 1 Pitch .25 .60
310 Utley Ties Reggie .25 .60
311 Matsui Knocks in 6 .40 1.00
312 Matsui Named MVP .40 1.00
313 The Winners Celebrate .40 1.00
314 H.Ramirez/E.Longoria .25 .60
315 Brandon Webb .25 .60
316 Kevin Youkilis .15 .40
317 Brent Dlugach (RC) .40 1.00
318 Aubrey Huff .15 .40
319 John Maine .15 .40
320 Pittsburgh Pirates .15 .40
321 Aramis Ramirez .15 .40
322 Michael Dunn RC .40 1.00
323 Shin-Soo Choo .25 .60
324 Mike Pelfrey .15 .40
325 Brett Gardner .25 .60
326 Nick Johnson .15 .40
327 Henry Rodriguez RC .40 1.00
328 Joe Nathan .15 .40
329 Mike Napoli .15 .40
330 Jamie Moyer .15 .40
331 Kyle Blanks .15 .40
332 Ryan Langerhans .15 .40
333 Travis Snider .15 .40
334 Wandy Rodriguez .15 .40
335 Carlos Gonzalez .25 .60
336 Francisco Rodriguez .25 .60
337 Mark Buehrle/Jake Peavy .25 .60
338 Ryan Zimmerman .25 .60
339 Michael Bourn .15 .40
340 Magglio Ordonez .25 .60
341 Brandon Morrow .15 .40
342 Daniel Murphy .30 .75
343 Ricky Romero .15 .40
344 Homer Bailey .15 .40
345 Nick Swisher .25 .60
346 Akinori Iwamura .15 .40
347 St. Louis Cardinals .25 .60
348 Julio Borbon .15 .40
349 Jose Guillen .15 .40
350 Scott Podsednik .15 .40
351 Bobby Crosby .15 .40
352 Ryan Ludwick .15 .40
353 Brett Cecil .15 .40
354 Minnesota Twins .15 .40
355 Ben Zobrist .25 .60
356 Dan Haren .15 .40
357 Vernon Wells .15 .40
358 Skip Schumaker .15 .40
359 Jose Lopez .15 .40
360a Vladimir Guerrero .25 .60
360b Vladimir Guerrero Dice Back SP 2.00 5.00
361 Checklist .15 .40
362 Brandon Allen (RC) .40 1.00
363 Joe Mauer .30 .75
Roy Halladay
364 Todd Helton .25 .60
365 J.J. Hardy .15 .40
366a CC Sabathia .25 .60
366b Sabath Grn-Yel Name SP 50.00 100.00
367 Yuniesky Betancourt .15 .40
368 Placido Polanco .15 .40
369 Josh Johnson .25 .60
370 Mark Reynolds .15 .40
371a Victor Martinez .25 .60
371b Victor Martinez Dice Back SP 3.00 8.00
372 Ian Stewart .15 .40
373 Boston Red Sox .25 .60
374 Brad Hawpe .15 .40
375 Ricky Nolasco .15 .40
376 Marco Scutaro .25 .60
377 Troy Tulowitzki .40 1.00
378 Francisco Liriano .15 .40
379 Randy Wells .15 .40
380 Jeff Francoeur .25 .60
381 Mike Lowell .15 .40
382 Hunter Pence .25 .60
383 T.Lincecum/M.Cain .25 .60
384 Scott Kazmir .15 .40
385 Hideki Matsui .40 1.00
386 Tim Wakefield .25 .60
387 Jeff Niemann .15 .40
388 John Smoltz .40 1.00
389 Franklin Gutierrez .15 .40
390 Matt LaPorta .15 .40
391 Melvin Mora .15 .40
392 Jeremy Bonderman .15 .40
393a Ryan Braun .25 .60
393b Ryan Braun Blue-Orange
Nameplate SP 30.00 60.00
394 Emilio Bonifacio .15 .40
395 Tommy Hanson .15 .40
396 Aaron Hill .15 .40
397 Micah Owings .15 .40
398 Jack Cust .15 .40
399 Jason Bartlett .15 .40
400 Brian McCann .25 .60
401 Babe Ruth BT 1.00 2.50
402 George Sisler BT .25 .60
403 Jackie Robinson BT .40 1.00
404 Rogers Hornsby BT .25 .60
405 Lou Gehrig BT .75 2.00
406 Mickey Mantle BT 1.25 3.00
407 Ty Cobb BT .60 1.50
408 Christy Mathewson BT .40 1.00
409 Walter Johnson BT .40 1.00
410 Honus Wagner BT .40 1.00
411 Pet/Pos/Jet/Riv 12.50 30.00
412 Joe Saunders .15 .40
413 Andrew Miller .25 .60
414 Alcides Escobar .25 .60
415 Luke Hochevar .15 .40
416 Gerardo Parra .15 .40
417 Garrett Atkins .15 .40
418 Jim Thome .25 .60
419 Michael Saunders .25 .60
420 Justin Morneau .25 .60
421 Dustin Pedroia .30 .75
422 Dioner Navarro .15 .40
423 Checklist .15 .40
424 Chien-Ming Wang .25 .60
425 Marcus Thames .15 .40
426 David Price SP 4.00 10.00
427a David Wright SP 2.50 6.00
427b David Wright Green
Yellow Nameplate SP 60.00 120.00
428 Tommy Manzella SP (RC) 2.50 6.00
429a Tim Lincecum SP 2.00 5.00
429b T.Lincecum Dice SP 2.00 5.00
430 Ken Griffey Jr. SP 5.00 12.00
431 Justin Masterson SP 2.50 6.00
432 Jermaine Dye SP 2.50 6.00
433 Casey McGehee SP 2.50 6.00
434 Brett Anderson SP 2.50 6.00
435 Matt Garza SP 2.50 6.00
436 Miguel Tejada SP 3.00 8.00
437 Checklist SP 2.50 6.00
438 Kurt Suzuki SP 2.50 6.00
439 Evan Longoria SP 3.00 8.00
440 Edinson Volquez SP 2.50 6.00
441 Doug Fister SP RC 2.50 6.00
442 Carlos Delgado SP 2.50 6.00
443 Philadelphia Phillies SP 2.50 6.00
444 Justin Duchscherer SP 2.50 6.00
445 Chris Volstad SP 2.50 6.00
446 Freddy Sanchez SP 2.50 6.00
447 Carlos Lee SP 2.50 6.00
448 Carlos Guillen SP 2.50 6.00
449 Hank Blalock SP 2.50 6.00
450 Ubaldo Jimenez SP 2.50 6.00
451 D.Jeter/J.Bartlett SP 5.00 12.00
452 Cliff Pennington SP 2.50 6.00
453 Miguel Montero SP 2.50 6.00
454 Corey Hart SP 2.50 6.00
455 Bronson Arroyo SP 2.50 6.00
456 Carlos Gomez SP 2.50 6.00
457 J.D. Drew SP 2.50 6.00
458 Kenshin Kawakami SP 3.00 8.00
459 Neftali Feliz SP 2.00 5.00
460 Bobby Abreu SP 2.50 6.00
461 Joe Maddon MG AS SP 2.50 6.00
462 Charlie Manuel MG AS SP 2.50 6.00
463a Mark Teixeira AS SP 3.00 8.00
463b Atlanta Braves SP 12.50 30.00
464 Albert Pujols AS SP 2.50 6.00
465 Aaron Hill AS SP 2.50 6.00
466 Chase Utley AS SP 3.00 8.00
467 Michael Young AS SP 2.00 5.00
468 David Wright AS SP 2.50 6.00
469 Derek Jeter AS SP 10.00 25.00
470 Hanley Ramirez AS SP 3.00 8.00
471 Jason Giambi SP 2.50 6.00
472 Ichiro Suzuki SP 3.00 8.00
473 Miguel Tejada SP 3.00 8.00
474 Alex Rodriguez SP 3.00 8.00
475 Justin Morneau SP 3.00 8.00
476 Dustin Pedroia SP 2.50 6.00
477 Albert Pujols SP 2.50 6.00
478 Jimmy Rollins SP 3.00 8.00
479 Ryan Howard SP 2.50 6.00
480 Cole Hamels SP 2.50 6.00
481 Manny Ramirez SP 3.00 8.00
482 Jermaine Dye SP 2.50 6.00
483 Mariano Rivera SP 6.00 15.00
484 Roy Oswalt SP 3.00 8.00
485 Matt Garza SP 2.50 6.00
486 Derek Jeter SP 8.00 20.00
487 Ichiro Suzuki AS SP 3.00 8.00
488 Raul Ibanez AS SP 3.00 8.00
489 Josh Hamilton AS SP 2.00 5.00
490 Shane Victorino AS SP 3.00 8.00
491 Jason Bay AS SP 3.00 8.00
492 Ryan Braun AS SP 3.00 8.00
493 Joe Mauer AS SP 2.50 6.00
494 Yadier Molina AS SP 5.00 12.00
495 Roy Halladay AS SP 3.00 8.00
496 Tim Lincecum AS SP 2.00 5.00
497 Mark Buehrle AS SP 4.00 10.00
498 Johan Santana AS SP 3.00 8.00
499 Mariano Rivera AS SP 6.00 15.00
500 Francisco Rodriguez AS SP 3.00 8.00

2010 Topps Heritage Advertising Panels

ISSUED AS BOX TOPPER
1 Rick Ankiel .40 1.00
Jarrod Washburn
Travis Hafner
2 Scott Baker 1.00 2.50
Miguel Cabrera
Reid Gorecki
3 Gordon Beckham .60 1.50
Zack Greinke
Prince Fielder
4 Lance Berkman 1.00 2.50
Josh Willingham
AL Strikeout LL
5 Josh Hamilton .60 1.50
Kevin Millwood
Chad Billingsley
6 Melky Cabrera .40 1.00
Mark DeRosa
Dave Trembley
7 Miguel Cabrera 1.00 2.50
Reid Gorecki
Melky Cabrera
8 Luis Castillo 1.00 2.50
Adam Dunn
Honus Wagner
9 Chris Coghlan .60 1.50
Lance Berkman
Josh Willingham
10 Nelson Cruz 1.00 2.50
Adam Jones
John Russell
11 Michael Cuddyer 1.00 2.50
Jim Thome
Adrian Beltre
12 Prince Fielder .60 1.50
Charlie Manuel
Juan Francisco
13 Gio Gonzalez .60 1.50
Jeff Samardzija
Brandon Morrow
14 Reid Gorecki .60 1.50
Melky Cabrera
Mark DeRosa
15 Zack Greinke .60 1.50
Prince Fielder
Charlie Manuel
16 Ozzie Guillen .40 1.00
Glen Perkins
Gordon Beckham
17 Jerry Hairston Jr. .60 1.50
Scott Rolen
Joakim Soria
18 Aaron Hill .40 1.00
Joe Saunders
Scott Podsednik
19 Huff/Santos/Kershaw 2.00 5.00
20 Chris Iannetta .60 1.50
Dexter Fowler
CC Sabathia
21 Edwin Jackson .60 1.50
Erick Aybar
Rogers Hornsby
22 Howie Kendrick .75 2.00
Willy Taveras
Joe Mauer
23 Kershaw/Butler/Owings 2.00 5.00
24 Mike Lowell .60 1.50
Chris Coghlan
Lance Berkman
25 Brandon Morrow .40 1.00
Aaron Hill
Joe Saunders
26 Daniel Murphy .75 2.00
Carlos Zambrano
Will Venable
27 Ricky Nolasco .40 1.00
Derek Holland
Felipe Lopez
28 Micah Owings .60 1.50
John Maine
Mat Latos
29 Hunter Pence .60 1.50
Luis Castillo
Adam Dunn
30 Glen Perkins .60 1.50
Gordon Beckham
Zack Greinke
31 A.J. Pierzynski .40 1.00
Yuniesky Betancourt
Matt LaPorta
32 Carlos Quentin 2.50 6.00
AL Batting Average LL
Nolan Reimold
33 Nolan Reimold .40 1.00
Baltimore Orioles
Edwin Jackson
34 Scott Rolen .60 1.50
Joakim Soria
Vernon Wells
35 Michael Saunders .40 1.00
Ricky Nolasco
Derek Holland
36 Gary Sheffield .40 1.00
Jose Guillen
Brad Hawpe
37 James Shields .40 1.00
Chase Headley
Howie Kendrick
38 Joakim Soria .40 1.00
Vernon Wells
Franklin Gutierrez
39 Will Venable 1.00 2.50
Scott Baker
Miguel Cabrera
40 Jarrod Washburn .40 1.00
Travis Hafner
David Hernandez
41 Josh Willingham 1.00 2.50
AL Strikeout LL
Alex Rodriguez
42 Carlos Zambrano .60 1.50
Will Venable
Scott Baker
43 Omir Santos 2.00 5.00
Clayton Kershaw
Billy Butler
44 Alfonso Soriano .60 1.50
Chris Iannetta
Dexter Fowler
45 Scott Podsednik .40 1.00
Rick Ankiel
Jarrod Washburn
46 Henry Rodriguez .60 1.50
Hunter Pence
Luis Castillo
47 Travis Snider 1.00 2.50
Nelson Cruz
Adam Jones
48 Paul Konerko .60 1.50
Mike Lowell
Chris Coglan

2010 Topps Heritage Chrome

COMPLETE SET (150) 125.00 250.00
1-100 STATED ODDS 1:5 HERITAGE HOBBY
101-150 ODDS 1:26 T.CHROME HOBBY
STATED PRINT RUN 1961 SER.#'d SETS
C1 Albert Pujols 2.50 6.00
C2 Joe Mauer 2.00 5.00
C3 Rajai Davis 1.50 4.00
C4 Adam Wainwright 2.00 5.00
C5 Grady Sizemore 2.00 5.00
C6 Alex Rodriguez 2.50 6.00
C7 Cole Hamels 2.00 5.00
C8 Matt Kemp 2.50 6.00
C9 Chris Tillman 1.50 4.00
C10 Reid Gorecki 2.00 5.00
C11 Chris Carpenter 1.50 4.00
C12 Jason Bay 2.00 5.00
C13 Gordon Beckham 1.25 3.00
C14 Curtis Granderson 2.50 6.00
C15 Daniel McCutchen 2.00 5.00
C16 Pablo Sandoval 2.00 5.00
C17 Jake Peavy 1.25 3.00
C18 Ryan Church 1.50 4.00
C19 Nick Markakis 2.00 5.00
C20 Josh Beckett 1.25 3.00
C21 Matt Cain 2.00 5.00
C22 Nate McLouth 1.50 4.00
C23 J.A. Happ 2.00 5.00
C24 Justin Upton 2.50 6.00
C25 Rick Porcello 2.50 6.00
C26 Mark Teixeira 1.50 4.00
C27 Raul Ibanez 2.00 5.00
C28 Zack Greinke 2.00 5.00
C29 Nolan Reimold 1.25 3.00
C30 Jimmy Rollins 2.00 5.00
C31 Jorge Posada 2.00 5.00
C32 Clayton Kershaw 5.00 12.00
C33 Buster Posey 25.00 60.00
C34 Adam Dunn 2.00 5.00
C35 Chipper Jones 2.50 6.00
C36 John Lackey 2.50 6.00
C37 Daniel Hudson 2.00 5.00
C38 Jacoby Ellsbury 2.00 5.00
C39 Mariano Rivera 3.00 8.00
C40 Jair Jurrjens 1.50 4.00
C41 Prince Fielder 1.50 4.00
C42 Shane Victorino 2.00 5.00
C43 Mark Buehrle 2.00 5.00
C44 Madison Bumgarner 8.00 20.00
C45 Yunel Escobar 1.50 4.00
C46 Chris Coghlan 1.50 4.00
C47 Justin Verlander 3.00 8.00
C48 Michael Brantley 2.50 6.00
C49 Matt Holliday 2.50 6.00
C50 Chase Utley 1.50 4.00
C51 Adam Jones 2.00 5.00
C52 Kendry Morales 1.50 4.00
C53 Denard Span 1.50 4.00
C54 Nyjer Morgan 1.50 4.00
C55 Adrian Gonzalez 2.50 6.00
C56 Daisuke Matsuzaka 1.25 3.00
C57 Joey Votto 2.50 6.00
C58 Jered Weaver 2.50 6.00
C59 Lance Berkman 2.00 5.00
C60 Andre Ethier 2.00 5.00
C61 Mat Latos 2.50 6.00
C62 Derek Jeter 10.00 25.00
C63 Johan Santana 1.50 4.00
C64 Max Scherzer 4.00 10.00
C65 Ian Kinsler 2.00 5.00
C66 Elvis Andrus 2.00 5.00
C67 Adam Lind 2.00 5.00
C68 Ichiro Suzuki 2.50 6.00
C69 Ryan Howard 1.50 4.00
C70 Dan Uggla 1.25 3.00
C71 Cliff Lee 2.00 5.00
C72 Andrew McCutchen 2.50 6.00
C73 Nelson Cruz 3.00 8.00
C74 Stephen Drew 1.25 3.00
C75 Koji Uehara 1.25 3.00
C76 Roy Halladay 1.50 4.00
C77 Felix Hernandez 1.50 4.00
C78 Josh Hamilton 1.50 4.00
C79 Hanley Ramirez 1.50 4.00
C80 Kevin Youkilis 1.25 3.00
C81 Kyle Blanks 1.50 4.00
C82 Ryan Zimmerman 2.00 5.00
C83 Ricky Romero 1.50 4.00
C84 Julio Borbon 1.50 4.00
C85 Ben Zobrist 2.50 6.00
C86 Vladimir Guerrero 1.50 4.00
C87 CC Sabathia 2.00 5.00
C88 Josh Johnson 2.00 5.00
C89 Mark Reynolds 1.50 4.00
C90 Troy Tulowitzki 3.00 8.00
C91 Hunter Pence 2.00 5.00
C92 Ryan Braun 1.25 3.00
C93 Tommy Hanson 1.25 3.00
C94 Aaron Hill 1.50 4.00
C95 Brian McCann 2.00 5.00
C96 David Wright 1.50 4.00
C97 Tim Lincecum 1.25 3.00
C98 Evan Longoria 1.25 3.00
C99 Ubaldo Jimenez 1.25 3.00
C100 Neftali Feliz 1.50 4.00
C101 Brian Roberts 1.50 4.00
C102 A.J. Burnett 1.25 3.00
C103 Ryan Dempster 1.50 4.00
C104 Russell Martin 1.50 4.00
C105 Jay Bruce 2.00 5.00
C106 Jayson Werth 2.00 5.00
C107 Michael Cuddyer 1.50 4.00
C108 Alfonso Soriano 2.00 5.00
C109 Martin Prado 1.50 4.00
C110 Miguel Cabrera 2.50 6.00
C111 Yadier Molina 3.00 8.00
C112 Kosuke Fukudome 1.50 4.00
C113 Andy Pettitte 2.00 5.00
C114 Johnny Cueto 2.50 6.00
C115 Alex Rios 1.25 3.00
C116 Howie Kendrick 1.50 4.00
C117 Robinson Cano 1.50 4.00
C118 Chad Billingsley 2.50 6.00
C119 Torii Hunter 1.50 4.00
C120 Brandon Phillips 1.50 4.00
C121 Carlos Pena 2.00 5.00
C122 Chone Figgins 2.00 5.00
C123 Alexei Ramirez 2.50 6.00
C124 Carlos Quentin 1.25 3.00
C125 Jose Reyes 2.00 5.00
C126 Manny Ramirez 2.50 6.00
C127 David Ortiz 3.00 8.00
C128 Carlos Beltran 2.50 6.00
C129 Michael Young 1.50 4.00
C130 Roy Oswalt 2.00 5.00
C131 Erick Aybar 1.50 4.00
C132 Yovani Gallardo 1.50 4.00
C133 Carlos Zambrano 2.00 5.00
C134 Carl Crawford 2.00 5.00
C135 Aramis Ramirez 1.50 4.00
C136 Shin-Soo Choo 1.50 4.00
C137 Wandy Rodriguez 1.50 4.00
C138 Magglio Ordonez 2.00 5.00
C139 Dan Haren 1.50 4.00
C140 Victor Martinez 2.00 5.00
C141 Ian Stewart 1.50 4.00
C142 Francisco Liriano 1.50 4.00
C143 Scott Kazmir 1.50 4.00
C144 Hideki Matsui 2.50 6.00
C145 Justin Morneau 1.50 4.00
C146 Dustin Pedroia 1.50 4.00
C147 David Price 2.00 5.00
C148 Ken Griffey Jr. 4.00 10.00
C149 Carlos Lee 1.50 4.00
C150 Bobby Abreu 1.50 4.00

2010 Topps Heritage Chrome Black Refractors

101-150 ODDS 1:816 T.CHROME HOBBY
1-100 ODDS 1:255 HERITAGE HOBBY
STATED PRINT RUN 61SER.#'d SETS
C1 Albert Pujols 25.00 60.00
C2 Joe Mauer 15.00 40.00
C3 Rajai Davis 8.00 20.00
C4 Adam Wainwright 12.00 30.00
C5 Grady Sizemore 12.00 30.00
C6 Alex Rodriguez 25.00 60.00
C7 Cole Hamels 15.00 40.00
C8 Matt Kemp 15.00 40.00
C9 Chris Tillman 8.00 20.00
C10 Reid Gorecki 12.00 30.00
C11 Chris Carpenter 12.00 30.00
C12 Jason Bay 12.00 30.00
C13 Gordon Beckham 8.00 20.00
C14 Curtis Granderson 15.00 40.00
C15 Daniel McCutchen 12.00 30.00
C16 Pablo Sandoval 12.00 30.00
C17 Jake Peavy 8.00 20.00
C18 Ryan Church 8.00 20.00
C19 Nick Markakis 15.00 40.00
C20 Josh Beckett 8.00 20.00
C21 Matt Cain 12.00 30.00
C22 Nate McLouth 8.00 20.00
C23 J.A. Happ 12.00 30.00
C24 Justin Upton 12.00 30.00
C25 Rick Porcello 12.00 30.00
C26 Mark Teixeira 12.00 30.00
C27 Raul Ibanez 12.00 30.00
C28 Zack Greinke 12.00 30.00
C29 Nolan Reimold 8.00 20.00
C30 Jimmy Rollins 12.00 30.00
C31 Jorge Posada 12.00 30.00
C32 Clayton Kershaw 40.00 100.00
C33 Buster Posey 60.00 150.00
C34 Adam Dunn 12.00 30.00
C35 Chipper Jones 20.00 50.00
C36 John Lackey 12.00 30.00
C37 Daniel Hudson 12.00 30.00
C38 Jacoby Ellsbury 15.00 40.00
C39 Mariano Rivera 25.00 60.00
C40 Jair Jurrjens 8.00 20.00
C41 Prince Fielder 12.00 30.00
C42 Shane Victorino 12.00 30.00
C43 Mark Buehrle 12.00 30.00
C44 Madison Bumgarner 60.00 150.00
C45 Yunel Escobar 8.00 20.00
C46 Chris Coghlan 8.00 20.00
C47 Justin Verlander 20.00 50.00
C48 Michael Brantley 12.00 30.00
C49 Matt Holliday 20.00 50.00
C50 Chase Utley 12.00 30.00
C51 Adam Jones 12.00 30.00
C52 Kendry Morales 8.00 20.00
C53 Denard Span 8.00 20.00
C54 Nyjer Morgan 8.00 20.00
C55 Adrian Gonzalez 15.00 40.00
C56 Daisuke Matsuzaka 12.00 30.00
C57 Joey Votto 20.00 50.00
C58 Jered Weaver 12.00 30.00
C59 Lance Berkman 12.00 30.00
C60 Andre Ethier 12.00 30.00
C61 Mat Latos 12.00 30.00
C62 Derek Jeter 50.00 125.00
C63 Johan Santana 12.00 30.00
C64 Max Scherzer 20.00 50.00
C65 Ian Kinsler 12.00 30.00
C66 Elvis Andrus 12.00 30.00
C67 Adam Lind 12.00 30.00
C68 Ichiro Suzuki 25.00 60.00
C69 Ryan Howard 15.00 40.00
C70 Dan Uggla 8.00 20.00
C71 Cliff Lee 12.00 30.00
C72 Andrew McCutchen 20.00 50.00
C73 Nelson Cruz 20.00 50.00
C74 Stephen Drew 8.00 20.00
C75 Koji Uehara 8.00 20.00
C76 Roy Halladay 12.00 30.00
C77 Felix Hernandez 12.00 30.00
C78 Josh Hamilton 12.00 30.00
C79 Hanley Ramirez 12.00 30.00
C80 Kevin Youkilis 8.00 20.00
C81 Kyle Blanks 8.00 20.00
C82 Ryan Zimmerman 12.00 30.00
C83 Ricky Romero 12.00 30.00
C84 Julio Borbon 8.00 20.00
C85 Ben Zobrist 12.00 30.00
C86 Vladimir Guerrero 12.00 30.00
C87 CC Sabathia 12.00 30.00
C88 Josh Johnson 12.00 30.00
C89 Mark Reynolds 8.00 20.00
C90 Troy Tulowitzki 20.00 50.00
C91 Hunter Pence 12.00 30.00
C92 Ryan Braun 12.00 30.00
C93 Tommy Hanson 12.00 30.00
C94 Aaron Hill 8.00 20.00
C95 Brian McCann 12.00 30.00
C96 David Wright 15.00 40.00
C97 Tim Lincecum 12.00 30.00
C98 Evan Longoria 12.00 30.00
C99 Ubaldo Jimenez 8.00 20.00
C100 Neftali Feliz 8.00 20.00
C101 Brian Roberts 8.00 20.00
C102 A.J. Burnett 8.00 20.00
C103 Ryan Dempster 8.00 20.00
C104 Russell Martin 8.00 20.00
C105 Jay Bruce 12.00 30.00
C106 Jayson Werth 12.00 30.00
C107 Michael Cuddyer 8.00 20.00
C108 Alfonso Soriano 12.00 30.00
C109 Martin Prado 8.00 20.00
C110 Miguel Cabrera 20.00 50.00
C111 Yadier Molina 20.00 50.00
C112 Kosuke Fukudome 12.00 30.00
C113 Andy Pettitte 12.00 30.00
C114 Johnny Cueto 12.00 30.00
C115 Alex Rios 8.00 20.00
C116 Howie Kendrick 8.00 20.00
C117 Robinson Cano 12.00 30.00
C118 Chad Billingsley 12.00 30.00
C119 Torii Hunter 8.00 20.00
C120 Brandon Phillips 8.00 20.00
C121 Carlos Pena 12.00 30.00
C122 Chone Figgins 8.00 20.00
C123 Alexei Ramirez 12.00 30.00
C124 Carlos Quentin 8.00 20.00
C125 Jose Reyes 12.00 30.00
C126 Manny Ramirez 20.00 50.00
C127 David Ortiz 20.00 50.00
C128 Carlos Beltran 12.00 30.00
C129 Michael Young 8.00 20.00
C130 Roy Oswalt 12.00 30.00
C131 Erick Aybar 8.00 20.00
C132 Yovani Gallardo 8.00 20.00
C133 Carlos Zambrano 12.00 30.00
C134 Carl Crawford 12.00 30.00
C135 Aramis Ramirez 8.00 20.00
C136 Shin-Soo Choo 12.00 30.00
C137 Wandy Rodriguez 8.00 20.00
C138 Magglio Ordonez 12.00 30.00
C139 Dan Haren 8.00 20.00
C140 Victor Martinez 12.00 30.00
C141 Ian Stewart 8.00 20.00
C142 Francisco Liriano 8.00 20.00
C143 Scott Kazmir 8.00 20.00
C144 Hideki Matsui 20.00 50.00
C145 Justin Morneau 12.00 30.00
C146 Dustin Pedroia 15.00 40.00
C147 David Price 15.00 40.00
C148 Ken Griffey Jr. 40.00 100.00
C149 Carlos Lee 8.00 20.00
C150 Bobby Abreu 8.00 20.00

2010 Topps Heritage Chrome Refractors

*REF: .6X TO 1.5X BASIC INSERTS
1-100 ODDS 1:18 HERITAGE HOBBY
101-150 ODDS 1:88 T.CHROME HOBBY
STATED PRINT RUN 561 SER.#'d SETS

2010 Topps Heritage Baseball Flashbacks

COMPLETE SET (10) 6.00 15.00
STATED ODDS 1:12 HOBBY
BF1 Roger Maris 1.25 3.00
BF2 Warren Spahn .75 2.00
BF3 Whitey Ford .75 2.00
BF4 Frank Robinson .75 2.00
BF5 Whitey Ford .75 2.00
BF6 Candlestick Park .50 1.25
BF7 Carl Yastrzemski 2.00 5.00
BF8 Luis Aparicio .75 2.00
BF9 Al Kaline 1.25 3.00
BF10 Angels/Senators .50 1.25

2010 Topps Heritage Clubhouse Collection Relics

STATED ODDS 1:29 HOBBY
AE Andre Ethier 3.00 8.00
AK Adam Kennedy 2.00 5.00
AL Adam Lind 3.00 8.00
AP Albert Pujols 6.00 15.00
AR Aramis Ramirez 2.00 5.00
AW Adam Wainwright 3.00 8.00
BJ Bobby Jenks 2.00 5.00
BW Billy Wagner 2.00 5.00
CB Clay Buchholz 2.00 5.00
CG Cristian Guzman 2.00 5.00
CH Cole Hamels 4.00 10.00
CM Carlos Marmol 3.00 8.00
CS CC Sabathia 3.00 8.00
CZ Carlos Zambrano 3.00 8.00
DH Dan Haren 2.00 5.00
DN Dioner Navarro 2.00 5.00
DO David Ortiz 5.00 12.00
DU Dan Uggla 2.00 5.00
EL Evan Longoria 3.00 8.00
EV Edinson Volquez 2.00 5.00
GB Gordon Beckham 2.00 5.00
GS Grady Sizemore 3.00 8.00
HK Hiroki Kuroda 2.00 5.00
JB Jason Bulger 2.00 5.00
JC Jose Contreras
JD Jermaine Dye 2.00 5.00
JF Jeff Francis 2.00 5.00
JL James Loney 2.00 5.00
JV Joey Votto 5.00 12.00
JW Jered Weaver 3.00 8.00
KJ Kenji Johjima 2.00 5.00
KM Kendry Morales 2.00 5.00
KW Kerry Wood 2.00 5.00
LB Lance Berkman 3.00 8.00
MB Mark Buehrle 3.00 8.00
ME Mark Ellis 2.00 5.00
MK Matt Kemp 4.00 10.00
MT Miguel Tejada 3.00 8.00
MY Michael Young 3.00 8.00
NM Nate McLouth 3.00 8.00
PK Paul Konerko 3.00 8.00
PS Pablo Sandoval 3.00 8.00
RB Rocco Baldelli 2.00 5.00
RD Ryan Dempster 2.00 5.00
RH Ryan Howard 4.00 10.00
RL Ryan Ludwick 2.00 5.00
RM Russell Martin 2.00 5.00
VG Vladimir Guerrero 3.00 8.00
AJP A.J. Pierzynski 2.00 5.00
ARA Alexei Ramirez 3.00 8.00
BWE Brandon Webb 3.00 8.00
CHE Chase Headley 2.00 5.00

HCK Hong-Chih Kuo 2.00 5.00
JCR Joe Crede 2.00 5.00
KMI Kevin Millwood 2.00 5.00

2010 Topps Heritage Clubhouse Collection Dual Relics

STATED ODDS 1:6150 HOBBY
STATED PRINT RUN 61 SER.#'d SETS
AR L.Aparicio/A.Ramirez 10.00 25.00
BM B.Robinson/N.Markakis 12.50 30.00
MR R.Maris/A.Rodriguez 100.00 200.00
MT M.Mantle/M.Teixeira 100.00 200.00
YE C.Yastrzemski/J.Ellsbury 40.00 80.00

2010 Topps Heritage Cut Signatures

STATED ODDS 1:285,000
STATED PRINT RUN 1 SER.#'d SET

2010 Topps Heritage Flashback Stadium Relics

STATED ODDS 1:475 HOBBY
AK Al Kaline 6.00 15.00
BG Bob Gibson 4.00 10.00
EB Ernie Banks 12.00 30.00
FR Frank Robinson 40.00 100.00
JP Jim Piersall 2.50 6.00
LA Luis Aparicio 4.00 10.00
MM Mickey Mantle 25.00 60.00
RM Roger Maris 20.00 50.00
RS Brooks Robinson 4.00 10.00
SM Stan Musial 10.00 25.00

2010 Topps Heritage Framed Dual Stamps

STATED ODDS 1:193 HOBBY
STATED PRINT RUN 50 SER.#'d SETS
AD Brett Anderson 6.00 15.00
Adam Dunn
AH Bronson Arroyo 4.00 10.00
Luke Hochevar
AP Garret Anderson 6.00 15.00
Andy Pettitte
BA Casey Blake 6.00 15.00
Elvis Andrus
BE Mark Buehrle 6.00 15.00
Yunel Escobar
BF R.Braun/G.Floyd 6.00 15.00
BG Jay Bruce 8.00 20.00
Curtis Granderson
BL Carlos Beltran 6.00 15.00
John Lackey
BT Marlon Byrd 6.00 15.00
Josh Thole
BU Kyle Blanks 6.00 15.00
B.J. Upton
CB Jorge Cantu 4.00 10.00
Scott Baker
CE Michael Cuddyer 6.00 15.00
Andre Either
CG Johnny Cueto 6.00 15.00
Zack Greinke
CH1 M.Cabrera/F.Hernandez 10.00 25.00
CH2 Chris Coghlan 6.00 15.00
Felix Hernandez
CJ M.Cabrera/G.Jones 10.00 25.00
CK Matt Cain 6.00 15.00
Paul Konerko
CL Melky Cabrera 6.00 15.00
Mat Latos
CM Orlando Cabrera 10.00 25.00
Yadier Molina
CR Shin-Soo Choo 6.00 15.00
Francisco Rodriguez
DA Adam Dunn 6.00 15.00
Bobby Abreu
DF Zach Duke 6.00 15.00
Tyler Flowers
DG David DeJesus 6.00 15.00
Reid Gorecki
DI Johnny Damon 6.00 15.00
Raul Ibanez
DR Rajai Davis 4.00 10.00
Mark Reynolds
DY Ryan Dempster 4.00 10.00
Michael Young
EC Andre Either 6.00 15.00
Robinson Cano
FB Pedro Feliz 10.00 25.00
Adrian Beltre
FG Jeff Francoeur 6.00 15.00
Carlos Guillen
GB Cristian Guzman 6.00 15.00
Chad Billingsley
GC Adrian Gonzalez 8.00 20.00
Carl Crawford
GF Matt Garza 6.00 15.00
Prince Fielder
GG Curtis Granderson 8.00 20.00
Adrian Gonzalez
GH Carlos Guillen 4.00 10.00
Rich Harden
GR Zack Greinke 6.00 15.00
Hanley Ramirez
GS Reid Gorecki 6.00 15.00
Joe Saunders
GW Vladimir Guerrero 8.00 20.00
David Wright
HA Orlando Hudson 4.00 10.00
Erick Aybar
HB Rich Harden 4.00 10.00
Marlon Byrd
HC J.Happ/M.Cabrera 10.00 25.00
HM Matt Holliday 10.00 25.00
Justin Morneau
HR Aaron Hill 6.00 15.00
Jimmy Rollins
HU Roy Halladay 6.00 15.00
Justin Upton
IL Raul Ibanez 6.00 15.00
Jon Lester
IU Ian Kinsler 8.00 20.00
Chase Utley
JL Jair Jurrjens 6.00 15.00
Adam Lind
JM Josh Johnson 6.00 15.00
Victor Martinez
JN Garrett Jones 4.00 10.00
Jeff Neimann
JO Ubaldo Jimenez 6.00 15.00
Magglio Ordonez
JZ Adam Jones 6.00 15.00
Ryan Zimmerman
KA Howie Kendrick 4.00 10.00
Bronson Arroyo
KD Jason Kubel 4.00 10.00
Stephen Drew
KJ Paul Konerko 6.00 15.00
Ubaldo Jimenez
KK Matt Kemp 8.00 20.00
Scott Kazmir
KM Scott Kazmir 4.00 10.00
Nate McLouth
KP Hiroki Kuroda 4.00 10.00
Chris Pettit
KQ Kenshin Kawakami 6.00 15.00
Carlos Quentin
KR C.Kershaw/A.Ramirez 20.00 50.00
LC Derek Lowe 4.00 10.00
Orlando Cabrera
LG T.Lincecum/M.Garza 6.00 15.00
LL Adam Lind 6.00 15.00
Felipe Lopez
LM Cliff Lee 10.00 25.00
Hideki Matsui
LT Mat Latos 6.00 15.00
Chris Tillman
LW Jon Lester 6.00 15.00
Jayson Werth
LZ Jose Lopez 6.00 15.00
Jordan Zimmermann
MB Kevin Millwood 4.00 10.00
Casey Blake
MD Yadier Molina 10.00 25.00
David DeJesus
ME Nate McLouth 8.00 20.00
Jacoby Ellsbury
MG M.Montero/K.Griffey 20.00 50.00
ML Hideki Matsui 10.00 25.00
James Loney
MM Kendry Morales 10.00 25.00
Andrew McCutchen
MU Justin Morneau 6.00 15.00
Dan Uggla
MV McCutchen/Verlander 10.00 25.00
NF Ricky Nolasco 4.00 10.00
Scott Feldman
NG Jeff Niemann 4.00 10.00
Cristian Guzman
NL Joe Nathan 4.00 10.00
Derek Lowe
OA Roy Oswalt 6.00 15.00
Brett Anderson
OO Magglio Ordonez 6.00 15.00
Roy Oswalt
OW David Ortiz 10.00 25.00
Brandon Webb
PB D.Pedroia/C.Beltran 8.00 20.00
PF Andy Pettitte 6.00 15.00
Pedro Feliz
PG Hunter Pence 6.00 15.00
Franklin Gutierrez
PR Mike Pelfrey 4.00 10.00
Dustin Richardson
PS David Price 10.00 25.00
Max Scherzer
QP Carlos Quentin 4.00 10.00
Gerardo Parra
RB M.Ramirez/G.Beckham 10.00 25.00
RJ Hanley Ramirez 6.00 15.00
Adam Jones
RL A.Rodriguez/T.Lincecum 12.00 30.00
RM Dustin Richardson 6.00 15.00
Brian McCann
RR J.Reyes/A.Rodriguez 12.00 30.00
RT Mark Reynolds 6.00 15.00
Mark Teixeira
SB I.Suzuki/R.Braun 12.00 30.00
SC Grady Sizemore 6.00 15.00
Johnny Cueto
SD Johan Santana 6.00 15.00
Rajai Davis
SG Pablo Sandoval 6.00 15.00
Vladimir Guerrero
SJ Denard Span 4.00 10.00
Jair Jurrjens
SK K.Suzuki/C.Kershaw 20.00 50.00
SY Nick Swisher 6.00 15.00
Eric Young Jr.
TD Ryan Theriot 6.00 15.00
Johnny Damon
TS Troy Tulowitzki 10.00 25.00
Grady Sizemore
TZ Chris Tillman 6.00 15.00
Carlos Zambrano
UC Koji Uehara 4.00 10.00
Jorge Cantu
UH Dan Uggla 4.00 10.00
Torii Hunter
UK Justin Upton 6.00 15.00
Ian Kinsler
UM B.J. Upton 6.00 15.00
Miguel Montero
UY Chase Utley 6.00 15.00
Kevin Youkilis
VH J.Verlander/R.Howard 10.00 25.00
VM Joey Votto 10.00 25.00
Nick Markakis
VR Shane Victorino 6.00 15.00
Brian Roberts
WF Jered Weaver 6.00 15.00
Dexter Fowler
WL Jayson Werth 6.00 15.00
Jose Lopez
WR Brandon Webb 6.00 15.00
Nolan Reimold
YC Eric Young Jr. 4.00 10.00
Melky Cabrera
YH Michael Young 10.00 25.00
Matt Holliday
YT Kevin Youkilis 10.00 25.00
Troy Tulowitzki
ZL Zimmerman/E.Longoria 6.00 15.00
ZO Carlos Zambrano 10.00 25.00
David Ortiz
ZU Jordan Zimmermann 6.00 15.00
Koji Uehara
AR1 Elvis Andrus 6.00 15.00
Colby Rasmus
AR2 Erick Aybar 4.00 10.00
Jorge De La Rosa
AV1 Bobby Abreu 6.00 15.00
Shane Victorino
AV2 Brandon Allen 4.00 10.00
Will Venable
BB1 Jason Bay 6.00 15.00
Lance Berkman
BB2 Adrian Beltre 10.00 25.00
Kyle Blanks
BB3 Chad Billingsley 6.00 15.00
Nick Blackburn
BH1 Scott Baker 4.00 10.00
Dan Haren
BH2 Gordon Beckham 4.00 10.00
Tommy Hanson
BM1 Jason Bartlett 6.00 15.00
Daniel McCutchen
BM2 Lance Berkman 6.00 15.00
Daisuke Matsuzaka
BP1 Josh Beckett 6.00 15.00
Hunter Pence
BP2 A.J. Burnett 4.00 10.00
Joel Pineiro
BV1 Nick Blackburn 10.00 25.00
Joey Votto
BV2 Billy Butler 4.00 10.00
Javier Vazquez
CD1 Robinson Cano 6.00 15.00
Carlos Delgado
CD2 Carl Crawford 6.00 15.00
Ryan Dempster
DB1 Jorge De La Rosa 4.00 10.00
Jason Bartlett
DB2 Carlos Delgado 4.00 10.00
Billy Butler
DS1 Mark Derosa 4.00 10.00
James Shields
DS2 Stephen Drew 6.00 15.00
CC Sabathia
EP1 J.Ellsbury/B.Posey 50.00 125.00
EP2 Yunel Escobar 6.00 15.00
Rick Porcello
FM1 Prince Fielder 6.00 15.00
Kendry Morales
FM2 Tyler Flowers 8.00 20.00
Daniel Murphy
FS1 Gavin Floyd 6.00 15.00
Alfonso Soriano
FS2 Dexter Fowler 6.00 15.00
Denard Span
FT1 Scott Feldman 4.00 10.00
Ryan Theriot
FT2 Chone Figgins 6.00 15.00
Miguel Tejada
GD1 K.Griffey/Z.Duke 20.00 50.00
GD2 Franklin Gutierrez 4.00 10.00
Mark Derosa
HF1 Tommy Hanson 4.00 10.00
Chone Figgins
HF2 Luke Hochevar 6.00 15.00
Jeff Francoeur
HH1 Brad Hawpe 6.00 15.00
Daniel Hudson
HH2 Felix Hernandez 6.00 15.00
Orlando Hudson
HJ1 Josh Hamilton 10.00 25.00
Chipper Jones
HJ2 Daniel Hudson 6.00 15.00
Nick Johnson
HK1 Cole Hamels 8.00 20.00
Jason Kubel
HK2 Todd Helton 6.00 15.00
Howie Kendrick
HK3 Torii Hunter 8.00 20.00
Matt Kemp
HP1 Dan Haren 4.00 10.00
Placido Polanco
HP2 R.Howard/D.Pedroia 8.00 20.00
JS1 D.Jeter/P.Sandoval 25.00 60.00
JS2 Nick Johnson 6.00 15.00
Nick Swisher
JS3 C.Jones/I.Suzuki 12.00 30.00
LB1 John Lackey 6.00 15.00
Jay Bruce
LB2 Derrek Lee 6.00 15.00
Mark Buehrle
LB3 Felipe Lopez 4.00 10.00
A.J. Burnett
LR1 E.Longoria/J.Reyes 6.00 15.00
LR2 James Loney 4.00 10.00
Juan Rivera
MP1 Nick Markakis 8.00 20.00
David Price
MP2 J.Mauer/A.Pujols 12.00 30.00
MR1 Victor Martinez 10.00 25.00
Manny Ramirez
MR2 Daisuke Matsuzaka 6.00 15.00
Aramis Ramirez
MR3 Brian McCann 12.00 30.00
Mariano Rivera
MR4 Daniel Murphy 8.00 20.00
Ricky Romero
MW1 John Maine 4.00 10.00
Vernon Wells
MW2 Daniel McCutchen 6.00 15.00
Jered Weaver
PA1 Jake Peavy 4.00 10.00
Garret Anderson
PA2 Rick Porcello 6.00 15.00
Brandon Allen
PC1 Carlos Pena 6.00 15.00
Matt Cain
PC2 Joel Pineiro 6.00 15.00
Shin-Soo Choo
PJ1 Jorge Posada 6.00 15.00
Josh Johnson
PJ2 A.Pujols/D.Jeter 25.00 60.00
PM1 Chris Pettit 4.00 10.00
John Maine
PM2 Placido Polanco 4.00 10.00
Kevin Millwood
PP1 Gerardo Parra 4.00 10.00
Jake Peavy
PP2 B.Posey/J.Posada 30.00 80.00
RH1 Alexi Ramirez 6.00 15.00
Brad Hawpe
RH2 Colby Rasmus 6.00 15.00
J.A. Happ
RK1 Nolan Reimold 6.00 15.00
Kenshin Kawakami
RK2 Ricky Romero 4.00 10.00
Hiroki Kuroda
RN1 Juan Rivera 4.00 10.00
Ricky Nolasco
RN2 Francisco Rodriguez 6.00 15.00
Joe Nathan
RP1 Aramis Ramirez 6.00 15.00
Carlos Pena
RP2 Brian Roberts 4.00 10.00
Mike Pelfrey
RS1 Mariano Rivera 12.00 30.00
Johan Santana
RS2 Jimmy Rollins 6.00 15.00
Kurt Suzuki
SH1 Max Scherzer 10.00 25.00
Aaron Hill
SH2 James Shields 8.00 20.00
Cole Hamels
SH3 Alfonso Soriano 6.00 15.00
Roy Halladay
SL1 CC Sabathia 6.00 15.00
Derrek Lee
SL2 Joe Saunders 6.00 15.00
Cliff Lee
TC1 Mark Teixeira 6.00 15.00
Chris Coghlan
TC2 Miguel Tejada 6.00 15.00
Michael Cuddyer
VB1 Javier Vazquez 4.00 10.00
Josh Beckett
VB2 Will Venable 6.00 15.00
Jason Bay
WH1 Vernon Wells 6.00 15.00
Todd Helton
WH2 David Wright 8.00 20.00
Josh Hamilton

2010 Topps Heritage Mantle Chase 61

COMPLETE SET (15) 30.00 60.00
COMMON MANTLE 3.00 8.00
RANDOM INSERTS IN TARGET PACKS
MM1 Mickey Mantle 3.00 8.00
MM2 Mickey Mantle 3.00 8.00
MM3 Mickey Mantle 3.00 8.00
MM4 Mickey Mantle 3.00 8.00
MM5 Mickey Mantle 3.00 8.00
MM6 Mickey Mantle 3.00 8.00
MM7 Mickey Mantle 3.00 8.00
MM8 Mickey Mantle 3.00 8.00
MM9 Mickey Mantle 3.00 8.00
MM10 Mickey Mantle 3.00 8.00
MM11 Mickey Mantle 3.00 8.00
MM12 Mickey Mantle 3.00 8.00
MM13 Mickey Mantle 3.00 8.00
MM14 Mickey Mantle 3.00 8.00
MM15 Mickey Mantle 3.00 8.00

2010 Topps Heritage Maris Chase 61

COMPLETE SET (15) 60.00 120.00
COMMON MARIS 5.00 12.00
RANDOM INSERTS IN WAL-MART PACKS
RM1 Roger Maris 5.00 12.00
RM2 Roger Maris 5.00 12.00
RM3 Roger Maris 5.00 12.00
RM4 Roger Maris 5.00 12.00
RM5 Roger Maris 5.00 12.00
RM6 Roger Maris 5.00 12.00
RM7 Roger Maris 5.00 12.00
RM8 Roger Maris 5.00 12.00
RM9 Roger Maris 5.00 12.00
RM10 Roger Maris 5.00 12.00
RM11 Roger Maris 5.00 12.00
RM12 Roger Maris 5.00 12.00
RM13 Roger Maris 5.00 12.00
RM14 Roger Maris 5.00 12.00
RM15 Roger Maris 5.00 12.00

2010 Topps Heritage New Age Performers

COMPLETE SET (15) 15.00 40.00
STATED ODDS 1:15 HOBBY
NA1 Justin Upton .60 1.50
NA2 Jacoby Ellsbury .75 2.00
NA3 Gordon Beckham .40 1.00
NA4 Tommy Hanson .40 1.00
NA5 Hanley Ramirez .60 1.50
NA6 Joe Mauer .75 2.00
NA7 Ichiro Suzuki 1.25 3.00
NA8 Derek Jeter 2.50 6.00
NA9 Albert Pujols 1.25 3.00
NA10 Ryan Howard .75 2.00
NA11 Zack Greinke .60 1.50
NA12 Matt Kemp .75 2.00
NA13 Miguel Cabrera 1.00 2.50
NA14 Mariano Rivera 1.25 3.00
NA15 Prince Fielder .60 1.50

2010 Topps Heritage News Flashbacks

COMPLETE SET (10) 5.00 12.00
2009 Topps Heritage News Flashbacks
NF1 Peace Corps .50 1.25
NF2 John F. Kennedy 1.25 3.00
NF3 Ham the Chimp .50 1.25
NF4 Venera 1 .50 1.25
NF5 Hassan II .50 1.25
NF6 Twenty Third Amendment .50 1.25
NF7 Apollo Program Announce .50 1.25
NF8 Berlin Wall .50 1.25
NF9 Vostok 1 .50 1.25
NF10 Ty Cobb 1.25 3.00

2010 Topps Heritage Real One Autographs

STATED ODDS 1:357 HOBBY
*RED INK/61: .5X TO 1.2X BASIC
AN Al Neiger 30.00 60.00
AR Al Rosen 20.00 50.00
BG Bob Gibson 30.00 60.00
BH Billy Harrell 10.00 25.00
BHA Bob Hale 10.00 25.00
BM Bobby Malkmus 30.00 60.00
BP Buster Posey 100.00 200.00
CB Collin Balester 10.00 25.00
DK Danny Kravitz 20.00 50.00
DP Dustin Pedroia 20.00 50.00
FR Frank Robinson 40.00 80.00
GB Gordon Beckham 12.00 30.00
GL Gene Leek 20.00 50.00
JB Jay Bruce 12.00 30.00
JB Julio Becquer 15.00 40.00
JC Jerry Casale 10.00 25.00
JD Joe DeMaestri 20.00 50.00
JG Joe Ginsberg 20.00 50.00
JJ Johnny James 15.00 40.00
JR Jim Rivera 12.00 30.00
JU Justin Upton 10.00 25.00
JW Jim Woods 10.00 25.00
LA Luis Aparicio 30.00 60.00
MH Matt Holliday 40.00 100.00
NG Ned Garver 20.00 50.00
RB Reno Bertoia 10.00 25.00
RB Rocky Bridges 30.00 60.00
RI Raul Ibanez 20.00 50.00
RL Ralph Lumenti 10.00 25.00
RS Ray Semproch 10.00 25.00
RS Red Schoendienst 30.00 60.00
RS R.C. Stevens 12.00 30.00
TB Tom Borland 10.00 25.00
TB Tom Brewer 12.00 30.00
TL Ted Lepcio 20.00 50.00
WD Walt Dropo 10.00 25.00

2010 Topps Heritage Ruth Chase 61

COMPLETE SET (15) 6.00 15.00
COMMON RUTH 1.25 3.00
RANDOM INSERTS IN HOBBY PACKS
BR1 Babe Ruth 1.25 3.00
BR2 Babe Ruth 1.25 3.00
BR3 Babe Ruth 1.25 3.00
BR4 Babe Ruth 1.25 3.00
BR5 Babe Ruth 1.25 3.00
BR6 Babe Ruth 1.25 3.00
BR7 Babe Ruth 1.25 3.00
BR8 Babe Ruth 1.25 3.00
BR9 Babe Ruth 1.25 3.00
BR10 Babe Ruth 1.25 3.00
BR11 Babe Ruth 1.25 3.00
BR12 Babe Ruth 1.25 3.00
BR13 Babe Ruth 1.25 3.00
BR14 Babe Ruth 1.25 3.00
BR15 Babe Ruth 1.25 3.00

2010 Topps Heritage Team Stamp Panels

1 Anaheim Angels 2.00 5.00
2 Arizona Diamondbacks 2.00 5.00
3 Atlanta Braves 3.00 8.00
4 Baltimore Orioles 2.50 6.00
5 Boston Red Sox 2.50 6.00
6 Chicago Cubs 2.00 5.00
7 Chicago White Sox 2.00 5.00
8 Cincinnati Reds 3.00 8.00
9 Cleveland Indians 2.00 5.00
10 Colorado Rockies 3.00 8.00
11 Detroit Tigers 3.00 8.00
12 Florida Marlins 2.00 5.00
13 Houston Astros 2.00 5.00
14 Kansas City Royals 2.00 5.00
15 Los Angeles Dodgers 3.00 8.00
16 Milwaukee Brewers 2.00 5.00
17 Minnesota Twins 2.50 6.00
18 New York Mets 2.50 6.00
19 New York Yankees 8.00 20.00
20 Oakland Athletics 1.25 3.00
21 Philadelphia Phillies 2.50 6.00
22 Pittsburgh Pirates 3.00 8.00
23 San Diego Padres 2.50 6.00
24 San Francisco Giants 2.00 5.00
25 Seattle Mariners 6.00 15.00
26 St. Louis Cardinals 4.00 10.00
27 Tampa Bay Rays 2.50 6.00
28 Texas Rangers 2.00 5.00
29 Toronto Blue Jays 2.00 5.00
30 Washington Nationals 2.00 5.00

2010 Topps Heritage Then and Now

STATED ODDS 1:15 HOBBY
TN1 R.Maris/A.Pujols 1.00 2.50
TN2 Roger Maris/Prince Fielder 1.25 3.00
TN3 Al Kaline/Joe Mauer 1.25 3.00
TN4 Luis Aparicio/Jacoby Ellsbury 1.00 2.50
TN5 M.Mantle/A.Gonzalez 2.00 5.00
TN6 Whitey Ford/Zack Greinke .75 2.00
TN7 Ford/JVerlander 1.25 3.00
TN8 Whitey Ford/Felix Hernandez .75 2.00
TN9 Ford/JVerlander 1.25 3.00
TN10 Whitey Ford/Roy Halladay .75 2.00

2010 Topps Heritage '60 National Convention VIP

COMPLETE SET (5) 10.00 25.00
573 Mickey Mantle 3.00 8.00
574 Mickey Mantle 3.00 8.00
575 Cal Ripken Jr. 3.00 8.00
576 Yogi Berra 1.00 2.50
577 Nolan Ryan 3.00 8.00

2011 Topps Heritage

COMP.SET w/o SP's (425) 25.00 60.00
COMMON CARD (1-425) .15 .40
COMMON ROOKIE (1-425) .40 1.00
COMPLETE J.ROB SET (10) 50.00 100.00
COMMON J.ROB SP (135-144) 5.00 12.00
STATED J.ROB ODDS 1:50 HOBBY
COMMON SP (426-500) 2.50 6.00
SP ODDS 1:3 HOBBY
1 Josh Hamilton .25 .60
2 Francisco Cordero .15 .40
3 David Ortiz .40 1.00
4 Ben Zobrist .25 .60
5 Clayton Kershaw .75 2.00
6 Brian Roberts .15 .40
7 Carlos Beltran .25 .60
8 John Danks .15 .40
9 Juan Uribe .15 .40
10 Andrew McCutchen .40 1.00
11 Joe Nathan .15 .40
12 Brad Mills MG .15 .40
13 Cliff Pennington .15 .40
14 Carlos Pena .25 .60
15 Fausto Carmona .15 .40
16 John Jaso .15 .40
17 Jayson Werth .25 .60
18 A.Pujols/R.Braun .50 1.25
19 Jake McGee (RC) .40 1.00
20 Johnny Damon .25 .60
21 Carl Pavano .15 .40
22 San Diego Padres .15 .40
23 Carlos Lee .15 .40
24 Detroit Tigers .15 .40
25 Starlin Castro .25 .60
26 Josh Thole .15 .40
27 Adam Kennedy .15 .40
28 Vernon Wells .15 .40
29 Terry Collins MG .15 .40
30 Chipper Jones .40 1.00
31 Ozzie Martinez RC .40 1.00
32 Russell Martin .15 .40
33 Barry Zito .25 .60
34 Ian Kinsler .25 .60
35 Stephen Strasburg .40 1.00
36 Mark Reynolds .15 .40
37 D.Jeter/R.Cano 1.00 2.50
38 Coco Crisp .15 .40
39 Erick Aybar .15 .40
40 Pablo Sandoval .25 .60
41 Chris Valaika RC .40 1.00
42 Nelson Cruz .40 1.00
43 Los Angeles Dodgers .25 .60
44 Justin Upton .25 .60
45 Evan Longoria .25 .60
46 Cole Hamels .30 .75
47 Kosuke Fukudome .25 .60
48 CC Sabathia .25 .60
49 Jordan Brown (RC) .40 1.00
50 Albert Pujols .50 1.25
51 Ham/Cabrera/Mauer/Beltre .40 1.00
52 Carlos Gonzalez/Joey Votto/Omar Infante
Troy Tulowitzki .40 1.00
53 Bautista/Kon/Cabr/Teix .40 1.00
54 Pujols/Dunn/Votto .50 1.25
55 Felix Hernandez/Clay Buchholz/David
Price/Trevor Cahill .30 .75
56 Josh Johnson/Adam Wainwright/Roy
Halladay/Jaime Garcia .25 .60
57 CC Sabathia/David Price/Jon Lester .30 .75
58 Roy Halladay/Adam Wainwright
Ubaldo Jimenez .25 .60
59 Wea/Felix/Lest/Verlan .40 1.00
60 Lin/Hal/Jim/Wain .25 .60
61 Milwaukee Brewers .15 .40
62 Brandon Inge .15 .40
63 Tommy Hanson .15 .40
64 Nick Markakis .30 .75
65 Robinson Cano .25 .60
66 Geovany Soto .25 .60
67 Zach Duke .15 .40
68 Travis Snider .15 .40
69 Cory Luebke RC .40 1.00
70 Justin Morneau .25 .60
71 Jonathan Sanchez .15 .40
72 Jimmy Rollins/Chase Utley .25 .60
73 Gordon Beckham .15 .40
74 Hanley Ramirez .25 .60
75 Chris Tillman .15 .40
76 Freddie Freeman RC 6.00 15.00
77 Chase Utley .25 .60
78 Matt LaPorta .15 .40
79 Jordan Zimmermann .25 .60
80 Jay Bruce .25 .60
81 Jason Varitek .40 1.00
82 Kevin Kouzmanoff .15 .40
83 Chris Carpenter .25 .60
84 Denard Span .15 .40
85 Ike Davis .15 .40
86 Alex Presley RC .60 1.50
87 Manny Ramirez .40 1.00
88 Joe Girardi MG .25 .60
89 Jake Peavy .15 .40
90 Julio Borbon .15 .40
91 Gaby Sanchez .15 .40
92 Armando Galarraga .15 .40
93 Nick Swisher .25 .60
94 R.A. Dickey .25 .60
95 Ryan Zimmerman .25 .60
96 Jered Weaver .25 .60
97 Grady Sizemore .25 .60
98 Minnesota Twins .15 .40
99 Brandon Snyder (RC) .40 1.00
100 David Price .30 .75
101 Jacoby Ellsbury .30 .75
102 Matt Capps .15 .40
103 Brandon Phillips .15 .40
104 Domonic Brown .30 .75
105 Max Scherzer .40 1.00
106 Yadier Molina .40 1.00
107 Madison Bumgarner .30 .75
108 Matt Kemp .30 .75
109 Ted Lilly .15 .40
110 Mark Teixeira .25 .60
111 Brad Lidge .15 .40
112 Luke Scott .15 .40
113 Chicago White Sox .15 .40
114 Kyle Drabek RC .60 1.50
115 Alfonso Soriano .25 .60
116 Gavin Floyd .15 .40
117 Alex Rios .15 .40
118 Skip Schumaker .15 .40
119 Scott Cousins RC .40 1.00
120 Bronson Arroyo .15 .40
121 Buck Showalter MG .15 .40
122 Trevor Cahill .15 .40
123 Aaron Hill .15 .40
124 Brian Duensing .15 .40
125A Vladimir Guerrero .25 .60
125B V.Guerrero SP 50.00 100.00
126 James Shields .15 .40
127 Dallas Braden/Trevor Cahill .15 .40
128 Joel Pineiro .15 .40
129 Carlos Quentin .15 .40
130 Omar Infante .15 .40
131 Brett Sinkbeil RC .40 1.00
132 Los Angeles Angels .15 .40
133 Andres Torres .15 .40
134 Brett Cecil .15 .40
135A Babe Ruth 1.00 2.50
135B Jackie Robinson/Displays Athletic Talents At
An Early Age SP 5.00 12.00
136A Babe Ruth 1.00 2.50
136B Jackie Robinson
Emerges As College Star SP 5.00 12.00
137A Babe Ruth 1.00 2.50
137B Jackie Robinson
Serves Three Years In The Army SP 5.00 12.00
138A Babe Ruth 1.00 2.50
138B Jackie Robinson
Breaks The Game's Color Barrier SP 5.00 12.00
139A Babe Ruth 1.00 2.50
139B Jackie Robinson
Takes ROY Honors, Then MVP SP 5.00 12.00
139C Joba Chamberlain SP 40.00 80.00
140A Babe Ruth 1.00 2.50
140B Jackie Robinson
Wraps Up Hall Of Fame Career SP 5.00 12.00
141A Babe Ruth 1.00 2.50

141B Jackie Robinson
Legacy Lives On SP 5.00 12.00
142A Babe Ruth 1.00 2.50
142B Jackie Robinson/Racks 'Em Up SP 5.00 12.00
143A Babe Ruth 1.00 2.50
143B Jackie Robinson
Robinson Shines in the Fall SP 5.00 12.00
144A Babe Ruth 1.00 2.50
144B Jackie Robinson/The Resume SP 5.00 12.00
145 Dallas Braden .15 .40
146 Placido Polanco .15 .40
147 Joakim Soria .15 .40
148 Jonny Gomes .15 .40
149 Ryan Franklin .15 .40
150 Miguel Cabrera .40 1.00
151 Arthur Rhodes .15 .40
152 Jim Riggleman MG .15 .40
153 Marco Scutaro .25 .60
154 Brennan Boesch .25 .60
155 Brian Wilson .40 1.00
156 Hank Conger RC .60 1.50
157 Shane Victorino .25 .60
158 Atlanta Braves .15 .40
159 Joba Chamberlain .15 .40
160 Garrett Jones .15 .40
161 Bobby Jenks .15 .40
162 Alex Gordon .25 .60
163 M.Teixeira/A.Rodriguez .50 1.25
164 Jason Kendall .15 .40
165 Adam Jones .25 .60
166 Kevin Slowey .15 .40
167 Wilson Ramos .15 .40
168 Rajai Davis .15 .40
169 Curtis Granderson .30 .75
170 Aramis Ramirez .15 .40
171 Edinson Volquez .15 .40
172 Dusty Baker MG .15 .40
173 Jhonny Peralta .15 .40
174 Jon Garland .15 .40
175 Adam Dunn .25 .60
176 Chase Headley .15 .40
177 J.A. Happ .25 .60
178 A.J. Pierzynski .15 .40
179 Mat Latos .25 .60
180 Jim Thome .25 .60
181 Dillon Gee RC .60 1.50
182 Cody Ross .15 .40
183 Mike Pelfrey .15 .40
184 Kurt Suzuki .15 .40
185 Mariano Rivera .50 1.25
186 Rick Ankiel .15 .40
187 Jon Lester .25 .60
188 Freddy Sanchez .15 .40
189 Heath Bell .15 .40
190 Todd Helton .25 .60
191 Ryan Dempster .15 .40
192 Florida Marlins .15 .40
193 Miguel Tejada .25 .60
194 Jordan Walden RC .40 1.00
195 Paul Konerko .25 .60
196 Jose Valverde .15 .40
197 Casey Blake .15 .40
198 Tony La Russa MG .25 .60
199 Aroldis Chapman RC 1.25 3.00
200 Derek Jeter 1.00 2.50
201 Josh Beckett .15 .40
202 Corey Hart .15 .40
203 Kevin Millwood .15 .40
204 Brian Bogusevic (RC) .40 1.00
205 Scott Rolen .25 .60
206 Washington Nationals .15 .40
207 C.J. Wilson .15 .40
208 Rickie Weeks .15 .40
209 Andrew Romine RC .40 1.00
210 Evan Meek .15 .40
211 Elvis Andrus/Ian Kinsler .25 .60
212 Roy Oswalt .25 .60
213 Angel Pagan .15 .40
214 Chris Sale RC 2.50 6.00
215 Asdrubal Cabrera .25 .60
216 David Aardsma .15 .40
217 Don Mattingly MG .75 2.00
218 Buster Posey .50 1.25
219 Jeremy Hellickson RC 1.00 2.50
220 Ryan Howard .30 .75
221 Jeremy Guthrie .15 .40
222 Franklin Gutierrez .15 .40
223 Ryan Theriot .15 .40
224 Casey Coleman RC .40 1.00
225 Adrian Beltre .40 1.00
226 San Francisco Giants .15 .40
227 Cliff Lee .25 .60
228 Marlon Byrd .15 .40
229 Pedro Ciriaco RC .60 1.50
230 Francisco Liriano .15 .40
231 Chone Figgins .15 .40
232 Giants Win Opener HL .15 .40
233 Cain Dominates HL .25 .60
234 Rangers Retaliate HL .15 .40
235 Bumgarner Baffles HL .30 .75
236 Giants Crush Rangers HL .15 .40
237 Winners Celebrate HL .25 .60
238 Ichiro Suzuki .50 1.25
239 Brandon Beachy RC 1.00 2.50
240 Xavier Nady .15 .40
241 Josh Johnson .25 .60
242 Manny Acta MG .15 .40
243 A.J. Burnett .15 .40
244 Lars Anderson RC .60 1.50
245 Jason Bartlett .15 .40
246 Andrew Bailey .15 .40
247 Jonathan Lucroy .25 .60
248 Chris Johnson .15 .40
249 Vance Worley (RC) 1.50 4.00
250 Joe Mauer .30 .75
251 Texas Rangers .15 .40
252 James McDonald .15 .40
253 Lou Marson .15 .40
254 Chris Carter
255 Edwin Jackson .15 .40
256 Ruben Tejada .15 .40
257 Scott Kazmir .15 .40
258 Ryan Braun .25 .60
259 Kelly Johnson .15 .40
260 Matt Cain .25 .60
261 Reid Brignac .15 .40
262 Ivan Rodriguez .25 .60
263 Josh Hamilton/Nelson Cruz .40 1.00
264 Jeff Niemann .15 .40
265 Derrek Lee .15 .40
266 Jose Ceda RC .40 1.00
267 B.J. Upton .25 .60
268 Ervin Santana .15 .40
269 Lance Berkman .25 .60
270 Ronny Cedeno .15 .40
271 Jeremy Jeffress RC .40 1.00
272 Delmon Young .25 .60
273 Chris Perez .15 .40
274 Will Venable .15 .40
275 Billy Butler .15 .40
276 Darwin Barney RC 1.25 3.00
277 Pedro Alvarez RC .30 .75
278 Derek Lowe .15 .40
279A Bengie Molina .15 .40
280 Hiroki Kuroda .15 .40
281 Eduardo Nunez RC 1.00 2.50
282 Aaron Harang .15 .40
283 Danny Valencia .25 .60
284 Jimmy Rollins .25 .60
285 Adam Wainwright .25 .60
286 Ozzie Guillen MG .15 .40
287 Neftali Feliz .15 .40
288 Mike Stanton .40 1.00
289 Darren Ford RC .40 1.00
290 Ty Wigginton .15 .40
291 Bobby Cramer RC .40 1.00
292 Orlando Hudson .15 .40
293 Jonathon Niese .15 .40
294 Philadelphia Phillies .15 .40
295 Paul Maholm .15 .40
296 Ian Desmond .15 .40
297 Jonathan Broxton .15 .40
298 Jason Kubel .15 .40
299 Daniel Descalso RC .40 1.00
300 Carl Crawford .25 .60
301 Clay Buchholz .15 .40
302 Ramon Hernandez .15 .40
303 Daric Barton .15 .40
304 Brett Myers .15 .40
305 Mike Aviles .15 .40
306 D.Ortiz/D.Pedroia .40 1.00
307 Jair Jurrjens .15 .40
308 Jason Bay .25 .60
309 Yonder Alonso RC .60 1.50
310 Andy Pettitte .25 .60
311 Derek Jeter IA 1.00 2.50
312 Roy Halladay IA .25 .60
313 Jose Bautista IA .25 .60
314 Miguel Cabrera IA .40 1.00
315 CC Sabathia IA .25 .60
316 Joe Mauer IA .30 .75
317 Ichiro Suzuki IA .50 1.25
318 Mark Teixeira IA .25 .60
319 Tim Lincecum IA .25 .60
320 Jason Heyward .30 .75
321 Matt Mangini RC .40 1.00
322 Bruce Bochy MG .25 .60
323 Jon Jay .15 .40
324 Tommy Hunter .25 .60
325 Alexei Ramirez .25 .60
326 Gregory Infante RC .40 1.00
327 Jose Lopez .25 .60
328 Raul Ibanez .25 .60
329 Yovani Gallardo .15 .40
330 Mike Napoli .15 .40
331 Mike Leake .25 .60
332 Alcides Escobar .25 .60
333 Lucas Duda RC 1.00 2.50
334 Tampa Bay Rays .15 .40
335 Austin Jackson .15 .40
336 John Lackey .25 .60
337 Adam LaRoche .15 .40
338 Brett Gardner .25 .60
339 J.J. Hardy .15 .40
340 Chad Billingsley .25 .60
341 Lorenzo Cain .15 .40
342 Zack Greinke .25 .60
343 Bobby Abreu .15 .40
344 Fernando Salas (RC) .60 1.50
345 Dustin Pedroia .30 .75
346 Felix Hernandez .25 .60
347 Nyjer Morgan .15 .40
348 Eric Sogard RC .40 1.00
349 Jeremy Bonderman .15 .40
350 Joey Votto .40 1.00
351 Justin Morneau/Joe Mauer .30 .75
352 Ricky Nolasco .15 .40
353 Neil Walker .25 .60
354 Hunter Pence .25 .60
355 Brian Matusz .15 .40
356 Jose Bautista .25 .60
357 Brett Anderson .15 .40
358 Andre Ethier .25 .60
359 Carlos Zambrano .25 .60
360 Jorge Posada .25 .60
361 Randy Wolf .15 .40
362 Greg Halman RC .60 1.50
363 Nick Hundley .15 .40
364 Russell Branyan .15 .40
365 Howie Kendrick .15 .40
366 Rick Porcello .25 .60
367 Dan Uggla .25 .60
368 J.P. Arencibia .15 .40
369 Dan Haren .15 .40
370 Matt Holliday .40 1.00
371 Victor Martinez .25 .60
372 Jaime Garcia .25 .60
373 Carlos Gonzalez .25 .60
374 Charlie Manuel MG .15 .40
375 James Loney .15 .40
376 Phil Hughes .15 .40
377 Carlos Santana .40 1.00
378 Ubaldo Jimenez .15 .40
379 Travis Hafner .15 .40
380 Tim Hudson .25 .60
381 Orlando Cabrera .15 .40
382 Casey McGehee .15 .40
383 Daniel Hudson .15 .40
384 Oakland Athletics .15 .40
385 Mark Buehrle .25 .60
386 Michael Cuddyer .15 .40
387 Desmond Jennings RC .60 1.50
388 Rafael Soriano .15 .40
389 Ryan Doumit .15 .40
390 Albert Pujols AS .50 1.25
391 Martin Prado AS .15 .40
392A Ryan Zimmerman AS .25 .60
392B R.Zimmerman SP 100.00 200.00
393 Hanley Ramirez AS .25 .60
394 Ryan Braun AS .25 .60
395 Matt Holliday AS .40 1.00
396 Carlos Gonzalez AS .25 .60
397 Brian McCann AS .25 .60
398 Joey Votto AS .40 1.00
399 Roy Halladay AS .25 .60
400 Mark Teixeira .25 .60
401 Matt Kemp/Andre Ethier .30 .75
402 David DeJesus .15 .40
403 Jonathan Papelbon .25 .60
404 Mark Trumbo (RC) 1.00 2.50
405 Gio Gonzalez .25 .60
406 Tyler Colvin .15 .40
407 Wade Davis .15 .40
408 Chris Coghlan .15 .40
409 Pittsburgh Pirates .15 .40
410 Juan Pierre .15 .40
411 Michael Young .15 .40
412 Colby Rasmus .25 .60
413 Chris Young .15 .40
414 Jarrod Dyson RC .60 1.50
415 Dexter Fowler .25 .60
416 Jim Leyland MG .15 .40
417 Lucas May RC .40 1.00
418 Ian Stewart .15 .40
419 Wandy Rodriguez .15 .40
420 Miguel Montero .15 .40
421 Francisco Rodriguez .25 .60
422 Kendry Morales .15 .40
423 B.Wilson/B.Posey .50 1.25
424 Leo Nunez .15 .40
425 Kevin Youkilis .15 .40
426 Brent Morel SP RC 2.50 6.00
427 Will Rhymes SP 2.50 6.00
428 Josh Willingham SP 4.00 10.00
429 Tim Lincecum SP 2.00 5.00
430 Troy Tulowitzki SP 5.00 12.00
431 Welington Castillo SP (RC) 2.50 6.00
432 Michael Bourn SP 2.50 6.00
433 Kyle Davies SP 2.50 6.00
434 Carlos Ruiz SP 2.50 6.00
435 Huston Street SP 2.50 6.00
436 Jose Reyes SP 3.00 8.00
437 Adrian Gonzalez SP 4.00 10.00
438 Shaun Marcum SP 2.50 6.00
439 Stephen Drew SP 2.50 6.00
440 Ricky Romero SP 2.50 6.00
441 Jorge de la Rosa SP 2.50 6.00
442 Kevin Gregg SP 2.50 6.00
443 Brian McCann SP 3.00 8.00
444 Rafael Furcal SP 2.50 6.00
445 Prince Fielder SP 3.00 8.00
446 Carlos Marmol SP 3.00 8.00
447 Shin-Soo Choo SP 2.00 5.00
448 Clayton Richard SP 2.50 6.00
449 Elvis Andrus SP 3.00 8.00
450 Johnny Cueto SP 4.00 10.00
451 Ben Revere SP RC 3.00 8.00
452 Adam Lind SP 3.00 8.00
453 Roy Halladay SP 2.00 5.00
454 Jose Tabata SP 2.50 6.00
455 Joe Saunders SP 2.50 6.00
456 Jeff Keppinger SP 2.50 6.00
457 J.D. Drew SP 2.50 6.00
458 Ian Kennedy SP 2.50 6.00
459 John Buck SP 2.50 6.00
460 Justin Verlander SP 5.00 12.00
461 Russ Mitchell SP RC 2.50 6.00
462 Magglio Ordonez SP 3.00 8.00
463 Bob Geren MG SP 2.50 6.00
464 Johan Santana SP 2.00 5.00
465 Cincinnati Reds SP 2.50 6.00
466 Miguel Cabrera AS SP 3.00 8.00
467 Robinson Cano AS SP 2.00 5.00
468 Evan Longoria AS SP 2.50 6.00
469 Evan Longoria AS SP 4.00 10.00
470 Carl Crawford AS SP 3.00 8.00
471 Josh Hamilton AS SP 2.00 5.00
472 Jose Bautista AS SP 3.00 8.00
473 Joe Mauer AS SP 2.50 6.00
474 Vladimir Guerrero AS SP 2.00 5.00
475 Felix Hernandez AS SP 2.00 5.00
476 Baltimore Orioles SP 2.50 6.00
477 Yunel Escobar SP 2.50 6.00
478A David Wright SP 2.50 6.00
478B D.Wright Reds SP 75.00 150.00
479 Lucas Harrell SP (RC) 2.50 6.00
480 Aubrey Huff SP 2.50 6.00
481 Kila Ka'aihue SP 2.50 6.00
482 Ron Gardenhire MG SP 2.50 6.00
483 Trevor Hoffman SP 3.00 8.00
484 David Eckstein SP 2.50 6.00
485 Matt Garza SP 2.50 6.00
486 Martin Prado SP 2.50 6.00
487 Drew Stubbs SP 2.50 6.00
488 Koji Uehara SP 2.50 6.00
489 Brandon Morrow SP 2.50 6.00
490A Alex Rodriguez SP 4.00 10.00
490B A.Rodriguez Rev.Neg SP 60.00 120.00
491 Torii Hunter SP 2.50 6.00
492 Jason Castro SP 2.50 6.00
493 Josh Tomlin/Jeanmar Gomez/Felix
Doubront/Jake Arrieta/Andy Oliver SP 5.00 12.00
494 Barry Enright RC/Mike Minor/Travis Wood/Alex
Sanabia/Drew Storen SP 2.50 6.00
495 Andrew Cashner/Jonny Venters/Kenley
Jansen/Jenrry Mejia/John Axford SP 4.00 10.00
496 Michael McKenry RC/Max St. Pierre/Chris
Hatcher RC/Mike Nickeas
Steve Hill SP RC 4.00 10.00
497 Argenis Diaz/Brett Wallace/Brandon Hicks
Lance Zawadzki SP 2.50 6.00
498 Josh Bell/Danny Worth
Luke Hughes/Trevor Plouffe SP 2.50 6.00
499 Dayan Viciedo/Jason Donald/Steve
Tolleson/Mitch Moreland SP 2.50 6.00
500 Peter Bourjos/Ryan Kalish/Daniel Nava
Chris Heisey/Logan Morrison SP 3.00 8.00

2011 Topps Heritage Blue Tint

110 Mark Teixeira 4.00 10.00
111 Brad Lidge 2.50 6.00
112 Luke Scott 2.50 6.00
113 Chicago White Sox 2.50 6.00
114 Kyle Drabek 4.00 10.00
115 Alfonso Soriano 4.00 10.00
116 Gavin Floyd 2.50 6.00
117 Alex Rios 2.50 6.00
118 Skip Schumaker 2.50 6.00
119 Scott Cousins 2.50 6.00
120 Bronson Arroyo 2.50 6.00
121 Buck Showalter MG 2.50 6.00
122 Trevor Cahill 2.50 6.00
123 Aaron Hill 2.50 6.00
124 Brian Duensing 2.50 6.00
125 Vladimir Guerrero 4.00 10.00
126 James Shields 2.50 6.00
127 Dallas Braden/Trevor Cahill 2.50 6.00
128 Joel Pineiro 2.50 6.00
129 Carlos Quentin 2.50 6.00
130 Omar Infante 2.50 6.00
131 Brett Sinkbeil 2.50 6.00
132 Los Angeles Angels 2.50 6.00
133 Andres Torres 2.50 6.00
134 Brett Cecil 2.50 6.00
135 Babe Ruth 10.00 25.00
136 Babe Ruth 10.00 25.00
137 Babe Ruth 10.00 25.00
138 Babe Ruth 10.00 25.00
139A Babe Ruth 10.00 25.00
139C Joba Chamberlain 2.50 6.00
140 Babe Ruth 10.00 25.00
141 Babe Ruth 10.00 25.00
142 Babe Ruth 10.00 25.00
143 Babe Ruth 10.00 25.00
144 Babe Ruth 10.00 25.00
145 Dallas Braden 2.50 6.00
146 Placido Polanco 2.50 6.00
147 Joakim Soria 2.50 6.00
148 Jonny Gomes 2.50 6.00
149 Ryan Franklin 2.50 6.00
150 Miguel Cabrera 6.00 15.00
151 Arthur Rhodes 2.50 6.00
152 Jim Riggleman MG 2.50 6.00
153 Marco Scutaro 4.00 10.00
154 Brennan Boesch 4.00 10.00
155 Brian Wilson 6.00 15.00
156 Hank Conger 4.00 10.00
157 Shane Victorino 4.00 10.00
158 Atlanta Braves 2.50 6.00
160 Garrett Jones 2.50 6.00
161 Bobby Jenks 2.50 6.00
162 Alex Gordon 4.00 10.00
163 M.Teixeira/A.Rodriguez 8.00 20.00
164 Jason Kendall 2.50 6.00
165 Adam Jones 4.00 10.00
166 Kevin Slowey 2.50 6.00
167 Wilson Ramos 2.50 6.00
168 Rajai Davis 2.50 6.00
169 Curtis Granderson 5.00 12.00
170 Aramis Ramirez 2.50 6.00
171 Edinson Volquez 2.50 6.00
172 Dusty Baker MG 2.50 6.00
173 Jhonny Peralta 2.50 6.00
174 Jon Garland 2.50 6.00
175 Adam Dunn 4.00 10.00
176 Chase Headley 2.50 6.00
177 J.A. Happ 4.00 10.00
178 A.J. Pierzynski 2.50 6.00
179 Mat Latos 4.00 10.00
180 Jim Thome 4.00 10.00
181 Dillon Gee 4.00 10.00
182 Cody Ross 2.50 6.00
183 Mike Pelfrey 2.50 6.00
184 Kurt Suzuki 2.50 6.00
185 Mariano Rivera 8.00 20.00
186 Rick Ankiel 2.50 6.00
187 Jon Lester 4.00 10.00
188 Freddy Sanchez 2.50 6.00
189 Heath Bell 2.50 6.00
190 Todd Helton 4.00 10.00
191 Ryan Dempster 2.50 6.00
192 Florida Marlins 2.50 6.00
193 Miguel Tejada 4.00 10.00
194 Jordan Walden 2.50 6.00
195 Paul Konerko 4.00 10.00
196 Jose Valverde 2.50 6.00

2011 Topps Heritage Green Tint

110 Mark Teixeira 2.50 6.00
111 Brad Lidge 1.50 4.00
112 Luke Scott 1.50 4.00
113 Chicago White Sox 2.00 5.00
114 Kyle Drabek 2.50 6.00
115 Alfonso Soriano 2.50 6.00
116 Gavin Floyd 1.50 4.00
117 Alex Rios 1.50 4.00
118 Skip Schumaker 1.50 4.00
119 Scott Cousins 1.50 4.00
120 Bronson Arroyo 1.50 4.00
121 Buck Showalter MG 1.50 4.00
122 Trevor Cahill 1.50 4.00
123 Aaron Hill 1.50 4.00
124 Brian Duensing 1.50 4.00
125 Vladimir Guerrero 2.50 6.00
126 James Shields 1.50 4.00
127 Dallas Braden/Trevor Cahill 1.50 4.00
128 Joel Pineiro 1.50 4.00
129 Carlos Quentin 1.50 4.00
130 Omar Infante 1.50 4.00
131 Brett Sinkbeil 1.50 4.00
132 Los Angeles Angels 2.00 5.00
133 Andres Torres 1.50 4.00
134 Brett Cecil 1.50 4.00
135 Babe Ruth 10.00 25.00
136 Babe Ruth 10.00 25.00
137 Babe Ruth 10.00 25.00
138 Babe Ruth 10.00 25.00
139A Babe Ruth 10.00 25.00
139C Joba Chamberlain 1.50 4.00
140 Babe Ruth 10.00 25.00
141 Babe Ruth 10.00 25.00
142 Babe Ruth 10.00 25.00
143 Babe Ruth 10.00 25.00
144 Babe Ruth 10.00 25.00
145 Dallas Braden 1.50 4.00
146 Placido Polanco 1.50 4.00
147 Joakim Soria 1.50 4.00
148 Jonny Gomes 1.50 4.00
149 Ryan Franklin 1.50 4.00
150 Miguel Cabrera 4.00 10.00
151 Arthur Rhodes 1.50 4.00
152 Jim Riggleman MG 1.50 4.00
153 Marco Scutaro 2.50 6.00
154 Brennan Boesch 2.50 6.00
155 Brian Wilson 4.00 10.00
156 Hank Conger 2.50 6.00
157 Shane Victorino 2.50 6.00
158 Atlanta Braves 2.50 5.00
160 Garrett Jones 1.50 4.00
161 Bobby Jenks 1.50 4.00
162 Alex Gordon 2.50 6.00
163 M.Teixeira/A.Rodriguez 20.00 30.00
164 Jason Kendall 1.50 4.00
165 Adam Jones 2.50 6.00
166 Kevin Slowey 1.50 4.00
167 Wilson Ramos 1.50 4.00
168 Rajai Davis 1.50 4.00
169 Curtis Granderson 3.00 8.00
170 Aramis Ramirez 1.50 4.00
171 Edinson Volquez 1.50 4.00
172 Dusty Baker MG 1.50 4.00
173 Jhonny Peralta 1.50 4.00
174 Jon Garland 1.50 4.00
175 Adam Dunn 2.50 6.00
176 Chase Headley 1.50 4.00
177 J.A. Happ 2.50 6.00
178 A.J. Pierzynski 1.50 4.00
179 Mat Latos 2.50 6.00
180 Jim Thome 2.50 6.00
181 Dillon Gee 2.50 6.00
182 Cody Ross 1.50 4.00
183 Mike Pelfrey 1.50 4.00
184 Kurt Suzuki 1.50 4.00
185 Mariano Rivera 5.00 12.00
186 Rick Ankiel 1.50 4.00
187 Jon Lester 2.50 6.00
188 Freddy Sanchez 1.50 4.00
189 Heath Bell 1.50 4.00
190 Todd Helton 2.50 6.00
191 Ryan Dempster 1.50 4.00
192 Florida Marlins 2.00 5.00
193 Miguel Tejada 2.50 6.00
194 Jordan Walden 1.50 4.00
195 Paul Konerko 2.50 6.00
196 Jose Valverde 1.50 4.00

2011 Topps Heritage Red Tint

110 Mark Teixeira 5.00 12.00
111 Brad Lidge 3.00 8.00
112 Luke Scott 3.00 8.00
113 Chicago White Sox 3.00 8.00
114 Kyle Drabek 5.00 12.00
115 Alfonso Soriano 5.00 12.00
116 Gavin Floyd 3.00 8.00
117 Alex Rios 3.00 8.00
118 Skip Schumaker 3.00 8.00
119 Scott Cousins 3.00 8.00
120 Bronson Arroyo 3.00 8.00
121 Buck Showalter MG 3.00 8.00
122 Trevor Cahill 3.00 8.00
123 Aaron Hill 3.00 8.00
124 Brian Duensing 3.00 8.00
125 Vladimir Guerrero 5.00 12.00
126 James Shields 3.00 8.00
127 Dallas Braden/Trevor Cahill 3.00 8.00
128 Joel Pineiro 3.00 8.00
129 Carlos Quentin 3.00 8.00
130 Omar Infante 3.00 8.00
131 Brett Sinkbeil 3.00 8.00
132 Los Angeles Angels 3.00 8.00
133 Andres Torres 3.00 8.00
134 Brett Cecil 3.00 8.00
135 Babe Ruth 8.00 20.00
136 Babe Ruth 8.00 20.00
137 Babe Ruth 8.00 20.00
138 Babe Ruth 8.00 20.00
139A Babe Ruth 8.00 20.00
139C Joba Chamberlain 3.00 8.00
140 Babe Ruth 8.00 20.00
141 Babe Ruth 8.00 20.00
142 Babe Ruth 8.00 20.00
143 Babe Ruth 8.00 20.00
144 Babe Ruth 8.00 20.00
145 Dallas Braden 3.00 8.00
146 Placido Polanco 3.00 8.00
147 Joakim Soria 3.00 8.00
148 Jonny Gomes 3.00 8.00
149 Ryan Franklin 3.00 8.00
150 Miguel Cabrera 8.00 20.00
151 Arthur Rhodes 3.00 8.00
152 Jim Riggleman MG 3.00 8.00
153 Marco Scutaro 5.00 12.00
154 Brennan Boesch 5.00 12.00
155 Brian Wilson 8.00 20.00
156 Hank Conger 5.00 12.00
157 Shane Victorino 5.00 12.00
158 Atlanta Braves 3.00 8.00
160 Garrett Jones 3.00 8.00
161 Bobby Jenks 3.00 8.00
162 Alex Gordon 5.00 12.00
163 M.Teixeira/A.Rodriguez 10.00 25.00
164 Jason Kendall 3.00 8.00
165 Adam Jones 5.00 12.00
166 Kevin Slowey 3.00 8.00
167 Wilson Ramos 3.00 8.00
168 Rajai Davis 3.00 8.00
169 Curtis Granderson 6.00 15.00
170 Aramis Ramirez 3.00 8.00
171 Edinson Volquez 3.00 8.00
172 Dusty Baker MG 3.00 8.00
173 Jhonny Peralta 3.00 8.00
174 Jon Garland 3.00 8.00
175 Adam Dunn 5.00 12.00
176 Chase Headley 3.00 8.00
177 J.A. Happ 5.00 12.00
178 A.J. Pierzynski 3.00 8.00
179 Mat Latos 5.00 12.00
180 Jim Thome 5.00 12.00
181 Dillon Gee 5.00 12.00
182 Cody Ross 3.00 8.00
183 Mike Pelfrey 3.00 8.00
184 Kurt Suzuki 3.00 8.00
185 Mariano Rivera 10.00 25.00
186 Rick Ankiel 3.00 8.00
187 Jon Lester 5.00 12.00
188 Freddy Sanchez 3.00 8.00
189 Heath Bell 3.00 8.00
190 Todd Helton 5.00 12.00
191 Ryan Dempster 3.00 8.00
192 Florida Marlins 3.00 8.00
193 Miguel Tejada 5.00 12.00
194 Jordan Walden 3.00 8.00
195 Paul Konerko 5.00 12.00
196 Jose Valverde 3.00 8.00

2011 Topps Heritage '62 Mint Coins

STATED ODDS 1:263 HOBBY
AO 1st American Orbits 15.00 40.00
BF Bob Feller 50.00 100.00
BR Brooks Robinson 40.00 80.00
CE U.S.-Cuba Embargo 12.50 30.00
CM Missile Crisis Begins 12.50 30.00
DS Duke Snider 10.00 25.00
DST Darryl Strawberry 10.00 25.00
EB Ernie Banks 20.00 50.00
ED Eric Davis 15.00 40.00
EK Ed Kranepool 5.00 12.00
FT Frank Thomas 30.00 60.00
GP Gaylord Perry 10.00 25.00
HK Harmon Killebrew 30.00 60.00
JM Jamie Moyer 12.50 30.00
JR Jackie Robinson 50.00 100.00
MM Mickey Mantle 20.00 50.00
NS SEALs Activated 15.00 40.00
SF Sid Fernandez 10.00 25.00
WS Warren Spahn 15.00 40.00
WST Willie Stargell 10.00 25.00

2011 Topps Heritage Advertising Panels

ISSUED AS BOX TOPPER
1 Atlanta Braves .40 1.00
Tyler Colvin
Matt Capps
2 Chris Carter .60 1.50
Ben Zobrist
Billy Butler
3 Jose Cerda 1.25 3.00
Carlos Pena
Ichiro Suzuki
4 Joba Chamberlain .60 1.50
Colby Rasmus
Gavin Floyd
5 Johnny Damon .60 1.50
Rafael Soriano
Jered Weaver
6 John Danks .60 1.50
Adam Wainwright
Adam Kennedy
7 Brian Duensing .40 1.00
A.J. Pierzynski
Rick Ankiel
8 Ryan Howard .75 2.00
Jason Kendall
Leo Nunez
9 Gregory Infante 1.00 2.50
Felix Hernandez
Clay Buchholz
David Price
Trevor Cahill
Joey Votto AS
10 Derek Jeter 2.50 6.00
Robinson Cano
Travis Hafner
Gaby Sanchez
11 Clayton Kershaw 2.00 5.00
Ronny Cedeno
John Jaso
12 Victor Martinez 1.00 2.50
Zach Duke
Mark Trumbo
13 Kendry Morales 1.25 3.00
Brian Wilson
Buster Posey
Brett Cecil
14 Mike Napoli .75 2.00
Nick Markakis
Jonathan Lucroy
15 Ricky Nolasco .60 1.50
Geovany Soto
Wade Davis
16 Cliff Pennington .40 1.00
Brett Myers
Vernon Wells
17 Andy Pettitte .60 1.50
Ian Kinsler
B.J. Upton
18 Joel Pineiro .60 1.50
Marco Scutaro
Andrew Romine
19 Albert Pujols 1.25 3.00
Adam Dunn
Joey Votto
Derek Lowe
San Diego Padres
20 Hanley Ramirez 2.50 6.00
Ted Lilly
Babe Ruth Special
21 Scott Rolen .60 1.50
Rangers Retaliate
Mat Latos
22 Jimmy Rollins .60 1.50
Carlos Lee
Carlos Gonzalez
23 Cody Ross 1.00 2.50
Brandon Beachy
Bruce Bochy
24 Babe Ruth Special 2.50 6.00
Mark Buehrle
Armando Galarraga
25 CC Sabathia .75 2.00
David Price
Jon Lester
Joe Mauer
Francisco Cordero
26 Grady Sizemore .60 1.50
Chris Young
Buck Showalter
27 Brandon Snyder 2.50 6.00
Babe Ruth Special
Francisco Liriano
28 Jim Thome .60 1.50
Franklin Gutierrez
Ryan Theriot
29 Ryan Dempster 1.00 2.50
Jeremy Hellickson
Brian Wilson
30 Luke Scott .40 1.00
Arthur Rhodes
Giants TC
31 Jose Ceda 1.25 3.00
Carlos Pena
Ichiro Suzuki

2011 Topps Heritage Baseball Bucks

RANDOMLY INSERTED BOX TOPPER
BB1 Justin Upton 3.00 8.00
BB2 Miguel Montero 2.00 5.00
BB3 Daniel Hudson 2.00 5.00
BB4 Torii Hunter 2.00 5.00
BB5 Jered Weaver 3.00 8.00
BB6 Kendry Morales 2.00 5.00
BB7 Chipper Jones 5.00 12.00
BB8 Jason Heyward 4.00 10.00
BB9 Martin Prado 2.00 5.00
BB10 Adam Jones 3.00 8.00
BB11 Nick Markakis 4.00 10.00
BB12 Brian Roberts 2.00 5.00
BB13 David Ortiz 5.00 12.00
BB14 Victor Martinez 3.00 8.00
BB15 Clay Buchholz 2.00 5.00

BB16 Starlin Castro 3.00 8.00
BB17 Aramis Ramirez 2.00 5.00
BB18 Tyler Colvin 2.00 5.00
BB19 Manny Ramirez 5.00 12.00
BB20 Carlos Quentin 2.00 5.00
BB21 John Danks 2.00 5.00
BB22 Joey Votto 5.00 12.00
BB23 Brandon Phillips 2.00 5.00
BB24 Jay Bruce 3.00 8.00
BB25 Shin-Soo Choo 3.00 8.00
BB26 Grady Sizemore 3.00 8.00
BB27 Carlos Santana 5.00 12.00
BB28 Troy Tulowitzki 5.00 12.00
BB29 Ubaldo Jimenez 2.00 5.00
BB30 Carlos Gonzalez 3.00 8.00
BB31 Miguel Cabrera 5.00 12.00
BB32 Justin Verlander 5.00 12.00
BB33 Austin Jackson 2.00 5.00
BB34 Hanley Ramirez 3.00 8.00
BB35 Mike Stanton 5.00 12.00
BB36 Logan Morrison 2.00 5.00
BB37 Hunter Pence 3.00 8.00
BB38 Wandy Rodriguez 2.00 5.00
BB39 Brett Wallace 2.00 5.00
BB40 Lorenzo Cain 2.00 5.00
BB41 Billy Butler 2.00 5.00
BB42 Joakim Soria 2.00 5.00
BB43 Clayton Kershaw 10.00 25.00
BB44 Andre Ethier 3.00 8.00
BB45 Matt Kemp 4.00 10.00
BB46 Ryan Braun 3.00 8.00
BB47 Yovani Gallardo 2.00 5.00
BB48 Casey McGehee 2.00 5.00
BB49 Joe Mauer 4.00 10.00
BB50 Justin Morneau 3.00 8.00
BB51 Danny Valencia 3.00 8.00
BB52 David Wright 4.00 10.00
BB53 Johan Santana 3.00 8.00
BB54 Ike Davis 2.00 5.00
BB55 Derek Jeter 12.00 30.00
BB56 CC Sabathia 3.00 8.00
BB57 Alex Rodriguez 6.00 15.00
BB58 Trevor Cahill 2.00 5.00
BB59 Kurt Suzuki 2.00 5.00
BB60 Brett Anderson 2.00 5.00
BB61 Roy Halladay 3.00 8.00
BB62 Ryan Howard 4.00 10.00
BB63 Domonic Brown 4.00 10.00
BB64 Andrew McCutchen 5.00 12.00
BB65 Jose Tabata 2.00 5.00
BB66 Neil Walker 3.00 8.00
BB67 Adrian Gonzalez 4.00 10.00
BB68 Heath Bell 2.00 5.00
BB69 Mat Latos 3.00 8.00
BB70 Tim Lincecum 3.00 8.00
BB71 Brian Wilson 5.00 12.00
BB72 Pablo Sandoval 3.00 8.00
BB73 Buster Posey 6.00 15.00
BB74 Matt Cain 3.00 8.00
BB75 Cody Ross 2.00 5.00
BB76 Ichiro Suzuki 6.00 15.00
BB77 Felix Hernandez 3.00 8.00
BB78 Franklin Gutierrez 2.00 5.00
BB79 Albert Pujols 6.00 15.00
BB80 Adam Wainwright 3.00 8.00
BB81 Yadier Molina 5.00 12.00
BB82 Evan Longoria 3.00 8.00
BB83 David Price 4.00 10.00
BB84 Jeremy Hellickson 5.00 12.00
BB85 Josh Hamilton 3.00 8.00
BB86 Neftali Feliz 2.00 5.00
BB87 Elvis Andrus 3.00 8.00
BB88 Michael Young 2.00 5.00
BB89 Ian Kinsler 3.00 8.00
BB90 Nelson Cruz 5.00 12.00
BB91 Vernon Wells 2.00 5.00
BB92 Jose Bautista 3.00 8.00
BB93 Brandon Morrow 2.00 5.00
BB94 Ryan Zimmerman 3.00 8.00
BB95 Jordan Zimmermann 3.00 8.00
BB96 Ian Desmond 2.00 5.00

2011 Topps Heritage Baseball Flashbacks

COMPLETE SET (10) 6.00 15.00
STATED ODDS 1:12 HOBBY
BF1 Mickey Mantle 3.00 8.00
BF2 Brooks Robinson .60 1.50
BF3 Roger Maris 1.00 2.50
BF4 Robin Roberts .60 1.50
BF5 Carl Yastrzemski 1.50 4.00
BF6 Whitey Ford .60 1.50
BF7 Harmon Killebrew 1.00 2.50
BF8 Warren Spahn .60 1.50
BF9 Frank Robinson .60 1.50
BF10 Bob Gibson .60 1.50

2011 Topps Heritage Black

*BLACK: .75X TO 2X BASIC CHROME

2011 Topps Heritage Checklists

COMPLETE SET (6) 1.50 4.00
COMMON CHECKLIST .40 1.00

2011 Topps Heritage Chrome

HERITAGE ODDS 1:11 HOBBY
TOPPS CHROME ODDS 1:7 HOBBY
STATED PRINT RUN 1962 SER.#'d SETS
1-100 ISSUED IN TOPPS HERITAGE
101-200 ISSUED IN TOPPS CHROME
C1 Andrew McCutchen 2.50 6.00
C2 Joe Nathan 1.00 2.50
C3 Jake McGee 1.00 2.50
C4 Miguel Cabrera 2.50 6.00
C5 Starlin Castro 1.50 4.00
C6 Josh Thole 1.00 2.50
C7 Russell Martin 1.00 2.50
C8 Mark Reynolds 1.00 2.50
C9 Nelson Cruz 2.50 6.00
C10 Cole Hamels 2.00 5.00
C11 CC Sabathia 1.50 4.00
C12 Carlos Gonzalez/Joey Votto
Omar Infante/Troy Tulowitzki 2.50 6.00
C13 Bautista/Kon/Cabr/Teix 2.50 6.00
C14 Weav/Felix/Lest/Verland 2.00 5.00
C15 Lin/Hal/Jim/Wain 1.25 3.00
C16 Tommy Hanson 1.00 2.50
C17 Travis Snider 1.00 2.50
C18 Jonathan Sanchez 1.00 2.50
C19 Ike Davis 1.00 2.50
C20 Nick Swisher 1.50 4.00
C21 Jacoby Ellsbury 2.00 5.00
C22 Brad Lidge 1.00 2.50
C23 Ryan Braun 1.25 3.00
C24 Kyle Drabek 1.50 4.00
C25 Bronson Arroyo 1.00 2.50
C26 Aaron Hill 1.00 2.50
C27 Omar Infante 1.00 2.50
C28 Babe Ruth 5.00 12.00
C29 Jonny Gomes 1.00 2.50
C30 Clay Buchholz 1.00 2.50
C31 Jhonny Peralta 1.00 2.50
C32 Mike Pelfrey 1.00 2.50
C33 Kurt Suzuki 1.00 2.50
C34 Paul Konerko 1.50 4.00
C35 Casey Blake 1.00 2.50
C36 Josh Beckett 1.00 2.50
C37 Corey Hart 1.00 2.50
C38 Kevin Millwood 1.00 2.50
C39 Evan Longoria 1.25 3.00
C40 Rickie Weeks 1.00 2.50
C41 Roy Oswalt 1.50 4.00
C42 Asdrubal Cabrera 1.50 4.00
C43 Don Mattingly 4.00 10.00
C44 Casey Coleman 1.00 2.50
C45 Adrian Beltre 2.50 6.00
C46 Cliff Lee 1.50 4.00
C47 Marlon Byrd 1.00 2.50
C48 Chone Figgins 1.00 2.50
C49 Giants Win Opener HL 1.00 2.50
C50 Giants Crush Rangers HL 1.00 2.50
C51 Xavier Nady 1.00 2.50
C52 Josh Johnson 1.50 4.00
C53 Chris Johnson 1.00 2.50
C54 Vance Worley 4.00 10.00
C55 Lou Marson 1.00 2.50
C56 Edwin Jackson 1.00 2.50
C57 Ruben Tejada 1.00 2.50
C58 Josh Hamilton/Nelson Cruz 2.50 6.00
C59 Delmon Young 1.50 4.00
C60 Will Venable 1.00 2.50
C61 Pedro Alvarez 2.00 5.00
C62 Hiroki Kuroda 1.00 2.50
C63 Neftali Feliz 1.00 2.50
C64 Mike Stanton 2.50 6.00
C65 Ty Wigginton 1.00 2.50
C66 Bobby Cramer 1.00 2.50
C67 Jason Kubel 1.00 2.50
C68 Daniel Descalso 1.00 2.50
C69 Ramon Hernandez 1.00 2.50
C70 Mike Aviles 1.00 2.50
C71 D.Ortiz/D.Pedroia 2.00 5.00
C72 Jason Bay 1.50 4.00
C73 CC Sabathia 1.50 4.00
C74 Joe Mauer 2.00 5.00
C75 Tommy Hunter 1.00 2.50
C76 Alexei Ramirez 1.50 4.00
C77 Raul Ibanez 1.50 4.00
C78 Lucas Duda 2.50 6.00
C79 Chad Billingsley 1.50 4.00
C80 Bobby Abreu 1.00 2.50
C81 Fernando Salas 1.50 4.00
C82 Nyjer Morgan 1.00 2.50
C83 Justin Morneau/Joe Mauer 2.00 5.00
C84 Hunter Pence 1.50 4.00
C85 Jose Bautista 1.50 4.00
C86 Brett Anderson 1.00 2.50
C87 Carlos Zambrano 1.50 4.00
C88 Greg Halman 1.50 4.00
C89 Nick Hundley 1.00 2.50
C90 J.P. Arencibia 1.00 2.50
C91 Dan Haren 1.00 2.50
C92 James Loney 1.00 2.50
C93 Phil Hughes 1.00 2.50
C94 Ubaldo Jimenez 1.00 2.50
C95 Michael Cuddyer 1.00 2.50
C96 Desmond Jennings 1.50 4.00
C97 Ryan Doumit 1.00 2.50
C98 Mark Teixeira 1.50 4.00
C99 Lucas May 1.00 2.50
C100 Wandy Rodriguez 1.00 2.50
C101 A.Pujols/R.Braun 2.50 6.00
C102 D.Jeter/R.Cano 5.00 12.00
C103 M.Teixeira/A.Rodriguez 2.50 6.00
C104 Matt Kemp/Andre Ethier 2.00 5.00
C105 Derek Jeter 5.00 12.00
C106 Roy Halladay 1.50 4.00
C107 Jose Bautista 1.50 4.00
C108 Miguel Cabrera 2.50 6.00
C109 Ichiro Suzuki 2.50 6.00
C110 Mark Teixeira 1.50 4.00
C111 Tim Lincecum 1.25 3.00
C112 Cory Luebke 1.00 2.50
C113 Freddie Freeman 6.00 15.00
C114 Scott Cousins 1.00 2.50
C115 Hank Conger 1.50 4.00
C116 Jordan Walden 1.00 2.50
C117 Aroldis Chapman 2.50 6.00
C118 Chris Sale 6.00 15.00
C119 Jeremy Hellickson 2.00 5.00
C120 Brandon Beachy 2.00 5.00
C121 Eric Sogard 1.00 2.50
C122 Mark Trumbo 2.50 6.00
C123 Brent Morel 1.00 2.50
C124 Stephen Strasburg 2.00 5.00
C125 Gaby Sanchez 1.00 2.50
C126 Buster Posey 2.50 6.00
C127 Danny Valencia 1.50 4.00
C128 Jason Heyward 1.50 4.00
C129 Austin Jackson 1.00 2.50
C130 Neil Walker 1.50 4.00
C131 Jaime Garcia 1.50 4.00
C132 Jose Tabata 1.00 2.50
C133 Josh Hamilton 1.50 4.00
C134 David Ortiz 2.50 6.00
C135 Clayton Kershaw 5.00 12.00
C136 Carlos Beltran 1.50 4.00
C137 Carlos Pena 1.50 4.00
C138 Jayson Werth 1.50 4.00
C139 Vernon Wells 1.00 2.50
C140 Chipper Jones 2.50 6.00
C141 Ian Kinsler 1.50 4.00
C142 Pablo Sandoval 1.50 4.00
C143 Justin Upton 1.50 4.00
C144 Kosuke Fukudome 1.50 4.00
C145 Albert Pujols 2.50 6.00
C146 Nick Markakis 2.00 5.00
C147 Robinson Cano 1.50 4.00
C148 Justin Morneau 1.50 4.00
C149 Gordon Beckham 1.00 2.50
C150 Hanley Ramirez 1.50 4.00
C151 Chase Utley 1.50 4.00
C152 Jay Bruce 1.50 4.00
C153 Nelson Cruz 2.50 6.00
C154 Ryan Zimmerman 1.50 4.00
C155 Jered Weaver 1.50 4.00
C156 David Price 2.00 5.00
C157 Domonic Brown 2.00 5.00
C158 Madison Bumgarner 2.00 5.00
C159 Matt Kemp 2.00 5.00
C160 Mark Teixeira 1.50 4.00
C161 Alfonso Soriano 1.50 4.00
C162 Carlos Quentin 1.00 2.50
C163 Miguel Cabrera 2.50 6.00
C164 Adam Jones 1.50 4.00
C165 Curtis Granderson 2.00 5.00
C166 Adam Dunn 1.50 4.00
C167 Jim Thome 1.50 4.00
C168 Mariano Rivera 3.00 8.00
C169 Jon Lester 1.50 4.00
C170 Derek Jeter 5.00 12.00
C171 Ryan Howard 1.50 4.00
C172 Francisco Liriano 1.00 2.50
C173 Ichiro Suzuki 2.50 6.00
C174 Joe Mauer 2.00 5.00
C175 Ryan Braun 1.25 3.00
C176 Matt Cain 1.50 4.00
C177 Carl Crawford 1.50 4.00
C178 Zack Greinke 1.50 4.00
C179 Dustin Pedroia 1.50 4.00
C180 Felix Hernandez 1.50 4.00
C181 Joey Votto 2.50 6.00
C182 Andre Ethier 1.50 4.00
C183 Jorge Posada 1.50 4.00
C184 Dan Uggla 1.00 2.50
C185 Matt Holliday 2.50 6.00
C186 Victor Martinez 1.50 4.00
C187 Carlos Gonzalez 1.50 4.00
C188 Carlos Santana 2.50 6.00
C189 Kevin Youkilis 1.00 2.50
C190 Tim Lincecum 1.25 3.00
C191 Troy Tulowitzki 2.50 6.00
C192 Jose Reyes 1.50 4.00
C193 Adrian Gonzalez 2.00 5.00
C194 Brian McCann 1.50 4.00
C195 Prince Fielder 1.50 4.00
C196 Roy Halladay 1.50 4.00
C197 David Wright 1.50 4.00
C198 Martin Prado 1.00 2.50
C199 Drew Stubbs 1.00 2.50
C200 Alex Rodriguez 2.50 6.00

2011 Topps Heritage Chrome Refractors

*REF: .6X TO 1.5X BASIC CHROME
HERITAGE ODDS 1:137 HOBBY
TOPPS CHROME ODDS 1:22 HOBBY
STATED PRINT RUN 562 SER.#'d SETS
1-100 ISSUED IN TOPPS HERITAGE
101-200 ISSUED IN TOPPS CHROME

2011 Topps Heritage Chrome Black Refractors

HERITAGE ODDS 1:334 HOBBY
TOPPS CHROME ODDS 1:148 HOBBY
STATED PRINT RUN 62 SER.#'d SETS
1-100 ISSUED IN TOPPS HERITAGE
101-200 ISSUED IN TOPPS CHROME
C1 Andrew McCutchen 12.00 30.00
C2 Joe Nathan 5.00 12.00
C3 Jake McGee 5.00 12.00
C4 Miguel Cabrera 12.00 30.00
C5 Starlin Castro 8.00 20.00
C6 Josh Thole 5.00 12.00
C7 Russell Martin 5.00 12.00
C8 Mark Reynolds 5.00 12.00
C9 Nelson Cruz 12.00 30.00
C10 Cole Hamels 10.00 25.00
C11 CC Sabathia 8.00 20.00
C12 Carlos Gonzalez/Joey Votto/Omar Infante
Troy Tulowitzki 12.00 30.00
C13 Bautista/Kon/Cabr/Teix 12.00 30.00
C14 Weav/Felix/Lest/Verland 12.00 30.00
C15 Lin/Hal/Jim/Wain 8.00 20.00
C16 Tommy Hanson 5.00 12.00
C17 Travis Snider 5.00 12.00
C18 Jonathan Sanchez 5.00 12.00
C19 Ike Davis 5.00 12.00
C20 Nick Swisher 8.00 20.00
C21 Jacoby Ellsbury 10.00 25.00
C22 Brad Lidge 5.00 12.00
C23 Ryan Braun 8.00 20.00
C24 Kyle Drabek 8.00 20.00
C25 Bronson Arroyo 5.00 12.00
C26 Aaron Hill 5.00 12.00
C27 Omar Infante 5.00 12.00
C28 Babe Ruth 30.00 80.00
C29 Jonny Gomes 5.00 12.00
C30 Clay Buchholz 5.00 12.00
C31 Jhonny Peralta 5.00 12.00
C32 Mike Pelfrey 5.00 12.00
C33 Kurt Suzuki 5.00 12.00
C34 Paul Konerko 8.00 20.00
C35 Casey Blake 5.00 12.00
C36 Josh Beckett 5.00 12.00
C37 Corey Hart 5.00 12.00
C38 Kevin Millwood 5.00 12.00
C39 Evan Longoria 8.00 20.00
C40 Rickie Weeks 5.00 12.00
C41 Roy Oswalt 8.00 20.00
C42 Asdrubal Cabrera 8.00 20.00
C43 Don Mattingly 25.00 60.00
C44 Casey Coleman 5.00 12.00
C45 Adrian Beltre 12.00 30.00
C46 Cliff Lee 8.00 20.00
C47 Marlon Byrd 5.00 12.00
C48 Chone Figgins 5.00 12.00
C49 Giants Win Opener HL 5.00 12.00
C50 Giants Crush Rangers HL 5.00 12.00
C51 Xavier Nady 5.00 12.00
C52 Josh Johnson 8.00 20.00
C53 Chris Johnson 5.00 12.00
C54 Vance Worley 20.00 50.00
C55 Lou Marson 5.00 12.00
C56 Edwin Jackson 5.00 12.00
C57 Ruben Tejada 5.00 12.00
C58 Josh Hamilton/Nelson Cruz 12.00 30.00
C59 Delmon Young 8.00 20.00
C60 Will Venable 5.00 12.00
C61 Pedro Alvarez 10.00 25.00
C62 Hiroki Kuroda 5.00 12.00
C63 Neftali Feliz 5.00 12.00
C64 Mike Stanton 12.00 30.00
C65 Ty Wigginton 5.00 12.00
C66 Bobby Cramer 5.00 12.00
C67 Jason Kubel 5.00 12.00
C68 Daniel Descalso 5.00 12.00
C69 Ramon Hernandez 5.00 12.00
C70 Mike Aviles 5.00 12.00
C71 D.Ortiz/D.Pedroia 12.00 30.00
C72 Jason Bay 8.00 20.00
C73 CC Sabathia 8.00 20.00
C74 Joe Mauer 10.00 25.00
C75 Tommy Hunter 5.00 12.00
C76 Alexei Ramirez 8.00 20.00
C77 Raul Ibanez 8.00 20.00
C78 Lucas Duda 12.00 30.00
C79 Chad Billingsley 8.00 20.00
C80 Bobby Abreu 5.00 12.00
C81 Fernando Salas 8.00 20.00
C82 Nyjer Morgan 5.00 12.00
C83 Justin Morneau/Joe Mauer 10.00 25.00
C84 Hunter Pence 8.00 20.00
C85 Jose Bautista 8.00 20.00
C86 Brett Anderson 5.00 12.00
C87 Carlos Zambrano 8.00 20.00
C88 Greg Halman 8.00 20.00
C89 Nick Hundley 5.00 12.00
C90 J.P. Arencibia 5.00 12.00
C91 Dan Haren 5.00 12.00
C92 James Loney 5.00 12.00
C93 Phil Hughes 5.00 12.00
C94 Ubaldo Jimenez 5.00 12.00
C95 Michael Cuddyer 5.00 12.00
C96 Desmond Jennings 8.00 20.00
C97 Ryan Doumit 5.00 12.00
C98 Mark Teixeira 8.00 20.00
C99 Lucas May 5.00 12.00
C100 Wandy Rodriguez 5.00 12.00
C101 A.Pujols/R.Braun 15.00 40.00
C102 D.Jeter/R.Cano 30.00 80.00
C103 Teixeira/ARod 15.00 40.00
C104 Matt Kemp/Andre Ethier 10.00 25.00
C105 Derek Jeter 30.00 80.00
C106 Roy Halladay 8.00 20.00
C107 Jose Bautista 8.00 20.00
C108 Miguel Cabrera 12.00 30.00
C109 Ichiro Suzuki 15.00 40.00
C110 Mark Teixeira 8.00 20.00
C111 Tim Lincecum 8.00 20.00
C112 Cory Luebke 5.00 12.00
C113 Freddie Freeman 30.00 80.00
C114 Scott Cousins 5.00 12.00
C115 Hank Conger 8.00 20.00
C116 Jordan Walden 5.00 12.00
C117 Aroldis Chapman 15.00 40.00
C118 Chris Sale 30.00 80.00
C119 Jeremy Hellickson 12.00 30.00
C120 Brandon Beachy 12.00 30.00
C121 Eric Sogard 5.00 12.00
C122 Mark Trumbo 12.00 30.00
C123 Brent Morel 5.00 12.00
C124 Stephen Strasburg 12.00 30.00
C125 Gaby Sanchez 5.00 12.00
C126 Buster Posey 15.00 40.00
C127 Danny Valencia 8.00 20.00
C128 Jason Heyward 10.00 25.00
C129 Austin Jackson 5.00 12.00
C130 Neil Walker 8.00 20.00
C131 Jaime Garcia 8.00 20.00
C132 Jose Tabata 5.00 12.00
C133 Josh Hamilton 8.00 20.00
C134 David Ortiz 12.00 30.00
C135 Clayton Kershaw 25.00 60.00
C136 Carlos Beltran 8.00 20.00
C137 Carlos Pena 8.00 20.00
C138 Jayson Werth 8.00 20.00
C139 Vernon Wells 5.00 12.00
C140 Chipper Jones 12.00 30.00
C141 Ian Kinsler 8.00 20.00
C142 Pablo Sandoval 8.00 20.00
C143 Justin Upton 8.00 20.00
C144 Kosuke Fukudome 8.00 20.00
C145 Albert Pujols 15.00 40.00
C146 Nick Markakis 10.00 25.00
C147 Robinson Cano 8.00 20.00
C148 Justin Morneau 8.00 20.00
C149 Gordon Beckham 5.00 12.00
C150 Hanley Ramirez 8.00 20.00
C151 Chase Utley 8.00 20.00
C152 Jay Bruce 8.00 20.00
C153 Nelson Cruz 12.00 30.00
C154 Ryan Zimmerman 8.00 20.00
C155 Jered Weaver 8.00 20.00
C156 David Price 10.00 25.00
C157 Domonic Brown 10.00 25.00
C158 Madison Bumgarner 10.00 25.00
C159 Matt Kemp 10.00 25.00
C160 Mark Teixeira 8.00 20.00
C161 Alfonso Soriano 8.00 20.00
C162 Carlos Quentin 5.00 12.00
C163 Miguel Cabrera 12.00 30.00
C164 Adam Jones 8.00 20.00
C165 Curtis Granderson 10.00 25.00
C166 Adam Dunn 8.00 20.00
C167 Jim Thome 8.00 20.00
C168 Mariano Rivera 15.00 40.00
C169 Jon Lester 8.00 20.00
C170 Derek Jeter 30.00 80.00
C171 Ryan Howard 10.00 25.00
C172 Francisco Liriano 5.00 12.00
C173 Ichiro Suzuki 15.00 40.00
C174 Joe Mauer 10.00 25.00
C175 Ryan Braun 8.00 20.00
C176 Matt Cain 8.00 20.00
C177 Carl Crawford 8.00 20.00
C178 Zack Greinke 8.00 20.00
C179 Dustin Pedroia 10.00 25.00
C180 Felix Hernandez 8.00 20.00
C181 Joey Votto 12.00 30.00
C182 Andre Ethier 8.00 20.00
C183 Jorge Posada 8.00 20.00
C184 Dan Uggla 5.00 12.00
C185 Matt Holliday 12.00 30.00
C186 Victor Martinez 8.00 20.00
C187 Carlos Gonzalez 8.00 20.00
C188 Carlos Santana 12.00 30.00
C189 Kevin Youkilis 5.00 12.00
C190 Tim Lincecum 8.00 20.00
C191 Troy Tulowitzki 12.00 30.00
C192 Jose Reyes 8.00 20.00
C193 Adrian Gonzalez 10.00 25.00
C194 Brian McCann 8.00 20.00
C195 Prince Fielder 8.00 20.00
C196 Roy Halladay 8.00 20.00
C197 David Wright 10.00 25.00
C198 Martin Prado 5.00 12.00
C199 Drew Stubbs 5.00 12.00
C200 Alex Rodriguez 15.00 40.00

2011 Topps Heritage Chrome Green Refractors

*GREEN REF: .75X TO 2X BASIC CHROME

2011 Topps Heritage Clubhouse Collection Dual Relic Autographs

STATED ODDS 1:14,883 HOBBY
STATED PRINT RUN 10 SER.#'d SETS
NO PRICING DUE TO SCARCITY
EXCHANGE DEADLINE 2/28/2014

2011 Topps Heritage Clubhouse Collection Dual Relics

STATED ODDS 1:7600 HOBBY
STATED PRINT RUN 62 SER.#'d SETS
FS W.Ford/C.Sabathia 15.00 40.00
GH B.Gibson/R.Halladay 50.00 100.00
KC A.Kaline/M.Cabrera 75.00 200.00
RV F.Robinson/J.Votto 15.00 40.00
RW B.Robinson/D.Wright 20.00 50.00

2011 Topps Heritage Clubhouse Collection Relics

STATED ODDS 1:29 HOBBY
AP Albert Pujols 6.00 15.00
AR Alex Rios 2.00 5.00
BG Brett Gardner 3.00 8.00
CB Carlos Beltran 3.00 8.00
CBU Clay Buchholz 2.00 5.00
CC Carl Crawford 3.00 8.00
CK Clayton Kershaw 10.00 25.00
CL Carlos Lee 2.00 5.00
CS Carlos Santana 5.00 12.00
CU Chase Utley 3.00 8.00
DU Dan Uggla 2.00 5.00
DW David Wright 4.00 10.00
EL Evan Longoria 3.00 8.00
FH Felix Hernandez 3.00 8.00
FL Francisco Liriano 2.00 5.00
GS Gaby Sanchez 2.00 5.00
HR Hanley Ramirez 3.00 8.00
ID Ike Davis 2.00 5.00
IK Ian Kinsler 3.00 8.00
IS Ichiro Suzuki 6.00 15.00
JB Jason Bartlett 2.00 5.00
JBA Jason Bay 3.00 8.00
JE Jacoby Ellsbury 4.00 10.00
JH Josh Hamilton 3.00 8.00
JJ Josh Johnson 3.00 8.00
JM Joe Mauer 4.00 10.00
JMO Justin Morneau 3.00 8.00
JP Jorge Posada 3.00 8.00
JR Jose Reyes 3.00 8.00
JS Johan Santana 3.00 8.00
JT Jim Thome 3.00 8.00
JTA Jose Tabata 2.00 5.00
JV Joey Votto 5.00 12.00
JW Jayson Werth 3.00 8.00
JWI Josh Willingham 3.00 8.00
MC Miguel Cabrera 5.00 12.00
MR Manny Ramirez 5.00 12.00
MRE Mark Reynolds 2.00 5.00
MT Mark Teixeira 3.00 8.00
PF Prince Fielder 3.00 8.00
PP Placido Polanco 2.00 5.00
RB Ryan Braun 3.00 8.00
RC Robinson Cano 3.00 8.00
RH Ryan Howard 4.00 10.00
SR Scott Rolen 3.00 8.00
TT Troy Tulowitzki 5.00 12.00
VG Vladimir Guerrero 3.00 8.00
VM Victor Martinez 3.00 8.00
YM Yadier Molina 5.00 12.00
ZG Zack Greinke 3.00 8.00

2011 Topps Heritage Flashback Stadium Relics

STATED ODDS 1:1175 HOBBY
AK Al Kaline 15.00 40.00
BG Roger Maris 10.00 25.00
BM Bill Mazeroski 15.00 40.00
BR Brooks Robinson 10.00 25.00
FR Luis Aparicio 10.00 25.00
FT Frank Thomas 12.50 30.00
HK Harmon Killebrew 10.00 25.00
HW Hoyt Wilhelm 10.00 25.00
MM Mickey Mantle 20.00 50.00
RR Robin Roberts 10.00 25.00

2011 Topps Heritage Framed Dual Stamps

STATED ODDS 1:211 HOBBY
STATED PRINT RUN 62 SER.#'d SETS
1 Bobby Abreu
Cole Hamels 6.00 15.00
2 Brett Anderson/Vernon Wells 6.00 15.00
3 Elvis Andrus/Curtis Granderson 6.00 15.00
4 Bronson Arroyo/Brad Lidge 8.00 20.00
5 Jason Bartlett/Adam Wainwright 8.00 20.00
6 Daric Barton/Carl Pavano 6.00 15.00
7 Jose Bautista/Clay Buchholz 6.00 15.00
8 Gordon Beckham/Howie Kendrick 6.00 15.00
9 Heath Bell/Alex Rios 6.00 15.00
10 Adrian Beltre/Denard Span 6.00 15.00
11 Chad Billingsley/Kendry Morales 10.00 25.00
12 Michael Bourn/Francisco Liriano 8.00 20.00
13 Dallas Braden/Will Venable 6.00 15.00
14 Ryan Braun/Gaby Sanchez 10.00 25.00
15 Domonic Brown/Stephen Drew 6.00 15.00
16 J.Bruce/M.Cabrera 6.00 15.00
17 Clay Buchholz/Yovani Gallardo 8.00 20.00
18 Billy Butler/Brett Gardner 6.00 15.00
19 Marlon Byrd/Mat Latos 6.00 15.00
20 M.Cabrera/R.Zimmerman 10.00 25.00
21 Trevor Cahill/Jose Tabata 8.00 20.00
22 M.Cain/E.Longoria 15.00 40.00
23 Robinson Cano/Ian Desmond 8.00 20.00
24 M.Capps/A.Jones 12.50 30.00
25 Chris Carpenter/Felix Hernandez 10.00 25.00
26 Starlin Castro/Francisco Cordero 10.00 25.00
27 Choo/L.Morrison 12.50 30.00
28 Chris Coghlan/Carlos Marmol 8.00 20.00
29 Tyler Colvin/Edwin Jackson 6.00 15.00
30 Francisco Cordero/Mike Napoli 6.00 15.00
31 Carl Crawford/Aaron Hill 8.00 20.00
32 Nelson Cruz/Brett Myers 6.00 15.00
33 Michael Cuddyer/Omar Infante 10.00 25.00
34 John Danks/Jorge Posada 8.00 20.00
35 I.Davis/D.Uggla 15.00 40.00
36 Ryan Dempster/Chris Young 6.00 15.00
37 Ian Desmond/Ben Zobrist 6.00 15.00
38 Stephen Drew/Roy Halladay 8.00 20.00
39 Adam Dunn/Adrian Beltre 8.00 20.00
40 J.Ellsbury/C.Rasmus 12.50 30.00
41 Andre Ethier/Wandy Rodriguez 6.00 15.00
42 Neftali Feliz/Alfonso Soriano 8.00 20.00
43 Prince Fielder/Corey Hart 10.00 25.00
44 Yovani Gallardo/Carl Crawford 6.00 15.00
45 Jaime Garcia/Jim Thome 10.00 25.00
46 Brett Gardner/Miguel Tejada 10.00 25.00
47 Matt Garza/Jayson Werth 6.00 15.00
48 Adrian Gonzalez/Jonathan Papelbon 10.00 25.00
49 Carlos Gonzalez/Trevor Cahill 8.00 20.00
50 Gio Gonzalez/Andre Ethier 6.00 15.00
51 C.Granderson/B.Posey 12.50 30.00
52 Vladimir Guerrero/Justin Morneau 8.00 20.00
53 Franklin Gutierrez/Juan Pierre 6.00 15.00
54 Roy Halladay/Daric Barton 8.00 20.00
55 Cole Hamels/Danny Valencia 8.00 20.00
56 J.Hamilton/H.Ramirez 12.50 30.00
57 Tommy Hanson/Vladimir Guerrero 8.00 20.00
58 Dan Haren/Franklin Gutierrez 6.00 15.00
59 Corey Hart/Yadier Molina 8.00 20.00
60 Chase Headley/Josh Johnson 6.00 15.00
61 Felix Hernandez/Matt Kemp 8.00 20.00
62 Jason Heyward/Chase Headley 8.00 20.00
63 Aaron Hill/Kelly Johnson 6.00 15.00
64 M.Holliday/D.Price 12.50 30.00
65 R.Howard/I.Suzuki 12.50 30.00
66 Daniel Hudson/James Shields 6.00 15.00
67 Tim Hudson/Adam Lind 10.00 25.00
68 A.Huff/I.Davis 15.00 40.00
69 Phil Hughes/Torii Hunter 6.00 15.00
70 Torii Hunter/Casey McGehee 8.00 20.00
71 O.Infante/D.Pedroia 15.00 40.00
72 Austin Jackson/Mariano Rivera 8.00 20.00
73 Edwin Jackson/Michael Bourn 6.00 15.00
75 D.Jeter/B.Upton 20.00 50.00
76 Ubaldo Jimenez/Angel Pagan 8.00 20.00
77 Josh Johnson/Ian Kinsler 6.00 15.00
78 Kelly Johnson/Ivan Rodriguez 6.00 15.00
79 Adam Jones/Chris Coghlan 10.00 25.00
80 C.Jones/R.Cano 30.00 60.00
81 Jair Jurrjens/Nick Markakis 8.00 20.00
82 Matt Kemp/John Lackey 8.00 20.00
83 Howie Kendrick/David Ortiz 6.00 15.00
84 C.Kershaw/J.Rollins 10.00 25.00
85 Ian Kinsler/Rafael Soriano 10.00 25.00
86 Paul Konerko/Manny Ramirez 8.00 20.00
87 John Lackey/Tommy Hanson 10.00 25.00
88 Mat Latos/Matt Holliday 6.00 15.00
89 Cliff Lee/Kevin Youkilis 10.00 25.00
90 Derrek Lee/C.J. Wilson 6.00 15.00
91 J.Lester/A.Torres 12.50 30.00
92 Brad Lidge/Bobby Abreu 6.00 15.00
93 T.Lincecum/C.Ruiz 12.50 30.00
94 Adam Lind/Carlos Quentin 8.00 20.00
95 Liriano/Verlander 10.00 25.00
96 J.Loney/A.Rodriguez 30.00 60.00
97 E.Longoria/D.Jeter 30.00 60.00
98 Derek Lowe/Joey Votto 10.00 25.00
99 N.Markakis/A.Gonzalez 12.50 30.00
100 Carlos Marmol/Barry Zito 6.00 15.00
101 Victor Martinez/Jay Bruce 6.00 15.00
102 Brian Matusz/Dallas Braden 10.00 25.00
103 J.Mauer/K.Suzuki 12.50 30.00
104 Brian McCann/Aubrey Huff 8.00 20.00
105 Andrew McCutchen/Max Scherzer 10.00 25.00
106 Casey McGehee/Derrek Lee 6.00 15.00
107 Jenrry Mejia/Brian Roberts 6.00 15.00
108 Yadier Molina/Jason Bartlett 8.00 20.00
109 Miguel Montero/Brett Wallace 6.00 15.00
110 Kendry Morales/Brandon Morrow 8.00 20.00
111 J.Morneau/P.Sandoval 12.50 30.00
112 Logan Morrison/Drew Stubbs 8.00 20.00
113 Brandon Morrow/Jonathan Sanchez 8.00 20.00
114 Brett Myers/Daniel Hudson 6.00 15.00
115 Mike Napoli/CC Sabathia 8.00 20.00
116 David Ortiz/Joakim Soria 15.00 40.00
117 Roy Oswalt/Jaime Garcia 10.00 25.00
118 A.Pagan/M.Cuddyer 12.50 30.00
119 J.Papelbon/D.Young 12.50 30.00
120 Carl Pavano/Grady Sizemore 8.00 20.00
121 D.Pedroia/B.Wilson 15.00 40.00
122 Mike Pelfrey/Domonic Brown 8.00 20.00
123 Hunter Pence/Josh Hamilton 10.00 25.00
124 A.Pettitte/M.Teixeira 15.00 40.00
125 Brandon Phillips/Johan Santana 10.00 25.00
126 Juan Pierre/Jon Jay 6.00 15.00
127 Jorge Posada/Tyler Colvin 10.00 25.00
128 B.Posey/C.Kershaw 15.00 40.00
129 Martin Prado/Elvis Andrus 8.00 20.00
130 David Price/Andy Pettitte 10.00 25.00
131 A.Pujols/M.Garza 20.00 50.00
132 Carlos Quentin/Bronson Arroyo 8.00 20.00
133 Alexei Ramirez/Mike Pelfrey 6.00 15.00
134 Aramis Ramirez/Michael Young 6.00 15.00
135 H.Ramirez/N.Swisher 12.50 30.00

136 Manny Ramirez/Cliff Lee 15.00 40.00
137 C.Rasmus/A.Dunn 12.50 30.00
138 Jose Reyes/Jose Bautista 10.00 25.00
139 Mark Reynolds/Andrew McCutchen 8.00 20.00
140 Alex Rios/Victor Martinez 8.00 20.00
141 Mariano Rivera/Dan Haren 10.00 25.00
142 Brian Roberts/Heath Bell 6.00 15.00
143 A.Rodriguez/J.Jurrjens 15.00 40.00
144 Ivan Rodriguez/Jose Reyes 10.00 25.00
145 Wandy Rodriguez/Billy Butler 6.00 15.00
146 J.Rollins/T.Lincecum 20.00 50.00
147 Ricky Romero/Jered Weaver 6.00 15.00
148 Carlos Ruiz/Martin Prado 6.00 15.00
149 C.Sabathia/A.Pujols 20.00 50.00
150 Gaby Sanchez/Ricky Romero 6.00 15.00
151 Jonathan Sanchez/Nelson Cruz 10.00 25.00
152 P.Sandoval/C.Carpenter 15.00 40.00
153 Carlos Santana/Jon Lester 8.00 20.00
154 Ervin Santana/Shin-Soo Choo 8.00 20.00
155 Johan Santana/Miguel Montero 8.00 20.00
156 M.Scherzer/J.Heyward 15.00 40.00
157 Luke Scott/Mike Stanton 8.00 20.00
158 James Shields/Chad Billingsley 6.00 15.00
159 Grady Sizemore/Alexei Ramirez 8.00 20.00
160 Joakim Soria/Ervin Santana 6.00 15.00
161 Alfonso Soriano/Prince Fielder 8.00 20.00
162 Rafael Soriano/Mark Reynolds 6.00 15.00
163 Denard Span/Carlos Santana 10.00 25.00
164 Mike Stanton/Matt Capps 12.50 30.00
165 Drew Stubbs/Gordon Beckham 10.00 25.00
166 Ichiro Suzuki/Justin Upton 10.00 25.00
167 Kurt Suzuki/Gio Gonzalez 8.00 20.00
168 Nick Swisher/Brian Matusz 10.00 25.00
169 Jose Tabata/Phil Hughes 8.00 20.00
170 Mark Teixeira/Ryan Dempster 10.00 25.00
171 M.Tejada/J.Mauer 15.00 40.00
172 Jim Thome/Brett Anderson 10.00 25.00
173 A.Torres/J.Ellsbury 12.50 30.00
174 Troy Tulowitzki/Hunter Pence 8.00 20.00
175 D.Uggla/M.Cain 12.50 30.00
176 B.J. Upton/Brian McCann 6.00 15.00
177 Justin Upton/Roy Oswalt 8.00 20.00
178 Chase Utley/Luke Scott 8.00 20.00
179 Danny Valencia/Tim Hudson 10.00 25.00
180 Will Venable/Troy Tulowitzki 8.00 20.00
181 Verlander/Victorino 8.00 20.00
182 Shane Victorino/John Danks 8.00 20.00
183 Joey Votto/Austin Jackson 10.00 25.00
184 A.Wainwright/R.Weeks 12.50 30.00
185 Neil Walker/James Loney 10.00 25.00
186 Brett Wallace/Ryan Braun 10.00 25.00
187 Jered Weaver/Brandon Phillips 6.00 15.00
188 Rickie Weeks/Neftali Feliz 8.00 20.00
189 Vernon Wells/Ryan Howard 8.00 20.00
190 J.Werth/D.Wright 12.50 30.00
191 B.Wilson/A.Ramirez 12.50 30.00
192 C.J. Wilson/Carlos Gonzalez 10.00 25.00
193 D.Wright/S.Castro 12.50 30.00
194 K.Youkilis/C.Jones 20.00 50.00
195 Chris Young/Marlon Byrd 6.00 15.00
196 Delmon Young/Neil Walker 10.00 25.00
197 Michael Young/Ubaldo Jimenez 6.00 15.00
198 Ryan Zimmerman/Jenrry Mejia 6.00 15.00
199 Barry Zito/Chase Utley 10.00 25.00
200 Ben Zobrist/Paul Konerko 8.00 20.00

2011 Topps Heritage Jackie Robinson Special Memorabilia

COMMON ROBINSON 20.00 50.00
STATED ODDS 1:1777 HOBBY
STATED PRINT RUN 42 SER.#'d SETS
135 Jackie Robinson 20.00 50.00
136 Jackie Robinson 20.00 50.00
137 Jackie Robinson 20.00 50.00
138 Jackie Robinson 20.00 50.00
139 Jackie Robinson 20.00 50.00
140 Jackie Robinson 20.00 50.00
141 Jackie Robinson 20.00 50.00
142 Jackie Robinson 20.00 50.00
143 Jackie Robinson 20.00 50.00
144 Jackie Robinson 20.00 50.00

2011 Topps Heritage New Age Performers

COMPLETE SET (15) 15.00 40.00
STATED ODDS 1:15 HOBBY
NAP1 Cliff Lee .60 1.50
NAP2 Jim Thome .60 1.50
NAP3 Josh Hamilton .60 1.50
NAP4 Roy Halladay .60 1.50
NAP5 Miguel Cabrera 1.00 2.50
NAP6 Ubaldo Jimenez .40 1.00
NAP7 Joey Votto 1.00 2.50
NAP8 CC Sabathia .60 1.50
NAP9 David Price .75 2.00
NAP10 Alex Rodriguez 1.25 3.00
NAP11 Evan Longoria .60 1.50
NAP12 Carlos Gonzalez .60 1.50
NAP13 Robinson Cano .60 1.50
NAP14 Felix Hernandez .60 1.50
NAP15 Albert Pujols 1.25 3.00

2011 Topps Heritage News Flashbacks

COMPLETE SET (10) 4.00 10.00
COMMON CARD .40 1.00
STATED ODDS 1:12 HOBBY
NF8 Mets Join National League .60 1.50
NF10 Jackie Robinson Enshrined 1.00 2.50

2011 Topps Heritage Real One Autographs

STATED ODDS 1:303
EXCHANGE DEADLINE 2/28/2014
AD Art Ditmar 10.00 25.00
AJ David Wright 30.00 60.00
AK Al Kaline 50.00 120.00
BC Bob Cerv 10.00 25.00
BG Bob Gibson 40.00 80.00
BP Bill Pierce 10.00 25.00
BR Brooks Robinson 30.00 60.00
DB Don Buddin 10.00 25.00
DD Dan Dobbek 10.00 25.00
DG Dick Gernert 8.00 20.00
DGI Don Gile 6.00 15.00
DH Dave Hillman 6.00 15.00
EB Ernie Banks 40.00 80.00
EBO Ed Bouchee 8.00 20.00
EL Evan Longoria 20.00 50.00
EY Eddie Yost 6.00 15.00
FT Frank Thomas 6.00 15.00
GWI Gordon Windhorn 10.00 25.00
HA Hank Aaron 200.00 400.00
HB Howie Bedell 10.00 25.00
HN Hal Naragon 6.00 15.00
HR Hanley Ramirez 10.00 25.00
HS Hal Stowe 15.00 40.00
JA Jim Archer 10.00 25.00
JD Jim Donohue 10.00 25.00
JDE John DeMerit 8.00 20.00
JH Joe Hicks 6.00 15.00
LP Leo Posada 6.00 15.00
MK Marty Kutyna 10.00 25.00
MS Mike Stanton 20.00 50.00
NC Neil Chrisley 10.00 25.00
RR Ray Rippelmeyer 6.00 15.00
SC Starlin Castro 10.00 25.00
SK Sandy Koufax 500.00 700.00
SM Stan Musial 125.00 250.00
TP Tom Parsons 10.00 25.00
TW Ted Wills 6.00 15.00

2011 Topps Heritage Real One Autographs Red Ink

*RED: 5.X TO 1.2X BASIC
STATED ODDS 1:700 HOBBY
STATED PRINT RUN 62 SER.#'d SETS
SM Stan Musial 150.00 300.00

2011 Topps Heritage Then and Now

COMPLETE SET (10) 8.00 20.00
STATED ODDS 1:15 HOBBY
TN1 Harmon Killebrew/Jose Bautista 1.00 2.50
TN2 F.Robinson/M.Cabrera 1.00 2.50
TN3 Frank Robinson/Josh Hamilton .60 1.50
TN4 Luis Aparicio/Juan Pierre .60 1.50
TN5 M.Mantle/P.Fielder 3.00 8.00
TN6 Robin Roberts/Felix Hernandez .60 1.50
TN7 Bob Gibson/Jered Weaver .60 1.50
TN8 Juan Marichal/CC Sabathia .60 1.50
TN9 Warren Spahn/Roy Halladay .60 1.50
TN10 Bob Gibson/Roy Halladay .60 1.50

2011 Topps Heritage Triple Stamp Box Topper

RANDOMLY INSERTED BOX TOPPER
TSBL1 Jered Weaver
Torii Hunter/Dan Haren 2.50 6.00
TSBL2 Stephen Drew/Justin Upton
Miguel Montero 2.50 6.00
TSBL3 McCann/Heyward/Prado 3.00 8.00
TSBL4 Brian Matusz/Adam Jones
Nick Markakis 3.00 8.00
TSBL5 Pedroia/Ortiz/Lester 4.00 10.00
TSBL6 Alfonso Soriano
Starlin Castro/Carlos Marmol 2.50 6.00
TSBL7 Alex Rios/Gordon Beckham
Alexei Ramirez 2.50 6.00
TSBL8 Brandon Phillips
Joey Votto/Jay Bruce 4.00 10.00
TSBL9 Shin-Soo Choo/Carlos Santana
Grady Sizemore 4.00 10.00
TSBL10 Troy Tulowitzki/Carlos Gonzalez
Ubaldo Jimenez 4.00 10.00
TSBL11 Verlander/Cabrera/Jackson 4.00 10.00
TSBL12 Stntn/Rmrz/Jhnsn 4.00 10.00
TSBL13 Michael Bourn/Hunter Pence
Wandy Rodriguez 2.50 6.00
TSBL14 Billy Butler/Lorezno Cain
Joakim Soria 1.50 4.00
TSBL15 Ethier/Kershaw/Kemp 8.00 20.00
TSBL16 Fielder/Braun/Gallardo 2.50 6.00
TSBL17 Justin Morneau/Joe Mauer
Francisco Liriano 3.00 8.00
TSBL18 Santana/Wright/Reyes 3.00 8.00
TSBL19 Cano/Jeter/Sabathia 10.00 25.00
TSBL20 Brett Anderson/Trevor Cahill
Gio Gonzalez 2.50 6.00
TSBL21 Howard/Halladay/Utley 3.00 8.00
TSBL22 Tbt/McCtchn/Wlkr 4.00 10.00
TSBL23 Mat Latos/Chase Headley
Heath Bell 2.50 6.00
TSBL24 Lincecum/Posey/Wilson 5.00 12.00
TSBL25 Hernandez/Ichiro/Gutierrez 5.00 12.00
TSBL26 Holl/Pujols/Wain 5.00 12.00
TSBL27 Price/Longoria/Upton 3.00 8.00
TSBL28 Nelson Cruz/Josh Hamilton
Ian Kinsler 4.00 10.00
TSBL29 Jose Bautista/Ricky Romero
Brandon Morrow 2.50 6.00
TSBL30 Jayson Werth/Ryan Zimmerman
Ian Desmond 2.50 6.00

2012 Topps Heritage

COMP.SET w/o SPs (425) 20.00 50.00
COMP.HN.FACT.SET (101) 300.00 500.00
COMP.HN SET (100) 75.00 150.00
COMMON CARD (1-425) .15 .40
COMMON ROOKIE (1-425) .40 1.00
COMMON SP (426-500) 2.50 6.00
SP ODDS 1:3 HOBBY
ERR SP'S ARE ERROR CARDS
COMMON BW SP (1-425) 2.50 6.00
BW SP FEATURE BLACK/WHITE MAIN PHOTO
COMMON CS SP (1-425) 12.50 30.00
CS SP FEATURE COLOR VARIATIONS
COMMON HN (H576-H675) .50 1.25
COMMON HN RC (H576-H675) .60 1.50
HN FACT SETS SOLD ONLY ON TOPPS.COM
1 NL Batting Leaders .40 1.00
2 AL Batting Leaders .40 1.00
3 NL HR Leaders .50 1.25
4 Jose Bautista/Curtis Granderson/Mark
Teixeira/Mark Reynolds/Adrian Beltre/I.40 1.00
5 Kersh/Halla/Lee/Vogel/Lince LL .75 2.00
6 AL ERA Leaders .40 1.00
7 Kenn/Kersh/Halla/Gallar/Lee/Gre .75 2.00
8 AL Pitching Leaders .40 1.00
9 Kersh/Lee/Halla/Lince/Gallar LL .75 2.00
10 AL Strikeout Leaders .40 1.00
11 Francisco Rodriguez .30 .75
12 Jim Johnson .15 .40
13 Philadelphia Phillies TC .15 .40
14A Justin Masterson .25 .60
15A Darwin Barney .25 .60
15B Darwin Barney ERR SP 30.00 60.00
16 Juan Pierre .25 .60
17 Mike Moustakas .30 .75
18 David Ortiz/Adrian Gonzalez .40 1.00
19 Zach Britton .30 .75
20A Derek Jeter 1.00 2.50
20B Derek Jeter CS SP 50.00 100.00
21 Drew Stubbs .25 .60
22A Edwin Jackson .25 .60
23 Ned Yost MG .15 .40
24 Mark Melancon .25 .60
25 Delmon Young .30 .75
26 Scott Baker .25 .60
27 Josh Thole .25 .60
28 Josh Beckett .25 .60
29A Pea RC/Mes RC/De Fra RC/Sav RC.75 2.00
29B Pea/Mes/De Fra/Sav ERR SP 60.00 120.00
30 Cody Ross .25 .60
31 Jeff Samardzija .25 .60
32A Domonic Brown .30 .75
33 Tyler Chatwood .25 .60
34A Josh Collmenter .30 .75
35 Chris Sale .40 1.00
36 Jason Kipnis .30 .75
37 Yonder Alonso .25 .60
38 Andrew Brackman .15 .40
39 Bronson Arroyo .25 .60
40 Chris Parmelee .25 .60
41 John Buck .25 .60
42 David Robertson .25 .60
43 M.Rivera/J.Girardi .50 1.25
44A Justin Verlander .40 1.00
44B Justin Verlander BW SP 4.00 10.00
45 Jimmy Paredes .25 .60
46 Michael Bourn .25 .60
47 Jayson Werth .30 .75
48 Manny Acta MG .15 .40
49 Jordan Walden .25 .60
50 Madison Bumgarner .30 .75
51 Alex Gordon .30 .75
52A Dustin Pedroia .30 .75
52B Dustin Pedroia BW SP 4.00 10.00
53 Freddie Freeman .50 1.25
54A Ga RC/Re RC/Ch RC/Be RC 1.00 2.50
54B Gaub/Reed/Cham/Bet ERR SP 20.00 50.00
55 Alex Presley .25 .60
56A Cliff Lee .30 .75
56B Cliff Lee BW SP 3.00 8.00
57 Howie Kendrick .25 .60
58 Marlon Byrd .25 .60
59 R.A. Dickey .30 .75
60A Jesus Montero .25 .60
61 Aubrey Huff .25 .60
62 Eric O'Flaherty .25 .60
63 Cincinnati Reds TC .15 .40
64 Victor Martinez .30 .75
65 Nick Markakis .30 .75
66 Sergio Santos .25 .60
67 J.P. Arencibia .25 .60
68 Ryan Vogelsong/Andre Ethier .30 .75
69 Michael Morse .25 .60
70 Homer Bailey .25 .60
71 Placido Polanco .25 .60
72A Carlos Santana .30 .75
73 Fredi Gonzalez MG .15 .40
74 Randy Wolf .25 .60
75 Aaron Crow .25 .60
76A Jon Lester .25 .60
77 J.B. Shuck .15 .40
78 Daniel Murphy .30 .75
79 Kendrys Morales .25 .60
80 Jamey Carroll .25 .60
81 Geovany Soto .30 .75
82 Greg Holland .75 2.00
83A Lance Berkman .30 .75
83B Lance Berkman CS SP 20.00 50.00
84A Doug Fister .25 .60
85A Buster Posey .50 1.25
85B Buster Posey CS SP 20.00 50.00
86 Dayan Viciedo .25 .60
87A Andrew McCutchen .40 1.00
87B Andrew McCutchen CS SP 30.00 60.00
88 J.J. Hardy .25 .60
89 Liam Hendriks .25 .60
90A Joey Votto .40 1.00
90B Joey Votto CS SP 30.00 60.00
91A Roy Halladay .30 .75
91B Roy Halladay BW SP 3.00 8.00
92 Austin Romine .25 .60
93 Johan Santana .30 .75
94 Wilson Ramos .25 .60
95 Joe Benson RC/Adron Chambers RC/Corey
Brown RC/Michael Taylor RC 1.00 2.50
96A Carl Crawford .30 .75
97 Kyle Lohse .25 .60
98A Torii Hunter .30 .75
99 Wandy Rodriguez .25 .60
100A Paul Konerko .25 .60
101 Jeff Karstens .25 .60
102 Ron Washington MG .15 .40
103 Michael Brantley .25 .60
104 Danny Duffy .25 .60
105 James Loney .25 .60
106A Tim Lincecum .30 .75
106B Tim Lincecum BW SP 3.00 8.00
107 Ruben Tejada .25 .60
108 Vladimir Guerrero .30 .75
109 Wade Davis .30 .75
110 Chase Headley .25 .60
111 Jeremy Hellickson .25 .60
112 New York Mets TC .25 .60
113A Kerry Wood .25 .60
113B Kerry Wood ERR SP 10.00 25.00
114 St. Louis Cardinals TC .25 .60
115A Jacoby Ellsbury .30 .75
115B Jacoby Ellsbury CS SP 15.00 40.00
116 Vance Worley .30 .75
117 Vernon Wells .25 .60
118 A.J. Pierzynski .25 .60
119 Matt Downs .25 .60
120 Nick Swisher .30 .75
121 Drew Storen .25 .60
122A Hanley Ramirez .30 .75
123 Andre Ethier .30 .75
124 Alcides Escobar .30 .75
125 Ron Gardenhire MG .15 .40
126 Jonathan Lucroy .30 .75
127 Willie Bloomquist .25 .60
128 Seth Smith .25 .60
129 Chris Perez .25 .60
130A David Freese .25 .60
131 Kevin Gregg .25 .60
132 Cole Hamels .30 .75
133 Todd Frazier .30 .75
134 Jim Leyland MG .15 .40
135 Chris Parmelee RC/Steve Lombardozzi
RC/Pedro Florimon RC
Jordan Pacheco RC .60 1.50
136 Jonathan Papelbon .30 .75
137A Nyjer Morgan .25 .60
137B Nyjer Morgan CS SP 20.00 50.00
138 Dan Uggla/Chipper Jones .40 1.00
139 Carlos Ruiz .25 .60
140 Max Scherzer .40 1.00
141 Carlos Lee .25 .60
142 Allen Craig WS HL .30 .75
143 Neftali Feliz WS HL .25 .60
144 Albert Pujols WS HL .50 1.25
145 Derek Holland WS HL .25 .60
146 Mike Napoli WS HL .25 .60
147 David Freese WS HL .25 .60
148 St. Louis Cardinals WS HL .15 .40
149 Ian Desmond .25 .60
150 Hiroki Kuroda .25 .60
151 Pittsburgh Pirates TC .15 .40
152 Nick Hagadone .25 .60
153 Miguel Montero .25 .60
154 Don Mattingly MG .75 2.00
155 Rafael Soriano .25 .60
156 Yuniesky Betancourt .25 .60
157 Melky Cabrera .25 .60
158 Lomb RC/Flor RC
Domin RC/Mes RC .75 2.00
159 Ryan Doumit .25 .60
160 Mark Buehrle .30 .75
161 Ryan Howard .30 .75
162 Minnesota Twins TC .15 .40
163 Matt Cain .30 .75
164A Austin Jackson .30 .75
165 C.J. Wilson .25 .60
166 Kirk Gibson MG .15 .40
167 Erick Aybar .25 .60
168 Ryan Lavarnway .25 .60
169 Luis Marte RC/Brett Pill RC/Efren Navarro
RC/Jared Hughes RC 1.00 2.50
170 Lonnie Chisenhall .25 .60
171 Jordan Zimmermann .30 .75
172A Yadier Molina .40 1.00
173 Bronx Bombers Best 1.00 2.50
174A Jose Reyes .25 .60
175 Matt Garza .25 .60
176 Michael Taylor .25 .60
177A Evan Longoria .30 .75
177B Evan Longoria CS SP 20.00 50.00
178 Devin Mesoraco .25 .60
179 Shaun Marcum .25 .60
180 Mitch Moreland .25 .60
181 Brent Morel .25 .60
182 Peter Bourjos .25 .60
183A Mark Teixeira .30 .75
183B Mark Teixeira BW SP 3.00 8.00
184 Jared Hughes .25 .60
185A Freddy Sanchez .40 1.00
186A Joe Mauer .30 .75
186B Joe Mauer BW SP 3.00 8.00
187 Shelley Duncan .25 .60
188 Marco Scutaro .30 .75
189 Wilton Lopez .40 1.00
190A Matt Holliday .40 1.00
191 He RC/Li RC/Mo RC/Sc RC 1.00 2.50
192 Justin De Fratus .25 .60
193A Starlin Castro .30 .75
193B Starlin Castro BW SP 3.00 8.00
194 Francisco Cordero .25 .60
195 Desmond Jennings .30 .75
196 Tim Federowicz .25 .60
197A Ian Kennedy .25 .60
197B Ian Kennedy BW SP 3.00 8.00
198 Joe Benson .25 .60
199 Jeff Keppinger .25 .60
200A Curtis Granderson .30 .75
200B Curtis Granderson BW SP 3.00 8.00
201A Yovani Gallardo .30 .75
201B Yovani Gallardo CS SP 20.00 50.00
202 Boston Red Sox TC .25 .60
203 Scott Rolen .30 .75
204 Chris Schwinden .30 .75
205 Robert Andino .25 .60
206 Lance Lynn .25 .60
207 Mike Trout 75.00 200.00
208 Pi RC/Ch RC/Fi RC/Po RC 1.00 2.50
209 Chris Iannetta .25 .60
210A Clayton Kershaw .75 2.00
211 Mark Trumbo .25 .60
212 Carlos Marmol .25 .60
213 Buck Showalter MG .15 .40
214 Joakim Soria .25 .60
215A B.J. Upton .30 .75
215B B.J. Upton CS SP 30.00 60.00
216 Kyle Weiland .15 .40
217A Dexter Fowler .30 .75
217B Dexter Fowler CS SP 30.00 60.00
218 Tigers Twirlers .40 1.00
219 Shin-Soo Choo .30 .75
220 Ricky Romero .25 .60
221A Chase Utley .30 .75
222 Jed Lowrie .25 .60
223 Addison Reed .25 .60
224A Alex Avila .25 .60
225A Aroldis Chapman .40 1.00
226 Skip Schumaker .25 .60
227A Ubaldo Jimenez .25 .60
228 Nick Hagadone RC/Josh Satin RC/Jared Hughes
RC/Joe Benson RC .75 2.00
229 Brandon Beachy .25 .60
230 Brett Wallace .25 .60
231A Dan Haren .25 .60
231B Dan Haren ERR SP 15.00 40.00
232A Kevin Youkilis .40 1.00
233 Terry Collins MG .15 .40
234 Alejandro De Aza .25 .60
235 Ryan Vogelsong .25 .60
236 Salvador Perez .30 .75
237 Ivan Nova .30 .75
238 Jose Constanza RC .60 1.50
239 Cleveland Indians TC .15 .40
240 Andy Dirks .25 .60
241 Johnny Cueto .30 .75
242 Jay Bruce/Justin Upton .30 .75
243 Jordan Pacheco .25 .60
244 Jason Motte .25 .60
245 Lucas Duda .30 .75
246A Felix Hernandez .30 .75
246B Felix Hernandez BW SP 3.00 8.00
247 Jarrod Parker RC .75 2.00
248 Kosuke Fukudome .30 .75
249 Alberto Callaspo .25 .60
250A Jon Jay .40 1.00
251 Clay Buchholz .25 .60
252 Aramis Ramirez .25 .60
253 Po RC/Re RC/Li RC/Ta RC .60 1.50
254 Carlos Quentin .25 .60
255 John Axford .25 .60
256 Johnny Giavotella .25 .60
257 Jacob Turner .30 .75
258 Bruce Bochy MG .25 .60
259 Neil Walker .30 .75
260A Anthony Rizzo .60 1.50
261 Javy Guerra .25 .60
262 J.D. Martinez .40 1.00
263 Tyler Clippard .25 .60
264A Robinson Cano .30 .75
264B Robinson Cano CS SP 12.50 30.00
265 Adron Chambers RC/Steve Lombardozzi RC/Tim
Federowicz RC/Brad Peacock RC 1.00 2.50
266 Travis Hafner .25 .60
267 Nick Hundley .25 .60
268 Hunter Pence .30 .75
269 Justin Morneau .30 .75
270 Nate Schierholtz .25 .60
271 Alexei Ramirez .30 .75
272 David Murphy .25 .60
273 Wilin Rosario .25 .60
274 Justin De Fratus RC/Jared Hughes RC/Alex
Liddi RC/Kyle Waldrop (RC) .60 1.50
275A Dan Uggla .30 .75
276A Ryan Braun .25 .60
276B Ryan Braun BW SP 4.00 10.00
277A David Price .30 .75
277B David Price CS SP 12.50 30.00
278 Jhonny Peralta .25 .60
279A Matt Kemp .30 .75
279B Matt Kemp BW SP 3.00 8.00
280 Brett Lawrie RC .75 2.00
281 Jason Marquis .25 .60
282A Jeff Francoeur .30 .75
282B Jeff Francoeur CS SP 30.00 60.00
283 Brad Lidge .15 .40
284 Matt Harrison .25 .60
285A Adrian Gonzalez .30 .75
285B Adrian Gonzalez CS SP 12.50 30.00
286 Mi RC/Re RC/Mo RC/Be RC 1.00 2.50
287 Yorvit Torrealba .15 .40
288 Chicago White Sox TC .15 .40
289A Mariano Rivera .50 1.25
289B Mariano Rivera BW SP 3.00 8.00
290A Albert Pujols .50 1.25
290B Albert Pujols CS SP 30.00 60.00
291 Stephen Strasburg .40 1.00
292 Justin Turner .30 .75
293 Tim Stauffer .25 .60
294 Mike Scioscia MG .15 .40
295 Cory Luebke .25 .60
296A Jim Thome .30 .75
297 Derek Holland .25 .60
298 Martin Prado .25 .60
299 Steve Delabar RC/Tom Milone RC/Luis Marte
RC/Jared Hughes RC .60 1.50
300 Carlos Beltran .30 .75
301 Gio Gonzalez .30 .75
302 Brennan Boesch .25 .60
303 Alexi Ogando .25 .60
304 Brandon Phillips .25 .60
305 Ryan Roberts .25 .60
306 Yadier Molina/Brian McCann .40 1.00
307 J.J. Putz .25 .60
308 Brian McCann .30 .75
309 Ryan Dempster .25 .60
310 Jerry Sands .25 .60
311 Brad Peacock .25 .60
312 Tampa Bay Rays TC .15 .40
313 Jaime Garcia .30 .75
314 Alexi Casilla .25 .60
315 Hector Noesi .25 .60
316 Billy Butler .25 .60
317 Jason Donald .25 .60
318 Charlie Manuel MG .15 .40
319A Adam Jones .30 .75
320 Zack Greinke .30 .75
321 Po RC/Sp (RC)/Br RC/Ch RC 1.00 2.50
322 Ervin Santana .25 .60
323 Chase d'Arnaud .25 .60
324 Jesus Montero RC/Austin Romine RC/Tim
Federowicz RC/Wilin Rosario RC .60 1.50
325A Brian Wilson .40 1.00
326 Ramon Hernandez .25 .60
327 Rick Porcello .25 .60
328 Elvis Andrus .30 .75
329 Francisco Cervelli .25 .60
330 Jorge Posada .25 .60
331 World Series Foes .50 1.25
332 Jorge De La Rosa .25 .60
333 Joe Benson RC/Liam Hendriks RC/Chris
Parmelee RC/Kyle Waldrop (RC) .60 1.50
334 Mat Latos .30 .75
335 Bobby Abreu .25 .60
336 Fernando Salas .25 .60
337 Adam Dunn .30 .75
338 Brandon McCarthy .25 .60
339 Guillermo Moscoso RC .75 2.00
340 Russell Martin .25 .60
341A Ryan Madson .25 .60
341B R.Madson Red ERR SP 50.00 100.00
341C R.Madson White ERR SP 75.00 150.00
342 Chris Coghlan .25 .60
343 Joe Maddon MG .15 .40
344 Anibal Sanchez .25 .60
345 Mark Reynolds .25 .60
346 Santiago Casilla .25 .60
347 Chipper Jones .40 1.00
348A Miguel Cabrera .40 1.00
348B Miguel Cabrera BW SP 3.00 8.00
349 Alex Gonzalez .25 .60
350 Tommy Hanson .25 .60
351 Danny Espinosa .25 .60
352 Mike Adams .25 .60
353 Cameron Maybin .25 .60
354 Jemile Weeks RC .60 1.50
355 Josh Reddick .25 .60
356A Adrian Beltre .40 1.00
356B David Ortiz CS SP 60.00 120.00
357 Allen Craig .30 .75
358 Steve Delabar .25 .60
359 Cliff Pennington .25 .60
360 Chad Billingsley .25 .60
361 Alex Rodriguez .50 1.25
362 Matt Dominguez RC/Chris Schwinden RC/Joe
Savery RC/Brad Peacock RC .75 2.00
363 Aaron Harang .25 .60
364 Jose Tabata .25 .60
365 Jose Valverde .30 .75
366 Dustin Ackley .25 .60
367 Trayvon Robinson .25 .60
368 Andrew Bailey .25 .60
369 Jason Kubel .25 .60
370 Koji Uehara .25 .60
371 Brett Gardner .30 .75
372 Scott Downs .25 .60
373A Michael Young .25 .60
373B Michael Young CS SP 40.00 80.00
374 Tom Milone .25 .60
375 Daniel Descalso .25 .60
376 Trevor Cahill .25 .60
377 Baltimore Orioles TC .15 .40
378 Jeff Niemann .25 .60
379 Joaquin Benoit .25 .60
380A Carlos Pena .30 .75
380B Carlos Pena ERR VAR SP 75.00 150.00
381 Blake Beavan .25 .60
382 Joe Girardi MG .25 .60
383 Jason Vargas .25 .60
384 Blake DeWitt .15 .40
385 Logan Morrison .25 .60
386 Mo RC/Br RC/Ro RC/Be RC 1.00 2.50
387 Ricky Nolasco .25 .60
388 Pablo Sandoval .30 .75
389 Drew Pomeranz .25 .60
390 Jason Heyward .30 .75
391 Matt Moore RC 1.00 2.50
392 Asdrubal Cabrera/Carlos Santana.30 .75
393 Clint Hurdle MG .15 .40
394 Tim Hudson .30 .75
395 Daniel Hudson .25 .60
396 Emilio Bonifacio .25 .60
397 Kansas City Royals TC .15 .40
398 Craig Kimbrel .30 .75
399 Mike Minor .25 .60
400 Jay Bruce .30 .75
401 Freddy Garcia .25 .60
402 Davey Johnson MG .15 .40
403 Colby Lewis .25 .60
404 Adam Lind .30 .75
405 Michael Pineda .25 .60
406 Al Alburquerque .15 .40
407 Domin RC/Moore RC
Meso RC/Taylor RC .75 2.00
408A Ian Kinsler .30 .75
408B Ian Kinsler CS SP 20.00 50.00
409 Jair Jurrjens .25 .60
410 Jesus Guzman .25 .60
411 Nathan Eovaldi .30 .75
412 Kemp/Ethier/Kershaw .75 2.00
413 Huston Street .25 .60
414A Corey Hart .25 .60
414B Corey Hart CS SP 20.00 50.00
415A Chris Carpenter .30 .75
415B Chris Carpenter BW SP 3.00 8.00
415C Chris Carpenter CS SP 30.00 60.00
416 Stephen Drew .25 .60
417 Jeremy Guthrie .25 .60
418 Johnny Damon .30 .75
419 Casey Janssen .15 .40
420 Eduardo Nunez .25 .60
421 Kyle Farnsworth .30 .75
422 Dusty Baker MG .15 .40
423 Neftali Feliz .25 .60
424 Matt Dominguez .30 .75
425 Wilson Betemit .25 .60
426 Frank Francisco SP 2.50 6.00
427 Dee Gordon SP 3.00 8.00
428 Eric Thames SP 2.50 6.00
429 Jonny Venters SP 2.50 6.00
430 Ben Zobrist SP 2.50 6.00
431 Jerry Hairston SP 2.50 6.00
432 Matt Joyce SP 2.50 6.00
433 Rickie Weeks SP 3.00 8.00
434 Shane Victorino SP 3.00 8.00
435 Asdrubal Cabrera SP 3.00 8.00
436 Ike Davis SP 3.00 8.00
437 Chris Denorfia SP 2.50 6.00
438 Juan Nicasio SP 2.50 6.00
439 Aaron Miles SP 2.50 6.00
440 Jonathan Sanchez SP 2.50 6.00
441 Paul Goldschmidt SP 3.00 8.00
442 Jason Bartlett SP 2.50 6.00
443 Endy Chavez SP 2.50 6.00
444 Brandon League SP 2.50 6.00
445A Gaby Sanchez SP 2.50 6.00
446 CC Sabathia SP 3.00 8.00
447 Jose Iglesias SP 2.50 6.00
448 Heath Bell SP 3.00 8.00
449 Gerardo Parra SP 2.50 6.00
450 Leo Nunez SP 2.50 6.00
451 Steve Lombardozzi SP 2.50 6.00
452 Fautino De Los Santos SP 2.50 6.00
453A Troy Tulowitzki SP 3.00 8.00
453B Troy Tulowitzki BW SP 3.00 8.00
454A Julio Teheran SP 2.50 6.00
454B Julio Teheran ERR SP 40.00 80.00
455 Jimmy Rollins SP 3.00 8.00
456 Greg Dobbs SP 2.50 6.00
457 Dellin Betances SP 3.00 8.00
458 Adron Chambers SP 3.00 8.00
459 Alex Liddi SP 3.00 8.00
460 Brett Pill SP 3.00 8.00
461 Jose Altuve SP 2.50 6.00
462 Chris Young SP 2.50 6.00
463 Edwin Encarnacion SP 2.50 6.00
464 Omar Infante SP 2.50 6.00
465 John Mayberry Jr. SP 2.50 6.00
466 Kyle Seager SP 2.50 6.00
467 David Wright SP 4.00 10.00
468A Nelson Cruz SP 3.00 8.00
468B Nelson Cruz BW SP 3.00 8.00
468C Nelson Cruz CS SP 12.50 30.00
469 Jeremy Affeldt SP 2.50 6.00
470 Ben Revere SP 3.00 8.00
471 Yunel Escobar SP 2.50 6.00
472 Alfonso Soriano SP 3.00 8.00
473 Carlos Zambrano SP 3.00 8.00
474 Barry Zito SP 2.50 6.00
475 Jason Bay SP 3.00 8.00
476A Prince Fielder SP 3.00 8.00

476B Prince Fielder BW SP 3.00 8.00
477 Derrek Lee SP 2.50 6.00
478 Roy Oswalt SP 3.00 8.00
479 Eric Hosmer SP 4.00 10.00
480A Carlos Gonzalez SP 3.00 8.00
480B Carlos Gonzalez CS SP 20.00 50.00
481A Justin Upton SP 3.00 8.00
481B Justin Upton BW SP 3.00 8.00
482 David Ortiz SP 3.00 8.00
483A Mike Stanton SP 3.00 8.00
483B Mike Stanton BW SP 3.00 8.00
483D Stntn ERR VAR SP 60.00 120.00
484A Todd Helton SP 3.00 8.00
485A Mike Napoli SP 3.00 8.00
485B Mike Napoli CS SP 20.00 50.00
486A Josh Hamilton SP 3.00 8.00
486B Josh Hamilton BW SP 3.00 8.00
487 Casey Kotchman SP 2.50 6.00
488 Ryan Adams SP 2.50 6.00
489A Jose Bautista SP 3.00 8.00
489B Jose Bautista BW SP 3.00 8.00
490 Brandon Belt SP 3.00 8.00
491 Ichiro Suzuki SP 4.00 10.00
492 Joel Hanrahan SP 2.50 6.00
493 Josh Willingham SP 2.50 6.00
494A Ryan Zimmerman SP 3.00 8.00
494B Ryan Zimmerman BW SP 3.00 8.00
495A James Shields SP 2.50 6.00
495B James Shields CS SP 12.00 30.00
496 Josh Johnson SP 3.00 8.00
497A Jered Weaver SP 2.50 6.00
497B Jered Weaver BW SP 2.50 6.00
498 Jhoulys Chacin SP 2.50 6.00
499 Jason Bourgeois SP 2.50 6.00
500 Michael Cuddyer SP 2.50 6.00
H576 Adam Wainwright 1.00 2.50
H577 Tsuyoshi Wada RC 1.00 2.50
H578 J.A. Happ 1.00 2.50
H579 Brian Matusz .75 2.00
H580 Chris Capuano .75 2.00
H581 Cody Ross .75 2.00
H582 Jarrod Saltalamacchia .75 2.00
H583 Ryan Hanigan .75 2.00
H584 Wade Miley 1.00 2.50
H585 Jonathon Niese .75 2.00
H586 Mike Aviles .75 2.00
H587 Bryan LaHair .75 2.00
H588 Jake Arrieta 1.00 2.50
H589 Hisashi Iwakuma RC 2.00 5.00
H590 Garrett Richards RC 1.50 4.00
H591 John Danks .75 2.00
H592 Brandon Morrow .75 2.00
H593 Ernesto Frieri .75 2.00
H594 Kenley Jansen 1.00 2.50
H595 Felix Doubront .75 2.00
H596 Vinnie Pestano .75 2.00
H597 Jake Peavy .75 2.00
H598 Jonathan Broxton .75 2.00
H599 Brian Dozier RC 3.00 8.00
H600 Yu Darvish RC 2.50 6.00
H601 Philip Humber .75 2.00
H602 Derek Lowe .75 2.00
H603 Drew Smyly RC 1.00 2.50
H604 Matt Capps .75 2.00
H605 Jamie Moyer .75 2.00
H606 Ichiro Suzuki 1.50 4.00
H607 Jerome Williams .75 2.00
H608 Bruce Chen .75 2.00
H609 Wei-Yin Chen RC 2.50 6.00
H610 Joe Saunders .75 2.00
H611 Alfredo Aceves .75 2.00
H612 Tyler Pastornicky RC 1.00 2.50
H613 Angel Pagan .75 2.00
H614 Juan Pierre .75 2.00
H615 Pedro Alvarez .75 2.00
H616 Sean Marshall .75 2.00
H617 Jack Hannahan .75 2.00
H618 Brett Myers .75 2.00
H619 Zack Cozart (RC) 1.00 2.50
H620 Fernando Rodney .75 2.00
H621 Chris Davis .75 2.00
H622 Reed Johnson .75 2.00
H623 Gordon Beckham .75 2.00
H624 Andrew Cashner .75 2.00
H625 Alex Rios 1.00 2.50
H626 Lorenzo Cain .75 2.00
H627 Wily Peralta RC 1.00 2.50
H628 Andres Torres .75 2.00
H629 Andruw Jones .75 2.00
H630 Denard Span .75 2.00
H631 Raul Ibanez 1.00 2.50
H632 Ryan Sweeney .75 2.00
H633 Cesar Izturis .75 2.00
H634 Chris Getz .75 2.00
H635 Francisco Liriano .75 2.00
H636 Daniel Bard .75 2.00
H637 Daisuke Matsuzaka 1.00 2.50
H638 Matt Adams RC 8.00 20.00
H639 Andy Pettitte 1.00 2.50
H640 Norichika Aoki RC 1.25 3.00
H641 Jordany Valdespin RC 1.25 3.00
H642 Andrelton Simmons RC 1.50 4.00
H643 Johnny Damon 1.00 2.50
H644 Colby Rasmus 1.00 2.50
H645 Bartolo Colon .50 1.25
H646 Kirk Nieuwenhuis RC 1.00 2.50
H647 A.J. Burnett .75 2.00
H648 Edinson Volquez .75 2.00
H649 Jake Westbrook .75 2.00
H650 Bryce Harper RC 250.00 500.00
H651 Will Middlebrooks RC 1.25 3.00
H652 Yoenis Cespedes RC 2.50 6.00
H653 Grant Balfour .75 2.00
H654 Edwin Jackson .75 2.00
H655 Henry Rodriguez .75 2.00
H656 Brandon Inge .75 2.00
H657 Trevor Bauer RC 3.00 8.00
H658 Chris Iannetta .75 2.00
H659 Garrett Jones .75 2.00
H660 Matt Hague RC 1.00 2.50
H661 Rafael Furcal .75 2.00
H662 Luke Scott .75 2.00
H663 Kelly Johnson .75 2.00
H664 Jonny Gomes .75 2.00
H665 Sean Rodriguez .75 2.00
H666 Carl Pavano .75 2.00
H667 Joe Nathan .75 2.00
H668 Juan Uribe .75 2.00
H669 Bobby Abreu .75 2.00
H670 Marco Scutaro 1.00 2.50
H671 Gavin Floyd .75 2.00
H672 Ted Lilly .75 2.00
H673 Drew Hutchison RC 1.25 3.00
H674 Leonys Martin RC 1.00 2.50
H675 Adam LaRoche .75 2.00

2012 Topps Heritage '63 Mint

STATED ODDS 1:288 HOBBY
JFK STATED ODDS 1:26,520 HOBBY
EXCHANGE DEADLINE 02/28/2015
63AK Al Kaline EXCH 15.00 40.00
63AZ Alcatraz 10.00 25.00
63BG Bob Gibson EXCH 10.00 25.00
63CY Carl Yastrzemski EXCH 25.00 60.00
63DS Duke Snider EXCH 15.00 40.00
63EM Eddie Mathews 20.00 50.00
63EMZ Edgar Martinez 8.00 20.00
63JFK John F. Kennedy EXCH 100.00 200.00
63JM Juan Marichal 12.50 30.00
63JM Joe Morgan 10.00 25.00
63MM Mickey Mantle EXCH 50.00 100.00
63PO Paul O'Neill 12.50 30.00
63RC Bob Clemente 40.00 80.00
63SK Sandy Koufax 20.00 50.00
63SM Stan Musial 20.00 50.00
63UA University of Alabama 8.00 20.00
63WF Whitey Ford EXCH 20.00 50.00
63WM Willie Mays 40.00 80.00
63WS Willie Stargell EXCH 15.00 40.00
63WS Warren Spahn EXCH 20.00 50.00
63YB Yogi Berra EXCH 20.00 50.00

2012 Topps Heritage Advertising Panels

ISSUED AS A BOX TOPPER
1 Bobby Abreu .75 2.00
Desmond Jennings
Allen Craig
2 AL HR Leader 1.00 2.50
Matt Holliday
Ramon Hernandez
3 AL Pitching Leaders .60 1.50
Tim Federowicz
Ron Washington
4 Bronson Arroyo .75 2.00
Cameron Maybin
Craig Kimbrel
5 Joaquin Benoit .75 2.00
Placido Polanco
Nathan Eovaldi
6 Joe Benson 1.00 2.50
Adron Chambers
Corey Brown
Michael Taylor
Jon Jay
Dodgers Big Three
7 Wilson Betemit .60 1.50
David Freese
Drew Pomeranz
8 Emilio Bonifacio .75 2.00
Johan Santana
Tom Milone
9 Alexi Casilla .75 2.00
Craig Pinches Rangers In Opener
Adrian Gonzalez
10 Josh Collmenter .75 2.00
Joaquin Benoit
Placido Polanco
11 Allen Craig .75 2.00
Edwin Jackson
Blake DeWitt
12 Craig Pinches Rangers In Opener 1.00 2.50
Adrian Gonzalez
Joe Benson
Adron Chambers
Corey Brown
Michael Taylor
13 Justin De Fratus .60 1.50
Wilson Betemit
David Freese
14 Deep Freese Makes Texas Toast .75 2.00
Jim Thome
Matt Dominguez
Jeremy Moore
Devin Mesoraco
Michael Taylor
15 Ian Desmond .75 2.00
Jesus Guzman
Vladimir Guerrero
16 Matt Dominguez 1.00 2.50
Jeremy Moore
Devin Mesoraco
Michael Taylor
Brad Lidge
Brett Pill
Ardon Chambers
Thomas Field
Drew Pomeranz
17 Tim Federowicz .60 1.50
Ron Washington
Lance Lynn
18 Rafael Finishes Off For Texas .60 1.50
Yorvit Torrealba
Ryan Dempster
19 Frmn/Cvlli/Arncba 1.25 3.00
20 David Freese .60 1.50
Drew Pomeranz
Liam Hendricks
21 Adrian Gonzalez 1.00 2.50
Joe Benson
Adron Chambers
Corey Brown
Michael Taylor
Jon Jay
22 Kevin Gregg .75 2.00
Emilio Bonifacio
Johan Santana
23 Vladimir Guerrero .75 2.00
Jason Vargas
J.B. Shuck
24 Jesus Guzman .75 2.00
Vladimir Guerrero
Jason Vargas
25 Jeremy Hellickson .75 2.00
Cliff Pennington
Josh Collmenter
26 Ramon Hernandez .60 1.50
Ryan Roberts
Justin De Fratus
Jared Hughes
Alex Liddi
Kyle Waldrop
27 Matt Holliday 1.00 2.50
Ramon Hernandez
Ryan Roberts
28 Jared Hughes .60 1.50
AL Pitching Leaders
Tim Federowicz
29 Edwin Jackson .60 1.50
Blake DeWitt
Kendrys Morales
30 Desmond Jennings .75 2.00
Allen Craig
Edwin Jackson
31 Davey Johnson .60 1.50
Jordan Pacheco
Jim Leyland
32 Clayton Kershaw 2.00 5.00
NL ERA Leaders
Justin De Fratus
33 Craig Kimbrel .75 2.00
Alexi Casilla
Craig Pinches Rangers In Opener
34 Jason Kubel .75 2.00
Jordan Walden
Mat Latos
35 Mat Latos .75 2.00
Jeremy Hellickson
Cliff Pennington
36 Ldge/Pill/Chmbrs/Fld/Mrntz 1.00 2.50
37 Wilson Lopez .60 1.50
Veteran Masters
Ian Desmond
38 Steve Lombardozzi .75 2.00
Pedro Florimon
Matt Dominguez
Devin Mesoraco
Carlos Quentin
Kirk Gibson
39 Carlos Marmol .60 1.50
NL Home Run Leaders
Wilton Lopez
40 Mrtnz/Hrdle/Cnstnza 1.00 2.50
41 Don Mattingly 2.00 5.00
Carlos Marmol
NL Home Run Leaders
42 Joe Mauer .75 2.00
Red Sox Smashers
Kevin Gregg
43 Cameron Maybin .75 2.00
Craig Kimbrel
Alexei Casilla
44 Milone/Freeman/Cervelli 1.25 3.00
45 Yadier Molina 1.00 2.50
Bobby Abreu
Desmond Jennings
46 Jesus Montero .60 1.50
Austin Romine
Tim Federowicz
Wilin Rosario
David Murphy
Feliz Finishes Off For Texas
47 Kendrys Morales .75 2.00
Michael Pineda
Tim Lincecum
48 Mitch Moreland .75 2.00
Deep Freese Makes Texas Toast
Jim Thome
49 David Murphy .60 1.50
Feliz Finishes Off For Texas
Yorvit Torrealba
50 NL Batting Leaders .75 2.00
Joe Mauer
Red Sox Smashers
51 NL ERA Leaders .60 1.50
Justin De Fratus
Wilson Betemit
52 NL Home Run Leaders .40 1.00
Wilton Lopez
Veteran Masters
53 Jordan Pacheco 2.00 5.00
Jim Leyland
Clayton Kershaw
54 Jarrod Parker 1.00 2.50
Nate Spears
Corey Brown
Drew Pomeranz
Adron Chambers
Nate Schierholtz
55 Brad Peacock 1.00 2.50
Devin Mesoraco
Justin DeFratus
Joe Savery
Jarrod Parker
Nate Spears
Corey Brown
Drew Pomeranz
Adron Chambers
56 Pill/Chmbrs/Fld/Pmrnz/Mrtnz/Hrdle 1.00 2.50
57 Michael Pineda .75 2.00
Tim Lincecum
Eduardo Nunez
58 Placido Polanco .75 2.00
Nathan Eovaldi
Wade Davis
59 Power Plus .60 1.50
Michael Taylor
AL Home Run Leaders
60 Pride of NL .60 1.50
Rafael Soriano
Power Plus
61 Carlos Quentin .60 1.50
Kirk Gibson
Joakim Soria
62 Hanely Ramirez .60 1.50
Jesus Montero
Austin Romine
Tim Federowicz
Wilin Rosario
David Murphy
63 Red Sox Smashers .60 1.50
Kevin Gregg
Emilio Bonifacio
64 Ryan Roberts .60 1.50
Justin De Fratus
Jared Hughes
Alex Liddi
Kyle Waldrop
Nick Hundley
65 Santana/Milone/Freeman 1.25 3.00
66 Rafael Soriano .60 1.50
Power Plus
Michael Taylor
67 Nate Spears 1.00 2.50
Corey Brown
Drew Pomeranz
Adron Chambers
Nate Schierholtz
Tigers Twirlers
68 Jose Tabata .60 1.50
Bronson Arroyo
Cameron Maybin
69 Michael Taylor 1.00 2.50
AL Home Run Leaders
Matt Holliday
70 Jim Thome .75 2.00
Matt Dominguez
Jeremy Moore
Devin Mesoraco
Michael Taylor
Brad Lidge
71 Yorvit Torrealba .75 2.00
Ryan Dempster
Steve Lombardozzi
Pedro Florimon
Matt Dominguez
Devin Mesoraco
72 Veteran Masters .60 1.50
Ian Desmond
Jesus Guzman
73 Jordan Walden .75 2.00
Mat Latos
Jeremy Hellickson
74 Ron Washington .75 2.00
Lance Lynn
Brad Peacock
Devin Mesoraco
Justin De Fratus
Joe Savery
75 World Series Foes .60 1.50
Mitch Moreland
Deep Freese Makes Texas Toast

2012 Topps Heritage Baseball Flashbacks

COMPLETE SET (10) 6.00 15.00
STATED ODDS 1:12 HOBBY
AK Al Kaline 1.00 2.50
EB Ernie Banks 1.00 2.50
EW Early Wynn .60 1.50
HA Hank Aaron 2.00 5.00
JM Juan Marichal .60 1.50
SK Sandy Koufax 2.00 5.00
SM Stan Musial 1.50 4.00
WM Willie Mays 2.00 5.00
SKO Sandy Koufax 2.00 5.00
WMC Willie McCovey .60 1.50

2012 Topps Heritage Black

INSERTED IN RETAIL PACKS
HP1 Matt Kemp 1.50 4.00
HP2 Ryan Braun 1.25 3.00
HP3 Adrian Gonzalez 1.50 4.00
HP4 Jacoby Ellsbury 1.50 4.00
HP5 Miguel Cabrera 2.00 5.00
HP6 Joey Votto 2.00 5.00
HP7 Curtis Granderson 1.50 4.00
HP8 Albert Pujols 2.50 6.00
HP9 Dustin Pedroia 1.50 4.00
HP10 Robinson Cano 1.50 4.00
HP11 Michael Young 1.25 3.00
HP12 Alex Gordon 1.50 4.00
HP13 Lance Berkman 1.50 4.00
HP14 Paul Konerko 1.25 3.00
HP15 Ian Kinsler 1.50 4.00
HP16 Aramis Ramirez 1.25 3.00
HP17 Hunter Pence 1.50 4.00
HP18 Jose Reyes 1.50 4.00
HP19 Hanley Ramirez 1.50 4.00
HP20 Victor Martinez 1.50 4.00
HP21 Ryan Howard 1.50 4.00
HP22 Melky Cabrera 1.25 3.00
HP23 Nick Swisher 1.50 4.00
HP24 Jay Bruce 1.50 4.00
HP25 Michael Bourn 1.25 3.00
HP26 Billy Butler 1.25 3.00
HP27 Dan Uggla 1.50 4.00
HP28 Evan Longoria 1.50 4.00
HP29 Adrian Beltre 2.00 5.00
HP30 Elvis Andrus 1.50 4.00
HP31 Mark Reynolds 1.25 3.00
HP32 Neil Walker 1.50 4.00
HP33 Derek Jeter 5.00 12.00
HP34 Torii Hunter 1.50 4.00
HP35 Nick Markakis 1.50 4.00
HP36 Howie Kendrick 1.25 3.00
HP37 Nyjer Morgan 1.25 3.00
HP38 Andre Ethier 1.50 4.00
HP39 Chris Iannetta 1.25 3.00
HP40 Austin Jackson 1.50 4.00
HP41 J.J. Hardy 1.25 3.00
HP42 Danny Espinosa 1.25 3.00
HP43 Alex Rodriguez 2.50 6.00
HP44 Marco Scutaro 1.50 4.00
HP45 Adam Jones 1.50 4.00
HP46 Jayson Werth 1.50 4.00
HP47 Ian Kennedy 1.25 3.00
HP48 Cole Hamels 1.50 4.00
HP49 Josh Beckett 1.25 3.00
HP50 Dan Haren 1.25 3.00
HP51 Ricky Romero 1.25 3.00
HP52 Tim Lincecum 1.50 4.00
HP53 Matt Cain 1.50 4.00
HP54 Felix Hernandez 1.50 4.00
HP55 Doug Fister 1.25 3.00
HP56 Johnny Cueto 1.50 4.00
HP57 Jeremy Hellickson 1.25 3.00
HP58 Justin Masterson 1.25 3.00
HP59 Jon Lester 1.25 3.00
HP60 Tim Hudson 1.50 4.00
HP61 David Price 1.50 4.00
HP62 Daniel Hudson 1.25 3.00
HP63 Vance Worley 1.50 4.00
HP64 Jair Jurrjens 1.25 3.00
HP65 Gio Gonzalez 1.25 3.00
HP66 Madison Bumgarner 1.50 4.00
HP67 Shaun Marcum 1.25 3.00
HP68 Ervin Santana 1.25 3.00
HP69 Ryan Vogelsong 1.25 3.00
HP70 Yovani Gallardo 1.50 4.00
HP71 Matt Harrison 1.50 4.00
HP72 Randy Wolf 1.25 3.00
HP73 Zack Greinke 1.50 4.00
HP74 Derek Holland 1.50 4.00
HP75 Jordan Zimmermann 1.50 4.00
HP76 Hiroki Kuroda 1.25 3.00
HP77 Mark Teixeira 1.50 4.00
HP78 Carlos Beltran 1.50 4.00
HP79 Andrew McCutchen 2.00 5.00
HP80 Starlin Castro 1.50 4.00
HP81 Matt Holliday 2.00 5.00
HP82 Pablo Sandoval 1.50 4.00
HP83 Michael Morse 1.25 3.00
HP84 Brandon Phillips 1.25 3.00
HP85 Alex Avila 1.25 3.00
HP86 Carlos Santana 1.50 4.00
HP87 Chris Carpenter 1.50 4.00
HP88 Max Scherzer 2.00 5.00
HP89 Rick Porcello 1.25 3.00
HP90 Jaime Garcia 1.50 4.00
HP91 Michael Pineda 1.25 3.00
HP92 AL Batting Leaders 2.00 5.00
HP93 NL Home Run Leaders 2.50 6.00
HP94 Kenn/Kersh/Halla/Gallar/Lee/Gre 4.00 10.00
HP95 AL Pitching Leaders 2.00 5.00
HP96 Ga/Re/Ch/Be 2.00 5.00
HP97 Steve Lombardozzi/Pedro Florimon/Matt Dominguez/Devin Mesoraco 1.50 4.00
HP98 Pi/Ch/Fi/Pom 2.00 5.00
HP99 Mil/Ree/Moo/Bet 2.00 5.00
HP100 Chris Parmelee/Steve Lombardozzi/Pedro Florimon/Jordan Pacheco 1.25 3.00

2012 Topps Heritage Chrome

COMPLETE SET (100) 150.00 300.00
STATED ODDS 1:11 HOBBY
STATED PRINT RUN 1963 SER.#'d SETS
HP1 Matt Kemp 2.00 5.00
HP2 Ryan Braun 1.50 4.00
HP3 Adrian Gonzalez 2.00 5.00
HP4 Jacoby Ellsbury 2.00 5.00
HP5 Miguel Cabrera 2.50 6.00
HP6 Joey Votto 2.50 6.00
HP7 Curtis Granderson 2.00 5.00
HP8 Albert Pujols 3.00 8.00
HP9 Dustin Pedroia 2.00 5.00
HP10 Robinson Cano 2.00 5.00
HP11 Michael Young 1.50 4.00
HP12 Alex Gordon 2.00 5.00
HP13 Lance Berkman 2.00 5.00
HP14 Paul Konerko 1.50 4.00
HP15 Ian Kinsler 2.00 5.00
HP16 Aramis Ramirez 1.50 4.00
HP17 Hunter Pence 2.00 5.00
HP18 Jose Reyes 2.00 5.00
HP19 Hanley Ramirez 2.00 5.00
HP20 Victor Martinez 2.00 5.00
HP21 Ryan Howard 2.00 5.00
HP22 Melky Cabrera 1.50 4.00
HP23 Nick Swisher 2.00 5.00
HP24 Jay Bruce 2.00 5.00
HP25 Michael Bourn 1.50 4.00
HP26 Billy Butler 1.50 4.00
HP27 Dan Uggla 2.00 5.00
HP28 Evan Longoria 2.00 5.00
HP29 Adrian Beltre 2.50 6.00
HP30 Elvis Andrus 2.00 5.00
HP31 Mark Reynolds 1.50 4.00
HP32 Neil Walker 2.00 5.00
HP33 Derek Jeter 6.00 15.00
HP34 Torii Hunter 2.00 5.00
HP35 Nick Markakis 2.00 5.00
HP36 Howie Kendrick 1.50 4.00
HP37 Nyjer Morgan 1.50 4.00
HP38 Andre Ethier 2.00 5.00
HP39 Chris Iannetta 1.50 4.00
HP40 Austin Jackson 2.00 5.00
HP41 J.J. Hardy 1.50 4.00
HP42 Danny Espinosa 1.50 4.00
HP43 Alex Rodriguez 3.00 8.00
HP44 Marco Scutaro 2.00 5.00
HP45 Adam Jones 2.00 5.00
HP46 Jayson Werth 2.00 5.00
HP47 Ian Kennedy 1.50 4.00
HP48 Cole Hamels 2.00 5.00
HP49 Josh Beckett 1.50 4.00
HP50 Dan Haren 1.50 4.00
HP51 Ricky Romero 1.50 4.00
HP52 Tim Lincecum 2.00 5.00
HP53 Matt Cain 2.00 5.00
HP54 Felix Hernandez 2.00 5.00
HP55 Doug Fister 1.50 4.00
HP56 Johnny Cueto 2.00 5.00
HP57 Jeremy Hellickson 1.50 4.00
HP58 Justin Masterson 1.50 4.00
HP59 Jon Lester 1.50 4.00
HP60 Tim Hudson 2.00 5.00
HP61 David Price 2.00 5.00
HP62 Daniel Hudson 1.50 4.00
HP63 Vance Worley 2.00 5.00
HP64 Jair Jurrjens 1.50 4.00
HP65 Gio Gonzalez 1.50 4.00
HP66 Madison Bumgarner 2.00 5.00
HP67 Shaun Marcum 1.50 4.00
HP68 Ervin Santana 1.50 4.00
HP69 Ryan Vogelsong 1.50 4.00
HP70 Yovani Gallardo 2.00 5.00
HP71 Matt Harrison 2.00 5.00
HP72 Randy Wolf 1.50 4.00
HP73 Zack Greinke 2.00 5.00
HP74 Derek Holland 1.50 4.00
HP75 Jordan Zimmermann 2.00 5.00
HP76 Hiroki Kuroda 1.50 4.00
HP77 Mark Teixeira 2.00 5.00
HP78 Carlos Beltran 2.00 5.00
HP79 Andrew McCutchen 2.50 6.00
HP80 Starlin Castro 2.00 5.00
HP81 Matt Holliday 2.50 6.00
HP82 Pablo Sandoval 2.00 5.00
HP83 Michael Morse 1.50 4.00
HP84 Brandon Phillips 1.50 4.00
HP85 Alex Avila 1.50 4.00
HP86 Carlos Santana 2.00 5.00
HP87 Chris Carpenter 2.00 5.00
HP88 Max Scherzer 2.50 6.00
HP89 Rick Porcello 1.50 4.00
HP90 Jaime Garcia 2.00 5.00
HP91 Michael Pineda 1.50 4.00
HP92 AL Batting Leaders 2.50 6.00
HP93 NL HR Leaders 3.00 8.00
HP94 Kenn/Kersh/Halla/Gallar/Lee/Gre 5.00 12.00
HP95 AL ERA Leaders 2.50 6.00
HP96 Gaub/Reed/Chamb/Betan 2.50 6.00
HP97 Lomb/Florimon/Doming/Mesor 2.00 5.00
HP98 Pill/Chamb/Field/Pomeranz 2.50 6.00
HP99 Milone/Reed/Moore/Betan 2.50 6.00
HP100 Chris Parmelee/Steve Lombardozzi/Pedro Florimon/Jordan Pacheco 1.50 4.00

2012 Topps Heritage Chrome Black Refractors

*BLACK REF: 4X TO 10X BASIC
STATED ODDS 1:329 HOBBY
STATED PRINT RUN 63 SER.#'d SETS
HP1 Matt Kemp 20.00 50.00
HP4 Jacoby Ellsbury 15.00 40.00
HP10 Robinson Cano 40.00 80.00
HP48 Cole Hamels 15.00 40.00
HP55 Doug Fister 12.50 30.00
HP58 Justin Masterson 15.00 40.00
HP64 Jair Jurrjens 20.00 50.00
HP84 Brandon Phillips 15.00 40.00
HP85 Alex Avila 30.00 60.00
HP89 Rick Porcello 15.00 40.00
HP93 NL HR Leaders 30.00 60.00
HP95 AL ERA Leaders 15.00 40.00
HP96 Gaub/Reed/Chamb/Betan 25.00 60.00
HP97 Lomb/Florimon/Doming/Mesor 20.00 50.00
HP98 Pill/Chamb/Field/Pomeranz 20.00 50.00
HP100 Parm/Lomb/Flor/Pacheco 12.50 30.00

2012 Topps Heritage Chrome Refractors

*REF: .6X TO 1.5X BASIC
STATED ODDS 1:37 HOBBY
STATED PRINT RUN 563 SER.#'d SETS

2012 Topps Heritage Clubhouse Collection Dual Relics

STATED ODDS 1:9280 HOBBY
STATED PRINT RUN 63 SER.#'d SETS
BC E.Banks/S.Castro 30.00 80.00
KC A.Kaline/M.Cabrera 30.00 60.00
MG R.Maris/C.Granderson 30.00 60.00
MP W.Mays/B.Posey 60.00 150.00
YE Yastrzemski/Ellsbury 50.00 100.00

2012 Topps Heritage Clubhouse Collection Relics

The short printed cards in this insert set are designed vertically and feature black and white photographs. They are also serial numbered to 63. The regularly inserted cards are desigend horizontally, feature color photography and are not serial numbered.

STATED ODDS 1:29 HOBBY
SP VAR PRINT RUN 63 SER.#'d SETS
AB Adrian Beltre 3.00 8.00
AC Aroldis Chapman 3.00 8.00
AJ Adam Jones 3.00 8.00
AM Andrew McCutchen 3.00 8.00
AR Aramis Ramirez 3.00 8.00
BJU B.J. Upton 3.00 8.00
BPH Brandon Phillips 3.00 8.00
CB Carlos Beltran 3.00 8.00
CC1 Chris Carpenter 3.00 8.00
CC2 Chris Carpenter SP 15.00 40.00
CCR Carl Crawford 3.00 8.00
CGO Carlos Gonzalez 3.00 8.00
CH Cole Hamels 4.00 10.00
CJW C.J. Wilson 3.00 8.00
CL1 Cliff Lee 4.00 10.00
CL2 Cliff Lee SP 8.00 20.00
CS Carlos Santana 3.00 8.00
CU Chase Utley 4.00 10.00
DH Dan Haren 3.00 8.00
DHU Daniel Hudson 3.00 8.00
DO1 David Ortiz 3.00 8.00
DO2 David Ortiz SP 20.00 50.00
DP1 Dustin Pedroia 4.00 10.00
DP2 Dustin Pedroia SP 20.00 50.00
DPR David Price 3.00 8.00
DU Dan Uggla 3.00 8.00
DW David Wright 3.00 8.00
EA Elvis Andrus 3.00 8.00
EL1 Evan Longoria 3.00 8.00
EL2 Evan Longoria SP 30.00 60.00
FH1 Felix Hernandez 3.00 8.00
FH2 Felix Hernandez SP 10.00 25.00
HP Hunter Pence 4.00 10.00
IK1 Ian Kennedy 3.00 8.00
IK2 Ian Kennedy SP 12.50 30.00
JB1 Jose Bautista 3.00 8.00
JB2 Jose Bautista SP 20.00 50.00
JBR Jay Bruce 3.00 8.00
JE1 Jacoby Ellsbury 5.00 12.00
JE2 Jacoby Ellsbury SP 20.00 50.00
JG Jaime Garcia 3.00 8.00
JH1 Josh Hamilton 4.00 10.00
JH2 Josh Hamilton SP 20.00 50.00
JM1 Joe Mauer 4.00 10.00
JM2 Joe Mauer SP 12.50 30.00
JR Jose Reyes 3.00 8.00
JRO Jimmy Rollins 4.00 10.00
JS James Shields 3.00 8.00
JU1 Justin Upton 3.00 8.00
JU2 Justin Upton SP 10.00 25.00
JV Justin Verlander 12.50 30.00
JW1 Jered Weaver 3.00 8.00
JW2 Jered Weaver SP 12.50 30.00
JWE Jayson Werth 3.00 8.00
LM Logan Morrison 3.00 8.00
MB Madison Bumgarner 4.00 10.00
MC1 Miguel Cabrera 4.00 10.00
MC2 Miguel Cabrera SP 15.00 40.00
MCA Matt Cain 3.00 8.00
MCB Melky Cabrera 3.00 8.00
MG Matt Garza 3.00 8.00
MH Matt Holliday 3.00 8.00
MK Matt Kemp 5.00 12.00
MR1 Mariano Rivera 4.00 10.00
MR2 Mariano Rivera SP 20.00 50.00
MS1 Mike Stanton 3.00 8.00
MS2 Mike Stanton SP 20.00 50.00
MT1 Mark Teixeira 4.00 10.00
MT2 Mark Teixeira SP 20.00 50.00
NC1 Nelson Cruz 3.00 8.00
NC2 Nelson Cruz SP 30.00 60.00
NM Nyjer Morgan 3.00 8.00
NS Nick Swisher 3.00 8.00
PF1 Prince Fielder 3.00 8.00
PF2 Prince Fielder SP 10.00 25.00
PK Paul Konerko 3.00 8.00
PS Pablo Sandoval 3.00 8.00
RB1 Ryan Braun 5.00 12.00

RB2 Ryan Braun SP 20.00 50.00
RH Roy Halladay SP 20.00 50.00
RHO Ryan Howard 4.00 10.00
RV Ryan Vogelsong 3.00 8.00
RW Rickie Weeks 3.00 8.00
RZ1 Ryan Zimmerman 3.00 8.00
RZ2 Ryan Zimmerman SP 15.00 40.00
SC1 Starlin Castro 5.00 12.00
SC2 Starlin Castro SP 12.50 30.00
TH Tommy Hanson 3.00 8.00
THU Tim Hudson 3.00 8.00
TL1 Tim Lincecum 5.00 12.00
TL2 Tim Lincecum SP 30.00 60.00
TT1 Troy Tulowitzki 3.00 8.00
TT2 Troy Tulowitzki SP 20.00 50.00
VM Victor Martinez 3.00 8.00
YG Yovani Gallardo 3.00 8.00
ZG Zack Greinke 3.00 8.00

2012 Topps Heritage Flashback Stadium Relics

STATED ODDS 1:1459 HOBBY
BG Bob Gibson 12.50 30.00
CY Carl Yastrzemski 12.00 30.00
EB Ernie Banks 15.00 40.00
EM Eddie Mathews 12.50 30.00
FR Frank Robinson 20.00 50.00
HA Hank Aaron 12.50 30.00
RC Bob Clemente 30.00 60.00
RM Roger Maris 12.50 30.00
SM Stan Musial 12.50 30.00
WM Willie Mays 20.00 50.00
YB Yogi Berra 12.50 30.00
MMA Mickey Mantle 15.00 40.00

2012 Topps Heritage JFK Stamp Collection

STATED ODDS 1:2950 HOBBY
STATED PRINT RUN 63 SER.#'d SETS
1 Problems 15.00 40.00
2 Liberty 15.00 40.00
3 Risks 15.00 40.00
4 The America 15.00 40.00
5 Our Common Common Link 15.00 40.00
6 A Free Society 15.00 40.00
7 Ask Not 15.00 40.00

2012 Topps Heritage New Age Performers

COMPLETE SET (15) 10.00 25.00
STATED ODDS 1:15 HOBBY
AP Albert Pujols 1.25 3.00
CJ Chipper Jones 1.00 2.50
CL Cliff Lee .75 2.00
DJ Derek Jeter 2.50 6.00
JB Jose Bautista .75 2.00
JB Josh Beckett .60 1.50
JV Joey Votto 1.00 2.50
JW Jered Weaver .75 2.00
MC Miguel Cabrera 1.00 2.50
MK Matt Kemp .75 2.00
RB Ryan Braun .60 1.50
RC Robinson Cano .75 2.00
RH Roy Halladay .75 2.00
TL Tim Lincecum .75 2.00
VM Victor Martinez .75 2.00

2012 Topps Heritage News Flashbacks

COMPLETE SET (10) 5.00 12.00
STATED ODDS 1:12 HOBBY
A Alcatraz .40 1.00
JK John F. Kennedy 1.00 2.50
MK Martin Luther King Jr. .60 1.50
PP Pope Paul VI .40 1.00
PS Penn Station .40 1.00
UA University of Alabama .40 1.00
UC U.S. Cuba Cuba .40 1.00
VT Valentina Tereshkova .40 1.00
JKE John F. Kennedy 1.00 2.50
MKI Martin Luther King Jr. .60 1.50

2012 Topps Heritage Real One Autographs

STATED ODDS 1:289 HOBBY
HN CARDS ISSUED IN HN.FACT.SETS
EXCHANGE DEADLINE 02/28/2015
AG Adrian Gonzalez 10.00 25.00
AGR Alex Grammas 8.00 20.00
AJ Adam Jones 15.00 40.00
AM Andrew McCutchen 30.00 80.00
AP Andy Pettitte HN 100.00 175.00
BA Bob Anderson 8.00 20.00
BD Bobby Del Greco 8.00 20.00
BG Bob Gibson 40.00 80.00
BGA Billy Gardner 8.00 20.00
BH Bryce Harper HN 400.00 800.00
BT Bob Turley 10.00 25.00
BV Bill Virdon 12.50 30.00
CA Craig Anderson 10.00 25.00
CBO Carl Boles 10.00 25.00
CE Chuck Essegian 8.00 20.00
CF Chico Fernandez 8.00 20.00
CG Chris Getz HN 10.00 25.00
CH Carroll Hardy 8.00 20.00
CK Clayton Kershaw 40.00 80.00
CM Charley Maxwell 8.00 20.00
CR Cody Ross HN 15.00 40.00
DB Daniel Bard HN 12.50 30.00
DH Drew Hutchison HN 20.00 50.00
DS Daryl Spencer 15.00 40.00
DST Dean Stone 8.00 20.00
DZ Brian Dozier HN 30.00 80.00
EA Earl Averill 12.50 30.00
EB Ed Bauta 10.00 25.00
EG Eli Grba 12.00 30.00
EK Eddie Kasko 10.00 25.00
ER Ed Roebuck 10.00 25.00
EV Edinson Volquez HN 40.00 100.00
FF Freddie Freeman 15.00 40.00
FR Fernando Rodney HN 30.00 60.00
FS Frank Sullivan 10.00 25.00
FTO Frank Torre 8.00 20.00
GB Gordon Beckham HN 15.00 40.00
GJ Garrett Jones HN 8.00 20.00
HL Hobie Landrith 15.00 40.00
ID Ike Delock 10.00 25.00
JB Jim Brosnan 10.00 25.00
JC Joe Cunningham 10.00 25.00
JK Jerry Kindall 10.00 25.00
JL Johnny Logan 10.00 25.00
JM Juan Marichal 40.00 100.00
JMO Jesus Montero 12.50 30.00
JV Jordany Valdespin HN 15.00 40.00
KN Kirk Nieuwenhuis HN 15.00 40.00
LA Luis Aparicio 15.00 40.00
MH Matt Holliday 20.00 50.00
MHA Matt Hague HN 12.50 30.00
MK Matt Kemp 12.00 30.00
MM Minnie Minoso 20.00 50.00
MMC Mike McCormick 8.00 20.00
OC Orlando Cepeda 60.00 150.00
RK Russ Kemmerer 10.00 25.00
RS Red Schoendienst 10.00 25.00
RZ Ryan Zimmerman 12.50 30.00
SC Starlin Castro 10.00 25.00
SM Stan Musial 40.00 100.00
TB Trevor Bauer HN 30.00 60.00
TC Tex Clevenger 8.00 20.00
TP Tyler Pastornicky HN 8.00 20.00
WM Will Middlebrooks HN 50.00 100.00
WM Willie Mays EXCH 250.00 500.00
WMC Willie McCovey 50.00 100.00
WP Wily Peralta HN 8.00 20.00
YC Yoenis Cespedes HN 60.00 120.00
YD Yu Darvish HN 50.00 120.00
ZC Zack Cozart HN 15.00 40.00

2012 Topps Heritage Real One Autographs Red Ink

*RED: .6X TO 1.5X BASIC
STATED ODDS 1:738 HOBBY
PRINT RUNS B/WN 10-63 COPIES PER
NO PRICING ON QTY 25 OR LESS
EXCHANGE DEADLINE 02/28/2015
AM Andrew McCutchen 75.00 200.00
CK Clayton Kershaw 125.00 250.00

2012 Topps Heritage Stick-Ons

COMPLETE SET (46) 40.00 80.00
STATED ODDS 1:8 HOBBY
1 Miguel Cabrera 1.00 2.50
2 Nelson Cruz 1.00 2.50
3 Jose Bautista .75 2.00
4 David Wright .75 2.00
5 Jose Reyes .75 2.00
6 Carlos Gonzalez .75 2.00
7 Josh Hamilton .75 2.00
8 Pablo Sandoval .75 2.00
9 Jacoby Ellsbury .75 2.00
10 Madison Bumgarner .75 2.00
11 David Price .75 2.00
12 Starlin Castro .75 2.00
13 Robinson Cano .75 2.00
14 Chris Carpenter .75 2.00
15 Matt Kemp .75 2.00
16 Andrew McCutchen 1.00 2.50
17 Ryan Zimmerman .75 2.00
18 Tim Lincecum .75 2.00
19 Ian Kinsler .75 2.00
20 Albert Pujols 1.25 3.00
21 Ryan Braun .60 1.50
22 Evan Longoria .75 2.00
23 Mark Teixeira .75 2.00
24 Ian Kennedy .60 1.50
25 David Ortiz 1.00 2.50
26 Justin Upton .75 2.00
27 Ryan Howard .75 2.00
28 Mike Stanton 1.00 2.50
29 Mariano Rivera 1.25 3.00
30 Roy Halladay .75 2.00
31 Curtis Granderson .75 2.00
32 Felix Hernandez .75 2.00
33 Troy Tulowitzki 1.00 2.50
34 Adrian Beltre 1.00 2.50
35 Joe Mauer .75 2.00
36 Chase Utley .75 2.00
37 Jimmy Rollins .75 2.00
38 Cliff Lee .75 2.00
39 Hunter Pence .75 2.00
40 Dustin Pedroia .75 2.00
41 Victor Martinez .75 2.00
42 Justin Verlander 1.00 2.50
43 James Shields .60 1.50
44 Buster Posey 1.25 3.00
45 Matt Moore 1.00 2.50
46 Jesus Montero .60 1.50

2012 Topps Heritage The JFK Story

COMPLETE SET (7) 40.00 80.00
COMMON CARD 6.00 15.00
JFK1 Kennedy at Cambridge 6.00 15.00
JFK2 A Profile in Courage 6.00 15.00
JFK3 Senate's Shining Stars 6.00 15.00
JFK4 Jack and Jackie 6.00 15.00
JFK5 The 35th President 6.00 15.00
JFK6 Call to Serve 6.00 15.00
JFK7 Cuban Crisis 6.00 15.00

2012 Topps Heritage Then and Now

COMPLETE SET (10) 6.00 15.00
STATED ODDS 1:15 HOBBY
AB Luis Aparicio/Michael Bourn .60 1.50
AK H.Aaron/M.Kemp 2.00 5.00
KB Harmon Killebrew/Jose Bautista 1.00 2.50
KK S.Koufax/C.Kershaw 2.00 5.00
KV S.Koufax/J.Verlander 2.00 5.00
MB Eddie Mathews/Jose Bautista 1.00 2.50
MS Juan Marichal/James Shields .60 1.50
MV J.Marichal/J.Verlander 1.00 2.50
SL Warren Spahn/Cliff Lee .75 2.00
YC Yastrzemski/Cabrera 1.50 4.00

2010 Topps Heritage Strasburg National Convention

DIST.AT 2010 NATIONAL CONVENTION
STATED PRINT RUN 999 SER.#'d SETS
NCC1 Stephen Strasburg 12.00 30.00

2011 Topps Heritage National Convention

COMPLETE SET (5) 15.00 40.00
DISTRIBUTED AT 2011 NATIONAL CON.
STATED PRINT RUN 299 SER.#'d SETS
NC1 Dustin Ackley 3.00 8.00
NC2 Dee Gordon 3.00 8.00
NC3 Mike Moustakas 5.00 12.00
NC4 Michael Pineda 5.00 12.00
NC5 Zach Britton 5.00 12.00

2013 Topps Heritage

COMP.SET w/o SPs (425) 20.00 50.00
COMP.HN.FACT.SET (101) 100.00 150.00
COMP.HN SET (100) 50.00 100.00
SP ODDS 1:3 HOBBY
ERROR SP ODDS 1:1567 HOBBY
SENATOR SP ODDS 1:13,058 HOBBY
NO SENATOR PRICING DUE TO SCARCITY
ACTION SP ODDS 1:26 HOBBY
COLOR SP ODDS 1:155 HOBBY
HN FACT SETS SOLD ONLY ON TOPPS.COM
1 Kershaw/Dickey/Cueto .75 2.00
2 Price/Verlander/Weaver .40 1.00
3 Gio Gonzalez .30 .75
R.A. Dickey
Johnny Cueto
Lance Lynn
4A David Price/Jered Weaver
Matt Harrison .30 .75
4B Price/Weav/Har Error SP 20.00 50.00
5 Dickey/Kershaw/Hamels .75 2.00
6 Verlan/Scher/Hernandez .40 1.00
7 Pos/McCut/Brn/Cbrr .50 1.25
8 Cabrera/Trout/Beltre 3.00 8.00
9 Ryan Braun .30 .75
Giancarlo Stanton
Jay Bruce
Adam LaRoche
10 Cabrera/Granderson/Hamilton .40 1.00
11 Chase Headley/Ryan Braun
Alfonso Soriano .30 .75
12 Cabrera/Ham/Encarnacion .40 1.00
13 Adam LaRoche .25 .60
14 Josh Wall RC/Paco Rodriguez RC .40 1.00
15 Drew Storen .25 .60
16 Cliff Lee .30 .75
17 Nick Markakis .30 .75
18 Adam Lind .30 .75
19 Alex Avila .30 .75
20 James McDonald .25 .60
21 Joe Girardi .30 .75
22 Andrelton Simmons .25 .60
23 Josh Johnson .30 .75
24 Anibal Sanchez .25 .60
25 Andrew Cashner .25 .60
26 Angel Pagan .25 .60
27 Joe Maddon .15 .40
28 Anthony Gose .25 .60
29 Norichika Aoki .25 .60
30 Chad Billingsley .30 .75
31 Asdrubal Cabrera .30 .75
32 C.J. Wilson .25 .60
33 Didi Gregorius RC
Todd Redmond RC .60 1.50
34 Ricky Romero .25 .60
35 Michael Bourn .25 .60
36 Ben Zobrist .30 .75
37 Brandon Crawford .30 .75
38 J.D. Martinez .40 1.00
39 Brandon League .25 .60
40 Carlos Beltran .30 .75
41 D.Jeter/M.Trout 3.00 8.00
42 Tommy Milone .25 .60
43 Brandon Morrow .25 .60
44 Ike Davis .25 .60
45 Brandon Phillips .25 .60
46A Ian Desmond .25 .60
47 Francisco Peguero RC
Jean Machi RC .60 1.50
48 Peter Bourjos .25 .60
49 Brett Jackson .25 .60
50 Curtis Granderson .30 .75
51 Kenley Jansen .30 .75
52 Jayson Werth .30 .75
53 Tyler Pastornicky .15 .40
54 Ron Gardenhire .15 .40
55 Brett Lawrie .30 .75
56A Ross Detwiler .25 .60
57 Brett Wallace .25 .60
58 Austin Jackson .25 .60
59 Adam Wainwright .30 .75
60 Will Middlebrooks .25 .60
61 Kirk Nieuwenhuis .25 .60
62 Starling Marte .30 .75
63 Jason Grilli .25 .60
64 Brian Wilson .40 1.00
65 Carlos Quentin .25 .60
66 Bruce Chen .25 .60
67 Davey Johnson .15 .40
68 Cameron Maybin .25 .60
69 Alex Rodriguez .50 1.25
70 Brian McCann .30 .75
71 Carlos Gomez .25 .60
72 Chase Utley .30 .75
73 Steve Lombardozzi .15 .40
74 Brock Holt RC/Kyle McPherson RC.75 2.00
75 Chris Carpenter .30 .75
76 Ron Washington .15 .40
77 Justin Masterson .25 .60
78 Mike Napoli .25 .60
79 Chris Johnson .25 .60
80A Jay Bruce .30 .75
80B J.Bruce Color SP 10.00 25.00
81 M.Kemp/C.Kershaw .75 2.00
82 Pablo Sandoval .30 .75
83 Carlos Ruiz .25 .60
84 Jonathon Niese .25 .60
85 Todd Frazier .30 .75
86 Ivan Nova .30 .75
87 Bruce Bochy .30 .75
88 A.J. Ellis .25 .60
89A Jose Bautista .30 .75
89B Jose Bautista Action SP 5.00 12.00
90A Joe Mauer .30 .75
90B Joe Mauer Action SP 5.00 12.00
90C J.Mauer Color SP 10.00 25.00
91 Chris Nelson .25 .60
92 Chris Young .25 .60
93 Christian Friedrich .25 .60
94 H.Rod RC/Cingrani RC 1.25 3.00
95 B.J. Upton .30 .75
96 Jeff Samardzija .25 .60
97 Erick Aybar .25 .60
98 Quintin Berry .15 .40
99 Tim Lincecum .30 .75
100A Robinson Cano .30 .75
100B Robinson Cano Action SP 5.00 12.00
100C R.Cano Color SP 10.00 25.00
101 Don Mattingly .75 2.00
102 Kirk Gibson .15 .40
103 Gordon Beckham .25 .60
104 Jonathan Papelbon .30 .75
105 Shin-Soo Choo .30 .75
106 Mike Leake .25 .60
107 Brian Omogrosso RC
Deunte Heath RC .60 1.50
108 Jarrod Parker .25 .60
109 Zack Cozart .25 .60
110 Mark Trumbo .25 .60
111 Clayton Richard .25 .60
112 Jarrod Saltalamacchia .25 .60
113 Johan Santana .30 .75
114 Cody Ross .25 .60
115 Dan Uggla .25 .60
116 Chris Herrmann RC
Nick Maronde RC .75 2.00
117 Colby Rasmus .30 .75
118 Robin Ventura .25 .60
119 Corey Hart .25 .60
120 Josh Beckett .25 .60
121 Ned Yost .15 .40
122 Hisashi Iwakuma .30 .75
123 Yunel Escobar .25 .60
124 Ryan Cook .25 .60
125A Yu Darvish .40 1.00
125B Y.Darvish Action SP 6.00 15.00
125C Y.Darvish Color SP 12.00 30.00
125D Yu Darvish Error SP 30.00 60.00
126A Craig Kimbrel .30 .75
126B Craig Kimbrel Action SP 5.00 12.00
127 Edwin Jackson .25 .60
128 Doug Fister .25 .60
129 Ruben Tejada .25 .60
130 Philip Humber .25 .60
131 Dan Haren .25 .60
132 Rickie Weeks .25 .60
133 Chris Perez .25 .60
134 Daniel Descalso .25 .60
135 Domonic Brown .30 .75
136 Pablo Sandoval .30 .75
137 Madison Bumgarner .30 .75
138 Gregor Blanco .25 .60
139 San Francisco Giants .15 .40
140 Carlos Pena .30 .75
141 Daniel Hudson .25 .60
142 Daniel Murphy .30 .75
143 Clint Hurdle .15 .40
144 Darwin Barney .25 .60
145 David DeJesus .25 .60
146 Thomas Neal RC/Jaye Chapman RC.60 1.50
147 Kyle Lohse .25 .60
148 A.J. Pierzynski .25 .60
149 Zack Greinke .30 .75
150 Melky Cabrera .25 .60
151 Brett Gardner .30 .75
152 Tim Hudson .30 .75
153 David Murphy .25 .60
154 Dee Gordon .25 .60
155 W.Middlebrooks/D.Ortiz .40 1.00
156 Dayan Viciedo .25 .60
157 Charlie Manuel .15 .40
158 Denard Span .25 .60
159 Desmond Jennings .30 .75
160 David Freese .25 .60
161 Jason Hammel .30 .75
162 B.Harper/C.Jones .60 1.50
163 Gaby Sanchez .25 .60
164 Dexter Fowler .30 .75
165 Omar Infante .25 .60
166 Dustin Ackley .25 .60
167 Christian Garcia (RC)/Eury Perez RC.75 2.00
168 Addison Reed .25 .60
169 Elvis Andrus .30 .75
170 Jon Lester .30 .75
171 Derek Holland .25 .60
172 Emilio Bonifacio .25 .60
173 Bud Black .25 .60
174 Derek Norris .25 .60
175 Alfonso Soriano .30 .75
176 Ervin Santana .25 .60
177 Ben Revere .25 .60
178 Everth Cabrera .25 .60
179 Justin Maxwell .25 .60
180 Carl Crawford .30 .75
181 Jose Valverde .25 .60
182 Felix Doubront .25 .60
183A Fernando Rodney .25 .60
183B Fernando Rodney Color SP 8.00 20.00
184 Franklin Gutierrez .25 .60
185 Ian Kennedy .25 .60
186 Casper Wells .25 .60
187 Tyler Clippard .25 .60
188 Matt Harvey .30 .75
189 Freddie Freeman .50 1.25
190A Derek Jeter 1.00 2.50
190B D.Jeter Action SP 40.00 100.00
191 Anthony Rizzo .60 1.50
192 Brandon McCarthy .25 .60
193 Garrett Jones .25 .60
194 Mike Moustakas .30 .75
195 Alex Rios .30 .75
196 Chris Carter .15 .40
197 Mark Buehrle .30 .75
198 Gavin Floyd .25 .60
199 Greg Dobbs .25 .60
200A Clayton Kershaw .75 2.00
200B C.Kershaw Color SP 15.00 40.00
201 Machado RC/Bundy RC 4.00 10.00
202 Luke Hochevar .25 .60
203 Alcides Escobar .30 .75
204 Gregor Blanco .25 .60
205 Howie Kendrick .25 .60
206 Huston Street .25 .60
207 Dusty Baker .25 .60
208 Juan Pierre .25 .60
209 Kyle Seager .25 .60
210 Jacoby Ellsbury .30 .75
211 Lance Lynn .25 .60
212 Edinson Volquez .25 .60
213 Michael Morse .25 .60
214 Jean Segura .30 .75
215 Francisco Liriano .25 .60
216 Jason Kipnis .30 .75
217 Alex Gordon .30 .75
218 Brandon Beachy .25 .60
219 S.Strasburg/G.Gonzalez .40 1.00
220 Matt Garza .25 .60
221 J.J. Hardy .25 .60
222 J.P. Arencibia .25 .60
223 James Loney .30 .75
224 Jamey Carroll .25 .60
225 Jason Kubel .25 .60
226 Steven Lerud (RC) .60 1.50
Luis Antonio Jimenez RC
227 Jason Motte .25 .60
228 Jason Vargas .25 .60
229 Jed Lowrie .25 .60
230 Mark Reynolds .25 .60
231 Jeff Francoeur .30 .75
232 Bob Melvin .15 .40
233 Jeremy Hellickson .25 .60
234 Adeiny Hechavarria (RC)
Tyson Brummett RC .75 2.00
235 Jhonny Peralta .25 .60
236 Jim Johnson .25 .60
237 Jimmy Rollins .30 .75
238 Joe Nathan .25 .60
239 Joel Hanrahan .25 .60
240 Allen Craig .30 .75
241 Geovany Soto .30 .75
242 John Jaso .25 .60
243 Ruf RC/Cloyd RC 1.25 3.00
244 Jon Jay .25 .60
245 Jordan Pacheco .25 .60
246A Josh Hamilton .30 .75
246B Josh Hamilton Action SP 5.00 12.00
246C J.Hamilton Color SP 10.00 25.00
247 Josh Reddick .25 .60
248 Jim Leyland .15 .40
249 Josh Thole .25 .60
250A Prince Fielder .30 .75
250B Prince Fielder Action SP 5.00 12.00
250C P.Fielder Color SP 10.00 25.00
251 Juan Nicasio .25 .60
252 Yonder Alonso .25 .60
253 Sergio Romo .25 .60
254 Nathan Eovaldi .30 .75
255 Salvador Perez .30 .75
256 Torii Hunter .25 .60
257 Rick Porcello .30 .75
258 Michael Young .25 .60
259 Miguel Montero .25 .60
260 Drew Stubbs .25 .60
261 Olt RC/Profar RC .75 2.00
262 Miller RC/Rosenthal (RC) 1.50 4.00
263 Vance Worley .30 .75
264 Vernon Wells .25 .60
265 Lorenzo Cain .25 .60
266 Lucas Duda .30 .75
267 Marco Estrada .25 .60
268 Justin Ruggiano .25 .60
269 Justin Smoak .25 .60
270 Trevor Plouffe .25 .60
271 Matt Dominguez .25 .60
272 Matt Joyce .25 .60
273 Matt Moore .30 .75
274 Justin Morneau .30 .75
275 Kevin Youkilis .25 .60
276 Nick Swisher .30 .75
277 Seth Smith .25 .60
278 Shaun Marcum .25 .60
279 Victor Martinez .30 .75
280 Ryan Vogelsong .25 .60
281 Adam Warren RC/Melky Mesa RC.75 2.00
282 Wandy Rodriguez .25 .60
283 Wily Peralta .25 .60
284 Yasmani Grandal .25 .60
285 Ricky Nolasco .25 .60
286 Tom Wilhelmsen .25 .60
287 A.J. Ramos RC/Rob Brantly RC .75 2.00
288 Logan Morrison .25 .60
289 Lonnie Chisenhall .25 .60
290 Josh Willingham .30 .75
291 Ryan Ludwick .25 .60
292 Trevor Cahill .25 .60
293 Ubaldo Jimenez .25 .60
294 Liam Hendriks .25 .60
295 Mitch Moreland .25 .60
296 Rafael Soriano .25 .60
297 Jordan Lyles .25 .60
298 Buck Showalter .15 .40
299 Garrett Richards .30 .75
300 Jason Heyward .30 .75
301 Ernesto Frieri .25 .60
302 Neil Walker .30 .75
303 Grant Balfour .25 .60
304 Paul Goldschmidt .40 1.00
305 Todd Helton .30 .75
306 Pablo Sandoval/Hunter Pence .30 .75
307 Dan Straily .25 .60
308 J.J. Putz .25 .60
309 Michael Cuddyer .25 .60
310 Mark Ellis .25 .60
311 Tyler Colvin .25 .60
312 Avisail Garcia RC/Hernan Perez RC.75 2.00
313 Stephen Drew .25 .60
314 Shane Victorino .30 .75
315 Rajai Davis .25 .60
316 Aaron Crow .25 .60
317 Lance Berkman .30 .75
318 Kendrys Morales .25 .60
319 Jason Isringhausen .25 .60
320 Coco Crisp .25 .60
321 Trevor Bauer .40 1.00
322 Scott Baker .25 .60
323 Danny Espinosa .25 .60
324 Terry Collins .25 .60
325A Rafael Betancourt .25 .60
325B Rafael Betancourt Error SP 20.00 50.00
326 Gerardo Parra .25 .60
327 Heath Bell .25 .60
328 Patrick Corbin .30 .75
329 Drew Pomeranz .30 .75
330 Johnny Cueto .30 .75
331 A.Rodriguez/R.Cano .50 1.25
332 John McDonald .15 .40
333 Mike Minor .25 .60
334 Kurt Suzuki .25 .60
335A Jonny Venters .25 .60
335B Jonny Venters Error SP 30.00 60.00
336 Nolan Reimold .25 .60
337 Kevin Mattison RC/Tom Koehler RC.60 1.50
338 Tommy Hunter .25 .60
339 David Robertson .25 .60
340 Paul Konerko .30 .75
341 Luis Ayala .25 .60
342 Homer Bailey .25 .60
343 Daniel Nava .25 .60
344 Andrew Bailey .25 .60
345 Pedro Ciriaco .25 .60
346 Rafael Dolis .25 .60
347 Carlos Marmol .25 .60
348 Miguel Gonzalez .25 .60
349 Ian Stewart .25 .60
350 Matt Cain .30 .75
351 Matt Thornton .25 .60
352 Alexei Ramirez .30 .75
353 Chris Heisey .25 .60
354 Sean Marshall .25 .60
355A Chris Tillman .25 .60
355B Chris Tillman Error SP 20.00 50.00
356 Adam Eaton RC/Tyler Skaggs RC 1.00 2.50
357 Ryan Hanigan .25 .60
358 Casey Kotchman .25 .60
359 Wilton Lopez .15 .40
360 Mark Teixeira .30 .75
361 Vinnie Pestano .25 .60
362 Ezequiel Carrera .25 .60
363 Neftali Feliz .25 .60
364 Russell Martin .25 .60
365 Phil Coke .25 .60
366 Jason Castro .25 .60
367 Jeremy Guthrie .25 .60
368 Ryan Dempster .25 .60
369 Greg Holland .25 .60
370 Bud Norris .25 .60
371 Cole De Vries .25 .60
372 Joe Blanton .25 .60
373 Ted Lilly .25 .60
374 Luis Cruz .25 .60
375 Austin Kearns .25 .60
376 Steve Cishek .25 .60
377 John Axford .25 .60
378 Rafael Ortega RC/Rob Scahill RC .60 1.50
379 Nyjer Morgan .25 .60
380 Phil Hughes .25 .60
381 Fernando Martinez .25 .60
382 Mike Fiers .25 .60
383 Mike Scioscia .15 .40
384 Ryan Doumit .25 .60
385 Glen Perkins .25 .60
386 Jared Burton .25 .60
387 Bobby Parnell .25 .60
388 Ali Solis RC/Casey Kelly RC .75 2.00
389 Frank Francisco .15 .40
390 Brandon Belt .30 .75
391 Andy Pettitte .30 .75
392 Mike Baxter .25 .60
393 Pat Neshek .25 .60
394 Brandon Inge .25 .60
395 Jemile Weeks .25 .60
396 Jeff Karstens .25 .60
397 Clint Barmes .25 .60
398 Jeurys Familia RC
Collin McHugh RC 1.00 2.50
399 Dale Sveum .15 .40
400 Kris Medlen .30 .75
401 Alex Presley .25 .60
402 Will Venable .25 .60
403 Luke Gregerson .25 .60
404 Barry Zito .30 .75
405 Brendan Ryan .25 .60
406 Jaime Garcia .30 .75
407 Rafael Furcal .25 .60
408 David Lough RC/Jake Odorizzi RC.75 2.00
409 Pete Kozma .25 .60
410 John Lackey .30 .75
411 Chris Archer .25 .60
412 Casey Janssen .25 .60
413 Mike Matheny .15 .40
414 Chris Iannetta .25 .60
415 Tommy Hanson .25 .60
416 Paul Maholm .25 .60
417 Juan Francisco .25 .60
418 Bryan Morris RC/Justin Wilson RC.60 1.50
419 Joe Saunders .25 .60
420 Bronson Arroyo .25 .60
421 Welington Castillo .25 .60
422 Eduardo Nunez .25 .60
423 M.Cain/B.Posey .50 1.25
424 Logan Forsythe .25 .60
425A Joey Votto .40 1.00
425B J.Votto Color SP 12.00 30.00
426A Miguel Cabrera SP 3.00 8.00
426B M.Cabrera Action SP 15.00 40.00
427 Andre Ethier SP 4.00 10.00
428A Ryan Howard SP 2.50 6.00
428B Ryan Howard Color SP 10.00 25.00
429 Aramis Ramirez SP 4.00 10.00
430A Mike Trout SP 40.00 100.00
430B M.Trout Action SP 200.00 400.00
430C M.Trout Color SP 200.00 400.00
431 Hunter Pence SP 4.00 10.00
432A Ryan Zimmerman SP 4.00 10.00
433 Adam Jones SP 4.00 10.00
434 Dustin Pedroia SP 2.50 6.00
435 Carlos Santana SP 5.00 12.00
436 Michael Brantley SP 4.00 10.00
437 Billy Butler SP 4.00 10.00
438A Andrew McCutchen SP 3.00 8.00
438B Andrew McCutchen Action SP 6.00 15.00
439 Evan Longoria SP 4.00 10.00
440A Bryce Harper SP 10.00 25.00
440B B.Harper Action SP 50.00 120.00
440C B.Harper Color SP 30.00 80.00
440D Bryce Harper Error SP 125.00 250.00
441 Jordan Zimmermann SP 5.00 12.00
442 Hanley Ramirez SP 4.00 10.00
443 Hiroki Kuroda SP 4.00 10.00
444 Adrian Beltre SP 6.00 15.00
445 Lucas Harrell SP 4.00 10.00
446 Jose Reyes SP 4.00 10.00
447A Felix Hernandez SP 2.50 6.00
447B Hernandez Action SP 10.00 25.00
447C Felix Hernandez Color SP 10.00 25.00
448A Cole Hamels SP 4.00 10.00
448B C.Hamels Color SP 10.00 25.00
449 Jered Weaver SP 4.00 10.00
450A Matt Kemp SP 2.50 6.00
450B Matt Kemp Action SP 5.00 12.00
450C Matt Kemp Color SP 10.00 25.00
451 Jake Peavy SP 4.00 10.00
452 Troy Tulowitzki SP 3.00 8.00
453 Justin Upton SP 4.00 10.00

454 Gio Gonzalez SP 4.00 10.00
455A Chris Sale SP 5.00 12.00
455B Chris Sale Color SP 12.00 30.00
456A CC Sabathia SP 4.00 10.00
456B CC Sabathia Action SP 5.00 12.00
457 Mat Latos SP 4.00 10.00
458A David Price SP 4.00 10.00
458B David Price Color SP 10.00 25.00
459A Yoenis Cespedes SP 3.00 8.00
459B Y.Cespedes Action SP 6.00 15.00
459C Y.Cespedes Color SP 12.00 30.00
460A Ryan Braun SP 2.50 6.00
460B Ryan Braun Action SP 5.00 12.00
461 Marco Scutaro SP 4.00 10.00
462 Roy Halladay SP 4.00 10.00
463A Giancarlo Stanton SP 3.00 8.00
463B G.Stanton Action SP 15.00 40.00
463C Giancarlo Stanton Color SP 12.00 30.00
464A R.A. Dickey SP 4.00 10.00
464B R.A. Dickey Action SP 5.00 12.00
465A David Wright SP 2.50 6.00
465B David Wright Color SP 10.00 25.00
466 Carlos Gonzalez SP 4.00 10.00
467A Chase Headley SP 4.00 10.00
467B Chase Headley Color SP 8.00 20.00
468 Mariano Rivera SP 4.00 10.00
469 Max Scherzer SP 6.00 15.00
470A Albert Pujols SP 4.00 10.00
470B A.Pujols Action SP 8.00 20.00
471 Matt Holliday SP 3.00 8.00
472 Adrian Gonzalez SP 2.50 6.00
473 Matt Harrison SP 4.00 10.00
474A Wade Miley SP 3.00 8.00
474B Wade Miley Action SP 4.00 10.00
474C Wade Miley Color SP 8.00 20.00
475 Edwin Encarnacion SP 6.00 15.00
476 Yovani Gallardo SP 4.00 10.00
477A Yadier Molina SP 3.00 8.00
477B Y.Molina Action SP 8.00 20.00
478 Madison Bumgarner SP 2.50 6.00
479 Ian Kinsler SP 4.00 10.00
480A Stephen Strasburg SP 3.00 8.00
480B S.Strasburg Action SP 6.00 15.00
480C Stephen Strasburg Color SP 12.00 30.00
481 Martin Prado SP 4.00 10.00
482 Nelson Cruz SP 5.00 12.00
483 James Shields SP 4.00 10.00
484A Adam Dunn SP 4.00 10.00
484B Adam Dunn Action SP 5.00 12.00
485A Starlin Castro SP 2.00 5.00
485B Starlin Castro Color SP 8.00 20.00
486 David Ortiz SP 5.00 12.00
487 Jose Altuve SP 4.00 10.00
488 Wilin Rosario SP 4.00 10.00
489 Aaron Hill SP 4.00 10.00
490A Buster Posey SP 4.00 10.00
490B B.Posey Action SP 8.00 20.00
490C B.Posey Color SP 15.00 40.00
491 Wei-Yin Chen SP 2.00 5.00
492 Eric Hosmer SP 4.00 10.00
493 Aroldis Chapman SP 5.00 12.00
494 A.J. Burnett SP 3.00 8.00
495 Scott Diamond SP 4.00 10.00
496 Clay Buchholz SP 3.00 8.00
497 Jonathan Lucroy SP 5.00 12.00
498 Pedro Alvarez SP 3.00 8.00
499 Jesus Montero SP 4.00 10.00
500 Justin Verlander SP 3.00 8.00
H501 Evan Gattis RC 2.00 5.00
H502 Devin Mesoraco .75 2.00
H503 Hyun-Jin Ryu RC 2.50 6.00
H504 Jose Fernandez RC 2.50 6.00
H505 Marcell Ozuna RC 2.50 6.00
H506 Jedd Gyorko RC 1.25 3.00
H507 Carlos Martinez RC 1.50 4.00
H508 Matt Adams .75 2.00
H509 Anthony Rendon RC 10.00 25.00
H510 Allen Webster RC 1.25 3.00
H511 Jackie Bradley Jr. RC 2.50 6.00
H512 Bruce Rondon RC 1.00 2.50
H513 Drew Smyly .75 2.00
H514 Aaron Hicks RC 1.50 4.00
H515 Oswaldo Arcia RC 1.00 2.50
H516 Michael Pineda .75 2.00
H517 Brandon Maurer RC 1.25 3.00
H518 Alex Cobb .75 2.00
H519 Nolan Arenado RC 12.00 30.00
H520 Eric Chavez .75 2.00
H521 Jorge De La Rosa .75 2.00
H522 Nate Karns RC 1.00 2.50
H523 Kyle Gibson RC 1.50 4.00
H524 Travis Wood .75 2.00
H525 Jarred Cosart RC 1.25 3.00
H526 Matt Magill RC 1.00 2.50
H527 Juan Uribe .75 2.00
H528 Alex Sanabia .75 2.00
H529 Chris Coghlan .75 2.00
H530 Jim Henderson RC 1.25 3.00
H531 Julio Teheran 1.00 2.50
H532 John Buck 1.00 2.50
H533 Mike Zunino RC 1.50 4.00
H534 Jonathan Pettibone RC 1.50 4.00
H535 John Mayberry Jr. .75 2.00
H536 Christian Yelich RC 25.00 60.00
H537 Jeff Locke .75 2.00
H538 Jose Tabata .75 2.00
H539 Kyle Blanks .75 2.00
H540 Edward Mujica .75 2.00
H541 Brett Cecil .75 2.00
H542 Hank Conger .75 2.00
H543 Freddy Garcia .50 1.25
H544 Brian Matusz .75 2.00
H545 Chris Davis 1.00 2.50
H546 Nate McLouth .75 2.00
H547 Koji Uehara .75 2.00
H548 Jose Iglesias 1.00 2.50
H549 Dylan Axelrod .75 2.00
H550 Jose Quintana .75 2.00
H551 Steve Delabar .75 2.00
H552 Tyler Flowers .75 2.00
H553 Alejandro De Aza .75 2.00
H554 Raul Ibanez 1.00 2.50
H555 Scott Kazmir .75 2.00
H556 Zach McAllister .75 2.00
H557 Corey Kluber RC 3.00 8.00
H558 Jason Giambi .75 2.00
H559 Mark Melancon .75 2.00
H560 Andy Dirks .75 2.00
H561 Erik Bedard .75 2.00
H562 Jose Veras .75 2.00
H563 Matt Carpenter 1.25 3.00
H564 Wil Myers RC 1.25 3.00
H565 Wade Davis .75 2.00
H566 Henry Urrutia RC 1.25 3.00
H567 Miguel Tejada .75 2.00
H568 Zack Wheeler RC 2.00 5.00
H569 Josh Donaldson 1.00 2.50
H570 Mike Pelfrey .75 2.00
H571 Pedro Hernandez RC 1.00 2.50
H572 Josh Phegley RC 1.00 2.50
H573 Boone Logan .75 2.00
H574 Preston Claiborne RC 1.00 2.50
H575 Austin Romine .75 2.00
H576 Travis Hafner .75 2.00
H577 Alex Wood RC 1.25 3.00
H578 Bartolo Colon .75 2.00
H579 A.J. Griffin .75 2.00
H580 Brett Anderson .75 2.00
H581 Nick Franklin RC 1.25 3.00
H582 Aaron Harang .75 2.00
H583 Cody Asche RC 1.50 4.00
H584 Yasiel Puig RC 4.00 10.00
H585 Roberto Hernandez .50 1.25
H586 Jake McGee .75 2.00
H587 Alex Colome RC 1.00 2.50
H588 Brad Miller RC 1.25 3.00
H589 Luke Scott .75 2.00
H590 Justin Grimm RC 1.00 2.50
H591 Alexi Ogando .75 2.00
H592 Leury Garcia RC 1.00 2.50
H593 Leonys Martin .75 2.00
H594 Michael Wacha RC 1.25 3.00
H595 J.A. Happ 1.00 2.50
H596 Gerrit Cole RC 10.00 25.00
H597 Maicer Izturis .75 2.00
H598 Brad Ziegler .75 2.00
H599 Mike Kickham RC 1.00 2.50
H600 Kevin Gausman RC 1.50 4.00

2013 Topps Heritage Mini

STATED ODDS 1:235 HOBBY
STATED PRINT RUN 100 SER.#'d SETS
13 Adam LaRoche 6.00 15.00
35 Michael Bourn 6.00 15.00
40 Carlos Beltran 8.00 20.00
43 Brandon Morrow 6.00 15.00
50 Curtis Granderson 8.00 20.00
58 Austin Jackson 6.00 15.00
80 Jay Bruce 8.00 20.00
89 Jose Bautista 8.00 20.00
90 Joe Mauer 8.00 20.00
100 Robinson Cano 12.50 30.00
108 Jarrod Parker 6.00 15.00
110 Mark Trumbo 10.00 25.00
125 Yu Darvish 10.00 25.00
147 Kyle Lohse 6.00 15.00
160 David Freese 12.50 30.00
183 Fernando Rodney 6.00 15.00
190 Derek Jeter 60.00 120.00
200 Clayton Kershaw 20.00 50.00
210 Jacoby Ellsbury 8.00 20.00
217 Alex Gordon 8.00 20.00
236 Jim Johnson 10.00 25.00
240 Allen Craig 8.00 20.00
246 Josh Hamilton 8.00 20.00
247 Josh Reddick 6.00 15.00
250 Prince Fielder 10.00 25.00
259 Miguel Montero 6.00 15.00
280 Ryan Vogelsong 10.00 25.00
290 Josh Willingham 8.00 20.00
330 Johnny Cueto 6.00 15.00
340 Paul Konerko 8.00 20.00
350 Matt Cain 12.50 30.00
360 Mark Teixeira 8.00 20.00
400 Kris Medlen 6.00 15.00
425 Joey Votto 12.50 30.00
426 Miguel Cabrera 10.00 25.00
427 Andre Ethier 6.00 15.00
428 Ryan Howard 8.00 20.00
429 Aramis Ramirez 6.00 15.00
430 Mike Trout 40.00 100.00
431 Hunter Pence 10.00 25.00
432 Ryan Zimmerman 12.50 30.00
433 Adam Jones 8.00 20.00
434 Dustin Pedroia 8.00 20.00
435 Carlos Santana 6.00 15.00
436 Michael Brantley 6.00 15.00
437 Billy Butler 6.00 15.00
438 Andrew McCutchen 10.00 25.00
439 Evan Longoria 10.00 25.00
440 Bryce Harper 15.00 40.00
441 Jordan Zimmermann 6.00 15.00
442 Hanley Ramirez 8.00 20.00
443 Hiroki Kuroda 6.00 15.00
444 Adrian Beltre 10.00 25.00
446 Jose Reyes 8.00 20.00
447 Felix Hernandez 8.00 20.00
448 Cole Hamels 8.00 20.00
449 Jered Weaver 8.00 20.00
450 Matt Kemp 8.00 20.00
451 Jake Peavy 6.00 15.00
452 Troy Tulowitzki 10.00 25.00
453 Justin Upton 8.00 20.00
454 Gio Gonzalez 8.00 20.00
455 Chris Sale 10.00 25.00
456 CC Sabathia 8.00 20.00
457 Mat Latos 8.00 20.00
458 David Price 8.00 20.00
459 Yoenis Cespedes 10.00 25.00
460 Ryan Braun 8.00 20.00
461 Marco Scutaro 10.00 25.00
462 Roy Halladay 8.00 20.00
463 Giancarlo Stanton 10.00 25.00
464 R.A. Dickey 8.00 20.00
465 David Wright 12.50 30.00
466 Carlos Gonzalez 8.00 20.00
467 Chase Headley 6.00 15.00
468 Mariano Rivera 20.00 50.00
469 Max Scherzer 10.00 25.00
470 Albert Pujols 25.00 60.00
471 Matt Holliday 12.50 30.00
472 Adrian Gonzalez 6.00 15.00
473 Matt Harrison 6.00 15.00
474 Wade Miley 6.00 15.00
475 Edwin Encarnacion 10.00 25.00
476 Yovani Gallardo 6.00 15.00
477 Yadier Molina 10.00 25.00
478 Madison Bumgarner 8.00 20.00
479 Ian Kinsler 8.00 20.00
480 Stephen Strasburg 15.00 40.00
481 Martin Prado 6.00 15.00
482 Nelson Cruz 10.00 25.00
483 James Shields 6.00 15.00
484 Adam Dunn 8.00 20.00
485 Starlin Castro 12.50 30.00
486 David Ortiz 10.00 25.00
488 Wilin Rosario 6.00 15.00
490 Buster Posey 25.00 60.00
492 Eric Hosmer 8.00 20.00
493 Aroldis Chapman 10.00 25.00
499 Jesus Montero 6.00 15.00
500 Justin Verlander 15.00 40.00

2013 Topps Heritage Target Red Border Variations

89 Jose Bautista 1.50 4.00
126 Craig Kimbrel 1.50 4.00
190 Derek Jeter 5.00 12.00
210 Jacoby Ellsbury 1.50 4.00
330 Johnny Cueto 1.50 4.00
350 Matt Cain 1.50 4.00
425 Joey Votto 2.00 5.00
426 Miguel Cabrera 2.00 5.00
428 Ryan Howard 1.50 4.00
438 Andrew McCutchen 2.00 5.00
439 Evan Longoria 1.50 4.00
440 Bryce Harper 3.00 8.00
449 Jered Weaver 1.50 4.00
452 Troy Tulowitzki 2.00 5.00
454 Gio Gonzalez 1.50 4.00
455 Chris Sale 2.00 5.00
456 CC Sabathia 1.50 4.00
458 David Price 1.50 4.00
459 Yoenis Cespedes 2.00 5.00
462 Roy Halladay 1.50 4.00
463 Giancarlo Stanton 2.00 5.00
465 David Wright 1.50 4.00
467 Chase Headley 1.25 3.00
470 Albert Pujols 2.50 6.00
477 Yadier Molina 2.00 5.00

2013 Topps Heritage Venezuelan

*BASIC VENEZUELAN: 3X TO 8X BASIC
NO ERROR PRICING DUE TO SCARCITY
NO SENATOR PRICING DUE TO SCARCITY
NO COLOR PRICING DUE TO SCARCITY
8 Cabrera/Trout/Beltre 3.00 8.00
41 D.Jeter/M.Trout 15.00 40.00
89B Jose Bautista Action SP 6.00 15.00
90B Joe Mauer Action SP 6.00 15.00
100B Robinson Cano Action SP 6.00 15.00
125B Y.Darvish Action SP 8.00 20.00
126B Craig Kimbrel Action SP 6.00 15.00
162 B.Harper/C.Jones 6.00 15.00
190A Derek Jeter 20.00 50.00
190B D.Jeter Action SP 20.00 50.00
246B Josh Hamilton Action SP 6.00 15.00
250B Prince Fielder Action SP 6.00 15.00
426A Miguel Cabrera SP 6.00 15.00
426B Miguel Cabrera Action SP 8.00 20.00
427 Andre Ethier SP 5.00 12.00
428A Ryan Howard SP 5.00 12.00
429 Aramis Ramirez SP 4.00 10.00
430A Mike Trout SP 40.00 100.00
430B M.Trout Action SP 200.00 400.00
431 Hunter Pence SP 5.00 12.00
432A Ryan Zimmerman SP 5.00 12.00
433 Adam Jones SP 5.00 12.00
434 Dustin Pedroia SP 5.00 12.00
435 Carlos Santana SP 5.00 12.00
436 Michael Brantley SP 4.00 10.00
437 Billy Butler SP 4.00 10.00
438A Andrew McCutchen SP 6.00 15.00
438B Andrew McCutchen Action SP 8.00 20.00
439 Evan Longoria SP 5.00 12.00
440A Bryce Harper SP 10.00 25.00
440B B.Harper Action SP 12.00 30.00
441 Jordan Zimmermann SP 5.00 12.00
442 Hanley Ramirez SP 5.00 12.00
443 Hiroki Kuroda SP 4.00 10.00
444 Adrian Beltre SP 6.00 15.00
445 Lucas Harrell SP 4.00 10.00
446 Jose Reyes SP 5.00 12.00
447A Felix Hernandez SP 5.00 12.00
447B Felix Hernandez Action SP 6.00 15.00
448A Cole Hamels SP 5.00 12.00
449 Jered Weaver SP 5.00 12.00
450A Matt Kemp SP 5.00 12.00
450B Matt Kemp Action SP 6.00 15.00
451 Jake Peavy SP 4.00 10.00
452 Troy Tulowitzki SP 6.00 15.00
453 Justin Upton SP 5.00 12.00
454 Gio Gonzalez SP 5.00 12.00
455A Chris Sale SP 6.00 15.00
456A CC Sabathia SP 5.00 12.00
456B CC Sabathia Action SP 6.00 15.00
457 Mat Latos SP 5.00 12.00
458A David Price SP 5.00 12.00
459A Yoenis Cespedes SP 6.00 15.00
459B Y.Cespedes Action SP 8.00 20.00
460A Ryan Braun SP 5.00 12.00
460B Ryan Braun Action SP 6.00 15.00
461 Marco Scutaro SP 5.00 12.00
462 Roy Halladay SP 5.00 12.00
463A Giancarlo Stanton SP 6.00 15.00
463B Giancarlo Stanton Action SP 8.00 20.00
464A R.A. Dickey SP 5.00 12.00
464B R.A. Dickey Action SP 6.00 15.00
465A David Wright SP 5.00 12.00
466 Carlos Gonzalez SP 5.00 12.00
467A Chase Headley SP 4.00 10.00
468 Mariano Rivera SP 8.00 20.00
469 Max Scherzer SP 6.00 15.00
470A Albert Pujols SP 8.00 20.00
470B A.Pujols Action SP 10.00 25.00
471 Matt Holliday SP 6.00 15.00
472 Adrian Gonzalez SP 5.00 12.00
473 Matt Harrison SP 4.00 10.00
474A Wade Miley SP 4.00 10.00
474B Wade Miley Action SP 5.00 12.00
475 Edwin Encarnacion SP 6.00 15.00
476 Yovani Gallardo SP 4.00 10.00
477A Yadier Molina SP 6.00 15.00
477B Yadier Molina Action SP 8.00 20.00
478 Madison Bumgarner SP 5.00 12.00
479 Ian Kinsler SP 5.00 12.00
480A Stephen Strasburg SP 6.00 15.00
480B S.Strasburg Action SP 8.00 20.00
481 Martin Prado SP 4.00 10.00
482 Nelson Cruz SP 6.00 15.00
483 James Shields SP 4.00 10.00
484A Adam Dunn SP 5.00 12.00
484B Adam Dunn Action SP 6.00 15.00
485A Starlin Castro SP 6.00 15.00
486 David Ortiz SP 6.00 15.00
487 Jose Altuve SP 5.00 12.00
488 Wilin Rosario SP 4.00 10.00
489 Aaron Hill SP 4.00 10.00
490A Buster Posey SP 8.00 20.00
490B B.Posey Action SP 10.00 25.00
491 Wei-Yin Chen SP 4.00 10.00
492 Eric Hosmer SP 5.00 12.00
493 Aroldis Chapman SP 6.00 15.00
494 A.J. Burnett SP 4.00 10.00
495 Scott Diamond SP 4.00 10.00
496 Clay Buchholz SP 5.00 12.00
497 Jonathan Lucroy SP 5.00 12.00
498 Pedro Alvarez SP 4.00 10.00
499 Jesus Montero SP 5.00 12.00
500 Justin Verlander SP 6.00 15.00

2013 Topps Heritage Wal-Mart Blue Border Variations

80 Jay Bruce 1.50 4.00
90 Joe Mauer 1.50 4.00
100 Robinson Cano 1.50 4.00
125 Yu Darvish 2.00 5.00
160 David Freese 1.25 3.00
183 Fernando Rodney 1.25 3.00
200 Clayton Kershaw 4.00 10.00
246 Josh Hamilton 1.50 4.00
250 Prince Fielder 1.50 4.00
430 Mike Trout 60.00 150.00
433 Adam Jones 1.50 4.00
434 Dustin Pedroia 1.50 4.00
447 Felix Hernandez 1.50 4.00
448 Cole Hamels 1.50 4.00
450 Matt Kemp 1.50 4.00
460 Ryan Braun 1.50 4.00
464 R.A. Dickey 1.50 4.00
471 Matt Holliday 2.00 5.00
472 Adrian Gonzalez 1.50 4.00
474 Wade Miley 1.25 3.00
480 Stephen Strasburg 2.00 5.00
484 Adam Dunn 1.50 4.00
485 Starlin Castro 1.25 3.00
490 Buster Posey 2.50 6.00
500 Justin Verlander 2.00 5.00

2013 Topps Heritage Black

INSERTED IN RETAIL PACKS
13 Adam LaRoche 1.25 3.00
35 Michael Bourn 1.25 3.00
40 Carlos Beltran 1.50 4.00
43 Brandon Morrow 1.25 3.00
50 Curtis Granderson 1.50 4.00
58 Austin Jackson 1.25 3.00
74 Brock Holt/Kyle McPherson 1.50 4.00
80 Jay Bruce 1.50 4.00
89 Jose Bautista 1.50 4.00
90 Joe Mauer 1.50 4.00
100 Robinson Cano 1.50 4.00
108 Jarrod Parker 1.25 3.00
110 Mark Trumbo 1.25 3.00
125 Yu Darvish 2.00 5.00
137 Madison Bumgarner 1.50 4.00
147 Kyle Lohse 1.25 3.00
160 David Freese 1.25 3.00
183 Fernando Rodney 1.25 3.00
190 Derek Jeter 8.00 20.00
200 Clayton Kershaw 4.00 10.00
201 M.Machado/D.Bundy 8.00 20.00
210 Jacoby Ellsbury 1.50 4.00
217 Alex Gordon 1.50 4.00
236 Jim Johnson 1.25 3.00
240 Allen Craig 1.50 4.00
243 D.Ruf/T.Cloyd 2.50 6.00
246 Josh Hamilton 1.50 4.00
247 Josh Reddick 1.25 3.00
250 Prince Fielder 1.50 4.00
259 Miguel Montero 1.25 3.00
261 M.Olt/J.Profar 1.50 4.00
262 S.Miller/T.Rosenthal 3.00 8.00
280 Ryan Vogelsong 1.25 3.00
290 Josh Willingham 1.50 4.00
330 Johnny Cueto 1.50 4.00
340 Paul Konerko 1.50 4.00
350 Matt Cain 1.50 4.00
356 Adam Eaton/Tyler Skaggs 2.00 5.00
398 Jeurys Familia/Collin McHugh 2.00 5.00
400 Kris Medlen 1.50 4.00
426 Miguel Cabrera 2.00 5.00
427 Andre Ethier 1.50 4.00
428 Ryan Howard 1.50 4.00
429 Aramis Ramirez 1.25 3.00
430 Mike Trout 300.00 600.00
431 Hunter Pence 1.50 4.00
432 Ryan Zimmerman 1.50 4.00
433 Adam Jones 1.50 4.00
434 Dustin Pedroia 1.50 4.00
435 Carlos Santana 1.50 4.00
437 Billy Butler 1.25 3.00
438 Andrew McCutchen 2.00 5.00
439 Evan Longoria 1.50 4.00
440 Bryce Harper 3.00 8.00
441 Jordan Zimmermann 1.25 3.00
442 Hanley Ramirez 1.50 4.00
443 Hiroki Kuroda 1.25 3.00
444 Adrian Beltre 2.00 5.00
446 Jose Reyes 1.50 4.00
447 Felix Hernandez 1.50 4.00
448 Cole Hamels 1.50 4.00
449 Jered Weaver 1.50 4.00
450 Matt Kemp 1.50 4.00
451 Jake Peavy 1.25 3.00
452 Troy Tulowitzki 2.00 5.00
453 Justin Upton 1.50 4.00
454 Gio Gonzalez 1.50 4.00
455 Chris Sale 2.00 5.00
456 CC Sabathia 1.50 4.00
457 Mat Latos 1.50 4.00
458 David Price 1.50 4.00
459 Yoenis Cespedes 2.00 5.00
460 Ryan Braun 1.50 4.00
461 Marco Scutaro 1.50 4.00
462 Roy Halladay 1.50 4.00
463 Giancarlo Stanton 2.00 5.00
464 R.A. Dickey 1.50 4.00
465 David Wright 1.50 4.00
466 Carlos Gonzalez 1.50 4.00
467 Chase Headley 1.25 3.00
468 Mariano Rivera 2.50 6.00
469 Max Scherzer 2.00 5.00
470 Albert Pujols 2.50 6.00
471 Matt Holliday 2.50 6.00
472 Adrian Gonzalez 1.50 4.00
473 Matt Harrison 1.25 3.00
474 Wade Miley 1.25 3.00
475 Edwin Encarnacion 2.00 5.00
476 Yovani Gallardo 1.25 3.00
477 Yadier Molina 2.00 5.00
479 Ian Kinsler 1.50 4.00
480 Stephen Strasburg 2.00 5.00
481 Martin Prado 1.25 3.00
482 Nelson Cruz 2.00 5.00
483 James Shields 1.25 3.00
484 Adam Dunn 1.50 4.00
485 Starlin Castro 1.25 3.00
488 Wilin Rosario 1.25 3.00
490 Buster Posey 2.50 6.00
500 Justin Verlander 2.00 5.00

2013 Topps Heritage Advertising Panels

ISSUED AS A BOX TOPPER
1 Bronson Arroyo .60 1.50
Josh Wall
Paco Rodriguez
Chris Johnson
2 Homer Bailey .75 2.00
Allen Craig
Matt Dominguez
3 Mike Baxter .60 1.50
Ross Detwiler
Garrett Jones
4 Bud Black .75 2.00
Josh Willingham
Alexei Ramirez
5 Stephen Drew .75 2.00
Christian Garcia
Eury Perez
AL Strikeout Leaders
6 Lucas Duda .75 2.00
Joe Saunders
Chris Nelson
7 Rafael Furcal .75 2.00
Joe Mauer
Gerardo Parra
8 Paul Goldschmidt 1.00 2.50
Johan Santana
John Axford
9 Joel Hanrahan .75 2.00
Andrelton Simmons
Shane Victorino
10 Edwin Jackson .60 1.50
Bryan Morris
Justin Wilson
Buck Showalter
11 John Jaso .75 2.00
Brian McCann
Dee Gordon
12 Kenley Jansen .75 2.00
Jon Lester
Anthony Gose
13 Desmond Jennings .75 2.00
Marco Estrada
Andrew Bailey
14 Ubaldo Jiminez .75 2.00
Brandon Crawford
Ruben Tejada
15 Howie Kendrick .60 1.50
Luis Ayala
Carlos Ruiz
16 Kyle Lohse .75 2.00
Torii Hunter
Todd Frazier
17 Jed Lowrie 1.00 2.50
Nyjer Morgan
Brian Wilson
18 Shaun Marcum .60 1.50
Jose Valverde
Ron Washington
19 Mrtnz/Mstks/Crrra 1.00 2.50
20 Mitch Moreland .60 1.50
Tyler Colvin
Sandoval Pokes Three
21 Glen Perkins .75 2.00
Jonathan Papelbon
Patrick Corbin
22 A.J. Pierzynski .60 1.50
Rafael Ortega
Rob Scahill
Mike Matheny
23 Henry Rodriguez 1.25 3.00
Tony Cingrani
Will Venable
Mark Teixeira
24 Seth Smith 1.25 3.00
AL RBI Leaders
Darin Ruf
Tyler Cloyd
25 Drew Storen .60 1.50
Gaby Sanchez
Jason Grilli
26 Robin Ventura .75 2.00
Curtis Granderson
Elvis Andrus

2013 Topps Heritage Baseball Flashbacks

COMPLETE SET (10) 4.00 10.00
STATED ODDS 1:12 HOBBY
AK Al Kaline .60 1.50
BG Bob Gibson .50 1.25
CY Carl Yastrzemski 1.00 2.50
EB Ernie Banks .60 1.50
FR Frank Robinson .50 1.25
HA Hank Aaron 1.25 3.00
JM Juan Marichal .50 1.25
SK Sandy Koufax 1.25 3.00
SS Shea Stadium .25 .60
WM Willie Mays 1.25 3.00

2013 Topps Heritage Bazooka

AM Andrew McCutchen 10.00 25.00
BG Bob Gibson 30.00 60.00
BH Bryce Harper 30.00 60.00
BP Buster Posey 15.00 40.00
BR Brooks Robinson 12.50 30.00
CY Carl Yastrzemski 20.00 50.00
DJ Derek Jeter 20.00 50.00
EB Ernie Banks 15.00 40.00
EM Eddie Mathews 10.00 25.00
FH Felix Hernandez 8.00 20.00
HK Harmon Killebrew 15.00 40.00
JM Juan Marichal 30.00 60.00
JV Justin Verlander 20.00 50.00
MC Miguel Cabrera 15.00 40.00
MT Mike Trout 30.00 60.00
RB Ryan Braun 15.00 40.00
RC Roberto Clemente 20.00 50.00
SK Sandy Koufax 15.00 40.00
WM Willie Mays 15.00 40.00
YC Yoenis Cespedes 15.00 40.00

2013 Topps Heritage Chrome

STATED ODDS 1:24 HOBBY
STATED PRINT RUN 999 SER.#'d SETS
HC1 Miguel Cabrera 2.50 6.00
HC2 Derek Jeter 6.00 15.00
HC3 Evan Longoria 2.00 5.00
HC4 Yadier Molina 2.50 6.00
HC5 Albert Pujols 3.00 8.00
HC6 Ryan Howard 2.00 5.00
HC7 Joe Mauer 2.00 5.00
HC8 Hunter Pence 2.00 5.00
HC9 Ian Kinsler 2.00 5.00
HC10 Mike Trout 75.00 200.00
HC11 Ryan Zimmerman 2.00 5.00
HC12 Adam Jones 2.00 5.00
HC13 Hanley Ramirez 2.00 5.00
HC14 Martin Prado 1.50 4.00
HC15 Dustin Pedroia 2.00 5.00
HC16 Andre Ethier 2.00 5.00
HC17 Nelson Cruz 2.50 6.00
HC18 Matt Cain 2.00 5.00
HC19 Jose Bautista 2.00 5.00
HC20 Buster Posey 3.00 8.00
HC21 Billy Butler 1.50 4.00
HC22 Andrew McCutchen 2.50 6.00
HC23 David Freese 1.50 4.00
HC24 Robinson Cano 2.00 5.00
HC25 Clayton Kershaw 5.00 12.00
HC26 Kyle Lohse 1.50 4.00
HC27 Matt Kemp 2.00 5.00
HC28 Hiroki Kuroda 1.50 4.00
HC29 Adrian Beltre 2.50 6.00
HC30 Justin Verlander 2.50 6.00
HC31 Josh Willingham 2.00 5.00
HC32 Jay Bruce 2.00 5.00
HC33 James Shields 1.50 4.00
HC34 Felix Hernandez 2.00 5.00
HC35 Cole Hamels 2.00 5.00
HC36 Jered Weaver 2.00 5.00
HC37 Stephen Strasburg 2.50 6.00
HC38 Jarrod Parker 1.50 4.00
HC39 Alex Gordon 2.00 5.00
HC40 Yu Darvish 2.50 6.00
HC41 Carlos Santana 2.00 5.00
HC42 Mariano Rivera 3.00 8.00
HC43 Jim Johnson 1.50 4.00
HC44 Jake Peavy 1.50 4.00
HC45 Troy Tulowitzki 2.50 6.00
HC46 Jacoby Ellsbury 2.00 5.00
HC47 Gio Gonzalez 2.00 5.00
HC48 Adam Dunn 2.00 5.00
HC49 Chris Sale 2.50 6.00
HC50 Bryce Harper 4.00 10.00
HC51 Carlos Beltran 2.00 5.00
HC52 CC Sabathia 2.00 5.00
HC53 Adam LaRoche 1.50 4.00
HC54 Matt Harrison 1.50 4.00
HC55 Mat Latos 2.00 5.00
HC56 Fernando Rodney 1.50 4.00
HC57 Johnny Cueto 2.00 5.00
HC58 Wilin Rosario 1.50 4.00
HC59 Marco Scutaro 2.00 5.00
HC60 David Price 2.00 5.00
HC61 Yoenis Cespedes 2.50 6.00
HC62 Max Scherzer 2.50 6.00
HC63 Aramis Ramirez 1.50 4.00
HC64 Starlin Castro 1.50 4.00
HC65 Mark Trumbo 1.50 4.00
HC66 Roy Halladay 2.00 5.00
HC67 Giancarlo Stanton 2.50 6.00
HC68 Justin Upton 2.00 5.00
HC69 Kris Medlen 2.00 5.00
HC70 R.A. Dickey 2.00 5.00
HC71 David Wright 2.00 5.00
HC72 Jose Reyes 2.00 5.00
HC73 Jordan Zimmermann 2.00 5.00
HC74 Carlos Gonzalez 2.00 5.00
HC75 Prince Fielder 2.00 5.00
HC76 Miguel Montero 1.50 4.00
HC77 Chase Headley 1.50 4.00
HC78 Paul Konerko 2.00 5.00
HC79 Brandon Morrow 1.50 4.00
HC80 Ryan Braun 2.00 5.00
HC81 Madison Bumgarner 2.00 5.00
HC82 Matt Holliday 2.50 6.00
HC83 Adrian Gonzalez 2.00 5.00
HC84 Curtis Granderson 2.00 5.00
HC85 Michael Bourn 1.50 4.00
HC86 Wade Miley 1.50 4.00
HC87 Allen Craig 2.00 5.00
HC88 Edwin Encarnacion 2.50 6.00
HC89 Yovani Gallardo 1.50 4.00
HC90 Josh Hamilton 2.00 5.00
HC91 Ryan Vogelsong 1.50 4.00
HC92 Josh Reddick 1.50 4.00
HC93 Austin Jackson 1.50 4.00
HC94 M.Machado/D.Bundy 10.00 25.00
HC95 M.Olt/J.Profar 2.00 5.00
HC96 S.Miller/T.Rosenthal 4.00 10.00
HC97 Adam Eaton/Tyler Skaggs 2.50 6.00
HC98 D.Ruf/T.Cloyd 3.00 8.00
HC99 Collin McHugh/Jeurys Familia 2.50 6.00
HC100 Brock Holt/Kyle McPherson 2.00 5.00

2013 Topps Heritage Chrome Black Refractors

*BLACK REF: 2X TO 5X BASIC
STATED ODDS 1:368 HOBBY
STATED PRINT RUN 64 SER.#'d SETS
HC2 Derek Jeter 125.00 250.00
HC10 Mike Trout 300.00 600.00
HC50 Bryce Harper 75.00 150.00

2013 Topps Heritage Chrome Purple Refractors

*PURPLE REF: .4X TO 1X BASIC

2013 Topps Heritage Chrome Refractors

*REF: .5X TO 1.2X BASIC
STATED ODDS 1:42 HOBBY
STATED PRINT RUN 554 SER.#'d SETS

2013 Topps Heritage Clubhouse Collection Dual Relics

STATED ODDS 1:5003 HOBBY
STATED PRINT RUN 64 SER.#'d SETS
CM R.Clemente/A.McCutchen 75.00 150.00
KC A.Kaline/M.Cabrera 60.00 120.00
KM H.Killebrew/J.Mauer 40.00 80.00
MP W.Mays/B.Posey 75.00 150.00
YE C.Yastrzemski/J.Ellsbury 40.00 80.00

2013 Topps Heritage Clubhouse Collection Relics

STATED ODDS 1:38 HOBBY
AB Adrian Beltre 3.00 8.00
AD Adam Dunn 3.00 8.00
AG Alex Gordon 3.00 8.00
AJ Adam Jones 3.00 8.00
AW Adam Wainwright 3.00 8.00
BB Brandon Beachy 3.00 8.00
BBE Brandon Belt 4.00 10.00
BBU Billy Butler 3.00 8.00
BM Brandon McCarthy 3.00 8.00
BMO Brandon Morrow 3.00 8.00
BP Brandon Phillips 3.00 8.00
BU B.J. Upton 3.00 8.00
CD Chris Davis 6.00 15.00
CG Carlos Gonzalez 3.00 8.00
CR Colby Rasmus 3.00 8.00
CS Carlos Santana 3.00 8.00
CW C.J. Wilson 3.00 8.00
DE Danny Espinosa 3.00 8.00
DG Dee Gordon 3.00 8.00
DH Dan Haren 3.00 8.00
DJ Desmond Jennings 3.00 8.00
DM Devin Mesoraco 3.00 8.00
DS Drew Stubbs 3.00 8.00
EA Elvis Andrus 3.00 8.00
EE Edwin Encarnacion 3.00 8.00
EL Evan Longoria 4.00 10.00
ID Ian Desmond 3.00 8.00
IK Ian Kinsler 3.00 8.00
IKE Ian Kennedy 3.00 8.00
JB Jay Bruce 4.00 10.00
JC Johnny Cueto 3.00 8.00
JCH Jhoulys Chacin 3.00 8.00
JG Jaime Garcia 3.00 8.00
JH Jason Heyward 4.00 10.00
JHA Josh Hamilton 3.00 8.00
JJ Jon Jay 3.00 8.00
JM Jesus Montero 3.00 8.00
JMO Jason Motte 3.00 8.00
JP Jake Peavy 3.00 8.00
JPA Jordan Pacheco 3.00 8.00
JPE Jhonny Peralta 3.00 8.00
JS Johan Santana 3.00 8.00
JV Justin Verlander 8.00 20.00
JZ Jordan Zimmermann 3.00 8.00
MB Madison Bumgarner 5.00 12.00
MC Matt Cain 4.00 10.00
MG Matt Garza 3.00 8.00
ML Mike Leake 3.00 8.00
MM Mike Moustakas
MMI Mike Minor 3.00 8.00
MMO Miguel Montero 3.00 8.00
MN Mike Napoli 3.00 8.00
MS Max Scherzer 3.00 8.00
MT Mike Trout 15.00 40.00
MY Michael Young 3.00 8.00
NC Nelson Cruz 3.00 8.00
NF Neftali Feliz 3.00 8.00
NM Nick Markakis 3.00 8.00
PA Pedro Alvarez 3.00 8.00
PK Paul Konerko 3.00 8.00
RP Rick Porcello 3.00 8.00
RZ Ryan Zimmerman 3.00 8.00
SC Starlin Castro 3.00 8.00
SM Shaun Marcum 3.00 8.00
SSC Shin-Soo Choo 3.00 8.00
TC Trevor Cahill 3.00 8.00
TH Tim Hudson 3.00 8.00
THA Tommy Hanson 3.00 8.00
THU Torii Hunter 3.00 8.00
WR Wilin Rosario 3.00 8.00
YA Yonder Alonso 3.00 8.00
YC Yoenis Cespedes 4.00 10.00
YG Yovani Gallardo 3.00 8.00

2013 Topps Heritage Clubhouse Collection Relics Gold

STATED ODDS 1:225 HOBBY
STATED PRINT RUN 99 SER.#'d SETS

2013 Topps Heritage Framed Stamps

STATED ODDS 1:4701 HOBBY
STATED PRINT RUN 50 SER.#'d SETS
S Shakespeare 12.50 30.00
AR Amateur Radio 12.50 30.00
CM C.M. Russell 15.00 40.00
DM Doctors Mayo 12.50 30.00
FA Fine Arts 12.50 30.00
HK Harmon Killebrew 15.00 40.00
JFK John F. Kennedy 20.00 50.00
JM John Muir 15.00 40.00
LA Luis Aparicio 15.00 40.00
MW Maury Wills 20.00 50.00
NJ N.J. Tricentenary 12.50 30.00
NS Nevada Statehood 15.00 40.00
RC Roberto Clemente 15.00 40.00
RG Robert H. Goddard 12.50 30.00
SH Sam Houston 12.50 30.00
UC U.S. Customs 15.00 40.00
UH U.S. Homemakers 12.50 30.00
UV U.S. Volte 30.00 60.00
VB Verrazano Bridge 15.00 40.00
WF World's Fair 15.00 40.00

2013 Topps Heritage Giants

STATED ODDS 1:36 HOBBY BOXES
AM Andrew McCutchen 12.00 30.00
BG Bob Gibson 20.00 50.00
BH Bryce Harper 20.00 50.00
DJ Derek Jeter 40.00 80.00
EB Ernie Banks 12.00 30.00
EM Eddie Mathews 30.00 60.00
FH Felix Hernandez 10.00 25.00
GS Giancarlo Stanton 12.00 30.00
HK Harmon Killebrew 15.00 40.00
JB Jose Bautista 10.00 25.00
JV Justin Verlander 12.00 30.00
MC Miguel Cabrera 12.00 30.00
MCA Matt Cain 10.00 25.00
MT Mike Trout 100.00 250.00
RA R.A. Dickey 10.00 25.00
RB Ryan Braun 10.00 25.00
RC Robinson Cano 15.00 40.00
WM Willie Mays 25.00 60.00
YC Yoenis Cespedes 12.00 30.00
YD Yu Darvish 12.00 30.00

2013 Topps Heritage Memorable Moments

COMPLETE SET (15) 6.00 15.00
STATED ODDS 1:12 HOBBY
BH Bryce Harper 1.00 2.50
CB Carlos Beltran .50 1.25
DJ Derek Jeter 1.50 4.00
DO David Ortiz .60 1.50
DP David Price .50 1.25
FH Felix Hernandez .50 1.25
JS Johan Santana .50 1.25
MC Miguel Cabrera .60 1.50
MCA Matt Cain .50 1.25
MM Manny Machado 2.50 6.00
MT Mike Trout 5.00 12.00
PF Prince Fielder .50 1.25
RA R.A. Dickey .50 1.25
TR Teddy Roosevelt .25 .60
YU Yu Darvish .60 1.50

2013 Topps Heritage New Age Performers

COMPLETE SET (30) 12.50 30.00
STATED ODDS 1:8 HOBBY
AB Adrian Beltre .60 1.50
AM Andrew McCutchen .60 1.50
AP Albert Pujols .75 2.00
BB Billy Butler .40 1.00
BH Bryce Harper 1.00 2.50
BP Buster Posey .75 2.00
CG Curtis Granderson .50 1.25
CK Clayton Kershaw 1.25 3.00
DP David Price .50 1.25
DW David Wright .50 1.25
FH Felix Hernandez .50 1.25
GG Gio Gonzalez .50 1.25
JM Joe Mauer .50 1.25
JV Justin Verlander .60 1.50
KM Kris Medlen .50 1.25
MC Miguel Cabrera .60 1.50
MK Matt Kemp .50 1.25
MM Manny Machado 2.50 6.00
MT Mike Trout 5.00 12.00
PF Prince Fielder .50 1.25
RB Ryan Braun .50 1.25
RC Robinson Cano .50 1.25
RD R.A. Dickey .50 1.25
SC Starlin Castro .40 1.00
SS Stephen Strasburg .60 1.50
WM Wade Miley .40 1.00
YC Yoenis Cespedes .60 1.50
YD Yu Darvish .60 1.50
YM Yadier Molina .60 1.50
MCA Matt Cain .50 1.25

2013 Topps Heritage News Flashbacks

COMPLETE SET (10) 3.00 8.00
STATED ODDS 1:12 HOBBY
J Jeopardy .25 .60
CRA Civil Rights Act of 1964 .25 .60
FM Ford Mustang .25 .60
LBJ Lyndon B. Johnson .25 .60
MLK Dr. Martin Luther King Jr. .40 1.00
MP Mary Poppins .25 .60
RS The Rolling Stones .60 1.50
SP Sidney Poitier .25 .60
TB The Beatles .60 1.50
WF 1964 World's Fair .25 .60

2013 Topps Heritage Real One Autographs

STATED ODDS 1:124 HOBBY
HN CARDS ISSUED IN HN.FACT.SETS
EXCHANGE DEADLINE 1/31/2016
HN EXCH.DEADLINE 11/30/2016
AE Adam Eaton HN 6.00 15.00
AG Anthony Gose 6.00 15.00
AH Aaron Hicks HN 10.00 25.00
AHE Adeiny Hechavarria HN 6.00 15.00
AM Al Moran 10.00 25.00
AR Anthony Rendon HN 100.00 250.00
AS Anibal Sanchez 12.50 30.00
ASA Amado Samuel 6.00 15.00
BD Bill Dailey 6.00 15.00
BF Bill Fischer 6.00 15.00
BG Bob Gibson 20.00 50.00
BJ Brett Jackson 6.00 15.00
BL Bob Lillis 10.00 25.00
BM Brandon Maurer HN 6.00 15.00
BP Bill Pierce 12.00 30.00
BR Bruce Rondon HN 10.00 25.00
BR Bobby Richardson 10.00 25.00
BS Bobby Shantz 10.00 25.00
CA Chris Archer 12.00 30.00
CB Carl Bouldin 6.00 15.00
CD Charlie Dees 10.00 25.00
CK Casey Kelly HN 6.00 15.00
CM Charlie Maxwell 10.00 25.00
DF David Freese 15.00 40.00
DG Didi Gregorius HN 30.00 80.00
DG Dick Groat 6.00 15.00
DL Don Leppert 10.00 25.00
DP Dan Pfister 6.00 15.00
DR Darin Ruf HN 6.00 15.00
EB Ernie Banks 50.00 100.00
EBU Ellis Burton 6.00 15.00
EG Evan Gattis HN 6.00 15.00
FF Frank Funk 6.00 15.00
FR Frank Robinson 30.00 60.00
GC Gene Conley 6.00 15.00
GC Gerrit Cole HN 40.00 80.00
GH Glen Hobbie 6.00 15.00
HA Hank Aaron 200.00 400.00
HB Hal Brown 6.00 15.00
HF Hank Foiles 6.00 15.00
HR Hyun-Jin Ryu HN 50.00 100.00
JB Jose Bautista 15.00 40.00
JB Jackie Bradley Jr. HN 25.00 60.00
JC Jim Campbell 6.00 15.00
JF Jose Fernandez HN 40.00 100.00
JG Jedd Gyorko HN 8.00 20.00
JG John Goryl 10.00 25.00
JH Jay Hook 6.00 15.00
JL Jeoff Long 6.00 15.00
JM Juan Marichal 20.00 50.00
JP Jurickson Profar HN 40.00 80.00
JSH James Shields 6.00 15.00
JSP Jack Spring 6.00 15.00
JW Jerry Walker 6.00 15.00
KF Kyuji Fujikawa HN 6.00 15.00
KM Ken MacKenzie 6.00 15.00
LL Lance Lynn 10.00 25.00
LT Luis Tiant 6.00 15.00
MA Matt Adams HN
MJ Mike Joyce 6.00 15.00
MM Mike Morse 10.00 25.00
MM Manny Machado HN 150.00 400.00
MMI Minnie Minoso 8.00 20.00
MO Marcell Ozuna HN 25.00 60.00
MOL Mike Olt HN 8.00 20.00
MR Mike Roarke 10.00 25.00
MT Mark Trumbo 6.00 15.00
MW Maury Wills 6.00 15.00
MZ Mike Zunino HN 8.00 20.00
NA Nolan Arenado HN
NF Nick Franklin HN EXCH 6.00 15.00
OA Oswaldo Arcia HN
OC Orlando Cepeda 10.00 25.00
PB Paul Brown 6.00 15.00
PF Paul Foytack 6.00 15.00
PG Paul Goldschmidt 50.00 120.00
PGR Pumpsie Green 12.00 30.00
PR Paco Rodriguez HN 8.00 20.00
RM Roman Mejias 12.00 30.00
SD Scott Diamond 6.00 15.00
SM Stan Musial 150.00 300.00
SM Shelby Miller HN 6.00 15.00
SMA Starling Marte 6.00 15.00
TB Ted Bowsfield 6.00 15.00
TBR Tom Brown 6.00 15.00
TC Tony Cingrani HN 6.00 15.00
TF Todd Frazier 6.00 15.00
TH Tim Harkness 6.00 15.00
WM Willie Mays 200.00 400.00
WM Wil Myers HN 20.00 50.00
WMI Will Middlebrooks 10.00 25.00
YG Yasmani Grandal 6.00 15.00
YP Yasiel Puig HN EXCH 400.00 600.00
ZW Zack Wheeler HN 8.00 20.00

2013 Topps Heritage Real One Autographs Red Ink

*RED: .6X TO 1.5X BASIC
STATED ODDS 1:480 HOBBY
HN CARDS FOUND IN HIGH NUMBER BOXES
PRINT RUNS B/WN 10-64 COPIES PER
HN PRINT RUN 10 SER.#'d SETS
NO HIGH NUMBER PRICING AVAILABLE
EXCHANGE DEADLINE 1/31/2016
HN EXCH.DEADLINE 11/30/2016

2013 Topps Heritage Then and Now

COMPLETE SET (10) 5.00 12.00
STATED ODDS 1:15 HOBBY
AT L.Aparicio/M.Trout 5.00 12.00
BV J.Bunning/J.Verlander .60 1.50
CP R.Clemente/B.Posey 1.50 4.00
FH Whitey Ford/Felix Hernandez .50 1.25
GV B.Gibson/J.Verlander .60 1.50
KC H.Killebrew/M.Cabrera .60 1.50
KK S.Koufax/C.Kershaw 1.25 3.00
MD Eddie Mathews/Adam Dunn .60 1.50
MG Juan Marichal/Gio Gonzalez .50 1.25
RC B.Robinson/M.Cabrera .60 1.50

2014 Topps Heritage

COMP.SET w/o SPs (425) 20.00 50.00
COMP.HN FACT.SET (101) 60.00 120.00
COMP.HN SET (100) 50.00 100.00
SP ODDS 1:3 HOBBY
ACTION SP ODDS 1:23 HOBBY
LOGO SP ODDS 1:135 HOBBY
THROWBACK SP ODDS 1:3175 HOBBY
ERROR SP ODDS 1:1473 HOBBY
HN FACT SETS SOLD ONLY
1 Trout/Mauer/Cabrera 1.25 3.00
2 Freeman/Johnson/Cuddyer .30 .75
3 Encarnacion/Cabrera/Davis .25 .60
4 Alvarez/Bruce/Brown/Goldschmidt .25 .60
5 Cano/Jones/Cabrera/Davis .25 .60
6 Frmn/Bruce/Gldschmdt .30 .75
7 A.Sanchez/B.Colon .15 .40
8 J.Fernandez/C.Kershaw .50 1.25
9 Tillman/Wilson/Moore/Colon/Scherzer .20 .50
10 Kershaw/Zimmermann/Wain .50 1.25
11 Sale/Darvish/Scherzer .25 .60
12 Samardzija/Kershaw/Lee .50 1.25
13 Ross Ohlendorf .15 .40
14 Brian Roberts .15 .40
15 Asdrubal Cabrera .20 .50
16 Carlos Ruiz .15 .40
17 John Mayberry .15 .40
18 Felix Doubront .15 .40
19 Jeff Locke .15 .40
20 Cliff Lee .20 .50
21 Jon Jay .15 .40
22 A.J. Ellis .15 .40
23 Joaquin Benoit .15 .40
24 E.Adrianza RC/Z.Walters RC .40 1.00
25 Kyle Lohse .15 .40
26 Ryan Wheeler .15 .40
27 Jarrod Saltalamacchia .15 .40
28 Jose Altuve .20 .50
29 Derek Norris .15 .40
30 Hiroki Kuroda .15 .40
31 Salvador Perez .20 .50
32 Bruce Bochy MG .20 .50
33 Michael Cuddyer .15 .40
34 A.J. Burnett .15 .40
35 Ryan Vogelsong .15 .40
36 Coco Crisp .15 .40
37 Logan Morrison .15 .40
38 Brett Lawrie .20 .50
39 Chris Carter .15 .40
40 Carl Crawford .20 .50
41 A.Rienzo RC/E.Johnson RC .40 1.00
42 Matt Joyce .15 .40
43A Carlos Beltran .20 .50
43B C.Beltran SP ERR 12.00 30.00
44 Aaron Hill .15 .40
45 Brett Wallace .15 .40
46 Stephen Drew .15 .40
47 Rex Brothers .15 .40
48 Marlon Byrd .15 .40
49 J.Schoop RC/X.Bogaerts RC 1.25 3.00
50 Matt Cain .20 .50
51 Denard Span .15 .40
52 Daniel Nava .15 .40
53A Giancarlo Stanton .25 .60
53B Giancarlo Stanton Logo SP 8.00 20.00
54 Andrew Cashner .15 .40
55 Matt Garza .15 .40
56 Alexi Ogando .15 .40
57 Ryne Sandberg .50 1.25
58 A.J. Pierzynski .15 .40
59 Adam Lind .15 .40
60 Aroldis Chapman .25 .60
61 Nate Eovaldi .20 .50
62A Kevin Correia .15 .40
62B K.Correia SP ERR 10.00 25.00
63 Jacob Turner .20 .50
64 Alex Rodriguez .30 .75
65 Garrett Richards .20 .50
66 Joe Maddon MG .15 .40
67 Nick Franklin .15 .40
68 Jake Odorizzi .15 .40
69 Gaby Sanchez .15 .40
70 Paul Konerko .20 .50
71 Heath Bell .15 .40
72 Homer Bailey .15 .40
73 Francisco Liriano .15 .40
74 C.Leesman RC/M.Belfiore RC .40 1.00
75 Cody Asche .20 .50
76 Chris Capuano .15 .40
77 Austin Romine .15 .40
78 Adam Jones .20 .50
79 Dan Haren .15 .40
80 Brett Oberholtzer .15 .40
81 Jed Lowrie .15 .40
82 C.Bethancourt RC/D.Hale RC .40 1.00
83 Justin Smoak .15 .40
84A Hyun-Jin Ryu .20 .50
84B Hyun-Jin Ryu Action SP 2.50 6.00
85 Alex Rios .20 .50
86 Wei-Yin Chen .15 .40
87 Daniel Murphy .20 .50
88 Ricky Nolasco .15 .40
89 Kyle Gibson .20 .50
90 Trevor Plouffe .15 .40
91 Clint Hurdle MG .15 .40
92 C.J. Wilson .15 .40
93 Jenrry Mejia .15 .40
94 Hector Santiago .15 .40
95 Brandon McCarthy .15 .40
96 Andres Torres .15 .40
97 Chris Heisey .15 .40
98 Mark Buehrle .20 .50
99 Walt Weiss MG .15 .40
100A Adam Wainwright .20 .50
100C Adam Wainwright Action SP 2.50 6.00
101 Brian Wilson .25 .60
102 Howie Kendrick .15 .40
103 Alex Gordon .20 .50
104 J.Butler RC/J.Adduci RC .40 1.00
105 Daniel Hudson .15 .40
106 Nick Markakis .20 .50
107 E.Martin RC/C.Rupp RC .40 1.00
108 Justin Masterson .15 .40
109 Miguel Montero .15 .40
110 Starlin Castro .15 .40
111 Yunel Escobar .15 .40
112 Marcell Ozuna .25 .60
113 Lance Berkman .20 .50
114 Addison Reed .15 .40
115 Ubaldo Jimenez .15 .40
116 K.Wong RC/A.Perez RC .50 1.25
117 Chase Headley .15 .40
118 Justin Ruggiano .15 .40
119 Chase Utley .20 .50
120 Shin-Soo Choo .20 .50
121 Kendrys Morales .15 .40
122 Tyler Chatwood .15 .40
123 Johnny Cueto .20 .50
124 Aramis Ramirez .15 .40
125 Nate Schierholtz .15 .40
126 Mike Matheny MG .15 .40
127 Matt Adams .15 .40
128 Mike Leake .15 .40
129 Alejandro De Aza .15 .40
130 Austin Jackson .15 .40
131 Joe Girardi .20 .50
132 World Series Game 1 .25 .60
133 World Series Game 2 .25 .60
134 World Series Game 3 .25 .60
135 World Series Game 4 .25 .60
136 World Series Game 5 .25 .60
137 World Series Game 6 .25 .60
137 Anthony Gose .15 .40
139 Melky Cabrera .15 .40
140A Jered Weaver .20 .50
140B Jered Weaver Action SP 2.50 6.00
141 Torii Hunter .15 .40
142 Michael Saunders .20 .50
143 A.Lambo RC/S.Pimentel RC .40 1.00
144 Brad Miller .20 .50
145 Edwin Encarnacion .25 .60
146 Juan Pierre .15 .40
147 Johan Santana .20 .50
148A Freddie Freeman .30 .75
148B F.Freeman TB SP 100.00 250.00
148C Freddie Freeman Action SP 4.00 10.00
149A Buster Posey .30 .75
149B B.Posey Logo SP 15.00 40.00
150A Manny Machado .25 .60
150B Machado Action SP 3.00 8.00
151 Kirk Gibson .15 .40
152 Todd Frazier .20 .50
153 Joe Kelly .15 .40
154 Kris Medlen .20 .50
155 Gio Gonzalez .20 .50
156 Mark Ellis .15 .40
157 Kyle Seager .15 .40
158 John Gibbons MG .15 .40
159 Clint Barmes .15 .40
160A Andrew McCutchen .25 .60
160B McCutchen Logo SP 10.00 25.00
160C McCutchen SP ERR 20.00 50.00
161 Brett Gardner .20 .50
162 Cameron Maybin .15 .40
163 Wily Peralta .15 .40
164 John Danks .15 .40
165 Gerardo Parra .15 .40
166 A.Almonte RC/L.Watkins RC .40 1.00
167 Raul Ibanez .20 .50
168 Ike Davis .15 .40
169 Brian Dozier .20 .50
170A Justin Upton .20 .50
170B J.Upton TB SP 75.00 150.00
170C Justin Upton Action SP 2.50 6.00
171 Gordon Beckham .15 .40
172 Ivan Nova .20 .50
173 Ryan Ludwick .15 .40
174 Carlos Martinez .20 .50
175 Dayan Viciedo .15 .40
176 J.B. Shuck .15 .40
177 Dan Straily .15 .40
178 Jose Quintana .15 .40
179 Rafael Betancourt .15 .40
180 Oswaldo Arcia .15 .40
181 T.Gosewisch RC/N.Christiani RC .40 1.00
182 Jake Peavy .15 .40
183 Robbie Grossman .15 .40
184 Kole Calhoun .15 .40
185 Matt Holliday .25 .60
186 Jon Niese .15 .40
187 Terry Collins .15 .40
188 Eric Sogard .15 .40
189 T.Medica RC/R.Fuentes RC .40 1.00
190 Allen Craig .20 .50
191 Tommy Milone .15 .40
192 Luke Hochevar .15 .40
193 Ian Kennedy .15 .40
194 B.Boshers RC/M.Shoemaker RC .60 1.50
195 John Jaso .15 .40
196 Jose Iglesias .15 .40
197A Josh Reddick .15 .40
197B J.Reddick TB SP 75.00 150.00
198A Eric Hosmer .20 .50
198B E.Hosmer TB SP 150.00 250.00
199 Jeremy Hefner .15 .40
200A Jason Heyward .20 .50
200B J.Heyward TB SP 75.00 150.00
201 Z.Rosscup RC/J.Pinto RC .40 1.00
202 Wade Miley .15 .40
203 Leonys Martin .15 .40
204 Jonathan Papelbon .20 .50
205 Starling Marte .20 .50
206 John Lackey .20 .50
207 David Murphy .15 .40
208 Roy Halladay .20 .50
209 Jason Vargas .15 .40
210 Erick Aybar .15 .40
211 Bronson Arroyo .15 .40
212 Steve Cishek .15 .40
213 Clay Buchholz .15 .40
214 Doug Fister .15 .40
215 Matt Harrison .15 .40
216 Patrick Corbin .20 .50
217 Don Mattingly .50 1.25
218 Juan Nicasio .15 .40
219 Michael Young .15 .40
220 Junior Lake .15 .40
221 Bartolo Colon .15 .40
222 Desmond Jennings .20 .50
223 Miguel Gonzalez .15 .40
224 Brandon Moss .15 .40
225 Juan Francisco .15 .40
226 C.Cabral RC/J.Murphy RC .40 1.00
227 Jonny Venters .15 .40
228 Mitch Moreland .15 .40
229 Colby Rasmus .20 .50
230 Lance Lynn .15 .40
231 Chris Johnson .15 .40
232 J.P. Arencibia .15 .40
233 Daniel Descalso .15 .40
234 Jonny Gomes .15 .40
235 Kevin Gregg .15 .40
236 Jorge De La Rosa .15 .40
237 Phil Hughes .15 .40
238 Josh Beckett .15 .40
239 Chris Perez .15 .40
240 Jarred Cosart .15 .40
241 Drew Stubbs .15 .40
242 Ross Detwiler .15 .40
243 N.Castellanos RC/B.Hamilton RC 1.25 3.00
244 Mike Napoli .15 .40
245 Neftali Feliz .15 .40
246 Jeremy Guthrie .15 .40
247 Mat Latos .20 .50
248 Pete Kozma .15 .40
249 Martin Prado .15 .40
250A Mike Trout 1.25 3.00
250B M.Trout TB SP 100.00 200.00
250C M.Trout Action SP 25.00 60.00
250D M.Trout Logo SP 20.00 50.00
251 John Farrell MG .15 .40
252 Dan Uggla .15 .40
253 Justin Maxwell .15 .40
254 Charlie Morton .25 .60
255 Darin Ruf .20 .50
256 Wilson Ramos .15 .40
257 Koji Uehara .15 .40
258 Rick Porcello .20 .50
259 T.Beckham RC/E.Romero RC .60 1.50
260 Zack Greinke .20 .50
261 Jose Molina .15 .40
262 Casey Janssen .15 .40
263 Jonathan Lucroy .20 .50
264 Fernando Rodney .15 .40
265 James Loney .15 .40
266 Adam Dunn .20 .50
267 Jason Grilli .15 .40
268 Christian Yelich .30 .75
269 Albert Pujols .30 .75
270 Jim Johnson .15 .40
271 Grant Balfour .15 .40
272 Eric Stults .15 .40
273 C.Bettis RC/D.Holmberg RC .40 1.00
274 Ron Washington MG .15 .40
275 Julio Teheran .20 .50
276 Ryan Dempster .15 .40
277 Will Venable .15 .40
278 David Lough .15 .40
279 Evan Gattis .15 .40
280 Ryan Howard .20 .50
281 Gregor Blanco .15 .40
282 K.Siegrist RC/H.Hembree RC .75 2.00
283 Josh Donaldson .20 .50
284A David Wright .20 .50
284B David Wright Action SP 2.50 6.00
285 Scooter Gennett .20 .50
286 A.Caminero RC/K.Johnson RC .40 1.00
287 Juan Uribe .15 .40
288 Jhonny Peralta .15 .40
289 Will Middlebrooks .15 .40
290 Chris Tillman .15 .40
291 Carlos Quentin .15 .40
292 Jim Henderson .15 .40
293 Shane Victorino .20 .50
294 David Robertson .15 .40
295 Kyle Blanks .15 .40
296 Randall Delgado .15 .40
297 Khris Davis .25 .60
298 Corey Hart .15 .40
299 Mike Moustakas .20 .50
300A Clayton Kershaw .50 1.25
300B Kershaw Action SP 6.00 15.00
301 Terry Francona MG .20 .50
302 Adam Eaton .15 .40
303 Prince Fielder .20 .50
304 Marco Estrada .15 .40
305 Garrett Jones .15 .40
306 R.A. Dickey .20 .50
307 Jonathan Villar .15 .40
308 T.d'Arnaud RC/W.Flores RC .50 1.25
309 Brandon Barnes .15 .40
310A Domonic Brown .20 .50
310B Domonic Brown Logo SP 6.00 15.00
311 Brandon Morrow .15 .40
312 Munenori Kawasaki .20 .50
313 Yonder Alonso .15 .40
314 Avisail Garcia .20 .50
315 Mike Pelfrey .15 .40
316 Ben Zobrist .20 .50
317 Neil Walker .20 .50
318 Dillon Gee .15 .40
319 David Price .20 .50
320 Shelby Miller .20 .50
321 Jason Castro .15 .40
322 Brandon Crawford .20 .50
323 Buck Showalter MG .15 .40
324 Devin Mesoraco .15 .40
325 Alexei Ramirez .20 .50
326 Elvis Andrus .20 .50
327 D.J. LeMahieu .25 .60
328 Jeremy Hellickson .15 .40
329 Ervin Santana .15 .40
330 CC Sabathia .20 .50
331 O.Garcia RC/N.Buss RC .40 1.00
332 Ryan Raburn .15 .40
333 Mark Melancon .15 .40
334 Alcides Escobar .20 .50
335 Tyler Pastornicky .15 .40
336 Andy Dirks .15 .40
337 Jimmy Rollins .20 .50
338 Corey Kluber .20 .50
339 Zack Cozart .15 .40
340 Josh Willingham .20 .50
341 Glen Perkins .15 .40
342 Matt Carpenter .25 .60
343 Russell Martin .15 .40
344 Justin Morneau .20 .50
345 Jose Bautista .20 .50
346 Fredi Gonzalez MG .15 .40
347 Jhoulys Chacin .15 .40
348 Kyuji Fujikawa .20 .50
349 Yovani Gallardo .15 .40
350 Alfonso Soriano .20 .50
351 Adam LaRoche .15 .40
352 Edward Mujica .15 .40
353 Rickie Weeks .15 .40
354 J.Paxton RC/T.Walker RC .60 1.50
355 Cody Ross .15 .40
356 Victor Martinez .20 .50
357 Lonnie Chisenhall .15 .40
358 Vernon Wells .15 .40
359 Huston Street .15 .40
360 Brandon Belt .20 .50
361 M.Choice RC/J.Marisnick RC .40 1.00
362 Eduardo Nunez .15 .40
363 Norichika Aoki .15 .40
364 Darwin Barney .15 .40
365 Adeiny Hechavarria .15 .40
366 A.J. Griffin .15 .40
367 Alex Cobb .15 .40
368 M.Davidson RC/C.Owings RC .40 1.00
369 Omar Infante .15 .40
370A Matt Kemp .20 .50
370B Matt Kemp Action SP 2.50 6.00
371 Edwin Jackson .15 .40
372 Chris Rusin .15 .40
373 Ben Revere .15 .40
374 W.Tovar RC/M.Robles RC .40 1.00
375 Yasmani Grandal .15 .40
376 Michael Brantley .20 .50
377 Kevin Gausman .20 .50
378 Trevor Rosenthal .20 .50
379 Trevor Cahill .15 .40
380 Michael Bourn .15 .40
381 Dustin Ackley .15 .40
382 Bobby Parnell .15 .40
383 Ryan Doumit .15 .40
384 Andre Ethier .20 .50
385 Nate McLouth .15 .40
386 Y.Ventura RC/J.Nelson RC .50 1.25
387 Jedd Gyorko .15 .40
388 Matt Dominguez .15 .40
389 Marco Scutaro .20 .50
390 Alex Avila .20 .50
391 Bob Melvin MG .15 .40
392 Travis Wood .15 .40
393 Lorenzo Cain .15 .40
394 Dexter Fowler .20 .50
395 Brian McCann .20 .50
396 Everth Cabrera .15 .40
397 Peter Bourjos .15 .40
398 D.Webb RC/C.Robinson RC .40 1.00
399 Nick Swisher .20 .50
400A Bryce Harper .40 1.00
400B B.Harper TB SP 200.00 400.00
400C B.Harper Action SP 10.00 25.00
400D B.Harper Logo SP 15.00 40.00
401 Jose Lobaton .15 .40
402 Jayson Werth .20 .50
403 Kenley Jansen .20 .50
404 Charlie Blackmon .25 .60
405 Danny Salazar .20 .50
406 Rajai Davis .15 .40
407A Michael Wacha .20 .50
407B M.Wacha Action SP 2.50 6.00
407C M.Wacha Logo SP 6.00 15.00
408 Didi Gregorius .20 .50
409 J.DeLeon RC/M.Stassi RC .40 1.00
410 J.J. Hardy .15 .40
411 Mike Minor .15 .40
412 Jose Tabata .15 .40
413 A.J. Pollock .20 .50
414 Robin Ventura MG .15 .40
415 Mike Zunino .15 .40
416 Emilio Bonifacio .15 .40
417 Bud Norris .15 .40
418 Joe Nathan .15 .40
419 Aaron Hicks .20 .50
420 Jeff Samardzija .15 .40
421 K.Pillar RC/R.Goins RC .50 1.25
422 Brad Ziegler .15 .40
423 Alex Wood .15 .40
424 Zack Wheeler .20 .50
425A Yoenis Cespedes .25 .60
425B Y.Cespedes TB SP 75.00 150.00
426A Yasiel Puig SP 8.00 20.00
426B Y.Puig Action SP 10.00 25.00
426C Y.Puig Logo SP 8.00 20.00
427 Jurickson Profar SP 2.00 5.00
428 Madison Bumgarner SP 2.00 5.00
429 Sonny Gray SP 2.00 5.00

430A Justin Verlander SP 2.50 6.00
430B Verlander Action SP 3.00 8.00
431 Jon Lester SP 2.00 5.00
432 Jay Bruce SP 2.00 5.00
433A Derek Jeter SP 10.00 25.00
433B DJeter TB SP 450.00 700.00
433C D.Jeter Action SP 12.00 30.00
434 Pedro Alvarez SP 1.50 4.00
435 Andrelton Simmons SP 1.50 4.00
436 Nelson Cruz SP 2.50 6.00
437A Hanley Ramirez SP 2.00 5.00
437B Hanley Ramirez Action SP 2.50 6.00
438 Mark Teixeira SP 2.00 5.00
439 Jose Fernandez SP 2.50 6.00
440 Tim Lincecum SP 2.00 5.00
441A David Ortiz SP 2.50 6.00
441B David Ortiz Action SP 3.00 8.00
442A Mark Trumbo SP 1.50 4.00
442B M.Trumbo SP ERR 20.00 50.00
443 Rafael Soriano SP 1.50 4.00
444A Yu Darvish SP 2.50 6.00
444B Yu Darvish Action SP 3.00 8.00
444C Yu Darvish Logo SP 8.00 20.00
445 Pablo Sandoval SP 2.00 5.00
446A Wil Myers SP 1.50 4.00
446B W.Myers Action SP 2.00 5.00
447A Dustin Pedroia SP 2.50 6.00
447B Dustin Pedroia Logo SP 8.00 20.00
448 Jason Kipnis SP 2.00 5.00
449 James Shields SP 1.50 4.00
450 David Freese SP 1.50 4.00
451 Matt Moore SP 2.00 5.00
452 Anibal Sanchez SP 1.50 4.00
453 Ian Desmond SP 1.50 4.00
454 Jacoby Ellsbury SP 2.00 5.00
455A Jose Reyes SP 2.00 5.00
455B Jose Reyes Logo SP 6.00 15.00
456 Brandon Phillips SP 1.50 4.00
457A Carlos Gomez SP 1.50 4.00
457B C.Gomez TB SP 50.00 100.00
457C Carlos Gomez Logo SP 5.00 12.00
458A Anthony Rizzo SP 4.00 10.00
458B Anthony Rizzo Logo SP 12.00 30.00
459 Ian Kinsler SP 2.00 5.00
460 Josh Hamilton SP 2.00 5.00
461A Evan Longoria SP 2.00 5.00
461B E.Longoria TB SP 150.00 250.00
461C Evan Longoria Action SP 2.50 6.00
461D Evan Longoria Logo SP 6.00 15.00
462A Jarrod Parker SP 1.50 4.00
462B J.Parker SP ERR 20.00 50.00
463A Paul Goldschmidt SP 2.50 6.00
463B Goldschmidt TB SP 75.00 150.00
463C Paul Goldschmidt Action SP 3.00 8.00
463D Paul Goldschmidt Logo SP 8.00 20.00
464A Joe Mauer SP 2.00 5.00
464B J.Mauer TB SP 150.00 250.00
464C Joe Mauer Logo SP 6.00 15.00
465 Anthony Rendon SP 2.50 6.00
466 Chris Archer SP 1.50 4.00
467A Ryan Braun SP 2.00 5.00
467B R.Braun TB SP 150.00 250.00
468A Carlos Santana SP 2.00 5.00
468B Carlos Santana Logo SP 6.00 15.00
469A Ryan Zimmerman SP 2.00 5.00
469B Zimmerman TB SP 150.00 250.00
470 Stephen Strasburg SP 2.50 6.00
471A Chris Sale SP 2.50 6.00
471B C.Sale TB SP 150.00 250.00
471C Chris Sale Logo SP 8.00 20.00
472A Joey Votto SP 2.50 6.00
472B J.Votto TB SP 150.00 250.00
472C Joey Votto Action SP 3.00 8.00
472D J.Votto SP ERR 50.00 100.00
473 Adrian Gonzalez SP 2.00 5.00
474 Billy Butler SP 1.50 4.00
475A Chris Davis SP 1.50 4.00
475B Chris Davis Action SP 2.00 5.00
475C Chris Davis Logo SP 5.00 12.00
476 Adrian Beltre SP 2.50 6.00
477A Robinson Cano SP 2.00 5.00
477B Robinson Cano Logo SP 6.00 15.00
478 Nolan Arenado SP 3.00 8.00
479 Hunter Pence SP 2.00 5.00
480 Craig Kimbrel SP 2.00 5.00
481 Wilin Rosario SP 1.50 4.00
482A Felix Hernandez SP 2.00 5.00
482B Felix Hernandez Logo SP 6.00 15.00
483 Cole Hamels SP 2.00 5.00
484 B.J. Upton SP 2.00 5.00
485 Derek Holland SP 1.50 4.00
486 Angel Pagan SP 1.50 4.00
487 Troy Tulowitzki SP 2.50 6.00
488 Sergio Romo SP 1.50 4.00
489 Jean Segura SP 2.00 5.00
490A Matt Harvey SP 2.00 5.00
490B Matt Harvey Logo SP 6.00 15.00
491A Yadier Molina SP 2.50 6.00
491B Y.Molina TB SP 200.00 300.00
491C Yadier Molina Logo SP 10.00 25.00
492 Jordan Zimmermann SP 2.00 5.00
493A Max Scherzer SP 2.50 6.00
493B Max Scherzer Action SP 3.00 8.00
494A Carlos Gonzalez SP 2.00 5.00
494B Carlos Gonzalez Logo SP 6.00 15.00
495 Hisashi Iwakuma SP 2.00 5.00
496 Tony Cingrani SP 2.00 5.00
497 Curtis Granderson SP 2.00 5.00
498 Greg Holland SP 1.50 4.00
499 Gerrit Cole SP 2.50 6.00
500A Miguel Cabrera SP 2.50 6.00
500B M.Cabrera TB SP 150.00 250.00
500C M.Cabrera Action SP 3.00 8.00
500D M.Cabrera Logo SP 8.00 20.00
H501 Masahiro Tanaka RC 1.50 4.00
H502 Dee Gordon .40 1.00
H503 James Paxton RC .75 2.00
H504 Edinson Volquez .40 1.00
H505 Jonathan Schoop RC .50 1.25
H506 Enny Romero RC .50 1.25
H507 James Jones RC .50 1.25
H508 Michael Choice RC .50 1.25
H509 Taijuan Walker RC .50 1.25
H510 Jimmy Nelson RC .50 1.25
H511 Tommy La Stella RC .50 1.25
H512 Jackie Bradley Jr. .60 1.50
H513 Martin Perez .50 1.25
H514 Marcus Semien RC .50 1.25
H515 Tommy Medica RC .50 1.25
H516 Collin McHugh .40 1.00
H517 Oscar Taveras RC .60 1.50
H518 Daisuke Matsuzaka .50 1.25
H519 Randal Grichuk RC 4.00 10.00
H520 Garin Cecchini RC .50 1.25
H521 Jon Singleton RC .60 1.50
H522 Tyson Ross .40 1.00
H523 Eddie Butler RC .50 1.25
H524 Sean Doolittle .40 1.00
H525 Billy Hamilton RC .60 1.50
H526 Josmil Pinto RC .50 1.25
H527 Gregory Polanco RC .75 2.00
H528 Luis Sardinas RC .50 1.25
H529 Kyle Parker RC .60 1.50
H530 Onelki Garcia RC .50 1.25
H531 John Ryan Murphy RC .50 1.25
H532 Tanner Roark .40 1.00
H533 Andrew Heaney RC .50 1.25
H534 Rougned Odor RC 1.00 2.50
H535 Joe Panik RC .75 2.00
H536 Pat Neshek .40 1.00
H537 Mike Morse .40 1.00
H538 Andre Rienzo RC .50 1.25
H539 Casey McGehee .40 1.00
H540 Michael Pineda .40 1.00
H541 Kevin Kiermaier RC .75 2.00
H542 Nelson Cruz .60 1.50
H543 Yangervis Solarte RC .50 1.25
H544 Jesse Hahn RC .60 1.50
H545 Rafael Montero RC .50 1.25
H546 Mike Olt .40 1.00
H547 Alex Guerrero RC .60 1.50
H548 Chris Owings RC .50 1.25
H549 Jacob deGrom RC 6.00 15.00
H550 Xander Bogaerts RC 1.50 4.00
H551 Erisbel Arruebarrena RC .50 1.25
H552 Nick Castellanos RC 1.50 4.00
H553 Jesse Chavez .40 1.00
H554 Stephen Vogt RC .50 1.25
H555 Ken Giles RC .60 1.50
H556 Scott Kazmir .40 1.00
H557 George Springer RC 2.00 5.00
H558 Mookie Betts RC 60.00 150.00
H559 Christian Vasquez RC UER .50 1.25
Last name misspelled
H560 Eric Young Jr. .40 1.00
H561 Kevin Siegrist (RC) .50 1.25
H562 Tom Koehler .40 1.00
H563 Arismendy Alcantara RC .50 1.25
H564 Dellin Betances .50 1.25
H565 Shane Greene RC 1.50 4.00
H566 Kennys Vargas RC .50 1.25
H567 Christian Bethancourt RC .50 1.25
H568 Steve Pearce .40 1.00
H569 Jake Marisnick RC .50 1.25
H570 David Phelps .40 1.00
H571 Kyle Hendricks RC 1.50 4.00
H572 Marcus Stroman RC .75 2.00
H573 Zach Walters RC .50 1.25
H574 Brock Holt .40 1.00
H575 LaTroy Hawkins .40 1.00
H576 Fernando Rodney .40 1.00
H577 Andrew Lambo RC .50 1.25
H578 Wilmer Flores RC .60 1.50
H579 Aaron Sanchez RC .60 1.50
H580 Erik Johnson RC .50 1.25
H581 Jesus Aguilar RC 1.50 4.00
H582 Matt Davidson RC .60 1.50
H583 Yordano Ventura RC .60 1.50
H584 Josh Harrison .40 1.00
H585 Kolten Wong RC .60 1.50
H586 Danny Santana RC .60 1.50
H587 Chris Colabello .40 1.00
H588 Eric Campbell RC .60 1.50
H589 Zach Britton .50 1.25
H590 Jose Ramirez RC 4.00 10.00
H591 Jeff Samardzija .40 1.00
H592 Travis d'Arnaud RC .60 1.50
H593 C.J. Cron RC .50 1.25
H594 Alfredo Simon .40 1.00
H595 Dylan Bundy .50 1.25
H596 Chase Whitley RC .50 1.25
H597 Stefen Romero RC .50 1.25
H598 Yan Gomes .40 1.00
H599 Cody Allen .40 1.00
H600 Jose Abreu RC 4.00 10.00

2014 Topps Heritage Mini

STATED ODDS 1:220 HOBBY
STATED PRINT RUN 100 SER.#'d SETS
20 Cliff Lee 12.00 30.00
160 Andrew McCutchen 15.00 40.00
250 Mike Trout 250.00 350.00
442 Mark Trumbo 12.00 30.00
444 Yu Darvish 12.00 30.00
479 Hunter Pence 15.00 40.00

2014 Topps Heritage Black Border

THC20 Cliff Lee 2.50 6.00
THC30 Hiroki Kuroda 2.00 5.00
THC33 Michael Cuddyer 2.00 5.00
THC43 Carlos Beltran 2.50 6.00
THC49 J.Schoop/X.Bogaerts 6.00 15.00
THC50 Matt Cain 2.50 6.00
THC53 Giancarlo Stanton 3.00 8.00
THC60 Aroldis Chapman 3.00 8.00
THC73 Francisco Liriano 2.00 5.00
THC78 Adam Jones 2.50 6.00
THC84 Hyun-Jin Ryu 2.50 6.00
THC100 Adam Wainwright 2.50 6.00
THC140 Jered Weaver 2.50 6.00
THC145 Edwin Encarnacion 3.00 8.00
THC148 Freddie Freeman 4.00 10.00
THC149 Buster Posey 4.00 10.00
THC150 Manny Machado 3.00 8.00
THC160 Andrew McCutchen 3.00 8.00
THC170 Justin Upton 2.50 6.00
THC190 Allen Craig 2.50 6.00
THC200 Jason Heyward 2.50 6.00
THC205 Starling Marte 2.50 6.00
THC213 Clay Buchholz 2.00 5.00
THC216 Patrick Corbin 2.50 6.00
THC243 N.Castellanos/B.Hamilton 6.00 15.00
THC250 Mike Trout 15.00 40.00
THC260 Zack Greinke 2.50 6.00
THC269 Albert Pujols 4.00 10.00
THC275 Julio Teheran 2.50 6.00
THC284 David Wright 2.50 6.00
THC300 Clayton Kershaw 6.00 15.00
THC303 Prince Fielder 2.50 6.00
THC310 Domonic Brown 2.50 6.00
THC320 Shelby Miller 2.50 6.00
THC330 CC Sabathia 2.50 6.00
THC342 Matt Carpenter 3.00 8.00
THC345 Jose Bautista 2.50 6.00
THC350 Alfonso Soriano 2.50 6.00
THC354 J.Paxton/T.Walker 3.00 8.00
THC370 Matt Kemp 2.50 6.00
THC400 Bryce Harper 5.00 12.00
THC407 Michael Wacha 2.50 6.00
THC425 Yoenis Cespedes 3.00 8.00
THC426 Yasiel Puig 3.00 8.00
THC427 Jurickson Profar 2.50 6.00
THC428 Madison Bumgarner 2.50 6.00
THC430 Justin Verlander 3.00 8.00
THC431 Jon Lester 2.50 6.00
THC432 Jay Bruce 2.50 6.00
THC433 Derek Jeter 8.00 20.00
THC434 Pedro Alvarez 2.00 5.00
THC435 Andrelton Simmons 2.00 5.00
THC436 Nelson Cruz 3.00 8.00
THC437 Hanley Ramirez 2.50 6.00
THC439 Jose Fernandez 2.50 6.00
THC441 David Ortiz 3.00 8.00
THC442 Mark Trumbo 2.00 5.00
THC444 Yu Darvish 3.00 8.00
THC445 Pablo Sandoval 2.50 6.00
THC446 Wil Myers 2.00 5.00
THC447 Dustin Pedroia 3.00 8.00
THC448 Jason Kipnis 2.50 6.00
THC449 James Shields 2.00 5.00
THC451 Matt Moore 2.50 6.00
THC453 Ian Desmond 2.50 6.00
THC454 Jacoby Ellsbury 2.50 6.00
THC456 Brandon Phillips 2.00 5.00
THC457 Carlos Gomez 2.00 5.00
THC458 Anthony Rizzo 5.00 12.00
THC459 Ian Kinsler 2.50 6.00
THC460 Josh Hamilton 2.50 6.00
THC461 Evan Longoria 2.50 6.00
THC463 Paul Goldschmidt 3.00 8.00
THC464 Joe Mauer 2.50 6.00
THC467 Ryan Braun 2.50 6.00
THC468 Carlos Santana 2.50 6.00
THC469 Ryan Zimmerman 2.50 6.00
THC470 Stephen Strasburg 2.50 6.00
THC471 Chris Sale 3.00 8.00
THC472 Joey Votto 3.00 8.00
THC473 Adrian Gonzalez 2.50 6.00
THC474 Billy Butler 2.00 5.00
THC475 Chris Davis 2.00 5.00
THC476 Adrian Beltre 3.00 8.00
THC477 Robinson Cano 2.50 6.00
THC478 Nolan Arenado 4.00 10.00
THC479 Hunter Pence 2.50 6.00
THC480 Craig Kimbrel 2.50 6.00
THC482 Felix Hernandez 2.50 6.00
THC487 Troy Tulowitzki 3.00 8.00
THC489 Jean Segura 2.50 6.00
THC490 Matt Harvey 2.50 6.00
THC491 Yadier Molina 3.00 8.00
THC492 Jordan Zimmermann 2.50 6.00
THC493 Max Scherzer 3.00 8.00
THC494 Carlos Gonzalez 2.50 6.00
THC495 Hisashi Iwakuma 2.50 6.00
THC497 Curtis Granderson 2.50 6.00
THC499 Gerrit Cole 3.00 8.00
THC500 Miguel Cabrera 3.00 8.00

2014 Topps Heritage Blue Border

FOUND IN WALMART PACKS
149 Buster Posey 3.00 8.00
160 Andrew McCutchen 2.50 6.00
170 Justin Upton 2.00 5.00
275 Julio Teheran 2.00 5.00
284 David Wright 2.00 5.00
300 Clayton Kershaw 5.00 12.00
303 Prince Fielder 2.00 5.00
407 Michael Wacha 2.00 5.00
426 Yasiel Puig 2.50 6.00
430 Justin Verlander 2.50 6.00
432 Jay Bruce 2.00 5.00
434 Pedro Alvarez 1.50 4.00
439 Jose Fernandez 2.50 6.00
444 Yu Darvish 2.50 6.00
447 Dustin Pedroia 2.50 6.00
457 Carlos Gomez 1.50 4.00
461 Evan Longoria 2.00 5.00
463 Paul Goldschmidt 2.50 6.00
468 Carlos Santana 2.00 5.00
471 Chris Sale 2.50 6.00
475 Chris Davis 1.50 4.00
477 Robinson Cano 2.00 5.00
482 Felix Hernandez 2.00 5.00
487 Troy Tulowitzki 2.50 6.00
499 Gerrit Cole 2.50 6.00

2014 Topps Heritage Red Border

FOUND IN TARGET PACKS
53 Giancarlo Stanton 1.50 4.00
78 Adam Jones 1.25 3.00
84 Hyun-Jin Ryu 1.25 3.00
140 Jered Weaver 1.25 3.00
150 Manny Machado 1.50 4.00
205 Starling Marte 1.25 3.00
250 Mike Trout 8.00 20.00
260 Zack Greinke 1.25 3.00
310 Domonic Brown 1.25 3.00
320 Shelby Miller 1.25 3.00
330 CC Sabathia 1.25 3.00
400 Bryce Harper 2.50 6.00
431 Jon Lester 1.25 3.00
433 Derek Jeter 4.00 10.00
437 Hanley Ramirez 1.25 3.00
446 Wil Myers 1.00 2.50
458 Anthony Rizzo 2.50 6.00
464 Joe Mauer 1.25 3.00
470 Stephen Strasburg 1.50 4.00
472 Joey Votto 1.50 4.00
480 Craig Kimbrel 1.25 3.00
491 Yadier Molina 1.50 4.00
493 Max Scherzer 1.50 4.00
494 Carlos Gonzalez 1.25 3.00
500 Miguel Cabrera 1.50 4.00

2014 Topps Heritage Advertising Panels

ISSUED AS A BOX TOPPER
1 AL Batting Leaders .40 1.00
Dayan Viciedo
Luke Hochevar
2 AL RBI Leaders 3.00 8.00
Brian McCann
Mike Trout
3 Altuve/Showalter/Dempster .50 1.25
4 Cody Asche .50 1.25
Rick Porcello
Martin Prado
5 Peter Bourjos .40 1.00
Andrew Lambo
Stolmy Pimentel
Chris Rusin
6 Chris Capuano .40 1.00
Chris Perez
Ron Washington
7 Cardinals Dealt Losing Hand .40 1.00
Ross Ohlendorf
Matt Joyce
8 Michael Cuddyer .50 1.25
A.J. Burnett
R.A. Dickey
9 A.J. Ellis .50 1.25
Nate Eovaldi
Nate McLouth
10 Edwin Encarnacion .60 1.50
Buddy Boshers
Matt Shoemaker
Juan Uribe
11 Prince Fielder .50 1.25
Torii Hunter
Jonathan Papelbon
12 Todd Frazier .50 1.25
James Loney
Kolten Wong
Audry Perez
13 Jedd Gyorko 1.00 2.50
Brad Miller
Bryce Harper
14 J.J. Hardy .50 1.25
Trevor Rosenthal
Miguel Gonzalez
15 Jeremy Hefner .60 1.50
Manny Machado
Garrett Richards
16 Jeremy Hellickson .60 1.50
Eric Stults
Giancarlo Stanton
17 Omar Infante .40 1.00
Glen Perkins
Kirk Gibson
18 Mat Latos .50 1.25
Shane Victorino
Neil Walker
19 Mike Moustakas .50 1.25
Cody Ross
David Holmberg
Chad Bettis
20 NL Pitching Leaders .40 1.00
Ryan Doumit
Michael Young
21 Derek Norris .50 1.25
Scooter Gennett
Brad Ziegler
22 Papi Pops Two Hs .40 1.00
Joe Kelly
Stephen Drew
23 Tyler Pastornicky .60 1.50
Matt Holliday
Jason Castro
24 Jhonny Peralta .40 1.00
Edward Mujica
Mike Minor
25 Jarrod Saltalamacchia .40 1.00
Yasmani Grandal
Logan Morrison
26 Johan Santana .50 1.25
Jose Tabata
Patrick Corbin
27 Drew Stubbs .40 1.00
Gordon Beckham
Terry Collins
28 Andres Torres .50 1.25
Alfonso Soriano
Dan Straily
29 Jered Weaver .60 1.50
Taijuan Walker
James Paxton
Marco Estrada
30 Jayson Werth .50 1.25
Devin Mesoraco
Nick Christiani
Tuffy Gosewisch

2014 Topps Heritage Baseball Flashbacks

COMPLETE SET (10) 4.00 10.00
STATED ODDS 1:12 HOBBY
BFA Astrodome .30 .75
BFAK Al Kaline .50 1.25
BFBG Bob Gibson .40 1.00
BFEB Ernie Banks .50 1.25
BFHK Frank Robinson .40 1.00
BFJM Juan Marichal .40 1.00
BFJP Jim Palmer .40 1.00
BFRC Roberto Clemente 1.25 3.00
BFSK Sandy Koufax 1.00 2.50
BFWM Willie Mays 1.00 2.50

2014 Topps Heritage Bazooka

STATED PRINT RUN 25 SER.#'d SETS
65BAM Andrew McCutchen 10.00 25.00
65BBH Bryce Harper 12.00 30.00
65BCD Chris Davis 10.00 25.00
65BCG Carlos Gomez 12.00 30.00
65BCK Clayton Kershaw 8.00 20.00
65BCS CC Sabathia 10.00 25.00
65BDJ Derek Jeter 25.00 60.00
65BDW David Wright 12.00 30.00
65BFH Felix Hernandez 5.00 12.00
65BGC Gerrit Cole 6.00 15.00
65BHJR Hyun-Jin Ryu 5.00 12.00
65BJF Jose Fernandez 6.00 15.00
65BJH Josh Hamilton 5.00 12.00
65BJU Justin Upton 5.00 12.00
65BJV Justin Verlander 6.00 15.00
65BMC Miguel Cabrera 12.00 30.00
65BMH Matt Harvey 8.00 20.00
65BMM Manny Machado 12.00 30.00
65BMT Mike Trout 30.00 80.00
65BPF Prince Fielder 5.00 12.00
65BSM Starling Marte 12.00 30.00
65BWM Wil Myers 4.00 10.00
65BYD Yu Darvish 6.00 15.00
65BYM Yadier Molina 6.00 15.00
65BYP Yasiel Puig 6.00 15.00

2014 Topps Heritage Chrome

STATED ODDS 1:14 HOBBY
STATED PRINT RUN 999 SER.#'d SETS
20 Cliff Lee 1.50 4.00
30 Hiroki Kuroda 1.25 3.00
33 Michael Cuddyer 1.25 3.00
43 Carlos Beltran 1.50 4.00
49 J.Schoop/X.Bogaerts 3.00 8.00
50 Matt Cain 1.50 4.00
53 Giancarlo Stanton 2.00 5.00
60 Aroldis Chapman 2.00 5.00
73 Francisco Liriano 1.25 3.00
78 Adam Jones 1.50 4.00
84 Hyun-Jin Ryu 1.50 4.00
100 Adam Wainwright 1.50 4.00
140 Jered Weaver 1.50 4.00
145 Edwin Encarnacion 2.00 5.00
148 Freddie Freeman 2.50 6.00
149 Buster Posey 2.50 6.00
150 Manny Machado 2.00 5.00
160 Andrew McCutchen 2.00 5.00
170 Justin Upton 1.50 4.00
190 Allen Craig 1.50 4.00
200 Jason Heyward 1.50 4.00
205 Starling Marte 1.50 4.00
213 Clay Buchholz 1.25 3.00
216 Patrick Corbin 1.50 4.00
243 N.Castellanos/B.Hamilton 4.00 10.00
250 Mike Trout 10.00 25.00
260 Zack Greinke 1.50 4.00
269 Albert Pujols 2.50 6.00
275 Julio Teheran 1.50 4.00
284 David Wright 1.50 4.00
300 Clayton Kershaw 4.00 10.00
303 Prince Fielder 1.50 4.00
310 Domonic Brown 1.50 4.00
320 Shelby Miller 1.50 4.00
330 CC Sabathia 1.50 4.00
342 Matt Carpenter 2.00 5.00
345 Jose Bautista 1.50 4.00
350 Alfonso Soriano 1.50 4.00
354 J.Paxton/T.Walker 2.00 5.00
370 Matt Kemp 1.50 4.00
400 Bryce Harper 3.00 8.00
407 Michael Wacha 1.50 4.00
425 Yoenis Cespedes 2.00 5.00
427 Jurickson Profar 1.50 4.00
428 Madison Bumgarner 1.50 4.00
430 Justin Verlander 2.00 5.00
431 Jon Lester 1.50 4.00
432 Jay Bruce 1.50 4.00
433 Derek Jeter 10.00 25.00
434 Pedro Alvarez 1.25 3.00
435 Andrelton Simmons 1.25 3.00
436 Nelson Cruz 2.00 5.00
437 Hanley Ramirez 1.50 4.00
439 Jose Fernandez 2.00 5.00
441 David Ortiz 2.00 5.00
442 Mark Trumbo 1.25 3.00
444 Yu Darvish 2.00 5.00
445 Pablo Sandoval 1.50 4.00
446 Wil Myers 1.25 3.00
447 Dustin Pedroia 2.00 5.00
448 Jason Kipnis 1.50 4.00
449 James Shields 1.25 3.00
451 Matt Moore 1.50 4.00
453 Ian Desmond 1.25 3.00
454 Jacoby Ellsbury 1.50 4.00
456 Brandon Phillips 1.25 3.00
457 Carlos Gomez 1.25 3.00
458 Anthony Rizzo 3.00 8.00
459 Ian Kinsler 1.50 4.00
460 Josh Hamilton 1.50 4.00
461 Evan Longoria 1.50 4.00
463 Paul Goldschmidt 2.00 5.00
464 Joe Mauer 1.50 4.00
467 Ryan Braun 1.50 4.00
468 Carlos Santana 1.50 4.00
469 Ryan Zimmerman 1.50 4.00
470 Stephen Strasburg 2.00 5.00
471 Chris Sale 2.00 5.00
472 Joey Votto 2.00 5.00
473 Adrian Gonzalez 1.50 4.00
474 Billy Butler 1.25 3.00
475 Chris Davis 1.25 3.00
476 Adrian Beltre 2.00 5.00
477 Robinson Cano 1.50 4.00
478 Nolan Arenado 2.50 6.00
479 Hunter Pence 1.50 4.00
480 Craig Kimbrel 1.50 4.00
482 Felix Hernandez 1.50 4.00
487 Troy Tulowitzki 2.00 5.00
489 Jean Segura 1.50 4.00
490 Matt Harvey 1.50 4.00
491 Yadier Molina 2.00 5.00
492 Jordan Zimmermann 1.50 4.00
493 Max Scherzer 2.00 5.00
494 Carlos Gonzalez 1.50 4.00
495 Hisashi Iwakuma 1.50 4.00
497 Curtis Granderson 1.50 4.00
499 Gerrit Cole 2.00 5.00
500 Miguel Cabrera 2.00 5.00

2014 Topps Heritage Chrome Black Refractors

*BLACK REF: 2.5X TO 6X BASIC
STATED ODDS 1:225 HOBBY
STATED PRINT RUN 65 SER.#'d SETS
400 Bryce Harper 50.00 100.00
433 Derek Jeter 150.00 250.00
435 Andrelton Simmons 20.00 50.00
461 Evan Longoria 15.00 40.00
470 Stephen Strasburg 20.00 50.00
490 Matt Harvey 25.00 60.00
500 Miguel Cabrera 30.00 80.00

2014 Topps Heritage Chrome Purple Refractors

*PURPLE: .4X TO 1X BASIC

2014 Topps Heritage Chrome Refractors

*REFRACTORS: .75X TO 2X BASIC
STATED ODDS 1:27 HOBBY
STATED PRINT RUN 565 SER.#'d SETS
433 Derek Jeter 25.00 60.00

2014 Topps Heritage Clubhouse Collection Dual Relics

STATED ODDS 1:4451 HOBBY
STATED PRINT RUN 25 SER.#'d SETS
CCDRBC J.Bench/T.Cingrani 25.00 60.00
CCDRGM B.McCann/E.Gattis 20.00 50.00
CCDRLB E.Longoria/W.Boggs 20.00 50.00
CCDRMA P.Alvarez/A.McCutchen 25.00 60.00
CCDRYS C.Yelich/G.Sheffield 30.00 80.00

2014 Topps Heritage Clubhouse Collection Relic Autographs

STATED ODDS 1:5965 HOBBY
STATED PRINT RUN 25 SER.#'d SETS
EXCHANGE DEADLINE 1/31/2017
CCARAG Anthony Gose 60.00 120.00
CCARAH Aaron Hicks 40.00 80.00
CCARCS Chris Sale EXCH 60.00 120.00
CCARDF David Freese 20.00 50.00
CCAREE E.Encarnacion EXCH 30.00 60.00
CCARJK Jason Kipnis 40.00 80.00
CCARMA Matt Adams 60.00 120.00
CCARMC Miguel Cabrera 300.00 400.00
CCARPG P.Goldschmidt EXCH 75.00 150.00
CCARWR Wilin Rosario 40.00 80.00

2014 Topps Heritage Clubhouse Collection Relics

STATED ODDS 1:35 HOBBY
CCRAJ Adam Jones 3.00 8.00
CCRAM Andrew McCutchen 4.00 10.00
CCRAP Andy Pettitte 3.00 8.00
CCRAW Adam Wainwright 3.00 8.00
CCRBH Bryce Harper 6.00 15.00
CCRBL Brett Lawrie 3.00 8.00
CCRBP Buster Posey 5.00 12.00
CCRBR Bruce Rondon 2.50 6.00
CCRBU B.J. Upton 3.00 8.00
CCRCS Chris Sale 4.00 10.00
CCRDB Domonic Brown 3.00 8.00
CCRDP Dustin Pedroia 4.00 10.00
CCRDS Drew Stubbs 2.50 6.00
CCRFH Felix Hernandez 3.00 8.00
CCRFM Fred McGriff 3.00 8.00
CCRHK Howie Kendrick 2.50 6.00
CCRIN Ivan Nova 3.00 8.00
CCRJA Jose Altuve 3.00 8.00
CCRJB Jose Bautista 3.00 8.00
CCRJBR Jay Bruce 3.00 8.00
CCRJS Jean Segura 3.00 8.00
CCRJT Julio Teheran 3.00 8.00
CCRJV Justin Verlander 4.00 10.00
CCRJW Jayson Werth 3.00 8.00
CCRMJ Matt Joyce 2.50 6.00
CCRMM Mike Moustakas 3.00 8.00
CCRMSC Mike Schmidt 6.00 15.00
CCRMT Mike Trout 30.00 60.00
CCRNF Neftali Feliz 2.50 6.00
CCRNFR Nick Franklin 2.50 6.00
CCRPS Pablo Sandoval 2.50 6.00
CCRRC Robinson Cano 3.00 8.00
CCRRD R.A. Dickey 3.00 8.00
CCRSP Salvador Perez 3.00 8.00
CCRTL Tim Lincecum 3.00 8.00
CCRTT Troy Tulowitzki 4.00 10.00
CCRWB Wade Boggs 3.00 8.00
CCRWR Wilin Rosario 2.50 6.00
CCRYO Yonder Alonso 2.50 6.00
CCRZC Zack Cozart 2.50 6.00

2014 Topps Heritage Clubhouse Collection Relics Gold

*GOLD: .6X TO 1.5X BASIC
STATED ODDS 1:365 HOBBY
STATED PRINT RUN 99 SER.#'d SETS

2014 Topps Heritage Clubhouse Collection Triple Relics

STATED ODDS 1:11,650 HOBBY
STATED PRINT RUN 25 SER.#'d SETS
CCTRCMS Star/Clem/McCut 200.00 300.00
CCTRGGE GregorEaton/Goldsch 90.00 150.00
CCTRHJC Jack/Hend/Cesped 90.00 150.00
CCTRKCF Cabrer/Fielder/Kaline 90.00 150.00
CCTRSMG Glav/Smoltz/Maddux 90.00 150.00

2014 Topps Heritage First Draft

COMPLETE SET (4) 2.00 5.00
STATED ODDS 1:12 HOBBY
65MLBGN Graig Nettles .30 .75
65MLBJB Johnny Bench .50 1.25
65MLBNR Nolan Ryan 1.50 4.00
65MLBJB2 Johnny Bench .50 1.25

2014 Topps Heritage Flashback Relic Autographs

STATED ODDS 1:5965 HOBBY
STATED PRINT RUN 25 SER.#'d SETS
EXCHANGE DEADLINE 1/31/2017
FARAK Al Kaline EXCH 75.00 200.00
FARBW B.Williams EXCH 90.00 150.00
FAREB Ernie Banks 200.00 300.00
FARFR Frank Robinson 75.00 150.00
FARJM J.Marichal EXCH 60.00 120.00
FARLT Luis Tiant 20.00 50.00
FARMW Maury Wills 60.00 120.00
FAROC Orlando Cepeda 25.00 60.00
FARWM Willie Mays EXCH 250.00 400.00

2014 Topps Heritage Framed Stamps

STATED ODDS 1:1885 HOBBY
STATED PRINT RUN 50 SER.#'d SETS
65USAK Al Kaline 20.00 50.00
65USBG Bob Gibson 20.00 50.00
65USEB Ernie Banks 25.00 60.00
65USFR Frank Robinson 20.00 50.00
65USJB Johnny Bench 20.00 50.00
65USJBU Jim Bunning 12.00 30.00
65USJM Juan Marichal 20.00 50.00
65USJP Jim Palmer 20.00 50.00
65USLB Lou Brock 12.00 30.00
65USMW Maury Wills 20.00 50.00
65USOC Orlando Cepeda 20.00 50.00
65USRC Roberto Clemente 50.00 120.00
65USSK Sandy Koufax 30.00 60.00
65USWM Willie Mays 20.00 50.00
65USWS Willie Stargell 20.00 50.00
65USYB Yogi Berra 25.00 60.00

2014 Topps Heritage New Age Performers

COMPLETE SET (20) 8.00 20.00
STATED ODDS 1:8 HOBBY
NAPBH Bryce Harper .75 2.00
NAPCD Chris Davis .30 .75
NAPCG Carlos Gomez .30 .75
NAPCGO Carlos Gonzalez .40 1.00
NAPCK Clayton Kershaw 1.00 2.50
NAPGS Giancarlo Stanton .50 1.25
NAPHR Hyun-Jin Ryu .40 1.00
NAPJF Jose Fernandez .50 1.25
NAPMC Miguel Cabrera .50 1.25
NAPMH Matt Harvey .40 1.00
NAPMS Max Scherzer .50 1.25
NAPMT Mike Trout 2.50 6.00
NAPMW Michael Wacha .40 1.00
NAPPA Pedro Alvarez .30 .75

NAPPG Paul Goldschmidt .50 1.25
NAPSS Stephen Strasburg .40 1.00
NAPWM Wil Myers .30 .75
NAPXB Xander Bogaerts 1.00 2.50
NAPYD Yu Darvish .50 1.25
NAPYP Yasiel Puig .50 1.25

2014 Topps Heritage News Flashbacks

COMPLETE SET (10) 3.00 8.00
STATED ODDS 1:12 HOBBY
NFAL Aleksei Leonov .30 .75
NFBC Bill Cosby .50 1.25
NFGA Gateway Arch .30 .75
NFJN Joe Namath .60 1.50
NFMA Muhammad Ali 1.00 2.50
NFMX The Autobiography of Malcolm X .30 .75
NFTB The Beatles .50 1.25
NFTRS The Rolling Stones .50 1.25
NFTSOM The Sound of Music .30 .75
NFVRA Voting Rights Act of 1965 .30 .75

2014 Topps Heritage Embossed Box Loaders

STATED ODDS 1:35 HOBBY BOX
AK Al Kaline 15.00 40.00
BG Bob Gibson 12.00 30.00
BH Bryce Harper 30.00 80.00
BJ Bo Jackson 15.00 40.00
CB Craig Biggio 12.00 30.00
CC CC Sabathia 12.00 30.00
CD Chris Davis 10.00 25.00
CK Clayton Kershaw 30.00 80.00
DW David Wright 20.00 50.00
EG Evan Gattis 10.00 25.00
JB Johnny Bench 15.00 40.00
JP Jim Palmer 12.00 30.00
JPA Jarrod Parker 10.00 25.00
KG Kevin Gausman 12.00 30.00
MM Mike Mussina 12.00 30.00
MMA Manny Machado 20.00 50.00
MZ Mike Zunino 10.00 25.00
RH Rickey Henderson 15.00 40.00
TG Tom Glavine 12.00 30.00
YD Yu Darvish 15.00 40.00

2014 Topps Heritage Embossed Box Loaders Relics

STATED ODDS 1:70 HOBBY BOXES
STATED PRINT RUN 25 SER.#'d SETS
AKR Al Kaline 30.00 80.00
BGR Bob Gibson 25.00 60.00
BHR Bryce Harper 50.00 120.00
BJR Bo Jackson 30.00 80.00
CBR Craig Biggio 25.00 60.00
CCR CC Sabathia 25.00 60.00
CDR Chris Davis 20.00 50.00
CKR Clayton Kershaw 60.00 150.00
DWR David Wright 25.00 60.00
JBR Johnny Bench 30.00 80.00
JPAR Jarrod Parker 20.00 50.00
KGR Kevin Gausman 25.00 60.00
MMAR Manny Machado 60.00 150.00
MMR Mike Mussina 25.00 60.00
RHR Rickey Henderson 30.00 80.00
TGR Tom Glavine 25.00 60.00

2014 Topps Heritage Mystery Redemption Autograph

MRAJA Jose Abreu 60.00 150.00

2014 Topps Heritage Real One Autographs

STATED ODDS 1:141 HOBBY
OLBERMANN STATED ODDS 1:15,000 HOBBY
HN CARDS ISSUED IN HN.FACT.SETS
EXCHANGE DEADLINE 1/31/2017
HN EXCH.DEADLINE 10/31/2017
ROAAA Arismendy Alcantara HN 8.00 20.00
ROAAG Alex Guerrero HN 10.00 25.00
ROAAH Andrew Heaney HN 8.00 20.00
ROAAS Aaron Sanchez HN 8.00 20.00
ROABD Bennie Daniels 8.00 20.00
ROABDA Bud Daley 8.00 20.00
ROABH Billy Hamilton HN 12.00 30.00
ROABM Billy Moran 8.00 20.00
ROABP Bill Pleis 8.00 20.00
ROABS Bill Spanswick 8.00 20.00
ROABSC Barney Schultz 8.00 20.00
ROABV Bill Virdon 8.00 20.00
ROACJ Chipper Jones 60.00 120.00
ROACJA Charlie James 8.00 20.00
ROACO Chris Owings HN 12.00 30.00
ROADC Dave Concepcion 15.00 40.00
ROADE Doc Edwards 8.00 20.00
ROADG Dallas Green 8.00 20.00
ROADL Don Larsen 10.00 25.00
ROADLE Don Lee 8.00 20.00
ROADLO Davey Lopes 8.00 20.00
ROADM Don Mattingly 40.00 80.00
ROADST Dave Stenhouse 8.00 20.00
ROADV Dave Vineyard 10.00 25.00
ROADZ Don Zimmer 15.00 40.00
ROAEA Erisbel Arruebarrena HN 12.00 30.00
ROAEB Ernie Banks 75.00 150.00
ROAED Eric Davis 12.00 30.00
ROAEG Evan Gattis 8.00 20.00
ROAER Ed Roebuck 8.00 20.00
ROAFB Frank Baumann 8.00 20.00
ROAFBO Frank Bolling 8.00 20.00
ROAFL Frank Lary 8.00 20.00
ROAFT Frank Thomas 8.00 20.00
ROAGP Gregory Polanco HN 12.00 30.00
ROAGS George Springer HN 30.00 80.00
ROAHA Hank Aaron/65 200.00 300.00
ROAHS Herm Starrette 8.00 20.00
ROAJA Jose Abreu HN 90.00 150.00
ROAJA2 Jose Abreu HN 90.00 150.00
ROAJB Jay Bruce 10.00 25.00
ROAJD Jim Duffalo 8.00 20.00
ROAJD Jacob deGrom HN 100.00 250.00
ROAJF Jerry Fosnow 8.00 20.00
ROAJM Jake Marisnick HN 8.00 20.00
ROAJN Jimmy Nelson HN 8.00 20.00
ROAJO Jake Odorizzi 8.00 20.00
ROAJP Josmil Pinto HN 8.00 20.00
ROAJPA Joe Panik HN 15.00 40.00
ROAJR Jose Ramirez HN 12.00 30.00
ROAJR Jay Ritchie 8.00 20.00
ROAJRI Jim Rice 15.00 40.00
ROAJRM John Ryan Murphy HN 12.00 30.00
ROAJS Jonathan Schoop HN 15.00 40.00
ROAKG Kevin Gausman 10.00 25.00
ROAKM Ken McBride 8.00 20.00
ROAKO Keith Olbermann 60.00 120.00
ROAKO2 Keith Olbermann 60.00 120.00
ROAKR Ken Retzer 8.00 20.00
ROAKS Kevin Siegrist HN 8.00 20.00
ROAKW Kolten Wong HN 15.00 40.00
ROALB Leo Burke 8.00 20.00
ROALS Luis Sardinas HN 8.00 20.00
ROALY Larry Yellen 8.00 20.00
ROAMA Matt Adams 8.00 20.00
ROAMB Mookie Betts HN 150.00 400.00
ROAMC Michael Choice HN 10.00 25.00
ROAMD Matt Davidson HN 10.00 25.00
ROAMST Marcus Stroman HN 12.00 30.00
ROAMW Maury Wills 12.00 30.00
ROAMWA Michael Wacha 10.00 25.00
ROAMZ Mike Zunino 10.00 25.00
ROANC Nick Castellanos HN 25.00 60.00
ROANG Nomar Garciaparra 25.00 60.00
ROANM Nelson Mathews 8.00 20.00
ROAOT Oscar Taveras HN 10.00 25.00
ROAPO Paul O'Neill 15.00 40.00
ROARP Rafael Palmeiro 10.00 25.00
ROARS Roy Sievers 8.00 20.00
ROATD Travis d'Arnaud HN 10.00 25.00
ROATM Tommy Medica HN 8.00 20.00
ROATW Taijuan Walker HN 10.00 25.00
ROATW Ted Wills 8.00 20.00
ROAWF Wilmer Flores HN 10.00 25.00
ROAWM Willie Mays/65 200.00 400.00
ROAWMY Wil Myers 12.00 30.00
ROAYS Yangervis Solarte HN 15.00 40.00
ROAYV Yordano Ventura HN 15.00 40.00

2014 Topps Heritage Real One Autographs Dual

STATED ODDS 1:3386 HOBBY
EXCHANGE DEADLINE 1/31/2017
RODABL Longoria/Boggs 100.00 175.00
RODABP Bench/Posey EXCH 150.00 300.00
RODAGH Griffey/Harper EXCH 350.00 500.00
RODAMB Marich/Bumg EXCH 75.00 200.00
RODAMF McGrff/Frmn 60.00 150.00
RODAMG Glts/McCnn EXCH 40.00 80.00
RODARB Brce/Rbnsn EXCH 75.00 150.00
RODARM Mchdo/Rpkn EXCH 250.00 350.00

2014 Topps Heritage Real One Autographs Red Ink

*RED INK: .6X TO 1.5X BASIC
STATED ODDS 1:372 HOBBY
HN CARDS FOUND IN HIGH NUMBER BOXES
PRINT RUNS B/WN 10-65 COPIES PER
NO HIGH NUMBER PRICING AVAILABLE
EXCHANGE DEADLINE 1/31/2017
ROACJ Chipper Jones 75.00 200.00
ROADM Don Mattingly 100.00 250.00
ROAPO Paul O'Neill 25.00 60.00
ROAWM Willie Mays EXCH 300.00 600.00

2014 Topps Heritage Then and Now

COMPLETE SET (10) 3.00 8.00
STATED ODDS 1:10 HOBBY
TANCC R.Clemente/M.Cabrera 1.25 3.00
TANGW B.Gibson/A.Wainwright .40 1.00
TANKD S.Koufax/Y.Darvish 1.00 2.50
TANKK S.Koufax/C.Kershaw 1.00 2.50
TANMC J.Marichal/B.Colon .40 1.00
TANMD W.Mays/C.Davis 1.00 2.50
TANMS J.Marichal/M.Scherzer .50 1.25
TANMV W.McCovey/J.Votto .50 1.25
TANRD F.Robinson/C.Davis .40 1.00
TANWE M.Wills/J.Ellsbury .40 1.00

2015 Topps Heritage

COMP.SET w/o SPs (425) 30.00 80.00
SP ODDS 1:3 HOBBY
HN SP ODDS 1:3 HOBBY
ACTION SP ODDS 1:24 HOBBY
HN ACTION SP ODDS 1:22 HOBBY
COLOR SWAP SP ODDS 1:140 HOBBY
CLR SWAP HN SP ODDS 1:76 HOBBY
THROWBACK SP ODDS 1:3310 HOBBY
ERROR SP ODDS 1:840 HOBBY
TRADED SP ODDS 1:2310 HOBBY
1A Buster Posey .30 .75
1B Posey Action SP 4.00 10.00
1C Posey Color SP 8.00 20.00
2 Melky Cabrera .15 .40
3 Ned Yost MG .15 .40
4 Danny Duffy .15 .40
5 Ryan Vogelsong .15 .40
6 Zach Britton .20 .50
7 Ian Kennedy .15 .40
8 Asdrubal Cabrera .20 .50
9 Jenrry Mejia .15 .40
10A Julio Teheran .20 .50
10B Teheran Thrwbck SP 75.00 150.00
11 Taylor RC/Pederson RC .75 2.00
12 Jean Segura .20 .50
13 Stephen Vogt .20 .50
14 Kyle Lohse .15 .40
15 Roenis Elias .15 .40
16 Anibal Sanchez .15 .40
17 Jason Hammel .15 .40
18 David Freese .15 .40
19 San Francisco Giants .20 .50
20 J.D. Martinez .25 .60
21 Mark Teixeira .20 .50
22 Kolten Wong .20 .50
23 Brad Ziegler .15 .40
24 Wil Myers .15 .40
25A Jose Abreu .25 .60
25B Abreu Action SP 3.00 8.00
25C Abreu Color SP 6.00 15.00
26 Ryan Zimmerman .20 .50
27 Cordier (RC)/Garces RC .40 1.00
28 Jason Castro .15 .40
29 Avisail Garcia .20 .50
30A Brandon Phillips .15 .40
30B B.Phillips ERR SP 12.00 30.00
31 Andrew Susac .15 .40
32 Andrelton Simmons .15 .40
33 Dan Haren .15 .40
34 Bob Melvin MG .15 .40
35 Mike Leake .15 .40
36A Sean Doolittle .15 .40
36B S.Doolittle ERR SP 12.00 30.00
37 John Farrell MG .15 .40
38 B.J. Upton .15 .40
39 Marcus Stroman .20 .50
40 Phil Hughes .15 .40
41 Wilmer Flores .20 .50
42 Jonathon Niese .15 .40
43 Juan Uribe .15 .40
44 Escobar RC/Barnes RC .40 1.00
45 Mookie Betts .40 1.00
46 Jason Vargas .15 .40
47 Jeff Locke .15 .40
48 Jeremy Guthrie .15 .40
49 Spangenberg RC/Liriano RC .40 1.00
50 Jacoby Ellsbury .20 .50
51 Francisco Rodriguez .20 .50
52 M.Trout/M.Cabrera 1.25 3.00
53 Hiroki Kuroda .15 .40
54 Lorenzo Cain .15 .40
55 Justin Turner .20 .50
56 Kris Medlen .15 .40
57 Carlos Ruiz .15 .40
58 Brandon Moss .15 .40
59 Cincinnati Reds .15 .40
60 Matt Holliday .25 .60
61 Russell Martin .15 .40
62 Lance Lynn .15 .40
63 Brett Lawrie .20 .50
64 Kelvin Herrera .15 .40
65 Logan Morrison .15 .40
66 Patrick Corbin .20 .50
67 Goeddel RC/Herrera RC .50 1.25
68A George Springer .20 .50
68B Springer Thrwbck SP 150.00 300.00
69 Angel Pagan .15 .40
70B Y.Cespedes Trade SP 20.00 50.00
70A Yoenis Cespedes .20 .50
71 Mark Buehrle .20 .50
72 Nolan Arenado .30 .75
73 Collin McHugh .15 .40
74A Jarrod Parker .15 .40
74B J.Parker ERR SP 12.00 30.00
75 Matt Kemp .20 .50
76 Mike Matheny .15 .40
77 Casey Janssen .15 .40
78 Joe Panik .20 .50
79 Emilio Bonifacio .15 .40
80 Cody Asche .20 .50
81 Jake McGee .15 .40
82 Scott Kazmir .15 .40
83 Matt Shoemaker .20 .50
84 Brentz RC/Moya RC .50 1.25
85 Derek Holland .15 .40
86A Norichika Aoki .15 .40
86B Aoki Thrwbck SP 150.00 300.00
87 Torii Hunter .15 .40
88 Butler RC/Rivero RC .40 1.00
89 Eduardo Escobar .15 .40
90A Jonathan Schoop .15 .40
90B Schoop Thrwbck SP 150.00 300.00
91 Nick Markakis .20 .50
92 New York Yankees .20 .50
93 Wilin Rosario .15 .40
94 Ken Giles .15 .40
95 Scooter Gennett .20 .50
96 Tim Lincecum .20 .50
97 Wade Davis .15 .40
98 Clay Buchholz .15 .40
99 M.Trout/A.Pujols 1.25 3.00
100A Clayton Kershaw .50 1.25
100B Kershaw Action SP 6.00 15.00
100C Kershaw Color SP 12.00 30.00
101 Bruce Bochy .15 .40
102 Tim Hudson .20 .50
103 Drew Storen .15 .40
104 Miguel Montero .15 .40
105 Marcell Ozuna .25 .60
106 Ender Inciarte RC .40 1.00
107 McCann RC/Ryan RC .60 1.50
108 James Loney .15 .40
109 Didi Gregorius .20 .50
110A Anthony Rizzo .40 1.00
110B Rizzo Thrwbck SP 150.00 400.00
111 Garin Cecchini .15 .40
112 Jeremy Hellickson .15 .40
113 Jake Peavy .15 .40
114 Josh Reddick .15 .40
115 Steve Pearce .25 .60
116 Don Mattingly .50 1.25
117 Matt Joyce .15 .40
118 Jonathan Papelbon .20 .50
119 Trevor Rosenthal .20 .50
120 Brian Dozier .20 .50
121 Kevin Kiermaier .20 .50
122 John Danks .15 .40
123 Holdzkom RC/Alvarez RC .40 1.00
124 Yovani Gallardo .15 .40
125 Jon Jay .15 .40
126A Chris Tillman .15 .40
126B C.Tillman ERR SP 12.00 30.00
127 Chafin RC/Lamb RC .60 1.50
128 Juan Perez .15 .40
129 Alex Avila .20 .50
130 Evan Gattis .15 .40
131 Los Angeles Angels .15 .40
132 Travis Ishikawa .15 .40
133 Mike Minor .15 .40
134 Yan Gomes .15 .40
135 Conor Gillaspie .20 .50
136 Jose Iglesias .20 .50
137 Domonic Brown .20 .50
138 Tony Gwynn Jr. .15 .40
139 Soler RC/Baez RC 3.00 8.00
140 Aroldis Chapman .25 .60
141 Dillon Gee .15 .40
142 Jake Petricka .15 .40
143 Joe Nathan .15 .40
144 Aaron Hill .15 .40
145 Ben Zobrist .20 .50
146 Rodriguez RC/Bonilla RC .40 1.00
147 Lloyd McClendon MG .15 .40
148 Cody Allen .15 .40
149 John Jaso .15 .40
150 Michael Brantley .20 .50
151 Andre Ethier .20 .50
152 Joe Kelly .15 .40
153 Tyler Clippard .15 .40
154 Chris Johnson .15 .40
155 Michael Cuddyer .15 .40
156 S.Castro/J.Baez 1.25 3.00
157 Francisco Liriano .15 .40
158 Trevor Cahill .15 .40
159 Joaquin Benoit .15 .40
160 Michael Pineda .15 .40
161 Adeiny Hechavarria .15 .40
162 Brad Miller .20 .50
163 Dexter Fowler .20 .50
164 Rogers RC/Szczur RC .50 1.25
165 Kennys Vargas .15 .40
166 Jhonny Peralta .15 .40
167 Bud Norris .15 .40
168 Jarred Cosart .15 .40
169 Brandon McCarthy .15 .40
170 Chase Utley .20 .50
171 A.J. Ellis .15 .40
172 New York Mets .15 .40
173 Trevor Plouffe .15 .40
174 Neftali Feliz .15 .40
175A Josh Donaldson .20 .50
175B J.Donaldson Trade SP 20.00 50.00
176 Adam Eaton .15 .40
177 Drew Hutchison .15 .40
178 Jake Odorizzi .15 .40
179 Tuivailala RC/Scruggs RC .40 1.00
180 Jay Bruce .20 .50
181 Gio Gonzalez .20 .50
182 Chris Owings .15 .40
183 Terry Francona .20 .50
184 Yasmani Grandal .15 .40
185 Bartolo Colon .15 .40
186 Trevor Bauer .25 .60
187 Brad Ausmus .15 .40
188 Brandon Crawford .20 .50
189 Casey McGehee .15 .40
190 Oswaldo Arcia .15 .40
191 Carlos Carrasco .15 .40
192A Kole Calhoun .15 .40
192B K.Calhoun ERR SP 12.00 30.00
193 Chris Iannetta .15 .40
194 Washington Nationals .15 .40
195 Edinson Volquez .15 .40
196 Matt Moore .20 .50
197 Mark Trumbo .15 .40
198 Derek Norris .15 .40
199 Mrte/Hrrsn/McCtchn .25 .60
200A Freddie Freeman .30 .75
200B Freddie Freeman Color SP 8.00 20.00
201A Jason Heyward .20 .50
201B J.Heyward Trade SP 20.00 50.00
202 Martin Perez .20 .50
203 Jed Lowrie .15 .40
204 Chicago Cubs .15 .40
205 Jorge De La Rosa .15 .40
206 Jarrod Dyson .15 .40
207 Chase Headley .15 .40
208 Devin Mesoraco .15 .40
209 Farmer RC/Lobstein RC .40 1.00
210 Neil Walker .20 .50
211 C.J. Cron .15 .40
212A Matt Carpenter .25 .60
212B Carpenter Thrwbck SP 250.00 400.00
213 Joakim Soria .15 .40
214 Allen Craig .15 .40
215 Mrn/McCtchn/Hrrsn .25 .60
216 Brantley/Altuve/Martinez .20 .50
217 Duda/Rizzo/Stanton .40 1.00
218 Carter/Abreu/Cruz .25 .60
219 Upton/Stanton/Gonzalez .25 .60
220 Cruz/Cabrera/Trout 1.25 3.00
221 Cto/Wnwrght/Krshw .50 1.25
222 Kluber/Sale/Hernandez .25 .60
223 Wnwght/Krshw/Cto .50 1.25
224 Scherzer/Weaver/Kluber .25 .60
225 Krshw/Cto/Strsbrg .50 1.25
226 Hernandez/Scherzer/Kluber/Price .25 .60
227 Austin Jackson .15 .40
228 Yonder Alonso .15 .40
229 Buck Showalter MG .15 .40
230 Ben Revere .15 .40
231 Brock Holt .15 .40
232 Martin Prado .15 .40
233 Patton RC/Jokisch RC .40 1.00
234 Pirela RC/Mitchell RC .40 1.00
235 Kevin Gausman .15 .40
236 Ervin Santana .15 .40
237 Dustin Ackley .20 .50
238 Los Angeles Dodgers .20 .50
239 LaTroy Hawkins .15 .40
240 Kurt Suzuki .15 .40
241 Ivan Nova .20 .50
242 Kendrys Morales .15 .40
243 Pablo Sandoval .20 .50
244 Tropeano RC/Foltynewicz RC .40 1.00
245 Matt Adams .15 .40
246 Kyle Gibson .20 .50
247 A.J. Pollock .20 .50
248 Wade Miley .15 .40
249 Mike Scioscia .15 .40
250A Johnny Cueto .20 .50
250B Johnny Cueto Color SP 5.00 12.00
251 David Peralta .15 .40
252 Chase Anderson .15 .40
253 Arismendy Alcantara .15 .40
254 Franco RC/Gonzalez RC .50 1.25
255 Drew Stubbs .15 .40
256 Starling Marte .20 .50
257 Danny Salazar .20 .50
258 Chris Archer .15 .40
259 Boston Red Sox .20 .50
260A Madison Bumgarner .20 .50
260B Bumgarner Thrwbck SP 150.00 300.00
260C Bmgrnr Action SP 2.50 6.00
261 Mark Melancon .15 .40
262 Huston Street .15 .40
263 Randal Grichuk .15 .40
264 May RC/Achter RC .40 1.00
265 Marlon Byrd .15 .40
266A Lonnie Chisenhall .15 .40
266B L.Chisenhall ERR SP 12.00 30.00
267 Santiago Casilla .15 .40
268A Nick Castellanos .25 .60
268B Castellanos Thrwbck SP 75.00 150.00
269 Bryan Price .15 .40
270 Hyun-Jin Ryu .20 .50
271 J.J. Hardy .15 .40
272 Wei-Yin Chen .15 .40
273 C.Kershaw/A.Wainwright .50 1.25
274 Hector Rondon .15 .40
275 Yadier Molina .25 .60
276 Addison Reed .15 .40
277 Josh Collmenter .15 .40
278 Mike Morse .15 .40
279 John Gibbons .15 .40
280 Howie Kendrick .15 .40
281 Mike Napoli .15 .40
282 Tanner Roark .15 .40
283 Daniel Hudson .15 .40
284 Nathan Eovaldi .20 .50
285 Omar Infante .15 .40
286 Colby Lewis .15 .40
287 R.A. Dickey .20 .50
288 Mercedes RC/Garcia RC .40 1.00
289 Will Middlebrooks .15 .40
290 Luis Valbuena .15 .40
291 John Lackey .20 .50
292 Taijuan Walker .20 .50
293 Rick Porcello .20 .50
294 J.A. Happ .15 .40
295 Jayson Werth .20 .50
296 Joe Girardi .20 .50
297 Colby Rasmus .20 .50
298 Carlos Martinez .20 .50
299 Justin Morneau .20 .50
300A Andrew McCutchen .25 .60
300B A.McCutchen Action SP 3.00 8.00
300C A.McCutchen Color SP 6.00 15.00
301 Erick Aybar .15 .40
302 Miguel Gonzalez .15 .40
303 Cleveland Indians .15 .40
304 Yusmeiro Petit .15 .40
305 Chris Young .15 .40
306 Williams RC/Ynoa RC .40 1.00
307 Alfredo Simon .15 .40
308 Salvador Perez .20 .50
309 Dioner Navarro .15 .40
310A Adam Jones .20 .50
310B Adam Jones Action SP 2.50 6.00
310C Adam Jones Color SP 5.00 12.00
311 Corcino RC/Rodriguez RC .40 1.00
312 Jon Singleton .20 .50
313 Gregor Blanco .15 .40
314 Alex Rios .20 .50
315 Koji Uehara .15 .40
316 Hector Santiago .15 .40
317 Tommy La Stella .15 .40
318 Clint Hurdle .15 .40
319 Mike Zunino .15 .40
320 Michael Wacha .20 .50
321 Aramis Ramirez .15 .40
322 Tsuyoshi Wada .15 .40
323 Andrew Cashner .15 .40
324 Alexei Ramirez .20 .50
325A Michael Bourn .15 .40
325B Bourn Thrwbck SP 125.00 300.00
326 Atlanta Braves .15 .40
327 Elvis Andrus .20 .50
328 Denard Span .15 .40
329 Michael Saunders .20 .50
330 Carl Crawford .20 .50
331A Henderson Alvarez .15 .40
331B Alvarez Thrwbck SP 125.00 300.00
332 Brian McCann .20 .50
333 Pompey RC/Norris RC .50 1.25
334 Alex Wood .15 .40
335 Charlie Blackmon .25 .60
336 Fernando Rodney .15 .40
337 Billy Butler .15 .40
338 Pat Neshek .15 .40
339 Alcides Escobar .20 .50
340 Garrett Richards .20 .50
341 Terry Collins .15 .40
342 Tyler Matzek .15 .40
343 Cliff Lee .20 .50
344 Jedd Gyorko .15 .40
345 Scott Van Slyke .20 .50
346 Jurickson Profar .20 .50
347 Danny Santana .15 .40
348 Baltimore Orioles .15 .40
349 Dallas Keuchel .20 .50
350A Masahiro Tanaka .20 .50
350B Tanaka Action SP 2.50 6.00
350C Tanaka Color SP 5.00 12.00
351 Aaron Sanchez .20 .50
352 Seth Smith .15 .40
353 CC Sabathia .20 .50
354 James Paxton .20 .50
355 David Robertson .20 .50
356 Rndo RC/Cstllo RC .50 1.25
357 Khris Davis .25 .60
358 Shane Greene .15 .40
359 Steve Cishek .15 .40
360 Daniel Murphy .20 .50
361 Zack Wheeler .20 .50
362 Carlos Beltran .20 .50
363 Bud Black .15 .40
364 Ryan Howard .20 .50
365A Brett Gardner .20 .50
365B B.Gardner ERR SP 15.00 40.00
366 Alex Cobb .15 .40
367 Kyle Hendricks .25 .60
368 Chris Coghlan .15 .40
369 Brandon Belt .20 .50
370 Zack Cozart .15 .40
371 Homer Bailey .15 .40
372 Juan Lagares .15 .40
373 Brown RC/Strickland RC .40 1.00
374 Jimmy Rollins .20 .50
375 Josh Harrison .15 .40
376 Wily Peralta .15 .40
377 Nick Swisher .20 .50
378 Ricky Nolasco .15 .40
379 St. Louis Cardinals .20 .50
380 Daniel Nava .15 .40
381 Eric Hosmer .20 .50
382 Mat Latos .20 .50
383 Mike Moustakas .20 .50
384 Jake Arrieta .20 .50
385 Wilson Ramos .15 .40
386 Matt Williams .15 .40
387A Shelby Miller .20 .50
387B S.Miller Trade SP 20.00 50.00
388 Dellin Betances .20 .50
389A Shin-Soo Choo .20 .50
389B Choo Thrwbck SP 125.00 300.00
390 Chris Davis .15 .40
391 Christian Vazquez .15 .40
392 Frias RC/Graveman RC .60 1.50
393 Tyson Ross .15 .40
394 Pedro Alvarez .15 .40
395 Lucas Duda .20 .50
396 Jose Quintana .15 .40
397 Kyle Kendrick .15 .40
398 Travis Wood .15 .40
399 Tony Watson .15 .40
400A Joe Mauer .20 .50
400B Mauer Thrwbck SP 125.00 300.00
401 Neris RC/Heston RC .40 1.00
402 Dayan Viciedo .15 .40
403 Adam Lind .20 .50
404 Pittsburgh Pirates .20 .50
405 C.J. Wilson .15 .40
406 Tom Koehler .15 .40
407 Scott Feldman .15 .40
408 Coco Crisp .15 .40
409 Jarrod Saltalamacchia .15 .40
410 Rajai Davis .15 .40
411 Ryne Sandberg MG .50 1.25
412 Rougned Odor .20 .50
413 Travis d'Arnaud .20 .50
414 Alex Rodriguez .30 .75
415 David Murphy .15 .40
416 Glen Perkins .15 .40
417 O'Malley RC/Diaz RC .15 .40
418 Matt Garza .15 .40
419 Vance Worley .15 .40
420 Matt Cain .20 .50
421 Gerardo Parra .15 .40
422 Curtis Granderson .20 .50
423 Matt den Dekker .15 .40
424 Finnegan RC/Gore RC .40 1.00
425 Gerrit Cole .25 .60
426A Giancarlo Stanton SP 2.50 6.00
426B Giancarlo Stanton Action SP 3.00 8.00
426C Giancarlo Stanton Color SP 6.00 15.00
427 Xander Bogaerts SP 2.50 6.00
428A Evan Longoria SP 2.00 5.00
428B Evan Longoria Action SP 2.50 6.00
428C Evan Longoria Color SP 5.00 12.00
429 Jacob deGrom SP 2.50 6.00
430 Prince Fielder SP 2.00 5.00
431 Billy Hamilton SP 2.00 5.00
432 Adam LaRoche SP 1.50 4.00
433 Jered Weaver SP 2.00 5.00
434 Todd Frazier SP 2.00 5.00
435 Gregory Polanco SP 2.00 5.00
436A Justin Upton SP 2.00 5.00
436B Justin Upton Color SP 5.00 12.00
437 Josh Hamilton SP 2.00 5.00
438 Hanley Ramirez SP 2.00 5.00
439 Carlos Gonzalez SP 2.00 5.00
440A Bryce Harper SP 4.00 10.00
440B Harper Action SP 5.00 12.00
440C Harper Color SP 10.00 25.00
441 Dee Gordon SP 1.50 4.00
442A Robinson Cano SP 2.00 5.00
442B Cano Thrwbck SP 100.00 200.00
442C Robinson Cano Color SP 5.00 12.00
443 Kenley Jansen SP 2.00 5.00
444A Jose Bautista SP 2.00 5.00
444B Jose Bautista Action SP 2.50 6.00
444C Jose Bautista Color SP 5.00 12.00
445A Jonathan Lucroy SP 2.00 5.00
445B Jonathan Lucroy Color SP 5.00 12.00
446 Adrian Beltre SP 2.50 6.00
447A Chris Sale SP 2.50 6.00
447B Chris Sale Action SP 3.00 8.00
447C Chris Sale Color SP 6.00 15.00
447D C.Sale ERR SP 40.00 100.00
448 Carlos Santana SP 2.00 5.00
449 Matt Harvey SP 2.50 6.00
450A Yasiel Puig SP 2.50 6.00
450B Puig Action SP 3.00 8.00
451 Joey Votto SP 2.50 6.00
452 Jordan Zimmermann SP 2.00 5.00
453A Troy Tulowitzki SP 2.50 6.00
453B Troy Tulowitzki Color SP 6.00 15.00
454 Manny Machado SP 2.50 6.00
455A Jose Altuve SP 2.00 5.00
455B Altuve Thrwbck SP 125.00 300.00
455C Jose Altuve Action SP 2.50 6.00
455D Jose Altuve Color SP 5.00 12.00
456 Doug Fister SP 1.50 4.00
457 Ian Kinsler SP 2.00 5.00
458 Jon Lester SP 2.00 5.00
459A David Wright SP 2.00 5.00
459B David Wright Color SP 5.00 12.00
460 James Shields SP 1.50 4.00
461 Anthony Rendon SP 2.50 6.00
462A Felix Hernandez SP 2.00 5.00
462B Felix Hernandez Action SP 2.50 6.00
462C Felix Hernandez Color SP 5.00 12.00
463 Jose Fernandez SP 2.50 6.00
464 Jose Reyes SP 2.00 5.00
465 David Price SP 2.00 5.00
466 Corey Dickerson SP 1.50 4.00
467A Paul Goldschmidt SP 2.50 6.00
467B Paul Goldschmidt Action SP 3.00 8.00
468 Zack Greinke SP 2.50 6.00
469 Max Scherzer SP 2.50 6.00
470 Nelson Cruz SP 2.50 6.00
471A Alex Gordon SP 2.00 5.00
471B Gordon Thrwbck SP 125.00 300.00
472A Craig Kimbrel SP 2.00 5.00
472B Craig Kimbrel Action SP 2.50 6.00
473A Adrian Gonzalez SP 2.00 5.00
473B Adrian Gonzalez Action SP 2.50 6.00
474 Ryan Braun SP 2.00 5.00
475A Miguel Cabrera SP 2.50 6.00
475B Cabrera Thrwbck SP 150.00 300.00
475C Cabrera Action SP 3.00 8.00
475D Cabrera Color SP 6.00 15.00
476 Greg Holland SP 1.50 4.00
477 Ian Desmond SP 1.50 4.00
478 Sonny Gray SP 2.00 5.00
479 Yordano Ventura SP 2.00 5.00
480A David Ortiz SP 2.50 6.00
480B David Ortiz Action SP 3.00 8.00
480C David Ortiz Color SP 6.00 15.00
481 Hisashi Iwakuma SP 2.00 5.00
482 Carlos Gomez SP 1.50 4.00
483A Adam Wainwright SP 2.00 5.00
483B Adam Wainwright Action SP 2.50 6.00
484A Corey Kluber SP 2.00 5.00
484B Corey Kluber Color SP 5.00 12.00
485 Chris Carter SP 1.50 4.00
486 Christian Yelich SP 3.00 8.00
487 Edwin Encarnacion SP 2.50 6.00
488 Hunter Pence SP 2.00 5.00
489 Jason Kipnis SP 2.00 5.00
490 Cole Hamels SP 2.00 5.00
491A Victor Martinez SP 2.00 5.00
491B Martinez Thrwbck SP 75.00 150.00
491C Victor Martinez Action SP 2.50 6.00
492A Jeff Samardzija SP 1.50 4.00
492B Jeff Samardzija Color SP 4.00 10.00
493 Kyle Seager SP 1.50 4.00
494A Starlin Castro SP 1.50 4.00
494B Castro Thrwbck SP 125.00 300.00
495 Justin Verlander SP 2.50 6.00
496 Albert Pujols SP 3.00 8.00
497A Yu Darvish SP 2.50 6.00
497B Darvish Thrwbck SP 125.00 300.00
497C Yu Darvish Action SP 3.00 8.00
498A Stephen Strasburg SP 2.50 6.00
498B Stephen Strasburg Action SP 3.00 8.00
499 Dustin Pedroia SP 2.50 6.00
500A Mike Trout SP 6.00 15.00

500B Trout Thrwbck SP 500.00 800.00
500C Trout Action SP 30.00 80.00
500D Trout Color SP 30.00 80.00
501 Christian Walker RC .75 2.00
502 Brett Cecil .15 .40
503 Ryan Rua RC .40 1.00
504 Ike Davis .15 .40
505 Jesse Chavez .15 .40
506 David Buchanan .15 .40
507 Chi Chi Gonzalez RC .60 1.50
508 Angel Nesbitt RC .40 1.00
509 Casey McGehee .15 .40
510 Justin Nicolino RC .40 1.00
511 Nick Ahmed .15 .40
512 Ruben Tejada .15 .40
513 Brad Boxberger .15 .40
514 Grant Balfour .15 .40
515 Zach McAllister .15 .40
516 Vincent Velasquez RC .60 1.50
517 Colby Rasmus .20 .50
518 Jason Marquis .15 .40
519 Cameron Maybin .15 .40
520 A.J. Burnett .15 .40
521 Shane Greene .15 .40
522 Anthony Ranaudo RC .40 1.00
523 Seth Smith .15 .40
524A Alex Rios .20 .50
524B Alex Rios Color SP 5.00 12.00
525 Jimmy Paredes .15 .40
526 Jordan Lyles .15 .40
527 Eduardo Rodriguez RC .40 1.00
528 Taylor Featherston RC .40 1.00
529 Rickie Weeks .15 .40
530 Norichika Aoki .15 .40
531 Mike Aviles .15 .40
532 Daniel Descalso .15 .40
533 Logan Forsythe .15 .40
534 T.J. House .15 .40
535 Dan Uggla .15 .40
536 Jose Urena RC .40 1.00
537 Anthony Gose .15 .40
538 Mike Fiers .15 .40
539 Matt Joyce .15 .40
540 Rafael Betancourt .15 .40
541 John Ryan Murphy .15 .40
542 Brayan Pena .15 .40
543 Tyler Clippard .15 .40
544 Yangervis Solarte .15 .40
545 Asher Wojciechowski RC .40 1.00
546 Will Venable .15 .40
547 J.R. Graham RC .40 1.00
548 Jacob Lindgren RC .50 1.25
549 David Ross .15 .40
550 Sergio Romo .15 .40
551 Grady Sizemore .20 .50
552 Aaron Harang .15 .40
553 Carlos Perez RC .40 1.00
554 Desmond Jennings .20 .50
555 James Shields .15 .40
556 A.J. Pierzynski .15 .40
557 Danny Muno RC .40 1.00
558 Carlos Sanchez .15 .40
559 Joba Chamberlain .15 .40
560 Pat Venditte RC .40 1.00
561 David Phelps .15 .40
562 Jack Leathersich RC .40 1.00
563A Carlos Correa RC 2.00 5.00
563B Correa Action SP 10.00 25.00
563C Correa Color SP 20.00 50.00
564 Delmon Young .20 .50
565 Jordy Mercer .15 .40
566 Yunel Escobar .15 .40
567 Tommy Pham RC .50 1.25
568 Mikie Mahtook RC .40 1.00
569 Jeurys Familia .20 .50
570 Dixon Machado RC .50 1.25
571 Odrisamer Despaigne .15 .40
572 Jonny Gomes .15 .40
573 Ryan Madson .15 .40
574 Sean Rodriguez .15 .40
575A Nathan Eovaldi .20 .50
575B Nathan Eovaldi Color SP 5.00 12.00
576 Tim Beckham .20 .50
577 Tommy Milone .15 .40
578 Ryan Flaherty .15 .40
579 Garrett Jones .15 .40
580 Bobby Parnell .15 .40
581 Chris Capuano .15 .40
582 Joe Smith .15 .40
583 Mitch Moreland .15 .40
584 Shawn Tolleson RC .40 1.00
585 Yasmani Grandal .15 .40
586 Billy Burns RC .40 1.00
587 Jason Grilli .15 .40
588 Jerome Williams .15 .40
589 Mason Williams RC .50 1.25
590 Taylor Jungmann RC .40 1.00
591A Roberto Osuna RC .40 1.00
591B Roberto Osuna Color SP 4.00 10.00
592 Kevin Plawecki RC .40 1.00
593 Matt Wisler RC .40 1.00
594 Gordon Beckham .15 .40
595 Trevor Cahill .15 .40
596 Freddy Galvis .15 .40
597 Justin Masterson .15 .40
598 Travis Snider .15 .40
599A Archie Bradley RC .40 1.00
599B Archie Bradley Action SP 2.00 5.00
599C Archie Bradley Color SP 4.00 10.00
600 Sean Gilmartin RC .40 1.00
601 Michael Blazek .15 .40
602 Justin Maxwell .15 .40
603 Martin Prado .15 .40
604 Pedro Strop .15 .40
605 Lance McCullers Jr. RC .40 1.00
606 Alex Meyer RC .40 1.00
607 Jordan Schafer .15 .40
608 Paulo Orlando RC .60 1.50
609 Leonys Martin .15 .40
610 Everth Cabrera .15 .40
611 Jed Lowrie .15 .40
612 Hansel Robles RC .40 1.00
613 Tyler Olson RC .40 1.00
614 Tyler Moore .15 .40
615 Nick Franklin .15 .40
616 Justin Bour RC .60 1.50
617A Micah Johnson RC .40 1.00
617B Micah Johnson Color SP 4.00 10.00
618A Noah Syndergaard RC .75 2.00
618B Sndgrd Action SP 4.00 10.00
618C Sndgrd Color SP 8.00 20.00
619 Melvin Upton Jr. .20 .50
620 Caleb Joseph RC .40 1.00
621 Wil Myers .15 .40
622 Will Middlebrooks .15 .40
623 Sam Fuld .15 .40
624 Johnny Giavotella .15 .40
625 Kelly Johnson .15 .40
626 Mike Olt .15 .40
627 Tony Cingrani .20 .50
628 Matt den Dekker .15 .40
629 Shane Victorino .20 .50
630 Steven Matz RC .60 1.50
631 Jimmy Nelson .15 .40
632 Marlon Byrd .15 .40
633 A.J. Cole RC .40 1.00
634 Emilio Bonifacio .15 .40
635 Drew Pomeranz .20 .50
636 Eric Sogard .15 .40
637 Brandon Morrow .15 .40
638 Eddie Butler .15 .40
639 Corey Hart .15 .40
640 Steven Souza Jr. .20 .50
641 DJ LeMahieu .25 .60
642 Mark Canha RC .60 1.50
643 Alex Torres .15 .40
644 Rene Rivera .15 .40
645 Ubaldo Jimenez .15 .40
646 A.J. Ramos .15 .40
647A Joey Gallo RC .75 2.00
647B Gallo Action SP 4.00 10.00
648 Leonel Campos RC .40 1.00
649 Nick Hundley .15 .40
650 Anthony DeSclafani .15 .40
651 Kyle Blanks .15 .40
652 Eric Young Jr. .15 .40
653 Nate Karns .15 .40
654 Christian Bethancourt .15 .40
655 Mark Reynolds .15 .40
656 Mike Pelfrey .15 .40
657 Stephen Drew .15 .40
658 Nick Martinez .15 .40
659 J.T. Realmuto RC 2.50 6.00
660 Michael Lorenzen RC .40 1.00
661 Roberto Hernandez .15 .40
662 Marcus Semien .15 .40
663 Robinson Chirinos .15 .40
664 Tyler Flowers .15 .40
665 Justin Smoak .15 .40
666 Odubel Herrera RC .60 1.50
667 Gregorio Petit .15 .40
668 Evan Scribner .15 .40
669 Luke Gregerson .15 .40
670 Austin Adams .15 .40
671 Adam Warren .15 .40
672 Tuffy Gosewisch .15 .40
673 Collin Cowgill .15 .40
674 Eddie Rosario RC .75 2.00
675 Jace Peterson .15 .40
676 Williams Perez RC .50 1.25
677 Ervin Santana .15 .40
678 Tim Cooney RC .40 1.00
679 Luis Valbuena .15 .40
680 Alexi Amarista .15 .40
681 Kevin Pillar .15 .40
682 Wilmer Difo RC .40 1.00
683 Eric Campbell .20 .50
684 Jose Ramirez .20 .50
685 Brandon Guyer .15 .40
686 David DeJesus .15 .40
687 Asdrubal Cabrera .20 .50
688 Rubby De La Rosa .15 .40
689 Ross Detwiler .15 .40
690 Jake Marisnick .15 .40
691 Slade Heathcott RC .50 1.25
692 Marco Gonzales RC .50 1.25
693 Francisco Cervelli .15 .40
694 Preston Tucker RC .60 1.50
695 Alex Guerrero .20 .50
696 Brett Anderson .15 .40
697 Orlando Calixte RC .40 1.00
698 John Jaso .15 .40
699 Delino DeShields Jr. RC .40 1.00
700 Casey Janssen .20 .50
701A Matt Kemp SP 1.25 3.00
701B Matt Kemp Color SP 5.00 12.00
702A Justin Upton SP 1.25 3.00
702B Justin Upton Action SP 2.50 6.00
702C Justin Upton Color SP 5.00 12.00
703 Edinson Volquez SP 1.00 2.50
704 Ben Zobrist SP 1.25 3.00
705A Yasmany Tomas SP RC 1.25 3.00
705B Tomas Action SP 2.50 6.00
705C Tomas Color SP 5.00 12.00
706A Ichiro Suzuki SP 2.00 5.00
706B Suzuki Action SP 4.00 10.00
706C Suzuki Color SP 8.00 20.00
707A Evan Gattis SP 1.00 2.50
707B Evan Gattis Color SP 4.00 10.00
708A Max Scherzer SP 1.50 4.00
708B Max Scherzer Action SP 3.00 8.00
708C Max Scherzer Color SP 6.00 15.00
709 Jesse Hahn SP 1.00 2.50
710A Carlos Rodon SP RC 1.50 4.00
710B Rodon Action SP 3.00 8.00
710C Rodon Color SP 6.00 15.00
711 Andrew Miller SP 1.25 3.00
712A Blake Swihart SP RC 1.25 3.00
712B Blake Swihart Action SP 2.50 6.00
712C Blake Swihart Color SP 5.00 12.00
713A Raisel Iglesias SP RC 1.25 3.00
713B Raisel Iglesias Color SP 5.00 12.00
714A Jung Ho Kang SP RC 1.00 2.50
714B Kang Color SP 4.00 10.00
715A Dexter Fowler SP 1.25 3.00
715B Dexter Fowler Color SP 5.00 12.00
716A Devon Travis SP RC 1.00 2.50
716B Devon Travis Color SP 4.00 10.00
717A Francisco Lindor SP RC 6.00 15.00
717B Lindor Action SP 12.00 30.00
717C Lindor Color SP 25.00 60.00
718A Addison Russell SP RC 3.00 8.00
718B Russell Action SP 6.00 15.00
718C Russell Color SP 12.00 30.00
719 Mike Foltynewicz SP RC 1.00 2.50
720 Austin Hedges SP RC 1.00 2.50
721A Jimmy Rollins SP 1.25 3.00
721B Jimmy Rollins Color SP 5.00 12.00
722A Craig Kimbrel SP 1.25 3.00
722B Craig Kimbrel Action SP 2.50 6.00
723A Yovani Gallardo SP 1.00 2.50
723B Yovani Gallardo Color SP 4.00 10.00
724A Byron Buxton SP RC 1.50 4.00
724B Buxton Action SP 3.00 8.00
724C Buxton Color SP 6.00 15.00
725A Kris Bryant SP RC 6.00 15.00
725B Bryant Action SP 12.00 30.00
725C Bryant Color SP 25.00 60.00

2015 Topps Heritage Gum Stained Back

*GUM BACK VET: 6X TO 15X BASIC
*GUM BACK RC: 2.5X TO 6X BASIC RC
*GUM BACK SP: .6X TO 1.5X BASIC SP
*GUM BACK 701-725: 1X TO 2.5X BASIC SP
HN STATED ODDS 1:43 HOBBY

25 Jose Abreu 12.00 30.00
52 Mike Trout 8.00 20.00
Miguel Cabrera
78 Joe Panik 12.00 30.00
99 Mike Trout 8.00 20.00
Albert Pujols
220 Nelson Cruz 8.00 20.00
Miguel Cabrera
Mike Trout
411 Ryne Sandberg 6.00 15.00
429 Jacob deGrom 10.00 25.00
440 Bryce Harper 20.00 50.00
449 Matt Harvey 10.00 25.00
451 Joey Votto 12.00 30.00
454 Manny Machado 10.00 25.00
500 Mike Trout 25.00 60.00
563 Carlos Correa 25.00 60.00
725 Kris Bryant 30.00 80.00

2015 Topps Heritage '66 Punchboards

STATED ODDS 1:137 HOBBY BOXES
HN ODDS 1:40 HOBBY BOXES
STATED PRINT RUN 50 SER.#'d SETS

66P1 J.Altuve/J.Morneau 6.00 15.00
66P2 Abreu/Gonzalez 8.00 20.00
66P3 Trout/Harper 30.00 80.00
66P4 J.Reyes/S.Castro 6.00 15.00
66P5 J.Bautista/G.Stanton 8.00 20.00
66P6 Cespedes/Puig 8.00 20.00
66P7 Jeter/Wright 30.00 80.00
66P8 Cabrera/Goldschmidt 8.00 20.00
66P9 Trout/Mays 30.00 80.00
66P10 Kaline/McCutchen 15.00 40.00
66P11 B.Robinson/E.Banks 8.00 20.00
66P12 I.Desmond/L.Aparicio 6.00 15.00
66P13 Killebrew/Goldschmidt 20.00 50.00
66P14 Hamilton/Ellsbury 6.00 15.00
66P15 Mazeroski/Cano 20.00 50.00
66P16 Perez/Posey 10.00 25.00
66P17 J.Altuve/J.Morgan 6.00 15.00
66P18 A.Jones/J.Upton 6.00 15.00
66P19 Soler/Castillo 6.00 15.00
66P20 Cepeda/Encarnacion 8.00 20.00
66P21 Donaldson/Bryant HN 25.00 60.00
66P22 Russell/Travis HN 10.00 25.00
66P23 Plawecki/Swihart HN 20.00 50.00
66P24 Upton/Gattis HN 6.00 15.00
66P25 Abreu/Bryant HN 25.00 60.00
66P26 Griffey Jr./Suzuki HN 30.00 80.00
66P27 Killebrew/Pederson HN 30.00 80.00
66P28 Harper/Cruz HN 20.00 50.00
66P29 Kaline/Clemente HN 30.00 80.00
66P30 Tomas/Castillo HN 12.00 30.00

2015 Topps Heritage '66 Punchboards Relics

STATED ODDS 1:85 HOBBY BOXES
HN ODDS 1:113 HOBBY BOXES
STATED PRINT RUN 25 SER.#'d SETS

66PRAC Aroldis Chapman HN 25.00 60.00
66PRAM Andrew McCutchen HN 30.00 80.00
66PRAR Anthony Rizzo 25.00 60.00
66PRAW Adam Wainwright HN 15.00 40.00
66PRCY Christian Yelich 15.00 40.00
66PRDW David Wright 20.00 50.00
66PRHJR Hyun-Jin Ryu 20.00 50.00
66PRJD Josh Donaldson 25.00 60.00
66PRJE Jacoby Ellsbury HN 30.00 80.00
66PRJT Julio Teheran 8.00 20.00
66PRJU Justin Upton 8.00 20.00
66PRMC Miguel Cabrera HN 25.00 60.00
66PRMM Manny Machado 25.00 60.00
66PRMP Mike Piazza 40.00 100.00
66PRMT Mark Teixeira 8.00 20.00
66PRPS Pablo Sandoval 20.00 50.00
66PRRB Ryan Braun 25.00 60.00
66PRRC Robinson Cano HN 20.00 50.00
66PRRJ Randy Johnson 30.00 80.00
66PRSM Shelby Miller 25.00 60.00
66PRSS Stephen Strasburg 40.00 100.00
66PRYP Yasiel Puig 10.00 25.00
66PRZG Zack Greinke HN 15.00 40.00

2015 Topps Heritage A Legend Begins

RANDOM INSERTS IN RETAIL PACKS

NR1 Nolan Ryan 3.00 8.00
NR2 Nolan Ryan 3.00 8.00
NR3 Nolan Ryan 3.00 8.00
NR4 Nolan Ryan 3.00 8.00
NR5 Nolan Ryan 3.00 8.00
NR6 Nolan Ryan 3.00 8.00
NR7 Nolan Ryan 3.00 8.00
NR8 Nolan Ryan 3.00 8.00
NR9 Nolan Ryan 3.00 8.00
NR10 Nolan Ryan 3.00 8.00
NR11 Nolan Ryan 3.00 8.00
NR12 Nolan Ryan 3.00 8.00
NR13 Nolan Ryan 3.00 8.00
NR14 Nolan Ryan 3.00 8.00
NR15 Nolan Ryan 3.00 8.00

2015 Topps Heritage A Legend Retires

RANDOM INSERTS IN RETAIL PACKS

SK1 Sandy Koufax 3.00 8.00
SK2 Sandy Koufax 3.00 8.00
SK3 Sandy Koufax 3.00 8.00
SK4 Sandy Koufax 3.00 8.00
SK5 Sandy Koufax 3.00 8.00
SK6 Sandy Koufax 3.00 8.00
SK7 Sandy Koufax 3.00 8.00
SK8 Sandy Koufax 3.00 8.00
SK9 Sandy Koufax 3.00 8.00
SK10 Sandy Koufax 3.00 8.00
SK11 Sandy Koufax 3.00 8.00
SK12 Sandy Koufax 3.00 8.00
SK13 Sandy Koufax 3.00 8.00
SK14 Sandy Koufax 3.00 8.00
SK15 Sandy Koufax 3.00 8.00

2015 Topps Heritage Award Winners

COMPLETE SET (10) 5.00 12.00
STATED ODDS 1:8 HOBBY

AW1 Mike Trout 2.50 6.00
AW2 Clayton Kershaw 1.00 2.50
AW3 Corey Kluber .40 1.00
AW4 Clayton Kershaw 1.00 2.50
AW5 Jose Abreu .50 1.25
AW6 Jacob deGrom .50 1.25
AW7 Buck Showalter .30 .75
AW8 Matt Williams .30 .75
AW9 Mike Trout 2.50 6.00
AW10 Madison Bumgarner .40 1.00

2015 Topps Heritage Baseball Flashbacks

COMPLETE SET (10) 5.00 12.00
STATED ODDS 1:12 HOBBY

BF1 Ernie Banks .50 1.25
BF2 Luis Aparicio .40 1.00
BF3 Lou Brock .40 1.00
BF4 Steve Carlton .40 1.00
BF5 Orlando Cepeda .40 1.00
BF6 Al Kaline .50 1.25
BF7 Juan Marichal .40 1.00
BF8 Brooks Robinson .40 1.00
BF9 Willie Mays 1.00 2.50
BF10 Sandy Koufax 1.00 2.50

2015 Topps Heritage Bazooka

COMPLETE SET (35)
RANDOM INSERTS IN PACKS

66BAC Aroldis Chapman 4.00 10.00
66BAG Adrian Gonzalez 3.00 8.00
66BAJ Adam Jones 3.00 8.00
66BAM Andrew McCutchen 4.00 10.00
66BAR Addison Russell HN 8.00 20.00
66BAW Adam Wainwright 3.00 8.00
66BBB Byron Buxton HN 4.00 10.00
66BBP Buster Posey 5.00 12.00
66BBS Blake Swihart HN 3.00 8.00
66BCC Carlos Correa HN 12.00 30.00
66BCK Clayton Kershaw 8.00 20.00
66BCR Carlos Rodon HN 4.00 10.00
66BCS Chris Sale 4.00 10.00
66BDO David Ortiz 4.00 10.00
66BFH Felix Hernandez 3.00 8.00
66BGS Giancarlo Stanton 4.00 10.00
66BJA Jose Abreu 4.00 10.00
66BJAL Jose Altuve 3.00 8.00
66BJB Javier Baez 20.00 50.00
66BJBA Jose Bautista 3.00 8.00
66BJF Jose Fernandez 4.00 10.00
66BJU Justin Upton HN 3.00 8.00
66BKB Kris Bryant HN 15.00 40.00
66BMB Madison Bumgarner 3.00 8.00
66BMC Miguel Cabrera 4.00 10.00
66BMK Matt Kemp HN 3.00 8.00
66BMS Max Scherzer HN 4.00 10.00
66BMT Mike Trout 30.00 80.00
66BMTA Masahiro Tanaka 3.00 8.00
66BPG Paul Goldschmidt 4.00 10.00
66BSS Stephen Strasburg 4.00 10.00
66BVM Victor Martinez 3.00 8.00
66BYD Yu Darvish 4.00 10.00
66BYP Yasiel Puig 4.00 10.00
66BYT Yasmany Tomas HN 3.00 8.00

2015 Topps Heritage Chrome

1-100 ODDS 1:23 HOBBY
101-150 ODDS 1:17 HOBBY
STATED PRINT RUN 999 SER.#'d SETS

THC1 Buster Posey 2.50 6.00
THC10 Julio Teheran 1.50 4.00
THC25 Jose Abreu 2.00 5.00
THC50 Jacoby Ellsbury 1.50 4.00
THC60 Matt Holliday 2.00 5.00
THC70 Yoenis Cespedes 1.50 4.00
THC75 Matt Kemp 1.50 4.00
THC100 Clayton Kershaw 4.00 10.00
THC110 Anthony Rizzo 3.00 8.00
THC139 J.Baez/J.Soler 10.00 25.00
THC140 Aroldis Chapman 2.00 5.00
THC150 Michael Brantley 1.50 4.00
THC175 Josh Donaldson 1.50 4.00
THC200 Freddie Freeman 2.50 6.00
THC250 Johnny Cueto 1.50 4.00
THC260 Madison Bumgarner 1.50 4.00
THC270 Hyun-Jin Ryu 1.50 4.00
THC275 Yadier Molina 2.00 5.00
THC300 Andrew McCutchen 2.00 5.00
THC310 Adam Jones 1.50 4.00
THC320 Michael Wacha 1.50 4.00
THC340 Garrett Richards 1.50 4.00
THC350 Masahiro Tanaka 1.50 4.00
THC356 Ranaudo/Castillo 1.50 4.00
THC375 Josh Harrison 1.25 3.00
THC400 Joe Mauer 1.50 4.00
THC426 Giancarlo Stanton 2.00 5.00
THC427 Xander Bogaerts 2.00 5.00
THC428 Evan Longoria 1.50 4.00
THC429 Jacob deGrom 2.00 5.00
THC430 Prince Fielder 1.50 4.00
THC431 Billy Hamilton 1.50 4.00
THC432 Adam LaRoche 1.25 3.00
THC433 Jered Weaver 1.50 4.00
THC434 Todd Frazier 1.25 3.00
THC435 Gregory Polanco 1.50 4.00
THC436 Justin Upton 1.50 4.00
THC437 Josh Hamilton 1.50 4.00
THC438 Hanley Ramirez 1.50 4.00
THC439 Carlos Gonzalez 1.50 4.00
THC440 Bryce Harper 3.00 8.00
THC441 Dee Gordon 1.25 3.00
THC442 Robinson Cano 1.50 4.00
THC443 Kenley Jansen 1.50 4.00
THC444 Jose Bautista 1.50 4.00
THC445 Jonathan Lucroy 1.50 4.00
THC446 Adrian Beltre 2.00 5.00
THC447 Chris Sale 2.00 5.00
THC448 Carlos Santana 1.50 4.00
THC449 Matt Harvey 1.50 4.00
THC450 Yasiel Puig 2.00 5.00
THC451 Joey Votto 2.00 5.00
THC452 Jordan Zimmermann 1.50 4.00
THC453 Troy Tulowitzki 2.00 5.00
THC454 Manny Machado 2.00 5.00
THC455 Jose Altuve 1.50 4.00
THC457 Ian Kinsler 1.50 4.00
THC458 Jon Lester 1.50 4.00
THC459 David Wright 1.50 4.00
THC460 James Shields 1.25 3.00
THC461 Anthony Rendon 2.00 5.00
THC462 Felix Hernandez 1.50 4.00
THC463 Jose Fernandez 2.00 5.00
THC464 Jose Reyes 1.50 4.00
THC465 David Price 1.50 4.00
THC466 Corey Dickerson 1.25 3.00
THC467 Paul Goldschmidt 2.00 5.00
THC468 Zack Greinke 2.00 5.00
THC469 Max Scherzer 2.00 5.00
THC470 Nelson Cruz 2.00 5.00
THC471 Alex Gordon 1.50 4.00
THC472 Craig Kimbrel 1.50 4.00
THC473 Adrian Gonzalez 1.50 4.00
THC474 Ryan Braun 1.50 4.00
THC475 Miguel Cabrera 2.00 5.00
THC476 Greg Holland 1.25 3.00
THC477 Ian Desmond 1.25 3.00
THC478 Sonny Gray 1.50 4.00
THC479 Yordano Ventura 1.50 4.00
THC480 David Ortiz 2.00 5.00
THC481 Hisashi Iwakuma 1.50 4.00
THC482 Carlos Gomez 1.25 3.00
THC483 Adam Wainwright 1.50 4.00
THC484 Corey Kluber 1.50 4.00
THC485 Chris Carter 1.25 3.00
THC486 Christian Yelich 2.50 6.00
THC487 Edwin Encarnacion 2.00 5.00
THC488 Hunter Pence 1.50 4.00
THC489 Jason Kipnis 1.50 4.00
THC490 Cole Hamels 1.50 4.00
THC491 Victor Martinez 1.50 4.00
THC492 Jeff Samardzija 1.25 3.00
THC493 Kyle Seager 1.25 3.00
THC494 Starlin Castro 1.25 3.00
THC495 Justin Verlander 2.00 5.00
THC496 Albert Pujols 2.50 6.00
THC497 Yu Darvish 2.00 5.00
THC498 Stephen Strasburg 2.00 5.00
THC499 Dustin Pedroia 2.00 5.00
THC500 Mike Trout 10.00 25.00
THC501 Christian Walker 2.50 6.00
THC522 Anthony Ranaudo 1.25 3.00
THC523 Seth Smith 1.25 3.00
THC524 Alex Rios 1.50 4.00
THC530 Norichika Aoki 1.25 3.00
THC548 Jacob Lindgren 1.50 4.00
THC555 James Shields 1.25 3.00
THC563 Carlos Correa 6.00 15.00
THC575 Nathan Eovaldi 1.50 4.00
THC585 Yasmani Grandal 1.25 3.00
THC587 Jason Grilli 1.25 3.00
THC591 Roberto Osuna 1.25 3.00
THC592 Kevin Plawecki 1.25 3.00
THC599 Archie Bradley 1.25 3.00
THC603 Martin Prado 1.25 3.00
THC611 Jed Lowrie 1.25 3.00
THC617 Micah Johnson 1.25 3.00
THC618 Noah Syndergaard 2.50 6.00
THC621 Wil Myers 1.25 3.00
THC622 Will Middlebrooks 1.25 3.00
THC640 Steven Souza Jr. 1.50 4.00
THC647 Joey Gallo 2.50 6.00
THC654 Christian Bethancourt 1.25 3.00
THC662 Marcus Semien 1.25 3.00
THC674 Eddie Rosario 2.50 6.00
THC687 Asdrubal Cabrera 1.50 4.00
THC701 Matt Kemp 1.50 4.00
THC702 Justin Upton 1.50 4.00
THC703 Edinson Volquez 1.25 3.00
THC704 Ben Zobrist 1.50 4.00
THC705 Yasmany Tomas 1.50 4.00
THC706 Ichiro Suzuki 2.50 6.00
THC707 Evan Gattis 1.25 3.00
THC708 Max Scherzer 2.00 5.00
THC709 Jesse Hahn 1.25 3.00
THC710 Carlos Rodon 2.00 5.00
THC711 Andrew Miller 1.50 4.00
THC712 Blake Swihart 1.50 4.00
THC713 Raisel Iglesias 1.50 4.00
THC714 Jung Ho Kang 1.25 3.00
THC715 Dexter Fowler 1.50 4.00
THC716 Devon Travis 1.25 3.00
THC717 Francisco Lindor 8.00 20.00
THC718 Addison Russell 4.00 10.00
THC719 Mike Foltynewicz 1.25 3.00
THC721 Jimmy Rollins 1.50 4.00
THC722 Craig Kimbrel 1.50 4.00
THC723 Yovani Gallardo 1.25 3.00
THC724 Byron Buxton 2.00 5.00
THC725 Kris Bryant 60.00 150.00

2015 Topps Heritage Chrome Black Refractors

*BLACK REF: 2X TO 5X BASIC
STATED ODDS 1:350 HOBBY
HN ODDS 1:256 HOBBY
STATED PRINT RUN 66 SER.#'d SETS

THC100 Clayton Kershaw 30.00 80.00
THC139 J.Baez/J.Soler 50.00 120.00
THC275 Yadier Molina 20.00 50.00
THC300 Andrew McCutchen 20.00 50.00
THC426 Giancarlo Stanton 20.00 50.00
THC429 Jacob deGrom 25.00 60.00
THC440 Bryce Harper 50.00 120.00
THC449 Matt Harvey 20.00 50.00
THC500 Mike Trout 75.00 150.00
THC563 Carlos Correa 75.00 150.00
THC618 Noah Syndergaard 25.00 60.00
THC706 Ichiro Suzuki 30.00 80.00
THC724 Byron Buxton 30.00 80.00
THC725 Kris Bryant 400.00 600.00

2015 Topps Heritage Chrome Purple Refractors

*PURPLE REF: .4X TO 1X BASIC
RANDOM INSERTS IN RETAIL PACKS

2015 Topps Heritage Chrome Refractors

*REFRACTORS: .6X TO 1.5X BASIC
STATED ODDS 1:41 HOBBY
HN ODDS 1:30 HOBBY
STATED PRINT RUN 566 SER.#'d SETS

2015 Topps Heritage Chrome Retail Foil

*RETAIL FOIL: .4X TO 1X BASIC
RANDOM INSERTS IN RETAIL PACKS

2015 Topps Heritage Clubhouse Collection Dual Relics

STATED ODDS 1:6950 HOBBY
HN ODDS 1:1491 HOBBY
STATED PRINT RUN 66 SER.#'d SETS

CCDRAH H.Aaron/J.Heyward 25.00 60.00
CCDRBB Baez/Banks HN 25.00 60.00
CCDRBC Castro/Banks HN 25.00 60.00
CCDRBH Bnnng/Hamels HN 25.00 60.00
CCDRCM McCtchn/Clmnte HN 50.00 120.00
CCDRCM Y.Molina/O.Cepeda 40.00 100.00
CCDRCW Cepeda/Wong HN 25.00 60.00
CCDRMB J.Marichal/M.Bumgarner 25.00 60.00
CCDRMJ D.Jeter/R.Maris 30.00 80.00
CCDRPG Plmr/Gsmn HN 20.00 50.00
CCDRRM Mchdo/Rbnsn HN 15.00 40.00
CCDRSM W.Stargell/A.McCutchen 50.00 120.00

2015 Topps Heritage Clubhouse Collection Relic Autographs

STATED ODDS 1:9100 HOBBY
HN ODDS 1:3346 HOBBY
STATED PRINT RUN 25 SER.#'d SETS
EXCHANGE DEADLINE 2/28/2018
HN EXCH DEADLINE 8/31/2017

CCARAR Anthony Rizzo 60.00 150.00
CCARBP Buster Posey 150.00 250.00
CCARDW David Wright 90.00 150.00
CCARFF Freddie Freeman 30.00 80.00
CCARHA H.Aaron HN EXCH 350.00 700.00
CCARJB Javier Baez HN 100.00 200.00
CCARJP J.Pederson HN EXCH 75.00 200.00
CCARJS Jorge Soler HN 75.00 150.00
CCARKW K.Wong HN EXCH 50.00 120.00
CCARMF Maikel Franco HN 30.00 80.00
CCARMM Manny Machado 100.00 200.00
CCARMT Mike Trout 250.00 400.00
CCARMT Michael Taylor HN 50.00 120.00
CCARTW T.Walker HN EXCH 30.00 80.00
CCARYP Yasiel Puig 30.00 80.00

2015 Topps Heritage Clubhouse Collection Relics

STATED ODDS 1:31 HOBBY
HN ODDS 1:38 HOBBY

CCRAB Adrian Beltre 3.00 8.00
CCRAC Aroldis Chapman 3.00 8.00
CCRAC Alex Cobb HN 2.00 5.00
CCRAJ Adam Jones 2.50 6.00
CCRAM Andrew McCutchen HN 5.00 12.00
CCRAW Alex Wood HN 2.00 5.00
CCRAW Adam Wainwright 2.50 6.00
CCRBH Bryce Harper 6.00 15.00
CCRBHA Billy Hamilton 2.50 6.00
CCRCA Chris Archer 2.00 5.00
CCRCD Chris Davis HN 2.00 5.00
CCRCG Carlos Gonzalez HN 2.50 6.00
CCRCK Clayton Kershaw 5.00 12.00
CCRCS Chris Sale HN 3.00 8.00
CCRCY Christian Yelich 4.00 10.00
CCRDB Dellin Betances HN 2.50 6.00
CCRDJ Derek Jeter 12.00 30.00
CCRDO David Ortiz 3.00 8.00
CCRDP Dustin Pedroia 3.00 8.00
CCRDW David Wright 2.50 6.00
CCREG Evan Gattis 2.00 5.00
CCRFF Freddie Freeman 4.00 10.00
CCRFH Felix Hernandez 2.50 6.00
CCRGS Giancarlo Stanton 3.00 8.00
CCRGS Giancarlo Stanton HN 3.00 8.00
CCRHI Hisashi Iwakuma HN 2.50 6.00
CCRHJR Hyun-Jin Ryu 2.50 6.00
CCRHR Hanley Ramirez 2.50 6.00
CCRIK Ian Kinsler HN 2.50 6.00
CCRJA Jose Abreu HN 2.50 6.00
CCRJAL Jose Altuve HN 2.50 6.00
CCRJB Javier Baez HN 15.00 40.00
CCRJB Jose Bautista 2.50 6.00
CCRJC Johnny Cueto HN 2.50 6.00
CCRJD Jacob deGrom HN 3.00 8.00
CCRJF Jose Fernandez HN 3.00 8.00
CCRJH Jason Heyward 2.50 6.00
CCRJMA Joe Mauer 2.50 6.00
CCRJV Justin Verlander 3.00 8.00
CCRJV Justin Verlander HN 3.00 8.00
CCRKW Kolten Wong HN 2.50 6.00
CCRMB Mookie Betts HN 5.00 12.00
CCRMC Miguel Cabrera HN 3.00 8.00
CCRMC Miguel Cabrera 3.00 8.00
CCRMH Matt Harvey HN 2.50 6.00
CCRMK Matt Kemp 2.50 6.00
CCRMM Manny Machado 3.00 8.00
CCRMM Manny Machado HN 3.00 8.00
CCRMS Max Scherzer 3.00 8.00
CCRMT Mike Trout 15.00 40.00
CCRMTA Michael Taylor HN 2.00 5.00
CCRMW Michael Wacha HN 2.50 6.00
CCRNR Nolan Ryan HN 10.00 25.00
CCROC Orlando Cepeda HN 2.50 6.00
CCRPG Paul Goldschmidt 3.00 8.00
CCRPS Pablo Sandoval HN 3.00 8.00
CCRRB Ryan Braun 2.50 6.00
CCRRC Robinson Cano HN 2.50 6.00
CCRTL Tim Lincecum HN 2.50 6.00
CCRTT Troy Tulowitzki 3.00 8.00
CCRTW Taijuan Walker HN 2.00 5.00
CCRXB Xander Bogaerts 2.50 6.00
CCRYD Yu Darvish 3.00 8.00
CCRYM Yadier Molina HN 3.00 8.00
CCRYP Yasiel Puig 3.00 8.00
CCRYV Yordano Ventura HN 2.50 6.00
CCRZG Zack Greinke 2.50 6.00
CCRZW Zack Wheeler 2.50 6.00

2015 Topps Heritage Clubhouse Collection Relics Gold

*GOLD: .8X TO 2X BASIC
STATED ODDS 1:550 HOBBY
HN ODDS 1:266 HOBBY
STATED PRINT RUN 99 SER.#'d SETS

CCRDJ Derek Jeter 50.00 120.00
CCREB Ernie Banks 20.00 50.00
CCRHA Hank Aaron 30.00 80.00
CCRJM Juan Marichal 5.00 12.00
CCRRM Roger Maris 40.00 100.00
CCRWM Willie Mays 40.00 100.00

2015 Topps Heritage Clubhouse Collection Triple Relics

STATED ODDS 1:18,688 HOBBY
HN ODDS 1:5018 HOBBY
STATED PRINT RUN 25 SER.#'d SETS

CCTRAHJ Aaron/Upton/Hywrd 50.00 120.00
CCTRATF Am/Frmn/Thm HN 50.00 120.00
CCTRBBC Baez/Cstro/Bnks HN 20.00 50.00
CCTRBJT Banks/Jeter/Tulo 100.00 200.00
CCTRCMS McCtchn/Clmnte
Strgll HN 125.00 250.00
CCTRCMW Wnwrght/Cpda/Mlna HN 50.00 120.00
CCTRMMA Maris/Mays/Aaron 250.00 350.00
CCTRMMP Mays/Psy/Mrchl HN 100.00 200.00
CCTRMPB Posey/Bmgmr/Mrchl 60.00 150.00

TRRJM Mchdo/Rbnsn/Jones HN 60.00 150.00
TRSMM McCtchn/Strgll/Marte 100.00 200.00

2015 Topps Heritage Combo Cards

MPLETE SET (10) 5.00 12.00
ATED ODDS 1:8 HOBBY
1 Sandoval/Ramirez/Ortiz .50 1.25
2 J.Bautista/J.Donaldson .40 1.00
3 Cincinnati Reds Mascots .30 .75
4 A.Miller/B.McCann .40 1.00
5 J.Altuve/G.Springer .40 1.00
6 M.Machado/C.Davis .50 1.25
7 A.Gordon/E.Hosmer .40 1.00
8 K.Plawecki/N.Syndergaard .60 1.50
9 K.Bryant/A.Russell 2.00 5.00
10 Myers/Upton/Kemp .40 1.00

015 Topps Heritage Flashback Relic Autographs

ATED ODDS 1:18,688 HOBBY
ATED PRINT RUN 25 SER.#'d SETS
CHANGE DEADLINE 2/28/2018
RHA Hank Aaron EXCH 200.00 300.00
RSC Steve Carlton 150.00 250.00

2015 Topps Heritage Framed Stamps

ATED ODDS 1:2310 HOBBY
ATED PRINT RUN 50 SER.#'d SETS
USAK Al Kaline 30.00 80.00
USBM Bill Mazeroski 25.00 60.00
USBR Brooks Robinson 25.00 60.00
USEB Ernie Banks 30.00 80.00
USEM Eddie Mathews 30.00 80.00
6USFJ Fergie Jenkins 25.00 60.00
6USHK Harmon Killebrew 30.00 80.00
6USJB Jim Bunning 25.00 60.00
6USJM Joe Morgan 25.00 60.00
6USJMA Juan Marichal 50.00 120.00
6USLA Luis Aparicio 25.00 60.00
6USLB Lou Brock 25.00 60.00
5USNR Nolan Ryan 100.00 250.00
6USOC Orlando Cepeda 25.00 60.00
6USPN Phil Niekro 25.00 60.00
6USSC Steve Carlton 25.00 60.00
6USTP Tony Perez 25.00 60.00
6USWF Whitey Ford 25.00 60.00
6USWM Willie McCovey 25.00 60.00
6USWMA Willie Mays 50.00 120.00

2015 Topps Heritage Mini

MINI: 1.2X TO 3X BASIC CHROME
STATED ODDS 1:231 HOBBY
HN ODDS 1:169 HOBBY
STATED PRINT RUN 100 SER.#'d SETS
Buster Posey 30.00 80.00
300 Andrew McCutchen 15.00 40.00
440 Bryce Harper 20.00 50.00
500 Mike Trout 75.00 200.00
725 Kris Bryant 150.00 400.00

2015 Topps Heritage New Age Performers

COMPLETE SET (20) 10.00 25.00
STATED ODDS 1:8 HOBBY
NAP1 Clayton Kershaw 1.00 2.50
NAP2 Jose Abreu .50 1.25
NAP3 Billy Hamilton .40 1.00
NAP4 Giancarlo Stanton .50 1.25
NAP5 Mike Trout 2.50 6.00
NAP6 Bryce Harper .75 2.00
NAP7 Yu Darvish .50 1.25
NAP8 Buster Posey .60 1.50
NAP9 Miguel Cabrera .50 1.25
NAP10 Andrew McCutchen .50 1.25
NAP11 Adam Jones .40 1.00
NAP12 Felix Hernandez .40 1.00
NAP13 Masahiro Tanaka .40 1.00
NAP14 Evan Longoria .40 1.00
NAP15 Javier Baez 2.50 6.00
NAP16 Aroldis Chapman .50 1.25
NAP17 Yasiel Puig .50 1.25
NAP18 Troy Tulowitzki .50 1.25
NAP19 Jacob deGrom .50 1.25
NAP20 Chris Sale .50 1.25

2015 Topps Heritage News Flashbacks

COMPLETE SET (10) 3.00 8.00
STATED ODDS 1:12 HOBBY
NF1 Batman .50 1.25
NF2 Lunar Orbiter 1 .40 1.00
NF3 Star Trek .75 2.00
NF4 Metropolitan Opera House .40 1.00
NF5 Jimi Hendrix Experience .40 1.00
NF6 Ronald Reagan .40 1.00
NF7 NFL/AFL Merger .40 1.00
NF8 Indira Gandhi .40 1.00
NF9 Marvin Miller .40 1.00
NF10 Sheila Scott .40 1.00

2015 Topps Heritage Now and Then

COMPLETE SET (15) 5.00 12.00
STATED ODDS 1:8 HOBBY
NT1 Corey Kluber .40 1.00
NT2 Steven Matz .50 1.25
NT3 Giancarlo Stanton .50 1.25
NT4 Mike Trout 2.50 6.00
NT5 Alex Rodriguez .60 1.50
NT6 Adrian Beltre .50 1.25
NT7 Miguel Cabrera .50 1.25
NT8 Felix Hernandez .40 1.00
NT9 Clayton Kershaw 1.00 2.50
NT10 Ryan Zimmerman .40 1.00
NT11 Eddie Rosario .60 1.50
NT12 Jose Altuve .40 1.00
NT13 Yasmani Grandal .30 .75
NT14 Andrew Miller .40 1.00
NT15 Bryce Harper .75 2.00

2015 Topps Heritage Real One Autographs

STATED ODDS 1:258 HOBBY
HN ODDS 1:167 HOBBY BOXES
EXCHANGE DEADLINE 2/28/2018
HN EXCH DEADLINE 8/31/2017
ROAAG Aubrey Gatewood 6.00 15.00
ROAAK Al Kaline 30.00 80.00
ROAAM Art Mahaffey 6.00 15.00
ROAAP Albie Pearson 6.00 15.00
ROAAS Aaron Sanchez 8.00 20.00
ROAAST Al Stanek 6.00 15.00
ROABF Bob Friend 6.00 15.00
ROABR Bobby Richardson 6.00 15.00
ROABS Bob Sadowski 6.00 15.00
ROABW Bill Wakefield 6.00 15.00
ROACCC Choo Choo Coleman 20.00 50.00
ROACS Chuck Schilling 12.00 30.00
ROACW Carl Warwick 6.00 15.00
ROADB Dellin Betances 10.00 25.00
ROADS Dick Stigman 6.00 15.00
ROAEB Ernie Bowman 6.00 15.00
ROAEBR Ernie Broglio 6.00 15.00
ROAFC Frank Carpin 6.00 15.00
ROAFK Frank Kreutzer 6.00 15.00
ROAFM Frank Malzone 6.00 15.00
ROAGB Greg Bollo 6.00 15.00
ROAGK Gary Kroll 6.00 15.00
ROAGR Gordon Richardson 6.00 15.00
ROAJAC Jack Cullen 12.00 30.00
ROAJB Javier Baez 30.00 80.00
Signed in red ink
ROAJC Joe Christopher 6.00 15.00
ROAJD Jim Dickson 6.00 15.00
ROAJG Joe Gaines 6.00 15.00
ROAJGE Jim Gentile 6.00 15.00
ROAJH John Herrnstein 12.00 30.00
ROAJM Juan Marichal 30.00 80.00
ROAKH Ken Hamlin 6.00 15.00
ROALB Lou Brock 40.00 100.00
ROAMB Mike Brumley 6.00 15.00
ROAMK Marty Keough 8.00 20.00
ROAOC Orlando Cepeda 30.00 80.00
ROAPN Phil Niekro 30.00 80.00
ROARC Roger Craig 10.00 25.00
ROARCA Rusney Castillo 20.00 50.00
ROARH Ray Herbert 6.00 15.00
ROARN Ron Nischwitz 12.00 30.00
ROASM Shelby Miller 15.00 40.00
ROATS Tracy Stallard 6.00 15.00
ROAHAB Archie Bradley HN 10.00 25.00
ROAHAK Al Kaline HN 40.00 100.00
ROAHAR Addison Russell HN 40.00 100.00
ROAHBB Byron Buxton HN 30.00 80.00
ROAHBS Blake Swihart HN 8.00 20.00
ROAHCC Carlos Correa HN 100.00 250.00
ROAHCR Carlos Rodon HN EXCH 10.00 25.00
ROAHDH Dilson Herrera HN 8.00 20.00
ROAHDN Daniel Norris HN 6.00 15.00
ROAHDP Dalton Pompey HN 8.00 20.00
ROAHFL Francisco Lindor HN 30.00 80.00
ROAHFR Frank Robinson HN 50.00 120.00
ROAHHR Hanley Ramirez HN 10.00 25.00
ROAHJA Jose Abreu HN 15.00 40.00
ROAHJL Jake Lamb HN 10.00 25.00
ROAHJP Joe Panik HN 15.00 40.00
ROAHJS Jorge Soler HN 10.00 25.00
ROAHKB Kris Bryant HN 250.00 500.00
ROAHKP Kevin Plawecki HN 6.00 15.00
ROAHMJ Micah Johnson HN 6.00 15.00
ROAHMS Max Scherzer HN 25.00 60.00
ROAHMT Michael Taylor HN 6.00 15.00
ROAHNR Nolan Ryan HN 125.00 300.00
ROAHNS Noah Syndergaard HN 25.00 60.00
ROAHPN Phil Niekro HN 15.00 40.00
ROAHRC Rusney Castillo HN 8.00 20.00
ROAHRI Raisel Iglesias HN 12.00 30.00
ROAHRO Roberto Osuna HN 6.00 15.00
ROAHSC Steve Carlton HN 40.00 100.00
ROAHYT Yasmany Tomas HN 8.00 20.00
ROAHJHE Jason Heyward HN 30.00 80.00
ROAHJHK Jung Ho Kang HN 6.00 15.00
ROAHJLE Jon Lester HN 12.00 30.00
ROAHJPE Joc Pederson HN 15.00 40.00
ROAHMFR Maikel Franco HN 12.00 30.00

2015 Topps Heritage Real One Autographs Red Ink

*RED INK: .6X TO 1.5X BASIC
STATED ODDS 1:390 HOBBY
HN ODDS 1:245 HOBBY
STATED PRINT RUN 66 SER.#'d SETS
EXCHANGE DEADLINE 2/28/2018
HN EXCH DEADLINE 8/31/2017
ROABH Bryce Harper 200.00 400.00
ROABRO Brooks Robinson 125.00 250.00
ROAMR Mariano Rivera 400.00 600.00
ROAOC Orlando Cepeda 50.00 120.00
ROASC Steve Carlton 150.00 250.00
ROASK Sandy Koufax EXCH 500.00 800.00
ROAHCK Clayton Kershaw HN 125.00 250.00

2015 Topps Heritage Real One Autographs Dual

STATED ODDS 1:3515 HOBBY
HN ODDS 1:5132 HOBBY
STATED PRINT RUN 25 SER.#'d SETS
EXCHANGE DEADLINE 2/28/2018
HN EXCH DEADLINE 8/31/2017
RODAAF Aaron/Freeman EXCH 125.00 300.00
RODABA L.Brock/M.Adams 100.00 200.00
RODABC Brck/Crpntr HN EXCH 60.00 150.00
RODACH Cpda/Hywrd HN EXCH 60.00 150.00
RODACM O.Cepeda/S.Miller 60.00 150.00
RODACW S.Carlton/M.Wacha 60.00 150.00
RODACW Wng/Cpda HN EXCH 50.00 120.00
RODAKC Cspds/Klne HN EXCH 100.00 250.00
RODAKC A.Kaline/M.Cabrera 125.00 300.00
RODAKK Kfx/Krshw HN EXCH 900.00 1200.00
RODANM Nkro/Mllr HN EXCH 60.00 150.00
RODANT Niekro/Teheran EXCH 60.00 150.00
RODAPJ Palmer/Jenkins EXCH 100.00 200.00
RODARG dGrm/Ryan HN EXCH 200.00 400.00
RODARJ Rbnsn/Jns HN 100.00 250.00
RODAWB Hywrd/Brk HN EXCH 50.00 120.00

2015 Topps Heritage Rookie Performers

COMPLETE SET (15) 10.00 25.00
STATED ODDS 1:8 HOBBY
RP1 Jorge Soler .50 1.25
RP2 Francisco Lindor 2.00 5.00
RP3 Joc Pederson .60 1.50
RP4 Kris Bryant 2.00 5.00
RP5 Addison Russell 1.00 2.50
RP6 Archie Bradley .30 .75
RP7 Carlos Rodon .50 1.25
RP8 Daniel Norris .30 .75
RP9 Javier Baez 2.50 6.00
RP10 Byron Buxton .50 1.25
RP11 Blake Swihart .40 1.00
RP12 Noah Syndergaard .60 1.50
RP13 Yasmany Tomas .40 1.00
RP14 Joey Gallo .60 1.50
RP15 Carlos Correa 1.50 4.00

2015 Topps Heritage Then and Now

COMPLETE SET (10) 5.00 12.00
STATED ODDS 1:10 HOBBY
TAN1 N.Cruz/H.Killebrew .50 1.25
TAN2 A.Gonzalez/W.Mays 1.00 2.50
TAN3 J.Altuve/W.Stargell .40 1.00
TAN4 D.Gordon/L.Brock .40 1.00
TAN5 C.Santana/H.Killebrew .50 1.25
TAN6 C.Kershaw/S.Koufax 1.00 2.50
TAN7 D.Price/S.Koufax 1.00 2.50
TAN8 C.Kershaw/S.Koufax 1.00 2.50
TAN9 S.Koufax/D.Price 1.00 2.50
TAN10 A.Wainwright/S.Koufax 1.00 2.50

2016 Topps Heritage

SP ODDS 1:3 HOBBY
HN SP ODDS 1:3 HOBBY
HN ACTION ODDS 1:25 HOBBY
HN CLR SWP ODDS 1:89 HOBBY
HN THRWBCK ODDS 1:1535 HOBBY
HN ERROR ODDS 1:430 HOBBY
1 Moustakas/Escobar/Hosmer .20 .50
2 Logan Forsythe .15 .40
3 Brad Miller .20 .50
4 Jeremy Hellickson .15 .40
5 Nick Hundley .15 .40
6 Aaron Hicks .20 .50
7 Alcides Escobar .20 .50
8A Shin-Soo Choo .20 .50
8B Choo Thrwbck SP 200.00 300.00
9 Wil Myers .15 .40
10 Gregory Polanco .20 .50
11 Francisco Rodriguez .20 .50
12 Andre Ethier .20 .50
13 Wily Peralta .15 .40
14 Jhonny Peralta .15 .40
15 Yan Gomes .15 .40
16 Nathan Karns .15 .40
17 Brayan Pena .15 .40
18 Luke Gregerson .15 .40
19 Ian Desmond .15 .40
20 Matt Adams .15 .40
21A Didi Gregorius .20 .50
21B Didi Gregorius Action SP 2.50 6.00
22 J.T. Realmuto .25 .60
23A Brandon Phillips .15 .40
23B Phillips Thrwbck SP 150.00 250.00
24 Rajai Davis .15 .40
25A Brian McCann .20 .50
25B Brian McCann Color SP 5.00 12.00
26 Drew Smyly .15 .40
27 Desmond Jennings .20 .50
28 David Freese .15 .40
29 Anthony Gose .15 .40
30 J.D. Martinez .25 .60
31A Alfredo Simon .15 .40
31B Simon Thrwbck SP 150.00 250.00
32 Jered Weaver .20 .50
33 Jason Grilli .15 .40
34 Kevin Kiermaier .20 .50
35 Jeurys Familia .20 .50
36 Carlos Martinez .20 .50
37 Santiago Casilla .15 .40
38 Adrian Gonzalez .20 .50
39 Jake Lamb .20 .50
40 Kole Calhoun .15 .40
41 Francisco Cervelli .15 .40
42 Justin Bour .20 .50
43 Adam Lind .20 .50
44 Jung Ho Kang .15 .40
45A Hanley Ramirez .20 .50
45B Hanley Ramirez Color SP 5.00 12.00
45C Ramirez ERR SP 20.00 50.00
46 Marcus Semien .15 .40
47 Darin Ruf .15 .40
48 Miguel Montero .15 .40
49 Yonder Alonso .15 .40
50A Byron Buxton .20 .50
50B Buxton Color SP 5.00 12.00
51 Kyle Seager .15 .40
52 Jason Hammel .20 .50
53 Cameron Maybin .15 .40
54 Asdrubal Cabrera .20 .50
55 Jeff Locke .15 .40
56 Robinson Chirinos .15 .40
57 Trevor Plouffe .15 .40
58A C.J. Cron .15 .40
58B Cron ERR SP 25.00 60.00
59 Kyle Hendricks .25 .60
60 Chris Davis .15 .40
61 Pat Venditte .15 .40
62 Steven Matz .20 .50
63 Piscotty/Carpenter .25 .60
64 Nick Ahmed .15 .40
65 Nick Martinez .15 .40
66 Eddie Rosario .20 .50
67 Gerardo Parra .15 .40
68 Wellington Castillo .15 .40
69 Freddy Galvis .15 .40
70A Kris Bryant .30 .75
70B Bryant Color SP 30.00 80.00
70C Bryant Thrwbck SP 400.00 800.00
71 Caleb Joseph .15 .40
72 Mark Trumbo .15 .40
73 Jonathan Papelbon .20 .50
74 Brock Holt .15 .40
75 Yangervis Solarte .15 .40
76 Daniel Murphy .20 .50
77A Evan Gattis .15 .40
77B Evan Gattis Color SP 4.00 10.00
78A Jake Arrieta .20 .50
78B Jake Arrieta Action SP 2.50 6.00
79 Jose Iglesias .20 .50
80 Aroldis Chapman .25 .60
81 Kendall Graveman .15 .40
82 Ryan Zimmerman .20 .50
83 Colby Rasmus .20 .50
84 Yasmani Grandal .15 .40
85 Bryan Morris .15 .40
86 Alexei Ramirez .20 .50
87 Jon Lester .20 .50
88A Xander Bogaerts .25 .60
88B Xander Bogaerts Action SP 3.00 8.00
89 Trevor Rosenthal .20 .50
90 Sonny Gray .20 .50
91 Jackie Bradley Jr. .25 .60
92 Jesse Hahn .15 .40
93 Mitch Moreland .15 .40
94 Mark Buehrle .20 .50
95 Chris Heston .15 .40
96 Blake Swihart .20 .50
97 Carlos Beltran .20 .50
98 Matt Wisler .15 .40
99 Roberto Osuna .15 .40
100A Adam Jones .20 .50
100B Adam Jones Color SP 5.00 12.00
101 Nick Castellanos .25 .60
102 Scott Kazmir .15 .40
103 Andrew Cashner .15 .40
104 Jean Segura .20 .50
105 Kendrys Morales .15 .40
106 Anibal Sanchez .15 .40
107 Jeanmar Gomez .15 .40
108 Rougned Odor .20 .50
109 Lindor/Kipnis .25 .60
110 Brandon Belt .20 .50
111 Eugenio Suarez .20 .50
112 Kyle Gibson .20 .50
113 Erick Aybar .15 .40
114 Kevin Gausman .15 .40
115 Hisashi Iwakuma .20 .50
116 Wade Miley .15 .40
117 James Loney .15 .40
118 Giovanny Urshela .25 .60
119 Joaquin Benoit .15 .40
120A Billy Hamilton .20 .50
120B Billy Hamilton Action SP 2.50 6.00
121 Carlos Carrasco .15 .40
122 Derek Norris .15 .40
123 Billy Butler .15 .40
124 Derek Dietrich .20 .50
125 Zach Britton .20 .50
126 Starlin Castro .15 .40
127 David Wright .20 .50
128A Mike Moustakas .20 .50
128B Moustakas ERR SP 30.00 80.00
129 Cesar Hernandez .15 .40
130 Zack Greinke .20 .50
131 Russell Martin .15 .40
132A Ichiro Suzuki .30 .75
132B Ichiro Action SP 4.00 10.00
133 Jeremy Jeffress .15 .40
134 Bartolo Colon .15 .40
135 Nick Swisher .20 .50
136 John Danks .15 .40
137 Jonathan Schoop .15 .40
138 Carlos Ruiz .15 .40
139 Jacob Lindgren .20 .50
140 Starling Marte .20 .50
141 Scooter Gennett .20 .50
142 Melky Cabrera .15 .40
143 Josh Reddick .15 .40
144 Michael Cuddyer .15 .40
145 Collin McHugh .15 .40
146 Kelvin Herrera .15 .40
147 Jace Peterson .15 .40
148 Will Smith .15 .40
149 R.A. Dickey .20 .50
150 Jacoby Ellsbury .20 .50
151A Eric Hosmer .20 .50
151B E.Hosmer Colorized SP 5.00 12.00
152A Johnny Cueto .20 .50
152B Cueto Colorized SP 20.00 50.00
153A Salvador Perez .20 .50
153B Perez Colorized SP 20.00 50.00
154A Wade Davis .15 .40
154B Davis Colorized SP 20.00 50.00
155A Kansas City Royals .20 .50
155B Royals Colorized SP 20.00 50.00
156 Mark Melancon .15 .40
157A Manny Machado .25 .60
157B Manny Machado Action SP 3.00 8.00
158 Yovani Gallardo .15 .40
159 Jose Reyes .20 .50
160 Joc Pederson .20 .50
161A Schwarber RC/Edwards RC 1.00 2.50
161B Kyle Schwarber SP 12.00 30.00
162 P.O'Brien RC/B.Drury RC .50 1.25
163 Mnts RC/Thmpsn RC .50 1.25
164 K.Waldrop RC/K.Sampson RC .40 1.00
165 G.Soto RC/S.Armstrong RC .40 1.00
166 T.Murphy RC/J.Gray RC .30 .75
167 S.Alexander RC/M.Almonte RC .30 .75
168A Seager RC/Peraza RC 2.50 6.00
168B Corey Seager SP 20.00 50.00
169 B.Ellington RC/C.Reed RC .30 .75
170 A.Pena RC/N.Ashley RC .30 .75
171 Pazos RC/Bird RC .40 1.00
172 R.Dull RC/C.Blair RC .30 .75
173 C.Murray RC/J.Eickhoff RC .50 1.25
174 C.Decker RC/T.Jankowski RC .30 .75
175 J.Hicks RC/K.Marte RC .60 1.50
176 L.Maile RC/R.Shaffer RC .30 .75
177A G.Sanchez RC/R.Mondesi RC 1.00 2.50
177B Snchz/Mndsi ERR SP 40.00 100.00
178 D.Alvarez RC/H.Owens RC .40 1.00
179 Z.Godley RC/S.Brito RC .30 .75
180 Turner RC/Olivera RC 1.00 2.50
181A Conforto RC/Nola RC .60 1.50
181B Aaron Nola SP 6.00 15.00
182 L.Jackson RC/T.Duffey RC .30 .75
183A Sweeney RC/Piscotty RC .50 1.25
183B Stephen Piscotty SP 8.00 20.00
184 E.Diaz RC/N.Ogando RC .30 .75
185 C.Hall RC/R.Lazo RC .30 .75
186 C.Granderson/J.Lagares .20 .50
187 T.Brown RC/M.Williamson RC .40 1.00
188 P.Severino RC/T.Tartamella RC .30 .75
189 Trrys RC/Brxtn RC .60 1.50
190A Severino RC/Sano RC .50 1.25
190B Luis Severino SP 6.00 15.00
191 Jimmy Rollins .20 .50
192 Rick Porcello .20 .50
193 A.J. Pierzynski .15 .40
194 Tommy Milone .15 .40
195A Nolan Arenado .30 .75
195B Nolan Arenado Action SP 4.00 10.00
195C Nolan Arenado Color SP 8.00 20.00
196 Jorge De La Rosa .15 .40
197 Erasmo Ramirez .15 .40
198 Jimmy Paredes .15 .40
199 Shawn Tolleson .15 .40
200A Hunter Pence .20 .50
200B Pence ERR SP 50.00 120.00
201 Luis Valbuena .15 .40
202 Chris Colabello .15 .40
203 Lonnie Chisenhall .15 .40
204 Adam LaRoche .15 .40
205 Khris Davis .25 .60
206 Kevin Pillar .15 .40
207 Brett Lawrie .20 .50
208 Jarrod Dyson .15 .40
209 Ubaldo Jimenez .15 .40
210A Michael Wacha .20 .50
210B Michael Wacha Color SP 5.00 12.00
211 Aaron Harang .15 .40
212 J.J. Hardy .15 .40
213 Brad Ziegler .15 .40
214 Gio Gonzalez .20 .50
215 John Jaso .15 .40
216 Kinsler/Cabrera .25 .60
217 J.P. Howell .15 .40
218 Matt Shoemaker .20 .50
219 Carson Smith .15 .40
220 Matt Duffy .15 .40
221 Christian Bethancourt .15 .40
222 Chris Iannetta .15 .40
223A Mike Zunino .15 .40
223B Zunino ERR SP 40.00 100.00
224 Jedd Gyorko .15 .40
225 Ken Giles .15 .40
226A Carlos Rodon .25 .60
226B Rodon Thrwbck SP 75.00 200.00
227 Carlos Gomez .15 .40
228 Ben Revere .15 .40
229 Ian Kennedy .15 .40
230 James Shields .15 .40
231 Tim Lincecum .20 .50
232 Sergio Romo .15 .40
233 Price/Gray/Keuchel .20 .50
234 Krshw/Grnke/Arrta .50 1.25
235 Price/McHugh/Keuchel .20 .50
236 Bmgrnr/Cole/Grnke/Arrta .25 .60
237 Sale/Archer/Kluber .25 .60
238 Arrieta/Scherzer/Kershaw .50 1.25
239 Altuive/Bogaerts/Cabrera .25 .60
240 Harper/Goldschmidt/Gordon .40 1.00
241 Jose Bautista .20 .50
Chris Davis
Josh Donaldson
242 Rizzo/Arenado/Goldschmidt .40 1.00
243 Cruz/Trout/Davis 1.25 3.00
244 Gonzalez/Harper/Arenado .40 1.00
245 Marco Estrada .15 .40
246 Logan Morrison .15 .40
247 Hector Santiago .15 .40
248 A.J. Ramos .15 .40
249 Lucas Duda .20 .50
250 Nick Markakis .20 .50
251 Yadier Molina .25 .60
252 Jeff Francoeur .20 .50
253 Michael Brantley .20 .50
254A Dee Gordon .15 .40
254B Gordon ERR SP 20.00 50.00
255 Jorge Soler .25 .60
256 Josh Harrison .15 .40
257 Skip Schumaker .15 .40
258 Rubby De La Rosa .15 .40
259 A.Houser RC/M.Reed RC .30 .75
260 Justin Turner .20 .50
261 Chip Hale MG .15 .40
262 Buck Showalter MG .15 .40
263 Joe Maddon MG .15 .40
264 Terry Francona MG .20 .50
265 A.J. Hinch MG .15 .40
266 Marte/McCutchen .25 .60
267 Mike Scioscia MG .15 .40
268 Fredi Gonzalez MG .15 .40
269 Paul Molitor .25 .60
270 Terry Collins MG .15 .40
271 Joe Girardi MG .20 .50
272 Walt Weiss MG .15 .40
273 Clint Hurdle MG .15 .40
274 Bruce Bochy MG .15 .40
275 Bryan Price MG .15 .40
276 Mike Matheny MG .15 .40
277 Kevin Cash MG .15 .40
278 John Gibbons MG .15 .40
279 Jeff Banister MG .15 .40
280 Craig Counsell MG .15 .40
281 Anthony DeSclafani .15 .40
282 Trevor Bauer .25 .60
283 Huston Street .15 .40
284 Stephen Strasburg .25 .60
285 Mike Leake .15 .40
286 Wei-Yin Chen .15 .40
287 Mark Canha .15 .40
288 Slade Heathcott .20 .50
289 Nathan Eovaldi .20 .50
290 Ryan Howard .20 .50
291 John Lackey .20 .50
292 Edwin Encarnacion .25 .60
293 Wade Davis .15 .40
294 Justin Morneau .20 .50
295 Avisail Garcia .20 .50
296 Eduardo Rodriguez .15 .40
297 Joe Panik .20 .50
298 Yohan Flande .15 .40
299 Ervin Santana .15 .40
300 Glen Perkins .15 .40
301 Mike Aviles .15 .40
302A Salvador Perez .20 .50
302B Salvador Perez Color SP 5.00 12.00
303 David Murphy .15 .40
304 Carlos Santana .20 .50
305 Chase Utley .20 .50
306 Yunel Escobar .15 .40
307 Martin Prado .15 .40
308 Chris Carter .15 .40
309 M.Franco/R.Howard .20 .50
310A Chris Sale .25 .60
310B Chris Sale Color SP 6.00 15.00
311 Jason Motte .15 .40
312 Vidal Nuno .15 .40
313 Seth Smith .15 .40
314 Delino DeShields Jr. .15 .40
315 Kolten Wong .20 .50
316 Steven Souza Jr. .20 .50
317 Colby Lewis .15 .40
318 Dexter Fowler .20 .50
319 Archie Bradley .15 .40
320 Madison Bumgarner .20 .50
321 Garrett Richards .20 .50
322A Giancarlo Stanton .25 .60
322B Giancarlo Stanton Action SP 3.00 8.00
322C Giancarlo Stanton Color SP 6.00 15.00
323 Nori Aoki .15 .40
324 Anthony Rendon .25 .60
325 Matt Holliday .25 .60
326A Francisco Liriano .15 .40
326B Liriano ERR SP 50.00 120.00
327A Matt Carpenter .25 .60
327B Carpenter Thrwbck SP 150.00 250.00
328 Denard Span .15 .40
329 Zack Cozart .15 .40
330 Kenley Jansen .20 .50
331 Brad Boxberger .15 .40
332 Ben Paulsen .15 .40
333A Craig Kimbrel .20 .50
333B Kimbrel Traded SP 60.00 150.00
334 Sano/Buxton .25 .60
335 Adam Eaton .15 .40
336 Drew Pomeranz .20 .50
337A Yordano Ventura .20 .50
337B Ventura Thrwbck SP 125.00 250.00
338 Jay Bruce .20 .50
339 Darren O'Day .15 .40
340 Mark Teixeira .20 .50
341 Baltimore Orioles .15 .40
342 Boston Red Sox .20 .50
343 New York Yankees .20 .50
344 Tampa Bay Rays .15 .40
345 Toronto Blue Jays .15 .40
346 Chicago White Sox .15 .40
347 Cleveland Indians .15 .40
348 Detroit Tigers .15 .40
349 Kansas City Royals .20 .50
350 Minnesota Twins .15 .40
351 Houston Astros .15 .40
352 Los Angeles Angels .15 .40
353 Oakland Athletics .15 .40
354 Seattle Mariners .15 .40
355 Texas Rangers .15 .40
356 Atlanta Braves .15 .40
357 Miami Marlins .15 .40
358 New York Mets .20 .50
359 Philadelphia Phillies .15 .40
360 Washington Nationals .15 .40
361 Chicago Cubs .20 .50
362 Cincinnati Reds .15 .40
363 Milwaukee Brewers .15 .40
364 Pittsburgh Pirates .15 .40
365 St. Louis Cardinals .20 .50
366 Arizona Diamondbacks .15 .40
367 Colorado Rockies .15 .40
368 Los Angeles Dodgers .20 .50
369 San Diego Padres .15 .40
370 San Francisco Giants .20 .50
371A Yasmany Tomas .15 .40
371B Yasmany Tomas Color SP 4.00 10.00
372 Cody Allen .15 .40
373 Marcell Ozuna .25 .60
374A Joe Mauer .20 .50
374B Mauer ERR SP 40.00 100.00
375 Tom Wilhelmsen .15 .40
376 Neil Walker .20 .50
377 Andres Blanco .15 .40
378 Jason Castro .15 .40
379 Drew Storen .15 .40
380 Phil Hughes .15 .40
381 Arodys Vizcaino .15 .40
382 Brett Gardner .20 .50
383 John Axford .15 .40
384 David Robertson .15 .40
385 Victor Martinez .20 .50
386 Hector Rondon .15 .40
387 Elvis Andrus .20 .50
388 Jordan Zimmermann .20 .50
389 Jeff Samardzija .15 .40
390 George Springer .20 .50
391 Mike Fiers .15 .40
392 Coco Crisp .15 .40
393 James McCann .20 .50
394 Ender Inciarte .15 .40
395 Jordy Mercer .15 .40
396 Freeman/Markakis .30 .75
397 Kevin Siegrist .15 .40
398 Wilmer Flores .20 .50
399 J.J. Hoover .15 .40
400A Andrew McCutchen .25 .60
400B McCtchn Action SP 3.00 8.00
401 Curtis Granderson .20 .50
402 Joe Kelly .15 .40
403 Danny Salazar .20 .50
404A Daniel Norris .15 .40
404B Norris Thrwbck SP
405 Adrian Beltre .25 .60
406 Alexi Amarista .15 .40
407 Ryan Flaherty .15 .40
408 Tom Koehler .15 .40
409 Pablo Sandoval .20 .50
410A Yasiel Puig .25 .60
410B Puig Action SP 3.00 8.00
411 Lance Lynn .15 .40
412 Andrew Miller .20 .50
413 Michael Pineda .15 .40
414 Clay Buchholz .15 .40
415 CC Sabathia .20 .50
416 Aaron Sanchez .20 .50
417A Julio Teheran .20 .50
417B Teheran ERR SP 40.00 100.00
418 Sean Doolittle .15 .40
419 DJ LeMahieu .25 .60
420 Justin Verlander .25 .60
421 Taijuan Walker .15 .40
422 Ned Yost .15 .40
423 Brandon Belt .20 .50
424 Domonic Brown .20 .50
425A Gerrit Cole .25 .60
425B Gerrit Cole Color SP 6.00 15.00
426A Clayton Kershaw SP 5.00 12.00
426B Kershaw Color SP 12.00 30.00
427 Brian Dozier SP 2.00 5.00
428 Corey Kluber SP 2.00 5.00
429 Jake Odorizzi SP 1.50 4.00
430A Dallas Keuchel SP 2.00 5.00
430B Keuchel Thrwbck SP 400.00 600.00
431A Jose Bautista SP 2.00 5.00
431B Jose Bautista Color SP 5.00 12.00
432A Robinson Cano SP 2.00 5.00
432B Robinson Cano Action SP 2.50 6.00
432C Cano Thrwbck SP 300.00 500.00
433 Prince Fielder SP 2.00 5.00
434 Jonathan Lucroy SP 2.00 5.00
435A Chris Archer SP 1.50 4.00
435B Chris Archer Color SP 4.00 10.00
436A Masahiro Tanaka SP 2.00 5.00
436B Masahiro Tanaka Color SP 5.00 12.00
437 Addison Russell SP 2.50 6.00
438A David Ortiz SP 2.50 6.00
438B Ortiz Thrwbck SP 300.00 500.00
439 Andrelton Simmons SP 1.50 4.00
440 Alex Rodriguez SP 3.00 8.00
441 Greg Holland SP 1.50 4.00
442 Jose Fernandez SP 2.50 6.00
443A Yu Darvish SP 2.50 6.00
443B Yu Darvish Color SP 6.00 15.00
444 Anthony Rizzo SP 4.00 10.00
445 Justin Upton SP 2.00 5.00
446A Troy Tulowitzki SP 2.50 6.00
446B Troy Tulowitzki Action SP 3.00 8.00

447 Brandon Crawford SP 2.00 5.00
448 Tyson Ross SP 1.50 4.00
449A Matt Kemp SP 2.00 5.00
449B Kemp Thrwbck SP 300.00 500.00
450A Bryce Harper SP 4.00 10.00
450B Harper Action SP 15.00 40.00
450C Harper Color SP 25.00 60.00
451 Stephen Vogt SP 2.00 5.00
452A Jose Abreu SP 2.50 6.00
452B Abreu Thrwbck SP 125.00 250.00
453 Michael Taylor SP 1.50 4.00
454 Ian Kinsler SP 2.00 5.00
455 Carlos Gonzalez SP 2.00 5.00
456 Dustin Pedroia SP 2.50 6.00
457 Nelson Cruz SP 2.50 6.00
458A Jason Kipnis SP 2.00 5.00
458B Kipnis Thrwbck SP
459 Max Scherzer SP 2.50 6.00
460A Buster Posey SP 3.00 8.00
460B Posey Action SP 4.00 10.00
460C Posey Color SP 8.00 20.00
461 Felix Hernandez SP 2.00 5.00
462 Dellin Betances SP 2.00 5.00
463 Josh Hamilton SP 2.00 5.00
464A Shelby Miller SP 2.00 5.00
464B Miller Traded SP 30.00 80.00
465A Paul Goldschmidt SP 2.50 6.00
465B Goldschmidt Thrwbck SP 400.00 600.00
466 A.J. Pollock SP 1.50 4.00
467 Christian Yelich SP 3.00 8.00
468 Yoenis Cespedes SP 2.50 6.00
469A Mookie Betts SP 4.00 10.00
469B Betts Actions SP 5.00 12.00
469C Betts Thrwbck SP 300.00 600.00
470 Jose Altuve SP 2.00 5.00
471 Randal Grichuk SP 1.50 4.00
472A Todd Frazier SP 2.00 5.00
472B Todd Frazier Color SP 5.00 12.00
473A Maikel Franco SP 2.00 5.00
473B Franco Thrwbck SP 200.00 400.00
474A Joey Votto SP 2.50 6.00
474B Votto ERR SP 50.00 120.00
474C Votto Throwback SP
475A Carlos Correa SP 2.50 6.00
475B Correa Action SP 12.00 30.00
475C Correa Thrwbck SP 300.00 600.00
476 David Peralta SP 1.50 4.00
477 David Price SP 2.00 5.00
478A Miguel Cabrera SP 2.50 6.00
478B Cabrera Color SP 15.00 40.00
479A Lorenzo Cain SP 1.50 4.00
479B Lorenzo Cain Action SP 2.00 5.00
480 Pedro Alvarez SP 1.50 4.00
481A Albert Pujols SP 3.00 8.00
481B Pujols Color SP 8.00 20.00
482A Francisco Lindor SP 2.50 6.00
482B Lindor Action SP 3.00 8.00
483A Josh Donaldson SP 2.00 5.00
483B Josh Donaldson Color SP 5.00 12.00
484 Billy Burns SP 1.50 4.00
485 Cole Hamels SP 2.00 5.00
486 Rusney Castillo SP 1.50 4.00
487 Freddie Freeman SP 3.00 8.00
488 Joey Gallo SP 2.00 5.00
489 Taylor Jungmann SP 1.50 4.00
490 Eric Hosmer SP 2.00 5.00
491 Edinson Volquez SP 1.50 4.00
492A Noah Syndergaard SP 2.00 5.00
492B Syndrgrd Action SP 2.50 6.00
493 Matt Harvey SP 2.00 5.00
494 Evan Longoria SP 2.00 5.00
495A Jacob deGrom SP 2.50 6.00
495B deGrom Color SP 6.00 15.00
496 Ryan Braun SP 2.00 5.00
497 Charlie Blackmon SP 2.50 6.00
498 Odubel Herrera SP 2.00 5.00
499 Jason Heyward SP 2.00 5.00
500A Mike Trout SP 12.00 30.00
500B Trout Action SP 15.00 40.00
501 Hank Conger .15 .40
502 Juan Lagares .15 .40
503 Travis Shaw .15 .40
504 Danny Valencia .20 .50
505 Willson Contreras RC 1.50 4.00
506 Joe Smith .15 .40
507 Jeimer Candelario RC .40 1.00
508 Pedro Alvarez .15 .40
509 Derek Holland .15 .40
510 Corey Dickerson .15 .40
511 Austin Jackson .15 .40
512 Jim Henderson .15 .40
513 Rich Hill .15 .40
514A Lucas Giolito RC .50 1.25
514B Giolito ERR SP Golto 25.00 60.00
515 Melvin Upton Jr. .20 .50
516 Shawn Morimando RC .15 .40
517 Jon Jay .15 .40
518A Jayson Werth .20 .50
518B Jayson Werth Action SP 2.50 6.00
518C Jayson Werth Color SP 5.00 12.00
519 Joaquin Benoit .15 .40
520A Ben Revere .15 .40
520B Revere Thrwbck SP 100.00 200.00
521 Aaron Hill .15 .40
522 Keon Broxton RC .30 .75
523 Logan Verrett .15 .40
524 David Ross .15 .40
525 Alex Presley .15 .40
526 Travis d'Arnaud .20 .50
527 Jed Lowrie .15 .40
528A Scott Kazmir .15 .40
528B Scott Kazmir Color SP 4.00 10.00
529 Enrique Hernandez .20 .50
530 Ezequiel Carrera .15 .40
531 Ryan Dull .15 .40
532 Justin Upton .20 .50
533 Adam Conley .15 .40
534 Gavin Floyd .15 .40
535 Chris Young .15 .40
536 Ryan Madson .15 .40
537 Phil Gosselin .15 .40
538 Wei-Yin Chen .15 .40
539 Vance Worley .15 .40
540 Matt Buschmann RC .30 .75
541 Joe Ross .15 .40
542 Chris Coghlan .15 .40
543 Daniel Castro .15 .40
544 Chris Carter .15 .40
545 Peter Bourjos .15 .40
546 Matt Wieters .25 .60
547 Michael Saunders .20 .50
548 Charlie Morton .25 .60
549A Ian Kennedy .15 .40
549B Kennedy Thrwbck SP 200.00 400.00
550 Jonathan Broxton .15 .40
551 Tyler Clippard .15 .40
552 Jon Niese .15 .40
553 Joe Blanton .15 .40
554 Matt Joyce .15 .40
555 Tanner Roark .15 .40
556 Joe Biagini RC .30 .75
557 Chris Tillman .15 .40
558 Mike Napoli .15 .40
559A Edwin Diaz RC .60 1.50
559B Diaz Thrwbck SP 150.00 300.00
560 Charlie Culberson .15 .40
561 David Freese .15 .40
562 Ryan Vogelsong .15 .40
563 Ryan Goins .15 .40
564A Ben Zobrist .20 .50
564B Ben Zobrist Action SP 2.50 6.00
564C Ben Zobrist Color SP 5.00 12.00
564D Zobrist Thrwbck SP 200.00 400.00
565 A.J. Griffin .15 .40
566A Joey Rickard RC .30 .75
566B Joey Rickard Action SP 2.00 5.00
566C Joey Rickard Color SP 4.00 10.00
567 Wilson Ramos .15 .40
568 Angel Pagan .15 .40
569 Craig Breslow .15 .40
570 John Jaso .15 .40
571 Jeff Francoeur .20 .50
572 Doug Fister .15 .40
573 Lance McCullers RC .30 .75
574 Bud Norris .15 .40
575 Howie Kendrick .15 .40
576 Drew Storen .15 .40
577 Nick Tropeano .15 .40
578 Alejandro De Aza .15 .40
579 Will Harris .15 .40
580 Mike Leake .15 .40
581 Patrick Corbin .20 .50
582A Jonathan Villar .15 .40
582B Jonathan Villar Color SP 4.00 10.00
582C Villar Thrwbck SP 200.00 400.00
583 Rickie Weeks .15 .40
584 Yusmeiro Petit .15 .40
585A Jeremy Hazelbaker RC .40 1.00
585B Jeremy Hazelbaker Color SP 5.00 12.00
586 J.A. Happ .20 .50
587 Munenori Kawasaki .15 .40
588A Johnny Cueto .20 .50
588B Johnny Cueto Action SP 2.50 6.00
588C Johnny Cueto Color SP 5.00 12.00
589 Josh Phegley .15 .40
590 Pat Neshek .15 .40
591 Matt Moore .20 .50
592 Adeiny Hechavarria .15 .40
593 Leonys Martin .15 .40
594 Stephen Drew .15 .40
595 Jimmy Nelson .15 .40
596 Adam Warren .15 .40
597 Jabari Blash RC .30 .75
598 Matt Szczur .20 .50
599 Ji-Man Choi RC .40 1.00
600A Julio Urias RC 1.00 2.50
600B Urias Color SP 12.00 30.00
600C Urias ERR SP No Sig 30.00 80.00
601 Devin Mesoraco .15 .40
602 Tony Cingrani .20 .50
603 Brandon Finnegan .15 .40
604 Raisel Iglesias .20 .50
605 Jake McGee .15 .40
606A Alexei Ramirez .15 .40
606B Alexei Ramirez Action SP 2.50 6.00
607 Mark Reynolds .15 .40
608 Cody Reed RC .30 .75
609 Luke Hochevar .15 .40
610 Jarrod Saltalamacchia .15 .40
611 Yovani Gallardo .15 .40
612 Eduardo Nunez .15 .40
613 Fernando Abad .15 .40
614A Drew Pomeranz .20 .50
614B Pomeranz Thrwbck SP 200.00 400.00
615 Junichi Tazawa .15 .40
616 Adonis Garcia .15 .40
617 Jose Quintana .15 .40
618 Chris Capuano .15 .40
619 Johnny Barbato RC .30 .75
620 Matthew Bowman RC .30 .75
621 Chris Johnson .15 .40
622 Khris Davis .25 .60
623 Denard Span .15 .40
624 Ian Desmond .15 .40
625 Gerardo Parra .15 .40
626 Mark Lowe .15 .40
627 Kurt Suzuki .15 .40
628 Jean Segura .20 .50
629 Steve Cishek .15 .40
630A Jameson Taillon RC .40 1.00
630B Jameson Taillon Color SP 5.00 12.00
630C Taillon Thrwbck SP 200.00 400.00
631 Tim Lincecum .20 .50
632 Michael Ynoa RC .30 .75
633 Jason Grilli .15 .40
634 Tyrell Jenkins RC .30 .75
635A Albert Almora RC .40 1.00
635B Albert Almora Color SP 5.00 12.00
636 Jake Barrett RC .30 .75
637 A.J. Reed RC .30 .75
638 Matt Purke RC .30 .75
639 Mike Clevinger RC .60 1.50
640 Adam Wainwright .20 .50
641 Colin Moran RC .30 .75
642 Matt Bush (RC) .20 .50
643 Luis Cessa RC .30 .75
644A Daniel Murphy .20 .50
644B Daniel Murphy Color SP 5.00 12.00
644C Murphy ERR NE Mets 20.00 50.00
645 Pat Dean RC .30 .75
646 Ryan O'Rourke RC .30 .75
647 Carlos Estevez RC .30 .75
648A Michael Fulmer RC .50 1.25
648B Fulmer Action SP 3.00 8.00
648C Fulmer Color SP 6.00 15.00
648D Fulmer ERR SP Pithcer 25.00 60.00
649 Matt Barnes .15 .40
650 Ben Gamel RC .40 1.00
651 Allen Hanson RC .40 1.00
652 Tony Kemp RC .30 .75
653A Steven Wright .15 .40
653B Steven Wright Color SP 4.00 10.00
654 Brad Ziegler .15 .40
655 Matt Reynolds RC .30 .75
656A Adam Duvall .50 1.25
656B Duvall Color SP 12.00 30.00
656C Duvall Thrwbck SP 200.00 400.00
657A James Loney .15 .40
657B Loney Thrwbck SP 150.00 300.00
658 Cameron Rupp .15 .40
659 Zach Eflin RC .40 1.00
660A Johnny Giavotella .15 .40
660B Giavotella Thrwbck SP 150.00 300.00
661 Geovany Soto .15 .40
662 Paulo Orlando .15 .40
663 Sean Manaea RC .30 .75
664 Darwin Barney .15 .40
665 Jurickson Profar .20 .50
666 Fernando Rodney .15 .40
667 Tyler Goeddel RC .30 .75
668 Chad Kuhl RC .30 .75
669 Mychal Givens .15 .40
670 Danny Santana .15 .40
671A Kevin Plawecki .15 .40
671B Kevin Plawecki Action SP 2.00 5.00
672 Rafael Ortega .15 .40
673 Hunter Cervenka RC .30 .75
674A Tim Anderson RC 1.25 3.00
674B Tim Anderson Color SP 15.00 40.00
674C Anderson Thrwbck SP 200.00 400.00
675 Blaine Boyer .15 .40
676 Brandon Moss .15 .40
677 Michael Bourn .15 .40
678 Drew Stubbs .15 .40
679 Josh Tomlin .15 .40
680 Tyler Chatwood .15 .40
681 Josh Rutledge .15 .40
682A Sandy Leon RC .40 1.00
682B Leon Thrwbck SP 200.00 400.00
683 Whit Merrifield RC 6.00 15.00
684 Nolan Reimold .15 .40
685 Taylor Motter RC .30 .75
686 Tommy Joseph RC .60 1.50
687 Tim Adleman RC .30 .75
688 Tony Barnette RC .30 .75
689 Sam Dyson .15 .40
690 Ivan Nova .20 .50
691 Dillon Gee .15 .40
692 Steven Moya .15 .40
693 C.J. Wilson .15 .40
694 Ryan Hanigan .15 .40
695 Chris Herrmann .15 .40
696 Brad Brach .15 .40
697 Derek Law RC .40 1.00
698 Jose Ramirez .20 .50
699 Hector Neris .15 .40
700 David Price .20 .50
701A Kenta Maeda SP RC 2.00 5.00
701B Maeda Action SP 4.00 10.00
701C Maeda Color SP 8.00 20.00
701D Maeda ERR SP Blank back 25.00 60.00
702 Aaron Blair SP RC 1.00 2.50
703A Seung-hwan Oh SP RC 2.50 6.00
703B Oh Color SP 10.00 25.00
703C Oh Thrwbck SP 150.00 300.00
704A Nomar Mazara SP RC 1.50 4.00
704B Mazara Action SP 3.00 8.00
704C Mazara Color SP 6.00 15.00
705A Blake Snell SP RC 1.25 3.00
705B Blake Snell Color SP 8.00 20.00
706 Robert Stephenson SP RC 1.00 2.50
707A Trevor Story SP RC 4.00 10.00
707B Story Action SP 8.00 20.00
707C Story Color SP 15.00 40.00
707D Story ERR SP No Line 25.00 60.00
708A Byung-Ho Park SP RC 1.25 3.00
708B Byung-Ho Park Color SP 6.00 15.00
709 Jose Berrios SP RC 1.25 3.00
710 Tyler White SP RC 1.00 2.50
711A Marcus Stroman SP 1.25 3.00
711B Marcus Stroman Action SP 2.50 6.00
712 Mallex Smith SP RC 1.00 2.50
713A Aledmys Diaz SP RC 4.00 10.00
713B Diaz Action SP 8.00 20.00
713C Diaz Color SP 20.00 50.00
713D Diaz Thrwbck SP 400.00 600.00
714A Tyler Naquin SP RC 1.25 3.00
714B Tyler Naquin Color SP 5.00 12.00
714C Naquin Thrwbck SP 300.00 500.00
715A Vince Velasquez SP 1.00 2.50
715B Vince Velasquez Color SP 4.00 10.00
716A Christian Vazquez SP 1.00 2.50
716B Christian Vazquez Action SP 2.00 5.00
717 Max Kepler SP RC 1.50 4.00
718A Aroldis Chapman SP 1.50 4.00
718B Aroldis Chapman Action SP 3.00 8.00
718C Aroldis Chapman Color SP 6.00 15.00
719 Domingo Santana SP 1.25 3.00
720 Ross Stripling SP RC 1.00 2.50
721A Hyun Soo Kim SP RC 1.50 4.00
721B Hyun Soo Kim Action SP 3.00 8.00
722 Aaron Sanchez SP 1.25 3.00
723 Javier Baez SP 2.00 5.00
724 Jeff Samardzija SP 1.00 2.50
725 Chase Headley SP 1.00 2.50

2016 Topps Heritage Black

INSERTED IN HN RETAIL PACKS
505 Willson Contreras 3.00 8.00
511 Austin Jackson .50 1.25
514 Lucas Giolito .75 2.00
528 Scott Kazmir .50 1.25
532 Justin Upton .60 1.50
541 Joe Ross .50 1.25
559 Edwin Diaz 1.00 2.50
566 Joey Rickard .50 1.25
588 Johnny Cueto .60 1.50
590 Pat Neshek .50 1.25
600 Julio Urias 1.50 4.00
606 Alexei Ramirez .60 1.50
611 Yovani Gallardo .50 1.25
614 Drew Pomeranz .60 1.50
628 Jean Segura .60 1.50
630 Jameson Taillon .60 1.50
635 Albert Almora .60 1.50
640 Adam Wainwright .60 1.50
644 Daniel Murphy .60 1.50
648 Michael Fulmer .75 2.00
649 Tanner Roark .50 1.25
653 Steven Wright .50 1.25
668 Ben Zobrist .60 1.50
674 Tim Anderson 2.00 5.00
693 C.J. Wilson .50 1.25
701 Kenta Maeda 1.00 2.50
702 Aaron Blair .50 1.25
703 Seung-hwan Oh 1.25 3.00
704 Nomar Mazara .75 2.00
705 Blake Snell .60 1.50
706 Robert Stephenson .50 1.25
707 Trevor Story 2.00 5.00
708 Byung-Ho Park .60 1.50
709 Jose Berrios .60 1.50
710 Tyler White .50 1.25
711 Marcus Stroman .60 1.50
712 Mallex Smith .50 1.25
713 Aledmys Diaz .75 2.00
714 Tyler Naquin .60 1.50
715 Vince Velasquez .50 1.25
716 Christian Vazquez .50 1.25
717 Max Kepler .75 2.00
718 Aroldis Chapman .75 2.00
719 Domingo Santana .60 1.50
720 Ross Stripling .50 1.25
721 Hyun Soo Kim .75 2.00
722 Aaron Sanchez .60 1.50
723 Javier Baez 1.00 2.50
724 Jeff Samardzija .50 1.25
725 Chase Headley .50 1.25

2016 Topps Heritage Gum Stained Back

*GUM BACK VET: 4X TO 10X BASIC
*GUM BACK RC: 2X TO 5X BASIC RC
*GUM BACK SP: .4X TO 1X BASIC SP
RANDOM INSERTS IN PACKS
HN STATED ODDS 1:50 HOBBY
70 Kris Bryant 25.00 60.00
168 Seager/Peraza 12.00 30.00
243 Cruz/Trout/Davis 5.00 12.00
450 Bryce Harper 30.00 80.00
460 Buster Posey 10.00 25.00
475 Carlos Correa 20.00 50.00
500 Mike Trout 30.00 80.00

2016 Topps Heritage '67 Poster Boxloader

STATED ODDS 1:34 HOBBY BOXES
ANNCD PRINT RUN 50 COPIES PER
67PBAG Adrian Gonzalez 8.00 20.00
67PBBH Bryce Harper 25.00 60.00
67PBBP Buster Posey 20.00 50.00
67PBCC Carlos Correa 20.00 50.00
67PBCH Cole Hamels 10.00 25.00
67PBCK Corey Kluber 10.00 25.00
67PBCKE Clayton Kershaw 20.00 50.00
67PBDO David Ortiz 20.00 50.00
67PBGS Giancarlo Stanton 30.00 80.00
67PBJD Josh Donaldson 8.00 20.00
67PBJL Jon Lester 8.00 20.00
67PBJS James Shields 10.00 25.00
67PBKB Kris Bryant 40.00 100.00
67PBMH Matt Harvey 15.00 40.00
67PBMT Mark Teixeira 12.00 30.00
67PBMTR Mike Trout 60.00 150.00
67PBMW Michael Wacha 15.00 40.00
67PBPG Paul Goldschmidt 20.00 50.00
67PBPS Pablo Sandoval 12.00 30.00
67PBSG Sonny Gray 8.00 20.00

2016 Topps Heritage '67 Punch Outs Boxloader

STATED ODDS 1:34 HOBBY BOXES
HN STATED ODDS 1:47 HOBBY BOXES
ANNCD PRINT RUN 50 COPIES PER
67PBPAG D/G/N/L/M/C/R/R/H 5.00 12.00
67PBPCY G/G/S/W/K/M/H/P/Y 10.00 25.00
67PBPFL C/H/L/O/R/B/D/W/J 6.00 15.00
67PBPFR R/V/Z/N/P/S/S/N/B 10.00 25.00
67PBPGS R/P/T/S/D/S/R/S/D 6.00 15.00
67PBPJC J/T/C/H/C/R/S/O/R 6.00 15.00
67BPJF G/F/D/D/J/D/F/P/P 12.00 30.00
67BPMS M/S/F/S/W/C/G/S/R 5.00 12.00
67BPRC S/P/V/C/G/B/R/C/M 8.00 20.00
67BPTT F/G/T/R/L/F/M/P/O 6.00 15.00
67POBAM H/C/C/K/M/S/K/W/K/R 10.00 25.00
67POBAN D/Y/G/P/N/P/O/D/R 8.00 20.00
67POBAP S/C/M/H/B/P/P/C/K 8.00 20.00
67POBAR E/G/V/H/R/A/P/E/B 8.00 20.00
67POBBH H/C/C/W/U/H/W/P/F 10.00 25.00
67POBBP P/R/B/L/d/U/P/P/B 8.00 20.00
67POBCC E/C/C/B/C/G/M/D/M 6.00 15.00
67POBCK K/H/M/C/M/G/P/S/D 12.00 30.00
67POBCS S/G/S/C/C/S/D/B/N 30.00 80.00
67POBDO H/O/S/D/S/S/K/C/P/D 6.00 15.00
67POBJD G/D/A/J/C/A/B/M/K 6.00 15.00
67POBKB S/B/R/M/G/U/S/M/H 8.00 20.00
67POBKS A/S/G/C/H/T/P/A/A 12.00 30.00
67POBLS S/S/E/B/H/A/I/S/T 5.00 12.00
67POBMB F/P/F/M/L/B/C/F/M/L 8.00 20.00
67POBMC M/G/L/I/S/C/T/V/R 6.00 15.00
67POBMH M/M/H/G/P/W/A/E/M 5.00 12.00
67POBMT C/B/T/G/D/C/B/G/P 30.00 80.00
67POBSP M/R/S/P/B/B/F/E/G 6.00 15.00
67POBZG A/Z/E/I/B/H/G/G/B 5.00 12.00

2016 Topps Heritage '67 Punch Outs Boxloader Patches

STATED ODDS 1:67 HOBBY BOXES
HN STATED ODDS 1:307 HOBBY BOXES
STATED PRINT RUN 25 SER.#'d SETS
67PJPRNC Nelson Cruz 12.00 30.00
67PJPRVM Victor Martinez 10.00 25.00
67PJPRYC Yoenis Cespedes 40.00 100.00
67POBPRAC Aroldis Chapman 12.00 30.00
67POBPRAJ Adam Jones 50.00 120.00
67POBPRAM Andrew McCutchen 50.00 120.00
67POBPRAW Adam Wainwright 10.00 25.00
67POBPRCA Chris Archer 8.00 20.00
67POBPRCD Chris Davis 8.00 20.00
67POBPRDP Dustin Pedroia 25.00 60.00
67POBPRFF Freddie Freeman 15.00 40.00
67POBPRGC Gerrit Cole 12.00 30.00
67POBPRI Ichiro Suzuki 15.00 40.00
67POBPRJP Joc Pederson 20.00 50.00
67POBPRJVE Justin Verlander 12.00 30.00
67POBPRJVO Joey Votto 25.00 60.00
67POBPRMC Miguel Cabrera 20.00 50.00
67POBPRNA Nolan Arenado 25.00 60.00
67POBPRRZ Ryan Zimmerman 10.00 25.00
67POBPRSP Salvador Perez 20.00 50.00
67POBPRSS Stephen Strasburg 20.00 50.00
67POBPRTF Todd Frazier 20.00 50.00
67POBPRWF Wilmer Flores 25.00 60.00

2016 Topps Heritage Award Winners

COMPLETE SET (10) 5.00 12.00
HN ODDS 1:8 HOBBY
AW1 Josh Donaldson .40 1.00
AW2 Bryce Harper .75 2.00
AW3 Dallas Keuchel .40 1.00
AW4 Jake Arrieta .40 1.00
AW5 Carlos Correa .50 1.25
AW6 Kris Bryant .60 1.50
AW7 Jeff Banister .30 .75
AW8 Joe Maddon .30 .75
AW9 Salvador Perez .40 1.00
AW10 Mike Trout 2.50 6.00

2016 Topps Heritage Baseball Flashbacks

COMPLETE SET (10) 3.00 8.00
STATED ODDS 1:12 HOBBY
BFBG Bob Gibson .40 1.00
BFCH Catfish Hunter .40 1.00
BFEM Eddie Mathews .50 1.25
BFOC Orlando Cepeda .40 1.00
BFRCA Rod Carew .40 1.00
BFRCL Roberto Clemente 1.25 3.00
BFRM Roger Maris .50 1.25
BFTP Tony Perez .40 1.00
BFTS Tom Seaver .40 1.00
BFWF Whitey Ford .40 1.00

2016 Topps Heritage Bazooka

INSERTED IN RETAIL PACKS
STATED PRINT RUN 25 SER.#'d SETS
HN CARDS ARE NOT SERIAL NUMBERED
67BAM Andrew McCutchen 10.00 25.00
67BAP Albert Pujols 12.00 30.00
67BARI Anthony Rizzo 15.00 40.00
67BARO Alex Rodriguez 12.00 30.00
67BBH Bryce Harper 30.00 80.00
67BBP Buster Posey 20.00 50.00
67BCA Chris Archer 6.00 15.00
67BCC Carlos Correa 25.00 60.00
67BCK Clayton Kershaw 25.00 60.00
67BCS Chris Sale HN 10.00 25.00
67BDK Dallas Keuchel 8.00 20.00
67BDO David Ortiz HN 10.00 25.00
67BDPE Dustin Pedroia 15.00 40.00
67BDPR David Price 8.00 20.00
67BJA Jake Arrieta 8.00 20.00
67BJD Josh Donaldson 8.00 20.00
67BJV Joey Votto 10.00 25.00
67BKB Kris Bryant 30.00 80.00
67BKM Kenta Maeda HN 12.00 30.00
67BLC Lorenzo Cain 6.00 15.00
67BMB Madison Bumgarner 8.00 20.00
67BMC Miguel Cabrera 20.00 50.00
67BMF Michael Fulmer HN 10.00 25.00
67BMH Matt Harvey 12.00 30.00
67BMT Mike Trout 40.00 100.00
67BNA Nolan Arenado HN 12.00 30.00
67BNC Nelson Cruz 10.00 25.00
67BNM Nomar Mazara HN 10.00 25.00
67BNS Noah Syndergaard HN 8.00 20.00
67BPG Paul Goldschmidt 10.00 25.00
67BSS Stephen Strasburg HN 10.00 25.00
67BTS Trevor Story HN 25.00 60.00
67BXB Xander Bogaerts HN 10.00 25.00
67BYM Yadier Molina 10.00 25.00
67BZG Zack Greinke 8.00 20.00

2016 Topps Heritage Chrome

STATED ODDS 1:25 HOBBY
HN ODDS 1:22 HOBBY
STATED PRINT RUN 999 SER.#'d SETS
*PRPLE REF: .4X TO 1X BASIC
*REF/567: .6X TO 1.5X BASIC
THC40 Kole Calhoun 1.25 3.00
THC50 Byron Buxton 1.50 4.00
THC60 Chris Davis 1.25 3.00
THC70 Kris Bryant 2.50 6.00
THC80 Aroldis Chapman 2.00 5.00
THC90 Sonny Gray 1.50 4.00
THC100 Adam Jones 1.50 4.00
THC130 Zack Greinke 1.50 4.00
THC140 Starling Marte 1.50 4.00
THC157 Manny Machado 2.00 5.00
THC161 Schwarber/Edwards Jr. 4.00 10.00
THC190 Luis Severino Miguel Sano 2.00 5.00
THC210 Michael Wacha 1.50 4.00
THC220 Matt Duffy 1.25 3.00
THC253 Michael Brantley 1.50 4.00
THC290 Ryan Howard 1.50 4.00
THC310 Chris Sale 2.00 5.00
THC320 Madison Bumgarner 1.50 4.00
THC322 Giancarlo Stanton 2.00 5.00
THC340 Mark Teixeira 1.50 4.00
THC390 George Springer 1.50 4.00
THC400 Andrew McCutchen 2.00 5.00
THC410 Yasiel Puig 2.00 5.00
THC420 Justin Verlander 2.00 5.00
THC425 Gerrit Cole 2.00 5.00
THC426 Clayton Kershaw 4.00 10.00
THC427 Brian Dozier 1.50 4.00
THC428 Corey Kluber 1.50 4.00
THC429 Jake Odorizzi 1.25 3.00
THC430 Dallas Keuchel 1.50 4.00
THC431 Jose Bautista 1.50 4.00
THC432 Robinson Cano 1.50 4.00
THC433 Prince Fielder 1.50 4.00
THC434 Jonathan Lucroy 1.50 4.00
THC435 Chris Archer 1.25 3.00
THC436 Masahiro Tanaka 1.50 4.00
THC437 Addison Russell 2.00 5.00
THC438 David Ortiz 2.00 5.00
THC439 Andrelton Simmons 1.25 3.00
THC440 Alex Rodriguez 2.50 6.00
THC441 Greg Holland 1.25 3.00
THC442 Jose Fernandez 2.00 5.00
THC443 Yu Darvish 2.00 5.00
THC444 Anthony Rizzo 3.00 8.00
THC445 Justin Upton 1.50 4.00
THC446 Troy Tulowitzki 2.00 5.00
THC447 Brandon Crawford 1.50 4.00
THC448 Tyson Ross 1.25 3.00
THC449 Matt Kemp 1.50 4.00
THC450 Bryce Harper 3.00 8.00
THC451 Stephen Vogt 1.50 4.00
THC452 Jose Abreu 2.00 5.00
THC453 Michael Taylor 1.25 3.00
THC454 Ian Kinsler 1.50 4.00
THC455 Carlos Gonzalez 1.50 4.00
THC456 Dustin Pedroia 2.00 5.00
THC457 Nelson Cruz 2.00 5.00
THC458 Jason Kipnis 1.50 4.00
THC459 Max Scherzer 2.00 5.00
THC460 Buster Posey 2.50 6.00
THC461 Felix Hernandez 1.50 4.00
THC462 Dellin Betances 1.50 4.00
THC463 Josh Hamilton 1.50 4.00
THC464 Shelby Miller 1.50 4.00
THC465 Paul Goldschmidt 2.00 5.00
THC466 A.J. Pollock 1.25 3.00
THC467 Christian Yelich 2.50 6.00
THC468 Yoenis Cespedes 2.00 5.00
THC469 Mookie Betts 3.00 8.00
THC470 Jose Altuve 1.50 4.00
THC471 Randal Grichuk 1.25 3.00
THC472 Todd Frazier 1.50 4.00
THC473 Maikel Franco 1.50 4.00
THC474 Joey Votto 2.00 5.00
THC475 Carlos Correa 2.00 5.00
THC476 David Peralta 1.25 3.00
THC477 David Price 1.50 4.00
THC478 Miguel Cabrera 2.00 5.00
THC479 Lorenzo Cain 1.25 3.00
THC480 Pedro Alvarez 1.25 3.00
THC481 Albert Pujols 2.50 6.00
THC482 Francisco Lindor 2.00 5.00
THC483 Josh Donaldson 1.50 4.00
THC484 Billy Burns 1.25 3.00
THC485 Cole Hamels 1.50 4.00
THC486 Rusney Castillo 1.25 3.00
THC487 Freddie Freeman 2.50 6.00
THC488 Joey Gallo 1.50 4.00
THC489 Taylor Jungmann 1.25 3.00
THC490 Eric Hosmer 1.50 4.00
THC491 Edinson Volquez 1.25 3.00
THC492 Noah Syndergaard 1.50 4.00
THC493 Matt Harvey 1.50 4.00
THC494 Evan Longoria 1.50 4.00
THC495 Jacob deGrom 2.00 5.00
THC496 Ryan Braun 1.50 4.00
THC497 Charlie Blackmon 2.00 5.00
THC498 Odubel Herrera 1.50 4.00
THC499 Jason Heyward 1.50 4.00
THC500 Mike Trout 10.00 25.00
THC505 Willson Contreras 3.00 8.00
THC511 Austin Jackson 1.25 3.00
THC514 Lucas Giolito 2.00 5.00
THC528 Scott Kazmir 1.25 3.00
THC532 Justin Upton 1.50 4.00
THC541 Joe Ross 1.25 3.00
THC559 Edwin Diaz 2.50 6.00
THC566 Joey Rickard 1.25 3.00
THC588 Johnny Cueto 1.50 4.00
THC590 Pat Neshek 1.25 3.00
THC600 Julio Urias 4.00 10.00
THC606 Alexei Ramirez 1.50 4.00
THC611 Yovani Gallardo 1.25 3.00
THC614 Drew Pomeranz 1.50 4.00
THC628 Jean Segura 1.50 4.00
THC630 Jameson Taillon 1.50 4.00
THC635 Albert Almora 1.50 4.00
THC640 Adam Wainwright 1.50 4.00
THC644 Daniel Murphy 1.50 4.00
THC648 Michael Fulmer 2.00 5.00
THC649 Tanner Roark 1.25 3.00
THC653 Steven Wright 1.25 3.00
THC668 Ben Zobrist 1.50 4.00
THC674 Tim Anderson 5.00 12.00
THC693 C.J. Wilson 1.25 3.00
THC701 Kenta Maeda 2.50 6.00
THC702 Aaron Blair 1.25 3.00
THC703 Seung-hwan Oh 3.00 8.00
THC704 Nomar Mazara 2.00 5.00
THC705 Blake Snell 1.50 4.00
THC706 Robert Stephenson 1.25 3.00
THC707 Trevor Story 5.00 12.00
THC708 Byung-Ho Park 1.50 4.00
THC709 Jose Berrios 1.50 4.00
THC710 Tyler White 1.25 3.00
THC711 Marcus Stroman 1.50 4.00
THC712 Mallex Smith 1.25 3.00
THC713 Aledmys Diaz 5.00 12.00
THC714 Tyler Naquin 1.50 4.00
THC715 Vince Velasquez 1.25 3.00
THC716 Christian Vazquez 1.25 3.00
THC717 Max Kepler 2.00 5.00
THC718 Aroldis Chapman 2.00 5.00
THC719 Domingo Santana 1.50 4.00
THC720 Ross Stripling 1.25 3.00
THC721 Hyun-Soo Kim 2.00 5.00
THC722 Aaron Sanchez 1.50 4.00
THC723 Javier Baez 2.50 6.00
THC724 Jeff Samardzija 1.25 3.00
THC725 Chase Headley 1.25 3.00

2016 Topps Heritage Chrome Black Refractors

*BLACK REF: 2.5X TO 6X BASIC
STATED ODDS 1:359 HOBBY
HN ODDS 1:321 HOBBY
STATED PRINT RUN 67 SER.#'d SETS
THC50 Byron Buxton 20.00 50.00
THC70 Kris Bryant 150.00 300.00
THC190 L.Severino/M.Sano 25.00 60.00
THC320 Madison Bumgarner 20.00 50.00
THC440 Alex Rodriguez 25.00 60.00
THC460 Buster Posey 25.00 60.00
THC475 Carlos Correa 75.00 150.00
THC478 Miguel Cabrera 30.00 80.00
THC492 Noah Syndergaard 25.00 60.00
THC493 Matt Harvey 10.00 25.00
THC500 Mike Trout 100.00 200.00

2016 Topps Heritage Clubhouse Collection Dual Relics

STATED ODDS 1:7211 HOBBY
HN STATED ODDS 1:2451 HOBBY
STATED PRINT RUN 67 SER.#'d SETS
CCDRCW S.Carlton/A.Wainwright 30.00 80.00
CCDRFV T.Frazier/J.Votto 25.00 60.00
CCDRHW D.Wright/M.Harvey 20.00 50.00
CCDRMA J.Altuve/J.Morgan 30.00 80.00
CCDRMP B.Posey/W.Mays 25.00 60.00
CCDRPB M.Bumgarner/B.Posey 30.00 80.00
CCDRPJ J.Pederson/Y.Puig 25.00 60.00
CCDRPV T.Perez/J.Votto 30.00 80.00
CCDRTP A.Pujols/M.Trout 50.00 120.00
CCDRYO D.Ortiz/C.Yastrzemski 25.00 60.00

2016 Topps Heritage Clubhouse Collection Relic Autographs

STATED ODDS 1:9645 HOBBY
HN STATED ODDS 1:3248 HOBBY
STATED PRINT RUN 25 SER.#'d SETS
EXCHANGE DEADLINE 2/28/2018
HN EXCH DEADLINE 8/31/2018
CCARAG Alex Gordon
CCARBH Bryce Harper EXCH 250.00 400.00
CCARBP Buster Posey 200.00 300.00
CCARCK Clayton Kershaw EXCH 250.00 400.00
CCARCR Carlos Rodon 30.00 80.00

CARDG Dee Gordon
CARFL Francisco Lindor 40.00 100.00
CARHR Hanley Ramirez EXCH 12.00 30.00
CARJA Jose Altuve 150.00 400.00
CARJH Jason Heyward 100.00 250.00
CARKB Kris Bryant 300.00 500.00
CARKS Kyle Schwarber 60.00 150.00
CARLS Luis Severino 100.00 200.00
CARMM Manny Machado 125.00 250.00
CARMS Miguel Sano 100.00 200.00
CARMT Mike Trout
CARNA Nolan Arenado 125.00 250.00
CARNS Noah Syndergaard 50.00 120.00
CARPS Pablo Sandoval 40.00 100.00

2016 Topps Heritage Clubhouse Collection Relics

STATED ODDS 1:33 HOBBY
HN STATED ODDS 1:45 HOBBY
CCRI Ichiro Suzuki HN 4.00 10.00
CCRI Ichiro Suzuki 4.00 10.00
CCRAG Adrian Gonzalez 2.50 6.00
CCRAG Adrian Gonzalez HN 2.50 6.00
CCRAJ Adam Jones HN 2.50 6.00
CCRAM Andrew McCutchen HN 3.00 8.00
CCRAM Andrew McCutchen 3.00 8.00
CCRAP Albert Pujols HN 4.00 10.00
CCRAPU Albert Pujols 4.00 10.00
CCRAR Anthony Rizzo HN 5.00 12.00
CCRARI Anthony Rizzo HN 5.00 12.00
CCRARU Addison Russell HN 3.00 8.00
CCRAW Adam Wainwright HN 2.50 6.00
CCRBH Bryce Harper HN 5.00 12.00
CCRBHAM Billy Hamilton 2.50 6.00
CCRBP Buster Posey 4.00 10.00
CCRBPH Brandon Phillips HN 2.00 5.00
CCRBPO Buster Posey HN 4.00 10.00
CCRCB Charlie Blackmon 3.00 8.00
CCRCD Chris Davis 2.00 5.00
CCRCD Chris Davis HN 2.00 5.00
CCRCH Cole Hamels HN 2.50 6.00
CCRCKE Clayton Kershaw HN 6.00 15.00
CCRCKE Clayton Kershaw 6.00 15.00
CCRCKI Craig Kimbrel HN 2.50 6.00
CCRCKL Corey Kluber 2.50 6.00
CCRCS Chris Sale 3.00 8.00
CCRCS Chris Sale HN 3.00 8.00
CCRDK Dallas Keuchel 2.50 6.00
CCRDO David Ortiz 3.00 8.00
CCRDO David Ortiz HN 3.00 8.00
CCRDP David Price HN 2.50 6.00
CCRDP David Price 2.50 6.00
CCRDW David Wright HN 2.50 6.00
CCRFF Freddie Freeman 4.00 10.00
CCRFH Felix Hernandez HN 2.50 6.00
CCRGC Gerrit Cole HN 3.00 8.00
CCRGC Gerrit Cole 3.00 8.00
CCRGS Giancarlo Stanton HN 3.00 8.00
CCRHR Hanley Ramirez 2.50 6.00
CCRJAB Jose Abreu 3.00 8.00
CCRJAB Jose Abreu HN 3.00 8.00
CCRJC Johnny Cueto HN 2.50 6.00
CCRJDE Jacob deGrom 3.00 8.00
CCRJH Jason Heyward HN 2.50 6.00
CCRJKA Jung Ho Kang 2.00 5.00
CCRJKI Jason Kipnis 2.00 5.00
CCRJM Joe Mauer HN 2.50 6.00
CCRJP Joc Pederson 2.50 6.00
CCRJS Jonathan Schoop 2.00 5.00
CCRJU Justin Upton 2.50 6.00
CCRJU Justin Upton HN 2.50 6.00
CCRJVE Justin Verlander HN 3.00 8.00
CCRJVE Justin Verlander 3.00 8.00
CCRJVO Joey Votto 3.00 8.00
CCRJVO Joey Votto HN 3.00 8.00
CCRKB Kris Bryant 4.00 10.00
CCRKS Kyle Schwarber
CCRLS Luis Severino 2.50 6.00
CCRMA Matt Adams 2.00 5.00
CCRMBR Michael Brantley HN 2.50 6.00
CCRMBU Madison Bumgarner 2.50 6.00
CCRMC Miguel Cabrera 3.00 8.00
CCRMC Matt Carpenter HN 3.00 8.00
CCRMCA Miguel Cabrera HN 3.00 8.00
CCRMH Matt Harvey HN 2.50 6.00
CCRMH Matt Harvey 2.50 6.00
CCRMK Matt Kemp HN 2.50 6.00
CCRMM Manny Machado HN 3.00 8.00
CCRMM Manny Machado 3.00 8.00
CCRMS Max Scherzer HN 3.00 8.00
CCRMSA Miguel Sano HN 3.00 8.00
CCRMT Mike Trout HN 8.00 20.00
CCRMTE Mark Teixeira 2.50 6.00
CCRMTR Mike Trout 8.00 20.00
CCRNA Nolan Arenado 4.00 10.00
CCRNS Noah Syndergaard 2.50 6.00
CCRNS Noah Syndergaard HN 2.50 6.00
CCRPF Prince Fielder HN 2.50 6.00
CCRPF Prince Fielder 2.50 6.00
CCRPG Paul Goldschmidt 3.00 8.00
CCRPG Paul Goldschmidt HN 3.00 8.00
CCRRB Ryan Braun 2.50 6.00
CCRRC Robinson Cano 2.50 6.00
CCRRC Robinson Cano HN 2.50 6.00
CCRRP Rick Porcello 2.50 6.00
CCRSMAR Starling Marte 2.50 6.00
CCRSMAT Steven Matz 2.50 6.00
CCRSMI Shelby Miller 2.50 6.00
CCRSPE Salvador Perez 2.50 6.00
CCRSS Stephen Strasburg 3.00 8.00
CCRTF Todd Frazier 2.50 6.00
CCRTT Troy Tulowitzki HN 3.00 8.00
CCRVM Victor Martinez 2.50 6.00
CCRYC Yoenis Cespedes HN 3.00 8.00
CCRYD Yu Darvish 3.00 8.00
CCRYM Yadier Molina HN 3.00 8.00
CCRYP Yasiel Puig HN 3.00 8.00

2016 Topps Heritage Clubhouse Collection Relics Gold

*GOLD: .6X TO 1.5X BASIC
STATED ODDS 1:405 HOBBY
HN STATED ODDS 1:194 HOBBY
STATED PRINT RUN 99 SER.#'d SETS
CCRKB Kris Bryant 20.00 50.00
CCRKS Kyle Schwarber 15.00 40.00

2016 Topps Heritage Clubhouse Collection Triple Relics

STATED ODDS 1:19,289 HOBBY
HN STATED ODDS 1:6617 HOBBY
STATED PRINT RUN 25 SER.#'d SETS
CCTRBRA Arrieta/Bryant/Rizzo 100.00 200.00
CCTRCVM Martinez/Cabrera/Verlander 30.00 80.00
CCTRFCV Frazier/Votto/Chapman 60.00 150.00
CCTRHDS Syndergaard Harvey/deGrom 100.00 200.00
CCTRHDS Harvey/deGrom Syndergaard 60.00 150.00
CCTRHSZ Harper/Zimmerman Strasburg 100.00 200.00
CCTRPBP Bumgarner/Posey/Pence 100.00 200.00
CCTRRSB Schwarber/Bryant/Rizzo 100.00 200.00
CCTRTPF Pujols/Freese/Trout 100.00 200.00
CCTRVCU Upton/Verlander/Cabrera 100.00 200.00

2016 Topps Heritage Combo Cards

COMPLETE SET (20) 8.00 20.00
HN ODDS 1:8 HOBBY
CC1 B.Harper/M.Scherzer .75 2.00
CC2 J.Panik/B.Posey .60 1.50
CC3 R.Cano/N.Cruz .50 1.25
CC4 A.Pujols/M.Trout 2.50 6.00
CC5 A.Jones/M.Machado .50 1.25
CC6 A.Gonzalez/J.Pederson .40 1.00
CC7 N.Mazara/A.Beltre .50 1.25
CC8 T.Story/N.Arenado 1.25 3.00
CC9 W.Castillo/P.Goldschmidt .50 1.25
CC10 D.Pedroia/H.Ramirez .50 1.25
CC11 X.Bogaerts/M.Betts .75 2.00
CC12 M.Prado/I.Suzuki .60 1.50
CC13 S.Matz/N.Syndergaard .40 1.00
CC14 J.Votto/B.Phillips .50 1.25
CC15 D.Gregorius/S.Castro .40 1.00
CC16 Y.Cespedes/D.Wright .50 1.25
CC17 J.Bautista/J.Donaldson .40 1.00
CC18 T.Frazier/A.Eaton .40 1.00
CC19 J.Altuve/C.Correa .50 1.25
CC20 J.Arrieta/D.Ross .40 1.00

2016 Topps Heritage Discs

RANDOM INSERTS IN PACKS
67TDCAM Andrew McCutchen 1.50 4.00
67TDCBH Bryce Harper 2.50 6.00
67TDCBP Buster Posey 2.00 5.00
67TDCCC Carlos Correa 1.50 4.00
67TDCCK Clayton Kershaw 3.00 8.00
67TDCJA Jake Arrieta 1.00 2.50
67TDCJD Josh Donaldson 1.25 3.00
67TDCKB Kris Bryant 2.00 5.00
67TDCKS Kyle Schwarber 3.00 8.00
67TDCMB Madison Bumgarner 1.25 3.00
67TDCMC Miguel Cabrera 1.50 4.00
67TDCMH Matt Harvey 1.25 3.00
67TDCMT Mike Trout 8.00 20.00
67TDCSP Stephen Piscotty 1.50 4.00
67TDCZG Zack Greinke 1.25 3.00

2016 Topps Heritage Flashback Relic Autographs

STATED ODDS 1:9645 HOBBY
STATED PRINT RUN 25 SER.#'d SETS
EXCHANGE DEADLINE 2/28/2018
FARAK Al Kaline 125.00 300.00
FARFR Frank Robinson EXCH 100.00 250.00
FARJB Johnny Bench 75.00 200.00
FARJM Juan Marichal
FARLB Lou Brock 75.00 200.00
FARNR Nolan Ryan 200.00 400.00
FARPN Phil Niekro 60.00 150.00
FARRC Rod Carew 75.00 200.00
FARRJ Reggie Jackson EXCH 100.00 250.00
FARTP Tony Perez EXCH 60.00 150.00

2016 Topps Heritage Mini

RANDOM INSERTS IN PACKS
STATED ODDS 1:215 HOBBY
STATED PRINT RUN 100 SER.#'d SETS
10 Gregory Polanco 5.00 12.00
23 Brandon Phillips 4.00 10.00
34 Kevin Kiermaier 5.00 12.00
38 Adrian Gonzalez 5.00 12.00
43 Adam Lind 5.00 12.00
44 Jung Ho Kang 10.00 25.00
50 Byron Buxton 10.00 25.00
60 Chris Davis 4.00 10.00
66 Eddie Rosario 8.00 20.00
70 Kris Bryant 75.00 150.00
77 Evan Gattis 4.00 10.00
78 Jake Arrieta 10.00 25.00
80 Aroldis Chapman 6.00 15.00
87 Jon Lester 5.00 12.00
88 Xander Bogaerts 8.00 20.00
90 Sonny Gray 5.00 12.00
100 Adam Jones 5.00 12.00
110 Brandon Belt 5.00 12.00
123 Billy Butler 4.00 10.00
130 Zack Greinke 5.00 12.00
132 Ichiro Suzuki 8.00 20.00
157 Manny Machado 12.00 30.00
195 Nolan Arenado 8.00 20.00
226 Carlos Rodon 6.00 15.00
230 James Shields 4.00 10.00
251 Yadier Molina 10.00 25.00
255 Jorge Soler 6.00 15.00
256 Josh Harrison 4.00 10.00
284 Stephen Strasburg 6.00 15.00
290 Ryan Howard 5.00 12.00
292 Edwin Encarnacion 6.00 15.00
302 Salvador Perez 5.00 12.00
304 Carlos Santana 5.00 12.00
310 Chris Sale 6.00 15.00
320 Madison Bumgarner 20.00 50.00
322 Giancarlo Stanton 6.00 15.00
337 Yordano Ventura 5.00 12.00
371 Yasmany Tomas 4.00 10.00
374 Joe Mauer 6.00 15.00
376 Neil Walker 8.00 20.00
390 George Springer 5.00 12.00
400 Andrew McCutchen 6.00 15.00
405 Adrian Beltre 6.00 15.00
410 Yasiel Puig 6.00 15.00
420 Justin Verlander 12.00 30.00
426 Clayton Kershaw 20.00 50.00
427 Brian Dozier 5.00 12.00
428 Corey Kluber 5.00 12.00
430 Dallas Keuchel 5.00 12.00
431 Jose Bautista 5.00 12.00
432 Robinson Cano 5.00 12.00
433 Prince Fielder 5.00 12.00
435 Chris Archer 4.00 10.00
436 Masahiro Tanaka 5.00 12.00
438 David Ortiz 8.00 20.00
439 Andrelton Simmons 4.00 10.00
440 Alex Rodriguez 8.00 20.00
442 Jose Fernandez 6.00 15.00
443 Yu Darvish 6.00 15.00
444 Anthony Rizzo 10.00 25.00
445 Justin Upton 5.00 12.00
447 Brandon Crawford 5.00 12.00
448 Tyson Ross 4.00 10.00
450 Bryce Harper 40.00 100.00
451 Stephen Vogt 5.00 12.00
452 Jose Abreu 5.00 12.00
454 Ian Kinsler 5.00 12.00
456 Dustin Pedroia 10.00 25.00
457 Nelson Cruz 6.00 15.00
459 Max Scherzer 6.00 15.00
460 Buster Posey 12.00 30.00
461 Felix Hernandez 5.00 12.00
462 Dellin Betances 5.00 12.00
464 Shelby Miller 5.00 12.00
465 Paul Goldschmidt 10.00 25.00
466 A.J. Pollock 4.00 10.00
468 Yoenis Cespedes 6.00 15.00
469 Mookie Betts 10.00 25.00
470 Jose Altuve 8.00 20.00
473 Maikel Franco 5.00 12.00
474 Joey Votto 10.00 25.00
475 Carlos Correa 30.00 80.00
477 David Price 10.00 25.00
478 Miguel Cabrera 20.00 50.00
479 Lorenzo Cain 4.00 10.00
481 Albert Pujols 8.00 20.00
482 Francisco Lindor 6.00 15.00
483 Josh Donaldson 5.00 12.00
485 Cole Hamels 5.00 12.00
487 Freddie Freeman 8.00 20.00
490 Eric Hosmer 5.00 12.00
492 Noah Syndergaard 10.00 25.00
493 Matt Harvey 10.00 25.00
494 Evan Longoria 5.00 12.00
495 Jacob deGrom 10.00 25.00
496 Ryan Braun 5.00 12.00
497 Charlie Blackmon 6.00 15.00
498 Odubel Herrera 5.00 12.00
499 Jason Heyward 5.00 12.00
500 Mike Trout 75.00 150.00
515 Melvin Upton Jr. 5.00 12.00
518 Jayson Werth 5.00 12.00
526 Travis d'Arnaud 5.00 12.00
528 Scott Kazmir 4.00 10.00
532 Justin Upton 5.00 12.00
541 Joe Ross 4.00 10.00
546 Matt Wieters 6.00 15.00
555 Tanner Roark 4.00 10.00
566 Joey Rickard 4.00 10.00
581 Patrick Corbin 5.00 12.00
588 Johnny Cueto 5.00 12.00
590 Pat Neshek 4.00 10.00
598 Matt Szczur 5.00 12.00
600 Julio Urias 12.00 30.00
606 Alexei Ramirez 5.00 12.00
622 Chris Davis 6.00 15.00
624 Ian Desmond 4.00 10.00
628 Jean Segura 5.00 12.00
632 Mike Clevinger 8.00 20.00
640 Adam Wainwright 5.00 12.00
644 Daniel Murphy 5.00 12.00
648 Michael Fulmer 6.00 15.00
649 Matt Barnes 4.00 10.00
651 Alen Hanson 5.00 12.00
656 Adam Duvall 12.00 30.00
663 Sean Manaea 4.00 10.00
668 Ben Zobrist 5.00 12.00
679 Josh Tomlin 4.00 10.00
693 C.J. Wilson 4.00 10.00
701 Kenta Maeda 8.00 20.00
702 Aaron Blair 4.00 10.00
703 Seung-hwan Oh 10.00 25.00
704 Nomar Mazara 6.00 15.00
705 Blake Snell 5.00 12.00
707 Trevor Story 15.00 40.00
708 Byung-Ho Park 5.00 12.00
709 Jose Berrios 5.00 12.00
710 Tyler White 4.00 10.00
711 Marcus Stroman 5.00 12.00
712 Mallex Smith 4.00 10.00
713 Aledmys Diaz 15.00 40.00
714 Tyler Naquin 5.00 12.00
716 Christian Vazquez 4.00 10.00
717 Max Kepler 6.00 15.00
718 Aroldis Chapman 6.00 15.00
720 Ross Stripling 4.00 10.00
721 Hyun Soo Kim 6.00 15.00
723 Javier Baez 8.00 20.00
724 Jeff Samardzija 4.00 10.00

2016 Topps Heritage New Age Performers

COMPLETE SET (20) 6.00 15.00
STATED ODDS 1:8 HOBBY
NAPAP A.J. Pollock .30 .75
NAPBH Bryce Harper .75 2.00
NAPCA Chris Archer .30 .75
NAPGS Giancarlo Stanton .50 1.25
NAPJA Jose Abreu .50 1.25
NAPJD Josh Donaldson .40 1.00
NAPJE Jacoby Ellsbury .40 1.00
NAPKB Kris Bryant .60 1.50
NAPKS Kyle Schwarber 1.00 2.50
NAPLC Lorenzo Cain .30 .75
NAPMMA Manny Machado .50 1.25
NAPMME Mark Melancon .30 .75
NAPMSA Miguel Sano .50 1.25
NAPMSC Max Scherzer .50 1.25
NAPNS Noah Syndergaard .40 1.00
NAPSG Sonny Gray .40 1.00
NAPSP Stephen Piscotty .50 1.25
NAPTT Troy Tulowitzki .50 1.25
NAPYD Yu Darvish .50 1.25
NAPYP Yasiel Puig .50 1.25

2016 Topps Heritage News Flashbacks

COMPLETE SET (10) 2.50 6.00
STATED ODDS 1:12 HOBBY
NFCG Che Guevara .40 1.00
NFEK Evel Knievel .40 1.00
NFJH Jimmy Hoffa .40 1.00
NFPW Presley Wedding .40 1.00
NFRM RMS Queen Mary .40 1.00
NFRR Ronald Reagan .40 1.00
NFSV Saturn V .40 1.00
NFTM Thurgood Marshall .40 1.00
NFSOL Summer of Love .40 1.00
NFB737 Boeing 737 .40 1.00

2016 Topps Heritage Now and Then

COMPLETE SET (15) 5.00 12.00
HN ODDS 1:8 HOBBY
NT1 Trevor Story 1.25 3.00
NT2 Victor Martinez .40 1.00
NT3 Ichiro Suzuki .60 1.50
NT4 Bartolo Colon .30 .75
NT5 David Ortiz .50 1.25
NT6 Jake Arrieta .40 1.00
NT7 Max Scherzer .50 1.25
NT8 Michael Fulmer .50 1.25
NT9 Carlos Beltran .40 1.00
NT10 Kenley Jansen .40 1.00
NT11 Freddie Freeman .60 1.50
NT12 Willson Contreras 1.25 3.00
NT13 Jackie Bradley Jr .50 1.25
NT14 Clayton Kershaw 1.00 2.50
NT15 Khris Davis .50 1.25

2016 Topps Heritage Postal Stamps

STATED ODDS 1:2404 HOBBY
STATED PRINT RUN 50 SER.#'d SETS
67USPSRAK Al Kaline 30.00 80.00
67USPSRBM Bill Mazeroski 25.00 60.00
67USPSRBR Brooks Robinson 25.00 60.00
67USPSRBW Billy Williams 15.00 40.00
67USPSRFJ Fergie Jenkins 12.00 30.00
67USPSRFR Frank Robinson 25.00 60.00
67USPSRHK Harmon Killebrew 25.00 60.00
67USPSRJB Jim Bunning 20.00 50.00
67USPSRJM Juan Marichal 20.00 50.00
67USPSRLA Luis Aparicio 15.00 40.00
67USPSRLB Lou Brock 25.00 60.00
67USPSROC Orlando Cepeda 15.00 40.00
67USPSRPN Phil Niekro 20.00 50.00
67USPSRRC Rod Carew 20.00 50.00
67USPSRTP Tony Perez 25.00 60.00
67USPSRTS Tom Seaver 25.00 60.00
67USPSRWF Whitey Ford 25.00 60.00
67USPSRWMA Willie Mays 40.00 100.00
67USPSRWMC Willie McCovey 25.00 60.00
67USPSRWS Willie Stargell 25.00 60.00

2016 Topps Heritage Real One Autographs

STATED ODDS 1:142 HOBBY
HN STATED ODDS 1:119 HOBBY
EXCHANGE DEADLINE 2/28/2018
HN EXCH DEADLINE 8/31/2018
ROAAA Albert Almora HN 15.00 40.00
ROAAB Aaron Blair HN 6.00 15.00
ROAAD Aledmys Diaz HN 15.00 40.00
ROAAK Al Kaline 50.00 120.00
ROAAN Aaron Nola 25.00 60.00
ROAARE A.J. Reed HN 6.00 15.00
ROABB Bob Bruce 6.00 15.00
ROABBR Bruce Brubaker 6.00 15.00
ROABD Bob Duliba 6.00 15.00
ROABD Brandon Drury HN 10.00 25.00
ROABH Bryce Harper HN
ROABH Bill Hepler 6.00 15.00
ROABL Barry Latman 6.00 15.00
ROABO Billy O'Dell 6.00 15.00
ROABPA Byung-Ho Park HN 8.00 20.00
ROABPO Buster Posey HN EXCH 75.00 200.00
ROABS Blake Snell HN 30.00 80.00
ROACC Carlos Correa HN 60.00 150.00
ROACC Carlos Correa 150.00 300.00
ROACHA Cole Hamels 8.00 20.00
ROACRO Carlos Rodon HN 10.00 25.00
ROACS Curt Simmons 6.00 15.00
ROACSE Corey Seager 125.00 250.00
ROACY Carl Yastrzemski HN
ROADCL Doug Clemens 6.00 15.00
ROADGO Dee Gordon 6.00 15.00
ROADGR Derrell Griffith 6.00 15.00
ROADO David Ortiz HN 60.00 150.00
ROADP Dustin Pedroia HN 25.00 60.00
ROADS Don Schwall 6.00 15.00
ROADSI Dwight Siebler 6.00 15.00
ROAEB Ed Bressoud 6.00 15.00
ROAEL Evan Longoria HN 20.00 50.00
ROAFM Frankie Montas HN 8.00 20.00
ROAFR Frank Robinson HN 60.00 150.00
ROAGA George Altman 6.00 15.00
ROAHA Hank Aaron HN 250.00 500.00
ROAHF Hank Fischer 6.00 15.00
ROAHO Henry Owens 8.00 20.00
ROAHOL Hector Olivera 10.00 25.00
ROAI Ichiro Suzuki HN 400.00 800.00
ROAJA Jose Altuve 30.00 80.00
Signed in red ink
ROAJB Jackie Brandt 6.00 15.00
ROAJBEN Johnny Bench HN 60.00 150.00
ROAJBER Jose Berrios HN 10.00 25.00
ROAJC Jim Coates 6.00 15.00
ROAJG Jon Gray 6.00 15.00
ROAJH Josh Harrison 6.00 15.00
ROAJHJ Jason Heyward HN 15.00 40.00
ROAJHA Jason Hammel HN 8.00 20.00
ROAJL Jim Landis 6.00 15.00
ROAJM John Miller 6.00 15.00
ROAJOR John Orsino 6.00 15.00
ROAJOT Jim O'Toole 6.00 15.00
ROAJOW Jim Owens 6.00 15.00
ROAJP Jose Peraza HN 12.00 30.00
ROAJSU John Sullivan 6.00 15.00
ROAJTR J.T. Realmuto 30.00 80.00
ROAJU Julio Urias HN 30.00 80.00
ROAJW Jake Wood 6.00 15.00
ROAKB Kris Bryant 150.00 300.00
ROAKB Kris Bryant HN 100.00 250.00
ROAKC Kole Calhoun 6.00 15.00
ROAKMAE Kenta Maeda HN 10.00 25.00
ROAKS Kyle Schwarber 20.00 50.00
ROALG Lucas Giolito HN 12.00 30.00
ROALS Luis Severino 30.00 80.00
ROAMDH Mike de la Hoz 6.00 15.00
ROAMK Max Kepler HN 10.00 25.00
ROAMR Matt Reynolds HN 6.00 15.00
ROAMS Miguel Sano 12.00 30.00
ROAMT Mike Trout HN 300.00 500.00
ROANA Nolan Arenado HN 40.00 100.00
ROANM Nomar Mazara HN 20.00 50.00
ROANR Nolan Ryan 150.00 250.00
ROANS Noah Syndergaard HN 25.00 60.00
ROAPN Phil Niekro HN 12.00 30.00
ROAPO Peter O'Brien HN 6.00 15.00
ROAPS Pablo Sandoval 8.00 20.00
ROARC Rod Carew HN 60.00 150.00
ROARJ Reggie Jackson HN 75.00 200.00
ROAROS Robert Stephenson HN 6.00 15.00
ROARR Rob Refsnyder HN 8.00 20.00
ROARST Ross Stripling HN 6.00 15.00
ROASM Shelby Miller 12.00 30.00
ROASMA Steven Matz 25.00 60.00
ROASP Stephen Piscotty 30.00 80.00
ROATA Tim Anderson HN 50.00 120.00
ROATN Tyler Naquin HN 12.00 30.00
ROATS Trevor Story HN 25.00 60.00
ROATTUL Troy Tulowitzki HN 30.00 80.00
ROATTUR Trea Turner HN 75.00 200.00
ROATW Tyler White HN 6.00 15.00
ROAVL Vern Law 6.00 15.00
ROAYC Yoenis Cespedes HN 20.00 50.00
ROAYG Yan Gomes 6.00 15.00

2016 Topps Heritage Real One Autographs Red Ink

*RED INK: .6X TO 1.5X BASIC
STATED ODDS 1:589 HOBBY
HN STATED ODDS 1:219 HOBBY
STATED PRINT RUN 67 SER.#'d SETS
EXCHANGE DEADLINE 2/28/2018
HN EXCH DEADLINE 8/31/2018
ROACC Carlos Correa 300.00 500.00
ROAKB Kris Bryant 300.00 500.00
ROAMT Mike Trout HN 400.00 600.00

2016 Topps Heritage Real One Autographs Dual

STATED ODDS 1:3229 HOBBY
HN STATED ODDS 1:2197 HOBBY
STATED PRINT RUN 25 SER.#'d SETS
EXCHANGE DEADLINE 2/28/2018
HN EXCH DEADLINE 8/31/2018
RODAAC M.Adams/O.Cepeda
RODAAT Tulo/Alomar EXCH 60.00 150.00
RODABB B.Buxton/R.Carew
RODABM Belt/Mrchl EXCH 50.00 125.00
RODABME J.Bench/D.Mesoraco
RODACB Correa/Biggio EXCH 100.00 250.00
RODACK Correa/Keuchel EXCH 100.00 250.00
RODACS Carew/Sano EXCH 100.00 250.00
RODADW deGrom/Wright EXCH 60.00 150.00
RODAHB Brck/Hyward EXCH 50.00 125.00
RODAHR Ryan/Harvey EXCH 150.00 300.00
RODAJR Robinson/Jones 125.00 250.00
RODAMK V.Martinez/A.Kaline
RODAMP Psy/Mrchl EXCH 75.00 150.00
RODAMR Robinson/Machado 200.00 300.00
RODAPK Park/Kim EXCH 125.00 300.00
RODAPM W.Mays/B.Posey
RODAPP Phllps/Prz EXCH 50.00 125.00
RODAPS Pdrsn/Seager EXCH 300.00 800.00
RODARB Bryant/Rizzo EXCH 100.00 250.00
RODASB Schwrbr/Bryant EXCH 200.00 500.00
RODASM P.Niekro/S.Miller 50.00 125.00

2016 Topps Heritage Rookie Performers

COMPLETE SET (15) 6.00 15.00
STATED ODDS 1:8 HOBBY
RPAD Aledmys Diaz 1.50 4.00
RPAN Aaron Nola .60 1.50
RPBS Blake Snell .40 1.00
RPCS Corey Seager 2.50 6.00
RPJB Jose Berrios .40 1.00
RPJU Julio Urias 1.00 2.50
RPKS Kyle Schwarber 1.00 2.50
RPMC Michael Conforto .40 1.00
RPMF Michael Fulmer .50 1.25
RPMS Miguel Sano .50 1.25
RPNM Nomar Mazara .50 1.25
RPSP Stephen Piscotty .50 1.25
RPTN Tyler Naquin .40 1.00
RPTS Trevor Story 1.25 3.00
RPTT Trayce Thompson .50 1.25

2016 Topps Heritage Stand Ups

COMMON CARD 1.00 2.50
SEMISTARS 1.25 3.00
UNLISTED STARS 1.50 4.00
RANDOM INSERTS IN PACKS
1 Bryce Harper 2.50 6.00
2 Madison Bumgarner 1.25 3.00
3 Clayton Kershaw 3.00 8.00
4 Josh Donaldson 1.25 3.00
5 Buster Posey 2.00 5.00
6 Andrew McCutchen 1.50 4.00
7 Carlos Correa 1.50 4.00
8 Zack Greinke 1.25 3.00
9 Kris Bryant 2.00 5.00
10 Jake Arrieta 1.25 3.00
11 Stephen Piscotty 1.50 4.00
12 Matt Harvey 1.25 3.00
13 Kyle Schwarber 2.50 6.00
14 Mike Trout 8.00 20.00
15 Miguel Cabrera 1.50 4.00

2016 Topps Heritage Then and Now

COMPLETE SET (10) 3.00 8.00
STATED ODDS 1:10 HOBBY
TANBG L.Brock/D.Gordon .40 1.00
TANBK C.Kershaw/J.Bunning 1.00 2.50
TANBS J.Bunning/M.Scherzer .50 1.25
TANCC M.Cabrera/R.Clemente 1.25 3.00
TANCK S.Carlton/C.Kershaw 1.00 2.50
TANJA J.Arrieta/F.Jenkins .40 1.00
TANKV J.Votto/H.Killebrew .50 1.25
TANNG P.Niekro/Z.Greinke .40 1.00
TANYA Yastrzemski/Arenado .75 2.00
TANYD C.Davis/C.Yastrzemski .75 2.00

2017 Topps Heritage

COMP.SET w/o SPs (600)
SP ODDS 1:3 HOBBY
SP HN ODDS 1:3 HOBBY
ACTION ODDS 1:25 HOBBY
ACTION HN ODDS 1:31 HOBBY
CLR SWP ODDS 1:147 HOBBY
CLR SWP HN ODDS 1:110 HOBBY
ERROR ODDS 1:1057 HOBBY
ERROR ODDS 1:273 WM HANGER
ERROR HN ODDS 1:461 HOBBY
TRADED ODDS 1:1057 HOBBY
TRADED ODDS 1:273 WM HANGER
TRADED HN ODDS 1:461 HOBBY
THRWBCK ODDS 1:1505 HOBBY
THRWBCK ODDS 1:1304 WM HANGER
THRWBCK HN ODDS 1:1648 HOBBY
NO THROWBACK PRICING DUE TO SCARCITY
1 LeMahieu/Votto/Murphy .25 .60
2 Pedroia/Betts/Altuve .40 1.00
3 Kemp/Rizzo/Arenado .40 1.00
4 Encarnacion/Pujols/Ortiz .30 .75
5 Carter/Arenado/Bryant .30 .75
6 Trumbo/Cruz/Davis .25 .60
7 Hendricks/Lester/Syndergaard .25 .60
8 Verlander/Sanchez/Tanaka .25 .60
9 Scherzer/Arrieta/Lester .25 .60
10A Kluber/Happ/Porcello .20 .50
10B Klbr/Hpp/Prcllo ERR SP 15.00 40.00
11 Ray/Bumgarner/Scherzer .25 .60
12 Verlander/Sale/Archer .25 .60
13 Francisco Cervelli .15 .40
14 Logan Forsythe .15 .40
15 Logan Morrison .15 .40
16 M.Margot RC/H.Renfroe RC .40 1.00
17 Rougned Odor .20 .50
18 Nate Jones .15 .40
19 Corey Dickerson .15 .40
20 Adam Jones .20 .50
21 Lonnie Chisenhall .15 .40
22 Keon Broxton .15 .40
23 David Wright .20 .50
24 Ryan Schimpf RC .30 .75
25 Aaron Hicks .20 .50
26 Howie Kendrick .15 .40
27 Tampa Bay Rays TC .15 .40
28 Jorge Soler .25 .60
29 A.Plutko RC/P.Garner RC .30 .75
30 Tyler Flowers .15 .40
31 Justin Grimm .15 .40
32 Jorge Polanco .15 .40
33 Jhonny Peralta .15 .40
34 Ryan Madson .15 .40
35 Anthony DeSclafani .15 .40
36 J.Bell RC/T.Glasnow RC .75 2.00
37 Mike Napoli .15 .40
38 Philadelphia Phillies TC .15 .40
39 Yasmany Tomas .15 .40
40 Jordan Zimmermann .20 .50
41 Melky Cabrera .15 .40
42 A.Brice RC/Y.Perez RC .50 1.25
43 Arodys Vizcaino .15 .40
44 Eduardo Nunez .15 .40
45 Scott Kazmir .15 .40
46 Lucas Duda .20 .50
47 Collin McHugh .15 .40
48 Seth Smith .15 .40
49 Danny Espinosa .15 .40
50 Denard Span .15 .40
51 Derek Norris .15 .40
52 Wellington Castillo .15 .40
53 C.J. Cron .15 .40
54 J.T. Realmuto .25 .60
55 Josh Phegley .15 .40
56 Hernan Perez .15 .40
57A Cameron Maybin .15 .40
57B Cameron Maybin TRD
SP*Trade with Tigers 8.00 20.00
58 Tony Watson .15 .40
59 Jose Peraza .20 .50
60 Carl Edwards Jr. .15 .40
61 Marco Estrada .15 .40
62 Nick Markakis .20 .50
63 Alex Wilson .15 .40
64 Russell Martin .15 .40
65 Cody Allen .15 .40
66 Kyle Hendricks .25 .60
67 Sean Doolittle .15 .40
68 Yunel Escobar .15 .40
69 T.Renda RC/W.Peralta RC .30 .75
70 Gerrit Cole .25 .60
71A Pat Neshek .15 .40
71B Pat Neshek Traded SP 8.00 20.00
Trade with Astros
72 Jonathan Villar .15 .40
73 Nick Hundley .15 .40
74 Matt Wieters .25 .60
75 Brandon Finnegan .15 .40
76A D.Swanson RC/R.Ruiz RC .75 2.00
76B Swanson Actn SP 15.00 40.00
77 Yadier Molina .25 .60
78 Pedro Baez .15 .40
79 Adrian Gonzalez .20 .50
80 Eddie Rosario .20 .50
81 Adam Rosales .15 .40
82 Leonys Martin .15 .40
83 G.Dayton RC/J.De Leon RC .30 .75
84 Evan Longoria .20 .50
85 Brett Gardner .20 .50
86A Danny Valencia .20 .50
86B Danny Valencia TRD
SP*Trade with A's 10.00 25.00
87 Starlin Castro .15 .40
88 Kyle Seager .15 .40
89 Wilson Ramos .15 .40
90A Billy Hamilton .20 .50
90B Billy Hamilton Throwback SP
'70's V-Neck Jersey
91 J.Lester/J.Arrieta .20 .50
92 R.A. Dickey .20 .50
93 Aaron Nola .20 .50
94 Francisco Liriano .15 .40
95 Eduardo Escobar .15 .40
96 Gerardo Parra .15 .40
97 Javier Baez .30 .75
98 Jace Peterson .15 .40
99 Christian Bethancourt .15 .40
100 Adam Wainwright .20 .50
101 Jose Iglesias .20 .50
102 Richie Shaffer .15 .40
103 Miguel Montero .15 .40
104 Carlos Santana .20 .50
105 Adam Lind .20 .50
106 Dexter Fowler .20 .50
107 Roberto Osuna .15 .40
108 Seung-Hwan Oh .30 .75
109 Chris Iannetta .15 .40
110 Mallex Smith .15 .40
111 Tanner Roark .15 .40
112 Matt Wisler .15 .40
113A A.Bregman RC/Y.Gurriel RC 1.25 3.00
113B Bregman Actn SP 15.00 40.00
114 Tom Koehler .15 .40
115 Elvis Andrus .20 .50
116 Asdrubal Cabrera .20 .50
117A C.Fulmer RC/Y.Moncada RC 1.00 2.50
117B Moncada Actn SP 6.00 15.00
118 Travis Shaw .15 .40
119 Carlos Beltran .20 .50
120 CC Sabathia .20 .50
121 Jeff Samardzija .15 .40
122 Brandon Drury .15 .40
123 Cam Bedrosian .15 .40
124 Chad Qualls .15 .40
125 Steven Wright .15 .40
126 Matt Duffy .15 .40

127 J.Querecuto RC/E.Gamboa RC .30 .75
128 Minnesota Twins TC .15 .40
129 Colorado Rockies TC .15 .40
130 Eugenio Suarez .20 .50
131 Andre Ethier .20 .50
132 Cheslor Cuthbert RC .30 .75
133 Arizona Diamondbacks TC .15 .40
134 Angel Pagan .15 .40
135 Phil Gosselin .15 .40
136 Ricky Nolasco .15 .40
137 Adeiny Hechavarria .15 .40
138 Justin Turner .20 .50
139 J.A. Happ .20 .50
140 Brock Holt .15 .40
141 Glen Perkins .15 .40
142 Byung-Ho Park .15 .40
143 Marwin Gonzalez .15 .40
144 Ryan Zimmerman .20 .50
145 New York Mets TC .15 .40
146 Stephen Vogt .20 .50
147 Chicago White Sox TC .15 .40
148 Clay Buchholz .15 .40
149 Oakland Athletics TC .15 .40
150 Jung Ho Kang .15 .40
151 Corey Kluber WSH .20 .50
152 Kyle Schwarber WSH .25 .60
153 Coco Crisp WSH .15 .40
154 Jason Kipnis WSH .20 .50
155 Aroldis Chapman WSH .25 .60
156 Addison Russell WSH .25 .60
157 Ben Zobrist WSH .20 .50
158 Chicago Cubs WSH .15 .40
159 J.J. Hardy .15 .40
160 Anibal Sanchez .15 .40
161 David Freese .15 .40
162A Weaver RC/Reyes RC .40 1.00
162B Alex Reyes Actn SP 2.50 6.00
163 Brett Wallace .15 .40
164 Tyler Chatwood .15 .40
165 D.Molleken RC/J.Jones RC .40 1.00
166 Jason Heyward .20 .50
167 Billy Butler .15 .40
168 Brett Lawrie .20 .50
169 Chad Bettis .15 .40
170 Andrelton Simmons .15 .40
171 Chicago Cubs TC .15 .40
172 Cristhian Adames .15 .40
173 Matt Shoemaker .20 .50
174 Chris Capuano .15 .40
175 Michael Saunders .20 .50
176 Brandon Phillips .15 .40
177 G.Cecchini RC/R.Gsellman RC .30 .75
178 James Shields .15 .40
179 J.Beresford RC/A.Wimmers RC .30 .75
180 Stephen Piscotty .20 .50
181 Corey Kluber .20 .50
182 Jacoby Ellsbury .20 .50
183 Jose Quintana .15 .40
184 Jeanmar Gomez .15 .40
185 Trayce Thompson .20 .50
186 Henry Owens .15 .40
187 Chase Utley .20 .50
188 Jedd Gyorko .15 .40
189 San Francisco Giants TC .15 .40
190 Tommy Joseph .25 .60
191 Alexi Amarista .15 .40
192 Zack Cozart .15 .40
193 Devon Travis .15 .40
194 Edwin Jackson .15 .40
195 Drew Pomeranz .20 .50
196 Brandon Crawford .20 .50
196B Ichiro ERR SP*Pitcher on front; card number 196 25.00 60.00
197 New York Yankees TC 1.25 3.00
198 Zack Greinke .20 .50
199 J.Cotton RC/R.Healy RC .40 1.00
200 Randal Grichuk .15 .40
201 Martin Maldonado .15 .40
202 Seattle Mariners TC .15 .40
203 H.Dozier RC/M.Strahm RC .30 .75
204 Tyler Thornburg .15 .40
205 Cincinnati Reds TC .15 .40
206 Robbie Grossman .15 .40
207 Chris Tillman .15 .40
208 Andrew Miller .20 .50
209 Nick Castellanos .25 .60
210 Carlos Rodon .20 .50
211 Jake Barrett .15 .40
212 Kevin Pillar .15 .40
213 Jeremy Hellickson .15 .40
214A A.Judge RC/T.Austin RC 4.00 10.00
214B Judge Actn SP 8.00 20.00
215 Freddy Galvis .15 .40
216 Baltimore Orioles TC .15 .40
217 Avisail Garcia .20 .50
218 Jim Johnson .15 .40
219 Pedro Alvarez .15 .40
220 Joe Mauer .20 .50
221 Toronto Blue Jays TC .15 .40
222 John Jaso .15 .40
223 Chris Archer .15 .40
224 Matt Szczur .20 .50
225 Francisco Rodriguez .20 .50
226 Jed Lowrie .15 .40
227 Steven Souza Jr. .20 .50
228 Jonathan Lucroy .20 .50
229 Luke Gregerson .15 .40
230 Adam Duvall .25 .60
231 Matt Garza .15 .40
232 Michael Conforto .20 .50
233 Scott Schebler .20 .50
234 St. Louis Cardinals TC .15 .40
235 Melvin Upton Jr. .20 .50
236 Ryan Vogelsong .15 .40
237 Kole Calhoun .15 .40
238A Joe Panik .20 .50
238B Joe Panik Throwback SP '70 Orange Jersey
239 Salvador Perez .20 .50
240 J.D. Martinez .25 .60
241 Travis Jankowski .15 .40
242 James McCann .20 .50
243 Byron Buxton .20 .50
244 Hanley Ramirez .20 .50
245 Tucker Barnhart .15 .40
246 Neil Walker .20 .50
247A Odubel Herrera .20 .50
247B Odubel Herrera Throwback SP '76 Jersey
248 Peter Bourjos .15 .40
249 Justin Bour .20 .50
250 Chris Young .15 .40
251 Victor Martinez .20 .50
252 Ender Inciarte .25 .60
253A Lorenzo Cain .15 .40
253B Lorenzo Cain Throwback SP '76 Baby blue jersey
254 Johnny Cueto .20 .50
255 Yasmani Grandal .25 .60
256 Matt Harvey .20 .50
257 Houston Astros TC .15 .40
258 R.Tapia RC/D.Dahl RC .40 1.00
259 Ken Giles .15 .40
260 Colby Rasmus .20 .50
261 Mitch Moreland .15 .40
262 Scooter Gennett .20 .50
263 K.Bryant/B.Harper .40 1.00
264 Joc Pederson .20 .50
265 Michael Taylor .15 .40
266 Los Angeles Angels TC .15 .40
267 O.Arcia RC/B.Suter RC .50 1.25
268 Garrett Richards .20 .50
269 Michael Brantley .20 .50
270 Jordy Mercer .15 .40
271 Jason Castro .15 .40
272 Wei-Yin Chen .15 .40
273 Chris Owings .15 .40
274 Nelson Cruz .25 .60
275 R.Quinn RC/J.Thompson RC .30 .75
276 Paulo Orlando .15 .40
277 Jason Motte .15 .40
278 Jeurys Familia .20 .50
279 Washington Nationals TC .15 .40
280 Chase Headley .15 .40
281 Brian McCann .20 .50
282A Bartolo Colon .15 .40
282B Bartolo Colon TRD SP*Signed with Braves 8.00 20.00
283 Pittsburgh Pirates TC .15 .40
284 Alcides Escobar .20 .50
285 Tyler Lyons .15 .40
286 Dellin Betances .20 .50
287A Adrian Beltre .25 .60
287B Adrian Beltre Throwback SP '90's Jersey
288 Jarrod Dyson .15 .40
289 Atlanta Braves TC .15 .40
290 Brandon Belt .20 .50
291 Wily Peralta .15 .40
292 Carlos Ruiz .15 .40
293 Didi Gregorius .20 .50
294 Cesar Hernandez .15 .40
295 Maikel Franco .20 .50
296 Jurickson Profar .20 .50
297 Ezequiel Carrera .15 .40
298 Ichiro Suzuki .30 .75
299 Cliff Pennington .15 .40
300 Nori Aoki .15 .40
301 Martin Prado .15 .40
302 Khris Davis .25 .60
303 Gio Gonzalez .20 .50
304 Kennys Vargas .15 .40
305 Kansas City Royals TC .15 .40
306A Adam Eaton .25 .60
306B Adam Eaton TRD SP*Trade with White Sox 12.00 30.00
307 Yordano Ventura .20 .50
308 Marcus Stroman .20 .50
309 A.J. Ramos .15 .40
310 Tyler Saladino .15 .40
311 Rajai Davis .15 .40
312 Darwin Barney .15 .40
313 Max Kepler .20 .50
314A R.Scott RC/A.Benintendi RC 1.00 2.50
314B Benintendi Actn SP 20.00 50.00
315 Detroit Tigers TC .15 .40
316 Kendrys Morales .15 .40
317 Andrew Romine .15 .40
318 Rick Porcello .15 .40
319 B.Goodwin RC/S.Kieboom RC .30 .75
320 Jayson Werth .20 .50
321 Evan Gattis .15 .40
322 Jonathan Schoop .15 .40
323 Los Angeles Dodgers TC .15 .40
324 Chris Carter .15 .40
325 Chris Davis .15 .40
326 Ben Zobrist .20 .50
327 Hisashi Iwakuma .20 .50
328 Ketel Marte .20 .50
329 Brad Miller .20 .50
330 Matt Holliday .25 .60
331 Joe Musgrove .15 .40
332 Jose Reyes .20 .50
333 John Lackey .20 .50
334 Justin Smoak .15 .40
335 Carlos Gomez .15 .40
336 D.LeMahieu/C.Blackmon .25 .60
337 Ervin Santana .15 .40
338 Ryan Rua .15 .40
339 Alex Gordon .20 .50
340 Jose Ramirez .20 .50
341 Patrick Corbin .20 .50
342 Curtis Granderson .20 .50
343 Marcus Semien .15 .40
344 Kolten Wong .20 .50
345 Jarred Cosart .15 .40
346 Craig Kimbrel .20 .50
347 Miami Marlins TC .15 .40
348 Julio Teheran .20 .50
349 Jake McGee .15 .40
350 David Robertson .15 .40
351 Michael Bourn .15 .40
352 Kevin Kiermaier .20 .50
353 Zach Britton .20 .50
354 Sandy Leon .15 .40
355 Anthony Rendon .25 .60
356 Huston Street .15 .40
357 Mark Reynolds .15 .40
358 San Diego Padres TC .15 .40
359 Sonny Gray .20 .50
360 Tyler Collins .15 .40
361 David Ortiz TNAS .25 .60
362 Mookie Betts TNAS .40 1.00
363 Mike Trout TNAS 1.25 3.00
364 Miguel Cabrera TNAS .25 .60
365 Josh Donaldson TNAS .20 .50
366 Carlos Correa TNAS .25 .60
367 Corey Seager TNAS .25 .60
368 Manny Machado TNAS .25 .60
369 Robinson Cano TNAS .20 .50
370 Jose Altuve TNAS .20 .50
371 Kris Bryant TNAS .30 .75
372 Anthony Rizzo TNAS .40 1.00
373 Nolan Arenado TNAS .30 .75
374 Clayton Kershaw TNAS .50 1.25
375 Buster Posey TNAS .30 .75
376 Madison Bumgarner TNAS .20 .50
377 Bryce Harper TNAS .40 1.00
378 Max Scherzer TNAS .25 .60
379 Noah Syndergaard TNAS .20 .50
380 Corey Kluber TNAS .20 .50
381 Matt Carpenter .25 .60
382 Boston Red Sox TC .15 .40
383 Robbie Ray .15 .40
384 B.Shipley RC/M.Koch RC .30 .75
385 Cleveland Indians TC .15 .40
386 A.J. Pollock .15 .40
387 Mike Moustakas .20 .50
388 Yonder Alonso .15 .40
389 DJ LeMahieu .25 .60
390 Josh Harrison .15 .40
391 Matt Moore .20 .50
392 Rickie Weeks Jr. .15 .40
393 D.Barnes RC/M.Dermody RC .30 .75
394 Texas Rangers TC .15 .40
395 Travis Wood .15 .40
396 Hart RC/Mancini RC .60 1.50
397 Milwaukee Brewers TC .15 .40
398 Yasiel Puig .25 .60
399 Sean Manaea .15 .40
400A Clayton Kershaw .50 1.25
400B Kershaw Actn SP 6.00 15.00
400C Clayton Kershaw Color SP 12.00 30.00
401A Giancarlo Stanton SP 2.00 5.00
401B Giancarlo Stanton Clr SP 6.00 15.00
402A Andrew McCutchen SP 2.00 5.00
402B McCutchen Clr SP 10.00 25.00
402C Andrew McCutchen Throwback SP '90's Jersey
403A Nolan Arenado SP 2.50 6.00
403B Nolan Arenado Actn SP 4.00 10.00
403C Nolan Arenado Clr SP 8.00 20.00
404A Max Scherzer SP 2.00 5.00
404B Max Scherzer Clr SP 6.00 15.00
405A Chris Sale SP 2.00 5.00
405B Chris Sale TRD SP*Trade with White Sox 12.00 30.00
406A Yoenis Cespedes SP 2.00 5.00
406B Cespedes Clr SP 10.00 25.00
407A Stephen Strasburg SP 2.00 5.00
407B Stephen Strasburg Clr SP 6.00 15.00
408A Felix Hernandez SP 1.50 4.00
408B Felix Hernandez Clr SP 5.00 12.00
409A Eric Hosmer SP 1.50 4.00
409B Eric Hosmer Clr SP 5.00 12.00
410A Anthony Rizzo SP 3.00 8.00
410B Anthony Rizzo Actn SP 5.00 12.00
410C Rizzo Clr SP 12.00 30.00
410D Anthony Rizzo Throwback SP 1916 Jersey
411 Matt Kemp SP 1.50 4.00
412A David Ortiz SP 3.00 8.00
412B Ortiz Clr SP 10.00 25.00
412C David Ortiz Throwback SP '36 Jersey
413A Albert Pujols SP 2.50 6.00
413B Pujols Actn SP 4.00 10.00
413C Pujols Clr SP 8.00 20.00
414 Masahiro Tanaka SP 1.50 4.00
415A Kenta Maeda SP 1.50 4.00
415B Maeda Clr SP 8.00 20.00
415C Kenta Maeda Throwback SP Brooklyn Hat
416 Yu Darvish SP 2.00 5.00
417 Justin Verlander SP 2.00 5.00
418 Miguel Cabrera SP 2.00 5.00
419A Francisco Lindor SP 2.00 5.00
419B Lindor Actn SP 3.00 8.00
420A Manny Machado SP 2.00 5.00
420B Manny Machado Actn SP 3.00 8.00
420C Machado Clr SP 12.00 30.00
420D Manny Machado Throwback SP '66 Jersey
421 Jacob deGrom SP 2.00 5.00
422A Robinson Cano SP 1.50 4.00
422B Robinson Cano Actn SP 2.50 6.00
423 Kyle Schwarber SP 2.00 5.00
424 Addison Russell SP 2.00 5.00
425 Jose Altuve SP 1.50 4.00
426 Paul Goldschmidt SP 2.00 5.00
427A Bryce Harper SP 3.00 8.00
427B Harper Actn SP 10.00 25.00
427C Harper Clr SP 20.00 50.00
427D Bryce Harper ERR SP 60.00 150.00 Nationals in white
427E Bryce Harper Throwback SP Homestead Grays Jersey
428A Mookie Betts SP 3.00 8.00
428B Betts Actn SP 5.00 12.00
429 Jose Abreu SP 2.00 5.00
430A Carlos Correa SP 2.00 5.00
430B Correa Actn SP 3.00 8.00
430C Correa Clr SP 15.00 40.00
431 Joey Votto SP 2.00 5.00
432 George Springer SP 1.50 4.00
433 Charlie Blackmon SP 2.00 5.00
434 Troy Tulowitzki SP 2.00 5.00
435 Todd Frazier SP 1.50 4.00
436 Miguel Sano SP 1.50 4.00
437 Carlos Gonzalez SP 1.50 4.00
438 Justin Upton SP 1.50 4.00
439 Hunter Pence SP 1.50 4.00
440A Corey Seager SP 2.00 5.00
440B Seager Actn SP 8.00 20.00
440C Seager Clr SP 30.00 80.00
440D Corey Seager ERR SP*no Rookie Cup;wrong birthday 60.00 150.00
441A Xander Bogaerts SP 2.00 5.00
441B Xander Bogaerts Clr SP 6.00 15.00
442A Wil Myers SP 1.25 3.00
442B Wil Myers Throwback SP '90's Jersey
443 Trevor Story SP 2.00 5.00
444A Gary Sanchez SP 2.00 5.00
444B Sanchez Actn SP 6.00 15.00
445 Edwin Encarnacion SP 2.00 5.00
446 Jose Bautista SP 1.50 4.00
447 Dee Gordon SP 1.50 4.00
448 Jason Kipnis SP 1.50 4.00
449 Freddie Freeman SP 2.50 6.00
450A Mike Trout SP 10.00 25.00
450B Trout Actn SP 15.00 40.00
450C Trout Clr SP 30.00 80.00
450D Mike Trout Throwback SP '70's Jersey
451 Ryan Braun SP 1.50 4.00
452 Ian Kinsler SP 1.50 4.00
453 Jay Bruce SP 1.50 4.00
454 Dustin Pedroia SP 2.00 5.00
455 Marcell Ozuna SP 2.00 5.00
456 Jean Segura SP 1.50 4.00
457 Daniel Murphy SP 1.50 4.00
458 Ian Desmond SP 1.25 3.00
459 Starling Marte SP 1.50 4.00
460A Madison Bumgarner SP 1.50 4.00
460B Bumgarner Actn SP 2.50 6.00
460C Bumgarner Clr SP 5.00 12.00
460D Madison Bumgarner ERR SP*Giants in white 15.00 40.00
461 Mark Trumbo SP 1.25 3.00
462 Jackie Bradley Jr. SP 2.00 5.00
463 Jon Gray SP 1.25 3.00
464 Jake Lamb SP 1.50 4.00
465 Brian Dozier SP 2.00 5.00
466 Christian Yelich SP 2.50 6.00
467 Gregory Polanco SP 1.50 4.00
468 Aaron Sanchez SP 1.50 4.00
469 Jon Lester SP 1.50 4.00
470A Noah Syndergaard SP 1.50 4.00
470B Syndergaard Actn SP 2.50 6.00
470C Syndergaard Clr SP 10.00 25.00
471 Danny Salazar SP 1.50 4.00
472 Aroldis Chapman SP 2.00 5.00
473 Cole Hamels SP 1.50 4.00
474A Danny Duffy SP 1.25 3.00
474B Danny Duffy Throwback SP K.C. Monarchs Jersey
475A Buster Posey SP 2.50 6.00
475B Posey Actn SP 4.00 10.00
475C Posey Clr SP 8.00 20.00
476A Lucas Giolito SP 1.50 4.00
476B Lucas Giolito TRD SP*Trade with Nationals 10.00 25.00
477A Julio Urias SP 2.00 5.00
477B Julio Urias Actn SP 3.00 8.00
478 Jameson Taillon SP 1.50 4.00
479 A.J. Reed SP 1.25 3.00
480A David Price SP 1.50 4.00
480B Price Clr SP 8.00 20.00
480C David Price Throwback SP
481 Willson Contreras SP 2.00 5.00
482 Albert Almora SP 1.50 4.00
483 Nomar Mazara SP 1.25 3.00
484 Michael Fulmer SP 1.25 3.00
485 Trea Turner SP 1.50 4.00
486 Ji-Man Choi SP 1.25 3.00
487 Mike Fiers SP 1.25 3.00
488 Greg Bird SP 1.50 4.00
489 Daniel Norris SP 1.25 3.00
490A Josh Donaldson SP 1.50 4.00
490B Josh Donaldson Actn SP 2.50 6.00
490C Josh Donaldson Clr SP 5.00 12.00
491 Jason Hammel SP 1.50 4.00
492 Aledmys Diaz SP 1.50 4.00
493 Sam Dyson SP 1.25 3.00
494 Alex Colome SP 1.25 3.00
495 Jerad Eickhoff SP 1.25 3.00
496 Jake Odorizzi SP 1.25 3.00
497 Kevin Gausman SP 1.25 3.00
498 Dan Straily SP 1.25 3.00
499A Jake Arrieta SP 1.50 4.00
499B Arrieta Clr SP 8.00 20.00
500A Kris Bryant SP 2.50 6.00
500B Bryant Actn SP 20.00 50.00
500C Bryant Clr SP 40.00 100.00
501 Yan Gomes .25 .60
502 Mike Zunino .15 .40
503 Joey Gallo .20 .50
504 Pierce Johnson RC .30 .75
505 Hunter Strickland .15 .40
506 Fernando Rodney .15 .40
507 Brandon McCarthy .15 .40
508A Christian Arroyo RC .50 1.25
508B Arroyo Actn SP 3.00 8.00
508C Arroyo Clr SP 6.00 15.00
508D Christian Arroyo ERR SP*Giants in white 20.00 50.00
509 Mike Montgomery .15 .40
510A Yovani Gallardo .15 .40
510B Yovani Gallardo TRD SP*Trade w/Orioles 8.00 20.00
511 Jose Martinez RC .50 1.25
512 Wade Miley .15 .40
513A Amir Garrett RC .30 .75
513B Amir Garrett ERR SP*Reds in yellow 12.00 30.00
514 Andrew Cashner .15 .40
515 Matt Adams .15 .40
516 Mallex Smith .15 .40
517A Jesse Winker RC .30 .75
517B Winker Actn SP 2.00 5.00
517C Winker Clr SP 4.00 10.00
517D Jesse Winker ERR SP*Reds in yellow 12.00 30.00
518 Lance Lynn .15 .40
519 Gift Ngoepe RC .30 .75
520 Carlos Asuaje RC .30 .75
521 Hector Neris .15 .40
522 Eduardo Rodriguez .15 .40
523A Antonio Senzatela RC .30 .75
523B Senzatela Actn SP 2.00 5.00
523C Antonio Senzatela ERR SP*Rockies in white 12.00 30.00
524 Zach Davies .15 .40
525 Nick Hundley .15 .40
526 Josh Smoker RC .30 .75
527 Mat Latos .20 .50
528A Logan Forsythe .15 .40
528B Logan Forsythe TRD SP*Trade w/Rays 8.00 20.00
529A Reynaldo Lopez RC .30 .75
529B Lopez Clr SP 4.00 10.00
529C Reynaldo Lopez TRD SP*Trade w/Nationals 8.00 20.00
530 Junior Guerra .15 .40
531 Andrew Toles RC .30 .75
532 Derek Dietrich .20 .50
533 Cameron Rupp .15 .40
534A Brandon Phillips .15 .40
534B Phillips Actn SP 2.00 5.00
534C Phillips Clr SP 4.00 10.00
534D Brandon Phillips TRD SP*Trade w/Reds 8.00 20.00
535A Eric Thames .20 .50
535B Thames Actn SP 2.50 6.00
536 Joe Ross .15 .40
537 Rob Zastryzny RC .30 .75
538 Rob Segedin RC .30 .75
539 Andrew Albers RC .30 .75
540 Michael Wacha .20 .50
541A Yangervis Solarte .15 .40
541B Yangervis Solarte Throwback SP '80's Jersey
542 Mychal Givens .15 .40
543 Austin Hedges .15 .40
544 Jaime Garcia .15 .40
545 Frankie Montas .15 .40
546 James Paxton .20 .50
547A Dan Straily .15 .40
547B Dan Straily TRD SP*Trade w/Reds 8.00 20.00
548 Danny Santana .15 .40
549 Brad Brach .15 .40
550 Adalberto Mejia RC .30 .75
551 Phil Ervin RC .30 .75
552 Archie Bradley .15 .40
553 Steve Pearce .25 .60
554 Brandon Kintzler .15 .40
555 Martin Perez .20 .50
556 Mauricio Cabrera RC .30 .75
557 Gabriel Ynoa RC .30 .75
558 Jesus Aguilar .25 .60
559 Jorge Bonifacio RC .30 .75
560 Stephen Cardullo RC .30 .75
561 Daniel Nava .15 .40
562 Phil Hughes .15 .40
563 Andrew Triggs .15 .40
564 Carlos Carrasco .15 .40
565 Chris Taylor .20 .50
566 Jose Berrios .20 .50
567 Joe Jimenez RC .30 .75
568A Koda Glover RC .30 .75
568B Glover Actn SP 2.00 5.00
568C Glover Clr SP 4.00 10.00
569 Allen Cordoba RC .30 .75
570 Abraham Almonte .15 .40
571 Hector Santiago .15 .40
572A Addison Reed .15 .40
572B Addison Reed Throwback SP V-neck Jersey
573 Drew Storen .15 .40
574 Colby Rasmus .20 .50
575 J.T. Riddle RC .30 .75
576A Bradley Zimmer RC .40 1.00
576B Zimmer Actn SP 2.50 6.00
576C Zimmer Clr SP 5.00 12.00
576D Bradley Zimmer ERR SP*Indians in white 15.00 40.00
577 Kurt Suzuki .15 .40
578 Jered Weaver .20 .50
579 Adam Lind .20 .50
580 Hector Rondon .15 .40
581 Darren O'Day .15 .40
582 Brad Ziegler .15 .40
583 Rafael Bautista RC .30 .75
584 Bruce Maxwell RC .30 .75
585 Joe Biagini .15 .40
586 Tyler Naquin .15 .40
587A Domingo Santana .20 .50
587B Domingo Santana Throwback SP '80's Jersey
588 Daniel Robertson RC .30 .75
589A Drew Smyly .15 .40
589B Drew Smyly TRD SP*Trade w/Rays 8.00 20.00
590 Travis d'Arnaud .20 .50
591 Alex Meyer .15 .40
592 Sergio Romo .15 .40
593A Hyun-Soo Kim .20 .50
593B Hyun-Soo Kim Throwback SP wearing elbow pad
594 Michael Saunders .20 .50
595 Koji Uehara .15 .40
596 Matt Joyce .15 .40
597 Jeremy Jeffress .15 .40
598 Bronson Arroyo .15 .40
599 Renato Nunez RC .60 1.50
600 Erick Aybar .15 .40
601 Blake Snell .20 .50
602 Alex Wood .15 .40
603 Dovydas Neverauskas RC .30 .75
604A Matt Cain .15 .40
604B Matt Cain Throwback SP Orange Jersey
605 Shelby Miller .20 .50
606 Ian Kennedy .15 .40
607 Mark Canha .15 .40
608 Chris Devenski .15 .40
609 Matt Carasiti RC .30 .75
610 Boog Powell RC .30 .75
611 Devin Mesoraco .15 .40
612 Brandon Moss .15 .40
613A Dan Vogelbach RC .50 1.25
613B Vogelbach Clr SP 6.00 15.00
614 Chad Pinder RC .30 .75
615 Brandon Guyer .15 .40
616A Whit Merrifield .25 .60
616B Whit Merrifield Throwback SP baby blue jersey
617 Seth Lugo RC .30 .75
618 Wade Davis .15 .40
619A Raisel Iglesias .20 .50
619B Raisel Iglesias Throwback SP '30's Jersey
620 Joe Kelly .15 .40
621 Tyson Ross .15 .40
622 Sal Romano RC .30 .75
623 Edinson Volquez .15 .40
624 Kendall Graveman .15 .40
625 Brock Stassi RC .40 1.00
626 Austin Jackson .15 .40
627 Neftali Feliz .15 .40
628 Tony Wolters .15 .40
629 Mac Williamson .15 .40
630 Mark Melancon .15 .40
631 Derek Norris .15 .40
632 Joaquin Benoit .15 .40
633A David Peralta .15 .40
633B David Peralta Throwback SP Pinstripe uniform
634 Matt Albers .15 .40
635 Mike Pelfrey .15 .40
636 Stuart Turner RC .30 .75
637 Ben Gamel .20 .50
638 Jason Grilli .15 .40
639A Jorge Alfaro RC .40 1.00
639B Alfaro Clr SP 5.00 12.00
640A Miguel Gonzalez .15 .40
640B Miguel Gonzalez Throwback SP '80's Jersey
641 Ivan Nova .20 .50
642A Jose De Leon RC .30 .75
642B De Leon Actn SP 2.00 5.00
642C De Leon Clr SP 4.00 10.00
642D Jose De Leon ERR SP*Rays in white 12.00 30.00
642E Jose De Leon TRD SP*Trade w/Dodgers 8.00 20.00
643 Jarlin Garcia RC .30 .75
644A Chase Anderson .15 .40
644B Chase Anderson Throwback SP 90's Uniform
645 Chih-Wei Hu RC .30 .75
646A Jordan Montgomery RC .50 1.25
646B Jordan Montgomery ERR SP*Yankees in white 12.00 30.00
647A Matt Wieters .25 .60
647B Wieters Actn SP 3.00 8.00
647C Wieters Clr SP 6.00 15.00
647D Matt Wieters TRD SP*Trade w/Nationals 12.00 30.
648 Delino DeShields .15
649A Mike Clevinger .20
649B Mike Clevinger Throwback SP Buckeyes Jersey
650 Tyler Clippard .15
651A Jeff Hoffman RC .30
651B Hoffman Clr SP 4.00 10.
652 Derek Holland .15
653 Jon Jay .15
654 Teoscar Hernandez RC 1.00 2.5
655 Craig Breslow .15
656 Daniel Descalso .15
657 Nathan Eovaldi .20
658 Wilmer Difo .15
659 Ty Blach RC .30
660A Ian Happ RC .60 1.5
660B Happ Actn SP 4.00 10.0
660C Happ Clr SP 8.00 20.0
660D Ian Happ ERR SP*Cubs in yellow 20.00 50.0
661 Derek Law .15
662 Martin Maldonado .15
663 Mike Minor .15
664A Edwin Encarnacion .25
664B Encrncn Actn SP 3.00 8.0
664C Encrncn Clr SP 6.00 15.0
664D Edwin Encarnacion TRD SP*Signed w/Indians 12.00 30.0
665 Trevor Plouffe .15
666 Kyle Freeland RC .40 1.
667 Aaron Altherr .15
668A Steve Cishek .15
668B Steve Cishek Throwback SP '80's Jersey
669 Adam Frazier RC .30 .7
670 Jeff Mathis .20 .5
671 Rajai Davis .15
672 Hansel Robles .15
673 Nick Ahmed .15
674 Magneuris Sierra RC .50 1.2
675 Joakim Soria .15
676A Mitch Haniger RC .50 1.2
676B Haniger Actn SP 3.00 8.0
676C Haniger Clr SP 6.00 15.0
676D Mitch Haniger ERR SP*Mariners in white 15.00 40.0
677 Brandon Nimmo .20 .5
678A Cody Bellinger RC 6.00 15.0
678B Bellinger Actn SP 40.00 100.0
678C Bellinger Clr SP 60.00 150.0
678D Cody Bellinger ERR SP*Dodgers in white 100.00 250.0
679 Jett Bandy .15 .4
680 Jarrod Dyson .15 .4
681 Matt Olson RC .50 1.2
682 Rene Rivera .15 .4
683 Brad Peacock .15 .4
684 Santiago Casilla .15 .4
685 German Marquez RC .50 1.2
686A Aroldis Chapman .25 .6
686B Chapman Actn SP 3.00 8.0
686C Chapman Clr SP 6.00 15.0
686D Aroldis Chapman TRD SP*Signed w/Yankees 12.00 30.0
687 Adam Ottavino .15 .4
688 Ben Revere .15 .4
689 Jason Vargas .15 .4
690 Anthony Alford RC .30 .7
691 Jose Osuna RC .30 .7
692 Pat Valaika RC .40 1.0
693 Corey Knebel .15 .4
694 Ronald Torreyes .15 .4
695 Christian Vazquez .15 .4
696 Luke Maile .15 .4
697 T.J. Rivera RC .50 1.2
698 Adam Conley .15 .4
699 Matt Bush .20 .5
700 Brett Anderson .15 .4
701 Tim Anderson SP 2.00 5.0
702 Edwin Diaz SP 1.50 4.0
703 Tom Murphy SP 1.25 3.0
704 Alex Cobb SP 1.25 3.0
705A Vince Velasquez SP 1.25 3.0
705B Vince Velasquez Throwback SP '80's Jersey
706A Carlos Martinez SP 1.50 4.0
706B Martinez Actn SP 2.50 6.0
706C Martinez Clr SP 5.00 12.0
707A Steven Matz SP 1.50 4.0
707B Matz Clr SP 5.00 12.0
708 Zack Wheeler SP 1.25 3.0
709 Michael Pineda SP 1.25 3.0
710 Luis Severino SP 1.50 4.0
711 Rich Hill SP 1.25 3.0
712A Kenley Jansen SP 1.50 4.0
712B Jansen Clr SP 5.00 12.0
713A Dylan Bundy SP 1.50 4.0
713B Bundy Clr SP 10.00 25.0
714 Kelvin Herrera SP 1.25 3.0
715A Trevor Bauer SP 2.00 5.0
715B Bauer Clr SP 6.00 15.0
716A Pablo Sandoval SP 1.50 4.0
716B Sandoval Clr SP 5.00 12.0
717A Shin-Soo Choo SP 1.50 4.0
717B Choo Clr SP 5.00 12.0
717C Shin-Soo Choo Throwback SP '90's Jersey
718 Taijuan Walker SP 1.25 3.0
719A Dallas Keuchel SP 1.50 4.0
719B Keuchel Clr SP 5.00 12.0
720A Lance McCullers SP 1.25 3.0
720B McCullers Clr SP 4.00 10.0
721 Josh Reddick SP 1.25 3.0

722 Greg Holland SP 1.25 3.00
723A Mike Leake SP 1.25 3.00
723B Mike Leake Throwback SP
'56 Jersey
724 Trevor Cahill SP 1.25 3.00
725 Jared Hughes SP 1.25 3.00

2017 Topps Heritage Blue

*BLUE: 8X TO 20X BASIC
*BLUE RC: 4X TO 10X BASIC RC
*BLUE SP: 1X TO 2.5X BASIC SP
STATED ODDS 1:37 HOBBY
STATED HN ODDS 1:61 HOBBY
ANNCD PRINT RUN OF 50 COPIES EACH
5 Carter/Arenado/Bryant 8.00 20.00
76 D.Swanson/R.Ruiz 15.00 40.00
117 C.Fulmer/Y.Moncada 12.00 30.00
177 Cecchini/Gsellman 8.00 20.00
197 New York Yankees TC 10.00 25.00
214 A.Judge/T.Austin 12.00 30.00
298 Ichiro Suzuki 8.00 20.00
314 R.Scott/A.Benintendi 40.00 100.00
363 Mike Trout TNAS 12.00 30.00
364 Miguel Cabrera TNAS 10.00 25.00
367 Corey Seager TNAS 15.00 40.00
368 Manny Machado TNAS 6.00 15.00
371 Kris Bryant TNAS 25.00 60.00
377 Bryce Harper TNAS 8.00 20.00
379 Noah Syndergaard TNAS 10.00 25.00
412 David Ortiz 8.00 20.00
418 Miguel Cabrera 10.00 25.00
420 Manny Machado 12.00 30.00
427 Bryce Harper 10.00 25.00
431 Joey Votto 8.00 20.00
440 Corey Seager 25.00 60.00
444 Gary Sanchez 10.00 25.00
450 Mike Trout 30.00 80.00
470 Noah Syndergaard 8.00 20.00
481 Willson Contreras 10.00 25.00
500 Kris Bryant 30.00 80.00
660 Ian Happ 20.00 50.00
678 Cody Bellinger 100.00 250.00

2017 Topps Heritage Bright Yellow Back

*YELLOW: 10X TO 25X BASIC
*YELLOW RC: 5X TO 25X BASIC RC
*YELLOW SP: 1.2X TO 3X BASIC SP
STATED ODDS 1:212 HOBBY
STATED ODDS 1:55 WM HANGER
STATED HN ODDS 1:205 HOBBY
ANNCD PRINT RUN OF 25 COPIES EACH
5 Carter/Arenado/Bryant 10.00 25.00
76 D.Swanson/R.Ruiz 20.00 50.00
117 C.Fulmer/Y.Moncada 15.00 40.00
177 Cecchini/Gsellman 10.00 25.00
197 New York Yankees TC 12.00 30.00
214 A.Judge/T.Austin 15.00 40.00
298 Ichiro Suzuki 10.00 25.00
314 R.Scott/A.Benintendi 50.00 120.00
363 Mike Trout TNAS 15.00 40.00
364 Miguel Cabrera TNAS 12.00 30.00
367 Corey Seager TNAS 20.00 50.00
368 Manny Machado TNAS 8.00 20.00
371 Kris Bryant TNAS 30.00 80.00
377 Bryce Harper TNAS 10.00 25.00
379 Noah Syndergaard TNAS 12.00 30.00
412 David Ortiz 10.00 25.00
418 Miguel Cabrera 12.00 30.00
427 Bryce Harper 12.00 30.00
431 Joey Votto 10.00 25.00
440 Corey Seager 30.00 80.00
444 Gary Sanchez 12.00 30.00
450 Mike Trout 40.00 100.00
470 Noah Syndergaard 10.00 25.00
481 Willson Contreras 12.00 30.00
500 Kris Bryant 40.00 100.00
660 Ian Happ 25.00 60.00
678 Cody Bellinger 125.00 300.00

2017 Topps Heritage Mini

STATED ODDS 1:204 HOBBY
STATED ODDS 1:53 WM HANGER
STATED HN ODDS 1:231 HOBBY
STATED PRINT RUN 100 SER.#'d SETS
17 Rougned Odor 5.00 12.00
20 Adam Jones 6.00 15.00
23 David Wright 5.00 12.00
67 Sean Doolittle 4.00 10.00
70 Gerrit Cole 6.00 15.00
77 Yadier Molina 6.00 15.00
79 Adrian Gonzalez 5.00 12.00
84 Evan Longoria 5.00 12.00
88 Kyle Seager 4.00 10.00
93 Aaron Nola 5.00 12.00
100 Adam Wainwright 5.00 12.00
106 Dexter Fowler 6.00 15.00
115 Elvis Andrus 5.00 12.00
119 Carlos Beltran 5.00 12.00
166 Jason Heyward 5.00 12.00
180 Stephen Piscotty 5.00 12.00
181 Corey Kluber 8.00 20.00
196 Brandon Crawford 5.00 12.00
198 Zack Greinke 5.00 12.00
208 Andrew Miller 5.00 12.00
220 Joe Mauer 5.00 12.00
223 Chris Archer 4.00 10.00
228 Jonathan Lucroy 5.00 12.00
239 Salvador Perez 5.00 12.00
240 J.D. Martinez 6.00 15.00
243 Byron Buxton 5.00 12.00
244 Hanley Ramirez 5.00 12.00
251 Victor Martinez 5.00 12.00
254 Johnny Cueto 5.00 12.00
256 Matt Harvey 5.00 12.00
274 Nelson Cruz 6.00 15.00
287 Adrian Beltre 6.00 15.00
295 Maikel Franco 5.00 12.00
302 Khris Davis 6.00 15.00
308 Marcus Stroman 5.00 12.00
318 Rick Porcello 5.00 12.00
325 Chris Davis 4.00 10.00
326 Ben Zobrist 5.00 12.00
359 Sonny Gray 5.00 12.00
381 Matt Carpenter 6.00 15.00
386 A.J. Pollock 4.00 10.00
400 Clayton Kershaw 12.00 30.00
401 Giancarlo Stanton 6.00 15.00
402 Andrew McCutchen 6.00 15.00
403 Nolan Arenado 8.00 20.00
404 Max Scherzer 6.00 15.00
405 Chris Sale 10.00 25.00
406 Yoenis Cespedes 6.00 15.00
407 Stephen Strasburg 6.00 15.00
408 Felix Hernandez 5.00 12.00
409 Eric Hosmer 5.00 12.00
410 Anthony Rizzo 10.00 25.00
411 Matt Kemp 5.00 12.00
412 David Ortiz 10.00 25.00
413 Albert Pujols 8.00 20.00
414 Masahiro Tanaka 5.00 12.00
415 Kenta Maeda 5.00 12.00
416 Yu Darvish 6.00 15.00
417 Justin Verlander 6.00 15.00
418 Miguel Cabrera 20.00 50.00
419 Francisco Lindor 10.00 25.00
420 Manny Machado 10.00 25.00
421 Jacob deGrom 8.00 20.00
422 Robinson Cano 5.00 12.00
423 Kyle Schwarber 6.00 15.00
424 Addison Russell 6.00 15.00
425 Jose Altuve 12.00 30.00
426 Paul Goldschmidt 8.00 20.00
427 Bryce Harper 25.00 60.00
428 Mookie Betts 10.00 25.00
429 Jose Abreu 6.00 15.00
430 Carlos Correa 6.00 15.00
431 Joey Votto 6.00 15.00
432 George Springer 5.00 12.00
433 Charlie Blackmon 6.00 15.00
434 Troy Tulowitzki 6.00 15.00
435 Todd Frazier 5.00 12.00
436 Miguel Sano 5.00 12.00
437 Carlos Gonzalez 5.00 12.00
438 Justin Upton 5.00 12.00
439 Hunter Pence 5.00 12.00
440 Corey Seager 20.00 50.00
441 Xander Bogaerts 6.00 15.00
442 Wil Myers 4.00 10.00
443 Trevor Story 6.00 15.00
444 Gary Sanchez 25.00 60.00
445 Edwin Encarnacion 6.00 15.00
446 Jose Bautista 10.00 25.00
447 Dee Gordon 4.00 10.00
448 Jason Kipnis 5.00 12.00
449 Freddie Freeman 8.00 20.00
450 Mike Trout 40.00 100.00
451 Ryan Braun 5.00 12.00
452 Ian Kinsler 5.00 12.00
453 Jay Bruce 5.00 12.00
454 Dustin Pedroia 10.00 25.00
455 Marcell Ozuna 5.00 12.00
456 Jean Segura 5.00 12.00
457 Daniel Murphy 5.00 12.00
458 Ian Desmond 4.00 10.00
459 Starling Marte 5.00 12.00
460 Madison Bumgarner 5.00 12.00
461 Mark Trumbo 4.00 10.00
462 Jackie Bradley Jr. 6.00 15.00
463 Jon Gray 4.00 10.00
464 Jake Lamb 5.00 12.00
465 Brian Dozier 5.00 12.00
466 Christian Yelich 8.00 20.00
467 Gregory Polanco 5.00 12.00
468 Aaron Sanchez 5.00 12.00
469 Jon Lester 5.00 12.00
470 Noah Syndergaard 5.00 12.00
471 Danny Salazar 8.00 20.00
472 Aroldis Chapman 6.00 15.00
473 Cole Hamels 5.00 12.00
474 Danny Duffy 4.00 10.00
475 Buster Posey 8.00 20.00
476 Lucas Giolito 5.00 12.00
477 Julio Urias 8.00 20.00
478 Jameson Taillon 5.00 12.00
479 A.J. Reed 4.00 10.00
480 David Price 5.00 12.00
481 Willson Contreras 6.00 15.00
482 Albert Almora 4.00 10.00
483 Nomar Mazara 4.00 10.00
484 Michael Fulmer 4.00 10.00
485 Trea Turner 5.00 12.00
490 Josh Donaldson 5.00 12.00
499 Jake Arrieta 5.00 12.00
500 Kris Bryant 30.00 80.00
508 Christian Arroyo 6.00 15.00
513 Amir Garrett 4.00 10.00
517 Jesse Winker 4.00 10.00
529 Reynaldo Lopez 4.00 10.00
531 Andrew Toles 4.00 10.00
534 Brandon Phillips 4.00 10.00
537 Rob Zastryzny 4.00 10.00
538 Rob Segedin 4.00 10.00
550 Adalberto Mejia 8.00 20.00
556 Mauricio Cabrera 4.00 10.00
567 Joe Jimenez 4.00 10.00
568 Koda Glover 4.00 10.00
576 Bradley Zimmer 10.00 25.00
584 Bruce Maxwell 4.00 10.00
589 Drew Smyly 4.00 10.00
595 Koji Uehara 4.00 10.00
599 Renato Nunez 8.00 20.00
601 Blake Snell 5.00 12.00
613 Dan Vogelbach 6.00 15.00
617 Seth Lugo 4.00 10.00
639 Jorge Alfaro 5.00 12.00
642 Jose De Leon 4.00 10.00
647 Matt Wieters 12.00 30.00
651 Jeff Hoffman 4.00 10.00
654 Teoscar Hernandez 12.00 30.00
659 Ty Blach 4.00 10.00
660 Ian Happ 8.00 20.00
664 Edwin Encarnacion 10.00 25.00
676 Mitch Haniger 6.00 15.00
678 Cody Bellinger 75.00 200.00
681 Matt Olson 6.00 15.00
685 German Marquez 6.00 15.00
686 Aroldis Chapman 6.00 15.00
697 T.J. Rivera 6.00 15.00
701 Tim Anderson 6.00 15.00
702 Edwin Diaz 5.00 12.00
705 Vince Velasquez 4.00 10.00
706 Carlos Martinez 5.00 12.00
707 Steven Matz 5.00 12.00
708 Zack Wheeler 5.00 12.00
709 Michael Pineda 4.00 10.00
710 Luis Severino 5.00 12.00
712 Kenley Jansen 5.00 12.00
713 Dylan Bundy 10.00 25.00
715 Trevor Bauer 6.00 15.00
716 Pablo Sandoval 5.00 12.00
717 Shin-Soo Choo 5.00 12.00
719 Dallas Keuchel 5.00 12.00
720 Lance McCullers 4.00 10.00
721 Josh Reddick 4.00 10.00

2017 Topps Heritage '68 Poster Boxloader

STATED ODDS 1:39 HOBBY BOXES
STATED HN ODDS 1:29 HOBBY BOXES
68PAB Alex Bregman HN 30.00 80.00
68PAK Al Kaline 20.00 50.00
68PAM Andrew McCutchen HN 30.00 80.00
68PBH Bryce Harper 20.00 50.00
68PBP Buster Posey 15.00 40.00
68PBR Brooks Robinson HN 30.00 80.00
68PCC Carlos Correa 12.00 30.00
68PCK Clayton Kershaw 25.00 60.00
68PCY Carl Yastrzemski 30.00 80.00
68PDP David Price 10.00 25.00
68PDS Dansby Swanson HN 20.00 50.00
68PFL Francisco Lindor 15.00 40.00
68PFR Frank Robinson HN 30.00 80.00
68PGS Gary Sanchez HN 40.00 100.00
68PGS Giancarlo Stanton HN 30.00 80.00
68PHA Hank Aaron 20.00 50.00
68PJA Jake Arrieta 10.00 25.00
68PJB Johnny Bench 30.00 80.00
68PJD Josh Donaldson HN 30.00 80.00
68PJP Jim Palmer HN 30.00 80.00
68PJV Joey Votto HN 25.00 60.00
68PKB Kris Bryant 30.00 80.00
68PKS Kyle Schwarber HN 25.00 60.00
68PLB Lou Brock HN 30.00 80.00
68PMB Mookie Betts HN 25.00 60.00
68PMB Madison Bumgarner 20.00 50.00
68PMC Miguel Cabrera HN 25.00 60.00
68PMM Manny Machado 30.00 80.00
68PMS Max Scherzer HN 30.00 80.00
68PMT Mike Trout 30.00 80.00
68PNR Nolan Ryan 40.00 100.00
68PNS Noah Syndergaard 25.00 60.00
68PRC Rod Carew 20.00 50.00
68PRJ Reggie Jackson HN 60.00 150.00
68PSC Steve Carlton HN 30.00 80.00
68PYM Yoan Moncada HN 25.00 60.00
68PYS Yoenis Cespedes HN 20.00 50.00
68PABR Andrew Benintendi HN 25.00 60.00
68PARI Anthony Rizzo 20.00 50.00
68PCSE Corey Seager 20.00 50.00

2017 Topps Heritage 3D

STATED ODDS 1:12 HOBBY BOXES
683DAR Anthony Rizzo 12.00 30.00
683DBH Bryce Harper 20.00 50.00
683DBP Buster Posey 12.00 30.00
683DCC Carlos Correa 12.00 30.00
683DCK Clayton Kershaw 12.00 30.00
683DCS Corey Seager 20.00 50.00
683DDO David Ortiz 10.00 25.00
683DGS Giancarlo Stanton 8.00 20.00
683DJA Jake Arrieta 5.00 12.00
683DJD Josh Donaldson 8.00 20.00
683DKB Kris Bryant 40.00 100.00
683DMBU Madison Bumgarner 12.00 30.00
683DMM Manny Machado 15.00 40.00
683DMT Mike Trout 30.00 80.00
683DNS Noah Syndergaard 12.00 30.00

2017 Topps Heritage Award Winners

COMPLETE SET (10) 4.00 10.00
STATED HN ODDS 1:8 HOBBY
AW1 Rick Porcello .50 1.25
AW2 Max Scherzer .60 1.50
AW3 Corey Seager .60 1.50
AW4 Michael Fulmer .40 1.00
AW5 Kris Bryant .75 2.00
AW6 Mike Trout 3.00 8.00
AW7 Eric Hosmer .50 1.25
AW8 Ben Zobrist .50 1.25
AW9 Kris Bryant .75 2.00
AW10 David Ortiz .60 1.50

2017 Topps Heritage Baseball Flashbacks

COMPLETE SET (15) 8.00 20.00
STATED ODDS 1:20 HOBBY
STATED ODDS 1:7 WM HANGER
BFBR Brooks Robinson .50 1.25
BFBW Billy Williams .50 1.25
BFCH Catfish Hunter .50 1.25
BFCY Carl Yastrzemski 1.00 2.50
BFFJ Fergie Jenkins .50 1.25
BFFR Frank Robinson .50 1.25
BFHA Hank Aaron 1.25 3.00
BFHK Harmon Killebrew .60 1.50
BFJB Johnny Bench .60 1.50
BFJM Joe Morgan .50 1.25
BFLB Lou Brock .50 1.25
BFNR Nolan Ryan 2.00 5.00
BFRJ Reggie Jackson .50 1.25
BFWM Willie McCovey .50 1.25
BFWS Willie Stargell .50 1.25

2017 Topps Heritage Bazooka

STATED ODDS 1:76 WM HANGER
68BAM Andrew McCutchen 5.00 12.00
68BAR Anthony Rizzo 8.00 20.00
68BBH Bryce Harper 15.00 40.00
68BBP Buster Posey 6.00 15.00
68BCC Carlos Correa 5.00 12.00
68BCK Clayton Kershaw 10.00 25.00
68BCS Chris Sale HN 8.00 20.00
68BCS Corey Seager 10.00 25.00
68BDO David Ortiz 5.00 12.00
68BDP David Price 4.00 10.00
68BEH Eric Hosmer 4.00 10.00
68BFF Freddie Freeman HN 8.00 20.00
68BFH Felix Hernandez 4.00 10.00
68BFL Francisco Lindor HN 10.00 25.00
68BGS Giancarlo Stanton 8.00 20.00
68BJA Jose Altuve HN 12.00 30.00
68BJA Jake Arrieta 4.00 10.00
68BJB Jose Bautista HN 8.00 20.00
68BJD Josh Donaldson 8.00 20.00
68BJU Julio Urias HN 8.00 20.00
68BJV Justin Verlander HN 8.00 20.00
68BJVO Joey Votto HN 10.00 25.00
68BKB Kris Bryant 20.00 50.00
68BKS Kyle Schwarber HN 5.00 12.00
68BMB Mookie Betts 8.00 20.00
68BMBU Madison Bumgarner 4.00 10.00
68BMC Miguel Cabrera 10.00 25.00
68BMM Manny Machado 5.00 12.00
68BMS Max Scherzer 5.00 12.00
68BMT Mike Trout 25.00 60.00
68BNA Nolan Arenado 10.00 25.00
68BNS Noah Syndergaard 4.00 10.00
68BRC Robinson Cano 4.00 10.00
68BTT Trea Turner HN 8.00 20.00
68BYC Yoenis Cespedes 5.00 12.00

2017 Topps Heritage Chrome

STATED ODDS 1:27 HOBBY
STATED ODDS 1:7 WM HANGER
STATED HN ODDS 1:24 HOBBY
STATED PRINT RUN 999 SER.#'d SETS
*PRPLE REF: .4X TO 1X BASIC
*REF/568: .6X TO 1.5X BASIC
16 M.Margot/H.Renfroe 1.50 4.00
36 J.Bell/T.Glasnow 3.00 8.00
76 D.Swanson/R.Ruiz 5.00 12.00
113 A.Bregman/Y.Gurriel 5.00 12.00
117 C.Fulmer/Y.Moncada 4.00 10.00
162 L.Weaver/A.Reyes 1.50 4.00
177 G.Cecchini/R.Gsellman 1.25 3.00
199 J.Cotton/R.Healy 1.50 4.00
214 A.Judge/T.Austin 30.00 80.00
258 R.Tapia/D.Dahl 1.50 4.00
THC400 Clayton Kershaw 4.00 10.00
THC401 Giancarlo Stanton 2.00 5.00
THC402 Andrew McCutchen 2.00 5.00
THC403 Nolan Arenado 2.50 6.00
THC404 Max Scherzer 2.00 5.00
THC405 Chris Sale 2.00 5.00
THC406 Yoenis Cespedes 2.00 5.00
THC407 Stephen Strasburg 2.00 5.00
THC408 Felix Hernandez 1.50 4.00
THC409 Eric Hosmer 1.50 4.00
THC410 Anthony Rizzo 3.00 8.00
THC411 Matt Kemp 1.50 4.00
THC412 David Ortiz 2.00 5.00
THC413 Albert Pujols 2.50 6.00
THC414 Masahiro Tanaka 1.50 4.00
THC415 Kenta Maeda 1.50 4.00
THC416 Yu Darvish 2.00 5.00
THC417 Justin Verlander 2.00 5.00
THC418 Miguel Cabrera 2.00 5.00
THC419 Francisco Lindor 2.00 5.00
THC420 Manny Machado 2.00 5.00
THC421 Jacob deGrom 2.00 5.00
THC422 Robinson Cano 1.50 4.00
THC423 Kyle Schwarber 1.50 4.00
THC424 Addison Russell 2.00 5.00
THC425 Jose Altuve 1.50 4.00
THC426 Paul Goldschmidt 2.00 5.00
THC427 Bryce Harper 4.00 10.00
THC428 Mookie Betts 3.00 8.00
THC429 Jose Abreu 2.00 5.00
THC430 Carlos Correa 2.00 5.00
THC431 Joey Votto 2.00 5.00
THC432 George Springer 1.50 4.00
THC433 Charlie Blackmon 2.00 5.00
THC434 Troy Tulowitzki 2.00 5.00
THC435 Todd Frazier 1.50 4.00
THC436 Miguel Sano 1.50 4.00
THC437 Carlos Gonzalez 1.50 4.00
THC438 Justin Upton 1.50 4.00
THC439 Hunter Pence 1.50 4.00
THC440 Corey Seager 5.00 12.00
THC441 Xander Bogaerts 2.00 5.00
THC442 Wil Myers 1.25 3.00
THC443 Trevor Story 2.00 5.00
THC444 Gary Sanchez 2.00 5.00
THC445 Edwin Encarnacion 2.00 5.00
THC446 Jose Bautista 1.50 4.00
THC447 Dee Gordon 1.25 3.00
THC448 Jason Kipnis 1.50 4.00
THC449 Freddie Freeman 2.50 6.00
THC450 Mike Trout 10.00 25.00
THC451 Ryan Braun 1.50 4.00
THC452 Ian Kinsler 1.50 4.00
THC453 Jay Bruce 1.50 4.00
THC454 Dustin Pedroia 2.00 5.00
THC455 Marcell Ozuna 2.00 5.00
THC456 Jean Segura 1.50 4.00
THC457 Daniel Murphy 1.50 4.00
THC458 Ian Desmond 1.25 3.00
THC459 Starling Marte 1.50 4.00
THC460 Madison Bumgarner 1.50 4.00
THC461 Mark Trumbo 1.25 3.00
THC462 Jackie Bradley Jr. 2.00 5.00
THC463 Jon Gray 1.25 3.00
THC464 Jake Lamb 1.50 4.00
THC465 Brian Dozier 2.00 5.00
THC466 Christian Yelich 2.50 6.00
THC467 Gregory Polanco 1.50 4.00
THC468 Aaron Sanchez 1.50 4.00
THC469 Jon Lester 1.50 4.00
THC470 Noah Syndergaard 1.50 4.00
THC471 Danny Salazar 1.50 4.00
THC472 Aroldis Chapman 2.00 5.00
THC473 Cole Hamels 1.50 4.00
THC474 Danny Duffy 1.25 3.00
THC475 Buster Posey 2.50 6.00
THC476 Lucas Giolito 1.50 4.00
THC477 Julio Urias 2.00 5.00
THC478 Jameson Taillon 1.50 4.00
THC479 A.J. Reed 1.25 3.00
THC480 David Price 1.50 4.00
THC481 Willson Contreras 2.00 5.00
THC482 Albert Almora 1.25 3.00
THC483 Nomar Mazara 1.25 3.00
THC484 Michael Fulmer 1.25 3.00
THC485 Trea Turner 1.50 4.00
THC490 Josh Donaldson 1.50 4.00
THC492 Aledmys Diaz 1.50 4.00
THC499 Jake Arrieta 1.50 4.00
THC500 Kris Bryant 12.00 30.00
THC508 Christian Arroyo 2.00 5.00
THC513 Amir Garrett 1.25 3.00
THC517 Jesse Winker 1.25 3.00
THC529 Reynaldo Lopez 1.25 3.00
THC531 Andrew Toles 1.25 3.00
THC534 Brandon Phillips 1.25 3.00
THC537 Rob Zastryzny 1.25 3.00
THC538 Rob Segedin 1.25 3.00
THC550 Adalberto Mejia 1.25 3.00
THC556 Mauricio Cabrera 1.25 3.00
THC567 Joe Jimenez 1.25 3.00
THC568 Koda Glover 1.25 3.00
THC576 Bradley Zimmer 1.50 4.00
THC584 Bruce Maxwell 1.25 3.00
THC589 Drew Smyly 1.25 3.00
THC599 Renato Nunez 2.50 6.00
THC601 Blake Snell 1.50 4.00
THC613 Dan Vogelbach 2.00 5.00
THC617 Seth Lugo 1.25 3.00
THC622 Sal Romano 1.25 3.00
THC639 Jorge Alfaro 1.50 4.00
THC642 Jose De Leon 1.25 3.00
THC647 Matt Wieters 2.00 5.00
THC651 Jeff Hoffman 1.25 3.00
THC654 Teoscar Hernandez 4.00 10.00
THC659 Ty Blach 1.25 3.00
THC660 Ian Happ 2.50 6.00
THC664 Edwin Encarnacion 2.00 5.00
THC666 Kyle Freeland 1.50 4.00
THC676 Mitch Haniger 2.00 5.00
THC677 Brandon Nimmo 1.50 4.00
THC678 Cody Bellinger 25.00 60.00
THC681 Matt Olson 2.00 5.00
THC685 German Marquez 2.00 5.00
THC686 Aroldis Chapman 2.00 5.00
THC691 Jose Osuna 1.25 3.00
THC697 T.J. Rivera 2.00 5.00
THC706 Carlos Martinez 1.50 4.00
THC707 Steven Matz 1.50 4.00
THC708 Zack Wheeler 1.50 4.00
THC709 Michael Pineda 1.25 3.00
THC710 Luis Severino 1.50 4.00
THC712 Kenley Jansen 1.50 4.00
THC713 Dylan Bundy 1.50 4.00
THC715 Trevor Bauer 2.00 5.00
THC716 Pablo Sandoval 1.50 4.00
THC717 Shin-Soo Choo 1.50 4.00
THC719 Dallas Keuchel 1.50 4.00
THC720 Lance McCullers 1.25 3.00
THC721 Josh Reddick 1.25 3.00

2017 Topps Heritage Chrome Blue Refractors

*BLUE REF: 2X TO 5X BASIC
STATED ODDS 1:389 HOBBY
STATED ODDS 1:100 WM HANGER
STATED HN ODDS 1:339 HOBBY
STATED PRINT RUN 68 SER.#'d SETS
THC418 Miguel Cabrera 30.00 80.00
THC423 Kyle Schwarber 25.00 60.00
THC427 Bryce Harper 40.00 100.00
THC440 Corey Seager 50.00 120.00
THC444 Gary Sanchez 30.00 80.00
THC470 Noah Syndergaard 15.00 40.00
THC500 Kris Bryant 100.00 250.00

2017 Topps Heritage Clubhouse Collection Dual Relics

STATED ODDS 1:5045 HOBBY
STATED ODDS 1:3354 WM HANGER
STATED HN ODDS 1:2667 HOBBY
STATED PRINT RUN 68 SER.#'d SETS
CCDRBV J.Votto/J.Bench 30.00 80.00
CCDRCB Buxton/Carew HN 20.00 50.00
CCDRCM A.McCutchen/R.Clemente 60.00 150.00
CCDRMA J.Altuve/J.Morgan 25.00 60.00
CCDRMOC Correa/Morgan HN 25.00 60.00
CCDRMP McCvy/Posey HN 40.00 100.00
CCDRPV Votto/Perez HN 30.00 80.00
CCDRRM Mchdo/Rbnsn HN 30.00 80.00
CCDRRS N.Ryan/N.Syndergaard 60.00 150.00
CCDRYO C.Yastrzemski/D.Ortiz 50.00 125.00

2017 Topps Heritage Clubhouse Collection Relic Autographs

STATED ODDS 1:6764 HOBBY
STATED ODDS 1:4471 WM HANGER
STATED HN ODDS 1:3190 HOBBY
STATED PRINT RUN 25 SER.#'d SETS
EXCHANGE DEADLINE 1/31/2019
HN EXCH DEADLINE 7/31/2019
CCARAB Benintendi HN 125.00 300.00
CCARABR Bregman HN EXCH 100.00 250.00
CCARAJ Adam Jones HN/25 60.00 150.00
CCARAJU Judge HN 150.00 400.00
CCARARI Anthony Rizzo/25 150.00 250.00
CCARBH Bryce Harper/25 250.00 400.00
CCARCC Carlos Correa/25
CCARCK Corey Kluber HN/25 50.00 210.00
CCARCSE Corey Seager/25 75.00 200.00
CCARDJ Derek Jeter HN/5
CCARDP David Price EXCH/25 30.00 80.00
CCARDS Swanson HN EXCH 60.00 150.00
CCARFF Freddie Freeman HN/25 50.00 125.00
CCARFL Francisco Lindor HN/25 75.00 200.00
CCARJD Donaldson HN EXCH 40.00 100.00
CCARKB Kris Bryant/25 250.00 500.00
CCARMM Manny Machado/25 150.00 300.00
CCARMT Mike Trout/25 200.00 400.00
CCARNS Noah Syndergaard/25 75.00 200.00

2017 Topps Heritage Clubhouse Collection Relics

STATED ODDS 1:36 HOBBY
STATED ODDS 1:24 WM HANGER
STATED HN ODDS 1:47 HOBBY
*GOLD/99: .5X TO 1.2X BASIC
CCRABE Andrew Benintendi HN 5.00 12.00
CCRABR Alex Bregman HN 4.00 10.00
CCRAC Aroldis Chapman HN 3.00 8.00
CCRAG Adrian Gonzalez HN 2.50 6.00
CCRAG Adrian Gonzalez 2.50 6.00
CCRAJ Adam Jones HN 2.50 6.00
CCRAJU Aaron Judge HN 25.00 60.00
CCRAM Andrew McCutchen HN 3.00 8.00
CCRAM Andrew McCutchen 3.00 8.00
CCRAP Albert Pujols 4.00 10.00
CCRAR Anthony Rizzo 5.00 12.00
CCRAR Alex Reyes HN 3.00 8.00
CCRARI Anthony Rizzo HN 5.00 12.00
CCRARU Addison Russell 3.00 8.00
CCRAW Adam Wainwright 2.50 6.00
CCRBB Byron Buxton HN 2.50 6.00
CCRBH Billy Hamilton 2.50 6.00
CCRBHA Bryce Harper 5.00 12.00
CCRBP Brandon Phillips 2.00 5.00
CCRBP Buster Posey HN 4.00 10.00
CCRBPO Buster Posey 4.00 10.00
CCRBZ Ben Zobrist HN 2.50 6.00
CCRCC Carlos Correa 3.00 8.00
CCRCG Carlos Gonzalez 2.50 6.00
CCRCH Cole Hamels 2.50 6.00
CCRCK Clayton Kershaw 6.00 15.00
CCRCK Clayton Kershaw HN 6.00 15.00
CCRCKL Corey Kluber 2.50 6.00
CCRCS Chris Sale HN 3.00 8.00
CCRCSE Corey Seager HN 3.00 8.00
CCRCY Christian Yelich HN 4.00 10.00
CCRDB Dellin Betances 2.50 6.00
CCRDG Dee Gordon 2.00 5.00
CCRDJ Derek Jeter HN 30.00 80.00
CCRDM Daniel Murphy HN 2.50 6.00
CCRDO David Ortiz 3.00 8.00
CCRDP David Price 2.50 6.00
CCRDP Dustin Pedroia HN 4.00 10.00
CCRDS Dansby Swanson HN 5.00 12.00
CCRDW David Wright 2.50 6.00
CCREH Eric Hosmer 2.50 6.00
CCREL Evan Longoria 2.50 6.00
CCRFF Freddie Freeman 4.00 10.00
CCRFH Felix Hernandez 2.50 6.00
CCRFL Francisco Lindor HN 3.00 8.00
CCRGC Gerrit Cole 3.00 8.00
CCRGP Gregory Polanco HN 2.50 6.00
CCRGS Gary Sanchez HN 3.00 8.00
CCRGS George Springer 2.50 6.00
CCRGST Giancarlo Stanton 3.00 8.00
CCRHP Hunter Pence HN 2.50 6.00
CCRHR Hanley Ramirez 2.50 6.00
CCRIK Ian Kinsler 2.50 6.00
CCRI Ichiro 4.00 10.00
CCRI Ichiro HN 4.00 10.00
CCRJA Jake Arrieta HN 2.50 6.00
CCRJA Jose Abreu 3.00 8.00
CCRJAL Jose Altuve 2.50 6.00
CCRJB Javier Baez 4.00 10.00
CCRJB Jose Bautista HN 2.50 6.00
CCRJBR Jackie Bradley Jr. HN 3.00 8.00
CCRJD Jacob deGrom HN 3.00 8.00
CCRJDO Josh Donaldson HN 2.50 6.00
CCRJE Jacoby Ellsbury HN 2.50 6.00
CCRJH Jason Heyward HN 2.50 6.00
CCRJL Jon Lester 4.00 10.00
CCRJM Joe Mauer 2.50 6.00
CCRJM J.D. Martinez HN 3.00 8.00
CCRJP Joc Pederson 2.50 6.00
CCRJT Jameson Taillon HN 2.50 6.00
CCRJU Justin Upton 2.50 6.00
CCRJV Justin Verlander 3.00 8.00
CCRJV Justin Verlander HN 3.00 8.00
CCRJVO Joey Votto 3.00 8.00
CCRKB Kris Bryant 10.00 25.00
CCRKB Kris Bryant HN 10.00 25.00
CCRKM Kenta Maeda HN 2.50 6.00
CCRKS Kyle Seager 2.00 5.00
CCRMB Mookie Betts HN 5.00 12.00
CCRMC Miguel Cabrera HN 3.00 8.00
CCRMC Miguel Cabrera 3.00 8.00
CCRMCA Matt Carpenter HN 3.00 8.00
CCRMF Michael Fulmer HN 2.00 5.00
CCRMH Matt Harvey 2.50 6.00
CCRMM Manny Machado 4.00 10.00
CCRMM Manny Machado HN 4.00 10.00
CCRMS Miguel Sano 2.50 6.00
CCRMST Marcus Stroman HN 2.50 6.00
CCRMT Masahiro Tanaka HN 2.50 6.00
CCRMTR Mike Trout HN 15.00 40.00
CCRMTR Mike Trout 15.00 40.00
CCRNA Nolan Arenado 4.00 10.00
CCRNC Nelson Cruz 3.00 8.00
CCRNS Noah Syndergaard 4.00 10.00
CCRNS Noah Syndergaard HN 4.00 10.00
CCRPG Paul Goldschmidt 3.00 8.00
CCRRB Ryan Braun 2.50 6.00
CCRRC Robinson Cano 2.50 6.00
CCRRO Rougned Odor 2.50 6.00
CCRRP Rick Porcello 2.50 6.00
CCRSG Sonny Gray HN 2.50 6.00
CCRSM Starling Marte 2.50 6.00
CCRSP Salvador Perez 2.50 6.00
CCRSP Stephen Piscotty HN 2.50 6.00
CCRTG Tyler Glasnow HN 2.50 6.00
CCRTS Trevor Story HN 3.00 8.00
CCRTT Troy Tulowitzki HN 3.00 8.00
CCRTTU Trea Turner HN 2.50 6.00
CCRVM Victor Martinez 2.50 6.00
CCRWM Wil Myers 2.00 5.00
CCRXB Xander Bogaerts HN 3.00 8.00
CCRYC Yoenis Cespedes 3.00 8.00
CCRYG Yulieski Gurriel HN 3.00 8.00
CCRYM Yadier Molina 3.00 8.00
CCRZG Zack Greinke HN 2.50 6.00

2017 Topps Heritage Clubhouse Collection Triple Relics

STATED ODDS 1:13,852 HOBBY
STATED ODDS 1:9389 WM HANGER
STATED HN ODDS 1:6139 HOBBY
STATED PRINT RUN 25 SER.#'d SETS
CCTRBBR Rzzo/Brnks/Brnt HN 100.00 250.00
CCTRBMC Brock/Molina/Carpenter HN 30.00 80.00
CCTRCAM Morgan/Altuve/Correa 75.00 200.00
CCTRJHM Jcksn/Hndrsn/McGwre HN 50.00 120.00
CCTRMBA Bggo/Altve/Mrgn HN 75.00 200.00
CCTRMJF Frmn/Chppr/Mthws HN 100.00 250.00
CCTROYB Yaz/Ortiz/Betts HN 75.00 200.00
CCTROYG Ortiz/Nomar/Yaz 75.00 200.00
CCTRPMB Bmgrnr/Posey/McCvy 75.00 200.00
CCTRSRD deGrom/Ryan/Sndrgrd 75.00 200.00
CCTRVBP Bench/Votto/Perez 50.00 120.00

2017 Topps Heritage Combo Cards

COMPLETE SET (15) 25.00 60.00
STATED HN ODDS 1:20 HOBBY
CC1 A.Rizzo/K.Bryant 2.00 5.00
CC2 A.Judge/G.Sanchez 10.00 25.00
CC3 G.Springer/C.Correa 1.25 3.00
CC4 G.Stanton/M.Ozuna 1.25 3.00
CC5 R.Zimmerman/D.Murphy 1.00 2.50
CC6 D.Santana/E.Thames 1.00 2.50
CC7 J.Kipnis/F.Lindor 1.25 3.00
CC8 A.Benintendi/M.Betts 2.50 6.00
CC9 J.Turner/C.Bellinger 5.00 12.00
CC10 Y.Alonso/K.Davis 1.25 3.00
CC11 B.Hamilton/J.Votto 1.25 3.00
CC12 M.Sano/J.Mauer 1.00 2.50
CC13 P.Goldschmidt/J.Lamb 1.25 3.00
CC14 E.Hosmer/S.Perez 1.00 2.50
CC15 J.Abreu/A.Garcia 1.25 3.00

2017 Topps Heritage Discs

COMPLETE SET (30) 40.00 100.00
STATED ODDS 1:2 WM HANGER
68TDC1 David Price .75 2.00
68TDC2 Anthony Rizzo 1.50 4.00
68TDC3 Manny Machado 1.00 2.50
68TDC4 Corey Seager 1.00 2.50
68TDC5 Noah Syndergaard .75 2.00
68TDC6 Giancarlo Stanton 1.00 2.50
68TDC7 Nolan Arenado 1.25 3.00
68TDC8 Max Scherzer 1.00 2.50
68TDC9 Mookie Betts 1.50 4.00
68TDC10 Yoenis Cespedes 1.00 2.50
68TDC11 Felix Hernandez .75 2.00
68TDC12 Eric Hosmer .75 2.00
68TDC13 Robinson Cano .75 2.00
68TDC14 David Ortiz 1.00 2.50
68TDC15 Gary Sanchez 1.00 2.50
68TDC16 Joey Votto 1.00 2.50
68TDC17 Bryce Harper 1.50 4.00

68TDC18 Clayton Kershaw 2.00 5.00
68TDC19 Josh Donaldson .75 2.00
68TDC20 Buster Posey 1.25 3.00
68TDC21 Andrew McCutchen 1.00 2.50
68TDC22 Kris Bryant 1.25 3.00
68TDC23 Carlos Correa 1.00 2.50
68TDC24 Kyle Schwarber 1.00 2.50
68TDC25 Mike Trout 5.00 12.00
68TDC26 Miguel Cabrera 1.00 2.50
68TDC27 Jose Altuve .75 2.00
68TDC28 Trea Turner .75 2.00
68TDC29 Francisco Lindor 1.00 2.50
68TDC30 Justin Verlander 1.00 2.50

2017 Topps Heritage Flashback Relic Autographs

STATED ODDS 1:6764 HOBBY
STATED ODDS 1:4471 WM HANGER
STATED PRINT RUN 25 SER.#'d SETS
EXCHANGE DEADLINE 1/31/2019
FARAK Al Kaline 100.00 250.00
FARBR Brooks Robinson 100.00 250.00
FARCY Carl Yastrzemski 100.00 250.00
FARHA Hank Aaron EXCH 300.00 500.00
FARJB Johnny Bench 75.00 200.00
FARLB Lou Brock 60.00 150.00
FARNR Nolan Ryan 200.00 400.00
FARPN Phil Niekro 25.00 60.00
FARRC Rod Carew 75.00 200.00
FARRF Rollie Fingers 25.00 60.00
FARRJ Reggie Jackson 200.00 400.00
FARSC Steve Carlton 100.00 250.00

2017 Topps Heritage High Number Topps Game Rookies

1 Manny Margot 1.25 3.00
2 Hunter Dozier 1.25 3.00
3 Jose De Leon 1.25 3.00
4 Mitch Haniger 2.00 5.00
5 Jorge Alfaro 1.50 4.00
6 Trey Mancini 2.50 6.00
7 JaCoby Jones 1.50 4.00
8 Christian Arroyo 2.00 5.00
9 Cody Bellinger 20.00 50.00
10 Raimel Tapia 1.50 4.00
11 Reynaldo Lopez 1.25 3.00
12 Joe Musgrove 1.25 3.00
13 Andrew Toles 1.25 3.00
14 Gavin Cecchini 1.25 3.00
15 Jharel Cotton 1.25 3.00

2017 Topps Heritage New Age Performers

COMPLETE SET (25) 10.00 25.00
STATED ODDS 1:12 HOBBY
STATED ODDS 1:4 WM HANGER
NAP1 DJ LeMahieu .60 1.50
NAP2 Nolan Arenado .75 2.00
NAP3 Mookie Betts 1.00 2.50
NAP4 Jean Segura .40 1.00
NAP5 Mike Trout 3.00 8.00
NAP6 Corey Seager .60 1.50
NAP7 Kenta Maeda .50 1.25
NAP8 Manny Machado .60 1.50
NAP9 Jose Altuve .50 1.25
NAP10 Carlos Correa .60 1.50
NAP11 Francisco Lindor .60 1.50
NAP12 Kris Bryant .75 2.00
NAP13 Anthony Rizzo 1.00 2.50
NAP14 Kyle Hendricks .60 1.50
NAP15 Christian Yelich .75 2.00
NAP16 Noah Syndergaard .50 1.25
NAP17 Danny Duffy .40 1.00
NAP18 Dellin Betances .50 1.25
NAP19 Gary Sanchez .60 1.50
NAP20 Orlando Arcia .50 1.25
NAP21 Michael Fulmer .40 1.00
NAP22 Starling Marte .50 1.25
NAP23 Blake Snell .50 1.25
NAP24 Khris Davis .60 1.50
NAP25 Wil Myers .40 1.00

2017 Topps Heritage News Flashbacks

COMPLETE SET (15) 6.00 15.00
STATED ODDS 1:20 HOBBY
STATED ODDS 1:7 WM HANGER
NF1 Vietnam War .40 1.00
NF2 MLK Assassination .40 1.00
NF3 Kennedy Assassination .40 1.00
NF4 President Johnson .40 1.00
NF5 60 Minutes .40 1.00
NF6 Apollo 8 .40 1.00
NF7 1968 Summer Games .40 1.00
NF8 Special Olympics Founded .40 1.00
NF9 2001: A Space Odyssey .40 1.00
NF10 The Beatles .60 1.50
NF11 First U.S. Heart Transplant .40 1.00
NF12 Civil Rights Act of 1968 .40 1.00
NF13 Ivy League Schools
Start going co-ed .40 1.00
NF14 Computer Mouse Invented .40 1.00
NF15 Arthur Ashe .40 1.00

2017 Topps Heritage Postal Stamps

STATED ODDS 1:1715 HOBBY
STATED ODDS 1:1145 WN HANGER
STATED PRINT RUN 50 SER.#'d SETS
68PSRBM Bill Mazeroski 20.00 50.00
68PSRBR Brooks Robinson 20.00 50.00
68PSRBW Billy Williams 15.00 40.00
68PSRCH Catfish Hunter 20.00 50.00
68PSRCY Carl Yastrzemski 30.00 80.00
68PSRFJ Fergie Jenkins 20.00 50.00
68PSRFR Frank Robinson 20.00 50.00
68PSRHA Hank Aaron 25.00 60.00
68PSRHK Harmon Killebrew 25.00 60.00
68PSRJB Johnny Bench 30.00 80.00
68PSRJM Joe Morgan 20.00 50.00
68PSRLA Luis Aparicio 20.00 50.00
68PSRLB Lou Brock 20.00 50.00
68PSRNR Nolan Ryan 80.00 200.00
68PSROC Orlando Cepeda 20.00 50.00
68PSRRC Rod Carew 20.00 50.00
68PSRRJ Reggie Jackson 20.00 50.00
68PSRTP Tony Perez 20.00 50.00
68PSRWM Willie McCovey 20.00 50.00
68PSRWS Willie Stargell 20.00 50.00

2017 Topps Heritage Real One Autographs

STATED ODDS 1:173 HOBBY
STATED ODDS 1:112 WM HANGER
STATED HN ODDS 106 HOBBY
EXCHANGE DEADLINE 1/31/2019
HN EXCH DEADLINE 7/31/2019
ROAAB Adrian Beltre HN 40.00 100.00
ROAABE Andrew Benintendi HN 60.00 150.00
ROAABE Andrew Benintendi 150.00 300.00
ROAABR Alex Bregman 50.00 120.00
ROAABR Alex Bregman HN 40.00 100.00
ROAAD Aledmys Diaz HN 10.00 25.00
ROAAG Amir Garrett HN 5.00 12.00
ROAAJ Aaron Judge 600.00 800.00
ROAAK Al Kaline 75.00 200.00
ROAARE Alex Reyes 12.00 30.00
ROAARI Anthony Rizzo
Signed in red ink
ROAAT Andrew Toles HN 5.00 12.00
ROAAW Al Worthington 10.00 25.00
ROABB Bill Bryan 8.00 20.00
ROABB Byron Buxton HN 25.00 60.00
ROABD Bill Denehy 8.00 20.00
ROABH Bryce Harper 75.00 200.00
ROABLE Bob Lee 10.00 25.00
ROABLO Bobby Locke 8.00 20.00
ROABR Brooks Robinson 50.00 120.00
ROABSA Bob Saverine 8.00 20.00
ROABSH Braden Shipley 10.00 25.00
ROABZ Bradley Zimmer HN 6.00 15.00
ROACA Christian Arroyo HN 15.00 40.00
ROACB Cody Bellinger HN 150.00 400.00
ROACC Carlos Correa 60.00 150.00
ROACFU Carson Fulmer 8.00 20.00
ROACJ Clarence Jones 8.00 20.00
ROACKL Corey Kluber HN 30.00 80.00
ROACS Chris Sale HN 40.00 100.00
ROACSE Corey Seager HN 75.00 200.00
ROACSE Corey Seager 75.00 200.00
ROACY Carl Yastrzemski HN
ROADD David Dahl 10.00 30.00
ROADJ Derek Jeter EXCH 600.00 900.00
ROADJ Derek Jeter HN
ROADN Dick Nen 8.00 20.00
ROADSW Dansby Swanson 60.00 150.00
ROADSW Dansby Swanson HN 30.00 80.00
ROADV Dan Vogelbach HN 8.00 20.00
ROAFB Franklin Barreto HN 5.00 12.00
ROAFF Freddie Freeman HN 25.00 60.00
ROAFL Francisco Lindor 25.00 60.00
ROAFRO Frank Robinson 40.00 100.00
ROAFV Fred Valentine 8.00 20.00
ROAGC Gavin Cecchini HN 5.00 12.00
ROAGM German Marquez HN 8.00 20.00
ROAGR Garry Roggenburk 8.00 20.00
ROAGS George Springer 10.00 25.00
ROAHA Hank Aaron HN
ROAHD Hunter Dozier HN 8.00 20.00
ROAHR Hunter Renfroe 20.00 50.00
ROAIH Ian Happ HN 50.00 120.00
ROAJA Jorge Alfaro HN 10.00 25.00
ROAJAL Jose Altuve HN 60.00 150.00
ROAJB Javier Baez HN 40.00 100.00
ROAJBE Johnny Bench 150.00 300.00
ROAJBO Jim Bouton 10.00 25.00
ROAJBU Jerry Buchek 8.00 20.00
ROAJC Jharel Cotton HN 5.00 12.00
ROAJD Jose De Leon HN 8.00 20.00
ROAJD Jacob deGrom 25.00 60.00
ROAJDE Jose De Leon 10.00 25.00
ROAJDO Josh Donaldson HN 30.00 80.00
ROAJHO Jeff Hoffman HN 5.00 12.00
ROAJJ Joe Jimenez HN 5.00 12.00
ROAJJO JaCoby Jones HN 6.00 15.00
ROAJM Joe Musgrove 8.00 20.00
ROAJS Jimmie Schaffer 8.00 20.00
ROAJT Jake Thompson 8.00 20.00
ROAJV Joey Votto HN 40.00 100.00
ROAJW Jesse Winker HN 10.00 25.00
ROAKB Kris Bryant HN 30.00 400.00
ROAKB Kris Bryant 300.00 600.00
ROAKM Kenta Maeda HN 12.00 30.00
ROALB Lewis Brinson HN 15.00 40.00
ROALBR Lou Brock 25.00 60.00
ROALG Lucas Giolito 10.00 25.00
ROALT Lee Thomas 8.00 20.00
ROALW Luke Weaver HN 6.00 15.00
ROAMF Michael Fulmer HN 15.00 40.00
ROAMM Manny Machado HN 150.00 300.00
ROAMMA Manny Margot HN 8.00 20.00
ROAMO Matt Olson HN 25.00 60.00
ROAMS Miguel Sano 12.00 30.00
ROAMT Mike Trout 250.00 400.00
ROAMT Mike Trout HN 300.00 500.00
ROANR Nolan Ryan 200.00 400.00
ROANS Noah Syndergaard 25.00 60.00
ROAOC Orlando Cepeda 15.00 40.00
ROAPC Pete Cimino 8.00 20.00
ROAPG Paul Goldschmidt HN 15.00 40.00
ROAPN Phil Niekro 15.00 40.00
ROARCA Rod Carew 75.00 200.00
ROARH Ryon Healy HN 6.00 15.00
ROARJ Reggie Jackson 150.00 300.00
ROARL Rene Lachemann 8.00 20.00
ROARL Reynaldo Lopez HN 8.00 20.00
ROART Raimel Tapia HN 6.00 15.00
ROASC Steve Carlton 25.00 60.00
ROASK Sandy Koufax HN
ROASN Sean Newcomb HN 6.00 15.00
ROASP Stephen Piscotty HN 10.00 25.00
ROATA Tyler Austin HN 10.00 25.00
ROATB Ty Blach HN 6.00 15.00
ROATG Tyler Glasnow 12.00 30.00
ROATM Trey Mancini HN 20.00 50.00
ROATST Trevor Story 8.00 20.00
ROAYG Yulieski Gurriel HN 12.00 30.00
ROAYM Yoan Moncada HN 75.00 200.00
ROAYM Yoan Moncada 150.00 300.00

2017 Topps Heritage Real One Autographs Red Ink

*RED INK: .6X TO 1.5X BASIC
*RED INK HN: 1X TO 2.5X BASIC
STATED ODDS 1:488 HOBBY
STATED ODDS 1:326 WM HANGER
STATED HN ODDS 1:269 HOBBY
PRINT RUNS B/WN 25-68 COPIES PER
EXCHANGE DEADLINE 1/31/2019
HN EXCH DEADLINE 7/31/2019
ROAAB Adrian Beltre HN 60.00 150.00
ROAABE Andrew Benintendi HN 250.00 400.00
Signed in gold ink
ROAABE Andrew Benintendi/68 300.00 600.00
ROAABR Alex Bregman/68 100.00 250.00
ROAABR Alex Bregman HN 60.00 150.00
ROAAD Aledmys Diaz HN 15.00 40.00
ROAAJ Aaron Judge/68 3000.00 5000.00
ROABB Byron Buxton HN 40.00 100.00
ROACB Cody Bellinger HN 800.00 1200.00
ROACS Chris Sale HN 60.00 150.00
ROACSE Corey Seager HN 125.00 300.00
ROACY Carl Yastrzemski/25 HN 200.00 400.00
ROADSW Dansby Swanson HN 50.00 120.00
ROADSW Dansby Swanson/68 200.00 400.00
ROAFB Franklin Barreto HN 12.00 30.00
ROAGC Gavin Cecchini HN 12.00 30.00
ROAIH Ian Happ HN 75.00 200.00
ROAJA Jorge Alfaro HN 30.00 80.00
ROAJAL Jose Altuve HN 75.00 200.00
ROAJB Javier Baez HN 60.00 150.00
ROAJBE Johnny Bench/25 300.00 500.00
ROAJDO Josh Donaldson/25 HN 50.00 120.00
ROAKB Kris Bryant/25 HN 800.00 1200.00
ROAKB Kris Bryant/25 1000.00 1500.00
ROAKM Kenta Maeda HN 20.00 50.00
ROAMF Michael Fulmer HN 25.00 60.00
ROAMM Manny Machado/25 HN 200.00 400.00
ROAMT Mike Trout/25 HN 800.00 1200.00
ROAMT Mike Trout/25 500.00 800.00
ROANR Nolan Ryan/25 500.00 800.00
ROANS Noah Syndergaard/68 50.00 120.00
ROASC Steve Carlton/68 75.00 200.00
ROASN Sean Newcomb HN 15.00 40.00
ROASP Stephen Piscotty HN 15.00 40.00
ROATA Tyler Austin HN 20.00 50.00

2017 Topps Heritage Real One Autographs Dual

STATED ODDS 1:3592 HOBBY
STATED HN ODDS 1:2624 HOBBY
STATED PRINT RUN 25 SER.#'d SETS
EXCHANGE DEADLINE 1/31/2019
HN EXCH DEADLINE 7/31/2019
RODAJ Jeter/Aaron HN EX
RODABC Brck/Critn HN EX 75.00 200.00
RODACB Brgmn/Crra HN EX 125.00 300.00
RODACB Brock/Cepeda 100.00 250.00
RODADR Ryan/deGrom EXCH 200.00 400.00
RODAFS Swnsn/Frmn HN EX 60.00 150.00
RODAGF Gray/Fingers EXCH 75.00 200.00
RODAKS Seager/Kershaw HN 400.00 600.00
RODAMR Robinson/Machado 100.00 250.00
RODAMRO F.Rob/Machado 100.00 250.00
RODAMY Yaz/Moncada 200.00 400.00
RODAPB Pdra/Bnntndi HN EX 100.00 250.00
RODARB Ryan/Bench 800.00 1300.00
RODARC Carlton/Reyes 100.00 250.00
RODARJ Jones/Robinson HN 125.00 300.00
RODARK Kershaw/Ryan HN EX
RODARP Plmr/Rbnsn HN EX 125.00 300.00
RODARR Rbnsn/RpknHN EX 125.00 300.00
RODASC Sano/Carew 100.00 250.00
RODASR Ryan/Sndrgrd 100.00 250.00
RODATM Thms/Mncda HN 150.00 400.00
RODAYF Fisk/Yaz HN 150.00 400.00

2017 Topps Heritage Then and Now

COMPLETE SET (15) 10.00 25.00
STATED ODDS 1:20 HOBBY
STATED ODDS 1:7 WM HANGER
TAN1 M.Trumbo/F.Howard .40 1.00
TAN2 N.Arenado/F.Howard .75 2.00
TAN3 D.LeMahieu/C.Yastrzemski 1.00 2.50
TAN4 J.Villar/L.Brock .50 1.25
TAN5 M.Trout/C.Yastrzemski 3.00 8.00
TAN6 K.Hendricks/F.Jenkins .60 1.50
TAN7 F.Jenkins/M.Scherzer .60 1.50
TAN8 R.Porcello/J.Marichal .50 1.25
TAN9 D.Price/J.Marichal .50 1.25
TAN10 C.Kershaw/J.Marichal 1.25 3.00
TAN11 C.Yastrzemski/J.Altuve 1.00 2.50
TAN12 F.Howard/E.Encarnacion .60 1.50
TAN13 L.Brock/R.Davis .50 1.25
TAN14 M.Scherzer/J.Marichal .60 1.50
TAN15 J.Verlander/F.Jenkins .60 1.50

2017 Topps Heritage Topps Game

COMPLETE SET (30) 25.00 60.00
STATED ODDS 1:10 HOBBY
STATED ODDS 1:4 WM HANGER
1 Max Scherzer .60 1.50
2 Jose Altuve .50 1.25
3 Clayton Kershaw 1.25 3.00
4 Mike Trout 3.00 8.00
5 Kris Bryant .75 2.00
6 Bryce Harper 1.00 2.50
7 Buster Posey .75 2.00
8 Anthony Rizzo 1.00 2.50
9 Manny Machado .60 1.50
10 Carlos Correa .60 1.50
11 Corey Seager .60 1.50
12 Jake Arrieta .50 1.25
13 Madison Bumgarner .50 1.25
14 Noah Syndergaard .50 1.25
15 Josh Donaldson .50 1.25
16 Giancarlo Stanton .60 1.50
17 Andrew McCutchen .60 1.50
18 Nolan Arenado .75 2.00
19 Mookie Betts 1.00 2.50
20 Yoenis Cespedes .60 1.50
21 Miguel Cabrera .60 1.50
22 Felix Hernandez .50 1.25
23 Eric Hosmer .50 1.25
24 Robinson Cano .50 1.25
25 David Ortiz .60 1.50
26 Gary Sanchez .60 1.50
27 Trea Turner .50 1.25
28 Aledmys Diaz .50 1.25
29 Addison Russell .60 1.50
30 Brian Dozier .60 1.50

2017 Topps Heritage Topps Game Rookies

1 Josh Bell 5.00 12.00
2 Tyler Glasnow 2.50 6.00
3 Orlando Arcia 3.00 8.00
4 Alex Bregman 5.00 12.00
5 David Dahl 2.50 6.00
6 Luke Weaver 2.50 6.00
7 Yulieski Gurriel 3.00 8.00
8 Andrew Benintendi 6.00 15.00
9 Yoan Moncada 5.00 12.00
10 Aaron Judge 25.00 60.00
11 Alex Reyes 2.50 6.00
12 Dansby Swanson 5.00 12.00
13 Hunter Renfroe 2.50 6.00
14 Jake Thompson 2.00 5.00
15 Ryon Healy 2.50 6.00

2018 Topps Heritage

SP ODDS 1:3 HOBBY
1 Altve/Hsmr/Rmrz/Grca LL .20 .50
2 Charlie Blackmon .25 .60
Justin Turner
Daniel Murphy LL
3 Judge/Cruz/Davis LL .60 1.50
4 Arndo/Stntn/Ozna LL .30 .75
5 Judge/Gallo/Davis LL .60 1.50
6 Bickmn/Arndo/Bllngr/Stntn LL .50 1.25
7 Kluber/Sale/Severino .25 .60
8 Schrzr/Strsbrg/Krshw LL .50 1.25
9 Jason Vargas .20 .50
Carlos Carrasco
Corey Kluber LL
10 Dvs/Krshw/Grnke LL .50 1.25
11 Archer/Sale/Kluber .25 .60
12 Robbie Ray .25 .60
Max Scherzer
Jacob deGrom LL
13 Domingo Santana .20 .50
14 Alex Mejia RC .30 .75
Sandy Alcantara RC
15 Chris Davis .15 .40
16 Ryder Jones RC .30 .75
Reyes Moronta RC
Miguel Gomez RC
17 Zach Davies .15 .40
18 Matt Carpenter .25 .60
19 Wilmer Flores .20 .50
20 Anthony Rizzo .40 1.00
21 Mitch Haniger .20 .50
22 Bryce Harper .40 1.00
23 Sean Manaea .15 .40
24 Charlie Blackmon .25 .60
25 Aaron Judge .60 1.50
26 Tommy Pham .15 .40
27 Jacoby Ellsbury .20 .50
28 Craig Kimbrel .20 .50
29 Andrelton Simmons .15 .40
30 Miguel Sano .20 .50
31 Dominic Smith RC .40 1.00
Amed Rosario RC
32 Steven Souza Jr. .20 .50
33 Gio Gonzalez .20 .50
34 Tommy Joseph .25 .60
35 Jose Altuve .20 .50
36 Chris Owings .15 .40
37 Adam Jones .20 .50
38 Fernando Rodney .15 .40
39 Ty Blach .15 .40
40 Miguel Cabrera .25 .60
41 Anthony Rendon .25 .60
42 David Wright .20 .50
43 Jon Lester .20 .50
44 Gregory Polanco .20 .50
45 Corey Seager .25 .60
46 Paul Goldschmidt .25 .60
47 Mike Trout 1.25 3.00
48 Joey Gallo .20 .50
49 Stephen Vogt .20 .50
50 Andrew McCutchen .25 .60
51 Brandon Crawford .20 .50
52 Bryce Harper .40 1.00
53 Dansby Swanson .25 .60
54 Blake Snell .20 .50
55 Aaron Sanchez .20 .50
56 Derek Fisher .15 .40
57 Mike Trout CL 1.25 3.00
58 Justin Verlander .25 .60
59 Albert Pujols .30 .75
60 Justin Upton .20 .50
61 Bradley Zimmer .15 .40
62 Eric Thames .20 .50
63 Ian Happ .20 .50
64 Johnny Cueto .20 .50
65 DJ LeMahieu .25 .60
66 Sisco RC/Hays RC .50 1.25
67 Max Scherzer .25 .60
68 Mikie Mahtook .15 .40
69 James Paxton .20 .50
70 Joey Votto .25 .60
71 Eric Hosmer .20 .50
72 Jacob deGrom .25 .60
73 Max Kepler .20 .50
74 Giancarlo Stanton .25 .60
75 Jonathan Schoop .15 .40
76 Greg Holland .15 .40
77 Brian McCann .20 .50
78 Jose Altuve .20 .50
79 Anthony Banda RC .30 .75
Jimmie Sherfy RC
80 Kris Bryant .30 .75
81 Luiz Gohara RC 1.25 3.00
Max Fried RC
82 Yonder Alonso .15 .40
83 Dexter Fowler .20 .50
84 Mike Clevinger .20 .50
85 Mike Zunino .15 .40
86 Gradewine RC/Calhoun RC .40 1.00
87 Starlin Castro .15 .40
88 Corey Dickerson .15 .40
89 Adam Duvall .25 .60
90 Noah Syndergaard .20 .50
91 Josh Donaldson .20 .50
92 Stephen Strasburg .25 .60
93 Mike Moustakas .20 .50
94 Kenta Maeda .20 .50
95 Kevin Gausman .15 .40
96 Jonathan Lucroy .20 .50
97 Jose Abreu .25 .60
98 Troy Tulowitzki .25 .60
99 Jorge RC/Granite RC .30 .75
100 Felix Hernandez .20 .50
101 Salvador Perez .20 .50
102 Edwin Diaz .20 .50
103 Justin Upton .20 .50
104 Trea Turner .20 .50
105 Josh Harrison .15 .40
106 Rizzo/Bryant .40 1.00
107 Kris Bryant CL .30 .75
108 Billy Hamilton .20 .50
109 Chris Sale .25 .60
110 Rougned Odor .20 .50
111 Michael Pineda .15 .40
112 Nolan Arenado .30 .75
113 Justin Bour .15 .40
114 Frazier RC/Andujar RC 1.25 3.00
115 Kendall Graveman .15 .40
116 Stephen Piscotty .15 .40
117 auchman RC/McMahon RC 1.50 4.00
118 Cody Bellinger .50 1.25
119 Alex Bregman .25 .60
120 Brad Peacock .15 .40
121 Kolten Wong .15 .40
122 Ian Desmond .15 .40
123 Carson Fulmer .15 .40
124 Kendrys Morales .15 .40
125 Nicholas Castellanos .25 .60
126 Jose Quintana .15 .40
127 Carlos Correa .25 .60
128 Ender Inciarte .15 .40
129 Randal Grichuk .15 .40
130 Andrew Benintendi .25 .60
131 Scott Schebler .15 .40
132 Maikel Franco .20 .50
133 Rick Porcello .20 .50
134 Kevin Kiermaier .20 .50
135 Raudy Read RC .30 .75
Erick Fedde RC
136 Bader RC/Flaherty RC .50 1.25
137 Martin Prado .15 .40
138 Aaron Hicks .20 .50
139 Jose Bautista .20 .50
140 Aroldis Chapman .25 .60
141 Johan Camargo .15 .40
142 Danny Duffy .15 .40
143 A.J. Pollock .15 .40
144 Travis d'Arnaud .20 .50
145 Francisco Lindor .25 .60
146 Hanley Ramirez .20 .50
147 Jharel Cotton .15 .40
148 Carlos Beltran .20 .50
149 Andrew Cashner .15 .40
150 Josh Hader .15 .40
151 Manny Machado .25 .60
152 Tim Anderson .25 .60
153 Elvis Andrus .20 .50
154 Devon Travis .15 .40
155 Orlando Arcia .15 .40
156 Jordy Mercer .15 .40
157 Cody Allen .15 .40
158 Joe Mauer .20 .50
159 Jay Bruce .20 .50
160 O'Koyea Dickson RC .30 .75
Kyle Farmer RC
Tim Locastro RC
161 Yu Darvish .25 .60
162 Kershaw WS HL .50 1.25
163 George Springer WS HL .20 .50
Game 2
164 Lance McCullers .15 .40
Brad Peacock WS HL
Game 3
165 Bellinger WS HL .50 1.25
166 Alex Bregman WS HL .25 .60
Game 5
167 Joc Pederson WS HL .20 .50
Game 6
168 George Springer WS HL .20 .50
Game 7
169 Astros Celebration WS HL .15 .40
170 Marcell Ozuna .25 .60
171 Javier Baez .30 .75
172 Jean Segura .15 .40
173 Nicky Delmonico RC .30 .75
Aaron Bummer RC
174 Welington Castillo .15 .40
175 Gerrit Cole .25 .60
176 Corey Kluber .20 .50
177 Sonny Gray .20 .50
178 Archie Bradley .15 .40
179 Gary Sanchez .25 .60
180 Jordan Montgomery .25 .60
181 Mark Reynolds .15 .40
182 Mookie Betts .40 1.00
183 Sanchez/Judge .60 1.50
184 Hector Neris .15 .40
185 Starling Marte .20 .50
186 Guillermo Heredia .15 .40
187 Joey Votto .25 .60
188 Aaron Nola .20 .50
189 Martin RC/Devers RC 1.00 2.50
190 Dinelson Lamet .15 .40
191 Gary Sanchez .25 .60
192 Tanner Roark .15 .40
193 Taijuan Walker .15 .40
194 Roberto Osuna .15 .40
195 Adam Wainwright .20 .50
196 Evan Gattis .15 .40
197 Jeff Samardzija .15 .40
198 Hunter Renfroe .15 .40
199 Jason Kipnis .20 .50
200 Pat Neshek .15 .40
201 Yoan Moncada .25 .60
202 Dallas Keuchel .20 .50
203 Carlos Asuaje .15 .40
204 Travis Shaw .15 .40
205 Cameron Maybin .15 .40
206 Hoskins RC/Williams RC 1.25 3.00
207 Jorge Polanco .15 .40
208 Yuli Gurriel .20 .50
209 Dee Gordon .15 .40
210 Jesse Winker .15 .40
211 Brandon Nimmo .20 .50
212 Didi Gregorius .20 .50
213 Ervin Santana .15 .40
214 Carlos Correa CL .25 .60
215 Brett Gardner .20 .50
216 Clayton Kershaw .50 1.25
217 A.J. Ramos .15 .40
218 Masahiro Tanaka .20 .50
219 Freddie Freeman .30 .75
220 Carlos Carrasco .15 .40
221 Yoenis Cespedes .25 .60
222 Steve Pearce .25 .60
223 Caleb Joseph .15 .40
224 Parker Bridwell RC .30 .75
Troy Scribner RC
225 Sean Newcomb .20 .50
226 Giancarlo Stanton .25 .60
227 Delino DeShields .15 .40
228 Wilson Ramos .15 .40
229 Matt Holliday .25 .60
230 Ryan Zimmerman .20 .50
231 Kole Calhoun .15 .40
232 Yadier Molina .25 .60
233 Kyle Seager .15 .40
234 Zack Greinke .20 .50
235 Buster Posey .30 .75
236 Joc Pederson .20 .50
237 Chris Rusin .15 .40
238 Corey Kluber .20 .50
239 Mike Foltynewicz .15 .40
240 Justin Smoak .15 .40
241 Addison Russell .20 .50
242 Jimmy Nelson .15 .40
243 Keon Broxton .15 .40
244 Francisco Mejia RC .40 1.00
Greg Allen RC
245 C.J. Cron .15 .40
246 Jose Reyes UER .20 .50
Missing career stats
247 Willson Contreras .25 .60
248 CC Sabathia .20 .50
249 Marcus Stroman .20 .50
250 Trey Mancini .20 .50
251 Matt Kemp .20 .50
252 Matt Davidson .20 .50
253 Luke Weaver .20 .50
254 Joe Panik .20 .50
255 Adam Eaton .25 .60
256 Clayton Kershaw .50 1.25
257 Hunter Pence .20 .50
258 Tyler Glasnow .15 .40
259 Brandon McCarthy .15 .40
260 Khris Davis .25 .60
261 Kyle Barraclough .15 .40
262 Eddie Rosario .25 .60
263 Alex Wood .15 .40
264 Carl Edwards Jr. .15 .40
265 Carlos Martinez .20 .50
266 Buehler RC/Verdugo RC 1.50 4.00
267 Trevor Bauer .25 .60
268 Kyle Schwarber .25 .60
269 Ken Giles .15 .40
270 Matt Adams .15 .40
271 Christian Vazquez .15 .40
272 Matt Moore .20 .50
273 Crwfrd RC/Arano RC/Rios RC .30 .75
274 Jon Gray .15 .40
275 Mike Trout 1.25 3.00
276 Trevor Story .25 .60
277 Russell Martin .15 .40
278 Aaron Judge .60 1.50
279 Jose Peraza .20 .50
280 Raisel Iglesias .20 .50
281 Cory Spangenberg .15 .40
282 Francisco Cervelli .15 .40
283 Brett Phillips .15 .40
284 Robles RC/Stevenson RC .75 2.00
285 Ian Kinsler .20 .50
286 Chris Archer .15 .40
287 Andrew Miller .20 .50
288 Jake Arrieta .20 .50
289 Dellin Betances .20 .50
290 Jose Berrios .20 .50
291 Jose Ramirez .20 .50
292 Manny Machado .25 .60
293 Buster Posey .30 .75
294 J.D. Martinez .25 .60
295 Corey Seager .25 .60
296 Reynaldo Lopez .20 .50
297 Taylor Davis RC .30 .75
Dillon Maples RC
Jen-Ho Tseng RC
298 Cody Bellinger .50 1.25
299 Andrew Heaney .15 .40
300 Ichiro .30 .75
301 Robinson Cano .20 .50
302 Matt Olson .15 .40
303 Luis Severino .20 .50
304 Christian Villanueva RC .30 .75
Kyle McGrath RC
305 Josh Bell .20 .50
306 Odubel Herrera .20 .50
307 David Robertson .15 .40
308 James Shields .15 .40
309 Charlie Morton .25 .60
310 Kyle Freeland .20 .50
311 Jed Lowrie .15 .40
312 Justin Turner .20 .50
313 Corey Knebel .15 .40
314 Cody Bellinger CL .50 1.25
315 Sean Doolittle .15 .40
316 Chad Green .15 .40
317 Taylor Rogers RC .40 1.00
318 Lance McCullers .15 .40
319 Brandon Belt .20 .50
320 Paul DeJong .25 .60
321 Tyler Wade RC .40 1.00
Garrett Cooper RC
322 Nelson Cruz .25 .60
323 Jack Reinheimer RC .40 1.00
Ildemaro Vargas RC
324 David Price .20 .50
325 Edwin Encarnacion .25 .60
326 Daniel Murphy .20 .50
327 Yasiel Puig .25 .60
328 Avisail Garcia .20 .50
329 Aaron Altherr .15 .40
330 Mookie Betts .40 1.00
331 Albies RC/Sims RC 1.00 2.50
332 Franklin Barreto .15 .40
333 Jedd Gyorko .15 .40
334 Zack Godley .15 .40
335 Nomar Mazara .15 .40
336 Howie Kendrick .15 .40
337 Byron Buxton .20 .50
338 Alex Colome .15 .40
339 Tyler Mahle RC .40 1.00
Jackson Stephens RC
340 Carlos Santana .20 .50
341 Christian Yelich .30 .75
342 Jacob Faria .15 .40
343 Martin Maldonado .15 .40
344 Manny Pina .15 .40
345 Robbie Ray .15 .40
346 Marcus Semien .15 .40
347 Dylan Bundy .20 .50
348 German Marquez .15 .40
349 Dustin Pedroia .25 .60
350 Yan Gomes .25 .60
351 Nolan Arenado .30 .75
352 Jorge Alfaro .15 .40
353 Pat Valaika .15 .40
354 Felipe Rivero .20 .50
355 Brandon Kintzler .15 .40
356 Brian Dozier .20 .50
357 Lucas Giolito .20 .50
358 Dustin Fowler RC .30 .75
Paul Blackburn RC
359 Wilmer Difo .15 .40
360 George Springer .20 .50
361 Aaron Judge CL .60 1.50
362 Kris Bryant .30 .75
363 Ian Kennedy .15 .40

Card	Low	High
364 Michael Conforto	.20	.50
365 Matt Chapman	.25	.60
366 Chris Taylor	.20	.50
367 Greg Bird	.20	.50
368 Jason Heyward	.20	.50
369 Paul Goldschmidt	.25	.60
370 Melky Cabrera	.15	.40
371 Brad Brach	.15	.40
372 Michael Taylor	.15	.40
373 Enrique Hernandez	.20	.50
374 Austin Hedges	.15	.40
375 Whit Merrifield	.25	.60
376 Manny Margot	.15	.40
377 Jose Abreu	.25	.60
378 Magneuris Sierra	.25	.60
379 Carlos Ramirez RC	.50	1.25
Chris Rowley RC		
Richard Urena RC		
380 Eric Sogard	.15	.40
381 Carlos Correa	.25	.60
382 Michael Fulmer	.15	.40
383 Jose de Leon	.15	.40
384 Jake Lamb	.20	.50
385 Michael Brantley	.20	.50
386 Alex Gordon	.20	.50
387 Wil Myers	.15	.40
388 J.T. Realmuto	.25	.60
389 Shelby Miller	.20	.50
390 Amir Garrett	.15	.40
391 Jackie Bradley Jr.	.25	.60
392 Jerad Eickhoff	.15	.40
393 Marco Estrada	.15	.40
394 Brandon Woodruff RC	.40	1.00
Aaron Wilkerson RC		
Taylor Williams RC		
395 Dillon Peters RC	.40	1.00
Brian Anderson RC		
396 Kevin Pillar	.15	.40
397 Evan Longoria	.20	.50
398 J.A. Happ	.20	.50
399 Bryce Harper CL	.40	1.00
400 Carlos Gomez	.15	.40
401 Scooter Gennett SP	1.50	4.00
402 Logan Morrison SP	1.25	3.00
403 Ben Zobrist SP	1.50	4.00
404 Drew Pomeranz SP	1.25	3.00
405 Xander Bogaerts SP	2.00	5.00
406 Ryan Braun SP	1.50	4.00
407 Lewis Brinson SP	1.25	3.00
408 Cole Hamels SP	1.50	4.00
409 Kelvin Herrera SP	1.25	3.00
410 Chad Kuhl SP	1.25	3.00
411 Albert Almora SP	1.50	4.00
412 Carlos Gonzalez SP	1.50	4.00
413 Todd Frazier SP	1.50	4.00
414 James McCann SP	1.50	4.00
415 Matt Wieters SP	2.00	5.00
416 Matt Harvey SP	1.50	4.00
417 Jason Vargas SP	1.25	3.00
418 Steven Matz SP	1.50	4.00
419 Brandon Drury SP	1.25	3.00
420 Martin Perez SP	1.50	4.00
421 Brandon Finnegan SP	1.25	3.00
422 Yolmer Sanchez SP	1.25	3.00
423 Kyle Hendricks SP	2.00	5.00
424 Kenley Jansen SP	1.50	4.00
425 Marwin Gonzalez SP	1.25	3.00
426 Rich Hill SP	1.25	3.00
427 Victor Martinez SP	1.50	4.00
428 Lorenzo Cain SP	1.25	3.00
429 Mike Leake SP	1.25	3.00
430 Wade Davis SP	1.25	3.00
431 Dan Straily SP	1.25	3.00
432 Chase Anderson SP	1.25	3.00
433 Hyun-Jin Ryu SP	1.50	4.00
434 Jeimer Candelario SP	1.50	4.00
435 Brad Ziegler SP	1.25	3.00
436 Carlos Rodon SP	1.50	4.00
437 Nick Pivetta SP	1.25	3.00
438 Matt Boyd SP	1.25	3.00
439 Lance Lynn SP	1.25	3.00
440 Seung-Hwan Oh SP	1.50	4.00
441 Zach Britton SP	1.25	3.00
442 Josh Reddick SP	1.25	3.00
443 Danny Salazar SP	1.50	4.00
444 Eugenio Suarez SP	1.50	4.00
445 Alcides Escobar SP	1.50	4.00
446 Michael Wacha SP	1.50	4.00
447 Zack Cozart SP	1.25	3.00
448 Jayson Werth SP	1.50	4.00
449 Ryon Healy SP	1.25	3.00
450 Christian Arroyo SP	1.25	3.00
451 Brad Hand SP	1.25	3.00
452 Garrett Richards SP	1.50	4.00
453 Ben Gamel SP	1.50	4.00
454 Shin-Soo Choo SP	1.50	4.00
455 Drew Smyly SP	1.25	3.00
456 Aledmys Diaz SP	1.50	4.00
457 Ivan Nova SP	1.50	4.00
458 Jonathan Villar SP	1.25	3.00
459 Jorge Bonifacio SP	1.25	3.00
460 Patrick Corbin SP	1.50	4.00
461 Jameson Taillon SP	1.50	4.00
462 Mike Napoli SP	1.25	3.00
463 Adrian Beltre SP	2.00	5.00
464 Alex Reyes SP	1.50	4.00
465 Kyle Gibson SP	1.50	4.00
466 Mark Trumbo SP	1.25	3.00
467 Julio Teheran SP	1.50	4.00
468 Alex Cobb SP	1.25	3.00
469 Julio Urias SP	2.00	5.00
470 Yasmani Grandal SP	1.25	3.00
471 Ricky Nolasco SP	1.25	3.00
472 Brandon Phillips SP	1.25	3.00
473 Matt Shoemaker SP	1.50	4.00
474 Yasmany Tomas SP	1.25	3.00
475 Kurt Suzuki SP	1.25	3.00
476 Nick Markakis SP	1.50	4.00
477 R.A. Dickey SP	1.50	4.00
478 Eduardo Rodriguez SP	1.25	3.00
479 Michael Lorenzen SP	1.25	3.00
480 Anthony DeSclafani SP	1.25	3.00
481 Lonnie Chisenhall SP	1.25	3.00
482 Josh Tomlin SP	1.25	3.00
483 Raimel Tapia SP	1.25	3.00
484 Antonio Senzatela SP	1.25	3.00
485 Tyler Anderson SP	1.25	3.00
486 Chad Bettis SP	1.25	3.00
487 Jose Iglesias SP	1.50	4.00
488 Jake Marisnick SP	1.25	3.00
489 Joe Musgrove SP	1.25	3.00
490 Adrian Gonzalez SP	1.50	4.00
491 Jose Urena SP	1.25	3.00
492 Edinson Volquez SP	1.25	3.00
493 Hernan Perez SP	1.25	3.00
494 Jeurys Familia SP	1.50	4.00
495 Bruce Maxwell SP	1.25	3.00
496 Vince Velasquez SP	1.25	3.00
497 David Freese SP	1.25	3.00
498 Yangervis Solarte SP	1.25	3.00
499 Luis Perdomo SP	1.25	3.00
500 Jose Pirela SP	1.25	3.00
501 Jordan Zimmermann	.20	.50
502 Juan Soto RC	6.00	15.00
503 Franchy Cordero	.15	.40
504 Ketel Marte	.20	.50
505 Mallex Smith	.15	.40
506 Braxton Lee RC	.30	.75
507 Jacob Barnes RC	.30	.75
508 Pedro Alvarez	.15	.40
509 Alex Blandino RC	.30	.75
510 Pablo Sandoval	.20	.50
511 Scott Kingery RC	.50	1.25
512 Yoshihisa Hirano RC	.50	1.25
513 Jaime Garcia	.15	.40
514 Matt Duffy	.15	.40
515 Hunter Strickland	.15	.40
516 Hector Velazquez	.25	.60
517 Jonathan Lucroy	.20	.50
518 John Axford	.15	.40
519 Eduardo Nunez	.15	.40
520 Tony Cingrani	.20	.50
521 Seth Lugo	.15	.40
522 Chris Iannetta	.15	.40
523 Danny Farquhar	.15	.40
524 Tyler Beede RC	.30	.75
525 Daniel Mengden	.15	.40
526 Steven Souza Jr.	.20	.50
527 Corey Dickerson	.15	.40
528 Matt Szczur	.20	.50
529 Mitch Garver RC	.30	.75
530 Trayce Thompson	.20	.50
531 Blake Swihart	.20	.50
532 J.D. Davis RC	.40	1.00
533 Trevor Cahill	.15	.40
534 Niko Goodrum RC	.50	1.25
535 Pedro Severino	.15	.40
536 Asdrubal Cabrera	.20	.50
537 Matt Adams	.15	.40
538 Eduardo Escobar	.15	.40
539 Jakob Junis	.15	.40
540 David Bote RC	.75	2.00
541 Freddy Peralta RC	.30	.75
542 Marco Gonzales	.15	.40
543 Ryan Yarbrough RC	.50	1.25
544 Fernando Rodney	.15	.40
545 Preston Tucker	.15	.40
546 Tommy La Stella	.15	.40
547 Clayton Richard	.15	.40
548 Dixon Machado	.15	.40
549 Jose Martinez	.15	.40
550 Leonys Martin	.15	.40
551 Tyler Clippard	.15	.40
552 Adeiny Hechavarria	.15	.40
553 Mark Melancon	.15	.40
554 Richard Bleier	.15	.40
555 Matt Moore	.20	.50
556 Mike Fiers	.15	.40
557 Trevor Williams	.15	.40
558 Jaime Schultz RC	.30	.75
559 Miles Mikolas RC	.40	1.00
560 P.J. Conlon RC	.30	.75
561 Ryan Flaherty	.15	.40
562 Joe Kelly	.15	.40
563 Garrett Cooper RC	.30	.75
564 Teoscar Hernandez	.25	.60
565 Dan Otero	.15	.40
566 Adam Ottavino	.15	.40
567 Craig Gentry	.15	.40
568 Austin Meadows RC	.50	1.25
569 Greg Holland	.15	.40
570 Adam Engel	.15	.40
571 Bryan Shaw	.15	.40
572 Tyler Skaggs	.15	.40
573 Max Stassi	.15	.40
574 Miguel Montero	.15	.40
575 Alen Hanson	.20	.50
576 Brandon Morrow	.15	.40
577 Jesse Biddle RC	.40	1.00
578 Victor Caratini RC	.40	1.00
579 Gift Ngoepe	.15	.40
580 Ronald Acuna Jr. RC	10.00	25.00
581 Sal Romano	.15	.40
582 Brian Johnson	.15	.40
583 Francisco Liriano	.15	.40
584 Jurickson Profar	.20	.50
585 Brian Goodwin	.15	.40
586 Mike Gerber RC	.30	.75
587 Brandon McCarthy	.15	.40
588 Lucas Duda	.20	.50
589 Rene Rivera	.15	.40
590 Dereck Rodriguez RC	.40	1.00
591 Kevin Plawecki	.15	.40
592 Yairo Munoz RC	.30	.75
593 Jaime Barria RC	.40	1.00
594 Harrison Musgrave RC	.30	.75
595 Freddy Galvis	.15	.40
596 Hector Rondon	.15	.40
597 Luis Valbuena	.15	.40
598 Jarrod Dyson	.15	.40
599 Tony Watson	.15	.40
600 Shohei Ohtani RC	2.00	5.00
601 Matt Albers	.15	.40
602 Cesar Hernandez	.15	.40
603 Gleyber Torres RC	3.00	8.00
604 Taylor Motter	.15	.40
605 Marcus Walden RC	.40	1.00
606 Bartolo Colon	.15	.40
607 Addison Reed	.15	.40
608 Jarlin Garcia	.15	.40
609 Keone Kela	.15	.40
610 C.J. Cron	.15	.40
611 Ronald Guzman RC	.30	.75
612 Tyler O'Neill RC	.50	1.25
613 Christian Arroyo	.15	.40
614 Will Smith	.25	.60
615 Matt Koch	.15	.40
616 Tim Beckham	.20	.50
617 Shane Greene	.15	.40
618 Denard Span	.15	.40
619 Austin Gomber RC	.40	1.00
620 Jordan Hicks RC	.60	1.50
621 Ross Stripling	.15	.40
622 Jake Odorizzi	.15	.40
623 Mark Canha	.15	.40
624 Nick Ahmed	.15	.40
625 Mitch Moreland	.15	.40
626 Rajai Davis	.15	.40
627 Colin Moran	.15	.40
628 Cameron Maybin	.15	.40
629 Andrew Suarez RC	.30	.75
630 Tyler Naquin	.15	.40
631 Robert Gsellman	.15	.40
632 Sergio Romo	.15	.40
633 Pat Neshek	.15	.40
634 Dylan Cozens RC	.30	.75
635 Austin Romine	.15	.40
636 JaCoby Jones	.20	.50
637 Joe Jimenez	.15	.40
638 Logan Forsythe	.15	.40
639 Anibal Sanchez	.15	.40
640 Anthony Santander RC	.30	.75
641 Andrew Romine	.15	.40
642 Ronald Torreyes	.15	.40
643 Willy Adames RC	.40	1.00
644 Joey Wendle	.15	.40
645 Tyson Ross	.15	.40
646 Dwight Smith Jr.	.15	.40
647 Caleb Smith	.15	.40
648 Austin Jackson	.15	.40
649 Tyler Chatwood	.15	.40
650 Tomas Nido RC	.30	.75
651 Nick Kingham RC	.30	.75
652 Seung-Hwan Oh	.20	.50
653 Steve Cishek	.15	.40
654 Brandon Drury	.15	.40
655 Joey Lucchesi RC	.30	.75
656 Jorge Soler	.25	.60
657 Mike Soroka RC	1.00	2.50
658 Jon Jay	.15	.40
659 Logan Morrison	.15	.40
660 Austin Barnes	.20	.50
661 Darren O'Day	.15	.40
662 Bud Norris	.15	.40
663 Billy McKinney RC	.40	1.00
664 Jeremy Jeffress	.15	.40
665 Chase Utley	.20	.50
666 Alex Avila	.20	.50
667 Jeremy Hellickson	.15	.40
668 Shane Carle RC	.40	1.00
669 A.J. Minter RC	.40	1.00
670 Yonny Chirinos RC	.30	.75
671 Carlos Gomez	.15	.40
672 Joe Musgrove	.15	.40
673 Blake Treinen	.15	.40
674 Isiah Kiner-Falefa RC	.30	.75
675 Colby Rasmus	.20	.50
676 Keynan Middleton	.30	.75
677 Jacob Nottingham RC	.30	.75
678 Drew Robinson	.15	.40
679 Carson Smith	.15	.40
680 Cheslor Cuthbert	.15	.40
681 Kelby Tomlinson	.15	.40
682 Lance Lynn	.15	.40
683 Andrew Cashner	.15	.40
684 Lourdes Gurriel Jr. RC	.60	1.50
685 Eric Lauer RC	.40	1.00
686 Mark Leiter	.20	.50
687 Roberto Perez	.15	.40
688 Fernando Romero RC	.30	.75
689 Wade Davis	.15	.40
690 Derek Holland	.15	.40
691 Brock Holt	.15	.40
692 Steven Brault	.15	.40
693 Daniel Palka RC	.30	.75
694 Tucker Barnhart	.15	.40
695 David Peralta	.15	.40
696 Tyler Austin	.25	.60
697 Brad Boxberger	.15	.40
698 Merandy Gonzalez RC	.30	.75
699 Miguel Rojas	.15	.40
700 Dan Vogelbach	.15	.40
701 Stephen Piscotty SP	1.25	3.00
702 Randal Grichuk SP	1.25	3.00
703 Jay Bruce SP	1.50	4.00
704 Yonder Alonso SP	1.25	3.00
705 Andrew McCutchen SP	2.00	5.00
706 Lorenzo Cain SP	1.25	3.00
707 Yu Darvish SP	2.00	5.00
708 Neil Walker SP	1.50	4.00
709 Eric Hosmer SP	1.50	4.00
710 J.D. Martinez SP	2.00	5.00
711 Carlos Santana SP	1.50	4.00
712 Eduardo Nunez SP	1.25	3.00
713 Matt Kemp SP	1.50	4.00
714 Anthony Banda SP	1.25	3.00
715 Gerrit Cole SP	2.00	5.00
716 Ichiro SP	2.50	6.00
717 Arodys Vizcaino SP	1.25	3.00
718 Todd Frazier SP	1.50	4.00
719 Curtis Granderson SP	1.50	4.00
720 Christian Yelich SP	2.50	6.00
721 Jake Arrieta SP	1.50	4.00
722 Lewis Brinson SP	1.25	3.00
723 Alex Cobb SP	1.25	3.00
724 Brandon Morrow SP	1.25	3.00
725 Evan Longoria SP	1.50	4.00

2018 Topps Heritage '69 Bazooka Ad Panel Boxloader

STATED ODDS 1:3 HOBBY BOXES

Card	Low	High
1 Carlos Correa	1.00	2.50
2 Mike Trout	5.00	12.00
3 Bryce Harper	1.50	4.00
4 Kris Bryant	1.25	3.00
5 Giancarlo Stanton	1.00	2.50
6 Manny Machado	1.00	2.50
7 Anthony Rizzo	1.50	4.00
8 Amed Rosario	.75	2.00
9 Aaron Judge	2.50	6.00
10 Clint Frazier	1.25	3.00
11 Cody Bellinger	2.00	5.00
12 Rhys Hoskins	2.50	6.00
13 Andrew Benintendi	1.00	2.50
14 Rafael Devers	2.00	5.00
15 Clayton Kershaw	2.00	5.00

2018 Topps Heritage '69 Bazooka All Time Greats

RANDOM INSERTS IN PACKS

Card	Low	High
69BG1 Adrian Beltre	6.00	15.00
69BG2 Albert Pujols	15.00	40.00
69BG3 Mike Trout	30.00	80.00
69BG4 Ichiro	10.00	25.00
69BG5 Miguel Cabrera	6.00	15.00
69BG6 Max Scherzer	6.00	15.00
69BG7 Joey Votto	6.00	15.00
69BG8 Clayton Kershaw	12.00	30.00
69BG9 Buster Posey	8.00	20.00
69BG10 Robinson Cano	5.00	12.00
69BG11 Yadier Molina	6.00	15.00
69BG12 Justin Verlander	6.00	15.00
69BG13 Felix Hernandez	5.00	12.00
69BG14 Bryce Harper	25.00	60.00
69BG15 Giancarlo Stanton	6.00	15.00
69BG16 Carl Yastrzemski	10.00	25.00
69BG17 Willie McCovey	10.00	25.00
69BG18 Orlando Cepeda	8.00	20.00
69BG19 Nolan Ryan	12.00	30.00
69BG20 Harmon Killebrew	10.00	25.00
69BG21 Bob Gibson	10.00	25.00
69BG22 Rollie Fingers	10.00	25.00
69BG23 Willie Stargell	10.00	25.00
69BG24 Reggie Jackson	10.00	25.00
69BG25 Roberto Clemente	12.00	30.00
69BG26 Tom Seaver	12.00	30.00
69BG27 Jim Palmer	10.00	25.00
69BG28 Brooks Robinson	12.00	30.00
69BG29 Steve Carlton	10.00	25.00
69BG30 Johnny Bench	15.00	40.00

2018 Topps Heritage '69 Collector Cards

RANDOM INSERTS IN PACKS

Card	Low	High
69CCAB Adrian Beltre HN	.75	2.00
69CCAJ Aaron Judge	2.00	5.00
69CCAM Andrew McCutchen HN	.75	2.00
69CCAR Anthony Rizzo	1.25	3.00
69CCARO Amed Rosario	.60	1.50
69CCBH Bryce Harper	1.25	3.00
69CCBP Buster Posey HN	1.25	3.00
69CCCB Cody Bellinger	1.50	4.00
69CCCC Carlos Correa HN	.75	2.00
69CCCK Clayton Kershaw HN	1.50	4.00
69CCCS Corey Seager HN	.75	2.00
69CCGS Giancarlo Stanton	.75	2.00
69CCGT Gleyber Torres HN	5.00	12.00
69CCI Ichiro HN	1.00	2.50
69CCJA Jose Altuve	.60	1.50
69CCJV Justin Verlander HN	.75	2.00
69CCJV Joey Votto	.75	2.00
69CCKB Kris Bryant	1.00	2.50
69CCMB Mookie Betts	1.25	3.00
69CCMM Manny Machado	.75	2.00
69CCMS Miguel Sano HN	.60	1.50
69CCMS Max Scherzer	.75	2.00
69CCMT Mike Trout	4.00	10.00
69CCNA Nolan Arenado HN	1.00	2.50
69CCNS Noah Syndergaard HN	.60	1.50
69CCOA Ozzie Albies HN	1.50	4.00
69CCPG Paul Goldschmidt HN	.75	2.00
69CCRD Rafael Devers	1.50	4.00
69CCRH Rhys Hoskins	2.00	5.00
69CCSO Shohei Ohtani HN	3.00	8.00

2018 Topps Heritage '69 Postal Stamps

STATED ODDS 1:3524 HOBBY
STATED PRINT RUN 50 SER.#'d SETS

Card	Low	High
69PSRAK Al Kaline	30.00	80.00
69PSRBR Brooks Robinson	30.00	80.00
69PSRBW Billy Williams	25.00	60.00
69PSRCH Catfish Hunter	30.00	80.00
69PSRFJ Fergie Jenkins	30.00	80.00
69PSRHA Hank Aaron	30.00	80.00
69PSRHK Harmon Killebrew	30.00	80.00
69PSRJB Johnny Bench	40.00	100.00
69PSRJM Joe Morgan	25.00	60.00
69PSRJP Jim Palmer	30.00	80.00
69PSRLB Lou Brock	30.00	80.00
69PSRNR Nolan Ryan	50.00	125.00
69PSROC Orlando Cepeda	25.00	60.00
69PSRRC Rod Carew	25.00	60.00
69PSRRJ Reggie Jackson	30.00	80.00
69PSRSC Steve Carlton		
69PSRTP Tony Perez	30.00	80.00
69PSRTS Tom Seaver	30.00	80.00
69PSRWM Willie McCovey	50.00	120.00
69PSRWS Willie Stargell	30.00	80.00

2018 Topps Heritage '69 Poster Boxloader

STATED ODDS 1:36 HOBBY BOXES
ANNCD PRINT RUN OF 50 COPIES EACH

Card	Low	High
69PA Angels	75.00	200.00
69PAB Braves	30.00	80.00
69PAD Diamondbacks	25.00	60.00
69PBO Orioles	30.00	80.00
69PBR Red Sox	50.00	120.00
69PCC Cubs	50.00	120.00
69PCI Indians	50.00	120.00
69PCR Reds	30.00	80.00
69PCW White Sox	30.00	80.00
69PDT Tigers	30.00	80.00
69PHA Astros	30.00	80.00
69PMB Brewers	30.00	80.00
69PMM Marlins	25.00	60.00
69PMT Twins	30.00	80.00
69POA A's	30.00	80.00
69PPP Phillies	40.00	100.00
69PSM Mariners	25.00	60.00
69PTR Rangers	30.00	80.00
69PWN Nationals	40.00	100.00
69PCOR Rockies	25.00	60.00
69PKCR Royals	30.00	80.00
69PLAD Dodgers	30.00	80.00
69PNYM Mets	40.00	100.00
69PNYY Yankees	40.00	100.00
69PPIP Pirates	25.00	60.00
69PSDP Padres	20.00	50.00
69PSFG Giants	30.00	80.00
69PSLC Cardinals	40.00	100.00
69PTBJ Blue Jays	20.00	50.00
69PTBR Rays	25.00	60.00

2018 Topps Heritage '69 Topps Decals

RANDOM INSERTS IN PACKS

Card	Low	High
1 Carlos Correa	1.25	3.00
2 Mike Trout	6.00	15.00
3 Bryce Harper	2.00	5.00
4 Kris Bryant	1.50	4.00
5 Giancarlo Stanton	1.25	3.00
6 Manny Machado	1.25	3.00
7 Anthony Rizzo	2.00	5.00
8 Amed Rosario	1.00	2.50
9 Aaron Judge	3.00	8.00
10 Clint Frazier	1.50	4.00
11 Cody Bellinger	2.50	6.00
12 Rhys Hoskins	3.00	8.00
13 Andrew Benintendi	1.25	3.00
14 Rafael Devers	2.50	6.00
15 Clayton Kershaw	2.50	6.00

2018 Topps Heritage '69 Topps Deckle Edge

Card	Low	High
COMPLETE SET (30)	30.00	80.00
STATED ODDS 1:10 HOBBY		
1 Mike Trout	5.00	12.00
2 Jose Altuve	.75	2.00
3 Carlos Correa	1.00	2.50
4 Aaron Judge	2.50	6.00
5 Francisco Lindor	1.00	2.50
6 Clayton Kershaw	2.00	5.00
7 Bryce Harper	1.50	4.00
8 Buster Posey	1.25	3.00
9 Cody Bellinger	2.00	5.00
10 Joey Votto	1.00	2.50
11 Ozzie Albies	2.00	5.00
12 Yadier Molina	1.00	2.50
13 Salvador Perez	.75	2.00
14 Mookie Betts	1.50	4.00
15 Gary Sanchez	1.00	2.50
16 Giancarlo Stanton	1.00	2.50
17 Andrew Benintendi	1.00	2.50
18 Kris Bryant	1.25	3.00
19 Anthony Rizzo	1.50	4.00
20 Manny Machado	1.00	2.50
21 Rafael Devers	2.00	5.00
22 Clint Frazier	1.25	3.00
23 Rhys Hoskins	2.50	6.00
24 Amed Rosario	.75	2.00
25 Victor Robles	1.50	4.00
26 Chris Sale	1.00	2.50
27 Nolan Arenado	1.25	3.00
28 Max Scherzer	1.00	2.50
29 Paul Goldschmidt	1.00	2.50
30 Corey Seager	1.00	2.50

2018 Topps Heritage 100th Anniversary

*100TH: 10X TO 25X BASIC
*100TH RC: 5X TO 12X BASIC RC
*100TH SP: 1.2X TO 3X BASIC SP
STATED ODDS 1:277 HOBBY
STATED HN ODDS 1:370 HOBBY
STATED PRINT RUN 25 SER.#'d SETS

Card	Low	High
22 Bryce Harper	25.00	60.00
25 Aaron Judge	100.00	250.00
502 Juan Soto	200.00	500.00
511 Scott Kingery	12.00	30.00
540 David Bote	25.00	60.00
580 Ronald Acuna Jr.	150.00	400.00
600 Shohei Ohtani	125.00	300.00
603 Gleyber Torres	100.00	250.00
716 Ichiro	12.00	30.00

2018 Topps Heritage Action Variations

STATED ODDS 1:35 HOBBY
STATED HN ODDS 1:24 HOBBY

Card	Low	High
17 Shohei Ohtani	125.00	300.00
20 Anthony Rizzo	6.00	15.00
22 Bryce Harper	10.00	20.00
25 Aaron Judge	25.00	60.00
31 Amed Rosario	10.00	25.00
35 Jose Altuve	3.00	8.00
45 Corey Seager	4.00	10.00
70 Joey Votto	4.00	10.00
80 Kris Bryant	5.00	12.00
114 Clint Frazier	5.00	12.00
118 Cody Bellinger	10.00	25.00
130 Andrew Benintendi	8.00	20.00
145 Francisco Lindor	4.00	10.00
151 Manny Machado	4.00	10.00
189 Rafael Devers	20.00	50.00
191 Gary Sanchez	4.00	10.00
206 Rhys Hoskins	15.00	40.00
216 Clayton Kershaw	8.00	20.00
275 Mike Trout	25.00	60.00
284 Victor Robles	12.00	30.00
293 Buster Posey	5.00	12.00
330 Mookie Betts	6.00	15.00
351 Nolan Arenado	5.00	12.00
369 Paul Goldschmidt	4.00	10.00
381 Carlos Correa	4.00	10.00
511 Scott Kingery	4.00	10.00
517 Jonathan Lucroy	3.00	8.00
549 Jose Martinez	2.50	6.00
580 Ronald Acuna Jr.	100.00	250.00
600 Shohei Ohtani	30.00	80.00
603 Gleyber Torres	50.00	120.00
606 Bartolo Colon	2.50	6.00
612 Tyler O'Neill	4.00	10.00
620 Jordan Hicks	5.00	12.00
636 JaCoby Jones	3.00	8.00
684 Lourdes Gurriel Jr.	5.00	12.00
696 Tyler Austin	4.00	10.00
701 Stephen Piscotty	2.50	6.00
705 Andrew McCutchen	4.00	10.00
706 Lorenzo Cain	2.50	6.00
707 Yu Darvish	4.00	10.00
709 Eric Hosmer	3.00	8.00
710 J.D. Martinez	4.00	10.00
711 Carlos Santana	3.00	8.00
713 Matt Kemp	3.00	8.00
715 Gerrit Cole	4.00	10.00
716 Ichiro	5.00	12.00
718 Todd Frazier	3.00	8.00
720 Christian Yelich	5.00	12.00
721 Jake Arrieta	3.00	8.00

2018 Topps Heritage Black Border

*BLACK: 8X TO 20X BASIC
*BLACK RC: 4X TO 10X BASIC RC
*BLACK SP: 1X TO 2.5X BASIC SP
STATED ODDS 1:52 HOBBY
STATED HN ODDS 1:77 HOBBY
ANNCD PRINT RUN OF 50 COPIES EACH

Card	Low	High
22 Bryce Harper	20.00	50.00
25 Aaron Judge	75.00	200.00
502 Juan Soto	150.00	400.00
540 David Bote	20.00	50.00
580 Ronald Acuna Jr.	200.00	500.00
600 Shohei Ohtani	100.00	250.00
603 Gleyber Torres	75.00	200.00
716 Ichiro	10.00	25.00

2018 Topps Heritage Error Variations

RANDOM INSERTS IN PACKS
STATED HN ODDS 1:1663 HOBBY

Card	Low	High
22 Harper Birth year	60.00	150.00
25 Judge Name clr	75.00	200.00
74 Stanton Rev Neg	60.00	150.00
80 Bryant Name clr	75.00	200.00
275 Trout Bat Boy	60.00	150.00
580 AcunaBlue lst nme	125.00	300.00
600 Ohtani Red lst nme	125.00	300.00
603 Torres Blue lst nme	50.00	120.00
705 McCtchn Cubs back	30.00	80.00
716 Ichiro Rvrse neg	30.00	80.00

2018 Topps Heritage Mini

STATED ODDS 1:262 HOBBY
STATED HN ODDS 1:416 HOBBY
STATED PRINT RUN 100 SER.#'d SETS

Card	Low	High
13 Domingo Santana	5.00	12.00
15 Chris Davis	4.00	10.00
17 Zach Davies	4.00	10.00
18 Matt Carpenter	6.00	15.00
20 Anthony Rizzo	10.00	25.00
21 Mitch Haniger	5.00	12.00
22 Bryce Harper	40.00	100.00
23 Sean Manaea	4.00	10.00
24 Charlie Blackmon	6.00	15.00
25 Aaron Judge	60.00	150.00
26 Tommy Pham	4.00	10.00
30 Miguel Sano	5.00	12.00
35 Jose Altuve	5.00	12.00
37 Adam Jones	5.00	12.00
40 Miguel Cabrera	20.00	50.00
43 Jon Lester	5.00	12.00
45 Corey Seager	6.00	15.00
48 Joey Gallo	5.00	12.00
50 Andrew McCutchen	6.00	15.00
51 Brandon Crawford	5.00	12.00
53 Dansby Swanson	6.00	15.00
58 Justin Verlander	6.00	15.00
59 Albert Pujols	12.00	30.00
60 Justin Upton	5.00	12.00
61 Bradley Zimmer	4.00	10.00
62 Eric Thames	5.00	12.00
63 Ian Happ	5.00	12.00
64 Johnny Cueto	5.00	12.00
67 Max Scherzer	6.00	15.00
70 Joey Votto	6.00	15.00
71 Eric Hosmer	5.00	12.00
72 Jacob deGrom	6.00	15.00
74 Giancarlo Stanton	20.00	50.00
75 Jonathan Schoop	4.00	10.00
80 Kris Bryant	40.00	100.00
83 Dexter Fowler	5.00	12.00
87 Starlin Castro	4.00	10.00
90 Noah Syndergaard	5.00	12.00
91 Josh Donaldson	5.00	12.00
92 Stephen Strasburg	6.00	15.00
93 Mike Moustakas	5.00	12.00
94 Kenta Maeda	5.00	12.00
97 Jose Abreu	6.00	15.00
100 Felix Hernandez	5.00	12.00
101 Salvador Perez	5.00	12.00
104 Trea Turner	5.00	12.00
105 Josh Harrison	4.00	10.00
108 Billy Hamilton	5.00	12.00
109 Chris Sale	6.00	15.00
118 Cody Bellinger	12.00	30.00
119 Alex Bregman	6.00	15.00
124 Kendrys Morales	4.00	10.00
128 Ender Inciarte	4.00	10.00
130 Andrew Benintendi	25.00	60.00
134 Kevin Kiermaier	5.00	12.00
139 Jose Bautista	5.00	12.00
140 Aroldis Chapman	6.00	15.00
143 A.J. Pollock	4.00	10.00
145 Francisco Lindor	6.00	15.00
150 Josh Hader	4.00	10.00
151 Manny Machado	12.00	30.00
153 Elvis Andrus	5.00	12.00
155 Orlando Arcia	4.00	10.00
161 Yu Darvish	6.00	15.00
170 Marcell Ozuna	6.00	15.00
171 Javier Baez	8.00	20.00
176 Corey Kluber	10.00	25.00
180 Jordan Montgomery	6.00	15.00
185 Starling Marte	5.00	12.00
188 Aaron Nola	5.00	12.00
191 Gary Sanchez	6.00	15.00
198 Hunter Renfroe	4.00	10.00
201 Yoan Moncada	6.00	15.00
202 Dallas Keuchel	5.00	12.00
208 Yuli Gurriel	5.00	12.00
209 Dee Gordon	4.00	10.00
212 Didi Gregorius	5.00	12.00
216 Clayton Kershaw	20.00	50.00
218 Masahiro Tanaka	5.00	12.00
219 Freddie Freeman	8.00	20.00
220 Carlos Carrasco	4.00	10.00
221 Yoenis Cespedes	6.00	15.00
230 Ryan Zimmerman	5.00	12.00
232 Yadier Molina	6.00	15.00
233 Kyle Seager	4.00	10.00
234 Zack Greinke	5.00	12.00
240 Justin Smoak	4.00	10.00
241 Addison Russell	5.00	12.00
247 Willson Contreras	6.00	15.00
249 Marcus Stroman	5.00	12.00
250 Trey Mancini	5.00	12.00
260 Khris Davis	6.00	15.00
262 Eddie Rosario	6.00	15.00
265 Carlos Martinez	5.00	12.00
267 Trevor Bauer	6.00	15.00
268 Kyle Schwarber	6.00	15.00
275 Mike Trout	60.00	150.00
286 Chris Archer	4.00	10.00
288 Jake Arrieta	5.00	12.00
290 Jose Berrios	5.00	12.00
291 Jose Ramirez	5.00	12.00
293 Buster Posey	8.00	20.00
294 J.D. Martinez	6.00	15.00
300 Ichiro	8.00	20.00
301 Robinson Cano	5.00	12.00
302 Matt Olson	4.00	10.00
303 Luis Severino	5.00	12.00
305 Josh Bell	5.00	12.00
320 Paul DeJong	6.00	15.00
322 Nelson Cruz	6.00	15.00
325 Edwin Encarnacion	6.00	15.00
326 Daniel Murphy	5.00	12.00
327 Yasiel Puig	6.00	15.00
330 Mookie Betts	10.00	25.00
337 Byron Buxton	5.00	12.00
341 Christian Yelich	8.00	20.00
344 Manny Pina	4.00	10.00
345 Robbie Ray	4.00	10.00
348 German Marquez	4.00	10.00
349 Dustin Pedroia	6.00	15.00

351 Nolan Arenado 8.00 20.00
356 Brian Dozier 5.00 12.00
360 George Springer 5.00 12.00
364 Michael Conforto 5.00 12.00
365 Matt Chapman 6.00 15.00
366 Chris Taylor 5.00 12.00
369 Paul Goldschmidt 6.00 15.00
375 Whit Merrifield 6.00 15.00
381 Carlos Correa 6.00 15.00
384 Jake Lamb 5.00 12.00
387 Wil Myers 4.00 10.00
397 Evan Longoria 5.00 12.00
502 Juan Soto 75.00 200.00
511 Scott Kingery 6.00 15.00
517 Jonathan Lucroy 5.00 12.00
526 Steven Souza Jr. 5.00 12.00
527 Corey Dickerson 4.00 10.00
537 Matt Adams 4.00 10.00
541 Freddy Peralta 4.00 10.00
549 Jose Martinez 4.00 10.00
555 Matt Moore 5.00 12.00
562 Joe Kelly 4.00 10.00
568 Austin Meadows 6.00 15.00
570 Adam Engel 4.00 10.00
580 Ronald Acuna Jr. 75.00 200.00
583 Francisco Liriano 4.00 10.00
588 Lucas Duda 5.00 12.00
600 Shohei Ohtani 60.00 150.00
603 Gleyber Torres 40.00 100.00
613 Christian Arroyo 4.00 10.00
616 Tim Beckham 5.00 12.00
620 Jordan Hicks 8.00 20.00
622 Jake Odorizzi 4.00 10.00
633 Pat Neshek 4.00 10.00
655 Joey Lucchesi 4.00 10.00
659 Logan Morrison 4.00 10.00
672 Joe Musgrove 4.00 10.00
689 Wade Davis 4.00 10.00
694 Tucker Barnhart 4.00 10.00
701 Stephen Piscotty 4.00 10.00
703 Jay Bruce 5.00 12.00
704 Yonder Alonso 4.00 10.00
705 Andrew McCutchen 12.00 30.00
706 Lorenzo Cain 4.00 10.00
707 Yu Darvish 6.00 15.00
708 Neil Walker 5.00 12.00
709 Eric Hosmer 5.00 12.00
710 J.D. Martinez 6.00 15.00
711 Carlos Santana 5.00 12.00
712 Eduardo Nunez 4.00 10.00
713 Matt Kemp 5.00 12.00
714 Anthony Banda 4.00 10.00
715 Gerrit Cole 6.00 15.00
716 Ichiro 8.00 20.00
717 Arodys Vizcaino 4.00 10.00
718 Todd Frazier 5.00 12.00
719 Curtis Granderson 5.00 12.00
720 Christian Yelich 8.00 20.00
721 Jake Arrieta 5.00 12.00
722 Lewis Brinson 4.00 10.00
724 Brandon Morrow 4.00 10.00
725 Evan Longoria 5.00 12.00

2018 Topps Heritage Nickname Variations

RANDOM INSERTS IN PACKS
STATED HN ODDS 1:1663 HOBBY
22 Bryce Harper 60.00 150.00
25 Aaron Judge 150.00 400.00
50 Andrew McCutchen 20.00 50.00
80 Kris Bryant 60.00 150.00
90 Noah Syndergaard 15.00 40.00
114 Clint Frazier 40.00 100.00
118 Cody Bellinger 30.00 80.00
130 Andrew Benintendi 20.00 50.00
145 Francisco Lindor 20.00 50.00
151 Manny Machado 40.00 100.00
189 Rafael Devers 75.00 200.00
216 Clayton Kershaw 40.00 100.00
275 Mike Trout 100.00 250.00
369 Paul Goldschmidt 20.00 50.00
381 Carlos Correa 20.00 50.00
600 Shohei Ohtani 100.00 250.00
707 Yu Darvish 20.00 50.00
716 Ichiro 25.00 60.00
718 Todd Frazier 15.00 40.00
725 Evan Longoria 15.00 40.00

2018 Topps Heritage Rookie Cup Variations

RANDOM INSERTS IN PACKS
25 Aaron Judge 75.00 200.00
63 Ian Happ 12.00 30.00
118 Cody Bellinger 30.00 80.00
130 Andrew Benintendi 30.00 80.00
150 Josh Hader 10.00 25.00
180 Jordan Montgomery 15.00 40.00
189 Rafael Devers 40.00 100.00
250 Trey Mancini 12.00 30.00
320 Paul DeJong 20.00 50.00
348 German Marquez 10.00 25.00

2018 Topps Heritage Team Color Swap Variations

STATED ODDS 1:205 HOBBY
STATED HN ODDS 1:139 HOBBY
20 Anthony Rizzo 15.00 40.00
22 Bryce Harper 25.00 60.00
25 Aaron Judge 60.00 150.00
31 Amed Rosario 15.00 40.00
67 Max Scherzer 8.00 20.00
70 Joey Votto 12.00 30.00
74 Giancarlo Stanton 25.00 60.00
80 Kris Bryant 10.00 25.00
101 Salvador Perez 6.00 15.00
109 Chris Sale 8.00 20.00
114 Clint Frazier 20.00 50.00
118 Cody Bellinger 20.00 50.00
130 Andrew Benintendi 20.00 50.00
145 Francisco Lindor 8.00 20.00
151 Manny Machado 8.00 20.00
189 Rafael Devers 50.00 120.00
191 Gary Sanchez 15.00 40.00
206 Rhys Hoskins 40.00 60.00
216 Clayton Kershaw 20.00 50.00
232 Yadier Molina 8.00 20.00
275 Mike Trout 40.00 100.00
284 Victor Robles 25.00 60.00
293 Buster Posey 15.00 40.00
330 Mookie Betts 12.00 30.00
381 Carlos Correa 8.00 20.00
510 Pablo Sandoval 6.00 15.00
511 Scott Kingery 8.00 20.00
517 Jonathan Lucroy 6.00 15.00
580 Ronald Acuna Jr. 50.00 120.00
600 Shohei Ohtani 30.00 80.00
603 Gleyber Torres 50.00 125.00
620 Jordan Hicks 10.00 25.00
655 Joey Lucchesi 5.00 12.00
684 Lourdes Gurriel Jr. 10.00 25.00
689 Wade Davis 5.00 12.00
696 Tyler Austin 8.00 20.00
701 Stephen Piscotty 5.00 12.00
705 Andrew McCutchen 8.00 20.00
707 Yu Darvish 8.00 20.00
709 Eric Hosmer 6.00 15.00
710 J.D. Martinez 15.00 40.00
713 Matt Kemp 6.00 15.00
715 Gerrit Cole 8.00 20.00
716 Ichiro 10.00 25.00
718 Todd Frazier 6.00 15.00
719 Curtis Granderson 6.00 15.00
720 Christian Yelich 10.00 25.00
721 Jake Arrieta 6.00 15.00
724 Brandon Morrow 5.00 12.00
725 Evan Longoria 6.00 15.00

2018 Topps Heritage Traded Variations

RANDOM INSERTS IN PACKS
STATED HN ODDS 1:831 HOBBY
58 Justin Verlander 12.00 30.00
60 Justin Upton 10.00 25.00
74 Giancarlo Stanton 50.00 120.00
126 Jose Quintana 8.00 20.00
159 Jay Bruce 10.00 25.00
161 Yu Darvish 12.00 30.00
177 Sonny Gray 10.00 25.00
294 J.D. Martinez 12.00 30.00
315 Sean Doolittle 8.00 20.00
472 Brandon Phillips 8.00 20.00
600 Shohei Ohtani 40.00 100.00
701 Stephen Piscotty 8.00 20.00
705 Andrew McCutchen 12.00 30.00
713 Matt Kemp 10.00 25.00
715 Gerrit Cole 12.00 30.00
716 Ichiro 15.00 40.00
718 Todd Frazier 10.00 25.00
721 Jake Arrieta 10.00 25.00
725 Evan Longoria 10.00 25.00

2018 Topps Heritage Amazin' Mets Autographs

STATED HN ODDS 1:1095 HOBBY
STATED PRINT RUN 69 SER.#'d SETS
EXCHANGE DEADLINE 8/31/2020
AMAAW Al Weis 20.00 50.00
AMACJ Cleon Jones 30.00 80.00
AMAEK Ed Kranepool 75.00 200.00
AMANR Nolan Ryan 300.00 600.00
AMARS Ron Swoboda 25.00 60.00
AMAWG Wayne Garrett 75.00 200.00

2018 Topps Heritage Baseball Flashbacks

COMPLETE SET (15) 8.00 20.00
STATED ODDS 1:20 HOBBY
BFBR Brooks Robinson .50 1.25
BFFJ Fergie Jenkins .50 1.25
BFHA Hank Aaron 1.25 3.00
BFHK Harmon Killebrew .60 1.50
BFJB Johnny Bench .60 1.50
BFJM Juan Marichal .50 1.25
BFJP Jim Palmer .50 1.25
BFLB Lou Brock .50 1.25
BFRC Rod Carew .50 1.25
BFRCL Roberto Clemente 1.50 4.00
BFRJ Reggie Jackson .50 1.25
BFSC Steve Carlton .50 1.25
BFTS Tom Seaver .50 1.25
BFWM Willie McCovey .50 1.25
BFWS Willie Stargell .50 1.25

2018 Topps Heritage Chrome

STATED ODDS 1:35 HOBBY
STATED HN ODDS 1:42 HOBBY
STATED PRINT RUN 999 SER.#'d SETS
*PRPLE REF: .4X TO 1X BASIC
*REF/569: .6X TO 1.5X BASIC
THC15 Chris Davis 1.25 3.00
THC17 Zach Davies 1.25 3.00
THC18 Matt Carpenter 2.00 5.00
THC20 Anthony Rizzo 2.50 6.00
THC22 Bryce Harper 3.00 8.00
THC23 Sean Manaea 1.25 3.00
THC24 Charlie Blackmon 2.00 5.00
THC25 Aaron Judge 5.00 12.00
THC30 Miguel Sano 1.50 4.00
THC31 Dominic Smith 1.50 4.00
Amed Rosario
THC35 Jose Altuve 1.50 4.00
THC37 Adam Jones 1.50 4.00
THC40 Miguel Cabrera 2.00 5.00
THC43 Jon Lester 1.50 4.00
THC45 Corey Seager 2.00 5.00
THC48 Joey Gallo 1.50 4.00
THC50 Andrew McCutchen 2.00 5.00
THC53 Dansby Swanson 2.00 5.00
THC58 Justin Verlander 2.00 5.00
THC59 Albert Pujols 2.50 6.00
THC61 Bradley Zimmer 1.25 3.00
THC62 Eric Thames 1.50 4.00
THC63 Ian Happ 1.50 4.00
THC64 Johnny Cueto 1.50 4.00
THC66 Sisco/Hays 2.00 5.00
THC67 Max Scherzer 2.00 5.00
THC70 Joey Votto 2.00 5.00
THC71 Eric Hosmer 1.50 4.00
THC72 Jacob deGrom 2.00 5.00
THC74 Giancarlo Stanton 2.00 5.00
THC80 Kris Bryant 2.50 6.00
THC87 Starlin Castro 1.25 3.00
THC90 Noah Syndergaard 1.50 4.00
THC91 Josh Donaldson 1.50 4.00
THC92 Stephen Strasburg 2.00 5.00
THC93 Mike Moustakas 1.50 4.00
THC94 Kenta Maeda 1.50 4.00
THC97 Jose Abreu 2.00 5.00
THC100 Freddie Freeman 2.50 6.00
THC109 Chris Sale 2.00 5.00
THC114 Frazier/Andujar 5.00 12.00
THC119 Alex Bregman 2.00 5.00
THC124 Kendrys Morales 1.25 3.00
THC125 Carlos Correa 2.00 5.00
THC128 Ender Inciarte 1.25 3.00
THC130 Andrew Benintendi 2.00 5.00
THC145 Francisco Lindor 2.00 5.00
THC150 Cody Bellinger 4.00 10.00
THC151 Manny Machado 2.00 5.00
THC153 Elvis Andrus 1.50 4.00
THC161 Yu Darvish 2.00 5.00
THC170 Marcell Ozuna 2.00 5.00
THC171 Javier Baez 2.50 6.00
THC176 Corey Kluber 1.50 4.00
THC188 Aaron Nola 1.50 4.00
THC189 Martin/Devers 4.00 10.00
THC191 Gary Sanchez 2.00 5.00
THC202 Dallas Keuchel 1.50 4.00
THC206 Williams/Hoskins 5.00 12.00
THC208 Yuli Gurriel 1.50 4.00
THC209 Dee Gordon 1.25 3.00
THC212 Didi Gregorius 1.50 4.00
THC216 Clayton Kershaw 4.00 10.00
THC220 Carlos Carrasco 1.25 3.00
THC221 Yoenis Cespedes 2.00 5.00
THC230 Ryan Zimmerman 1.50 4.00
THC232 Yadier Molina 2.00 5.00
THC233 Kyle Seager 1.25 3.00
THC247 Willson Contreras 2.00 5.00
THC250 Trey Mancini 1.50 4.00
THC254 Zack Greinke 1.50 4.00
THC260 Khris Davis 2.00 5.00
THC266 Buehler/Verdugo 6.00 15.00
THC267 Trevor Bauer 2.00 5.00
THC268 Kyle Schwarber 2.00 5.00
THC275 Mike Trout 10.00 25.00
THC284 Stevenson/Robles 3.00 8.00
THC288 Jake Arrieta 1.50 4.00
THC290 Jose Berrios 1.50 4.00
THC291 Jose Ramirez 1.50 4.00
THC293 Buster Posey 2.50 6.00
THC294 J.D. Martinez 2.00 5.00
THC300 Ichiro 2.50 6.00
THC301 Robinson Cano 1.50 4.00
THC320 Paul DeJong 2.00 5.00
THC322 Nelson Cruz 2.00 5.00
THC325 Edwin Encarnacion 2.00 5.00
THC326 Daniel Murphy 1.50 4.00
THC327 Yasiel Puig 2.00 5.00
THC330 Mookie Betts 3.00 8.00
THC331 Albies/Sims 6.00 15.00
THC349 Dustin Pedroia 2.00 5.00
THC351 Nolan Arenado 2.50 6.00
THC356 Brian Dozier 1.50 4.00
THC360 George Springer 1.50 4.00
THC364 Michael Conforto 1.50 4.00
THC369 Paul Goldschmidt 2.00 5.00
THC384 Jake Lamb 1.50 4.00
THC387 Wil Myers 1.25 3.00
THC397 Evan Longoria 1.50 4.00
THC502 Juan Soto 75.00 200.00
THC511 Scott Kingery 2.00 5.00
THC517 Jonathan Lucroy 1.50 4.00
THC526 Steven Souza Jr. 1.50 4.00
THC527 Corey Dickerson 1.25 3.00
THC537 Matt Adams 1.25 3.00
THC544 Fernando Rodney 1.25 3.00
THC549 Jose Martinez 1.25 3.00
THC555 Matt Moore 1.25 3.00
THC568 Austin Meadows 2.00 5.00
THC580 Ronald Acuna Jr. 40.00 100.00
THC583 Francisco Liriano 1.25 3.00
THC588 Lucas Duda 1.25 3.00
THC600 Shohei Ohtani 8.00 20.00
THC603 Gleyber Torres 12.00 30.00
THC612 Tyler O'Neill 2.00 5.00
THC613 Christian Arroyo 1.25 3.00
THC616 Tim Beckham 1.25 3.00
THC618 Denard Span 1.25 3.00
THC620 Jordan Hicks 2.50 6.00
THC622 Jake Odorizzi 1.25 3.00
THC633 Pat Neshek 1.25 3.00
THC634 Dylan Cozens 1.25 3.00
THC643 Willy Adames 1.50 4.00
THC655 Joey Lucchesi 1.25 3.00
THC659 Logan Morrison 1.25 3.00
THC689 Wade Davis 1.25 3.00
THC701 Stephen Piscotty 1.25 3.00
THC703 Jay Bruce 1.50 4.00
THC704 Yonder Alonso 1.25 3.00
THC705 Andrew McCutchen 2.00 5.00
THC706 Lorenzo Cain 1.25 3.00
THC707 Yu Darvish 2.00 5.00
THC708 Neil Walker 1.50 4.00
THC709 Eric Hosmer 1.50 4.00
THC710 J.D. Martinez 2.00 5.00
THC711 Carlos Santana 1.50 4.00
THC712 Eduardo Nunez 1.25 3.00
THC713 Matt Kemp 1.50 4.00
THC714 Anthony Banda 1.25 3.00
THC715 Gerrit Cole 2.00 5.00
THC716 Ichiro 2.50 6.00
THC717 Arodys Vizcaino 1.25 3.00
THC718 Todd Frazier 1.50 4.00
THC719 Curtis Granderson 1.50 4.00
THC720 Christian Yelich 2.50 6.00
THC721 Jake Arrieta 1.50 4.00
THC722 Lewis Brinson 1.25 3.00
THC724 Brandon Morrow 1.25 3.00
THC725 Evan Longoria 1.50 4.00

2018 Topps Heritage Chrome Black Refractors

*BLACK REF: 2X TO 5X BASIC
STATED ODDS 1:501 HOBBY
STATED HN ODDS 1:602 HOBBY
STATED PRINT RUN 69 SER.#'d SETS
THC22 Bryce Harper 40.00 100.00
THC25 Aaron Judge 200.00 400.00
THC189 Kyle Martin 30.00 80.00
Rafael Devers
THC266 Buehler/Verdugo 40.00 100.00
THC275 Mike Trout 75.00 200.00
THC502 Juan Soto 500.00 1200.00
THC580 Ronald Acuna Jr. 500.00 1000.00
THC600 Shohei Ohtani 200.00 500.00
THC603 Gleyber Torres 125.00 300.00
THC716 Ichiro 15.00 40.00

2018 Topps Heritage Clubhouse Collection Autograph Relics

STATED ODDS 1:8151 HOBBY
STATED HN ODDS 1:3021 HOBBY
STATED PRINT RUN 25 SER.#'d SETS
EXCHANGE DEADLINE 1/31/2020
HN EXCH DEADLINE 8/31/2020
CCARAB Alex Bregman HN EXCH 50.00 120.00
CCARABE Andrew Benintendi HN 60.00 150.00
CCARAJ Aaron Judge
CCARAR Amed Rosario HN EXCH 40.00 100.00
CCARAR Anthony Rizzo
CCARBG Bob Gibson HN 50.00 120.00
CCARBP Buster Posey HN 60.00 150.00
CCARCB Charlie Blackmon HN
CCARCC Carlos Correa
CCARCK Clayton Kershaw EXCH 100.00 250.00
CCARCS Chris Sale 50.00 120.00
CCARDP Dustin Pedroia HN EXCH 40.00 100.00
CCARIH Ian Happ
CCARJA Jose Altuve HN 40.00 100.00
CCARJD Jacob deGrom 30.00 80.00
CCARJV Joey Votto
CCARKB Kris Bryant 150.00 400.00
CCARMM Manny Machado 100.00 250.00
CCARMT Mike Trout 300.00 600.00
CCARNS Noah Syndergaard EXCH 50.00 120.00
CCARPG Paul Goldschmidt HN EXCH 40.00 100.00
CCARRJ Reggie Jackson HN 50.00 120.00
CCARSM Starling Marte HN
CCARVR Victor Robles HN 25.00 60.00
CCARYM Yadier Molina HN EXCH 125.00 300.00

2018 Topps Heritage Clubhouse Collection Dual Relics

STATED ODDS 1:8490 HOBBY
STATED HN ODDS 1:3356 HOBBY
STATED PRINT RUN 69 SER.#'d SETS
CCDRBV Bench/Votto HN 20.00 50.00
CCDRBV Votto/Bench 40.00 100.00
CCDRCS Carew/Sano 40.00 100.00
CCDRGM Gibson/Molina HN 30.00 80.00
CCDRMA Altuve/Morgan 50.00 120.00
CCDRMC Correa/Morgan 20.00 50.00
CCDRRS Syndergaard/Ryan 75.00 200.00
CCDRSB Stargell/Bell HN 25.00 60.00
CCDRSS Seaver/Syndrgrd HN 15.00 40.00
CCDRYB Yaz/Benint. HN 25.00 60.00

2018 Topps Heritage Clubhouse Collection Relics

STATED ODDS 1:33 HOBBY
STATED HN ODDS 1:45 HOBBY
*GOLD/99: .5X TO 1.2X BASIC
CCRAB Adrian Beltre HN 3.00 8.00
CCRABE Andrew Benintendi HN 4.00 10.00
CCRABR Alex Bregman HN 3.00 8.00
CCRAM Andrew McCutchen 3.00 8.00
CCRAP Albert Pujols 4.00 10.00
CCRAR Anthony Rendon HN 3.00 8.00
CCRAR Anthony Rizzo 5.00 12.00
CCRARI Anthony Rizzo HN 5.00 12.00
CCRARO Amed Rosario HN 2.50 6.00
CCRARU Addison Russell 2.50 6.00
CCRAW Adam Wainwright 2.50 6.00
CCRBH Bryce Harper HN 5.00 12.00
CCRBH Billy Hamilton 2.50 6.00
CCRBHA Bryce Harper 10.00 25.00
CCRBP Buster Posey HN 4.00 10.00
CCRBPO Buster Posey 4.00 10.00
CCRBS Blake Snell HN 2.50 6.00
CCRCA Chris Archer 2.00 5.00
CCRCB Charlie Blackmon 3.00 8.00
CCRCBE Cody Bellinger 6.00 15.00
CCRCC Carlos Correa 3.00 8.00
CCRCF Clint Frazier HN 4.00 10.00
CCRCG Carlos Gonzalez 2.50 6.00
CCRCH Cole Hamels 2.50 6.00
CCRCK Clayton Kershaw HN 6.00 15.00
CCRCK Clayton Kershaw 6.00 15.00
CCRCKI Craig Kimbrel HN 2.50 6.00
CCRCS CC Sabathia HN 2.50 6.00
CCRCS Chris Sale 3.00 8.00
CCRCSE Corey Seager 3.00 8.00
CCRDD Danny Duffy HN 2.00 5.00
CCRDG Dee Gordon 2.00 5.00
CCRDK Dallas Keuchel HN 2.50 6.00
CCRDK Dallas Keuchel 2.50 6.00
CCRDL DJ LeMahieu HN 3.00 8.00
CCRDM Daniel Murphy HN 2.50 6.00
CCRDP David Price 2.50 6.00
CCRDW David Wright 2.50 6.00
CCREA Elvis Andrus HN 2.50 6.00
CCREH Eric Hosmer 2.50 6.00
CCREI Ender Inciarte HN 2.00 5.00
CCREL Evan Longoria 2.50 6.00
CCRFB Franklin Barreto HN 2.00 5.00
CCRFF Freddie Freeman 4.00 10.00
CCRFH Felix Hernandez 2.50 6.00
CCRFM Francisco Mejia HN 2.50 6.00
CCRGC Gerrit Cole 3.00 8.00
CCRGP Gregory Polanco 2.50 6.00
CCRGS George Springer 2.50 6.00
CCRGSA Gary Sanchez 3.00 8.00
CCRGST Giancarlo Stanton 3.00 8.00
CCRGT Gleyber Torres HN 6.00 15.00
CCRHR Hanley Ramirez 2.50 6.00
CCRIK Ian Kinsler 2.50 6.00
CCRIS Ichiro HN 4.00 10.00
CCRI Ichiro 4.00 10.00
CCRJA Jose Abreu 3.00 8.00
CCRJAL Jose Altuve 2.50 6.00
CCRJB Josh Bell HN 2.50 6.00
CCRJB Javier Baez 4.00 10.00
CCRJBE Jose Berrios HN 2.50 6.00
CCRJC J.P. Crawford HN 2.00 5.00
CCRJD Jacob deGrom HN 3.00 8.00
CCRJDO Josh Donaldson HN 2.50 6.00
CCRJG Jon Gray 2.00 5.00
CCRJGA Joey Gallo 2.50 6.00
CCRJL Jon Lester 2.50 6.00
CCRJM Joe Mauer 2.50 6.00
CCRJR Jose Ramirez HN 2.50 6.00
CCRJT Justin Turner HN 2.50 6.00
CCRJU Justin Upton 2.50 6.00
CCRJV Justin Verlander 3.00 8.00
CCRJVO Joey Votto 3.00 8.00
CCRKB Kris Bryant HN 5.00 12.00
CCRKB Kris Bryant 6.00 15.00
CCRKD Khris Davis 3.00 8.00
CCRKS Kyle Seager 2.00 5.00
CCRKSC Kyle Schwarber 3.00 8.00
CCRLC Lorenzo Cain 2.00 5.00
CCRLS Luis Severino HN 2.50 6.00
CCRMB Mookie Betts 5.00 12.00
CCRMC Miguel Cabrera 3.00 8.00
CCRMCO Michael Conforto 2.50 6.00
CCRMF Michael Fulmer HN 2.00 5.00
CCRMM Manny Machado HN 3.00 8.00
CCRMM Manny Machado 3.00 8.00
CCRMS Miguel Sano 2.50 6.00
CCRMSC Max Scherzer 3.00 8.00
CCRMT Masahiro Tanaka HN 2.50 6.00
CCRMTR Mike Trout HN 10.00 25.00
CCRMTR Mike Trout 15.00 40.00
CCRNA Nolan Arenado 4.00 10.00
CCRNC Nelson Cruz 3.00 8.00
CCRNS Noah Syndergaard 2.50 6.00
CCROA Ozzie Albies HN 4.00 10.00
CCRPG Paul Goldschmidt HN 3.00 8.00
CCRPG Paul Goldschmidt 3.00 8.00
CCRRA Ronald Acuna Jr. HN 12.00 30.00
CCRRB Ryan Braun 2.50 6.00
CCRRD Rafael Devers HN 6.00 15.00
CCRRH Rhys Hoskins HN 5.00 12.00
CCRRI Raisel Iglesias HN 2.50 6.00
CCRRO Rougned Odor 2.50 6.00
CCRSM Starling Marte 2.50 6.00
CCRSP Salvador Perez 2.50 6.00
CCRSS Stephen Strasburg 3.00 8.00
CCRWM Whit Merrifield HN 3.00 8.00
CCRWM Wil Myers 2.00 5.00
CCRYC Yoenis Cespedes 3.00 8.00
CCRYM Yadier Molina 3.00 8.00
CCRYP Yasiel Puig HN 3.00 8.00
CCRZD Zach Davies HN 2.00 5.00
CCRZG Zack Greinke 2.50 6.00

2018 Topps Heritage Clubhouse Collection Triple Relics

STATED ODDS 1:23,511 HOBBY
STATED HN ODDS 1:9247 HOBBY
STATED PRINT RUN 25 SER.#'d SETS
CCTRCAM Correa/Altuve/Morgan 60.00 150.00
CCTRJMJ Jtr/Mttngly/Jcksn HN 75.00 200.00
CCTRPMM Mrchl/Posey/McCvy 200.00 400.00
CCTRRMC Reyes/Martinez/Carlton 100.00 200.00
CCTRRMR B.Rob/Murray/CRJ HN 125.00 300.00
CCTRSGS Svr/Gdn/Sndrgrd HN 30.00 80.00
CCTRSPK Sttn/Pzza/Krshw HN 40.00 100.00
CCTRSRD Ryan/deGrom/Sndrgrd 60.00 150.00
CCTRVBP Bench/Votto/Perez 60.00 150.00
CCTRWSR Williams/Sndbrg/Rizzo HN 40.00 100.00

2018 Topps Heritage Flashbacks Autograph Relics

STATED ODDS 1:11,986 HOBBY
STATED HN ODDS 1:32,937 HOBBY
PRINT RUNS B/WN 19-25 COPIES PER
EXCHANGE DEADLINE 1/31/2020
FARAK Al Kaline/25 100.00 250.00
FARCY Carl Yastrzemski/25 75.00 200.00
FARHA Hank Aaron/25 250.00 400.00
FARJB Johnny Bench/25 75.00 200.00
FARJP Jim Palmer/25 60.00 150.00
FARLB Lou Brock/19 50.00 120.00
FARNR Nolan Ryan
FARPN Phil Niekro/25 25.00 60.00
FARRC Rod Carew/25 60.00 150.00
FARRJ Reggie Jackson/25 60.00 150.00
FARSC Steve Carlton/25 60.00 150.00

2018 Topps Heritage High Number '69 Bazooka Ad Panel Boxloader

STATED ODDS 1:2 HOBBY BOXES
1 Ian Happ .60 1.50
2 Shohei Ohtani 3.00 8.00
3 Ichiro 1.00 2.50
4 George Springer .60 1.50
5 Giancarlo Stanton .75 2.00
6 Ryan Braun .60 1.50
7 Shohei Ohtani 3.00 8.00
8 Didi Gregorius .60 1.50
9 Adrian Beltre .75 2.00
10 Adam Jones .60 1.50
11 Andrew McCutchen .75 2.00
12 Xander Bogaerts .75 2.00
13 Jameson Taillon .60 1.50
14 Max Scherzer .75 2.00
15 Walker Buehler 2.50 6.00

2018 Topps Heritage High Number '69 Topps Decals

RANDOM INSERTS IN PACKS
69TDBB Byron Buxton 1.00 2.50
69TDBP Buster Posey 1.50 4.00
69TDCS Corey Seager 1.25 3.00
69TDFL Francisco Lindor 1.25 3.00
69TDJA Jose Altuve 1.00 2.50
69TDJV Joey Votto 1.25 3.00
69TDNR Nolan Ryan 4.00 10.00
69TDNS Noah Syndergaard 1.00 2.50
69TDNW Nick Williams 1.00 2.50
69TDOA Ozzie Albies 2.50 6.00
69TDRC Robinson Cano 1.00 2.50
69TDRJ Reggie Jackson 1.00 2.50
69TDSO Shohei Ohtani 4.00 10.00
69TDTS Tom Seaver 1.00 2.50
69TDVR Victor Robles 2.00 5.00

2018 Topps Heritage High Number '69 Topps Deckle Edge

COMPLETE SET (30) 30.00 80.00
STATED HN ODDS 1:10 HOBBY
1 Shohei Ohtani 4.00 10.00
2 Ichiro 1.25 3.00
3 Andrew McCutchen 1.00 2.50
4 Charlie Blackmon 1.00 2.50
5 Albert Pujols 1.25 3.00
6 Justin Verlander 1.00 2.50
7 Josh Donaldson .75 2.00
8 Freddie Freeman 1.25 3.00
9 Corey Kluber .75 2.00
10 Noah Syndergaard .75 2.00
11 Joe Mauer .75 2.00
12 Miguel Cabrera .75 2.00
13 Eric Hosmer .75 2.00
14 Mike Moustakas .75 2.00
15 Javier Baez 1.25 3.00
16 Stephen Piscotty .60 1.50
17 Scott Kingery 1.00 2.50
18 Jordan Hicks 1.25 3.00
19 Alex Bregman 1.00 2.50
20 Christian Yelich 1.25 3.00
21 Adrian Beltre 1.00 2.50
22 Matt Chapman 1.00 2.50
23 Didi Gregorius .75 2.00
24 Jose Abreu 1.00 2.50
25 Starling Marte .75 2.00
26 Trey Mancini .75 2.00
27 Gleyber Torres 5.00 12.00
28 Dansby Swanson 1.00 2.50
29 Patrick Corbin .75 2.00
30 Christian Villanueva .60 1.50

2018 Topps Heritage Miracle of '69

COMPLETE SET (5) 4.00 10.00
STATED HN ODDS 1:24 HOBBY
MO69AW Al Weis .40 1.00
MO69CJ Cleon Jones .40 1.00
MO69NR Nolan Ryan 2.00 5.00
MO69RS Ron Swoboda .40 1.00
MO69TS Tom Seaver .50 1.25

2018 Topps Heritage New Age Performers

COMPLETE SET (25) 12.00 30.00
STATED ODDS 1:12 HOBBY
NAP1 Mookie Betts 1.00 2.50
NAP2 Mike Trout 3.00 8.00
NAP3 Jose Altuve .50 1.25
NAP4 Carlos Correa .60 1.50
NAP5 Aaron Judge 1.50 4.00
NAP6 Francisco Lindor .60 1.50
NAP7 Clayton Kershaw 1.00 2.50
NAP8 Bryce Harper 1.00 2.50
NAP9 Buster Posey .75 2.00
NAP10 Cody Bellinger 1.25 3.00
NAP11 Paul Goldschmidt .60 1.50
NAP12 Corey Seager .60 1.50
NAP13 Joey Votto .60 1.50
NAP14 Nolan Arenado .75 2.00
NAP15 Gary Sanchez .60 1.50
NAP16 Giancarlo Stanton .60 1.50
NAP17 Andrew Benintendi .60 1.50
NAP18 Kris Bryant .75 2.00
NAP19 Anthony Rizzo 1.00 2.50
NAP20 Manny Machado .60 1.50
NAP21 Rafael Devers 1.25 3.00
NAP22 Rhys Hoskins 1.50 4.00
NAP23 Amed Rosario .50 1.25
NAP24 Chris Sale .60 1.50
NAP25 Clint Frazier .75 2.00

2018 Topps Heritage News Flashbacks

2017 Topps Heritage News Flashbacks 8.00 20.00
2017 Topps Heritage News Flashbacks
NF1 Apollo 11 Moon Landing .60 1.50
NF2 Woodstock Music & Art Fair .60 1.50
NF3 The Beatles' Abbey Road Album Released .60 1.50
NF4 Dodge Charger Daytona: American Muscle .60 1.50
NF5 Boeing 747 Jumbo Jet Debuts .60 1.50
NF6 Concorde Test Flight .60 1.50
NF7 Automated Teller Machine .60 1.50
NF8 Apollo 12 .60 1.50
NF9 The Brady Bunch .60 1.50
NF10 Richard Nixon .60 1.50
NF11 Vietnam War Draft Lottery .60 1.50
NF12 Project Blue Book Confirms no UFO's .60 1.50
NF13 Vietnam War Protest March on Washington .60 1.50
NF14 Stonewall Riot .60 1.50
NF15 Sesame Street Debut .60 1.50

2018 Topps Heritage Real One Autographs

STATED ODDS 1:154 HOBBY
STATED HN ODDS 1:118 HOBBY
EXCHANGE DEADLINE 1/31/2020
HN EXCH DEADLINE 8/31/2020
ROAAB Anthony Banda HN 5.00 12.00
ROAABE Andrew Benintendi HN 25.00 60.00
ROAAH Austin Hays 12.00 30.00
ROAAK Al Kaline 50.00 120.00
ROAAN Aaron Nola HN 20.00 50.00
ROAAO Amed Rosario HN 20.00 50.00
ROAAR Anthony Rizzo HN 25.00 60.00
ROAAR Anthony Rizzo 60.00 150.00
ROAARO Amed Rosario 20.00 50.00
ROAAV Alex Verdugo 25.00 60.00
ROABA Brian Anderson HN 10.00 25.00
ROABB Byron Buxton HN 10.00 25.00
ROABP Buster Posey HN 100.00 250.00
ROABRO Bob Rodgers 10.00 25.00
ROABRP Bryce Harper HN 100.00 250.00
ROABW Brandon Woodruff HN 8.00 20.00
ROACC Carlos Correa 30.00 80.00
ROACF Clint Frazier 20.00 50.00
ROACK Corey Kluber HN 20.00 50.00
ROACS Chris Sale 25.00 60.00
ROACSI Chance Sisco 10.00 25.00
ROACT Chris Taylor HN 8.00 20.00
ROACY Carl Yastrzemski 100.00 250.00
ROADF Dustin Fowler 8.00 20.00
ROADG Didi Gregorius 15.00 40.00
ROADH Dick Hughes 8.00 20.00
ROADJ Derek Jeter HN
ROADS Dominic Smith 25.00 60.00
ROADT Dick Tracewski 8.00 20.00
ROAFF Freddie Freeman 30.00 80.00
ROAFM Francisco Mejia 12.00 30.00
ROAFP Freddie Patek HN 10.00 25.00
ROAGA Greg Allen HN 10.00 25.00
ROAGC Garrett Cooper HN 5.00 12.00
ROAGT Gleyber Torres HN 250.00 600.00
ROAHA Hank Aaron HN 200.00 500.00
ROAHA Hank Aaron
ROAHB Harrison Bader 8.00 20.00
ROAIH Ian Happ HN 6.00 15.00
ROAJB Johnny Bench 150.00 400.00
ROAJBR Jose Berrios HN 6.00 15.00
ROAJC J.P. Crawford HN 10.00 25.00
ROAJD J.D. Davis HN 6.00 15.00
ROAJE Jackson Stephens HN 5.00 12.00
ROAJF Jack Flaherty 12.00 30.00
ROAJL Jake Lamb HN 6.00 15.00
ROAJP Jim Palmer 50.00 120.00
ROAJS Justin Smoak HN 8.00 20.00
ROAJSO Juan Soto HN 350.00 700.00
ROAJV Joey Votto HN 40.00 100.00
ROAKB Kris Bryant HN 125.00 300.00
ROAKB Kris Bryant 150.00 400.00
ROAKD Khris Davis 20.00 50.00
ROALB Lou Brock 50.00 120.00
ROALS Lucas Sims 8.00 20.00
ROAMA Miguel Andujar HN 60.00 150.00
ROAMF Max Fried HN 10.00 25.00
ROAMM Manny Machado 60.00 150.00
ROAMO Matt Olson HN 12.00 30.00
ROAMT Mike Trout HN 500.00 800.00
ROAMT Mike Trout
ROAND Nicky Delmonico 8.00 20.00
ROANR Nolan Ryan 300.00 500.00
ROANS Noah Syndergaard HN 20.00 50.00
ROAOA Ozzie Albies HN 75.00 200.00
ROAOC Orlando Cepeda 25.00 60.00
ROAPB Paul Blackburn HN 5.00 12.00
ROAPD Paul DeJong HN 15.00 40.00

OAPG Paul Goldschmidt 25.00 60.00
OAPN Phil Niekro HN 10.00 25.00
OARA Ronald Acuna HN 800.00 1200.00
OARC Rod Carew 40.00 100.00
OARD Rafael Devers 60.00 150.00
OARF Rollie Fingers HN 20.00 50.00
OARFA Roy Face HN 10.00 25.00
OARH Rhys Hoskins HN 40.00 100.00
OARJ Reggie Jackson 150.00 400.00
OARM Ryan McMahon 10.00 25.00
OARU Richard Urena HN 6.00 15.00
OASA Sandy Alcantara HN 6.00 15.00
OASC Steve Carlton 20.00 50.00
OASG Sonny Gray HN 6.00 15.00
OASK Scott Kingery HN 15.00 40.00
OASO Shohei Ohtani HN 300.00 600.00
OASO Shohei Ohtani 1200.00 1600.00
OATM Trey Mancini 10.00 25.00
OATMA Tyler Mahle 10.00 25.00
OATW Tyler Wade HN 10.00 25.00
OAVR Victor Robles HN 50.00 120.00
OAVR Victor Robles 20.00 50.00
OAWB Walker Buehler 50.00 120.00
OAWC Willson Contreras HN 25.00 60.00
OAZG Zack Granite HN 5.00 12.00

2018 Topps Heritage Real One Autographs Red Ink

RED INK: .75X TO 2X BASIC
RED INK NH: .6X TO 1.5X BASIC
TATED ODDS 1:1003 HOBBY
STATED HN ODDS 1:277 HOBBY
PRINT RUNS B/WN 25-69 COPIES PER
XCHANGE DEADLINE 1/31/2020
N EXCH DEADLINE 8/31/2020
OAABE Andrew Benintendi HN 100.00 250.00
ROAARO Amed Rosario/69 50.00 120.00
ROAAV Alex Verdugo/69 60.00 150.00
ROABA Brian Anderson HN 30.00 80.00
ROACF Clint Frazier/69 75.00 200.00
ROAFM Francisco Mejia/69 40.00 100.00
ROAJSO Juan Soto HN/69 1000.00 1500.00
ROAJV Joey Votto HN/25 125.00 300.00
ROARA Ronald Acuna HN 1500.00 2000.00
ROARH Rhys Hoskins HN 100.00 250.00
ROASO Shohei Ohtani HN 1200.00 2000.00
ROASO Shohei Ohtani/69 5000.00 8000.00
ROAVR Victor Robles/69 30.00 80.00
ROAWB Walker Buehler/69 125.00 300.00

2018 Topps Heritage Real One Dual Autographs

STATED ODDS 1:5045 HOBBY
STATED HN ODDS 1:3371 HOBB8Y
STATED PRINT RUN 25 SER.#'d SETS
HN EXCH DEADLINE 8/31/2020
EXCHANGE DEADLINE 1/31/2020
RODABC Carlton/Brock
RODABV Votto/Bench EXCH 200.00 400.00
RODACN Cepeda/Niekro 75.00 200.00
RODAFA Frmn/Acna HN EX 300.00 500.00
RODAFE Eckersley/Fingers 75.00 200.00
RODAJH Henderson/Jackson 300.00 500.00
RODAJJ Judge/Jackson 300.00 500.00
RODAJM Jcksn/McGwre HN 200.00 400.00
RODAJT Judge/Torres HN 300.00 600.00
RODAKB Krshw/Bllngr HN EX 300.00 500.00
RODAOD Ortz/Dvrs HN EX 75.00 200.00
RODARM Rbnsn/Mchdo EXCH 150.00 300.00
RODARP Plmr/Rbnsn EXCH 150.00 300.00
RODARS Ryan/Svr HN EX 600.00 1000.00
RODASR Syndrgrd/Rsro HN EX 60.00 150.00

2018 Topps Heritage Reggie Jackson Highlights

COMPLETE SET (5) 5.00 12.00
STATED HN ODDS 1:24 HOBBY
RJH1 Reggie Jackson 1.00 2.50
RJH2 Reggie Jackson 1.00 2.50
RJH3 Reggie Jackson 1.00 2.50
RJH4 Reggie Jackson 1.00 2.50
RJH5 Reggie Jackson 1.00 2.50

2018 Topps Heritage Rookie Performers

COMPLETE SET (15) 6.00 15.00
STATED HN ODDS 1:8 HOBBY
RPAR Amed Rosario .30 .75
RPCS Chance Sisco .30 .75
RPCV Christian Villanueva .25 .60
RPGT Gleyber Torres 2.50 6.00
RPJH Jordan Hicks .50 1.25
RPJL Joey Lucchesi .25 .60
RPMA Miguel Andujar 1.00 2.50
RPOA Ozzie Albies .75 2.00
RPRA Ronald Acuna Jr. 5.00 12.00
RPRD Rafael Devers .75 2.00
RPRH Rhys Hoskins 1.00 2.50
RPSK Scott Kingery .40 1.00
RPSO Shohei Ohtani 1.50 4.00
RPVR Victor Robles .60 1.50
RPWB Walker Buehler 1.25 3.00

2018 Topps Heritage Seattle Pilots Autographs

STATED ODDS 1:3464 HOBBY
EXCHANGE DEADLINE 1/31/2020
SPABE Bill Edgerton 40.00 100.00
SPABP Bill Parsons 30.00 80.00
SPABR Bob Richmond 30.00 80.00
SPABS Bernie Smith 30.00 80.00
SPABST Buzz Stephen 30.00 80.00
SPADB Dick Baney 30.00 80.00
SPADBA Dick Bates 30.00 80.00
SPAFK Frank Kimball 30.00 80.00
SPAFS Fred Stanley 30.00 80.00
SPAJB Jim Bouton 75.00 200.00
SPAMR Mike Rollyson 30.00 80.00
SPAPK Pete Koegel 30.00 80.00
SPARH Roric Harrison 30.00 80.00
SPARK Ron Kotick 30.00 80.00
SPARP Ray Peters 40.00 100.00

2018 Topps Heritage Then and Now

COMPLETE SET (15) 12.00 30.00
STATED ODDS 1:20 HOBBY
TN1 Seaver/Kershaw 1.25 3.00
TN2 Corey Kluber .50 1.25
Jim Palmer
TN3 Kershaw/Marichal 1.25 3.00
TN4 Corey Kluber .50 1.25
Jim Palmer
TN5 Judge/Killebrew 1.50 4.00
TN6 Stanton/McCovey .60 1.50
TN7 Harmon Killebrew .60 1.50
Nelson Cruz
TN8 Stanton/McCovey .60 1.50
TN9 Altuve/Carew .50 1.25
TN10 Blackmon/Clemente 1.50 4.00
TN11 Dee Gordon .50 1.25
Lou Brock
TN12 Corey Kluber .50 1.25
Jim Palmer
TN13 Juan Marichal .50 1.25
Carlos Martinez
TN14 Max Scherzer .60 1.50
Fergie Jenkins
TN15 Sale/Hunter .60 1.50

2019 Topps Heritage

SP ODDS 1:3 HOBBY
1 Boston Red Sox WS Champs .25 .60
2 Felix Hernandez .20 .50
3 Jared Hughes .15 .40
4 Kole Calhoun .15 .40
5 Alex Wood .15 .40
6 Nick Pivetta .15 .40
7 Kopech RC/Fiare RC .00 1.50
8 Josh Harrison .15 .40
9 Brandon Lowe RC .50 1.25
Michael Perez RC
10 Jackie Bradley Jr. .25 .60
11 Daniel Mengden .15 .40
12 Jordan Zimmermann .20 .50
13 Chris Stratton .15 .40
14 Adam Eaton .25 .60
15 Roberto Osuna .15 .40
16 Jake Junis .15 .40
17 Sean Newcomb .15 .40
18 Lucas Giolito .20 .50
19 Russell Martin .15 .40
20 Alex Cobb .15 .40
21 Martini RC/Laureano RC .60 1.50
22 Jose Peraza .20 .50
23 CC Sabathia .20 .50
24 Zach Eflin .15 .40
25 Eddie Rosario .20 .50
26 Juan Lagares .15 .40
27 Leonys Martin .15 .40
28 Tommy Hunter .15 .40
29 Andrelton Simmons .15 .40
30 Gregory Polanco .20 .50
31 Jhoulys Chacin .15 .40
32 Brad Peacock .15 .40
33 Jeimer Candelario .15 .40
34 Cody Bellinger .50 1.25
35 Ketel Marte .20 .50
36 Blake Trahan RC .30 .75
Jesus Reyes RC
37 Danny Duffy .15 .40
38 Randal Grichuk .15 .40
39 Brock Holt .15 .40
40 Jose Martinez .15 .40
41 Yusmeiro Petit .15 .40
42 Evan Longoria .20 .50
43 Luke Voit .40 1.00
44 Joey Lucchesi .15 .40
45 Jonathan Villar .15 .40
46 Kyle Hendricks .25 .60
47 Zack Godley .15 .40
48 Jesse Biddle .15 .40
49 Howie Kendrick .15 .40
50 Yoenis Cespedes .25 .60
51 Robbie Ray .15 .40
52 Chris Archer .15 .40
53 Orlando Arcia .15 .40
54 Ross Stripling .15 .40
55 Lou Trivino .15 .40
56 Ranger Suarez RC .30 .75
Enyel de los Santos RC
57 David Peralta .15 .40
58 Gorkys Hernandez .15 .40
59 Mike Clevinger .20 .50
60 Josh Reddick .15 .40
61 Ylch/Fmn/Gennett LL .30 .75
62 Altuve/Betts/Martinez LL .40 1.00
63 Baez/Aglr/Stry/Ylch/Arndo LL .30 .75
64 Encrncn/Mrtnz/Davis LL .25 .60
65 Ylch/Crpntr/Story/Arndo LL .30 .75
66 Gallo/Mrtnz/Davis LL .25 .60
67 Max Scherzer .25 .60
Aaron Nola
Jacob deGrom LL
68 Justin Verlander .25 .60
Trevor Bauer
Blake Snell LL
69 Kyle Freeland .25 .60
Aaron Nola
Miles Mikolas
Jon Lester
Max Scherzer LL
70 Corey Kluber .20 .50
Luis Severino
Blake Snell LL
71 Jacob deGrom .25 .60
Patrick Corbin
Max Scherzer LL
72 Sale/Vrlndr/Cole LL .25 .60
73 Tyler Mahle .15 .40
74 David Fletcher RC 1.00 2.50
Taylor Ward RC
75 Jake Lamb .20 .50
76 Dexter Fowler .20 .50
77 Tony Watson .15 .40
78 Mookie Betts .40 1.00
79 Clayton Richard .15 .40
80 Ian Happ .20 .50
81 Archie Bradley .15 .40
82 Austin Romine .15 .40
83 Noah Syndergaard .20 .50
84 Wilmer Difo .15 .40
85 Chris Iannetta .15 .40
86 Martin Prado .15 .40
87 Ken Giles .15 .40
88 Nate Orf RC .50 1.25
Corbin Burnes RC
89 Adalberto Mondesi .20 .50
90 J.P. Crawford .15 .40
91 Yolmer Sanchez .15 .40
92 Jack Flaherty .20 .50
93 Brian Anderson .15 .40
94 Francisco Cervelli .15 .40
95 Joe Jimenez .15 .40
96 Dakota Hudson RC .50 1.25
Daniel Poncedeleon RC
97 Rich Hill .15 .40
98 Nicholas Castellanos .25 .60
99 Jay Bruce .20 .50
100 Masahiro Tanaka .20 .50
101 Tim Beckham .20 .50
102 Mark Canha .15 .40
103 Miguel Rojas .15 .40
104 Christian Vazquez .15 .40
105 Ender Inciarte .15 .40
106 Stephen Strasburg .25 .60
107 Joe Panik .20 .50
108 Alex Gordon .20 .50
109 Rowdy Tellez RC .50 1.25
Reese McGuire RC
110 Kyle Crick .15 .40
111 Ryan Braun .20 .50
112 Shane Bieber .25 .60
113 Lance McCullers Jr. .15 .40
114 Didi Gregorius .20 .50
115 Billy Hamilton .20 .50
116 Derek Dietrich .20 .50
117 Kyle Schwarber .25 .60
118 Kyle Barraclough .15 .40
119 Michael Wacha .20 .50
120 Matt Chapman .25 .60
121 Duane Underwood Jr. RC .30 .75
James Norwood RC
122 Julio Teheran .20 .50
123 Sandy Alcantara .15 .40
124 Marcus Stroman .20 .50
125 Maikel Franco .20 .50
126 Max Stassi .15 .40
127 Jurickson Profar .20 .50
128 Robinson Chirinos .15 .40
129 James McCann .20 .50
130 Hunter Renfroe .15 .40
131 Dennis Santana RC .40 1.00
Caleb Ferguson RC
132 Blake Parker .15 .40
133 Sal Romano .15 .40
134 Nelson Cruz .25 .60
135 Alen Hanson .20 .50
136 Carlos Carrasco .15 .40
137 Michael Conforto .20 .50
138 James Paxton .20 .50
139 Jedd Gyorko .15 .40
140 Dustin Fowler .15 .40
141 Nick Burdi RC .30 .75
Alex McRae RC
142 Sonny Gray .20 .50
143 Chasen Shreve .15 .40
144 Joey Gallo .20 .50
145 Adam Duvall .20 .50
146 Nate Jones .15 .40
147 Yangervis Solarte .15 .40
148 Ronald Guzman .15 .40
149 Vince Velasquez .15 .40
150 Mallex Smith .15 .40
151 Craig Stammen .15 .40
152 Matt Boyd .15 .40
153 Seth Lugo .15 .40
154 Austin Voth RC .30 .75
Jimmy Cordero RC
155 Collin McHugh .15 .40
156 Matt Shoemaker .20 .50
157 Enrique Hernandez .20 .50
158 Mike Zunino .15 .40
159 Michael Lorenzen .15 .40
160 Shane Carle .15 .40
161 Joey Wendle .15 .40
162 Kolten Wong .20 .50
163 Rafael Devers .30 .75
164 Aledmys Diaz .15 .40
165 Jorge Soler .25 .60
166 Trevor Williams .15 .40
167 Dellin Betances .20 .50
168 Victor Arano .15 .40
169 Matt Duffy .15 .40
170 Albert Almora Jr. .20 .50
171 Darren O'Day .15 .40
172 Chad Sobotka RC .40 1.00
Bryse Wilson RC
173 Jaime Barria .15 .40
174 Justin Turner .20 .50
175 Daniel Robertson .15 .40
176 Will Smith .15 .40
177 Niko Goodrum .20 .50
178 Hector Rondon .15 .40
179 Manny Margot .15 .40
180 Daniel Palka .15 .40
181 Ryan Yarbrough .15 .40
182 Andrew Cashner .15 .40
183 Wilmer Flores .20 .50
184 Yan Gomes .25 .60
185 Ryon Healy .15 .40
186 Scott Kingery .20 .50
187 Whit Merrifield .25 .60
188 Corey Dickerson .15 .40
189 Adams RC/Loaisiga RC .40 1.00
190 Luke Weaver .15 .40
191 David Price .20 .50
192 Jason Heyward .20 .50
193 Devon Travis .15 .40
194 Tommy Pham .15 .40
195 Justin Turner Playoff HL .20 .50
196 Cody Bellinger Playoff HL .50 1.25
197 Clayton Kershaw Playoff HL .50 1.25
198 Yasiel Puig Playoff HL .25 .60
199 Jackie Bradley Playoff HL .25 .60
200 Jackie Bradley Playoff HL .25 .60
201 Andrew Benintendi Playoff HL .25 .60
202 David Price Playoff HL .20 .50
203 Andrew Heaney .15 .40
204 C.J. Cron .15 .40
205 Marcus Semien .15 .40
206 Johan Camargo .15 .40
207 Dawel Lugo RC .50 1.25
Christin Stewart RC
208 Tony Kemp .15 .40
209 Roberto Perez .15 .40
210 Mark Melancon .15 .40
211 Willy Adames .15 .40
212 Hyun-Jin Ryu .20 .50
213 Mark Trumbo .15 .40
214 Todd Frazier .20 .50
215 Steven Wright .15 .40
216 Josh Bell .20 .50
217 Tim Anderson .25 .60
218 Nick Williams .15 .40
219 Jesus Sucre RC .30 .75
220 Marcell Ozuna .25 .60
221 Kendrys Morales .15 .40
222 Hunter Dozier .15 .40
223 Ben Zobrist .20 .50
224 Chase Anderson .15 .40
225 Scott Schebler .20 .50
226 Miguel Sano .20 .50
227 Tucker RC/Perez RC .60 1.50
228 Kaleb Cowart .15 .40
229 Freddy Peralta .25 .60
230 Chris Davis .15 .40
231 Travis Shaw .15 .40
232 A.J. Minter .20 .50
233 Blake Treinen .15 .40
234 Travis Jankowski .15 .40
235 Ryan Zimmerman .20 .50
236 Jameson Taillon .20 .50
237 Eduardo Rodriguez .15 .40
238 Brandon Drury .15 .40
239 Avisail Garcia .20 .50
240 Yu Darvish .25 .60
241 Viloria RC/O'Hearn RC .30 .75
242 Ian Desmond .15 .40
243 Richard Urena .15 .40
244 Ty Buttrey RC .50 1.25
Francisco Arcia RC
Williams Jerez RC
245 Wade Davis .15 .40
246 Steven Matz .20 .50
247 Jason Kipnis .20 .50
248 Gerardo Parra .15 .40
249 Jeremy Jeffress .15 .40
250 Brandon Belt .20 .50
251 Dustin Pedroia .25 .60
252 Pat Neshek .15 .40
253 Kyle Freeland .20 .50
254 Luis Castillo .20 .50
255 Jon Gray .15 .40
256 David Dahl .15 .40
257 Brad Hand .15 .40
258 Cole Hamels .20 .50
259 Chad Pinder .15 .40
260 German Marquez .15 .40
261 Lewis Brinson .15 .40
262 Nix RC/Urias RC .50 1.25
263 Welington Castillo .15 .40
264 Colin Moran .15 .40
265 Steve Pearce .25 .60
266 Rosell Herrera .15 .40
267 Steven Duggar RC .40 1.00
Ray Black RC
268 Brad Boxberger .15 .40
269 Shane Greene .15 .40
270 Jorge Alfaro .15 .40
271 Kyle Seager .15 .40
272 Tyler White .15 .40
273 Willie Calhoun .15 .40
274 Carlos Rodon .20 .50
275 Yoshihisa Hirano .15 .40
276 Pablo Sandoval .20 .50
277 Cam Bedrosian .15 .40
278 Josh Donaldson .20 .50
279 Rick Porcello .20 .50
280 Nick Ahmed .15 .40
281 Rougned Odor .20 .50
282 Harrison Bader .20 .50
283 Adam Conley .15 .40
284 Austin Hedges .15 .40
285 Isiah Kiner-Falefa .15 .40
286 Edmundo Sosa RC .40 1.00
Adolis Garcia RC
287 Mike Fiers .15 .40
288 Cesar Hernandez .15 .40
289 Mike Leake .15 .40
290 Jose Leclerc .15 .40
291 Steve Cishek .15 .40
292 Steven Souza Jr. .20 .50
293 Kevin Pillar .15 .40
294 Justin Anderson .15 .40
295 Kevin Gausman .15 .40
296 Tucker Barnhart .15 .40
297 Greg Bird .20 .50
298 Dereck Rodriguez .15 .40
299 Nicky Delmonico .15 .40
300 Zack Wheeler .20 .50
301 Ben Gamel .20 .50
302 Seranthony Dominguez .15 .40
303 Elvis Andrus .20 .50
304 Chris Taylor .20 .50
305 Eduardo Nunez WS HL .15 .40
306 J.D. Martinez WS HL .25 .60
307 Max Muncy WS HL .20 .50
308 Steve Pearce WS HL .25 .60
309 David Price WS HL .20 .50
310 Boston Red Sox WS HL .25 .60
311 Fernando Rodney .15 .40
312 Yairo Munoz .15 .40
313 Michael Fulmer .15 .40
314 Matt Strahm .15 .40
315 Yoan Moncada .25 .60
316 Dansby Swanson .25 .60
317 Joffroy Springs RC .30 .75
Jose Trevino RC
318 Carl Edwards Jr. .15 .40
319 Dylan Bundy .20 .50
320 Raisel Iglesias .15 .40
321 Arodys Vizcaino .15 .40
322 Ivan Nova .20 .50
323 Robinson Cano .20 .50
324 Justin Bour .15 .40
325 Frankie Montas .15 .40
326 Tyler Skaggs .15 .40
327 Mike Foltynewicz .25 .60
328 Anthony Rendon .25 .60
329 Robbie Erlin .15 .40
330 John Gant .15 .40
331 Matt Olson .15 .40
332 Hernan Perez .15 .40
333 Manny Pina .15 .40
334 Jose Quintana .15 .40
335 Josh Hader .15 .40
336 Ervin Santana .15 .40
337 Reyes Moronta .15 .40
338 Jarrod Dyson .15 .40
339 Denard Span .15 .40
340 Eduardo Nunez .15 .40
341 Corey Seager .25 .60
342 Alex Colome .15 .40
343 Cedric Mullins RC .50 1.25
Paul Fry RC
Austin Wynns RC
344 Joe Musgrove .15 .40
345 Kirby Yates .20 .50
346 Pedro Strop .15 .40
347 David Bote .20 .50
348 McNeil RC/Smith RC .75 2.00
349 Chris Shaw RC .50 1.25
Aramis Garcia RC
350 Chris Sale AS .25 .60
351 Salvador Perez AS .20 .50
352 Jose Abreu AS .25 .60
353 Jose Altuve AS .20 .50
354 Manny Machado AS .25 .60
355 Jose Ramirez AS .20 .50
356 Aaron Judge AS .60 1.50
357 Mike Trout AS 1.25 3.00
358 Mookie Betts AS .40 1.00
359 J.D. Martinez AS .25 .60
360 Max Scherzer AS .25 .60
361 Willson Contreras AS .20 .50
362 Freddie Freeman AS .30 .75
363 Javier Baez AS .30 .75
364 Brandon Crawford AS .20 .50
365 Nolan Arenado AS .30 .75
366 Matt Kemp AS .20 .50
367 Bryce Harper AS .40 1.00
368 Nick Markakis AS .20 .50
369 Paul Goldschmidt AS .25 .60
370 Mike Moustakas .20 .50
371 Heath Fillmyer RC .30 .75
Brad Keller RC
372 Kevin Newman RC .50 1.25
Kevin Kramer RC
373 Aaron Hicks .20 .50
374 Robert Gsellman .15 .40
375 Brandon Morrow .15 .40
376 Ryan Borucki RC .30 .75
Danny Jansen RC
Sean Reid-Foley RC
377 Marco Gonzales .15 .40
378 Max Kepler .20 .50
379 Jorge Polanco .15 .40
380 Jesse Winker .15 .40
381 Andrew Velazquez RC .30 .75
Nick Ciuffo RC
382 Yuli Gurriel .20 .50
383 Mitch Garver .15 .40
384 Keone Kela .15 .40
385 Mitch Moreland .15 .40
386 Kohl Stewart RC .40 1.00
Willians Astudillo RC
Stephen Gonsalves RC
387 Brent Suter .15 .40
388 Carlos Santana .20 .50
389 Mike Minor .15 .40
390 Joc Pederson .20 .50
391 Austin Dean RC .30 .75
Isaac Galloway RC
Pablo Lopez RC
392 Ryne Stanek .15 .40
393 Wade LeBlanc .15 .40
394 Joakim Soria .15 .40
395 Matt Davidson .20 .50
396 Garrett Hampson RC .30 .75
Sam Howard RC
Yency Almonte RC
397 Zack Cozart .15 .40
398 Teoscar Hernandez .25 .60
399 Wright RC/Tssnt RC/Allard RC .50 1.25
400 Dean Deetz RC .50 1.25
Framber Valdez RC
Josh James RC
401 Francisco Lindor SP 2.00 5.00
402 Salvador Perez SP 1.50 4.00
403 Jake Arrieta SP 1.50 4.00
404 Kris Bryant SP 2.50 6.00
405 Jon Lester SP 1.50 4.00
406 Anthony Rizzo SP 3.00 8.00
407 George Springer SP 1.50 4.00
408 Sean Manaea SP 1.25 3.00
409 Jose Altuve SP 1.50 4.00
410 Christian Yelich SP 2.50 6.00
411 Blake Snell SP 1.50 4.00
412 Trevor Bauer SP 2.00 5.00
413 Gleyber Torres SP 4.00 10.00
414 Paul DeJong SP 2.00 5.00
415 Bryce Harper SP 3.00 8.00
416 Luis Severino SP 1.50 4.00
417 Jordan Hicks SP 1.50 4.00
418 Gary Sanchez SP 2.00 5.00
419 Jacob deGrom SP 2.00 5.00
420 Kenley Jansen SP 1.50 4.00
421 Justin Upton SP 1.50 4.00
422 Albert Pujols SP 2.50 6.00
423 Carlos Correa SP 2.00 5.00
424 Alex Bregman SP 2.00 5.00
425 Franmil Reyes SP 1.25 3.00
426 Justin Verlander SP 2.00 5.00
427 Walker Buehler SP 2.50 6.00
428 Trey Mancini SP 1.50 4.00
429 Gerrit Cole SP 2.00 5.00
430 Shohei Ohtani SP 2.50 6.00
431 Brandon Nimmo SP 1.50 4.00
432 Khris Davis SP 2.00 5.00
433 Justin Smoak SP 1.25 3.00
434 Stephen Piscotty SP 1.25 3.00
435 Miles Mikolas SP 2.00 5.00
436 Ozzie Albies SP 2.00 5.00
437 Lorenzo Cain SP 1.25 3.00
438 Matt Carpenter SP 2.00 5.00
439 Yadier Molina SP 2.00 5.00
440 Javier Baez SP 2.50 6.00
441 Paul Goldschmidt SP 2.00 5.00
442 Zack Greinke SP 1.50 4.00
443 Matt Kemp SP 1.50 4.00
444 Kenta Maeda SP 1.50 4.00
445 Buster Posey SP 2.50 6.00
446 Max Muncy SP 1.50 4.00
447 Edwin Encarnacion SP 2.00 5.00
448 Corey Kluber SP 1.50 4.00
449 Dee Gordon SP 1.25 3.00
450 Jean Segura SP 2.00 5.00
451 Edwin Diaz SP 1.50 4.00
452 Starlin Castro SP 1.25 3.00
453 J.T. Realmuto SP 2.00 5.00
454 Max Scherzer SP 2.00 5.00
455 Trea Turner SP 1.50 4.00
456 Jonathan Schoop SP 1.25 3.00
457 Eric Hosmer SP 1.50 4.00
458 Rhys Hoskins SP 2.50 6.00
459 Aaron Nola SP 1.50 4.00
460 Felipe Vasquez SP 1.25 3.00
461 Shin-Soo Choo SP 1.50 4.00
462 Nomar Mazara SP 1.25 3.00
463 Kevin Kiermaier SP 1.50 4.00
464 Chris Sale SP 2.00 5.00
465 Joey Votto SP 2.00 5.00
466 Scooter Gennett SP 1.50 4.00
467 Eugenio Suarez SP 1.50 4.00
468 Nolan Arenado SP 2.50 6.00
469 Trevor Story SP 2.00 5.00
470 Starling Marte SP 1.50 4.00
471 Charlie Blackmon SP 2.00 5.00
472 Miguel Cabrera SP 2.00 5.00
473 Miguel Andujar SP 2.00 5.00
474 Giancarlo Stanton SP 2.00 5.00
475 J.D. Martinez SP 2.00 5.00
476 Jesus Aguilar SP 1.25 3.00
477 Mitch Haniger SP 1.50 4.00
478 Brandon Crawford SP 1.50 4.00
479 Jose Berrios SP 1.50 4.00
480 Lourdes Gurriel Jr. SP 1.50 4.00
481 Juan Soto SP 5.00 12.00
482 Carlos Martinez SP 1.50 4.00
483 Jose Abreu SP 2.00 5.00
484 Andrew Benintendi SP 2.00 5.00
485 Mike Trout SP 10.00 25.00
486 Adam Jones SP 1.50 4.00
487 Xander Bogaerts SP 2.00 5.00
488 Odubel Herrera SP 1.50 4.00
489 Freddie Freeman SP 2.50 6.00
490 Clayton Kershaw SP 4.00 10.00
491 Jose Ramirez SP 1.50 4.00
492 Willson Contreras SP 1.50 4.00
493 Aroldis Chapman SP 2.00 5.00
494 Wil Myers SP 1.25 3.00
495 Sean Doolittle SP 1.25 3.00
496 Eric Thames SP 1.25 3.00
497 Yonder Alonso SP 1.25 3.00
498 Amed Rosario SP 1.50 4.00
499 Aaron Judge SP 5.00 12.00
500 Ronald Acuna Jr. SP 8.00 20.00
501 Michael Chavis RC .50 1.25
502 Charlie Morton .25 .60
503 Michael Brantley .20 .50
504 Vladimir Guerrero Jr. RC 4.00 10.00
505 Nick Markakis .20 .50
506 Yasmani Grandal .15 .40
507 Nick Senzel RC 1.00 2.50
508 Brendan Rodgers RC .50 1.25
509 Derek Holland .15 .40
510 Lonnie Chisenhall .15 .40
511 Phil Ervin .15 .40
512 Keston Hiura RC 1.00 2.50
513 Kurt Suzuki .15 .40
514 Eric Stamets RC .30 .75
515 Sam Gaviglio .15 .40
516 Eloy Jimenez RC 1.25 3.00
517 Fernando Tatis Jr. RC 6.00 15.00
518 Bradley Zimmer .15 .40
519 Pete Alonso RC 3.00 8.00
520 Manny Machado .25 .60
521 Andrew Miller .20 .50
522 A.J. Pollock .15 .40
523 Carter Kieboom RC .50 1.25
524 Griffin Canning RC .50 1.25
525 Justus Sheffield RC .50 1.25
526 Yusei Kikuchi RC .50 1.25
527 Jorge Alfaro .15 .40
528 Joe Kelly .15 .40
529 Brian Dozier .20 .50
530 Patrick Corbin .20 .50
531 Taylor Clarke RC .30 .75
532 Richie Martin RC .30 .75
533 Jon Duplantier RC .30 .75
534 Bryce Harper .40 1.00
535 J.T. Realmuto .25 .60
536 Trevor Cahill .15 .40
537 Austin Meadows .20 .50
538 Tyler Glasnow .15 .40
539 Byron Buxton .20 .50
540 Alex Verdugo .20 .50
541 Yasiel Puig .25 .60
542 Nicky Lopez RC .50 1.25
543 Sonny Gray .20 .50
544 Daniel Murphy .20 .50
545 Troy Tulowitzki .25 .60
546 DJ LeMahieu .25 .60
547 J.A. Happ .20 .50
548 Adam Ottavino .15 .40
549 Zack Britton .15 .40
550 Brian Goodwin .15 .40
551 Ian Kinsler .20 .50
552 Josh Harrison .15 .40
553 Marwin Gonzalez .15 .40
554 Tim Beckham .20 .50
555 Jurickson Profar .20 .50
556 Jake Bauers RC .50 1.25
557 Jed Lowrie .15 .40
558 Wilson Ramos .15 .40
559 Jeurys Familia .20 .50
560 Robinson Chirinos .15 .40
561 Lance Lynn .15 .40
562 Wade Miley .15 .40
563 Danny Salazar .20 .50
564 Tyler O'Neill .20 .50
565 Matt Davidson .20 .50
566 Jonathan Lucroy .20 .50
567 Alex Wood .15 .40
568 Nathan Eovaldi .20 .50
569 Cody Allen .15 .40
570 Josh Phegley .15 .40
571 Kendrys Morales .15 .40
572 Clay Buchholz .15 .40
573 Matt Shoemaker .20 .50
574 Craig Kimbrel .20 .50
575 Freddy Galvis .15 .40
576 Elvis Luciano RC .50 1.25
577 Max Fried .25 .60
578 Alex Jackson RC .50 1.25
579 Brian McCann .20 .50
580 Brandon Woodruff .15 .40
581 Zach Davies .15 .40
582 Ben Gamel .20 .50
583 John Brebbia .15 .40
584 Adam Wainwright .20 .50
585 Alex Reyes .20 .50
586 Daniel Descalso .15 .40
587 Victor Caratini .15 .40
588 Brad Brach .15 .40
589 Eduardo Escobar .15 .40
590 Wilmer Flores .20 .50
591 Christian Walker .20 .50
592 Carson Kelly .15 .40
593 Greg Holland .15 .40
594 Merrill Kelly RC .30 .75
595 Corbin Martin RC .50 1.25
596 Russell Martin .15 .40
597 Austin Barnes .15 .40
598 Kevin Pillar .15 .40

599 Gerardo Parra .15 .40
600 Jeff Samardzija .15 .40
601 Drew Pomeranz .15 .40
602 Cohnor Joe RC .30 .75
603 Tyler Naquin .15 .40
604 Nate Lowe RC .40 1.00
605 Adam Cimber .15 .40
606 Domingo Santana .20 .50
607 Omar Narvaez .20 .50
608 Braden Bishop RC .40 1.00
609 Curtis Granderson .20 .50
610 Neil Walker .20 .50
611 Sergio Romo .15 .40
612 Trevor Richards RC .30 .75
613 Cal Quantrill RC .30 .75
614 Austin Riley RC 1.50 4.00
615 Skye Bolt RC .40 1.00
616 Jorge Lopez .15 .40
617 J.D. Davis .15 .40
618 Matt Adams .15 .40
619 Jeremy Hellickson .15 .40
620 Dwight Smith Jr. .15 .40
621 Drew Jackson RC .30 .75
622 David Hess .15 .40
623 Rio Ruiz .15 .40
624 Francisco Mejia .20 .50
625 Nick Margevicius RC .30 .75
626 Eric Lauer .15 .40
627 David Robertson .15 .40
628 Jason Martin RC .40 1.00
629 Melky Cabrera .15 .40
630 Jung Ho Kang .15 .40
631 Adam Frazier .15 .40
632 Francisco Liriano .15 .40
633 Delino DeShields .15 .40
634 Asdrubal Cabrera .20 .50
635 Logan Forsythe .15 .40
636 Yandy Diaz .20 .50
637 Ji-Man Choi .15 .40
638 Avisail Garcia .20 .50
639 Jose Alvarado .15 .40
640 Blake Swihart .20 .50
641 Matt Barnes .15 .40
642 Curt Casali .15 .40
643 Jose Iglesias .20 .50
644 Derek Dietrich .20 .50
645 Tanner Roark .15 .40
646 Amir Garrett .15 .40
647 Josh Fuentes RC .50 1.25
648 Mark Reynolds .15 .40
649 Ryan McMahon .15 .40
650 Homer Bailey .15 .40
651 Martin Maldonado .15 .40
652 Richard Lovelady RC .30 .75
653 Kyle Zimmer RC .30 .75
654 Ian Kennedy .15 .40
655 JaCoby Jones .20 .50
656 Jordy Mercer .15 .40
657 Matt Moore .20 .50
658 Tyson Ross .15 .40
659 Grayson Greiner .15 .40
660 Jake Cave RC .40 1.00
661 Kyle Gibson .20 .50
662 Michael Pineda .15 .40
663 Brett Gardner .20 .50
664 Domingo German .20 .50
665 John Means RC .50 1.25
666 Jesus Sucre .15 .40
667 Brandon Kintzler .15 .40
668 Leury Garcia .15 .40
669 Kelvin Herrera .15 .40
670 Kevin Plawecki .15 .40
671 Max Moroff .15 .40
672 Brandon Brennan RC .30 .75
673 Hansel Robles .15 .40
674 Matt Harvey .20 .50
675 Tommy La Stella .15 .40
676 Ryan Pressly .15 .40
677 Brett Anderson .15 .40
678 Billy McKinney .15 .40
679 Aaron Sanchez .20 .50
680 Clayton Richard .15 .40
681 Cole Tucker RC .50 1.25
682 Charlie Culberson .15 .40
683 Junior Guerra .15 .40
684 Pedro Avila RC .30 .75
685 Anthony DeSclafani .15 .40
686 Shelby Miller .20 .50
687 Scott Oberg .15 .40
688 Jake Marisnick .15 .40
689 Terrance Gore .15 .40
690 Scott Alexander .15 .40
691 David Freese .15 .40
692 Nick Anderson RC .30 .75
693 Renato Nunez .20 .50
694 Ryan Brasier .15 .40
695 Raimel Tapia .15 .40
696 Josh Sborz RC .30 .75
697 Travis Bergen RC .30 .75
698 Joe Harvey RC .30 .75
699 Caleb Smith .15 .40
700 Nick Kingham .15 .40
701 Victor Robles SP 2.50 6.00
702 Andrew McCutchen SP 2.00 5.00
703 Chris Paddack SP RC 2.50 6.00
704 Hunter Pence SP 1.50 4.00
705 Adam Jones SP 1.50 4.00
706 Daniel Vogelbach SP 1.25 3.00
707 Dominic Smith SP 1.25 3.00
708 Clint Frazier SP 1.50 4.00
709 Gio Gonzalez SP 1.50 4.00
710 Cameron Maybin SP 1.25 3.00
711 Johnny Cueto SP 1.50 4.00
712 Hunter Strickland SP 1.25 3.00
713 Chris Devenski SP 1.25 3.00
714 Franklin Barreto SP 1.25 3.00
715 Thomas Pannone SP RC 2.00 5.00
716 Alen Hanson SP 1.50 4.00
717 Ryan Helsley SP RC 1.50 4.00
718 Erik Swanson SP RC 1.25 3.00
719 Tayron Guerrero SP RC 1.25 3.00
720 Anibal Sanchez SP 1.25 3.00
721 Mychal Givens SP 1.25 3.00
722 Hector Neris SP 1.25 3.00
723 Dominic Leone SP 1.25 3.00
724 Luis Cessa SP 1.25 3.00
725 Ichiro SP 2.50 6.00

2019 Topps Heritage Action Variations

STATED ODDS 1:41 HOBBY
STATED HN ODDS 1:26 HOBBY
78 Mookie Betts 6.00 15.00
384 Michael Kopech 10.00 25.00
387 Luis Urias 6.00 15.00
392 Danny Jansen 2.50 6.00
393 Corbin Burnes 4.00 10.00
394 Kyle Tucker 10.00 25.00
401 Francisco Lindor 4.00 10.00
404 Kris Bryant 5.00 12.00
406 Anthony Rizzo 6.00 15.00
409 Jose Altuve 3.00 8.00
410 Christian Yelich 5.00 12.00
413 Gleyber Torres 8.00 20.00
415 Bryce Harper 6.00 15.00
419 Jacob deGrom 4.00 10.00
424 Alex Bregman 4.00 10.00
430 Shohei Ohtani 12.00 30.00
436 Ozzie Albies 4.00 10.00
440 Javier Baez 5.00 12.00
458 Rhys Hoskins 5.00 12.00
468 Nolan Arenado 5.00 12.00
475 J.D. Martinez 4.00 10.00
481 Juan Soto 25.00 60.00
485 Mike Trout 25.00 60.00
499 Aaron Judge 10.00 25.00
500 Ronald Acuna Jr. 25.00 60.00
501 Michael Chavis 4.00 10.00
504 Vladimir Guerrero Jr. 40.00 100.00
506 Yasmani Grandal 2.50 6.00
507 Nick Senzel 8.00 20.00
508 Brendan Rodgers 4.00 10.00
512 Keston Hiura 20.00 50.00
516 Eloy Jimenez 15.00 40.00
517 Fernando Tatis Jr. 40.00 100.00
519 Pete Alonso 40.00 100.00
520 Manny Machado 4.00 10.00
523 Carter Kieboom 4.00 10.00
526 Yusei Kikuchi 4.00 10.00
527 Jorge Alfaro 2.50 6.00
534 Bryce Harper 6.00 15.00
535 J.T. Realmuto 4.00 10.00
537 Austin Meadows 3.00 8.00
539 Byron Buxton 3.00 8.00
540 Alex Verdugo 3.00 8.00
545 Troy Tulowitzki 4.00 10.00
591 Christian Walker 3.00 8.00
701 Victor Robles 5.00 12.00
702 Andrew McCutchen 4.00 10.00
703 Chris Paddack 5.00 12.00
708 Clint Frazier 3.00 8.00
725 Ichiro 5.00 12.00

2019 Topps Heritage Black Border

*BLACK: 10X TO 25X BASIC
*BLACK RC: 5X TO 12X BASIC RC
*BLACK SP: 1.2X TO 3X BASIC SP
STATED ODDS 1:62 HOBBY
STATED HN ODDS 1:86 HOBBY
ANNCD PRINT RUN OF 50 COPIES EACH
357 Mike Trout AS 40.00 100.00
413 Gleyber Torres 20.00 50.00
430 Shohei Ohtani 40.00 100.00
481 Juan Soto 40.00 100.00
485 Mike Trout 75.00 200.00
499 Aaron Judge 60.00 150.00
500 Ronald Acuna Jr. 125.00 300.00
504 Vladimir Guerrero Jr. 75.00 200.00
512 Keston Hiura 25.00 60.00
516 Eloy Jimenez 60.00 150.00
517 Fernando Tatis Jr. 200.00 500.00
519 Pete Alonso 125.00 300.00

2019 Topps Heritage French Text

*FRENCH: 10X TO 25X BASIC
*FRENCH RC: 5X TO 12X BASIC RC
*FRENCH SP: 1.2X TO 3X BASIC SP
STATED ODDS 1:164 HOBBY
STATED HN ODDS 1:345 HOBBY
485 Mike Trout 40.00 100.00
516 Eloy Jimenez 25.00 60.00
517 Fernando Tatis Jr. 50.00 120.00
519 Pete Alonso 50.00 120.00

2019 Topps Heritage Silver Metal

STATED ODDS 1:817 HOBBY
STATED HN ODDS 1:689 HOBBY
ANNCD PRINT RUN 70 SER.#'d SETS
52 Chris Archer 5.00 12.00
78 Mookie Betts 12.00 30.00
83 Noah Syndergaard 6.00 15.00
98 Nicholas Castellanos 8.00 20.00
117 Kyle Schwarber 8.00 20.00
163 Rafael Devers 10.00 25.00
347 David Bote 6.00 15.00
401 Francisco Lindor 8.00 20.00
402 Salvador Perez 6.00 15.00
403 Jake Arrieta 6.00 15.00
404 Kris Bryant 10.00 25.00
405 Jon Lester 6.00 15.00
406 Anthony Rizzo 12.00 30.00
407 George Springer 6.00 15.00
408 Sean Manaea 5.00 12.00
409 Jose Altuve 6.00 15.00
410 Christian Yelich 10.00 25.00
411 Blake Snell 6.00 15.00
412 Trevor Bauer 8.00 20.00
413 Gleyber Torres 30.00 80.00
414 Paul DeJong 8.00 20.00
415 Bryce Harper 30.00 80.00
416 Luis Severino 6.00 15.00
417 Jordan Hicks 6.00 15.00
418 Gary Sanchez 8.00 20.00
419 Jacob deGrom 8.00 20.00
421 Justin Upton 6.00 15.00
422 Albert Pujols 10.00 25.00
423 Carlos Correa 8.00 20.00
424 Alex Bregman 8.00 20.00
425 Franmil Reyes 5.00 12.00
426 Justin Verlander 8.00 20.00
427 Walker Buehler 10.00 25.00
428 Trey Mancini 6.00 15.00
429 Gerrit Cole 8.00 20.00
430 Shohei Ohtani 40.00 100.00
431 Brandon Nimmo 6.00 15.00
432 Khris Davis 8.00 20.00
433 Justin Smoak 5.00 12.00
434 Stephen Piscotty 5.00 12.00
435 Miles Mikolas 8.00 20.00
436 Ozzie Albies 8.00 20.00
437 Lorenzo Cain 5.00 12.00
438 Matt Carpenter 8.00 20.00
439 Yadier Molina 8.00 20.00
440 Javier Baez 10.00 25.00
441 Paul Goldschmidt 8.00 20.00
442 Zack Greinke 6.00 15.00
443 Matt Kemp 6.00 15.00
444 Kenta Maeda 6.00 15.00
445 Buster Posey 10.00 25.00
446 Max Muncy 6.00 15.00
447 Edwin Encarnacion 8.00 20.00
448 Corey Kluber 6.00 15.00
449 Dee Gordon 5.00 12.00
450 Jean Segura 8.00 20.00
451 Edwin Diaz 6.00 15.00
452 Starlin Castro 5.00 12.00
453 J.T. Realmuto 8.00 20.00
454 Max Scherzer 8.00 20.00
455 Trea Turner 6.00 15.00
456 Jonathan Schoop 5.00 12.00
457 Eric Hosmer 6.00 15.00
458 Rhys Hoskins 10.00 25.00
459 Aaron Nola 6.00 15.00
460 Felipe Vasquez 5.00 12.00
461 Shin-Soo Choo 6.00 15.00
462 Nomar Mazara 5.00 12.00
463 Kevin Kiermaier 6.00 15.00
464 Chris Sale 8.00 20.00
465 Joey Votto 8.00 20.00
466 Scooter Gennett 6.00 15.00
467 Eugenio Suarez 6.00 15.00
468 Nolan Arenado 10.00 25.00
469 Trevor Story 8.00 20.00
470 Starling Marte 6.00 15.00
471 Charlie Blackmon 8.00 20.00
472 Miguel Cabrera 8.00 20.00
473 Miguel Andujar 8.00 20.00
474 Giancarlo Stanton 8.00 20.00
475 J.D. Martinez 8.00 20.00
476 Jesus Aguilar 5.00 12.00
477 Mitch Haniger 6.00 15.00
478 Brandon Crawford 6.00 15.00
479 Jose Berrios 6.00 15.00
480 Lourdes Gurriel Jr. 6.00 15.00
481 Juan Soto 25.00 60.00
483 Jose Abreu 8.00 20.00
484 Andrew Benintendi 8.00 20.00
485 Mike Trout 125.00 300.00
486 Adam Jones 6.00 15.00
487 Xander Bogaerts 8.00 20.00
488 Odubel Herrera 6.00 15.00
490 Clayton Kershaw 15.00 40.00
491 Jose Ramirez 6.00 15.00
493 Aroldis Chapman 8.00 20.00
494 Wil Myers 5.00 12.00
498 Amed Rosario 6.00 15.00
499 Aaron Judge 100.00 250.00
500 Ronald Acuna Jr. 50.00 120.00
501 Michael Chavis 8.00 20.00
502 Charlie Morton 8.00 20.00
503 Michael Brantley 6.00 15.00
504 Vladimir Guerrero Jr. 125.00 300.00
505 Nick Markakis 6.00 15.00
506 Yasmani Grandal 5.00 12.00
507 Nick Senzel 15.00 40.00
508 Brendan Rodgers 12.00 30.00
512 Keston Hiura 30.00 80.00
516 Eloy Jimenez 30.00 80.00
517 Fernando Tatis Jr. 200.00 500.00
519 Pete Alonso 125.00 300.00
520 Manny Machado 8.00 20.00
521 Andrew Miller 6.00 15.00
522 A.J. Pollock 5.00 12.00
523 Carter Kieboom 8.00 20.00
525 Justus Sheffield 8.00 20.00
526 Yusei Kikuchi 8.00 20.00
527 Jorge Alfaro 5.00 12.00
529 Brian Dozier 6.00 15.00
530 Patrick Corbin 6.00 15.00
533 Jon Duplantier 5.00 12.00
534 Bryce Harper 30.00 80.00
535 J.T. Realmuto 8.00 20.00
537 Austin Meadows 6.00 15.00
538 Tyler Glasnow 5.00 12.00
539 Byron Buxton 6.00 15.00
540 Alex Verdugo 6.00 15.00
541 Yasiel Puig 8.00 20.00
542 Nicky Lopez 8.00 20.00
543 Sonny Gray 6.00 15.00
544 Daniel Murphy 6.00 15.00
545 Troy Tulowitzki 8.00 20.00
546 DJ LeMahieu 8.00 20.00
547 J.A. Happ 6.00 15.00
548 Adam Ottavino 5.00 12.00
549 Zack Britton 5.00 12.00
551 Ian Kinsler 6.00 15.00
566 Jonathan Lucroy 6.00 15.00
575 Freddy Galvis 5.00 12.00
577 Max Fried 8.00 20.00
580 Brandon Woodruff 5.00 12.00
595 Corbin Martin 8.00 20.00
598 Kevin Pillar 5.00 12.00
624 Francisco Mejia 6.00 15.00
664 Domingo German 6.00 15.00
701 Victor Robles 10.00 25.00
702 Andrew McCutchen 8.00 20.00
703 Chris Paddack 10.00 25.00
725 Ichiro 10.00 25.00

2019 Topps Heritage Team Color Swap Variations

STATED ODDS 1:245 HOBBY
STATED HN ODDS 1:154 HOBBY
78 Mookie Betts 8.00 20.00
401 Francisco Lindor 8.00 20.00
404 Kris Bryant 6.00 15.00
406 Anthony Rizzo 8.00 20.00
409 Jose Altuve 4.00 10.00
410 Christian Yelich 6.00 15.00
413 Gleyber Torres 15.00 40.00
415 Bryce Harper 8.00 20.00
419 Jacob deGrom 5.00 12.00
424 Alex Bregman 5.00 12.00
426 Justin Verlander 5.00 12.00
430 Shohei Ohtani 6.00 15.00
432 Khris Davis 5.00 12.00
436 Ozzie Albies 5.00 12.00
440 Javier Baez 6.00 15.00
442 Zack Greinke 4.00 10.00
451 Edwin Diaz 4.00 10.00
454 Max Scherzer 5.00 12.00
458 Rhys Hoskins 6.00 15.00
468 Nolan Arenado 6.00 15.00
475 J.D. Martinez 5.00 12.00
481 Juan Soto 20.00 40.00
485 Mike Trout 40.00 100.00
499 Aaron Judge 20.00 80.00
500 Ronald Acuna Jr. 25.00 60.00
501 Michael Chavis 5.00 12.00
504 Vladimir Guerrero Jr. 25.00 60.00
506 Yasmani Grandal 3.00 8.00
507 Nick Senzel 10.00 25.00
508 Brendan Rodgers 8.00 20.00
512 Keston Hiura 15.00 40.00
516 Eloy Jimenez 20.00 50.00
517 Fernando Tatis Jr. 40.00 100.00
519 Pete Alonso 25.00 60.00
520 Manny Machado 5.00 12.00
523 Carter Kieboom 5.00 12.00
526 Yusei Kikuchi 5.00 12.00
527 Jorge Alfaro 6.00 15.00
534 Bryce Harper 8.00 20.00
535 J.T. Realmuto 5.00 12.00
537 Austin Meadows 4.00 10.00
539 Byron Buxton 6.00 15.00
540 Alex Verdugo 4.00 10.00
545 Troy Tulowitzki 5.00 12.00
591 Christian Walker 4.00 10.00
701 Victor Robles 6.00 15.00
702 Andrew McCutchen 5.00 12.00
703 Chris Paddack 6.00 15.00
708 Clint Frazier 6.00 15.00
725 Ichiro 8.00 20.00

2019 Topps Heritage '70 Postal Stamps

STATED ODDS 1:5718 HOBBY
STATED PRINT RUN 50 SER.#'d SETS
70USAK Al Kaline 30.00 80.00
70USBR Brooks Robinson 20.00 50.00
70USBW Billy Williams 20.00 50.00
70USFJ Fergie Jenkins 20.00 50.00
70USHA Hank Aaron 40.00 100.00
70USHK Harmon Killebrew 30.00 80.00
70USJB Johnny Bench 30.00 80.00
70USJM Joe Morgan 20.00 50.00
70USJP Jim Palmer 30.00 80.00
70USLA Luis Aparicio 20.00 50.00
70USLB Lou Brock 20.00 50.00
70USNR Nolan Ryan 50.00 120.00
70USOC Orlando Cepeda 20.00 50.00
70USRC Rod Carew 20.00 50.00
70USRJ Reggie Jackson 30.00 80.00
70USSC Steve Carlton 20.00 50.00
70USTP Tony Perez 30.00 80.00
70USTS Tom Seaver 30.00 80.00
70USWM Willie McCovey 30.00 80.00
70USWS Willie Stargell 30.00 80.00

2019 Topps Heritage '70 Poster Boxloader

STATED ODDS 1:31 HOBBY BOX
STATED HN ODDS 1:19 HOBBY BOX
1 Shohei Ohtani 20.00 50.00
2 Jose Altuve 12.00 30.00
3 Khris Davis 10.00 25.00
4 Justin Smoak 15.00 40.00
5 Ronald Acuna Jr. 25.00 60.00
6 Christian Yelich 12.00 30.00
7 Matt Carpenter 15.00 40.00
8 Kris Bryant 12.00 30.00
9 Paul Goldschmidt 20.00 50.00
10 Clayton Kershaw 20.00 50.00
11 Buster Posey 25.00 60.00
12 Francisco Lindor 10.00 25.00
13 Edwin Diaz 8.00 20.00
14 Starlin Castro 6.00 15.00
15 Noah Syndergaard 8.00 20.00
16 Juan Soto 20.00 50.00
17 Trey Mancini 12.00 30.00
18 Eric Hosmer 8.00 20.00
19 Rhys Hoskins 15.00 40.00
20 Starling Marte 12.00 30.00
21 Adrian Beltre 15.00 40.00
22 Blake Snell 12.00 30.00
23 Mookie Betts 15.00 40.00
24 Joey Votto 20.00 50.00
25 Nolan Arenado 12.00 30.00
26 Salvador Perez 8.00 20.00
27 Miguel Cabrera 25.00 60.00
28 Joe Mauer 30.00 50.00
29 Jose Abreu 15.00 40.00
30 Aaron Judge 20.00 50.00
31 Mike Trout 60.00 150.00
32 Carlos Correa 15.00 40.00
33 Stephen Piscotty 6.00 15.00
34 Vladimir Guerrero Jr. 25.00 60.00
35 Freddie Freeman 12.00 30.00
36 Lorenzo Cain 6.00 15.00
37 Yadier Molina 15.00 40.00
38 Anthony Rizzo 15.00 40.00
39 Zack Greinke 8.00 20.00
40 Corey Seager 10.00 25.00
41 Evan Longoria 20.00 50.00
42 Jose Ramirez 8.00 20.00
43 Yusei Kikuchi 15.00 40.00
44 Brian Anderson 6.00 15.00
45 Jacob deGrom 10.00 25.00
46 Max Scherzer 15.00 40.00
47 Jonathan Villar 6.00 15.00
48 Manny Machado 10.00 25.00
49 Bryce Harper 15.00 40.00
50 Felipe Vasquez 6.00 15.00
51 Joey Gallo 8.00 20.00
52 Austin Meadows 8.00 20.00
53 J.D. Martinez 15.00 40.00
54 Yasiel Puig 15.00 40.00
55 Trevor Story 10.00 25.00
56 Whit Merrifield 15.00 40.00
57 Nicholas Castellanos 15.00 40.00
58 Jose Berrios 15.00 40.00
59 Eloy Jimenez 25.00 60.00
60 Giancarlo Stanton 10.00 25.00

2019 Topps Heritage '70 Super Boxloader

STATED ODDS 1:3 HOBBY BOX
STATED HN ODDS 1:3 HOBBY BOX
1 Gleyber Torres 4.00 10.00
2 Mookie Betts 3.00 8.00
3 Mike Trout 10.00 25.00
4 Shohei Ohtani 2.50 6.00
5 Juan Soto 6.00 15.00
6 Kris Bryant 2.50 6.00
7 Ronald Acuna Jr. 10.00 25.00
8 Carl Yastrzemski 8.00 20.00
9 Nolan Ryan 6.00 15.00
10 Bob Gibson 1.50 4.00
11 Al Kaline 5.00 12.00
12 Brooks Robinson 1.50 4.00
13 Johnny Bench 5.00 12.00
14 Roberto Clemente 10.00 25.00
15 Thurman Munson 5.00 12.00
16 Aaron Judge 5.00 12.00
17 Cody Bellinger 4.00 10.00
18 Bryce Harper 3.00 8.00
19 Christian Yelich 2.50 6.00
20 Manny Machado 2.00 5.00
21 Ichiro 5.00 12.00
22 Hank Aaron 4.00 10.00
23 Willie Mays 4.00 10.00
24 Jim Palmer 1.50 4.00
25 Carter Kieboom 2.00 5.00
26 Yusei Kikuchi 2.00 5.00
27 Eloy Jimenez 6.00 15.00
28 Fernando Tatis Jr. 12.00 30.00
29 Pete Alonso 10.00 25.00
30 Vladimir Guerrero Jr. 8.00 20.00

2019 Topps Heritage '70 Topps Candy Lids

STATED ODDS 1:8 RETAIL
1 Max Scherzer .50 1.25
2 Mike Trout 2.50 6.00
3 Aaron Nola .40 1.00
4 Giancarlo Stanton .50 1.25
5 Anthony Rizzo .75 2.00
6 Joey Votto .50 1.25
7 Ozzie Albies .50 1.25
8 Francisco Lindor .50 1.25
9 Jose Altuve .40 1.00
10 Matt Carpenter .50 1.25
11 Blake Snell .40 1.00
12 Buster Posey .60 1.50
13 Carlos Correa .50 1.25
14 Miguel Andujar .50 1.25
15 Bryce Harper .75 2.00
16 Kris Bryant .60 1.50
17 Shohei Ohtani .60 1.50
18 Aaron Judge 1.50 4.00
19 Mookie Betts .75 2.00
20 Pete Alonso 2.50 6.00
21 Fernando Tatis Jr. 3.00 8.00
22 Christian Yelich .60 1.50
23 Eloy Jimenez 1.25 3.00
24 Cody Bellinger 1.00 2.50
25 Ronald Acuna Jr. 2.50 6.00
26 Juan Soto 1.50 4.00
27 Manny Machado .50 1.25
28 Paul Goldschmidt .50 1.25
29 Rhys Hoskins .60 1.50
30 Vladimir Guerrero Jr. 2.00 5.00

2019 Topps Heritage '70 Topps Player Story Booklets

STATED ODDS 1:972 RETAIL
ANNCD PRINT RUN 250 COPIES PER
1 Aaron Judge 25.00 60.00
2 Miguel Cabrera 8.00 20.00
3 Salvador Perez 6.00 15.00
4 Jose Altuve 6.00 15.00
5 Mike Trout 30.00 80.00
6 Felix Hernandez 6.00 15.00
7 Adrian Beltre 8.00 20.00
8 Freddie Freeman 10.00 25.00
9 Rhys Hoskins 10.00 25.00
10 Kris Bryant 15.00 40.00
11 Joey Votto 8.00 20.00
12 Yadier Molina 12.00 30.00
13 Buster Posey 10.00 25.00
14 Nolan Arenado 10.00 25.00
15 Clayton Kershaw 15.00 40.00
16 Mookie Betts 12.00 30.00
17 Jacob deGrom 8.00 20.00
18 Christian Yelich 10.00 25.00
19 Manny Machado 8.00 20.00
20 Jose Berrios 6.00 15.00
21 Juan Soto 12.00 30.00
22 Blake Snell 6.00 15.00
23 Francisco Lindor 8.00 20.00
24 Khris Davis 8.00 20.00
25 Lewis Brinson 5.00 12.00
26 Trey Mancini 12.00 30.00
27 Eloy Jimenez 10.00 25.00
28 Zack Greinke 6.00 15.00
29 Vladimir Guerrero Jr. 20.00 50.00
30 Starling Marte 6.00 15.00

2019 Topps Heritage '70 Topps Scratch Offs

STATED ODDS 1:24 HOBBY
1 Mike Trout 3.00 8.00
2 Jose Altuve .50 1.25
3 Khris Davis .60 1.50
4 Justin Smoak .40 1.00
5 Freddie Freeman .75 2.00
6 Lorenzo Cain .40 1.00
7 Yadier Molina .60 1.50
8 Anthony Rizzo 1.00 2.50
9 Paul Goldschmidt .60 1.50
10 Clayton Kershaw 1.25 3.00
11 Buster Posey .75 2.00
12 Francisco Lindor .60 1.50
13 Robinson Cano .50 1.25
14 Starlin Castro .40 1.00
15 Noah Syndergaard .50 1.25
16 Max Scherzer .60 1.50
17 Trey Mancini .50 1.25
18 Eric Hosmer .60 1.50
19 Rhys Hoskins .75 2.00
20 Starling Marte .50 1.25
21 Elvis Andrus .50 1.25
22 Blake Snell .50 1.25
23 Mookie Betts 1.00 2.50
24 Joey Votto .60 1.50
25 Nolan Arenado .75 2.00
26 Salvador Perez .50 1.25
27 Miguel Cabrera .60 1.50
28 Jose Berrios .50 1.25
29 Jose Abreu .60 1.50
30 Aaron Judge 1.50 4.00

2019 Topps Heritage '70 Topps Stickers

INSERTED IN WALMART PACKS
1 Aaron Judge 1.50 4.00
2 Kris Bryant .75 2.00
3 Clayton Kershaw 1.25 3.00
4 Juan Soto 2.00 5.00
5 Gleyber Torres 1.25 3.00
6 Mookie Betts 1.00 2.50
7 Ronald Acuna Jr. 3.00 8.00
8 Paul Goldschmidt .60 1.50
9 Jose Ramirez .60 1.50
10 J.D. Martinez .60 1.50
11 Jacob deGrom .60 1.50
12 Rhys Hoskins .75 2.00
13 Khris Davis .60 1.50
14 Justin Verlander .60 1.50
15 Nolan Arenado .75 2.00
16 Shohei Ohtani .75 2.00
17 Eloy Jimenez 1.50 4.00
18 Fernando Tatis Jr. 10.00 25.00
19 Pete Alonso 3.00 8.00
20 Manny Machado .60 1.50
21 Yusei Kikuchi .60 1.50
22 Bryce Harper 1.00 2.50
23 Ichiro .75 2.00
24 Cody Bellinger 1.25 3.00
25 Christian Yelich .75 2.00
26 Mike Trout 5.00 12.00
27 Jose Altuve .50 1.25
28 Victor Robles .75 2.00
29 Vladimir Guerrero Jr. 2.50 6.00
30 Javier Baez .75 2.00

2019 Topps Heritage Award Winners

STATED HN ODDS 1:8 HOBBY
AW1 Mookie Betts .60 1.50
AW2 Christian Yelich .50 1.25
AW3 Blake Snell .30 .75
AW4 Jacob deGrom .40 1.00
AW5 Shohei Ohtani .50 1.25
AW6 Ronald Acuna Jr. 2.00 5.00
AW7 Steve Pearce .40 1.00
AW8 Alex Bregman .40 1.00
AW9 J.D. Martinez .40 1.00
AW10 Christian Yelich .50 1.25

2019 Topps Heritage Baseball Flashbacks

COMPLETE SET (15) 8.00 20.00
STATED ODDS 1:18 HOBBY
BFAK Al Kaline .60 1.50
BFBG Bob Gibson .50 1.25
BFBR Brooks Robinson .50 1.25
BFCY Carl Yastrzemski 1.00 2.50
BFHA Hank Aaron 1.25 3.00
BFJB Johnny Bench .60 1.50
BFJM Juan Marichal .50 1.25
BFJT Joe Torre .50 1.25
BFNR Nolan Ryan 2.00 5.00
BFRC Rod Carew .50 1.25
BFRJ Reggie Jackson .50 1.25
BFSC Steve Carlton .50 1.25
BFTM Thurman Munson .60 1.50
BFTS Tom Seaver .50 1.25
BFWM Willie McCovey .50 1.25

2019 Topps Heritage Brew Crew Autographs

STATED ODDS 1:3738 HOBBY
STATED PRINT RUN 100 SER.#'d SETS
EXCHANGE DEADLINE 1/31/2021
IBCBL Bob Locker 50.00 210.00
IBCBM Bob Meyer 50.00 120.00
IBCBS Bud Selig 75.00 200.00
IBCDB Dave Baldwin 50.00 120.00
IBCFS Fred Stanley 50.00 120.00
IBCKS Ken Sanders 50.00 120.00
IBCLK Lew Krausse 60.00 150.00
IBCMA Max Alvis 50.00 120.00
IBCRP Ray Peters 60.00 150.00
IBCWC Wayne Comer 50.00 120.00

2019 Topps Heritage Chrome

STATED ODDS 1:58 HOBBY
STATED HN ODDS 1:49 HOBBY
STATED PRINT RUN 999 SER.#'d SETS
*PRPLE REF: .4X TO 1X BASIC
*REF/569: .6X TO 1.5X BASIC
THC2 Felix Hernandez MB 1.50 4.00
THC7 Kopech/Frare 2.50 6.00
THC17 Sean Newcomb MB 1.25 3.00
THC19 Russell Martin MB 1.25 3.00
THC25 Eddie Rosario MB 1.50 4.00
THC29 Andrelton Simmons MB 1.25 3.00
THC30 Gregory Polanco MB 1.50 4.00
THC34 Cody Bellinger MB 4.00 10.00
THC39 Brock Holt MB 1.25 3.00
THC42 Evan Longoria MB 1.50 4.00
THC43 Luke Voit MB 3.00 8.00
THC50 Yoenis Cespedes MB 1.50 4.00
THC52 Chris Archer 1.25 3.00
THC53 Orlando Arcia MB 1.25 3.00
THC55 Lou Trivino MB 1.25 3.00
THC78 Mookie Betts 3.00 8.00
THC80 Ian Happ MB 1.50 4.00
THC83 Noah Syndergaard 1.50 4.00
THC89 Adalberto Mondesi MB 1.50 4.00
THC92 Jack Flaherty MB 1.50 4.00
THC93 Jorge Polanco MB 1.25 3.00
THC98 Nicholas Castellanos MB 2.00 5.00
THC100 Masahiro Tanaka MB 1.50 4.00
THC101 Tim Beckham MB 1.25 3.00
THC105 Ender Inciarte MB 1.25 3.00
THC106 Stephen Strasburg MB 2.00 5.00
THC108 Alex Gordon MB 1.50 4.00
THC111 Ryan Braun MB 1.50 4.00
THC115 Billy Hamilton MB 1.50 4.00
THC117 Kyle Schwarber MB 2.00 5.00
THC119 Michael Wacha MB 1.50 4.00
THC120 Matt Chapman MB 2.00 5.00
THC124 Marcus Stroman MB 1.50 4.00
THC125 Maikel Franco MB 1.25 3.00
THC127 Jurickson Profar MB 1.50 4.00
THC130 Hunter Renfroe MB 1.25 3.00
THC136 Carlos Carrasco MB 1.25 3.00
THC138 James Paxton MB 1.50 4.00
THC144 Joey Gallo MB 1.50 4.00
THC148 Ronald Guzman MB 1.25 3.00
THC163 Rafael Devers 2.50 6.00
THC179 Manny Margot MB 1.25 3.00
THC180 Daniel Palka MB 1.25 3.00
THC181 Ryan Yarbrough MB 1.25 3.00
THC186 Scott Kingery MB 1.50 4.00
THC187 Whit Merrifield MB 2.00 5.00
THC188 Corey Dickerson MB 1.25 3.00
THC189 Adams/Loaisiga 1.50 4.00
THC191 David Price MB 1.50 4.00
THC194 Tommy Pham MB 1.25 3.00
THC211 Willy Adames MB 1.25 3.00
THC213 Mark Trumbo MB 1.25 3.00
THC214 Todd Frazier MB 1.50 4.00
THC216 Josh Bell MB 1.50 4.00
THC220 Marcell Ozuna MB 2.00 5.00
THC223 Ben Zobrist MB 1.50 4.00
THC226 Miguel Sano MB 1.50 4.00

HC227 Perez/Tucker 2.50 6.00
HC229 Freddy Peralta MB 2.00 5.00
HC231 Travis Shaw MB 1.25 3.00
HC232 A.J. Minter MB 1.50 4.00
HC233 Blake Treinen MB 1.25 3.00
HC235 Ryan Zimmerman MB 1.50 4.00
HC236 Jameson Taillon MB 1.50 4.00
HC239 Avisail Garcia MB 1.50 4.00
HC240 Yu Darvish MB 2.00 5.00
HC245 Wade Davis MB 1.25 3.00
HC247 Jason Kipnis MB 1.50 4.00
HC249 Jeremy Jeffress MB 1.25 3.00
HC250 Brandon Belt MB 1.50 4.00
HC252 Pat Neshek MB 1.25 3.00
HC253 Kyle Freeland MB 1.50 4.00
HC254 Luis Castillo MB 1.50 4.00
HC256 David Dahl MB 1.25 3.00
HC258 Cole Hamels MB 1.50 4.00
HC260 German Marquez MB 1.25 3.00
HC261 Lewis Brinson MB 1.25 3.00
HC262 Nix/Urias 2.00 5.00
HC269 Shane Greene MB 1.25 3.00
HC270 Jorge Alfaro MB 1.25 3.00
HC271 Kyle Seager MB 1.25 3.00
HC276 Pablo Sandoval MB 1.50 4.00
HC279 Rick Porcello MB 1.50 4.00
HC281 Rougned Odor MB 1.50 4.00
HC282 Harrison Bader MB 1.50 4.00
HC288 Cesar Hernandez MB 1.25 3.00
HC290 Jose Leclerc MB 1.25 3.00
HC293 Kevin Pillar MB 1.25 3.00
HC295 Kevin Gausman MB 1.25 3.00
HC298 Dereck Rodriguez MB 1.25 3.00
HC300 Zack Wheeler MB 1.50 4.00
HC302 Seranthony Dominguez MB 1.25 3.00
HC303 Elvis Andrus MB 1.50 4.00
HC313 Michael Fulmer MB 1.25 3.00
HC315 Yoan Moncada MB 2.00 5.00
HC316 Dansby Swanson MB 2.00 5.00
HC320 Raisel Iglesias MB 1.25 3.00
HC323 Robinson Cano MB 1.50 4.00
HC327 Mike Foltynewicz MB 2.00 5.00
HC331 Matt Olson MB 1.25 3.00
HC335 Josh Hader MB 1.25 3.00
HC340 Eduardo Nunez MB 1.25 3.00
HC341 Corey Seager MB 2.00 5.00
HC373 Aaron Hicks MB 1.50 4.00
HC382 Yuli Gurriel MB 1.50 4.00
HC388 Carlos Santana MB 1.50 4.00
HC390 Joc Pederson MB 1.50 4.00
HC401 Francisco Lindor 2.00 5.00
HC402 Salvador Perez 1.50 4.00
HC403 Jake Arrieta 1.50 4.00
THC404 Kris Bryant 2.50 6.00
THC405 Jon Lester 1.50 4.00
THC406 Anthony Rizzo 3.00 8.00
THC407 George Springer 1.50 4.00
THC408 Sean Manaea 1.25 3.00
THC409 Jose Altuve 1.50 4.00
THC410 Christian Yelich 2.50 6.00
THC411 Blake Snell 1.50 4.00
THC412 Trevor Bauer 2.00 5.00
THC413 Gleyber Torres 4.00 10.00
THC414 Paul DeJong 2.00 5.00
THC415 Bryce Harper 3.00 8.00
THC416 Luis Severino 1.50 4.00
THC417 Jordan Hicks 1.50 4.00
THC418 Gary Sanchez 2.00 5.00
THC419 Jacob deGrom 2.00 5.00
THC420 Kenley Jansen MB 1.50 4.00
THC421 Justin Upton 1.50 4.00
THC422 Albert Pujols 2.50 6.00
THC423 Carlos Correa 2.00 5.00
THC424 Alex Bregman 2.00 5.00
THC426 Justin Verlander 2.00 5.00
THC427 Walker Buehler 2.50 6.00
THC428 Trey Mancini 1.50 4.00
THC429 Gerrit Cole 2.00 5.00
THC430 Shohei Ohtani 2.50 6.00
THC431 Brandon Nimmo 1.50 4.00
THC432 Khris Davis 2.00 5.00
THC433 Justin Smoak 1.50 4.00
THC434 Stephen Piscotty 1.25 3.00
THC435 Miles Mikolas 2.00 5.00
THC436 Ozzie Albies 2.00 5.00
THC437 Lorenzo Cain 1.25 3.00
THC438 Matt Carpenter 2.00 5.00
THC439 Yadier Molina 2.00 5.00
THC440 Javier Baez 2.50 6.00
THC441 Paul Goldschmidt 2.00 5.00
THC442 Zack Greinke 1.50 4.00
THC443 Matt Kemp 1.50 4.00
THC444 Kenta Maeda 1.50 4.00
THC445 Buster Posey 2.50 6.00
THC446 Max Muncy 1.50 4.00
THC447 Edwin Encarnacion 2.00 5.00
THC448 Corey Kluber 1.50 4.00
THC449 Dee Gordon 1.25 3.00
THC450 Jean Segura 2.00 5.00
THC451 Edwin Diaz 1.50 4.00
THC452 Starlin Castro 1.25 3.00
THC453 J.T. Realmuto 2.00 5.00
THC454 Max Scherzer 2.00 5.00
THC455 Trea Turner 1.50 4.00
THC456 Jonathan Schoop 1.25 3.00
THC457 Eric Hosmer 1.50 4.00
THC458 Rhys Hoskins 2.50 6.00
THC459 Aaron Nola 1.50 4.00
THC460 Felipe Vasquez 1.25 3.00
THC461 Shin-Soo Choo 1.50 4.00
THC462 Nomar Mazara 1.25 3.00
THC463 Kevin Kiermaier 1.50 4.00
THC464 Chris Sale 2.00 5.00
THC465 Joey Votto 2.00 5.00
THC466 Scooter Gennett 1.50 4.00
THC467 Eugenio Suarez 1.50 4.00
THC468 Nolan Arenado 2.50 6.00
THC469 Trevor Story 2.00 5.00
THC470 Starling Marte 1.50 4.00
THC471 Charlie Blackmon 2.00 5.00
THC472 Miguel Cabrera 2.00 5.00
THC473 Miguel Andujar 2.00 5.00
THC474 Giancarlo Stanton 2.00 5.00
THC475 J.D. Martinez 2.00 5.00
THC476 Jesus Aguilar 1.25 3.00
THC477 Mitch Haniger 1.50 4.00
THC478 Brandon Crawford 1.50 4.00
THC479 Jose Berrios 1.50 4.00
THC480 Lourdes Gurriel Jr. 1.50 4.00
THC481 Juan Soto 15.00 40.00
THC483 Jose Abreu 2.00 5.00
THC484 Andrew Benintendi 2.00 5.00
THC485 Mike Trout 20.00 50.00
THC486 Adam Jones 1.50 4.00
THC487 Xander Bogaerts 2.00 5.00
THC488 Odubel Herrera 1.50 4.00
THC490 Clayton Kershaw 4.00 10.00
THC491 Jose Ramirez 1.50 4.00
THC493 Aroldis Chapman 2.00 5.00
THC494 Wil Myers 1.25 3.00
THC498 Amed Rosario 1.50 4.00
THC499 Aaron Judge 5.00 12.00
THC500 Ronald Acuna Jr. 15.00 40.00
THC501 Michael Chavis 2.00 5.00
THC502 Charlie Morton 2.00 5.00
THC503 Michael Brantley 1.50 4.00
THC504 Vladimir Guerrero Jr. 20.00 50.00
THC505 Nick Markakis 1.50 4.00
THC506 Yasmani Grandal 1.25 3.00
THC507 Nick Senzel 4.00 10.00
THC508 Brendan Rodgers 2.00 5.00
THC512 Keston Hiura 10.00 25.00
THC516 Eloy Jimenez 12.00 30.00
THC517 Fernando Tatis Jr 40.00 100.00
THC519 Pete Alonso 20.00 50.00
THC520 Manny Machado 2.00 5.00
THC521 Andrew Miller 1.50 4.00
THC522 A.J. Pollock 1.25 3.00
THC523 Carter Kieboom 4.00 10.00
THC524 Griffin Canning MB 2.00 5.00
THC525 Justus Sheffield 2.00 5.00
THC526 Yusei Kikuchi 2.00 5.00
THC527 Jorge Alfaro 1.25 3.00
THC529 Brian Dozier 1.50 4.00
THC530 Patrick Corbin 1.50 4.00
THC532 Richie Martin 1.25 3.00
THC533 Jon Duplantier 1.25 3.00
THC534 Bryce Harper 3.00 8.00
THC535 J.T. Realmuto 2.00 5.00
THC537 Austin Meadows 1.50 4.00
THC538 Tyler Glasnow 1.25 3.00
THC539 Byron Buxton 1.50 4.00
THC540 Alex Verdugo 1.50 4.00
THC541 Yasiel Puig 2.00 5.00
THC542 Nicky Lopez 2.00 5.00
THC543 Sonny Gray 1.50 4.00
THC544 Daniel Murphy 1.50 4.00
THC545 Troy Tulowitzki 2.00 5.00
THC546 DJ LeMahieu 2.00 5.00
THC547 J.A. Happ 1.50 4.00
THC548 Adam Ottavino 1.25 3.00
THC549 Zack Britton 1.25 3.00
THC551 Ian Kinsler 1.50 4.00
THC556 Jake Bauers 2.00 5.00
THC558 Wilson Ramos 1.25 3.00
THC560 Robinson Chirinos MB 1.25 3.00
THC562 Wade Miley MB 1.25 3.00
THC563 Danny Salazar 1.50 4.00
THC564 Tyler O'Neill 1.50 4.00
THC568 Nathan Eovaldi 1.50 4.00
THC573 Matt Shoemaker MB 1.50 4.00
THC575 Freddy Galvis MB 1.25 3.00
THC577 Max Fried MB 2.00 5.00
THC579 Brian McCann MB 1.50 4.00
THC580 Brandon Woodruff MB 1.25 3.00
THC581 Zach Davies MB 1.25 3.00
THC584 Adam Wainwright MB 1.50 4.00
THC585 Alex Reyes MB 1.50 4.00
THC591 Christian Walker MB 1.50 4.00
THC594 Merrill Kelly MB 1.25 3.00
THC595 Corbin Martin MB 2.00 5.00
THC596 Russell Martin MB 1.25 3.00
THC598 Kevin Pillar MB 1.25 3.00
THC600 Jeff Samardzija MB 1.25 3.00
THC604 Nate Lowe MB 1.50 4.00
THC605 Adam Cimber MB 1.25 3.00
THC606 Domingo Santana MB 1.50 4.00
THC624 Francisco Mejia MB 1.50 4.00
THC625 Nick Margevicius MB 1.25 3.00
THC629 Melky Cabrera MB 1.25 3.00
THC636 Yandy Diaz MB 1.50 4.00
THC637 Ji-Man Choi MB 1.25 3.00
THC639 Jose Alvarado MB 1.25 3.00
THC646 Amir Garrett MB 1.25 3.00
THC649 Ryan McMahon MB 1.25 3.00
THC654 Ian Kennedy MB 1.25 3.00
THC661 Kyle Gibson MB 1.50 4.00
THC663 Brett Gardner MB 1.50 4.00
THC664 Domingo German MB 1.50 4.00
THC672 Brandon Brennan MB 1.25 3.00
THC676 Ryan Pressly MB 1.25 3.00
THC683 Junior Guerra MB 1.25 3.00
THC692 Nick Anderson MB 1.25 3.00
THC694 Ryan Brasier MB 1.25 3.00
THC699 Caleb Smith MB 1.25 3.00
THC701 Victor Robles 2.50 6.00
THC702 Andrew McCutchen 2.00 5.00
THC703 Chris Paddack 2.50 6.00
THC704 Hunter Pence MB 1.50 4.00
THC705 Adam Jones MB 1.50 4.00
THC706 Daniel Vogelbach MB 1.25 3.00
THC707 Dominic Smith MB 1.25 3.00
THC708 Clint Frazier MB 1.50 4.00
THC709 Gio Gonzalez 1.50 4.00
THC710 Cameron Maybin 1.25 3.00
THC711 Johnny Cueto MB 1.50 4.00
THC712 Hunter Strickland MB 1.25 3.00
THC713 Chris Devenski MB 1.25 3.00
THC714 Franklin Barreto MB 1.25 3.00
THC719 Tayron Guerrero MB 1.25 3.00
THC721 Mychal Givens MB 1.25 3.00
THC722 Hector Neris MB 1.25 3.00
THC725 Ichiro 2.50 6.00

2019 Topps Heritage Chrome Black Refractors

*BLACK REF: 2X TO 5X BASIC
STATED ODDS 1:817 HOBBY
STATED HN ODDS 1:699 HOBBY
THC2-THC500 PRINT RUN 70 SER.#'d SETS
THC501-THC725 PRINT RUN 69 SER.#'d SETS
THC504 Vladimir Guerrero Jr. 200.00 500.00
THC512 Keston Hiura 100.00 250.00
THC516 Eloy Jimenez 100.00 250.00
THC517 Fernando Tatis Jr. 600.00 1200.00
THC519 Pete Alonso 300.00 600.00

2019 Topps Heritage Chrome Refractors

*REF: .6X TO 1.5X BASIC
STATED ODDS 1:101 HOBBY
STATED HN ODDS 1:85 HOBBY
THC2-THC500 PRINT RUN 570 SER.#'d SETS
THC501-THC725 PRINT RUN 569 SER.#'d SETS
THC504 Vladimir Guerrero Jr. 60.00 150.00
THC517 Fernando Tatis Jr. 125.00 300.00
THC523 Carter Kieboom 10.00 25.00

2019 Topps Heritage Clubhouse Collection Autograph Relics

STATED ODDS 1:14,867 HOBBY
STATED HN ODDS 1:6555 HOBBY
HN EXCH DEADLINE 7/31/2021
STATED PRINT RUN 25 SER.#'d SETS
EXCHANGE DEADLINE 1/31/2021
CCARAJ Aaron Judge 150.00 400.00
CCARAK Al Kaline HN 75.00 200.00
CCARBS Blake Snell 20.00 50.00
CCARBS Blake Snell HN 20.00 50.00
CCARCY Carl Yastrzemski HN 75.00 200.00
CCARDG Didi Gregorius 50.00 120.00
CCARDS Don Sutton HN EXCH 40.00 100.00
CCARFL Francisco Lindor HN 30.00 80.00
CCARGT Gleyber Torres 100.00 250.00
CCARJA Jose Altuve 30.00 80.00
CCARJD Jacob deGrom HN 25.00 60.00
CCARJR Jose Ramirez 15.00 40.00
CCARJS Juan Soto HN 75.00 200.00
CCARKB Kris Bryant 75.00 200.00
CCARKB Kris Bryant HN 75.00 200.00
CCARLS Luis Severino
CCARMA Miguel Andujar HN
CCARMC Matt Carpenter HN 50.00 120.00
CCARMM Miles Mikolas HN 30.00 80.00
CCARMT Mike Trout 300.00 600.00
CCARNR Nolan Ryan HN
CCARPG Paul Goldschmidt 25.00 60.00
CCARRA Ronald Acuna Jr. 125.00 300.00
CCARRD Rafael Devers EXCH 50.00 120.00
CCARRH Rhys Hoskins 50.00 120.00
CCARRH Rhys Hoskins HN 50.00 120.00
CCARSO Shohei Ohtani 100.00 250.00
CCARSO Shohei Ohtani HN 100.00 250.00
CCARTP Tony Perez HN 40.00 100.00

2019 Topps Heritage Clubhouse Collection Dual Relics

STATED ODDS 1:16,318 HOBBY
STATED HN ODDS 1:6,934 HOBBY
STATED PRINT RUN 70 SER.#'d SETS
CCDRBR Rizzo/Bryant HN 30.00 80.00
CCDRBV Bench/Votto/HN 15.00 40.00
CCDRCS Stargell/Clemente HN 40.00 100.00
CCDRJS Stanton/Judge HN 30.00 80.00
CCDRKC Kaline/Cabrera 30.00 80.00
CCDRLR Lindor/Ramirez 25.00 60.00
CCDRMB Munson/Bench 30.00 80.00
CCDRTP Trout/Pujols 60.00 150.00
CCDRYB Yaz/Betts 40.00 100.00
CCDRYM Martinez/Yaz HN 25.00 60.00

2019 Topps Heritage Clubhouse Collection Relics

STATED ODDS 1:35 HOBBY
STATED HN ODDS 1:40 HOBBY
*GOLD/99: .6X TO 1.5X BASIC
CCRAA Albert Almora Jr. HN 2.50 6.00
CCRAB Andrew Benintendi 3.00 8.00
CCRAB Andrew Benintendi HN 3.00 8.00
CCRABE Adrian Beltre 3.00 8.00
CCRAC Aroldis Chapman HN 3.00 8.00
CCRAJ Aaron Judge 8.00 20.00
CCRAM Adalberto Mondesi HN 2.50 6.00
CCRAP Albert Pujols 4.00 10.00
CCRAR Anthony Rizzo 5.00 12.00
CCRBB Brandon Belt HN 2.50 6.00
CCRBH Bryce Harper 5.00 12.00
CCRBP Buster Posey 4.00 10.00
CCRBP Buster Posey HN 4.00 10.00
CCRBT Blake Treinen HN 2.00 5.00
CCRBZ Ben Zobrist 2.50 6.00
CCRCB Cody Bellinger HN 6.00 15.00
CCRCC Carlos Correa 3.00 8.00
CCRCC Carlos Correa HN 3.00 8.00
CCRCK Clayton Kershaw 6.00 15.00
CCRCM Carlos Martinez 2.50 6.00
CCRCS Chris Sale 3.00 8.00
CCRCS CC Sabathia HN 2.50 6.00
CCRCSE Corey Seager 3.00 8.00
CCRCY Christian Yelich 4.00 10.00
CCRDB Dellin Betances 2.50 6.00
CCRDG Dee Gordon HN 2.00 5.00
CCRDP David Price 2.50 6.00
CCRDS Dansby Swanson 3.00 8.00
CCREA Elvis Andrus HN 2.50 6.00
CCREE Edwin Encarnacion 3.00 8.00
CCREH Eric Hosmer HN 2.50 6.00
CCREL Evan Longoria 2.50 6.00
CCRER Eddie Rosario 2.50 6.00
CCRFF Freddie Freeman 4.00 10.00
CCRFL Francisco Lindor 3.00 8.00
CCRFL Francisco Lindor HN 3.00 8.00
CCRGC Gerrit Cole HN 3.00 8.00
CCRGS George Springer 2.50 6.00
CCRGS Giancarlo Stanton HN 3.00 8.00
CCRGT Gleyber Torres 6.00 15.00
CCRHR Hyun-Jin Ryu HN 2.50 6.00
CCRI Ichiro HN 4.00 10.00
CCRJA Jose Abreu 3.00 8.00
CCRJA Jesus Aguilar HN 2.00 5.00
CCRJAL Jose Altuve 2.50 6.00
CCRJB Javier Baez HN 4.00 10.00
CCRJD Jacob deGrom 3.00 8.00
CCRJD Josh Donaldson HN 2.50 6.00
CCRJG Joey Gallo HN 2.50 6.00
CCRJH Josh Hader HN 2.00 5.00
CCRJHA Josh Harrison 2.00 5.00
CCRJL Jon Lester 2.50 6.00
CCRJM J.D. Martinez 3.00 8.00
CCRJP James Paxton 2.50 6.00
CCRJR Jose Ramirez 2.50 6.00
CCRJS Justin Smoak HN 2.00 5.00
CCRJT Jameson Taillon 2.50 6.00
CCRJT Julio Teheran HN 2.50 6.00
CCRJU Justin Upton HN 2.50 6.00
CCRJV Joey Votto 3.00 8.00
CCRJV Justin Verlander HN 3.00 8.00
CCRKB Kris Bryant 4.00 10.00
CCRKB Kris Bryant HN 4.00 10.00
CCRKF Kyle Freeland HN 2.50 6.00
CCRKM Ketel Marte HN 2.50 6.00
CCRKS Kyle Schwarber 3.00 8.00
CCRKS Kyle Seager HN 2.00 5.00
CCRLB Lewis Brinson HN 2.00 5.00
CCRLC Lorenzo Cain HN 2.00 5.00
CCRLM Lance McCullers Jr. 2.00 5.00
CCRLS Luis Severino 2.50 6.00
CCRLU Luis Urias HN 3.00 8.00
CCRMA Miguel Andujar HN 3.00 8.00
CCRMB Mookie Betts HN 5.00 12.00
CCRMB Mookie Betts 5.00 12.00
CCRMC Miguel Cabrera 3.00 8.00
CCRMCH Matt Chapman 3.00 8.00
CCRMM Manny Machado HN 3.00 8.00
CCRMMI Miles Mikolas 3.00 8.00
CCRMO Marcell Ozuna HN 3.00 8.00
CCRMS Miguel Sano HN 2.50 6.00
CCRMT Masahiro Tanaka 2.50 6.00
CCRMT Mike Trout HN 10.00 25.00
CCRMTR Mike Trout 10.00 25.00
CCRNA Nolan Arenado 4.00 10.00
CCRNC Nicholas Castellanos 3.00 8.00
CCRNE Nathan Eovaldi HN 2.50 6.00
CCRNM Nick Markakis 2.50 6.00
CCRNMA Nomar Mazara 2.00 5.00
CCRNS Noah Syndergaard 2.50 6.00
CCRNS Noah Syndergaard HN 2.50 6.00
CCROA Ozzie Albies HN 3.00 8.00
CCRPA Pete Alonso HN 12.00 30.00
CCRPG Paul Goldschmidt HN 3.00 8.00
CCRRB Ryan Braun 2.50 6.00
CCRRD Rafael Devers 4.00 10.00
CCRRH Rhys Hoskins HN 4.00 10.00
CCRRI Raisel Iglesias HN 2.00 5.00
CCRRP Rick Porcello 2.50 6.00
CCRSC Shin-Soo Choo 2.50 6.00
CCRSG Scooter Gennett 2.50 6.00
CCRSM Starling Marte 2.50 6.00
CCRSO Shohei Ohtani 4.00 10.00
CCRSO Shohei Ohtani HN 4.00 10.00
CCRSP Salvador Perez 2.50 6.00
CCRSS Stephen Strasburg 3.00 8.00
CCRTG Tyler Glasnow HN 2.00 5.00
CCRTM Trey Mancini 2.50 6.00
CCRTT Touki Toussaint HN 2.50 6.00
CCRVG Vladimir Guerrero Jr. HN 8.00 20.00
CCRVR Victor Robles HN 4.00 10.00
CCRWC Willson Contreras HN 2.50 6.00
CCRWM Wil Myers 2.00 5.00
CCRWME Whit Merrifield 3.00 8.00
CCRXB Xander Bogaerts 3.00 8.00
CCRYC Yoenis Cespedes 3.00 8.00
CCRYM Yadier Molina 3.00 8.00
CCRYP Yasiel Puig HN 3.00 8.00
CCRZG Zack Greinke 2.50 6.00
CCRABR Alex Bregman HN 3.00 8.00
CCRAPU Albert Pujols HN 4.00 10.00
CCRBBU Byron Buxton HN 2.50 6.00
CCRJAL Jose Altuve HN 2.50 6.00
CCRJBE Jose Berrios HN 2.50 6.00
CCRJBR Jackie Bradley Jr. HN 3.00 8.00
CCRJHA Josh Harrison HN 2.00 5.00
CCRJSO Juan Soto HN 10.00 25.00
CCRTTU Trea Turner HN 2.50 6.00
ECCRAB Andrew Benintendi 3.00 8.00
ECCRAJ Aaron Judge 8.00 20.00
ECCRAP Albert Pujols 4.00 10.00
ECCRAR Anthony Rizzo 5.00 12.00
ECCRBP Buster Posey 4.00 10.00
ECCRCC Carlos Correa 3.00 8.00
ECCRCK Clayton Kershaw 6.00 15.00
ECCRCS Chris Sale 3.00 8.00
ECCRDP David Price 2.50 6.00
ECCRFL Francisco Lindor 3.00 8.00
ECCRJA Jose Altuve 2.50 6.00
ECCRJM J.D. Martinez 3.00 8.00
ECCRJV Justin Verlander 3.00 8.00
ECCRKB Kris Bryant 4.00 10.00
ECCRKD Khris Davis 3.00 8.00
ECCRMA Miguel Andujar 3.00 8.00
ECCRMB Mookie Betts 5.00 12.00
ECCRMC Miguel Cabrera 3.00 8.00
ECCRMS Max Scherzer 3.00 8.00
ECCRMT Mike Trout 10.00 25.00
ECCRSO Shohei Ohtani 4.00 10.00
ECCRTS Trevor Story 3.00 8.00
ECCRYM Yadier Molina 3.00 8.00
ECCRABR Alex Bregman 3.00 8.00
ECCRARO Amed Rosario 2.50 6.00

2019 Topps Heritage Clubhouse Collection Triple Relics

STATED ODDS 1:46,148 HOBBY
STATED HN ODDS 1:19,511 HOBBY
STATED PRINT RUN 25 SER.#'d SETS
CCTRACB Altuve/Bregman/Correa HN 30.00 80.00
CCTRBPV Perez/Votto/Bench HN 50.00 120.00
CCTRBRB Bryant/Rizzo/Baez 75.00 200.00
CCTRGSM Gibson/Smith/Molina 75.00 200.00
CCTRJMD Jackson/McGwire/Davis 75.00 200.00
CCTRMJJ Munson/Jeter/Judge HN
CCTRMMJ Munson/Mattingly/Jeter 100.00 250.00
CCTRTOP Pujols/Trout/Ohtani HN 60.00 150.00
CCTRYBB Yaz/Betts/Benintendi 40.00 100.00
CCTRYOB Ortiz/Yaz/Betts HN 40.00 100.00

2019 Topps Heritage Combo Cards

STATED ODDS 1:20 HOBBY
CC1 Tatis Jr/Machado 4.00 10.00
CC2 Harper/Hoskins 1.00 2.50
CC3 Torres/Andujar 1.25 3.00
CC4 Yusei Kikuchi .60 1.50
Ichiro
CC5 Goldschmidt/Molina .60 1.50
CC6 Verlander/Altuve .60 1.50
CC7 Robinson Cano .50 1.25
Amed Rosario
CC8 Muncy/Bellinger 1.25 3.00
CC9 Joey Votto .60 1.50
Yasiel Puig
CC10 Yelich/Cain .75 2.00

2019 Topps Heritage Flashback Autograph Relics

2019 Topps Heritage Action Variations
STATED PRINT RUN 25 SER.#'d SETS
EXCHANGE DEADLINE 1/31/2021
FARAK Al Kaline 150.00 400.00
FARBG Bob Gibson 60.00 150.00
FARCY Carl Yastrzemski
FARJB Johnny Bench 125.00 300.00
FARJT Joe Torre 125.00 300.00
FARNR Nolan Ryan 125.00 300.00
FARRJ Reggie Jackson 100.00 250.00
FARSC Steve Carlton 100.00 250.00

2019 Topps Heritage Mini

STATED ODDS 1:434 HOBBY
STATED HN ODDS 1:482 HOBBY
STATED PRINT RUN 100 SER.#'d SETS
17 Sean Newcomb 5.00 12.00
25 Eddie Rosario 6.00 15.00
29 Andrelton Simmons 5.00 12.00
34 Cody Bellinger 15.00 40.00
47 Zack Godley 5.00 12.00
52 Chris Archer 5.00 12.00
54 Ross Stripling 5.00 12.00
55 Lou Trivino 5.00 12.00
78 Mookie Betts 12.00 30.00
83 Noah Syndergaard 6.00 15.00
98 Nicholas Castellanos 8.00 20.00
100 Masahiro Tanaka 6.00 15.00
113 Lance McCullers Jr. 5.00 12.00
114 Didi Gregorius 6.00 15.00
117 Kyle Schwarber 8.00 20.00
120 Matt Chapman 8.00 20.00
125 Maikel Franco 6.00 15.00
136 Carlos Carrasco 5.00 12.00
138 James Paxton 6.00 15.00
163 Rafael Devers 10.00 25.00
174 Justin Turner 6.00 15.00
188 Corey Dickerson 5.00 12.00
191 David Price 6.00 15.00
253 Kyle Freeland 6.00 15.00
278 Josh Donaldson 6.00 15.00
279 Rick Porcello 6.00 15.00
298 Dereck Rodriguez 5.00 12.00
300 Zack Wheeler 6.00 15.00
335 Josh Hader 6.00 15.00
341 Corey Seager 8.00 20.00
347 David Bote 6.00 15.00
370 Mike Moustakas 6.00 15.00
401 Francisco Lindor 8.00 20.00
402 Salvador Perez 6.00 15.00
403 Jake Arrieta 6.00 15.00
404 Kris Bryant 10.00 25.00
405 Jon Lester 6.00 15.00
406 Anthony Rizzo 12.00 30.00
407 George Springer 6.00 15.00
408 Sean Manaea 5.00 12.00
409 Jose Altuve 6.00 15.00
410 Christian Yelich 10.00 25.00
411 Blake Snell 6.00 15.00
412 Trevor Bauer 8.00 20.00
413 Gleyber Torres 15.00 40.00
414 Paul DeJong 8.00 20.00
415 Bryce Harper 12.00 30.00
416 Luis Severino 6.00 15.00
417 Jordan Hicks 6.00 15.00
418 Gary Sanchez 8.00 20.00
419 Jacob deGrom 8.00 20.00
420 Kenley Jansen 6.00 15.00
421 Justin Upton 6.00 15.00
422 Albert Pujols 10.00 25.00
423 Carlos Correa 8.00 20.00
424 Alex Bregman 8.00 20.00
425 Franmil Reyes 5.00 12.00
426 Justin Verlander 8.00 20.00
427 Walker Buehler 10.00 25.00
428 Trey Mancini 6.00 15.00
429 Gerrit Cole 8.00 20.00
430 Shohei Ohtani 10.00 25.00
431 Brandon Nimmo 6.00 15.00
432 Khris Davis 8.00 20.00
433 Justin Smoak 5.00 12.00
434 Stephen Piscotty 5.00 12.00
435 Miles Mikolas 8.00 20.00
436 Ozzie Albies 8.00 20.00
437 Lorenzo Cain 5.00 12.00
438 Matt Carpenter 8.00 20.00
439 Yadier Molina 8.00 20.00
440 Javier Baez 10.00 25.00
441 Paul Goldschmidt 8.00 20.00
442 Zack Greinke 6.00 15.00
443 Matt Kemp 6.00 15.00
444 Kenta Maeda 6.00 15.00
445 Buster Posey 10.00 25.00
446 Max Muncy 6.00 15.00
447 Edwin Encarnacion 8.00 20.00
448 Corey Kluber 6.00 15.00
449 Dee Gordon 5.00 12.00
450 Jean Segura 8.00 20.00
451 Edwin Diaz 6.00 15.00
452 Starlin Castro 5.00 12.00
453 J.T. Realmuto 8.00 20.00
454 Max Scherzer 8.00 20.00
455 Trea Turner 6.00 15.00
456 Jonathan Schoop 5.00 12.00
457 Eric Hosmer 6.00 15.00
458 Rhys Hoskins 10.00 25.00
459 Aaron Nola 6.00 15.00
460 Felipe Vasquez 5.00 12.00
461 Shin-Soo Choo 6.00 15.00
462 Nomar Mazara 5.00 12.00
463 Kevin Kiermaier 6.00 15.00
464 Chris Sale 8.00 20.00
465 Joey Votto 8.00 20.00
466 Scooter Gennett 6.00 15.00
467 Eugenio Suarez 6.00 15.00
468 Nolan Arenado 10.00 25.00
469 Trevor Story 8.00 20.00
470 Starling Marte 6.00 15.00
471 Charlie Blackmon 8.00 20.00
472 Miguel Cabrera 8.00 20.00
473 Miguel Andujar 8.00 20.00
474 Giancarlo Stanton 8.00 20.00
475 J.D. Martinez 8.00 20.00
476 Jesus Aguilar 5.00 12.00
477 Mitch Haniger 6.00 15.00
478 Brandon Crawford 6.00 15.00
479 Jose Berrios 6.00 15.00
480 Lourdes Gurriel Jr. 6.00 15.00
481 Juan Soto 25.00 60.00
482 Carlos Martinez 6.00 15.00
483 Jose Abreu 8.00 20.00
484 Andrew Benintendi 8.00 20.00
485 Mike Trout 100.00 250.00
486 Adam Jones 6.00 15.00
487 Xander Bogaerts 8.00 20.00
488 Odubel Herrera 6.00 15.00
489 Freddie Freeman 10.00 25.00
490 Clayton Kershaw 15.00 40.00
491 Jose Ramirez 6.00 15.00
492 Willson Contreras 6.00 15.00
493 Aroldis Chapman 8.00 20.00
494 Wil Myers 5.00 12.00
495 Sean Doolittle 5.00 12.00
496 Eric Thames 5.00 12.00
497 Yonder Alonso 5.00 12.00
498 Amed Rosario 6.00 15.00
499 Aaron Judge 20.00 50.00
500 Ronald Acuna Jr. 40.00 100.00
501 Michael Chavis 8.00 20.00
502 Charlie Morton 8.00 20.00
503 Michael Brantley 6.00 15.00
504 Vladimir Guerrero Jr. 30.00 80.00
505 Nick Markakis 6.00 15.00
506 Yasmani Grandal 5.00 12.00
507 Nick Senzel 15.00 40.00
508 Brendan Rodgers 8.00 20.00
512 Keston Hiura 30.00 80.00
516 Eloy Jimenez 30.00 80.00
517 Fernando Tatis Jr. 50.00 120.00
519 Pete Alonso 50.00 120.00
520 Manny Machado 8.00 20.00
521 Andrew Miller 6.00 15.00
522 A.J. Pollock 5.00 12.00
523 Carter Kieboom 8.00 20.00
525 Justus Sheffield 8.00 20.00
526 Yusei Kikuchi 8.00 20.00
527 Jorge Alfaro 5.00 12.00
529 Brian Dozier 6.00 15.00
530 Patrick Corbin 6.00 15.00
533 Jon Duplantier 5.00 12.00
534 Bryce Harper 12.00 30.00
535 J.T. Realmuto 8.00 20.00
537 Austin Meadows 6.00 15.00
538 Tyler Glasnow 5.00 12.00
539 Byron Buxton 6.00 15.00
540 Alex Verdugo 6.00 15.00
541 Yasiel Puig 8.00 20.00
543 Sonny Gray 6.00 15.00
544 Daniel Murphy 6.00 15.00
545 Troy Tulowitzki 8.00 20.00
546 DJ LeMahieu 8.00 20.00
547 J.A. Happ 6.00 15.00
548 Adam Ottavino 5.00 12.00
549 Zack Britton 5.00 12.00
551 Ian Kinsler 6.00 15.00
558 Wilson Ramos 5.00 12.00
563 Danny Salazar 6.00 15.00
574 Craig Kimbrel 6.00 15.00
577 Max Fried 8.00 20.00
580 Brandon Woodruff 5.00 12.00
595 Corbin Martin 8.00 20.00
598 Kevin Pillar 5.00 12.00
624 Francisco Mejia 6.00 15.00
664 Domingo German 6.00 15.00
701 Victor Robles 10.00 25.00
702 Andrew McCutchen 8.00 20.00
703 Chris Paddack 10.00 25.00
725 Ichiro 10.00 25.00

2019 Topps Heritage Mystery Autograph Redemptions

RANDOM INSERTS IN PACKS
EXCHANGE DEADLINE 9/26/2020
TBAA Vladimir Guerrero 300.00 500.00
Mystery EXCH Player A
TBAB Eloy Jimenez 300.00 500.00
Mystery EXCH Player B

2019 Topps Heritage New Age Performers

COMPLETE SET (25) 15.00 40.00
STATED ODDS 1:6 HOBBY
NAP1 Blake Snell .50 1.25
NAP2 Mookie Betts 1.00 2.50
NAP3 J.D. Martinez .60 1.50
NAP4 Miguel Andujar .60 1.50
NAP5 Aaron Judge 1.50 4.00
NAP6 Gleyber Torres 1.25 3.00
NAP7 Francisco Lindor .60 1.50
NAP8 Jose Ramirez .50 1.25
NAP9 Mitch Haniger .50 1.25
NAP10 Khris Davis .60 1.50
NAP11 Alex Bregman .60 1.50
NAP12 Justin Verlander .60 1.50
NAP13 Mike Trout 3.00 8.00
NAP14 Shohei Ohtani .75 2.00
NAP15 Juan Soto 2.00 5.00
NAP16 Max Scherzer .60 1.50
NAP17 Ronald Acuna Jr. 3.00 8.00
NAP18 Ozzie Albies .60 1.50
NAP19 Jacob deGrom .60 1.50
NAP20 Aaron Nola .50 1.25
NAP21 Javier Baez .75 2.00
NAP22 Nolan Arenado .75 2.00
NAP23 Trevor Story .60 1.50
NAP24 Christian Yelich .75 2.00
NAP25 Walker Buehler .75 2.00

2019 Topps Heritage News Flashbacks

COMPLETE SET (15) 8.00 20.00
STATED ODDS 1:18 HOBBY
NF1 Music World Loses Jimi Hendrix .60 2.00
NF2 Janis Joplin Passes Away .60 1.50
NF3 First Earth Day Celebration .60 1.50
NF4 Apollo 13 Mission .60 1.50
NF5 American Top 40 Premieres .60 1.50
NF6 PBS Begins Broadcasting .60 1.50
NF7 Isle of Wight Music Festival .60 1.50
NF8 Establishment of Environmental Protection Agency .60 1.50
NF9 Voting Age Lowered to 18 .60 1.50
NF10 President Nixon Meets with Elvis Presley .60 1.50
NF11 The Beatles Break Up .60 1.50
NF12 Venera 7 Lands on Venus .60 1.50
NF13 First Women Promoted to U.S. Army Generals .60 1.50
NF14 Marshall University Football .60 1.50
NF15 Diana Ross & The Supremes' Final Concert .60 1.50

2019 Topps Heritage Now and Then

STATED ODDS 1:8 HOBBY
NT1 Paul Goldschmidt .60 1.50
NT2 Christian Yelich .75 2.00
NT3 Elvis Luciano .60 1.50
NT4 Zack Greinke .50 1.25
NT5 Jacob deGrom .60 1.50
NT6 Trevor Bauer .60 1.50
NT7 Ryan Braun .50 1.25
NT8 Shane Greene .40 1.00
NT9 Khris Davis .60 1.50
NT10 Taylor Clarke .40 1.00
NT11 Nolan Arenado .75 2.00
NT12 Vladimir Guerrero Jr. 2.50 6.00
NT13 Cody Bellinger 1.25 3.00
NT14 Carter Kieboom .60 1.50
NT15 Albert Pujols .75 2.00

2019 Topps Heritage Real One Autographs

STATED ODDS 1:106 HOBBY
STATED HN ODDS 1:86 HOBBY
EXCHANGE DEADLINE 1/31/2021
HN EXCH DEADLINE 7/31/2021

ROAAB Alex Bregman 25.00 60.00
ROAAJ Aaron Judge 150.00 400.00
ROAAJ Aaron Judge HN 100.00 250.00
ROAAK Al Kaline 50.00 120.00
ROAAK Al Kaline HN 30.00 80.00
ROAAR Anthony Rizzo HN 20.00 50.00
ROABBL Bert Blyleven 15.00 40.00
ROABD Bill Dillman 8.00 20.00
ROABG Bob Gibson 30.00 80.00
ROABG Bob Gibson HN 30.00 80.00
ROABR Brendan Rodgers HN EXCH 15.00 40.00
ROABS Blake Snell 10.00 25.00
ROACA Chance Adams 8.00 20.00
ROACBU Corbin Burnes 12.00 30.00
ROACC Cisco Carlos 8.00 20.00
ROACK Carter Kieboom HN 20.00 50.00
ROACM Cedric Mullins HN 12.00 30.00
ROACP Chris Paddack HN EXCH 20.00 50.00
ROACS Chris Sale 12.00 30.00
ROACY Carl Yastrzemski 75.00 200.00
ROACY Carl Yastrzemski HN 40.00 100.00
ROACYE Christian Yelich 40.00 100.00
ROADH Dakota Hudson HN 12.00 30.00
ROADJA Danny Jansen 8.00 20.00
ROADM Danny Murphy 8.00 20.00
ROADP David Price HN 10.00 25.00
ROADR Dereck Rodriguez HN 8.00 20.00
ROADS Don Sutton HN EXCH 15.00 40.00
ROAEJ Eloy Jimenez HN 40.00 100.00
ROAEJ Eloy Jimenez Mystery 75.00 200.00
ROAFF Freddie Freeman 25.00 60.00
ROAFH Frank Howard HN 8.00 20.00
ROAFL Francisco Lindor HN 20.00 50.00
ROAFT Fernando Tatis Jr. HN 500.00 1200.00
ROAGA Gerry Arrigo 8.00 20.00
ROAHA Hank Aaron HN 200.00 500.00
ROAJA Jose Altuve 20.00 50.00
ROAJA Jose Altuve HN 20.00 50.00
ROAJB Jack Baldschun 8.00 20.00
ROAJBA Jake Bauers 12.00 30.00
ROAJBE Johnny Bench 75.00 200.00
ROAJD Jacob deGrom 20.00 50.00
ROAJD Jacob deGrom HN 20.00 50.00
ROAJH Josh Hader HN 8.00 20.00
ROAJHI Jim Hicks 8.00 20.00
ROAJJ Josh James HN 12.00 30.00
ROAJM Jeff McNeil HN 20.00 50.00
ROAJMA Juan Marichal HN 40.00 100.00
ROAJN Gerry Nyman 8.00 20.00
ROAJS Justus Sheffield 12.00 30.00
ROAJS Justus Sheffield HN 12.00 30.00
ROAJSO Juan Soto 75.00 200.00
ROAJSO Juan Soto HN 75.00 200.00
ROAJT Joe Torre 40.00 100.00
ROAKA Kolby Allard 12.00 30.00
ROAKB Kris Bryant 100.00 250.00
ROAKH Keston Hiura HN 40.00 100.00
ROAKK Kevin Kramer HN 10.00 25.00
ROAKT Kyle Tucker 20.00 50.00
ROAKW Kyle Wright HN 12.00 30.00
ROALB Lou Brock 30.00 80.00
ROALGU Lourdes Gurriel Jr. 8.00 20.00
ROALK Lou Klimchock 8.00 20.00
ROALU Luis Urias 8.00 20.00
ROAMA Max Alvis 10.00 25.00
ROAMA Miguel Andujar HN 20.00 50.00
ROAMCA Miguel Cabrera HN 60.00 150.00
ROAMCH Michael Chavis HN 20.00 50.00
ROAMK Matt Kemp HN 10.00 25.00
ROAMKE Mitch Keller HN 8.00 20.00
ROAMKO Michael Kopech 15.00 40.00
ROAMM Miles Mikolas 12.00 30.00
ROAMMU Max Muncy 10.00 25.00
ROAMO Marcell Ozuna HN 15.00 40.00
ROAMT Mike Trout 400.00 800.00
ROAMT Mike Trout HN 400.00 800.00
ROANR Nolan Ryan 75.00 200.00
ROANR Nolan Ryan HN 75.00 200.00
ROANS Noah Syndergaard HN 10.00 25.00
ROANSE Nick Senzel HN 25.00 60.00
ROAOA Ozzie Albies HN EXCH 20.00 50.00
ROAPA Pete Alonso HN 60.00 150.00
ROAPC Patrick Corbin HN 10.00 25.00
ROAPD Paul DeJong 8.00 20.00
ROAPG Paul Goldschmidt HN 25.00 60.00
ROARA Ronald Acuna Jr. HN 250.00 500.00
ROARC Rod Carew 20.00 50.00
ROARC Rod Carew HN 20.00 50.00
ROARD Rafael Devers HN 30.00 80.00
ROARF Rollie Fingers HN 15.00 40.00
ROARH Rhys Hoskins 25.00 60.00
ROARH Rhys Hoskins HN 25.00 60.00
ROARJ Reggie Jackson HN 50.00 120.00
ROARN Rich Nye 8.00 20.00
ROARP Rico Petrocelli 8.00 20.00
ROART Rowdy Tellez HN 12.00 30.00
ROARW Ray Washburn 8.00 20.00
ROASC Steve Carlton HN 25.00 60.00
ROASG Scooter Gennett HN
ROASO Shohei Ohtani 100.00 250.00
ROASO Shohei Ohtani HN 100.00 250.00
ROASW Steve Whitaker 8.00 20.00
ROATB Trevor Bauer HN 15.00 40.00
ROATO Tony Oliva HN 15.00 40.00
ROATP Tony Perez HN 20.00 50.00
ROATST Trevor Story 12.00 30.00
ROAVF Vern Fuller 10.00 25.00
ROAVG Vladimir Guerrero Jr. HN 150.00 400.00
ROAVG Vladimir Guerrero Jr Mystery 150.00 400.00
ROAWA Willy Adames HN 8.00 20.00
ROAWAS Willians Astudillo HN 8.00 20.00
ROAWC Willson Contreras 10.00 25.00
ROAYK Yusei Kikuchi HN 12.00 30.00

2019 Topps Heritage Real One Autographs Red Ink

*RED INK: .75X TO 2X BASIC
STATED ODDS 1:1404 HOBBY
STATED HN ODDS 1:348 HOBBY
PRINT RUNS B/WN 25-70 COPIES PER
EXCHANGE DEADLINE 1/31/2021
HN EXCH DEADLINE 7/31/2021
ROAAJ Aaron Judge 500.00 1000.00
ROACK Carter Kieboom HN 100.00 250.00
ROAEJ Eloy Jimenez HN 150.00 400.00
ROAEJ Eloy Jimenez Mystery 250.00 600.00
ROAJS Justus Sheffield 25.00 60.00
ROAKH Keston Hiura HN 150.00 400.00
ROAMKO Michael Kopech 60.00 150.00
ROAMT Mike Trout 600.00 1200.00
ROAMT Mike Trout/25 HN 800.00 1500.00
ROAPA Pete Alonso HN 800.00 1200.00
ROASG Scooter Gennett HN 20.00 50.00
ROASO Shohei Ohtani 150.00 400.00
ROASO Shohei Ohtani/25 HN 200.00 500.00
ROAVG Vladimir Guerrero Jr Mystery 400.00 800.00

2019 Topps Heritage Real One Dual Autographs

STATED ODDS 1:5947 HOBBY
STATED ODDS HN 1:3763 HOBBY
STATED PRINT RUN 25 SER.#'d SETS
EXCHANGE DEADLINE 1/31/2021
HN EXCH DEADLINE 7/31/2021
RODAAA Aaron/Acuna 700.00 1000.00
RODAAB Brgmn/Altve HN EXCH 100.00 250.00
RODAAS Acuna/Soto HN 400.00 800.00
RODABR Bryant/Rizzo 125.00 300.00
RODACO Carew/Oliva HN EXCH 75.00 200.00
RODACR Carew/Rosario 50.00 120.00
RODAGB Ryan/Gibson 300.00 600.00
RODAGC Carlton/Gibson HN 125.00 300.00
RODAJA Judge/Andjr HN EXCH
RODAJD Jackson/Davis 100.00 250.00
RODAMG Gldschmdt/Mina HN EXCH 75.00 200.00
RODAMP Marichal/Posey HN 75.00 200.00
RODAPP Piniella/Perez 40.00 100.00
RODAPV Voto/Perez HN 75.00 200.00
RODARD Ryan/deGrom HN 150.00 400.00
RODASP Price/Sale HN EXCH 75.00 200.00
RODATM Torre/Molina EXCH 75.00 200.00
RODATO Trout/Ohtani 1200.00 1600.00
RODATO Ohtani/Trout HN
RODAYD Yaz./Devers 125.00 300.00
RODAYO Yaz./Ortiz 150.00 400.00

2019 Topps Heritage Rookie Performers

STATED ODDS 1:8 HOBBY
RP1 Vladimir Guerrero Jr. 1.50 4.00
RP2 Yusei Kikuchi .40 1.00
RP3 Pete Alonso 2.00 5.00
RP4 Chris Paddack .50 1.25
RP5 Jon Duplantier .25 .60
RP6 Kyle Tucker .50 1.25
RP7 Eloy Jimenez 1.00 2.50
RP8 Brendan Rodgers .40 1.00
RP9 Nick Senzel .75 2.00
RP10 Michael Chavis .40 1.00
RP11 Willians Astudillo .25 .60
RP12 Fernando Tatis Jr. 2.50 6.00
RP13 Touki Toussaint .30 .75
RP14 Keston Hiura .75 2.00
RP15 Carter Kieboom .40 1.00

2019 Topps Heritage Teammates Boxloader

STATED ODDS 1:51 HOBBY BOX
1 Product Development Team 8.00 20.00
2 Licensing Team 8.00 20.00
3 Art/Packaging Team 8.00 20.00
4 Production Team 8.00 20.00
5 Marketing Team 8.00 20.00
6 Customer Service Team 8.00 20.00
7 E-Commerce Team 8.00 20.00
8 Quality Assurance Team 8.00 20.00
9 Finance Team 8.00 20.00
10 BOM/Logistics Team 8.00 20.00
11 Legal/HR Team 8.00 20.00
12 Sales Team 8.00 20.00
13 Executive Team 8.00 20.00
14 Information Technology Team 8.00 20.00
15 Corporate Finance Team 8.00 20.00
16 Fulfillment Team 8.00 20.00
17 Acquistion Team 8.00 20.00
18 Planning/Manufacturing Team 8.00 20.00

2019 Topps Heritage The Hammer's Greatest Hits

STATED HN ODDS 1:24 HOBBY
THGH1 Hank Aaron 1.00 2.50
THGH2 Hank Aaron 1.00 2.50
THGH3 Hank Aaron 1.00 2.50
THGH4 Hank Aaron 1.00 2.50
THGH5 Hank Aaron 1.00 2.50
THGH6 Hank Aaron 1.00 2.50
THGH7 Hank Aaron 1.00 2.50
THGH8 Hank Aaron 1.00 2.50
THGH9 Hank Aaron 1.00 2.50
THGH10 Hank Aaron 1.00 2.50
THGH11 Hank Aaron 1.00 2.50
THGH12 Hank Aaron 1.00 2.50
THGH13 Hank Aaron 1.00 2.50
THGH14 Hank Aaron 1.00 2.50
THGH15 Hank Aaron 1.00 2.50

2019 Topps Heritage The Hammer's Greatest Hits Autographs

STATED HN ODDS 1:12,338 HOBBY
STATED PRINT RUN 5 SER.#'d SETS
HN EXCH DEADLINE 7/31/2021
THGH1 Hank Aaron 300.00 600.00
THGH2 Hank Aaron 300.00 600.00
THGH3 Hank Aaron 300.00 600.00
THGH4 Hank Aaron 300.00 600.00
THGH5 Hank Aaron 300.00 600.00
THGH6 Hank Aaron 300.00 600.00
THGH7 Hank Aaron 300.00 600.00
THGH8 Hank Aaron 300.00 600.00
THGH9 Hank Aaron 300.00 600.00
THGH10 Hank Aaron 300.00 600.00
THGH11 Hank Aaron 300.00 600.00
THGH12 Hank Aaron 300.00 600.00
THGH13 Hank Aaron 300.00 600.00
THGH14 Hank Aaron 300.00 600.00
THGH15 Hank Aaron 300.00 600.00

2019 Topps Heritage Then and Now

COMPLETE SET (15) 6.00 15.00
STATED ODDS 1:18 HOBBY
TN1 Bob Gibson Max Scherzer .60 1.50
TN2 Jim Perry Blake Snell .50 1.25
TN3 Tom Seaver Jacob deGrom .60 1.50
TN4 Jim Palmer Blake Snell .50 1.25
TN5 Harmon Killebrew Khris Davis .60 1.50
TN6 Johnny Bench Nolan Arenado .75 2.00
TN7 Killebrew/Martinez .60 1.50
TN8 Bench/Baez .75 2.00
TN9 Ystrzmski/Betts 1.00 2.50
TN10 Torre/Yelich .75 2.00
TN11 Lou Brock Whit Merrifield .60 1.50
TN12 Jim Palmer Justin Verlander .60 1.50
TN13 Bob Gibson Max Scherzer .60 1.50
TN14 Tom Seaver Max Scherzer .60 1.50
TN15 Jim Palmer Justin Verlander .60 1.50

2020 Topps Heritage

SP ODDS 1:3 HOBBY
1 Washington Nationals WS Champs .15 .40
2 Trevor Bauer .25 .60
3 Jesse Winker .15 .40
4 Adam Frazier .15 .40
5 Gary Sanchez .25 .60
6 Derek Dietrich .20 .50
7 Seth Lugo .15 .40
8 Gio Urshela .25 .60
9 Donovan Solano .25 .60
10 Jedd Gyorko .15 .40
11 Tom Murphy .15 .40
12 Tony Wolters .15 .40
13 Cease RC/Collins RC .60 1.50
14 Matt Beaty .20 .50
15 Anibal Sanchez .15 .40
16 Johnny Cueto .20 .50
17 Yuli Gurriel .20 .50
18 Josh Reddick .15 .40
19 Vince Velasquez .15 .40
20 Shed Long .20 .50
21 Steven Matz .20 .50
22 Julio Teheran .20 .50
23 Scott Kingery .20 .50
24 Mike Moustakas .20 .50
25 Taylor Rogers .15 .40
26 Jose Quintana .15 .40
27 D.Agrazal RC/J.Marvel RC .40 1.00
28 Omar Narvaez .15 .40
29 Adam Ottavino .15 .40
30 Justin Turner .20 .50
31 Victor Caratini .15 .40
32 Evan Longoria .20 .50
33 Ender Inciarte .15 .40
34 Orlando Arcia .15 .40
35 Jorge Soler .25 .60
36 Kenley Jansen .20 .50
37 Luke Jackson .15 .40
38 Rougned Odor .20 .50
39 J.Rogers RC/T.Alexander RC .50 1.25
40 Joey Votto .25 .60
41 Miguel Cabrera .25 .60
42 Albert Almora .20 .50
43 Emilio Pagan .15 .40
44 Brendan Rodgers .25 .60
45 Kyle Tucker .50 1.25
46 Adam Engel .15 .40
47 J.A. Happ .20 .50
48 Matt Adams .15 .40
49 Harold Ramirez .15 .40
50 Chris Bassitt .15 .40
51 Mitch Haniger .20 .50
52 Bichette RC/Kay RC 2.50 6.00
53 Aaron Nola .25 .60
54 Alvarez RC/Aquino RC 1.50 4.00
55 Cavan Biggio .30 .75
56 Carlos Santana .20 .50
57 Chris Taylor .20 .50
58 Andrew Miller .15 .40
59 Scott Oberg .15 .40
60 Mark Canha .15 .40
61 Tim Anderson Yoan Moncada DJ LeMahieu LL .25 .60
62 Rndn/Ylch/Mrte LL .30 .75
63 Jorge Soler Jose Abreu Xander Bogaerts LL .25 .60
64 Alnso/Frmn/Rndn LL .60 1.50
65 Soler/Brgmn/Cruz/Trout LL 1.25 3.00
66 Srz/Bllngr/Alnso LL .60 1.50
67 Vrlndr/Mrtn/Cole LL .40 1.00
68 Mike Soroka Jacob deGrom Hyun-Jin Ryu LL .25 .60
69 Rdrgz/Vrlndr/Cole LL .40 1.00
70 Krshw/Hdsn/Fried/Strsbrg LL .50 1.25
71 Vrlndr/Bbr/Cole LL .40 1.00
72 Max Scherzer Jacob deGrom Stephen Strasburg LL .25 .60
73 Antonio Senzatela .15 .40
74 L.Thorpe RC/B.Graterol RC .50 1.25
75 J.T. Realmuto .25 .60
76 Touki Toussaint .20 .50
77 Dylan Bundy .20 .50
78 Albert Pujols .30 .75
79 Jay Bruce .20 .50
80 Harrison Bader .20 .50
81 Khris Davis .25 .60
82 Max Scherzer .25 .60
83 Bradley RC/Civale RC .50 1.25
84 David Bote .20 .50
85 Christin Stewart .15 .40
86 Colin Moran .15 .40
87 Josh Hader .15 .40
88 Dexter Fowler .20 .50
89 Carlos Carrasco .15 .40
90 Robinson Cano .20 .50
91 Mike Foltynewicz .15 .40
92 Carson Kelly .15 .40
93 Gallen RC/Young RC .75 2.00
94 Marco Gonzales .15 .40
95 Pedro Severino .15 .40
96 Mitch Garver .15 .40
97 Wil Myers .15 .40
98 Marcus Semien .15 .40
99 Tommy La Stella .15 .40
100 Nick Markakis .20 .50
101 Brad Hand .15 .40
102 Abreu RC/Armntrs RC/Toro RC .40 1.00
103 Adalberto Mondesi .25 .60
104 Austin Hedges .15 .40
105 Josh VanMeter .15 .40
106 James McCann .20 .50
107 Tucker Barnhart .15 .40
108 Tyler Flowers .15 .40
109 Joey Lucchesi .15 .40
110 Pablo Sandoval .20 .50
111 Rojas RC/Leyba RC .40 1.00
112 Nick Ahmed .15 .40
113 Eduardo Rodriguez .15 .40
114 Caleb Smith .15 .40
115 Cal Quantrill .15 .40
116 Grisham RC/Dubon RC 1.25 3.00
117 Marcus Stroman .20 .50
118 Whit Merrifield .25 .60
119 Maikel Franco .20 .50
120 Willians Astudillo .15 .40
121 Hoerner RC/Alzolay RC 1.25 3.00
122 Brandon Dixon .15 .40
123 Hilliard RC/Nunez RC .50 1.25
124 Kolten Wong .20 .50
125 Ross Stripling .20 .50
126 Edwin Encarnacion .25 .60
127 Yan Gomes .25 .60
128 Josh James .25 .60
129 Oscar Mercado .20 .50
130 Clint Frazier .20 .50
131 Luke Voit .30 .75
132 Jose Martinez .15 .40
133 Buster Posey .30 .75
134 Willie Calhoun .15 .40
135 Raimel Tapia .15 .40
136 Cesar Hernandez .15 .40
137 Rio Ruiz .15 .40
138 Kyle Seager .15 .40
139 Kevin Newman .20 .50
140 Nathan Eovaldi .20 .50
141 Brandon Belt .20 .50
142 Javier Baez .30 .75
143 Ildemaro Vargas .15 .40
144 Miguel Rojas .15 .40
145 Rafael Devers .30 .75
146 Mallex Smith .15 .40
147 Tyler Naquin .15 .40
148 Adam Plutko .15 .40
149 Zack Greinke .20 .50
150 Shane Greene .15 .40
151 Jon Gray .15 .40
152 M.Thaiss RC/P.Sandoval RC .50 1.25
153 Sandy Alcantara .15 .40
154 Trea Turner .20 .50
155 Jarlin Garcia .15 .40
156 Ranger Suarez .15 .40
157 Ben Gamel .20 .50
158 Daniel Murphy .20 .50
159 Garrett Cooper .15 .40
160 Domingo Santana .20 .50
161 Brosseau RC/McKay RC .50 1.25
162 David Price .20 .50
163 Tyler Beede .15 .40
164 Sam Coonrod .15 .40
165 Kurt Suzuki .15 .40
166 Joe Panik .20 .50
167 Max Muncy .20 .50
168 Ken Giles .15 .40
169 Lance Lynn .15 .40
170 Justin Wilson .15 .40
171 Andrew Stevenson .15 .40
172 Pedro Baez .15 .40
173 Trevor Richards .15 .40
174 Christian Yelich .30 .75
175 Danny Santana .15 .40
176 Dinelson Lamet .15 .40
177 Wellington Castillo .15 .40
178 Brandon Crawford .20 .50
179 Austin Dean .15 .40
180 Byron Buxton .20 .50
181 Solak RC/Burke RC .50 1.25
182 Chris Paddack .25 .60
183 Ketel Marte .20 .50
184 Manny Margot .15 .40
185 Luis Severino .20 .50
186 Nelson Cruz .25 .60
187 John Gant .15 .40
188 Lux RC/May RC 2.00 5.00
189 Leury Garcia .15 .40
190 Ronald Guzman .15 .40
191 Francisco Mejia .20 .50
192 Victor Reyes .15 .40
193 Brandon Nimmo .20 .50
194 Craig Kimbrel .20 .50
195 Gleyber Torres PO HL .50 1.25
196 Carlos Correa PO HL .25 .60
197 Gerrit Cole PO HL .40 1.00
198 George Springer Carlos Correa PO HL .25 .60
199 James Paxton PO HL .20 .50
200 Jose Altuve PO HL .20 .50
201 Houston Astros PO HL .15 .40
202 Anibal Sanchez PO HL .20 .50
203 Max Scherzer .25 .60
204 Stephen Strasburg PO HL .25 .60
205 Patrick Corbin PO HL .20 .50
206 Washington Nationals PO HL .15 .40
207 Travis d'Arnaud .20 .50
208 Juan Lagares .15 .40
209 Austin Slater .15 .40
210 Ian Kinsler .20 .50
211 Cam Bedrosian .15 .40
212 Teoscar Hernandez .25 .60
213 Ian Kennedy .15 .40
214 Griffin Canning .25 .60
215 Justin Upton .20 .50
216 Arzrna RC/Frnndz RC 2.50 6.00
217 Archie Bradley .15 .40
218 Lourdes Gurriel Jr. .20 .50
219 Danny Jansen .15 .40
220 Nate Lowe .15 .40
221 Jacob Stallings RC .40 1.00
222 Anthony DeSclafani .15 .40
223 Jordan Hicks .20 .50
224 Joc Pederson .20 .50
225 Zach Davies .15 .40
226 Ji-Man Choi .15 .40
227 Drew VerHagen .15 .40
228 Mike Fiers .15 .40
229 Dakota Hudson .15 .40
230 Patrick Corbin .20 .50
231 L.Allen RC/Y.Chang RC .50 1.25
232 Joe Musgrove .15 .40
233 Joey Gallo .25 .60
234 Jose Osuna .15 .40
235 Mike Freeman RC .30 .75
236 Jorge Polanco .20 .50
237 Mychal Givens .15 .40
238 Jose Berrios .15 .40
239 Jose Peraza .20 .50
240 Brian Anderson .15 .40
241 Willson Contreras .15 .40
242 Michael Lorenzen .15 .40
243 Aaron Sanchez .20 .50
244 George Springer .25 .60
245 Mike Soroka .25 .60
246 Jesus Aguilar .15 .40
247 Starling RC/Staumont RC .60 1.50
248 Sean Manaea .15 .40
249 Jackie Bradley Jr. .25 .60
250 Erick Fedde .15 .40
251 Ryan Zimmerman .20 .50
252 Nick Wittgren RC .50 1.25
253 Joe Jimenez .15 .40
254 Zach Plesac .25 .60
255 Brandon Lowe .25 .60
256 Brad Peacock .15 .40
257 Cody Bellinger .50 1.25
258 Brad Keller .15 .40
259 Lewis Brinson .15 .40
260 Ryan Pressly .15 .40
261 Jack Flaherty .25 .60
262 A.Munoz RC/M.Baez RC .40 1.00
263 Freddie Freeman .30 .75
264 Jose Altuve .20 .50
265 Keone Kela .15 .40
266 Delino DeShields Jr. .15 .40
267 Ryan Yarbrough .15 .40
268 Tommy Pham .15 .40
269 John Means .15 .40
270 Raisel Iglesias .15 .40
271 Andrew Cashner .15 .40
272 Eugenio Suarez .20 .50
273 Gregory Polanco .20 .50
274 Wilmer Flores .20 .50
275 Franmil Reyes .15 .40
276 L.Webb RC/T.Rogers RC .40 1.00
277 Richie Martin .15 .40
278 Wilson Ramos .15 .40
279 Starlin Castro .15 .40
280 Kirby Yates .15 .40
281 Enrique Hernandez .20 .50
282 Randal Grichuk .15 .40
283 Eric Hosmer .20 .50
284 Mike Minor .15 .40
285 Will Smith .30 .75
286 Ozzie Albies .25 .60
287 Jake Arrieta .20 .50
288 Miles Mikolas .15 .40
289 Willy Adames .15 .40
290 Ian Desmond .15 .40
291 Kris Bryant .30 .75
292 Luis Arraez .30 .75
293 Mike Leake .15 .40
294 Trent Thornton .15 .40
295 Zach Eflin .15 .40
296 Eric Lauer .15 .40
297 Brandon Workman .15 .40
298 Ryan McMahon .15 .40
299 Cam Gallagher .15 .40
300 Renato Nunez .20 .50
301 Freddy Galvis .15 .40
302 Phil Ervin .15 .40
303 Masahiro Tanaka .25 .60
304 Tommy Edman .25 .60
305 Nicky Lopez .15 .40
306 Nomar Mazara .15 .40
307 Kolby Allard .15 .40
308 Manny Machado .25 .60
309 Martin Perez .20 .50
310 Michael Conforto .20 .50
311 Chris Archer .15 .40
312 Carlos Correa .25 .60
313 Thairo Estrada .20 .50
314 Kenta Maeda .20 .50
315 Luke Weaver .15 .40
316 Nick Anderson .15 .40
317 Lzrdo RC/Puk RC/Brwn RC .60 1.50
318 Andrew Heaney .15 .40
319 Kevin Kiermaier .20 .50
320 Adam Eaton .25 .60
321 Ryan Braun .20 .50
322 Nolan Arenado .30 .75
323 Edwin Diaz .20 .50
324 Jose Ramirez .20 .50
325 Jason Kipnis .25 .60
326 Austin Hays .25 .60
327 Juan Soto WS HL .75 2.00
328 Kurt Suzuki WS HL .15 .40
329 Zack Greinke WS HL .25 .60
330 Alex Bregman WS HL .25 .60
331 Gerrit Cole WS HL .40 1.00
332 Stephen Strasburg WS HL .25 .60
333 Howie Kendrick WS HL .15 .40
334 Washington Nationals WS HL .15 .40
335 Sean Murphy .20 .50
336 Shin-Soo Choo .20 .50
337 Jake Marisnick .15 .40
338 Hector Neris .15 .40
339 Sean Doolittle .15 .40
340 CC Sabathia .20 .50
341 Mike Clevinger .20 .50
342 Jake Junis .15 .40
343 Gonsolin RC/Sborz RC 1.25 3.00
344 Reynaldo Lopez .20 .50
345 Xander Bogaerts .25 .60
346 Trey Mancini .25 .60
347 Jurickson Profar .20 .50
348 Chad Pinder .15 .40
349 C.J. Cron .20 .50
350 Trevor Story .25 .60
351 Ty France .25 .60
352 Mike Tauchman .25 .60
353 J.P. Crawford .15 .40
354 Yoan Moncada .25 .60
355 Amed Rosario .20 .50
356 Jordan Luplow .15 .40
357 Chance Sisco .15 .40
358 Mike Ford .25 .60
359 Roberto Perez .15 .40
360 Andrelton Simmons .15 .40
361 Merrill Kelly .15 .40
362 D.Tate RC/H.Harvey RC .50 1.25
363 Josh Naylor .15 .40
364 Alex Dickerson .15 .40
365 Tyler Glasnow .20 .50
366 Jake Lamb .20 .50
367 Gerrit Cole .40 1.00
368 Junior Guerra .15 .40
369 Yamamoto RC/Diaz RC .50 1.25
370 Matt Carpenter .25 .60
371 Adam Haseley .25 .60
372 Yolmer Sanchez .15 .40
373 Anthony Rizzo .40 1.00
374 Brandon Woodruff .15 .40
375 Hansel Robles .15 .40
376 T.Zeuch RC/J.Romano RC .50 1.25
377 Alex Colome .15 .40
378 Tyler Chatwood .15 .40
379 Rowdy Tellez .20 .50
380 Mark Melancon .15 .40
381 Darwinzon Hernandez .15 .40
382 Austin Romine .15 .40
383 Bryan Reynolds .20 .50
384 Chase Anderson .15 .40
385 Clayton Kershaw .50 1.25
386 Dominic Smith .15 .40
387 Matt Boyd .15 .40
388 Niko Goodrum .20 .50
389 Ian Happ .20 .50
390 Dansby Swanson .25 .60
391 Dunn RC/Nola RC/Lewis RC 2.50 6.00
392 Freddy Peralta .15 .40
393 Anthony Santander .15 .40
394 Kevin Pillar .15 .40
395 Aaron Judge .60 1.50
396 Hanser Alberto .15 .40
397 Eric Thames .15 .40
398 Luis Urias .20 .50
399 Jeff Samardzija .15 .40
400 Yadier Molina .25 .60
401 Elvis Andrus SP 1.50 4.00
402 Jorge Alfaro SP 1.25 3.00
403 Juan Soto SP 6.00 15.00
404 Marwin Gonzalez SP 1.25 3.00
405 Dee Gordon SP 1.25 3.00
406 Jacob deGrom SP 2.00 5.00
407 Matt Olson SP 1.25 3.00
408 Yusei Kikuchi SP 1.50 4.00
409 Kyle Schwarber SP 2.00 5.00
410 Corey Seager SP 2.00 5.00
411 Alex Gordon SP 1.50 4.00
412 A.J. Pollock SP 1.25 3.00
413 Keston Hiura SP 2.50 6.00
414 Vladimir Guerrero Jr. SP 4.00 10.00
415 DJ LeMahieu SP 2.00 5.00
416 Lucas Giolito SP 1.50 4.00
417 Blake Snell SP 1.50 4.00
418 Justus Sheffield SP 2.00 5.00
419 Andrew Benintendi SP 2.00 5.00
420 Charlie Blackmon SP 2.00 5.00
421 Stephen Piscotty SP 1.25 3.00
422 Josh Bell SP 1.50 4.00
423 J.D. Martinez SP 2.00 5.00
424 Yasmani Grandal SP 1.25 3.00
425 Michael Brantley SP 1.50 4.00
426 Mike Yastrzemski SP 3.00 8.00
427 Jason Heyward SP 1.50 4.00
428 Noah Syndergaard SP 1.50 4.00
429 Giovanny Gallegos SP 1.25 3.00
430 Sean Newcomb SP 1.25 3.00
431 Robbie Ray SP 1.25 3.00
432 Eddie Rosario SP 1.50 4.00
433 Shohei Ohtani SP 2.50 6.00
434 Dwight Smith Jr. SP 1.25 3.00
435 Lorenzo Cain SP 1.25 3.00
436 Tim Anderson SP 2.00 5.00
437 Fernando Tatis Jr. SP 8.00 20.00
438 German Marquez SP 2.00 5.00
439 Luis Castillo SP 1.50 4.00
440 Jonathan Villar SP 1.25 3.00
441 Miguel Sano SP 1.50 4.00
442 Francisco Lindor SP 2.00 5.00
443 Giancarlo Stanton SP 2.00 5.00
444 Kyle Hendricks SP 2.00 5.00
445 J.D. Davis SP 1.25 3.00
446 Jose Leclerc SP 1.25 3.00
447 Bryce Harper SP 3.00 8.00
448 Amir Garrett SP 1.25 3.00
449 Jon Duplantier SP 1.25 3.00
450 Carlos Martinez SP 1.50 4.00
451 Chris Sale SP 2.00 5.00
452 David Peralta SP 1.25 3.00
453 Alex Bregman SP 2.00 5.00
454 Shane Bieber SP 2.00 5.00
455 Sonny Gray SP 1.50 4.00
456 Andrew McCutchen SP 2.00 5.00
457 Pete Alonso SP 5.00 12.00
458 Jean Segura SP 1.50 4.00
459 Alex Verdugo SP 1.50 4.00
460 Zack Britton SP 1.25 3.00
461 Daniel Vogelbach SP 1.25 3.00
462 Starling Marte SP 1.50 4.00
463 Kole Calhoun SP 1.25 3.00
464 Ronald Acuna Jr. SP 8.00 20.00
465 Max Fried SP 2.00 5.00
466 Mike Trout SP 10.00 25.00
467 Paul Goldschmidt SP 2.00 5.00
468 Matt Chapman SP 2.00 5.00
469 Julio Urias SP 2.00 5.00
470 Ryan O'Hearn SP 1.25 3.00
471 Christian Vazquez SP 1.25 3.00
472 Liam Hendriks SP 1.25 3.00
473 Justin Verlander SP 2.00 5.00
474 Eduardo Escobar SP 1.25 3.00
475 Yu Darvish SP 2.00 5.00
476 Paul DeJong SP 2.00 5.00
477 Hunter Renfroe SP 1.25 3.00
478 David Dahl SP 1.25 3.00
479 Max Kepler SP 1.50 4.00
480 James Paxton SP 1.50 4.00
481 Austin Meadows SP 1.50 4.00
482 Nick Senzel SP 2.00 5.00
483 Gleyber Torres SP 4.00 10.00
484 Aroldis Chapman SP 2.00 5.00
485 David Fletcher SP 2.00 5.00
486 Jon Lester SP 1.50 4.00
487 Hunter Dozier SP 1.25 3.00
488 Christian Walker SP 1.50 4.00
489 Aaron Hicks SP 1.50 4.00
490 Rhys Hoskins SP 2.50 6.00
491 Austin Riley SP 3.00 8.00
492 Jeff McNeil SP 1.50 4.00
493 Mookie Betts SP 4.00 10.00
494 Eloy Jimenez SP 4.00 10.00
495 Ramon Laureano SP 2.00 5.00
496 Walker Buehler SP 2.50 6.00
497 Victor Robles SP 2.50 6.00
498 Charlie Morton SP 2.00 5.00
499 Roberto Osuna SP 1.25 3.00
500 Michael Chavis SP 1.50 4.00
501 Gerrit Cole .40 1.00
502 Mookie Betts .50 1.25

503 Josh Donaldson .20 .50
504 James Karinchak RC .50 1.25
505 Ben Zobrist .20 .50
506 Jonathan Hernandez RC .30 .75
507 Chad Wallach RC .30 .75
508 Corey Kluber .20 .50
509 Brock Holt .15 .40
510 Collin McHugh .15 .40
511 Hunter Pence .20 .50
512 Luis Robert RC 6.00 15.00
513 Freddy Galvis .15 .40
514 Rich Hill .15 .40
515 Jose Rodriguez RC .30 .75
516 Julio Teheran .20 .50
517 Kole Calhoun .15 .40
518 Felix Hernandez .20 .50
519 Chris Davis .15 .40
520 Dallas Keuchel .20 .50
521 Jeremy Jeffress .15 .40
522 Jharel Cotton .15 .40
523 Danny Mendick RC .40 1.00
524 Delino DeShields Jr. .15 .40
525 Rangel Ravelo RC .40 1.00
526 Willi Castro RC .50 1.25
527 Shogo Akiyama .25 .60
528 Robert Dugger RC .30 .75
529 Maikel Franco .20 .50
530 Edwin Rios RC .75 2.00
531 Tom Eshelman RC .40 1.00
532 Francisco Cervelli .15 .40
533 Justin Smoak .15 .40
534 Randy Dobnak RC .60 1.50
535 Dellin Betances .20 .50
536 Michael Wacha .20 .50
537 Tommy Kahnle .15 .40
538 Kenta Maeda .20 .50
539 Sheldon Neuse RC .40 1.00
540 Jon Berti RC .30 .75
541 Kean Wong RC .40 1.00
542 Zack Wheeler .20 .50
543 Garrett Stubbs RC .30 .75
544 Kwang-Hyun Kim .50 1.25
545 Emilio Pagan .15 .40
546 Jaylin Davis RC .50 1.25
547 Jake Fraley RC .40 1.00
548 Yoshi Tsutsugo .20 .50
549 Shun Yamaguchi .20 .50
550 Mitch Moreland .15 .40
551 Miguel Andujar .25 .60
552 Chad Green .15 .40
553 Anthony Rendon .25 .60
554 Yandy Diaz .20 .50
555 Nick Castellanos .25 .60
556 Cole Hamels .20 .50
557 Yasiel Puig .25 .60
558 Stephen Strasburg .25 .60
559 Salvador Perez .20 .50
560 Jose Iglesias .20 .50
561 Jonathan Lucroy .20 .50
562 Andrew Cashner .15 .40
563 Didi Gregorius .20 .50
564 Jose Martinez .15 .40
565 David Price .20 .50
566 Hyun-Jin Ryu .20 .50
567 Michael Kopech .30 .75
568 Robel Garcia RC .30 .75
569 Nomar Mazara .15 .40
570 Corey Dickerson .20 .50
571 Wade Miley .15 .40
572 Jonathan Schoop .15 .40
573 Homer Bailey .15 .40
574 Joey Wendle .15 .40
575 LaMonte Wade Jr. RC .50 1.25
576 Manuel Margot .15 .40
577 Eric Thames .15 .40
578 Steven Souza Jr. .15 .40
579 Austin Dean .15 .40
580 Brad Miller .15 .40
581 Yoenis Cespedes .25 .60
582 Kevin Pillar .15 .40
583 Junior Guerra .15 .40
584 Franchy Cordero .15 .40
585 Jack Mayfield RC .30 .75
586 Tony Kemp .15 .40
587 Edwin Encarnacion .25 .60
588 Carlos Rodon .20 .50
589 Josh Harrison .15 .40
590 Cameron Maybin .15 .40
591 C.J. Cron .15 .40
592 Todd Frazier .20 .50
593 Kyle Gibson .15 .40
594 Kyle Higashioka .15 .40
595 Ehire Adrianza .15 .40
596 Ryan McBroom RC .40 1.00
597 Myles Straw .25 .60
598 Patrick Wisdom .15 .40
599 Eric Lauer .15 .40
600 Ronny Rodriguez .15 .40
601 Brusdar Graterol RC .50 1.25
602 Emmanuel Clase RC .40 1.00
603 Tyrone Taylor RC .30 .75
604 Frankie Montas .15 .40
605 Scott Heineman RC .30 .75
606 Tim Lopes RC .40 1.00
607 Seth Mejias-Brean RC .30 .75
608 Reggie McClain RC .50 1.25
609 Jarrod Dyson .15 .40
610 Brian O'Grady RC .30 .75
611 David Bednar RC .30 .75
612 Tyler Beede .15 .40
613 Carlos Gonzalez .20 .50
614 Tyler Duffey .15 .40
615 Danny Duffy .15 .40
616 Yangervis Solarte .15 .40
617 Wilmer Flores .20 .50
618 Brian Goodwin .15 .40
619 Carl Edwards Jr. .15 .40
620 DJ Stewart .15 .40
621 Michael Taylor .15 .40
622 Lane Thomas .15 .40
623 Daniel Descalso .15 .40
624 Cy Sneed RC .30 .75
625 Trey Wingenter RC .30 .75
626 Alex Avila .15 .40
627 Jason Castro .15 .40
628 Jesus Tinoco RC .30 .75
629 Ryne Harper .15 .40
630 Adolis Garcia .15 .40
631 Zach Davies .15 .40
632 Dustin Garneau .15 .40
633 Robbie Grossman .15 .40
634 Kelvin Herrera .15 .40
635 Brian Dozier .20 .50
636 Matt Joyce .15 .40
637 Franklin Barreto .15 .40
638 Kyle Farmer .15 .40
639 Travis d'Arnaud .20 .50
640 Peter Fairbanks RC .50 1.25
641 Jeff Hoffman .15 .40
642 Luis Torrens .15 .40
643 Tyler Mahle .15 .40
644 Jimmy Nelson .15 .40
645 Jake Diekman .15 .40
646 Greg Bird .20 .50
647 Tanner Roark .15 .40
648 Adrian Houser .15 .40
649 Pedro Strop .15 .40
650 Yohander Mendez RC .30 .75
651 Chris Devenski .15 .40
652 Jalen Beeks .15 .40
653 Jason Kipnis .20 .50
654 Cody Stashak RC .30 .75
655 Drew Steckenrider .15 .40
656 Kevin Ginkel RC .30 .75
657 Matt Wisler .15 .40
658 Keynan Middleton .15 .40
659 Aaron Bummer .15 .40
660 Jeimer Candelario .15 .40
661 Steve Cishek .15 .40
662 Carter Kieboom .20 .50
663 Alex Wood .15 .40
664 Blake Treinen .15 .40
665 Martin Maldonado .15 .40
666 Austin Allen .20 .50
667 Garrett Hampson .15 .40
668 Brad Wieck RC .50 1.25
669 Domingo Santana .20 .50
670 Kevin Kramer .15 .40
671 Matt Strahm .15 .40
672 Johan Camargo .15 .40
673 Howie Kendrick .15 .40
674 Seby Zavala RC .50 1.25
675 Luis Rengifo .15 .40
676 Omar Narvaez .15 .40
677 Brandon Drury .15 .40
678 JaCoby Jones .20 .50
679 Brandon Kintzler .15 .40
680 Robinson Chirinos .15 .40
681 Austin Pruitt .20 .50
682 Luis Guillorme .15 .40
683 Eric Sogard .15 .40
684 Ryan Cordell .15 .40
685 Tyler Clippard .15 .40
686 Luis Cessa .15 .40
687 Sergio Romo .15 .40
688 Josh Phegley .15 .40
689 Shawn Armstrong .15 .40
690 Jeff Mathis .20 .50
691 Roman Quinn .15 .40
692 Jake Bauers .20 .50
693 Jake Marisnick .15 .40
694 Daniel Hudson .15 .40
695 Austin Voth .15 .40
696 Tommy Milone .15 .40
697 Jimmy Cordero .15 .40
698 Tim Locastro .15 .40
699 Tommy Hunter .15 .40
700 Hernan Perez .15 .40
701 Joe Kelly SP 1.25 3.00
702 Rick Porcello SP 1.50 4.00
703 Starling Marte SP 1.50 4.00
704 Ivan Nova SP 1.25 3.00
705 Yonathan Daza SP RC 1.50 4.00
706 Lance McCullers Jr. SP 1.25 3.00
707 Jose Abreu SP 2.00 5.00
708 Kyle Garlick SP RC 2.00 5.00
709 Starlin Castro SP 1.25 3.00
710 Jake Cave SP 1.50 4.00
711 Alec Mills SP RC 1.25 3.00
712 Lucas Sims SP 1.25 3.00
713 Luis Urias SP 1.50 4.00
714 Daniel Ponce de Leon SP 1.25 3.00
715 Wade Davis SP 1.25 3.00
716 Kevin Gausman SP 1.25 3.00
717 Nestor Cortes SP 1.25 3.00
718 Jordan Lyles SP 1.25 3.00
719 Francisco Liriano SP 1.25 3.00
720 Wilmer Difo SP 1.25 3.00
721 Alex Blandino SP 1.25 3.00
722 Tyler O'Neill SP 1.50 4.00
723 Marcell Ozuna SP 2.00 5.00
724 Drew Pomeranz SP 1.25 3.00
725 Alex Verdugo SP 1.50 4.00

2020 Topps Heritage Action Variations

STATED ODDS 1:27 HOBBY
52 Bo Bichette 30.00 80.00
54 Yordan Alvarez 25.00 60.00
54 Aristides Aquino 10.00 25.00
121 Nico Hoerner 8.00 20.00
142 Javier Baez 4.00 10.00
145 Rafael Devers 4.00 10.00
174 Christian Yelich 4.00 10.00
188 Gavin Lux 20.00 50.00
257 Cody Bellinger 6.00 15.00
291 Kris Bryant 4.00 10.00
308 Manny Machado 3.00 8.00
322 Nolan Arenado 4.00 10.00
385 Clayton Kershaw 6.00 15.00
403 Juan Soto 10.00 25.00
414 Vladimir Guerrero Jr. 8.00 20.00
430 Shohei Ohtani 4.00 10.00
437 Fernando Tatis Jr. 12.00 30.00
442 Francisco Lindor 4.00 10.00
447 Bryce Harper 5.00 12.00
453 Alex Bregman 4.00 10.00
457 Pete Alonso 10.00 25.00
464 Ronald Acuna Jr. 12.00 30.00
466 Mike Trout 30.00 80.00
473 Justin Verlander 3.00 8.00
493 Mookie Betts 6.00 15.00

2020 Topps Heritage French Text

*FRENCH: 6X TO 15X BASIC
*FRENCH RC: 3X TO 8X BASIC RC
STATED ODDS 1:243 HOBBY
40 Joey Votto 10.00 25.00
41 Miguel Cabrera 12.00 30.00
52 Bichette/Kay 40.00 100.00
54 Alvarez/Aquino 75.00 200.00
145 Rafael Devers 8.00 20.00
174 Christian Yelich 12.00 30.00
188 Lux/May 50.00 120.00
257 Cody Bellinger 25.00 60.00
291 Kris Bryant 10.00 25.00
317 Luzardo/Puk/Brown 20.00 50.00

2020 Topps Heritage Missing Signature Variations

STATED ODDS 1:2009 HOBBY
145 Rafael Devers 25.00 60.00
174 Christian Yelich 25.00 60.00
257 Cody Bellinger 25.00 60.00
395 Aaron Judge 50.00 120.00
403 Juan Soto 25.00 60.00
414 Vladimir Guerrero Jr. 30.00 80.00
437 Fernando Tatis Jr. 60.00 150.00
453 Alex Bregman 20.00 50.00
457 Pete Alonso 50.00 120.00
464 Ronald Acuna Jr. 60.00 150.00
466 Mike Trout 100.00 250.00
483 Gleyber Torres 30.00 80.00

2020 Topps Heritage Nickname Variations

STATED ODDS 1:2414 HOBBY
174 Christian Yelich 25.00 60.00
257 Cody Bellinger 25.00 60.00
395 Aaron Judge 60.00 150.00
414 Vladimir Guerrero Jr. 30.00 80.00
447 Bryce Harper 30.00 80.00
453 Alex Bregman 20.00 50.00
457 Pete Alonso 30.00 80.00
464 Ronald Acuna Jr. 30.00 80.00
466 Mike Trout 100.00 250.00
483 Gleyber Torres 30.00 80.00
501 Gerrit Cole
502 Josh Donaldson
512 Luis Robert
553 Anthony Rendon
723 Marcell Ozuna

2020 Topps Heritage Silver Team Name Variations

STATED ODDS 1:265 HOBBY
82 Max Scherzer 8.00 20.00
142 Javier Baez 10.00 25.00
145 Rafael Devers 10.00 25.00
257 Cody Bellinger 15.00 40.00
264 Jose Altuve 6.00 15.00
291 Kris Bryant 12.00 30.00
373 Anthony Rizzo 12.00 30.00
385 Clayton Kershaw 15.00 40.00
395 Aaron Judge 20.00 50.00
403 Juan Soto 25.00 60.00
414 Vladimir Guerrero Jr. 15.00 40.00
415 DJ LeMahieu 8.00 20.00
423 J.D. Martinez 8.00 20.00
433 Shohei Ohtani 10.00 25.00
437 Fernando Tatis Jr. 30.00 80.00
442 Francisco Lindor 8.00 20.00
453 Alex Bregman 8.00 20.00
457 Pete Alonso 20.00 50.00
464 Ronald Acuna Jr. 30.00 80.00
466 Mike Trout 50.00 210.00
473 Justin Verlander 8.00 20.00
483 Gleyber Torres 15.00 40.00
490 Rhys Hoskins 10.00 25.00
494 Eloy Jimenez 15.00 40.00

2020 Topps Heritage White Border

*WHITE: 10X TO 25X BASIC
*WHITE RC: 6X TO 15X BASIC RC
*WHITE SP: 1.2X TO 3X BASIC SP
STATED ODDS 1:67 HOBBY
ANNCD PRINT RUN 50 SER.#'d SETS
5 Gary Sanchez 10.00 25.00
13 Cease/Collins 20.00 50.00
39 Rogers/Alexander 10.00 25.00
40 Joey Votto 15.00 40.00
41 Miguel Cabrera 20.00 50.00
52 Bichette/Kay 60.00 510.00
54 Alvarez/Aquino 125.00 300.00
145 Rafael Devers 12.00 30.00
174 Christian Yelich 20.00 50.00
188 Lux/May 75.00 200.00
257 Cody Bellinger 40.00 100.00
291 Kris Bryant 15.00 40.00
317 Luzardo/Puk/Brown 30.00 80.00
395 Aaron Judge 60.00 150.00
400 Yadier Molina 15.00 40.00
403 Juan Soto 25.00 60.00
414 Vladimir Guerrero Jr. 40.00 100.00
433 Shohei Ohtani 20.00 50.00
437 Fernando Tatis Jr. 50.00 120.00
447 Bryce Harper 25.00 60.00
457 Pete Alonso 30.00 80.00
464 Ronald Acuna Jr. 75.00 200.00
466 Mike Trout 200.00 500.00
483 Gleyber Torres 25.00 60.00
493 Mookie Betts 15.00 40.00
496 Walker Buehler 25.00 60.00

2020 Topps Heritage '20 Sticker Collection Preview

1 Mike Trout 6.00 15.00
2 Yordan Alvarez 4.00 10.00
3 Gleyber Torres 2.50 6.00
4 Vladimir Guerrero Jr. 2.50 6.00
5 Max Scherzer 1.25 3.00
6 Paul Goldschmidt 1.25 3.00
7 Christian Yelich 1.50 4.00
8 Ronald Acuna Jr. 5.00 12.00
9 Clayton Kershaw 2.50 6.00
10 Francisco Lindor 1.25 3.00

2020 Topps Heritage '71 Bazooka Numbered Test

STATED ODDS 1:8 BLASTER PACKS
1 Mike Trout 8.00 20.00
2 Alex Bregman 1.50 4.00
3 Matt Chapman 1.50 4.00
4 Vladimir Guerrero Jr. 3.00 8.00
5 Ronald Acuna Jr. 6.00 15.00
6 Christian Yelich 2.00 5.00
7 Paul Goldschmidt 1.50 4.00
8 Javier Baez 2.00 5.00
9 Ketel Marte 1.25 3.00
10 Cody Bellinger 3.00 8.00
11 Buster Posey 2.00 5.00
12 Francisco Lindor 1.50 4.00
13 Daniel Vogelbach 1.00 2.50
14 Brian Anderson 1.00 2.50
15 Pete Alonso 4.00 10.00
16 Juan Soto 5.00 12.00
17 Trey Mancini 1.50 4.00
18 Fernando Tatis Jr. 6.00 15.00
19 Bryce Harper 2.50 6.00
20 Josh Bell 1.25 3.00
21 Rougned Odor 1.25 3.00
22 Austin Meadows 1.25 3.00
23 Rafael Devers 2.00 5.00
24 Aristides Aquino 2.00 5.00
25 Nolan Arenado 2.00 5.00

2020 Topps Heritage '71 Postal Stamps

STATED ODDS 1:6044 HOBBY
STATED PRINT RUN 50 SER.#'d SETS
71USAK Al Kaline 60.00 150.00
71USBG Bob Gibson
71USBR Brooks Robinson 50.00 120.00
71USCY Carl Yastrzemski 30.00 80.00
71USFJ Fergie Jenkins 20.00 50.00
71USHA Hank Aaron 50.00 120.00
71USHK Harmon Killebrew 25.00 60.00
71USJB Johnny Bench 40.00 100.00
71USJP Jim Palmer
71USJT Joe Torre 20.00 50.00
71USLB Lou Brock 20.00 50.00
71USNR Nolan Ryan 50.00 120.00
71USRC Rod Carew 40.00 100.00
71USRCL Roberto Clemente 75.00 200.00
71USRJ Reggie Jackson 25.00 60.00
71USSC Steve Carlton 40.00 100.00
71USTS Tom Seaver 25.00 60.00
71USWM Willie Mays 60.00 150.00
71USWMC Willie McCovey 50.00 120.00
71USWS Willie Stargell 40.00 100.00

2020 Topps Heritage '71 Topps Baseball Tattoos

STATED ODDS 1:728 BLSTR PACKS
1 Yordan Alvarez 12.00 30.00
2 Vladimir Guerrero Jr. 8.00 20.00
3 S.Ohtani/M.Trout 40.00 100.00
4 Christian Yelich 15.00 40.00
5 Paul Goldschmidt 6.00 15.00
6 M.Chapman/R.Laureano 8.00 20.00
7 Zack Greinke 3.00 8.00
8 Buster Posey 12.00 30.00
9 A.Riley/R.Acuna Jr. 25.00 60.00
10 Francisco Lindor 8.00 20.00
11 Pete Alonso 25.00 60.00
12 K.Bryant/J.Baez 15.00 40.00
13 Max Scherzer 10.00 25.00
14 Fernando Tatis Jr. 12.00 30.00
15 C.Bellinger/C.Kershaw 15.00 40.00
16 Josh Bell 8.00 20.00
17 Elvis Andrus 8.00 20.00
18 D.Gordon/D.Vogelbach 8.00 20.00
19 Blake Snell 6.00 15.00
20 Nick Senzel 12.00 30.00
21 J.Yamamoto/J.Alfaro 6.00 15.00
22 Nolan Arenado 8.00 20.00
23 Whit Merrifield 6.00 15.00
24 G.Torres/A.Judge 30.00 80.00
25 Miguel Cabrera 10.00 25.00
26 Mookie Betts 10.00 25.00
27 B.Harper/R.Hoskins 12.00 30.00
28 Eloy Jimenez 8.00 20.00
29 Trey Mancini 8.00 20.00
30 J.Berrios/M.Kepler 20.00 50.00

2020 Topps Heritage '71 Topps Greatest Moments Boxloader

STATED ODDS 1:3 HOBBY BOXES
1 Roberto Clemente 20.00 50.00
2 Tony Oliva 10.00 25.00
3 Joe Torre 6.00 15.00
4 Willie Stargell 8.00 20.00
5 Harmon Killebrew 8.00 20.00
6 Fergie Jenkins 8.00 20.00
7 Lou Brock 6.00 15.00
8 Tom Seaver 8.00 20.00
9 Brooks Robinson 10.00 25.00
10 Hank Aaron 10.00 25.00
11 Johnny Bench 10.00 25.00
12 Bob Gibson 20.00 50.00
13 Reggie Jackson 15.00 40.00
14 Jim Palmer 8.00 20.00
15 Willie Mays 15.00 40.00
16 Rod Carew 10.00 25.00
17 Catfish Hunter 8.00 20.00
18 Al Kaline 12.00 30.00
19 Willie McCovey 10.00 25.00
20 Tony Perez 6.00 15.00
21 Mike Trout 15.00 40.00
22 Alex Bregman 5.00 12.00
23 Vladimir Guerrero Jr. 6.00 15.00
24 Justin Verlander 5.00 12.00
25 Ronald Acuna Jr. 8.00 20.00
26 Christian Yelich 6.00 15.00
27 Yadier Molina 6.00 15.00
28 Kris Bryant 8.00 20.00
29 Max Scherzer 8.00 20.00
30 Cody Bellinger 10.00 25.00
31 Buster Posey 6.00 15.00
32 Francisco Lindor 5.00 12.00
33 Clayton Kershaw 10.00 25.00
34 Pete Alonso 15.00 40.00
35 Juan Soto 10.00 25.00
36 Fernando Tatis Jr. 8.00 20.00
37 Bryce Harper 8.00 20.00
38 Nolan Arenado 6.00 15.00
39 Anthony Rizzo 8.00 20.00
40 Aaron Judge 10.00 25.00
41 Jacob deGrom 5.00 12.00
42 Rafael Devers 6.00 15.00
43 Miguel Cabrera 8.00 20.00
44 Mookie Betts 6.00 15.00
45 Shohei Ohtani 6.00 15.00
46 Manny Machado 5.00 12.00
47 Gleyber Torres 5.00 12.00
48 Keston Hiura 4.00 10.00
49 Rhys Hoskins 6.00 15.00
50 Aristides Aquino 6.00 15.00
51 Yordan Alvarez 8.00 20.00
52 Bo Bichette 8.00 20.00
53 Brendan McKay 4.00 10.00
54 Gavin Lux 5.00 12.00
55 Kyle Lewis 6.00 15.00

2020 Topps Heritage '71 Topps Scratch Offs

1 Shohei Ohtani .75 2.00
2 Yordan Alvarez 2.00 5.00
3 Matt Chapman .60 1.50
4 Vladimir Guerrero Jr. 1.25 3.00
5 Ronald Acuna Jr. 2.50 6.00
6 Christian Yelich .75 2.00
7 Paul Goldschmidt .60 1.50
8 Kris Bryant .75 2.00
9 Ketel Marte .50 1.25
10 Cody Bellinger 1.25 3.00
11 Evan Longoria .50 1.25
12 Francisco Lindor .60 1.50
13 Dee Gordon .40 1.00
14 Brian Anderson .40 1.00
15 Pete Alonso 1.50 4.00

2020 Topps Heritage '71 Topps Super Baseball Boxloader

STATED ODDS 1:5 HOBBY BOXES
1 Vladimir Guerrero Jr. 3.00 8.00
2 Fernando Tatis Jr. 6.00 15.00
3 Ronald Acuna Jr. 6.00 15.00
4 Yordan Alvarez 6.00 15.00
5 Mike Trout 8.00 20.00
6 Max Scherzer 1.50 4.00
7 Javier Baez 4.00 10.00
8 Eloy Jimenez 5.00 12.00
9 Christian Yelich 2.00 5.00
10 Clayton Kershaw 3.00 8.00
11 Shohei Ohtani 4.00 10.00
12 Cody Bellinger 6.00 15.00
13 Pete Alonso 4.00 10.00
14 Aaron Judge 8.00 20.00
15 Bo Bichette 8.00 20.00

2020 Topps Heritage '71 Topps Super Baseball Boxloader Autographs

STATED ODDS 1:383 HOBBY BOXES
STATED PRINT RUN 25 SER.#'d SETS
EXCHANGE DEADLINE 1/31/2022
1 Vladimir Guerrero Jr. 100.00 250.00
4 Yordan Alvarez 300.00 600.00

2020 Topps Heritage 20 Gigantic Seasons

COMPLETE SET (20) 15.00 40.00
STATED ODDS 1:14 HOBBY
1 Willie Mays 1.25 3.00
2 Willie Mays 1.25 3.00
3 Willie Mays 1.25 3.00
4 Willie Mays 1.25 3.00
5 Willie Mays 1.25 3.00
6 Willie Mays 1.25 3.00
7 Willie Mays 1.25 3.00
8 Willie Mays 1.25 3.00
9 Willie Mays 1.25 3.00
10 Willie Mays 1.25 3.00
11 Willie Mays 1.25 3.00
12 Willie Mays 1.25 3.00
13 Willie Mays 1.25 3.00
14 Willie Mays 1.25 3.00
15 Willie Mays 1.25 3.00
16 Willie Mays 1.25 3.00
17 Willie Mays 1.25 3.00
18 Willie Mays 1.25 3.00
19 Willie Mays 1.25 3.00
20 Willie Mays 1.25 3.00

2020 Topps Heritage Baseball Flashbacks

COMPLETE SET (15) 8.00 20.00
STATED ODDS 1:18 HOBBY
BF1 Hank Aaron 1.25 3.00
BF2 Bert Blyleven .50 1.25
BF3 Bob Gibson .50 1.25
BF4 Johnny Bench .60 1.50
BF5 Rod Carew .50 1.25
BF6 Reggie Jackson .50 1.25
BF7 Nolan Ryan 2.00 5.00
BF8 Don Sutton .50 1.25
BF9 Carlton Fisk .50 1.25
BF10 Carl Yastrzemski 1.00 2.50
BF11 Roberto Clemente 1.50 4.00
BF12 Joe Torre .50 1.25
BF13 Willie Stargell .50 1.25
BF14 Tom Seaver .50 1.25
BF15 Brooks Robinson .50 1.25

2020 Topps Heritage Chrome

STATED ODDS 1:60 HOBBY
STATED PRINT RUN 999 SER.#'d SETS
*PURPLE REF: .4X TO 1X BASIC
THC8 Gio Urshela 2.00 5.00
THC17 Yuli Gurriel 1.50 4.00
THC18 Josh Reddick 1.25 3.00
THC22 Julio Teheran 1.50 4.00
THC23 Scott Kingery 1.50 4.00
THC24 Mike Moustakas 1.50 4.00
THC32 Evan Longoria 1.50 4.00
THC35 Jorge Soler 2.00 5.00
THC41 Miguel Cabrera 2.00 5.00
THC52 Bo Bichette 10.00 25.00
Anthony Kay
THC53 Aaron Nola 2.00 5.00
THC54 Y.Alvarez/A.Aquino 15.00 40.00
THC56 Carlos Santana 1.50 4.00
THC75 J.T. Realmuto 2.00 5.00
THC78 Albert Pujols 2.50 6.00
THC82 Max Scherzer 2.00 5.00
THC118 Whit Merrifield 2.00 5.00
THC121 N.Hoerner/A.Alzolay 5.00 12.00
THC142 Javier Baez 2.50 6.00
THC145 Rafael Devers 2.50 6.00
THC149 Zack Greinke 1.50 4.00
THC154 Trea Turner 1.50 4.00
THC167 Max Muncy 1.50 4.00
THC174 Christian Yelich 2.50 6.00
THC175 Danny Santana 1.25 3.00
THC182 Chris Paddack 2.00 5.00
THC183 Ketel Marte 1.50 4.00
THC188 G.Lux/D.May 8.00 20.00
THC194 Craig Kimbrel 1.50 4.00
THC229 Dakota Hudson 1.50 4.00
THC230 Patrick Corbin 1.50 4.00
THC236 Jorge Polanco 1.50 4.00
THC240 Brian Anderson 1.25 3.00
THC241 Willson Contreras 2.00 5.00
THC244 George Springer 1.50 4.00
THC245 Mike Soroka 2.00 5.00
THC257 Cody Bellinger 4.00 10.00
THC260 Ryan Pressly 1.25 3.00
THC261 Jack Flaherty 1.50 4.00
THC272 Eugenio Suarez 1.50 4.00
THC285 Will Smith 2.50 6.00
THC286 Ozzie Albies 2.00 5.00
THC310 Michael Conforto 1.50 4.00
THC312 Carlos Correa 2.00 5.00
THC317 Luzardo/Puk/Brown 2.50 6.00
THC320 Adam Eaton 2.00 5.00
THC321 Ryan Braun 1.50 4.00
THC322 Nolan Arenado 2.50 6.00
THC341 Mike Clevinger 1.50 4.00
THC345 Xander Bogaerts 2.00 5.00
THC346 Trey Mancini 2.00 5.00
THC350 Trevor Story 2.00 5.00
THC373 Anthony Rizzo 3.00 8.00
THC383 Bryan Reynolds 1.50 4.00
THC394 Kevin Pillar 1.25 3.00
THC395 Aaron Judge 5.00 12.00
THC401 Elvis Andrus 1.50 4.00
THC403 Juan Soto 6.00 15.00
THC406 Jacob deGrom 2.00 5.00
THC407 Matt Olson 1.25 3.00
THC410 Corey Seager 2.00 5.00
THC413 Keston Hiura 2.50 6.00
THC414 Vladimir Guerrero Jr. 4.00 10.00
THC415 DJ LeMahieu 2.00 5.00
THC416 Lucas Giolito 1.50 4.00
THC419 Andrew Benintendi 2.00 5.00
THC422 Josh Bell 1.50 4.00
THC423 J.D. Martinez 2.00 5.00
THC425 Michael Brantley 1.50 4.00
THC426 Mike Yastrzemski 3.00 8.00
THC432 Eddie Rosario 1.50 4.00
THC433 Shohei Ohtani 2.50 6.00
THC436 Tim Anderson 2.00 5.00
THC437 Fernando Tatis Jr. 8.00 20.00
THC439 Luis Castillo 1.50 4.00
THC442 Francisco Lindor 2.00 5.00
THC445 J.D. Davis 1.25 3.00
THC447 Bryce Harper 3.00 8.00
THC451 Chris Sale 2.00 5.00
THC457 Pete Alonso 5.00 12.00
THC461 Daniel Vogelbach 1.25 3.00
THC464 Ronald Acuna Jr. 8.00 20.00
THC465 Max Fried 2.00 5.00
THC466 Mike Trout 25.00 60.00
THC467 Paul Goldschmidt 2.00 5.00
THC468 Matt Chapman 2.00 5.00
THC473 Justin Verlander 2.00 5.00
THC474 Eduardo Escobar 1.25 3.00
THC476 Paul DeJong 2.00 5.00
THC478 David Dahl 1.25 3.00
THC479 Max Kepler 1.50 4.00
THC481 Austin Meadows 1.50 4.00
THC482 Nick Senzel 2.00 5.00
THC483 Gleyber Torres 4.00 10.00
THC488 Christian Walker 1.50 4.00
THC492 Jeff McNeil 1.50 4.00
THC494 Eloy Jimenez 4.00 10.00
THC495 Ramon Laureano 2.00 5.00
THC496 Walker Buehler 2.50 6.00
THC498 Charlie Morton 2.00 5.00
THC501 Gerrit Cole 3.00 8.00
THC502 Mookie Betts 15.00 40.00
THC503 Josh Donaldson 1.50 4.00
THC505 Ben Zobrist 1.50 4.00
THC508 Corey Kluber 1.50 4.00
THC509 Brock Holt 1.25 3.00
THC510 Collin McHugh 1.25 3.00
THC511 Hunter Pence 1.50 4.00
THC512 Luis Robert 75.00 200.00
THC513 Freddy Galvis 1.25 3.00
THC514 Rich Hill 1.25 3.00
THC515 Jose Rodriguez 1.25 3.00
THC516 Julio Teheran 1.50 4.00
THC517 Kole Calhoun 1.25 3.00
THC518 Felix Hernandez 1.50 4.00
THC519 Chris Davis 1.25 3.00
THC521 Jeremy Jeffress 1.25 3.00
THC522 Jharel Cotton 1.25 3.00
THC523 Danny Mendick 1.50 4.00
THC524 Delino DeShields 1.25 3.00
THC526 Willi Castro 2.00 5.00
THC527 Shogo Akiyama 2.00 5.00
THC529 Maikel Franco 1.50 4.00
THC530 Edwin Rios 3.00 8.00
THC532 Francisco Cervelli 1.25 3.00
THC533 Justin Smoak 1.25 3.00
THC534 Randy Dobnak 2.50 6.00
THC535 Dellin Betances 1.50 4.00
THC536 Michael Wacha 1.50 4.00
THC537 Tommy Kahnle 1.25 3.00
THC538 Kenta Maeda 1.50 4.00
THC539 Sheldon Neuse 1.50 4.00
THC540 Jon Berti 1.25 3.00
THC541 Kean Wong 1.50 4.00
THC542 Zack Wheeler 1.50 4.00
THC543 Garrett Stubbs 1.25 3.00
THC544 Kwang-Hyun Kim 4.00 10.00
THC545 Emilio Pagan 1.25 3.00
THC546 Jaylin Davis 2.00 5.00
THC547 Jake Fraley 1.50 4.00
THC548 Yoshi Tsutsugo 1.50 4.00
THC549 Shun Yamaguchi 1.50 4.00
THC702 Rick Porcello 1.50 4.00
THC705 Yonathan Daza 1.50 4.00
THC706 Lance McCullers Jr. 1.25 3.00
THC707 Jose Abreu 2.00 5.00
THC708 Kyle Garlick 2.00 5.00
THC709 Starlin Castro 1.25 3.00
THC723 Marcell Ozuna 2.00 5.00
THC725 Alex Verdugo 1.50 4.00

2020 Topps Heritage Chrome Refractors

*REF: .6X TO 1.5X BASIC
STATED ODDS 1:106 HOBBY
STATED PRINT RUN 571 SER.#'d SETS

2020 Topps Heritage Chrome White Refractors

*WHITE REF: 2X TO 5X BASIC
STATED ODDS 1:849 HOBBY
STATED PRINT RUN 71 SER.#'d SETS
THC464 Ronald Acuna Jr. 75.00 200.00

2020 Topps Heritage Chrome Spring Mega Box

INSERTED IN
STATED PRINT RUN 999 SER.#'d SETS
THC2 Trevor Bauer 2.00 5.00
THC5 Gary Sanchez 2.00 5.00
THC30 Justin Turner 1.50 4.00
THC33 Ender Inciarte 1.25 3.00
THC36 Kenley Jansen 1.50 4.00
THC40 Joey Votto 2.00 5.00
THC44 Brendan Rodgers 2.00 5.00
THC60 Mark Canha 1.25 3.00
THC81 Khris Davis 2.00 5.00
THC86 Colin Moran 1.25 3.00
THC87 Josh Hader 1.25 3.00

THC93 Z.Gallen/A.Young 3.00 8.00
THC94 Marco Gonzales 1.25 3.00
THC96 Mitch Garver 1.25 3.00
THC98 Marcus Semien 1.25 3.00
THC101 Brad Hand 1.25 3.00
THC103 Adalberto Mondesi 2.00 5.00
THC106 James McCann 1.50 4.00
THC112 Nick Ahmed 1.25 3.00
THC113 Eduardo Rodriguez 1.25 3.00
THC116 T.Grisham/M.Dubon 5.00 12.00
THC117 Marcus Stroman 1.50 4.00
THC120 Willians Astudillo 1.25 3.00
THC124 Kolten Wong 1.50 4.00
THC126 Edwin Encarnacion 2.00 5.00
THC130 Clint Frazier 1.50 4.00
THC131 Luke Voit 2.50 6.00
THC133 Buster Posey 2.50 6.00
THC139 Kevin Newman 1.50 4.00
THC160 Domingo Santana 1.50 4.00
THC162 David Price 1.50 4.00
THC168 Ken Giles 1.25 3.00
THC187 John Gant 1.25 3.00
THC218 Lourdes Gurriel Jr. 1.50 4.00
THC224 Joc Pederson 1.50 4.00
THC228 Mike Fiers 1.25 3.00
THC233 Joey Gallo 2.00 5.00
THC238 Jose Berrios 1.50 4.00
THC242 Michael Lorenzen 1.25 3.00
THC263 Freddie Freeman 2.50 6.00
THC264 Jose Altuve 1.50 4.00
THC267 Ryan Yarbrough 1.25 3.00
THC269 John Means 1.25 3.00
THC278 Wilson Ramos 1.25 3.00
THC279 Starlin Castro 1.25 3.00
THC280 Kirby Yates 1.25 3.00
THC282 Randal Grichuk 1.25 3.00
THC283 Eric Hosmer 1.50 4.00
THC284 Mike Minor 1.25 3.00
THC291 Kris Bryant 2.50 6.00
THC292 Luis Arraez 2.50 6.00
THC298 Ryan McMahon 1.25 3.00
THC300 Renato Nunez 1.50 4.00
THC303 Masahiro Tanaka 2.00 5.00
THC306 Nomar Mazara 1.25 3.00
THC308 Manny Machado 2.00 5.00
THC324 Jose Ramirez 1.50 4.00
THC336 Shin-Soo Choo 1.50 4.00
THC354 Yoan Moncada 2.00 5.00
THC355 Amed Rosario 1.50 4.00
THC360 Andrelton Simmons 1.25 3.00
THC374 Brandon Woodruff 1.25 3.00
THC385 Clayton Kershaw 4.00 10.00
THC387 Matt Boyd 1.25 3.00
THC390 Dansby Swanson 2.00 5.00
THC396 Hanser Alberto 1.25 3.00
THC397 Eric Thames 1.25 3.00
THC400 Yadier Molina 2.00 5.00
THC402 Jorge Alfaro 1.25 3.00
THC405 Dee Gordon 1.25 3.00
THC408 Yusei Kikuchi 1.50 4.00
THC409 Kyle Schwarber 2.00 5.00
THC417 Blake Snell 1.50 4.00
THC420 Charlie Blackmon 2.00 5.00
THC424 Yasmani Grandal 1.50 4.00
THC427 Jason Heyward 1.50 4.00
THC428 Noah Syndergaard 1.50 4.00
THC431 Robbie Ray 1.25 3.00
THC435 Lorenzo Cain 1.25 3.00
THC441 Miguel Sano 1.50 4.00
THC443 Giancarlo Stanton 2.00 5.00
THC444 Kyle Hendricks 2.00 5.00
THC453 Alex Bregman 2.00 5.00
THC454 Shane Bieber 2.00 5.00
THC455 Sonny Gray 1.50 4.00
THC458 Jean Segura 1.50 4.00
THC459 Alex Verdugo 1.50 4.00
THC462 Starling Marte 1.50 4.00
THC463 Kole Calhoun 1.25 3.00
THC472 Liam Hendriks 1.25 3.00
THC477 Hunter Renfroe 1.25 3.00
THC484 Aroldis Chapman 2.00 5.00
THC485 David Fletcher 1.25 3.00
THC486 Jon Lester 1.50 4.00
THC487 Hunter Dozier 1.25 3.00
THC490 Rhys Hoskins 2.50 6.00
THC491 Austin Riley 3.00 8.00
THC493 Mookie Betts 4.00 10.00
THC497 Victor Robles 2.50 6.00
THC500 Michael Chavis 1.50 4.00
THC520 Dallas Keuchel 1.50 4.00
THC553 Anthony Rendon 2.00 5.00
THC555 Nick Castellanos 2.00 5.00
THC556 Cole Hamels 1.50 4.00
THC557 Yasiel Puig 2.00 5.00
THC558 Stephen Strasburg 2.00 5.00
THC559 Salvador Perez 1.50 4.00
THC560 Jose Iglesias 1.50 4.00
THC561 Jonathan Lucroy 1.50 4.00
THC562 Andrew Cashner 1.25 3.00
THC563 Didi Gregorius 1.50 4.00
THC565 David Price 1.50 4.00
THC566 Hyun-Jin Ryu 1.50 4.00
THC567 Michael Kopech 2.50 6.00
THC568 Robel Garcia 1.25 3.00
THC569 Nomar Mazara 1.25 3.00
THC570 Corey Dickerson 1.50 4.00
THC571 Wade Miley 1.25 3.00
THC572 Jonathan Schoop 1.25 3.00
THC573 Homer Bailey 1.25 3.00
THC575 LaMonte Wade Jr. 2.00 5.00
THC576 Manuel Margot 1.25 3.00
THC577 Eric Thames 1.25 3.00
THC578 Steven Souza Jr. 1.25 3.00
THC579 Austin Dean 1.25 3.00
THC580 Brad Miller 1.25 3.00
THC581 Yoenis Cespedes 2.00 5.00
THC582 Kevin Pillar 1.25 3.00
THC583 Junior Guerra 1.25 3.00
THC584 Franchy Cordero 1.25 3.00
THC585 Jack Mayfield 1.25 3.00
THC586 Tony Kemp 1.25 3.00
THC587 Edwin Encarnacion 2.00 5.00
THC588 Carlos Rodon 1.50 4.00
THC589 Josh Harrison 1.25 3.00
THC590 Cameron Maybin 1.25 3.00
THC591 C.J. Cron 1.25 3.00
THC592 Todd Frazier 1.50 4.00
THC593 Kyle Gibson 1.25 3.00
THC594 Kyle Higashioka 1.25 3.00
THC595 Ehire Adrianza 1.25 3.00
THC596 Ryan McBroom 1.50 4.00
THC597 Myles Straw 2.00 5.00
THC598 Patrick Wisdom 1.25 3.00
THC599 Eric Lauer 1.25 3.00
THC600 Ronny Rodriguez 1.25 3.00
THC601 Brusdar Graterol 2.00 5.00
THC602 Emmanuel Clase 1.50 4.00
THC703 Starling Marte 1.50 4.00
THC704 Ivan Nova 1.25 3.00

2020 Topps Heritage Clubhouse Collection Autograph Relics

STATED ODDS 1:15,948 HOBBY
EXCHANGE DEADLINE 1/31/2022
CCARAA Aristides Aquino HN
CCARAB Andrew Benintendi EXCH 75.00 200.00
CCARAJ Aaron Judge HN
CCARAR Anthony Rizzo 50.00 120.00
CCARBB Bo Bichette HN
CCARBH Bryce Harper HN
CCARCK Clayton Kershaw EXCH 60.00 150.00
CCARCY Christian Yelich 75.00 200.00
CCARDL DJ LeMahieu HN
CCARFT Fernando Tatis Jr. EXCH
CCARGT Gleyber Torres 125.00 300.00
CCARJL Jesus Luzardo HN
CCARKH Keston Hiura HN
CCARLR Luis Robert HN
CCARMT Mike Trout 250.00 600.00
CCARNA Nolan Arenado 60.00 150.00
CCAROA Ozzie Albies EXCH 50.00 120.00
CCARPG Paul Goldschmidt HN
CCARRA Ronald Acuna Jr. HN
CCARRA Ronald Acuna Jr. 250.00 600.00
CCARRD Rafael Devers 75.00 200.00
CCARRH Rhys Hoskins HN
CCARSO Shohei Ohtani HN
CCARVG Vladimir Guerrero Jr. HN
CCARVG Vladimir Guerrero Jr. 100.00 250.00
CCARXB Xander Bogaerts HN
CCARYA Yordan Alvarez 125.00 300.00

2020 Topps Heritage Clubhouse Collection Dual Relics

STATED ODDS 1:17,063 HOBBY
STATED PRINT RUN 71 SER.#'d SETS
CCDRAA R.Acuna Jr./H.Aaron 50.00 120.00
CCDRBA A.Bregman/Y.Alvarez 60.00 150.00
CCDRBV Joey Votto
Johnny Bench HN
CCDRCS R.Clemente/W.Stargell 100.00 250.00
CCDRMA Jose Altuve
Joe Morgan HN
CCDRMJ Thurman Munson
Aaron Judge HN
CCDRRD Nolan Ryan
Jacob deGrom HN
CCDRSA P.Alonso/T.Seaver 50.00 120.00
CCDRSH Mike Schmidt
Bryce Harper HN
CCDRYD R.Devers/C.Yastrzemski 30.00 80.00

2020 Topps Heritage Clubhouse Collection Relics

STATED ODDS 1:34 HOBBY
*GOLD/99: .6X TO 1.5X BASIC
CCRAA Albert Almora HN
CCRAA Aristides Aquino 8.00 20.00
CCRAB Alex Bregman 3.00 8.00
CCRAB Alex Bregman HN
CCRAJ Aaron Judge HN
CCRAJ Aaron Judge 8.00 20.00
CCRAM Andrew McCutchen HN
CCRAN Aaron Nola HN
CCRAN Aaron Nola 3.00 8.00
CCRAP Albert Pujols 4.00 10.00
CCRAR Anthony Rizzo 5.00 12.00
CCRAR Anthony Rizzo HN
CCRARO Amed Rosario 2.50 6.00
CCRBB Bo Bichette 6.00 15.00
CCRBB Bo Bichette HN
CCRBC Brandon Crawford HN
CCRBH Bryce Harper HN
CCRBH Bryce Harper 5.00 12.00
CCRBP Buster Posey 5.00 12.00
CCRBP Buster Posey HN
CCRCB Charlie Blackmon HN
CCRCB Cody Bellinger HN
CCRCB Cody Bellinger 6.00 15.00
CCRCBL Charlie Blackmon 3.00 8.00
CCRCC Carlos Correa HN
CCRCK Clayton Kershaw HN
CCRCK Clayton Kershaw 6.00 15.00
CCRCM Charlie Morton 3.00 8.00
CCRCP Chris Paddack 4.00 10.00
CCRCS Chris Sale HN
CCRCY Christian Yelich HN
CCRCY Christian Yelich 4.00 10.00
CCRDL DJ LeMahieu HN
CCRDL DJ LeMahieu 3.00 8.00
CCRDS Dansby Swanson HN
CCRDV Daniel Vogelbach 2.00 5.00
CCREA Elvis Andrus 3.00 8.00
CCREL Evan Longoria 3.00 8.00
CCRFB Franklin Barreto HN
CCRFL Francisco Lindor HN
CCRFT Fernando Tatis Jr. HN
CCRFT Fernando Tatis Jr. 6.00 15.00
CCRGS Gary Sanchez HN
CCRGS George Springer 2.50 6.00
CCRGT Gleyber Torres HN
CCRGT Gleyber Torres 4.00 10.00
CCRGU Gio Urshela 3.00 8.00
CCRHR Hyun-Jin Ryu HN
CCRHR Hyun-Jin Ryu 2.50 6.00
CCRJA Jose Altuve HN
CCRJA Jose Altuve 4.00 10.00
CCRJB Javier Baez HN
CCRJB Javier Baez 4.00 10.00
CCRJD Jacob deGrom HN
CCRJG Joey Gallo 3.00 8.00
CCRJM Jeff McNeil HN
CCRJM J.D. Martinez 3.00 8.00
CCRJMC Jeff McNeil 2.50 6.00
CCRJR Jose Ramirez HN
CCRJR Jose Ramirez 2.50 6.00
CCRJRE J.T. Realmuto 3.00 8.00
CCRJS Juan Soto HN
CCRJV Justin Verlander 3.00 8.00
CCRKB Kris Bryant HN
CCRKB Kris Bryant 4.00 10.00
CCRKH Keston Hiura 4.00 10.00
CCRKK Kevin Kiermaier HN
CCRKM Ketel Marte 2.50 6.00
CCRKS Kyle Schwarber 3.00 8.00
CCRLC Lorenzo Cain HN
CCRLG Lucas Giolito 4.00 10.00
CCRMB Mookie Betts HN
CCRMB Mookie Betts 6.00 15.00
CCRMBR Michael Brantley 2.50 6.00
CCRMC Matt Chapman 4.00 10.00
CCRMCO Michael Conforto 4.00 10.00
CCRMF Max Fried 4.00 10.00
CCRMH Mitch Haniger 4.00 10.00
CCRMK Max Kepler 4.00 10.00
CCRMS Max Scherzer HN
CCRMT Mike Trout HN
CCRMT Mike Trout 15.00 40.00
CCRNA Nolan Arenado HN
CCRNA Nolan Arenado 4.00 10.00
CCRNH Nico Hoerner HN
CCRNS Nick Solak HN
CCRNS Noah Syndergaard 4.00 10.00
CCROA Ozzie Albies HN
CCROA Ozzie Albies 4.00 10.00
CCRPA Pete Alonso HN
CCRPA Pete Alonso 8.00 20.00
CCRPC Patrick Corbin 2.50 6.00
CCRPG Paul Goldschmidt HN
CCRPG Paul Goldschmidt 4.00 10.00
CCRRA Ronald Acuna Jr. HN
CCRRA Ronald Acuna Jr. 12.00 30.00
CCRRD Rafael Devers HN
CCRRD Rafael Devers 4.00 10.00
CCRRH Rhys Hoskins HN
CCRRH Rhys Hoskins 4.00 10.00
CCRSO Shohei Ohtani HN
CCRSO Shohei Ohtani 12.00 30.00
CCRSS Stephen Strasburg 3.00 8.00
CCRTM Trey Mancini HN
CCRTM Trey Mancini 4.00 10.00
CCRTS Trevor Story HN
CCRTT Trea Turner 2.50 6.00
CCRVG Vladimir Guerrero Jr. HN
CCRVG Vladimir Guerrero Jr. 4.00 10.00
CCRVR Victor Robles HN
CCRWB Walker Buehler HN
CCRWB Walker Buehler 4.00 10.00
CCRWC Willson Contreras HN
CCRWC Willson Contreras 3.00 8.00
CCRXB Xander Bogaerts 3.00 8.00
CCRYA Yordan Alvarez HN
CCRYA Yordan Alvarez 8.00 20.00
CCRYM Yadier Molina HN
CCRYM Yadier Molina 3.00 8.00
CCRZG Zack Greinke 4.00 10.00
CCRAAQ Aristides Aquino HN
CCRJAB Jose Abreu HN
CCRJBE Jose Berrios HN
CCRJBJ Jackie Bradley Jr. HN
CCRJRE J.T. Realmuto HN
CCRKMA Ketel Marte HN
CCRMSA Miguel Sano HN
CCRMSM Mallex Smith HN

2020 Topps Heritage Clubhouse Collection Triple Relics

STATED ODDS 1:48,345 HOBBY
STATED PRINT RUN 25 SER.#'d SETS
CCTRAJA Acuna Jr./Aaron/Jones 60.00 150.00
CCTRCSB Bell/Stargell/Clemente 150.00 400.00
CCTRBMA Morgan/Biggio/Altuve 50.00 120.00
CCTRTMG Molina/Goldschmidt/Torre 125.00 300.00
CCTRYOD Devers/Yastrzemski/Ortiz 50.00 120.00

2020 Topps Heritage Flashback Autograph Relics

STATED ODDS 1:24,173 HOBBY
PRINT RUNS B/WN 10-25 COPIES PER
NO PRICING ON QTY 10
EXCHANGE DEADLINE 1/31/2022
FARBB Bert Blyleven/25 100.00 250.00
FARBG Bob Gibson/25 125.00 300.00
FARCF Carlton Fisk/25 75.00 200.00
FARCY Carl Yastrzemski/25 100.00 250.00
FARDS Don Sutton EXCH 50.00 120.00
FARJB Johnny Bench
FARNR Nolan Ryan/25 125.00 300.00
FARRC Rod Carew EXCH 100.00 250.00
FARRJ Reggie Jackson/25 200.00 500.00

2020 Topps Heritage Mini

STATED ODDS 1:457 HOBBY
STATED PRINT RUN 100 SER.#'d SETS
5 Gary Sanchez 8.00 20.00
8 Gio Urshela 8.00 20.00
17 Yuli Gurriel 6.00 15.00
32 Evan Longoria 6.00 15.00
35 Jorge Soler 8.00 20.00
40 Joey Votto 10.00 25.00
41 Miguel Cabrera 25.00 60.00
53 Aaron Nola 8.00 20.00
56 Carlos Santana 6.00 15.00
75 J.T. Realmuto 8.00 20.00
78 Albert Pujols 10.00 25.00
82 Max Scherzer 12.00 30.00
87 Josh Hader 5.00 12.00
96 Mitch Garver 5.00 12.00
98 Marcus Semien 5.00 12.00
118 Whit Merrifield 8.00 20.00
131 Luke Voit 10.00 25.00
142 Javier Baez 10.00 25.00
145 Rafael Devers 10.00 25.00
149 Zack Greinke 6.00 15.00
154 Trea Turner 6.00 15.00
167 Max Muncy 6.00 15.00
174 Christian Yelich 10.00 25.00
182 Chris Paddack 8.00 20.00
183 Ketel Marte 6.00 15.00
185 Luis Severino 6.00 15.00
220 Nate Lowe 5.00 12.00
224 Joc Pederson 6.00 15.00
230 Patrick Corbin 6.00 15.00
236 Jorge Polanco 6.00 15.00
238 Jose Berrios 6.00 15.00
240 Brian Anderson 5.00 12.00
241 Willson Contreras 8.00 20.00
244 George Springer 6.00 15.00
245 Mike Soroka 8.00 20.00
257 Cody Bellinger 15.00 40.00
263 Freddie Freeman 10.00 25.00
264 Jose Altuve 10.00 25.00
272 Eugenio Suarez 6.00 15.00
280 Kirby Yates 5.00 12.00
283 Eric Hosmer 6.00 15.00
285 Will Smith 10.00 25.00
286 Ozzie Albies 8.00 20.00
291 Kris Bryant 12.00 30.00
300 Renato Nunez 6.00 15.00
303 Masahiro Tanaka 8.00 20.00
308 Manny Machado 8.00 20.00
310 Michael Conforto 6.00 15.00
312 Carlos Correa 8.00 20.00
321 Ryan Braun 6.00 15.00
322 Nolan Arenado 10.00 25.00
324 Jose Ramirez 6.00 15.00
341 Mike Clevinger 8.00 20.00
345 Xander Bogaerts 8.00 20.00
346 Trey Mancini 8.00 20.00
350 Trevor Story 8.00 20.00
354 Yoan Moncada 8.00 20.00
355 Amed Rosario 6.00 15.00
373 Anthony Rizzo 12.00 30.00
383 Bryan Reynolds 6.00 15.00
385 Clayton Kershaw 15.00 40.00
394 Kevin Pillar 5.00 12.00
395 Aaron Judge 30.00 80.00
400 Yadier Molina 10.00 25.00
401 Elvis Andrus 6.00 15.00
403 Juan Soto 25.00 60.00
406 Jacob deGrom 8.00 20.00
407 Matt Olson 5.00 12.00
408 Yusei Kikuchi 6.00 15.00
409 Kyle Schwarber 8.00 20.00
410 Corey Seager 8.00 20.00
413 Keston Hiura 10.00 25.00
414 Vladimir Guerrero Jr. 30.00 80.00
415 DJ LeMahieu 8.00 20.00
416 Lucas Giolito 6.00 15.00
417 Blake Snell 6.00 15.00
419 Andrew Benintendi 8.00 20.00
420 Charlie Blackmon 8.00 20.00
422 Josh Bell 6.00 15.00
423 J.D. Martinez 8.00 20.00
424 Yasmani Grandal 5.00 12.00
425 Michael Brantley 6.00 15.00
426 Mike Yastrzemski 12.00 30.00
428 Noah Syndergaard 6.00 15.00
432 Eddie Rosario 6.00 15.00
433 Shohei Ohtani 10.00 25.00
435 Lorenzo Cain 5.00 12.00
436 Tim Anderson 8.00 20.00
437 Fernando Tatis Jr. 30.00 80.00
439 Luis Castillo 6.00 15.00
440 Jonathan Villar 5.00 12.00
441 Miguel Sano 6.00 15.00
442 Francisco Lindor 8.00 20.00
443 Giancarlo Stanton 15.00 40.00
447 Bryce Harper 12.00 30.00
451 Chris Sale 8.00 20.00
453 Alex Bregman 12.00 30.00
454 Shane Bieber 10.00 25.00
455 Sonny Gray 6.00 15.00
456 Andrew McCutchen 8.00 20.00
457 Pete Alonso 20.00 50.00
458 Jean Segura 6.00 15.00
459 Alex Verdugo 6.00 15.00
461 Daniel Vogelbach 5.00 12.00
462 Starling Marte 6.00 15.00
464 Ronald Acuna Jr. 50.00 120.00
465 Max Fried 8.00 20.00
466 Mike Trout 100.00 250.00
467 Paul Goldschmidt 8.00 20.00
468 Matt Chapman 8.00 20.00
472 Liam Hendriks 5.00 12.00
473 Justin Verlander 8.00 20.00
474 Eduardo Escobar 5.00 12.00
476 Paul DeJong 10.00 25.00
478 David Dahl 5.00 12.00
479 Max Kepler 8.00 20.00
480 James Paxton 6.00 15.00
481 Austin Meadows 6.00 15.00
482 Nick Senzel 8.00 20.00
483 Gleyber Torres 15.00 40.00
484 Aroldis Chapman 8.00 20.00
487 Hunter Dozier 5.00 12.00
488 Christian Walker 6.00 15.00
490 Rhys Hoskins 10.00 25.00
491 Austin Riley 12.00 30.00
492 Jeff McNeil 6.00 15.00
493 Mookie Betts 15.00 40.00
494 Eloy Jimenez 15.00 40.00
495 Ramon Laureano 8.00 20.00
496 Walker Buehler 12.00 30.00
497 Victor Robles 10.00 25.00
500 Michael Chavis 6.00 15.00

2020 Topps Heritage New Age Performers

COMPLETE SET (25) 15.00 40.00
STATED ODDS 1:11 HOBBY
NAP1 Eugenio Suarez .50 1.25
NAP2 Yordan Alvarez 2.00 5.00
NAP3 Mike Soroka .60 1.50
NAP4 Jorge Soler .60 1.50
NAP5 Keston Hiura .75 2.00
NAP6 Lucas Giolito .50 1.25
NAP7 Pete Alonso 1.50 4.00
NAP8 Ketel Marte .50 1.25
NAP9 Jose Berrios .50 1.25
NAP10 Vladimir Guerrero Jr. 1.25 3.00
NAP11 Gio Urshela .60 1.50
NAP12 Josh Hader .40 1.00
NAP13 Shane Bieber .60 1.50
NAP14 Matt Chapman .60 1.50
NAP15 Bo Bichette 2.50 6.00
NAP16 Tim Anderson .60 1.50
NAP17 J.T. Realmuto .60 1.50
NAP18 Mike Yastrzemski 1.00 2.50
NAP19 Josh Bell .50 1.25
NAP20 George Springer .50 1.25
NAP21 Jack Flaherty .50 1.25
NAP22 Austin Meadows .50 1.25
NAP23 Max Fried .60 1.50
NAP24 Fernando Tatis Jr. 2.50 6.00
NAP25 Luis Castillo .50 1.25

2020 Topps Heritage News Flashbacks

STATED ODDS 1:18 HOBBY
NF1 Walt Disney World opens .60 1.50
NF2 First Starbucks opens .60 1.50
NF3 The Ed Sullivan show airs
last episode .60 1.50
NF4 Evel Knievel jumps 19 cars .60 1.50
NF5 NASDAQ is founded .60 1.50
NF6 Fight of the Century .60 1.50
NF7 Apollo 14 launches .60 1.50
NF8 Willy Wonka and the Chocolate
Factory is released .60 1.50
NF9 Jim Morrison dies at 27 .60 1.50
NF10 Mariner 9 enters Mars' orbit .60 1.50
NF11 First microprocessor released .60 1.50
NF12 All in the Family debuts .60 1.50
NF13 Lunar Roving Vehicle
used on moon .60 1.50
NF14 The Mystery of D.B. Cooper .60 1.50
NF15 Louie Armstrong passes away .60 1.50

2020 Topps Heritage Real One Autographs

STATED ODDS 1:110 HOBBY
EXCHANGE DEADLINE 1/31/2022
ROAAA Adbert Alzolay 8.00 20.00
ROAAQ Aristides Aquino 20.00 50.00
ROAAF Al Ferrara 6.00 15.00
ROAAK Anthony Kay 6.00 15.00
ROAAM Austin Meadows HN
ROAAN Aaron Nola HN
ROAAP A.J. Puk 10.00 25.00
ROAAR Anthony Rendon HN
ROAAR Austin Riley 15.00 40.00
ROAARI Anthony Rizzo 20.00 50.00
ROABB Bert Blyleven HN
ROABB Bo Bichette 100.00 250.00
ROABBR Bobby Bradley 8.00 20.00
ROABBU Bill Burbach 6.00 15.00
ROABG Bob Gibson HN
ROABH Bryce Harper HN
ROABL Brandon Lowe 10.00 25.00
ROABM Brendan McKay 10.00 25.00
ROABR Bryan Reynolds 8.00 20.00
ROACB Cavan Biggio HN
ROACK Corey Kluber HN
ROACR Claude Raymond 10.00 25.00
ROACY Carl Yastrzemski 50.00 120.00
ROACYE Christian Yelich 40.00 100.00
ROADC Dylan Cease 10.00 25.00
ROADL DJ LeMahieu HN
ROADM Dustin May 25.00 60.00
ROADW Devin Williams HN
ROAEJ Eloy Jimenez 25.00 60.00
ROAFL Francisco Lindor 25.00 60.00
ROAFT Fernando Tatis Jr. EXCH 200.00 500.00
ROAGC Gerrit Cole HN
ROAGL Gavin Lux 75.00 200.00
ROAGS George Springer 15.00 40.00
ROAGT Gleyber Torres 30.00 80.00
ROAGTH George Thomas 6.00 15.00
ROAHA Hank Aaron 300.00 600.00
ROAJA Jose Altuve 25.00 60.00
ROAJB Johnny Bench 100.00 250.00
ROAJD Justin Dunn 8.00 20.00
ROAJF Jim French 6.00 15.00
ROAJG John Gelnar 10.00 25.00
ROAJGI Jake Gibbs 6.00 15.00
ROAJL Jesus Luzardo 15.00 40.00
ROAJM Juan Marichal HN
ROAJM Joe Moeller 10.00 25.00
ROAJR Jose Ramirez HN
ROAJS Juan Soto HN
ROAJT Joe Torre 40.00 100.00
ROAJY Jordan Yamamoto 8.00 20.00
ROAKB Kris Bryant HN
ROAKH Ken Harrelson 20.00 50.00
ROAKHI Keston Hiura 20.00 50.00
ROAKL Kyle Lewis 50.00 120.00
ROAKM Ketel Marte HN
ROALA Luis Arraez HN
ROALA Logan Allen 6.00 15.00
ROALB Lou Brock HN
ROALG Lucas Giolito HN
ROALR Luis Robert HN
ROALT Luis Tiant HN
ROAMC Miguel Cabrera HN
ROAMK Max Kepler HN
ROAML Marcel Lachemann 6.00 15.00
ROAMS Mike Soroka HN
ROAMT Masahiro Tanaka HN
ROAMT Mike Trout 250.00 600.00
ROAMW Maury Wills HN
ROANA Nolan Arenado 30.00 80.00
ROANH Nico Hoerner 12.00 30.00
ROANR Nolan Ryan 125.00 300.00
ROAOM Oscar Mercado HN
ROAPA Pete Alonso HN
ROAPA Pete Alonso 75.00 200.00
ROAPC Patrick Corbin HN
ROAPD Paul DeJong 10.00 25.00
ROAPG Paul Goldschmidt HN
ROARA Ronald Acuna Jr. HN
ROARA Ronald Acuna Jr. 100.00 250.00
ROARC Rod Carew HN
ROARD Rafael Devers 30.00 80.00
ROARF Rollie Fingers HN
ROARH Rhys Hoskins 25.00 60.00
ROARJ Reggie Jackson 60.00 125.00
ROASB Seth Brown 6.00 15.00
ROASC Sal Campisi 6.00 15.00
ROASCA Steve Carlton 30.00 80.00
ROASO Shohei Ohtani EXCH 100.00 250.00
ROASY Shun Yamaguchi HN
ROATC Ty Cline 8.00 20.00
ROATD Tommy Dean 10.00 25.00
ROATE Tommy Edman HN
ROATG Trent Grisham HN
ROATO Tony Oliva HN
ROATP Tony Perez HN
ROATT Tom Tischinski 10.00 25.00
ROAVB Vida Blue HN
ROAVG Vladimir Guerrero Jr. HN
ROAVG Vladimir Guerrero Jr. 40.00 100.00
ROAWB Walker Buehler 30.00 80.00
ROAWS Will Smith 15.00 40.00
ROAWW Woody Woodward 12.00 30.00
ROAYA Yordan Alvarez 50.00 120.00
ROAYG Yuli Gurriel HN
ROAZW Zack Wheeler HN
ROAAMO Adalberto Mondesi HN
ROABPR Bob Priddy HN
ROACBE Cody Bellinger HN
ROADCO Danny Coombs HN
ROADSW Dansby Swanson HN
ROAFJO Frank Johnson HN
ROAJDM J.D. Martinez HN
ROAJMC Jeff McNeil HN
ROAJRE J.T. Realmuto HN
ROAJSO Jorge Soler HN

2020 Topps Heritage Real One Autographs Red Ink

*RED INK: 1X TO 2.5X BASIC
STATED ODDS 1:1274 HOBBY
STATED PRINT RUN 71 SER.#'d SETS
EXCHANGE DEADLINE 1/31/2022
ROAAR Austin Riley
ROABB Bo Bichette 400.00 1000.00
ROAHA Hank Aaron/25 400.00 800.00
ROAJB Johnny Bench 150.00 400.00
ROAJT Joe Torre 50.00 120.00
ROAMT Mike Trout 300.00 800.00
ROANA Nolan Arenado
ROANH Nico Hoerner
ROANR Nolan Ryan 200.00 500.00
ROAPA Pete Alonso 125.00 300.00

2020 Topps Heritage Real One Dual Autographs

STATED ODDS 1:6446 HOBBY
STATED PRINT RUN 25 SER.#'d SETS
EXCHANGE DEADLINE 1/31/2022
RODAAA Y.Alvarez/J.Altuve 150.00 400.00
RODAAR A.Riley/R.Acuna Jr. 150.00 400.00
RODABS N.Senzel/J.Bench 150.00 400.00
RODAKC A.Kaline/M.Cabrera 250.00 600.0
RODATM J.Torre/Y.Molina 100.00 250.0
RODATO S.Ohtani/M.Trout
RODAYB A.Benintendi/C.Yastrzemski 150.00 400.00
RODAAS Ronald Acuna Jr.
Juan Soto HN
RODAJT Judge/Torres
RODACM Joe Mauer
Rod Carew HN
RODAGB Bob Gibson
Lou Brock HN
RODAJR Luis Robert
Eloy Jimenez HN
RODAJT Aaron Judge
Gleyber Torres HN
RODAYH Christian Yelich
Keston Hiura HN

2020 Topps Heritage Senators Final Season Autographs

STATED ODDS 1:6684 HOBBY
STATED PRINT RUN 25 SER.#'d SETS
EXCHANGE DEADLINE 1/31/2022
WSFSBG Bill Gogolewski 60.00 150.0
WSFSDB Dick Billings 60.00 150.0
WSFSDBO Dick Bosman 60.00 150.0
WSFSDK Darold Knowles 40.00 100.0
WSFSDM Denny McLain 60.00 150.0
WSFSEM Elliott Maddox 60.00 150.0
WSFSFH Frank Howard 75.00 200.0
WSFSJB Jeff Burroughs 60.00 150.0
WSFSJF Jim French 60.00 150.0

2020 Topps Heritage Then and Now

COMPLETE SET (15) 6.00 15.0
STATED ODDS 1:18 HOBBY
TN1 Fergie Jenkins .60 1.5
Stephen Strasburg
TN2 Verlander/Hunter .60 1.5
TN3 Hyun-Jin Ryu .50 1.2
Tom Seaver
TN4 Gerrit Cole 1.00 2.5
Jim Palmer
TN5 Alonso/Stargell 1.50 4.0
TN6 Jorge Soler .60 1.5
Reggie Jackson
TN7 Joe Torre .60 1.5
Anthony Rendon
TN8 Jose Abreu .60 1.5
Harmon Killebrew
TN9 Yelich/Torre .75 2.0
TN10 Tim Anderson .60 1.5
Tony Oliva
TN11 Mallex Smith .50 1.2
Lou Brock
TN12 Stephen Strasburg .60 1.5
Fergie Jenkins
TN13 Palmer/Verlander .60 1.5
TN14 Jacob deGrom .60 1.5
Tom Seaver
TN15 Gerrit Cole 1.00 2.5
Bert Blyleven

2015 Topps Heritage '51 Collection

COMPLETE SET (104) 15.00 40.0
ONE COMPLETE BASE SET PER BOX
1 Mike Trout 1.50 4.0
2 Felix Hernandez .25 .6
3 Miguel Cabrera .30 .7
4 Madison Bumgarner .25 .6
5 Masahiro Tanaka .25 .6
6 Joey Votto .30 .7
7 David Price .25 .6
8 Mookie Betts .50 1.2
9 Jake Lamb RC .60 1.5
10 Yasmany Tomas RC .50 1.2
11 Archie Bradley RC .40 1.0
12 Todd Frazier .25 .6
13 Michael Pineda .20 .5
14 Taijuan Walker .20 .5
15 Starling Marte .25 .6
16 Dalton Pompey RC .50 1.2
17 Eric Hosmer .25 .6
18 Paul Goldschmidt .30 .7
19 Kolten Wong .25 .6
20 Kevin Plawecki RC .40 1.0
21 Jorge Soler RC .60 1.5
22 Devon Travis RC .40 1.0
23 Max Scherzer .30 .7
24 Ian Desmond .20 .5
25 Kris Bryant RC 2.50 6.0
26 Steven Souza Jr. .25 .6
27 Joc Pederson RC .75 2.0
28 Jason Heyward .25 .6
29 Justin Upton .25 .6
30 Craig Kimbrel .25 .6
31 Jose Altuve .25 .6
32 Michael Brantley .25 .6
33 Ian Kinsler .25 .6
34 Hanley Ramirez .25 .6
35 Matt Harvey .25 .6
36 Yoenis Cespedes .25 .6
37 Ryan Braun .25 .6
38 George Springer .25 .6
39 Hunter Pence .25 .6
40 Carlos Gonzalez .25 .6
41 Manny Machado .30 .7
42 Corey Kluber .25 .6
43 Daniel Norris RC .40 1.0
44 Joey Gallo RC .75 2.0
45 Jose Bautista .25 .6
46 Albert Pujols .40 1.0
47 Michael Wacha .25 .6

ristian Yelich .40 1.00
ck Greinke .25 .60
yce Harper .50 1.25
asiel Puig .30 .75
ff Samardzija .20 .50
obinson Cano .25 .60
arlos Rodon RC .60 1.50
nthony Rizzo .50 1.25
sh Donaldson .25 .60
sney Castillo RC .50 1.25
oah Syndergaard RC .75 2.00
ames Shields .20 .50
iancarlo Stanton .30 .75
avid Ortiz .30 .75
oy Tulowitzki .30 .75
ablo Sandoval .25 .60
randon Finnegan RC .40 1.00
ucas Duda .25 .60
hris Sale .30 .75
arlos Correa RC 2.00 5.00
nthony Rendon .30 .75
ndrew McCutchen .30 .75
ole Hamels .25 .60
an Longoria .25 .60
acoby Ellsbury .25 .60
drian Gonzalez .25 .60
yron Buxton RC .60 1.50
rancisco Lindor RC 2.50 6.00
yle Seager .20 .50
ddison Russell RC 1.25 3.00
acob deGrom .30 .75
tephen Strasburg .30 .75
ndrew Miller .25 .60
illy Hamilton .25 .60
dam Jones .25 .60
avid Wright .25 .60
aron Sanchez .25 .60
hris Archer .20 .50
onny Gray .25 .60
drian Beltre .30 .75
eddie Freeman .40 1.00
att Kemp .25 .60
rince Fielder .25 .60
lex Cobb .20 .50
ustin Pedroia .30 .75
ordan Zimmermann .25 .60
ohnny Cueto .25 .60
dwin Encarnacion .30 .75
on Lester .25 .60
uster Posey .40 1.00
elson Cruz .30 .75
ose Abreu .30 .75
Clayton Kershaw .60 1.50
Starlin Castro .20 .50
Eduardo Rodriguez RC .40 1.00
Blake Swihart RC .50 1.25
Aroldis Chapman .30 .75

2015 Topps Heritage '51 Collection Mini Black Back
ACK: 3X TO 8X BASIC
ACK RC: 1.5X TO 4X BASIC
MINI BLACK PER BOX SET

2015 Topps Heritage '51 Collection Mini Blue Back
UE: 1.5X TO 4X BASIC
UE RC: .75X TO 2X BASIC
E MINI BLUE PER BOX SET

2015 Topps Heritage '51 Collection Mini Gold Back
LD: 6X TO 15X BASIC
LD RC: 3X TO 8X BASIC
E MINI GOLD PER BOX SET
ike Trout 25.00 60.00

2015 Topps Heritage '51 Collection Mini Green Back
EEN: 2X TO 5X BASIC
EEN RC: 1X TO 2.5X BASIC
EE MINI GREEN PER BOX SET

2015 Topps Heritage '51 Collection Mini Red Back
D: 1.2X TO 3X BASIC
D RC: .6X TO 1.5X BASIC
MINI RED PER BOX SET

2015 Topps Heritage '51 Collection Autographs
ERALL ONE AUTO PER BOX SET
NT RUNS B/WN 50-250 COPIES PER
CHANGE DEADLINE 10/31/2017
UE/25: .6X TO 1.5X BASIC
AAB Archie Bradley/250 5.00 12.00
AAR Addison Russell/250 15.00 40.00
ABB Byron Buxton/250 15.00 40.00
ABH Bryce Harper/50 125.00 250.00
ABP Buster Posey 40.00 100.00
ACC Carlos Correa/50 100.00 250.00
ACR Carlos Rodon 8.00 20.00
ADP Dalton Pompey/250 6.00 15.00
ADW David Wright/100 25.00 60.00
AER Eduardo Rodriguez/250 5.00 12.00
AFL Francisco Lindor/250 25.00 60.00
AJA Jose Abreu/250 8.00 20.00
AJD Jacob deGrom/250 10.00 25.00
AJL Jake Lamb/250 8.00 20.00
AJP Joc Pederson/250 8.00 20.00
AJS Jorge Soler/250 10.00 25.00
AKB Kris Bryant/210 100.00 250.00
AKP Kevin Plawecki/250 5.00 12.00
ALD Lucas Duda EXCH 6.00 15.00
AMT Mike Trout/50 200.00 300.00
ANS Noah Syndergaard/250 20.00 50.00
ARC Rusney Castillo/250 6.00 15.00
H51ASG Sonny Gray/250 6.00 15.00
H51ASS Steven Souza Jr./250 6.00 15.00
H51ATW Taijuan Walker/250 5.00 12.00
H51AYT Yasmany Tomas EXCH 6.00 15.00

2014 Topps High Tek Wave
*SPIRAL: .5X TO 1.2X WAVE
*SCRIBBLE: .6X TO 1.5X WAVE
*LG SHATTERED: 1.5X TO 4X WAVE
*SMALL MAZE: 3X TO 8X WAVE
HTAB Albert Belle .60 1.50
HTAJ Adam Jones .75 2.00
HTAP Albert Pujols 1.25 3.00
HTBJ Bo Jackson 1.00 2.50
HTCF Carlton Fisk .75 2.00
HTCR Cal Ripken Jr. 3.00 8.00
HTCS Chris Sale 1.00 2.50
HTDE Dennis Eckersley .75 2.00
HTDPE Dustin Pedroia 1.00 2.50
HTEL Evan Longoria .75 2.00
HTEM Edgar Martinez .75 2.00
HTFM Fred McGriff .75 2.00
HTFT Frank Thomas 1.00 2.50
HTGS George Springer RC 2.50 6.00
HTIR Ivan Rodriguez .75 2.00
HTJA Jose Abreu RC 5.00 12.00
HTJC Jose Canseco .75 2.00
HTJG Juan Gonzalez .60 1.50
HTJM Joe Mauer .75 2.00
HTJSI Jon Singleton RC .75 2.00
HTKG Ken Griffey Jr. 2.00 5.00
HTMC Miguel Cabrera 1.00 2.50
HTMM Mike Mussina .75 2.00
HTMN Mike Napoli .60 1.50
HTMR Mariano Rivera 1.25 3.00
HTMS Marcus Stroman RC 1.00 2.50
HTMSC Max Scherzer 1.00 2.50
HTMT Mike Trout 5.00 12.00
HTMTA Masahiro Tanaka RC 2.00 5.00
HTNC Nick Castellanos RC 2.00 5.00
HTNG Nomar Garciaparra .75 2.00
HTNR Nolan Ryan 3.00 8.00
HTOH Orlando Hernandez .60 1.50
HTOV Omar Vizquel .75 2.00
HTPF Prince Fielder .75 2.00
HTPM Pedro Martinez .75 2.00
HTPO Paul O'Neill .75 2.00
HTRA Roberto Alomar .75 2.00
HTRC Robinson Cano .75 2.00
HTRCL Roger Clemens 1.25 3.00
HTRE Roenis Elias RC .60 1.50
HTRH Rickey Henderson 1.00 2.50
HTRJA Reggie Jackson .75 2.00
HTRP Rafael Palmeiro .75 2.00
HTRY Robin Yount 1.00 2.50
HTSG Sonny Gray .60 1.50
HTTW Taijuan Walker RC .60 1.50
HTWB Wade Boggs .75 2.00
HTWM Wil Myers .60 1.50
HTYC Yoenis Cespedes 1.00 2.50
HTYD Yu Darvish 1.00 2.50
HTYS Yangervis Solarte RC .60 1.50
HTYV Yordano Ventura RC .75 2.00

2014 Topps High Tek Wave Clouds Diffractor 25
*CLOUDS: 3X TO 8X BASIC
STATED ODDS 1:10 PACKS
STATED PRINT RUN 25 SER.#'d SETS
HTCR Cal Ripken Jr. 20.00 50.00
HTKG Ken Griffey Jr. 20.00 50.00
HTMT Mike Trout 30.00 80.00
HTRH Rickey Henderson 10.00 25.00
HTRJA Reggie Jackson 8.00 20.00

2014 Topps High Tek Wave Disco Diffractor 50
*DISCO: 1.2X TO 3X BASIC
STATED ODDS 1:5 PACKS
STATED PRINT RUN 50 SER.#'d SETS
HTKG Ken Griffey Jr. 8.00 20.00
HTMT Mike Trout 15.00 40.00
HTRH Rickey Henderson 4.00 10.00
HTRJA Reggie Jackson 3.00 8.00

2014 Topps High Tek Wave Gold Diffractor 99
*GOLD: 1.2X TO 3X BASIC
STATED ODDS 1:3 PACKS
STATED PRINT RUN 99 SER.#'d SETS
HTKG Ken Griffey Jr. 8.00 20.00
HTMT Mike Trout 15.00 40.00
HTRH Rickey Henderson 4.00 10.00
HTRJA Reggie Jackson 3.00 8.00

2014 Topps High Tek Wave Ice Diffractor 75
*ICE: 1.2X TO 3X BASIC
STATED ODDS 1:4 PACKS
STATED PRINT RUN 75 SER.#'d SETS
HTKG Ken Griffey Jr. 8.00 20.00
HTMT Mike Trout 15.00 40.00
HTRH Rickey Henderson 4.00 10.00
HTRJA Reggie Jackson 3.00 8.00

2014 Topps High Tek Spiral Bricks
*SPIRAL: .5X TO 1.2X SPIRAL BRICK
*NET: .5X TO 1.2X SPIRAL BRICK
*SHATTER: .5X TO 1.2X SPIRAL BRICK
*LG MAZE: 2X TO 5X SPIRAL BRICK
2014 Topps High Tek Net
*ZIGZAG: 4X TO 10X SPIRAL BRICK
HTAG Alex Guerrero RC .75 2.00
HTAGO Adrian Gonzalez .75 2.00
HTAH Andrew Heaney RC .60 1.50
HTAS Andrelton Simmons .60 1.50
HTBH Bryce Harper 1.50 4.00
HTBPO Buster Posey 1.25 3.00
HTCB Craig Biggio .75 2.00
HTCG Carlos Gonzalez .75 2.00
HTCJ Chipper Jones 1.00 2.50
HTCK Clayton Kershaw 2.00 5.00
HTCO Chris Owings RC .60 1.50
HTCY Christian Yelich 1.25 3.00
HTDW David Wright .75 2.00
HTEB Ernie Banks 1.00 2.50
HTEBU Eddie Butler RC .60 1.50
HTFF Freddie Freeman 1.25 3.00
HTFV Fernando Valenzuela .60 1.50
HTGM Greg Maddux 1.25 3.00
HTGP Gregory Polanco RC 1.00 2.50
HTGST Giancarlo Stanton 1.00 2.50
HTHA Hank Aaron 2.00 5.00
HTHR Hanley Ramirez .75 2.00
HTJB Jeff Bagwell .75 2.00
HTJCU Johnny Cueto .75 2.00
HTJF Jose Fernandez 1.00 2.50
HTJH Jason Heyward .75 2.00
HTJS Jean Segura .75 2.00
HTJT Julio Teheran .75 2.00
HTJV Joey Votto 1.00 2.50
HTMIS Mike Schmidt 1.50 4.00
HTMMC Mark McGwire 2.00 5.00
HTMP Mike Piazza 1.00 2.50
HTMW Michael Wacha .75 2.00
HTOT Oscar Taveras RC .75 2.00
HTPG Paul Goldschmidt 1.00 2.50
HTRB Ryan Braun .75 2.00
HTRJ Randy Johnson 1.00 2.50
HTSK Sandy Koufax 2.00 5.00
HTSM Shelby Miller .75 2.00
HTTG Tom Glavine .75 2.00
HTTGW Tony Gwynn 1.00 2.50
HTTP Terry Pendleton .60 1.50
HTTT Troy Tulowitzki 1.00 2.50
HTVG Vladimir Guerrero .75 2.00
HTWMA Willie Mays 2.00 5.00
HTYM Yadier Molina 1.00 2.50
HTYP Yasiel Puig 1.00 2.50

2014 Topps High Tek Spiral Bricks Clouds Diffractor 25
*CLOUDS: 2.5X TO 6X BASIC
STATED ODDS 1:10 PACKS
STATED PRINT RUN 25 SER.#'d SETS
HTMMC Mark McGwire 20.00 50.00
HTMP Mike Piazza 15.00 40.00
HTTGW Tony Gwynn 12.00 30.00
HTYM Yadier Molina 10.00 25.00

2014 Topps High Tek Spiral Bricks Disco Diffractor 50
*DISCO: 1X TO 2.5X BASIC
STATED ODDS 1:5 PACKS
STATED PRINT RUN 50 SER.#'d SETS
HTMMC Mark McGwire 8.00 20.00
HTMP Mike Piazza 6.00 15.00
HTTGW Tony Gwynn 5.00 12.00
HTYM Yadier Molina 4.00 10.00

2014 Topps High Tek Spiral Bricks Gold Diffractor 99
*GOLD: 1X TO 2.5X BASIC
STATED ODDS 1:3 PACKS
STATED PRINT RUN 99 SER.#'d SETS
HTMMC Mark McGwire 8.00 20.00
HTMP Mike Piazza 6.00 15.00
HTTGW Tony Gwynn 5.00 12.00
HTYM Yadier Molina 4.00 10.00

2014 Topps High Tek Spiral Bricks Ice Diffractor 75
*ICE: 1X TO 2.5X BASIC
STATED ODDS 1:4 PACKS
STATED PRINT RUN 75 SER.#'d SETS
HTMMC Mark McGwire 8.00 20.00
HTMP Mike Piazza 6.00 15.00
HTTGW Tony Gwynn 5.00 12.00
HTYM Yadier Molina 4.00 10.00

2014 Topps High Tek '00 TEKtonics Diffractors
STATED ODDS 1:24 PACKS
STATED PRINT RUN 50 SER.#'d SETS
TDAB Albert Belle 2.00 5.00
TDAM Andrew McCutchen 3.00 8.00
TDBH Bryce Harper 5.00 12.00
TDCJ Chipper Jones 10.00 25.00
TDCR Cal Ripken Jr. 10.00 25.00
TDDE Dennis Eckersley 2.50 6.00
TDDJ Derek Jeter 25.00 60.00
TDDW David Wright 2.50 6.00
TDJA Jose Abreu 15.00 40.00
TDMP Mike Piazza 3.00 8.00
TDMT Masahiro Tanaka 6.00 15.00
TDNG Nomar Garciaparra 2.50 6.00
TDNR Nolan Ryan 10.00 25.00
TDPF Prince Fielder 2.50 6.00
TDPG Paul Goldschmidt 3.00 8.00
TDPM Pedro Martinez 2.50 6.00
TDRC Robinson Cano 2.50 6.00
TDVG Vladimir Guerrero 2.50 6.00
TDWM Willie Mays 6.00 15.00
TDYD Yu Darvish 3.00 8.00

2014 Topps High Tek '99 TEKnicians Diffractors
STATED ODDS 1:19 PACKS
STATED PRINT RUN 50 SER.#'d SETS
99TAC Aroldis Chapman 6.00 15.00
99TAM Andrew McCutchen 6.00 15.00
99TBM Brian McCann 5.00 12.00
99TCS Chris Sale 6.00 15.00
99TFT Frank Thomas 12.00 30.00
99TGC Gerrit Cole 6.00 15.00
99TGM Greg Maddux 20.00 50.00
99TGS Giancarlo Stanton 6.00 15.00
99THJR Hyun-Jin Ryu 5.00 12.00
99THR Hanley Ramirez 5.00 12.00
99TJH Josh Hamilton 5.00 12.00
99TKG Ken Griffey Jr. 15.00 40.00
99TMC Miguel Cabrera 6.00 15.00
99TMM Mark McGwire 12.00 30.00
99TMS Max Scherzer 6.00 15.00
99TMT Mike Trout 30.00 80.00
99TPG Paul Goldschmidt 6.00 15.00
99TPO Paul O'Neill 5.00 12.00
99TRC Roger Clemens 8.00 20.00
99TRH Rickey Henderson 6.00 15.00
99TRJ Randy Johnson 6.00 15.00
99TRP Rafael Palmeiro 5.00 12.00
99TTG Tom Glavine 5.00 12.00
99TXB Xander Bogaerts 10.00 25.00
99TYP Yasiel Puig 10.00 25.00

2014 Topps High Tek Autographs
OVERALL AUTO ODDS 1:1 PACKS
EXCHANGE DEADLINE 11/30/2017
HTAG Alex Guerrero 5.00 12.00
HTAGA Andres Galarraga 5.00 12.00
HTAGO Adrian Gonzalez 10.00 25.00
HTAH Andrew Heaney 4.00 10.00
HTBP Brandon Phillips 5.00 12.00
HTCB Craig Biggio 15.00 40.00
HTCF Carlton Fisk 15.00 40.00
HTCJ Chipper Jones 40.00 80.00
HTCO Chris Owings 4.00 10.00
HTCS Chris Sale 8.00 20.00
HTCY Christian Yelich 30.00 80.00
HTDE Dennis Eckersley 8.00 20.00
HTDW David Wright 15.00 40.00
HTEBU Eddie Butler 4.00 10.00
HTEM Edgar Martinez 10.00 25.00
HTFF Freddie Freeman 6.00 15.00
HTFM Fred McGriff 6.00 15.00
HTFT Frank Thomas 40.00 80.00
HTFV Fernando Valenzuela 15.00 40.00
HTGP Gregory Polanco 6.00 15.00
HTGS George Springer 20.00 50.00
HTHR Hanley Ramirez 8.00 20.00
HTIR Ivan Rodriguez 10.00 25.00
HTJA Jose Abreu 8.00 20.00
HTJC Jose Canseco 6.00 15.00
HTJF Jose Fernandez 12.00 30.00
HTJG Juan Gonzalez 6.00 15.00
HTJH Jason Heyward 6.00 15.00
HTMB Madison Bumgarner 20.00 50.00
HTMN Mike Napoli 4.00 10.00
HTMS Marcus Stroman 6.00 15.00
HTMSC Max Scherzer 15.00 40.00
HTMW Michael Wacha 8.00 20.00
HTNC Nick Castellanos 12.00 30.00
HTNG Nomar Garciaparra 12.00 30.00
HTOH Orlando Hernandez 4.00 10.00
HTOT Oscar Taveras 5.00 12.00
HTOV Omar Vizquel 5.00 12.00
HTPG Paul Goldschmidt 10.00 25.00
HTPO Paul O'Neill 5.00 12.00
HTRA Roberto Alomar 6.00 15.00
HTRB Ryan Braun 8.00 20.00
HTRC Robinson Cano 15.00 40.00
HTRE Roenis Elias 4.00 10.00
HTRG Ron Gant 4.00 10.00
HTRP Rafael Palmeiro 6.00 15.00
HTRY Robin Yount 25.00 60.00
HTSG Sonny Gray 5.00 12.00
HTSM Shelby Miller 5.00 12.00
HTTG Tom Glavine 10.00 25.00
HTTP Terry Pendleton 6.00 15.00
HTTW Taijuan Walker 4.00 10.00
HTWM Wil Myers 6.00 15.00
HTYC Yoenis Cespedes 8.00 20.00
HTYS Yangervis Solarte 4.00 10.00
HTYV Yordano Ventura 5.00 12.00
HTZW Zack Wheeler 5.00 12.00

2014 Topps High Tek Autographs Clouds Diffractor 25
*CLOUDS 25: .6X TO 1.5X BASIC
STATED ODDS 1:13 PACKS
STATED PRINT RUN 25 SER.#'d SETS
EXCHANGE DEADLINE 11/30/2017
HTBJ Bo Jackson 40.00 100.00
HTCK Clayton Kershaw 60.00 120.00
HTEL Evan Longoria 15.00 40.00
HTGST Giancarlo Stanton 30.00 80.00
HTJT Julio Teheran 10.00 25.00
HTJV Joey Votto 25.00 60.00
HTMC Miguel Cabrera 50.00 100.00
HTMIS Mike Schmidt 30.00 60.00
HTMMC Mark McGwire 75.00 150.00
HTMR Mariano Rivera 75.00 150.00
HTMT Mike Trout 200.00 400.00
HTNR Nolan Ryan 100.00 200.00
HTRJA Reggie Jackson 30.00 60.00
HTTT Troy Tulowitzki 12.00 30.00
HTVG Vladimir Guerrero 20.00 50.00
HTWB Wade Boggs 20.00 50.00
HTYD Yu Darvish 60.00 120.00
HTYP Yasiel Puig 60.00 120.00

2014 Topps High Tek Autographs Disco Diffractor 50
*DISCO 50: .5X TO 1.2X BASIC
STATED ODDS 1:8 PACKS
STATED PRINT RUN 50 SER.#'d SETS
EXCHANGE DEADLINE 11/30/2017
HTBJ Bo Jackson 30.00 80.00
HTCG Carlos Gonzalez 8.00 20.00
HTCK Clayton Kershaw 50.00 100.00
HTGST Giancarlo Stanton 25.00 60.00
HTJT Julio Teheran 8.00 20.00
HTJV Joey Votto 20.00 50.00
HTMT Mike Trout 150.00 300.00
HTTT Troy Tulowitzki 10.00 25.00
HTVG Vladimir Guerrero 15.00 40.00

2014 Topps High Tek Low Tek Diffractors
STATED ODDS 1:14 PACKS
STATED PRINT RUN 50 SER.#'d SETS
LTAJ Adam Jones 5.00 12.00
LTCB Craig Biggio 5.00 12.00
LTCF Carlton Fisk 5.00 12.00
LTCG Carlos Gonzalez 5.00 12.00
LTDJ Derek Jeter 20.00 50.00
LTDO David Ortiz 6.00 15.00
LTDP Dustin Pedroia 8.00 20.00
LTEB Ernie Banks 6.00 15.00
LTFF Freddie Freeman 8.00 20.00
LTFH Felix Hernandez 5.00 12.00
LTGS Giancarlo Stanton 6.00 15.00
LTHA Hank Aaron 12.00 30.00
LTIR Ivan Rodriguez 5.00 12.00
LTJA Jose Abreu 12.00 30.00
LTJB Johnny Bench 6.00 15.00
LTJE Jacoby Ellsbury 5.00 12.00
LTJF Jose Fernandez 6.00 15.00
LTJG Juan Gonzalez 10.00 25.00
LTJS John Smoltz 6.00 15.00
LTJU Justin Upton 5.00 12.00
LTJV Justin Verlander 6.00 15.00
LTKG Ken Griffey Jr. 15.00 40.00
LTMM Mike Mussina 12.00 30.00
LTMT Mike Trout 30.00 80.00
LTRA Roberto Alomar 5.00 12.00
LTRB Ryan Braun 5.00 12.00
LTSG Sonny Gray 5.00 12.00
LTSK Sandy Koufax 10.00 25.00
LTSS Stephen Strasburg 6.00 15.00
LTTG Tony Gwynn 6.00 15.00
LTTT Troy Tulowitzki 6.00 15.00
LTWB Wade Boggs 10.00 25.00
LTYD Yu Darvish 6.00 15.00
LTYP Yasiel Puig 10.00 25.00

2015 Topps High Tek
GROUP A = GRASS PATTERN
GROUP B = WAVES PATTERN
HTABY Archie Bradley B RC .75 2.00
HTAG Alex Gordon A 1.00 2.50
HTAJO Adam Jones A 1.00 2.50
HTAJS Andruw Jones A .75 2.00
HTAL Al Leiter B .75 2.00
HTAM Andrew McCutchen A 1.25 3.00
HTAP Albert Pujols A 1.50 4.00
HTAR Addison Russell A RC 2.50 6.00
HTARI Anthony Rizzo A 2.00 5.00
HTBB Byron Buxton A RC 1.25 3.00
HTBC Brandon Crawford B 1.00 2.50
HTBF Brandon Finnegan B RC .75 2.00
HTBH Bryce Harper A 2.00 5.00
HTBJ Bo Jackson A 1.25 3.00
HTBL Barry Larkin B 1.00 2.50
HTBP Buster Posey B 1.50 4.00
HTBS Blake Swihart B RC 1.00 2.50
HTBW Bernie Williams A 1.00 2.50
HTCB Craig Biggio A 1.00 2.50
HTCC Carlos Correa B RC 4.00 10.00
HTCD Carlos Delgado A .75 2.00
HTCJ Chipper Jones B 1.25 3.00
HTCKR Corey Kluber B 1.00 2.50
HTCKW Clayton Kershaw B 2.50 6.00
HTCRN Cal Ripken Jr. B 4.00 10.00
HTCRO Carlos Rodon B RC 1.25 3.00
HTCSE Chris Sale B 1.25 3.00
HTCY Christian Yelich A 1.50 4.00
HTDB Dellin Betances B 1.00 2.50
HTDF Doug Fister B .75 2.00
HTDH Dilson Herrera A RC 1.00 2.50
HTDJ Derek Jeter B 3.00 8.00
HTDN Daniel Norris B RC .75 2.00
HTDO David Ortiz A 1.25 3.00
HTDPA Dustin Pedroia A 1.25 3.00
HTDPY Dalton Pompey A RC 1.25 3.00
HTDT Devon Travis A RC .75 2.00
HTEE Edwin Encarnacion A 1.25 3.00
HTEM Edgar Martinez A 1.25 3.00
HTFF Freddie Freeman A 1.50 4.00
HTFH Felix Hernandez B 1.25 3.00
HTFL Francisco Lindor B RC 5.00 12.00
HTFR Frank Robinson A 1.25 3.00
HTFT Frank Thomas A 1.25 3.00
HTGM Greg Maddux B 1.50 4.00
HTGR Garrett Richards B 1.00 2.50
HTGS George Springer A 1.25 3.00
HTGSS Giancarlo Stanton A 1.25 3.00
HTHA Hank Aaron A 2.50 6.00
HTI Ichiro A 1.50 4.00
HTJAE Jose Altuve A 1.00 2.50
HTJAU Jose Abreu A 1.25 3.00
HTJB Javier Baez A RC 6.00 15.00
HTJB Johnny Bench B 1.25 3.00
HTJC Jose Canseco A 1.00 2.50
HTJDM Jacob deGrom B 1.25 3.00
HTJF Jose Fernandez B 1.25 3.00
HTJGZ Juan Gonzalez A .75 2.00
HTJK Jung-Ho Kang B RC .75 2.00
HTJL Jon Lester B 1.00 2.50
HTJM Joe Mauer A 1.00 2.50
HTJPK Joe Panik A 1.00 2.50
HTJPN Joc Pederson A RC 1.50 4.00
HTJSR Jorge Soler A RC 1.25 3.00
HTJSS James Shields B .75 2.00
HTJSZ John Smoltz B 1.25 3.00
HTKB Kris Bryant B RC 10.00 25.00
HTKG Ken Griffey Jr. A 2.50 6.00
HTKP Kevin Plawecki B RC .75 2.00
HTMBR Madison Bumgarner B 1.00 2.50
HTMBS Matt Barnes B RC .75 2.00
HTMC Miguel Cabrera A 1.25 3.00
HTMFO Maikel Franco B RC 1.00 2.50
HTMGE Mark Grace A 1.00 2.50
HTMGM Marquis Grissom A .75 2.00
HTMHY Matt Harvey B 1.00 2.50
HTMJ Micah Johnson A RC .75 2.00
HTMME Mark McGwire A 2.00 5.00
HTMPA Mike Piazza B 1.25 3.00
HTMPR Mark Prior B 1.00 2.50
HTMR Mariano Rivera B 1.50 4.00
HTMSR Matt Shoemaker B 1.00 2.50
HTMSZ Max Scherzer B 1.25 3.00
HTMTA Masahiro Tanaka B 1.00 2.50
HTMTR Michael Taylor A RC .75 2.00
HTMTT Mike Trout A 6.00 15.00
HTNG Nomar Garciaparra B 1.00 2.50
HTNR Nolan Ryan B 4.00 10.00
HTNS Noah Syndergaard B RC 1.50 4.00
HTOS Ozzie Smith B 1.50 4.00
HTOV Omar Vizquel B 1.00 2.50
HTPG Paul Goldschmidt A 1.25 3.00
HTPS Pablo Sandoval B 1.00 2.50
HTRA Roberto Alomar A 1.00 2.50
HTRCA Rusney Castillo A RC 1.00 2.50
HTRCO Robinson Cano A 1.00 2.50
HTRCS Roger Clemens B 1.50 4.00
HTRH Rickey Henderson A 1.25 3.00
HTRI Raisel Iglesias B RC 1.00 2.50
HTRJA Reggie Jackson A 1.00 2.50
HTRJO Randy Johnson B 1.25 3.00
HTRO Roberto Osuna B RC .75 2.00
HTSGY Sonny Gray B 1.00 2.50
HTSK Sandy Koufax B 2.50 6.00
HTSMA Steven Moya A RC 1.00 2.50
HTSME Starling Marte A 1.00 2.50
HTSP Salvador Perez B 1.00 2.50
HTTG Tom Glavine B 1.00 2.50
HTVC Vinny Castilla B .75 2.00
HTVM Victor Martinez A 1.00 2.50
HTYP Yasiel Puig A 1.25 3.00
HTYT Yasmany Tomas A RC 1.00 2.50

2015 Topps High Tek Blade
*BLADE: 2.5X TO 6X BASIC
STATED ODDS 1:24 HOBBY

2015 Topps High Tek Chain Link
*CHAIN LINK: .75X TO 2X BASIC
STATED ODDS 1:3 HOBBY

2015 Topps High Tek Circuit Board
*CIRCUIT BOARD: .5X TO 1.2X BASIC
RANDOM INSERTS IN PACKS

2015 Topps High Tek Clouds Diffractor
*CLDS DFFRCTR: 2.5X TO 6X BASIC
STATED ODDS 1:10 HOBBY
STATED PRINT RUN 25 SER.#'d SETS

2015 Topps High Tek Confetti Diffractor
*CNFTTI DFFRCTR: 1.2X TO 3X BASIC
STATED ODDS 1:5 HOBBY
STATED PRINT RUN 99 SER.#'d SETS

2015 Topps High Tek Cubes
*CUBES: .75X TO 2X BASIC
STATED ODDS 1:3 HOBBY

2015 Topps High Tek Diamonds
*DIAMONDS: 1.2X TO 3X BASIC
STATED ODDS 1:6 HOBBY

2015 Topps High Tek Dots
*DOTS: .4X TO 1X BASIC
RANDOM INSERTS IN PACKS

2015 Topps High Tek Gold Rainbow
*GOLD RNBW: 2X TO 5X BASIC
STATED ODDS 1:7 HOBBY
STATED PRINT RUN 35 SER.#'d SETS

2015 Topps High Tek Grid
*GRID: 1.5X TO 4X BASIC
STATED ODDS 1:12 HOBBY
HTKB Kris Bryant 60.00 150.00

2015 Topps High Tek Home Uniform Photo Variations
*UNIFORM: 2.5X TO 6X BASIC
STATED ODDS 1:42 HOBBY
HTBP Buster Posey 30.00 80.00
HTCKW Clayton Kershaw 25.00 60.00
HTDJ Derek Jeter 40.00 100.00
HTMTT Mike Trout 60.00 150.00
HTOV Omar Vizquel 75.00 150.00

2015 Topps High Tek Pipes
*PIPES: .5X TO 1.2X BASIC
RANDOM INSERTS IN PACKS

2015 Topps High Tek Purple Rainbow
*PRPLE RNBW: .5X TO 1.2X BASIC
STATED ODDS 1:3 HOBBY

2015 Topps High Tek Pyramids
*PYRAMIDS: 1.2X TO 3X BASIC
STATED ODDS 1:6 HOBBY

2015 Topps High Tek Spiral
*SPIRAL: .4X TO 1X BASIC
RANDOM INSERTS IN PACKS

2015 Topps High Tek Stripes
*STRIPES: 1.5X TO 4X BASIC
STATED ODDS 1:12 HOBBY

2015 Topps High Tek Tidal Diffractor
*TDL DFFRCTR: 1.5X TO 4X BASIC
STATED ODDS 1:7 HOBBY
STATED PRINT RUN 75 SER.#'d SETS

2015 Topps High Tek Autographs
OVERALL AUTO ODDS 1:1 HOBBY
EXCHANGE DEADLINE 9/30/2017
HTABY Archie Bradley 3.00 8.00
HTAG Alex Gordon 4.00 10.00
HTAJS Andruw Jones 3.00 8.00
HTAL Al Leiter 4.00 10.00
HTAR Addison Russell 10.00 25.00
HTBB Byron Buxton 5.00 12.00
HTBC Brandon Crawford 5.00 12.00
HTBJ Bo Jackson 25.00 60.00
HTBL Barry Larkin 15.00 40.00
HTBS Blake Swihart 4.00 10.00
HTBW Bernie Williams 10.00 25.00
HTCB Craig Biggio 8.00 20.00
HTCC Carlos Correa 75.00 200.00
HTCD Carlos Delgado 3.00 8.00
HTCJ Chipper Jones 25.00 60.00
HTCKR Corey Kluber 4.00 10.00
HTCKW Clayton Kershaw 25.00 60.00
HTCSE Chris Sale 10.00 25.00
HTDB Dellin Betances 4.00 10.00
HTDF Doug Fister 3.00 8.00
HTDO David Ortiz 15.00 40.00
HTDPA Dustin Pedroia 12.00 30.00
HTDT Devon Travis 3.00 8.00
HTEE Edwin Encarnacion 5.00 12.00
HTEM Edgar Martinez 10.00 25.00
HTFL Francisco Lindor 20.00 50.00
HTFR Frank Robinson 15.00 40.00
HTGR Garrett Richards 4.00 10.00
HTGS George Springer 10.00 25.00
HTI Ichiro Suzuki 250.00 400.00
HTJAE Jose Altuve 12.00 30.00
HTJAU Jose Abreu 12.00 30.00
HTJB Javier Baez 20.00 50.00
HTJC Jose Canseco 10.00 25.00
HTJDM Jacob deGrom 15.00 40.00
HTJGZ Juan Gonzalez 3.00 8.00
HTJL Jon Lester 8.00 20.00
HTJPK Joe Panik 4.00 10.00
HTJPN Joc Pederson 6.00 15.00
HTJSR Jorge Soler 5.00 12.00
HTJSS James Shields 3.00 8.00
HTJSZ John Smoltz 12.00 30.00
HTKP Kevin Plawecki 3.00 8.00
HTMBS Matt Barnes 3.00 8.00
HTMFO Maikel Franco 4.00 10.00
HTMGE Mark Grace 4.00 10.00
HTMGM Marquis Grissom 3.00 8.00
HTMHY Matt Harvey 20.00 50.00
HTMJ Micah Johnson 3.00 8.00
HTMPR Mark Prior 4.00 10.00
HTMSR Matt Shoemaker 4.00 10.00
HTMTR Michael Taylor 3.00 8.00
HTNG Nomar Garciaparra 10.00 25.00
HTNS Noah Syndergaard 12.00 30.00
HTOS Ozzie Smith 15.00 40.00
HTOV Omar Vizquel 4.00 10.00
HTPG Paul Goldschmidt 12.00 30.00
HTRA Roberto Alomar 10.00 25.00
HTRCA Rusney Castillo 4.00 10.00
HTRI Raisel Iglesias 4.00 10.00
HTRO Roberto Osuna 3.00 8.00
HTSGY Sonny Gray 4.00 10.00
HTSME Starling Marte 5.00 12.00
HTSP Salvador Perez 10.00 25.00
HTTG Tom Glavine 10.00 25.00
HTVC Vinny Castilla 3.00 8.00

2015 Topps High Tek Autographs Clouds Diffractor
*CLDS DFFRCTR: .75X TO 2X BASIC
STATED ODDS 1:20 HOBBY
STATED PRINT RUN 25 SER.#'d SETS
EXCHANGE DEADLINE 9/30/2017
HTBH Bryce Harper EXCH 150.00 250.00
HTBP Buster Posey EXCH 100.00 200.00
HTCRN Cal Ripken Jr. 50.00 120.00
HTCRO Carlos Rodon 10.00 25.00
HTFF Freddie Freeman EXCH 12.00 30.00
HTJB Johnny Bench 30.00 80.00
HTJK Jung-Ho Kang EXCH 30.00 80.00
HTMME Mark McGwire 125.00 250.00
HTRH Rickey Henderson 40.00 100.00
HTRJ Randy Johnson EXCH 60.00 150.00
HTYT Yasmany Tomas 30.00 80.00

2015 Topps High Tek Autographs Gold Rainbow
*GLD RNBW: .6X TO 1.5X BASIC
STATED ODDS 1:10 HOBBY
STATED PRINT RUN 50 SER.#'d SETS
EXCHANGE DEADLINE 9/30/2017
HTCRN Cal Ripken Jr. 40.00 100.00
HTCRO Carlos Rodon 8.00 20.00
HTFF Freddie Freeman EXCH 10.00 25.00
HTJB Johnny Bench 25.00 60.00
HTJK Jung-Ho Kang EXCH 25.00 60.00

2015 Topps High Tek Autographs Tidal Diffractor
*TDL DFFRCTR: .5X TO 1.2X BASIC
STATED ODDS 1:5 HOBBY
STATED PRINT RUN 99 SER.#'d SETS
EXCHANGE DEADLINE 9/30/2017
HTCRO Carlos Rodon 6.00 15.00
HTFF Freddie Freeman EXCH 8.00 20.00

2015 Topps High Tek Bright Horizons
STATED ODDS 1:63 HOBBY
STATED PRINT RUN 50 SER.#'d SETS
BHBH Bryce Harper 8.00 20.00
BHGS George Springer 4.00 10.00
BHJA Jose Abreu 5.00 12.00
BHJD Jacob deGrom 5.00 12.00
BHJP Joc Pederson 6.00 15.00
BHJS Jorge Soler 5.00 12.00
BHKB Kris Bryant 25.00 60.00
BHMT Mike Trout 25.00 60.00
BHRC Rusney Castillo 4.00 10.00
BHTW Taijuan Walker 3.00 8.00

2015 Topps High Tek Bright Horizons Autographs
STATED ODDS 1:122 HOBBY
STATED PRINT RUN 50 SER.#'d SETS
EXCHANGE DEADLINE 9/30/2017
BHJA Jose Abreu 20.00 50.00
BHJD Jacob deGrom 30.00 80.00
BHJP Joc Pederson 12.00 30.00
BHJS Jorge Soler 10.00 25.00
BHRC Rusney Castillo 8.00 20.00

2015 Topps High Tek DramaTEK Performers
STATED ODDS 1:42 HOBBY
STATED PRINT RUN 50 SER.#'d SETS
DTPAG Adrian Gonzalez 4.00 10.00
DTPAJ Adam Jones 4.00 10.00
DTPAR Anthony Rizzo 8.00 20.00
DTPBP Buster Posey 6.00 15.00
DTPCK Clayton Kershaw 10.00 25.00
DTPCS Chris Sale 5.00 12.00
DTPDW David Wright 4.00 10.00
DTPEE Edwin Encarnacion 5.00 12.00
DTPFF Freddie Freeman 6.00 15.00
DTPGS Giancarlo Stanton 5.00 12.00
DTPHR Hanley Ramirez 4.00 10.00
DTPMT Mike Trout 25.00 60.00
DTPPG Paul Goldschmidt 5.00 12.00
DTPRC Robinson Cano 4.00 10.00
DTPTT Troy Tulowitzki 5.00 12.00

2015 Topps High Tek DramaTEK Performers Autographs
STATED ODDS 1:122 HOBBY
STATED PRINT RUN 25 SER.#'d SETS
EXCHANGE DEADLINE 9/30/2017
DTPAJ Adam Jones 12.00 30.00
DTPAR Anthony Rizzo 50.00 120.00
DTPBP Buster Posey 125.00 250.00
DTPDW David Wright EXCH 12.00 30.00
DTPFF Freddie Freeman 50.00 120.00
DTPMT Mike Trout 250.00 350.00
DTPPG Paul Goldschmidt 25.00 60.00

2015 Topps High Tek Low TEK Diffractors
STATED ODDS 1:42 HOBBY
STATED PRINT RUN 50 SER.#'d SETS
LTBL Barry Larkin 2.50 6.00
LTBP Buster Posey 4.00 10.00
LTCR Cal Ripken Jr. 10.00 25.00
LTJL Jon Lester 2.50 6.00
LTMM Mark McGwire 5.00 12.00
LTMP Mike Piazza 3.00 8.00
LTNT Nolan Ryan 10.00 25.00
LTOS Ozzie Smith 4.00 10.00
LTRC Roger Clemens 4.00 10.00
LTRS Ryne Sandberg 6.00 15.00
LTWM Willie Mays 6.00 15.00
LTCKR Corey Kluber 2.50 6.00
LTCKW Clayton Kershaw 6.00 15.00
LTRJA Reggie Jackson 2.50 6.00
LTRJO Randy Johnson 3.00 8.00

2015 Topps High Tek Low TEK Diffractors Autographs
STATED ODDS 1:122 HOBBY
STATED PRINT RUN 25 SER.#'d SETS
EXCHANGE DEADLINE 9/30/2017
LTBL Barry Larkin 30.00 80.00
LTBP Buster Posey 100.00 250.00
LTJL Jon Lester 12.00 30.00
LTMP Mike Piazza 50.00 120.00
LTNR Nolan Ryan 100.00 250.00
LTRS Ryne Sandberg 30.00 80.00
LTCKR Corey Kluber 12.00 30.00
LTCKW Clayton Kershaw 60.00 150.00
LTRJA Reggie Jackson 40.00 100.00
LTRJO Randy Johnson 50.00 120.00

2016 Topps High Tek
GROUP A = SPIRAL PATTERN
GROUP B = MAZE PATTERN
PRINTING PROOF ODDS 1:63 HOBBY
PLATE PRINT RUN 1 SET PER COLOR
BLACK-CYAN-MAGENTA-YELLOW ISSUED
NO PLATE PRICING DUE TO SCARCITY
HTAB Aaron Blair A RC .60 1.50
HTAC Aroldis Chapman B 1.00 2.50
HTAG Andres Galarraga A .75 2.00
HTAJ Adam Jones A .75 2.00
HTAM Andrew McCutchen B 1.00 2.50
HTAN Aaron Nola B RC 1.25 3.00
HTAP A.J. Pollock A .60 1.50
HTAPE Andy Pettitte B .75 2.00
HTAPU Albert Pujols A 1.25 3.00
HTAR Anthony Rizzo A 1.50 4.00
HTBH Bryce Harper B 1.50 4.00
HTBHP Byung-Ho Park B RC .75 2.00
HTBP Buster Posey B 1.25 3.00
HTBR Babe Ruth B 2.50 6.00
HTBS Blake Snell B RC .75 2.00
HTBW Billy Wagner A .60 1.50
HTBWI Bernie Williams B .75 2.00
HTCB Craig Biggio A .75 2.00
HTCC Carlos Correa A 1.00 2.50
HTCE Carl Edwards Jr. A RC .75 2.00
HTCJ Chipper Jones A 1.00 2.50
HTCK Clayton Kershaw B 2.00 5.00
HTCR Cal Ripken Jr. A 3.00 8.00
HTCRO Carlos Rodon A 1.00 2.50
HTCS Curt Schilling A .75 2.00
HTCSA Chris Sale A 1.00 2.50
HTCSE Corey Seager B RC 5.00 12.00
HTDG Dee Gordon B .60 1.50
HTDO David Ortiz A 1.00 2.50
HTDP David Price A .75 2.00
HTDW David Wright B .75 2.00
HTER Eddie Rosario B .75 2.00
HTFH Felix Hernandez B .75 2.00
HTFL Francisco Lindor A 1.00 2.50
HTFM Frankie Montas B RC .75 2.00
HTFT Frank Thomas A 1.00 2.50
HTGM Greg Maddux A 1.25 3.00
HTGR Garrett Richards A .75 2.00
HTGS Giancarlo Stanton B 1.00 2.50
HTHA Hank Aaron A 2.00 5.00
HTHO Henry Owens A RC .75 2.00
HTHOL Hector Olivera A RC .75 2.00
HTI Ichiro Suzuki B 1.25 3.00
HTIR Ivan Rodriguez B .75 2.00
HTJAR Jake Arrieta A .75 2.00
HTJB Johnny Bench A 1.00 2.50
HTJBA Jose Bautista B .75 2.00
HTJBE Jose Berrios B RC .75 2.00
HTJC Jose Canseco B .75 2.00
HTJD Johnny Damon A .75 2.00
HTJDE Jacob deGrom B 1.00 2.50
HTJDO Josh Donaldson B .75 2.00
HTJG Jon Gray A RC .60 1.50
HTJGO Juan Gonzalez B .60 1.50
HTJH Jason Heyward A .75 2.00
HTJM J.D. Martinez A 1.00 2.50
HTJP Jose Peraza A RC .75 2.00
HTJR Jackie Robinson A 1.00 2.50
HTJS John Smoltz A 1.00 2.50
HTJV Jason Varitek A 1.00 2.50
HTKB Kris Bryant A 1.25 3.00
HTKG Ken Griffey Jr. B 2.00 5.00
HTKM Kenta Maeda B RC 1.25 3.00
HTKMA Ketel Marte B RC 1.25 3.00
HTKS Kyle Schwarber A RC 2.00 5.00
HTLG Luis Gonzalez A .75 2.00
HTLS Luis Severino B RC .75 2.00
HTMB Madison Bumgarner B .75 2.00
HTMC Miguel Cabrera A 1.00 2.50
HTMCO Michael Conforto B RC .75 2.00
HTMF Michael Fulmer A RC 1.00 2.50
HTMH Matt Harvey B .75 2.00
HTMK Max Kepler B RC 1.00 2.50
HTMKE Matt Kemp B .75 2.00
HTMM Manny Machado A 1.00 2.50
HTMMC Mark McGwire B 1.50 4.00
HTMP Mike Piazza B 1.00 2.50
HTMS Mallex Smith A RC .60 1.50
HTMS Miguel Sano B RC 1.00 2.50
HTMSC Max Scherzer B 1.00 2.50
HTMST Marcus Stroman B .75 2.00
HTMT Mike Trout A 5.00 12.00
HTMTA Masahiro Tanaka B .75 2.00
HTNA Nolan Arenado A 1.25 3.00
HTNC Nelson Cruz B 1.00 2.50
HTNG Nomar Garciaparra A .75 2.00
HTNM Nomar Mazara B RC 1.00 2.50
HTNS Noah Syndergaard B .75 2.00
HTOV Omar Vizquel A .75 2.00
HTPG Paul Goldschmidt A 1.00 2.50
HTRA Roberto Alomar A .75 2.00
HTRB Ryan Braun B .75 2.00
HTRC Roger Clemens A 1.25 3.00
HTRJ Randy Johnson A 1.00 2.50
HTRP Rafael Palmeiro A .75 2.00
HTRS Robert Stephenson A RC .60 1.50
HTSG Sonny Gray B .75 2.00
HTSK Sandy Koufax B 2.00 5.00
HTSM Sean Manaea B RC .60 1.50
HTSP Stephen Piscotty B RC 1.00 2.50
HTTG Tom Glavine A .75 2.00
HTTS Trevor Story A RC 2.50 6.00
HTTT Troy Tulowitzki B 1.00 2.50
HTTTU Trea Turner B RC 2.00 5.00
HTTW Ted Williams A 2.00 5.00
HTTYW Tyler White A RC .60 1.50
HTVG Vladimir Guerrero B .75 2.00
HTWB Wade Boggs B .75 2.00
HTYC Yoenis Cespedes B 1.00 2.50
HTYD Yu Darvish B 1.00 2.50
HTZG Zack Greinke A .75 2.00

2016 Topps High Tek Arrows
*ARROWS: 1X TO 2.5X BASIC
STATED ODDS 1:6 HOBBY
HTCR Cal Ripken Jr. 12.00 30.00
HTKB Kris Bryant 15.00 40.00

2016 Topps High Tek Buckle
*BUCKLE: .4X TO 1X BASIC
RANDOM INSERTS IN PACKS

2016 Topps High Tek Cubes
*CUBES: .4X TO 1X BASIC
RANDOM INSERTS IN PACKS

2016 Topps High Tek Diamonds
*DIAMONDS: 2.5X TO 6X BASIC
STATED ODDS 1:24 HOBBY
HTCR Cal Ripken Jr. 30.00 80.00
HTKB Kris Bryant 40.00 100.00

2016 Topps High Tek Gold Rainbow
*GOLD RAINBOW: 1X TO 2.5X BASIC
RANDOM INSERTS IN PACKS
STATED PRINT RUN 60 SER.#'d SETS
HTCR Cal Ripken Jr. 20.00 50.00
HTCSE Corey Seager 12.00 30.00
HTKB Kris Bryant 20.00 50.00

2016 Topps High Tek Grass
*GRASS: .6X TO 1.5X BASIC
STATED ODDS 1:3 HOBBY
HTCR Cal Ripken Jr. 8.00 20.00
HTKB Kris Bryant 10.00 25.00

2016 Topps High Tek Green Rainbow
*GREEN RAINBOW: 1X TO 2.5X BASIC
STATED ODDS 1:3 HOBBY
STATED PRINT RUN 99 SER.#'d SETS
HTCSE Corey Seager 12.00 30.00
HTKB Kris Bryant 20.00 50.00
HTMT Mike Trout 20.00 50.00

2016 Topps High Tek Lines
*LINES: 1.5X TO 4X BASIC
STATED ODDS 1:12 HOBBY
HTCR Cal Ripken Jr. 20.00 50.00
HTKB Kris Bryant 25.00 60.00

2016 Topps High Tek Orange Magma Diffractor
*ORANGE MAGMA: 3X TO 8X BASIC
STATED ODDS 1:10 HOBBY
STATED PRINT RUN 25 SER.#'d SETS
HTCSE Corey Seager 25.00 60.00
HTKB Kris Bryant 40.00 100.00

2016 Topps High Tek Peak
*PEAK: 1X TO 2.5X BASIC
STATED ODDS 1:6 HOBBY
HTCSE Corey Seager 15.00 40.00
HTSK Sandy Koufax 10.00 25.00

2016 Topps High Tek Red Orbit Diffractor
*RED ORBIT: 4X TO 10X BASIC
STATED ODDS 1:13 HOBBY
HTCSE Corey Seager 30.00 80.00
HTKB Kris Bryant 50.00 120.00

2016 Topps High Tek Tidal Diffractor
*TIDAL: .5X TO 1.2X BASIC
STATED ODDS 1:2 HOBBY

2016 Topps High Tek Triangles
*TRIANGLES: 1.5X TO 4X BASIC
STATED ODDS 1:12 HOBBY
HTCSE Corey Seager 25.00 60.00
HTSK Sandy Koufax 15.00 40.00

2016 Topps High Tek Waves
*WAVES: .6X TO 1.5X BASIC
STATED ODDS 1:3 HOBBY
HTCSE Corey Seager 10.00 25.00
HTSK Sandy Koufax 5.00 12.00

2016 Topps High Tek '66 Short Prints
STATED ODDS 1:19 HOBBY
66FR Frank Robinson 3.00 8.00
66HA Hank Aaron 8.00 20.00
66LB Lou Brock 3.00 8.00
66RC Roberto Clemente 10.00 25.00
66SK Sandy Koufax 8.00 20.00
66WM Willie Mays 8.00 20.00

2016 Topps High Tek '66 Short Prints Autographs
STATED ODDS 1:421 HOBBY
STATED PRINT RUN 35 SER.#'d SETS
EXCHANGE DEADLINE 10/31/2018
66FR Frank Robinson 40.00 100.00
66HA Hank Aaron 125.00 300.00
66LB Lou Brock 40.00 100.00

2016 Topps High Tek Home Uniform Photo Variations
*UNIFORM: 2.5X TO 6X BASIC
STATED ODDS 1:38 HOBBY
STATED PRINT RUN 50 SER.#'d SETS

2016 Topps High Tek Home Uniform Photo Variations Autographs
STATED ODDS 1:85 HOBBY
PRINT RUNS B/WN 15-50 COPIES PER
NO PRICING ON QTY 15
EXCHANGE DEADLINE 10/31/2018
HTAR Anthony Rizzo/50 60.00 150.00
HTBP Buster Posey/20 60.00 150.00
HTCSA Chris Sale/50 10.00 25.00
HTJDE Jacob deGrom/50 12.00 30.00
HTJH Jason Heyward/35 20.00 50.00
HTNA Nolan Arenado/50 20.00 50.00
HTRB Ryan Braun/35 15.00 40.00
HTTT Troy Tulowitzki

2016 Topps High Tek Autographs
PRINTING PROOF ODDS 1:99 HOBBY
PLATE PRINT RUN 1 SET PER COLOR
NO PLATE PRICING DUE TO SCARCITY
EXCHANGE DEADLINE 10/31/2018
HTAB Aaron Blair 3.00 8.00
HTAG Andres Galarraga 5.00 12.00
HTAN Aaron Nola 6.00 15.00
HTAPE Andy Pettitte 12.00 30.00
HTAR Anthony Rizzo 25.00 60.00
HTBH Bryce Harper 75.00 200.00
HTBP Buster Posey
HTBS Blake Snell 5.00 12.00
HTBW Billy Wagner 3.00 8.00
HTBWI Bernie Williams 20.00 50.00
HTCB Craig Biggio 10.00 25.00
HTCC Carlos Correa 25.00 60.00
HTCE Carl Edwards Jr. 4.00 10.00
HTCJ Chipper Jones 25.00 60.00
HTCK Clayton Kershaw 30.00 80.00
HTCR Cal Ripken Jr.
HTCRO Carlos Rodon 5.00 12.00
HTCS Curt Schilling 8.00 20.00
HTCSA Chris Sale 12.00 30.00
HTCSE Corey Seager
HTDO David Ortiz 30.00 80.00
HTDP David Price 6.00 15.00
HTER Eddie Rosario 4.00 10.00
HTFL Francisco Lindor 20.00 50.00
HTFM Frankie Montas 4.00 10.00
HTGM Greg Maddux 40.00 100.00
HTHA Hank Aaron
HTHO Henry Owens 4.00 10.00
HTI Ichiro Suzuki
HTIR Ivan Rodriguez 10.00 25.00
HTJAR Jake Arrieta EXCH
HTJB Johnny Bench
HTJBE Jose Berrios 4.00 10.00
HTJC Jose Canseco 6.00 15.00
HTJD Johnny Damon 4.00 10.00
HTJDE Jacob deGrom 5.00 12.00
HTJG Jon Gray 3.00 8.00
HTJGO Juan Gonzalez 5.00 12.00
HTJH Jason Heyward 6.00 15.00
HTJM J.D. Martinez 10.00 25.00
HTJP Jose Peraza 4.00 10.00
HTJS John Smoltz 10.00 25.00
HTJV Jason Varitek 5.00 12.00
HTKB Kris Bryant
HTKG Ken Griffey Jr. 125.00 250.00
HTKM Kenta Maeda
HTKMA Ketel Marte 6.00 15.00
HTKS Kyle Schwarber 15.00 40.00
HTLG Luis Gonzalez 4.00 10.00
HTLS Luis Severino 8.00 20.00
HTMF Michael Fulmer 8.00 20.00
HTMK Max Kepler 5.00 12.00
HTMMC Mark McGwire
HTMP Mike Piazza
HTMS Mallex Smith 3.00 8.00
HTMS Miguel Sano 5.00 12.00
HTMT Mike Trout 150.00 300.00
HTMTA Masahiro Tanaka
HTNA Nolan Arenado 12.00 30.00
HTNG Nomar Garciaparra 10.00 25.00
HTNM Nomar Mazara 6.00 15.00
HTNS Noah Syndergaard 12.00 30.00
HTOV Omar Vizquel 5.00 12.00
HTPG Paul Goldschmidt 5.00 12.00
HTRA Roberto Alomar 5.00 12.00
HTRB Ryan Braun 6.00 15.00
HTRC Roger Clemens 20.00 50.00
HTRJ Randy Johnson 25.00 60.00
HTRP Rafael Palmeiro 4.00 10.00
HTRS Robert Stephenson 3.00 8.00
HTSK Sandy Koufax
HTSP Stephen Piscotty 5.00 12.00
HTTG Tom Glavine 12.00 30.00
HTTS Trevor Story 12.00 30.00
HTTT Troy Tulowitzki 8.00 20.00
HTTTU Trea Turner 10.00 25.00
HTTYW Tyler White 3.00 8.00
HTVG Vladimir Guerrero 12.00 30.00
HTWB Wade Boggs 10.00 25.00

2016 Topps High Tek Autographs Gold Rainbow
*GOLD RAINBOW: .6X TO 1.5X BASIC
STATED ODDS 1:9 HOBBY
STATED PRINT RUN 50 SER.#'d SETS
EXCHANGE DEADLINE 10/31/2018
HTBP Buster Posey 50.00 120.00
HTCR Cal Ripken Jr. 60.00 150.00
HTCSE Corey Seager 75.00 200.00
HTGM Greg Maddux
HTHA Hank Aaron
HTI Ichiro Suzuki
HTJAR Jake Arrieta EXCH 25.00 60.00
HTJB Johnny Bench 30.00 80.00
HTKB Kris Bryant 150.00 300.00
HTKG Ken Griffey Jr.
HTKM Kenta Maeda 25.00 60.00
HTMMC Mark McGwire 50.00 120.00
HTMP Mike Piazza
HTMT Mike Trout 200.00 400.00
HTMTA Masahiro Tanaka 200.00 400.00
HTOV Omar Vizquel
HTRC Roger Clemens
HTRJ Randy Johnson
HTSK Sandy Koufax

2016 Topps High Tek Autographs Orange Magma Diffractor
*ORANGE MAGMA: .75X TO 2X BASIC
STATED ODDS 1:16 HOBBY
STATED PRINT RUN 25 SER.#'d SETS
EXCHANGE DEADLINE 10/31/2018
HTBP Buster Posey 60.00 150.00
HTCR Cal Ripken Jr. 75.00 200.00
HTCSE Corey Seager 100.00 250.00
HTHA Hank Aaron 150.00 400.00
HTI Ichiro Suzuki 300.00 500.00
HTJAR Jake Arrieta EXCH 30.00 80.00
HTJB Johnny Bench 40.00 100.00
HTKB Kris Bryant 200.00 400.00
HTKG Ken Griffey Jr. 200.00 400.00
HTKM Kenta Maeda 30.00 80.00
HTMMC Mark McGwire 60.00 150.00
HTMP Mike Piazza 75.00 200.00
HTMT Mike Trout 250.00 500.00
HTMTA Masahiro Tanaka 250.00 500.00

2016 Topps High Tek Autographs Sky Rainbow
*SKY RAINBOW: .75X TO 2X BASIC
RANDOM INSERTS IN ASIA PACKS
STATED PRINT RUN 20 SER.#'d SETS
EXCHANGE DEADLINE 10/31/2018
HTBP Buster Posey 60.00 150.00
HTCR Cal Ripken Jr. 75.00 200.00
HTCSE Corey Seager 100.00 250.00
HTHA Hank Aaron 150.00 400.00
HTI Ichiro Suzuki 300.00 500.00
HTJAR Jake Arrieta EXCH 30.00 80.00
HTJB Johnny Bench 40.00 100.00
HTKB Kris Bryant 200.00 400.00
HTKG Ken Griffey Jr. 200.00 400.00
HTKM Kenta Maeda 30.00 80.00
HTMMC Mark McGwire 60.00 150.00
HTMP Mike Piazza 75.00 200.00
HTMT Mike Trout 250.00 500.00
HTMTA Masahiro Tanaka 250.00 500.00

2016 Topps High Tek Bright Horizons
STATED ODDS 1:56 HOBBY
STATED PRINT RUN 50 SER.#'d SETS
BHBP Byung-Ho Park 2.50 6.00
BHBS Blake Snell 3.00 8.00
BHCC Carlos Correa 4.00 10.00
BHCS Corey Seager 20.00 50.00
BHFL Francisco Lindor 4.00 10.00
BHKM Kenta Maeda 5.00 12.00
BHKS Kyle Schwarber 8.00 20.00
BHLS Luis Severino 3.00 8.00
BHMC Michael Conforto 3.00 8.00
BHMS Miguel Sano 4.00 10.00

2016 Topps High Tek Bright Horizons Autographs
STATED ODDS 1:119 HOBBY
STATED PRINT RUN 50 SER.#'d SETS
EXCHANGE DEADLINE 10/31/2018
BHCC Carlos Correa 40.00 100.00
BHCS Corey Seager
BHFL Francisco Lindor 30.00 80.00
BHKM Kenta Maeda 20.00 50.00
BHKS Kyle Schwarber 50.00 120.00
BHMS Miguel Sano 10.00 25.00

2016 Topps High Tek Highlights
STATED ODDS 1:23 HOBBY
STATED PRINT RUN 50 SER.#'d SETS
HAP Albert Pujols 4.00 10.00
HBH Bryce Harper 5.00 12.00
HCB Craig Biggio 2.50 6.00
HCC Carlos Correa 3.00 8.00
HCJ Chipper Jones 3.00 8.00
HCK Clayton Kershaw 6.00 15.00
HCR Cal Ripken Jr. 20.00 50.00
HFH Felix Hernandez 2.50 6.00
HFT Frank Thomas 3.00 8.00
HGM Greg Maddux 4.00 10.00
HHA Hank Aaron 6.00 15.00
HIR Ivan Rodriguez 2.50 6.00
HIS Ichiro Suzuki 4.00 10.00
HJD Jacob deGrom 3.00 8.00
HJS John Smoltz 3.00 8.00
HKB Kris Bryant 15.00 40.00
HKG Ken Griffey Jr. 15.00 40.00
HMM Manny Machado 3.00 8.00
HMP Mike Piazza 3.00 8.00
HMT Mike Trout 15.00 40.00
HNG Nomar Garciaparra 2.50 6.00
HRJ Randy Johnson 3.00 8.00
HTT Troy Tulowitzki 3.00 8.00
HVG Vladimir Guerrero 2.50 6.00
HAPE Andy Pettitte 2.50 6.00

2016 Topps High Tek Highlights Autographs
STATED ODDS 1:79 HOBBY
STATED PRINT RUN 25 SER.#'d SETS
EXCHANGE DEADLINE 10/31/2018
HBH Bryce Harper 150.00 300.00
HCB Craig Biggio 15.00 40.00
HCC Carlos Correa 30.00 80.00
HCJ Chipper Jones 60.00 150.00
HCR Cal Ripken Jr. 75.00 200.00
HFH Felix Hernandez 20.00 50.00
HGM Greg Maddux 60.00 150.00
HHA Hank Aaron 150.00 300.00
HIR Ivan Rodriguez
HIS Ichiro Suzuki 300.00 500.00
HJD Jacob deGrom 12.00 30.00
HJS John Smoltz 60.00 150.00
HKB Kris Bryant 125.00 300.00
HKG Ken Griffey Jr. EXCH 200.00 400.00
HMT Mike Trout 175.00 350.00
HNG Nomar Garciaparra
HRJ Randy Johnson 50.00 120.00
HVG Vladimir Guerrero 25.00 60.00
HAPE Andy Pettitte 30.00 80.00

2017 Topps High Tek
GROUP A = BASEBALL GRUNGE
GROUP B = PIXEL CIRCLE
HTAB Adrian Beltre A .75 2.00
HTABE Andrew Benintendi B RC 1.50 4.00
HTABO Aaron Boone A .50 1.25
HTABR Alex Bregman A RC 2.00 5.00
HTAD Aledmys Diaz A .60 1.50
HTAG Amir Garrett B RC .50 1.25
HTAJ Aaron Judge B RC 6.00 15.00
HTANP Andy Pettitte B .60 1.50
HTAP Albert Pujols A 1.00 2.50
HTAR Addison Russell A .75 2.00
HTARI Anthony Rizzo A 1.25 3.00
HTBA Bobby Abreu B .50 1.25
HTBH Bryce Harper B 1.25 3.00
HTBP Buster Posey B 1.00 2.50
HTBZ Ben Zobrist B .60 1.50
HTCA Christian Arroyo A .75 2.00
HTCBE Cody Bellinger A RC 2.50 6.00
HTCC Carlos Correa A .75 2.00
HTCCC Carlos Carrasco B .50 1.25
HTCK Clayton Kershaw B 1.50 4.00
HTCKL Corey Kluber B .60 1.50
HTCP Chad Pinder A RC .50 1.25
HTCRJ Cal Ripken Jr. A 2.50 6.00
HTCS Corey Seager A .75 2.00
HTCSA Chris Sale B .75 2.00
HTDG Didi Gregorius A .60 1.50
HTDJ Derek Jeter A 2.00 5.00
HTDL Derrek Lee A .50 1.25
HTDM Daniel Murphy A .60 1.50
HTDO David Ortiz A .75 2.00
HTDP Dustin Pedroia A .75 2.00
HTDPR David Price B .60 1.50
HTDS Dansby Swanson A RC 1.25 3.00
HTDV Dan Vogelbach A RC .75 2.00
HTER Edgar Renteria A .50 1.25
HTET Eric Thames A .60 1.50
HTFF Freddie Freeman A 1.00 2.50
HTFL Francisco Lindor A .75 2.00
HTGM Greg Maddux B 1.00 2.50
HTGS Gary Sheffield B .50 1.25
HTGSP George Springer B .60 1.50
HTGST Giancarlo Stanton B .75 2.00
HTHA Hank Aaron B 1.50 4.00
HTHO Henry Owens B .50 1.25
HTHR Hunter Renfroe B RC .60 1.50
HTIH Ian Happ B RC 1.00 2.50
HTIR Ivan Rodriguez B .60 1.50
HTI Ichiro B 1.00 2.50
HTJA Jose Altuve A .60 1.50
HTJAB Jose Abreu A .75 2.00
HTJB Jeff Bagwell A 1.00 2.50
HTJBA Javier Baez A 1.00 2.50
HTJBE Josh Bell A 1.25 3.00
HTJCO Jharel Cotton B RC .50 1.25
HTJD Josh Donaldson A .60 1.50
HTJDA Johnny Damon B .60 1.50
HTJDE Jacob deGrom B .75 2.00
HTJDL Jose De Leon B RC .50 1.25
HTJE Jim Edmonds B .50 1.25
HTJJ Joe Jimenez B RC .50 1.25
HTJS John Smoltz B .75 2.00
HTJT Jim Thome A .60 1.50
HTJU Julio Urias B .75 2.00
HTJV Jonathan Villar A .50 1.25
HTJVO Joey Votto A .75 2.00
HTJW Jesse Winker B RC .75 2.00
HTKB Kris Bryant A 1.00 2.50
HTKGJ Ken Griffey Jr. B 1.50 4.00
HTKH Kelvin Herrera B .50 1.25
HTKS Kyle Seager A .50 1.25
HTKSC Kyle Schwarber B .75 2.00
HTLG Lucas Giolito B .60 1.50
HTLS Luis Severino B .60 1.50
HTLW Luke Weaver B RC .60 1.50
HTMAT Masahiro Tanaka B .60 1.50
HTMB Mookie Betts B 1.25 3.00
HTMC Matt Carpenter A .75 2.00
HTMCA Miguel Cabrera A .75 2.00
HTMF Maikel Franco A .60 1.50
HTMFU Michael Fulmer B .50 1.25
HTMH Mitch Haniger B RC .75 2.00
HTMM Manny Machado A .75 2.00
HTMMA Manny Margot B RC .50 1.25
HTMMC Mark McGwire A 1.25 3.00
HTMP Mike Piazza B .75 2.00
HTMS Max Scherzer B .75 2.00
HTMT Mike Trout B 4.00 10.00
HTNA Nolan Arenado A 1.00 2.50
HTNG Nomar Garciaparra A .60 1.50
HTNS Noah Syndergaard B .60 1.50
HTOA Orlando Arcia A RC .75 2.00
HTPG Paul Goldschmidt A .75 2.00
HTPK Paul Konerko A .60 1.50
HTPM Pedro Martinez B .60 1.50
HTRA Roberto Alomar A .60 1.50
HTRC Roger Clemens B 1.00 2.50
HTRT Raimel Tapia B .60 1.50
HTSK Sandy Koufax B 1.50 4.00
HTSL Seth Lugo B RC .50 1.25
HTSS Stephen Strasburg B .75 2.00
HTTA Tyler Austin A RC .75 2.00
HTTF Todd Frazier A .60 1.50
HTTG Tyler Glasnow B RC .60 1.50
HTTGL Tom Glavine B .60 1.50
HTTM Trey Mancini A RC 1.00 2.50
HTTR Tim Raines B .60 1.50
HTTS Trevor Story A .75 2.00
HTTT Trea Turner A .60 1.50
HTWM Wil Myers A .50 1.25
HTXB Xander Bogaerts A .75 2.00
HTYG Yulieski Gurriel A RC .75 2.00
HTYM Yoan Moncada A RC 1.50 4.00

2017 Topps High Tek Blacko
*BLACKOUT: .6X TO 1.5X BASIC
RANDOM INSERTS IN PACKS

2017 Topps High Tek Blacko Braid
*BLCKOUT BRAID: .6X TO 1.5X BASIC
RANDOM INSERTS IN PACKS

2017 Topps High Tek Blacko Chainlink Hexagon
*BLCK CHNLNK HXGN: .6X TO 1.5X BASIC
RANDOM INSERTS IN PACKS

2017 Topps High Tek Blue Rainbow
*BLUE RAINBOW: 1.2X TO 3X BASIC
STATED ODDS 1:2 HOBBY
STATED PRINT RUN 75 SER.#'d SETS
HTCBE Cody Bellinger A 25.00 6

2017 Topps High Tek Braid
*BRAID: .5X TO 1.2X BASIC
RANDOM INSERTS IN PACKS

2017 Topps High Tek Cam Stripes
*CAMO STRIPES: .5X TO 1.2X BASIC
RANDOM INSERTS IN PACKS

2017 Topps High Tek Chainl Hexagon
*CHNLNK HXGN: .5X TO 1.2X BASIC
RANDOM INSERTS IN PACKS

2017 Topps High Tek Diamon
*DIAMOND X: 1.2X TO 3X BASIC
RANDOM INSERTS IN PACKS

2017 Topps High Tek Green Rainbow
*GREEN RAINBOW: 1X TO 2.5X BASIC
STATED ODDS 1:2 HOBBY
STATED PRINT RUN 99 SER.#'d SETS
HTCBE Cody Bellinger A 20.00 5

2017 Topps High Tek Hexag Circle
*HXGN CIRCLE: .6X TO 1.5X BASIC
RANDOM INSERTS IN PACKS

2017 Topps High Tek Lightni
*LIGHTNING: .5X TO 1.2X BASIC
RANDOM INSERTS IN PACKS

2017 Topps High Tek Orang Magma
*ORANGE MAGMA: 3X TO 8X BASIC
STATED ODDS 1:6 HOBBY
STATED PRINT RUN 25 SER.#'d SETS
HTCBE Cody Bellinger A 60.00 15

2017 Topps High Tek Shatte
*SHATTER: 1X TO 2.5X BASIC
RANDOM INSERTS IN PACKS

2017 Topps High Tek Spiral D
*SPIRAL DOTS: .6X TO 1.5X BASIC
RANDOM INSERTS IN PACKS

2017 Topps High Tek Spiral G
*SPIRAL GRID: 1.2X TO 3X BASIC
RANDOM INSERTS IN PACKS

2017 Topps High Tek Squigg
*SQUIGGLE: .75X TO 2X BASIC
RANDOM INSERTS IN PACKS

2017 Topps High Tek Stadiu
*STADIUM: 1X TO 2.5X BASIC
RANDOM INSERTS IN PACKS

2017 Topps High Tek Tidal Diffractors
*TIDAL DIFFRACTORS: .75X TO 2X BASIC
RANDOM INSERTS IN PACKS
STATED PRINT RUN 250 SER.#'d SETS
HTCBE Cody Bellinger A 15.00 4

2017 Topps High Tek Wave
*WAVE: .75X TO 2X BASIC
RANDOM INSERTS IN PACKS

2017 Topps High Tek Clubhou Images
STATED ODDS 1:31 HOBBY
STATED PRINT RUN 50 SER.#'d SETS
CIAR Anthony Rizzo 8.00 2
CIBH Bryce Harper 25.00 6
CICC Carlos Correa 4.00 1
CICS Corey Seager 4.00 1
CIDP David Price 3.00 8
CIFL Francisco Lindor 4.00 1
CIKB Kris Bryant 15.00 4
CIMT Mike Trout 25.00 6
CINS Noah Syndergaard 3.00 8

2017 Topps High Tek Clubhou Images Autographs
STATED ODDS 1:61 HOBBY
PRINT RUNS B/WN 10-50 COPIES PER
NO PRICING ON QTY 10
EXCHANGE DEADLINE 10/31/2019
CICC Carlos Correa/25 60.00 15
CIDP David Price/40 8.00 2
CIFL Francisco Lindor/50 20.00 5
CINS Noah Syndergaard EXCH 15.00 4

2017 Topps High Tek Jubilati
STATED ODDS 1:20 HOBBY
STATED PRINT RUN 50 SER.#'d SETS
JAB Alex Bregman 10.00 2
JABE Andrew Benintendi 20.00 5
JAJ Aaron Judge 50.00 12
JBH Bryce Harper 6.00 1
JCC Carlos Correa 6.00 1
JCK Clayton Kershaw 8.00 2
JDS Dansby Swanson 5.00 1
JFL Francisco Lindor 4.00 1

A Jose Altuve 6.00 15.00
) Josh Donaldson 6.00 15.00
B Kris Bryant 12.00 30.00
IB Mookie Betts 6.00 15.00
IM Manny Machado 4.00 10.00
IS Max Scherzer 4.00 10.00
IT Mike Trout 25.00 60.00
C Robinson Cano 3.00 8.00

017 Topps High Tek Jubilation Autographs
TATED ODDS 1:43 HOBBY
TATED PRINT RUN 35 SER.#'d SETS
XCHANGE DEADLINE 10/31/2019
B Alex Bregman 20.00 50.00
BE Andrew Benintendi 25.00 120.00
H Bryce Harper 125.00 300.00
C Carlos Correa 60.00 150.00
L Francisco Lindor 20.00 50.00
D Josh Donaldson 30.00 80.00
B Kris Bryant 100.00 250.00
MM Manny Machado 20.00 50.00
MT Mike Trout 250.00 400.00

2017 Topps High Tek Rookie Tek
TATED ODDS 1:20 HOBBY
TATED PRINT RUN 50 SER.#'d SETS
TAB Alex Bregman 10.00 25.00
TABE Andrew Benintendi 20.00 50.00
TAJ Aaron Judge 50.00 120.00
TAR Alex Reyes 3.00 8.00
TDD David Dahl 3.00 8.00
TDS Dansby Swanson 5.00 12.00
THR Hunter Renfroe 3.00 8.00
TJA Jorge Alfaro 3.00 8.00
TJC Jharel Cotton 2.50 6.00
TJDL Jose De Leon 2.50 6.00
TLW Luke Weaver 3.00 8.00
TOA Orlando Arcia 4.00 10.00
TTG Tyler Glasnow 3.00 8.00
TYG Yulieski Gurriel 4.00 10.00
TYM Yoan Moncada 5.00 12.00

2017 Topps High Tek Rookie Tek Autographs
TATED ODDS 1:30 HOBBY
TATED PRINT RUN 50 SER.#'d SETS
XCHANGE DEADLINE 10/31/2019
TAB Alex Bregman 20.00 50.00
TABE Andrew Benintendi 50.00 120.00
TAJ Aaron Judge 100.00 250.00
TAR Alex Reyes 8.00 20.00
TDD David Dahl 8.00 20.00
TDS Dansby Swanson 10.00 25.00
THR Hunter Renfroe 5.00 12.00
TLW Luke Weaver 5.00 12.00
TTG Tyler Glasnow 5.00 12.00
TYG Yulieski Gurriel 10.00 25.00

2017 Topps High Tek TwiliTEK
TATED ODDS 1:21 HOBBY
TATED PRINT RUN 50 SER.#'d SETS
WAB Alex Bregman 10.00 25.00
WABE Andrew Benintendi 20.00 50.00
WBZ Ben Zobrist 3.00 8.00
WCC Carlos Correa 6.00 15.00
WCS Corey Seager 4.00 10.00
WGS Giancarlo Stanton 4.00 10.00
WGSA Gary Sanchez 4.00 10.00
WI Ichiro 5.00 12.00
WKB Kris Bryant 12.00 30.00
WMAT Masahiro Tanaka 3.00 8.00
WMT Mike Trout 25.00 60.00
WNA Nolan Arenado 5.00 12.00
WPG Paul Goldschmidt 4.00 10.00
WTS Trevor Story 4.00 10.00
WYM Yoan Moncada 5.00 12.00

2017 Topps High Tek TwiliTEK Autographs
STATED ODDS 1:41 HOBBY
PRINT RUNS B/WN 10-50 COPIES PER
NO PRICING ON QTY 10
EXCHANGE DEADLINE 10/31/2019
WAB Alex Bregman/50 20.00 50.00
WBZ Ben Zobrist/50 20.00 50.00
WCC Carlos Correa/25
WCS Corey Seager EXCH 20.00 50.00
WPG Paul Goldschmidt/40
WTS Trevor Story/50 10.00 25.00

2017 Topps High Tek Autographs
RANDOM INSERTS IN PACKS
EXCHANGE DEADLINE 10/31/2019
HTAB Adrian Beltre 15.00 40.00
HTABE Andrew Benintendi 25.00 60.00
HTABO Aaron Boone 4.00 10.00
HTABR Alex Bregman 15.00 40.00
HTAD Aledmys Diaz 3.00 8.00
HTAG Amir Garrett 2.50 6.00
HTAJ Aaron Judge 75.00 200.00
HTANP Andy Pettitte 12.00 30.00
HTAP Albert Pujols 60.00 150.00
HTAR Addison Russell 4.00 10.00
HTARI Anthony Rizzo 15.00 40.00
HTBH Bryce Harper 75.00 200.00
HTBP Buster Posey 30.00 80.00
HTBZ Ben Zobrist 12.00 30.00
HTCA Christian Arroyo 4.00 10.00
HTCBE Cody Bellinger 40.00 100.00
HTCC Carlos Carrasco 2.50 6.00
HTCC Carlos Correa 25.00 60.00
HTCKL Corey Kluber 8.00 20.00
HTCP Chad Pinder 2.50 6.00
HTCS Corey Seager 20.00 50.00
HTCSA Chris Sale 12.00 30.00
HTDG Didi Gregorius 10.00 25.00
HTDJ Derek Jeter 300.00 500.00
HTDO David Ortiz 20.00 50.00
HTDPR David Price 5.00 12.00
HTDV Dan Vogelbach 4.00 10.00
HTER Edgar Renteria 4.00 10.00
HTET Eric Thames 3.00 8.00
HTFF Freddie Freeman 8.00 20.00
HTFL Francisco Lindor 12.00 30.00
HTGM Greg Maddux 30.00 80.00
HTGS Gary Sheffield 4.00 10.00
HTHA Hank Aaron 100.00 250.00
HTHR Hunter Renfroe 3.00 8.00
HTI Ichiro 150.00 300.00
HTIH Ian Happ 5.00 12.00
HTIR Ivan Rodriguez 10.00 25.00
HTJA Jose Altuve 12.00 30.00
HTJBA Javier Baez 15.00 40.00
HTJCO Jharel Cotton 2.50 6.00
HTJD Josh Donaldson 6.00 15.00
HTJDE Jacob deGrom 10.00 25.00
HTJJ Joe Jimenez 2.50 6.00
HTJT Jim Thome 25.00 60.00
HTJU Julio Urias 5.00 12.00
HTJV Jonathan Villar 2.50 6.00
HTJW Jesse Winker 2.50 6.00
HTKB Kris Bryant 30.00 80.00
HTKH Kelvin Herrera 2.50 6.00
HTKS Kyle Seager 2.50 6.00
HTLG Lucas Giolito 3.00 8.00
HTLS Luis Severino 3.00 8.00
HTLW Luke Weaver 3.00 8.00
HTMF Maikel Franco 3.00 8.00
HTMFU Michael Fulmer 2.50 6.00
HTMH Mitch Haniger 4.00 10.00
HTMM Manny Machado 20.00 50.00
HTMMA Manny Margot 2.50 6.00
HTMMC Mark McGwire 40.00 100.00
HTMT Mike Trout 150.00 400.00
HTNG Nomar Garciaparra 10.00 25.00
HTNS Noah Syndergaard 10.00 25.00
HTPK Paul Konerko 8.00 20.00
HTPM Pedro Martinez 20.00 50.00
HTRA Roberto Alomar 10.00 25.00
HTRC Roger Clemens 20.00 50.00
HTRT Raimel Tapia 3.00 8.00
HTSK Sandy Koufax
HTSL Seth Lugo 2.50 6.00
HTTA Tyler Austin 4.00 10.00
HTTG Tyler Glasnow 3.00 8.00
HTTGL Tom Glavine 5.00 12.00
HTTM Trey Mancini 5.00 12.00
HTTR Tim Raines 5.00 12.00
HTTS Trevor Story 4.00 10.00
HTWM Wil Myers 2.50 6.00
HTYG Yulieski Gurriel 5.00 12.00

2017 Topps High Tek Autographs Blackout
*BLACKOUT: .5X TO 1.2X BASIC
STATED ODDS 1:7 HOBBY
STATED PRINT RUN 50 SER.#'d SETS
EXCHANGE DEADLINE 10/31/2019

2017 Topps High Tek Autographs Blue Rainbow
*BLUE RAINBOW: .5X TO 1.2X BASIC
STATED ODDS 1:6 HOBBY
STATED PRINT RUN 50 SER.#'d SETS
EXCHANGE DEADLINE 10/31/2019

2017 Topps High Tek Autographs Green Rainbow
*GREEN RAINBOW: .5X TO 1.2X BASIC
RANDOM INSERTS IN PACKS
STATED PRINT RUN 75 SER.#'d SETS
EXCHANGE DEADLINE 10/31/2019

2017 Topps High Tek Autographs Orange Magma
*ORANGE MAGMA: .6X TO 1.5X BASIC
STATED ODDS 1:10 HOBBY
STATED PRINT RUN 25 SER.#'d SETS
EXCHANGE DEADLINE 10/31/2019
HTFF Freddie Freeman 20.00 50.00
HTJVO Joey Votto 40.00 100.00

2018 Topps High Tek
GROUP A = WAVES
GROUP B = DIAGONALS
HTAA Aaron Altherr B .40 1.00
HTAB Anthony Banda A RC .40 1.00
HTABE Andrew Benintendi A .60 1.50
HTAH Austin Hays A RC .60 1.50
HTAJ Aaron Judge A 1.50 4.00
HTAP Andy Pettitte A .50 1.25
HTAR Anthony Rizzo B 1.00 2.50
HTARD Alex Rodriguez A .75 2.00
HTARO Amed Rosario B RC .50 1.25
HTAS Andrew Stevenson B RC .40 1.00
HTASA Anthony Santander A RC .40 1.00
HTAV Alex Verdugo B RC .60 1.50
HTBB Byron Buxton A .50 1.25
HTBD Brian Dozier A .50 1.25
HTBH Bryce Harper B 1.00 2.50
HTBW Brandon Woodruff B RC .50 1.25
HTBWI Bernie Williams A .50 1.25
HTCB Charlie Blackmon B .60 1.50
HTCBE Cody Bellinger B 1.25 3.00
HTCC Carlos Correa A .60 1.50
HTCF Clint Frazier A RC .75 2.00
HTCJ Chipper Jones B .60 1.50
HTCK Clayton Kershaw B 1.25 3.00
HTCKE Carson Kelly B .40 1.00
HTCR Cal Ripken Jr. A 2.00 5.00
HTCS Carlos Santana B .50 1.25
HTCSE Corey Seager B .60 1.50
HTCSI Chance Sisco A RC .50 1.25
HTDF Dustin Fowler A RC .40 1.00
HTDG Didi Gregorius A .50 1.25
HTDGO Dwight Gooden A .40 1.00
HTDJ Derek Jeter A 1.50 4.00
HTDM Don Mattingly A 1.25 3.00
HTDO David Ortiz A .60 1.50
HTDS Dominic Smith B RC .40 1.00
HTDST Darryl Strawberry B .40 1.00
HTEM Edgar Martinez A .50 1.25
HTFF Freddie Freeman B .75 2.00
HTFL Francisco Lindor A .60 1.50
HTFM Francisco Mejia A RC .50 1.25
HTGA Greg Allen A RC .40 1.00
HTGS Gary Sanchez A .60 1.50
HTGSP George Springer A .50 1.25
HTGST Giancarlo Stanton A .60 1.50
HTGT Gleyber Torres A RC 4.00 10.00
HTHA Hank Aaron B 1.25 3.00
HTJA Jose Altuve A .50 1.25
HTJB Jeff Bagwell B .50 1.25
HTJBE Johnny Bench B .60 1.50
HTJC J.P. Crawford B RC .40 1.00
HTJCA Jose Canseco A .50 1.25
HTJD Jacob deGrom B .60 1.50
HTJDA J.D. Davis A RC .50 1.25
HTJE Jim Edmonds B .40 1.00
HTJF Jack Flaherty B RC .60 1.50
HTJL Jordan Luplow B RC .40 1.00
HTJM Jordan Montgomery A .60 1.50
HTJR Jose Ramirez A .50 1.25
HTJS Justin Smoak A .40 1.00
HTJT Jim Thome A .50 1.25
HTJU Justin Upton A .50 1.25
HTKB Kris Bryant B .75 2.00
HTKBR Keon Broxton B .40 1.00
HTKS Kyle Schwarber B .60 1.50
HTMA Miguel Andujar A RC 1.50 4.00
HTMB Mookie Betts A 1.00 2.50
HTMM Mark McGwire B 1.00 2.50
HTMMA Manny Machado A .60 1.50
HTMO Marcell Ozuna B .60 1.50
HTMOS Matt Olson A .40 1.00
HTMR Mariano Rivera A .75 2.00
HTMS Max Scherzer B .60 1.50
HTMT Mike Trout A 3.00 8.00
HTNA Nolan Arenado B .75 2.00
HTND Nicky Delmonico A RC .40 1.00
HTNG Nomar Garciaparra A .50 1.25
HTNR Nolan Ryan A 2.00 5.00
HTNS Noah Syndergaard B .50 1.25
HTNW Nick Williams B RC .50 1.25
HTOA Ozzie Albies B RC 1.25 3.00
HTPB Paul Blackburn A RC .40 1.00
HTPBR Parker Bridwell A RC .40 1.00
HTPD Paul DeJong B .60 1.50
HTPG Paul Goldschmidt B .60 1.50
HTPM Pedro Martinez B .50 1.25
HTRA Ronald Acuna Jr. B RC 8.00 20.00
HTRC Roger Clemens A .75 2.00
HTRD Rafael Devers A RC 1.25 3.00
HTRH Rhys Hoskins B RC 1.50 4.00
HTRI Raisel Iglesias B .50 1.25
HTRJ Randy Johnson B .60 1.50
HTRJA Reggie Jackson A .50 1.25
HTSA Sandy Alcantara B RC .40 1.00
HTSD Sean Doolittle B .40 1.00
HTSK Sandy Koufax B 1.25 3.00
HTSKI Scott Kingery B RC .60 1.50
HTSO Shohei Ohtani A RC 2.50 6.00
HTTG Tom Glavine B .50 1.25
HTTM Tyler Mahle B RC .50 1.25
HTTN Tomas Nido B RC .40 1.00
HTTP Tommy Pham B .40 1.00
HTTT Trea Turner B .50 1.25
HTTV Thyago Vieira A RC .40 1.00
HTTW Ted Williams A 1.25 3.00
HTVR Victor Robles B RC 1.00 2.50
HTWB Walker Buehler B RC 2.00 5.00
HTWBO Wade Boggs A .50 1.25
HTWC Will Clark A .50 1.25
HTWM Whit Merrifield A .60 1.50
HTYM Yadier Molina B .60 1.50
HTZC Zack Cozart A .40 1.00
HTZG Zack Godley B .40 1.00

2018 Topps High Tek Black
*BLACK: 1.2X TO 3X BASIC
*BLACK RC: 1.2X TO 3X BASIC
STATED ODDS 1:3 HOBBY
STATED PRINT RUN 50 SER.#'d SETS

2018 Topps High Tek Blue
*BLUE: .75X TO 2X BASIC
*BLUE RC: .75X TO 2X BASIC
RANDOM INSERTS IN PACKS
STATED PRINT RUN 150 SER.#'d SETS

2018 Topps High Tek Circuit Board
*CIRCUIT BOARD: .6X TO 1.5X BASIC
APPX.FOUR PER PACK

2018 Topps High Tek Diamond Grid
*DIAMOND GRID: .5X TO 1.2X BASIC
APPX.SIX PER PACK

2018 Topps High Tek Dot Grid
*DOTS GRID: .5X TO 1.2X BASIC
APPX.EIGHT PER PACK

2018 Topps High Tek Galactic Wave
*GALACTIC WAVE: .6X TO 1.5X BASIC
APPX.FOUR PER PACK

2018 Topps High Tek Green
*GREEN: 1X TO 2.5X BASIC
*GREEN RC: 1X TO 2.5X BASIC
STATED ODDS 1:2 HOBBY
STATED PRINT RUN 99 SER.#'d SETS

2018 Topps High Tek Lightning
*LIGHTNING: .5X TO 1.2X BASIC
APPX.EIGHT PER PACK

2018 Topps High Tek Orange
*ORANGE: 2.5X TO 6X BASIC
*ORANGE RC: 2.5X TO 6X BASIC
STATED ODDS 1:6 HOBBY
STATED PRINT RUN 25 SER.#'d SETS
HTDJ Derek Jeter A 15.00 40.00
HTDM Don Mattingly A 20.00 50.00

2018 Topps High Tek Triangles
*TRIANGLES: .5X TO 1.2X BASIC
APPX.SIX PER PACK

2018 Topps High Tek Black and White Variations
STATED ODDS 1:67 HOBBY
STATED PRINT RUN 50 SER.#'d SETS
HTAJ Aaron Judge 10.00 25.00
HTKB Kris Bryant 5.00 12.00
HTMR Mariano Rivera 5.00 12.00
HTMT Mike Trout 20.00 50.00
HTSO Shohei Ohtani 15.00 40.00

2018 Topps High Tek Black and White Variations Autographs
STATED ODDS 1:107 HOBBY
PRINT RUNS B/WN 20-40 COPIES PER
EXCHANGE DEADLINE 9/30/2020
HTAJ Aaron Judge EXCH
HTKB Kris Bryant/30 60.00 150.00
HTMR Mariano Rivera/20 75.00 200.00
HTMT Mike Trout/20 250.00 500.00
HTSO Shohei Ohtani/40 100.00 250.00

2018 Topps High Tek Autographs
RANDOM INSERTS IN PACKS
EXCHANGE DEADLINE 9/30/2020
HTAA Aaron Altherr 2.50 6.00
HTAH Austin Hays 4.00 10.00
HTAJ Aaron Judge 60.00 150.00
HTAR Anthony Rizzo 12.00 30.00
HTARD Alex Rodriguez 30.00 80.00
HTARO Amed Rosario 3.00 8.00
HTAV Alex Verdugo 8.00 20.00
HTBB Byron Buxton 3.00 8.00
HTBD Brian Dozier 3.00 8.00
HTBH Bryce Harper 60.00 150.00
HTBWI Bernie Williams 12.00 30.00
HTCB Charlie Blackmon 6.00 15.00
HTCF Clint Frazier 6.00 15.00
HTCJ Chipper Jones 40.00 100.00
HTCK Clayton Kershaw 25.00 60.00
HTCKE Carson Kelly 2.50 6.00
HTCR Cal Ripken Jr. 40.00 100.00
HTCS Carlos Santana 3.00 8.00
HTDF Dustin Fowler 2.50 6.00
HTDGO Dwight Gooden 5.00 12.00
HTDJ Derek Jeter 150.00 400.00
HTDS Dominic Smith 2.50 6.00
HTDST Darryl Strawberry 5.00 12.00
HTFL Francisco Lindor 12.00 30.00
HTFM Francisco Mejia 3.00 8.00
HTGS Gary Sanchez 10.00 25.00
HTGSP George Springer 6.00 15.00
HTGT Gleyber Torres 30.00 80.00
HTHA Hank Aaron 125.00 300.00
HTJA Jose Altuve 12.00 30.00
HTJB Jeff Bagwell 12.00 30.00
HTJCA Jose Canseco 10.00 25.00
HTJDA J.D. Davis 3.00 8.00
HTJM Jordan Montgomery 4.00 10.00
HTJS Justin Smoak 2.50 6.00
HTJT Jim Thome 20.00 50.00
HTJU Justin Upton 3.00 8.00
HTKB Kris Bryant 40.00 100.00
HTKBR Keon Broxton 2.50 6.00
HTMA Miguel Andujar 10.00 25.00
HTMM Mark McGwire 30.00 80.00
HTMO Marcell Ozuna 4.00 10.00
HTMOS Matt Olson 2.50 6.00
HTMR Mariano Rivera 40.00 100.00
HTMT Mike Trout 125.00 300.00
HTND Nicky Delmonico 2.50 6.00
HTNG Nomar Garciaparra 10.00 25.00
HTNS Noah Syndergaard 5.00 12.00
HTNW Nick Williams 3.00 8.00
HTPB Paul Blackburn 2.50 6.00
HTPD Paul DeJong 4.00 10.00
HTPM Pedro Martinez 20.00 50.00
HTRA Ronald Acuna 60.00 150.00
HTRC Roger Clemens 20.00 50.00
HTRH Rhys Hoskins 15.00 40.00
HTRI Raisel Iglesias 3.00 8.00
HTRJA Reggie Jackson 20.00 50.00
HTSA Sandy Alcantara 2.50 6.00
HTSD Sean Doolittle 2.50 6.00
HTSK Sandy Koufax 100.00 250.00
HTSKI Scott Kingery 4.00 10.00
HTSO Shohei Ohtani 125.00 300.00
HTTM Tyler Mahle 3.00 8.00
HTTN Tomas Nido 2.50 6.00
HTTV Thyago Vieira 2.50 6.00
HTVR Victor Robles 8.00 20.00
HTWBO Wade Boggs 10.00 25.00
HTWC Will Clark 6.00 15.00
HTWM Whit Merrifield 4.00 10.00
HTYM Yadier Molina EXCH 20.00 50.00
HTZC Zack Cozart 2.50 6.00
HTZG Zack Godley 2.50 6.00

2018 Topps High Tek Autographs Black Orbit Diffractors
*BLACK ORBIT: .5X TO 1.2X BASIC
RANDOM INSERTS IN PACKS
STATED PRINT RUN 50 SER.#'d SETS
EXCHANGE DEADLINE 9/30/2020
HTGA Greg Allen 10.00 25.00
HTOA Ozzie Albies 15.00 40.00
HTWB Walker Buehler 20.00 50.00

2018 Topps High Tek Autographs Blue
*BLUE: .5X TO 1.2X BASIC
RANDOM INSERTS IN PACKS
STATED PRINT RUN 75 SER.#'d SETS
EXCHANGE DEADLINE 9/30/2020
HTGA Greg Allen 10.00 25.00
HTOA Ozzie Albies 15.00 40.00
HTWB Walker Buehler 20.00 50.00

2018 Topps High Tek Autographs Green
*GREEN: .5X TO 1.2X BASIC
RANDOM INSERTS IN PACKS
STATED PRINT RUN 99 SER.#'d SETS
EXCHANGE DEADLINE 9/30/2020
HTGA Greg Allen 10.00 25.00
HTOA Ozzie Albies 15.00 40.00
HTWB Walker Buehler 20.00 50.00

2018 Topps High Tek Autographs Orange Orbit Diffractors
*ORANGE ORBIT: .6X TO 1.5X BASIC
STATED ODDS 1:10 HOBBY
STATED PRINT RUN 25 SER.#'d SETS
EXCHANGE DEADLINE 9/30/2020
HTGA Greg Allen 12.00 30.00
HTOA Ozzie Albies 20.00 50.00
HTWB Walker Buehler 25.00 60.00

2018 Topps High Tek Galactic Diffractors
*GLCTC DFFRCTRS: .6X TO 1.5X BASIC
*GLCTC DFFRCTRS RC: .6X TO 1.5X BASIC
APPX.ONE GALACTIC PER PACK

2018 Topps High Tek Galactic Diffractors Orange
*GALA ORANGE: 2.5X TO 6X BASIC
*GALA ORANGE RC: 2.5X TO 6X BASIC
STATED ODDS 1:6 HOBBY
STATED PRINT RUN 25 SER.#'d SETS
HTDJ Derek Jeter A 15.00 40.00
HTDM Don Mattingly A 20.00 50.00

2018 Topps High Tek Magma Diffractors
*MGMA DFFRCTRS: .5X TO 1.2X BASIC
*MGMA DFFRCTRS RC: .5X TO 1.2X BASIC
APPX.EIGHT MAGMA PER PACK

2018 Topps High Tek Magma Diffractors Black
*MAG BLACK: 1.2X TO 3X BASIC
*MAG BLACK RC: 1.2X TO 3X BASIC
STATED ODDS 1:3 HOBBY
STATED PRINT RUN 50 SER.#'d SETS

2018 Topps High Tek Magma Diffractors Green
*MAG GREEN: 1X TO 2.5X BASIC
*MAG GREEN RC: 1X TO 2.5X BASIC
STATED ODDS 1:2 HOBBY
STATED PRINT RUN 99 SER.#'d SETS

2018 Topps High Tek Magma Diffractors Orange
*MAGMA ORANGE: 2.5X TO 6X BASIC
*MAGMA ORANGE RC: 2.5X TO 6X BASIC
STATED ODDS 1:6 HOBBY
STATED PRINT RUN 25 SER.#'d SETS
HTDJ Derek Jeter A 15.00 40.00
HTDM Don Mattingly A 20.00 50.00

2018 Topps High Tek Orbit Diffractors
*ORBT DFFRCTRS: .5X TO 1.2X BASIC
*ORBT DFFRCTRS RC: .5X TO 1.2X BASIC
APPX.TWO ORBIT PER PACK

2018 Topps High Tek Orbit Diffractors Black
*ORBIT BLACK: 1.2X TO 3X BASIC
*ORBIT BLACK RC: 1.2X TO 3X BASIC
STATED ODDS 1:3 HOBBY
STATED PRINT RUN 50 SER.#'d SETS

2018 Topps High Tek Orbit Diffractors Orange
*ORBIT ORANGE: 2.5X TO 6X BASIC
*ORBIT ORANGE RC: 2.5X TO 6X BASIC
STATED ODDS 1:6 HOBBY
STATED PRINT RUN 25 SER.#'d SETS
HTDJ Derek Jeter A 15.00 40.00
HTDM Don Mattingly A 20.00 50.00

2018 Topps High Tek PortraiTEK
STATED ODDS 1:16 HOBBY
STATED PRINT RUN 50 SER.#'d SETS
*ORANGE/25: .6X TO 1.5X BASIC
PTAR Amed Rosario 2.50 6.00
PTARI Anthony Rizzo 5.00 12.00
PTBH Bryce Harper 5.00 12.00
PTCJ Chipper Jones 3.00 8.00
PTCR Cal Ripken Jr. 10.00 25.00
PTDJ Derek Jeter 8.00 20.00
PTGS Gary Sanchez 3.00 8.00
PTHA Hank Aaron 6.00 15.00
PTJA Jose Altuve 2.50 6.00
PTJB Jeff Bagwell 2.50 6.00
PTJT Jim Thome 2.50 6.00
PTKB Kris Bryant 4.00 10.00
PTMM Mark McGwire 5.00 12.00
PTMMA Manny Machado 3.00 8.00
PTMR Mariano Rivera 4.00 10.00
PTMT Mike Trout 15.00 40.00
PTPM Pedro Martinez 2.50 6.00
PTRC Roger Clemens 4.00 10.00
PTRD Rafael Devers 6.00 15.00
PTSO Shohei Ohtani 12.00 30.00
PTYM Yadier Molina 3.00 8.00

2018 Topps High Tek PortraiTEK Autographs
STATED ODDS 1:21 HOBBY
PRINT RUNS B/WN 20-99 COPIES PER
EXCHANGE DEADLINE 9/30/2020
PTAR Amed Rosario/99 5.00 12.00
PTBH Bryce Harper 75.00 200.00
PTCJ Chipper Jones/75 30.00 80.00
PTCR Cal Ripken Jr./75 50.00 120.00
PTDJ Derek Jeter
PTHA Hank Aaron/20 125.00 300.00
PTJA Jose Altuve/99 15.00 40.00
PTJT Jim Thome/99 20.00 50.00
PTKB Kris Bryant/55 50.00 120.00
PTMM Mark McGwire/75 40.00 100.00
PTMR Mariano Rivera/30 60.00 150.00
PTMT Mike Trout/25 250.00 500.00
PTPM Pedro Martinez/60 30.00 80.00
PTRD Rafael Devers 12.00 30.00
PTSO Shohei Ohtani/75 100.00 250.00
PTYM Yadier Molina EXCH 25.00 60.00

2018 Topps High Tek PortraiTEK Autographs Black
*BLACK: .4X TO 1X BASIC
STATED ODDS 1:21 HOBBY
STATED PRINT RUN 50 SER.#'d SETS
EXCHANGE DEADLINE 9/30/2020
PTRC Roger Clemens 25.00 60.00

2018 Topps High Tek PyroTEKnics
STATED ODDS 1:12 HOBBY
STATED PRINT RUN 99 SER.#'d SETS
*ORANGE/25: .6X TO 1.5X BASIC
PYTAR Amed Rosario 2.00 5.00
PYTBH Bryce Harper 4.00 10.00
PYTCF Clint Frazier 3.00 8.00
PYTCK Clayton Kershaw 5.00 12.00
PYTFL Francisco Lindor 2.50 6.00
PYTGS Giancarlo Stanton 2.50 6.00
PYTJA Jose Altuve 2.00 5.00
PYTKB Kris Bryant 3.00 8.00
PYTMB Mookie Betts 4.00 10.00
PYTMM Manny Machado 2.50 6.00
PYTMT Mike Trout 12.00 30.00
PYTRD Rafael Devers 5.00 12.00
PYTSO Shohei Ohtani 10.00 25.00
PYTVR Victor Robles 4.00 10.00
PYTYM Yadier Molina 2.50 6.00

2018 Topps High Tek PyroTEKnics Autographs
STATED ODDS 1:54 HOBBY
PRINT RUNS B/WN 20-50 COPIES PER
EXCHANGE DEADLINE 9/30/2020
PYTAR Amed Rosario/25 10.00 25.00
PYTBH Bryce Harper/20 75.00 200.00
PYTCF Clint Frazier/50 12.00 30.00
PYTFL Francisco Lindor/50 20.00 50.00
PYTJA Jose Altuve/50 15.00 40.00
PYTKB Kris Bryant/40 60.00 150.00
PYTMT Mike Trout/20 250.00 500.00
PYTSO Shohei Ohtani/20 300.00 600.00
PYTVR Victor Robles/50 15.00 40.00
PYTYM Yadier Molina EXCH 30.00 80.00

2018 Topps High Tek Rookie Tek
STATED ODDS 1:12 HOBBY
STATED PRINT RUN 99 SER.#'d SETS
*ORANGE/25: .6X TO 1.5X BASIC
RTAH Austin Hays 2.00 5.00
RTAR Amed Rosario 1.50 4.00
RTAV Alex Verdugo 2.00 5.00
RTCF Clint Frazier 2.50 6.00
RTDS Dominic Smith 1.25 3.00
RTFM Francisco Mejia 1.50 4.00
RTJC J.P. Crawford 1.25 3.00
RTMA Miguel Andujar 5.00 12.00
RTNW Nick Williams 1.50 4.00
RTOA Ozzie Albies 4.00 10.00
RTRD Rafael Devers 4.00 10.00
RTRH Rhys Hoskins 5.00 12.00
RTSK Scott Kingery 2.00 5.00
RTSO Shohei Ohtani 25.00 60.00
RTVR Victor Robles 3.00 8.00

2018 Topps High Tek Rookie Tek Autographs
STATED ODDS 1:33 HOBBY
STATED PRINT RUN 50 SER.#'d SETS
EXCHANGE DEADLINE 9/30/2020
RTAH Austin Hays 6.00 15.00
RTAR Amed Rosario 5.00 12.00
RTAV Alex Verdugo
RTCF Clint Frazier 8.00 20.00
RTFM Francisco Mejia 5.00 12.00
RTNW Nick Williams 5.00 12.00
RTOA Ozzie Albies 12.00 30.00
RTRH Rhys Hoskins 20.00 50.00
RTSK Scott Kingery
RTSO Shohei Ohtani 250.00 500.00
RTVR Victor Robles 12.00 30.00

2019 Topps High Tek
1 Cal Ripken Jr. 2.00 5.00
2 Cedric Mullins RC .60 1.50
3 Trey Mancini .50 1.25
4 Roberto Alomar .50 1.25
5 Mookie Betts 1.00 2.50
6 Andrew Benintendi .60 1.50
7 Rafael Devers .75 2.00
8 Chris Sale .60 1.50
9 David Ortiz .60 1.50
10 Pedro Martinez .50 1.25
11 J.D. Martinez .60 1.50
12 Frank Thomas .60 1.50
13 Michael Kopech RC .75 2.00
14 Jose Abreu .60 1.50
15 Francisco Lindor .60 1.50
16 Jose Ramirez .50 1.25
17 Corey Kluber .50 1.25
18 Miguel Cabrera .60 1.50
19 Christin Stewart RC .50 1.25
20 Jeff Bagwell .50 1.25
21 Jose Altuve .50 1.25
22 Carlos Correa .60 1.50
23 Alex Bregman .60 1.50
24 Justin Verlander .60 1.50
25 Gerrit Cole .60 1.50
26 George Springer .50 1.25
27 Whit Merrifield .60 1.50
28 Salvador Perez .50 1.25
29 Ryan O'Hearn RC .40 1.00
30 George Brett 1.25 3.00
31 Mike Trout 3.00 8.00
32 Shohei Ohtani .75 2.00
33 Albert Pujols .75 2.00
34 Nolan Ryan 2.00 5.00
35 Jose Berrios .50 1.25
36 Miguel Sano .50 1.25
37 Eddie Rosario .50 1.25
38 Derek Jeter 1.50 4.00
39 Tino Martinez .50 1.25
40 Aaron Judge 1.50 4.00
41 Gleyber Torres 1.25 3.00
42 Miguel Andujar .60 1.50
43 Mariano Rivera .75 2.00
44 Luis Severino .50 1.25
45 Khris Davis .60 1.50
46 Matt Chapman .60 1.50
47 Rickey Henderson .60 1.50
48 Ken Griffey Jr. 1.25 3.00
49 Yusei Kikuchi RC .60 1.50
50 Justus Sheffield RC .60 1.50
51 Ichiro .75 2.00
52 Edgar Martinez .50 1.25
53 Blake Snell .50 1.25
54 Austin Meadows .50 1.25
55 Jose Canseco .50 1.25
56 Joey Gallo .50 1.25
57 Nomar Mazara .40 1.00
58 Ivan Rodriguez .50 1.25
59 Rowdy Tellez RC .60 1.50
60 Danny Jansen RC .40 1.00
61 Roy Halladay .50 1.25
62 Randy Johnson .60 1.50
63 Zack Greinke .50 1.25
64 Robbie Ray .40 1.00
65 Chipper Jones .60 1.50
66 Ronald Acuna Jr. 3.00 8.00
67 Touki Toussaint RC .50 1.25
68 Kolby Allard RC .60 1.50
69 John Smoltz .60 1.50
70 Kris Bryant .75 2.00
71 Anthony Rizzo 1.00 2.50
72 Javier Baez .75 2.00
73 Kyle Schwarber .60 1.50
74 Joey Votto .60 1.50
75 Yasiel Puig .60 1.50
76 Scooter Gennett .50 1.25
77 Nolan Arenado .75 2.00
78 Trevor Story .60 1.50
79 Charlie Blackmon .60 1.50
80 Todd Helton .50 1.25
81 Clayton Kershaw 1.25 3.00
82 Sandy Koufax 1.25 3.00
83 Walker Buehler .75 2.00
84 Corey Seager .60 1.50
85 Cody Bellinger 1.25 3.00
86 Max Muncy .50 1.25
87 Brian Anderson .40 1.00
88 Jorge Alfaro .40 1.00
89 Christian Yelich .75 2.00
90 Lorenzo Cain .40 1.00
91 Josh Hader .40 1.00
92 Noah Syndergaard .50 1.25
93 Jacob deGrom .60 1.50
94 Bryce Harper 1.00 2.50
95 Robinson Cano .50 1.25
96 Rhys Hoskins .75 2.00
97 Andrew McCutchen .60 1.50
98 Aaron Nola .50 1.25
99 J.T. Realmuto .60 1.50
100 Starling Marte .60 1.50
101 Chris Archer .40 1.00
102 Gregory Polanco .50 1.25
103 Manny Machado .60 1.50
104 Luis Urias RC .60 1.50
105 Tony Gwynn .60 1.50
106 Buster Posey .75 2.00
107 Brandon Crawford .50 1.25
108 Paul Goldschmidt .60 1.50
109 Yadier Molina .60 1.50
110 Juan Soto 2.00 5.00
111 Victor Robles .75 2.00
112 Max Scherzer .60 1.50

2019 Topps High Tek Black
*BLACK: 1.2X TO 3X BASIC
*BLACK RC: 1.2X TO 3X BASIC
STATED ODDS 1:10 HOBBY
STATED PRINT RUN 50 SER.#'d SETS
38 Derek Jeter 10.00 25.00
48 Ken Griffey Jr. 12.00 30.00

2019 Topps High Tek Green
*GREEN: .8X TO 2X BASIC
*GREEN RC: .8X TO 2X BASIC
STATED ODDS 1:4 HOBBY
STATED PRINT RUN 150 SER.#'d SETS
48 Ken Griffey Jr. 6.00 15.00

2019 Topps High Tek Orange
*ORANGE: 2.5X TO 6X BASIC
*ORANGE RC: 2.5X TO 6X BASIC
STATED ODDS 1:19 HOBBY
STATED PRINT RUN 25 SER.#'d SETS
38 Derek Jeter 20.00 50.00
48 Ken Griffey Jr. 30.00 80.00

2019 Topps High Tek Pink
*PINK: 1X TO 2.5X BASIC
*PINK RC: 1X TO 2.5X BASIC
STATED ODDS 1:6 HOBBY
STATED PRINT RUN 75 SER.#'d SETS
38 Derek Jeter 8.00 20.00
48 Ken Griffey Jr. 8.00 20.00

2019 Topps High Tek Purple
*PURPLE: 1X TO 2.5X BASIC
*PURPLE RC: 1X TO 2.5X BASIC
STATED ODDS 1:5 HOBBY
STATED PRINT RUN 99 SER.#'d SETS
38 Derek Jeter 8.00 20.00
48 Ken Griffey Jr. 8.00 20.00

2019 Topps High Tek CelebraTEK
STATED ODDS 1:34 HOBBY
STATED PRINT RUN 99 SER.#'d SETS
*ORANGE/25: .6X TO 1.5X BASIC
CTAB Alex Bregman 5.00 12.00
CTAJ Aaron Judge 12.00 30.00
CTCY Christian Yelich 6.00 15.00
CTFL Francisco Lindor 2.50 6.00
CTJD Jacob deGrom 4.00 10.00
CTJR Jose Ramirez 2.00 5.00
CTJS Juan Soto 8.00 20.00
CTKB Kris Bryant 5.00 12.00
CTKS Kyle Schwarber 4.00 10.00
CTMT Mike Trout 12.00 30.00
CTNS Noah Syndergaard 4.00 10.00
CTOA Ozzie Albies 4.00 10.00
CTRA Ronald Acuna Jr. 15.00 40.00
CTRH Rhys Hoskins 3.00 8.00
CTSO Shohei Ohtani 3.00 8.00

2019 Topps High Tek CelebraTEK Orange
*ORANGE: .6X TO 1.5X BASIC
STATED ODDS 1:135 HOBBY
STATED PRINT RUN 25 SER.#'d SETS
CTAB Alex Bregman 15.00 40.00
CTOA Ozzie Albies 10.00 25.00

2019 Topps High Tek CelebraTEK Autographs
STATED ODDS 1:198 HOBBY
PRINT RUNS B/WN 15-50 COPIES PER
NO PRICING QTY 15 OR LESS
EXCHANGE DEADLINE 10/31/2021
CTAJ Aaron Judge/20 40.00 100.00
CTCY Christian Yelich EXCH
CTFL Francisco Lindor EXCH
CTJS Juan Soto/30 50.00 120.00
CTKS Kyle Schwarber/45 10.00 25.00
CTOA Ozzie Albies/50 15.00 40.00
CTRA Ronald Acuna Jr./25 100.00 250.00
CTRH Rhys Hoskins/30 25.00 60.00

2019 Topps High Tek Future TEK
STATED ODDS 1:34 HOBBY
STATED PRINT RUN 99 SER.#'d SETS
*ORANGE/25: .6X TO 1.5X BASIC
FTCP Cionel Perez 1.50 4.00
FTDB David Bote 4.00 10.00
FTEJ Eloy Jimenez 6.00 15.00
FTJH Josh Hader 1.50 4.00
FTJS Justus Sheffield 2.50 6.00
FTKT Kyle Tucker 3.00 8.00
FTLU Luis Urias 2.50 6.00
FTMC Mike Clevinger 2.00 5.00
FTMK Michael Kopech 3.00 8.00
FTRL Ramon Laureano 3.00 8.00
FTRT Rowdy Tellez 2.50 6.00
FTTT Touki Toussaint 2.00 5.00
FTVG Vladimir Guerrero Jr. 10.00 25.00
FTWA Willy Adames 1.50 4.00
FTYK Yusei Kikuchi 2.50 6.00

2019 Topps High Tek Future TEK Orange
*ORANGE: .6X TO 1.5X BASIC
STATED ODDS 1:135 HOBBY
STATED PRINT RUN 25 SER.#'d SETS
FTKT Kyle Tucker 12.00 30.00
FTRL Ramon Laureano 8.00 20.00

2019 Topps High Tek Future TEK Autographs
STATED ODDS 1:99 HOBBY
STATED PRINT RUN 50 SER.#'d SETS
EXCHANGE DEADLINE 10/31/2021
FTEJ Eloy Jimenez 20.00 50.00
FTJS Justus Sheffield 6.00 15.00
FTRT Rowdy Tellez 6.00 15.00
FTVG Vladimir Guerrero Jr. 60.00 150.00

2019 Topps High Tek PortraiTEK
STATED ODDS 1:49 HOBBY
STATED PRINT RUN 50 SER.#'d SETS
*ORANGE/25: .5X TO 1.2X BASIC
PTBH Bryce Harper 10.00 25.00
PTCR Cal Ripken Jr. 15.00 40.00
PTCS Chris Sale 3.00 8.00
PTCY Christian Yelich 8.00 20.00
PTDJ Derek Jeter 15.00 40.00
PTDO David Ortiz 3.00 8.00
PTFL Francisco Lindor 6.00 15.00
PTFT Frank Thomas 6.00 15.00
PTI Ichiro 6.00 15.00
PTJD Jacob deGrom 3.00 8.00
PTJS Juan Soto 10.00 25.00
PTKG Ken Griffey Jr. 30.00 80.00
PTMA Miguel Andujar 3.00 8.00
PTMM Manny Machado 3.00 8.00
PTMT Mike Trout 15.00 40.00
PTPG Paul Goldschmidt 3.00 8.00
PTRA Ronald Acuna Jr. 15.00 40.00
PTRD Rafael Devers 4.00 10.00
PTRJ Randy Johnson 3.00 8.00
PTSO Shohei Ohtani 4.00 10.00
PTSS Sammy Sosa 3.00 8.00

2019 Topps High Tek PortraiTEK Orange
*ORANGE: .5X TO 1.2X BASIC
STATED ODDS 1:96 HOBBY
STATED PRINT RUN 25 SER.#'d SETS
PTDJ Derek Jeter 30.00 80.00
PTFT Frank Thomas 15.00 40.00
PTI Ichiro 10.00 25.00
PTMT Mike Trout 25.00 60.00
PTSS Sammy Sosa 4.00 10.00

2019 Topps High Tek PortraiTEK Autographs
STATED ODDS 1:56 HOBBY
PRINT RUNS B/WN 25-99 COPIES PER
EXCHANGE DEADLINE 10/31/2021
*BLACK: .4X TO 1X p/r 60-70
PTBH Bryce Harper/25 75.00 200.00
PTCR Cal Ripken Jr./60 30.00 80.00
PTCS Chris Sale/70 6.00 15.00
PTCY Christian Yelich EXCH 30.00 80.00
PTDO David Ortiz/60 20.00 50.00
PTFL Francisco Lindor EXCH 20.00 50.00
PTFT Frank Thomas/65 30.00 80.00
PTI Ichiro/25 100.00 250.00
PTJS Juan Soto/70 50.00 120.00
PTMA Miguel Andujar/70 10.00 25.00
PTMT Mike Trout/25 200.00 500.00
PTPG Paul Goldschmidt/65 15.00 40.00
PTRA Ronald Acuna Jr./70 50.00 120.00
PTRD Rafael Devers/70 15.00 40.00
PTRJ Randy Johnson/60 25.00 60.00
PTSO Shohei Ohtani/25 100.00 250.00

2019 Topps High Tek ReflecTEK
STATED ODDS 1:202 HOBBY
STATED PRINT RUN 50 SER.#'d SETS
RTCR Cal Ripken Jr. 10.00 25.00
RTDJ Derek Jeter 15.00 40.00
RTKG Ken Griffey Jr. 30.00 80.00
RTMR Mariano Rivera 10.00 25.00
RTPM David Ortiz 3.00 8.00

2019 Topps High Tek ReflecTEK Autographs
STATED ODDS 1:393 HOBBY
PRINT RUNS B/WN 25-35 COPIES PER
EXCHANGE DEADLINE 10/31/2021
RTDO David Ortiz/35 25.00 60.00
RTKG Ken Griffey Jr./25 150.00 400.00

2019 Topps High Tek Autographs
STATED ODDS 1 PER HOBBY
EXCHANGE DEADLINE 10/31/2021
HTAAG Aramis Garcia 4.00 10.00
HTAAJ Andruw Jones 10.00 25.00
HTAAJU Aaron Judge 50.00 120.00
HTAAM Austin Meadows 5.00 12.00
HTAAR Anthony Rizzo 15.00 40.00
HTABB Byron Buxton 3.00 8.00
HTABH Bryce Harper 75.00 200.00
HTABK Brad Keller 2.50 6.00
HTABL Brandon Lowe 6.00 15.00
HTABT Blake Treinen 2.50 6.00
HTABW Bryse Wilson 8.00 20.00
HTACC Carlos Carrasco 2.50 6.00
HTACK Carter Kieboom 10.00 25.00
HTACT Cole Tucker 4.00 10.00
HTADH Darwinzon Hernandez 2.50 6.00
HTADS DJ Stewart 3.00 8.00
HTAEJ Eloy Jimenez 15.00 40.00
HTAEL Elvis Luciano 4.00 10.00
HTAEM Edgar Martinez 6.00 15.00
HTAFT Fernando Tatis Jr. EXCH 75.00 200.00
HTAFV Framber Valdez 8.00 20.00
HTAHM Hideki Matsui 30.00 80.00
HTAI Ichiro 100.00 250.00
HTAJC Jose Canseco 8.00 20.00
HTAJDA Johnny Damon 5.00 12.00
HTAJDU Jon Duplantier 2.50 6.00
HTAJG Juan Gonzalez 5.00 12.00
HTAJM Jose Martinez 2.50 6.00
HTAJP Jorge Posada 8.00 20.00
HTAJS Justus Sheffield 4.00 10.00
HTAJSM John Smoltz 10.00 25.00
HTAJSO Juan Soto 50.00 120.00
HTAKB Kris Bryant 30.00 80.00
HTAKH Keston Hiura 15.00 40.00
HTAKN Kevin Newman 4.00 10.00
HTAKS Kyle Schwarber 6.00 15.00
HTAKW Kyle Wright 10.00 25.00
HTALM Lance McCullers Jr. 4.00 10.00
HTALT Lane Thomas 4.00 10.00
HTALV Luke Voit 15.00 40.00
HTAMA Miguel Andujar 10.00 25.00
HTAMC Miguel Cabrera 20.00 50.00
HTAMF Mike Foltynewicz 4.00 10.00
HTAMK Merrill Kelly 2.50 6.00
HTAMMU Max Muncy 6.00 15.00
HTAMT Mike Trout 150.00 400.00
HTANL Nate Lowe EXCH 3.00 8.00
HTANM Nick Margevicius 2.50 6.00
HTANR Nolan Ryan 50.00 120.00
HTAOA Ozzie Albies 10.00 25.00
HTAPC Patrick Corbin 3.00 8.00
HTAPD Paul DeJong 4.00 10.00
HTAPG Paul Goldschmidt 15.00 40.00
HTARA Ronald Acuna Jr. 50.00 120.00
HTARAN Rick Ankiel 4.00 10.00
HTARC Roger Clemens 25.00 60.00
HTARD Rafael Devers 12.00 30.00
HTARH Rickey Henderson 25.00 60.00
HTARJ Randy Johnson 40.00 100.00
HTARM Reese McGuire 4.00 10.00
HTART Rowdy Tellez 4.00 10.00
HTASB Skye Bolt 3.00 8.00
HTASK Sandy Koufax 100.00 250.00
HTASKI Scott Kingery 4.00 10.00
HTASO Shohei Ohtani 60.00 150.00
HTATE Thairo Estrada 6.00 15.00
HTATM Tino Martinez 8.00 20.00
HTATP Thomas Pannone 4.00 10.00
HTATT Touki Toussaint 3.00 8.00
HTATTH Trent Thornton 2.50 6.00
HTATW Taylor Ward 2.50 6.00
HTAVG Vladimir Guerrero Jr. 40.00 100.00

2019 Topps High Tek Autographs Black
*BLACK: .5X TO 1.2X BASIC
STATED ODDS 1:14 HOBBY
STATED PRINT RUN 50 SER.#'d SETS
EXCHANGE DEADLINE 10/31/2021
HTAEM Edgar Martinez 12.00 30.00
HTAFL Francisco Lindor EXCH 15.00 40.00
HTAFT Fernando Tatis Jr. EXCH 150.00 400.00
HTAJC Jose Canseco 12.00 30.00
HTAJP Jorge Posada 15.00 40.00
HTALM Lance McCullers Jr. 6.00 15.00
HTANS Nick Senzel EXCH 20.00 50.00
HTAPA Pete Alonso EXCH 100.00 250.00

2019 Topps High Tek Autographs Orange
*ORANGE: .6X TO 1.5X BASIC
STATED ODDS 1:28 HOBBY
STATED PRINT RUN 25 SER.#'d SETS
EXCHANGE DEADLINE 10/31/2021
HTAEJ Eloy Jimenez 30.00 80.00
HTAEM Edgar Martinez 15.00 40.00
HTAFT Fernando Tatis Jr. EXCH 250.00 600.00
HTAJC Jose Canseco 10.00 25.00
HTAJDA Johnny Damon 10.00 25.00
HTAJG Juan Gonzalez 10.00 25.00
HTAJP Jorge Posada 20.00 50.00
HTAKH Keston Hiura 40.00 100.00
HTALM Lance McCullers Jr. 8.00 20.00
HTANS Nick Senzel EXCH 40.00 100.00
HTAPA Pete Alonso EXCH 125.00 300.00
HTAXB Xander Bogaerts 15.00 40.00

2019 Topps High Tek Autographs Pink
*PINK: .5X TO 1.2X BASIC
STATED ODDS 1:11 HOBBY
STATED PRINT RUN 75 SER.#'d SETS
EXCHANGE DEADLINE 10/31/2021
HTAEM Edgar Martinez 12.00 30.00
HTALM Lance McCullers Jr. 6.00 15.00

2019 Topps High Tek Autographs Purple
*PURPLE: .5X TO 1.2X BASIC
STATED ODDS 1:9 HOBBY
STATED PRINT RUN 99 SER.#'d SETS
EXCHANGE DEADLINE 10/31/2021
HTALM Lance McCullers Jr. 6.00 15.00

2017 Topps Inception
COMP.SET w/o AU's (100) 75.00 200.00
AU RC PRINT RUNS B/WN 149-299 COPIES PER
PRINTING PLATE ODDS 1:106 HOBBY
PLATE PRINT RUN 1 SET PER COLOR
BLACK-CYAN-MAGENTA-YELLOW ISSUED
NO PLATE PRICING DUE TO SCARCITY
EXCHANGE DEADLINE 4/30/2019
1 Mike Trout 4.00 10.00
2 Jose Altuve .60 1.50
3 Mookie Betts 1.25 3.00
4 Nolan Arenado 1.00 2.50
5 Paul Goldschmidt .75 2.00
6 Manny Machado .75 2.00
7 Anthony Rizzo 1.25 3.00
8 Josh Donaldson .60 1.50
9 Bryce Harper 1.25 3.00
10 Clayton Kershaw 1.50 4.00
11 Xander Bogaerts .75 2.00
12 Carlos Correa .75 2.00
13 Chris Sale .75 2.00
14 Starling Marte .60 1.50
15 Francisco Lindor .75 2.00
16 Wil Myers .50 1.25
17 Brian Dozier .75 2.00
18 Jake Arrieta .60 1.50
19 Carlos Gonzalez .60 1.50
20 Noah Syndergaard .60 1.50
21 Daniel Murphy .60 1.50
22 Christian Yelich 1.00 2.50
23 J.D. Martinez .75 2.00
24 Jacob deGrom .75 2.00
25 Stephen Strasburg .75 2.00
26 George Springer .60 1.50
27 Jose Abreu .75 2.00
28 A.J. Pollock .50 1.25
29 Dee Gordon .50 1.25
30 Rougned Odor .60 1.50
31 Billy Hamilton .60 1.50
32 Yu Darvish .75 2.00
33 Dellin Betances .60 1.50
34 Buster Posey 1.00 2.50
35 Maikel Franco .60 1.50
36 Giancarlo Stanton .75 2.00
37 Andrew McCutchen .75 2.00
38 Kris Bryant 1.00 2.50
39 Joey Votto .75 2.00
40 Miguel Cabrera .75 2.00
41 Freddie Freeman 1.00 2.50
42 Julio Urias .75 2.00
43 Gregory Polanco .60 1.50
44 Chris Archer .50 1.25
45 Carlos Martinez .60 1.50
46 Jonathan Villar .50 1.25
47 Kyle Hendricks .75 2.00
48 Jean Segura .60 1.50
49 Matt Harvey .60 1.50
50 Gerrit Cole .75 2.00
51 Jackie Bradley Jr. .75 2.00
52 Masahiro Tanaka .60 1.50
53 Marcell Ozuna .75 2.00
54 Rick Porcello .60 1.50
55 Randal Grichuk .50 1.25
56 Joc Pederson .60 1.50
57 Willson Contreras .75 2.00
58 Gary Sanchez .75 2.00
59 Corey Seager .75 2.00
60 Byron Buxton .60 1.50
61 Javier Baez 1.00 2.50
62 Max Scherzer .75 2.00
63 Robinson Cano .60 1.50
64 Kyle Seager .50 1.25
65 Yoenis Cespedes .75 2.00
66 Jason Kipnis .60 1.50
67 Aaron Sanchez .60 1.50
68 Lucas Giolito .60 1.50
69 Michael Conforto .60 1.50
70 Marcus Stroman .60 1.50
71 Felix Hernandez .60 1.50
72 Kenta Maeda .60 1.50
73 Lance McCullers .50 1.25
74 Danny Duffy .50 1.25
75 Sonny Gray .60 1.50
76 Yasmany Tomas .50 1.25
77 Kyle Schwarber .75 2.00
78 Jon Gray .50 1.25
79 Jameson Taillon .60 1.50
80 Carlos Rodon .60 1.50
81 Miguel Sano .60 1.50
82 Luis Severino .60 1.50
83 Trevor Story .75 2.00
84 Trea Turner .60 1.50
85 Stephen Piscotty .60 1.50
86 Aledmys Diaz .60 1.50
87 Tyler Naquin .50 1.25
88 Nomar Mazara .50 1.25
89 Addison Russell .75 2.00
90 Aaron Nola .60 1.50
91 Jake Lamb .60 1.50
92 Michael Fulmer .50 1.25
93 Steven Matz .50 1.25
94 Yasiel Puig .75 2.00
95 Jurickson Profar .60 1.50
96 Vince Velasquez .50 1.25
97 Blake Snell .60 1.50
98 A.J. Reed .50 1.25
99 David Price .60 1.50
100 Eric Hosmer .60 1.50
101 Yoan Moncada AU/149 RC 25.00 60.00
102 Orlando Arcia AU/249 RC 4.00 10.00
103 Dansby Swanson AU/199 RC 12.00 30.00
104 Alex Bregman AU/199 RC 25.00 60.00
105 Yulieski Gurriel AU/199 RC 8.00 20.00
106 Andrew Benintendi AU/199 RC 30.00 80.00
107 Jose De Leon AU/199 RC 3.00 8.00
108 Hunter Dozier AU/199 RC 6.00 15.00
109 Hunter Renfroe AU/199 RC 4.00 10.00
110 Jake Thompson AU/299 RC 3.00 8.00
111 Jorge Alfaro AU/199 RC 4.00 10.00
112 Aaron Judge AU/199 RC 100.00 250.00
114 David Dahl AU/199 RC 4.00 15.00
115 Alex Reyes AU/199 RC 4.00 10.00
116 JaCoby Jones AU/199 RC 4.00 10.00
117 Manny Margot AU/249 RC 5.00 12.00
118 Luke Weaver AU/249 RC 4.00 10.00
120 Raimel Tapia AU/199 RC 4.00 10.00
121 Braden Shipley AU/249 RC 3.00 8.00
122 Reynaldo Lopez AU/249 RC 3.00 8.00
123 Joe Musgrove AU/299 RC 3.00 8.00
124 Teoscar Hernandez AU/299 RC 10.00 25.00
125 Jharel Cotton AU/299 RC 3.00 8.00
127 Dan Vogelbach AU/249 RC 5.00 12.00
128 Ty Blach AU/299 RC 5.00 12.00
129 Matt Olson AU/299 RC 5.00 12.00
130 Rob Zastryzny AU/299 RC 3.00 8.00
131 Ryon Healy AU/299 RC 5.00 12.00
132 Robert Gsellman AU/299 RC 3.00 8.00
134 Trey Mancini AU/299 RC 10.00 25.00
135 Carson Fulmer AU/199 RC 5.00 12.00
136 Bruce Maxwell AU/299 RC 3.00 8.00
137 Tyler Austin AU/299 RC 5.00 12.00
138 Matt Strahm AU/299 RC 4.00 10.00
139 German Marquez AU/299 RC 5.00 12.00
140 Seth Lugo AU/299 RC 3.00 8.00
141 Renato Nunez AU/299 RC 6.00 15.00
142 Donnie Hart AU/299 RC 4.00 10.00
145 Chad Pinder AU/299 RC 4.00 10.00

2017 Topps Inception Blue
*BLUE 1-100: 3X TO 8X BASIC
*BLUE 101-145: .75X TO 2X BASIC
1-100 STATED ODDS 1:17 HOBBY
101-145 STATED ODDS 1:33 HOBBY
STATED PRINT RUN 25 SER.#'d SETS
EXCHANGE DEADLINE 4/30/2019
1 Mike Trout 30.00 80.00
38 Kris Bryant 30.00 80.00

2017 Topps Inception Green
*GREEN: .5X TO 1.2X BASIC
RANDOM INSERTS IN PACKS

2017 Topps Inception Magenta
*MAGENTA 1-100: 1.5X TO 4X BASIC
*MAGENTA 101-145: .5X TO 1.2X BASIC
1-100 STATED ODDS 1:5 HOBBY
101-145 STATED ODDS 1:9 HOBBY
STATED PRINT RUN 99 SER.#'d SETS
EXCHANGE DEADLINE 4/30/2019

2017 Topps Inception Orange
*ORANGE 1-100: 2.5X TO 6X BASIC
*ORANGE 101-145: .6X TO 1.5X BASIC
1-100 STATED ODDS 1:9 HOBBY
101-145 STATED ODDS 1:17 HOBBY
STATED PRINT RUN 50 SER.#'d SETS
EXCHANGE DEADLINE 4/30/2019
1 Mike Trout 25.00 60.00
38 Kris Bryant 25.00 60.00

2017 Topps Inception Purple
*PURPLE: 1.2X TO 3X BASIC
STATED ODDS 1:3 HOBBY
STATED PRINT RUN 150 SER.#'d SETS

2017 Topps Inception Red
*RED 1-100: 2X TO 5X BASIC
*RED 101-145: .5X TO 1.2X BASIC
1-100 STATED ODDS 1:6 HOBBY
101-145 STATED ODDS 1:11 HOBBY
STATED PRINT RUN 75 SER.#'d SETS
EXCHANGE DEADLINE 4/30/2019

2017 Topps Inception Autograph Jumbo Patches
STATED ODDS 1:25 HOBBY
PRINT RUNS B/WN 30-75 COPIES PER
EXCHANGE DEADLINE 4/30/2019
*ORANGE/25: .5X TO 1.2X BASIC
IAJAB Andrew Benintendi
IAJABR Alex Bregman/75 25.00 60.00
IAJAD Aledmys Diaz/75 12.00 30.00
IAJAJ Aaron Judge/45 200.00 400.00
IAJAR Alex Reyes/75 12.00 30.00
IAJCC Carlos Correa/50 30.00 80.00
IAJCF Carson Fulmer/30 10.00 25.00
IAJCS Corey Seager/50 40.00 100.00
IAJDD David Dahl/75 12.00 30.00
IAJDS Dansby Swanson/75 20.00 50.00
IAJFL Francisco Lindor/50 50.00 120.00
IAJHR Hunter Renfroe/75 15.00 40.00
IAJJC Jharel Cotton/75 10.00 25.00
IAJJM Joe Musgrove/75 10.00 25.00
IAJJT Jake Thompson/75 10.00 25.00
IAJJU Julio Urias/75 25.00 60.00
IAJKS Kyle Schwarber/75 30.00 80.00
IAJLW Luke Weaver/75 12.00 30.00
IAJMM Manny Machado/50 50.00 120.00
IAJMT Mike Trout/50 150.00 400.00
IAJNS Noah Syndergaard/75 40.00 100.00
IAJRH Ryon Healy/75 12.00 30.00
IAJTG Tyler Glasnow/75 12.00 30.00
IAJTT Trea Turner/75 12.00 30.00
IAJYG Yulieski Gurriel/75 15.00 40.00
IAJYM Yoan Moncada

2017 Topps Inception Autograph Patches
STATED ODDS 1:7 HOBBY
PRINT RUNS B/WN 50-199 COPIES PER
EXCHANGE DEADLINE 4/30/20109
*MAGENTA/50: .6X TO 1.5X BASIC
*RED/25: .75X TO 2X BASIC
IAPAB Andrew Benintendi/199 30.00 80.00
IAPABR Alex Bregman/199 20.00 50.00
IAPAD Aledmys Diaz/199 4.00 10.00
IAPAJ Aaron Judge/199 75.00 200.00
IAPAN Aaron Nola/199 15.00 40.00
IAPARE Alex Reyes/199 6.00 15.00
IAPBSN Blake Snell/199 5.00 12.00
IAPCC Carlos Correa/50 30.00 80.00
IAPCF Carson Fulmer/199 4.00 10.00
IAPCS Corey Seager/50 40.00 100.00
IAPDD David Dahl/199 5.00 12.00
IAPDS Dansby Swanson/149 25.00 60.00
IAPFL Francisco Lindor/149 15.00 40.00
IAPHR Hunter Renfroe/149 6.00 15.00
IAPJA Jorge Alfaro/199 6.00 15.00
IAPJC Jharel Cotton/199 4.00 10.00
IAPJM Joe Musgrove/199 4.00 10.00
IAPJT Jameson Taillon/199 8.00 20.00
IAPJU Julio Urias/199 8.00 20.00
IAPKS Kyle Schwarber EXCH 30.00 80.00
IAPLS Luis Severino/199 10.00 25.00
IAPLW Luke Weaver/199 5.00 12.00
IAPMM Manny Machado/50 30.00 80.00
IAPMS Miguel Sano EXCH 20.00 50.00
IAPMT Mike Trout/50 200.00 400.00
IAPNS Noah Syndergaard/149 10.00 25.00
IAPRG Robert Gsellman EXCH 6.00 15.00
IAPRH Ryon Healy/199 5.00 12.00
IAPSM Steven Matz/199 5.00 12.00
IAPSP Stephen Piscotty/199 5.00 12.00
IAPTA Tim Anderson/199 6.00 15.00
IAPTAU Tyler Austin/199 8.00 20.00
IAPTG Tyler Glasnow/199 15.00 40.00
IAPTTU Trea Turner/199 12.00 30.00
IAPWC Willson Contreras/199 12.00 30.00
IAPYG Yulieski Gurriel/149 10.00 25.00
IAPYM Yoan Moncada/65 30.00 80.00

2017 Topps Inception Legendary Debut Autographs
STATED ODDS 1:138 HOBBY
PRINT RUNS B/WN 10-35 COPIES PER
NO PRICING ON QTY 15 OR LESS
EXCHANGE DEADLINE 4/30/2019
LDABH Bryce Harper/10 50.00 110.00
LDABP Buster Posey/10 60.00 150.00
LDACC Carlos Correa/15 30.00 80.00
LDACS Chris Sale/35 20.00 50.00
LDADP Dustin Pedroia/20 25.00 60.00
LDAFF Freddie Freeman/20 40.00 100.00
LDAFL Francisco Lindor EXCH 30.00 80.00
LDAJA Jose Altuve/35 25.00 60.00
LDAKB Kris Bryant/15
LDAKS Kyle Schwarber EXCH 20.00 50.00
LDAMM Manny Machado/25 50.00 120.00
LDANS Noah Syndergaard/35 30.00 80.00
LDARB Ryan Braun/20 12.00 30.00

2017 Topps Inception Silver Signings
STATED ODDS 1:23 HOBBY
PRINT RUNS B/WN 10-99 COPIES PER
NO PRICING ON QTY 10
EXCHANGE DEADLINE 4/30/20109
*GOLD/25: .5X TO 1.2X BASIC
SSAB Andrew Benintendi/99 30.00 80.00
SSABR Alex Bregman/75 25.00 60.00
SSAD Aledmys Diaz/99 10.00 25.00
SSAJ Aaron Judge/99 200.00 400.00
SSAR Alex Reyes/99 12.00 30.00
SSARU Addison Russell/50 12.00 30.00
SSBH Bryce Harper EXCH
SSCC Carlos Correa EXCH
SSCS Corey Seager/20 75.00 200.00
SSDD David Dahl/99 8.00 20.00
SSDS Dansby Swanson/75 50.00 120.00
SSFL Francisco Lindor/75 30.00 80.00
SSHR Hunter Renfroe/75 12.00 30.00
SSJC Jharel Cotton/50 6.00 15.00
SSJD Jose De Leon/75 6.00 15.00
SSJG Jon Gray/50 10.00 25.00
SSJT Jameson Taillon/50 12.00 30.00
SSJTH Jake Thompson/75 6.00 15.00
SSJU Julio Urias EXCH 15.00 40.00
SSKB Kris Bryant EXCH
SSKS Kyle Schwarber EXCH 10.00 25.00
SSLW Luke Weaver/99 10.00 25.00
SSMC Manny Machado/20
SSMM Manny Margot/50 6.00 15.00
SSMS Miguel Sano EXCH 8.00 20.00
SSNM Nomar Mazara/50 12.00 30.00
SSNS Noah Syndergaard EXCH 25.00 60.00
SSTG Tyler Glasnow EXCH 8.00 20.00
SSTS Trevor Story/99 10.00 25.00
SSTT Trea Turner/99 15.00 40.00
SSYG Yulieski Gurriel/75 10.00 25.00
SSYM Yoan Moncada/25

2017 Topps Inception Stars Autographs
RANDOM INSERTS IN PACKS
PRINT RUNS B/WN 15-299 COPIES PER
NO PRICING ON QTY 15
EXCHANGE DEADLINE 4/30/20109
BSAAD Aledmys Diaz
BSAAN Aaron Nola/75 5.00 12.00
BSAARU Addison Russell
BSABH Bryce Harper EXCH
BSACC Carlos Correa EXCH
BSACS Corey Seager/50 60.00 150.00
BSAJBA Javier Baez EXCH
BSAJT Jameson Taillon EXCH 10.00 25.00
BSAJU Julio Urias EXCH 10.00 25.00
BSAKB Kris Bryant/25 125.00 250.00
BSAKG Ken Giles/199 4.00 10.00
BSAKS Kyle Schwarber EXCH 12.00 30.00
BSALG Lucas Giolito/299 5.00 12.00
BSALS Luis Severino/299 10.00 25.00
BSAMFU Michael Fulmer/75
BSAMM Manny Machado/50 20.00 50.00
BSAMSA Miguel Sano/75 8.00 20.00
BSANS Noah Syndergaard EXCH 15.00 40.00
BSASM Steven Matz/75 5.00 12.00
BSATN Tyler Naquin/75 4.00 10.00
BSATS Trevor Story/75
BSATTU Trea Turner/75 5.00 12.00
BSAZW Zack Wheeler

2017 Topps Inception Stars Autographs Blue
*BLUE: .5X TO 1.2X BASIC
STATED ODDS 1:33 HOBBY
STATED PRINT RUN 25 SER.#'d SETS
EXCHANGE DEADLINE 4/30/2019
BSAAD Aledmys Diaz 15.00 40.00
BSAARU Addison Russell 20.00 50.00
BSAJBA Javier Baez EXCH 25.00 60.00
BSAMFU Michael Fulmer 15.00 40.00
BSAMM Manny Machado 50.00 120.00
BSATS Trevor Story 10.00 25.00
BSAZW Zack Wheeler 6.00 15.00

2017 Topps Inception Stars Autographs Magenta
*MAGENTA: .4X TO 1X BASIC
STATED ODDS 1:9 HOBBY
STATED PRINT RUN 99 SER.#'d SETS
EXCHANGE DEADLINE 4/30/2019
BSAZW Zack Wheeler 5.00 12.00

2017 Topps Inception Stars Autographs Orange
*ORANGE: .4X TO 1X BASIC
STATED ODDS 1:17 HOBBY
STATED PRINT RUN 50 SER.#'d SETS
EXCHANGE DEADLINE 4/30/2019
BSAAD Aledmys Diaz 12.00 30.00
BSAARU Addison Russell 15.00 40.00
BSAJBA Javier Baez EXCH 20.00 50.00
BSAMFU Michael Fulmer 12.00 30.00
BSAMM Manny Machado 40.00 100.00
BSATS Trevor Story 8.00 20.00
BSAZW Zack Wheeler 5.00 12.00

2017 Topps Inception Stars Autographs Red
*RED: .4X TO 1X BASIC
STATED ODDS 1:11 HOBBY
STATED PRINT RUN 75 SER.#'d SETS
EXCHANGE DEADLINE 4/30/2019
BSAAD Aledmys Diaz 12.00 30.00
BSAARU Addison Russell 15.00 40.00
BSAMFU Michael Fulmer 12.00 30.00
BSATS Trevor Story 8.00 20.00
BSAZW Zack Wheeler 5.00 12.00

2018 Topps Inception
1 Aaron Judge 2.00 5.00
2 Luis Severino .60 1.50
3 Jack Flaherty RC 1.00 2.50
4 Noah Syndergaard .60 1.50
5 Nicky Delmonico RC .60 1.50
6 Jacob Faria .50 1.25
7 Ryan McMahon RC .75 2.00
8 Tzu-Wei Lin RC .75 2.00
9 Ryon Healy .50 1.25
10 Max Fried RC 2.50 6.00
11 Zack Greinke .60 1.50
12 Trey Mancini .60 1.50
13 Jose Berrios .60 1.50
14 Harrison Bader RC 1.00 2.50
15 Dustin Fowler RC .60 1.50
16 Andrew Stevenson RC .60 1.50
17 Bryce Harper 1.25 3.00
18 Joe Jimenez .50 1.25
19 Kenley Jansen .60 1.50
20 Sean Newcomb .60 1.50
21 Paul Blackburn RC .60 1.50
22 Garrett Cooper RC .60 1.50
23 Ichiro 1.00 2.50
24 Francisco Lindor .75 2.00
25 Victor Robles RC 1.50 4.00
26 Greg Allen RC .60 1.50
27 Anthony Banda RC .60 1.50
28 Nick Williams RC .75 2.00
29 Keon Broxton .50 1.25
30 Brett Phillips .50 1.25
31 Jonathan Schoop .50 1.25
32 Brandon Woodruff RC .75 2.00
33 Jose Altuve .60 1.50
34 Lewis Brinson .50 1.25
35 Tyler Austin .75 2.00
36 Alex Verdugo RC 1.00 2.50
37 Corey Seager .75 2.00
38 Raimel Tapia .50 1.25
39 Clayton Kershaw 1.50 4.00
40 Tyler Wade RC .75 2.00
41 Nolan Arenado 1.00 2.50
42 Dominic Smith RC .60 1.50
43 German Marquez .50 1.25
44 Freddie Freeman 1.00 2.50
45 Carlos Correa .75 2.00
46 Matt Olson .50 1.25
47 Jordan Montgomery .75 2.00
48 Austin Hays RC 1.00 2.50
49 Domingo Santana .60 1.50
50 Rafael Devers RC 2.00 5.00
51 Luiz Gohara RC .60 1.50
52 Miguel Gomez RC .60 1.50
53 Hunter Renfroe .50 1.25
54 Miguel Andujar RC 2.50 6.00
55 Andrew Benintendi .75 2.00
56 Tyler Mahle RC .75 2.00
57 Alex Bregman .75 2.00
58 Rhys Hoskins RC 2.50 6.00
59 J.D. Davis RC .75 2.00
60 Brian Anderson RC .75 2.00
61 George Springer .60 1.50
62 Walker Buehler RC 3.00 8.00
63 Adrian Beltre .75 2.00
64 Bradley Zimmer .50 1.25
65 Lucas Sims RC .60 1.50
66 Anthony Rizzo 1.25 3.00
67 Zack Granite RC .60 1.50
68 Francisco Mejia RC .75 2.00
69 Steven Souza Jr. .60 1.50
70 Chance Sisco RC .75 2.00
71 Sandy Alcantara RC .60 1.50
72 Jose Ramirez .60 1.50
73 Ozzie Albies RC 2.00 5.00
74 Billy Hamilton .60 1.50
75 Giancarlo Stanton .75 2.00
76 Cody Bellinger 1.50 4.00
77 Gary Sanchez .75 2.00
78 J.P. Crawford RC .60 1.50
79 Manny Machado .75 2.00
80 Paul DeJong .75 2.00

Jake Lamb .60 1.50
2 Jacob deGrom .75 2.00
3 Franklin Barreto .50 1.25
4 Jose Abreu .75 2.00
5 Luke Weaver .60 1.50
6 Kris Bryant 1.00 2.50
7 Willie Calhoun RC .75 2.00
8 Clint Frazier RC 1.25 3.00
9 Mike Clevinger .60 1.50
0 Mookie Betts 1.25 3.00
1 Lucas Giolito .60 1.50
2 Christian Arroyo .50 1.25
3 Josh Donaldson .60 1.50
4 Parker Bridwell RC .60 1.50
5 Erick Fedde RC .60 1.50
6 Felix Jorge RC .60 1.50
7 Manny Margot .50 1.25
8 Ian Happ .60 1.50
9 Amed Rosario RC .75 2.00
00 Mike Trout 4.00 10.00

2018 Topps Inception Magenta

MAGENTA: 1X TO 2.5X BASIC
MAGENTA RC: .75X TO 2X BASIC
TATED ODDS 1:6 HOBBY
TATED PRINT RUN 99 SER.#'d SETS
Aaron Judge 15.00 40.00
00 Mike Trout 12.00 30.00

2018 Topps Inception Orange

ORANGE: 2X TO 5X BASIC
ORANGE RC: 1.5X TO 4X BASIC
TATED ODDS 1:11 HOBBY
TATED PRINT RUN 50 SER.#'d SETS
Aaron Judge 25.00 60.00
00 Mike Trout 20.00 50.00

2018 Topps Inception Purple

PURPLE: .75X TO 2X BASIC
PURPLE RC: .6X TO 1.5X BASIC
TATED ODDS 1:4 HOBBY
TATED PRINT RUN 150 SER.#'d SETS
Aaron Judge 12.00 30.00
00 Mike Trout 10.00 25.00

2018 Topps Inception Red

*RED: 1.5X TO 4X BASIC
*RED RC: 1.2X TO 3X BASIC
TATED ODDS 1:7 HOBBY
TATED PRINT RUN 75 SER.#'d SETS
Aaron Judge 20.00 50.00
00 Mike Trout 15.00 40.00

2018 Topps Inception Blue

*BLUE: 2.5X TO 6X BASIC
*BLUE RC: 2X TO 5X BASIC
TATED ODDS 1:21 HOBBY
TATED PRINT RUN 25 SER.#'d SETS
1 Aaron Judge 30.00 80.00
100 Mike Trout 25.00 60.00

2018 Topps Inception Green

*GREEN: .6X TO 1.5X BASIC
*GREEN RC: .5X TO 1.2X BASIC
RANDOM INSERTS IN PACKS

2018 Topps Inception Jumbo Patch Autographs

STATED ODDS 1:22 HOBBY
PRINT RUNS B/WN 14-150 COPIES PER
NO PRICING ON QTY 14
EXCHANGE DEADLINE 5/31/2020
IAJAB Anthony Banda/150 8.00 20.00
IAJAH Austin Hays/123 10.00 25.00
IAJAS Andrew Stevenson/150 8.00 20.00
IAJBW Brandon Woodruff/60 10.00 25.00
IAJBZ Bradley Zimmer/99 8.00 20.00
IAJCF Clint Frazier/140 15.00 40.00
IAJCS Chance Sisco/150 10.00 25.00
IAJDF Dustin Fowler/70 12.00 30.00
IAJFM Francisco Mejia/80 12.00 30.00
IAJGD Greg Bird/99 10.00 25.00
IAJGC Garrett Cooper/150 8.00 20.00
IAJHR Hunter Renfroe/25 12.00 30.00
IAJIH Ian Happ/70 15.00 40.00
IAJJC J.P. Crawford/150 15.00 40.00
IAJJFL Jack Flaherty/40 12.00 30.00
IAJMO Matt Olson/150 10.00 25.00
IAJOA Ozzie Albies/80 60.00 150.00
IAJPD Paul DeJong/99 15.00 40.00
IAJRD Rafael Devers/99 40.00 100.00
IAJSO Shohei Ohtani/80 300.00 600.00
IAJTM Tyler Mahle/99 12.00 30.00
IAJVR Victor Robles/70 25.00 60.00
IAJZG Zack Granite/60 8.00 20.00

2018 Topps Inception Jumbo Patch Autographs Orange

*ORNGE: .6X TO 1.5X BASE p/r 40-150
*ORNGE: .4X TO 1X BASE p/r 25
STATED ODDS 1:69 HOBBY
STATED PRINT RUN 25 SER.#'d SETS
EXCHANGE DEADLINE 5/31/2020
IAJAR Amed Rosario 15.00 40.00
IAJAV Alex Verdugo 30.00 80.00
IAJFL Francisco Lindor 40.00 100.00
IAJMF Michael Fulmer 12.00 30.00
IAJMM Manny Machado 40.00 100.00
IAJMT Mike Trout 400.00 600.00
IAJSO Shohei Ohtani 400.00 800.00

2018 Topps Inception Legendary Debut Autographs

STATED ODDS 1:161 HOBBY
STATED PRINT RUN 20 SER.#'d SETS
EXCHANGE DEADLINE 5/31/2020
LDAAB Adrian Beltre 30.00 80.00
LDAAD Adam Duvall
LDAAJ Adam Jones
LDAAR Anthony Rizzo 25.00 60.00
LDAARU Addison Russell 15.00 40.00
LDACK Corey Kluber
LDACS Corey Seager 30.00 80.00
LDADJ Derek Jeter 400.00 600.00
LDADP David Price
LDAEE Edwin Encarnacion
LDAEL Evan Longoria 15.00 40.00
LDAET Eric Thames
LDAGS George Springer
LDAJD Josh Donaldson 15.00 40.00
LDAJV Joey Votto 60.00 150.00
LDAPG Paul Goldschmidt 25.00 60.00

2018 Topps Inception Patch Autographs

STATED ODDS 1:7 HOBBY
PRINT RUNS B/WN 20-299 COPIES PER
EXCHANGE DEADLINE 5/31/2020
IAPAB Anthony Banda/99 5.00 12.00
IAPAH Austin Hays/249 12.00 30.00
IAPAR Amed Rosario/122 10.00 25.00
IAPAS Andrew Stevenson/99 5.00 12.00
IAPAT Andrew Toles/199 5.00 12.00
IAPAV Alex Verdugo/109 8.00 20.00
IAPBA Brian Anderson/299 8.00 20.00
IAPBS Blake Snell/249 8.00 20.00
IAPBW Brandon Woodruff/299 6.00 15.00
IAPBZ Bradley Zimmer/199 8.00 20.00
IAPCC Carlos Correa
IAPCF Clint Frazier/249 15.00 40.00
IAPCS Corey Seager
IAPCSI Chance Sisco/249 6.00 15.00
IAPDD David Dahl/30 12.00 30.00
IAPDF Dustin Fowler/249 5.00 12.00
IAPFM Francisco Mejia/99 6.00 15.00
IAPGC Garrett Cooper/99 5.00 12.00
IAPHB Harrison Bader/249 8.00 20.00
IAPHR Hunter Renfroe
IAPIH Ian Happ/99 6.00 15.00
IAPJA Jorge Alfaro/199 8.00 20.00
IAPJC J.P. Crawford/249 10.00 25.00
IAPJFL Jack Flaherty/214 25.00 60.00
IAPKB Kris Bryant
IAPLS Lucas Sims/299 6.00 15.00
IAPLW Luke Weaver/249 6.00 15.00
IAPMA Miguel Andujar/249 25.00 60.00
IAPMF Michael Fulmer/90 10.00 25.00
IAPMG Miguel Gomez/299 6.00 15.00
IAPMM Manny Machado/65 30.00 80.00
IAPMMA Manny Margot/149 5.00 12.00
IAPMO Matt Olson/249 5.00 12.00
IAPND Nicky Delmonico/299 10.00 25.00
IAPNS Noah Syndergaard/30 20.00 50.00
IAPOA Ozzie Albies/99 30.00 80.00
IAPPD Paul DeJong/205 12.00 30.00
IAPRD Rafael Devers/205 30.00 80.00
IAPRM Ryan McMahon/199 6.00 15.00
IAPSO Shohei Ohtani/99 150.00 400.00
IAPTAN Tim Anderson/25 15.00 40.00
IAPTM Trey Mancini/249 6.00 15.00
IAPTMA Tyler Mahle/299 6.00 15.00
IAPTW Tyler Wade/99 12.00 30.00
IAPVR Victor Robles/99 12.00 30.00
IAPYM Yoan Moncada/20 15.00 40.00
IAPZG Zack Granite/299 5.00 12.00

2018 Topps Inception Patch Autographs Magenta

*MAGENTA: .4X TO 1X BASIC
STATED ODDS 1:17 HOBBY
PRINT RUNS B/WN 50-75 COPIES PER
EXCHANGE DEADLINE 5/31/2020
IAPABR Alex Bregman/75 20.00 50.00
IAPDS Dominic Smith/75 10.00 25.00
IAPFL Francisco Lindor/75 25.00 60.00
IAPKB Kris Bryant/50 75.00 200.00
IAPMT Mike Trout/75 300.00 600.00

2018 Topps Inception Patch Autographs Red

*RED: .75X TO 2X BASE p/r 50-199
*RED: .4X TO 1X BASE p/r 30
STATED ODDS 1:45 HOBBY
STATED PRINT RUN 25 SER.#'d SETS
EXCHANGE DEADLINE 5/31/2020
IAPABR Alex Bregman 40.00 100.00
IAPDS Dominic Smith 20.00 50.00
IAPFL Francisco Lindor 50.00 120.00
IAPKB Kris Bryant 125.00 300.00
IAPMT Mike Trout 400.00 800.00
IAPSO Shohei Ohtani 300.00 600.00

2018 Topps Inception Rookies and Emerging Stars Autographs

PRINT RUNS B/WN 230-299 COPIES PER
EXCHANGE DEADLINE 5/31/2020
RESAB Alex Bregman/299 20.00 50.00
RESABA Anthony Banda/230 2.50 6.00
RESAG Amir Garrett/299 2.50 6.00
RESAR Amed Rosario/230 3.00 8.00
RESAS Andrew Stevenson/230 2.50 6.00
RESAV Alex Verdugo/230 6.00 15.00
RESBM Bruce Maxwell/299 2.50 6.00
RESBP Brett Phillips/230 2.50 6.00
RESBW Brandon Woodruff/230 3.00 8.00
RESBZ Bradley Zimmer/230 3.00 8.00
RESCA Christian Arroyo/230 2.50 6.00
RESCF Clint Frazier/230 10.00 25.00
RESCFU Carson Fulmer/299 2.50 6.00
RESCS Chance Sisco/230 6.00 15.00
RESDF Dustin Fowler/230 2.50 6.00
RESFB Franklin Barreto/230 2.50 6.00
RESGA Greg Allen/230 3.00 8.00
RESGCO Garrett Cooper/230 2.50 6.00
RESGM German Marquez/230 2.50 6.00
RESHR Hunter Renfroe/230 2.50 6.00
RESIH Ian Happ/230 3.00 8.00
RESJCR J.P. Crawford/230 2.50 6.00
RESJD J.D. Davis/230 3.00 8.00
RESJF Jacob Faria/230 2.50 6.00
RESJFL Jack Flaherty/230 4.00 10.00
RESJW Jesse Winker/299 4.00 10.00
RESLB Lewis Brinson/230 2.50 6.00
RESLS Lucas Sims/230 3.00 8.00
RESLW Luke Weaver/230 3.00 8.00
RESMA Miguel Andujar/230 10.00 25.00
RESMC Mike Clevinger/230 3.00 8.00
RESMF Max Fried/230 10.00 25.00
RESMM Manny Margot/230 2.50 6.00
RESMO Matt Olson/230 5.00 12.00
RESND Nicky Delmonico/299 2.50 6.00
RESOA Ozzie Albies/230 12.00 30.00
RESPB Parker Bridwell/230 2.50 6.00
RESPBL Paul Blackburn/230 2.50 6.00
RESPD Paul DeJong/230 5.00 12.00
RESRD Rafael Devers/230 15.00 40.00
RESRG Robert Gsellman/299 2.50 6.00
RESRH Ryon Healy/230 2.50 6.00
RESRHO Rhys Hoskins/230 15.00 40.00
RESRM Ryan McMahon/230 3.00 8.00
RESRQ Roman Quinn/299 2.50 6.00
RESRT Raimel Tapia/230 2.50 6.00
RESSA Sandy Alcantara/230 4.00 10.00
RESSL Seth Lugo/299 2.50 6.00
RESSN Sean Newcomb/230 6.00 15.00
RESTA Tyler Austin/230 4.00 10.00
RESTB Ty Blach/299 2.50 6.00
RESTG Tyler Glasnow/299 2.50 6.00
RESTM Trey Mancini/230 3.00 8.00
RESTMA Tyler Mahle/230 3.00 8.00
RESTR T.J. Rivera/299 2.50 6.00
RESTW Tyler Wade/230 6.00 15.00
RESVR Victor Robles/230 10.00 25.00
RESWB Walker Buehler/230 12.00 30.00
RESYG Yulieski Gurriel/299 5.00 12.00
RESZG Zack Granite/230 2.50 6.00

2018 Topps Inception Rookies and Emerging Stars Autographs Blue

*BLUE: .75X TO 2X BASIC
STATED ODDS 1:33 HOBBY
STATED PRINT RUN 25 SER.#'d SETS
EXCHANGE DEADLINE 5/31/2020
RESAH Austin Hays 12.00 30.00
RESAJ Aaron Judge EXCH
RESDS Dominic Smith 5.00 12.00
RESHB Harrison Bader 8.00 20.00
RESJT Jake Thompson 5.00 12.00
RESYM Yoan Moncada 15.00 40.00

2018 Topps Inception Rookies and Emerging Stars Autographs Magenta

*MAGENTA: .5X TO 1.2X BASIC
STATED ODDS 1:9 HOBBY
STATED PRINT RUN 99 SER.#'d SETS
EXCHANGE DEADLINE 5/31/2020
RESAH Austin Hays 8.00 20.00
RESDS Dominic Smith 3.00 8.00
RESHB Harrison Bader 5.00 12.00
RESYM Yoan Moncada 10.00 25.00

2018 Topps Inception Rookies and Emerging Stars Autographs Orange

*ORANGE: .6X TO 1.5X BASIC
STATED ODDS 1:17 HOBBY
STATED PRINT RUN 50 SER.#'d SETS
EXCHANGE DEADLINE 5/31/2020
RESAH Austin Hays 10.00 25.00
RESAJ Aaron Judge EXCH
RESDS Dominic Smith 4.00 10.00
RESHB Harrison Bader 6.00 15.00
RESJT Jake Thompson 4.00 10.00
RESYM Yoan Moncada 12.00 30.00

2018 Topps Inception Rookies and Emerging Stars Autographs Red

*RED: .5X TO 1.2X BASIC
STATED ODDS 1:11 HOBBY
STATED PRINT RUN 75 SER.#'d SETS
EXCHANGE DEADLINE 5/31/2020
RESAH Austin Hays 8.00 20.00
RESDS Dominic Smith 3.00 8.00
RESHB Harrison Bader 5.00 12.00
RESJT Jake Thompson 3.00 8.00
RESYM Yoan Moncada 10.00 25.00

2018 Topps Inception Silver Signings

STATED ODDS 1:18 HOBBY
PRINT RUNS B/WN 25-99 COPIES PER
EXCHANGE DEADLINE 5/31/2020
*GOLD INK/25: .5X TO 1.2X BASIC
SSAB Alex Bregman/99 15.00 40.00
SSAR Amed Rosario/99 8.00 20.00
SSAV Alex Verdugo/90 20.00 50.00
SSBH Bryce Harper/25 200.00 400.00
SSBZ Bradley Zimmer/90 10.00 25.00
SSCA Christian Arroyo/99 6.00 15.00
SSCC Carlos Correa/90 25.00 60.00
SSCS Corey Seager/90 15.00 40.00
SSDF Dustin Fowler/99 6.00 15.00
SSDS Dominic Smith/90 6.00 15.00
SSFB Franklin Barreto/99 6.00 15.00
SSHB Harrison Bader/99 10.00 25.00
SSHR Hunter Renfroe/99 6.00 15.00
SSIH Ian Happ/90 20.00 50.00
SSJC J.P. Crawford
SSJF Jack Flaherty/90 10.00 25.00
SSKB Kris Bryant/90 75.00 200.00
SSLB Lewis Brinson/99 6.00 15.00
SSLW Luke Weaver/99 8.00 20.00
SSMA Miguel Andujar/99 40.00 100.00
SSMF Michael Fulmer/99 10.00 25.00
SSMM Manny Machado/90 20.00 50.00
SSMMA Manny Margot/99 6.00 15.00
SSMT Mike Trout/25 300.00 600.00
SSNS Noah Syndergaard/90 12.00 30.00
SSOA Ozzie Albies/90 20.00 50.00
SSPD Paul DeJong/90 10.00 25.00
SSRD Rafael Devers/90 15.00 40.00
SSRHO Rhys Hoskins/90 40.00 100.00
SSRM Ryan McMahon/90 8.00 20.00
SSRT Raimel Tapia/99 6.00 15.00
Signed in gold ink
SSSN Sean Newcomb/90 8.00 20.00
SSTM Trey Mancini/90 10.00 25.00
SSTW Tyler Wade/99 12.00 30.00
SSVR Victor Robles/90 15.00 40.00
SSYM Yoan Moncada/99 25.00 60.00

2019 Topps Inception

1 Mike Trout 4.00 10.00
2 Max Scherzer .75 2.00
3 Nicholas Ciuffo RC .60 1.50
4 Freddie Freeman 1.00 2.50
5 Francisco Arcia RC 1.00 2.50
6 Aaron Nola .60 1.50
7 Luis Urias RC 1.00 2.50
8 Carlos Correa .75 2.00
9 Kohl Stewart RC .75 2.00
10 Eddie Rosario .60 1.50
11 Clayton Kershaw 1.50 4.00
12 Nick Burdi RC .60 1.50
13 Khris Davis .75 2.00
14 Enyel De Los Santos RC .60 1.50
15 Michael Kopech RC 1.25 3.00
16 Bryce Harper 1.25 3.00
17 Francisco Lindor .75 2.00
18 Dawel Lugo RC 1.00 2.50
19 Daniel Poncedeleon RC 1.00 2.50
20 Cedric Mullins RC 1.00 2.50
21 Christian Yelich 1.00 2.50
22 Bryse Wilson RC .75 2.00
23 Kyle Wright RC 1.00 2.50
24 George Springer .60 1.50
25 Kyle Tucker RC 1.25 3.00
26 Javier Baez 1.00 2.50
27 Sean Reid-Foley RC .60 1.50
28 Miguel Andujar .75 2.00
29 Justin Verlander .75 2.00
30 Chris Shaw RC 1.00 2.50
31 Corey Seager .75 2.00
32 Ryan Borucki RC .60 1.50
33 Aramis Garcia RC .60 1.50
34 Mitch Haniger .60 1.50
35 Kolby Allard RC 1.00 2.50
36 Kevin Newman RC 1.00 2.50
37 Dennis Santana RC .60 1.50
38 Paul Goldschmidt .75 2.00
39 Alex Bregman .75 2.00
40 Mookie Betts 1.25 3.00
41 Blake Snell .60 1.50
42 Giancarlo Stanton .75 2.00
43 Noah Syndergaard .60 1.50
44 Rhys Hoskins 1.00 2.50
45 Trevor Richards RC .60 1.50
46 Trea Turner .60 1.50
47 Edwin Encarnacion .75 2.00
48 Kevin Kramer RC .75 2.00
49 Jonathan Loaisiga RC .75 2.00
50 Shohei Ohtani 1.00 2.50
51 Edwin Diaz .60 1.50
52 Whit Merrifield .75 2.00
53 David Fletcher RC 2.00 5.00
54 Heath Fillmyer RC .60 1.50
55 Jake Cave RC .75 2.00
56 Joey Votto .75 2.00
57 Ramon Laureano RC 1.25 3.00
58 Steven Duggar RC .75 2.00
59 Chance Adams RC .60 1.50
60 Ozzie Albies .75 2.00
61 Touki Toussaint RC .75 2.00
62 Jose Ramirez .60 1.50
63 Adolis Garcia RC .60 1.50
64 Corbin Burnes RC 1.00 2.50
65 Matt Carpenter .75 2.00
66 Jeff McNeil RC 1.50 4.00
67 Luis Severino .60 1.50
68 Pablo Lopez RC .60 1.50
69 Josh Hader .50 1.25
70 Josh Rogers RC .60 1.50
71 Jacob deGrom .75 2.00
72 Eugenio Suarez .60 1.50
73 Ray Black RC .60 1.50
74 Masahiro Tanaka .60 1.50
75 Juan Soto 2.50 6.00
76 Charlie Blackmon .75 2.00
77 Jacob Nix RC .75 2.00
78 Christin Stewart RC .75 2.00
79 Jose Altuve .60 1.50
80 Rowdy Tellez RC 1.00 2.50
81 Aaron Judge 2.00 5.00
82 Taylor Ward RC .60 1.50
83 Nolan Arenado 1.00 2.50
84 Andrew Benintendi .75 2.00
85 Brandon Lowe RC 1.00 2.50
86 Jake Bauers RC 1.00 2.50
87 Jalen Beeks RC .60 1.50
88 Gerrit Cole .75 2.00
89 Adam Cimber RC .60 1.50
90 Anthony Rizzo 1.25 3.00
91 Josh James RC 1.00 2.50
92 Chris Sale .75 2.00
93 J.D. Martinez .75 2.00
94 Justus Sheffield RC 1.00 2.50
95 Ryan O'Hearn RC .60 1.50
96 Brad Keller RC .60 1.50
97 Kris Bryant 1.00 2.50
98 Gleyber Torres 1.50 4.00
99 Danny Jansen RC .60 1.50
100 Ronald Acuna Jr. 4.00 10.00

2019 Topps Inception Blue

*BLUE: 3X TO 8X BASIC
*BLUE RC: 2.5X TO 6X BASIC
STATED ODDS 1:23 HOBBY
STATED PRINT RUN 25 SER.#'d SETS
1 Mike Trout 50.00 120.00
50 Shohei Ohtani 40.00 100.00
75 Juan Soto 25.00 60.00
81 Aaron Judge 50.00 120.00
100 Ronald Acuna Jr. 25.00 60.00

2019 Topps Inception Green

*GREEN: .6X TO 1.5X BASIC
*GREEN RC: .5X TO 1.2X BASIC
RANDOM INSERTS IN PACKS

2019 Topps Inception Magenta

*MAGENTA: 1.5X TO 4X BASIC
*MAGENTA RC: 1.2X TO 3X BASIC
STATED ODDS 1:6 HOBBY
STATED PRINT RUN 99 SER.#'d SETS

2019 Topps Inception Orange

*ORANGE: 2X TO 5X BASIC
*ORANGE RC: 1.5X TO 4X BASIC
STATED ODDS 1:12 HOBBY
STATED PRINT RUN 50 SER.#'d SETS
1 Mike Trout 30.00 80.00
75 Juan Soto 15.00 40.00
81 Aaron Judge 30.00 80.00
100 Ronald Acuna Jr. 15.00 40.00

2019 Topps Inception Purple

*PURPLE: 1.2X TO 3X BASIC
*PURPLE RC: 1X TO 2.5X BASIC
STATED ODDS 1:4 HOBBY
STATED PRINT RUN 150 SER.#'d SETS

2019 Topps Inception Red

*RED: 2X TO 5X BASIC
*RED RC: 1.5X TO 4X BASIC
STATED ODDS 1:8 HOBBY
STATED PRINT RUN 75 SER.#'d SETS

2019 Topps Inception Jumbo Patch Autographs

STATED ODDS 1:22 HOBBY
PRINT RUNS B/WN 15-125 COPIES PER
NO PRICING ON QTY 15
EXCHANGE DEADLINE 2/28/2021
*ORANGE/25: .6X TO1.5X BASIC
IAJAB Alex Bregman EXCH 40.00 100.00
IAJAJ Aaron Judge/20 125.00 300.00
IAJAM Austin Meadows/110 10.00 25.00
IAJBK Brad Keller/125 12.00 30.00
IAJBN Brandon Nimmo/110 10.00 25.00
IAJBW Bryse Wilson/125 10.00 25.00
IAJCA Chance Adams/99 8.00 20.00
IAJCB Corbin Burnes/99 12.00 30.00
IAJCM Cedric Mullins/99 12.00 30.00
IAJCS Chris Shaw/99 12.00 30.00
IAJJA Jesus Aguilar/110 8.00 20.00
IAJJB Jake Bauers/99 12.00 30.00
IAJJSH Justus Sheffield/99 12.00 30.00
IAJKA Kolby Allard/125 12.00 30.00
IAJKT Kyle Tucker/99 15.00 40.00
IAJKW Kyle Wright/125 12.00 30.00
IAJLU Luis Urias/99 12.00 30.00
IAJMH Mitch Haniger/110 12.00 30.00
IAJMK Michael Kopech/99 20.00 50.00
IAJMM Miles Mikolas/110 10.00 25.00
IAJOA Ozzie Albies/40 30.00 80.00
IAJRAJ Ronald Acuna Jr./40 75.00 200.00
IAJRH Rhys Hoskins/40 40.00 100.00
IAJROH Ryan O'Hearn/125 8.00 20.00
IAJRT Rowdy Tellez/99 10.00 25.00
IAJSO Shohei Ohtani/125 125.00 300.00

2019 Topps Inception Legendary Debut Autographs

STATED ODDS 1:226 HOBBY
STATED PRINT RUN 20 SER.#'d SETS
EXCHANGE DEADLINE 2/28/2021
LDAAJ Aaron Judge
LDAAM Andrew McCutchen 60.00 150.00
LDAAP Andy Pettitte 60.00 150.00
LDAAPU Albert Pujols
LDADG Didi Gregorius 12.00 30.00
LDADO David Ortiz
LDAER Eddie Rosario 12.00 30.00
LDAHM Hideki Matsui
LDAJA Jesus Aguilar
LDAJD Jacob deGrom 30.00 80.00
LDAJU Justin Upton 12.00 30.00
LDAKD Khris Davis 15.00 40.00
LDAMH Mitch Haniger 25.00 60.00
LDASO Shohei Ohtani
LDATH Torii Hunter 25.00 60.00
LDATS Trevor Story 25.00 60.00
LDAVG Yadier Molina 50.00 120.00

2019 Topps Inception Mystery Redemption Autographs

RANDOM INSERTS IN PACKS
EXCHANGE DEADLINE 2/28/2021
*ORANGE: .5X TO 1.2X BASIC
*BLUE: .6X TO 1.5X BASIC

2019 Topps Inception Patch Autographs

STATED ODDS 1:7 HOBBY
PRINT RUNS B/WN 15-199 COPIES PER
EXCHANGE DEADLINE 2/28/2021
IAPAG Aramis Garcia/199 5.00 12.00
IAPAJ Aaron Judge/30 100.00 250.00
IAPAM Austin Meadows EXCH 10.00 25.00
IAPBK Brad Keller/199 10.00 25.00
IAPBL Brandon Lowe/199 10.00 25.00
IAPBT Blake Treinen/199 10.00 25.00
IAPBW Bryse Wilson/199 10.00 25.00
IAPCB Corbin Burnes/199 8.00 20.00
IAPCM Cedric Mullins/100 10.00 25.00
IAPCS Chris Shaw/199 8.00 20.00
IAPDC Dylan Cozens/199 5.00 12.00
IAPDF David Fletcher/199 15.00 40.00
IAPDH Dakota Hudson/199 10.00 25.00
IAPDJ Danny Jansen/199 10.00 25.00
IAPDL Dawel Lugo/199 8.00 20.00
IAPDS Dennis Santana/199 5.00 12.00
IAPHD Hunter Dozier/199 5.00 12.00
IAPHF Heath Fillmyer/199 5.00 12.00
IAPIKF Isiah Kiner-Falefa/199 5.00 12.00
IAPJA Jesus Aguilar/199 5.00 12.00
IAPJB Jake Bauers/199 8.00 20.00
IAPJM Jeff McNeil/199 20.00 50.00
IAPJN Jacob Nix/199 6.00 15.00
IAPJSH Justus Sheffield/160 8.00 20.00
IAPKA Kolby Allard/199 8.00 20.00
IAPKT Kyle Tucker/199 10.00 25.00
IAPKWR Kyle Wright/199 8.00 20.00
IAPLGJ Lourdes Gurriel Jr./199 8.00 20.00
IAPLU Luis Urias/199 8.00 20.00
IAPMH Mitch Haniger/50 15.00 40.00
IAPMK Michael Kopech/75 12.00 30.00
IAPMM Miles Mikolas/150 8.00 20.00
IAPNK Nick Kingham/199 5.00 12.00
IAPOA Ozzie Albies/99 20.00 50.00
IAPRAJ Ronald Acuna Jr./199 75.00 200.00
IAPRB Ryan Borucki/199 10.00 25.00
IAPRH Rhys Hoskins/199 30.00 80.00
IAPRL Ramon Laureano/199 15.00 40.00
IAPROH Ryan O'Hearn/199 5.00 12.00
IAPRT Rowdy Tellez/199 8.00 20.00
IAPSD Steven Duggar/199 6.00 15.00
IAPSK Scott Kingery/199 6.00 15.00
IAPSO Shohei Ohtani/50 100.00 250.00
IAPTA Tim Anderson/199 8.00 20.00
IAPTM Tyler Mahle/199 5.00 12.00
IAPTP Tommy Pham/199 5.00 12.00
IAPTW Taylor Ward/199 5.00 12.00

2019 Topps Inception Patch Autographs Magenta

*MAGENTA: .4X TO 1X BASIC
STATED ODDS 1:17 HOBBY
STATED PRINT RUN 75 SER.#'d SETS
EXCHANGE DEADLINE 2/28/2021
IAPBN Brandon Nimmo 10.00 25.00
IAPCA Chance Adams 10.00 25.00

2019 Topps Inception Patch Autographs Red

*RED: .75X TO 2X BASE p/r 50-199
*RED: .4X TO 1X BASE p/r 30
STATED ODDS 1:45 HOBBY
STATED PRINT RUN 25 SER.#'d SETS
EXCHANGE DEADLINE 2/28/2021
IAPAB Alex Bregman EXCH 40.00 100.00
IAPBN Brandon Nimmo 20.00 50.00
IAPCA Chance Adams 20.00 50.00

2019 Topps Inception Rookie and Emerging Stars Autographs

PRINT RUNS B/WN 30-250 COPIES PER
EXCHANGE DEADLINE 2/28/2021
*MAGENTA/99: .5X TO 1.2X BASIC
*RED/75: .5X TO 1.2X BASIC
*ORANGE/50: .6X TO 1.5X BASIC
*BLUE/25: .75X TO 2X p/r 60-250
*BLUE/25: .5X TO 1.2X p/r 30
RESAC Adam Cimber/250 2.50 6.00
RESAG Adolis Garcia/225 4.00 10.00
RESAGA Aramis Garcia/225 2.50 6.00
RESAJ Aaron Judge/30 100.00 250.00
RESAM Austin Meadows/200 4.00 10.00
RESAR Amed Rosario/125 6.00 15.00
RESBA Brian Anderson/225 2.50 6.00
RESBK Brad Keller/200 8.00 20.00
RESBKE Brad Keller/200 8.00 20.00
RESBL Brandon Lowe/200 12.00 30.00
RESBW Bryse Wilson/200 8.00 20.00
RESCA Chance Adams/225 5.00 12.00
RESCB Corbin Burnes/225 5.00 12.00
RESCK Carson Kelly/200 2.50 6.00
RESCM Cedric Mullins/200 6.00 15.00
RESCS Christin Stewart/200 12.00 30.00
RESCSH Chris Shaw/200 5.00 12.00
RESDC Dylan Cozens/200 5.00 12.00
RESDJ Danny Jansen/200 6.00 15.00
RESDL Dawel Lugo/225 4.00 10.00
RESDP Daniel Poncedeleon/225 4.00 10.00
RESDS Dennis Santana/225 2.50 6.00
RESEDL Enyel De Los Santos/225 4.00 10.00
RESEJ Eloy Jimenez/125 30.00 80.00
Mystery
RESFA Francisco Arcia/225 4.00 10.00
RESFL Francisco Lindor/60 15.00 40.00
RESFP Freddy Peralta/200 4.00 10.00
RESFR Franmil Reyes/200 5.00 12.00
RESHB Harrison Bader/200 3.00 8.00
RESHF Heath Fillmyer/225 4.00 10.00
RESIKF Isiah Kiner-Faleta/200 3.00 8.00
RESJB Jake Bauers/200 5.00 12.00
RESJBE Jalen Beeks 2.50 6.00
RESJC Johan Camargo/225 10.00 25.00
RESJCA Jake Cave/225 8.00 20.00
RESJF Jack Flaherty/200 10.00 25.00
RESJM Jeff McNeil/225 10.00 25.00
RESJN Jacob Nix/200 3.00 8.00
RESJR Josh Rogers/225 8.00 20.00
RESJS Juan Soto/125 50.00 120.00
RESJSH Justus Sheffield/200 8.00 20.00
RESKA Kolby Allard/200 4.00 10.00
RESKB Kris Bryant EXCH 50.00 120.00
RESKK Kevin Kramer/225 3.00 8.00
RESKN Kevin Newman/200 4.00 10.00
RESKS Kohl Stewart/200 3.00 8.00
RESKT Kyle Tucker/200 12.00 30.00
RESKW Kyle Wright/200 8.00 20.00
RESLGJ Lourdes Gurriel Jr./200 8.00 20.00
RESLU Luis Urias/200 10.00 25.00
RESMC Matt Chapman/200 10.00 25.00
RESMK Michael Kopech/200 8.00 20.00
RESMM Miles Mikolas/200 8.00 20.00
RESMT Mike Trout/30 200.00 500.00
RESNB Nick Burdi/225 2.50 6.00
RESND Nicky Delmonico/200 2.50 6.00
RESNK Nick Kingham/200 2.50 6.00
RESNW Nick Williams/125 2.50 6.00
RESPL Pablo Lopez/225 5.00 12.00
RESPW Patrick Wisdom/225 3.00 8.00
RESRAJ Ronald Acuna Jr./125 50.00 120.00
RESRB Ryan Borucki/200 3.00 8.00
RESRBL Ray Black/225 3.00 8.00
RESRL Ramon Laureano/225 12.00 30.00
RESRMG Reese McGuire/225 6.00 15.00
RESROH Ryan O'Hearn/225 2.50 6.00
RESRT Rowdy Tellez/200 4.00 10.00
RESSA Sandy Alcantara/200 2.50 6.00
RESSD Steven Duggar/225 3.00 8.00
RESSK Scott Kingery/200 5.00 12.00
RESSM Sean Manaea/200 4.00 10.00
RESSO Shohei Ohtani/30 75.00 200.00
RESSRF Sean Reid-Foley/225 2.50 6.00
RESTT Touki Toussaint/200 3.00 8.00
RESTW Tyler Wade/225 5.00 12.00
RESTWA Taylor Ward/225 2.50 6.00
RESWA Willy Adames/200 4.00 10.00
RESVGJ Vladimir Guerrero Jr./125 100.00 250.00
Mystery

2019 Topps Inception Silver Signings

STATED ODDS 1:18 HOBBY
PRINT RUNS B/WN 10-99 COPIES PER
NO PRICING ON QTY 15 OR LESS
EXCHANGE DEADLINE 2/28/2021
*GOLD INK/25: .5X TO 1.2X BASIC
SSAM Austin Meadows EXCH 12.00 30.00
SSAR Amed Rosario EXCH 8.00 20.00
SSBA Brian Anderson/99 6.00 15.00
SSCA Chance Adams/99 10.00 25.00
SSCB Corbin Burnes/99 12.00 30.00
SSCM Cedric Mullins/99 12.00 30.00
SSCS Christin Stewart/99 20.00 50.00
SSCSH Chris Shaw/99 12.00 30.00
SSDC Dylan Cozens/99 6.00 15.00
SSDJ Danny Jansen/99 15.00 40.00
SSFA Francisco Arcia/99 12.00 30.00
SSFL Francisco Lindor/30 30.00 80.00
SSHB Harrison Bader/99 8.00 20.00
SSJB Jake Bauers/99 10.00 25.00
SSJF Jack Flaherty/99 8.00 20.00
SSJL Jonathan Loaisiga/99 20.00 50.00
SSJS Juan Soto/60 40.00 100.00
SSJSH Justus Sheffield/99 10.00 25.00
SSKA Kolby Allard/99 10.00 25.00
SSKB Kris Bryant EXCH 60.00 150.00
SSKT Kyle Tucker/90 12.00 30.00
SSKW Kyle Wright/90 20.00 50.00
SSLGJ Lourdes Gurriel Jr./99 12.00 30.00
SSLU Luis Urias/90 10.00 25.00
SSMK Michael Kopech/90 25.00 60.00
SSMM Miles Mikolas/99 8.00 20.00
SSRAJ Ronald Acuna Jr./60 100.00 250.00
SSRB Ryan Borucki/99 10.00 25.00
SSSD Steven Duggar/99 10.00 25.00
SSSK Scott Kingery/90 12.00 30.00
SSSM Sean Manaea/99 12.00 30.00
SSSO Shohei Ohtani
SSTT Touki Toussaint/99 8.00 20.00
SSWA Willy Adames/99 10.00 25.00

2020 Topps Inception

1 Ronald Acuna Jr. 3.00 8.00
2 Matt Thaiss RC .75 2.00
3 Jose Altuve .60 1.50
4 Juan Soto 2.50 6.00
5 Max Scherzer .75 2.00
6 Carlos Correa .75 2.00
7 Abraham Toro RC .75 2.00
8 Robel Garcia RC .60 1.50
9 Sean Murphy RC 1.00 2.50
10 Austin Nola RC 1.00 2.50
11 Logan Allen RC .60 1.50
12 Bryce Harper 1.25 3.00
13 Francisco Lindor .75 2.00
14 Edwin Rios RC 1.50 4.00
15 Josh Hader .50 1.25
16 A.J. Puk RC 1.25 3.00
17 Sam Hilliard RC 1.00 2.50
18 Michel Baez RC .60 1.50
19 Kris Bryant 1.00 2.50
20 Aaron Civale RC 1.00 2.50
21 Tony Gonsolin RC 2.50 6.00
22 Gleyber Torres 1.50 4.00
23 Gavin Lux RC 4.00 10.00

24 Victor Robles 1.00 2.50
25 Yordan Alvarez RC 3.00 8.00
26 Walker Buehler 1.00 2.50
27 Sheldon Neuse RC .75 2.00
28 Trent Grisham RC 2.50 6.00
29 J.T. Realmuto .75 2.00
30 Rafael Devers 1.00 2.50
31 Aaron Judge 2.00 5.00
32 Randy Arozarena RC 5.00 12.00
33 Alex Bregman .75 2.00
34 Cody Bellinger 1.50 4.00
35 Rogelio Armenteros RC .75 2.00
36 Bobby Bradley RC .75 2.00
37 George Springer .60 1.50
38 Adbert Alzolay RC .75 2.00
39 Eloy Jimenez 1.50 4.00
40 Seth Brown RC .60 1.50
41 Trevor Story .75 2.00
42 Isan Diaz RC 1.00 2.50
43 DJ LeMahieu .75 2.00
44 Noah Syndergaard .60 1.50
45 Aristides Aquino RC 1.25 3.00
46 Luis Castillo .60 1.50
47 Charlie Blackmon .75 2.00
48 Nico Hoerner RC 2.50 6.00
49 Dustin May RC 2.50 6.00
50 Christian Yelich 1.00 2.50
51 Justin Dunn RC .75 2.00
52 Jacob deGrom .75 2.00
53 Anthony Kay RC .60 1.50
54 Shane Bieber .75 2.00
55 Jordan Yamamoto RC .75 2.00
56 Shohei Ohtani 1.00 2.50
57 Bo Bichette RC 5.00 12.00
58 Domingo Leyba RC .75 2.00
59 Jack Flaherty .60 1.50
60 Dylan Cease RC 1.25 3.00
61 Brusdar Graterol RC 1.00 2.50
62 Zac Gallen RC 1.50 4.00
63 Josh Staumont RC .60 1.50
64 Pete Alonso 2.00 5.00
65 Manny Machado .75 2.00
66 Brock Burke RC .60 1.50
67 Nick Solak RC 1.00 2.50
68 Joey Gallo .75 2.00
69 Tom Eshelman RC .75 2.00
70 Keston Hiura 1.00 2.50
71 Jake Rogers RC .60 1.50
72 Andres Munoz RC .75 2.00
73 Fernando Tatis Jr. 3.00 8.00
74 Willi Castro RC 1.00 2.50
75 Anthony Rizzo 1.25 3.00
76 Hunter Harvey RC 1.00 2.50
77 Javier Baez 1.00 2.50
78 Josh Bell .60 1.50
79 Jose Urquidy RC .75 2.00
80 Travis Demeritte RC .75 2.00
81 Junior Fernandez RC .60 1.50
82 Justin Verlander .75 2.00
83 Jesus Luzardo RC 1.25 3.00
84 Blake Snell .60 1.50
85 Zack Collins RC .75 2.00
86 Mauricio Dubon RC .75 2.00
87 Adrian Morejon RC .60 1.50
88 Tyler Alexander RC 1.00 2.50
89 Eddie Rosario .60 1.50
90 Paul Goldschmidt .75 2.00
91 Chris Paddack .75 2.00
92 Kyle Lewis RC 5.00 12.00
93 Nolan Arenado 1.00 2.50
94 Freddie Freeman 1.00 2.50
95 Patrick Corbin .60 1.50
96 Giancarlo Stanton .75 2.00
97 Mookie Betts 1.50 4.00
98 Jose Ramirez .60 1.50
99 Ozzie Albies .75 2.00
100 Mike Trout 4.00 10.00

2020 Topps Inception Blue

*BLUE: 3X TO 8X BASIC
*BLUE RC: 2.5X TO 6X BASIC
STATED ODDS 1:25 HOBBY
STATED PRINT RUN 25 SER.#'d SETS
100 Mike Trout 40.00 100.00

2020 Topps Inception Green

*GREEN: .6X TO 1.5X BASIC
*GREEN RC: .5X TO 1.2X BASIC
RANDOM INSERTS IN PACKS

2020 Topps Inception Magenta

*MAGENTA: 1.5X TO 4X BASIC
*MAGENTA RC: 1.2X TO 3X BASIC
STATED ODDS 1:7 HOBBY
STATED PRINT RUN 99 SER.#'d SETS
100 Mike Trout 20.00 50.00

2020 Topps Inception Orange

*ORANGE: 2X TO 5X BASIC
*ORANGE RC: 1.5X TO 4X BASIC
STATED ODDS 1:13 HOBBY
STATED PRINT RUN 50 SER.#'d SETS
100 Mike Trout 25.00 60.00

2020 Topps Inception Purple

*PURPLE: 1.2X TO 3X BASIC
*PURPLE RC: 1X TO 2.5X BASIC
STATED ODDS 1:5 HOBBY
STATED PRINT RUN 150 SER.#'d SETS
100 Mike Trout 15.00 40.00

2020 Topps Inception Red

*RED: 2X TO 5X BASIC
*RED RC: 1.5X TO 4X BASIC
STATED ODDS 1:9 HOBBY
STATED PRINT RUN 75 SER.#'d SETS
100 Mike Trout 25.00 60.00

2020 Topps Inception Dawn of Greatness Autographs

STATED ODDS 1:200 HOBBY
STATED PRINT RUN 20 SER.#'d SETS
EXCHANGE DEADLINE 2/29/2022
DOGAAJ Aaron Judge 150.00 400.00
DOGAAR Anthony Rizzo 25.00 60.00
DOGABH Bryce Harper
DOGACCS CC Sabathia 30.00 80.00
DOGACY Christian Yelich
DOGAHA Hank Aaron
DOGAJA Jose Altuve 25.00 60.00
DOGAJC Jose Canseco 30.00 80.00
DOGAJDM J.D. Martinez 20.00 50.00
DOGAKGJ Ken Griffey Jr.
DOGAMC Miguel Cabrera 75.00 200.00
DOGAMM Mike Mussina 50.00 120.00
DOGAMT Mike Trout
DOGARH Rhys Hoskins 30.00 80.00
DOGASK Sandy Koufax
DOGASO Shohei Ohtani
DOGATM Tino Martinez 20.00 50.00
DOGAWM Whit Merrifield 20.00 50.00
DOGAXB Xander Bogaerts 30.00 80.00

2020 Topps Inception Jumbo Patch Autographs

STATED ODDS 1:28 HOBBY
PRINT RUNS B/WN 10-125 COPIES PER
NO PRICING ON QTY 10
EXCHANGE DEADLINE 2/29/2022
IAJPAA Aristides Aquino/90 50.00 120.00
IAJPAR Austin Riley/90 20.00 50.00
IAJPAY Alex Young/90 10.00 25.00
IAJPBB Bo Bichette/90 60.00 150.00
IAJPBM Brendan McKay/90 20.00 50.00
IAJPCB Cavan Biggio/90 30.00 80.00
IAJPDC Dylan Cease/90 15.00 40.00
IAJPDM Dustin May/90 25.00 60.00
IAJPFTJ Fernando Tatis Jr./90 100.00 250.00
IAJPGL Gavin Lux/90 40.00 100.00
IAJPJC Jake Cave/90 10.00 25.00
IAJPJM Jeff McNeil/90 20.00 50.00
IAJPKH Keston Hiura/90 30.00 80.00
IAJPKL Kyle Lewis/90 40.00 100.00
IAJPLA Logan Allen/45 12.00 30.00
IAJPMD Mauricio Dubon/90 10.00 25.00
IAJPMT Matt Thaiss/90 15.00 40.00
IAJPNH Nico Hoerner/90 20.00 50.00
IAJPPA Pete Alonso/90 60.00 510.00
IAJPRAJ Ronald Acuna Jr./90 75.00 200.00
IAJPRD Rafael Devers/90 20.00 50.00
IAJPTA Tim Anderson/90 25.00 60.00
IAJPVGJ Vladimir Guerrero Jr./90 60.00 150.00
IAJPWS Will Smith/90 15.00 40.00
IAJPYA Yordan Alvarez/90 40.00 100.00

2020 Topps Inception Jumbo Patch Autographs Orange

*ORANGE: .5X TO 1.2X BASIC
STATED ODDS 1:79 HOBBY
STATED PRINT RUN 25 SER.#'d SETS
EXCHANGE DEADLINE 2/29/2022
IAJPAAL Adbert Alzolay 12.00 30.00
IAJPAC Aaron Civale 15.00 40.00
IAJPAJ Aaron Judge 125.00 300.00
IAJPJY Jordan Yamamoto 30.00 80.00
IAJPKB Kris Bryant 75.00 200.00
IAJPRH Rhys Hoskins 40.00 100.00

2020 Topps Inception Patch Autographs

STATED ODDS 1:7 HOBBY
PRINT RUNS B/WN 50-199 COPIES PER
EXCHANGE DEADLINE 2/29/2022
IAPAA Adbert Alzolay/155 8.00 20.00
IAPAAQ Aristides Aquino/199 20.00 50.00
IAPAC Aaron Civale/155 10.00 25.00
IAPAJ Aaron Judge/50 75.00 200.00
IAPAMU Andres Munoz/155 5.00 12.00
IAPAN Austin Nola/155 10.00 25.00
IAPAP A.J. Puk/155 12.00 30.00
IAPAR Austin Riley/199 10.00 25.00
IAPAT Abraham Toro/199 5.00 12.00
IAPAY Alex Young/155 8.00 20.00
IAPBB Bobby Bradley/199 10.00 25.00
IAPBBI Bo Bichette/155 75.00 200.00
IAPBM Brendan McKay/155 12.00 30.00
IAPBR Brendan Rodgers/199 10.00 25.00
IAPCB Cavan Biggio/155 20.00 50.00
IAPCK Carter Kieboom/155 15.00 40.00
IAPDC Dylan Cease/155 10.00 25.00
IAPDL Domingo Leyba/155 5.00 12.00
IAPDM Dustin May/155 20.00 50.00
IAPFTJ Fernando Tatis Jr./155 75.00 200.00
IAPGL Gavin Lux/155 60.00 150.00
IAPGT Gleyber Torres/186 50.00 120.00
IAPID Isan Diaz/199 10.00 25.00
IAPJC Jake Cave/199 8.00 20.00
IAPJL Jesus Luzardo/199 20.00 50.00
IAPJM Jeff McNeil/199 15.00 40.00
IAPJR Jake Rogers/155 10.00 25.00
IAPJS Justus Sheffield/148 10.00 25.00
IAPJST Josh Staumont/165 4.00 10.00
IAPJY Jordan Yamamoto/155 10.00 25.00
IAPKB Kris Bryant
IAPKH Keston Hiura/199 25.00 60.00
IAPKL Kyle Lewis/199 25.00 60.00
IAPKN Kevin Newman/199 10.00 25.00
IAPLA Logan Allen/75 5.00 12.00
IAPMB Michael Brosseau/155 8.00 20.00
IAPMC Michael Chavis/155 5.00 12.00
IAPMD Mauricio Dubon/199 5.00 12.00
IAPMT Matt Thaiss/199 5.00 12.00
IAPNH Nico Hoerner/155 30.00 80.00
IAPNS Nick Senzel/155 15.00 40.00
IAPNSO Nick Solak/155 15.00 40.00
IAPPA Pete Alonso/155 50.00 120.00
IAPPS Patrick Sandoval/155 6.00 15.00
IAPRAJ Ronald Acuna Jr./155 60.00 150.00
IAPRAR Rogelio Armenteros/155 5.00 12.00
IAPRD Rafael Devers/155 20.00 50.00
IAPRG Robel Garcia/199 10.00 25.00
IAPRH Rhys Hoskins
IAPRL Ramon Laureano/199 15.00 40.00
IAPTA Tim Anderson/199 20.00 50.00
IAPTD Travis Demeritte/155 5.00 12.00
IAPVGJ Vladimir Guerrero Jr./155 50.00 120.00
IAPWC Willson Contreras/145 20.00 50.00
IAPWS Will Smith/155 15.00 40.00
IAPYA Yordan Alvarez/199 40.00 100.00

2020 Topps Inception Patch Autographs Magenta

*MAGENTA/75: .5X TO 1.2X BASIC
*MAGENTA/35: .6X TO 1.5X BASIC
STATED ODDS 1:16 HOBBY
PRINT RUNS B/WN 35-75 COPIES PER
EXCHANGE DEADLINE 2/29/2022
IAPRH Rhys Hoskins/75 25.00 60.00

2020 Topps Inception Patch Autographs Red

*RED/25: .6X TO 1.5X BASIC
STATED ODDS 1:45 HOBBY
PRINT RUNS B/WN 15-25 COPIES PER
NO PRICING ON QTY 15
EXCHANGE DEADLINE 2/29/2022
IAPRH Rhys Hoskins/25 30.00 80.00

2020 Topps Inception Rookie and Emerging Stars Autographs

RANDOM INSERTS IN PACKS
PRINT RUNS B/WN 100-249 COPIES PER
EXCHANGE DEADLINE 2/29/2022
RESAAA Adbert Alzolay/249 3.00 8.00
RESAAAQ Aristides Aquino/249 30.00 80.00
RESAAC Aaron Civale/245 5.00 12.00
RESAAJP A.J. Puk/245 8.00 20.00
RESAAK Anthony Kay/245 5.00 12.00
RESAAMU Andres Munoz/245 5.00 12.00
RESAAN Austin Nola/245 6.00 15.00
RESAAR Austin Riley/245 10.00 25.00
RESAAT Abraham Toro/245 3.00 8.00
RESAAY Alex Young/245 2.50 6.00
RESABB Bobby Bradley/245 3.00 8.00
RESABBI Bo Bichette/245 50.00 120.00
RESABM Brendan McKay/245 10.00 25.00
RESABR Brendan Rodgers/245 5.00 12.00
RESABRE Bryan Reynolds/245 8.00 20.00
RESACA Chance Adams/245 2.50 6.00
RESACK Carter Kieboom/245 10.00 25.00
RESACT Cole Tucker/220 4.00 10.00
RESADC Dylan Cease/245 8.00 20.00
RESADF David Fletcher/220 4.00 10.00
RESADJ Danny Jansen/245 2.50 6.00
RESADL Domingo Leyba/245 3.00 8.00
RESADM Dustin May/245 15.00 40.00
RESADSJ Dwight Smith Jr./245 2.50 6.00
RESAGC Griffin Canning/220 4.00 10.00
RESAGH Garrett Hampson/220 2.50 6.00
RESAGL Gavin Lux/245 50.00 120.00
RESAHH Hunter Harvey/245 4.00 10.00
RESAID Isan Diaz/245 4.00 10.00
RESAJAM James Marvel/245 2.50 6.00
RESAJB Jake Bauers/245 3.00 8.00
RESAJD Jon Duplantier/245 2.50 6.00
RESAJL Jesus Luzardo/245 12.00 30.00
RESAJME John Means/245 6.00 15.00
RESAJN Josh Naylor/220 2.50 6.00
RESAJR Jake Rogers/245 6.00 15.00
RESAJST Josh Staumont/220 2.50 6.00
RESAJU Jose Urquidy/245 10.00 25.00
RESAJY Jordan Yamamoto/245 6.00 15.00
RESAKH Keston Hiura/245 15.00 40.00
RESAKN Kevin Newman/245 3.00 8.00
RESALA Logan Allen/245 2.50 6.00
RESALAR Luis Arraez/245 12.00 30.00
RESALR Luis Robert EXCH 150.00 400.00
RESAMBE Matt Beaty/245 6.00 15.00
RESAMBR Michael Brosseau/220 5.00 12.00
RESAMC Michael Chavis/245 10.00 25.00
RESAMD Mauricio Dubon/245 10.00 25.00
RESAMK Mitch Keller/245 4.00 10.00
RESAMKE Merrill Kelly/220 2.50 6.00
RESAMT Matt Thaiss/245 3.00 8.00
RESAMTA Mike Tauchman/245 15.00 40.00
RESAMY Mike Yastrzemski/245 15.00 40.00
RESANH Nico Hoerner/245 10.00 25.00
RESANS Nick Senzel/100 12.00 30.00
RESANSO Nick Solak/245 8.00 20.00
RESARA Rogelio Armenteros/220 3.00 8.00
RESARG Robel Garcia/245 6.00 15.00
RESASA Shaun Anderson/220 4.00 10.00
RESASB Seth Brown/245 5.00 12.00
RESASL Shed Long/245 5.00 12.00
RESASM Sean Murphy/245 6.00 15.00
RESATA Tyler Alexander/220 4.00 10.00
RESATD Travis Demeritte/220 3.00 8.00
RESATE Thairo Estrada/245 3.00 8.00
RESATES Tom Eshelman/220 3.00 8.00
RESATG Trent Grisham/245 6.00 15.00
RESATGO Tony Gonsolin/245 8.00 20.00
RESATW Taylor Ward/220 4.00 10.00
RESAVGJ Vladimir Guerrero Jr./100 40.00 100.00
RESAVR Victor Robles/245 10.00 25.00
RESAWA Willians Astudillo/245 5.00 12.00
RESAWS Will Smith/245 10.00 25.00
RESAYA Yordan Alvarez/245 50.00 120.00
RESAYC Yu Chang/245 EXCH 10.00 25.00
RESAZC Zack Collins/245 3.00 8.00
RESAZP Zach Plesac/220 5.00 12.00

2020 Topps Inception Rookie and Emerging Stars Autographs Blue

*BLUE: .75X TO 2X BASIC
STATED ODDS 1:31 HOBBY
STATED PRINT RUN 25 SER.#'d SETS
EXCHANGE DEADLINE 2/29/2022
RESACP Chris Paddack 20.00 50.00
RESAGT Gleyber Torres 60.00 150.00
RESAJSO Juan Soto EXCH 60.00 150.00
RESAMBE Matt Beaty 25.00 60.00
RESASO Shohei Ohtani EXCH 100.00 250.00

2020 Topps Inception Rookie and Emerging Stars Autographs Magenta

*MAGENTA: .5X TO 1.2X BASIC
STATED ODDS 1:8 HOBBY
STATED PRINT RUN 99 SER.#'d SETS
EXCHANGE DEADLINE 2/29/2022
RESACP Chris Paddack 12.00 30.00
RESAGT Gleyber Torres 40.00 100.00
RESAJSO Juan Soto EXCH 40.00 100.00

2020 Topps Inception Rookie and Emerging Stars Autographs Orange

*ORANGE: .6X TO 1.5X BASIC
STATED ODDS 1:16 HOBBY
STATED PRINT RUN 50 SER.#'d SETS
EXCHANGE DEADLINE 2/29/2022
RESACP Chris Paddack 15.00 40.00
RESAGT Gleyber Torres 50.00 120.00
RESAJSO Juan Soto EXCH 50.00 120.00
RESAMBE Matt Beaty 20.00 50.00
RESASO Shohei Ohtani EXCH 75.00 200.00

2020 Topps Inception Rookie and Emerging Stars Autographs Red

*RED: .5X TO 1.2X BASIC
STATED ODDS 1:11 HOBBY
STATED PRINT RUN 75 SER.#'d SETS
EXCHANGE DEADLINE 2/29/2022
RESACP Chris Paddack 12.00 30.00
RESAGT Gleyber Torres 40.00 100.00
RESAJSO Juan Soto EXCH 40.00 100.00

2020 Topps Inception Silver Signings

STATED ODDS 1:21 HOBBY
PRINT RUNS B/WN 50-99 COPIES PER
EXCHANGE DEADLINE 2/29/2022
SSAA Adbert Alzolay/99 8.00 20.00
SSAAQ Aristides Aquino/99 40.00 100.00
SSAMU Andres Munoz/90 8.00 20.00
SSAN Austin Nola/90 10.00 25.00
SSAP A.J. Puk/99 20.00 50.00
SSAR Austin Riley/70 30.00 80.00
SSBB Bo Bichette/70 100.00 250.00
SSBM Brendan McKay/60 10.00 25.00
SSCK Carter Kieboom/99 15.00 40.00
SSDC Dylan Cease/99 15.00 40.00
SSDF David Fletcher/90 12.00 30.00
SSDM Dustin May/99 20.00 50.00
SSFTJ Fernando Tatis Jr./70 150.00 400.00
SSGL Gavin Lux/99 75.00 200.00
SSGT Gleyber Torres/50 75.00 200.00
SSID Isan Diaz/99 10.00 25.00
SSJB Jake Bauers/90 8.00 20.00
SSJL Jesus Luzardo/99 30.00 80.00
SSJM Jordan Yamamoto/99 12.00 30.00
SSJME John Means/90 6.00 15.00
SSJN Josh Naylor/90 6.00 15.00
SSJR Jake Rogers/99 8.00 20.00
SSKH Keston Hiura/99 40.00 100.00
SSLA Logan Allen/99 6.00 15.00
SSLAR Luis Arraez/90 30.00 80.00
SSMB Michael Brosseau/90 8.00 20.00
SSMC Michael Chavis/99 20.00 50.00
SSMT Mike Tauchman/99 10.00 25.00
SSNS Nick Senzel/70 20.00 50.00
SSPA Pete Alonso/50 75.00 200.00
SSRAJ Ronald Acuna Jr./50 60.00 150.00
SSRG Robel Garcia/99 6.00 15.00
SSSM Sean Murphy/99 10.00 25.00
SSTG Trent Grisham/99 12.00 30.00
SSTGO Tony Gonsolin/99 15.00 40.00
SSVGJ Vladimir Guerrero Jr./70 75.00 200.00
SSYA Yordan Alvarez/70 75.00 200.00

2020 Topps Inception Silver Signings Gold Ink

*GOLD INK: .5X TO 1.2X BASIC
STATED ODDS 1:66 HOBBY
STATED PRINT RUN 25 SER.#'d SETS
EXCHANGE DEADLINE 2/29/2022
SSCP Chris Paddack 50.00 120.00
SSSO Shohei Ohtani EXCH 75.00 200.00
SSZC Zack Collins 10.00 25.00

2020 Topps Inception Sock Autographs

STATED ODDS 1:200 HOBBY
STATED PRINT RUN 25 SER.#'d SETS
EXCHANGE DEADLINE 2/29/2022
IAGSAA Adbert Alzolay 12.00 30.00
IAGSAAQ Aristides Aquino 60.00 150.00
IAGSAC Aaron Civale 15.00 40.00
IAGSAJP A.J. Puk 25.00 60.00
IAGSAY Alex Young 10.00 25.00
IAGSBB Bobby Bradley 12.00 30.00
IAGSBBI Bo Bichette 80.00 200.00
IAGSDC Dylan Cease 20.00 50.00
IAGSDL Domingo Leyba 12.00 30.00
IAGSDM Dustin May 40.00 100.00
IAGSGL Gavin Lux 100.00 250.00
IAGSID Isan Diaz 25.00 60.00
IAGSJR Jake Rogers 10.00 25.00
IAGSJY Jordan Yamamoto 25.00 60.00
IAGSLA Logan Allen 10.00 25.00
IAGSMB Michael Brosseau 20.00 50.00
IAGSMD Mauricio Dubon 50.00 120.00
IAGSRG Robel Garcia 10.00 25.00
IAGSSM Sean Murphy 40.00 100.00
IAGSYC Yu Chang 20.00 50.00

2018 Topps Living

ISSUED VIA TOPPS.COM
ANNCD PRINT RUNS B/WN 2678-46,809 COPIES PER
1 Aaron Judge/13,256* 15.00 40.00
2 Joe Panik/3650* 75.00 200.00
3 Nicholas Castellanos/3639* 40.00 100.00
4 Rhys Hoskins/5446* 15.00 40.00
5 Ian Happ/3042* 75.00 200.00
6 Nick Markakis/2678* 125.00 300.00
7 Shohei Ohtani/20,966* 6.00 15.00
8 Russell Martin/3953* 12.00 30.00
9 Jackie Bradley Jr./3959* 25.00 60.00
10 Derek Jeter/10,692* 6.00 15.00
11 Alex Gordon/4143* 10.00 25.00
12 Jean Segura/4052* 8.00 20.00
13 Bryce Harper/9515* 4.00 10.00
14 Mallex Smith/4529* 8.00 20.00
15 A.J. Pollock/4221* 12.00 30.00
16 Jose Altuve/6185* 6.00 15.00
17 Chris Taylor/4837* 5.00 12.00
18 Paul DeJong/4936* 6.00 15.00
19 Ronald Acuna/46,809* 5.00 12.00
20 Jose Ramirez/9671* 4.00 10.00
21 Matt Olson/9631* 4.00 10.00
22 Albert Pujols/9403* 5.00 12.00
23 Amed Rosario/7637* 5.00 12.00
24 Chase Headley/6752* 5.00 12.00
25 Ichiro Suzuki/10,713* 5.00 12.00
26 Yoan Moncada/6382* 5.00 12.00
27 Jose Berrios/6065* 5.00 12.00
28 Rickey Henderson/6851* 5.00 12.00
29 Rafael Devers/8403* 5.00 12.00
30 Brandon Morrow/5585* 3.00 8.00
31 Charlie Blackmon/6585* 4.00 10.00
32 Ozzie Albies/14,036* 3.00 8.00
33 Lewis Brinson/5549* 3.00 8.00
34 Gleyber Torres/28,550* 5.00 12.00
35 Adam Duvall/5766* 3.00 8.00
36 Jordy Mercer/5731* 3.00 8.00
37 Manny Machado/6516* 4.00 10.00
38 Christian Villanueva/5296* 3.00 8.00
39 Eric Sogard/4690* 4.00 10.00
40 Scott Kingery/7277* 6.00 15.00
41 Joey Rickard/5731* 3.00 8.00
42 Jackie Robinson/13,147* 4.00 10.00
43 Juan Soto/28,572* 5.00 12.00
44 Bartolo Colon/5630* 4.00 10.00
45 Brad Peacock/5440* 3.00 8.00
46 Hank Aaron/11,233* 4.00 10.00
47 Jordan Hicks/6099* 3.00 8.00
48 Kevin Pillar/5505* 3.00 8.00
49 Miguel Andujar/12,794* 6.00 15.00
50 Noah Syndergaard/6167* 5.00 12.00
51 Austin Hedges/5354* 3.00 8.00
52 Max Scherzer/6277* 5.00 12.00
53 Walker Buehler/7503* 5.00 12.00
54 Mitch Haniger/5218* 4.00 10.00
55 Ted Williams/10,927* 5.00 12.00
56 Brian Anderson/5218* 4.00 10.00
57 Sean Manaea/4792* 4.00 10.00
58 Giancarlo Stanton/7626* 4.00 10.00
59 Freddy Peralta/4915 4.00 10.00
60 Pat Neshek/12,736* 5.00 12.00
61 Francisco Lindor/6714* 5.00 12.00
62 Andrew Benintendi/6239* 5.00 12.00
63 Austin Meadows/5639* 5.00 12.00
64 Ryne Sandberg/7212* 4.00 10.00
65 Dustin Fowler/4808* 4.00 10.00
66 Yasiel Puig/4886* 4.00 10.00
67 Anthony Rizzo/5568* 4.00 10.00
68 Daniel Murphy/4586* 4.00 10.00
69 Willy Adames/4974* 5.00 12.00
70 Bo Jackson/7321* 4.00 10.00
71 Jake Arrieta/5060* 4.00 10.00
72 Dereck Rodriguez/5798* 4.00 10.00
73 Cody Bellinger/5273* 4.00 10.00
74 Lourdes Gurriel Jr./5094* 3.00 8.00
75 Joe Mauer/4725* 3.00 8.00
76 Roberto Clemente/10,922* 4.00 10.00
77 Tyler O'Neill/4851* 5.00 12.00
78 Avisail Garcia/4520* 5.00 12.00
79 Jacob deGrom/5302* 4.00 10.00
80 Victor Robles/6104* 4.00 10.00
81 Jed Lowrie/4348* 6.00 15.00
82 Joey Votto/4915* 4.00 10.00
83 David Bote/5345* 4.00 10.00
84 Trevor Story/4576* 4.00 10.00
85 Don Mattingly/6785* 4.00 10.00
86 Nick Williams/4733* 3.00 8.00
87 David Wright/5524* 4.00 10.00
88 Manny Machado/4802* 4.00 10.00
89 Jack Flaherty/4754* 4.00 10.00
90 Adrian Beltre/4585* 4.00 10.00
91 J.D. Martinez/4532* 6.00 15.00
92 Francisco Mejia/5096* 4.00 10.00
93 Evan Gattis/3990* 10.00 25.00
94 Christian Yelich/5025* 5.00 12.00
95 Clayton Kershaw/5872* 5.00 12.00
96 Ryan McMahon/4549* 5.00 12.00
97 Chris Sale/4622* 5.00 12.00
98 Dominic Smith/4035* 5.00 12.00
99 Ender Inciarte/4248* 4.00 10.00
100 Babe Ruth/14,976* 4.00 10.00
101 Sandy Alcantara/4771* 4.00 10.00
102 Victor Martinez/4634* 4.00 10.00
103 Javier Baez/4499* 4.00 10.00
104 Alex Verdugo/3911* 5.00 12.00
105 Ketel Marte/3644* 10.00 25.00
106 Cal Ripken Jr./6423* 6.00 15.00
107 Blake Snell/4173* 4.00 10.00
108 JP Crawford/4180* 4.00 10.00
109 Nolan Arenado/4065* 5.00 12.00
110 Clint Frazier/4365* 5.00 12.00
111 Andrew Heaney/3602* 10.00 25.00
112 Ralph Kiner/4114* 4.00 10.00
113 Daniel Palka/3923* 4.00 10.00
114 Billy Hamilton/3837* 5.00 12.00

2017 Topps Luminaries Hit Kings Autographs

STATED PRINT RUN 15 SER.#'d SETS
EXCHANGE DEADLINE 10/31/2019
HKAB Alex Bregman 25.00 60.00
HKABE Andrew Benintendi 30.00 80.00
HKAJ Aaron Judge 125.00 300.00
HKAJU Aaron Judge 125.00 300.00
HKANB Andrew Benintendi 30.00 80.00
HKAP Albert Pujols
HKAR Anthony Rizzo 40.00 100.00
HKBH Bryce Harper EXCH 100.00 250.00
HKBL Barry Larkin 25.00 60.00
HKBLA Barry Larkin 25.00 60.00
HKBP Buster Posey 40.00 100.00
HKCB Craig Biggio 20.00 50.00
HKCBI Craig Biggio 20.00 50.00
HKCC Carlos Correa 40.00 100.00
HKCJ Chipper Jones 50.00 120.00
HKCR Cal Ripken Jr. 60.00 150.00
HKCS Corey Seager 30.00 80.00
HKCSE Corey Seager 30.00 80.00
HKCY Carl Yastrzemski 40.00 100.00
HKDJ Derek Jeter
HKDS Dansby Swanson 20.00 50.00
HKDSW Dansby Swanson 20.00 50.00
HKFL Francisco Lindor 20.00 50.00
HKFLI Francisco Lindor 20.00 50.00
HKFR Frank Robinson 30.00 80.00
HKFRO Frank Robinson 30.00 80.00
HKFT Frank Thomas 40.00 100.00
HKFTH Frank Thomas 40.00 100.00
HKHA Hank Aaron 150.00 400.00
HKIR Ivan Rodriguez 30.00 80.00
HKI Ichiro 250.00 400.00
HKJB Johnny Bench 40.00 100.00
HKKB Kris Bryant 75.00 200.00
HKMM Manny Machado 25.00 60.00
HKMMA Manny Machado 25.00 60.00
HKMT Mike Trout 125.00 300.00
HKNG Nomar Garciaparra 20.00 50.00
HKNGA Nomar Garciaparra 20.00 50.00
HKOS Ozzie Smith 25.00 60.00
HKOV Omar Vizquel 12.00 30.00
HKOVI Omar Vizquel 12.00 30.00
HKRA Roberto Alomar 20.00 50.00
HKRC Rod Carew 20.00 50.00
HKRCA Rod Carew 20.00 50.00
HKRH Rickey Henderson 60.00 150.00
HKRJ Reggie Jackson 40.00 100.00
HKWB Wade Boggs 40.00 100.00
HKYG Yulieski Gurriel 20.00 50.00
HKYGU Yulieski Gurriel 20.00 50.00
HKYMO Yoan Moncada 20.00 50.00

2017 Topps Luminaries Hit Kings Relic Autographs

STATED PRINT RUN 15 SER.#'d SETS
EXCHANGE DEADLINE 10/31/2019
HKRAB Alex Bregman 25.00 60.00
HKRABE Andrew Benintendi 30.00 80.00
HKRABR Alex Bregman 25.00 60.00
HKRANB Andrew Benintendi 30.00 80.00
HKRAP Albert Pujols
HKRAR Anthony Rizzo 40.00 100.00
HKRBH Bryce Harper EXCH 100.00 250.00
HKRBL Barry Larkin 15.00 40.00
HKRBP Buster Posey 40.00 100.00
HKRCB Craig Biggio 20.00 50.00
HKRCC Carlos Correa 40.00 100.00
HKRCJ Chipper Jones 50.00 120.00
HKRCR Cal Ripken Jr. 60.00 150.00
HKRCS Corey Seager 30.00 80.00
HKRCY Carl Yastrzemski 40.00 100.00
HKRDJ Derek Jeter
HKRDO David Ortiz 40.00 100.00
HKRDP Dustin Pedroia 25.00 60.00
HKRDS Dansby Swanson 20.00 50.00
HKRFL Francisco Lindor 20.00 50.00
HKRFT Frank Thomas 40.00 100.00
HKRHA Hank Aaron 150.00 400.00
HKRIR Ivan Rodriguez 30.00 80.00
HKRI Ichiro 250.00 400.00
HKRJB Johnny Bench 40.00 100.00
HKRJBA Jeff Bagwell 30.00 80.00
HKRKB Kris Bryant 75.00 200.00
HKRMM Manny Machado 25.00 60.00
HKRMT Mike Trout 125.00 300.00
HKRNG Nomar Garciaparra 20.00 50.00
HKROS Ozzie Smith 25.00 60.00
HKRRA Roberto Alomar 20.00 50.00
HKRRC Rod Carew 20.00 50.00
HKRRH Rickey Henderson 60.00 150.00
HKRRJ Reggie Jackson 40.00 100.00
HKRRS Ryne Sandberg 40.00 100.00
HKRWB Wade Boggs 40.00 100.00
HKRYG Yulieski Gurriel 20.00 50.00

2017 Topps Luminaries Home Run Kings Autographs

STATED PRINT RUN 15 SER.#'d SETS
EXCHANGE DEADLINE 10/31/2019
HRKAB Alex Bregman 25.00 60.00
HRKABE Andrew Benintendi 30.00 80.00
HRKABR Alex Bregman 25.00 60.00
HRKAJ Aaron Judge 125.00 300.00
HRKAJU Aaron Judge 125.00 300.00
HRKANB Andrew Benintendi 30.00 80.00
HRKAP Albert Pujols
HRKAPU Albert Pujols
HRKAR Alex Rodriguez 75.00 200.00
HRKARI Anthony Rizzo 40.00 100.00
HRKBH Bryce Harper 100.00 250.00
HRKBJ Bo Jackson 60.00 150.00
HRKBJA Bo Jackson 60.00 150.00
HRKBP Buster Posey 40.00 100.00
HRKBW Bernie Williams 20.00 50.00
HRKCC Carlos Correa 40.00 100.00
HRKCCO Carlos Correa 40.00 100.00
HRKCJ Chipper Jones 50.00 120.00
HRKCJO Chipper Jones 50.00 120.00
HRKCRJ Cal Ripken Jr. 60.00 150.00
HRKCS Corey Seager 30.00 80.00
HRKCSE Corey Seager 30.00 80.00
HRKCY Carl Yastrzemski 40.00 100.00
HRKDD David Dahl 12.00 30.00
HRKDO David Ortiz 40.00 100.00
HRKDOR David Ortiz 40.00 100.00
HRKDW Dave Winfield 25.00 60.00
HRKFL Francisco Lindor 20.00 50.00
HRKFR Frank Robinson 30.00 80.00
HRKFT Frank Thomas 40.00 100.00
HRKFTH Frank Thomas 40.00 100.00
HRKHA Hank Aaron 150.00 400.00
HRKIR Ivan Rodriguez 30.00 80.00
HRKIRO Ivan Rodriguez 30.00 80.00
HRKJA Jose Altuve 40.00 100.00
HRKJB Johnny Bench 40.00 100.00
HRKJBA Jeff Bagwell 30.00 80.00
HRKJBG Jeff Bagwell 30.00 80.00
HRKJD Josh Donaldson 15.00 40.00
HRKJDO Josh Donaldson 15.00 40.00
HRKKB Kris Bryant 75.00 200.00
HRKKBR Kris Bryant 75.00 200.00
HRKKS Kyle Schwarber 12.00 30.00
HRKKSC Kyle Schwarber 12.00 30.00
HRKMAM Manny Machado 25.00 60.00
HRKMM Mark McGwire 50.00 120.00
HRKMMA Manny Machado 25.00 60.00
HRKMP Mike Piazza 50.00 120.00
HRKMT Mike Trout 125.00 300.00
HRKRC Robinson Cano 20.00 50.00
HRKRJ Reggie Jackson 40.00 100.00
HRKTS Trevor Story 12.00 30.00
HRKTST Trevor Story 12.00 30.00
HRKDAW Dave Winfield 25.00 60.00

2017 Topps Luminaries Home Run Kings Relic Autographs

STATED PRINT RUN 15 SER.#'d SETS
EXCHANGE DEADLINE 10/31/2019
HRKRAB Alex Bregman 25.00 60.00
HRKRAJ Aaron Judge 125.00 300.00
HRKRAP Albert Pujols
HRKRAR Alex Rodriguez 75.00 200.00
HRKRBH Bryce Harper EXCH 100.00 250.00
HRKRBJ Bo Jackson 60.00 150.00
HRKRBP Buster Posey 40.00 100.00
HRKRCJ Chipper Jones 50.00 120.00
HRKRCR Cal Ripken Jr. 60.00 150.00
HRKRCS Corey Seager 30.00 80.00
HRKRCY Carl Yastrzemski 40.00 100.00
HRKRDO David Ortiz 40.00 100.00
HRKRDW Dave Winfield 25.00 60.00
HRKRFT Frank Thomas 40.00 100.00
HRKRHA Hank Aaron 150.00 400.00
HRKRJD Josh Donaldson 15.00 40.00
HRKRKB Kris Bryant 75.00 200.00
HRKRMM Mark McGwire 50.00 120.00
HRKRMP Mike Piazza 50.00 120.00
HRKRMT Mike Trout 125.00 300.00
HRKRRC Robinson Cano 20.00 50.00
HRKRRJ Reggie Jackson 40.00 100.00
HRKRALB Alex Bregman 25.00 60.00
HRKRARI Anthony Rizzo 40.00 100.00
HRKRCCO Carlos Correa 40.00 100.00
HRKRCJO Chipper Jones 50.00 120.00
HRKRDOR David Ortiz 40.00 100.00
HRKRKBR Kris Bryant 75.00 200.00
HRKRMAM Manny Machado 25.00 60.00
HRKRMMA Manny Machado 25.00 60.00

2017 Topps Luminaries Masters of the Mound Autographs

STATED PRINT RUN 15 SER.#'d SETS
EXCHANGE DEADLINE 10/31/2019
MMCK Clayton Kershaw EXCH 60.00 150.00
MMCS Chris Sale
MMGM Greg Maddux 75.00 200.00
MMJS John Smoltz 25.00 60.00
MMJSM John Smoltz 25.00 60.00
MMKM Kenta Maeda 15.00 40.00
MMLG Lucas Giolito 15.00 40.00
MMMT Masahiro Tanaka 75.00 200.00
MMNR Nolan Ryan 100.00 250.00
MMNS Noah Syndergaard 15.00 40.00
MMPM Pedro Martinez 40.00 100.00
MMPMA Pedro Martinez 40.00 100.00
MMRC Roger Clemens 40.00 100.00

IRCL Roger Clemens 40.00 100.00
IRJ Randy Johnson 50.00 120.00
ISK Sandy Koufax
ITG Tyler Glasnow 15.00 40.00

017 Topps Luminaries Masters f the Mound Relic Autographs

TED PRINT RUN 15 SER.#'d SETS
CHANGE DEADLINE 10/31/2019
IRCK Clayton Kershaw EXCH 100.00 250.00
IRGM Greg Maddux EXCH 75.00 200.00
IRJS John Smoltz
IRMT Masahiro Tanaka 75.00 200.00
IRNR Nolan Ryan
IRNS Noah Syndergaard 25.00 60.00
IRPM Pedro Martinez 40.00 100.00
IRRC Roger Clemens 40.00 100.00
IRRJ Randy Johnson 50.00 120.00
IRTG Tom Glavine 20.00 50.00

2018 Topps Luminaries Hit Kings Autograph Relics

TED ODDS 1:12 HOBBY
TED PRINT RUN 15 SER.#'d SETS
CHANGE DEADLINE 7/31/2020
ARAD Andre Dawson 20.00 50.00
ARADA Andre Dawson 20.00 50.00
ARAJ Aaron Judge 50.00 120.00
ARAP Albert Pujols 75.00 200.00
ARAR Anthony Rizzo 30.00 80.00
ARARO Amed Rosario 15.00 40.00
ARBH Bryce Harper 100.00 250.00
ARBL Barry Larkin EXCH 20.00 50.00
ARBLA Barry Larkin EXCH 20.00 50.00
ARBP Buster Posey 30.00 80.00
ARCB Craig Biggio 20.00 50.00
ARCF Clint Frazier 40.00 100.00
ARCJ Chipper Jones
ARCR Cal Ripken Jr. 60.00 150.00
ARDJ Derek Jeter
ARDM Don Mattingly 100.00 250.00
ARDO David Ortiz 30.00 80.00
ARFL Francisco Lindor 30.00 80.00
KARFT Frank Thomas 60.00 150.00
KARGT Gleyber Torres 100.00 250.00
KARHA Hank Aaron
KARHM Hideki Matsui 75.00 200.00
KARJA Jose Altuve 15.00 40.00
KARJAL Jose Altuve 15.00 40.00
KARJB Johnny Bench 40.00 100.00
KARJR Jose Ramirez
KARJV Joey Votto 30.00 80.00
KARKB Kris Bryant EXCH 60.00 150.00
KARMM Manny Machado 30.00 80.00
KARMT Mike Trout
KARNG Nomar Garciaparra 20.00 50.00
KAROA Ozzie Albies 40.00 100.00
KAROS Ozzie Smith
KARRA Roberto Alomar 20.00 50.00
KARRAC Ronald Acuna 300.00 500.00
KARRC Rod Carew 20.00 50.00
KARRD Rafael Devers 40.00 100.00
KARRDE Rafael Devers 40.00 100.00
KARRH Rhys Hoskins 40.00 100.00
KARRJ Reggie Jackson 30.00 80.00
KARRJA Reggie Jackson 30.00 80.00
KARVR Victor Robles 20.00 50.00
KARWB Wade Boggs 30.00 80.00

2018 Topps Luminaries Hit Kings Autographs

TATED ODDS 1:10 HOBBY
TATED PRINT RUN 15 SER.#'d SETS
XCHANGE DEADLINE 7/31/2020
KAB Adrian Beltre 30.00 80.00
KAD Andre Dawson 20.00 50.00
KAJ Aaron Judge 50.00 120.00
KAK Al Kaline 40.00 100.00
KAMR Amed Rosario 15.00 40.00
KAP Albert Pujols 60.00 150.00
KAR Anthony Rizzo 30.00 80.00
KBH Bryce Harper 100.00 250.00
KBL Barry Larkin EXCH 20.00 50.00
KBLA Barry Larkin EXCH 20.00 50.00
KBP Buster Posey 30.00 80.00
KBR Brooks Robinson EXCH 25.00 60.00
KCB Craig Biggio 20.00 50.00
KCBI Craig Biggio 15.00 40.00
KCJ Chipper Jones 40.00 100.00
KCJO Chipper Jones 40.00 100.00
KCR Cal Ripken Jr. 60.00 150.00
KCRJ Cal Ripken Jr. 60.00 150.00
KDJ Derek Jeter
KDM Don Mattingly 60.00 150.00
KDO David Ortiz 30.00 80.00
KFR Frank Robinson 20.00 50.00
KFRB Frank Robinson 20.00 50.00
KFT Frank Thomas 40.00 100.00
KGT Gleyber Torres 100.00 250.00
KHA Hank Aaron 125.00 300.00
KHM Hideki Matsui 75.00 200.00
KI Ichiro 150.00 400.00
KJA Jose Altuve 15.00 40.00
KJB Johnny Bench 40.00 100.00
KJBE Johnny Bench 40.00 100.00
KJR Jose Ramirez EXCH 15.00 40.00
KJVO Joey Votto 30.00 80.00
KKB Kris Bryant EXCH 60.00 150.00
KLB Lou Brock 20.00 50.00
KLBR Lou Brock 20.00 50.00
KMM Manny Machado 30.00 80.00
KMT Mike Trout 150.00 400.00
KNG Nomar Garciaparra
KOA Ozzie Albies 40.00 100.00
KOAL Ozzie Albies 40.00 100.00

HKOS Ozzie Smith 25.00 60.00
HKOSM Ozzie Smith 25.00 60.00
HKRA Roberto Alomar 20.00 50.00
HKRAC Ronald Acuna 300.00 500.00
HKRC Rod Carew 20.00 50.00
HKRCA Rod Carew 20.00 50.00
HKRD Rafael Devers 40.00 100.00
HKRDE Rafael Devers 40.00 100.00
HKRH Rhys Hoskins 40.00 100.00
HKRJ Reggie Jackson 30.00 80.00
HKRY Robin Yount 60.00 150.00
HKSO Shohei Ohtani 300.00 600.00
HKVRO Victor Robles 20.00 50.00
HKWB Wade Boggs 30.00 80.00

2018 Topps Luminaries Home Run Kings Autograph Relics

STATED ODDS 1:14 HOBBY
STATED PRINT RUN 15 SER.#'d SETS
EXCHANGE DEADLINE 7/31/2020
HRKRAD Andre Dawson 20.00 50.00
HRKRAJ Aaron Judge 50.00 120.00
HRKRAP Albert Pujols 75.00 200.00
HRKRAR Alex Rodriguez EXCH 75.00 200.00
HRKRARI Anthony Rizzo 30.00 80.00
HRKRBH Bryce Harper EXCH 100.00 250.00
HRKRBJA Bo Jackson 60.00 150.00
HRKRBP Buster Posey 30.00 80.00
HRKRCF Clint Frazier 40.00 100.00
HRKRCJ Chipper Jones
HRKRCR Cal Ripken Jr. 60.00 150.00
HRKRDM Don Mattingly 100.00 250.00
HRKRDO David Ortiz 30.00 80.00
HRKRDW Dave Winfield 30.00 80.00
HRKRFL Francisco Lindor 30.00 80.00
HRKRFT Frank Thomas 60.00 150.00
HRKRGS Gary Sanchez 30.00 80.00
HRKRGSP George Springer 15.00 40.00
HRKRHA Hank Aaron
HRKRHM Hideki Matsui 75.00 200.00
HRKRJA Jose Altuve 15.00 40.00
HRKRJB Johnny Bench 40.00 100.00
HRKRJBA Jeff Bagwell 40.00 100.00
HRKRJV Joey Votto 30.00 80.00
HRKRKB Kris Bryant 60.00 150.00
HRKRMM Mark McGwire 30.00 80.00
HRKRMMA Manny Machado 30.00 80.00
HRKRMMC Mark McGwire 30.00 80.00
HRKRMP Mike Piazza 40.00 100.00
HRKRMPI Mike Piazza 40.00 100.00
HRKRMT Mike Trout
HRKRPG Paul Goldschmidt 20.00 50.00
HRKRRD Rafael Devers 40.00 100.00
HRKRRH Rhys Hoskins 40.00 100.00
HRKRRJ Reggie Jackson 30.00 80.00

2018 Topps Luminaries Home Run Kings Autographs

STATED ODDS 1:8 HOBBY
STATED PRINT RUN 15 SER.#'d SETS
EXCHANGE DEADLINE 7/31/2020
HRKABE Adrian Beltre 30.00 80.00
HRKAD Andre Dawson 20.00 50.00
HRKADA Andre Dawson 20.00 50.00
HRKAJ Aaron Judge 50.00 120.00
HRKAK Al Kaline 40.00 100.00
HRKAKA Al Kaline 40.00 100.00
HRKANR Anthony Rizzo 30.00 80.00
HRKAP Albert Pujols 60.00 150.00
HRKAR Alex Rodriguez EXCH 75.00 200.00
HRKARI Anthony Rizzo 30.00 80.00
HRKBH Bryce Harper 100.00 250.00
HRKBJ Bo Jackson 60.00 150.00
HRKBJA Bo Jackson 60.00 150.00
HRKBP Buster Posey 30.00 80.00
HRKBPO Buster Posey 30.00 80.00
HRKBW Bernie Williams 20.00 50.00
HRKBWI Bernie Williams 20.00 50.00
HRKCF Clint Frazier 15.00 40.00
HRKCFI Carlton Fisk
HRKCJ Chipper Jones 40.00 100.00
HRKCJO Chipper Jones 40.00 100.00
HRKCR Cal Ripken Jr. 60.00 150.00
HRKCRJ Cal Ripken Jr. 60.00 150.00
HRKDM Don Mattingly 60.00 150.00
HRKDO David Ortiz 30.00 80.00
HRKDOR David Ortiz 30.00 80.00
HRKDW Dave Winfield
HRKFL Francisco Lindor 30.00 80.00
HRKFR Frank Robinson 20.00 50.00
HRKFRO Frank Robinson 20.00 50.00
HRKFT Frank Thomas 40.00 100.00
HRKGS Gary Sanchez 30.00 80.00
HRKGSP George Springer
HRKHA Hank Aaron 125.00 300.00
HRKHM Hideki Matsui 75.00 200.00
HRKHMA Hideki Matsui 75.00 200.00
HRKJA Jose Altuve 15.00 40.00
HRKJAL Jose Altuve 15.00 40.00
HRKJB Johnny Bench 40.00 100.00
HRKJBA Jeff Bagwell 40.00 100.00
HRKJBE Johnny Bench 40.00 100.00
HRKJEF Jeff Bagwell 40.00 100.00
HRKJV Joey Votto 30.00 80.00
HRKKB Kris Bryant 60.00 150.00
HRKKBR Kris Bryant 60.00 150.00
HRKMM Mark McGwire 30.00 80.00
HRKMMA Manny Machado 30.00 80.00
HRKMMC Manny Machado 30.00 80.00
HRKMP Mike Piazza 40.00 100.00
HRKMPI Mike Piazza 40.00 100.00
HRKMT Mike Trout 150.00 400.00
HRKPG Paul Goldschmidt 20.00 50.00
HRKPGO Paul Goldschmidt 20.00 50.00

HRKRA Ronald Acuna 300.00 500.00
HRKRD Rafael Devers 40.00 100.00
HRKRDE Rafael Devers 40.00 100.00
HRKRH Rhys Hoskins 40.00 100.00
HRKRJ Reggie Jackson 30.00 80.00
HRKRJA Reggie Jackson 30.00 80.00
HRKRS Ryne Sandberg 30.00 80.00
HRKSO Shohei Ohtani 300.00 600.00

2018 Topps Luminaries Masters of the Mound Autograph Relics

STATED ODDS 1:32 HOBBY
STATED PRINT RUN 15 SER.#'d SETS
EXCHANGE DEADLINE 7/31/2020
MOTMARAND Andy Pettitte 25.00 60.00
MOTMARAP Andy Pettitte 25.00 60.00
MOTMARCK Clayton Kershaw EXCH 60.00 150.00
MOTMARCS Chris Sale 20.00 50.00
MOTMARGM Greg Maddux EXCH 40.00 100.00
MOTMARJS John Smoltz 20.00 50.00
MOTMARMR Mariano Rivera 125.00 300.00
MOTMARNR Nolan Ryan 75.00 200.00
MOTMARNS Noah Syndergaard 15.00 40.00
MOTMARPM Pedro Martinez 40.00 100.00
MOTMARPMA Pedro Martinez 40.00 100.00
MOTMARRJ Randy Johnson 40.00 100.00
MOTMARSC Steve Carlton 20.00 50.00
MOTMARTG Tom Glavine 20.00 50.00

2018 Topps Luminaries Masters of the Mound Autographs

STATED ODDS 1:18 HOBBY
STATED PRINT RUN 15 SER.#'d SETS
EXCHANGE DEADLINE 7/31/2020
MMANP Andy Pettitte 25.00 60.00
MMAP Andy Pettitte 25.00 60.00
MMCK Clayton Kershaw EXCH 60.00 150.00
MMCS Chris Sale 20.00 50.00
MMCSA Chris Sale 20.00 50.00
MMGM Greg Maddux 40.00 100.00
MMGMA Greg Maddux 40.00 100.00
MMGRE Greg Maddux 40.00 100.00
MMJP Jim Palmer EXCH 15.00 40.00
MMJPA Jim Palmer EXCH 15.00 40.00
MMJS John Smoltz 20.00 50.00
MMJSM John Smoltz 20.00 50.00
MMMR Mariano Rivera 75.00 200.00
MMNOL Nolan Ryan 75.00 200.00
MMNR Nolan Ryan 75.00 200.00
MMNRY Nolan Ryan 75.00 200.00
MMNS Noah Syndergaard 15.00 40.00
MMNSY Noah Syndergaard 15.00 40.00
MMPM Pedro Martinez 40.00 100.00
MMPMA Pedro Martinez 40.00 100.00
MMRJ Randy Johnson
MMRJO Randy Johnson
MMSC Steve Carlton 20.00 50.00
MMSCA Steve Carlton 20.00 50.00
MMSK Sandy Koufax
MMSO Shohei Ohtani EXCH 300.00 600.00
MMTG Tom Glavine 20.00 50.00
MMTGL Tom Glavine 20.00 5.00

2019 Topps Luminaries Hit Kings Autograph Patches

STATED ODDS 1:XX HOBBY
STATED PRINT RUN 15 SER.#'d SETS
EXCHANGE DEADLINE 7/31/2021
HKAPAR Alex Rodriguez 60.00 150.00
HKAPARI Anthony Rizzo 40.00 100.00
HKAPARO Alex Rodriguez 60.00 150.00
HKAPBP Buster Posey 40.00 100.00
HKAPCF Carlton Fisk 40.00 100.00
HKAPCRJ Cal Ripken Jr. 100.00 250.00
HKAPDO David Ortiz 50.00 120.00
HKAPGS George Springer 40.00 100.00
HKAPGSP George Springer 40.00 100.00
HKAPIR Ivan Rodriguez 40.00 100.00
HKAPIRO Ivan Rodriguez 40.00 100.00
HKAPJA Jose Altuve 30.00 80.00
HKAPJAL Jose Altuve 30.00 80.00
HKAPJS Juan Soto 60.00 150.00
HKAPJSO Juan Soto 20.00 50.00
HKAPJV Joey Votto 30.00 80.00
HKAPKB Kris Bryant 75.00 200.00
HKAPKGJ Ken Griffey Jr. 150.00 400.00
HKAPMC Miguel Cabrera 60.00 150.00
HKAPMP Mike Piazza 75.00 200.00
HKAPMT Mike Trout 400.00 800.00
HKAPMTR Mike Trout 400.00 800.00
HKAPRC Rod Carew 25.00 60.00
HKAPRH Rickey Henderson 50.00 120.00
HKAPRHO Rhys Hoskins 30.00 80.00
HKAPRHS Rhys Hoskins 30.00 80.00
HKAPRJ Reggie Jackson 50.00 120.00
HKAPVGJ Vladimir Guerrero Jr. 150.00 400.00
HKAPVGU Vladimir Guerrero 30.00 80.00
HKAPVLG Vladimir Guerrero Jr. 150.00 400.00

2019 Topps Luminaries Hit Kings Autograph Relics

STATED ODDS 1:XX HOBBY
STATED PRINT RUN 15 SER.#'d SETS
EXCHANGE DEADLINE 7/31/2021
*BLUE/10: .4X TO 1X BASIC
HKARAD Andre Dawson 25.00 60.00
HKARAK Al Kaline 40.00 100.00
HKARAR Anthony Rizzo 30.00 80.00
HKARBL Barry Larkin
HKARBP Buster Posey 30.00 80.00
HKARBW Bernie Williams 25.00 60.00
HKARCF Carlton Fisk 30.00 80.00
HKARCRJ Cal Ripken Jr. 75.00 200.00
HKARDJ Derek Jeter 250.00 500.00
HKARDM Don Mattingly 75.00 200.00
HKARDO David Ortiz 40.00 100.00

HKARFF Freddie Freeman 40.00 100.00
HKARFT Frank Thomas 60.00 150.00
HKARFTJ Fernando Tatis Jr. 200.00 500.00
HKARGS George Springer 30.00 80.00
HKARHA Hank Aaron 125.00 300.00
HKARHM Hideki Matsui 50.00 120.00
HKARIR Ivan Rodriguez 30.00 80.00
HKARI Ichiro 125.00 300.00
HKARJA Jose Altuve 25.00 60.00
HKARJB Johnny Bench 50.00 120.00
HKARJBA Jeff Bagwell 30.00 80.00
HKARJP Jorge Posada 50.00 120.00
HKARJS Juan Soto 50.00 120.00
HKARJV Joey Votto 25.00 60.00
HKARKB Kris Bryant 60.00 150.00
HKARKGJ Ken Griffey Jr. 200.00 500.00
HKARMC Miguel Cabrera 50.00 120.00
HKARMP Mike Piazza 60.00 150.00
HKARMT Mike Trout 300.00 600.00
HKAROS Ozzie Smith
HKARRAJ Ronald Acuna Jr.
HKARRC Rod Carew 20.00 50.00
HKARRH Rickey Henderson 40.00 100.00
HKARRHO Rhys Hoskins 25.00 60.00
HKARRJ Reggie Jackson 40.00 100.00
HKARSO Shohei Ohtani 100.00 250.00
HKARVGJ Vladimir Guerrero Jr. 125.00 300.00
HKARVGS Vladimir Guerrero 25.00 60.00

2019 Topps Luminaries Hit Kings Autographs

STATED ODDS 1:XX HOBBY
STATED PRINT RUN 15 SER.#'d SETS
EXCHANGE DEADLINE 7/31/2021
*RED/10: .4X TO 1X BASIC
HKAB Adrian Beltre 25.00 60.00
HKABE Andrew Benintendi 40.00 100.00
HKAD Andre Dawson 20.00 50.00
HKAJ Aaron Judge 75.00 200.00
HKAK Al Kaline 50.00 120.00
HKAR Alex Rodriguez 50.00 120.00
HKARI Anthony Rizzo 20.00 50.00
HKBJ Bo Jackson 50.00 120.00
HKBL Barry Larkin 20.00 50.00
HKBP Buster Posey 30.00 80.00
HKBW Bernie Williams 20.00 50.00
HKCF Carlton Fisk 20.00 50.00
HKCJ Chipper Jones 40.00 100.00
HKCRJ Cal Ripken Jr. 60.00 150.00
HKCY Christian Yelich EXCH 75.00 200.00
HKDJ Derek Jeter 250.00 500.00
HKDM Don Mattingly 60.00 150.00
HKDO David Ortiz 30.00 80.00
HKEJ Eloy Jimenez 60.00 150.00
HKFF Freddie Freeman 25.00 60.00
HKFL Francisco Lindor 25.00 60.00
HKFT Frank Thomas 40.00 100.00
HKFTA Fernando Tatis Jr. 200.00 500.00
HKGS George Springer
HKHA Hank Aaron 100.00 250.00
HKHM Hideki Matsui 40.00 100.00
HKIR Ivan Rodriguez 25.00 60.00
HKI Ichiro 150.00 400.00
HKJA Jose Altuve 30.00 80.00
HKJB Johnny Bench 40.00 100.00
HKJBA Jeff Bagwell 25.00 60.00
HKJP Jorge Posada 20.00 50.00
HKJS Juan Soto 50.00 100.00
HKJT Jim Thome 30.00 80.00
HKJV Joey Votto 20.00 50.00
HKKB Kris Bryant 40.00 100.00
HKKGJ Ken Griffey Jr. 125.00 300.00
HKMC Miguel Cabrera 40.00 100.00
HKMP Mike Piazza 30.00 80.00
HKMT Mike Trout 250.00 500.00
HKOA Ozzie Albies 25.00 60.00
HKOS Ozzie Smith 25.00 60.00
HKPG Paul Goldschmidt 20.00 50.00
HKRAJ Ronald Acuna Jr. 100.00 250.00
HKRC Rod Carew 20.00 50.00
HKRD Rafael Devers 25.00 60.00
HKRH Rickey Henderson 50.00 120.00
HKRHO Rhys Hoskins 40.00 100.00
HKRJ Reggie Jackson 30.00 80.00
HKRS Ryne Sandberg 50.00 120.00
HKSO Shohei Ohtani 125.00 300.00
HKTR Tim Raines 15.00 40.00
HKVGJ Vladimir Guerrero Jr. 100.00 250.00
HKVGS Vladimir Guerrero 25.00 60.00

2019 Topps Luminaries Home Run Kings Autograph Patches

STATED ODDS 1:XX HOBBY
STATED PRINT RUN 15 SER.#'d SETS
EXCHANGE DEADLINE 7/31/2021
HRKAPMC Alex Rodriguez 60.00 150.00
HRKAPARO Alex Rodriguez 60.00 150.00
HRKAPBP Buster Posey 40.00 100.00
HRKAPBPO Buster Posey 40.00 100.00
HRKAPCF Carlton Fisk 40.00 100.00
HRKAPCR Cal Ripken Jr. 100.00 250.00
HRKAPDO David Ortiz 50.00 120.00
HRKAPDOR David Ortiz 50.00 120.00
HRKAPFF Freddie Freeman 50.00 120.00
HRKAPFTA Fernando Tatis Jr. 250.00 600.00
HRKAPJS Juan Soto 60.00 150.00
HRKAPKB Kris Bryant 75.00 200.00
HRKAPKBR Kris Bryant 75.00 200.00
HRKAPKGJ Ken Griffey Jr. 150.00 400.00
HRKAPMC Miguel Cabrera 60.00 150.00
HRKAPMP Mike Piazza 75.00 200.00
HRKAPMPI Mike Piazza 75.00 200.00
HRKAPMT Mike Trout 400.00 800.00
HRKAPMTR Mike Trout 400.00 800.00

HRKAPRH Rhys Hoskins 30.00 80.00
HRKAPRJ Reggie Jackson 50.00 120.00
HRKAPVGJ Vladimir Guerrero Jr. 150.00 400.00
HRKAPVLG Vladimir Guerrero 30.00 80.00

2019 Topps Luminaries Home Run Kings Autograph Relics

STATED ODDS 1:XX HOBBY
STATED PRINT RUN 15 SER.#'d SETS
EXCHANGE DEADLINE 7/31/2021
*BLUE/10: .4X TO 1X BASIC
HRKARAD Andre Dawson 25.00 60.00
HRKARAK Al Kaline 40.00 100.00
HRKARAR Alex Rodriguez 50.00 120.00
HRKARARI Anthony Rizzo 30.00 80.00
HRKARARO Alex Rodriguez 50.00 120.00
HRKARBJ Bo Jackson 50.00 120.00
HRKARCF Carlton Fisk 30.00 80.00
HRKARCRJ Cal Ripken Jr. 75.00 200.00
HRKARDM Don Mattingly 75.00 200.00
HRKARDO David Ortiz 40.00 100.00
HRKARFF Freddie Freeman 40.00 100.00
HRKARFT Frank Thomas 60.00 150.00
HRKARFTJ Fernando Tatis Jr. 200.00 500.00
HRKARGS George Springer 30.00 80.00
HRKARHM Hideki Matsui 50.00 120.00
HRKARI Ichiro 125.00 300.00
HRKARJB Johnny Bench 50.00 120.00
HRKARJP Jorge Posada 50.00 120.00
HRKARJS Juan Soto 50.00 120.00
HRKARKB Kris Bryant 60.00 150.00
HRKARKGJ Ken Griffey Jr. 125.00 300.00
HRKARMC Miguel Cabrera 50.00 120.00
HRKARMT Mike Trout 300.00 600.00
HRKARRD Rafael Devers
HRKARRH Rhys Hoskins 25.00 60.00
HRKARRJ Reggie Jackson 40.00 100.00
HRKARSO Shohei Ohtani 100.00 250.00
HRKARVGJ Vladimir Guerrero Jr. 125.00 300.00
HRKARVGS Vladimir Guerrero 25.00 60.00

2019 Topps Luminaries Home Run Kings Autographs

STATED ODDS 1:XX HOBBY
STATED PRINT RUN 15 SER.#'d SETS
EXCHANGE DEADLINE 7/31/2021
*RED/10: .4X TO 1X BASIC
HRKAB Adrian Beltre 25.00 60.00
HRKAJ Aaron Judge 75.00 200.00
HRKAJU Aaron Judge 75.00 200.00
HRKAK Al Kaline 50.00 120.00
HRKAM Andrew McCutchen 40.00 100.00
HRKAR Alex Rodriguez 50.00 120.00
HRKARI Anthony Rizzo 20.00 50.00
HRKARZ Anthony Rizzo 20.00 50.00
HRKBJ Bo Jackson 50.00 120.00
HRKBP Buster Posey 30.00 80.00
HRKBW Bernie Williams 20.00 50.00
HRKBWI Bernie Williams 20.00 50.00
HRKCF Carlton Fisk 20.00 50.00
HRKCJ Chipper Jones 40.00 100.00
HRKCJO Chipper Jones 40.00 100.00
HRKCR Cal Ripken Jr. 60.00 150.00
HRKCY Christian Yelich EXCH 75.00 200.00
HRKDM Don Mattingly 60.00 150.00
HRKDMA Don Mattingly 60.00 150.00
HRKDMU Dale Murphy 30.00 80.00
HRKDO David Ortiz 30.00 80.00
HRKDOR David Ortiz 30.00 80.00
HRKEJ Eloy Jimenez 60.00 150.00
HRKFF Freddie Freeman 25.00 60.00
HRKFL Francisco Lindor 25.00 60.00
HRKFLI Francisco Lindor 25.00 60.00
HRKFT Frank Thomas 40.00 100.00
HRKFTA Fernando Tatis Jr. 200.00 500.00
HRKFTH Frank Thomas 40.00 100.00
HRKFTJ Fernando Tatis Jr. 200.00 500.00
HRKHA Hank Aaron 100.00 250.00
HRKHM Hideki Matsui 40.00 100.00
HRKHMA Hideki Matsui 40.00 100.00
HRKIR Ivan Rodriguez 20.00 50.00
HRKI Ichiro 150.00 400.00
HRKJB Johnny Bench 40.00 100.00
HRKJBA Jeff Bagwell 25.00 60.00
HRKJBG Jeff Bagwell 25.00 60.00
HRKJP Jorge Posada 20.00 50.00
HRKJPO Jorge Posada 20.00 50.00
HRKJS Juan Soto 50.00 120.00
HRKJSO Juan Soto 50.00 120.00
HRKJT Jim Thome 30.00 80.00
HRKJV Joey Votto 20.00 50.00
HRKKB Kris Bryant 40.00 100.00
HRKKGJ Ken Griffey Jr. 125.00 300.00
HRKMC Miguel Cabrera 40.00 100.00
HRKMP Mike Piazza 30.00 80.00
HRKMPI Mike Piazza 30.00 80.00
HRKMT Mike Trout 250.00 500.00
HRKPG Paul Goldschmidt 20.00 50.00
HRKRAC Ronald Acuna Jr. 100.00 250.00
HRKRAJ Ronald Acuna Jr. 100.00 250.00
HRKRH Rhys Hoskins 40.00 100.00
HRKRJ Reggie Jackson 30.00 80.00
HRKRJA Reggie Jackson 30.00 80.00
HRKSO Shohei Ohtani 125.00 300.00
HRKVGJ Vladimir Guerrero Jr. 100.00 250.00
HRKVGR Vladimir Guerrero Jr. 100.00 250.00
HRKVGS Vladimir Guerrero 25.00 60.00
HRKVLG Vladimir Guerrero 25.00 60.00

2019 Topps Luminaries Masters of the Mound Autograph Patches

STATED ODDS 1:XX HOBBY
STATED PRINT RUN 15 SER.#'d SETS
EXCHANGE DEADLINE 7/31/2021

MOMAPANP Andy Pettitte 25.00 60.00
MOMAPAP Andy Pettitte 25.00 60.00
MOMAPCK Clayton Kershaw 75.00 200.00
MOMAPJD Jacob deGrom 30.00 80.00
MOMAPJDE Jacob deGrom 30.00 80.00
MOMAPMR Mariano Rivera 125.00 300.00
MOMAPMRI Mariano Rivera 125.00 300.00
MOMAPNS Noah Syndergaard 20.00 50.00
MOMAPNSY Noah Syndergaard 20.00 50.00
MOMAPRJ Randy Johnson 50.00 120.00

2019 Topps Luminaries Masters of the Mound Autograph Relics

STATED ODDS 1:XX HOBBY
STATED PRINT RUN 15 SER.#'d SETS
EXCHANGE DEADLINE 7/31/2021
*BLUE/10: .4X TO 1X BASIC
MOMARANP Andy Pettitte 20.00 50.00
MOMARAP Andy Pettitte 20.00 50.00
MOMARCK Clayton Kershaw 60.00 150.00
MOMARJD Jacob deGrom 25.00 60.00
MOMARLS Luis Severino
MOMARMR Mariano Rivera 125.00 300.00
MOMARPM Pedro Martinez 30.00 80.00
MOMARRC Roger Clemens 75.00 200.00
MOMARRJ Randy Johnson 40.00 100.00
MOMARSO Shohei Ohtani 100.00 250.00

2019 Topps Luminaries Masters of the Mound Autographs

STATED ODDS 1:XX HOBBY
STATED PRINT RUN 15 SER.#'d SETS
EXCHANGE DEADLINE 7/31/2021
*RED/10: .4X TO 1X BASIC
MOMAP Andy Pettitte 25.00 60.00
MOMBG Bob Gibson 25.00 60.00
MOMCK Clayton Kershaw 50.00 120.00
MOMCS Chris Sale 20.00 50.00
MOMCSA Chris Sale 20.00 50.00
MOMJD Jacob deGrom 20.00 50.00
MOMJM Juan Marichal
MOMJS John Smoltz 25.00 60.00
MOMLS Luis Severino 25.00 60.00
MOMMR Mariano Rivera 75.00 200.00
MOMNR Nolan Ryan 75.00 200.00
MOMPM Pedro Martinez 40.00 100.00
MOMPMA Pedro Martinez 40.00 100.00
MOMRC Roger Clemens 50.00 120.00
MOMRJ Randy Johnson 50.00 120.00
MOMSK Sandy Koufax 150.00 400.00
MOMSO Shohei Ohtani 125.00 300.00
MOMYK Yusei Kikuchi 20.00 50.00

2020 Topps Luminaries Hit Kings Autographs

STATED ODDS 1:XX HOBBY
STATED PRINT RUN 15 SER.#'d SETS
EXCHANGE DEADLINE 7/31/22
*RED/10: .4X TO 1X BASIC
HKI Ichiro 200.00 500.00
HKAA Aristides Aquino 25.00 60.00
HKAB Andrew Benintendi 20.00 50.00
HKAJ Aaron Judge 100.00 250.00
HKAR Alex Rodriguez 60.00 150.00
HKBH Bryce Harper 100.00 250.00
HKBL Barry Larkin 40.00 100.00
HKBP Buster Posey 40.00 100.00
HKCJ Chipper Jones 4.00 150.00
HKCY Carl Yastrzemski 75.00 200.00
HKDJ Derek Jeter 400.00 800.00
HKDM Don Mattingly 50.00 120.00
HKDO David Ortiz 50.00 120.00
HKEM Edgar Martinez 25.00 60.00
HKFT Frank Thomas 60.00 150.00
HKGS George Springer 20.00 50.00
HKGT Gleyber Torres 60.00 150.00
HKHA Hank Aaron 150.00 4001.00
HKJA Jose Altuve 20.00 50.00
HKJB Johnny Bench 50.00 120.00
HKJS Juan Soto 100.00 250.00
HKJT Jim Thome 30.00 80.00
HKJV Joey Votto 20.00 50.00
HKKB Kris Bryant 40.00 100.00
HKKH Keston Hiura 25.00 60.00
HKLR Luis Robert 200.00 500.00
HKMM Mark McGwire 50.00 120.00
HKMS Mike Schmidt 60.00 150.00
HKMT Mike Trout 400.00 800.00
HKNH Nico Hoerner 50.00 125.00
HKOS Ozzie Smith 40.00 100.00
HKPA Pete Alonso 50.00 125.00
HKRA Roberto Alomar 25.00 60.00
HKRC Rod Carew 25.00 60.00
HKRD Rafael Devers 30.00 80.00
HKRH Rickey Henderson 60.00 150.00
HKRS Ryne Sandberg 50.00 120.00
HKRY Robin Yount 50.00 120.00
HKSO Shohei Ohtani 100.00 250.00
HKTR Tim Raines 15.00 40.00
HKWB Wade Boggs 40.00 100.00
HKXB Xander Bogaerts 40.00 100.00
HKYA Yordan Alvarez 60.00 150.00
HKAAQ Aristides Aquino 25.00 60.00
HKARI Anthony Rizzo 30.00 80.00
HKBBI Bo Bichette 100.00 250.00
HKCRJ Cal Ripken Jr. 75.00 200.00
HKCYE Christian Yelich 50.00 120.00
HKDMA Don Mattingly 50.00 120.00
HKFTJ Fernando Tatis Jr. 125.00 300.00
HKGSP George Springer 20.00 50.00
HKJBA Jeff Bagwell 30.00 80.00
HKJSO Juan Soto 100.00 250.00
HKKGJ Ken Griffey Jr. 200.00 500.00
HKKHI Keston Hiura 25.00 60.00
HKMMC Mark McGwire 50.00 120.00

HKPAL Pete Alonso 50.00 125.00
HKRAJ Ronald Acuna Jr. 80.00 200.00
HKRHO Rhys Hoskins 25.00 60.00
HKROA Ronald Acuna Jr. 80.00 200.00
HKVGJ Vladimir Guerrero Jr. 40.00 100.00
HKVLG Vladimir Guerrero Jr. 40.00 100.00

2020 Topps Luminaries Hit Kings Autograph Patches

STATED ODDS 1:XX HOBBY
STATED PRINT RUN 15 SER.#'d SETS
EXCHANGE DEADLINE 7/31/22
HKAPAA Aristides Aquino 30.00 80.00
HKAPAR Alex Rodriguez 125.00 300.00
HKAPBH Bryce Harper 150.00 400.00
HKAPBP Buster Posey 50.00 120.00
HKAPCY Christian Yelich 75.00 200.00
HKAPDO David Ortiz 50.00 120.00
HKAPGS George Springer 20.00 50.00
HKAPIS Ichiro 150.00 400.00
HKAPJA Jose Altuve 20.00 50.00
HKAPJT Jim Thome 50.00 120.00
HKAPKH Keston Hiura 40.00 100.00
HKAPMT Mike Trout 400.00 800.00
HKAPRA Roberto Alomar 50.00 120.00
HKAPRC Rod Carew 40.00 100.00
HKAPRH Rhys Hoskins 40.00 100.00
HKAPRY Robin Yount 75.00 200.00
HKAPSO Shohei Ohtani 125.00 300.00
HKAPWB Wade Boggs 50.00 120.00
HKAPXB Xander Bogaerts 40.00 100.00
HKAPYA Yordan Alvarez 80.00 200.00
HKAPAAQ Aristides Aquino 30.00 80.00
HKAPBBI Bo Bichette 125.00 300.00
HKAPDOR David Ortiz 50.00 120.00
HKAPFTJ Fernando Tatis Jr. 150.00 400.00
HKAPKGJ Ken Griffey Jr. 400.00 800.00
HKAPMTE Mark Teixeira 40.00 100.00
HKAPRAJ Ronald Acuna Jr. 100.00 250.00

2020 Topps Luminaries Hit Kings Autograph Relics

STATED ODDS 1:XX HOBBY
STATED PRINT RUN 15 SER.#'d SETS
EXCHANGE DEADLINE 7/31/22
HKARI Ichiro 200.00 500.00
HKARAA Aristides Aquino 25.00 60.00
HKARAB Andrew Benintendi 20.00 50.00
HKARAJ Aaron Judge 100.00 250.00
HKARBH Bryce Harper 125.00 300.00
HKARBL Barry Larkin 30.00 80.00
HKARBP Buster Posey 25.00 60.00
HKARCJ Chipper Jones 75.00 200.00
HKARCY Carl Yastrzemski 60.00 150.00
HKARDM Don Mattingly 60.00 150.00
HKARDO David Ortiz 40.00 100.00
HKAREM Edgar Martinez 50.00 120.00
HKARFT Frank Thomas 75.00 200.00
HKARGS George Springer 20.00 50.00
HKARGT Gleyber Torres 60.00 150.00
HKARHA Hank Aaron 150.00 400.00
HKARJA Jose Altuve 25.00 60.00
HKARJB Johnny Bench 60.00 150.00
HKARJS Juan Soto 75.00 200.00
HKARJT Jim Thome 30.00 80.00
HKARJV Joey Votto 40.00 100.00
HKARKB Kris Bryant 50.00 120.00
HKARMT Mike Trout 400.00 800.00
HKARPA Pete Alonso 75.00 200.00
HKARRC Rod Carew 25.00 60.00
HKARRH Rickey Henderson 50.00 120.00
HKARSO Shohei Ohtani 75.00 200.00
HKARVG Vladimir Guerrero 40.00 100.00
HKARYA Yordan Alvarez 75.00 200.00
HKARARO Alex Rodriguez 100.00 250.00
HKARBBI Bo Bichette 100.00 250.00
HKARCRJ Cal Ripken Jr. 75.00 200.00
HKARKGJ Ken Griffey Jr. 200.00 500.00
HKARMTE Mark Teixeira 40.00 100.00
HKARRAJ Ronald Acuna Jr. 80.00 200.00
HKARRAL Roberto Alomar 40.00 100.00
HKARRHO Rhys Hoskins 25.00 60.00
HKARVGJ Vladimir Guerrero Jr. 60.00 150.00

2020 Topps Luminaries Home Run Kings Autograph Patches

STATED ODDS 1:XX HOBBY
STATED PRINT RUN 15 SER.#'d SETS
EXCHANGE DEADLINE 7/31/22
HRKAPAA Aristides Aquino 30.00 80.00
HRKAPBH Bryce Harper 150.00 400.00
HRKAPBP Buster Posey 50.00 120.00
HRKAPCY Christian Yelich 75.00 200.00
HRKAPDO David Ortiz 50.00 120.00
HRKAPFT Frank Thomas 100.00 250.00
HRKAPGS George Springer 20.00 50.00
HRKAPIR Ivan Rodriguez 50.00 120.00
HRKAPJA Jose Altuve 20.00 50.00
HRKAPMT Mike Trout 400.00 800.00
HRKAPRA Ronald Acuna Jr. 100.00 250.00
HRKAPRH Rhys Hoskins 40.00 100.00
HRKAPSO Shohei Ohtani 125.00 300.00
HRKAPYA Yordan Alvarez 80.00 200.00
HRKAPBBI Bo Bichette 125.00 300.00
HRKAPBHA Bryce Harper 150.00 400.00
HRKAPBOB Bo Bichette 125.00 300.00
HRKAPCYE Christian Yelich 75.00 200.00
HRKAPIRO Ivan Rodriguez 50.00 120.00
HRKAPKGJ Ken Griffey Jr. 400.00 800.00
HRKAPMTE Mark Teixeira 40.00 100.00
HRKAPMTR Mike Trout 400.00 800.00
HRKAPRAJ Ronald Acuna Jr. 100.00 250.00
HRKAPYAL Yordan Alvarez 80.00 200.00

2020 Topps Luminaries Home Run Kings Autograph Relics

STATED ODDS 1:XX HOBBY

STATED PRINT RUN 15 SER.#'d SETS
EXCHANGE DEADLINE 7/31/22
HRKARAA Aristides Aquino 25.00 60.00
HRKARAB Andrew Benintendi 20.00 50.00
HRKARAJ Aaron Judge 100.00 250.00
HRKARAR Alex Rodriguez 100.00 250.00
HRKARBH Bryce Harper 125.00 300.00
HRKARCJ Chipper Jones 75.00 200.00
HRKARCY Carl Yastrzemski 60.00 150.00
HRKARDO David Ortiz 40.00 100.00
HRKAREM Edgar Martinez 50.00 120.00
HRKARFT Frank Thomas 75.00 200.00
HRKARGT Gleyber Torres 60.00 150.00
HRKARHA Hank Aaron 150.00 400.00
HRKARIR Ivan Rodriguez 20.00 50.00
HRKARJA Jose Altuve 25.00 60.00
HRKARJS Juan Soto 75.00 200.00
HRKARKB Kris Bryant 50.00 120.00
HRKARMT Mike Trout 400.00 800.00
HRKARNA Nolan Arenado 75.00 200.00
HRKARPA Pete Alonso 75.00 200.00
HRKARPG Paul Goldschmidt 25.00 60.00
HRKARRH Rhys Hoskins 25.00 60.00
HRKARSO Shohei Ohtani 75.00 200.00
HRKARSS Sammy Sosa 125.00 300.00
HRKARVG Vladimir Guerrero 40.00 100.00
HRKARYA Yordan Alvarez 75.00 200.00
HRKARBBi Bo Bichette 100.00 250.00
HRKARCRJ Cal Ripken Jr. 75.00 200.00
HRKARCYE Christian Yelich 125.00 300.00
HRKARKGJ Ken Griffey Jr. 200.00 500.00
HRKARRAJ Ronald Acuna Jr. 80.00 200.00
HRKARVGJ Vladimir Guerrero Jr. 60.00 150.00

2020 Topps Luminaries Home Run Kings Autographs

STATED ODDS 1:XX HOBBY
STATED PRINT RUN 15 SER.#'d SETS
EXCHANGE DEADLINE 7/31/22
*RED/10: .4X TO 1X BASIC
HRKAA Aristides Aquino 25.00 60.00
HRKAB Andrew Benintendi 20.00 50.00
HRKAD Andre Dawson 30.00 80.00
HRKAJ Aaron Judge 100.00 250.00
HRKAR Alex Rodriguez 60.00 150.00
HRKBH Bryce Harper 100.00 250.00
HRKBP Buster Posey 40.00 100.00
HRKBW Bernie Williams 30.00 80.00
HRKCF Carlton Fisk 20.00 50.00
HRKCJ Chipper Jones 60.00 150.00
HRKCY Carl Yastrzemski 75.00 200.00
HRKDO David Ortiz 50.00 120.00
HRKDW David Wright 40.00 100.00
HRKEJ Eloy Jimenez 40.00 100.00
HRKEM Edgar Martinez 40.00 100.00
HRKFT Frank Thomas 60.00 150.00
HRKGS George Springer 20.00 50.00
HRKGT Gleyber Torres 60.00 150.00
HRKHA Hank Aaron 150.00 400.00
HRKIR Ivan Rodriguez 25.00 60.00
HRKJA Jose Altuve 20.00 50.00
HRKJB Johnny Bench 50.00 120.00
HRKJR Jim Rice 25.00 60.00
HRKJS Juan Soto 100.00 250.00
HRKJT Jim Thome 30.00 80.00
HRKJV Joey Votto 40.00 100.00
HRKKB Kris Bryant 40.00 100.00
HRKLR Luis Robert 200.00 500.00
HRKMM Mark McGwire 50.00 120.00
HRKMS Mike Schmidt 60.00 150.00
HRKMT Mike Trout 400.00 800.00
HRKNA Nolan Arenado 50.00 120.00
HRKPA Pete Alonso 50.00 125.00
HRKPG Paul Goldschmidt 30.00 80.00
HRKRH Rhys Hoskins 25.00 60.00
HRKRJ Reggie Jackson 30.00 80.00
HRKSO Shohei Ohtani 75.00 200.00
HRKVG Vladimir Guerrero 40.00 100.00
HRKYA Yordan Alvarez 60.00 150.00
HRKARI Anthony Rizzo 30.00 80.00
HRKBBI Bo Bichette 100.00 250.00
HRKCRJ Cal Ripken Jr. 75.00 200.00
HRKFTH Frank Thomas 60.00 150.00
HRKJAL Jose Altuve 20.00 50.00
HRKJBA Jeff Bagwell 30.00 80.00
HRKJBE Johnny Bench 50.00 120.00
HRKJDM J.D. Martinez 20.00 50.00
HRKJSO Juan Soto 100.00 250.00
HRKKGJ Ken Griffey Jr. 200.00 500.00
HRKMTE Mark Teixeira 30.00 80.00
HRKPAL Pete Alonso 50.00 125.00
HRKRAJ Ronald Acuna Jr. 80.00 200.00
HRKRHO Rhys Hoskins 25.00 60.00
HRKRJA Reggie Jackson 30.00 80.00
HRKROA Ronald Acuna Jr. 80.00 200.00
HRKVGJ Vladimir Guerrero Jr. 40.00 100.00
HRKVLJ Vladimir Guerrero Jr. 40.00 100.00
HRKYAL Yordan Alvarez 60.00 150.00

2020 Topps Luminaries Masters of the Mound Autograph Patches

STATED ODDS 1:XX HOBBY
STATED PRINT RUN 15 SER.#'d SETS
EXCHANGE DEADLINE 7/31/22
MOMAPCK Clayton Kershaw 100.00 250.00
MOMAPGC Gerrit Cole 60.00 150.00
MOMAPMR Mariano Rivera 125.00 300.00
MOMAPMS Max Scherzer 75.00 200.00
MOMAPMT Masahiro Tanaka 50.00 120.00
MOMAPPM Pedro Martinez 60.00 150.00
MOMAPSO Shohei Ohtani 125.00 300.00
MOMAPCKE Clayton Kershaw 100.00 250.00
MOMAPMRI Mariano Rivera 125.00 300.00
MOMAPMPA Pedro Martinez 60.00 150.00

2020 Topps Luminaries Masters of the Mound Autograph Relics

STATED ODDS 1:XX HOBBY
STATED PRINT RUN 15 SER.#'d SETS
EXCHANGE DEADLINE 7/31/22
MOMARAP Andy Pettitte 50.00 120.00
MOMARBB Bert Blyleven 30.00 80.00
MOMARCK Clayton Kershaw 100.00 250.00
MOMARJS John Smoltz 30.00 80.00
MOMARMR Mariano Rivera 125.00 300.00
MOMARMT Masahiro Tanaka 100.00 250.00
MOMARPM Pedro Martinez 40.00 100.00
MOMARRC Roger Clemens 75.00 200.00
MOMARSC Steve Carlton 30.00 80.00
MOMARSO Shohei Ohtani 75.00 200.00
MOMARCCS CC Sabathia 40.00 100.00

2020 Topps Luminaries Masters of the Mound Autographs

STATED ODDS 1:XX HOBBY
STATED PRINT RUN 15 SER.#'d SETS
EXCHANGE DEADLINE 7/31/22
*RED/10: .4X TO 1X BASIC
MOMAP Andy Pettitte 25.00 60.00
MOMBB Bert Blyleven 25.00 60.00
MOMBG Bob Gibson 40.00 100.00
MOMGC Gerrit Cole 100.00 250.00
MOMJM Juan Marichal 30.00 80.00
MOMJS John Smoltz 20.00 50.00
MOMMM Mike Mussina 50.00 120.00
MOMMR Mariano Rivera
MOMMS Max Scherzer 50.00 120.00
MOMNR Nolan Ryan 100.00 250.00
MOMPM Pedro Martinez 40.00 100.00
MOMRC Roger Clemens 40.00 100.00
MOMRJ Randy Johnson 60.00 150.00
MOMSC Steve Carlton 25.00 60.00
MOMSK Sandy Koufax 150.00 400.00
MOMSO Shohei Ohtani 75.00 200.00
MOMCCS CC Sabathia 30.00 80.00

2020 Topps Luminaries Spark of Light Autograph Patches

STATED ODDS 1:XX HOBBY
STATED PRINT RUN 15 SER.#'d SETS
EXCHANGE DEADLINE 7/31/22
SLPAA Aristides Aquino 30.00 80.00
SLPBB Bo Bichette 125.00 300.00
SLPEJ Eloy Jimenez 50.00 125.00
SLPGT Gleyber Torres 75.00 200.00
SLPKH Keston Hiura 40.00 100.00
SLPRH Rhys Hoskins 40.00 100.00
SLPSO Shohei Ohtani 125.00 300.00
SLPYA Yordan Alvarez 80.00 200.00
SLPRAJ Ronald Acuna Jr. 100.00 250.00
SLPVGJ Vladimir Guerrero Jr. 50.00 125.00

2020 Topps Luminaries Spark of Light Dual Autograph Patches

STATED ODDS 1:XX HOBBY
STATED PRINT RUN 15 SER.#'d SETS
EXCHANGE DEADLINE 7/31/22
SLDPBL G.Lux/B.Bichette EXCH 200.00 500.00

2020 Topps Luminaries Spark of Light Dual Autographs

STATED ODDS 1:XX HOBBY
STATED PRINT RUN 15 SER.#'d SETS
EXCHANGE DEADLINE 7/31/22
SLDAAS R.Acuna/J.Soto 200.00 500.00
SLDAJC D.Cease/E.Jimenez 40.00 100.00
SLDATA G.Torres/P.Alonso 200.00 500.00

2012 Topps Museum Collection

COMMON CARD (1-100) .40 1.00
COMMON RC (1-120) .40 1.00
1 Jeremy Hellickson .60 1.50
2 Albert Pujols 1.25 3.00
3 Carlos Santana .75 2.00
4 Jay Bruce .75 2.00
5 Don Mattingly 2.00 5.00
6 Justin Upton .75 2.00
7 Buster Posey 1.25 3.00
8 Stan Musial 1.50 4.00
9 Cole Hamels .75 2.00
10 Dan Haren .60 1.50
11 Carl Crawford .75 2.00
12 Cal Ripken 3.00 8.00
13 Nolan Ryan 3.00 8.00
14 Adrian Gonzalez .75 2.00
15 Derek Jeter 2.50 6.00
16 Prince Fielder .75 2.00
17 Clayton Kershaw 2.00 5.00
18 Joe Mauer .75 2.00
19 Ryne Sandberg 2.00 5.00
20 Matt Holliday 1.00 2.50
21 Joey Votto 1.00 2.50
22 Lou Gehrig 2.00 5.00
23 Tony Gwynn 1.00 2.50
24 Matt Moore RC 1.00 2.50
25 Matt Kemp .75 2.00
26 Curtis Granderson .75 2.00
27 Roberto Clemente 2.50 6.00
28 Carlos Gonzalez .75 2.00
29 Craig Kimbrel .75 2.00
30 Jim Palmer .60 1.50
31 Evan Longoria .75 2.00
32 Babe Ruth 2.50 6.00
33 David Wright .75 2.00
34 Robinson Cano .75 2.00
35 Jesus Montero RC .60 1.50
36 Jose Reyes .60 1.50
37 Stephen Strasburg 1.00 2.50
38 Edgar Martinez .60 1.50
39 Eric Hosmer .75 2.00
40 Frank Robinson .60 1.50
41 Mark Teixeira .75 2.00
42 Mickey Mantle 3.00 8.00
43 Mark Trumbo .60 1.50
44 Eddie Murray .60 1.50
45 Dustin Ackley .60 1.50
46 Mike Stanton 1.00 2.50
47 CC Sabathia .75 2.00
48 Rollie Fingers .60 1.50
49 Elvis Andrus .75 2.00
50 Aramis Ramirez .60 1.50
51 Dustin Pedroia .75 2.00
52 Drew Stubbs .60 1.50
53 Lou Brock .60 1.50
54 Justin Verlander 1.00 2.50
55 David Price .75 2.00
56 Jered Weaver .75 2.00
57 Neftali Feliz .60 1.50
58 Cliff Lee .75 2.00
59 Josh Hamilton .75 2.00
60 Carlton Fisk .60 1.50
61 Ian Kinsler .75 2.00
62 Roberto Alomar .60 1.50
63 Ryan Braun .60 1.50
64 Roy Halladay .75 2.00
65 Adrian Beltre 1.00 2.50
66 Andrew McCutchen 1.00 2.50
67 Victor Martinez .75 2.00
68 Julio Teheran .75 2.00
69 Felix Hernandez .75 2.00
70 Ty Cobb 1.50 4.00
71 Willie Mays 3.00 8.00
72 Hanley Ramirez .75 2.00
73 Paul Molitor 1.00 2.50
74 Troy Tulowitzki 1.00 2.50
75 Paul Konerko .60 1.50
76 Michael Pineda .60 1.50
77 Pablo Sandoval .75 2.00
78 Sandy Koufax 2.00 5.00
79 Ryan Zimmerman .75 2.00
80 Phil Niekro .60 1.50
81 Joe DiMaggio 2.00 5.00
82 Jackie Robinson 1.00 2.50
83 Mike Trout 60.00 150.00
84 Dan Uggla .75 2.00
85 Reggie Jackson .60 1.50
86 Starlin Castro .75 2.00
87 Jaime Garcia .75 2.00
88 Bob Gibson .60 1.50
89 Ichiro Suzuki 1.25 3.00
90 Alex Rodriguez 1.25 3.00
91 Paul O'Neill .60 1.50
92 Johnny Bench 1.00 2.50
93 Carl Yastrzemski 1.50 4.00
94 Brooks Robinson .60 1.50
95 Hunter Pence .60 1.50
96 Jacoby Ellsbury .75 2.00
97 Jose Bautista .75 2.00
98 Steve Carlton .60 1.50
99 Tim Lincecum .75 2.00
100 Miguel Cabrera 1.00 2.50

2012 Topps Museum Collection Blue

*BLUE: 1X TO 2.5X BASIC
STATED ODDS 1:6 PACKS
STATED PRINT RUN 99 SER.#'d SETS

2012 Topps Museum Collection Copper

*COPPER: .5X TO 1.2X BASIC
STATED PRINT RUN 299 SER.#'d SETS

2012 Topps Museum Collection Green

*GREEN: .6X TO 1.5X BASIC
STATED ODDS 1:3 PACKS
STATED PRINT RUN 199 SER.#'d SETS

2012 Topps Museum Collection Archival Autographs

STATED ODDS 1:5 PACKS
PRINT RUN B/WN 25-399 COPIES PER
EXCHANGE DEADLINE 3/31/2015
AC Aroldis Chapman/299 10.00 25.00
AC2 Aroldis Chapman/399 10.00 25.00
AG Adrian Gonzalez/25 12.50 30.00
AK Al Kaline/25 60.00 150.00
AM Andrew McCutchen/299 20.00 50.00
AO Alexi Ogando/399 6.00 15.00
AO2 Alexi Ogando/399 6.00 15.00
AP Andy Pettitte/25 40.00 80.00
APU Albert Pujols/25 75.00 150.00
AR Anthony Rizzo/399 20.00 50.00
ARA Aramis Ramirez/100 6.00 15.00
BB Brandon Belt/399 4.00 10.00
BP Buster Posey/25 100.00 200.00
CC Carl Crawford/25 8.00 20.00
CF Carlton Fisk/25 20.00 50.00
CGO Carlos Gonzalez/25 15.00 40.00
CK Clayton Kershaw/100 40.00 80.00
CK2 Clayton Kershaw/100 40.00 80.00
CS CC Sabathia EXCH 30.00 60.00
CY Carl Yastrzemski/25 50.00 100.00
DM Don Mattingly/25 50.00 100.00
DP Drew Pomeranz/299 6.00 15.00
DP2 Drew Pomeranz/299 6.00 15.00
DPE Dustin Pedroia/25 15.00 40.00
DW David Wright/25 12.00 30.00
EA Elvis Andrus/299 6.00 15.00
EH Eric Hosmer/100 10.00 25.00
EH2 Eric Hosmer/100 10.00 25.00
EH3 Eric Hosmer/100 10.00 25.00
EL Evan Longoria/25 30.00 60.00
EM Edgar Martinez/25 12.00 30.00
FF Freddie Freeman/25 20.00 50.00
FH Felix Hernandez/25 30.00 60.00
IK Ian Kennedy/100 8.00 20.00
JB Jay Bruce/100 8.00 20.00
JBE Johnny Bench EXCH 50.00 100.00
JG Jaime Garcia/399 6.00 15.00
JH Jeremy Hellickson/299 6.00 15.00
JH2 Jeremy Hellickson/299 6.00 15.00
JHA Josh Hamilton/25 20.00 50.00
JM Jesus Montero/25 12.50 30.00
JMA Joe Mauer EXCH 30.00 60.00
JR Jim Rice/100 8.00 20.00
JT Julio Teheran/399 8.00 20.00
JW Jered Weaver EXCH 6.00 15.00
KG Ken Griffey Jr. EXCH 300.00 400.00
MC Miguel Cabrera 60.00 120.00
MK Matt Kemp EXCH 30.00 60.00
MK2 Matt Kemp EXCH 30.00 60.00
MM Matt Moore/399 6.00 15.00
MMO Mike Moustakas/299 8.00 20.00
MP Michael Pineda/299 6.00 15.00
MP2 Michael Pineda/299 6.00 15.00
MS Mike Stanton/25 40.00 80.00
MT Mark Trumbo/399 10.00 25.00
MT2 Mark Trumbo/399 10.00 25.00
MT3 Mark Trumbo/399 10.00 25.00
MTR Mike Trout/25 300.00 800.00
NF Neftali Feliz/299 6.00 15.00
NR Nolan Ryan/25 200.00 300.00
PF Prince Fielder/25 10.00 25.00
PO Paul O'Neill/25 12.50 30.00
RC Robinson Cano EXCH 50.00 100.00
RH Roy Halladay EXCH 60.00 120.00
RJ Reggie Jackson/25 50.00 100.00
RR Ricky Romero/399 6.00 15.00
RR2 Ricky Romero/399 6.00 15.00
RZ Ryan Zimmerman/25 40.00 80.00
SC Starlin Castro/100 8.00 20.00
SK Sandy Koufax/25 350.00 500.00
SP Salvador Perez/399 15.00 40.00
WM Willie Mays EXCH 175.00 350.00
YU Yu Darvish EXCH 500.00 1000.00

2012 Topps Museum Collection Canvas Collection

APPX.ODDS 1:4 PACKS
CC1 Babe Ruth 6.00 15.00
CC2 Lou Gehrig 5.00 12.00
CC3 Ty Cobb 4.00 10.00
CC4 Stan Musial 4.00 10.00
CC5 Adrian Gonzalez 2.00 5.00
CC6 Willie Mays 5.00 12.00
CC7 Mickey Mantle 8.00 20.00
CC8 Warren Spahn 1.50 4.00
CC9 Bob Gibson 1.50 4.00
CC10 Johnny Bench 2.50 6.00
CC11 Miguel Cabrera 2.50 6.00
CC12 Frank Robinson 1.50 4.00
CC13 Tom Seaver 1.50 4.00
CC14 Roberto Clemente 6.00 15.00
CC15 Steve Carlton 1.50 4.00
CC16 Yogi Berra 2.50 6.00
CC17 Jim Thome 2.00 5.00
CC18 Jackie Robinson 2.50 6.00
CC19 Ken Griffey 5.00 12.00
CC20 Rickey Henderson 2.50 6.00
CC21 Nolan Ryan 8.00 20.00
CC22 Eddie Mathews 2.50 6.00
CC23 Cal Ripken Jr. 8.00 20.00
CC24 Tony Gwynn 2.50 6.00
CC25 Ichiro Suzuki 3.00 8.00
CC26 Carl Yastrzemski 4.00 10.00
CC27 Joe Mauer 2.00 5.00
CC28 Josh Hamilton 2.00 5.00
CC29 Ozzie Smith 3.00 8.00
CC30 Ryan Braun 1.50 4.00
CC31 Willie McCovey 1.50 4.00
CC32 Jim Palmer 1.50 4.00
CC33 Rod Carew 1.50 4.00
CC34 Derek Jeter 6.00 15.00
CC35 Duke Snider 1.50 4.00
CC36 Al Kaline 2.50 6.00
CC37 Alex Rodriguez 3.00 8.00
CC38 Harmon Killebrew 2.50 6.00
CC39 Reggie Jackson 1.50 4.00
CC40 Vladimir Guerrero 2.00 5.00
CC41 Robinson Cano 2.00 5.00
CC42 Robin Yount 2.50 6.00
CC43 Roy Halladay 2.00 5.00
CC44 Wade Boggs 1.50 4.00
CC45 Eddie Murray 1.00 2.50
CC46 Johan Santana 2.00 5.00
CC47 Mariano Rivera 3.00 8.00
CC48 Carlton Fisk 1.50 4.00

2012 Topps Museum Collection Jumbo Lumber

STATED ODDS 1:38 PACKS
STATED PRINT RUN 30 SER.#'d SETS
AE Andre Ethier 12.00 30.00
AG Adrian Gonzalez 10.00 25.00
AJ Adam Jones 8.00 20.00
AK Al Kaline 20.00 50.00
AR Alexei Ramirez 10.00 25.00
BU B.J. Upton 8.00 20.00
CF Carlton Fisk 12.00 30.00
CG Carlos Gonzalez 6.00 15.00
CP Carlos Pena 8.00 20.00
DU Dan Uggla 6.00 15.00
DW David Wright 15.00 40.00
EL Evan Longoria 10.00 25.00
EM Eddie Murray 12.00 30.00
FR Frank Robinson 10.00 25.00
GB George Brett 12.00 30.00
GS Gary Sheffield 12.00 30.00
HR Hanley Ramirez 10.00 25.00
IR Ivan Rodriguez 10.00 25.00
JB Jose Bautista 12.00 30.00
JD Joe DiMaggio 40.00 100.00
JE Jacoby Ellsbury 12.00 30.00
JH Jason Heyward 6.00 15.00
JV Joey Votto 15.00 40.00
MD Matt Dominguez 6.00 15.00
MK Matt Kemp 15.00 40.00
MS Mike Stanton 10.00 25.00
MT Mark Teixeira 8.00 20.00
OC Orlando Cepeda 10.00 25.00
OS Ozzie Smith 20.00 50.00
PF Prince Fielder 10.00 25.00
RC Rod Carew 10.00 25.00
RI Raul Ibanez 8.00 20.00
RJ Reggie Jackson 10.00 25.00
SC Starlin Castro 10.00 25.00
TG Tony Gwynn 12.00 30.00
TT Troy Tulowitzki 8.00 20.00
VG Vladimir Guerrero 10.00 25.00
WB Wade Boggs 15.00 40.00
YG Yovani Gallardo 10.00 25.00
ARO Alex Rodriguez 15.00 40.00
JBU Jay Bruce 10.00 25.00
MCA Miguel Cabrera 15.00 40.00
NMO Nyjer Morgan 10.00 25.00

2012 Topps Museum Collection Momentous Material Jumbo Relics

STATED ODDS 1:11 PACKS
STATED PRINT RUN 50 SER.#'d SETS
AB Albert Belle 6.00 15.00
ABE Adrian Beltre 6.00 15.00
ABU A.J. Burnett 4.00 10.00
AC Allen Craig 8.00 20.00
ACH Aroldis Chapman 8.00 20.00
AET Andre Ethier 12.00 30.00
AJ Adam Jones 12.00 30.00
AK Al Kaline 10.00 25.00
AM Andrew McCutchen 10.00 25.00
AP Andy Pettitte 8.00 20.00
APU Albert Pujols 15.00 40.00
AR Aramis Ramirez 4.00 10.00
AS Alfonso Soriano 8.00 20.00
BBU Billy Butler 5.00 12.00
BG Brett Gardner 10.00 25.00
BM Brian McCann 4.00 10.00
BP Buster Posey 10.00 25.00
BS Bruce Sutter 5.00 12.00
BU B.J. Upton 4.00 10.00
BW Brian Wilson 10.00 25.00
CB Clay Buchholz 5.00 12.00
CBE Carlos Beltran 5.00 12.00
CC Carl Crawford 6.00 15.00
CCA Chris Carpenter 8.00 20.00
CF Carlton Fisk 8.00 20.00
CG Curtis Granderson 10.00 25.00
CH Cole Hamels 10.00 25.00
CHA Corey Hart 8.00 20.00
CK Craig Kimbrel 6.00 15.00
CLE Cliff Lee 8.00 20.00
CS CC Sabathia 6.00 15.00
CU Chase Utley 8.00 20.00
CW C.J. Wilson 5.00 12.00
DG Dwight Gooden 10.00 25.00
DHA Dan Haren 4.00 10.00
DJ Derek Jeter 30.00 80.00
DM Don Mattingly 10.00 25.00
DO David Ortiz 10.00 25.00
DP Dustin Pedroia 10.00 25.00
DSN Duke Snider 12.50 30.00
DU Dan Uggla 10.00 25.00
DW David Wright 8.00 20.00
EA Elvis Andrus 5.00 12.00
EL Evan Longoria 8.00 20.00
EL2 Evan Longoria 8.00 20.00
FF Freddie Freeman 5.00 12.00
FH Felix Hernandez 5.00 12.00
GB Gordon Beckham 8.00 20.00
HP Hunter Pence 10.00 25.00
HR Hanley Ramirez 5.00 12.00
I Ichiro Suzuki 12.00 30.00
IK Ian Kennedy 5.00 12.00
IKI Ian Kinsler 5.00 12.00
IR Ivan Rodriguez 8.00 20.00
JB Jose Bautista 10.00 25.00
JBR Jay Bruce 8.00 20.00
JE Jacoby Ellsbury 12.00 30.00
JH Josh Hamilton 10.00 25.00
JH Joel Hanrahan 6.00 15.00
JHE Jeremy Hellickson 5.00 12.00
JJH J.J. Hardy 6.00 15.00
JMO Jesus Montero 10.00 25.00
JP Jorge Posada 10.00 25.00
JR Jose Reyes 12.00 30.00
JRO Jimmy Rollins 6.00 15.00
JU Justin Upton 5.00 12.00
LB Lance Berkman 12.00 30.00
LBR Lou Brock 6.00 15.00
LM Logan Morrison 4.00 10.00
MAC Matt Cain 10.00 25.00
MC Miguel Cabrera 12.00 30.00
MH Matt Holliday 5.00 12.00
MK Matt Kemp 12.00 30.00
MMO Matt Moore 10.00 25.00
MR Mariano Rivera 15.00 40.00
MS Mike Stanton 8.00 20.00
NF Neftali Feliz 5.00 12.00
NS Nick Swisher 10.00 25.00
NW Neil Walker 10.00 25.00
PF Prince Fielder 6.00 15.00
PF2 Prince Fielder 6.00 15.00
PN Phil Niekro 6.00 15.00
PO Paul O'Neill 10.00 25.00
RB Ryan Braun 10.00 25.00
RC Robinson Cano 10.00 25.00
RCA Rod Carew 6.00 15.00
RH Roy Halladay 15.00 40.00
RHO Ryan Howard 10.00 25.00
RM Russell Martin 10.00 25.00
RO Roy Oswalt 6.00 15.00
SC Starlin Castro 10.00 25.00
TG Tony Gwynn 8.00 20.00
THE Todd Helton 8.00 20.00
THU Torii Hunter 4.00 10.00
TL Tim Lincecum 10.00 25.00
UJ Ubaldo Jimenez 6.00 15.00
WS Willie Stargell 12.00 30.00
YG Yovani Gallardo 4.00 10.00
YM Yadier Molina 15.00 40.00
ZG Zack Greinke 4.00 10.00

2012 Topps Museum Collection Momentous Material Jumbo Relics Gold 35

*GOLD 35: .4X TO 1X BASIC
STATED ODDS 1:15 PACKS
STATED PRINT RUN 35 SER.#'d SETS

2012 Topps Museum Collection Primary Pieces Four Player Quad Relics

STATED ODDS 1:34 PACKS
STATED PRINT RUN 99 SER.#'d SETS
BWKR Heath Bell 8.00 20.00
Brian Wilson
Craig Kimbrel
Mariano Rivera
CGOF Miguel Cabrera 10.00 25.00
Adrian Gonzalez
David Ortiz
Prince Fielder
CHKA Allen Craig 6.00 15.00
Matt Holliday
Ian Kinsler
Elvis Andrus
CPUU Robinson Cano 8.00 20.00
Dustin Pedroia
Dan Uggla
Chase Utley
GHPT Gonz/How/Puj/Teix 8.00 20.00
GLGB Curtis Granderson 8.00 20.00
Evan Longoria
Adrian Gonzalez
Jose Bautista
LRUV Lee/Rol/Utley/Vict 12.50 30.00
MPRO Matt/Pett/Rivera/O'Neill 10.00 25.00
PCEO Ped/Craw/Ells/Ortiz 12.50 30.00
RHSS Ryan/Hall/CC/Seaver 10.00 25.00
RMKF Aramis Ramirez 6.00 15.00
Brian McCann
Matt Kemp
Prince Fielder
RRTC Jimmy Rollins 8.00 20.00
Hanley Ramirez
Troy Tulowitzki
Starlin Castro
TRAR Troy Tulowitzki 8.00 20.00
Hanley Ramirez
Elvis Andrus
Jose Reyes
VLHK Justin Verlander 10.00 25.00
Cliff Lee
Jeremy Hellickson
Craig Kimbrel
WRJR Wright/Rey/Jeter/ARod 12.50 30.00

2012 Topps Museum Collection Primary Pieces Four Player Quad Relics Red 75

*RED 75: .4X TO 1X BASIC
STATED ODDS 1:45 PACKS
STATED PRINT RUN 75 SER.#'d SETS

2012 Topps Museum Collection Primary Pieces Quad Relics

STATED ODDS 1:12 PACKS
STATED PRINT RUN 99 SER.#'d SETS
AG Adrian Gonzalez 6.00 15.00
AM Andrew McCutchen 10.00 25.00
AP Albert Pujols 12.50 30.00
BW Brian Wilson 12.50 30.00
CC Carl Crawford 8.00 20.00
CG Carlos Gonzalez 6.00 15.00
CL Cliff Lee 8.00 20.00
CU Chase Utley 10.00 25.00
DO David Ortiz 10.00 25.00
DP Dustin Pedroia 12.50 30.00
DU Dan Uggla 8.00 20.00
DW David Wright 8.00 20.00
EA Elvis Andrus 8.00 20.00
EL Evan Longoria 6.00 15.00
FH Felix Hernandez 8.00 20.
IK Ian Kennedy 6.00 15.
IR Ivan Rodriguez 8.00 20.
JB Jose Bautista 12.50 30.
JE Jacoby Ellsbury 10.00 25.
JR Jose Reyes 10.00 25.
JW Jered Weaver 10.00 25.
MC Miguel Cabrera 10.00 25.
MH Matt Holliday 10.00 25.
MK Matt Kemp 12.50 30.
MR Mariano Rivera 12.50 30.
MS Mike Stanton 10.00 25.
MT Mark Teixeira 8.00 20.
PF Prince Fielder 8.00 20.
RB Ryan Braun 20.00 50.
RC Robinson Cano 10.00 25.
RH Roy Halladay 10.00 25.
SC Starlin Castro 12.50 30.
SV Shane Victorino 10.00 25.
TH Todd Helton 6.00 15.
TL Tim Lincecum 10.00 25.
TT Troy Tulowitzki 12.50 30.
CKI Craig Kimbrel 10.00 25.
IKI Ian Kinsler 6.00 15.
JBE Josh Beckett 6.00 15.
JBR Jay Bruce 6.00 15.
JHE Jeremy Hellickson 6.00 15.
JMO Jesus Montero 8.00 20.
JRO Jimmy Rollins 8.00 20.
JVO Joey Votto 10.00 25.
RHO Ryan Howard 8.00 20.

2012 Topps Museum Collection Primary Pieces Quad Relics Re[d] 75

*RED 75: .4X TO 1X BASIC
STATED ODDS 1:15 PACKS
STATED PRINT RUN 75 SER.#'d SETS

2012 Topps Museum Collection Signature Swatches Dual Relic Autographs

STATED ODDS 1:9 PACKS
PRINT RUN B/WN 30-250 COPIES PER
EXCHANGE DEADLINE 3/31/2015
AC Allen Craig/179 8.00 20.
ACH Aroldis Chapman/99 30.00 60.
AE Andre Ethier/50 15.00 40.
AM Andrew McCutchen/70 40.00 80.
AR Aramis Ramirez/70 10.00 25.
BB Brandon Belt/250 6.00 15.
BBU Billy Butler/70 6.00 15.
BG Brett Gardner EXCH 15.00 40.
BM Brian McCann/50 20.00 50.
BP Brandon Phillips/70 10.00 25.
BU B.J. Upton/70 10.00 25.
CB Clay Buchholz/50 6.00 15.
CC Carl Crawford/30 8.00 20.
CF Carlton Fisk/30 30.00 60.
CH Chris Heisey/250 6.00 15.
CH2 Chris Heisey/250 6.00 15.
CHA Cole Hamels EXCH 12.50 30.
CK Craig Kimbrel/179 12.50 30.
CK2 Craig Kimbrel/30 20.00 50.
CKE Clayton Kershaw/70 50.00 100.
DA Dustin Ackley/70 10.00 25.
DE Danny Espinosa/179 6.00 15.
DGE Dillon Gee/250 6.00 15.
DP Dustin Pedroia/30 40.00 80.
DS Drew Storen/250 6.00 15.
DSN Duke Snider/30 10.00 25.
DU Dan Uggla/50 6.00 15.
GB Gordon Beckham/50 8.00 20.
GC Gary Carter/50 30.00 60.
GS Gary Sheffield/99 6.00 15.
HP Hunter Pence EXCH 40.00 80.
JB Jay Bruce/70 12.50 30.
JBA Jose Bautista/30 20.00 50.
JC Johnny Cueto/179 8.00 20.
JC2 Johnny Cueto/250 8.00 20.
JG Jaime Garcia/179 8.00 20.
JH Jeremy Hellickson/179 6.00 15.
JJ Jon Jay/250 6.00 15.
JW Jemile Weeks/250 6.00 15.
JWA Jordan Walden/179 6.00 15.
MB Madison Bumgarner/70 40.00 100.
MMO Matt Moore/99 10.00 25.
MS Mike Stanton/50 40.00 80.
MT Mark Trumbo/250 6.00 15.
NC Nelson Cruz/50 10.00 25.
NF Neftali Feliz/179 6.00 15.
PF Prince Fielder/30 10.00 25.
PS Pablo Sandoval/70 12.50 30.
RP Rick Porcello/70 10.00 25.
RZ Ryan Zimmerman/50 12.50 30.
SC Starlin Castro/70 6.00 15.
SV Shane Victorino/70 12.50 30.
VW Vernon Wells/30 8.00 20.

2012 Topps Museum Collection Signature Swatches Triple Relic Autographs

STATED ODDS 1:18 PACKS
PRINT RUNS B/WN 30-235 COPIES PER
EXCHANGE DEADLINE 3/31/2012
AC Allen Craig/209 12.50 30.
AG Adrian Gonzalez/30 12.50 30.
AR Anthony Rizzo/235 10.00 25.
BB Brandon Belt/209 10.00 25.
BBU Billy Butler/59 8.00 20.
CF Carlton Fisk/30 15.00 40.
CG Carlos Gonzalez/59 15.00 40.

Chris Heisey/235 6.00 15.00
Craig Kimbrel/175 15.00 40.00
Daniel Bard/235 8.00 20.00
Derek Holland/175 10.00 25.00
Duke Snider/30 30.00 60.00
Gary Carter/59 20.00 50.00
Hector Noesi/235 6.00 15.00
Hunter Pence EXCH 40.00 80.00
Jose Bautista/30 15.00 40.00
Jeremy Hellickson/59 6.00 15.00
Jesus Montero/175 12.50 30.00
Mike Stanton/59 20.00 50.00
Mark Trumbo/209 8.00 20.00
Neil Walker/209 10.00 25.00
Starlin Castro/59 10.00 25.00
Shane Victorino/59 6.00 15.00

013 Topps Museum Collection

erek Jeter 2.00 5.00
eorge Brett 1.50 4.00
uan Marichal .60 1.50
ed Williams 1.50 4.00
ob Gibson .60 1.50
ylan Bundy RC 1.25 3.00
rank Thomas .75 2.00
uster Posey 1.00 2.50
ackie Robinson .75 2.00
Gary Carter .60 1.50
Adrian Gonzalez .60 1.50
Bryce Harper 1.25 3.00
Starlin Castro .50 1.25
Troy Tulowitzki .75 2.00
Ryu Hyun-Jin RC 1.25 3.00
Wade Boggs .60 1.50
Giancarlo Stanton .75 2.00
Matt Cain .60 1.50
Hank Aaron 1.50 4.00
Will Middlebrooks .50 1.25
David Price .60 1.50
Miguel Cabrera .75 2.00
Yu Darvish .75 2.00
Felix Hernandez .60 1.50
Chris Sale .75 2.00
Bill Mazeroski .60 1.50
Robin Yount .75 2.00
Adam Jones .60 1.50
Johnny Bench .75 2.00
Ken Griffey Jr. 1.50 4.00
Matt Kemp .60 1.50
Stan Musial 1.25 3.00
Johnny Cueto .60 1.50
Willie McCovey .60 1.50
Carlos Gonzalez .60 1.50
Joe Mauer .60 1.50
Reggie Jackson .60 1.50
Yoenis Cespedes .75 2.00
Lou Brock .60 1.50
Cole Hamels .60 1.50
Chase Headley .50 1.25
Jose Bautista .60 1.50
Cal Ripken Jr. 2.50 6.00
John Smoltz .75 2.00
Al Kaline .75 2.00
Mike Trout 6.00 15.00
Justin Verlander .75 2.00
Dustin Pedroia .60 1.50
Gio Gonzalez .60 1.50
Stephen Strasburg .75 2.00
Nolan Ryan 2.50 6.00
Paul Molitor .75 2.00
Lou Gehrig 1.50 4.00
Prince Fielder .60 1.50
Willie Stargell .60 1.50
Norichika Aoki .50 1.25
Anthony Rizzo 1.25 3.00
Gary Sheffield .50 1.25
Brooks Robinson .60 1.50
David Wright .60 1.50
Joey Votto .75 2.00
Adrian Beltre .75 2.00
Ryne Sandberg 1.50 4.00
Joe Morgan .60 1.50
Ryan Braun .60 1.50
Pablo Sandoval .60 1.50
Aroldis Chapman .75 2.00
Babe Ruth 2.00 5.00
Sandy Koufax 1.50 4.00
Manny Machado RC 3.00 8.00
Clayton Kershaw 1.50 4.00
Albert Pujols 1.00 2.50
Justin Upton .60 1.50
Duke Snider .60 1.50
Billy Butler .50 1.25
Will Clark .60 1.50
Mike Schmidt 1.25 3.00
Ty Cobb 1.25 3.00
Jurickson Profar RC .60 1.50
Jake Peavy .50 1.25
Evan Longoria .60 1.50
R.A. Dickey .60 1.50
Eddie Murray .60 1.50
Albert Belle .50 1.25
Tom Seaver .60 1.50
Yadier Molina .75 2.00
Josh Hamilton .60 1.50
Rickey Henderson .75 2.00
Ozzie Smith 1.00 2.50
Bob Feller .60 1.50
Ernie Banks .75 2.00
Alex Rodriguez 1.00 2.50
93 Jered Weaver .60 1.50
94 Carlos Beltran .60 1.50
95 Harmon Killebrew .75 2.00
96 Jose Reyes .60 1.50
97 Andrew McCutchen .75 2.00
98 Roy Halladay .60 1.50
99 Tony Gwynn .75 2.00
100 Willie Mays 1.50 4.00

2013 Topps Museum Collection Blue

*BLUE VET: 1.5X TO 4X BASIC
*BLUE RC: 1.5X TO 4X BASIC RC
STATED ODDS 1:8 PACKS
STATED PRINT RUN 99 SER.#'d SETS

2013 Topps Museum Collection Copper

*COPPER VET: .5X TO 1.2X BASIC
*COPPER RC: .5X TO 1.2X BASIC RC
STATED PRINT RUN 424 SER.#'d SETS

2013 Topps Museum Collection Green

*GREEN VET: .75X TO 2X BASIC
*GREEN RC: .75X TO 2X BASIC RC
STATED ODDS 1:4 PACKS
STATED PRINT RUN 199 SER.#'d SETS

2013 Topps Museum Collection Autographs

PRINT RUNS B/WN 27-399 COPIES PER
EXCHANGE DEADLINE 5/31/2016
AB Albert Belle/50 6.00 15.00
AD Andre Dawson/50 8.00 20.00
AG Adrian Gonzalez/25 10.00 25.00
AH Drew Hutchison/399 5.00 12.00
AJ Adam Jones/50 10.00 25.00
AK Al Kaline/50 20.00 50.00
AR Anthony Rizzo/399 15.00 40.00
BB Bill Buckner/399 6.00 15.00
BBL Bert Blyleven/199 8.00 20.00
BBU Billy Butler/399 6.00 15.00
BG Bob Gibson EXCH 20.00 50.00
BS Bruce Sutter/50 10.00 25.00
BW Billy Williams/199 10.00 25.00
CB Craig Biggio/25 30.00 60.00
CF Cecil Fielder/199 6.00 15.00
CKI Craig Kimbrel/50 20.00 50.00
CW C.J. Wilson/399 5.00 12.00
DBU Dylan Bundy/399 5.00 12.00
DE Dennis Eckersley/50 12.00 30.00
DH Derek Holland/399 5.00 12.00
DM Don Mattingly/20 40.00 80.00
DME Devin Mesoraco/399 5.00 12.00
DMU Dale Murphy/50 20.00 50.00
DP Dustin Pedroia/25 30.00 60.00
DS Dave Stewart/159 6.00 15.00
DST Drew Storen/399 5.00 12.00
DSU Don Sutton/399 6.00 15.00
DW David Wright/20 50.00 100.00
EL Evan Longoria/20 50.00 100.00
GS Giancarlo Stanton/199 25.00 60.00
HA Hank Aaron/20 125.00 250.00
JA Jim Abbott/399 5.00 12.00
JB Johnny Bench/110 30.00 80.00
JBA Jose Bautista/25 12.00 30.00
JC Johnny Cueto/50 5.00 12.00
JH Jason Heyward/50 12.00 30.00
JK John Kruk/199 6.00 15.00
JPA Jarrod Parker/399 5.00 12.00
JPR Jurickson Profar/399 5.00 12.00
JR Jim Rice/399 6.00 15.00
JS John Smoltz/25 30.00 60.00
JSE Jean Segura/399 6.00 15.00
JW Jered Weaver/25 15.00 40.00
KG Ken Griffey Jr. EXCH 100.00 200.00
MA Matt Adams/399 5.00 12.00
MC Miguel Cabrera/20 125.00 250.00
MMA Manny Machado/50 30.00 60.00
MMO Matt Moore/399 5.00 12.00
MT Mike Trout/27 175.00 350.00
MW Maury Wills/399 5.00 12.00
NE Nate Eovaldi/399 5.00 12.00
PF Prince Fielder/20 30.00 60.00
PG Paul Goldschmidt/399 12.00 30.00
RD R.A. Dickey/50 12.00 30.00
RV Robin Ventura/199 8.00 20.00
SM Starling Marte/399 6.00 15.00
TB Trevor Bauer/399 6.00 15.00
TF Todd Frazier/399 5.00 12.00
TR Tim Raines/199 8.00 20.00
TSK Tyler Skaggs/399 5.00 12.00
VB Vida Blue/399 5.00 12.00
WC Will Clark/399 12.00 30.00
WJ Wally Joyner/399 6.00 15.00
WM Will Middlebrooks/399 5.00 12.00
WMA Willie Mays/20 150.00 250.00
WMI Wade Miley/399 5.00 12.00
WP Wily Peralta/399 5.00 12.00
WR Wilin Rosario/399 5.00 12.00
YA Yonder Alonso/399 5.00 12.00
YC Yoenis Cespedes/399 6.00 15.00
YD Yu Darvish/25 75.00 150.00
YG Yovani Gallardo/50 6.00 15.00

2013 Topps Museum Collection Canvas Collection

STATED ODDS 1:4 PACKS
1 Albert Pujols 1.25 3.00
2 Andrew McCutchen 1.00 2.50
3 Stephen Strasburg 1.00 2.50
4 David Price .75 2.00
5 Bryce Harper 1.50 4.00
6 Buster Posey 1.25 3.00
7 Prince Fielder .75 2.00
8 Mike Trout 8.00 20.00
9 Willie Mays 2.00 5.00
10 Cal Ripken Jr. 3.00 8.00
11 Ryan Braun .75 2.00
12 Reggie Jackson .75 2.00
13 Johnny Bench 1.00 2.50
14 Roberto Clemente 2.50 6.00
15 Mike Schmidt 1.50 4.00
16 Carlton Fisk .75 2.00
17 Yu Darvish 1.00 2.50
18 Clayton Kershaw 2.00 5.00
19 R.A. Dickey .75 2.00
20 Nolan Ryan 3.00 8.00
21 Tony Gwynn 1.00 2.50
22 Derek Jeter 2.50 6.00
23 Ernie Banks 1.00 2.50
24 Ozzie Smith 1.25 3.00
25 George Brett 2.00 5.00
26 Will Clark .75 2.00
27 Stan Musial 1.50 4.00
28 Miguel Cabrera 1.00 2.50
29 Ken Griffey Jr. 2.00 5.00
30 Ted Williams 2.00 5.00
31 John Smoltz 1.00 2.50
32 Tom Seaver .75 2.00
33 Felix Hernandez .75 2.00
34 Orlando Cepeda .75 2.00
35 Lou Gehrig 2.00 5.00

2013 Topps Museum Collection Jumbo Lumber

STATED ODDS 1:35 PACKS
STATED PRINT RUN 30 SER.#'d SETS
AB Albert Belle 10.00 25.00
AD Adam Dunn 6.00 15.00
AG Anthony Gose 8.00 20.00
AJ Adam Jones 10.00 25.00
AK Al Kaline 15.00 40.00
AP Albert Pujols 10.00 25.00
AROD Alex Rodriguez 15.00 40.00
BB Bill Buckner 8.00 20.00
BE Brandon Belt 12.50 30.00
BM Bill Mazeroski 12.50 30.00
BR Brooks Robinson 20.00 50.00
BW Brett Wallace 6.00 15.00
CF Carlton Fisk 6.00 15.00
CFI Cecil Fielder 12.50 30.00
CH Chris Heisey 5.00 12.00
CK Clayton Kershaw 8.00 20.00
CP Carlos Pena 5.00 12.00
CR Cal Ripken Jr. 30.00 60.00
CRO Cody Ross 5.00 12.00
DD David DeJesus 5.00 12.00
DGO Dee Gordon 5.00 12.00
DH Daniel Hudson 8.00 20.00
DJU David Justice 12.50 30.00
DMA Don Mattingly 30.00 60.00
DME Devin Mesoraco 6.00 15.00
DS Darryl Strawberry 12.50 30.00
DST Drew Stubbs 5.00 12.00
DU Dan Uggla 5.00 12.00
DWR David Wright 10.00 25.00
EA Elvis Andrus 6.00 15.00
EBA Ernie Banks 15.00 40.00
EE Edwin Encarnacion EXCH 6.00 15.00
EL Evan Longoria 8.00 20.00
EM Eddie Murray 12.50 30.00
FJE Fergie Jenkins 5.00 12.00
GG Goose Gossage 10.00 25.00
GSH Gary Sheffield 5.00 12.00
HP Hunter Pence 12.50 30.00
HR Hanley Ramirez 10.00 25.00
ID Ian Desmond 5.00 12.00
IK Ian Kinsler 8.00 20.00
JB Johnny Bench 15.00 40.00
JBR Jay Bruce 8.00 20.00
JC Johnny Cueto 5.00 12.00
JH Josh Hamilton 10.00 25.00
JHE Jason Heyward 12.50 30.00
JJA Jon Jay 10.00 25.00
JK Jason Kubel 5.00 12.00
JL James Loney 15.00 40.00
JR Jim Rice 10.00 25.00
JV Joey Votto 10.00 25.00
JZ Jordan Zimmermann 10.00 25.00
LB Lou Brock 20.00 50.00
MC Melky Cabrera 5.00 12.00
MD Matt Dominguez 5.00 12.00
MK Matt Kemp 8.00 20.00
MM Mike Morse 5.00 12.00
MP Martin Prado 5.00 12.00
MS Mike Schmidt 12.50 30.00
MTE Mark Teixeira 12.50 30.00
NC Nelson Cruz 5.00 12.00
OS Ozzie Smith 10.00 25.00
PS Pablo Sandoval 8.00 20.00
RC Rod Carew 10.00 25.00
RJ Reggie Jackson 12.50 30.00
RY Robin Yount 10.00 25.00
SC Starlin Castro 10.00 25.00
SG Steve Garvey 50.00 100.00
SV Shane Victorino 8.00 20.00
TG Tony Gwynn 10.00 25.00
TL Tim Lincecum 12.50 30.00
TW Ted Williams 40.00 80.00
UJ Ubaldo Jimenez 5.00 12.00
WB Wade Boggs 12.50 30.00
ZG Zack Greinke 6.00 15.00

2013 Topps Museum Collection Momentous Material Jumbo Relics

STATED ODDS 1:11 PACKS
STATED PRINT RUN 50 SER.#'d SETS
AD Adam Dunn 5.00 12.00
AE Andre Ethier 3.00 8.00
AGO Adrian Gonzalez 4.00 10.00
AJ Austin Jackson 5.00 12.00
AJO Adam Jones 6.00 15.00
AK Al Kaline 15.00 40.00
AM Andrew McCutchen 10.00 25.00
APE Andy Pettitte 6.00 15.00
AR Anthony Rizzo 10.00 25.00
AROD Alex Rodriguez 15.00 40.00
AS Alfonso Soriano 4.00 10.00
AW Adam Wainwright 8.00 20.00
BB Billy Butler 4.00 10.00
BF Bob Feller 15.00 40.00
BG Bob Gibson 10.00 25.00
BGA Brett Gardner 6.00 15.00
BH Bryce Harper 12.50 30.00
BM Brandon Morrow 5.00 12.00
BMC Brian McCann 6.00 15.00
BP Brandon Phillips 8.00 20.00
BR Brooks Robinson 15.00 40.00
BW Brett Wallace 3.00 8.00
CBI Chad Billingsley 5.00 12.00
CCS CC Sabathia 10.00 25.00
CF Carlton Fisk 8.00 20.00
CG Carlos Gonzalez 5.00 12.00
CH Cole Hamels 6.00 15.00
CJ Chipper Jones 10.00 25.00
CK Clayton Kershaw 8.00 20.00
CKI Craig Kimbrel 4.00 10.00
CL Cliff Lee 5.00 12.00
CM Carlos Marmol 3.00 8.00
CP Carlos Pena 3.00 8.00
CR Cal Ripken Jr. 12.50 30.00
CRA Colby Rasmus 3.00 8.00
CSA Carlos Santana 6.00 15.00
DA Dustin Ackley 5.00 12.00
DF David Freese 8.00 20.00
DJ Derek Jeter 20.00 50.00
DJE Desmond Jennings 3.00 8.00
DM Don Mattingly 15.00 40.00
DP David Price 3.00 8.00
DS Darryl Strawberry 6.00 15.00
DW David Wright 12.50 30.00
DYB Dylan Bundy 12.50 30.00
EA Elvis Andrus 4.00 10.00
EL Evan Longoria 5.00 12.00
EM Eddie Murray 5.00 12.00
FF Freddie Freeman 6.00 15.00
FH Felix Hernandez 6.00 15.00
GB George Brett 12.50 30.00
GG Gio Gonzalez 4.00 10.00
HK Harmon Killebrew 15.00 40.00
HR Hanley Ramirez 4.00 10.00
HW Hoyt Wilhelm 10.00 25.00
ID Ike Davis 4.00 10.00
IDE Ian Desmond 4.00 10.00
IK Ian Kinsler 4.00 10.00
IKE Ian Kennedy 3.00 8.00
JA Jose Altuve 5.00 12.00
JAR J.P. Arencibia 5.00 12.00
JAX John Axford 4.00 10.00
JB Johnny Bench 10.00 25.00
JBR Jay Bruce 5.00 12.00
JC Johnny Cueto 4.00 10.00
JG Jaime Garcia 5.00 12.00
JH Josh Hamilton 8.00 20.00
JHE Jason Heyward 8.00 20.00
JJ Josh Johnson 4.00 10.00
JK Jason Kipnis 8.00 20.00
JKU Jason Kubel 3.00 8.00
JL Jon Lester 5.00 12.00
JM Justin Morneau 5.00 12.00
JMA Joe Mauer 4.00 10.00
JMC James McDonald 3.00 8.00
JMO Jesus Montero 3.00 8.00
JOZ Jordan Zimmermann 5.00 12.00
JP Jarrod Parker 4.00 10.00
JPE Jake Peavy 3.00 8.00
JR Jose Reyes 6.00 15.00
JRE Josh Reddick 5.00 12.00
JRO Jimmy Rollins 5.00 12.00
JS Johan Santana 5.00 12.00
JSM John Smoltz 6.00 15.00
JT Jacob Turner 3.00 8.00
JU Justin Upton 5.00 12.00
JV Justin Verlander 12.50 30.00
JVO Joey Votto 10.00 25.00
JW Jered Weaver 5.00 12.00
JWE Jemile Weeks 3.00 8.00
LL Lance Lynn 6.00 15.00
MB Madison Bumgarner 12.50 30.00
MC Miguel Cabrera 12.50 30.00
MCA Matt Cain 6.00 15.00
MCB Melky Cabrera 3.00 8.00
MH Matt Harvey 10.00 25.00
MMI Mike Minor 6.00 15.00
MMO Mike Moustakas 4.00 10.00
MS Mike Schmidt 10.00 25.00
MSC Max Scherzer 6.00 15.00
MT Mike Trout 12.00 30.00
MTR Mark Trumbo 8.00 20.00
NC Nelson Cruz 4.00 10.00
NF Neftali Feliz 3.00 8.00
NM Nick Markakis 8.00 20.00
NS Nick Swisher 5.00 12.00
NW Neil Walker 5.00 12.00
PA Pedro Alvarez 5.00 12.00
PF Prince Fielder 8.00 20.00
PK Paul Konerko 4.00 10.00
PN Phil Niekro 6.00 15.00
RB Ryan Braun 6.00 15.00
RC Rod Carew 6.00 15.00
RD R.A. Dickey 4.00 10.00
RH Rickey Henderson 12.50 30.00
RHA Roy Halladay 5.00 12.00
RHO Ryan Howard 5.00 12.00
RJ Reggie Jackson 12.50 30.00
RP Rick Porcello 5.00 12.00
RS Ryne Sandberg 15.00 40.00
RY Robin Yount 10.00 25.00
SC Starlin Castro 8.00 20.00
SM Stan Musial 30.00 60.00
SMA Shaun Marcum 3.00 8.00
SMR Starling Marte 10.00 25.00
SS Stephen Strasburg 6.00 15.00
TG Tony Gwynn 8.00 20.00
TH Torii Hunter 5.00 12.00
TL Tim Lincecum 10.00 25.00
TM Tommy Milone 3.00 8.00
TT Troy Tulowitzki 6.00 15.00
TW Ted Williams 40.00 80.00
VM Victor Martinez 5.00 12.00
WB Wade Boggs 10.00 25.00
WD Wade Davis 3.00 8.00
WMI Will Middlebrooks 6.00 15.00
WR Wilin Rosario 3.00 8.00
YA Yonder Alonso 3.00 8.00
YC Yoenis Cespedes 8.00 20.00
YD Yu Darvish 15.00 40.00
YG Yovani Gallardo 3.00 8.00

2013 Topps Museum Collection Momentous Material Jumbo Relics Gold

*GOLD: .4X TO 1X BASIC
STATED ODDS 1:15 PACKS
STATED PRINT RUN 35 SER.#'d SETS

2013 Topps Museum Collection Primary Pieces Four Player Quad Relics

STATED ODDS 1:32 PACKS
STATED PRINT RUN 99 SER.#'d SETS
1 Mattingly/Strawberry/CC/ARod 15.00 40.00
2 Weaver/Wilson/Trout/Trumbo 12.50 30.00
3 Phillips/Votto/Bench/Bruce 12.50 30.00
4 Koufax/Garvey/Ethier/Kemp 10.00 25.00
5 Prince/Mur/Ripk/Miggy 10.00 25.00
6 Rob/Cano/Kins/Pedr 20.00 50.00
7 Bog/Wright/Schm/Miggy 10.00 25.00
8 Ben/McC/Sant/Mauer 15.00 40.00
9 Uggla/Smoltz/Ryan/Kinsler 10.00 25.00
10 Mays/Griffey/Harper/Trout 50.00 100.00
11 Tulo/Jeter/ARod/Ripken 20.00 50.00
12 Bruce/Votto/Choo/Phillips 15.00 40.00
13 Dickey/Harvey/Sant/Seaver 20.00 50.00
14 Linc/Koufax/Kershaw/Cain 10.00 25.00
15 Smoltz/Posey/Heyward/Cain 15.00 40.00
16 David Ortiz 10.00 25.00
Ryan Howard
Chase Utley
Wade Boggs
17 Yonder Alonso 8.00 20.00
Tony Gwynn
Adrian Gonzalez
Andre Ethier
18 David Price 10.00 25.00
Matt Cain
Justin Verlander
Madison Bumgarner
19 Buster Posey 12.50 30.00
Tim Lincecum
Ian Kinsler
Yu Darvish
20 Andrew McCutchen 12.50 30.00
Yoenis Cespedes
Reggie Jackson
Willie Stargell
21 Mays/Lincecum/Cain/Posey 15.00 40.00
22 Garcia/Gibs/Holl/Musial 12.50 30.00
23 Gio/Zimm/Harper/Strasburg 12.50 30.00
24 Stras/Hernan/Darvish/Price 10.00 25.00
25 Cesped/Darv/Harp/Trout 12.00 30.00

2013 Topps Museum Collection Primary Pieces Four Player Quad Relics Copper

*COPPER: .4X TO 1X BASIC
STATED ODDS 1:42 HOBBY
STATED PRINT RUN 75 SER.#'d SETS

2013 Topps Museum Collection Primary Pieces Quad Relics

STATED ODDS 1:12 PACKS
STATED PRINT RUN 99 SER.#'d SETS
AB Adrian Beltre 4.00 10.00
AC Aroldis Chapman 5.00 12.00
AG Alex Gordon 6.00 15.00
AJ Austin Jackson 8.00 20.00
AM Andrew McCutchen 10.00 25.00
AP Albert Pujols 10.00 25.00
AROD Alex Rodriguez 6.00 15.00
BB Brandon Beachy 4.00 10.00
BBU Billy Butler 4.00 10.00
BP Brandon Phillips 6.00 15.00
BU B.J. Upton 4.00 10.00
CB Chad Billingsley 4.00 10.00
CH Cole Hamels 6.00 15.00
CK Clayton Kershaw 10.00 25.00
CR Colby Rasmus 4.00 10.00
CS Chris Sale 5.00 12.00
CSA Carlos Santana 4.00 10.00
CW C.J. Wilson 4.00 10.00
DA Dustin Ackley 4.00 10.00
DG Dee Gordon 4.00 10.00
DH Dan Haren 4.00 10.00
DO David Ortiz 8.00 20.00
DP Dustin Pedroia 5.00 12.00
DPR David Price 5.00 12.00
DS Drew Stubbs 4.00 10.00
DU Dan Uggla 4.00 10.00
DW David Wright 12.50 30.00
FH Felix Hernandez 6.00 15.00
GB Gordon Beckham 4.00 10.00
GG Gio Gonzalez 4.00 10.00
GS Giancarlo Stanton 6.00 15.00
HI Hisashi Iwakuma 4.00 10.00
HR Hanley Ramirez 6.00 15.00
IK Ian Kinsler 4.00 10.00
IKE Ian Kennedy 4.00 10.00
JBR Jay Bruce 5.00 12.00
JH Jason Heyward 8.00 20.00
JK Jason Kipnis 4.00 10.00
JM Jesus Montero 4.00 10.00
JR Josh Reddick 4.00 10.00
JU Justin Upton 6.00 15.00
JV Joey Votto 6.00 15.00
JVE Justin Verlander 8.00 20.00
JW Jered Weaver 5.00 12.00
MC Miguel Cabrera 12.50 30.00
MCA Matt Cain 6.00 15.00
MH Matt Holliday 8.00 20.00
MK Matt Kemp 4.00 10.00
MM Matt Moore 5.00 12.00
MTE Mark Teixeira 5.00 12.00
MTR Mark Trumbo 12.50 30.00
NA Norichika Aoki 10.00 25.00
NC Nelson Cruz 5.00 12.00
PA Pedro Alvarez 6.00 15.00
PF Prince Fielder 5.00 12.00
RB Ryan Braun 6.00 15.00
RD R.A. Dickey 4.00 10.00
RH Roy Halladay 6.00 15.00
RHO Ryan Howard 6.00 15.00
RZ Ryan Zimmerman 5.00 12.00
SC Starlin Castro 6.00 15.00
TH Tommy Hanson 4.00 10.00
TM Tommy Milone 4.00 10.00
TS Tyler Skaggs 4.00 10.00
TT Troy Tulowitzki 6.00 15.00
VM Victor Martinez 5.00 12.00
YC Yoenis Cespedes 5.00 12.00
YG Yovani Gallardo 4.00 10.00

2013 Topps Museum Collection Primary Pieces Quad Relics Copper

*COPPER: .4X TO 1X BASIC
STATED ODDS 1:16 PACKS
STATED PRINT RUN 75 SER.#'d SETS

2013 Topps Museum Collection Signature Swatches Dual Relic Autographs

STATED ODDS 1:10 PACKS
PRINT RUNS B/WN 25-299 COPIES PER
EXCHANGE DEADLINE 5/31/2016
AA Alex Avila EXCH 6.00 15.00
AC Alex Cobb/299 5.00 12.00
ACA Andrew Cashner/299 5.00 12.00
AE Andre Ethier/50 10.00 25.00
AG Adrian Gonzalez/25 15.00 40.00
AJ Austin Jackson EXCH 8.00 20.00
AK Al Kaline/50 25.00 50.00
AR Anthony Rizzo/99 40.00 100.00
BB Billy Butler/299 6.00 15.00
BBE Brandon Beachy EXCH 8.00 20.00
BG Brett Gardner EXCH 10.00 25.00
BH Bryce Harper/50 125.00 250.00
BP Brandon Phillips/50 10.00 25.00
BS Bruce Sutter/50 15.00 40.00
CG Carlos Gonzalez/50 5.00 12.00
CK Clayton Kershaw/50 30.00 80.00
CKI Craig Kimbrel/50 12.50 30.00
CRA Colby Rasmus/99 6.00 15.00
CS Carlos Santana/99 5.00 12.00
CW C.J. Wilson/50 8.00 20.00
DB Domonic Brown/99 5.00 12.00
DF David Freese/50 20.00 50.00
DH Derek Holland/50 6.00 15.00
DM Devin Mesoraco/299 5.00 12.00
DO David Ortiz/50 20.00 50.00
DP Dustin Pedroia/50 20.00 50.00
DW David Wright/50 20.00 50.00
EA Elvis Andrus/99 6.00 15.00
EL Evan Longoria/50 10.00 25.00
FH Felix Hernandez/50 20.00 50.00
GS Giancarlo Stanton/50 30.00 60.00
GSH Gary Sheffield/99 8.00 20.00
HR Hanley Ramirez/50 12.50 30.00
IN Ivan Nova/99 5.00 12.00
JB Jay Bruce/50 15.00 40.00
JC Johnny Cueto/50 4.00 10.00
JG Jaime Garcia EXCH 5.00 12.00
JH Josh Hamilton/50 12.50 30.00
JJ Jon Jay EXCH 5.00 12.00
JK Jason Kipnis/299 5.00 12.00
JMO Jesus Montero/99 6.00 15.00
JN Jeff Niemann/299 5.00 12.00
JP Jhonny Peralta/99 4.00 10.00
JPA Jarrod Parker/299 5.00 12.00
JR Josh Reddick EXCH 8.00 20.00
JS John Smoltz/85 30.00 60.00
JSE Jean Segura EXCH 15.00 40.00
JZ Jordan Zimmermann/50 5.00 12.00
MB Madison Bumgarner/50 30.00 80.00
MC Miguel Cabrera/50 30.00 80.00
MCA Matt Cain EXCH 15.00 40.00
MH Matt Holliday EXCH 15.00 40.00
MM Manny Machado/50 30.00 60.00
MMO Mike Moustakas EXCH 10.00 25.00
MO Mike Olt/212 5.00 12.00
MP Michael Pineda/99 10.00 25.00
MT Mike Trout/50 125.00 250.00
MTR Mark Trumbo/99 5.00 12.00
NE Nate Eovaldi/299 5.00 12.00
NF Neftali Feliz/99 4.00 10.00
PF Prince Fielder/50 10.00 25.00
PS Pablo Sandoval EXCH 25.00 60.00
RB Ryan Braun EXCH 10.00 25.00
RD R.A. Dickey/50 10.00 25.00
RZ Ryan Zimmerman/50 12.50 30.00
SC Starlin Castro/50 10.00 25.00
SM Starling Marte/50 8.00 20.00
TM Tommy Milone/299 6.00 15.00
TS Tyler Skaggs/299 5.00 12.00
WC Will Clark/50 30.00 60.00
WR Wilin Rosario/299 5.00 12.00
YA Yonder Alonso/99 6.00 15.00
YC Yoenis Cespedes/50 20.00 50.00
YG Yovani Gallardo/99 6.00 15.00
ZC Zack Cozart/299 5.00 12.00

2013 Topps Museum Collection Signature Swatches Triple Relic Autographs

STATED ODDS 1:15 PACKS
PRINT RUNS B/WN 50-299 COPIES PER
EXCHANGE DEADLINE 5/31/2016
AG Adrian Gonzalez/50 15.00 40.00
AK Al Kaline/50 25.00 50.00
BB Billy Butler/299 8.00 20.00
BG Brett Gardner EXCH 10.00 25.00
BP Brandon Phillips/50 12.50 30.00
BS Bruce Sutter/50 15.00 40.00
CG Carlos Gonzalez/50 15.00 40.00
CK Clayton Kershaw/50 50.00 100.00
CR Colby Rasmus/99 5.00 12.00
CSA Carlos Santana/299 4.00 10.00
CW C.J. Wilson/50 8.00 20.00
DH Derek Holland/99 6.00 15.00
DM Devin Mesoraco/299 5.00 12.00
DP Dustin Pedroia/50 20.00 50.00
FD Felix Doubront EXCH 5.00 12.00
GG Gio Gonzalez/50 5.00 12.00
ID Ian Desmond EXCH 8.00 20.00
JH Josh Hamilton/50 4.00 10.00
JJ Jon Jay/50 5.00 12.00
JP Jarrod Parker/299 5.00 12.00
JZ Jordan Zimmermann/50 12.00 30.00
KG Ken Griffey Jr. EXCH 100.00 200.00
KN Kirk Nieuwenhuis/299 5.00 12.00
MA Matt Adams/299 10.00 25.00
MC Miguel Cabrera/50 75.00 150.00
MCA Matt Cain EXCH 15.00 40.00
MH Matt Holliday EXCH 15.00 40.00
MM Manny Machado/99 30.00 60.00
MMO Mike Moustakas EXCH 10.00 25.00
MP Michael Pineda/99 8.00 20.00
PF Prince Fielder/50 20.00 50.00
RB Ryan Braun EXCH 10.00 25.00
RD R.A. Dickey/50 12.00 30.00
RZ Ryan Zimmerman/50 15.00 40.00
SM Starling Marte/99 8.00 20.00
TM Tommy Milone/299 5.00 12.00
TS Tyler Skaggs/299 6.00 15.00
WR Wilin Rosario/299 5.00 12.00
YA Yonder Alonso/224 4.00 10.00
YG Yovani Gallardo/50 6.00 15.00

2014 Topps Museum Collection

COMPLETE SET (100) 30.00 80.00
1 Avisail Garcia .50 1.25
2 Christian Yelich .75 2.00
3 Yasiel Puig .60 1.50
4 Nick Castellanos RC 1.25 3.00
5 Andre Dawson .50 1.25
6 Billy Hamilton RC .50 1.25
7 Wade Miley .40 1.00
8 Didi Gregorius .50 1.25
9 Xander Bogaerts RC 1.25 3.00
10 David Ortiz .60 1.50
11 Wilin Rosario .40 1.00
12 Julio Teheran .50 1.25
13 Travis d'Arnaud RC .50 1.25
14 Matt Adams .40 1.00
15 Jose Fernandez .60 1.50
16 Taijuan Walker RC .40 1.00
17 Todd Frazier .50 1.25
18 Ricky Nolasco .40 1.00
19 Mike Zunino .40 1.00
20 Paul Goldschmidt .60 1.50
21 Steve Carlton .50 1.25
22 Starling Marte .50 1.25
23 Kris Medlen .50 1.25
24 Jurickson Profar .50 1.25
25 Wil Myers .40 1.00
26 Juan Gonzalez .40 1.00

27 Yoenis Cespedes .60 1.50
28 Jason Kipnis .50 1.25
29 Shelby Miller .50 1.25
30 Allen Craig .50 1.25
31 David Freese .40 1.00
32 Jordan Zimmermann .50 1.25
33 Paul O'Neill .50 1.25
34 Chris Davis .40 1.00
35 James Shields .40 1.00
36 Jim Rice .50 1.25
37 Rafael Palmeiro .50 1.25
38 Albert Belle .40 1.00
39 Chris Sale .60 1.50
40 Will Clark .50 1.25
41 Adrian Gonzalez .50 1.25
42 Dustin Pedroia .60 1.50
43 Mike Mussina .50 1.25
44 Clayton Kershaw 1.25 3.00
45 Jeff Bagwell .50 1.25
46 Jered Weaver .50 1.25
47 Ivan Rodriguez .50 1.25
48 Manny Machado .60 1.50
49 Tom Glavine .50 1.25
50 Lou Brock .50 1.25
51 Yadier Molina .60 1.50
52 Ozzie Smith .75 2.00
53 Prince Fielder .50 1.25
54 Bob Gibson .50 1.25
55 John Smoltz .60 1.50
56 Don Mattingly 1.25 3.00
57 Nomar Garciaparra .50 1.25
58 Rod Carew .50 1.25
59 Bo Jackson .60 1.50
60 Babe Ruth 1.50 4.00
61 Miguel Cabrera .60 1.50
62 Mike Schmidt 1.00 2.50
63 Roger Clemens .75 2.00
64 Mike Trout 3.00 8.00
65 Pedro Martinez .50 1.25
66 Nolan Ryan 2.00 5.00
67 Robin Yount .50 1.25
68 Randy Johnson .60 1.50
69 Troy Tulowitzki .60 1.50
70 Rickey Henderson .60 1.50
71 Greg Maddux .75 2.00
72 Bryce Harper 1.00 2.50
73 Willie Mays 1.25 3.00
74 Mark McGwire 1.25 3.00
75 Yu Darvish .60 1.50
76 Sandy Koufax 1.25 3.00
77 Ken Griffey Jr. 1.25 3.00
78 Andrew Lambo RC .40 1.00
79 Cal Ripken Jr. 2.00 5.00
80 Hank Aaron 1.25 3.00
81 Devin Mesoraco .40 1.00
82 Oswaldo Arcia .40 1.00
83 Tony Cingrani .50 1.25
84 Mike Olt .40 1.00
85 Alex Cobb .40 1.00
86 Hisashi Iwakuma .50 1.25
87 Jean Segura .50 1.25
88 Felix Doubront .40 1.00
89 Jedd Gyorko .40 1.00
90 Yonder Alonso .40 1.00
91 Domonic Brown .50 1.25
92 Ryan Braun .50 1.25
93 R.A. Dickey .50 1.25
94 Anthony Rizzo 1.00 2.50
95 Gio Gonzalez .50 1.25
96 Johnny Bench .60 1.50
97 Josh Hamilton .50 1.25
98 Matt Moore .50 1.25
99 Trevor Bauer .60 1.50
100 Tony Gwynn .60 1.50

2014 Topps Museum Collection Blue

*BLUE: 2X TO 5X BASIC
*BLUE RC: 2X TO 5X BASIC RC
STATED ODDS 1:8 PACKS
STATED PRINT RUN 99 SER.#'d SETS
9 Xander Bogaerts 12.00 30.00
64 Mike Trout 12.00 30.00
66 Nolan Ryan 12.00 30.00

2014 Topps Museum Collection Copper

*COPPER: .6X TO 1.5X BASIC
*COPPER RC: .6X TO 1.5X BASIC RC

2014 Topps Museum Collection Green

*GREEN: 1.2X TO 3X BASIC
*GREEN RC: 1.2X TO 3X BASIC RC
STATED ODDS 1:4 PACKS
STATED PRINT RUN 199 SER.#'d SETS

2014 Topps Museum Collection Autographs

PRINT RUNS B/WN 10-399 COPIES PER
NO PRICING ON QTY 15 OR LESS
EXCHANGE DEADLINE 2/24/2016
AAABE Albert Belle/99 6.00 15.00
AAACO Alex Cobb/399 4.00 10.00
AAACR Allen Craig/399 6.00 15.00
AAAGO Adrian Gonzalez/25 6.00 15.00
AAAGOS Anthony Gose/399 4.00 10.00
AAAR Anthony Rizzo/399 15.00 40.00
AABHAM Billy Hamilton/399 5.00 12.00
AACK Clayton Kershaw/25 50.00 120.00
AACR Cal Ripken Jr. EXCH 90.00 150.00
AACS Chris Sale/99 12.00 30.00
AACY Christian Yelich/399 20.00 50.00
AADF David Freese/99 4.00 10.00
AADG Didi Gregorius/399 6.00 15.00
AADME Devin Mesoraco/399 6.00 15.00
AADO David Ortiz/199 40.00 100.00
AADP Dustin Pedroia/25 40.00 80.00
AADR Darin Ruf/399 5.00 12.00
AAFD Felix Doubront/399 4.00 10.00
AAHA Hank Aaron EXCH 150.00 250.00
AAHI Hisashi Iwakuma/199 8.00 20.00
AAJA Jose Abreu/25 20.00 50.00
AAJC Jose Canseco/99 12.00 30.00
AAJH Josh Hamilton/199 5.00 12.00
AAJK Jason Kipnis/399 5.00 12.00
AAJP Jurickson Profar/399 6.00 15.00
AAJR Jim Rice/99 6.00 15.00
AAJS Jean Segura/199 5.00 12.00
AAJSH James Shields/99 4.00 10.00
AAJTE Julio Teheran/399 5.00 12.00
AAJZ Jordan Zimmermann/99 5.00 12.00
AAKM Kris Medlen/399 5.00 12.00
AAKS Kyle Seager/399 4.00 10.00
AALB Lou Brock/99 20.00 50.00
AAMA Matt Adams/399 4.00 10.00
AAMMO Matt Moore/399 5.00 12.00
AAMMU Mike Mussina EXCH 15.00 40.00
AAMO Mike Olt/399 4.00 10.00
AAMZ Mike Zunino/399 4.00 10.00
AANC Nick Castellanos/399 12.00 30.00
AAPG Paul Goldschmidt/399 25.00 60.00
AAPO Paul O'Neill/99 12.00 30.00
AARB Ryan Braun/49 10.00 25.00
AARN Ricky Nolasco/399 4.00 10.00
AARP Rafael Palmeiro/99 8.00 20.00
AASC Steve Carlton/99 10.00 25.00
AASCI Steve Cishek/399 4.00 10.00
AASMI Shelby Miller/399 5.00 12.00
AATB Trevor Bauer/399 6.00 15.00
AATC Tony Cingrani/399 5.00 12.00
AATD Travis d'Arnaud/399 6.00 15.00
AATF Todd Frazier/399 5.00 12.00
AATGL Tom Glavine EXCH 30.00 60.00
AATGW Tony Gwynn/49 30.00 60.00
AATS Tyler Skaggs/399 4.00 10.00
AATW Taijuan Walker/399 4.00 10.00
AAWC Will Clark/99 15.00 40.00
AAWMI Wade Miley/399 4.00 10.00
AAWMY Wil Myers/260 4.00 10.00
AAWR Wilin Rosario/399 4.00 10.00
AAYC Yoenis Cespedes/399 4.00 10.00
AAZW Zack Wheeler/399 5.00 12.00

2014 Topps Museum Collection Canvas Collection

STATED ODDS 1:4 PACKS
CCR1 Mike Trout 5.00 12.00
CCR2 Deion Sanders .75 2.00
CCR3 Yu Darvish 1.00 2.50
CCR4 Bo Jackson 1.00 2.50
CCR5 Joe Mauer .75 2.00
CCR6 Stephen Strasburg 1.00 2.50
CCR7 Nolan Ryan 3.00 8.00
CCR8 Roberto Clemente 2.50 6.00
CCR9 Robinson Cano .75 2.00
CCR10 Mark McGwire 2.00 5.00
CCR11 Miguel Cabrera 1.00 2.50
CCR12 Yoenis Cespedes 1.00 2.50
CCR13 Don Mattingly 2.00 5.00
CCR14 Bryce Harper 1.50 4.00
CCR15 Tommy Lasorda .75 2.00
CCR16 Andrew McCutchen 1.00 2.50
CCR17 Tony Gwynn 1.00 2.50
CCR18 Matt Harvey .75 2.00
CCR19 Pedro Martinez .75 2.00
CCR20 Ernie Banks 1.00 2.50
CCR21 Tom Seaver .75 2.00
CCR22 Wade Boggs .75 2.00
CCR23 David Ortiz 1.00 2.50
CCR24 Brooks Robinson .75 2.00
CCR25 Ozzie Smith 1.25 3.00
CCR26 CC Sabathia .75 2.00
CCR27 Randy Johnson 1.00 2.50
CCR28 Ted Williams 2.00 5.00
CCR29 Jimmie Foxx 1.00 2.50
CCR30 Lou Brock .75 2.00
CCR31 Rickey Henderson 1.00 2.50
CCR32 Yogi Berra 1.00 2.50
CCR33 Dwight Gooden .60 1.50
CCR34 Paul Molitor 1.00 2.50
CCR35 Jackie Robinson 1.00 2.50
CCR36 Robin Yount 1.00 2.50
CCR37 Johnny Bench 1.00 2.50
CCR38 Ty Cobb 1.50 4.00
CCR39 Cal Ripken Jr. 3.00 8.00
CCR40 Justin Verlander 1.00 2.50
CCR41 Yogi Berra 1.00 2.50
CCR42 Reggie Jackson .75 2.00
CCR43 Lou Gehrig 2.00 5.00
CCR44 Johnny Bench 1.00 2.50
CCR45 Buster Posey 1.25 3.00
CCR46 Jose Fernandez 1.00 2.50
CCR47 Darryl Strawberry .60 1.50
CCR48 Lou Brock .75 2.00
CCR49 Joey Votto 1.00 2.50
CCR50 David Wright .75 2.00

2014 Topps Museum Collection Canvas Collection Jumbo

STATED ODDS 1:39 BOXES
STATED PRINT RUN 25 SER.#'d SETS
EXCAHNGE DEADLINE 2/24/2016
CCFAAM Andrew McCutchen EXCH 30.00 80.00
CCFABH Bryce Harper 25.00 60.00
CCFABJ Bo Jackson 30.00 80.00
CCFABP Buster Posey 30.00 80.00
CCFACR Cal Ripken Jr. 30.00 80.00
CCFADM Don Mattingly 20.00 50.00
CCFADO David Ortiz EXCH 30.00 80.00
CCFADS Deion Sanders EXCH 25.00 60.00
CCFAEB Ernie Banks 25.00 60.00
CCFAMC Miguel Cabrera EXCH 20.00 50.00
CCFAMM Mark McGwire 40.00 100.00
CCFAMT Mike Trout 50.00 120.00
CCFANR Nolan Ryan 30.00 80.00
CCFARC Robinson Cano 8.00 20.00
CCFARH Rickey Henderson 20.00 50.00
CCFARJ Randy Johnson EXCH 25.00 60.00
CCFATG Tony Gwynn 20.00 50.00
CCFATS Tom Seaver 15.00 40.00
CCFAYC Yoenis Cespedes 15.00 40.00
CCFAYD Yu Darvish EXCH 25.00 60.00

2014 Topps Museum Collection Jumbo Lumber

STATED ODDS 1:41 PACKS
STATED PRINT RUN 25 SER.#'d SETS
MMJLAB Adrian Beltre 10.00 25.00
MMJLABE Albert Belle 8.00 20.00
MMJLAD Andre Dawson 10.00 25.00
MMJLAJ Adam Jones 12.00 30.00
MMJLBP Brandon Phillips 10.00 25.00
MMJLBR Brooks Robinson 15.00 40.00
MMJLCB Carlos Beltran 8.00 20.00
MMJLCD Chris Davis 15.00 40.00
MMJLCDA Chris Davis 15.00 40.00
MMJLCG Cole Gillespie 6.00 15.00
MMJLCK Clayton Kershaw 20.00 50.00
MMJLCR Cal Ripken Jr. 20.00 50.00
MMJLDJ Derek Jeter 30.00 80.00
MMJLDJE Derek Jeter 30.00 80.00
MMJLDJT Derek Jeter 30.00 80.00
MMJLDM Don Mattingly 25.00 60.00
MMJLDMA Don Mattingly 25.00 60.00
MMJLDO David Ortiz 12.00 30.00
MMJLDOR David Ortiz 12.00 30.00
MMJLDS Drew Stubbs 6.00 15.00
MMJLDW David Wright 20.00 50.00
MMJLEL Evan Longoria 8.00 20.00
MMJLELO Evan Longoria 8.00 20.00
MMJLEM Eddie Mathews 20.00 50.00
MMJLEMD Eddie Murray 10.00 25.00
MMJLEMU Eddie Murray 10.00 25.00
MMJLFM Fred McGriff 10.00 25.00
MMJLHR Hyun-jin Ryu 8.00 20.00
MMJLIK Ian Kinsler 8.00 20.00
MMJLIR Ivan Rodriguez 8.00 20.00
MMJLJB Jay Bruce 10.00 25.00
MMJLJBE Johnny Bench 12.00 30.00
MMJLJBR Jay Bruce 10.00 25.00
MMJLJF Juan Francisco 6.00 15.00
MMJLJG Juan Gonzalez 30.00 80.00
MMJLJJ Jon Jay 8.00 20.00
MMJLJU Justin Upton 8.00 20.00
MMJLJUP Justin Upton 8.00 20.00
MMJLJV Joey Votto 20.00 50.00
MMJLJZ Jordan Zimmermann 8.00 20.00
MMJLMH Matt Harvey 8.00 20.00
MMJLMK Matt Kemp 8.00 20.00
MMJLMM Manny Machado 10.00 25.00
MMJLMN Mike Napoli 12.00 30.00
MMJLMS Mike Schmidt 15.00 40.00
MMJLMSC Mike Schmidt 15.00 40.00
MMJLMSI Mike Schmidt 15.00 40.00
MMJLMT Mark Teixeira 8.00 20.00
MMJLMTE Mark Teixeira 8.00 20.00
MMJLMTR Mike Trout 50.00 120.00
MMJLMZ Mike Zunino 12.00 30.00
MMJLNR Nolan Ryan 50.00 120.00
MMJLNRY Nolan Ryan 50.00 120.00
MMJLNS Nick Swisher 10.00 25.00
MMJLOC Orlando Cepeda 15.00 40.00
MMJLPF Prince Fielder 12.00 30.00
MMJLPM Paul Molitor 8.00 20.00
MMJLRC Roberto Clemente 100.00 175.00
MMJLRC Rod Carew 8.00 20.00
MMJLRH Ryan Howard 20.00 50.00
MMJLRJ Reggie Jackson 12.00 30.00
MMJLRY Robin Yount 8.00 20.00
MMJLSC Starlin Castro 6.00 15.00
MMJLSG Steve Garvey 30.00 80.00
MMJLTD Travis d'Arnaud 8.00 20.00
MMJLTG Tony Gwynn 15.00 40.00
MMJLTGW Tony Gwynn 15.00 40.00
MMJLTGY Tony Gwynn 15.00 40.00
MMJLTT Troy Tulowitzki 10.00 25.00
MMJLWB Wade Boggs 10.00 25.00
MMJLWM Willie McCovey 15.00 40.00
MMJLWMA Willie Mays 30.00 60.00
MMJLWMC Willie McCovey 15.00 40.00
MMJLWMI Willie McCovey 15.00 40.00
MMJLZW Zack Wheeler 8.00 20.00

2014 Topps Museum Collection Momentous Material Jumbo Relics

STATED ODDS 1:10 PACKS
STATED PRINT RUN 50 SER.#'d SETS
MMJRAB Adrian Beltre 6.00 15.00
MMJRAC Alex Cobb 4.00 10.00
MMJRACH Aroldis Chapman 6.00 15.00
MMJRAD Adam Dunn 5.00 12.00
MMJRAE Adam Eaton 4.00 10.00
MMJRAEL A.J. Ellis 4.00 10.00
MMJRAG Alex Gordon 8.00 20.00
MMJRAH Adeiny Hechavarria 4.00 10.00
MMJRAL Adam Lind 5.00 12.00
MMJRAM Andrew McCutchen 25.00 60.00
MMJRAMC Andrew McCutchen 25.00 60.00
MMJRAP Andy Pettitte 5.00 12.00
MMJRAPU Albert Pujols 8.00 20.00
MMJRAR Alex Rodriguez 8.00 20.00
MMJRAW Adam Wainwright 5.00 12.00
MMJRBB Billy Butler 4.00 10.00
MMJRBBE Brandon Beachy 4.00 10.00
MMJRBG Brett Gardner 8.00 20.00
MMJRBH Billy Hamilton 8.00 20.00
MMJRBHA Bryce Harper 10.00 25.00
MMJRBHI Billy Hamilton 8.00 20.00
MMJRBL Brett Lawrie 5.00 12.00
MMJRBM Brian McCann 5.00 12.00
MMJRBMO Brandon Morrow 4.00 10.00
MMJRBP Buster Posey 8.00 20.00
MMJRBR Bruce Rondon 4.00 10.00
MMJRBU B.J. Upton 5.00 12.00
MMJRCA Chris Archer 4.00 10.00
MMJRCB Chad Billingsley 5.00 12.00
MMJRCBE Carlos Beltran 6.00 15.00
MMJRCBU Clay Buchholz 4.00 10.00
MMJRCC CC Sabathia 5.00 12.00
MMJRCG Curtis Granderson 5.00 12.00
MMJRCGO Carlos Gonzalez 5.00 12.00
MMJRCH Chase Headley 4.00 10.00
MMJRCHA Cole Hamels 5.00 12.00
MMJRCK Craig Kimbrel 5.00 12.00
MMJRCO Chris Owings 4.00 10.00
MMJRCR Carlos Ruiz 4.00 10.00
MMJRCS Chris Sale 6.00 15.00
MMJRCSA Carlos Santana 5.00 12.00
MMJRCW C.J. Wilson 4.00 10.00
MMJRDB Domonic Brown 5.00 12.00
MMJRDF David Freese 4.00 10.00
MMJRDG Didi Gregorius 5.00 12.00
MMJRDGR Didi Gregorius 5.00 12.00
MMJRDJ Derek Jeter 40.00 80.00
MMJRDJE Desmond Jennings 5.00 12.00
MMJRDO David Ortiz 8.00 20.00
MMJRDS Drew Storen 4.00 10.00
MMJRDW David Wright 12.00 30.00
MMJRDWR David Wright 12.00 30.00
MMJREA Elvis Andrus 5.00 12.00
MMJREE Edwin Encarnacion 6.00 15.00
MMJREH Eric Hosmer 6.00 15.00
MMJREL Evan Longoria 6.00 15.00
MMJRELO Evan Longoria 6.00 15.00
MMJREN Eduardo Nunez 4.00 10.00
MMJRFF Freddie Freeman 10.00 25.00
MMJRFFR Freddie Freeman 10.00 25.00
MMJRFH Felix Hernandez 6.00 15.00
MMJRFM Fred McGriff 5.00 12.00
MMJRGB Gordon Beckham 4.00 10.00
MMJRGC Gerrit Cole 8.00 20.00
MMJRGS Gary Sheffield 6.00 15.00
MMJRGST Giancarlo Stanton 6.00 15.00
MMJRHK Hiroki Kuroda 8.00 20.00
MMJRHP Hunter Pence 8.00 20.00
MMJRHR Hanley Ramirez 5.00 12.00
MMJRID Ike Davis 4.00 10.00
MMJRIN Ivan Nova 5.00 12.00
MMJRJA Jose Altuve 5.00 12.00
MMJRJB Jackie Bradley Jr. 8.00 20.00
MMJRJBA Jose Bautista 5.00 12.00
MMJRJBR Jay Bruce 5.00 12.00
MMJRJC Jhoulys Chacin 4.00 10.00
MMJRJCH Joba Chamberlain 4.00 10.00
MMJRJH Jeremy Hellickson 4.00 10.00
MMJRJHA Josh Hamilton 5.00 12.00
MMJRJL Jon Lester 5.00 12.00
MMJRJM Justin Masterson 4.00 10.00
MMJRJN Joe Nathan 4.00 10.00
MMJRJPA Jarrod Parker 4.00 10.00
MMJRJPE Jhonny Peralta 4.00 10.00
MMJRJPH Jordan Pacheco 4.00 10.00
MMJRJS Jean Segura 5.00 12.00
MMJRJSA Jarrod Saltalamacchia 4.00 10.00
MMJRJU Justin Upton 6.00 15.00
MMJRJV Joey Votto 6.00 15.00
MMJRJVE Justin Verlander 6.00 15.00
MMJRJW Jayson Werth 5.00 12.00
MMJRJZ Jordan Zimmermann 5.00 12.00
MMJRJZI Jordan Zimmermann 5.00 12.00
MMJRKH Kelvin Herrera 4.00 10.00
MMJRKHE Kelvin Herrera 4.00 10.00
MMJRKM Kris Medlen 8.00 20.00
MMJRKN Kirk Nieuwenhuis 4.00 10.00
MMJRKS Kyle Seager 4.00 10.00
MMJRLM Logan Morrison 4.00 10.00
MMJRMA Matt Adams 6.00 15.00
MMJRMAD Matt Adams 6.00 15.00
MMJRMB Madison Bumgarner 8.00 20.00
MMJRMC Matt Cain 8.00 20.00
MMJRMH Matt Harvey 10.00 25.00
MMJRMHA Matt Harrison 4.00 10.00
MMJRMHO Matt Holliday 10.00 25.00
MMJRMK Matt Kemp 8.00 20.00
MMJRML Mat Latos 5.00 12.00
MMJRMM Manny Machado 12.00 30.00
MMJRMMI Mike Minor 4.00 10.00
MMJRMMO Mitch Moreland 4.00 10.00
MMJRMMU Mike Mussina 5.00 12.00
MMJRMR Mariano Rivera 8.00 20.00
MMJRMS Max Scherzer 8.00 20.00
MMJRMT Mike Trout 25.00 60.00
MMJRMV Matt Davidson 5.00 12.00
MMJRMW Michael Wacha 10.00 25.00
MMJRNA Nolan Arenado 6.00 15.00
MMJRNAR Nolan Arenado 6.00 15.00
MMJRNC Nick Castellanos 8.00 20.00
MMJRNCA Nick Castellanos 8.00 20.00
MMJRNF Nick Franklin 4.00 10.00
MMJRPA Pedro Alvarez 8.00 20.00
MMJRPC Patrick Corbin 5.00 12.00
MMJRPF Prince Fielder 5.00 12.00
MMJRPG Paul Goldschmidt 10.00 25.00
MMJRPGO Paul Goldschmidt 10.00 25.00
MMJRPH Phil Hughes 4.00 10.00
MMJRPS Pablo Sandoval 8.00 20.00
MMJRRB Ryan Braun 5.00 12.00
MMJRRBR Rob Brantly 4.00 10.00
MMJRRC Roberto Clemente 50.00 100.00
MMJRRD R.A. Dickey 5.00 12.00
MMJRRHO Ryan Howard 8.00 20.00
MMJRRV Ryan Vogelsong 6.00 15.00
MMJRRW Rickie Weeks 4.00 10.00
MMJRRZ Ryan Zimmerman 6.00 15.00
MMJRRZI Ryan Zimmerman 6.00 15.00
MMJRSM Shelby Miller 10.00 25.00
MMJRSMA Starling Marte 10.00 25.00
MMJRSP Salvador Perez 5.00 12.00
MMJRSS Stephen Strasburg 8.00 20.00
MMJRTC Tony Cingrani 5.00 12.00
MMJRTD Travis d'Arnaud 5.00 12.00
MMJRTG Tony Gwynn 10.00 25.00
MMJRTH Torii Hunter 4.00 10.00
MMJRTL Tim Lincecum 5.00 12.00
MMJRTT Troy Tulowitzki 6.00 15.00
MMJRUJ Ubaldo Jimenez 4.00 10.00
MMJRVM Victor Martinez 6.00 15.00
MMJRWB Wade Boggs 10.00 25.00
MMJRWM Wade Miley 4.00 10.00
MMJRWMY Wil Myers 12.00 30.00
MMJRWR Wilin Rosario 4.00 10.00
MMJRYA Yonder Alonso 4.00 10.00
MMJRYM Yadier Molina 12.00 30.00
MMJRZC Zack Cozart 4.00 10.00
MMJRZW Zack Wheeler 5.00 12.00

2014 Topps Museum Collection Momentous Material Jumbo Relics Gold

*GOLD: .4X TO 1X BASIC
STATED ODDS 1:14 PACKS
STATED PRINT RUN 35 SER.#'d SETS

2014 Topps Museum Collection Primary Pieces Four Player Quad Relics

STATED ODDS 1:32 PACKS
STATED PRINT RUN 99 SER.#'d SETS
PPFQR1 Parker/Miller/Ryu/Sale 8.00 20.00
PPFQR3 Rosario/McCann/Santana/Perez 6.00 15.00
PPFQR4 Field/Puj/Freem/Goldsc 10.00 25.00
PPFQR5 Utley/Carpenter/Cano/Pedroia 8.00 20.00
PPFQR6 Lngria/Bltr/Cab/Wright 8.00 20.00
PPFQR8 Hey/Slant/Gonz/Harp 12.00 30.00
PPFQR9 Jones/Ellsb/McCut/Trout 40.00 80.00
PPFQR10 Bourn/Upton Granderson/Kemp 6.00 15.00
PPFQR11 Myers/Price/Hellic/Cobb 6.00 15.00
PPFQR14 Matt/Riv/Jeter/Pettitte 30.00 80.00
PPFQR15 d'Arn/Davis/Harv/Wheel 12.00 30.00
PPFQR16 Pujols/Trum/Trout/Ham 20.00 50.00
PPFQR17 Jone/Dav/Gaus/Mach 20.00 50.00
PPFQR18 Arcia/Hicks/Mauer/Parmelee 6.00 15.00
PPFQR19 Swish/Kip/Bourn/Sant 8.00 20.00
PPFQR20 Scher/Verlan/Field/Cab 15.00 40.00
PPFQR21 Darvish/Sale Hernandez/Kershaw 10.00 25.00
PPFQR22 McCut/Alvar/Cole/Marte 25.00 60.00
PPFQR23 Beltre/Kinsler/Darvish/Andrus 8.00 20.00
PPFQR24 Belt/Wain/Frees/Miller 6.00 15.00
PPFQR25 Tulowitzki/Gonzalez Rosario/Chacin 10.00 25.00
PPFQR26 Rasmus/Morrow Encarnacion/Bautista 8.00 20.00
PPFQR27 Roll/Utley/Hamel/Halla 12.00 30.00
PPFQR28 Beltre/Darvish Gonzalez/Rodriguez 8.00 20.00
PPFQR30 Grnk/Krshw/Puig/Kemp 15.00 40.00

2014 Topps Museum Collection Primary Pieces Four Player Quad Relics Copper

*COPPER: .4X TO 1X BASIC
STATED ODDS 1:41 PACKS
STATED PRINT RUN 75 SER.#'d SETS

2014 Topps Museum Collection Primary Pieces Four Player Quad Relics Gold

*GOLD: .5X TO 1.2X BASIC
STATED ODDS 1:123 PACKS
STATED PRINT RUN 25 SER.#'d SETS

2014 Topps Museum Collection Primary Pieces Legends Quad Relics

STATED ODDS 1:154 PACKS
STATED PRINT RUN 25 SER.#'d SETS
PPQRLBR Brooks Robinson 15.00 40.00
PPQRLBRU Babe Ruth 250.00 350.00
PPQRLCR Cal Ripken Jr. 30.00 80.00
PPQRLDM Don Mattingly 25.00 60.00
PPQRLDS Duke Snider 20.00 50.00
PPQRLEM Eddie Murray 10.00 25.00
PPQRLFJ Fergie Jenkins 10.00 25.00
PPQRLFM Fred McGriff 10.00 25.00
PPQRLMR Mariano Rivera 20.00 50.00
PPQRLMS Mike Schmidt 20.00 50.00
PPQRLOC Orlando Cepeda 10.00 25.00
PPQRLRC Rod Carew 10.00 25.00
PPQRLRCL Roberto Clemente 75.00 150.00
PPQRLRJ Randy Johnson 12.00 30.00
PPQRLRK Ralph Kiner 10.00 25.00
PPQRLSC Steve Carlton 10.00 25.00
PPQRLTGY Tony Gwynn 12.00 30.00
PPQRLWB Wade Boggs 20.00 50.00
PPQRLWM Willie McCovey 20.00 50.00

2014 Topps Museum Collection Primary Pieces Quad Relics

STATED ODDS 1:12 PACKS
STATED PRINT RUN 99 SER.#'d SETS
PPQRAC Alex Cobb 4.00 10.00
PPQRAM Andrew McCutchen 30.00 80.00
PPQRAP Andy Pettitte 8.00 20.00
PPQRAPJ Albert Pujols 10.00 25.00
PPQRAR Alex Rodriguez 10.00 25.00
PPQRARI Alexei Ramirez 5.00 12.00
PPQRARZ Aramis Ramirez 4.00 10.00
PPQRBH Bryce Harper 15.00 40.00
PPQRBHM Billy Hamilton 5.00 12.00
PPQRBM Brian McCann 5.00 12.00
PPQRBP Buster Posey 12.00 30.00
PPQRBPH Troy Tulowitzki 10.00 25.00
PPQRCB Carlos Beltran 8.00 20.00
PPQRCC CC Sabathia 5.00 12.00
PPQRCCS CC Sabathia 5.00 12.00
PPQRCD Chris Davis 12.00 30.00
PPQRCG Curtis Granderson 5.00 12.00
PPQRCGO Carlos Gonzalez 5.00 12.00
PPQRCH Cole Hamels 5.00 12.00
PPQRCK Craig Kimbrel 10.00 25.00
PPQRCKE Clayton Kershaw 6.00 15.00
PPQRCS Chris Sale 6.00 15.00
PPQRDB Domonic Brown 5.00 12.00
PPQRDH Dan Haren 4.00 10.00
PPQRDO David Ortiz 10.00 25.00
PPQRDS Darryl Strawberry 6.00 15.00
PPQRDS Drew Stubbs 4.00 10.00
PPQRDW David Wright 8.00 20.00
PPQREC Edwin Encarnacion 6.00 15.00
PPQRFF Freddie Freeman 8.00 20.00
PPQRFH Felix Hernandez 6.00 15.00
PPQRGC Gerrit Cole 8.00 20.00
PPQRGG Gio Gonzalez 5.00 12.00
PPQRHC Hank Conger 4.00 10.00
PPQRHP Hunter Pence 8.00 20.00
PPQRJB Jay Bruce 5.00 12.00
PPQRJBU Jose Bautista 5.00 12.00
PPQRJH Jeremy Hellickson 4.00 10.00
PPQRJS James Shields 4.00 10.00
PPQRJV Joey Votto 8.00 20.00
PPQRJVE Justin Verlander 10.00 25.00
PPQRKM Kris Medlen 5.00 12.00
PPQRMA Matt Adams 6.00 15.00
PPQRMC Matt Cain 5.00 12.00
PPQRMH Matt Harvey 12.00 30.00
PPQRMK Matt Kemp 8.00 20.00
PPQRML Mike Leake 4.00 10.00
PPQRMM Manny Machado 12.00 30.00
PPQRMR Mariano Rivera 15.00 40.00
PPQRMS Max Scherzer 6.00 15.00
PPQRPG Paul Goldschmidt 10.00 25.00
PPQRPS Pablo Sandoval 6.00 15.00
PPQRRW Rickie Weeks 4.00 10.00
PPQRSM Starling Marte 8.00 20.00
PPQRSML Shelby Miller 5.00 12.00
PPQRSP Salvador Perez 12.00 30.00
PPQRSS Stephen Strasburg 8.00 20.00
PPQRTG Tony Gwynn 6.00 15.00
PPQRTL Tim Lincecum 5.00 12.00
PPQRYM Yadier Molina 10.00 25.00
PPQRYP Yasiel Puig 10.00 25.00
PPQRZG Zack Greinke 5.00 12.00
PPQRZW Zack Wheeler 10.00 25.00
PPQRMSC Mike Schmidt 10.00 25.00

2014 Topps Museum Collection Primary Pieces Quad Relics Copper

*COPPER: .4X TO 1X BASIC
STATED ODDS 1:16 PACKS
STATED PRINT RUN 75 SER.#'d SETS

2014 Topps Museum Collection Primary Pieces Quad Relics Gold

*GOLD: .5X TO 1.2X BASIC
STATED ODDS 1:146 PACKS
STATED PRINT RUN 25 SER.#'d SETS

2014 Topps Museum Collection Signature Swatches Dual Relic Autographs

STATED ODDS 1:10 PACKS
PRINT RUNS B/WN 50-299 COPIES PER
EXCHANGE DEADLINE 2/24/2016
SSDAB Albert Belle/99 10.00 25.00
SSDAC Allen Craig/99 6.00 15.00
SSDAGA Avisail Garcia/299 6.00 15.00
SSDAGO Adrian Gonzalez/50 15.00 40.00
SSDBH Billy Hamilton/299 6.00 15.00
SSDCK Clayton Kershaw EXCH 40.00 80.00
SSDCS Chris Sale/99 15.00 40.00
SSDCY Christian Yelich/299 25.00 60.00
SSDDB Domonic Brown/50 12.00 30.00
SSDDF David Freese/99 5.00 12.00
SSDDG Didi Gregorius/99 6.00 15.00
SSDDMS Devin Mesoraco/299 8.00 20.00
SSDDO David Ortiz/99 30.00 60.00
SSDDP Dustin Pedroia/50 20.00 50.00
SSDDW David Wright/50 20.00 50.00
SSDFD Felix Doubront/299 5.00 12.00
SSDIR Ivan Rodriguez/50 12.00 30.00
SSDJB Jeff Bagwell/50 20.00 50.00
SSDJBC Johnny Bench/99 20.00 50.00
SSDJG Juan Gonzalez/99 10.00 25.00
SSDJGK Jedd Gyorko/299 5.00 12.00
SSDJH Josh Hamilton/99 10.00 25.00
SSDJP Jurickson Profar/189 6.00 15.00
SSDJR Jim Rice/99 10.00 25
SSDJS James Shields/99 5.00 12
SSDJSE Jean Segura/99 4.00 10
SSDJSM John Smoltz/50 60.00 120
SSDJZ Jordan Zimmermann/99 6.00 15
SSDKM Kris Medlen/99 8.00 20
SSDKS Kyle Seager/299 5.00 12
SSDMA Matt Adams/299 5.00 12
SSDMM Manny Machado/50 50.00 100
SSDMMU Mike Mussina EXCH 15.00 40
SSDMO Mike Olt/99 8.00 20
SSDMZ Mike Zunino/199 8.00 20
SSDNC Nick Castellanos/299 15.00 40
SSDNG Nomar Garciaparra/50 12.00 30
SSDOS Ozzie Smith/50 30.00 60
SSDPG Paul Goldschmidt/199 12.00 30
SSDPO Paul O'Neill EXCH 12.00 30
SSDRB Ryan Braun/99 15.00 40
SSDRC Rod Carew/50 15.00 40.
SSDRN Ricky Nolasco/106 5.00 12.
SSDSC Steve Carlton/99 12.00 30
SSDSM Shelby Miller/99 6.00 15.
SSDSMA Starling Marte/99 15.00 40
SSDTC Tony Cingrani/299 6.00 15.
SSDTD Travis d'Arnaud/299 10.00 25.
SSDTF Todd Frazier/199 6.00 15.
SSDTG Tom Glavine/50 15.00 40
SSDTT Troy Tulowitzki 8.00 20
SSDTTU Troy Tulowitzki/299 8.00 20
SSDTW Taijuan Walker/299 6.00 15.
SSDWC Will Clark/99 12.00 30.
SSDWME Wil Myers/99 10.00 25
SSDWR Wilin Rosario/299 5.00 12.
SSDYC Yoenis Cespedes/99 10.00 25.
SSDYD Yu Darvish/25 60.00 150.
SSDYM Yadier Molina EXCH 30.00 60.

2014 Topps Museum Collectic Signature Swatches Triple Rel Autographs

STATED ODDS 1:14 PACKS
PRINT RUNS B/WN 30-299 COPIES PER
EXCHANGE DEADLINE 2/24/2016
SSTAB Albert Belle EXCH 10.00 25.
SSTAC Allen Craig/50 10.00 25.
SSTBHL Billy Hamilton EXCH 12.00 30.
SSTBHL2 Billy Hamilton EXCH 12.00 30.
SSTBHL3 Billy Hamilton EXCH 12.00 30.
SSTBJ Bo Jackson EXCH 40.00 80.
SSTCS Chris Sale/299 10.00 25.
SSTCS2 Chris Sale/121 15.00 40.
SSTCY Christian Yelich/70 20.00 50.
SSTDF David Freese EXCH 5.00 12.
SSTDFR David Freese EXCH 5.00 12.
SSTDG Didi Gregorius/299 6.00 15.
SSTDM Devin Mesoraco/299 8.00 20.
SSTDM2 Devin Mesoraco/70 8.00 20.
SSTDO David Ortiz 30.00 60.
SSTDP Dustin Pedroia/50 20.00 50.
SSTEL Evan Longoria/50 30.00 60.
SSTFD Felix Doubront/299 5.00 12.
SSTFD2 Felix Doubront/70 5.00 12.
SSTIR Ivan Rodriguez/110 12.00 30.
SSTJG Juan Gonzalez/110 10.00 25.
SSTJH Josh Hamilton/110 15.00 40.
SSTJS Jean Segura/299 8.00 20.
SSTMA Matt Adams/70 10.00 25.
SSTMO Mike Olt/299 5.00 12.
SSTMO2 Mike Olt/70 5.00 12.
SSTNC Nick Castellanos/299 10.00 25.
SSTSC Steve Carlton/150 12.00 30.
SSTTD Travis d'Arnaud/289 10.00 25.
SSTTD2 Travis d'Arnaud/70 10.00 25.
SSTTG Tony Cingrani/299 8.00 20.
SSTTG2 Tony Cingrani/269 8.00 20.
SSTTGY Tony Gwynn/30 30.00 60.
SSTWR Wilin Rosario/299 5.00 12.
SSTWR2 Wilin Rosario/70 5.00 12.
SSTYC Yoenis Cespedes/50 15.00 40.
SSTYUD Yu Darvish EXCH 75.00 150.

2014 Topps Museum Collectio Signature Swatches Triple Rel Autographs Gold

*GOLD: .5X TO 1.2X BASIC
STATED ODDS 1:77 PACKS
STATED PRINT RUN 25 SER.#'d SETS
EXCHANGE DEADLINE 2/24/2016

2015 Topps Museum Collectio

1 David Ortiz .75 2.0
2 Eric Hosmer .60 1.5
3 Roger Maris .75 2.0
4 Mariano Rivera 1.00 2.5
5 Yu Darvish .75 2.0
6 Shin-Soo Choo .60 1.5
7 Anthony Rendon .75 2.0
8 Anthony Rizzo 1.25 3.0
9 Adrian Beltre .75 2.0
10 Buster Posey 1.00 2.5
11 Ian Kinsler .60 1.5
12 Daniel Norris .50 1.2
13 Dilson Herrera .60 1.5
14 Brandon Belt .60 1.5
15 Matt Adams .50 1.2
16 Albert Pujols 1.00 2.5
17 Jose Altuve .60 1.5
18 Randy Johnson .75 2.0
19 Sandy Koufax 1.50 4.0
20 Joc Pederson RC 1.25 3.0

21 Rusney Castillo RC .75 2.00
22 Cal Ripken Jr. 2.50 6.00
23 Giancarlo Stanton .75 2.00
24 Maikel Franco RC .75 2.00
25 Derek Jeter 2.00 5.00
26 Roberto Clemente 2.00 5.00
27 Jimmie Foxx .75 2.00
28 Mark Teixeira .60 1.50
29 Madison Bumgarner .60 1.50
30 Stephen Strasburg .75 2.00
31 Brandon Finnegan .50 1.25
32 James Shields .50 1.25
33 Mike Schmidt 1.25 3.00
34 Miguel Cabrera .75 2.00
35 Dalton Pompey RC .75 2.00
36 Paul Goldschmidt .75 2.00
37 Warren Spahn .60 1.50
38 Nolan Ryan 2.50 6.00
39 Ryan Howard .60 1.50
40 Dustin Pedroia .75 2.00
41 Masahiro Tanaka .60 1.50
42 Mike Piazza .75 2.00
43 Matt Holliday .75 2.00
44 Jason Heyward .60 1.50
45 Johnny Cueto .60 1.50
46 Hyun-Jin Ryu .60 1.50
47 Yadier Molina .75 2.00
48 Reggie Jackson .60 1.50
49 Greg Maddux 1.00 2.50
50 Gregory Polanco .60 1.50
51 Mike Trout 4.00 10.00
52 Jonathan Lucroy .60 1.50
53 Yasiel Puig .75 2.00
54 Roger Clemens 1.00 2.50
55 Prince Fielder .60 1.50
56 Phil Niekro .60 1.50
57 Michael Taylor .50 1.25
58 Fernando Rodney .50 1.25
59 Ken Griffey Jr. 1.50 4.00
60 Lou Gehrig 1.50 4.00
61 Clayton Kershaw 1.50 4.00
62 Ernie Banks .75 2.00
63 Felix Hernandez .60 1.50
64 Joe DiMaggio 1.50 4.00
65 Pablo Sandoval .60 1.50
66 Mike Moustakas .60 1.50
67 Max Scherzer .75 2.00
68 Joey Votto .75 2.00
69 Nelson Cruz .75 2.00
70 Tony Gwynn .75 2.00
71 David Wright .60 1.50
72 Freddie Freeman 1.00 2.50
73 Adam Wainwright .60 1.50
74 Bryce Harper 1.25 3.00
75 Robinson Cano .60 1.50
76 Jacob deGrom .75 2.00
77 Jacoby Ellsbury .60 1.50
78 Andrew McCutchen .75 2.00
79 Troy Tulowitzki .75 2.00
80 Jackie Robinson .75 2.00
81 Adrian Gonzalez .60 1.50
82 Yoenis Cespedes .60 1.50
83 Ted Williams 1.50 4.00
84 Ryan Braun .60 1.50
85 Manny Machado .75 2.00
86 Francisco Liriano .50 1.25
87 Jeff Bagwell .60 1.50
88 Ty Cobb 1.25 3.00
89 Jose Bautista .60 1.50
90 Victor Martinez .60 1.50
91 Babe Ruth 2.00 5.00
92 Willie Mays 1.50 4.00
93 Hank Aaron 1.50 4.00
94 Johnny Bench .75 2.00
95 Jose Abreu .75 2.00
96 Javier Baez RC 5.00 12.00
97 Tom Seaver .60 1.50
98 Hanley Ramirez .60 1.50
99 Jorge Soler RC 1.00 2.50
100 Adam Jones .60 1.50

2015 Topps Museum Collection Blue

*BLUE: 2X TO 5X BASIC
*BLUE RC: 1.5X TO 4X BASIC RC
STATED ODDS 1:7 MINI BOXES
STATED PRINT RUN 99 SER.#'d SETS

2015 Topps Museum Collection Copper

*COPPER: .6X TO 1.5X BASIC
*COPPER RC: .5X TO 1.2X BASIC RC
RANDOM INSERTS IN MINI BOXES

2015 Topps Museum Collection Green

*GREEN: 1.2X TO 3X BASIC
*GREEN RC: 1X TO 2.5X BASIC RC
STATED ODDS 1:4 MINI BOXES
STATED PRINT RUN 199 SER.#'d SETS

2015 Topps Museum Collection Archival Autographs

PRINT RUNS B/WN 15-399 COPIES PER
NO PRICING ON QTY 15 OR LESS
EXCHANGE DEADLINE 3/31/2018
AAAD Andre Dawson/99 12.00 30.00
AAAG Adrian Gonzalez/99 5.00 12.00
AAARA Anthony Ranaudo/399 4.00 10.00
AAARI Anthony Rizzo/399 15.00 40.00
AABF Brandon Finnegan/399 4.00 10.00
AABJ Bo Jackson/25 50.00 120.00
AACA Chris Archer/399 4.00 10.00
AACB Craig Biggio/99 10.00 25.00
AACJC C.J. Cron/399 4.00 10.00
AACK Clayton Kershaw/99 50.00 120.00
AACR Cal Ripken Jr./25 40.00 100.00
AACS Chris Sale/99 8.00 20.00
AACY Christian Yelich/399 15.00 40.00
AADB Dellin Betances/399 5.00 12.00
AADC David Cone/199 4.00 10.00
AADE Dennis Eckersley/99 8.00 20.00
AADH Dilson Herrera/399 5.00 12.00
AADMT Don Mattingly/49 20.00 50.00
AADN Daniel Norris/399 4.00 10.00
AADO David Ortiz/25 25.00 60.00
AADP Dustin Pedroia/99 12.00 30.00
AADPO Dalton Pompey/399 5.00 12.00
AADW David Wright/25 12.00 30.00
AAFF Freddie Freeman/199 8.00 20.00
AAFV Fernando Valenzuela/99 15.00 40.00
AAGM Greg Maddux/25 60.00 150.00
AAJA Jose Abreu/99 20.00 50.00
AAJBZ Javier Baez/199 8.00 20.00
AAJC Jose Canseco/199 5.00 12.00
AAJDG Jacob deGrom/299 8.00 20.00
AAJF Jose Fernandez/99 15.00 40.00
AAJGO Juan Gonzalez/299 5.00 12.00
AAJH Jason Heyward/99 8.00 20.00
AAJP Joe Panik/399 5.00 12.00
AAJPE Joc Pederson/299 6.00 15.00
AAJPO Jorge Posada/99 20.00 50.00
AAJR Jim Rice/399 6.00 15.00
AAJS Jorge Soler/399 4.00 10.00
AAJSM John Smoltz/99 15.00 40.00
AAKG Ken Griffey Jr./25 150.00 250.00
AAKV Kennys Vargas/399 4.00 10.00
AAKW Kolten Wong/399 5.00 12.00
AAMAD Matt Adams/399 4.00 10.00
AAMBA Matt Barnes/399 4.00 10.00
AAMC Matt Carpenter/399 6.00 15.00
AAMMC Mark McGwire/25 60.00 150.00
AAMRI Mariano Rivera/25 75.00 200.00
AAMSC Mike Schmidt/25 50.00 120.00
AAMSH Max Scherzer/99 20.00 50.00
AAMTR Mike Trout/25 150.00 250.00
AAMW Michael Wacha/199 5.00 12.00
AANG Nomar Garciaparra/59 20.00 50.00
AAOH Orlando Hernandez/249 4.00 10.00
AAOS Ozzie Smith/59 25.00 60.00
AAOV Omar Vizquel/399 5.00 12.00
AAPG Paul Goldschmidt/199 8.00 20.00
AAPO Paul O'Neill/299 8.00 20.00
AAPP Yasiel Puig/25 40.00 100.00
AARA Roberto Alomar/99 10.00 25.00
AARB Ryan Braun/49 10.00 25.00
AARCA Robinson Cano/25 12.00 30.00
AARCR Rod Carew/99 12.00 30.00
AARCS Rusney Castillo/99 5.00 12.00
AARJO Randy Johnson/25 50.00 120.00
AARY Robin Yount/25 30.00 80.00
AASG Sonny Gray/399 6.00 15.00
AASMA Starling Marte/399 6.00 15.00
AATG Tom Glavine/99 15.00 40.00
AAVG Vladimir Guerrero/99 15.00 40.00
AAYC Yoenis Cespedes/99 10.00 25.00
AAYV Yordano Ventura/399 12.00 30.00

2015 Topps Museum Collection Canvas Collection

STATED ODDS 1:4 MINI BOXES
CCR01 Mike Piazza 1.00 2.50
CCR02 Ken Griffey Jr. 2.00 5.00
CCR03 John Smoltz 1.00 2.50
CCR04 Ken Griffey Jr. 2.00 5.00
CCR05 Nolan Ryan 3.00 8.00
CCR06 Dave Winfield .75 2.00
CCR07 Ivan Rodriguez .75 2.00
CCR08 Stephen Strasburg 1.00 2.50
CCR09 Mike Piazza 1.00 2.50
CCR10 Duke Snider .75 2.00
CCR11 Ozzie Smith 1.25 3.00
CCR12 Warren Spahn .75 2.00
CCR13 Wade Boggs .75 2.00
CCR14 Nolan Ryan 3.00 8.00
CCR15 Ozzie Smith 1.25 3.00
CCR16 Dave Winfield .75 2.00
CCR17 Nolan Ryan 3.00 8.00
CCR18 Johnny Bench 1.00 2.50
CCR19 Derek Jeter 2.50 6.00
CCR20 Harmon Killebrew 1.00 2.50
CCR21 Tom Seaver .75 2.00
CCR22 Jim Palmer .75 2.00
CCR23 Warren Spahn .75 2.00
CCR24 Phil Niekro .75 2.00
CCR25 Al Kaline 1.00 2.50
CCR26 Whitey Ford .75 2.00
CCR27 Wade Boggs .75 2.00
CCR28 George Brett 2.00 5.00
CCR29 Willie Mays 2.00 5.00
CCR30 Steve Carlton .75 2.00
CCR31 Roberto Clemente 2.50 6.00
CCR32 Mariano Rivera 1.25 3.00
CCR33 Don Mattingly 2.00 5.00
CCR34 Randy Johnson 1.00 2.50
CCR35 Chipper Jones 1.00 2.50
CCR36 Masahiro Tanaka .75 2.00
CCR37 Giancarlo Stanton 1.00 2.50
CCR38 Andrew McCutchen 1.00 2.50
CCR39 Clayton Kershaw 2.00 5.00
CCR40 Yasiel Puig 1.00 2.50
CCR41 Miguel Cabrera 1.00 2.50
CCR42 Albert Pujols 1.25 3.00
CCR43 David Ortiz 1.00 2.50
CCR44 Jose Abreu 1.00 2.50
CCR45 Yu Darvish 1.00 2.50
CCR46 Robinson Cano .75 2.00
CCR47 Jose Bautista .75 2.00
CCR48 Buster Posey 1.25 3.00
CCR49 Bryce Harper 1.50 4.00
CCR50 Manny Machado 1.00 2.50

2015 Topps Museum Collection Momentous Material Jumbo Relics

STATED ODDS 1:9 PACKS
STATED PRINT RUN 50 SER.#'d SETS
*COPPER/35: .4X TO 1X BASIC
MMJRAAA Alex Avila 6.00 15.00
MMJRABE Adrian Beltre 6.00 15.00
MMJRABL Adrian Beltre 6.00 15.00
MMJRACH Aroldis Chapman 6.00 15.00
MMJRAGN Alex Gordon 5.00 12.00
MMJRAGO Adrian Gonzalez 5.00 12.00
MMJRAGR Alex Gordon 5.00 12.00
MMJRAGZ Adrian Gonzalez 5.00 12.00
MMJRAJO Adam Jones 5.00 12.00
MMJRALD Adam Lind 5.00 12.00
MMJRAMN Andrew McCutchen 20.00 50.00
MMJRAMU Andrew McCutchen 20.00 50.00
MMJRARD Alex Rodriguez 10.00 25.00
MMJRARE Anthony Rendon 6.00 15.00
MMJRARN Anthony Rendon 6.00 15.00
MMJRARO Anthony Rizzo 10.00 25.00
MMJRARY Anthony Rizzo 10.00 25.00
MMJRARZ Alex Rodriguez 10.00 25.00
MMJRASI Andrelton Simmons 6.00 15.00
MMJRASZ Aaron Sanchez 5.00 12.00
MMJRAWR Adam Wainwright 8.00 20.00
MMJRBBR Billy Butler 4.00 10.00
MMJRBBU Billy Butler 4.00 10.00
MMJRBHA Bryce Harper 10.00 25.00
MMJRBHM Billy Hamilton 5.00 12.00
MMJRBHN Billy Hamilton 5.00 12.00
MMJRBM Brad Miller 5.00 12.00
MMJRBPS Brandon Phillips 4.00 10.00
MMJRCAN Aroldis Chapman 6.00 15.00
MMJRCBG Craig Biggio 8.00 20.00
MMJRCBO Craig Biggio 8.00 20.00
MMJRCBZ Clay Buchholz 4.00 10.00
MMJRCGN Carlos Gonzalez 5.00 12.00
MMJRCGO Carlos Gomez 4.00 10.00
MMJRCGZ Carlos Gonzalez 5.00 12.00
MMJRCJO Chipper Jones 8.00 20.00
MMJRCJS Chipper Jones 8.00 20.00
MMJRCKI Craig Kimbrel 5.00 12.00
MMJRCKL Craig Kimbrel 5.00 12.00
MMJRCKW Clayton Kershaw 12.00 30.00
MMJRCOS Chris Owings 4.00 10.00
MMJRCSA CC Sabathia 6.00 15.00
MMJRCSB CC Sabathia 6.00 15.00
MMJRCSE Chris Sale 6.00 15.00
MMJRCSL Chris Sale 6.00 15.00
MMJRCYE Christian Yelich 8.00 20.00
MMJRDJS Desmond Jennings 5.00 12.00
MMJRDMU Daniel Murphy 5.00 12.00
MMJRDMY Daniel Murphy 5.00 12.00
MMJRDOR David Ortiz 6.00 15.00
MMJRDOZ David Ortiz 6.00 15.00
MMJRDPD Dustin Pedroia 6.00 15.00
MMJRDPR David Price 6.00 15.00
MMJRDSN Drew Storen 4.00 10.00
MMJRDWR David Wright 12.00 30.00
MMJRDWT David Wright 12.00 30.00
MMJREAN Elvis Andrus 5.00 12.00
MMJREAS Elvis Andrus 5.00 12.00
MMJREHO Eric Hosmer 8.00 20.00
MMJRELA Evan Longoria 5.00 12.00
MMJRELO Evan Longoria 5.00 12.00
MMJRFFN Freddie Freeman 8.00 20.00
MMJRFFR Freddie Freeman 8.00 20.00
MMJRFHE Felix Hernandez 6.00 15.00
MMJRFHZ Felix Hernandez 6.00 15.00
MMJRGCE Gerrit Cole 6.00 15.00
MMJRGCO Gerrit Cole 6.00 15.00
MMJRGGZ Gio Gonzalez 5.00 12.00
MMJRGPL Gregory Polanco 8.00 20.00
MMJRGPO Gregory Polanco 8.00 20.00
MMJRGSN Giancarlo Stanton 8.00 20.00
MMJRGST Giancarlo Stanton 8.00 20.00
MMJRHER Eric Hosmer 8.00 20.00
MMJRHIW Hisashi Iwakuma 5.00 12.00
MMJRHRU Hyun-Jin Ryu 8.00 20.00
MMJRIKR Ian Kinsler 6.00 15.00
MMJRJBA Jose Bautista 5.00 12.00
MMJRJBC Jay Bruce 10.00 25.00
MMJRJBE Jay Bruce 10.00 25.00
MMJRJBG Jeff Bagwell 8.00 20.00
MMJRJBL Jeff Bagwell 8.00 20.00
MMJRJCO Johnny Cueto 5.00 12.00
MMJRJFE Jose Fernandez 6.00 15.00
MMJRJFZ Jose Fernandez 6.00 15.00
MMJRJHD Jason Heyward 6.00 15.00
MMJRJJY Jon Jay 4.00 10.00
MMJRJMA Joe Mauer 6.00 15.00
MMJRJMR Joe Mauer 6.00 15.00
MMJRJMY John Ryan Murphy 6.00 15.00
MMJRJPA Jorge Posada 5.00 12.00
MMJRJPI Joe Panik 20.00 50.00
MMJRJPK Joe Panik 20.00 50.00
MMJRJRK Josh Reddick 4.00 10.00
MMJRJRS Jose Reyes 5.00 12.00
MMJRJSA Jean Segura 5.00 12.00
MMJRJSG Jon Singleton 5.00 12.00
MMJRJSN Jon Singleton 5.00 12.00
MMJRJSP Jonathan Schoop 4.00 10.00
MMJRJUP Justin Upton 5.00 12.00
MMJRJVO Joey Votto 8.00 20.00
MMJRKUA Koji Uehara 4.00 10.00
MMJRMCA Miguel Cabrera 6.00 15.00
MMJRMCB Miguel Cabrera 6.00 15.00
MMJRMCD Michael Cuddyer 8.00 20.00
MMJRMCP Matt Carpenter 10.00 25.00
MMJRMCR Matt Carpenter 10.00 25.00
MMJRMCY Michael Cuddyer 8.00 20.00
MMJRMFO Maikel Franco 5.00 12.00
MMJRMHO Matt Holliday 6.00 15.00
MMJRMHY Matt Holliday 6.00 15.00
MMJRMKE Matt Kemp 5.00 12.00
MMJRMKP Matt Kemp 5.00 12.00
MMJRMLS Mat Latos 5.00 12.00
MMJRMMC Mark McGwire 10.00 25.00
MMJRMME Mark McGwire 10.00 25.00
MMJRMMK Mike Moustakas 5.00 12.00
MMJRMMO Manny Machado 10.00 25.00
MMJRMPA Mike Piazza 12.00 30.00
MMJRMPI Mike Piazza 12.00 30.00
MMJRMSR Max Scherzer 6.00 15.00
MMJRMSZ Max Scherzer 6.00 15.00
MMJRMTT Mike Trout 25.00 60.00
MMJRMWA Michael Wacha 5.00 12.00
MMJRNAO Nolan Arenado 8.00 20.00
MMJRNAR Nolan Arenado 8.00 20.00
MMJRNCR Nelson Cruz 6.00 15.00
MMJRNCS Nick Castellanos 6.00 15.00
MMJRNCZ Nelson Cruz 6.00 15.00
MMJRNGP Nomar Garciaparra 8.00 20.00
MMJRNWR Neil Walker 6.00 15.00
MMJRPGO Paul Goldschmidt 6.00 15.00
MMJRPGT Paul Goldschmidt 6.00 15.00
MMJRPKK Paul Konerko 8.00 20.00
MMJRPKO Paul Konerko 8.00 20.00
MMJRPSA Pablo Sandoval 5.00 12.00
MMJRPSL Pablo Sandoval 5.00 12.00
MMJRRHD Ryan Howard 5.00 12.00
MMJRRHO Ryan Howard 5.00 12.00
MMJRROR Rougned Odor 5.00 12.00
MMJRSCA Starlin Castro 4.00 10.00
MMJRSCH Shin-Soo Choo 5.00 12.00
MMJRSCO Shin-Soo Choo 5.00 12.00
MMJRSCS Starlin Castro 4.00 10.00
MMJRSGY Sonny Gray 5.00 12.00
MMJRSPE Salvador Perez 5.00 12.00
MMJRSPZ Salvador Perez 5.00 12.00
MMJRSSG Stephen Strasburg 6.00 15.00
MMJRSST Stephen Strasburg 6.00 15.00
MMJRTDA Travis d'Arnaud 6.00 15.00
MMJRTFR Todd Frazier 8.00 20.00
MMJRTHR Torii Hunter 4.00 10.00
MMJRTLM Tim Lincecum 5.00 12.00
MMJRVMA Victor Martinez 8.00 20.00
MMJRVMZ Victor Martinez 8.00 20.00
MMJRWBS Wade Boggs 5.00 12.00
MMJRWFL Wilmer Flores 5.00 12.00
MMJRWFS Wilmer Flores 5.00 12.00
MMJRWMS Will Middlebrooks 4.00 10.00
MMJRWMY Wil Myers 4.00 10.00
MMJRXBO Xander Bogaerts 10.00 25.00
MMJRXBS Xander Bogaerts 10.00 25.00
MMJRYCE Yoenis Cespedes 5.00 12.00
MMJRYCS Yoenis Cespedes 5.00 12.00
MMJRYDA Yu Darvish 10.00 25.00
MMJRYDH Yu Darvish 10.00 25.00
MMJRYPG Yasiel Puig 8.00 20.00
MMJRZGE Zack Greinke 5.00 12.00
MMJRZWR Zack Wheeler 5.00 12.00

2015 Topps Museum Collection Premium Prints Autographs

STATED ODDS 1:110 MINI BOXES
STATED PRINT RUN 25 SER.#'d SETS
EXCHANGE DEADLINE 3/31/2018
PPAD Andre Dawson 20.00 50.00
PPBJ Bo Jackson 60.00 150.00
PPBP Buster Posey EXCH 100.00 250.00
PPCB Craig Biggio 20.00 50.00
PPDMA Don Mattingly 40.00 100.00
PPDW David Wright 20.00 50.00
PPHA Hank Aaron 125.00 250.00
PPJA Jose Abreu 30.00 80.00
PPJB Jeff Bagwell EXCH 40.00 100.00
PPJC Jose Canseco 20.00 50.00
PPJG Juan Gonzalez 15.00 40.00
PPJP Jorge Posada 20.00 50.00
PPJR Jim Rice 20.00 50.00
PPJS John Smoltz 40.00 100.00
PPMC Miguel Cabrera EXCH 60.00 150.00
PPMS Mike Schmidt 60.00 150.00
PPNG Nomar Garciaparra 60.00 150.00
PPOS Ozzie Smith 30.00 80.00
PPRC Rod Carew 20.00 50.00
PPTG Tom Glavine 20.00 50.00

2015 Topps Museum Collection Primary Pieces Four Player Quad Relics

STATED ODDS 1:35 PACKS
STATED PRINT RUN 99 SER.#'d SETS
PRICING FOR BASIC JSY SWATCHES
*COPPER/75: .4X TO 1X BASIC
*GOLD/25: .5X TO 1.2X BASIC
PPFQAT Abru/dGrm/Hmltn/Tnka 8.00 20.00
PPFQBC Nva/Crg/Btts/Cstllo 12.00 30.00
PPFQBH Hsmr/Mstks/Btlr/Prz 12.00 30.00
PPFQCM Crpntr/Mlna/Adms/Mllr 12.00 30.00
PPFQDG Gry/Rddck/Dnldsn/Nrrs 10.00 25.00
PPFQDS Dvs/Schp/Crz/Jns 10.00 25.00
PPFQFC Fielder/Darvish/Choo/Choice 8.00 20.00
PPFQFS Smmns/Hywrd/Thrn/Frmn 10.00 25.00
PPFQKC Clayton Kershaw
Felix Hernandez
Johnny Cueto
Chris Sale
PPFQKP Rmrz/Krshw/Pg/Gnzlz 15.00 40.00
PPFQLH Lee/Hamels/Howard/Utley 6.00 15.00
PPFQMM Cle/McCtchn/Mrte/Plnco 20.00 50.00
PPFQMP d'Arnd/Mrinz/dGrm/Pizza 15.00 40.00
PPFQPK Hmltn/Pjls/Kndrck/Trt 15.00 40.00
PPFQRH Rosenthal/Holland
Kimbrel/Rodney 6.00 15.00
PPFQRS Sabathia/Ellsbury
Teixeira/Rodriguez 8.00 20.00
PPFQSM Dnld/Stn/Trt/McCtch 30.00 80.00
PPFQSR Bz/Rzzo/Cstro/Slr 30.00 80.00
PPFQVS Cbrra/Vrlndr/Mrtnz/Schrzr 8.00 20.00
PPFQ1WH Hrvy/Whlr/dGrm/d'Arnd 20.00 50.00

2015 Topps Museum Collection Primary Pieces Quad Relics

STATED ODDS 1:12 PACKS
STATED PRINT RUN 99 SER.#'d SETS
*COPPER/75: .4X TO 1X BASIC
*GOLD/25: .5X TO 1.2X BASIC
PPQRAC Aroldis Chapman 6.00 15.00
PPQRAGN Alex Gordon 6.00 15.00
PPQRAGZ Adrian Gonzalez 4.00 10.00
PPQRAJ Adam Jones 6.00 15.00
PPQRAM Andrew McCutchen 15.00 40.00
PPQRAW Adam Wainwright 4.00 10.00
PPQRBB Billy Butler 3.00 8.00
PPQRBHN Billy Hamilton 4.00 10.00
PPQRCBO Craig Biggio 6.00 15.00
PPQRCBZ Clay Buchholz 3.00 8.00
PPQRCGN Carlos Gonzalez 4.00 10.00
PPQRCJ Chipper Jones 5.00 12.00
PPQRCKL Craig Kimbrel 4.00 10.00
PPQRCKW Clayton Kershaw 12.00 30.00
PPQRCSA CC Sabathia 4.00 10.00
PPQRCSE Chris Sale 5.00 12.00
PPQRDO David Ortiz 6.00 15.00
PPQRDPA Dustin Pedroia 5.00 12.00
PPQREA Elvis Andrus 4.00 10.00
PPQREHO Eric Hosmer 4.00 10.00
PPQREL Evan Longoria 4.00 10.00
PPQRFF Freddie Freeman 6.00 15.00
PPQRFH Felix Hernandez 4.00 10.00
PPQRGC Gerrit Cole 5.00 12.00
PPQRGP Gregory Polanco 4.00 10.00
PPQRGSN Giancarlo Stanton 5.00 12.00
PPQRHER Eric Hosmer 4.00 10.00
PPQRHR Hanley Ramirez 4.00 10.00
PPQRJBA Jose Bautista 4.00 10.00
PPQRJBL Jeff Bagwell 6.00 15.00
PPQRJF Jose Fernandez 10.00 25.00
PPQRJM Joe Mauer 6.00 15.00
PPQRJPK Joe Panik 10.00 25.00
PPQRJPN Joc Pederson 5.00 12.00
PPQRJRS Jose Reyes 4.00 10.00
PPQRJSN Jon Singleton 4.00 10.00
PPQRJV Joey Votto 5.00 12.00
PPQRMBS Mookie Betts 8.00 20.00
PPQRMCA Miguel Cabrera 5.00 12.00
PPQRMK Matt Kemp 4.00 10.00
PPQRMMO Manny Machado 5.00 12.00
PPQRMMS Mike Moustakas 4.00 10.00
PPQRMP Mike Piazza 10.00 25.00
PPQRMS Max Scherzer 5.00 12.00
PPQRMW Michael Wacha 6.00 15.00
PPQRNCS Nick Castellanos 5.00 12.00
PPQRNCZ Nelson Cruz 5.00 12.00
PPQRNG Nomar Garciaparra 4.00 10.00
PPQRPG Paul Goldschmidt 5.00 12.00
PPQRPK Paul Konerko 8.00 20.00
PPQRPS Pablo Sandoval 4.00 10.00
PPQRRH Ryan Howard 4.00 10.00
PPQRSCH Shin-Soo Choo 4.00 10.00
PPQRSS Stephen Strasburg 5.00 12.00
PPQRTG Tony Gwynn 8.00 20.00
PPQRTT Troy Tulowitzki 5.00 12.00
PPQRVM Victor Martinez 10.00 25.00
PPQRWB Wade Boggs 4.00 10.00
PPQRXB Xander Bogaerts 5.00 12.00
PPQRYC Yoenis Cespedes 4.00 10.00
PPQRYD Yu Darvish 5.00 12.00
PPQRYP Yasiel Puig 5.00 12.00

2015 Topps Museum Collection Primary Pieces Quad Relics Legends

STATED ODDS 1:137 PACKS
STATED PRINT RUN 25 SER.#'d SETS
PPQLBD Bobby Doerr 30.00 80.00
PPQLBF Bob Feller 25.00 60.00
PPQLBR Babe Ruth 200.00 300.00
PPQLDS Duke Snider 30.00 80.00
PPQLEB Ernie Banks 30.00 80.00
PPQLEM Eddie Mathews 20.00 50.00
PPQLES Enos Slaughter 25.00 60.00
PPQLHA Hank Aaron 90.00 150.00
PPQLJD Joe DiMaggio 90.00 150.00
PPQLJM Juan Marichal 30.00 80.00
PPQLJR Jackie Robinson 50.00 120.00
PPQLMT Masahiro Tanaka 12.00 30.00
PPQLRC Roberto Clemente 90.00 150.00
PPQLRK Ralph Kiner 30.00 80.00
PPQLTC Ty Cobb 50.00 120.00
PPQLTS Tom Seaver 12.00 30.00
PPQLTW Ted Williams 100.00 200.00
PPQLWS Warren Spahn 30.00 80.00
PPQLWMS Willie Mays 60.00 150.00

2015 Topps Museum Collection Signature Swatches Dual Relic Autographs

STATED ODDS 1:9 PACKS
PRINT RUNS B/WN 25-299 COPIES PER
EXCHANGE DEADLINE 3/31/2018
PRICING FOR BASIC JSY SWATCHES
*GOLD: .4X TO 1X BASIC p/r 25-30
*GOLD: .5X TO 1.2X BASIC p/r 50-99
*GOLD: .6X TO 1.5X BASIC p/r 109-299
SSDAC Allen Craig/125 5.00 12.00
SSDARA Anthony Ranaudo/299 5.00 12.00
SSDAS Andrelton Simmons/299 5.00 12.00
SSDBC Brandon Crawford/299 4.00 10.00
SSDBM Brian McCann/75 6.00 15.00
SSDBPS Brandon Phillips/75 5.00 12.00
SSDCAC Chris Archer/299 5.00 12.00
SSDCAR Chris Archer/299 5.00 12.00
SSDCC C.J. Cron/299 5.00 12.00
SSDCK Clayton Kershaw/30 60.00 150.00
SSDCR Cal Ripken Jr./25 60.00 150.00
SSDCSE Chris Sale/99 10.00 25.00
SSDDMO Devin Mesoraco/299 5.00 12.00
SSDDN Daniel Nava/109 5.00 12.00
SSDDPA Dustin Pedroia/25 30.00 80.00
SSDDPY Dalton Pompey/299 6.00 15.00
SSDDW David Wright/30 25.00 60.00
SSDEG Evan Gattis/299 5.00 12.00
SSDFF Freddie Freeman/75 10.00 25.00
SSDGP Gregory Polanco/125 10.00 25.00
SSDHAZ Henderson Alvarez/299 5.00 12.00
SSDJD Jacob deGrom/299 20.00 50.00
SSDJH Jason Heyward/75 6.00 15.00
SSDJPK Joe Panik/189 5.00 12.00
SSDJPN Joc Pederson/299 15.00 40.00
SSDJR Jim Rice/75 6.00 15.00
SSDJT Junichi Tazawa/299 5.00 12.00
SSDKV Kennys Vargas/299 5.00 12.00
SSDKW Kolten Wong/299 6.00 15.00
SSDLH Livan Hernandez/199 5.00 12.00
SSDMBS Matt Barnes/299 6.00 15.00
SSDMC Matt Carpenter/125 10.00 25.00
SSDMFO Maikel Franco/299 6.00 15.00
SSDMMA Mike Mussina/30 25.00 60.00
SSDMMR Mike Minor/299 5.00 12.00
SSDMN Mike Napoli/299 5.00 12.00
SSDMSN Marcus Stroman/241 6.00 15.00
SSDMSR Max Scherzer/50 15.00 40.00
SSDNG Nomar Garciaparra/30 20.00 50.00
SSDRCO Rusney Castillo/75 6.00 15.00
SSDRCS Roger Clemens/30 25.00 60.00
SSDSME Starling Marte/65 20.00 50.00
SSDSMR Shelby Miller/125 6.00 15.00
SSDYV Yordano Ventura/299 12.00 30.00

2015 Topps Museum Collection Signature Swatches Triple Relic Autographs

STATED ODDS 1:14 PACKS
PRINT RUNS B/WN 25-349 COPIES PER
EXCHANGE DEADLINE 3/31/2018
PRICING FOR BASIC JSY SWATCHES
*GOLD: .4X TO 1X BASIC p/r 25-30
*GOLD: .5X TO 1.2X BASIC p/r 50-99
*GOLD: .6X TO 1.5X BASIC p/r 109-349
SSTARO Anthony Ranaudo/75 5.00 12.00
SSTAS Andrelton Simmons/249 12.00 30.00
SSTBH Bryce Harper/25 150.00 300.00
SSTBM Brian McCann/30 8.00 20.00
SSTCC C.J. Cron/249 5.00 12.00
SSTCK Clayton Kershaw/30 60.00 150.00
SSTCSE Chris Sale/50 8.00 20.00
SSTDPA Dustin Pedroia/30 25.00 60.00
SSTEG Evan Gattis/249 5.00 12.00
SSTFF Freddie Freeman/50 20.00 50.00
SSTGM Greg Maddux/30 40.00 100.00
SSTGP Gregory Polanco/50 12.00 30.00
SSTJD Jacob deGrom/249 20.00 50.00
SSTJH Jason Heyward/50 8.00 20.00
SSTJR Jim Rice/199 8.00 20.00
SSTJT Junichi Tazawa/239 5.00 12.00
SSTKV Kennys Vargas/249 5.00 12.00
SSTKW Kolten Wong/349 6.00 15.00
SSTLH Livan Hernandez/249 5.00 12.00
SSTMC Matt Carpenter/199 10.00 25.00
SSTMFO Maikel Franco/249 15.00 40.00
SSTMME Mark McGwire/30 60.00 150.00
SSTMMR Mike Minor/249 5.00 12.00
SSTMN Mike Napoli/249 5.00 12.00
SSTMPA Mike Piazza/30 50.00 120.00
SSTMSN Marcus Stroman/349 6.00 15.00
SSTMSR Max Scherzer/30 20.00 50.00
SSTNG Nomar Garciaparra/30 12.00 30.00
SSTRCS Roger Clemens/30 25.00 60.00
SSTSMR Shelby Miller/199 6.00 15.00
SSTYP Yasiel Puig/30 60.00 150.00
SSTYV Yordano Ventura/329 6.00 15.00

2016 Topps Museum Collection

1 Buster Posey 1.00 2.50
2 Jean Segura .60 1.50
3 Kyle Seager .50 1.25
4 Noah Syndergaard .60 1.50
5 Bryce Harper 1.25 3.00
6 Miguel Cabrera .75 2.00
7 J.D. Martinez .75 2.00
8 Eric Hosmer .60 1.50
9 Kyle Schwarber RC 2.00 5.00
10 Mike Trout 4.00 10.00
11 Starling Marte .60 1.50
12 Carlos Martinez .60 1.50
13 Max Scherzer .75 2.00
14 Lorenzo Cain .50 1.25
15 Joc Pederson .60 1.50
16 Rob Refsnyder RC .75 2.00
17 A.J. Pollock .50 1.25
18 Kaleb Cowart RC .60 1.50
19 Luis Severino RC .75 2.00
20 Ryan Braun .60 1.50
21 Xander Bogaerts .75 2.00
22 Jorge Soler .75 2.00
23 Hector Olivera RC .75 2.00
24 David Price .60 1.50
25 Chris Davis .50 1.25
26 Dee Gordon .50 1.25
27 Craig Kimbrel .60 1.50
28 Hanley Ramirez .60 1.50
29 Yasiel Puig .75 2.00
30 Todd Frazier .60 1.50
31 Jon Gray RC .60 1.50
32 Carlos Carrasco .50 1.25
33 Trevor Rosenthal .60 1.50
34 Addison Russell .75 2.00
35 Billy Hamilton .60 1.50
36 Giancarlo Stanton .75 2.00
37 Zack Greinke .60 1.50
38 Byron Buxton .60 1.50
39 Jake Arrieta .60 1.50
40 Kris Bryant 1.00 2.50
41 Jose Altuve .60 1.50
42 Josh Reddick .50 1.25
43 Nolan Arenado 1.00 2.50
44 Jordan Zimmermann .60 1.50
45 Madison Bumgarner .60 1.50
46 Roberto Clemente 2.00 5.00
47 Jose Fernandez .75 2.00
48 Stephen Strasburg .75 2.00
49 Joey Votto .75 2.00
50 Clayton Kershaw 1.50 4.00
51 Corey Kluber .60 1.50
52 Carlos Gomez .50 1.25
53 Chris Sale .75 2.00
54 Prince Fielder .60 1.50
55 Corey Seager RC 5.00 12.00
56 Mookie Betts 1.25 3.00
57 Felix Hernandez .60 1.50
58 Trea Turner RC 2.00 5.00
59 Justin Upton .60 1.50
60 Kenley Jansen .60 1.50
61 Andrew McCutchen .75 2.00
62 Stephen Piscotty RC 1.00 2.50
63 Francisco Lindor .75 2.00
64 Miguel Sano RC 1.00 2.50
65 Chris Archer .50 1.25
66 Maikel Franco .60 1.50
67 Rougned Odor .60 1.50
68 Michael Conforto RC .75 2.00
69 Gerrit Cole .75 2.00
70 Jose Abreu .75 2.00
71 Carlos Correa .75 2.00
72 Jose Bautista .60 1.50
73 Paul Goldschmidt .75 2.00
74 George Springer .60 1.50
75 Michael Brantley .60 1.50
76 Matt Harvey .60 1.50
77 Aaron Nola RC 1.25 3.00
78 Manny Machado .75 2.00
79 Corey Dickerson .50 1.25
80 Sonny Gray .60 1.50
81 Anthony Rizzo 1.25 3.00
82 Josh Donaldson .60 1.50
83 Michael Wacha .60 1.50
84 Dellin Betances .60 1.50
85 Jacoby Ellsbury .60 1.50
86 Carlos Rodon .75 2.00
87 Charlie Blackmon .75 2.00
88 Kolten Wong .60 1.50
89 Evan Longoria .60 1.50
90 Yoenis Cespedes .75 2.00
91 Jacob deGrom .75 2.00
92 Danny Salazar .60 1.50
93 Jason Kipnis .60 1.50
94 Anthony Rendon .75 2.00
95 Adam Jones .60 1.50
96 Freddie Freeman 1.00 2.50
97 Gregory Polanco .60 1.50
98 Edwin Encarnacion .75 2.00
99 Troy Tulowitzki .75 2.00
100 Christian Yelich 1.00 2.50

2016 Topps Museum Collection Blue

*BLUE: 1X TO 2.5X BASIC
*BLUE RC: .75X TO 2X BASIC RC
STATED ODDS 1:8 MINI BOXES
STATED PRINT RUN 99 SER.#'d SETS

2016 Topps Museum Collection Copper

*COPPER: .6X TO 1.5X BASIC
*COPPER RC: .5X TO 1.2X BASIC RC
RANDOM INSERTS IN MINI BOXES

2016 Topps Museum Collection Green

*GREEN: .75X TO 2X BASIC
*GREEN RC: .6X TO 1.5X BASIC RC
STATED ODDS 1:4 MINI BOXES
STATED PRINT RUN 199 SER.#'d SETS

2016 Topps Museum Collection Archival Autographs

RANDOM INSERTS IN MINI BOXES
PRINT RUNS B/WN 25-399 COPIES PER
EXCHANGE DEADLINE 2/28/2018
AAAC Alex Colome/299 3.00 8.00
AAACB Alex Cobb/299 3.00 8.00
AAAD Andre Dawson/50 10.00 25.00
AAAG Andres Galarraga/199 6.00 15.00
AAAGO Alex Gordon EXCH 20.00 50.00
AAAGZ Adrian Gonzalez/75 4.00 10.00
AAAJ Andruw Jones/299 5.00 12.00

AAAN Aaron Nola/299 6.00 15.00
AAARZ Anthony Rizzo/125 20.00 50.00
AABBE Brandon Belt/299 5.00 12.00
AABH Bryce Harper/25 250.00 400.00
AABJ Bo Jackson/25 50.00 120.00
AABL Barry Larkin/50 4.00 10.00
AABS Blake Swihart/299 4.00 10.00
AABW Bernie Williams/75 20.00 50.00
AACH Cole Hamels/75 6.00 15.00
AACK Clayton Kershaw/50 60.00 150.00
AACKL Corey Kluber/299 10.00 25.00
AACM Carlos Martinez/299 5.00 12.00
AACR Carlos Rodon/125 8.00 20.00
AACRJ Cal Ripken Jr./25 60.00 150.00
AACS Corey Seager/125 30.00 80.00
AADC David Cone/125 3.00 8.00
AADF Doug Fister/199 3.00 8.00
AADG Dee Gordon/125 5.00 12.00
AADGR Didi Gregorius/299 6.00 15.00
AADL DJ LeMahieu/299 12.00 30.00
AADM Don Mattingly/50
AADO David Ortiz/25 40.00 100.00
AAEL Evan Longoria/50 4.00 10.00
AAEMA Edgar Martinez/99 4.00 10.00
AAFF Freddie Freeman/75 6.00 15.00
AAFL Francisco Lindor/299 12.00 30.00
AAFV Fernando Valenzuela/75 10.00 25.00
AAGH Greg Holland/299 3.00 8.00
AAGM Greg Maddux EXCH 50.00 120.00
AAGS George Springer/299 4.00 10.00
AAHA Hank Aaron EXCH 150.00 300.00
AAHO Hector Olivera/299 4.00 10.00
AAHOW Henry Owens/125 4.00 10.00
AAI Ichiro Suzuki/25 200.00 300.00
AAJA Jose Altuve/125 25.00 60.00
AAJC Jose Canseco/99 12.00 30.00
AAJD Jacob deGrom/75 10.00 25.00
AAJG Juan Gonzalez/125 8.00 20.00
AAJGR Jon Gray/150 3.00 8.00
AAJHE Jason Heyward EXCH 12.00 30.00
AAJHM Jason Hammel/299 5.00 12.00
AAJS James Shields/125 3.00 8.00
AAJSO Jorge Soler/199 5.00 12.00
AAJSZ John Smoltz/75 15.00 40.00
AAKB Kris Bryant/75 60.00 150.00
AAKC Kole Calhoun/299 5.00 12.00
AAKSC Kyle Schwarber/199 10.00 25.00
AAKSZ Kurt Suzuki/299 3.00 8.00
AALG Luis Gonzalez/125 4.00 10.00
AALS Luis Severino/150 4.00 10.00
AAMA Matt Adams/199 3.00 8.00
AAMC Matt Carpenter/199 5.00 12.00
AAMCA Matt Cain/75 6.00 15.00
AAMCO Michael Conforto EXCH 15.00 40.00
AAMG Mark Grace/125 8.00 20.00
AAMGR Marquis Grissom/299 3.00 8.00
AAMP Mike Piazza/25 60.00 150.00
AAMS Miguel Sano/299 5.00 12.00
AAMT Mike Trout/25 150.00 300.00
AAMW Matt Williams/299 3.00 8.00
AANS Noah Syndergaard/125 20.00 50.00
AAPM Paul Molitor/125 10.00 25.00
AAPO Paul O'Neill/99 10.00 25.00
AAPS Pablo Sandoval/75 4.00 10.00
AARC Rod Carew/75 12.00 30.00
AARI Raisel Iglesias/299 4.00 10.00
AARK Ryan Klesko/299 5.00 12.00
AARPA Rafael Palmeiro/75 6.00 15.00
AARY Robin Yount EXCH 25.00 60.00
AASG Sonny Gray/199 6.00 15.00
AASGR Shawn Green/199 3.00 8.00
AASK Sandy Koufax EXCH 150.00 300.00
AASM Steven Matz/299 6.00 15.00
AASP Stephen Piscotty/299 5.00 12.00
AASS Steven Souza Jr./299 4.00 10.00
AATT Troy Tulowitzki/50 10.00 25.00
AATTU Trea Turner/299 10.00 25.00
AATW Taijuan Walker/199 3.00 8.00
AAVC Vinny Castilla/299 3.00 8.00
AAWM Wil Myers/125 3.00 8.00

2016 Topps Museum Collection Canvas Collection

STATED ODDS 1:4 MINI BOXES
CC1 Hank Aaron 2.00 5.00
CC2 Bernie Williams .75 2.00
CC3 George Brett 2.00 5.00
CC4 Buster Posey 1.25 3.00
CC5 Ichiro Suzuki 1.25 3.00
CC6 Kris Bryant 1.25 3.00
CC7 Noah Syndergaard .75 2.00
CC8 Frank Thomas 1.00 2.50
CC9 Ichiro Suzuki 1.25 3.00
CC10 Bryce Harper 1.50 4.00
CC11 Cal Ripken Jr. 3.00 8.00
CC12 Clayton Kershaw 2.00 5.00
CC13 Mike Trout 5.00 12.00
CC14 Rollie Fingers .75 2.00
CC15 Jose Bautista .75 2.00
CC16 Greg Maddux 1.25 3.00
CC17 Kris Bryant 1.25 3.00
CC18 Reggie Jackson .75 2.00
CC19 David Ortiz 1.00 2.50
CC20 Carl Yastrzemski 1.50 4.00
CC21 Ken Griffey Jr. 2.00 5.00
CC22 Mike Piazza 1.00 2.50
CC23 Andrew McCutchen 1.00 2.50
CC24 Matt Harvey .75 2.00
CC25 Yu Darvish 1.00 2.50

2016 Topps Museum Collection Meaningful Material Prime Relics

STATED ODDS 1:9 PACKS
STATED PRINT RUN 50 SER.#'d SETS
*GOLD/35: .4X TO 1X BASIC
MMPRABE Adrian Beltre 8.00 20.00
MMPRABR Archie Bradley 5.00 12.00
MMPRACH Aroldis Chapman 8.00 20.00
MMPRACO Alex Cobb 5.00 12.00
MMPRAGO Alex Gordon 6.00 15.00
MMPRAGZ Adrian Gonzalez 6.00 15.00
MMPRAJ Adam Jones 6.00 15.00
MMPRAL Adam Lind 6.00 15.00
MMPRAMC Andrew McCutchen 15.00 40.00
MMPRAMI Andrew Miller 6.00 15.00
MMPRARE Anthony Rendon 8.00 20.00
MMPRARI Anthony Rizzo 12.00 30.00
MMPRARU Addison Russell 8.00 20.00
MMPRAS Andrelton Simmons 5.00 12.00
MMPRAW Adam Wainwright 6.00 15.00
MMPRBB Byron Buxton 6.00 15.00
MMPRBBE Brandon Belt 6.00 15.00
MMPRBBU Billy Butler 5.00 12.00
MMPRBC Brandon Crawford 6.00 15.00
MMPRBG Brett Gardner 6.00 15.00
MMPRBHM Billy Hamilton 6.00 15.00
MMPRBM Brian McCann 6.00 15.00
MMPRBPH Brandon Phillips 5.00 12.00
MMPRBPO Buster Posey 10.00 25.00
MMPRBS Blake Swihart 6.00 15.00
MMPRCA Chris Archer 5.00 12.00
MMPRCBE Carlos Beltran 6.00 15.00
MMPRCBL Charlie Blackmon 8.00 20.00
MMPRCBU Clay Buchholz 5.00 12.00
MMPRCCR Carl Crawford 6.00 15.00
MMPRCCS CC Sabathia 6.00 15.00
MMPRCD Chris Davis 5.00 12.00
MMPRCGR Curtis Granderson 6.00 15.00
MMPRCK Clayton Kershaw 15.00 40.00
MMPRCKL Corey Kluber 6.00 15.00
MMPRCM Carlos Martinez 6.00 15.00
MMPRCSA Chris Sale 8.00 20.00
MMPRCSE Corey Seager 15.00 40.00
MMPRDB Dellin Betances 6.00 15.00
MMPRDD Delino DeShields Jr. 5.00 12.00
MMPRDFI Doug Fister 5.00 12.00
MMPRDFR David Freese 5.00 12.00
MMPRDGO Dee Gordon 5.00 12.00
MMPRDGR Didi Gregorius 6.00 15.00
MMPRDK Dallas Keuchel 6.00 15.00
MMPRDL DJ LeMahieu 8.00 20.00
MMPRDME Devin Mesoraco 5.00 12.00
MMPRDO David Ortiz 8.00 20.00
MMPRDPE Dustin Pedroia 8.00 20.00
MMPRDW David Wright 6.00 15.00
MMPREA Elvis Andrus 6.00 15.00
MMPREG Evan Gattis 5.00 12.00
MMPREH Eric Hosmer 6.00 15.00
MMPREI Ender Inciarte 5.00 12.00
MMPREL Evan Longoria 6.00 15.00
MMPRFF Freddie Freeman 10.00 25.00
MMPRFH Felix Hernandez 6.00 15.00
MMPRFL Francisco Lindor 8.00 20.00
MMPRFM Frankie Montas 6.00 15.00
MMPRFR Fernando Rodney 5.00 12.00
MMPRGC Gerrit Cole 8.00 20.00
MMPRGG Gio Gonzalez 6.00 15.00
MMPRGH Greg Holland 5.00 12.00
MMPRGP Gregory Polanco 6.00 15.00
MMPRGSA Gary Sanchez 15.00 40.00
MMPRGSP George Springer 6.00 15.00
MMPRGST Giancarlo Stanton 8.00 20.00
MMPRHI Hisashi Iwakuma 6.00 15.00
MMPRHJR Hyun-Jin Ryu 6.00 15.00
MMPRHO Henry Owens 6.00 15.00
MMPRHP Hunter Pence 10.00 25.00
MMPRID Ian Desmond 5.00 12.00
MMPRIK Ian Kinsler 6.00 15.00
MMPRJBA Javier Baez 10.00 25.00
MMPRJBR Jay Bruce 6.00 15.00
MMPRJD Josh Donaldson 6.00 15.00
MMPRJDG Jacob deGrom 8.00 20.00
MMPRJE Jacoby Ellsbury 6.00 15.00
MMPRJFA Jeurys Familia 6.00 15.00
MMPRJFE Jose Fernandez 8.00 20.00
MMPRJHA Josh Harrison 5.00 12.00
MMPRJHK Jung Ho Kang 5.00 12.00
MMPRJHM Josh Hamilton 6.00 15.00
MMPRJJ Jon Jay 5.00 12.00
MMPRJK Jason Kipnis 6.00 15.00
MMPRJLE Jon Lester 6.00 15.00
MMPRJLU Jonathan Lucroy 6.00 15.00
MMPRJMA Joe Mauer 6.00 15.00
MMPRJMC James McCann 12.00 30.00
MMPRJMR J.D. Martinez 8.00 20.00
MMPRJPD Joc Pederson 6.00 15.00
MMPRJRE Josh Reddick 5.00 12.00
MMPRJRO Jimmy Rollins 6.00 15.00
MMPRJS Jonathan Schoop 5.00 12.00
MMPRJT Julio Teheran 6.00 15.00
MMPRJU Justin Upton 6.00 15.00
MMPRJV Joey Votto 8.00 20.00
MMPRJW Jayson Werth 6.00 15.00
MMPRKB Kris Bryant 10.00 25.00
MMPRKC Kole Calhoun 5.00 12.00
MMPRKJ Kenley Jansen 6.00 15.00
MMPRKM Ketel Marte 10.00 25.00
MMPRKSE Kyle Seager 5.00 12.00
MMPRKW Kolten Wong 6.00 15.00
MMPRLC Lorenzo Cain 5.00 12.00
MMPRLD Lucas Duda 6.00 15.00
MMPRLL Lance Lynn 5.00 12.00
MMPRLS Luis Severino 6.00 15.00
MMPRMA Matt Adams 5.00 12.00
MMPRMBE Mookie Betts 12.00 30.00
MMPRMBR Michael Brantley 6.00 15.00
MMPRMBU Madison Bumgarner 6.00 15.00
MMPRMCA Matt Cain 6.00 15.00
MMPRMCB Miguel Cabrera 8.00 20.00
MMPRMCH Michael Choice 5.00 12.00
MMPRMCO Michael Conforto 6.00 15.00
MMPRMCR Matt Carpenter 8.00 20.00
MMPRMD Matt Duffy 5.00 12.00
MMPRMF Maikel Franco 6.00 15.00
MMPRMHA Matt Harvey 6.00 15.00
MMPRMHO Matt Holliday 8.00 20.00
MMPRMMA Manny Machado 15.00 40.00
MMPRMME Mark Melancon 5.00 12.00
MMPRMP Michael Pineda 5.00 12.00
MMPRMST Marcus Stroman 6.00 15.00
MMPRMTR Mike Trout 40.00 100.00
MMPRMTX Mark Teixeira 6.00 15.00
MMPRMW Michael Wacha 8.00 20.00
MMPRNA Nolan Arenado 10.00 25.00
MMPRNCA Nick Castellanos 8.00 20.00
MMPRNCR Nelson Cruz 8.00 20.00
MMPRNS Noah Syndergaard 6.00 15.00
MMPRPA Pedro Alvarez 5.00 12.00
MMPRPF Prince Fielder 6.00 15.00
MMPRPG Paul Goldschmidt 8.00 20.00
MMPRPS Pablo Sandoval 6.00 15.00
MMPRRA Roberto Alomar 6.00 15.00
MMPRRB Ryan Braun 6.00 15.00
MMPRRC Robinson Cano 6.00 15.00
MMPRRD R.A. Dickey 6.00 15.00
MMPRRH Ryan Howard 6.00 15.00
MMPRRM Russell Martin 5.00 12.00
MMPRROD Rougned Odor 6.00 15.00
MMPRROS Roberto Osuna 5.00 12.00
MMPRRP Rick Porcello 6.00 15.00
MMPRRZ Ryan Zimmerman 6.00 15.00
MMPRSC Starlin Castro 5.00 12.00
MMPRSG Sonny Gray 6.00 15.00
MMPRSMI Shelby Miller 6.00 15.00
MMPRSMR Starling Marte 6.00 15.00
MMPRSMZ Steven Matz 6.00 15.00
MMPRSPE Salvador Perez 6.00 15.00
MMPRSS Stephen Strasburg 8.00 20.00
MMPRSSC Shin-Soo Choo 6.00 15.00
MMPRSV Stephen Vogt 6.00 15.00
MMPRTD Travis d'Arnaud 6.00 15.00
MMPRTF Todd Frazier 6.00 15.00
MMPRTH Torii Hunter 5.00 12.00
MMPRTR Trevor Rosenthal 6.00 15.00
MMPRVM Victor Martinez 6.00 15.00
MMPRWD Wade Davis 5.00 12.00
MMPRWF Wilmer Flores 6.00 15.00
MMPRXB Xander Bogaerts 8.00 20.00
MMPRYC Yoenis Cespedes 8.00 20.00
MMPRYD Yu Darvish 8.00 20.00
MMPRYG Yasmani Grandal 5.00 12.00
MMPRYM Yadier Molina 10.00 25.00
MMPRYP Yasiel Puig 8.00 20.00
MMPRYT Yasmany Tomas 5.00 12.00
MMPRZG Zack Greinke 6.00 15.00
MMPRZW Zack Wheeler 6.00 15.00

2016 Topps Museum Collection Premium Prints Autographs

STATED ODDS 1:109 MINI BOX
STATED PRINT RUN 25 SER.#'d SETS
EXCHANGE DEADLINE 2/28/2018
PPBBE Brandon Belt
PPBH Bryce Harper 200.00 400.00
PPBL Barry Larkin 20.00 50.00
PPBP Buster Posey 50.00 120.00
PPBW Bernie Williams EXCH 25.00 60.00
PPCC Carlos Correa 200.00 400.00
PPCK Corey Kluber 10.00 25.00
PPCR Cal Ripken Jr. 75.00 200.00
PPDG Dee Gordon EXCH 8.00 20.00
PPDP Dustin Pedroia 25.00 60.00
PPFL Franciso Lindor 30.00 80.00
PPGM Greg Maddux EXCH 40.00 100.00
PPHA Hank Aaron 150.00 300.00
PPHR Hanley Ramirez EXCH 10.00 25.00
PPJAL Jose Altuve 25.00 60.00
PPJS Jorge Soler
PPKB Kris Bryant EXCH 150.00 300.00
PPKS Kyle Schwarber 25.00 60.00
PPMAD Matt Adams 8.00 20.00
PPMMA Manny Machado 60.00 150.00
PPPMO Paul Molitor 12.00 30.00
PPSK Sandy Koufax EXCH 150.00 400.00
PPTG Tom Glavine 20.00 50.00

2016 Topps Museum Collection Primary Pieces Four Player Quad Relics

STATED ODDS 1:36 PACKS
STATED PRINT RUN 99 SER.#'d SETS
PRICING FOR BASIC JSY SWATCHES
*COPPER/75: .4X TO 1X BASIC
*GOLD/25: .5X TO 1.2X BASIC
PPFQASSE Sam/Sal/Eat/Abr 6.00 15.00
PPFQCALW Ada/Lyn/Car/Wac 6.00 15.00
PPFQCCHI Iwk/Cru/Hrn/Can 8.00 20.00
PPFQCKVC Ver/Cas/Cab/Kin 12.00 30.00
PPFQDSBE Bau/Str/Don/Enc 6.00 15.00
PPFQFHDC Fie/Ham/Cho/DeS 5.00 12.00
PPFQFVHC Cha/Ham/Fra/Vot 15.00 40.00
PPFQGHHV Hos/Hol/Ven/Gor 12.00 30.00
PPFQHDSM deG/Har/Mat/Syn 30.00 80.00
PPFQJDMH Mac/Dav/Jon/Har 12.00 30.00
PPFQKGGP Gre/Gon/Ker/Pui 12.00 30.00
PPFQLKBS Lin/Bra/Klu/San 6.00 15.00
PPFQMKCM Col/Mar/Kan/McC 25.00 60.00
PPFQPBPC Cai/Pos/Pen/Bum 8.00 20.00
PPFQPSMB Mil/Ser/Pin/Bet 5.00 12.00
PPFQSBPO San/Bog/Ort/Ped 10.00 25.00
PPFQSRBR Sol/Rus/Bry/Riz 20.00 50.00
PPFQTCPF Puj/Tro/Cal/Fre 12.00 30.00
PPFQTTEB Tei/Tan/Bel/Ell 10.00 25.00
PPFQWCGD Wri/Con/Dud/Gra 5.00 12.00

2016 Topps Museum Collection Primary Pieces Quad Relics

STATED ODDS 1:12 PACKS
STATED PRINT RUN 99 SER.#'d SETS
*COPPER/75: .4X TO 1X BASIC
*GOLD/25: .5X TO 1.2X BASIC
PPQRI Ichiro Suzuki 12.00 30.00
PPQRAB Adrian Beltre 6.00 15.00
PPQRAC Aroldis Chapman 5.00 12.00
PPQRAG Adrian Gonzalez 4.00 10.00
PPQRAMC Andrew McCutchen 10.00 25.00
PPQRAMU Andrew McCutchen 10.00 25.00
PPQRAP Albert Pujols 6.00 15.00
PPQRAR Anthony Rizzo 8.00 20.00
PPQRAW Adam Wainwright 6.00 15.00
PPQRBB Byron Buxton 4.00 10.00
PPQRBP Buster Posey 6.00 15.00
PPQRCA Chris Archer 3.00 8.00
PPQRCBI Craig Biggio 4.00 10.00
PPQRCBU Clay Buchholz 3.00 8.00
PPQRCH Cole Hamels 4.00 10.00
PPQRCJ Chipper Jones 10.00 25.00
PPQRCK Clayton Kershaw 8.00 20.00
PPQRCR Cal Ripken Jr. 15.00 40.00
PPQRDM Don Mattingly 10.00 25.00
PPQRDO David Ortiz 10.00 25.00
PPQREA Elvis Andrus 5.00 12.00
PPQRFF Freddie Freeman 6.00 15.00
PPQRFH Felix Hernandez 4.00 10.00
PPQRGC Gerrit Cole 5.00 12.00
PPQRGS Giancarlo Stanton 5.00 12.00
PPQRJAB Jose Abreu 5.00 12.00
PPQRJBA Jose Bautista 4.00 10.00
PPQRJBE Javier Baez 6.00 15.00
PPQRJD Josh Donaldson 4.00 10.00
PPQRJDG Jacob deGrom 5.00 12.00
PPQRJE Jacoby Ellsbury 4.00 10.00
PPQRJF Jose Fernandez 5.00 12.00
PPQRJH Josh Hamilton 4.00 10.00
PPQRJM Joe Mauer 4.00 10.00
PPQRJP Joc Pederson 4.00 10.00
PPQRJV Justin Verlander 8.00 20.00
PPQRKB Kris Bryant 15.00 40.00
PPQRLC Lorenzo Cain 3.00 8.00
PPQRLL Lance Lynn 3.00 8.00
PPQRMA Matt Adams 3.00 8.00
PPQRMB Madison Bumgarner 4.00 10.00
PPQRMCB Miguel Cabrera 8.00 20.00
PPQRMCR Matt Carpenter 5.00 12.00
PPQRMHA Matt Harvey 6.00 15.00
PPQRMHO Matt Holliday 5.00 12.00
PPQRMM Manny Machado 5.00 12.00
PPQRMP Mike Piazza 10.00 25.00
PPQRMT Mike Trout 20.00 50.00
PPQRNA Nolan Arenado 8.00 20.00
PPQROV Omar Vizquel 75.00 200.00
PPQRPA Pedro Alvarez 3.00 8.00
PPQRPF Prince Fielder 4.00 10.00
PPQRPG Paul Goldschmidt 6.00 15.00
PPQRRA Roberto Alomar 4.00 10.00
PPQRRC Roger Clemens 6.00 15.00
PPQRRH Rickey Henderson 8.00 20.00
PPQRSS Stephen Strasburg 5.00 12.00
PPQRTF Todd Frazier 4.00 10.00
PPQRTG Tony Gwynn 15.00 40.00
PPQRVM Victor Martinez 4.00 10.00
PPQRYD Yu Darvish 5.00 12.00
PPQRYM Yadier Molina 8.00 20.00
PPQRYP Yasiel Puig 5.00 12.00
PPQRYV Yordano Ventura 4.00 10.00

2016 Topps Museum Collection Primary Pieces Quad Relics Legends

STATED ODDS 1:140 MINI BOX
STATED PRINT RUN 25 SER.#'d SETS
PPQLBD Bobby Doerr 10.00 25.00
PPQLBF Bob Feller 20.00 50.00
PPQLBL Bob Lemon 10.00 25.00
PPQLCY Carl Yastrzemski 20.00 50.00
PPQLEM Eddie Murray 10.00 25.00
PPQLHA Hank Aaron 60.00 150.00
PPQLJB Jim Bunning 10.00 25.00
PPQLJM Juan Marichal 10.00 25.00
PPQLJP Jim Palmer 10.00 25.00
PPQLJR Jackie Robinson 40.00 100.00
PPQLOC Orlando Cepeda 10.00 25.00
PPQLOS Ozzie Smith 30.00 80.00
PPQLRC Rod Carew 10.00 25.00
PPQLRF Rollie Fingers 20.00 50.00
PPQLRJ Reggie Jackson 20.00 50.00
PPQLRM Roger Maris 40.00 100.00
PPQLSC Steve Carlton 25.00 60.00
PPQLTP Tony Perez 20.00 50.00
PPQLTW Ted Williams 60.00 150.00
PPQLWM Willie Mays 60.00 150.00

2016 Topps Museum Collection Signature Swatches Dual Relic Autographs

STATED ODDS 1:9 PACKS
PRINT RUNS B/WN 30-399 COPIES PER
EXCHANGE DEADLINE 2/28/2018
PRICING FOR BASIC JSY SWATCHES
*GOLD: .4X TO 1X BASIC p/r 30
*GOLD: .5X TO 1.2X BASIC p/r 50-99
*GOLD: .6X TO 1.5X BASIC p/r 150-399
SSDAE Alcides Escobar/199 8.00 20.00
SSDAGN Adrian Gonzalez/99 8.00 20.00
SSDAJO Adam Jones/99 10.00 25.00
SSDAM Andrew Miller/299 6.00 15.00
SSDBB Byron Buxton/99 6.00 15.00
SSDBH Brock Holt/299 5.00 12.00
SSDBP Buster Posey/30 40.00 100.00
SSDBZ Brad Ziegler/90 15.00 40.00
SSDCK Clayton Kershaw/30 50.00 120.00
SSDCKE Clayton Kershaw/50 40.00 100.00
SSDCS Corey Seager/225 30.00 80.00
SSDDG Dee Gordon/299 5.00 12.00
SSDDK Dallas Keuchel/225 6.00 15.00
SSDDL DJ LeMahieu/299 12.00 30.00
SSDDW David Wright/50 8.00 20.00
SSDEL Evan Longoria/30 10.00 25.00
SSDGH Greg Holland/354 5.00 12.00
SSDHOL Hector Olivera/249 6.00 15.00
SSDHOW Henry Owens/299 6.00 15.00
SSDJD Jacob deGrom/199 12.00 30.00
SSDJFA Jeurys Familia/399 6.00 15.00
SSDJK Jung Ho Kang/299 10.00 25.00
SSDJL Jon Lester/99 10.00 25.00
SSDKB Kris Bryant/50 75.00 200.00
SSDKP Kevin Plawecki/399 5.00 12.00
SSDKS Kyle Schwarber/299 20.00 50.00
SSDLS Luis Severino/299 6.00 15.00
SSDMCA Matt Cain/99 6.00 15.00
SSDMCO Michael Conforto/199 25.00 60.00
SSDMH Matt Harvey EXCH 30.00 80.00
SSDMM Mark McGwire/50 50.00 120.00
SSDMTE Mark Teixeira/99 8.00 20.00
SSDMTR Mike Trout/30 150.00 400.00
SSDNS Noah Syndergaard/99 25.00 60.00
SSDPF Prince Fielder/30 10.00 25.00
SSDRC Robinson Cano/30 12.00 30.00
SSDRR Rob Refsnyder/299 6.00 15.00
SSDSH Slade Heathcott/399 6.00 15.00
SSDSMA Steven Matz/399 6.00 15.00
SSDSMI Shelby Miller/225 6.00 15.00
SSDSPE Salvador Perez/30 15.00 40.00
SSDSPI Stephen Piscotty/299 8.00 20.00
SSDTT Troy Tulowitzki/50 12.00 30.00
SSDWM Wil Myers/99 5.00 12.00
SSDYT Yasmany Tomas/99 5.00 12.00
SSDZW Zack Wheeler/299 6.00 15.00

2016 Topps Museum Collection Signature Swatches Triple Relic Autographs

STATED ODDS 1:15 PACKS
PRINT RUNS B/WN 25-299 COPIES PER
EXCHANGE DEADLINE 2/28/2018
PRICING FOR BASIC JSY SWATCHES
*GOLD: .4X TO 1X BASIC p/r 25
*GOLD: .5X TO 1.2X BASIC p/r 50-99
*GOLD: .6X TO 1.5X BASIC p/r 150-299
SSTAM Andrew Miller/179 6.00 15.00
SSTBB Byron Buxton/50 12.00 30.00
SSTBH Brock Holt/299 5.00 12.00
SSTBP Buster Posey/25 60.00 150.00
SSTCS Corey Seager/99 30.00 80.00
SSTDK Dallas Keuchel/99 10.00 25.00
SSTDL DJ LeMahieu/299 12.00 30.00
SSTDW David Wright/55 12.00 30.00
SSTGH Greg Holland/175 5.00 12.00
SSTHOL Hector Olivera/99 6.00 15.00
SSTHOW Henry Owens/299 6.00 15.00
SSTJD Jacob deGrom/99 20.00 50.00
SSTJF Jeurys Familia/299 6.00 15.00
SSTJK Jung Ho Kang/299 12.00 30.00
SSTKP Kevin Plawecki/299 5.00 12.00
SSTKS Kyle Schwarber/150 20.00 50.00
SSTLS Luis Severino/99 6.00 15.00
SSTMC Michael Conforto/99 25.00 60.00
SSTMF Maikel Franco/299 6.00 15.00
SSTMM Mark McGwire/50
SSTMTR Mike Trout/50 150.00 400.00
SSTMTX Mark Teixeira/50 10.00 25.00
SSTNS Noah Syndergaard/99 25.00 60.00
SSTRR Rob Refsnyder/299 6.00 15.00
SSTSH Slade Heathcott/99 6.00 15.00
SSTSMA Steven Matz/299 15.00 40.00
SSTSMI Shelby Miller/99 6.00 15.00
SSTSPE Salvador Perez/99 15.00 40.00
SSTWM Wil Myers/50 5.00 12.00
SSTYD Yu Darvish/50 25.00 60.00
SSTYT Yasmany Tomas/50 5.00 12.00
SSTZW Zack Wheeler/99 6.00 15.00

2017 Topps Museum Collection

1 Kris Bryant 1.00 2.50
2 Mike Trout 4.00 10.00
3 Paul Goldschmidt .75 2.00
4 Manny Machado .75 2.00
5 Mookie Betts 1.25 3.00
6 Anthony Rizzo 1.25 3.00
7 Kyle Schwarber .75 2.00
8 Joey Votto .75 2.00
9 Nolan Arenado 1.00 2.50
10 Miguel Cabrera .75 2.00
11 Justin Verlander .75 2.00
12 Carlos Correa .75 2.00
13 Eric Hosmer .60 1.50
14 Clayton Kershaw 1.50 4.00
15 Corey Seager .75 2.00
16 Julio Urias .75 2.00
17 Giancarlo Stanton .75 2.00
18 Ichiro 1.00 2.50
19 Noah Syndergaard .60 1.50
20 Masahiro Tanaka .60 1.50
21 Gary Sanchez .75 2.00
22 Carl Yastrzemski 1.25 3.00
23 Buster Posey 1.00 2.50
24 Felix Hernandez .60 1.50
25 Robinson Cano .60 1.50
26 Aledmys Diaz .60 1.50
27 Yu Darvish .75 2.00
28 Josh Donaldson .60 1.50
29 Jose Bautista .60 1.50
30 Bryce Harper 1.25 3.00
31 Max Scherzer .75 2.00
32 Francisco Lindor .75 2.00
33 Chris Sale .75 2.00
34 Addison Russell .75 2.00
35 Javier Baez 1.00 2.50
36 Jacob deGrom .75 2.00
37 Andrew McCutchen .75 2.00
38 Wil Myers .50 1.25
39 Albert Pujols 1.00 2.50
40 Yoenis Cespedes .75 2.00
41 Jose Altuve .60 1.50
42 Jake Arrieta .60 1.50
43 Edwin Encarnacion .75 2.00
44 David Price .60 1.50
45 Ryan Braun .60 1.50
46 Freddie Freeman 1.00 2.50
47 Troy Tulowitzki .75 2.00
48 Matt Carpenter .75 2.00
49 Carlos Gonzalez .60 1.50
50 Adrian Beltre .75 2.00
51 Hunter Pence .60 1.50
52 Corey Kluber .60 1.50
53 Trea Turner .60 1.50
54 Kenta Maeda .60 1.50
55 Stephen Strasburg .75 2.00
56 Matt Kemp .60 1.50
57 David Wright .60 1.50
58 Xander Bogaerts .75 2.00
59 Adam Jones .60 1.50
60 Daniel Murphy .60 1.50
61 Ken Griffey Jr. 1.50 4.00
62 Roberto Clemente 2.00 5.00
63 Cal Ripken Jr. 2.50 6.00
64 Hank Aaron 1.50 4.00
65 Ted Williams 1.50 4.00
66 Jackie Robinson .75 2.00
67 Sandy Koufax 1.50 4.00
68 Babe Ruth 2.00 5.00
69 Ernie Banks .75 2.00
70 Derek Jeter 2.00 5.00
71 David Ortiz .75 2.00
72 Mark McGwire 1.25 3.00
73 Randy Johnson .75 2.00
74 Honus Wagner .75 2.00
75 Roger Maris .75 2.00
76 Ty Cobb 1.25 3.00
77 Lou Gehrig 1.50 4.00
78 Reggie Jackson .60 1.50
79 George Brett 1.50 4.00
80 Don Mattingly 1.50 4.00
81 Frank Thomas .75 2.00
82 Bo Jackson .75 2.00
83 Johnny Bench .75 2.00
84 Greg Maddux 1.00 2.50
85 Roger Clemens 1.00 2.50
86 Mike Piazza .75 2.00
87 Nolan Ryan 2.50 6.00
88 Brooks Robinson .60 1.50
89 Chipper Jones .75 2.00
90 Ozzie Smith 1.00 2.50
91 Dansby Swanson RC 1.50 4.00
92 Andrew Benintendi RC 2.00 5.00
93 Yoan Moncada RC 2.00 5.00
94 Alex Bregman RC 2.50 6.00
95 Aaron Judge RC 10.00 25.00
96 Tyler Glasnow RC .75 2.00
97 Hunter Renfroe RC .75 2.00
98 Alex Reyes RC .75 2.00
99 Yulieski Gurriel RC 1.00 2.50
100 David Dahl RC .75 2.00

2017 Topps Museum Collection Blue

*BLUE: .75X TO 2X BASIC
*BLUE RC: ..6X TO 1.5X BASIC RC
STATED ODDS 1:6 HOBBY
STATED PRINT RUN 150 SER.#'d SETS
70 Derek Jeter 8.00 20.00
95 Aaron Judge 15.00 40.00

2017 Topps Museum Collection Copper

*COPPER: .6X TO 1.5X BASIC
*COPPER RC: .5X TO 1.2X BASIC RC
RANDOM INSERTS IN PACKS
70 Derek Jeter 6.00 15.00

2017 Topps Museum Collection Purple

*PURPLE: 1X TO 2.5X BASIC
*PURPLE RC: .75X TO 2X BASIC RC
STATED ODDS 1:8 HOBBY
STATED PRINT RUN 99 SER.#'d SETS
70 Derek Jeter 10.00 25.00
95 Aaron Judge 20.00 50.00

2017 Topps Museum Collection Red

*RED: 1.5X TO 4X BASIC
*RED RC: 1.2X TO 3X BASIC RC
STATED ODDS 1:16 HOBBY
STATED PRINT RUN 50 SER.#'d SETS
70 Derek Jeter 15.00 40.00
95 Aaron Judge 30.00 80.00

2017 Topps Museum Collection Archival Autographs

STATED ODDS 1:8 HOBBY
PRINT RUNS B/WN 75-299 COPIES PER
EXCHANGE DEADLINE 5/31/2019
AAAB Alex Bregman/299 20.00 50.00
AAADI Aledmys Diaz/199 4.00 10.00
AAAGA Andres Galarraga/99 4.00 10.00
AAAJU Aaron Judge/299 100.00 250.00
AAAK Al Kaline/99 15.00 40.00
AAAN Aaron Nola/199 4.00 10.00
AAARE Alex Reyes/299 4.00 10.00
AAARI Anthony Rizzo/99 20.00 50.00
AAARU Addison Russell/149 12.00 30.00
AABA Bobby Abreu EXCH 5.00 12.00
AABW Billy Wagner/99 5.00 12.00
AACB Craig Biggio/75 12.00 30.00
AACFL Carson Fulmer/299 3.00 8.00
AACSA Chris Sale/75 5.00 12.00
AACSE Corey Seager/75 25.00 60.00
AADD David Dahl/299 4.00 10.00
AADF Dexter Fowler EXCH 10.00 25.00
AADL Derrek Lee/99 3.00 8.00
AADS Dansby Swanson/299 15.00 40.00
AAFL Francisco Lindor/299 15.00 40.00
AAFV Fernando Valenzuela/99 10.00 25.00
AAHO Henry Owens/150 3.00 8.00
AAIR Ivan Rodriguez/75 12.00 30.00
AAJAL Jose Altuve/199 20.00 50.00
AAJCA Jose Canseco/199 6.00 15.00
AAJDG Jacob deGrom/99 10.00 25.00
AAJDL Jose De Leon/299 3.00 8.00
AAJR Jim Rice/199 4.00 10.00
AAJTA Jameson Taillon/75 4.00 10.00
AAJTH Jake Thompson/299 3.00 8.00
AAJTU Justin Turner/199 12.00 30.00
AAJV Jason Varitek/75 12.00 30.00
AAKH Kelvin Herrera/299 3.00 8.00
AAKMA Kenta Maeda/75 6.00 15.00
AAKMO Kendrys Morales/199 3.00 8.00
AAKS Kyle Schwarber/99 12.00 30.00
AALG Lucas Giolito/75 4.00 10.00
AALS Luis Severino/150 10.00 25.00
AAMC Matt Carpenter/199 8.00 20.00
AAMFR Maikel Franco/75 5.00 12.00
AAMFU Michael Fulmer/199 6.00 15.00
AAMMU Mark Mulder/99 5.00 12.00
AAMSA Miguel Sano/75 4.00 10.00
AAMTR Mike Trout
AANM Nomar Mazara/75 6.00 15.00
AANS Noah Syndergaard/199 12.00 30.00
AAOS Ozzie Smith/75 20.00 50.00
AAOV Omar Vizquel/99 6.00 15.00
AAPK Paul Konerko/99 10.00 25.00
AARA Roberto Alomar/75 10.00 25.00
AARCR Rod Carew/75 10.00 25.00
AARF Rollie Fingers/199 4.00 10.00
AARO Roy Oswalt/99 4.00 10.00
AASMZ Steven Matz/99 4.00 10.00
AASW Steven Wright/199 3.00 8.00
AATA Tyler Austin/299 5.00 12.00
AATGS Tyler Glasnow/299 4.00 10.00
AATGV Tom Glavine/75 12.00 30.00
AATS Trevor Story/199 8.00 20.00
AATTH Trayce Thompson/299 4.00 10.00
AATTU Trea Turner/199 10.00 25.00
AAWC Willson Contreras/199 12.00 30.00
AAYG Yulieski Gurriel/299 8.00 20.00
AAYM Yoan Moncada/99 15.00 40.00

2017 Topps Museum Collection Archival Autographs Copper

*COPPER: .5X TO 1.2X BASIC
STATED ODDS 1:22 HOBBY
STATED PRINT RUN 50 SER.#'d SETS
EXCHANGE DEADLINE 5/31/2019
AAAGO Adrian Gonzalez 5.00 12.00
AAAJO Adam Jones 6.00 15.00
AACC Carlos Correa 40.00 100.00
AADM Don Mattingly 25.00 60.00
AADPE Dustin Pedroia 10.00 25.00
AADPR David Price 10.00 25.00
AAJU Julio Urias 8.00 20.00
AAKB Kris Bryant 75.00 200.00
AAMWI Matt Wieters 8.00 20.00

2017 Topps Museum Collection Archival Autographs Gold

*GOLD: .6X TO 1.5X BASIC
STATED ODDS 1:42 HOBBY
STATED PRINT RUN 25 SER.#'d SETS
EXCHANGE DEADLINE 5/31/2019
AAAGO Adrian Gonzalez 6.00 15.00
AAAJO Adam Jones 8.00 20.00
AABH Bryce Harper 150.00 300.00
AACC Carlos Correa 50.00 120.00
AACK Clayton Kershaw 60.00 150.00
AACR Carlos Rodon EXCH 6.00 15.00
AADM Don Mattingly 30.00 80.00
AADPE Dustin Pedroia 12.00 30.00
AADPR David Price 12.00 30.00
AAJU Julio Urias 10.00 25.00
AAKB Kris Bryant 100.00 250.00
AAMMA Manny Machado 30.00 80.00
AAMWI Matt Wieters 10.00 25.00

2017 Topps Museum Collection Canvas Collection

STATED ODDS 1:4 HOBBY
CCRAB Alex Bregman 2.50 6.00
CCRAJ Aaron Judge 8.00 20.00
CCRAM Andrew McCutchen 1.00 2.50
CCRAR Anthony Rizzo 1.50 4.00

CCRBH Bryce Harper 1.50 4.00
CCRCC Carlos Correa 1.00 2.50
CCRCO Carlos Correa 1.00 2.50
CCRCK Clayton Kershaw 2.00 5.00
CCRCKE Clayton Kershaw 2.00 5.00
CCRCKR Clayton Kershaw 2.00 5.00
CCRCS Corey Seager 1.00 2.50
CCRCSS Corey Seager 1.00 2.50
CCRDM Don Mattingly 2.00 5.00
CCRDO David Ortiz 1.00 2.50
CCRDW David Wright .75 2.00
CCRFL Francisco Lindor 1.00 2.50
CCRGC Gary Carter .75 2.00
CCRGS Giancarlo Stanton 1.00 2.50
CCRGSA Gary Sanchez 1.00 2.50
CCRGST Giancarlo Stanton 1.00 2.50
CCRHA Hank Aaron 2.00 5.00
CCRJA Jose Altuve .75 2.00
CCRJAR Jake Arrieta .75 2.00
CCRKB Kris Bryant 1.25 3.00
CCRKG Ken Griffey Jr. 2.00 5.00
CCRKM Kenta Maeda .75 2.00
CCRKMA Kenta Maeda .75 2.00
CCRKS Kyle Schwarber 1.00 2.50
CCRKSC Kyle Schwarber 1.00 2.50
CCRMB Mookie Betts 1.50 4.00
CCRMC Miguel Cabrera 1.00 2.50
CCRMCA Miguel Cabrera 1.00 2.50
CCRMCB Miguel Cabrera 1.00 2.50
CCRMM Manny Machado 1.00 2.50
CCRMP Mike Piazza 1.00 2.50
CCRMS Max Scherzer 1.00 2.50
CCRMT Mike Trout 5.00 12.00
CCRNA Nolan Arenado 1.25 3.00
CCRNR Nolan Ryan 3.00 8.00
CCRNS Noah Syndergaard .75 2.00
CCRNSN Noah Syndergaard .75 2.00
CCRRC Rod Carew .75 2.00
CCRRJ Reggie Jackson .75 2.00
CCRRM Roger Maris 1.00 2.50
CCRRMA Roger Maris 1.00 2.50
CCRSK Sandy Koufax 2.00 5.00
CCRWB Wade Boggs .75 2.00
CCRWF Whitey Ford .75 2.00
CCRXB Xander Bogaerts 1.00 2.50
CCRYC Yoenis Cespedes 1.00 2.50

2017 Topps Museum Collection Meaningful Materials Relics

STATED ODDS 1:10 HOBBY
STATED PRINT RUN 50 SER.#'d SETS
*COPPER/35: .4X TO 1X BASIC
MRAC Aroldis Chapman 5.00 12.00
MRAD Adam Duvall 20.00 50.00
MRAG Adrian Gonzalez 4.00 10.00
MRAJ Adam Jones 4.00 10.00
MRAN Aaron Nola 4.00 10.00
MRAS Aaron Sanchez 4.00 10.00
MRBH Bryce Harper 15.00 40.00
MRBM Brandon Moss 3.00 8.00
MRBP Buster Posey 6.00 15.00
MRBS Blake Snell 4.00 10.00
MRBZ Ben Zobrist 8.00 20.00
MRCB Charlie Blackmon 5.00 12.00
MRDG Dee Gordon 3.00 8.00
MRDL DJ LeMahieu 5.00 12.00
MRDO David Ortiz 6.00 15.00
MRDP Dustin Pedroia 8.00 20.00
MRDT Devon Travis 3.00 8.00
MREL Evan Longoria 4.00 10.00
MRFF Freddie Freeman 6.00 15.00
MRGP Gregory Polanco UER 4.00 10.00
Wrong Player
MRGS George Springer 4.00 10.00
MRHI Hisashi Iwakuma 4.00 10.00
MRHR Hyun-Jin Ryu 4.00 10.00
MMAE Alcides Escobar 4.00 10.00
MMAJ Adam Jones 4.00 10.00
MMAM Andrew McCutchen 8.00 20.00
MMAR Anthony Rendon 6.00 15.00
MMARU Addison Russell 5.00 12.00
MMAW Adam Wainwright 4.00 10.00
MMBF Brandon Finnegan 3.00 8.00
MMBG Brett Gardner 5.00 12.00
MMBH Billy Hamilton 4.00 10.00
MMBP Brandon Phillips 3.00 8.00
MMCA Chris Archer 3.00 8.00
MMCD Chris Davis 6.00 15.00
MMCDI Corey Dickerson 3.00 8.00
MMCG Curtis Granderson 4.00 10.00
MMCGO Carlos Gonzalez 4.00 10.00
MMCH Cole Hamels 4.00 10.00
MMCK Corey Kluber 4.00 10.00
MMCM Carlos Martinez 4.00 10.00
MMCR Carlos Rodon 4.00 10.00
MMCS Carlos Santana 4.00 10.00
MMCY Christian Yelich 6.00 15.00
MMDB Dylan Bundy 6.00 15.00
MMDBE Dellin Betances 4.00 10.00
MMDD Danny Duffy 6.00 15.00
MMDK Dallas Keuchel 4.00 10.00
MMDW David Wright 4.00 10.00
MMEG Evan Gattis 3.00 8.00
MMEH Eric Hosmer 6.00 15.00
MMEL Evan Longoria 4.00 10.00
MMFF Freddie Freeman 6.00 15.00
MMFH Felix Hernandez 4.00 10.00
MMGC Gerrit Cole 6.00 15.00
MMGG Gio Gonzalez 4.00 10.00
MMGP Gregory Polanco 4.00 10.00
MMGR Garrett Richards 4.00 10.00
MMGS George Springer 4.00 10.00
MMGST Giancarlo Stanton 5.00 12.00
MMHR Hanley Ramirez 4.00 10.00
MMHRY Hyun-Jin Ryu 4.00 10.00
MMIK Ian Kinsler 6.00 15.00
MRI Ichiro 10.00 25.00
MMJD Jacob deGrom 5.00 12.00
MMJF Jeurys Familia 4.00 10.00
MMJG Jon Gray 3.00 8.00
MMJH Jason Hammel 4.00 10.00
MMJHA Josh Harrison 8.00 20.00
MMJK Jason Kipnis 6.00 15.00
MMJKA Jung Ho Kang 3.00 8.00
MMJM J.D. Martinez 5.00 12.00
MMJO Jake Odorizzi 3.00 8.00
MMJP Jurickson Profar 4.00 10.00
MMJS Jonathan Schoop 6.00 15.00
MMJT Julio Teheran 4.00 10.00
MMJV Joey Votto 5.00 12.00
MMJVE Justin Verlander 5.00 12.00
MMJW Jayson Werth 4.00 10.00
MMJZ Jordan Zimmermann 4.00 10.00
MMKG Kevin Gausman 6.00 15.00
MMKK Kevin Kiermaier 4.00 10.00
MMKS Kyle Seager 3.00 8.00
MMKU Koji Uehara 3.00 8.00
MMKW Kolten Wong 4.00 10.00
MMLC Lorenzo Cain 10.00 25.00
MMLCH Lonnie Chisenhall 10.00 25.00
MMMA Matt Adams 3.00 8.00
MMMB Mookie Betts 6.00 15.00
MMMC Michael Conforto 4.00 10.00
MMMCA Miguel Cabrera 5.00 12.00
MMMH Matt Harvey 4.00 10.00
MMMM Manny Machado 8.00 20.00
MMMW Matt Wieters 6.00 15.00
MMMWA Michael Wacha 4.00 10.00
MMNC Nelson Cruz 5.00 12.00
MMNCA Nick Castellanos 5.00 12.00
MMNS Noah Syndergaard 4.00 10.00
MMPF Prince Fielder 4.00 10.00
MMPG Paul Goldschmidt 10.00 25.00
MMRI Raisel Iglesias 4.00 10.00
MMRO Roberto Osuna 3.00 8.00
MMROD Rougned Odor 8.00 20.00
MMRP Rick Porcello 4.00 10.00
MMRZ Ryan Zimmerman 4.00 10.00
MMSC Shin-Soo Choo 4.00 10.00
MMSD Sean Doolittle 3.00 8.00
MMSG Sonny Gray 4.00 10.00
MMSM Steven Matz 4.00 10.00
MMSMA Starling Marte 4.00 10.00
MMSP Salvador Perez 6.00 15.00
MMTL Tim Lincecum 12.00 30.00
MMVM Victor Martinez 4.00 10.00
MMWM Wil Myers 3.00 8.00
MMYC Yoenis Cespedes 5.00 12.00
MMZW Zack Wheeler 4.00 10.00
MRAGO Alex Gordon 4.00 10.00
MRARA A.J. Ramos 3.00 8.00
MRBHA Billy Hamilton 4.00 10.00
MRCCA Chris Carpenter 6.00 15.00
MRCKI Craig Kimbrel 4.00 10.00
MRCKL Corey Kluber 4.00 10.00
MRDPR David Price 4.00 10.00
MRGST Giancarlo Stanton 5.00 12.00
MRJB Jackie Bradley Jr. 5.00 12.00
MRJBA Jose Bautista 4.00 10.00
MRJC Johnny Cueto 6.00 15.00
MRJE Jacoby Ellsbury 4.00 10.00
MRJF Jeurys Familia 4.00 10.00
MRJL Jon Lester 5.00 12.00
MRJS Jeff Samardzija 3.00 8.00
MRJT Julio Teheran 4.00 10.00
MRJU Justin Upton 4.00 10.00
MRJV Justin Verlander 5.00 12.00
MRKJ Kenley Jansen 6.00 15.00
MRKSE Kyle Seager 3.00 8.00
MRMBE Mookie Betts 6.00 15.00
MRMCA Matt Cain 4.00 10.00
MRMCB Miguel Cabrera 5.00 12.00
MRME Marco Estrada 3.00 8.00
MRMH Matt Harvey 4.00 10.00
MRMM Manny Machado 8.00 20.00
MRMO Marcell Ozuna 5.00 12.00
MRMP Michael Pineda 3.00 8.00
MRMSA Michael Saunders 4.00 10.00
MRMTA Masahiro Tanaka 4.00 10.00
MRPF Prince Fielder 4.00 10.00
MRRB Ryan Braun 4.00 10.00
MRRBR Ryan Braun 4.00 10.00
MRRC Robinson Cano 4.00 10.00
MRRH Ryan Howard 4.00 10.00
MRSM Starling Marte 4.00 10.00
MRSPE Salvador Perez 6.00 15.00
MRSR Sergio Romo 8.00 20.00
MRSS Stephen Strasburg 5.00 12.00
MRSV Stephen Vogt 5.00 12.00
MRTB Trevor Bauer 5.00 12.00
MRTF Todd Frazier 4.00 10.00
MRWF Wilmer Flores 4.00 10.00
MRWM Wil Myers 3.00 8.00
MRXB Xander Bogaerts 12.00 30.00
MRYC Yoenis Cespedes 5.00 12.00
MRYM Yadier Molina 12.00 30.00
MRYP Yasiel Puig 5.00 12.00
MRZB Zach Britton 6.00 15.00
MRZC Zack Cozart 3.00 8.00
MRZG Zack Greinke 4.00 10.00
MRZW Zack Wheeler 4.00 10.00

2017 Topps Museum Collection Premium Prints Autographs

STATED ODDS 1:100 HOBBY
STATED PRINT RUN 25 SER.#'d SETS
EXCHANGE DEADLINE 5/31/2019
PPAB Alex Bregman 60.00 150.00
PPAG Andres Galarraga 12.00 30.00
PPAN Aaron Nola 12.00 30.00
PPARI Anthony Rizzo
PPARU Addison Russell 20.00 50.00
PPBH Bryce Harper
PPBP Buster Posey 60.00 150.00
PPCC Carlos Correa 50.00 120.00
PPCSE Corey Seager 40.00 100.00
PPDD David Dahl 12.00 30.00
PPDM Don Mattingly 50.00 120.00
PPDP David Price 12.00 30.00
PPDS Dansby Swanson 50.00 120.00
PPFL Francisco Lindor 40.00 100.00
PPFT Frank Thomas 60.00 150.00
PPJC Jose Canseco 30.00 80.00
PPJDG Jacob deGrom 20.00 50.00
PPJU Julio Urias 15.00 40.00
PPJV Jason Varitek 15.00 40.00
PPKB Kris Bryant 200.00 400.00
PPKG Ken Griffey Jr. 200.00 400.00
PPKM Kenta Maeda 20.00 50.00
PPKS Kyle Schwarber 15.00 40.00
PPMM Manny Machado 30.00 80.00
PPMT Mike Trout 200.00 400.00
PPNS Noah Syndergaard 20.00 50.00
PPOS Ozzie Smith 20.00 50.00
PPOV Omar Vizquel 12.00 30.00
PPRA Roberto Alomar 15.00 40.00
PPRB Ryan Braun 20.00 50.00
PPTGS Tyler Glasnow 15.00 40.00
PPTS Trevor Story 15.00 40.00

2017 Topps Museum Collection Primary Pieces Four Player Quad Relics

STATED ODDS 1:46 PACKS
STATED PRINT RUN 75 SER.#'d SETS
PRICING FOR BASIC JSY SWATCHES
*COPPER/75: .4X TO 1X BASIC
*GOLD/25: .5X TO 1.2X BASIC
FPQBBBR Be/Br/Ha/Xa 20.00 50.00
FPQBBGW Br/Bu/Wi/Ga 12.00 30.00
FPQBBRP Ha/Xa/Du/Be 20.00 50.00
FPQCASB Co/Al/Sp/Br 40.00 100.00
FPQCGCS Sy/Co/Ce/Gr 15.00 40.00
FPQCHSC He/Se/Cr/Ca 15.00 40.00
FPQCKVM Ma/Ca/Ki/Ve 15.00 40.00
FPQGHCP Ho/Go/Ca/Pe 25.00 60.00
FPQKCMU Ma/Ca/Up/Ki 10.00 25.00
FPQKCVU Up/Ve/Ca/Ki 6.00 15.00
FPQMCPM Co/Mc/Po/Ma 40.00 100.00
FPQOPPR Pr/Or/Pe/Ra 20.00 50.00
FPQPPOB Or/Be/Po/Pr 20.00 50.00
FPQSCSW Ce/de/Sy/Wr 15.00 40.00
FPQSGYO Go/St/Oz/Ye 15.00 40.00
FPQVPDH Du/Ph/Vo/Ha 20.00 50.00
FPQWCMM Mo/Ca/Ma/Wa 12.00 30.00

2017 Topps Museum Collection Primary Pieces Quad Relics

STATED ODDS 1:14 PACKS
STATED PRINT RUN 99 SER.#'d SETS
*COPPER/75: .4X TO 1X BASIC
SPRAG Alex Gordon 4.00 10.00
SPRAJ Adam Jones 5.00 12.00
SPRAM Andrew McCutchen 20.00 50.00
SPRAR Anthony Rizzo 8.00 20.00
SPRARU Addison Russell 8.00 20.00
SPRBH Bryce Harper
SPRBPO Buster Posey 6.00 15.00
SPRCC Carlos Correa 6.00 15.00
SPRCD Chris Davis 3.00 8.00
SPRCG Curtis Granderson 4.00 10.00
SPRCGO Carlos Gonzalez 5.00 12.00
SPRCK Clayton Kershaw
SPRCSE Corey Seager
SPRDB Dellin Betances 4.00 10.00
SPRDM Daniel Murphy 4.00 10.00
SPRDO David Ortiz 5.00 12.00
SPRDP David Price 4.00 10.00
SPRDPE Dustin Pedroia 8.00 20.00
SPRDW David Wright 4.00 10.00
SPREH Eric Hosmer 12.00 30.00
SPREL Evan Longoria 4.00 10.00
SPRFF Freddie Freeman 6.00 15.00
SPRFH Felix Hernandez 4.00 10.00
SPRFL Francisco Lindor 5.00 12.00
SPRGC Gerrit Cole 8.00 20.00
SPRGS George Springer 8.00 20.00
SPRGST Giancarlo Stanton 5.00 12.00
SPRHR Hanley Ramirez 4.00 10.00
SPRIK Ian Kinsler 4.00 10.00
SPRI Ichiro 8.00 20.00
SPRJA Jake Arrieta 8.00 20.00
SPRJAL Jose Altuve 10.00 25.00
SPRJC Johnny Cueto 4.00 10.00
SPRJD Jacob deGrom 6.00 15.00
SPRJDO Josh Donaldson 4.00 10.00
SPRJV Joey Votto 8.00 20.00
SPRJVE Justin Verlander 5.00 12.00
SPRKB Kris Bryant
SPRKM Kenta Maeda 4.00 10.00
SPRKS Kyle Seager 3.00 8.00
SPRKSC Kyle Schwarber 5.00 12.00
SPRMB Mookie Betts 10.00 25.00
SPRMC Miguel Cabrera 10.00 25.00
SPRMCA Matt Carpenter 5.00 12.00
SPRMH Matt Harvey 4.00 10.00
SPRMM Manny Machado 5.00 12.00
SPRMT Masahiro Tanaka 4.00 10.00
SPRMTR Mike Trout
SPRNA Nolan Arenado 10.00 25.00
SPRNC Nelson Cruz 5.00 12.00
SPRPG Paul Goldschmidt 5.00 12.00
SPRRB Ryan Braun 4.00 10.00
SPRRC Robinson Cano 4.00 10.00
SPRRP Rick Porcello 4.00 10.00
SPRSM Starling Marte 4.00 10.00
SPRSP Salvador Perez 10.00 25.00
SPRSPI Stephen Piscotty 4.00 10.00
SPRTS Trevor Story 5.00 12.00
SPRTT Troy Tulowitzki 5.00 12.00
SPRVM Victor Martinez 4.00 10.00
SPRWM Wil Myers 3.00 8.00
SPRXB Xander Bogaerts 5.00 12.00
SPRYC Yoenis Cespedes 5.00 12.00

2017 Topps Museum Collection Primary Pieces Quad Relics Gold

STATED ODDS 1:50 MINI BOXES
STATED PRINT RUN 25 SER.#'d SETS
SPRBH Bryce Harper 20.00 50.00
SPRCK Clayton Kershaw 15.00 40.00
SPRGC Gerrit Cole 30.00 80.00
SPRKB Kris Bryant 30.00 80.00
SPRMTR Mike Trout 30.00 80.00

2017 Topps Museum Collection Primary Pieces Quad Relics Legends

STATED ODDS 1:153 MINI BOX
STATED PRINT RUN 25 SER.#'d SETS
SPQCB Craig Biggio 4.00 10.00
SPQCJ Chipper Jones 12.00 30.00
SPQCR Cal Ripken Jr. 40.00 100.00
SPQCY Carl Yastrzemski 40.00 100.00
SPQDM Don Mattingly 30.00 80.00
SPQGM Greg Maddux 25.00 60.00
SPQHA Hank Aaron 40.00 100.00
SPQJB Johnny Bench 15.00 40.00
SPQJS John Smoltz 12.00 30.00
SPQKG Ken Griffey Jr. 30.00 80.00
SPQMM Mark McGwire 25.00 60.00
SPQMP Mike Piazza 12.00 30.00
SPQNR Nolan Ryan 30.00 80.00
SPQOS Ozzie Smith 20.00 50.00
SPQRA Roberto Alomar 15.00 40.00
SPQRC Rod Carew 4.00 10.00
SPQRH Rickey Henderson 25.00 60.00
SPQRJ Reggie Jackson 15.00 40.00
SPQRY Robin Yount 20.00 50.00
SPQTW Ted Williams 40.00 100.00

2017 Topps Museum Collection Primary Pieces World Baseball Classic Patches

STATED ODDS 1:57 HOBBY
STATED PRINT RUN 75 SER.#'d SETS
*COPPER/45: .4X TO 1X BASIC
WBCPRBCR Brandon Crawford 8.00 20.00
WBCPRBN Brandon Nimmo 5.00 12.00
WBCPRBP Buster Posey
WBCPRCA Chris Archer 4.00 10.00
WBCPRCM Carlos Martinez 5.00 12.00
WBCPRCY Christian Yelich 6.00 15.00
WBCPRDB Dellin Betances 5.00 12.00
WBCPRDG Didi Gregorius 10.00 25.00
WBCPRDM Daniel Murphy 8.00 20.00
WBCPRGC Gavin Cecchini 4.00 10.00
WBCPRHS Hayato Sakamoto 25.00 60.00
WBCPRIK Ian Kinsler 8.00 20.00
WBCPRJA Jose Altuve 15.00 40.00
WBCPRJP Jurickson Profar 8.00 20.00
WBCPRJQ Jose Quintana 4.00 10.00
WBCPRJT Julio Teheran 6.00 15.00
WBCPRKT Kohsuke Tanaka 8.00 20.00
WBCPRMM Manny Machado
WBCPRNA Norichika Aoki
WBCPRNC Nelson Cruz 6.00 15.00
WBCPRRC Robinson Cano 8.00 20.00
WBCPRSM Starling Marte 20.00 50.00
WBCPRSS Seiya Suzuki 20.00 50.00
WBCPRST Shota Takeda
WBCPRYM Yuki Matsui 8.00 20.00

2017 Topps Museum Collection Primary Pieces World Baseball Classic Quad Relics

STATED ODDS 1:43 HOBBY
STATED PRINT RUN 99 SER.#'d SETS
*COPPER/50: .4X TO 1X BASIC
WBCQRABR Alex Bregman
WBCQRAG Adrian Gonzalez 4.00 10.00
WBCQRAJ Adam Jones 4.00 10.00
WBCQRAM Andrew McCutchen 15.00 40.00
WBCQRBP Buster Posey
WBCQRCG Carlos Gonzalez 4.00 10.00
WBCQREH Eric Hosmer 12.00 30.00
WBCQRGP Gregory Polanco
WBCQRGS Giancarlo Stanton 6.00 15.00
WBCQRJB Javier Baez 6.00 15.00
WBCQRJBA Jose Bautista 4.00 10.00
WBCQRMC Miguel Cabrera 12.00 30.00
WBCQRMM Manny Machado 5.00 12.00
WBCQRMS Marcus Stroman 4.00 10.00
WBCQRPG Paul Goldschmidt 6.00 15.00
WBCQRRC Robinson Cano 4.00 10.00
WBCQRSF Shintaro Fujinami 4.00 10.00
WBCQRSP Salvador Perez 10.00 25.00
WBCQRTN Takahiro Norimoto 6.00 15.00
WBCQRTS Tomoyuki Sugano 6.00 15.00
WBCQRTY Tetsuto Yamada 6.00 15.00
WBCQRVM Victor Martinez 4.00 10.00
WBCQRXB Xander Bogaerts 10.00 25.00
WBCQRYM Yadier Molina 12.00 30.00
WBCQRYT Yoshitomo Tsutsugo 10.00 25.00

2017 Topps Museum Collection Signature Swatches Dual Relic Autographs

STATED ODDS 1:9 PACKS
PRINT RUNS B/WN 75-299 COPIES PER
EXCHANGE DEADLINE 5/31/2019
PRICING FOR BASIC JSY SWATCHES
*COPPER/50: .4X TO 1X p/r 75-99
*COPPER/50: .5X TO 1.2X p/r 149-299
*GOLD/25: .5X TO 1.2X p/r 75-99
*GOLD/25: .6X TO 1.5X p/r 149-299
DRAABN Andrew Benintendi/299 20.00 50.00
DRAAG Alex Gordon/199 8.00 20.00
DRAANO Aaron Nola/299 5.00 12.00
DRAARD A.J. Reed/299 4.00 10.00
DRAARY Alex Reyes/199 6.00 15.00
DRACCO Carlos Correa/75 30.00 80.00
DRACD Chris Davis/99 8.00 20.00
DRACK Corey Kluber/199 12.00 30.00
DRACKE Clayton Kershaw/75 50.00 120.00
DRACS Corey Seager/99 8.00 20.00
DRAEL Evan Longoria/75 10.00 25.00
DRAFF Freddie Freeman/149 12.00 30.00
DRAFL Francisco Lindor/299 12.00 30.00
DRAHR Hunter Renfroe/299 5.00 12.00
DRAIK Ian Kinsler/99 8.00 20.00
DRAJA Jose Altuve/299 25.00 60.00
DRAJBR Jackie Bradley Jr./149 12.00 30.00
DRAJD Jacob deGrom/199 10.00 25.00
DRAJMA J.D. Martinez/75 10.00 25.00
DRAJPA Joe Panik/299 5.00 12.00
DRAJPE Joc Pederson/299 5.00 12.00
DRAKB Kris Bryant/75 75.00 200.00
DRAKK Kevin Kiermaier/299 5.00 12.00
DRAKMA Kenta Maeda/199 5.00 12.00
DRAKS Kyle Schwarber/199 10.00 25.00
DRALS Luis Severino/299 10.00 25.00
DRALW Luke Weaver/299 5.00 12.00
DRAMC Matt Carpenter/299 6.00 15.00
DRAMCO Michael Conforto/199 12.00 30.00
DRAMM Manny Machado/99 20.00 50.00
DRAMSA Miguel Sano/299 6.00 15.00
DRANA Nolan Arenado
DRANM Nomar Mazara/299 6.00 15.00
DRANS Noah Syndergaard/199 12.00 30.00
DRAPF Prince Fielder 5.00 12.00
DRARB Ryan Braun/75 8.00 20.00
DRARH Ryon Healy/299 6.00 15.00
DRARP Rick Porcello/299 5.00 12.00
DRASMR Starling Marte/199 5.00 12.00
DRASP Stephen Piscotty/299 6.00 15.00
DRATST Trevor Story/199 6.00 15.00
DRAWM Wil Myers/99 5.00 12.00
DRAYC Yoenis Cespedes/99 8.00 20.00

2017 Topps Museum Collection Signature Swatches Triple Relic Autographs

STATED ODDS 1:19 PACKS
PRINT RUNS B/WN 30-199 COPIES PER
EXCHANGE DEADLINE 5/31/2019
PRICING FOR BASIC JSY SWATCHES
*COPPER/25: .5X TO 1.2X p/r 30-99
*COPPER/25: .6X TO 1.5X p/r 149-199
TRAAPU Albert Pujols
TRAAR Anthony Rendon/199 8.00 20.00
TRAARI Anthony Rizzo/99 20.00 50.00
TRABB Brandon Belt/199 5.00 12.00
TRABH Bryce Harper
TRABPO Buster Posey/35 40.00 100.00
TRACC Carlos Correa/99 30.00 80.00
TRACH Cole Hamels/99 8.00 20.00
TRACR Carlos Rodon/99 6.00 15.00
TRADB Dellin Betances/99 6.00 15.00
TRADO David Ortiz/35 40.00 100.00
TRAEE Edwin Encarnacion/35 8.00 20.00
TRAFH Felix Hernandez
TRAFL Francisco Lindor/199 12.00 30.00
TRAFT Frank Thomas/30 25.00 60.00
TRAGB Greg Bird/75 6.00 15.00
TRAGP Gregory Polanco/99 6.00 15.00
TRAHI Hisashi Iwakuma/149 5.00 12.00
TRAJA Jose Abreu/99 8.00 20.00
TRAJBA Javier Baez/99 20.00 50.00
TRAJGR Jon Gray/99 8.00 20.00
TRAJH Jason Heyward/99 10.00 25.00
TRAJM Joe Mauer
TRAJTA Jameson Taillon/199 5.00 12.00
TRAKB Kris Bryant/99 75.00 200.00
TRAKSC Kyle Schwarber/149 10.00 25.00
TRAKSE Kyle Seager/99 8.00 20.00
TRALS Luis Severino/99 15.00 40.00
TRAMC Matt Carpenter/199 6.00 15.00
TRAMFL Michael Fulmer/99 10.00 25.00
TRAMFR Maikel Franco/99 6.00 15.00
TRAMM Manny Machado
TRAMSA Miguel Sano/199 8.00 20.00
TRAMT Mike Trout/35 150.00 300.00
TRANS Noah Syndergaard/199 12.00 30.00
TRASM Steven Matz/99 6.00 15.00
TRATS Trevor Story/199 6.00 15.00
TRATTL Troy Tulowitzki/35 8.00 20.00
TRAVM Victor Martinez/99 8.00 20.00
TRAWC Willson Contreras/99 12.00 30.00
TRAYT Yasmany Tomas/50 5.00 12.00

2018 Topps Museum Collection

1 Bryce Harper 1.25 3.00
2 Kris Bryant 1.00 2.50
3 Mike Trout 4.00 10.00
4 Paul Goldschmidt .75 2.00
5 Manny Machado .75 2.00
6 Mookie Betts 1.25 3.00
7 Anthony Rizzo 1.25 3.00
8 Kyle Schwarber .75 2.00
9 Joey Votto .75 2.00
10 Nolan Arenado 1.00 2.50
11 Miguel Cabrera .75 2.00
12 Justin Verlander .75 2.00
13 Carlos Correa .75 2.00
14 Eric Hosmer .60 1.50
15 Clayton Kershaw 1.50 4.00
16 Corey Seager .75 2.00
17 Cody Bellinger 1.50 4.00
18 Giancarlo Stanton .75 2.00
19 Ichiro 1.00 2.50
20 Noah Syndergaard .60 1.50
21 Masahiro Tanaka .60 1.50
22 Gary Sanchez .75 2.00
23 Aaron Judge 2.00 5.00
24 Buster Posey 1.00 2.50
25 Felix Hernandez .60 1.50
26 Robinson Cano .60 1.50
27 Yu Darvish .75 2.00
28 Josh Donaldson .60 1.50
29 Max Scherzer .75 2.00
30 Francisco Lindor .75 2.00
31 Chris Sale .75 2.00
32 Jacob deGrom .75 2.00
33 Andrew McCutchen .75 2.00
34 Wil Myers .50 1.25
35 Albert Pujols 1.00 2.50
36 Yoenis Cespedes .75 2.00
37 Jose Altuve .60 1.50
38 Adrian Beltre .75 2.00
39 Corey Kluber .60 1.50
40 Trea Turner .60 1.50
41 Stephen Strasburg .75 2.00
42 Xander Bogaerts .75 2.00
43 Adam Jones .60 1.50
44 Daniel Murphy .60 1.50
45 Roberto Clemente 2.00 5.00
46 Cal Ripken Jr. 2.50 6.00
47 Hank Aaron 1.50 4.00
48 Ted Williams 1.50 4.00
49 Jackie Robinson .75 2.00
50 Sandy Koufax 1.50 4.00
51 Babe Ruth 2.00 5.00
52 Ernie Banks .75 2.00
53 Derek Jeter 2.00 5.00
54 David Ortiz .75 2.00
55 Mark McGwire 1.25 3.00
56 Randy Johnson .75 2.00
57 Honus Wagner .75 2.00
58 Roger Maris .75 2.00
59 Ty Cobb 1.25 3.00
60 Lou Gehrig 1.50 4.00
61 Reggie Jackson .60 1.50
62 George Brett 1.50 4.00
63 Don Mattingly 1.50 4.00
64 Frank Thomas .75 2.00
65 Bo Jackson .75 2.00
66 Johnny Bench .75 2.00
67 Greg Maddux 1.00 2.50
68 Roger Clemens 1.00 2.50
69 Mike Piazza .75 2.00
70 Nolan Ryan 2.50 6.00
71 Byron Buxton .60 1.50
72 Pedro Martinez .60 1.50
73 Ryne Sandberg 1.50 4.00
74 Barry Larkin .60 1.50
75 Chipper Jones .75 2.00
76 Ozzie Smith 1.00 2.50
77 Luis Severino .60 1.50
78 Andrew Benintendi .75 2.00
79 George Springer .60 1.50
80 J.D. Martinez .75 2.00
81 Rhys Hoskins RC 2.50 6.00
82 Michael Conforto .60 1.50
83 Clint Frazier RC 1.25 3.00
84 Trey Mancini .60 1.50
85 Alex Bregman .75 2.00
86 Freddie Freeman 1.00 2.50
87 Ozzie Albies RC 2.00 5.00
88 Rafael Devers RC 2.00 5.00
89 Justin Upton .60 1.50
90 Marcell Ozuna .75 2.00
91 Edwin Encarnacion .75 2.00
92 Javier Baez 1.00 2.50
93 Ryan Braun .60 1.50
94 Miguel Sano .60 1.50
95 Victor Robles RC 1.50 4.00
96 Francisco Mejia RC .75 2.00
97 Salvador Perez .60 1.50
98 Yoan Moncada .75 2.00
99 Mariano Rivera 1.00 2.50
100 Shohei Ohtani RC 4.00 10.00

2018 Topps Museum Collection Copper

*COPPER: .6X TO 1.5X BASIC
*COPPER RC: .5X TO 1.2X BASIC RC
RANDOM INSERTS IN PACKS

2018 Topps Museum Collection Ruby

*RUBY: 1.5X TO 4X BASIC
*RUBY RC: 1.2X TO 3X BASIC RC
STATED ODDS 1:17 HOBBY
STATED PRINT RUN 50 SER.#'d SETS
100 Shohei Ohtani 40.00 100.00

2018 Topps Museum Collection Sapphire

*SAPPHIRE: .75X TO 2X BASIC
*SAPPHIRE RC: .6X TO 1.5X BASIC RC
STATED ODDS 1:6 HOBBY
STATED PRINT RUN 150 SER.#'d SETS

2018 Topps Museum Collection Amethyst

*PURPLE: 1X TO 2.5X BASIC
*PURPLE RC: .75X TO 2X BASIC RC
STATED ODDS 1:9 HOBBY
STATED PRINT RUN 99 SER.#'d SETS

2018 Topps Museum Collection Archival Autographs

STATED ODDS 1:8 HOBBY
PRINT RUNS B/WN 75-299 COPIES PER
EXCHANGE DEADLINE 5/31/2020
AABR Alex Bregman/199 20.00 50.00
AAD Andre Dawson/299 8.00 20.00
AAH Austin Hays/299 5.00 12.00
AAK Al Kaline/75 20.00 50.00
AAN Aaron Nola/299 4.00 10.00
AARO Amed Rosario/299 4.00 10.00
AABB Byron Buxton/199 4.00 10.00
AABD Brian Dozier/299 6.00 15.00
AABW Brandon Woodruff/299 4.00 10.00
AACKI Craig Kimbrel/299 6.00 15.00
AACKL Corey Kluber/75 10.00 25.00
AACSA Chris Sale/99 12.00 30.00
AACSI Chance Sisco/299 4.00 10.00
AACT Chris Taylor/299 4.00 10.00
AADG Didi Gregorius/299 6.00 15.00
AADSM Dominic Smith/99 3.00 8.00
AADST Darryl Strawberry/199 8.00 20.00
AAET Eric Thames/299 4.00 10.00
AAFF Freddie Freeman/299 12.00 30.00
AAFL Francisco Lindor EXCH 20.00 50.00
AAFM Francisco Mejia/299 6.00 15.00
AAGSP George Springer/75 8.00 20.00
AAJC J.P. Crawford/299 3.00 8.00
AAJCA Jose Canseco/299 10.00 25.00
AAJD J.D. Davis/299 4.00 10.00
AAJDE Jacob deGrom/299 10.00 25.00
AAJF Jack Flaherty/299 5.00 12.00
AAJL Jake Lamb/299 4.00 10.00
AAJR Jose Ramirez/299 12.00 30.00
AAJS Jean Segura/299 3.00 8.00
AAKD Khris Davis/299 8.00 20.00
AAKS Kyle Schwarber/199 5.00 12.00
AALB Lou Brock/299 15.00 40.00
AALS Luis Severino/299 8.00 20.00
AALSI Lucas Sims/299 3.00 8.00
AAMO Matt Olson/299 3.00 8.00
AANS Noah Syndergaard/99 10.00 25.00
AAOA Ozzie Albies/299 10.00 25.00
AAPD Paul DeJong/299 5.00 12.00
AARD Rafael Devers/299 15.00 40.00
AARH Rhys Hoskins/299 15.00 40.00
AARM Ryan McMahon/299 4.00 10.00
AASG Sonny Gray/299 4.00 10.00
AASM Starling Marte/299 4.00 10.00
AASO Shohei Ohtani/99 250.00 500.00
AATG Tom Glavine/299 8.00 20.00
AATM Tyler Mahle/299 4.00 10.00
AATMA Trey Mancini/299 4.00 10.00
AATP Tommy Pham/299 3.00 8.00
AATS Travis Shaw/299 3.00 8.00
AAVR Victor Robles/299 15.00 40.00
AAWCO Willson Contreras/199 5.00 12.00
AAWM Whit Merrifield/299 5.00 12.00

2018 Topps Museum Collection Archival Autographs Copper

*COPPER: .5X TO 1.2X BASIC
STATED ODDS 1:21 HOBBY
STATED PRINT RUN 50 SER.#'d SETS
EXCHANGE DEADLINE 5/31/2020
AAAB Adrian Beltre 20.00 50.00
AAAP Andy Pettitte 12.00 30.00
AABL Barry Larkin 15.00 40.00
AADM Don Mattingly 25.00 60.00
AAJA Jose Altuve 20.00 50.00
AAJSM John Smoltz 20.00 50.00
AARA Roberto Alomar 10.00 25.00
AARC Rod Carew 12.00 30.00
AASC Steve Carlton 12.00 30.00

2018 Topps Museum Collection Archival Autographs Gold

*GOLD: .6X TO 1.5X BASIC
STATED ODDS 1:42 HOBBY
STATED PRINT RUN 25 SER.#'d SETS
EXCHANGE DEADLINE 5/31/2020
AAAB Adrian Beltre 25.00 60.00
AAAP Andy Pettitte 15.00 40.00
AAAR Anthony Rizzo 25.00 60.00
AABH Bryce Harper 125.00 300.00
AABL Barry Larkin 20.00 50.00
AADM Don Mattingly 30.00 80.00
AAI Ichiro 200.00 400.00
AAJA Jose Altuve 25.00 60.00
AAJSM John Smoltz 25.00 60.00
AAJV Joey Votto 40.00 100.00
AAKB Kris Bryant EXCH 75.00 200.00
AAMM Manny Machado 30.00 80.00
AAMTR Mike Trout 400.00 600.00
AARA Roberto Alomar 12.00 30.00
AARC Rod Carew 15.00 40.00
AASC Steve Carlton 15.00 40.00

2018 Topps Museum Collection Canvas Collection

STATED ODDS 1:4 HOBBY
CC1 Roberto Clemente 2.50 6.00
CC2 Mariano Rivera 1.25 3.00
CC3 Harmon Killebrew 1.00 2.50
CC4 Ted Williams 2.00 5.00
CC5 Nolan Arenado 1.25 3.00
CC6 Jimmie Foxx 1.00 2.50
CC7 Frank Thomas 1.00 2.50
CC8 Bryce Harper 1.50 4.00
CC9 Babe Ruth 2.50 6.00
CC10 Mike Trout 5.00 12.00
CC11 Rickey Henderson 1.00 2.50
CC12 Jose Altuve .75 2.00
CC13 Cody Bellinger 2.00 5.00
CC14 Nelson Cruz 1.00 2.50
CC15 Bo Jackson 1.00 2.50
CC16 Aaron Judge 2.50 6.00
CC17 Derek Jeter 2.50 6.00
CC18 Willie Stargell .75 2.00
CC19 Ozzie Smith 1.25 3.00
CC20 Jim Thome .75 2.00
CC21 Giancarlo Stanton 1.00 2.50
CC22 Bryce Harper 1.50 4.00
CC23 Noah Syndergaard .75 2.00
CC24 Wade Boggs .75 2.00
CC25 Mike Piazza 1.00 2.50
CC26 Shohei Ohtani 4.00 10.00
CC27 David Ortiz 1.00 2.50
CC28 Mariano Rivera 1.25 3.00
CC29 Rod Carew .75 2.00
CC30 Roberto Clemente 2.50 6.00
CC31 Reggie Jackson .75 2.00
CC32 Willie McCovey .75 2.00
CC33 Ryne Sandberg 2.00 5.00
CC34 Sandy Koufax 2.00 5.00
CC35 Alex Rodriguez 1.25 3.00
CC36 Chipper Jones 1.00 2.50
CC37 Dave Winfield .75 2.00
CC38 Barry Larkin .75 2.00
CC39 Al Kaline 1.00 2.50
CC40 Nolan Ryan 3.00 8.00
CC41 George Brett 2.00 5.00
CC42 Mike Trout 5.00 12.00
CC43 Babe Ruth 2.50 6.00
CC44 Shohei Ohtani 4.00 10.00
CC45 Derek Jeter 2.50 6.00
CC46 Bryce Harper 1.50 4.00
CC47 Aaron Judge 2.50 6.00
CC48 Mariano Rivera 1.25 3.00
CC49 Mike Piazza 1.00 2.50
CC50 Kris Bryant 1.25 3.00

2018 Topps Museum Collection Dual Meaningful Material Relics

STATED PRINT 1:65 HOBBY
STATED PRINT RUN 50 SER.#'d SETS
*COPPER/35: .4X TO 1X BASIC
DAAC McCutchen/Harrison 20.00 50.00
DAAJ Russell/Baez 20.00 50.00
DABC Arenado/Blackmon 10.00 25.00
DABH Pence/Crawford 10.00 25.00
DABM Buxton/Sano 8.00 20.00
DACC Sale/Kimbrel 15.00 40.00
DACD deGrom/Conforto 10.00 25.00
DACS Kershaw/Seager 15.00 40.00
DADT Murphy/Turner 8.00 20.00
DAES Hosmer/Perez 8.00 20.00
DAFH Hernandez/Cruz 10.00 25.00
DAGA Bregman/Springer 12.00 30.00
DAJS Bell/Marte 12.00 30.00
DAKE Kluber/Encarnacion 10.00 25.00
DAMB Benintendi/Betts
DAMN Castellanos/Cabrera 10.00 25.00
DAMS Strasburg/Scherzer 12.00 30.00
DAMSC Schoop/Machado 10.00 25.00
DAMT Stroman/Tulowitzki 10.00 25.00
DAMY Cespedes/Conforto 10.00 25.00
DAPJ Lamb/Goldschmidt 15.00 40.00
DARN Cruz/Cano 10.00 25.00
DAWF Wainwright/Fowler 8.00 20.00
DAXM Bogaerts/Betts 20.00 50.00
DAYC Molina/Martinez 10.00 25.00

2018 Topps Museum Collection Meaningful Material Relics

STATED ODDS 1:12 HOBBY
STATED PRINT RUN 50 SER.#'d SETS
*COPPER/35: .4X TO 1X BASIC
*GOLD/25: .5X TO 1.2X BASIC
MMRAB Andrew Benintendi 5.00 12.00
MMRABE Adrian Beltre 5.00 12.00
MMRAC Aroldis Chapman 5.00 12.00
MMRAD Adam Duvall 5.00 12.00
MMRAM Andrew McCutchen 12.00 30.00
MMRAN Aaron Nola 4.00 10.00
MMRAP A.J. Pollock 3.00 8.00
MMRAR Addison Russell 4.00 10.00
MMRARE Anthony Rendon 5.00 12.00
MMRARU Addison Russell 4.00 10.00
MMRAS Aaron Sanchez 4.00 10.00
MMRAW Adam Wainwright 4.00 10.00
MMRAWA Adam Wainwright 4.00 10.00
MMRBC Brandon Crawford 10.00 25.00
MMRBCR Brandon Crawford 10.00 25.00
MMRBD Brian Dozier 4.00 10.00
MMRBG Brett Gardner 4.00 10.00
MMRBGA Brett Gardner 4.00 10.00
MMRBH Billy Hamilton 4.00 10.00
MMRBHA Billy Hamilton 4.00 10.00
MMRBHR Bryce Harper
MMRBP Buster Posey 6.00 15.00
MMRBZ Ben Zobrist 4.00 10.00
MMRCA Chris Archer 3.00 8.00
MMRCB Charlie Blackmon 5.00 12.00
MMRCC Carlos Correa 5.00 12.00
MMRCG Carlos Gonzalez 4.00 10.00
MMRCH Cole Hamels 4.00 10.00
MMRCKI Craig Kimbrel 4.00 10.00
MMRCM Carlos Martinez 4.00 10.00
MMRCMA Carlos Martinez 4.00 10.00
MMRCSL Chris Sale 5.00 12.00
MMRCYE Christian Yelich 6.00 15.00
MMRDB Dylan Bundy 4.00 10.00
MMRDBE Dellin Betances 4.00 10.00
MMRDD Danny Duffy 3.00 8.00
MMRDF Dexter Fowler 4.00 10.00
MMRDFO Dexter Fowler 4.00 10.00
MMRDGR Didi Gregorius 4.00 10.00
MMRDK Dallas Keuchel 4.00 10.00
MMRDKE Dallas Keuchel 4.00 10.00
MMRDM Daniel Murphy 4.00 10.00
MMRDO David Ortiz 5.00 12.00
MMRDP Dustin Pedroia 5.00 12.00
MMRDPE Dustin Pedroia 5.00 12.00
MMRDPR David Price 4.00 10.00
MMREG Evan Gattis 3.00 8.00
MMREH Eric Hosmer 4.00 10.00
MMREI Ender Inciarte 3.00 8.00
MMRFFR Freddie Freeman 6.00 15.00
MMRFH Felix Hernandez 4.00 10.00
MMRFHE Felix Hernandez 4.00 10.00
MMRGG Gio Gonzalez 4.00 10.00
MMRGP Gregory Polanco 4.00 10.00
MMRGPO Gregory Polanco 4.00 10.00
MMRGR Garrett Richards 4.00 10.00
MMRGS Giancarlo Stanton 6.00 15.00
MMRGSP George Springer 4.00 10.00
MMRGST Giancarlo Stanton 6.00 15.00
MMRHP Hunter Pence 4.00 10.00
MMRHR Hyun-Jin Ryu 4.00 10.00
MMRHRA Hanley Ramirez 4.00 10.00
MMRHRY Hyun-Jin Ryu 4.00 10.00
MMRI Ichiro 12.00 30.00
MMRJAR Jake Arrieta 4.00 10.00
MMRJB Josh Bell 6.00 15.00
MMRJBA Jose Bautista 4.00 10.00
MMRJBE Josh Bell 6.00 15.00
MMRJBJ Jackie Bradley Jr. 5.00 12.00
MMRJBO Justin Bour 3.00 8.00
MMRJC Johnny Cueto 4.00 10.00
MMRJCU Johnny Cueto 4.00 10.00
MMRJD Josh Donaldson 4.00 10.00
MMRJDE Jacob deGrom 6.00 15.00
MMRJE Jacoby Ellsbury 4.00 10.00
MMRJEL Jacoby Ellsbury 4.00 10.00
MMRJF Jeurys Familia 4.00 10.00
MMRJG Jon Gray 3.00 8.00
MMRJGR Jon Gray 3.00 8.00
MMRJH Josh Harrison 3.00 8.00
MMRJHA Josh Harrison 3.00 8.00
MMRJHE Jason Heyward 4.00 10.00
MMRJK Jason Kipnis 5.00 12.00
MMRJL Jon Lester 4.00 10.00
MMRJP Joe Panik 4.00 10.00
MMRJPA Joe Panik 4.00 10.00
MMRJS Jonathan Schoop 3.00 8.00
MMRJSA Jeff Samardzija 3.00 8.00
MMRJSC Jonathan Schoop 3.00 8.00
MMRJT Julio Teheran 4.00 10.00
MMRJVO Joey Votto 5.00 12.00
MMRJW Jayson Werth 4.00 10.00
MMRKB Kris Bryant 15.00 40.00
MMRKG Kevin Gausman 3.00 8.00
MMRKK Kevin Kiermaier 4.00 10.00
MMRKKI Kevin Kiermaier 4.00 10.00
MMRKSC Kyle Schwarber 5.00 12.00
MMRKSE Kyle Seager 3.00 8.00
MMRMB Mookie Betts 10.00 25.00
MMRMBE Mookie Betts 10.00 25.00
MMRMC Miguel Cabrera 5.00 12.00
MMRMCA Miguel Cabrera 5.00 12.00
MMRMCB Miguel Cabrera 5.00 12.00
MMRMCO Michael Conforto 4.00 10.00
MMRME Marco Estrada 3.00 8.00
MMRMF Michael Fulmer 3.00 8.00
MMRMH Matt Harvey 4.00 10.00
MMRMHA Matt Harvey 4.00 10.00
MMRMK Max Kepler 4.00 10.00
MMRMM Manny Machado 8.00 20.00
MMRMMA Manny Machado 8.00 20.00
MMRMO Matt Olson 3.00 8.00
MMRMS Max Scherzer 6.00 15.00
MMRMT Mike Trout 30.00 80.00
MMRMTA Masahiro Tanaka 4.00 10.00
MMRMW Michael Wacha 4.00 10.00
MMRNC Nelson Cruz 5.00 12.00
MMRNCA Nick Castellanos 5.00 12.00
MMRNCR Nelson Cruz 5.00 12.00
MMRNS Noah Syndergaard 4.00 10.00
MMRPGO Paul Goldschmidt 5.00 12.00
MMRRBR Ryan Braun 4.00 10.00
MMRRC Robinson Cano 4.00 10.00
MMRRO Rougned Odor 4.00 10.00
MMRRZ Ryan Zimmerman 4.00 10.00
MMRSC Shin-Soo Choo 4.00 10.00
MMRSD Sean Doolittle 3.00 8.00
MMRSG Sonny Gray 4.00 10.00
MMRSMA Starling Marte 4.00 10.00
MMRSMT Steven Matz 4.00 10.00
MMRSP Salvador Perez 8.00 20.00
MMRSPE Salvador Perez 8.00 20.00
MMRSS Steven Souza Jr. 4.00 10.00
MMRSST Stephen Strasburg 5.00 12.00
MMRTP Tommy Pham 3.00 8.00
MMRVM Victor Martinez 4.00 10.00
MMRVMA Victor Martinez 4.00 10.00
MMRWM Wil Myers 3.00 8.00
MMRWMY Wil Myers 3.00 8.00
MMRXB Xander Bogaerts 5.00 12.00
MMRYC Yoenis Cespedes 5.00 12.00
MMRYCE Yoenis Cespedes 5.00 12.00
MMRYG Yuli Gurriel 4.00 10.00
MMRYM Yadier Molina 6.00 15.00
MMRZG Zack Greinke 4.00 10.00

2018 Topps Museum Collection Premium Print Autographs

STATED ODDS 1:105 HOBBY
STATED PRINT RUN 25 SER.#'d SETS
EXCHANGE DEADLINE 5/31/2020
PPAARO Amed Rosario 12.00 30.00
PPABB Byron Buxton 12.00 30.00
PPABH Bryce Harper 150.00 400.00
PPABJ Bo Jackson 50.00 120.00
PPABL Barry Larkin 20.00 50.00
PPACJ Chipper Jones 75.00 200.00
PPACKL Corey Kluber 20.00 50.00
PPACR Cal Ripken Jr. 60.00 150.00
PPACS Chris Sale 20.00 50.00
PPADM Don Mattingly 50.00 120.00
PPADS Dominic Smith 5.00 12.00
PPAFF Freddie Freeman 30.00 80.00
PPAFL Francisco Lindor EXCH
PPAFT Frank Thomas 30.00 80.00
PPAHM Hideki Matsui 100.00 250.00
PPAJA Jose Altuve 60.00 150.00
PPAJS John Smoltz
PPAJV Joey Votto
PPAKB Kris Bryant EXCH 75.00 200.00
PPALS Luis Severino 50.00 120.00
PPAMT Mike Trout 400.00 800.00
PPANS Noah Syndergaard 20.00 50.00
PPAOA Ozzie Albies 75.00 200.00
PPARD Rafael Devers 40.00 100.00
PPARHO Rhys Hoskins 60.00 150.00
PPASG Sonny Gray 6.00 15.00
PPAVR Victor Robles 40.00 100.00

2018 Topps Museum Collection Primary Pieces Four Player Quad Relics

STATED PRINT 1:41 HOBBY
STATED PRINT RUN 99 SER.#'d SETS
*COPPER/75: .4X TO 1X BASIC
*GOLD/25: .75X TO 2X BASIC
FPQRARI Goldschmidt
Pollock/Lamb/Greinke 5.00 12.00
FPQRBSN Betts/Bgrts/Pdra/Rmrz 8.00 20.00
FPQRCHI Rssll/Schwrbr/Brynt/Rzzo 8.00 20.00
FPQRCUB Happ/Schwrbr/Baez/Rssll 10.00 25.00
FPQRHOU Sprngr/Crra/Brgmn/Altve 25.00 60.00
FPQRKEE Grgrs/Grdnr/Snchz/Bird 10.00 25.00
FPQRLAA Pjos/Uptn/Clhn/Trt 25.00 60.00
FPQRMIL Braun/Arcia/Thames/Santana 4.00 10.00
FPQRMIN Buxton/Sano/Rosario/Mauer 5.00 12.00
FPQRNAT Trnr/Stasbrg/Mrphy/Schrzr 10.00 25.00
FPQRNYM Cnfrto/Sndrgrd/Cspds/dGrm 10.0025.00
FPQRNYY Btncs/Grgrs/Snchz/Tnka 8.00 20.00
FPQRSEA Cruz/Cano/Hernandez/Seager 5.00 12.00
FPQRSFG Pnk/Psy/Pnce/Crwfrd 10.00 25.00
FPQRSOX Bnntndi/Btts/Sale/Kmbrl 10.00 25.00
FPQRSTL Carpenter/Wainwright
Martinez/Molina 12.00 30.00
FPQRTEX Odor/Gallo/Hamels/Beltre 5.00 12.00
FPQRTOR Smoak/Stroman
Tulowitzki/Donaldson 5.00 12.00
FPQRWAS Trnr/Hrpr/Strsbrg/Schrzr 8.00 20.00
FPQRYAN Svrno/Chpmn/Gray/Tnka 8.00 20.00

2018 Topps Museum Collection Primary Pieces Quad Relics

STATED ODDS 1:11 HOBBY
STATED PRINT RUN 99 SER.#'d SETS
*COPPER/75: .4X TO 1X BASIC
*GOLD/25: .6X TO 1.5X BASIC
SPQRABE Adrian Beltre 4.00 10.00
SPQRABN Andrew Benintendi 4.00 10.00
SPQRAC Aroldis Chapman 4.00 10.00
SPQRAJ Adam Jones 3.00 8.00
SPQRAM Andrew McCutchen 4.00 10.00
SPQRAN Aaron Nola 3.00 8.00
SPQRARI Anthony Rizzo 6.00 15.00
SPQRARU Addison Russell 3.00 8.00
SPQRAW Adam Wainwright 3.00 8.00
SPQRBC Brandon Crawford 3.00 8.00
SPQRBG Brett Gardner 3.00 8.00
SPQRBHA Bryce Harper 6.00 15.00
SPQRBP Buster Posey 5.00 12.00
SPQRCC Carlos Correa 4.00 10.00
SPQRCD Chris Davis 2.50 6.00
SPQRCG Carlos Gonzalez 3.00 8.00
SPQRCH Cole Hamels 3.00 8.00
SPQRCK Craig Kimbrel 3.00 8.00
SPQRCKE Clayton Kershaw 8.00 20.00
SPQRCM Carlos Martinez 3.00 8.00
SPQRCS Corey Seager 4.00 10.00
SPQRCSA Chris Sale 4.00 10.00
SPQRCY Christian Yelich 5.00 12.00
SPQRDK Dallas Keuchel 3.00 8.00
SPQRDO David Ortiz 4.00 10.00
SPQRDP Dustin Pedroia 4.00 10.00
SPQRDW David Wright 3.00 8.00
SPQREL Evan Longoria 3.00 8.00
SPQRFF Freddie Freeman 5.00 12.00
SPQRFH Felix Hernandez 3.00 8.00
SPQRGP Gregory Polanco 3.00 8.00
SPQRHJR Hyun-Jin Ryu 3.00 8.00
SPQRHP Hunter Pence 3.00 8.00
SPQRHR Hanley Ramirez 3.00 8.00
SPQRI Ichiro 8.00 20.00
SPQRIK Ian Kinsler 3.00 8.00
SPQRJB Josh Bell 3.00 8.00
SPQRJBA Javier Baez 8.00 20.00
SPQRJD Josh Donaldson 3.00 8.00
SPQRJDE Jacob deGrom 6.00 15.00
SPQRJH Josh Harrison 2.50 6.00
SPQRJM J.D. Martinez 4.00 10.00
SPQRJS Jonathan Schoop 2.50 6.00
SPQRJU Justin Upton 3.00 8.00
SPQRJV Justin Verlander 5.00 12.00
SPQRJVO Joey Votto 4.00 10.00
SPQRKB Kris Bryant 5.00 12.00
SPQRKSC Kyle Schwarber 4.00 10.00
SPQRLS Luis Severino 3.00 8.00
SPQRMB Mookie Betts 8.00 20.00
SPQRMC Miguel Cabrera 4.00 10.00
SPQRMCO Michael Conforto 3.00 8.00
SPQRMF Michael Fulmer 2.50 6.00
SPQRMM Manny Machado 4.00 10.00
SPQRMO Marcell Ozuna 4.00 10.00
SPQRMS Max Scherzer 4.00 10.00
SPQRMT Mike Trout 25.00 60.00
SPQRMTA Masahiro Tanaka 3.00 8.00
SPQRNCR Nelson Cruz 4.00 10.00
SPQRNS Noah Syndergaard 3.00 8.00
SPQRPG Paul Goldschmidt 4.00 10.00
SPQRRB Ryan Braun 3.00 8.00
SPQRRC Robinson Cano 3.00 8.00
SPQRRP Rick Porcello 3.00 8.00
SPQRRZ Ryan Zimmerman 3.00 8.00
SPQRSG Sonny Gray 3.00 8.00
SPQRSMA Starling Marte 3.00 8.00
SPQRSP Salvador Perez 3.00 8.00
SPQRSS Stephen Strasburg 4.00 10.00
SPQRTT Trea Turner 3.00 8.00
SPQRWM Wil Myers 2.50 6.00
SPQRXB Xander Bogaerts 4.00 10.00
SPQRYC Yoenis Cespedes 4.00 10.00
SPQRYG Yuli Gurriel 3.00 8.00
SPQRYM Yadier Molina 5.00 12.00
SPQRYP Yasiel Puig 4.00 10.00
SPQRZG Zack Greinke 3.00 8.00

2018 Topps Museum Collection Primary Pieces Quad Relics Legends

STATED ODDS 1:160 HOBBY
STATED PRINT RUN 25 SER.#'d SETS
SPQLAK Al Kaline
SPQLBL Barry Larkin 5.00 12.00
SPQLCR Cal Ripken Jr. 30.00 80.00
SPQLDJ Derek Jeter 20.00 50.00
SPQLDM Don Mattingly 25.00 60.00
SPQLGB George Brett 25.00 60.00
SPQLGM Greg Maddux 20.00 50.00
SPQLHA Hank Aaron 60.00 150.00
SPQLJB Johnny Bench
SPQLMM Mark McGwire 20.00 50.00
SPQLMP Mike Piazza
SPQLNR Nolan Ryan 30.00 80.00
SPQLOS Ozzie Smith 8.00 20.00
SPQLRCE Roger Clemens
SPQLRCL Roberto Clemente 75.00 200.00
SPQLRH Rickey Henderson 12.00 30.00
SPQLRJA Reggie Jackson
SPQLTS Tom Seaver 12.00 30.00
SPQLTW Ted Williams
SPQLWB Wade Boggs 15.00 40.00

2018 Topps Museum Collection Signature Swatches Dual Relic Autographs

STATED ODDS 1:10 HOBBY
PRINT RUNS B/WN 60-299 COPIES PER
NO PRICING DUE TO SCARCITY
EXCHANGE DEADLINE 5/31/2020
*COPPER/50: .4X TO 1X BASIC
*GOLD/25: .6X TO 1.5X BASIC
DRAAB Alex Bregman/199 12.00 30.00
DRAAD Adam Duvall/299 6.00 15.00
DRAAN Aaron Nola/299 10.00 25.00
DRAAR Addison Russell/99 10.00 25.00
DRAARO Amed Rosario/199 5.00 12.00
DRAAW Alex Wood/299 6.00 15.00
DRABD Brian Dozier/99 6.00 15.00
DRABS Blake Snell/299 5.00 12.00
DRACR Carlos Rodon
DRACS Carlos Santana/99 5.00 12.00
DRADG Dee Gordon/60 4.00 10.00
DRADGR Didi Gregorius/299 12.00 30.00
DRADP David Price
DRADS Domingo Santana/299 5.00 12.00
DRAER Eddie Rosario/299 8.00 20.00
DRAET Eric Thames/99 5.00 12.00
DRAGB Greg Bird/299 5.00 12.00
DRAGSA Gary Sanchez
DRAGSE Gary Sheffield/199 8.00 20.00
DRAGSH Gary Sheffield/99 8.00 20.00
DRAIH Ian Happ/199 5.00 12.00
DRAJB Justin Bour/299 4.00 10.00
DRAJC J.P. Crawford/299 5.00 12.00
DRAJD Jacob deGrom/99 10.00 25.00
DRAJDA Johnny Damon/99 8.00 20.00
DRAJH Josh Harrison/299 4.00 10.00
DRAJL Jake Lamb/199 5.00 12.00
DRAJP Joc Pederson/99 5.00 12.00
DRAJSM Justin Smoak/99 4.00 10.00
DRAJT Jameson Taillon/74 5.00 12.00
DRAKD Khris Davis/199 6.00 15.00
DRAKS Kyle Seager/199 4.00 10.00
DRAMC Matt Carpenter/199 6.00 15.00
DRAMF Michael Fulmer/199 4.00 10.00
DRANM Nomar Mazara/175 4.00 10.00
DRANS Noah Syndergaard
DRAOA Ozzie Albies/299 12.00 30.00
DRAPD Paul DeJong
DRARD Rafael Devers/199 20.00 50.00
DRASM Starling Marte/299 5.00 12.00
DRASMA Steven Matz/299 5.00 12.00
DRATM Trey Mancini
DRATP Tommy Pham/299 4.00 10.00
DRATS Trevor Story EXCH 10.00 25.00
DRATSH Travis Shaw/299 6.00 15.00
DRAWM Whit Merrifield/299 6.00 15.00

2018 Topps Museum Collection Signature Swatches Triple Relic Autographs

STATED ODDS 1:15 HOBBY
PRINT RUNS B/WN 45-149 COPIES PER
NO PRICING DUE TO SCARCITY
EXCHANGE DEADLINE 5/31/2020
*COPPER/25: .5X TO 1.2X BASIC
TRAAB Anthony Banda/149 4.00 10.00
TRAABR Alex Bregman/149 15.00 40.00
TRAAD Adam Duvall/149 6.00 15.00
TRAAJ Adam Jones/149 8.00 20.00
TRAAN Aaron Nola/149 6.00 15.00
TRAAR Amed Rosario/149 8.00 20.00
TRABD Brian Dozier/149 10.00 25.00
TRACC Carlos Correa/99 25.00 60.00
TRACF Clint Frazier/149 12.00 30.00
TRACK Corey Kluber/45 25.00 60.00
TRACKI Craig Kimbrel/149 10.00 25.00
TRADGO Dee Gordon/149 4.00 10.00
TRADGR Didi Gregorius/149 15.00 40.00
TRADSM Dominic Smith/149 4.00 10.00
TRAFF Freddie Freeman/149 15.00 40.00
TRAGB Greg Bird/45 5.00 12.00
TRAGS Gary Sanchez/149 15.00 40.00
TRAIH Ian Happ/149 10.00 25.00
TRAJA Jose Altuve/149 25.00 60.00
TRAJB Jose Berrios/149 5.00 12.00
TRAJBA Javier Baez EXCH 25.00 60.00
TRAJC J.P. Crawford/149 4.00 10.00
TRAJD Josh Donaldson/45 12.00 30.00
TRAJF Jack Flaherty/149 6.00 15.00
TRAJH Josh Harrison/149 4.00 10.00
TRAJL Jake Lamb/149 5.00 12.00
TRAJS Justin Smoak/149 10.00 25.00
TRAKB Kris Bryant/149 60.00 150.00
TRAKD Khris Davis/149 10.00 25.00
TRAKS Kyle Seager/149 4.00 10.00
TRAMM Manny Machado/149 25.00 60.00
TRANS Noah Syndergaard/149 10.00 25.00
TRAPG Paul Goldschmidt/149 12.00 30.00
TRARH Rhys Hoskins/149 15.00 40.00
TRASD Sean Doolittle/149 6.00 15.00
TRASM Steven Matz/99 5.00 12.00
TRATP Tommy Pham/45 4.00 10.00
TRAWC Willson Contreras/149 10.00 25.00
TRAYG Yuli Gurriel/149 5.00 12.00

2019 Topps Museum Collection

1 Mike Trout 4.00 10.00
2 Albert Pujols 1.00 2.50
3 Shohei Ohtani 1.00 2.50
4 Freddie Freeman 1.00 2.50
5 Ozzie Albies .75 2.00
6 Ronald Acuna Jr. 4.00 10.00
7 Josh Donaldson .60 1.50
8 Chipper Jones .75 2.00
9 Deion Sanders .60 1.50
10 Cal Ripken Jr. 2.50 6.00
11 Mookie Betts 1.25 3.00
12 Chris Sale .75 2.00
13 Andrew Benintendi .75 2.00
14 J.D. Martinez .75 2.00
15 Ted Williams 1.50 4.00
16 David Ortiz .75 2.00
17 Roger Clemens 1.00 2.50
18 Jackie Robinson .75 2.00
19 Kris Bryant 1.00 2.50
20 Anthony Rizzo 1.25 3.00
21 Javier Baez 1.00 2.50
22 Ernie Banks .75 2.00
23 Ryne Sandberg 1.50 4.00
24 Michael Kopech RC 1.25 3.00
25 Frank Thomas .75 2.00
26 Joey Votto .75 2.00
27 Johnny Bench .75 2.00
28 Barry Larkin .60 1.50
29 Francisco Lindor .75 2.00
30 Corey Kluber .60 1.50
31 Trevor Bauer .75 2.00
32 Jose Ramirez .60 1.50
33 Nolan Arenado 1.00 2.50
34 Charlie Blackmon .75 2.00
35 Trevor Story .75 2.00
36 Miguel Cabrera .75 2.00
37 Justin Verlander .75 2.00
38 Carlos Correa .75 2.00
39 Jose Altuve .60 1.50
40 George Springer .60 1.50
41 Alex Bregman .75 2.00
42 Kyle Tucker RC 1.25 3.00
43 Nolan Ryan 2.50 6.00
44 Salvador Perez .60 1.50
45 Whit Merrifield .75 2.00
46 Bo Jackson .75 2.00
47 Clayton Kershaw 1.50 4.00
48 Corey Seager .75 2.00
49 Cody Bellinger 1.50 4.00
50 Sandy Koufax 1.50 4.00
51 Walker Buehler 1.00 2.50
52 Christian Yelich 1.00 2.50
53 Noah Syndergaard .60 1.50
54 Jacob deGrom .75 2.00
55 Robinson Cano .60 1.50
56 Mike Piazza .75 2.00
57 Giancarlo Stanton .75 2.00
58 Masahiro Tanaka .60 1.50
59 Gary Sanchez .75 2.00
60 Aaron Judge 2.00 5.00
61 Luis Severino .60 1.50
62 Gleyber Torres 1.50 4.00
63 Miguel Andujar .75 2.00
64 Hideki Matsui .75 2.00
65 Derek Jeter 2.00 5.00
66 Don Mattingly 1.50 4.00
67 Mariano Rivera 1.00 2.50
68 Khris Davis .75 2.00
69 Matt Chapman .75 2.00
70 Rickey Henderson .75 2.00
71 Mark McGwire 1.25 3.00
72 Rhys Hoskins 1.00 2.50
73 Aaron Nola .60 1.50
74 Andrew McCutchen .75 2.00
75 J.T. Realmuto .75 2.00
76 Roberto Clemente 2.00 5.00
77 Chris Archer .50 1.25
78 Manny Machado .75 2.00
79 Pete Alonso RC 6.00 15.00
80 Luis Urias RC 1.00 2.50
81 Tony Gwynn .75 2.00
82 Buster Posey 1.00 2.50
83 Ichiro 1.00 2.50
84 Ken Griffey Jr. 1.50 4.00
85 Yusei Kikuchi RC 1.00 2.50
86 Paul Goldschmidt .75 2.00
87 Fernando Tatis Jr. RC 6.00 15.00
88 Yadier Molina .75 2.00
89 Ozzie Smith 1.00 2.50
90 Blake Snell .60 1.50
91 Adrian Beltre .75 2.00
92 Eloy Jimenez RC 2.50 6.00
93 Roberto Alomar .60 1.50
94 Bryce Harper 1.25 3.00
95 Max Scherzer .75 2.00
96 Trea Turner .60 1.50
97 Stephen Strasburg .75 2.00
98 Juan Soto 2.50 6.00
99 Matt Carpenter .75 2.00
100 Vladimir Guerrero Jr. RC 4.00 10.00

2019 Topps Museum Collection Amethyst

*AMETHYST: 1X TO 2.5X BASIC
*AMETHYST RC: .75X TO 2X BASIC RC
STATED ODDS 1:9 HOBBY
STATED PRINT RUN 99 SER.#'d SETS
79 Pete Alonso 20.00 50.00
87 Fernando Tatis Jr. 12.00 30.00
100 Vladimir Guerrero Jr. 15.00 40.00

2019 Topps Museum Collection Ruby

*RUBY: 1.5X TO 4X BASIC
*RUBY RC: 1.2X TO 3X BASIC RC
STATED ODDS 1:18 HOBBY
STATED PRINT RUN 50 SER.#'d SETS
79 Pete Alonso 30.00 80.00
87 Fernando Tatis Jr. 20.00 50.00
100 Vladimir Guerrero Jr. 30.00 80.00

2019 Topps Museum Collection Sapphire

*SAPPHIRE: .75X TO 2X BASIC
*SAPPHIRE RC: ..6X TO 1.5X BASIC RC
STATED ODDS 1:6 HOBBY
STATED PRINT RUN 150 SER.#'d SETS
79 Pete Alonso 15.00 40.00
87 Fernando Tatis Jr. 6.00 15.00

2019 Topps Museum Collection Archival Autographs

STATED ODDS 1:7 HOBBY
PRINT RUNS B/WN 99-299 COPIES PER
EXCHANGE DEADLINE 5/31/2021
*COPPER/50: .5X TO 1.2X BASIC
*GOLD: .6X TO 1.5X BASIC
AAAD Andre Dawson 8.00 20.00
AAAK Al Kaline/99 15.00 40.00
AABG Bob Gibson/199 40.00 100.00
AABN Brandon Nimmo/299 4.00 10.00
AACM Cedric Mullins/299 5.00 12.00
AACST Christin Stewart/299 4.00 10.00
AADE Dennis Eckersley/199 6.00 15.00
AADMU Dale Murphy/199 12.00 30.00
AADS Don Sutton/299 4.00 10.00
AADST Darryl Strawberry/199 8.00 20.00
AAEJ Eloy Jimenez/299 25.00 60.00
AAFF Freddie Freeman/99 25.00 60.00
AAFL Francisco Lindor/99 12.00 30.00
AAFT Fernando Tatis Jr./299 100.00 250.00
AAJAG Jesus Aguilar/299 3.00 8.00
AAJCA Jose Canseco/299 10.00 25.00
AAJDE Jacob deGrom/199 10.00 25.00
AAJG Juan Gonzalez/199 3.00 8.00
AAJHA Josh Hader/299 6.00 15.00
AAJM Jose Martinez/299 3.00 8.00
AAJMA Juan Marichal/199 10.00 25.00
AAJR Jim Rice/299 4.00 10.00
AAJRO Jose Ramirez/199 10.00 25.00
AAJSH Justus Sheffield/299 5.00 12.00
AAJSO Juan Soto/199 50.00 120.00
AAJVA Jason Varitek/199 10.00 25.00
AAKS Kyle Schwarber/199 6.00 15.00
AAKTU Kyle Tucker/299 10.00 25.00
AAKW Kyle Wright/299 5.00 12.00
AALB Lou Brock/99 12.00 30.00
AALS Luis Severino/199 6.00 15.00
AAMA Miguel Andujar/99 8.00 20.00
AAMH Mitch Haniger/299 4.00 10.00
AAMK Michael Kopech/299 6.00 15.00
AAMKE Matt Kemp/199 4.00 10.00
AAMMU Max Muncy/299 4.00 10.00
AANS Noah Syndergaard/99 4.00 10.00
AAOA Ozzie Albies/299 20.00 50.00
AAPA Peter Alonso/299 60.00 150.00
AAPCO Patrick Corbin/299 4.00 10.00
AAPD Paul DeJong/299 5.00 12.00
AARAJ Ronald Acuna Jr./199 40.00 100.00
AARH Rhys Hoskins/199 8.00 20.00
AASGE Scooter Gennett/299 4.00 10.00
AASM Steven Matz/299 4.00 10.00
AASMA Sean Manaea 3.00 8.00
AATH Torii Hunter/199 6.00 15.00
AATMA Trey Mancini/299 4.00 10.00
AATP Tommy Pham/299 3.00 8.00
AATST Trevor Story/299 12.00 30.00
AATT Touki Toussaint/299 4.00 10.00
AAVG Vladimir Guerrero Jr./299 30.00 80.00
AAWC Willson Contreras/199 4.00 10.00
AAWCL Will Clark/199 15.00 40.00
AAWM Whit Merrifield/299 5.00 12.00

2019 Topps Museum Collection Archival Autographs Copper

*COPPER: .5X TO 1.2X BASIC
STATED ODDS 1:27 HOBBY
STATED PRINT RUN 50 SER.#'d SETS
EXCHANGE DEADLINE 5/31/2021
AAAB Adrian Beltre 20.00 50.00
AAAP Andy Pettitte 10.00 25.00
AACF Carlton Fisk 12.00 30.00
AACSA Chris Sale 6.00 15.00
AADM Don Mattingly 30.00 80.00
AAGSP George Springer 5.00 12.00
AAJA Jose Altuve 12.00 30.00
AAJG Juan Gonzalez 8.00 20.00
AARA Roberto Alomar 10.00 25.00
AARC Rod Carew 12.00 30.00
AASC Steve Carlton 15.00 40.00

2019 Topps Museum Collection Archival Autographs Gold

*GOLD: .6X TO 1.5X BASIC
STATED ODDS 1:48 HOBBY
STATED PRINT RUN 25 SER.#'d SETS
EXCHANGE DEADLINE 5/31/2021
AAAK Al Kaline 30.00 80.00
AAAR Anthony Rizzo 15.00 40.00
AAI Ichiro 125.00 300.00
AAJG Juan Gonzalez 20.00 50.00
AAJV Joey Votto 25.00 60.00
AAKB Kris Bryant 60.00 150.00
AAMTR Mike Trout 300.00 600.00
AASO Shohei Ohtani 75.00 200.00
AATG Tom Glavine 25.00 60.00
AATH Torii Hunter 20.00 50.00

2019 Topps Museum Collection Canvas Collection

STATED ODDS 1:4 HOBBY
CC1 Javier Baez 1.25 3.00
CC2 Tony Gwynn 1.00 2.50
CC3 Joey Votto 1.00 2.50
CC4 Mike Trout 5.00 12.00
CC5 Alex Bregman 1.00 2.50
CC6 Mark McGwire 1.50 4.00
CC7 Derek Jeter 2.50 6.00
CC8 Ronald Acuna Jr. 5.00 12.00
CC9 Jose Altuve .75 2.00
CC10 Juan Soto 3.00 8.00
CC11 Mookie Betts 1.50 4.00
CC12 Luis Severino .75 2.00
CC13 Nolan Arenado 1.25 3.00
CC14 Don Mattingly 2.00 5.00
CC15 Aaron Judge 2.50 6.00
CC16 Yadier Molina 1.00 2.50
CC17 Jacob deGrom 1.00 2.50
CC18 Francisco Lindor 1.00 2.50
CC19 Anthony Rizzo 1.50 4.00
CC20 Kris Bryant 1.25 3.00
CC21 Bryce Harper 1.50 4.00
CC22 David Wright .75 2.00
CC23 Gleyber Torres 2.00 5.00
CC24 Max Scherzer 1.00 2.50
CC25 Paul Goldschmidt 1.00 2.50
CC26 Shohei Ohtani 1.25 3.00
CC27 Roberto Clemente 2.50 6.00
CC28 Mariano Rivera 1.25 3.00
CC29 Chris Sale 1.00 2.50
CC30 J.D. Martinez 1.00 2.50
CC31 Andrew Benintendi 6.00 15.00
CC32 Bo Jackson 1.00 2.50
CC33 Rhys Hoskins 1.25 3.00
CC34 Babe Ruth 2.50 6.00
CC35 Albert Pujols 1.25 3.00
CC36 Christian Yelich 1.25 3.00
CC37 Victor Robles 1.25 3.00
CC38 Honus Wagner 1.00 2.50
CC39 Manny Machado 1.00 2.50
CC40 Cal Ripken Jr. 3.00 8.00
CC41 Nolan Ryan 3.00 8.00
CC42 Buster Posey 1.25 3.00
CC43 Ozzie Smith 1.25 3.00
CC44 Hideki Matsui 1.00 2.50
CC45 Rickey Henderson 1.00 2.50
CC46 Ken Griffey Jr. 2.00 5.00
CC47 Ichiro 1.25 3.00
CC48 Lou Gehrig 2.00 5.00
CC49 Ty Cobb 1.50 4.00
CC50 Clayton Kershaw 2.00 5.00

2019 Topps Museum Collection Dual Meaningful Material Relics

STATED PRINT 1:64 HOBBY

TED PRINT RUN 50 SER.#'d SETS
PPER/35: .5X TO 1.2X BASIC
RAB Bregman/Altuve 6.00 15.00
RAC Altuve/Correa 6.00 15.00
RAJ Chris Archer 5.00 12.00
sh Bell
RAM Cabrera/Benintendi 8.00 20.00
RAS Trevor Story 8.00 20.00
olan Arenado
RBB Betts/Benintendi 10.00 25.00
RBR Bryant/Rizzo 15.00 40.00
RCA Nicholas Castellanos 6.00 15.00
iguel Cabrera
RCC Michael Conforto 6.00 15.00
oenis Cespedes
RCR Amed Rosario 6.00 15.00
oenis Cespedes
RFS Freeman/Swanson 8.00 20.00
RGM Nomar Mazara 5.00 12.00
oey Gallo
RHH Felix Hernandez 5.00 12.00
Mitch Haniger
RHM Eric Hosmer 5.00 12.00
Wil Myers
RLH Jason Heyward 5.00 12.00
on Lester
RLR Jose Ramirez 6.00 15.00
Francisco Lindor
ROP Dustin Pedroia 6.00 15.00
David Ortiz
RPB Xander Bogaerts 6.00 15.00
Dustin Pedroia
RPC Crawford/Posey 8.00 20.00
RPM Salvador Perez 6.00 15.00
Whit Merrifield
RSC Aroldis Chapman 6.00 15.00
Luis Severino
RSL Stephen Strasburg 6.00 15.00
Max Scherzer
RSS Justin Smoak 5.00 12.00
Marcus Stroman
RST Stephen Strasburg 6.00 15.00
Trea Turner
RTA Torres/Andujar 12.00 30.00
RTM Jameson Taillon 5.00 12.00
Starling Marte
RVG Scooter Gennett 6.00 15.00
Joey Votto

2019 Topps Museum Collection Dual Meaningful Material Relics Copper

COPPER: .5X TO 1.2X BASIC
TATED ODDS 1:111 HOBBY
TATED PRINT RUN 35 SER.#'d SETS
MRAM Cabrera/Pujols 12.00 30.00
MRFS Freeman/Swanson 20.00 50.00

2019 Topps Museum Collection Meaningful Material Relics

STATED ODDS 1:12 HOBBY
STATED PRINT RUN 50 SER.#'d SETS
*COPPER/35: .5X TO 1.2X BASIC
*GOLD/25: .5X TO 1.2X BASIC
MMRAA Albert Almora 4.00 10.00
MMRAB Andrew Benintendi 5.00 12.00
MMRAC Aroldis Chapman 5.00 12.00
MMRAM Andrew McCutchen 5.00 12.00
MMRAR Addison Russell 4.00 10.00
MMRAW Adam Wainwright 4.00 10.00
MMRBB Brandon Belt 4.00 10.00
MMRBC Brandon Crawford 4.00 10.00
MMRBM Brian McCann 4.00 10.00
MMRBN Brandon Nimmo 4.00 10.00
MMRBP Buster Posey 6.00 15.00
MMRCA Chris Archer 3.00 8.00
MMRCB Cody Bellinger 10.00 25.00
MMRCC Carlos Correa 5.00 12.00
MMRCD Corey Dickerson 3.00 8.00
MMRCK Craig Kimbrel 4.00 10.00
MMRCM Carlos Martinez 4.00 10.00
MMRCS CC Sabathia 4.00 10.00
MMRCT Chris Taylor 4.00 10.00
MMRCY Christian Yelich 6.00 15.00
MMRDB Dellin Betances 4.00 10.00
MMRDG Dee Gordon 3.00 8.00
MMRDO David Ortiz 5.00 12.00
MMRDP David Price 4.00 10.00
MMRDS Dansby Swanson 5.00 12.00
MMREH Eric Hosmer 4.00 10.00
MMREI Ender Inciarte 3.00 8.00
MMREL Evan Longoria 4.00 10.00
MMRER Eddie Rosario 4.00 10.00
MMRET Eric Thames 3.00 8.00
MMRFB Franklin Barreto 3.00 8.00
MMRFF Freddie Freeman 6.00 15.00
MMRFH Felix Hernandez 4.00 10.00
MMRGP Gregory Polanco 4.00 10.00
MMRGS Giancarlo Stanton 5.00 12.00
MMRHR Hyun-Jin Ryu 4.00 10.00
MMRIH Ian Happ 4.00 10.00
MMRJA Jose Abreu 5.00 12.00
MMRJB Jackie Bradley Jr. 5.00 12.00
MMRJC Johnny Cueto 4.00 10.00
MMRJd Jacob deGrom 5.00 12.00
MMRJE Jacoby Ellsbury 4.00 10.00
MMRJG Joey Gallo 4.00 10.00
MMRJH Jason Heyward 4.00 10.00
MMRJL Jake Lamb 4.00 10.00
MMRJM Joe Mauer 4.00 10.00
MMRJP Joe Panik 4.00 10.00
MMRJS Jeff Samardzija 3.00 8.00
MMRJT Jameson Taillon 4.00 10.00
MMRJV Joey Votto 5.00 12.00
MMRJW Jesse Winker 3.00 8.00
MMRKF Kyle Freeland 4.00 10.00
MMRKK Kevin Kiermaier 4.00 10.00
MMRKM Kenta Maeda 4.00 10.00
MMRKS Kyle Seager 3.00 8.00
MMRKW Kolten Wong 4.00 10.00
MMRLS Luis Severino 4.00 10.00
MMRMA Miguel Andujar 5.00 12.00
MMRMB Mookie Betts 8.00 20.00
MMRMC Miguel Cabrera 5.00 12.00
MMRMF Max Fried 5.00 12.00
MMRMK Max Kepler 4.00 10.00
MMRMO Matt Olson 3.00 8.00
MMRMS Marcus Stroman 4.00 10.00
MMRMW Michael Wacha 4.00 10.00
MMRNA Nolan Arenado 6.00 15.00
MMRNC Nicholas Castellanos 5.00 12.00
MMRNM Nomar Mazara 3.00 8.00
MMRNS Noah Syndergaard 4.00 10.00
MMRPD Paul DeJong 5.00 12.00
MMRPG Paul Goldschmidt 5.00 12.00
MMRRB Ryan Braun 4.00 10.00
MMRRD Rafael Devers 6.00 15.00
MMRRI Raisel Iglesias 3.00 8.00
MMRRO Rougned Odor 4.00 10.00
MMRRP Rick Porcello 4.00 10.00
MMRRZ Ryan Zimmerman 4.00 10.00
MMRSC Shin-Soo Choo 4.00 10.00
MMRSD Sean Doolittle 3.00 8.00
MMRSG Scooter Gennett 4.00 10.00
MMRSM Starling Marte 4.00 10.00
MMRSP Salvador Perez 4.00 10.00
MMRSS Stephen Strasburg 5.00 12.00
MMRTM Trey Mancini 4.00 10.00
MMRTP Tommy Pham 3.00 8.00
MMRTS Travis Shaw 3.00 8.00
MMRTT Trea Turner 4.00 10.00
MMRVM Victor Martinez 4.00 10.00
MMRWM Wil Myers 3.00 8.00
MMRXB Xander Bogaerts 5.00 12.00
MMRYC Yoenis Cespedes 5.00 12.00
MMRYM Yadier Molina 5.00 12.00
MMRYP Yasiel Puig 5.00 12.00
MMRZG Zack Greinke 4.00 10.00
MMRZW Zack Wheeler 4.00 10.00
MMRAMC Andrew McCutchen 5.00 12.00
MMRARE Anthony Rendon 5.00 12.00
MMRARN Anthony Rendon 5.00 12.00
MMRARO Amed Rosario 4.00 10.00
MMRARU Addison Russell 4.00 10.00
MMRAWA Adam Wainwright 4.00 10.00
MMRBBU Byron Buxton 4.00 10.00
MMRBBX Byron Buxton 4.00 10.00
MMRBCR Brandon Crawford 4.00 10.00
MMRCAR Chris Archer 3.00 8.00
MMRCKI Craig Kimbrel 4.00 10.00
MMRCMA Carlos Martinez 4.00 10.00
MMRCSA Chris Sale 5.00 12.00
MMRDBE Dellin Betances 4.00 10.00
MMRDBU Dylan Bundy 4.00 10.00
MMRDGR Didi Gregorius 4.00 10.00
MMRDPD Dustin Pedroia 5.00 12.00
MMRDPE Dustin Pedroia 5.00 12.00
MMRDPR David Price 4.00 10.00
MMRDSW Dansby Swanson 5.00 12.00
MMRELO Evan Longoria 4.00 10.00
MMRGSP George Springer 4.00 10.00
MMRHRY Hyun-Jin Ryu 4.00 10.00
MMRJAG Jesus Aguilar 3.00 8.00
MMRJAL Jose Altuve 4.00 10.00
MMRJBE Josh Bell 4.00 10.00
MMRJBI Jose Berrios 4.00 10.00
MMRJBL Josh Bell 4.00 10.00
MMRJBR Jackie Bradley Jr. 5.00 12.00
MMRJCU Johnny Cueto 4.00 10.00
MMRJDO Josh Donaldson 4.00 10.00
MMRJFL Jack Flaherty 4.00 10.00
MMRJHE Jason Heyward 4.00 10.00
MMRJLE Jon Lester 4.00 10.00
MMRJMA Joe Mauer 4.00 10.00
MMRJMR J.D. Martinez 5.00 12.00
MMRJPD Joc Pederson 4.00 10.00
MMRJPE Jose Peraza 4.00 10.00
MMRJSM Justin Smoak 3.00 8.00
MMRJTA Jameson Taillon 4.00 10.00
MMRJTH Julio Teheran 4.00 10.00
MMRJVE Justin Verlander 5.00 12.00
MMRJVR Justin Verlander 5.00 12.00
MMRKKI Kevin Kiermaier 4.00 10.00
MMRKSE Kyle Seager 3.00 8.00
MMRMBE Mookie Betts 8.00 20.00
MMRMCA Miguel Cabrera 5.00 12.00
MMRMCN Michael Conforto 4.00 10.00
MMRMCO Michael Conforto 4.00 10.00
MMRMFU Michael Fulmer 3.00 8.00
MMRMMI Miles Mikolas 5.00 12.00
MMRMSA Miguel Sano 4.00 10.00
MMRMSC Max Scherzer 5.00 12.00
MMRMST Marcus Stroman 4.00 10.00
MMRNMA Nick Markakis 4.00 10.00
MMRRPO Rick Porcello 4.00 10.00
MMRSGA Sonny Gray 4.00 10.00
MMRSMA Steven Matz 4.00 10.00
MMRSMR Starling Marte 4.00 10.00
MMRSST Stephen Strasburg 5.00 12.00
MMRTMA Trey Mancini 4.00 10.00
MMRWMR Whit Merrifield 5.00 12.00
MMRWMY Wil Myers 3.00 8.00
MMRXBO Xander Bogaerts 5.00 12.00
MMRYCE Yoenis Cespedes 5.00 12.00
MMRYPU Yasiel Puig 5.00 12.00

2019 Topps Museum Collection Meaningful Material Relics Copper

*COPPER: .5X TO 1.2X BASIC
STATED ODDS 1:17 HOBBY
STATED PRINT RUN 35 SER.#'d SETS
MMRBP Buster Posey 10.00 25.00

2019 Topps Museum Collection Meaningful Material Relics Gold

*GOLD: .5X TO 1.2X BASIC
STATED ODDS 1:22 HOBBY
STATED PRINT RUN 25 SER.#'d SETS
MMRAB Andrew Benintendi 15.00 40.00
MMRAP Albert Pujols 8.00 20.00
MMRBP Buster Posey 12.00 30.00
MMRABR Alex Bregman 10.00 25.00

2019 Topps Museum Collection Primary Pieces Four Player Quad Relics

STATED PRINT 1:35 HOBBY
STATED PRINT RUN 99 SER.#'d SETS
*COPPER/75: .4X TO 1X BASIC
*GOLD/25: .75X TO 2X BASIC
FPRABCS Altve/Brgmn/Crra/Sprngr 5.00 12.00
FPRABMT Starling Marte 4.00 10.00
Jameson Taillon
Josh Bell
Chris Archer
FPRBASD Charlie Blackmon 6.00 15.00
David Dahl
Trevor Story
Nolan Arenado
FPRBBRS Brynt/Schwrbr/Rzzo/Baez 12.00 30.00
FPRBPBB Betts/Bgrts/Pdra/Bnntndi 8.00 20.00
FPRBSBM Sale/Mrtnz/Bnntndi/Btts 8.00 20.00
FPRCARN Alnso/Rsro/Nmmo/Cnfrto 25.00 60.00
FPRCDOM Matt Chapman 5.00 12.00
Sean Manaea
Matt Olson
Khris Davis
FPRCPLB Belt/Lngra/Crwfrd/Psy 6.00 15.00
FPRFDSA Frmn/Dnldsn/Swnsn/Albs 6.00 15.00
FPRHMKU Myrs/Knslr/Uris/Hsmr 5.00 12.00
FPRKPBM Krshw/Pdrsn/Bllngr/Muncy 10.00 25.00
FPRLRKB Trevor Bauer 5.00 12.00
Corey Kluber
Jose Ramirez
Francisco Lindor
FPRMGMC Mlna/Gldschmdt
Crpntr/Mrtnz 5.00 12.00
FPRRASC Ryan Braun 4.00 10.00
Jesus Aguilar
Lorenzo Cain
Travis Shaw
FPRRSLH Hywrd/Lstr/Schwrbr/Rizzo 8.00 20.00
FPRSATG Snchz/Trrs/Andjr/Grgous 10.00 25.00
FPRSPBB Prce/Bnntndi/Btts/Sale 8.00 20.00
FPRSSAT Gary Sanchez 5.00 12.00
Luis Severino
Masahiro Tanaka
Miguel Andujar
FPRSSTS Soto/Schrzr/Trnr/Strsbrg 15.00 40.00
FPRSTSC CC Sabathia 5.00 12.00
Masahiro Tanaka
Aroldis Chapman
Luis Severino
FPRTPOU Ohtni/Pjls/Trt/Uptn 25.00 60.00
FPRTRGC Ryan/Trout/Grrro/Crw 25.00 60.00
FPRZTSR Soto/Rndn/Trnr/Zmmrmn 15.00 40.00

2019 Topps Museum Collection Primary Pieces Four Player Quad Relics Copper

*COPPER: .4X TO 1X BASIC
STATED ODDS 1:46 HOBBY
STATED PRINT RUN 75 SER.#'d SETS
FPRMTO Shohei Ohtani 25.00 60.00
Masahiro Tanaka
Ichiro
Hideki Matsui

2019 Topps Museum Collection Primary Pieces Quad Relics

STATED ODDS 1:12 HOBBY
STATED PRINT RUN 99 SER.#'d SETS
*COPPER/75: .4X TO 1X BASIC
*GOLD/25: .6X TO 1.5X BASIC
SPQRAB Andrew Benintendi 4.00 10.00
SPQRAC Aroldis Chapman 4.00 10.00
SPQRAP Albert Pujols 6.00 15.00
SPQRAR Anthony Rizzo 6.00 15.00
SPQRAW Adam Wainwright 3.00 8.00
SPQRBB Byron Buxton 3.00 8.00
SPQRBC Brandon Crawford 3.00 8.00
SPQRBP Buster Posey 5.00 12.00
SPQRCA Chris Archer 2.50 6.00
SPQRCB Charlie Blackmon 4.00 10.00
SPQRCC Carlos Correa 4.00 10.00
SPQRCK Clayton Kershaw 8.00 20.00
SPQRCM Carlos Martinez 3.00 8.00
SPQRCS Chris Sale 4.00 10.00
SPQRDG Didi Gregorius 3.00 8.00
SPQRDP David Price 3.00 8.00
SPQRDS Dansby Swanson 4.00 10.00
SPQREA Elvis Andrus 3.00 8.00
SPQREH Eric Hosmer 3.00 8.00
SPQREL Evan Longoria 3.00 8.00
SPQRFF Freddie Freeman 5.00 12.00
SPQRFL Francisco Lindor 4.00 10.00
SPQRGS George Springer 3.00 8.00
SPQRJA Jose Abreu 4.00 10.00
SPQRJB Javier Baez 5.00 12.00
SPQRJG Joey Gallo 3.00 8.00
SPQRJH Jason Heyward 3.00 8.00
SPQRJL Jon Lester 3.00 8.00
SPQRJM J.D. Martinez 4.00 10.00
SPQRJR Jose Ramirez 3.00 8.00
SPQRJS Justin Smoak 2.50 6.00
SPQRJU Justin Upton 3.00 8.00
SPQRJV Joey Votto 4.00 10.00
SPQRKB Kris Bryant 5.00 12.00
SPQRKK Kevin Kiermaier 3.00 8.00
SPQRKS Kyle Seager 2.50 6.00
SPQRLS Luis Severino 3.00 8.00
SPQRMA Miguel Andujar 4.00 10.00
SPQRMB Mookie Betts 6.00 15.00
SPQRMC Miguel Cabrera 4.00 10.00
SPQRMO Marcell Ozuna 4.00 10.00
SPQRMS Marcus Stroman 3.00 8.00
SPQRNA Nolan Arenado 5.00 12.00
SPQRNC Nicholas Castellanos 4.00 10.00
SPQRNS Noah Syndergaard 3.00 8.00
SPQROA Ozzie Albies 4.00 10.00
SPQRPD Paul DeJong 4.00 10.00
SPQRRB Ryan Braun 3.00 8.00
SPQRRD Rafael Devers 5.00 12.00
SPQRRH Rhys Hoskins 5.00 12.00
SPQRRZ Ryan Zimmerman 3.00 8.00
SPQRSM Starling Marte 3.00 8.00
SPQRSP Salvador Perez 3.00 8.00
SPQRSS Stephen Strasburg 4.00 10.00
SPQRTB Trevor Bauer 4.00 10.00
SPQRTM Trey Mancini 3.00 8.00
SPQRTS Trevor Story 4.00 10.00
SPQRTT Trea Turner 3.00 8.00
SPQRVR Victor Robles 5.00 12.00
SPQRWM Whit Merrifield 4.00 10.00
SPQRXB Xander Bogaerts 4.00 10.00
SPQRYG Yuli Gurriel 3.00 8.00
SPQRYM Yadier Molina 4.00 10.00
SPQRZG Zack Greinke 3.00 8.00
SPQRABR Alex Bregman 6.00 15.00
SPQRARE Anthony Rendon 4.00 10.00
SPQRCBE Cody Bellinger 8.00 20.00
SPQRCSA Carlos Santana 3.00 8.00
SPQRDGO Dee Gordon 2.50 6.00
SPQRDPE Dustin Pedroia 4.00 10.00
SPQRGSA Gary Sanchez 4.00 10.00
SPQRJAL Jose Altuve 3.00 8.00
SPQRJSO Juan Soto 12.00 30.00
SPQRMCA Matt Carpenter 4.00 10.00
SPQRMCO Michael Conforto 3.00 8.00
SPQRMSC Max Scherzer 4.00 10.00
SPQRMTA Masahiro Tanaka 3.00 8.00
SPQRWMY Wil Myers 2.50 6.00

2019 Topps Museum Collection Primary Pieces Quad Relics Gold

*GOLD: .6X TO 1.5X BASIC
STATED ODDS 1:44 HOBBY
STATED PRINT RUN 25 SER.#'d SETS
SPQRFF Freddie Freeman 12.00 30.00
SPQRMB Mookie Betts 12.00 30.00
SPQRMT Mike Trout 40.00 100.00

2019 Topps Museum Collection Primary Pieces Quad Relics Legends

STATED ODDS 1:122 HOBBY
STATED PRINT RUN 25 SER.#'d SETS
SPQLAK Al Kaline 12.00 30.00
SPQLBL Barry Larkin 8.00 20.00
SPQLCR Cal Ripken Jr. 20.00 50.00
SPQLCY Carl Yastrzemski 20.00 50.00
SPQLDJ Derek Jeter 30.00 80.00
SPQLDM Don Mattingly 20.00 50.00
SPQLEM Eddie Mathews 10.00 25.00
SPQLFT Frank Thomas 15.00 40.00
SPQLGB George Brett 20.00 50.00
SPQLJB Johnny Bench 15.00 40.00
SPQLJM Johnny Mize 40.00 100.00
SPQLKG Ken Griffey Jr. 20.00 50.00
SPQLMM Mark McGwire 15.00 40.00
SPQLMP Mike Piazza 25.00 60.00
SPQLNR Nolan Ryan 20.00 50.00
SPQLOS Ozzie Smith 15.00 40.00
SPQLPM Pedro Martinez 5.00 12.00
SPQLPR Pee Wee Reese 5.00 12.00
SPQLRH Rickey Henderson 15.00 40.00
SPQLRJ Reggie Jackson 10.00 25.00
SPQLRY Robin Yount 10.00 25.00
SPQLTG Tony Gwynn 40.00 100.00
SPQLTW Ted Williams 40.00 100.00
SPQLWB Wade Boggs 15.00 40.00
SPQLRCL Roger Clemens 8.00 20.00
SPQLRHO Rogers Hornsby 25.00 60.00
SPQLTSP Tris Speaker 30.00 80.00

2019 Topps Museum Collection Signature Swatches Dual Relic Autographs

STATED ODDS 1:9 HOBBY
PRINT RUNS B/WN 99-299 COPIES PER
EXCHANGE DEADLINE 5/31/2021
*COPPER/50: .5X TO 1.2X BASIC
*GOLD/25: .6X TO 1.5X BASIC
SSDABN Brandon Nimmo/299 5.00 12.00
SSDABS Blake Snell/299 5.00 12.00
SSDACF Clint Frazier/199 5.00 12.00
SSDACM Cedric Mullins/299 6.00 15.00
SSDACS Carlos Santana/299 5.00 12.00
SSDADG Didi Gregorius/299 6.00 15.00
SSDAER Eddie Rosario/199 5.00 12.00
SSDAFR Franmil Reyes/299 4.00 10.00
SSDAHB Harrison Bader/299 5.00 12.00
SSDAJA Jesus Aguilar/199 4.00 10.00
SSDAJB Jose Berrios/299 5.00 12.00
SSDAJF Jack Flaherty/299 5.00 12.00
SSDAJH Josh Hader/199 4.00 10.00
SSDAJM Jose Martinez/299 4.00 10.00
SSDAJS Justin Smoak/149 4.00 10.00
SSDAKD Khris Davis/199 6.00 15.00
SSDALG Lourdes Gurriel Jr./299 5.00 12.00
SSDALV Luke Voit/299 25.00 60.00
SSDAMC Matt Chapman/191 6.00 15.00
SSDAMH Mitch Haniger/199 5.00 12.00
SSDAMM Max Muncy/199 5.00 12.00
SSDAMO Marcell Ozuna/99 6.00 15.00
SSDAOA Ozzie Albies/199 6.00 15.00
SSDAOH Odubel Herrera/199 5.00 12.00
SSDAPD Paul DeJong/299 6.00 15.00
SSDARL Ramon Laureano/299 10.00 25.00
SSDARO Ryan O'Hearn/299 4.00 10.00
SSDASG Scooter Gennett/299 5.00 12.00
SSDASP Salvador Perez/99 5.00 12.00
SSDATM Trey Mancini/199 5.00 12.00
SSDATP Tommy Pham/199 4.00 10.00
SSDATT Touki Toussaint/299 5.00 12.00
SSDAVR Victor Robles/199 8.00 20.00
SSDAWA Willy Adames/299 4.00 10.00
SSDAWM Whit Merrifield/199 6.00 15.00
SSDAZW Zack Wheeler/249 5.00 12.00
SSDAJSE Jean Segura/299 6.00 15.00
SSDAMKO Michael Kopech/299 8.00 20.00
SSDASMA Steven Matz/299 5.00 12.00
SSDATSH Travis Shaw/199 4.00 10.00

2019 Topps Museum Collection Signature Swatches Dual Relic Autographs Copper

*COPPER: .5X TO 1.2X BASIC
STATED ODDS 1:39 HOBBY
STATED PRINT RUN 50 SER.#'d SETS
EXCHANGE DEADLINE 5/31/2021
SSDAET Eric Thames 5.00 12.00
SSDASM Sean Manaea 5.00 12.00
SSDAWC Willson Contreras 6.00 15.00
SSDAGSP George Springer 12.00 30.00
SSDAMCA Matt Carpenter 8.00 20.00

2019 Topps Museum Collection Signature Swatches Dual Relic Autographs Gold

*GOLD: .6X TO 1.5X BASIC
STATED ODDS 1:73 HOBBY
STATED PRINT RUN 25 SER.#'d SETS
EXCHANGE DEADLINE 5/31/2021
SSDAAR Anthony Rizzo 20.00 50.00
SSDAJAL Jose Altuve 15.00 40.00

2019 Topps Museum Collection Signature Swatches Triple Relic Autographs

STATED ODDS 1:18 HOBBY
PRINT RUNS B/WN 80-299 COPIES PER
EXCHANGE DEADLINE 5/31/2021
*COPPER: .6X TO 1.5X BASIC
SSTAAM Adalberto Mondesi 12.00 30.00
SSTACB Charlie Blackmon/199 6.00 15.00
SSTACK Corey Kluber/99 5.00 12.00
SSTACS Chris Sale/99 12.00 30.00
SSTADB Dellin Betances/199 10.00 25.00
SSTADD David Dahl/99 4.00 10.00
SSTADJ Danny Jansen/299 4.00 10.00
SSTAEL Evan Longoria/99 5.00 12.00
SSTAFB Franklin Barreto/199 4.00 10.00
SSTAFF Freddie Freeman 20.00 50.00
SSTAFL Francisco Lindor/99 20.00 50.00
SSTAJd Jacob deGrom/99 6.00 15.00
SSTAJR Jim Rice/99 5.00 12.00
SSTAJU Justin Upton/199 5.00 12.00
SSTAKS Kyle Schwarber/99 6.00 15.00
SSTALS Luis Severino/149 5.00 12.00
SSTALU Luis Urias/299 6.00 15.00
SSTAMA Miguel Andujar/99 6.00 15.00
SSTAMF Maikel Franco/99 5.00 12.00
SSTAMG Mark Grace/149 10.00 25.00
SSTAMK Matt Kemp/199 5.00 12.00
SSTAMO Matt Olson/99 4.00 10.00
SSTANS Noah Syndergaard/99 8.00 20.00
SSTARD Rafael Devers/199 15.00 40.00
SSTARH Rhys Hoskins/99 15.00 40.00
SSTARM Jeff McNeil/299 10.00 25.00
SSTASG Shawn Green/99 6.00 15.00
SSTASP Stephen Piscotty/99 4.00 10.00
SSTAVG Vladimir Guerrero/99 12.00 30.00
SSTAARE Anthony Rendon/95 12.00 30.00
SSTAJHI Jordan Hicks/299 5.00 12.00
SSTAJSO Juan Soto/99 25.00 60.00

2019 Topps Museum Collection Superstar Showpieces Autographs

STATED ODDS 1:112 HOBBY
STATED PRINT RUN 25 SER.#'d SETS
EXCHANGE DEADLINE 5/31/2021
SSAJ Aaron Judge 100.00 250.00
SSBL Barry Larkin 25.00 60.00
SSCR Cal Ripken Jr. 50.00 120.00
SSCS Chris Sale 10.00 25.00
SSCY Christian Yelich EXCH 50.00 120.00
SSDM Don Mattingly 25.00 60.00
SSDO David Ortiz 30.00 80.00
SSFF Freddie Freeman 40.00 100.00
SSFL Francisco Lindor 10.00 25.00
SSFT Frank Thomas 30.00 80.00
SSHM Hideki Matsui 50.00 120.00
SSJA Jose Altuve 15.00 40.00
SSJd Jacob deGrom 30.00 80.00
SSJR Jose Ramirez 8.00 20.00
SSJS John Smoltz 20.00 50.00
SSJV Joey Votto 30.00 80.00
SSKB Kris Bryant 60.00 150.00
SSLS Luis Severino 8.00 20.00
SSMA Miguel Andujar 10.00 25.00
SSMT Mike Trout 300.00 600.00
SSOA Ozzie Albies 10.00 25.00
SSOS Ozzie Smith 25.00 60.00
SSRA Ronald Acuna Jr. 125.00 300.00
SSRH Rhys Hoskins 30.00 80.00
SSTS Trevor Story 10.00 25.00
SSWC Will Clark 25.00 60.00
SSYM Yadier Molina EXCH 40.00 100.00
SSJSO Juan Soto 25.00 60.00

2020 Topps Museum Collection

1 Willie Mays 1.50 4.00
2 Nolan Arenado 1.00 2.50
3 Ted Williams 1.50 4.00
4 Jose Ramirez .60 1.50
5 Robinson Cano .60 1.50
6 Mariano Rivera 1.00 2.50
7 J.D. Martinez .75 2.00
8 Fernando Tatis Jr. 3.00 8.00
9 Matt Chapman .75 2.00
10 Tony Gwynn .75 2.00
11 Ichiro 1.00 2.50
12 Aaron Judge 4.00 10.00
13 Juan Soto 2.50 6.00
14 Manny Machado .75 2.00
15 Noah Syndergaard .60 1.50
16 Kyle Lewis RC 6.00 15.00
17 Don Mattingly 1.50 4.00
18 Nico Hoerner RC 2.50 6.00
19 Joey Votto .75 2.00
20 Trevor Story .75 2.00
21 Kris Bryant 1.00 2.50
22 Babe Ruth 2.00 5.00
23 Whit Merrifield .75 2.00
24 Mike Trout 4.00 10.00
25 Cal Ripken Jr. 2.50 6.00
26 Bryce Harper 1.25 3.00
27 Alex Bregman .75 2.00
28 Aristides Aquino RC 5.00 12.00
29 Charlie Blackmon .75 2.00
30 Ryne Sandberg 1.50 4.00
31 Anthony Rendon .75 2.00
32 Giancarlo Stanton .75 2.00
33 Rhys Hoskins 1.00 2.50
34 Jacob deGrom .75 2.00
35 Roberto Clemente 4.00 10.00
36 Bo Bichette RC 5.00 12.00
37 Jack Flaherty .60 1.50
38 Ernie Banks .75 2.00
39 Justin Verlander .75 2.00
40 Carlos Correa .75 2.00
41 Ken Griffey Jr. 5.00 12.00
42 Christian Yelich 1.00 2.50
43 Ozzie Albies .75 2.00
44 Walker Buehler 1.00 2.50
45 Cody Bellinger 1.50 4.00
46 Sandy Koufax 1.50 4.00
47 Buster Posey 1.00 2.50
48 Paul Goldschmidt .75 2.00
49 Shane Bieber .75 2.00
50 Mark McGwire 1.25 3.00
51 Hideki Matsui .75 2.00
52 Pete Alonso 2.00 5.00
53 Luis Robert RC 6.00 15.00
54 Keston Hiura 1.00 2.50
55 Ronald Acuna Jr. 4.00 10.00
56 Johnny Bench .75 2.00
57 David Ortiz .75 2.00
58 Josh Bell .60 1.50
59 Vladimir Guerrero Jr. 1.50 4.00
60 Sonny Gray .60 1.50
61 Freddie Freeman 1.00 2.50
62 Clayton Kershaw 1.50 4.00
63 Rickey Henderson .75 2.00
64 Trea Turner .60 1.50
65 Roberto Alomar .60 1.50
66 Masahiro Tanaka .75 2.00
67 Mike Schmidt 1.25 3.00
68 Eloy Jimenez 1.50 4.00
69 Chipper Jones .75 2.00
70 Roger Clemens 1.00 2.50
71 Mookie Betts 1.50 4.00
72 Javier Baez 1.00 2.50
73 George Springer .60 1.50
74 Lou Gehrig 1.50 4.00
75 Gleyber Torres 1.50 4.00
76 George Brett 1.50 4.00
77 Randy Johnson .75 2.00
78 Jesus Luzardo RC 1.25 3.00
79 Albert Pujols 1.00 2.50
80 Stephen Strasburg .75 2.00
81 Anthony Rizzo 1.25 3.00
82 Max Scherzer .75 2.00
83 Brendan McKay RC 1.00 2.50
84 Yordan Alvarez RC 5.00 12.00
85 Andrew McCutchen .75 2.00
86 Yadier Molina .75 2.00
87 Gavin Lux RC 4.00 10.00
88 Barry Larkin .60 1.50
89 Rafael Devers 1.00 2.50
90 Gerrit Cole 1.25 3.00
91 Shohei Ohtani 1.00 2.50
92 Nolan Ryan 2.50 6.00
93 Jackie Robinson .75 2.00
94 Ozzie Smith 1.00 2.50
95 Chris Sale .75 2.00
96 Frank Thomas .75 2.00
97 Jose Altuve .60 1.50
98 J.T. Realmuto .75 2.00
99 Francisco Lindor .75 2.00
100 Miguel Cabrera .75 2.00

2020 Topps Museum Collection Amethyst

*AMETHYST: 1X TO 2.5X BASIC
*AMETHYST RC: .75X TO 2X BASIC RC
STATED ODDS 1:9 HOBBY
STATED PRINT RUN 99 SER.#'d SETS
16 Kyle Lewis 15.00 40.00
24 Mike Trout 20.00 50.00
36 Bo Bichette 20.00 50.00
87 Gavin Lux 12.00 30.00

2020 Topps Museum Collection Ruby

*RUBY: 1.5X TO 4X BASIC
*RUBY RC: 1.2X TO 3X BASIC RC
STATED ODDS 1:18 HOBBY
STATED PRINT RUN 50 SER.#'d SETS
16 Kyle Lewis 25.00 60.00
24 Mike Trout 30.00 80.00
36 Bo Bichette 30.00 80.00
87 Gavin Lux 30.00 80.00

2020 Topps Museum Collection Sapphire

*SAPPHIRE: .75X TO 2X BASIC
*SAPPHIRE RC: ..6X TO 1.5X BASIC RC
STATED ODDS 1:6 HOBBY
STATED PRINT RUN 150 SER.#'d SETS
16 Kyle Lewis 12.00 30.00
24 Mike Trout 15.00 40.00
87 Gavin Lux 10.00 25.00

2020 Topps Museum Collection Archival Autographs

STATED ODDS 1: HOBBY
PRINT RUNS B/WN 99-299 COPIES PER
EXCHANGE DEADLINE 5/31/22
AAAA Adbert Alzolay 6.00 15.00
AAAC Aaron Civale 8.00 20.00
AAAD Andre Dawson 15.00 40.00
AAAH Aaron Hicks 10.00 25.00
AAAN Aaron Nola 10.00 25.00
AAAQ Aristides Aquino 12.00 30.00
AAAR Austin Riley 12.00 30.00
AAAY Alex Young 3.00 8.00
AABB Bo Bichette 50.00 120.00
AABM Brendan McKay 5.00 12.00
AADC Dylan Cease 6.00 15.00
AADE Dennis Eckersley 10.00 25.00
AADL DJ LeMahieu 40.00 100.00
AADM Dustin May 20.00 50.00
AADS Dansby Swanson 10.00 25.00
AAEJ Eloy Jimenez 20.00 50.00
AAFT Fernando Tatis Jr. 75.00 200.00
AAGL Gavin Lux 25.00 60.00
AAJL Jesus Luzardo 6.00 15.00
AAJR Jake Rogers 3.00 8.00
AAJS Jorge Soler 5.00 12.00
AAKH Kyle Hendricks 15.00 40.00
AAKL Kyle Lewis 40.00 100.00
AALA Logan Allen 3.00 8.00
AALB Lou Brock 25.00 60.00
AALG Lucas Giolito 10.00 25.00
AALR Luis Robert 125.00 300.00
AALW Logan Webb 4.00 10.00
AAMD Mauricio Dubon 4.00 10.00
AAMK Max Kepler 4.00 10.00
AAMS Mike Soroka 15.00 40.00
AAMY Mike Yastrzemski 20.00 50.00
AANH Nico Hoerner 12.00 30.00
AANS Nick Solak 5.00 12.00
AARG Robel Garcia 3.00 8.00
AARH Rhys Hoskins 12.00 30.00
AASB Seth Brown 3.00 8.00
AASM Sean Murphy 5.00 12.00
AATA Tim Anderson 8.00 20.00
AATG Trent Grisham 10.00 25.00
AAWC Willson Contreras 6.00 15.00
AAWM Whit Merrifield 6.00 15.00
AAYA Yordan Alvarez 25.00 60.00
AAYG Yasmani Grandal 3.00 8.00
AABRO Brendan Rodgers 5.00 12.00
AADMU Dale Murphy 12.00 30.00
AADST Darryl Strawberry 15.00 40.00
AAJAY Jaylin Davis 5.00 12.00
AAJCA Jose Canseco 15.00 40.00
AAJFL Jack Flaherty 12.00 30.00
AAJMA Juan Marichal 12.00 30.00
AAJMC Jeff McNeil 10.00 25.00
AAJRI Jim Rice 12.00 30.00
AAJSO Juan Soto 50.00 120.00
AAJTR J.T. Realmuto 12.00 30.00
AAJVA Jason Varitek 20.00 50.00
AAKHI Keston Hiura 10.00 25.00
AAMMU Max Muncy 8.00 20.00
AANSE Nick Senzel 8.00 20.00
AAPCO Patrick Corbin 4.00 10.00
AAWCL Will Clark 20.00 50.00

2020 Topps Museum Collection Archival Autographs Copper

AAAR Austin Riley 20.00 50.00
AACF Carlton Fisk 20.00 50.00
AAGT Gleyber Torres 40.00 100.00
AAJA Jose Altuve 5.00 12.00
AAMK Max Kepler 12.00 30.00
AAPA Pete Alonso 40.00 100.00
AARA Roberto Alomar 20.00 50.00
AARC Rod Carew 15.00 40.00
AASC Steve Carlton 15.00 40.00
AAVG Vladimir Guerrero Jr. 30.00 80.00
AADMA Don Mattingly 30.00 80.00
AAJSM John Smoltz 25.00 60.00
AAPET Andy Pettitte 20.00 50.00
AARAJ Ronald Acuna Jr. 50.00 120.00
AATGL Tom Glavine 20.00 50.00

2020 Topps Museum Collection Archival Autographs Gold

*GOLD/25: .6X TO 1.5X BASIC
STATED ODDS 1: HOBBY
STATED PRINT RUN 25 SER.#'d SETS
EXCHANGE DEADLINE 5/31/22
AAI Ichiro 10.00 25.00
AAAR Austin Riley 25.00 60.00
AAKB Kris Bryant 40.00 100.00
AAMK Max Kepler 15.00 40.00
AAMTR Mike Trout 400.00 800.00

2020 Topps Museum Collection Canvas Collection Reprints

STATED ODDS 1:4 HOBBY
CCR1 Juan Soto 3.00 8.00
CCR2 Mookie Betts 5.00 12.00
CCR3 Mike Trout 5.00 12.00
CCR4 Vladimir Guerrero Jr. 2.00 5.00
CCR5 Ronald Acuna Jr. 4.00 10.00
CCR6 Don Mattingly 6.00 15.00
CCR7 Ernie Banks 4.00 10.00
CCR8 Jacob deGrom 1.00 2.50
CCR9 Gleyber Torres 8.00 20.00
CCR10 Max Scherzer 1.00 2.50
CCR11 Paul Goldschmidt 1.00 2.50
CCR12 Christian Yelich 1.25 3.00
CCR13 Ken Griffey Jr. 8.00 20.00
CCR14 Ty Cobb 8.00 20.00
CCR15 Gerrit Cole 6.00 15.00
CCR16 Rod Carew .75 2.00
CCR17 Frank Thomas 1.00 2.50
CCR18 Cody Bellinger 2.00 5.00
CCR19 Pete Alonso 2.50 6.00
CCR20 Bryce Harper 10.00 25.00
CCR21 Rafael Devers 8.00 20.00
CCR22 Cal Ripken Jr. 5.00 12.00
CCR23 Yordan Alvarez 3.00 8.00
CCR24 Anthony Rendon 10.00 25.00
CCR25 Eloy Jimenez 4.00 10.00
CCR26 Roberto Clemente 6.00 15.00
CCR27 Mike Piazza 6.00 15.00
CCR28 Gavin Lux 4.00 10.00
CCR29 Albert Pujols 1.25 3.00
CCR30 Bo Bichette 10.00 25.00
CCR31 Willie Mays 5.00 12.00
CCR32 Fernando Tatis Jr. 4.00 10.00
CCR33 Shohei Ohtani 1.25 3.00
CCR34 Andre Dawson .75 2.00
CCR35 Ryne Sandberg 2.00 5.00
CCR36 Anthony Rizzo 1.50 4.00
CCR37 Ichiro 5.00 12.00
CCR38 Hank Aaron 5.00 12.00
CCR39 Reggie Jackson 4.00 10.00
CCR40 Ozzie Smith 4.00 10.00
CCR41 Roberto Alomar .75 2.00
CCR42 Nolan Arenado 4.00 10.00
CCR43 Keston Hiura 5.00 12.00
CCR44 Francisco Lindor 5.00 12.00
CCR45 Mike Schmidt 5.00 12.00
CCR46 Wade Boggs 5.00 12.00
CCR47 Luis Robert 15.00 40.00
CCR48 Lou Gehrig 2.00 5.00
CCR49 Jackie Robinson 5.00 12.00
CCR50 Gary Carter 4.00 10.00

2020 Topps Museum Collection Dual Meaningful Material Relics

STATED ODDS 1: HOBBY
STATED PRINT RUN 50 SER.#'d SETS
DMRAC C.Correa/J.Altuve 6.00 15.00
DMRAM A.Pujols/M.Cabrera 10.00 25.00
DMRAS N.Arenado/T.Story 12.00 30.00
DMRBC W.Contreras/J.Baez 10.00 25.00
DMRBD X.Bogaerts/R.Devers 12.00 30.00
DMRBR K.Bryant/A.Rizzo 10.00 25.00
DMRBS A.Bregman/G.Springer 6.00 15.00
DMRFO F.Freeman/O.Albies 8.00 20.00
DMRGA J.Gallo/E.Andrus 6.00 15.00
DMRGB V.Guerrero Jr./B.Bichette 10.00 25.00
DMRHB B.Harper/K.Bryant 10.00 25.00
DMRMM R.Acuna Jr./M.Trout 30.00 80.00
DMROB M.Betts/D.Ortiz 12.00 30.00
DMROP D.Ortiz/D.Pedroia 6.00 15.00
DMRSC L.Severino/A.Chapman 6.00 15.00
DMRSL S.Strasburg/M.Scherzer 6.00 15.00
DMRST T.Turner/S.Strasburg 6.00 15.00
DMRTA G.Torres/M.Andujar 12.00 30.00
DMRTH B.Harper/M.Trout 30.00 80.00
DMRVG J.Votto/S.Gray 10.00 25.00
DMRBAL A.Bregman/J.Altuve 6.00 15.00
DMRBAR C.Archer/J.Bell 5.00 12.00
DMRBBU C.Bellinger/W.Buehler 20.00 50.00
DMRHVO D.Vogelbach/M.Haniger 12.00 30.00
DMRKSA M.Sano/M.Kepler 5.00 12.00
DMRMBO X.Bogaerts/J.Martinez 6.00 15.00
DMRPLO B.Posey/E.Longoria 8.00 20.00
DMRPSA C.Sabathia/A.Pettitte 5.00 12.00
DMRSCO M.Conforto/N.Syndergaard 5.00 12.00
DMRVTJ V.Guerrero Jr./F.Tatis Jr. 30.00 80.00

2020 Topps Museum Collection Dual Meaningful Material Relics Copper

*COPPER/35: .4X TO 1X BASIC
STATED ODDS 1: HOBBY
STATED PRINT RUN 35 SER.#'d SETS
DMRAS N.Arenado/T.Story 25.00 60.00
DMRSL S.Strasburg/M.Scherzer 15.00 40.00
DMRKSA M.Sano/M.Kepler 12.00 30.00
DMRMBO X.Bogaerts/J.Martinez 12.00 30.00
DMRPSA C.Sabathia/A.Pettitte 12.00 30.00

2020 Topps Museum Collection Meaningful Material Relics

STATED ODDS 1: HOBBY
STATED PRINT RUN 50 SER.#'d SETS
MMRAB Andrew Benintendi 5.00 12.00
MMRAC Aroldis Chapman 5.00 12.00
MMRAM Andrew McCutchen 12.00 30.00
MMRAR Austin Riley 8.00 20.00
MMRBC Brandon Crawford 4.00 10.00
MMRBH Bryce Harper 8.00 20.00
MMRBN Brandon Nimmo 4.00 10.00
MMRBP Buster Posey 6.00 15.00
MMRCA Chris Archer 3.00 8.00
MMRCB Cody Bellinger 10.00 25.00
MMRCC Carlos Correa 5.00 12.00
MMRCP Chris Paddack 5.00 12.00
MMRCS CC Sabathia 4.00 10.00
MMRCT Chris Taylor 4.00 10.00
MMRCY Christian Yelich 6.00 15.00
MMRDO David Ortiz 5.00 12.00
MMRDS Dansby Swanson 5.00 12.00
MMREL Evan Longoria 4.00 10.00
MMRFF Freddie Freeman 6.00 15.00
MMRFH Felix Hernandez 6.00 15.00
MMRJB Jackie Bradley Jr. 5.00 12.00
MMRJG Joey Gallo 5.00 12.00
MMRJH Jason Heyward 4.00 10.00
MMRJM Joe Mauer 4.00 10.00
MMRJS Jeff Samardzija 3.00 8.00
MMRJV Craig Kimbrel 4.00 10.00
MMRKK Kevin Kiermaier 4.00 10.00
MMRKM Kenta Maeda 4.00 10.00
MMRKW Kolten Wong 6.00 15.00
MMRKY Kirby Yates 3.00 8.00
MMRLS Luis Severino 4.00 10.00
MMRLV Luke Voit 6.00 15.00
MMRMA Miguel Andujar 5.00 12.00
MMRMB Mookie Betts 10.00 25.00
MMRMC Miguel Cabrera 5.00 12.00
MMRMF Max Fried 10.00 25.00
MMRMT Mike Trout 25.00 60.00
MMRNA Nolan Arenado 6.00 15.00
MMROA Ozzie Albies 5.00 12.00
MMRRB Ryan Braun 6.00 15.00
MMRRD Rafael Devers 6.00 15.00
MMRRO Rougned Odor 4.00 10.00
MMRRZ Ryan Zimmerman 8.00 20.00
MMRSC Shin-Soo Choo 4.00 10.00
MMRSS Stephen Strasburg 5.00 12.00
MMRTM Trey Mancini 5.00 12.00
MMRTT Trea Turner 4.00 10.00
MMRXB Xander Bogaerts 5.00 12.00
MMRYK Yusei Kikuchi 4.00 10.00
MMRAAQ Aristides Aquino 6.00 15.00
MMRABR Alex Bregman 5.00 12.00
MMRAHI Aaron Hicks 4.00 10.00
MMRAME Austin Meadows 4.00 10.00
MMRAMO Adalberto Mondesi 5.00 12.00
MMRANO Aaron Nola 10.00 25.00
MMRARO Amed Rosario 4.00 10.00
MMRBCR Brandon Crawford 4.00 10.00
MMRBLO Brandon Lowe 5.00 12.00
MMRBRO Brendan Rodgers 5.00 12.00
MMRCBL Charlie Blackmon 5.00 12.00
MMRCCA Carlos Carrasco 3.00 8.00
MMRCCS CC Sabathia 4.00 10.00
MMRCHA Matt Chapman 5.00 12.00
MMRCKE Clayton Kershaw 10.00 25.00
MMRDDA David Dahl 3.00 8.00
MMRDHU Dakota Hudson 4.00 10.00
MMRDJ1 DJ LeMahieu 5.00 12.00
MMRDJL DJ LeMahieu 5.00 12.00
MMRDO1 David Ortiz 5.00 12.00
MMRDPD Dustin Pedroia 5.00 12.00
MMRDPE Dustin Pedroia 5.00 12.00
MMRDPR David Price 4.00 10.00
MMRDSM Dominic Smith 5.00 12.00
MMREAN Elvis Andrus 4.00 10.00
MMRELO Evan Longoria 4.00 10.00
MMRESU Eugenio Suarez 4.00 10.00
MMRFFR Freddie Freeman 6.00 15.00
MMRFTJ Fernando Tatis Jr. 20.00 50.00
MMRGM1 German Marquez 5.00 12.00
MMRGSA Gary Sanchez 5.00 12.00
MMRGSP George Springer 4.00 10.00
MMRGTO Gleyber Torres 10.00 25.00
MMRGUR Gio Urshela 5.00 12.00
MMRHDO Hunter Dozier 3.00 8.00
MMRHRY Justus Sheffield 5.00 12.00
MMRJAL Jose Altuve 4.00 10.00
MMRJAR Jake Arrieta 4.00 10.00
MMRJBA Javier Baez 6.00 15.00
MMRJBE Josh Bell 4.00 10.00
MMRJBI Jose Berrios 4.00 10.00
MMRJBR Jackie Bradley Jr. 5.00 12.00
MMRJFL Jack Flaherty 4.00 10.00
MMRJHA Josh Hader 3.00 8.00
MMRJHI Jordan Hicks 4.00 10.00
MMRJLE Jon Lester 4.00 10.00
MMRJLU Joey Lucchesi 3.00 8.00
MMRJMC Jeff McNeil 4.00 10.00
MMRJMR J.D. Martinez 5.00 12.00
MMRJPD Joc Pederson 4.00 10.00
MMRJPO Jorge Polanco 4.00 10.00
MMRJRA Jose Ramirez 4.00 10.00
MMRJSE Jean Segura 6.00 15.00
MMRJTA Jameson Taillon 4.00 10.00
MMRJTR J.T. Realmuto 6.00 15.00
MMRJVR Justin Verlander 5.00 12.00
MMRKDA Khris Davis 5.00 12.00
MMRKHI Keston Hiura 6.00 15.00
MMRKSE Kyle Seager 3.00 8.00
MMRLC1 Lorenzo Cain 3.00 8.00
MMRLCA Lorenzo Cain 3.00 8.00
MMRLG1 Lourdes Gurriel Jr. 4.00 10.00
MMRLGU Lourdes Gurriel Jr. 4.00 10.00
MMRMBE Mookie Betts 10.00 25.00
MMRMCA Miguel Cabrera 5.00 12.00
MMRMCN Michael Conforto 4.00 10.00
MMRMFO Mike Foltynewicz 3.00 8.00
MMRMGA Mitch Garver 3.00 8.00
MMRMHA Mitch Haniger 4.00 10.00
MMRMMI Miles Mikolas 3.00 8.00
MMRMS1 Miguel Sano 4.00 10.00
MMRMSA Miguel Sano 4.00 10.00
MMRMSC Max Scherzer 5.00 12.00
MMRMSE Marcus Semien 3.00 8.00
MMRMSO Mike Soroka 10.00 25.00
MMRMST Marcus Stroman 4.00 10.00
MMRMT1 Mike Trout 25.00 60.00
MMRMTA Masahiro Tanaka 6.00 15.00
MMRNSE Nick Senzel 5.00 12.00
MMROME Oscar Mercado 4.00 10.00
MMRRAJ Ronald Acuna Jr. 20.00 50.00
MMRRHO Rhys Hoskins 6.00 15.00
MMRRLA Ramon Laureano 8.00 20.00
MMRSGA Sonny Gray 4.00 10.00
MMRSKI Scott Kingery 4.00 10.00
MMRSST Stephen Strasburg 5.00 12.00
MMRTEX Mark Teixeira 4.00 10.00
MMRTGL Tyler Glasnow 3.00 8.00
MMRTMA Trey Mancini 5.00 12.00
MMRTSO Trevor Story 5.00 12.00
MMRTST Trevor Story 5.00 12.00
MMRVGJ Vladimir Guerrero Jr. 10.00 25.00
MMRWAS Willians Astudillo 3.00 8.00
MMRWMR Whit Merrifield 5.00 12.00
MMRWSM Will Smith 6.00 15.00
MMRYGU Yuli Gurriel 10.00 25.00
MMRGSA1 Gary Sanchez 5.00 12.00
MMRJMC1 Jeff McNeil 4.00 10.00
MMRLCAS Luis Castillo 4.00 10.00
MMRMCH1 Michael Chavis 4.00 10.00

2020 Topps Museum Collection Meaningful Material Relics Copper

*COPPER/35: .4X TO 1X BASIC
STATED ODDS 1: HOBBY
STATED PRINT RUN 35 SER.#'d SETS
MMRDS Dansby Swanson 12.00 30.00
MMRJG Joey Gallo 10.00 25.00
MMRJM Joe Mauer 12.00 30.00
MMRKW Kolten Wong 8.00 20.00
MMRMF Max Fried 12.00 30.00
MMROA Ozzie Albies 10.00 25.00
MMRRB Ryan Braun 8.00 20.00
MMRCBL Charlie Blackmon 10.00 25.00
MMRCCA Carlos Carrasco 8.00 20.00
MMRCHA Matt Chapman 15.00 40.00
MMRJLE Jon Lester 10.00 25.00
MMRRHO Rhys Hoskins 12.00 30.00

2020 Topps Museum Collection Meaningful Material Relics Gold

*GOLD/25: .5X TO 1.2X BASIC
STATED ODDS 1: HOBBY
STATED PRINT RUN 25 SER.#'d SETS
MMRAM Andrew McCutchen 25.00 60.00
MMRDS Dansby Swanson 15.00 40.00
MMRJG Joey Gallo 12.00 30.00
MMRJM Joe Mauer 15.00 40.00
MMRKW Kolten Wong 10.00 25.00
MMRMF Max Fried 15.00 40.00
MMROA Ozzie Albies 12.00 30.00
MMRRB Ryan Braun 10.00 25.00
MMRCBL Charlie Blackmon 12.00 30.00
MMRCCA Carlos Carrasco 10.00 25.00
MMRCHA Matt Chapman 20.00 50.00
MMRJLE Jon Lester 15.00 40.00
MMRRHO Rhys Hoskins 15.00 40.00

2020 Topps Museum Collection Primary Pieces Four Player Quad Relics

FPRAAJM Andrsn/Jimnz/Abru/Moncda 10.00 25.00
FPRAFAS Albes/Freman/Acuna/Swnsn 15.00 40.00
FPRASBD Dahl/Story/Arnado/Blkmn 6.00 15.00
FPRBACS Corra/Sprngr/Altve/Brgmn 5.00 12.00
FPRBASV Sprngr/Altve/Brgmn/Vrlndr 5.00 12.00
FPRBBTA Tailln/Rynlds/Bell/Archr 4.00 10.00
FPRCGSB Sano/Cruz/Berios/Grvr 5.00 12.00
FPRCOML Manea/Chpmn/Olsn/Lzrdo 6.00 15.00
FPRDASC dGrm/Syndrgrd/Alnso/Cnfrto 12.00 30.00
FPRGACO Gallo/Choo/Andrus/Odor 5.00 12.00
FPRGBBG GureroJr. Bchtte/Bigio/GurielJr. 15.00 40.00
FPRHHNM Hskns/Hrpr/Nola/Relmto 8.00 20.00
FPRJTSL LeMahu/Tores/Stntn/Judge 12.00 30.00
FPRKBBS Seagr/Belli/Krshw/Buhlr 10.00 25.00
FPRLRSR Santna/Lndor/Rmirz/Reyes 5.00 12.00
FPRMBDB Mrtnz/Devrs/Bentndi/Bgarts 6.00 15.00
FPRMSMP Perz/Mondsi/Solr/Merifield 5.00 12.00
FPRMTPM TatisJr./Machdo/Myrs/Padak 20.00 50.00
FPRRBBC Rizzo/Baez/Contreras/Bryant 8.00 20.00
FPRRBBS Rizzo/Schwrbr/Bryant/Baez 8.00 20.00
FPRSAGT Soto/AcunaJr. GureroJr./TatisJr. 100.00 250.00
FPRSBDM Mrtnez/Devers/Bogarts/Sale 6.00 15.00
FPRSSST Schrzr/Soto/Strsbrg/Turnr 15.00 40.00
FPRTPOU Upton/Pujols/Ohtani/Trout 25.00 60.00
FPRVSAS Votto/Senzl/Suarez/Aquino 6.00 15.00
FPRYGFD DeJng/Flhrty Gldschmdt/Molina 5.00 12.00
FPRYHCB Cain/Hiura/Yelich/Braun 6.00 15.00
FPRZSTR Zimermn/Turnr/Robls/Strsbrg 6.00 15.00

2020 Topps Museum Collection Primary Pieces Four Player Quad Relics Gold

*GOLD/25: .8X TO 2X BASIC
STATED ODDS 1:1221 HOBBY
STATED PRINT RUN 25 SER.#'d SETS
FPRIMTO Ohtani/Ichiro/Matsui/Tanaka 75.00 200.00

2020 Topps Museum Collection Primary Pieces Quad Relics

STATED ODDS 1: HOBBY
STATED PRINT RUN 99 SER.#'d SETS
SPQRAB Andrew Benintendi 8.00 20.00
SPQRAC Aroldis Chapman 8.00 20.00
SPQRAJ Aaron Judge 20.00 50.00
SPQRAM Andrew McCutchen 10.00 25.00
SPQRAP Albert Pujols 8.00 20.00
SPQRAR Anthony Rizzo 12.00 30.00
SPQRBC Brandon Crawford 8.00 20.00
SPQRBH Bryce Harper 20.00 50.00
SPQRBP Buster Posey 8.00 20.00
SPQRCA Chris Archer 2.50 6.00
SPQRCB Charlie Blackmon 8.00 20.00
SPQRCC Carlos Correa 8.00 20.00
SPQRCK Clayton Kershaw 8.00 20.00
SPQRCS Chris Sale 4.00 10.00
SPQRCY Christian Yelich 10.00 25.00
SPQRDP David Price 3.00 8.00
SPQRDS Dansby Swanson 8.00 20.00
SPQREA Elvis Andrus 3.00 8.00
SPQREL Evan Longoria 5.00 12.00
SPQRFF Freddie Freeman 5.00 12.00
SPQRGS George Springer 3.00 8.00
SPQRJA Jose Abreu 4.00 10.00
SPQRJB Javier Baez 5.00 12.00
SPQRJG Joey Gallo 4.00 10.00
SPQRJH Jason Heyward 8.00 20.00
SPQRJL Jon Lester 3.00 8.00
SPQRJM J.D. Martinez 4.00 10.00
SPQRJR Jose Ramirez 8.00 20.00
SPQRJS Lourdes Gurriel Jr. 3.00 8.00
SPQRJU Justin Upton 3.00 8.00
SPQRKK Kevin Kiermaier 3.00 8.00
SPQRKW Kolten Wong 8.00 20.00
SPQRLS Luis Severino 3.00 8.00
SPQRMA Miguel Andujar 4.00 10.00
SPQRMC Miguel Cabrera 8.00 20.00
SPQRMH Mitch Haniger 6.00 15.00
SPQRMS Marcus Stroman 3.00 8.00
SPQRMT Mike Trout 25.00 60.00
SPQRNA Nolan Arenado 5.00 12.00
SPQROA Ozzie Albies 8.00 20.00
SPQRPD Paul DeJong 4.00 10.00
SPQRPG Paul Goldschmidt 8.00 20.00
SPQRRB Ryan Braun 3.00 8.00
SPQRRD Rafael Devers 5.00 12.00
SPQRRH Rhys Hoskins 8.00 20.00
SPQRRZ Ryan Zimmerman 3.00 8.00
SPQRSC Shin-Soo Choo 3.00 8.00
SPQRSG Sonny Gray 10.00 25.00
SPQRSM Starling Marte 3.00 8.00
SPQRSS Stephen Strasburg 6.00 15.00
SPQRTM Trey Mancini 4.00 10.00
SPQRTS Trevor Story 4.00 10.00
SPQRTT Trea Turner 3.00 8.00
SPQRVR Victor Robles 5.00 12.00
SPQRXB Xander Bogaerts 4.00 10.00
SPQRYG Yuli Gurriel 3.00 8.00
SPQRYK Yusei Kikuchi 3.00 8.00
SPQRABR Alex Bregman 4.00 10.00
SPQRAME Austin Meadows 6.00 15.00
SPQRAMO Adalberto Mondesi 4.00 10.00
SPQRBLO Brandon Lowe 4.00 10.00
SPQRCBE Cody Bellinger 15.00 40.00
SPQRCPA Chris Paddack 4.00 10.00
SPQRCSA Carlos Santana 3.00 8.00
SPQRDJL DJ LeMahieu 10.00 25.00
SPQRDPE Dustin Pedroia 10.00 25.00
SPQRGSA Gary Sanchez 6.00 15.00
SPQRJAL Jose Altuve 3.00 8.00
SPQRJHA Josh Hader 2.50 6.00
SPQRJMA Joe Mauer 10.00 25.00
SPQRJMc Jeff McNeil 8.00 20.00
SPQRJTA Jameson Taillon 3.00 8.00
SPQRKHI Keston Hiura 8.00 20.00
SPQRLCA Lorenzo Cain 2.50 6.00
SPQRMCA Matt Carpenter 4.00 10.00
SPQRMCH Michael Chavis 3.00 8.00
SPQRMCO Michael Conforto 3.00 8.00
SPQRMSA Miguel Sano 3.00 8.00
SPQRMSC Max Scherzer 6.00 15.00
SPQRMSO Mike Soroka 10.00 25.00
SPQRMTA Masahiro Tanaka 4.00 10.00

2020 Topps Museum Collection Primary Pieces Quad Relics Copper

*COPPER/75: .4X TO 1X BASIC
STATED ODDS 1:15 HOBBY
STATED PRINT RUN 75 SER.#'d SETS
SPQRRA Ronald Acuna Jr. 15.00 40.00

2020 Topps Museum Collection Primary Pieces Quad Relics Gold

*GOLD/25: .6X TO 1.5X BASIC
STATED ODDS 1:43 HOBBY
STATED PRINT RUN 25 SER.#'d SETS
SPQRMT Mike Trout 75.00 200.00
SPQRRA Ronald Acuna Jr. 75.00 200.00

2020 Topps Museum Collection Primary Pieces Quad Relics Legends

STATED ODDS 1: HOBBY
STATED PRINT RUN 50 SER.#'d SETS
SPQLBL Barry Larkin 12.00 30.00
SPQLCR Cal Ripken Jr. 30.00 80.00
SPQLCY Carl Yastrzemski 25.00 60.00
SPQLDM Don Mattingly 25.00 60.00
SPQLEM Eddie Mathews 20.00 50.00
SPQLFT Frank Thomas 20.00 50.00
SPQLGB George Brett 30.00 80.00
SPQLJB Johnny Bench 25.00 60.00
SPQLKG Ken Griffey Jr. 30.00 80.00
SPQLMP Mark McGwire 20.00 50.00
SPQLNR Nolan Ryan 25.00 60.00
SPQLOS Ozzie Smith 20.00 50.00
SPQLPM Pedro Martinez 6.00 15.00
SPQLRH Rickey Henderson 25.00 60.00
SPQLRJ Reggie Jackson 15.00 40.00
SPQLRY Robin Yount 15.00 40.00
SPQLTG Tony Gwynn 15.00 40.00
SPQLTS Tom Seaver 15.00 40.00
SPQLTW Ted Williams 50.00 120.00
SPQLWB Wade Boggs 25.00 60.00
SPQLBRO Brooks Robinson 40.00 100.00
SPQLJMO Joe Morgan 10.00 25.00
SPQLKGJ Ken Griffey Jr. 50.00 120.00
SPQLRCL Roger Clemens 15.00 40.00
SPQLRHO Willie McCovey 15.00 40.00
SPQLRJA Reggie Jackson 15.00 40.00
SPQLRJO Randy Johnson 12.00 30.00

2020 Topps Museum Collection Signature Swatches Dual Relic Autographs

STATED ODDS 1: HOBBY
PRINT RUNS B/WN 99-299 COPIES PER
EXCHANGE DEADLINE 5/31/22
SSDAAH Aaron Hicks 5.00 12.00
SSDAAM Austin Meadows 5.00 12.00
SSDAAN Aaron Nola 12.00 30.00
SSDABN Nico Hoerner 15.00 40.00
SSDABW Brandon Woodruff 4.00 10.00
SSDACP Chris Paddack 10.00 25.00
SSDADL DJ LeMahieu 30.00 80.00
SSDAEJ Eloy Jimenez 20.00 50.00
SSDAES Eugenio Suarez 12.00 30.00
SSDAGS Gary Sheffield 10.00 25.00
SSDAHD Hunter Dozier 4.00 10.00
SSDAHK Howie Kendrick 4.00 10.00
SSDAJA Keston Hiura 10.00 25.00
SSDAJB Jose Berrios 5.00 12.00
SSDAJH Josh Hader 4.00 10.00
SSDAJP Jorge Polanco 6.00 15.00
SSDAJS Cavan Biggio 12.00 30.00
SSDAKH Kyle Hendricks 10.00 25.00
SSDAKY Kirby Yates 4.00 10.00
SSDALC Luis Castillo 5.00 12.00
SSDALG Lourdes Gurriel Jr. 5.00 12.00
SSDALV Luke Voit 25.00 60.00
SSDAMG Mitch Garver 4.00 10.00
SSDAMH Mitch Haniger 5.00 12.00
SSDAMK Max Kepler 5.00 12.00
SSDAMM Max Muncy 8.00 20.00
SSDAMS Mike Soroka 15.00 40.00
SSDANA Nolan Arenado EXCH 30.00 80.00
SSDANS Nick Solak 6.00 15.00
SSDAPC Patrick Corbin 5.00 12.00
SSDAPD Paul DeJong 6.00 15.00
SSDARH Ryan Howard 10.00 25.00
SSDARL Ramon Laureano 10.00 25.00
SSDASG Sonny Gray 10.00 25.00
SSDASM Sean Murphy 6.00 15.00
SSDATA Tim Anderson 12.00 30.00
SSDATE Tommy Edman 10.00 25.00
SSDATP Tommy Pham 4.00 10.00
SSDAVR Victor Robles 8.00 20.00
SSDAYG Yuli Gurriel 10.00 25.00
SSDALGI Lucas Giolito 8.00 20.00
SSDASGR Shawn Green 8.00 20.00
SSDAWSM Will Smith 10.00 25.00
SSDAYGR Yasmani Grandal 4.00 10.00

2020 Topps Museum Collection Signature Swatches Dual Relic Autographs Copper

*COPPER/50: .5X TO 1.2X BASIC
STATED ODDS 1: HOBBY
STATED PRINT RUN 50 SER.#'d SETS
EXCHANGE DEADLINE 5/31/22
SSDAAJ Andruw Jones 20.00 50.00
SSDAJM J.D. Martinez 15.00 40.00
SSDATL Tim Lincecum 25.00 60.00
SSDATM Trey Mancini 12.00 30.00
SSDAGSP George Springer 10.00 25.00
SSDAJLU Jesus Luzardo 10.00 25.00
SSDAJMA Joe Mauer 20.00 50.00
SSDASMA Sean Manaea 5.00 12.00

2020 Topps Museum Collection Signature Swatches Dual Relic Autographs Gold

*GOLD/25: .6X TO 1.5X BASIC
STATED ODDS 1: HOBBY
STATED PRINT RUN 25 SER.#'d SETS
EXCHANGE DEADLINE 5/31/22
SSDADG Didi Gregorius 10.00 25.00
SSDAWM Whit Merrifield 10.00 25.00

2020 Topps Museum Collection Signature Swatches Triple Relic Autographs

COMMON CARD p/r 99-299 4.00 10.00
SEMISTARS p/r 99-299 5.00 12.00
UNLISTED STARS p/r 99-299 6.00 15.00
COMMON CARD p/r 50 5.00 12.00
SEMISTARS p/r 50 6.00 15.00
UNLISTED STARS p/r 50 8.00 20.00
STATED ODDS 1: HOBBY
PRINT RUNS B/WN 50-299 COPIES PER
EXCHANGE DEADLINE 5/31/22
SSTAAA Aristides Aquino 15.00 40.00
SSTABB Byron Buxton 5.00 12.00
SSTABR Brendan Rodgers 6.00 15.00
SSTACB Charlie Blackmon 15.00 40.00
SSTACF Clint Frazier 10.00 25.00
SSTACS Chris Sale 15.00 40.00
SSTAJd Jacob deGrom, 10.00 25.00
SSTAJF Jack Flaherty 12.00 30.00
SSTAJG Juan Gonzalez 10.00 25.00
SSTAJR Jose Ramirez 10.00 25.00
SSTAJS Jorge Soler 8.00 20.00
SSTAJU Justin Upton 5.00 12.00
SSTALS Luis Severino 12.00 30.00
SSTAMA Miguel Andujar 10.00 25.00
SSTAMS Max Scherzer 30.00 80.00
SSTAPG Paul Goldschmidt 20.00 50.00
SSTARA Ronald Acuna Jr. 75.00 200.00
SSTARD Rafael Devers 15.00 40.00
SSTARH Rhys Hoskins 10.00 25.00
SSTATB Trevor Bauer 12.00 301.00
SSTAWC Willson Contreras 12.00 30.00
SSTAXB Xander Bogaerts 15.00 40.00
SSTAYA Yordan Alvarez 30.00 80.00
SSTAAMC Andrew McCutchen 30.00 80.00
SSTAARI Austin Riley 10.00 25.00
SSTACSA Carlos Santana 5.00 12.00
SSTAJSO Juan Soto 50.00 120.00
SSTAJTR J.T. Realmuto 12.00 30.00
SSTAMOZ Marcell Ozuna 20.00 50.00
SSTANSE Nick Senzel 10.00 25.00
SSTASSC Shin-Soo Choo 12.00 30.00

2020 Topps Museum Collection Signature Swatches Triple Relic Autographs Copper

*COPPER/50: .5X TO 1.2X p/r 99-299
*COPPER/25: .5X TO 1.2X p/r 50
STATED ODDS 1: HOBBY
PRINT RUNS B/WN 25-50 COPIES PER
EXCHANGE DEADLINE 5/31/22
SSTAAB Adrian Beltre 30.00 80.00
SSTAAR Anthony Rizzo 40.00 100.00
SSTABM Brendan McKay 10.00 25.00
SSTACY Christian Yelich 60.00 150.00
SSTAGL Gavin Lux 60.00 150.00
SSTAGS Gary Sanchez 25.00 60.00
SSTAJA Jose Altuve 20.00 50.00
SSTAMC Miguel Cabrera 50.00 120.00
SSTAMM Manny Machado 25.00 60.00
SSTAVG Vladimir Guerrero 20.00 50.00

2020 Topps Museum Collection Signature Swatches Triple Relic Autographs Gold

*GOLD/25: .6X TO 1.5X p/r 99-299
STATED ODDS 1: HOBBY
PRINT RUNS B/WN 5-25 COPIES PER
NO PRICING ON QTY 15 OR LESS
EXCHANGE DEADLINE 5/31/22

2020 Topps Museum Collection Superstar Showpieces Autographs

STATED ODDS 1:116 HOBBY
STATED PRINT RUN 25 SER.#'d SETS
SSAA Aristides Aquino 12.00 30.00
SSAR Anthony Rizzo 30.00 80.00
SSBB Bo Bichette 125.00 300.00
SSDM Don Mattingly 40.00 100.00
SSDO David Ortiz 40.00 100.00
SSEJ Eloy Jimenez 20.00 50.00
SSFT Frank Thomas 30.00 80.00
SSGL Gavin Lux 40.00 100.00
SSGS George Springer 15.00 40.00
SSGT Gleyber Torres 60.00 150.00
SSHM Hideki Matsui 40.00 100.00
SSJA Jose Altuve 15.00 40.00
SSJF Jack Flaherty 8.00 20.00
SSJV Joey Votto 25.00 60.00
SSKB Kris Bryant 60.00 150.00
SSMT Mike Trout 400.00 100.00
SSNH Nico Hoerner 25.00 60.00
SSOS Ozzie Smith 40.00 100.00
SSPA Pete Alonso 75.00 200.00
SSPG Paul Goldschmidt 20.00 50.00
SSRA Ronald Acuna Jr. 100.00 250.00
SSRD Rafael Devers
SSRH Rhys Hoskins 25.00 60.00
SSSO Shohei Ohtani 100.00 250.00
SSWC Will Clark 40.00 100.00
SSYA Yordan Alvarez 125.00 300.00
SSFTJ Fernando Tatis Jr. 125.00 300.00
SSJSO Juan Soto 75.00 200.00

1998 Topps Opening Day

COMPLETE SET (165) 20.00 50.00
*OPEN.DAY: .75X TO 2X BASIC TOPPS
ISSUED IN OPENING DAY PACKS

1999 Topps Opening Day

COMPLETE SET (165) 15.00 40.0
*OPEN.DAY: .75X TO 2X BASIC TOPPS
ISSUED IN OPENING DAY PACKS
AARON AUTO STATED ODDS 1:29,642
1 Hank Aaron 1.00 2.5
HA Hank Aaron AU 175.00 350.0

1999 Topps Opening Day Oversize

Randomly inserted one per retail box of 1999 Topp Opening Day base set, this three-card set features color player photos printed on 4 1/2" by 3 1/4" cards.

COMPLETE SET (3) 3.00 8.0
1 Sammy Sosa .50 1.2
2 Mark McGwire 1.25 3.0
3 Ken Griffey Jr. 1.00 2.5

2000 Topps Opening Day

COMPLETE SET (165) 15.00 40.0
*OPEN.DAY: .75X TO 2X BASIC TOPPS
ISSUED IN OPENING DAY PACKS
NO MM VARIATIONS IN OPENING DAY

2000 Topps Opening Day Autographs

Randomly inserted in packs, this insert set features autographs of five major league players. There were three levels of autographs. Level A were inserted int packs at one in 4207, Level B were inserted at one i 48074, Level C were inserted at one in 6280. Card backs carry an "ODA" prefix.

GROUP B STATED ODDS 1:48074
GROUP C STATED ODDS 1:6280
ODA1 Edgardo Alfonzo A 6.00 15.00
ODA2 Wade Boggs A 50.00 100.00
ODA3 Robin Ventura A 6.00 15.00
ODA4 Josh Hamilton 12.00 30.00
ODA5 Vernon Wells C 15.00 40.00

2001 Topps Opening Day

COMPLETE SET (165) 15.00 40.00
*OPEN.DAY: .75X TO 2X BASIC TOPPS
ISSUED IN OPENING DAY PACKS

2001 Topps Opening Day Autographs

Randomly inserted into packs, this 4-card insert set features authentic autographs from four of the Major League's top players. The set is broken down into four groups: Group A is Chipper Jones (1:31,680), Group B is Todd Helton (1:15,020), Group C is Magglio Ordonez (1:10,004), and Group D is Corey Patterson (1:5,940). Card backs carry an "ODA" prefix followed by the player's initials.

GROUP A ODDS 1:31,680
GROUP B ODDS 1:15,020
GROUP C ODDS 1:10,004
GROUP D ODDS 1:5,940
ODACJ Chipper Jones A 60.00 120.00
ODACP Corey Patterson D 10.00 25.00
ODAMO Magglio Ordonez C 10.00 24.00
ODATH Todd Helton B 12.00 30.00

2001 Topps Opening Day Stickers

Randomly inserted into packs at approximately one in two, this 30-card insert features stickers of all 30 Major League Franchises. Card backs are not numbered and are listed below in alphabetical order for convenience.

COMPLETE SET (30) 2.50 6.00
COMMON TEAM (1-30) .08 .25

2002 Topps Opening Day

COMPLETE SET (165) 15.00 40.00
*OPEN.DAY: .75X TO X2 BASIC TOPPS
ISSUED IN OPENING DAY PACKS

2002 Topps Opening Day Autographs

Randomly inserted into packs, these three cards feature autographs of players in the Opening Day set. These cards were all inserted at differening odds and we have notated that information next to the player's name.
GROUP A STATED ODDS 1:6069
GROUP B STATED ODDS 1:3036
GROUP C STATED ODDS 1:2014
NO PRICING DUE TO SCARCITY

2003 Topps Opening Day

COMPLETE SET (165) 15.00 40.00
*OPEN.DAY: .75X TO 2X BASIC TOPPS
ISSUED IN OPENING DAY PACKS

2003 Topps Opening Day Stickers

Issued one per pack, these 72 cards partially parallel the Opening Day set. Each of the fronts is designed exactly as the basic 2003 Topps card.
*OD STICKERS: 1.5X TO 4X BASIC TOPPS
ONE PER PACK
CARDS LISTED ALPHABETICALLY

2003 Topps Opening Day Autographs

Inserted at different odds depending on which group the players were assigned to, these cards feature authentic autographs of the featured players.
GROUP A ODDS 1:10,623
GROUP B ODDS 1:3539
GROUP C ODDS 1:2654
JD Johnny Damon B 15.00 40.00
LB Lance Berkman A 20.00 50.00
RF Rafael Furcal C 10.00 25.00

2004 Topps Opening Day

COMPLETE SET (165) 15.00 40.00
*OPEN.DAY 1-165: .75X TO 2X BASIC TOPPS
ISSUED IN OPENING DAY PACKS

2004 Topps Opening Day Autographs

STATED ODDS 1:629
AT Andres Torres 6.00 15.00
DW Dontrelle Willis 15.00 40.00
JD Jeff Duncan 6.00 15.00
JW Jerome Williams 6.00 15.00
RH Rich Harden 10.00 25.00
RW Ryan Wagner 6.00 15.00

2005 Topps Opening Day

This 165-card set was released early in 2005. The set features a mix of players from either series of the 2005 basic Topps set with the only difference being an opening day logo on the card.
COMPLETE SET (165) 15.00 40.00
COMMON CARD (1-165) .15 .40
ISSUED IN OPENING DAY PACKS
1 Alex Rodriguez .50 1.25
2 Placido Polanco .15 .40
3 Torii Hunter .15 .40
4 Lyle Overbay .15 .40
5 Johnny Damon .25 .60
6 Mike Cameron .15 .40
7 Ichiro Suzuki .50 1.25
8 Francisco Rodriguez .25 .60
9 Bobby Crosby .15 .40
10 Sammy Sosa .40 1.00
11 Randy Wolf .15 .40
12 Jason Bay .15 .40
13 Mike Lieberthal .15 .40
14 Paul Konerko .25 .60
15 Brian Giles .15 .40
16 Luis Gonzalez .15 .40
17 Jim Edmonds .25 .60
18 Carlos Lee .15 .40
19 Corey Patterson .15 .40
20 Hank Blalock .15 .40
21 Sean Casey .15 .40
22 Dmitri Young .15 .40
23 Mark Mulder .15 .40
24 Bobby Abreu .15 .40
25 Jim Thome .25 .60
26 Jason Kendall .15 .40
27 Jason Giambi .15 .40
28 Vinny Castilla .15 .40
29 Tony Batista .15 .40
30 Ivan Rodriguez .25 .60
31 Craig Biggio .25 .60
32 Chris Carpenter .25 .60
33 Adrian Beltre .40 1.00
34 Scott Podsednik .15 .40
35 Cliff Floyd .15 .40
36 Chad Tracy .15 .40
37 John Smoltz .40 1.00
38 Shingo Takatsu .15 .40
39 Jack Wilson .15 .40
40 Gary Sheffield .15 .40
41 Lance Berkman .25 .60
42 Carl Crawford .25 .60
43 Carlos Guillen .15 .40
44 David Bell .15 .40
45 Kazuo Matsui .15 .40
46 Jason Schmidt .15 .40
47 Jason Marquis .15 .40
48 Melvin Mora .15 .40
49 David Ortiz .40 1.00
50 Andruw Jones .15 .40
51 Miguel Tejada .25 .60
52 Bartolo Colon .15 .40
53 Derrek Lee .15 .40
54 Eric Gagne .15 .40
55 Miguel Cabrera .40 1.00
56 Travis Hafner .15 .40
57 Jose Valentin .15 .40
58 Mark Prior .25 .60
59 Phil Nevin .15 .40
60 Jose Vidro .15 .40
61 Khalil Greene .15 .40
62 Carlos Zambrano .25 .60
63 Erubiel Durazo .15 .40
64 Michael Young UER .15 .40
65 Woody Williams .15 .40
66 Edgardo Alfonzo .15 .40
67 Troy Glaus .15 .40
68 Garret Anderson .15 .40
69 Richie Sexson .15 .40
70 Curt Schilling .25 .60
71 Randy Johnson .40 1.00
72 Chipper Jones .40 1.00
73 J.D. Drew .15 .40
74 Russ Ortiz .15 .40
75 Frank Thomas .40 1.00
76 Jimmy Rollins .25 .60
77 Barry Zito .25 .60
78 Rafael Palmeiro .25 .60
79 Brad Wilkerson .15 .40
80 Adam Dunn .25 .60
81 Doug Mientkiewicz .15 .40
82 Manny Ramirez .40 1.00
83 Pedro Martinez .25 .60
84 Moises Alou .15 .40
85 Mike Sweeney .15 .40
86 Boston Red Sox WC .40 1.00
87 Matt Clement .15 .40
88 Nomar Garciaparra .25 .60
89 Magglio Ordonez .25 .60
90 Bret Boone .15 .40
91 Mark Loretta .15 .40
92 Jose Contreras .15 .40
93 Randy Winn .15 .40
94 Austin Kearns .15 .40
95 Ken Griffey Jr. .75 2.00
96 Jake Westbrook .15 .40
97 Kazuhito Tadano .15 .40
98 C.C. Sabathia .25 .60
99 Todd Helton .25 .60
100 Albert Pujols .50 1.25
101 Jose Molina .15 .40
Bengie Molina
102 Aaron Miles .15 .40
103 Mike Lowell .15 .40
104 Paul Lo Duca .15 .40
105 Juan Pierre .15 .40
106 Dontrelle Willis .15 .40
107 Jeff Bagwell .25 .60
108 Carlos Beltran .25 .60
109 Ronnie Belliard .15 .40
110 Roy Oswalt .25 .60
111 Zack Greinke .40 1.00
112 Steve Finley .15 .40
113 Kazuhisa Ishii .15 .40
114 Justin Morneau .25 .60
115 Ben Sheets .15 .40
116 Johan Santana .25 .60
117 Billy Wagner .15 .40
118 Mariano Rivera .50 1.25
119 Corey Koskie .15 .40
120 Akinori Otsuka .15 .40
121 Joe Mauer .30 .75
122 Jacque Jones .15 .40
123 Joe Nathan .15 .40
124 Nick Johnson .15 .40
125 Vernon Wells .15 .40
126 Mike Piazza .40 1.00
127 Jose Guillen .15 .40
128 Jose Reyes .25 .60
129 Marcus Giles .15 .40
130 Javy Lopez .15 .40
131 Kevin Millar .15 .40
132 Jorge Posada .25 .60
133 Carl Pavano .15 .40
134 Bernie Williams .25 .60
135 Kerry Wood .15 .40
136 Matt Holliday .40 1.00
137 Kevin Brown .15 .40
138 Derek Jeter 1.00 2.50
139 Barry Bonds .60 1.50
140 Jeff Kent .15 .40
141 Mark Kotsay .15 .40
142 Shawn Green .15 .40
143 Tim Hudson .25 .60
144 Shannon Stewart .15 .40
145 Pat Burrell .15 .40
146 Gavin Floyd .15 .40
147 Mike Mussina .25 .60
148 Eric Chavez .15 .40
149 Jon Lieber .15 .40
150 Vladimir Guerrero .25 .60
151 Vicente Padilla .15 .40
152 Ryan Klesko .15 .40
153 Jake Peavy .15 .40
154 Scott Rolen .25 .60
155 Greg Maddux .50 1.25
156 Edgar Renteria .15 .40
157 Larry Walker .25 .60
158 Scott Kazmir .40 1.00
159 B.J. Upton .25 .60
160 Mark Teixeira .25 .60
161 Ken Harvey .15 .40
162 Alfonso Soriano .25 .60
163 Carlos Delgado .15 .40
164 Alexis Rios .15 .40
165 Checklist .15 .40

2005 Topps Opening Day Chrome

*REF: .6X TO 1.5X BASIC
ODC1 Albert Pujols 1.25 3.00
ODC2 Alex Rodriguez 1.25 3.00
ODC3 Ivan Rodriguez .60 1.50
ODC4 Jim Thome .60 1.50
ODC5 Sammy Sosa 1.00 2.50
ODC6 Vladimir Guerrero .60 1.50
ODC7 Alfonso Soriano .60 1.50
ODC8 Ichiro Suzuki 1.25 3.00
ODC9 Derek Jeter 2.50 6.00
ODC10 Chipper Jones 1.00 2.50

2005 Topps Opening Day Autographs

GROUP A ODDS 1:852
GROUP B ODDS 1:1192
EXCHANGE DEADLINE 02/28/07
AH Aaron Hill B 4.00 10.00
AW Anthony Whittington A 4.00 10.00
CC Chad Cordero A 6.00 15.00
OQ Omar Quintanilla B 6.00 15.00
PM Paul Maholm A 4.00 10.00

2005 Topps Opening Day MLB Game Worn Jersey Collection

RANDOM INSERTS IN TARGET RETAIL
37 Vladimir Guerrero 3.00 8.00
38 Albert Pujols 6.00 15.00
39 Torii Hunter 2.00 5.00
40 Alfonso Soriano 2.00 5.00
41 Bobby Abreu 2.00 5.00
42 Moises Alou 2.00 5.00
43 Sean Burroughs 2.00 5.00
44 Shannon Stewart 2.00 5.00
45 Troy Glaus 2.00 5.00
46 Fernando Vina 2.00 5.00
47 Dan Wilson 2.00 5.00
48 Paul Konerko 2.00 5.00
49 Jimmy Rollins 2.00 5.00
50 Livan Hernandez 2.00 5.00
51 Sean Casey 2.00 5.00
52 Paul LoDuca 2.00 5.00
53 Richie Sexson 2.00 5.00
54 Aubrey Huff 2.00 5.00

2006 Topps Opening Day

This 165-card set was released in March, 2006. This set was issued six-card hobby and retail packs with an 99 cent SRP which came 36 packs to a box and 20 boxes to a case. Cards numbered 1-134 feature veterans while cards 135-164 feature players who qualified for the rookie card status in 2006.
COMPLETE SET (165) 15.00 40.00
COMMON CARD (1-165) .15 .40
OVERALL PLATE SER.1 ODDS 1:246 HTA
PLATE PRINT RUN 1 SET PER COLOR
BLACK-CYAN-MAGENTA-YELLOW ISSUED
NO PLATE PRICING DUE TO SCARCITY
1 Alex Rodriguez .50 1.25
2 Jhonny Peralta .15 .40
3 Garrett Atkins .15 .40
4 Vernon Wells .15 .40
5 Carl Crawford .25 .60
6 Josh Beckett .15 .40
7 Mickey Mantle 1.25 3.00
8 Willy Taveras .15 .40
9 Ivan Rodriguez .25 .60
10 Clint Barmes .15 .40
11 Jose Reyes .25 .60
12 Travis Hafner .15 .40
13 Tadahito Iguchi .15 .40
14 Barry Zito .25 .60
15 Brian Roberts .15 .40
16 David Wright .30 .75
17 Mark Teixeira .25 .60
18 Roy Halladay .25 .60
19 Scott Rolen .25 .60
20 Bobby Abreu .15 .40
21 Lance Berkman .25 .60
22 Moises Alou .15 .40
23 Chone Figgins .15 .40
24 Aaron Rowand .15 .40
25 Chipper Jones .40 1.00
26 Johnny Damon .25 .60
27 Matt Clement .15 .40
28 Nick Johnson .15 .40
29 Freddy Garcia .15 .40
30 Jon Garland .15 .40
31 Torii Hunter .15 .40
32 Mike Sweeney .15 .40
33 Mike Lieberthal .15 .40
34 Rafael Furcal .15 .40
35 Brad Wilkerson .15 .40
36 Brad Penny .15 .40
37 Jorge Cantu .15 .40
38 Paul Konerko .25 .60
39 Rickie Weeks .15 .40
40 Jorge Posada .25 .60
41 Albert Pujols .50 1.25
42 Zack Greinke .25 .60
43 Jimmy Rollins .25 .60
44 Mark Prior .25 .60
45 Greg Maddux .50 1.25
46 Jeff Francis .15 .40
47 Felipe Lopez .15 .40
48 Dan Johnson .15 .40
49 B.J. Ryan .15 .40
50 Manny Ramirez .40 1.00
51 Melvin Mora .15 .40
52 Javy Lopez .15 .40
53 Garret Anderson .15 .40
54 Jason Bay .15 .40
55 Joe Mauer .25 .60
56 C.C. Sabathia .25 .60
57 Bartolo Colon .15 .40
58 Ichiro Suzuki .50 1.25
59 Andruw Jones .15 .40
60 Rocco Baldelli .15 .40
61 Jeff Kent .15 .40
62 Cliff Floyd .15 .40
63 John Smoltz .40 1.00
64 Shawn Green .15 .40
65 Nomar Garciaparra .25 .60
66 Miguel Cabrera .40 1.00
67 Vladimir Guerrero .25 .60
68 Gary Sheffield .15 .40
69 Jake Peavy .15 .40
70 Carlos Lee .15 .40
71 Tom Glavine .25 .60
72 Craig Biggio .25 .60
73 Steve Finley .15 .40
74 Adrian Beltre .40 1.00
75 Eric Gagne .15 .40
76 Aubrey Huff .15 .40
77 Livan Hernandez .15 .40
78 Scott Podsednik .15 .40
79 Todd Helton .25 .60
80 Kerry Wood .15 .40
81 Randy Johnson .40 1.00
82 Huston Street .15 .40
83 Pedro Martinez .25 .60
84 Roger Clemens .50 1.25
85 Hank Blalock .15 .40
86 Carlos Beltran .25 .60
87 Chien-Ming Wang .25 .60
88 Rich Harden .15 .40
89 Mike Mussina .25 .60
90 Mark Buehrle .25 .60
91 Michael Young .15 .40
92 Mark Mulder .15 .40
93 Khalil Greene .15 .40
94 Johan Santana .25 .60
95 Andy Pettitte .25 .60
96 Derek Jeter 1.00 2.50
97 Jack Wilson .15 .40
98 Ben Sheets .15 .40
99 Miguel Tejada .25 .60
100 Barry Bonds .60 1.50
101 Dontrelle Willis .15 .40
102 Curt Schilling .25 .60
103 Jose Contreras .15 .40
104 Jeremy Bonderman .15 .40
105 David Ortiz .40 1.00
106 Lyle Overbay .15 .40
107 Robinson Cano .25 .60
108 Tim Hudson .25 .60
109 Paul Lo Duca .15 .40
110 Mariano Rivera .50 1.25
111 Derrek Lee .15 .40
112 Morgan Ensberg .15 .40
113 Wily Mo Pena .15 .40
114 Roy Oswalt .25 .60
115 Adam Dunn .25 .60
116 Hideki Matsui .40 1.00
117 Pat Burrell .15 .40
118 Jason Schmidt .15 .40
119 Alfonso Soriano .25 .60
120 Aramis Ramirez .15 .40
121 Jason Giambi .15 .40
122 Orlando Hernandez .15 .40
123 Magglio Ordonez .25 .60
124 Troy Glaus .15 .40
125 Carlos Delgado .15 .40
126 Kevin Millwood .15 .40
127 Shannon Stewart .15 .40
128 Luis Castillo .15 .40
129 Jim Edmonds .25 .60
130 Richie Sexson .15 .40
131 Dmitri Young .15 .40
132 Russ Adams .15 .40
133 Nick Swisher .25 .60
134 Jermaine Dye .15 .40
135 Anderson Hernandez (RC) .15 .40
136 Justin Huber (RC) .15 .40
137 Jason Botts (RC) .15 .40
138 Jeff Mathis (RC) .15 .40
139 Ryan Garko (RC) .15 .40
140 Charlton Jimerson (RC) .15 .40
141 Chris Denorfia (RC) .15 .40
142 Anthony Reyes (RC) .15 .40
143 Bryan Bullington (RC) .15 .40
144 Chuck James (RC) .15 .40
145 Danny Sandoval RC .15 .40
146 Walter Young (RC) .15 .40
147 Fausto Carmona (RC) .15 .40
148 Francisco Liriano (RC) .40 1.00
149 Hong-Chih Kuo (RC) .40 1.00
150 Joe Saunders (RC) .15 .40
151 John Koronka (RC) .15 .40
152 Robert Andino RC .15 .40
153 Shaun Marcum (RC) .15 .40
154 Tom Gorzelanny (RC) .15 .40
155 Craig Breslow RC .15 .40
156 Chris Demaria RC .15 .40
157 Brayan Pena (RC) .15 .40
158 Rich Hill (RC) .40 1.00
159 Rick Short (RC) .15 .40
160 Darrell Rasner (RC) .15 .40
161 C.J. Wilson (RC) .25 .60
162 Brandon Watson (RC) .15 .40
163 Paul McAnulty (RC) .15 .40
164 Marshall McDougall (RC) .15 .40
165 Checklist .15 .40

2006 Topps Opening Day Red Foil

*RED FOIL: 3X TO 8X BASIC
*RED FOIL: 3X TO 8X BASIC RC
STATED ODDS 1:8 HOBBY, 1:11 RETAIL
STATED PRINT RUN 2006 SERIAL #'d SETS

2006 Topps Opening Day Autographs

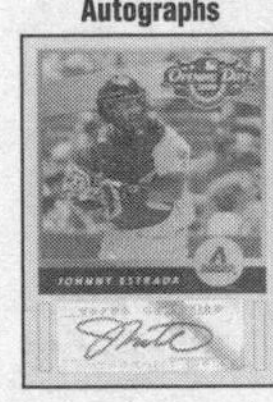

GROUP A ODDS 1:10928 H, 1:11668 R
GROUP B ODDS 1:3491 H, 1:3491 R
GROUP C ODDS 1:978 H, 1:1185 R
BE Brad Eldred B 4.00 10.00
EM Eli Marrero C 4.00 10.00
JE Johnny Estrada A 6.00 15.00
MK Mark Kotsay B 6.00 15.00
TH Toby Hall C 4.00 10.00
VZ Victor Zambrano C 4.00 10.00

2006 Topps Opening Day Sports Illustrated For Kids

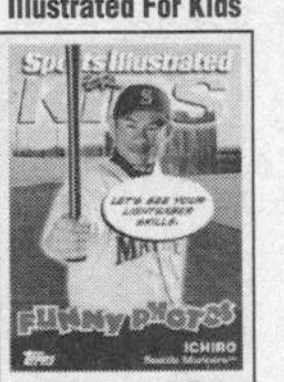

COMPLETE SET (25) 4.00 10.00
STATED ODDS 1:1
1 Vladimir Guerrero .40 1.00
2 Marcus Giles .25 .60
3 Michael Young .25 .60
4 Derek Jeter 1.50 4.00
5 Darry Donds 1.00 2.50
6 Ivan Rodriguez .40 1.00
7 Miguel Cabrera .60 1.50
8 Jim Edmonds .40 1.00
9 Jack Wilson .25 .60
10 Khalil Greene .25 .60
11 Miguel Tejada .40 1.00
12 Eric Chavez .25 .60
13 Shannon Stewart .25 .60
14 Julio Lugo .25 .60
15 Andruw Jones .25 .60
16 N.Johnson .60 1.50
R.Johnson
17 T.Iguchi .40 1.00
I.Rodriguez
18 R.Oswalt .40 1.00
J.Reyes
19 M.Ramirez .60 1.50
R.Belliard
20 T.Helton .40 1.00
K.Greene
21 D.Ortiz .60 1.50
D.Willis
22 I.Suzuki .75 2.00
J.Damon
23 C.Biggio .40 1.00
J.Wilson
24 B.Roberts .25 .60
R.Sexson
25 C.Jones .60 1.50
M.Giles

2007 Topps Opening Day

This 220-card set was released in March, 2007. This set was issued in six-card packs, with an 99 cent SRP, which came 36 packs to a box and 20 boxes to a case. The Derek Jeter (#46) card, which featured Mickey Mantle and President George W Bush in the regular Topps set; did not feature either personage in the background.
COMPLETE SET (220) 20.00 50.00
COMMON CARD (1-220) .15 .40
COMMON RC .15 .40
OVERALL PLATE ODDS 1:370 HOBBY
PLATE PRINT RUN 1 SET PER COLOR
BLACK-CYAN-MAGENTA-YELLOW ISSUED
NO PLATE PRICING DUE TO SCARCITY
1 Bobby Abreu .15 .40
2 Mike Piazza .40 1.00
3 Jake Westbrook .15 .40
4 Zach Duke .15 .40
5 David Wright .30 .75
6 Adrian Gonzalez .30 .75
7 Mickey Mantle 1.25 3.00
8 Bill Hall .15 .40
9 Robinson Cano .25 .60
10 Dontrelle Willis .15 .40
11 J.D. Drew .15 .40
12 Paul Konerko .25 .60
13 Austin Kearns .15 .40
14 Mike Lowell .15 .40
15 Magglio Ordonez .25 .60
16 Rafael Furcal .15 .40
17 Matt Cain .25 .60
18 Craig Monroe .15 .40
19 Matt Holliday .40 1.00
20 Edgar Renteria .15 .40
21 Mark Buehrle .25 .60
22 Carlos Quentin .15 .40
23 C.C. Sabathia .25 .60
24 Nick Markakis .30 .75
25 Chipper Jones .40 1.00
26 Jason Giambi .15 .40
27 Barry Zito .25 .60
28 Jake Peavy .15 .40
29 Hank Blalock .15 .40
30 Johnny Damon .25 .60
31 Chad Tracy .15 .40
32 Nick Swisher .25 .60
33 Willy Taveras .15 .40
34 Chuck James .15 .40
35 Carlos Delgado .15 .40
36 Livan Hernandez .15 .40
37 Freddy Garcia .15 .40
38 Bronson Arroyo .15 .40
39 Jack Wilson .15 .40
40 Dan Uggla .15 .40
41 Chris Carpenter .25 .60
42 Jorge Posada .25 .60
43 Joe Mauer .30 .75
44 Corey Patterson .15 .40
45 Chien-Ming Wang .25 .60
46 Derek Jeter 1.00 2.50
47 Carlos Beltran .25 .60
48 Jim Edmonds .25 .60
49 Jeremy Sowers .15 .40
50 Randy Johnson .40 1.00
51 Jered Weaver .25 .60
52 Josh Barfield .15 .40
53 Scott Rolen .25 .60
54 Ryan Shealy .15 .40
55 Freddy Sanchez .15 .40
56 Javier Vazquez .15 .40
57 Jeremy Bonderman .15 .40
58 Miguel Cabrera .40 1.00
59 Kazuo Matsui .15 .40
60 Curt Schilling .25 .60
61 Alfonso Soriano .25 .60
62 Orlando Hernandez .15 .40
63 Joe Blanton .15 .40
64 Aramis Ramirez .15 .40
65 Ben Sheets .15 .40
66 Jimmy Rollins .25 .60
67 Mark Loretta .15 .40
68 Cole Hamels .30 .75
69 Albert Pujols .50 1.25
70 Moises Alou .15 .40
71 Mark Teahen .15 .40
72 Roy Halladay .25 .60
73 Cory Sullivan .15 .40
74 Frank Thomas .40 1.00
75 Ryan Howard .30 .75
76 Rocco Baldelli .15 .40
77 Manny Ramirez .40 1.00
78 Ray Durham .15 .40
79 Gary Sheffield .15 .40
80 Jay Gibbons .15 .40
81 Todd Helton .25 .60
82 Gary Matthews .15 .40
83 Brandon Inge .15 .40
84 Jonathan Papelbon .40 1.00
85 John Smoltz .40 1.00
86 Chone Figgins .15 .40
87 Hideki Matsui .40 1.00
88 Carlos Lee .15 .40
89 Jose Reyes .25 .60
90 Lyle Overbay .15 .40
91 Johan Santana .25 .60
92 Ian Kinsler .25 .60
93 Scott Kazmir .25 .60
94 Hanley Ramirez .25 .60
95 Greg Maddux .50 1.25
96 Johnny Estrada .15 .40
97 B.J. Upton .15 .40
98 Francisco Liriano .15 .40
99 Chase Utley .25 .60
100 Preston Wilson .15 .40
101 Marcus Giles .15 .40
102 Jeff Kent .15 .40
103 Grady Sizemore .25 .60
104 Ken Griffey .75 2.00
105 Garret Anderson .15 .40
106 Brian McCann .15 .40
107 Jon Garland .15 .40
108 Troy Glaus .15 .40
109 Brandon Webb .25 .60

110 Jason Schmidt .15 .40
111 Ramon Hernandez .15 .40
112 Justin Morneau .25 .60
113 Mike Cameron .15 .40
114 Andruw Jones .15 .40
115 Russell Martin .15 .40
116 Vernon Wells .15 .40
117 Orlando Hudson .15 .40
118 Derek Lowe .15 .40
119 Alex Rodriguez .50 1.25
120 Chad Billingsley .25 .60
121 Kenji Johjima .40 1.00
122 Nick Johnson .15 .40
123 Dan Haren .15 .40
124 Mark Teixeira .25 .60
125 Jeff Francoeur .40 1.00
126 Ted Lilly .15 .40
127 Jhonny Peralta .15 .40
128 Aaron Harang .15 .40
129 Ryan Zimmerman .25 .60
130 Jermaine Dye .15 .40
131 Orlando Cabrera .15 .40
132 Juan Pierre .15 .40
133 Brian Giles .15 .40
134 Jason Bay .25 .60
135 David Ortiz .40 1.00
136 Chris Capuano .15 .40
137 Carlos Zambrano .25 .60
138 Luis Gonzalez .15 .40
139 Jeff Weaver .15 .40
140 Lance Berkman .25 .60
141 Raul Ibanez .25 .60
142 Jim Thome .25 .60
143 Jose Contreras .15 .40
144 David Eckstein .15 .40
145 Adam Dunn .25 .60
146 Alex Rios .15 .40
147 Garrett Atkins .15 .40
148 A.J. Burnett .15 .40
149 Jeremy Hermida .15 .40
150 Conor Jackson .15 .40
151 Adrian Beltre .40 1.00
152 Torii Hunter .15 .40
153 Andrew Miller RC .60 1.50
154 Ichiro Suzuki .50 1.25
155 Mark Redman .15 .40
156 Paul LoDuca .15 .40
157 Xavier Nady .15 .40
158 Stephen Drew .15 .40
159 Eric Chavez .15 .40
160 Pedro Martinez .25 .60
161 Derrek Lee .15 .40
162 David DeJesus .15 .40
163 Troy Tulowitzki (RC) .50 1.25
164 Vinny Rottino (RC) .15 .40
165 Philip Humber (RC) .15 .40
166 Jerry Owens (RC) .15 .40
167 Ubaldo Jimenez (RC) .50 1.25
168 Michael Young .15 .40
169 Ryan Braun RC .15 .40
170 Kevin Kouzmanoff (RC) .15 .40
171 Oswaldo Navarro RC .15 .40
172 Miguel Montero (RC) .15 .40
173 Roy Oswalt .25 .60
174 Shane Youman RC .15 .40
175 Josh Fields (RC) .15 .40
176 Adam Lind (RC) .15 .40
177 Miguel Tejada .25 .60
178 Delwyn Young (RC) .15 .40
179 Scott Moore (RC) .15 .40
180 Fred Lewis (RC) .25 .60
181 Glen Perkins (RC) .15 .40
182 Vladimir Guerrero .25 .60
183 Drew Anderson RC .15 .40
184 Jeff Salazar (RC) .15 .40
185 Tom Gordon .15 .40
186 The Bird .15 .40
187 Justin Verlander .40 1.00
188 Delmon Young (RC) .25 .60
189 Homer .15 .40
190 Wally the Green Monster .15 .40
191 Southpaw .15 .40
192 Dinger .15 .40
193 Carl Crawford .25 .60
194 Slider .15 .40
195 Gapper .15 .40
196 Paws .15 .40
197 Billy the Marlin .15 .40
198 Ivan Rodriguez .25 .60
199 Slugger .15 .40
200 Junction Jack .15 .40
201 Bernie Brewer .15 .40
202 Travis Hafner .15 .40
203 Stomper .15 .40
204 Mr. Met .15 .40
205 The Moose .15 .40
206 Phillie Phanatic .15 .40
207 Prince Fielder .25 .60
208 Julio Lugo .15 .40
209 Pirate Parrot .15 .40
210 Joel Zumaya .15 .40
211 Swinging Friar .15 .40
212 Jay Payton .15 .40
213 Lou Seal .15 .40
214 Fredbird .15 .40
215 Screech .15 .40
216 TC Bear .15 .40
217 Andre Ethier .25 .60
218 Ervin Santana .15 .40
219 Melvin Mora .15 .40
220 Checklist .15 .40

2007 Topps Opening Day Gold

COMPLETE SET (219) 75.00 150.00
*GOLD: 1.2X TO 3X BASIC
*GOLD: 1.2X TO 3X BASIC RC
STATED ODDS APPX. 1 PER HOBBY PACK
STATED PRINT RUN 2007 SERIAL #'d SETS

2007 Topps Opening Day Autographs

STATED ODDS 1:965 HOBBY, 1:965 RETAIL
EF Emiliano Fruto 10.00 25.00
HK Howie Kendrick 20.00 50.00
JM Juan Morillo 6.00 15.00
MC Matt Cain 5.00 12.00
MK Matt Kemp 5.00 12.00
OH Orlando Hudson 10.00 25.00
SS Shannon Stewart 6.00 15.00

2007 Topps Opening Day Diamond Stars

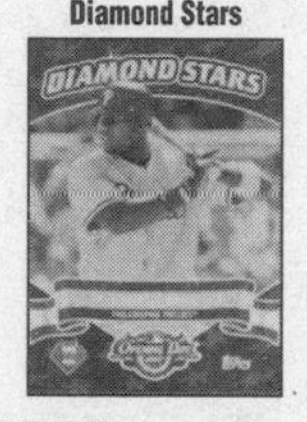

COMPLETE SET (25) 6.00 15.00
STATED ODDS 1:4 HOBBY, 1:4 RETAIL
DS1 Ryan Howard .50 1.25
DS2 Alfonso Soriano .40 1.00
DS3 Alex Rodriguez .75 2.00
DS4 David Ortiz .60 1.50
DS5 Raul Ibanez .40 1.00
DS6 Matt Holliday .60 1.50
DS7 Delmon Young .40 1.00
DS8 Derrick Turnbow .25 .60
DS9 Freddy Sanchez .25 .60
DS10 Troy Glaus .25 .60
DS11 A.J. Pierzynski .25 .60
DS12 Dontrelle Willis .25 .60
DS13 Justin Morneau .40 1.00
DS14 Jose Reyes .40 1.00
DS15 Derek Jeter 1.50 4.00
DS16 Ivan Rodriguez .40 1.00
DS17 Jay Payton .25 .60
DS18 Adrian Gonzalez .50 1.25
DS19 David Eckstein .25 .60
DS20 Chipper Jones .60 1.50
DS21 Aramis Ramirez .25 .60
DS22 David Wright .50 1.25
DS23 Mark Teixeira .40 1.00
DS24 Stephen Drew .25 .60
DS25 Ichiro Suzuki .75 2.00

2007 Topps Opening Day Movie Gallery

STATED ODDS 1:6 HOBBY
NNO Alex Rodriguez .12 .30

2007 Topps Opening Day Puzzle

COMPLETE SET (28) 6.00 15.00
STATED ODDS 1:3 HOBBY, 1:3 RETAIL
P1 Adam Dunn .40 1.00
P2 Adam Dunn .40 1.00
P3 Miguel Tejada .40 1.00
P4 Miguel Tejada .40 1.00
P5 Hanley Ramirez .40 1.00
P6 Hanley Ramirez .40 1.00
P7 Johan Santana .40 1.00
P8 Johan Santana .40 1.00
P9 Brandon Webb .40 1.00
P10 Brandon Webb .40 1.00
P11 David Wright .50 1.25
P12 David Wright .50 1.25
P13 Alex Rodriguez .75 2.00
P14 Alex Rodriguez .75 2.00
P15 Ryan Howard .50 1.25
P16 Ryan Howard .50 1.25
P17 Albert Pujols .75 2.00
P18 Albert Pujols .75 2.00
P19 Andruw Jones .25 .60
P20 Andruw Jones .25 .60
P21 Alfonso Soriano .40 1.00
P22 Alfonso Soriano .40 1.00
P23 Vladimir Guerrero .40 1.00
P24 Vladimir Guerrero .40 1.00
P25 David Ortiz .60 1.50
P26 David Ortiz .60 1.50
P27 Ichiro Suzuki .75 2.00
P28 Ichiro Suzuki .75 2.00

2008 Topps Opening Day

COMPLETE SET (220) 15.00 40.00
COMMON CARD (1-194) .12 .30
COMMON RC (195-220) .20 .50
OVERALL PLATE ODDS 1:546 HOBBY
PLATE PRINT RUN 1 SET PER COLOR
BLACK-CYAN-MAGENTA-YELLOW ISSUED
NO PLATE PRICING DUE TO SCARCITY
1 Alex Rodriguez .40 1.00
2 Barry Zito .20 .50
3 Jeff Suppan .12 .30
4 Placido Polanco .12 .30
5 Scott Kazmir .20 .50
6 Ivan Rodriguez .20 .50
7 Mickey Mantle 1.00 2.50
8 Stephen Drew .12 .30
9 Ken Griffey Jr. .60 1.50
10 Miguel Cabrera .30 .75
11 Yorvit Torrealba .12 .30
12 Daisuke Matsuzaka .20 .50
13 Kyle Kendrick .12 .30
14 Jimmy Rollins .20 .50
15 Joe Mauer .25 .60
16 Cole Hamels .25 .60
17 Yovani Gallardo .12 .30
18 Miguel Tejada .20 .50
19 Corey Hart .12 .30
20 Nick Markakis .25 .60
21 Zack Greinke .20 .50
22 Orlando Cabrera .20 .50
23 Jake Peavy .12 .30
24 Erik Bedard .12 .30
25 Trevor Hoffman .20 .50
26 Derrek Lee .12 .30
27 Hank Blalock .12 .30
28 Victor Martinez .20 .50
29 Chris Young .12 .30
30 Jose Reyes .20 .50
31 Mike Lowell .12 .30
32 Curtis Granderson .12 .30
33 Dan Uggla .12 .30
34 Mike Piazza .30 .75
35 Garrett Atkins .12 .30
36 Felix Hernandez .20 .50
37 Alex Rios .12 .30
38 Mark Reynolds .12 .30
39 Jason Bay .20 .50
40 Josh Beckett .12 .30
41 Jack Cust .12 .30
42 Vladimir Guerrero .20 .50
43 Marcus Giles .12 .30
44 Kenny Lofton .12 .30
45 John Lackey .20 .50
46 Ryan Howard .20 .50
47 Kevin Youkilis .12 .30
48 Gary Sheffield .12 .30
49 Justin Morneau .20 .50
50 Albert Pujols .40 1.00
51 Ubaldo Jimenez .12 .30
52 Johan Santana .20 .50
53 Chuck James .12 .30
54 Jeremy Hermida .12 .30
55 Andruw Jones .12 .30
56 Jason Varitek .30 .75
57 Tim Hudson .20 .50
58 Justin Upton .20 .50
59 Brad Penny .12 .30
60 Robinson Cano .20 .50
61 Johnny Estrada .12 .30
62 Brandon Webb .20 .50
63 Chris Duncan .12 .30
64 Aaron Hill .12 .30
65 Alfonso Soriano .20 .50
66 Carlos Zambrano .20 .50
67 Ben Sheets .12 .30
68 Andy LaRoche .12 .30
69 Tim Lincecum .20 .50
70 Phil Hughes .12 .30
71 Magglio Ordonez .20 .50
72 Scott Rolen .20 .50
73 John Maine .12 .30
74 Delmon Young .20 .50
75 Chase Utley .20 .50
76 Jose Valverde .12 .30
77 Tadahito Iguchi .12 .30
78 Checklist .12 .30
79 Russell Martin .12 .30
80 B.J. Upton .20 .50
81 Orlando Hudson .12 .30
82 Jim Edmonds .20 .50
83 J.J. Hardy .12 .30
84 Todd Helton .20 .50
85 Melky Cabrera .12 .30
86 Adrian Beltre .30 .75
87 Manny Ramirez .30 .75
88 Rafael Furcal .12 .30
89 Gil Meche .12 .30
90 Grady Sizemore .20 .50
91 Jeff Kent .12 .30
92 David DeJesus .12 .30
93 Lyle Overbay .12 .30
94 Moises Alou .12 .30
95 Frank Thomas .30 .75
96 Ryan Garko .12 .30
97 Kevin Kouzmanoff .12 .30
98 Roy Oswalt .20 .50
99 Mark Buehrle .20 .50
100 David Ortiz .30 .75
101 Hunter Pence .20 .50
102 David Wright .20 .50
103 Dustin Pedroia .20 .50
104 Roy Halladay .20 .50
105 Derek Jeter .75 2.00
106 Casey Blake .12 .30
107 Rich Harden .12 .30
108 Shane Victorino .12 .30
109 Richie Sexson .12 .30
110 Jim Thome .20 .50
111 Akinori Iwamura .12 .30
112 Dan Haren .12 .30
113 Jose Contreras .12 .30
114 Jonathan Papelbon .20 .50
115 Prince Fielder .20 .50
116 Dan Johnson .12 .30
117 Dmitri Young .12 .30
118 Brandon Phillips .12 .30
119 Brett Myers .12 .30
120 James Loney .12 .30
121 C.C. Sabathia .20 .50
122 Jermaine Dye .12 .30
123 Aubrey Huff .12 .30
124 Carlos Ruiz .12 .30
125 Hanley Ramirez .20 .50
126 Edgar Renteria .12 .30
127 Mark Loretta .20 .50
128 Brian McCann .20 .50
129 Paul Konerko .20 .50
130 Jorge Posada .20 .50
131 Chien-Ming Wang .20 .50
132 Jose Vidro .12 .30
133 Carlos Delgado .12 .30
134 Kelvim Escobar .12 .30
135 Pedro Martinez .20 .50
136 Jeremy Guthrie .12 .30
137 Ramon Hernandez .12 .30
138 Ian Kinsler .20 .50
139 Ichiro Suzuki .40 1.00
140 Garret Anderson .12 .30
141 Tom Gorzelanny .12 .30
142 Bobby Crosby .12 .30
143 Jeff Francoeur .20 .50
144 Josh Hamilton .20 .50
145 Mark Teixeira .20 .50
146 Fausto Carmona .12 .30
147 Alex Gordon .20 .50
148 Nick Swisher .20 .50
149 Justin Verlander .30 .75
150 Pat Burrell .12 .30
151 Chris Carpenter .20 .50
152 Matt Holliday .30 .75
153 Adam Dunn .20 .50
154 Curt Schilling .20 .50
155 Kelly Johnson .12 .30
156 Aaron Rowand .12 .30
157 Brian Roberts .12 .30
158 Bobby Abreu .12 .30
159 Carlos Beltran .20 .50
160 Lance Berkman .20 .50
161 Gary Matthews .12 .30
162 Jeff Francis .12 .30
163 Vernon Wells .12 .30
164 Dontrelle Willis .12 .30
165 Travis Hafner .12 .30
166 Brian Bannister .12 .30
167 Carlos Pena .20 .50
168 Raul Ibanez .20 .50
169 Aramis Ramirez .12 .30
170 Eric Byrnes .12 .30
171 Greg Maddux .40 1.00
172 John Smoltz .30 .75
173 Jarrod Saltalamacchia .12 .30
174 Hideki Okajima .20 .50
175 Javier Vazquez .12 .30
176 Aaron Harang .12 .30
177 Jhonny Peralta .12 .30
178 Carlos Lee .12 .30
179 Ryan Braun .20 .50
180 Torii Hunter .12 .30
181 Hideki Matsui .30 .75
182 Eric Chavez .12 .30
183 Freddy Sanchez .12 .30
184 Adrian Gonzalez .20 .50
185 Bengie Molina .12 .30
186 Kenji Johjima .12 .30
187 Carl Crawford .20 .50
188 Chipper Jones .30 .75
189 Chris Young .12 .30
190 Michael Young .12 .30
191 Troy Glaus .20 .50
192 Ryan Zimmerman .20 .50
193 Brian Giles .12 .30
194 Troy Tulowitzki .30 .75
195 Chin-Lung Hu (RC) .20 .50
196 Seth Smith (RC) .20 .50
197 Wladimir Balentien (RC) .20 .50
198 Rich Thompson RC .30 .75
199 Radhames Liz RC .30 .75
200 Ross Detwiler RC .30 .75
201 Sam Fuld RC .60 1.50
202 Clint Sammons (RC) .20 .50
203 Ross Ohlendorf RC .30 .75
204 Jonathan Albaladejo RC .30 .75
205 Brandon Jones RC .50 1.25
206 Steve Pearce RC 1.00 2.50
207 Kevin Hart (RC) .20 .50
208 Luke Hochevar RC .30 .75
209 Troy Patton (RC) .20 .50
210 Josh Anderson (RC) .20 .50
211 Clay Buchholz (RC) .30 .75
212 Joe Koshansky (RC) .20 .50
213 Bronson Sardinha (RC) .20 .50
214 Emilio Bonifacio RC .50 1.25
215 Daric Barton (RC) .20 .50
216 Lance Broadway (RC) .20 .50
217 Jeff Clement (RC) .20 .50
218 Joey Votto (RC) .75 2.00
219 J.R. Towles RC .30 .75
220 Nyjer Morgan (RC) .20 .50

2008 Topps Opening Day Gold

COMPLETE SET (220) 50.00 100.00
*GOLD VET: 1X TO 2.5X BASIC
*GOLD RC: 1X TO 2.5X BASIC RC
STATED ODDS APPX. ONE PER PACK
STATED PRINT RUN 2007 SERIAL #'d SETS
7 Mickey Mantle 3.00 8.00

2008 Topps Opening Day Autographs

GROUP A ODDS 1:359
GROUP B ODDS 1:7800
AAL Adam Lind A 6.00 15.00
AL Anthony Lerew A 6.00 15.00
GP Glen Perkins A 3.00 8.00
JAB Jason Bartlett A 3.00 8.00
JB Jeff Baker A 3.00 8.00
JCB Jason Botts B 6.00 15.00
JRB John Buck A 3.00 8.00
KG Kevin Gregg A 5.00 12.00
NS Nate Schierholtz A 5.00 12.00

2008 Topps Opening Day Flapper Cards

COMPLETE SET (18) 6.00 15.00
STATED ODDS 1:8
AP Albert Pujols .75 2.00
AR Alex Rodriguez .75 2.00
CJ Chipper Jones .60 1.50
DJ Derek Jeter 1.50 4.00
DM Daisuke Matsuzaka .40 1.00
DO David Ortiz .60 1.50
DW David Wright .40 1.00
GM Greg Maddux .75 2.00
IS Ichiro Suzuki .75 2.00
JB Josh Beckett .25 .60
JR Jose Reyes .40 1.00
KG Ken Griffey Jr 1.25 3.00
MM Mickey Mantle 1.50 4.00
MR Manny Ramirez .60 1.50
PF Prince Fielder .40 1.00
RC Roger Clemens .75 2.00
RH Ryan Howard .40 1.00
VG Vladimir Guerrero .40 1.00

2008 Topps Opening Day Puzzle

COMPLETE SET (28) 5.00 12.00
STATED ODDS 1:3
1 Matt Holliday .50 1.25
2 Matt Holliday .50 1.25
3 Vladimir Guerrero .30 .75
4 Vladimir Guerrero .30 .75
5 Jose Reyes .30 .75
6 Jose Reyes .30 .75
7 Josh Beckett .20 .50
8 Josh Beckett .20 .50
9 Albert Pujols .60 1.50
10 Albert Pujols .60 1.50
11 Alex Rodriguez .60 1.50
12 Alex Rodriguez .60 1.50
13 Jake Peavy .20 .50
14 Jake Peavy .20 .50
15 David Ortiz .50 1.25
16 David Ortiz .50 1.25
17 Ryan Howard .30 .75
18 Ryan Howard .30 .75
19 Ichiro Suzuki .60 1.50
20 Ichiro Suzuki .60 1.50
21 Hanley Ramirez .30 .75
22 Hanley Ramirez .30 .75
23 Grady Sizemore .30 .75
24 Grady Sizemore .30 .75
25 David Wright .30 .75
26 David Wright .30 .75
27 Alex Rios .20 .50
28 Alex Rios .20 .50

2008 Topps Opening Day Tattoos

STATED ODDS 1:12
AB Atlanta Braves .60 1.50
AD Arizona Diamondbacks .60 1.50
BB Bernie Brewer .60 1.50
BM Billy the Marlin .60 1.50
BRS Boston Red Sox .60 1.50
CC Chicago Cubs .60 1.50
CI Cleveland Indians .60 1.50
CR Cincinnati Reds .60 1.50
CWS Chicago White Sox .60 1.50
FB Fredbird .60 1.50
FM Florida Marlins .60 1.50
JJ Junction Jack .60 1.50
LAA Los Angeles Angels .60 1.50
LS Lou Seal .60 1.50
MM Mr. Met .60 1.50
NYM New York Mets .60 1.50
NYY New York Yankees .60 1.50
PIP Pirate Parrot .60 1.50
PP Phillie Phanatic .60 1.50
PW Paws .60 1.50
SF Swinging Friar .60 1.50
SFG San Francisco Giants .60 1.50
SL Slider .60 1.50
ST Stomper .60 1.50
TB TC Bear .60 1.50
TBJ Toronto Blue Jays .60 1.50
TDR Tampa Bay Rays .60 1.50
TM The Moose .60 1.50
TR Texas Rangers .60 1.50
WM Wally the Green Monster .60 1.50

2010 Topps Opening Day

COMPLETE SET (220) 15.00 40.00
COMMON CARD (1-205/220) .12 .30
COMMON RC (206-219) .20 .50
OVERALL PLATE ODDS 1:2119 HOBBY
1 Prince Fielder .20 .50
2 Derrek Lee .12 .30
3 Clayton Kershaw .60 1.50
4 Orlando Cabrera .12 .30
5 Ted Lilly .12 .30
6 Bobby Abreu .12 .30
7 Mickey Mantle 1.00 2.50
8 Johnny Cueto .20 .50
9 Dexter Fowler .20 .50
10 Felipe Lopez .12 .30
11 Tommy Hanson .12 .30
12 Cristian Guzman .12 .30
13 Shane Victorino .20 .50
14 John Maine .12 .30
15 Adam Jones .20 .50
16 Aubrey Huff .12 .30
17 Victor Martinez .20 .50
18 Rick Porcello .20 .50
19 Garret Anderson .12 .30
20 Josh Johnson .20 .50
21 Marco Scutaro .20 .50
22 Howie Kendrick .12 .30
23 Joey Votto .30 .75
24 Jorge De La Rosa .12 .30
25 Zack Greinke .20 .50
26 Eric Young Jr .12 .30
27 Billy Butler .12 .30
28 John Lackey .20 .50
29 Manny Ramirez .30 .75
30 CC Sabathia .20 .50
31 Kyle Blanks .12 .3
32 David Wright .25 .6
33 Kevin Millwood .12 .3
34 Nick Swisher .20 .5
35 Matt LaPorta .12 .3
36 Brandon Inge .20 .5
37 Cole Hamels .25 .6
38 Adrian Gonzalez .25 .6
39 Joe Saunders .12 .3
40 Kenshin Kawakami .20 .5
41 Tim Lincecum .20 .5
42 Ken Griffey Jr. .60 1.5
43 Ian Kinsler .20 .5
44 Ivan Rodriguez .20 .5
45 Carl Crawford .20 .5
46 Jon Garland .12 .3
47 Albert Pujols .40 1.0
48 Daniel Murphy .25 .6
49 Scott Hairston .12 .30
50 Justin Masterson .12 .30
51 Andrew McCutchen .30 .75
52 Gordon Beckham .12 .30
53 David DeJesus .12 .30
54 Jorge Posada .20 .50
55 Brett Anderson .12 .30
56 Ichiro Suzuki .40 1.00
57 Hank Blalock .12 .30
58 Vladimir Guerrero .20 .50
59 Cliff Lee .20 .50
60 Freddy Sanchez .12 .30
61 Ryan Dempster .12 .30
62 Adam Wainwright .20 .50
63 Matt Holliday .30 .75
64 Chone Figgins .12 .30
65 Tim Hudson .20 .50
66 Rich Harden .12 .30
67 Justin Upton .20 .50
68 Yunel Escobar .12 .30
69 Joe Mauer .25 .60
70 Jeff Niemann .12 .30
71 Vernon Wells .12 .30
72 Miguel Tejada .20 .50
73 Denard Span .12 .30
74 Brandon Phillips .12 .30
75 Jason Bay .20 .50
76 Kendry Morales .12 .30
77 Josh Hamilton .20 .50
78 Yovani Gallardo .12 .30
79 Adam Lind .20 .50
80 Nick Johnson .12 .30
81 Coco Crisp .12 .30
82 Jeff Francoeur .20 .50
83 Hideki Matsui .30 .75
84 Will Venable .12 .30
85 Adrian Beltre .30 .75
86 Pablo Sandoval .20 .50
87 Mat Latos .20 .50
88 James Shields .12 .30
89 R.Halladay UER 2.50 6.00
90 Chris Coghlan .12 .30
91 Colby Rasmus .20 .50
92 Alexei Ramirez .20 .50
93 Josh Beckett .12 .30
94 Kelly Shoppach .12 .30
95 Magglio Ordonez .20 .50
96 Matt Kemp .25 .60
97 Max Scherzer .30 .75
98 Curtis Granderson .25 .60
99 David Price .25 .60
100 Neftali Feliz .12 .30
101 Ian Stewart .12 .30
102 Ricky Romero .12 .30
103 Barry Zito .20 .50
104 Lance Berkman .20 .50
105 Andre Ethier .20 .50
106 Mark Teixeira .20 .50
107 Bengie Molina .12 .30
108 Edwin Jackson .12 .30
109 Akinori Iwamura .12 .30
110 Jermaine Dye .12 .30
111 Jair Jurrjens .12 .30
112 Stephen Drew .12 .30
113 Carlos Delgado .12 .30
114 Mark DeRosa .12 .30
115 Kurt Suzuki .12 .30
116 Javier Vazquez .12 .30
117 Lyle Overbay .12 .30
118 Orlando Hudson .12 .30
119 Adam Dunn .20 .50
120 Kevin Youkilis .12 .30
121 Ben Zobrist .20 .50
122 Chase Utley .20 .50
123 Jack Cust .12 .30
124 Gerald Laird .12 .30
125 Elvis Andrus .20 .50
126 Jason Kubel .12 .30
127 Scott Kazmir .12 .30
128 Ryan Doumit .12 .30
129 Brian McCann .20 .50
130 Jim Thome .20 .50
131 Alex Rios .12 .30
132 Jered Weaver .20 .50
133 Carlos Lee .12 .30
134 Mark Buehrle .20 .50
135 Chipper Jones .30 .75
136 Robinson Cano .20 .50
137 Mark Reynolds .12 .30
138 David Ortiz .30 .75
139 Carlos Gonzalez .20 .50
140 Torii Hunter .12 .30
141 Nick Markakis .25 .60
142 Jose Reyes .20 .50
143 Johnny Damon .20 .50

44 Roy Oswalt .20 .50
45 Alfonso Soriano .20 .50
46 Jimmy Rollins .20 .50
47 Matt Garza .12 .30
48 Michael Cuddyer .12 .30
49 Rick Ankiel .12 .30
50 Miguel Cabrera .30 .75
51 Mike Napoli .12 .30
52 Josh Willingham .20 .50
53 Chris Carpenter .20 .50
154 Paul Konerko .20 .50
155 Jake Peavy .12 .30
156 Nate McLouth .12 .30
157 Daisuke Matsuzaka .20 .50
158 Brad Hawpe .12 .30
159 Johan Santana .20 .50
160 Grady Sizemore .20 .50
161 Chad Billingsley .20 .50
162 Corey Hart .12 .30
163 A.J. Burnett .12 .30
164 Kosuke Fukudome .20 .50
165 Justin Verlander .30 .75
166 Jayson Werth .20 .50
167 Matt Cain .20 .50
168 Carlos Pena .20 .50
169 Hunter Pence .20 .50
170 Russell Martin .12 .30
171 Carlos Quentin .12 .30
172 Jacoby Ellsbury .25 .60
173 Todd Helton .20 .50
174 Derek Jeter .75 2.00
175 Dan Haren .12 .30
176 Nelson Cruz .30 .75
177 Jose Lopez .12 .30
178 Carlos Zambrano .20 .50
179 Hanley Ramirez .20 .50
180 Aaron Hill .12 .30
181 Ubaldo Jimenez .12 .30
182 Brian Roberts .12 .30
183 Jon Lester .20 .50
184 Ryan Braun .20 .50
185 Jay Bruce .20 .50
186 Aramis Ramirez .12 .30
187 Dustin Pedroia .25 .60
188 Troy Tulowitzki .30 .75
189 Justin Morneau .20 .50
190 Jorge Cantu .12 .30
191 Scott Rolen .20 .50
192 B.J. Upton .20 .50
193 Yadier Molina .30 .75
194 Alex Rodriguez .40 1.00
195 Felix Hernandez .20 .50
196 Raul Ibanez .20 .50
197 Travis Snider .12 .30
198 Brandon Webb .20 .50
199 Ryan Howard .25 .60
200 Michael Young .12 .30
201 Rajai Davis .12 .30
202 Ryan Zimmerman .20 .50
203 Carlos Beltran .20 .50
204 Evan Longoria .20 .50
205 Dan Uggla .12 .30
206 Brandon Allen (RC) .20 .50
207 Buster Posey RC 3.00 8.00
208 Drew Stubbs RC .50 1.25
209 Madison Bumgarner RC 1.50 4.00
210 Reid Gorecki (RC) .30 .75
211 Wade Davis (RC) .30 .75
212 Neil Walker (RC) .30 .75
213 Ian Desmond (RC) .30 .75
214 Josh Thole RC .30 .75
215 Chris Pettit RC .20 .50
216 Daniel McCutchen RC .30 .75
217 Daniel Hudson RC .30 .75
218 Michael Brantley RC .30 .75
219 Tyler Flowers RC .30 .75
220 Checklist .12 .30

2010 Topps Opening Day Blue

*GOLD VET: 1.5X TO 4X BASIC
*GOLD RC: 1.2X TO 3X BASIC RC
STATED ODDS 1:5 HOBBY
STATED PRINT RUN 2010 SERIAL #'d SETS

2010 Topps Opening Day Attax

COMPLETE SET (25) 10.00 25.00
STATED ODDS 1:6 HOBBY
ODTA1 Tim Lincecum .60 1.50
ODTA2 Ichiro Suzuki 1.25 3.00
ODTA3 Miguel Cabrera 1.00 2.50
ODTA4 Ryan Braun .60 1.50
ODTA5 Zack Greinke .60 1.50
ODTA6 Alex Rodriguez 1.25 3.00
ODTA7 Albert Pujols 1.25 3.00
ODTA8 Evan Longoria .60 1.50
ODTA9 Roy Halladay .60 1.50
ODTA10 Ryan Howard .75 2.00
ODTA11 Josh Beckett .40 1.00
ODTA12 Hanley Ramirez .60 1.50
ODTA13 Lance Berkman .60 1.50
ODTA14 Dan Haren .40 1.00
ODTA15 Joe Mauer .75 2.00
ODTA16 Adrian Gonzalez .75 2.00
ODTA17 Vladimir Guerrero .60 1.50
ODTA18 Felix Hernandez .60 1.50
ODTA19 Matt Kemp .75 2.00
ODTA20 Mariano Rivera 1.25 3.00
ODTA21 Grady Sizemore .60 1.50
ODTA22 Nick Markakis .75 2.00
ODTA23 CC Sabathia .60 1.50
ODTA24 Ian Kinsler .60 1.50
ODTA25 David Wright .75 2.00

2010 Topps Opening Day Autographs

STATED ODDS 1:746 HOBBY
ODAAC Aaron Cunningham 4.00 10.00
ODACP Cliff Pennington 4.00 10.00
ODACV Chris Volstad 4.00 10.00
ODADS Denard Span 8.00 20.00
ODADSC Daniel Schlereth 6.00 15.00
ODAGP Gerardo Parra 5.00 12.00
ODAMT Matt Tolbert 8.00 20.00

2010 Topps Opening Day Mascots

COMPLETE SET (25) 6.00 15.00
STATED ODDS 1:4 HOBBY
M1 Baxter the Bobcat .40 1.00
M2 Homer the Brave .40 1.00
M3 The Oriole Bird .40 1.00
M4 Wally the Green Monster .40 1.00
M5 Southpaw .40 1.00
M6 Gapper .40 1.00
M7 Slider .40 1.00
M8 Dinger .40 1.00
M9 Paws .40 1.00
M10 Billy the Marlin .40 1.00
M11 Junction Jack .40 1.00
M12 Sluggerrr .40 1.00
M13 Bernie Brewer .40 1.00
M14 TC the Bear .40 1.00
M15 Mr. Met .40 1.00
M16 Stomper .40 1.00
M17 Phillie Phanatic .40 1.00
M18 The Pirate Parrot .40 1.00
M19 The Swinging Friar .40 1.00
M20 Mariner Moose .40 1.00
M21 Fredbird .40 1.00
M22 Raymond .40 1.00
M23 Rangers Captain .40 1.00
M24 ACE .40 1.00
M25 Screech the Eagle .40 1.00

2010 Topps Opening Day Superstar Celebrations

COMPLETE SET (10) 4.00 10.00
STATED ODDS 1:9 HOBBY
SC1 Ryan Braun .40 1.00
SC2 Mark Buehrle .40 1.00
SC3 Alex Rodriguez .75 2.00
SC4 Ichiro Suzuki .75 2.00
SC5 Ryan Zimmerman .40 1.00
SC6 Colby Rasmus .40 1.00
SC7 Andre Ethier .40 1.00
SC8 Michael Young .25 .60
SC9 Evan Longoria .40 1.00
SC10 Aramis Ramirez .25 .60

2010 Topps Opening Day Topps Town Stars

COMPLETE SET (25) 5.00 12.00
STATED ODDS 1:3 HOBBY
TTS1 Vladimir Guerrero .30 .75
TTS2 Justin Upton .30 .75
TTS3 Chipper Jones .50 1.25
TTS4 Nick Markakis .40 1.00
TTS5 David Ortiz .50 1.25
TTS6 Alfonso Soriano .30 .75
TTS7 Jake Peavy .20 .50
TTS8 Jay Bruce .30 .75
TTS9 Grady Sizemore .30 .75
TTS10 Troy Tulowitzki .50 1.25
TTS11 Miguel Cabrera .50 1.25
TTS12 Hanley Ramirez .30 .75
TTS13 Hunter Pence .30 .75
TTS14 Zack Greinke .30 .75
TTS15 Manny Ramirez .50 1.25
TTS16 Prince Fielder .30 .75
TTS17 Joe Mauer .40 1.00
TTS18 David Wright .40 1.00
TTS19 Mark Teixeira .30 .75
TTS20 Evan Longoria .30 .75
TTS21 Ryan Howard .40 1.00
TTS22 Albert Pujols .60 1.50
TTS23 Adrian Gonzalez .40 1.00
TTS24 Tim Lincecum .30 .75
TTS25 Ichiro Suzuki .60 1.50

2010 Topps Opening Day Where'd You Go Bazooka Joe

COMPLETE SET (10) 5.00 12.00
STATED ODDS 1:9 HOBBY
WBJ1 David Wright .50 1.25
WBJ2 Ryan Howard .50 1.25
WBJ3 Miguel Cabrera .60 1.50
WBJ4 Albert Pujols .75 2.00
WBJ5 CC Sabathia .40 1.00
WBJ6 Prince Fielder .40 1.00
WBJ7 Evan Longoria .40 1.00
WBJ8 Chipper Jones .60 1.50
WBJ9 Grady Sizemore .40 1.00
WBJ10 Ian Kinsler .40 1.00

2011 Topps Opening Day

COMPLETE SET (220) 15.00 40.00
COMMON CARD (1-220) .12 .30
COMMON RC (1-220) .20 .50
OVERALL PLATE ODDS 1:2660
PLATE PRINT RUN 1 SET PER COLOR
BLACK-CYAN-MAGENTA-YELLOW ISSUED
NO PLATE PRICING DUE TO SCARCITY
1 Carlos Gonzalez .20 .50
2 Shin-Soo Choo .20 .50
3 Jon Lester .20 .50
4 Jason Kubel .12 .30
5 David Wright .25 .60
6 Aramis Ramirez .12 .30
7 Mickey Mantle 1.00 2.50
8 Hanley Ramirez .20 .50
9 Michael Cuddyer .12 .30
10 Joey Votto .30 .75
11 Jaime Garcia .20 .50
12 Neil Walker .20 .50
13 Carl Crawford .20 .50
14 Ben Zobrist .20 .50
15 David Price .25 .60
16 Max Scherzer .30 .75
17 Ryan Dempster .12 .30
18 Justin Upton .20 .50
19 Carlos Marmol .20 .50
20 Mariano Rivera .40 1.00
21 Martin Prado .12 .30
22 Hunter Pence .20 .50
23 Chris Johnson .12 .30
24 Andrew Cashner .12 .30
25 Johan Santana .20 .50
26 Gaby Sanchez .12 .30
27 Andrew McCutchen .30 .75
28 Edinson Volquez .12 .30
29 Jonathan Papelbon .20 .50
30 Alex Rodriguez .40 1.00
31 Chris Sale RC 1.25 3.00
32 James McDonald .12 .30
33 Kyle Drabek RC .30 .75
34 Jair Jurrjens .12 .30
35 Vladimir Guerrero .20 .50
36 Daniel Descalso RC .20 .50
37 Tim Hudson .20 .50
38 Mike Stanton .30 .75
39 Kurt Suzuki .12 .30
40 CC Sabathia .20 .50
41 Aubrey Huff .12 .30
42 Greg Halman RC .30 .75
43 Jered Weaver .20 .50
44 Omar Infante .12 .30
45 Desmond Jennings RC .30 .75
46 Yadier Molina .30 .75
47 Phil Hughes .12 .30
48 Paul Konerko .20 .50
49 Yonder Alonso RC .30 .75
50 Albert Pujols .40 1.00
51 Ben Revere RC .30 .75
52 Placido Polanco .12 .30
53 Bronson Arroyo .12 .30
54 Ian Stewart .12 .30
55 Cliff Lee .20 .50
56 Brian Bogusevic (RC) .20 .50
57 Zack Greinke .20 .50
58 Howie Kendrick .12 .30
59 Russell Martin .12 .30
60 Aroldis Chapman RC .60 1.50
61 Jason Bay .20 .50
62 Mat Latos .20 .50
63 Manny Ramirez .30 .75
64 Miguel Tejada .20 .50
65 Mike Stanton .30 .75
66 Brett Anderson .12 .30
67 Johnny Cueto .20 .50
68 Jeremy Jeffress RC .12 .30
69 Lance Berkman .20 .50
70 Freddie Freeman RC 3.00 8.00
71 Jon Niese .12 .30
72 Ricky Romero .12 .30
73 David Aardsma .12 .30
74 Fausto Carmona .12 .30
75 Buster Posey .40 1.00
76 Chris Perez .12 .30
77 Koji Uehara .12 .30
78 Garrett Jones .12 .30
79 Heath Bell .12 .30
80 Jeremy Hellickson RC .50 1.25
81 Jay Bruce .20 .50
82 Brennan Boesch .20 .50
83 Daniel Hudson .12 .30
84 Brian Matusz .12 .30
85 Carlos Santana .30 .75
86 Stephen Strasburg .30 .75
87 Brandon Morrow .12 .30
88 Carl Pavano .12 .30
89 Pablo Sandoval .20 .50
90 Chase Utley .20 .50
91 Andres Torres .12 .30
92 Nick Markakis .25 .60
93 Aaron Hill .12 .30
94 Jimmy Rollins .20 .50
95 Josh Johnson .20 .50
96 James Shields .12 .30
97 Mike Napoli .12 .30
98 Angel Pagan .12 .30
99 Clay Buchholz .12 .30
100 Miguel Cabrera .30 .75
101 Brian Wilson .30 .75
102 Carlos Ruiz .12 .30
103 Jose Bautista .20 .50
104 Victor Martinez .20 .50
105 Roy Oswalt .20 .50
106 Todd Helton .20 .50
107 Scott Rolen .20 .50
108 Jonathan Sanchez .12 .30
109 Mark Buehrle .20 .50
110 Ichiro Suzuki .40 1.00
111 Nelson Cruz .30 .75
112 Andre Ethier .20 .50
113 Wandy Rodriguez .12 .30
114 Ervin Santana .12 .30
115 Starlin Castro .20 .50
116 Torii Hunter .12 .30
117 Tyler Colvin .12 .30
118 Rafael Soriano .12 .30
119 Alexei Ramirez .20 .50
120 Roy Halladay .20 .50
121 John Danks .12 .30
122 Rickie Weeks .12 .30
123 Stephen Drew .12 .30
124 Clayton Kershaw .60 1.50
125 Adam Dunn .20 .50
126 Brian Duensing .12 .30
127 Nick Swisher .20 .50
128 Andrew Bailey .12 .30
129 Ike Davis .12 .30
130 Justin Morneau .20 .50
131 Chris Carpenter .20 .50
132 Miguel Montero .12 .30
133 Alex Rios .12 .30
134 Ian Desmond .12 .30
135 David Ortiz .30 .75
136 Gaby Sanchez .12 .30
137 Joel Pineiro .12 .30
138 Chris Young .12 .30
139 Michael Young .12 .30
140 Derek Jeter .75 2.00
141 Brent Morel RC .20 .50
142 C.J. Wilson .12 .30
143 Jeremy Guthrie .12 .30
144 Brett Gardner .20 .50
145 Ubaldo Jimenez .12 .30
146 Gavin Floyd .12 .30
147 Josh Hamilton .20 .50
148 Kevin Youkilis .12 .30
149 Tommy Hanson .12 .30
150 Matt Cain .20 .50
151 Adam Wainwright .20 .50
152 Mark Reynolds .12 .30
153 Kendry Morales .12 .30
154 Dan Haren .12 .30
155 Cole Hamels .25 .60
156 Ryan Zimmerman .20 .50
157 Adam Lind .20 .50
158 Brian McCann .20 .50
159 Dan Uggla .12 .30
160 Carlos Lee .12 .30
161 Jose Tabata .12 .30
162 Gordon Beckham .12 .30
163 Chad Billingsley .20 .50
164 Grady Sizemore .20 .50
165 Carlos Zambrano .20 .50
166 Ian Kinsler .20 .50
167 Geovany Soto .20 .50
168 Tim Lincecum .20 .50
169 Felix Hernandez .20 .50
170 Logan Morrison .12 .30
171 Yovani Gallardo .12 .30
172 Jorge Posada .20 .50
173 Joakim Soria .12 .30
174 Buster Posey .40 1.00
175 Adam Jones .20 .50
176 Jason Heyward .25 .60
177 Magglio Ordonez .20 .50
178 Joe Mauer .25 .60
179 Prince Fielder .20 .50
180 Colby Rasmus .20 .50
181 Josh Beckett .12 .30
182 Troy Tulowitzki .30 .75
183 Jacoby Ellsbury .25 .60
184 Austin Jackson .12 .30
185 Billy Butler .12 .30
186 Evan Longoria .20 .50
187 Brandon Phillips .12 .30
188 Justin Verlander .30 .75
189 B.J. Upton .20 .50
190 Elvis Andrus .20 .50
191 Corey Hart .12 .30
192 Dustin Pedroia .25 .60
193 Trevor Cahill .12 .30
194 Delmon Young .20 .50
195 Shaun Marcum .12 .30
196 Brian Roberts .12 .30
197 Kelly Johnson .12 .30
198 Adrian Gonzalez .25 .60
199 Francisco Liriano .12 .30
200 Robinson Cano .20 .50
201 Madison Bumgarner .25 .60
202 Mike Leake .20 .50
203 Neftali Feliz .12 .30
204 Carlos Beltran .20 .50
205 Carlos Quentin .12 .30
206 Rafael Furcal .12 .30
207 Kosuke Fukudome .20 .50
208 Matt Kemp .25 .60
209 Shane Victorino .20 .50
210 Drew Stubbs .12 .30
211 Ricky Nolasco .12 .30
212 Vernon Wells .12 .30
213 Matt Holliday .30 .75
214 Bobby Abreu .12 .30
215 Mark Teixeira .20 .50
216 Jose Reyes .20 .50
217 Andy Pettitte .20 .50
218 Ryan Howard .25 .60
219 Matt Garza .12 .30
220 Alfonso Soriano .20 .50

2011 Topps Opening Day Blue

*BLUE VET: 3X TO 8X BASIC
*BLUE RC: 1.5X TO 4X BASIC RC
STATED ODDS 1:5
STATED PRINT RUN 2011 SER.#'d SETS

2011 Topps Opening Day Autographs

STATED ODDS 1:480
CC Chris Carter 10.00 25.00
CM Casey McGehee 6.00 15.00
DM Dustin Moseley 10.00 25.00
HK Howie Kendrick 8.00 20.00
JG Justin Germano 8.00 20.00
JM Jose Mijares 8.00 20.00
PH Philip Humber 6.00 15.00
TB Taylor Buchholz 4.00 10.00
JMO Jose Morales 6.00 15.00
JVE Jonathan Van Every 8.00 20.00

2011 Topps Opening Day Mascots

COMPLETE SET (25) 12.50 30.00
STATED ODDS 1:4
M1 Arizona Diamondbacks .60 1.50
M2 Atlanta Braves .60 1.50
M3 Baltimore Orioles .60 1.50
M4 Wally the Green Monster .60 1.50
M5 Chicago White Sox .60 1.50
M6 Gapper .60 1.50
M7 Slider .60 1.50
M8 Dinger .60 1.50
M9 Paws .60 1.50
M10 Billy the Marlin .60 1.50
M11 Junction Jack .60 1.50
M12 Kansas City Royals .60 1.50
M13 Bernie Brewer .60 1.50
M14 TC .60 1.50
M15 Mr. Met .60 1.50
M16 Oakland Athletics .60 1.50
M17 Phillie Phanatic .60 1.50
M18 Pirate Parrot .60 1.50
M19 Swinging Friar .60 1.50
M20 Mariner Moose .60 1.50
M21 Fredbird .60 1.50
M22 Raymond .60 1.50
M23 Rangers Captain .60 1.50
M24 Toronto Blue Jays .60 1.50
M25 Screech .60 1.50

2011 Topps Opening Day Presidential First Pitch

COMPLETE SET (10) 4.00 10.00
STATED ODDS 1:6
PFP1 Barack Obama 1.00 2.50
PFP2 Harry Truman .40 1.00
PFP3 Calvin Coolidge .40 1.00
PFP4 Ronald Reagan .75 2.00
PFP5 Richard Nixon .40 1.00
PFP6 Woodrow Wilson .40 1.00
PFP7 George W. Bush .75 2.00
PFP8 George W. Bush .75 2.00
PFP9 John F. Kennedy .75 2.00
PFP10 Barack Obama 1.00 2.50

2011 Topps Opening Day Spot the Error

COMPLETE SET (10) 4.00 10.00
STATED ODDS 1:6
1 Mark Teixeira .30 .75
2 Jason Heyward .40 1.00
3 Jose Bautista .30 .75
4 Chase Utley .30 .75
5 David Ortiz .50 1.25
6 Ubaldo Jimenez .20 .50
7 David Wright .40 1.00
8 Hanley Ramirez .30 .75
9 Buster Posey .60 1.50
10 Derek Jeter 1.25 3.00

2011 Topps Opening Day Stadium Lights

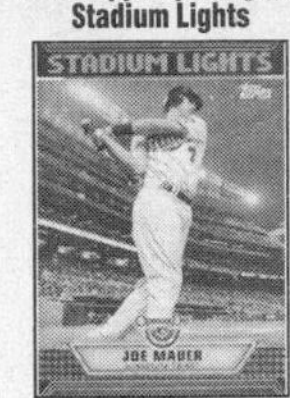

COMPLETE SET (10) 4.00 10.00
STATED ODDS 1:9
UL1 Joe Mauer .50 1.25
UL2 Troy Tulowitzki .60 1.50
UL3 Robinson Cano .40 1.00
UL4 Alex Rodriguez .75 2.00
UL5 Miguel Cabrera .60 1.50
UL6 Chase Utley .40 1.00
UL7 Pedro Alvarez .50 1.25
UL8 Adrian Gonzalez .50 1.25
UL9 Jason Heyward .50 1.25
UL10 Ryan Braun .40 1.00

2011 Topps Opening Day Stars

COMPLETE SET (10) 5.00 12.00
STATED ODDS 1:12
ODS1 Roy Halladay .40 1.00
ODS2 Carlos Gonzalez .40 1.00
ODS3 Alex Rodriguez .75 2.00
ODS4 Josh Hamilton .40 1.00
ODS5 Miguel Cabrera .60 1.50
ODS6 CC Sabathia .40 1.00
ODS7 Joe Mauer .50 1.25
ODS8 Joey Votto .60 1.50
ODS9 David Price .50 1.25
ODS10 Albert Pujols .75 2.00

2011 Topps Opening Day Superstar Celebrations

COMPLETE SET (25) 5.00 12.00
STATED ODDS 1:4
SC1 Jason Heyward .30 .75
SC2 Buster Posey .50 1.25
SC3 David Ortiz .40 1.00
SC4 Jay Bruce .25 .60
SC5 Ubaldo Jimenez .15 .40
SC6 Evan Longoria .25 .60
SC7 Jim Thome .25 .60
SC8 Vladimir Guerrero .25 .60
SC9 Nick Markakis .30 .75
SC10 Carlos Pena .25 .60
SC11 Jimmy Rollins .25 .60
SC12 Matt Garza .15 .40
SC13 Albert Pujols .50 1.25
SC14 David Wright .30 .75
SC15 Alex Rodriguez .50 1.25
SC16 Jose Reyes .25 .60
SC17 Prince Fielder .25 .60
SC18 Derek Jeter 1.00 2.50
SC19 Bobby Abreu .15 .40
SC20 Ichiro Suzuki .50 1.25
SC21 Matt Holliday .50 1.25
SC22 Cliff Lee .25 .60
SC23 Ryan Braun .25 .60
SC24 Troy Tulowitzki .40 1.00
SC25 Matt Kemp .30 .75

2011 Topps Opening Day Topps Town Codes

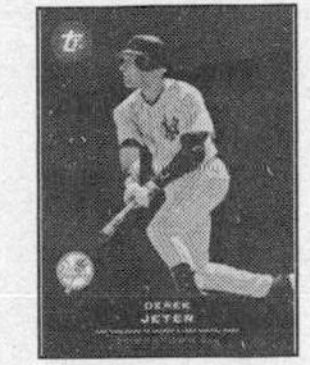

COMPLETE SET (25) 8.00 20.00
TTOD1 Clayton Kershaw 1.25 3.00
TTOD2 Hunter Pence .40 1.00
TTOD3 Trevor Cahill .25 .60
TTOD4 Jose Bautista .40 1.00
TTOD5 Jon Lester .40 1.00
TTOD6 Matt Holliday .60 1.50
TTOD7 Carlos Marmol .40 1.00
TTOD8 Justin Upton .40 1.00
TTOD9 Jered Weaver .40 1.00
TTOD10 Tim Lincecum .40 1.00
TTOD11 Logan Morrison .25 .60
TTOD12 Ike Davis .25 .60
TTOD13 Ian Desmond .25 .60
TTOD14 Brian Matusz .25 .60
TTOD15 Justin Morneau .40 1.00
TTOD16 Jose Tabata .25 .60
TTOD17 Ian Kinsler .40 1.00
TTOD18 Desmond Jennings .40 1.00
TTOD19 Martin Prado .25 .60
TTOD20 Alex Rodriguez .75 2.00
TTOD21 Austin Jackson .25 .60
TTOD22 Carlos Ruiz .25 .60
TTOD23 Gordon Beckham .25 .60
TTOD24 Jay Bruce .40 1.00
TTOD25 Derek Jeter 1.50 4.00

2011 Topps Opening Day Toys R Us Geoffrey the Giraffe

COMPLETE SET (5) 3.00 8.00
INSERT IN TRU PACKS
TRU1 Geoffrey 1.50 4.00
TRU2 Geoffrey 1.50 4.00
TRU3 Geoffrey 1.50 4.00
TRU4 Geoffrey 1.50 4.00
TRU5 Geoffrey 1.50 4.00

2012 Topps Opening Day

COMPLETE SET (220) 15.00 40.00
COMMON CARD (1-220) .12 .30
COMMON RC (1-220) .20 .50
OVERALL PLATE ODDS 1:3226 RETAIL
PLATE PRINT RUN 1 SET PER COLOR
BLACK-CYAN-MAGENTA-YELLOW ISSUED
NO PLATE PRICING DUE TO SCARCITY
1 Ryan Braun .12 .30
2 Stephen Drew .12 .30
3 Nelson Cruz .20 .50
4 Jacoby Ellsbury .15 .40
5 Roy Halladay .15 .40
6 Bud Norris .12 .30
7 Mickey Mantle .60 1.50
8 Jordan Zimmermann .15 .40
9 Chris Young .12 .30
10 Jose Valverde .15 .40
11 Michael Morse .12 .30
12 Jason Heyward .15 .40
13 Bobby Abreu .12 .30
14 Buster Posey .25 .60
15 Jeremy Hellickson .12 .30
16 Torii Hunter .15 .40
17 Pedro Alvarez .12 .30
18 David Ortiz .20 .50
19 Mat Latos .15 .40
20 Howie Kendrick .12 .30
21 Matt Moore RC .30 .75
22 Aroldis Chapman .20 .50
23 Troy Tulowitzki .20 .50
24 Brandon Morrow .12 .30
25 Eric Hosmer .15 .40
26 Drew Stubbs .12 .30
27 Chase Utley .15 .40
28 Michael Young .12 .30
29 Mike Napoli .12 .30
30 Shane Victorino .15 .40
31 Evan Longoria .15 .40
32 Anibal Sanchez .12 .30
33 Nick Markakis .15 .40
34 James McDonald .12 .30
35 Brennan Boesch .12 .30
36 Dexter Fowler .15 .40
37 Josh Beckett .12 .30
38 Brett Myers .12 .30
39 Michael Cuddyer .12 .30
40 Domonic Brown .15 .40
41 J.J. Hardy .12 .30
42 Mark Reynolds .12 .30

43 Angel Pagan .12 .30
44 Jay Bruce .15 .40
45 Mark Melancon .12 .30
46 Chris Sale .20 .50
47 Nick Swisher .15 .40
48 Adrian Beltre .20 .50
49 Melky Cabrera .12 .30
50 Ichiro Suzuki .25 .60
51 Prince Fielder .15 .40
52 Matt Joyce .12 .30
53 Alex Rodriguez .25 .60
54 Asdrubal Cabrera .15 .40
55 Miguel Cabrera .20 .50
56 Vance Worley .15 .40
57 Adam Lind .15 .40
58 Justin Masterson .12 .30
59 Alcides Escobar .12 .30
60 Adam Wainwright .15 .40
61 C.J. Wilson .12 .30
62 Ervin Santana .12 .30
63 Pablo Sandoval .15 .40
64 Dan Haren .12 .30
65 Dustin Ackley .12 .30
66 Adam Jones .15 .40
67 Billy Butler .12 .30
68 Shaun Marcum .12 .30
69 Tim Lincecum .15 .40
70 Madison Bumgarner .15 .40
71 Ian Kennedy .12 .30
72 Derek Holland .12 .30
73 Kevin Youkilis .20 .50
74 Cameron Maybin .12 .30
75 Justin Upton .15 .40
76 Gio Gonzalez .15 .40
77 Jimmy Rollins .15 .40
78 Matt Holliday .20 .50
79 Hanley Ramirez .15 .40
80 Joe Mauer .15 .40
81 Brandon Beachy .12 .30
82 Phil Hughes .12 .30
83 Carlos Gonzalez .15 .40
84 Dan Uggla .15 .40
85 Mike Trout 6.00 15.00
86 Jon Lester .12 .30
87 Ryan Howard .15 .40
88 John Axford .12 .30
89 Drew Pomeranz .12 .30
90 Derek Jeter .50 1.25
91 Jayson Werth .15 .40
92 Mike Stanton .20 .50
93 Tim Hudson .15 .40
94 Doug Fister .12 .30
95 Victor Martinez .15 .40
96 Chris Carpenter .15 .40
97 David Price .15 .40
98 Ben Zobrist .15 .40
99 Robinson Cano .15 .40
100 Matt Kemp .15 .40
101 Todd Helton .15 .40
102 Jesus Montero RC .20 .50
103 Mike Leake .12 .30
104 Alexi Ogando .12 .30
105 Curtis Granderson .15 .40
106 Josh Johnson .15 .40
107 Rickie Weeks .12 .30
108 Roy Oswalt .15 .40
109 Brett Gardner .15 .40
110 Scott Rolen .15 .40
111 Carlos Santana .15 .40
112 Dee Gordon .12 .30
113 Justin Verlander .20 .50
114 Paul Konerko .12 .30
115 Yunel Escobar .12 .30
116 Josh Hamilton .15 .40
117 Brandon Belt .15 .40
118 Miguel Montero .12 .30
119 Ricky Nolasco .12 .30
120 Matt Garza .12 .30
121 Mark Teixeira .15 .40
122 Neftali Feliz .12 .30
123 Ryan Roberts .12 .30
124 Grady Sizemore .15 .40
125 Matt Cain .15 .40
126 Danny Valencia .12 .30
127 J.P. Arencibia .12 .30
128 Lance Berkman .15 .40
129 Alex Rios .15 .40
130 Brett Wallace .12 .30
131 Scott Baker .12 .30
132 Kurt Suzuki .12 .30
133 Sergio Santos .12 .30
134 Chipper Jones .20 .50
135 Josh Reddick .12 .30
136 Justin Morneau .15 .40
137 B.J. Upton .15 .40
138 Russell Martin .12 .30
139 Trevor Cahill .12 .30
140 Erick Aybar .12 .30
141 Drew Storen .12 .30
142 Tommy Hanson .12 .30
143 Craig Kimbrel .15 .40
144 Andrew McCutchen .20 .50
145 CC Sabathia .15 .40
146 Ian Desmond .12 .30
147 Corey Hart .12 .30
148 Shin-Soo Choo .15 .40
149 Adrian Gonzalez .15 .40
150 Jose Bautista .15 .40
151 Johnny Cueto .15 .40
152 Neil Walker .15 .40
153 Aramis Ramirez .12 .30
154 Yadier Molina .20 .50
155 Juan Nicasio .12 .30
156 Joey Votto .20 .50
157 Ubaldo Jimenez .12 .30
158 Mark Trumbo .12 .30
159 Max Scherzer .20 .50
160 Carlos Ruiz .12 .30
161 Hunter Pence .15 .40
162 Ricky Romero .12 .30
163 Heath Bell .12 .30
164 Nyjer Morgan .12 .30
165 Yovani Gallardo .15 .40
166 Peter Bourjos .12 .30
167 Orlando Hudson .12 .30
168 Jose Tabata .12 .30
169 Ian Kinsler .15 .40
170 Brian Wilson .20 .50
171 Jaime Garcia .15 .40
172 Dustin Pedroia .15 .40
173 Michael Pineda .12 .30
174 Brian McCann .15 .40
175 Jason Bay .15 .40
176 Geovany Soto .15 .40
177 Jhonny Peralta .12 .30
178 Desmond Jennings .15 .40
179 Zack Greinke .15 .40
180 Ted Lilly .12 .30
181 Clayton Kershaw .40 1.00
182 Seth Smith .12 .30
183 Cliff Lee .15 .40
184 Michael Bourn .12 .30
185 Jeff Niemann .12 .30
186 Martin Prado .12 .30
187 David Wright .15 .40
188 Paul Goldschmidt .20 .50
189 Mariano Rivera .25 .60
190 Stephen Strasburg .20 .50
191 Ivan Nova .15 .40
192 James Shields .12 .30
193 Casey McGehee .12 .30
194 Alex Gordon .15 .40
195 Ike Davis .12 .30
196 Cole Hamels .15 .40
197 Elvis Andrus .15 .40
198 Carl Crawford .15 .40
199 Felix Hernandez .15 .40
200 Albert Pujols .25 .60
201 Jose Reyes .12 .30
202 Starlin Castro .15 .40
203 John Danks .12 .30
204 Cory Luebke .12 .30
205 Chad Billingsley .12 .30
206 David Freese .12 .30
207 Brandon McCarthy .12 .30
208 James Loney .12 .30
209 Jered Weaver .15 .40
210 Freddie Freeman .25 .60
211 Ben Revere .15 .40
212 Daniel Hudson .12 .30
213 Jhoulys Chacin .12 .30
214 Alex Avila .12 .30
215 Colby Lewis .12 .30
216 Jason Kipnis .25 .60
217 Ryan Zimmerman .25 .60
218 Clay Buchholz .20 .50
219 Brandon Phillips .20 .50
220 Carlos Lee UER .20 .50
No card number
CL Christian Lopez SP 50.00 100.00

2012 Topps Opening Day Blue

*BLUE VET: 3X TO 8X BASIC
*BLUE RC: 1.5X TO 4X BASIC RC
STATED ODDS 1:6 RETAIL
STATED PRINT RUN 2012 SER.#'d SETS

2012 Topps Opening Day Autographs

STATED ODDS 1:568 RETAIL
AC Andrew Cashner 10.00 25.00
AE Alcides Escobar 8.00 20.00
BA Brett Anderson 6.00 15.00
CC Chris Coghlan 5.00 12.00
CH Chris Heisey 5.00 12.00
DB Daniel Bard 5.00 12.00
DM Daniel McCutchen 5.00 12.00
JJ Jon Jay 12.50 30.00
JN Jon Niese 5.00 12.00
MM Mitch Moreland 8.00 20.00
NF Neftali Feliz 8.00 20.00
NW Neil Walker 6.00 15.00

2012 Topps Opening Day Box Bottom

NNO Justin Verlander 1.50 4.00

2012 Topps Opening Day Elite Skills

COMPLETE SET (25) 5.00 12.00
STATED ODDS 1:4 RETAIL
ES1 Jose Reyes .40 1.00
ES2 Alex Gordon .50 1.25
ES3 Prince Fielder .50 1.25
ES4 Ian Kinsler .50 1.25
ES5 James Shields .40 1.00
ES6 Andrew McCutchen .60 1.50
ES7 Justin Verlander .60 1.50
ES8 Felix Hernandez .50 1.25
ES9 Barry Zito .50 1.25
ES10 R.A. Dickey .50 1.25
ES11 Roy Halladay .50 1.25
ES12 Ichiro Suzuki .75 2.00
ES13 David Wright .50 1.25
ES14 Troy Tulowitzki .60 1.50
ES15 Jose Bautista .50 1.25
ES16 Joey Votto .60 1.50
ES17 Joe Mauer .50 1.25
ES18 Mark Teixeira .50 1.25
ES19 Mike Stanton .60 1.50
ES20 Yadier Molina .60 1.50
ES21 Ryan Zimmerman .50 1.25
ES22 Jacoby Ellsbury .50 1.25
ES23 Carlos Gonzalez .50 1.25
ES24 Jered Weaver .50 1.25
ES25 Elvis Andrus .50 1.25

2012 Topps Opening Day Fantasy Squad

COMPLETE SET (30) 6.00 15.00
STATED ODDS 1:4 RETAIL
FS1 Albert Pujols .75 2.00
FS2 Miguel Cabrera .60 1.50
FS3 Adrian Gonzalez .50 1.25
FS4 Robinson Cano .50 1.25
FS5 Dustin Pedroia .50 1.25
FS6 Ian Kinsler .50 1.25
FS7 Troy Tulowitzki .60 1.50
FS8 Starlin Castro .50 1.25
FS9 Jose Reyes .40 1.00
FS10 David Wright .50 1.25
FS11 Evan Longoria .50 1.25
FS12 Hanley Ramirez .50 1.25
FS13 Victor Martinez .50 1.25
FS14 Brian McCann .50 1.25
FS15 Joe Mauer .50 1.25
FS16 David Ortiz .60 1.50
FS17 Billy Butler .40 1.00
FS18 Michael Young .40 1.00
FS19 Ryan Braun .40 1.00
FS20 Carlos Gonzalez .50 1.25
FS21 Josh Hamilton .50 1.25
FS22 Curtis Granderson .50 1.25
FS23 Matt Kemp .50 1.25
FS24 Jacoby Ellsbury .50 1.25
FS25 Jose Bautista .50 1.25
FS26 Justin Upton .50 1.25
FS27 Mike Stanton .60 1.50
FS28 Justin Verlander .60 1.50
FS29 Roy Halladay .50 1.25
FS30 Tim Lincecum .50 1.25

2012 Topps Opening Day Mascots

COMPLETE SET (25) 10.00 25.00
STATED ODDS 1:4 RETAIL
M1 Bernie Brewer .60 1.50
M2 Baltimore Orioles .60 1.50
M3 Toronto Blue Jays .60 1.50
M4 Arizona Diamondbacks .60 1.50
M5 Fredbird .60 1.50
M6 Raymond .60 1.50
M7 Mr. Met .60 1.50
M8 Atlanta Braves .60 1.50
M9 Rangers Captain .60 1.50
M10 Pirate Parrot .60 1.50
M11 Billy the Marlin .60 1.50
M12 Paws .60 1.50
M13 Dinger .60 1.50
M14 Phillie Phanatic .60 1.50
M15 Kansas City Royals .60 1.50
M16 Wally the Green Monster .60 1.50
M17 Gapper .60 1.50
M18 Slider .60 1.50
M19 TC .60 1.50
M20 Swinging Firar .60 1.50
M21 Chicago White Sox .60 1.50
M22 Screech .60 1.50
M23 Mariner Moose .60 1.50
M24 Oakland Athletics .60 1.50
M25 Junction Jack .60 1.50

2012 Topps Opening Day Stars

COMPLETE SET (25) 12.50 30.00
STATED ODDS 1:8 RETAIL
ODS1 Ryan Braun .60 1.50
ODS2 Albert Pujols 1.25 3.00
ODS3 Miguel Cabrera 1.00 2.50
ODS4 Adrian Gonzalez .75 2.00
ODS5 Troy Tulowitzki 1.00 2.50
ODS6 Matt Kemp .75 2.00
ODS7 Justin Verlander 1.00 2.50
ODS8 Jose Bautista .75 2.00
ODS9 Robinson Cano .75 2.00
ODS10 Roy Halladay .75 2.00
ODS11 Jacoby Ellsbury .75 2.00
ODS12 Prince Fielder .75 2.00
ODS13 Justin Upton .75 2.00
ODS14 Hanley Ramirez .75 2.00
ODS15 Clayton Kershaw 2.00 5.00
ODS16 Felix Hernandez .75 2.00
ODS17 David Wright .75 2.00
ODS18 Mark Teixeira .75 2.00
ODS19 Josh Hamilton .75 2.00
ODS20 Jered Weaver .75 2.00
ODS21 Joey Votto 1.00 2.50
ODS22 Evan Longoria .75 2.00
ODS23 Carlos Gonzalez .75 2.00
ODS24 Dustin Pedroia .75 2.00
ODS25 Tim Lincecum .75 2.00

2012 Topps Opening Day Superstar Celebrations

COMPLETE SET (20) 4.00 10.00
STATED ODDS 1:4 RETAIL
SC1 Matt Kemp .40 1.00
SC2 Justin Upton .40 1.00
SC3 Dan Uggla .40 1.00
SC4 Geovany Soto .40 1.00
SC5 Joey Votto .50 1.25
SC6 Alex Rios .40 1.00
SC7 Eric Hosmer .40 1.00
SC8 Troy Tulowitzki .50 1.25
SC9 Ryan Zimmerman .40 1.00
SC10 J.J. Putz .30 .75
SC11 Jacoby Ellsbury .40 1.00
SC12 Ian Kinsler .40 1.00
SC13 David Wright .40 1.00
SC14 Ryan Braun .30 .75
SC15 Miguel Cabrera .50 1.25
SC16 Nelson Cruz .50 1.25
SC17 Adam Jones .40 1.00
SC18 Brett Lawrie .40 1.00
SC19 Mark Trumbo .30 .75
SC20 Martin Prado .30 .75

2013 Topps Opening Day

COMP.SET w/o SP's (220) 12.50 30.00
1A Buster Posey .40 1.00
1B Posey SP Celebrate
2 Ricky Romero .20 .50
3 CC Sabathia .25 .60
4 Matt Dominguez .20 .50
5 Eric Hosmer .25 .60
6 David Wright .25 .60
7 Adrian Beltre .30 .75
8 Ryan Braun .25 .60
9 Mark Buehrle .25 .60
10 Mat Latos .25 .60
11 Hanley Ramirez .25 .60
12 Aroldis Chapman .30 .75
13 Carlos Beltran .25 .60
14 Josh Willingham .25 .60
15 Jim Johnson .20 .50
16 Jesus Montero .20 .50
17 John Axford .20 .50
18 Jemile Weeks .20 .50
19 Joey Votto .30 .75
20 Jacoby Ellsbury .25 .60
21 Yovani Gallardo .20 .50
22 Felix Hernandez .25 .60
23 Logan Morrison .20 .50
24 Tommy Milone .20 .50
25 Jonathan Papelbon .25 .60
26 Howie Kendrick .20 .50
27 Mike Trout 2.50 6.00
28A Prince Fielder .25 .60
28B Fielder SP Celebrate 12.00 30.00
29 Bronson Arroyo .20 .50
30 Jayson Werth .25 .60
31 Jeremy Hellickson .20 .50
32 Jered Weaver .25 .60
33 Trevor Plouffe .20 .50
34 Gerardo Parra .20 .50
35 Justin Verlander .30 .75
36 Tommy Hanson .20 .50
37 Jurickson Profar RC .40 1.00
38 Albert Pujols .40 1.00
39 Heath Bell .20 .50
40 Carlos Quentin .20 .50
41 Dustin Pedroia .25 .60
42 Jon Lester .25 .60
43 Pedro Alvarez .20 .50
44 Gio Gonzalez .25 .60
45 Clayton Kershaw .60 1.50
46A Zack Greinke .25 .60
46B Greinke SP Press 12.00 30.00
47 Jake Peavy .20 .50
48 Ike Davis .20 .50
49 Grant Balfour .20 .50
50A Bryce Harper .50 1.25
50B Harper SP w/Fans 40.00 80.00
51 Elvis Andrus .25 .60
52 Dylan Bundy RC .75 2.00
53 Addison Reed .20 .50
54 Starlin Castro .20 .50
55 Darwin Barney .20 .50
56A Josh Hamilton .25 .60
56B Hamilton SP Press 12.00 30.00
57 Cliff Lee .25 .60
58 Chris Davis .25 .60
59 Matt Harvey .25 .60
60 Carl Crawford .25 .60
61 Drew Hutchison .20 .50
62 Jason Kubel .20 .50
63 Jonathon Niese .20 .50
64 Justin Masterson .20 .50
65 Will Venable .20 .50
66 Shin-Soo Choo .25 .60
67 Marco Scutaro .25 .60
68 Barry Zito .25 .60
69 Brett Gardner .25 .60
70 Danny Espinosa .20 .50
71 Victor Martinez .25 .60
72 Shelby Miller RC .75 2.00
73 Ryan Vogelsong .20 .50
74 Jason Kipnis .25 .60
75 Trevor Cahill .20 .50
76 Adam Jones .25 .60
77 Mark Trumbo .20 .50
78 Hisashi Iwakuma .25 .60
79 Tyler Colvin .20 .50
80 Anthony Rizzo .50 1.25
81 Miguel Cabrera .30 .75
82 Carlos Santana .25 .60
83 Wilin Rosario .20 .50
84 Yonder Alonso .20 .50
85 Jeff Samardzija .20 .50
86 Brandon League .20 .50
87 Adrian Gonzalez .25 .60
88 Edwin Encarnacion .30 .75
89 Drew Stubbs .20 .50
90A Nick Swisher .25 .60
90B Swisher SP Press 40.00 80.00
91 Adam Wainwright .25 .60
92 Aramis Ramirez .20 .50
93A Justin Upton .25 .60
93B Upton SP Press 12.00 30.00
94A James Shields .20 .50
94B Shields SP Press
95 Daniel Murphy .25 .60
96 Jordan Zimmermann .25 .60
97A Matt Cain .25 .60
97B Cain SP w/Mic 8.00 20.00
98 Paul Goldschmidt .30 .75
99 Vernon Wells .20 .50
100 Matt Kemp .25 .60
101 Adeiny Hechavarria RC .40 1.00
102 Andrew McCutchen .30 .75
103 Desmond Jennings .25 .60
104 Tim Lincecum .25 .60
105 James McDonald .20 .50
106 Trevor Bauer .30 .75
107 Lance Berkman .25 .60
108 Hunter Pence .25 .60
109 Ian Desmond .20 .50
110 Corey Hart .20 .50
111 Jean Segura .25 .60
112 Chase Utley .25 .60
113 Carlos Gonzalez .25 .60
114 Mike Olt RC .40 1.00
115A B.J. Upton .25 .60
115B Upton SP Press
116 Norichika Aoki .20 .50
117 Michael Young .20 .50
118 Max Scherzer .30 .75
119 Angel Pagan .20 .50
120 Alex Rodriguez .40 1.00
121 Nick Markakis .25 .60
122 Aaron Hill .20 .50
123 John Danks .20 .50
124 Josh Reddick .20 .50
125 Bartolo Colon .20 .50
126 Todd Frazier .25 .60
127 Edinson Volquez .20 .50
128 A.J. Burnett .20 .50
129 Sergio Romo .20 .50
130 Chase Headley .20 .50
131A Jose Reyes .25 .60
131B Reyes SP Press 12.00 30.00
132 David Freese .20 .50
133 Billy Butler .20 .50
134 Cameron Maybin .20 .50
135 Josh Johnson .25 .60
136 Ian Kennedy .20 .50
137A Yoenis Cespedes .30 .75
137B Cespedes SP w/Fans
138 Joe Mauer .25 .60
139 Mark Teixeira .25 .60
140 Tyler Skaggs RC .50 1.25
141 Yadier Molina .30 .75
142 Jarrod Parker .20 .50
143 David Ortiz .30 .75
144 Matt Holliday .30 .75
145 Giancarlo Stanton .30 .75
146 Alex Cobb .20 .50
147 Ryan Zimmerman .25 .60
148 Alex Rios .25 .60
149 C.J. Wilson .20 .50
150 Derek Jeter .75 2.00
151A Torii Hunter .20 .50
151B Hunter SP Press 12.00 30.00
152 Brian Wilson .30 .75
153 Andre Ethier .25 .60
154 Nelson Cruz .30 .75
155 Brandon Crawford .25 .60
156 Adam Dunn .25 .60
157 Madison Bumgarner .25 .60
158 J.J. Putz .20 .50
159 Mike Moustakas .25 .60
160 Johan Santana .25 .60
161 Dan Uggla .20 .50
162 Roy Halladay .25 .60
163 Justin Morneau .25 .60
164 Jose Altuve .25 .60
165 Yu Darvish .30 .75
166 Tyler Clippard .20 .50
167 Starling Marte .25 .60
168 Miguel Montero .20 .50
169 Robinson Cano .25 .60
170 Stephen Strasburg .30 .75
171 Jarrod Saltalamacchia .20 .50
172 Manny Machado RC 2.00 5.00
173 Zack Cozart .20 .50
174 Kendrys Morales .20 .50
175 Brandon Phillips .20 .50
176 Mariano Rivera .40 1.00
177 Chris Sale .30 .75
178 Ben Zobrist .25 .60
179 Wade Miley .20 .50
180 Jason Heyward .25 .60
181 Neftali Feliz .20 .50
182 Freddie Freeman .40 1.00
183 Fernando Rodney .20 .50
184 Denard Span .20 .50
185 Curtis Granderson .25 .60
186 Paul Konerko .25 .60
187 Huston Street .20 .50
188 Coco Crisp .20 .50
189 Austin Jackson .20 .50
190 Chris Carpenter .25 .60
191 Johnny Cueto .25 .60
192 Josh Beckett .20 .50
193 Alex Gordon .25 .60
194 Rickie Weeks .20 .50
195 Tim Hudson .25 .60
196 Kyle Seager .20 .50
197 Jhonny Peralta .20 .50
198 Ryan Howard .25 .60
199 Craig Kimbrel .25 .60
200 Evan Longoria .25 .60
201 Ervin Santana .20 .50
202 Jason Motte .20 .50
203 Daniel Hudson .20 .50
204 Jay Bruce .25 .60
205 Doug Fister .20 .50
206 Cole Hamels .25 .60
207 Jose Bautista .25 .60
208 Jimmy Rollins .25 .60
209 Drew Storen .20 .50
210 Will Middlebrooks .20 .50
211 Allen Craig .25 .60
212A Pablo Sandoval .25 .60
212B Sandoval SP Celebrate 12.00 30.00
213A R.A. Dickey .25 .60
213B Dickey SP Press 12.00 30.00
214 Ian Kinsler .25 .60
215 Ivan Nova .25 .60
216 Kris Medlen .25 .60
217 Carlos Ruiz .20 .50
218 David Price .25 .60
219 Troy Tulowitzki .30 .75
220 Brett Lawrie .25 .60

2013 Topps Opening Day Blue

*BLUE VET: 2.5X TO 6X BASIC
*BLUE RC: 1.5X TO 4X BASIC RC
STATED PRINT RUN 2013 SER.#'d SETS

2013 Topps Opening Day Toys R Us Purple Border

*BLUE VET: 6X TO 15X BASIC
*BLUE RC: 4X TO 10X BASIC RC

2013 Topps Opening Day Autographs

BL Boone Logan 4.00 10.00
CG Craig Gentry 4.00 10.00
DC David Cooper 4.00 10.00
DW David Wright 12.00 30.00
HR Hanley Ramirez 10.00 25.00
ID Ike Davis 4.00 10.00
JT Justin Turner 25.00 60.00
JV Josh Vitters 5.00 12.00
RP Rick Porcello 5.00 12.00
WM Will Middlebrooks 4.00 10.00

2013 Topps Opening Day Ballpark Fun

COMPLETE SET (25) 4.00 10.00
BF1 Dustin Pedroia .40 1.00
BF2 Josh Reddick .30 .75
BF3 Jay Bruce .40 1.00
BF4 Prince Fielder .40 1.00
BF5 Matt Kemp .40 1.00
BF6 Adam Jones .40 1.00
BF7 Manny Machado 2.00 5.00
BF8 Johan Santana .40 1.00
BF9 Bryce Harper .75 2.00
BF10 Miguel Cabrera .50 1.25
BF11 Evan Longoria .40 1.00
BF12 David Ortiz .50 1.25
BF13 Albert Pujols .60 1.50
BF14 Jayson Werth .40 1.00
BF15 Derek Jeter 1.25 3.00
BF16 Elvis Andrus .40 1.00
BF17 Aaron Hill .30 .75
BF18 Darwin Barney .30 .75
BF19 Brandon Phillips .30 .75
BF20 Alfonso Soriano .40 1.00
BF21 Jurickson Profar .40 1.00
BF22 David Price .40 1.00
BF23 Aroldis Chapman .50 1.25
BF24 Hanley Ramirez .40 1.00
BF25 Coco Crisp .30 .75

2013 Topps Opening Day Highlights

ODH1 Ryan Zimmerman 1.25 3.00
ODH2 Miguel Cabrera 1.50 4.00
ODH3 Felix Hernandez 1.25 3.00
ODH4 Jason Heyward 1.25 3.00
ODH5 Jose Altuve 1.25 3.00
ODH6 CC Sabathia 1.25 3.00
ODH7 Clayton Kershaw 3.00 8.00
ODH8 Roy Halladay 1.25 3.00
ODH9 Jay Bruce 1.25 3.00
ODH10 Jose Bautista 1.25 3.00

2013 Topps Opening Day Mascot Autographs

MA1 Mr. Met 30.00 80.00
MA2 Phillie Phanatic 40.00 80.00
MA3 Mariner Moose 15.00 40.00
MA4 Fredbird 15.00 40.00
MA5 Rangers Captain 10.00 25.00

2013 Topps Opening Day Mascots

COMPLETE SET (24) 12.50 30.00
M1 Mr. Met .75 2.00
M2 Phillie Phanatic .75 2.00
M3 Mariner Moose .75 2.00
M4 Fredbird .75 2.00
M5 Rangers Captain .75 2.00
M6 Oakland Athletics .75 2.00
M7 Screech .75 2.00
M8 Bernie Brewer .75 2.00
M9 Chicago White Sox .75 2.00
M10 Swinging Friar .75 2.00
M11 TC .75 2.00
M12 Baltimore Orioles .75 2.00
M13 Atlanta Braves .75 2.00
M14 Raymond .75 2.00
M15 Pirate Parrot .75 2.00
M16 Orbit .75 2.00
M17 Paws .75 2.00
M18 Dinger .75 2.00
M19 Toronto Blue Jays .75 2.00
M20 Arizona Diamondbacks .75 2.00
M21 Kansas City Royals .75 2.00
M22 Wally the Green Monster .75 2.00
M23 Gapper .75 2.00
M24 Slider .75 2.00

2013 Topps Opening Day Play Hard

COMPLETE SET (25) 8.00 20.00
PH1 Buster Posey .75 2.00
PH2 Bryce Harper 1.00 2.50
PH3 Mike Trout 5.00 12.00
PH4 Ian Kinsler .50 1.25
PH5 Brett Lawrie .50 1.25
PH6 Jason Heyward .50 1.25
PH7 Dustin Pedroia .50 1.25
PH8 Josh Reddick .40 1.00
PH9 Starlin Castro .40 1.00
PH10 Miguel Cabrera .60 1.50
PH11 David Ortiz .60 1.50
PH12 Joe Mauer .50 1.25
PH13 Albert Pujols .75 2.00
PH14 David Wright .50 1.25
PH15 Andrew McCutchen .60 1.50
PH16 Matt Kemp .50 1.25
PH17 Jay Bruce .50 1.25
PH18 Carlos Ruiz .40 1.00
PH19 Prince Fielder .50 1.25
PH20 Yadier Molina .60 1.50
PH21 David Freese .40 1.00
PH22 Paul Goldschmidt .60 1.50
PH23 Hanley Ramirez .50 1.25
PH24 Alex Rodriguez .50 1.25
PH25 Alex Gordon .50 1.25

2013 Topps Opening Day Stars

COMPLETE SET (25) 12.50 30.00
ODS1 Prince Fielder .60 1.50
ODS2 Justin Verlander .75 2.00
ODS3 Miguel Cabrera .75 2.00
ODS4 Buster Posey 1.00 2.50
ODS5 Derek Jeter 2.00 5.00
ODS6 Robinson Cano .60 1.50
ODS7 Evan Longoria .60 1.50
ODS8 David Ortiz .75 2.00
ODS9 Joe Mauer .60 1.50
ODS10 Albert Pujols 1.00 2.50
ODS11 Mike Trout 6.00 15.00
ODS12 Josh Hamilton .60 1.50
ODS13 Yu Darvish .75 2.00
ODS14 Felix Hernandez .60 1.50
ODS15 David Wright .60 1.50
ODS16 R.A. Dickey .60 1.50
ODS17 Adrian Gonzalez .60 1.50
ODS18 Cole Hamels .60 1.50
ODS19 Bryce Harper 1.25 3.00
ODS20 Stephen Strasburg .75 2.00
ODS21 Joey Votto .75 2.00
ODS22 Ryan Braun .60 1.50
ODS23 Andrew McCutchen .75 2.00
ODS24 Matt Kemp .60 1.50
ODS25 Yadier Molina .75 2.00

2013 Topps Opening Day Superstar Celebrations

COMPLETE SET (25) 8.00 20.00
SC1 Matt Kemp .50 1.25
SC2 Billy Butler .40 1.00
SC3 Albert Pujols .75 2.00
SC4 Joey Votto .60 1.50
SC5 Giancarlo Stanton .60 1.50
SC6 Adam Jones .50 1.25
SC7 Josh Reddick .40 1.00
SC8 Ryan Zimmerman .50 1.25
SC9 Bryce Harper 1.00 2.50
SC10 Joe Mauer .50 1.25
SC11 Jayson Werth .50 1.25
SC12 Justin Morneau .50 1.25
SC13 Corey Hart .40 1.00
SC14 Chipper Jones .60 1.50
SC15 Felix Hernandez .50 1.25

C16 Mike Olt .50 1.25
C17 Chase Headley .40 1.00
C18 Josh Willingham .50 1.25
C19 Alfonso Soriano .50 1.25
C20 Prince Fielder .50 1.25
C21 Buster Posey .75 2.00
C22 Miguel Cabrera
C23 Mike Trout 5.00 12.00
C24 Justin Verlander .60 1.50
C25 David Ortiz .60 1.50

2014 Topps Opening Day

COMP.SET w/o SP's (220) 12.00 30.00
SP VARIATION ODDS 1:222
PRINTING PLATE ODDS 1:1575
PLATE PRINT RUN 1 SET PER COLOR
BLACK-CYAN-MAGENTA-YELLOW ISSUED
NO PLATE PRICING DUE TO SCARCITY
1A Mike Trout 1.00 2.50
1B Trout SP w/Glove 25.00 60.00
2A Dustin Pedroia .20 .50
2B Pedroia SP Red jsy 20.00 50.00
3 James Paxton RC .30 .75
4 Yordano Ventura RC .25 .60
5 Freddie Freeman .25 .60
6 Adrian Beltre .20 .50
7A Jacoby Ellsbury .15 .40
7B Ellsbury SP Press 15.00 40.00
8 Mike Napoli .12 .30
9 R.A. Dickey .15 .40
10 Pedro Alvarez .12 .30
11 Josh Donaldson .15 .40
12 Mark Teixeira .15 .40
13 Gerrit Cole .20 .50
14 Trevor Rosenthal .15 .40
15 Martin Perez .15 .40
16 Carlos Gonzalez .15 .40
17 Aaron Hicks .15 .40
18 Jered Weaver .15 .40
19A Koji Uehara .12 .30
19B Uehara SP w/Ortiz 10.00 25.00
20 Mike Minor .12 .30
21 Stephen Strasburg .20 .50
22 Clay Buchholz .12 .30
23 Felix Hernandez .15 .40
24 Michael Wacha .15 .40
25 Torii Hunter .12 .30
26 Jonathan Papelbon .15 .40
27 Doug Fister .12 .30
28 Kyle Seager .12 .30
29 C.J. Wilson .12 .30
30 Jason Heyward .15 .40
31 Hunter Pence .15 .40
32 Sergio Romo .12 .30
33 Ben Revere .12 .30
34 Jeremy Hellickson .12 .30
35 Junior Lake .12 .30
36 Wilin Rosario .12 .30
37 Brandon Belt .15 .40
38 Michael Cuddyer .12 .30
39 Allen Craig .15 .40
40 Wil Myers .12 .30
41 Roy Halladay .15 .40
42A Mariano Rivera .25 .60
42B Rivera SP Tipping cap 25.00 60.00
43 Victor Martinez .15 .40
44 Wade Miley .12 .30
45 Carl Crawford .15 .40
46 Todd Helton .15 .40
47 Matt Harvey .15 .40
48 Paul Goldschmidt .20 .50
49 Ian Desmond .12 .30
50A Clayton Kershaw .40 1.00
50B Kershaw SP Horizontal 20.00 50.00
51A David Ortiz .20 .50
51B Ortiz SP w/Trophy 20.00 50.00
52 Carlos Santana .15 .40
53 Paul Konerko .15 .40
54 Christian Yelich .25 .60
55 Nelson Cruz .20 .50
56 Jedd Gyorko .12 .30
57 Andrelton Simmons .12 .30
58 Justin Upton .15 .40
59 Francisco Liriano .12 .30
60 Alex Rios .15 .40
61 Yonder Alonso .12 .30
62 Matt Adams .12 .30
63 Starling Marte .15 .40
64 Tyler Skaggs .12 .30
65 Brett Gardner .15 .40
66 Albert Pujols .25 .60
67 Evan Gattis .12 .30
68 Patrick Corbin .15 .40
69 Jason Grilli .12 .30
70 Craig Kimbrel .15 .40
71 Jordan Zimmermann .15 .40
72A Jose Fernandez .20 .50
72B Fernandez SP w/Dino 20.00 50.00
73 Joe Mauer .15 .40
74 Matt Carpenter .20 .50
75 Will Middlebrooks .12 .30
76 Hisashi Iwakuma .15 .40
77 Jose Reyes .15 .40
78 Chris Davis .12 .30
79A Nick Castellanos RC .60 1.50
79B Castellanos SP Dugout 40.00 80.00
80A Justin Verlander .20 .50
80B Verlander SP Arm up 10.00 25.00
81 Hiroki Kuroda .12 .30
82 Rafael Soriano .12 .30
83 Cole Hamels .15 .40
84 Desmond Jennings .12 .30
85 Mike Leake .12 .30
86 Jeff Samardzija .12 .30
87 Jayson Werth .15 .40
88 Yoenis Cespedes .20 .50
89 Julio Teheran .15 .40
90 Jurickson Profar .15 .40
91 Matt Cain .15 .40
92 Coco Crisp .12 .30
93 Elvis Andrus .15 .40
94 Jim Henderson .12 .30
95 Todd Frazier .15 .40
96 Andre Rienzo RC .20 .50
97 Wilmer Flores RC .25 .60
98 Jose Altuve .15 .40
99 Pablo Sandoval .15 .40
100A Miguel Cabrera .20 .50
100B Cabrera SP Dugout 40.00 80.00
101 Zack Wheeler .15 .40
102 James Shields .12 .30
103A Adam Jones .15 .40
103B Jones SP w/Fans 12.00 30.00
104 Jason Kipnis .15 .40
105 Brian Dozier .15 .40
106 Matt Moore .15 .40
107 Joe Nathan .12 .30
108 Troy Tulowitzki .20 .50
109 Jay Bruce .15 .40
110 Jonny Gomes .12 .30
111 Aroldis Chapman .20 .50
112 Billy Butler .12 .30
113 Jon Lester .15 .40
114 Adam Dunn .15 .40
115 Max Scherzer .20 .50
116 Yunel Escobar .12 .30
117 Michael Choice RC .20 .50
118 J.J. Hardy .12 .30
119 Chase Utley .15 .40
120 Shin-Soo Choo .15 .40
121 Brandon Phillips .12 .30
122 Yadier Molina .20 .50
123 Lance Lynn .12 .30
124 Madison Bumgarner .15 .40
125 Tim Lincecum .15 .40
126 David Price .15 .40
127 Adam LaRoche .12 .30
128 Manny Machado .20 .50
129 Joey Votto .20 .50
130 Nick Swisher .15 .40
131 CC Sabathia .15 .40
132A Prince Fielder .15 .40
132B Fielder SP Press 20.00 50.00
133 Greg Holland .12 .30
134 David Wright .15 .40
135 Zack Greinke .15 .40
136 Anthony Rizzo .30 .75
137 Austin Jackson .12 .30
138 Enny Romero RC .20 .50
139 Jarred Cosart .12 .30
140A Brian McCann .15 .40
140B McCann SP Press 20.00 50.00
141A Kolten Wong RC .25 .60
141B Wong SP Arms up 20.00 50.00
142 Starlin Castro .12 .30
143A Taijuan Walker RC .20 .50
143B Walker SP No ball 12.00 30.00
144 Carlos Gomez .12 .30
145 Carlos Beltran .15 .40
146 Howie Kendrick .12 .30
147 Bobby Parnell .12 .30
148A Yu Darvish .20 .50
148B Darvish SP Blue shirt 15.00 40.00
149 Alex Rodriguez .25 .60
150A Buster Posey .25 .60
150B Posey SP Fielding 20.00 50.00
151 Chris Sale .20 .50
152 Darwin Barney .12 .30
153 Chris Archer .12 .30
154 Anthony Rendon .20 .50
155 Kendrys Morales .12 .30
156 Kris Medlen .15 .40
157 Jimmy Rollins .15 .40
158 Nolan Arenado .25 .60
159 Adam Wainwright .15 .40
160 Nate Schierholtz .12 .30
161 Nick Markakis .15 .40
162 Edwin Encarnacion .20 .50
163 Chris Johnson .12 .30
164 Sonny Gray .15 .40
165 Jose Iglesias .15 .40
166 Jose Bautista .15 .40
167 Sean Doolittle .12 .30
168 Kyle Lohse .12 .30
169 Martin Prado .12 .30
170A Billy Hamilton RC .25 .60
170B Hamilton SP Vertical 30.00 60.00
171 Ryan Zimmerman .15 .40
172 Josh Hamilton .15 .40
173 Josh Reddick .12 .30
174 Matt Davidson RC .25 .60
175 Trevor Plouffe .12 .30
176 Yovani Gallardo .12 .30
177 Nick Franklin .12 .30
178A Xander Bogaerts RC .60 1.50
178B Bogaerts SP Sliding 40.00 80.00
179 Johnny Cueto .15 .40
180 Alex Gordon .15 .40
181 Jean Segura .15 .40
182 Adrian Gonzalez .15 .40
183 Aramis Ramirez .12 .30
184 Ubaldo Jimenez .12 .30
185 Ian Kinsler .15 .40
186 Jonathan Schoop RC .20 .50
187 Giancarlo Stanton .20 .50
188 Andrew Lambo RC .20 .50
189 Matt Holliday .20 .50
190A Andrew McCutchen .20 .50
190B McCutch SP Fielding 15.00 40.00
191 Derek Holland .12 .30
192 Kevin Gausman .15 .40
193 Matt Kemp .15 .40
194 Shane Victorino .15 .40
195A Robinson Cano .15 .40
195B Cano SP Press 15.00 40.00
196 Mike Zunino .12 .30
197 David Freese .12 .30
198 Evan Longoria .15 .40
199 Ryan Braun .15 .40
200A Bryce Harper .30 .75
200B Harper SP Horizontal 20.00 50.00
201 Tony Cingrani .15 .40
202 Jake Marisnick RC .20 .50
203 Ryan Howard .15 .40
204 Shelby Miller .15 .40
205 Domonic Brown .15 .40
206 Carlos Ruiz .12 .30
207 Joe Kelly .12 .30
208 Hanley Ramirez .15 .40
209 Alfonso Soriano .15 .40
210 Eric Hosmer .15 .40
211 Mat Latos .15 .40
212 Mark Trumbo .12 .30
213 Hyun-Jin Ryu .15 .40
214 Travis d'Arnaud RC .25 .60
215 Cliff Lee .15 .40
216 Chase Headley .12 .30
217 Robbie Erlin RC .20 .50
218 Everth Cabrera .12 .30
219A Yasiel Puig .20 .50
219B Puig SP Throwing 50.00 100.00
220A Derek Jeter .50 1.25
220B Jeter SP w/Ball 50.00 120.00

2014 Topps Opening Day Blue

*BLUE: 2.5X TO 6X BASIC
*BLUE RC: 1.5X TO 4X BASIC RC
STATED ODDS 1:3
STATED PRINT RUN 2014 SER.#'d SETS

2014 Topps Opening Day Toys R Us Purple Border

*BLUE VET: 4X TO 10X BASIC
*BLUE RC: 2.5X TO 6X BASIC RC
220 Derek Jeter 12.00 30.00

2014 Topps Opening Day Autographs

STATED ODDS 1:278
ODAAL Andrew Lambo 6.00 15.00
ODAGP Glen Perkins 6.00 15.00
ODAJL Junior Lake 10.00 25.00
ODAKS Kyle Seager 6.00 15.00
ODAMO Marcell Ozuna 10.00 25.00
ODASC Steve Cishek 6.00 15.00
ODASD Steve Delabar 6.00 15.00
ODATF Todd Frazier 8.00 20.00
ODAWM Wil Myers 6.00 15.00
ODAZA Zoilo Almonte 8.00 20.00

2014 Topps Opening Day Between Innings

COMPLETE SET (10) 15.00 40.00
STATED ODDS 1:36
BI1 Racing Presidents 2.00 5.00
BI2 Pierogie Race 2.00 5.00
BI3 Hot Dog Race 2.00 5.00
BI4 Cincinnati Mascot Races 2.00 5.00
BI5 Hot Dog Cannon 2.00 5.00
BI6 Famous Racing Sausages 2.00 5.00
BI7 Prank the Opponent 2.00 5.00
BI8 Hug a Mascot 2.00 5.00
BI9 Thank the Fans 2.00 5.00
BI10 Start a Cheer 2.00 5.00

2014 Topps Opening Day Breaking Out

COMPLETE SET (20) 5.00 12.00
STATED ODDS 1:5
BO1 Jason Heyward .30 .75
BO2 Clayton Kershaw .75 2.00
BO3 Bryce Harper .60 1.50
BO4 Mike Trout 2.00 5.00
BO5 Buster Posey .50 1.25
BO6 Yoenis Cespedes .40 1.00
BO7 David Wright .30 .75
BO8 Evan Longoria .30 .75
BO9 Joe Mauer .30 .75
BO10 Jay Bruce .30 .75
BO11 Joey Votto .40 1.00
BO12 Troy Tulowitzki .40 1.00
BO13 Stephen Strasburg .40 1.00
BO14 Andrew McCutchen .40 1.00
BO15 Ryan Braun .30 .75
BO16 Robinson Cano .30 .75
BO17 Justin Verlander .40 1.00
BO18 Felix Hernandez .30 .75
BO19 Manny Machado .40 1.00
BO20 Paul Goldschmidt .40 1.00

2014 Topps Opening Day Fired Up

COMPLETE SET (30) 6.00 15.00
STATED ODDS 1:5
UP1 Bryce Harper .60 1.50
UP2 Yasiel Puig .40 1.00
UP3 Dustin Pedroia .40 1.00
UP4 Jon Lester .30 .75
UP5 Sergio Romo .25 .60
UP6 Jonathan Papelbon .30 .75
UP7 Justin Verlander .40 1.00
UP8 Felix Hernandez .30 .75
UP9 Yadier Molina .40 1.00
UP10 Yu Darvish .40 1.00
UP11 Jacoby Ellsbury .30 .75
UP12 Jered Weaver .30 .75
UP13 Matt Kemp .30 .75
UP14 Koji Uehara .25 .60
UP15 David Wright .30 .75
UP16 Eric Hosmer .30 .75
UP17 Hanley Ramirez .30 .75
UP18 Brandon Phillips .25 .60
UP19 CC Sabathia .30 .75
UP20 David Price .30 .75
UP21 Mike Trout 2.00 5.00
UP22 Allen Craig .30 .75
UP23 Matt Carpenter .40 1.00
UP24 Jason Grilli .25 .60
UP25 Brett Lawrie .30 .75
UP26 Adam Wainwright .30 .75
UP27 Craig Kimbrel .30 .75
UP28 Hunter Pence .30 .75
UP29 Adrian Gonzalez .30 .75
UP30 Jason Kipnis .30 .75

2014 Topps Opening Day Mascot Autographs

STATED ODDS 1:555
MABO Baltimore Orioles 20.00 50.00
MAPP Pirate Parrot 12.00 30.00
MAPAW Paws 12.00 30.00
MARAY Raymond 12.00 30.00
MAWGM Wally the Green Monster 20.00 50.00

2014 Topps Opening Day Mascots

COMPLETE SET (25) 12.00 30.00
COMMON CARD .75 2.00
STATED ODDS 1:5
M1 Kansas City Royals .75 2.00
M2 Orbit .75 2.00
M3 Baltimore Orioles .75 2.00
M4 Bernie Brewer .75 2.00
M5 Oakland Athletics .75 2.00
M6 Fredbird .75 2.00
M7 Chicago White Sox .75 2.00
M8 TC Bear .75 2.00
M9 Raymond .75 2.00
M10 Dinger .75 2.00
M11 Gapper .75 2.00
M12 Wally the Green Monster 1.00 2.50
M13 Phillie Phanatic 1.00 2.50
M14 Rangers Captain .75 2.00
M15 Screech .75 2.00
M16 Atlanta Braves .75 2.00
M17 Paws .75 2.00
M18 Baxter the Bobcat .75 2.00
M19 Slider .75 2.00
M20 Toronto Blue Jays .75 2.00
M21 Pirate Parrot .75 2.00
M22 Swinging Friar .75 2.00
M23 Mariner Moose .75 2.00
M24 Billy the Marlin .75 2.00
M25 Mr. Met 1.00 2.50

2014 Topps Opening Day Relics

STATED ODDS 1:278
ODRAG Alex Gordon 3.00 8.00
ODRDJ Desmond Jennings 3.00 8.00
ODRDJ Derek Jeter 30.00 60.00
ODRFF Freddie Freeman 4.00 10.00
ODRJB Jose Bautista 3.00 8.00
ODRKU Koji Uehara 6.00 15.00
ODRMK Matt Kemp 3.00 8.00
ODRSM Starling Marte 5.00 12.00
ODRTH Torii Hunter 2.50 6.00
ODRJBR Jay Bruce 4.00 10.00

2014 Topps Opening Day Stars

COMPLETE SET (25) 12.00 30.00
STATED ODDS 1:5
ODS1 Mike Trout 3.00 8.00
ODS2 Miguel Cabrera .60 1.50
ODS3 Andrew McCutchen .60 1.50
ODS4 Paul Goldschmidt .60 1.50
ODS5 Ryan Braun .50 1.25
ODS6 Clayton Kershaw 1.25 3.00
ODS7 Carlos Gonzalez .50 1.25
ODS8 Chris Davis .40 1.00
ODS9 Troy Tulowitzki .60 1.50
ODS10 Joe Mauer .50 1.25
ODS11 Buster Posey .75 2.00
ODS12 Stephen Strasburg .60 1.50
ODS13 Felix Hernandez .50 1.25
ODS14 David Ortiz .60 1.50
ODS15 Yasiel Puig .60 1.50
ODS16 Matt Kemp .50 1.25
ODS17 Dustin Pedroia .60 1.50
ODS18 Bryce Harper 1.00 2.50
ODS19 Yu Darvish .60 1.50
ODS20 David Wright .50 1.25
ODS21 Joey Votto .60 1.50
ODS22 Justin Upton .50 1.25
ODS23 Giancarlo Stanton .60 1.50
ODS24 Evan Longoria .50 1.25
ODS25 Derek Jeter 1.50 4.00

2014 Topps Opening Day Superstar Celebrations

COMPLETE SET (25) 5.00 12.00
COMMON CARD .25 .60
SEMISTARS .30 .75
UNLISTED STARS .40 1.00
STATED ODDS 1:5
SC1 Jay Bruce .30 .75
SC2 Alex Gordon .30 .75
SC3 Torii Hunter .25 .60
SC4 Freddie Freeman .50 1.25
SC5 Jose Bautista .30 .75
SC6 Chris Johnson .25 .60
SC7 Barry Zito .30 .75
SC8 Buster Posey .50 1.25
SC9 Chris Davis .25 .60
SC10 Adam Dunn .30 .75
SC11 Salvador Perez .30 .75
SC12 Carl Crawford .30 .75
SC13 Aramis Ramirez .25 .60
SC14 Yoenis Cespedes .40 1.00
SC15 Mike Napoli .25 .60
SC16 Jason Kipnis .30 .75
SC17 Nick Swisher .30 .75
SC18 Justin Upton .30 .75
SC19 Pablo Sandoval .30 .75
SC20 Andrelton Simmons .25 .60
SC21 Paul Goldschmidt .40 1.00
SC22 Bryce Harper .60 1.50
SC23 Josh Donaldson .30 .75
SC24 Jonny Gomes .25 .60
SC25 Yasiel Puig .40 1.00

2015 Topps Opening Day

COMP.SET w/o SP's (200) 12.00 30.00
SP VARIATION ODDS 1:307 HOBBY
PRINTING PLATE ODDS 1:2391 HOBBY
PLATE PRINT RUN 1 SET PER COLOR
BLACK-CYAN-MAGENTA-YELLOW ISSUED
NO PLATE PRICING DUE TO SCARCITY
1 Homer Bailey .12 .30
2 Curtis Granderson .15 .40
3 Todd Frazier .15 .40
4 Lonnie Chisenhall .12 .30
5A Jose Altuve .15 .40
5B Altuve SP w/Fans 15.00 40.00
6 Matt Carpenter .20 .50
7 Matt Garza .12 .30
8 Starling Marte .15 .40
9 Yu Darvish .20 .50
10 Pat Neshek .12 .30
11 Anthony Rizzo .30 .75
12 Chris Tillman .12 .30
13 Drew Hutchison .12 .30
14 Michael Taylor RC .20 .50
15 Gregory Polanco .15 .40
16 Jake Lamb RC .30 .75
17 David Ortiz .20 .50
18A Pablo Sandoval .15 .40
18B Sndvl SP w/Mascot 20.00 50.00
19 Adam Jones .15 .40
20 Miguel Cabrera .20 .50
21 Evan Gattis .12 .30
22 Gerrit Cole .20 .50
23 Greg Holland .12 .30
24 Tim Lincecum .15 .40
25 Jorge Soler RC .30 .75
26A Buster Posey .25 .60
26B Posey SP Parade 25.00 60.00
27 George Springer .15 .40
28 Jedd Gyorko .12 .30
29 John Lackey .15 .40
30A Danny Santana .12 .30
30B Sntna SP In dugout 12.00 30.00
31 David Wright .15 .40
32 Jordan Zimmermann .15 .40
33A Eric Hosmer .15 .40
33B Hosmer SP w/Fans 25.00 60.00
34 Michael Pineda .12 .30
35 Travis d'Arnaud .15 .40
36 Clay Buchholz .12 .30
37 Chris Archer .12 .30
38A Johnny Cueto .15 .40
38B Johnny Cueto SP Sunglasses 15.00 40.00
39 Albert Pujols .25 .60
40A Clayton Kershaw .40 1.00
40B Kershaw SP Celebrate 50.00 120.00
41 Carlos Gonzalez .15 .40
42 Anthony Rendon .20 .50
43 Nick Castellanos .20 .50
44 Jonathan Lucroy .15 .40
45 Bryce Harper .30 .75
46 Chris Owings .12 .30
47 Jacoby Ellsbury .15 .40
48 Alex Rodriguez .25 .60
49 Jonny Gomes .12 .30
50 Rougned Odor .15 .40
51 Aramis Ramirez .12 .30
52 Roenis Elias .12 .30
53 Jean Segura .15 .40
54 Jeff Samardzija .12 .30
55 Francisco Liriano .12 .30
56 Elvis Andrus .15 .40
57 Salvador Perez .15 .40
58 Starlin Castro .12 .30
59 Paul Goldschmidt .20 .50
60 Ryan Braun .15 .40
61 Yovani Gallardo .12 .30
62 Jose Bautista .15 .40
63 Adrian Gonzalez .15 .40
64 Anibal Sanchez .12 .30
65 Michael Wacha .15 .40
66A Andrew McCutchen .20 .50
66B McCtchn SP On deck 30.00 80.00
67 Josh Harrison .12 .30
68A Joe Mauer .15 .40
68B Mauer SP In dugout 15.00 40.00
69 James Shields .12 .30
70 Alfredo Simon .12 .30
71 J.D. Martinez .20 .50
72 Coco Crisp .12 .30
73 Kyle Seager .12 .30
74A Derek Norris .12 .30
74B Ellsbury SP Stretching 30.00 80.00
75 Jimmy Rollins .15 .40
76 Matt Shoemaker .15 .40
77A Mike Trout 1.00 2.50
77B Trout SP On deck 400.00 800.00
78 Garrett Richards .15 .40
79 Jered Weaver .15 .40
80 Alexei Ramirez .15 .40
81 Aroldis Chapman .20 .50
82 Joey Votto .20 .50
83 Corey Kluber .15 .40
84 Troy Tulowitzki .20 .50
85 Zack Greinke .15 .40
86 Giancarlo Stanton .20 .50
87 Josh Hamilton .15 .40
88 Christian Yelich .25 .60
89 Brian Dozier .15 .40
90 Daniel Murphy .15 .40
91 Brett Gardner .15 .40
92 Mark Teixeira .15 .40
93 Carlos Beltran .15 .40
94 Sonny Gray .15 .40
95 Jonathan Papelbon .15 .40
96A Madison Bumgarner .15 .40
96B Bmgrnr SP Parade 30.00 80.00
97 Lance Lynn .12 .30
98 Adam Wainwright .15 .40
99 Evan Longoria .15 .40
100 Shin-Soo Choo .15 .40
101 Edwin Encarnacion .20 .50
102 Gio Gonzalez .15 .40
103 Ryan Zimmerman .15 .40
104 Anthony Ranaudo RC .20 .50
105A Jose Abreu .20 .50
105B Abreu SP Pinstripes 20.00 50.00
106A Jacob deGrom .20 .50
106B deGrom SP Blue jacket 20.00 50.00
107 Erick Aybar .12 .30
108 R.A. Dickey .15 .40
109A Brandon Finnegan RC .20 .50
109B Fnngn SP Gatorade 30.00 80.00
110 Dalton Pompey RC .25 .60
111 Dilson Herrera RC .25 .60
112 Bryce Brentz RC .20 .50
113 Matt Barnes RC .20 .50
114 Hunter Pence .15 .40
115 Jason Kipnis .15 .40
116 David Freese .12 .30
117 Hector Santiago .12 .30
118 Mookie Betts .30 .75
119A Craig Kimbrel .15 .40
119B Kmbrl SP w/Award 15.00 40.00
120 Jay Bruce .15 .40
121 Mike Leake .12 .30
122A Justin Verlander .20 .50
122B Vrlndr SP w/Fans 25.00 60.00
123A Victor Martinez .15 .40
123B Mrtnz SP Press conference 15.00 40.00
124 Henderson Alvarez .12 .30
125 Adeiny Hechavarria .12 .30
126 Oswaldo Arcia .12 .30
127 Francisco Cervelli .12 .30
128 Chase Headley .12 .30
129 Angel Pagan .12 .30
130 Matt Holliday .20 .50
131 Yadier Molina .20 .50
132 Peter Bourjos .12 .30
133 Jose Molina .12 .30
134 Stephen Strasburg .20 .50
135 Stephen Drew .12 .30
136 Drew Smyly .12 .30
137 Dellin Betances .15 .40
138 Gregor Blanco .12 .30
139 Marcell Ozuna .20 .50
140A Hanley Ramirez .15 .40
140B Rmrz SP Press conference 15.00 40.00
141 Julio Teheran .15 .40
142 Zack Wheeler .15 .40
143 Freddie Freeman .25 .60
144A Robinson Cano .15 .40
144B Cano SP Signing 30.00 80.00
145 Kolten Wong .15 .40
146 Ben Zobrist .15 .40
147 Carlos Martinez .15 .40
148 Ryan Howard .15 .40
149 Jason Castro .12 .30
150 Hisashi Iwakuma .15 .40
151A Rusney Castillo RC .25 .60
151B Cstllo SP w/Ortiz 25.00 60.00
152 Ian Desmond .12 .30
153 Cole Hamels .15 .40
154 Tanner Roark .12 .30
155 Xander Bogaerts .20 .50
156 Daniel Corcino RC .20 .50
157 Cory Spangenberg RC .20 .50
158 Wilmer Flores .15 .40
159A Justin Morneau .15 .40
159B Morneau SP w/ Puig 20.00 50.00
160 Kevin Kiermaier .15 .40
161 Arismendy Alcantara .12 .30
162 Chris Davis .12 .30
163 Rafael Montero .12 .30
164 Jose Reyes .15 .40
165 Ian Kinsler .15 .40
166 Masahiro Tanaka .15 .40
167 Mike Minor .12 .30
168 Kennys Vargas .12 .30
169 Matt Adams .12 .30
170 Marcus Stroman .15 .40
171 Andrelton Simmons .12 .30
172A David Price .15 .40
172B Price SP Glasses 25.00 60.00
173 Alex Cobb .12 .30
174 Michael Brantley .15 .40
175 Manny Machado .20 .50
176 Lucas Duda .15 .40
177 Billy Hamilton .15 .40
178 Carlos Santana .15 .40
179 David Robertson .15 .40
180 Doug Fister .12 .30
181 Jose Fernandez .20 .50
182 Adrian Beltre .20 .50
183 Dustin Pedroia .20 .50
184 Guilder Rodriguez RC .20 .50
185 Maikel Franco RC .25 .60
186 Felix Hernandez .15 .40
187 Daniel Norris RC .20 .50
188A Javier Baez RC 1.50 4.00
188B Baez SP Sunglasses 30.00 80.00
189 CC Sabathia .15 .40
190 Cliff Lee .15 .40
191 Jayson Werth .15 .40
192 Allen Craig .12 .30
193 Joc Pederson RC .40 1.00
194 Andrew Cashner .12 .30
195 Carlos Gomez .12 .30
196 Brandon Phillips .12 .30
197 Brian McCann .15 .40
198A Yasiel Puig .20 .50
198B Puig SP w/Fans 25.00 60.00
199 Aaron Sanchez .15 .40
200 Desmond Jennings .15 .40

2015 Topps Opening Day Blue Foil

*BLUE: 2.5X TO 6X BASIC
*BLUE RC: 1.5X TO 4X BASIC RC
STATED ODDS 1:5 HOBBY

2015 Topps Opening Day Toys R Us Purple Border

*PURPLE VET: 4X TO 10X BASIC
*PURPLE RC: 2.5X TO 6X BASIC RC

2015 Topps Opening Day Autographs

STATED ODDS 1:383 HOBBY
ODAAA Arismendy Alcantara 4.00 10.00
ODACO Chris Owings 4.00 10.00
ODAJB Javier Baez 20.00 50.00
ODAJP Joe Panik 20.00 50.00
ODAJS Jonathan Schoop 12.00 30.00
ODALD Lucas Duda 5.00 12.00
ODAMB Mookie Betts 30.00 80.00
ODAMF Mike Foltynewicz 6.00 15.00
ODAMZ Mike Zunino 4.00 10.00
ODARC Rusney Castillo 12.00 30.00
ODARD Rubby De La Rosa 4.00 10.00
ODARE Roenis Elias 4.00 10.00
ODATT Troy Tulowitzki 20.00 50.00

2015 Topps Opening Day Franchise Flashbacks

COMPLETE SET (20) 4.00 10.00
STATED ODDS 1:5 HOBBY
FF01 Craig Kimbrel .25 .60
FF02 Ryan Braun .25 .60
FF03 George Springer .25 .60
FF04 Robinson Cano .25 .60
FF05 Anthony Rizzo .50 1.25
FF06 Manny Machado .30 .75
FF07 Gregor Blanco .20 .50
FF08 Julio Teheran .25 .60
FF09 Alex Gordon .25 .60
FF10 Tim Lincecum .25 .60
FF11 Adrian Beltre .30 .75
FF12 Nick Castellanos .30 .75
FF13 Jose Altuve .25 .60
FF14 Jered Weaver .20 .50
FF15 Danny Santana .20 .50
FF16 Jonathan Lucroy .25 .60
FF17 Starlin Castro .20 .50
FF18 Chase Utley .25 .60
FF19 Freddie Freeman .40 1.00
FF20 Mike Trout 1.50 4.00

2015 Topps Opening Day Hit the Dirt

COMPLETE SET (15) 4.00 10.00
STATED ODDS 1:5 HOBBY
HTD01 Bryce Harper .60 1.50
HTD02 Lorenzo Cain .25 .60
HTD03 Billy Hamilton .25 .60
HTD04 Mike Trout 2.00 5.00
HTD05 Jacoby Ellsbury .30 .75
HTD06 Ian Kinsler .30 .75
HTD07 Jose Reyes .30 .75
HTD08 Carlos Gomez .25 .60
HTD09 George Springer .30 .75
HTD10 Ben Revere .25 .60
HTD11 Starling Marte .30 .75
HTD12 Yasiel Puig .40 1.00
HTD13 Elvis Andrus .30 .75
HTD14 Denard Span .25 .60
HTD15 Dustin Pedroia .40 1.00

2015 Topps Opening Day Mascot Autographs

STATED ODDS 1:776 HOBBY
MABT Billy the Marlin 12.00 30.00
MAPP Phillie Phanatic 20.00 50.00
MARC Rangers Captain 12.00 30.00
MATB TC Bear 12.00 30.00
MATR Theodore Roosevelt 12.00 30.00

2015 Topps Opening Day Mascots

COMPLETE SET (25) 10.00 25.00
STATED ODDS 1:5 HOBBY
M01 Baxter the Bobcat .60 1.50
M02 Atlanta Braves .60 1.50
M03 Baltimore Orioles .60 1.50

M04 Wally the Green Monster .75 2.00
M05 Clark .60 1.50
M06 Chicago White Sox .60 1.50
M07 Gapper .60 1.50
M08 Rosie Red .60 1.50
M09 Slider .60 1.50
M10 Dinger .60 1.50
M11 Paws .60 1.50
M12 Billy the Marlin .60 1.50
M13 Orbit .60 1.50
M14 Kansas City Royals .60 1.50
M15 TC Bear .60 1.50
M16 Bernie Brewer .60 1.50
M17 Mr. Met .75 2.00
M18 Phillie Phanatic .75 2.00
M19 Pirate Parrot .60 1.50
M20 Swinging Friar .60 1.50
M21 Mariner Moose .60 1.50
M22 Fredbird .60 1.50
M23 Raymond .60 1.50
M24 Rangers Captain .60 1.50
M25 Theodore Roosevelt .60 1.50

2015 Topps Opening Day Relics

STATED ODDS 1:383 HOBBY
ODRAM Andrew McCutchen 6.00 15.00
ODRBP Buster Posey 6.00 15.00
ODRDO David Ortiz 5.00 12.00
ODRDW David Wright 4.00 10.00
ODRKW Kolten Wong 6.00 15.00
ODRMC Miguel Cabrera 6.00 15.00
ODRNC Nick Castellanos 6.00 15.00
ODRTT Troy Tulowitzki 5.00 12.00
ODRYP Yasiel Puig 5.00 12.00
ODRYV Yordano Ventura 6.00 15.00

2015 Topps Opening Day Stadium Scenes

COMPLETE SET (15) 2.50 6.00
STATED ODDS 1:5 HOBBY
STABS Ben Shaw .25 .60
STACP Cameron Payne .25 .60
STADA Dylan Abruscato .25 .60
STADD David Joseph Dick Jr. .25 .60
STADR Donny Racz .25 .60
STAJB Jim Brady .25 .60
STAJF Jordyn Fernandez .25 .60
STAJFJ Juan Fernandez Jr. .25 .60
STAJW Joey Wright .25 .60
STAKR Kevin Ransom .25 .60
STALD Luca Djelosevic .25 .60
STALM Lance McKinnon .25 .60
STARG Robert Grunbaum .25 .60
STARGM Ryan Groose-Meils .25 .60
STATC Tom Cicotello .25 .60
STATCC Tim Culin-Couwels .25 .60
STATV Tony Voda .25 .60

2015 Topps Opening Day Stars

COMPLETE SET (25) 20.00 50.00
STATED ODDS 1:24 HOBBY
ODS01 Mike Trout 5.00 12.00
ODS02 Miguel Cabrera 1.00 2.50
ODS03 Andrew McCutchen 1.00 2.50
ODS04 Jose Abreu 1.00 2.50
ODS05 Clayton Kershaw 2.00 5.00
ODS06 Yasiel Puig 1.00 2.50
ODS07 Felix Hernandez .75 2.00
ODS08 Robinson Cano .75 2.00
ODS09 David Ortiz 1.00 2.50
ODS10 Freddie Freeman 1.25 3.00
ODS11 Buster Posey 1.25 3.00
ODS12 Masahiro Tanaka .75 2.00
ODS13 Paul Goldschmidt 1.00 2.50
ODS14 Bryce Harper 1.50 4.00
ODS15 Yadier Molina 1.00 2.50
ODS16 Adam Jones .75 2.00
ODS17 Evan Longoria .75 2.00
ODS18 David Wright .75 2.00
ODS19 Matt Harvey .75 2.00
ODS20 Joe Mauer .75 2.00
ODS21 Ryan Braun .75 2.00
ODS22 Yu Darvish 1.00 2.50
ODS23 Prince Fielder .75 2.00
ODS24 Troy Tulowitzki 1.00 2.50
ODS25 Jacob deGrom 1.00 2.50

2015 Topps Opening Day Superstar Celebrations

COMPLETE SET (25) 5.00 12.00
STATED ODDS 1:5 HOBBY
SC01 Mike Trout 2.00 5.00
SC02 Madison Bumgarner .30 .75
SC03 Salvador Perez .30 .75
SC04 Giancarlo Stanton .40 1.00
SC05 Tim Lincecum .30 .75
SC06 Rajai Davis .25 .60
SC07 Jordan Zimmermann .30 .75
SC08 Bryce Harper .60 1.50
SC09 Clayton Kershaw .75 2.00
SC10 Chase Utley .30 .75
SC11 Jose Abreu .40 1.00
SC12 Tommy Hunter .25 .60
SC13 Miguel Cabrera .40 1.00
SC14 Albert Pujols .50 1.25
SC15 Anthony Rizzo .60 1.50
SC16 Kolten Wong .30 .75
SC17 Michael Brantley .30 .75
SC18 Mike Napoli .25 .60
SC19 Mike Moustakas .30 .75
SC20 Edwin Encarnacion .40 1.00
SC21 Coco Crisp .25 .60
SC22 Kyle Seager .25 .60
SC23 Jason Castro .25 .60
SC24 Adrian Beltre .40 1.00
SC25 Evan Gattis .25 .60

2015 Topps Opening Day Team Spirit

COMPLETE SET (10) 8.00 20.00
STATED ODDS 1:36 HOBBY
TS01 Mike Trout 4.00 10.00
TS02 Phillie Phanatic .75 2.00
TS03 Madison Bumgarner .60 1.50
TS04 Greg Holland .50 1.25
TS05 Miguel Cabrera .75 2.00
TS06 Clayton Kershaw 1.50 4.00
TS07 Bryce Harper 1.25 3.00
TS08 TC Bear .75 2.00
TS09 Jorge Soler .75 2.00
TS10 Adam Eaton .50 1.25

2016 Topps Opening Day

COMP.SET w/o SP's (200) 10.00 25.00
SP VARIATION ODDS 1:393 HOBBY
PRINTING PLATE ODDS 1:3070 HOBBY
PLATE PRINT RUN 1 SET PER COLOR
BLACK-CYAN-MAGENTA-YELLOW ISSUED
NO PLATE PRICING DUE TO SCARCITY
OD1 Mike Trout 1.00 2.50
OD2A Noah Syndergaard .15 .40
OD2B Syndrgrd SP w/Team 25.00 60.00
OD3 Carlos Santana .15 .40
OD4 Derek Norris .12 .30
OD5A Kenley Jansen .15 .40
OD5B Jansen SP Peace 12.00 30.00
OD6 Luke Jackson RC .20 .50
OD7 Brian Johnson RC .20 .50
OD8 Russell Martin .12 .30
OD9 Rick Porcello .15 .40
OD10 Felix Hernandez .15 .40
OD11 Danny Salazar .15 .40
OD12A Dellin Betances .15 .40
OD12B Btncs SP T-shirt 20.00 50.00
OD13 Rob Refsnyder RC .25 .60
OD14 James Shields .12 .30
OD15 Brandon Crawford .15 .40
OD16 Tom Murphy RC .20 .50
OD17A Kris Bryant .25 .60
OD17B Bryant SP Celebrate 50.00 120.00
OD18 Richie Shaffer RC .20 .50
OD19 Brandon Belt .15 .40
OD20 Anthony Rizzo .30 .75
OD21A Mike Moustakas .15 .40
OD21B Mstaks SP Goggles 12.00 30.00
OD22 Roberto Osuna .12 .30
OD23 Jimmy Nelson .12 .30
OD24 Luis Severino RC .25 .60
OD25 Justin Verlander .20 .50
OD26 Ryan Braun .15 .40
OD27 Chris Tillman .12 .30
OD28A Alex Rodriguez .25 .60
OD28B Rdrgz SP Signing autos 20.00 50.00
OD29A Ichiro Suzuki .25 .60
OD29B Ichiro SP Pitching
OD30 R.A. Dickey .15 .40
OD31 Alex Gordon .15 .40
OD32A Raul Mondesi RC .25 .60
OD32B Mndsi SP w/Trophy
OD33 Josh Reddick .12 .30
OD34 Wilson Ramos .12 .30
OD35 Julio Teheran .15 .40
OD36 Colin Rea RC .20 .50
OD37 Stephen Vogt .15 .40
OD38 Jon Gray RC .20 .50
OD39 DJ LeMahieu .20 .50
OD40 Michael Taylor .12 .30
OD41 Ketel Marte RC .40 1.00
OD42 Albert Pujols .25 .60
OD43 Max Kepler RC .30 .75
OD44 Lorenzo Cain .12 .30
OD45 Carlos Beltran .15 .40
OD46 Carl Edwards Jr. RC .25 .60
OD47A Kyle Schwarber RC .60 1.50
OD47B Schwrbr SP Celebrate 30.00 80.00
OD48 Corey Seager RC 1.50 4.00
OD49 Erasmo Ramirez .12 .30
OD50A Josh Donaldson .15 .40
OD50B Dnldsn SP Press conf 12.00 30.00
OD51A Andrew McCutchen .20 .50
OD51B McCtchn SP Clmnte Awrd 60.00 150.00
OD52A Miguel Sano RC .30 .75
OD52B Sano SP Glasses 40.00 100.00
OD53 Joc Pederson .15 .40
OD54 Marco Estrada .12 .30
OD55 Carlos Rodon .15 .40
OD56 Didi Gregorius .15 .40
OD57 Chris Sale .20 .50
OD58A Carlos Correa .20 .50
OD58B Correa SP Signing autos 15.00 40.00
OD59 David Peralta .12 .30
OD60 Andrew Miller .15 .40
OD61A Adeiny Hechavarria .12 .30
OD61B Hchvrra SP w/Teammate 10.00 25.00
OD62 Yadier Molina .20 .50
OD63 Freddie Freeman .25 .60
OD64 Dalton Pompey .15 .40
OD65 Hector Rondon .12 .30
OD66 Sonny Gray .15 .40
OD67 Max Scherzer .20 .50
OD68 Jacob deGrom .20 .50
OD69 Yordano Ventura .15 .40
OD70 Aaron Nola RC .40 1.00
OD71 Robbie Ray .12 .30
OD72 Michael Conforto RC .25 .60
OD73 George Springer .15 .40
OD74 Brett Gardner .15 .40
OD75A Prince Fielder .15 .40
OD75B Fielder SP w/Teammate 12.00 30.00
OD76 Adam Jones .15 .40
OD77A Xander Bogaerts .20 .50
OD77B Bogaerts SP w/Fans 25.00 60.00
OD78 Joey Gallo .15 .40
OD79 A.J. Pollock .12 .30
OD80 Jung Ho Kang .12 .30
OD81 Maikel Franco .15 .40
OD82 Delino DeShields Jr. .12 .30
OD83 Chris Heston .12 .30
OD84 Yasmany Tomas .12 .30
OD85 Carlos Carrasco .12 .30
OD86 Devon Travis .12 .30
OD87 Yasmani Grandal .12 .30
OD88 Odubel Herrera .15 .40
OD89 J.D. Martinez .20 .50
OD90 Jonathan Lucroy .15 .40
OD91A Madison Bumgarner .15 .40
OD91B Bmgrnr SP w/Teammate 12.00 30.00
OD92 Jean Segura .15 .40
OD93 Corey Kluber .15 .40
OD94 Lucas Duda .15 .40
OD95 Jon Lester .15 .40
OD96 Gregory Polanco .15 .40
OD97 Joe Mauer .15 .40
OD98 Jackie Bradley Jr. .20 .50
OD99A Ruben Tejada .12 .30
OD99B Tjda SP Tipping cap 10.00 25.00
OD100 Clayton Kershaw .40 1.00
OD101 Jose Iglesias .15 .40
OD102 Josh Hamilton .15 .40
OD103 Brock Holt .12 .30
OD104 Manny Machado .20 .50
OD105 Kolten Wong .15 .40
OD106 Victor Martinez .15 .40
OD107A Matt Reynolds RC .20 .50
OD107B Rynlds SP Hand on hip 20.00 50.00
OD108 Adam Wainwright .15 .40
OD109 Michael Reed RC .20 .50
OD110A Francisco Lindor .20 .50
OD110B Lindor SP Signing autos 25.00 60.00
OD111 Edwin Encarnacion .20 .50
OD112 Mookie Betts .30 .75
OD113 Alex Cobb .12 .30
OD114 Michael Brantley .15 .40
OD115 Carlos Gomez .12 .30
OD116 Jason Kipnis .15 .40
OD117 Michael Pineda .12 .30
OD118 Mike Foltynewicz .12 .30
OD119 Yasiel Puig .20 .50
OD120A Wil Myers .12 .30
OD120B Myers SP No bat 10.00 25.00
OD121 Addison Russell .20 .50
OD122A Masahiro Tanaka .15 .40
OD122B Tanaka SP Goggles 12.00 30.00
OD123 Johnny Giavotella .12 .30
OD124 Trevor Plouffe .12 .30
OD125 Hector Olivera RC .25 .60
OD126 Ian Kinsler .15 .40
OD127 Matt Harvey .15 .40
OD128A Salvador Perez .15 .40
OD128B Perez SP w/Trophy 20.00 50.00
OD129 Dee Gordon .12 .30
OD130 Brian McCann .15 .40
OD131 Carlos Martinez .15 .40
OD132 Brandon Drury RC .30 .75
OD133 Greg Holland .12 .30
OD134 Joe Panik .15 .40
OD135 Adrian Gonzalez .15 .40
OD136 Starling Marte .15 .40
OD137 Mike Fiers .12 .30
OD138 David Ortiz .20 .50
OD139 Dustin Pedroia .20 .50
OD140 Glen Perkins .12 .30
OD141 Christian Yelich .25 .60
OD142 Miguel Almonte RC .20 .50
OD143 Evan Gattis .12 .30
OD144 Adrian Beltre .20 .50
OD145 Domonic Brown .15 .40
OD146 Gary Sanchez RC .60 1.50
OD147 Jose Altuve .15 .40
OD148 Robinson Cano .15 .40
OD149 Nick Markakis .15 .40
OD150 Miguel Cabrera .20 .50
OD151 Kyle Barraclough RC .20 .50
OD152A Carlos Gonzalez .15 .40
OD152B Gnzlz SP Celebrate 12.00 30.00
OD153 Danny Valencia .15 .40
OD154 Trea Turner RC .60 1.50
OD155 Jake Odorizzi .12 .30
OD156 Greg Bird RC .25 .60
OD157 Odrisamer Despaigne .12 .30
OD158 Peter O'Brien RC .20 .50
OD159 James McCann .15 .40
OD160 Anthony Gose .12 .30
OD161 Stephen Piscotty RC .30 .75
OD162 Frankie Montas RC .25 .60
OD163 Gerrit Cole .20 .50
OD164 Joey Votto .20 .50
OD165 Matt Kemp .15 .40
OD166 Hanley Ramirez .15 .40
OD167 Henry Owens RC .25 .60
OD168 Nick Castellanos .20 .50
OD169 Taylor Jungmann .12 .30
OD170 Jose Quintana .12 .30
OD171 Lance McCullers .12 .30
OD172 Randal Grichuk .12 .30
OD173 Miguel Castro .12 .30
OD174 J.T. Realmuto .20 .50
OD175 Alex Rios .15 .40
OD176 Steven Matz .15 .40
OD177 Eduardo Rodriguez .12 .30
OD178 Drew Smyly .12 .30
OD179 Daniel Norris .12 .30
OD180 Pedro Alvarez .12 .30
OD181 Justin Bour .15 .40
OD182 Matt Adams .12 .30
OD183A Buster Posey .25 .60
OD183B Posey SP Batting 40.00 100.00
OD184 Giancarlo Stanton .20 .50
OD185 Tyson Ross .12 .30
OD186 Jacoby Ellsbury .15 .40
OD187 Jose Bautista .15 .40
OD188 Troy Tulowitzki .20 .50
OD189 Kyle Seager .12 .30
OD190 Billy Hamilton .15 .40
OD191 Jose Fernandez .20 .50
OD192 Luis Valbuena .12 .30
OD193 Hector Santiago .12 .30
OD194 Stephen Strasburg .20 .50
OD195 Jake Arrieta .15 .40
OD196 Jason Castro .12 .30
OD197 Aroldis Chapman .20 .50
OD198 Avisail Garcia .15 .40
OD199 Paul Goldschmidt .20 .50
OD200 Bryce Harper .30 .75

2016 Topps Opening Day Blue Foil

*BLUE: 3X TO 8X BASIC
*BLUE RC: 2X TO 5X BASIC RC
STATED ODDS 1:7 HOBBY

2016 Topps Opening Day Toys R Us Purple Foil

*PURPLE: 10X TO 25X BASIC
*PURPLE RC: 6X TO 15X BASIC RC
INSERTED IN TOYS R US PACKS

2016 Topps Opening Day Alternate Reality

COMPLETE SET (15) 4.00 10.00
STATED ODDS 1:5 HOBBY
AR1 Manny Machado .30 .75
AR2 Mookie Betts .50 1.25
AR3 Troy Tulowitzki .30 .75
AR4 Matt Harvey .25 .60
AR5 Bryce Harper .50 1.25
AR6 Kris Bryant .40 1.00
AR7 Andrew McCutchen .30 .75
AR8 Mike Trout 1.50 4.00
AR9 Eric Hosmer .25 .60
AR10 Miguel Sano .30 .75
AR11 Carlos Correa .30 .75
AR12 Clayton Kershaw .60 1.50
AR13 Buster Posey .40 1.00
AR14 Jose Abreu .30 .75
AR15 Freddie Freeman .40 1.00

2016 Topps Opening Day Autographs

STATED ODDS 1:491 HOBBY
ODAAB Archie Bradley 4.00 10.00
ODAAN Aaron Nola 8.00 20.00
ODABB Brandon Belt 6.00 15.00
ODACC Carlos Correa 100.00 200.00
ODACR Carlos Rodon
ODACS Corey Seager 50.00 100.00
ODADF Doug Fister 4.00 10.00
ODADL DJ LeMahieu 8.00 20.00
ODAFL Francisco Lindor 15.00 40.00
ODAJHA Jesse Hahn 4.00 10.00
ODAJHM Jason Hammel 5.00 12.00
ODAKB Kris Bryant 100.00 200.00
ODAKS Kyle Schwarber 20.00 50.00
ODAKW Kolten Wong 5.00 12.00
ODALS Luis Severino
ODAMC Michael Conforto 25.00 60.00
ODAMS Miguel Sano 20.00 50.00
ODAMSC Matt Shoemaker 5.00 12.00
ODARR Rob Refsnyder

2016 Topps Opening Day Bubble Trouble

COMPLETE SET (10) 12.00 30.00
STATED ODDS 1:36 HOBBY
BT1 Robinson Cano 1.00 2.50
BT2 Felix Hernandez 1.00 2.50
BT3 Salvador Perez 1.00 2.50
BT4 Chris Archer .75 2.00
BT5 Albert Pujols 1.50 4.00
BT6 Manny Machado 1.25 3.00
BT7 Adam Eaton .75 2.00
BT8 Domonic Brown 1.00 2.50
BT9 Nick Castellanos 1.25 3.00
BT10 Troy Tulowitzki 1.25 3.00

2016 Topps Opening Day Heavy Hitters

COMPLETE SET (20) 4.00 10.00
STATED ODDS 1:5 HOBBY
HH1 Bryce Harper .50 1.25
HH2 Giancarlo Stanton .30 .75
HH3 Miguel Cabrera .30 .75
HH4 Kyle Schwarber .60 1.50
HH5 Miguel Sano .30 .75
HH6 Chris Davis .20 .50
HH7 Nelson Cruz .30 .75
HH8 Nolan Arenado .40 1.00
HH9 Jose Bautista .25 .60
HH10 Mike Trout 1.50 4.00
HH11 David Ortiz .30 .75
HH12 Paul Goldschmidt .30 .75
HH13 Joey Votto .30 .75
HH14 Jose Abreu .30 .75
HH15 Prince Fielder .25 .60

2016 Topps Opening Day Mascot Autographs

STATED ODDS 1:482 HOBBY
MAC Clark 15.00 40.00
MAO Orbit 12.00 30.00
MABM Billy the Marlin 12.00 30.00
MAGW George Washington 20.00 50.00
MAMM Mariner Moose 12.00 30.00
MAMR Mr. Red 15.00 40.00
MAWM Wally the Green Monster 12.00 30.00
MAPPA Pirate Parrot 15.00 40.00

2016 Topps Opening Day Mascots

COMPLETE SET (25) 8.00 20.00
STATED ODDS 1:5 HOBBY
M1 Paws .60 1.50
M2 Billy the Marlin .60 1.50
M3 Rally Monkey .60 1.50
M4 Wally the Green Monster .60 1.50
M5 Mr. Red .60 1.50
M6 Diamondbacks Mascot .60 1.50
M7 Orbit .60 1.50
M8 Clark .60 1.50
M9 Mrs. Met .60 1.50
M10 TC Bear .60 1.50
M11 Braves Mascot .60 1.50
M12 Slider .60 1.50
M13 Dinger .60 1.50
M14 Royals Mascot .60 1.50
M15 Hank the Ballpark Pup .60 1.50
M16 Phillie Phanatic .60 1.50
M17 Pirate Parrot .60 1.50
M18 Swinging Friar .60 1.50
M19 Mariner Moose .60 1.50
M20 Fredbird .60 1.50
M21 White Sox Mascot .60 1.50
M22 A's Mascot .60 1.50
M23 Raymond .60 1.50
M24 Rangers Captain .60 1.50
M25 Blue Jays Mascot .60 1.50

2016 Topps Opening Day Relics

STATED ODDS 1:491 HOBBY
ODRI Ichiro Suzuki 6.00 15.00
ODRAR Anthony Rizzo 6.00 15.00
ODRBP Buster Posey 6.00 15.00
ODRCK Clayton Kershaw 10.00 25.00
ODRDO David Ortiz 5.00 12.00
ODRFF Freddie Freeman 6.00 15.00
ODRJM Joe Mauer 4.00 10.00
ODRMW Michael Wacha 4.00 10.00
ODRPF Prince Fielder 4.00 10.00
ODRPS Pablo Sandoval 6.00 15.00
ODRRC Robinson Cano 4.00 10.00

2016 Topps Opening Day Stars

COMPLETE SET (25) 25.00 60.00
STATED ODDS 1:24 HOBBY
ODS1 Mike Trout 5.00 12.00
ODS2 Bryce Harper 1.50 4.00
ODS3 Paul Goldschmidt 1.00 2.50
ODS4 Josh Donaldson .75 2.00
ODS5 Clayton Kershaw 2.00 5.00
ODS6 Nolan Arenado 1.25 3.00
ODS7 Carlos Correa 1.00 2.50
ODS8 Kris Bryant 1.25 3.00
ODS9 Manny Machado 1.00 2.50
ODS10 Ryan Braun .75 2.00
ODS11 Miguel Cabrera 1.00 2.50
ODS12 Andrew McCutchen 1.00 2.50
ODS13 Buster Posey 1.25 3.00
ODS14 Jacob deGrom 1.00 2.50
ODS15 Jose Abreu 1.00 2.50
ODS16 Salvador Perez .75 2.00
ODS17 David Ortiz 1.00 2.50
ODS18 Luis Severino .75 2.00
ODS19 Evan Longoria .75 2.00
ODS20 Freddie Freeman 1.25 3.00
ODS21 Giancarlo Stanton 1.00 2.50
ODS22 Joey Votto 1.00 2.50
ODS23 Miguel Sano 1.00 2.50
ODS24 Yadier Molina 1.00 2.50
ODS25 Prince Fielder .75 2.00

2016 Topps Opening Day Striking Distance

COMPLETE SET (15) 4.00 10.00
STATED ODDS 1:5 HOBBY
SD1 Ichiro Suzuki .40 1.00
SD2 Robinson Cano .25 .60
SD3 Alex Rodriguez .40 1.00
SD4 Miguel Cabrera .30 .75
SD5 Albert Pujols .40 1.00
SD6 David Ortiz .30 .75
SD7 Felix Hernandez .25 .60
SD8 Justin Verlander .30 .75
SD9 Francisco Rodriguez .25 .60
SD10 John Lackey .25 .60
SD11 Ian Kinsler .25 .60
SD12 Ryan Howard .25 .60
SD13 Ichiro Suzuki .40 1.00
SD14 Mark Teixeira .25 .60
SD15 Cole Hamels .25 .60

2016 Topps Opening Day Superstar Celebrations

COMPLETE SET (20) 4.00 10.00
STATED ODDS 1:5 HOBBY
SC1 Mike Trout 1.50 4.00
SC2 Chris Davis .20 .50
SC3 Wilmer Flores .25 .60
SC4 Salvador Perez .25 .60
SC5 Jake Arrieta .25 .60
SC6 Daniel Murphy .25 .60
SC7 Dallas Keuchel .25 .60
SC8 Kris Bryant .40 1.00
SC9 Michael Brantley .25 .60
SC10 Ryan Zimmerman .25 .60
SC11 Brian Dozier .25 .60
SC12 Ian Kinsler .25 .60
SC13 Josh Reddick .20 .50
SC14 Robinson Chirinos .20 .50
SC15 Josh Donaldson .25 .60
SC16 Pedro Alvarez .20 .50
SC17 Derek Norris .20 .50
SC18 Carlos Gonzalez .25 .60
SC19 Andre Ethier .25 .60
SC20 Justin Bour .25 .60

2017 Topps Opening Day

COMP.SET w/o SP's (200) 10.00 25.00
SP VARIATION ODDS 1:256 HOBBY
PRINTING PLATE ODDS 1:3269 HOBBY
PLATE PRINT RUN 1 SET PER COLOR
BLACK-CYAN-MAGENTA-YELLOW ISSUED
NO PLATE PRICING DUE TO SCARCITY
1A Kris Bryant .30 .75
1B Bryant SP WS shirt 40.00 100.00
2 Reynaldo Lopez RC .20 .50
3 Aaron Sanchez .20 .50
4 Justin Turner .20 .50
5A Trevor Story .25 .60
5B Story SP Gray Jrsy 15.00 40.00
6 Robinson Cano .20 .50
7 Drew Smyly .15 .40
8 Victor Martinez .20 .50
9A Max Scherzer .25 .60
9B Schrzr SP High five 10.00 25.00
10 Luke Weaver RC .25 .60
11 Kyle Hendricks .25 .60
12 Marcell Ozuna .25 .60
13 JaCoby Jones RC .25 .60
14 Alex Gordon .20 .50
15 Ben Zobrist .20 .50
16A Ichiro .30 .75
16B Ichiro SP Dugout 40.00 100.00
17 Maikel Franco .20 .50
18A Adam Jones .20 .50
18B Jones SP Cage 8.00 20.00
19A Alex Bregman RC .75 2.00
19B Bregman SP Thrwbc 30.00 80.00
20A Bryce Harper .40 1.00
20B Harper SP Laughing 40.00 100.00
20C Harper SP Stppng out 40.00 100.00
21 Ryan Zimmerman .20 .50
22 Lucas Giolito .20 .50
23A Salvador Perez .20 .50
23B Perez SP Mantis cage 8.00 20.00
24 Randal Grichuk .15 .40
25 Adam Eaton .25 .60
26A Freddie Freeman .30 .75
26B Freeman SP White Jrsy 15.00 40.00
27 Nelson Cruz .25 .60
28 Jon Gray .15 .40
29 Wilson Ramos .15 .40
30 Jason Kipnis .20 .50
31 George Springer .20 .50
32 Aaron Nola .20 .50
33 Joey Votto .25 .60
34 David Ortiz .25 .60
35 Nolan Arenado .30 .75
36 Rougned Odor .20 .50
37 Justin Upton .20 .50
38 David Wright .20 .50
39 Aledmys Diaz .20 .50
40 Adam Duvall .25 .60
41 Jose Bautista .20 .50
42 Yulieski Gurriel RC .30 .75
43 Joe Musgrove RC .30 .75
44 Danny Salazar .20 .50
45 Jake Lamb .20 .50
46 Kendrys Morales .15 .40
47 Sean Doolittle .15 .40
48 Yadier Molina .25 .60
49 Hunter Pence .20 .50
50A Clayton Kershaw .50 1.25
50B Kershaw SP w/Bat 20.00 50.00
51 Kevin Gausman .15 .40
52 Andrew Miller .20 .50
53 Chase Utley .20 .50
54 Lance McCullers .15 .40
55 Robbie Ray .15 .40
56 Zack Greinke .20 .50
57 Josh Bell RC .50 1.25
58A Andrew Benintendi RC .60 1.50
58B Benintendi SP In chair 75.00 200.00
59 Marcus Semien .15 .40
60A Hanley Ramirez .20 .50
60B Ramirez SP Crouching 15.00 40.00
61 Kenta Maeda .20 .50
62 Carlos Rodon .20 .50
63A Corey Kluber .20 .50
63B Kluber SP Soccer 8.00 20.00
64 Zach Britton .20 .50
65 Adam Wainwright .20 .50
66 Willson Contreras .25 .60
67 Ryan Braun .20 .50
68 Stephen Piscotty .20 .50
69 Jon Lester .20 .50
70 Jay Bruce .20 .50
71 Jacob deGrom .25 .60
72 Yoenis Cespedes .25 .60
73 Joe Mauer .20 .50
74 Yoan Moncada RC .60 1.50
75A Mike Trout 1.25 3.00
75B Trout SP Into dugout 40.00 100.00
75C Trout SP Puppy 40.00 100.00
76 Felix Hernandez .20 .50
77 Nomar Mazara .15 .40
78 Ian Kinsler .20 .50
79 Sonny Gray .20 .50
80A Manny Machado .25 .60
80B Machado SP Black shirt 15.00 40.00
81 Jean Segura .20 .50
82 Jose De Leon RC .20 .50
83 Carlos Martinez .20 .50
84 James Shields .15 .40
85 Braden Shipley RC .20 .50
86A Addison Russell .25 .60
86B Russell SP High Five 10.00 25.00
87A Jose Altuve .20 .50
87B Altuve SP w/o Jrsy 8.00 20.00
88 Jose Reyes .20 .50
89 Matt Harvey .20 .50
90 Matt Strahm RC .20 .50
91 Tim Anderson .25 .60
92 Masahiro Tanaka .20 .50
93 Michael Fulmer .15 .40
94 Anthony DeSclafani .15 .40
95 Kyle Seager .15 .40
96A Anthony Rizzo .40 1.00
96B Rizzo SP Parade 20.00 50.00
97 Brett Gardner .20 .50
98 Lorenzo Cain .15 .40
99 Christian Yelich .30 .75
100 Jonathan Villar .15 .40
101 Starling Marte .20 .50
102 Adrian Beltre .25 .60
103A Daniel Murphy .20 .50
103B Murphy SP Gray jrsy 15.00 40.00
104 Chris Archer .15 .40
105 Danny Duffy .15 .40
106 Xander Bogaerts .25 .60
107 Tommy Joseph .25 .60
108 Tyler Glasnow RC .25 .60
109 Tyler Austin RC .30 .75
110A Giancarlo Stanton .25 .60
110B Stanton SP Cage 10.00 25.00
111 Craig Kimbrel .20 .50
112 Dustin Pedroia .25 .60
113A Mookie Betts .40 1.00
113B Betts SP Cage 15.00 40.00
114 Jackie Bradley Jr. .25 .60
115 Carlos Gonzalez .25 .60
116 Chris Sale .25 .60
117A Jake Arrieta .20 .50
117B Arrieta SP Red coat 15.00 40.00
118 Curtis Granderson .20 .50
119 Cameron Maybin .15 .40
120A Andrew McCutchen .25 .60
120B McCtchn SP Thrwbck 20.00 50.00
121 Carson Fulmer RC .20 .50
122A Francisco Lindor .25 .60
122B Lindor SP WS shirt 20.00 50.00
123 Khris Davis .25 .60
124 Cole Hamels .20 .50
125 Jake Thompson RC .20 .50
126 David Dahl RC .25 .60
127 Wil Myers .15 .40
128A Eric Hosmer .20 .50
128B Hosmer SP Blue jrsy 8.00 20.00
129A Trea Turner .20 .50
129B Turner SP Gray jrsy 8.00 20.00
130 Jose Abreu .25 .60
131 Orlando Arcia RC .30 .75
132A David Price .20 .50
132B Price SP Glasses 8.00 20.00
133A Javier Baez .30 .75
133B Baez SP Pullover 12.00 30.00
134A Miguel Sano .25 .60
134B Sano SP Dugout 8.00 20.00
135A Madison Bumgarner .20 .50
135B Bumgarner SP Btlng 20.00 50.00
136 Jeff Hoffman RC .20 .50
137 Jonathan Lucroy .20 .50
138 Marcus Stroman .20 .50
139 Rick Porcello .20 .50
140 Albert Pujols .30 .75
141A Evan Longoria .20 .50
141B Longoria SP Football 8.00 20.00
142 Elvis Andrus .20 .50
143 Brandon Finnegan .15 .40
144 Gerrit Cole .25 .60
145 Robert Gsellman RC .25 .60
146 Corey Seager .25 .60
147A Aaron Judge RC 2.50 6.00
147B Judge SP w/Bat 125.00 300.00
148A Miguel Cabrera .25 .60
148B Cabrera SP Open mouth 10.00 25.00
149 Troy Tulowitzki .25 .60
150A Kyle Schwarber .25 .60
150B Schwrbr SP WS shirt 15.00 40.00
151A Justin Verlander .25 .60
151B Verlander SP Cage 15.00 40.00
152 Brandon Belt .20 .50
153 Matt Moore .20 .50
154 Sean Manaea .15 .40
155 Brandon Phillips .15 .40
156A Matt Carpenter .25 .60
156B Carpenter SP High five 10.00 25.00
157 Gregory Polanco .20 .50
158 Carlos Carrasco .15 .40
159 Ryon Healy RC .25 .60
160 Adrian Gonzalez .20 .50
161 Brian McCann .20 .50
162 Brian Dozier .25 .60
163 Mike Moustakas .20 .50
164 Travis Jankowski .15 .40
165 Alex Reyes RC .25 .60
166 Tyler Naquin .15 .40
167 Byron Buxton .20 .50
168 Brandon Crawford .20 .50
169 Paul Goldschmidt .25 .60
170A Gary Sanchez .25 .60
170B Snchz SP Wearing gear 40.00 100.00
171 Dallas Keuchel .25 .60
172 J.D. Martinez .25 .60

Edwin Encarnacion .25 .60
Stephen Strasburg .25 .60
Carlos Santana .20 .50
Teoscar Hernandez RC .60 1.50
Tanner Roark .15 .40
Mark Trumbo .15 .40
Ryan Schimpf .15 .40
Jameson Taillon .20 .50
Dee Gordon .15 .40
Seung-Hwan Oh RC .40 1.00
Chris Davis .15 .40
Johnny Cueto .20 .50
A.J. Pollock .15 .40
Julio Urias .25 .60
Jason Heyward .20 .50
Yu Darvish .25 .60
Todd Frazier .20 .50
A Noah Syndergaard .20 .50
B Syndrgrd SP Dugout 25.00 60.00
Dellin Betances .20 .50
Charlie Blackmon .25 .60
Kenley Jansen .20 .50
A Josh Donaldson .20 .50
B Donaldson SP w/Fans 25.00 60.00
Dansby Swanson RC .50 1.25
Jacoby Ellsbury .20 .50
A Carlos Correa .25 .60
B Correa SP Ornge Jrsy 10.00 25.00
Matt Kemp .20 .50
Billy Hamilton .20 .50
Buster Posey .30 .75

2017 Topps Opening Day Blue Foil

UE: 3X TO 8X BASIC
UE RC: 2X TO 5X BASIC RC
ATED ODDS 1:7 HOBBY

017 Topps Opening Day Toys R Us Purple Border

URPLE: 3X TO 8X BASIC
URPLE RC: 3X TO 8X BASIC RC
SUED IN TRU PACKS

2017 Topps Opening Day Autographs

TATED ODDS 1:654 HOBBY
DAABE Andrew Benintendi 40.00 100.00
DAABR Alex Bregman 25.00 60.00
DAAD Aledmys Diaz 30.00 80.00
DAAJ Aaron Judge 100.00 250.00
DAAN Aaron Nola 8.00 20.00
DAARU Addison Russell 25.00 60.00
DACC Carlos Correa
DADD David Dahl 6.00 15.00
DAGB Greg Bird 8.00 20.00
DAJM Joe Musgrove 6.00 15.00
DAKB Kris Bryant 100.00 250.00
DANS Noah Syndergaard 20.00 50.00
DATA Tim Anderson 6.00 15.00
DATS Trevor Story 15.00 40.00
DATT Trea Turner 15.00 40.00
DAYM Yoan Moncada 100.00 250.00

2017 Topps Opening Day Incredible Eats

OMPLETE SET (18) 4.00 10.00
TATED ODDS 1:8 HOBBY
E1 Italian sausage .30 .75
E2 Peanuts .30 .75
E3 Fresh Popcorn .30 .75
E4 South Philly Dog .30 .75
E5 Cheesy Corn Brisket-acho .30 .75
E6 Chicken and Waffle Cone .30 .75
E7 Classic Pastrami .30 .75
E8 Foot-long Hot Dog .30 .75
E9 Nacho bowl .30 .75
E10 Soft Pretzels .30 .75
E11 Cotton Candy .30 .75
E12 Corn on a Stick .30 .75
E13 Hot Dogs & Onions .30 .75
E14 Broomstick Hot Dog .30 .75
E15 Bacon Mac & Cheese .30 .75
E16 Kayem Fenway Frank .30 .75
E17 Cracker Jack & Mac Dog .30 .75
E18 Buffalo Cauliflower Poutine .30 .75

2017 Topps Opening Day Mascot Autographs

STATED ODDS 1:747 HOBBY
MAB Billy the Marlin 12.00 30.00
MAC Clark 20.00 50.00
MAF Fredbird 20.00 50.00
MAO Orbit 15.00 40.00
MAS Slider 15.00 40.00
MAPIP Pirate Parrot 12.00 30.00
MAWGM Wally the Green Monster 20.00 50.00

2017 Topps Opening Day Mascot Relics

STATED ODDS 1:2097 HOBBY
MRB Billy the Marlin 12.00 30.00
MRC Clark 25.00 60.00
MRF Fredbird 20.00 50.00
MRS Slider 25.00 60.00
MRWGM Wally the Green Monster 20.00 50.00

2017 Topps Opening Day Mascots

COMPLETE SET (25) 5.00 12.00
STATED ODDS 1:3 HOBBY
M1 Paws .30 .75
M2 Billy the Marlin .30 .75
M3 Rally Monkey .30 .75
M4 Mr. Red .30 .75
M5 Mr. Met .30 .75
M6 TC Bear .30 .75
M7 Braves Mascot .30 .75
M8 Slider .30 .75
M9 Dinger .30 .75
M10 Royals Mascot .30 .75
M11 Phillie Phanatic .30 .75
M12 Pirate Parrot .30 .75
M13 Swinging Friar .30 .75
M14 Mariner Moose .30 .75
M15 Fredbird .30 .75
M16 White Sox Mascot .30 .75
M17 Athletics Mascot .30 .75
M18 Raymond .30 .75
M19 Rangers Captain .30 .75
M20 Blue Jays Mascot .30 .75
M21 Hank the Ballpark Pup .30 .75
M22 Orbit .30 .75
M23 Clark .30 .75
M24 Wally the Green Monster .30 .75
M25 Brewers Mascot .30 .75

2017 Topps Opening Day MLB Sticker Collection Stars

COMPLETE SET (4)
STATED ODDS 1:288 HOBBY
2 Mike Trout 6.00 15.00
83 David Ortiz 1.25 3.00
194 Kris Bryant 1.50 4.00
212 Clayton Kershaw 2.50 6.00

2017 Topps Opening Day National Anthem

COMPLETE SET (25)
STATED ODDS 1:210 HOBBY
NA1 Addison Russell 3.00 8.00
NA2 Andrew McCutchen 3.00 8.00
NA3 Anthony Rizzo 10.00 25.00
NA4 Bryce Harper 10.00 25.00
NA5 Josh Donaldson 2.50 6.00
NA6 Miguel Cabrera 3.00 8.00
NA7 Carlos Correa 3.00 8.00
NA8 Clayton Kershaw 8.00 20.00
NA9 Felix Hernandez 2.50 6.00
NA10 Francisco Lindor 8.00 20.00
NA11 Jose Altuve 2.50 6.00
NA12 Manny Machado 12.00 30.00
NA13 Mookie Betts 8.00 20.00
NA14 Noah Syndergaard 8.00 20.00
NA15 Robinson Cano 2.50 6.00
NA16 David Ortiz 8.00 20.00
NA17 Khris Davis 3.00 8.00
NA18 Jayson Werth 2.50 6.00
NA19 Jon Lester 2.50 6.00
NA20 Aaron Judge 20.00 50.00
NA21 Eric Hosmer 8.00 20.00
NA22 Mike Trout 15.00 40.00
NA23 Kyle Schwarber 3.00 8.00
NA24 Madison Bumgarner 2.50 6.00
NA25 Adam Jones 6.00 15.00

2017 Topps Opening Day Opening Day

COMPLETE SET (15) 4.00 10.00
STATED ODDS 1:5 HOBBY
ODB1 Pittsburgh Pirates .40 1.00
ODB2 Tampa Bay Rays .40 1.00
ODB3 Kansas City Royals .40 1.00
ODB4 Milwaukee Brewers .40 1.00
ODB5 Baltimore Orioles .40 1.00
ODB6 Texas Rangers .40 1.00
ODB7 Cincinnati Reds .40 1.00
ODB8 Atlanta Braves .40 1.00
ODB9 San Diego Padres .40 1.00
ODB10 Arizona Diamondbacks .40 1.00
ODB11 Los Angeles Angels .40 1.00
ODB12 Oakland Athletics .40 1.00
ODB13 New York Yankees .40 1.00
ODB14 Cleveland Indians .40 1.00
ODB15 Miami Marlins .40 1.00

2017 Topps Opening Day Opening Day Stars

COMPLETE SET (44) 50.00 120.00
STATED ODDS 1:27 HOBBY
ODS1 Adam Jones 1.00 2.50
ODS2 Addison Russell 1.25 3.00
ODS3 Ichiro 1.50 4.00
ODS4 Javier Baez 1.50 4.00
ODS5 Andrew McCutchen 1.25 3.00
ODS6 Anthony Rizzo 2.00 5.00
ODS7 Brandon Phillips .75 2.00
ODS8 Justin Verlander 1.25 3.00
ODS9 Bryce Harper 2.00 5.00
ODS10 Josh Donaldson 1.00 2.50
ODS11 Miguel Cabrera 1.25 3.00
ODS12 Bryce Harper 2.00 5.00
ODS13 Buster Posey 1.50 4.00
ODS14 Max Scherzer 1.25 3.00
ODS15 Clayton Kershaw 2.50 6.00
ODS16 Corey Seager 1.25 3.00
ODS17 Eric Hosmer 1.00 2.50
ODS18 Evan Longoria 1.00 2.50
ODS19 Felix Hernandez 1.00 2.50
ODS20 Hanley Ramirez 1.00 2.50
ODS21 Freddie Freeman 1.50 4.00
ODS22 Jake Arrieta 1.00 2.50
ODS23 Giancarlo Stanton 1.25 3.00
ODS24 Jose Altuve 1.00 2.50
ODS25 Kris Bryant 8.00 20.00
ODS26 Kyle Schwarber 1.25 3.00
ODS27 Gary Sanchez 1.25 3.00
ODS28 Francisco Lindor 1.25 3.00
ODS29 Madison Bumgarner 1.00 2.50
ODS30 Manny Machado 1.25 3.00
ODS31 Matt Carpenter 1.25 3.00
ODS32 Miguel Sano 1.00 2.50
ODS33 Mike Trout 8.00 20.00
ODS34 Mookie Betts 2.00 5.00
ODS35 Noah Syndergaard 1.00 2.50
ODS36 Nolan Arenado 1.50 4.00
ODS37 Paul Goldschmidt 1.25 3.00
ODS38 Robinson Cano 1.00 2.50
ODS39 Ryan Braun 1.00 2.50
ODS40 Salvador Perez 1.00 2.50
ODS41 Trea Turner 1.00 2.50
ODS42 Trevor Story 1.25 3.00
ODS43 Corey Kluber 1.00 2.50
ODS44 Carlos Correa 1.25 3.00

2017 Topps Opening Day Relics

STATED ODDS 1:525 HOBBY
ODRAM Andrew McCutchen 6.00 15.00
ODRBH Bryce Harper 10.00 25.00
ODRBP Buster Posey 6.00 15.00
ODRCC Carlos Correa 5.00 12.00
ODRCK Clayton Kershaw 6.00 15.00
ODRDW David Wright 4.00 10.00
ODRJA Jose Altuve 4.00 10.00
ODRMT Mike Trout
ODRARI Anthony Rizzo 6.00 15.00
ODRJVE Justin Verlander 5.00 12.00

2017 Topps Opening Day Stadium Signatures

COMPLETE SET (25)
STATED ODDS 1:420 HOBBY
SS1 Jose Altuve 5.00 12.00
SS2 Corey Seager 20.00 50.00
SS3 Dee Gordon 4.00 10.00
SS4 Jon Gray 10.00 25.00
SS5 Paul Goldschmidt 6.00 15.00
SS6 Carlos Correa
SS7 Ichiro 25.00 60.00
SS8 Ben Zobrist 20.00 50.00
SS9 David Price 5.00 12.00
SS10 Tyler Naquin 12.00 30.00
SS11 Trevor Story 12.00 30.00
SS12 Mike Trout 60.00 150.00
SS13 Julio Urias 12.00 30.00
SS14 Francisco Lindor 25.00 60.00
SS15 Addison Russell 12.00 30.00
SS16 Michael Conforto 5.00 12.00
SS17 Maikel Franco 5.00 12.00
SS18 Jason Heyward 8.00 20.00
SS19 Bryce Harper 20.00 50.00
SS20 Kyle Schwarber 12.00 30.00
SS21 Trea Turner 20.00 50.00
SS22 Kris Bryant 60.00 150.00
SS23 Nolan Arenado 8.00 20.00
SS24 Charlie Blackmon 10.00 25.00
SS25 Miguel Sano 20.00 50.00

2017 Topps Opening Day Superstar Celebrations

COMPLETE SET (25) 5.00 12.00
STATED ODDS 1:3 HOBBY
SC1 Brian Dozier .30 .75
SC2 Khris Davis .30 .75
SC3 Javier Baez .40 1.00
SC4 Anthony Rizzo .50 1.25
SC5 Francisco Lindor .30 .75
SC6 Jayson Werth .25 .60
SC7 Josh Harrison .20 .50
SC8 Carlos Santana .25 .60
SC9 Andrew McCutchen .30 .75
SC10 Rougned Odor .25 .60
SC11 Adam Eaton .30 .75
SC12 Addison Russell .30 .75
SC13 Robinson Cano .25 .60
SC14 Troy Tulowitzki .30 .75
SC15 David Ortiz .30 .75
SC16 Jonathan Lucroy .25 .60
SC17 Russell Martin .20 .50
SC18 Edwin Encarnacion .30 .75
SC19 Gregory Polanco .25 .60
SC20 Carlos Correa .30 .75
SC21 Giancarlo Stanton .30 .75
SC22 Jose Ramirez .25 .60
SC23 Bryce Harper .50 1.25
SC24 Jackie Bradley Jr. .30 .75
SC25 Yunel Escobar .20 .50

2017 Topps Opening Day Wacky Packages

COMPLETE SET (9)
STATED ODDS 1:1169 HOBBY
WP1 Clam Chowder 8.00 20.00
WP2 Deep Dish Pizza 15.00 40.00
WP3 Alphabet Chili 8.00 20.00
WP4 Royals Mustard 8.00 20.00
WP5 Sssssssarsaparilla 8.00 20.00
WP6 Kielbasa 12.00 30.00
WP7 Hot Salsa 8.00 20.00
WP8 Tuna Steak Marinade 4.00 10.00
WP9 MLB Draft 8.00 20.00

2018 Topps Opening Day

COMPLETE SET (200) 12.00 30.00
PRINTING PLATE ODDS 1:4680 BLASTER
PLATE PRINT RUN 1 SET PER COLOR
BLACK-CYAN-MAGENTA-YELLOW ISSUED
NO PLATE PRICING DUE TO SCARCITY
1 Clayton Kershaw .50 1.25
2 Rafael Devers RC .60 1.50
3 Kris Bryant .30 .75
4 Mike Trout 1.25 3.00
5 Buster Posey .30 .75
6 Anthony Rizzo .40 1.00
7 Carlos Correa .25 .60
8 A.J. Pollock .15 .40
9 Jake Lamb .20 .50
10 J.D. Martinez .25 .60
11 Matt Kemp .20 .50
12 Nick Markakis .20 .50
13 Ozzie Albies RC .60 1.50
14 Dansby Swanson .25 .60
15 Adam Jones .20 .50
16 Manny Machado .25 .60
17 Jonathan Schoop .15 .40
18 Trey Mancini .20 .50
19 Craig Kimbrel .20 .50
20 Chris Sale .25 .60
21 Christian Vazquez .15 .40
22 Mookie Betts .40 1.00
23 Willson Contreras .25 .60
24 Kyle Schwarber .25 .60
25 Jon Lester .20 .50
26 Javier Baez .30 .75
27 Ian Happ .20 .50
28 Avisail Garcia .20 .50
29 Carlos Rodon .20 .50
30 Jose Abreu .25 .60
31 Yoan Moncada .25 .60
32 Raisel Iglesias .15 .40
33 Zack Cozart .15 .40
34 Billy Hamilton .20 .50
35 Andrew Miller .20 .50
36 Jason Kipnis .20 .50
37 Carlos Carrasco .15 .40
38 Danny Salazar .20 .50
39 Francisco Lindor .25 .60
40 Raimel Tapia .15 .40
41 Nolan Arenado .30 .75
42 Jon Gray .15 .40
43 Antonio Senzatela .15 .40
44 David Dahl .15 .40
45 Trevor Story .25 .60
46 Miguel Cabrera .25 .60
47 Michael Fulmer .15 .40
48 George Springer .20 .50
49 Yulieski Gurriel .20 .50
50 Jose Altuve .20 .50
51 Dallas Keuchel .20 .50
52 Justin Verlander .25 .60
53 Alex Bregman .25 .60
54 Danny Duffy .15 .40
55 Mike Moustakas .20 .50
56 Salvador Perez .25 .60
57 Yasiel Puig .25 .60
58 Cody Bellinger .50 1.25
59 Corey Seager .25 .60
60 Giancarlo Stanton .25 .60
61 Ichiro .30 .75
62 Ryan Braun .20 .50
63 Jonathan Villar .15 .40
64 Byron Buxton .20 .50
65 Joe Mauer .20 .50
66 Miguel Sano .20 .50
67 Michael Conforto .20 .50
68 Noah Syndergaard .20 .50
69 Jacob deGrom .25 .60
70 Amed Rosario RC .25 .60
71 Aaron Judge .60 1.50
72 Gary Sanchez .25 .60
73 Masahiro Tanaka .20 .50
74 Todd Frazier .20 .50
75 Luis Severino .20 .50
76 Khris Davis .25 .60
77 Jharel Cotton .15 .40
78 Sean Manaea .15 .40
79 Odubel Herrera .20 .50
80 Maikel Franco .20 .50
81 Aaron Nola .20 .50
82 Rhys Hoskins RC .75 2.00
83 Andrew McCutchen .25 .60
84 Starling Marte .25 .60
85 Gregory Polanco .20 .50
86 Wil Myers .15 .40
87 Hunter Renfroe .15 .40
88 Johnny Cueto .20 .50
89 Jeff Samardzija .15 .40
90 Hunter Pence .20 .50
91 Nelson Cruz .25 .60
92 Robinson Cano .20 .50
93 Felix Hernandez .20 .50
94 Adam Wainwright .20 .50
95 Dexter Fowler .20 .50
96 Yadier Molina .25 .60
97 Kevin Kiermaier .25 .60
98 Corey Dickerson .15 .40
99 Chris Archer .15 .40
100 Joey Gallo .20 .50
101 Elvis Andrus .20 .50
102 Adrian Beltre .25 .60
103 Rougned Odor .25 .60
104 Nomar Mazara .20 .50
105 Kendrys Morales .15 .40
106 Troy Tulowitzki .20 .50
107 Josh Donaldson .20 .50
108 Marcus Stroman .20 .50
109 Anthony Rendon .25 .60
110 Trea Turner .20 .50
111 Daniel Murphy .20 .50
112 Max Scherzer .25 .60
113 Stephen Strasburg .25 .60
114 Bryce Harper .40 1.00
115 Ryan McMahon RC .60 1.50
116 Jackie Bradley Jr. .25 .60
117 Clint Frazier RC .40 1.00
118 Willie Calhoun RC .25 .60
119 Dominic Smith RC .20 .50
120 Nick Williams RC .25 .60
121 Greg Allen RC .20 .50
122 Brandon Woodruff RC .25 .60
123 Chance Sisco RC .25 .60
124 Nicky Delmonico RC .20 .50
125 Austin Hays RC .30 .75
126 J.P. Crawford RC .20 .50
127 Victor Robles RC .50 1.25
128 Alex Verdugo RC .30 .75
129 Francisco Mejia RC .25 .60
130 Jack Flaherty RC .30 .75
131 Brian Anderson RC .25 .60
132 Walker Buehler RC 1.00 2.50
133 Erick Fedde RC .20 .50
134 Harrison Bader RC .30 .75
135 Andrew Stevenson RC .20 .50
136 Anthony Banda RC .20 .50
137 Miguel Andujar RC .75 2.00
138 Luiz Gohara RC .20 .50
139 Joey Votto .25 .60
140 Albert Pujols .30 .75
141 Zack Greinke .20 .50
142 Paul Goldschmidt .25 .60
143 Freddie Freeman .30 .75
144 Julio Teheran .20 .50
145 Zach Britton .15 .40
146 Chris Davis .15 .40
147 Hanley Ramirez .20 .50
148 David Price .20 .50
149 Xander Bogaerts .25 .60
150 Andrew Benintendi .25 .60
151 Jason Heyward .20 .50
152 Jake Arrieta .20 .50
153 Addison Russell .20 .50
154 Tim Anderson .25 .60
155 Melky Cabrera .15 .40
156 Adam Duvall .25 .60
157 Jesse Winker .15 .40
158 Corey Kluber .20 .50
159 Edwin Encarnacion .25 .60
160 Jose Ramirez .20 .50
161 Charlie Blackmon .25 .60
162 DJ LeMahieu .25 .60
163 Ian Kinsler .20 .50
164 Brian McCann .20 .50
165 Alcides Escobar .20 .50
166 Justin Turner .25 .60
167 Chris Taylor .20 .50
168 Yu Darvish .25 .60
169 Kenley Jansen .20 .50
170 Dee Gordon .15 .40
171 Justin Bour .15 .40
172 Eric Thames .20 .50
173 Jose Berrios .20 .50
174 Eddie Rosario .25 .60
175 Didi Gregorius .25 .60
176 Aroldis Chapman .25 .60
177 Sonny Gray .20 .50
178 Ryon Healy .15 .40
179 Matt Olson .20 .50
180 Jeremy Hellickson .15 .40
181 Aaron Altherr .15 .40
182 Josh Bell .20 .50
183 Gerrit Cole .25 .60
184 Yangervis Solarte .15 .40
185 Brandon Crawford .20 .50
186 Kyle Seager .15 .40
187 Matt Carpenter .25 .60
188 Paul DeJong .25 .60
189 Steven Souza Jr. .20 .50
190 Cole Hamels .20 .50
191 Matt Wieters .25 .60
192 Whit Merrifield .25 .60
193 Robbie Ray .15 .40
194 Alex Colome .15 .40
195 Marcell Ozuna .25 .60
196 Alex Wood .15 .40
197 Parker Bridwell RC .20 .50
198 Mark Reynolds .15 .40
199 Jose Quintana .15 .40
200 Shohei Ohtani RC 5.00 12.00

2018 Topps Opening Day Blue Foil

*BLUE: 2X TO 5X BASIC
*BLUE RC: 1.5X TO 4X BASIC RC
STATED ODDS 1:9 BLASTER
ANNCD PRINT RUN 2018 SETS
200 Shohei Ohtani 12.00 30.00

2018 Topps Opening Day Variations

STATED ODDS 1:477 BLASTER
1 Kershaw Hoodie 30.00 80.00
3 Bryant Hat on 30.00 80.00
4 Trout Red jsy 60.00 150.00
5 Posey Mask on 20.00 50.00
7 Correa Helmet 15.00 40.00
16 Machado White jsy 30.00 80.00
30 Abreu No hat 15.00 40.00
39 Lindor Blue jsy 8.00 20.00
41 Arenado Pnstp jsy 8.00 20.00
46 Cabrera Sunglasses 25.00 60.00
55 Moustakas Wht jsy 15.00 40.00
60 Stanton No hat 20.00 50.00
63 Villar Pullover 10.00 25.00
64 Buxton Hat on 15.00 40.00
70 Rosario No helmet 15.00 40.00
71 Judge Pnstp Jsy 125.00 300.00
82 Hoskins High fives 40.00 100.00
83 McCutchen Blk jsy 25.00 60.00
87 Renfroe Diving 8.00 20.00
93 Hernandez Pullover 8.00 20.00
99 Archer Tshirt 8.00 20.00
100 Gallo Hat on 8.00 20.00
107 Donaldson Blue jsy 10.00 25.00
112 Scherzer Ski mask 10.00 25.00
139 Votto Wht jsy 20.00 50.00
142 Goldschmidt Hat on 12.00 30.00
143 Freeman Wht Jsy 20.00 50.00
150 Benintendi Navy jsy 30.00 80.00
179 Olson In dugout 20.00 50.00
187 Carpenter High fives 10.00 25.00

2018 Topps Opening Day At The Ballpark

STATED ODDS 1:6 BLASTER
ODBA Los Angeles Angels .40 1.00
ODBAB Atlanta Braves .40 1.00
ODBAD Arizona Diamondbacks .40 1.00
ODBBO Baltimore Orioles .40 1.00
ODBCC Chicago Cubs .40 1.00
ODBCI Cleveland Indians .40 1.00
ODBCR Cincinnati Reds .40 1.00
ODBDT Detroit Tigers .40 1.00
ODBHA Houston Astros .40 1.00
ODBMB Milwaukee Brewers .40 1.00
ODBPP Pittsburgh Pirates .40 1.00
ODBTR Texas Rangers .40 1.00
ODBWN Washington Nationals .40 1.00
ODBBRS Boston Red Sox .40 1.00
ODBCOR Colorado Rockies .40 1.00
ODBLAD Los Angeles Dodgers .40 1.00
ODBNYM New York Mets .40 1.00
ODBNYY New York Yankees .40 1.00
ODBSLC St. Louis Cardinals .40 1.00
ODBTBR Tampa Bay Rays .40 1.00

2018 Topps Opening Day Autographs

STATED ODDS 1:701 BLASTER
ODAAR Amed Rosario 12.00 30.00
ODACB Charlie Blackmon 10.00 25.00
ODACC Carlos Correa 25.00 60.00
ODAET Eric Thames 4.00 10.00
ODAHB Harrison Bader 5.00 12.00
ODAJB Javier Baez 20.00 50.00
ODAJL Jake Lamb 4.00 10.00
ODAJU Julio Urias 8.00 20.00
ODAKS Kyle Schwarber 15.00 40.00
ODAMK Max Kepler 4.00 10.00
ODAMT Mike Trout
ODANS Noah Syndergaard 20.00 50.00
ODARD Rafael Devers 20.00 50.00
ODART Raimel Tapia 3.00 8.00

2018 Topps Opening Day Before Opening Day

COMPLETE SET (20) 4.00 10.00
STATED ODDS 1:5 BLASTER
BODAB Andrew Benintendi .50 1.25
BODAJ Aaron Judge 1.25 3.00
BODAR Anthony Rizzo .75 2.00
BODBB Byron Buxton .40 1.00
BODBH Bryce Harper .75 2.00
BODBP Buster Posey .60 1.50
BODCB Cody Bellinger 1.00 2.50
BODCD Chris Davis .30 .75
BODCS Chris Sale .50 1.25
BODCV Christian Vazquez .30 .75
BODDK Dallas Keuchel .40 1.00
BODI Ichiro .60 1.50
BODKB Kris Bryant .60 1.50
BODMB Mookie Betts .75 2.00
BODMG Marwin Gonzalez .30 .75
BODMK Mikie Mahtook .30 .75
BODMS Miguel Sano .40 1.00
BODMT Mike Trout 2.50 6.00
BODSP Salvador Perez .40 1.00
BODYP Yasiel Puig .50 1.25

2018 Topps Opening Day Diamond Relics

STATED ODDS 1:1772 BLASTER
DRAB Andrew Benintendi 10.00 25.00
DRAM Andrew McCutchen 20.00 50.00
DRAN Aaron Nola 10.00 25.00
DRCA Chris Archer 8.00 20.00
DRDD Danny Duffy 10.00 25.00
DREL Evan Longoria 8.00 20.00
DRET Eric Thames
DRFL Francisco Lindor 10.00 25.00
DRJD Josh Donaldson 12.00 30.00
DRKB Kris Bryant 12.00 30.00
DRMC Miguel Cabrera 10.00 25.00
DRNA Nolan Arenado 12.00 30.00
DRNC Nicholas Castellanos 15.00 30.00
DRNS Noah Syndergaard 8.00 20.00
DRRB Ryan Braun 12.00 30.00
DRRH Rhys Hoskins 20.00 60.00
DRSM Starling Marte 12.00 30.00
DRTS Trevor Story 10.00 25.00
DRVM Victor Martinez 8.00 20.00
DRYC Yoenis Cespedes 10.00 25.00
DRYM Yadier Molina 15.00 40.00

2018 Topps Opening Day Dugout Peeks

STATED ODDS 1:1791 BLASTER
DPAJ Aaron Judge 50.00 120.00
DPBC Brandon Crawford 15.00 40.00
DPBH Bryce Harper 50.00 120.00
DPBZ Ben Zobrist 15.00 40.00
DPCC Carlos Carrasco 12.00 30.00
DPEE Edwin Encarnacion 20.00 50.00
DPID Ian Desmond 12.00 30.00
DPJA Jose Altuve 15.00 40.00
DPJB Josh Bell 15.00 40.00
DPJS Jonathan Schoop 25.00 60.00
DPKM Kenta Maeda 15.00 40.00
DPMT Mark Trumbo 12.00 30.00
DPPB Parker Bridwell 12.00 30.00
DPRB Ryan Braun 20.00 50.00
DPRH Rhys Hoskins 50.00 125.00
DPRP Rick Porcello
DPTB Tim Beckham
DPWM Wil Myers 12.00 30.00
DPXB Xander Bogaerts 20.00 50.00
DPYP Yasiel Puig 20.00 50.00

2018 Topps Opening Day Mascot Autographs

STATED ODDS 1:1560 BLASTER
MAS Sluggerrr 12.00 30.00
MABB Bernie Brewer 15.00 40.00
MABTM Billy the Marlin 8.00 20.00
MATCB TC Bear 25.00 60.00
MAWGM Wally the Green Monster 15.00 40.00

2018 Topps Opening Day Mascot Relics

STATED ODDS 1:4951 BLASTER
MRC Clark 8.00 20.00
MRF Fredbird 8.00 20.00
MRS Sluggerrr 8.00 20.00
MRBB Bernie Brewer 20.00 50.00
MRBTM Billy the Marlin 8.00 20.00
MRTCB TC Bear 15.00 40.00
MRWGM Wally the Green Monster 15.00 40.00

2018 Topps Opening Day Mascots

COMPLETE SET (25) 6.00 15.00
STATED ODDS 1:4 BLASTER
M1 Sluggerrr .40 1.00
M2 Wally the Green Monster .40 1.00
M3 Tessie .40 1.00
M4 Clark .40 1.00
M5 Gapper .40 1.00
M6 Mr. Red .40 1.00
M7 Mr. Redlegs .40 1.00
M8 Rosie Red .40 1.00
M9 Slider .40 1.00
M10 Dinger .40 1.00
M11 Paws .40 1.00
M12 Billy the Marlin .40 1.00
M13 Orbit .40 1.00
M14 Rally Monkey .40 1.00
M15 TC Bear .40 1.00
M16 Bernie Brewer .40 1.00
M17 Mr. Met .40 1.00
M18 Phillie Phanatic .40 1.00
M19 Pirate Parrot .40 1.00
M20 Swinging Friar .40 1.00
M21 Mariner Moose .40 1.00
M22 Fredbird .40 1.00
M23 Raymond .40 1.00
M24 Rangers Captain .40 1.00
M25 Screech .40 1.00

2018 Topps Opening Day MLB Sticker Collection Stars

STATED ODDS 1:288 BLASTER
ODV1 Aaron Judge 4.00 10.00
ODV2 Francisco Lindor 1.25 3.00
ODV3 Bryce Harper 2.00 5.00
ODV4 Clayton Kershaw 2.50 6.00

2018 Topps Opening Day National Anthem

STATED ODDS 1:286 BLASTER
NAAB Alex Bregman 4.00 10.00
NAAN Andrew Benintendi 10.00 25.00
NACC Carlos Correa 4.00 10.00
NACF Clint Frazier 8.00 20.00
NACH Cesar Hernandez 2.50 6.00
NACS Chris Sale 6.00 15.00
NADF Dexter Fowler 3.00 8.00
NAEE Edwin Encarnacion 4.00 10.00
NAEH Eric Hosmer 6.00 15.00
NAFL Francisco Lindor 4.00 10.00
NAHR Hanley Ramirez 5.00 12.00
NAJA Jose Altuve 3.00 8.00
NAJB Jackie Bradley Jr. 6.00 15.00
NAJC J.P. Crawford 6.00 15.00
NAJD Jacob deGrom 6.00 15.00
NAJK Jason Kipnis 3.00 8.00
NAJM James McCann 6.00 15.00
NAJT Justin Turner 3.00 8.00
NAKD Khris Davis 4.00 10.00
NAKP Kevin Pillar 2.50 6.00
NAKS Kyle Seager 2.50 6.00
NAMB Mookie Betts 6.00 15.00
NAMM Mikie Mahtook 2.50 6.00
NAMT Mike Trout 15.00 40.00
NAYP Yasiel Puig 4.00 10.00

2018 Topps Opening Day Relics

STATED ODDS 1:707 BLASTER
ODRAP Albert Pujols 5.00 12.00
ODRAR Anthony Rizzo 6.00 15.00
ODRCC Carlos Correa 5.00 12.00
ODRCK Clayton Kershaw 6.00 15.00
ODRCS Corey Seager 5.00 12.00
ODRJV Joey Votto 6.00 15.00
ODRKB Kris Bryant 8.00 20.00
ODRMM Manny Machado 5.00 12.00
ODRMS Max Scherzer 5.00 12.00
ODRMT Mike Trout 25.00 60.00

2018 Topps Opening Day Stadium Signatures

STATED ODDS 1:572 BLASTER
SSAJ Aaron Judge 40.00 100.00
SSAP A.J. Pollock 4.00 10.00
SSBB Byron Buxton 5.00 12.00
SSBH Bryce Harper 15.00 40.00
SSCB Cody Bellinger 8.00 20.00
SSCK Clayton Kershaw 8.00 20.00
SSDD Delino Deshields Jr. 4.00 10.00
SSFL Francisco Lindor 6.00 15.00
SSGP Gregory Polanco 5.00 12.00
SSJL Jake Lamb 6.00 15.00
SSJM Joe Musgrove 4.00 10.00
SSKB Kris Bryant 25.00 60.00

SSKM Kenta Maeda 5.00 12.00
SSMB Mookie Betts 10.00 25.00
SSMF Maikel Franco 5.00 12.00
SSMH Matt Shoemaker 5.00 12.00
SSMK Matt Kemp 4.00 10.00
SSMM Manny Machado 15.00 40.00
SSMS Marcus Stroman 5.00 12.00
SSMT Mike Trout 25.00 60.00
SSNA Nolan Arenado 15.00 40.00
SSNC Nicholas Castellanos 6.00 15.00
SSRC Robinson Cano 5.00 12.00
SSTB Tim Beckham 10.00 25.00
SSTM Trey Mancini 12.00 30.00

2018 Topps Opening Day Stars

STATED ODDS 1:27 BLASTER
ODSAD Adam Duvall 1.25 3.00
ODSAG Alex Gordon 1.00 2.50
ODSAJ Adam Jones 1.00 2.50
ODSAP Albert Pujols 1.50 4.00
ODSAS Antonio Senzatela .75 2.00
ODSAU Aaron Judge 3.00 8.00
ODSAV Alex Verdugo 1.25 3.00
ODSBB Brandon Belt 1.00 2.50
ODSBD Brian Dozier 1.00 2.50
ODSCB Charlie Blackmon 1.25 3.00
ODSCF Clint Frazier 1.50 4.00
ODSCH Cole Hamels 1.00 2.50
ODSCI Chance Sisco 1.00 2.50
ODSCK Corey Kluber 1.00 2.50
ODSCS Corey Seager 1.25 3.00
ODSDP Dustin Pedroia 1.25 3.00
ODSDS Dominic Smith .75 2.00
ODSDW Dansby Swanson 1.25 3.00
ODSFM Francisco Mejia 1.00 2.50
ODSGS George Springer 1.00 2.50
ODSJC J.P. Crawford .75 2.00
ODSJd Jacob deGrom 1.25 3.00
ODSJH Josh Harrison .75 2.00
ODSJV Justin Verlander 1.25 3.00
ODSKE Kyle Seager .75 2.00
ODSKJ Kenley Jansen 1.00 2.50
ODSKK Kevin Kiermaier 1.00 2.50
ODSKM Kendrys Morales .75 2.00
ODSKS Kyle Schwarber 1.25 3.00
ODSNC Nicholas Castellanos 1.25 3.00
ODSNW Nick Williams 1.00 2.50
ODSOA Ozzie Albies 2.50 6.00
ODSOR Orlando Arcia .75 2.00
ODSPD Paul DeJong 1.25 3.00
ODSRD Rafael Devers 2.50 6.00
ODSRH Rhys Hoskins 3.00 8.00
ODSSM Sean Manaea .75 2.00
ODSSS Stephen Strasburg 1.25 3.00
ODSVR Victor Robles 2.00 5.00
ODSWB Walker Buehler 4.00 10.00
ODSWC Willie Calhoun 1.00 2.50
ODSWM Wil Myers .75 2.00
ODSYM Yoan Moncada 1.25 3.00
ODSZG Zack Greinke 1.00 2.50

2018 Topps Opening Day Team Traditions and Celebrations

COMPLETE SET (15) 4.00 10.00
STATED ODDS 1:4 BLASTER
TTCCH Clydesdale Horses .40 1.00
TTCHA Home Run Apple .40 1.00
TTCHS Home Run Slide .40 1.00
TTCHT Home Run Train .40 1.00
TTCKC King's Court .40 1.00
TTCMC McCovey Cove .40 1.00
TTCMS Minnie and Paul Sign .40 1.00
TTCPR Racing Presidents .40 1.00
TTCRM Rally Monkey .40 1.00
TTCSC Sweet Caroline .40 1.00
TTCTF The Freeze .40 1.00
TTCYD Y.M.C.A. Dance .40 1.00
TTCODP Opening Day Parade .40 1.00
TTCOTD Old Timers Day .40 1.00
TTCTMO Take Me Out to the Ballgame .40 1.00

2019 Topps Opening Day

COMPLETE SET (200) 12.00 30.00
PRINTING PLATE ODDS 1:XXX
PLATE PRINT RUN 1 SET PER COLOR
BLACK-CYAN-MAGENTA-YELLOW ISSUED
NO PLATE PRICING DUE TO SCARCITY
1 Billy Hamilton .20 .50
2 Kyle Freeland .20 .50
3 Justin Verlander .25 .60
4 Ryan O'Hearn RC .20 .50
5 Corey Seager .25 .60
6 Scooter Gennett .20 .50
7 Adalberto Mondesi .20 .50
8 Freddie Freeman .30 .75
9 Niko Goodrum .20 .50
10 Jordan Zimmermann .20 .50
11 Nicholas Castellanos .25 .60
12 Zack Greinke .20 .50
13 Kyle Schwarber .25 .60
14 Rick Porcello .20 .50
15 Aaron Judge .60 1.50
16 Brian Anderson .15 .40
17 Sandy Alcantara .15 .40
18 Kyle Tucker RC .40 1.00
19 Charlie Blackmon .25 .60
20 Jon Lester .20 .50
21 Kenley Jansen .20 .50
22 Bryce Harper .40 1.00
23 Miguel Cabrera .25 .60
24 Mike Trout 1.25 3.00
25 Michael Lorenzen .15 .40
26 Zack Godley .15 .40
27 Raisel Iglesias .15 .40
28 Mark Trumbo .15 .40
29 David Dahl .15 .40
30 Eugenio Suarez .20 .50
31 Nolan Arenado .30 .75
32 Derek Dietrich .20 .50
33 Mookie Betts .40 1.00
34 Trevor Story .25 .60
35 Andrew Benintendi .25 .60
36 Trevor Bauer .25 .60
37 Jose Abreu .25 .60
38 Dansby Swanson .25 .60
39 Christian Yelich .30 .75
40 George Springer .20 .50
41 Jose Altuve .20 .50
42 Rafael Devers .30 .75
43 David Price .20 .50
44 Trey Mancini .20 .50
45 Kris Bryant .30 .75
46 Clayton Kershaw .50 1.25
47 Xander Bogaerts .25 .60
48 Matt Kemp .20 .50
49 Willson Contreras .20 .50
50 Mike Clevinger .20 .50
51 Ronald Acuna Jr. 1.25 3.00
52 Corey Kluber .20 .50
53 Carlos Correa .25 .60
54 Mike Foltynewicz .20 .50
55 Yusei Kikuchi RC .30 .75
56 Justin Upton .20 .50
57 Carlos Rodon .20 .50
58 Alex Gordon .20 .50
59 Joey Votto .25 .60
60 J.T. Realmuto .25 .60
61 Albert Almora .20 .50
62 Ketel Marte .20 .50
63 Avisail Garcia .20 .50
64 Tim Beckham .20 .50
65 Albert Pujols .30 .75
66 Matt Davidson .20 .50
67 Max Muncy .20 .50
68 Christin Stewart RC .25 .60
69 Alex Bregman .25 .60
70 Edwin Encarnacion .25 .60
71 Whit Merrifield .25 .60
72 Carlos Carrasco .15 .40
73 Gerrit Cole .25 .60
74 Jonathan Schoop .15 .40
75 Salvador Perez .20 .50
76 Cedric Mullins RC .30 .75
77 Jose Ramirez .20 .50
78 Andrelton Simmons .15 .40
79 Justin Turner .20 .50
80 Dylan Bundy .20 .50
81 Jeimer Candelario .15 .40
82 Jonathan Villar .15 .40
83 Kole Calhoun .15 .40
84 Francisco Lindor .25 .60
85 German Marquez .15 .40
86 Anthony Rizzo .40 1.00
87 Starlin Castro .15 .40
88 Justus Sheffield RC .30 .75
89 Yoan Moncada .25 .60
90 Jaime Barria .15 .40
91 Brad Keller RC .20 .50
92 David Peralta .15 .40
93 J.D. Martinez .25 .60
94 Paul Goldschmidt .25 .60
95 Javier Baez .30 .75
96 Kevin Gausman .15 .40
97 Brad Boxberger .15 .40
98 Ozzie Albies .25 .60
99 Daniel Palka .15 .40
100 Shohei Ohtani .30 .75
101 Jose Berrios .20 .50
102 Yadier Molina .25 .60
103 Mitch Garver .15 .40
104 Shane Bieber .25 .60
105 Buster Posey .30 .75
106 Gleyber Torres .50 1.25
107 Rhys Hoskins .30 .75
108 Jose Martinez .15 .40
109 Carlos Martinez .20 .50
110 Jorge Polanco .15 .40
111 Tommy Pham .15 .40
112 Rowdy Tellez RC .30 .75
113 Edwin Diaz .20 .50
114 Matt Duffy .15 .40
115 Josh Hader .15 .40
116 Dakota Hudson RC .25 .60
117 Cionel Perez RC .20 .50
118 Dereck Rodriguez .15 .40
119 Randal Grichuk .15 .40
120 Dee Gordon .15 .40
121 Orlando Arcia .15 .40
122 Ryan Zimmerman .20 .50
123 Eric Hosmer .20 .50
124 Stephen Strasburg .25 .60
125 Franmil Reyes .15 .40
126 Noah Syndergaard .20 .50
127 Mitch Haniger .20 .50
128 Juan Soto .75 2.00
129 Justin Smoak .15 .40
130 Lourdes Gurriel Jr. .20 .50
131 Michael Kopech RC .40 1.00
132 Kevin Pillar .15 .40
133 Jeff McNeil RC .50 1.25
134 Jameson Taillon .20 .50
135 Matt Chapman .25 .60
136 Jesus Aguilar .15 .40
137 Odubel Herrera .15 .40
138 Luis Urias RC .30 .75
139 Jack Flaherty .20 .50
140 Wil Myers .15 .40
141 Ryan Yarbrough .15 .40
142 Eddie Rosario .20 .50
143 Sean Manaea .15 .40
144 Miguel Andujar .25 .60
145 Luis Severino .20 .50
146 Blake Treinen .15 .40
147 Carlos Santana .20 .50
148 Chris Archer .15 .40
149 Todd Frazier .20 .50
150 Jacob deGrom .25 .60
151 Rougned Odor .25 .60
152 Matt Olson .15 .40
153 Willians Astudillo RC .20 .50
154 Sean Doolittle .15 .40
155 Jose Leclerc .15 .40
156 Aledmys Diaz .15 .40
157 Lorenzo Cain .15 .40
158 Gregory Polanco .20 .50
159 Nick Martini RC .20 .50
160 Ramon Laureano RC .40 1.00
161 Brandon Nimmo .20 .50
162 Jean Segura .25 .60
163 Will Smith .15 .40
164 Willy Adames .15 .40
165 Joey Lucchesi .15 .40
166 Didi Gregorius .20 .50
167 Tyler Glasnow .15 .40
168 Matt Carpenter .25 .60
169 Brandon Belt .20 .50
170 Kyle Gibson .20 .50
171 Corey Dickerson .15 .40
172 Max Kepler .20 .50
173 Amed Rosario .20 .50
174 Harrison Bader .20 .50
175 Hunter Renfroe .15 .40
176 Joey Gallo .20 .50
177 Jake Bauers RC .30 .75
178 Touki Toussaint RC .25 .60
179 Jake Arrieta .20 .50
180 Elvis Andrus .20 .50
181 Josh James RC .30 .75
182 Anthony Rendon .25 .60
183 Max Scherzer .25 .60
184 Maikel Franco .20 .50
185 Khris Davis .20 .50
186 Starling Marte .20 .50
187 Evan Longoria .15 .40
188 Robinson Cano .20 .50
189 Michael Conforto .20 .50
190 Miles Mikolas .25 .60
191 Joey Wendle .15 .40
192 Nomar Mazara .15 .40
193 Masahiro Tanaka .20 .50
194 Stephen Piscotty .15 .40
195 James Paxton .20 .50
196 Blake Snell .20 .50
197 Felipe Vazquez .15 .40
198 Aaron Nola .20 .50
199 Brandon Crawford .20 .50
200 Shin-Soo Choo .20 .50

2019 Topps Opening Day Blue Foil

*BLUE: 2X TO 5X BASIC
*BLUE RC: 1.5X TO 4X BASIC RC
STATED ODDS 1:XX
ANNCD PRINT RUN 2019 SETS

2019 Topps Opening Day Purple Foil

*PURPLE: 5X TO 12X BASIC
*PURPLE RC: 4X TO 10X BASIC RC
FOUND IN MEIJER BLISTER PACKS

2019 Topps Opening Day Red Foil

*RED: 5X TO 12X BASIC
*RED RC: 4X TO 10X BASIC RC
FOUND IN TARGET MEGA BOX

2019 Topps Opening Day Photo Variations

STATED ODDS 1:XXX
15 Judge Blk Jrsy 60.00 150.00
22 Harper Portrait 20.00 50.00
24 Trout w/Bat 150.00 400.00
39 Yelich Tip cap
41 Altuve Sitting
45 Bryant Snglsses 20.00 50.00
51 Acuna At wall
53 Correa Dugout
67 Muncy Run
84 Lindor Salute 8.00 20.00
95 Baez Blue Jrsy 25.00 60.00
102 Molina Point 30.00 80.00
106 Torres Smile 30.00 80.00
128 Soto Dugout 40.00 100.00
150 deGrom Yllw Jckt 30.00 80.00

2019 Topps Opening Day 150 Years of Fun

COMPLETE SET (25)
STATED ODDS 1:XX
YOF1 Ty Cobb .60 1.50
YOF2 Jackie Robinson .40 1.00
YOF3 Lou Gehrig .75 2.00
YOF4 Ted Williams .75 2.00
YOF5 Babe Ruth 1.00 2.50
YOF6 Hank Aaron .75 2.00
YOF7 Sandy Koufax .75 2.00
YOF8 Roberto Clemente 1.00 2.50
YOF9 Ernie Banks .40 1.00
YOF10 Ozzie Smith .50 1.25
YOF11 Gary Carter .30 .75
YOF12 Joe Morgan .30 .75
YOF13 Tom Seaver .30 .75
YOF14 Jim Palmer .30 .75
YOF15 Reggie Jackson .30 .75
YOF16 Frank Thomas .40 1.00
YOF17 Nolan Ryan 1.25 3.00
YOF18 Cal Ripken Jr. 1.25 3.00
YOF19 Pedro Martinez .30 .75
YOF20 David Ortiz .40 1.00
YOF21 Ichiro .50 1.25
YOF22 Derek Jeter 1.00 2.50
YOF23 Francisco Lindor .40 1.00
YOF24 Ronald Acuna Jr. 2.00 5.00
YOF25 Mike Trout 2.00 5.00

2019 Topps Opening Day Autographs

STATED ODDS 1:XXX
EXCHANGE DEADLINE 1/31/2021
ODAAJ Aaron Judge 75.00 200.00
ODAAR Anthony Rizzo 25.00 60.00
ODABN Brandon Nimmo 12.00 30.00
ODABW Brandon Woodruff 3.00 8.00
ODADR Dereck Rodriguez 10.00 25.00
ODAFL Francisco Lindor 20.00 50.00
ODAJA Jesus Aguilar 3.00 8.00
ODAJAL Jose Altuve 20.00 50.00
ODAJH Josh Hader 8.00 20.00
ODAJS Jean Segura 12.00 30.00
ODAKF Kyle Freeland 4.00 10.00
ODALG Lourdes Gurriel Jr. 6.00 15.00
ODAMC Matt Chapman 5.00 12.00
ODAMK Michael Kopech 6.00 15.00
ODAMMU Max Muncy 8.00 20.00
ODARA Ronald Acuna Jr. 40.00 100.00
ODASB Shane Bieber 5.00 12.00
ODASO Shohei Ohtani 100.00 250.00
ODAWA Willy Adames 3.00 8.00

2019 Topps Opening Day Diamond Autograph Relics

STATED ODDS 1:XXX
STATED PRINT RUN 50 SER.#'d SETS
EXCHANGE DEADLINE 1/31/2021
DARBS Blake Snell 20.00 50.00
DARKD Khris Davis
DARMH Mitch Haniger 20.00 50.00
DARMK Michael Kopech
DARRA Ronald Acuna Jr.
DARRH Rhys Hoskins 60.00 150.00
DARSO Shohei Ohtani
DARSP Salvador Perez
DARTM Trey Mancini 25.00 60.00
DARTS Trevor Story

2019 Topps Opening Day Diamond Relics

STATED ODDS 1:XXX
DRAB Adrian Beltre 10.00 25.00
DRABR Alex Bregman 20.00 50.00
DRAR Anthony Rizzo 15.00 40.00
DRBP Buster Posey 12.00 30.00
DRBS Blake Snell 8.00 20.00
DRCK Clayton Kershaw 20.00 50.00
DRCY Christian Yelich
DREH Eric Hosmer 8.00 20.00
DRGP Gregory Polanco 8.00 20.00
DRJD Jacob deGrom 10.00 25.00
DRJR Jose Ramirez 8.00 20.00
DRJV Joey Votto 10.00 25.00
DRKD Khris Davis 10.00 25.00
DRMB Mookie Betts 15.00 40.00
DRMC Matt Carpenter 10.00 25.00
DRMH Mitch Haniger 8.00 20.00
DRMK Michael Kopech 12.00 30.00
DRNC Nicholas Castellanos 10.00 25.00
DRRA Ronald Acuna Jr. 25.00 60.00
DRRH Rhys Hoskins 15.00 40.00
DRSC Starlin Castro
DRSO Shohei Ohtani 12.00 30.00
DRSP Salvador Perez 15.00 40.00
DRTM Trey Mancini 8.00 20.00
DRTS Trevor Story 10.00 25.00

2019 Topps Opening Day Dugout Peeks

STATED ODDS 1:XXX
DP1 Francisco Lindor 30.00 80.00
DP2 Jose Altuve 30.00 80.00
DP3 David Wright 30.00 80.00
DP4 Manny Machado 20.00 50.00
DP5 Starlin Castro 10.00 25.00
DP6 Ichiro 50.00 120.00
DP7 David Price 20.00 50.00
DP8 Marwin Gonzalez 6.00 15.00
DP9 Aaron Judge
DP10 Didi Gregorius 25.00 60.00
DP11 Khris Davis
DP12 Shohei Ohtani 60.00 150.00
DP13 Ronald Acuna Jr.
DP14 Mike Trout 125.00 300.00
DP15 Jose Altuve 30.00 80.00
DP16 Jake Arrieta
DP17 Odubel Herrera 15.00 40.00
DP18 Corey Dickerson 10.00 25.00
DP19 Ronald Acuna Jr.
DP20 Tim Beckham 20.00 50.00

2019 Topps Opening Day Mascot Autograph Relics

STATED ODDS 1:XXX
EXCHANGE DEADLINE 1/31/2021
MARB Blooper
MARO Orbit 30.00 80.00
MARS Screech
MARCC Clark 30.00 80.00
MARMM Mariner Moose
MARSL Slider 30.00 80.00
MARTCB TC Bear 30.00 80.00

2019 Topps Opening Day Mascot Autographs

STATED ODDS 1:XXX
EXCHANGE DEADLINE 1/31/2021
MAB Blooper 20.00 50.00
MAO Orbit 25.00 60.00
MAS Screech 15.00 40.00
MACC Clark 15.00 40.00
MAMM Mariner Moose 12.00 30.00
MAPP Pirate Parrot 12.00 30.00
MASF Swinging Friar 12.00 30.00
MASL Slider 12.00 30.00
MATCB TC Bear 12.00 30.00

2019 Topps Opening Day Mascot Relics

STATED ODDS 1:XXX
MRB Blooper 6.00 15.00
MRO Orbit 6.00 15.00
MRS Screech 6.00 15.00
MRBB Bernie Brewer 6.00 15.00
MRCC Clark the Cub 6.00 15.00
MRMM Mariner Moose 6.00 15.00
MRSL Slider 6.00 15.00
MRTCB TC Bear 6.00 15.00
MRWGM Wally the Green Monster 10.00 25.00

2019 Topps Opening Day Mascots

COMPLETE SET (25) 6.00 15.00
STATED ODDS 1:XX
M1 Blooper .40 1.00
M2 Slider .40 1.00
M3 Clark .40 1.00
M4 Pirate Parrot .40 1.00
M5 Screech .40 1.00
M6 Orbit .40 1.00
M7 Mariner Moose .40 1.00
M8 TC Bear .40 1.00
M9 Swinging Friar .40 1.00
M10 Mascot .40 1.00
M11 Mascot .40 1.00
M12 Rangers Captain .40 1.00
M13 Paws .40 1.00
M14 Sluggerrr .40 1.00
M15 Wally the Green Monster .40 1.00
M16 Mr. Red .40 1.00
M17 Dinger .40 1.00
M18 Billy the Marlin .40 1.00
M19 Bernie Brewer .40 1.00
M20 Mr. Met .40 1.00
M21 Phillie Phanatic .40 1.00
M22 Fredbird .40 1.00
M23 Raymond .40 1.00
M24 Mascot .40 1.00
M25 Mascot .40 1.00

2019 Topps Opening Day Opening Day

COMPLETE SET (15) 4.00 10.00
STATED ODDS 1:XX
ODBAB Atlanta Braves .40 1.00
ODBAD Arizona Diamondbacks .40 1.00
ODBBO Baltimore Orioles .40 1.00
ODBCR Cincinnati Reds .40 1.00
ODBDT Detroit Tigers .40 1.00
ODBMM Miami Marlins .40 1.00
ODBOA Oakland Athletics .40 1.00
ODBSM Seattle Mariners .40 1.00
ODBTR Texas Rangers .40 1.00
ODBKCR Kansas City Royals .40 1.00
ODBLAD Los Angeles Dodgers .40 1.00
ODBNYM New York Mets .40 1.00
ODBSDP San Diego Padres .40 1.00
ODBTBJ Toronto Blue Jays .40 1.00
ODBTBR Tampa Bay Rays .40 1.00

2019 Topps Opening Day Rally Time

STATED ODDS 1:XXX
RTA Ozzie Albies 8.00 20.00
RTB Mookie Betts 12.00 30.00
RTC Matt Davidson 6.00 15.00
RTL Clayton Kershaw 15.00 40.00
RTM Christian Yelich 10.00 25.00
RTS Matt Adams 5.00 12.00
RTAB Alex Bregman 15.00 40.00
RTAJ Aaron Judge 40.00 100.00
RTAR Anthony Rizzo 12.00 30.00
RTCY Christian Yelich 10.00 25.00
RTDB David Bote 12.00 30.00
RTEE Enrique Hernandez 6.00 15.00
RTEH Eric Hosmer 6.00 15.00
RTJJ Jeremy Jeffress 5.00 12.00
RTJK Jason Kipnis 6.00 15.00
RTJP Jurickson Profar 6.00 15.00
RTMT Max Kepler 6.00 15.00
RTRA Ronald Acuna Jr. 40.00 100.00
RTRH Rhys Hoskins 10.00 25.00
RTRO Rougned Odor 6.00 15.00
RTSL Matt Carpenter 8.00 20.00
RTWC Willson Contreras 6.00 15.00
RTXB Xander Bogaerts 8.00 20.00
RTYC Yoenis Cespedes 8.00 20.00
RTYM Yadier Molina 15.00 40.00

2019 Topps Opening Day Relics

STATED ODDS 1:XXX
ODRAJ Aaron Judge 20.00 50.00
ODRAP Albert Pujols 5.00 12.00
ODRAR Anthony Rizzo 6.00 15.00
ODRBP Buster Posey 5.00 12.00
ODRCC Carlos Correa 4.00 10.00
ODRCK Clayton Kershaw 8.00 20.00
ODRDG Didi Gregorius 3.00 8.00
ODRJA Jose Abreu 4.00 10.00
ODRJM J.D. Martinez 6.00 15.00
ODRJS Juan Soto 12.00 30.00
ODRJV Justin Verlander 4.00 10.00
ODRKB Kris Bryant 10.00 25.00
ODRMC Miguel Cabrera 4.00 10.00
ODRMS Max Scherzer 4.00 10.00
ODRMT Mike Trout 20.00 50.00
ODRNA Nolan Arenado 5.00 12.00
ODRRH Rhys Hoskins 5.00 12.00
ODRSO Shohei Ohtani 5.00 12.00
ODRYM Yadier Molina 4.00 10.00
ODRJAL Jose Altuve 3.00 8.00
ODRJVO Joey Votto 4.00 10.00

2019 Topps Opening Day Sock it To Me

STATED ODDS 1:XX
SM1 Bryce Harper 30.00 80.00
SM2 Aaron Judge 25.00 60.00
SM3 Javier Baez 12.00 30.00
SM4 Mookie Betts 30.00 80.00
SM5 Ronald Acuna Jr. 50.00 125.00
SM6 Juan Soto 20.00 50.00
SM7 Rhys Hoskins 12.00 30.00
SM8 Jose Altuve 8.00 20.00
SM9 Mike Trout 75.00 200.00
SM10 Francisco Lindor 10.00 25.00
SM11 Trevor Story 10.00 25.00
SM12 Khris Davis 10.00 25.00
SM13 Anthony Rizzo 15.00 40.00
SM14 Chris Archer 6.00 15.00
SM15 Amed Rosario 12.00 30.00
SM16 Joey Votto 10.00 25.00
SM17 Harrison Bader 8.00 20.00
SM18 Chris Taylor 8.00 20.00
SM19 Ozzie Albies 10.00 25.00
SM20 Corey Kluber 8.00 20.00
SM21 Jose Berrios 8.00 20.00
SM22 Andrew Benintendi 10.00 25.00
SM23 Ben Zobrist 8.00 20.00
SM24 Kyle Schwarber 10.00 25.00
SM25 Dee Gordon 6.00 15.00

2019 Topps Opening Day Team Traditions and Celebrations

COMPLETE SET (10) 3.00 8.00
STATED ODDS 1:XX
TTCBM Bobblehead Museum .40 1.00
TTCCS California Spectacular .40 1.00
TTCES Eutaw Street .40 1.00
TTCLB Liberty Bell .40 1.00
TTCOP Outfield Pool .40 1.00
TTCSB Western Metal Building .40 1.00
TTCSF Stadium Fountains .40 1.00
TTCSP Scoreboard Pinwheels .40 1.00
TTCWF Tiger Merry-Go-Round .40 1.00
TTCTGS Tony Gwynn Statue .60 1.50

2020 Topps Opening Day

COMP.SET w/o SP (200) 12.00 30.00
1 Brendan McKay RC .30 .75
2 Jonathan Villar .15 .40
3 Garrett Cooper .15 .40
4 Brandon Woodruff .15 .40
5 Mike Moustakas .20 .50
6 Sean Doolittle .15 .40
7 James Paxton .20 .50
8 Domingo Santana .20 .50
9 Joc Pederson .20 .50
10 Yasmani Grandal .15 .40
11 Luis Arraez .30 .75
12 Nico Hoerner RC .75 2.00
13 Brian Anderson .15 .40
14 Alex Verdugo .20 .50
15 J.T. Realmuto .25 .60
16 Zac Gallen RC .50 1.25
17 Kyle Lewis RC 1.50 4.00
18 Lance Lynn .15 .40
19 Tim Anderson .25 .60
20 Max Scherzer .25 .60
21 Gerrit Cole .40 1.00
22 Anthony Rizzo .40 1.00
23 Eduardo Rodriguez .15 .40
24 Willson Contreras .25 .60
25 Omar Narvaez .15 .40
26 Sean Murphy RC .30 .75
27 Juan Soto .75 2.00
28 Mookie Betts .50 1.25
29 Jordan Yamamoto RC .25 .60
30 Nick Solak RC .30 .75
31 Aaron Judge .60 1.50
32 J.D. Martinez .25 .60
33 Vladimir Guerrero Jr. .50 1.25
34 Jeff McNeil .20 .50
35 Trea Turner .20 .50
36 Ken Giles .15 .40
37 Justin Turner .20 .50
38 Nolan Arenado .30 .75
39 Carter Kieboom .20 .50
40 Mitch Garver .15 .40
41 Patrick Corbin .20 .50
42 Max Fried .25 .60
43 Shohei Ohtani .30 .75
44 Albert Pujols .30 .75
45 Dakota Hudson .20 .50
46 Franmil Reyes .15 .40
47 Jose Ramirez .20 .50
48 Francisco Lindor .25 .60
49 Sandy Alcantara .15 .40
50 Kenta Maeda .20 .50
51 Ramon Laureano .20 .60
52 David Dahl .15 .40
53 Jon Lester .20 .50
54 Adalberto Mondesi .25 .60
55 Abraham Toro RC .25 .60
56 Mike Soroka .25
57 Dustin May RC .75 2
58 Mike Fiers .15
59 Gary Sanchez .25
60 Lourdes Gurriel Jr. .20
61 Keston Hiura .30
62 Michel Baez RC .20
63 Yordan Alvarez RC 1.00 2
64 Mike Yastrzemski .40 1
65 Justin Verlander .25
66 Paul Goldschmidt .25
67 Ronald Acuna Jr. 1.00 2
68 Dominic Smith .15
69 Tommy La Stella .15
70 Gavin Lux RC 1.25 3.
71 Ozzie Albies .25
72 Jorge Soler .25
73 Amed Rosario .20
74 Tommy Pham .15
75 Craig Kimbrel .20
76 Jack Flaherty .20
77 Bryan Reynolds .20
78 Matt Chapman .25
79 DJ LeMahieu .25
80 Michael Conforto .20
81 Evan Longoria .20 .5
82 Orlando Arcia .15 .4
83 Eric Hosmer .20 .5
84 Kyle Seager .15 .4
85 Elvis Andrus .20 .5
86 Anthony Rendon .25 .6
87 Giancarlo Stanton .25 .6
88 Matt Carpenter .25 .6
89 Jose Altuve .20 .5
90 Mike Trout 1.25 3.0
91 Marco Gonzales .15 .4
92 Zach Plesac .25 .6
93 Nelson Cruz .25 .6
94 Liam Hendriks .15 .4
95 Eduardo Escobar .15 .4
96 Aroldis Chapman .25 .6
97 Eugenio Suarez .20 .5
98 Oscar Mercado .20 .5
99 Nick Senzel .25 .6
100 John Means .15 .4
101 Kenley Jansen .20 .5
102 Scott Kingery .20 .5
103 Hanser Alberto .15 .4
104 Matthew Boyd .15 .40
105 Jesus Luzardo RC .40 1.00
106 Tyler Glasnow .15 .40
107 Max Muncy .20 .50
108 Corey Seager .25 .60
109 Trevor Story .25 .60
110 Merrill Kelly .15 .40
111 Miguel Cabrera .25 .60
112 Victor Robles .30 .75
113 Charlie Morton .25 .60
114 Randal Grichuk .15 .40
115 Yusei Kikuchi .20 .50
116 Dansby Swanson .25 .60
117 Kris Bryant .30 .75
118 Yoan Moncada .25 .60
119 Joey Lucchesi .15 .40
120 Hunter Dozier .15 .40
121 Zack Greinke .20 .50
122 Jorge Alfaro .15 .40
123 Trey Mancini .25 .60
124 Carlos Correa .25 .60
125 Luis Castillo .20 .50
126 Andres Munoz RC .25 .60
127 Kirby Yates .15 .40
128 Javier Baez .30 .75
129 Cody Bellinger .50 1.25
130 Yadier Molina .25 .60
131 Eddie Rosario .20 .50
132 Clayton Kershaw .50 1.25
133 Christian Walker .20 .50
134 Michael Brantley .20 .50
135 Tommy Edman .25 .60
136 Shane Bieber .25 .60
137 Gregory Polanco .20 .50
138 Eloy Jimenez .50 1.25
139 Paul DeJong .25 .60
140 Michael Chavis .20 .50
141 Lucas Giolito .20 .50
142 Carlos Santana .20 .50
143 Kyle Schwarber .25 .60
144 Buster Posey .30 .75
145 Freddie Freeman .30 .75
146 George Springer .20 .50
147 Aristides Aquino RC .40 1.00
148 Jorge Polanco .20 .50
149 Charlie Blackmon .25 .60
150 Will Smith .30 .75
151 Ian Kennedy .15 .40
152 Marcus Stroman .20 .50
153 Josh Hader .15 .40
154 Whit Merrifield .25 .60
155 J.D. Davis .15 .40
156 Rhys Hoskins .30 .75
157 Pete Alonso .60 1.50
158 Mike Clevinger .20 .50
159 Luke Voit .30 .75
160 Ryan Braun .20 .50
161 Ketel Marte .20 .50
162 Max Kepler .20 .50
163 Christian Yelich .30 .75
164 Alex Bregman .25 .60
165 Brandon Lowe .25 .60
166 Andrew Benintendi .25 .60
167 Adbert Alzolay RC .25 .60
168 A.J. Puk RC .40 1.00

169 Rafael Devers	.30	.75
170 Starling Marte	.20	.50
171 Joey Votto	.25	.60
172 Walker Buehler	.30	.75
173 Bo Bichette RC	1.50	4.00
174 Sonny Gray	.20	.50
175 Austin Meadows	.20	.50
176 Jean Segura	.20	.50
177 Masahiro Tanaka	.25	.60
178 Marcus Semien	.15	.40
179 Niko Goodrum	.20	.50
180 Austin Riley	.40	1.00
181 Starlin Castro	.15	.40
182 Jameson Taillon	.20	.50
183 Yuli Gurriel	.20	.50
184 Matt Olson	.15	.40
185 Aaron Nola	.25	.60
186 Gleyber Torres	.50	1.25
187 Jacob deGrom	.25	.60
188 Bryce Harper	.40	1.00
189 Fernando Tatis Jr.	1.00	2.50
190 Trent Grisham RC	.75	2.00
191 Hunter Renfroe	.15	.40
192 Dee Gordon	.15	.40
193 Cavan Biggio	.30	.75
194 Emilio Pagan	.15	.40
195 Brad Hand	.15	.40
196 Chris Paddack	.25	.60
197 Josh Bell	.20	.50
198 Dan Vogelbach	.15	.40
199 Jose Berrios	.20	.50
200 Manny Machado	.25	.60
201 Luis Robert SP RC	25.00	60.00

2020 Topps Opening Day Blue Foil

*BLUE: 1.5X TO 4X BASIC
*BLUE RC: 1.2X TO 3X BASIC RC

2020 Topps Opening Day Blue Jays Maple Leaf Red

DISTRIBUTED IN CANADA

33 Vladimir Guerrero Jr.	5.00	12.00
36 Ken Giles	1.50	4.00
60 Lourdes Gurriel Jr.	2.00	5.00
114 Randal Grichuk	1.50	4.00
173 Bo Bichette	15.00	40.00
193 Cavan Biggio	3.00	8.00

2020 Topps Opening Day Purple Foil

*PURPLE: 3X TO 8X BASIC
*PURPLE RC: 2.5X TO 6X BASIC RC

2020 Topps Opening Day Red Foil

*RED: 2X TO 5X BASIC
*RED RC: 1.5X TO 4X BASIC RC

2020 Topps Opening Day Photo Variations

1 Brendan McKay	8.00	20.00
24 Willson Contreras	15.00	40.00
27 Juan Soto	50.00	120.00
33 Vladimir Guerrero Jr.	15.00	40.00
38 Nolan Arenado	10.00	25.00
39 Carter Kieboom	10.00	25.00
43 Shohei Ohtani	25.00	60.00
61 Keston Hiura	10.00	25.00
63 Yordan Alvarez	25.00	60.00
67 Ronald Acuna Jr.	30.00	80.00
78 Matt Chapman	8.00	20.00
79 DJ LeMahieu	15.00	40.00
105 Jesus Luzardo	10.00	25.00
107 Max Muncy	12.00	30.00
116 Dansby Swanson	8.00	20.00
117 Kris Bryant	12.00	30.00
138 Eloy Jimenez	15.00	40.00
147 Aristides Aquino	20.00	50.00
156 Rhys Hoskins	10.00	25.00
157 Pete Alonso	60.00	150.00
161 Ketel Marte	10.00	25.00
163 Christian Yelich	10.00	25.00
165 Brandon Lowe	10.00	25.00
169 Rafael Devers	30.00	80.00
172 Walker Buehler	10.00	25.00
173 Bo Bichette	50.00	120.00
186 Gleyber Torres	15.00	40.00
187 Jacob deGrom	12.00	30.00
188 Bryce Harper	12.00	30.00
199 Jose Berrios	10.00	25.00

2020 Topps Opening Day Autographs

ODAAA Aristides Aquino	10.00	25.00
ODAAP A.J. Puk	6.00	15.00
ODABB Bo Bichette	40.00	100.00
ODACB Cavan Biggio	10.00	25.00
ODAGL Gavin Lux	30.00	80.00
ODAGT Gleyber Torres	30.00	80.00
ODAJF Jack Flaherty	10.00	25.00
ODAJS Juan Soto	50.00	120.00
ODAJSO Jorge Soler	10.00	25.00
ODAKH Keston Hiura	15.00	40.00
ODAKL Kyle Lewis	50.00	120.00
ODAMK Max Kepler	6.00	15.00
ODAMS Max Scherzer	15.00	40.00
ODAMSO Mike Soroka	10.00	25.00
ODAMT Mike Trout	150.00	400.00
ODAMY Mike Yastrzemski	12.00	30.00
ODARA Ronald Acuna Jr.	60.00	150.00
ODAWA Willians Astudillo	6.00	15.00
ODAWS Will Smith	12.00	30.00
ODAYA Yordan Alvarez	75.00	200.00

2020 Topps Opening Day Ballpark Profile Autographs

BPACC Chip Caray	20.00	50.00
BPADB Dan Baker	12.00	30.00
BPADBR Dick Bremer	25.00	60.00
BPADG Drew Goodman	12.00	30.00
BPADO Don Orsillo	12.00	30.00
BPAGP Gary Pressy	25.00	60.00
BPAJD Jacques Doucet	15.00	40.00
BPAJJ Jaime Jarrin	30.00	80.00
BPAJK John Keating	20.00	50.00
BPARBM Renel Brooks-Moon	15.00	40.00
BPATC Tom Caron	12.00	30.00

2020 Topps Opening Day Diamond Autograph Relics

DARAA Aristides Aquino/40	12.00	30.00
DARBR Bryan Reynolds/49	30.00	80.00
DARCP Chris Paddack/50	20.00	50.00
DARKH Keston Hiura/50	50.00	120.00
DARKL Kyle Lewis/40	15.00	40.00
DARKM Ketel Marte/50	20.00	50.00
DARMCH Matt Chapman/50	15.00	40.00
DARMM Max Muncy/50	20.00	50.00
DARPA Pete Alonso/30	60.00	150.00
DARYA Yordan Alvarez/40	75.00	200.00

2020 Topps Opening Day Diamond Relics

DRAA Aristides Aquino	15.00	40.00
DRBH Bryce Harper	15.00	40.00
DRBR Bryan Reynolds	5.00	12.00
DRCB Clayton Kershaw	12.00	30.00
DRCK Cody Bellinger	10.00	25.00
DRCP Chris Paddack	6.00	15.00
DRCY Christian Yelich	8.00	20.00
DRFF Freddie Freeman	8.00	20.00
DRFT Fernando Tatis Jr.	12.00	30.00
DRJB Javier Baez	8.00	20.00
DRJF Jack Flaherty	10.00	25.00
DRKH Keston Hiura	10.00	25.00
DRKL Kyle Lewis	8.00	20.00
DRKM Ketel Marte	5.00	12.00
DRMC Miguel Cabrera	12.00	30.00
DRMCH Matt Chapman	12.00	30.00
DRMT Mike Trout	30.00	80.00
DRNA Nolan Arenado	8.00	20.00
DRPA Pete Alonso	20.00	50.00
DRPG Paul Goldschmidt	6.00	15.00
DRRA Ronald Acuna Jr.	15.00	40.00
DRRH Rhys Hoskins	8.00	20.00
DRRO Rougned Odor	5.00	12.00
DRSC Shin-Soo Choo	5.00	12.00
DRSO Shohei Ohtani	8.00	20.00
DRYA Yordan Alvarez	25.00	60.00

2020 Topps Opening Day Dugout Peeks

DP1 Ronald Acuna Jr.	60.00	150.00
DP2 Bryce Harper	30.00	80.00
DP3 Nelson Cruz	20.00	50.00
DP4 Kris Bryant	12.00	30.00
DP5 Alex Bregman	10.00	25.00
DP6 Cody Bellinger	20.00	50.00
DP7 Juan Soto	30.00	80.00
DP8 Pete Alonso	40.00	100.00
DP9 Aaron Judge	25.00	60.00
DP10 Mike Trout	150.00	400.00
DP11 Aristides Aquino	40.00	100.00
DP12 Manny Machado	10.00	25.00
DP13 Francisco Lindor	25.00	60.00
DP14 Eloy Jimenez	20.00	50.00
DP15 Ketel Marte	15.00	40.00
DP16 Nolan Arenado	12.00	30.00
DP17 Vladimir Guerrero Jr.	40.00	100.00
DP18 Joey Votto	20.00	50.00
DP19 Mookie Betts	20.00	50.00
DP20 Matt Chapman	10.00	25.00

2020 Topps Opening Day Major League Mementos Relics

MLMBH Bryce Harper	8.00	20.00
MLMBM Brendan McKay	5.00	12.00
MLMBP Buster Posey	6.00	15.00
MLMCY Christian Yelich	6.00	15.00
MLMKB Kris Bryant	6.00	15.00
MLMMT Mike Trout	25.00	60.00
MLMPA Pete Alonso	12.00	30.00
MLMRD Rafael Devers	10.00	25.00

2020 Topps Opening Day Mascot Autograph Relics

MARBB Bernie Brewer	40.00	100.00
MARC Clark	40.00	100.00
MARFB Fredbird	40.00	100.00
MARS Sluggerrr	40.00	100.00
MARWGM Wally the Green Monster	40.00	100.00

2020 Topps Opening Day Mascot Autographs

MABB Bernie Brewer	15.00	40.00
MACC Clark	12.00	30.00
MAFB Fredbird	12.00	30.00
MAMM Mr. Met	25.00	60.00
MAR Raymond	10.00	25.00
MAS Sluggerrr	10.00	25.00
MAWGM Wally the Green Monster	12.00	30.00

2020 Topps Opening Day Mascot Patches

STATED PRINT RUN 99 SER.#'d SETS

MPRCC Clark	30.00	80.00
MPRD Dinger	20.00	50.00
MPRMM Mr. Met	20.00	50.00
MPRMM Mariner Moose	20.00	50.00
MPRO Orbit	20.00	50.00
MPRR Raymond	20.00	50.00
MPRS Screech	20.00	50.00
MPRTCB TC Bear	20.00	50.00
MPRWGM Wally the Green Monster	20.00	50.00

2020 Topps Opening Day Mascot Relics

MRBB Bernie Brewer	8.00	20.00
MRCC Clark	8.00	20.00
MRF Fredbird	8.00	20.00
MRS Sluggerrr	8.00	20.00
MRWGM Wally the Green Monster	8.00	20.00

2020 Topps Opening Day Mascots

COMPLETE SET (24)	6.00	15.00
STATED ODDS 1:XX		
M1 Clark	.40	1.00
M2 Wally the Green Monster	.40	1.00
M3 Mr. Met	.40	1.00
M4 Dinger	.40	1.00
M5 Fredbird	.40	1.00
M6 Paws	.40	1.00
M7 Sluggerrr	.40	1.00
M8 Bernie Brewer	.40	1.00
M9 Raymond	.40	1.00
M10 Rosie Red	.40	1.00
M11 Blooper	.40	1.00
M12 Slider	.40	1.00
M13 Pirate Parrot	.40	1.00
M14 Screech	.40	1.00
M15 Orbit	.40	1.00
M16 Mariner Moose	.40	1.00
M17 TC Bear	.40	1.00
M18 Swinging Friar	.40	1.00
M19 Rangers Captain	.40	1.00
M20 Mr. Red	.40	1.00
M21 Billy the Marlin	.40	1.00
M22 Mascot	.40	1.00
M23 Mrs. Met	.40	1.00
M24 Mascot	.40	1.00

2020 Topps Opening Day Opening Day

COMPLETE SET (15)	4.00	10.00
COMMON CARD	.40	1.00
OD1 Cincinnati Reds	.40	1.00
OD2 Kansas City Royals	.40	1.00
OD3 Los Angeles Dodgers	.40	1.00
OD4 Miami Marlins	.40	1.00
OD5 Milwaukee Brewers	.40	1.00
OD6 Minnesota Twins	.40	1.00
OD7 New York Yankees	.40	1.00
OD8 Oakland Athletics	.40	1.00
OD9 Philadelphia Phillies	.40	1.00
OD10 San Diego Padres	.40	1.00
OD11 Seattle Mariners	.40	1.00
OD12 Tampa Bay Rays	.40	1.00
OD13 Texas Rangers	.40	1.00
OD14 Toronto Blue Jays	.40	1.00
OD15 Washington Nationals	.40	1.00

2020 Topps Opening Day Relics

ODRAA Aristides Aquino	10.00	25.00
ODRAB Alex Bregman	4.00	10.00
ODRAJ Aaron Judge	10.00	25.00
ODRAR Anthony Rizzo	8.00	20.00
ODRBH Bryce Harper	10.00	25.00
ODRCB Cody Bellinger	6.00	15.00
ODRCK Clayton Kershaw	8.00	20.00
ODRCY Christian Yelich	8.00	20.00
ODRFT Fernando Tatis Jr.	8.00	20.00
ODRGT Gleyber Torres	8.00	20.00
ODRJB Javier Baez	6.00	15.00
ODRJV Justin Verlander	6.00	15.00
ODRKB Kris Bryant	5.00	12.00
ODRKH Keston Hiura	5.00	12.00
ODRMC Miguel Cabrera	8.00	20.00
ODRMS Max Scherzer	6.00	15.00
ODRMT Mike Trout	25.00	60.00
ODRNS Nick Senzel	4.00	10.00
ODRPA Pete Alonso	10.00	25.00
ODRRA Ronald Acuna Jr.	12.00	30.00
ODRRH Rhys Hoskins	6.00	15.00
ODRSO Shohei Ohtani	8.00	20.00
ODRVG Vladimir Guerrero Jr.	8.00	20.00
ODRYA Yordan Alvarez	15.00	40.00
ODRYM Yadier Molina	6.00	15.00

2020 Topps Opening Day Spring Has Sprung

COMPLETE SET (25)	8.00	20.00
SHS1 Babe Ruth	.75	2.00
SHS2 Roberto Clemente	.75	2.00
SHS3 Ted Williams	.60	1.50
SHS4 Sandy Koufax	.60	1.50
SHS5 Willie Mays	.60	1.50
SHS6 George Brett	.60	1.50
SHS7 Reggie Jackson	.25	.60
SHS8 Ken Griffey Jr.	.60	1.50
SHS9 Cal Ripken Jr.	1.00	2.50
SHS10 Mark McGwire	.50	1.25
SHS11 Frank Thomas	.30	.75
SHS12 Aaron Judge	.75	2.00
SHS13 Cody Bellinger	.60	1.50
SHS14 Bryce Harper	.50	1.25
SHS15 Ronald Acuna Jr.	1.25	3.00
SHS16 Mike Trout	1.50	4.00
SHS17 Javier Baez	.40	1.00
SHS18 Clayton Kershaw	.60	1.50
SHS19 Juan Soto	1.00	2.50
SHS20 Rafael Devers	.40	1.00
SHS21 Vladimir Guerrero Jr.	.60	1.50
SHS22 Fernando Tatis Jr.	1.25	3.00
SHS23 Yordan Alvarez	1.00	2.50
SHS24 Bo Bichette	1.50	4.00
SHS25 Gavin Lux	1.25	3.00

2020 Topps Opening Day Sticker Collection Preview

COMPLETE SET (10)	4.00	10.00
SP1 Justin Verlander	.30	.75
SP2 Javier Baez	.40	1.00
SP3 Pete Alonso	.75	2.00
SP4 Bo Bichette	1.50	4.00
SP5 Nolan Arenado	.40	1.00
SP6 Aaron Judge	.75	2.00
SP7 Juan Soto	1.00	2.50
SP8 Cody Bellinger	.60	1.50
SP9 Mookie Betts	.60	1.50
SP10 Bryce Harper	.50	1.25

2020 Topps Opening Day Team Traditions and Celebrations

COMPLETE SET (10)	3.00	8.00
TTC1 Judge's Court	.75	2.00
TTC2 Jackie Robinson Statue	.30	.75
TTC3 Pesky's Pole	.20	.50
TTC4 Hand-turned Scoreboard		
TTC5 Stan Musial Statue	.50	1.25
TTC6 Crown Vision		
TTC7 Outfield Cable Car		
TTC8 Willie Mays Statue	.60	1.50
TTC9 Monument Garden		
TTC10 Baseball Bat Chandelier		

2020 Topps Opening Day The Lighter Side of Baseball

LSB1 Ronald Acuna Jr.	15.00	40.00
LSB2 Derek Dietrich	8.00	20.00
LSB3 Gerardo Parra	3.00	8.00
LSB4 Francisco Lindor	6.00	15.00
LSB5 Mookie Betts	10.00	25.00
LSB6 Juan Soto	15.00	40.00
LSB7 Vladimir Guerrero Jr.	10.00	25.00
LSB8 Jose Altuve	10.00	25.00
LSB9 Cody Bellinger	10.00	25.00
LSB10 Fernando Tatis Jr.	8.00	20.00
LSB11 Bryce Harper	8.00	20.00
LSB12 Eugenio Suarez	6.00	15.00
LSB13 Tim Anderson	6.00	15.00
LSB14 Anthony Rizzo	10.00	25.00
LSB15 Anthony Rendon	5.00	12.00
LSB16 Shohei Ohtani	6.00	15.00
LSB17 Nelson Cruz	6.00	15.00
LSB18 Walker Buehler	6.00	15.00
LSB19 Pete Alonso	20.00	50.00
LSB20 Max Scherzer	6.00	15.00
LSB21 Mike Trout	30.00	80.00
LSB22 Alex Bregman	8.00	20.00
LSB23 Christian Yelich	8.00	20.00
LSB24 Rafael Devers	6.00	15.00
LSB25 Javier Baez	10.00	25.00

2020 Topps Opening Day Walk This Way

WW1 Ronald Acuna Jr.	20.00	50.00
WW2 Max Muncy	3.00	8.00
WW3 Matt Olson	2.50	6.00
WW4 Keston Hiura	8.00	20.00
WW5 Bryce Harper	6.00	15.00
WW6 Will Smith	5.00	12.00
WW7 Pete Alonso	15.00	40.00
WW8 DJ LeMahieu	4.00	10.00
WW9 Bo Bichette	20.00	50.00
WW10 Christian Yelich	5.00	12.00
WW11 Miguel Sano	3.00	8.00
WW12 Harold Ramirez	2.50	6.00
WW13 Mallex Smith	2.50	6.00
WW14 Tim Locastro	8.00	20.00
WW15 Rafael Devers	5.00	12.00
WW16 Trevor Story	4.00	10.00
WW17 Dominic Smith	6.00	15.00
WW18 Bryan Reynolds	3.00	8.00
WW19 Kurt Suzuki	2.50	6.00
WW20 Harrison Bader	3.00	8.00
WW21 Kevin Newman	3.00	8.00
WW22 Joc Pederson	3.00	8.00
WW23 Nolan Arenado	5.00	12.00
WW24 Carlos Santana	3.00	8.00
WW25 Mike Yastrzemski	6.00	15.00

2020 Topps Project 2020

1 Ichiro/1334*	1250.00	2500.00
2 Sandy Koufax/1135*	200.00	500.00
3 Jackie Robinson/1302*	250.00	600.00
4 Mike Trout/2911*	300.00	800.00
5 Cal Ripken Jr./1205*	250.00	600.00
6 Ken Griffey Jr./2504*	200.00	500.00
7 Bob Gibson/1205*	200.00	500.00
8 Mariano Rivera/1617*	150.00	400.00
9 Ted Williams/1385*	125.00	300.00
10 Roberto Clemente/1844*	250.00	600.00
11 George Brett/1227*	200.00	500.00
12 Dwight Gooden/1065*	300.00	800.00
13 Don Mattingly/1686*	150.00	400.00
14 Rickey Henderson/1221*	150.00	400.00
15 Willie Mays/1464*	125.00	300.00
16 Tony Gwynn/1302*	125.00	300.00
17 Mark McGwire/1456*	100.00	250.00
18 Nolan Ryan/2623*	100.00	250.00
19 Roberto Clemente/1819*	100.00	250.00
20 Cal Ripken Jr./1576*	75.00	200.00
21 Rickey Henderson/2104*	100.00	250.00
22 Ichiro/1972*	100.00	250.00
23 Frank Thomas/2836*	125.00	300.00
24 Tony Gwynn/1441*	100.00	250.00
25 Ken Griffey Jr./3707*	25.00	60.00
26 Dwight Gooden/1101*	200.00	500.00
27 Willie Mays/1480*	100.00	250.00
28 Mark McGwire/1199*	150.00	400.00
29 Derek Jeter/9873*	12.00	30.00
30 Nolan Ryan/2215*	100.00	250.00
31 Jackie Robinson/2741*	50.00	120.00
32 Ichiro/1798*	100.00	250.00
33 Don Mattingly/2409*	75.00	200.00
34 Ted Williams/1131*	75.00	200.00
35 Mike Trout/13200*	12.00	30.00
36 Sandy Koufax/2488*	40.00	100.00
37 Cal Ripken Jr./2621*	30.00	80.00
38 Dwight Gooden/1864*	100.00	250.00
39 Derek Jeter/9322*	12.00	30.00
40 Tony Gwynn/2319*	40.00	100.00
41 Mariano Rivera/2452*	20.00	50.00
42 Jackie Robinson/2980*	25.00	60.00
43 George Brett/2360*	40.00	100.00
44 Frank Thomas/1480*	60.00	150.00
45 Roberto Clemente/1910*	60.00	150.00
46 Bob Gibson/1268*	100.00	250.00
47 Don Mattingly/2763*	40.00	100.00
48 Willie Mays/1556*	100.00	250.00
49 Sandy Koufax/2149*	50.00	120.00
50 Cal Ripken Jr./2369*	75.00	200.00
51 Mike Trout/34950*	10.00	25.00
52 Nolan Ryan/4103*	30.00	80.00
53 Ken Griffey Jr./4236*	20.00	50.00
54 Bob Gibson/1451*	125.00	300.00
55 George Brett/1992*	50.00	120.00
56 Mariano Rivera/1127*	125.00	300.00
57 Rickey Henderson/3819*	12.00	30.00
58 Ted Williams/4859*	15.00	40.00
59 Derek Jeter/6511*	10.00	25.00
60 Mark McGwire/2687*	20.00	50.00
61 Willie Mays/5459*	8.00	20.00
62 Ichiro/6207*	10.00	25.00
63 Mike Trout/16430*	6.00	15.00
64 Tony Gwynn/3368*	20.00	50.00
65 Dwight Gooden/5041*	10.00	25.00
66 Ken Griffey Jr./9536*	10.00	25.00
67 Nolan Ryan/7383*	10.00	25.00
68 Roberto Clemente/8518*	8.00	20.00
69 Don Mattingly/7900*	6.00	15.00
70 Bob Gibson/6757*	15.00	40.00
71 Rickey Henderson/15741*	10.00	25.00
72 Mariano Rivera/9545*	6.00	15.00
73 Frank Thomas/11969*	8.00	20.00
74 Ted Williams/8897*	8.00	20.00
75 George Brett/5638*	10.00	25.00
76 Sandy Koufax/6607*	8.00	20.00
77 Ichiro /11425*	6.00	15.00
78 Roberto Clemente/8610*	6.00	15.00
79 Jackie Robinson/11643*	6.00	15.00
80 Willie Mays/10480*	8.00	20.00
81 Mark McGwire/18205*	6.00	15.00
82 Derek Jeter/20974*	6.00	15.00
83 Frank Thomas/8806*	8.00	20.00
84 Bob Gibson/14867*	6.00	15.00
85 Mike Trout/33818*	5.00	12.00
86 Dwight Gooden/25928*	5.00	12.00
87 Nolan Ryan/*64629	6.00	15.00
88 Ken Griffey Jr./99177*	5.00	12.00
89 Sandy Koufax/43147*	5.00	10.00
90 Ted Williams/41407*	5.00	12.00
91 Mariano Rivera/35330*	6.00	15.00
92 Cal Ripken Jr/41392*	12.00	30.00
93 Derek Jeter/48465*	5.00	12.00
94 Tony Gwynn/31030*	6.00	15.00
95 Don Mattingly/27299*	5.00	12.00
96 Frank Thomas/22911*	5.00	12.00
97 Mark McGwire/19894*	6.00	15.00
98 Jackie Robinson/20219*	6.00	15.00
99 Sandy Koufax/21535*	6.00	15.00
100 Mike Trout/74862*	8.00	20.00
101 Willie Mays/10568*	5.00	12.00
102 George Brett/10757*	6.00	15.00
103 Roberto Clemente/11577*	6.00	15.00
104 Rickey Henderson/11578*	10.00	25.00
105 Nolan Ryan/12874*	6.00	15.00
106 Dwight Gooden/8854*	5.00	10.00
107 Derek Jeter/24908*	6.00	15.00
108 Bob Gibson/11395*	6.00	15.00
109 Cal Ripken Jr./36466*	25.00	60.00
110 Roberto Clemente/12077*	8.00	20.00
111 Mark McGwire/9169*	6.00	15.00
112 George Brett/6558*	8.00	20.00
113 Tony Gwynn/8401*	6.00	15.00
114 Jackie Robinson/14067*	8.00	20.00
115 Frank Thomas/6763*	6.00	15.00
116 Ken Griffey Jr./10957*	15.00	40.00
117 Mariano Rivera/7460*	10.00	25.00
118 Don Mattingly/8469*	8.00	20.00
119 Dwight Gooden/5868*	6.00	15.00
120 Ichiro/8333*	6.00	15.00
121 Mike Trout/20961*	10.00	25.00
122 Ted Williams/9507*	6.00	15.00
123 Rickey Henderson/4966*	8.00	20.00
124 Bob Gibson/6090*	8.00	20.00
125 Sandy Koufax/4966*	8.00	20.00
126 Nolan Ryan/4859*	12.00	30.00
127 Ken Griffey Jr./10472*	8.00	20.00
128 Willie Mays/7195*	6.00	15.00
129 Rickey Henderson/6609*	8.00	20.00
130 Ichiro/6238*	6.00	15.00
131 Mariano Rivera/9468*	8.00	20.00
132 Derek Jeter/64088*	8.00	20.00
133 George Brett/7757*	12.00	30.00
134 Mark McGwire/5092*	8.00	20.00
135 Tony Gwynn/4863*	8.00	20.00
136 Cal Ripken Jr./4976*	10.00	25.00
137 Dwight Gooden/7141*	12.00	30.00
138 Roberto Clemente/6507*	12.00	30.00
139 Don Mattingly/4682*	8.00	20.00
140 Jackie Robinson/6068*	10.00	25.00
141 Frank Thomas/6678*	8.00	20.00
142 Mike Trout/14821*	10.00	25.00
143 Willie Mays/5930*	8.00	20.00
144 Bob Gibson/4367*	10.00	25.00
145 Sandy Koufax/6385*	10.00	25.00
146 Ted Williams/4693*	10.00	25.00
147 Nolan Ryan/3781*	10.00	25.00
148 Ken Griffey Jr./6021*	8.00	20.00
149 Ichiro/6042*	8.00	20.00
150 George Brett/4085*	10.00	25.00
151 Mariano Rivera/12611*	10.00	25.00
152 Mark McGwire/6977*	12.00	30.00
153 Rickey Henderson/5155*	12.00	30.00
154 Roberto Clemente/5916*	10.00	25.00
155 Don Mattingly/4292*	10.00	25.00
156 Jackie Robinson/4046*	12.00	30.00
157 Derek Jeter/8413*	6.00	15.00
158 Ted Williams/4404*	10.00	25.00
159 Cal Ripken Jr./4158*	10.00	25.00
160 Frank Thomas/5101*	10.00	25.00
161 Tony Gwynn/5543*	10.00	25.00
162 Sandy Koufax/4009*	10.00	25.00
163 Bob Gibson/3484*	10.00	25.00
164 Dwight Gooden/3175*	10.00	25.00
165 Nolan Ryan/4146*	15.00	40.00
166 Willie Mays/3609*	10.00	25.00
167 Mike Trout/11658*	10.00	25.00
168 Rickey Henderson/6650*	12.00	30.00
169 Ichiro/6640*	12.00	30.00
170 Don Mattingly/10210*	12.00	30.00
171 Derek Jeter/6009*	12.00	30.00
172 Ted Williams/3484*	12.00	30.00
173 Cal Ripken Jr./4509*	8.00	20.00
174 Frank Thomas/4239*	10.00	25.00
175 George Brett/3278*	8.00	20.00
176 Jackie Robinson/3253*	10.00	25.00
177 Ken Griffey Jr./6527*	10.00	25.00
178 Mark McGwire/3224*	10.00	25.00
179 Mariano Rivera/3154*	10.00	25.00
180 Tony Gwynn/4292*	10.00	25.00
181 Sandy Koufax/4369*	12.00	30.00
182 Roberto Clemente/3592*	12.00	30.00
183 Ichiro/3652*	10.00	25.00
184 Dwight Gooden/3554*	10.00	25.00
185 Rickey Henderson/4046*	15.00	40.00
186 Nolan Ryan/2981*	15.00	40.00
187 Mike Trout/11405*	10.00	25.00
188 Willie Mays/3858*	10.00	25.00
189 Ted Williams/4684*	10.00	25.00
190 Don Mattingly/3550*	10.00	25.00
191 Mark McGwire/9758*	10.00	25.00
192 George Brett/3851*	10.00	25.00
193 Frank Thomas/3781*	15.00	40.00
194 Jackie Robinson/3268*	10.00	25.00
195 Cal Ripken Jr./4055*	12.00	30.00
196 Ichiro/3930*	10.00	25.00
197 Roberto Clemente/4280*	12.00	30.00
198 Tony Gwynn/3567*	15.00	40.00
199 Mariano Rivera/4952*	15.00	40.00
200 Derek Jeter/7285*	12.00	30.00

2006 Topps Sterling

This 200-card set was releasedIn November, 2006. The set was issued in a special "cherry wood player specific box" which had three base cards plus an autographed relic or relic card of the featured player,. In addition, each box had an mystery pack with either an cut signature or an framed parallel card of the featured player. These "boxes" had an $250 SRP and were issued 10 to a case. Each base card in this set had a stated print run of 250 serial numbered sets.

B.BONDS (1-19)	5.00	12.00
B.BONDS ODDS 1:10		
M.MANTLE (20-39)	8.00	20.00
M.MANTLE ODDS 1:10		
J.GIBSON (40-43)	12.50	30.00
J.GIBSON ODDS 1:191		
R.HENDERSON (44-53)	4.00	10.00
R.HENDERSON ODDS 1:22		
T.WILLIAMS (54-62)	5.00	12.00
T.WILLIAMS ODDS 1:27		
R.CLEMENTE (63-67)	10.00	25.00
R.CLEMENTE ODDS 1:40		
N.RYAN (68-77)	8.00	20.00
N.RYAN ODDS 1:20		
C.RIPKEN (78-96)	8.00	20.00
C.RIPKEN ODDS 1:10		
S.MUSIAL (97-101)	4.00	10.00
S.MUSIAL ODDS 1:40		
R.JACKSON (102-106)	4.00	10.00
R.JACKSON ODDS 1:40		
J.BENCH (107-111)	4.00	10.00
J.BENCH ODDS 1:43		
G.BRETT (112-121)	4.00	10.00
G.BRETT ODDS 1:20		
D.MATTINGLY (122-131)	5.00	12.00
D.MATTINGLY ODDS 1:20		
R.MARIS (132-136)	5.00	12.00
R.MARIS ODDS 1:40		
R.CAREW (137-146)	4.00	10.00
R.CAREW ODDS 1:20		
Y.BERRA (147-151)	4.00	10.00
Y.BERRA ODDS 1:40		
M.SCHMIDT (152-156)	4.00	10.00
M.SCHMIDT ODDS 1:40		
C.YASTRZEMSKI (157-175)	4.00	10.00
C.YASTRZEMSKI ODDS 1:10		
T.GWYNN (176-185	4.00	10.00
T.GWYNN ODDS 1:20		
R.SANDBERG (186-190)	4.00	10.00
R.SANDBERG ODDS 1:40		
O.SMITH (191-200)	4.00	10.00
O.SMITH ODDS 1:20		
STATED PRINT RUN 250 SER.#'d SETS		

2006 Topps Sterling Framed Burgundy

B.BONDS (1-19)	30.00	60.00
M.MANTLE (20-39)	50.00	100.00
J.GIBSON (40-43)	30.00	60.00
R.HENDERSON (44-53)	20.00	50.00
T.WILLIAMS (54-62)	30.00	60.00
R.CLEMENTE (63-67)	40.00	80.00
N.RYAN (68-77)	75.00	150.00
C.RIPKEN (78-96)	75.00	150.00
S.MUSIAL (97-101)	20.00	50.00
R.JACKSON (102-106)	20.00	50.00
J.BENCH (107-111)	20.00	50.00
G.BRETT (112-121)	30.00	60.00
D.MATTINGLY (122-131)	30.00	60.00
R.MARIS (132-136)	30.00	60.00
R.CAREW (137-146)	10.00	25.00
Y.BERRA (147-151)	20.00	50.00
M.SCHMIDT (152-156)	20.00	50.00
C.YASTRZEMSKI (157-175)	20.00	50.00
T.GWYNN (176-185	20.00	50.00
R.SANDBERG (186-190)	20.00	50.00
O.SMITH (191-200)	20.00	50.00
RANDOM INSERTS IN BONUS PACKS		
STATED PRINT RUN 10 SER.#'d SETS		

2006 Topps Sterling Framed White

*FRAMED WHITE: .6X TO 1.5X BASIC
RANDOM INSERTS IN BONUS PACKS
STATED PRINT RUN 50 SER.#'d SETS

2006 Topps Sterling Baseball Cut Signatures

OVERALL CUT SIGNATURE ODDS 1:5		
AK Al Kaline	40.00	100.00
BF Bob Feller	15.00	40.00
BG Bob Gibson	40.00	80.00
BR Brooks Robinson	40.00	80.00
CF Carlton Fisk	30.00	60.00
DS Duke Snider	15.00	40.00
EW Earl Weaver	15.00	40.00
GC Gary Carter	20.00	50.00
GK George Kell	15.00	40.00
GP Gaylord Perry	15.00	40.00
HK Harmon Killebrew	50.00	100.00
JB Johnny Bench	30.00	80.00
JMO Joe Morgan	15.00	40.00
JP Jim Palmer	15.00	40.00
LA Luis Aparicio	30.00	60.00
LB Lou Brock	30.00	60.00
MI Monte Irvin	15.00	40.00
OC Orlando Cepeda	15.00	40.00
PN Phil Niekro	15.00	40.00
RC Rod Carew	20.00	50.00
RF Rollie Fingers	15.00	40.00
RK Ralph Kiner	20.00	50.00
RR Robin Roberts	30.00	60.00
RS Ryne Sandberg	20.00	50.00
RSH Red Schoendienst	15.00	40.00
RY Robin Yount	30.00	60.00
SA Sparky Anderson	20.00	50.00
SC Steve Carlton	30.00	60.00
TP Tony Perez	30.00	60.00

2006 Topps Sterling Cut Signatures

OVERALL CUT SIGNATURE ODDS 1:5
67 Lloyd Waner 20.00 50.00
68 Sal Maglie 20.00 50.00
69 Waite Hoyt 40.00 80.00
70 Warren Spahn 75.00 150.00
72 A.B. Chandler 40.00 80.00
73 Al Barlick 20.00 50.00
74 Bill Dickey 60.00 120.00
75 Bill Terry 20.00 50.00
76 Billy Herman 30.00 60.00
77 Bob Lemon 20.00 50.00
78 Buck Leonard 20.00 50.00
79 Charles Gehringer 60.00 120.00
82 Hoyt Wilhelm 20.00 50.00
83 Catfish Hunter 50.00 100.00
84 Joe Sewell 30.00 60.00
85 Judy Johnson 20.00 50.00
86 Carl Hubbell 30.00 60.00
87 Lou Boudreau 40.00 80.00
88 Luke Appling 20.00 50.00
89 Ray Dandridge 20.00 50.00
90 Rick Ferrell 30.00 60.00
91 Stan Coveleski 40.00 80.00
92 Willie Stargell 50.00 100.00

2006 Topps Sterling Moments Relics

B.BONDS 30.00 80.00
M.MANTLE 3 or 4 RELIC 75.00 150.00
M.MANTLE 5 or 6 RELIC 125.00 250.00
J.GIBSON 500.00 800.00
R.HENDERSON 40.00 100.00
T.WILLIAMS 25.00 60.00
R.CLEMENTE 125.00 250.00
N.RYAN 60.00 150.00
C.RIPKEN 40.00 80.00
S.MUSIAL 25.00 60.00
R.JACKSON 25.00 60.00
J.BENCH 25.00 60.00
G.BRETT 25.00 60.00
R.MARIS 50.00 120.00
Y.BERRA 30.00 80.00
M.SCHMIDT 25.00 60.00
C.YASTRZEMSKI 20.00 50.00
T.GWYNN 25.00 60.00
R.SANDBERG 25.00 60.00
OVERALL AU/GU ODDS 1:3
STATED PRINT RUN 10 SER.#'d SETS
PRIME PRIME RUN 1 SER.#'d SET
NO PRIME PRICING DUE TO SCARCITY

2006 Topps Sterling Moments Relics Autographs

R.HENDERSON 125.00 250.00
N.RYAN 100.00 200.00
C.RIPKEN 150.00 300.00
S.MUSIAL 90.00 150.00
R.JACKSON 40.00 80.00
J.BENCH 75.00 150.00
G.BRETT 75.00 150.00
D.MATTINGLY 75.00 150.00
R.CAREW 40.00 80.00
Y.BERRA 90.00 150.00
M.SCHMIDT 75.00 150.00
C.YASTRZEMSKI 60.00 120.00
T.GWYNN 50.00 100.00
R.SANDBERG 75.00 150.00
O.SMITH 75.00 150.00
OVERALL AU-GU ODDS 1:3
STATED PRINT RUN 10 SERIAL #'d SETS
NO BONDS PRICING DUE TO SCARCITY
PRIME PRINT RUN 1 SER.#'d SET
NO PRIME PRICING DUE TO SCARCITY

2006 Topps Sterling Triple Relics Autographs

OVERALL AU/GU ODDS 1:3
STATED PRINT RUN 10 SERIAL #'d SETS
NO PRICING DUE TO SCARCITY
PRIME PRINT RUN 10 SERIAL #'d SETS
NO PRIME PRICING DUE TO SCARCITY
STER.SIL. PRINT RUN 1 SER. #'d SET
NO STER.SIL. PRICING DUE TO SCARCITY
SS PRIME PRINT RUN 1 SER.#'d SET
NO SS PRIME PRICING DUE TO SCARCITY

2007 Topps Sterling

This 254-card set was released in December, 2007. The set was issued in "box" form which consisted of a player specific wood box and a mystery pack which also pertained to the player one recieved in the wood box. Each full box had five total cards in them and those boxes came five per carton and two cartons per full case.

COMMON MANTLE (1-24) 5.00 12.00
COMMON BONDS (25-48) 5.00 12.00
COMMON ICHIRO (49-56) 4.00 10.00
COMMON YAZ (57-64) 3.00 8.00
COMMON WRIGHT (65-76) 3.00 8.00
COMMON CLEMENTE (77-81) 6.00 15.00
COMMON SANTANA (82-89) 3.00 8.00
COMMON MORNEAU (90-101) 3.00 8.00
COMMON R.JACKSON (102-109) 3.00 8.00
COMMON CLEMENS (110-117) 4.00 10.00
COMMON T.WILLIAMS (118-122) 5.00 12.00
COMMON BERRA (123-130) 3.00 8.00
COMMON MATSUI (131-135) 3.00 8.00
COMMON HOWARD (136-143) 3.00 8.00
COMMON GWYNN (144-151) 3.00 8.00
COMMON ORTIZ (152-159) 2.50 6.00
COMMON SEAVER (160-167) 2.50 6.00
COMMON PUJOLS (168-175) 4.00 10.00
COMMON MUSIAL (176-183) 3.00 8.00
COMMON WANG (184-191) 5.00 12.00
COMMON SANDBERG (192-199) 4.00 10.00
COMMON N.RYAN (200-207) 8.00 20.00
COMMON B.GIBSON (208-215) 2.50 6.00
COMMON MARIS (216-220) 3.00 8.00
COMMON M.RAMIREZ (221-228) 3.00 8.00
COMMON SCHMIDT (229-236) 4.00 10.00
COMMON A.ROD (237-244) 3.00 8.00
COMMON MATSUZAKA (245-249) 6.00 15.00
COMMON DIMAGGIO (250-254) 4.00 10.00
THREE BASE CARDS PER BOX
STATED PRINT RUN 250 SER.#'d SETS
1 Mickey Mantle 5.00 12.00
2 Mickey Mantle 5.00 12.00
3 Mickey Mantle 5.00 12.00
4 Mickey Mantle 5.00 12.00
5 Mickey Mantle 5.00 12.00
6 Mickey Mantle 5.00 12.00
7 Mickey Mantle 5.00 12.00
8 Mickey Mantle 5.00 12.00
9 Mickey Mantle 5.00 12.00
10 Mickey Mantle 5.00 12.00
11 Mickey Mantle 5.00 12.00
12 Mickey Mantle 5.00 12.00
13 Mickey Mantle 5.00 12.00
14 Mickey Mantle 5.00 12.00
15 Mickey Mantle 5.00 12.00
16 Mickey Mantle 5.00 12.00
17 Mickey Mantle 5.00 12.00
18 Mickey Mantle 5.00 12.00
19 Mickey Mantle 5.00 12.00
20 Mickey Mantle 5.00 12.00
21 Mickey Mantle 5.00 12.00
22 Mickey Mantle 5.00 12.00
23 Mickey Mantle 5.00 12.00
24 Mickey Mantle 5.00 12.00
25 Barry Bonds 5.00 12.00
26 Barry Bonds 5.00 12.00
27 Barry Bonds 5.00 12.00
28 Barry Bonds 5.00 12.00
29 Barry Bonds 5.00 12.00
30 Barry Bonds 5.00 12.00
31 Barry Bonds 5.00 12.00
32 Barry Bonds 5.00 12.00
33 Barry Bonds 5.00 12.00
34 Barry Bonds 5.00 12.00
35 Barry Bonds 5.00 12.00
36 Barry Bonds 5.00 12.00
37 Barry Bonds 5.00 12.00
38 Barry Bonds 5.00 12.00
39 Barry Bonds 5.00 12.00
40 Barry Bonds 5.00 12.00
41 Barry Bonds 5.00 12.00
42 Barry Bonds 5.00 12.00
43 Barry Bonds 5.00 12.00
44 Barry Bonds 5.00 12.00
45 Barry Bonds 5.00 12.00
46 Barry Bonds 5.00 12.00
47 Barry Bonds 5.00 12.00
48 Barry Bonds 5.00 12.00
49 Ichiro Suzuki 4.00 10.00
50 Ichiro Suzuki 4.00 10.00
51 Ichiro Suzuki 4.00 10.00
52 Ichiro Suzuki 4.00 10.00
53 Ichiro Suzuki 4.00 10.00
54 Ichiro Suzuki 4.00 10.00
55 Ichiro Suzuki 4.00 10.00
56 Ichiro Suzuki 4.00 10.00
57 Carl Yastrzemski 3.00 8.00
58 Carl Yastrzemski 3.00 8.00
59 Carl Yastrzemski 3.00 8.00
60 Carl Yastrzemski 3.00 8.00
61 Carl Yastrzemski 3.00 8.00
62 Carl Yastrzemski 3.00 8.00
63 Carl Yastrzemski 3.00 8.00
64 Carl Yastrzemski 3.00 8.00
65 David Wright 3.00 8.00
66 David Wright 3.00 8.00
67 David Wright 3.00 8.00
68 David Wright 3.00 8.00
69 David Wright 3.00 8.00
70 David Wright 3.00 8.00
71 David Wright 3.00 8.00
72 David Wright 3.00 8.00
73 David Wright 3.00 8.00
74 David Wright 3.00 8.00
75 David Wright 3.00 8.00
76 David Wright 3.00 8.00
77 Roberto Clemente 6.00 15.00
78 Roberto Clemente 6.00 15.00
79 Roberto Clemente 6.00 15.00
80 Roberto Clemente 6.00 15.00
81 Roberto Clemente 6.00 15.00
82 Johan Santana 3.00 8.00
83 Johan Santana 3.00 8.00
84 Johan Santana 3.00 8.00
85 Johan Santana 3.00 8.00
86 Johan Santana 3.00 8.00
87 Johan Santana 3.00 8.00
88 Johan Santana 3.00 8.00
89 Johan Santana 3.00 8.00
90 Justin Morneau 3.00 8.00
91 Justin Morneau 3.00 8.00
92 Justin Morneau 3.00 8.00
93 Justin Morneau 3.00 8.00
94 Justin Morneau 3.00 8.00
95 Justin Morneau 3.00 8.00
96 Justin Morneau 3.00 8.00
97 Justin Morneau 3.00 8.00
98 Justin Morneau 3.00 8.00
99 Justin Morneau 3.00 8.00
100 Justin Morneau 3.00 8.00
101 Justin Morneau 3.00 8.00
102 Reggie Jackson 3.00 8.00
103 Reggie Jackson 3.00 8.00
104 Reggie Jackson 3.00 8.00
105 Reggie Jackson 3.00 8.00
106 Reggie Jackson 3.00 8.00
107 Reggie Jackson 3.00 8.00
108 Reggie Jackson 3.00 8.00
109 Reggie Jackson 3.00 8.00
110 Roger Clemens 4.00 10.00
111 Roger Clemens 4.00 10.00
112 Roger Clemens 4.00 10.00
113 Roger Clemens 4.00 10.00
114 Roger Clemens 4.00 10.00
115 Roger Clemens 4.00 10.00
116 Roger Clemens 4.00 10.00
117 Roger Clemens 4.00 10.00
118 Ted Williams 5.00 12.00
119 Ted Williams 5.00 12.00
120 Ted Williams 5.00 12.00
121 Ted Williams 5.00 12.00
122 Ted Williams 5.00 12.00
123 Yogi Berra 3.00 8.00
124 Yogi Berra 3.00 8.00
125 Yogi Berra 3.00 8.00
126 Yogi Berra 3.00 8.00
127 Yogi Berra 3.00 8.00
128 Yogi Berra 3.00 8.00
129 Yogi Berra 3.00 8.00
130 Yogi Berra 3.00 8.00
131 Hideki Matsui 3.00 8.00
132 Hideki Matsui 3.00 8.00
133 Hideki Matsui 3.00 8.00
134 Hideki Matsui 3.00 8.00
135 Hideki Matsui 3.00 8.00
136 Ryan Howard 3.00 8.00
137 Ryan Howard 3.00 8.00
138 Ryan Howard 3.00 8.00
139 Ryan Howard 3.00 8.00
140 Ryan Howard 3.00 8.00
141 Ryan Howard 3.00 8.00
142 Ryan Howard 3.00 8.00
143 Ryan Howard 3.00 8.00
144 Tony Gwynn 3.00 8.00
145 Tony Gwynn 3.00 8.00
146 Tony Gwynn 3.00 8.00
147 Tony Gwynn 3.00 8.00
148 Tony Gwynn 3.00 8.00
149 Tony Gwynn 3.00 8.00
150 Tony Gwynn 3.00 8.00
151 Tony Gwynn 3.00 8.00
152 David Ortiz 2.50 6.00
153 David Ortiz 2.50 6.00
154 David Ortiz 2.50 6.00
155 David Ortiz 2.50 6.00
156 David Ortiz 2.50 6.00
157 David Ortiz 2.50 6.00
158 David Ortiz 2.50 6.00
159 David Ortiz 2.50 6.00
160 Tom Seaver 2.50 6.00
161 Tom Seaver 2.50 6.00
162 Tom Seaver 2.50 6.00
163 Tom Seaver 2.50 6.00
164 Tom Seaver 2.50 6.00
165 Tom Seaver 2.50 6.00
166 Tom Seaver 2.50 6.00
167 Tom Seaver 2.50 6.00
168 Albert Pujols 4.00 10.00
169 Albert Pujols 4.00 10.00
170 Albert Pujols 4.00 10.00
171 Albert Pujols 4.00 10.00
172 Albert Pujols 4.00 10.00
173 Albert Pujols 4.00 10.00
174 Albert Pujols 4.00 10.00
175 Albert Pujols 4.00 10.00
176 Stan Musial 3.00 8.00
177 Stan Musial 3.00 8.00
178 Stan Musial 3.00 8.00
179 Stan Musial 3.00 8.00
180 Stan Musial 3.00 8.00
181 Stan Musial 3.00 8.00
182 Stan Musial 3.00 8.00
183 Stan Musial 3.00 8.00
184 Chien-Ming Wang 5.00 12.00
185 Chien-Ming Wang 5.00 12.00
186 Chien-Ming Wang 5.00 12.00
187 Chien-Ming Wang 5.00 12.00
188 Chien-Ming Wang 5.00 12.00
189 Chien-Ming Wang 5.00 12.00
190 Chien-Ming Wang 5.00 12.00
191 Chien-Ming Wang 5.00 12.00
192 Ryne Sandberg 4.00 10.00
193 Ryne Sandberg 4.00 10.00
194 Ryne Sandberg 4.00 10.00
195 Ryne Sandberg 4.00 10.00
196 Ryne Sandberg 4.00 10.00
197 Ryne Sandberg 4.00 10.00
198 Ryne Sandberg 4.00 10.00
199 Ryne Sandberg 4.00 10.00
200 Nolan Ryan 8.00 20.00
201 Nolan Ryan 8.00 20.00
202 Nolan Ryan 8.00 20.00
203 Nolan Ryan 8.00 20.00
204 Nolan Ryan 8.00 20.00
205 Nolan Ryan 8.00 20.00
206 Nolan Ryan 8.00 20.00
207 Nolan Ryan 8.00 20.00
208 Bob Gibson 2.50 6.00
209 Bob Gibson 2.50 6.00
210 Bob Gibson 2.50 6.00
211 Bob Gibson 2.50 6.00
212 Bob Gibson 2.50 6.00
213 Bob Gibson 2.50 6.00
214 Bob Gibson 2.50 6.00
215 Bob Gibson 2.50 6.00
216 Roger Maris 3.00 8.00
217 Roger Maris 3.00 8.00
218 Roger Maris 3.00 8.00
219 Roger Maris 3.00 8.00
220 Roger Maris 3.00 8.00
221 Manny Ramirez 3.00 8.00
222 Manny Ramirez 3.00 8.00
223 Manny Ramirez 3.00 8.00
224 Manny Ramirez 3.00 8.00
225 Manny Ramirez 3.00 8.00
226 Manny Ramirez 3.00 8.00
227 Manny Ramirez 3.00 8.00
228 Manny Ramirez 3.00 8.00
229 Mike Schmidt 4.00 10.00
230 Mike Schmidt 4.00 10.00
231 Mike Schmidt 4.00 10.00
232 Mike Schmidt 4.00 10.00
233 Mike Schmidt 4.00 10.00
234 Mike Schmidt 4.00 10.00
235 Mike Schmidt 4.00 10.00
236 Mike Schmidt 4.00 10.00
237 Alex Rodriguez 3.00 8.00
238 Alex Rodriguez 3.00 8.00
239 Alex Rodriguez 3.00 8.00
240 Alex Rodriguez 3.00 8.00
241 Alex Rodriguez 3.00 8.00
242 Alex Rodriguez 3.00 8.00
243 Alex Rodriguez 3.00 8.00
244 Alex Rodriguez 3.00 8.00
245 Daisuke Matsuzaka RC 6.00 15.00
246 Daisuke Matsuzaka RC 6.00 15.00
247 Daisuke Matsuzaka RC 6.00 15.00
248 Daisuke Matsuzaka RC 6.00 15.00
249 Daisuke Matsuzaka RC 6.00 15.00
250 Joe DiMaggio 4.00 10.00
251 Joe DiMaggio 4.00 10.00
252 Joe DiMaggio 4.00 10.00
253 Joe DiMaggio 4.00 10.00
254 Joe DiMaggio 4.00 10.00

2007 Topps Sterling Framed Burgundy

COMMON MANTLE (1-24) 20.00 50.00
COMMON BONDS (25-48) 12.50 30.00
COMMON ICHIRO (49-56) 12.50 30.00
COMMON YAZ (57-64) 12.50 30.00
COMMON WRIGHT (65-76) 10.00 25.00
COMMON CLEMENTE (77-81) 20.00 50.00
COMMON SANTANA (82-89) 8.00 20.00
COMMON MORNEAU (90-101) 6.00 15.00
COMMON R.JACKSON (102-109) 10.00 25.00
COMMON CLEMENS (110-117) 10.00 25.00
COMMON T.WILLIAMS (118-122) 12.50 30.00
COMMON BERRA (123-130) 6.00 15.00
COMMON MATSUI (131-135) 8.00 20.00
COMMON HOWARD (136-143) 10.00 25.00
COMMON GWYNN (144-151) 20.00 50.00
COMMON ORTIZ (152-159) 6.00 15.00
COMMON SEAVER (160-167) 8.00 20.00
COMMON PUJOLS (168-175) 12.50 30.00
COMMON MUSIAL (176-183) 10.00 25.00
COMMON WANG (184-191) 15.00 40.00
COMMON SANDBERG (192-199) 12.50 30.00
COMMON N.RYAN (200-207) 30.00 60.00
COMMON B.GIBSON (208-215) 8.00 20.00
COMMON MARIS (216-220) 12.50 30.00
COMMON M.RAMIREZ (221-228) 6.00 15.00
COMMON SCHMIDT (229-236) 15.00 40.00
COMMON A.ROD (237-244) 20.00 50.00
COMMON MATSUZAKA (245-249) 20.00 50.00
COMMON DIMAGGIO (250-254) 15.00 40.00
RANDOMLY INSERTED IN MYSTERY PACKS
STATED PRINT RUN 14 SER.#'d SETS

2007 Topps Sterling Framed Gold

COMMON MANTLE (1-24) 40.00 80.00
COMMON BONDS (25-48) 30.00 60.00
COMMON ICHIRO (49-56) 20.00 50.00
COMMON YAZ (57-64) 15.00 40.00
COMMON WRIGHT (65-76) 15.00 40.00
COMMON CLEMENTE (77-81) 30.00 60.00
COMMON SANTANA (82-89) 10.00 25.00
COMMON MORNEAU (90-101) 6.00 15.00
COMMON R.JACKSON (102-109) 12.50 30.00
COMMON CLEMENS (110-117) 12.50 30.00
COMMON T.WILLIAMS (118-122) 15.00 40.00
COMMON BERRA (123-130) 10.00 25.00
COMMON MATSUI (131-135) 15.00 40.00
COMMON HOWARD (136-143) 12.50 30.00
COMMON GWYNN (144-151) 30.00 60.00
COMMON ORTIZ (152-159) 8.00 20.00
COMMON SEAVER (160-167) 10.00 25.00
COMMON PUJOLS (168-175) 20.00 50.00
COMMON MUSIAL (176-183) 12.50 30.00
COMMON WANG (184-191) 30.00 60.00
COMMON SANDBERG (192-199) 15.00 40.00
COMMON N.RYAN (200-207) 30.00 60.00
COMMON B.GIBSON (208-215) 12.50 30.00
COMMON MARIS (216-220) 12.50 30.00
COMMON M.RAMIREZ (221-228) 8.00 20.00
COMMON SCHMIDT (229-236) 20.00 50.00
COMMON A.ROD (237-244) 20.00 50.00
COMMON MATSUZAKA (245-249) 30.00 60.00
COMMON DIMAGGIO (250-254) 20.00 50.00
RANDOMLY INSERTED IN MYSTERY PACKS
STATED PRINT RUN 9 SER.#'d SETS

2007 Topps Sterling Framed White Suede

*FRAMED WHITE: .6X TO 1.5X BASIC
RANDOM INSERTS IN MYSTERY PACKS
STATED PRINT RUN 50 SER.#'d SETS

2007 Topps Sterling Career Stats Relics Five

COMMON MANTLE 100.00 175.00
COMMON BONDS 30.00 60.00
COMMON ICHIRO 75.00 150.00
COMMON YAZ 30.00 60.00
COMMON WRIGHT 40.00 80.00
COMMON CLEMENTE 90.00 150.00
COMMON MORNEAU 12.50 30.00
COMMON CLEMENS 20.00 50.00
COMMON T.WILLIAMS 75.00 150.00
COMMON MATSUI 50.00 100.00
COMMON HOWARD 30.00 60.00
COMMON ORTIZ 20.00 50.00
COMMON PUJOLS 30.00 60.00
COMMON WANG 40.00 80.00
COMMON RYAN 50.00 100.00
COMMON GIBSON 20.00 50.00
COMMON MARIS 50.00 100.00
COMMON M.RAMIREZ 15.00 40.00
COMMON SCHMIDT 12.50 30.00
COMMON A.ROD 60.00 120.00
COMMON MATSUZAKA 60.00 120.00
COMMON DIMAGGIO 60.00 120.00
RANDOM INSERTS IN BOXES
OVERALL ONE AUTO OR MEM PER BOX
STATED PRINT RUN 10 SER.#'d SETS
NO BERRA,GWYNN PRICING
NO SEAVER,SANDBERG PRICING

2007 Topps Sterling Career Stats Relics Quad

COMMON MANTLE 100.00 175.00
COMMON BONDS 20.00 50.00
COMMON ICHIRO 60.00 120.00
COMMON YAZ 30.00 60.00
COMMON CLEMENTE 90.00 150.00
COMMON SANTANA 15.00 40.00
COMMON CLEMENS 20.00 50.00
COMMON T.WILLIAMS 40.00 80.00
COMMON MATSUI 40.00 80.00
COMMON ORTIZ 15.00 40.00
COMMON SEAVER 30.00 60.00
COMMON PUJOLS 20.00 50.00
COMMON GIBSON 20.00 50.00
COMMON MARIS 50.00 100.00
COMMON SCHMIDT 40.00 80.00
COMMON MATSUZAKA 60.00 120.00
COMMON DIMAGGIO 60.00 120.00
RANDOM INSERTS IN BOXES
OVERALL ONE AUTO OR MEM PER BOX
STATED PRINT RUN 10 SER.#'d SETS
NO WRIGHT,MORNEAU,JACKSON PRICING
NO HOWARD,MUSIAL,WANG PRICING
NO SANDBERG PRICING

2007 Topps Sterling Career Stats Relics Six

COMMON MANTLE 75.00 150.00
COMMON BONDS 30.00 60.00
COMMON ICHIRO 75.00 150.00
COMMON D.WRIGHT 40.00 80.00
COMMON CLEMENTE 100.00 200.00
COMMON SANTANA 20.00 50.00
COMMON MORNEAU 12.50 30.00
COMMON R.JACKSON 30.00 60.00
COMMON CLEMENS 20.00 50.00
COMMON T.WILLIAMS 40.00 80.00
COMMON MATSUI 50.00 100.00
COMMON ORTIZ 20.00 50.00
COMMON PUJOLS 40.00 80.00
COMMON WANG 50.00 100.00
COMMON SANDBERG 20.00 50.00
COMMON RYAN 50.00 100.00
COMMON MARIS 50.00 100.00
COMMON M.RAMIREZ 20.00 50.00
COMMON SCHMIDT 40.00 80.00
COMMON AROD 75.00 150.00
COMMON MATSUZAKA 75.00 150.00
COMMON DIMAGGIO 75.00 150.00
RANDOM INSERTS IN BOXES
OVERALL ONE AUTO OR MEM PER BOX
STATED PRINT RUN 10 SER.#'d SETS
NO YAZ,BERRA,GWYNN PRICING
NO MUSIAL OR GIBSON PRICING

2007 Topps Sterling Career Stats Relics Triple

COMMON MANTLE 90.00 150.00
COMMON BONDS 20.00 50.00
COMMON ICHIRO 60.00 120.00
COMMON D.WRIGHT 30.00 60.00
COMMON CLEMENTE 75.00 150.00
COMMON MORNEAU 10.00 25.00
COMMON CLEMENS 15.00 40.00
COMMON T.WILLIAMS 50.00 100.00
COMMON BERRA 30.00 60.00
COMMON MATSUI 30.00 60.00
COMMON ORTIZ 15.00 40.00
COMMON SEAVER 20.00 50.00
COMMON PUJOLS 20.00 50.00
COMMON MUSIAL 30.00 60.00
COMMON GIBSON 15.00 40.00
COMMON MARIS 40.00 80.00
COMMON SCHMIDT 40.00 80.00
COMMON MATSUZAKA 60.00 120.00
COMMON DIMAGGIO 60.00 120.00
RANDOM INSERTS IN BOXES
OVERALL ONE AUTO OR MEM PER BOX
STATED PRINT RUN 10 SER.#'d SETS
NO YAZ,JACKSON,GWYNN PRICING
NO SANDBERG,RYAN PRICING

2007 Topps Sterling Career Stats Relics Autographs Quad

COMMON YAZ 50.00 100.00
COMMON D.WRIGHT 20.00 50.00
COMMON SANTANA 12.00 30.00
COMMON MORNEAU 20.00 50.00
COMMON R.JACKSON 40.00 80.00
COMMON R.CLEMENS 60.00 120.00
COMMON Y.BERRA 60.00 120.00
COMMON R.HOWARD 50.00 100.00
COMMON T.GWYNN 60.00 120.00
COMMON ORTIZ 50.00 100.00
COMMON T.SEAVER 40.00 80.00
COMMON PUJOLS 175.00 300.00
COMMON MUSIAL 60.00 120.00
COMMON WANG 60.00 120.00
COMMON SANDBERG 60.00 120.00
COMMON RYAN 75.00 150.00
COMMON GIBSON 30.00 60.00
COMMON M.RAMIREZ 40.00 80.00
COMMON SCHMIDT 40.00 80.00
COMMON AROD 175.00 300.00
RANDOM INSERTS IN BOXES
OVERALL ONE AUTO OR MEM PER BOX
STATED PRINT RUN 10 SER.#'d SETS
NO MATSUI PRICING DUE TO SCARCITY

2007 Topps Sterling Career Stats Relics Autographs Triple

COMMON BONDS 175.00 300.00
COMMON YAZ 40.00 80.00
COMMON D.WRIGHT 15.00 40.00
COMMON SANTANA 20.00 50.00
COMMON MORNEAU 20.00 50.00
COMMON R.JACKSON 30.00 60.00
COMMON R.CLEMENS 60.00 120.00
COMMON Y.BERRA 50.00 100.00
COMMON R.HOWARD 30.00 60.00
COMMON T.GWYNN 50.00 100.00
COMMON ORTIZ 40.00 80.00
COMMON T.SEAVER 40.00 80.00
COMMON PUJOLS 175.00 300.00
COMMON MUSIAL 75.00 150.00
COMMON WANG 150.00 250.00
COMMON SANDBERG 50.00 100.00
COMMON RYAN 60.00 120.00
COMMON GIBSON 30.00 60.00
COMMON M.RAMIREZ 30.00 60.00
COMMON SCHMIDT 40.00 80.00
COMMON AROD 175.00 300.00
RANDOM INSERTS IN BOXES
OVERALL ONE AUTO OR MEM PER BOX
STATED PRINT RUN 10 SER.#'d SETS

2007 Topps Sterling Moments Relics Eight

COMMON MANTLE 275.00 375.00
COMMON BONDS 150.00 250.00
COMMON MATSUI 75.00 150.00
COMMON ORTIZ 40.00 80.00
RANDOM INSERTS IN BOXES
OVERALL ONE AUTO OR MEM PER BOX
STATED PRINT RUN 10 SER.#'d SETS
NO PRICING ON MOST DUE TO SCARCITY

2007 Topps Sterling Moments Relics Five

COMMON MANTLE 100.00 175.00
COMMON BONDS 30.00 60.00
COMMON ICHIRO 75.00 150.00
COMMON YAZ 30.00 60.00
COMMON WRIGHT 40.00 80.00
COMMON CLEMENTE 90.00 150.00
COMMON MORNEAU 12.50 30.00
COMMON CLEMENS 20.00 50.00
COMMON T.WILLIAMS 75.00 150.00
COMMON MATSUI 50.00 100.00
COMMON HOWARD 30.00 60.00
COMMON ORTIZ 20.00 50.00
COMMON PUJOLS 30.00 60.00
COMMON WANG 40.00 80.00
COMMON RYAN 50.00 100.00
COMMON GIBSON 20.00 50.00
COMMON MARIS 50.00 100.00
COMMON M.RAMIREZ 15.00 40.00
COMMON SCHMIDT 12.50 30.00
COMMON A.ROD 60.00 120.00
COMMON MATSUZAKA 60.00 120.00
COMMON DIMAGGIO 60.00 120.00
RANDOM INSERTS IN BOXES
OVERALL ONE AUTO OR MEM PER BOX
STATED PRINT RUN 10 SER.#'d SETS
NO JOHAN,SEAVER,MUSIAL PRICING

2007 Topps Sterling Moments Relics Quad

COMMON MANTLE 100.00 175.00
COMMON BONDS 20.00 50.00
COMMON ICHIRO 60.00 120.00
COMMON YAZ 30.00 60.00
COMMON CLEMENTE 90.00 150.00
COMMON SANTANA 15.00 40.00
COMMON CLEMENS 20.00 50.00
COMMON T.WILLIAMS 40.00 80.00
COMMON MATSUI 40.00 80.00
COMMON ORTIZ 15.00 40.00
COMMON SEAVER 30.00 60.00
COMMON PUJOLS 20.00 50.00
COMMON GIBSON 20.00 50.00
COMMON MARIS 50.00 100.00
COMMON SCHMIDT 40.00 80.00
COMMON MATSUZAKA 60.00 120.00
COMMON DIMAGGIO 60.00 120.00
RANDOM INSERTS IN BOXES
OVERALL ONE AUTO OR MEM PER BOX
STATED PRINT RUN 10 SER.#'d SETS
NO WRIGHT,MORNEAU,BERRA PRICING
NO GWYNN OR MUSIAL PRICING

2007 Topps Sterling Moments Relics Six

COMMON MANTLE 75.00 150.00
COMMON BONDS 30.00 60.00
COMMON ICHIRO 75.00 150.00
COMMON D.WRIGHT 40.00 100.00
COMMON CLEMENTE 100.00 200.00
COMMON SANTANA 20.00 50.00
COMMON MORNEAU 12.50 30.00
COMMON R.JACKSON 30.00 60.00
COMMON CLEMENS 20.00 50.00
COMMON T.WILLIAMS 40.00 80.00
COMMON MATSUI 50.00 100.00
COMMON ORTIZ 20.00 50.00
COMMON PUJOLS 40.00 80.00
COMMON WANG 50.00 100.00
COMMON SANDBERG 20.00 50.00
COMMON RYAN 50.00 100.00
COMMON MARIS 50.00 100.00
COMMON M.RAMIREZ 20.00 50.00
COMMON SCHMIDT 40.00 80.00
COMMON AROD 75.00 150.00
COMMON MATSUZAKA 75.00 150.00
COMMON DIMAGGIO 75.00 150.00
RANDOM INSERTS IN BOXES
OVERALL ONE AUTO OR MEM PER BOX
STATED PRINT RUN 10 SER.#'d SETS
NO HOWARD PRICING

2007 Topps Sterling Moments Relics Triple

COMMON MANTLE 90.00 150.00
COMMON BONDS 20.00 50.00
COMMON ICHIRO 60.00 120.00
COMMON D.WRIGHT 30.00 60.00
COMMON CLEMENTE 75.00 150.00
COMMON MORNEAU 10.00 25.00
COMMON CLEMENS 15.00 40.00
COMMON T.WILLIAMS 50.00 100.00
COMMON BERRA 30.00 60.00
COMMON MATSUI 30.00 60.00
COMMON ORTIZ 15.00 40.00
COMMON SEAVER 20.00 50.00
COMMON PUJOLS 20.00 50.00
COMMON MUSIAL 30.00 60.00
COMMON GIBSON 15.00 40.00
COMMON MARIS 40.00 80.00
COMMON SCHMIDT 40.00 80.00
COMMON MATSUZAKA 60.00 120.00
COMMON DIMAGGIO 60.00 120.00
RANDOM INSERTS IN BOXES
OVERALL ONE AUTO OR MEM PER BOX
STATED PRINT RUN 10 SER.#'d SETS
NO JACKSON OR GWYNN PRICING

2007 Topps Sterling Moments Relics Autographs Eight

COMMON M.RAMIREZ 60.00 120.00
RANDOM INSERTS IN BOXES
OVERALL ONE AUTO OR MEM PER BOX
STATED PRINT RUN 10 SER.#'d SETS
NO PRICING ON MOST DUE TO SCARCITY

2007 Topps Sterling Moments Relics Autographs Quad

COMMON YAZ 50.00 100.00
COMMON D.WRIGHT 20.00 50.00
COMMON SANTANA 12.00 30.00
COMMON MORNEAU 20.00 50.00
COMMON R.JACKSON 40.00 80.00
COMMON R.CLEMENS 60.00 120.00
COMMON Y.BERRA 60.00 120.00
COMMON R.HOWARD 50.00 100.00
COMMON T.GWYNN 60.00 120.00
COMMON ORTIZ 50.00 100.00
COMMON T.SEAVER 40.00 80.00
COMMON PUJOLS 175.00 300.00
COMMON MUSIAL 60.00 120.00
COMMON WANG 60.00 120.00
COMMON SANDBERG 60.00 120.00
COMMON RYAN 75.00 150.00
COMMON GIBSON 30.00 60.00
COMMON M.RAMIREZ 40.00 80.00
COMMON SCHMIDT 40.00 80.00
COMMON AROD 175.00 300.00
RANDOM INSERTS IN BOXES
OVERALL ONE AUTO OR MEM PER BOX
STATED PRINT RUN 10 SER.#'d SETS
NO BONDS PRICING DUE TO SCARCITY

2007 Topps Sterling Moments Relics Autographs Triple

COMMON BONDS 175.00 300.00
COMMON YAZ 40.00 80.00
COMMON D.WRIGHT 15.00 40.00
COMMON SANTANA 20.00 50.00
COMMON MORNEAU 20.00 50.00
COMMON R.JACKSON 30.00 60.00
COMMON R.CLEMENS 60.00 120.00
COMMON Y.BERRA 50.00 100.00
COMMON R.HOWARD 30.00 60.00
COMMON T.GWYNN 50.00 100.00
COMMON ORTIZ 40.00 80.00
COMMON T.SEAVER 40.00 80.00
COMMON PUJOLS 175.00 300.00
COMMON MUSIAL 75.00 150.00
COMMON WANG 150.00 250.00
COMMON SANDBERG 50.00 100.00
COMMON RYAN 60.00 120.00
COMMON GIBSON 30.00 60.00
COMMON M.RAMIREZ 30.00 60.00
COMMON SCHMIDT 40.00 80.00
COMMON AROD 175.00 300.00
RANDOM INSERTS IN BOXES
OVERALL ONE AUTO OR MEM PER BOX
STATED PRINT RUN 10 SER.#'d SETS

2007 Topps Sterling Stardom Relics Eight

COMMON MANTLE 275.00 375.00
COMMON BONDS 150.00 250.00
COMMON MATSUI 75.00 150.00
COMMON ORTIZ 40.00 80.00
RANDOM INSERTS IN BOXES
OVERALL ONE AUTO OR MEM PER BOX
STATED PRINT RUN 10 SER.#'d SETS
NO PRICING ON MOST DUE TO SCARCITY

2007 Topps Sterling Stardom Relics Five

COMMON MANTLE 100.00 175.00
COMMON BONDS 30.00 60.00
COMMON ICHIRO 75.00 150.00
COMMON YAZ 30.00 60.00
COMMON WRIGHT 40.00 80.00
COMMON CLEMENTE 90.00 150.00
COMMON MORNEAU 12.50 30.00
COMMON CLEMENS 20.00 50.00
COMMON T.WILLIAMS 75.00 150.00
COMMON MATSUI 50.00 100.00
COMMON HOWARD 30.00 60.00
COMMON ORTIZ 20.00 50.00
COMMON PUJOLS 30.00 60.00
COMMON WANG 40.00 80.00
COMMON RYAN 50.00 100.00
COMMON GIBSON 20.00 50.00
COMMON MARIS 50.00 100.00
COMMON M.RAMIREZ 15.00 40.00
COMMON SCHMIDT 12.50 30.00
COMMON A.ROD 60.00 120.00
COMMON MATSUZAKA 60.00 120.00
COMMON DIMAGGIO 60.00 120.00
RANDOM INSERTS IN BOXES
OVERALL ONE AUTO OR MEM PER BOX
STATED PRINT RUN 10 SER.#'d SETS
NO JOHAN,JACKSON,BERRA PRICING

2007 Topps Sterling Stardom Relics Quad

COMMON MANTLE 100.00 175.00
COMMON BONDS 20.00 50.00
COMMON ICHIRO 60.00 120.00
COMMON YAZ 30.00 60.00
COMMON CLEMENTE 90.00 150.00
COMMON SANTANA 15.00 40.00
COMMON CLEMENS 20.00 50.00
COMMON T.WILLIAMS 40.00 80.00
COMMON MATSUI 40.00 80.00
COMMON ORTIZ 15.00 40.00
COMMON SEAVER 30.00 60.00
COMMON PUJOLS 20.00 50.00
COMMON GIBSON 20.00 50.00
COMMON MARIS 50.00 100.00
COMMON SCHMIDT 40.00 80.00
COMMON MATSUZAKA 60.00 120.00
COMMON DIMAGGIO 60.00 120.00
RANDOM INSERTS IN BOXES
OVERALL ONE AUTO OR MEM PER BOX
STATED PRINT RUN 10 SER.#'d SETS
NO BERRA,HOWARD,GWYNN PRICING
NO WANG,SANDBERG, AROD PRICING

2007 Topps Sterling Stardom Relics Six

COMMON MANTLE 75.00 150.00
COMMON BONDS 30.00 60.00
COMMON ICHIRO 75.00 150.00
COMMON D.WRIGHT 40.00 100.00
COMMON CLEMENTE 100.00 200.00
COMMON SANTANA 20.00 50.00
COMMON MORNEAU 12.50 30.00
COMMON R.JACKSON 30.00 60.00
COMMON CLEMENS 20.00 50.00
COMMON T.WILLIAMS 40.00 80.00
COMMON MATSUI 50.00 100.00
COMMON ORTIZ 20.00 50.00
COMMON PUJOLS 40.00 80.00
COMMON WANG 50.00 100.00
COMMON SANDBERG 20.00 50.00
COMMON RYAN 50.00 100.00
COMMON MARIS 50.00 100.00
COMMON M.RAMIREZ 20.00 50.00
COMMON SCHMIDT 40.00 80.00
COMMON AROD 75.00 150.00
COMMON MATSUZAKA 75.00 150.00
COMMON DIMAGGIO 75.00 150.00
RANDOM INSERTS IN BOXES
OVERALL ONE AUTO OR MEM PER BOX
STATED PRINT RUN 10 SER.#'d SETS
NO HOWARD PRICING

2007 Topps Sterling Stardom Relics Triple

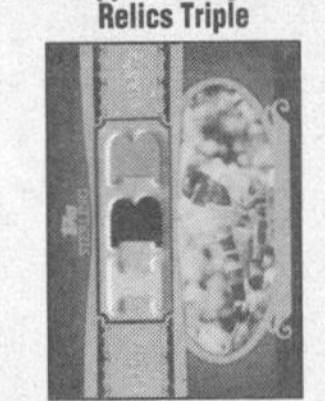

COMMON MANTLE 90.00 150.00
COMMON BONDS 20.00 50.00
COMMON ICHIRO 60.00 120.00
COMMON D.WRIGHT 30.00 60.00
COMMON CLEMENTE 75.00 150.00
COMMON MORNEAU 10.00 25.00
COMMON CLEMENS 15.00 40.00
COMMON T.WILLIAMS 50.00 100.00
COMMON BERRA 30.00 60.00
COMMON MATSUI 30.00 60.00
COMMON ORTIZ 15.00 40.00
COMMON SEAVER 20.00 50.00
COMMON PUJOLS 20.00 50.00
COMMON MUSIAL 30.00 60.00
COMMON GIBSON 15.00 40.00
COMMON MARIS 40.00 80.00
COMMON SCHMIDT 40.00 80.00
COMMON MATSUZAKA 60.00 120.00
COMMON DIMAGGIO 60.00 120.00
RANDOM INSERTS IN BOXES
OVERALL ONE AUTO OR MEM PER BOX
STATED PRINT RUN 10 SER.#'d SETS
NO YAZ OR RYAN PRICING

2007 Topps Sterling Stardom Relics Autographs Eight

COMMON M.RAMIREZ 60.00 120.00
RANDOM INSERTS IN BOXES
OVERALL ONE AUTO OR MEM PER BOX
STATED PRINT RUN 10 SER.#'d SETS
NO PRICING ON MOST DUE TO SCARCITY

2007 Topps Sterling Stardom Relics Autographs Quad

COMMON YAZ 50.00 100.00
COMMON D.WRIGHT 20.00 50.00
COMMON SANTANA 12.00 30.00
COMMON MORNEAU 20.00 50.00
COMMON R.JACKSON 40.00 80.00
COMMON R.CLEMENS 60.00 120.00
COMMON Y.BERRA 60.00 120.00
COMMON R.HOWARD 50.00 100.00
COMMON T.GWYNN 60.00 120.00
COMMON ORTIZ 50.00 100.00
COMMON T.SEAVER 40.00 80.00
COMMON PUJOLS 175.00 300.00
COMMON MUSIAL 60.00 120.00
COMMON WANG 60.00 120.00
COMMON SANDBERG 60.00 120.00
COMMON RYAN 75.00 150.00
COMMON GIBSON 30.00 60.00
COMMON M.RAMIREZ 40.00 80.00
COMMON SCHMIDT 40.00 80.00
COMMON AROD 175.00 300.00
RANDOM INSERTS IN BOXES
OVERALL ONE AUTO OR MEM PER BOX
STATED PRINT RUN 10 SER.#'d SETS
NO BONDS OR MATSUI PRICING

2007 Topps Sterling Stardom Relics Autographs Triple

COMMON BONDS 175.00 300.00
COMMON YAZ 40.00 80.00
COMMON D.WRIGHT 15.00 40.00
COMMON SANTANA 20.00 50.00
COMMON MORNEAU 20.00 50.00
COMMON R.JACKSON 30.00 60.00
COMMON R.CLEMENS 60.00 120.00
COMMON Y.BERRA 50.00 100.00
COMMON R.HOWARD 30.00 60.00
COMMON T.GWYNN 50.00 100.00
COMMON ORTIZ 40.00 80.00
COMMON T.SEAVER 40.00 80.00
COMMON PUJOLS 175.00 300.00
COMMON MUSIAL 75.00 150.00
COMMON WANG 150.00 250.00
COMMON SANDBERG 50.00 100.00
COMMON RYAN 60.00 120.00
COMMON GIBSON 30.00 60.00
COMMON M.RAMIREZ 30.00 60.00
COMMON SCHMIDT 40.00 80.00
COMMON AROD 175.00 300.00
RANDOM INSERTS IN BOXES
OVERALL ONE AUTO OR MEM PER BOX
STATED PRINT RUN 10 SER.#'d SETS

2008 Topps Sterling

This set was released on December 24, 2008. The base set consists of 282 cards.

COMMON MANTLE (1-4) 5.00 12.00
COMMON RUTH (5-8) 6.00 15.00
COMMON OTT (9-12) 2.00 5.00
COMMON BENCH (13-23) 3.00 8.00
COMMON FOXX (24-27) 2.50 6.00
COMMON MURRAY (28-38) 2.00 5.00
COMMON J.ROBINSON (39-42) 3.00 8.00
COMMON SNIDER (43-53) 2.50 6.00
COMMON GIBSON (54-64) 2.50 6.00
COMMON BERRA (65-75) 3.00 8.00
COMMON MUSIAL (76-86) 4.00 10.00
COMMON HORNSBY (87-90) 2.50 6.00
COMMON SEAVER (91-101) 2.50 6.00
COMMON FORD (102-112) 2.50 6.00
COMMON MARIS (124-127) 2.50 6.00
COMMON MUNSON (128-131) 2.50 6.00
COMMON PALMER (132-142) 2.00 5.00
COMMON R.JACKSON (143-153) 2.50 6.00
COMMON SCHMIDT (154-164) 2.50 6.00
COMMON YAZ (165-175) 2.50 6.00
COMMON MATTINGLY (176-186) 3.00 8.00
COMMON CAMPANELLA (187-190) 2.00 5.00
COMMON RYAN (191-201) 6.00 15.00
COMMON COBB (213-216) 3.00 8.00
COMMON YOUNT (217-227) 2.50 6.00
COMMON RIPKEN (228-231) 5.00 12.00
COMMON GEHRIG (232-235) 4.00 10.00
COMMON CLEMENTE (236-239) 5.00 12.00
COMMON SANDBERG (240-250) 3.00 8.00
COMMON T.WILLIAMS (251-254) 3.00 8.00
COMMON F.ROBINSON (255-265) 2.00 5.00
COMMON T.GWYNN (266-276) 2.50 6.00
COMMON BANKS (277-287) 3.00 8.00
COMMON WAGNER (288-291) 2.50 6.00
COMMON MOLITOR (296-308) 2.50 6.00
THREE BASE CARDS PER PACK
STATED PRINT RUN 250 SER.#'d SETS

2008 Topps Sterling Framed Burgundy

COMMON MANTLE (1-4) 30.00 60.00
COMMON RUTH (5-8) 40.00 80.00
COMMON OTT (9-12) 12.50 30.00
COMMON BENCH (13-23) 15.00 40.00
COMMON FOXX (24-27) 12.50 30.00
COMMON MURRAY (28-38) 15.00 40.00
COMMON J.ROBINSON (39-42) 20.00 50.00
COMMON SNIDER (43-53) 10.00 25.00
COMMON GIBSON (54-64) 12.50 30.00
COMMON BERRA (65-75) 20.00 50.00
COMMON MUSIAL (76-86) 12.50 30.00
COMMON HORNSBY (87-90) 10.00 25.00
COMMON SEAVER (91-101) 12.50 30.00
COMMON FORD (102-112) 10.00 25.00
COMMON MARIS (124-127) 20.00 50.00
COMMON MUNSON (128-131) 12.50 30.00
COMMON PALMER (132-142) 10.00 25.00
COMMON R.JACKSON (143-153) 12.50 30.00
COMMON SCHMIDT (154-164) 12.50 30.00
COMMON YAZ (165-175) 12.50 30.00
COMMON MATTINGLY (176-186) 20.00 50.00
COMMON CAMPANELLA (187-190) 12.50 30.00
COMMON RYAN (191-201) 50.00 100.00
COMMON COBB (213-216) 40.00 80.00
COMMON YOUNT (217-227) 15.00 40.00
COMMON RIPKEN (228-231) 60.00 120.00
COMMON GEHRIG (232-235) 20.00 50.00
COMMON CLEMENTE (236-239) 40.00 80.00
COMMON SANDBERG (240-250) 12.50 30.00
COMMON T.WILLIAMS (251-254) 20.00 50.00
COMMON F.ROBINSON (255-265) 10.00 25.00
COMMON T.GWYNN (266-276) 20.00 50.00
COMMON BANKS (277-287) 20.00 50.00
COMMON WAGNER (288-291) 10.00 25.00
COMMON MOLITOR (296-308) 10.00 25.00
RANDOMLY INSERTED IN MYSTERY PACKS
STATED PRINT RUN 10 SER.#'d SETS

2008 Topps Sterling Framed Gold

COMMON MANTLE (1-4) 60.00 120.00
COMMON RUTH (5-8) 75.00 150.00
COMMON OTT (9-12) 30.00 60.00
COMMON BENCH (13-23) 30.00 60.00
COMMON FOXX (24-27) 40.00 80.00
COMMON MURRAY (28-38) 20.00 50.00
COMMON J.ROBINSON (39-42) 30.00 60.00
COMMON SNIDER (43-53) 20.00 50.00
COMMON GIBSON (54-64) 20.00 50.00
COMMON BERRA (65-75) 30.00 60.00
COMMON MUSIAL (76-86) 20.00 50.00
COMMON HORNSBY (87-90) 15.00 40.00
COMMON SEAVER (91-101) 15.00 40.00
COMMON FORD (102-112) 12.50 30.00
COMMON MARIS (124-127) 30.00 60.00
COMMON MUNSON (128-131) 30.00 60.00
COMMON PALMER (132-142) 20.00 50.00
COMMON R.JACKSON (143-153) 40.00 80.00
COMMON SCHMIDT (154-164) 30.00 60.00
COMMON YAZ (165-175) 20.00 50.00
COMMON MATTINGLY (176-186) 50.00 100.00
COMMON CAMPANELLA (187-190) 15.00 40.00
COMMON RYAN (191-201) 100.00 200.00
COMMON COBB (213-216) 50.00 100.00
COMMON YOUNT (217-227) 20.00 50.00
COMMON RIPKEN (228-231) 100.00 175.00
COMMON GEHRIG (232-235) 40.00 80.00
COMMON CLEMENTE (236-239) 75.00 150.00
COMMON SANDBERG (240-250) 40.00 80.00
COMMON T.WILLIAMS (251-254) 30.00 60.00
COMMON F.ROBINSON (255-265) 20.00 50.00
COMMON T.GWYNN (266-276) 30.00 60.00
COMMON BANKS (277-287) 40.00 80.00
COMMON WAGNER (288-291) 30.00 60.00
COMMON MOLITOR (296-308) 30.00 60.00
RANDOMLY INSERTED IN MYSTERY PACKS
STATED PRINT RUN 5 SER.#'d SETS

2008 Topps Sterling Framed White

COMMON MANTLE (1-4) 12.50 30.00
COMMON RUTH (5-8) 12.50 30.00
COMMON OTT (9-12) 8.00 20.00
COMMON BENCH (13-23) 6.00 15.00
COMMON FOXX (24-27) 5.00 12.00
COMMON MURRAY (28-38) 5.00 12.00
COMMON J.ROBINSON (39-42) 8.00 20.00
COMMON SNIDER (43-53) 5.00 12.00
COMMON GIBSON (54-64) 6.00 15.00
COMMON BERRA (65-75) 6.00 15.00
COMMON MUSIAL (76-86) 8.00 20.00
COMMON HORNSBY (87-90) 5.00 12.00
COMMON SEAVER (91-101) 5.00 12.00
COMMON FORD (102-112) 5.00 12.00
COMMON MARIS (124-127) 6.00 15.00
COMMON MUNSON (128-131) 6.00 15.00
COMMON PALMER (132-142) 5.00 12.00
COMMON R.JACKSON (143-153) 5.00 12.00
COMMON SCHMIDT (154-164) 5.00 12.00
COMMON YAZ (165-175) 5.00 12.00
COMMON MATTINGLY (176-186) 5.00 12.00
COMMON CAMPANELLA (187-190) 5.00 12.00
COMMON RYAN (191-201) 12.50 30.00
COMMON COBB (213-216) 8.00 20.00
COMMON YOUNT (217-227) 6.00 15.00
COMMON RIPKEN (228-231) 25.00 60.00
COMMON GEHRIG (232-235) 10.00 25.00
COMMON CLEMENTE (236-239) 15.00 40.00
COMMON SANDBERG (240-250) 6.00 15.00
COMMON T.WILLIAMS (251-254) 8.00 20.00
COMMON F.ROBINSON (255-265) 5.00 12.00
COMMON T.GWYNN (266-276) 8.00 20.00
COMMON BANKS (277-287) 8.00 20.00
COMMON WAGNER (288-291) 6.00 15.00
COMMON MOLITOR (296-308) 5.00 12.00
RANDOMLY INSERTED IN MYSTERY PACKS
STATED PRINT RUN 50 SER.#'d SETS

2008 Topps Sterling Career Stats Relics Five

COMMON MANTLE 75.00 150.00
COMMON RUTH 150.00 250.00
COMMON OTT 50.00 100.00
COMMON BENCH 20.00 50.00
COMMON FOXX 60.00 120.00
COMMON J.ROBINSON 40.00 80.00
COMMON MUSIAL 20.00 50.00
COMMON HORNSBY 40.00 80.00
COMMON SEAVER 15.00 40.00
COMMON MARIS 50.00 100.00
COMMON MUNSON 30.00 60.00
COMMON R.JACKSON 10.00 25.00
COMMON YAZ 20.00 50.00
COMMON CAMPANELLA 30.00 60.00
COMMON RYAN 50.00 100.00
COMMON COBB 100.00 175.00
COMMON RIPKEN 100.00 175.00
COMMON GEHRIG 150.00 250.00
COMMON CLEMENTE 60.00 120.00
COMMON T.WILLIAMS 60.00 120.00
COMMON F.ROBINSON 15.00 40.00
COMMON T.GWYNN 20.00 50.00
COMMON BANKS 15.00 40.00
COMMON WAGNER 100.00 200.00
OVERALL ONE AUTO OR MEM PER BOX
STATED PRINT RUN 10 SER.#'d SETS
5CS1 Mickey Mantle 75.00 150.00
5CS2 Mickey Mantle 75.00 150.00
5CS3 Babe Ruth 150.00 250.00
5CS4 Babe Ruth 150.00 250.00
5CS5 Mel Ott 50.00 100.00
5CS6 Mel Ott 50.00 100.00
5CS7 Johnny Bench 20.00 50.00
5CS8 Johnny Bench 20.00 50.00
5CS9 Johnny Bench 20.00 50.00
5CS10 Johnny Bench 20.00 50.00
5CS11 Jimmie Foxx 60.00 120.00
5CS12 Jimmie Foxx 60.00 120.00
5CS13 Jackie Robinson 40.00 80.00
5CS14 Jackie Robinson 40.00 80.00
5CS15 Stan Musial 20.00 50.00
5CS16 Stan Musial 20.00 50.00
5CS17 Stan Musial 20.00 50.00
5CS18 Stan Musial 20.00 50.00
5CS19 Rogers Hornsby 40.00 80.00
5CS20 Rogers Hornsby 40.00 80.00
5CS21 Tom Seaver 15.00 40.00
5CS22 Tom Seaver 15.00 40.00
5CS23 Tom Seaver 15.00 40.00
5CS24 Tom Seaver 15.00 40.00
5CS29 Roger Maris 50.00 100.00
5CS30 Roger Maris 50.00 100.00
5CS31 Thurman Munson 30.00 60.00
5CS32 Thurman Munson 30.00 60.00
5CS33 Reggie Jackson 10.00 25.00
5CS34 Reggie Jackson 10.00 25.00
5CS35 Reggie Jackson 10.00 25.00
5CS36 Reggie Jackson 10.00 25.00
5CS37 Carl Yastrzemski 20.00 50.00
5CS38 Carl Yastrzemski 20.00 50.00
5CS39 Carl Yastrzemski 20.00 50.00
5CS40 Carl Yastrzemski 20.00 50.00
5CS41 Roy Campanella 30.00 60.00
5CS42 Roy Campanella 30.00 60.00
5CS43 Nolan Ryan 50.00 100.00
5CS44 Nolan Ryan 50.00 100.00
5CS45 Nolan Ryan 50.00 100.00
5CS46 Nolan Ryan 50.00 100.00
5CS51 Ty Cobb 100.00 175.00
5CS52 Ty Cobb 100.00 175.00
5CS53 Cal Ripken 100.00 175.00
5CS54 Lou Gehrig 150.00 250.00
5CS55 Lou Gehrig 150.00 250.00
5CS56 Roberto Clemente 60.00 120.00
5CS57 Roberto Clemente 60.00 120.00
5CS58 Ted Williams 60.00 120.00
5CS59 Ted Williams 60.00 120.00
5CS60 Frank Robinson 15.00 40.00
5CS61 Frank Robinson 15.00 40.00
5CS62 Frank Robinson 15.00 40.00
5CS63 Frank Robinson 15.00 40.00
5CS64 Tony Gwynn 20.00 50.00
5CS65 Tony Gwynn 20.00 50.00
5CS66 Tony Gwynn 20.00 50.00
5CS67 Tony Gwynn 20.00 50.00
5CS68 Ernie Banks 15.00 40.00
5CS69 Ernie Banks 15.00 40.00
5CS70 Ernie Banks 15.00 40.00
5CS71 Ernie Banks 15.00 40.00
5CS72 Honus Wagner 100.00 200.00
5CS73 Honus Wagner 100.00 200.00

2008 Topps Sterling Career Stats Relics Quad

COMMON MANTLE 75.00 150.00
COMMON RUTH 200.00 350.00
COMMON OTT 50.00 100.00
COMMON BENCH 20.00 50.00
COMMON FOXX 40.00 80.00
COMMON J.ROBINSON 40.00 80.00
COMMON MUSIAL 30.00 60.00
COMMON HORNSBY 30.00 60.00
COMMON SEAVER 15.00 40.00
COMMON MARIS 50.00 100.00
COMMON MUNSON 30.00 60.00
COMMON R.JACKSON 15.00 40.00
COMMON YAZ 15.00 40.00
COMMON CAMPANELLA 30.00 60.00
COMMON COBB 40.00 80.00
COMMON RIPKEN 90.00 150.00
COMMON GEHRIG 100.00 250.00
COMMON CLEMENTE 60.00 120.00
COMMON T.WILLIAMS 40.00 80.00
COMMON F.ROBINSON 15.00 40.00
COMMON T.GWYNN 15.00 40.00
COMMON WAGNER 100.00 200.00
OVERALL ONE AUTO OR MEM PER BOX
STATED PRINT RUN 10 SER.#'d SETS
NO RYAN PRICING AVAILABLE
4CS1 Mickey Mantle 75.00 150.00
4CS2 Mickey Mantle 75.00 150.00
4CS3 Babe Ruth 200.00 350.00
4CS4 Babe Ruth 200.00 350.00
4CS5 Mel Ott 50.00 100.00
4CS6 Mel Ott 50.00 100.00
4CS7 Johnny Bench 20.00 50.00
4CS9 Johnny Bench 20.00 50.00
4CS11 Jimmie Foxx 40.00 80.00
4CS12 Jimmie Foxx 40.00 80.00
4CS13 Jackie Robinson 40.00 80.00
4CS14 Jackie Robinson 40.00 80.00
4CS15 Stan Musial 30.00 60.00
4CS16 Stan Musial 30.00 60.00
4CS17 Stan Musial 30.00 60.00
4CS19 Rogers Hornsby 30.00 60.00
4CS20 Rogers Hornsby 30.00 60.00
4CS21 Tom Seaver 15.00 40.00
4CS22 Tom Seaver 15.00 40.00
4CS23 Tom Seaver 15.00 40.00
4CS24 Tom Seaver 15.00 40.00
4CS29 Roger Maris 50.00 100.00
4CS30 Roger Maris 50.00 100.00
4CS31 Thurman Munson 30.00 60.00
4CS32 Thurman Munson 30.00 60.00
4CS34 Reggie Jackson 15.00 40.00
4CS35 Reggie Jackson 15.00 40.00
4CS36 Reggie Jackson 15.00 40.00
4CS40 Carl Yastrzemski 15.00 40.00
4CS41 Roy Campanella 30.00 60.00
4CS42 Roy Campanella 30.00 60.00
4CS54 Ty Cobb 40.00 80.00
4CS55 Ty Cobb 40.00 80.00
4CS56 Cal Ripken 90.00 150.00
4CS57 Lou Gehrig 100.00 250.00
4CS58 Lou Gehrig 100.00 250.00
4CS59 Roberto Clemente 60.00 120.00
4CS60 Roberto Clemente 60.00 120.00
4CS61 Ted Williams 40.00 80.00
4CS62 Ted Williams 40.00 80.00
4CS63 Frank Robinson 15.00 40.00
4CS64 Frank Robinson 15.00 40.00
4CS66 Frank Robinson 15.00 40.00
4CS67 Tony Gwynn 15.00 40.00
4CS68 Tony Gwynn 15.00 40.00
4CS69 Tony Gwynn 15.00 40.00
4CS70 Tony Gwynn 15.00 40.00
4CS77 Honus Wagner 100.00 200.00
4CS78 Honus Wagner 100.00 200.00

2008 Topps Sterling Career Stats Relics Six

COMMON MANTLE 100.00 200.00
COMMON RUTH 250.00 400.00
COMMON OTT 50.00 100.00
COMMON BENCH 20.00 50.00
COMMON FOXX 50.00 100.00
COMMON MURRAY 20.00 50.00
COMMON J.ROBINSON 50.00 100.00
COMMON SNIDER 30.00 60.00
COMMON GIBSON 20.00 50.00
COMMON BERRA 30.00 60.00
COMMON MUSIAL 30.00 60.00
COMMON HORNSBY 40.00 80.00
COMMON SEAVER 20.00 50.00
COMMON FORD 20.00 50.00
COMMON MARIS 60.00 120.00
COMMON MUNSON 40.00 80.00
COMMON PALMER 12.50 30.00
COMMON R.JACKSON 20.00 50.00
COMMON SCHMIDT 20.00 50.00
COMMON YAZ 20.00 50.00
COMMON MATTINGLY 40.00 80.00
COMMON CAMPANELLA 20.00 50.00
COMMON RYAN 30.00 60.00
COMMON COBB 150.00 250.00
COMMON YOUNT 20.00 50.00
COMMON RIPKEN 75.00 150.00
COMMON GEHRIG 175.00 300.00
COMMON CLEMENTE 75.00 150.00
COMMON SANDBERG 20.00 50.00
COMMON T.WILLIAMS 75.00 150.00
COMMON F.ROBINSON 20.00 50.00
COMMON T.GWYNN 20.00 50.00
COMMON BANKS 15.00 40.00
COMMON WAGNER 150.00 250.00
OVERALL ONE AUTO OR MEM PER BOX
STATED PRINT RUN 10 SER.#'d SETS
6CS1 Mickey Mantle 100.00 200.00
6CS2 Mickey Mantle 100.00 200.00

6CS3 Babe Ruth 250.00 400.00
6CS4 Babe Ruth 250.00 400.00
6CS5 Mel Ott 50.00 100.00
6CS6 Mel Ott 50.00 100.00
6CS7 Johnny Bench 20.00 50.00
6CS8 Johnny Bench 20.00 50.00
6CS9 Jimmie Foxx 50.00 100.00
6CS10 Jimmie Foxx 50.00 100.00
6CS11 Eddie Murray 20.00 50.00
6CS12 Jackie Robinson 50.00 100.00
6CS13 Jackie Robinson 50.00 100.00
6CS14 Duke Snider 30.00 60.00
6CS15 Bob Gibson 20.00 50.00
6CS16 Yogi Berra 30.00 60.00
6CS17 Stan Musial 30.00 60.00
6CS18 Stan Musial 30.00 60.00
6CS19 Rogers Hornsby 40.00 80.00
6CS20 Rogers Hornsby 40.00 80.00
6CS21 Tom Seaver 20.00 50.00
6CS22 Tom Seaver 20.00 50.00
6CS23 Whitey Ford 20.00 50.00
6CS26 Roger Maris 60.00 120.00
6CS27 Roger Maris 60.00 120.00
6CS28 Thurman Munson 40.00 80.00
6CS29 Thurman Munson 40.00 80.00
6CS30 Jim Palmer 12.50 30.00
6CS31 Reggie Jackson 20.00 50.00
6CS32 Reggie Jackson 20.00 50.00
6CS33 Mike Schmidt 20.00 50.00
6CS34 Carl Yastrzemski 20.00 50.00
6CS35 Carl Yastrzemski 20.00 50.00
6CS36 Don Mattingly 40.00 80.00
6CS37 Roy Campanella 20.00 50.00
6CS38 Roy Campanella 20.00 50.00
6CS39 Nolan Ryan 30.00 60.00
6CS40 Nolan Ryan 30.00 60.00
6CS41 Nolan Ryan 30.00 60.00
6CS42 Nolan Ryan 30.00 60.00
6CS43 Nolan Ryan 30.00 60.00
6CS44 Nolan Ryan 30.00 60.00
6CS51 Ty Cobb 150.00 250.00
6CS52 Ty Cobb 150.00 250.00
6CS53 Robin Yount 20.00 50.00
6CS54 Cal Ripken 75.00 150.00
6CS55 Cal Ripken 75.00 150.00
6CS56 Lou Gehrig 175.00 300.00
6CS57 Lou Gehrig 175.00 300.00
6CS58 Roberto Clemente 75.00 150.00
6CS59 Roberto Clemente 75.00 150.00
6CS60 Ryne Sandberg 20.00 50.00
6CS61 Ted Williams 75.00 150.00
6CS62 Ted Williams 75.00 150.00
6CS63 Frank Robinson 20.00 50.00
6CS64 Frank Robinson 20.00 50.00
6CS65 Tony Gwynn 20.00 50.00
6CS66 Tony Gwynn 20.00 50.00
6CS67 Ernie Banks 15.00 40.00
6CS68 Ernie Banks 15.00 40.00
6CS69 Ernie Banks 15.00 40.00
6CS70 Ernie Banks 15.00 40.00
6CS71 Ernie Banks 15.00 40.00
6CS72 Honus Wagner 150.00 250.00
6CS73 Honus Wagner 150.00 250.00

2008 Topps Sterling Career Stats Relics Triple

COMMON MANTLE 60.00 120.00
COMMON RUTH 125.00 250.00
COMMON OTT 40.00 80.00
COMMON FOXX 30.00 60.00
COMMON J.ROBINSON 40.00 80.00
COMMON GIBSON 40.00 80.00
COMMON MARIS 40.00 80.00
COMMON MUNSON 50.00 100.00
COMMON CAMPANELLA 20.00 50.00
COMMON COBB 75.00 150.00
COMMON RIPKEN 90.00 150.00
COMMON GEHRIG 150.00 250.00
COMMON CLEMENTE 50.00 100.00
COMMON T.WILLIAMS 40.00 80.00
COMMON WAGNER 90.00 150.00
OVERALL ONE AUTO OR MEM PER BOX
STATED PRINT RUN 10 SER.#'d SETS
3CS1 Mickey Mantle 60.00 120.00
3CS2 Mickey Mantle 60.00 120.00
3CS3 Mickey Mantle 60.00 120.00
3CS4 Babe Ruth 125.00 250.00
3CS5 Babe Ruth 125.00 250.00
3CS6 Babe Ruth 125.00 250.00
3CS7 Mel Ott 40.00 80.00
3CS8 Mel Ott 40.00 80.00
3CS9 Mel Ott 40.00 80.00
3CS13 Jimmie Foxx 30.00 60.00
3CS14 Jimmie Foxx 30.00 60.00
3CS15 Jimmie Foxx 30.00 60.00
3CS16 Jackie Robinson 40.00 80.00
3CS17 Jackie Robinson 40.00 80.00
3CS18 Jackie Robinson 40.00 80.00
3CS22 Rogers Hornsby 40.00 80.00
3CS23 Rogers Hornsby 40.00 80.00
3CS24 Rogers Hornsby 40.00 80.00
3CS31 Roger Maris 40.00 80.00
3CS32 Roger Maris 40.00 80.00
3CS33 Roger Maris 40.00 80.00
3CS34 Thurman Munson 50.00 100.00
3CS35 Thurman Munson 50.00 100.00
3CS36 Thurman Munson 50.00 100.00
3CS43 Roy Campanella 20.00 50.00
3CS44 Roy Campanella 20.00 50.00
3CS45 Roy Campanella 20.00 50.00
3CS54 Ty Cobb 75.00 150.00
3CS55 Ty Cobb 75.00 150.00
3CS56 Ty Cobb 75.00 150.00
3CS57 Cal Ripken 90.00 150.00
3CS58 Lou Gehrig 150.00 250.00
3CS59 Lou Gehrig 150.00 250.00
3CS60 Lou Gehrig 150.00 250.00
3CS61 Roberto Clemente 50.00 100.00
3CS62 Roberto Clemente 50.00 100.00
3CS63 Roberto Clemente 50.00 100.00
3CS64 Ted Williams 40.00 80.00
3CS65 Ted Williams 40.00 80.00
3CS66 Ted Williams 40.00 80.00
3CS77 Honus Wagner 90.00 150.00
3CS78 Honus Wagner 90.00 150.00
3CS79 Honus Wagner 90.00 150.00

2008 Topps Sterling Career Stats Relics Autographs Quad

COMMON BENCH 40.00 80.00
COMMON MURRAY 30.00 60.00
COMMON SNIDER 30.00 60.00
COMMON GIBSON 40.00 80.00
COMMON BERRA 50.00 100.00
COMMON MUSIAL 75.00 150.00
COMMON SEAVER 30.00 60.00
COMMON FORD 40.00 80.00
COMMON PALMER 20.00 50.00
COMMON R.JACKSON 40.00 80.00
COMMON SCHMIDT 40.00 80.00
COMMON YAZ 50.00 100.00
COMMON MATTINGLY 50.00 100.00
COMMON RYAN 100.00 200.00
COMMON YOUNT 40.00 80.00
COMMON RIPKEN 100.00 200.00
COMMON SANDBERG 40.00 80.00
COMMON F.ROBINSON 20.00 50.00
COMMON T.GWYNN 40.00 80.00
COMMON BANKS 30.00 60.00
COMMON MOLITOR 30.00 60.00
OVERALL ONE AUTO OR MEM PER BOX
STATED PRINT RUN 10 SER.#'d SETS
4CSA1 Johnny Bench 40.00 80.00
4CSA2 Johnny Bench 40.00 80.00
4CSA3 Johnny Bench 40.00 80.00
4CSA4 Eddie Murray 30.00 60.00
4CSA5 Eddie Murray 30.00 60.00
4CSA6 Eddie Murray 30.00 60.00
4CSA7 Eddie Murray 30.00 60.00
4CSA8 Eddie Murray 30.00 60.00
4CSA9 Eddie Murray 30.00 60.00
4CSA10 Eddie Murray 30.00 60.00
4CSA11 Eddie Murray 30.00 60.00
4CSA12 Eddie Murray 30.00 60.00
4CSA13 Eddie Murray 30.00 60.00
4CSA15 Eddie Murray 30.00 60.00
4CSA16 Duke Snider 30.00 60.00
4CSA17 Duke Snider 30.00 60.00
4CSA18 Duke Snider 30.00 60.00
4CSA19 Duke Snider 30.00 60.00
4CSA20 Duke Snider 30.00 60.00
4CSA21 Duke Snider 30.00 60.00
4CSA22 Duke Snider 30.00 60.00
4CSA23 Duke Snider 30.00 60.00
4CSA24 Duke Snider 30.00 60.00
4CSA25 Duke Snider 30.00 60.00
4CSA26 Duke Snider 30.00 60.00
4CSA27 Bob Gibson 40.00 80.00
4CSA28 Bob Gibson 40.00 80.00
4CSA29 Bob Gibson 40.00 80.00
4CSA30 Bob Gibson 40.00 80.00
4CSA31 Bob Gibson 40.00 80.00
4CSA32 Bob Gibson 40.00 80.00
4CSA33 Bob Gibson 40.00 80.00
4CSA34 Bob Gibson 40.00 80.00
4CSA35 Bob Gibson 40.00 80.00
4CSA36 Bob Gibson 40.00 80.00
4GSA37 Bob Gibson 40.00 80.00
4CSA38 Bob Gibson 40.00 80.00
4CSA39 Yogi Berra 50.00 120.00
4CSA40 Yogi Berra 50.00 120.00
4CSA41 Yogi Berra 50.00 120.00
4CSA42 Yogi Berra 50.00 120.00
4CSA43 Yogi Berra 50.00 120.00
4CSA44 Yogi Berra 50.00 120.00
4CSA45 Yogi Berra 50.00 120.00
4CSA46 Yogi Berra 50.00 120.00
4CSA47 Yogi Berra 50.00 120.00
4CSA48 Yogi Berra 50.00 120.00
4CSA49 Yogi Berra 50.00 120.00
4CSA50 Stan Musial 75.00 150.00
4CSA51 Stan Musial 75.00 150.00
4CSA52 Stan Musial 75.00 150.00
4CSA53 Stan Musial 75.00 150.00
4CSA54 Tom Seaver 30.00 80.00
4CSA55 Tom Seaver 30.00 80.00
4CSA56 Tom Seaver 30.00 80.00
4CSA57 Whitey Ford 40.00 80.00
4CSA58 Whitey Ford 40.00 80.00
4CSA59 Whitey Ford 40.00 80.00
4CSA60 Whitey Ford 40.00 80.00
4CSA61 Whitey Ford 40.00 80.00
4CSA62 Whitey Ford 40.00 80.00
4CSA63 Whitey Ford 40.00 80.00
4CSA64 Whitey Ford 40.00 80.00
4CSA65 Whitey Ford 40.00 80.00
4CSA66 Whitey Ford 40.00 80.00
4CSA67 Whitey Ford 40.00 80.00
4CSA68 Whitey Ford 40.00 80.00
4CSA73 Jim Palmer 20.00 50.00
4CSA74 Jim Palmer 20.00 50.00
4CSA75 Jim Palmer 20.00 50.00
4CSA76 Jim Palmer 20.00 50.00
4CSA77 Jim Palmer 20.00 50.00
4CSA78 Jim Palmer 20.00 50.00
4CSA79 Jim Palmer 20.00 50.00
4CSA80 Jim Palmer 20.00 50.00
4CSA81 Jim Palmer 20.00 50.00
4CSA82 Jim Palmer 20.00 50.00
4CSA83 Jim Palmer 20.00 50.00
4CSA84 Reggie Jackson 40.00 80.00
4CSA85 Reggie Jackson 40.00 80.00
4CSA86 Reggie Jackson 40.00 80.00
4CSA87 Mike Schmidt 40.00 80.00
4CSA88 Mike Schmidt 40.00 80.00
4CSA89 Mike Schmidt 40.00 80.00
4CSA90 Mike Schmidt 40.00 80.00
4CSA91 Mike Schmidt 40.00 80.00
4CSA92 Mike Schmidt 40.00 80.00
4CSA93 Mike Schmidt 40.00 80.00
4CSA94 Mike Schmidt 40.00 80.00
4CSA95 Mike Schmidt 40.00 80.00
4CSA96 Mike Schmidt 40.00 80.00
4CSA97 Mike Schmidt 40.00 80.00
4CSA98 Mike Schmidt 40.00 80.00
4CSA99 Carl Yastrzemski 50.00 100.00
4CSA100 Carl Yastrzemski 50.00 100.00
4CSA101 Carl Yastrzemski 50.00 100.00
4CSA102 Don Mattingly 50.00 100.00
4CSA103 Don Mattingly 50.00 100.00
4CSA104 Don Mattingly 50.00 100.00
4CSA105 Don Mattingly 50.00 100.00
4CSA106 Don Mattingly 50.00 100.00
4CSA107 Don Mattingly 50.00 100.00
4CSA108 Don Mattingly 50.00 100.00
4CSA109 Don Mattingly 50.00 100.00
4CSA110 Don Mattingly 50.00 100.00
4CSA111 Don Mattingly 50.00 100.00
4CSA112 Don Mattingly 50.00 100.00
4CSA113 Nolan Ryan 100.00 200.00
4CSA114 Nolan Ryan 100.00 200.00
4CSA117 Robin Yount 40.00 80.00
4CSA118 Robin Yount 40.00 80.00
4CSA119 Robin Yount 40.00 80.00
4CSA120 Robin Yount 40.00 80.00
4CSA121 Robin Yount 40.00 80.00
4CSA122 Robin Yount 40.00 80.00
4CSA123 Robin Yount 40.00 80.00
4CSA124 Robin Yount 40.00 80.00
4CSA125 Robin Yount 40.00 80.00
4CSA126 Robin Yount 40.00 80.00
4CSA127 Robin Yount 40.00 80.00
4CSA128 Cal Ripken 100.00 200.00
4CSA129 Ryne Sandberg 40.00 80.00
4CSA130 Ryne Sandberg 40.00 80.00
4CSA131 Ryne Sandberg 40.00 80.00
4CSA132 Ryne Sandberg 40.00 80.00
4CSA133 Ryne Sandberg 40.00 80.00
4CSA134 Ryne Sandberg 40.00 80.00
4CSA135 Ryne Sandberg 40.00 80.00
4CSA136 Ryne Sandberg 40.00 80.00
4CSA137 Ryne Sandberg 40.00 80.00
4CSA138 Ryne Sandberg 40.00 80.00
4CSA139 Ryne Sandberg 40.00 80.00
4CSA140 Frank Robinson 20.00 50.00
4CSA141 Frank Robinson 20.00 50.00
4CSA142 Frank Robinson 20.00 50.00
4CSA143 Frank Robinson 20.00 50.00
4CSA144 Tony Gwynn 40.00 80.00
4CSA145 Tony Gwynn 40.00 80.00
4CSA146 Tony Gwynn 40.00 80.00
4CSA147 Ernie Banks 30.00 60.00
4CSA148 Ernie Banks 30.00 60.00
4CSA149 Paul Molitor 30.00 60.00
4CSA150 Paul Molitor 30.00 60.00
4CSA153 Paul Molitor 30.00 60.00
4CSA155 Paul Molitor 30.00 60.00
4CSA157 Paul Molitor 30.00 60.00
4CSA160 Paul Molitor 30.00 60.00

2008 Topps Sterling Career Stats Relics Autographs Triple

COMMON BENCH 40.00 80.00
COMMON MURRAY 30.00 60.00
COMMON SNIDER 30.00 60.00
COMMON GIBSON 40.00 80.00
COMMON BERRA 40.00 80.00
COMMON SEAVER 30.00 60.00
COMMON FORD 40.00 80.00
COMMON PALMER 20.00 50.00
COMMON R.JACKSON 30.00 60.00
COMMON SCHMIDT 40.00 80.00
COMMON YAZ 30.00 60.00
COMMON MATTINGLY 60.00 120.00
COMMON RYAN 75.00 150.00
COMMON YOUNT 40.00 80.00
COMMON RIPKEN 125.00 250.00
COMMON SANDBERG 40.00 80.00
COMMON T.GWYNN 50.00 100.00
COMMON BANKS 40.00 80.00
COMMON MOLITOR 30.00 60.00
OVERALL ONE AUTO OR MEM PER BOX
STATED PRINT RUN 10 SER.#'d SETS
3CSA3 Johnny Bench 40.00 80.00
3CSA4 Johnny Bench 40.00 80.00
3CSA5 Eddie Murray 30.00 60.00
3CSA6 Eddie Murray 30.00 60.00
3CSA13 Eddie Murray 30.00 60.00
3CSA14 Eddie Murray 30.00 60.00
3CSA15 Eddie Murray 30.00 60.00
3CSA16 Duke Snider 30.00 60.00
3CSA17 Duke Snider 30.00 60.00
3CSA21 Duke Snider 30.00 60.00
3CSA23 Duke Snider 30.00 60.00
3CSA24 Duke Snider 30.00 60.00
3CSA28 Bob Gibson 40.00 80.00
3CSA29 Bob Gibson 40.00 80.00
3CSA31 Bob Gibson 40.00 80.00
3CSA34 Bob Gibson 40.00 80.00
3CSA37 Bob Gibson 40.00 80.00
3CSA40 Yogi Berra 40.00 100.00
3CSA42 Yogi Berra 40.00 100.00
3CSA43 Yogi Berra 40.00 100.00
3CSA45 Yogi Berra 40.00 100.00
3CSA47 Yogi Berra 40.00 100.00
3CSA48 Yogi Berra 40.00 100.00
3CSA49 Yogi Berra 40.00 100.00
3CSA54 Tom Seaver 30.00 80.00
3CSA56 Tom Seaver 30.00 80.00
3CSA59 Whitey Ford 40.00 80.00
3CSA61 Whitey Ford 40.00 80.00
3CSA64 Whitey Ford 40.00 80.00
3CSA66 Whitey Ford 40.00 80.00
3CSA72 Jim Palmer 20.00 50.00
3CSA74 Jim Palmer 20.00 50.00
3CSA76 Jim Palmer 20.00 50.00
3CSA77 Jim Palmer 20.00 50.00
3CSA78 Jim Palmer 20.00 50.00
3CSA82 Jim Palmer 20.00 50.00
3CSA86 Reggie Jackson 30.00 60.00
3CSA89 Mike Schmidt 40.00 80.00
3CSA92 Mike Schmidt 40.00 80.00
3CSA93 Mike Schmidt 40.00 80.00
3CSA98 Mike Schmidt 40.00 80.00
3CSA102 Carl Yastrzemski 30.00 60.00
3CSA103 Don Mattingly 60.00 120.00
3CSA105 Don Mattingly 60.00 120.00
3CSA106 Don Mattingly 60.00 120.00
3CSA108 Don Mattingly 60.00 120.00
3CSA110 Don Mattingly 60.00 120.00
3CSA114 Don Mattingly 60.00 120.00
3CSA115 Nolan Ryan 75.00 150.00
3CSA118 Robin Yount 40.00 80.00
3CSA120 Robin Yount 40.00 80.00
3CSA121 Robin Yount 40.00 80.00
3CSA124 Robin Yount 40.00 80.00
3CSA125 Robin Yount 40.00 80.00
3CSA128 Cal Ripken 125.00 250.00
3CSA130 Ryne Sandberg 40.00 80.00
3CSA133 Ryne Sandberg 40.00 80.00
3CSA136 Ryne Sandberg 40.00 80.00
3CSA139 Ryne Sandberg 40.00 80.00
3CSA140 Ryne Sandberg 40.00 80.00
3CSA146 Tony Gwynn 50.00 100.00
3CSA148 Ernie Banks 40.00 80.00
3CSA157 Paul Molitor 30.00 60.00
3CSA158 Paul Molitor 30.00 60.00
3CSA159 Paul Molitor 30.00 60.00

2008 Topps Sterling Moments Relics Five

COMMON MANTLE 75.00 150.00
COMMON RUTH 150.00 250.00
COMMON OTT 50.00 100.00
COMMON BENCH 20.00 50.00
COMMON FOXX 60.00 120.00
COMMON J.ROBINSON 40.00 80.00
COMMON MUSIAL 20.00 50.00
COMMON HORNSBY 40.00 80.00
COMMON SEAVER 15.00 40.00
COMMON MARIS 50.00 100.00
COMMON MUNSON 30.00 60.00
COMMON R.JACKSON 10.00 25.00
COMMON YAZ 20.00 50.00
COMMON CAMPANELLA 30.00 60.00
COMMON RYAN 50.00 100.00
COMMON COBB 100.00 175.00
COMMON RIPKEN 100.00 175.00
COMMON GEHRIG 150.00 250.00
COMMON CLEMENTE 60.00 120.00
COMMON T.WILLIAMS 60.00 120.00
COMMON F.ROBINSON 15.00 40.00
COMMON T.GWYNN 20.00 50.00
COMMON BANKS 15.00 40.00
COMMON WAGNER 100.00 200.00
OVERALL ONE AUTO OR MEM PER BOX
STATED PRINT RUN 10 SER.#'d SETS
5SM1 Mickey Mantle 75.00 150.00
5SM2 Mickey Mantle 75.00 150.00
5SM3 Babe Ruth 150.00 250.00
5SM4 Babe Ruth 150.00 250.00
5SM5 Mel Ott 50.00 100.00
5SM6 Mel Ott 50.00 100.00
5SM7 Johnny Bench 20.00 50.00
5SM8 Johnny Bench 20.00 50.00
5SM9 Johnny Bench 20.00 50.00
5SM10 Johnny Bench 20.00 50.00
5SM11 Johnny Bench 20.00 50.00
5SM12 Jimmie Foxx 60.00 120.00
5SM13 Jimmie Foxx 60.00 120.00
5SM14 Jackie Robinson 40.00 80.00
5SM15 Jackie Robinson 40.00 80.00
5SM16 Stan Musial 20.00 50.00
5SM17 Stan Musial 20.00 50.00
5SM18 Stan Musial 20.00 50.00
5SM19 Stan Musial 20.00 50.00
5SM20 Stan Musial 20.00 50.00
5SM21 Rogers Hornsby 40.00 80.00
5SM22 Rogers Hornsby 40.00 80.00
5SM23 Tom Seaver 15.00 40.00
5SM24 Tom Seaver 15.00 40.00
5SM25 Tom Seaver 15.00 40.00
5SM26 Tom Seaver 15.00 40.00
5SM27 Tom Seaver 15.00 40.00
5SM33 Roger Maris 50.00 100.00
5SM34 Roger Maris 50.00 100.00
5SM35 Thurman Munson 30.00 60.00
5SM36 Thurman Munson 30.00 60.00
5SM37 Reggie Jackson 10.00 25.00
5SM38 Reggie Jackson 10.00 25.00
5SM39 Reggie Jackson 10.00 25.00
5SM40 Reggie Jackson 10.00 25.00
5SM41 Reggie Jackson 10.00 25.00
5SM42 Carl Yastrzemski 20.00 50.00
5SM43 Carl Yastrzemski 20.00 50.00
5SM44 Carl Yastrzemski 20.00 50.00
5SM45 Carl Yastrzemski 20.00 50.00
5SM46 Carl Yastrzemski 20.00 50.00
5SM47 Roy Campanella 30.00 60.00
5SM48 Roy Campanella 30.00 60.00
5SM51 Nolan Ryan 50.00 100.00
5SM52 Nolan Ryan 50.00 100.00
5SM58 Ty Cobb 100.00 175.00
5SM59 Ty Cobb 100.00 175.00
5SM60 Cal Ripken 100.00 175.00
5SM61 Lou Gehrig 150.00 250.00
5SM62 Lou Gehrig 150.00 250.00
5SM63 Roberto Clemente 60.00 120.00
5SM64 Roberto Clemente 60.00 120.00
5SM65 Ted Williams 60.00 120.00
5SM66 Ted Williams 60.00 120.00
5SM67 Frank Robinson 15.00 40.00
5SM68 Frank Robinson 15.00 40.00
5SM69 Frank Robinson 15.00 40.00
5SM70 Frank Robinson 15.00 40.00
5SM71 Frank Robinson 15.00 40.00
5SM72 Tony Gwynn 20.00 50.00
5SM73 Tony Gwynn 20.00 50.00
5SM74 Tony Gwynn 20.00 50.00
5SM75 Tony Gwynn 20.00 50.00
5SM76 Tony Gwynn 20.00 50.00
5SM77 Ernie Banks 15.00 40.00
5SM78 Ernie Banks 15.00 40.00
5SM79 Ernie Banks 15.00 40.00
5SM80 Ernie Banks 15.00 40.00
5SM81 Ernie Banks 15.00 40.00
5SM82 Honus Wagner 100.00 200.00
5SM83 Honus Wagner 100.00 200.00

2008 Topps Sterling Moments Relics Quad

COMMON MANTLE 75.00 150.00
COMMON RUTH 200.00 350.00
COMMON OTT 50.00 100.00
COMMON BENCH 20.00 50.00
COMMON FOXX 40.00 80.00
COMMON J.ROBINSON 40.00 80.00
COMMON MUSIAL 30.00 60.00
COMMON HORNSBY 30.00 60.00
COMMON SEAVER 15.00 40.00
COMMON MARIS 50.00 100.00
COMMON MUNSON 30.00 60.00
COMMON R.JACKSON 15.00 40.00
COMMON YAZ 15.00 40.00
COMMON CAMPANELLA 30.00 60.00
COMMON COBB 40.00 80.00
COMMON RIPKEN 90.00 150.00
COMMON GEHRIG 100.00 250.00
COMMON CLEMENTE 60.00 120.00
COMMON T.WILLIAMS 40.00 80.00
COMMON F.ROBINSON 12.50 30.00
COMMON T.GWYNN 12.50 30.00
COMMON WAGNER 100.00 200.00
OVERALL ONE AUTO OR MEM PER BOX
STATED PRINT RUN 10 SER.#'d SETS
NO BANKS PRICING AVAILABLE
4SM1 Mickey Mantle 75.00 150.00
4SM2 Mickey Mantle 75.00 150.00
4SM3 Babe Ruth 200.00 350.00
4SM4 Babe Ruth 200.00 350.00
4SM5 Mel Ott 50.00 100.00
4SM6 Mel Ott 50.00 100.00
4SM8 Johnny Bench 20.00 50.00
4SM10 Johnny Bench 20.00 50.00
4SM13 Jimmie Foxx 40.00 80.00
4SM14 Jimmie Foxx 40.00 80.00
4SM15 Jackie Robinson 40.00 80.00
4SM16 Jackie Robinson 40.00 80.00
4SM17 Stan Musial 30.00 60.00
4SM19 Stan Musial 30.00 60.00
4SM20 Stan Musial 30.00 60.00
4SM23 Rogers Hornsby 30.00 60.00
4SM24 Rogers Hornsby 30.00 60.00
4SM27 Tom Seaver 15.00 40.00
4SM29 Tom Seaver 15.00 40.00
4SM37 Roger Maris 50.00 100.00
4SM38 Roger Maris 50.00 100.00
4SM39 Thurman Munson 30.00 60.00
4SM40 Thurman Munson 30.00 60.00
4SM41 Reggie Jackson 15.00 40.00
4SM42 Reggie Jackson 15.00 40.00
4SM43 Reggie Jackson 15.00 40.00
4SM45 Reggie Jackson 15.00 40.00
4SM46 Reggie Jackson 15.00 40.00
4SM48 Carl Yastrzemski 15.00 40.00
4SM50 Carl Yastrzemski 15.00 40.00
4SM51 Carl Yastrzemski 15.00 40.00
4SM52 Carl Yastrzemski 15.00 40.00
4SM53 Roy Campanella 30.00 60.00
4SM54 Roy Campanella 30.00 60.00
4SM65 Ty Cobb 40.00 80.00
4SM66 Ty Cobb 40.00 80.00
4SM67 Cal Ripken 90.00 150.00
4SM68 Lou Gehrig 100.00 250.00
4SM69 Lou Gehrig 100.00 250.00
4SM70 Roberto Clemente 60.00 120.00
4SM71 Roberto Clemente 60.00 120.00
4SM72 Ted Williams 40.00 80.00
4SM73 Ted Williams 40.00 80.00
4SM74 Frank Robinson 12.50 30.00
4SM76 Frank Robinson 12.50 30.00
4SM78 Frank Robinson 12.50 30.00
4SM79 Frank Robinson 12.50 30.00
4SM82 Tony Gwynn 12.50 30.00
4SM83 Tony Gwynn 12.50 30.00
4SM84 Tony Gwynn 12.50 30.00
4SM92 Honus Wagner 100.00 200.00
4SM93 Honus Wagner 100.00 200.00

2008 Topps Sterling Moments Relics Six

COMMON MANTLE 100.00 200.00
COMMON RUTH 250.00 400.00
COMMON OTT 50.00 100.00
COMMON BENCH 20.00 50.00
COMMON FOXX 50.00 100.00
COMMON MURRAY 20.00 50.00
COMMON J.ROBINSON 50.00 100.00
COMMON SNIDER 30.00 60.00
COMMON GIBSON 20.00 50.00
COMMON BERRA 30.00 60.00
COMMON MUSIAL 30.00 60.00
COMMON HORNSBY 40.00 80.00
COMMON SEAVER 20.00 50.00
COMMON FORD 20.00 50.00
COMMON MARIS 60.00 120.00
COMMON MUNSON 40.00 80.00
COMMON PALMER 12.50 30.00
COMMON R.JACKSON 20.00 50.00
COMMON SCHMIDT 20.00 50.00
COMMON YAZ 20.00 50.00
COMMON MATTINGLY 40.00 80.00
COMMON CAMPANELLA 20.00 50.00
COMMON RYAN 30.00 60.00
COMMON COBB 150.00 250.00
COMMON YOUNT 20.00 50.00
COMMON RIPKEN 75.00 150.00
COMMON GEHRIG 175.00 300.00
COMMON CLEMENTE 75.00 150.00
COMMON SANDBERG 20.00 50.00
COMMON T.WILLIAMS 75.00 150.00
COMMON F.ROBINSON 20.00 50.00
COMMON T.GWYNN 20.00 50.00
COMMON BANKS 15.00 40.00
COMMON WAGNER 150.00 250.00
COMMON MOLITOR 20.00 50.00
OVERALL ONE AUTO OR MEM PER BOX
STATED PRINT RUN 10 SER.#'d SETS
6SM1 Mickey Mantle 100.00 200.00
6SM2 Babe Ruth 250.00 400.00
6SM3 Mel Ott 50.00 100.00
6SM4 Johnny Bench 20.00 50.00
6SM5 Johnny Bench 20.00 50.00
6SM6 Johnny Bench 20.00 50.00
6SM7 Jimmie Foxx 50.00 100.00
6SM8 Eddie Murray 20.00 50.00
6SM9 Jackie Robinson 50.00 100.00
6SM10 Duke Snider 30.00 60.00
6SM11 Bob Gibson 20.00 50.00
6SM12 Yogi Berra 30.00 60.00
6SM13 Stan Musial 30.00 60.00
6SM14 Stan Musial 30.00 60.00
6SM15 Stan Musial 30.00 60.00
6SM16 Rogers Hornsby 40.00 80.00
6SM17 Tom Seaver 20.00 50.00
6SM18 Tom Seaver 20.00 50.00
6SM19 Tom Seaver 20.00 50.00
6SM20 Whitey Ford 20.00 50.00
6SM24 Roger Maris 60.00 120.00
6SM25 Thurman Munson 40.00 80.00
6SM26 Jim Palmer 12.50 30.00
6SM27 Reggie Jackson 20.00 50.00
6SM28 Reggie Jackson 20.00 50.00
6SM29 Reggie Jackson 20.00 50.00
6SM30 Mike Schmidt 20.00 50.00
6SM31 Carl Yastrzemski 20.00 50.00
6SM32 Carl Yastrzemski 20.00 50.00
6SM33 Carl Yastrzemski 20.00 50.00
6SM34 Don Mattingly 40.00 80.00
6SM35 Roy Campanella 20.00 50.00
6SM36 Nolan Ryan 30.00 60.00
6SM37 Nolan Ryan 30.00 60.00
6SM38 Nolan Ryan 30.00 60.00
6SM39 Nolan Ryan 30.00 60.00
6SM40 Nolan Ryan 30.00 60.00
6SM41 Nolan Ryan 30.00 60.00
6SM42 Nolan Ryan 30.00 60.00
6SM43 Nolan Ryan 30.00 60.00
6SM44 Nolan Ryan 30.00 60.00
6SM45 Nolan Ryan 30.00 60.00
6SM46 Nolan Ryan 30.00 60.00
6SM47 Nolan Ryan 30.00 60.00
6SM48 Nolan Ryan 30.00 60.00
6SM60 Ty Cobb 150.00 250.00
6SM61 Robin Yount 20.00 50.00
6SM62 Cal Ripken 75.00 150.00
6SM63 Lou Gehrig 175.00 300.00
6SM64 Roberto Clemente 75.00 150.00
6SM65 Ryne Sandberg 20.00 50.00
6SM66 Ted Williams 75.00 150.00
6SM67 Frank Robinson 20.00 50.00
6SM68 Frank Robinson 20.00 50.00
6SM69 Frank Robinson 20.00 50.00
6SM70 Tony Gwynn 20.00 50.00
6SM71 Tony Gwynn 20.00 50.00
6SM72 Tony Gwynn 20.00 50.00
6SM73 Ernie Banks 15.00 40.00
6SM74 Ernie Banks 15.00 40.00
6SM75 Ernie Banks 15.00 40.00
6SM76 Ernie Banks 15.00 40.00
6SM77 Ernie Banks 15.00 40.00
6SM78 Ernie Banks 15.00 40.00
6SM79 Ernie Banks 15.00 40.00
6SM80 Ernie Banks 15.00 40.00
6SM81 Ernie Banks 15.00 40.00
6SM82 Ernie Banks 15.00 40.00
6SM83 Ernie Banks 15.00 40.00
6SM84 Honus Wagner 150.00 250.00
6SM88 Paul Molitor 20.00 50.00

2008 Topps Sterling Moments Relics Triple

COMMON MANTLE 60.00 120.00
COMMON RUTH 125.00 250.00
COMMON OTT 40.00 80.00
COMMON FOXX 30.00 60.00
COMMON J.ROBINSON 40.00 80.00
COMMON HORNSBY 40.00 80.00
COMMON MARIS 40.00 80.00
COMMON MUNSON 50.00 100.00
COMMON CAMPANELLA 20.00 50.00
COMMON COBB 75.00 150.00
COMMON RIPKEN 90.00 150.00
COMMON GEHRIG 150.00 250.00
COMMON CLEMENTE 50.00 100.00
COMMON T.WILLIAMS 40.00 80.00
COMMON WAGNER 90.00 150.00
OVERALL ONE AUTO OR MEM PER BOX
STATED PRINT RUN 10 SER.#'d SETS
NO SEAVER PRICING AVAILABLE
3SM1 Mickey Mantle 60.00 120.00
3SM2 Mickey Mantle 60.00 120.00
3SM3 Mickey Mantle 60.00 120.00
3SM4 Babe Ruth 125.00 250.00
3SM5 Babe Ruth 125.00 250.00
3SM6 Babe Ruth 125.00 250.00
3SM7 Mel Ott 40.00 80.00
3SM8 Mel Ott 40.00 80.00
3SM9 Mel Ott 40.00 80.00
3SM14 Jimmie Foxx 30.00 60.00
3SM15 Jimmie Foxx 30.00 60.00
3SM16 Jimmie Foxx 30.00 60.00
3SM17 Jackie Robinson 40.00 80.00
3SM18 Jackie Robinson 40.00 80.00
3SM19 Jackie Robinson 40.00 80.00
3SM24 Rogers Hornsby 40.00 80.00
3SM25 Rogers Hornsby 40.00 80.00
3SM26 Rogers Hornsby 40.00 80.00
3SM35 Roger Maris 40.00 80.00
3SM36 Roger Maris 40.00 80.00
3SM37 Roger Maris 40.00 80.00
3SM38 Thurman Munson 50.00 100.00
3SM39 Thurman Munson 50.00 100.00
3SM40 Thurman Munson 50.00 100.00
3SM49 Roy Campanella 20.00 50.00
3SM50 Roy Campanella 20.00 50.00
3SM51 Roy Campanella 20.00 50.00
3SM62 Ty Cobb 75.00 150.00
3SM63 Ty Cobb 75.00 150.00
3SM64 Ty Cobb 75.00 150.00
3SM65 Cal Ripken 90.00 150.00
3SM66 Lou Gehrig 150.00 250.00
3SM67 Lou Gehrig 150.00 250.00
3SM68 Lou Gehrig 150.00 250.00
3SM69 Roberto Clemente 50.00 100.00
3SM70 Roberto Clemente 50.00 100.00
3SM71 Roberto Clemente 50.00 100.00
3SM72 Ted Williams 40.00 80.00
3SM73 Ted Williams 40.00 80.00
3SM74 Ted Williams 40.00 80.00
3SM90 Honus Wagner 90.00 150.00
3SM91 Honus Wagner 90.00 150.00
3SM92 Honus Wagner 90.00 150.00

2008 Topps Sterling Moments Relics Autographs Eight

COMMON BENCH 60.00 120.00
COMMON MURRAY 60.00 120.00
COMMON SNIDER 50.00 100.00
COMMON GIBSON 40.00 80.00
COMMON BERRA 75.00 150.00
COMMON MUSIAL 75.00 150.00
COMMON SEAVER 40.00 80.00
COMMON FORD 50.00 100.00
COMMON PALMER 30.00 60.00
COMMON R.JACKSON 40.00 80.00
COMMON SCHMIDT 60.00 120.00
COMMON YAZ 75.00 150.00
COMMON MATTINGLY 75.00 150.00
COMMON RYAN 100.00 175.00
COMMON YOUNT 60.00 120.00
COMMON RIPKEN 100.00 200.00
COMMON SANDBERG 60.00 120.00
COMMON F.ROBINSON 50.00 100.00
COMMON T.GWYNN 75.00 150.00
COMMON BANKS 75.00 150.00
COMMON MOLITOR 50.00 100.00
OVERALL ONE AUTO OR MEM PER BOX
STATED PRINT RUN 10 SER.#'d SETS
8SMA1 Johnny Bench 60.00 120.00
8SMA2 Johnny Bench 60.00 120.00
8SMA3 Eddie Murray 60.00 120.00
8SMA4 Duke Snider 50.00 100.00
8SMA5 Duke Snider 50.00 100.00
8SMA6 Bob Gibson 40.00 80.00
8SMA7 Yogi Berra 75.00 200.00
8SMA8 Stan Musial 75.00 150.00
8SMA9 Stan Musial 75.00 150.00
8SMA10 Tom Seaver 40.00 100.00
8SMA11 Tom Seaver 40.00 100.00
8SMA12 Whitey Ford 50.00 100.00
8SMA14 Jim Palmer 30.00 60.00
8SMA15 Jim Palmer 30.00 60.00
8SMA16 Reggie Jackson 40.00 80.00
8SMA17 Mike Schmidt 60.00 120.00
8SMA18 Carl Yastrzemski 75.00 150.00
8SMA19 Carl Yastrzemski 75.00 150.00
8SMA20 Don Mattingly 75.00 150.00
8SMA21 Nolan Ryan 100.00 175.00
8SMA23 Robin Yount 60.00 120.00

4SMA24 Robin Yount 60.00 120.00
4SMA25 Cal Ripken 100.00 200.00
4SMA26 Ryne Sandberg 60.00 120.00
4SMA27 Ryne Sandberg 60.00 120.00
4SMA28 Frank Robinson 50.00 100.00
4SMA29 Tony Gwynn 75.00 150.00
4SMA30 Ernie Banks 75.00 150.00
4SMA31 Paul Molitor 50.00 100.00

2008 Topps Sterling Moments Relics Autographs Quad

COMMON BENCH 40.00 80.00
COMMON MURRAY 30.00 60.00
COMMON SNIDER 30.00 60.00
COMMON GIBSON 40.00 80.00
COMMON BERRA 50.00 100.00
COMMON MUSIAL 75.00 150.00
COMMON SEAVER 30.00 60.00
COMMON FORD 40.00 80.00
COMMON PALMER 20.00 50.00
COMMON R.JACKSON 40.00 80.00
COMMON SCHMIDT 40.00 80.00
COMMON YAZ 50.00 100.00
COMMON MATTINGLY 50.00 100.00
COMMON RYAN 100.00 200.00
COMMON YOUNT 30.00 60.00
COMMON RIPKEN 100.00 200.00
COMMON SANDBERG 40.00 80.00
COMMON F.ROBINSON 20.00 50.00
COMMON T.GWYNN 40.00 80.00
COMMON BANKS 30.00 60.00
COMMON MOLITOR 30.00 60.00
OVERALL ONE AUTO OR MEM PER BOX
STATED PRINT RUN 10 SER.#'d SETS
4SMA1 Johnny Bench 40.00 80.00
4SMA2 Johnny Bench 40.00 80.00
4SMA3 Johnny Bench 40.00 80.00
4SMA4 Eddie Murray 30.00 60.00
4SMA5 Eddie Murray 30.00 60.00
4SMA6 Eddie Murray 30.00 60.00
4SMA7 Eddie Murray 30.00 60.00
4SMA8 Eddie Murray 30.00 60.00
4SMA9 Eddie Murray 30.00 60.00
4SMA10 Eddie Murray 30.00 60.00
4SMA11 Eddie Murray 30.00 60.00
4SMA12 Eddie Murray 30.00 60.00
4SMA13 Eddie Murray 30.00 60.00
4SMA14 Eddie Murray 30.00 60.00
4SMA15 Eddie Murray 30.00 60.00
4SMA16 Eddie Murray 30.00 60.00
4SMA17 Eddie Murray 30.00 60.00
4SMA18 Duke Snider 30.00 60.00
4SMA19 Duke Snider 30.00 60.00
4SMA20 Duke Snider 30.00 60.00
4SMA21 Duke Snider 30.00 60.00
4SMA22 Duke Snider 30.00 60.00
4SMA23 Duke Snider 30.00 60.00
4SMA24 Duke Snider 30.00 60.00
4SMA25 Duke Snider 30.00 60.00
4SMA26 Duke Snider 30.00 60.00
4SMA27 Duke Snider 30.00 60.00
4SMA28 Duke Snider 30.00 60.00
4SMA29 Duke Snider 30.00 60.00
4SMA30 Duke Snider 30.00 60.00
4SMA31 Duke Snider 30.00 60.00
4SMA32 Bob Gibson 40.00 80.00
4SMA33 Bob Gibson 40.00 80.00
4SMA34 Bob Gibson 40.00 80.00
4SMA35 Bob Gibson 40.00 80.00
4SMA36 Bob Gibson 40.00 80.00
4SMA37 Bob Gibson 40.00 80.00
4SMA38 Bob Gibson 40.00 80.00
4SMA39 Bob Gibson 40.00 80.00
4SMA40 Bob Gibson 40.00 80.00
4SMA41 Bob Gibson 40.00 80.00
4SMA42 Bob Gibson 40.00 80.00
4SMA43 Bob Gibson 40.00 80.00
4SMA44 Bob Gibson 40.00 80.00
4SMA45 Bob Gibson 40.00 80.00
4SMA46 Yogi Berra 50.00 120.00
4SMA47 Yogi Berra 50.00 120.00
4SMA48 Yogi Berra 50.00 120.00
4SMA49 Yogi Berra 50.00 120.00
4SMA50 Yogi Berra 50.00 120.00
4SMA51 Yogi Berra 50.00 120.00
4SMA52 Yogi Berra 50.00 120.00
4SMA53 Yogi Berra 50.00 120.00
4SMA54 Yogi Berra 50.00 120.00
4SMA55 Yogi Berra 50.00 120.00
4SMA56 Yogi Berra 50.00 120.00
4SMA57 Yogi Berra 50.00 120.00
4SMA58 Yogi Berra 50.00 120.00
4SMA59 Yogi Berra 50.00 120.00
4SMA60 Stan Musial 75.00 150.00
4SMA61 Stan Musial 75.00 150.00
4SMA62 Stan Musial 75.00 150.00
4SMA63 Tom Seaver 30.00 80.00
4SMA64 Tom Seaver 30.00 80.00
4SMA65 Tom Seaver 30.00 80.00
4SMA66 Whitey Ford 40.00 80.00
4SMA67 Whitey Ford 40.00 80.00
4SMA68 Whitey Ford 40.00 80.00
4SMA69 Whitey Ford 40.00 80.00
4SMA70 Whitey Ford 40.00 80.00
4SMA71 Whitey Ford 40.00 80.00
4SMA72 Whitey Ford 40.00 80.00
4SMA73 Whitey Ford 40.00 80.00
4SMA74 Whitey Ford 40.00 80.00
4SMA75 Whitey Ford 40.00 80.00
4SMA76 Whitey Ford 40.00 80.00
4SMA77 Whitey Ford 40.00 80.00
4SMA78 Whitey Ford 40.00 80.00
4SMA79 Whitey Ford 40.00 80.00
4SMA84 Jim Palmer 20.00 50.00
4SMA85 Jim Palmer 20.00 50.00
4SMA86 Jim Palmer 20.00 50.00
4SMA87 Jim Palmer 20.00 50.00
4SMA88 Jim Palmer 20.00 50.00
4SMA89 Jim Palmer 20.00 50.00
4SMA90 Jim Palmer 20.00 50.00
4SMA91 Jim Palmer 20.00 50.00
4SMA92 Jim Palmer 20.00 50.00
4SMA93 Jim Palmer 20.00 50.00
4SMA94 Jim Palmer 20.00 50.00
4SMA95 Jim Palmer 20.00 50.00
4SMA96 Jim Palmer 20.00 50.00
4SMA97 Jim Palmer 20.00 50.00
4SMA98 Reggie Jackson 40.00 80.00
4SMA99 Reggie Jackson 40.00 80.00
4SMA100 Reggie Jackson 40.00 80.00
4SMA101 Mike Schmidt 40.00 80.00
4SMA102 Mike Schmidt 40.00 80.00
4SMA103 Mike Schmidt 40.00 80.00
4SMA104 Mike Schmidt 40.00 80.00
4SMA105 Mike Schmidt 40.00 80.00
4SMA106 Mike Schmidt 40.00 80.00
4SMA107 Mike Schmidt 40.00 80.00
4SMA108 Mike Schmidt 40.00 80.00
4SMA109 Mike Schmidt 40.00 80.00
4SMA110 Mike Schmidt 40.00 80.00
4SMA111 Mike Schmidt 40.00 80.00
4SMA112 Mike Schmidt 40.00 80.00
4SMA113 Mike Schmidt 40.00 80.00
4SMA114 Mike Schmidt 40.00 80.00
4SMA115 Carl Yastrzemski 50.00 100.00
4SMA116 Carl Yastrzemski 50.00 100.00
4SMA117 Carl Yastrzemski 50.00 100.00
4SMA118 Don Mattingly 50.00 100.00
4SMA119 Don Mattingly 50.00 100.00
4SMA120 Don Mattingly 50.00 100.00
4SMA121 Don Mattingly 50.00 100.00
4SMA122 Don Mattingly 50.00 100.00
4SMA123 Don Mattingly 50.00 100.00
4SMA124 Don Mattingly 50.00 100.00
4SMA125 Don Mattingly 50.00 100.00
4SMA126 Don Mattingly 50.00 100.00
4SMA127 Don Mattingly 50.00 100.00
4SMA128 Don Mattingly 50.00 100.00
4SMA129 Don Mattingly 50.00 100.00
4SMA130 Don Mattingly 50.00 100.00
4SMA131 Don Mattingly 50.00 100.00
4SMA132 Nolan Ryan 100.00 200.00
4SMA133 Nolan Ryan 100.00 200.00
4SMA135 Robin Yount 40.00 80.00
4SMA136 Robin Yount 40.00 80.00
4SMA137 Robin Yount 40.00 80.00
4SMA138 Robin Yount 40.00 80.00
4SMA139 Robin Yount 40.00 80.00
4SMA140 Robin Yount 40.00 80.00
4SMA141 Robin Yount 40.00 80.00
4SMA142 Robin Yount 40.00 80.00
4SMA143 Robin Yount 40.00 80.00
4SMA144 Robin Yount 40.00 80.00
4SMA145 Robin Yount 40.00 80.00
4SMA146 Robin Yount 40.00 80.00
4SMA147 Robin Yount 40.00 80.00
4SMA148 Robin Yount 40.00 80.00
4SMA149 Cal Ripken 100.00 200.00
4SMA150 Cal Ripken 100.00 200.00
4SMA151 Ryne Sandberg 40.00 80.00
4SMA152 Ryne Sandberg 40.00 80.00
4SMA153 Ryne Sandberg 40.00 80.00
4SMA154 Ryne Sandberg 40.00 80.00
4SMA155 Ryne Sandberg 40.00 80.00
4SMA156 Ryne Sandberg 40.00 80.00
4SMA157 Ryne Sandberg 40.00 80.00
4SMA158 Ryne Sandberg 40.00 80.00
4SMA159 Ryne Sandberg 40.00 80.00
4SMA160 Ryne Sandberg 40.00 80.00
4SMA161 Ryne Sandberg 40.00 80.00
4SMA162 Ryne Sandberg 40.00 80.00
4SMA163 Ryne Sandberg 40.00 80.00
4SMA164 Ryne Sandberg 40.00 80.00
4SMA165 Frank Robinson 20.00 50.00
4SMA166 Frank Robinson 20.00 50.00
4SMA167 Frank Robinson 20.00 50.00
4SMA168 Tony Gwynn 40.00 80.00
4SMA169 Tony Gwynn 40.00 80.00
4SMA170 Tony Gwynn 40.00 80.00
4SMA171 Ernie Banks 30.00 60.00
4SMA172 Ernie Banks 30.00 60.00
4SMA174 Paul Molitor 30.00 60.00
4SMA176 Paul Molitor 30.00 60.00
4SMA177 Paul Molitor 30.00 60.00
4SMA178 Paul Molitor 30.00 60.00
4SMA180 Paul Molitor 30.00 60.00

2008 Topps Sterling Moments Relics Autographs Triple

COMMON BENCH 40.00 80.00
COMMON MURRAY 30.00 60.00
COMMON SNIDER 30.00 60.00
COMMON GIBSON 40.00 80.00
COMMON BERRA 40.00 80.00
COMMON MUSIAL 75.00 150.00
COMMON SEAVER 30.00 60.00
COMMON FORD 40.00 80.00
COMMON PALMER 20.00 50.00
COMMON R.JACKSON 30.00 60.00
COMMON SCHMIDT 40.00 80.00
COMMON YAZ 30.00 60.00
COMMON MATTINGLY 60.00 120.00
COMMON RYAN 75.00 150.00
COMMON YOUNT 40.00 80.00
COMMON RIPKEN 125.00 250.00
COMMON SANDBERG 40.00 80.00
COMMON F.ROBINSON 20.00 50.00
COMMON T.GWYNN 50.00 100.00
COMMON BANKS 40.00 80.00
COMMON MOLITOR 30.00 60.00
OVERALL ONE AUTO OR MEM PER BOX
STATED PRINT RUN 10 SER.#'d SETS
3SMA2 Johnny Bench 40.00 80.00
3SMA6 Eddie Murray 30.00 60.00
3SMA7 Eddie Murray 30.00 60.00
3SMA10 Eddie Murray 30.00 60.00
3SMA11 Eddie Murray 30.00 60.00
3SMA16 Eddie Murray 30.00 60.00
3SMA17 Eddie Murray 30.00 60.00
3SMA20 Duke Snider 30.00 60.00
3SMA21 Duke Snider 30.00 60.00
3SMA26 Duke Snider 30.00 60.00
3SMA27 Duke Snider 30.00 60.00
3SMA28 Duke Snider 30.00 60.00
3SMA34 Bob Gibson 40.00 80.00
3SMA37 Bob Gibson 40.00 80.00
3SMA39 Bob Gibson 40.00 80.00
3SMA40 Bob Gibson 40.00 80.00
3SMA42 Bob Gibson 40.00 80.00
3SMA43 Bob Gibson 40.00 80.00
3SMA47 Yogi Berra 40.00 100.00
3SMA48 Yogi Berra 40.00 100.00
3SMA49 Yogi Berra 40.00 100.00
3SMA52 Yogi Berra 40.00 100.00
3SMA58 Stan Musial 75.00 150.00
3SMA60 Stan Musial 75.00 150.00
3SMA62 Tom Seaver 30.00 80.00
3SMA64 Tom Seaver 30.00 80.00
3SMA67 Whitey Ford 40.00 80.00
3SMA68 Whitey Ford 40.00 80.00
3SMA71 Whitey Ford 40.00 80.00
3SMA75 Whitey Ford 40.00 80.00
3SMA76 Whitey Ford 40.00 80.00
3SMA77 Whitey Ford 40.00 80.00
3SMA82 Jim Palmer 20.00 50.00
3SMA89 Jim Palmer 20.00 50.00
3SMA90 Jim Palmer 20.00 50.00
3SMA93 Jim Palmer 20.00 50.00
3SMA94 Jim Palmer 20.00 50.00
3SMA97 Reggie Jackson 30.00 60.00
3SMA101 Reggie Jackson 30.00 60.00
3SMA102 Mike Schmidt 40.00 80.00
3SMA105 Mike Schmidt 40.00 80.00
3SMA106 Mike Schmidt 40.00 80.00
3SMA109 Mike Schmidt 40.00 80.00
3SMA111 Mike Schmidt 40.00 80.00
3SMA112 Mike Schmidt 40.00 80.00
3SMA115 Carl Yastrzemski 30.00 60.00
3SMA116 Carl Yastrzemski 30.00 60.00
3SMA123 Don Mattingly 60.00 120.00
3SMA126 Don Mattingly 60.00 120.00
3SMA127 Don Mattingly 60.00 120.00
3SMA130 Don Mattingly 60.00 120.00
3SMA132 Don Mattingly 60.00 120.00
3SMA133 Nolan Ryan 75.00 150.00
3SMA136 Robin Yount 40.00 80.00
3SMA138 Robin Yount 40.00 80.00
3SMA139 Robin Yount 40.00 80.00
3SMA141 Robin Yount 40.00 80.00
3SMA143 Robin Yount 40.00 80.00
3SMA145 Robin Yount 40.00 80.00
3SMA146 Robin Yount 40.00 80.00
3SMA148 Cal Ripken 125.00 250.00
3SMA149 Ryne Sandberg 40.00 80.00
3SMA154 Ryne Sandberg 40.00 80.00
3SMA156 Ryne Sandberg 40.00 80.00
3SMA161 Ryne Sandberg 40.00 80.00
3SMA163 Frank Robinson 20.00 50.00
3SMA165 Frank Robinson 20.00 50.00
3SMA170 Tony Gwynn 50.00 100.00
3SMA172 Ernie Banks 40.00 80.00
3SMA174 Paul Molitor 30.00 60.00
3SMA176 Paul Molitor 30.00 60.00

2008 Topps Sterling Stardom Relics Eight

RANDOM INSERTS IN BOXES
OVERALL ONE AUTO OR MEM PER BOX
STATED PRINT RUN 10 SER.#'d SETS
NO PRICING DUE TO SCARCITY

2008 Topps Sterling Stardom Relics Five

COMMON MANTLE 75.00 150.00
COMMON RUTH 150.00 250.00
COMMON OTT 50.00 100.00
COMMON BENCH 20.00 50.00
COMMON FOXX 60.00 120.00
COMMON J.ROBINSON 40.00 80.00
COMMON MUSIAL 20.00 50.00
COMMON HORNSBY 40.00 80.00
COMMON SEAVER 15.00 40.00
COMMON MARIS 50.00 100.00
COMMON MUNSON 30.00 60.00
COMMON R.JACKSON 10.00 25.00
COMMON YAZ 20.00 50.00
COMMON CAMPANELLA 30.00 60.00
COMMON RYAN 50.00 100.00
COMMON COBB 100.00 175.00
COMMON RIPKEN 100.00 175.00
COMMON GEHRIG 150.00 250.00
COMMON CLEMENTE 60.00 120.00
COMMON T.WILLIAMS 60.00 120.00
COMMON F.ROBINSON 15.00 40.00
COMMON T.GWYNN 20.00 50.00
COMMON BANKS 15.00 40.00
COMMON WAGNER 100.00 200.00
OVERALL ONE AUTO OR MEM PER BOX
STATED PRINT RUN 10 SER.#'d SETS
5SS1 Mickey Mantle 75.00 150.00
5SS2 Mickey Mantle 75.00 150.00
5SS3 Babe Ruth 150.00 250.00
5SS4 Babe Ruth 150.00 250.00
5SS5 Mel Ott 50.00 100.00
5SS6 Mel Ott 50.00 100.00
5SS7 Johnny Bench 20.00 50.00
5SS8 Johnny Bench 20.00 50.00
5SS9 Johnny Bench 20.00 50.00
5SS10 Johnny Bench 20.00 50.00
5SS11 Johnny Bench 20.00 50.00
5SS12 Jimmie Foxx 60.00 120.00
5SS13 Jimmie Foxx 60.00 120.00
5SS14 Jackie Robinson 40.00 80.00
5SS15 Jackie Robinson 40.00 80.00
5SS16 Stan Musial 20.00 50.00
5SS17 Stan Musial 20.00 50.00
5SS18 Stan Musial 20.00 50.00
5SS19 Stan Musial 20.00 50.00
5SS20 Stan Musial 20.00 50.00
5SS21 Rogers Hornsby 40.00 80.00
5SS22 Rogers Hornsby 40.00 80.00
5SS23 Tom Seaver 15.00 40.00
5SS24 Tom Seaver 15.00 40.00
5SS25 Tom Seaver 15.00 40.00
5SS26 Tom Seaver 15.00 40.00
5SS27 Tom Seaver 15.00 40.00
5SS33 Roger Maris 50.00 100.00
5SS34 Roger Maris 50.00 100.00
5SS35 Thurman Munson 30.00 60.00
5SS36 Thurman Munson 30.00 60.00
5SS37 Reggie Jackson 10.00 25.00
5SS38 Reggie Jackson 10.00 25.00
5SS39 Reggie Jackson 10.00 25.00
5SS40 Reggie Jackson 10.00 25.00
5SS41 Reggie Jackson 10.00 25.00
5SS42 Carl Yastrzemski 20.00 50.00
5SS43 Carl Yastrzemski 20.00 50.00
5SS44 Carl Yastrzemski 20.00 50.00
5SS45 Carl Yastrzemski 20.00 50.00
5SS46 Carl Yastrzemski 20.00 50.00
5SS47 Roy Campanella 30.00 60.00
5SS48 Roy Campanella 30.00 60.00
5SS49 Nolan Ryan 50.00 100.00
5SS50 Nolan Ryan 50.00 100.00
5SS51 Nolan Ryan 50.00 100.00
5SS52 Nolan Ryan 50.00 100.00
5SS53 Nolan Ryan 50.00 100.00
5SS59 Ty Cobb 100.00 175.00
5SS60 Ty Cobb 100.00 175.00
5SS61 Cal Ripken 100.00 175.00
5SS62 Lou Gehrig 150.00 250.00
5SS63 Lou Gehrig 150.00 250.00
5SS64 Roberto Clemente 60.00 120.00
5SS65 Roberto Clemente 60.00 120.00
5SS66 Ted Williams 60.00 120.00
5SS67 Ted Williams 60.00 120.00
5SS68 Frank Robinson 15.00 40.00
5SS69 Frank Robinson 15.00 40.00
5SS70 Frank Robinson 15.00 40.00
5SS71 Frank Robinson 15.00 40.00
5SS72 Frank Robinson 15.00 40.00
5SS73 Tony Gwynn 20.00 50.00
5SS74 Tony Gwynn 20.00 50.00
5SS75 Tony Gwynn 20.00 50.00
5SS76 Tony Gwynn 20.00 50.00
5SS77 Ernie Banks 15.00 40.00
5SS78 Ernie Banks 15.00 40.00
5SS79 Ernie Banks 15.00 40.00
5SS80 Ernie Banks 15.00 40.00
5SS81 Ernie Banks 15.00 40.00
5SS82 Honus Wagner 100.00 200.00
5SS83 Honus Wagner 100.00 200.00

2008 Topps Sterling Stardom Relics Quad

COMMON MANTLE 75.00 150.00
COMMON RUTH 200.00 350.00
COMMON OTT 50.00 100.00
COMMON BENCH 20.00 50.00
COMMON FOXX 40.00 80.00
COMMON J.ROBINSON 40.00 80.00
COMMON MUSIAL 30.00 60.00
COMMON HORNSBY 30.00 60.00
COMMON SEAVER 15.00 40.00
COMMON MARIS 50.00 100.00
COMMON MUNSON 30.00 60.00
COMMON R.JACKSON 15.00 40.00
COMMON YAZ 15.00 40.00
COMMON CAMPANELLA 30.00 60.00
COMMON COBB 40.00 80.00
COMMON RIPKEN 90.00 150.00
COMMON GEHRIG 100.00 250.00
COMMON CLEMENTE 60.00 120.00
COMMON T.WILLIAMS 40.00 80.00
COMMON F.ROBINSON 15.00 40.00
COMMON T.GWYNN 15.00 40.00
COMMON WAGNER 100.00 200.00
OVERALL ONE AUTO OR MEM PER BOX
STATED PRINT RUN 10 SER.#'d SETS
NO RYAN PRICING AVAILABLE
4SS1 Mickey Mantle 75.00 150.00
4SS2 Mickey Mantle 75.00 150.00
4SS3 Babe Ruth 200.00 350.00
4SS4 Babe Ruth 200.00 350.00
4SS5 Mel Ott 50.00 100.00
4SS6 Mel Ott 50.00 100.00
4SS7 Johnny Bench 20.00 50.00
4SS8 Johnny Bench 20.00 50.00
4SS10 Johnny Bench 20.00 50.00
4SS11 Johnny Bench 20.00 50.00
4SS12 Jimmie Foxx 40.00 80.00
4SS13 Jimmie Foxx 40.00 80.00
4SS14 Jackie Robinson 40.00 80.00
4SS15 Jackie Robinson 40.00 80.00
4SS16 Stan Musial 30.00 60.00
4SS17 Stan Musial 30.00 60.00
4SS19 Stan Musial 30.00 60.00
4SS21 Stan Musial 30.00 60.00
4SS22 Rogers Hornsby 30.00 60.00
4SS23 Rogers Hornsby 30.00 60.00
4SS24 Tom Seaver 15.00 40.00
4SS27 Tom Seaver 15.00 40.00
4SS35 Roger Maris 50.00 100.00
4SS36 Roger Maris 50.00 100.00
4SS37 Thurman Munson 30.00 60.00
4SS38 Thurman Munson 30.00 60.00
4SS41 Reggie Jackson 15.00 40.00
4SS42 Reggie Jackson 15.00 40.00
4SS44 Carl Yastrzemski 15.00 40.00
4SS46 Carl Yastrzemski 15.00 40.00
4SS47 Carl Yastrzemski 15.00 40.00
4SS48 Carl Yastrzemski 15.00 40.00
4SS49 Carl Yastrzemski 15.00 40.00
4SS50 Roy Campanella 30.00 60.00
4SS51 Roy Campanella 30.00 60.00
4SS63 Ty Cobb 40.00 80.00
4SS64 Ty Cobb 40.00 80.00
4SS65 Cal Ripken 90.00 150.00
4SS66 Lou Gehrig 100.00 250.00
4SS67 Lou Gehrig 100.00 250.00
4SS68 Roberto Clemente 60.00 120.00
4SS69 Roberto Clemente 60.00 120.00
4SS70 Ted Williams 40.00 80.00
4SS71 Ted Williams 40.00 80.00
4SS72 Frank Robinson 15.00 40.00
4SS74 Frank Robinson 15.00 40.00
4SS76 Frank Robinson 15.00 40.00
4SS78 Tony Gwynn 15.00 40.00
4SS81 Tony Gwynn 15.00 40.00
4SS82 Tony Gwynn 15.00 40.00
4SS87 Honus Wagner 100.00 200.00
4SS88 Honus Wagner 100.00 200.00

2008 Topps Sterling Stardom Relics Six

COMMON MANTLE 100.00 200.00
COMMON RUTH 250.00 400.00
COMMON OTT 50.00 100.00
COMMON BENCH 20.00 50.00
COMMON FOXX 50.00 100.00
COMMON MURRAY 20.00 50.00
COMMON J.ROBINSON 50.00 100.00
COMMON SNIDER 30.00 60.00
COMMON GIBSON 20.00 50.00
COMMON BERRA 30.00 60.00
COMMON MUSIAL 30.00 60.00
COMMON HORNSBY 40.00 80.00
COMMON SEAVER 20.00 50.00
COMMON FORD 20.00 50.00
COMMON MARIS 60.00 120.00
COMMON MUNSON 40.00 80.00
COMMON PALMER 12.50 30.00
COMMON R.JACKSON 20.00 50.00
COMMON SCHMIDT 20.00 50.00
COMMON YAZ 20.00 50.00
COMMON MATTINGLY 40.00 80.00
COMMON CAMPANELLA 20.00 50.00
COMMON RYAN 30.00 60.00
COMMON COBB 150.00 250.00
COMMON YOUNT 20.00 50.00
COMMON RIPKEN 75.00 150.00
COMMON GEHRIG 175.00 300.00
COMMON CLEMENTE 75.00 150.00
COMMON SANDBERG 20.00 50.00
COMMON T.WILLIAMS 75.00 150.00
COMMON F.ROBINSON 20.00 50.00
COMMON T.GWYNN 20.00 50.00
COMMON BANKS 15.00 40.00
COMMON WAGNER 150.00 250.00
COMMON MOLITOR 20.00 50.00
OVERALL ONE AUTO OR MEM PER BOX
STATED PRINT RUN 10 SER.#'d SETS
6SS1 Mickey Mantle 100.00 200.00
6SS2 Babe Ruth 250.00 400.00
6SS3 Mel Ott 50.00 100.00
6SS4 Johnny Bench 20.00 50.00
6SS5 Johnny Bench 20.00 50.00
6SS6 Johnny Bench 20.00 50.00
6SS7 Johnny Bench 20.00 50.00
6SS8 Jimmie Foxx 50.00 100.00
6SS9 Eddie Murray 20.00 50.00
6SS10 Jackie Robinson 50.00 100.00
6SS11 Duke Snider 30.00 60.00
6SS12 Bob Gibson 20.00 50.00
6SS13 Yogi Berra 30.00 60.00
6SS14 Stan Musial 30.00 60.00
6SS15 Stan Musial 30.00 60.00
6SS16 Stan Musial 30.00 60.00
6SS17 Stan Musial 30.00 60.00
6SS18 Rogers Hornsby 40.00 80.00
6SS19 Tom Seaver 20.00 50.00
6SS20 Tom Seaver 20.00 50.00
6SS21 Tom Seaver 20.00 50.00
6SS22 Tom Seaver 20.00 50.00
6SS23 Whitey Ford 20.00 50.00
6SS28 Roger Maris 60.00 120.00
6SS29 Thurman Munson 40.00 80.00
6SS30 Jim Palmer 12.50 30.00
6SS31 Reggie Jackson 20.00 50.00
6SS32 Reggie Jackson 20.00 50.00
6SS33 Reggie Jackson 20.00 50.00
6SS34 Reggie Jackson 20.00 50.00
6SS35 Mike Schmidt 20.00 50.00
6SS36 Carl Yastrzemski 20.00 50.00
6SS37 Carl Yastrzemski 20.00 50.00
6SS38 Carl Yastrzemski 20.00 50.00
6SS39 Carl Yastrzemski 20.00 50.00
6SS40 Don Mattingly 40.00 80.00
6SS41 Roy Campanella 20.00 50.00
6SS42 Nolan Ryan 30.00 60.00
6SS43 Nolan Ryan 30.00 60.00
6SS44 Nolan Ryan 30.00 60.00
6SS45 Nolan Ryan 30.00 60.00
6SS46 Nolan Ryan 30.00 60.00
6SS47 Nolan Ryan 30.00 60.00
6SS48 Nolan Ryan 30.00 60.00
6SS49 Nolan Ryan 30.00 60.00
6SS50 Nolan Ryan 30.00 60.00
6SS60 Ty Cobb 150.00 250.00
6SS61 Robin Yount 20.00 50.00
6SS62 Cal Ripken 75.00 150.00
6SS63 Lou Gehrig 175.00 300.00
6SS64 Roberto Clemente 75.00 150.00
6SS65 Ryne Sandberg 20.00 50.00
6SS66 Ted Williams 75.00 150.00
6SS67 Frank Robinson 20.00 50.00
6SS68 Frank Robinson 20.00 50.00
6SS69 Frank Robinson 20.00 50.00
6SS70 Frank Robinson 20.00 50.00
6SS71 Tony Gwynn 20.00 50.00
6SS72 Tony Gwynn 20.00 50.00
6SS73 Tony Gwynn 20.00 50.00
6SS74 Tony Gwynn 20.00 50.00
6SS75 Ernie Banks 15.00 40.00
6SS76 Ernie Banks 15.00 40.00
6SS77 Ernie Banks 15.00 40.00
6SS78 Ernie Banks 15.00 40.00
6SS79 Ernie Banks 15.00 40.00
6SS80 Ernie Banks 15.00 40.00
6SS81 Ernie Banks 15.00 40.00
6SS82 Ernie Banks 15.00 40.00
6SS83 Ernie Banks 15.00 40.00
6SS84 Honus Wagner 150.00 250.00
6SS87 Paul Molitor 20.00 50.00
6SS94 Paul Molitor 20.00 50.00

2008 Topps Sterling Stardom Relics Triple

COMMON MANTLE 60.00 120.00
COMMON RUTH 125.00 250.00
COMMON OTT 40.00 80.00
COMMON FOXX 30.00 60.00
COMMON J.ROBINSON 40.00 80.00
COMMON HORNSBY 40.00 80.00
COMMON MARIS 40.00 80.00
COMMON MUNSON 50.00 100.00
COMMON CAMPANELLA 20.00 50.00
COMMON COBB 75.00 150.00
COMMON RIPKEN 90.00 150.00
COMMON GEHRIG 150.00 250.00
COMMON CLEMENTE 50.00 100.00
COMMON T.WILLIAMS 40.00 80.00
COMMON WAGNER 90.00 150.00
OVERALL ONE AUTO OR MEM PER BOX
STATED PRINT RUN 10 SER.#'d SETS
NO RYAN PRICING AVAILABLE
3SS1 Mickey Mantle 60.00 120.00
3SS2 Mickey Mantle 60.00 120.00
3SS3 Mickey Mantle 60.00 120.00
3SS4 Babe Ruth 125.00 250.00
3SS5 Babe Ruth 125.00 250.00
3SS6 Babe Ruth 125.00 250.00
3SS7 Mel Ott 40.00 80.00
3SS8 Mel Ott 40.00 80.00
3SS9 Mel Ott 40.00 80.00
3SS14 Jimmie Foxx 30.00 60.00
3SS15 Jimmie Foxx 30.00 60.00
3SS16 Jimmie Foxx 30.00 60.00
3SS17 Jackie Robinson 40.00 80.00
3SS18 Jackie Robinson 40.00 80.00
3SS19 Jackie Robinson 40.00 80.00
3SS24 Rogers Hornsby 40.00 80.00
3SS25 Rogers Hornsby 40.00 80.00
3SS26 Rogers Hornsby 40.00 80.00
3SS35 Roger Maris 40.00 80.00
3SS36 Roger Maris 40.00 80.00
3SS37 Roger Maris 40.00 80.00
3SS38 Thurman Munson 50.00 100.00
3SS39 Thurman Munson 50.00 100.00
3SS40 Thurman Munson 50.00 100.00
3SS49 Roy Campanella 20.00 50.00
3SS50 Roy Campanella 20.00 50.00
3SS51 Roy Campanella 20.00 50.00
3SS60 Ty Cobb 75.00 150.00
3SS61 Ty Cobb 75.00 150.00
3SS62 Ty Cobb 75.00 150.00
3SS63 Cal Ripken 90.00 150.00
3SS64 Lou Gehrig 150.00 250.00
3SS65 Lou Gehrig 150.00 250.00
3SS66 Lou Gehrig 150.00 250.00
3SS67 Roberto Clemente 50.00 100.00
3SS68 Roberto Clemente 50.00 100.00
3SS69 Roberto Clemente 50.00 100.00
3SS70 Ted Williams 40.00 80.00
3SS71 Ted Williams 40.00 80.00
3SS72 Ted Williams 40.00 80.00
3SS85 Honus Wagner 90.00 150.00
3SS86 Honus Wagner 90.00 150.00
3SS87 Honus Wagner 90.00 150.00

2008 Topps Sterling Stardom Relics Autographs Eight

COMMON BENCH 60.00 120.00
COMMON MURRAY 60.00 120.00
COMMON SNIDER 50.00 100.00
COMMON GIBSON 40.00 80.00
COMMON BERRA 75.00 150.00
COMMON MUSIAL 75.00 150.00
COMMON SEAVER 40.00 80.00
COMMON FORD 50.00 100.00
COMMON PALMER 30.00 60.00
COMMON R.JACKSON 40.00 80.00
COMMON SCHMIDT 60.00 120.00
COMMON YAZ 75.00 150.00
COMMON MATTINGLY 75.00 150.00
COMMON RYAN 100.00 175.00
COMMON YOUNT 60.00 120.00
COMMON RIPKEN 100.00 200.00
COMMON SANDBERG 60.00 120.00
COMMON F.ROBINSON 50.00 100.00
COMMON T.GWYNN 75.00 150.00
COMMON BANKS 75.00 150.00
COMMON MOLITOR 50.00 100.00
OVERALL ONE AUTO OR MEM PER BOX
STATED PRINT RUN 10 SER.#'d SETS
8SSA1 Johnny Bench 60.00 120.00
8SSA2 Johnny Bench 60.00 120.00
8SSA3 Eddie Murray 60.00 120.00
8SSA4 Duke Snider 50.00 100.00
8SSA5 Bob Gibson 40.00 80.00
8SSA6 Bob Gibson 40.00 80.00
8SSA7 Yogi Berra 75.00 200.00
8SSA8 Stan Musial 75.00 150.00
8SSA9 Stan Musial 75.00 150.00
8SSA10 Tom Seaver 40.00 100.00
8SSA11 Whitey Ford 50.00 100.00
8SSA14 Jim Palmer 30.00 60.00
8SSA15 Reggie Jackson 40.00 80.00
8SSA16 Mike Schmidt 60.00 120.00
8SSA17 Carl Yastrzemski 75.00 150.00
8SSA18 Carl Yastrzemski 75.00 150.00
8SSA19 Don Mattingly 75.00 150.00
8SSA20 Don Mattingly 75.00 150.00
8SSA21 Nolan Ryan 100.00 175.00
8SSA23 Robin Yount 60.00 120.00
8SSA24 Cal Ripken 100.00 200.00
8SSA25 Ryne Sandberg 60.00 120.00
8SSA26 Frank Robinson 50.00 100.00
8SSA27 Frank Robinson 50.00 100.00
8SSA28 Tony Gwynn 75.00 150.00
8SSA29 Tony Gwynn 75.00 150.00
8SSA30 Ernie Banks 75.00 150.00
8SSA31 Paul Molitor 50.00 100.00

2008 Topps Sterling Stardom Relics Autographs Quad

COMMON BENCH 40.00 80.00
COMMON MURRAY 30.00 60.00
COMMON SNIDER 30.00 60.00
COMMON GIBSON 40.00 80.00
COMMON BERRA 50.00 100.00
COMMON MUSIAL 75.00 150.00
COMMON SEAVER 30.00 60.00
COMMON FORD 40.00 80.00
COMMON PALMER 20.00 50.00
COMMON R.JACKSON 40.00 80.00
COMMON SCHMIDT 40.00 80.00
COMMON YAZ 50.00 100.00
COMMON MATTINGLY 50.00 100.00
COMMON RYAN 100.00 200.00
COMMON YOUNT 30.00 60.00
COMMON RIPKEN 100.00 200.00
COMMON SANDBERG 40.00 80.00
COMMON F.ROBINSON 20.00 50.00
COMMON T.GWYNN 40.00 80.00
COMMON BANKS 30.00 60.00
COMMON MOLITOR 30.00 60.00
OVERALL ONE AUTO OR MEM PER BOX
STATED PRINT RUN 10 SER.#'d SETS
4SSA1 Johnny Bench 40.00 80.00
4SSA2 Johnny Bench 40.00 80.00
4SSA3 Johnny Bench 40.00 80.00
4SSA4 Johnny Bench 40.00 80.00
4SSA5 Johnny Bench 40.00 80.00
4SSA6 Johnny Bench 40.00 80.00
4SSA7 Eddie Murray 30.00 60.00
4SSA8 Eddie Murray 30.00 60.00
4SSA9 Eddie Murray 30.00 60.00
4SSA10 Eddie Murray 30.00 60.00
4SSA11 Eddie Murray 30.00 60.00
4SSA12 Eddie Murray 30.00 60.00
4SSA13 Eddie Murray 30.00 60.00
4SSA14 Eddie Murray 30.00 60.00
4SSA15 Eddie Murray 30.00 60.00
4SSA16 Eddie Murray 30.00 60.00
4SSA17 Eddie Murray 30.00 60.00
4SSA18 Eddie Murray 30.00 60.00
4SSA19 Duke Snider 30.00 60.00
4SSA20 Duke Snider 30.00 60.00
4SSA21 Duke Snider 30.00 60.00
4SSA22 Duke Snider 30.00 60.00
4SSA23 Duke Snider 30.00 60.00
4SSA24 Duke Snider 30.00 60.00
4SSA25 Duke Snider 30.00 60.00
4SSA26 Duke Snider 30.00 60.00
4SSA27 Duke Snider 30.00 60.00
4SSA28 Duke Snider 30.00 60.00
4SSA29 Duke Snider 30.00 60.00
4SSA30 Duke Snider 30.00 60.00
4SSA31 Bob Gibson 40.00 80.00
4SSA32 Bob Gibson 40.00 80.00
4SSA33 Bob Gibson 40.00 80.00
4SSA34 Bob Gibson 40.00 80.00
4SSA35 Bob Gibson 40.00 80.00
4SSA36 Bob Gibson 40.00 80.00
4SSA37 Bob Gibson 40.00 80.00
4SSA38 Bob Gibson 40.00 80.00
4SSA39 Bob Gibson 40.00 80.00
4SSA40 Bob Gibson 40.00 80.00
4SSA41 Bob Gibson 40.00 80.00
4SSA42 Bob Gibson 40.00 80.00
4SSA43 Yogi Berra 50.00 120.00
4SSA44 Yogi Berra 50.00 120.00

4SSA45 Yogi Berra 50.00 120.00
4SSA46 Yogi Berra 50.00 120.00
4SSA47 Yogi Berra 50.00 120.00
4SSA48 Yogi Berra 50.00 120.00
4SSA49 Yogi Berra 50.00 120.00
4SSA50 Yogi Berra 50.00 120.00
4SSA51 Yogi Berra 50.00 120.00
4SSA52 Yogi Berra 50.00 120.00
4SSA53 Yogi Berra 50.00 120.00
4SSA54 Yogi Berra 50.00 120.00
4SSA55 Stan Musial 75.00 150.00
4SSA56 Stan Musial 75.00 150.00
4SSA57 Stan Musial 75.00 150.00
4SSA58 Stan Musial 75.00 150.00
4SSA59 Stan Musial 75.00 150.00
4SSA60 Tom Seaver 30.00 80.00
4SSA61 Tom Seaver 30.00 80.00
4SSA62 Tom Seaver 30.00 80.00
4SSA63 Tom Seaver 30.00 80.00
4SSA64 Tom Seaver 30.00 80.00
4SSA65 Whitey Ford 40.00 80.00
4SSA66 Whitey Ford 40.00 80.00
4SSA67 Whitey Ford 40.00 80.00
4SSA68 Whitey Ford 40.00 80.00
4SSA69 Whitey Ford 40.00 80.00
4SSA70 Whitey Ford 40.00 80.00
4SSA71 Whitey Ford 40.00 80.00
4SSA72 Whitey Ford 40.00 80.00
4SSA73 Whitey Ford 40.00 80.00
4SSA74 Whitey Ford 40.00 80.00
4SSA75 Whitey Ford 40.00 80.00
4SSA76 Whitey Ford 40.00 80.00
4SSA82 Jim Palmer 20.00 50.00
4SSA83 Jim Palmer 20.00 50.00
4SSA84 Jim Palmer 20.00 50.00
4SSA85 Jim Palmer 20.00 50.00
4SSA86 Jim Palmer 20.00 50.00
4SSA87 Jim Palmer 20.00 50.00
4SSA88 Jim Palmer 20.00 50.00
4SSA89 Jim Palmer 20.00 50.00
4SSA90 Jim Palmer 20.00 50.00
4SSA91 Jim Palmer 20.00 50.00
4SSA92 Jim Palmer 20.00 50.00
4SSA93 Jim Palmer 20.00 50.00
4SSA94 Reggie Jackson 40.00 80.00
4SSA95 Reggie Jackson 40.00 80.00
4SSA96 Reggie Jackson 40.00 80.00
4SSA97 Reggie Jackson 40.00 80.00
4SSA98 Reggie Jackson 40.00 80.00
4SSA99 Reggie Jackson 40.00 80.00
4SSA100 Mike Schmidt 40.00 80.00
4SSA101 Mike Schmidt 40.00 80.00
4SSA102 Mike Schmidt 40.00 80.00
4SSA103 Mike Schmidt 40.00 80.00
4SSA104 Mike Schmidt 40.00 80.00
4SSA105 Mike Schmidt 40.00 80.00
4SSA106 Mike Schmidt 40.00 80.00
4SSA107 Mike Schmidt 40.00 80.00
4SSA108 Mike Schmidt 40.00 80.00
4SSA109 Mike Schmidt 40.00 80.00
4SSA110 Mike Schmidt 40.00 80.00
4SSA111 Mike Schmidt 40.00 80.00
4SSA112 Carl Yastrzemski 50.00 100.00
4SSA113 Carl Yastrzemski 50.00 100.00
4SSA114 Carl Yastrzemski 50.00 100.00
4SSA115 Carl Yastrzemski 50.00 100.00
4SSA116 Carl Yastrzemski 50.00 100.00
4SSA117 Don Mattingly 50.00 100.00
4SSA118 Don Mattingly 50.00 100.00
4SSA119 Don Mattingly 50.00 100.00
4SSA120 Don Mattingly 50.00 100.00
4SSA121 Don Mattingly 50.00 100.00
4SSA122 Don Mattingly 50.00 100.00
4SSA123 Don Mattingly 50.00 100.00
4SSA124 Don Mattingly 50.00 100.00
4SSA125 Don Mattingly 50.00 100.00
4SSA126 Don Mattingly 50.00 100.00
4SSA127 Don Mattingly 50.00 100.00
4SSA128 Don Mattingly 50.00 100.00
4SSA129 Nolan Ryan 100.00 200.00
4SSA132 Robin Yount 40.00 80.00
4SSA133 Robin Yount 40.00 80.00
4SSA134 Robin Yount 40.00 80.00
4SSA135 Robin Yount 40.00 80.00
4SSA136 Robin Yount 40.00 80.00
4SSA137 Robin Yount 40.00 80.00
4SSA138 Robin Yount 40.00 80.00
4SSA139 Robin Yount 40.00 80.00
4SSA140 Robin Yount 40.00 80.00
4SSA141 Robin Yount 40.00 80.00
4SSA142 Robin Yount 40.00 80.00
4SSA143 Cal Ripken 100.00 200.00
4SSA144 Cal Ripken 100.00 200.00
4SSA145 Ryne Sandberg 40.00 80.00
4SSA146 Ryne Sandberg 40.00 80.00
4SSA147 Ryne Sandberg 40.00 80.00
4SSA148 Ryne Sandberg 40.00 80.00
4SSA149 Ryne Sandberg 40.00 80.00
4SSA150 Ryne Sandberg 40.00 80.00
4SSA151 Ryne Sandberg 40.00 80.00
4SSA152 Ryne Sandberg 40.00 80.00
4SSA153 Ryne Sandberg 40.00 80.00
4SSA154 Ryne Sandberg 40.00 80.00
4SSA155 Ryne Sandberg 40.00 80.00
4SSA156 Ryne Sandberg 40.00 80.00
4SSA157 Frank Robinson 20.00 50.00
4SSA158 Frank Robinson 20.00 50.00
4SSA159 Frank Robinson 20.00 50.00
4SSA160 Frank Robinson 20.00 50.00
4SSA161 Frank Robinson 20.00 50.00
4SSA162 Frank Robinson 20.00 50.00
4SSA163 Tony Gwynn 40.00 80.00
4SSA164 Tony Gwynn 40.00 80.00
4SSA165 Tony Gwynn 40.00 80.00
4SSA166 Tony Gwynn 40.00 80.00
4SSA167 Tony Gwynn 40.00 80.00
4SSA168 Tony Gwynn 40.00 80.00
4SSA169 Ernie Banks 30.00 60.00
4SSA170 Ernie Banks 30.00 60.00
4SSA173 Paul Molitor 30.00 60.00
4SSA176 Paul Molitor 30.00 60.00

2008 Topps Sterling Stardom Relics Autographs Triple

COMMON BENCH 40.00 80.00
COMMON MURRAY 30.00 60.00
COMMON SNIDER 30.00 60.00
COMMON GIBSON 40.00 80.00
COMMON BERRA 40.00 80.00
COMMON MUSIAL 75.00 150.00
COMMON SEAVER 30.00 60.00
COMMON FORD 40.00 80.00
COMMON PALMER 20.00 50.00
COMMON R.JACKSON 30.00 60.00
COMMON SCHMIDT 40.00 80.00
COMMON YAZ 30.00 60.00
COMMON MATTINGLY 60.00 120.00
COMMON RYAN 75.00 150.00
COMMON YOUNT 40.00 80.00
COMMON RIPKEN 125.00 250.00
COMMON SANDBERG 40.00 80.00
COMMON F.ROBINSON 20.00 50.00
COMMON T.GWYNN 50.00 100.00
COMMON BANKS 40.00 80.00
OVERALL ONE AUTO OR MEM PER BOX
STATED PRINT RUN 10 SER.#'d SETS
3SSA1 Johnny Bench 40.00 80.00
3SSA9 Eddie Murray 30.00 60.00
3SSA11 Eddie Murray 30.00 60.00
3SSA12 Eddie Murray 30.00 60.00
3SSA14 Eddie Murray 30.00 60.00
3SSA16 Eddie Murray 30.00 60.00
3SSA21 Duke Snider 30.00 60.00
3SSA24 Duke Snider 30.00 60.00
3SSA26 Duke Snider 30.00 60.00
3SSA28 Duke Snider 30.00 60.00
3SSA30 Duke Snider 30.00 60.00
3SSA34 Bob Gibson 40.00 80.00
3SSA40 Bob Gibson 40.00 80.00
3SSA41 Bob Gibson 40.00 80.00
3SSA45 Yogi Berra 40.00 100.00
3SSA49 Yogi Berra 40.00 100.00
3SSA51 Yogi Berra 40.00 100.00
3SSA53 Yogi Berra 40.00 100.00
3SSA54 Yogi Berra 40.00 100.00
3SSA59 Stan Musial 75.00 150.00
3SSA62 Stan Musial 75.00 150.00
3SSA63 Tom Seaver 30.00 80.00
3SSA65 Tom Seaver 30.00 80.00
3SSA71 Whitey Ford 40.00 80.00
3SSA73 Whitey Ford 40.00 80.00
3SSA76 Whitey Ford 40.00 80.00
3SSA77 Whitey Ford 40.00 80.00
3SSA79 Whitey Ford 40.00 80.00
3SSA89 Jim Palmer 20.00 50.00
3SSA91 Jim Palmer 20.00 50.00
3SSA94 Jim Palmer 20.00 50.00
3SSA97 Jim Palmer 20.00 50.00
3SSA101 Reggie Jackson 30.00 60.00
3SSA103 Reggie Jackson 30.00 60.00
3SSA107 Reggie Jackson 30.00 60.00
3SSA111 Mike Schmidt 40.00 80.00
3SSA113 Mike Schmidt 40.00 80.00
3SSA114 Mike Schmidt 40.00 80.00
3SSA115 Mike Schmidt 40.00 80.00
3SSA119 Mike Schmidt 40.00 80.00
3SSA120 Carl Yastrzemski 30.00 60.00
3SSA125 Carl Yastrzemski 30.00 60.00
3SSA128 Don Mattingly 60.00 120.00
3SSA129 Don Mattingly 60.00 120.00
3SSA134 Don Mattingly 60.00 120.00
3SSA135 Don Mattingly 60.00 120.00
3SSA139 Nolan Ryan 75.00 150.00
3SSA142 Robin Yount 40.00 80.00
3SSA148 Robin Yount 40.00 80.00
3SSA149 Robin Yount 40.00 80.00
3SSA153 Cal Ripken 125.00 250.00
3SSA155 Ryne Sandberg 40.00 80.00
3SSA156 Ryne Sandberg 40.00 80.00
3SSA158 Ryne Sandberg 40.00 80.00
3SSA159 Ryne Sandberg 40.00 80.00
3SSA162 Ryne Sandberg 40.00 80.00
3SSA163 Ryne Sandberg 40.00 80.00
3SSA165 Ryne Sandberg 40.00 80.00
3SSA168 Frank Robinson 20.00 50.00
3SSA171 Frank Robinson 20.00 50.00
3SSA176 Tony Gwynn 50.00 100.00
3SSA178 Tony Gwynn 50.00 100.00
3SSA179 Tony Gwynn 50.00 100.00
3SSA180 Ernie Banks 40.00 80.00

2009 Topps Sterling

COMMON CARD .75 2.00
THREE BASE CARDS PER BOX
STATED PRINT RUN 250 SER.#'d SETS
1 Babe Ruth 5.00 12.00
2 Bob Feller 1.25 3.00
3 Orlando Cepeda 1.25 3.00
4 Curt Schilling 1.25 3.00
5 Mickey Mantle 6.00 15.00
6 Joey Votto 2.00 5.00
7 Koji Uehara RC 2.00 5.00
8 Mel Ott 2.00 5.00
9 Miguel Cabrera 2.00 5.00
10 Prince Fielder 1.25 3.00
11 Jose Reyes 1.25 3.00
12 Carlos Beltran 1.25 3.00
13 David Price RC 1.50 4.00
14 Tommy Hanson RC 2.00 5.00
15 Roger Maris 2.00 5.00
16 Roger Maris 2.00 5.00
17 Mike Schmidt 3.00 8.00
18 Lou Gehrig 4.00 10.00
19 Ozzie Smith 2.50 6.00
20 Reggie Jackson 1.25 3.00
21 Reggie Jackson 1.25 3.00
22 Reggie Jackson 1.25 3.00
23 Tim Lincecum 1.25 3.00
24 Warren Spahn 1.25 3.00
25 Duke Snider 1.25 3.00
26 Yogi Berra 2.00 5.00
27 Ty Cobb 3.00 8.00
28 Stan Musial 3.00 8.00
29 Jimmie Foxx 2.00 5.00
30 Jimmie Foxx 2.00 5.00
31 Rick Porcello RC 2.50 6.00
32 Dwight Gooden .75 2.00
33 Ichiro Suzuki 2.50 6.00
34 CC Sabathia 1.25 3.00
35 Willie McCovey 1.25 3.00
36 Albert Pujols 2.50 6.00
37 Gary Sheffield .75 2.00
38 Cal Ripken Jr. 6.00 15.00
39 Daisuke Matsuzaka 1.25 3.00
40 Gary Carter 1.25 3.00
41 Josh Hamilton 1.25 3.00
42 Joe Mauer 1.50 4.00
43 Pedro Martinez 1.25 3.00
44 Whitey Ford 1.25 3.00
45 Johnny Damon 1.25 3.00
46 Frank Thomas 2.00 5.00
47 Dale Murphy 2.00 5.00
48 George Sisler 1.25 3.00
50 Lou Brock 1.25 3.00
51 Paul Molitor 2.00 5.00
52 David Ortiz 2.00 5.00
53 Tris Speaker 1.25 3.00
54 Tris Speaker 1.25 3.00
55 Carl Yastrzemski 3.00 8.00
56 Nolan Ryan 6.00 15.00
57 Nolan Ryan 6.00 15.00
58 Nolan Ryan 6.00 15.00
59 Eddie Mathews 2.00 5.00
60 Joe Morgan 1.25 3.00
61 Honus Wagner 2.00 5.00
62 Andre Dawson 1.25 3.00
63 Justin Morneau 1.25 3.00
64 Manny Ramirez 2.00 5.00
65 Manny Ramirez 2.00 5.00
66 Manny Ramirez 2.00 5.00
67 Vladimir Guerrero 1.25 3.00
68 Hanley Ramirez 1.25 3.00
69 Ryan Braun 1.25 3.00
70 Dan Haren .75 2.00
71 Dave Winfield 1.25 3.00
72 Robin Yount 2.00 5.00
73 Ryne Sandberg 4.00 10.00
74 Johnny Mize 1.25 3.00
75 Johnny Mize 1.25 3.00
76 Johnny Mize 1.25 3.00
77 Don Mattingly 4.00 10.00
78 Ivan Rodriguez 1.25 3.00
79 Ralph Kiner 1.25 3.00
80 Steve Garvey .75 2.00
81 Carlos Delgado .75 2.00
82 Dustin Pedroia 1.50 4.00
83 Hank Greenberg 2.00 5.00
84 Al Kaline 2.00 5.00
85 Fergie Jenkins 1.25 3.00
86 David Wright 1.50 4.00
87 Frank Robinson 1.25 3.00
88 Brandon Webb 1.25 3.00
89 Colby Rasmus (RC) 1.25 3.00
90 Alfonso Soriano 1.25 3.00
91 Jackie Robinson 2.00 5.00
92 Lance Berkman 1.25 3.00
93 Chase Utley 1.25 3.00
94 Mark Teixeira 1.25 3.00
95 Mike Piazza 2.00 5.00
96 Johan Santana 1.25 3.00
97 Rogers Hornsby 1.25 3.00
98 Rogers Hornsby 1.25 3.00
99 Dennis Eckersley 1.25 3.00
100 Evan Longoria 1.25 3.00
101 Bob Gibson 1.25 3.00
102 Tom Seaver 1.25 3.00
103 Tony Gwynn 2.00 5.00
104 Johnny Bench 2.00 5.00
105 Carlton Fisk 1.25 3.00
106 Ernie Banks 2.00 5.00
107 Mariano Rivera 2.50 6.00
108 Tony Perez 1.25 3.00
109 Roy Campanella 2.00 5.00
110 Francisco Rodriguez 1.25 3.00
111 Luis Aparicio 1.25 3.00
112 Monte Irvin 1.25 3.00
113 Zack Greinke 1.25 3.00
114 Jim Thome 1.25 3.00
115 Jimmy Piersall .75 2.00
116 Eddie Murray 1.25 3.00
117 Jim Palmer 1.25 3.00
118 Carl Erskine .75 2.00
119 Juan Marichal 1.25 3.00
120 Joba Chamberlain .75 2.00
121 Chipper Jones 2.00 5.00
122 Johnny Podres .75 2.00
123 Wade Boggs 1.25 3.00
124 Michael Young .75 2.00
125 Steve Carlton 1.25 3.00
126 Ryan Howard 1.50 4.00
127 Jay Bruce 1.25 3.00
128 Alex Rodriguez 2.50 6.00
129 Alex Rodriguez 2.50 6.00
130 Alex Rodriguez 2.50 6.00

2009 Topps Sterling Framed White

*WHITE VET: 1X TO 2.5X BASIC
*WHITE RC: 1X TO 2.5X BASIC RC
OVERALL PARALLEL ODDS 1:1
STATED PRINT RUN 50 SER.#'d SETS

2009 Topps Sterling Career Chronicles Relics Quad

OVERALL MEM ODDS 1:1
STATED PRINT RUN 25 SER.#'d SETS
ALL VARIATIONS PRICED EQUALLY
10 PRINT RUN 10 SER.#'d SETS
NO 10 PRICING DUE TO SCARCITY
SS PRINT RUN 1 SER.#'d SET
NO SS PRICING DUE TO SCARCITY
1 Babe Ruth 200.00 400.00
2 Ichiro Suzuki 30.00 60.00
3 Ichiro Suzuki 30.00 60.00
4 Jackie Robinson 30.00 60.00
5 Jackie Robinson 30.00 60.00
6 Cal Ripken Jr. 30.00 60.00
7 Cal Ripken Jr. 30.00 60.00
8 David Ortiz 8.00 20.00
9 David Ortiz 8.00 20.00
10 Vladimir Guerrero 8.00 20.00
11 Vladimir Guerrero 8.00 20.00
12 Reggie Jackson 15.00 40.00
13 Reggie Jackson 15.00 40.00
14 Prince Fielder 10.00 25.00
15 Prince Fielder 10.00 25.00
16 Chase Utley 15.00 40.00
17 Chase Utley 15.00 40.00
18 Francisco Rodriguez 8.00 20.00
19 Francisco Rodriguez 8.00 20.00
20 Lou Brock 15.00 40.00
21 Lou Brock 15.00 40.00
22 Carl Yastrzemski 12.50 30.00
23 Carl Yastrzemski 12.50 30.00
24 Jimmie Foxx 20.00 50.00
25 Jimmie Foxx 20.00 50.00
26 Eddie Mathews 15.00 40.00
27 Eddie Mathews 15.00 40.00
28 Yogi Berra 20.00 50.00
29 Yogi Berra 20.00 50.00
30 Mike Schmidt 12.50 30.00
31 Mike Schmidt 12.50 30.00
32 Tim Lincecum 20.00 50.00
33 Tim Lincecum 20.00 50.00
34 Mark Teixeira 10.00 25.00
35 Mark Teixeira 10.00 25.00
36 Ernie Banks 12.50 30.00
37 Ernie Banks 12.50 30.00
38 Joe Morgan 8.00 20.00
39 Joe Morgan 8.00 20.00
40 Al Kaline 15.00 40.00
41 Al Kaline 15.00 40.00
42 Carlos Beltran 8.00 20.00
43 Carlos Beltran 8.00 20.00
44 Mel Ott 20.00 50.00
45 Mickey Mantle 60.00 120.00
46 Mickey Mantle 60.00 120.00
47 Albert Pujols 20.00 50.00
48 Albert Pujols 20.00 50.00
49 Chipper Jones 12.50 30.00
50 Chipper Jones 12.50 30.00
51 Daisuke Matsuzaka 10.00 25.00
52 Daisuke Matsuzaka 10.00 25.00
53 Carlos Delgado 8.00 20.00
54 Carlos Delgado 8.00 20.00
55 Joba Chamberlain 10.00 25.00
56 Joba Chamberlain 10.00 25.00
57 Dennis Eckersley 8.00 20.00
58 Dennis Eckersley 8.00 20.00
59 Luis Aparicio 10.00 25.00
60 Luis Aparicio 10.00 25.00
61 CC Sabathia 10.00 25.00
62 CC Sabathia 10.00 25.00
63 Evan Longoria 12.50 30.00
64 Evan Longoria 12.50 30.00
65 Honus Wagner 60.00 120.00
66 Ryan Howard 15.00 40.00
67 Ryan Howard 15.00 40.00
68 Mariano Rivera 15.00 40.00
69 Mariano Rivera 15.00 40.00
70 Ty Cobb 50.00 100.00
71 Nolan Ryan 30.00 60.00
72 Nolan Ryan 30.00 60.00
73 Lou Gehrig 100.00 175.00
74 Dale Murphy 20.00 50.00
75 Dale Murphy 20.00 50.00
76 Eddie Murray 12.50 30.00
77 Eddie Murray 12.50 30.00
78 Don Mattingly 15.00 40.00
79 Don Mattingly 15.00 40.00
80 Johnny Bench 10.00 25.00
81 Johnny Bench 10.00 25.00
82 Joe Mauer 15.00 40.00
83 Joe Mauer 15.00 40.00
84 Dave Winfield 10.00 25.00
85 Dave Winfield 10.00 25.00
86 David Wright 10.00 25.00
87 David Wright 10.00 25.00
88 Carlton Fisk 10.00 25.00
89 Carlton Fisk 10.00 25.00
90 Frank Robinson 8.00 20.00
91 Frank Robinson 8.00 20.00
92 Johan Santana 8.00 20.00
93 Johan Santana 8.00 20.00
94 Duke Snider 12.50 30.00
95 Duke Snider 12.50 30.00
96 Bob Gibson 10.00 25.00
97 Bob Gibson 10.00 25.00
98 Tom Seaver 10.00 25.00
99 Tom Seaver 10.00 25.00
100 Warren Spahn 15.00 40.00
101 Warren Spahn 15.00 40.00
102 Paul Molitor 10.00 25.00
103 Paul Molitor 10.00 25.00
104 Orlando Cepeda 8.00 20.00
105 Orlando Cepeda 8.00 20.00
106 Roger Maris 30.00 60.00
107 Roger Maris 30.00 60.00
108 Tris Speaker 30.00 60.00
109 Manny Ramirez 12.50 30.00
110 Manny Ramirez 12.50 30.00
111 Hank Greenberg 20.00 50.00
112 Hank Greenberg 20.00 50.00
113 Rogers Hornsby 20.00 50.00
114 Tony Gwynn 15.00 40.00
115 Tony Gwynn 15.00 40.00
116 Ozzie Smith 20.00 50.00
117 Ozzie Smith 20.00 50.00
118 Stan Musial 15.00 40.00
119 Stan Musial 15.00 40.00
120 George Sisler 30.00 60.00
121 Roy Campanella 15.00 40.00
122 Roy Campanella 15.00 40.00
123 Jim Palmer 10.00 25.00
124 Jim Palmer 10.00 25.00
125 Ryan Braun 10.00 25.00
126 Ryan Braun 10.00 25.00
127 Johnny Mize 10.00 25.00
128 Johnny Mize 10.00 25.00
129 Ryne Sandberg 12.50 30.00
130 Ryne Sandberg 12.50 30.00
131 Robin Yount 12.50 30.00
132 Robin Yount 12.50 30.00
133 Juan Marichal 15.00 40.00
134 Juan Marichal 15.00 40.00
135 Alex Rodriguez 30.00 60.00
136 Alex Rodriguez 30.00 60.00

2009 Topps Sterling Career Chronicles Relics Triple

OVERALL MEM ODDS 1:1
STATED PRINT RUN 25 SER.#'d SETS
ALL VARIATIONS PRICED EQUALLY
10 PRINT RUN 10 SER.#'d SETS
NO 10 PRICING DUE TO SCARCITY
SS PRINT RUN 1 SER.#'d SET
NO SS PRICING DUE TO SCARCITY
1 Babe Ruth 150.00 300.00
2 Babe Ruth 150.00 300.00
3 Babe Ruth 150.00 300.00
4 Ichiro Suzuki 20.00 50.00
5 Ichiro Suzuki 20.00 50.00
6 Ichiro Suzuki 20.00 50.00
7 Jackie Robinson 30.00 60.00
8 Jackie Robinson 30.00 60.00
9 Jackie Robinson 30.00 60.00
10 Cal Ripken Jr. 20.00 50.00
11 Cal Ripken Jr. 20.00 50.00
12 Cal Ripken Jr. 20.00 50.00
13 David Ortiz 6.00 15.00
14 David Ortiz 6.00 15.00
15 David Ortiz 6.00 15.00
16 Vladimir Guerrero 6.00 15.00
17 Vladimir Guerrero 6.00 15.00
18 Vladimir Guerrero 6.00 15.00
19 Reggie Jackson 12.50 30.00
20 Reggie Jackson 12.50 30.00
21 Reggie Jackson 12.50 30.00
22 Prince Fielder 10.00 25.00
23 Prince Fielder 10.00 25.00
24 Chase Utley 15.00 40.00
25 Chase Utley 15.00 40.00
26 Francisco Rodriguez 8.00 20.00
27 Francisco Rodriguez 8.00 20.00
28 Lou Brock 15.00 40.00
29 Lou Brock 15.00 40.00
30 Carl Yastrzemski 10.00 25.00
31 Carl Yastrzemski 10.00 25.00
32 Carl Yastrzemski 10.00 25.00
33 Jimmie Foxx 20.00 50.00
34 Jimmie Foxx 20.00 50.00
35 Eddie Mathews 15.00 40.00
36 Eddie Mathews 15.00 40.00
37 Yogi Berra 15.00 40.00
38 Yogi Berra 15.00 40.00
39 Yogi Berra 15.00 40.00
40 Mike Schmidt 10.00 25.00
41 Mike Schmidt 10.00 25.00
42 Mike Schmidt 10.00 25.00
43 Tim Lincecum 15.00 40.00
44 Tim Lincecum 15.00 40.00
45 Tim Lincecum 15.00 40.00
46 Mark Teixeira 10.00 25.00
47 Mark Teixeira 10.00 25.00
48 Ernie Banks 10.00 25.00
49 Ernie Banks 10.00 25.00
50 Ernie Banks 10.00 25.00
51 Joe Morgan 8.00 20.00
52 Joe Morgan 8.00 20.00
53 Al Kaline 15.00 40.00
54 Al Kaline 15.00 40.00
55 Carlos Beltran 8.00 20.00
56 Carlos Beltran 8.00 20.00
57 Mel Ott 15.00 40.00
58 Mel Ott 15.00 40.00
59 Mel Ott 15.00 40.00
60 Mickey Mantle 50.00 100.00
61 Mickey Mantle 50.00 100.00
62 Mickey Mantle 50.00 100.00
63 Albert Pujols 15.00 40.00
64 Albert Pujols 15.00 40.00
65 Albert Pujols 15.00 40.00
66 Chipper Jones 12.50 30.00
67 Chipper Jones 12.50 30.00
68 Daisuke Matsuzaka 8.00 20.00
69 Daisuke Matsuzaka 8.00 20.00
70 Daisuke Matsuzaka 8.00 20.00
71 Carlos Delgado 8.00 20.00
72 Carlos Delgado 8.00 20.00
73 Joba Chamberlain 8.00 20.00
74 Joba Chamberlain 8.00 20.00
75 Joba Chamberlain 8.00 20.00
76 Dennis Eckersley 8.00 20.00
77 Dennis Eckersley 8.00 20.00
78 Luis Aparicio 10.00 25.00
79 Luis Aparicio 10.00 25.00
80 CC Sabathia 10.00 25.00
81 CC Sabathia 10.00 25.00
82 Evan Longoria 12.50 30.00
83 Evan Longoria 12.50 30.00
84 Honus Wagner 60.00 120.00
85 Honus Wagner 60.00 120.00
86 Honus Wagner 60.00 120.00
87 Ryan Howard 12.50 30.00
88 Ryan Howard 12.50 30.00
89 Ryan Howard 12.50 30.00
90 Mariano Rivera 12.50 30.00
91 Mariano Rivera 12.50 30.00
92 Mariano Rivera 12.50 30.00
93 Ty Cobb 40.00 80.00
94 Ty Cobb 40.00 80.00
95 Ty Cobb 40.00 80.00
96 Nolan Ryan 20.00 50.00
97 Nolan Ryan 20.00 50.00
98 Nolan Ryan 20.00 50.00
99 Lou Gehrig 75.00 150.00
100 Lou Gehrig 75.00 150.00
101 Lou Gehrig 75.00 150.00
102 Dale Murphy 8.00 20.00
103 Dale Murphy 8.00 20.00
104 Dale Murphy 8.00 20.00
105 Eddie Murray 12.50 30.00
106 Eddie Murray 12.50 30.00
107 Don Mattingly 12.50 30.00
108 Don Mattingly 12.50 30.00
109 Don Mattingly 12.50 30.00
110 Johnny Bench 10.00 25.00
111 Johnny Bench 10.00 25.00
112 Johnny Bench 10.00 25.00
113 Joe Mauer 15.00 40.00
114 Joe Mauer 15.00 40.00
115 Dave Winfield 10.00 25.00
116 Dave Winfield 10.00 25.00
117 David Wright 10.00 25.00
118 David Wright 10.00 25.00
119 Carlton Fisk 10.00 25.00
120 Carlton Fisk 10.00 25.00
121 Frank Robinson 6.00 15.00
122 Frank Robinson 6.00 15.00
123 Frank Robinson 6.00 15.00
124 Johan Santana 8.00 20.00
125 Johan Santana 8.00 20.00
126 Duke Snider 12.50 30.00
127 Duke Snider 12.50 30.00
128 Bob Gibson 8.00 20.00
129 Bob Gibson 8.00 20.00
130 Bob Gibson 8.00 20.00
131 Tom Seaver 8.00 20.00
132 Tom Seaver 8.00 20.00
133 Tom Seaver 8.00 20.00
134 Warren Spahn 15.00 40.00
135 Warren Spahn 15.00 40.00
136 Paul Molitor 10.00 25.00
137 Paul Molitor 10.00 25.00
138 Orlando Cepeda 8.00 20.00
139 Orlando Cepeda 8.00 20.00
140 Roger Maris 30.00 60.00
141 Roger Maris 30.00 60.00
142 Roger Maris 30.00 60.00
143 Tris Speaker 20.00 50.00
144 Tris Speaker 20.00 50.00
145 Tris Speaker 20.00 50.00
146 Manny Ramirez 10.00 25.00
147 Manny Ramirez 10.00 25.00
148 Manny Ramirez 10.00 25.00
149 Hank Greenberg 20.00 50.00
150 Hank Greenberg 20.00 50.00
151 Rogers Hornsby 15.00 40.00
152 Rogers Hornsby 15.00 40.00
153 Rogers Hornsby 15.00 40.00
154 Tony Gwynn 15.00 40.00
155 Tony Gwynn 15.00 40.00
156 Ozzie Smith 15.00 40.00
157 Ozzie Smith 15.00 40.00
158 Ozzie Smith 15.00 40.00
159 Stan Musial 15.00 40.00
160 Stan Musial 15.00 40.00
161 Stan Musial 15.00 40.00
162 George Sisler 20.00 40.00
163 George Sisler 20.00 50.00
164 George Sisler 20.00 50.00
165 Roy Campanella 12.50 30.00
166 Roy Campanella 12.50 30.00
167 Roy Campanella 12.50 30.00
168 Jim Palmer 10.00 25.00
169 Jim Palmer 10.00 25.00
170 Ryan Braun 10.00 25.00
171 Ryan Braun 10.00 25.00
172 Johnny Mize 10.00 25.00
173 Johnny Mize 10.00 25.00
174 Ryne Sandberg 10.00 25.00
175 Ryne Sandberg 10.00 25.00
176 Ryne Sandberg 10.00 25.00
177 Robin Yount 12.50 30.00
178 Robin Yount 12.50 30.00
179 Juan Marichal 15.00 40.00
180 Juan Marichal 15.00 40.00
181 Alex Rodriguez 20.00 50.00
182 Alex Rodriguez 20.00 50.00
183 Alex Rodriguez 20.00 50.00

2009 Topps Sterling Jumbo Swatch Relic Autographs

OVERALL AUTO ODDS 1:1
STATED PRINT RUN 10 SER.#'d SETS
NO PRICING DUE TO SCARCITY

2010 Topps Sterling

COMMON CARD .75 2.00
COMMON RC 1.50 4.00
THREE BASE CARDS PER BOX
STATED PRINT RUN 250 SER.#'d SETS
1 Honus Wagner 2.00 5.00
2 Babe Ruth 5.00 12.00
3 Babe Ruth 5.00 12.00
4 Lou Gehrig 4.00 10.00
5 Christy Mathewson 2.00 5.00
6 Starlin Castro RC 4.00 10.00
7 Mickey Mantle 6.00 15.00
8 Carl Yastrzemski 3.00 8.00
9 Clayton Kershaw 4.00 10.00
10 Cal Ripken Jr. 6.00 15.00
11 Willie McCovey 1.25 3.00
12 Johnny Podres .75 2.00
13 Curt Schilling 1.25 3.00
14 Ernie Banks 2.00 5.00
15 Thurman Munson 2.00 5.00
16 Reggie Jackson 1.25 3.00
17 Reggie Jackson 1.25 3.00
18 Reggie Jackson 1.25 3.00
19 Tony Gwynn 2.00 5.00
20 Mike Schmidt 3.00 8.00
21 Ian Kinsler 1.25 3.00
22 Jason Heyward 3.00 8.00
23 Wade Boggs 1.25 3.00
24 Ryan Braun 1.25 3.00
25 Eddie Mathews 2.00 5.00
26 Chase Utley 1.25 3.00
27 Manny Ramirez 2.00 5.00
28 Manny Ramirez 2.00 5.00
29 Manny Ramirez 2.00 5.00
30 Ty Cobb 3.00 8.00
31 Ty Cobb 3.00 8.00
32 Steve Carlton 1.25 3.00
33 Steve Carlton 1.25 3.00
34 Frank Thomas 2.00 5.00
35 Hank Greenberg 2.00 5.00
36 Red Schoendienst 1.25 3.00
37 Stephen Strasburg RC 12.00 30.00
38 Fergie Jenkins 1.25 3.00
39 Roy Campanella 2.00 5.00
40 Mel Ott 2.00 5.00
41 Brooks Robinson 1.25 3.00
42 Jackie Robinson 2.00 5.00
43 Larry Walker 1.25 3.00
44 Juan Marichal 1.25 3.00
45 Bob Gibson 1.25 3.00
46 Duke Snider 1.25 3.00
47 Kevin Youkilis .75 2.00
48 Mike Piazza 2.00 5.00
49 Mike Piazza 2.00 5.00
50 Albert Pujols 2.50 6.00
51 Ichiro Suzuki 2.50 6.00
52 Robin Yount 2.00 5.00
53 Ozzie Smith 2.50 6.00
54 Ozzie Smith 2.50 6.00
55 Tim Lincecum 1.25 3.00
56 Paul Molitor 2.00 5.00
57 Paul Molitor 2.00 5.00
58 Rickey Henderson 2.00 5.00
59 Rickey Henderson 2.00 5.00
60 Joe Mauer 1.50 4.00
61 Willie Stargell 1.25 3.00
62 Joe Morgan 1.25 3.00
63 Johnny Mize 1.25 3.00
64 Johnny Mize 1.25 3.00
65 Johnny Mize 1.25 3.00
66 Whitey Ford 1.25 3.00
67 Carlton Fisk 1.25 3.00
68 Carlton Fisk 1.25 3.00
69 Harmon Killebrew 2.00 5.00
70 Jimmie Foxx 2.00 5.00
71 Jimmie Foxx 2.00 5.00
72 Bernie Williams 1.25 3.00
73 Justin Upton 1.25 3.00
74 Dale Murphy 2.00 5.00
75 Alex Rodriguez 2.50 6.00
76 Alex Rodriguez 2.50 6.00
77 Alex Rodriguez 2.50 6.00
78 Al Kaline 2.00 5.00
79 Justin Morneau 1.25 3.00
80 Yogi Berra 2.00 5.00
81 Dennis Eckersley 1.25 3.00

82 David Ortiz 2.00 5.00
83 Barry Larkin 1.25 3.00
84 Chipper Jones 2.00 5.00
85 Cy Young 2.00 5.00
86 Roberto Alomar 1.25 3.00
87 Tris Speaker 1.25 3.00
88 Eddie Murray 1.25 3.00
89 Adrian Gonzalez 1.50 4.00
90 Roger Maris 2.00 5.00
91 Roger Maris 2.00 5.00
92 Vladimir Guerrero 1.25 3.00
93 Vladimir Guerrero 1.25 3.00
94 Vladimir Guerrero 1.25 3.00
95 Pee Wee Reese 1.25 3.00
96 Robin Roberts 1.25 3.00
97 Johnny Bench 2.00 5.00
98 Josh Hamilton 1.25 3.00
99 Robinson Cano 1.25 3.00
100 Stan Musial 3.00 8.00
101 Dave Winfield 1.25 3.00
102 Dave Winfield 1.25 3.00
103 Mike Stanton RC 12.00 30.00
104 Orlando Cepeda 1.25 3.00
105 Evan Longoria 1.25 3.00
106 Dustin Pedroia 1.50 4.00
107 Luis Aparicio 1.25 3.00
108 Catfish Hunter 1.25 3.00
109 Bill Mazeroski 1.25 3.00
110 Frank Robinson 1.25 3.00
111 Frank Robinson 1.25 3.00
112 Phil Rizzuto 1.25 3.00
113 Prince Fielder 1.25 3.00
114 Gary Carter 1.25 3.00
115 Ryne Sandberg 4.00 10.00
116 Andre Ethier 1.25 3.00
117 Mark Teixeira 1.25 3.00
118 Mark Teixeira 1.25 3.00
119 Victor Martinez 1.25 3.00
120 George Sisler 1.25 3.00
121 Rod Carew 1.25 3.00
122 CC Sabathia 1.25 3.00
123 Craig Biggio 1.25 3.00
124 David Wright 1.50 4.00
125 Ryan Howard 1.50 4.00
126 Miguel Cabrera 2.00 5.00
127 Don Mattingly 4.00 10.00
128 Bob Feller 1.25 3.00
129 Rogers Hornsby 1.25 3.00
130 Rogers Hornsby 1.25 3.00
131 Greg Maddux 2.50 6.00
132 Greg Maddux 2.50 6.00
133 Ralph Kiner 1.25 3.00
134 Roy Halladay 1.25 3.00
135 Walter Johnson 2.00 5.00
136 Warren Spahn 1.25 3.00
137 Andre Dawson 1.25 3.00
138 Andre Dawson 1.25 3.00
139 Tom Seaver 1.25 3.00
140 Tom Seaver 1.25 3.00
141 Tom Seaver 1.25 3.00
142 Mariano Rivera 2.50 6.00
143 Hanley Ramirez 1.25 3.00
144 Ubaldo Jimenez .75 2.00
145 Jim Palmer 1.25 3.00
146 Monte Irvin 1.25 3.00
147 Nolan Ryan 6.00 15.00
148 Nolan Ryan 6.00 15.00
149 Nolan Ryan 6.00 15.00
150 Nolan Ryan 6.00 15.00

2010 Topps Sterling Framed White

*WHITE VET: .75X TO 2X BASIC
*WHITE RC: .5X TO 1.2X BASIC RC
OVERALL PARALLEL ODDS 1:1
STATED PRINT RUN 50 SER.#'d SETS

2010 Topps Sterling Career Chronicles Relics Five

OVERALL MEM ODDS 1:1
STATED PRINT RUN 25 SER.#'d SETS
ALL VARIATIONS PRICED EQUALLY
10 PRINT RUN 10 SER.#'d SETS
SS PRINT RUN 1 SER.#'d SET
CCR1 Ryan Braun 10.00 25.00
CCR2 Ryan Braun 10.00 25.00
CCR3 Harmon Killebrew 20.00 50.00
CCR4 Harmon Killebrew 20.00 50.00
CCR5 Wade Boggs 12.50 30.00
CCR6 Evan Longoria 12.50 30.00
CCR7 Mickey Mantle 60.00 120.00
CCR8 Mickey Mantle 60.00 120.00
CCR9 Cal Ripken Jr. 30.00 60.00
CCR10 Cal Ripken Jr. 30.00 60.00
CCR11 Yogi Berra 15.00 40.00
CCR12 Yogi Berra 15.00 40.00
CCR13 Roy Halladay 15.00 40.00
CCR14 Roy Halladay 15.00 40.00
CCR15 Joe Mauer 12.50 30.00
CCR16 Joe Mauer 12.50 30.00
CCR17 Rogers Hornsby 20.00 50.00
CCR18 Hank Greenberg 20.00 50.00
CCR19 Albert Pujols 30.00 60.00
CCR20 Albert Pujols 30.00 60.00
CCR21 George Sisler 20.00 50.00
CCR22 George Sisler 20.00 50.00
CCR23 Jackie Robinson 30.00 60.00
CCR24 Jackie Robinson 30.00 60.00
CCR25 Manny Ramirez 15.00 40.00
CCR26 Jimmie Foxx 50.00 100.00
CCR27 Carl Yastrzemski 15.00 40.00
CCR28 Carl Yastrzemski 15.00 40.00
CCR29 Hanley Ramirez 12.50 30.00
CCR30 Hanley Ramirez 12.50 30.00
CCR31 Stan Musial 30.00 60.00
CCR32 Stan Musial 30.00 60.00
CCR33 Nolan Ryan 30.00 60.00
CCR34 Nolan Ryan 30.00 60.00
CCR35 Ty Cobb 60.00 120.00
CCR36 Pee Wee Reese 20.00 50.00
CCR37 Reggie Jackson 12.50 30.00
CCR38 Reggie Jackson 12.50 30.00
CCR39 Mike Schmidt 20.00 50.00
CCR40 Jim Palmer 10.00 25.00
CCR41 Miguel Cabrera 10.00 25.00
CCR42 Whitey Ford 15.00 40.00
CCR43 Honus Wagner 50.00 100.00
CCR44 Honus Wagner 50.00 100.00
CCR45 Frank Robinson 10.00 25.00
CCR46 Roy Campanella 20.00 50.00
CCR47 Alex Rodriguez 10.00 25.00
CCR48 Kevin Youkilis 12.50 30.00
CCR49 Mel Ott 20.00 50.00
CCR50 Tom Seaver 15.00 40.00
CCR51 Warren Spahn 12.50 30.00
CCR52 Roger Maris 30.00 60.00
CCR53 Tim Lincecum 15.00 40.00
CCR54 Tim Lincecum 15.00 40.00
CCR55 Johnny Mize 12.50 30.00
CCR56 Johnny Mize 12.50 30.00
CCR57 Lou Gehrig 75.00 150.00
CCR58 Lou Gehrig 75.00 150.00
CCR59 Ichiro Suzuki 40.00 80.00
CCR60 Ichiro Suzuki 40.00 80.00

2010 Topps Sterling Career Chronicles Relics Quad

OVERALL MEM ODDS 1:1
STATED PRINT RUN 25 SER.#'d SETS
ALL VARIATIONS PRICED EQUALLY
10 PRINT RUN 10 SER.#'d SETS
SS PRINT RUN 1 SER.#'d SET
CCR1 Babe Ruth
CCR2 Babe Ruth
CCR3 Harmon Killebrew 15.00 40.00
CCR4 Harmon Killebrew 15.00 40.00
CCR5 Wade Boggs 10.00 25.00
CCR6 Evan Longoria 10.00 25.00
CCR7 Mickey Mantle 50.00 100.00
CCR8 Mickey Mantle 50.00 100.00
CCR9 Cal Ripken Jr. 20.00 50.00
CCR10 Cal Ripken Jr. 20.00 50.00
CCR11 Yogi Berra 12.50 30.00
CCR12 Yogi Berra 12.50 30.00
CCR13 Roy Halladay 12.50 30.00
CCR14 Roy Halladay 12.50 30.00
CCR15 Joe Mauer 10.00 25.00
CCR16 Joe Mauer 10.00 25.00
CCR17 Rogers Hornsby 15.00 40.00
CCR18 Hank Greenberg 15.00 40.00
CCR19 Albert Pujols 20.00 50.00
CCR20 Albert Pujols 20.00 50.00
CCR21 George Sisler 12.50 30.00
CCR22 George Sisler 12.50 30.00
CCR23 Jackie Robinson 20.00 50.00
CCR24 Jackie Robinson 20.00 50.00
CCR25 Manny Ramirez 12.50 30.00
CCR26 Jimmie Foxx 15.00 40.00
CCR27 Carl Yastrzemski 12.50 30.00
CCR28 Carl Yastrzemski 12.50 30.00
CCR29 Hanley Ramirez 10.00 25.00
CCR30 Hanley Ramirez 10.00 25.00
CCR31 Stan Musial 20.00 50.00
CCR32 Stan Musial 20.00 50.00
CCR33 Nolan Ryan 20.00 50.00
CCR34 Nolan Ryan 20.00 50.00
CCR35 Ty Cobb 40.00 80.00
CCR36 Pee Wee Reese 15.00 40.00
CCR37 Reggie Jackson 10.00 25.00
CCR38 Reggie Jackson 10.00 25.00
CCR39 Mike Schmidt 15.00 40.00
CCR40 Jim Palmer 8.00 20.00
CCR41 Miguel Cabrera 8.00 20.00
CCR42 Whitey Ford 12.50 30.00
CCR43 Honus Wagner 40.00 80.00
CCR44 Honus Wagner 40.00 80.00
CCR45 Frank Robinson 8.00 20.00
CCR46 Roy Campanella 15.00 40.00
CCR47 Alex Rodriguez 12.50 30.00
CCR48 Kevin Youkilis 10.00 25.00
CCR49 Mel Ott 15.00 40.00
CCR50 Tom Seaver 12.50 30.00
CCR51 Warren Spahn 10.00 25.00
CCR52 Roger Maris 20.00 50.00
CCR53 Tim Lincecum 12.50 30.00
CCR54 Tim Lincecum 12.50 30.00
CCR55 Johnny Mize 10.00 25.00
CCR56 Johnny Mize 10.00 25.00
CCR57 Lou Gehrig 60.00 120.00
CCR58 Lou Gehrig 60.00 120.00
CCR59 Ichiro Suzuki 30.00 60.00
CCR60 Ichiro Suzuki 30.00 60.00

2010 Topps Sterling Career Chronicles Relics Triple

OVERALL MEM ODDS 1:1
STATED PRINT RUN 25 SER.#'d SETS
ALL VARIATIONS PRICED EQUALLY
10 PRINT RUN 10 SER.#'d SETS
SS PRINT RUN 1 SER.#'d SET
CCR1 Ryan Braun 8.00 20.00
CCR2 Ryan Braun 8.00 20.00
CCR3 Harmon Killebrew 15.00 40.00
CCR4 Harmon Killebrew 15.00 40.00
CCR5 Wade Boggs 10.00 25.00
CCR6 Evan Longoria 10.00 25.00
CCR7 Mickey Mantle 50.00 100.00
CCR8 Mickey Mantle 50.00 100.00
CCR9 Cal Ripken Jr. 20.00 50.00
CCR10 Cal Ripken Jr. 20.00 50.00
CCR11 Yogi Berra 12.50 30.00
CCR12 Yogi Berra 12.50 30.00
CCR13 Roy Halladay 12.50 30.00
CCR14 Roy Halladay 12.50 30.00
CCR15 Joe Mauer 10.00 25.00
CCR16 Joe Mauer 10.00 25.00
CCR17 Rogers Hornsby 15.00 40.00
CCR18 Hank Greenberg 15.00 40.00
CCR19 Albert Pujols 10.00 25.00
CCR20 Albert Pujols 10.00 25.00
CCR21 George Sisler 12.50 30.00
CCR22 George Sisler 12.50 30.00
CCR23 Jackie Robinson 20.00 50.00
CCR24 Jackie Robinson 20.00 50.00
CCR25 Manny Ramirez 12.50 30.00
CCR26 Jimmie Foxx 15.00 40.00
CCR27 Carl Yastrzemski 12.50 30.00
CCR28 Carl Yastrzemski 12.50 30.00
CCR29 Hanley Ramirez 10.00 25.00
CCR30 Hanley Ramirez 10.00 25.00
CCR31 Stan Musial 20.00 50.00
CCR32 Stan Musial 20.00 50.00
CCR33 Nolan Ryan 20.00 50.00
CCR34 Nolan Ryan 20.00 50.00
CCR35 Ty Cobb 40.00 80.00
CCR36 Pee Wee Reese 15.00 40.00
CCR37 Reggie Jackson 10.00 25.00
CCR38 Reggie Jackson 10.00 25.00
CCR39 Mike Schmidt 15.00 40.00
CCR40 Jim Palmer 8.00 20.00
CCR41 Miguel Cabrera 8.00 20.00
CCR42 Whitey Ford 12.50 30.00
CCR43 Honus Wagner 40.00 80.00
CCR44 Honus Wagner 40.00 80.00
CCR45 Frank Robinson 8.00 20.00
CCR46 Roy Campanella 15.00 40.00
CCR47 Alex Rodriguez 12.50 30.00
CCR48 Kevin Youkilis 10.00 25.00
CCR49 Mel Ott 15.00 40.00
CCR50 Tom Seaver 12.50 30.00
CCR51 Warren Spahn 10.00 25.00
CCR52 Roger Maris 10.00 25.00
CCR53 Tim Lincecum 12.50 30.00
CCR54 Tim Lincecum 12.50 30.00
CCR55 Johnny Mize 10.00 25.00
CCR56 Johnny Mize 10.00 25.00
CCR57 Lou Gehrig 60.00 120.00
CCR58 Lou Gehrig 60.00 120.00
CCR59 Ichiro Suzuki 30.00 60.00
CCR60 Ichiro Suzuki 30.00 60.00

2010 Topps Sterling Legendary Leather Relics Five

OVERALL MEM ODDS 1:1
STATED PRINT RUN 25 SER.#'d SETS
ALL VARIATIONS PRICED EQUALLY
10 PRINT RUN 10 SER.#'d SETS
SS PRINT RUN 1 SER.#'d SET
LLR1 Babe Ruth 125.00 250.00
LLR2 Babe Ruth 125.00 250.00
LLR3 Mike Schmidt 20.00 50.00
LLR4 Mike Schmidt 20.00 50.00
LLR5 Joe Mauer 12.50 30.00
LLR6 Rickey Henderson 40.00 80.00
LLR7 Mickey Mantle 60.00 120.00
LLR8 Mickey Mantle 60.00 120.00
LLR9 Mark Teixeira 12.50 30.00
LLR10 Mark Teixeira 12.50 30.00
LLR11 Carl Yastrzemski 15.00 40.00
LLR12 Carl Yastrzemski 15.00 40.00
LLR13 David Wright 15.00 40.00
LLR14 David Wright 15.00 40.00
LLR15 Bob Gibson 15.00 40.00
LLR16 Bob Gibson 15.00 40.00
LLR17 Pee Wee Reese 20.00 50.00
LLR18 Pee Wee Reese 20.00 50.00
LLR19 Luis Aparicio 10.00 25.00
LLR20 Luis Aparicio 10.00 25.00
LLR21 Roberto Alomar 30.00 60.00
LLR22 Roberto Alomar 30.00 60.00
LLR23 Ernie Banks 12.50 30.00
LLR24 Rogers Hornsby 20.00 50.00
LLR25 Greg Maddux 15.00 40.00
LLR26 Greg Maddux 15.00 40.00
LLR27 Yogi Berra 15.00 40.00
LLR28 Johnny Bench 10.00 25.00
LLR29 Alex Rodriguez 10.00 25.00
LLR30 Dave Winfield 10.00 25.00
LLR31 Tony Gwynn 10.00 25.00
LLR32 Tony Gwynn 10.00 25.00
LLR33 Robinson Cano 15.00 40.00
LLR34 Robinson Cano 15.00 40.00
LLR35 Duke Snider 20.00 50.00
LLR36 Duke Snider 20.00 50.00
LLR37 Barry Larkin 10.00 25.00
LLR38 Barry Larkin 10.00 25.00
LLR39 Evan Longoria 12.50 30.00
LLR40 Evan Longoria 12.50 30.00
LLR41 Joe Morgan 10.00 25.00
LLR42 Roy Campanella 20.00 50.00
LLR43 Craig Biggio 12.50 30.00
LLR44 Craig Biggio 12.50 30.00
LLR45 Brooks Robinson 12.50 30.00
LLR46 Brooks Robinson 12.50 30.00
LLR47 Eddie Murray 12.50 30.00
LLR48 Thurman Munson 10.00 25.00
LLR49 Don Mattingly 20.00 50.00
LLR50 Don Mattingly 20.00 50.00
LLR51 Andre Dawson 12.50 30.00
LLR52 Andre Dawson 12.50 30.00
LLR53 Al Kaline 15.00 40.00
LLR54 Al Kaline 15.00 40.00
LLR55 Albert Pujols 30.00 60.00
LLR56 Albert Pujols 30.00 60.00
LLR57 Ichiro Suzuki 40.00 80.00
LLR58 Ichiro Suzuki 40.00 80.00
LLR59 Ozzie Smith 10.00 25.00
LLR60 Phil Rizzuto 10.00 25.00

2010 Topps Sterling Legendary Leather Relics Quad

OVERALL MEM ODDS 1:1
STATED PRINT RUN 25 SER.#'d SETS
ALL VARIATIONS PRICED EQUALLY
10 PRINT RUN 10 SER.#'d SETS
SS PRINT RUN 1 SER.#'d SET
LLR1 Babe Ruth 100.00 200.00
LLR2 Babe Ruth 100.00 200.00
LLR3 Mike Schmidt 15.00 40.00
LLR4 Mike Schmidt 15.00 40.00
LLR5 Joe Mauer 10.00 25.00
LLR6 Rickey Henderson 30.00 60.00
LLR7 Mickey Mantle 50.00 100.00
LLR8 Mickey Mantle 50.00 100.00
LLR9 Mark Teixeira 10.00 25.00
LLR10 Mark Teixeira 10.00 25.00
LLR11 Carl Yastrzemski 12.50 30.00
LLR12 Carl Yastrzemski 12.50 30.00
LLR13 David Wright 12.50 30.00
LLR14 David Wright 12.50 30.00
LLR15 Bob Gibson 12.50 30.00
LLR16 Bob Gibson 12.50 30.00
LLR18 Pee Wee Reese 15.00 40.00
LLR19 Luis Aparicio 8.00 20.00
LLR20 Luis Aparicio 8.00 20.00
LLR21 Roberto Alomar 20.00 50.00
LLR22 Roberto Alomar 20.00 50.00
LLR23 Ernie Banks 10.00 25.00
LLR24 Rogers Hornsby 15.00 40.00
LLR25 Greg Maddux 12.50 30.00
LLR26 Greg Maddux 12.50 30.00
LLR27 Mike Piazza 10.00 25.00
LLR28 Yogi Berra 12.50 30.00
LLR29 Alex Rodriguez 12.50 30.00
LLR30 Dave Winfield 8.00 20.00
LLR31 Tony Gwynn 12.50 30.00
LLR32 Tony Gwynn 12.50 30.00
LLR33 Robinson Cano 12.50 30.00
LLR34 Robinson Cano 12.50 30.00
LLR35 Duke Snider 15.00 40.00
LLR36 Duke Snider 15.00 40.00
LLR37 Barry Larkin 8.00 20.00
LLR38 Barry Larkin 8.00 20.00
LLR39 Evan Longoria 10.00 25.00
LLR40 Evan Longoria 10.00 25.00
LLR41 Joe Morgan 8.00 20.00
LLR42 Roy Campanella 15.00 40.00
LLR43 Craig Biggio 10.00 25.00
LLR44 Craig Biggio 10.00 25.00
LLR45 Brooks Robinson 10.00 25.00
LLR46 Brooks Robinson 10.00 25.00
LLR47 Eddie Murray 10.00 25.00
LLR48 Thurman Munson 15.00 40.00
LLR49 Don Mattingly 15.00 40.00
LLR50 Don Mattingly 15.00 40.00
LLR51 Andre Dawson 10.00 25.00
LLR52 Andre Dawson 10.00 25.00
LLR53 Al Kaline 12.50 30.00
LLR54 Honus Wagner 40.00 80.00
LLR55 Albert Pujols 20.00 50.00
LLR56 Albert Pujols 20.00 50.00
LLR57 Ichiro Suzuki 30.00 60.00
LLR58 Ichiro Suzuki 30.00 60.00
LLR59 Ozzie Smith 20.00 50.00
LLR60 Phil Rizzuto 15.00 40.00

2010 Topps Sterling Legendary Leather Relics Triple

OVERALL MEM ODDS 1:1
STATED PRINT RUN 25 SER.#'d SETS
ALL VARIATIONS PRICED EQUALLY
10 PRINT RUN 10 SER.#'d SETS
SS PRINT RUN 1 SER.#'d SET
LLR1 Babe Ruth 100.00 200.00
LLR2 Babe Ruth 100.00 200.00
LLR3 Mike Schmidt 15.00 40.00
LLR4 Mike Schmidt 15.00 40.00
LLR5 Joe Mauer 10.00 25.00
LLR6 Rickey Henderson 30.00 60.00
LLR7 Mickey Mantle 50.00 100.00
LLR8 Mickey Mantle 50.00 100.00
LLR9 Mark Teixeira 10.00 25.00
LLR10 Mark Teixeira 10.00 25.00
LLR11 Carl Yastrzemski 12.50 30.00
LLR12 Carl Yastrzemski 12.50 30.00
LLR13 David Wright 12.50 30.00
LLR14 David Wright 12.50 30.00
LLR15 Bob Gibson 12.50 30.00
LLR16 Bob Gibson 12.50 30.00
LLR18 Pee Wee Reese 15.00 40.00
LLR19 Luis Aparicio 8.00 20.00
LLR20 Luis Aparicio 8.00 20.00
LLR21 Roberto Alomar 20.00 50.00
LLR22 Roberto Alomar 20.00 50.00
LLR23 Ernie Banks 10.00 25.00
LLR24 Rogers Hornsby 15.00 40.00
LLR25 Greg Maddux 12.50 30.00
LLR26 Greg Maddux 12.50 30.00
LLR27 Yogi Berra 12.50 30.00
LLR28 Mike Piazza 30.00 60.00
LLR29 Alex Rodriguez 12.50 30.00
LLR30 Dave Winfield 8.00 20.00
LLR31 Tony Gwynn 12.50 30.00
LLR32 Tony Gwynn 12.50 30.00
LLR33 Robinson Cano 12.50 30.00
LLR34 Robinson Cano 12.50 30.00
LLR35 Duke Snider 15.00 40.00
LLR36 Duke Snider 15.00 40.00
LLR37 Barry Larkin 8.00 20.00
LLR38 Barry Larkin 8.00 20.00
LLR39 Evan Longoria 10.00 25.00
LLR40 Evan Longoria 10.00 25.00
LLR41 Joe Morgan 8.00 20.00
LLR42 Roy Campanella 15.00 40.00
LLR43 Craig Biggio 10.00 25.00
LLR44 Craig Biggio 10.00 25.00
LLR45 Brooks Robinson 10.00 25.00
LLR46 Brooks Robinson 10.00 25.00
LLR47 Eddie Murray 10.00 25.00
LLR48 Thurman Munson 15.00 40.00
LLR49 Don Mattingly 15.00 40.00
LLR50 Don Mattingly 15.00 40.00
LLR51 Andre Dawson 10.00 25.00
LLR52 Andre Dawson 10.00 25.00
LLR53 Al Kaline 12.50 30.00
LLR54 Al Kaline 12.50 30.00
LLR55 Albert Pujols 10.00 25.00
LLR56 Albert Pujols 10.00 25.00
LLR57 Ichiro Suzuki 30.00 60.00
LLR58 Ichiro Suzuki 30.00 60.00
LLR59 Ozzie Smith 20.00 50.00
LLR60 Phil Rizzuto 15.00 40.00

2010 Topps Sterling Sterling Stats Relics Six

OVERALL MEM ODDS 1:1
STATED PRINT RUN 25 SER.#'d SETS
ALL VARIATIONS PRICED EQUALLY
10 PRINT RUN 10 SER.#'d SETS
SS PRINT RUN 1 SER.#'d SET
SSR3 Babe Ruth 150.00 300.00
SSR4 Babe Ruth 150.00 300.00
SSR5 Rickey Henderson 40.00 80.00
SSR6 Rickey Henderson 40.00 80.00
SSR7 Cal Ripken Jr. 30.00 60.00
SSR8 Cal Ripken Jr. 30.00 60.00
SSR9 George Sisler 50.00 100.00
SSR10 George Sisler 50.00 100.00
SSR11 Al Kaline 15.00 40.00
SSR12 Al Kaline 15.00 40.00
SSR13 Carl Yastrzemski 15.00 40.00
SSR14 Carl Yastrzemski 15.00 40.00
SSR15 Dale Murphy 12.50 30.00
SSR16 Dale Murphy 12.50 30.00
SSR17 Honus Wagner 50.00 100.00
SSR18 Honus Wagner 50.00 100.00
SSR19 Craig Biggio 12.50 30.00
SSR20 Craig Biggio 12.50 30.00
SSR21 Johnny Mize 12.50 30.00
SSR22 Johnny Mize 12.50 30.00
SSR23 Ryan Braun 10.00 25.00
SSR24 Ryan Braun 10.00 25.00
SSR25 Manny Ramirez 15.00 40.00
SSR26 Manny Ramirez 15.00 40.00
SSR27 Alex Rodriguez 12.50 30.00
SSR28 Alex Rodriguez 12.50 30.00
SSR29 Carlton Fisk 12.50 30.00
SSR30 Carlton Fisk 12.50 30.00
SSR31 Lou Gehrig 75.00 150.00
SSR32 Lou Gehrig 75.00 150.00
SSR33 Ozzie Smith 12.50 30.00
SSR34 Ozzie Smith 12.50 30.00
SSR35 Hank Greenberg 20.00 50.00
SSR36 Hank Greenberg 20.00 50.00
SSR37 Roy Campanella 20.00 50.00
SSR38 Roy Campanella 20.00 50.00
SSR39 Ernie Banks 10.00 25.00
SSR40 Ernie Banks 10.00 25.00
SSR41 Jackie Robinson 30.00 60.00
SSR42 Jackie Robinson 30.00 60.00
SSR43 Phil Rizzuto 20.00 50.00
SSR44 Phil Rizzuto 20.00 50.00
SSR45 Harmon Killebrew 20.00 50.00
SSR46 Harmon Killebrew 20.00 50.00
SSR47 Yogi Berra 15.00 40.00
SSR48 Yogi Berra 15.00 40.00
SSR49 Tom Seaver 10.00 25.00
SSR50 Tom Seaver 10.00 25.00
SSR51 Rogers Hornsby 40.00 80.00
SSR52 Rogers Hornsby 40.00 80.00
SSR53 Dustin Pedroia 20.00 50.00
SSR54 Dustin Pedroia 20.00 50.00
SSR55 Reggie Jackson 12.50 30.00
SSR56 Reggie Jackson 12.50 30.00
SSR57 Miguel Cabrera 10.00 25.00
SSR58 Miguel Cabrera 10.00 25.00
SSR59 Mel Ott 20.00 50.00
SSR60 Mel Ott 20.00 50.00
SSR61 Roger Maris 30.00 60.00
SSR62 Roger Maris 30.00 60.00
SSR63 Prince Fielder 8.00 20.00
SSR64 Prince Fielder 8.00 20.00
SSR65 Eddie Murray 12.50 30.00
SSR66 Eddie Murray 12.50 30.00
SSR67 Johnny Bench 12.50 30.00
SSR68 Johnny Bench 12.50 30.00
SSR69 Frank Robinson 10.00 25.00
SSR70 Frank Robinson 10.00 25.00
SSR71 Greg Maddux 15.00 40.00
SSR72 Greg Maddux 15.00 40.00
SSR73 Ty Cobb 60.00 120.00
SSR74 Ty Cobb 60.00 120.00
SSR75 Mike Schmidt 10.00 25.00
SSR76 Mike Schmidt 10.00 25.00
SSR77 Warren Spahn 40.00 80.00
SSR78 Warren Spahn 40.00 80.00
SSR79 Bob Gibson 15.00 40.00
SSR80 Bob Gibson 15.00 40.00
SSR81 Mark Teixeira 12.50 30.00
SSR82 Mark Teixeira 12.50 30.00
SSR83 Andre Dawson 12.50 30.00
SSR84 Andre Dawson 12.50 30.00
SSR85 Ryan Howard 15.00 40.00
SSR86 Ryan Howard 15.00 40.00
SSR87 Brooks Robinson 12.50 30.00
SSR88 Brooks Robinson 12.50 30.00
SSR89 Joe Morgan 10.00 25.00
SSR90 Joe Morgan 10.00 25.00
SSR91 Roy Halladay 15.00 40.00
SSR92 Roy Halladay 15.00 40.00
SSR93 Stan Musial 30.00 60.00
SSR94 Stan Musial 30.00 60.00
SSR95 Evan Longoria 12.50 30.00
SSR96 Evan Longoria 12.50 30.00
SSR97 Nolan Ryan 30.00 60.00
SSR98 Nolan Ryan 30.00 60.00
SSR99 Chase Utley 10.00 25.00
SSR100 Chase Utley 10.00 25.00
SSR101 Pee Wee Reese 10.00 25.00
SSR102 Pee Wee Reese 10.00 25.00
SSR103 Jim Palmer 10.00 25.00
SSR104 Jim Palmer 10.00 25.00
SSR105 Dave Winfield 10.00 25.00
SSR106 Dave Winfield 10.00 25.00
SSR107 David Ortiz 8.00 20.00
SSR108 David Ortiz 8.00 20.00
SSR109 Hanley Ramirez 12.50 30.00
SSR110 Hanley Ramirez 12.50 30.00
SSR111 Thurman Munson 20.00 50.00
SSR112 Thurman Munson 20.00 50.00
SSR113 David Wright 15.00 40.00
SSR114 David Wright 15.00 40.00
SSR115 Tim Lincecum 10.00 25.00
SSR116 Tim Lincecum 10.00 25.00
SSR117 Chipper Jones 15.00 40.00
SSR118 Chipper Jones 15.00 40.00
SSR119 Wade Boggs 12.50 30.00
SSR120 Wade Boggs 12.50 30.00
SSR121 Don Mattingly 50.00 100.00
SSR122 Don Mattingly 50.00 100.00
SSR123 Vladimir Guerrero 8.00 20.00
SSR124 Vladimir Guerrero 8.00 20.00
SSR125 Jimmie Foxx 20.00 50.00
SSR126 Jimmie Foxx 20.00 50.00
SSR127 CC Sabathia 8.00 20.00
SSR128 CC Sabathia 8.00 20.00
SSR129 Tony Gwynn 15.00 40.00
SSR130 Tony Gwynn 15.00 40.00
SSR133 Mariano Rivera 15.00 40.00
SSR134 Mariano Rivera 15.00 40.00
SSR135 Duke Snider 10.00 25.00
SSR136 Duke Snider 10.00 25.00
SSR137 Whitey Ford 10.00 25.00
SSR138 Whitey Ford 10.00 25.00
SSR139 Jason Heyward 20.00 50.00
SSR140 Jason Heyward 20.00 50.00

2020 Topps Sterling Sterling Seasons Relic Autographs

STATED ODDS 1:xx HOBBY
PRINT RUNS B/WN 15-25 COPIES PER
NO PRICING ON QTY 15 OR LESS
EXCHANGE DEADLINE 6/30/22
SSARI Ichiro
SSARAJ Aaron Judge
SSARAR Alex Rodriguez
SSARBB Bo Bichette RC EXCH 100.00 250.00
SSARBG Bob Gibson 50.00 120.00
SSARBL Barry Larkin 30.00 80.00
SSARBP Buster Posey
SSARCR Cal Ripken Jr. 75.00 200.00
SSARCS CC Sabathia 25.00 60.00
SSARCY Carl Yastrzemski 60.00 150.00
SSARDM Dale Murphy 30.00 80.00
SSARDW David Wright 30.00 80.00
SSARFT Frank Thomas 60.00 150.00
SSARGS George Springer 20.00 50.00
SSARHA Hank Aaron
SSARHM Hideki Matsui 40.00 100.00
SSARIC Ichiro
SSARJA Jose Altuve 25.00 60.00
SSARJB Jeff Bagwell 40.00 100.00
SSARJd Jacob deGrom 50.00 120.00
SSARJS John Smoltz 30.00 80.00
SSARJV Joey Votto 30.00 80.00
SSARKB Kris Bryant 75.00 200.00
SSARKG Ken Griffey Jr.
SSARMC Miguel Cabrera 60.00 150.00
SSARMM Mark McGwire 40.00 100.00
SSARMS Max Scherzer
SSARMT Mike Trout
SSARPA Pete Alonso 75.00 200.00
SSARPM Pedro Martinez
SSARRA Ronald Acuna Jr. 100.00 250.00
SSARRH Rickey Henderson 75.00 200.00
SSARRJ Randy Johnson
SSARRS Ryne Sandberg 60.00 150.00
SSARRY Robin Yount 30.00 80.00
SSARSC Steve Carlton 30.00 80.00
SSARSO Shohei Ohtani
SSARTG Tom Glavine 30.00 80.00
SSARTL Tim Lincecum
SSARVG Vladimir Guerrero 40.00 100.00
SSARWB Wade Boggs 30.00 80.00
SSARWC Will Clark 30.00 80.00
SSARYA Yordan Alvarez RC 60.00 150.00
SSARAAQ Aristides Aquino RC 40.00 100.00
SSARCYE Christian Yelich 50.00 120.00
SSARDMA Don Mattingly 50.00 120.00
SSARDOR David Ortiz 50.00 120.00
SSARJBE Johnny Bench 50.00 120.00
SSARJSO Juan Soto 100.00 250.00
SSARKGR Ken Griffey Jr.
SSARMMC Mark McGwire 40.00 100.00
SSARMSC Mike Schmidt 60.00 150.00
SSARMTR Mike Trout
SSARNRY Nolan Ryan 100.00 250.00
SSARPMA Pedro Martinez
SSARRAL Roberto Alomar 30.00 80.00
SSARRCA Rod Carew 40.00 100.00
SSARRCL Roger Clemens
SSARRHE Rickey Henderson 75.00 200.00
SSARRJA Reggie Jackson
SSARRJO Randy Johnson
SSARVGR Vladimir Guerrero Jr. 40.00 100.00

2020 Topps Sterling Sterling Strikes Relic Autographs

STATED ODDS 1:xx HOBBY
PRINT RUNS B/WN 15-25 COPIES PER
NO PRICING ON QTY 15 OR LESS
EXCHANGE DEADLINE 6/30/22
STARAP Andy Pettitte 30.00 80.00
STARBG Bob Gibson 10.00 25.00
STARBM Brendan McKay 15.00 40.00
STARCC CC Sabathia 25.00 60.00
STARCS Chris Sale 25.00 60.00
STARDM Dustin May 75.00 200.00
STARJd Jacob deGrom 50.00 120.00
STARJL Jesus Luzardo 15.00 40.00
STARJS John Smoltz 30.00 80.00
STARMR Mariano Rivera
STARMT Masahiro Tanaka 50.00 120.00
STARNR Nolan Ryan
STARRJ Randy Johnson
STARSC Steve Carlton 30.00 80.00
STARSO Shohei Ohtani
STARTG Tom Glavine 30.00 80.00
STARTL Tim Lincecum 60.00 150.00
STARWB Walker Buehler 40.00 100.00
STARCKE Clayton Kershaw
STARMSC Max Scherzer
STARPMA Pedro Martinez
STARRCL Roger Clemens
STARRJO Randy Johnson

2020 Topps Sterling Sterling Swings Relic Autographs

STATED ODDS 1:xx HOBBY
PRINT RUNS B/WN 15-25 COPIES PER
NO PRICING ON QTY 15 OR LESS
EXCHANGE DEADLINE 6/30/22
SWARAA Aristides Aquino 40.00 100.00
SWARAK Al Kaline
SWARBL Barry Larkin 30.00 80.00
SWARBP Buster Posey
SWARCJ Chipper Jones 75.00 200.00
SWARCR Cal Ripken Jr. 75.00 200.00
SWARCY Christian Yelich 50.00 120.00
SWARDM Don Mattingly 50.00 120.00
SWARDO David Ortiz 50.00 120.00
SWAREM Edgar Martinez 30.00 80.00
SWARGL Gavin Lux 100.00 250.00
SWARGS George Springer 20.00 50.00
SWARHA Hank Aaron
SWARHM Hideki Matsui 40.00 100.00
SWARJB Jeff Bagwell 40.00 100.00
SWARJS Juan Soto 100.00 250.00
SWARJV Joey Votto 30.00 80.00
SWARMC Miguel Cabrera 60.00 150.00
SWARMM Mark McGwire 40.00 100.00
SWARMT Mike Trout
SWARNA Nolan Arenado 60.00 150.00
SWARPA Pete Alonso 75.00 200.00
SWARPG Paul Goldschmidt 30.00 80.00
SWARRA Roberto Alomar 30.00 80.00
SWARRC Rod Carew 40.00 100.00
SWARRD Rafael Devers 25.00 60.00
SWARRS Ryne Sandberg 60.00 150.00
SWARRY Robin Yount 30.00 80.00
SWARSO Shohei Ohtani
SWARVG Vladimir Guerrero 40.00 100.00

SWARWB Wade Boggs 30.00 80.00
SWARWC Will Clark 30.00 80.00
SWARYA Yordan Alvarez 60.00 150.00
SWARARI Anthony Rizzo 40.00 100.00
SWARBBI Bo Bichette 100.00 250.00
SWARCYA Carl Yastrzemski 60.00 150.00
SWARDMU Dale Murphy 30.00 80.00
SWARDWR David Wright 30.00 80.00
SWARFTH Frank Thomas 60.00 150.00
SWARGTO Gleyber Torres 200.00 500.00
SWARJAL Jose Altuve 25.00 60.00
SWARJBE Johnny Bench 50.00 120.00
SWARKBR Kris Bryant
SWARMSC Mike Schmidt 60.00 150.00
SWARRAJ Ronald Acuna Jr. 100.00 250.00
SWARRHE Rickey Henderson 75.00 200.00
SWARRHO Rhys Hoskins 40.00 100.00
SWARVGJ Vladimir Guerrero Jr. 40.00 100.00

2011 Topps Tier One

COMMON CARD (1-100) .60 1.50
COMMON RC (1-100) .60 1.50
STATED PRINT RUN 799 SER.#'d SETS
1 Joe DiMaggio 3.00 8.00
2 Derek Jeter 4.00 10.00
3 Babe Ruth 4.00 10.00
4 Lou Gehrig 3.00 8.00
5 Ty Cobb 2.50 6.00
6 Stan Musial 2.50 6.00
7 Mickey Mantle 5.00 12.00
8 Ryan Braun 1.00 2.50
9 Roger Maris 1.50 4.00
10 Albert Pujols 2.00 5.00
11 Luis Aparicio 1.00 2.50
12 Starlin Castro 1.00 2.50
13 Alex Rodriguez 2.00 5.00
14 Justin Verlander 1.50 4.00
15 Thurman Munson 1.50 4.00
16 Cliff Lee 1.00 2.50
17 Matt Holliday 1.50 4.00
18 Clayton Kershaw 3.00 8.00
19 Tony Gwynn 1.50 4.00
20 Frank Robinson 1.00 2.50
21 Paul O'Neill 1.00 2.50
22 Jim Palmer 1.00 2.50
23 Don Mattingly 3.00 8.00
24 Rickey Henderson 1.50 4.00
25 Matt Kemp 1.25 3.00
26 Chipper Jones 1.50 4.00
27 Juan Marichal 1.00 2.50
28 Bert Blyleven 1.00 2.50
29 Mark Teixeira 1.00 2.50
30 Johnny Mize 1.00 2.50
31 Dustin Pedroia 1.25 3.00
32 Sandy Koufax 3.00 8.00
33 Eddie Murray 1.00 2.50
34 Nolan Ryan 5.00 12.00
35 Frank Thomas 1.50 4.00
36 Michael Pineda RC 1.50 4.00
37 Jose Reyes 1.00 2.50
38 Buster Posey 2.00 5.00
39 Roy Campanella 1.50 4.00
40 Mel Ott 1.50 4.00
41 Tom Seaver 1.00 2.50
42 Jackie Robinson 1.50 4.00
43 Prince Fielder 1.00 2.50
44 Hank Aaron 3.00 8.00
45 Bob Gibson 1.00 2.50
46 Ryne Sandberg 3.00 8.00
47 Duke Snider 1.00 2.50
48 Joe Morgan 1.00 2.50
49 Tim Lincecum 1.00 2.50
50 Walter Johnson 1.50 4.00
51 Ichiro Suzuki 2.00 5.00
52 Cole Hamels 1.25 3.00
53 Zach Britton RC 1.50 4.00
54 Carl Crawford 1.00 2.50
55 Johnny Bench 1.50 4.00
56 Adrian Gonzalez 1.25 3.00
57 Paul Konerko 1.00 2.50
58 Anthony Rizzo RC 6.00 15.00
59 Felix Hernandez 1.00 2.50
60 Jimmie Foxx 1.50 4.00
61 Troy Tulowitzki 1.50 4.00
62 Jay Bruce 1.00 2.50
63 Mariano Rivera 2.00 5.00
64 Roberto Alomar 1.00 2.50
65 Willie McCovey 1.00 2.50
66 Ryan Howard 1.25 3.00
67 Mike Moustakas RC 1.50 4.00
68 Andre Dawson 1.00 2.50
69 Jose Bautista 1.00 2.50
70 Rogers Hornsby 1.00 2.50
71 Ozzie Smith 2.00 5.00
72 Carlton Fisk 1.00 2.50
73 Hunter Pence 1.00 2.50
74 Justin Upton 1.00 2.50
75 Robinson Cano 1.00 2.50
76 Brian Wilson 1.50 4.00
77 CC Sabathia 1.00 2.50
78 Hanley Ramirez 1.00 2.50
79 David Ortiz 1.50 4.00
80 Cal Ripken Jr. 5.00 12.00
81 Barry Larkin 1.00 2.50
82 Roy Halladay 1.00 2.50
83 Tris Speaker 1.00 2.50
84 David Wright 1.25 3.00
85 Brooks Robinson 1.00 2.50
86 Paul Molitor 1.50 4.00
87 Andrew McCutchen 1.50 4.00
88 Reggie Jackson 1.00 2.50
89 Evan Longoria 1.00 2.50
90 Christy Mathewson 1.50 4.00
91 Pee Wee Reese 1.00 2.50
92 Dustin Ackley RC 1.00 2.50
93 Carlos Gonzalez 1.00 2.50
94 Ryan Zimmerman 1.00 2.50
95 Mike Schmidt 2.50 6.00
96 Miguel Cabrera 1.50 4.00
97 Joe Mauer 1.25 3.00
98 Josh Hamilton 1.00 2.50
99 Honus Wagner 1.50 4.00
100 Eric Hosmer RC 4.00 10.00

2011 Topps Tier One Black

*BLACK VET: 1X TO 2.5X BASIC VET
*BLACK RC: 1X TO 2.5X BASIC RC
STATED ODDS 1:11 BOXES
STATED PRINT RUN 50 SER.#'d SETS

2011 Topps Tier One Blue

*BLUE VET: .75X TO 2X BASIC VET
*BLUE RC: .75X TO 2X BASIC RC
STATED ODDS 1:6 BOXES
STATED PRINT RUN 199 SER.#'d SETS

2011 Topps Tier One Crowd Pleaser Autographs

OVERALL AUTO ODDS 2:1 BOXES
PRINT RUNS B/WN 50-699 COPIES PER
GOLD STATED ODDS 1:18 BOXES
GOLD STATED PRINT RUN 25 SER.#'d SETS
NO GOLD PRICING DUE TO SCARCITY
EXCHANGE DEADLINE 11/30/2014
AB Albert Belle/75 6.00 15.00
AE Andre Ethier EXCH 3.00 8.00
AJ Adam Jones/75 10.00 25.00
AK Al Kaline/50 25.00 50.00
AL Adam Lind/649 3.00 8.00
AP Angel Pagan/499 4.00 10.00
AR Aramis Ramirez/50 6.00 15.00
BB Bert Blyleven/50 15.00 40.00
BBU Billy Butler EXCH 10.00 25.00
BG Brett Gardner EXCH 15.00 40.00
BJU B.J. Upton/75 8.00 20.00
BM Brian McCann/50 5.00 12.00
BP Brandon Phillips/75 10.00 25.00
CB Clay Buchholz/50 8.00 20.00
CC Carl Crawford 6.00 15.00
CG Carlos Gonzalez EXCH 12.00 30.00
CJ Chipper Jones/50 40.00 100.00
CK Clayton Kershaw/75 30.00 80.00
CL Cliff Lee EXCH 30.00 60.00
CY Chris Young/75 6.00 15.00
DM Don Mattingly/50 25.00 60.00
DP Dustin Pedroia/50 12.00 30.00
EA Elvis Andrus/50 5.00 12.00
EM Edgar Martinez/75 12.00 30.00
ES Ervin Santana/549 6.00 15.00
FJ Fergie Jenkins/50 15.00 40.00
GF George Foster/50 5.00 12.00
GG Gio Gonzalez/699 5.00 12.00
HR Hanley Ramirez/50 10.00 25.00
IK Ian Kinsler EXCH 10.00 25.00
IKN Ian Kennedy EXCH 5.00 12.00
JB Jay Bruce/75 3.00 8.00
JC Johnny Cueto/699 3.00 8.00
JJ Josh Johnson/50 4.00 10.00
JM Joe Morgan EXCH 20.00 50.00
JP Jhonny Peralta/699 3.00 8.00
JW Jered Weaver/50 15.00 40.00
LA Luis Aparicio/50 20.00 50.00
MC Matt Cain EXCH 40.00 80.00
MG Matt Garza/75 10.00 25.00
MK Matt Kemp/75 6.00 15.00
ML Mat Latos EXCH 8.00 20.00
OS Ozzie Smith EXCH 30.00 60.00
PM Paul Molitor/50 8.00 20.00
PO Paul O'Neill/75 8.00 20.00
PS Pablo Sandoval/699 8.00 20.00
RA Roberto Alomar/50 30.00 60.00
RB Ryan Braun EXCH 6.00 15.00
RED Red Schoendienst/75 12.00 30.00
RN Ricky Nolasco/699 3.00 8.00
RS Ryne Sandberg/50 40.00 80.00
RZ Ryan Zimmerman/75 8.00 20.00
TC Trevor Cahill/699 4.00 10.00
UJ Ubaldo Jimenez/50 8.00 20.00

2011 Topps Tier One On The Rise Autographs

OVERALL AUTO ODDS 2:1 BOXES
PRINT RUNS B/WN 99-999 COPIES PER
GOLD STATED ODDS 1:18 BOXES
GOLD STATED PRINT RUN 25 SER.#'d SETS
NO GOLD PRICING DUE TO SCARCITY
EXCHANGE DEADLINE 11/30/2014
AC Alex Cobb/999 3.00 8.00
ACH Aroldis Chapman/99 12.00 30.00
ACR Allen Craig/999 3.00 8.00
AJ Austin Jackson/99 8.00 20.00
AM Andrew McCutchen/99 30.00 60.00
AO Alexi Ogando/999 3.00 8.00
AR Anthony Rizzo/999 20.00 50.00
AW Alex White/999 3.00 8.00
BB Brandon Belt/699 3.00 8.00
BBE Brandon Beachy/999 3.00 8.00
BC Brandon Crawford/999 3.00 8.00
BG Brandon Guyer/999 4.00 10.00
BH Brad Hand/999 3.00 8.00
BM Brent Morel/699 3.00 8.00
BW Brett Wallace/399 4.00 10.00
CC Carlos Carrasco/999 6.00 15.00
CJ Chris Johnson/699 5.00 12.00
CK Craig Kimbrel/699 6.00 15.00
CP Carlos Peguero/999 3.00 8.00
CR Colby Rasmus/349 5.00 12.00
CS Carlos Santana/399 3.00 8.00
CSA Chris Sale/599 12.00 30.00
DA Dustin Ackley/399 5.00 12.00
DC David Cooper/999 3.00 8.00
DD Danny Duffy/999 5.00 12.00
DG Dee Gordon/999 6.00 15.00
DGE Dillon Gee/999 4.00 10.00
DH Daniel Hudson/699 6.00 15.00
DS Drew Storen/699 4.00 10.00
DV Danny Valencia/999 4.00 10.00
EH Eric Hosmer/399 15.00 40.00
EN Eduardo Nunez/999 3.00 8.00
ES Eric Sogard/999 3.00 8.00
ET Eric Thames/999 15.00 40.00
FF Freddie Freeman/99 10.00 25.00
FM Fernando Martinez/499 3.00 8.00
GS Gaby Sanchez/399 5.00 12.00
HN Hector Noesi/999 3.00 8.00
JH Jason Heyward/99 6.00 15.00
JHE Jeremy Hellickson EXCH 10.00 25.00
JI Jose Iglesias/499 10.00 25.00
JS Jordan Schafer/999 3.00 8.00
JT Josh Thole/999 3.00 8.00
JZ Jordan Zimmermann/999 6.00 15.00
LF Logan Forsythe/999 3.00 8.00
MB Madison Bumgarner/99 30.00 60.00
MM Mike Minor/699 3.00 8.00
MP Michael Pineda/99 12.00 30.00
MS Mike Stanton EXCH 20.00 50.00
MSC Max Scherzer EXCH 20.00 50.00
MT Mark Trumbo/399 3.00 8.00
RT Ruben Tejada/699 4.00 10.00
SC Starlin Castro/99 12.50 30.00
TC Tyler Colvin/999 3.00 8.00
TR Tyson Ross/999 3.00 8.00
ZB Zach Britton/99 5.00 12.00

2011 Topps Tier One Top Shelf Relics

OVERALL RELIC ODDS 1:1 BOXES
STATED PRINT RUN 399 SER.#'d SETS
EXCHANGE DEADLINE 9/30/2014
TSR1 Ichiro Suzuki 8.00 20.00
TSR2 Roberto Alomar 4.00 10.00
TSR3 Thurman Munson 8.00 20.00
TSR4 Carlton Fisk 4.00 10.00
TSR5 Joe DiMaggio 20.00 50.00
TSR6 Jimmie Foxx 10.00 25.00
TSR7 Rogers Hornsby 12.00 30.00
TSR8 Ryan Braun 4.00 10.00
TSR9 Roy Campanella 6.00 15.00
TSR10 Roy Halladay 6.00 15.00
TSR11 Johnny Mize 8.00 20.00
TSR12 Aramis Ramirez 3.00 8.00
TSR13 Pee Wee Reese 8.00 20.00
TSR14 George Sisler 6.00 15.00
TSR15 Tris Speaker 10.00 25.00
TSR16 Babe Ruth 60.00 120.00
TSR17 Carl Crawford 3.00 8.00
TSR18 Ian Kinsler 3.00 8.00
TSR19 Johnny Bench 6.00 15.00
TSR20 Reggie Jackson 4.00 10.00
TSR21 Carlos Beltran 4.00 10.00
TSR22 Ty Cobb 30.00 60.00
TSR23 Joey Votto 5.00 12.00
TSR24 Jose Reyes 4.00 10.00
TSR25 Cole Hamels 4.00 10.00
TSR26 Rickey Henderson EXCH 6.00 15.00
TSR27 Lou Gehrig 40.00 80.00
TSR28 Jered Weaver 3.00 8.00
TSR29 Paul Molitor 4.00 10.00
TSR30 Tim Lincecum 6.00 15.00
TSR31 David Wright 4.00 10.00
TSR32 Jacoby Ellsbury 4.00 10.00
TSR33 Sandy Koufax 15.00 40.00
TSR34 Dustin Pedroia 4.00 10.00
TSR35 Eddie Murray 4.00 10.00
TSR36 Mickey Mantle 30.00 80.00
TSR37 Stan Musial 12.00 30.00
TSR38 Ubaldo Jimenez 3.00 8.00
TSR39 Paul O'Neill 4.00 10.00
TSR40 Willie McCovey 6.00 15.00
TSR41 Brian McCann 3.00 8.00
TSR42 Albert Pujols 10.00 25.00
TSR43 Don Mattingly 12.00 30.00
TSR44 Hank Aaron 10.00 25.00
TSR45 Brooks Robinson 5.00 12.00
TSR46 Ryne Sandberg EXCH 10.00 25.00
TSR47 Tom Seaver 5.00 12.00
TSR48 Willie Mays 12.00 30.00
TSR49 Chipper Jones 5.00 12.00
TSR50 Cal Ripken Jr. 6.00 15.00

2011 Topps Tier One Top Shelf Relics Dual

STATED ODDS 1:6 BOXES
STATED PRINT RUN 99 SER.#'d SETS
EXCHANGE DEADLINE 9/30/2014
TSR1 Ichiro Suzuki 10.00 25.00
TSR2 Roberto Alomar 5.00 12.00
TSR3 Thurman Munson 15.00 40.00
TSR4 Carlton Fisk 4.00 10.00
TSR5 Joe DiMaggio 20.00 50.00
TSR6 Jimmie Foxx 12.00 30.00
TSR7 Rogers Hornsby 12.00 30.00
TSR8 Ryan Braun 5.00 12.00
TSR9 Roy Campanella 10.00 25.00
TSR10 Roy Halladay 6.00 15.00
TSR11 Johnny Mize 10.00 25.00
TSR12 Aramis Ramirez 4.00 10.00
TSR13 Pee Wee Reese 10.00 25.00
TSR14 George Sisler 8.00 20.00
TSR15 Tris Speaker 12.00 30.00
TSR16 Babe Ruth 75.00 150.00
TSR17 Carl Crawford 6.00 15.00
TSR18 Ian Kinsler 4.00 10.00
TSR19 Johnny Bench 10.00 25.00
TSR20 Reggie Jackson 8.00 20.00
TSR21 Carlos Beltran 4.00 10.00
TSR22 Ty Cobb 40.00 80.00
TSR23 Joey Votto 6.00 15.00
TSR24 Jose Reyes 6.00 15.00
TSR25 Cole Hamels 4.00 10.00
TSR26 Rickey Henderson EXCH 8.00 20.00
TSR27 Lou Gehrig 30.00 60.00
TSR28 Jered Weaver 4.00 10.00
TSR29 Paul Molitor 6.00 15.00
TSR30 Tim Lincecum 8.00 20.00
TSR31 David Wright 5.00 12.00
TSR32 Jacoby Ellsbury 10.00 25.00
TSR33 Sandy Koufax 40.00 80.00
TSR34 Dustin Pedroia 8.00 20.00
TSR35 Eddie Murray 8.00 20.00
TSR36 Mickey Mantle 30.00 60.00
TSR37 Stan Musial 8.00 20.00
TSR38 Ubaldo Jimenez 4.00 10.00
TSR39 Paul O'Neill 6.00 15.00
TSR40 Willie McCovey 6.00 15.00
TSR41 Brian McCann 5.00 12.00
TSR42 Albert Pujols 12.00 30.00
TSR43 Don Mattingly 12.00 30.00
TSR44 Hank Aaron 20.00 50.00
TSR45 Brooks Robinson 12.00 30.00
TSR46 Ryne Sandberg EXCH 10.00 25.00
TSR47 Tom Seaver 8.00 20.00
TSR48 Willie Mays 10.00 25.00
TSR49 Chipper Jones 10.00 25.00
TSR50 Cal Ripken Jr. 8.00 20.00

2011 Topps Tier One Top Tier Autographs

STATED ODDS 1:13 BOXES
PRINT RUNS B/WN 99-199 COPIES PER
PACQUIAO NOT SERIAL NUMBERED
GOLD STATED ODDS 1:120 BOXES
GOLD PRINT RUN B/WN 10-25 COPIES PER
NO GOLD PRICING DUE TO SCARCITY
EXCHANGE DEADLINE 11/30/2014
AG Adrian Gonzalez/99 10.00 25.00
AP Albert Pujols EXCH 150.00 300.00
BG Bob Gibson/99 20.00 50.00
CF Carlton Fisk/99 15.00 40.00
EL Evan Longoria/99 20.00 50.00
FH Felix Hernandez/99 20.00 50.00
FR Frank Robinson/99 15.00 40.00
HA Hank Aaron EXCH 150.00 400.00
JB Johnny Bench/99 30.00 60.00
JH Josh Hamilton/99 10.00 25.00
MC Miguel Cabrera/99 50.00 100.00
MP Manny Pacquiao 100.00 200.00
MS Mike Schmidt/99 20.00 50.00
NR Nolan Ryan EXCH 75.00 150.00
PF Prince Fielder/99 10.00 25.00
RH Rickey Henderson/99 50.00 150.00
RH Roy Halladay EXCH 100.00 250.00
RJ Reggie Jackson/99 15.00 40.00
SK Sandy Koufax/199 125.00 250.00
SM Stan Musial/99 60.00 120.00
TG Tony Gwynn/99 60.00 120.00

2012 Topps Tier One Autograph Relics

STATED ODDS 1:11 HOBBY
STATED PRINT RUN 99 SER.#'d SETS
EXCHANGE DEADLINE 05/31/2015
CC Carl Crawford 6.00 15.00
CH Chris Heisey 6.00 15.00
DG Dee Gordon 10.00 25.00
DU Dan Uggla 10.00 25.00
EL Evan Longoria 10.00 25.00
GB Gordon Beckham 6.00 15.00
GS Gary Sheffield 6.00 15.00
GST Giancarlo Stanton 25.00 60.00
JHE Jason Heyward 4.00 10.00
JJ Jon Jay 12.50 30.00
JJO Josh Johnson 8.00 20.00
MK Matt Kemp 8.00 20.00
MT Mark Trumbo 12.00 30.00
NF Neftali Feliz 6.00 15.00
PF Prince Fielder 20.00 50.00
PO Paul O'Neill 12.50 30.00
RB Ryan Braun 12.50 30.00
SC Starlin Castro 8.00 20.00
TG Tony Gwynn 30.00 60.00

2012 Topps Tier One Autographs

STATED ODDS 1:21 HOBBY
PRINT RUNS B/WN 50-225 COPIES PER
EXCHANGE DEADLINE 05/31/2015
AP Albert Pujols EXCH 150.00 250.00
CF Carlton Fisk 20.00 50.00
CR Cal Ripken Jr. 75.00 150.00
CY Carl Yastrzemski 30.00 60.00
DM Don Mattingly 50.00 100.00
EB Ernie Banks 30.00 60.00
FR Frank Robinson 30.00 60.00
HA Hank Aaron 150.00 300.00
JB Johnny Bench 30.00 60.00
JH Josh Hamilton 20.00 50.00
KG Ken Griffey Jr. 125.00 250.00
MS Mike Schmidt 50.00 120.00
NR Nolan Ryan 75.00 150.00
RH Roy Halladay 20.00 50.00
RJ Reggie Jackson 30.00 60.00
RS Ryne Sandberg 30.00 60.00
SK Sandy Koufax 200.00 300.00
WMC Willie McCovey 30.00 60.00
YD Yu Darvish 60.00 150.00

2012 Topps Tier One Clear Rookie Reprint Autographs

STATED ODDS 1:82 HOBBY
STATED PRINT RUN 25 SER.#'d SETS
EXCHANGE DEADLINE 05/31/2015
CJ Chipper Jones 300.00 500.00
CR Cal Ripken Jr. 200.00 400.00
CS CC Sabathia 30.00 60.00
DM Don Mattingly 150.00 250.00
EB Ernie Banks 60.00 150.00
JH Josh Hamilton 150.00 250.00
KG Ken Griffey Jr. 300.00 600.00
MC Miguel Cabrera 75.00 200.00
RS Ryne Sandberg 60.00 150.00
WM Willie Mays 200.00 400.00

2012 Topps Tier One Crowd Pleaser Autographs

PRINT RUNS B/WN 50-399 COPIES PER
EXCHANGE DEADLINE 05/31/2015
AB Albert Belle/50 12.00 30.00
AD Andre Dawson/50 10.00 25.00
AE Andre Ethier/50 6.00 15.00
AK Al Kaline/50 20.00 50.00
AL Adam Lind/99 5.00 12.00
ALI Adam Lind/399 5.00 12.00
AM Andrew McCutchen/50 30.00 60.00
AP Andy Pettitte/50 40.00 80.00
AR Aramis Ramirez/75 4.00 10.00
BB Billy Butler/75 4.00 10.00
BG Brett Gardner/245 6.00 15.00
BM Brian McCann/50 10.00 25.00
BP Boog Powell/399 6.00 15.00
BPH Brandon Phillips/75 6.00 15.00
BPO Buster Posey/50 60.00 120.00
BW Billy Williams/50 12.50 30.00
CC Carl Crawford/50 8.00 20.00
CH Cole Hamels/50 12.50 30.00
CJ Chipper Jones/50 50.00 120.00
DP Dustin Pedroia/50 20.00 50.00
DU Dan Uggla/50 8.00 20.00
DW David Wright EXCH 30.00 60.00
EA Elvis Andrus/245 6.00 15.00
EK Ed Kranepool/399 6.00 15.00
EL Evan Longoria/50 20.00 50.00
EM Edgar Martinez/50 12.00 30.00
GF George Foster/75 10.00 25.00
GS Gaby Sanchez/399 4.00 10.00
GSA Gaby Sanchez/399 4.00 10.00
HK Howie Kendrick/245 5.00 12.00
HKE Howie Kendrick/245 5.00 12.00
HR Hanley Ramirez EXCH 10.00 25.00
ID Ike Davis/75 10.00 25.00
JB Jay Bruce/75 4.00 10.00
JC Johnny Cueto/245 6.00 15.00
JCU Johnny Cueto/245 6.00 15.00
JH Joel Hanrahan/399 6.00 15.00
JHA Joel Hanrahan/399 6.00 15.00
JJ Josh Johnson/50 6.00 15.00
JM Joe Mauer/50 20.00 50.00
JMO Jason Motte/399 5.00 12.00
JMT Jason Motte/399 5.00 12.00
JP Jhonny Peralta/245 6.00 15.00
JPE Jhonny Peralta/245 6.00 15.00
JR Jim Rice/75 12.50 30.00
JV Jose Valverde/399 8.00 20.00
JVA Jose Valverde/399 8.00 20.00
LT Luis Tiant/245 6.00 15.00
MB Marlon Byrd/399 4.00 10.00
MBY Marlon Byrd/399 4.00 10.00
MCA Miguel Cabrera/50 75.00 150.00
MGA Matt Garza/75 6.00 15.00
MH Matt Holliday EXCH 20.00 50.00
MK Matt Kemp/50 12.00 30.00
MM Mike Moustakas/75 8.00 20.00
MMO Mike Morse/399 5.00 12.00
MMS Mike Morse/399 5.00 12.00
NC Nelson Cruz/50 10.00 25.00
PF Prince Fielder/50 10.00 25.00
PM Paul Molitor/50 10.00 25.00
PO Paul O'Neill/50 12.00 30.00
RB Ryan Braun/50 20.00 50.00
RC Robinson Cano/50 20.00 50.00
RS Red Schoendienst/75 15.00 40.00
RZ Ryan Zimmerman/50 10.00 25.00
SC Starlin Castro/75 5.00 12.00
THU Tim Hudson/50 10.00 25.00
UJ Ubaldo Jimenez/50 6.00 15.00
WC Will Clark/245 10.00 25.00
WJ Wally Joyner/399 5.00 12.00
YG Yovani Gallardo/50 8.00 20.00

2012 Topps Tier One Crowd Pleaser Autographs White Ink

STATED ODDS 1:10 HOBBY
STATED PRINT RUN 25 SER.#'d SETS
NO PRICING ON MOST DUE TO SCARCITY
EXCHANGE DEADLINE 05/31/2015
AL Adam Lind 8.00 20.00
ALI Adam Lind 8.00 20.00
GS Gaby Sanchez 8.00 20.00
GSA Gaby Sanchez 8.00 20.00
HK Howie Kendrick 10.00 25.00
HKE Howie Kendrick 10.00 25.00
JC Johnny Cueto 15.00 40.00
JCU Johnny Cueto 15.00 40.00
JH Joel Hanrahan 20.00 50.00
JHA Joel Hanrahan 20.00 50.00
JMO Jason Motte 10.00 25.00
JMT Jason Motte 10.00 25.00
JP Jhonny Peralta 10.00 25.00
JPE Jhonny Peralta 10.00 25.00
JV Jose Valverde 15.00 40.00
JVA Jose Valverde 15.00 40.00
MB Marlon Byrd 5.00 12.00
MBY Marlon Byrd 5.00 12.00
MMO Mike Morse 10.00 25.00
MMS Mike Morse 10.00 25.00
PM Paul Molitor 15.00 40.00

2012 Topps Tier One Dual Relics

STATED ODDS 1:7 HOBBY
STATED PRINT RUN 50 SER.#'d SETS
I Ichiro Suzuki 10.00 25.00
AB Adrian Beltre 4.00 10.00
AE Andre Ethier 4.00 10.00
AG Adrian Gonzalez 4.00 10.00
AM Andrew McCutchen 10.00 25.00
AP Albert Pujols 10.00 25.00
APE Andy Pettitte 8.00 20.00
AR Alex Rodriguez 8.00 20.00
AW Adam Wainwright 4.00 10.00
BP Buster Posey 10.00 25.00
BS Bruce Sutter 12.00 30.00
BW Brian Wilson 6.00 15.00
CF Carlton Fisk 5.00 12.00
CJ Chipper Jones 8.00 20.00
CJ2 Chipper Jones 8.00 20.00
CR Cal Ripken Jr. 122.00 30.00
CS CC Sabathia 6.00 15.00
DH Dan Haren 4.00 10.00
DJ Derek Jeter 15.00 40.00
DO David Ortiz 5.00 12.00
DU Dan Uggla 4.00 10.00
DW David Wright 5.00 12.00
EM Eddie Murray 6.00 15.00
FF Freddie Freeman 5.00 12.00
FT Frank Thomas 10.00 25.00
GB George Bell 5.00 12.00
IK Ian Kennedy 4.00 10.00
IKI Ian Kinsler 4.00 10.00
JBR Jay Bruce 8.00 20.00
JE Jacoby Ellsbury 5.00 12.00
JH Jason Heyward 4.00 10.00
JHE Jeremy Hellickson 4.00 10.00
JJ Josh Johnson 4.00 10.00
JL Jon Lester 5.00 12.00
JM Jason Motte 4.00 10.00
JRI Jim Rice 5.00 12.00
JS James Shields 4.00 10.00
JV Justin Verlander 8.00 20.00
JVO Joey Votto 8.00 20.00
KY Kevin Youkilis 5.00 12.00
MC Miguel Cabrera 6.00 15.00
MR Mariano Rivera 8.00 20.00
MT Mark Trumbo 12.00 30.00
MTR Mike Trout 50.00 120.00
MY Michael Young 4.00 10.00
PF Prince Fielder 4.00 10.00
PK Paul Konerko 5.00 12.00
PM Paul Molitor 5.00 12.00
PO Paul O'Neill 10.00 25.00
RCW Rod Carew 5.00 12.00
RH Ryan Howard 5.00 12.00
RO Roy Oswalt 4.00 10.00
RZ Ryan Zimmerman 5.00 12.00
SC Steve Carlton 4.00 10.00
SCA Starlin Castro 4.00 10.00
SS Stephen Strasburg 12.00 30.00
THU Tim Hudson 6.00 15.00
TL Tim Lincecum 6.00 15.00
TT Troy Tulowitzki 6.00 15.00
UJ Ubaldo Jimenez 5.00 12.00
YG Yovanni Gallardo 4.00 10.00

2012 Topps Tier One Elevated Ink

STATED PRINT RUN 250 SER.#'d SETS
DM Devin Mesoraco 6.00 15.00
HI Hisashi Iwakuma 15.00 40.00
JB Jay Bruce 6.00 15.00

2012 Topps Tier One Legends Relics

STATED ODDS 1:28 HOBBY
STATED PRINT RUN 50 SER.#'d SETS
FR Frank Robinson 10.00 25.00
HK Harmon Killebrew 8.00 20.00
JM Joe Morgan 6.00 15.00
LB Lou Brock 6.00 15.00
MM Mickey Mantle 40.00 80.00
MS Mike Schmidt 6.00 15.00
OS Ozzie Smith 12.50 30.00
RC Roberto Clemente 30.00 60.00
RJ Reggie Jackson 6.00 15.00
RS Ryne Sandberg 12.50 30.00
TC Ty Cobb 30.00 60.00
WB Wade Boggs 6.00 15.00
WM Willie McCovey 10.00 25.00
WS Willie Stargell 10.00 25.00
WMA Willie Mays 20.00 50.00

2012 Topps Tier One On The Rise Autographs

PRINT RUNS B/WN 50-395 COPIES PER
EXCHANGE DEADLINE 05/31/2015
AA Alex Avila/235 6.00 15.00
AC Allen Craig/235 8.00 20.00
ACH Aroldis Chapman/75 15.00 40.00
AJO Adam Jones/50 6.00 15.00
AO Alexi Ogando/75 6.00 15.00
AR Anthony Rizzo/235 10.00 25.00
ARI Anthony Rizzo/235 10.00 25.00
BA Brett Anderson/235 5.00 12.00
BAN Brett Anderson/235 5.00 12.00
BBE Brandon Belt/235 6.00 15.00
BH Bryce Harper EXCH 250.00 400.00
BL Brett Lawrie/50 8.00 20.00
BM Brent Morel/235 5.00 12.00
BP Brad Peacock/350 5.00 12.00
BPE Brad Peacock/350 5.00 12.00
BR Ben Revere/235 5.00 12.00
BRE Ben Revere/235 5.00 12.00
CGO Carlos Gonzalez/50 20.00 50.00
CH Chris Heisey/235 5.00 12.00
CHE Chris Heisey/235 5.00 12.00
CK Craig Kimbrel/50 10.00 25.00
CKE Clayton Kershaw/50 20.00 50.00
CR Colby Rasmus/75 3.00 8.00
CS Carlos Santana/50 3.00 8.00
CSA Chris Sale/75 15.00 40.00
DA Dustin Ackley/50 12.50 30.00
DB Darwin Barney/235 6.00 15.00
DBA Daniel Bard/235 5.00 12.00
DBD Daniel Bard/235 5.00 12.00
DE Danny Espinosa/235 3.00 8.00
DGO Dee Gordon/75 5.00 12.00
DH Derek Holland/75 8.00 20.00
DHU Daniel Hudson/235 3.00 8.00
DM Devin Mesoraco/75 6.00 15.00
DME Devin Mesoraco/75 6.00 15.00
DP Drew Pomeranz/75 6.00 15.00
DS Drew Storen/75 6.00 15.00
DST Drew Stubbs/75 8.00 20.00
EH Eric Hosmer/50 15.00 40.00
EN Eduardo Nunez/75 6.00 15.00
ENU Eduardo Nunez/75 6.00 15.00
FF Freddie Freeman/50 12.50 30.00
GB Gordon Beckham EXCH 8.00 20.00
GG Gio Gonzalez/50 15.00 40.00
HN Hector Noesi/315 4.00 10.00
IN Ivan Nova/75 6.00 15.00
INO Ivan Nova/75 6.00 15.00
JA J.P. Arencibia/75 5.00 12.00
JAR J.P. Arencibia/75 5.00 12.00
JDM J.D. Martinez/350 10.00 25.00
JG Johnny Giavotella/395 5.00 12.00
JH Jeremy Hellickson/50 8.00 20.00
JJ Jon Jay/235 6.00 15.00
JK Jason Kipnis/75 6.00 15.00
JMA J.D. Martinez/350 10.00 25.00
JMO Jesus Montero/50 10.00 25.00
JN Jon Niese/235 4.00 10.00
JP Jarrod Parker/235 3.00 8.00
JPA Jimmy Paredes/350 4.00 10.00
JPR Jimmy Paredes/350 4.00 10.00
JR Josh Reddick/350 8.00 20.00
JRE Josh Reddick/350 8.00 20.00
JTE Julio Teheran/235 5.00 12.00
JW Jemile Weeks/235 6.00 15.00
JWA Jordan Walden/75 4.00 10.00
JWE Jemile Weeks/235 5.00 12.00
JZ Jordan Zimmermann/235 6.00 15.00
KS Kyle Seager/235 6.00 15.00
KSE Kyle Seager/395 6.00 15.00
LM Logan Morrison/50 6.00 15.00
MB Madison Bumgarner/50 50.00 100.00
MM Mitch Moreland/350 5.00 12.00
MMO Matt Moore/75 6.00 15.00
MMR Mitch Moreland/350 5.00 12.00
MP Michael Pineda/75 10.00 25.00
MST Giancarlo Stanton/50 20.00 50.00
MT Mark Trumbo/50 6.00 15.00
MTM Mark Trumbo/50 6.00 15.00
MTR Mike Trout/50 200.00 500.00
NE Nathan Eovaldi/395 4.00 10.00
NF Neftali Feliz/75 5.00 12.00
NW Neil Walker/235 3.00 8.00
PG Paul Goldschmidt/75 8.00 20.00
RD Randall Delgado/395 5.00 12.00
RR Ricky Romero/75 6.00 15.00
SP Salvador Perez/350 10.00 25.00
SPE Salvador Perez/350 10.00 25.00
TC Trevor Cahill/75 6.00 15.00
TW Travis Wood/235 5.00 12.00
VW Vance Worley/355 5.00 12.00
VWO Vance Worley/355 5.00 12.00
WR Wilson Ramos/75 8.00 20.00
YC Yoenis Cespedes/50 20.00 50.00
ZB Zach Britton/50 8.00 20.00

2012 Topps Tier One On The Rise Autographs White Ink

STATED ODDS 1:9 HOBBY
STATED PRINT RUN 25 SER.#'d SETS
NO PRICING ON MOST DUE TO SCARCITY
EXCHANGE DEADLINE 05/31/2015
AR Anthony Rizzo 30.00 60.00
ARI Anthony Rizzo 30.00 60.00
BA Brett Anderson 10.00 25.00
BAN Brett Anderson 10.00 25.00

BP Brad Peacock 10.00 25.00
BPE Brad Peacock 10.00 25.00
BR Ben Revere 10.00 25.00
BRE Ben Revere 10.00 25.00
CH Chris Heisey 8.00 20.00
CHE Chris Heisey 8.00 20.00
DBA Daniel Bard 12.50 30.00
DBD Daniel Bard 12.50 30.00
DM Devin Mesoraco 20.00 50.00
DME Devin Mesoraco 20.00 50.00
EN Eduardo Nunez 8.00 20.00
ENU Eduardo Nunez 8.00 20.00
IN Ivan Nova 12.50 30.00
INO Ivan Nova 12.50 30.00
JA J.P. Arencibia 8.00 20.00
JAR J.P. Arencibia 8.00 20.00
JDM J.D. Martinez 15.00 40.00
JMA J.D. Martinez 15.00 40.00
JPA Jimmy Paredes 10.00 25.00
JPR Jimmy Paredes 10.00 25.00
JR Josh Reddick 15.00 40.00
JRE Josh Reddick 15.00 40.00
JW Jemile Weeks 8.00 20.00
JWE Jemile Weeks 8.00 20.00
KS Kyle Seager 30.00 60.00
KSE Kyle Seager 30.00 60.00
MM Mitch Moreland 10.00 25.00
MMR Mitch Moreland 10.00 25.00
MT Mark Trumbo 15.00 40.00
MTM Mark Trumbo 15.00 40.00
SP Salvador Perez 15.00 40.00
SPE Salvador Perez 15.00 40.00
VW Vance Worley 15.00 40.00
VWO Vance Worley 15.00 40.00

2012 Topps Tier One Relics

PRINT RUNS B/WN 150-399 COPIES PER
I Ichiro Suzuki/150 8.00 20.00
AB Adrian Beltre/399 3.00 8.00
AE Andre Ethier/399 4.00 10.00
AG Adrian Gonzalez/399 4.00 10.00
AM Andrew McCutchen/399 6.00 15.00
AP Albert Pujols/150 6.00 15.00
APE Andy Pettitte/150 5.00 12.00
AR Alex Rodriguez/399 8.00 20.00
AW Adam Wainwright/399 4.00 10.00
BP Buster Posey/399 6.00 15.00
BS Bruce Sutter/150 4.00 10.00
BW Brian Wilson/399 4.00 10.00
CF Carlton Fisk/150 4.00 10.00
CJ Chipper Jones/399 5.00 12.00
CJ2 Chipper Jones/399 5.00 12.00
CR Cal Ripken Jr./150 10.00 25.00
CS CC Sabathia/399 4.00 10.00
DH Dan Haren/399 3.00 8.00
DJ Derek Jeter/150 12.50 30.00
DO David Ortiz/399 4.00 10.00
DU Dan Uggla/399 3.00 8.00
DW David Wright/399 4.00 10.00
EM Eddie Murray/150 4.00 10.00
FF Freddie Freeman/399 3.00 8.00
FT Frank Thomas/150 6.00 15.00
GB George Bell/150 5.00 12.00
IK Ian Kennedy/399 3.00 8.00
IKI Ian Kinsler/399 3.00 8.00
JBR Jay Bruce/399 4.00 10.00
JE Jacoby Ellsbury/399 4.00 10.00
JH Jason Heyward/399 3.00 8.00
JHE Jeremy Hellickson/399 3.00 8.00
JJ Josh Johnson/399 3.00 8.00
JL Jon Lester/399 3.00 8.00
JM Jason Motte/399 3.00 8.00
JRI Jim Rice/150 5.00 12.00
JS James Shields/399 3.00 8.00
JV Justin Verlander/150 5.00 12.00
JVO Joey Votto/399 6.00 15.00
KY Kevin Youkilis/399 3.00 8.00
MC Miguel Cabrera/399 5.00 12.00
MR Mariano Rivera/150 8.00 20.00
MT Mark Trumbo/399 10.00 25.00
MTR Mike Trout/399 40.00 100.00
MY Michael Young/399 3.00 8.00
PF Prince Fielder/399 4.00 10.00
PK Paul Konerko/399 3.00 8.00
PM Paul Molitor/150 5.00 12.00
PO Paul O'Neill/150 4.00 10.00
RCW Rod Carew/150 4.00 10.00
RH Ryan Howard/399 4.00 10.00
RO Roy Oswalt/399 3.00 8.00
RZ Ryan Zimmerman/399 3.00 8.00
SC Steve Carlton/150 4.00 10.00
SCA Starlin Castro/399 3.00 8.00
SS Stephen Strasburg/399 4.00 10.00
THU Tim Hudson/399 3.00 8.00
TL Tim Lincecum/399 5.00 12.00
TT Troy Tulowitzki/399 3.00 8.00
UJ Ubaldo Jimenez/399 3.00 8.00
YG Yovani Gallardo/399 3.00 8.00

2013 Topps Tier One Relics

STATED PRINT RUN 399 SER.#'d SETS
AB Albert Belle 3.00 8.00
AC Aroldis Chapman 3.00 8.00
AG Adrian Gonzalez 3.00 8.00
AJ Adam Jones 3.00 8.00
AK Al Kaline 5.00 12.00
AM Andrew McCutchen 4.00 10.00
AW Adam Wainwright 4.00 10.00
BB Billy Butler 3.00 8.00
BP Buster Posey 4.00 10.00
CB Craig Biggio 3.00 8.00
CCS CC Sabathia 3.00 8.00
CG Carlos Gonzalez 3.00 8.00
CK Clayton Kershaw 6.00 15.00
CRJ Cal Ripken Jr. 8.00 20.00
CS Chris Sale 3.00 8.00
DF David Freese 3.00 8.00
DG Dwight Gooden 3.00 8.00
DO David Ortiz 4.00 10.00
DP Dustin Pedroia 3.00 8.00
DW David Wright 4.00 10.00
EH Eric Hosmer 3.00 8.00
EL Evan Longoria 3.00 8.00
FH Felix Hernandez 3.00 8.00
FT Frank Thomas 6.00 15.00
GSH Gary Sheffield 3.00 8.00
IK Ian Kinsler 3.00 8.00
JB Johnny Bench 5.00 12.00
JBR Jay Bruce 3.00 8.00
JBT Jose Bautista 3.00 8.00
JC Johnny Cueto 3.00 8.00
JH Jason Heyward 3.00 8.00
JK Jason Kipnis 3.00 8.00
JL Jon Lester 3.00 8.00
JM Joe Mauer 3.00 8.00
JP Jake Peavy 3.00 8.00
JR Jim Rice 3.00 8.00
JS John Smoltz 3.00 8.00
JU Justin Upton 3.00 8.00
JV Joey Votto 4.00 10.00
JVR Justin Verlander 5.00 12.00
KGJ Ken Griffey Jr. 8.00 20.00
LB Lou Brock 4.00 10.00
MC Miguel Cabrera 5.00 12.00
MCN Matt Cain 3.00 8.00
MH Matt Harvey 5.00 12.00
MK Matt Kemp 3.00 8.00
MTR Mark Trumbo 3.00 8.00
NC Nelson Cruz 3.00 8.00
NG Nomar Garciaparra 3.00 8.00
OC Orlando Cepeda 3.00 8.00
PA Pedro Alvarez 3.00 8.00
PF Prince Fielder 3.00 8.00
PM Pedro Martinez 5.00 12.00
PO Paul O'Neill 3.00 8.00
PS Pablo Sandoval 3.00 8.00
RAD R.A. Dickey 4.00 10.00
RB Ryan Braun 3.00 8.00
RH Rickey Henderson 5.00 12.00
RHD Ryan Howard 3.00 8.00
RHY Roy Halladay 3.00 8.00
RZ Ryan Zimmerman 3.00 8.00
SC Starlin Castro 3.00 8.00
SCR Steve Carlton 3.00 8.00
SS Stephen Strasburg 5.00 12.00
TF Todd Frazier 3.00 8.00
TG Tony Gwynn 3.00 8.00
TL Tim Lincecum 3.00 8.00
TM Tommy Milone 3.00 8.00
TT Troy Tulowitzki 3.00 8.00
YD Yu Darvish 5.00 12.00
YG Yasmani Grandal 3.00 8.00

2013 Topps Tier One Dual Relics

DUAL: .5X TO 1.5X BASIC
STATED ODDS 1:9 HOBBY
STATED PRINT RUN 50 SER.#'d SETS
CRJ Cal Ripken Jr. 12.50 30.00
KGJ Ken Griffey Jr. 12.50 30.00
RH Rickey Henderson 12.50 30.00

2013 Topps Tier One Triple Relics

*TRIPLE: .75X TO 2X BASIC
STATED ODDS 1:17 HOBBY
STATED PRINT RUN 25 SER.#'d SETS
CRJ Cal Ripken Jr. 40.00 80.00
KGJ Ken Griffey Jr. 30.00 60.00
RH Rickey Henderson 20.00 50.00

2013 Topps Tier One Autograph Dual Relics

STATED ODDS 1:46 HOBBY
STATED PRINT RUN 25 SER.#'d SETS
EXCHANGE DEADLINE 07/31/2016
CB Craig Biggio EXCH 30.00 60.00
CG Carlos Gonzalez EXCH 10.00 25.00
CRJ Cal Ripken Jr. 100.00 200.00
CS Chris Sale 30.00 60.00
CST Carlos Santana 20.00 50.00
DF David Freese 25.00 60.00
DP David Price EXCH 15.00 40.00
DW David Wright 50.00 100.00
EA Elvis Andrus EXCH 12.50 30.00
EL Evan Longoria 40.00 80.00
JS Jean Segura EXCH 20.00 50.00
KGJ Ken Griffey Jr. 200.00 500.00
MB Madison Bumgarner EXCH 25.00 60.00
MC Miguel Cabrera 75.00 150.00
MM Matt Moore 40.00 80.00
MO Mike Olt 15.00 40.00
NR Nolan Ryan 125.00 250.00
PF Prince Fielder EXCH 30.00 60.00
PG Paul Goldschmidt 60.00 120.00
RB Ryan Braun 12.50 30.00
RZ Ryan Zimmerman 10.00 25.00
TS Tyler Skaggs EXCH 8.00 20.00
YD Yu Darvish 100.00 200.00

2013 Topps Tier One Autograph Relics

STATED ODDS 1:12 HOBBY
STATED PRINT RUN 99 SER.#'d SETS
EXCHANGE DEADLINE 07/31/2016
CB Craig Biggio 20.00 50.00
CG Carlos Gonzalez EXCH 6.00 15.00
CRJ Cal Ripken Jr. 50.00 100.00
CS Chris Sale 12.50 30.00
CST Carlos Santana 10.00 25.00
DF David Freese 6.00 15.00
DP David Price 10.00 25.00
DW David Wright 40.00 80.00
EA Elvis Andrus EXCH 6.00 15.00
EL Evan Longoria 20.00 50.00
JS Jean Segura EXCH 10.00 25.00
KGJ Ken Griffey Jr. 125.00 300.00
MB Madison Bumgarner EXCH 40.00 80.00
MC Miguel Cabrera 60.00 120.00
MH Matt Holliday EXCH 12.50 30.00
MM Matt Moore 12.50 30.00
MO Mike Olt 10.00 25.00
NR Nolan Ryan 60.00 120.00
PF Prince Fielder EXCH 15.00 40.00
PG Paul Goldschmidt 15.00 40.00
RB Ryan Braun 10.00 25.00
RZ Ryan Zimmerman 12.50 30.00
SC Starlin Castro 12.50 30.00
TS Tyler Skaggs EXCH 6.00 15.00
YD Yu Darvish 30.00 80.00

2013 Topps Tier One Autographs

STATED ODDS 1:19 HOBBY
PRINT RUNS B/WN 50-199 COPIES PER
EXCHANGE DEADLINE 07/31/2016
AD Andre Dawson EXCH 12.50 30.00
BG Bob Gibson/69 20.00 50.00
CK Clayton Kershaw/90 30.00 80.00
CRJ Cal Ripken Jr./50 60.00 120.00
DM Don Mattingly/199 20.00 50.00
EB Ernie Banks/50 30.00 60.00
FT Frank Thomas 50.00 100.00
HA Hank Aaron EXCH 100.00 200.00
JB Johnny Bench EXCH 30.00 60.00
JH Josh Hamilton/99 10.00 25.00
KGJ Ken Griffey Jr./50 100.00 200.00
MC Miguel Cabrera/50 50.00 100.00
MS Mike Schmidt/50 40.00 80.00
NR Nolan Ryan/50 60.00 120.00
OS Ozzie Smith/199 30.00 60.00
P Pele/50 200.00 300.00
PF Prince Fielder EXCH 15.00 40.00
RB Ryan Braun/50 6.00 15.00
RH Rickey Henderson/50 25.00 60.00
RJ Reggie Jackson EXCH 20.00 50.00
SK Sandy Koufax/50 150.00 300.00
TG Tony Gwynn/50 15.00 40.00
TS Tom Seaver EXCH 50.00 120.00
WM Willie Mays/50 100.00 200.00
YD Yu Darvish EXCH 60.00 120.00

2013 Topps Tier One Clear Reprint Autographs

STATED ODDS 1:46 HOBBY
STATED PRINT RUN 25 SER.#'d SETS
EXCHANGE DEADLINE 07/31/2016
AK Al Kaline 75.00 200.00
BG Bob Gibson 100.00 200.00
BP Buster Posey 150.00 300.00
CRJ Cal Ripken Jr. 125.00 300.00
EL Evan Longoria 60.00 120.00
FT Frank Thomas 150.00 300.00
HA Hank Aaron 500.00 800.00
JB Johnny Bench 60.00 200.00
JH Josh Hamilton 50.00 100.00
JW Jered Weaver 60.00 120.00
MC Miguel Cabrera 200.00 300.00
MS Mike Schmidt 75.00 150.00
MT Mike Trout 300.00 500.00
NG N.Garciaparra EXCH 50.00 100.00
NR Nolan Ryan 175.00 350.00
OS Ozzie Smith 150.00 300.00
PF Prince Fielder 60.00 120.00
PO Paul O'Neill 50.00 100.00
RB Ryan Braun 50.00 100.00
RH Rickey Henderson 200.00 300.00
RJ Reggie Jackson 50.00 80.00
SK Sandy Koufax 400.00 800.00
TG Tony Gwynn 100.00 200.00
TS Tom Seaver 100.00 250.00
WM Willie Mays 300.00 400.00

2013 Topps Tier One Crowd Pleaser Autographs

PRINT RUNS B/WN 50-399 COPIES PER
ALL VERSIONS EQUALLY PRICED
EXCHANGE DEADLINE 07/31/2016
AA1 Alex Avila/299 5.00 12.00
AB1 Albert Belle/299 5.00 12.00
AB2 Albert Belle/299 5.00 12.00
AC1 Allen Craig/299 8.00 20.00
AC2 Allen Craig/299 8.00 20.00
AG Adrian Gonzalez/50 20.00 50.00
AJO Adam Jones/99 8.00 20.00
AK Al Kaline/50 25.00 50.00
BB1 Bill Buckner/299 6.00 15.00
BB2 Bill Buckner/299 6.00 15.00
BBU Billy Butler/206 4.00 10.00
BM Brian McCann/99 10.00 25.00
BP Buster Posey/50 40.00 80.00
BP1 Brandon Phillips/299 6.00 15.00
BP2 Brandon Phillips/299 6.00 15.00
BS Bruce Sutter/99 8.00 20.00
CB Craig Biggio EXCH 20.00 50.00
CF Cecil Fielder/199 10.00 25.00
CG Carlos Gonzalez EXCH 10.00 25.00
CH1 Chase Headley/299 4.00 10.00
CH2 Chase Headley/299 4.00 10.00
CJW C.J. Wilson/99 4.00 10.00
CR Carlos Ruiz/299 4.00 10.00
DF1 Dexter Fowler/299 4.00 10.00
DH1 Derek Holland/299 4.00 10.00
DH2 Derek Holland/299 4.00 10.00
DM Dale Murphy/99 10.00 25.00
DO David Ortiz/50 20.00 50.00
DP David Price/50 8.00 20.00
DPD Dustin Pedroia EXCH 15.00 40.00
DS1 Don Sutton/299 6.00 15.00
DS2 Don Sutton/299 6.00 15.00
DST Dave Stewart/299 4.00 10.00
DST2 Dave Stewart/299 4.00 10.00
DW David Wright/50 15.00 40.00
EL Evan Longoria/50 10.00 25.00
FH Felix Hernandez EXCH 12.50 30.00
FL1 Fred Lynn/99 6.00 15.00
FL2 Fred Lynn/180 6.00 15.00
GB1 Grant Balfour/299 5.00 12.00
GB2 Grant Balfour/299 5.00 12.00
GG Gio Gonzalez EXCH 4.00 10.00
GJ1 Garrett Jones/299 5.00 12.00
GJ2 Garrett Jones/299 5.00 12.00
HI1 Hisashi Iwakuma/299 6.00 15.00
JA1 Jim Abbott/299 5.00 12.00
JA2 Jim Abbott/299 5.00 12.00
JB Jose Bautista/50 12.00 30.00
JBR Jay Bruce/99 6.00 15.00
JC Johnny Cueto/99 4.00 10.00
JJ1 Jon Jay/299 5.00 12.00
JJ2 Jon Jay/299 5.00 12.00
JM Juan Marichal/99 10.00 25.00
JP1 Jhonny Peralta/299 4.00 10.00
JP2 Jhonny Peralta/299 4.00 10.00
JR1 Jim Rice/299 6.00 15.00
JR2 Jim Rice/299 6.00 15.00
JS John Smoltz EXCH 15.00 40.00
JS1 James Shields/299 4.00 10.00
JS2 James Shields/299 4.00 10.00
JU Justin Upton 6.00 15.00
KL Kenny Lofton/59 12.00 30.00
LA Luis Aparicio EXCH 10.00 25.00
MC Matt Cain/50 12.50 30.00
MH Matt Holliday EXCH 12.50 30.00
MH1 Matt Harrison/299 4.00 10.00
MH2 Matt Harrison/299 4.00 10.00
MM Mike Mussina EXCH 12.50 30.00
MMO Mike Morse/299 4.00 10.00
MN1 Mike Napoli/299 10.00 25.00
MN2 Mike Napoli/299 10.00 25.00
MW Maury Wills/299 5.00 12.00
NC Nelson Cruz/99 4.00 10.00
NG Nomar Garciaparra/99 12.00 30.00
PM Pedro Martinez/50 75.00 150.00
PO Paul O'Neill/299 6.00 15.00
RAD R.A. Dickey EXCH 6.00 15.00
RV Robin Ventura/299 4.00 10.00
RZ Ryan Zimmerman/99 8.00 20.00
SM1 Shaun Marcum/299 4.00 10.00
SM2 Shaun Marcum/299 4.00 10.00
TG Tom Glavine EXCH 20.00 50.00
TH Tim Hudson/99 6.00 15.00
TR1 Tim Raines/299 6.00 15.00
TR2 Tim Raines/299 6.00 15.00
VB1 Vida Blue/299 5.00 12.00
VB2 Vida Blue/299 5.00 12.00
WC Will Clark/99 12.50 30.00
WJ Wally Joyner/299 5.00 12.00
YG Yovani Gallardo EXCH 4.00 10.00
YP Yasiel Puig EXCH 200.00 400.00

2013 Topps Tier One Dual Autographs

STATED ODDS 1:76 HOBBY
STATED PRINT RUN 25 SER.#'d SETS
BC Banks/Castro EXCH 60.00 120.00
BM Bundy/Machado EXCH 75.00 150.00
BS Banks/Smith 50.00 120.00
FK Fielder/Kinsler 40.00 100.00
KA Aaron/Koufax EXCH 600.00 800.00
KM Kimbrel/Medlen 40.00 80.00
MC Musial/Craig 50.00 100.00
RD Darvish/Ryan EXCH 75.00 200.00
RT Rizzo/Thomas EXCH 60.00 120.00
SL Schmidt/Longoria 50.00 100.00
TH Henderson/Trout EXCH 150.00 400.00
THR Trout/Harper EXCH 500.00 700.00
WB Bundy/Hyun-Jin EXCH 40.00 80.00
WK Kershaw/Weaver EXCH 60.00 120.00
WW Weaver/Wilson EXCH 40.00 80.00

2013 Topps Tier One Legends Dual Relics

*DUAL: .5X TO 1.2X BASIC
STATED ODDS 1:76 HOBBY
STATED PRINT RUN 25 SER.#'d SETS

2013 Topps Tier One Legends Relics

STATED ODDS 1:21 HOBBY
PRINT RUNS B/WN 44-99 COPIES PER
BG Bob Gibson 5.00 12.00
BR Babe Ruth/44 60.00 120.00
CRJ Cal Ripken Jr. 15.00 40.00
EB Ernie Banks/45 12.50 30.00
GB George Brett 10.00 25.00
JR Jackie Robinson 15.00 40.00
KGR Ken Griffey Jr. 12.50 30.00
NR1 Nolan Ryan 15.00 40.00
OC Orlando Cepeda 8.00 20.00
OS Ozzie Smith 12.50 30.00
RC Rod Carew 5.00 12.00
RJ Reggie Jackson 5.00 12.00
TW Ted Williams 15.00 40.00
WM Willie Mays 10.00 25.00
YB Yogi Berra 8.00 20.00

2013 Topps Tier One On the Rise Autographs

PRINT RUNS B/WN 50-399 COPIES PER
ALL VERSIONS EQUALLY PRICED
EXCHANGE DEADLINE 07/31/2016
AC Andrew Cashner/399 3.00 8.00
AC1 Alex Cobb/399 3.00 8.00
AC2 Alex Cobb/399 3.00 8.00
ACS1 Andrew Cashner/399 3.00 8.00
AE1 Adam Eaton/399 3.00 8.00
AE2 Adam Eaton/399 3.00 8.00
AG1 Anthony Gose/399 3.00 8.00
AG2 Anthony Gose/399 3.00 8.00
AGR1 Avisail Garcia/399 6.00 15.00
AGR2 Avisail Garcia/399 6.00 15.00
AR Anthony Rizzo 20.00 50.00
BH Bryce Harper 125.00 250.00
BH1 Brock Holt/399 10.00 25.00
BH2 Brock Holt/399 10.00 25.00
BJ1 Brett Jackson/399 3.00 8.00
BJ2 Brett Jackson/399 3.00 8.00
CA1 Chris Archer/399 4.00 10.00
CA2 Chris Archer/399 4.00 10.00
CK Craig Kimbrel/50 30.00 60.00
CK1 Casey Kelly/399 3.00 8.00
CK2 Casey Kelly/399 3.00 8.00
CS Chris Sale/50 10.00 25.00
CST Carlos Santana/299 4.00 10.00
DBY1 Dylan Bundy/99 8.00 20.00
DBY2 Dylan Bundy/99 8.00 20.00
DF David Freese/50 12.50 30.00
DM Devin Mesoraco/399 3.00 8.00
DS Drew Storen/299 3.00 8.00
DS1 Drew Smyly/399 4.00 10.00
DS2 Drew Smyly/399 4.00 10.00
FD1 Felix Doubront/399 5.00 12.00
FD2 Felix Doubront/399 5.00 12.00
JF1 Jeurys Familia/399 3.00 8.00
JF2 Jeurys Familia/399 3.00 8.00
JK Jason Kipnis/99 8.00 20.00
JP1 Jurickson Profar/99 10.00 25.00
JP2 Jurickson Profar/99 10.00 25.00
JPK Jarrod Parker/199 4.00 10.00
JR Josh Reddick/399 4.00 10.00
JRT Josh Rutledge/399 4.00 10.00
JS1 Jean Segura/399 6.00 15.00
JS2 Jean Segura/399 6.00 15.00
JZ1 Jordan Zimmermann/199 4.00 10.00
JZ2 Jordan Zimmermann/199 4.00 10.00
KM Kris Medlen/99 15.00 40.00
KN1 Kirk Nieuwenhuis/399 3.00 8.00
KN2 Kirk Nieuwenhuis/399 3.00 8.00
LL Lance Lynn/99 3.00 8.00
MA Matt Adams/399 4.00 10.00
MB Madison Bumgarner/50 20.00 50.00
MF1 Michael Fiers/399 4.00 10.00
MM Matt Moore/99 3.00 8.00
MM1 Manny Machado/99 30.00 80.00
MM2 Manny Machado/99 30.00 80.00
MO1 Mike Olt/399 4.00 10.00
MO2 Mike Olt/399 4.00 10.00
MP Michael Pineda/199 5.00 12.00
MT Mike Trout/50 100.00 200.00
MTR Mark Trumbo/99 8.00 20.00
NE1 Nate Eovaldi/399 3.00 8.00
NE2 Nate Eovaldi/399 3.00 8.00
NF Neftali Feliz/199 3.00 8.00
PG Paul Goldschmidt/99 12.50 30.00
SD1 Scott Diamond/399 3.00 8.00
SD2 Scott Diamond/399 3.00 8.00
SM Starling Marte/399 4.00 10.00
SM1 Shelby Miller/99 8.00 20.00
SP1 Salvador Perez/399 8.00 20.00
SP2 Salvador Perez/399 8.00 20.00
TF Todd Frazier/299 6.00 15.00
TM1 Tommy Milone/399 3.00 8.00
TM2 Tommy Milone/399 3.00 8.00
TS1 Tyler Skaggs/300 4.00 10.00
TS2 Tyler Skaggs/399 4.00 10.00
WM Will Middlebrooks EXCH 8.00 20.00
WM1 Wil Myers/199 5.00 12.00
WM2 Wil Myers/399 4.00 10.00
WMY Wade Miley/99 4.00 10.00
WP1 Wily Peralta/399 3.00 8.00
WP2 Wily Peralta/399 3.00 8.00
WR Wilin Rosario/399 3.00 8.00
YC1 Yoenis Cespedes/99 12.50 30.00
YC2 Yoenis Cespedes/99 12.50 30.00
YG1 Yasmani Grandal/399 3.00 8.00
ZC1 Zack Cozart/399 4.00 10.00
ZC2 Zack Cozart/399 4.00 10.00

2014 Topps Tier One Relics

PRINT RUNS B/WN 199-399 COPIES PER
TORABE Adrian Beltre/299 4.00 10.00
TORABL Albert Belle/299 2.50 6.00
TORAC Aroldis Chapman/299 4.00 10.00
TORAD Andre Dawson/399 3.00 8.00
TORAG Adrian Gonzalez/254 3.00 8.00
TORAJ Adam Jones/299 3.00 8.00
TORAK Al Kaline/254 4.00 10.00
TORBBU Billy Butler/299 2.50 6.00
TORBP Buster Posey/254 5.00 12.00
TORBW Billy Williams/299 3.00 8.00
TORBZ Ben Zobrist/399 3.00 8.00
TORCA Chris Archer/299 2.50 6.00
TORCDA Chris Davis/249 2.50 6.00
TORCH Cole Hamels/299 3.00 8.00
TORCKE Clayton Kershaw/254 8.00 20.00
TORCKI Craig Kimbrel/254 3.00 8.00
TORCR Colby Rasmus/254 3.00 8.00
TORCW C.J. Wilson/399 2.50 6.00
TORDJ Derek Jeter/254 10.00 25.00
TORDM Dale Murphy/254 4.00 10.00
TORDOR David Ortiz/199 4.00 10.00
TORDPD Dustin Pedroia/254 4.00 10.00
TORDPE Dustin Pedroia/254 4.00 10.00
TORDSA Deion Sanders/254 3.00 8.00
TORDWR David Wright/254 3.00 8.00
TOREEC Edwin Encarnacion/399 4.00 10.00
TOREEN Edwin Encarnacion/399 4.00 10.00
TORELN Evan Longoria/399 3.00 8.00
TORELO Evan Longoria/399 3.00 8.00
TORFF Freddie Freeman/254 5.00 12.00
TORFH Felix Hernandez/254 3.00 8.00
TORFJ Fergie Jenkins/254 3.00 8.00
TORFM Fred McGriff/254 3.00 8.00
TORHP Hunter Pence/254 3.00 8.00
TORHRA Hanley Ramirez/254 3.00 8.00
TORHRY Hyun-Jin Ryu/254 3.00 8.00
TORJBA Jose Bautista/299 3.00 8.00
TORJBR Jackie Bradley Jr./299 4.00 10.00
TORJBU Jay Bruce/299 3.00 8.00
TORJCA Jose Canseco/299 3.00 8.00
TORJCE Johnny Cueto/299 3.00 8.00
TORJCH Jhoulys Chacin/299 2.50 6.00
TORJCU Johnny Cueto/299 3.00 8.00
TORJEV Joey Votto/254 4.00 10.00
TORJHA Josh Hamilton/254 3.00 8.00
TORJHE Jason Heyward/254 3.00 8.00
TORJOV Joey Votto/254 4.00 10.00
TORJPA Jarrod Parker/254 2.50 6.00
TORJPO Jorge Posada/399 3.00 8.00
TORJSH James Shields/399 2.50 6.00
TORJSM John Smoltz/254 4.00 10.00
TORJVO Joey Votto/254 4.00 10.00
TORJVT Joey Votto/254 4.00 10.00
TORJW Jayson Werth/254 3.00 8.00
TORJZ Jordan Zimmermann/254 3.00 8.00
TORKU Koji Uehara/254 2.50 6.00
TORMB Michael Bourn/299 2.50 6.00
TORMCA Miguel Cabrera/299 4.00 10.00
TORMCB Miguel Cabrera/254 4.00 10.00
TORMMA Manny Machado/254 4.00 10.00
TORMT Mark Trumbo/399 2.50 6.00
TORPF Prince Fielder/254 3.00 8.00
TORPG Paul Goldschmidt/254 4.00 10.00
TORRBR Ryan Braun/299 3.00 8.00
TORRD R.A. Dickey/299 3.00 8.00
TORSC Shin Soo Choo/299 3.00 8.00
TORTC Tony Cingrani/299 3.00 8.00
TORTG Tom Glavine/254 3.00 8.00
TORTL Tim Lincecum/299 3.00 8.00
TORTTL Troy Tulowitzki/254 4.00 10.00
TORTTU Troy Tulowitzki/254 4.00 10.00
TORYC Yoenis Cespedes/399 4.00 10.00
TORYD Yu Darvish/199 4.00 10.00
TORYM Yadier Molina/399 4.00 10.00
TORZW Zack Wheeler/254 3.00 8.00

2014 Topps Tier One Dual Relics

STATED ODDS 1:7 HOBBY
STATED PRINT RUN 50 SER.#'d SETS
TORDJ Derek Jeter 20.00 50.00
TORYM Yadier Molina 10.00 25.00

2014 Topps Tier One Triple Relics

STATED ODDS 1:13 HOBBY
STATED PRINT RUN 25 SER.#'d SETS
TORDJ Derek Jeter 30.00 80.00
TORYM Yadier Molina 15.00 40.00

2014 Topps Tier One Acclaimed Autographs

PRINT RUNS B/WN 50-299 COPIES PER
EXCHANGE DEADLINE 5/31/2017
AABL Albert Belle/299 5.00 12.00
AAD Andre Dawson/50 12.00 30.00
AAG Adrian Gonzalez/50 10.00 25.00
AAJN Adam Jones/100 8.00 20.00
AAJO Adam Jones/100 8.00 20.00
AAKA Al Kaline/299 15.00 40.00
AAKL Al Kaline/299 15.00 40.00
AABBU Billy Butler/299 4.00 10.00
AABZ Ben Zobrist/299 5.00 12.00
AACBA Carlos Baerga/299 4.00 10.00
AACKE Clayton Kershaw/50 30.00 80.00
AACRA Colby Rasmus/299 5.00 12.00
AACRS Colby Rasmus/299 5.00 12.00
AACWI C.J. Wilson/50 4.00 10.00
AACWL C.J. Wilson/50 4.00 10.00
AADBA Dusty Baker/299 6.00 15.00
AADBK Dusty Baker/299 6.00 15.00
AADFR David Freese/100 4.00 10.00
AADM Dale Murphy/100 8.00 20.00
AADO David Ortiz/50 20.00 50.00
AADP Dustin Pedroia/50 20.00 50.00
AADW David Wright/50 15.00 40.00
AAEDA Eric Davis/299 8.00 20.00
AAEDV Eric Davis/299 8.00 20.00
AAEL Evan Longoria/50 8.00 20.00
AAEM Edgar Martinez/299 5.00 12.00
AAFL Fred Lynn/100 5.00 12.00
AAFMC Fred McGriff/50 6.00 15.00
AAFMG Fred McGriff/50 6.00 15.00
AAGNE Graig Nettles/299 5.00 12.00
AAGNT Graig Nettles/299 5.00 12.00
AAIR Ivan Rodriguez/50 20.00 50.00
AAJB Jeff Bagwell/50 25.00 60.00
AAJCA Jose Canseco/299 10.00 25.00
AAJCN Jose Canseco/299 10.00 25.00
AAJCU Johnny Cueto/299 6.00 15.00
AAJGO Juan Gonzalez/50 12.00 30.00
AAJGZ Juan Gonzalez/50 12.00 30.00
AAJHA Josh Hamilton/50 6.00 15.00
AAJHE Jason Heyward/50 10.00 25.00
AAJM Juan Marichal/50 8.00 20.00
AAJPA Jim Palmer/100 10.00 25.00
AAJPO Jorge Posada/50 15.00 40.00
AAJR Jim Rice/299 6.00 15.00
AAJSH James Shields/299 4.00 10.00
AAJSI James Shields/299 4.00 10.00
AAJSM John Smoltz/50 15.00 40.00
AAJUI Juan Uribe/299 5.00 12.00
AAJUR Juan Uribe/299 5.00 12.00
AAJV Joey Votto/50 12.00 30.00
AAKL Kenny Lofton/50 4.00 10.00
AALB Lou Brock/50 15.00 40.00
AALGN Luis Gonzalez/299 4.00 10.00
AALGO Luis Gonzalez/299 4.00 10.00
AALHE Livan Hernandez/299 4.00 10.00
AALSI Lee Smith/299 5.00 12.00
AAMCA Miguel Cabrera/50 40.00 100.00
AAMCU Michael Cuddyer/299 8.00 20.00
AAMGE Mike Greenwell/299 8.00 20.00
AAMGR Mike Greenwell/299 8.00 20.00
AAMTR Mark Trumbo/299 4.00 10.00
AAMTU Mark Trumbo/299 4.00 10.00
AAMWI Matt Williams/299 5.00 12.00
AAMWL Matt Williams/299 5.00 12.00
AANG Nomar Garciaparra/50 15.00 40.00
AAOC Orlando Cepeda/50 12.00 30.00
AAOHE Orlando Hernandez/299 10.00 25.00
AAOHR Orlando Hernandez/299 10.00 25.00
AAPGO Paul Goldschmidt/299 10.00 25.00
AAPOE Paul O'Neill/299 8.00 20.00
AAPON Paul O'Neill/299 8.00 20.00
AARB Ryan Braun/50 10.00 25.00
AARD R.A. Dickey/50 6.00 15.00
AARNO Ricky Nolasco/299 4.00 10.00
AARPA Rafael Palmeiro/50 8.00 20.00
AARPL Rafael Palmeiro/50 8.00 20.00
AARZI Ryan Zimmerman/50 8.00 20.00
AATG Tom Glavine/50 15.00 40.00
AATRA Tim Raines/50 5.00 12.00
AATT Troy Tulowitzki EXCH 10.00 25.00
AAYC Yoenis Cespedes/299 8.00 20.00
AAYM Yadier Molina EXCH 40.00 100.00

2014 Topps Tier One Acclaimed Autographs Bronze Ink

*BRONZE: .6X TO 1.5X BASIC
STATED ODDS 1:11 HOBBY
STATED PRINT RUN 25 SER.#'d SETS
EXCHANGE DEADLINE 5/31/2017

2014 Topps Tier One Acetate Autographs

STATED ODDS 1:19 HOBBY
PRINT RUNS B/WN 30-99 COPIES PER
EXCHANGE DEADLINE 5/31/2017
TOABJ Bo Jackson/99 40.00 100.00
TOACR Cal Ripken Jr./30 100.00 200.00
TOAEBA Ernie Banks/99 30.00 80.00
TOAGM Greg Maddux/30 100.00 200.00
TOAHA Hank Aaron/30 125.00 250.00
TOAJB Johnny Bench/99 40.00 100.00
TOAKG Ken Griffey Jr./30 75.00 200.00
TOAMM Mark McGwire/45 125.00 250.00
TOAMR Mariano Rivera/69 60.00 150.00
TOAMSH Mike Schmidt/99 30.00 80.00
TOANR Nolan Ryan/45 100.00 200.00
TOAOSI Ozzie Smith/99 20.00 50.00
TOAPM Pedro Martinez/99 40.00 100.00
TOARH Rickey Henderson/99 40.00 100.00
TOARJA Reggie Jackson/45 50.00 100.00
TOARJO Randy Johnson/30 60.00 150.00
TOASCR Steve Carlton/99 25.00 60.00
TOASK Sandy Koufax 150.00 250.00
TOATGW Tony Gwynn/99 30.00 80.00

2014 Topps Tier One Acetate Autographs Bronze Ink

*BRONZE: .4X TO 1X BASIC
STATED ODDS 1:49 HOBBY
STATED PRINT RUN 25 SER.#'d SETS
EXCHANGE DEADLINE 5/31/2017
TOAWM Mays Signed in Black 125.00 250.00

2014 Topps Tier One Autograph Relics

STATED ODDS 1:10 HOBBY
STATED PRINT RUN 99 SER.#'d SETS
EXCHANGE DEADLINE 5/31/2017
TOARAC Alex Cobb 4.00 10.00
TOARAS A.Simmons EXCH 15.00 40.00
TOARBH Billy Hamilton EXCH 12.00 30.00
TOARBJ Bo Jackson 40.00 100.00
TOARBP Buster Posey 40.00 100.00
TOARCA Chris Archer EXCH 4.00 10.00
TOARCS Chris Sale 6.00 15.00
TOARDO David Ortiz 25.00 60.00
TOAREG Evan Gattis 4.00 10.00
TOARFF Freddie Freeman 12.00 30.00
TOARGM Greg Maddux 25.00 60.00
TOARJBA Jose Bautista 12.00 30.00
TOARJG Juan Gonzalez 4.00 10.00
TOARJH Jason Heyward 8.00 20.00
TOARJP Jorge Posada 20.00 50.00
TOARJV Joey Votto 12.00 30.00
TOARJZ Jordan Zimmermann 10.00 25.00
TOARKU Koji Uehara 4.00 10.00
TOARMT Mike Trout 125.00 250.00
TOARRH Rickey Henderson 40.00 100.00
TOARRJ Reggie Jackson 25.00 60.00
TOARSC Steve Carlton 15.00 40.00
TOARTGL Tom Glavine 25.00 60.00
TOARWB Wade Boggs 10.00 25.00
TOARYD Yu Darvish 50.00 120.00

2014 Topps Tier One Autograph Dual Relics

STATED ODDS 1:39 HOBBY
STATED PRINT RUN 25 SER.#'d SETS
EXCHANGE DEADLINE 5/31/2017

2014 Topps Tier One Dual Autographs

STATED ODDS 1:65 HOBBY
STATED PRINT RUN 25 SER.#'d SETS
EXCHANGE DEADLINE 5/31/2017

DABB Biggio/Bagwell EXCH 100.00 200.00
DACT Trout/Cabrera EXCH 300.00 500.00
DAGB Garciapar/Boggs EXCH 40.00 100.00
DAHJ R.Jackson/R.Henderson 10.00 100.00
DAJM Johnson/Martinez EXCH 100.00 200.00
DAMC Cepeda/Marichal EXCH 40.00 100.00
DAMJ Jones/Machado EXCH 75.00 150.00
DAML W.Myers/E.Longoria 40.00 100.00
DAMP Molina/Posey EXCH 100.00 200.00
DAPV B.Phillips/J.Votto 40.00 100.00
DARG IRod/Gonzalez EXCH 40.00 100.00
DARP M.Rivera/J.Posada 300.00 400.00
DASG J.Smoltz/T.Glavine 100.00 200.00
DASJ Jackson/Sanders EXCH 75.00 150.00
DASR Ryan/Seaver EXCH 125.00 300.00

2014 Topps Tier One Legends Relics

STATED ODDS 1:13 HOBBY
STATED PRINT RUN 99 SER.#'d SETS
TORLAB Albert Belle 4.00 10.00
TORLBJ Bo Jackson 8.00 20.00
TORLBR Babe Ruth 50.00 120.00
TORLCR Cal Ripken Jr. 8.00 20.00
TORLDS Deion Sanders 6.00 15.00
TORLGM Greg Maddux 8.00 20.00
TORLGS Gary Sheffield 4.00 10.00
TORLJG Juan Gonzalez 5.00 12.00
TORLJM Joe Morgan 5.00 12.00
TORLJP Jorge Posada 5.00 12.00
TORLMM Mark McGwire 12.00 30.00
TORLMR Manny Ramirez 6.00 15.00
TORLNG Nomar Garciaparra 5.00 12.00
TORLOC Orlando Cepeda 5.00 12.00
TORLRJA Reggie Jackson 5.00 12.00
TORLRJO Randy Johnson 6.00 15.00
TORLSCA Steve Carlton 5.00 12.00
TORLSCR Steve Carlton 5.00 12.00
TORLTGL Tom Glavine 5.00 12.00
TORLTGY Tony Gwynn 6.00 15.00

2014 Topps Tier One Legends Dual Relics

STATED ODDS 1:49 HOBBY
STATED PRINT RUN 25 SER.#'d SETS

2014 Topps Tier One New Guard Autographs

PRINT RUNS B/WN 50-399 COPIES PER
EXCHANGE DEADLINE 5/31/2017
NGAACO Alex Cobb/399 4.00 10.00
NGAACR Allen Craig/50 5.00 12.00
NGAAG Anthony Gose/399 4.00 10.00
NGAALM Andrew Lambo/399 4.00 10.00
NGAAR Anthony Rizzo/50 10.00 25.00
NGAASI Andrelton Simmons/99 12.00 30.00
NGAASM Andrelton Simmons/99 12.00 30.00
NGAAWE Allen Webster/399 4.00 10.00
NGABHA Billy Hamilton 5.00 12.00
NGABHR Bryce Harper/50 75.00 150.00
NGABMI Brad Miller/399 5.00 12.00
NGACAH Cody Asche/399 6.00 15.00
NGACAR Chris Archer/181 4.00 10.00
NGACSA Chris Sale/50 10.00 25.00
NGACSN Carlos Santana/50 6.00 15.00
NGACY Christian Yelich/181 20.00 50.00
NGADB Dylan Bundy/50 12.00 30.00
NGADG Didi Gregorius/399 5.00 12.00
NGADSA Danny Salazar/399 5.00 12.00
NGAEGA Evan Gattis/182 4.00 10.00
NGAEJ Erik Johnson/399 4.00 10.00
NGAER Enny Romero/399 4.00 10.00
NGAFF Freddie Freeman/50 15.00 40.00
NGAHAL Henderson Alvarez/399 4.00 10.00
NGAJA Jose Abreu/399 8.00 20.00
NGAJCO Jarred Cosart/399 4.00 10.00
NGAJKE Joe Kelly/399 4.00 10.00
NGAJKI Jason Kipnis/50 5.00 12.00
NGAJLA Junior Lake/399 6.00 15.00
NGAJLK Junior Lake/399 6.00 15.00
NGAJN Jimmy Nelson/399 4.00 10.00
NGAJOD Jake Odorizzi/399 4.00 10.00
NGAJPR Jurickson Profar/50 5.00 12.00
NGAJSC Jonathan Schoop/399 4.00 10.00
NGAJSE Jean Segura/182 5.00 12.00
NGAJTE Julio Teheran/182 5.00 12.00
NGAKSE Kyle Seager/399 4.00 10.00
NGAKW Kolten Wong/399 5.00 12.00
NGAMAA Matt Adams/399 6.00 15.00
NGAMAD Matt Adams/399 6.00 15.00
NGAMB Madison Bumgarner/50 25.00 60.00
NGAMCA Matt Carpenter/50 20.00 50.00
NGAMCR Matt Carpenter/50 10.00 25.00
NGAMD Matt Davidson/399 6.00 15.00
NGAMMA Manny Machado/50 20.00 50.00
NGAMMI Mike Minor/182 4.00 10.00
NGAMMN Mike Minor/182 4.00 10.00
NGAMOL Mike Olt/399 4.00 10.00
NGAMT Mike Trout/50 100.00 250.00
NGAMWC Michael Wacha/399 10.00 25.00
NGAMWH Michael Wacha/399 10.00 25.00
NGAMZN Mike Zunino/50 6.00 15.00
NGAMZU Mike Zunino/50 6.00 15.00
NGAPBO Peter Bourjos/399 5.00 12.00
NGAPBU Peter Bourjos/399 5.00 12.00
NGAPCO Patrick Corbin/50 5.00 12.00
NGAPCR Patrick Corbin/50 6.00 15.00
NGASGA Sonny Gray/399 8.00 20.00
NGASGR Sonny Gray/399 8.00 20.00
NGASMA Starling Marte/399 6.00 15.00
NGASMI Shelby Miller/50 12.00 30.00
NGASML Shelby Miller/50 12.00 30.00
NGASPE Salvador Perez/399 12.00 30.00
NGATBA Trevor Bauer/50 8.00 20.00
NGATBU Trevor Bauer/50 8.00 20.00
NGATCI Tony Cingrani/399 5.00 12.00
NGATCN Tony Cingrani/399 5.00 12.00
NGATD Travis d'Arnaud/182 5.00 12.00
NGATFR Todd Frazier/99 12.00 30.00
NGATJO Taylor Jordan/399 4.00 10.00
NGATTH Tyler Thornburg/399 4.00 10.00
NGATTO Tyler Thornburg/399 4.00 10.00
NGATW Taijuan Walker/182 4.00 10.00
NGAWFL Wilmer Flores/399 5.00 12.00
NGAWFO Wilmer Flores/399 5.00 12.00
NGAWME Wil Myers/50 10.00 25.00
NGAWMI Wade Miley/399 4.00 10.00
NGAWMY Wil Myers/50 10.00 25.00
NGAWR Wilin Rosario/399 4.00 10.00
NGAXB Xander Bogaerts/399 12.00 30.00
NGAYD Yu Darvish EXCH 50.00 120.00
NGAYV Yordano Ventura/399 8.00 20.00
NGAZWE Zack Wheeler/50 8.00 20.00
NGAZWH Zack Wheeler/50 8.00 20.00

2014 Topps Tier One New Guard Autographs Bronze Ink

*BRONZE: .6X TO 1.5X BASIC
STATED ODDS 1:11 HOBBY
STATED PRINT RUN 25 SER.#'d SETS
EXCHANGE DEADLINE 5/31/2017

2015 Topps Tier One Relics

RANDOM INSERTS IN PACKS
PRINT RUNS B/WN 175-399 COPIES PER
*DUAL/50: .6X TO 1.5 SNGL RELIC
*TRIPLE/25: .75X TO 2X SNGL RELIC
TSRACG Allen Craig/399 2.50 6.00
TSRAD Andre Dawson/199 3.00 8.00
TSRAGZ Adrian Gonzalez/399 3.00 8.00
TSRAJ Adam Jones/399 3.00 8.00
TSRAM Andrew McCutchen/175 10.00 25.00
TSRAP Albert Pujols/249 5.00 12.00
TSRAW Adam Wainwright/399 3.00 8.00
TSRBHN Billy Hamilton/399 3.00 8.00
TSRBHR Bryce Harper/199 10.00 25.00
TSRBJ Bo Jackson/199 6.00 15.00
TSRBP Buster Posey/299 5.00 12.00
TSRCBN Charlie Blackmon/399 4.00 10.00
TSRCBO Craig Biggio/199 3.00 8.00
TSRCD Chris Davis/399 2.50 6.00
TSRCF Carlton Fisk/199 3.00 8.00
TSRCJ Chipper Jones/299 4.00 10.00
TSRCR Cal Ripken Jr./199 8.00 20.00
TSRCS CC Sabathia/399 3.00 8.00
TSRCU Chase Utley/399 3.00 8.00
TSRDJ Derek Jeter/399 10.00 25.00
TSRDM Don Mattingly/199 6.00 15.00
TSRDW David Wright/399 3.00 8.00
TSREA Elvis Andrus/399 3.00 8.00
TSREL Evan Longoria/399 3.00 8.00
TSRFF Freddie Freeman/199 5.00 12.00
TSRFH Felix Hernandez/399 3.00 8.00
TSRFT Frank Thomas/199 4.00 10.00
TSRGC Gerrit Cole/399 4.00 10.00
TSRGS Giancarlo Stanton/399 4.00 10.00
TSRHRU Hyun-Jin Ryu/399 3.00 8.00
TSRHRZ Hanley Ramirez/249 3.00 8.00
TSRJA Jose Abreu/199 5.00 12.00
TSRJBA Jose Bautista/399 3.00 8.00
TSRJBE Jay Bruce/399 3.00 8.00
TSRJD Jacob deGrom/399 6.00 15.00
TSRJE Jacoby Ellsbury/399 3.00 8.00
TSRJF Jose Fernandez/399 4.00 10.00
TSRJG Juan Gonzalez/199 2.50 6.00
TSRJH Jason Heyward/399 3.00 8.00
TSRJR Jim Rice/199 3.00 8.00
TSRJVR Justin Verlander/399 4.00 10.00
TSRKG Ken Griffey Jr./199 8.00 20.00
TSRMBR Madison Bumgarner/199 6.00 15.00
TSRMBS Mookie Betts/399 6.00 15.00
TSRMC Miguel Cabrera/399 4.00 10.00
TSRMK Matt Kemp/399 3.00 8.00
TSRMM Mark McGwire/199 10.00 25.00
TSRMP Mike Piazza/249 5.00 12.00
TSRMTA Masahiro Tanaka/399 3.00 8.00
TSRMTT Mike Trout/199 15.00 40.00
TSRNCS Nick Castellanos/399 4.00 10.00
TSRPF Prince Fielder/399 3.00 8.00
TSRPG Paul Goldschmidt/199 4.00 10.00
TSRPS Pablo Sandoval/399 3.00 8.00
TSRRB Ryan Braun/399 3.00 8.00
TSRRC Roger Clemens/199 5.00 12.00
TSRRHD Ryan Howard/399 3.00 8.00
TSRRHN Rickey Henderson/399 4.00 10.00
TSRRJA Reggie Jackson/199 3.00 8.00
TSRRJO Randy Johnson/199 4.00 10.00
TSRRS Ryne Sandberg/199 5.00 12.00
TSRSCH Shin-Soo Choo/399 3.00 8.00
TSRSM Shelby Miller/399 3.00 8.00
TSRSS Stephen Strasburg/399 4.00 10.00
TSRTGE Tom Glavine/199 3.00 8.00
TSRTGN Tony Gwynn/199 5.00 12.00
TSRTL Tim Lincecum/399 4.00 10.00
TSRTR Tim Raines/299 3.00 8.00
TSRTT Troy Tulowitzki/399 4.00 10.00
TSRVG Vladimir Guerrero/199 3.00 8.00
TSRWB Wade Boggs/199 5.00 12.00
TSRXB Xander Bogaerts/399 4.00 10.00
TSRYC Yoenis Cespedes/199 3.00 8.00
TSRYD Yu Darvish/199 4.00 10.00
TSRYP Yasiel Puig/249 4.00 10.00
TSRZG Zack Greinke/299 3.00 8.00

2015 Topps Tier One Acclaimed Autographs

RANDOM INSERTS IN PACKS
PRINT RUNS B/WN 50-399 COPIES PER
EXCHANGE DEADLINE 4/30/2018
AAAC Allen Craig/299 4.00 10.00
AAAD Andre Dawson/50 10.00 25.00
AAAG Adrian Gonzalez/50 5.00 12.00
AAAGA Andres Galarraga/399 4.00 10.00
AAAJ Adam Jones/50 10.00 25.00
AABC Brandon Crawford/399 6.00 15.00
AABMN Brian McCann/149 6.00 15.00
AABMO Brandon Moss/399 3.00 8.00
AABMS Brandon Moss/399 3.00 8.00
AABPS Brandon Phillips/199 6.00 15.00
AACB Carlos Baerga/399 3.00 8.00
AACD Carlos Delgado/399 3.00 8.00
AACFD Cliff Floyd/399 3.00 8.00
AACFK Carlton Fisk/50 20.00 50.00
AACHS Cole Hamels/299 12.00 30.00
AACHY Chase Headley/299 5.00 12.00
AACJ Chris Johnson/399 3.00 8.00
AADC David Cone/299 3.00 8.00
AADEN David Eckstein/299 3.00 8.00
AADEY Dennis Eckersley/149 5.00 12.00
AADF David Freese/149 3.00 8.00
AADMP Dale Murphy/149 10.00 25.00
AADMY Don Mattingly/50 30.00 80.00
AADN Daniel Nava/399 3.00 8.00
AADO David Ortiz/50 20.00 50.00
AADPA Dustin Pedroia/50 12.00 30.00
AADW David Wright/50 15.00 40.00
AAED Eric Davis/399 6.00 15.00
AAEL Evan Longoria/50 5.00 12.00
AAEM Edgar Martinez/149 6.00 15.00
AAFM Fred McGriff/50 5.00 12.00
AAFV Fernando Valenzuela/50 10.00 25.00
AAGS Giancarlo Stanton EXCH 20.00 50.00
AAGV Greg Vaughn/399 3.00 8.00
AAHR Hanley Ramirez/50 5.00 12.00
AAHS Hector Santiago/399 3.00 8.00
AAJCA Jose Canseco/175 12.00 30.00
AAJG Juan Gonzalez/299 5.00 12.00
AAJML Juan Marichal/149 10.00 25.00
AAJMR Joe Mauer EXCH 12.00 30.00
AAJR Jim Rice/299 6.00 15.00
AAJS John Smoltz/50 15.00 40.00
AAJV Joey Votto/50 15.00 40.00
AAKGS Ken Griffey Sr./299 6.00 15.00
AAKU Koji Uehara/299 6.00 15.00
AALB Lou Brock/149 15.00 40.00
AALG Luis Gonzalez/249 3.00 8.00
AALH Livan Hernandez/399 3.00 8.00
AAMC Michael Cuddyer/249 3.00 8.00
AAMMY Mike Matheny/299 10.00 25.00
AAMN Mike Napoli/149 3.00 8.00
AAMT Mark Teixeira/149 12.00 30.00
AAMWN Mookie Wilson/399 6.00 15.00
AAMWS Matt Williams/399 3.00 8.00
AANG Nomar Garciaparra/50 12.00 30.00
AAOC Orlando Cepeda/149 10.00 25.00
AAOH Orlando Hernandez/299 3.00 8.00
AAOV Omar Vizquel/299 6.00 15.00
AAPG Paul Goldschmidt/149 6.00 15.00
AAPN Phil Niekro/149 8.00 20.00
AARA Roberto Alomar/50 15.00 40.00
AARB Ryan Braun/50 10.00 25.00
AARCO Robinson Cano/50 15.00 40.00
AARCW Rod Carew/50 12.00 30.00
AARD Rob Dibble/399 3.00 8.00
AARG Ron Gant/399 3.00 8.00
AARP Rafael Palmeiro/149 4.00 10.00
AARW Rondell White/399 3.00 8.00
AARY Robin Yount/50 25.00 60.00
AARZ Ryan Zimmerman/149 4.00 10.00
AATG Tom Glavine/50 12.00 30.00
AATP Terry Pendleton/399 3.00 8.00
AATR Tim Raines/50 6.00 15.00
AATT Troy Tulowitzki/50 12.00 30.00
AAUJ Ubaldo Jimenez/149 3.00 8.00
AAVC Vinny Castilla/399 3.00 8.00
AAVG Vladimir Guerrero/50 10.00 25.00

2015 Topps Tier One Acclaimed Autographs Bronze Ink

*BRONZE: X TO X BASIC
STATED ODDS 1:12 HOBBY
STATED PRINT RUN 25 SER.#'d SETS
NO PRICING DUE TO SCARCITY
EXCHANGE DEADLINE 4/30/2018

2015 Topps Tier One Autograph Relics

STATED ODDS 1:12 HOBBY
STATED PRINT RUN 99 SER.#'d SETS
EXCHANGE DEADLINE 4/30/2018
*DUAL/25: .6X TO 1.5X BASIC
TOARAGO Adrian Gonzalez 10.00 25.00
TOARAR Anthony Rizzo 30.00 80.00
TOARCD Carlos Delgado 8.00 20.00
TOARDB Dellin Betances 10.00 25.00
TOARDWR David Wright 15.00 40.00
TOARDWT David Wright 15.00 40.00
TOAREL Evan Longoria 10.00 25.00
TOARFF Freddie Freeman 15.00 40.00
TOARFV Fernando Valenzuela 15.00 40.00
TOARHR Hanley Ramirez 10.00 25.00
TOARJD Jacob deGrom 12.00 30.00
TOARJH Jason Heyward 10.00 25.00
TOARMA Matt Adams 8.00 20.00
TOARMCR Matt Carpenter 12.00 30.00
TOARMG Mark Grace 15.00 40.00
TOARMTA Mark Teixeira 15.00 40.00
TOARPG Paul Goldschmidt 15.00 40.00
TOARRC Rusney Castillo 10.00 25.00
TOARSG Sonny Gray 10.00 25.00
TOARSM Starling Marte 10.00 25.00
TOARYV Yordano Ventura 12.00 30.00

2015 Topps Tier One Autographs

STATED PRINT RUN 1:20 HOBBY
PRINT RUNS B/WN 30-99 COPIES PER
EXCHANGE DEADLINE 4/30/2018
TOABJ Bo Jackson/30 40.00 100.00
TOABP Buster Posey/99 40.00 100.00
TOACJ Chipper Jones/30 50.00 120.00
TOACK Clayton Kershaw/99 40.00 100.00
TOACR Cal Ripken Jr./30 60.00 150.00
TOAFT Frank Thomas/99 25.00 60.00
TOAGM Greg Maddux/30 30.00 80.00
TOAHA Hank Aaron/30 150.00 250.00
TOAJA Jose Abreu/99 6.00 15.00
TOAJB Johnny Bench/30 30.00 80.00
TOAKB Kris Bryant/75 60.00 150.00
TOAMC Miguel Cabrera/30 60.00 150.00
TOAMM Mark McGwire/30 50.00 125.00
TOAMP Mike Piazza/30 60.00 150.00
TOAMR Mariano Rivera/30 75.00 150.00
TOAMS Mike Schmidt/30 50.00 100.00
TOAMTT Mike Trout/30 150.00 250.00
TOANR Nolan Ryan/30 90.00 150.00
TOAOS Ozzie Smith/99 20.00 50.00
TOARC Roger Clemens/30 40.00 100.00
TOARH Rickey Henderson/30 30.00 80.00
TOARJA Reggie Jackson/30 25.00 60.00
TOARJO Randy Johnson/30 30.00 80.00
TOASC Steve Carlton/99 12.00 30.00
TOASK Sandy Koufax/30 200.00 300.00
TOAWB Wade Boggs/99 20.00 50.00
TOAYP Yasiel Puig/30 40.00 100.00

2015 Topps Tier One Autographs Bronze Ink

*BRONZE: .4X TO 1X BASIC p/r 30
*BRONZE: .6X TO 1.5X BASIC p/r 99
STATED ODDS 1:37 HOBBY
STATED PRINT RUN 25 SER.#'d SETS
NO PRICING DUE TO SCARCITY
EXCHANGE DEADLINE 4/30/2018

2015 Topps Tier One Clear One Autographs

STATE ODDS 1:52 HOBBY
STATED PRINT RUN 25 SER.#'d SETS
EXCHANGE DEADLINE 4/30/2018
COABJ Bo Jackson 40.00 100.00
COABP Buster Posey 60.00 150.00
COACJ Chipper Jones EXCH 60.00 150.00
COACK Clayton Kershaw EXCH 100.00 200.00
COADO David Ortiz 12.00 30.00
COAFT Frank Thomas 40.00 100.00
COAJA Jose Abreu 12.00 30.00
COAJF Jose Fernandez EXCH 25.00 60.00
COAJR Jim Rice 10.00 25.00
COAKG Ken Griffey Jr. 100.00 250.00
COAMC Michael Cuddyer EXCH 8.00 20.00
COANG Nomar Garciaparra 10.00 25.00
COAOS Ozzie Smith 15.00 40.00
COARY Robin Yount 30.00 80.00
COASC Steve Carlton 10.00 25.00
COATT Troy Tulowitzki 12.00 30.00
COAWM Wil Myers 8.00 20.00

2015 Topps Tier One Dual Autographs

STATE ODDS 1:69 HOBBY
STATED PRINT RUN 25 SER.#'d SETS
EXCHANGE DEADLINE 4/30/2018
DAAB Baez/Abreu EXCH 150.00 400.00
DAAM Adms/McGwre EXCH 50.00 120.00
DAFO D.Ortiz/C.Fisk 30.00 80.00
DAGJ L.Gonzalez/R.Johnson 40.00 100.00
DAGR A.Gonzalez/H.Ramirez 25.00 60.00
DAJG T.Glavine/C.Jones 150.00 300.00
DAMG Gonzalez/Mattingly 60.00 150.00
DAMT Txra/Mttngly EXCH 60.00 150.00
DAPW D.Wright/M.Piazza 60.00 150.00
DARP J.Posada/M.Rivera 150.00 250.00
DART M.Teixeira/A.Rizzo 50.00 120.00
DATP M.Trout/Y.Puig 175.00 350.00
DAWJ Jones/Wright EXCH 150.00 250.00

2015 Topps Tier One Legends Relics

STATE ODDS 1:14 HOBBY
STATED PRINT RUN 99 SER.#'d SETS
*DUAL/25: .6X TO 1.5X SNGL RELIC
TORLBD Bobby Doerr 6.00 15.00
TORLDS Duke Snider 6.00 15.00
TORLEB Ernie Banks 10.00 25.00
TORLES Enos Slaughter 6.00 15.00
TORLEW Early Wynn 6.00 15.00
TORLFR Frank Robinson 6.00 15.00
TORLHA Hank Aaron 12.00 30.00
TORLHW Hoyt Wilhelm 12.00 30.00
TORLJB Jim Bunning 6.00 15.00
TORLJD Joe DiMaggio 25.00 60.00
TORLJM Juan Marichal 10.00 25.00
TORLJR Jackie Robinson 20.00 50.00
TORLRC Roberto Clemente 30.00 80.00
TORLRF Rick Ferrell 8.00 20.00
TORLRS Red Schoendienst 6.00 15.00
TORLTC Ty Cobb 25.00 60.00
TORLTW Ted Williams 25.00 60.00
TORLWMS Willie Mays 20.00 50.00
TORLWSL Willie Stargell 10.00 25.00

2015 Topps Tier One New Guard Autographs

RANDOM INSERTS IN PACKS
PRINT RUNS B/WN 50-399 COPIES PER
EXCHANGE DEADLINE 4/30/2018
NGAAAA Arismendy Alcantara/399 3.00 8.00
NGAAAY Arismendy Alcantara/399 3.00 8.00
NGAACB Alex Cobb/299 3.00 8.00
NGAACO Alex Cobb/299 3.00 8.00
NGAARA Anthony Ranaudo/399 3.00 8.00
NGAARI Anthony Rizzo/50 20.00 50.00
NGAASA Aaron Sanchez/399 4.00 10.00
NGAASN Andrelton Simmons EXCH 8.00 20.00
NGAASZ Aaron Sanchez/399 4.00 10.00
NGABH Bryce Harper EXCH 125.00 250.00
NGABOB Brett Oberholtzer/299 3.00 8.00
NGABOZ Brett Oberholtzer/299 3.00 8.00
NGACA Chris Archer/199 3.00 8.00
NGACCJ C.J. Cron/399 3.00 8.00
NGACCN C.J. Cron/399 3.00 8.00
NGACK Corey Kluber/199 6.00 15.00
NGACR Carlos Rodon EXCH 20.00 50.00
NGACSE Chris Sale/50 10.00 25.00
NGACSG Cory Spangenberg/399 3.00 8.00
NGACY Christian Yelich/99 10.00 25.00
NGADBE Dellin Betances/349 4.00 10.00
NGADBS Dellin Betances/349 4.00 10.00
NGADH Dilson Herrera/349 4.00 10.00
NGADMO Devin Mesoraco/99 8.00 20.00
NGADN Daniel Norris/349 3.00 8.00
NGAFF Freddie Freeman/99 10.00 25.00
NGAGP Gregory Polanco/50 5.00 12.00
NGAHAL Henderson Alvarez/349 3.00 8.00
NGAHAZ Henderson Alvarez/349 3.00 8.00
NGAJBA Javier Baez/299 8.00 20.00
NGAJBZ Javier Baez/299 8.00 20.00
NGAJCS Jarred Cosart/399 3.00 8.00
NGAJDM Jacob deGrom/299 15.00 40.00
NGAJDN Josh Donaldson/50 5.00 12.00
NGAJF Jose Fernandez/50 25.00 60.00
NGAJHA Josh Harrison/299 10.00 25.00
NGAJHD Jason Heyward/50 5.00 12.00
NGAJHN Josh Harrison/299 10.00 25.00
NGAJKY Joe Kelly/349 3.00 8.00
NGAJLG Juan Lagares/399 6.00 15.00
NGAJPA Joe Panik/399 12.00 30.00
NGAJPE Joc Pederson/349 6.00 15.00
NGAJPK Joe Panik/399 4.00 10.00
NGAJPN Joc Pederson/349 6.00 15.00
NGAJSC Jonathan Schoop/299 3.00 8.00
NGAJSO Jorge Soler/349 5.00 12.00
NGAJSP Jonathan Schoop/299 3.00 8.00
NGAJSR Jorge Soler/349 10.00 25.00
NGAJT Julio Teheran/50 5.00 12.00
NGAKCN Kole Calhoun/349 3.00 8.00
NGAKGA Kevin Gausman/299 3.00 8.00
NGAKGN Kevin Gausman/299 3.00 8.00
NGAKSE Kyle Seager/225 3.00 8.00
NGAKSR Kyle Seager/225 3.00 8.00
NGAKVA Kennys Vargas/399 3.00 8.00
NGAKVG Kennys Vargas/399 3.00 8.00
NGAMA Matt Adams/199 3.00 8.00
NGAMC Matt Carpenter/50 12.00 30.00
NGAMFO Maikel Franco/349 4.00 10.00
NGAMFR Maikel Franco/349 4.00 10.00
NGAMFZ Mike Foltynewicz/399 3.00 8.00
NGAMSN Marcus Stroman/399 4.00 10.00
NGAMST Marcus Stroman/399 4.00 10.00
NGAMTA Michael Taylor/349 3.00 8.00
NGAMTY Michael Taylor/349 3.00 8.00
NGANC Nick Castellanos/50 12.00 30.00
NGAPC Patrick Corbin/50 5.00 12.00
NGARC Rusney Castillo/50 5.00 12.00
NGARDA Rubby De La Rosa/349 3.00 8.00
NGARDE Rubby De La Rosa/349 3.00 8.00
NGARMN Rafael Montero/399 3.00 8.00
NGARMO Rafael Montero/399 3.00 8.00
NGASDE Sean Doolittle/349 3.00 8.00
NGASDO Sean Doolittle/349 3.00 8.00
NGASGE Shane Greene/349 3.00 8.00
NGASGR Shane Greene/349 3.00 8.00
NGASGY Sonny Gray/99 8.00 20.00
NGASMA Starling Marte/225 8.00 20.00
NGASME Starling Marte/225 8.00 20.00
NGATRO Tyson Ross/225 3.00 8.00
NGATRS Tyson Ross/225 3.00 8.00
NGATW Taijuan Walker/99 8.00 20.00
NGAWM Wil Myers/50 4.00 10.00
NGAYV Yordano Ventura/199 6.00 15.00
NGAZW Zack Wheeler/50 5.00 12.00

2015 Topps Tier One New Guard Autographs Bronze Ink

*BRONZE: X TO X BASIC
STATED ODDS 1:11 HOBBY
STATED PRINT RUN 25 SER.#'d SETS
EXCHANGE DEADLINE 4/30/2018

2016 Topps Tier One Relics

RANDOM INSERTS IN PACKS
PRINT RUNS B/WN 99-399 COPIES PER
*DUAL/50: .6X TO 1.5 SNGL RELIC
*TRIPLE/25: .75X TO 2X SNGL RELIC
T1RAGN Adrian Gonzalez/399 3.00 8.00
T1RAGR Alex Gordon/205 3.00 8.00
T1RAM Andrew McCutchen/99 6.00 15.00
T1RAPO A.J. Pollock/299 2.50 6.00
T1RAPU Albert Pujols/299 5.00 12.00
T1RARI Anthony Rizzo/299 6.00 15.00
T1RARU Addison Russell/199 4.00 10.00
T1RAW Adam Wainwright/199 3.00 8.00
T1RBG Brett Gardner/399 3.00 8.00
T1RBH Bryce Harper/299 6.00 15.00
T1RBM Brian McCann/299 3.00 8.00
T1RBPH Brandon Phillips/299 2.50 6.00
T1RBPO Buster Posey/299 5.00 12.00
T1RCBE Carlos Beltran/399 3.00 8.00
T1RCKE Clayton Kershaw/299 8.00 20.00
T1RCM Carlos Martinez/299 3.00 8.00
T1RCSA Carlos Santana/199 3.00 8.00
T1RCY Christian Yelich/199 5.00 12.00
T1RDK Dallas Keuchel/199 3.00 8.00
T1RDO David Ortiz/299 4.00 10.00
T1RDP Dustin Pedroia/299 4.00 10.00
T1RDW David Wright/199 3.00 8.00
T1REE Edwin Encarnacion/399 4.00 10.00
T1REL Evan Longoria/299 3.00 8.00
T1RFH Felix Hernandez/199 3.00 8.00
T1RFL Francisco Lindor/299 4.00 10.00
T1RGSP George Springer/199 3.00 8.00
T1RGST Giancarlo Stanton/199 4.00 10.00
T1RHP Hunter Pence/299 3.00 8.00
T1RHR Hanley Ramirez/299 3.00 8.00
T1RI Ichiro Suzuki/199 5.00 12.00
T1RJAB Jose Abreu/399 4.00 10.00
T1RJBU Jose Bautista/399 3.00 8.00
T1RJBZ Javier Baez/399 5.00 12.00
T1RJC Jose Canseco/99 6.00 15.00
T1RJDA Johnny Damon/399 3.00 8.00
T1RJDE Jacob deGrom/399 4.00 10.00
T1RJE Jacoby Ellsbury/399 3.00 8.00
T1RJF Jose Fernandez/399 4.00 10.00
T1RJH Josh Harrison/299 2.50 6.00
T1RJK Jung Ho Kang/99 2.50 6.00
T1RJLE Jon Lester/299 3.00 8.00
T1RJLU Jonathan Lucroy/299 3.00 8.00
T1RJS Jorge Soler/199 4.00 10.00
T1RJVE Justin Verlander/199 4.00 10.00
T1RJVO Joey Votto/199 4.00 10.00
T1RKB Kris Bryant/399 8.00 20.00
T1RKC Kole Calhoun/399 2.50 6.00
T1RKP Kevin Plawecki/299 2.50 6.00
T1RKSE Kyle Seager/199 2.50 6.00
T1RKSU Kurt Suzuki/199 2.50 6.00
T1RKW Kolten Wong/199 3.00 8.00
T1RLD Lucas Duda/399 3.00 8.00
T1RMCA Miguel Cabrera/399 4.00 10.00
T1RMCR Matt Carpenter/299 4.00 10.00
T1RMH Matt Harvey/299 3.00 8.00
T1RMMA Manny Machado/299 4.00 10.00
T1RMMC Mark McGwire/299 6.00 15.00
T1RMPI Michael Pineda/299 2.50 6.00
T1RMTA Masahiro Tanaka/199 3.00 8.00
T1RMTE Mark Teixeira/199 3.00 8.00
T1RMTR Mike Trout/199 10.00 25.00
T1RNA Nolan Arenado/399 5.00 12.00
T1RPF Prince Fielder/399 3.00 8.00
T1RPG Paul Goldschmidt/399 4.00 10.00
T1RPS Pablo Sandoval/199 3.00 8.00
T1RRCA Robinson Cano/369 3.00 8.00
T1RRCL Roger Clemens/399 5.00 12.00
T1RRCS Rusney Castillo/99 2.50 6.00
T1RRH Ryan Howard/299 3.00 8.00
T1RSC Shin-Soo Choo/399 3.00 8.00
T1RSM Steven Matz/299 3.00 8.00
T1RTD Travis D'Arnaud/399 3.00 8.00
T1RTT Troy Tulowitzki/99 4.00 10.00
T1RVG Vladimir Guerrero/399 3.00 8.00
T1RVM Victor Martinez/299 3.00 8.00
T1RYM Yadier Molina/299 4.00 10.00
T1RYT Yasmany Tomas/199 2.50 6.00
T1RZW Zack Wheeler/199 3.00 8.00

2016 Topps Tier One Autograph Relics

STATED ODDS 1:10 MINI BOX
PRINT RUNS B/WN 50-149 COPIES PER
EXCHANGE DEADLINE 5/31/2018
*DUAL: .6X TO 1.5X BASIC
AT1RAG Alex Gordon/50 10.00 25.00
AT1RAJ Adam Jones/149 10.00 25.00
AT1RBB Byron Buxton/50 5.00 12.00
AT1RBP Buster Posey/50 40.00 100.00
AT1RCK Clayton Kershaw/50 50.00 120.00
AT1RCSA Chris Sale/149 12.00 30.00
AT1RCSE Corey Seager/149 30.00 80.00
AT1RDG Didi Gregorius/149 5.00 12.00
AT1RDK Dallas Keuchel/149 20.00 50.00
AT1RDL DJ LeMahieu/149 8.00 20.00
AT1RDO David Ortiz/99 40.00 100.00
AT1RDP Dustin Pedroia/149 15.00 40.00
AT1RDW David Wright/99 10.00 25.00
AT1RHO Henry Owens/149 5.00 12.00
AT1RKB Kris Bryant/50 75.00 200.00
AT1RKS Kyle Schwarber/149 12.00 30.00
AT1RMCA Matt Cain/50 5.00 12.00
AT1RMH Matt Harvey
AT1RMM Manny Machado/99 40.00 100.00
AT1RMT Mike Trout/50 150.00 400.00
AT1RNS Noah Syndergaard/75 25.00 60.00
AT1RRB Ryan Braun/99 10.00 25.00
AT1RRR Rob Refsnyder/149 5.00 12.00
AT1RSP Stephen Piscotty/149 6.00 15.00
AT1RWM Wil Myers/149 10.00 25.00

2016 Topps Tier One Autographs

STATED ODDS 1:23 MINI BOX
PRINT RUNS B/WN 30-99 COPIES PER
EXCHANGE DEADLINE 5/31/2018
T1ABH Bryce Harper/30 200.00 400.00
T1ABJ Bo Jackson/50 40.00 100.00
T1ABP Buster Posey/30 60.00 150.00
T1ACB Craig Biggio/75 10.00 25.00
T1ACC Carlos Correa/75 40.00 100.00
T1ACJ Chipper Jones/50 40.00 100.00
T1ACK Clayton Kershaw/75 40.00 100.00
T1ACR Cal Ripken Jr./50 50.00 120.00
T1ACY Carl Yastrzemski/75 40.00 100.00
T1AFT Frank Thomas/50 30.00 80.00
T1AGM Greg Maddux/30 40.00 100.00
T1AHA Hank Aaron
T1AI Ichiro Suzuki
T1AJB Johnny Bench/50 25.00 60.00
T1AKB Kris Bryant/75 75.00 200.00
T1AKG Ken Griffey Jr./30 75.00 200.00
T1AMM Mark McGwire/30 60.00 150.00
T1AMP Mike Piazza/30 50.00 120.00
T1AMT Mike Trout/50 150.00 400.00
T1ANR Nolan Ryan
T1AOS Ozzie Smith/50 15.00 40.00
T1ARC Roger Clemens/30 25.00 60.00
T1ARH Rickey Henderson/50 40.00 100.00
T1ARJA Reggie Jackson/30 25.00 60.00
T1ARJO Randy Johnson/30 25.00 60.00
T1ASC Steve Carlton/75 10.00 25.00
T1ASK Sandy Koufax/50 150.00 300.00
T1AYD Yu Darvish/30 40.00 100.00

2016 Topps Tier One Autographs Copper Ink

*COPPER: .6X TO 1.5X BASE p/r 75-99
STATED ODDS 1:32 MINI BOX
STATED PRINT RUN 25 SER.#'d SETS
EXCHANGE DEADLINE 5/31/2018
T1AHA Hank Aaron 125.00 250.00
T1AI Ichiro Suzuki 300.00 500.00
T1ANR Nolan Ryan 60.00 150.00

2016 Topps Tier One Breakout Autographs

RANDOM INSERTS IN PACKS
PRINT RUNS B/WN 99-299 COPIES PER
EXCHANGE DEADLINE 5/31/2018
*COPPER/25: .6X TO 1.5X BASIC
BOAAC Alex Colome/299 3.00 8.00
BOAANL Aaron Nola/299 8.00 20.00
BOAANO Aaron Nola/299 8.00 20.00
BOABD Brandon Drury/299 5.00 12.00
BOABDR Brandon Drury/249 5.00 12.00
BOABH Brock Holt/299 5.00 12.00
BOABJ Brian Johnson/299 3.00 8.00
BOABSI Blake Swihart/299 4.00 10.00
BOABSW Blake Swihart/299 4.00 10.00
BOABYP Byung-Ho Park/249 4.00 10.00
BOACED Carl Edwards Jr./299 4.00 10.00
BOACEJ Carl Edwards Jr./249 4.00 10.00
BOACEW Carl Edwards Jr./299 4.00 10.00
BOACHE Chris Heston/299 3.00 8.00
BOACHS Chris Heston/299 3.00 8.00
BOACM Carlos Martinez/249 5.00 12.00
BOACRA Colin Rea/249 3.00 8.00
BOACRE Colin Rea/299 3.00 8.00
BOACRO Carlos Rodon/149 5.00 12.00
BOACSA Corey Seager/149 30.00 80.00
BOACSE Corey Seager/149 30.00 80.00
BOADP Dalton Pompey/299 4.00 10.00
BOADT Devon Travis/299 3.00 8.00
BOAER Eduardo Rodriguez/299 3.00 8.00
BOAFL Francisco Lindor/199 10.00 25.00
BOAGBI Greg Bird/249 4.00 10.00
BOAGBR Greg Bird/249 4.00 10.00
BOAHOE Henry Owens/299 4.00 10.00
BOAHOI Hector Olivera/299 4.00 10.00
BOAHOL Hector Olivera/299 4.00 10.00
BOAHOW Henry Owens/249 4.00 10.00
BOAJD Jacob deGrom/99 20.00 50.00
BOAJFA Jeurys Familia/299 4.00 10.00
BOAJGR Jon Gray/159 3.00 8.00
BOAJHA Jesse Hahn/299 3.00 8.00
BOAJPA Joe Panik/249 4.00 10.00
BOAJPD Joc Pederson/199 8.00 20.00
BOAJR J.T. Realmuto/299 20.00 50.00
BOAJS Jorge Soler/199 5.00 12.00
BOAKM Ketel Marte/299 6.00 15.00
BOAKMA Kenta Maeda/99 8.00 20.00
BOAKP Kevin Plawecki/299 3.00 8.00
BOAKSC Kyle Schwarber/199 15.00 40.00
BOAKWA Kyle Waldrop/299 4.00 10.00
BOAKWL Kyle Waldrop/249 4.00 10.00
BOAKWO Kolten Wong/299 4.00 10.00
BOALJ Luke Jackson/299 3.00 8.00
BOALSE Luis Severino/249 12.00 30.00
BOAMAL Miguel Almonte/299 3.00 8.00
BOAMCN Michael Conforto/199 8.00 20.00
BOAMDF Matt Duffy/299 6.00 15.00
BOAMDU Matt Duffy/299 6.00 15.00
BOAMRE Michael Reed/249 3.00 8.00
BOAMRY Matt Reynolds/249 3.00 8.00
BOAMSA Miguel Sano/199 8.00 20.00
BOAMSE Marcus Semien/299 3.00 8.00
BOAMSH Matt Shoemaker/299 4.00 10.00
BOAMSN Miguel Sano/199 8.00 20.00
BOAMT Michael Taylor/299 3.00 8.00
BOAMWI Matt Wisler/299 4.00 10.00
BOAMWM Mac Williamson/299 3.00 8.00
BOANS Noah Syndergaard/199 15.00 40.00
BOAPOB Peter O'Brien/299 3.00 8.00
BOARMO Raul Mondesi/249 4.00 10.00
BOARRF Rob Refsnyder/299 4.00 10.00
BOARRS Rob Refsnyder/299 4.00 10.00
BOARSA Richie Shaffer/249 3.00 8.00
BOARSH Richie Shaffer/299 3.00 8.00
BOASG Sonny Gray/199 4.00 10.00
BOASH Slade Heathcott/299 4.00 10.00
BOASMA Steven Matz/299 10.00 25.00
BOASMT Steven Matz/299 10.00 25.00
BOASPI Stephen Piscotty/299 5.00 12.00
BOASPS Stephen Piscotty/299 5.00 12.00
BOATH T.J. House/299 3.00 8.00
BOATMU Tom Murphy/249 3.00 8.00
BOATTR Trea Turner/249 8.00 20.00
BOATTU Trea Turner/249 8.00 20.00
BOAZL Zach Lee/299 3.00 8.00
BOAZLE Zach Lee/249 3.00 8.00
BOAZW Zack Wheeler/199 5.00 12.00

2016 Topps Tier One Clear One Autographs

STATED ODDS 1:48 MINI BOX
STATED PRINT RUN 25 SER.#'d SETS
EXCHANGE DEADLINE 5/31/2018

AAJ Adam Jones	15.00	40.00
AAM Andrew Miller	20.00	50.00
ABL Barry Larkin	25.00	60.00
ABW Bernie Williams	12.00	30.00
ACC Carlos Correa	25.00	60.00
ACS Corey Seager	25.00	60.00
ADK Dallas Keuchel	10.00	25.00
ADM Don Mattingly	25.00	60.00
ADP Dustin Pedroia	25.00	60.00
AHO Hector Olivera	6.00	15.00
AJA Jose Abreu	10.00	25.00
AJC Jose Canseco	20.00	50.00
AJF Jeurys Familia	15.00	40.00
AKS Kyle Schwarber	25.00	60.00
ALS Luis Severino	12.00	30.00
AMS Miguel Sano	8.00	20.00
AMT Mike Trout		
APM Paul Molitor	15.00	40.00
APS Pablo Sandoval	6.00	15.00
ARC Rod Carew	15.00	40.00
ATT Troy Tulowitzki	10.00	25.00

2016 Topps Tier One Dual Autographs

ATED ODDS 1:63 MINI BOX
ATED PRINT RUN 25 SER.#'d SETS
CHANGE DEADLINE 5/31/2018

AAG Alou/Galarraga EXCH	20.00	50.00
ABA Biggio/Altuve EXCH	60.00	150.00
ACA Altuve/Correa EXCH	40.00	100.00
AET Encrncn/Tulo EXCH	25.00	60.00
AGJ Gordon/Jackson	60.00	150.00
AJR Jones/Robinson	50.00	120.00
AKK Krshw/Kfx EXCH	600.00	1000.00
ALP Larkin/Phillips	50.00	120.00
AOJ Jones/Olivera	25.00	60.00
ARG Gregorius/Refsnyder	20.00	50.00
ASM Syndrgrd/Matz EXCH	75.00	200.00
ATA Aaron/Trout	500.00	800.00

2016 Topps Tier One Legends Relics

ATED ODDS 1:16 MINI BOX
RINT RUNS B/WN 75-149 COPIES PER
UAL/25: .6X TO 1.5X SNGL RELIC

1RLBD Bobby Doerr/75	6.00	15.00
1RLBF Bob Feller/75	8.00	20.00
1RLCB Craig Biggio/149	5.00	12.00
1RLCF Carlton Fisk/75	6.00	15.00
1RLCR Cal Ripken Jr./149	8.00	20.00
1RLGB George Brett/75	20.00	50.00
1RLHA Hank Aaron/75	12.00	30.00
1RLJG Josh Gibson/75	60.00	150.00
1RLRA Roberto Alomar/149	6.00	15.00
1RLRC Roberto Clemente		
1RLRFE Rick Ferrell/75	4.00	10.00
1RLRFI Rollie Fingers/75	5.00	12.00
1RLRM Roger Maris/75	12.00	30.00
1RLSC Steve Carlton/75	5.00	12.00
1RLTGW Tony Gwynn/149	5.00	12.00
1RLTW Ted Williams/75	15.00	40.00
1RLWB Wade Boggs/75	5.00	12.00
1RLWSP Warren Spahn/75	5.00	12.00

2016 Topps Tier One Prime Performers Autographs

RANDOM INSERTS IN PACKS
PRINT RUNS B/WN 50-299 COPIES PER
EXCHANGE DEADLINE 5/31/2018
*CPPR/25: .6X TO 1.5X BASE p/r 99-299
*CPPR/25: .5X TO 1.2X BASE p/r 50

PPAD Andre Dawson/50	10.00	25.00
PPAE Alcides Escobar/249	6.00	15.00
PPAGA Andres Galarraga/249	5.00	12.00
PPAGN Adrian Gonzalez/50	6.00	15.00
PPAGO Alex Gordon/149	4.00	10.00
PPAJ Adam Jones/50	12.00	30.00
PPAK Al Kaline/99	12.00	30.00
PPAMI Andrew Miller/249	5.00	12.00
PPBBO Bret Boone/299	3.00	8.00
PPBL Barry Larkin/50	20.00	50.00
PPBMC Brian McCann/50	5.00	12.00
PPBMO Brandon Moss/249	3.00	8.00
PPBP Brandon Phillips/149	5.00	12.00
PPBW Bernie Williams/50	12.00	30.00
PPCDE Carlos Delgado/249	3.00	8.00
PPCDL Carlos Delgado/299	3.00	8.00
PPCF Carlton Fisk/50	12.00	30.00
PPCHA Cole Hamels/50	15.00	40.00
PPCHE Chase Headley/249	5.00	12.00
PPCK Corey Kluber/149	5.00	12.00
PPCSA Chris Sale/50	10.00	25.00
PPCSL Chris Sale/50	10.00	25.00
PPCY Christian Yelich/249	20.00	50.00
PPDE Dennis Eckersley/149	5.00	12.00
PPDGO Dee Gordon/249	3.00	8.00
PPDGR Didi Gregorius/249	4.00	10.00
PPDKE Dallas Keuchel/249	4.00	10.00
PPDMA Don Mattingly/50	25.00	60.00
PPDME Devin Mesoraco/249	3.00	8.00
PPDP Dustin Pedroia/50	15.00	40.00
PPDWR David Wright/50	10.00	25.00
PPEE Edwin Encarnacion/50	6.00	15.00
PPEL Evan Longoria/50	8.00	20.00
PPEM Edgar Martinez/149	6.00	15.00
PPFF Freddie Freeman/50	10.00	25.00
PPFM Fred McGriff/50	8.00	20.00
PPFR Frank Robinson/50	15.00	40.00
PPFVA Fernando Valenzuela/50	10.00	25.00
PPFVL Fernando Valenzuela/50	10.00	25.00
PPGR Garrett Richards EXCH	4.00	10.00
PPHR Hanley Ramirez/50	5.00	12.00
PPJA Jose Altuve/249	12.00	30.00
PPJG Juan Gonzalez/249	5.00	12.00
PPJHA Josh Harrison/249	3.00	8.00
PPJPA Jimmy Paredes/249	3.00	8.00
PPJR Jim Rice/249	6.00	15.00
PPJSH James Shields/249	3.00	8.00
PPJSM John Smoltz/50	15.00	40.00
PPKSE Kyle Seager/249	3.00	8.00
PPKSU Kurt Suzuki/299	3.00	8.00
PPLD Lucas Duda/249	4.00	10.00
PPLG Luis Gonzalez/249	4.00	10.00
PPMCA Matt Cain/50	5.00	12.00
PPMMA Mike Matheny/249	8.00	20.00
PPMMC Manny Machado/50	30.00	80.00
PPMP Mark Prior/249	4.00	10.00
PPMT Mark Teixeira/99	4.00	10.00
PPMWI Matt Williams/229	4.00	10.00
PPMZ Mike Zunino/249	3.00	8.00
PPNEO Nathan Eovaldi/299	4.00	10.00
PPNEV Nathan Eovaldi/249	4.00	10.00
PPNG Nomar Garciaparra/50	20.00	50.00
PPOC Orlando Cepeda/149	4.00	10.00
PPOVI Omar Vizquel/249	6.00	15.00
PPOVZ Omar Vizquel/249	6.00	15.00
PPPMO Paul Molitor/50	10.00	25.00
PPPN Phil Niekro/99	6.00	15.00
PPPO Paul O'Neill/149	8.00	20.00
PPPS Pablo Sandoval/50	5.00	12.00
PPRA Roberto Alomar/50	15.00	40.00
PPRB Ryan Braun/50	10.00	25.00
PPRCA Rod Carew/50	15.00	40.00
PPRCN Robinson Cano/50	12.00	30.00
PPRPA Rafael Palmeiro/99	6.00	15.00
PPRPO Rick Porcello/249	4.00	10.00
PPRS Ryne Sandberg/50	20.00	50.00
PPRY Robin Yount/50	20.00	50.00
PPSGE Shawn Green/299	3.00	8.00
PPSGR Shawn Green/249	3.00	8.00
PPSMA Starling Marte/249	5.00	12.00
PPSMT Starling Marte/299	5.00	12.00
PPTG Tom Glavine/50	12.00	30.00
PPTT Troy Tulowitzki/50	6.00	15.00
PPVCO Vince Coleman/249	5.00	12.00
PPVV Vince Coleman/249	5.00	12.00
PPWMY Wil Myers/99	3.00	8.00
PPYGO Yan Gomes/249	3.00	8.00
PPYGR Yasmani Grandal/249	5.00	12.00

2017 Topps Tier One Relics

RANDOM INSERTS IN PACKS
PRINT RUNS B/WN 225-331 COPIES PER
*DUAL/25: .6X TO 1.5X SNGL RELIC

T1RAB Alex Bregman/331	5.00	12.00
T1RABE Andrew Benintendi/331	8.00	20.00
T1RAJ Aaron Judge/331	20.00	50.00
T1RAM Andrew McCutchen/331	5.00	12.00
T1RAPU Albert Pujols/331	4.00	10.00
T1RAR Anthony Rizzo/331	5.00	12.00
T1RARE Alex Reyes/331	2.50	6.00
T1RARU Addison Russell/331	3.00	8.00
T1RBB Brandon Belt/331	2.50	6.00
T1RBD Brian Dozier/331	3.00	8.00
T1RBH Bryce Harper/331	5.00	12.00
T1RBHA Billy Hamilton/331	2.50	6.00
T1RBP Buster Posey/331	4.00	10.00
T1RBZ Ben Zobrist/331	3.00	8.00
T1RCA Chris Archer/331	2.00	5.00
T1RCC Carlos Correa/331	3.00	8.00
T1RCD Chris Davis/225	2.00	5.00
T1RCG Carlos Gonzalez/331	2.50	6.00
T1RCK Clayton Kershaw/331	4.00	10.00
T1RCKL Corey Kluber/331	2.50	6.00
T1RCSE Corey Seager/331	3.00	8.00
T1RCY Christian Yelich/331	4.00	10.00
T1RDB Dellin Betances/331	2.50	6.00
T1RDD David Dahl/331	2.50	6.00
T1RDL DJ LeMahieu/331	3.00	8.00
T1RDM Daniel Murphy/331	2.50	6.00
T1RDP Dustin Pedroia/331	3.00	8.00
T1RDS Dansby Swanson/331	5.00	12.00
T1REH Eric Hosmer/331	2.50	6.00
T1RFF Freddie Freeman/331	4.00	10.00
T1RFH Felix Hernandez/331	2.50	6.00
T1RGP Gregory Polanco/331	2.50	6.00
T1RGS Giancarlo Stanton/331	3.00	8.00
T1RGSA Gary Sanchez/331	6.00	15.00
T1RGSP George Springer/331	2.50	6.00
T1RHR Hunter Renfroe/331	2.50	6.00
T1RJA Jake Arrieta/331	2.50	6.00
T1RJB Jackie Bradley Jr./331	3.00	8.00
T1RJC Johnny Cueto/331	2.50	6.00
T1RJD Josh Donaldson/331	2.50	6.00
T1RJDE Jacob deGrom/331	3.00	8.00
T1RJL Jon Lester/331	2.50	6.00
T1RJM J.D. Martinez/331	3.00	8.00
T1RJV Joey Votto/331	3.00	8.00
T1RJVE Justin Verlander/331	3.00	8.00
T1RKB Kris Bryant/331	4.00	10.00
T1RKS Kyle Seager/331	2.00	5.00
T1RKSC Kyle Schwarber/331	3.00	8.00
T1RLW Luke Weaver/331	2.50	6.00
T1RMB Mookie Betts/331	5.00	12.00
T1RMC Miguel Cabrera/331	3.00	8.00
T1RMCA Matt Carpenter/331	3.00	8.00
T1RMM Manny Machado/331	3.00	8.00
T1RMS Max Scherzer		
T1RMT Mike Trout/331	15.00	40.00
T1RMTA Masahiro Tanaka/331	2.50	6.00
T1RNA Nolan Arenado/331	4.00	10.00
T1RNC Nelson Cruz/331	3.00	8.00
T1RNS Noah Syndergaard/331	2.50	6.00
T1RPG Paul Goldschmidt/331	3.00	8.00
T1RRB Ryan Braun/331	2.50	6.00
T1RRC Robinson Cano/331	2.50	6.00
T1RRG Randal Grichuk/331	2.00	5.00
T1RRO Rougned Odor/331	2.50	6.00
T1RSM Starling Marte/331	2.50	6.00
T1RSP Stephen Piscotty/331	2.50	6.00
T1RSS Stephen Strasburg/331	3.00	8.00
T1RTF Todd Frazier/331	2.50	6.00
T1RTG Tyler Glasnow/331	2.50	6.00
T1RTS Trevor Story/331	3.00	8.00
T1RWM Wil Myers/331	2.00	5.00
T1RXB Xander Bogaerts/331	3.00	8.00
T1RYG Yulieski Gurriel/331	3.00	8.00
T1RZB Zach Britton/331	2.50	6.00
T1RZG Zack Greinke/331	2.50	6.00

2017 Topps Tier One Autograph Relics

STATED ODDS 1:9 HOBBY
PRINT RUNS B/WN 20-100 COPIES PER
EXCHANGE DEADLINE 5/31/2018
*DUAL/25: .6X TO 1.5X BASIC

T1ARABE Andrew Benintendi/75	30.00	80.00
T1ARABR Alex Bregman/65	20.00	50.00
T1ARAG Alex Gordon/50	10.00	25.00
T1ARAJ Aaron Judge/100	100.00	250.00
T1ARARD A.J. Reed/100	4.00	10.00
T1ARARE Alex Reyes/75	5.00	12.00
T1ARARY Alex Reyes/75	5.00	12.00
T1ARBB Brandon Belt/75	5.00	12.00
T1ARCC Carlos Correa/30	30.00	80.00
T1ARCD Chris Davis/30	10.00	25.00
T1ARCH Cole Hamels/20	12.00	30.00
T1ARCKE Clayton Kershaw/30	50.00	120.00
T1ARCKL Corey Kluber/40	15.00	40.00
T1ARCS Corey Seager/30	30.00	80.00
T1ARDD David Dahl/75	6.00	15.00
T1ARDP David Price/50	8.00	20.00
T1AREL Evan Longoria/30	10.00	25.00
T1ARFF Freddie Freeman/30	20.00	50.00
T1ARJA Jose Altuve/65	30.00	80.00
T1ARJBE Josh Bell		
T1ARJC Jose Canseco/100	20.00	50.00
T1ARJD Jacob deGrom/50	15.00	40.00
T1ARJMR J.D. Martinez/75	15.00	40.00
T1ARJPA Joe Panik/75	5.00	12.00
T1ARJPE Joc Pederson/35	10.00	25.00
T1ARJT Julio Teheran/100	6.00	15.00
T1ARKB Kris Bryant/30	60.00	150.00
T1ARKK Kevin Kiermaier/60	6.00	15.00
T1ARKMA Kenta Maeda/60		
T1ARKS Kyle Schwarber		
T1ARLS Luis Severino/75	10.00	25.00
T1ARLW Luke Weaver/100	5.00	12.00
T1ARMCA Matt Carpenter/65	6.00	15.00
T1ARMCO Michael Conforto/65	12.00	30.00
T1ARMFR Maikel Franco/30	15.00	40.00
T1ARMFU Michael Fulmer/70	8.00	20.00
T1ARMM Manny Machado/30	50.00	120.00
T1ARMST Marcus Stroman/40	8.00	20.00
T1ARNM Nomar Mazara/75	4.00	10.00
T1ARNS Noah Syndergaard/50	10.00	25.00
T1ARPF Prince Fielder/30		
T1ARRB Ryan Braun/30	10.00	25.00
T1ARRP Rick Porcello/75	5.00	12.00
T1ARSMA Starling Marte/30	5.00	12.00
T1ARSMZ Steven Matz/100	5.00	12.00
T1ARSP Stephen Piscotty/75	5.00	12.00
T1ARTG Tyler Glasnow/100	5.00	12.00
T1ARWC Willson Contreras/30	12.00	30.00
T1ARWM Wil Myers/26		
T1ARYC Yoenis Cespedes/30	10.00	25.00

2017 Topps Tier One Autographs

STATED ODDS 1:20 HOBBY
PRINT RUNS B/WN 11-99 COPIES PER
EXCHANGE DEADLINE 6/30/2019
NO PRICING ON QTY 11
*CPPR/25: .6X TO 1.5X BASE p/r 99
*CPPR/25: .5X TO 1.2X BASE p/r 30
*CPPR/25: .4X TO 1X BASE p/r 25

T1ABH Bryce Harper/20	75.00	200.00
T1ABJ Bo Jackson/30	30.00	80.00
T1ABP Buster Posey/25	60.00	150.00
T1ACC Carlos Correa/99	20.00	50.00
T1ACJ Chipper Jones/30	40.00	100.00
T1ACK Clayton Kershaw/30	40.00	100.00
T1ACR Cal Ripken Jr./30	60.00	150.00
T1ADJ Derek Jeter/11		
T1ADM Don Mattingly/99	25.00	60.00
T1ADO David Ortiz/75	20.00	50.00
T1AFT Frank Thomas/99	20.00	50.00
T1AGM Greg Maddux/20	40.00	100.00
T1AI Ichiro/20	200.00	400.00
T1AIR Ivan Rodriguez/99	12.00	30.00
T1AJB Johnny Bench/30	30.00	80.00
T1AKB Kris Bryant/30	75.00	200.00
T1AKG Ken Griffey Jr./20	150.00	300.00
T1AMMA Manny Machado/30	15.00	40.00
T1AMMG Mark McGwire/30	40.00	100.00
T1AMP Mike Piazza/30		
T1AMTA Masahiro Tanaka/20	150.00	300.00
T1AMTR Mike Trout/20	200.00	400.00
T1ANR Nolan Ryan/30	60.00	150.00
T1AOV Omar Vizquel/30	5.00	12.00
T1ARB Ryan Braun/30	8.00	20.00
T1ARCA Rod Carew/30	12.00	30.00
T1ARCL Roger Clemens/20	40.00	100.00
T1ARH Rickey Henderson/30	25.00	60.00
T1ARJA Reggie Jackson/30	25.00	60.00
T1ARJO Randy Johnson/20	30.00	80.00
T1ARS Ryne Sandberg/99	20.00	50.00
T1ASC Steve Carlton/30	12.00	30.00
T1ASK Sandy Koufax		
T1ATG Tom Glavine/99	12.00	30.00

2017 Topps Tier One Break Out Autographs

RANDOM INSERTS IN PACKS
PRINT RUNS B/WN 50-300 COPIES PER
EXCHANGE DEADLINE 6/30/2019
*CPPR/25: .6X TO 1.5X BASE p/r 60-300
*CPPR/25: .5X TO 1.2X BASE p/r 50

BOAAB Andrew Benintendi/90	40.00	100.00
BOAABR Alex Bregman/60	25.00	60.00
BOAAC Adam Conley/300	3.00	8.00
BOAADA Aledmys Diaz/140	4.00	10.00
BOAADI Aledmys Diaz/140	4.00	10.00
BOAAJD Aaron Judge/140	200.00	400.00
BOAAJR A.J. Reed/300	3.00	8.00
BOAAJU Aaron Judge/140	200.00	400.00
BOAANL Aaron Nola/300	4.00	10.00
BOAANO Aaron Nola/300	4.00	10.00
BOAARD A.J. Reed/300	3.00	8.00
BOAARE Alex Reyes/140	4.00	10.00
BOAARY Alex Reyes/140	4.00	10.00
BOABM Bruce Maxwell/300	3.00	8.00
BOABS Blake Snell/300	4.00	10.00
BOABSN Blake Snell/300	4.00	10.00
BOACF Carson Fulmer/150	3.00	8.00
BOACP Chad Pinder/300	3.00	8.00
BOACRD Cody Reed/300	3.00	8.00
BOACRE Cody Reed/300	3.00	8.00
BOADDA David Dahl/140	4.00	10.00
BOADDH David Dahl/140	4.00	10.00
BOADG Didi Gregorius/140	20.00	50.00
BOADS Dansby Swanson/60	20.00	50.00
BOAEDD Eddie Rosario/300	4.00	10.00
BOAEI Ender Inciarte/171	8.00	20.00
BOAER Eddie Rosario/300	4.00	10.00
BOAGB Greg Bird/180	4.00	10.00
BOAGM German Marquez/297	5.00	12.00
BOAHD Hunter Dozier/140	4.00	10.00
BOAHOE Henry Owens EXCH	3.00	8.00
BOAHOW Henry Owens EXCH	3.00	8.00
BOAHR Hunter Renfroe/180	5.00	12.00
BOAHRE Hunter Renfroe/200	5.00	12.00
BOAJA Jorge Alfaro/300	4.00	10.00
BOAJDA Javier Baez/65	10.00	25.00
BOAJBZ Javier Baez/65	10.00	25.00
BOAJCO Jharel Cotton/300	3.00	8.00
BOAJCT Jharel Cotton/300	3.00	8.00
BOAJD Jose De Leon/90	3.00	8.00
BOAJG Jon Gray/85	3.00	8.00
BOAJH Jeremy Hazelbaker/300	4.00	10.00
BOAJHO Jeff Hoffman/200	6.00	15.00
BOAJJ JaCoby Jones/140	6.00	15.00
BOAJM Joe Musgrove/300	3.00	8.00
BOAJPA Joe Panik/120	4.00	10.00
BOAJPN Joe Panik/120	4.00	10.00
BOAJT Jameson Taillon/85	4.00	10.00
BOAJU Julio Urias/50	5.00	12.00
BOAKG Ken Giles/300	3.00	8.00
BOAKS Kyle Schwarber/65	15.00	40.00
BOALG Lucas Giolito/65	8.00	20.00
BOALSE Luis Severino/90	8.00	20.00
BOALSV Luis Severino/90	8.00	20.00
BOALWA Luke Weaver/200	4.00	10.00
BOALWE Luke Weaver/200	4.00	10.00
BOAMFA Maikel Franco/100	4.00	10.00
BOAMFL Michael Fulmer/150	8.00	20.00
BOAMFR Maikel Franco/100	4.00	10.00
BOAMFU Michael Fulmer/150	8.00	20.00
BOAMK Max Kepler/300	4.00	10.00
BOAMKE Max Kepler/300	4.00	10.00
BOAMM Manny Margot/300	3.00	8.00
BOAMO Matt Olson/300	6.00	15.00
BOAMSA Miguel Sano/90	6.00	15.00
BOANM Nomar Mazara/85	6.00	15.00
BOARG Randal Grichuk/200	8.00	20.00
BOARGE Robert Gsellman/300	3.00	8.00
BOARGR Randal Grichuk/200	8.00	20.00
BOARGS Robert Gsellman/300	3.00	8.00
BOARHA Ryon Healy/300	4.00	10.00
BOARHE Ryon Healy/300	4.00	10.00
BOARLO Reynaldo Lopez/300	3.00	8.00
BOARLP Reynaldo Lopez/300	3.00	8.00
BOARQI Roman Quinn/300	3.00	8.00
BOARQU Roman Quinn/300	3.00	8.00
BOARSC Ryan Schimpf/300	3.00	8.00
BOARST Robert Stephenson/300	3.00	8.00
BOART Raimel Tapia/200	4.00	10.00
BOASLU Seth Lugo/300	3.00	8.00
BOASP Stephen Piscotty/85	4.00	10.00
BOASPI Stephen Piscotty/85	4.00	10.00
BOATAS Tyler Austin/300	5.00	12.00
BOATAU Tyler Austin/300	5.00	12.00
BOATB Ty Blach/295	3.00	8.00
BOATCN Tim Cooney/300	3.00	8.00
BOATCO Tim Cooney/300	3.00	8.00
BOATG Tyler Glasnow/200	4.00	10.00
BOATGL Tyler Glasnow/200	4.00	10.00
BOATMA Trey Mancini/300	15.00	40.00
BOATMN Trey Mancini/300	15.00	40.00
BOATNA Tyler Naquin/300	3.00	8.00
BOATNQ Tyler Naquin/300	3.00	8.00
BOATSO Trevor Story/140	5.00	12.00
BOATST Trevor Story/140	5.00	12.00
BOATTH Trayce Thompson/300	4.00	10.00
BOATTO Trayce Thompson/300	4.00	10.00
BOATTR Trea Turner/200	10.00	25.00
BOATTU Trea Turner/200	10.00	25.00
BOAWC Willson Contreras/50	12.00	30.00
BOAWCO Willson Contreras/50	12.00	30.00
BOAYG Yulieski Gurriel/65	10.00	25.00
BOAYMO Yoan Moncada		

2017 Topps Tier One Dual Autographs

STATED ODDS 1:67 MINI BOX
STATED PRINT RUN 25 SER.#'d SETS
EXCHANGE DEADLINE 6/30/2019

DABS Crra/Brgmn EXCH	75.00	200.00
DAFS Swanson/Freeman	100.00	250.00
DAGB Griffey/Bonds EXCH	700.00	900.00
DAGR Gnzlz/Rdrgz EXCH	60.00	150.00
DAGV Glrrga/Vizquel EXCH	30.00	80.00
DAHT Harper/Turner		
DAJS Smoltz/Jones EXCH		
DAKS Seager/Kershaw	300.00	500.00
DAMB Mncda/Bnntndi EXCH	150.00	400.00
DAOW Oswalt/Wagner	12.00	30.00
DASG Glavine/Smoltz	60.00	150.00
DATB Bryant/Trout		
DAVL Lndr/Vzql EXCH		
DAVU Valenzuela/Urias	25.00	60.00

2017 Topps Tier One Legend Relics

STATED ODDS 1:7 MINI BOX
PRINT RUNS B/WN 25-200 COPIES PER

T1RLBR Babe Ruth/30	60.00	150.00
T1RLCJ Chipper Jones/200	4.00	10.00
T1RLCR Cal Ripken Jr./200	8.00	20.00
T1RLCY Carl Yastrzemski/200	5.00	12.00
T1RLDJ Derek Jeter/200	15.00	40.00
T1RLDS Duke Snider		
T1RLEB Ernie Banks/25	15.00	40.00
T1RLES Enos Slaughter/200	4.00	10.00
T1RLFT Frank Thomas/200	4.00	10.00
T1RLGB George Brett/200	8.00	20.00
T1RLGC Gary Carter/100	3.00	8.00
T1RLGM Greg Maddux/200	5.00	12.00
T1RLHA Hank Aaron/200	10.00	25.00
T1RLJB Johnny Bench/200	5.00	12.00
T1RLJR Jackie Robinson/40	20.00	50.00
T1RLKGJ Ken Griffey Jr./200	10.00	25.00
T1RLMM Mark McGwire/200	6.00	15.00
T1RLMP Mike Piazza/200	4.00	10.00
T1RLNR Nolan Ryan/200	8.00	20.00
T1RLPR Phil Rizzuto/100	5.00	12.00
T1RLRC Roberto Clemente/200	20.00	50.00
T1RLRJ Randy Johnson/200	4.00	10.00
T1RLRM Roger Maris		
T1RLTC Ty Cobb/60	30.00	80.00
T1RLTW Ted Williams/200	12.00	30.00
T1RLWS Willie Stargell		

2017 Topps Tier One Legend Dual Relics

*DUAL: .6X TO 1.5X BASIC
STATED ODDS 1:41 MINI BOX
STATED PRINT RUN 25 SER.#'d SETS

T1RLBR Babe Ruth	125.00	300.00
T1RLCR Cal Ripken Jr.	30.00	80.00
T1RLCY Carl Yastrzemski	20.00	50.00
T1RLDJ Derek Jeter	60.00	150.00
T1RLGB George Brett	20.00	50.00
T1RLHA Hank Aaron	40.00	100.00
T1RLNR Nolan Ryan	20.00	50.00
T1RLRM Roger Maris	10.00	25.00
T1RLTW Ted Williams	30.00	80.00
T1RLWS Willie Stargell	25.00	60.00

2017 Topps Tier One Prime Performers Autographs

RANDOM INSERTS IN PACKS
PRINT RUNS B/WN 30-300 COPIES PER
EXCHANGE DEADLINE 6/30/2019
*CPPR/25: .6X TO 1.5X BASE p/r 65-300
*CPPR/25: .4X TO 1X BASE p/r 30-40

PPAADU Adam Duvall/300	6.00	15.00
PPAADV Adam Duvall/300	6.00	15.00
PPAAGA Andres Galarraga/200	4.00	10.00
PPAAGR Andres Galarraga/200	4.00	10.00
PPAAJ Adam Jones/65	8.00	20.00
PPAAPE Andy Pettitte/40	20.00	50.00
PPAARI Anthony Rizzo/75	20.00	50.00
PPABA Bobby Abreu/100	6.00	15.00
PPABF Brandon Finnegan/300	4.00	10.00
PPABL Barry Larkin EXCH	15.00	40.00
PPACCO Carlos Correa EXCH	40.00	100.00
PPACCR Carlos Carrasco/300	5.00	12.00
PPACJ Chipper Jones/30	40.00	100.00
PPACSA Chris Sale/65	20.00	50.00
PPACSC Curt Schilling/40	6.00	15.00
PPACSE Corey Seager/40	30.00	80.00
PPADBE Dellin Betances/200	4.00	10.00
PPADBT Dellin Betances/200	4.00	10.00
PPADDF Danny Duffy/300	3.00	8.00
PPADDU Danny Duffy/300	3.00	8.00
PPADFO Dexter Fowler/100	6.00	15.00
PPADFW Dexter Fowler/100	6.00	15.00
PPADGR Dee Gordon/100	3.00	8.00
PPADL Derrek Lee/200	4.00	10.00
PPADMA Don Mattingly/30	30.00	80.00
PPADO David Ortiz/30	40.00	100.00
PPADPE Dustin Pedroia/40	15.00	40.00
PPADPM Drew Pomeranz/200	5.00	12.00
PPADPO Drew Pomeranz/200	5.00	12.00
PPADPR David Price/40	10.00	25.00
PPAEE Edwin Encarnacion EXCH	10.00	25.00
PPAFF Freddie Freeman/65	15.00	40.00
PPAFLI Francisco Lindor EXCH	20.00	50.00
PPAFLN Francisco Lindor EXCH	20.00	50.00
PPAFR Frank Robinson/30	20.00	50.00
PPAFT Frank Thomas/30	20.00	50.00
PPAFV Fernando Valenzuela/65	15.00	40.00
PPAGS George Springer/200	12.00	30.00
PPAIR Ivan Rodriguez/40	15.00	40.00
PPAJAL Jose Altuve/100	20.00	50.00
PPAJAT Jose Altuve/100	20.00	50.00
PPAJCA Jose Canseco/300	8.00	20.00
PPAJCN Jose Canseco/300	8.00	20.00
PPAJDE Jacob deGrom EXCH	12.00	30.00
PPAJDG Jacob deGrom EXCH	12.00	30.00
PPAJFA Jeurys Familia/300	4.00	10.00
PPAJFM Jeurys Familia/300	4.00	10.00
PPAJH Jason Heyward/40	5.00	12.00
PPAJMA J.D. Martinez/100	12.00	30.00
PPAJMR J.D. Martinez/175	12.00	30.00
PPAJOE John Olerud/300	10.00	25.00
PPAJOL John Olerud/300	10.00	25.00
PPAJRC Jim Rice/100	5.00	12.00
PPAJRI Jim Rice/100	5.00	12.00
PPAJS John Smoltz/40	12.00	30.00
PPAJTR Justin Turner/300	10.00	25.00
PPAJTU Justin Turner/300	10.00	25.00
PPAJV Jason Varitek/40	10.00	25.00
PPAKB Kris Bryant EXCH	75.00	200.00
PPAKDA Khris Davis/300	5.00	12.00
PPAKDV Khris Davis/300	5.00	12.00
PPAKH Kelvin Herrera/300	4.00	10.00
PPAKMA Kenta Maeda/65	8.00	20.00
PPAKMO Kendrys Morales/200	3.00	8.00
PPAKSA Kyle Seager/200	3.00	8.00
PPAKSE Kyle Seager/200	3.00	8.00
PPALB Lou Brock/65	12.00	30.00
PPAMCA Matt Carpenter/100	5.00	12.00
PPAMCR Matt Carpenter/100	5.00	12.00
PPAMMA Manny Machado/30	60.00	150.00
PPAMML Mark Mulder/300	3.00	8.00
PPAMMU Mark Mulder/300	3.00	8.00
PPAMW Matt Wieters/40	6.00	15.00
PPANSN Noah Syndergaard/85	15.00	40.00
PPANSY Noah Syndergaard/85	15.00	40.00
PPAOG Ozzie Guillen/200	5.00	12.00
PPAOS Ozzie Smith/40	15.00	40.00
PPAOVI Omar Vizquel/200	4.00	10.00
PPAOVZ Omar Vizquel/200	4.00	10.00
PPAPF Prince Fielder/30	6.00	15.00
PPAPK Paul Konerko/65	8.00	20.00
PPAPN Phil Niekro/65	4.00	10.00
PPARA Roberto Alomar/40	12.00	30.00
PPARB Ryan Braun/40	10.00	25.00
PPARC Rod Carew/40	15.00	40.00
PPARO Roy Oswalt/200	5.00	12.00
PPARS Ryne Sandberg/30	20.00	50.00
PPARY Robin Yount/30	25.00	60.00
PPASA Sandy Alomar Jr./300	5.00	12.00
PPASMA Steven Matz/300	4.00	10.00
PPASME Starling Marte/200	4.00	10.00
PPASMR Starling Marte/200	4.00	10.00
PPASMT Steven Matz/300	4.00	10.00
PPASWI Steven Wright/300	3.00	8.00
PPASWR Steven Wright/300	3.00	8.00
PPAWB Wade Boggs/30	15.00	40.00
PPAWDA Wade Davis/300	3.00	8.00
PPAWDV Wade Davis/300	3.00	8.00

2018 Topps Tier One Relics

RANDOM INSERTS IN PACKS
PRINT RUNS B/WN 335-400 COPIES PER
*DUAL/25: .6X TO 1.5X SNGL RELIC

T1RAB Andrew Benintendi/335	4.00	10.00
T1RABR Alex Bregman/335	3.00	8.00
T1RAD Adam Duvall/335	3.00	8.00
T1RAJO Adam Jones/335	2.50	6.00
T1RAM Andrew McCutchen/335	3.00	8.00
T1RAMI Andrew Miller/335	2.50	6.00
T1RAN Aaron Nola/335	2.50	6.00
T1RAP A.J. Pollock/335	2.00	5.00
T1RAR Amed Rosario/400	2.50	6.00
T1RARE Anthony Rondon/335	3.00	8.00
T1RARU Addison Russell/335	2.50	6.00
T1RBB Byron Buxton/335	2.50	6.00
T1RBH Bryce Harper/400	5.00	12.00
T1RBP Buster Posey/335	4.00	10.00
T1RBZ Ben Zobrist/335	2.50	6.00
T1RCA Chris Archer/335	2.00	5.00
T1RCB Charlie Blackmon/400	3.00	8.00
T1RCBE Cody Bellinger/335	5.00	12.00
T1RCC Carlos Correa/335	3.00	8.00
T1RCF Clint Frazier/400	4.00	10.00
T1RCK Clayton Kershaw/335	6.00	15.00
T1RCKI Craig Kimbrel/335	2.50	6.00
T1RCKL Corey Kluber/335	2.50	6.00
T1RCM Carlos Martinez/335	2.50	6.00
T1RCS Chris Sale/400	3.00	8.00
T1RCSE Corey Seager/335	3.00	8.00
T1RCY Christian Yelich/335	4.00	10.00
T1RDB Dellin Betances/335	2.50	6.00
T1RDG Didi Gregorius/335	2.50	6.00
T1RDK Dallas Keuchel/335	2.50	6.00
T1RDM Daniel Murphy/335	2.50	6.00
T1RDP Drew Pomeranz/335	2.00	5.00
T1RDS Dominic Smith/335	2.00	5.00
T1RGS Giancarlo Stanton/335	4.00	10.00
T1RGSP George Springer/335	2.50	6.00
T1RIH Ian Happ/335	2.50	6.00
T1RIK Ian Kinsler/335	2.50	6.00
T1RJA Jose Altuve/400	2.50	6.00
T1RJD Josh Donaldson/335	2.50	6.00
T1RJF Jack Flaherty/335	3.00	8.00
T1RJG Joey Gallo/335	2.50	6.00
T1RJH Josh Harrison/335	2.00	5.00
T1RJL Jake Lamb/335	2.50	6.00
T1RJLE Jon Lester/335	2.50	6.00
T1RJS Jonathan Schoop/335	2.00	5.00
T1RJT Justin Turner/335	2.50	6.00
T1RJV Joey Votto/335	3.00	8.00
T1RKB Kris Bryant/400	6.00	15.00
T1RKJ Kenley Jansen/335	2.50	6.00
T1RKS Kyle Seager/335	2.00	5.00
T1RLM Lance McCullers/335	2.00	5.00
T1RLS Luis Severino/400	2.50	6.00
T1RMB Mookie Betts/400	5.00	12.00
T1RMBR Michael Brantley/335	2.50	6.00
T1RMC Miguel Cabrera/335	2.50	6.00
T1RMCO Michael Conforto/335	2.50	6.00
T1RMF Michael Fulmer/335	2.00	5.00
T1RMM Manny Machado/400	3.00	8.00
T1RMO Marcell Ozuna/335	3.00	8.00
T1RMOL Matt Olson/335	2.00	5.00
T1RMS Max Scherzer/400	3.00	8.00
T1RMSA Miguel Sano/335	2.50	6.00
T1RMT Mike Trout/400	12.00	30.00
T1RMTA Masahiro Tanaka/335	2.50	6.00
T1RNA Nolan Arenado/400	4.00	10.00
T1RNC Nelson Cruz/335	3.00	8.00
T1RNS Noah Syndergaard/335	2.50	6.00
T1RPG Paul Goldschmidt/400	3.00	8.00
T1RRC Robinson Cano/335	2.50	6.00
T1RRD Rafael Devers/400	4.00	10.00
T1RRH Rhys Hoskins/335	5.00	12.00
T1RRI Raisel Iglesias/335	2.50	6.00
T1RRM Ryan McMahon/335	2.50	6.00
T1RRO Roberto Osuna/335	2.00	5.00
T1RROD Rougned Odor/335	2.50	6.00
T1RSC Starlin Castro/335	2.00	5.00
T1RSN Sean Newcomb/335	2.50	6.00
T1RSP Salvador Perez/335	2.50	6.00
T1RSS Stephen Strasburg/335	3.00	8.00
T1RSSO Steven Souza Jr./335	2.50	6.00
T1RTP Tommy Pham/335	2.00	5.00
T1RTS Trevor Story/335	3.00	8.00
T1RVR Victor Robles/335	4.00	10.00
T1RWC Willson Contreras/335	3.00	8.00
T1RWM Wil Myers/335	2.00	5.00
T1RYG Yuli Gurriel/335	2.50	6.00
T1RYM Yadier Molina/335	3.00	8.00
T1RYP Yasiel Puig/335	3.00	8.00
T1RZG Zack Greinke/335	2.50	6.00

2018 Topps Tier One Autograph Relics

STATED ODDS 1:9 HOBBY
PRINT RUNS B/WN 5-100 COPIES PER
NO PRICING ON QTY 10 OR LESS
EXCHANGE DEADLINE 4/30/2020

ATRAD Adrian Beltre/35	25.00	60.00
ATRABR Alex Bregman/60	12.00	30.00
ATRAP Andy Pettitte/35	15.00	40.00
ATRAPO A.J. Pollock/25	6.00	15.00
ATRAR Amed Rosario/70	5.00	12.00
ATRARE Anthony Rendon/100	12.00	30.00
ATRBG Brett Gardner/60	10.00	25.00
ATRBS Blake Snell/100	8.00	20.00
ATRCB Charlie Blackmon/90	8.00	20.00
ATRCC Carlos Correa		
ATRCF Clint Frazier/80	12.00	30.00
ATRCK Craig Kimbrel/55	8.00	20.00
ATRCSA Chris Sale/45	10.00	25.00
ATRCSI Chance Sisco/100	5.00	12.00
ATRDG Didi Gregorius/100	15.00	40.00
ATRDP David Price/35	8.00	20.00
ATRDPO Drew Pomeranz/90	4.00	10.00
ATRDW Dave Winfield/15	20.00	50.00
ATRFF Freddie Freeman/45	12.00	30.00
ATRFM Fred McGriff/35	15.00	40.00
ATRGS Gary Sanchez/55	15.00	40.00
ATRHB Harrison Bader/100	6.00	15.00
ATRJB Jose Berrios/70	5.00	12.00
ATRJC J.P. Crawford/100	8.00	20.00
ATRJG Joey Gallo/70	5.00	12.00
ATRJH Josh Harrison/100	5.00	12.00
ATRJJ JaCoby Jones/100	5.00	12.00
ATRKB Kris Bryant/15	75.00	200.00
ATRKGJ Ken Griffey Jr.		
ATRLS Lucas Sims/100	4.00	10.00
ATRMF Michael Fulmer/62	4.00	10.00
ATRMK Max Kepler/100	5.00	12.00
ATRNS Noah Syndergaard/35	12.00	30.00
ATRRA Roberto Alomar/35	20.00	50.00
ATRRD Rafael Devers/80	12.00	30.00
ATRRG Randal Grichuk/24	4.00	10.00
ATRRJ Reggie Jackson/15	30.00	80.00
ATRRM Ryan McMahon/100	5.00	12.00
ATRRT Raimel Tapia/100	4.00	10.00
ATRSN Sean Newcomb/100	5.00	12.00
ATRST Sam Travis/100	4.00	10.00
ATRTM Trey Mancini/100	5.00	12.00
ATRTP Tommy Pham/100	4.00	10.00
ATRWM Whit Merrifield/100	8.00	20.00

2018 Topps Tier One Autograph Dual Relics

ATRCC Carlos Correa	40.00	100.00
ATRJC J.P. Crawford	25.00	60.00

2018 Topps Tier One Autographs

OVERALL AUTO ODDS 1:19 HOBBY
PRINT RUNS B/WN 15-125 COPIES PER
EXCHANGE DEADLINE 4/30/2020

T1AAJ Aaron Judge/40	100.00	250.00
T1AAP Andy Pettitte/125	12.00	30.00
T1AAR Anthony Rizzo/60	20.00	50.00
T1AARO Alex Rodriguez/20	75.00	200.00
T1ABH Bryce Harper/30	125.00	300.00
T1ABJ Bo Jackson/30	40.00	100.00
T1ABL Barry Larkin/55	15.00	40.00
T1ACJ Chipper Jones/50	30.00	80.00
T1ACR Cal Ripken Jr./50	40.00	100.00
T1ACS Chris Sale EXCH	10.00	25.00
T1ADJ Derek Jeter/15	600.00	1000.00
T1ADM Don Mattingly/80	30.00	80.00
T1ADW Dave Winfield/60	12.00	30.00
T1AFL Francisco Lindor/110	12.00	30.00
T1AFT Frank Thomas/80	25.00	60.00
T1AGM Greg Maddux/30	50.00	120.00
T1AGS Gary Sanchez/110	10.00	25.00
T1AHA Hank Aaron/15	300.00	600.00
T1AI Ichiro/30	200.00	400.00
T1AJB Johnny Bench/45	25.00	60.00
T1AJP Jim Palmer/90	12.00	30.00

T1AKB Kris Bryant EXCH 60.00 150.00
T1AMM Mark McGwire/50 50.00 120.00
T1AMMA Manny Machado/80 12.00 30.00
T1AMR Mariano Rivera/30 75.00 200.00
T1AMT Mike Trout/20 300.00 500.00
T1ANG Nomar Garciaparra/90 15.00 40.00
T1ANR Nolan Ryan/50 50.00 120.00
T1AOS Ozzie Smith/125 20.00 50.00
T1ARC Roger Clemens/30 30.00 80.00
T1ARCA Rod Carew/90 12.00 30.00
T1ARH Rickey Henderson/50 40.00 100.00
T1ARJ Randy Johnson/30 50.00 120.00
T1ARJA Reggie Jackson/50 30.00 80.00
T1ASC Steve Carlton/90 12.00 30.00
T1ASK Sandy Koufax/15
T1ATG Tom Glavine/90 10.00 25.00

2018 Topps Tier One Autographs Bronze Ink

*BRONZE: .6X TO 1.5X BASIC
STATED ODDS 1:49 HOBBY
STATED PRINT RUN 25 SER.#'d SETS
EXCHANGE DEADLINE 4/30/2020
T1AFT Frank Thomas 30.00 80.00

2018 Topps Tier One Break Out Autographs

OVERALL AUTO ODDS 1:19 HOBBY
PRINT RUNS B/WN 45-275 COPIES PER
EXCHANGE DEADLINE 4/30/2020
BAAB Anthony Banda/275 3.00 8.00
BAAG Amir Garrett/275 3.00 8.00
BAAH Austin Hays/275 5.00 12.00
BAAR Amed Rosario/100 6.00 15.00
BAARO Amed Rosario/100 6.00 15.00
BAAS Andrew Stevenson/275 3.00 8.00
BAAV Alex Verdugo/275 5.00 12.00
BABG Ben Gamel/275 4.00 10.00
BABP Brett Phillips/275 3.00 8.00
BABPH Brett Phillips/275 3.00 8.00
BABS Blake Snell/275 4.00 10.00
BABSN Blake Snell/275 4.00 10.00
BABW Brandon Woodruff/275 4.00 10.00
BABZ Bradley Zimmer/225 3.00 8.00
BACAR Christian Arroyo/275 3.00 8.00
BACF Clint Frazier/275 10.00 25.00
BACFR Clint Frazier/275 10.00 25.00
BACS Chance Sisco/275 4.00 10.00
BACT Chris Taylor/275 8.00 20.00
BADF Derek Fisher/275 3.00 8.00
BADFI Derek Fisher/275 3.00 8.00
BADFO Dustin Fowler/275 3.00 8.00
BADUF Dustin Fowler/275 3.00 8.00
BADL Dinelson Lamet/275 3.00 8.00
BADOS Domingo Santana/275 4.00 10.00
BADSA Domingo Santana/275 4.00 10.00
BADR Daniel Robertson/275 3.00 8.00
BADRO Daniel Robertson/275 3.00 8.00
BADS Dominic Smith/100 3.00 8.00
BADSM Dominic Smith/275 3.00 8.00
BAFJ Felix Jorge/275 3.00 8.00
BAFM Francisco Mejia/275 4.00 10.00
BAGB Greg Bird/275 4.00 10.00
BAGC Garrett Cooper/275 3.00 8.00
BAGCO Garrett Cooper/275 3.00 8.00
BAHB Harrison Bader/275 5.00 12.00
BAHBA Harrison Bader/275 5.00 12.00
BAJC J.P. Crawford/250 3.00 8.00
BAJF Jack Flaherty/275 5.00 12.00
BAJFL Jack Flaherty/275 5.00 12.00
BAJFA Jacob Faria/275 3.00 8.00
BAJH Josh Hader/275 3.00 8.00
BAJJ JaCoby Jones/275 4.00 10.00
BAJJI Joe Jimenez/275 3.00 8.00
BAJR Jose Ramirez/100 12.00 30.00
BAJW Jesse Winker/275 3.00 8.00
BAKB Keon Broxton/275 3.00 8.00
BALC Luis Castillo/275 4.00 10.00
BALG Lucas Giolito/100 4.00 10.00
BALGI Lucas Giolito/100 4.00 10.00
BALS Lucas Sims/275 3.00 8.00
BALSI Lucas Sims/275 3.00 8.00
BALW Luke Weaver/275 4.00 10.00
BALWE Luke Weaver/275 4.00 10.00
BAMA Miguel Andujar/275 30.00 80.00
BAMAN Miguel Andujar/275 30.00 80.00
BAMAF Max Fried/275 12.00 30.00
BAMFR Max Fried/275 12.00 30.00
BAMF Michael Fulmer/225 3.00 8.00
BAMFU Michael Fulmer/275 3.00 8.00
BAMK Max Kepler/275 4.00 10.00
BAMKE Max Kepler/275 4.00 10.00
BAND Nicky Delmonico/275 3.00 8.00
BANDO Nicky Delmonico/265 3.00 8.00
BAOA Ozzie Albies/225 30.00 80.00
BAOAL Ozzie Albies/225 30.00 80.00
BAPD Paul DeJong/275 5.00 12.00
BARD Rafael Devers/100 20.00 50.00
BARDE Rafael Devers/275 20.00 50.00
BARH Rhys Hoskins/225 15.00 40.00
BARHO Rhys Hoskins/275 15.00 40.00
BARI Raisel Iglesias/265 4.00 10.00
BARM Ryan McMahon/275 4.00 10.00
BARMC Ryan McMahon/275 4.00 10.00
BART Raimel Tapia/275 3.00 8.00
BARTA Raimel Tapia/275 3.00 8.00
BARTO Ronald Torreyes/275 12.00 30.00
BASN Sean Newcomb/275 6.00 15.00
BASNE Sean Newcomb/275 6.00 15.00
BASO Shohei Ohtani 400.00 800.00
BAST Sam Travis/275 3.00 8.00
BASTR Sam Travis/275 3.00 8.00
BATB Tim Beckham/265 4.00 10.00
BATM Trey Mancini/225 4.00 10.00
BATMA Tyler Mahle/275 5.00 12.00
BATP Tommy Pham/275 3.00 8.00
BATS Travis Shaw/275 3.00 8.00
BATW Tyler Wade/275 5.00 12.00
BATWL Tzu-Wei Lin/275 10.00 25.00
BAVR Victor Robles/250 20.00 50.00
BAWB Walker Buehler/275 15.00 40.00

2018 Topps Tier One Break Out Autographs Bronze Ink

*BRONZE: .6X TO 1.5X BASIC
STATED ODDS 1:18 HOBBY
STATED PRINT RUN 25 SER.#'d SETS
EXCHANGE DEADLINE 4/30/2020
BAAH Austin Hays 20.00 50.00
BAJH Josh Hader 5.00 12.00
BAMA Miguel Andujar 60.00 150.00
BAMAN Miguel Andujar 60.00 150.00
BARH Rhys Hoskins 40.00 100.00
BARHO Rhys Hoskins 40.00 100.00
BATWL Tzu-Wei Lin 20.00 50.00
BAWB Walker Buehler 60.00 150.00

2018 Topps Tier One Dual Autographs

STATED ODDS 1:81 HOBBY
STATED PRINT RUN 25 SER.#'d SETS
EXCHANGE DEADLINE 4/30/2020
T1DAAJ Jones/Albies EXCH 125.00 300.00
T1DABT M.Trout/K.Bryant
T1DAFD Devers/Frazier EXCH 30.00 80.00
T1DAJM R.Johnson/P.Martinez 75.00 200.00
T1DAJR M.Rivera/D.Jeter
T1DAKA Koufax/Aaron EXCH 500.00 1000.00
T1DARS Smith/Rosario EXCH 40.00 100.00
T1DASC Clemens/Sale EXCH 60.00 150.00
T1DASD P.DeJong/O.Smith 75.00 200.00

2018 Topps Tier One Legend Relics

STATED ODDS 1:9 MINI BOX
PRINT RUNS B/WN 7-175 COPIES PER
NO PRICING ON QTY 7
T1RLBJ Bo Jackson/175 4.00 10.00
T1RLBRO Brooks Robinson/100 8.00 20.00
T1RLDJ Derek Jeter/175 12.00 30.00
T1RLDM Don Mattingly/175 4.00 10.00
T1RLDS Duke Snider/100 8.00 20.00
T1RLDW Dave Winfield/175 4.00 10.00
T1RLFT Frank Thomas/175 4.00 10.00
T1RLGB George Brett
T1RLGM Greg Maddux/175 5.00 12.00
T1RLHA Hank Aaron/75 12.00 30.00
T1RLHW Honus Wagner/50 30.00 80.00
T1RLJR Jackie Robinson/30 15.00 40.00
T1RLMM Mark McGwire/175 6.00 15.00
T1RLMP Mike Piazza/175 4.00 10.00
T1RLNR Nolan Ryan/175 8.00 20.00
T1RLOS Ozzie Smith/175 6.00 15.00
T1RLPM Pedro Martinez/175 5.00 12.00
T1RLRA Roberto Alomar/175 5.00 12.00
T1RLRC Roberto Clemente/100 25.00 60.00
T1RLRJ Reggie Jackson/175 4.00 10.00
T1RLRJO Randy Johnson/50 4.00 10.00
T1RLTC Ty Cobb
T1RLTW Ted Williams/175 20.00 50.00
T1RLWS Warren Spahn/100 6.00 15.00

2018 Topps Tier One Legend Dual Relics

*DUAL: .75X TO 2X BASIC
STATED ODDS 1:50 MINI BOX
STATED PRINT RUN 25 SER.#'d SETS
T1RLGB George Brett 40.00 100.00

2018 Topps Tier One Prime Performers Autographs

OVERALL AUTO ODDS 1:19 HOBBY
PRINT RUNS B/WN 50-285 COPIES PER
EXCHANGE DEADLINE 4/30/2020
PPAAB Adrian Beltre/80 15.00 40.00
PPAABR Alex Bregman/145 20.00 50.00
PPAAD Adam Duvall/285 5.00 12.00
PPAAG Andres Galarraga/270 4.00 10.00
PPAAK Al Kaline/90 20.00 50.00
PPAAP Andy Pettitte/80 12.00 30.00
PPAAR Alex Rodriguez
PPAARI Anthony Rizzo/60 20.00 50.00
PPAAW Alex Wood/285 3.00 8.00
PPABD Brian Dozier/285 4.00 10.00
PPABW Bernie Williams/50 20.00 50.00
PPABZ Ben Zobrist/110 12.00 30.00
PPACBL Charlie Blackmon/250 10.00 25.00
PPACCA Carlos Carrasco/285 3.00 8.00
PPACJ Chipper Jones/70 30.00 80.00
PPACK Clayton Kershaw/60 40.00 100.00
PPACKI Craig Kimbrel/130 10.00 25.00
PPACRK Craig Kimbrel/130 10.00 25.00
PPACS Corey Seager
PPACSA Chris Sale/90 10.00 25.00
PPADB Dellin Betances/285 4.00 10.00
PPADBE Dellin Betances/275 4.00 10.00
PPADE Dennis Eckersley/90 4.00 10.00
PPADG Didi Gregorius EXCH 8.00 20.00
PPADP David Price/80 5.00 12.00
PPADPR David Price/80 5.00 12.00
PPADPO Drew Pomeranz/250 3.00 8.00
PPADRP Drew Pomeranz/270 3.00 8.00
PPAEE Edwin Encarnacion/90 8.00 20.00
PPAEM Edgar Martinez/130 8.00 20.00
PPAET Eric Thames/270 4.00 10.00
PPAFL Francisco Lindor/110 20.00 50.00
PPAGS Gary Sanchez/110 12.00 30.00
PPAGSH Gary Sheffield/130 5.00 12.00
PPAGSP George Springer/145 12.00 30.00
PPAIH Ian Happ/270 8.00 20.00
PPAIHA Ian Happ/270 8.00 20.00
PPAJA Jose Altuve/110 20.00 50.00
PPAJB Johnny Bench/70 25.00 60.00
PPAJBA Javier Baez/145 20.00 50.00
PPAJBE Jose Berrios/285 4.00 10.00
PPAJOB Jose Berrios/285 4.00 10.00
PPAJC Jose Canseco/285 10.00 25.00
PPAJDA Johnny Damon/90 8.00 20.00
PPAJDE Jacob deGrom/110 12.00 30.00
PPAJDG Jacob deGrom/90 12.00 30.00
PPAJG Juan Gonzalez/250 5.00 12.00
PPAJH Josh Harrison/285 3.00 8.00
PPAJHA Josh Harrison/275 3.00 8.00
PPAJL Jake Lamb/145 4.00 10.00
PPAJP Jim Palmer/50 12.00 30.00
PPAJR Jim Rice/125 6.00 15.00
PPAJS Justin Smoak/120 6.00 15.00
PPAJT Jim Thome/90 25.00 60.00
PPAKB Kris Bryant/70 60.00 150.00
PPAKD Khris Davis/285 8.00 20.00
PPAKS Kyle Schwarber/130 10.00 25.00
PPAKSC Kyle Schwarber/130 10.00 25.00
PPAKSE Kyle Seager/285 3.00 8.00
PPAMG Marwin Gonzalez/275 3.00 8.00
PPAMGO Marwin Gonzalez/275 3.00 8.00
PPAMM Manny Machado/60 25.00 60.00
PPAOG Ozzie Guillen/275 3.00 8.00
PPAOV Omar Vizquel/130 5.00 12.00
PPAPG Paul Goldschmidt/90 12.00 30.00
PPAPK Paul Konerko/110 8.00 20.00
PPARC Rod Carew/80 12.00 30.00
PPARF Rollie Fingers/250 8.00 20.00
PPASG Sonny Gray/145 5.00 12.00
PPASM Starling Marte/275 4.00 10.00
PPATR Tim Raines/70 8.00 20.00
PPATS Trevor Story/285 5.00 12.00
PPATW Tim Wakefield/250 6.00 15.00
PPAWC Willson Contreras/130 10.00 25.00
PPAYA Yonder Alonso/145 3.00 8.00
PPAYAL Yonder Alonso/125 3.00 8.00
PPAYC Yoenis Cespedes/80 8.00 20.00

2018 Topps Tier One Prime Performers Autographs Bronze Ink

*BRONZE: .6X TO 1.5X BASIC
STATED ODDS 1:19 HOBBY
STATED PRINT RUN 25 SER.#'d SETS
EXCHANGE DEADLINE 4/30/2020
PPACS Corey Seager 30.00 80.00

2018 Topps Tier One Talent Autographs

OVERALL AUTO ODDS 1:19 HOBBY
PRINT RUNS B/WN 30-295 COPIES PER
EXCHANGE DEADLINE 4/30/2020
TTAAB Adrian Beltre/80 15.00 40.00
TTAABR Alex Bregman/160 10.00 25.00
TTAAG Andres Galarraga/275 4.00 10.00
TTAAMR Amed Rosario/245 6.00 15.00
TTAAP Andy Pettitte/90 12.00 30.00
TTAAR Anthony Rizzo/60 20.00 50.00
TTAARO Alex Rodriguez
TTAARU Addison Russell
TTAAV Alex Verdugo/295 5.00 12.00
TTABD Brian Dozier/275 4.00 10.00
TTABS Blake Snell/295 8.00 20.00
TTABZ Bradley Zimmer/295 3.00 8.00
TTABZO Ben Zobrist/90 15.00 40.00
TTACA Christian Arroyo/295 3.00 8.00
TTACF Clint Frazier/295 12.00 30.00
TTACJ Chipper Jones/60 30.00 80.00
TTACK Craig Kimbrel/160 8.00 20.00
TTACR Cal Ripken Jr./60 40.00 100.00
TTACS Corey Seager
TTACSA Chris Sale/130 10.00 25.00
TTACT Chris Taylor/275 4.00 10.00
TTADB Dellin Betances/295 4.00 10.00
TTADM Don Mattingly/60 30.00 80.00
TTADP David Price/80 15.00 40.00
TTADPO Drew Pomeranz/275 3.00 8.00
TTADS Dominic Smith/160 3.00 8.00
TTADW Dave Winfield/60 12.00 30.00
TTAEE Edwin Encarnacion/130 8.00 20.00
TTAEM Edgar Martinez/160 8.00 20.00
TTAET Eric Thames/295 4.00 10.00
TTAFL Francisco Lindor/130 20.00 50.00
TTAFLI Francisco Lindor/160 20.00 50.00
TTAFT Frank Thomas/60 25.00 60.00
TTAGS Gary Sanchez/160 15.00 40.00
TTAGSH Gary Sheffield/110 5.00 12.00
TTAGSP George Springer/245 10.00 25.00
TTAHB Harrison Bader/275 5.00 12.00
TTAIH Ian Happ/295 4.00 10.00
TTAJA Jose Altuve/160 20.00 50.00
TTAJB Javier Baez/245 15.00 40.00
TTAJBE Johnny Bench/40 25.00 60.00
TTAJDE Jacob deGrom/160 15.00 40.00
TTAJL Jake Lamb/245 4.00 10.00
TTAJR Jose Ramirez/245 4.00 10.00
TTAJT Jim Thome/130 20.00 50.00
TTAKS Kyle Schwarber/160 10.00 25.00
TTALG Lucas Giolito/245 4.00 10.00
TTAMF Michael Fulmer/295 3.00 8.00
TTAMG Marwin Gonzalez/160 3.00 8.00
TTAMM Manny Machado/60 15.00 40.00
TTAMMC Mark McGwire/30 50.00 120.00
TTAMP Mike Piazza
TTANR Nolan Ryan/60 50.00 120.00
TTAOA Ozzie Albies/295 15.00 40.00
TTAOS Ozzie Smith/50 20.00 50.00
TTAOV Omar Vizquel/110 5.00 12.00
TTAPD Paul DeJong/295 5.00 12.00
TTAPG Paul Goldschmidt/70 12.00 30.00
TTAPK Paul Konerko/90 4.00 10.00
TTARC Rod Carew/80 15.00 40.00
TTARD Rafael Devers/245 15.00 40.00
TTARHE Rickey Henderson/30 40.00 100.00
TTARHO Rhys Hoskins/295 8.00 20.00
TTARJ Randy Johnson/60 40.00 100.00
TTARJA Reggie Jackson/60 20.00 50.00
TTASG Sonny Gray/245 5.00 12.00
TTASK Sandy Koufax
TTASN Sean Newcomb/295 4.00 10.00
TTATM Trey Mancini/295 4.00 10.00
TTATP Tommy Pham/275 3.00 8.00
TTAVR Victor Robles/295 8.00 20.00
TTAWC Willson Contreras/160 5.00 12.00
TTAYA Yonder Alonso/150 3.00 8.00
TTAYC Yoenis Cespedes/80 10.00 25.00

2018 Topps Tier One Talent Autographs Bronze Ink

*BRONZE: .6X TO 1.5X BASIC
STATED ODDS 1:19 HOBBY
STATED PRINT RUN 25 SER.#'d SETS
EXCHANGE DEADLINE 4/30/2020
TTAARU Addison Russell 20.00 50.00
TTABH Bryce Harper 150.00 400.00
TTACS Corey Seager 30.00 80.00
TTAFT Frank Thomas 30.00 80.00
TTAMR Mariano Rivera 75.00 200.00
TTARJ Randy Johnson 50.00 120.00

2019 Topps Tier One Relics

RANDOM INSERTS IN PACKS
PRINT RUNS B/WN 200-399 COPIES PER
T1RAA Albert Almora/375 2.50 6.00
T1RAB Andrew Benintendi/375 3.00 8.00
T1RABR Alex Bregman/399 3.00 8.00
T1RAC Aroldis Chapman/375 3.00 8.00
T1RAM Andrew McCutchen/375 3.00 8.00
T1RAN Aaron Nola/375 2.50 6.00
T1RAP Albert Pujols/399 4.00 10.00
T1RARI Anthony Rizzo/399 5.00 12.00
T1RBP Buster Posey/375 4.00 10.00
T1RCB Charlie Blackmon/375 3.00 8.00
T1RCBE Cody Bellinger/375 6.00 15.00
T1RCC Carlos Correa/399 3.00 8.00
T1RCCS CC Sabathia/375 2.50 6.00
T1RCK Corey Kluber/375 2.50 6.00
T1RCKE Clayton Kershaw/399 6.00 15.00
T1RCKI Craig Kimbrel/375 2.50 6.00
T1RCS Chris Sale/375 3.00 8.00
T1RCY Carl Yastrzemski/399 5.00 12.00
T1RDB Dellin Betances/375 2.50 6.00
T1RDG Didi Gregorius/375 2.50 6.00
T1RDGO Dee Gordon/399 2.00 5.00
T1RDP David Price/399 2.50 6.00
T1REE Edwin Encarnacion/375 3.00 8.00
T1REH Eric Hosmer/375 2.50 6.00
T1REL Evan Longoria/375 2.50 6.00
T1RER Eddie Rosario/399 2.50 6.00
T1RES Eugenio Suarez/375 2.50 6.00
T1RFF Freddie Freeman/375 4.00 10.00
T1RFL Francisco Lindor/200 3.00 8.00
T1RGP Gregory Polanco/375 2.50 6.00
T1RGS George Springer/375 2.50 6.00
T1RGSA Gary Sanchez/399 3.00 8.00
T1RGT Gleyber Torres/399 6.00 15.00
T1RJA Jose Altuve/375 2.50 6.00
T1RJAB Jose Abreu/375 3.00 8.00
T1RJAG Jesus Aguilar/399 2.00 5.00
T1RJAR Jake Arrieta/399 2.50 6.00
T1RJB Javier Baez/375 4.00 10.00
T1RJBJ Jackie Bradley Jr./375 3.00 8.00
T1RJG Joey Gallo/375 2.50 6.00
T1RJM Joe Mauer/375 2.50 6.00
T1RJMA J.D. Martinez/399 3.00 8.00
T1RJR Jose Ramirez/399 2.50 6.00
T1RJS Justin Smoak/375 2.00 5.00
T1RJSO Juan Soto/399 5.00 12.00
T1RJU Justin Upton/375 2.50 6.00
T1RJV Joey Votto/375 3.00 8.00
T1RJVE Justin Verlander/399 3.00 8.00
T1RKB Kris Bryant/375 4.00 10.00
T1RKD Khris Davis/375 3.00 8.00
T1RKS Kyle Schwarber/399 3.00 8.00
T1RKSE Kyle Seager/399 2.00 5.00
T1RLC Lorenzo Cain/375 2.00 5.00
T1RLS Luis Severino/375 2.50 6.00
T1RMB Mookie Betts/399 5.00 12.00
T1RMC Miguel Cabrera/375 3.00 8.00
T1RMCA Matt Carpenter/375 3.00 8.00
T1RMCH Matt Chapman/375 3.00 8.00
T1RMH Mitch Haniger/375 2.50 6.00
T1RMK Max Kepler/375 2.50 6.00
T1RMKO Michael Kopech/375 2.50 6.00
T1RMO Matt Olson/399 2.00 5.00
T1RMS Max Scherzer/375 3.00 8.00
T1RMST Marcus Stroman/375 2.50 6.00
T1RMT Mike Trout/375 15.00 40.00
T1RMTA Masahiro Tanaka/375 2.50 6.00
T1RNA Nolan Arenado/375 4.00 10.00
T1RNC Nicholas Castellanos/375 3.00 8.00
T1ROA Ozzie Albies/375 3.00 8.00
T1ROH Odubel Herrera/399 2.50 6.00
T1RPG Paul Goldschmidt/375 3.00 8.00
T1RRAJ Ronald Acuna Jr./375 15.00 40.00
T1RRO Rougned Odor/375 2.50 6.00
T1RRP Rick Porcello/375 2.50 6.00
T1RSK Scott Kingery/399 2.50 6.00
T1RSM Starling Marte/375 2.50 6.00
T1RSP Salvador Perez/399 2.50 6.00
T1RSS Stephen Strasburg/375 3.00 8.00
T1RTB Trevor Bauer/375 3.00 8.00
T1RTST Trevor Story/375 3.00 8.00
T1RTT Trea Turner/375 2.50 6.00
T1RWC Willson Contreras/375 2.50 6.00
T1RWM Whit Merrifield/375 3.00 8.00
T1RXB Xander Bogaerts/375 3.00 8.00
T1RYA Yonder Alonso/375 2.00 5.00
T1RYM Yadier Molina/399 3.00 8.00

2019 Topps Tier One Dual Relics

*DUAL: 1X TO 2.5X SNGL RELIC
STATE ODDS 1:16 HOBBY
STATED PRINT RUN 25 SER.#'d SETS
T1RBS Blake Snell 6.00 15.00
T1RJD Jacob deGrom 8.00 20.00
T1RNS Noah Syndergaard 6.00 15.00
T1RTS Travis Shaw 5.00 12.00
T1RWMY Wil Myers 5.00 12.00

2019 Topps Tier One Autograph Relics

STATED ODDS 1:12 HOBBY
PRINT RUNS B/WN 5-100 COPIES PER
NO PRICING ON QTY 15 OR LESS
EXCHANGE DEADLINE 4/30/2021
*DUAL/25: .75X TO 2X BASIC
T1ATRAB Adrian Beltre/30 20.00 50.00
T1ATRAK Al Kaline/50 25.00 50.00
T1ATRAM Andrew McCutchen/30 15.00 40.00
T1ATRAN Aaron Nola/45 20.00 50.00
T1ATRBG Bob Gibson/40 20.00 50.00
T1ATRBS Blake Snell/100 8.00 20.00
T1ATRCK Corey Kluber/50
T1ATRCT Chris Taylor/100 6.00 15.00
T1ATRDM Dale Murphy/70 12.00 30.00
T1ATRFL Francisco Lindor/50 20.00 50.00
T1ATRFT Frank Thomas/30 30.00 80.00
T1ATRFV Felipe Vazquez/100 5.00 12.00
T1ATRGS George Springer/40 25.00 60.00
T1ATRIH Ian Happ/70 5.00 12.00
T1ATRJA Jose Altuve/30 30.00 80.00
T1ATRJAG Jesus Aguilar/100 4.00 10.00
T1ATRJB Jeff Bagwell/40 20.00 50.00
T1ATRJC Jose Canseco/100 10.00 25.00
T1ATRJD Jacob deGrom/50 12.00 30.00
T1ATRJS Jean Segura/100 6.00 15.00
T1ATRJU Justin Upton/50 10.00 25.00
T1ATRLS Luis Severino/50 5.00 12.00
T1ATRMC Matt Carpenter/70 8.00 20.00
T1ATRMCH Matt Chapman/100 10.00 25.00
T1ATRMCO Michael Conforto/100 10.00 25.00
T1ATRMG Marwin Gonzalez/100 6.00 15.00
T1ATRMH Mitch Haniger/100 10.00 25.00
T1ATRMK Michael Kopech/100 10.00 25.00
T1ATROA Ozzie Albies/100 20.00 50.00
T1ATRPG Paul Goldschmidt/40 20.00 50.00
T1ATRRA Roberto Alomar/50 20.00 50.00
T1ATRRCA Rod Carew/50 12.00 30.00
T1ATRRYH Rhys Hoskins/70 20.00 50.00
T1ATRSO Shohei Ohtani/5
T1ATRSP Salvador Perez/70 10.00 25.00
T1ATRTL Tommy Lasorda/40 5.00 12.00
T1ATRVG Vladimir Guerrero/30
T1ATRWM Whit Merrifield/100 20.00 50.00
T1ATRYM Yadier Molina/50 40.00 100.00

2019 Topps Tier One Autographs

OVERALL AUTO ODDS 1:14 HOBBY
PRINT RUNS B/WN 15-125 COPIES PER
NO PRICING ON QTY 15
EXCHANGE DEADLINE 4/30/2021
*BRONZE/25: .6X TO 1.5X p/r 30-125
T1AAB Adrian Beltre/60 20.00 50.00
T1AAJ Aaron Judge/30 100.00 250.00
T1AAK Al Kaline/90 20.00 50.00
T1AAP Andy Pettitte/90 12.00 30.00
T1AAR Anthony Rizzo/40 20.00 50.00
T1ABG Bob Gibson/80 20.00 50.00
T1ACF Carlton Fisk/90 12.00 30.00
T1ACJ Chipper Jones/50 40.00 100.00
T1ADM Don Mattingly/70 25.00 60.00
T1ADO David Ortiz/50 30.00 80.00
T1ADS Deion Sanders/50 30.00 80.00
T1AEJ Eloy Jimenez/125 20.00 50.00
T1AFT Frank Thomas/70 20.00 50.00
T1AHM Hideki Matsui/50 50.00 120.00
T1AI Ichiro/25 150.00 400.00
T1AJA Jose Altuve/70 15.00 40.00
T1AJB Johnny Bench/50 25.00 60.00
T1AJD Jacob deGrom/125 10.00 25.00
T1AJS Juan Soto/125 30.00 80.00
T1AKB Kris Bryant EXCH 50.00 120.00
T1ALS Luis Severino/125 4.00 10.00
T1AMA Miguel Andujar/125 6.00 15.00
T1AMR Mariano Rivera/30 100.00 250.00
T1AMT Mike Trout/25 200.00 500.00
T1ANR Nolan Ryan/50 40.00 100.00
T1ANS Noah Syndergaard/90 10.00 25.00
T1AOA Ozzie Albies/125 12.00 30.00
T1AOS Ozzie Smith/90 12.00 30.00
T1APM Pedro Martinez/40 30.00 80.00
T1ARAJ Ronald Acuna Jr./125 50.00 120.00
T1ARH Rickey Henderson/50 40.00 100.00
T1ASO Shohei Ohtani/25 100.00 250.00
T1ATH Trevor Hoffman/125 8.00 20.00
T1AVG Vladimir Guerrero/70 20.00 50.00

2019 Topps Tier One Break Out Autographs

RANDOM INSERTS IN PACKS
PRINT RUNS B/WN 15-250 COPIES PER
NO PRICING ON QTY 15
EXCHANGE DEADLINE 4/30/2021
*BRONZE/25: .6X TO 1.5X p/r 100-250
BAAG Adolis Garcia/250 3.00 8.00
BAAM Austin Meadows/250 8.00 20.00
BAAME Austin Meadows/250 8.00 20.00
BAAR Amed Rosario/100 5.00 12.00
BAARO Amed Rosario/100 5.00 12.00
BABA Brian Anderson/250 3.00 8.00
BABK Brad Keller/250 3.00 8.00
BABKE Brad Keller/250 3.00 8.00
BABL Brandon Lowe/250 8.00 20.00
BABLO Brandon Lowe/250 8.00 20.00
BABN Brandon Nimmo/250 4.00 10.00
BABNI Brandon Nimmo/250 4.00 10.00
BABW Bryse Wilson/250 4.00 10.00
BABWI Bryse Wilson/250 4.00 10.00
BACA Chance Adams/250 3.00 8.00
BACAD Chance Adams/250 3.00 8.00
BACB Corbin Burnes/250 5.00 12.00
BACBU Corbin Burnes/250 5.00 12.00
BACK Carson Kelly/250 3.00 8.00
BACM Cedric Mullins/250 5.00 12.00
BACMU Cedric Mullins/250 5.00 12.00
BADC Dylan Cozens/250 3.00 8.00
BADCO Dylan Cozens/250 3.00 8.00
BADF Dustin Fowler/250 3.00 8.00
BADJ Danny Jansen/250 3.00 8.00
BADJA Danny Jansen/250 3.00 8.00
BADP Daniel Poncedeleon/250 5.00 12.00
BADS Dennis Santana/250 3.00 8.00
BAEDL Enyel De Los Santos/250 3.00 8.00
BAEJ Eloy Jimenez/100 20.00 50.00
BAFA Francisco Arcia/250 5.00 12.00
BAFAR Francisco Arcia/250 5.00 12.00
BAFR Franmil Reyes/250 3.00 8.00
BAFRE Franmil Reyes/250 3.00 8.00
BAFRO Fernando Romero/250 3.00 8.00
BAFTJ Fernando Tatis Jr./100 75.00 200.00
BAHB Harrison Bader/250 4.00 10.00
BAHFI Heath Fillmyer/250 3.00 8.00
BAIG Isaac Galloway/250 3.00 8.00
BAJB Jake Bauers/250 5.00 12.00
BAJBI Jesse Biddle/250 3.00 8.00
BAJF Jack Flaherty/250 4.00 10.00
BAJM Jeff McNeil/250 12.00 30.00
BAJMC Jeff McNeil/250 12.00 30.00
BAJN Jacob Nix/250 4.00 10.00
BAJR Josh Rogers/250 3.00 8.00
BAJS Juan Soto/100 30.00 80.00
BAJSO Juan Soto/100 30.00 80.00
BAKA Kolby Allard/250 5.00 12.00
BAKAL Kolby Allard/250 5.00 12.00
BAKN Kevin Newman/250 5.00 12.00
BAKT Kyle Tucker/200 8.00 20.00
BAKTU Kyle Tucker/200 8.00 20.00
BAKW Kyle Wright/200 5.00 12.00
BALGJ Lourdes Gurriel Jr./250 4.00 10.00
BALS Lucas Sims EXCH 3.00 8.00
BALV Luke Voit/250 25.00 60.00
BAMA Miguel Andujar/100 10.00 25.00
BAMK Michael Kopech/200 8.00 20.00
BAMKO Michael Kopech/200 8.00 20.00
BAMM Miles Mikolas/250 5.00 12.00
BAOA Ozzie Albies/100 12.00 30.00
BAOAL Ozzie Albies/100 12.00 30.00
BAPA Pete Alonso EXCH 60.00 150.00
BARAJ Ronald Acuna Jr./100 50.00 120.00
BARB Ryan Borucki/250 3.00 8.00
BARBO Ryan Borucki/250 3.00 8.00
BARD Rafael Devers/100 10.00 25.00
BARL Ramon Laureano/250 8.00 20.00
BAROH Ryan O'Hearn/250 3.00 8.00
BART Ronald Torreyes/250 3.00 8.00
BARTE Rowdy Tellez/250 5.00 12.00
BARYH Ryan O'Hearn/250 3.00 8.00
BASA Sandy Alcantara/250 3.00 8.00
BASD Steven Duggar/250 4.00 10.00
BASK Scott Kingery/200 4.00 10.00
BASKI Scott Kingery/200 4.00 10.00
BASM Sean Manaea/250 3.00 8.00
BASMA Sean Manaea/250 3.00 8.00
BASRF Sean Reid-Foley/250 3.00 8.00
BATG Tayron Guerrero/250 3.00 8.00
BATM Tyler Mahle/250 3.00 8.00
BATRW Trevor Williams/250 3.00 8.00
BATT Touki Toussaint/250 4.00 10.00
BATW Taylor Ward/250 3.00 8.00
BATWA Taylor Ward/250 3.00 8.00
BATWI Trevor Williams/250 3.00 8.00
BAWA Willy Adames/250 3.00 8.00
BAWAD Willy Adames/250 3.00 8.00
BAYK Yusei Kikuchi/250 5.00 12.00
BAVGJ Guerrero Jr Mstry EX 150.00 400.00

2019 Topps Tier One Dual Autographs

STATED ODDS 1:83 HOBBY
STATED PRINT RUN 25 SER.#'d SETS
EXCHANGE DEADLINE 4/30/2021
T1DAAA Acuna/Albies 100.00 250.00
T1DABBR Bagwell/Bregman 75.00 200.00
T1DABS Blackmon/Story 20.00 50.00
T1DACS Clemens/Sale
T1DAGD Guerrero/Dawson 60.00 150.00
T1DAHB Hunter/Buxton 30.00 80.00
T1DAIO Ichiro/Ohtani
T1DALR Lindor/Ramirez
T1DAMH McGwire/Henderson EXCH 100.00 250.00
T1DARH Rivera/Hoffman
T1DASA Soto/Acuna 150.00 400.00
T1DASD Syndergaard/deGrom 50.00 120.00
T1DASP Severino/Pettitte 25.00 60.00
T1DATB Trout/Bryant EXCH 300.00 600.00
T1DATM Tanaka/Matsui EXCH 150.00 400.00

2019 Topps Tier One Legends Relics

STATED ODDS 1:11 MINI BOX
PRINT RUNS B/WN 25-175 COPIES PER
*DUAL/25: 1X TO 2.5X p/r 50-175
*DUAL/25: .4X TO 1X p/r 25
T1RLAR Alex Rodriguez/175 5.00 12.00
T1RLBG Bob Gibson/175 3.00 8.00
T1RLCJ Chipper Jones/175 4.00 10.00
T1RLCRJ Cal Ripken Jr./175 10.00 25.00
T1RLCY Carl Yastrzemski/175 10.00 25.00
T1RLDJ Derek Jeter/175 12.00 30.00
T1RLDO David Ortiz/175 10.00 25.00
T1RLEB Ernie Banks/50
T1RLEM Eddie Mathews/175 5.00 12.00
T1RLHW Honus Wagner/50 25.00 60.00
T1RLJB Johnny Bench/175 5.00 12.00
T1RLJR Jackie Robinson/25 25.00 60.00
T1RLMP Mike Piazza/175 4.00 10.00
T1RLMR Mariano Rivera/175 5.00 12.00
T1RLRC Roger Clemens/175 5.00 12.00
T1RLRH Rickey Henderson/175 5.00 12.00
T1RLRJ Reggie Jackson/175 5.00 12.00
T1RLTW Ted Williams/175 20.00 50.00
T1RLVG Vladimir Guerrero/175 3.00 8.00
T1RLWM Willie McCovey/175 4.00 10.00

2019 Topps Tier One Prime Performers Autographs

RANDOM INSERTS IN PACKS
PRINT RUNS B/WN 50-299 COPIES PER
EXCHANGE DEADLINE 4/30/2021
PPAAK Al Kaline/100 20.00 50.00
PPAAKI Al Kaline/100 20.00 50.00
PPAAM Andrew McCutchen/70 30.00 80.00
PPAAMC Andrew McCutchen/70 30.00 80.00
PPAANP Andy Pettitte/60 12.00 30.00
PPAAP Andy Pettitte/60 12.00 30.00
PPAAR Alex Rodriguez
PPAAT Alan Trammell/120 15.00 40.00
PPAAW Alex Wood/299 3.00 8.00
PPAAWO Alex Wood/299 3.00 8.00
PPABB Byron Buxton/150 10.00 25.00
PPABBU Byron Buxton/150 10.00 25.00
PPABL Barry Larkin/70 15.00 40.00
PPABR Bobby Richardson/299 6.00 15.00
PPABRI Bobby Richardson/299 6.00 15.00
PPABS Blake Snell/299 5.00 12.00
PPABSN Blake Snell/299 5.00 12.00
PPABT Blake Treinen/299 3.00 8.00
PPABTR Blake Treinen/299 3.00 8.00
PPACF Carlton Fisk/60 12.00 30.00
PPACHY Christian Yelich/240 30.00 80.00
PPACI Carlton Fisk/60 12.00 30.00
PPACY Carl Yastrzemski/50 40.00 100.00
PPACYE Christian Yelich/240 30.00 80.00
PPADJ Derek Jeter
PPADM Dale Murphy/150 10.00 25.00
PPADMU Dale Murphy/150 10.00 25.00
PPADO David Ortiz/50 30.00 80.00
PPADS Deion Sanders/50 30.00 80.00
PPAER Eddie Rosario/299 8.00 20.00
PPAERO Eddie Rosario/299 8.00 20.00
PPAET Eric Thames/299 3.00 8.00
PPAETH Eric Thames/299 3.00 8.00
PPAFF Freddie Freeman/100 15.00 40.00
PPAFFR Freddie Freeman/100 15.00 40.00
PPAFL Francisco Lindor/100 15.00 40.00
PPAFLI Francisco Lindor/100 15.00 40.00
PPAGS George Springer/60 15.00 40.00
PPAGSP George Springer/60 15.00 40.00
PPAHM Hideki Matsui/50 50.00 120.00
PPAIK Ian Kinsler/150 4.00 10.00
PPAIR Ivan Rodriguez EXCH 15.00 40.00
PPAJA Jose Altuve/70 15.00 40.00
PPAJAG Jesus Aguilar/240 3.00 8.00
PPAJB Johnny Bench/65 30.00 80.00
PPAJBE Jose Berrios/299 4.00 10.00
PPAJD Johnny Damon/240 6.00 15.00
PPAJEA Jesus Aguilar/240 3.00 8.00
PPAJG Juan Gonzalez/299 6.00 15.00
PPAJGO Juan Gonzalez/299 6.00 15.00
PPAJOB Jose Berrios/299 4.00 10.00
PPAJP Jorge Posada/100 20.00 50.00
PPAJR Jose Ramirez/150 4.00 10.00
PPAJRA Jose Ramirez/150 4.00 10.00
PPAJS Jean Segura/299 5.00 12.00
PPAJSE Jean Segura/299 5.00 12.00
PPAJV Joey Votto/65 15.00 40.00
PPAKB Kris Bryant/65 50.00 120.00
PPAKBR Kris Bryant/65 50.00 120.00
PPAMC Matt Chapman/299 8.00 20.00
PPAMCA Matt Carpenter/240 8.00 20.00
PPAMCH Matt Chapman/299 8.00 20.00
PPAMM Mark McGwire/50 40.00 100.00
PPAMMU Max Muncy/299 8.00 20.00
PPAMO Marcell Ozuna/150 5.00 12.00
PPAMOZ Marcell Ozuna/150 5.00 12.00
PPANR Nolan Ryan
PPAOH Odubel Herrera/299 6.00 15.00
PPARA Roberto Alomar/70 10.00 25.00
PPARJ Reggie Jackson/50 20.00 50.00
PPASK Sandy Koufax
PPASP Salvador Perez/150 6.00 15.00
PPASPE Salvador Perez/150 6.00 15.00
PPATH Trevor Hoffman/150 8.00 20.00
PPATHO Trevor Hoffman/150 8.00 20.00
PPATS Trevor Story/299 5.00 12.00
PPATST Trevor Story/299 5.00 12.00
PPAYM Yadier Molina EXCH 30.00 80.00
PPAYMO Yadier Molina EXCH 30.00 80.00
PPAZW Zack Wheeler/240 4.00 10.00
PPAZWH Zack Wheeler/240 4.00 10.00

2019 Topps Tier One Prime Performers Autographs Bronze Ink

*BRONZE: .6X TO 1.5X BASIC
STATED ODDS 1:19 HOBBY
STATED PRINT RUN 25 SER.#'d SETS
EXCHANGE DEADLINE 4/30/2021

AAJ Aaron Judge 100.00 250.00
ARC Roger Clemens 30.00 80.00

2019 Topps Tier One Talent Autographs

NDOM INSERTS IN PACKS
RINT RUNS B/WN 10-299 COPIES PER
PRICING ON QTY 10
CHANGE DEADLINE 4/30/2021
RONZE/25: .6X TO 1.5X BASIC
AAB Adrian Beltre/70 20.00 50.00
AABR Alex Bregman EXCH 20.00 50.00
AAD Andre Dawson/60 10.00 25.00
AADA Andre Dawson/60 10.00 25.00
AAJ Andruw Jones/299 8.00 20.00
AAJO Andruw Jones/299 8.00 20.00
AALB Alex Bregman EXCH 20.00 50.00
AAP Albert Pujols
AAR Anthony Rizzo/70 20.00 50.00
ABB Bert Blyleven/200 8.00 20.00
ABBL Bert Blyleven/200 8.00 20.00
ABG Bob Gibson/60 15.00 40.00
ABGI Bob Gibson/60 15.00 40.00
ABJ Bo Jackson EXCH 60.00 150.00
ACB Charlie Blackmon/200 6.00 15.00
ACBL Charlie Blackmon/200 6.00 15.00
ACG Chad Green/299 5.00 12.00
ACGR Chad Green/299 5.00 12.00
ACJ Chipper Jones/50 40.00 100.00
ACK Corey Kluber/100 6.00 15.00
ACKL Corey Kluber/100 6.00 15.00
ACRJ Cal Ripken Jr./50 50.00 120.00
ACS Carlos Santana/240 4.00 10.00
ACSA Carlos Santana/240 4.00 10.00
ADG Didi Gregorius/240 8.00 20.00
ADGR Didi Gregorius/240 8.00 20.00
ADJ David Justice/299 6.00 15.00
ADJU David Justice/299 6.00 15.00
ADS Deion Sanders/50 30.00 80.00
AFB Franklin Barreto/299 3.00 8.00
AFBA Franklin Barreto/299 3.00 8.00
AFM Fred McGriff/100 10.00 25.00
AFMC Fred McGriff/100 10.00 25.00
AFT Frank Thomas/70 20.00 50.00
AFV Felipe Vazquez/299 3.00 8.00
AFVA Felipe Vazquez/299 3.00 8.00
AGS Gary Sanchez/70 20.00 50.00
AGSA Gary Sanchez/70 20.00 50.00
AI Ichiro
AJC Jose Canseco/299 8.00 20.00
AJCA Jose Canseco/299 8.00 20.00
TAJD Jacob deGrom/120 10.00 25.00
TAJDE Jacob deGrom/120 10.00 25.00
TAJH Josh Hader/299 5.00 12.00
TAJHA Josh Hader/299 5.00 12.00
TAJM Juan Marichal/100 15.00 40.00
TAJR Jim Rice/240 8.00 20.00
TAJSM Justin Smoak/200 3.00 8.00
TAJU Justin Upton EXCH 4.00 10.00
TAKD Khris Davis/299 6.00 15.00
TAKDA Khris Davis/299 6.00 15.00
TAKS Kyle Seager/299 3.00 8.00
TALS Luis Severino/120 8.00 20.00
TALSE Luis Severino/120 8.00 20.00
TAMAK Matt Kemp/200 4.00 10.00
TAMH Mitch Haniger/240 6.00 15.00
TAMHA Mitch Haniger/240 6.00 15.00
TAMK Max Kepler/299 4.00 10.00
TAMKE Max Kepler/299 4.00 10.00
TAMR Mariano Rivera
TAMT Mike Trout
TANS Noah Syndergaard/100 10.00 25.00
TANSY Noah Syndergaard/100 10.00 25.00
TAPG Paul Goldschmidt/60 10.00 25.00
TAPGO Paul Goldschmidt/60 10.00 25.00
TAPM Pedro Martinez/40 30.00 80.00
TARH Rickey Henderson/50 40.00 100.00
TATA Tim Anderson/299 5.00 12.00
TATG Tom Glavine/70 12.00 30.00
TATH Torii Hunter/100 8.00 20.00
TATHU Torii Hunter/100 8.00 20.00
TATS Travis Shaw/299 3.00 8.00
TATSH Travis Shaw/299 3.00 8.00
TAVG Vladimir Guerrero/70 20.00 50.00
TAWC Will Clark/100 20.00 50.00
TAWM Whit Merrifield/299 8.00 20.00
TAWME Whit Merrifield/299 8.00 20.00
TAZC Zack Cozart/299 3.00 8.00

2020 Topps Tier One Relics

RANDOM INSERTS IN PACKS
STATED PRINT RUN 395 SER.#'d SETS
T1RAA Aristides Aquino 5.00 12.00
T1RAB Andrew Benintendi 6.00 15.00
T1RAH Aaron Hicks 4.00 10.00
T1RAJ Aaron Judge 8.00 20.00
T1RAM Adrian Morejon 2.00 5.00
T1RAN Aaron Nola 3.00 8.00
T1RAP Albert Pujols 5.00 12.00
T1RAR Austin Riley 5.00 12.00
T1RBB Bobby Bradley 2.50 6.00
T1RBH Bryce Harper 6.00 15.00
T1RBM Brendan McKay 3.00 8.00
T1RBP Buster Posey 4.00 10.00
T1RBR Brendan Rodgers 3.00 8.00
T1RBW Brandon Woodruff 2.00 5.00
T1RCB Cavan Biggio 6.00 15.00
T1RCC Carlos Carrasco 2.00 5.00
T1RCK Clayton Kershaw 5.00 12.00
T1RCP Chris Paddack 5.00 12.00
T1RCS Chris Sale 3.00 8.00
T1RCY Christian Yelich 6.00 15.00
T1RDM Dustin May 8.00 20.00
T1REI Ender Inciarte 2.00 5.00
T1REJ Eloy Jimenez 6.00 15.00
T1RGL Gavin Lux 8.00 20.00
T1RGS George Springer 4.00 10.00
T1RGT Gleyber Torres 6.00 15.00
T1RGU Gio Urshela 3.00 8.00
T1RHD Hunter Dozier 2.00 5.00
T1RID Isan Diaz 4.00 10.00
T1RJA Jose Altuve 4.00 10.00
T1RJF Jack Flaherty 6.00 12.00
T1RJH Josh Hader 3.00 8.00
T1RJL Jesus Luzardo 4.00 10.00
T1RJM Jeff McNeil 5.00 12.00
T1RJR Jake Rogers 2.00 5.00
T1RJS Jorge Soler 3.00 8.00
T1RJV Joey Votto 4.00 10.00
T1RJY Jordan Yamamoto 2.50 6.00
T1RKH Keston Hiura 4.00 10.00
T1RKN Kevin Newman 2.50 6.00
T1RLC Lorenzo Cain 4.00 10.00
T1RLS Luis Severino 4.00 10.00
T1RLV Luke Voit 8.00 20.00
T1RMB Mookie Betts 6.00 15.00
T1RMC Michael Chavis 2.50 6.00
T1RMH Mitch Haniger 5.00 12.00
T1RMM Miles Mikolas 2.00 5.00
T1RMS Max Scherzer 3.00 8.00
T1RMT Mike Trout 12.00 30.00
T1RMY Mike Yastrzemski 5.00 12.00
T1RNL Nate Lowe 2.00 5.00
T1RNS Nick Senzel 5.00 12.00
T1ROA Ozzie Albies 3.00 8.00
T1RPG Paul Goldschmidt 6.00 15.00
T1RRD Rafael Devers 4.00 10.00
T1RRH Rhys Hoskins 4.00 10.00
T1RRL Ramon Laureano 3.00 8.00
T1RSB Shane Bieber 3.00 8.00
T1RSO Shohei Ohtani 5.00 12.00
T1RTS Trevor Story 6.00 15.00
T1RWC Willson Contreras 3.00 8.00
T1RXB Xander Bogaerts 4.00 10.00
T1RYA Yordan Alvarez 6.00 15.00
T1RYC Yu Chang 4.00 10.00
T1RYG Yuli Gurriel 2.50 6.00
T1RAAL Adbert Alzolay 2.50 6.00
T1RABR Alex Bregman 5.00 12.00
T1RAJP A.J. Puk 4.00 10.00
T1RAME Austin Meadows 4.00 10.00
T1RAMU Andres Munoz 2.50 6.00
T1RANO Austin Nola 4.00 10.00
T1RARI Anthony Rizzo 6.00 15.00
T1RBBI Bo Bichette 8.00 20.00
T1RCCO Carlos Correa 4.00 10.00
T1RCCS CC Sabathia 6.00 15.00
T1RCKI Carter Kieboom 2.50 6.00
T1RDJL DJ LeMahieu 3.00 8.00
T1RFTJ Fernando Tatis Jr. 8.00 20.00
T1RGSA Gary Sanchez 5.00 12.00
T1RJDM J.D. Martinez 3.00 8.00
T1RJHE Jason Heyward 2.50 6.00
T1RJME John Means 2.00 5.00
T1RLGJ Lourdes Gurriel Jr. 2.50 6.00
T1RMAC Matt Carpenter 3.00 8.00
T1RMBA Michel Baez 2.00 5.00
T1RMBE Matt Beaty 4.00 10.00
T1RMCA Miguel Cabrera 4.00 10.00
T1RMTA Masahiro Tanaka 3.00 8.00
T1RRAJ Ronald Acuna Jr. 8.00 20.00
T1RSSC Shin-Soo Choo 2.50 6.00
T1RVGJ Vladimir Guerrero Jr. 5.00 12.00

2020 Topps Tier One Dual Relics

*DUAL/25: 1X TO 2.5X BASIC
STATED ODDS 1:16 HOBBY
STATED PRINT RUN 25 SER.#'d SETS
T1RBH Bryce Harper 20.00 50.00
T1RSB Shane Bieber 12.00 30.00
T1RSO Shohei Ohtani 25.00 60.00
T1RWC Willson Contreras 15.00 40.00
T1RBBI Bo Bichette 25.00 60.00

2020 Topps Tier One Autograph Dual Relics

*DUAL/25: .6X TO 1.5X p/r 30-99
*DUAL/25: .4X TO 1X p/r 25
STATED ODDS 1:53 HOBBY
STATED PRINT RUN 25 SER.#'d SETS
T1ATRGL Gavin Lux 75.00 200.00
T1ATRHD Hunter Dozier 20.00 50.00
T1ATRJR Jake Rogers 20.00 50.00
T1ATRTM Tino Martinez 40.00 100.00
T1ATRSSC Shin-Soo Choo 50.00 120.00

2020 Topps Tier One Autograph Relics

STATED ODDS 1:13 HOBBY
PRINT RUNS B/WN 5-99 COPIES PER
NO PRICING ON QTY 15 OR LESS
EXCHANGE DEADLINE 5/31/2022
T1ATRAA Adbert Alzolay 6.00 15.00
T1ATRAM Andres Munoz 6.00 15.00
T1ATRAP A.J. Puk 10.00 25.00
T1ATRBB Bert Blyleven 10.00 25.00
T1ATRBM Brendan McKay 8.00 20.00
T1ATRBR Brendan Rodgers 8.00 20.00
T1ATRDM Dustin May 20.00 50.00
T1ATREM Edgar Martinez 15.00 40.00
T1ATRFM Fred McGriff 15.00 40.00
T1ATRFT Frank Thomas 30.00 80.00
T1ATRGL Gavin Lux 40.00 100.00
T1ATRGU Gio Urshela 10.00 25.00
T1ATRHD Hunter Dozier 5.00 12.00
T1ATRID Isan Diaz 8.00 20.00
T1ATRIR Ivan Rodriguez 15.00 40.00
T1ATRJA Jose Altuve 10.00 25.00
T1ATRJL Jesus Luzardo 10.00 25.00
T1ATRJM Jeff McNeil 10.00 25.00
T1ATRJR Jake Rogers 5.00 12.00
T1ATRJS Jorge Soler 8.00 20.00
T1ATRJY Jordan Yamamoto 6.00 15.00
T1ATRMB Michel Baez 5.00 12.00
T1ATRMH Mitch Haniger 6.00 15.00
T1ATRNS Nick Senzel 8.00 20.00
T1ATROS Ozzie Smith 25.00 60.00
T1ATRRA Roberto Alomar 25.00 60.00
T1ATRRL Ramon Laureano 12.00 30.00
T1ATRTM Tino Martinez 15.00 40.00
T1ATRXB Xander Bogaerts 25.00 60.00
T1ATRYA Yordan Alvarez 60.00 150.00
T1ATRAAQ Aristides Aquino 10.00 25.00
T1ATRARI Austin Riley 12.00 30.00
T1ATRCCS CC Sabathia 20.00 50.00
T1ATRCYE Christian Yelich 50.00 120.00
T1ATRJDM J.D. Martinez 20.00 50.00
T1ATRLGJ Lourdes Gurriel Jr. 6.00 15.00
T1ATRSSC Shin-Soo Choo 15.00 40.00

2020 Topps Tier One Autographs

STATED ODDS 1:15 HOBBY
PRINT RUNS B/WN 15-150 COPIES PER
NO PRICING ON QTY 15 OR LESS
EXCHANGE DEADLINE 5/31/2022
T1AI Ichiro 150.00 400.00
T1AAJ Aaron Judge 60.00 150.00
T1ABB Bo Bichette RC 50.00 120.00
T1ABH Bryce Harper 150.00 400.00
T1ACJ Chipper Jones 50.00 120.00
T1ACK Clayton Kershaw 40.00 100.00
T1ADJ Derek Jeter 400.00 800.00
T1ADM Don Mattingly 30.00 80.00
T1AFL Francisco Lindor 20.00 50.00
T1AFT Frank Thomas 25.00 60.00
T1AHA Hank Aaron
T1AJA Jose Altuve 20.00 50.00
T1AJB Johnny Bench 30.00 80.00
T1AJS Juan Soto 40.00 100.00
T1AMM Mark McGwire 50.00 120.00
T1AMR Mariano Rivera 100.00 250.00
T1AMT Mike Trout 300.00 600.00
T1ANR Nolan Ryan 50.00 120.00
T1AOS Ozzie Smith 20.00 50.00
T1APA Pete Alonso 40.00 100.00
T1ARH Rickey Henderson 50.00 120.00
T1ARJ Randy Johnson 60.00 150.00
T1ASC Steve Carlton 12.00 30.00
T1ASK Sandy Koufax
T1ASO Shohei Ohtani 100.00 250.00
T1ASS Sammy Sosa 60.00 150.00
T1AWC Willson Contreras 10.00 25.00
T1AXB Xander Bogaerts EXCH 20.00 50.00
T1AYA Yordan Alvarez RC 40.00 100.00
T1ACRJ Cal Ripken Jr. 50.00 120.00
T1ACYE Christian Yelich 40.00 100.00
T1AFTJ Fernando Tatis Jr. EXCH 60.00 150.00
T1AKGJ Ken Griffey Jr. 150.00 400.00
T1AMMU Mike Mussina 15.00 40.00
T1ARAJ Ronald Acuna Jr. 60.00 150.00
T1ARHO Rhys Hoskins 15.00 40.00
T1ARJA Reggie Jackson 30.00 80.00
T1AVGJ Vladimir Guerrero Jr. EXCH 40.00 100.00

2020 Topps Tier One Autographs Bronze Ink

*BRONZE/25: .6X TO 1.5X p/r 30-150
*BRONZE/25: .4X TO 1X p/r 25
STATED ODDS 1:98 HOBBY
STATED PRINT RUN 25 SER.#'d SETS
T1AYA Yordan Alvarez 125.00 300.00

2020 Topps Tier One Break Out Autographs

RANDOM INSERTS IN PACKS
PRINT RUNS B/WN 100-299 COPIES PER
EXCHANGE DEADLINE 5/31/2022
BOAAA Adbert Alzolay 4.00 10.00
BOAAC Aaron Civale 5.00 12.00
BOAAP A.J. Puk 6.00 15.00
BOAAR Austin Riley 15.00 40.00
BOAAY Alex Young 3.00 8.00
BOABB Bobby Bradley 4.00 10.00
BOABM Brendan McKay 5.00 12.00
BOABR Brendan Rodgers 5.00 12.00
BOACB Cavan Biggio 12.00 30.00
BOACK Carter Kieboom 4.00 10.00
BOACP Chris Paddack 10.00 25.00
BOADC Dylan Cease 6.00 15.00
BOADL Domingo Leyba 4.00 10.00
BOADM Dustin May 12.00 30.00
BOAEJ Eloy Jimenez 20.00 50.00
BOAGL Gavin Lux 30.00 80.00
BOAID Isan Diaz 8.00 20.00
BOAJB Jake Bauers 4.00 10.00
BOAJL Jesus Luzardo 15.00 40.00
BOAJM John Means 6.00 15.00
BOAJY Jordan Yamamoto 4.00 10.00
BOAKH Keston Hiura 10.00 25.00
BOAKL Kyle Lewis 25.00 60.00
BOAKN Kevin Newman 4.00 10.00
BOALA Logan Allen 3.00 8.00
BOALR Luis Robert 125.00 300.00
BOAMC Michael Chavis 4.00 10.00
BOAMD Mauricio Dubon 4.00 10.00
BOAMK Mitch Keller 5.00 12.00
BOAMT Matt Thaiss 6.00 15.00
BOAMY Mike Yastrzemski 20.00 50.00
BOANH Nico Hoerner 12.00 30.00
BOANS Nick Senzel 10.00 25.00
BOAPA Pete Alonso 40.00 100.00
BOARA Rogelio Armenteros 4.00 10.00
BOARG Robel Garcia 3.00 8.00
BOASA Shaun Anderson 3.00 8.00
BOASL Shed Long 4.00 10.00
BOATD Travis Demeritte 4.00 10.00
BOATG Trent Grisham 12.00 30.00
BOATW Taylor Ward 5.00 12.00
BOAWA Willians Astudillo 3.00 8.00
BOAWS Will Smith 6.00 15.00
BOAYA Yordan Alvarez 30.00 80.00
BOAYC Yu Chang 8.00 20.00
BOAZC Zack Collins 4.00 10.00
BOAZP Zach Plesac 8.00 20.00
BOAAAL Adbert Alzolay 4.00 10.00
BOAAAQ Aristides Aquino 15.00 40.00
BOAACI Aaron Civale 5.00 12.00
BOAAMU Andres Munoz 4.00 10.00
BOAAPU A.J. Puk 6.00 15.00
BOAARA Aristides Aquino 15.00 40.00
BOAARI Austin Riley 15.00 40.00
BOAAYO Alex Young 3.00 8.00
BOABBI Bo Bichette 25.00 60.00
BOABBR Bobby Bradley 4.00 10.00
BOABMC Brendan McKay 5.00 12.00
BOABOB Bo Bichette 25.00 60.00
BOABRE Bryan Reynolds 4.00 10.00
BOABRY Bryan Reynolds 4.00 10.00
BOACBI Cavan Biggio 12.00 30.00
BOACKI Carter Kieboom 4.00 10.00
BOADCE Dylan Cease 6.00 15.00
BOADLE Domingo Leyba 4.00 10.00
BOADMA Dustin May 12.00 30.00
BOADSJ Dwight Smith Jr. 3.00 8.00
BOAFTJ Fernando Tatis Jr. 60.00 150.00
BOAGAL Gavin Lux 30.00 80.00
BOAJYA Jordan Yamamoto 4.00 10.00
BOAKHI Keston Hiura 10.00 25.00
BOAKYL Kyle Lewis 25.00 60.00
BOALAL Logan Allen 3.00 8.00
BOALAR Luis Arraez 8.00 20.00
BOAMAB Matt Beaty 4.00 10.00
BOAMBE Matt Beaty 4.00 10.00
BOAMBR Michael Brosseau 6.00 15.00
BOAMEK Merrill Kelly 3.00 8.00
BOAMIT Mike Tauchman 5.00 12.00
BOAMKE Mitch Keller 5.00 12.00
BOAMTA Mike Tauchman 5.00 12.00
BOAPAL Pete Alonso 40.00 100.00
BOARGA Robel Garcia 3.00 8.00
BOATGR Trent Grisham 12.00 30.00
BOAWAS Willians Astudillo 3.00 8.00
BOAWSM Will Smith 6.00 15.00
BOAYAL Yordan Alvarez 30.00 80.00
BOAZCO Zack Collins 4.00 10.00

2020 Topps Tier One Break Out Autographs Bronze Ink

*BRONZE/25: .6X TO 1.5X BASIC
STATED ODDS 1:15 HOBBY
STATED PRINT RUN 25 SER.#'d SETS
EXCHANGE DEADLINE 5/31/2022
BOACP Chris Paddack 20.00 50.00
BOAGL Gavin Lux 75.00 200.00
BOAJM John Means 15.00 40.00
BOAKH Keston Hiura 25.00 60.00
BOAKN Kevin Newman 12.00 30.00
BOAMT Matt Thaiss 20.00 50.00
BOAAAQ Aristides Aquino 30.00 80.00
BOAARA Aristides Aquino 30.00 80.00
BOAGAL Gavin Lux 75.00 200.00
BOAKHI Keston Hiura 25.00 60.00

2020 Topps Tier One Dual Autographs

STATED ODDS 1:69 HOBBY
PRINT RUNS B/WN 5-25 COPIES PER
NO PRICING ON QTY 15 OR LESS
EXCHANGE DEADLINE 5/31/2022
T1DAAB Y.Alvarez/J.Bagwell 125.00 300.00
T1DAAR A.Riley/R.Acuna Jr. 125.00 300.00
T1DABM M.Muncy/M.Beaty 40.00 100.00
T1DAEP A.Puk/D.Eckersley 30.00 80.00
T1DAGS T.Glavine/J.Smoltz
T1DAHH B.Harper/R.Hoskins
T1DAIG K.Griffey Jr./Ichiro
T1DAJC D.Cease/E.Jimenez 100.00 250.00
T1DAKS C.Kieboom/J.Soto 75.00 200.00
T1DAMJ R.Johnson/P.Martinez
T1DAPC W.Clark/B.Posey 75.00 200.00
T1DARG V.Guerrero/T.Raines 50.00 120.00
T1DASM B.McKay/B.Snell 15.00 40.00
T1DATO S.Ohtani/M.Trout
T1DAWM B.Williams/T.Martinez 60.00 150.00

2020 Topps Tier One Legend Dual Relics

*DUAL/25: 1X TO 2.5X BASIC
STATED ODDS 1:68 HOBBY
STATED PRINT RUN 25 SER.#'d SETS
T1LRBR Babe Ruth 125.00 300.00
T1LRCJ Chipper Jones 25.00 60.00
T1LRDS Deion Sanders 20.00 50.00
T1LRFT Frank Thomas 20.00 50.00
T1LRHA Hank Aaron 40.00 100.00
T1LRTG Tony Gwynn 20.00 50.00
T1LRTM Thurman Munson 40.00 100.00
T1LRTW Ted Williams 30.00 80.00

2020 Topps Tier One Next Level Autographs

STATED ODDS 1:46 HOBBY
STATED PRINT RUN 50 SER.#'d SETS
EXCHANGE DEADLINE 5/31/2022
NLABB Bo Bichette EXCH 50.00 120.00
NLACY Carl Yastrzemski EXCH 50.00 120.00
NLADM Don Mattingly 40.00 100.00
NLAJB Johnny Bench 30.00 80.00
NLAJS Juan Soto 40.00 100.00
NLAPA Pete Alonso 40.00 100.00
NLARH Rickey Henderson 40.00 100.00
NLASS Sammy Sosa 50.00 120.00
NLAXB Xander Bogaerts EXCH 25.00 60.00
NLACRJ Cal Ripken Jr. 60.00 150.00
NLAFTJ Fernando Tatis Jr. EXCH 75.00 200.00
NLARHO Rhys Hoskins 25.00 60.00
NLAVGJ Vladimir Guerrero Jr. EXCH 40.00 100.00

2020 Topps Tier One Next Level Autographs Bronze

*BRONZE/25: .6X TO 1.5X BASIC
STATED ODDS 1:78 HOBBY
STATED PRINT RUN 25 SER.#'d SETS
EXCHANGE DEADLINE 5/31/2022
NLAAJ Aaron Judge 75.00 200.00
NLABH Bryce Harper
NLACJ Chipper Jones 60.00 150.00
NLADM Don Mattingly 75.00 200.00
NLAMR Mariano Rivera
NLAMT Mike Trout
NLASK Sandy Koufax
NLASO Shohei Ohtani
NLAFTJ Fernando Tatis Jr. EXCH 150.00 400.00
NLAKGJ Ken Griffey Jr. 150.00 400.00

2020 Topps Tier One Prime Performers Autographs

RANDOM INSERTS IN PACKS
PRINT RUNS B/WN 10-299 COPIES PER
NO PRICING ON QTY 15 OR LESS
EXCHANGE DEADLINE 5/31/2022
PPAAG Andres Galarraga 8.00 20.00
PPAAH Aaron Hicks 10.00 25.00
PPAAK Al Kaline 25.00 60.00
PPABB Bert Blyleven 4.00 10.00
PPABT Blake Treinen 3.00 8.00
PPABW Bernie Williams 15.00 40.00
PPACC Carlos Carrasco 3.00 8.00
PPACD Corey Dickerson 4.00 10.00
PPACS CC Sabathia 15.00 40.00
PPADC David Cone 6.00 15.00
PPADM Don Mattingly 30.00 80.00
PPAFL Francisco Lindor 20.00 50.00
PPAGS George Springer 8.00 20.00
PPAHM Hideki Matsui 40.00 100.00
PPAJA Jose Altuve 12.00 30.00
PPAJB Jeff Bagwell 20.00 50.00
PPAJL Jed Lowrie 6.00 15.00
PPAJR Jim Rice 10.00 25.00
PPAJS Juan Soto 40.00 100.00
PPAKB Kris Bryant 40.00 100.00
PPAMH Mitch Haniger 6.00 15.00
PPAMM Max Muncy 4.00 10.00
PPAMT Mark Teixeira 8.00 20.00
PPANA Nolan Arenado EXCH 30.00 12.00
PPAPC Patrick Corbin 4.00 10.00
PPAPD Paul DeJong 5.00 12.00
PPARC Rod Carew 15.00 40.00
PPASB Shane Bieber 5.00 12.00
PPASS Sammy Sosa 50.00 120.00
PPATH Todd Helton 12.00 30.00
PPAVG Vladimir Guerrero 20.00 50.00
PPAXB Xander Bogaerts 20.00 50.00
PPAZW Zack Wheeler 6.00 15.00
PPAAKA Al Kaline 25.00 60.00
PPAANR Anthony Rizzo 25.00 60.00
PPAARI Anthony Rizzo 25.00 60.00
PPABBL Bert Blyleven 4.00 10.00
PPABTR Blake Treinen 3.00 8.00
PPABWI Bernie Williams 15.00 40.00
PPACCA Carlos Carrasco 3.00 8.00
PPACCS CC Sabathia 15.00 40.00
PPACDI Corey Dickerson 4.00 10.00
PPACHS Chris Sale 8.00 20.00
PPACRJ Cal Ripken Jr. 50.00 120.00
PPACSA Chris Sale 8.00 20.00
PPADAM Dale Murphy 15.00 40.00
PPADCO David Cone 6.00 15.00
PPADMA Don Mattingly 30.00 80.00
PPADMU Dale Murphy 15.00 40.00
PPAFLI Francisco Lindor 20.00 50.00
PPAGSP George Springer 8.00 20.00
PPAJAL Jose Altuve 12.00 30.00
PPAJBA Jeff Bagwell 20.00 50.00
PPAJOS Jorge Soler 10.00 25.00
PPAJSO Juan Soto 40.00 100.00
PPALGJ Lourdes Gurriel Jr. 4.00 10.00
PPALGU Lourdes Gurriel Jr. 4.00 10.00
PPAMAC Matt Carpenter 5.00 12.00
PPAMCA Matt Carpenter 5.00 12.00
PPAMMG Mark McGwire 50.00 120.00
PPAMMI Miles Mikolas 3.00 8.00
PPAMMU Max Muncy 4.00 10.00
PPAMTE Mark Teixeira 8.00 20.00
PPANAR Nolan Arenado EXCH 30.00 12.00
PPAPCO Patrick Corbin 4.00 10.00
PPAPDE Paul DeJong 5.00 12.00
PPARCA Rod Carew 15.00 40.00
PPASBI Shane Bieber 5.00 12.00
PPATHE Todd Helton 12.00 30.00
PPAVLG Vladimir Guerrero 20.00 50.00
PPAXBO Xander Bogaerts 20.00 50.00

2020 Topps Tier One Prime Performers Autographs Bronze Ink

*BRONZE/25: .6X TO 1.5X BASIC
STATED ODDS 1:19 HOBBY
STATED PRINT RUN 25 SER.#'d SETS
EXCHANGE DEADLINE 5/31/2022
PPAAG Andres Galarraga 15.00 40.00
PPACK Clayton Kershaw 60.00 150.00
PPAMT Mark Teixeira 15.00 40.00
PPAKGJ Ken Griffey Jr. 300.00 600.00
PPAMTE Mark Teixeira 15.00 40.00

2020 Topps Tier One Talent Autographs

RANDOM INSERTS IN PACKS
PRINT RUNS B/WN 10-299 COPIES PER
NO PRICING ON QTY 15 OR LESS
EXCHANGE DEADLINE 5/31/2022
T1TAAD Andre Dawson 12.00 30.00
T1TAAM Austin Meadows 6.00 15.00
T1TAAN Aaron Nola 8.00 20.00
T1TABL Barry Larkin 20.00 50.00
T1TABP Buster Posey 30.00 80.00
T1TABS Blake Snell 4.00 10.00
T1TABW Brandon Woodruff 3.00 8.00
T1TACF Cecil Fielder 8.00 20.00
T1TACK Corey Kluber 4.00 10.00
T1TACY Carl Yastrzemski 40.00 100.00
T1TADE Dennis Eckersley 10.00 25.00
T1TAFM Fred McGriff 15.00 40.00
T1TAFT Frank Thomas 25.00 60.00
T1TAGT Gleyber Torres 40.00 100.00
T1TAHD Hunter Dozier 6.00 15.00
T1TAIR Ivan Rodriguez 15.00 40.00
T1TAJB Johnny Bench 30.00 80.00
T1TAJC Jose Canseco 10.00 25.00
T1TAJH Josh Hader 3.00 8.00
T1TAJM J.D. Martinez 12.00 30.00
T1TAJP Jorge Posada 15.00 40.00
T1TAJT Jim Thome 20.00 50.00
T1TAKW Kerry Wood 12.00 30.00
T1TALM Lance McCullers Jr. 3.00 8.00
T1TALV Luke Voit 15.00 40.00
T1TAMM Mike Mussina 12.00 30.00
T1TAOS Ozzie Smith 15.00 40.00
T1TARD Rafael Devers 15.00 40.00
T1TARF Rollie Fingers 8.00 20.00
T1TARH Rickey Henderson 30.00 80.00
T1TARJ Reggie Jackson 25.00 60.00
T1TARS Ryne Sandberg 20.00 50.00
T1TATA Tim Anderson 5.00 12.00
T1TATM Tino Martinez 12.00 30.00
T1TATR Tim Raines 8.00 20.00
T1TAVR Victor Robles 6.00 15.00
T1TAWC Will Clark 20.00 50.00
T1TAWM Whit Merrifield 5.00 12.00
T1TAYG Yuli Gurriel 8.00 20.00
T1TAADA Andre Dawson 12.00 30.00
T1TAANO Aaron Nola 8.00 20.00
T1TABLA Barry Larkin 20.00 50.00
T1TABSN Blake Snell 4.00 10.00
T1TABWO Brandon Woodruff 3.00 8.00
T1TACFI Cecil Fielder 8.00 20.00
T1TACKL Corey Kluber 4.00 10.00
T1TADEC Dennis Eckersley 10.00 25.00
T1TAFMC Fred McGriff 15.00 40.00
T1TAFTH Frank Thomas 25.00 60.00
T1TAGTO Gleyber Torres 40.00 100.00
T1TAJDM J.D. Martinez 12.00 30.00
T1TAJHA Josh Hader 3.00 8.00
T1TAJPO Jorge Posada 15.00 40.00
T1TAJTH Jim Thome 20.00 50.00
T1TAKWO Kerry Wood 12.00 30.00
T1TALMJ Lance McCullers Jr. 3.00 8.00
T1TALVO Luke Voit 15.00 40.00
T1TAMMU Mike Mussina 12.00 30.00
T1TAOSM Ozzie Smith 15.00 40.00
T1TARAJ Ronald Acuna Jr. 50.00 120.00
T1TARDE Rafael Devers 15.00 40.00
T1TARFI Rollie Fingers 8.00 20.00
T1TARHO Rhys Hoskins 12.00 30.00
T1TARHY Rhys Hoskins 12.00 30.00
T1TAROJ Ronald Acuna Jr. 50.00 120.00
T1TASSC Shin-Soo Choo 15.00 40.00
T1TATAN Tim Anderson 5.00 12.00
T1TATMA Tino Martinez 12.00 30.00
T1TATRA Tim Raines 8.00 20.00
T1TAVRO Victor Robles 6.00 15.00
T1TAWCL Will Clark 20.00 50.00
T1TAWCO Willson Contreras 8.00 20.00
T1TAWIC Willson Contreras 8.00 20.00
T1TAWME Whit Merrifield 5.00 12.00

2020 Topps Tier One Talent Autographs Bronze Ink

*BRONZE/25: .6X TO 1.5X BASIC
STATED ODDS 1:18 HOBBY
STATED PRINT RUN 25 SER.#'d SETS
EXCHANGE DEADLINE 5/31/2022
T1TAAJ Aaron Judge 20.00 50.00
T1TACJ Chipper Jones 60.00 150.00
T1TAMM Mike Mussina 30.00 80.00
T1TAMT Mike Trout 400.00 800.00
T1TAMMU Mike Mussina 30.00 80.00
T1TARHO Rhys Hoskins 30.00 80.00
T1TARHY Rhys Hoskins 30.00 80.00

2016 Topps Transcendent

STATED PRINT RUN 65 SER.#'d SETS
1 Babe Ruth 60.00 150.00
2 Kenta Maeda 25.00 60.00
3 Buster Posey 25.00 60.00
4 Julio Urias RC 40.00 100.00
5 Ty Cobb 40.00 100.00
6 Frank Robinson 20.00 50.00
7 Chipper Jones 20.00 50.00
8 Mark McGwire 25.00 60.00
9 Honus Wagner 40.00 100.00
10 Corey Seager RC 100.00 250.00
11 Manny Machado 30.00 80.00
12 Kris Bryant 20.00 50.00
13 Willie Mays 40.00 100.00
14 Clayton Kershaw 20.00 50.00
15 Mike Piazza 20.00 50.00
16 Randy Johnson 20.00 50.00
17 Albert Pujols 25.00 60.00
18 Madison Bumgarner 15.00 40.00
19 Frank Thomas 30.00 80.00
20 Carl Yastrzemski 30.00 80.00
21 Ken Griffey Jr. 30.00 80.00
22 Satchel Paige 40.00 100.00
23 Johnny Bench 25.00 60.00
24 Bryce Harper 40.00 100.00
25 Hank Aaron 40.00 100.00
26 Don Mattingly 40.00 100.00
27 Ichiro 25.00 60.00
28 Lou Gehrig 40.00 100.00
29 Nolan Ryan 50.00 120.00
30 Ozzie Smith 25.00 60.00
31 Eddie Mathews 20.00 50.00
32 Reggie Jackson 20.00 50.00
33 David Price 15.00 40.00
34 Felix Hernandez 15.00 40.00
35 Harmon Killebrew 20.00 50.00
36 Rickey Henderson 30.00 80.00
37 Kyle Schwarber RC 60.00 150.00
38 Roger Clemens 25.00 60.00
39 Mike Trout 100.00 250.00
40 Greg Maddux 25.00 60.00
41 Carlos Correa 20.00 50.00
42 Jackie Robinson 40.00 100.00
43 John Smoltz 20.00 50.00
44 Barry Larkin 20.00 50.00
45 Roberto Clemente 60.00 150.00
46 Roger Maris 25.00 60.00
47 Ted Williams 50.00 120.00
48 Ryne Sandberg 30.00 80.00
49 Cal Ripken Jr. 40.00 100.00
50 Sandy Koufax 40.00 100.00

2016 Topps Transcendent Autographs

STATED PRINT RUN 52 SER.#'d SETS
EXCHANGE DEADLINE 11/30/2018
*BLUE/25: .4X TO 1X BASIC
TCAAP Albert Pujols 100.00 250.00
TCAAR Alex Rodriguez 100.00 250.00
TCABB Barry Bonds 150.00 400.00
TCABH Bryce Harper 175.00 350.00
TCABP Buster Posey 60.00 150.00
TCACC Carlos Correa 100.00 250.00
TCACJ Chipper Jones 100.00 200.00
TCACK Clayton Kershaw 100.00 250.00
TCACR Cal Ripken Jr. 75.00 200.00
TCACS Corey Seager 200.00 400.00
TCACY Carl Yastrzemski 75.00 200.00
TCADJ Derek Jeter 300.00 600.00
TCADM Don Mattingly 75.00 200.00
TCADO David Ortiz 100.00 250.00
TCADR Daisy Ridley 300.00 600.00
TCAFR Frank Robinson 75.00 200.00
TCAFT Frank Thomas 30.00 80.00
TCAGM Greg Maddux 100.00 250.00
TCAHA Hank Aaron 200.00 400.00
TCAI Ichiro 300.00 500.00
TCAJB Johnny Bench 75.00 200.00
TCAJBA John Boyega 250.00 400.00
TCAKB Kris Bryant 400.00 800.00
TCAKGJ Ken Griffey Jr. 350.00 700.00
TCAKM Kenta Maeda 75.00 200.00
TCAKS Kyle Schwarber 60.00 150.00
TCAMM Mark McGwire 75.00 200.00
TCAMP Mike Piazza 60.00 150.00
TCAMT Mike Trout 400.00 800.00
TCAMTA Masahiro Tanaka 175.00 350.00
TCANR Nolan Ryan 100.00 250.00
TCAOS Ozzie Smith 60.00 150.00
TCAOV Omar Vizquel 40.00 100.00
TCAP Pele 200.00 400.00
TCAPM Pedro Martinez 75.00 200.00
TCARC Roger Clemens 75.00 200.00
TCARH Rickey Henderson 100.00 250.00
TCARJ Randy Johnson 75.00 200.00
TCARJA Reggie Jackson 60.00 150.00
TCARS Ryne Sandberg 75.00 200.00
TCASK Sandy Koufax 200.00 400.00
TCAVS Vin Scully 250.00 500.00

2016 Topps Transcendent Sketch Cards

STATED PRINT RUN 65 SER.#'d SETS
TSCR1 Willie Mays 40.00 100.00
TSCR2 Jackie Robinson 30.00 80.00
TSCR3 Eddie Mathews 15.00 40.00
TSCR4 Phil Rizzuto 12.00 30.00
TSCR5 Monte Irvin 15.00 40.00
TSCR6 Satchel Paige 30.00 80.00
TSCR7 Jackie Robinson 30.00 80.00
TSCR8 Hank Aaron 40.00 100.00
TSCR9 Ted Williams 30.00 80.00
TSCR10 Willie Mays 40.00 100.00
TSCR11 Al Kaline 30.00 80.00
TSCR12 Sandy Koufax 30.00 80.00
TSCR13 Roberto Clemente 40.00 100.00
TSCR14 Ted Williams 30.00 80.00
TSCR15 Jackie Robinson 30.00 80.00
TSCR16 Hank Aaron 40.00 100.00
TSCR17 Frank Robinson 15.00 40.00
TSCR18 Sandy Koufax 30.00 80.00
TSCR19 Roger Maris 30.00 80.00
TSCR20 Orlando Cepeda 15.00 40.00
TSCR21 Roberto Clemente 40.00 100.00
TSCR22 Carl Yastrzemski 25.00 60.00
TSCR23 Willie McCovey 20.00 50.00
TSCR24 Roger Maris 30.00 80.00
TSCR25 Jim Palmer 12.00 30.00
TSCR26 Steve Carlton 15.00 40.00
TSCR27 Rod Carew 15.00 40.00
TSCR28 Reggie Jackson 20.00 50.00
TSCR29 Johnny Bench 20.00 50.00

TSCR30 Nolan Ryan 40.00 100.00
TSCR31 Roberto Clemente 40.00 100.00
TSCR32 Joe Morgan 15.00 40.00
TSCR33 Dave Winfield 15.00 40.00
TSCR34 George Brett 30.00 80.00
TSCR35 Dennis Eckersley 12.00 30.00
TSCR36 Reggie Jackson 20.00 50.00
TSCR37 Robin Yount 20.00 50.00
TSCR38 Eddie Murray 15.00 40.00
TSCR39 Ozzie Smith 20.00 50.00
TSCR40 Rickey Henderson 40.00 100.00
TSCR41 Cal Ripken Jr. 40.00 100.00
TSCR42 Wade Boggs 20.00 50.00
TSCR43 Don Mattingly 30.00 80.00
TSCR44 Darryl Strawberry 15.00 40.00
TSCR45 Mark McGwire 25.00 60.00
TSCR46 Roger Clemens 20.00 50.00
TSCR47 Dwight Gooden 12.00 30.00
TSCR48 Greg Maddux 20.00 50.00
TSCR49 Ken Griffey Jr. 50.00 120.00
TSCR50 Randy Johnson 15.00 40.00
TSCR51 Frank Thomas 20.00 50.00
TSCR52 Chipper Jones 20.00 50.00
TSCR53 Mike Piazza 15.00 40.00
TSCR54 Nomar Garciaparra 20.00 50.00
TSCR55 Alex Rodriguez 20.00 50.00
TSCR56 Miguel Cabrera 15.00 40.00
TSCR57 Albert Pujols 20.00 50.00
TSCR58 Ichiro 20.00 50.00
TSCR59 Clayton Kershaw 20.00 50.00
TSCR60 Buster Posey 20.00 50.00
TSCR61 Mike Trout 60.00 150.00
TSCR62 Bryce Harper 25.00 60.00
TSCR63 Kris Bryant 75.00 200.00
TSCR64 Carlos Correa 20.00 50.00
TSCR65 Jose Bautista 20.00 50.00

2017 Topps Transcendent

STATED PRINT RUN 87 SER.#'d SETS
1 Jackie Robinson 20.00 50.00
2 Aaron Judge RC 25.00 60.00
3 Roberto Clemente 30.00 80.00
4 Bryce Harper 12.00 30.00
5 Randy Johnson 15.00 40.00
6 Alex Bregman RC 30.00 80.00
7 Kris Bryant 30.00 80.00
8 Francisco Lindor 15.00 40.00
9 Bo Jackson 25.00 60.00
10 Greg Maddux 20.00 50.00
11 Ted Williams 20.00 50.00
12 Rickey Henderson 20.00 50.00
13 Reggie Jackson 10.00 25.00
14 Roger Maris 20.00 50.00
15 Honus Wagner 10.00 25.00
16 Roger Clemens 10.00 25.00
17 Ernie Banks 20.00 50.00
18 Miguel Cabrera 15.00 40.00
19 Chris Sale 15.00 40.00
20 Yoan Moncada RC 30.00 80.00
21 Andrew Benintendi RC 60.00 150.00
22 Manny Machado 15.00 40.00
23 Carl Yastrzemski 20.00 50.00
24 Clayton Kershaw 20.00 50.00
25 Babe Ruth 40.00 100.00
26 Nolan Ryan 30.00 80.00
27 Carlos Correa 15.00 40.00
28 Dave Winfield 12.00 30.00
29 Anthony Rizzo 12.00 30.00
30 Albert Pujols 20.00 50.00
31 Mike Piazza 15.00 40.00
32 Hank Aaron 20.00 50.00
33 George Brett 25.00 60.00
34 Pedro Martinez 12.00 30.00
35 Jimmie Foxx 15.00 40.00
36 Cal Ripken Jr. 25.00 60.00
37 Chipper Jones 15.00 40.00
38 David Ortiz 15.00 40.00
39 Ichiro 20.00 50.00
40 Lou Gehrig 30.00 80.00
41 Ken Griffey Jr. 25.00 60.00
42 Hideki Matsui 15.00 40.00
43 Sandy Koufax 20.00 50.00
44 Ty Cobb 10.00 25.00
45 Mike Trout 25.00 60.00
46 Cody Bellinger RC 100.00 250.00
47 Corey Seager 20.00 50.00
48 Max Scherzer 10.00 250.00
49 Buster Posey 20.00 50.00
50 Derek Jeter 40.00 100.00

2017 Topps Transcendent Autographs

STATED PRINT RUN 25 SER.#'d SETS
EXCHANGE DEADLINE 11/30/2019
ALL VERSIONS EQUALLY PRICED
TCAAB Adrian Beltre 40.00 100.00
TCAAB Adrian Beltre 40.00 100.00
TCAABE Andrew Benintendi 125.00 300.00
TCAABE Andrew Benintendi 125.00 300.00
TCAABR Alex Bregman 100.00 250.00
TCAABR Alex Bregman 100.00 250.00
TCAAJ Aaron Judge 400.00 800.00
TCAAJ Aaron Judge 400.00 800.00
TCAARI Anthony Rizzo 60.00 150.00
TCAARI Anthony Rizzo 60.00 150.00
TCABH Bryce Harper 150.00 400.00
TCABH Bryce Harper 150.00 400.00
TCABJ Bo Jackson 75.00 200.00
TCABJ Bo Jackson 75.00 200.00
TCABL Barry Larkin 30.00 80.00
TCABL Barry Larkin 30.00 80.00
TCABP Buster Posey 75.00 200.00
TCABP Buster Posey 75.00 200.00
TCACBE Cody Bellinger EXCH 150.00 400.00
TCACBE Cody Bellinger VAR EXCH 150.00 400.00
TCACC Carlos Correa 60.00 150.00
TCACC Carlos Correa 60.00 150.00
TCACJ Chipper Jones 100.00 250.00
TCACJ Chipper Jones 100.00 250.00
TCACK Clayton Kershaw 75.00 200.00
TCACK Clayton Kershaw 75.00 200.00
TCACR Cal Ripken Jr. 75.00 200.00
TCACR Cal Ripken Jr. 75.00 200.00
TCADJ Derek Jeter 300.00 600.00
TCADJ Derek Jeter 300.00 600.00
TCADM Don Mattingly 60.00 150.00
TCADM Don Mattingly 60.00 150.00
TCADO David Ortiz 75.00 200.00
TCADO David Ortiz 75.00 200.00
TCADW Dave Winfield 40.00 100.00
TCADW Dave Winfield 40.00 100.00
TCAFL Francisco Lindor 40.00 100.00
TCAFL Francisco Lindor 40.00 100.00
TCAFMJ Floyd Mayweather Jr. 150.00 400.00
TCAFMJ Floyd Mayweather Jr. 150.00 400.00
TCAGM Greg Maddux 60.00 150.00
TCAGM Greg Maddux 60.00 150.00
TCAHA Hank Aaron 150.00 400.00
TCAHA Hank Aaron 150.00 400.00
TCAHM Hideki Matsui 100.00 250.00
TCAHM Hideki Matsui 100.00 250.00
TCAI Ichiro 300.00 600.00
TCAI Ichiro 300.00 600.00
TCAIH Ian Happ EXCH 40.00 100.00
TCAIH Ian Happ VAR EXCH 40.00 100.00
TCAJB Johnny Bench 60.00 150.00
TCAJB Johnny Bench 60.00 150.00
TCAJD Josh Donaldson 40.00 100.00
TCAJD Josh Donaldson 40.00 100.00
TCAJT Jim Thome 60.00 150.00
TCAJT Jim Thome 60.00 150.00
TCAKB Kris Bryant 125.00 300.00
TCAKB Kris Bryant 125.00 300.00
TCALV Lindsey Vonn EXCH 125.00 300.00
TCALV Lindsey Vonn VAR EXCH 125.00 300.00
TCAMM Manny Machado 60.00 150.00
TCAMM Manny Machado 60.00 150.00
TCAMMC Mark McGwire 75.00 200.00
TCAMMC Mark McGwire 75.00 200.00
TCAMP Mike Piazza 75.00 200.00
TCAMP Mike Piazza 75.00 200.00
TCAMR Mariano Rivera 125.00 300.00
TCAMR Mariano Rivera 125.00 300.00
TCAMT Mike Trout 250.00 500.00
TCAMT Mike Trout 250.00 500.00
TCANR Nolan Ryan 125.00 300.00
TCANR Nolan Ryan 125.00 300.00
TCANS Noah Syndergaard 50.00 120.00
TCANS Noah Syndergaard 50.00 120.00
TCAPM Pedro Martinez 60.00 150.00
TCAPM Pedro Martinez 60.00 150.00
TCARC Roger Clemens 75.00 200.00
TCARC Roger Clemens 75.00 200.00
TCARCA Rod Carew 50.00 120.00
TCARCA Rod Carew 50.00 120.00
TCARH Rickey Henderson 60.00 150.00
TCARH Rickey Henderson 60.00 150.00
TCARJ Randy Johnson 60.00 150.00
TCARJ Randy Johnson 60.00 150.00
TCARJA Reggie Jackson 50.00 120.00
TCARJA Reggie Jackson 50.00 120.00
TCASK Sandy Koufax 200.00 400.00
TCASK Sandy Koufax 200.00 400.00
TCATE Theo Epstein 75.00 200.00
TCATE Theo Epstein 75.00 200.00
TCATS Tom Seaver 60.00 150.00
TCATS Tom Seaver 60.00 150.00
TCAYM Yoan Moncada 60.00 150.00
TCAYM Yoan Moncada 60.00 150.00

2017 Topps Transcendent Autographs Purple

*PURPLE: .5X TO 1.2X BASIC
STATED PRINT RUN 10 SER.#'d SETS
EXCHANGE DEADLINE 11/30/2019

2017 Topps Transcendent Autographs Silver

*SILVER: .4X TO 1X BASIC
STATED PRINT RUN 15 SER.#'d SETS
EXCHANGE DEADLINE 11/30/2019

2017 Topps Transcendent MLB Moments Sketch Cards

STATED PRINT RUN 87 SER.#'d SETS
MLBMRAR Alex Rodriguez 15.00 40.00
MLBMRARO Alex Rodriguez 15.00 40.00
MLBMRBH Bryce Harper 40.00 100.00
MLBMRBJ Bo Jackson 40.00 100.00
MLBMRBM Bill Mazeroski 10.00 25.00
MLBMRBOS Boston Red Sox 15.00 40.00
MLBMRBR Babe Ruth 30.00 80.00
MLBMRBRI K.Bryant/A.Rizzo 75.00 200.00
MLBMRBRU Babe Ruth 30.00 80.00
MLBMRCB Craig Biggio 10.00 25.00
MLBMRCF Carlton Fisk 20.00 50.00
MLBMRCHI Chicago Cubs 50.00 120.00
MLBMRCK Clayton Kershaw 30.00 80.00
MLBMRCR Cal Ripken Jr. 30.00 80.00
MLBMRCRI Cal Ripken Jr. 30.00 80.00
MLBMRCS Curt Schilling 12.00 30.00
MLBMRCY Carl Yastrzemski 20.00 50.00
MLBMRDEJ Derek Jeter 50.00 120.00
MLBMRDJ Derek Jeter 50.00 120.00
MLBMRDJE Derek Jeter 50.00 120.00
MLBMRDJR Derek Jeter 50.00 120.00
MLBMRDJT Derek Jeter 50.00 120.00
MLBMRDO David Ortiz 20.00 50.00
MLBMREL Evan Longoria 10.00 25.00
MLBMRES Enos Slaughter 12.00 30.00
MLBMRGM Greg Maddux 15.00 40.00
MLBMRGWB George W. Bush 30.00 80.00
MLBMRHA Hank Aaron 30.00 80.00
MLBMRHM Hideki Matsui 12.00 30.00
MLBMRIR Ivan Rodriguez 10.00 25.00
MLBMRI Ichiro 20.00 50.00
MLBMRJB Jose Bautista 20.00 50.00
MLBMRJC Jose Canseco 40.00 100.00
MLBMRJG Josh Gibson 20.00 50.00
MLBMRJR Jackie Robinson 30.00 80.00
MLBMRJRO Jackie Robinson 30.00 80.00
MLBMRKG Ken Griffey Jr. 40.00 100.00
MLBMRKGR Ken Griffey Jr. 40.00 100.00
MLBMRLD Larry Doby 10.00 25.00
MLBMRLG Lou Gehrig 25.00 60.00
MLBMRLGH Lou Gehrig 25.00 60.00
MLBMRMM Manny Machado 20.00 50.00
MLBMRMMC Mark McGwire 20.00 50.00
MLBMRMP Mike Piazza 12.00 30.00
MLBMRMR Mariano Rivera 15.00 40.00
MLBMRMS Max Scherzer 12.00 30.00
MLBMRMT Mike Trout 30.00 80.00
MLBMRMTR Mike Trout 30.00 80.00
MLBMRNR Nolan Ryan 25.00 60.00
MLBMROS Ozzie Smith 15.00 40.00
MLBMROSM Ozzie Smith 15.00 40.00
MLBMRPM Pedro Martinez 12.00 30.00
MLBMRRC Roberto Clemente 40.00 100.00
MLBMRRCL Roger Clemens 15.00 40.00
MLBMRRH Rickey Henderson 15.00 40.00
MLBMRRHA Roy Halladay 20.00 50.00
MLBMRRJ Randy Johnson 12.00 30.00
MLBMRRJA Reggie Jackson 12.00 30.00
MLBMRRM Roger Maris 20.00 50.00
MLBMRRS Ryne Sandberg 30.00 80.00
MLBMRSK Sandy Koufax 25.00 60.00
MLBMRSP Satchel Paige 20.00 50.00
MLBMRTW Ted Williams 30.00 80.00
MLBMRTWI Ted Williams 30.00 80.00
MLBMRWB Wade Boggs 15.00 40.00

2018 Topps Transcendent

ONE COMPLETE SET PER BOX
STATED PRINT RUN 83 SER.#'d SETS
1 Sandy Koufax 10.00 25.00
2 Rhys Hoskins RC 12.00 30.00
3 Ryne Sandberg 10.00 25.00
4 Hideki Matsui 5.00 12.00
5 Gleyber Torres RC 150.00 400.00
6 Mariano Rivera 6.00 15.00
7 Mike Piazza 5.00 12.00
8 Jose Altuve 4.00 10.00
9 Frank Thomas 5.00 12.00
10 Shohei Ohtani RC 75.00 200.00
11 Johnny Bench 5.00 12.00
12 Francisco Lindor 5.00 12.00
13 George Brett 10.00 25.00
14 Roger Clemens 6.00 15.00
15 Tom Seaver 4.00 10.00
16 Aaron Judge 12.00 30.00
17 Lou Gehrig 10.00 25.00
18 Ty Cobb 8.00 20.00
19 Chipper Jones 5.00 12.00
20 Kris Bryant 6.00 15.00
21 Pedro Martinez 4.00 10.00
22 Greg Maddux 6.00 15.00
23 Clayton Kershaw 10.00 25.00
24 Randy Johnson 5.00 12.00
25 Derek Jeter 12.00 30.00
26 Bo Jackson 5.00 12.00
27 Rafael Devers RC 75.00 200.00
28 David Ortiz 5.00 12.00
29 Tommy Lasorda 4.00 10.00
30 Bryce Harper 8.00 20.00
31 Jimmie Foxx 5.00 12.00
32 Gary Sanchez 5.00 12.00
33 Alex Rodriguez 6.00 15.00
34 Ted Williams 10.00 25.00
35 Manny Machado 5.00 12.00
36 Rickey Henderson 5.00 12.00
37 Honus Wagner 5.00 12.00
38 Mark McGwire 8.00 20.00
39 Jackie Robinson 5.00 12.00
40 Ichiro 6.00 15.00
41 Roberto Clemente 12.00 30.00
42 Mike Trout 25.00 60.00
43 Reggie Jackson 4.00 10.00
44 Cal Ripken Jr. 15.00 40.00
45 Albert Pujols 6.00 15.00
46 Don Mattingly 10.00 25.00
47 Anthony Rizzo 8.00 20.00
48 Nolan Ryan 15.00 40.00
49 Ronald Acuna Jr. RC 500.00 1000.00
50 Hank Aaron 10.00 25.00

2018 Topps Transcendent Autographs

ONE COMPLETE SET PER BOX
STATED PRINT RUN 25 SER.#'d SETS
ALL VERSIONS EQUALLY PRICED
*EMERALD/15: .4X TO 1X BASIC
*PURPLE/10: .5X TO 1.2X BASIC
TCAI Ichiro V 150.00 400.00
TCAI Ichiro H 150.00 400.00
TCAAJ Aaron Judge V 125.00 300.00
TCAAJ Aaron Judge H 125.00 300.00
TCAAM Andrew McCutchen V 30.00 80.00
TCAAM Andrew McCutchen H 30.00 80.00
TCAAP Albert Pujols V 60.00 150.00
TCAAP Albert Pujols H 60.00 150.00
TCAAR Alex Rodriguez V 75.00 200.00
TCAAR Alex Rodriguez H 75.00 200.00
TCABH Bryce Harper V 125.00 300.00
TCABH Bryce Harper H 125.00 300.00
TCABJ Bo Jackson V 60.00 150.00
TCABJ Bo Jackson H 60.00 150.00
TCACJ Chipper Jones V 125.00 300.00
TCACJ Chipper Jones H 125.00 300.00
TCACK Clayton Kershaw V 60.00 150.00
TCACK Clayton Kershaw H 60.00 150.00
TCACR Cal Ripken Jr. V 60.00 150.00
TCACR Cal Ripken Jr. H 60.00 150.00
TCADJ Derek Jeter H 250.00 500.00
TCADM Don Mattingly V 50.00 120.00
TCADM Don Mattingly H 50.00 120.00
TCADO David Ortiz V 50.00 120.00
TCADO David Ortiz H 50.00 120.00
TCAFL Francisco Lindor V 40.00 100.00
TCAFL Francisco Lindor H 40.00 100.00
TCAFT Frank Thomas V 60.00 150.00
TCAFT Frank Thomas H 60.00 150.00
TCAGM Greg Maddux V 50.00 120.00
TCAGM Greg Maddux H 50.00 120.00
TCAGS Gary Sanchez V 30.00 80.00
TCAGS Gary Sanchez H 30.00 80.00
TCAGT Gleyber Torres V 60.00 150.00
TCAGT Gleyber Torres H 60.00 150.00
TCAHA Hank Aaron V 150.00 400.00
TCAHA Hank Aaron H 150.00 400.00
TCAHM Hideki Matsui V 60.00 150.00
TCAHM Hideki Matsui H 60.00 150.00
TCAJA Jose Altuve V 40.00 100.00
TCAJA Jose Altuve H 40.00 100.00
TCAJB Johnny Bench V 40.00 100.00
TCAJB Johnny Bench H 40.00 100.00
TCAJS Juan Soto V 250.00 500.00
TCAJS Juan Soto H 250.00 500.00
TCAJT Jim Thome V 50.00 120.00
TCAJT Jim Thome H 50.00 120.00
TCAKB Kris Bryant V 75.00 200.00
TCAKB Kris Bryant H 75.00 200.00
TCAMM Mark McGwire V 60.00 150.00
TCAMM Mark McGwire H 60.00 150.00
TCAMP Mike Piazza V 50.00 120.00
TCAMP Mike Piazza H 50.00 120.00
TCAMR Mariano Rivera V 125.00 300.00
TCAMR Mariano Rivera H 125.00 300.00
TCAMT Mike Trout V 300.00 500.00
TCAMT Mike Trout H 300.00 500.00
TCANR Nolan Ryan V 75.00 200.00
TCANR Nolan Ryan H 75.00 200.00
TCAPM Pedro Martinez V 30.00 80.00
TCAPM Pedro Martinez H 30.00 80.00
TCARC Roger Clemens V 60.00 150.00
TCARC Roger Clemens H 60.00 150.00
TCARD Rafael Devers V 40.00 100.00
TCARD Rafael Devers H 40.00 100.00
TCARH Rickey Henderson V 50.00 120.00
TCARH Rickey Henderson H 50.00 120.00
TCARJ Randy Johnson V 40.00 100.00
TCARJ Randy Johnson H 40.00 100.00
TCARS Ryne Sandberg V 50.00 120.00
TCARS Ryne Sandberg H 50.00 120.00
TCASK Sandy Koufax V 150.00 400.00
TCASK Sandy Koufax H 150.00 400.00
TCASO Shohei Ohtani V 300.00 600.00
TCASO Shohei Ohtani H 300.00 600.00
TCAYM Yadier Molina V 75.00 200.00
TCAYM Yadier Molina H 75.00 200.00
TCAANP Andy Pettitte V 20.00 50.00
TCAARI Anthony Rizzo V 30.00 80.00
TCAARI Anthony Rizzo H 30.00 80.00
TCABG Bob Gibson V 30.00 80.00
TCABG Bob Gibson H 30.00 80.00
TCAMMA Manny Machado V 40.00 100.00
TCAMMA Manny Machado H 40.00 100.00
TCARAC Ronald Acuna Jr. V 300.00 600.00
TCARAC Ronald Acuna Jr. H 300.00 600.00
TCARHO Rhys Hoskins V 50.00 120.00
TCARHO Rhys Hoskins H 50.00 120.00
TCARJA Reggie Jackson V 40.00 100.00
TCARJA Reggie Jackson H 40.00 100.00

2018 Topps Transcendent Mike Trout Through the Years Autographs

STATED ODDS ONE PER BOX
STATED PRINT RUN 1 SER.#'d SET
ALL VERSIONS EQUALLY PRICED
MT1952 Mike Trout 1200.00 2500.00
MT1953 Mike Trout 1200.00 2500.00
MT1954 Mike Trout 1200.00 2500.00
MT1955 Mike Trout 1200.00 2500.00
MT1956 Mike Trout 1200.00 2500.00
MT1957 Mike Trout 1200.00 2500.00
MT1958 Mike Trout 1200.00 2500.00
MT1959 Mike Trout 1200.00 2500.00
MT1960 Mike Trout 1200.00 2500.00
MT1961 Mike Trout 1200.00 2500.00
MT1962 Mike Trout 1200.00 2500.00
MT1963 Mike Trout 1200.00 2500.00
MT1964 Mike Trout 1200.00 2500.00
MT1965 Mike Trout 1200.00 2500.00
MT1966 Mike Trout 1200.00 2500.00
MT1967 Mike Trout 1200.00 2500.00
MT1968 Mike Trout 1200.00 2500.00
MT1969 Mike Trout 1200.00 2500.00
MT1970 Mike Trout 1200.00 2500.00
MT1971 Mike Trout 1200.00 2500.00
MT1972 Mike Trout 1200.00 2500.00
MT1973 Mike Trout 1200.00 2500.00
MT1974 Mike Trout 1200.00 2500.00
MT1975 Mike Trout 1200.00 2500.00
MT1976 Mike Trout 1200.00 2500.00
MT1977 Mike Trout 1200.00 2500.00
MT1978 Mike Trout 1200.00 2500.00
MT1979 Mike Trout 1200.00 2500.00
MT1980 Mike Trout 1200.00 2500.00
MT1981 Mike Trout 1200.00 2500.00
MT1982 Mike Trout 1200.00 2500.00
MT1983 Mike Trout 1200.00 2500.00
MT1984 Mike Trout 1200.00 2500.00
MT1985 Mike Trout 1200.00 2500.00
MT1986 Mike Trout 1200.00 2500.00
MT1987 Mike Trout 1200.00 2500.00
MT1988 Mike Trout 1200.00 2500.00
MT1989 Mike Trout 1200.00 2500.00
MT1990 Mike Trout 1200.00 2500.00
MT1991 Mike Trout 1200.00 2500.00
MT1992 Mike Trout 1200.00 2500.00
MT1993 Mike Trout 1200.00 2500.00
MT1994 Mike Trout 1200.00 2500.00
MT1995 Mike Trout 1200.00 2500.00
MT1996 Mike Trout 1200.00 2500.00
MT1997 Mike Trout 1200.00 2500.00
MT1998 Mike Trout 1200.00 2500.00
MT1999 Mike Trout 1200.00 2500.00
MT2000 Mike Trout 1200.00 2500.00
MT2001 Mike Trout 1200.00 2500.00
MT2002 Mike Trout 1200.00 2500.00
MT2003 Mike Trout 1200.00 2500.00
MT2004 Mike Trout 1200.00 2500.00
MT2005 Mike Trout 1200.00 2500.00
MT2006 Mike Trout 1200.00 2500.00
MT2007 Mike Trout 1200.00 2500.00
MT2008 Mike Trout 1200.00 2500.00
MT2009 Mike Trout 1200.00 2500.00
MT2010 Mike Trout 1200.00 2500.00
MT2011 Mike Trout 1200.00 2500.00
MT2012 Mike Trout 1200.00 2500.00
MT2013 Mike Trout 1200.00 2500.00
MT2014 Mike Trout 1200.00 2500.00
MT2015 Mike Trout 1200.00 2500.00
MT2016 Mike Trout 1200.00 2500.00
MT2017 Mike Trout 1200.00 2500.00
MT2018 Mike Trout 1200.00 2500.00
MT51RB Mike Trout 1200.00 2500.00
MT55BB Mike Trout 1200.00 2500.00
MT58AS Mike Trout 1200.00 2500.00
MT68TG Mike Trout 1200.00 2500.00
MT69TS Mike Trout 1200.00 2500.00
MT72IA Mike Trout 1200.00 2500.00
MT75TH Mike Trout 1200.00 2500.00
MT77TB Mike Trout 1200.00 2500.00
MT78RB Mike Trout 1200.00 2500.00
MT82IA Mike Trout 1200.00 2500.00
MT82TH Mike Trout 1200.00 2500.00
MT88AS Mike Trout 1200.00 2500.00
MT88RB Mike Trout 1200.00 2500.00
MT89RB Mike Trout 1200.00 2500.00
MT90RB Mike Trout 1200.00 2500.00
MT91AS Mike Trout 1200.00 2500.00

2018 Topps Transcendent Origins Sketch Reproductions

ONE COMPLETE SET PER BOX
STATED PRINT RUN 83 SER.#'d SETS
OSI Ichiro 12.00 30.00
OSAB Andrew Benintendi 10.00 25.00
OSAD Andre Dawson 8.00 20.00
OSAJ Aaron Judge 25.00 60.00
OSAP Albert Pujols 12.00 30.00
OSAR Alex Rodriguez 12.00 30.00
OSBF Bob Feller 8.00 20.00
OSBH Bryce Harper 15.00 40.00
OSBJ Bo Jackson 10.00 25.00
OSBP Buster Posey 12.00 30.00
OSBW Billy Williams 8.00 20.00
OSCB Cody Bellinger 20.00 50.00
OSCC Carlos Correa 10.00 25.00
OSCF Carlton Fisk 10.00 25.00
OSCS Corey Seager 10.00 25.00
OSDJ Derek Jeter 20.00 50.00
OSDP Dustin Pedroia 10.00 25.00
OSEM Eddie Murray 8.00 20.00
OSFL Francisco Lindor 10.00 25.00
OSFR Frank Robinson 8.00 20.00
OSGM Greg Maddux 12.00 30.00
OSGS Gary Sanchez 10.00 25.00
OSHA Hank Aaron 25.00 60.00
OSHM Hideki Matsui 10.00 25.00
OSIS Ichiro 12.00 30.00
OSJB Jeff Bagwell 12.00 30.00
OSJR Jackie Robinson 10.00 25.00
OSKB Kris Bryant 12.00 30.00
OSLA Luis Aparicio 8.00 20.00
OSLG Lou Gehrig 20.00 50.00
OSMC Miguel Cabrera 10.00 25.00
OSMM Manny Machado 10.00 25.00
OSMP Mike Piazza 10.00 25.00
OSMR Mariano Rivera 15.00 40.00
OSMT Mike Trout 25.00 60.00
OSNR Nolan Ryan 25.00 60.00
OSOC Orlando Cepeda 8.00 20.00
OSRC Roberto Clemente 30.00 80.00
OSRH Rhys Hoskins 20.00 50.00
OSRJ Randy Johnson 10.00 25.00
OSSK Sandy Koufax 20.00 50.00
OSSO Shohei Ohtani 25.00 60.00
OSTS Tom Seaver 8.00 20.00
OSTW Ted Williams 20.00 50.00
OSWM Willie McCovey 12.00 30.00
OSAAJ Aaron Judge 25.00 60.00
OSAJU Aaron Judge 25.00 60.00
OSARI Anthony Rizzo 15.00 40.00
OSBHA Bryce Harper 15.00 40.00
OSCAR Cal Ripken Jr. 25.00 60.00
OSCRJ Cal Ripken Jr. 25.00 60.00
OSDEJ Derek Jeter 20.00 50.00
OSDJE Derek Jeter 20.00 50.00
OSHMI Hideki Matsui 10.00 25.00
OSICS Ichiro 12.00 30.00
OSJBE Johnny Bench 10.00 25.00
OSJRO Jackie Robinson 10.00 25.00
OSKBR Kris Bryant 12.00 30.00
OSMIT Mike Trout 25.00 60.00
OSMMC Mark McGwire 15.00 40.00
OSMTR Mike Trout 25.00 60.00
OSRCA Rod Carew 15.00 40.00
OSRCL Roger Clemens 12.00 30.00
OSRHE Rickey Henderson 20.00 50.00
OSSOH Shohei Ohtani 25.00 60.00

2018 Topps Transcendent Japan

ISSUED IN ASIAN BOXES
STATED PRINT RUN 50 SER.#'d SETS
ALL VERSIONS EQUALLY PRICED
TI1 Ichiro 25.00 60.00
TI2 Ichiro 25.00 60.00
TI3 Ichiro 25.00 60.00
TI4 Ichiro 25.00 60.00
TI5 Ichiro 25.00 60.00
TI6 Ichiro 25.00 60.00
TI7 Ichiro 25.00 60.00
TI8 Ichiro 25.00 60.00
TI9 Ichiro 25.00 60.00
TI10 Ichiro 25.00 60.00
TI11 Ichiro 25.00 60.00
TI12 Ichiro 25.00 60.00
TI13 Ichiro 25.00 60.00
TI14 Ichiro 25.00 60.00
TI15 Ichiro 25.00 60.00
TI16 Ichiro 25.00 60.00
TI17 Ichiro 25.00 60.00
TI18 Ichiro 25.00 60.00
TI19 Ichiro 25.00 60.00
TI20 Ichiro 25.00 60.00
TSO1 Shohei Ohtani 30.00 80.00
TSO2 Shohei Ohtani 30.00 80.00
TSO3 Shohei Ohtani 30.00 80.00
TSO4 Shohei Ohtani 30.00 80.00
TSO5 Shohei Ohtani 30.00 80.00
TSO6 Shohei Ohtani 30.00 80.00
TSO7 Shohei Ohtani 30.00 80.00
TSO8 Shohei Ohtani 30.00 80.00
TSO9 Shohei Ohtani 30.00 80.00
TSO10 Shohei Ohtani 30.00 80.00
TSO11 Shohei Ohtani 30.00 80.00
TSO12 Shohei Ohtani 30.00 80.00
TSO13 Shohei Ohtani 30.00 80.00
TSO14 Shohei Ohtani 30.00 80.00
TSO15 Shohei Ohtani 30.00 80.00
TSO16 Shohei Ohtani 30.00 80.00
TSO17 Shohei Ohtani 30.00 80.00
TSO18 Shohei Ohtani 30.00 80.00
TSO19 Shohei Ohtani 30.00 80.00
TSO20 Shohei Ohtani 30.00 80.00
TSO21 Shohei Ohtani 30.00 80.00
TSO22 Shohei Ohtani 30.00 80.00
TSO23 Shohei Ohtani 30.00 80.00
TSO24 Shohei Ohtani 30.00 80.00
TSO25 Shohei Ohtani 30.00 80.00
TSO26 Shohei Ohtani 30.00 80.00
TSO27 Shohei Ohtani 30.00 80.00
TSO28 Shohei Ohtani 30.00 80.00
TSO29 Shohei Ohtani 30.00 80.00
TSO30 Shohei Ohtani 30.00 80.00

2018 Topps Transcendent Japan '17 Bowman Chrome Mega Box Ohtani Autographs

ISSUED IN ASIAN BOXES
STATED PRINT RUN 17 SER.#'d SETS
BCP31 S.Otani/17 UER 800.00 1200.00

2018 Topps Transcendent Japan Autographs

ISSUED IN ASIAN BOXES
STATED PRINT RUN 5 SER.#'d SETS
ALL VERSIONS EQUALLY PRICED
*EMERALD/3: .4X TO 1X BASIC
TAI1 Ichiro 250.00 500.00
TAI2 Ichiro 250.00 500.00
TAI3 Ichiro 250.00 500.00
TAI4 Ichiro 250.00 500.00
TAI5 Ichiro 250.00 500.00
TAI6 Ichiro 250.00 500.00
TAI7 Ichiro 250.00 500.00
TAI8 Ichiro 250.00 500.00
TAI9 Ichiro 250.00 500.00
TAI10 Ichiro 250.00 500.00
TAI11 Ichiro 250.00 500.00
TAI12 Ichiro 250.00 500.00
TAI13 Ichiro 250.00 500.00
TAI14 Ichiro 250.00 500.00
TAI15 Ichiro 250.00 500.00
TAI16 Ichiro 250.00 500.00
TAI17 Ichiro 250.00 500.00
TAI18 Ichiro 250.00 500.00
TAI19 Ichiro 250.00 500.00
TAI20 Ichiro 250.00 500.00
TASO1 Shohei Ohtani 400.00 800.00
TASO2 Shohei Ohtani 400.00 800.00
TASO3 Shohei Ohtani 400.00 800.00
TASO4 Shohei Ohtani 400.00 800.00
TASO5 Shohei Ohtani 400.00 800.00
TASO6 Shohei Ohtani 400.00 800.00
TASO7 Shohei Ohtani 400.00 800.00
TASO8 Shohei Ohtani 400.00 800.00
TASO9 Shohei Ohtani 400.00 800.00
TASO10 Shohei Ohtani 400.00 800.00
TASO11 Shohei Ohtani 400.00 800.00
TASO12 Shohei Ohtani 400.00 800.00
TASO13 Shohei Ohtani 400.00 800.00
TASO14 Shohei Ohtani 400.00 800.00
TASO15 Shohei Ohtani 400.00 800.00
TASO16 Shohei Ohtani 400.00 800.00
TASO17 Shohei Ohtani 400.00 800.00
TASO18 Shohei Ohtani 400.00 800.00
TASO19 Shohei Ohtani 400.00 800.00
TASO20 Shohei Ohtani 400.00 800.00
TASO21 Shohei Ohtani 400.00 800.00
TASO22 Shohei Ohtani 400.00 800.00
TASO23 Shohei Ohtani 400.00 800.00
TASO24 Shohei Ohtani 400.00 800.00
TASO25 Shohei Ohtani 400.00 800.00
TASO26 Shohei Ohtani 400.00 800.00
TASO27 Shohei Ohtani 400.00 800.00
TASO28 Shohei Ohtani 400.00 800.00
TASO29 Shohei Ohtani 400.00 800.00
TASO30 Shohei Ohtani 400.00 800.00

2018 Topps Transcendent Japan Shohei Ohtani Through the Years Autographs

ISSUED IN ASIAN BOXES
STATED PRINT RUN 1 SER.#'d SET
ALL VERSIONS EQUALLY PRICED
SO1952 Shohei Ohtani 1200.00 2500.00
SO1953 Shohei Ohtani 1200.00 2500.00
SO1954 Shohei Ohtani 1200.00 2500.00
SO1955 Shohei Ohtani 1200.00 2500.00
SO1956 Shohei Ohtani 1200.00 2500.00
SO1957 Shohei Ohtani 1200.00 2500.00
SO1958 Shohei Ohtani 1200.00 2500.00
SO1959 Shohei Ohtani 1200.00 2500.00
SO1960 Shohei Ohtani 1200.00 2500.00
SO1961 Shohei Ohtani 1200.00 2500.00
SO1962 Shohei Ohtani 1200.00 2500.00
SO1963 Shohei Ohtani 1200.00 2500.00
SO1964 Shohei Ohtani 1200.00 2500.00
SO1965 Shohei Ohtani 1200.00 2500.00
SO1966 Shohei Ohtani 1200.00 2500.00
SO1967 Shohei Ohtani 1200.00 2500.00
SO1968 Shohei Ohtani 1200.00 2500.00
SO1969 Shohei Ohtani 1200.00 2500.00
SO1970 Shohei Ohtani 1200.00 2500.00
SO1971 Shohei Ohtani 1200.00 2500.00
SO1972 Shohei Ohtani 1200.00 2500.00
SO1973 Shohei Ohtani 1200.00 2500.00
SO1975 Shohei Ohtani 1200.00 2500.00
SO1976 Shohei Ohtani 1200.00 2500.00
SO1977 Shohei Ohtani 1200.00 2500.00
SO1979 Shohei Ohtani 1200.00 2500.00
SO1981 Shohei Ohtani 1200.00 2500.00
SO1982 Shohei Ohtani 1200.00 2500.00
SO1983 Shohei Ohtani 1200.00 2500.00
SO1984 Shohei Ohtani 1200.00 2500.00
SO1985 Shohei Ohtani 1200.00 2500.00
SO1986 Shohei Ohtani 1200.00 2500.00
SO1987 Shohei Ohtani 1200.00 2500.00
SO1988 Shohei Ohtani 1200.00 2500.00
SO1989 Shohei Ohtani 1200.00 2500.00
SO1990 Shohei Ohtani 1200.00 2500.00
SO1991 Shohei Ohtani 1200.00 2500.00
SO1992 Shohei Ohtani 1200.00 2500.00
SO1995 Shohei Ohtani 1200.00 2500.00
SO1999 Shohei Ohtani 1200.00 2500.00
SO2001 Shohei Ohtani 1200.00 2500.00
SO2002 Shohei Ohtani 1200.00 2500.00
SO2003 Shohei Ohtani 1200.00 2500.00
SO2005 Shohei Ohtani 1200.00 2500.00
SO2007 Shohei Ohtani 1200.00 2500.00
SO2008 Shohei Ohtani 1200.00 2500.00
SO2010 Shohei Ohtani 1200.00 2500.00
SO2014 Shohei Ohtani 1200.00 2500.00
SO2017 Shohei Ohtani 1200.00 2500.00
SO2018 Shohei Ohtani 1200.00 2500.00

2018 Topps Transcendent VIP Party Aaron Judge Bunt

ISSUED AT TRANSCENDENT VIP PARTY
STATED PRINT RUN 87 SER.#'d SETS
NNO Aaron Judge 20.00 50.00

2018 Topps Transcendent VIP Party Aaron Judge History

ISSUED AT TRANSCENDENT VIP PARTY
STATED PRINT RUN 87 SER.#'d SETS
AJ55B Aaron Judge 60.00 150.00
AJ1952 Aaron Judge 200.00 400.00
AJ1953 Aaron Judge 150.00 300.00
AJ1954 Aaron Judge 75.00 200.00
AJ1955 Aaron Judge 60.00 150.00
AJ1956 Aaron Judge 60.00 150.00
AJ1957 Aaron Judge 40.00 100.00
AJ1958 Aaron Judge 40.00 100.00
AJ1959 Aaron Judge 40.00 100.00
AJ1960 Aaron Judge 40.00 100.00
AJ1961 Aaron Judge 40.00 100.00
AJ1962 Aaron Judge 40.00 100.00
AJ1963 Aaron Judge 40.00 100.00
AJ1964 Aaron Judge 40.00 100.00
AJ1965 Aaron Judge 40.00 100.00
AJ1966 Aaron Judge 40.00 100.00
AJ1967 Aaron Judge 40.00 100.00
AJ1968 Aaron Judge 40.00 100.00
AJ1969 Aaron Judge 40.00 100.00
AJ1970 Aaron Judge 40.00 100.00
AJ1971 Aaron Judge 40.00 100.00
AJ1972 Aaron Judge 40.00 100.00
AJ1973 Aaron Judge 40.00 100.00
AJ1974 Aaron Judge 40.00 100.00
AJ1975 Aaron Judge 40.00 100.00
AJ1976 Aaron Judge 40.00 100.00
AJ1977 Aaron Judge 40.00 100.00
AJ1978 Aaron Judge 40.00 100.00
AJ1979 Aaron Judge 40.00 100.00
AJ1980 Aaron Judge 40.00 100.00

AJ1981 Aaron Judge 40.00 100.00
AJ1982 Aaron Judge 40.00 100.00
AJ1983 Aaron Judge 40.00 100.00
AJ1984 Aaron Judge 40.00 100.00
AJ1985 Aaron Judge 40.00 100.00
AJ1986 Aaron Judge 40.00 100.00
AJ1987 Aaron Judge 40.00 100.00
AJ1988 Aaron Judge 40.00 100.00
AJ1989 Aaron Judge 40.00 100.00
AJ1990 Aaron Judge 40.00 100.00
AJ1991 Aaron Judge 40.00 100.00
AJ1992 Aaron Judge 40.00 100.00
AJ1993 Aaron Judge 40.00 100.00
AJ1994 Aaron Judge 40.00 100.00
AJ1995 Aaron Judge 40.00 100.00
AJ1996 Aaron Judge 40.00 100.00
AJ1997 Aaron Judge 40.00 100.00
AJ1998 Aaron Judge 40.00 100.00
AJ1999 Aaron Judge 40.00 100.00
AJ2000 Aaron Judge 40.00 100.00
AJ2001 Aaron Judge 40.00 100.00
AJ2002 Aaron Judge 40.00 100.00
AJ2003 Aaron Judge 40.00 100.00
AJ2004 Aaron Judge 40.00 100.00
AJ2005 Aaron Judge 40.00 100.00
AJ2006 Aaron Judge 40.00 100.00
AJ2007 Aaron Judge 40.00 100.00
AJ2008 Aaron Judge 40.00 100.00
AJ2009 Aaron Judge 40.00 100.00
AJ2010 Aaron Judge 40.00 100.00
AJ2011 Aaron Judge 40.00 100.00
AJ2012 Aaron Judge 40.00 100.00
AJ2013 Aaron Judge 40.00 100.00
AJ2014 Aaron Judge 40.00 100.00
AJ2015 Aaron Judge 40.00 100.00
AJ2016 Aaron Judge 40.00 100.00
AJ2017 Aaron Judge 40.00 100.00
AJ51PB Aaron Judge 40.00 100.00
AJ58AS Aaron Judge 40.00 100.00
AJ60RS Aaron Judge 40.00 100.00
AJ68TG Aaron Judge 40.00 100.00
AJ69TS Aaron Judge 40.00 100.00
AJ71TH Aaron Judge 40.00 100.00
AJ72IA Aaron Judge 40.00 100.00
AJ75TH Aaron Judge 40.00 100.00
AJ78RB Aaron Judge 40.00 100.00
AJ83TH Aaron Judge 40.00 100.00
AJ87FS Aaron Judge 40.00 100.00
AJ88AS Aaron Judge 40.00 100.00
AJ88RB Aaron Judge 40.00 100.00
AJ89RB Aaron Judge 40.00 100.00
AJ90DR Aaron Judge 40.00 100.00
AJ90TR Aaron Judge 40.00 100.00
AJ91AS Aaron Judge 40.00 100.00
AJ91RB Aaron Judge 40.00 100.00
AJ93CA Aaron Judge 40.00 100.00
AJ93DP Aaron Judge 40.00 100.00

2018 Topps Transcendent VIP Party Clint Frazier Autographs

ISSUED AT TRANSCENDENT VIP PARTY
STATED PRINT RUN 25 SER.#'d SETS
2018RC1 Clint Frazier 75.00 200.00
2018RC2 Clint Frazier 75.00 200.00
2018RC3 Clint Frazier 75.00 200.00
2018RC4 Clint Frazier 75.00 200.00

2018 Topps Transcendent VIP Party Hank Aaron Autographs Gold Frame

ISSUED AT TRANSCENDENT VIP PARTY
STATED PRINT RUN 15 SER.#'d SETS
VIP1 Hank Aaron 200.00 400.00
VIP2 Hank Aaron 200.00 400.00
VIP3 Hank Aaron 200.00 400.00
VIP4 Hank Aaron 200.00 400.00
VIP5 Hank Aaron 200.00 400.00
VIP6 Hank Aaron 200.00 400.00

2018 Topps Transcendent VIP Party Hank Aaron Autographs Silver Frame

ISSUED AT TRANSCENDENT VIP PARTY
STATED PRINT RUN 25 SER.#'d SETS
HANK1 Hank Aaron 200.00 400.00
HANK2 Hank Aaron 200.00 400.00
HANK3 Hank Aaron 200.00 400.00
HANK4 Hank Aaron 200.00 400.00

2019 Topps Transcendent

ONE COMPLETE SET PER CASE
STATED PRINT RUN 100 SER.#'d SETS
1 Babe Ruth 12.00 30.00
2 Nick Senzel RC 20.00 50.00
3 Francisco Lindor 10.00 25.00
4 Cody Bellinger 10.00 25.00
5 Roger Clemens 10.00 25.00
6 Giancarlo Stanton 5.00 12.00
7 Ken Griffey Jr. 25.00 60.00
8 Ernie Banks 6.00 15.00
9 Ronald Acuna Jr. 20.00 50.00
10 Bryce Harper 20.00 50.00
11 Christy Mathewson 10.00 25.00
12 Derek Jeter 20.00 50.00
13 Hank Aaron 12.00 30.00
14 Mookie Betts 8.00 20.00
15 Ty Cobb 12.00 30.00
16 Manny Machado 8.00 20.00
17 Jose Altuve 6.00 15.00
18 Rhys Hoskins 12.00 30.00
19 Lou Gehrig 12.00 30.00
20 Sammy Sosa 6.00 15.00
21 Rogers Hornsby 6.00 15.00
22 Pete Alonso RC 100.00 250.00
23 Carter Kieboom RC 30.00 80.00
24 Ted Williams 10.00 25.00
25 Vladimir Guerrero Jr. RC 100.00 250.00
26 Jacob deGrom 8.00 20.00
27 Shohei Ohtani 20.00 50.00
28 Aaron Judge 12.00 30.00
29 Cal Ripken Jr. 15.00 40.00
30 Thurman Munson 10.00 25.00
31 Mariano Rivera 10.00 25.00
32 Carl Yastrzemski 8.00 20.00
33 Honus Wagner 6.00 15.00
34 Juan Soto 15.00 40.00
35 Roberto Clemente 30.00 80.00
36 Deion Sanders 6.00 15.00
37 Vladimir Guerrero 6.00 15.00
38 Rickey Henderson 12.00 30.00
39 Johnny Bench 10.00 25.00
40 Christian Yelich 12.00 30.00
41 Tony Gwynn 12.00 30.00
42 Kris Bryant 12.00 30.00
43 Willie Mays 20.00 50.00
44 Eloy Jimenez RC 40.00 100.00
45 Nolan Ryan 25.00 60.00
46 Sandy Koufax 10.00 25.00
47 Ichiro 15.00 40.00
48 Jackie Robinson 10.00 25.00
49 Fernando Tatis Jr. RC 100.00 250.00
50 Mike Trout 40.00 100.00

2019 Topps Transcendent Autographs

FIFTY AUTOGRAPHS PER CASE
STATED PRINT RUN 25 SER.#'d SETS
*EMERALD/15: .4X TO 1X BASIC
*VAR/25: .4X TO 1X BASIC
*VAR.EMRLD/15: .4X TO 1X BASIC
TCAAB Adrian Beltre 30.00 80.00
TCAAJ Aaron Judge 60.00 150.00
TCAAP Albert Pujols 60.00 150.00
TCAARI Anthony Rizzo 30.00 80.00
TCABH Bryce Harper 100.00 250.00
TCABJ Bo Jackson 40.00 100.00
TCABL Barry Larkin 30.00 80.00
TCABP Buster Posey 40.00 100.00
TCACJ Chipper Jones 40.00 100.00
TCACRJ Cal Ripken Jr. 60.00 150.00
TCACY Carl Yastrzemski 40.00 100.00
TCACYE Christian Yelich 50.00 120.00
TCADJ Derek Jeter 200.00 500.00
TCADM Don Mattingly 40.00 100.00
TCADO David Ortiz 40.00 100.00
TCADS Deion Sanders 40.00 100.00
TCAEJ Eloy Jimenez 60.00 150.00
TCAEM Edgar Martinez 30.00 80.00
TCAFL Francisco Lindor
TCAFTH Frank Thomas 40.00 100.00
TCAFTJ Fernando Tatis Jr. 200.00 500.00
TCAHA Hank Aaron 125.00 300.00
TCAHM Hideki Matsui 40.00 100.00
TCAI Ichiro 125.00 300.00
TCAJA Jose Altuve 20.00 50.00
TCAJB Johnny Bench 30.00 80.00
TCAJM J.D. Martinez 25.00 60.00
TCAJS Juan Soto 75.00 200.00
TCAJV Joey Votto 25.00 60.00
TCAKB Kris Bryant 40.00 100.00
TCAKGJ Ken Griffey Jr. 150.00 400.00
TCAMC Miguel Cabrera 40.00 100.00
TCAMMC Mark McGwire 40.00 100.00
TCAMR Mariano Rivera 75.00 200.00
TCAMT Mike Trout 200.00 500.00
TCAMTA Masahiro Tanaka 40.00 100.00
TCANR Nolan Ryan 60.00 150.00
TCAOS Ozzie Smith 25.00 60.00
TCAPA Pete Alonso 100.00 250.00
TCAPM Pedro Martinez 60.00 150.00
TCARAJ Ronald Acuna Jr. 75.00 200.00
TCARC Roger Clemens 50.00 120.00
TCARH Rickey Henderson 40.00 100.00
TCARJ Randy Johnson 60.00 150.00
TCASK Sandy Koufax 150.00 400.00
TCASO Shohei Ohtani 75.00 200.00
TCASS Sammy Sosa 40.00 100.00
TCAXB Xander Bogaerts 30.00 80.00
TCARJA Reggie Jackson 25.00 60.00
TCAVGJ Vladimir Guerrero Jr. 100.00 250.00
TCAVGS Vladimir Guerrero 40.00 100.00

2019 Topps Transcendent Franchise Favorites Reproductions

ONE COMPLETE SET PER CASE
STATED PRINT RUN 100 SER.#'d SETS
FFRAB Adrian Beltre 5.00 12.00
FFRAD Andre Dawson 6.00 15.00
FFRAJ Aaron Judge 12.00 30.00
FFRAK Al Kaline 12.00 30.00
FFRAP Albert Pujols 10.00 25.00
FFRAT Alan Trammell 12.00 30.00
FFRBF Bob Feller 6.00 15.00
FFRBG Bob Gibson 4.00 10.00
FFRBH Bryce Harper 8.00 20.00
FFRBJ Bo Jackson 12.00 30.00
FFRBL Barry Larkin 8.00 20.00
FFRBP Buster Posey 12.00 30.00
FFRBR Babe Ruth 8.00 20.00
FFRBRU Babe Ruth 8.00 20.00
FFRBW Billy Williams 8.00 20.00
FFRCC Carlos Correa 8.00 20.00
FFRCJ Chipper Jones 12.00 30.00
FFRCK Clayton Kershaw 10.00 25.00
FFRCRJ Cal Ripken Jr. 15.00 40.00
FFRCY Carl Yastrzemski 8.00 20.00
FFRCYE Christian Yelich 8.00 20.00
FFRDE Dennis Eckersley 6.00 15.00
FFRDG Dwight Gooden 3.00 8.00
FFRDJ Derek Jeter 15.00 40.00
FFRDO David Ortiz 8.00 20.00
FFRDS Darryl Strawberry 6.00 15.00
FFRDSN Duke Snider 10.00 25.00
FFRDW Dave Winfield 4.00 10.00
FFREB Ernie Banks 12.00 30.00
FFREM Eddie Murray 10.00 25.00
FFREMA Edgar Martinez 6.00 15.00
FFRFL Francisco Lindor 5.00 12.00
FFRFR Frank Robinson 6.00 15.00
FFRFT Frank Thomas 12.00 30.00
FFRGB George Brett 15.00 40.00
FFRGC Gary Carter 8.00 20.00
FFRGCA Gary Carter 8.00 20.00
FFRGM Greg Maddux 10.00 25.00
FFRGS Giancarlo Stanton 5.00 12.00
FFRHA Hank Aaron 15.00 40.00
FFRHB Harold Baines 4.00 10.00
FFRHK Harmon Killebrew 10.00 25.00
FFRHW Honus Wagner 5.00 12.00
FFRIR Ivan Rodriguez 6.00 15.00
FFRIS Ichiro 12.00 30.00
FFRI Ichiro 12.00 30.00
FFRJB Jeff Bagwell 6.00 15.00
FFRJBE Johnny Bench 6.00 15.00
FFRJBU Jim Bunning 4.00 10.00
FFRJM Joe Morgan 6.00 15.00
FFRJMA Juan Marichal 8.00 20.00
FFRJP Jim Palmer 6.00 15.00
FFRJR Jackie Robinson 10.00 25.00
FFRJT Jim Thome 6.00 15.00
FFRJV Justin Verlander 8.00 20.00
FFRKGJ Ken Griffey Jr. 15.00 40.00
FFRLG Lou Gehrig 10.00 25.00
FFRMB Mookie Betts 8.00 20.00
FFRMC Miguel Cabrera 8.00 20.00
FFRMI Monte Irvin 4.00 10.00
FFRMP Mike Piazza 8.00 20.00
FFRMR Mariano Rivera 8.00 20.00
FFRMS Max Scherzer 6.00 15.00
FFRMT Mike Trout 20.00 50.00
FFRNA Nolan Arenado 8.00 20.00
FFRNOR Nolan Ryan 15.00 40.00
FFRNR Nolan Ryan 15.00 40.00
FFRNRY Nolan Ryan 15.00 40.00
FFROS Ozzie Smith 8.00 20.00
FFRPG Paul Goldschmidt 6.00 15.00
FFRPM Pedro Martinez 4.00 10.00
FFRRA Roberto Alomar 6.00 15.00
FFRRAJ Ronald Acuna Jr. 15.00 40.00
FFRRAN Randy Johnson 5.00 12.00
FFRRC Rod Carew 8.00 20.00
FFRRCL Roberto Clemente 20.00 50.00
FFRREJ Reggie Jackson 4.00 10.00
FFRRF Rollie Fingers 4.00 10.00
FFRRH Roy Halladay 6.00 15.00
FFRRIH Rickey Henderson 10.00 25.00
FFRRJ Reggie Jackson 4.00 10.00
FFRRJO Randy Johnson 5.00 12.00
FFRROY Roy Halladay 4.00 10.00
FFRRS Ryne Sandberg 10.00 25.00
FFRRY Robin Yount 8.00 20.00
FFRSC Steve Carlton 8.00 20.00
FFRSK Sandy Koufax 10.00 25.00
FFRSM Stan Musial 10.00 25.00
FFRSS Sammy Sosa 5.00 12.00
FFRTC Ty Cobb 8.00 20.00
FFRTG Tony Gwynn 12.00 30.00
FFRTH Todd Helton 4.00 10.00
FFRTHO Trevor Hoffman 4.00 10.00
FFRTM Thurman Munson 8.00 20.00
FFRTW Ted Williams 12.00 30.00
FFRVGS Vladimir Guerrero 8.00 20.00
FFRVLG Vladimir Guerrero 8.00 20.00
FFRWB Wade Boggs 8.00 20.00
FFRWM Willie McCovey 6.00 15.00
FFRWS Willie Stargell 8.00 20.00

2019 Topps Transcendent Ohtani VIP Party Autographs

ISSUED AT TOPPS VIP PARTY
PRINT RUNS B/WN 10-25 COPIES PER
NO PRICING ON QTY 10
SHAP1 Shohei Ohtani 60.00 150.00
SHAP2 Shohei Ohtani 60.00 150.00

2019 Topps Transcendent Ohtani VIP Party Bunt

ISSUED AT TOPPS VIP PARTY
STATED PRINT RUN 50 SER.#'d SETS
NNO Shohei Ohtani 10.00 25.00

2019 Topps Transcendent Ohtani VIP Party On Demand

ISSUED AT TOPPS VIP PARTY
STATED PRINT RUN 83 SER.#'d SETS
1 Shohei Ohtani 2.50 6.00
2 Shohei Ohtani 2.50 6.00
3 Shohei Ohtani 2.50 6.00
4 Shohei Ohtani 2.50 6.00
5 Shohei Ohtani 2.50 6.00
6 Shohei Ohtani 2.50 6.00
7 Shohei Ohtani 2.50 6.00
8 Shohei Ohtani 2.50 6.00
9 Shohei Ohtani 2.50 6.00
10 Shohei Ohtani 2.50 6.00

2019 Topps Transcendent Ohtani VIP Party Through the Years

ISSUED AT TOPPS VIP PARTY
STATED PRINT RUN 50 SER.#'d SETS
SO1952 Shohei Ohtani 8.00 20.00
SO1953 Shohei Ohtani 8.00 20.00
SO1954 Shohei Ohtani 8.00 20.00
SO1955 Shohei Ohtani 8.00 20.00
SO1956 Shohei Ohtani 8.00 20.00
SO1957 Shohei Ohtani 8.00 20.00
SO1958 Shohei Ohtani 8.00 20.00
SO1959 Shohei Ohtani 8.00 20.00
SO1960 Shohei Ohtani 8.00 20.00
SO1961 Shohei Ohtani 8.00 20.00
SO1962 Shohei Ohtani 8.00 20.00
SO1963 Shohei Ohtani 8.00 20.00
SO1964 Shohei Ohtani 8.00 20.00
SO1965 Shohei Ohtani 8.00 20.00
SO1966 Shohei Ohtani 8.00 20.00
SO1967 Shohei Ohtani 8.00 20.00
SO1968 Shohei Ohtani 8.00 20.00
SO1969 Shohei Ohtani 8.00 20.00
SO1970 Shohei Ohtani 8.00 20.00
SO1971 Shohei Ohtani 8.00 20.00
SO1972 Shohei Ohtani 8.00 20.00
SO1973 Shohei Ohtani 8.00 20.00
SO1975 Shohei Ohtani 8.00 20.00
SO1976 Shohei Ohtani 8.00 20.00
SO1977 Shohei Ohtani 8.00 20.00
SO1979 Shohei Ohtani 8.00 20.00
SO1981 Shohei Ohtani 8.00 20.00
SO1982 Shohei Ohtani 8.00 20.00
SO1983 Shohei Ohtani 8.00 20.00
SO1984 Shohei Ohtani 8.00 20.00
SO1985 Shohei Ohtani 8.00 20.00
SO1986 Shohei Ohtani 8.00 20.00
SO1987 Shohei Ohtani 8.00 20.00
SO1988 Shohei Ohtani 8.00 20.00
SO1989 Shohei Ohtani 8.00 20.00
SO1990 Shohei Ohtani 8.00 20.00
SO1991 Shohei Ohtani 8.00 20.00
SO1992 Shohei Ohtani 8.00 20.00
SO1995 Shohei Ohtani 8.00 20.00
SO1999 Shohei Ohtani 8.00 20.00
SO2001 Shohei Ohtani 8.00 20.00
SO2002 Shohei Ohtani 8.00 20.00
SO2003 Shohei Ohtani 8.00 20.00
SO2005 Shohei Ohtani 8.00 20.00
SO2007 Shohei Ohtani 8.00 20.00
SO2008 Shohei Ohtani 8.00 20.00
SO2010 Shohei Ohtani 8.00 20.00
SO2014 Shohei Ohtani 8.00 20.00
SO2017 Shohei Ohtani 8.00 20.00
SO2018 Shohei Ohtani 8.00 20.00

2019 Topps Transcendent VIP Party Mike Trout Autographs

ISSUED AT TOPPS VIP PARTY
PRINT RUNS B/WN 15-25 COPIES PER
MTA1 Mike Trout 300.00 500.00
MTA2 Mike Trout 300.00 500.00
MTA3 Mike Trout 300.00 500.00
MTA4 Mike Trout 300.00 500.00
MTA5 Mike Trout 300.00 500.00
MTA6 Mike Trout 300.00 500.00
MTAP1 Mike Trout 300.00 500.00
MTAP2 Mike Trout 300.00 500.00
MTAP3 Mike Trout 300.00 500.00
MTAP4 Mike Trout 300.00 500.00

2019 Topps Transcendent VIP Party Mike Trout Bunt

ISSUED AT TOPPS VIP PARTY
STATED PRINT RUN 83 SER.#'d SETS
NNO Mike Trout 20.00 50.00

2019 Topps Transcendent VIP Party Mike Trout On Demand

ISSUED AT TOPPS VIP PARTY
STATED PRINT RUN 83 SER.#'d SETS
1 Mike Trout 10.00 25.00
2 Mike Trout 10.00 25.00
3 Mike Trout 10.00 25.00
4 Mike Trout 10.00 25.00
5 Mike Trout 10.00 25.00
6 Mike Trout 10.00 25.00
7 Mike Trout 10.00 25.00
8 Mike Trout 10.00 25.00
9 Mike Trout 10.00 25.00
10 Mike Trout 10.00 25.00

2019 Topps Transcendent VIP Party Mike Trout Through the Years

ISSUED AT TOPPS VIP PARTY
STATED PRINT RUN 83 SER.#'d SETS
MT1952 Mike Trout 15.00 40.00
MT1953 Mike Trout 15.00 40.00
MT1954 Mike Trout 15.00 40.00
MT1955 Mike Trout 15.00 40.00
MT1956 Mike Trout 15.00 40.00
MT1957 Mike Trout 15.00 40.00
MT1958 Mike Trout 15.00 40.00
MT1959 Mike Trout 15.00 40.00
MT1960 Mike Trout 15.00 40.00
MT1961 Mike Trout 15.00 40.00
MT1962 Mike Trout 15.00 40.00
MT1963 Mike Trout 15.00 40.00
MT1964 Mike Trout 15.00 40.00
MT1965 Mike Trout 15.00 40.00
MT1966 Mike Trout 15.00 40.00
MT1967 Mike Trout 15.00 40.00
MT1968 Mike Trout 15.00 40.00
MT1969 Mike Trout 15.00 40.00
MT1970 Mike Trout 15.00 40.00
MT1971 Mike Trout 15.00 40.00
MT1972 Mike Trout 15.00 40.00
MT1973 Mike Trout 15.00 40.00
MT1974 Mike Trout 15.00 40.00
MT1975 Mike Trout 15.00 40.00
MT1976 Mike Trout 15.00 40.00
MT1977 Mike Trout 15.00 40.00
MT1978 Mike Trout 15.00 40.00
MT1979 Mike Trout 15.00 40.00
MT1980 Mike Trout 15.00 40.00
MT1981 Mike Trout 15.00 40.00
MT1982 Mike Trout 15.00 40.00
MT1983 Mike Trout 15.00 40.00
MT1984 Mike Trout 15.00 40.00
MT1985 Mike Trout 15.00 40.00
MT1986 Mike Trout 15.00 40.00
MT1987 Mike Trout 15.00 40.00
MT1988 Mike Trout 15.00 40.00
MT1989 Mike Trout 15.00 40.00
MT1990 Mike Trout 15.00 40.00
MT1991 Mike Trout 15.00 40.00
MT1992 Mike Trout 15.00 40.00
MT1993 Mike Trout 15.00 40.00
MT1994 Mike Trout 15.00 40.00
MT1995 Mike Trout 15.00 40.00
MT1996 Mike Trout 15.00 40.00
MT1997 Mike Trout 15.00 40.00
MT1998 Mike Trout 15.00 40.00
MT1999 Mike Trout 15.00 40.00
MT2000 Mike Trout 15.00 40.00
MT2001 Mike Trout 15.00 40.00
MT2002 Mike Trout 15.00 40.00
MT2003 Mike Trout 15.00 40.00
MT2004 Mike Trout 15.00 40.00
MT2005 Mike Trout 15.00 40.00
MT2006 Mike Trout 15.00 40.00
MT2007 Mike Trout 15.00 40.00
MT2008 Mike Trout 15.00 40.00
MT2009 Mike Trout 15.00 40.00
MT2010 Mike Trout 15.00 40.00
MT2011 Mike Trout 15.00 40.00
MT2012 Mike Trout 15.00 40.00
MT2013 Mike Trout 15.00 40.00
MT2014 Mike Trout 15.00 40.00
MT2015 Mike Trout 15.00 40.00
MT2016 Mike Trout 15.00 40.00
MT2017 Mike Trout 15.00 40.00
MT2018 Mike Trout 15.00 40.00
MT51PB Mike Trout 15.00 40.00
MT55BB Mike Trout 15.00 40.00
MT58AS Mike Trout 15.00 40.00
MT68TG Mike Trout 15.00 40.00
MT69TS Mike Trout 15.00 40.00
MT72IA Mike Trout 15.00 40.00
MT75TH Mike Trout 15.00 40.00
MT77TB Mike Trout 15.00 40.00
MT78RB Mike Trout 15.00 40.00
MT82IA Mike Trout 15.00 40.00
MT82TH Mike Trout 15.00 40.00
MT88AS Mike Trout 15.00 40.00
MT88RB Mike Trout 15.00 40.00
MT89RB Mike Trout 15.00 40.00
MT90RB Mike Trout 15.00 40.00
MT91AS Mike Trout 15.00 40.00

2020 Topps Transcendent Hall of Fame

ONE COMPLETE SET PER BOX
STATED PRINT RUN 50 SER.#'d SETS
1 Babe Ruth 15.00 40.00
2 Mike Mussina 8.00 20.00
3 Frank Thomas 15.00 40.00
4 Roberto Alomar 6.00 15.00
5 Johnny Bench 8.00 20.00
6 Jeff Bagwell 20.00 50.00
7 Harold Baines 8.00 20.00
8 George Brett 12.00 30.00
9 Edgar Martinez 6.00 15.00
10 Carl Yastrzemski 10.00 25.00
11 Cal Ripken Jr. 15.00 40.00
12 Tom Glavine 6.00 15.00
13 Al Kaline 10.00 25.00
14 Wade Boggs 8.00 20.00
15 Bert Blyleven 6.00 15.00
16 Ken Griffey Jr. 25.00 60.00
17 Jim Thome 6.00 15.00
18 Vladimir Guerrero 6.00 15.00
19 Juan Marichal 10.00 25.00
20 Nolan Ryan 20.00 50.00
21 Ivan Rodriguez 10.00 25.00
22 Rickey Henderson 10.00 25.00
23 Andre Dawson 8.00 20.00
24 Ryne Sandberg 15.00 40.00
25 Sandy Koufax 15.00 40.00
26 Ted Williams 12.00 30.00
27 Honus Wagner 10.00 25.00
28 Chipper Jones 12.00 30.00
29 Jackie Robinson 8.00 20.00
30 Craig Biggio 10.00 25.00
31 Steve Carlton 6.00 15.00
32 John Smoltz 8.00 20.00
33 Lou Gehrig 10.00 25.00
34 Ozzie Smith 10.00 25.00
35 Robin Yount 10.00 25.00
36 Tony Gwynn 10.00 25.00
37 Reggie Jackson 8.00 20.00
38 Bob Gibson 6.00 15.00
39 Barry Larkin 6.00 15.00
40 Randy Johnson 8.00 20.00
41 Rod Carew 6.00 15.00
42 Tony Perez 15.00 40.00
43 Stan Musial 12.00 30.00
44 Tim Raines 6.00 15.00
45 Carlton Fisk 10.00 25.00
46 Alan Trammell 20.00 50.00
47 Lou Brock 8.00 20.00
48 Dennis Eckersley 6.00 15.00
49 Mariano Rivera 12.00 30.00
50 Hank Aaron 12.00 30.00

2020 Topps Transcendent Hall of Fame Sketch Reproductions

ONE COMPLETE SET PER BOX
STATED PRINT RUN 50 SER.#'d SETS
HOFRAD Andre Dawson 8.00 20.00
HOFRBF Bob Feller 8.00 20.00
HOFRBG Bob Gibson 6.00 15.00
HOFRBL Barry Larkin 6.00 15.00
HOFRBR Babe Ruth 15.00 40.00
HOFRCJ Chipper Jones 12.00 30.00
HOFRCM Christy Mathewson 8.00 20.00
HOFRCRJ Cal Ripken Jr. 15.00 40.00
HOFRCY Carl Yastrzemski 10.00 25.00
HOFREB Ernie Banks 8.00 20.00
HOFREM Edgar Martinez 6.00 15.00
HOFRFT Frank Thomas 15.00 40.00
HOFRGB George Brett 12.00 30.00
HOFRGC Gary Carter 12.00 30.00
HOFRHA Hank Aaron 12.00 30.00
HOFRHK Harmon Killebrew 8.00 20.00
HOFRHW Honus Wagner 10.00 25.00
HOFRIR Ivan Rodriguez 10.00 25.00
HOFRJB Jeff Bagwell 20.00 50.00
HOFRJBE Johnny Bench 8.00 20.00
HOFRJM Joe Morgan 6.00 15.00
HOFRJR Jackie Robinson 8.00 20.00
HOFRJT Jim Thome 6.00 15.00
HOFRKGJ Ken Griffey Jr. 25.00 60.00
HOFRLG Lou Gehrig 10.00 25.00
HOFRMI Monte Irvin 6.00 15.00
HOFRMP Mike Piazza 10.00 25.00
HOFRMR Mariano Rivera 12.00 30.00
HOFRNR Nolan Ryan 20.00 50.00
HOFROS Ozzie Smith 10.00 25.00
HOFRPM Pedro Martinez 6.00 15.00
HOFRRA Roberto Alomar 6.00 15.00
HOFRRC Rod Carew 6.00 15.00
HOFRRCL Roberto Clemente 30.00 80.00
HOFRRH Rickey Henderson 10.00 25.00
HOFRRHO Rogers Hornsby 6.00 15.00
HOFRRJ Randy Johnson 8.00 20.00
HOFRRJA Reggie Jackson 8.00 20.00
HOFRSC Steve Carlton 6.00 15.00
HOFRSK Sandy Koufax 15.00 40.00
HOFRSM Stan Musial 12.00 30.00
HOFRTC Ty Cobb 10.00 25.00
HOFRTG Tom Glavine 6.00 15.00
HOFRTGW Tony Gwynn 10.00 25.00
HOFRTS Tris Speaker 8.00 20.00
HOFRTW Ted Williams 12.00 30.00
HOFRVG Vladimir Guerrero 6.00 15.00
HOFRWB Wade Boggs 8.00 20.00
HOFRWM Willie Mays 12.00 30.00
HOFRWMC Willie McCovey 10.00 25.00

2020 Topps Transcendent Hall of Fame Sandy Koufax Through the Years Autographs

OVERALL ONE KOUFAX AUTO PER BOX
STATED PRINT RUN 1 SER.#'d SET

2020 Topps Transcendent Hall of Fame Autographs

OVERALL FORTY AUTOS PER BOX
STATED PRINT RUN 25 SER.#'d SETS
THOFAD Andre Dawson 30.00 80.00
THOFAK Al Kaline 50.00 120.00
THOFBG Bob Gibson 40.00 100.00
THOFBL Barry Larkin 30.00 80.00
THOFCF Carlton Fisk 30.00 80.00
THOFCJ Chipper Jones 75.00 200.00
THOFCRJ Cal Ripken Jr. 75.00 200.00
THOFCY Carl Yastrzemski 50.00 120.00
THOFFT Frank Thomas 50.00 120.00
THOFHA Hank Aaron 200.00 500.00
THOFJB Johnny Bench 40.00 100.00
THOFJBA Jeff Bagwell 75.00 200.00
THOFJM Juan Marichal 30.00 80.00
THOFJS John Smoltz 40.00 100.00
THOFJT Jim Thome 50.00 120.00
THOFKGJ Ken Griffey Jr. 200.00 500.00
THOFMM Mike Mussina 40.00 100.00
THOFMR Mariano Rivera 100.00 250.00
THOFNR Nolan Ryan 100.00 250.00
THOFOS Ozzie Smith 40.00 100.00
THOFPM Paul Molitor 40.00 100.00
THOFRA Roberto Alomar 30.00 80.00
THOFRC Rod Carew 30.00 80.00
THOFRH Rickey Henderson 50.00 120.00
THOFRJ Randy Johnson 50.00 120.00
THOFRJA Reggie Jackson 40.00 100.00
THOFRS Ryne Sandberg 60.00 150.00
THOFRY Robin Yount 40.00 100.00
THOFSK Sandy Koufax 200.00 500.00
THOFTG Tom Glavine 30.00 80.00
THOFVG Vladimir Guerrero 30.00 80.00
THOFWB Wade Boggs 30.00 80.00

2020 Topps Transcendent Hall of Fame Collection Image Variation Autographs

OVERALL FORTY AUTOS PER BOX
STATED PRINT RUN 25 SER.#'d SETS
THOFVAD Andre Dawson 30.00 80.00
THOFVAK Al Kaline 50.00 210.00
THOFVBG Bob Gibson 40.00 100.00
THOFVBL Barry Larkin 30.00 80.00
THOFVCF Carlton Fisk 30.00 80.00
THOFVCJ Chipper Jones 75.00 200.00
THOFVCRJ Cal Ripken Jr. 75.00 200.00
THOFVCY Carl Yastrzemski 50.00 120.00
THOFVFT Frank Thomas 50.00 120.00
THOFVHA Hank Aaron 200.00 500.00
THOFVJB Johnny Bench 40.00 100.00
THOFVJBA Jeff Bagwell 75.00 200.00
THOFVJM Juan Marichal 30.00 80.00
THOFVJS John Smoltz 40.00 100.00
THOFVJT Jim Thome 50.00 120.00
THOFVKGJ Ken Griffey Jr. 200.00 500.00
THOFVMM Mike Mussina 40.00 100.00
THOFVMR Mariano Rivera 100.00 250.00
THOFVNR Nolan Ryan 100.00 250.00
THOFVOS Ozzie Smith 40.00 100.00
THOFVPM Paul Molitor 40.00 100.00
THOFVRA Roberto Alomar 30.00 80.00
THOFVRC Rod Carew 30.00 80.00
THOFVRH Rickey Henderson 50.00 120.00
THOFVRJ Randy Johnson 50.00 120.00
THOFVRJA Reggie Jackson 40.00 100.00
THOFVRS Ryne Sandberg 60.00 150.00
THOFVRY Robin Yount 40.00 100.00
THOFVSK Sandy Koufax 200.00 500.00
THOFVTG Tom Glavine 30.00 80.00
THOFVVG Vladimir Guerrero 30.00 80.00
THOFVWB Wade Boggs 30.00 80.00

2001 Topps Tribute

This hobby-only product was released in mid-December 2001, and featured a 90-card base set that honors Hall of Fame caliber players like Babe Ruth and Mickey Mantle. Each pack contained four-cards, and carried a suggested retail price of 40.00.

COMPLETE SET (90) 60.00 120.00
PSA-GRADED MANTLE EXCH ODDS 1:170
M.MANTLE REPURCHASED ODDS 1:426
J.ROBINSON REPURCHASED ODDS 1:426
T.WILLIAMS REPURCHASED ODDS 1:426
EXCHANGE DEADLINE 11/30/03
1 Pee Wee Reese 2.50 6.00
2 Babe Ruth 8.00 20.00
3 Ralph Kiner 2.00 5.00
4 Brooks Robinson 2.00 5.00
5 Don Sutton 2.00 5.00
6 Carl Yastrzemski 4.00 10.00
7 Roger Maris 2.50 6.00
8 Andre Dawson 2.00 5.00
9 Luis Aparicio 2.00 5.00
10 Wade Boggs 2.00 5.00
11 Johnny Bench 2.50 6.00
12 Ernie Banks 2.50 6.00
13 Thurman Munson 2.50 6.00
14 Harmon Killebrew 2.50 6.00
15 Ted Kluszewski 2.00 5.00
16 Bob Feller 2.00 5.00
17 Mike Schmidt 5.00 12.00
18 Warren Spahn 2.00 5.00
19 Jim Palmer 2.00 5.00
20 Don Mattingly 5.00 12.00
21 Willie Mays 5.00 12.00
22 Gil Hodges 2.50 6.00
23 Juan Marichal 2.00 5.00
24 Robin Yount 2.50 6.00
25 Nolan Ryan Angels 6.00 15.00
26 Dave Winfield 2.00 5.00
27 Hank Greenberg 2.50 6.00
28 Honus Wagner 3.00 8.00
29 Nolan Ryan Rangers 6.00 15.00
30 Phil Niekro 2.00 5.00
31 Robin Roberts 2.00 5.00
32 Casey Stengel Yankees 2.00 5.00
33 Willie McCovey 2.00 5.00
34 Roy Campanella 2.50 6.00
35 Rollie Fingers A's 2.00 5.00
36 Tom Seaver 2.00 5.00
37 Jackie Robinson 2.50 6.00
38 Hank Aaron Braves 5.00 12.00
39 Bob Gibson 2.00 5.00
40 Carlton Fisk Red Sox 2.00 5.00
41 Hank Aaron Brewers 5.00 12.00
42 George Brett 5.00 12.00
43 Orlando Cepeda 2.00 5.00
44 Red Schoendienst 2.00 5.00
45 Don Drysdale 2.00 5.00
46 Mel Ott 2.50 6.00
47 Casey Stengel Mets 2.50 6.00
48 Al Kaline 2.50 6.00
49 Reggie Jackson 2.50 6.00
50 Tony Perez 2.00 5.00
51 Ozzie Smith 4.00 10.00
52 Billy Martin 2.00 5.00
53 Bill Dickey 2.00 5.00
54 Catfish Hunter 2.00 5.00
55 Duke Snider 2.00 5.00
56 Dale Murphy 2.00 5.00
57 Bobby Doerr 2.00 5.00
58 Earl Averill 2.00 5.00
59 Carlton Fisk White Sox 2.00 5.00
60 Tom Lasorda 2.00 5.00
61 Lou Gehrig 5.00 12.00
62 Enos Slaughter 2.00 5.00
63 Jim Bunning 2.00 5.00
64 Rollie Fingers Brewers 2.00 5.00
65 Frank Robinson Reds 2.00 5.00
66 Earl Weaver 2.00 5.00
67 Eddie Mathews 2.50 6.00
68 Kirby Puckett 2.50 6.00
69 Phil Rizzuto 2.50 6.00
70 Lou Brock 2.00 5.00
71 Walt Alston 2.00 5.00

72 Billy Pierce 2.00 5.00
73 Joe Morgan 2.00 5.00
74 Roberto Clemente 6.00 15.00
75 Whitey Ford 2.00 5.00
76 Richie Ashburn 2.00 5.00
77 Elston Howard 2.00 5.00
78 Gary Carter 2.00 5.00
79 Carl Hubbell 2.00 5.00
80 Yogi Berra 2.50 6.00
81 Ken Boyer 2.00 5.00
82 Nolan Ryan Astros 6.00 15.00
83 Bill Mazeroski 2.00 5.00
84 Dizzy Dean 2.50 6.00
85 Nellie Fox 2.00 5.00
86 Stan Musial 4.00 10.00
87 Steve Carlton 2.00 5.00
88 Willie Stargell 2.00 5.00
89 Hal Newhouser 2.00 5.00
90 Frank Robinson Orioles 2.00 5.00

2001 Topps Tribute Dual Relics

This two-card set features relic cards of Casey Stengel and Frank Robinson. Each card was issued at 1:860 packs.

C.STENGEL ODDS 1:860
F.ROBINSON ODDS 1:860
CSYM Casey Stengel Jsy-Jsy 75.00 150.00
FRRO Frank Robinson Bat-Jsy 50.00 100.00

2001 Topps Tribute Franchise Figures Relics

This 19-card set features relic cards of franchise players from teams past. Please note that these cards were broken into two groups: Group A were inserted at a rate of 1:106, while, Group B were inserted at 1:34. Card backs carry a "RM" prefix.

GROUP A STATED ODDS 1:50
GROUP B STATED ODDS 1:106
OVERALL STATED ODDS 1:34
AL Alston/Lasorda A 15.00 40.00
CD Carter/Dawson B 15.00 40.00
FY Fisk/Yastrzemski A 75.00 150.00
JM R.Jackson/Martin A 40.00 80.00
KG Kaline/Greenberg A 30.00 60.00
MM Munson/Mattingly A 100.00 200.00
PK Puckett/Killebrew A 75.00 150.00
RG B.Ruth/L.Gehrig A 300.00 600.00
RR B.Rob/F.Rob A 60.00 120.00
AFF Aparicio/Fox/Fisk A 75.00 150.00
HDB Dickey/How/Berra A 125.00 200.00
HSS Hodges/Steng/Seav A 60.00 120.00
MCS Maz/Clem/Starg A 150.00 250.00
MMA Murphy/Math/Aaron A 40.00 80.00
MMC Mays/McCov/Cep A 60.00 120.00
RSC Reese/Duke/Campy A 40.00 80.00
SAC Schm/Ash/Carlton A 100.00 200.00
BPKRM Cincy Reds A 100.00 200.00
SBSM Ozzie Smith 75.00 150.00
Lou Brock
Red Schoendienst
Stan Musial A

2001 Topps Tribute Game Bat Relics

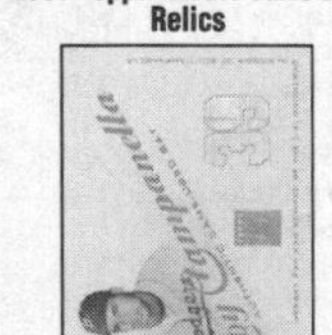

This 31-card set features bat relic cards of classic players like George Brett and Hank Aaron. Please note that these cards were broken into two groups: Group 1 were inserted at a rate of 1:2, while, Group 2 were inserted at 1:35. Card backs carry a "RB" prefix.

GROUP 1 STATED ODDS 1:2
GROUP 2 STATED ODDS 1:35
OVERALL STATED ODDS 1:2
BAT LOGO & STENCIL CUT-OUT SAME QTY
BAT LOGO & STENCIL CUT-OUT SAME VALUE
RBAK Al Kaline 1 10.00 25.00
RBBM Billy Martin 1 10.00 25.00
RBBR Babe Ruth 2 40.00 100.00
RBBRO Brooks Robinson 1 10.00 25.00
RBCFR Carlton Fisk Red Sox 1 10.00 25.00
RBCFW Carlton Fisk W.Sox 1 10.00 25.00
RBCS Casey Stengel 1 10.00 25.00
RBCY Carl Yastrzemski 1 10.00 25.00
RBDM Don Mattingly 1 10.00 25.00
RBFRR Frank Robinson Reds 1 10.00 25.00
RBGB George Brett 1 15.00 40.00
RBGH Gil Hodges 1 10.00 25.00
RBHA Hank Aaron Braves 1 12.50 30.00
RBHAB Hank Aaron Brewers 1 12.50 30.00
RBHG Hank Greenberg 1 10.00 25.00
RBHK Harmon Killebrew 1 10.00 25.00
RBHW Honus Wagner 1 20.00 50.00
RBKB Ken Boyer 1 6.00 15.00
RBLA Luis Aparicio 1 6.00 15.00
RBLB Lou Brock 1 20.00 50.00
RBLG Lou Gehrig 1 50.00 100.00
RBOS Ozzie Smith 1 10.00 25.00
RBPWR Pee Wee Reese 1 10.00 25.00
RBRA Richie Ashburn 1 10.00 25.00
RBRC Roy Campanella 1 12.50 30.00
RBRCL Roberto Clemente 1 30.00 80.00
RBRJ Reggie Jackson 1 10.00 25.00
RBRM Roger Maris 1 12.50 30.00
RBTM Thurman Munson 1 10.00 25.00
RBWM Willie McCovey 1 10.00 25.00

2001 Topps Tribute Game Patch-Number Relics

This 23-card set features swatches of actual game-used jersey patches. These cards were issued into packs at 1:61. Card backs carry a "RPN" prefix.

STATED ODDS 1:61
STATED PRINT RUN 30 SETS
CARDS ARE NOT SERIAL NUMBERED
PRINT RUN INFO PROVIDED BY TOPPS
RPNBD Bill Dickey 150.00 250.00
RPNBDO Bobby Doerr 90.00 150.00
RPNCY Carl Yastrzemski 125.00 250.00
RPNDM Don Mattingly 150.00 250.00
RPNDW Dave Winfield 90.00 150.00
RPNEM Eddie Mathews 125.00 200.00
RPNGB George Brett 125.00 200.00
RPNHK Harmon Killebrew 125.00 200.00
RPNJB Johnny Bench 125.00 200.00
RPNJM Juan Marichal 90.00 150.00
RPNJP Jim Palmer 90.00 150.00
RPNKB Kirby Puckett 125.00 200.00
RPNLB Lou Brock 90.00 150.00
RPNMS Mike Schmidt 150.00 300.00
RPNNRA Nolan Ryan Angels 100.00 200.00
RPNNRH Nolan Ryan Astros 100.00 200.00
RPNNRR Nolan Ryan Rgr 100.00 200.00
RPNRS Red Schoendienst 90.00 150.00
RPNRY Robin Yount 125.00 200.00
RPNTL Tom Lasorda 90.00 150.00
RPNWA Walt Alston 90.00 150.00
RPNWB Wade Boggs 125.00 200.00
RPNYB Yogi Berra 125.00 200.00

2001 Topps Tribute Game Worn Relics

This 39-card set features swatches of actual game-used jerseys. These cards were issued into packs in two different groups: Group 1 (1:282), and Group 2 (1:13) packs. Card backs carry a "RJ" prefix.

GROUP 1 STATED ODDS 1:282
GROUP 2 STATED ODDS 1:13
GROUP 3 STATED ODDS 1:42
GROUP 4 STATED ODDS 1:12
GROUP 5 STATED ODDS 1:9
OVERALL STATED ODDS 1:2
RJBD Bill Dickey 5 12.50 30.00
RJBDO Bobby Doerr 2 8.00 20.00
RJCS Casey Stengel 5 10.00 25.00
RJCY Carl Yastrzemski White 3 12.00 30.00
RJCYA Carl Yastrzemski Gray 3 15.00 40.00
RJDD Dizzy Dean Uni 4 12.00 30.00
RJDM Don Mattingly 2 10.00 25.00
RJDW Dave Winfield 2 8.00 20.00
RJEB Ernie Banks White 2 12.50 30.00
RJEM Eddie Mathews 2 12.50 30.00
RJEBA Ernie Banks Gray 2 12.50 30.00
RJFR Frank Robinson 2 8.00 20.00
RJGB George Brett 2 10.00 25.00
RJHK Harmon Killebrew 2 12.50 30.00
RJJB Johnny Bench White 2 8.00 20.00
RJJP Jim Palmer White 2 8.00 20.00
RJJR Jackie Robinson 1 50.00 100.00
RJJBE Johnny Bench Gray 2 8.00 20.00
RJJMG Juan Marichal 2 8.00 20.00
RJJPA Jim Palmer Gray 2 8.00 20.00
RJKP Kirby Puckett 2 15.00 40.00
RJLB Lou Brock 2 12.50 30.00
RJMSB Mike Schmidt Blue 2 15.00 40.00
RJMSW Mike Schmidt White 2 12.50 30.00
RJNF Nellie Fox 2 12.50 30.00
RJNRA Nolan Ryan Angels 2 12.50 30.00
RJNRH Nolan Ryan Astros 2 12.50 30.00
RJNRR Nolan Ryan Rangers 2 12.50 30.00
RJRS Red Schoendienst 2 8.00 20.00
RJRY Robin Yount 2 12.50 30.00
RJSC Steve Carlton 2 8.00 20.00
RJSM Stan Musial 2 12.50 30.00
RJTL Tom Lasorda 4 8.00 20.00
RJWA Walt Alston 4 8.00 20.00
RJWB Wade Boggs 2 12.50 30.00
RJWMF Willie Mays Gray 2 15.00 40.00
RJWMW Willie Mays White 2 15.00 40.00
RJWST Willie Stargell 2 12.50 30.00
RJYB Yogi Berra 2 12.50 30.00

2001 Topps Tribute Tri-Relic

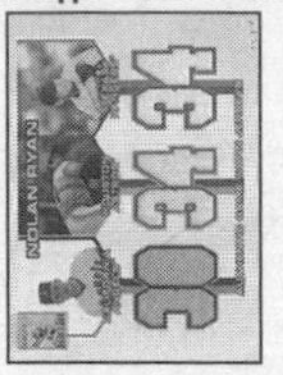

This one-card set features a tri-relic card of Nolan Ryan. This card was issued at 1:1292. Card backs carry a "NR" prefix.

2002 Topps Tribute

This 90 card set was released in November, 2002. These cards were issued in five card packs which came six packs to a box and four boxes to a case. Each of these packs had an SRP of $50 per pack.

COMPLETE SET (90) 40.00 80.00
1 Hank Aaron 4.00 10.00
2 Rogers Hornsby 1.25 3.00
3 Bobby Thomson 1.25 3.00
4 Eddie Collins 1.25 3.00
5 Joe Carter .75 2.00
6 Jim Palmer 1.25 3.00
7 Willie Mays 4.00 10.00
8 Willie Stargell 1.25 3.00
9 Vida Blue .75 2.00
10 Whitey Ford 1.25 3.00
11 Bob Gibson 1.25 3.00
12 Nellie Fox 1.25 3.00
13 Napoleon Lajoie 2.00 5.00
14 Frankie Frisch 1.25 3.00
15 Nolan Ryan 6.00 15.00
16 Brooks Robinson 1.25 3.00
17 Kirby Puckett 2.00 5.00
18 Fergie Jenkins 1.25 3.00
19 Edd Roush 1.25 3.00
20 Honus Wagner 2.00 5.00
21 Richie Ashburn 1.25 3.00
22 Bob Feller 1.25 3.00
23 Joe Morgan 1.25 3.00
24 Orlando Cepeda 1.25 3.00
25 Steve Garvey .75 2.00
26 Hank Greenberg 2.00 5.00
27 Stan Musial 3.00 8.00
28 Sam Crawford 1.25 3.00
29 Jim Rice 1.25 3.00
30 Hack Wilson 1.25 3.00
31 Lou Brock 1.25 3.00
32 Mickey Vernon .75 2.00
33 Chuck Klein .75 2.00
34 Tony Gwynn 2.00 5.00
35 Duke Snider 1.25 3.00
36 Ryne Sandberg 4.00 10.00
37 Johnny Bench 2.00 5.00
38 Sam Rice 1.25 3.00
39 Lou Gehrig 4.00 10.00
40 Robin Yount 2.00 5.00
41 Don Sutton 1.25 3.00
42 Jim Bottomley .75 2.00
43 Billy Herman .75 2.00
44 Zach Wheat 1.25 3.00
45 Juan Marichal 1.25 3.00
46 Bert Blyleven 1.25 3.00
47 Jackie Robinson 2.00 5.00
48 Gil Hodges 1.25 3.00
49 Mike Schmidt 3.00 8.00
50 Dale Murphy 2.00 5.00
51 Phil Rizzuto 1.25 3.00
52 Ty Cobb 3.00 8.00
53 Andre Dawson 1.25 3.00
54 Fred Lindstrom .75 2.00
55 Roy Campanella 2.00 5.00
56 Don Larsen .75 2.00
57 Harry Heilmann 1.25 3.00
58 Catfish Hunter 1.25 3.00
59 Frank Robinson 1.25 3.00
60 Bill Mazeroski 1.25 3.00
61 Roger Maris 2.00 5.00
62 Dave Winfield 1.25 3.00
63 Warren Spahn 1.25 3.00
64 Babe Ruth 5.00 12.00
65 Ernie Banks 2.00 5.00
66 Wade Boggs 1.25 3.00
67 Carl Yastrzemski 3.00 8.00
68 Ron Santo 1.25 3.00
69 Dennis Martinez .75 2.00
70 Yogi Berra 2.00 5.00
71 Paul Waner 1.25 3.00
72 George Brett 4.00 10.00
73 Eddie Mathews 2.00 5.00
74 Bill Dickey .75 2.00
75 Carlton Fisk 1.25 3.00
76 Thurman Munson 2.00 5.00
77 Reggie Jackson 1.25 3.00
78 Phil Niekro 1.25 3.00
79 Luis Aparicio 1.25 3.00
80 Steve Carlton 1.25 3.00
81 Tris Speaker 1.25 3.00
82 Johnny Mize 1.25 3.00
83 Tom Seaver 1.25 3.00
84 Heinie Manush .75 2.00
85 Tommy John .75 2.00
86 Joe Cronin .75 2.00
87 Don Mattingly 4.00 10.00
88 Kirk Gibson .75 2.00
89 Bo Jackson 2.00 5.00
90 Mel Ott 2.00 5.00

2002 Topps Tribute First Impressions

*1ST IMP p/r 50-100: .75X TO 2X
*1ST IMP p/r 36-48: 1X TO 2.5X
*1ST IMP p/r 26-31: 1.2X TO 3X
STATED ODDS 1:16
PRINT RUNS BASED ON PLAYER'S 1ST YR
NO PRICING ON QTY OF 25 OR LESS
FIRST IMPRESSIONS FEATURE BLUE FOIL

2002 Topps Tribute Lasting Impressions

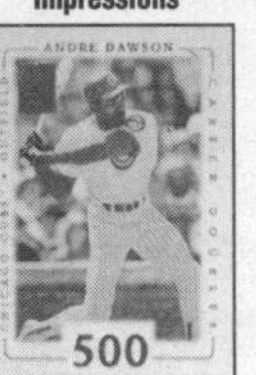

*LAST IMP p/r 53-99: .75X TO 2X
*LAST IMP p/r 36-47: 1X TO 2.5X
*LAST IMP p/r 27-35: 1.2X TO 3X
STATED ODDS 1:13
PRINT RUNS BASED ON PLAYER'S LAST YR
NO PRICING ON QTY OF 25 OR LESS
LASTING IMPRESSIONS FEATURE RED FOIL

2002 Topps Tribute The Catch Dual Relic

Inserted into packs at a stated rate of one in 1023, this card features relics from players involved in Willie Mays' legendary catch during the 1954 World Series when he ran down a well hit ball by Vic Wertz.

STATED ODDS 1:1023
JSY NUMBER ODDS 1:3161
JSY NUMBER PRINT RUN 24 #'d CARDS
NO JSY NUM.PRICING DUE TO SCARCITY
*SEASON: .6X TO 1.2X BASIC DUAL RELIC
SEASON ODDS 1:1391
SEASON PRINT RUN 54 SERIAL #'d CARDS
MW Wertz Bat/Mays Glove 150.00 300.00

2002 Topps Tribute Marks of Excellence Autograph

Inserted into packs at a stated rate of one in 61, these six cards feature players who signed cards honoring their signature moment.

STATED ODDS 1:61
DL Don Larsen 10.00 25.00
LB Lou Brock 15.00 40.00
MS Mike Schmidt 30.00 60.00
SC Steve Carlton 15.00 40.00
SM Stan Musial 40.00 80.00
WS Warren Spahn 15.00 40.00

2002 Topps Tribute Marks of Excellence Autograph Relics

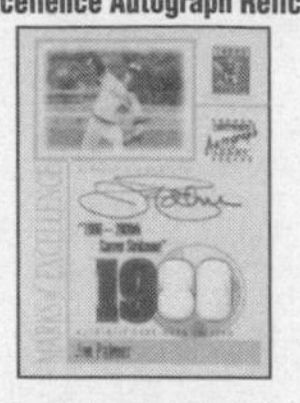

Inserted in packs at a stated rate of one in 61, these six cards feature game-used memorabilia pieces honoring players and their signature moment.

STATED ODDS 1:61
BR Brooks Robinson Bat 30.00 80.00
DM Don Mattingly Jsy 30.00 80.00
DS Duke Snider Uni 12.00 30.00
FJ Fergie Jenkins Jsy 10.00 25.00
JP Jim Palmer Uni 20.00 50.00
RY Robin Yount Uni 30.00 80.00

2002 Topps Tribute Matching Marks Dual Relics

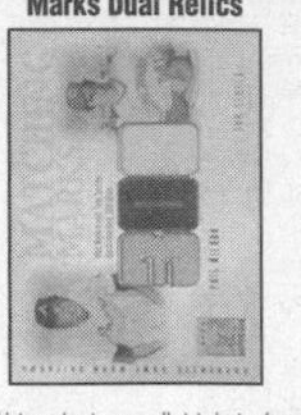

Inserted into packs at an overall stated rate of one in 11, these 22 cards feature two players and a game-used memorabilia piece from each of them.

GROUP A ODDS 1:134
GROUP B ODDS 1:368
GROUP C ODDS 1:123
GROUP D ODDS 1:43
GROUP E ODDS 1:105
GROUP F ODDS 1:82
GROUP G ODDS 1:31
OVERALL STATED ODDS 1:11
AR Aaron Bat 250.00 400.00
Ruth Bat A
BB Boggs Jsy/Brett Jsy C 20.00 50.00
BF Bench Bat/Fisk Bat A 30.00 60.00
BM V.Blue Jsy/D.Martinez Jsy G 6.00 15.00
BMA Brett Jsy/Mattingly Jsy A 75.00 150.00
BS Blyleven Jsy/Sutton Jsy C 8.00 20.00
GA G'berg Bat/Ashburn Bat A 60.00 120.00
GH Garvey Bat/Hodges Bat D 10.00 25.00
JS Jenkins Jsy/Seaver Jsy B 20.00 50.00
MA Mays Uni/Aaron Bat A 150.00 250.00
NS Niekro Uni/Seaver Uni G 6.00 15.00
PJ Palmer Jsy/John Jsy D 10.00 25.00
RJ F.Rob Uni/Reggie Bat A 30.00 60.00
RS Ryan Jsy/Seaver Jsy A 40.00 100.00
SB Speaker Bat/Brett Bat A 200.00 300.00
SBA Santo Bat/Banks Bat D 10.00 25.00
SM Snider Bat/Mays Uni A 50.00 100.00
SR Stargell Uni/Rice Uni E 8.00 20.00
WY Winfield Bat/Yaz Bat D 10.00 25.00
WYO Winfield Uni/Yount Uni F 8.00 20.00
YK Yastrzemski Bat/Klein Bat A 10.00 25.00
YP Yount Uni/Puckett Uni A 30.00 80.00

2002 Topps Tribute Memorable Materials

Inserted into packs at different rates depending on what group and game-used memorabilia piece, these 22 cards feature players from the tribute set as well as a memorabilia piece. We have notated next to the player's name what group this memorabilia piece belongs to.

BAT GROUP A ODDS 1:11,592
BAT GROUP B ODDS 1:6
JSY/UNI GROUP A ODDS 1:246
JSY/UNI GROUP B ODDS 1:12
BJ Bo Jackson Jsy B 10.00 25.00
BM Bill Mazeroski Uni B 8.00 20.00
BT Bobby Thomson Bat B 8.00 20.00
CF Carlton Fisk Bat B 10.00 25.00
CK Chuck Klein Bat B 15.00 40.00
CY Carl Yastrzemski Uni B 8.00 20.00
DM Don Mattingly Jsy B 8.00 20.00
GB George Brett Jsy B 8.00 20.00
HA Hank Aaron Bat B 10.00 25.00
HW Hack Wilson Bat B 12.00 30.00
JC Joe Carter Bat B 8.00 20.00
JM Joe Morgan Bat B 8.00 20.00
JR Jackie Robinson Bat B 20.00 50.00
KG Kirk Gibson Bat B 8.00 20.00
KP Kirby Puckett Bat B 10.00 25.00
NR Nolan Ryan Jsy A 10.00 25.00
PR Phil Rizzuto Bat B 15.00 40.00
RC Roy Campanella Bat B 15.00 40.00
RJ Reggie Jackson Bat B 10.00 25.00
RM Roger Maris Bat B 15.00 40.00
TM Thurman Munson Bat B 20.00 50.00

2002 Topps Tribute Memorable Materials Jersey Number

BAT STATED ODDS 1:208
JSY/UNI STATED ODDS 1:644
PRINT RUNS BASED ON JERSEY NUMBER
NO PRICING ON QTY OF 40 OR LESS
HA Hank Aaron Bat/44 12.00 30.00
JR Jackie Robinson Bat/42 50.00 120.00
RJ Reggie Jackson Bat/44 25.00 60.00

2002 Topps Tribute Memorable Materials Season

BAT STATED ODDS 1:72
JSY/UNI STATED ODDS 1:152
PRINT RUNS BASED ON KEY SEASON
NO PRICING ON QTY OF 40 OR LESS
BJ Bo Jackson Jsy/89 10.00 25.00
BM Bill Mazeroski Uni/60 15.00 40.00
BT Bobby Thomson Bat/51 15.00 40.00
CF Carlton Fisk Bat/75 15.00 40.00
CY Carl Yastrzemski Uni/75 UER 12.50 30.00
DM Don Mattingly Jsy/87 10.00 25.00
GB George Brett Jsy/83 12.00 30.00
HA Hank Aaron Bat/74 12.00 30.00
JC Joe Carter Bat/93 12.00 30.00
JM Joe Morgan Bat/76 12.00 30.00
JR Jackie Robinson Bat/47 20.00 50.00
KG Kirk Gibson Bat/88 12.00 30.00
KP Kirby Puckett Bat/91 10.00 25.00
NR Nolan Ryan Jsy/91 30.00 80.00
PR Phil Rizzuto Bat/50 30.00 80.00
RC Roy Campanella Bat/55 30.00 80.00
RJ Reggie Jackson Bat/77 15.00 40.00
RM Roger Maris Bat/61 30.00 80.00
TM Thurman Munson Bat/76 30.00 80.00

2002 Topps Tribute Milestone Materials

Inserted at different stated odds depending on whether it is a bat or a jersey/uniform piece, these 50 cards feature game-used memorabilia from the feature player's career.

BAT STATED ODDS 1:4
JSY/UNI STATED ODDS 1:5
AD Andre Dawson Jsy 6.00 15.00
BD Bill Dickey Uni 10.00 25.00
BF Bob Feller Bat 10.00 25.00
BG Bob Gibson Uni 8.00 20.00
BH Billy Herman Uni 6.00 15.00
BR Babe Ruth Bat 50.00 100.00
BRO Brooks Robinson Bat 10.00 25.00
CH Catfish Hunter Jsy 8.00 20.00
DM Dale Murphy Jsy 8.00 20.00
DS Duke Snider Uni 6.00 15.00
EB Ernie Banks Uni 10.00 25.00
EC Eddie Collins Bat 50.00 100.00
EM Eddie Mathews Jsy 10.00 25.00
ER Edd Roush Bat 20.00 50.00
FF Frankie Frisch Bat 10.00 25.00
FL Fred Lindstrom Uni 6.00 15.00
FR Frank Robinson Bat 10.00 25.00
HH Harry Heilmann Bat 12.00 30.00
HM Heinie Manush Bat 12.00 30.00
HW Honus Wagner Bat 40.00 80.00
JB Johnny Bench Jsy 10.00 25.00
JBO Jim Bottomley Bat 12.50 30.00
JC Joe Cronin Bat 10.00 25.00
JM Johnny Mize Uni 8.00 20.00
JMA Juan Marichal Jsy 6.00 15.00
JP Jim Palmer Uni 6.00 15.00
LA Luis Aparicio Bat 8.00 20.00
LG Lou Gehrig Bat 40.00 80.00
MO Mel Ott Bat 12.50 30.00
MV Mickey Vernon Bat 8.00 20.00
NF Nellie Fox Uni 10.00 25.00
NL Napoleon Lajoie Bat 50.00 100.00
NR Nolan Ryan Jsy 10.00 25.00
OC Orlando Cepeda Jsy 6.00 15.00
PW Paul Waner Bat 6.00 15.00
RH Rogers Hornsby Bat 10.00 25.00
RJ Reggie Jackson Jsy 8.00 20.00
RS Ryne Sandberg Bat 10.00 25.00
RY Robin Yount Uni 10.00 25.00
SC Sam Crawford Bat 10.00 25.00
SR Sam Rice Bat 15.00 40.00
TC Ty Cobb Bat 20.00 50.00
TS Tom Seaver Jsy 8.00 20.00
TSP Tris Speaker Bat 20.00 50.00
WB Wade Boggs Uni 8.00 20.00
WF Whitey Ford Uni 8.00 20.00
WM Willie Mays Uni 15.00 40.00
WS Willie Stargell Uni 8.00 20.00
YB Yogi Berra Jsy 10.00 25.00
ZW Zach Wheat Bat 15.00 40.00

2002 Topps Tribute Milestone Materials Jersey Number

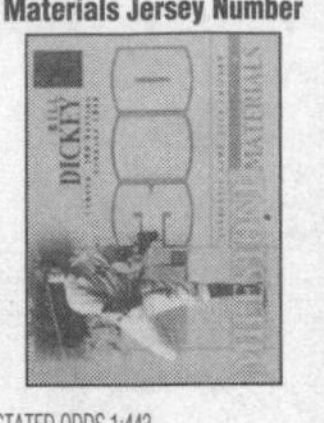

BAT STATED ODDS 1:443
JSY/UNI STATED ODDS 1:148
PRINT RUNS BASED ON JERSEY NUMBER
NO PRICING ON QTY OF 40 OR LESS
BG Bob Gibson Uni/45 20.00 50.00
EM Eddie Mathews Jsy/41 25.00 60.00
RJ Reggie Jackson Jsy/44 20.00 50.00
TS Tom Seaver Jsy/41 20.00 50.00

2002 Topps Tribute Milestone Materials Season

BAT STATED ODDS 1:73
JSY/UNI STATED ODDS 1:41
PRINT RUNS BASED ON KEY SEASON
NO PRICING ON QTY OF 40 OR LESS
AD Andre Dawson Jsy/95 12.50 30.00
BD Bill Dickey Uni/46 25.00 60.00
BF Bob Feller Bat/54 25.00 60.00
BG Bob Gibson Uni/74 15.00 40.00
BH Billy Herman Uni/47 15.00 40.00
BRO Brooks Robinson Bat/74 20.00 50.00
CH Catfish Hunter Jsy/79 15.00 40.00
DM Dale Murphy Jsy/91 20.00 50.00
DS Duke Snider Uni/63 15.00 40.00
EB Ernie Banks Uni/70 20.00 50.00
EM Eddie Mathews Jsy/67 25.00 60.00
FR Frank Robinson Bat/71 20.00 50.00
JB Johnny Bench Jsy/80 20.00 50.00
JC Joe Cronin Bat/45 25.00 60.00
JM Johnny Mize Uni/50 20.00 50.00
JP Jim Palmer Uni/82 12.50 30.00
LA Luis Aparicio Bat/73 15.00 40.00
MO Mel Ott Bat/45 60.00 150.00
MV Mickey Vernon Bat/56 20.00 50.00
NF Nellie Fox Uni/41 40.00 100.00
NR Nolan Ryan Jsy/89 20.00 50.00
OC Orlando Cepeda Jsy/73 12.50 30.00
PW Paul Waner Bat/42 12.00 30.00
RJ Reggie Jackson Jsy/84 15.00 40.00
RS Ryne Sandberg Bat/93 20.00 50.00
RY Robin Yount Uni/92 15.00 40.00
TS Tom Seaver Jsy/81 15.00 40.00
WB Wade Boggs Uni/99 15.00 40.00
WF Whitey Ford Uni/62 20.00 50.00
WM Willie Mays Uni/69 12.50 30.00
WS Willie Stargell Uni/80 15.00 40.00
YB Yogi Berra Jsy/61 25.00 60.00

2002 Topps Tribute Pastime Patches

Inserted into packs at a stated overall rate of one in 92, these 12 cards feature game-worn patch relic cards of these baseball legends.

*LOGO PATCHES: 2.5X VALUE
GROUP A ODDS 1:184
GROUP B ODDS 1:184
OVERALL ODDS 1:92
BD Bill Dickey B 50.00 100.00
CY Carl Yastrzemski B 125.00 200.00
DM Don Mattingly A 75.00 150.00
DW Dave Winfield A 30.00 60.00
EM Eddie Mathews A 40.00 80.00
GB George Brett A 30.00 60.00
JB Johnny Bench B 75.00 150.00

P Jim Palmer B 30.00 60.00
KP Kirby Puckett B 50.00 120.00
RY Robin Yount B 75.00 150.00
WB Wade Boggs B 75.00 150.00
NRR Nolan Ryan B 150.00 250.00

2002 Topps Tribute Signature Cuts

Inserted into packs at a stated rate of one in 9936, these four cards feature cut autographs of four of baseball's most legendary figures. According to Topps, each of these cards were issued to a print run of two cards.

2009 Topps Tribute

COMPLETE SET (100) 100.00 200.00
COMMON CARD (1-100) .60 1.50
COMMON RC (1-100) 1.00 2.50
PRINTING PLATE ODDS 1:91 HOBBY
PLATE PRINT RUN 1 SET PER COLOR
BLACK-CYAN-MAGENTA-YELLOW ISSUED
NO PLATE PRICING DUE TO SCARCITY
1 Babe Ruth 4.00 10.00
2 Christy Mathewson 1.50 4.00
3 Don Zimmer .60 1.50
4 Nolan Ryan 5.00 12.00
5 Dennis Eckersley 1.00 2.50
6 Carl Yastrzemski 2.50 6.00
7 Mickey Mantle 5.00 12.00
8 Tony Perez 1.00 2.50
9 Cal Ripken Jr. 5.00 12.00
10 Derek Jeter 4.00 10.00
11 Wade Boggs 1.00 2.50
12 Tom Seaver 1.00 2.50
13 Willie McCovey 1.00 2.50
14 Walter Johnson 1.50 4.00
15 Steve Garvey .60 1.50
16 George Sisler 1.00 2.50
17 Joe Morgan 1.00 2.50
18 Don Larson .60 1.50
19 Reggie Jackson 1.00 2.50
20 Thurman Munson 1.50 4.00
21 Howard Johnson .60 1.50
22 Johnny Bench 1.50 4.00
23 Bo Jackson 1.50 4.00
24 Ray Knight .60 1.50
25 Cy Young 1.50 4.00
26 Bruce Sutter 1.00 2.50
27 Mike Schmidt 2.50 6.00
28 Roy Campanella 1.50 4.00
29 John Smoltz 1.50 4.00
30 Bob Gibson 1.00 2.50
31 Roy Halladay 1.00 2.50
32 Tris Speaker 1.00 2.50
33 Tony Gwynn 1.50 4.00
34 Whitey Ford 1.00 2.50
35 Carlos Beltran 1.00 2.50
36 Manny Ramirez 1.50 4.00
37 Frank Thomas 1.50 4.00
38 Honus Wagner 1.50 4.00
39 Josh Beckett .60 1.50
40 Hanley Ramirez 1.00 2.50
41 Ty Cobb 2.50 6.00
42 Darryl Strawberry .60 1.50
43 Stan Musial 2.50 6.00
44 Duke Snider 1.00 2.50
45 Rollie Fingers 1.00 2.50
46 Juan Marichal 1.00 2.50
47 Eddie Mathews 1.50 4.00
48 Paul Molitor 1.50 4.00
49 Pee Wee Reese 1.00 2.50
50 Ryan Howard 1.25 3.00
51 Johnny Podres .60 1.50
52 Randy Johnson 1.50 4.00
53 Rogers Hornsby 1.00 2.50
54 Dwight Gooden .60 1.50
55 Ryne Sandberg 3.00 8.00
56 Robin Yount 1.50 4.00
57 Greg Maddux 2.00 5.00
58 Jackie Robinson 1.50 4.00
59 Adrian Gonzalez 1.25 3.00
60 Jim Palmer 1.00 2.50
61 David Wright 1.25 3.00
62 Ernie Banks 1.50 4.00
63 Chipper Jones 1.50 4.00
64 Gary Carter 1.00 2.50
65 Aramis Ramirez .60 1.50
66 Jimmie Foxx 1.50 4.00
67 Joe Mauer 1.25 3.00
68 Ozzie Smith 2.00 5.00
69 George Kell 1.00 2.50
70 Derrek Lee .60 1.50
71 Hank Greenberg 1.50 4.00
72 Joey Votto 1.50 4.00
73 Mel Ott 1.50 4.00
74 Clayton Kershaw 3.00 8.00
75 Josh Hamilton 1.00 2.50
76 Tommy Hanson RC 2.50 6.00
77 Alex Rodriguez 2.00 5.00
78 Andre Dawson 1.00 2.50
79 Johnny Mize 1.00 2.50
80 Sal Bando .60 1.50
81 Justin Morneau 1.00 2.50
82 Keith Hernandez .60 1.50
83 Lou Gehrig 3.00 8.00
84 Dustin Pedroia 1.25 3.00
85 Mark Teixeira 1.00 2.50
86 Jay Bruce 1.00 2.50
87 Chase Utley 1.00 2.50
88 Lance Berkman 1.00 2.50
89 Frank Robinson 1.00 2.50
90 Matt LaPorta RC 1.50 4.00
91 Albert Pujols 2.00 5.00
92 Mike Piazza 1.50 4.00
93 Robin Roberts 1.00 2.50
94 Evan Longoria 1.00 2.50
95 Ryan Braun 1.00 2.50
96 Rick Porcello RC 3.00 8.00
97 CC Sabathia 1.00 2.50
98 Brooks Robinson 1.00 2.50
99 Ichiro Suzuki 2.00 5.00
100 Ken Griffey Jr. 3.00 8.00

2009 Topps Tribute Black

*BLACK: .75X TO 2X BASIC
*BLACK RC: .6X TO 1.5X BASIC RC
STATED ODDS 1:4 HOBBY
STATED PRINT RUN 99 SER.#'d SETS

2009 Topps Tribute Blue

*BLUE: .5X TO 1.2X BASIC
*BLUE RC: .5X TO 1.2X BASIC RC
RANDOM INSERTS IN PACKS
STATED PRINT RUN 219 SER.#'d SETS

2009 Topps Tribute Gold

*GOLD: 1.5X TO 4X BASIC
*GOLD RC: .75X TO 2X BASIC RC
STATED ODDS 1:8 HOBBY
STATED PRINT RUN 50 SER.#'d SETS

2009 Topps Tribute Autograph Relics

STATED ODDS 1:7 HOBBY
STATED PRINT RUN 99 SER.#'d SETS
ALL VARIATIONS PRICED EQUALLY
JH Josh Hamilton 20.00 50.00
JM Juan Marichal 10.00 25.00
TS Tom Seaver 20.00 50.00
AD1 Andre Dawson 12.50 30.00
AD2 Andre Dawson 12.50 30.00
CC1 Carl Crawford 6.00 15.00
CC2 Carl Crawford 6.00 15.00
CK1 Clayton Kershaw 30.00 60.00
CK2 Clayton Kershaw 30.00 60.00
CK3 Clayton Kershaw 30.00 60.00
CK4 Clayton Kershaw 50.00 100.00
DP1 Dustin Pedroia 15.00 40.00
DP2 Dustin Pedroia 15.00 40.00
DP3 Dustin Pedroia 15.00 40.00
DP4 Dustin Pedroia 15.00 40.00
DS1 Duke Snider 12.50 30.00
DS2 Duke Snider 12.50 30.00
DS3 Duke Snider 12.50 30.00
DS4 Duke Snider 12.50 30.00
DW1 David Wright 15.00 40.00
DW2 David Wright 15.00 40.00
DW3 David Wright 15.00 40.00
DW4 David Wright 15.00 40.00
EL1 Evan Longoria 20.00 50.00
EL2 Evan Longoria 20.00 50.00
EL3 Evan Longoria 20.00 50.00
EL4 Evan Longoria 20.00 50.00
GC1 Gary Carter 15.00 40.00
GC2 Gary Carter 15.00 40.00
GC3 Gary Carter 15.00 40.00
GC4 Gary Carter 15.00 40.00
JB1 Jay Bruce 8.00 20.00
JB2 Jay Bruce 8.00 20.00
JB3 Jay Bruce 8.00 20.00
JB4 Jay Bruce 8.00 20.00
JP1 Johnny Podres 8.00 20.00
JP2 Johnny Podres 8.00 20.00
KH1 Keith Hernandez 6.00 15.00
KH2 Keith Hernandez 6.00 15.00
KH3 Keith Hernandez 6.00 15.00
KH4 Keith Hernandez 6.00 15.00
ML1 Matt LaPorta 12.50 30.00
RB1 Ryan Braun 10.00 25.00
RB2 Ryan Braun 10.00 25.00
RB3 Ryan Braun 10.00 25.00
RB4 Ryan Braun 10.00 25.00
RP1 Rick Porcello 6.00 15.00
RP2 Rick Porcello 6.00 15.00
RP3 Rick Porcello 6.00 15.00
RP4 Rick Porcello 6.00 15.00
SB1 Sal Bando 8.00 20.00
SB2 Sal Bando 8.00 20.00
SB3 Sal Bando 8.00 20.00
SB4 Sal Bando 8.00 20.00
TH1 Tommmy Hanson 6.00 15.00
TH2 Tommmy Hanson 6.00 15.00

2009 Topps Tribute Autograph Relics Black

*BLACK: .5X TO 1.2X BASIC
OVERALL ODDS 1:10 HOBBY
STATED PRINT RUN 50 SER.#'d SETS

2009 Topps Tribute Autograph Relics Blue

*BLUE: .4X TO 1X BASIC
OVERALL ODDS 1:7 HOBBY
STATED PRINT RUN 75 SER.#'d SETS

2009 Topps Tribute Autograph Dual Relics

STATED ODDS 1:21 HOBBY
STATED PRINT RUN 99 SER.#'d SETS
ALL VARIATIONS PRICED EQUALLY
AI Akinori Iwamura 6.00 15.00
AR Aramis Ramirez 6.00 15.00
BJ Bo Jackson 30.00 60.00
DG Dwight Gooden 10.00 25.00
DP Dustin Pedroia 20.00 50.00
DS Duke Snider 15.00 40.00
DS Darryl Strawberry 10.00 25.00
DW David Wright 10.00 25.00
EL Evan Longoria 12.50 30.00
GC Gary Carter 15.00 40.00
JB Jay Bruce 10.00 25.00
MC Melky Cabrera 6.00 15.00
PF Prince Fielder 15.00 40.00
RP Rick Porcello 6.00 15.00
DW2 David Wright 10.00 25.00
EL2 Evan Longoria 12.50 30.00
RC1 Robinson Cano 20.00 50.00
RC2 Robinson Cano 20.00 50.00

2009 Topps Tribute Autograph Dual Relics Black

*BLACK: .5X TO 1.2X BASIC
OVERALL ODDS 1:10 HOBBY
STATED PRINT RUN 50 SER.#'d SETS

2009 Topps Tribute Autograph Dual Relics Blue

*BLUE: .4X TO 1X BASIC
OVERALL ODDS 1:7 HOBBY
STATED PRINT RUN 75 SER.#'d SETS

2009 Topps Tribute Autograph Triple Relics

STATED ODDS 1:75 HOBBY
STATED PRINT RUN 99 SER.#'d SETS
AP Albert Pujols 50.00 120.00
CJ Chipper Jones 30.00 60.00
DM Don Mattingly 30.00 60.00
DW David Wright 20.00 50.00
RH Ryan Howard 6.00 15.00

2009 Topps Tribute Autograph Triple Relics Black

*BLACK: .5X TO 1.2X BASIC
OVERALL ODDS 1:10 HOBBY
STATED PRINT RUN 50 SER.#'d SETS

2009 Topps Tribute Autograph Triple Relics Blue

*BLUE: .4X TO 1X BASIC
OVERALL ODDS 1:7 HOBBY
STATED PRINT RUN 75 SER.#'d SETS

2009 Topps Tribute Relics

STATED ODDS 1:8 HOBBY
STATED PRINT RUN 99 SER.#'d SETS
1 Babe Ruth 60.00 120.00
4 Nolan Ryan 12.50 30.00
6 Carl Yastrzemski 5.00 12.00
7 Mickey Mantle 50.00 100.00
9 Cal Ripken Jr. 10.00 25.00
12 Tom Seaver 8.00 20.00
18 Don Larson 4.00 10.00
19 Reggie Jackson 6.00 15.00
20 Thurman Munson 8.00 20.00
22 Johnny Bench 5.00 12.00
23 Bo Jackson 8.00 20.00
27 Mike Schmidt 6.00 15.00
28 Roy Campanella 8.00 20.00
30 Bob Gibson 5.00 12.00
33 Tony Gwynn 5.00 12.00
34 Whitey Ford 8.00 20.00
36 Manny Ramirez 4.00 10.00
40 Hanley Ramirez 3.00 8.00
41 Ty Cobb 20.00 50.00
44 Duke Snider 5.00 12.00
46 Juan Marichal 3.00 8.00
47 Eddie Mathews 6.00 15.00
49 Pee Wee Reese 6.00 15.00
50 Ryan Howard 5.00 12.00
58 Jackie Robinson 20.00 50.00
61 David Wright 6.00 15.00
63 Chipper Jones 5.00 12.00
67 Joe Mauer 5.00 12.00
68 Ozzie Smith 5.00 12.00
72 Joey Votto 4.00 10.00
74 Clayton Kershaw 3.00 8.00
75 Josh Hamilton 4.00 10.00
76 Tommy Hanson 5.00 12.00
77 Alex Rodriguez 10.00 25.00
81 Justin Morneau 5.00 12.00
83 Lou Gehrig 60.00 120.00
84 Dustin Pedroia 4.00 10.00
85 Mark Teixeira 6.00 15.00
87 Chase Utley 5.00 12.00
88 Lance Berkman 3.00 8.00
91 Albert Pujols 6.00 15.00
92 Mike Piazza 6.00 15.00
94 Evan Longoria 5.00 12.00
95 Ryan Braun 4.00 10.00
96 Rick Porcello 3.00 8.00
97 CC Sabathia 3.00 8.00
99 Ichiro Suzuki 12.50 30.00

2009 Topps Tribute Relics Black

*BLACK: .5X TO 1.2X BASIC
STATED ODDS 1:11 HOBBY
STATED PRINT RUN 50 SER.#'d SETS

2009 Topps Tribute Relics Blue

*BLUE: .4X TO 1X BASIC
STATED ODDS 1:8 HOBBY
STATED PRINT RUN 75 SER.#'d SETS

2009 Topps Tribute Relics Dual

STATED ODDS 1:25 HOBBY
STATED PRINT RUN 99 SER.#'d SETS
1 Babe Ruth 75.00 150.00
9 Cal Ripken Jr. 12.50 30.00
19 Reggie Jackson 6.00 15.00
22 Johnny Bench 6.00 15.00
27 Mike Schmidt 10.00 25.00
33 Tony Gwynn 6.00 15.00
36 Manny Ramirez 5.00 12.00
41 Ty Cobb 40.00 80.00
44 Duke Snider 6.00 15.00
50 Ryan Howard 6.00 15.00
61 David Wright 6.00 15.00
76 Tommy Hanson 5.00 12.00
94 Evan Longoria 5.00 12.00
95 Ryan Braun 6.00 15.00
99 Ichiro Suzuki 12.50 30.00

2009 Topps Tribute Relics Dual Black

*BLACK: .5X TO 1.2X BASIC
STATED ODDS 1:11 HOBBY
STATED PRINT RUN 50 SER.#'d SETS

2009 Topps Tribute Relics Dual Blue

*BLUE: .4X TO 1X BASIC
STATED ODDS 1:8 HOBBY
STATED PRINT RUN 75 SER.#'d SETS

2009 Topps Tribute Relics Triple

STATED ODDS 1:75 HOBBY
STATED PRINT RUN 99 SER.#'d SETS
1 Babe Ruth 75.00 150.00
7 Mickey Mantle 60.00 120.00
58 Jackie Robinson 20.00 50.00
77 Alex Rodriguez 12.50 30.00
91 Albert Pujols 12.50 30.00

2009 Topps Tribute Relics Triple Black

*BLACK: .5X TO 1.2X BASIC
STATED ODDS 1:11 HOBBY
STATED PRINT RUN 50 SER.#'d SETS

2009 Topps Tribute Relics Triple Blue

*BLUE: .4X TO 1X BASIC
STATED ODDS 1:8 HOBBY
STATED PRINT RUN 75 SER.#'d SETS

2010 Topps Tribute

COMPLETE SET (100) 100.00 200.00
COMMON CARD (1-75) .60 1.50
COMMON CARD (75-90) .60 1.50
COMMON CARD (91-100) .60 1.50
PRINTING PLATE ODDS 1:161 HOBBY
1 Babe Ruth 4.00 10.00
2 Walter Johnson 1.50 4.00
3 Ty Cobb 2.50 6.00
4 Tris Speaker 1.00 2.50
5 Thurman Munson 1.50 4.00
6 Roy Campanella 1.50 4.00
7 Rogers Hornsby 1.00 2.50
8 Orlando Cepeda 1.00 2.50
9 Jackie Robinson 1.50 4.00
10 Mel Ott 1.50 4.00
11 Johnny Mize 1.00 2.50
12 Jimmie Foxx 1.50 4.00
13 Honus Wagner 1.50 4.00
14 Pee Wee Reese 1.00 2.50
15 Christy Mathewson 1.50 4.00
16 Carlton Fisk 1.00 2.50
17 Yogi Berra 1.50 4.00
18 Lou Gehrig 3.00 8.00
19 Jim Bunning 1.00 2.50
20 Reggie Jackson 1.00 2.50
21 Tony Gwynn 1.50 4.00
22 Al Kaline 1.50 4.00
23 Roger Maris 1.50 4.00
24 Harmon Killebrew 1.50 4.00
25 Eddie Mathews 1.50 4.00
26 Willie McCovey 1.00 2.50
27 Joe Morgan 1.00 2.50
28 Eddie Murray 1.00 2.50
29 Jim Palmer 1.00 2.50
30 Tony Perez 1.00 2.50
31 Gaylord Perry 1.00 2.50
32 Phil Rizzuto 1.00 2.50
33 Robin Roberts 1.00 2.50
34 Brooks Robinson 1.00 2.50
35 Nolan Ryan 5.00 12.00
36 Ryne Sandberg 3.00 8.00
37 Mike Schmidt 2.50 6.00
38 Red Schoendienst 1.00 2.50
39 Tom Seaver 1.00 2.50
40 Ozzie Smith 2.00 5.00
41 Warren Spahn 1.00 2.50
42 Willie Stargell 1.00 2.50
43 Stan Musial 2.50 6.00
44 Cy Young 1.50 4.00
45 Bob Gibson 1.00 2.50
46 Dizzy Dean 1.00 2.50
47 Frank Robinson 1.00 2.50
48 Hank Greenberg 1.50 4.00
49 Johnny Bench 1.50 4.00
50 Mickey Mantle 5.00 12.00
51 Albert Pujols 2.00 5.00
52 Ichiro Suzuki 2.00 5.00
53 Alex Rodriguez 2.00 5.00
54 Prince Fielder 1.00 2.50
55 Joe Mauer 1.25 3.00
56 Tim Lincecum 1.00 2.50
57 Hanley Ramirez 1.00 2.50
58 Chase Utley 1.00 2.50
59 Roy Halladay 1.00 2.50
60 Adrian Gonzalez 1.25 3.00
61 Manny Ramirez 1.50 4.00
62 Chipper Jones 1.50 4.00
63 Grady Sizemore 1.00 2.50
64 Mariano Rivera 2.00 5.00
65 Miguel Cabrera 1.50 4.00
66 Johan Santana 1.00 2.50
67 Ryan Braun 1.00 2.50
68 Zack Greinke 1.00 2.50
69 Ryan Howard 1.25 3.00
70 Dustin Pedroia 1.25 3.00
71 Ian Kinsler 1.00 2.50
72 Evan Longoria 1.00 2.50
73 David Wright 1.25 3.00
74 Vladimir Guerrero 1.00 2.50
75 Derek Jeter 4.00 10.00
76 L.Gehrig T205 3.00 8.00
77 I.Suzuki T205 2.00 5.00
78 Jackie Robinson T205 1.50 4.00
79 Cy Young T205 1.50 4.00
80 D.Jeter T205 4.00 10.00
81 T.Cobb T205 2.50 6.00
82 M.Mantle T205 5.00 12.00
83 N.Ryan T205 5.00 12.00
84 Joe Mauer T205 1.25 3.00
85 Honus Wagner T205 1.50 4.00
86 Frank Robinson T205 1.00 2.50
87 A.Pujols T205 2.00 5.00
88 T.Lincecum T205 1.00 2.50
89 B.Ruth T205 4.00 10.00
90 Tom Seaver T205 1.00 2.50
91 Hatfields vs. McCoys 1.00 2.50
92 David vs. Goliath 1.00 2.50
93 Moby Dick vs. Captain Ahab 1.00 2.50
94 Billy the Kid vs. Pat Garrett 1.00 2.50
95 John F. Kennedy vs Richard Nixon 1.50 4.00
96 Obama vs McCain 2.00 5.00
97 Abraham Lincoln vs Jefferson Davis 1.50 4.00
98 Montagues vs Capulets 1.00 2.50
99 USA vs. Russia 1.00 2.50
100 Tortoise vs The Hare 1.00 2.50

2010 Topps Tribute Black

*BLACK: .75X TO 2X BASIC
STATED ODDS 1:7 HOBBY
STATED PRINT RUN 99 SER.#'d SETS

2010 Topps Tribute Black and White

*BW: .75X TO 2X BASIC
STATED ODDS 1:7 HOBBY
STATED PRINT RUN 99 SER.#'d SETS

2010 Topps Tribute Blue

*BLUE: .5X TO 1.2X BASIC
RANDOM INSERTS IN PACKS
STATED PRINT RUN 399 SER.#'d SETS

2010 Topps Tribute Gold

*GOLD: 1.2X TO 3X BASIC
STATED ODDS 1:13 HOBBY
STATED PRINT RUN 50 SER.#'d SETS

2010 Topps Tribute Red

STATED ODDS 1:656 HOBBY
STATED PRINT RUN 1 SER.#'d SET

2010 Topps Tribute Autograph Relics

STATED ODDS 1:35 HOBBY
STATED PRINT RUN 99 SER.#'d SETS
EXCH DEADLINE 7/31/2013
SAME PLAYER VERSIONS EQUALLY PRICED
AH Aaron Hill 5.00 12.00
AI Akinori Iwamura 5.00 12.00
AJ Adam Jones 5.00 12.00
BM Bengie Molina 6.00 15.00
BMC Brian McCann 6.00 15.00
CF Chone Figgins 5.00 12.00
CP Carlos Pena 8.00 20.00
CS Curt Schilling 12.50 30.00
JHE Jason Heyward 4.00 10.00
JL Jon Lester 8.00 20.00
MCA Miguel Cabrera 50.00 100.00
MK M.Kemp 10.00 25.00
ML Mat Latos 6.00 15.00
NM N.Markakis EXCH 8.00 20.00
OC Orlando Cabrera 5.00 12.00
PF Prince Fielder 12.50 30.00
RK Ralph Kiner 12.50 30.00
SS S.Strasburg 20.00 50.00
TH Tommy Hanson 8.00 20.00
TL Tony LaRussa 15.00 40.00
AD1 Andre Dawson 10.00 25.00
AD2 Andre Dawson 10.00 25.00
AD3 Andre Dawson 10.00 25.00
AD4 Andre Dawson 10.00 25.00
BC B.Cox Red jrsy 30.00 60.00
BC B.Cox White jrsy 30.00 60.00
BM2 Bengie Molina 6.00 15.00
CK1 Clayton Kershaw 30.00 60.00
CK2 Clayton Kershaw 30.00 60.00
CK3 Clayton Kershaw 30.00 60.00
CK4 Clayton Kershaw 30.00 60.00
CL1 Cliff Lee 8.00 20.00
CL2 Cliff Lee 8.00 20.00
CL3 Cliff Lee 8.00 20.00
CL4 Cliff Lee 8.00 20.00
DG01 Dwight Gooden 8.00 20.00
DG02 Dwight Gooden 8.00 20.00
DP1 Dustin Pedroia 15.00 40.00
DP2 Dustin Pedroia 15.00 40.00
DP3 Dustin Pedroia 15.00 40.00
DP4 Dustin Pedroia 15.00 40.00
DSN1 Duke Snider 12.50 30.00
DS1 Darryl Strawberry 6.00 15.00
DS2 Darryl Strawberry 6.00 15.00
DSN2 Duke Snider 12.50 30.00
DSN3 Duke Snider 12.50 30.00
GC1 Gary Carter 10.00 25.00
GC2 Gary Carter 10.00 25.00
GS1 Gary Sheffield 6.00 15.00
GS2 Gary Sheffield 6.00 15.00
GS3 Gary Sheffield 6.00 15.00
GS4 Gary Sheffield 6.00 15.00
JG1 Joe Girardi 12.50 30.00
JG2 Joe Girardi 12.50 30.00
JH1 Josh Hamilton 12.50 30.00
JH2 Josh Hamilton 12.50 30.00
JH3 Josh Hamilton 12.50 30.00
JH4 Josh Hamilton 12.50 30.00
MK2 Matt Kemp 10.00 25.00
MK3 Matt Kemp 10.00 25.00
MK4 Matt Kemp 10.00 25.00
MS1 Max Scherzer 20.00 50.00
MS2 Max Scherzer 20.00 50.00
MS3 Max Scherzer 20.00 50.00
MS4 Max Scherzer 20.00 50.00
NM2 Nick Markakis 8.00 20.00
NM3 Nick Markakis 8.00 20.00
NM4 Nick Markakis 8.00 20.00
OC2 Orlando Cabrera 5.00 12.00
PS1 Pablo Sandoval 10.00 25.00
PS2 Pablo Sandoval 10.00 25.00
PS3 Pablo Sandoval 10.00 25.00
PS4 Pablo Sandoval 10.00 25.00
RC1 Robinson Cano 12.50 30.00
RC2 Robinson Cano 12.50 30.00
RC3 Robinson Cano 12.50 30.00
RC4 Robinson Cano 12.50 30.00
RP1 Rick Porcello 6.00 15.00
RP2 Rick Porcello 6.00 15.00
RP3 Rick Porcello 6.00 15.00
RP4 Rick Porcello 6.00 15.00
RZ1 Ryan Zimmerman 10.00 25.00
RZ2 Ryan Zimmerman 10.00 25.00
RZ3 Ryan Zimmerman 10.00 25.00
RZ4 Ryan Zimmerman 10.00 25.00
ST1 Starlin Castro 12.50 30.00
ST2 Starlin Castro 12.50 30.00
ST3 Starlin Castro 12.50 30.00
ST4 Starlin Castro 12.50 30.00
TL2 Tony LaRussa 15.00 40.00
TT1 Troy Tulowitzki 10.00 25.00
TT2 Troy Tulowitzki 10.00 25.00
TT3 Troy Tulowitzki 10.00 25.00
TT4 Troy Tulowitzki 10.00 25.00
ADU1 Adam Dunn 8.00 20.00
ADU2 Adam Dunn 8.00 20.00
ADU3 Adam Dunn 8.00 20.00
ADU4 Adam Dunn 8.00 20.00
DG03 Dwight Gooden 8.00 20.00
DSN4 Duke Snider 12.50 30.00

2010 Topps Tribute Autograph Relics Black

*BLACK: .5X TO 1.2X BASIC
STATED ODDS 1:11 HOBBY
STATED PRINT RUN 50 SER.#'d SETS
EXCH DEADLINE 7/31/2013

2010 Topps Tribute Autograph Relics Blue

*BLUE: .4X TO 1X BASIC
STATED ODDS 1:7 HOBBY
STATED PRINT RUN 75 SER.#'d SETS
EXCH DEADLINE 7/31/2013

2010 Topps Tribute Autograph Dual Relics

STATED ODDS 1:35 HOBBY
STATED PRINT RUN 99 SER.#'d SETS
EXCH DEADLINE 7/31/2013
AJ Adam Jones 10.00 25.00
DO David Ortiz 15.00 40.00
DW David Wright 10.00 25.00
EL Evan Longoria 8.00 20.00
GB Gordon Beckham 10.00 25.00
GC Gary Carter 20.00 50.00
GK George Kell 10.00 25.00
JH Josh Hamilton 10.00 25.00
JH Jason Heyward 40.00 80.00
JU Justin Upton 6.00 15.00
MH Matt Holliday 10.00 25.00
MK Matt Kemp 12.50 30.00
PF Prince Fielder 12.00 30.00
RB Ryan Braun 8.00 20.00
RP Rick Porcello 6.00 15.00
SS S.Strasburg 60.00 120.00
TH Tommy Hanson 6.00 15.00
TT Troy Tulowitzki 8.00 20.00
WM Willie McCovey 20.00 50.00

2010 Topps Tribute Autograph Dual Relics Black

*BLACK: .5X TO 1.2X BASIC
STATED ODDS 1:11 HOBBY
STATED PRINT RUN 50 SER.#'d SETS
EXCH DEADLINE 7/31/2013

2010 Topps Tribute Autograph Dual Relics Blue

*BLUE: .4X TO 1X BASIC
STATED ODDS 1:7 HOBBY
STATED PRINT RUN 75 SER.#'d SETS
EXCH DEADLINE 7/31/2013

2010 Topps Tribute Autograph Triple Relics

GROUP A ODDS 1:73 HOBBY
GROUP B ODDS 1:262 HOBBY
STATED PRINT RUN 99 SER.#'d SETS
EXCH DEADLINE 7/31/2013
AP Albert Pujols 75.00 150.00
AR Alex Rodriguez 100.00 200.00
CR Cal Ripken 50.00 100.00
DS Duke Snider 12.50 30.00
DW David Wright 12.00 30.00
EL Evan Longoria 15.00 40.00
HR Hanley Ramirez 8.00 20.00
MC Miguel Cabrera 50.00 100.00
MK Matt Kemp 10.00 25.00
MR Manny Ramirez 12.50 30.00
NM Nick Markakis 8.00 20.00
RC Robinson Cano 12.50 30.00
RC Rod Carew 15.00 40.00
RH Ryan Howard 12.00 30.00
VG Vladimir Guerrero 15.00 40.00

2010 Topps Tribute Autograph Triple Relics Black

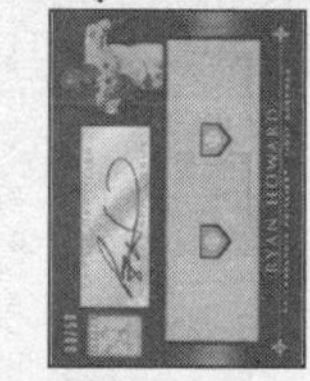

*BLACK: .5X TO 1.2X BASIC
STATED ODDS 1:11 HOBBY
STATED PRINT RUN 50 SER.#'d SETS
EXCH DEADLINE 7/31/2013

2010 Topps Tribute Autograph Triple Relics Blue

*BLUE: .4X TO 1X BASIC
STATED ODDS 1:7 HOBBY
STATED PRINT RUN 75 SER.#'d SETS
EXCH DEADLINE 7/31/2013

2010 Topps Tribute Buyback Relics

STATED ODDS 1:167 HOBBY
PRINT RUNS B/WN 10-50 COPIES PER
AP Albert Pujols/50 15.00 40.00
BR Babe Ruth/35 50.00 100.00
HA Hank Aaron/45 20.00 50.00

2010 Topps Tribute Relics

STATED ODDS 1:7 HOBBY
STATED PRINT RUN 99 SER.#'d SETS
AD Adrian Gonzalez 4.00 10.00
AK Al Kaline 10.00 25.00
AP Albert Pujols 10.00 25.00
AR Alex Rodriguez 6.00 15.00

BD Bobby Doerr 8.00 20.00
BF Bob Feller 6.00 15.00
BG Bob Gibson 6.00 15.00
BL Bob Lemon 5.00 12.00
BM Bill Mazeroski 10.00 25.00
BR Brooks Robinson 6.00 15.00
BS Bruce Sutter 6.00 15.00
BW Billy Williams 4.00 10.00
CF Carlton Fisk 5.00 12.00
CH Catfish Hunter 4.00 10.00
CJ Chipper Jones 8.00 20.00
CS CC Sabathia 6.00 15.00
CU Chase Utley 5.00 12.00
CY Carl Yastrzemski 8.00 20.00
DE Dennis Eckersley 3.00 8.00
DJ Derek Jeter 10.00 25.00
DJ2 Derek Jeter 10.00 25.00
DJ3 Derek Jeter 10.00 25.00
DJ4 Derek Jeter 10.00 25.00
DS Don Sutton 4.00 10.00
DW David Wright 6.00 15.00
EB Ernie Banks 6.00 15.00
EL Evan Longoria 5.00 12.00
EM Eddie Mathews 12.50 30.00
ES Enos Slaughter 8.00 20.00
EW Early Wynn 6.00 15.00
FJ Fergie Jenkins 4.00 10.00
FR Frank Robinson 4.00 10.00
GC Gary Carter 4.00 10.00
GK George Kell 4.00 10.00
GP Gaylord Perry 3.00 8.00
HG Hank Greenberg 10.00 25.00
HK Harmon Killebrew 8.00 20.00
HN Hal Newhouser 4.00 10.00
HR Hanley Ramirez 3.00 8.00
HW Hoyt Wilhelm 5.00 12.00
IS Ichiro Suzuki 12.50 30.00
JB Johnny Bench 8.00 20.00
JF Jimmie Foxx 12.50 30.00
JM Juan Marichal 4.00 10.00
JR Jackie Robinson 12.50 30.00
LA Luis Aparicio 4.00 10.00
LG Lou Gehrig 40.00 80.00
MC Miguel Cabrera 5.00 12.00
MI Monte Irvin 6.00 15.00
MM Mickey Mantle 30.00 60.00
MO Mel Ott 10.00 25.00
MR Mariano Rivera 8.00 20.00
MS Mike Schmidt 12.50 30.00
MT Mark Teixeira 6.00 15.00
NR Nolan Ryan 10.00 25.00
OC Orlando Cepeda 3.00 8.00
OS Ozzie Smith 6.00 15.00
PF Prince Fielder 4.00 10.00
PM Paul Molitor 5.00 12.00
PN Phil Niekro 3.00 8.00
PR Phil Rizzuto 6.00 15.00
RA Richie Ashburn 8.00 20.00
RB Ryan Braun 4.00 10.00
RC Rod Carew 4.00 10.00
RF Rick Ferrell 8.00 20.00
RH Rogers Hornsby 8.00 20.00
RJ Reggie Jackson 8.00 20.00
RK Ralph Kiner 6.00 15.00
RM Roger Maris 12.50 30.00
RR Robin Roberts 8.00 20.00
RS Ryne Sandberg 6.00 15.00
RY Robin Yount 8.00 20.00
SC Steve Carlton 6.00 15.00
SM Stan Musial 8.00 20.00
TC Ty Cobb 30.00 60.00
TG Tony Gwynn 6.00 15.00
TL Tim Lincecum 8.00 20.00
TM Thurman Munson 12.50 30.00
TP Tony Perez 4.00 10.00
TS Tom Seaver 6.00 15.00
VG Vladimir Guerrero 4.00 10.00
WM Willie McCovey 5.00 12.00
WS Warren Spahn 8.00 20.00
BRU Babe Ruth 60.00 120.00
EMU Eddie Murray 4.00 10.00
HWA Honus Wagner 40.00 80.00
JBU Jim Bunning 4.00 10.00
JMA Joe Mauer 6.00 15.00
JMI Johnny Mize 6.00 15.00
JMO Joe Morgan 4.00 10.00
JPI Jimmy Piersall 8.00 20.00
LBR Lou Brock 6.00 15.00
MRA Manny Ramirez 5.00 12.00
RCA Roy Campanella 8.00 20.00
RFI Rollie Fingers 3.00 8.00
RHO Ryan Howard 6.00 15.00
RSC Red Schoendienst 4.00 10.00
TSP Tris Speaker 15.00 40.00
WST Willie Stargell 8.00 20.00

2010 Topps Tribute Relics Black

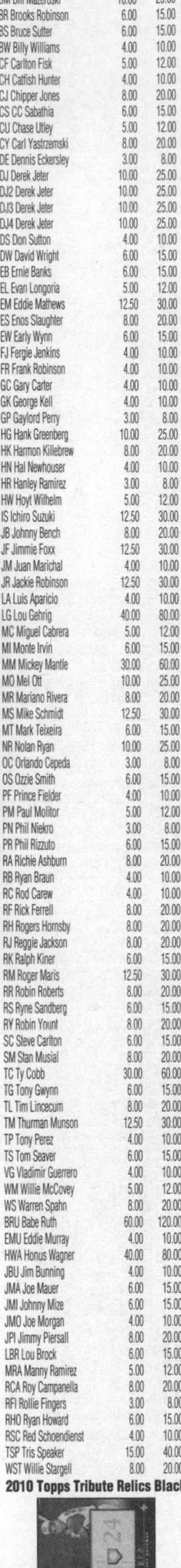

*BLACK: .5X TO 1.2X BASIC
STATED ODDS 1:10 HOBBY
STATED PRINT RUN 50 SER.#'d SETS

2010 Topps Tribute Relics Blue

*BLUE: .4X TO 1X BASIC
STATED ODDS 1:7 HOBBY
STATED PRINT RUN 75 SER.#'d SETS

2010 Topps Tribute Relics Dual

STATED ODDS 1:7 HOBBY
STATED PRINT RUN 99 SER.#'d SETS
AR Alex Rodriguez 10.00 25.00
CF Carlton Fisk 6.00 15.00
CS CC Sabathia 5.00 12.00
DJ Derek Jeter 12.50 30.00
DP Dustin Pedroia 6.00 15.00
DW David Wright 8.00 20.00
JB Johnny Bench 6.00 15.00
JE Jacoby Ellsbury 10.00 25.00
JP Jorge Posada 5.00 12.00
KY Kevin Youkilis 5.00 12.00
MR Mariano Rivera 8.00 20.00
MS Mike Schmidt 10.00 25.00
MT Mark Teixeira 6.00 15.00
NR Nolan Ryan 10.00 25.00
OS Ozzie Smith 6.00 15.00
RA Richie Ashburn 10.00 25.00
RB Ryan Braun 4.00 10.00
RH Ryan Howard 6.00 15.00
TG Tony Gwynn 4.00 10.00
VM Victor Martinez 4.00 10.00

2010 Topps Tribute Relics Dual Black

*BLACK: .5X TO 1.2X BASIC
STATED ODDS 1:10 HOBBY
STATED PRINT RUN 50 SER.#'d SETS

2010 Topps Tribute Relics Dual Blue

*BLUE: .4X TO 1X BASIC
STATED ODDS 1:7 HOBBY
STATED PRINT RUN 75 SER.#'d SETS

2010 Topps Tribute Relics Triple

STATED ODDS 1:7 HOBBY
STATED PRINT RUN 99 SER.#'d SETS
CR Cal Ripken 10.00 25.00
DJ Derek Jeter 15.00 40.00
JM Justin Morneau 5.00 12.00
PM Paul Molitor 5.00 12.00
RA Richie Ashburn 12.50 30.00
RG Reggie Jackson 4.00 10.00
RP Rick Porcello 4.00 10.00
RY Robin Yount 8.00 20.00
TG Tony Gwynn 5.00 12.00
TM Thurman Munson 12.50 30.00

2010 Topps Tribute Relics Triple Black

*BLACK: .5X TO 1.2X BASIC
STATED ODDS 1:10 HOBBY
STATED PRINT RUN 50 SER.#'d SETS

2010 Topps Tribute Relics Triple Blue

*BLUE: .4X TO 1X BASIC
STATED ODDS 1:7 HOBBY
STATED PRINT RUN 75 SER.#'d SETS

2011 Topps Tribute

COMPLETE SET (100) 150.00 250.00
COMMON CARD (1-100) .60 1.50
PLATES RANDOMLY INSERTED
PLATE PRINT RUN 1 SET PER COLOR
BLACK-CYAN-MAGENTA-YELLOW ISSUED
NO PLATE PRICING DUE TO SCARCITY
1 Babe Ruth 4.00 10.00
2 Cy Young 1.50 4.00
3 Joe Mauer 1.25 3.00
4 Honus Wagner 1.50 4.00
5 Justin Morneau 1.00 2.50
6 Nolan Ryan 5.00 12.00
7 David Wright 1.25 3.00
8 Evan Longoria 1.00 2.50
9 Troy Tulowitzki 1.50 4.00
10 Mark Teixeira 1.00 2.50
11 Stan Musial 2.50 6.00
12 Sandy Koufax 3.00 8.00
13 Ryan Howard 1.25 3.00
14 Joey Votto 1.50 4.00
15 Carlos Gonzalez 1.00 2.50
16 Roy Halladay 1.00 2.50
17 Brooks Robinson 1.00 2.50
18 Hoyt Wilhelm 1.00 2.50
19 Walter Johnson 1.50 4.00
20 Eddie Murray 1.00 2.50
21 Stephen Strasburg 1.50 4.00
22 Lou Gehrig 3.00 8.00
23 Derek Jeter 4.00 10.00
24 Rod Carew 1.00 2.50
25 Felix Hernandez 1.00 2.50
26 Robin Yount 1.50 4.00
27 Jason Heyward 1.25 3.00
28 Hanley Ramirez 1.00 2.50
29 Fergie Jenkins 1.00 2.50
30 Mickey Mantle 5.00 12.00
31 Josh Hamilton 1.00 2.50
32 Al Kaline 1.50 4.00
33 Hank Greenberg 1.50 4.00
34 Miguel Cabrera 1.50 4.00
35 Jackie Robinson 1.50 4.00
36 Cal Ripken Jr. 5.00 12.00
37 Bob Feller 1.00 2.50
38 Ryne Sandberg 3.00 8.00
39 Dizzy Dean 1.00 2.50
40 Catfish Hunter 1.00 2.50
41 Harmon Killebrew 1.50 4.00
42 Goose Gossage 1.00 2.50
43 Bill Mazeroski 1.00 2.50
44 Bob Gibson 1.00 2.50
45 Johnny Mize 1.00 2.50
46 Tom Seaver 1.00 2.50
47 Jim Bunning 1.00 2.50
48 CC Sabathia 1.00 2.50
49 Rogers Hornsby 1.00 2.50
50 Adam Wainwright 1.00 2.50
51 Thurman Munson 1.50 4.00
52 Albert Pujols 2.00 5.00
53 Willie Stargell 1.00 2.50
54 Tony Gwynn 1.50 4.00
55 Whitey Ford 1.00 2.50
56 Pee Wee Reese 1.00 2.50
57 Frank Robinson 1.00 2.50
58 Roy Campanella 1.50 4.00
59 Robin Roberts 1.00 2.50
60 George Sisler 1.00 2.50
61 Alex Rodriguez 2.00 5.00
62 Ozzie Smith 2.00 5.00
63 Jered Weaver 1.00 2.50
64 Lou Brock 1.00 2.50
65 Bobby Doerr 1.00 2.50
66 Josh Johnson 1.00 2.50
67 David Ortiz 1.50 4.00
68 Johan Santana 1.00 2.50
69 Buster Posey 2.00 5.00
70 Ubaldo Jimenez .60 1.50
71 Duke Snider 1.00 2.50
72 Josh Beckett .60 1.50
73 Vladimir Guerrero 1.00 2.50
74 Justin Verlander 1.50 4.00
75 Mike Schmidt 2.50 6.00
76 Chipper Jones 1.50 4.00
77 Jim Palmer 1.00 2.50
78 Ryan Braun 1.00 2.50
79 Tim Lincecum 1.00 2.50
80 Vernon Wells .60 1.50
81 Joe Morgan 1.00 2.50
82 David Price 1.25 3.00
83 Jon Lester 1.00 2.50
84 Reggie Jackson 1.00 2.50
85 Christy Mathewson 1.50 4.00
86 Prince Fielder 1.00 2.50
87 Johnny Bench 1.50 4.00
88 Tris Speaker 1.00 2.50
89 Juan Marichal 1.00 2.50
90 Ichiro Suzuki 2.00 5.00
91 Warren Spahn 1.00 2.50
92 Yogi Berra 1.50 4.00
93 Willie McCovey 1.00 2.50
94 Cliff Lee 1.00 2.50
95 Mel Ott 1.50 4.00
96 Ty Cobb 2.50 6.00
97 Rollie Fingers 1.00 2.50
98 Chase Utley 1.00 2.50
99 Early Wynn .60 1.50
100 Hank Aaron 3.00 8.00

2011 Topps Tribute Blue

*BLUE: .6X TO 1.5X BASIC
RANDOM INSERTS IN PACKS
STATED PRINT RUN 199 SER.#'d SETS

2011 Topps Tribute Gold

*GOLD: 1.5X TO 4X BASIC
STATED ODDS 1:7 HOBBY
STATED PRINT RUN 50 SER.#'d SETS

2011 Topps Tribute Green

*GREEN: 1X TO 2.5X BASIC
STATED ODDS 1:5 HOBBY
STATED PRINT RUN 75 SER.#'d SETS

2011 Topps Tribute Autograph Dual Relics

STATED ODDS 1:23 HOBBY
STATED PRINT RUN 99 SER.#'d SETS
EXCHANGE DEADLINE 3/31/2014
BP Buster Posey 50.00 100.00
BR Brooks Robinson 15.00 40.00
CB Clay Buchholz 10.00 25.00
DW David Wright 15.00 40.00
EB Ernie Banks 30.00 60.00
EL Evan Longoria 8.00 20.00
FR Frank Robinson 15.00 40.00
JR Jim Rice 10.00 25.00
MM Mike Mussina 8.00 20.00
NG Nomar Garciaparra 30.00 60.00
RH Ryan Howard 12.00 30.00
RS Ryne Sandberg 30.00 60.00
WF Whitey Ford 30.00 60.00
WM Willie McCovey 20.00 50.00
YB Yogi Berra EXCH 25.00 60.00

2011 Topps Tribute Autograph Dual Relics Green

*GREEN: .4X TO 1X BASIC
STATED ODDS 1:6 HOBBY
STATED PRINT RUN 75 SER.#'d SETS
EXCHANGE DEADLINE 3/31/2014

2011 Topps Tribute Autograph Relics

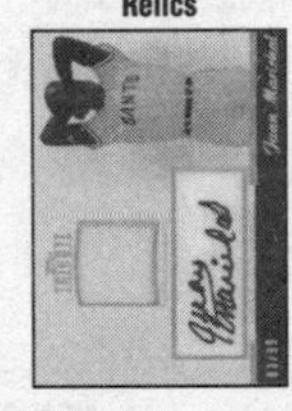

STATED ODDS 1:6 HOBBY
RC AU RELIC ODDS 1:110 HOBBY
STATED PRINT RUN 99 SER.#'d SETS
EXCHANGE DEADLINE 3/31/2014
AB Albert Belle 10.00 25.00
AC Aroldis Chapman 10.00 25.00
AK Al Kaline 25.00 50.00
BL Barry Larkin 20.00 50.00
BP Buster Posey 40.00 80.00
BW Bernie Williams 25.00 60.00
CR Cal Ripken Jr. 40.00 80.00
CS Curt Schilling 15.00 40.00
CU Chase Utley 15.00 40.00
CY Carl Yastrzemski 30.00 80.00
DC David Cone 6.00 15.00
DE Dennis Eckersley 10.00 25.00
DM Don Mattingly 30.00 60.00
DW Dave Winfield 12.50 30.00
EB Ernie Banks 30.00 60.00
FF Freddie Freeman 10.00 25.00
FT Frank Thomas 30.00 60.00
HR Hanley Ramirez 10.00 25.00
JH Josh Hamilton 6.00 15.00
JM Joe Morgan 12.50 30.00
JR Jim Rice 10.00 25.00
JS John Smoltz 15.00 40.00
MI Monte Irvin EXCH 10.00 25.00
MR Manny Ramirez 20.00 50.00
PO Paul O'Neill 15.00 40.00
RA Roberto Alomar 10.00 25.00
RB Ryan Braun 8.00 20.00
RC Robinson Cano 20.00 50.00
RG Ron Guidry 10.00 25.00
SK Sandy Koufax 125.00 250.00
TG Tony Gwynn 15.00 40.00
AB2 Albert Belle 6.00 15.00
AD1 Andre Dawson 10.00 25.00
BP2 Buster Posey 40.00 80.00
CBU Clay Buchholz 10.00 25.00
CBU2 Clay Buchholz 6.00 15.00
DM1 Dale Murphy 12.50 30.00
DS1 Duke Snider 8.00 20.00
DS2 Duke Snider 8.00 20.00
DW1 David Wright 20.00 50.00
DW2 David Wright 10.00 25.00
FJ1 Fergie Jenkins 10.00 25.00
GC1 Gary Carter 15.00 40.00
JHE Jason Heyward 10.00 25.00
JHEL Jeremy Hellickson 10.00 25.00
JMA Juan Marichal 10.00 25.00
JS2 John Smoltz 15.00 40.00
MMC Mike Mussina 12.50 30.00
MS1 Mike Stanton 20.00 50.00
MS2 Mike Stanton 20.00 50.00
OC1 Orlando Cepeda 10.00 25.00
OC2 Orlando Cepeda 10.00 25.00
PO2 Paul O'Neill 10.00 25.00
RA2 Roberto Alomar 10.00 25.00
RA3 Roberto Alomar 10.00 25.00
RG2 Ron Guidry 10.00 25.00
RH1 Ryan Howard 6.00 15.00
RH2 Ryan Howard 10.00 25.00
RK1 Ralph Kiner 12.00 30.00
RK2 Ralph Kiner 10.00 25.00
TP1 Tony Perez 15.00 40.00
YA1 Yonder Alonso 10.00 25.00
YA2 Yonder Alonso 10.00 25.00

2011 Topps Tribute Autograph Relics Green

*GREEN: .4X TO 1X BASIC
STATED ODDS 1:6 HOBBY
RC AU RELIC ODDS 1:145 HOBBY
STATED PRINT RUN 75 SER.#'d SETS
EXCHANGE DEADLINE 3/31/2014

2011 Topps Tribute Autograph Triple Relics

STATED ODDS 1:34 HOBBY
STATED PRINT RUN 99 SER.#'d SETS
EXCHANGE DEADLINE 3/31/2014
AP Albert Pujols 75.00 150.00
AR Alex Rodriguez 40.00 100.00
HA Hank Aaron 100.00 200.00
MR Mariano Rivera 100.00 200.00
NR Nolan Ryan 40.00 80.00
OS Ozzie Smith 30.00 60.00
RH Ryan Howard 10.00 25.00
RJ Reggie Jackson 40.00 80.00
TS Tom Seaver 25.00 60.00
CCS CC Sabathia 6.00 15.00

2011 Topps Tribute Autograph Triple Relics Green

*GREEN: .4X TO 1X BASIC
STATED ODDS 1:6 HOBBY
STATED PRINT RUN 75 SER.#'d SETS
EXCHANGE DEADLINE 3/31/2014

2011 Topps Tribute Dual Relics

STATED ODDS 1:7 HOBBY
STATED PRINT RUN 99 SER.#'d SETS
AB Albert Belle 4.00 10.00
AD Andre Dawson 4.00 10.00
AK Al Kaline 10.00 25.00
BD Bobby Doerr 6.00 15.00
BR Babe Ruth 75.00 150.00
CF Carlton Fisk 8.00 20.00
CR Cal Ripken Jr. 12.50 30.00
CY Carl Yastrzemski 10.00 25.00
DM Don Mattingly 12.50 30.00
DW Dave Winfield 5.00 12.00
EM Eddie Mathews 5.00 12.00
FR Frank Robinson 5.00 12.00
FT Frank Thomas 10.00 25.00
GS George Sisler 10.00 25.00
HA Hank Aaron 12.50 30.00
HG Hank Greenberg 10.00 25.00
HK Harmon Killebrew 10.00 25.00
HW Honus Wagner 50.00 100.00
JB Johnny Bench 8.00 20.00
JF Jimmie Foxx 10.00 25.00
JM Johnny Mize 8.00 20.00
JP Jim Palmer EXCH 8.00 20.00
JR Jackie Robinson 20.00 50.00
JS John Smoltz 5.00 12.00
LG Lou Gehrig 60.00 120.00
MM Mickey Mantle 50.00 100.00
MP Mike Piazza 6.00 15.00
MS Mike Schmidt 8.00 20.00
NR Nolan Ryan 15.00 40.00
OC Orlando Cepeda 8.00 20.00
OS Ozzie Smith 8.00 20.00
PR Phil Rizzuto 6.00 15.00
RA Roberto Alomar 8.00 20.00
RC Roy Campanella 8.00 20.00
RH Rogers Hornsby 12.50 30.00
RJ Reggie Jackson 8.00 20.00
RM Roger Maris 15.00 40.00
RR Robin Roberts EXCH 10.00 25.00
RS Ryne Sandberg 10.00 25.00
RY Robin Yount 6.00 15.00
SK Sandy Koufax 25.00 60.00
SM Stan Musial 20.00 50.00
TC Ty Cobb 30.00 60.00
TG Tony Gwynn 6.00 15.00
TM Thurman Munson 12.50 30.00
TP Tony Perez 4.00 10.00
TS Tris Speaker 12.50 30.00
WF Whitey Ford 5.00 12.00
WS Warren Spahn 5.00 12.00
YB Yogi Berra 10.00 25.00
BRO Brooks Robinson 10.00 25.00
DMU Dale Murphy 6.00 15.00
EMU Eddie Murray 5.00 12.00
RCA Rod Carew 6.00 15.00
TSE Tom Seaver 6.00 15.00
WST Willie Stargell 10.00 25.00

2011 Topps Tribute Dual Relics Green

*GREEN: .4X TO 1X BASIC
STATED ODDS 1:5 HOBBY
STATED PRINT RUN 75 SER.#'d SETS

2011 Topps Tribute Quad Relics

STATED ODDS 1:34 HOBBY
STATED PRINT RUN 99 SER.#'d SETS
AR Alex Rodriguez 10.00 25.00
BG Bob Gibson 8.00 20.00
DJ Derek Jeter 12.50 30.00
IS Ichiro Suzuki 20.00 50.00
JV Joey Votto 10.00 25.00
MO Mel Ott 12.50 30.00
NR Nolan Ryan 20.00 50.00
RH Roy Halladay 15.00 40.00
RH Ryan Howard 10.00 25.00
SS Stephen Strasburg 20.00 50.00

2011 Topps Tribute Quad Relics Green

*GREEN: .4X TO 1X BASIC
STATED ODDS 1:5 HOBBY
STATED PRINT RUN 75 SER.#'d SETS

2011 Topps Tribute Tribute to the Stars Dual Autographs

STATED ODDS 1:38 HOBBY
STATED PRINT RUN 74 SER.#'d SETS
DR A.Dawson/J.Rice 15.00 40.00
DS A.Dawson/R.Sandberg 50.00 100.00
GC D.Gooden/G.Carter 20.00 50.00
HU R.Howard/C.Utley 60.00 120.00
KZ G.Kell/R.Zimmerman 12.00 30.00
LH N.Cruz/J.Hamilton 30.00 60.00
MH D.Murphy/J.Heyward 20.00 50.00
MP B.Matusz/J.Palmer 12.50 30.00
PM A.Pujols/S.Musial 250.00 500.00
PS J.Podres/D.Snider 15.00 40.00
PSA B.Posey/C.Santana 30.00 60.00
SG D.Strawberry/D.Gooden 20.00 50.00

2011 Topps Tribute Tribute to the Stars Triple Autographs

STATED ODDS 1:124 HOBBY
STATED PRINT RUN 24 SER.#'d SETS
SRC Ozzie/Hanley/Starlin 30.00 80.00
FFM Podres/Ford/Marichal 60.00 150.00
HCR Hughes/Cano/Rivera 60.00 150.00
JDS Jenkins/Dawson/Sandberg 30.00 80.00
PKL Price/Kershaw/Lester 40.00 100.00
PSM Posey/Santana/McCann 40.00 100.00
PSN Podres/Snider/Newcombe 20.00 50.00
SBH Stanton/Brown/Heyward 40.00 100.00
SGH Strawberry/Gooden/Carter 40.00 100.00
UHV Utley/Howard/Victorino 60.00 150.00
WAB Wells/Alomar/Bautista 30.00 80.00
YMB Yount/Molitor/Braun 75.00 200.00

2011 Topps Tribute Triple Relics

STATED ODDS 1:23 HOBBY
STATED PRINT RUN 99 SER.#'d SETS
AB Albert Belle 5.00 12.00
AP Albert Pujols 12.50 30.00
CR Cal Ripken Jr. 20.00 50.00
DJ Derek Jeter 10.00 25.00
DM Don Mattingly 10.00 25.00
DW Dave Winfield 6.00 15.00
HA Hank Aaron 20.00 50.00
HK Harmon Killebrew 12.50 30.00
JB Johnny Bench 10.00 25.00
JS John Smoltz 6.00 15.00
LG Lou Gehrig 75.00 150.00
MR Mariano Rivera 10.00 25.00
RS Ryne Sandberg 10.00 25.00
TG Tony Gwynn 10.00 25.00
TS Tom Seaver 8.00 20.00

2011 Topps Tribute Triple Relics Green

*GREEN: .4X TO 1X BASIC
STATED ODDS 1:5 HOBBY
STATED PRINT RUN 75 SER.#'d SETS

2012 Topps Tribute

COMPLETE SET (100) 75.00 150.00
COMMON CARD .40 1.00
PLATES RANDOMLY INSERTED
PLATE PRINT RUN 1 SET PER COLOR
BLACK-CYAN-MAGENTA-YELLOW ISSUED
NO PLATE PRICING DUE TO SCARCITY
1 Hank Aaron 2.00 5.00
2 Luis Aparicio .60 1.50
3 Jose Bautista .75 2.00
4 Albert Belle .40 1.00
5 Johnny Bench 1.00 2.50
6 Lance Berkman .75 2.00
7 Ryan Braun .60 1.50
8 Ralph Kiner .60 1.50
9 Miguel Cabrera 1.00 2.50
10 Robinson Cano .75 2.00
11 Starlin Castro .75 2.00
12 Eddie Mathews 1.00 2.50
13 Ty Cobb 1.50 4.00
14 Yogi Berra 1.00 2.50
15 Andre Dawson .60 1.50
16 Joe DiMaggio 2.00 5.00
17 Duke Snider .60 1.50
18 Prince Fielder .75 2.00
19 Carlton Fisk .60 1.50
20 Orlando Cepeda .60 1.50
21 Yovani Gallardo .75 2.00
22 Lou Gehrig 2.00 5.00
23 Bob Gibson .60 1.50
24 Adrian Gonzalez .75 2.00
25 Carlos Gonzalez .75 2.00
26 Rollie Fingers .60 1.50
27 Roy Halladay .75 2.00
28 Josh Hamilton .75 2.00
29 Juan Marichal .60 1.50
30 Felix Hernandez .75 2.00
31 Mike Napoli .60 1.50
32 Matt Holliday 1.00 2.50
33 Ryan Howard .75 2.00
34 Reggie Jackson .60 1.50
35 Derek Jeter 2.50 6.00
36 Larry Doby .60 1.50
37 Al Kaline 1.00 2.50
38 Matt Kemp .75 2.00
39 Ian Kennedy .60 1.50
40 Clayton Kershaw 2.00 5.00
41 Ian Kinsler .75 2.00
42 Sandy Koufax 2.00 5.00
43 Harmon Killebrew 1.00 2.50
44 Cliff Lee .75 2.00
45 Nelson Cruz 1.00 2.50
46 Tim Lincecum .75 2.00
47 Evan Longoria .75 2.00
48 Mickey Mantle 3.00 8.00
49 Roger Maris 1.00 2.50
50 Edgar Martinez .60 1.50
51 Joe Mauer .75 2.00
52 Willie Mays 2.00 5.00
53 Willie McCovey .60 1.50
54 Michael Young .60 1.50
55 Paul Molitor 1.00 2.50
56 Wade Boggs .60 1.50
57 Stan Musial 1.50 4.00
58 Paul O'Neill .60 1.50
59 Dustin Pedroia .75 2.00
60 Andy Pettitte .75 2.00
61 Buster Posey 1.25 3.00
62 Albert Pujols 1.25 3.00
63 Tony Gwynn 1.00 2.50
64 Hanley Ramirez .75 2.00
65 Ken Griffey Jr. 2.00 5.00
66 Cal Ripken Jr. 3.00 8.00
67 Mariano Rivera 1.25 3.00
68 Brooks Robinson .60 1.50
69 Frank Robinson .60 1.50
70 Alex Rodriguez 1.25 3.00
71 Nolan Ryan 5.00 12.00
72 CC Sabathia .75 2.00
73 Ryne Sandberg 2.00 5.00
74 David Freese .60 1.50
75 Mike Schmidt 1.50 4.00
76 Red Schoendienst .60 1.50
77 Tom Seaver .60 1.50
78 John Smoltz 1.00 2.50
79 Mike Stanton 1.00 2.50
80 Mark Teixeira .75 2.00
81 Frank Thomas 1.00 2.50
82 Troy Tulowitzki 1.00 2.50
83 Justin Upton .75 2.00
84 Chase Utley .75 2.00
85 Justin Verlander 1.00 2.50
86 Joey Votto 1.00 2.50
87 Jered Weaver .75 2.00
88 Eddie Murray .60 1.50
89 Jacoby Ellsbury .75 2.00
90 Ryan Zimmerman .75 2.00
91 Roberto Clemente 2.50 6.00
92 Jackie Robinson 1.00 2.50
93 Babe Ruth 2.50 6.00
94 Ernie Banks 1.00 2.50
95 Warren Spahn .60 1.50
96 Carl Yastrzemski 1.50 4.00
97 Bob Feller .60 1.50
98 Rod Carew .60 1.50
99 Willie Stargell .60 1.50
100 Lou Brock .60 1.50

2012 Topps Tribute Black

*BLACK: 2.5X TO 6X BASIC
STATED PRINT RUN 60 SER.#'d SETS

2012 Topps Tribute Blue

*BLUE: .75X TO 2X BASIC
STATED PRINT RUN 199 SER.#'d SETS

2012 Topps Tribute Bronze

*BRONZE: .5X TO 1.2X BASIC
STATED PRINT RUN 299 SER.#'d SETS

2012 Topps Tribute Gold

GOLD: 4X TO 10X BASIC
STATED PRINT RUN 25 SER.#'d SETS

2012 Topps Tribute Green

*GREEN: 1.5X TO 4X BASIC
STATED PRINT RUN 75 SER.#'d SETS

2012 Topps Tribute Orange

*ORANGE: 2.5X TO 6X BASIC
STATED PRINT RUN 50 SER.#'d SETS

2012 Topps Tribute 1994 Topps Achives 1954 Buyback Aaron Autograph

STATED PRINT RUN 100 SER.#'d SETS
128 Hank Aaron 150.00 250.00

2012 Topps Tribute Autographs

PLATES RANDOMLY INSERTED
PLATE PRINT RUN 1 SET PER COLOR
BLACK-CYAN-MAGENTA-YELLOW ISSUED
NO PLATE PRICING DUE TO SCARCITY
EXCHANGE DEADLINE 02/28/2015
AB Albert Belle 10.00 25.00
AB1 Albert Belle 10.00 25.00
AC Alex Cobb 6.00 15.00

CH Aroldis Chapman 15.00 40.00
CH1 Aroldis Chapman 15.00 40.00
) Andre Dawson 12.50 30.00
: Andre Ethier 8.00 20.00
; Adrian Gonzalez 6.00 15.00
Adam Jones 10.00 25.00
1 Adam Jones 10.00 25.00
.1 Adam Lind 6.00 15.00
.2 Adam Lind 6.00 15.00
M1 Andrew McCutchen 25.00 60.00
M2 Andrew McCutchen 25.00 60.00
)1 Alexi Ogando 6.00 15.00
)2 Alexi Ogando 6.00 15.00
)3 Alexi Ogando 6.00 15.00
' Andy Pettitte 30.00 60.00
R2 Aramis Ramirez 6.00 15.00
RI Anthony Rizzo 8.00 20.00
RI2 Anthony Rizzo 8.00 20.00
31 Brandon Beachy 12.50 30.00
31 Bert Blyleven 10.00 25.00
32 Brandon Beachy 6.00 15.00
3E1 Brandon Belt 8.00 20.00
3E2 Brandon Belt 8.00 20.00
3L Bert Blyleven 10.00 25.00
G1 Brett Gardner 10.00 25.00
G1 Bob Gibson 20.00 50.00
MC Brian McCann 6.00 15.00
P Buster Posey 60.00 120.00
PH Brandon Phillips 10.00 25.00
C Carl Crawford 6.00 15.00
F Carlton Fisk 15.00 40.00
G Carlos Gonzalez 10.00 25.00
G1 Carlos Gonzalez 10.00 25.00
H Chris Heisey 6.00 15.00
KE1 Clayton Kershaw 50.00 100.00
KE2 Clayton Kershaw 50.00 100.00
RI Cal Ripken Jr./49 75.00 150.00
YA Carl Yastrzemski/49 50.00 100.00
A Dustin Ackley 12.50 30.00
A1 Dustin Ackley 12.50 30.00
E Danny Espinosa 6.00 15.00
E Dennis Eckersley 8.00 20.00
E1 Dennis Eckersley 8.00 20.00
G1 Dee Gordon 6.00 15.00
G2 Dee Gordon 6.00 15.00
H1 Daniel Hudson 6.00 15.00
H2 Daniel Hudson 6.00 15.00
M Don Mattingly 25.00 60.00
MU Dale Murphy 20.00 50.00
P Dustin Pedroia 20.00 50.00
P1 Dustin Pedroia 10.00 25.00
U1 Dan Uggla 6.00 15.00
A Elvis Andrus 10.00 25.00
B Ernie Banks 30.00 80.00
H1 Eric Hosmer 8.00 20.00
H2 Eric Hosmer 10.00 25.00
.1 Evan Longoria 20.00 50.00
M1 Edgar Martinez 10.00 25.00
M2 Edgar Martinez 10.00 25.00
N Eduardo Nunez 8.00 20.00
N1 Eduardo Nunez 8.00 20.00
N2 Eduardo Nunez 8.00 20.00
F Freddie Freeman 12.50 30.00
H Felix Hernandez 20.00 50.00
H1 Felix Hernandez 20.00 50.00
J Fergie Jenkins 10.00 25.00
R Frank Robinson/74 15.00 40.00
T Frank Thomas 40.00 80.00
F George Foster 6.00 15.00
G1 Gio Gonzalez 10.00 25.00
G2 Gio Gonzalez 10.00 25.00
A Hank Aaron/74 150.00 250.00
DA Ike Davis 8.00 20.00
KE Ian Kennedy 6.00 15.00
KE1 Ian Kennedy 6.00 15.00
KE2 Ian Kennedy 6.00 15.00
KI1 Ian Kinsler 8.00 20.00
KI2 Ian Kinsler 8.00 20.00
KI3 Ian Kinsler 8.00 20.00
N Ivan Nova 10.00 25.00
N1 Ivan Nova 10.00 25.00
A J.P. Arencibia 8.00 20.00
B Johnny Bench/74 20.00 50.00
BR Jay Bruce 10.00 25.00
BR1 Jay Bruce 10.00 25.00
C1 Johnny Cueto 6.00 15.00
C2 Johnny Cueto 6.00 15.00
G Jaime Garcia 6.00 15.00
G1 Jaime Garcia 6.00 15.00
G2 Jaime Garcia 6.00 15.00
H Jason Heyward 10.00 25.00
H1 Jeremy Hellickson 8.00 20.00
H2 Jeremy Hellickson 8.00 20.00
J Josh Johnson 6.00 15.00
J1 Jon Jay 6.00 15.00
J2 Jon Jay 6.00 15.00
MA Joe Mauer/74 20.00 50.00
MO Jesus Montero 6.00 15.00
MO1 Jesus Montero 6.00 15.00
MO2 Jesus Montero 6.00 15.00
R Jim Rice 8.00 20.00
R1 Jim Rice 8.00 20.00
S John Smoltz 15.00 40.00
TE Julio Teheran 8.00 20.00
TE1 Julio Teheran 8.00 20.00
U1 Justin Upton/49 10.00 25.00
W1 Jered Weaver 6.00 15.00
W2 Jered Weaver 6.00 15.00
WA Jordan Walden 6.00 15.00
WK Jemile Weeks 6.00 15.00
WK1 Jemile Weeks 6.00 15.00
Z1 Jordan Zimmermann 8.00 20.00
Z2 Jordan Zimmermann 8.00 20.00
KGJ Ken Griffey Jr./49 200.00 400.00
LA Luis Aparicio 10.00 25.00
LM Logan Morrison 6.00 15.00
MB1 Madison Bumgarner 20.00 50.00
MB2 Madison Bumgarner 20.00 50.00
MCA Miguel Cabrera 50.00 100.00
MG1 Matt Garza 6.00 15.00
MG2 Matt Garza 6.00 15.00
MH Matt Holliday/74 20.00 50.00
MK1 Matt Kemp 10.00 25.00
MK2 Matt Kemp 10.00 25.00
MK3 Matt Kemp 10.00 25.00
MM1 Mike Minor 6.00 15.00
MM2 Mike Minor 6.00 15.00
MMI1 Minnie Minoso 10.00 25.00
MMI1 Minnie Minoso 10.00 25.00
MML Mitch Moreland 8.00 20.00
MMO Matt Moore 6.00 15.00
MMO1 Matt Moore 6.00 15.00
MMO2 Matt Moore 6.00 15.00
MMS1 Mike Morse 8.00 20.00
MMS2 Mike Morse 8.00 20.00
MMU Mike Moustakas 10.00 25.00
MP1 Michael Pineda 10.00 25.00
MP2 Michael Pineda 10.00 25.00
MP3 Michael Pineda 10.00 25.00
MS Mike Schmidt 40.00 100.00
MST Mike Stanton 15.00 40.00
MT1 Mark Trumbo 8.00 20.00
MT2 Mark Trumbo 8.00 20.00
MT3 Mark Trumbo 8.00 20.00
MT4 Mark Trumbo 8.00 20.00
MTR Mike Trout 400.00 1000.00
MTR1 Mike Trout 400.00 1000.00
MTR2 Mike Trout 400.00 1000.00
NC Nelson Cruz 6.00 15.00
NE1 Nathan Eovaldi 6.00 15.00
NE2 Nathan Eovaldi 6.00 15.00
NE3 Nathan Eovaldi 6.00 15.00
NR Nolan Ryan 50.00 120.00
NW Neil Walker 8.00 20.00
PF Prince Fielder 12.00 30.00
PM Paul Molitor 10.00 25.00
PO1 Paul O'Neill 8.00 20.00
PO2 Paul O'Neill 8.00 20.00
PO3 Paul O'Neill 8.00 20.00
PS1 Pablo Sandoval 15.00 40.00
PS2 Pablo Sandoval 15.00 40.00
RB Ryan Braun 12.00 30.00
RC Robinson Cano 20.00 50.00
RC1 Robinson Cano 10.00 25.00
RD Randall Delgado 6.00 15.00
RJ Reggie Jackson 40.00 80.00
RS Red Schoendienst 15.00 40.00
RSA Ryne Sandberg 30.00 60.00
RZ Ryan Zimmerman 8.00 20.00
SC1 Starlin Castro 10.00 25.00
SC2 Starlin Castro 10.00 25.00
SC3 Starlin Castro 10.00 25.00
SK Sandy Koufax/49 200.00 400.00
SM Stan Musial 60.00 120.00
SP Salvador Perez 12.00 30.00
SP1 Salvador Perez 12.00 30.00
TH1 Tommy Hanson 6.00 15.00
TH2 Tommy Hanson 6.00 15.00
THU Tim Hudson 8.00 20.00
UJ Ubaldo Jimenez 6.00 15.00
WM Willie Mays/74 150.00 250.00
WMC Willie McCovey 30.00 60.00

2012 Topps Tribute Autographs Blue

*BLUE: .5X TO 1.2X BASIC
PRINT RUNS B/WN 8-50 COPIES PER
NO PRICING ON QTY 25 OR LESS
EXCHANGE DEADLINE 02/28/2015

2012 Topps Tribute Championship Material Dual Relics

STATED PRINT RUN 99 SER.#'d SETS
AR Alex Rodriguez 12.50 30.00
CC Chris Carpenter 10.00 25.00
CH Cole Hamels 12.50 30.00
CJ Chipper Jones 10.00 25.00
CS CC Sabathia 12.50 30.00
CU Chase Utley 10.00 25.00
DF David Freese 10.00 25.00
DJ Derek Jeter 30.00 60.00
DO David Ortiz 10.00 25.00
DP Dustin Pedroia 12.50 30.00
JE Jacoby Ellsbury 10.00 25.00
JP Jorge Posada 10.00 25.00
JR Jimmy Rollins 10.00 25.00
MC Miguel Cabrera 10.00 25.00
MR Mariano Rivera 15.00 40.00
MT Mark Teixeira 10.00 25.00
NS Nick Swisher 4.00 10.00
PK Paul Konerko 8.00 20.00
RH Ryan Howard 10.00 25.00
TL Tim Lincecum 12.00 30.00

2012 Topps Tribute Championship Material Dual Relics Blue

*BLUE: .4X TO 1X BASIC
STATED PRINT RUN 50 SER.#'d SETS

2012 Topps Tribute Debut Digit Relics

PRINT RUNS B/WN 49-99 COPIES PER
AG Adrian Gonzalez 5.00 12.00
AK Al Kaline 6.00 15.00
BL Bob Lemon 6.00 15.00
CB Carlos Beltran 5.00 12.00
CG Carlos Gonzalez 6.00 15.00
CJ Chipper Jones 6.00 15.00
CL Cliff Lee 5.00 12.00
DF David Freese 10.00 25.00
DM Don Mattingly 10.00 25.00
DO David Ortiz 6.00 15.00
FH Felix Hernandez 6.00 15.00
GB George Brett 20.00 50.00
GC Gary Carter 10.00 25.00
HA Hank Aaron 30.00 60.00
JB Jose Bautista 10.00 25.00
JD Joe DiMaggio 30.00 60.00
JH Josh Hamilton 10.00 25.00
JW Jered Weaver 10.00 25.00
LB Lance Berkman 8.00 20.00
MC Miguel Cabrera 10.00 25.00
MM Mickey Mantle 50.00 100.00
MT Mark Teixeira 8.00 20.00
RC Rod Carew 12.50 30.00
RC Robinson Cano 10.00 25.00
RH Ryan Howard 8.00 20.00
RK Ralph Kiner 10.00 25.00
LBR Lou Brock 10.00 25.00
RCL Roberto Clemente 40.00 80.00

2012 Topps Tribute Debut Digit Relics Blue

*BLUE: .4X TO 1X BASIC
STATED PRINT RUN 50 SER.#'d SETS

2012 Topps Tribute Positions of Power Relics

PRINT RUNS B/WN 49-99 COPIES PER
AB Adrian Beltre 6.00 15.00
AG Adrian Gonzalez 5.00 12.00
AR Alex Rodriguez 15.00 40.00
BM Brian McCann 10.00 25.00
CG Carlos Gonzalez 6.00 15.00
DU Dan Uggla 5.00 12.00
EL Evan Longoria 10.00 25.00
IK Ian Kinsler 5.00 12.00
JB Jose Bautista 8.00 20.00
JH Josh Hamilton 10.00 25.00
JU Justin Upton 8.00 20.00
JV Joey Votto 10.00 25.00
MC Miguel Cabrera 10.00 25.00
MS Mike Stanton 8.00 20.00
MT Mark Teixeira 10.00 25.00
NC Nelson Cruz 5.00 12.00
PF Prince Fielder 8.00 20.00
RB Ryan Braun 6.00 15.00
RH Ryan Howard 8.00 20.00
TT Troy Tulowitzki 5.00 12.00
CGR Curtis Granderson 8.00 20.00

2012 Topps Tribute Positions of Power Relics Blue

*BLUE: .4X TO 1X BASIC
STATED PRINT RUN 50 SER.#'d SETS

2012 Topps Tribute Retired Remnants Relics

PRINT RUNS B/WN 49-99 COPIES PER
AK Al Kaline 10.00 25.00
AP Andy Pettitte 8.00 20.00
BB Bert Blyleven 5.00 12.00
CR Cal Ripken Jr. 30.00 60.00
CY Carl Yastrzemski 10.00 25.00
DE Dennis Eckersley 8.00 20.00
DM Don Mattingly 15.00 40.00
DW Dave Winfield 5.00 12.00
EB Ernie Banks 10.00 25.00
GB George Brett 12.50 30.00
HA Hank Aaron 50.00 100.00
HK Harmon Killebrew 10.00 25.00
JB Johnny Bench 15.00 40.00
JD Joe DiMaggio 40.00 80.00
JR Jim Rice 6.00 15.00
MM Mickey Mantle 60.00 120.00
MS Mike Schmidt 10.00 25.00
PO Paul O'Neill 10.00 25.00
RC Rod Carew 8.00 20.00
RJ Reggie Jackson 10.00 25.00
RK Ralph Kiner 5.00 12.00
RM Roger Maris 10.00 25.00
RY Robin Yount 8.00 20.00
SC Steve Carlton 8.00 20.00
TG Tony Gwynn 8.00 20.00
WB Wade Boggs 8.00 20.00
WM Willie Mays 12.00 30.00
RCL Roberto Clemente 30.00 60.00

2012 Topps Tribute Retired Remnants Relics Blue

*BLUE: .4X TO 1X BASIC
PRINT RUNS B/WN 30-50 COPIES PER
EB Ernie Banks/30 15.00 40.00

2012 Topps Tribute Superstar Swatches

PRINT RUNS B/WN 79-99 COPIES PER
CG Carlos Gonzalez 8.00 20.00
CL Cliff Lee 5.00 12.00
CS CC Sabathia 12.50 30.00
DJ Derek Jeter 40.00 100.00
DO David Ortiz 10.00 25.00
DP Dustin Pedroia 12.50 30.00
EL Evan Longoria 10.00 25.00
FH Felix Hernandez 5.00 12.00
JB Jose Bautista 8.00 20.00
JE Jacoby Ellsbury 6.00 15.00
JH Josh Hamilton 10.00 25.00
JM Joe Mauer 10.00 25.00
JR Jose Reyes 8.00 20.00
JU Justin Upton 8.00 20.00
JW Jered Weaver 8.00 20.00
MC Miguel Cabrera 10.00 25.00
SS Stephen Strasburg 15.00 40.00
TL Tim Lincecum 8.00 20.00
TT Troy Tulowitzki 8.00 20.00
DPR David Price 5.00 12.00

2012 Topps Tribute Superstar Swatches Blue

*BLUE: .4X TO 1X BASIC
STATED PRINT RUN 50 SER.#'d SETS

2012 Topps Tribute Tribute to the Stars Autographs

PRINT RUNS B/WN 9-24 COPIES PER
NO PRICING ON QTY LESS THAN 24
EXCHANGE DEADLINE 02/28/2015
AG Adrian Gonzalez 12.00 30.00
BP Buster Posey 75.00 150.00
CC Carl Crawford 8.00 20.00
CCS CC Sabathia 20.00 50.00
CJ Chipper Jones 100.00 175.00
CK Clayton Kershaw 40.00 80.00
DG Doc Gooden 30.00 60.00
DG1 Doc Gooden 30.00 60.00
DJ David Justice 20.00 50.00
DJ1 David Justice 20.00 50.00
DO David Ortiz 50.00 100.00
DS Darryl Strawberry 60.00 120.00
DS1 Darryl Strawberry 20.00 50.00
DS2 Darryl Strawberry 20.00 50.00
DW David Wright 75.00 150.00
GC Gary Carter 50.00 100.00
GC1 Gary Carter 50.00 100.00
GC2 Gary Carter 50.00 100.00
HR Hanley Ramirez 20.00 50.00
JB Jose Bautista 30.00 60.00
MK Matt Kemp 12.00 30.00
MST Mike Stanton 25.00 60.00
NC Nelson Cruz 15.00 40.00
OC Orlando Cepeda 20.00 50.00
OC1 Orlando Cepeda 20.00 50.00
RK Ralph Kiner 50.00 100.00
RK1 Ralph Kiner 20.00 50.00
SC Steve Carlton 20.00 50.00
SG Steve Garvey 40.00 80.00
SG1 Steve Garvey 40.00 80.00
SG2 Steve Garvey 40.00 80.00

2012 Topps Tribute Tribute to the Stars Relics

STATED PRINT RUN 99 SER.#'d SETS
AM Andrew McCutchen 8.00 20.00
CG Carlos Gonzalez 4.00 10.00
CJ Chipper Jones 10.00 25.00
CL Cliff Lee 8.00 20.00
CU Chase Utley 6.00 15.00
DF David Freese 12.50 30.00
DO David Ortiz 6.00 15.00
DP Dustin Pedroia 8.00 20.00
DW David Wright 6.00 15.00
EL Evan Longoria 8.00 20.00
FH Felix Hernandez 4.00 10.00
IK Ian Kinsler 5.00 12.00
JB Jose Bautista 5.00 12.00
JE Jacoby Ellsbury 10.00 25.00
JH Josh Hamilton 10.00 25.00
JM Joe Mauer 8.00 20.00
JU Justin Upton 5.00 12.00
KY Kevin Youkilis 5.00 12.00
LB Lance Berkman 10.00 25.00
MC Miguel Cabrera 8.00 20.00
MH Matt Holliday 8.00 20.00
MM Matt Moore 10.00 25.00
MS Mike Stanton 8.00 20.00
MT Mark Teixeira 12.50 30.00
NC Nelson Cruz 4.00 10.00
RZ Ryan Zimmerman 5.00 12.00
SC Starlin Castro 8.00 20.00
TL Tim Lincecum 12.50 30.00
TT Troy Tulowitzki 6.00 15.00
DPR David Price 5.00 12.00
IKY Ian Kennedy 5.00 12.00
JMO Jesus Montero 8.00 20.00
JRO Jimmy Rollins 8.00 20.00
RHO Ryan Howard 6.00 15.00

2012 Topps Tribute Tribute to the Stars Relics Blue

*BLUE: .4X TO 1X BASIC
STATED PRINT RUN 50 SER.#'d SETS

2012 Topps Tribute World Series Swatches

PRINT RUNS B/WN 49-99 COPIES PER
AK Al Kaline 12.50 30.00
AP Andy Pettitte 6.00 15.00
BB Bert Blyleven 6.00 15.00
BL Bob Lemon 10.00 25.00
BS Bruce Sutter 15.00 40.00
CR Cal Ripken Jr. 40.00 80.00
DE Dennis Eckersley 6.00 15.00
DS Duke Snider 10.00 25.00
DW Dave Winfield 8.00 20.00
EM Eddie Murray 10.00 25.00
EM Eddie Mathews 10.00 25.00
GB George Brett 10.00 25.00
GC Gary Carter 10.00 25.00
HA Hank Aaron/49 40.00 80.00
HW Hoyt Wilhelm 8.00 20.00
JB Johnny Bench 12.50 30.00
JD Joe DiMaggio/49 20.00 50.00
LA Luis Aparicio 8.00 20.00
LB Lou Brock 10.00 25.00
LG Lou Gehrig/49 50.00 100.00
MS Mike Schmidt 10.00 25.00
OS Ozzie Smith 15.00 40.00
PM Paul Molitor 6.00 15.00
PO Paul O'Neill 10.00 25.00
PR Phil Rizzuto 10.00 25.00
RC Roberto Clemente 30.00 60.00
RJ Reggie Jackson/49 10.00 25.00
RM Roger Maris 12.50 30.00
SA Sparky Anderson 8.00 20.00
SC Steve Carlton 8.00 20.00
WB Wade Boggs 10.00 25.00
WM Willie Mays/49 20.00 50.00
WS Willie Stargell 10.00 25.00

2012 Topps Tribute World Series Swatches Blue

*BLUE: .4X TO 1X BASIC
STATED PRINT RUN 50 SER.#'d SETS

2013 Topps Tribute

COMPLETE SET (100) 75.00 150.00
PRINTING PLATE ODDS 1:227 HOBBY
1 Whitey Ford .75 2.00
2 Albert Pujols 1.25 3.00
3 Alex Rodriguez 1.25 3.00
4 Buster Posey 1.25 3.00
5 Andre Dawson .75 2.00
6 Carlos Gonzalez .75 2.00
7 CC Sabathia .75 2.00
8 Clayton Kershaw 2.00 5.00
9 Cliff Lee .75 2.00
10 Sandy Koufax 2.00 5.00
11 David Freese .60 1.50
12 Dustin Pedroia .75 2.00
13 Evan Longoria .75 2.00
14 Felix Hernandez .75 2.00
15 Carlton Fisk .75 2.00
16 Frank Thomas 1.00 2.50
17 Giancarlo Stanton 1.00 2.50
18 Hanley Ramirez .75 2.00
19 Jacoby Ellsbury .75 2.00
20 Roberto Clemente 2.50 6.00
21 Jered Weaver .75 2.00
22 Joe Mauer .75 2.00
23 Joey Votto 1.00 2.50
24 John Smoltz 1.00 2.50
25 Derek Jeter 2.50 6.00
26 Jose Bautista .75 2.00
27 Josh Hamilton .75 2.00
28 Justin Verlander 1.00 2.50
29 Ken Griffey Jr. 2.00 5.00
30 Ted Williams 2.00 5.00
31 Mark Teixeira .75 2.00
32 Matt Holliday 1.00 2.50
33 Matt Kemp .75 2.00
34 Miguel Cabrera 1.00 2.50
35 Ernie Banks 1.00 2.50
36 Nolan Ryan 3.00 8.00
37 Prince Fielder .75 2.00
38 Robinson Cano .75 2.00
39 Roy Halladay .75 2.00
40 Cal Ripken Jr. 3.00 8.00
41 Ryan Braun .75 2.00
42 Ryan Howard .75 2.00
43 Ryan Zimmerman .75 2.00
44 Stan Musial 1.50 4.00
45 Ryne Sandberg 2.00 5.00
46 Troy Tulowitzki 1.00 2.50
47 Willie Mays 2.00 5.00
48 Mike Trout 8.00 20.00
49 Bryce Harper 1.50 4.00
50 Babe Ruth 2.50 6.00
51 Don Mattingly 2.00 5.00
52 Billy Williams .75 2.00
53 Stephen Strasburg 1.00 2.50
54 Rickey Henderson 1.00 2.50
55 Mariano Rivera 1.25 3.00
56 David Price .75 2.00
57 Andrew McCutchen 1.00 2.50
58 David Wright .75 2.00
59 Yoenis Cespedes 1.00 2.50
60 Johnny Bench 1.00 2.50
61 Curtis Granderson .75 2.00
62 Juan Marichal .75 2.00
63 R.A. Dickey .75 2.00
64 Adam Jones .75 2.00
65 Mike Schmidt 1.50 4.00
66 Adrian Beltre 1.00 2.50
67 Frank Robinson .75 2.00
68 Chipper Jones 1.00 2.50
69 Madison Bumgarner .75 2.00
70 Al Kaline 1.00 2.50
71 Cole Hamels .75 2.00
72 Yu Darvish 1.00 2.50
73 Adam Wainwright .75 2.00
74 Fergie Jenkins .75 2.00
75 Reggie Jackson .75 2.00
76 Yadier Molina 1.00 2.50
77 Chris Sale 1.00 2.50
78 Aroldis Chapman 1.00 2.50
79 Bob Feller .75 2.00
80 Gary Carter .75 2.00
81 Bob Gibson .75 2.00
82 Dylan Bundy RC 1.50 4.00
83 Larry Doby .60 1.50
84 Lou Brock .75 2.00
85 Ozzie Smith 1.25 3.00
86 Johnny Cueto .75 2.00
87 Harmon Killebrew 1.00 2.50
88 Lou Gehrig 2.00 5.00
89 Matt Cain .75 2.00
90 Willie Stargell .75 2.00
91 Paul Molitor .75 2.00
92 Jurickson Profar RC .75 2.00
93 Manny Machado RC 4.00 10.00
94 George Kell .75 2.00
95 Robin Yount 1.00 2.50
96 Wade Boggs .75 2.00
97 Allen Craig .75 2.00
98 Adrian Gonzalez .75 2.00
99 Monte Irvin .60 1.50
100 Ty Cobb 1.50 4.00

2013 Topps Tribute Blue

*BLUE: 1.2X TO 3X BASIC
STATED ODDS 1:9 HOBBY
STATED PRINT RUN 99 SER.#'d SETS

2013 Topps Tribute Green

*GREEN: 1.2X TO 3X BASIC
STATED ODDS 1:12 HOBBY
STATED PRINT RUN 75 SER.#'d SETS

2013 Topps Tribute Orange

*ORANGE: 2.5X TO 6X BASIC
STATED ODDS 1:18 HOBBY
STATED PRINT RUN 50 SER.#'d SETS

2013 Topps Tribute Autographs

STATED ODDS 1:5 HOBBY
PRINT RUNS B/WN 24-99 COPIES PER
ALL VERSIONS EQUALLY PRICED
EXCHANGE DEADLINE 2/28/2016
AB Albert Belle 8.00 20.00
AB2 Albert Belle 8.00 20.00
AB3 Albert Belle 8.00 20.00
AD Andre Dawson 8.00 20.00
AE Andre Ethier 10.00 25.00
AG Anthony Gose 6.00 15.00
AG2 Anthony Gose 6.00 15.00
AGO Adrian Gonzalez 5.00 12.00
AJ Adam Jones 8.00 20.00
AJ2 Adam Jones 8.00 20.00
AJ3 Adam Jones 8.00 20.00
AP Albert Pujols 125.00 250.00
APE Andy Pettitte/31 30.00 60.00
AR Anthony Rizzo 8.00 20.00
AR2 Anthony Rizzo 8.00 20.00
AR3 Anthony Rizzo 10.00 25.00
BB Bill Buckner 8.00 20.00
BB2 Bill Buckner 8.00 20.00
BBU Billy Butler 6.00 15.00
BBU2 Billy Butler 6.00 15.00
BBU3 Billy Butler 6.00 15.00
BBU4 Billy Butler 6.00 15.00
BG Bob Gibson/31 20.00 50.00
BH Bryce Harper/24 125.00 250.00
BJ Brett Jackson 6.00 15.00
BJ2 Brett Jackson 6.00 15.00
BJ3 Brett Jackson 6.00 15.00
BL Brett Lawrie 6.00 15.00
BL2 Brett Lawrie 6.00 15.00
BL3 Brett Lawrie 6.00 15.00
BM Brian McCann 6.00 15.00
BP Buster Posey/31 75.00 150.00
BPH Brandon Phillips 10.00 25.00
CB Craig Biggio 10.00 25.00
CF Carlton Fisk 15.00 40.00
CFI Cecil Fielder 8.00 20.00
CG Carlos Gonzalez 10.00 25.00
CJ Chipper Jones/31 60.00 120.00
CK Clayton Kershaw 30.00 60.00
CK2 Clayton Kershaw 60.00 120.00
CKE Casey Kelly 6.00 15.00
CR Cal Ripken Jr./24 75.00 150.00
CRU Carlos Ruiz 8.00 20.00
CRU2 Carlos Ruiz 8.00 20.00
CS Chris Sale 8.00 20.00
CS2 Chris Sale 8.00 20.00
CW C.J. Wilson 6.00 15.00
CW2 C.J. Wilson 6.00 15.00
DB Dylan Bundy 10.00 25.00
DB2 Dylan Bundy 10.00 25.00
DE Dennis Eckersley 8.00 20.00
DF David Freese 8.00 20.00
DM Dale Murphy 8.00 20.00
DMA Don Mattingly/31 50.00 100.00
DP Dustin Pedroia 15.00 40.00
DP2 Dustin Pedroia 15.00 40.00
DS Dave Stewart 8.00 20.00
DST Darryl Strawberry 10.00 25.00
DW David Wright/31 10.00 25.00
EA Elvis Andrus 8.00 20.00
EB Ernie Banks/31 40.00 80.00
EE Edwin Encarnacion 6.00 15.00
EE2 Edwin Encarnacion 6.00 15.00
EH Eric Hosmer 10.00 25.00
EL Evan Longoria/31 10.00 25.00
EM Edgar Martinez 5.00 15.00
FF Freddie Freeman 10.00 25.00
FH Felix Hernandez 20.00 50.00
FJ Fergie Jenkins 6.00 15.00
FR Frank Robinson/31 30.00 80.00
FT Frank Thomas/31 40.00 80.00
GF George Foster 6.00 15.00
GG Gio Gonzalez 10.00 25.00
GS Giancarlo Stanton 40.00 100.00
HA Hank Aaron/24 150.00 300.00
IN Ivan Nova 6.00 15.00
JA Jim Abbott 8.00 20.00
JA2 Jim Abbott 8.00 20.00
JB Johnny Bench/31 25.00 60.00
JBA Jose Bautista 10.00 25.00
JBR Jay Bruce 6.00 15.00
JC Johnny Cueto 6.00 15.00
JC2 Johnny Cueto 6.00 15.00
JC3 Johnny Cueto 6.00 15.00
JH Jeremy Hellickson 8.00 20.00
JHA Josh Hamilton/31 10.00 25.00
JHE Jason Heyward 12.00 30.00
JK John Kruk 8.00 20.00
JM Juan Marichal 12.00 30.00
JMO Jesus Montero 8.00 20.00
JP Jim Palmer 10.00 25.00
JP2 Jim Palmer 10.00 25.00
JPR Jurickson Profar 10.00 25.00
JR Jim Rice 10.00 25.00
JS Jean Segura 6.00 15.00
JS2 Jean Segura 6.00 15.00
JSH James Shields 6.00 15.00
JSM John Smoltz 20.00 50.00
JT Jacob Turner 6.00 15.00
JW Jered Weaver 6.00 15.00
JW3 Jered Weaver 6.00 15.00
J7 Jordan Zimmermann 8.00 20.00
JZ2 Jordan Zimmermann 8.00 20.00
JZ3 Jordan Zimmermann 8.00 20.00
KG Ken Griffey Jr. 50.00 100.00
KGS Ken Griffey Sr. 8.00 20.00
KL Kenny Lofton 12.00 30.00
LL Lance Lynn 6.00 15.00
LL2 Lance Lynn 6.00 15.00
MA Matt Adams 10.00 25.00
MA2 Matt Adams 10.00 25.00
MB Madison Bumgarner 20.00 50.00
MC Miguel Cabrera/31 25.00 60.00
MCA Matt Cain 12.00 30.00
MK Matt Kemp 12.00 30.00
MM Matt Moore 8.00 20.00
MM2 Matt Moore 8.00 20.00
MM3 Matt Moore 8.00 20.00
MMA Manny Machado 15.00 40.00
MMI Minnie Minoso 15.00 40.00
MMO Mike Moustakas 8.00 20.00
MMU Mike Mussina 10.00 25.00
MN Mike Napoli 6.00 15.00
MO Mike Olt 6.00 15.00
MO2 Mike Olt 6.00 15.00
MS Mike Schmidt/31 30.00 60.00
MT Mike Trout/31 150.00 250.00
MT4 Mark Trumbo 8.00 20.00
MTR Mark Trumbo 8.00 20.00
MTR2 Mark Trumbo 8.00 20.00
MW Maury Wills 6.00 15.00
MW2 Maury Wills 6.00 15.00
NC Nelson Cruz 8.00 20.00
NG Nomar Garciaparra 15.00 40.00
NR Nolan Ryan/24 150.00 250.00
PF Prince Fielder 6.00 15.00
PG Paul Goldschmidt 15.00 40.00
PG2 Paul Goldschmidt 15.00 40.00
PG3 Paul Goldschmidt 15.00 40.00
PM Paul Molitor 6.00 15.00
PMA Pedro Martinez/24 60.00 150.00
PO Paul O'Neill 10.00 25.00
PS Pablo Sandoval 6.00 15.00
RB Ryan Braun 8.00 20.00
RC Robinson Cano 10.00 25.00
RD R.A. Dickey 8.00 20.00
RH Rickey Henderson/31 60.00 120.00
RJ Reggie Jackson 30.00 60.00
RS Ryne Sandberg/31 40.00 80.00
RV Robin Ventura 10.00 25.00
RZ Ryan Zimmerman 8.00 20.00
SC Starlin Castro 10.00 25.00
SD Scott Diamond 12.00 30.00
SK Sandy Koufax 150.00 300.00
SM Starling Marte 10.00 25.00
SM2 Starling Marte 10.00 25.00
SM3 Starling Marte 10.00 25.00
SMI Shelby Miller 6.00 15.00
SMU Stan Musial/24 75.00 200.00
SP Salvador Perez 6.00 15.00
SP2 Salvador Perez 6.00 15.00
SP3 Salvador Perez 10.00 25.00
TB Trevor Bauer 6.00 15.00
TB2 Trevor Bauer 6.00 15.00
TBA3 Trevor Bauer 6.00 15.00
TC Tony Cingrani 10.00 25.00
TC2 Tony Cingrani 10.00 25.00
TF Todd Frazier 6.00 15.00
TF2 Todd Frazier 6.00 15.00
TFR Todd Frazier 6.00 15.00
TG Tony Gwynn/31 50.00 120.00
TGL Tom Glavine 10.00 25.00
TH Tim Hudson 10.00 25.00
TP Terry Pendleton 8.00 20.00
TP2 Terry Pendleton 8.00 20.00
TR Tim Raines 10.00 25.00
TS Tom Seaver 25.00 60.00
TSK Tyler Skaggs 6.00 15.00
VB Vida Blue 10.00 25.00
VB2 Vida Blue 10.00 25.00
WC Will Clark 10.00 25.00
WC2 Will Clark 12.00 30.00
WM Will Middlebrooks 6.00 15.00
WM2 Will Middlebrooks 6.00 15.00
WM3 Will Middlebrooks 6.00 15.00
WM4 Will Middlebrooks 6.00 15.00
WMA Willie Mays 125.00 250.00
WMI Wade Miley 8.00 20.00
WMI2 Wade Miley 8.00 20.00
WR Wilin Rosario 6.00 15.00
WR2 Wilin Rosario 6.00 15.00
YA Yonder Alonso 6.00 15.00
YA2 Yonder Alonso 6.00 15.00
YC Yoenis Cespedes 15.00 40.00
YC3 Yoenis Cespedes 15.00 40.00
YD Yu Darvish 75.00 150.00
YG Yasmani Grandal 6.00 15.00
YG2 Yasmani Grandal 6.00 15.00
YGO Yovani Gallardo 6.00 15.00
YGO2 Yovani Gallardo 6.00 15.00
YGO3 Yovani Gallardo 6.00 15.00

2013 Topps Tribute Autographs Blue

*BLUE: .4X TO 1X BASIC
STATED ODDS 1:11 HOBBY
STATED PRINT RUN 50 SER.#'d SETS
ALL VERSIONS EQUALLY PRICED
EXCHANGE DEADLINE 2/28/2016

2013 Topps Tribute Autographs Orange

*ORANGE: .5X TO 1.2X BASIC #'d/99
*ORANGE: .4X TO 1X BASIC #'d/31
STATED ODDS 1:19 HOBBY
STATED PRINT RUN 25 SER.#'d SETS
ALL VERSIONS EQUALLY PRICED
EXCHANGE DEADLINE 2/28/2016

2013 Topps Tribute Autographs Sepia

*SEPIA: .5X TO 1.2X BASIC
STATED ODDS 1:15 HOBBY
STATED PRINT RUN 35 SER.#'d SETS
ALL VERSIONS EQUALLY PRICED
EXCHANGE DEADLINE 2/28/2016

2013 Topps Tribute Commemorative Cuts Relics

STATED ODDS 1:33 HOBBY
STATED PRINT RUN 99 SER.#'d SETS
AB Adrian Beltre 4.00 10.00
AG Adrian Gonzalez 8.00 20.00
AP Albert Pujols 10.00 25.00
BH Bryce Harper 10.00 25.00
CB Carlos Beltran 8.00 20.00
CGO Carlos Gonzalez 4.00 10.00
CS Chris Sale 5.00 12.00
DJ Derek Jeter 30.00 60.00
DO David Ortiz 5.00 12.00
FH Felix Hernandez 10.00 25.00
GS Giancarlo Stanton 6.00 15.00
JH Josh Hamilton 8.00 20.00
JS Johan Santana 4.00 10.00
JV Joey Votto 8.00 20.00
JW Jered Weaver 5.00 12.00
MC Matt Cain 8.00 20.00
MCA Miguel Cabrera 12.50 30.00
MK Matt Kemp 5.00 12.00
MM Manny Machado 12.50 30.00
MTE Mark Teixeira 5.00 12.00
PF Prince Fielder 6.00 15.00
PK Paul Konerko 4.00 10.00
RB Ryan Braun 5.00 12.00
RD R.A. Dickey 4.00 10.00
WM Wade Miley 4.00 10.00
WMI Will Middlebrooks 8.00 20.00
YC Yoenis Cespedes 10.00 25.00
YD Yu Darvish 10.00 25.00

2013 Topps Tribute Commemorative Cuts Relics Blue

*BLUE: .4X TO 1X BASIC
STATED ODDS 1:65 HOBBY
STATED PRINT RUN 50 SER.#'d SETS

2013 Topps Tribute Famous Four Baggers Relics

STATED ODDS 1:67 HOBBY
STATED PRINT RUN 99 SER.#'d SETS
AB Albert Belle 4.00 10.00
AD Adam Dunn 4.00 10.00
AG Adrian Gonzalez 4.00 10.00
AK Al Kaline 8.00 20.00
AP Albert Pujols 8.00 20.00
AR Alex Rodriguez 5.00 12.00
CF Cecil Fielder 10.00 25.00
CFI Carlton Fisk 5.00 12.00
CGO Carlos Gonzalez 4.00 10.00
CJ Chipper Jones 10.00 25.00
DK Dave Kingman 6.00 15.00
DO David Ortiz 4.00 10.00
EL Evan Longoria 4.00 10.00
EM Eddie Murray 5.00 12.00
GSH Gary Sheffield 4.00 10.00
JBE Johnny Bench 10.00 25.00
JH Josh Hamilton 6.00 15.00
JR Jim Rice 4.00 10.00
MC Miguel Cabrera 6.00 15.00
MK Matt Kemp 6.00 15.00
MS Mike Schmidt 8.00 20.00
MT Mark Teixeira 4.00 10.00
MTR Mark Trumbo 4.00 10.00
PF Prince Fielder 6.00 15.00
PK Paul Konerko 4.00 10.00
RB Ryan Braun 8.00 20.00
RH Ryan Howard 4.00 10.00

2013 Topps Tribute Famous Four Baggers Relics Blue

*BLUE: .4X TO 1X BASIC
STATED ODDS 1:67 HOBBY
STATED PRINT RUN 50 SER.#'d SETS

2013 Topps Tribute Prime Patches

STATED ODDS 1:79 HOBBY
PRINT RUNS B/WN 13-24 COPIES PER
NO PRICING ON QTY 13
AB Adrian Beltre 10.00 25.00
AC Aroldis Chapman 8.00 20.00
AM Andrew McCutchen 20.00 50.00
AR Alex Rodriguez 25.00 60.00
AW Adam Wainwright 25.00 60.00
BH Bryce Harper 25.00 60.00
BP Buster Posey 25.00 60.00
CG Carlos Gonzalez 10.00 25.00
CJ Chipper Jones 25.00 60.00
CK Clayton Kershaw 20.00 50.00
CL Cliff Lee 15.00 40.00
CS Chris Sale 15.00 40.00
DF David Freese 25.00 60.00
DJ Derek Jeter 100.00 200.00
DS Don Sutton 25.00 60.00
DW David Wright 20.00 50.00
EL Evan Longoria 15.00 40.00
FH Felix Hernandez 20.00 50.00
JH Josh Hamilton 15.00 40.00
JHE Jason Heyward 15.00 40.00
JM Joe Mauer 25.00 60.00
JP Jim Palmer 15.00 40.00
JS Johan Santana 10.00 25.00
JSM John Smoltz 20.00 50.00
JW Jered Weaver 10.00 25.00
LB Lou Brock 15.00 40.00
MH Matt Holliday 12.00 30.00
MK Matt Kemp 15.00 40.00
MT Mike Trout 50.00 120.00
OS Ozzie Smith 50.00 120.00
PF Prince Fielder 20.00 50.00
PK Paul Konerko 12.00 30.00
RB Ryan Braun 12.00 30.00
RC Robinson Cano 30.00 80.00
RCA Rod Carew 12.00 30.00
RD R.A. Dickey 12.00 30.00
RH Roy Halladay 15.00 40.00
RHE Rickey Henderson 40.00 100.00
RZ Ryan Zimmerman 15.00 40.00
SS Stephen Strasburg 15.00 40.00
TL Tim Lincecum 20.00 50.00
TLA Tommy LaSorda 20.00 50.00
TT Troy Tulowitzki 12.00 30.00
WB Wade Boggs 20.00 50.00
WM Willie Mays 50.00 120.00
YC Yoenis Cespedes 25.00 60.00
YD Yu Darvish 10.00 25.00

2013 Topps Tribute Retired Remnants Relics

STATED ODDS 1:26 HOBBY
STATED PRINT RUN 99 SER.#'d SETS
AD Andre Dawson 5.00 12.00
AK Al Kaline 10.00 25.00
BG Bob Gibson 6.00 15.00
BW Billy Williams 4.00 10.00
CF Carlton Fisk 5.00 12.00
CR Cal Ripken Jr. 10.00 25.00
DE Dennis Eckersley 5.00 12.00
DG Dwight Gooden 5.00 12.00
DM Don Mattingly 10.00 25.00
DS Darryl Strawberry 8.00 20.00
EM Eddie Murray 6.00 15.00
EMA Eddie Mathews 6.00 15.00
FJ Fergie Jenkins 5.00 12.00
GB George Brett 10.00 25.00
GC Gary Carter 6.00 15.00
JB Johnny Bench 8.00 20.00
JF Jimmie Foxx 12.50 30.00
JS John Smoltz 5.00 12.00
KG Ken Griffey Jr. 12.50 30.00
LB Lou Brock 6.00 15.00
MS Mike Schmidt 8.00 20.00
NR Nolan Ryan 15.00 40.00
PO Paul O'Neill 6.00 15.00
PR Phil Rizzuto 8.00 20.00
RC Roberto Clemente 20.00 50.00
RJ Reggie Jackson 8.00 20.00
RS Ryne Sandberg 8.00 20.00
RY Robin Yount 6.00 15.00
TC Ty Cobb 20.00 50.00
TG Tony Gwynn 8.00 20.00
TS Tom Seaver 6.00 15.00
TW Ted Williams 20.00 50.00
WM Willie Mays 20.00 50.00
WS Willie Stargell 8.00 20.00
WSP Warren Spahn 5.00 12.00
YB Yogi Berra 8.00 20.00

2013 Topps Tribute Retired Remnants Relics Blue

*BLUE: .4X TO 1X BASIC
STATED ODDS 1:52 HOBBY
STATED PRINT RUN 50 SER.#'d SETS

2013 Topps Tribute Superstar Swatches

STATED ODDS 1:21 HOBBY
STATED PRINT RUN 99 SER.#'d SETS
AB Adrian Beltre 4.00 10.00
AC Aroldis Chapman 5.00 12.00
AG Adrian Gonzalez 4.00 10.00
AM Andrew McCutchen 6.00 15.00
AR Alex Rodriguez 5.00 12.00
AW Adam Wainwright 5.00 12.00
BP Buster Posey 12.50 30.00
CG Carlos Gonzalez 4.00 10.00
CJ Chipper Jones 10.00 25.00
CK Clayton Kershaw 6.00 15.00
CL Cliff Lee 6.00 15.00
CS Chris Sale 4.00 10.00
DF David Freese 5.00 12.00
DJ Derek Jeter 20.00 50.00
DP Dustin Pedroia 8.00 20.00
DW David Wright 5.00 12.00
EL Evan Longoria 4.00 10.00
FH Felix Hernandez 6.00 15.00
HR Hanley Ramirez 4.00 10.00
IK Ian Kinsler 4.00 10.00
JE Jacoby Ellsbury 4.00 10.00
JH Josh Hamilton 6.00 15.00
JM Joe Mauer 8.00 20.00
JR Jose Reyes 4.00 10.00
JS Johan Santana 4.00 10.00
JV Joey Votto 8.00 20.00
JVE Justin Verlander 10.00 25.00
JW Jered Weaver 4.00 10.00
MC Matt Cain 6.00 15.00
MH Matt Holliday 8.00 20.00
MK Matt Kemp 6.00 15.00
MT Mike Trout 20.00 50.00
PF Prince Fielder 6.00 15.00
PK Paul Konerko 4.00 10.00
PS Pablo Sandoval 4.00 10.00
RC Robinson Cano 8.00 20.00
RH Roy Halladay 4.00 10.00
RHO Ryan Howard 4.00 10.00
RZ Ryan Zimmerman 5.00 12.00
SS Stephen Strasburg 10.00 25.00
TL Tim Lincecum 8.00 20.00
TT Troy Tulowitzki 5.00 12.00
YC Yoenis Cespedes 8.00 20.00

2013 Topps Tribute Superstar Swatches Blue

*BLUE: .4X TO 1X BASIC
STATED ODDS 1:42 HOBBY
STATED PRINT RUN 50 SER.#'d SETS

2013 Topps Tribute Transitions Relics

STATED ODDS 1:31 HOBBY
PRINT RUNS B/WN 67-99 COPIES PER
AB Albert Belle 6.00 15.00
AD Andre Dawson 8.00 20.00
AG Adrian Gonzalez 8.00 20.00
AJ Adam Jones 8.00 20.00
AR Alex Rodriguez 8.00 20.00
BS Bruce Sutter 8.00 20.00
CF Carlton Fisk 8.00 20.00
CG Carlos Gonzalez 8.00 20.00
DK Dave Kingman 6.00 15.00
DO David Ortiz 10.00 25.00
EM Eddie Murray 8.00 20.00
FJ Fergie Jenkins 8.00 20.00
FR Frank Robinson 8.00 20.00
HK Harmon Killebrew 12.00 30.00
HR Hanley Ramirez 8.00 20.00
JB Jose Bautista 8.00 20.00
JF Jimmie Foxx 12.00 30.00
JH Josh Hamilton 8.00 20.00
JR Jose Reyes 8.00 20.00
KG Ken Griffey Sr. 4.00 10.00
MC Miguel Cabrera 8.00 20.00
MH Matt Holliday 10.00 25.00
MT Mark Teixeira 8.00 20.00
PF Prince Fielder 8.00 20.00
PM Paul Molitor/67 10.00 25.00
RC Rod Carew 8.00 20.00
TS Tom Seaver 8.00 20.00
WB Wade Boggs 8.00 20.00
CFI Cecil Fielder 6.00 15.00

2013 Topps Tribute Tribute to the Stars Autographs

STATED ODDS 1:38 HOBBY
STATED PRINT RUN 24 SER.#'d SETS
ALL VERSIONS EQUALLY PRICED
EXCHANGE DEADLINE 02/28/2016
AD Andre Dawson 20.00 50.00
AG Adrian Gonzalez 30.00 60.00
AJ Adam Jones 10.00 25.00
BB Brandon Beachy 8.00 20.00
BG Bob Gibson 30.00 60.00
BP Buster Posey 75.00 150.00
BR Brooks Robinson 30.00 60.00
CC CC Sabathia 10.00 25.00
DG Dwight Gooden 10.00 25.00
DJ David Justice 15.00 40.00
DS Duke Snider 10.00 25.00
EE Edwin Encarnacion 10.00 25.00
EL Evan Longoria 20.00 50.00
FH Felix Hernandez 20.00 50.00
FJ Fergie Jenkins 12.00 30.00
FT Frank Thomas 50.00 100.00
GC Gary Carter 12.00 30.00
GF George Foster 12.00 30.00
GS Gary Sheffield 10.00 25.00
ID Ike Davis 12.00 30.00
JM Joe Mauer 20.00 50.00
JP Johnny Podres 12.00 30.00
JR Josh Reddick 12.00 30.00
JU Justin Upton 10.00 25.00
LA Luis Aparicio 10.00 25.00
MC Melky Cabrera 12.00 30.00
MH Matt Harrison 10.00 25.00
MI Monte Irvin 15.00 40.00
MM Manny Machado 60.00 50.00
MO Mike Olt EXCH 12.00 30.00
NM Nick Markakis EXCH 10.00 25.00
OC Orlando Cepeda 10.00 25.00
PM Paul Molitor 20.00 50.00
RB Ryan Braun 10.00 25.00
RC Robinson Cano EXCH 15.00 40.00
RJ Reggie Jackson EXCH 20.00 50.00
RK Ralph Kiner 20.00 50.00
RS Red Schoendienst 10.00 25.00
SG Steve Garvey 20.00 50.00
SV Shane Victorino 20.00 50.00
TB Trevor Bauer 20.00 50.00
WF Whitey Ford 30.00 60.00
AD2 Andre Dawson 20.00 50.00
ADA Adam Dunn 10.00 25.00
AG2 Adrian Gonzalez 30.00 60.00
AJA Austin Jackson 10.00 25.00
BG2 Bob Gibson 30.00 60.00
BP2 Buster Posey 75.00 150.00
DG2 Dwight Gooden 10.00 25.00
DG3 Dwight Gooden 10.00 25.00
DG4 Dwight Gooden 10.00 25.00
DG5 Dwight Gooden 10.00 25.00
DG6 Dwight Gooden 10.00 25.00
DJ2 David Justice 15.00 40.00
DS2 Duke Snider 10.00 25.00
DS3 Duke Snider 10.00 25.00
DS4 Duke Snider 10.00 25.00
DSU Don Sutton 12.00 30.00
DWR David Wright 15.00 40.00
EL2 Evan Longoria 12.00 30.00
FH2 Felix Hernandez 20.00 50.00
FJ2 Fergie Jenkins 12.00 30.00
FJ3 Fergie Jenkins 12.00 30.00
GC2 Gary Carter 12.00 30.00
GC3 Gary Carter 12.00 30.00
GC4 Gary Carter 12.00 30.00
GS2 Gary Sheffield 10.00 25.00
GS3 Gary Sheffield 10.00 25.00
GS4 Gary Sheffield 10.00 25.00
GS5 Gary Sheffield 10.00 25.00
GS6 Gary Sheffield 10.00 25.00
ID2 Ike Davis 12.00 30.00
ID3 Ike Davis 12.00 30.00
JMA Juan Marichal 10.00 25.00
JP2 Johnny Podres 12.00 30.00
JP3 Johnny Podres 12.00 30.00
JP4 Johnny Podres 12.00 30.00
JPA Jim Palmer 12.00 30.00
JU2 Justin Upton 10.00 25.00
JU3 Justin Upton 10.00 25.00
LA2 Luis Aparicio 10.00 25.00
MH2 Matt Harrison 10.00 25.00
MM2 Manny Machado 20.00 50.00
MO2 Mike Olt EXCH 12.00 30.00
NM2 Nick Markakis EXCH 10.00 25.00
OC2 Orlando Cepeda 10.00 25.00
OC3 Orlando Cepeda 10.00 25.00
RB2 Ryan Braun 10.00 25.00
RB3 Ryan Braun 10.00 25.00
RS2 Red Schoendienst 10.00 25.00
SG2 Steve Garvey 20.00 50.00
SG3 Steve Garvey 20.00 50.00
SV2 Shane Victorino 20.00 50.00
TB2 Trevor Bauer 20.00 50.00
WF2 Whitey Ford 30.00 60.00
DSU2 Don Sutton 12.50 30.00
DSU3 Don Sutton 12.50 25.00
JMA2 Juan Marichal 10.00 25.00
JPA2 Jim Palmer 12.00 30.00
JPA3 Jim Palmer 12.00 30.00

2013 Topps Tribute Tribute to the Stars Relics

STATED ODDS 1:15 HOBBY
STATED PRINT RUN 99 SER.#'d SETS
AB Adrian Beltre 4.00 10.00
AC Aroldis Chapman 4.00 10.00
AE Andre Ethier 4.00 10.00
AG Adrian Gonzalez 4.00 10.00
AJ Adam Jones 5.00 12.00
AM Andrew McCutchen 6.00 15.00
AR Alex Rodriguez 10.00 25.00
AW Adam Wainwright 6.00 15.00
BB Billy Butler 4.00 10.00
BG Bob Gibson 6.00 15.00
BH Bryce Harper 12.00 30.00
BP Buster Posey 10.00 25.00
BR Babe Ruth 50.00 120.00
CGO Carlos Gonzalez 4.00 10.00
CH Cole Hamels 4.00 10.00
CJ Chipper Jones 4.00 10.00
CK Clayton Kershaw 4.00 10.00
CL Cliff Lee 4.00 10.00
CR Carlos Ruiz 4.00 10.00
CS Chris Sale 4.00 10.00
CU Chase Utley 4.00 10.00
DF David Freese 4.00 10.00
DJ Derek Jeter 12.50 30.00
DP Dustin Pedroia 4.00 10.00
DPR David Price 4.00 10.00
DW David Wright 6.00 15.00
EL Evan Longoria 6.00 15.00
FH Felix Hernandez 5.00 12.00
HR Hanley Ramirez 4.00 10.00
IK Ian Kinsler 4.00 10.00
JB Jose Bautista 4.00 10.00
JC Johnny Cueto 4.00 10.00
JE Jacoby Ellsbury 4.00 10.00
JH Josh Hamilton 5.00 12.00
JHE Jason Heyward 4.00 10.00
JR Jose Reyes 4.00 10.00
JS Johan Santana 4.00 10.00
JV Joey Votto 4.00 10.00
JVE Justin Verlander 4.00 10.00
JW Jered Weaver 4.00 10.00
MB Madison Bumgarner 8.00 20.00
MC Matt Cain 5.00 12.00
MH Matt Holliday 4.00 10.00
MK Matt Kemp 5.00 12.00
MT Mike Trout 10.00 25.00
MTE Mark Teixeira 10.00 25.00
PF Prince Fielder 6.00 15.00
PK Paul Konerko 4.00 10.00
PO Paul O'Neill 6.00 15.00
PS Pablo Sandoval 6.00 15.00
RB Ryan Braun 5.00 12.00
RC Robinson Cano 8.00 20.00
RH Roy Halladay 4.00 10.00
RHO Ryan Howard 5.00 12.00
RZ Ryan Zimmerman 5.00 12.00
SS Stephen Strasburg 10.00 25.00
TL Tim Lincecum 4.00 10.00
TT Troy Tulowitzki 4.00 10.00
TW Ted Williams 20.00 50.00
YC Yoenis Cespedes 4.00 10.00
YD Yu Darvish 8.00 20.00

2013 Topps Tribute Tribute to the Stars Relics Green

*GREEN: .4X TO 1X BASIC
STATED ODDS 1:37 HOBBY
STATED PRINT RUN 40 SER.#'d SETS

2013 Topps Tribute Tribute to the Stars Relics Orange

*ORANGE: .4X TO 1X BASIC
STATED ODDS 1:30 HOBBY
STATED PRINT RUN 50 SER.#'d SETS

2014 Topps Tribute

PRINTING PLATE ODDS 1:238 HOBBY
PLATE PRINT RUN 1 SET PER COLOR
BLACK-CYAN-MAGENTA-YELLOW ISSUED
NO PLATE PRICING DUE TO SCARCITY
1 Buster Posey 1.25 3.00
2 Yoenis Cespedes 1.00 2.50
3 Whitey Ford .75 2.00
4 Willie Stargell .75 2.00
5 Giancarlo Stanton 1.00 2.50
6 Troy Tulowitzki 1.00 2.50
7 Adam Jones .75 2.00
8 Adrian Beltre 1.00 2.50
9 Shelby Miller .75 2.00
10 Jayson Werth .75 2.00
11 Lou Gehrig 2.00 5.00
12 Babe Ruth 2.50 6.00
13 Wade Boggs .75 2.00
14 Adam Wainwright .75 2.00
15 Ozzie Smith 1.25 3.00
16 Don Mattingly 2.00 5.00
17 Jose Bautista .75 2.00
18 Mike Schmidt 1.50 4.00
19 Roberto Clemente 2.50 6.00
20 Prince Fielder .75 2.00
21 Matt Cain .75 2.00
22 Derek Jeter 2.50 6.00
23 Ted Williams 2.00 5.00
24 Robinson Cano .75 2.00
25 Willie Mays 2.00 5.00
26 Miguel Cabrera 1.00 2.50
27 Josh Hamilton .75 2.00
28 Stan Musial 1.50 4.00
29 Bob Gibson .75 2.00
30 Andrew McCutchen 1.00 2.50
31 Joey Votto 1.00 2.50
32 CC Sabathia .75 2.00
33 Mike Trout 5.00 12.00
34 Monte Irvin .75 2.00
35 Cliff Lee .75 2.00
36 Randy Johnson 1.00 2.50
37 Clayton Kershaw 2.00 5.00
38 Matt Harvey .75 2.00
39 Robin Yount 1.00 2.50
40 John Smoltz 1.00 2.50
41 Ken Griffey Jr. 2.00 5.00
42 Al Kaline 1.00 2.50
43 Aroldis Chapman 1.00 2.50
44 Johnny Bench 1.00 2.50
45 Bryce Harper 1.50 4.00
46 Paul Molitor 1.00 2.50
47 Jose Fernandez 1.00 2.50
48 George Kell .75 2.00
49 Yadier Molina 1.00 2.50
50 Juan Marichal .75 2.00
51 Joe DiMaggio 2.00 5.00
52 R.A. Dickey .75 2.00
53 Jurickson Profar .75 2.00
54 Frank Robinson .75 2.00
55 Lou Brock .75 2.00
56 Evan Longoria .75 2.00
57 Bob Feller .75 2.00
58 Gary Carter .75 2.00
59 Harmon Killebrew 1.00 2.50
60 Carlos Gonzalez .75 2.00
61 Stephen Strasburg 1.00 2.50
62 Carlton Fisk .75 2.00
63 Andre Dawson .75 2.00
64 Mariano Rivera 1.25 3.00
65 Joe Mauer .75 2.00
66 Felix Hernandez .75 2.00
67 Ivan Rodriguez .75 2.00
68 Reggie Jackson .75 2.00
69 Manny Machado 1.00 2.50
70 Nolan Ryan 3.00 8.00
71 Ernie Banks 1.00 2.50
72 Adrian Gonzalez .75 2.00
73 Cal Ripken Jr. 3.00 8.00
74 Larry Doby .75 2.00
75 Dustin Pedroia 1.00 2.50
76 Billy Williams .75 2.00
77 Cole Hamels .75 2.00
78 Frank Thomas 1.00 2.50
79 Albert Pujols 1.25 3.00
80 Chipper Jones 1.00 2.50
81 Rickey Henderson 1.00 2.50
82 Sandy Koufax 2.00 5.00
83 Justin Verlander 1.00 2.50
84 David Price .75 2.00
85 Chris Sale 1.00 2.50
86 Jacoby Ellsbury .75 2.00
87 Ryne Sandberg 2.00 5.00
88 David Wright .75 2.00
89 Matt Kemp .75 2.00
90 Ty Cobb 1.50 4.00
91 Yu Darvish 1.00 2.50
92 Yasiel Puig 1.00 2.50
93 Bo Jackson 1.00 2.50
94 Gerrit Cole 1.00 2.50
95 Wil Myers .60 1.50
96 Mike Zunino .60 1.50
97 Zack Wheeler .75 2.00
98 Greg Maddux 1.25 3.00
99 Paul Goldschmidt 1.00 2.50
100 Chris Davis .60 1.50

2014 Topps Tribute Blue

*BLUE: 1.5X TO 4X BASIC
STATED ODDS 1:10 HOBBY
STATED PRINT RUN 99 SER.#'d SETS
1 Buster Posey 6.00 15.00
22 Derek Jeter 15.00 40.00
23 Ted Williams 6.00 15.00
25 Willie Mays 10.00 25.00
28 Stan Musial 5.00 12.00
49 Yadier Molina 5.00 12.00
51 Joe DiMaggio 8.00 20.00
64 Mariano Rivera 12.00 30.00
98 Greg Maddux 6.00 15.00

2014 Topps Tribute Gold

*GOLD: 3X TO 8X BASIC
STATED ODDS 1:39 HOBBY
STATED PRINT RUN 25 SER.#'d SETS
1 Buster Posey 15.00 40.00
22 Derek Jeter 40.00 100.00
23 Ted Williams 12.50 30.00
25 Willie Mays 20.00 50.00
28 Stan Musial 10.00 25.00
33 Mike Trout 30.00 80.00
49 Yadier Molina 10.00 25.00
51 Joe DiMaggio 15.00 40.00
64 Mariano Rivera 12.50 30.00
98 Greg Maddux 12.50 30.00

2014 Topps Tribute Green

*GREEN: 2X TO 5X BASIC
STATED ODDS 1:20 HOBBY
STATED PRINT RUN 50 SER.#'d SETS
1 Buster Posey 10.00 25.00
22 Derek Jeter 25.00 60.00
23 Ted Williams 8.00 20.00
25 Willie Mays 12.50 30.00
28 Stan Musial 6.00 15.00
49 Yadier Molina 6.00 15.00
51 Joe DiMaggio 10.00 25.00
64 Mariano Rivera 8.00 20.00
98 Greg Maddux 8.00 20.00

2014 Topps Tribute Autographs

PRINTING PLATE ODDS 1:948 HOBBY
PLATE PRINT RUN 1 SET PER COLOR
BLACK-CYAN-MAGENTA-YELLOW ISSUED
NO PLATE PRICING DUE TO SCARCITY
EXCHANGE DEADLINE 2/28/2017
TAAB Albert Belle 5.00 12.00
TAAG Adrian Gonzalez 10.00 25.00
TAAH Aaron Hicks 6.00 15.00
TAAJ Adam Jones 10.00 25.00
TAAR Anthony Rizzo 12.00 30.00
TABB Billy Butler 5.00 12.00
TABG Bob Gibson 20.00 50.00
TABPH Brandon Phillips 5.00 12.00
TABZ Ben Zobrist 6.00 15.00
TACF Carlton Fisk 10.00 25.00
TACH Cole Hamels 6.00 15.00
TACKE Clayton Kershaw 50.00 100.00
TACS Chris Sale 10.00 25.00
TACSA Carlos Santana 6.00 15.00
TACW C.J. Wilson 5.00 12.00
TACWI C.J. Wilson 5.00 12.00
TADB Dylan Bundy 8.00 20.00
TADF David Freese 5.00 12.00
TADG Didi Gregorius 6.00 15.00
TADH Derek Holland 5.00 12.00
TADM Dale Murphy 15.00 40.00
TADP Dustin Pedroia 15.00 40.00
TADST Dave Stewart 5.00 12.00
TADW David Wright 12.00 30.00
TAEB Ernie Banks 20.00 50.00
TAED Eric Davis 5.00 12.00
TAEG Evan Gattis 5.00 12.00
TAEL Evan Longoria 6.00 15.00
TAEM Edgar Martinez 10.00 25.00
TAFF Freddie Freeman 10.00 25.00
TAFL Fred Lynn 8.00 20.00
TAFM Fred McGriff 12.00 30.00
TAIR Ivan Rodriguez 8.00 20.00
TAJC Jose Canseco 12.00 30.00
TAJCU Johnny Cueto 6.00 15.00
TAJGR Jason Grilli 5.00 12.00
TAJH Jason Heyward 6.00 15.00
TAJP Jorge Posada 20.00 50.00
TAJR Jim Rice 6.00 15.00
TAJS Jean Segura 6.00 15.00
TAJSH James Shields 5.00 12.00
TAJT Julio Teheran 6.00 15.00
TAKM Kevin Mitchell 5.00 12.00
TAKME Kris Medlen 6.00 15.00
TALB Lou Brock 15.00 40.00
TALG Luis Gonzalez 5.00 12.00
TALL Lance Lynn 5.00 12.00
TALS Lee Smith 5.00 12.00
TAMB Madison Bumgarner 15.00 40.00
TAMM Matt Moore 6.00 15.00
TAMMI Mike Minor 5.00 12.00
TAMT Mark Trumbo 5.00 12.00
TAMW Matt Williams 10.00 25.00
TAPC Patrick Corbin 6.00 15.00
TAPG Paul Goldschmidt 10.00 25.00
TAPO Paul O'Neill 8.00 20.00
TARZ Ryan Zimmerman 6.00 15.00
TATB Trevor Bauer 8.00 20.00
TATC Tony Cingrani 6.00 15.00
TATD Travis d'Arnaud 6.00 15.00
TATR Tim Raines 6.00 15.00
TATS Tyler Skaggs 5.00 12.0
TAWC Will Clark 12.00 30.0
TAWM Wil Myers 12.00 30.0
TAWMI Will Middlebrooks 5.00 12.0
TAWR Wilin Rosario 5.00 12.0
TAZW Zack Wheeler 6.00 15.0

2014 Topps Tribute Autographs Blue

*BLUE: .4X TO 1X BASIC
STATED ODDS 1:31 HOBBY
STATED PRINT RUN 50 SER.#'d SETS
EXCHANGE DEADLINE 2/28/2017

2014 Topps Tribute Autographs Green

*GREEN: .6X TO 1.5X BASIC
STATED ODDS 1:57 HOBBY
STATED PRINT RUN 25 SER.#'d SETS
EXCHANGE DEADLINE 2/28/2017
TABJ Bo Jackson 50.00 120.0
TABP Buster Posey 60.00 150.0
TACR Cal Ripken Jr. 30.00 80.0
TADMA Don Mattingly 50.00 120.0
TAFJ Fergie Jenkins 12.00 30.0

2014 Topps Tribute Autographs Orange

*ORANGE: .4X TO 1X BASIC
STATED ODDS 1:39 HOBBY
STATED PRINT RUN 40 SER.#'d SETS
EXCHANGE DEADLINE 2/28/2017

2014 Topps Tribute Autographs Pink

*PINK: .4X TO 1X BASIC
STATED ODDS 1:34 HOBBY
STATED PRINT RUN 45 SER.#'d SETS
EXCHANGE DEADLINE 2/28/2017

2014 Topps Tribute Autographs Sepia

*SEPIA: .5X TO 1.2X BASIC
STATED ODDS 1:44 HOBBY
STATED PRINT RUN 35 SER.#'d SETS
EXCHANGE DEADLINE 2/28/2017

2014 Topps Tribute Autographs Yellow

*YELLOW: .5X TO 1.2X BASIC
STATED ODDS 1:51 HOBBY
STATED PRINT RUN 30 SER.#'d SETS
EXCHANGE DEADLINE 2/28/2017

2014 Topps Tribute Forever Young Relics

STATED ODDS 1:28 HOBBY
STATED PRINT RUN 99 SER.#'d SETS
FYRAC Aroldis Chapman 5.00 12.0
FYRBH Bryce Harper 8.00 20.0
FYRBHA Billy Hamilton 8.00 20.0
FYRBP Buster Posey 6.00 15.0
FYRCK Clayton Kershaw 10.00 25.0
FYRCS Chris Sale 5.00 12.0
FYRDB Domonic Brown 4.00 10.0
FYREH Eric Hosmer 4.00 10.0
FYRFF Freddie Freeman 6.00 15.0
FYRFH Felix Hernandez 4.00 10.0
FYRGC Gerrit Cole 6.00 15.0
FYRJF Jose Fernandez 4.00 10.0
FYRJH Jason Heyward 4.00 10.0
FYRJP Jurickson Profar 4.00 10.0
FYRJS Jean Segura 4.00 10.0
FYRJU Justin Upton 4.00 10.0
FYRJZ Jordan Zimmermann 4.00 10.0
FYRMH Matt Harvey 4.00 10.0
FYRMM Manny Machado 5.00 12.0
FYRMMO Matt Moore 4.00 10.0
FYRMT Mike Trout 25.00 60.0
FYRMW Michael Wacha 4.00 10.0
FYRPG Paul Goldschmidt 5.00 12.0
FYRRH Hyun-Jin Ryu 4.00 10.0
FYRSM Shelby Miller 4.00 10.0
FYRSS Stephen Strasburg 5.00 12.0
FYRTC Tony Cingrani 4.00 10.0
FYRTD Travis d'Arnaud 4.00 10.0
FYRTW Taijuan Walker 3.00 8.0
FYRWM Wil Myers 3.00 8.0
FYRXB Xander Bogaerts 12.00 30.0
FYRYC Yoenis Cespedes 5.00 12.0
FYRYP Yasiel Puig 10.00 25.0
FYRZW Zack Wheeler 4.00 10.0

2014 Topps Tribute Forever Young Relics Blue

*BLUE: .4X TO 1X BASIC
STATED ODDS 1:55 HOBBY
STATED PRINT RUN 50 SER.#'d SETS

2014 Topps Tribute Forever Young Relics Green

*GREEN: .5X TO 1.2X BASIC
STATED ODDS 1:108 HOBBY
STATED PRINT RUN 25 SER.#'d SETS

2014 Topps Tribute Forever Young Relics Sepia

*SEPIA: .5X TO 1.2X BASIC
STATED ODDS 1:78 HOBBY
STATED PRINT RUN 35 SER.#'d SETS

2014 Topps Tribute Mystery Redemption Autographs

EXCHANGE DEADLINE 2/28/2017
HAMR Hank Aaron 150.00 300.0

2014 Topps Tribute Prime Patches

STATED ODDS 1:79 HOBBY
STATED PRINT RUN 24 SER.#'d SETS
PPAB Adrian Beltre 12.00 30.0
PPAC Allen Craig 20.00 50.0

PAG Adrian Gonzalez 12.50 30.00
PAJ Adam Jones 20.00 50.00
PAM Andrew McCutchen 12.50 30.00
PAP Albert Pujols 40.00 80.00
PBH Bryce Harper 30.00 60.00
PBHA Billy Hamilton 15.00 40.00
PBP Buster Posey 20.00 50.00
PCC CC Sabathia 20.00 50.00
PCF Carlton Fisk 25.00 60.00
PCG Carlos Gonzalez 20.00 50.00
PCKE Clayton Kershaw 20.00 50.00
PCS Chris Sale 40.00 80.00
PDG Dwight Gooden 20.00 50.00
PDP David Price 12.50 30.00
PDPE Dustin Pedroia 15.00 40.00
PFF Freddie Freeman 12.00 30.00
PFH Felix Hernandez 20.00 50.00
PGC Gerrit Cole 40.00 80.00
PGS Giancarlo Stanton 20.00 50.00
PJF Jose Fernandez 20.00 50.00
PJR Jose Reyes 30.00 60.00
PJU Justin Upton 12.00 30.00
PJV Joey Votto 50.00 100.00
PJVE Justin Verlander 20.00 50.00
PMC Miguel Cabrera 12.00 30.00
PMH Matt Harvey 15.00 40.00
PMK Matt Kemp 12.50 30.00
PMM Manny Machado 50.00 100.00
PMMO Matt Moore 12.50 30.00
PMS Max Scherzer 12.50 30.00
PMT Mike Trout 75.00 200.00
PPF Prince Fielder 15.00 40.00
PPG Paul Goldschmidt 40.00 80.00
PSM Shelby Miller 15.00 40.00
PSS Stephen Strasburg 12.00 30.00
PTG Tony Gwynn 15.00 40.00
PTGL Tom Glavine 15.00 40.00
PTL Tim Lincecum 20.00 50.00
PTW Taijuan Walker 12.50 30.00
PWB Wade Boggs 20.00 50.00
PWM Wil Myers 15.00 40.00
PXB Xander Bogaerts 40.00 80.00
PYC Yoenis Cespedes 20.00 50.00
PYM Yadier Molina 30.00 60.00
PYP Yasiel Puig 12.00 30.00

2014 Topps Tribute Timeless Tribute Dual Autographs

STATED ODDS 1:394 HOBBY
STATED PRINT RUN 24 SER.#'d SETS
EXCHANGE DEADLINE 2/28/2017
TRASW Schmidt/Wright EXCH 90.00 150.00
TRABH Brock/Henderson 125.00 250.00
TRABP Bench/Posey 100.00 200.00
TRABR Bench/IRod 60.00 150.00
TRAGH Ham/Griffey Jr. EXCH 75.00 200.00
TRAHT Henderson/Trout 250.00 350.00
TRAJT Jackson/Trout 250.00 350.00
TRAKK Kouf/Kersh 400.00 600.00
TRART Tulowitzki/Ripken 125.00 250.00

2014 Topps Tribute Tribute Titans Relics

STATED ODDS 1:19 HOBBY
STATED PRINT RUN 99 SER.#'d SETS
TRAB Adrian Beltre 5.00 12.00
TRAC Allen Craig 4.00 10.00
TRACH Aroldis Chapman 5.00 12.00
TRAG Adrian Gonzalez 4.00 10.00
TRAJ Adam Jones 4.00 10.00
TRAM Andrew McCutchen 5.00 12.00
TRAP Albert Pujols 6.00 15.00
TRBH Bryce Harper 12.50 30.00
TRBP Buster Posey 6.00 15.00
TRCC CC Sabathia 4.00 10.00
TRCD Chris Davis 3.00 8.00
TRCG Carlos Gonzalez 4.00 10.00
TRCK Clayton Kershaw 10.00 25.00
TRCS Chris Sale 5.00 12.00
TRDF David Freese 3.00 8.00
TRDO David Ortiz 5.00 12.00
TRDP David Price 4.00 10.00
TRDPE Dustin Pedroia 10.00 25.00
TRDW David Wright 4.00 10.00
TREE Edwin Encarnacion 5.00 12.00
TREL Evan Longoria 4.00 10.00
TRFF Freddie Freeman 6.00 15.00
TRGC Gerrit Cole 8.00 20.00
TRGG Gio Gonzalez 4.00 10.00
TRJB Jose Bautista 4.00 10.00
TRJF Jose Fernandez 8.00 20.00
TRJH Jason Heyward 4.00 10.00
TRJP Jurickson Profar 4.00 10.00
TRJR Jose Reyes 4.00 10.00
TRJS Jean Segura 4.00 10.00
TRJU Justin Upton 4.00 10.00
TRJV Joey Votto 5.00 12.00
TRJVE Justin Verlander 5.00 12.00
TRMC Miguel Cabrera 12.50 30.00
TRMH Matt Harvey 4.00 10.00
TRMK Matt Kemp 4.00 10.00
TRMM Manny Machado 5.00 12.00
TRMMO Matt Moore 4.00 10.00
TRMT Mike Trout 25.00 60.00
TRMTE Mark Teixeira 4.00 10.00
TRPF Prince Fielder 4.00 10.00
TRPG Paul Goldschmidt 5.00 12.00
TRRD R.A. Dickey 4.00 10.00
TRRH Hyun-Jin Ryu 4.00 10.00
TRRHA Roy Halladay 4.00 10.00
TRRZ Ryan Zimmerman 4.00 10.00
TRSM Shelby Miller 4.00 10.00
TRSS Stephen Strasburg 5.00 12.00
TTRTT Troy Tulowitzki 5.00 12.00
TTRWM Wil Myers 3.00 8.00
TTRYP Yasiel Puig 10.00 25.00
TTRZG Zack Greinke 4.00 10.00

2014 Topps Tribute Tribute Titans Relics Blue

*BLUE: .4X TO 1X BASIC
STATED ODDS 1:37 HOBBY
STATED PRINT RUN 50 SER.#'d SETS

2014 Topps Tribute Tribute Titans Relics Green

*GREEN: .5X TO 1.2X BASIC
STATED ODDS 1:73 HOBBY
STATED PRINT RUN 25 SER.#'d SETS

2014 Topps Tribute Tribute Titans Relics Sepia

*SEPIA: .5X TO 1.2X BASIC
STATED ODDS 1:52 HOBBY
STATED PRINT RUN 35 SER.#'d SETS

2014 Topps Tribute Tribute to the Pastime Autographs

PRINTING PLATE ODDS 1:437 HOBBY
PLATE PRINT RUN 1 SET PER COLOR
BLACK-CYAN-MAGENTA-YELLOW ISSUED
NO PLATE PRICING DUE TO SCARCITY
EXCHANGE DEADLINE 2/28/2017
TPTAB Albert Belle 8.00 20.00
TPTAG Adrian Gonzalez 10.00 25.00
TPTAH Aaron Hicks 6.00 15.00
TPTAJ Adam Jones 10.00 25.00
TPTAR Anthony Rizzo 12.00 30.00
TPTBB Billy Butler 5.00 12.00
TPTBP Brandon Phillips 6.00 15.00
TPTBZ Ben Zobrist 6.00 15.00
TPTCS Chris Sale 8.00 20.00
TPTCSA Carlos Santana 6.00 15.00
TPTDC Dave Concepcion 5.00 12.00
TPTDF David Freese 5.00 12.00
TPTDG Didi Gregorius 6.00 15.00
TPTDH Derek Holland 5.00 12.00
TPTDP Dustin Pedroia 15.00 40.00
TPTDS Dave Stewart 5.00 12.00
TPTED Eric Davis 6.00 15.00
TPTEG Evan Gattis 5.00 12.00
TPTEM Edgar Martinez 6.00 15.00
TPTFF Freddie Freeman 10.00 25.00
TPTFL Fred Lynn 5.00 12.00
TPTFM Fred McGriff 10.00 25.00
TPTJC Johnny Cueto 6.00 15.00
TPTJGR Jason Grilli 5.00 12.00
TPTJR Jim Rice 6.00 15.00
TPTJS Jean Segura 6.00 15.00
TPTJSH James Shields 5.00 12.00
TPTJT Julio Teheran 6.00 15.00
TPTKM Kevin Mitchell 6.00 15.00
TPTKME Kris Medlen 6.00 15.00
TPTLL Lance Lynn 5.00 12.00
TPTLS Lee Smith 5.00 12.00
TPTMB Madison Bumgarner 40.00 80.00
TPTMMI Mike Minor 5.00 12.00
TPTMMO Matt Moore 6.00 15.00
TPTMT Mark Trumbo 5.00 12.00
TPTMW Matt Williams 6.00 15.00
TPTNG Nomar Garciaparra 10.00 25.00
TPTPC Patrick Corbin 6.00 15.00
TPTPG Paul Goldschmidt 10.00 25.00
TPTPO Paul O'Neill 10.00 25.00
TPTPS Pablo Sandoval 6.00 15.00
TPTRB Ryan Braun 6.00 15.00
TPTRZ Ryan Zimmerman 6.00 15.00
TPTSC Steve Carlton 12.00 30.00
TPTSM Shelby Miller 6.00 15.00
TPTSMA Starling Marte 6.00 15.00
TPTSP Salvador Perez 10.00 25.00
TPTTB Trevor Bauer 8.00 20.00
TPTTC Tony Cingrani 6.00 15.00
TPTTD Travis d'Arnaud 10.00 25.00
TPTTH Tim Hudson 6.00 15.00
TPTTR Tim Raines 6.00 15.00
TPTTSK Tyler Skaggs 5.00 12.00
TPTTT Troy Tulowitzki 12.00 30.00
TPTVG Vladimir Guerrero 6.00 15.00
TPTWC Will Clark 12.00 30.00
TPTWMY Wil Myers 12.00 30.00
TPTWR Wilin Rosario 5.00 12.00
TPTXB Xander Bogaerts 10.00 25.00
TPTYM Yadier Molina 30.00 80.00
TPTZW Zack Wheeler 10.00 25.00

2014 Topps Tribute Tribute to the Pastime Autographs Blue

*BLUE: .4X TO 1X BASIC
STATED ODDS 1:32 HOBBY
STATED PRINT RUN 50 SER.#'d SETS
EXCHANGE DEADLINE 2/28/2017

2014 Topps Tribute Tribute to the Pastime Autographs Green

*GREEN: .6X TO 1.5X BASIC
STATED ODDS 1:48 HOBBY
STATED PRINT RUN 25 SER.#'d SETS
EXCHANGE DEADLINE 2/28/2017
TPTGM Greg Maddux 75.00 200.00
TPTOC Orlando Cepeda 10.00 25.00
TPTPM Pedro Martinez 75.00 150.00
TPTRH Rickey Henderson 60.00 120.00
TPTRY Robin Yount 50.00 100.00
TPTSK Sandy Koufax 200.00 300.00
TPTTGW Tony Gwynn 20.00 50.00

2014 Topps Tribute Tribute to the Pastime Autographs Orange

*ORANGE: .4X TO 1X BASIC
STATED ODDS 1:39 HOBBY
STATED PRINT RUN 40 SER.#'d SETS
EXCHANGE DEADLINE 2/28/2017

2014 Topps Tribute Tribute to the Pastime Autographs Sepia

*SEPIA: .5X TO 1.2X BASIC
STATED ODDS 1:45 HOBBY
STATED PRINT RUN 35 SER.#'d SETS
EXCHANGE DEADLINE 2/28/2017

2014 Topps Tribute Tribute to the Pastime Autographs Yellow

*YELLOW: .5X TO 1.2X BASIC
STATED ODDS 1:52 HOBBY
STATED PRINT RUN 30 SER.#'d SETS
EXCHANGE DEADLINE 2/28/2017

2014 Topps Tribute Tribute to the Stars Autographs

STATED ODDS 1:51 HOBBY
STATED PRINT RUN 24 SER.#'d SETS
ALL VERSIONS EQUALLY PRICED
EXCHANGE DEADLINE 2/28/2017
TSAAR Anthony Rizzo 20.00 50.00
TSABB Billy Butler 10.00 25.00
TSABH Billy Hamilton 10.00 25.00
TSABH1 Billy Hamilton 10.00 25.00
TSABH2 Billy Hamilton 10.00 25.00
TSABH3 Billy Hamilton 10.00 25.00
TSABP Brandon Phillips 20.00 50.00
TSADM Dale Murphy 20.00 50.00
TSADS Duke Snider 10.00 25.00
TSADS1 Duke Snider 10.00 25.00
TSADS2 Duke Snider 10.00 25.00
TSAEG Evan Gattis 15.00 40.00
TSAEJ Erik Johnson 10.00 25.00
TSAEJ1 Erik Johnson 10.00 25.00
TSAEL Evan Longoria 15.00 40.00
TSAEL1 Evan Longoria 15.00 40.00
TSAFF Freddie Freeman 15.00 40.00
TSAFJ Fergie Jenkins 12.50 30.00
TSAFJ1 Fergie Jenkins 12.50 30.00
TSAFJ2 Fergie Jenkins 12.50 30.00
TSAFJ3 Fergie Jenkins 12.50 30.00
TSAGC Gary Carter 20.00 50.00
TSAGC1 Gary Carter 20.00 50.00
TSAGC2 Gary Carter 20.00 50.00
TSAGC3 Gary Carter 20.00 50.00
TSAGC4 Gary Carter 20.00 50.00
TSAGC5 Gary Carter 20.00 50.00
TSAGC6 Gary Carter 20.00 50.00
TSAGG Goose Gossage 12.50 30.00
TSAGG1 Goose Gossage 12.50 30.00
TSAGK George Kell 15.00 40.00
TSAGK1 George Kell 15.00 40.00
TSAGM Greg Maddux 90.00 150.00
TSAHI Hisashi Iwakuma 20.00 50.00
TSAHI1 Hisashi Iwakuma 20.00 50.00
TSAHI2 Hisashi Iwakuma 20.00 50.00
TSAJB Jose Bautista 15.00 40.00
TSAJB1 Jose Bautista 15.00 40.00
TSAJB2 Jose Bautista 15.00 40.00
TSAJP Johnny Podres 15.00 40.00
TSAJP1 Johnny Podres 15.00 40.00
TSAJW Jered Weaver 10.00 25.00
TSAJW1 Jered Weaver 10.00 25.00
TSAJW2 Jered Weaver 10.00 25.00
TSAMA Mariano Rivera 200.00 300.00
TSAMC Miguel Cabrera 75.00 150.00
TSAMM Mike Minor 10.00 25.00
TSAMMO Matt Moore 10.00 25.00
TSAMT Mike Trout 150.00 250.00
TSANC Nick Castellanos 12.00 30.00
TSANC1 Nick Castellanos 12.00 30.00
TSANC2 Nick Castellanos 12.00 30.00
TSAOS Ozzie Smith 30.00 60.00
TSARC Rod Carew 15.00 40.00
TSARC1 Rod Carew 15.00 40.00
TSASC Starlin Castro 10.00 25.00
TSASC1 Starlin Castro 10.00 25.00
TSASK Sandy Koufax 200.00 300.00
TSATB Trevor Bauer 10.00 25.00
TSATC Tony Cingrani 10.00 25.00
TSATD Travis d'Arnaud 10.00 25.00
TSATD1 Travis d'Arnaud 10.00 25.00
TSATG Tom Glavine 20.00 50.00
TSATG1 Tom Glavine 20.00 50.00
TSATR Tim Raines 10.00 25.00
TSATW Taijuan Walker 15.00 40.00
TSATW1 Taijuan Walker 15.00 40.00
TSATW2 Taijuan Walker 15.00 40.00
TSAWB Wade Boggs 50.00 100.00
TSAWM Wil Myers 15.00 40.00
TSAXB Xander Bogaerts 60.00 120.00
TSAXB1 Xander Bogaerts 60.00 120.00
TSAZW Zack Wheeler 12.50 30.00

2014 Topps Tribute Tribute to the Throne Relics

STATED ODDS 1:24 HOBBY
STATED PRINT RUN 99 SER.#'d SETS
EXCHANGE DEADLINE 2/28/2017
THRONEAD Andre Dawson 8.00 20.00
THRONEAK Al Kaline EXCH 10.00 25.00
THRONEBF Bob Feller 10.00 25.00
THRONEBR Babe Ruth 75.00 150.00
THRONECF Carlton Fisk 8.00 20.00
THRONECR Cal Ripken Jr. 10.00 25.00
THRONEDM Don Mattingly 10.00 25.00
THRONEDMU Dale Murphy 10.00 25.00
THRONEDS Don Sutton 8.00 20.00
THRONEEB Ernie Banks 10.00 25.00
THRONEEM Eddie Mathews 10.00 25.00
THRONEEMU Eddie Murray 8.00 20.00
THRONEFJ Fergie Jenkins 8.00 20.00
THRONEGB George Brett 10.00 25.00
THRONEHA Hank Aaron 12.00 30.00
THRONEHK Harmon Killebrew 10.00 25.00
THRONEIR Ivan Rodriguez 8.00 20.00
THRONEJB Johnny Bench 15.00 40.00
THRONEJD Joe DiMaggio 40.00 100.00
THRONEJR Jackie Robinson 20.00 50.00
THRONEKG Ken Griffey Jr. 10.00 25.00
THRONELB Lou Brock 12.00 30.00
THRONEMS Mike Schmidt 12.00 30.00
THRONEOC Orlando Cepeda 10.00 25.00
THRONEPN Phil Niekro 8.00 20.00
THRONERC Roberto Clemente 30.00 60.00
THRONERCA Rod Carew 8.00 20.00
THRONERH Rickey Henderson 10.00 25.00
THRONERJ Reggie Jackson 8.00 20.00
THRONERJO Randy Johnson 10.00 25.00
THRONERY Robin Yount 10.00 25.00
THRONESM Stan Musial 10.00 25.00
THRONETC Ty Cobb 20.00 50.00
THRONETG Tom Glavine 8.00 20.00
THRONETGW Tony Gwynn 10.00 25.00
THRONETW Ted Williams 20.00 50.00
THRONEWB Wade Boggs 8.00 20.00
THRONEWBO Wade Boggs 8.00 20.00
THRONEWM Willie Mays 15.00 40.00
THRONEWMC Willie McCovey 8.00 20.00
THRONEYB Yogi Berra 10.00 25.00

2014 Topps Tribute Tribute to the Throne Relics Blue

*BLUE: .4X TO 1X BASIC
STATED ODDS 1:47 HOBBY
STATED PRINT RUN 50 SER.#'d SETS
EXCHANGE DEADLINE 2/28/2017

2014 Topps Tribute Tribute to the Throne Relics Green

*GREEN: .5X TO 1.2X BASIC
STATED ODDS 1:93 HOBBY
STATED PRINT RUN 25 SER.#'d SETS
EXCHANGE DEADLINE 2/28/2017

2014 Topps Tribute Tribute to the Throne Relics Sepia

*SEPIA: .5X TO 1.2X BASIC
STATED ODDS 1:66 HOBBY
STATED PRINT RUN 35 SER.#'d SETS
EXCHANGE DEADLINE 2/28/2017

2014 Topps Tribute Tribute Traditions Autographs

PRINTING PLATE ODDS 1:580 HOBBY
PLATE PRINT RUN 1 SET PER COLOR
BLACK-CYAN-MAGENTA-YELLOW ISSUED
NO PLATE PRICING DUE TO SCARCITY
EXCHANGE DEADLINE 2/28/2017
TTAB Albert Belle 5.00 12.00
TTAG Adrian Gonzalez 8.00 20.00
TTAH Aaron Hicks 6.00 15.00
TTAJ Adam Jones 10.00 25.00
TTAR Anthony Rizzo 20.00 50.00
TTBB Billy Butler 5.00 12.00
TTBP Brandon Phillips 6.00 15.00
TTBZ Ben Zobrist 6.00 15.00
TTCS Chris Sale 10.00 25.00
TTCSA Carlos Santana 6.00 15.00
TTDC Dave Concepcion 10.00 25.00
TTDF David Freese 5.00 12.00
TTDG Didi Gregorius 6.00 15.00
TTDH Derek Holland 5.00 12.00
TTDP Dustin Pedroia 15.00 40.00
TTDS Dave Stewart 5.00 12.00
TTED Eric Davis 10.00 25.00
TTEG Evan Gattis 5.00 12.00
TTEM Edgar Martinez 6.00 15.00
TTFL Fred Lynn 5.00 12.00
TTFM Fred McGriff 15.00 40.00
TTGS Giancarlo Stanton 40.00 100.00
TTIR Ivan Rodriguez 12.00 30.00
TTJC Johnny Cueto 6.00 15.00
TTJGR Jason Grilli 6.00 15.00
TTJHE Jason Heyward 6.00 15.00
TTJM Juan Marichal 8.00 20.00
TTJP Jim Palmer 12.00 30.00
TTJR Jim Rice 6.00 15.00
TTJS John Smoltz 15.00 40.00
TTJSE Jean Segura 6.00 15.00
TTJSH James Shields 5.00 12.00
TTJU Justin Upton 6.00 15.00
TTKL Kenny Lofton 12.00 30.00
TTKM Kevin Mitchell 5.00 12.00
TTKME Kris Medlen 6.00 15.00
TTLL Lance Lynn 5.00 12.00
TTLS Lee Smith 5.00 12.00
TTMB Madison Bumgarner 40.00 50.00
TTMMI Mike Minor 5.00 12.00
TTMMO Matt Moore 6.00 15.00
TTMTR Mark Trumbo 5.00 12.00
TTMW Matt Williams 6.00 15.00
TTPC Patrick Corbin 6.00 15.00
TTPG Paul Goldschmidt 10.00 25.00
TTPM Paul Molitor 12.00 30.00
TTPO Paul O'Neill 10.00 25.00
TTRP Rafael Palmeiro 10.00 25.00
TTRZ Ryan Zimmerman 10.00 25.00
TTSM Starling Marte 6.00 15.00
TTSP Salvador Perez 10.00 25.00
TTTB Trevor Bauer 6.00 15.00
TTTC Tony Cingrani 6.00 15.00
TTTD Travis d'Arnaud 10.00 25.00
TTTR Tim Raines 6.00 15.00
TTTS Tyler Skaggs 5.00 12.00
TTWC Will Clark 12.00 30.00
TTWM Wil Myers 5.00 12.00
TTWMI Will Middlebrooks 5.00 12.00
TTWR Wilin Rosario 5.00 12.00
TTZW Zack Wheeler 10.00 25.00

2014 Topps Tribute Tribute Traditions Autographs Blue

*BLUE: .4X TO 1X BASIC
STATED ODDS 1:32 HOBBY
STATED PRINT RUN 50 SER.#'d SETS
EXCHANGE DEADLINE 2/28/2017

2014 Topps Tribute Tribute Traditions Autographs Green

*GREEN: .6X TO 1.5X BASIC
STATED ODDS 1:52 HOBBY
STATED PRINT RUN 25 SER.#'d SETS
EXCHANGE DEADLINE 2/28/2017
TTCJ Chipper Jones 100.00 200.00
TTJB Johnny Bench 50.00 120.00
TTKG Ken Griffey Jr. 125.00 250.00
TTMC Matt Cain 12.00 30.00
TTMCA Miguel Cabrera 75.00 150.00
TTMM Manny Machado 25.00 60.00
TTMMU Mike Mussina 20.00 50.00
TTNR Nolan Ryan 125.00 250.00
TTRJ Randy Johnson 75.00 150.00

2014 Topps Tribute Tribute Traditions Autographs Orange

*ORANGE: .4X TO 1X BASIC
STATED ODDS 1:39 HOBBY
STATED PRINT RUN 40 SER.#'d SETS
EXCHANGE DEADLINE 2/28/2017

2014 Topps Tribute Tribute Traditions Autographs Sepia

*SEPIA: .5X TO 1.2X BASIC
STATED ODDS 1:45 HOBBY
STATED PRINT RUN 35 SER.#'d SETS
EXCHANGE DEADLINE 2/28/2017

2014 Topps Tribute Tribute Traditions Autographs Yellow

*YELLOW: .5X TO 1.2X BASIC
STATED ODDS 1:52 HOBBY
STATED PRINT RUN 30 SER.#'d SETS
EXCHANGE DEADLINE 2/28/2017

2015 Topps Tribute

PRINTING PLATE RANDOMLY INSERTED
PLATE PRINT RUN 1 SET PER COLOR
NO PLATE PRICING DUE TO SCARCITY
1 Mike Trout 10.00 25.00
2 Rod Carew 1.50 4.00
3 Yadier Molina 2.00 5.00
4 Chris Sale 2.00 5.00
5 Nomar Garciaparra 1.50 4.00
6 Manny Machado 2.00 5.00
7 Roberto Alomar 1.50 4.00
8 Javier Baez RC 10.00 25.00
9 George Springer 1.50 4.00
10 Madison Bumgarner 1.50 4.00
11 Bryce Harper 3.00 8.00
12 Steve Carlton 1.50 4.00
13 Joe DiMaggio 4.00 10.00
14 Ted Williams 4.00 10.00
15 Albert Pujols 2.50 6.00
16 Joe Morgan 1.50 4.00
17 Tony Gwynn 2.00 5.00
18 Corey Kluber 1.50 4.00
19 Mike Piazza 2.00 5.00
20 Andre Dawson 1.50 4.00
21 Lou Brock 1.50 4.00
22 Jackie Robinson 2.00 5.00
23 Wade Boggs 1.50 4.00
24 Ernie Banks 2.00 5.00
25 Jose Abreu 2.00 5.00
26 Freddie Freeman 2.50 6.00
27 Nelson Cruz 2.00 5.00
28 Adrian Beltre 2.00 5.00
29 Masahiro Tanaka 1.50 4.00
30 Maikel Franco RC 1.50 4.00
31 Josh Donaldson 1.50 4.00
32 Bo Jackson 2.00 5.00
33 David Ortiz 2.00 5.00
34 Roger Clemens 2.50 6.00
35 Carlton Fisk 1.50 4.00
36 Carlos Gonzalez 1.50 4.00
37 Ian Desmond 1.25 3.00
38 Carlos Gomez 1.25 3.00
39 Stephen Strasburg 2.00 5.00
40 Eddie Murray 1.50 4.00
41 Felix Hernandez 1.50 4.00
42 Mariano Rivera 2.50 6.00
43 Reggie Jackson 1.50 4.00
44 David Price 1.50 4.00
45 Jorge Soler RC 6.00 15.00
46 Anthony Rizzo 3.00 8.00
47 Ozzie Smith 2.50 6.00
48 David Wright 1.50 4.00
49 Jonathan Lucroy 1.50 4.00
50 Clayton Kershaw 4.00 10.00
51 Joc Pederson RC 8.00 20.00
52 Michael Wacha 1.50 4.00
53 Johnny Bench 2.00 5.00
54 Victor Martinez 1.50 4.00
55 Mark McGwire 3.00 8.00
56 Dale Murphy 2.00 5.00
57 Rusney Castillo RC 1.50 4.00
58 Jose Fernandez 2.00 5.00
59 Buster Posey 2.50 6.00
60 Justin Upton 1.50 4.00
61 Dustin Pedroia 2.00 5.00
62 Max Scherzer 2.00 5.00
63 Robin Yount 2.00 5.00
64 Tom Seaver 1.50 4.00
65 Roger Maris 2.00 5.00
66 Justin Verlander 2.00 5.00
67 Ty Cobb 3.00 8.00
68 Adam Wainwright 1.50 4.00
69 Jose Altuve 1.50 4.00
70 Sandy Koufax 4.00 10.00
71 Cal Ripken Jr. 6.00 15.00
72 Craig Kimbrel 1.50 4.00
73 Jose Bautista 1.50 4.00
74 Jacoby Ellsbury 1.50 4.00
75 Miguel Cabrera 2.00 5.00
76 Andrew McCutchen 2.00 5.00
77 Yoenis Cespedes 1.50 4.00
78 Ryan Braun 1.50 4.00
79 Jose Reyes 1.50 4.00
80 Yu Darvish 2.00 5.00
81 Adam Jones 1.50 4.00
82 Nolan Ryan 5.00 12.00
83 Jim Palmer 1.50 4.00
84 Edwin Encarnacion 2.00 5.00
85 Jim Rice 1.50 4.00
86 George Brett 4.00 10.00
87 Hunter Pence 1.50 4.00
88 Lou Gehrig 4.00 10.00
89 Yasiel Puig 2.00 5.00
90 Mike Schmidt 3.00 8.00
91 Jon Lester 1.50 4.00
92 Paul Goldschmidt 2.00 5.00
93 Tom Glavine 1.50 4.00
94 Luis Aparicio 1.50 4.00
95 Gregory Polanco 1.50 4.00
96 Whitey Ford 1.50 4.00
97 Billy Hamilton 1.50 4.00
98 Robinson Cano 1.50 4.00
99 Evan Longoria 1.50 4.00
100 Babe Ruth 5.00 12.00

2015 Topps Tribute Black

*BLACK: 1.5X TO 4X BASIC
RANDOM INSERTS IN PACKS
STATED PRINT RUN 50 SER.#'d SETS

2015 Topps Tribute Green

*GREEN: .75X TO 2X BASIC
RANDOM INSERTS IN PACKS
STATED PRINT RUN 99 SER.#'d SETS

2015 Topps Tribute Diamond Cuts Jerseys

RANDOM INSERTS IN PACKS
STATED PRINT RUN 199 SER.#'d SETS
DCAC Aroldis Chapman 4.00 10.00
DCAG Adrian Gonzalez 3.00 8.00
DCAGO Alex Gordon 3.00 8.00
DCAM Andrew McCutchen 4.00 10.00
DCAP Albert Pujols 6.00 15.00
DCAW Adam Wainwright 3.00 8.00
DCBHA Billy Hamilton 3.00 8.00
DCBP Buster Posey 5.00 12.00
DCCC CC Sabathia 3.00 8.00
DCCG Carlos Gonzalez 3.00 8.00
DCCK Clayton Kershaw 8.00 20.00
DCCS Chris Sale 4.00 10.00
DCDO David Ortiz 4.00 10.00
DCDW David Wright 3.00 8.00
DCFF Freddie Freeman 5.00 12.00
DCGC Gerrit Cole 4.00 10.00
DCGP Gregory Polanco 3.00 8.00
DCGS Giancarlo Stanton 4.00 10.00
DCHR Hanley Ramirez 3.00 8.00
DCIK Ian Kinsler 3.00 8.00
DCJS Jorge Soler 4.00 10.00
DCJV Justin Verlander 4.00 10.00
DCJVO Joey Votto 4.00 10.00
DCKU Koji Uehara 2.50 6.00
DCMC Miguel Cabrera 4.00 10.00
DCMS Max Scherzer 4.00 10.00
DCPS Pablo Sandoval 3.00 8.00
DCRB Ryan Braun 3.00 8.00
DCSG Sonny Gray 3.00 8.00
DCTT Troy Tulowitzki 4.00 10.00
DCYD Yu Darvish 4.00 10.00
DCYM Yadier Molina 4.00 10.00
DCYP Yasiel Puig 4.00 10.00
DCYV Yordano Ventura 3.00 8.00
DCZG Zack Greinke 3.00 8.00

2015 Topps Tribute Diamond Cuts Jerseys Black

*BLACK: .4X TO 1X BASIC
RANDOM INSERTS IN PACKS
STATED PRINT RUN 50 SER.#'d SETS

2015 Topps Tribute Diamond Cuts Jerseys Gold Patch

*GOLD: 1.2X TO 3X BASIC
RANDOM INSERTS IN PACKS
STATED PRINT RUN 25 SER.#'d SETS

2015 Topps Tribute Diamond Cuts Jerseys Orange

*ORANGE: .4X TO 1X BASIC
RANDOM INSERTS IN PACKS
STATED PRINT RUN 75 SER.#'d SETS

2015 Topps Tribute Foundations of Greatness Autographs

RANDOM INSERTS IN PACKS
STATED PRINT RUN 89 SER.#'d SETS
EXCHANGE DEADLINE 2/28/2018
PRICING FOR NON-DAMAGED AUTOS
THENAD Andre Dawson 10.00 25.00
THENDC David Cone 8.00 20.00
THENDE Dennis Eckersley 10.00 25.00
THENDM Dale Murphy 20.00 50.00
THENEM Edgar Martinez 10.00 25.00
THENFM Fred McGriff 10.00 25.00
THENGP Gregory Polanco 10.00 25.00
THENJA Jose Abreu 8.00 20.00
THENJG Juan Gonzalez 10.00 25.00
THENJM Juan Marichal 12.00 30.00
THENJR Jim Rice 10.00 25.00
THENLB Lou Brock 20.00 50.00
THENLG Luis Gonzalez 8.00 20.00
THENOC Orlando Cepeda 10.00 25.00
THENOS Ozzie Smith 20.00 50.00
THENPN Phil Niekro 12.00 30.00
THENPO Paul O'Neill 8.00 20.00
THENSC Steve Carlton 15.00 40.00
THENSG Sonny Gray 10.00 25.00

2015 Topps Tribute Foundations of Greatness Autographs Black

*BLACK: .4X TO 1X BASIC
RANDOM INSERTS IN PACKS
STATED PRINT RUN 50 SER.#'d SETS
EXCHANGE DEADLINE 2/28/2018
PRICING FOR NON-DAMAGED AUTOS
THENCF Carlton Fisk 25.00 60.00
THENCK Clayton Kershaw 100.00 200.00
THENRC Rod Carew 15.00 40.00

2015 Topps Tribute Foundations of Greatness Autographs Gold

*GOLD: .5X TO 1.2X BASIC
RANDOM INSERTS IN PACKS
STATED PRINT RUN 25 SER.#'d SETS
EXCHANGE DEADLINE 2/28/2018
PRICING FOR NON-DAMAGED AUTOS
THENAG Adrian Gonzalez 12.00 30.00
THENCK Clayton Kershaw 125.00 250.00
THENNR Nolan Ryan 50.00 125.00

2015 Topps Tribute Framed Autographs

RANDOM INSERTS IN PACKS
STATED PRINT RUN 189 SER.#'d SETS
EXCHANGE DEADLINE 2/28/2018
PRICING FOR NON-DAMAGED AUTOS
TAAC Allen Craig 6.00 15.00
TAAD Andre Dawson 10.00 25.00
TAAJ Adam Jones 6.00 15.00
TAAR Anthony Rizzo 15.00 40.00
TAARA Anthony Ranaudo 6.00 15.00
TACA Chris Archer 6.00 15.00
TACB Craig Biggio 12.00 30.00
TACC Carlos Correa/150 50.00 120.00
TACH Chase Headley 12.00 30.00
TACS Chris Sale 10.00 25.00
TADC David Cone 10.00 25.00
TADE Dennis Eckersley 8.00 20.00
TADMU Dale Murphy 8.00 20.00
TADN Daniel Norris 15.00 40.00
TADPO Dalton Pompey 20.00 50.00
TAFF Freddie Freeman 10.00 25.00
TAFL Francisco Lindor 50.00 120.00
TAFM Fred McGriff 10.00 25.00
TAFV Fernando Valenzuela 10.00 25.00
TAGP Gregory Polanco 10.00 25.00
TAGSP George Springer 12.00 30.00
TAJA Jose Abreu 10.00 25.00
TAJB Javier Baez 20.00 50.00
TAJBA Javier Baez 20.00 50.00
TAJCA Jose Canseco 12.00 30.00
TAJD Josh Donaldson 10.00 25.00
TAJF Jose Fernandez 20.00 50.00
TAJG Juan Gonzalez 6.00 15.00
TAJM Juan Marichal 12.00 30.00
TAJOS Jorge Soler 25.00 60.00
TAJP Joc Pederson 25.00 60.00
TAJPE Joc Pederson 25.00 60.00
TAJR Jim Rice 10.00 25.00
TAJS Jon Singleton 10.00 25.00
TAJSM John Smoltz 10.00 25.00
TAJSO Jorge Soler 25.00 60.00
TAKU Koji Uehara 12.00 30.00
TAKW Kolten Wong 6.00 12.00
TALB Lou Brock 12.00 30.00
TALG Luis Gonzalez 6.00 15.00
TAMA Matt Adams 10.00 25.00
TAMC Matt Carpenter 10.00 25.00
TAMN Mike Napoli 6.00 15.00
TAMS Max Scherzer 15.00 40.00
TAMTA Michael Taylor 8.00 20.00
TAMW Michael Wacha 10.00 25.00
TAOC Orlando Cepeda 15.00 40.00
TAPG Paul Goldschmidt 12.00 30.00
TAPN Phil Niekro 10.00 25.00
TARUC Rusney Castillo 8.00 20.00
TARUS Rusney Castillo 8.00 20.00
TASG Sonny Gray 10.00 25.00
TATW Taijuan Walker 6.00 15.00
TAVG Vladimir Guerrero 10.00 25.00
TAYC Yoenis Cespedes 10.00 25.00
TAYVE Yordano Ventura 10.00 25.00

2015 Topps Tribute Framed Autographs Black

*BLACK: .4X TO 1X BASIC
RANDOM INSERTS IN PACKS
STATED PRINT RUN 50 SER.#'d SETS
EXCHANGE DEADLINE 2/28/2018
PRICING FOR NON-DAMAGED AUTOS

2015 Topps Tribute Framed Autographs Gold

*GOLD: .6X TO 1.5X BASIC
RANDOM INSERTS IN PACKS
STATED PRINT RUN 25 SER.#'d SETS
EXCHANGE DEADLINE 2/28/2018
PRICING FOR NON-DAMAGED AUTOS

2015 Topps Tribute Framed Autographs Green

*GREEN: .4X TO 1X BASIC
RANDOM INSERTS IN PACKS
STATED PRINT RUN 99 SER.#'d SETS

EXCHANGE DEADLINE 2/28/2018
PRICING FOR NON-DAMAGED AUTOS

2015 Topps Tribute Framed Autographs Orange

*ORANGE: X TO X BASIC
RANDOM INSERTS IN PACKS
STATED PRINT RUN 75 SER.#'d SETS
EXCHANGE DEADLINE 2/28/2018
PRICING FOR NON-DAMAGED AUTOS

2015 Topps Tribute Prime Patches

RANDOM INSERTS IN PACKS
STATED PRINT RUN 45 SER.#'d SETS

PPBP Buster Posey	20.00	50.00
PPCJ Chipper Jones	30.00	80.00
PPCK Clayton Kershaw	30.00	80.00
PPCR Cal Ripken Jr.	30.00	80.00
PPDP Dustin Pedroia	25.00	60.00
PPDW David Wright	12.00	30.00
PPEL Evan Longoria	12.00	30.00
PPFF Freddie Freeman	20.00	50.00
PPFT Frank Thomas	25.00	60.00
PPGM Greg Maddux	20.00	50.00
PPGS Giancarlo Stanton	15.00	40.00
PPJE Jacoby Ellsbury	12.00	30.00
PPJV Joey Votto	25.00	60.00
PPMC Miguel Cabrera	20.00	50.00
PPMM Mark McGwire	25.00	60.00
PPMP Mike Piazza	25.00	60.00
PPMTA Masahiro Tanaka	12.00	30.00
PPRB Ryan Braun	12.00	30.00
PPRCA Rod Carew	12.00	30.00
PPRCL Roger Clemens	20.00	50.00
PPRH Rickey Henderson	15.00	40.00
PPRJ Randy Johnson	15.00	40.00
PPROC Robinson Cano	12.00	30.00
PPRP Rafael Palmeiro	12.00	30.00
PPVG Vladimir Guerrero	12.00	30.00
PPWB Wade Boggs	12.00	30.00
PPYD Yu Darvish	15.00	40.00
PPYP Yasiel Puig	15.00	40.00

2015 Topps Tribute Relics

RANDOM INSERTS IN PACKS
STATED PRINT RUN 199 SER.#'d SETS

TRAD Andre Dawson	6.00	15.00
TRAM Andrew McCutchen	10.00	25.00
TRAP Albert Pujols	6.00	15.00
TRAW Adam Wainwright	4.00	10.00
TRBP Buster Posey	12.00	30.00
TRCB Craig Biggio	4.00	10.00
TRCK Clayton Kershaw	4.00	10.00
TRCR Cal Ripken Jr.	15.00	40.00
TRDO David Ortiz	6.00.	15.00
TRDP Dustin Pedroia	8.00	20.00
TRDW David Wright	4.00	10.00
TREL Evan Longoria	4.00	10.00
TRFF Freddie Freeman	6.00	15.00
TRFT Frank Thomas	10.00	25.00
TRGP Gregory Polanco	6.00	15.00
TRGS Giancarlo Stanton	5.00	12.00
TRHR Hanley Ramirez	4.00	10.00
TRJA Jose Abreu	5.00	12.00
TRJB Johnny Bench	5.00	12.00
TRJV Justin Verlander	6.00	15.00
TRKG Ken Griffey Jr.	15.00	40.00
TRMC Miguel Cabrera	5.00	12.00
TRMP Mike Piazza	10.00	25.00
TRMS Mike Schmidt	10.00	25.00
TRMSC Max Scherzer	5.00	12.00
TRMT Masahiro Tanaka	15.00	40.00
TRNR Nolan Ryan	15.00	40.00
TROS Ozzie Smith	10.00	25.00
TRRC Roger Clemens	6.00	15.00
TRRCA Rod Carew	4.00	10.00
TRRH Rickey Henderson	8.00	20.00
TRRJ Randy Johnson	8.00	20.00
TRRJA Reggie Jackson	8.00	20.00
TRRS Ryne Sandberg	10.00	25.00
TRRY Robin Yount	6.00	15.00
TRSS Stephen Strasburg	5.00	12.00
TRTT Troy Tulowitzki	5.00	12.00

2015 Topps Tribute Relics Black

*BLACK: .4X TO 1X BASIC
RANDOM INSERTS IN PACKS
STATED PRINT RUN 50 SER.#'d SETS

2015 Topps Tribute Relics Gold

*GOLD: 1.2X TO 3X BASIC
RANDOM INSERTS IN PACKS
STATED PRINT RUN 25 SER.#'d SETS

2015 Topps Tribute Relics Green

*GREEN: .4X TO 1X BASIC
RANDOM INSERTS IN PACKS
STATED PRINT RUN 150 SER.#'d SETS

2015 Topps Tribute Relics Orange

*ORANGE: .4X TO 1X BASIC
RANDOM INSERTS IN PACKS
STATED PRINT RUN 75 SER.#'d SETS

2015 Topps Tribute Rightful Recognition Autographs

RANDOM INSERTS IN PACKS
STATED PRINT RUN 89 SER.#'d SETS
EXCHANGE DEADLINE 2/28/2018
PRICING FOR NON-DAMAGED AUTOS

NOWAC Allen Craig	8.00	20.00
NOWAD Andre Dawson	10.00	25.00
NOWDC David Cone	10.00	25.00
NOWDE Dennis Eckersley	10.00	25.00
NOWDM Dale Murphy	10.00	25.00
NOWEM Edgar Martinez	10.00	25.00
NOWFM Fred McGriff	10.00	25.00
NOWGP Gregory Polanco	15.00	40.00
NOWJG Juan Gonzalez	10.00	25.00
NOWJM Juan Marichal	12.00	30.00
NOWJR Jim Rice	10.00	25.00
NOWLB Lou Brock	20.00	50.00
NOWLG Luis Gonzalez	8.00	20.00
NOWOC Orlando Cepeda	10.00	25.00
NOWOS Ozzie Smith	25.00	60.00
NOWPN Phil Niekro	12.00	30.00
NOWPO Paul O'Neill	15.00	40.00
NOWSC Steve Carlton	10.00	25.00
NOWSG Sonny Gray	10.00	25.00

2015 Topps Tribute Rightful Recognition Autographs Black

*BLACK: .4X TO 1X BASIC
RANDOM INSERTS IN PACKS
STATED PRINT RUN 50 SER.#'d SETS
EXCHANGE DEADLINE 2/28/2018
PRICING FOR NON-DAMAGED AUTOS

2015 Topps Tribute Rightful Recognition Autographs Gold

*GOLD: .5X TO 1.2X BASIC
RANDOM INSERTS IN PACKS
STATED PRINT RUN 25 SER.#'d SETS
EXCHANGE DEADLINE 2/28/2018
PRICING FOR NON-DAMAGED AUTOS

2015 Topps Tribute To The Victors Die Cut Autographs

RANDOM INSERTS IN PACKS
STATED PRINT RUN 30 SER.#'d SETS
EXCHANGE DEADLINE 2/28/2018
PRICING FOR NON-DAMAGED AUTOS

TTVCJ Chipper Jones	60.00	150.00
TTVDC David Cone	20.00	50.00
TTVDEC Dennis Eckersley	25.00	60.00
TTVFV Fernando Valenzuela	25.00	60.00
TTVHA Hank Aaron	200.00	300.00
TTVJB Johnny Bench	40.00	100.00
TTVJP Jim Palmer	40.00	100.00
TTVJPO Jorge Posada	40.00	100.00
TTVLB Lou Brock	30.00	80.00
TTVLG Luis Gonzalez	20.00	50.00
TTVMM Mark McGwire	200.00	300.00
TTVMR Mariano Rivera	100.00	250.00
TTVMS Mike Schmidt	100.00	200.00
TTVOC Orlando Cepeda	25.00	60.00
TTVOH Orlando Hernandez	25.00	60.00
TTVOS Ozzie Smith	20.00	50.00
TTVPM Pedro Martinez	20.00	50.00
TTVRA Roberto Alomar	30.00	80.00
TTVRJO Randy Johnson	125.00	250.00
TTVTS Tom Seaver	50.00	120.00

2016 Topps Tribute

PRINTING PLATE ODDS 1:185 HOBBY
PLATE PRINT RUN 1 SET PER COLOR
NO PLATE PRICING DUE TO SCARCITY

1 Mike Trout	5.00	12.00
2 Willie Stargell	.75	2.00
3 Chris Sale	1.00	2.50
4 Kris Bryant	1.25	3.00
5 David Price	.75	2.00
6 Rafael Palmeiro	.75	2.00
7 Paul Goldschmidt	1.00	2.50
8 Willie Mays	2.00	5.00
9 Ian Kinsler	.75	2.00
10 George Brett	2.00	5.00
11 Buster Posey	1.25	3.00
12 Carlos Correa	1.00	2.50
13 Joey Votto	1.00	2.50
14 Randy Johnson	1.00	2.50
15 Goose Gossage	.75	2.00
16 Doc Gooden	.60	1.50
17 Nolan Arenado	1.25	3.00
18 Zack Greinke	.75	2.00
19 David Peralta	.60	1.50
20 Michael Brantley	.75	2.00
21 Paul Molitor	1.00	2.50
22 Satchel Paige	1.00	2.50
23 Yadier Molina	1.00	2.50
24 Sonny Gray	.75	2.00
25 Babe Ruth	2.50	6.00
26 Felix Hernandez	.75	2.00
27 Larry Doby	.75	2.00
28 Bo Jackson	1.00	2.50
29 Cal Ripken Jr.	3.00	8.00
30 Warren Spahn	.75	2.00
31 Ralph Kiner	.75	2.00
32 Dee Gordon	.60	1.50
33 Wade Davis	.60	1.50
34 Trevor Rosenthal	.75	2.00
35 Adrian Gonzalez	.75	2.00
36 Jake Arrieta	.75	2.00
37 Tony Perez	.75	2.00
38 Gerrit Cole	1.00	2.50
39 Bryce Harper	1.50	4.00
40 Bert Blyleven	.75	2.00
41 Xander Bogaerts	1.00	2.50
42 Bobby Doerr	.75	2.00
43 Andrew McCutchen	1.00	2.50
44 Jose Abreu	1.00	2.50
45 Phil Rizzuto	.75	2.00
46 Matt Kemp	.75	2.00
47 Billy Williams	.75	2.00
48 David Ortiz	1.00	2.50
49 Ted Williams	2.00	5.00
50 Sandy Koufax	2.00	5.00
51 Albert Pujols	1.25	3.00
52 Jacob deGrom	1.00	2.50
53 Anthony Rizzo	1.50	4.00
54 Jose Bautista	.75	2.00
55 Eddie Murray	.75	2.00
56 Catfish Hunter	.75	2.00
57 Brooks Robinson	.75	2.00
58 Miguel Cabrera	1.00	2.50
59 Carlos Martinez	.75	2.00
60 Justin Upton	.75	2.00
61 Manny Machado	1.00	2.50
62 Wade Boggs	.75	2.00
63 Eddie Mathews	1.00	2.50
64 Adam Jones	.75	2.00
65 Hoyt Wilhelm	.75	2.00
66 Rollie Fingers	.75	2.00
67 Robin Roberts	.75	2.00
68 Stan Musial	1.50	4.00
69 Harmon Killebrew	1.00	2.50
70 Whitey Ford	.75	2.00
71 Chris Archer	.60	1.50
72 Bob Feller	.75	2.00
73 Honus Wagner	1.00	2.50
74 Josh Donaldson	.75	2.00
75 Bruce Sutter	.75	2.00
76 Jim Bunning	.75	2.00
77 Paul O'Neill	.75	2.00
78 Johnny Bench	1.00	2.50
79 Nelson Cruz	1.00	2.50
80 Dellin Betances	.75	2.00
81 Jim Palmer	.75	2.00
82 Dallas Keuchel	.75	2.00
83 Yoenis Cespedes	1.00	2.50
84 Max Scherzer	1.00	2.50
85 J.D. Martinez	1.00	2.50
86 Salvador Perez	.75	2.00
87 Matt Carpenter	1.00	2.50
88 Mark Teixeira	.75	2.00
89 Madison Bumgarner	.75	2.00
90 Clayton Kershaw	2.00	5.00

2016 Topps Tribute Green

*GREEN: 1X TO 2.5X BASIC
STATED ODDS 1:8 HOBBY
STATED PRINT RUN 99 SER.#'d SETS

1 Mike Trout	6.00	15.00

2016 Topps Tribute Purple

*PURPLE: 2X TO 5X BASIC
STATED ODDS 1:15 HOBBY
STATED PRINT RUN 50 SER.#'d SETS

2016 Topps Tribute '16 Rookies

STATED ODDS 1:24 HOBBY
PRINTING PLATE ODDS 1:1627 HOBBY
PLATE PRINT RUN 1 SET PER COLOR
NO PLATE PRICING DUE TO SCARCITY
*PURPLE: .6X TO 1.5X BASIC

16R1 Blake Snell	2.50	6.00
16R2 Corey Seager	15.00	40.00
16R3 Miguel Sano	3.00	8.00
16R4 Kyle Schwarber	6.00	15.00
16R5 Trevor Story	6.00	15.00
16R6 Luis Severino	2.50	6.00
16R7 Aaron Nola	4.00	10.00
16R8 Stephen Piscotty	3.00	8.00
16R9 Michael Conforto	2.50	6.00
16R10 Kenta Maeda	4.00	10.00

2016 Topps Tribute Ageless Accolades Autographs

STATED ODDS 1:66 HOBBY
STATED PRINT RUN 50 SER.#'d SETS
EXCHANGE DEADLINE 6/30/2018

AAI Ichiro Suzuki	250.00	400.00
AABL Barry Larkin	20.00	50.00
AABP Buster Posey	60.00	150.00
AACJ Chipper Jones	40.00	100.00
AACK Clayton Kershaw	50.00	120.00
AACR Cal Ripken Jr.	30.00	80.00
AADE Dennis Eckersley	10.00	25.00
AADM Don Mattingly	30.00	80.00
AADMU Dale Murphy	25.00	60.00
AADP Dustin Pedroia	15.00	40.00
AAFR Frank Robinson	12.00	30.00
AAFT Frank Thomas	25.00	60.00
AAJB Johnny Bench	25.00	60.00
AAJC Jose Canseco	15.00	40.00
AAJG Juan Gonzalez	15.00	40.00
AAJR Jim Rice	12.00	30.00
AAKG Ken Griffey Jr.	60.00	150.00
AAMT Mike Trout	200.00	400.00
AARB Ryan Braun	10.00	25.00
AARH Rickey Henderson	25.00	60.00
AARJ Reggie Jackson	25.00	60.00
AARY Robin Yount	25.00	60.00
AAVG Vladimir Guerrero	15.00	40.00

2016 Topps Tribute Autographs

PRINT RUNS B/WN 20-199 COPIES PER
*BLUE/150: .4X TO 1X BASIC
*GREEN/99: .5X TO 1.2X BASIC
*PURPLE/50: .5X TO 1.2X BASIC
*ORANGE/25: .6X TO 1.5X BASE p/r 50-199
*ORANGE/25: .4X TO 1X BASE p/r 30
EXCHANGE DEADLINE 6/30/2018

TAAD Andre Dawson/75	8.00	20.00
TAADG Adrian Gonzalez/75	6.00	15.00
TAAG Andres Galarraga/199	4.00	10.00
TAAGO Alex Gordon/199	6.00	15.00
TAAJ Andruw Jones/199	3.00	8.00
TAAN Aaron Nola/199	6.00	15.00
TAAW Alex Wood/199	3.00	8.00
TABC Brandon Crawford/199	5.00	12.00
TABH Bryce Harper/30	200.00	400.00
TABJ Brian Johnson/199	3.00	8.00
TABJA Bo Jackson/30	30.00	80.00
TABL Barry Larkin/50	20.00	50.00
TABP Buster Posey/30	50.00	120.00
TABPA Byung-Ho Park	4.00	10.00
TACC Carlos Correa/50	25.00	60.00
TACD Carlos Delgado/199	3.00	8.00
TACF Carlton Fisk/75	15.00	40.00
TACH Cole Hamels/75	4.00	10.00
TACK Corey Kluber/199	10.00	25.00
TACKE Clayton Kershaw/50	60.00	150.00
TACR Carlos Rodon/199	5.00	12.00
TACS Corey Seager/199	30.00	80.00
TADE Dennis Eckersley/199	4.00	10.00
TADG Dee Gordon/199	3.00	8.00
TADL DJ LeMahieu/199	10.00	25.00
TADM Don Mattingly/50	20.00	50.00
TADP Dustin Pedroia/75	12.00	30.00
TADW David Wright/50	10.00	25.00
TAEM Edgar Martinez/199	10.00	25.00
TAFV Fernando Valenzuela/75	10.00	25.00
TAGR Garrett Richards/199	4.00	10.00
TAHA Hank Aaron/20	200.00	400.00
TAHO Henry Owens/199	4.00	10.00
TAHOL Hector Olivera/199	4.00	10.00
TAI Ichiro Suzuki/20	250.00	400.00
TAJA Jose Altuve/199	15.00	40.00
TAJB Jeff Bagwell/75	20.00	50.00
TAJBE Jose Berrios/199	4.00	10.00
TAJC Jose Canseco/199	10.00	25.00
TAJD Jacob deGrom/199	5.00	12.00
TAJG Juan Gonzalez/199	3.00	8.00
TAJGR Jon Gray/199	3.00	8.00
TAJP Joe Panik/199	4.00	10.00
TAJRI Jim Rice/199	5.00	12.00
TAJSM John Smoltz/75	12.00	30.00
TAKB Kris Bryant		
TAKG Ken Griffey Jr.	125.00	250.00
TAKM Kenta Maeda	12.00	30.00
TAKS Kyle Schwarber/199	15.00	40.00
TAKW Kolten Wong/199	4.00	10.00
TALB Lou Brock/199	12.00	30.00
TALS Luis Severino/199	10.00	25.00
TAMCO Michael Conforto/199	12.00	30.00
TAMM Mark McGwire/30	50.00	120.00
TAMP Michael Pineda/199	3.00	8.00
TAMPI Mike Piazza/20	60.00	150.00
TAMSA Miguel Sano/199	5.00	12.00
TAMT Mike Trout/20	200.00	400.00
TANR Nolan Ryan/30	60.00	150.00
TANS Noah Syndergaard/199	10.00	25.00
TAOS Ozzie Smith/75	15.00	40.00
TAPM Paul Molitor/75	10.00	25.00
TAPO Paul O'Neill/199	8.00	20.00
TARB Ryan Braun/75	6.00	15.00
TARJ Reggie Jackson/30	20.00	50.00
TARM Raul Mondesi		
TARS Robert Stephenson/199	3.00	8.00
TASC Steve Carlton/75	12.00	30.00
TASG Sonny Gray/199	4.00	10.00
TASPI Stephen Piscotty/199	5.00	12.00
TATT Troy Tulowitzki/50	8.00	20.00
TATTU Trea Turner/199	10.00	25.00

2016 Topps Tribute Cuts From the Cloth Autographs

STATED ODDS 1:94 HOBBY
STATED PRINT RUN 50 SER.#'d SETS
EXCHANGE DEADLINE 6/30/2018

CFCAG Adrian Gonzalez	8.00	20.00
CFCCB Craig Biggio	15.00	40.00
CFCCR Cal Ripken Jr. EXCH	40.00	100.00
CFCFF Freddie Freeman EXCH	10.00	25.00
CFCFT Frank Thomas	25.00	60.00
CFCJA Jose Altuve	30.00	80.00
CFCJS John Smoltz	15.00	40.00
CFCKB Kris Bryant	100.00	250.00
CFCMM Mark McGwire	75.00	200.00
CFCOS Ozzie Smith	25.00	60.00
CFCRC Robinson Cano	12.00	30.00

2016 Topps Tribute Foundations of Greatness Autographs

STATED ODDS 1:47 HOBBY
STATED PRINT RUN 99 SER.#'d SETS
EXCHANGE DEADLINE 6/30/2018

THENAK Al Kaline/99	15.00	40.00
THENAR Anthony Rizzo/99	20.00	50.00
THENCB Craig Biggio/99	12.00	30.00
THENCS Chris Sale/99	10.00	25.00
THENDM Don Mattingly/99	20.00	50.00
THENI Ichiro Suzuki/10		
THENJB Jeff Bagwell/99	12.00	30.00
THENJP Joc Pederson/99	10.00	25.00
THENJS James Shields/99	3.00	8.00
THENMT Mark Teixeira/99	12.00	30.00
THENOV Omar Vizquel/99	6.00	15.00
THENPM Paul Molitor/99	12.00	30.00
THENRA Roberto Alomar/99	10.00	25.00
THENRP Rafael Palmeiro/99	6.00	15.00
THENTG Tom Glavine/99	12.00	30.00
THENVG Vladimir Guerrero/99	8.00	20.00

2016 Topps Tribute Foundations of Greatness Autographs Orange

*ORANGE: .6X TO 1.5X BASIC
STATED ODDS 1:105 HOBBY
STATED PRINT RUN 25 SER.#'d SETS
EXCHANGE DEADLINE 6/30/2018

THENBL Barry Larkin	25.00	60.00
THENBP Buster Posey	60.00	150.00
THENCJ Chipper Jones	40.00	100.00
THENCR Cal Ripken Jr. EXCH	60.00	150.00
THENDO David Ortiz	40.00	100.00
THENFT Frank Thomas	30.00	80.00
THENGM Greg Maddux	60.00	150.00
THENJBE Johnny Bench	30.00	80.00
THENNG Nomar Garciaparra	15.00	40.00
THENRH Rickey Henderson	30.00	80.00
THENRJ Randy Johnson	50.00	120.00
THENRS Ryne Sandberg	25.00	60.00
THENRY Robin Yount	25.00	60.00
THENWB Wade Boggs	20.00	50.00

2016 Topps Tribute Foundations of Greatness Autographs Purple

*PURPLE: .5X TO 1.2X BASIC
STATED ODDS 1:63 HOBBY
STATED PRINT RUN 50 SER.#'d SETS
EXCHANGE DEADLINE 6/30/2018

THENBL Barry Larkin	20.00	50.00
THENCJ Chipper Jones	30.00	80.00
THENDO David Ortiz	30.00	80.00
THENFT Frank Thomas	25.00	60.00
THENJBE Johnny Bench	25.00	60.00
THENNG Nomar Garciaparra	12.00	30.00
THENRH Rickey Henderson	25.00	60.00
THENRS Ryne Sandberg	20.00	50.00
THENRY Robin Yount	20.00	50.00
THENWB Wade Boggs	15.00	40.00

2016 Topps Tribute Prime Patches

STATED ODDS 1:89 HOBBY
STATED PRINT RUN 25 SER.#'d SETS

PPI Ichiro Suzuki	30.00	80.00
PPAM Andrew McCutchen	25.00	60.00
PPBH Bryce Harper	25.00	60.00
PPBP Buster Posey	20.00	50.00
PPCB Craig Biggio	8.00	20.00
PPCJ Chipper Jones	10.00	25.00
PPCK Clayton Kershaw	12.00	30.00
PPDG Doc Gooden	10.00	25.00
PPEM Eddie Murray	15.00	40.00
PPFH Felix Hernandez	8.00	20.00
PPFT Frank Thomas	25.00	60.00
PPGM Greg Maddux	12.00	30.00
PPJA Jose Altuve	8.00	20.00
PPJB Jose Bautista	12.00	30.00
PPJM Juan Marichal	15.00	40.00
PPJP Jim Palmer	10.00	25.00
PPJS John Smoltz	12.00	30.00
PPJV Joey Votto	15.00	40.00
PPKB Kris Bryant	30.00	80.00
PPKGJ Ken Griffey Jr.	30.00	80.00
PPMC Miguel Cabrera	10.00	25.00
PPMM Mark McGwire	40.00	100.00
PPMP Mike Piazza	20.00	50.00
PPMT Mike Trout	25.00	60.00
PPNR Nolan Ryan	20.00	50.00
PPRJ Randy Johnson	10.00	25.00
PPRJA Reggie Jackson	10.00	25.00
PPWB Wade Boggs	10.00	25.00
PPWS Warren Spahn	20.00	5.00
PPZG Zack Greinke	8.00	20.00

2016 Topps Tribute Relics

PRINT RUNS B/WN 196-199 COPIES PER
*GREEN/99: .4X TO 1X BASIC
*PURPLE/50: .5X TO 1.2X BASIC
*ORANGE/25: .75X TO 2X BASIC

TRI Ichiro Suzuki/199	8.00	20.00
TRAJ Adam Jones/196	3.00	8.00
TRAM Andrew McCutchen/199	5.00	12.00
TRAMI Andrew Miller/196	3.00	8.00
TRAP Albert Pujols/196	5.00	12.00
TRAW Adam Wainwright/196	3.00	8.00
TRBP Buster Posey/196	5.00	12.00
TRCA Chris Archer/196	2.50	6.00
TRCB Craig Biggio/196	3.00	8.00
TRCK Clayton Kershaw/199	5.00	12.00
TRCKL Corey Kluber/199	3.00	8.00
TRCR Cal Ripken Jr./196	6.00	15.00
TRCS Chris Sale/196	4.00	10.00
TRDG Dee Gordon/196	2.50	6.00
TREM Eddie Murray/196	3.00	8.00
TRFH Felix Hernandez/196	3.00	8.00
TRFM Fred McGriff/196	3.00	8.00
TRGC Gerrit Cole/196	4.00	10.00
TRGM Greg Maddux/196	5.00	12.00
TRJB Jeff Bagwell/196	3.00	8.00
TRJD Jacob deGrom/196	4.00	10.00
TRJE Jacoby Ellsbury/196	3.00	8.00
TRJG Juan Gonzalez/196	2.50	6.00
TRJM Juan Marichal/196	3.00	8.00
TRJP Jim Palmer/196	3.00	8.00
TRJS John Smoltz/196	4.00	10.00
TRKB Kris Bryant/196	8.00	20.00
TRKG Ken Griffey Jr./196	5.00	12.00
TRKS Kyle Schwarber/196	5.00	12.00
TRMB Madison Bumgarner/196	3.00	8.00
TRMC Miguel Cabrera/199	4.00	10.00
TRMH Matt Harvey/196	3.00	8.00
TRMM Manny Machado/199	5.00	12.00
TRMMC Mark McGwire/196	5.00	12.00
TRMP Mike Piazza/196	4.00	10.00
TRMS Max Scherzer/199	4.00	10.00
TRMT Mike Trout/199	20.00	50.00
TRNA Nolan Arenado/196	5.00	12.00
TRNR Nolan Ryan/196	8.00	20.00
TRPF Prince Fielder/196	3.00	8.00
TRPG Paul Goldschmidt/196	4.00	10.00
TRRB Ryan Braun/196	3.00	8.00
TRRC Rod Carew/196	3.00	8.00
TRRCA Robinson Cano/196	3.00	8.00
TRRJ Randy Johnson/196	4.00	10.00
TRRJA Reggie Jackson/196	3.00	8.00
TRSG Sonny Gray/196	3.00	8.00
TRSM Starling Marte/196	3.00	8.00
TRTD Todd Frazier/196	3.00	8.00
TRTW Ted Williams/196	12.00	30.00
TRYD Yu Darvish/196	4.00	10.00
TRYP Yasiel Puig/196	4.00	10.00
TRZG Zack Greinke/196	3.00	8.00

2016 Topps Tribute Rightful Recognition Autographs

STATED ODDS 1:47 HOBBY
PRINT RUNS B/WN 10-99 COPIES PER
NO PRICING ON QTY 10
EXCHANGE DEADLINE 6/30/2018

NOWAK Al Kaline/99	15.00	40.00
NOWAR Anthony Rizzo/99	20.00	50.00
NOWCB Craig Biggio/99	12.00	30.00
NOWCS Chris Sale/99	10.00	25.00
NOWDM Don Mattingly/99	20.00	50.00
NOWJB Jeff Bagwell/99	15.00	40.00
NOWJP Joc Pederson/99	8.00	20.00
NOWJS James Shields/99	3.00	8.00
NOWMT Mark Teixeira/99	12.00	30.00
NOWOV Omar Vizquel/99	6.00	15.00
NOWPM Paul Molitor/99	10.00	25.00
NOWRA Roberto Alomar/99	10.00	25.00
NOWRP Rafael Palmeiro/99	6.00	15.00
NOWTG Tom Glavine/99	12.00	30.00
NOWVG Vladimir Guerrero/99	10.00	25.00

2016 Topps Tribute Rightful Recognition Autographs Orange

*ORANGE: .6X TO 1.5X BASIC
STATED ODDS 1:105 HOBBY
STATED PRINT RUN 25 SER.#'d SETS
EXCHANGE DEADLINE 6/30/2018

NOWBL Barry Larkin	25.00	60.00
NOWBP Buster Posey	60.00	150.00
NOWCJ Chipper Jones	40.00	100.00
NOWCR Cal Ripken Jr.	60.00	150.00
NOWDO David Ortiz	50.00	120.00
NOWFT Frank Thomas	30.00	80.00
NOWGM Greg Maddux	60.00	150.00
NOWJBE Johnny Bench	30.00	80.00
NOWNG Nomar Garciaparra	15.00	40.00
NOWRH Rickey Henderson	30.00	80.00
NOWRJ Randy Johnson	60.00	150.00
NOWRS Ryne Sandberg	25.00	60.00
NOWRY Robin Yount	25.00	60.00
NOWWB Wade Boggs	20.00	50.00

2016 Topps Tribute Rightful Recognition Autographs Purple

*PURPLE: .5X TO 1.2X BASIC
STATED ODDS 1:63 HOBBY
STATED PRINT RUN 50 SER.#'d SETS
EXCHANGE DEADLINE 6/30/2018

NOWBL Barry Larkin	20.00	50.00
NOWCJ Chipper Jones	30.00	80.00
NOWDO David Ortiz	40.00	100.00
NOWFT Frank Thomas	25.00	60.00
NOWJBE Johnny Bench	25.00	60.00
NOWNG Nomar Garciaparra	12.00	30.00
NOWRH Rickey Henderson	25.00	60.00
NOWRS Ryne Sandberg	20.00	50.00
NOWRY Robin Yount	20.00	50.00
NOWWB Wade Boggs	15.00	40.00

2016 Topps Tribute Stamp of Approval Relics

STATED PRINT RUN 199 SER.#'d SETS
*GREEN/99: .4X TO 1X BASIC
*PURPLE/50: .5X TO 1.2X BASIC
*ORANGE/25: .75X TO 2X BASIC

SOAAC Aroldis Chapman	4.00	10.00
SOAAE Alcides Escobar	3.00	8.00
SOAAW Adam Wainwright	3.00	8.00
SOABH Billy Hamilton	3.00	8.00
SOACA Chris Archer	2.50	6.00
SOACK Corey Kluber	3.00	8.00
SOACM Carlos Martinez	3.00	8.00
SOACS Corey Seager	4.00	10.00
SOADP Dustin Pedroia	4.00	10.00
SOAEG Evan Gattis	2.50	6.00
SOAEL Evan Longoria	3.00	8.00
SOAGP Gregory Polanco	4.00	10.00
SOAJA Jose Altuve	6.00	15.00
SOAJB Jose Bautista	3.00	8.00
SOAJE Jacoby Ellsbury	3.00	8.00
SOAJHK Jung Ho Kang	2.50	6.00
SOAJP Joc Pederson	3.00	8.00
SOAJZ Jordan Zimmermann	3.00	8.00
SOAKJ Kenley Jansen	3.00	8.00
SOAKS Kyle Schwarber	5.00	12.00
SOAKSE Kyle Seager	2.50	6.00
SOAMB Mookie Betts	5.00	12.00
SOAMC Miguel Cabrera	4.00	10.00
SOAMCO Michael Conforto	3.00	8.00
SOAMT Michael Taylor	2.50	6.00
SOAMTR Mike Trout	20.00	50.00
SOANA Nolan Arenado	5.00	12.00
SOANS Noah Syndergaard	3.00	8.00
SOASM Starling Marte	3.00	8.00
SOASP Salvador Perez	3.00	8.00
SOAYC Yoenis Cespedes	4.00	10.00
SOAYD Yu Darvish	4.00	10.00

2016 Topps Tribute Tribute Tandems Autographs

STATED ODDS 1:516 HOBBY
STATED PRINT RUN 25 SER.#'d SETS
EXCHANGE DEADLINE 6/30/2018

TTAB J.Altuve/C.Biggio	75.00	200.00
TTBS K.Bryant/R.Sandberg	250.00	400.00
TTJR Rbnsn/Jns EXCH	60.00	150.00
TTPB J.Bench/B.Posey	150.00	300.00
TTSJ R.Johnson/C.Sale	60.00	150.00
TTTA H.Aaron/M.Trout	600.00	800.00
TTTM Txra/Mttngly EXCH	60.00	150.00

2016 Topps Tribute Triple Crown Memories Autographs

STATED ODDS 1:721 HOBBY
STATED PRINT RUN 15 SER.#'d SETS
EXCHANGE DEADLINE 6/30/2018

TCFR1 Frank Robinson	25.00	60.00
TCFR2 Frank Robinson	25.00	60.00
TCFR3 Frank Robinson	25.00	60.00
TCSK1 Sandy Koufax	200.00	300.00
TCSK2 Sandy Koufax	200.00	300.00
TCSK3 Sandy Koufax	200.00	300.00

2017 Topps Tribute

1 Babe Ruth	3.00	8.00
2 Justin Verlander	1.25	3.00
3 Whitey Ford	1.00	2.50
4 Andy Pettitte	1.00	2.50
5 Zach Britton	1.00	2.50
6 Yu Darvish	1.25	3.00
7 Wil Myers	.75	2.00
8 Duke Snider	1.00	2.50
9 Roger Maris	1.25	3.00
10 Ryne Sandberg	2.50	6.00
11 Jim Palmer	1.00	2.50
12 Tommy Lasorda	1.00	2.50
13 Corey Kluber	1.00	2.50
14 Trevor Story	1.25	3.00
15 Roberto Clemente	3.00	8.00
16 Gary Carter	1.00	2.50
17 Ozzie Smith	1.50	4.00
18 Jose Altuve	1.00	2.50
19 Daniel Murphy	1.00	2.50
20 Ichiro	1.50	4.00
21 Michael Fulmer	.75	2.00
22 Jose Bautista	1.00	2.50
23 Willie Stargell	1.00	2.50
24 Mookie Betts	2.00	5.00
25 Mike Trout	6.00	15.00
26 Sparky Anderson	1.00	2.50
27 Anthony Rizzo	2.00	5.00
28 Rod Carew	1.00	2.50
29 Lou Brock	1.00	2.50
30 Edwin Encarnacion	1.25	3.00
31 Randy Johnson	1.25	3.00
32 Jeurys Familia	1.00	2.50
33 Madison Bumgarner	1.00	2.50
34 Stephen Piscotty	1.00	2.50
35 Stephen Strasburg	1.25	3.00
36 Manny Machado	1.25	3.00
37 Mark Trumbo	.75	2.00
38 Danny Salazar	1.00	2.50
39 Nolan Arenado	1.50	4.00
40 Kris Bryant	1.50	4.00
41 Yoenis Cespedes	1.25	3.00
42 Noah Syndergaard	1.00	2.50
43 Kenta Maeda	1.00	2.50
44 Cole Hamels	1.00	2.50
45 Luis Aparicio	1.00	2.50
46 Starling Marte	1.00	2.50
47 Earl Weaver	1.00	2.50
48 Johnny Cueto	1.00	2.50
49 Corey Seager	1.25	3.00
50 Sandy Koufax	2.50	6.00
51 Carl Yastrzemski	2.00	5.00
52 Harmon Killebrew	1.25	3.00
53 David Price	1.00	2.50
54 Billy Williams	1.00	2.50
55 Xander Bogaerts	1.25	3.00
56 Ivan Rodriguez	1.00	2.50
57 Jackie Robinson	1.25	3.00
58 Buster Posey	1.50	4.00
59 Tom Glavine	1.00	2.50
60 Catfish Hunter	1.00	2.50
61 Joe Morgan	1.00	2.50
62 Bryce Harper	2.00	5.00
63 Giancarlo Stanton	1.25	3.00
64 Chris Sale	1.25	3.00
65 Ken Griffey Jr.	2.50	6.00
66 Ty Cobb	2.00	5.00
67 Clayton Kershaw	2.50	6.00
68 Jake Arrieta	1.00	2.50
69 Tony La Russa	1.00	2.50
70 Wade Boggs	1.00	2.50
71 Lorenzo Cain	.75	2.00
72 Jacob deGrom	1.25	3.00
73 Phil Rizzuto	1.00	2.50
74 Yadier Molina	1.25	3.00
75 David Ortiz	1.25	3.00
76 Eddie Mathews	1.25	3.00
77 Francisco Lindor	1.25	3.00
78 Andrew McCutchen	1.25	3.00
79 Mark McGwire	2.00	5.00
80 Carlos Correa	1.25	3.00
81 Nomar Mazara	.75	2.00
82 George Brett	2.50	6.00
83 Aledmys Diaz	1.00	2.50
84 Lou Gehrig	2.50	6.00
85 Albert Pujols	1.50	4.00
86 Mike Piazza	1.25	3.00
87 Brooks Robinson	1.00	2.50
88 Josh Donaldson	1.00	2.50
89 Max Scherzer	1.25	3.00
90 Hank Aaron	2.50	6.00

2017 Topps Tribute Green

*GREEN: 1X TO 2.5X BASIC
STATED ODDS 1:6 HOBBY
STATED PRINT RUN 99 SER.#'d SETS

2017 Topps Tribute Purple

*PURPLE: 1.2X TO 3X BASIC
STATED ODDS 1:15 HOBBY
STATED PRINT RUN 50 SER.#'d SETS

2017 Topps Tribute '17 Rookies

STATED ODDS 1:24 HOBBY
*PURPLE/50: .5X TO 1.2X BASIC

17R1 Alex Bregman	12.00	30.00
17R2 Jose De Leon	2.00	5.00
17R3 David Dahl	2.50	6.00

17R4 Andrew Benintendi 30.00 80.00
17R5 Orlando Arcia 5.00 12.00
17R6 Alex Reyes 2.50 6.00
17R7 Tyler Glasnow 2.50 6.00
17R8 Aaron Judge 12.00 30.00
17R9 Dansby Swanson 10.00 25.00
17R10 Yoan Moncada 8.00 20.00

2017 Topps Tribute Autograph Patches

STATED ODDS 1:89 HOBBY
STATED PRINT RUN 50 SER.#'d SETS
EXCHANGE DEADLINE 2/28/2019
TAPAJ Adam Jones EXCH 30.00 80.00
TAPCC Carlos Correa
TAPDF Dexter Fowler 30.00 80.00
TAPDO David Ortiz
TAPDPE Dustin Pedroia 30.00 80.00
TAPFF Freddie Freeman 20.00 50.00
TAPFL Francisco Lindor 50.00 120.00
TAPHR Hanley Ramirez EXCH 8.00 20.00
TAPI Ichiro
TAPJA Jose Altuve 30.00 80.00
TAPJM J.D. Martinez 25.00 60.00
TAPMF Michael Fulmer 20.00 50.00
TAPMM Manny Machado
TAPNM Nomar Mazara EXCH 30.00 80.00
TAPNS Noah Syndergaard 25.00 60.00
TAPSM Starling Marte EXCH 30.00 80.00

2017 Topps Tribute Autographs

STATE ODDS 1:7 HOBBY
PRINT RUNS B/WN 15-199 COPIES PER
*GREEN/99: .5X TO 1.2X BASIC
*BLUE/75: .5X TO 1.2X BASIC
*PURPLE/50: .4X TO 1X BASE p/r 50
*PURPLE/50: .5X TO 1.2X BASE p/r 90-199
*ORANGE/25: .4X TO 1X BASE p/r 20-30
*ORANGE/25: .6X TO 1.5X BASE p/r 90-199
NO PRICING ON QTY 15
EXCHANGE DEADLINE 2/28/2019
TAAB Alex Bregman/199 20.00 50.00
TAABE Andrew Benintendi/199 75.00 200.00
TAAC Adam Conley/199 3.00 8.00
TAAJU Aaron Judge/199 100.00 250.00
TAAP Andy Pettitte/30 12.00 30.00
TAAR Anthony Rizzo
TAARE Alex Reyes/199 4.00 10.00
TABB Barry Bonds/20
TABH Bryce Harper EXCH
TABP Buster Posey/30
TABS Blake Snell/199 4.00 10.00
TABSH Braden Shipley/199 4.00 10.00
TACC Carlos Correa/90 30.00 80.00
TACFU Carson Fulmer/199 3.00 8.00
TACR Cal Ripken Jr./30 60.00 150.00
TACRO Carlos Rodon EXCH 4.00 10.00
TACSE Corey Seager/199 20.00 50.00
TACY Carl Yastrzemski/30 40.00 100.00
TADD David Dahl/199 4.00 10.00
TADF Dexter Fowler/199 6.00 15.00
TADG Didi Gregorius/199 6.00 15.00
TADJ Derek Jeter EXCH
TADO David Ortiz/30 40.00 100.00
TADP David Price/199 8.00 20.00
TADS Dansby Swanson/199 10.00 25.00
TAFL Francisco Lindor/199 20.00 50.00
TAFLI Francisco Lindor/199 20.00 50.00
TAFV Fernando Valenzuela/50 8.00 20.00
TAGS George Springer/199 10.00 25.00
TAIR Ivan Rodriguez/199 12.00 30.00
TAJAL Jose Altuve/199 12.00 30.00
TAJD Jacob deGrom/199 10.00 25.00
TAJDL Jose De Leon/199 5.00 12.00
TAJM J.D. Martinez/199 12.00 30.00
TAJOA Jose Altuve/199 12.00 30.00
TAJP Joc Pederson/199 8.00 20.00
TAJT Jameson Taillon/199 6.00 15.00
TAJU Julio Urias EXCH 5.00 12.00
TAKB Kris Bryant/100 25.00 60.00
TAKGJ Ken Griffey Jr./30 125.00 300.00
TAKMO Kendrys Morales/199 3.00 8.00
TAKS Kyle Schwarber/199 12.00 30.00
TALW Luke Weaver/199 4.00 10.00
TAMAT Masahiro Tanaka EXCH 125.00 300.00
TAMF Michael Fulmer/199 3.00 8.00
TAMS Marcus Stroman/199 5.00 12.00
TAMW Matt Wieters/199 5.00 12.00
TANM Nomar Mazara/199 12.00 30.00
TANMA Nomar Mazara/199 12.00 30.00
TANR Nolan Ryan/30 100.00 250.00
TANS Noah Syndergaard/199 10.00 25.00
TAOS Ozzie Smith/145 20.00 50.00
TAOV Omar Vizquel/110 6.00 15.00
TAPK Paul Konerko/199 4.00 10.00
TARH Ryon Healy/199 6.00 15.00
TARJ Reggie Jackson/30 30.00 80.00
TARS Ryne Sandberg
TASG Sonny Gray/199 5.00 12.00
TASMA Steven Matz/199 4.00 10.00
TASP Stephen Piscotty/199 4.00 10.00
TASW Steven Wright/199 4.00 10.00
TATA Tim Anderson/199 4.00 10.00
TATG Tom Glavine/199 10.00 25.00
TATRS Trevor Story/199 8.00 20.00
TATS Trevor Story/199 8.00 20.00
TATT Trea Turner/199 12.00 30.00
TATTU Trea Turner/199 12.00 30.00
TAWC Willson Contreras/199 8.00 20.00
TAWD Wade Davis/199 3.00 8.00
TAYG Yulieski Gurriel/199 10.00 25.00
TAYM Yoan Moncada/100 30.00 80.00

2017 Topps Tribute Dual Relics

STATED ODDS 1:85 HOBBY
STATED PRINT RUN 50 SER.#'d SETS
EXCHANGE DEADLINE 2/28/2019
DRACA Abreu/Cabrera 5.00 12.00
DRBE Bautista/Encarnacion 20.00 50.00
DRCA Altuve/Correa
DRCE Cain/Escobar
DRCP Perez/Cain 12.00 30.00
DRCS Springer/Correa 12.00 30.00
DRFN Franco/Nola 10.00 25.00
DRFZI Fulmer/Zimmerman 12.00 30.00
DRHC Hernandez/Cano
DRJM Machado/Jones 20.00 50.00
DRKM Martinez/Kinsler
DRLG Gonzalez/LeMahieu
DRMH Mazara/Hamels 8.00 20.00
DRMM McCutchen/Marte 40.00 100.00
DRSW Wright/Syndergaard 20.00 50.00

2017 Topps Tribute Dual Autographs

STATED ODDS 1:356 HOBBY
STATED PRINT RUN 25 SER.#'d SETS
EXCHANGE DEADLINE 2/28/2019
DACG Tom Glavine 25.00 60.00
David Cone
DAJK John Kruk 60.00 150.00
Randy Johnson
DAJP Andy Pettitte 60.00 150.00
Randy Johnson
DAKA Hank Aaron
Sandy Koufax EXCH
DAKP Clayton Kershaw 75.00 200.00
Buster Posey
DAPS Andy Pettitte 60.00 150.00
John Smoltz
DARJ Nolan Ryan
Reggie Jackson

2017 Topps Tribute Generations of Excellence Autographs

STATE ODDS 1:34 HOBBY
STATED PRINT RUN 99 SER.#'d SETS
*PURPLE/50: .4X TO 1X BASIC
*ORANGE/25: .5X TO 1.2X BASIC
EXCHANGE DEADLINE 2/28/2019
GOEAD Andre Dawson 12.00 30.00
GOEAG Andres Galarraga 5.00 12.00
GOEAP Andy Pettitte 15.00 40.00
GOEBL Barry Larkin 25.00 60.00
GOEBW Billy Wagner 6.00 15.00
GOECB Craig Biggio 12.00 30.00
GOECY Carl Yastrzemski
GOEDC David Cone 10.00 25.00
GOEDE Dennis Eckersley 6.00 15.00
GOEDJ Derek Jeter
GOEDM Don Mattingly 40.00 100.00
GOEDO David Ortiz
GOEFT Frank Thomas 30.00 80.00
GOEHA Hank Aaron
GOEIR Ivan Rodriguez 15.00 40.00
GOEJB Johnny Bench
GOEJR Jim Rice 10.00 25.00
GOEJS John Smoltz 15.00 40.00
GOEMM Mark McGwire
GOEMP Mike Piazza
GOENR Nolan Ryan
GOEOS Ozzie Smith 40.00 100.00
GOEOV Omar Vizquel 5.00 12.00
GOEPK Paul Konerko 12.00 30.00
GOEPM Paul Molitor 10.00 25.00
GOEPO Paul O'Neill 12.00 30.00
GOERA Roberto Alomar 10.00 25.00
GOERJ Reggie Jackson
GOERO Roy Oswalt 6.00 15.00
GOERS Ryne Sandberg 25.00 60.00
GOESG Steve Garvey 12.00 30.00
GOESK Sandy Koufax
GOETG Tom Glavine 12.00 30.00

2017 Topps Tribute Relics

STATED ODDS 1:7 HOBBY
PRINT RUNS B/WN 196-199 COPIES PER
*GREEN/99: .4X TO 1X BASIC
*PURPLE/50: .5X TO 1.2X BASIC
*ORANGE/25: .75X TO 2X BASIC
TRAM Andrew McCutchen/192 6.00 15.00
TRAR Anthony Rizzo/199 5.00 12.00
TRARU Addison Russell/192 5.00 12.00
TRBH Bryce Harper/192 6.00 15.00
TRBL Barry Larkin/192 3.00 8.00
TRBP Buster Posey/192 5.00 12.00
TRCB Craig Biggio/192 3.00 8.00
TRCC Carlos Correa/192 6.00 15.00
TRCH Cole Hamels/192 3.00 8.00
TRCJ Chipper Jones/192 5.00 12.00
TRCR Cal Ripken Jr./192 10.00 25.00
TRCSA Carlos Santana/192 3.00 8.00
TRCSE Corey Seager/192 5.00 12.00
TRDB Dellin Betances/192 3.00 8.00
TRDM Don Mattingly/192 8.00 20.00
TRDO David Ortiz/199 4.00 10.00
TRFH Felix Hernandez/199 3.00 8.00
TRFL Francisco Lindor/192 4.00 10.00
TRGS Giancarlo Stanton/199 4.00 10.00
TRGSP George Springer/192 3.00 8.00
TRI Ichiro/192 5.00 12.00
TRJA Jose Altuve/192 3.00 8.00
TRJAR Jake Arrieta/192 3.00 8.00
TRJB Jose Bautista/192 3.00 8.00
TRJBJ Jackie Bradley Jr./192 4.00 10.00
TRJD Josh Donaldson/192 3.00 8.00
TRJDE Jacob deGrom/192 4.00 10.00
TRJFA Jeurys Familia/192 3.00 8.00
TRJS John Smoltz/192 4.00 10.00
TRJU Julio Urias/192 4.00 10.00
TRJV Joey Votto/192 4.00 10.00
TRKS Kyle Seager/192 2.50 6.00
TRKSC Kyle Schwarber/199 4.00 10.00
TRMB Madison Bumgarner/199 3.00 8.00
TRMC Miguel Cabrera/199 4.00 10.00
TRMCA Matt Carpenter/192 4.00 10.00
TRMM Manny Machado/192 4.00 10.00
TRMMC Mark McGwire/192 6.00 15.00
TRMP Mike Piazza/192 4.00 10.00
TRMT Mike Trout/199 20.00 50.00
TRMTA Masahiro Tanaka/192 6.00 15.00
TRNC Nelson Cruz/192 4.00 10.00
TRNM Nomar Mazara/192 2.50 6.00
TRNS Noah Syndergaard/192 5.00 12.00
TRPG Paul Goldschmidt/192 4.00 10.00
TRRC Robinson Cano/192 3.00 8.00
TRRCL Roger Clemens/192 5.00 12.00
TRRO Rougned Odor/199 3.00 8.00
TRTG Tom Glavine/192 3.00 8.00
TRXB Xander Bogaerts/199 4.00 10.00
TRYC Yoenis Cespedes/199 4.00 10.00

2017 Topps Tribute Stamp of Approval Relics

STATED ODDS 1:11 HOBBY
STATED PRINT RUN 199 SER.#'d SETS
*GREEN/99: .4X TO 1X BASIC
*PURPLE/50: .5X TO 1.2X BASIC
*ORANGE/25: .75X TO 2X BASIC
SOAAJ Adam Jones 3.00 8.00
SOAAM Andrew McCutchen 10.00 25.00
SOAAN Aaron Nola 3.00 8.00
SOABH Billy Hamilton 3.00 8.00
SOABZ Ben Zobrist 3.00 8.00
SOACC Carlos Correa 4.00 10.00
SOACH Cole Hamels 3.00 8.00
SOADF Dexter Fowler 3.00 8.00
SOAEE Edwin Encarnacion 4.00 10.00
SOAFH Felix Hernandez 3.00 8.00
SOAGS George Springer 3.00 8.00
SOAHR Hanley Ramirez 3.00 8.00
SOAI Ichiro 5.00 12.00
SOAJA Jose Altuve 3.00 8.00
SOAJAB Jose Abreu 4.00 10.00
SOAJBA Jose Bautista 3.00 8.00
SOAJOB Javier Baez 4.00 10.00
SOAJV Joey Votto 4.00 10.00
SOAJZ Jordan Zimmermann 3.00 8.00
SOALC Lorenzo Cain 2.50 6.00
SOAMC Melky Cabrera 2.50 6.00
SOAMF Michael Fulmer 2.50 6.00
SOAMFR Maikel Franco 3.00 8.00
SOAMM Manny Machado 4.00 10.00
SOANM Nomar Mazara 2.50 6.00
SOANS Noah Syndergaard 5.00 12.00
SOARC Robinson Cano 3.00 8.00
SOASM Starling Marte 8.00 20.00
SOASP Salvador Perez 3.00 8.00
SOAWM Wil Myers 2.50 6.00

2017 Topps Tribute Tandem Autograph Booklets

STATED ODDS 1:192 HOBBY
STATED PRINT RUN 25 SER.#'d SETS
EXCHANGE DEADLINE 2/28/2019
TTCB Biggio/Correa 100.00 250.00
TTFJ Jones/Freeman 125.00 300.00
TTHG Harper/Griffey
TTKK Kershaw/Koufax
TTLB Boggs/Longoria
TTLV Lindor/Vizquel 250.00 400.00
TTMK Kaline/Martinez 75.00 200.00
TTMR Machado/Ripken 250.00 400.00
TTPG Garciaparra/Pedroia
TTPR Posey/Pudge 50.00 120.00
TTSC Carlton/Sale EXCH 20.00 50.00
TTSR Ryan/Syndergaard EXCH 250.00 400.00
TTUV Valenzuela/Urias EXCH 125.00 300.00
TTVH Heyward/Dawson 40.00 100.00

2017 Topps Tribute to the Moment Autographs

STATE ODDS 1:40 HOBBY
PRINT RUNS B/WN 25-99 COPIES PER
*PURPLE/50: .4X TO 1X BASIC
*ORANGE/25: .5X TO 1.2X BASIC
EXCHANGE DEADLINE 2/28/2019
TTMAD Andre Dawson/99 10.00 25.00
TTMAK Al Kaline/99 20.00 50.00
TTMBB Barry Bonds/25 100.00 250.00
TTMCB Craig Biggio/99 12.00 30.00
TTMCK Clayton Kershaw/50 40.00 100.00
TTMCY Carl Yastrzemski 40.00 100.00
TTMDM Don Mattingly/60 40.00 100.00
TTMDP David Price/99 12.00 30.00
TTMFT Frank Thomas/50 25.00 60.00
TTMHA Hank Aaron
TTMIR Ivan Rodriguez/99 15.00 40.00
TTMI Ichiro/25
TTMJG Juan Gonzalez/99 6.00 15.00
TTMJR Jim Rice/99 10.00 25.00
TTMJS John Smoltz/99 8.00 20.00
TTMMM Manny Machado/99 25.00 60.00
TTMMP Mike Piazza/25 60.00 150.00
TTMMT Mike Trout/40 300.00 600.00
TTMNR Nolan Ryan/50 60.00 150.00
TTMPM Paul Molitor/99 12.00 30.00
TTMYM Yoan Moncada/50 40.00 100.00

2017 Topps Tribute Walk Off Autographs

STATE ODDS 1:104 HOBBY
STATED PRINT RUN 99 SER.#'d SETS
*ORANGE/25: .5X TO 1.2X BASIC
EXCHANGE DEADLINE 2/28/2019
WOAAB Aaron Boone 15.00 40.00
WOABW Bernie Williams 20.00 50.00
WOACF Carlton Fisk 25.00 60.00
WOACJ Chipper Jones 50.00 120.00
WOADO David Ortiz 40.00 100.00
WOAEM Edgar Martinez 15.00 40.00
WOAJB Johnny Bench 25.00 60.00
WOAKGJ Ken Griffey Jr.
WOALG Luis Gonzalez 20.00 50.00
WOAMM Mark McGwire 40.00 100.00
WOAOS Ozzie Smith 20.00
WOAOV Omar Vizquel 12.00 30.00

2013 Topps Tribute WBC

1 Miguel Cabrera 1.00 2.50
2 Andre Rienzo .60 1.50
3 Erisbel Arruebarruena 8.00 20.00
4 Mike Aviles .60 1.50
5 Hideaki Wakui .60 1.50
6 Yao-Hsun Yang 1.00 2.50
7 Jae Weong Seo .60 1.50
8 Andrelton Simmons .60 1.50
9 Anthony Rizzo 1.50 4.00
10 Shinnosuke Abe 1.00 2.50
11 Heath Bell .60 1.50
12 Jhoulys Chacin .60 1.50
13 Adam Jones .75 2.00
14 Marco Estrada .60 1.50
15 Yulieski Gourriel 1.25 3.00
16 John Axford .60 1.50
17 Carlos Gonzalez .75 2.00
18 Edwin Encarnacion 1.00 2.50
19 Toshiya Sugiuchi .60 1.50
20 Joe Mauer .75 2.00
21 Eddie Rosario 1.25 3.00
22 Anibal Sanchez .60 1.50
23 Salvador Perez .75 2.00
24 Kelvin Herrera .60 1.50
25 Xander Bogaerts 2.00 5.00
26 Takeru Imamura .40 1.00
27 Yadier Pedroso .40 1.00
28 Steve Cishek .60 1.50
29 Atsunori Inaba .60 1.50
30 Jose Reyes .75 2.00
31 Miguel Montero .60 1.50
32 Kenji Ohtonari 1.00 2.50
33 Angel Pagan .60 1.50
34 Carlos Zambrano .75 2.00
35 Che-Hsuan Lin 1.00 2.50
36 Eric Hosmer .75 2.00
37 Sergio Romo .60 1.50
38 Martin Prado .60 1.50
39 Atsushi Nohmi 1.00 2.50
40 Joey Votto 1.00 2.50
41 Jonatan Isenia 1.00 2.50
42 Yadier Molina 1.00 2.50
43 Giancarlo Stanton 1.00 2.50
44 Edinson Volquez .60 1.50
45 Masahiro Tanaka 6.00 15.00
46 Ben Zobrist .60 1.50
47 Philippe Aumont .60 1.50
48 Ryan Vogelsong .60 1.50
49 Dae Ho Lee 1.00 2.50
50 David Wright .75 2.00
51 Carlos Beltran .75 2.00
52 Fernando Rodney .60 1.50
53 Odrisamer Despaigne 8.00 20.00
54 Jose Fernandez 1.50 4.00
55 Dai-Kang Yang 2.50 6.00
56 Marco Scutaro .75 2.00
57 Kenta Maeda 4.00 10.00
58 Jameson Taillon .75 2.00
59 Kazuo Matsui .40 1.00
60 Robinson Cano .75 2.00
61 Adrian Gonzalez .75 2.00
62 J.P. Arencibia .60 1.50
63 Henderson Alvarez .60 1.50
64 Hayato Sakamoto 1.25 3.00
65 Justin Morneau .75 2.00
66 Wandy Rodriguez .60 1.50
67 Gio Gonzalez .75 2.00
68 Alex Rios .75 2.00
69 Freddy Alvarez 1.00 2.50
70 Jimmy Rollins .75 2.00
71 Yuichi Honda 1.00 2.50
72 Derek Holland .60 1.50
73 Erick Aybar .60 1.50
74 Chien-Ming Wang .75 2.00
75 Nelson Cruz 1.00 2.50
76 Suk-Min Yoon 1.00 2.50
77 Jose Berrios 1.00 2.50
78 Jonathan Lucroy .75 2.00
79 Elvis Andrus .75 2.00
80 R.A. Dickey .75 2.00
81 Yovani Gallardo .60 1.50
82 Tadashi Settsu 1.00 2.50
83 Jen-Ho Tseng 1.50 4.00
84 Carlos Santana .75 2.00
85 Craig Kimbrel .75 2.00
86 Asdrubal Cabrera .75 2.00
87 Alfredo Despaigne 1.00 2.50
88 Jonathan Schoop .60 1.50
89 Tetsuya Utsumi .60 1.50
90 Pablo Sandoval .75 2.00
91 Nobuhiro Matsuda 1.00 2.50
92 Shane Victorino .75 2.00
93 Jurickson Profar .75 2.00
94 Andruw Jones .60 1.50
95 Brandon Phillips .60 1.50
96 Ross Detwiler .60 1.50
97 Hanley Ramirez .75 2.00
98 Jose Abreu 10.00 25.00
99 Miguel Tejada .60 1.50
100 Ryan Braun .75 2.00

2013 Topps Tribute WBC Gold

*GOLD: 3X TO 8X BASIC
STATED ODDS 1:20 HOBBY
STATED PRINT RUN 25 SER.#'d SETS
25 Xander Bogaerts 10.00 25.00
30 Jose Reyes 10.00 25.00
42 Yadier Molina 15.00 40.00
53 Odrisamer Despaigne 30.00 60.00
98 Jose Abreu

2013 Topps Tribute WBC Autographs

STATED ODDS 1:4 HOBBY
ALL VERSIONS EQUALLY PRICED
EXCHANGE DEADLINE 06/30/2016
AC Asdrubal Cabrera 5.00 12.00
AC2 Asdrubal Cabrera 5.00 12.00
AG Adrian Gonzalez 8.00 20.00
AG2 Adrian Gonzalez 8.00 20.00
AJ Adam Jones 8.00 20.00
AJ2 Adam Jones 8.00 20.00
AJ3 Adam Jones 8.00 20.00
AR Andre Rienzo 4.00 10.00
AR2 Andre Rienzo 4.00 10.00
ARI Anthony Rizzo 8.00 20.00
ARI2 Anthony Rizzo 8.00 20.00
ARI3 Anthony Rizzo 10.00 25.00
AS Andrelton Simmons 10.00 25.00
AS2 Andrelton Simmons 10.00 25.00
BP Brandon Phillips 5.00 12.00
BP2 Brandon Phillips 5.00 12.00
BP3 Brandon Phillips 5.00 12.00
BZ Ben Zobrist 10.00 25.00
BZ2 Ben Zobrist 10.00 25.00
BZ3 Ben Zobrist 10.00 25.00
CK Craig Kimbrel 10.00 25.00
CK2 Craig Kimbrel 10.00 25.00
CS Carlos Santana 5.00 12.00
CS2 Carlos Santana 5.00 12.00
DHO Derek Holland 4.00 10.00
DHO2 Derek Holland 4.00 10.00
DHO3 Derek Holland 4.00 10.00
DW David Wright 12.50 30.00
EE Edwin Encarnacion 6.00 15.00
EE2 Edwin Encarnacion 6.00 15.00
ER Eddie Rosario 8.00 20.00
ER2 Eddie Rosario 8.00 20.00
FR Fernando Rodney EXCH 4.00 10.00
GG Gio Gonzalez EXCH 4.00 10.00
GP Glen Perkins 4.00 10.00
GP2 Glen Perkins 4.00 10.00
HA Henderson Alvarez 4.00 10.00
HA2 Henderson Alvarez 4.00 10.00
HR Hanley Ramirez 10.00 25.00
JA J.P. Arencibia 6.00 15.00
JA2 J.P. Arencibia 6.00 15.00
JAX John Axford 4.00 10.00
JAX2 John Axford 4.00 10.00
JB Jose Berrios 8.00 20.00
JB2 Jose Berrios 8.00 20.00
JG Jason Grilli 6.00 15.00
JG2 Jason Grilli 6.00 15.00
JL Jonathan Lucroy 8.00 20.00
JL2 Jonathan Lucroy 8.00 20.00
JP Jurickson Profar EXCH 8.00 20.00
JR Jose Reyes 6.00 15.00
JSC Jonathan Schoop 4.00 10.00
JSC2 Jonathan Schoop 4.00 10.00
JSC3 Jonathan Schoop 4.00 10.00
JT Jameson Taillon 6.00 15.00
JT2 Jameson Taillon 6.00 15.00
JT3 Jameson Taillon 6.00 15.00
KH Kelvin Herrera 4.00 10.00
KH2 Kelvin Herrera 4.00 10.00
LM Luis Mendoza 4.00 10.00
LM2 Luis Mendoza 4.00 10.00
MC Miguel Cabrera 20.00 50.00
MC2 Miguel Cabrera 20.00 50.00
MM Miguel Montero 4.00 10.00
MM2 Miguel Montero 4.00 10.00
MP Martin Prado 4.00 10.00
MP2 Martin Prado 4.00 10.00
NC Nelson Cruz 4.00 10.00
NC2 Nelson Cruz 4.00 10.00
NC3 Nelson Cruz 4.00 10.00
RD R.A. Dickey 5.00 12.00
RDE Ross Detwiler 4.00 10.00
RDE2 Ross Detwiler 4.00 10.00
RV Ryan Vogelsong 5.00 12.00
RV2 Ryan Vogelsong 5.00 12.00
SP Salvador Perez 6.00 15.00
SP2 Salvador Perez 6.00 15.00
SP3 Salvador Perez 6.00 15.00
SV Shane Victorino 6.00 15.00
SV2 Shane Victorino 6.00 15.00
WR Wandy Rodriguez 4.00 10.00
WR2 Wandy Rodriguez 4.00 10.00
YG Yovani Gallardo 6.00 15.00
YG2 Yovani Gallardo 6.00 15.00
YG3 Yovani Gallardo 6.00 15.00
YLW Yao-Lin Wang 5.00 12.00

2013 Topps Tribute WBC Autographs Blue

*BLUE: .5X TO 1.2X BASIC
STATED ODDS 1:9 HOBBY
STATED PRINT RUN 50 SER.#'d SETS
EXCHANGE DEADLINE 06/30/2016

2013 Topps Tribute WBC Autographs Orange

*ORANGE: .6X TO 1.5X BASIC
STATED ODDS 1:17 HOBBY
STATED PRINT RUN 25 SER.#'d SETS
EXCHANGE DEADLINE 06/30/2016

2013 Topps Tribute WBC Autographs Sepia

*SEPIA: .5X TO 1.2X BASIC
STATED ODDS 1:12 HOBBY
STATED PRINT RUN 35 SER.#'d SETS
EXCHANGE DEADLINE 06/30/2016

2013 Topps Tribute WBC Heroes Autographs

STATED ODDS 1:82 HOBBY
PRINT RUNS B/WN 20-200 COPIES PER
NO PRICING ON QTY 20 OR LESS
EXCHANGE DEADLINE 06/30/2016
AI Akinori Iwamura/200 5.00 12.00
HI Hisashi Iwakuma/100 20.00 50.00
KJ Kenji Johjima EXCH 10.00 25.00

2013 Topps Tribute WBC Prime Patches

PRINT RUNS B/WN 43-131 COPIES PER
AC Asdrubal Cabrera/131 5.00 12.00
AG Adrian Gonzalez/131 8.00 20.00
AIN Atsunori Inaba/43 20.00 50.00
AJ Andruw Jones/125 6.00 15.00
AJO Adam Jones/107 8.00 20.00
ALR Alex Rios/102 10.00 25.00
AP Angel Pagan/111 8.00 20.00
AR Andre Rienzo/95 6.00 15.00
ARI Anthony Rizzo/127 8.00 20.00
AS Andrelton Simmons/89 8.00 20.00
ASA Anibal Sanchez/131 5.00 12.00
BZ Ben Zobrist/126 8.00 20.00
CB Carlos Beltran/118 8.00 20.00
CGO Carlos Gonzalez/91 6.00 15.00
CHL Che-Hsuan Lin/101 8.00 20.00
CK Craig Kimbrel/131 10.00 25.00
CS Carlos Santana/120 6.00 15.00
DH Derek Holland/131 5.00 12.00
DHL Dae Ho Lee/67 10.00 25.00
DN Darien Nunez/117 5.00 12.00
DW David Wright/75 10.00 25.00
EAN Elvis Andrus/79 6.00 15.00
EAY Erick Aybar/87 5.00 12.00
EE Edwin Encarnacion/131 6.00 15.00
EH Eric Hosmer/131 6.00 15.00
ER Eddie Rosario/95 6.00 15.00
FC Frederich Cepeda/113 10.00 25.00
FR Fernando Rodney/131 5.00 12.00
GS Giancarlo Stanton/131 10.00 25.00
HR Hanley Ramirez/118 5.00 12.00
HWC Hung-Wen Chen/119 12.50 30.00
JB Jose Berrios/127 8.00 20.00
JF Jose Fernandez/85 8.00 20.00
JL Jonathan Lucroy/131 8.00 20.00
JM Justin Morneau/131 8.00 20.00
JMA Joe Mauer/55 12.50 30.00
JP J.P. Arencibia/101 10.00 25.00
JR Jose Reyes/53 10.00 25.00
JRO Jimmy Rollins/101 5.00 12.00
JS Jonathan Schoop/122 6.00 15.00
JT Jameson Taillon/131 8.00 20.00
JTT Jen-Ho Tseng/61 15.00 40.00
JV Joey Votto/118 12.50 30.00
JWS Jae Weong Seo/73 12.50 30.00
KM Kenta Maeda/43 40.00 100.00
KO Kenji Ohtonari/43 30.00 60.00
MC Miguel Cabrera/131 12.50 30.00
MM Miguel Montero/131 5.00 12.00
MS Marco Scutaro/129 6.00 15.00
MT Miguel Tejada/95 5.00 12.00
NC Nelson Cruz/95 5.00 12.00
NM Nobuhiro Matsuda/43 8.00 20.00
PA Philippe Aumont/131 5.00 12.00
RB Ryan Braun/81 6.00 15.00
RC Robinson Cano/131 15.00 40.00
RD R.A. Dickey/131 10.00 25.00
RDE Ross Detwiler/131 5.00 12.00
SP Salvador Perez/131 5.00 12.00
SR Sergio Romo/102 10.00 25.00
SV Shane Victorino/131 5.00 12.00
TI Takeru Imamura/43 8.00 20.00
TS Toshiya Sugiuchi/43 30.00 60.00
TU Tetsuya Utsumi/43 15.00 40.00
XB Xander Bogaerts/67 12.50 30.00
YG Yulieski Gourriel/76 10.00 25.00
YGA Yovani Gallardo/131 8.00 20.00
YH Yuichi Honda/43 20.00 50.00
YHY Yao-Hsun Yang/95 15.00 40.00
YLW Yao-Lin Wang/102 8.00 20.00
YM Yadier Molina/74 15.00 40.00

2013 Topps Tribute WBC Prime Patches Blue

*BLUE: .4X TO 1X BASIC
STATED PRINT RUN 50 SER.#'d SETS

2013 Topps Tribute WBC Prime Patches Green

*GREEN: .5X TO 1.2X BASIC
STATED PRINT RUN 35 SER.#'d SETS

2013 Topps Tribute WBC Prime Patches Orange

*ORANGE: .5X TO 1.2X BASIC
STATED PRINT RUN 25 SER.#'d SETS
NM Nobuhiro Matsuda 30.00 60.00
TU Tetsuya Utsumi 15.00 40.00

2018 Topps Tribute

1 Mike Trout 5.00 12.00
2 Clayton Kershaw 2.00 5.00
3 Kris Bryant 1.25 3.00
4 Monte Irvin .75 2.00
5 Andrew Benintendi 1.00 2.50
6 Jose Ramirez .75 2.00
7 Goose Gossage .75 2.00
8 Roberto Clemente 2.50 6.00
9 Buster Posey 1.25 3.00
10 Ernie Banks 1.00 2.50
11 Nolan Ryan 3.00 8.00
12 Corey Seager 1.00 2.50
13 Manny Machado 1.00 2.50
14 Bo Jackson 1.00 2.50
15 Paul DeJong 1.00 2.50
16 Jonathan Schoop .60 1.50
17 Lorenzo Cain .60 1.50
18 Jacob deGrom 1.00 2.50
19 Cody Bellinger 2.00 5.00
20 Bert Blyleven .75 2.00
21 Anthony Rizzo 1.50 4.00
22 Red Schoendienst .75 2.00
23 Domingo Santana .75 2.00
24 Luis Severino .75 2.00
25 Bryce Harper 1.50 4.00
26 Adrian Beltre 1.00 2.50
27 Craig Kimbrel .75 2.00
28 Carlos Correa 1.00 2.50
29 Johnny Bench 1.00 2.50
30 Nolan Arenado 1.25 3.00
31 Josh Donaldson .75 2.00
32 Honus Wagner 1.00 2.50
33 Tommy Lasorda .75 2.00
34 Freddie Freeman 1.25 3.00
35 Billy Hamilton .75 2.00
36 Tim Raines .75 2.00
37 Robinson Cano .75 2.00
38 Aaron Judge 2.50 6.00
39 Wade Boggs .75 2.00
40 Giancarlo Stanton 1.00 2.50
41 Jose Altuve .75 2.00
42 Jimmie Foxx 1.00 2.50
43 Alex Bregman 1.00 2.50
44 Ichiro 1.25 3.00
45 Catfish Hunter .75 2.00
46 Billy Williams .75 2.00
47 Jose Abreu 1.00 2.50
48 Chris Sale 1.00 2.50
49 Whitey Ford .75 2.00
50 Hank Aaron 2.00 5.00
51 Jake Lamb .75 2.00
52 George Brett 2.00 5.00
53 Brooks Robinson .75 2.00
54 Mookie Betts 1.50 4.00
55 John Smoltz 1.00 2.50
56 Max Scherzer 1.00 2.50
57 Nelson Cruz 1.00 2.50
58 Cal Ripken Jr. 3.00 8.00
59 Jim Palmer .75 2.00
60 Roger Clemens 1.25 3.00
61 Satchel Paige 1.00 2.50
62 Willie Stargell .75 2.00
63 Steven Souza Jr. .75 2.00
64 Kenley Jansen .75 2.00
65 Francisco Lindor 1.00 2.50
66 Pedro Martinez .75 2.00
67 Ted Williams 2.00 5.00
68 Jeff Bagwell .75 2.00
69 Corey Kluber .75 2.00
70 Noah Syndergaard .75 2.00
71 Matt Olson .60 1.50
72 Zack Greinke .75 2.00
73 Justin Verlander 1.00 2.50
74 Paul Goldschmidt 1.00 2.50
75 Don Sutton .75 2.00
76 Jim Edmonds .60 1.50
77 Stephen Strasburg 1.00 2.50
78 Jim Thome .75 2.00
79 Carlton Fisk .75 2.00
80 Rickey Henderson 1.00 2.50
81 Alex Rodriguez 1.25 3.00
82 Orlando Cepeda .75 2.00
83 Andrew McCutchen 1.00 2.50
84 Carlos Carrasco .60 1.50
85 Justin Upton .60 1.50
86 Salvador Perez .75 2.00
87 Mariano Rivera 1.25 3.00
88 Frank Thomas 1.00 2.50
89 Duke Snider .75 2.00
90 Sandy Koufax 2.00 5.00

2018 Topps Tribute Green

*GREEN: 1X TO 2.5X BASIC
STATED ODDS 1:9 HOBBY
STATED PRINT RUN 99 SER.#'d SETS

2018 Topps Tribute Purple

*PURPLE: 1.2X TO 3X BASIC
STATED ODDS 1:17 HOBBY
STATED PRINT RUN 50 SER.#'d SETS

2018 Topps Tribute '18 Rookies

STATED ODDS 1:30 HOBBY
STATED PRINT RUN 254 SER.#'d SETS
*GREEN/99: .5X TO 1.2X BASIC
*PURPLE/50: .6X TO 1.5X BASIC
18R1 Rafael Devers 4.00 10.00
18R2 Amed Rosario 1.50 4.00
18R3 Alex Verdugo 2.00 5.00
18R4 Ozzie Albies 4.00 10.00
18R5 Rhys Hoskins 10.00 25.00
18R6 J.P. Crawford 1.25 3.00
18R7 Dominic Smith 1.25 3.00
18R8 Clint Frazier 2.50 6.00
18R9 Nick Williams 1.50 4.00
18R10 Victor Robles 3.00 8.00

2018 Topps Tribute Autograph Patches

STATED ODDS 1:111 HOBBY
STATED PRINT RUN 50 SER.#'d SETS
EXCHANGE DEADLINE 1/31/2020
TAPAB Andrew Benintendi EXCH 40.00 100.00
TAPAR Anthony Rizzo

TAPBP Buster Posey
TAPCC Carlos Correa
TAPCJ Chipper Jones
TAPCRK Craig Kimbrel 25.00 60.00
TAPCSA Chris Sale 25.00 60.00
TAPDB Dellin Betances 10.00 25.00
TAPDJ Derek Jeter
TAPDM Daniel Murphy EXCH 15.00 40.00
TAPDP David Price 20.00 50.00
TAPEL Evan Longoria
TAPJV Joey Votto EXCH
TAPKD Khris Davis 12.00 30.00
TAPKS Kyle Seager 15.00 40.00
TAPLS Luis Severino 30.00 80.00
TAPMM Manny Machado
TAPMT Mike Trout

2018 Topps Tribute Autographs

STATED ODDS 1:6 HOBBY
PRINT RUNS B/WN 15-199 COPIES PER
NO PRICING ON QTY 15 OR LESS
EXCHANGE DEADLINE 1/31/2020
TAAB Adrian Beltre/110 20.00 50.00
TAABA Anthony Banda/199 3.00 8.00
TAABE Andrew Benintendi/199 20.00 50.00
TAABR Alex Bregman/193 20.00 50.00
TAAD Adam Duvall/196 5.00 12.00
TAAG Andres Galarraga/199 4.00 10.00
TAAJ Aaron Judge/100 100.00 250.00
TAAJU Aaron Judge/100 100.00 250.00
TAAK Al Kaline/199 20.00 50.00
TAAP Andy Pettitte/110 15.00 40.00
TAAR Anthony Rizzo/110 25.00 60.00
TAARO Amed Rosario/199 4.00 10.00
TAAV Alex Verdugo/199 5.00 12.00
TABA Bobby Abreu/190 3.00 8.00
TABJ Bo Jackson/85 30.00 80.00
TABRZ Bradley Zimmer/199 3.00 8.00
TABZI Bradley Zimmer/162 3.00 8.00
TABZ Ben Zobrist/191 10.00 25.00
TACA Christian Arroyo/199 3.00 8.00
TACAR Christian Arroyo/199 3.00 8.00
TACC Carlos Correa/80 15.00 40.00
TACCA Carlos Carrasco/199 3.00 8.00
TACF Clint Frazier/199 6.00 15.00
TACK Craig Kimbrel/199 10.00 25.00
TACRJ Cal Ripken Jr./40 50.00 120.00
TACSA Chris Sale/110 12.00 30.00
TADB Dellin Betances/199 4.00 10.00
TADBE Dellin Betances/199 4.00 10.00
TADDU Danny Duffy/195 3.00 8.00
TADF Derek Fisher/199 3.00 8.00
TADFO Dustin Fowler/199 3.00 8.00
TADG Didi Gregorius/199 4.00 10.00
TADJU David Justice/199 5.00 12.00
TADM Daniel Murphy EXCH 8.00 20.00
TADO David Ortiz/60 30.00 80.00
TADP David Price/110 8.00 20.00
TADS Dominic Smith/199 6.00 15.00
TADW Dave Winfield/85 15.00 40.00
TAET Eric Thames/199 4.00 10.00
TAETH Eric Thames/199 4.00 10.00
TAFB Franklin Barreto/199 3.00 8.00
TAFBA Franklin Barreto/199 3.00 8.00
TAFF Freddie Freeman/199 12.00 30.00
TAFME Francisco Mejia/199 10.00 25.00
TAFT Frank Thomas/100 25.00 60.00
TAHA Hank Aaron/20 100.00 400.00
TAHB Harrison Bader/199 5.00 12.00
TAIH Ian Happ/199 8.00 20.00
TAJC J.P. Crawford/199 8.00 20.00
TAJD Josh Donaldson/80 10.00 25.00
TAJDE Jacob deGrom/199 10.00 25.00
TAJT Jim Thome EXCH 20.00 50.00
TAKB Kris Bryant/85 40.00 100.00
TAKD Khris Davis/199 5.00 12.00
TAKDA Khris Davis/199 5.00 12.00
TAKS Kyle Schwarber/199 5.00 12.00
TALB Lewis Brinson/199 3.00 8.00
TALBR Lewis Brinson/198 3.00 8.00
TALG Lucas Giolito/199 4.00 10.00
TALW Luke Weaver/199 4.00 10.00
TAMCO Michael Conforto/186 4.00 10.00
TAMF Michael Fulmer/199 3.00 8.00
TAMFU Michael Fulmer/199 3.00 8.00
TAMH Mitch Haniger/199 8.00 20.00
TAMM Manny Machado/100 20.00 50.00
TAMP Mike Piazza/30 40.00 100.00
TAMR Mariano Rivera/30 60.00 150.00
TAMT Mike Trout/30 200.00 500.00
TANS Noah Syndergaard/110 12.00 30.00
TAOAL Ozzie Albies/199 20.00 50.00
TAPD Paul DeJong/199 5.00 12.00
TAPM Pedro Martinez/30 40.00 100.00
TARB Ryan Braun/152 5.00 12.00
TARD Rafael Devers/199 10.00 25.00
TARHO Rhys Hoskins/199 15.00 40.00
TARJ Reggie Jackson/40 15.00 40.00
TASK Sandy Koufax
TASN Sean Newcomb/199 4.00 10.00
TASNE Sean Newcomb/199 4.00 10.00
TATR Tim Raines/199 8.00 20.00
TAWC Willson Contreras/178 6.00 15.00

2018 Topps Tribute Autographs Blue

*BLUE: .4X TO 1X BASIC
STATED ODDS 1:20 HOBBY
PRINT RUNS B/WN 113-150 COPIES PER
EXCHANGE DEADLINE 1/31/2020
TALS Luis Severino/142 10.00 25.00

2018 Topps Tribute Autographs Green

*GREEN: .5X TO 1.2X BASIC
STATED ODDS 1:13 HOBBY
PRINT RUNS B/WN 78-99 COPIES PER
NO PRICING ON QTY 15 OR LESS
EXCHANGE DEADLINE 1/31/2020
TALS Luis Severino/81 12.00 30.00

2018 Topps Tribute Autographs Orange

*ORANGE: .6X TO 1.5X BASE p/r 100-199
*ORANGE: .5X TO 1.2X BASE p/r 30-85
STATED ODDS 1:39 HOBBY
PRINT RUNS B/WN 16-25 COPIES PER
NO PRICING ON QTY 19 OR LESS
EXCHANGE DEADLINE 1/31/2020
TALS Luis Severino/25 15.00 40.00
TASO Shohei Ohtani 1000.00 1500.00

2018 Topps Tribute Autographs Purple

*PURPLE: .5X TO 1.2X BASE p/r 100-199
*PURPLE: .4X TO 1X BASE p/r 30-85
STATED ODDS 1:22 HOBBY
PRINT RUNS B/WN 40-50 COPIES PER
NO PRICING ON QTY 15 OR LESS
EXCHANGE DEADLINE 1/31/2020
TALS Luis Severino/46 12.00 30.00
TASO Shohei Ohtani 800.00 1200.00

2018 Topps Tribute Dual Player Relics

RANDOM INSERTS IN PACKS
STATED PRINT RUN 150 SER.#'d SETS
*GREEN/99: .4X TO 1X BASIC
*PURPLE/50: .5X TO 1.2X BASIC
*ORANGE/25: 1X TO 2.5X BASIC
DRAB Nolan Arenado 6.00 15.00
Charlie Blackmon
DRBB Mookie Betts 8.00 20.00
Xander Bogaerts
DRBH Bryce Harper 8.00 20.00
Kris Bryant
DRBL Wade Boggs 5.00 12.00
Evan Longoria
DRCB Dellin Betances 5.00 12.00
Aroldis Chapman
DRCC Robinson Cano 5.00 12.00
Nelson Cruz
DRCS Sale/Clemens 6.00 15.00
DRCSE Carlos Correa 5.00 12.00
Corey Seager
DRCSP Carlos Correa 5.00 12.00
George Springer
DRDB Jose Bautista 4.00 10.00
Josh Donaldson
DRDT Yu Darvish 5.00 12.00
Masahiro Tanaka
DRGG Zack Greinke 5.00 12.00
Paul Goldschmidt
DRGM Ken Griffey Jr. 12.00 30.00
Mark McGwire
DRIS Ichiro 6.00 15.00
Giancarlo Stanton
DRJS Dansby Swanson 8.00 20.00
Chipper Jones
DRKJ Kenley Jansen 6.00 15.00
Clayton Kershaw
DROS Giancarlo Stanton 5.00 12.00
Marcell Ozuna
DRPC Mike Piazza 5.00 12.00
Yoenis Cespedes
DRPCR Brandon Crawford 6.00 15.00
Buster Posey
DRRB Bryant/Rizzo 8.00 20.00
DRRM Cal Ripken Jr. 10.00 25.00
Manny Machado
DRSD Noah Syndergaard 8.00 20.00
Jacob deGrom
DRTM Daniel Murphy 4.00 10.00
Trea Turner
DRTP Mike Trout 25.00 60.00
Albert Pujols

2018 Topps Tribute Dual Relics

STATED ODDS 1:12 HOBBY
STATED PRINT RUN 150 SER.#'d SETS
*GREEN/99: .4X TO 1X BASIC
*PURPLE/50: .5X TO 1.2X BASIC
*ORANGE/25: .75X TO 2X BASIC
DRABE Andrew Benintendi 4.00 10.00
DRABR Alex Bregman 4.00 10.00
DRBLA Barry Larkin 3.00 8.00
DRCF Clint Frazier 5.00 12.00
DRCK Craig Kimbrel 3.00 8.00
DRDO David Ortiz 4.00 10.00
DRFL Francisco Lindor 4.00 10.00
DRGS Gary Sanchez 5.00 12.00
DRJV Joey Votto 4.00 10.00
DRLS Luis Severino 3.00 8.00
DRMS Max Scherzer 4.00 10.00
DRNR Nolan Ryan 8.00 20.00
DRPM Pedro Martinez 3.00 8.00
DRRH Rickey Henderson 5.00 12.00
DRRJ Reggie Jackson 5.00 12.00
DRSS Stephen Strasburg 4.00 10.00

2018 Topps Tribute Generations of Excellence Autographs

STATED ODDS 1:56 HOBBY
PRINT RUNS B/WN X-X COPIES PER
NO PRICING ON QTY 15 OR LESS
EXCHANGE DEADLINE 1/31/2020
*ORANGE/23-25: .4X TO 1X BASE p/r 20-30
*ORANGE/23-25: .5X TO 1.2X BASE p/r 35-65
GOEAD Andre Dawson/40 20.00 50.00
GOEAG Andres Galarraga/65 6.00 15.00
GOEAK Al Kaline/65 25.00 50.00
GOEAP Andy Pettitte/40 12.00 30.00
GOEBJ Bo Jackson/30 40.00 100.00
GOEBW Bernie Williams/40 20.00 50.00
GOECJ Chipper Jones/30 60.00 150.00
GOECRJ Cal Ripken Jr./20 75.00 200.00
GOECY Carl Yastrzemski/20 30.00 120.00
GOEDC David Cone/65 10.00 25.00
GOEDE Dennis Eckersley/50 10.00 25.00
GOEDM Don Mattingly/30 50.00 120.00
GOEDO David Ortiz/30 30.00 80.00
GOEDW Dave Winfield/30 15.00 40.00
GOEEM Edgar Martinez/65 12.00 30.00
GOEFT Frank Thomas/30 30.00 80.00
GOEJB Jeff Bagwell/40 20.00 50.00
GOEJD Johnny Damon/65 5.00 12.00
GOEJG Juan Gonzalez/65 10.00 25.00
GOEJS John Smoltz/35 20.00 50.00
GOEJT Jim Thome EXCH 40.00 100.00
GOEMM Mark McGwire/20 50.00 120.00
GOENG Nomar Garciaparra/40 20.00 50.00
GOEOS Ozzie Smith/35 20.00 50.00
GOEOV Omar Vizquel/50 5.00 12.00
GOEPM Pedro Martinez/20 40.00 100.00
GOEPN Phil Niekro/65 12.00 30.00
GOERA Roberto Alomar/40 12.00 30.00
GOERCA Rod Carew/45 15.00 40.00
GOERF Rollie Fingers/65 10.00 25.00
GOERJA Reggie Jackson/20 40.00 100.00
GOETG Tom Glavine/35 20.00 50.00
GOETR Tim Raines/50 10.00 25.00
GOEWB Wade Boggs/30 25.00 60.00

2018 Topps Tribute Iconic Perspectives Autographs

STATED ODDS 1:40 HOBBY
PRINT RUNS B/WN 10-99 COPIES PER
NO PRICING ON QTY 15 OR LESS
EXCHANGE DEADLINE 1/31/2020
*ORANGE/23-25: .4X TO 1X BASE p/r 25-30
*ORANGE/23-25: .5X TO 1.2X BASE p/r 34-99
IPAB Adrian Beltre/35 20.00 50.00
IPAJ Aaron Judge/99 100.00 250.00
IPAK Al Kaline/99 25.00 50.00
IPAP Andy Pettitte/34 12.00 30.00
IPAR Anthony Rizzo/50 20.00 50.00
IPBJ Bo Jackson/30 40.00 100.00
IPCC Carlos Correa/40 40.00 100.00
IPCSA Chris Sale/50 10.00 25.00
IPDB Dellin Betances/99 5.00 12.00
IPDJU David Justice/97 10.00 25.00
IPDO David Ortiz/30 30.00 80.00
IPDP David Price/35 10.00 25.00
IPER Edgar Renteria/99 5.00 12.00
IPHA Hank Aaron
IPJB Jeff Bagwell/35 20.00 50.00
IPJD Josh Donaldson/50 15.00 40.00
IPJDA Johnny Damon/99 5.00 12.00
IPJDE Jacob deGrom/99 10.00 25.00
IPJT Jim Thome EXCH 25.00 60.00
IPKB Kris Bryant EXCH 75.00 200.00
IPKS Kyle Schwarber/99 12.00 30.00
IPMM Manny Machado/40 20.00 50.00
IPNS Noah Syndergaard/50 20.00 50.00
IPOV Omar Vizquel/99 5.00 12.00
IPPM Pedro Martinez/25 40.00 100.00
IPRC Rod Carew/35 15.00 40.00
IPRJ Randy Johnson/25 40.00 100.00
IPRJA Reggie Jackson/30 40.00 100.00
IPSP Stephen Piscotty/97 4.00 10.00
IPTR Tim Raines/50 10.00 25.00
IPWC Willson Contreras/99 12.00 30.00

2018 Topps Tribute League Inauguration Autographs

STATED ODDS 1:96 HOBBY
PRINT RUNS B/WN 69-75 COPIES PER
EXCHANGE DEADLINE 1/31/2020
*ORANGE/25: .5X TO 1.2X BASIC
LAAR Amed Rosario/75 12.00 30.00
LACF Clint Frazier/75 8.00 20.00
LADS Dominic Smith/75 4.00 10.00
LAHB Harrison Bader/75 6.00 15.00
LAJC J.P. Crawford/69 4.00 10.00
LAOA Ozzie Albies/75 25.00 60.00
LARD Rafael Devers/75 12.00 30.00
LARH Rhys Hoskins/75 60.00 150.00
LARM Ryan McMahon/75 8.00 20.00

2018 Topps Tribute Stamp of Approval Relics

STATED ODDS 1:14 HOBBY
STATED PRINT RUN 150 SER.#'d SETS
*GREEN/99: .4X TO 1X BASIC
*PURPLE/50: .5X TO 1.2X BASIC
*ORANGE/25: .75X TO 2X BASIC
SOAAB Andrew Benintendi/150 4.00 10.00
SOAABR Alex Bregman 4.00 10.00
SOAAR Anthony Rizzo/150 6.00 15.00
SOABH Bryce Harper/150 6.00 15.00
SOABP Buster Posey/150 5.00 12.00
SOACB Cody Bellinger/150 6.00 15.00
SOACBL Charlie Blackmon/150 4.00 10.00
SOACC Carlos Correa/150 4.00 10.00
SOACF Clint Frazier/150 5.00 12.00
SOACJ Chipper Jones/150 4.00 10.00
SOACK Clayton Kershaw/150 8.00 20.00
SOACKI Craig Kimbrel/150 3.00 8.00
SOACM Carlos Martinez/150 3.00 8.00
SOACS Corey Seager/150 4.00 10.00
SOACSA Chris Sale/150 4.00 10.00
SOADB Dellin Betances/150 3.00 8.00
SOADJ Derek Jeter/150 25.00 60.00
SOADM Daniel Murphy/150 3.00 8.00
SOADP David Price/150 3.00 8.00
SOADS Dansby Swanson/150 4.00 10.00
SOAEL Evan Longoria/150 3.00 8.00
SOAFL Francisco Lindor/150 4.00 10.00
SOAGS George Springer/150 3.00 8.00
SOAI Ichiro/140 5.00 12.00
SOAJA Jose Altuve/149 3.00 8.00
SOAJM J.D. Martinez/150 4.00 10.00
SOAJV Joey Votto/150 4.00 10.00
SOAKB Kris Bryant/150 5.00 12.00
SOAKD Khris Davis/150 4.00 10.00
SOAKS Kyle Seager/150 2.50 6.00
SOALS Luis Severino/150 3.00 8.00
SOAMAT Masahiro Tanaka/150 3.00 8.00
SOAMM Manny Machado/150 4.00 10.00
SOAMR Mariano Rivera/150 5.00 12.00
SOAMS Marcus Stroman/150 3.00 8.00
SOAMT Mike Trout/150 20.00 50.00
SOANA Nolan Arenado/150 5.00 12.00

2018 Topps Tribute Tandem Autograph Booklets

STATED ODDS 1:240 HOBBY
STATED PRINT RUN 25 SER.#'d SETS
EXCHANGE DEADLINE 1/31/2020
TTAB Altve/Biggo EXCH 30.00 80.00
TTBB Craig Biggio 40.00 100.00
Alex Bregman EXCH
TTDR dGrm/Ryn EXCH 75.00 200.00
TTET Encrncn/Thme EXCH 75.00 200.00
TTGB Bgwll/Gldschmdt EXCH 50.00 120.00
TTJJ Judge/Jeter
TTJJA Jackson/Judge 100.00 250.00
TTJW Winfield/Judge 150.00 400.00
TTPM Mrtnz/Prce EXCH 60.00 150.00
TTRS Sndbrg/Rssll EXCH 60.00 150.00
TTSC Sale/Clemens
TTSW Miguel Sano 30.00 80.00
Dave Winfield EXCH

2018 Topps Tribute Tribute to the Moment Autographs

STATED ODDS 1:62 HOBBY
PRINT RUNS B/WN 10-99 COPIES PER
NO PRICING ON QTY 10 OR LESS
EXCHANGE DEADLINE 1/31/2020
*PRPLE/47-50: .4X TO 1X BASE p/r 40-99
*ORNGE/23-25: .4X TO 1X BASE p/r 30
*ORNGE/23-25: .5X TO 1.2X BASE p/r 40-99
TTMAB Adrian Beltre/75 20.00 50.00
TTMAR Amed Rosario/99 10.00 25.00
TTMCF Carlton Fisk/67 20.00 50.00
TTMCFR Clint Frazier/99 8.00 20.00
TTMCJ Chipper Jones/40 50.00 120.00
TTMCRJ Cal Ripken Jr. EXCH 75.00 200.00
TTMCS Chris Sale/99 10.00 25.00
TTMJB Jeff Bagwell/75 20.00 50.00
TTMJT Jim Thome EXCH 30.00 80.00
TTMKB Kris Bryant/40 75.00 200.00
TTMOV Omar Vizquel/67 5.00 12.00
TTMRA Roberto Alomar/75 8.00 20.00
TTMRC Roger Clemens/30 25.00 60.00
TTMRCA Rod Carew/75 15.00 40.00
TTMRD Rafael Devers/99 12.00 30.00
TTMRF Rollie Fingers/65 10.00 25.00
TTMRJ Reggie Jackson/40 30.00 80.00
TTMRJO Randy Johnson/30 40.00 100.00
TTMTR Tim Raines/62 10.00 25.00
TTMWB Wade Boggs/40 20.00 50.00

2018 Topps Tribute Triple Relics

STATED ODDS 1:13 HOBBY
STATED PRINT RUN 150 SER.#'d SETS
*GREEN/99: .4X TO 1X BASIC
*PURPLE/50: .5X TO 1.2X BASIC
*ORANGE/25: .75X TO 2X BASIC
TTRAB Andrew Benintendi 4.00 10.00
TTRAC Aroldis Chapman 4.00 10.00
TTRAP Albert Pujols 5.00 12.00
TTRAR Anthony Rizzo 6.00 15.00
TTRBH Bryce Harper 6.00 15.00
TTRBL Barry Larkin 3.00 8.00
TTRBP Buster Posey 5.00 12.00
TTRCB Cody Bellinger 6.00 15.00
TTRCBL Charlie Blackmon 4.00 10.00
TTRCC Carlos Correa 4.00 10.00
TTRCJ Chipper Jones 5.00 12.00
TTRCK Clayton Kershaw 8.00 20.00
TTRCRJ Cal Ripken Jr. 12.00 30.00
TTRCS Chris Sale 4.00 10.00
TTRCSE Corey Seager 4.00 10.00
TTRER Edgar Renteria 2.50 6.00
TTRGS Gary Sanchez 5.00 12.00
TTRGST Giancarlo Stanton 5.00 12.00
TTRI Ichiro 5.00 12.00
TTRJA Jose Altuve 3.00 8.00
TTRJD Josh Donaldson 3.00 8.00
TTRJV Joey Votto 4.00 10.00
TTRKB Kris Bryant 5.00 12.00
TTRKGJ Ken Griffey Jr. 10.00 25.00
TTRMB Mookie Betts 6.00 15.00
TTRMM Manny Machado 4.00 10.00
TTRMP Mike Piazza 4.00 10.00
TTRMS Max Scherzer 4.00 10.00
TTRMT Masahiro Tanaka 3.00 8.00
TTRMTR Mike Trout 20.00 50.00
TTRNR Nolan Ryan 12.00 30.00
TTRNS Noah Syndergaard 3.00 8.00
TTRPM Pedro Martinez 3.00 8.00
TTRRC Robinson Cano 3.00 8.00
TTRRHE Rickey Henderson 5.00 12.00
TTRRJ Reggie Jackson 5.00 12.00
TTRTM Trey Mancini 3.00 8.00
TTRWB Wade Boggs 3.00 8.00
TTRYC Yoenis Cespedes 4.00 10.00

2019 Topps Tribute

1 Mike Trout 3.00 8.00
2 Gary Carter .50 1.25
3 Duke Snider .50 1.25
4 Khris Davis .60 1.50
5 Lou Gehrig 1.25 3.00
6 Giancarlo Stanton .60 1.50
7 Bo Jackson .60 1.50
8 Reggie Jackson .50 1.25
9 Eddie Murray .50 1.25
10 Ivan Rodriguez .50 1.25
11 Carl Yastrzemski 1.00 2.50
12 Max Scherzer .60 1.50
13 Will Clark .50 1.25
14 Phil Rizzuto .50 1.25
15 Vladimir Guerrero .50 1.25
16 Nolan Arenado .75 2.00
17 Josh Hader .40 1.00
18 Nolan Ryan 2.00 5.00
19 Warren Spahn .50 1.25
20 Noah Syndergaard .50 1.25
21 David Ortiz .60 1.50
22 Jacob deGrom .60 1.50
23 Miguel Andujar .60 1.50
24 Clayton Kershaw 1.25 3.00
25 Jackie Robinson .60 1.50
26 Justin Verlander .60 1.50
27 Gerrit Cole .60 1.50
28 Roberto Alomar .50 1.25
29 Catfish Hunter .50 1.25
30 Luis Severino .50 1.25
31 Roberto Clemente 1.50 4.00
32 Ronald Acuna Jr. 3.00 8.00
33 Mitch Haniger .50 1.25
34 Jose Altuve .50 1.25
35 Edwin Encarnacion .60 1.50
36 Francisco Lindor .60 1.50
37 Juan Soto 2.00 5.00
38 Javier Baez .75 2.00
39 Bryce Harper 1.00 2.50
40 Trea Turner .50 1.25
41 Corey Seager .60 1.50
42 Edwin Diaz .50 1.25
43 Red Schoendienst .50 1.25
44 Torii Hunter .40 1.00
45 Shohei Ohtani .75 2.00
46 Alex Bregman .60 1.50
47 Christian Yelich .75 2.00
48 Chris Sale .60 1.50
49 Ty Cobb 1.00 2.50
50 Mookie Betts 1.00 2.50
51 Joey Votto .60 1.50
52 Joe Morgan .50 1.25
53 George Springer .50 1.25
54 Sandy Koufax 1.25 3.00
55 Paul Goldschmidt .60 1.50
56 Ozzie Albies .60 1.50
57 Carlos Correa .60 1.50
58 Eddie Mathews .60 1.50
59 Roger Maris .60 1.50
60 Willie Stargell .50 1.25
61 Tommy Lasorda .50 1.25
62 Matt Carpenter .60 1.50
63 Aaron Nola .50 1.25
64 Goose Gossage .50 1.25
65 Hank Aaron 1.25 3.00
66 Don Mattingly 1.25 3.00
67 Whitey Ford .50 1.25
68 Derek Jeter 1.50 4.00
69 Kris Bryant .75 2.00
70 Jose Ramirez .50 1.25
71 Eugenio Suarez .50 1.25
72 Whit Merrifield .60 1.50
73 J.D. Martinez .60 1.50
74 Bob Feller .50 1.25
75 Aaron Judge 1.50 4.00
76 Freddie Freeman .75 2.00
77 Pedro Martinez .50 1.25
78 Anthony Rizzo 1.00 2.50
79 Rhys Hoskins .75 2.00
80 Harmon Killebrew .60 1.50
81 Blake Snell .50 1.25
82 Gleyber Torres 1.25 3.00
83 Enos Slaughter .50 1.25
84 Charlie Blackmon .60 1.50
85 Mike Piazza .60 1.50
86 Mark McGwire 1.00 2.50
87 George Brett 1.25 3.00
88 Andrew Benintendi .60 1.50
89 Eddie Rosario .50 1.25
90 Babe Ruth 1.50 4.00

2019 Topps Tribute Green

*GREEN: 1.2X TO 3X BASIC
STATED ODDS 1:9 HOBBY
STATED PRINT RUN 99 SER.#'d SETS

2019 Topps Tribute Purple

*PURPLE: 1.5X TO 4X BASIC
STATED ODDS 1:18 HOBBY
STATED PRINT RUN 50 SER.#'d SETS

2019 Topps Tribute '19 Rookies

STATED ODDS 1:18 HOBBY
STATED PRINT RUN 435 SER.#'d SETS
*GREEN/99: .5X TO 1.2X BASIC
*PURPLE/50: .6X TO 1.5X BASIC
19R1 Kyle Tucker 2.50 6.00
19R2 Rowdy Tellez 2.00 5.00
19R3 Cedric Mullins 2.00 5.00
19R4 Luis Urias 2.00 5.00
19R5 Ryan O'Hearn 1.25 3.00
19R6 Jake Bauers 2.00 5.00
19R7 Michael Kopech 2.50 6.00
19R8 Chance Adams 1.25 3.00
19R9 Kolby Allard 2.00 5.00
19R10 Justus Sheffield 2.00 5.00
19R11 Vladimir Guerrero Jr. 10.00 25.00
19R12 Fernando Tatis Jr. 6.00 15.00
19R13 Eloy Jimenez 5.00 12.00
19R14 Nick Senzel 4.00 10.00
19R15 Pete Alonso 10.00 25.00
19R16 Carter Kieboom 2.00 5.00

2019 Topps Tribute Autograph Patches

STATED ODDS 1:99 HOBBY
STATED PRINT RUN 50 SER.#'d SETS
EXCHANGE DEADLINE 7/31/2021
TAPAM Andrew McCutchen 25.00 60.00
TAPAR Amed Rosario 10.00 25.00
TAPDG Didi Gregorius 20.00 50.00
TAPER Eddie Rosario 8.00 20.00
TAPGS George Springer 15.00 40.00
TAPJD Jacob deGrom EXCH 20.00 50.00
TAPJV Joey Votto 30.00 80.00
TAPKS Kyle Schwarber 10.00 25.00
TAPLS Luis Severino 20.00 50.00
TAPMO Matt Olson 6.00 15.00
TAPNS Noah Syndergaard 15.00 40.00
TAPOA Ozzie Albies 20.00 50.00
TAPRI Raisel Iglesias 6.00 15.00
TAPTM Trey Mancini 15.00 40.00
TAPWM Whit Merrifield 12.00 30.00

2019 Topps Tribute Autographs

STATED ODDS 1:6 HOBBY
PRINT RUNS B/WN 5-199 COPIES PER
NO PRICING ON QTY 15 OR LESS
EXCHANGE DEADLINE 7/31/2021
*BLUE/150: .4X TO 1X p/r 125-199
*GREEN/99: .5X TO 1.2X p/r 125-199
*PURPLE/50: .5X TO 1.2X p/r 125-199
*PURPLE/50: .4X TO 1X p/r 30-90
*ORANGE/25: .6X TO 1.5X p/r 125-199
*ORANGE/25: .5X TO 1.2X p/r 30-90
TAAB Adrian Beltre/55 20.00 50.00
TAAJ Aaron Judge/40 60.00 150.00
TAAK Al Kaline/170 15.00 40.00
TAAM Andrew McCutchen/170 20.00 50.00
TAAME Austin Meadows/199 4.00 10.00
TAAP Andy Pettitte/170 8.00 20.00
TAAR Anthony Rizzo/60 20.00 50.00
TAARO Amed Rosario/199 4.00 10.00
TABB Byron Buxton/199 4.00 10.00
TABBL Bert Blyleven/199 4.00 10.00
TABG Bob Gibson/170 50.00 120.00
TABJ Bo Jackson
TABN Brandon Nimmo/199 8.00 20.00
TABP Buster Posey/45 30.00 80.00
TABW Bernie Williams/150 15.00 40.00
TACA Chance Adams/199 3.00 8.00
TACB Charlie Blackmon/199 5.00 12.00
TACBU Corbin Burnes/199 5.00 12.00
TACJ Chipper Jones/40 40.00 100.00
TACK Corey Kluber/170 4.00 10.00
TACY Carl Yastrzemski/40 40.00 100.00
TADE Dennis Eckersley/199 6.00 15.00
TADG Didi Gregorius/199 6.00 15.00
TADJ Derek Jeter/15
TADM Don Mattingly/170 30.00 80.00
TADO David Ortiz/40 25.00 60.00
TADS Deion Sanders EXCH 30.00 80.00
TAEM Edgar Martinez/199 10.00 25.00
TAER Eddie Rosario/199 4.00 10.00
TAFF Freddie Freeman/170 25.00 60.00
TAFT Frank Thomas/170 25.00 60.00
TAFTJ Fernando Tatis Jr./199 125.00 300.00
TAGM Greg Maddux/45 40.00 100.00
TAHM Hideki Matsui/40 40.00 100.00
TAIH Ian Happ/199 4.00 10.00
TAI Ichiro/25 150.00 400.00
TAJA Jose Altuve/170 15.00 40.00
TAJAB Jake Bauers/199 5.00 12.00
TAJAG Jesus Aguilar/199 3.00 8.00
TAJB Johnny Bench/66 20.00 50.00
TAJL Jonathan Loaisiga/199 4.00 10.00
TAJR Jim Rice/199 4.00 10.00
TAJRA Jose Ramirez/199 4.00 10.00
TAJS Juan Soto/199 25.00 60.00
TAJSH Justus Sheffield/199 5.00 12.00
TAJU Justin Upton/170 5.00 12.00
TAJV Joey Votto/60 15.00 40.00
TAKA Kolby Allard/199 5.00 12.00
TAKB Kris Bryant/60 50.00 120.00
TAKGJ Ken Griffey Jr. EXCH 125.00 300.00
TAKT Kyle Tucker
TALM Lance McCullers Jr./199 6.00 15.00
TALU Luis Urias/199 8.00 20.00
TAMA Miguel Andujar/199 8.00 20.00
TAMCA Miguel Cabrera/60 30.00 80.00
TAMH Mitch Haniger/199 4.00 10.00
TAMK Michael Kopech/199 6.00 15.00
TAMM Miles Mikolas/199 5.00 12.00
TAMO Marcell Ozuna/199 8.00 20.00
TAMOL Matt Olson/199 3.00 8.00
TAMP Mike Piazza/125 30.00 80.00
TAMR Mariano Rivera/30 100.00 250.00
TAMT Mike Trout/25 150.00 400.00
TAMTA Masahiro Tanaka/45 40.00 100.00
TANR Nolan Ryan/40 60.00 150.00
TANS Noah Syndergaard/170 10.00 25.00
TAOS Ozzie Smith/170 20.00 50.00
TAPA Peter Alonso/150 50.00 120.00
TAPD Paul DeJong/199 5.00 12.00
TAPDE Paul DeJong/199 5.00 12.00
TARAJ Ronald Acuna Jr./199 50.00 120.00
TARC Roger Clemens/35 30.00 80.00
TARCA Rod Carew/170 15.00 40.00
TARH Rhys Hoskins/199 6.00 15.00
TARJ Randy Johnson/40 50.00 120.00
TARJA Reggie Jackson/40 20.00 50.00
TASCK Scott Kingery/199 4.00 10.00
TASKI Scott Kingery/199 4.00 10.00
TASM Sean Manaea/199 3.00 8.00
TASO Shohei Ohtani/25 125.00 300.00
TATG Tom Glavine/90 10.00 25.00
TATH Trevor Hoffman/199 8.00 20.00
TATHU Torii Hunter/199 5.00 12.00
TATMA Tino Martinez/199 10.00 25.00
TATO Tyler O'Neill/199 4.00 10.00
TATR Tim Raines/170 6.00 15.00
TAVGJ Vladimir Guerrero Jr./199 40.00 100.00
TAWA Willy Adames/199 3.00 8.00
TAWB Walker Buehler/199 20.00 50.00
TAWC Willson Contreras/199 4.00 10.00
TAXB Xander Bogaerts EXCH 15.00 40.00
TAYK Yusei Kikuchi/199 8.00 20.00

2019 Topps Tribute Dual Player Relics

RANDOM INSERTS IN PACKS
STATED PRINT RUN 150 SER.#'d SETS
*GREEN/99: .4X TO 1X BASIC
*PURPLE/50: .5X TO 1.2X BASIC
*ORANGE/25: .75X TO 2X BASIC
DRAM Jose Abreu 4.00 10.00
Yoan Moncada
DRAS Ozzie Albies 4.00 10.00
Dansby Swanson
DRBA Nolan Arenado 5.00 12.00
Charlie Blackmon
DRBAN Brian Anderson 2.50 6.00
Justin Bour
DRBB Betts/Bogaerts 6.00 15.00
DRBR Eddie Rosario 3.00 8.00
Byron Buxton
DRBRI Bryant/Rizzo 6.00 15.00
DRBT Tucker/Bregman 5.00 12.00
DRCC Miguel Cabrera 4.00 10.00
Nicholas Castellanos
DRCM Matt Carpenter 4.00 10.00
Yadier Molina
DRCO Matt Chapman 4.00 10.00
Matt Olson
DRCS Carlos Correa 4.00 10.00
George Springer
DRDS Jacob deGrom 4.00 10.00
Noah Syndergaard
DREK Corey Kluber 4.00 10.00
Edwin Encarnacion
DRGM Joey Gallo 3.00 8.00
Nomar Mazara
DRGP Goldschmidt/Pollock 4.00 10.00
DRNA Aaron Nola 3.00 8.00
Jake Arrieta
DRPB Gregory Polanco 3.00 8.00
Josh Bell
DRPM Whit Merrifield 4.00 10.00
Salvador Perez
DRPMC Posey/McCutchen 5.00 12.00
DRPS Corey Seager 4.00 10.00
Yasiel Puig
DRSK Chris Sale 4.00 10.00
Craig Kimbrel
DRSS Marcus Stroman 3.00 8.00
Justin Smoak
DRST Masahiro Tanaka 3.00 8.00
Luis Severino
DRTP Trout/Pujols 12.00 30.00
DRVH Billy Hamilton 4.00 10.00
Joey Votto

2019 Topps Tribute Dual Relics

STATED ODDS 1:14 HOBBY
STATED PRINT RUN 150 SER.#'d SETS
*GREEN/99: .4X TO 1X BASIC
*PURPLE/50: .5X TO 1.2X BASIC
*ORANGE/25: .75X TO 2X BASIC
DRAP Andy Pettitte 2.50 6.00
DRAR Alex Rodriguez 4.00 10.00
DRCF Carlton Fisk 2.50 6.00
DRCRJ Cal Ripken Jr. 10.00 25.00
DRCY Carl Yastrzemski 5.00 12.00
DRDJ Derek Jeter 10.00 25.00
DRDW Dave Winfield 2.50 6.00
DRFT Frank Thomas 5.00 12.00
DRIR Ivan Rodriguez 2.50 6.00
DRI Ichiro 4.00 10.00
DRJB Johnny Bench 6.00 15.00
DRMP Mike Piazza 3.00 8.00
DRRC Roger Clemens 4.00 10.00
DRRH Rickey Henderson 10.00 25.00
DRRJ Reggie Jackson 6.00 15.00
DRSC Steve Carlton 2.50 6.00
DRWB Wade Boggs 2.50 6.00

2019 Topps Tribute Iconic Perspectives Autographs

STATED ODDS 1:42 HOBBY
PRINT RUNS B/WN 15-99 COPIES PER
NO PRICING ON TY 15 OR LESS
EXCHANGE DEADLINE 7/31/2021
*ORANGE/25: .5X TO 1.2X p/r 30-99
*ORANGE/25: .4X TO 1X p/r 25
IAPAB Adrian Beltre/30 20.00 50.00
IAPAD Andre Dawson/99 10.00 25.00
IAPBB Bert Blyleven/99 10.00 25.00
IAPCF Carlton Fisk/70 15.00 40.00
IAPCY Carl Yastrzemski/25 30.00 80.00
IAPDG Didi Gregorius/99 10.00 25.00
IAPDM Don Mattingly/30 30.00 80.00
IAPFF Freddie Freeman/99 20.00 50.00
IAPJB Johnny Bench/30 30.00 80.00

BA Jeff Bagwell/70 15.00 40.00
U Justin Upton/99 5.00 12.00
MO Marcell Ozuna/99 6.00 15.00
NR Nolan Ryan/25 125.00 300.00
OS Ozzie Smith/70 15.00 40.00
SK Scott Kingery/99 8.00 20.00
WC Willson Contreras/99 12.00 30.00
M Andrew McCutchen/30 15.00 40.00
ME Austin Meadows/99 5.00 12.00
P Andy Pettitte/70 12.00 30.00
R Anthony Rizzo
RO Amed Rosario/99 5.00 12.00
B Byron Buxton/99 8.00 20.00
G Bob Gibson/70 15.00 40.00
B Charlie Blackmon/99 6.00 15.00
J Derek Jeter
O David Ortiz/25 30.00 80.00
F Frank Thomas/30 25.00 60.00
A Hank Aaron
M Hideki Matsui/25 50.00 21.00
A Jose Altuve/30 15.00 40.00
S Juan Soto/99 30.00 80.00
B Kris Bryant/30 60.00 150.00
A Miguel Andujar/99 8.00 20.00
P Mike Piazza
T Mike Trout
S Noah Syndergaard/99 8.00 20.00
AJ Ronald Acuna Jr./99 60.00 150.00
C Roger Clemens
H Rhys Hoskins/99 12.00 30.00
J Reggie Jackson/25 30.00 80.00
H Trevor Hoffman/99 8.00 20.00
HU Torii Hunter/99 10.00 25.00

2019 Topps Tribute League Inauguration Autographs

ATED ODDS 1:149 HOBBY
ATED PRINT RUN 75 SER.#'d SETS
CHANGE DEADLINE 7/31/2021
RANGE/25: .5X TO 1.2X BASIC
CA Chance Adams 4.00 10.00
CB Corbin Burnes 6.00 15.00
EJ Eloy Jimenez 25.00 60.00
FTJ Fernando Tatis Jr. 75.00 200.00
JB Jake Bauers 6.00 15.00
JS Justus Sheffield 6.00 15.00
KA Kolby Allard 6.00 15.00
KT Kyle Tucker 20.00 50.00
LU Luis Urias 6.00 15.00
NS Nick Senzel
PA Peter Alonso 60.00 150.00
VGJ Vladimir Guerrero Jr. 100.00 250.00

2019 Topps Tribute Stamp of Approval Relics

ATED ODDS 1:14 HOBBY
ATED PRINT RUN 150 SER.#'d SETS
REEN/99: .4X TO 1X BASIC
URPLE/50: .5X TO 1.2X BASIC
RANGE/25: .75X TO 2X BASIC
AAB Adrian Beltre 3.00 8.00
AABR Alex Bregman 3.00 8.00
AAM Andrew McCutchen 3.00 8.00
AAR Anthony Rizzo 5.00 12.00
AARO Amed Rosario 2.50 6.00
ABP Buster Posey 4.00 10.00
ACC Carlos Correa 3.00 8.00
ACS Chris Sale 3.00 8.00
ADG Didi Gregorius 2.50 6.00
ADO David Ortiz 3.00 8.00
AEE Edwin Encarnacion 3.00 8.00
AER Eddie Rosario 2.50 6.00
AFF Freddie Freeman 4.00 10.00
AGS George Springer 2.50 6.00
AJA Jose Altuve 3.00 8.00
AJD Jacob deGrom 3.00 8.00
AJG Joey Gallo 2.50 6.00
AJH Josh Harrison 2.00 5.00
AJL Jake Lamb 2.50 6.00
AJS Justin Smoak 2.00 5.00
AJV Joey Votto 3.00 8.00
AKB Kris Bryant 4.00 10.00
AKD Khris Davis 3.00 8.00
AKS Kyle Schwarber 3.00 8.00
AKSE Kyle Seager 2.00 5.00
ALS Luis Severino 2.50 6.00
AMC Michael Conforto 2.50 6.00
AMO Matt Olson 2.00 5.00
AMT Masahiro Tanaka 2.50 6.00
AMTR Mike Trout 12.00 30.00
ANS Noah Syndergaard 2.50 6.00
AOA Ozzie Albies 3.00 8.00
ARI Raisel Iglesias 2.00 5.00
ASM Starling Marte 2.50 6.00
ASP Salvador Perez 2.50 6.00
ATM Trey Mancini 2.50 6.00
AWC Willson Contreras 2.50 6.00
AWM Whit Merrifield 3.00 8.00
AXB Xander Bogaerts 3.00 8.00

2019 Topps Tribute Tandem Autograph Booklets

ATED ODDS 1:647 HOBBY
ATED PRINT RUN 25 SER.#'d SETS
CHANGE DEADLINE 7/31/2021
AA Acuna/Aaron
BB Blyleven/Berrios 30.00 80.00
BH Buxton/Hunter 40.00 100.00
GR Gregorius/Richardson 40.00 100.00
HT Thome/Hoskins EXCH 75.00 200.00
JM Matsui/Judge
OB Ozuna/Brock 40.00 100.00
OR Ohtani/Ryan
PB Bench/Posey
RS Rizzo/Sandberg 100.00 250.00

TTSD Soto/Dawson 40.00 100.00
TTSR Syndergaard/Ryan 150.00 400.00
TTJA Trout/Jackson
TTTP Pettitte/Tanaka

2019 Topps Tribute Tribute to Enshrinement Autographs

STATED ODDS 1:57 HOBBY
PRINT RUNS B/WN 10-99 COPIES PER
NO PRICING ON TY 15 OR LESS
EXCHANGE DEADLINE 7/31/2021
*PURPLE/50: .4X TO 1X BASIC
*ORANGE/25: .5X TO 1.2X BASIC
HOFAD Andre Dawson/99 10.00 25.00
HOFAK Al Kaline/99 20.00 50.00
HOFAT Alan Trammell/99 25.00 60.00
HOFBB Bert Blyleven/99 10.00 25.00
HOFBG Bob Gibson/90 15.00 40.00
HOFCF Carlton Fisk/90 15.00 40.00
HOFCJ Chipper Jones/30 50.00 120.00
HOFCRJ Cal Ripken Jr./30 50.00 120.00
HOFCY Carl Yastrzemski/30 30.00 80.00
HOFEM Edgar Martinez/99 12.00 30.00
HOFFT Frank Thomas/40 25.00 60.00
HOFHA Hank Aaron
HOFJB Johnny Bench/30 30.00 80.00
HOFJBA Jeff Bagwell/70 15.00 40.00
HOFJM Juan Marichal
HOFNR Nolan Ryan/30 100.00 250.00
HOFOS Ozzie Smith/90 15.00 40.00
HOFRC Rod Carew/99 15.00 40.00
HOFRH Rickey Henderson
HOFRJ Randy Johnson
HOFRJA Reggie Jackson/30 25.00 60.00
HOFRY Robin Yount/40 30.00 80.00
HOFSC Steve Carlton/90 12.00 30.00
HOFTH Trevor Hoffman/99 8.00 20.00
HOFWB Wade Boggs/30 10.00 25.00

2019 Topps Tribute Tribute to the Postseason Autographs

STATED ODDS 1:48 HOBBY
PRINT RUNS B/WN 15-99 COPIES PER
NO PRICING ON TY 15 OR LESS
EXCHANGE DEADLINE 7/31/2021
*ORANGE/25: .5X TO 1.2X p/r 30-99
*ORANGE/25: .4X TO 1X p/r 20
TTPAB Adrian Beltre/50 25.00 60.00
TTPAK Al Kaline/99 20.00 50.00
TTPAP Andy Pettitte/99 15.00 40.00
TTPAR Anthony Rizzo/40 20.00 50.00
TTPBG Bob Gibson/99 20.00 50.00
TTPBW Bernie Williams/99
TTPCF Carlton Fisk/99 25.00 60.00
TTPCJ Chipper Jones/30 50.00 210.00
TTPCY Carl Yastrzemski/40 30.00 80.00
TTPDE Dennis Eckersley/99 10.00 25.00
TTPDG Didi Gregorius/99 15.00 40.00
TTPDJ Derek Jeter
TTPDO David Ortiz/40 25.00 60.00
TTPGS George Springer/99 12.00 30.00
TTPHM Hideki Matsui/40 50.00 120.00
TTPIR Ivan Rodriguez/99 10.00 25.00
TTPJA Jose Altuve/99 20.00 50.00
TTPJB Johnny Bench/40 30.00 80.00
TTPJD Johnny Damon/99 10.00 25.00
TTPJM Jack Morris/99 12.00 30.00
TTPJS John Smoltz/99 20.00 50.00
TTPKB Kris Bryant/40 60.00 150.00
TTPMR Mariano Rivera
TTPNR Nolan Ryan/40 100.00 250.00
TTPOS Ozzie Smith
TTPRJ Randy Johnson/20 40.00 100.00
TTPRJA Reggie Jackson/40 25.00 60.00
TTPSC Steve Carlton
TTPSK Sandy Koufax
TTPSP Salvador Perez/99 10.00 25.00
TTPTG Tom Glavine/99 20.00 50.00
TTPTH Torii Hunter/99 10.00 25.00
TTPTHO Trevor Hoffman/99 12.00 30.00
TTPVG Vladimir Guerrero/50 20.00 50.00

2019 Topps Tribute Triple Relics

STATED ODDS 1:15 HOBBY
STATED PRINT RUN 150 SER.#'d SETS
*GREEN/99: .4X TO 1X BASIC
*PURPLE/50: .5X TO 1.2X BASIC
*ORANGE/25: .75X TO 2X BASIC
TTRAB Andrew Benintendi 3.00 8.00
TTRABE Adrian Beltre 3.00 8.00
TTRAC Aroldis Chapman 3.00 8.00
TTRAJ Aaron Judge 8.00 20.00
TTRAP A.J. Pollock 2.00 5.00
TTRAR Anthony Rizzo 5.00 12.00
TTRBH Bryce Harper 5.00 12.00
TTRBP Buster Posey 4.00 10.00
TTRCB Charlie Blackmon 3.00 8.00
TTRCK Corey Kluber 2.50 6.00
TTRCKE Clayton Kershaw 6.00 15.00
TTRCS Chris Sale 3.00 8.00
TTRCSE Corey Seager 3.00 8.00
TTRDG Didi Gregorius 2.50 6.00
TTRDL DJ LeMahieu 3.00 8.00
TTREE Edwin Encarnacion 3.00 8.00
TTRER Eddie Rosario 2.50 6.00
TTRFF Freddie Freeman 4.00 10.00
TTRFL Francisco Lindor 3.00 8.00
TTRGS Gary Sanchez 3.00 8.00
TTRGSP George Springer 2.50 6.00
TTRJA Jose Altuve 2.50 6.00
TTRJAB Jose Abreu 3.00 8.00
TTRJB Josh Bell 2.50 6.00
TTRJBA Javier Baez 4.00 10.00
TTRJM J.D. Martinez 3.00 8.00

TTRJV Joey Votto 3.00 8.00
TTRKB Kris Bryant 4.00 10.00
TTRKS Kyle Schwarber 3.00 8.00
TTRKT Kyle Tucker 4.00 10.00
TTRLS Luis Severino 2.50 6.00
TTRMA Miguel Andujar 3.00 8.00
TTRMB Mookie Betts 5.00 12.00
TTRMC Miguel Cabrera 3.00 8.00
TTRMCA Matt Carpenter 3.00 8.00
TTRMS Max Scherzer 3.00 8.00
TTRMT Mike Trout 15.00 40.00
TTRNA Nolan Arenado 4.00 10.00
TTRNC Nicholas Castellanos 3.00 8.00
TTRNS Noah Syndergaard 2.50 6.00
TTROA Ozzie Albies 3.00 8.00
TTRPG Paul Goldschmidt 3.00 8.00
TTRRAJ Ronald Acuna Jr. 15.00 40.00
TTRRD Rafael Devers 4.00 10.00
TTRTS Trevor Story 3.00 8.00
TTRXB Xander Bogaerts 3.00 8.00
TTRYC Yoenis Cespedes 3.00 8.00
TTRYM Yadier Molina 3.00 8.00
TTRYP Yasiel Puig 3.00 8.00

2020 Topps Tribute

1 Mike Trout 3.00 8.00
2 Mike Mussina .50 1.25
3 Alex Rodriguez 2.00 5.00
4 DJ LeMahieu .60 1.50
5 Tom Seaver .50 1.25
6 Clayton Kershaw 1.25 3.00
7 David Cone .40 1.00
8 Khris Davis .60 1.50
9 Shohei Ohtani .75 2.00
10 Gleyber Torres 1.25 3.00
11 Joey Gallo .60 1.50
12 Justin Verlander .60 1.50
13 Chipper Jones .60 1.50
14 Alex Bregman .60 1.50
15 Eugenio Suarez .50 1.25
16 Pete Alonso 1.50 4.00
17 Hank Aaron 1.25 3.00
18 Cal Ripken Jr. 2.00 5.00
19 Willie Mays 1.25 3.00
20 Roger Clemens .75 2.00
21 Lou Gehrig 1.25 3.00
22 Ty Cobb 2.00 5.00
23 Harold Baines 1.50 4.00
24 Aaron Judge 1.50 4.00
25 Christian Yelich .75 2.00
26 Edgar Martinez .50 1.25
27 Bryce Harper 1.00 2.50
28 Eloy Jimenez .75 2.00
29 Hyun-Jin Ryu .50 1.25
30 Mookie Betts 1.25 3.00
31 Vladimir Guerrero .50 1.25
32 Don Mattingly 1.25 3.00
33 Austin Riley 1.00 2.50
34 Deion Sanders .50 1.25
35 Charlie Blackmon .60 1.50
36 Ramon Laureano .60 1.50
37 Mariano Rivera .75 2.00
38 Reggie Jackson .60 1.50
39 Yasiel Puig .60 1.50
40 Rhys Hoskins .75 2.00
41 Jose Altuve .60 1.50
42 Jacob deGrom .60 1.50
43 Ozzie Albies .60 1.50
44 Gary Sanchez .60 1.50
45 Walker Buehler .75 2.00
46 Ronald Acuna Jr. 2.50 6.00
47 Anthony Rizzo .60 1.50
48 Jackie Robinson .60 1.50
49 J.D. Martinez .60 1.50
50 Cody Bellinger 1.25 3.00
51 Josh Bell .50 1.25
52 Chris Sale .60 1.50
53 Ted Williams 1.25 3.00
54 Kris Bryant .75 2.00
55 Roberto Clemente 1.50 4.00
56 Sammy Sosa .60 1.50
57 Jeff McNeil .50 1.25
58 Rickey Henderson .60 1.50
59 Tony Gwynn .60 1.50
60 Juan Soto 2.00 5.00
61 Carl Yastrzemski 1.00 2.50
62 Trea Turner .50 1.25
63 Nick Senzel .60 1.50
65 Yoan Moncada .60 1.50
66 Max Scherzer .60 1.50
67 Roger Maris .60 1.50
68 Jose Abreu .60 1.50
69 George Brett 1.25 3.00
70 Manny Machado .60 1.50
71 Nolan Arenado .75 2.00
72 Francisco Lindor .60 1.50
73 Whit Merrifield .60 1.50
74 Wade Boggs .50 1.25
75 Javier Baez .75 2.00
76 Paul DeJong .60 1.50
77 Brandon Lowe .60 1.50
78 Freddie Freeman .75 2.00
79 Fernando Tatis Jr. 2.50 6.00
80 Paul Goldschmidt .60 1.50
81 Ichiro .75 2.00
82 Ken Griffey Jr. 1.25 3.00
83 Ernie Banks .60 1.50
84 Jim Thome .60 1.50
85 Vladimir Guerrero Jr. 1.25 3.00
86 Chris Paddack .60 1.50
87 Honus Wagner .60 1.50
88 Xander Bogaerts .60 1.50
89 Sandy Koufax 1.25 3.00

90 Babe Ruth 1.50 4.00
62A Gerrit Cole 1.00 2.50
62B Gerrit Cole 1.00 2.50

2020 Topps Tribute '20 Rookies

STATED ODDS 1:18 HOBBY
STATED PRINT RUN 450 SER.#'d SETS
20RAP A.J. Puk 2.50 6.00
20RBB Bo Bichette 12.00 30.00
20RBM Brendan McKay 2.50 6.00
20RDC Dylan Cease 3.00 8.00
20RGL Gavin Lux 15.00 40.00
20RJL Jesus Luzardo 2.50 6.00
20RKL Kyle Lewis 6.00 15.00
20RNH Nico Hoerner 5.00 12.00
20RYA Yordan Alvarez 15.00 40.00

2020 Topps Tribute '20 Rookies Green

*GREEN: .5X TO 1.2X BASIC
STATED ODDS 1:84 HOBBY
STATED PRINT RUN 99 SER.#'d SETS

2020 Topps Tribute '20 Rookies Purple

*PURPLE: .6X TO 1.5X BASIC
STATED ODDS 1:165 HOBBY
STATED PRINT RUN 50 SER.#'d SETS
20RYA Yordan Alvarez 30.00 80.00

2020 Topps Tribute Autograph Patches

STATED ODDS 1:86 HOBBY
STATED PRINT RUN 50 SER.#'d SETS
TAPAJ Aaron Judge
TAPAN Aaron Nola 20.00 50.00
TAPAR Anthony Rizzo 50.00 120.00
TAPBL Brandon Lowe 20.00 50.00
TAPBP Buster Posey
TAPBS Blake Snell 15.00 40.00
TAPGC Gerrit Cole 30.00 80.00
TAPGS George Springer 25.00 60.00
TAPJA Jose Altuve 25.00 60.00
TAPMC Miguel Cabrera 60.00 150.00
TAPMT Mike Trout
TAPOA Ozzie Albies EXCH 40.00 100.00
TAPRH Rhys Hoskins 25.00 60.00
TAPRT Rowdy Tellez 8.00 20.00
TAPVR Victor Robles 40.00 100.00
TAPWM Whit Merrifield 12.00 30.00
TAPFTJ Fernando Tatis Jr. 150.00 400.00
TAPLGJ Lourdes Gurriel Jr. 8.00 20.00

2020 Topps Tribute Autographs

STATED ODDS 1:8 HOBBY
PRINT RUNS B/WN 10-199 COPIES PER
NO PRICING ON QTY 15 OR LESS
EXCHANGE DEADLINE 1/31/22
TAAA Aristides Aquino/199 12.00 30.00
TAAG Andres Galarraga/199 4.00 10.00
TAAJ Aaron Judge/35 75.00 200.00
TAAK Al Kaline/150 20.00 50.00
TAAM Austin Meadows/199 8.00 20.00
TAAP Andy Pettitte/110 20.00 50.00
TAAPU A.J. Puk/199 6.00 15.00
TAAR Anthony Rizzo/60 25.00 60.00
TABB Bert Blyleven/199 8.00 20.00
TABBI Bo Bichette/199 60.00 150.00
TABDR Bobby Bradley/199 4.00 10.00
TABH Bryce Harper/30 150.00 400.00
TABM Brendan McKay/199 6.00 15.00
TABR Brendan Rodgers/199 6.00 15.00
TABS Blake Snell/199 4.00 10.00
TABW Bernie Williams/110 20.00 50.00
TACB Cavan Biggio/199 20.00 50.00
TACCS CC Sabathia/110 25.00 60.00
TACRJ Cal Ripken Jr./40 60.00 150.00
TACF Carlton Fisk/110 15.00 40.00
TACJ Chipper Jones/40 50.00 120.00
TACY Christian Yelich/110 25.00 60.00
TADC David Cone/199 15.00 40.00
TADCE Dylan Cease/199 8.00 20.00
TADE Dennis Eckersley/199 10.00 25.00
TADM Don Mattingly/60 40.00 100.00
TADMA Dustin May/199 20.00 50.00
TAEJ Eloy Jimenez/199 20.00 50.00
TAEM Edgar Martinez/150 15.00 40.00
TAFL Francisco Lindor/150 20.00 50.00
TAFT Frank Thomas/60 40.00 100.00
TAGL Gavin Lux/199 25.00 60.00
TAGS George Springer/160 8.00 20.00
TAHM Hideki Matsui/40 40.00 100.00
TAJA Jose Altuve/60 15.00 40.00
TAJB Johnny Bench/60 40.00 100.00
TAJC Jose Canseco/199 15.00 40.00
TAJDM J.D. Martinez/150 12.00 30.00
TAJL Jesus Luzardo/199 6.00 15.00
TAJP Jorge Posada/199 15.00 40.00
TAJR Jim Rice/199 10.00 25.00
TAJSM John Smoltz/110 15.00 40.00
TAJY Jordan Yamamoto/199 6.00 15.00
TAKB Kris Bryant/60 60.00 150.00
TAKH Keston Hiura/199 20.00 50.00
TAKHI Keston Hiura/199 20.00 50.00
TALA Logan Allen/199 3.00 8.00
TALMJ Lance McCullers Jr./199 6.00 15.00
TALR Luis Robert/199 100.00 250.00
TALV Luke Voit/199 15.00 40.00
TAMC Miguel Cabrera/60 60.00 150.00
TAMCH Michael Chavis/199 8.00 20.00
TAMMU Mike Mussina/110 25.00 60.00
TAMR Mariano Rivera/30 75.00 200.00
TAMT Mike Trout/25 800.00 1200.00
TAMUN Max Muncy/199 8.00 20.00
TANA Nolan Arenado/110 30.00 80.00
TANR Nolan Ryan/40 75.00 200.00

TANSZ Nick Senzel/199 8.00 20.00
TAOS Ozzie Smith/110 20.00 50.00
TAPD Paul DeJong/199 5.00 12.00
TARC Roger Clemens/35 50.00 120.00
TARCA Rod Carew/160 15.00 40.00
TARF Rollie Fingers/199 10.00 25.00
TARG Robel Garcia/199 3.00 8.00
TARH Rickey Henderson/40 60.00 150.00
TARHO Rhys Hoskins/199 6.00 15.00
TARJ Reggie Jackson/40 30.00 80.00
TASB Seth Brown/199 3.00 8.00
TASC Steve Carlton/110 15.00 40.00
TASM Sean Murphy/199 5.00 12.00
TASN Sheldon Neuse/199 4.00 10.00
TASO Shohei Ohtani/25 75.00 200.00
TATB Trevor Bauer/199 15.00 40.00
TATM Tino Martinez/199 20.00 50.00
TAVG Vladimir Guerrero/60 30.00 80.00
TAVGJ Vladimir Guerrero Jr./199 40.00 100.00
TAWC Willson Contreras/199 10.00 25.00
TAWM Whit Merrifield/199 5.00 12.00
TAWME Whit Merrifield/199 5.00 12.00
TAXB Xander Bogaerts/199 20.00 50.00
TAYA Yordan Alvarez/199 50.00 120.00

2020 Topps Tribute Autographs Blue

*BLUE/150: .4X TO 1X p/r 110-199
STATED ODDS 1:12 HOBBY
STATED PRINT RUN 150 SER.#'d SETS
TAFET Fernando Tatis Jr. 60.00 150.00
TAFTJ Fernando Tatis Jr. 60.00 150.00
TAJY Jordan Yamamoto 10.00 25.00

2020 Topps Tribute Autographs Green

*GREEN/99: .5X TO 1.2X p/r 110-199
STATED ODDS 1:18 HOBBY
STATED PRINT RUN 99 SER.#'d SETS
TAFET Fernando Tatis Jr. 75.00 200.00
TAFTJ Fernando Tatis Jr. 75.00 200.00
TAJY Jordan Yamamoto 12.00 30.00
TAPA Pete Alonso 50.00 120.00
TAPAL Pete Alonso 50.00 120.00
TARG Robel Garcia 8.00 20.00

2020 Topps Tribute Autographs Orange

*ORANGE/25: .6X TO 1.5X p/r 110-199
*ORANGE/25: .5X TO 1.2X p/r 30-60
*ORANGE/25: .4X TO 1X p/r 25
STATED ODDS 1:47 HOBBY
STATED PRINT RUN 25 SER.#'d SETS
TAAA Aristides Aquino 60.00 150.00
TAFET Fernando Tatis Jr. 100.00 250.00
TAFTJ Fernando Tatis Jr. 100.00 250.00
TAJY Jordan Yamamoto 15.00 40.00
TAMS Max Scherzer EXCH 50.00 120.00
TAMI Mike Trout 800.00 1200.00
TAPA Pete Alonso 60.00 150.00
TAPAL Pete Alonso 60.00 150.00
TARAJ Ronald Acuna Jr. 100.00 250.00
TARG Robel Garcia 12.00 30.00
TAYA Yordan Alvarez 100.00 250.00

2020 Topps Tribute Autographs Purple

*PURPLE/50: .5X TO 1.2X p/r 110-199
*PURPLE/50: .4X TO 1X p/r 30-60
STATED ODDS 1:27 HOBBY
STATED PRINT RUN 50 SER.#'d SETS
TAAA Aristides Aquino 30.00 80.00
TAFET Fernando Tatis Jr. 75.00 200.00
TAFTJ Fernando Tatis Jr. 75.00 200.00
TAJY Jordan Yamamoto 12.00 30.00
TAMS Max Scherzer EXCH 40.00 100.00
TAPA Pete Alonso 50.00 120.00
TAPAL Pete Alonso 50.00 120.00
TARAJ Ronald Acuna Jr. 75.00 200.00
TARG Robel Garcia 8.00 20.00
TAYA Yordan Alvarez 75.00 200.00

2020 Topps Tribute Dual Player Relics

STATED ODDS 1:14 HOBBY
STATED PRINT RUN 150 SER.#'d SETS
*GREEN/99: .4X TO 1X BASIC
*PURPLE/50: .5X TO 1.2X BASIC
*ORANGE/25: .8X TO 2X BASIC
DRAA O.Albies/R.Acuna Jr. 15.00 40.00
DRAC J.Altuve/C.Correa 6.00 15.00
DRAS N.Arenado/T.Story 6.00 15.00
DRAY C.Yelich/H.Aaron 15.00 40.00
DRBB X.Bogaerts/M.Betts 8.00 20.00
DRBP J.Bell/G.Polanco 6.00 15.00
DRBR A.Rizzo/J.Baez 15.00 40.00
DRCM J.McNeil/M.Conforto 3.00 8.00
DRGA V.Guerrero Jr./R.Alomar 8.00 20.00
DRGM K.Griffey Jr./E.Martinez 20.00 50.00
DRHH B.Harper/R.Hoskins 12.00 30.00
DRIK Ichiro/Y.Kikuchi 8.00 20.00
DRJH R.Henderson/R.Jackson 15.00 40.00
DRJS A.Judge/G.Stanton 10.00 25.00
DRLA W.Adames/B.Lowe 4.00 10.00
DRMO J.Martinez/D.Ortiz 4.00 10.00
DRMR C.Ripken Jr./E.Murray 12.00 30.00
DROT M.Trout/S.Ohtani 25.00 60.00
DRPS A.Pettitte/C.Sabathia 8.00 20.00
DRRC N.Ryan/G.Cole 12.00 30.00
DRRK C.Kershaw/H.Ryu 4.00 10.00
DRRS V.Robles/J.Soto 12.00 30.00
DRSB C.Seager/C.Bellinger 8.00 20.00
DRSR C.Santana/J.Ramirez 3.00 8.00
DRTR F.Tatis Jr./F.Reyes 8.00 20.00
DRGMA J.Gallo/N.Mazara 4.00 10.00
DRSBR K.Bryant/S.Sosa 10.00 25.00

2020 Topps Tribute Dual Relics

STATED ODDS 1:14 HOBBY
STATED PRINT RUN 150 SER.#'d SETS
*GREEN/99: .4X TO 1X BASIC
*PURPLE/50: .5X TO 1.2X BASIC
*ORANGE/25: .8X TO 2X BASIC
SDRAB Andrew Benintendi 3.00 8.00
SDRCS Carlos Santana 2.50 6.00
SDREM Eddie Murray 2.50 6.00
SDRFF Freddie Freeman 4.00 10.00
SDRHA Hank Aaron 6.00 15.00
SDRKS Kyle Schwarber 6.00 15.00
SDRMB Michael Brantley 2.50 6.00
SDRMC Michael Conforto 2.50 6.00
SDRNR Nolan Ryan 10.00 25.00
SDRRC Rod Carew 10.00 25.00
SDRRJ Randy Johnson 5.00 12.00
SDRXB Xander Bogaerts 10.00 25.00
SDRABR Alex Bregman 4.00 10.00
SDRCSE Corey Seager 4.00 10.00
SDRFTJ Fernando Tatis Jr. 10.00 25.00
SDRRJA Reggie Jackson 10.00 25.00
SDRVGJ Vladimir Guerrero Jr. 6.00 15.00

2020 Topps Tribute Franchise Best Autographs

STATED ODDS 1:150 HOBBY
PRINT RUNS B/WN 15-99 COPIES PER
NO PRICING ON QTY 15 OR LESS
EXCHANGE DEADLINE 1/31/22
FBAI Ichiro/15 300.00 600.00
FBAAJ Aaron Judge/15 150.00 400.00
FBAAP Andy Pettitte/50 25.00 60.00
FBABS Blake Snell/99 8.00 20.00
FBACF Carlton Fisk/50 20.00 50.00
FBACY Christian Yelich/50 50.00 120.00
FBADO David Ortiz/30 40.00 100.00
FBAFL Francisco Lindor/99 25.00 60.00
FBAHA Hank Aaron/15 150.00 400.00
FBAIR Ivan Rodriguez/50 30.00 80.00
FBAJB Johnny Bench/30 60.00 150.00
FBAKB Kris Bryant/30 75.00 200.00
FBAMC Miguel Cabrera/30 75.00 200.00
FBAMM Mike Mussina/50 30.00 80.00
FBAMR Mariano Rivera/15 200.00 500.00
FBAMS Max Scherzer/50 40.00 100.00
FBAMT Mike Trout/15 500.00 1000.00
FBANR Nolan Ryan/30 150.00 400.00
FBANS Nick Senzel/99 15.00 40.00
FBAOS Ozzie Smith/50 20.00 50.00
FBARC Rod Carew/99 20.00 50.00
FBARH Rhys Hoskins/99 20.00 50.00
FBARJ Reggie Jackson/50 40.00 100.00
FBAVG Vladimir Guerrero/50 30.00 80.00
FBAWB Walker Buehler/99 30.00 80.00
FBACCS CC Sabathia/50 30.00 80.00
FBACRJ Cal Ripken Jr./30 75.00 200.00
FBAJDM J.D. Martinez/99 15.00 40.00
FBAJSM John Smoltz/50 15.00 40.00
FBAKGJ Ken Griffey Jr./15 200.00 500.00
FBARAJ Ronald Acuna Jr./99 100.00 250.00
FBARCL Roger Clemens/15 50.00 120.00
FBAVGJ Vladimir Guerrero Jr./99 60.00 150.00

2020 Topps Tribute Franchise Best Autographs Orange

*ORANGE/25: .5X TO 1.2X p/r 30-99
STATED ODDS 1:191 HOBBY
STATED PRINT RUN 25 SER.#'d SETS
FBAAP Andy Pettitte 40.00 100.00
FBABS Blake Snell 12.00 30.00

2020 Topps Tribute Iconic Perspectives Autographs

STATED ODDS 1:28 HOBBY
PRINT RUNS B/WN 5-99 COPIES PER
NO PRICING ON QTY 15 OR LESS
EXCHANGE DEADLINE 1/31/22
IPAG Andres Galarraga/99 8.00 20.00
IPAJ Aaron Judge/15 125.00 300.00
IPAK Al Kaline/70 25.00 60.00
IPAM Austin Meadows/99 8.00 20.00
IPBS Blake Snell/99 8.00 20.00
IPBW Bernie Williams/50 25.00 60.00
IPCF Carlton Fisk/50 20.00 50.00
IPCY Christian Yelich/50 50.00 120.00
IPDC David Cone/99 20.00 50.00
IPDM Don Mattingly/45 40.00 100.00
IPDO David Ortiz/25 60.00 150.00
IPEJ Eloy Jimenez/99 20.00 50.00
IPFL Francisco Lindor/70 25.00 60.00
IPJA Jose Altuve/45 20.00 50.00
IPJC Jose Canseco/99 20.00 50.00
IPJP Jorge Posada/70 15.00 40.00
IPKH Keston Hiura/99 12.00 30.00
IPMC Michael Chavis/99 15.00 40.00
IPNA Nolan Arenado/50 40.00 100.00
IPNS Nick Senzel/99 15.00 40.00
IPOA Ozzie Albies EXCH/99 20.00 50.00
IPOS Ozzie Smith/50 50.00 120.00
IPPA Pete Alonso/99 50.00 120.00
IPPD Paul DeJong/99 6.00 15.00
IPRC Rod Carew/50 20.00 50.00
IPRF Rollie Fingers/99 10.00 25.00
IPRH Rhys Hoskins/80 10.00 25.00
IPSC Steve Carlton/50 20.00 50.00
IPTB Trevor Bauer/99 8.00 20.00
IPTM Tino Martinez/99 15.00 40.00
IPWB Walker Buehler/99 30.00 80.00
IPWC Willson Contreras/99 6.00 15.00
IPWM Whit Merrifield/99 10.00 25.00
IPXB Xander Bogaerts/80 15.00 40.00
IPCCS CC Sabathia/50 30.00 80.00
IPCRJ Cal Ripken Jr./25 75.00 200.00
IPFTJ Fernando Tatis Jr./99 75.00 200.00

IPJDM J.D. Martinez/70 15.00 40.00
IPJSM John Smoltz/50 15.00 40.00
IPLMJ Lance McCullers Jr./99 8.00 20.00
IPMMU Mike Mussina/50 30.00 80.00
IPMUN Max Muncy/99 12.00 30.00
IPRHE Rickey Henderson/25 50.00 120.00
IPVGJ Vladimir Guerrero Jr./99 60.00 150.00
IPWBO Wade Boggs/45 30.00 80.00

2020 Topps Tribute Iconic Perspectives Autographs Orange

*ORANGE/25: .5X TO 1.2X p/r 45-99
*ORANGE/25: .4X TO 1X p/r 25
STATED ODDS 1:102 HOBBY
STATED PRINT RUN 25 SER.#'d SETS
IPAG Andres Galarraga 15.00 40.00
IPAM Austin Meadows 15.00 40.00
IPBS Blake Snell 12.00 30.00
IPRF Rollie Fingers 15.00 40.00

2020 Topps Tribute League Inauguration Autographs

STATED ODDS 1:59 HOBBY
STATED PRINT RUN 99 SER.#'d SETS
EXCHANGE DEADLINE 1/31/22
*ORANGE/25: .5X TO 1.2X
LAAP A.J. Puk 8.00 20.00
LABB Bo Bichette 75.00 200.00
LABM Brendan McKay 12.00 30.00
LADC Dylan Cease 8.00 20.00
LAJL Jesus Luzardo 8.00 20.00
LAJY Jordan Yamamoto 5.00 12.00
LALA Logan Allen 4.00 10.00
LALR Luis Robert 125.00 300.00
LARG Robel Garcia 4.00 10.00
LASM Sean Murphy 6.00 15.00
LAYA Yordan Alvarez 75.00 200.00
LABBR Bobby Bradley 5.00 12.00

2020 Topps Tribute Stamp of Approval Relics

STATED ODDS 1:14 HOBBY
STATED PRINT RUN 150 SER.#'d SETS
*GREEN/99: .4X TO 1X BASIC
*PURPLE/50: .5X TO 1.2X BASIC
*ORANGE/25: .8X TO 2X BASIC
SOAAH Aaron Hicks 4.00 10.00
SOAAJ Aaron Judge 8.00 20.00
SOAAM Austin Meadows 4.00 10.00
SOAAN Aaron Nola 5.00 12.00
SOAAR Anthony Rizzo 6.00 15.00
SOABL Brandon Lowe 3.00 8.00
SOABP Buster Posey 6.00 15.00
SOABS Blake Snell 4.00 10.00
SOACB Cody Bellinger 6.00 15.00
SOACM Charlie Morton 3.00 8.00
SOACS Chris Sale 3.00 8.00
SOAFF Freddie Freeman 4.00 10.00
SOAGC Gerrit Cole 5.00 12.00
SOAGS George Springer 2.50 6.00
SOAJA Jose Altuve 2.50 6.00
SOAJH Josh Hader 4.00 10.00
SOAJV Joey Votto 5.00 12.00
SOAKH Keston Hiura 6.00 15.00
SOAMA Miguel Andujar 4.00 10.00
SOAMB Michael Brantley 2.50 6.00
SOAMC Miguel Cabrera 5.00 12.00
SOAMT Mike Trout 15.00 40.00
SOANS Noah Syndergaard 4.00 10.00
SOAOA Ozzie Albies 6.00 15.00
SOARH Rhys Hoskins 4.00 10.00
SOART Rowdy Tellez 3.00 8.00
SOATM Trey Mancini 3.00 8.00
SOATP Tommy Pham 5.00 12.00
SOATS Trevor Story 5.00 12.00
SOAVR Victor Robles 4.00 10.00
SOAWB Walker Buehler 4.00 10.00
SOAWM Whit Merrifield 5.00 12.00
SOAYK Yusei Kikuchi 4.00 10.00
SOACCS CC Sabathia 2.50 6.00
SOACSE Corey Seager 3.00 8.00
SOAFTJ Fernando Tatis Jr. 12.00 30.00
SOAJDM J.D. Martinez 3.00 8.00
SOALGJ Lourdes Gurriel Jr. 2.50 6.00
SOALMJ Lance McCullers Jr. 2.00 5.00
SOAMAT Masahiro Tanaka 6.00 15.00
SOANSE Nick Senzel 3.00 8.00

2020 Topps Tribute Tandem Autograph Booklets

STATED ODDS 1:269 HOBBY
STATED PRINT RUN 25 SER.#'d SETS
TTAG A.Galarraga/N.Arenado 75.00 200.00
TTCK M.Cabrera/A.Kaline 250.00 500.00
TTGA V.Guerrero Jr./R.Alomar 250.00 500.00
TTGG V.Guerrero Jr./V.Guerrero 250.00 500.00
TTNC S.Carlton/A.Nola 50.00 120.00
TTOC R.Carew/S.Ohtani
TTSP A.Pettitte/C.Sabathia 75.00 200.00
TTTS O.Smith/F.Tatis Jr. 250.00 600.00

2020 Topps Tribute Tribute to Great Hitters Autographs

STATED ODDS 1:60 HOBBY
PRINT RUNS B/WN 15-99 COPIES PER
NO PRICING ON QTY 20 OR LESS
EXCHANGE DEADLINE 1/31/22
*PURPLE/50: .4X TO 1X p/r 75-99
TGHAK Al Kaline/99 25.00 60.00
TGHCJ Chipper Jones/30 40.00 100.00
TGHCY Carl Yastrzemski/30 50.00 120.00
TGHDM Don Mattingly/95 40.00 100.00
TGHDO David Ortiz/30
TGHEM Edgar Martinez/99 20.00 50.00
TGHFL Francisco Lindor/99 25.00 60.00
TGHFT Frank Thomas/70 40.00 100.00

TGHHM Hideki Matsui/25 40.00 100.00
TGHJB Johnny Bench/40 40.00 100.00
TGHKB Kris Bryant/50 60.00 150.00
TGHMC Miguel Cabrera/50 60.00 150.00
TGHRC Rod Carew/70 20.00 50.00
TGHRH Rickey Henderson/30 40.00 100.00
TGHVG Vladimir Guerrero/75 30.00 80.00
TGHXB Xander Bogaerts/99 15.00 40.00
TGHCRJ Cal Ripken Jr./30 50.00 120.00
TGHCYE Christian Yelich/75 50.00 120.00
TGHRHS Rhys Hoskins/99 10.00 25.00
TGHVGJ Vladimir Guerrero Jr./99 60.00 150.00

2020 Topps Tribute Tribute to Great Hitters Autographs Orange

*ORANGE/25: .5X TO 1.2X p/r 30-99
*ORANGE/25: .4X TO 1X p/r 25
STATED ODDS 1:180 HOBBY
STATED PRINT RUN 25 SER.#'d SETS
TGHDO David Ortiz 40.00 100.00

2020 Topps Tribute Triple Relics

STATED ODDS 1:14 HOBBY
STATED PRINT RUN 150 SER.#'d SETS
*GREEN/99: .4X TO 1X BASIC
*PURPLE/50: .5X TO 1.2X BASIC
*ORANGE/25: .8X TO 2X BASIC
TTRAC Aroldis Chapman 6.00 15.00
TTRAJ Aaron Judge 12.00 30.00
TTRAP Andy Pettitte 6.00 15.00
TTRAR Anthony Rizzo 5.00 12.00
TTRBL Brandon Lowe 4.00 10.00
TTRCB Cody Bellinger 8.00 20.00
TTRCM Charlie Morton 3.00 8.00
TTRCS Chris Sale 3.00 8.00
TTRCY Christian Yelich 10.00 25.00
TTRDC David Cone 5.00 12.00
TTRDS Dansby Swanson 6.00 15.00
TTREH Eric Hosmer 2.50 6.00
TTREM Edgar Martinez 8.00 20.00
TTRER Eddie Rosario 2.50 6.00
TTRFR Franmil Reyes 2.00 5.00
TTRGC Gerrit Cole 5.00 12.00
TTRGS George Springer 4.00 10.00
TTRJB Josh Bell 2.50 6.00
TTRJR Jose Ramirez 2.50 6.00
TTRJS Juan Soto 10.00 25.00
TTRMB Mookie Betts 10.00 25.00
TTRMC Matt Chapman 10.00 25.00
TTRMS Mike Soroka 3.00 8.00
TTRMT Mike Trout 25.00 60.00
TTRNA Nolan Arenado 4.00 10.00
TTROA Ozzie Albies 5.00 12.00
TTRPG Paul Goldschmidt 3.00 8.00
TTRPM Pedro Martinez 6.00 15.00
TTRRH Rickey Henderson 12.00 30.00
TTRSC Steve Carlton 2.50 6.00
TTRSO Shohei Ohtani 10.00 25.00
TTRSS Sammy Sosa 8.00 20.00
TTRTM Thurman Munson 15.00 40.00
TTRTS Trevor Story 3.00 8.00
TTRVG Vladimir Guerrero 2.50 6.00
TTRVR Victor Robles 4.00 10.00
TTRWB Wade Boggs 5.00 12.00
TTRYA Yordan Alvarez 10.00 25.00
TTRYP Yasiel Puig 5.00 12.00
TTRCCS CC Sabathia 2.50 6.00
TTRCRJ Cal Ripken Jr. 12.00 30.00
TTRGST Giancarlo Stanton 8.00 20.00
TTRHJR Hyun-Jin Ryu 2.50 6.00
TTRJBA Javier Baez 12.00 30.00
TTRJDM J.D. Martinez 3.00 8.00
TTRKGJ Ken Griffey Jr. 20.00 50.00
TTRLMJ Lance McCullers Jr. 2.00 5.00
TTRRAJ Ronald Acuna Jr. 20.00 50.00
TTRRAL Roberto Alomar 6.00 15.00
TTRRHO Rhys Hoskins 4.00 10.00

2006 Topps Triple Threads

This 120-card set was released in April, 2006. The set was release solely through the hobby in six-card packs with an $80 SRP which came two packs to a box and 18 boxes to a case. The first 100-cards are a mix of veteran players and retired greats. With the exception of Don Mattingly, all of the retired players pictured are in the Hall of Fame. Cards numbered 101-120 feature younger players who both signed these cards and had some game-used memorabilia included on the card. These cards were issued to a stated print run of 225 serial numbered cards.

1-100 THREE PER PACK
101-120 ODDS 1:7 MINI
101-120 PRINT RUN 225 SERIAL #'d SETS
OVERALL 1-100 PLATE ODDS 1:80 MINI
PLATE PRINT RUN 1 SET PER COLOR
BLACK-CYAN-MAGENTA-YELLOW ISSUED
NO PLATE PRICING DUE TO SCARCITY
1 Hideki Matsui 2.00 5.00
2 Josh Gibson HOF 2.00 5.00
3 Roger Clemens 2.50 6.00
4 Paul Konerko 1.25 3.00
5 Brooks Robinson HOF 1.25 3.00
6 Stan Musial HOF 3.00 8.00
7 Dontrelle Willis .75 2.00
8 Yogi Berra HOF 2.00 5.00
9 John Smoltz 2.00 5.00
10 Brian Roberts .75 2.00
11 Gary Sheffield .75 2.00
12 Wade Boggs HOF 1.25 3.00
13 Alex Rodriguez 2.50 6.00
14 Ernie Banks HOF 2.00 5.00
15 Ichiro Suzuki 2.50 6.00
16 Whitey Ford HOF 1.25 3.00
17 Vladimir Guerrero 1.25 3.00
18 Tadahito Iguchi .75 2.00
19 Robin Yount HOF 2.00 5.00
20 Jason Schmidt .75 2.00
21 Roberto Clemente HOF 5.00 12.00
22 Andruw Jones .75 2.00
23 Don Mattingly 4.00 10.00
24 Joe Mauer 1.25 3.00
25 Barry Bonds 3.00 8.00
26 Johnny Damon 1.25 3.00
27 Chris Carpenter 1.25 3.00
28 Garret Anderson .75 2.00
29 Scott Rolen 1.25 3.00
30 Tim Hudson 1.25 3.00
31 Dave Winfield HOF 1.25 3.00
32 Steve Carlton HOF 1.25 3.00
33 Miguel Tejada 1.25 3.00
34 Nolan Ryan HOF 6.00 15.00
35 Mark Buehrle 1.25 3.00
36 Travis Hafner .75 2.00
37 Rickie Weeks .75 2.00
38 Sammy Sosa 2.00 5.00
39 Carlos Beltran 1.25 3.00
40 Todd Helton 1.25 3.00
41 Tom Seaver HOF 1.25 3.00
42 Ted Williams HOF 4.00 10.00
43 Alfonso Soriano 1.25 3.00
44 Reggie Jackson HOF 1.25 3.00
45 Pedro Martinez 1.25 3.00
46 Randy Johnson 2.00 5.00
47 Ted Williams HOF 4.00 10.00
48 Torii Hunter .75 2.00
49 Manny Ramirez 2.00 5.00
50 George Brett HOF 4.00 10.00
51 Chipper Jones 2.00 5.00
52 Nomar Garciaparra 1.25 3.00
53 Richie Sexson .75 2.00
54 David Ortiz 2.00 5.00
55 Derek Jeter 5.00 12.00
56 Mickey Mantle HOF 6.00 15.00
57 Michael Young .75 2.00
58 Aramis Ramirez .75 2.00
59 Bartolo Colon .75 2.00
60 Troy Glaus .75 2.00
61 Carlos Delgado .75 2.00
62 Mike Sweeney .75 2.00
63 Jorge Cantu .75 2.00
64 Mike Mussina 1.25 3.00
65 Hank Blalock .75 2.00
66 Frank Robinson HOF 1.25 3.00
67 Carl Yastrzemski HOF 3.00 8.00
68 Adam Dunn 1.25 3.00
69 Eric Chavez .75 2.00
70 Curt Schilling 1.25 3.00
71 Jeff Francoeur 2.00 5.00
72 C.C. Sabathia 1.25 3.00
73 Roy Oswalt 1.25 3.00
74 Carlos Lee .75 2.00
75 Barry Zito 1.25 3.00
76 Derrek Lee .75 2.00
77 Greg Maddux 2.50 6.00
78 Ivan Rodriguez 1.25 3.00
79 Jeff Kent .75 2.00
80 Gary Carter HOF 1.25 3.00
81 Jose Reyes 1.25 3.00
82 Johan Santana 1.25 3.00
83 Magglio Ordonez 1.25 3.00
84 Mark Prior 1.25 3.00
85 Johnny Bench HOF 2.00 5.00
86 Vernon Wells .75 2.00
87 Mark Mulder .75 2.00
88 Cal Ripken 6.00 15.00
89 Mark Teixeira 1.25 3.00
90 Miguel Cabrera 2.00 5.00
91 Duke Snider HOF 1.25 3.00
92 Jason Giambi .75 2.00
93 Albert Pujols 2.50 6.00
94 Carl Crawford 1.25 3.00
95 Jim Edmonds 1.25 3.00
96 Jose Contreras .75 2.00
97 Victor Martinez 1.25 3.00
98 Jeremy Bonderman .75 2.00
99 Lance Berkman 1.25 3.00
100 Rocco Baldelli .75 2.00
101 Zach Duke AU J-J 10.00 25.00
102 Felix Hernandez AU J-J 15.00 40.00
103 Dan Johnson AU J-J 6.00 15.00
104 Brandon McCarthy AU J-J 10.00 25.00
105 Huston Street AU J-J 6.00 15.00
106 Robinson Cano AU J-J 12.50 30.00
107 Jason Bay AU J-J 6.00 15.00
108 Ryan Howard AU B-B 15.00 40.00
109 Ervin Santana AU J-J 6.00 15.00
110 Rich Harden AU J-J 6.00 15.00
111 Aaron Hill AU J-J 6.00 15.00
112 David Wright AU J-J 12.50 30.00
113 Rich Hill AU J-J (RC) 6.00 15.00
114 Nelson Cruz AU J-J (RC) 15.00 40.00
115 F.Liriano AU J-J (RC) 6.00 15.00
116 Hong-Chih Kuo AU J-J (RC) 30.00 60.00
117 Ryan Garko AU J-J (RC) 10.00 25.00
118 Craig Hansen AU J-J RC 6.00 15.00
119 Shin-Soo Choo AU J-J (RC) 6.00 15.00
120 Darrell Rasner AU J-J (RC) 6.00 15.00

2006 Topps Triple Threads Emerald

*EMERALD 1-100: .75X TO 2X BASIC
1-100 ODDS 1:4 MINI
1-100 PRINT RUN 99 SERIAL #'d SETS
*EMERALD 101-112: .5X TO 1.2X BASIC AU
*EMERALD 113-120: .5X TO 1.2X BASIC AU
101-120 AU ODDS 1:21 MINI
101-120 AU PRINT RUN 75 SERIAL #'d SETS

2006 Topps Triple Threads Gold

*GOLD 1-100: 1.25X TO 3X BASIC
1-100 ODDS 1:7 MINI
1-100 PRINT RUN 50 SERIAL #'d SETS
*GOLD 101-112: .6X TO 1.5X BASIC AU
*GOLD 113-120: .6X TO 1.5X BASIC AU
101-120 AU ODDS 1:32 MINI
101-120 AU PRINT RUN 50 SERIAL #'d SETS
116 Hong-Chih Kuo AU J-J 75.00 150.00

2006 Topps Triple Threads Sapphire

*SAPHIRE 1-100: 2X TO 5X BASIC
1-100 ODDS 1:13 MINI
1-100 PRINT RUN 25 SERIAL #'d SETS
101-120 AU ODDS 1:63 MINI
101-120 AU PRINT RUN 25 SERIAL #'d SETS
101-120 NO PRICING DUE TO SCARCITY

2006 Topps Triple Threads Sepia

*SEPIA 1-100: .6X TO 1.5X BASIC
1-100 ODDS 1:3 MINI
1-100 PRINT RUN 150 SERIAL #'d SETS
*SEPIA 101-112: .4X TO 1X BASIC AU
*SEPIA 113-120: .4X TO 1X BASIC AU
101-120 AU ODDS 1:13 MINI
101-120 AU PRINT RUN 125 SERIAL #'d SETS

2006 Topps Triple Threads Heroes

COMM.T.WILL (1-5/42;1-5/47) 5.00 12.00
COMMON MANTLE (1-10) 6.00 15.00
COMMON F.ROB (1-10) .75 2.00
COMMON YAZ (1-10) 3.00 8.00
ONE BASIC OR DIE CUT HEROES PER PACK
*DIE CUT: 1X TO 2.5X BASIC
DIE CUT ODDS 1:16 MINI
DIE CUT PRINT RUN 50 SERIAL #'d SETS

2006 Topps Triple Threads Relic

STATED ODDS 1:7 MINI
STATED PRINT RUN 18 SERIAL #'d SETS
*GOLD: .5X TO 1.2X BASIC
GOLD ODDS 1:15 MINI
GOLD PRINT RUN 9 SERIAL #'d SETS
PLATINUM ODDS 1:43 MINI
PLATINUM PRINT RUN 3 SERIAL #'d SETS
NO PLATINUM PRICING DUE TO SCARCITY
1 Adam Dunn RBI 10.00 25.00
2 Adam Dunn CIN 10.00 25.00
3 Adrian Beltre LAD 10.00 25.00
4 Adrian Beltre SEA 10.00 25.00
5 Al Kaline GG 15.00 40.00
6 Al Kaline HOF 15.00 40.00
7 Al Kaline DET 15.00 40.00
8 Albert Pujols STL 30.00 60.00
9 Albert Pujols 300 30.00 60.00
10 Albert Pujols MVP 30.00 60.00
11 Albert Pujols ROY 30.00 60.00
12 Alex Rodriguez NYY 15.00 40.00
13 Alex Rodriguez #13 15.00 40.00
14 Alex Rodriguez MVP 15.00 40.00
15 Alex Rodriguez 400 15.00 40.00
16 Alex Rodriguez SEA 15.00 40.00
17 Alex Rodriguez 40/40 15.00 40.00
18 Alex Rodriguez TEX 15.00 40.00
19 Alex Rodriguez GG 15.00 40.00
20 Alex Rodriguez MVP 15.00 40.00
21 Alfonso Soriano NYY 10.00 25.00
22 Alfonso Soriano TEX 10.00 25.00
23 Andruw Jones GG 15.00 40.00
24 Andruw Jones ATL 15.00 40.00
25 Andy Pettitte ACE 15.00 40.00
26 Andy Pettitte HOU 15.00 40.00
27 Aramis Ramirez CHC 10.00 25.00
28 B.J. Upton MLB 10.00 25.00
29 Barry Bonds 40/40 40.00 80.00
30 Barry Bonds MVP 40.00 80.00
31 Barry Bonds PIT 40.00 80.00
32 Barry Bonds 700 40.00 80.00
33 Barry Bonds SFG 40.00 80.00
34 Barry Bonds 700 40.00 80.00
35 Barry Bonds #25 40.00 80.00
36 Barry Bonds 7MVP 40.00 80.00
37 Barry Zito OAK 10.00 25.00
38 Barry Zito CY 10.00 25.00
39 Ben Sheets USA 10.00 25.00
40 Bill Mazeroski PIT 15.00 40.00
41 Bob Feller HOF 15.00 40.00
42 Bobby Abreu PHI 10.00 25.00
43 Bobby Cox ATL 10.00 25.00
44 Bobby Doerr BOS 15.00 40.00
45 Brad Lidge HOU 10.00 25.00
46 Brian Giles SDP 10.00 25.00
47 Brian Roberts BAL 10.00 25.00
48 Cal Ripken CAL 40.00 80.00
49 Cal Ripken MVP 40.00 80.00
50 Cal Ripken BAL 40.00 80.00
51 Carl Yastrzemski YAZ 30.00 60.00
52 Carl Yastrzemski MVP 30.00 60.00
53 Carl Yastrzemski BOS 30.00 60.00
54 Carlos Beltran ROY 10.00 25.00
55 Carlos Beltran NYM 10.00 25.00
56 Carlos Delgado RBI 10.00 25.00
57 Carlton Fisk BOS 15.00 40.00
58 Carlton Fisk HOF 15.00 40.00
59 Carlton Fisk CWS 15.00 40.00
60 Chipper Jones MVP 30.00 60.00
61 Chipper Jones 300 30.00 60.00
62 Chipper Jones ATL 30.00 60.00
63 Chris Carpenter STL 15.00 40.00
64 Craig Biggio HBP 15.00 40.00
65 Craig Biggio HOU 15.00 40.00
66 Curt Schilling WS 10.00 25.00
67 Curt Schilling ACE 10.00 25.00
68 Curt Schilling WS 15.00 40.00
69 Curt Schilling BOS 10.00 25.00
70 Dale Murphy ATL 15.00 40.00
71 Darryl Strawberry NYM 10.00 25.00
72 Darryl Strawberry ROY 10.00 25.00
73 Dave Winfield GG 10.00 25.00
74 Dave Winfield NYY 10.00 25.00
75 Dave Winfield HOF 10.00 25.00
76 David Ortiz RBI 15.00 40.00
77 David Ortiz BOS 15.00 40.00
78 David Ortiz MIN 15.00 40.00
79 Derrek Lee CHC 15.00 40.00
80 Don Mattingly NYY 30.00 60.00
81 Don Mattingly #23 30.00 60.00
82 Don Mattingly MVP 30.00 60.00
83 Dontrelle Willis ROY 10.00 25.00
84 Dontrelle Willis FLA 10.00 25.00
85 Duke Snider HOF 15.00 40.00
86 Dwight Gooden Dr.K 10.00 25.00
87 Dwight Gooden ROY 10.00 25.00
88 Eric Chavez OAK 10.00 25.00
89 Ernie Banks CHC 20.00 50.00
90 Ernie Banks HOF 20.00 50.00
91 Ernie Banks 512 20.00 50.00
92 Frank Robinson 586 15.00 40.00
93 Frank Robinson MVP 15.00 40.00
94 Frankie Frisch HOF 20.00 50.00
95 Gary Carter NYM 10.00 25.00
96 Gary Sheffield NYY 10.00 25.00
97 Gary Sheffield RBI 10.00 25.00
98 George Brett KC5 40.00 80.00
99 George Brett MVP 40.00 80.00
100 Greg Maddux CHC 40.00 80.00
101 Hank Blalock TEX 10.00 25.00
102 Hank Greenberg HOF 60.00 120.00
103 Hank Greenberg DET 60.00 120.00
104 Hideki Matsui NYY 40.00 80.00
105 Hideki Matsui MLB 40.00 80.00
106 Hideki Matsui RBI 40.00 80.00
107 Ichiro Suzuki SEA 60.00 120.00
108 Ichiro Suzuki ROY 60.00 120.00
109 Ichiro Suzuki 262 60.00 120.00
110 Ivan Rodriguez GG 10.00 25.00
111 Ivan Rodriguez DET 10.00 25.00
112 Ivan Rodriguez FLA 10.00 25.00
113 Ivan Rodriguez TEX 10.00 25.00
114 Jake Peavy SDP 10.00 25.00
115 Javy Lopez BAL 10.00 25.00
116 Jeff Bagwell HOU 15.00 40.00
117 Jim Edmonds STL 10.00 25.00
118 Jim Thome PHI 15.00 40.00
119 Joe Mauer MIN 10.00 25.00
120 Joe Torre STL 10.00 25.00
121 Johan Santana CY 15.00 40.00
122 Johan Santana MIN 15.00 40.00
123 Johnny Bench ROY 30.00 60.00
124 Johnny Bench CIN 30.00 60.00
125 Johnny Damon BOS 15.00 40.00
126 Jon Garland WS 10.00 25.00
127 Jon Garland CWS 10.00 25.00
128 Jorge Posada NYY 8.00 20.00
129 Jorge Posada RBI 8.00 20.00
130 Jose Canseco ROY 40.00 80.00
131 Jose Reyes NYM 10.00 25.00
132 Juan Marichal SFG 10.00 25.00
133 Kerry Wood ROY 10.00 25.00
134 Kerry Wood CHC 10.00 25.00
135 Lance Berkman MLB 10.00 25.00
136 Lance Berkman HOU 10.00 25.00
137 Lloyd Waner HOF 40.00 80.00
138 Lloyd Waner PIT 40.00 80.00
139 Lou Brock HOF 15.00 40.00
140 Manny Ramirez RBI 15.00 40.00
141 Manny Ramirez BOS 15.00 40.00
142 Mariano Rivera NYY 30.00 60.00
143 Mariano Rivera SAV 30.00 60.00
144 Mark Buehrle CWS 10.00 25.00
145 Mark Mulder OAK 10.00 25.00
146 Mark Mulder STL 10.00 25.00
147 Mark Prior CHC 10.00 25.00
148 Mark Teixeira TEX 15.00 40.00
149 Michael Young TEX 10.00 25.00
150 Michael Young BAT 10.00 25.00
151 Mickey Mantle NYY 200.00 350.00
152 Mickey Mantle 536 200.00 350.00
153 Mickey Mantle HOF 200.00 350.00
154 Mickey Mantle NY7 200.00 350.00
155 Mickey Mantle 3MVP 200.00 350.00
156 Miguel Cabrera FLA 15.00 40.00
157 Miguel Tejada #10 10.00 25.00
158 Miguel Tejada RBI 10.00 25.00
159 Miguel Tejada BAL 10.00 25.00
160 Miguel Tejada MVP 10.00 25.00
161 Mike Mussina NYY 15.00 40.00
162 Mike Mussina ACE 15.00 40.00
163 Mike Piazza LAD 40.00 80.00
164 Mike Piazza NYM 40.00 80.00
165 Mike Piazza #31 30.00 60.00
166 Mike Schmidt 548 12.50 30.00
167 Mike Schmidt HOF 12.50 30.00
168 Mike Schmidt MVP 12.50 30.00
169 Monte Irvin HOF 15.00 40.00
170 Morgan Ensberg HOU 10.00 25.00
171 Nolan Ryan HOF 20.00 50.00
172 Nolan Ryan HOU 20.00 50.00
173 Nolan Ryan TEX 20.00 50.00
174 Nolan Ryan 324 20.00 50.00
175 Wade Boggs WS 15.00 40.00
176 Ozzie Smith GG 20.00 50.00
177 Ozzie Smith HOF 20.00 50.00
178 Pat Burrell PHI 10.00 25.00
179 Paul Konerko WS 10.00 25.00
180 Paul Konerko RBI 10.00 25.00
181 Paul Konerko CWS 10.00 25.00
182 Paul Molitor HOF 10.00 25.00
183 Pedro Martinez 3CY 15.00 40.00
184 Pedro Martinez NYM 15.00 40.00
185 Pedro Martinez ACE 15.00 40.00
186 Randy Johnson TC 15.00 40.00
187 Randy Johnson 5CY 15.00 40.00
188 Reggie Jackson OCT 20.00 50.00
189 Reggie Jackson 563 20.00 50.00
190 Rickey Henderson NYY 30.00 60.00
191 Rickey Henderson OAK 30.00 60.00
192 Rickey Henderson MVP 30.00 60.00
193 Rickey Henderson 130 30.00 60.00
194 Rickie Weeks MLB 10.00 25.00
195 Rickie Weeks MIL 10.00 25.00
196 Roberto Clemente 3000 100.00 175.00
197 Roberto Clemente MVP 100.00 175.00
198 Robin Yount 2MVP 30.00 60.00
199 Rod Carew ROY 15.00 40.00
200 Roger Clemens 7CY 30.00 60.00
201 Roger Clemens CY 30.00 60.00
202 Roger Clemens ERA 30.00 60.00
203 Roger Clemens HOU 30.00 60.00
204 Roger Clemens NYY 30.00 60.00
205 Roger Clemens CY 30.00 60.00
206 Roy Halladay CY 10.00 25.00
207 Roy Oswalt 20W 10.00 25.00
208 Roy Oswalt HOU 10.00 25.00
209 Ryne Sandberg HOF 40.00 80.00
210 Ryne Sandberg MVP 40.00 80.00
211 Sammy Sosa 500 30.00 60.00
212 Sammy Sosa BAL 30.00 60.00
213 Sammy Sosa MVP 30.00 60.00
214 Sammy Sosa CHC 30.00 60.00
215 Sammy Sosa 500 30.00 60.00
216 Scott Rolen ROY 15.00 40.00
217 Scott Rolen STL 15.00 40.00
218 Sean Burroughs SDP 10.00 25.00
219 Stan Musial 3MVP 30.00 60.00
220 Steve Carlton PHI 10.00 25.00
221 Steve Carlton 4CY 10.00 25.00
222 Steve Carlton 329 10.00 25.00
223 Steve Garvey MVP 10.00 25.00
224 Tadahito Iguchi CWS 10.00 25.00
225 Ted Williams .406 100.00 200.00
226 Ted Williams 521 100.00 200.00
227 Tim Hudson ATL 10.00 25.00
228 Tim Hudson OAK 10.00 25.00
229 Todd Helton GG 15.00 40.00
230 Todd Helton 300 15.00 40.00
231 Todd Helton COL 15.00 40.00
232 Tom Seaver 311 15.00 40.00
233 Tony Gwynn SDP 30.00 60.00
234 Tony Gwynn 300 30.00 60.00
235 Tony Gwynn 3000 30.00 60.00
236 Torii Hunter GG 10.00 25.00
237 Torii Hunter MIN 10.00 25.00
238 Travis Hafner CLE 10.00 25.00
239 Vladimir Guerrero MVP 20.00 50.00
240 Vladimir Guerrero RBI 20.00 50.00
241 Wade Boggs 3000 15.00 40.00
242 Willie Stargell HOF 15.00 40.00
243 Willie Stargell PIT 15.00 40.00
244 Willie Stargell POP 15.00 40.00
245 Willy Taveras HOU 10.00 25.00

2006 Topps Triple Threads Relic Autograph

STATED ODDS 1:14 MINI
STATED PRINT RUN 18 SERIAL #'d SETS
*GOLD: .5X TO 1.2X BASIC
GOLD ODDS 1:27 MINI
GOLD PRINT RUN 9 SERIAL #'d SETS
PLATINUM ODDS 1:81 MINI
PLATINUM PRINT RUN 3 SERIAL #'d SETS
NO PLATINUM PRICING DUE TO SCARCITY
1 Albert Pujols MVP 300.00 500.00
2 Albert Pujols ROY 300.00 500.00
3 Albert Pujols STL 100.00 200.00
4 Alex Rodriguez MVP 150.00 300.00
5 Alex Rodriguez 40/40 150.00 300.00
6 Alex Rodriguez MVP 150.00 300.00
7 Derrek Lee CHC 25.00 60.00
8 Barry Bonds 700 250.00 400.00
9 Ben Sheets MIL 15.00 40.00
10 Ben Sheets USA 15.00 40.00
11 Brad Lidge HOU 15.00 40.00
12 B.Lidge Pitcher-Ball 12.50 30.00
13 Cal Ripken BAL 100.00 200.00
14 Cal Ripken HIT 100.00 200.00
15 Cal Ripken MVP 100.00 200.00
16 Carl Yastrzemski BOS 60.00 120.00
17 Carl Yastrzemski MVP 60.00 120.00
18 Carl Yastrzemski YAZ 60.00 120.00
19 Chase Utley PHI 25.00 60.00
20 Chase Utley RBI 25.00 60.00
21 C.Wang Chinese 600.00 1000.00
22 Chien-Ming Wang ERA 300.00 500.00
23 Chien-Ming Wang NYY 300.00 500.00
24 C.Wang Pitcher-Ball 300.00 500.00
25 Chris Carpenter CY 60.00 120.00
26 Chris Carpenter STL 60.00 120.00
27 Clint Barmes COL 10.00 25.00
28 Clint Barmes MLB 10.00 25.00
29 Conor Jackson 1ST 25.00 60.00
30 Conor Jackson ARI 25.00 60.00
31 David Ortiz BOS 50.00 100.00
32 Don Mattingly #23 30.00 60.00
33 Don Mattingly MVP 30.00 60.00
34 Don Mattingly NYY 30.00 60.00
35 Duke Snider LAD 15.00 40.00
36 Duke Snider HOF 15.00 40.00
37 Ernie Banks CHC 75.00 150.00
38 Frank Robinson MVP 25.00 60.00
39 Frank Robinson CIN 25.00 60.00
40 Frank Robinson TC 25.00 60.00
41 Garrett Atkins 3RD 10.00 25.00
42 Garrett Atkins COL 10.00 25.00
43 Derrek Lee BAT 25.00 60.00
44 Derrek Lee LEE 25.00 60.00
45 Derrek Lee OPS 25.00 60.00
46 J.J. Hardy MIL 10.00 25.00
47 J.J. Hardy SS6 10.00 25.00
48 Jake Peavy ERA 25.00 60.00
49 Jake Peavy SDP 25.00 60.00
50 Jeff Francis COL 10.00 25.00
51 J.Francis Pitcher-Ball 10.00 25.00
52 Joe Mauer MIN 30.00 60
53 Joe Mauer RBI 30.00 60
54 Joey Devine ATL 15.00 40
55 J.Devine Pitcher-Ball 15.00 40
56 Johan Santana CY 8.00 20
57 Johan Santana ERA 8.00 20
58 Johan Santana MIN 8.00 20
59 Johan Santana KK 8.00 20
60 Johnny Bench CIN 50.00 100
61 Johnny Bench MVP 50.00 100
62 Johnny Bench ROY 50.00 100
63 Johnny Damon BOS 50.00 100
64 Jonny Gomes MLB 15.00 40
65 Jonny Gomes RBI 15.00 40
66 Jose Reyes MLB 20.00 50
67 Jose Reyes NYM 20.00 50
68 Justin Morneau 1ST 15.00 40
69 Justin Morneau MIN 15.00 40
70 Lou Brock 938 25.00 60
71 Lou Brock 3 Stars 25.00 60
72 Lou Brock HOF 25.00 60
73 Lou Brock STL 25.00 60
74 Manny Ramirez BOS 50.00 100
75 Mariano Rivera 0.81 125.00 200
76 Mark Prior CHC 15.00 40
77 Miguel Cabrera #24 50.00 100
78 Miguel Cabrera FLA 50.00 100
79 Miguel Cabrera 300 50.00 100
80 Miguel Cabrera RBI 50.00 100
81 Mike Schmidt HOF 50.00 100
82 Mike Schmidt MVP 50.00 100
83 Mike Schmidt PHI 50.00 100
84 Morgan Ensberg 3 Stars 15.00 40
85 Morgan Ensberg HOU 15.00 40
86 Nick Swisher OAK 15.00 40
87 Nick Swisher RBI 15.00 40
88 Nolan Ryan HOF 30.00 60
89 Nolan Ryan TEX 30.00 60
90 Nolan Ryan 7 NO NO 30.00 60
91 Zach Duke PIT 15.00 40
92 Zach Duke WIN 15.00 40
93 Ozzie Smith GG 50.00 100
94 Ozzie Smith HOF 50.00 100
95 Ozzie Smith STL 50.00 100
96 Pedro Martinez NYM 75.00 150
97 Robin Yount HOF 25.00 60
98 Robin Yount MIL 25.00 60
99 Robin Yount MVP 25.00 60
100 Rod Carew BAT 50.00 100
101 Rod Carew MIN 50.00 100
102 Rod Carew MVP 50.00 100
103 Rod Carew ROY 50.00 100
104 Roger Clemens CY 125.00 200
105 Roger Clemens CY 125.00 200
106 Ryan Langerhans ATL 20.00 50
107 Ryan Langerhans RBI 20.00 50
108 Ryne Sandberg CHC 50.00 100
109 Ryne Sandberg HOF 50.00 100
110 Ryne Sandberg MVP 50.00 100
111 Scott Kazmir ERA 15.00 40.
112 S.Kazmir Pitcher-Ball 15.00 40.
113 Stan Musial 3 Stars 60.00 120.
114 Stan Musial MVP 60.00 120.
115 Stan Musial STL 60.00 120.
116 Steve Carlton 329 15.00 40
117 Steve Carlton CY 15.00 40.
118 Steve Carlton PHI 15.00 40.
119 Steve Garvey LAD 20.00 50.
120 Steve Garvey MVP 20.00 50.
121 Tony Gwynn 300 50.00 100
122 Tony Gwynn HIT 50.00 100
123 Tony Gwynn SDP 50.00 100.
124 Travis Hafner CLE 15.00 40.
125 Travis Hafner RBI 15.00 40.
126 Victor Martinez CLE 15.00 40.
127 Victor Martinez RBI 15.00 40.
128 Wade Boggs BAT 25.00 60.
129 Wade Boggs BOS 25.00 60.
130 Wade Boggs RBI 25.00 60.

2006 Topps Triple Threads Rel[ic] Combos

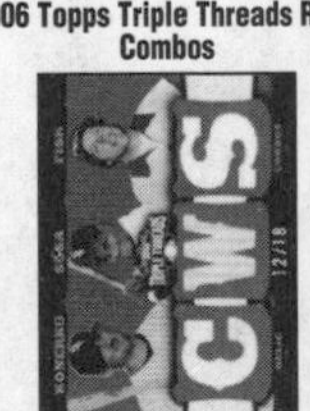

STATED ODDS 1:7 MINI
STATED PRINT RUN 18 SERIAL #'d SETS
*GOLD: .5X TO 1.2X BASIC
GOLD ODDS 1:14 MINI
GOLD PRINT RUN 9 SERIAL #'d SETS
PLATINUM ODDS 1:42 MINI
PLATINUM PRINT RUN 3 SERIAL #'d SETS
NO PLATINUM PRICING DUE TO SCARCITY
1 Pujols J/A-Rod PT/Bonds P 60.00 120.
2 A-Rod J/Bonds J/Pujols J 60.00 120.
3 Pujols P/A-Rod B/Manny J 15.00 40.
4 Pujols J/Bonds H/T.Will B 75.00 150.
5 A-Rod B/Bonds P/Chip J 20.00 50.
6 A-Rod J/Clem P/Bonds P 60.00 120.
7 A-Rod J/Vlad H/Ichiro J 50.00 100.
8 A-Rod B/Musial P/T.Will B 50.00 100.
9 Andruw H/A.Sor S/Vlad H 15.00 40.
10 Bonds B/Ichiro J/Clem B 75.00 150.
11 Bonds B/L.Waner B/Clem B 75.00 150.
12 Bonds B/Manny S/And BG 30.00 60.

onds P/Manny J/T.Will B 50.00 100.00
onds P/Clem B/Stargell H 75.00 150.00
az S/Moli S/Manny S 30.00 60.00
att J/Moli S/Boggs B 30.00 60.00
att J/Carew B/Gwy J 30.00 60.00
heff P/Vlad PT/I-Rod PT 15.00 40.00
berg B/Musial B/T.Will B 75.00 150.00
hiro J/Chip PT/Bonds P 50.00 100.00
hiro J/T.Will B/Clem P 150.00 250.00
organ H/Moli S/G.Cart H 15.00 40.00
anny J/Vlad B/Clem P 40.00 80.00
iaz BG/Moli BG/Hend BG 30.00 60.00
ajoie B/Musial B/T.Will B 75.00 150.00
Moli H/Andruw H/Yount H 20.00 50.00
Moli S/Andruw S/A.Sor S 15.00 40.00
eggie PT/Vlad PT/And PT 20.00 50.00
end S/Boggs S/Gwy S 30.00 60.00
lem B/T.Will B/Gwy B 75.00 150.00
usial B/T.Will B/Gwy B 50.00 100.00
Will B/Ichiro J/Boggs B 75.00 150.00
ujols J/T.Will B/Mantle J 60.00 120.00
ndruw H/Brett H/Chip H 20.00 50.00
Madd PT/Ryan B/Carlton P 30.00 60.00
Madd PT/Carlton P/Seav P 20.00 50.00
yan J/Carlton S/Seav B 20.00 50.00
yan J/Seav H/Roger J 40.00 80.00
oger H/Ryan J/Seav H 40.00 80.00
onds B/Hend S/Gwy S 30.00 60.00
ip P/Yaz J/Moli J 40.00 80.00
ip P/Brett B/Clem P 60.00 120.00
ip P/Brett B/Gwy S 40.00 80.00
ip J/Moli PT/Hend J 30.00 60.00
ip J/Moli J/Gwy J 30.00 60.00
rett B/Rip P/Carew B 40.00 80.00
rett B/Rip P/Carew PT 40.00 80.00
rett B/Yount J/Carew B 20.00 50.00
rett B/Carew PT/Musial B 30.00 60.00
rett B/Gwy J/Boggs B 30.00 60.00
oli H/Yount J/Boggs J 20.00 50.00
.Waner B/Hend S/Musial P 40.00 80.00
.Waner B/Fred P/Boggs B 25.00 60.00
.Wnr B/Carew B/Boggs B 15.00 40.00
lend J/Musial B/Boggs B 30.00 60.00
lem P/Yount H/Carew B 50.00 100.00
lem P/Yount H/Gwy S 50.00 100.00
lem B/Musial B/Gwy B 50.00 100.00
arew J/Musial P/Gwy J 20.00 50.00
Musial P/Gwy J/Boggs PT 20.00 50.00
Boggs B/Boggs B/Boggs B 20.00 50.00
Bonds B/Mantle B/F.Rob B 100.00 175.00
Bonds SU/T.Will B/Mant SU 200.00 350.00
Bonds B/F.Rob P/Reggie B 40.00 80.00
Bonds P/F.Rob B/Kill J 30.00 60.00
F.Rob B/Bonds P/Schmidt J 40.00 80.00
F.Rob B/Kill B/Mantle B 100.00 175.00
J.Gib B/Bonds B/Mantle PT 200.00 350.00
J.Gib B/Bonds J/T.Will B 125.00 200.00
Schmidt B/Kill J/Reggie B 30.00 60.00
Winfield J/Vlad B/Reggie J 15.00 40.00
Carew B/Reggie J/Vlad B 15.00 40.00
Andruw S/Chip PT/Franc J 30.00 60.00
Cox PT/Andruw S/Chip J 20.00 50.00
Chip PT/Madd PT/And PT 15.00 40.00
Roberts J/Sosa J/Tejada P 15.00 40.00
Brooks B/Rip P/Palm H 40.00 80.00
Brooks B/Palm J/F.Rob B 15.00 40.00
Rip P/Brooks B/Tejada P 30.00 60.00
Rip P/F.Rob B/Sosa J 30.00 60.00
F.Rob B/Reggie J/Brooks B 20.00 50.00
Palm J/F.Rob B/Reggie J 15.00 40.00
Palm P/Reggie J/Sosa J 30.00 60.00
Palm P/Sosa B/Tejada P 15.00 40.00
Tejada P/Roberts J/Rip P 10.00 25.00
Reggie J/F.Rob B/Sosa J 30.00 60.00
Doerr B/Yaz S/T.Will B 75.00 150.00
Yaz S/Ortiz J/Manny S 30.00 60.00
Yaz P/T.Will B/Ortiz J 75.00 150.00
Yaz J/T.Will B/Manny S 75.00 150.00
Schil J/Ortiz J/Damon J 15.00 40.00
Schil PT/Ortiz B/Manny J 15.00 40.00
Schil J/Manny B/Damon J 15.00 40.00
Ortiz B/Damon P/Manny B 15.00 40.00
Damon B/Manny J/T.Will B 40.00 80.00
Manny S/Ortiz J/Pedro PT 30.00 60.00
Manny J/T.Will B/Ortiz J 30.00 60.00
Pedro S/Roger H/Manny S 30.00 60.00
Madd J/Randy J/Roger J 20.00 50.00
0 Johan J/Pedro S/Roger J 20.00 50.00
1 Roger J/Roger J/Roger J 50.00 100.00
2 Roger J/Roger J/Roger J 75.00 150.00
3 Randy H/Schil J/Roger H 30.00 60.00
4 D.Lee J/Aramis B/Prior J 15.00 40.00
5 D.Lee J/Ryno B/Sosa J 40.00 80.00
6 Banks P/Ryno B/D.Lee J 40.00 80.00
7 Banks P/Ryno B/Sosa J 40.00 80.00
8 Madd J/Ryno B/Banks P 50.00 100.00
9 Prior J/Wood PT/Madd J 30.00 60.00
0 Sosa J/Banks P/D.Lee J 40.00 80.00
1 F.Rob P/Morgan H/Bench P 20.00 50.00
2 Bench P/F.Rob B/Seav H 20.00 50.00
3 Bench P/Seav H/Morgan J 20.00 50.00
4 Dye P/Pods B/Iguchi J 15.00 40.00
5 Thome B/Koner P/Iguchi B 30.00 60.00
6 Garland P/Pods B/Buehr P 15.00 40.00
7 Garland P/Iguchi J/Buehr P 15.00 40.00
8 Koner J/Sosa B/Fisk P 30.00 60.00
9 Koner P/Iguchi J/Dye P 15.00 40.00
0 Kaline B/I-Rod J/G'berg B 50.00 100.00
1 Madd BG/Johan J/Roger J 30.00 60.00
2 Marichal J/Ryan P/Roger P 30.00 60.00
3 Ryan P/Randy J/Ford B 30.00 60.00
4 Rip J/Ozzie B/Schmidt J 40.00 80.00
5 Schmidt B/Rip P/Ozzie B 40.00 80.00

126 Kaline B/F.Rob P/P.Wnr B 30.00 60.00
127 Kaline B/Kill P/F.Rob B 30.00 60.00
128 Kaline B/Mantle P/Reggie J 100.00 175.00
129 Kaline B/Reggie B/Musial B 40.00 80.00
130 Kaline B/Yount J/P.Waner B 30.00 60.00
131 Bond P/Chip PT/Manny WB 30.00 60.00
132 Feller P/Marichal J/Ryan J 20.00 50.00
133 Feller P/Ford B/Carlton P 15.00 40.00
134 Doerr B/T.Will B/Boggs B 40.00 80.00
135 Brooks B/Ozzie B/Ryno B 30.00 60.00
136 Yaz S/Brett B/Moli S 30.00 60.00
137 Fisk B/Yaz J/Boggs B 20.00 50.00
138 Morgan H/Brett H/Schmidt H 30.00 60.00
139 Berra FG/Fisk B/G.Cart H 20.00 50.00
140 Pettitte J/Ryan P/Lidge J 20.00 50.00
141 Pettitte J/Ryan B/Randy P 20.00 50.00
142 Pettitte J/Ryan P/Roger J 15.00 40.00
143 Pettitte J/Randy P/Lidge J 15.00 40.00
144 Pettitte J/Oswalt J/Roger J 30.00 60.00
145 Lidge J/Oswalt J/Pettitte J 15.00 40.00
146 Bigg PT/Bag H/Berk PT 20.00 50.00
147 Ryan P/Roger J/Randy P 50.00 100.00
148 Roger J/Lidge J/Pettitte J 20.00 50.00
149 Roger J/Randy P/Pettitte J 20.00 50.00
150 Ichiro J/Hideki J/Ichiro J 100.00 175.00
151 Ichiro B/Hideki J/Kaz B 100.00 175.00
152 Ichiro J/Iguchi J/Hideki J 100.00 175.00
153 Gagne PT/Piaz B/Snider P 20.00 50.00
154 Sheff P/Weeks B/Moli J 15.00 40.00
155 Moli P/Sheff P/Yount PT 20.00 50.00
156 Yount B/Moli J/Weeks B 15.00 40.00
157 Kill P/Carew B/Johan J 20.00 50.00
158 Kill B/Torii J/Carew B 20.00 50.00
159 Johan J/Mauer J/Torii J 15.00 40.00
160 Moli P/Carew B/Kill B 30.00 60.00
161 Pujols J/Ichiro J/Bonds P 75.00 150.00
162 A-Rod J/Bonds P/Brett PT 75.00 150.00
163 A-Rod J/Bonds P/Mantle J 125.00 200.00
164 A-Rod J/Ichiro J/Mantle J 75.00 150.00
165 A-Rod B/Reggie B/Berra B 40.00 80.00
166 A-Rod J/T.Will B/Mantle P 100.00 200.00
167 A-Rod J/Berra B/Matt P 60.00 120.00
168 A-Rod S/Bonds B/Matt P 50.00 100.00
169 A-Rod S/Rip P/Tejada P 40.00 80.00
170 Bonds B/Kill J/Reggie B 40.00 80.00
171 Bonds B/Clem P/Stargell B 75.00 150.00
172 Bonds P/A-Rod J/Pujols H 60.00 120.00
173 Bonds P/Rip J/Mantle P 75.00 150.00
174 Bonds P/J.Gib B/Pujols J 75.00 150.00
175 Bonds P/Vlad B/Ichiro J 50.00 100.00
176 Brooks B/Brett B/Schmidt B 30.00 60.00
177 Rip B/Bonds B/Ichiro B 100.00 175.00
178 Rip J/Matt J/Brett B 50.00 100.00
179 Rip P/Brett B/Matt J 50.00 100.00
180 Rip J/Schmidt B/Matt J 50.00 100.00
181 Rip P/Roger J/Matt P 50.00 100.00
182 Chip PT/Murphy B/Matt P 40.00 80.00
183 Matt J/Mantle P/Reggie B 125.00 200.00
184 Brett B/Bench P/Schmidt B 30.00 60.00
185 Brett B/Bench B/Schmidt B 30.00 60.00
186 Ichiro B/Bonds P/Mantle B 150.00 250.00
187 I-Rod P/Vlad B/Tejada P 15.00 40.00
188 I-Rod P/Berra J/Bench P 20.00 50.00
189 I-Rod P/Berra FG/Bench P 20.00 50.00
190 Bench P/Piaz B/Berra P 40.00 80.00
191 Mantle B/Bonds P/T.Will B 50.00 120.00
192 Mantle P/Ichiro J/Clem P 75.00 150.00
193 Mantle J/Clem P/Musial P 125.00 200.00
194 Mantle J/T.Will B/Clem P 100.00 200.00
195 Mantle P/Vlad B/Clem P 60.00 120.00
196 Tejada P/Reggie B/Hend P 20.00 50.00
197 Reggie B/A-Rod J/Berra B 30.00 60.00
198 Clem B/Mantle B/Bonds B 125.00 200.00
199 O'Neil B/J.Gib B/Irvin B 150.00 250.00
200 Beltran J/Delg B/Wright J 20.00 50.00
201 Beltran J/Delg B/Reyes J 15.00 40.00
202 Beltran J/Wright J/Pedro J 20.00 50.00
203 Straw B/Gooden J/G.Cart B 15.00 40.00
204 Wright J/Beltran PT/Piaz J 40.00 80.00
205 Wright B/Piaz PT/Reyes B 40.00 80.00
206 Reyes J/Kaz B/Wright J 15.00 40.00
207 A-Rod J/Matt J/Mantle J 150.00 250.00
208 A-Rod J/Hideki J/Torre P 50.00 100.00
209 A-Rod J/Hideki J/Mantle P 150.00 250.00
210 Matt J/Mantle J/Roger J 75.00 150.00
211 Hideki J/Sheff B/A-Rod J 50.00 100.00
212 Hideki J/Sheff B/Posada J 40.00 80.00
213 Posada J/Roger J/Muss P 50.00 100.00
214 Mantle J/Ford B/Berra FG 150.00 250.00
215 Muss P/Ford B/Roger J 30.00 60.00
216 Roger J/Mantle P/A-Rod J 150.00 250.00
217 Boggs S/Torre P/A.Sor S 15.00 40.00
218 Zito P/Mudd PT/Hudson J 15.00 40.00
219 Cans J/Reggie B/Hend S 20.00 50.00
220 Muld P/Tejada P/Hudson P 15.00 40.00
221 Abreu J/Burr B/Thome PT 15.00 40.00
222 Schil H/Schmidt B/Carlton P 20.00 50.00
223 Schmidt B/Burr B/Rolen B 20.00 50.00
224 Bonds B/Clem B/J.Gib B 100.00 175.00
225 P.Waner B/Clem P/L.Wnr B 100.00 200.00
226 Stargell P/Maz B/Clem P 60.00 120.00
227 Pujols P/Beltran B/Willis PT 30.00 60.00
228 Pujols B/Willis PT/Ichiro B 50.00 100.00
229 Rip J/Pujols P/Willis J 40.00 80.00
230 Rip J/Fisk B/Seav P 30.00 60.00
231 Rip P/Carew B/Fisk P 30.00 60.00
232 Rip P/Carew B/Fisk P 30.00 60.00
233 Bag H/Pujols B/Piaz H 30.00 60.00
234 Piaz B/Bag P/Rolen J 30.00 60.00
235 Hend S/Garvey B/Gwy J 30.00 60.00
236 Beltre B/Ichiro J/A-Rod B 50.00 100.00
237 Ichiro J/A-Rod B/Randy H 50.00 100.00
238 Bonds P/J.Mari J/Moises B 40.00 80.00
239 Marichal J/Irvin B/Moises B 15.00 40.00
240 Moises B/Irvin B/Bonds J 30.00 60.00
241 Pujols J/Frisch B/Musial P 50.00 100.00
242 Pujols J/Muld P/Rolen J 15.00 40.00
243 Rolen J/Edm J/Pujols J 40.00 80.00
244 Musial P/Ozzie B/Pujols P 40.00 80.00
245 A-Rod S/I-Rod PT/A.Sor S 20.00 50.00
246 A-Rod J/Teixeira J/A.Sor P 20.00 50.00
247 A-Rod S/Ryan J/A.Sor S 30.00 60.00
248 A.Sor P/Blal J/Teixeira J 15.00 40.00
249 A.Sor S/Blal J/Young J 15.00 40.00
250 Teixeira J/A.Sor S/Young J 15.00 40.00

2006 Topps Triple Threads Relic Combos Autograph

STATED ODDS 1:59 MINI
STATED PRINT RUN 18 SERIAL #'d SETS
*GOLD: .5X TO 1.2X BASIC
GOLD ODDS 1:116 MINI
GOLD PRINT RUN 9 SERIAL #'d SETS
PLATINUM ODDS 1:353 MINI
PLATINUM PRINT RUN 3 SERIAL #'d SETS
NO PLATINUM PRICING DUE TO SCARCITY
1 Pujols J/Bonds J/A-Rod J 400.00 800.00
2 Felix J/A-Rod J/Choo J 100.00 200.00
3 Ryan J/Roger J/Felix J 175.00 350.00
4 Damon B/A-Rod J/Cano P 150.00 300.00
5 Manny J/Yaz J/Ortiz J 100.00 200.00
6 Young J/Rip J/Ozzie S 125.00 250.00
7 Roberts J/Rip J/F.Rob B 100.00 200.00
8 Musial P/Ozzie B/Brock B 100.00 200.00
9 Ozzie S/Musial P/Brock B 100.00 200.00
10 Gwy J/Musial P/Carew PT 100.00 200.00
11 Brooks P/Rip J/Roberts J 100.00 200.00
12 Carew PT/Yount J/Moli J 60.00 120.00
13 D.Lee J/Ryno B/Prior J 50.00 100.00
14 Wang J/Carlton P/Willis PT 125.00 250.00
15 Lidge J/Rivera J/Street J 100.00 200.00
16 Ensb J/Boggs B/Wright J 60.00 120.00
17 Sheets J/Carlton P/Felix J 40.00 80.00
18 V.Mart J/Bench P/Mauer J 75.00 150.00
19 Wright J/Schmidt B/Hill J 40.00 80.00
20 Utley J/Schmidt S/How B 150.00 300.00
21 Felix J/Carlton P/McCar J 40.00 80.00
22 Wright J/Cabrera J/Bay J 50.00 100.00
23 Cano P/Matt J/Wang J 200.00 400.00
24 Morneau B/Matt J/Hafner J 75.00 150.00
25 Garvey B/Matt J/D.John J 30.00 60.00
26 Hafner PT/Cabrera J/Bay J 60.00 120.00
27 Sheets J/Johan J/Peavy J 50.00 100.00
28 Ervin J/Johan J/Sheets B 30.00 60.00
29 Carp J/Johan J/Harden J 40.00 80.00
30 Duke J/Johan J/McCar J 30.00 60.00

2007 Topps Triple Threads

This 204-card set was released in June, 2007. This set was issued in three-card mini-boxes with an $65 SRP. Those mini-boxes came two to an display box which came nine boxes to a carton and two cartons to a case. Cards numbered 1-125 feature veterans, while the rest of the set features either just game-used relic cards or game-used relic cards with an autograph as well.

COMP.SET w/o AU's (125) 125.00 200.00
COMMON CARD (1-125) .40 1.00
1-125 STATED PRINT RUN 1350 SER.#'d SETS
COMMON JSY AU 5.00 12.00
126-189 JSY AU ODDS 1:9 MINI
126-189 JSY AU VARIATION ODDS 1:38 MINI
126-189 JSY AU PRINT RUN 99 SER.#'d SETS
TEAM INITIAL DIECUTS ARE VARIATIONS
OVERALL 1-125 PLATE ODDS 1:113 MINI
PLATE PRINT RUN 1 SET PER COLOR
BLACK-CYAN-MAGENTA-YELLOW ISSUED
NO PLATE PRICING DUE TO SCARCITY
1 Alex Rodriguez 1.25 3.00
2 Barry Zito .60 1.50
3 Corey Patterson .40 1.00
4 Roberto Clemente 2.50 6.00
5 David Wright .75 2.00
6 Dontrelle Willis .40 1.00
7 Mickey Mantle 3.00 8.00
8 Adam Dunn .60 1.50
9 Richie Ashburn .60 1.50
10 Ryan Howard .75 2.00
11 Miguel Tejada .60 1.50
12 Ernie Banks 1.00 2.50
13 Ken Griffey Jr. 2.00 5.00
14 Johnny Bench 1.00 2.50
15 Ichiro Suzuki 1.25 3.00
16 Gil Meche .40 1.00
17 Kazuo Matsui .40 1.00
18 Matt Holliday 1.00 2.50
19 Juan Pierre .40 1.00
20 Yogi Berra 1.00 2.50
21 Bill Hall .40 1.00
22 Wade Boggs .60 1.50
23 Jason Bay .60 1.50
24 Troy Glaus .40 1.00
25 Paul Konerko .60 1.50
26 Rod Carew .60 1.50
27 Jay Gibbons .40 1.00
28 Frank Thomas 1.00 2.50
29 Joe Mauer .75 2.00
30 Carlos Beltran .60 1.50
31 Frank Robinson .60 1.50
32 Bobby Abreu .40 1.00
33 Roy Oswalt .60 1.50
34 Edgar Renteria .40 1.00
35 Magglio Ordonez .60 1.50
36 Mike Piazza 1.00 2.50
37 Trevor Hoffman .60 1.50
38 Eddie Mathews 1.00 2.50
39 Albert Pujols 1.25 3.00
40 Dennis Eckersley .40 1.00
41 Andruw Jones .40 1.00
42 Alfonso Soriano .60 1.50
43 Bob Feller .60 1.50
44 J.D. Drew .40 1.00
45 Jason Schmidt .40 1.00
46 Vladimir Guerrero .60 1.50
47 Reggie Jackson .60 1.50
48 Lance Berkman .60 1.50
49 Michael Young .40 1.00
50 Carlton Fisk .60 1.50
51 Brandon Webb .60 1.50
52 Adrian Beltre 1.00 2.50
53 Hideki Matsui 1.00 2.50
54 Bronson Arroyo .40 1.00
55 Tony Gwynn 1.00 2.50
56 Ray Durham .40 1.00
57 Garrett Atkins .40 1.00
58 Nolan Ryan 3.00 8.00
59 Daisuke Matsuzaka RC 1.50 4.00
60 Todd Helton .60 1.50
61 Carl Crawford .60 1.50
62 Jake Peavy .40 1.00
63 Rafael Furcal .40 1.00
64 Joe Morgan .60 1.50
65 Greg Maddux 1.25 3.00
66 Luis Aparicio .60 1.50
67 Derrek Lee .40 1.00
68 Johnny Damon .60 1.50
69 Mike Lowell .40 1.00
70 Roger Maris 1.00 2.50
71 Vernon Wells .40 1.00
72 Monte Irvin .60 1.50
73 Jermaine Dye .40 1.00
74 Miguel Cabrera 1.00 2.50
75 Barry Bonds 1.50 4.00
76 Stan Musial 1.50 4.00
77 Derek Lowe .40 1.00
78 Don Mattingly 2.00 5.00
79 Lyle Overbay .40 1.00
80 Chien-Ming Wang .60 1.50
81 Carlos Zambrano .60 1.50
82 Kei Igawa RC 1.00 2.50
83 Cole Hamels .75 2.00
84 Gary Sheffield .40 1.00
85 Nick Johnson .40 1.00
86 Brooks Robinson .60 1.50
87 Curt Schilling .60 1.50
88 Ryne Sandberg 2.00 5.00
89 Mike Cameron .40 1.00
90 Mike Schmidt 1.50 4.00
91 Chris Carpenter .60 1.50
92 Scott Rolen .60 1.50
93 Rocco Baldelli .40 1.00
94 C.C. Sabathia .60 1.50
95 Jeff Francis .40 1.00
96 Ozzie Smith 1.25 3.00
97 Aramis Ramirez .40 1.00
98 Aaron Harang .40 1.00
99 Duke Snider .60 1.50
100 David Ortiz 1.00 2.50
101 Raul Ibanez .60 1.50
102 Bruce Sutter .60 1.50
103 Gary Matthews .40 1.00
104 Chipper Jones 1.00 2.50
105 Craig Biggio .60 1.50
106 Roy Halladay .60 1.50
107 Hoyt Wilhelm .60 1.50
108 Manny Ramirez 1.00 2.50
109 Randy Johnson 1.00 2.50
110 Carl Yastrzemski 1.50 4.00
111 Mark Teixeira .60 1.50
112 Derek Jeter 2.50 6.00
113 Stephen Drew .40 1.00
114 Darryl Strawberry .40 1.00
115 Travis Hafner .40 1.00
116 Torii Hunter .40 1.00
117 Jim Edmonds .60 1.50
118 John Smoltz 1.00 2.50
119 Bo Jackson 1.00 2.50
120 Roger Clemens 1.25 3.00
121 Pedro Martinez .60 1.50
122 Rickey Henderson 1.00 2.50
123 Ivan Rodriguez .60 1.50
124 Robin Yount 1.00 2.50
125 Johan Santana .60 1.50
126a Robinson Cano Jsy AU 15.00 40.00
126b Robinson Cano Jsy AU 15.00 40.00
127a Jose Reyes Jsy AU 12.50 30.00
127b Jose Reyes Jsy AU 12.50 30.00
128a Justin Morneau Jsy AU 8.00 20.00
128b Justin Morneau Jsy AU 10.00 25.00
129a Curtis Granderson Jsy AU 6.00 15.00
129b Curtis Granderson Jsy AU 6.00 15.00
130a Justin Verlander Jsy AU 20.00 50.00
130b Justin Verlander Jsy AU 20.00 50.00
131 Prince Fielder Jsy AU 8.00 20.00
132a Ryan Zimmerman Jsy AU 10.00 25.00
132b Ryan Zimmerman Jsy AU 10.00 25.00
133 Mike Napoli Jsy AU 10.00 25.00
134 Melky Cabrera Jsy AU 10.00 25.00
135 Jonathan Papelbon Jsy AU 15.00 40.00
136a Nick Markakis Jsy AU 8.00 20.00
136b Nick Markakis Jsy AU BAL 8.00 20.00
137 B.J. Upton Jsy AU 12.50 30.00
138a Joel Zumaya Jsy AU 10.00 25.00
138b Joel Zumaya Jsy AU 10.00 25.00
140 Nick Swisher Jsy AU 10.00 25.00
141 Andre Ethier Jsy AU 10.00 25.00
142a Jered Weaver Jsy AU 8.00 20.00
142b Jered Weaver Jsy AU LAA 8.00 20.00
143 Matt Cain Jsy AU 8.00 20.00
144 Lastings Milledge Jsy AU 8.00 20.00
145 Brian McCann Jsy AU 8.00 20.00
146 Shin-Soo Choo Jsy AU 6.00 15.00
147a Dan Uggla Jsy AU 8.00 20.00
147b Dan Uggla Jsy AU 8.00 20.00
148 Hanley Ramirez Jsy AU 10.00 25.00
149 Russell Martin Jsy AU 5.00 12.00
150 Francisco Liriano Jsy AU 6.00 15.00
151 Anthony Reyes Jsy AU 5.00 12.00
152 Josh Barfield Jsy AU 6.00 15.00
153 Anibal Sanchez Jsy AU 5.00 12.00
154 Jeremy Hermida Jsy AU 6.00 15.00
155 Kendry Morales Jsy AU 6.00 15.00
156 Matt Kemp Jsy AU 20.00 50.00
157 Freddy Sanchez Jsy AU 6.00 15.00
158 Howie Kendrick Jsy AU 8.00 20.00
159 Scott Thorman Jsy AU 8.00 20.00
160 Franklin Gutierrez Bat AU 6.00 15.00
161 Jason Bartlett Jsy AU 6.00 15.00
162 Chris Duncan Jsy AU 6.00 15.00
163 Maicer Izturis Jsy AU 5.00 12.00
164 Jason Botts Jsy AU 5.00 12.00
165 Tony Gwynn Jr. Jsy AU 15.00 40.00
166 Jorge Cantu Jsy AU 5.00 12.00
167 Adam Jones Jsy AU 10.00 25.00
168 Edinson Volquez Jsy AU 8.00 20.00
169 Joey Gathright Jsy AU 5.00 12.00
170 Carlos Marmol Jsy AU 8.00 20.00
171 Ben Zobrist Jsy AU 10.00 25.00
172 Josh Willingham Jsy AU 5.00 12.00
173 Brad Thompson Jsy AU 10.00 25.00
174a Chris Ray Jsy AU 6.00 15.00
174b Ervin Santana Jsy AU 6.00 15.00
175 Ronny Paulino Jsy AU 5.00 12.00
176 Tyler Johnson Jsy AU 5.00 12.00
177 J.J. Hardy Jsy AU 5.00 12.00
178 Adrian Gonzalez Jsy AU 8.00 20.00
179 Scott Kazmir Jsy AU 6.00 15.00
180 Juan Morillo Jsy AU (RC) 5.00 12.00
181a Shawn Riggans JSY AU (RC) 5.00 12.00
181b Shawn Riggans JSY AU (RC) 5.00 12.00
182 Brian Stokes JSY AU (RC) 5.00 12.00
183 Delmon Young JSY AU (RC) 5.00 12.00
184a Troy Tulowitzki JSY AU (RC) 10.00 25.00
184b Troy Tulowitzki JSY AU (RC) 10.00 25.00
185 Adam Lind JSY AU (RC) 6.00 15.00
186 David Murphy JSY AU (RC) 6.00 15.00
187a Philip Humber JSY AU (RC) 6.00 15.00
187b Philip Humber JSY AU (RC) 6.00 15.00
188a Andrew Miller JSY AU RC 6.00 15.00
188b Andrew Miller JSY AU RC 6.00 15.00
189a Glen Perkins JSY AU (RC) 5.00 12.00
189b Glen Perkins JSY AU (RC) 5.00 12.00

2007 Topps Triple Threads Emerald

*EMERALD 1-125: .75X TO 2X BASIC
1-125 ODDS 1:2 MINI
1-125 PRINT RUN 239 SERIAL #'d SETS
*EMERALD AUTO: .5X TO 1.2X BASIC AU
*EMERLD VAR AUTO: .5X TO 1.2X BAS.AU VAR
126-189 AU ODDS 1:18 MINI
126-189 AU VARIATION ODDS 1:75 MINI
126-189 AU PRINT RUN 50 SERIAL #'d SETS
TEAM INITIAL DIECUTS ARE VARIATIONS

2007 Topps Triple Threads Gold

*GOLD 1-125: 1.25X TO 3X BASIC
1-125 ODDS 1:5 MINI
1-125 PRINT RUN 99 SERIAL #'d SETS
*GOLD AUTO: .75X TO 2X BASIC AU
*GOLD VAR AUTO: .75X TO 2X BASIC AU VAR
126-189 AU ODDS 1:35 MINI
126-189 AU VARIATION ODDS 1:149 MINI
126-189 AU PRINT RUN 25 SERIAL #'d SETS
TEAM INITIAL DIECUTS ARE VARIATIONS

2007 Topps Triple Threads Sapphire

*SAPPHIRE 1-125: 3X TO 8X BASIC
1-125 ODDS 1:19 MINI
1-125 PRINT RUN 25 SERIAL #'d SETS
126-189 JSY AU ODDS 1:88 MINI
126-189 JSY AU VAR.ODDS 1:372 MINI
126-189 AU PRINT RUN 10 SERIAL #'d SETS
TEAM INITIAL DIECUTS ARE VARIATIONS
NO SAPPHIRE JSY AUTO PRICING AVAILABLE

2007 Topps Triple Threads Sepia

*SEPIA 1-125: .5X TO 1.2X BASIC
1-125 ODDS XXX MINI
1-125 PRINT RUN 559 SERIAL #'d SETS
*SEPIA AUTO: .5X TO 1.2X BASIC AU
*SEPIA VAR AUTO: .5X TO 1.2X BASIC AU VAR
126-189 AU ODDS 1:12 MINI
126-189 AU VAR.ODDS 1:50 MINI
126-189 AU PRINT RUN 75 SERIAL #'d SETS
TEAM INITIAL DIECUTS ARE VARIATIONS

2007 Topps Triple Threads Relics

STATED ODDS 1:11 MINI
STATED PRINT RUN 36 SER.#'d SETS
EMERALD ODDS 1:21 MINI
GOLD ODDS 1:42 MINI
GOLD PRINT RUN 9 SER.#'d SETS
PLATINUM ODDS 1:373 MINI
PLATINUM PRINT RUN 1 SER.#'d SET
NO PLATINUM PRICING DUE TO SCARCITY
SAPPHIRE ODDS 1:125 MINI
SAPPHIRE PRINT RUN 3 SER.#'d SETS
NO SAPPHIRE PRICING DUE TO SCARCITY
*SEPIA: .4X TO 1X BASIC
SEPIA ODDS 1:14 MINI
SEPIA PRINT RUN 27 SER.#'d SETS
ALL DC VARIATIONS PRICED EQUALLY
1 Carl Yastrzemski 12.50 30.00
2 Carl Yastrzemski 12.50 30.00
3 Carl Yastrzemski 12.50 30.00
4 Roberto Clemente 75.00 150.00
5 Roberto Clemente 75.00 150.00
6 Roberto Clemente 75.00 150.00
7 Roberto Clemente 75.00 150.00
8 Roberto Clemente 75.00 150.00
9 Roberto Clemente 75.00 150.00
10 Alex Rodriguez 12.50 30.00
11 Alex Rodriguez 12.50 30.00
12 Alex Rodriguez 12.50 30.00
13 Alex Rodriguez 12.50 30.00
14 Alex Rodriguez 12.50 30.00
15 Alex Rodriguez 12.50 30.00
16 Ryan Howard 20.00 50.00
17 Ryan Howard 20.00 50.00
18 Ryan Howard 20.00 50.00
19 David Wright 10.00 25.00
20 David Wright 10.00 25.00
21 David Wright 10.00 25.00
22 Chien-Ming Wang 75.00 150.00
23 Chien-Ming Wang 75.00 150.00
24 Chien-Ming Wang 75.00 150.00
25 Ichiro Suzuki 60.00 120.00
26 Ichiro Suzuki 60.00 120.00
27 Ichiro Suzuki 60.00 120.00
28 Hideki Matsui 10.00 25.00
29 Hideki Matsui 10.00 25.00
30 Hideki Matsui 10.00 25.00
31 Luis Aparicio 8.00 20.00
32 Luis Aparicio 8.00 20.00
33 Luis Aparicio 8.00 20.00
34 Joe DiMaggio 40.00 80.00
35 Joe DiMaggio 40.00 80.00
36 Joe DiMaggio 40.00 80.00
37 Ted Williams 40.00 80.00
38 Ted Williams 40.00 80.00
39 Ted Williams 40.00 80.00
40 Mickey Mantle 75.00 150.00
41 Mickey Mantle 75.00 150.00
42 Mickey Mantle 75.00 150.00
43 Mickey Mantle 75.00 150.00
44 Mickey Mantle 75.00 150.00
45 Mickey Mantle 75.00 150.00
46 Mickey Mantle 75.00 150.00
47 Mickey Mantle 75.00 150.00
48 Mickey Mantle 75.00 150.00
49 David Ortiz 10.00 25.00
50 David Ortiz 10.00 25.00
51 David Ortiz 10.00 25.00
52 Albert Pujols 20.00 50.00
53 Albert Pujols 20.00 50.00
54 Albert Pujols 20.00 50.00
55 Justin Morneau 10.00 25.00
56 Justin Morneau 10.00 25.00
57 Justin Morneau 10.00 25.00
58 Nolan Ryan 25.00 60.00
59 Nolan Ryan 25.00 60.00
60 Nolan Ryan 25.00 60.00
61 Nolan Ryan 25.00 60.00
62 Nolan Ryan 25.00 60.00
63 Nolan Ryan 25.00 60.00
64 Manny Ramirez 10.00 25.00
65 Manny Ramirez 10.00 25.00
66 Manny Ramirez 10.00 25.00
67 Roger Maris 30.00 60.00
68 Roger Maris 30.00 60.00
69 Roger Maris 30.00 60.00
70 Daisuke Matsuzaka 10.00 25.00
71 Daisuke Matsuzaka 10.00 25.00
72 Daisuke Matsuzaka 10.00 25.00
73 Brian Cashman 8.00 20.00
74 Brian Cashman 8.00 20.00
75 Brian Cashman 8.00 20.00
76 Ernie Banks 20.00 50.00
77 Ernie Banks 20.00 50.00
78 Ernie Banks 20.00 50.00
79 Stan Musial 25.00 60.00
80 Stan Musial 25.00 60.00
81 Stan Musial 25.00 60.00
82 Duke Snider 12.50 30.00
83 Duke Snider 12.50 30.00
84 Duke Snider 12.50 30.00
85 Yogi Berra 20.00 50.00
86 Yogi Berra 20.00 50.00
87 Yogi Berra 20.00 50.00
88 Harmon Killebrew 15.00 40.00
89 Harmon Killebrew 15.00 40.00
90 Harmon Killebrew 15.00 40.00
91 Joe Mauer 8.00 20.00
92 Joe Mauer 8.00 20.00
93 Joe Mauer 8.00 20.00
94 Alfonso Soriano 10.00 25.00
95 Alfonso Soriano 10.00 25.00
96 Alfonso Soriano 10.00 25.00
97 Reggie Jackson 15.00 40.00
98 Reggie Jackson 15.00 40.00
99 Reggie Jackson 15.00 40.00
100 Reggie Jackson 15.00 40.00
101 Reggie Jackson 15.00 40.00
102 Reggie Jackson 15.00 40.00
103 Vladimir Guerrero 10.00 25.00
104 Vladimir Guerrero 10.00 25.00
105 Vladimir Guerrero 10.00 25.00
106 Pedro Martinez 10.00 25.00
107 Pedro Martinez 10.00 25.00
108 Pedro Martinez 10.00 25.00
109 Roger Clemens 12.50 30.00
110 Roger Clemens 12.50 30.00
111 Roger Clemens 12.50 30.00
112 Randy Johnson 10.00 25.00
113 Randy Johnson 10.00 25.00
114 Randy Johnson 10.00 25.00
115 Don Mattingly 15.00 40.00
116 Don Mattingly 15.00 40.00
117 Don Mattingly 15.00 40.00
118 Bill Dickey 20.00 50.00
119 Bill Dickey 20.00 50.00
120 Bill Dickey 20.00 50.00
121a Barry Bonds 30.00 60.00
121b Bruce Sutter 10.00 25.00
122a Barry Bonds 30.00 60.00
122b Bruce Sutter 10.00 25.00
123a Barry Bonds 30.00 60.00
123b Bruce Sutter 10.00 25.00
124 John F. Kennedy 150.00 250.00
125 John F. Kennedy 150.00 250.00
126 John F. Kennedy 150.00 250.00
127 Johnny Bench 12.50 30.00
128 Johnny Bench 12.50 30.00
129 Johnny Bench 12.50 30.00
130 Mark Teixeira 12.50 30.00
131 Mark Teixeira 12.50 30.00
132 Mark Teixeira 12.50 30.00
133 Johan Santana 10.00 25.00
134 Johan Santana 10.00 25.00
135 Johan Santana 10.00 25.00
136 Alex Rodriguez 12.50 30.00
137 Alex Rodriguez 12.50 30.00
138 Alex Rodriguez 12.50 30.00
139 Brooks Robinson 12.50 30.00
140 Brooks Robinson 12.50 30.00
141 Brooks Robinson 12.50 30.00
142 Rickey Henderson 12.50 30.00
143 Rickey Henderson 12.50 30.00
144 Rickey Henderson 12.50 30.00
145 Ozzie Smith 12.50 30.00
146 Ozzie Smith 12.50 30.00

147 Ozzie Smith 12.50 30.00
148 Chipper Jones 12.50 30.00
149 Chipper Jones 12.50 30.00
150 Chipper Jones 12.50 30.00

2007 Topps Triple Threads Relics Emerald

*EMERALD: .5X TO 1.2X BASIC
STATED ODDS 1:21 MINI
STATED PRINT RUN 18 SER.#'d SETS
ALL DC VARIATIONS PRICED EQUALLY
4 Roberto Clemente 75.00 150.00
40 Mickey Mantle 75.00 150.00
121a Barry Bonds 30.00 60.00
124 John F. Kennedy 150.00 250.00

2007 Topps Triple Threads Relics Gold

*GOLD: .6X TO 1.5X BASIC
STATED ODDS 1:42 MINI
STATED PRINT RUN 9 SER.#'d SETS
ALL DC VARIATIONS PRICED EQUALLY
25 Ichiro Suzuki 150.00 300.00
79 Stan Musial 40.00 80.00
118 Bill Dickey 30.00 60.00
121a Barry Bonds 30.00 60.00
124 John F. Kennedy 150.00 250.00
145 Ozzie Smith 15.00 40.00

2007 Topps Triple Threads Relics Autographs

STATED ODDS 1:18 MINI
STATED PRINT RUN 18 SER.#'d SETS
*GOLD: .5X TO 1.2X BASIC
GOLD ODDS 1:34 MINI
GOLD PRINT RUN 9 SER.#'d SETS
PLATINUM ODDS 1:472 MINI
PLATINUM PRINT RUN 1 SER.#'d SET
NO PLATINUM PRICING DUE TO SCARCITY
SAPPHIRE ODDS 1:104 MINI
SAPPHIRE PRINT RUN 3 SER.#'d SETS
NO SAPPHIRE PRICING DUE TO SCARCITY
WHITE WHALE ODDS 1:118 MINI
WHITE WHALE PRINT RUN 1 SER.#'d SET
NO WHITE WHALE PRICING DUE TO SCARCITY
ALL DC VARIATIONS PRICED EQUALLY
1 Alex Rodriguez 125.00 250.00
2 Alex Rodriguez 125.00 250.00
3 Alex Rodriguez 125.00 250.00
4 Chien-Ming Wang 30.00 60.00
5 Chien-Ming Wang 30.00 60.00
6 Chien-Ming Wang 30.00 60.00
7 David Ortiz 40.00 50.00
8 David Ortiz 40.00 80.00
9 David Ortiz 40.00 80.00
10 Manny Ramirez 60.00 120.00
11 Manny Ramirez 60.00 120.00
12 Manny Ramirez 60.00 120.00
13 Johnny Damon 30.00 60.00
14 Johnny Damon 30.00 60.00
15 Johnny Damon 30.00 60.00
16 Miguel Tejada 20.00 50.00
17 Miguel Tejada 20.00 50.00
18 Miguel Tejada 20.00 50.00
19 Carl Crawford 20.00 50.00
20 Carl Crawford 20.00 50.00
21 Carl Crawford 20.00 50.00
22 Johan Santana 15.00 40.00
23 Johan Santana 15.00 40.00
24 Johan Santana 15.00 40.00
25 Francisco Liriano 10.00 25.00
26 Francisco Liriano 10.00 25.00
27 Francisco Liriano 10.00 25.00
28 Bob Feller 40.00 80.00
29 Bob Feller 40.00 80.00
30 Bob Feller 40.00 80.00
31 Vladimir Guerrero 20.00 50.00
32 Vladimir Guerrero 20.00 50.00
33 Vladimir Guerrero 20.00 50.00
34 Ernie Banks 50.00 100.00
35 Ernie Banks 50.00 100.00
36 Ernie Banks 50.00 100.00
37 Yogi Berra 60.00 150.00
38 Yogi Berra 60.00 150.00
39 Yogi Berra 60.00 150.00
40 Nolan Ryan 100.00 200.00
41 Nolan Ryan 100.00 200.00
42 Nolan Ryan 100.00 200.00
43 Ozzie Smith 50.00 100.00
44 Ozzie Smith 50.00 100.00
45 Ozzie Smith 50.00 100.00
46 David Wright 20.00 50.00
47 David Wright 20.00 50.00
48 David Wright 20.00 50.00
49 Albert Pujols 200.00 350.00
50 Albert Pujols 200.00 350.00
51 Albert Pujols 200.00 350.00
52 Ryan Howard 20.00 50.00
53 Ryan Howard 20.00 50.00
54 Ryan Howard 20.00 50.00
55 Don Mattingly 50.00 100.00
56 Don Mattingly 50.00 100.00
57 Don Mattingly 50.00 100.00
58 Brooks Robinson 30.00 60.00
59 Brooks Robinson 30.00 60.00
60 Brooks Robinson 30.00 60.00
61 Robin Yount 30.00 60.00
62 Robin Yount 30.00 60.00
63 Robin Yount 30.00 60.00
64 Mike Schmidt 60.00 120.00
65 Mike Schmidt 60.00 120.00
66 Mike Schmidt 60.00 120.00
67 Carl Yastrzemski 50.00 100.00
68 Carl Yastrzemski 50.00 100.00
69 Carl Yastrzemski 50.00 100.00
70 Wade Boggs 40.00 80.00
71 Wade Boggs 40.00 80.00
72 Wade Boggs 40.00 80.00
73 Andre Dawson 30.00 60.00
74 Andre Dawson 30.00 60.00
75 Andre Dawson 30.00 60.00
76 Reggie Jackson 40.00 80.00
77 Reggie Jackson 40.00 80.00
78 Reggie Jackson 40.00 80.00
79 Miguel Cabrera 30.00 60.00
80 Miguel Cabrera 30.00 60.00
81 Miguel Cabrera 30.00 60.00
82 Tom Seaver 40.00 100.00
83 Tom Seaver 40.00 100.00
84 Tom Seaver 40.00 100.00
85 Ralph Kiner 30.00 60.00
86 Ralph Kiner 30.00 60.00
87 Ralph Kiner 30.00 60.00
88 Chipper Jones 50.00 100.00
89 Chipper Jones 50.00 100.00
90 Chipper Jones 50.00 100.00
91 Andruw Jones 10.00 25.00
92 Andruw Jones 10.00 25.00
93 Andruw Jones 10.00 25.00
94 Dontrelle Willis 20.00 50.00
95 Dontrelle Willis 20.00 50.00
96 Dontrelle Willis 20.00 50.00
97 Bob Gibson 30.00 60.00
98 Bob Gibson 30.00 60.00
99 Bob Gibson 30.00 60.00
100 Johnny Bench 40.00 80.00
101 Johnny Bench 40.00 80.00
102 Johnny Bench 40.00 80.00
103 Joe Morgan 20.00 50.00
104 Joe Morgan 20.00 50.00
105 Joe Morgan 20.00 50.00
106 Ryne Sandberg 50.00 100.00
107 Ryne Sandberg 50.00 100.00
108 Ryne Sandberg 50.00 100.00
109 Dwight Gooden 20.00 50.00
110 Dwight Gooden 20.00 50.00
111 Dwight Gooden 20.00 50.00
112 Johnny Podres 20.00 50.00
113 Johnny Podres 20.00 50.00
114 Johnny Podres 20.00 50.00
115 Monte Irvin 10.00 25.00
116 Monte Irvin 10.00 25.00
117 Monte Irvin 10.00 25.00
118 Orlando Cepeda 20.00 50.00
119 Orlando Cepeda 20.00 50.00
120 Orlando Cepeda 20.00 50.00
121 Bo Jackson 60.00 120.00
122 Bo Jackson 60.00 120.00
123 Bo Jackson 60.00 120.00
124 Gary Sheffield 20.00 50.00
125 Gary Sheffield 20.00 50.00
126 Gary Sheffield 20.00 50.00
127 Tom Glavine 20.00 50.00
128 Tom Glavine 20.00 50.00
129 Tom Glavine 20.00 50.00
130 Tony LaRussa 20.00 50.00
131 Tony LaRussa 20.00 50.00
132 Tony LaRussa 20.00 50.00
133 Jim Leyland 40.00 80.00
134 Jim Leyland 40.00 80.00
135 Jim Leyland 40.00 80.00
136 Joe Torre 40.00 80.00
137 Joe Torre 40.00 80.00
138 Joe Torre 40.00 80.00
139 Gary Carter 30.00 60.00
140 Gary Carter 30.00 60.00
141 Gary Carter 30.00 60.00
142 Roy Oswalt 20.00 50.00
143 Roy Oswalt 20.00 50.00
144 Roy Oswalt 20.00 50.00
145 Carlos Delgado 20.00 50.00
146 Carlos Delgado 20.00 50.00
147 Carlos Delgado 20.00 50.00
148 Jason Varitek 40.00 80.00
149 Jason Varitek 40.00 80.00
150 Jason Varitek 40.00 80.00
151 Bobby Abreu 20.00 50.00
152 Bobby Abreu 20.00 50.00
153 Bobby Abreu 20.00 50.00
154 Juan Marichal 20.00 50.00
155 Juan Marichal 20.00 50.00
156 Juan Marichal 20.00 50.00
157 Frank Robinson 30.00 60.00
158 Frank Robinson 30.00 60.00
159 Frank Robinson 30.00 60.00
160 Jorge Posada 50.00 100.00
161 Jorge Posada 50.00 100.00
162 Jorge Posada 50.00 100.00
163 Luis Aparicio 20.00 50.00
164 Luis Aparicio 20.00 50.00
165 Luis Aparicio 20.00 50.00
166 Carlton Fisk 30.00 60.00
167 Carlton Fisk 30.00 60.00
168 Carlton Fisk 30.00 60.00
169 Dale Murphy 75.00 150.00
170 Dale Murphy 75.00 150.00
171 Dale Murphy 75.00 150.00
172 Mark Teixeira 20.00 50.00
173 Mark Teixeira 20.00 50.00
174 Mark Teixeira 20.00 50.00
175 Darryl Strawberry 20.00 50.00
176 Darryl Strawberry 20.00 50.00
177 Darryl Strawberry 20.00 50.00
178 Justin Morneau 12.50 30.00
179 Justin Morneau 12.50 30.00
180 Justin Morneau 12.50 30.00

2007 Topps Triple Threads Relics Autographs Gold

*GOLD: .5X TO 1.2X BASIC
STATED ODDS 1:34 MINI
STATED PRINT RUN 9 SER.#'d SETS
ALL DC VARIATIONS PRICED EQUALLY
34 Ernie Banks 50.00 100.00
37 Yogi Berra 60.00 150.00
49 Albert Pujols 250.00 350.00
88 Chipper Jones 75.00 150.00
121 Bo Jackson 75.00 150.00

2007 Topps Triple Threads Relics Combos

STATED ODDS 1:16 MINI
STATED PRINT RUN 36 SER.#'d SETS
*EMERALD: .5X TO 1.2X BASIC
EMERALD ODDS 1:31 MINI
EMERALD PRINT RUN 18 SER.#'d SETS
GOLD ODDS 1:62 MINI
GOLD PRINT RUN 9 SER.#'d SETS
NO GOLD PRICING DUE TO SCARCITY
PLATINUM ODDS 1:558 MINI
PLATINUM PRINT RUN 1 SER.#'d SET
NO PLATINUM PRICING DUE TO SCARCITY
SAPPHIRE ODDS 1:186 MINI
SAPPHIRE PRINT RUN 3 SER.#'d SETS
NO SAPPHIRE PRICING DUE TO SCARCITY
*SEPIA: .4X TO 1X BASIC
SEPIA ODDS 1:21 MINI
SEPIA PRINT RUN 27 SER.#'d SETS
WHITE WHALE RANDOMLY INSERTED
WHITE WHALE PRINT RUN 1 SER.#'d SET
NO WHITE WHALE PRICING DUE TO SCARCITY
1 Pujols/Manny/Ortiz 20.00 50.00
2 Pujols/Pedro/Vlad 20.00 50.00
3 Pudge/Delgado/Clemente 60.00 120.00
4 Clemente/Bernie/Beltran 30.00 60.00
5 J.Reyes/Soriano/Tejada 8.00 20.00
6 Crawford/J.Reyes/Pierre 8.00 20.00
7 Hideki/Ichiro/Taguchi 40.00 80.00
8 Mig.Cabrera/J.Santana/Abreu 12.50 30.00
9 ARod/Mariano/Hideki 30.00 60.00
10 Reggie/ARod/Mattingly 30.00 60.00
11 Berra/Mattingly/Reggie 30.00 60.00
12 Ortiz/Boggs/Manny 12.50 30.00
13 Ortiz/Manny/Pedro 12.50 30.00
14 Tejada/Murray/Brooks 10.00 25.00
15 Mauer/Morneau/J.Santana 15.00 40.00
16 Killebrew/Mauer/Morneau 20.00 50.00
17 Verlander/Pudge/Zumaya 12.50 30.00
18 Zito/Eckersley/Street 8.00 20.00
19 Reggie/Carew/Vlad 10.00 25.00
20 Vlad/Pedro/Alou 12.50 30.00
21 Young/Teixeira/ARod 12.50 30.00
22 Edgar/Ichiro/ARod 40.00 80.00
23 Wright/Delgado/J.Reyes 12.50 30.00
24 J.Reyes/Pedro/Wright 15.00 40.00
25 J.Reyes/Beltran/Wright 10.00 25.00
26 Howard/Utley/Rollins 30.00 60.00
27 Francoeur/Chipper/McCann 8.00 20.00
28 Smoltz/Glavine/Maddux 20.00 50.00
29 Chipper/Francoeur/Andruw 15.00 40.00
30 Ryan/Pedro/Seaver 20.00 50.00
31 Schmidt/Thome/Howard 15.00 40.00
32 Musial/Pujols/Ozzie 30.00 60.00
33 Pujols/Eckstein/Edmonds 15.00 40.00
34 Berkman/Oswalt/Biggio 12.50 30.00
35 Clemens/Oswalt/Ryan 15.00 40.00
36 F.Robinson/Morgan/Bench 20.00 50.00
37 Molitor/Prince/Yount 15.00 40.00
38 Banks/Soriano/Sandberg 20.00 50.00
39 Ethier/Kemp/Jer.Weaver 8.00 20.00
40 Wang/ARod/Mariano 50.00 100.00
41 Pujols/Ichiro/Vlad 10.00 25.00
42 Pujols/ARod/Ichiro 40.00 80.00
43 Howard/Morneau/Pujols 15.00 40.00
44 Pujols/Clemente/Ichiro 50.00 100.00
45 Pujols/Clemente/Mantle 100.00 200.00
46 DiMaggio/Mantle/ARod 100.00 150.00
47 Williams/DiMaggio/Mantle 150.00 250.00
48 Clemente/Mantle/Reggie 75.00 150.00
49 Musial/Clemente/F.Robinson 50.00 100.00
50 Pujols/Bench/Mantle 40.00 80.00
51 Yaz/Williams/Mantle 100.00 150.00
52 Webb/Seaver/J.Santana 12.50 30.00
53 Clemens/Gooden/Pedro 15.00 40.00
54 J.Santana/Maddux/Clemens 12.50 30.00
55 J.Santana/Pedro/Clemens 12.50 30.00
56 Unit/Clemens/Glavine 12.50 30.00
57 Verlander/Howard/Suzuki 20.00 50.00
58 Willis/Beltran/Bay 8.00 20.00
59 Pujols/Rolen/Howard 12.50 30.00
60 Clemente/DiMaggio/Mantle 125.00 200.00
61 Musial/Banks/Mantle 60.00 120.00
62 Schmidt/Morgan/Bench 15.00 40.00
63 Brett/Yount/Ozzie 20.00 50.00
64 Pujols/Ichiro/Carew 30.00 60.00
65 Soriano/Mantle/ARod 30.00 60.00
66 Mattingly/Boggs/Gwynn 20.00 50.00
67 Carew/Vlad/G.Anderson 10.00 25.00
68 Gwynn/Boggs/Brett 30.00 60.00
69 Vlad/Soriano/Abreu 15.00 40.00
70 Strawberry/Beltran/H.Johnson 15.00 40.00
71 Thome/Manny/F.Thomas 12.50 30.00
72 Mantle/Piazza/Schmidt 60.00 120.00
73 Yaz/ARod/Winfield 20.00 50.00
74 J.Santana/Pedro/Clemens 12.50 30.00
75 Maddux/Ryan/Seaver 30.00 60.00
76 Gibson/Gooden/Maddux 20.00 50.00
77 Clemente/Reggie/Manny 30.00 60.00
78 Podres/Larsen/Burdette 10.00 25.00
79 Ichiro/Johjima/Iguchi 30.00 60.00
80 Molitor/Rollins/Utley 10.00 25.00
81 Carter/LoDuca/Piazza 30.00 60.00
82 Brett/ARod/Wright 30.00 60.00
83 Wilhelm/ Niekro/Wakefield 20.00 50.00
84 FDR/Truman/Eisenhower 30.00 60.00
85 Ichiro/Chavez/Hunter 12.50 30.00
86 Nixon/Reagan/Bush 60.00 120.00
87 Smoltz/Delgado/Edgar 8.00 20.00
88 Manny/Vlad/Ortiz 12.50 30.00
89 Livan/Hershiser/Stargell 10.00 25.00
90 Ortiz/Howard/Pujols 10.00 25.00
91 Wang/J.Santana/Garland 15.00 40.00
92 Deion/Bo/B.Jordan 15.00 40.00
93 FDR/JFK/Clinton 75.00 150.00
94 Vlad/Ichiro/Wells 10.00 25.00
95 Thome/Dye/Konerko 10.00 25.00
96 Pierzynski/Escobar/Paul 8.00 20.00
97 Carter/Rickey/Molitor 15.00 40.00
98 Gibson/Eckersley 20.00 50.00
99 L.Castillo/Alou/Prior 8.00 20.00
100 Mookie/Knight/Buckner 20.00 50.00

2007 Topps Triple Threads Relics Combos Autographs

STATED ODDS 1:94 MINI
STATED PRINT RUN 36 SER.#'d SETS
EMERALD: .5X TO 1.2X BASIC
EMERALD ODDS 1:185 MINI
EMERALD PRINT RUN 18 SER.#'d SETS
GOLD ODDS 1:371 MINI
GOLD PRINT RUN 9 SER.#'d SETS
NO GOLD PRICING DUE TO SCARCITY
PLATINUM ODDS 1:2996 MINI
PLATINUM PRINT RUN 1 SER.#'d SET
NO PLATINUM PRICING DUE TO SCARCITY
SAPPHIRE ODDS 1:1145 MINI
SAPPHIRE PRINT RUN 3 SER.#'d SETS
NO SAPPHIRE PRICING DUE TO SCARCITY
*SEPIA: .4X TO 1X BASIC
SEPIA ODDS 1:129 MINI
SEPIA PRINT RUN 27 SER.#'d SETS
WHITE WHALE ODDS 1:1219 MINI
WHITE WHALE PRINT RUN 1 SER.#'d SET
NO WHITE WHALE PRICING DUE TO SCARCITY
1 Brooks/Yount/Bench 40.00 80.00
2 Reggie/Morgan/Sandberg 75.00 150.00
3 Seaver/Gibson/Ryan 150.00 400.00
4 Pujols/ARod/Vlad 175.00 350.00
5 Seaver/Clemens/Gooden 60.00 150.00
6 J.Santana/Glavine/Clemens 40.00 80.00
7 ARod/Wang/Mattingly 100.00 200.00
8 Howard/Schmidt/Abreu 75.00 150.00
9 Howard/Ortiz/Pujols 100.00 200.00
10 ARod/Wright/J.Reyes 125.00 250.00
11 Mig.Cabrera/Manny/Ortiz 75.00 150.00
12 Verlander/Jer.Weaver/Wang 150.00 300.00
13 Kiner/Snider/Berra 125.00 250.00
14 Howard/ARod/Andruw 100.00 200.00
15 Lind/Stokes/Dav.Murphy 12.50 30.00
16 And.Miller/Stokes/Perkins 12.50 30.00
17 Riggans/Tulo/And.Miller 20.00 50.00
18 Perkins/Milledge/Tulo 20.00 50.00

2007 Topps Triple Threads Relics Combos Double

STATED ODDS 1:31 MINI
STATED PRINT RUN 36 SER.#'d SETS
*EMERALD: .4X TO 1X BASIC
EMERALD ODDS 1:62 MINI
EMERALD PRINT RUN 18 SER.#'d SETS
GOLD ODDS 1:125 MINI
PLATINUM ODDS 1:1140 MINI
PLATINUM PRINT RUN 1 SER.#'d SET
GOLD PRINT RUN 9 SER.#'d SETS
NO GOLD PRICING DUE TO SCARCITY
NO PLATINUM PRICING DUE TO SCARCITY
SAPPHIRE ODDS 1:372 MINI
SAPPHIRE PRINT RUN 3 SER.#'d SETS
NO SAPPHIRE PRICING DUE TO SCARCITY
*SEPIA: .4X TO 1X BASIC
SEPIA ODDS 1:42 MINI
SEPIA PRINT RUN 27 SER.#'d SETS
1 Mantle/DiMaggio 200.00 300.00
2 Yankees/Red Sox 125.00 175.00
3 Mets/Braves 30.00 60.00
4 David Wright 30.00 60.00
5 Albert Pujols 50.00 100.00
6 Chien-Ming Wang 100.00 200.00
7 Wright/Howard 30.00 60.00
8 Alex Rodriguez 50.00 100.00
9 Ryan Howard 12.50 30.00
10 Ichiro Suzuki 75.00 150.00
11 Dominican Republic 30.00 60.00
12 Japan 100.00 200.00
13 Puerto Rico 75.00 150.00
14 Venezuelan 40.00 80.00
15 Hall of Famers 150.00 300.00
16 MVPs 250.00 350.00
17 Yankees 60.00 120.00
18 Red Sox 40.00 80.00
19 Twins 50.00 100.00
20 Tigers 50.00 100.00
21 Athletics 60.00 120.00
22 Angels 20.00 50.00
23 Expos 30.00 60.00
24 Rangers 50.00 100.00
25 Mariners 60.00 120.00
26 Mets 20.00 50.00
27 Cardinals 50.00 100.00
28 Astros 100.00 200.00
29 Phillies 125.00 175.00
30 Braves 40.00 80.00
31 Cubs 40.00 80.00
32 Generation Now 20.00 50.00
33 David Ortiz 15.00 40.00
34 MVPs 60.00 120.00
35 Cardinals/Tigers 50.00 100.00
36 Cubs/White Sox 40.00 80.00
37 Mets/Yankees 15.00 40.00
38 06 AVG Leaders 30.00 60.00
39 06 HR Leaders 40.00 80.00
40 06 RBI Leaders 30.00 60.00
41 06 ERA Leaders 30.00 60.00
42 2006 Wins Leaders 50.00 100.00
43 2006 SO Leaders 12.50 30.00
44 LCS MVPs 30.00 60.00
45 Giants/Dodgers 50.00 100.00
46 03-05 HOF 40.00 80.00
47 White Sox 30.00 60.00
48 Active SO Leaders 40.00 80.00
49 Third Baseman 125.00 175.00
50 Active 30-30 40.00 80.00

2008 Topps Triple Threads

COMMON CARD (1-145) .40 1.00
1-145 PRINT RUN 1350 SER.#'d SETS
COMMON JSY AU RC (146-170) 4.00 10.00
JSY AU RC ODDS 1:11 MINI
JSY AU RC VAR.ODDS 1:20 MINI
JSY AU RC PRINT RUN 99 SER.#'d SETS
TEAM INITIAL DIECUTS ARE VARIATIONS
COMMON JSY AU (171-220) 4.00 10.00
JSY AU ODDS 1:11 MINI
JSY AU VAR.ODDS 1:20 MINI
JSY AU PRINT RUN 99 SER.#'d SETS
TEAM INITIAL DIECUTS ARE VARIATIONS
COMMON CARD (221-251) .40 1.00
221-251 PRINT RUN 1350 SER.#'d SETS
COMMON ROOKIE (221-251) .40 1.00
221-251 RC PRINT RUN 1350 SER.#'d SETS
OVERALL 1-145 PLATE ODDS 1:116 MINI
OVERALL 221-251 PLATE ODDS 1:116 MINI
PLATE PRINT RUN 1 SET PER COLOR
BLACK-CYAN-MAGENTA-YELLOW ISSUED
NO PLATE PRICING DUE TO SCARCITY
1 David Wright .60 1.50
2 Nolan Ryan 3.00 8.00
3 Johnny Damon .60 1.50
4 Joe Mauer .75 2.00
5 Francisco Rodriguez .60 1.50
6 Carlos Beltran .60 1.50
7 Mickey Mantle 3.00 8.00
8 Brian Roberts .40 1.00
9 Lou Gehrig 2.00 5.00
10 Babe Ruth 2.50 6.00
11 Ryne Sandberg 2.00 5.00
12 Bob Gibson .60 1.50
13 Greg Maddux 1.25 3.00
14 Jered Weaver .60 1.50
15 Johnny Bench 1.00 2.50
16 Maggio Ordonez .60 1.50
17 Carl Yastrzemski 1.50 4.00
18 Derek Jeter 2.50 6.00
19 Gil Meche .40 1.00
20 Hanley Ramirez .60 1.50
21 Edgar Martinez .60 1.50
22 Steve Carlton .60 1.50
23 C.C. Sabathia .60 1.50
24 Chase Utley .60 1.50
25 Francisco Cordero .40 1.00
26 Mark Ellis .40 1.00
27 Jeff Kent .40 1.00
28 Brian Fuentes .40 1.00
29 Johan Santana .60 1.50
30 Ichiro 1.25 3.00
31 Ken Griffey Jr. 2.00 5.00
32 Steve Garvey .40 1.00
33 Rafael Furcal .40 1.00
34 Chipper Jones 1.00 2.50
35 Roberto Clemente 2.50 6.00
36 Rich Harden .40 1.00
37 Cy Young 1.00 2.50
38 Albert Pujols 1.25 3.00
39 Dontrelle Willis .40 1.00
40 Mark Teixeira .60 1.50
41 Daisuke Matsuzaka .60 1.50
42 Harmon Killebrew 1.00 2.50
43 Darryl Strawberry .40 1.00
44 Eric Chavez .40 1.00
45 Don Larsen .40 1.00
46 Huston Street .60 1.50
47 Jake Peavy .40 1.00
48 Prince Fielder .60 1.50
49 Garret Anderson .40 1.00
50 Matt Holliday 1.00 2.50
51 Travis Buck .60 1.50
52 Ben Sheets .40 1.00
53 George Brett 2.00 5.00
54 Dmitri Young .40 1.00
55 Phil Rizzuto .60 1.50
56 Jimmy Rollins .60 1.50
57 Manny Ramirez 1.00 2.50
58 Ozzie Smith 1.25 3.00
59 Dale Murphy 1.00 2.50
60 Bobby Crosby .40 1.00
61 Trevor Hoffman .60 1.50
62 Chien-Ming Wang .60 1.50
63 Jose Reyes .60 1.50
64 Vladimir Guerrero .60 1.50
65 Vida Blue .40 1.00
66 Rod Carew .60 1.50
67 Aaron Rowand .40 1.00
68 Hong-Chih Kuo .40 1.00
69 Mike Schmidt 1.50 4.00
70 Rogers Hornsby .60 1.50
71 Alex Rodriguez 1.25 3.00
72 Roger Maris 1.00 2.50
73 Travis Hafner .40 1.00
74 Tom Glavine .60 1.50
75 Pat Burrell .40 1.00
76 Pedro Martinez .60 1.50
77 Joba Chamberlain .40 1.00
78 Jason Varitek 1.00 2.50
79 Hideo Nomo 1.00 2.50
80 Frank Thomas 1.00 2.50
81 Rollie Fingers .60 1.50
82 Carl Crawford .60 1.50
83 Bobby Jenks .40 1.00
84 Victor Martinez .60 1.50
85 Ernie Banks 1.00 2.50
86 Josh Beckett .40 1.00
87 Jose Valverde .40 1.00
88 Reggie Jackson .60 1.50
89 Duke Snider .60 1.50
90 Mike Lowell .40 1.00
91 Dom DiMaggio .40 1.00
92 Torii Hunter .40 1.00
93 Alfonso Soriano .60 1.50
94 Justin Morneau .60 1.50
95 Carlos Delgado .40 1.00
96 Ty Cobb 1.50 4.00
97 Andruw Jones .40 1.00
98 Yogi Berra 1.00 2.50
99 Joe DiMaggio 2.00 5.00
100 Willie Randolph .40 1.00
101 Miguel Cabrera 1.00 2.50
102 Grady Sizemore .60 1.50
103 Michael Young .40 1.00
104 Wade Boggs .60 1.50
105 Goose Gossage .60 1.50
106 Robin Roberts .60 1.50
107 Brooks Robinson .60 1.50
108 Jim Palmer .60 1.50
109 Jorge Posada .60 1.50
110 Keith Hernandez .40 1.00
111 Ivan Rodriguez .60 1
112 Carlos Lee .40 1
113 John Lackey .60 1
114 Alex Rios .40 1
115 Carlton Fisk .60 1
116 Gary Matthews .40 1
117 Billy Martin .60 1
118 Paul Molitor 1.00 2
119 Hideki Matsui 1.00 2
120 Al Kaline 1.00 2
121 Takashi Saito .40 1
122 Stan Musial 1.50 4
123 Ryan Howard .60 1
124 Whitey Ford .60 1
125 John Smoltz 1.00 2
126 Roy Oswalt .60 1
127 Jim Thome .60 1
128 Tony Gwynn 1.00 2
129 Dennis Eckersley .60 1
130 Ted Williams 2.00 5
131 Justin Verlander 1.00 2
132 David Ortiz 1.00 2
133 Tom Gordon .40 1
134 Tom Seaver .60 1
135 Red Schoendienst .60 1.
136 Johnny Podres .40 1
137 Paul Konerko .60 1
138 Robin Yount 1.00 2
139 Todd Helton .60 1.
140 Frank Robinson .60 1.
141 J.J. Putz .40 1.
142 Jackie Robinson 1.00 2
143 Brandon Webb .60 1.
144 Eddie Murray .60 1
145 Freddy Sanchez .40 1
146 Josh Anderson Jsy AU (RC) 5.00 12.
147a Daric Barton Jsy AU (RC) 5.00 12.
147b Daric Barton Jsy AU (RC) 5.00 12.
148 S.Pearce Jsy AU RC 40.00 100
149 C.Hu Jsy AU (RC) 5.00 12.
150a Buchholz Jsy AU (RC) 10.00 25
150b Buchholz Jsy AU (RC) 8.00 20.
151a J.Towles Jsy AU RC 6.00 15.
151b J.Towles Jsy AU RC 6.00 15.
152 Brandon Jones Jsy AU RC 5.00 12.
153 Broadway Jsy AU (RC) 6.00 15.
154a Nyjer Morgan Jsy AU (RC) 6.00 15.
154b Nyjer Morgan Jsy AU (RC) 6.00 15.
155a Ross Ohlendorf Jsy AU RC 5.00 12.
155b Ross Ohlendorf Jsy AU RC 5.00 12.
156 Chris Seddon Jsy AU (RC) 4.00 10.
157 Jonathan Albaladejo Jsy AU RC 5.00 12.
158a Seth Smith Jsy AU (RC) 4.00 10.
158b Seth Smith Jsy AU (RC) 4.00 10.
159a Kevin Hart Jsy AU (RC) 5.00 12.
159b Kevin Hart Jsy AU (RC) 5.00 12.
160 Bill White Jsy AU RC 5.00 12.
161 Wladimir Balentien Jsy AU (RC) 5.00 12.
162a Justin Ruggiano Jsy AU RC 4.00 10.
162b Justin Ruggiano Jsy AU RC 4.00 10.
163a Clint Sammons Jsy AU (RC) 5.00 12.
163b Clint Sammons Jsy AU (RC) 5.00 12.
164 Rich Thompson Jsy AU RC 5.00 12.
165 Dave Davidson Jsy AU RC 4.00 10.
166 Troy Patton Jsy AU (RC) 5.00 12.
167 Joe Koshansky Jsy AU (RC) 5.00 12.
168a Colt Morton Jsy AU RC 5.00 12.
168b Colt Morton Jsy AU RC 5.00 12.
169 Galarraga Jsy AU RC 12.50 30.
170a Sam Fuld Jsy AU RC 4.00 10.
170b Sam Fuld Jsy AU RC 4.00 10.
171 Dustin Moseley Bat AU 4.00 10.0
172 T.Lincecum Jsy AU 20.00 50.0
173a Ryan Braun Jsy AU 15.00 40.
173b Ryan Braun Jsy AU 15.00 40.
174 Phil Hughes Jsy AU 8.00 20.0
175a J.Chamberlain Jsy AU 8.00 20.0
175b J.Chamberlain Jsy AU 8.00 20.
176 H.Pence Jsy AU 12.00 30.0
177a F.Carmona Jsy AU 5.00 12.0
177b F.Carmona Jsy AU 5.00 12.0
178a U.Jimenez Jsy AU 6.00 15.0
178b Ubaldo Jimenez Jsy AU 6.00 15.0
179a C.Maybin Jsy AU 6.00 15.0
179b C.Maybin Jsy AU 6.00 15.0
180a Adam Jones Jsy AU 6.00 15.0
180b Adam Jones Jsy AU 6.00 15.0
181a Brian Bannister Jsy AU 5.00 12.0
181b Brian Bannister Jsy AU 5.00 12.0
182a Saltalamac Jsy AU 8.00 20.0
182b Saltalamac Jsy AU 5.00 12.0
183 Alex Gordon Jsy AU 8.00 20.0
184a R.Martin Jsy AU 6.00 15.0
184b R.Martin Jsy AU 6.00 15.0
185 John Maine Jsy AU 10.00 25.0
186a H.Okajima Jsy AU 5.00 12.0
186b H.Okajima Jsy AU 5.00 12.0
187a Granderson Jsy AU 10.00 25.0
187b Granderson Jsy AU 10.00 25.0
188 Delmon Young Jsy AU 5.00 12.0
189a Jo-Jo Reyes Jsy AU 5.00 12.0
189b Jo-Jo Reyes Jsy AU 5.00 12.0
190 Y.Gallardo Jsy AU 8.00 20.0
191a Zimmerman Jsy AU 10.00 25.0
191b Zimmerman Jsy AU 6.00 15.0
192 J.Guthrie Jsy AU 8.00 20.0
193a Dan Uggla Jsy AU 6.00 15.0
193b Dan Uggla Jsy AU 6.00 15.0
194a Andre Ethier Jsy AU 8.00 20.0
194b Andre Ethier Jsy AU 8.00 20.0
195a C.Young Jsy AU 6.00 15.0
195b C.Young Jsy AU 6.00 15.0
196a Elijah Dukes Jsy AU 5.00 12.0

b Elijah Dukes Jsy AU 5.00 12.00
'a N.Markakis Jsy AU 8.00 20.00
'b N.Markakis Jsy AU 8.00 20.00
a M.Cabrera Jsy AU 5.00 12.00
b M.Cabrera Jsy AU 5.00 12.00
Cole Hamels Jsy AU 12.50 30.00
J.Loney Jsy AU 5.00 12.00
a K.Slowey Jsy AU 8.00 20.00
b K.Slowey Jsy AU 8.00 20.00
. Carlos Marmol Jsy AU 6.00 15.00
3a A.Iwamura Jsy AU 10.00 25.00
b A.Iwamura Jsy AU 10.00 25.00
A.Gonzalez Jsy AU 6.00 15.00
a B.Phillips Jsy AU 5.00 12.00
b B.Phillips Jsy AU 5.00 12.00
5 J.J. Hardy Jsy AU 10.00 25.00
'a Tom Gorzelanny Jsy AU 4.00 10.00
'b Tom Gorzelanny Jsy AU 4.00 10.00
3a Matt Cain Jsy AU 10.00 25.00
3b Matt Cain Jsy AU 10.00 25.00
9a Matt Capps Jsy AU 5.00 12.00
9b Matt Capps Jsy AU 5.00 12.00
0a Jeff Francis Jsy AU 5.00 12.00
0b Jeff Francis Jsy AU 5.00 12.00
B.McCann Jsy AU 10.00 25.00
2 Matt Garza Jsy AU 8.00 20.00
3a R.Cano Jsy AU 20.00 50.00
3b R.Cano Jsy AU 20.00 50.00
F.Hernandez Jsy AU 10.00 25.00
5 Y.Escobar Jsy AU 8.00 20.00
5a F.Liriano Jsy AU 8.00 20.00
5b F.Liriano Jsy AU 8.00 20.00
7a Rich Hill Jsy AU 5.00 12.00
7b Rich Hill Jsy AU 5.00 12.00
3a Taylor Buchholz Jsy AU 4.00 10.00
3b Taylor Buchholz Jsy AU 4.00 10.00
9 Asdrubal Cabrera Jsy AU 6.00 15.00
0a Lastings Milledge Jsy AU 5.00 12.00
0b Lastings Milledge Jsy AU 5.00 12.00
1 Honus Wagner 1.00 2.50
2 Walter Johnson 1.00 2.50
3 Thurman Munson 1.00 2.50
4 Roy Campanella 1.00 2.50
5 George Sisler .60 1.50
6 Pee Wee Reese .60 1.50
7 Johnny Mize .60 1.50
8 Jimmie Foxx 1.00 2.50
9 Tris Speaker .60 1.50
0 Christy Mathewson 1.00 2.50
1 Mel Ott 1.00 2.50
2 Ralph Kiner .60 1.50
3 Joey Votto (RC) 1.50 4.00
4 Hiroki Kuroda RC 1.00 2.50
5 John Bowker (RC) .40 1.00
6 Lance Berkman .60 1.50
7 Aaron Harang .40 1.00
8 B.J. Upton .60 1.50
9 Zack Greinke .60 1.50
0 Cal Ripken Jr. 3.00 8.00
1 Justin Upton .60 1.50
2 Roy Halladay .60 1.50
3 Orlando Hudson .40 1.00
4 Scott Kazmir .60 1.50
5 Matt Kemp .75 2.00
6 Mark Buehrle .60 1.50
7 Adam Dunn .60 1.50
8 Erik Bedard .40 1.00
9 Carlos Zambrano .60 1.50
0 Jeff Francoeur .60 1.50
1 Brad Penny .40 1.00

2008 Topps Triple Threads Black

BLACK 1-145: 3X TO 8X BASIC
BLACK 221-251: 3X TO 8X BASIC
-145/221-251 ODDS 1:16 MINI
-145/221-251 PNT RUN 30 SER.#'d SETS

2008 Topps Triple Threads Emerald

EMERALD 1-145: .6X TO 1.5X BASIC
EMERALD 221-251: .6X TO 1.5X BASIC
-145/221-251 ODDS 1:2 MINI
-145/221-251 PNT RUN 240 SER.#'d SETS
EMERALD AUTO: .5X TO 1.2X BASIC AU
EMERALD VAR AU: .5X TO 1.2X BASIC AU
46-220 AU ODDS 1:22 MINI
46-220 AU VAR.ODDS 1:39 MINI
46-220 AU PRINT RUN 50 SERIAL #'d SETS
EAM INITIAL DIECUTS ARE VARIATIONS

2008 Topps Triple Threads Gold

GOLD 1-145: 1X TO 2.5X BASIC
GOLD 221-251: 1X TO 2.5X BASIC
-145/221-251 ODDS 1:5 MINI
-145/221-251 PNT RUN 99 SER.#'d SETS
GOLD AUTO: .6X TO 1.5X BASIC AU
GOLD VAR AU: .6X TO 1.5X BASIC AU
46-220 AU ODDS 1:43 MINI
46-220 AU VAR.ODDS 1:77 MINI
46-220 AU PRINT RUN 25 SERIAL #'d SETS
EAM INITIAL DIECUTS ARE VARIATIONS

2008 Topps Triple Threads Sapphire

SAPPHIRE 1-145: 3X TO 8X BASIC
SAPPHIRE 221-251: 3X TO 8X BASIC
-145/221-251 ODDS 1:19 MINI
-145/221-251 PNT RUN 25 SER.#'d SETS
46-220 JSY AU ODDS 1:107 MINI
46-220 JSY AU VAR.ODDS 1:190 MINI
46-220 AU PRINT RUN 10 SERIAL #'d SETS
EAM INITIAL DIECUTS ARE VARIATIONS
NO SAPPHIRE JSY AUTO PRICING AVAILABLE

2008 Topps Triple Threads Sepia

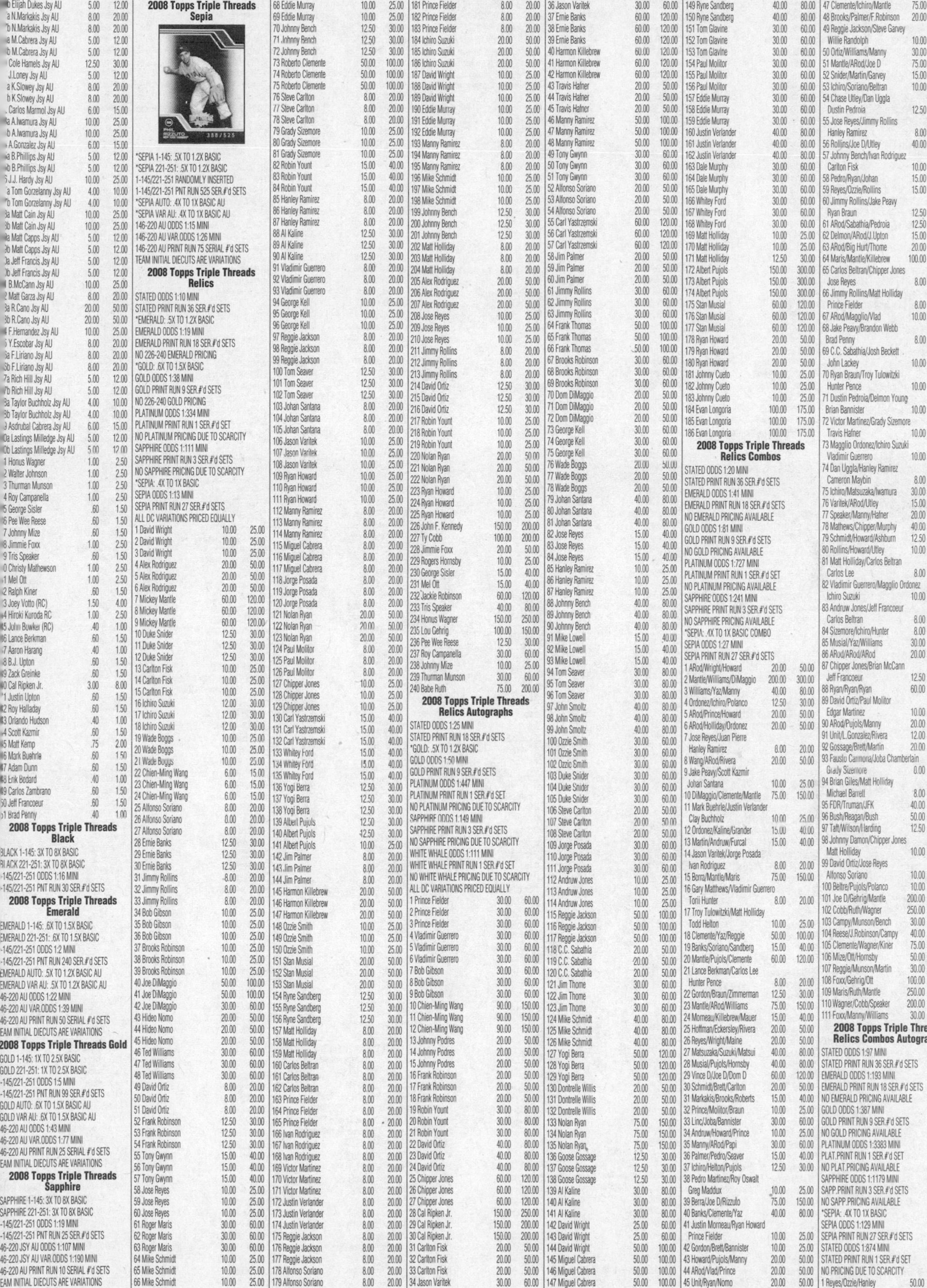

*SEPIA 1-145: .5X TO 1.2X BASIC
*SEPIA 221-251: .5X TO 1.2X BASIC
1-145/221-251 RANDOMLY INSERTED
1-145/221-251 PNT RUN 525 SER.#'d SETS
*SEPIA AUTO: .4X TO 1X BASIC AU
*SEPIA VAR AU: .4X TO 1X BASIC AU
146-220 AU ODDS 1:15 MINI
146-220 AU VAR.ODDS 1:26 MINI
146-220 AU PRINT RUN 75 SERIAL #'d SETS
TEAM INITIAL DIECUTS ARE VARIATIONS

2008 Topps Triple Threads Relics

STATED ODDS 1:10 MINI
STATED PRINT RUN 36 SER.#'d SETS
*EMERALD: .5X TO 1.2X BASIC
EMERALD ODDS 1:19 MINI
EMERALD PRINT RUN 18 SER.#'d SETS
NO 226-240 EMERALD PRICING
*GOLD: .6X TO 1.5X BASIC
GOLD ODDS 1:38 MINI
GOLD PRINT RUN 9 SER.#'d SETS
NO 226-240 GOLD PRICING
PLATINUM ODDS 1:334 MINI
PLATINUM PRINT RUN 1 SER.#'d SET
NO PLATINUM PRICING DUE TO SCARCITY
SAPPHIRE ODDS 1:111 MINI
SAPPHIRE PRINT RUN 3 SER.#'d SETS
NO SAPPHIRE PRICING DUE TO SCARCITY
*SEPIA: .4X TO 1X BASIC
SEPIA ODDS 1:13 MINI
SEPIA PRINT RUN 27 SER.#'d SETS
ALL DC VARIATIONS PRICED EQUALLY
1 David Wright 10.00 25.00
2 David Wright 10.00 25.00
3 David Wright 10.00 25.00
4 Alex Rodriguez 20.00 50.00
5 Alex Rodriguez 20.00 50.00
6 Alex Rodriguez 20.00 50.00
7 Mickey Mantle 60.00 120.00
8 Mickey Mantle 60.00 120.00
9 Mickey Mantle 60.00 120.00
10 Duke Snider 12.50 30.00
11 Duke Snider 12.50 30.00
12 Duke Snider 12.50 30.00
13 Carlton Fisk 10.00 25.00
14 Carlton Fisk 10.00 25.00
15 Carlton Fisk 10.00 25.00
16 Ichiro Suzuki 12.00 30.00
17 Ichiro Suzuki 12.00 30.00
18 Ichiro Suzuki 12.00 30.00
19 Wade Boggs 10.00 25.00
20 Wade Boggs 10.00 25.00
21 Wade Boggs 10.00 25.00
22 Chien-Ming Wang 6.00 15.00
23 Chien-Ming Wang 6.00 15.00
24 Chien-Ming Wang 6.00 15.00
25 Alfonso Soriano 8.00 20.00
26 Alfonso Soriano 8.00 20.00
27 Alfonso Soriano 8.00 20.00
28 Ernie Banks 12.50 30.00
29 Ernie Banks 12.50 30.00
30 Ernie Banks 12.50 30.00
31 Jimmy Rollins 8.00 20.00
32 Jimmy Rollins 8.00 20.00
33 Jimmy Rollins 8.00 20.00
34 Bob Gibson 10.00 25.00
35 Bob Gibson 10.00 25.00
36 Bob Gibson 10.00 25.00
37 Brooks Robinson 10.00 25.00
38 Brooks Robinson 10.00 25.00
39 Brooks Robinson 10.00 25.00
40 Joe DiMaggio 50.00 100.00
41 Joe DiMaggio 50.00 100.00
42 Joe DiMaggio 30.00 60.00
43 Hideo Nomo 20.00 50.00
44 Hideo Nomo 20.00 50.00
45 Hideo Nomo 20.00 50.00
46 Ted Williams 30.00 60.00
47 Ted Williams 30.00 60.00
48 Ted Williams 30.00 60.00
49 David Ortiz 8.00 20.00
50 David Ortiz 8.00 20.00
51 David Ortiz 8.00 20.00
52 Frank Robinson 12.50 30.00
53 Frank Robinson 12.50 30.00
54 Frank Robinson 12.50 30.00
55 Tony Gwynn 15.00 40.00
56 Tony Gwynn 15.00 40.00
57 Tony Gwynn 15.00 40.00
58 Jose Reyes 10.00 25.00
59 Jose Reyes 10.00 25.00
60 Jose Reyes 10.00 25.00
61 Roger Maris 30.00 60.00
62 Roger Maris 30.00 60.00
63 Roger Maris 30.00 60.00
64 Mike Schmidt 10.00 25.00
65 Mike Schmidt 10.00 25.00
66 Mike Schmidt 10.00 25.00
67 Eddie Murray 10.00 25.00
68 Eddie Murray 10.00 25.00
69 Eddie Murray 10.00 25.00
70 Johnny Bench 12.50 30.00
71 Johnny Bench 12.50 30.00
72 Johnny Bench 12.50 30.00
73 Roberto Clemente 50.00 100.00
74 Roberto Clemente 50.00 100.00
75 Roberto Clemente 50.00 100.00
76 Steve Carlton 8.00 20.00
77 Steve Carlton 8.00 20.00
78 Steve Carlton 8.00 20.00
79 Grady Sizemore 10.00 25.00
80 Grady Sizemore 10.00 25.00
81 Grady Sizemore 10.00 25.00
82 Robin Yount 15.00 40.00
83 Robin Yount 15.00 40.00
84 Robin Yount 15.00 40.00
85 Hanley Ramirez 8.00 20.00
86 Hanley Ramirez 8.00 20.00
87 Hanley Ramirez 8.00 20.00
88 Al Kaline 12.50 30.00
89 Al Kaline 12.50 30.00
90 Al Kaline 12.50 30.00
91 Vladimir Guerrero 8.00 20.00
92 Vladimir Guerrero 8.00 20.00
93 Vladimir Guerrero 8.00 20.00
94 George Kell 10.00 25.00
95 George Kell 10.00 25.00
96 George Kell 10.00 25.00
97 Reggie Jackson 8.00 20.00
98 Reggie Jackson 8.00 20.00
99 Reggie Jackson 8.00 20.00
100 Tom Seaver 12.50 30.00
101 Tom Seaver 12.50 30.00
102 Tom Seaver 12.50 30.00
103 Johan Santana 8.00 20.00
104 Johan Santana 8.00 20.00
105 Johan Santana 8.00 20.00
106 Jason Varitek 10.00 25.00
107 Jason Varitek 10.00 25.00
108 Jason Varitek 10.00 25.00
109 Ryan Howard 10.00 25.00
110 Ryan Howard 10.00 25.00
111 Ryan Howard 10.00 25.00
112 Manny Ramirez 8.00 20.00
113 Manny Ramirez 8.00 20.00
114 Manny Ramirez 8.00 20.00
115 Miguel Cabrera 8.00 20.00
116 Miguel Cabrera 8.00 20.00
117 Miguel Cabrera 8.00 20.00
118 Jorge Posada 8.00 20.00
119 Jorge Posada 8.00 20.00
120 Jorge Posada 8.00 20.00
121 Nolan Ryan 20.00 50.00
122 Nolan Ryan 20.00 50.00
123 Nolan Ryan 20.00 50.00
124 Paul Molitor 8.00 20.00
125 Paul Molitor 8.00 20.00
126 Paul Molitor 8.00 20.00
127 Chipper Jones 10.00 25.00
128 Chipper Jones 10.00 25.00
129 Chipper Jones 10.00 25.00
130 Carl Yastrzemski 15.00 40.00
131 Carl Yastrzemski 15.00 40.00
132 Carl Yastrzemski 15.00 40.00
133 Whitey Ford 15.00 40.00
134 Whitey Ford 15.00 40.00
135 Whitey Ford 15.00 40.00
136 Yogi Berra 12.50 30.00
137 Yogi Berra 12.50 30.00
138 Yogi Berra 12.50 30.00
139 Albert Pujols 12.50 30.00
140 Albert Pujols 12.50 30.00
141 Albert Pujols 10.00 25.00
142 Jim Palmer 8.00 20.00
143 Jim Palmer 8.00 20.00
144 Jim Palmer 8.00 20.00
145 Harmon Killebrew 20.00 50.00
146 Harmon Killebrew 20.00 50.00
147 Harmon Killebrew 20.00 50.00
148 Ozzie Smith 10.00 25.00
149 Ozzie Smith 10.00 25.00
150 Ozzie Smith 10.00 25.00
151 Stan Musial 20.00 50.00
152 Stan Musial 20.00 50.00
153 Stan Musial 20.00 50.00
154 Ryne Sandberg 12.50 30.00
155 Ryne Sandberg 12.50 30.00
156 Ryne Sandberg 12.50 30.00
157 Matt Holliday 8.00 20.00
158 Matt Holliday 8.00 20.00
159 Matt Holliday 8.00 20.00
160 Carlos Beltran 8.00 20.00
161 Carlos Beltran 8.00 20.00
162 Carlos Beltran 8.00 20.00
163 Prince Fielder 8.00 20.00
164 Prince Fielder 8.00 20.00
165 Prince Fielder 8.00 20.00
166 Ivan Rodriguez 8.00 20.00
167 Ivan Rodriguez 8.00 20.00
168 Ivan Rodriguez 8.00 20.00
169 Victor Martinez 8.00 20.00
170 Victor Martinez 8.00 20.00
171 Victor Martinez 8.00 20.00
172 Justin Verlander 8.00 20.00
173 Justin Verlander 8.00 20.00
174 Justin Verlander 8.00 20.00
175 Reggie Jackson 8.00 20.00
176 Reggie Jackson 8.00 20.00
177 Reggie Jackson 8.00 20.00
178 Alfonso Soriano 8.00 20.00
179 Alfonso Soriano 8.00 20.00
180 Alfonso Soriano 8.00 20.00
181 Prince Fielder 8.00 20.00
182 Prince Fielder 8.00 20.00
183 Prince Fielder 8.00 20.00
184 Ichiro Suzuki 20.00 50.00
185 Ichiro Suzuki 20.00 50.00
186 Ichiro Suzuki 20.00 50.00
187 David Wright 10.00 25.00
188 David Wright 10.00 25.00
189 David Wright 10.00 25.00
190 Eddie Murray 10.00 25.00
191 Eddie Murray 10.00 25.00
192 Eddie Murray 10.00 25.00
193 Manny Ramirez 8.00 20.00
194 Manny Ramirez 8.00 20.00
195 Manny Ramirez 8.00 20.00
196 Mike Schmidt 10.00 25.00
197 Mike Schmidt 10.00 25.00
198 Mike Schmidt 10.00 25.00
199 Johnny Bench 12.50 30.00
200 Johnny Bench 12.50 30.00
201 Johnny Bench 12.50 30.00
202 Matt Holliday 8.00 20.00
203 Matt Holliday 8.00 20.00
204 Matt Holliday 8.00 20.00
205 Alex Rodriguez 20.00 50.00
206 Alex Rodriguez 20.00 50.00
207 Alex Rodriguez 20.00 50.00
208 Jose Reyes 10.00 25.00
209 Jose Reyes 10.00 25.00
210 Jose Reyes 10.00 25.00
211 Jimmy Rollins 8.00 20.00
212 Jimmy Rollins 8.00 20.00
213 Jimmy Rollins 8.00 20.00
214 David Ortiz 12.50 30.00
215 David Ortiz 12.50 30.00
216 David Ortiz 12.50 30.00
217 Robin Yount 10.00 25.00
218 Robin Yount 10.00 25.00
219 Robin Yount 10.00 25.00
220 Nolan Ryan 20.00 50.00
221 Nolan Ryan 20.00 50.00
222 Nolan Ryan 20.00 50.00
223 Ryan Howard 10.00 25.00
224 Ryan Howard 10.00 25.00
225 Ryan Howard 10.00 25.00
226 John F. Kennedy 150.00 200.00
227 Ty Cobb 100.00 200.00
228 Jimmie Foxx 20.00 50.00
229 Rogers Hornsby 10.00 25.00
230 George Sisler 15.00 40.00
231 Mel Ott 15.00 40.00
232 Jackie Robinson 60.00 120.00
233 Tris Speaker 40.00 80.00
234 Honus Wagner 150.00 250.00
235 Lou Gehrig 100.00 150.00
236 Pee Wee Reese 12.50 30.00
237 Roy Campanella 30.00 60.00
238 Johnny Mize 10.00 25.00
239 Thurman Munson 30.00 60.00
240 Babe Ruth 75.00 200.00

2008 Topps Triple Threads Relics Autographs

STATED ODDS 1:25 MINI
STATED PRINT RUN 18 SER.#'d SETS
*GOLD: .5X TO 1.2X BASIC
GOLD ODDS 1:50 MINI
GOLD PRINT RUN 9 SER.#'d SETS
PLATINUM ODDS 1:447 MINI
PLATINUM PRINT RUN 1 SER.#'d SET
NO PLATINUM PRICING DUE TO SCARCITY
SAPPHIRE ODDS 1:149 MINI
SAPPHIRE PRINT RUN 3 SER.#'d SETS
NO SAPPHIRE PRICING DUE TO SCARCITY
WHITE WHALE ODDS 1:111 MINI
WHITE WHALE PRINT RUN 1 SER.#'d SET
NO WHITE WHALE PRICING DUE TO SCARCITY
ALL DC VARIATIONS PRICED EQUALLY
1 Prince Fielder 30.00 60.00
2 Prince Fielder 30.00 60.00
3 Prince Fielder 30.00 60.00
4 Vladimir Guerrero 30.00 60.00
5 Vladimir Guerrero 30.00 60.00
6 Vladimir Guerrero 30.00 60.00
7 Bob Gibson 30.00 60.00
8 Bob Gibson 30.00 60.00
9 Bob Gibson 30.00 60.00
10 Chien-Ming Wang 90.00 150.00
11 Chien-Ming Wang 90.00 150.00
12 Chien-Ming Wang 90.00 150.00
13 Johnny Podres 20.00 50.00
14 Johnny Podres 20.00 50.00
15 Johnny Podres 20.00 50.00
16 Frank Robinson 20.00 50.00
17 Frank Robinson 20.00 50.00
18 Frank Robinson 20.00 50.00
19 Robin Yount 30.00 80.00
20 Robin Yount 30.00 80.00
21 Robin Yount 30.00 80.00
22 David Ortiz 40.00 80.00
23 David Ortiz 40.00 80.00
24 David Ortiz 40.00 80.00
25 Chipper Jones 60.00 120.00
26 Chipper Jones 60.00 120.00
27 Chipper Jones 60.00 120.00
28 Cal Ripken Jr. 150.00 250.00
29 Cal Ripken Jr. 150.00 200.00
30 Cal Ripken Jr. 150.00 200.00
31 Carlton Fisk 20.00 50.00
32 Carlton Fisk 20.00 50.00
33 Carlton Fisk 20.00 50.00
34 Jason Varitek 30.00 60.00
35 Jason Varitek 30.00 60.00
36 Jason Varitek 30.00 60.00
37 Ernie Banks 60.00 120.00
38 Ernie Banks 60.00 120.00
39 Ernie Banks 60.00 120.00
40 Harmon Killebrew 60.00 120.00
41 Harmon Killebrew 60.00 120.00
42 Harmon Killebrew 60.00 120.00
43 Travis Hafner 20.00 50.00
44 Travis Hafner 20.00 50.00
45 Travis Hafner 20.00 50.00
46 Manny Ramirez 50.00 100.00
47 Manny Ramirez 50.00 100.00
48 Manny Ramirez 50.00 100.00
49 Tony Gwynn 30.00 60.00
50 Tony Gwynn 30.00 60.00
51 Tony Gwynn 30.00 60.00
52 Alfonso Soriano 20.00 50.00
53 Alfonso Soriano 20.00 50.00
54 Alfonso Soriano 20.00 50.00
55 Carl Yastrzemski 60.00 120.00
56 Carl Yastrzemski 60.00 120.00
57 Carl Yastrzemski 60.00 120.00
58 Jim Palmer 20.00 50.00
59 Jim Palmer 20.00 50.00
60 Jim Palmer 20.00 50.00
61 Jimmy Rollins 30.00 60.00
62 Jimmy Rollins 30.00 60.00
63 Jimmy Rollins 30.00 60.00
64 Frank Thomas 50.00 100.00
65 Frank Thomas 50.00 100.00
66 Frank Thomas 50.00 100.00
67 Brooks Robinson 30.00 60.00
68 Brooks Robinson 30.00 60.00
69 Brooks Robinson 30.00 60.00
70 Dom DiMaggio 20.00 50.00
71 Dom DiMaggio 20.00 50.00
72 Dom DiMaggio 20.00 50.00
73 George Kell 30.00 60.00
74 George Kell 30.00 60.00
75 George Kell 30.00 60.00
76 Wade Boggs 20.00 50.00
77 Wade Boggs 20.00 50.00
78 Wade Boggs 20.00 50.00
79 Johan Santana 40.00 80.00
80 Johan Santana 40.00 80.00
81 Johan Santana 40.00 80.00
82 Jose Reyes 15.00 40.00
83 Jose Reyes 15.00 40.00
84 Jose Reyes 15.00 40.00
85 Hanley Ramirez 10.00 25.00
86 Hanley Ramirez 10.00 25.00
87 Hanley Ramirez 10.00 25.00
88 Johnny Bench 40.00 80.00
89 Johnny Bench 40.00 80.00
90 Johnny Bench 40.00 80.00
91 Mike Lowell 15.00 40.00
92 Mike Lowell 15.00 40.00
93 Mike Lowell 15.00 40.00
94 Tom Seaver 30.00 80.00
95 Tom Seaver 30.00 80.00
96 Tom Seaver 30.00 80.00
97 John Smoltz 40.00 80.00
98 John Smoltz 40.00 80.00
99 John Smoltz 40.00 80.00
100 Ozzie Smith 30.00 60.00
101 Ozzie Smith 30.00 60.00
102 Ozzie Smith 30.00 60.00
103 Duke Snider 30.00 60.00
104 Duke Snider 30.00 60.00
105 Duke Snider 30.00 60.00
106 Steve Carlton 20.00 50.00
107 Steve Carlton 20.00 50.00
108 Steve Carlton 20.00 50.00
109 Jorge Posada 30.00 60.00
110 Jorge Posada 30.00 60.00
111 Jorge Posada 30.00 60.00
112 Andruw Jones 10.00 25.00
113 Andruw Jones 10.00 25.00
114 Andruw Jones 10.00 25.00
115 Reggie Jackson 50.00 100.00
116 Reggie Jackson 50.00 100.00
117 Reggie Jackson 50.00 100.00
118 C.C. Sabathia 20.00 50.00
119 C.C. Sabathia 20.00 50.00
120 C.C. Sabathia 20.00 50.00
121 Jim Thome 30.00 60.00
122 Jim Thome 30.00 60.00
123 Jim Thome 30.00 60.00
124 Mike Schmidt 40.00 80.00
125 Mike Schmidt 40.00 80.00
126 Mike Schmidt 40.00 80.00
127 Yogi Berra 50.00 120.00
128 Yogi Berra 50.00 120.00
129 Yogi Berra 50.00 120.00
130 Dontrelle Willis 20.00 50.00
131 Dontrelle Willis 20.00 50.00
132 Dontrelle Willis 20.00 50.00
133 Nolan Ryan 75.00 150.00
134 Nolan Ryan 75.00 150.00
135 Nolan Ryan 75.00 150.00
136 Goose Gossage 12.50 30.00
137 Goose Gossage 12.50 30.00
138 Goose Gossage 12.50 30.00
139 Al Kaline 30.00 80.00
140 Al Kaline 30.00 80.00
141 Al Kaline 30.00 80.00
142 David Wright 25.00 60.00
143 David Wright 25.00 60.00
144 David Wright 50.00 100.00
145 Miguel Cabrera 50.00 100.00
146 Miguel Cabrera 50.00 100.00
147 Miguel Cabrera 50.00 100.00
148 Ryne Sandberg 40.00 80.00
149 Ryne Sandberg 40.00 80.00
150 Ryne Sandberg 40.00 80.00
151 Tom Glavine 30.00 60.00
152 Tom Glavine 30.00 60.00
153 Tom Glavine 30.00 60.00
154 Paul Molitor 30.00 60.00
155 Paul Molitor 30.00 60.00
156 Paul Molitor 30.00 60.00
157 Eddie Murray 30.00 60.00
158 Eddie Murray 30.00 60.00
159 Eddie Murray 30.00 60.00
160 Justin Verlander 40.00 80.00
161 Justin Verlander 40.00 80.00
162 Justin Verlander 40.00 80.00
163 Dale Murphy 30.00 60.00
164 Dale Murphy 30.00 60.00
165 Dale Murphy 30.00 60.00
166 Whitey Ford 30.00 60.00
167 Whitey Ford 30.00 60.00
168 Whitey Ford 30.00 60.00
169 Matt Holliday 10.00 25.00
170 Matt Holliday 10.00 25.00
171 Matt Holliday 12.50 30.00
172 Albert Pujols 150.00 300.00
173 Albert Pujols 150.00 300.00
174 Albert Pujols 150.00 300.00
175 Stan Musial 60.00 120.00
176 Stan Musial 60.00 120.00
177 Stan Musial 60.00 120.00
178 Ryan Howard 20.00 50.00
179 Ryan Howard 20.00 50.00
180 Ryan Howard 20.00 50.00
181 Johnny Cueto 10.00 25.00
182 Johnny Cueto 10.00 25.00
183 Johnny Cueto 10.00 25.00
184 Evan Longoria 100.00 175.00
185 Evan Longoria 100.00 175.00
186 Evan Longoria 100.00 175.00

2008 Topps Triple Threads Relics Combos

STATED ODDS 1:20 MINI
STATED PRINT RUN 36 SER.#'d SETS
EMERALD ODDS 1:41 MINI
EMERALD PRINT RUN 18 SER.#'d SETS
NO EMERALD PRICING AVAILABLE
GOLD ODDS 1:81 MINI
GOLD PRINT RUN 9 SER.#'d SETS
NO GOLD PRICING AVAILABLE
PLATINUM ODDS 1:727 MINI
PLATINUM PRINT RUN 1 SER.#'d SET
NO PLATINUM PRICING AVAILABLE
SAPPHIRE ODDS 1:241 MINI
SAPPHIRE PRINT RUN 3 SER.#'d SETS
NO SAPPHIRE PRICING AVAILABLE
*SEPIA: .4X TO 1X BASIC COMBO
SEPIA ODDS 1:27 MINI
SEPIA PRINT RUN 27 SER.#'d SETS
1 ARod/Wright/Howard 20.00 50.00
2 Mantle/Williams/DiMaggio 200.00 300.00
3 Williams/Yaz/Manny 40.00 80.00
4 Ordonez/Ichiro/Polanco 12.50 30.00
5 ARod/Prince/Howard 20.00 50.00
6 ARod/Holliday/Ordonez 20.00 50.00
7 Jose Reyes/Juan Pierre
Hanley Ramirez 8.00 20.00
8 Wang/ARod/Rivera 20.00 50.00
9 Jake Peavy/Scott Kazmir
Johan Santana 10.00 25.00
10 DiMaggio/Clemente/Mantle 75.00 150.00
11 Mark Buehrle/Justin Verlander
Clay Buchholz 10.00 25.00
12 Ordonez/Kaline/Grander 15.00 40.00
13 Martin/Andruw/Furcal 15.00 40.00
14 Jason Varitek/Jorge Posada
Ivan Rodriguez 8.00 20.00
15 Berra/Mantle/Maris 75.00 150.00
16 Gary Matthews/Vladimir Guerrero
Torii Hunter 8.00 20.00
17 Troy Tulowitzki/Matt Holliday
Todd Helton 10.00 25.00
18 Clemente/Yaz/Reggie 50.00 100.00
19 Banks/Soriano/Sandberg 15.00 40.00
20 Mantle/Pujols/Clemente 60.00 120.00
21 Lance Berkman/Carlos Lee
Hunter Pence 8.00 20.00
22 Gordon/Braun/Zimmerman 12.50 30.00
23 Mantle/ARod/Williams 75.00 150.00
24 Morneau/Killebrew/Mauer 15.00 40.00
25 Hoffman/Eckersley/Rivera 20.00 50.00
26 Reyes/Wright/Maine 20.00 50.00
27 Matsuzaka/Suzuki/Matsui 40.00 80.00
28 Musial/Pujols/Hornsby 40.00 80.00
29 Vince D/Joe D/Dom D 60.00 120.00
30 Schmidt/Brett/Carlton 20.00 50.00
31 Markakis/Brooks/Roberts 15.00 40.00
32 Prince/Molitor/Braun 10.00 25.00
33 Linc/Joba/Bannister 30.00 60.00
34 Andruw/Howard/Prince 10.00 25.00
35 Manny/ARod/Papi 30.00 60.00
36 Palmer/Pedro/Seaver 15.00 40.00
37 Ichiro/Helton/Pujols 12.50 30.00
38 Pedro Martinez/Roy Oswalt
Greg Maddux 10.00 25.00
39 Berra/Joe D/Rizzuto 75.00 150.00
40 Banks/Clemente/Yaz 40.00 80.00
41 Justin Morneau/Ryan Howard
Prince Fielder 10.00 25.00
42 Gordon/Brett/Bannister 10.00 25.00
43 Howard/Pujols/Manny 20.00 50.00
44 ARod/Vlad/Prince 20.00 50.00
45 Unit/Ryan/Nomo 20.00 50.00
46 Fingers/Reggie/Blue 15.00 40.00
47 Clemente/Ichiro/Mantle 75.00 150.00
48 Brooks/Palmer/F.Robinson 20.00 50.00
49 Reggie Jackson/Steve Garvey
Willie Randolph 10.00 25.00
50 Ortiz/Williams/Manny 30.00 60.00
51 Mantle/ARod/Joe D 75.00 150.00
52 Snider/Martin/Garvey 15.00 40.00
53 Ichiro/Soriano/Beltran 10.00 25.00
54 Chase Utley/Dan Uggla
Dustin Pedroia 12.50 30.00
55 Jose Reyes/Jimmy Rollins
Hanley Ramirez 8.00 20.00
56 Rollins/Joe D/Utley 40.00 80.00
57 Johnny Bench/Ivan Rodriguez
Carlton Fisk 10.00 25.00
58 Pedro/Ryan/Johan 15.00 40.00
59 Reyes/Ozzie/Rollins 15.00 40.00
60 Jimmy Rollins/Jake Peavy
Ryan Braun 12.50 30.00
61 ARod/Sabathia/Pedroia 12.50 30.00
62 Delmon/ARod/J.Upton 15.00 40.00
63 ARod/Big Hurt/Thome 20.00 50.00
64 Maris/Mantle/Killebrew 100.00 200.00
65 Carlos Beltran/Chipper Jones
Jose Reyes 8.00 20.00
66 Jimmy Rollins/Matt Holliday
Prince Fielder 8.00 20.00
67 ARod/Magglio/Vlad 10.00 25.00
68 Jake Peavy/Brandon Webb
Brad Penny 8.00 20.00
69 C.C. Sabathia/Josh Beckett
John Lackey 10.00 25.00
70 Ryan Braun/Troy Tulowitzki
Hunter Pence 10.00 25.00
71 Dustin Pedroia/Delmon Young
Brian Bannister 10.00 25.00
72 Victor Martinez/Grady Sizemore
Travis Hafner 10.00 25.00
73 Magglio Ordonez/Ichiro Suzuki
Vladimir Guerrero 10.00 25.00
74 Dan Uggla/Hanley Ramirez
Cameron Maybin 8.00 20.00
75 Ichiro/Matsuzaka/Iwamura 30.00 60.00
76 Varitek/ARod/Utley 15.00 40.00
77 Speaker/Manny/Hafner 20.00 50.00
78 Mathews/Chipper/Murphy 40.00 80.00
79 Schmidt/Howard/Ashburn 12.50 30.00
80 Rollins/Howard/Utley 10.00 25.00
81 Matt Holliday/Carlos Beltran
Carlos Lee 8.00 20.00
82 Vladimir Guerrero/Magglio Ordonez
Ichiro Suzuki 10.00 25.00
83 Andruw Jones/Jeff Francoeur
Carlos Beltran 8.00 20.00
84 Sizemore/Ichiro/Hunter 8.00 20.00
85 Musial/Yaz/Williams 30.00 60.00
86 ARod/ARod/ARod 20.00 50.00
87 Chipper Jones/Brian McCann
Jeff Francoeur 12.50 30.00
88 Ryan/Ryan/Ryan 60.00 120.00
89 David Ortiz/Paul Molitor
Edgar Martinez 10.00 25.00
90 ARod/Pujols/Manny 20.00 50.00
91 Unit/L.Gonzalez/Rivera 12.50 30.00
92 Gossage/Brett/Martin 20.00 50.00
93 Fausto Carmona/Joba Chamberlain
Grady Sizemore 8.00 20.00
94 Brian Giles/Matt Holliday
Michael Barrett 8.00 20.00
95 FDR/Truman/JFK 40.00 80.00
96 Bush/Reagan/Bush 50.00 100.00
97 Taft/Wilson/Harding 12.50 30.00
98 Johnny Damon/Chipper Jones
Matt Holliday 10.00 25.00
99 David Ortiz/Jose Reyes
Alfonso Soriano 10.00 25.00
100 Beltre/Pujols/Polanco 10.00 25.00
101 Joe D/Gehrig/Mantle 200.00 300.00
102 Cobb/Ruth/Wagner 250.00 350.00
103 Campy/Munson/Bench 30.00 60.00
104 Reese/J.Robinson/Campy 40.00 80.00
105 Clemente/Wagner/Kiner 75.00 150.00
106 Mize/Ott/Hornsby 50.00 100.00
107 Reggie/Munson/Martin 30.00 60.00
108 Foxx/Gehrig/Ott 100.00 175.00
109 Maris/Ruth/Mantle 250.00 350.00
110 Wagner/Cobb/Speaker 200.00 300.00
111 Foxx/Manny/Williams 30.00 60.00

2008 Topps Triple Threads Relics Combos Autographs

STATED ODDS 1:97 MINI
STATED PRINT RUN 36 SER.#'d SETS
EMERALD ODDS 1:193 MINI
EMERALD PRINT RUN 18 SER.#'d SETS
NO EMERALD PRICING AVAILABLE
GOLD ODDS 1:387 MINI
GOLD PRINT RUN 9 SER.#'d SETS
NO GOLD PRICING AVAILABLE
PLATINUM ODDS 1:3383 MINI
PLAT.PRINT RUN 1 SER.#'d SET
NO PLAT.PRICING AVAILABLE
SAPPHIRE ODDS 1:1179 MINI
SAPP.PRINT RUN 3 SER.#'d SETS
NO SAPP.PRICING AVAILABLE
*SEPIA: .4X TO 1X BASIC
SEPIA ODDS 1:129 MINI
SEPIA PRINT RUN 27 SER.#'d SETS
STATED ODDS 1:874 MINI
STATED PRINT RUN 1 SER.#'d SET
NO PRICING DUE TO SCARCITY
1 Reyes/Ozzie/Hanley 50.00 100.00
2 Pujols/Manny/Vlad 125.00 250.00

3 Hernandez/Schmidt/Murphy 50.00 100.00
4 F.Robinson/Yaz/Killebrew 100.00 200.00
5 Gibson/Seaver/Carlton 60.00 150.00
6 Killebrew/Carew/Brooks 60.00 120.00
7 Wright/Howard/Pujols 100.00 250.00
8 Prince/Murray/Howard 20.00 50.00
9 Ryan/Brett/Yount 200.00 400.00
10 Bench/Pudge/Fisk 60.00 120.00
11 Berra/Ford/Posada 75.00 200.00
12 Gwynn/Murphy/Strawberry 50.00 100.00
13 Lowell/Manny/Papi 60.00 120.00
14 Joba/Posada/Wang 75.00 150.00
15 Jeff Francis/Taylor Buchholz
Ubaldo Jimenez 12.50 30.00
16 Melky/Ohlendorf/Cano 20.00 50.00
17 Uggla/Seddon/Hanley 12.00 30.00
18 Gordon/Longoria/Zimmerman 30.00 60.00
19 Chris Young/Melky Cabrera
Lastings Milledge 12.50 30.00
20 Rich Hill/Johnny Cueto
Tom Gorzelanny 12.50 30.00
21 Moseley/Liriano/King Felix 15.00 40.00
22 Hanley/Loney/Hardy 15.00 40.00
23 Armando Galarraga/Fausto Carmona
Troy Patton 12.50 30.00

2008 Topps Triple Threads Relics Combos Double

STATED ODDS 1:41 MINI
STATED PRINT RUN 36 SER.#'d SETS
EMERALD ODDS 1:81 MINI
EMERALD PRINT RUN 18 SER.#'d SETS
NO EMERALD PRICING AVAILABLE
GOLD ODDS 1:162 MINI
GOLD PRINT RUN 9 SER.#'d SETS
NO GOLD PRICING AVAILABLE
PLATINUM ODDS 1:1496 MINI
PLAT.PRINT RUN 1 SER.#'d SET
NO PLAT.PRICING AVAILABLE
SAPPHIRE ODDS 1:486 MINI
SAPP.PRINT RUN 3 SER.#'d SETS
NO SAPP.PRICING AVAILABLE
*SEPIA: .4X TO 1X BASIC
SEPIA ODDS 1:54 MINI
SEPIA PRINT RUN 27 SER.#'d SETS
1 Vintage OFs 125.00 250.00
2 Batting Avg LDR 250.00 350.00
3 Triple Play 30.00 60.00
4 Cardinals 60.00 120.00
5 Four Baggers 15.00 40.00
6 Vintage Pitchers 30.00 60.00
7 Base Stealers 15.00 40.00
8 Catchers 30.00 60.00
9 J.DiMaggio/M.Mantle 100.00 200.00
10 Vintage Yankees 100.00 200.00
11 MVP-HOF 100.00 200.00
12 Osw/Mun/Saar/Lid/DOt/Wag 20.00 50.00
13 Yanks/Sox/Mets/Phils 75.00 150.00
14 Yankees 50.00 100.00
15 Japanese Stars 50.00 100.00
16 Russell Martin 20.00 50.00
Jason Bay
Erik Bedard
Rich Harden
Justin Morneau
Shawn Hill
17 Carlos Beltran 30.00 60.00
David Wright
Carlos Delgado
Jose Reyes
Pedro Martinez
John Maine
18 Travis Hafner 10.00 25.00
Victor Martinez
Grady Sizemore
C.C. Sabathia
Fausto Carmona
Bob Feller
19 Brooks Robinson 20.00 50.00
Jim Palmer
Eddie Murray
Brian Roberts
Nick Markakis
Melvin Mora
20 Red Sox 40.00 80.00
21 Mariners 40.00 80.00
22 2007 Award Winners 30.00 60.00
23 Mickey Mantle 75.00 150.00
24 Joe DiMaggio 60.00 120.00
25 Roberto Clemente 60.00 120.00
26 Astros 30.00 60.00
27 Phillies 20.00 50.00
28 WS MVPs 40.00 80.00
29 Ted Williams 50.00 100.00
30 Twins 50.00 100.00
31 First Basemen 10.00 25.00
32 Tigers 50.00 100.00
33 Carlton Fisk 20.00 50.00
Jim Thome
Jermaine Dye
Mark Buehrle
Paul Konerko
Luis Aparicio
34 Keith Hernandez 20.00 50.00
Dwight Gooden
Darryl Strawberry
David Wright
Pedro Martinez
Jose Reyes
35 Braves 30.00 60.00
36 Yankees/Red Sox 40.00 80.00
37 R.Maris/M.Mantle 200.00 300.00
38 Ichiro Suzuki 40.00 80.00
39 Albert Pujols 12.00 30.00
40 Brewers 30.00 60.00
41 Rangers 30.00 60.00
42 Vladimir Guerrero 20.00 50.00
John Lackey
Jered Weaver
Garret Anderson
Torii Hunter
Gary Matthews
43 Tim Lincecum 20.00 50.00
Rich Aurilia
Barry Zito
Eric Chavez
Mark Ellis
Bobby Crosby
44 Russell Martin 20.00 50.00
Rafael Furcal
Andruw Jones
Matt Kemp
Jeff Kent
Hong-Chih Kuo
45 Mets/Phillies 20.00 50.00
46 Chien-Ming Wang 20.00 50.00
47 2007 All-Stars 30.00 60.00
48 2007 ALCS 20.00 50.00
49 Matt Holliday 20.00 50.00
Todd Helton
Troy Tulowitzki
Orlando Hudson
Stephen Drew
Chris Young
50 2007 World Series 30.00 60.00
51 A.Rodriguez/M.Mantle 40.00 80.00
52 Dominican Republic 30.00 60.00
53 All-Time Greats 450.00 650.00
54 STL/PHI/NYG/BRK 60.00 120.00
55 1955 World Series 100.00 200.00

2008 Topps Triple Threads Relics Pairs Rookie-Stars Autographs

STATED ODDS 1:160 MINI
STATED PRINT RUN 50 SER.#'d SETS
GLD ODDS 1:322 MINI
GLD.PRINT RUN 25 SER.#'d SETS
NO GLD.PRICING AVAILABLE
PLAT.ODDS 1:7781 MINI
PLAT.PRINT RUN 1 SER.#'d SET
NO PLAT.PRICING AVAILABLE
SAP.ODDS 1:802 MINI
SAP.PRINT RUN 10 SER.#'d SETS
NO SAP.PRICING AVAILABLE
1 S.Pearce/N.Morgan 15.00 40.00
2 C.Maybin/C.Granderson 12.50 30.00
3 M.Cabrera/R.Cano 30.00 60.00
4 L.Milledge/E.Dukes 10.00 25.00
5 R.Hill/S.Fuld 10.00 25.00
6 J.Towles/J.Saltalamacchia 10.00 25.00
7 C.Buchholz/F.Carmona 10.00 25.00
8 R.Braun/R.Zimmerman 15.00 40.00
9 P.Hughes/J.Chamberlain 15.00 40.00
10 B.Phillips/H.Bailey 12.50 30.00

2009 Topps Triple Threads

COMMON CARD (1-100) .40 1.00
1-100 PRINT RUN 1350 SER.#'d SETS
COMMON JSY AU RC (101-138) 6.00 15.00
JSY AU RC ODDS 1:11 MINI
JSY AU RC PRINT RUN 99 SER.#'d SETS
COMMON JSY AU (101-121) 6.00 15.00
JSY AU ODDS 1:11 MINI
JSY AU PRINT RUN 99 SER.#'d SETS
OVERALL 1-100 PLATE ODDS 1:97 MINI
OVERALL 101-138 PLATE ODDS 1:255 MINI
PLATE PRINT RUN 1 SET PER COLOR
BLACK-CYAN-MAGENTA-YELLOW ISSUED
NO PLATE PRICING DUE TO SCARCITY
1 Justin Upton .60 1.50
2 Brian McCann .60 1.50
3 Babe Ruth 2.50 6.00
4 Alfonso Soriano .60 1.50
5 Albert Pujols 1.25 3.00
6 Edinson Volquez .40 1.00
7 Todd Helton .60 1.50
8 Hanley Ramirez .60 1.50
9 Mickey Mantle 3.00 8.00
10 Manny Ramirez 1.00 2.50
11 Francisco Liriano .40 1.00
12 Lou Gehrig 2.00 5.00
13 Carlos Delgado .40 1.00
14 Walter Johnson 1.00 2.50
15 Alex Rodriguez 1.25 3.00
16 Ryan Howard .75 2.00
17 Nate McLouth .40 1.00
18 Cy Young 1.00 2.50
19 Ichiro Suzuki 1.25 3.00
20 Jorge Posada .60 1.50
21 Scott Kazmir .40 1.00
22 Michael Young .40 1.00
23 Brandon Webb .60 1.50
24 George Sisler .60 1.50
25 Chipper Jones 1.00 2.50
26 Adam Jones .60 1.50
27 David Ortiz 1.00 2.50
28 Geovany Soto .60 1.50
29 Tony Gwynn 1.00 2.50
30 Victor Martinez .60 1.50
31 Jose Lopez .40 1.00
32 Lance Berkman .60 1.50
33 Russell Martin .40 1.00
34 Cal Ripken 3.00 8.00
35 Dan Haren .40 1.00
36 Jose Reyes .60 1.50
37 Rogers Hornsby .60 1.50
38 Mark Teixeira .60 1.50
39 Ernie Banks 1.00 2.50
40 Jimmy Rollins .60 1.50
41 Jake Peavy .40 1.00
42 Jackie Robinson 1.00 2.50
43 B.J. Upton .60 1.50
44 Roy Halladay .60 1.50
45 Jimmie Foxx 1.00 2.50
46 Randy Johnson 1.00 2.50
47 Mel Ott 1.00 2.50
48 Carlos Lee .40 1.00
49 Nick Markakis .75 2.00
50 Dustin Pedroia .75 2.00
51 Nolan Ryan 3.00 8.00
52 Matt Cain .60 1.50
53 Grady Sizemore .60 1.50
54 Christy Mathewson 1.00 2.50
55 Miguel Cabrera 1.00 2.50
56 Roy Campanella 1.00 2.50
57 Prince Fielder .60 1.50
58 Ty Cobb 1.50 4.00
59 Carlos Beltran .60 1.50
60 Pee Wee Reese .60 1.50
61 A.J. Burnett .40 1.00
62 Carl Crawford .60 1.50
63 Chase Utley .60 1.50
64 Adrian Gonzalez .75 2.00
65 Thurman Munson 1.00 2.50
66 Felix Hernandez .60 1.50
67 Chris Carpenter .60 1.50
68 Carl Yastrzemski 1.50 4.00
69 Ian Kinsler .60 1.50
70 Vernon Wells .40 1.00
71 Matt Holliday 1.00 2.50
72 Tris Speaker .60 1.50
73 Roy Oswalt .60 1.50
74 Ozzie Smith 1.25 3.00
75 Daisuke Matsuzaka .60 1.50
76 David Wright .75 2.00
77 Kosuke Fukudome .60 1.50
78 Johan Santana .60 1.50
79 Curtis Granderson .75 2.00
80 Johnny Mize .60 1.50
81 Derek Jeter 2.50 6.00
82 Vladimir Guerrero .60 1.50
83 Dan Uggla .40 1.00
84 Hank Greenberg 1.00 2.50
85 Justin Morneau .60 1.50
86 CC Sabathia .60 1.50
87 Mike Schmidt 1.50 4.00
88 Cole Hamels .75 2.00
89 Alex Rios .40 1.00
90 Ryne Sandberg 2.00 5.00
91 Ryan Ludwick .60 1.50
92 Tim Lincecum .60 1.50
93 Honus Wagner 1.00 2.50
94 Carlos Quentin .40 1.00
95 Alexei Ramriez .60 1.50
96 Joe Mauer .75 2.00
97 Bob Gibson .60 1.50
98 Reggie Jackson .60 1.50
99 Carlos Zambrano .60 1.50
100 Stan Musial 1.50 4.00
101 R.Braun Jsy AU 15.00 40.00
102 J.Bruce Jsy AU 10.00 25.00
103 Fausto Carmona Jsy AU 6.00 15.00
104 M.Kemp Jsy AU 20.00 50.00
105 C.Maybin Jsy AU 8.00 20.00
106 J.Cueto Jsy AU 10.00 25.00
107 J.Hamilton Jsy AU 15.00 40.00
108 U.Jimenez Jsy AU 6.00 15.00
109 G.Soto Jsy AU 6.00 15.00
110 Jon Lester Jsy AU 15.00 40.00
111 C.Kershaw Jsy AU 50.00 100.00
112 L.Hochevar Jsy AU 6.00 15.00
113 E.Longoria Jsy AU 15.00 40.00
114 J.Masterson Jsy AU 6.00 15.00
115 B.DeWitt Jsy AU 6.00 15.00
116 D.Murphy Jsy AU RC 20.00 50.00
117 C.Billingsley Jsy AU 6.00 15.00
118 D.Pedroia Jsy AU 20.00 50.00
119 H.Pence Jsy AU 10.00 25.00
120 Joakim Soria Jsy AU 6.00 15.00
121 Justin Upton Jsy AU 20.00 50.00
122 F.Martinez Jsy AU RC 10.00 25.00
123 N.Reimold Jsy AU (RC) 6.00 15.00
124 M.Gamel Jsy AU RC 6.00 15.00
125 M.Bowden Jsy AU (RC) 6.00 15.00
126 D.Holland Jsy AU RC 6.00 15.00
127 E.Andrus Jsy AU RC 12.50 30.00
128 T.Cahill Jsy AU RC 8.00 20.00
129 Ryan Perry Jsy AU RC 6.00 15.00
130 J.Zimmermann Jsy AU RC 12.50 30.00
131 T.Hanson Jsy AU RC 6.00 15.00
132 D.Price Jsy AU RC 15.00 40.00
133 C.Rasmus Jsy AU (RC) 6.00 15.00
134 R.Porcello Jsy AU RC 12.00 30.00
135 B.Anderson Jsy AU RC 6.00 15.00
136 K.Uehara Jsy AU RC 15.00 40.00
137 L.Marson Jsy AU (RC) 6.00 15.00
138 Matt Tolbert Jsy AU 6.00 15.00

2009 Topps Triple Threads Emerald

*EMERALD 1-100: .6X TO 1.5X BASIC
1-100 ODDS 1:2 MINI
1-100 PRINT RUN 240 SER.#'d SETS
*EMERALD JSY AU: .4X TO 1X BASIC
EMERALD JSY AU ODDS 1:21 MINI
EM.JSY AU PRINT RUN 50 SER.#'d SETS

2009 Topps Triple Threads Gold

*GOLD 1-100: 1X TO 2.5X BASIC
1-100 ODDS 1:4 MINI
1-100 PRINT RUN 99 SER.#'d SETS
GOLD JSY AU ODDS 1:41 MINI
GOLD JSY AU PRINT RUN 25 SER.#'d SETS
NO GOLD JSY AU PRICING AVAILABLE

2009 Topps Triple Threads Legend Relics

STATED ODDS 1:72 MINI
STATED PRINT RUN 36 SER.#'d SETS
1 Babe Ruth 175.00 350.00
2 Rogers Hornsby 15.00 40.00
3 Pee Wee Reese 10.00 25.00
4 Lou Gehrig 150.00 250.00
5 Jimmie Foxx 10.00 25.00
6 Honus Wagner 100.00 175.00
7 Roy Campanella 20.00 50.00
8 Mickey Mantle 100.00 175.00
9 Mel Ott 40.00 80.00
10 Tris Speaker 15.00 40.00
11 Jackie Robinson 40.00 80.00
12 George Sisler 20.00 50.00
13 Ty Cobb 90.00 150.00
14 Thurman Munson 20.00 50.00
15 Johnny Mize 12.50 30.00

2009 Topps Triple Threads Relic Autographs

STATED ODDS 1:13 MINI
STATED PRINT RUN 18 SER.#'d SETS
ALL DC VARIATIONS PRICED EQUALLY
1 David Wright 30.00 60.00
2 David Wright 30.00 60.00
3 David Wright 30.00 60.00
4 David Ortiz 30.00 60.00
5 David Ortiz 30.00 60.00
6 David Ortiz 30.00 60.00
7 Jose Reyes 15.00 40.00
8 Jose Reyes 15.00 40.00
9 Jose Reyes 15.00 40.00
10 Zack Greinke 12.50 30.00
11 Zack Greinke 12.50 30.00
12 Zack Greinke 12.50 30.00
13 Miguel Cabrera 50.00 100.00
14 Miguel Cabrera 50.00 100.00
15 Miguel Cabrera 50.00 100.00
16 Matt Cain 20.00 50.00
17 Matt Cain 20.00 50.00
18 Matt Cain 20.00 50.00
19 Robinson Cano 20.00 50.00
20 Robinson Cano 20.00 50.00
21 Robinson Cano 20.00 50.00
22 Andre Ethier 15.00 40.00
23 Andre Ethier 15.00 40.00
24 Andre Ethier 15.00 40.00
25 Curtis Granderson 20.00 50.00
26 Curtis Granderson 20.00 50.00
27 Curtis Granderson 20.00 50.00
28 Manny Ramirez 50.00 100.00
29 Manny Ramirez 50.00 100.00
30 Manny Ramirez 50.00 100.00
31 Nick Markakis 12.50 30.00
32 Nick Markakis 12.50 30.00
33 Nick Markakis 12.50 30.00
34 Vladimir Guerrero 40.00 80.00
35 Vladimir Guerrero 40.00 80.00
36 Vladimir Guerrero 40.00 80.00
37 Matt Holliday 15.00 40.00
38 Matt Holliday 15.00 40.00
39 Matt Holliday 15.00 40.00
40 Ryan Howard 15.00 40.00
41 Ryan Howard 15.00 40.00
42 Ryan Howard 15.00 40.00
43 Chipper Jones 50.00 100.00
44 Chipper Jones 50.00 100.00
45 Chipper Jones 50.00 100.00
46 Scott Kazmir 10.00 25.00
47 Scott Kazmir 10.00 25.00
48 Scott Kazmir 10.00 25.00
49 Joba Chamberlain 20.00 50.00
50 Joba Chamberlain 20.00 50.00
51 Joba Chamberlain 20.00 50.00
52 Alfonso Soriano 15.00 40.00
53 Alfonso Soriano 15.00 40.00
54 Alfonso Soriano 15.00 40.00
55 Nick Swisher 20.00 50.00
56 Nick Swisher 20.00 50.00
57 Nick Swisher 20.00 50.00
58 Prince Fielder 40.00 80.00
59 Prince Fielder 40.00 80.00
60 Prince Fielder 40.00 80.00
61 Ryan Zimmerman 20.00 50.00
62 Ryan Zimmerman 20.00 50.00
63 Ryan Zimmerman 20.00 50.00
64 Johnny Podres 20.00 50.00
65 Johnny Podres 20.00 50.00
66 Johnny Podres 20.00 50.00
67 George Kell 20.00 50.00
68 George Kell 20.00 50.00
69 George Kell 20.00 50.00
70 Gary Carter 30.00 60.00
71 Gary Carter 30.00 60.00
72 Gary Carter 30.00 60.00
73 Whitey Ford 40.00 80.00
74 Whitey Ford 40.00 80.00
75 Whitey Ford 40.00 80.00
76 Bob Gibson 30.00 60.00
77 Bob Gibson 30.00 60.00
78 Bob Gibson 30.00 60.00
79 Juan Marichal 20.00 50.00
80 Juan Marichal 20.00 50.00
81 Juan Marichal 20.00 50.00
82 Duke Snider 30.00 60.00
83 Duke Snider 30.00 60.00
84 Duke Snider 30.00 60.00
85 Robin Yount 20.00 50.00
86 Robin Yount 20.00 50.00
87 Robin Yount 20.00 50.00
88 Jim Palmer 15.00 40.00
89 Jim Palmer 15.00 40.00
90 Jim Palmer 15.00 40.00
91 Bo Jackson 40.00 80.00
92 Bo Jackson 40.00 80.00
93 Bo Jackson 40.00 80.00
94 Don Larsen 30.00 60.00
95 Don Larsen 30.00 60.00
96 Don Larsen 30.00 60.00
97 Tony Gwynn 40.00 80.00
98 Tony Gwynn 40.00 80.00
99 Tony Gwynn 40.00 80.00
100 Brian McCann 12.00 30.00
101 Brian McCann 12.00 30.00
102 Brian McCann 12.00 30.00
103 Shane Victorino 40.00 80.00
104 Shane Victorino 40.00 80.00
105 Shane Victorino 40.00 80.00
106 Adrian Gonzalez 12.50 30.00
107 Adrian Gonzalez 12.50 30.00
108 Adrian Gonzalez 12.50 30.00
109 Garrett Atkins 8.00 20.00
110 Garrett Atkins 8.00 20.00
111 Garrett Atkins 8.00 20.00
112 Carl Yastrzemski 40.00 80.00
113 Carl Yastrzemski 40.00 80.00
114 Carl Yastrzemski 40.00 80.00
115 Carlos Delgado 15.00 40.00
116 Carlos Delgado 15.00 40.00
117 Carlos Delgado 15.00 40.00
118 Jason Varitek 20.00 50.00
119 Jason Varitek 20.00 50.00
120 Jason Varitek 20.00 50.00
121 Tom Seaver 40.00 100.00
122 Tom Seaver 40.00 100.00
123 Tom Seaver 40.00 100.00
124 Rich Harden 8.00 20.00
125 Rich Harden 8.00 20.00
126 Rich Harden 8.00 20.00
127 Aramis Ramirez 15.00 40.00
128 Aramis Ramirez 15.00 40.00
129 Aramis Ramirez 15.00 40.00
130 Chien-Ming Wang 90.00 150.00
131 Chien-Ming Wang 90.00 150.00
132 Chien-Ming Wang 90.00 150.00
133 Jayson Werth 20.00 50.00
134 Jayson Werth 20.00 50.00
135 Jayson Werth 20.00 50.00
136 Jonathan Papelbon 12.50 30.00
137 Jonathan Papelbon 12.50 30.00
138 Jonathan Papelbon 12.50 30.00
139 Alex Rodriguez 50.00 100.00
140 Alex Rodriguez 50.00 100.00
141 Alex Rodriguez 50.00 100.00
142 Johnny Bench 50.00 100.00
143 Johnny Bench 50.00 100.00
144 Johnny Bench 50.00 100.00
145 Mark Teixeira 90.00 150.00
146 Mark Teixeira 90.00 150.00
147 Mark Teixeira 90.00 150.00
148 Dan Haren 10.00 25.00
149 Dan Haren 10.00 25.00
150 Dan Haren 10.00 25.00
151 Ernie Banks 15.00 40.00
152 Ernie Banks 15.00 40.00
153 Ernie Banks 15.00 40.00
154 Lance Berkman 15.00 40.00
155 Lance Berkman 15.00 40.00
156 Lance Berkman 15.00 40.00
157 Cal Ripken 100.00 200.00
158 Cal Ripken 100.00 200.00
159 Cal Ripken 100.00 200.00
160 Paul Molitor 15.00 40.00
161 Paul Molitor 15.00 40.00
162 Paul Molitor 15.00 40.00
163 Mike Lowell 15.00 40.00
164 Mike Lowell 15.00 40.00
165 Mike Lowell 15.00 40.00
166 Dan Uggla 8.00 20.00
167 Dan Uggla 8.00 20.00
168 Dan Uggla 8.00 20.00
169 Aaron Hill 12.50 30.00
170 Aaron Hill 12.50 30.00
171 Aaron Hill 12.50 30.00
172 Johnny Damon 20.00 50.00
173 Johnny Damon 20.00 50.00
174 Johnny Damon 20.00 50.00

2009 Topps Triple Threads Relic Autographs Gold

*GOLD: .5X TO 1.2X BASIC
STATED ODDS 1:25 MINI
STATED PRINT RUN 9 SER.#'d SETS
ALL DC VARIATIONS PRICED EQUALLY

2009 Topps Triple Threads Relic Combo Autographs

STATED ODDS 1:51 MINI
STATED PRINT RUN 36 SER.#'d SETS
1 Soto/McCann/Martin 10.00 25.00
2 Hanley/Reyes/Tejada 30.00 60.00
3 Cueto/Silva/Soria 6.00 15.00
4 Halladay/Webb/Wang 50.00 100.00
5 Manny/Kemp/Ethier 50.00 100.00
6 F.Rob/Palmer/Murray 40.00 80.00
7 Kazmir/Joba/Lester 30.00 60.00
8 Howard/Pujols/Cabrera 150.00 300.00
9 Reggie/ARod/Cano 90.00 150.00
10 Molitor/Yount/Braun 60.00 120.00
11 Lester/Mast/Papel 30.00 60.00
12 Bruce/Hamilton/Pence 15.00 40.00
13 Ortiz/Varitek/Papel 40.00 80.00
14 Snider/Manny/Kemp 75.00 150.00
15 Roberts/Pedroia/Cano 30.00 60.00
16 Soriano/Aramis/Sandberg 40.00 80.00
17 Wright/Hanley/Pujols 150.00 250.00
18 Kazmir/Longoria/Price 40.00 80.00
19 Teixeira/Cano/ARod 175.00 350.00
20 Papel/Soria/Nathan 12.50 30.00
21 Torii/Vlad/Reggie 20.00 50.00

2009 Topps Triple Threads Relic Combos

STATED ODDS 1:24 MINI
STATED PRINT RUN 36 SER.#'d SETS
1 Seaver/Ryan/Santana 20.00 50.00
2 Howard/Schmidt/Utley 40.00 80.00
3 Posada/Mantle/Teixeira 30.00 60.00
4 Beckett/Lester/Smoltz 12.50 30.00
5 Reyes/Carter/Wright 20.00 50.00
6 Pujols/Cabrera/Howard 20.00 50.00
7 Sandberg/Schmidt/Ozzie 15.00 40.00
8 Matsuzaka/Ichiro/Matsui 30.00 60.00
9 Kawa/Matsuzaka/Uehara 30.00 60.00
10 Manny/Beltran/Soriano 10.00 25.00
11 Hamil/Kins/Young 8.00 20.00
12 Sizemore/Hamilton/Ichiro 15.00 40.00
13 Ramir/Roll/Reyes 8.00 20.00
14 Pedroi/Sand/Kins 10.00 25.00
15 Longoria/ARod/Chipper 15.00 40.00
16 Manny/Pujols/Howard 12.50 30.00
17 Thome/Manny/Sheff 8.00 20.00
18 Mantle/Ruth/Gehrig 200.00 400.00
20 Mantle/F.Rob/Yaz 50.00 100.00
21 Reese/J.Rob/Campy 40.00 80.00
22 Belt/Delg/Wright 10.00 25.00
23 Zimmerman/Wright/Longoria 12.50 30.00
24 Mauer/Bench/McCann 12.50 30.00
25 Howard/ARod/Wright 12.50 30.00
26 incecum/Peavy/Webb 12.50 30.00
27 Youk/Ortiz/Varitek 10.00 25.00
28 Mart/Manny/Kemp 10.00 25.00
29 Soto/Braun/Ramir 10.00 25.00
30 Pujols/Howard/Hanley 12.50 30.00
31 Gonz/Roll/Wright 10.00 25.00
32 Ripken/ARod/Chipper 30.00 60.00
33 Banks/Ozzie/Hanley 12.50 30.00
34 Gonzalez/Gwynn/Peavy 10.00 25.00
35 Banks/Ozzie/Ripken 20.00 50.00
36 Utley/Rollins/Howard 20.00 50.00
37 Reggie/Reggie/Reggie 15.00 40.00
38 Ryan/Ryan/Ryan 30.00 60.00
39 Prince/Pujols/Berkman 12.50 30.00
40 Cantu/Soria/Gonz 10.00 25.00
41 Felix/Ordonez/Cabrera 12.50 30.00
42 Roll/Oswa/Dunn 8.00 20.00
43 Lee/Lee/Choo 15.00 40.00
44 Aumont/Chapman/Lindsay 8.00 20.00
45 Cepeda/Gourriel/Cespedes 40.00 80.00
46 Ichiro/Darvish/Aoki 60.00 120.00

2009 Topps Triple Threads Relic Combos Sepia

*SEPIA: .4X TO 1X BASIC
STATED ODDS 1:32 MINI
STATED PRINT RUN 27 SER.#'d SETS
1 Tom Seaver 20.00 50.00
Nolan Ryan
Johan Santana
2 Ryan Howard 40.00 80.00
Mike Schmidt
Chase Utley
3 Jorge Posada 30.00 60.00
Mickey Mantle
Mark Teixeira
4 Josh Beckett 12.50 30.00
Jon Lester
John Smoltz
5 Jose Reyes 20.00 50.00
Gary Carter
David Wright
6 Albert Pujols 20.00 50.00
Miguel Cabrera
Ryan Howard
7 Ryne Sandberg 15.00 40.00
Mike Schmidt
Ozzie Smith
8 Daisuke Matsuzaka 30.00 60.00
Ichiro Suzuki
Hideki Matsui
9 Kenshin Kawakami 30.00 60.00
Daisuke Matsuzaka
Koji Uehara
10 Manny Ramirez 10.00 25.00
Carlos Beltran
Alfonso Soriano
11 Josh Hamilton 8.00 20.00
Ian Kinsler
Michael Young
12 Grady Sizemore 15.00 40.00
Josh Hamilton
Ichiro Suzuki
13 Hanley Ramirez 8.00 20.00
Jimmy Rollins
Jose Reyes
14 Dustin Pedroia 10.00 25.00
Ryne Sandberg
Ian Kinsler
15 Evan Longoria 15.00 40.00
Alex Rodriguez
Chipper Jones
16 Manny Ramirez 12.50 30.00
Albert Pujols
Ryan Howard
17 Jim Thome 8.00 20.00
Manny Ramirez
Gary Sheffield
18 Mickey Mantle 400.00 800.
Babe Ruth
Lou Gehrig
20 Mickey Mantle 50.00 100.
Frank Robinson
Carl Yastrzemski
21 Pee Wee Reese 40.00 80.
Jackie Robinson
Roy Campanella
22 Carlos Beltran 10.00 25.
Carlos Delgado
David Wright
23 Ryan Zimmerman 12.50 30.
David Wright
Evan Longoria
24 Joe Mauer 12.50 30.
Johnny Bench
Brian McCann
25 Ryan Howard 12.50 30.
Alex Rodriguez
David Wright
26 Tim Lincecum 12.50 30.
Jake Peavy
Brandon Webb
27 Kevin Youkilis 10.00 25.
David Ortiz
Jason Varitek
28 Russell Martin 10.00 25.
Manny Ramirez
Matt Kemp
29 Geovany Soto 10.00 25.
Ryan Braun
Hanley Ramirez
30 Albert Pujols 12.50 30.
Ryan Howard
Hanley Ramirez
31 Adrian Gonzalez 10.00 25.
Jimmy Rollins
David Wright
32 Cal Ripken 30.00 60.
Alex Rodriguez
Chipper Jones
33 Ernie Banks 12.50 30.
Ozzie Smith
Hanley Ramirez
34 Adrian Gonzalez 10.00 25.
Tony Gwynn
Jake Peavy
35 Ernie Banks 20.00 50.0
Ozzie Smith
Cal Ripken
36 Chase Utley 20.00 50.
Jimmy Rollins
Ryan Howard
37 Reggie Jackson 15.00 40.0
Reggie Jackson
Reggie Jackson
38 Nolan Ryan 30.00 60.
Nolan Ryan
Nolan Ryan
39 Prince Fielder 12.50 30.0
Albert Pujols
Lance Berkman
40 Jorge Cantu 10.00 25.0
Joakim Soria
Edgar Gonzalez
41 Felix Hernandez 12.50 30.0
Maggio Ordonez
Miguel Cabrera
42 Jimmy Rollins 8.00 20.0
Roy Oswalt
Adam Dunn
43 Dae Ho Lee 15.00 40.0
Jin Young Lee
Shin-Soo Choo
44 Phillippe Aumont 8.00 20.0
Aroldis Chapman
Dylan Lindsay
45 Frederich Cepeda 40.00 80.0
Yulieski Gourriel
Yoennis Cespedes
46 Ichiro Suzuki 60.00 120.0
Yu Darvish
Norichika Aoki

2009 Topps Triple Threads Reli[c] Combos Double

STATED ODDS 1:90 MINI
STATED PRINT RUN 36 SER.#'d SETS
1 M.Schmidt/R.Howard 30.00 60.0
2 Y.Gourriel/Y.Darvish 100.00 175.0
3 Ryan Howard 20.00 50.0
4 Dustin Pedroia 15.00 40.0
5 R.Howard/D.Pedroia 15.00 40.0
6 C.Ripken/A.Rodriguez 30.00 60.0
7 J.Peavy/T.Lincecum 12.50 30.0
8 Ichiro/D.Matsuzaka 30.00 60.0
9 Ram/Sor/How/Lon/Quen/Vlad 20.00 50.0
10 Riv/Pap/Hof/Nat/Rod/Eck 40.00 80.0
11 ARod/Lon/You/Rios/Mar/Boggs 20.00 50.0
12 Puj/Wri/Ram/ARod/Ham/Long 40.00 80.0

2009 Topps Triple Threads Reli[c] Combos Double Sepia

*SEPIA: .4X TO 1X BASIC
STATED ODDS 1:120 MINI
STATED PRINT RUN 27 SER.#'d SETS

2009 Topps Triple Threads Relics

STATED ODDS 1:10 MINI
STATED PRINT RUN 36 SER.#'d SETS
ALL DC VARIATIONS PRICED EQUALLY

m Lincecum 12.50 30.00
m Lincecum 12.50 30.00
m Lincecum 12.50 30.00
avid Wright 10.00 25.00
avid Wright 10.00 25.00
avid Wright 10.00 25.00
bert Pujols 20.00 50.00
bert Pujols 20.00 50.00
bert Pujols 20.00 50.00
Alex Rodriguez 12.50 30.00
Alex Rodriguez 12.50 30.00
Alex Rodriguez 12.50 30.00
David Ortiz 10.00 25.00
David Ortiz 10.00 25.00
David Ortiz 10.00 25.00
Manny Ramirez 12.50 30.00
Manny Ramirez 12.50 30.00
Manny Ramirez 12.50 30.00
chiro Suzuki 20.00 50.00
chiro Suzuki 20.00 50.00
chiro Suzuki 20.00 50.00
ladimir Guerrero 6.00 15.00
ladimir Guerrero 6.00 15.00
ladimir Guerrero 6.00 15.00
Ryan Braun 10.00 25.00
Ryan Braun 10.00 25.00
Ryan Braun 10.00 25.00
Chipper Jones 10.00 25.00
Chipper Jones 10.00 25.00
Chipper Jones 10.00 25.00
Evan Longoria 12.50 30.00
Evan Longoria 12.50 30.00
Evan Longoria 12.50 30.00
Dustin Pedroia 8.00 20.00
Dustin Pedroia 8.00 20.00
Dustin Pedroia 8.00 20.00
Alfonso Soriano 6.00 15.00
Alfonso Soriano 6.00 15.00
Alfonso Soriano 6.00 15.00
Miguel Cabrera 8.00 20.00
Miguel Cabrera 8.00 20.00
Miguel Cabrera 8.00 20.00
Nick Markakis 8.00 20.00
Nick Markakis 8.00 20.00
Nick Markakis 8.00 20.00
Josh Hamilton 8.00 20.00
Josh Hamilton 8.00 20.00
Josh Hamilton 8.00 20.00
Jose Reyes 8.00 20.00
Jose Reyes 8.00 20.00
Jose Reyes 8.00 20.00
Bob Gibson 10.00 25.00
Bob Gibson 10.00 25.00
Bob Gibson 10.00 25.00
Frank Robinson 10.00 25.00
Frank Robinson 10.00 25.00
Frank Robinson 10.00 25.00
Paul Molitor 10.00 25.00
Paul Molitor 10.00 25.00
Paul Molitor 10.00 25.00
Tom Seaver 10.00 25.00
Tom Seaver 10.00 25.00
Tom Seaver 10.00 25.00
Gary Carter 12.50 30.00
Gary Carter 12.50 30.00
Gary Carter 12.50 30.00
Stan Musial 20.00 50.00
Stan Musial 20.00 50.00
Stan Musial 20.00 50.00
Ryne Sandberg 10.00 25.00
Ryne Sandberg 10.00 25.00
Ryne Sandberg 10.00 25.00
Carl Yastrzemski 10.00 25.00
Carl Yastrzemski 10.00 25.00
Carl Yastrzemski 10.00 25.00
Duke Snider 12.50 30.00
Duke Snider 12.50 30.00
Duke Snider 12.50 30.00
Whitey Ford 15.00 40.00
Whitey Ford 15.00 40.00
Whitey Ford 15.00 40.00
Mike Schmidt 15.00 40.00
Mike Schmidt 15.00 40.00
Mike Schmidt 15.00 40.00
Daisuke Matsuzaka 10.00 25.00
Daisuke Matsuzaka 10.00 25.00
Daisuke Matsuzaka 10.00 25.00
8 Grady Sizemore 6.00 15.00
9 Grady Sizemore 6.00 15.00
0 Grady Sizemore 6.00 15.00
1 Chase Utley 12.50 30.00
2 Chase Utley 12.50 30.00
3 Chase Utley 12.50 30.00
4 Josh Beckett 8.00 20.00
5 Josh Beckett 8.00 20.00
6 Josh Beckett 8.00 20.00
7 Hanley Ramirez 8.00 20.00
8 Hanley Ramirez 8.00 20.00
9 Hanley Ramirez 8.00 20.00
00 Johan Santana 8.00 20.00
01 Johan Santana 8.00 20.00
02 Johan Santana 8.00 20.00
03 Ryan Howard 12.50 30.00
04 Ryan Howard 12.50 30.00
05 Ryan Howard 12.50 30.00
06 Bo Jackson 10.00 25.00
07 Bo Jackson 10.00 25.00
08 Bo Jackson 10.00 25.00
09 Carlos Quentin 6.00 15.00
10 Carlos Quentin 6.00 15.00
11 Carlos Quentin 6.00 15.00
12 Hideki Matsui 15.00 40.00
13 Hideki Matsui 15.00 40.00
114 Hideki Matsui 15.00 40.00
115 Rickey Henderson 20.00 50.00
116 Rickey Henderson 20.00 50.00
117 Rickey Henderson 20.00 50.00

2009 Topps Triple Threads Relics Emerald

*EMERALD: .5X TO 1.2X BASIC
STATED ODDS 1:19 MINI
STATED PRINT RUN 18 SER.#'d SETS
ALL DC VARIATIONS PRICED EQUALLY

2009 Topps Triple Threads Relics Gold

*GOLD: .6X TO 1.5X BASIC
STATED ODDS 1:37 MINI
STATED PRINT RUN 9 SER.#'d SETS
ALL DC VARIATIONS PRICED EQUALLY

2009 Topps Triple Threads Relics Sepia

*SEPIA: .4X TO 1X BASIC
STATED ODDS 1:13 MINI
STATED PRINT RUN 27 SER.#'d SETS
ALL DC VARIATIONS PRICED EQUALLY

2009 Topps Triple Threads WBC Relic Autographs

STATED ODDS 1:178 MINI
STATED PRINT RUN 36 SER.#'d SETS
BCAR1 Miguel Tejada 8.00 20.00
BCAR2 Jose Reyes 20.00 50.00
BCAR3 Geovany Soto 10.00 25.00
BCAR4 David Wright 60.00 150.00
BCAR5 Roy Oswalt 12.50 30.00
BCAR6 Miguel Cabrera 40.00 80.00

2009 Topps Triple Threads WBC Relic Autographs Sepia

*SEPIA: .4X TO 1X BASIC
STATED ODDS 1:239 MINI
STATED PRINT RUN 27 SER.#'d SETS

2010 Topps Triple Threads

COMMON CARD (1-120) .40 1.00
1-120 PRINT RUN 1350 SER.#'d SETS
COMMON JSY AU RC (121-189) 6.00 15.00
JSY AU RC ODDS 1:12 HOBBY
JSY AU RC PRINT RUN 99 SER.#'d SETS
COMMON JSY AU (121-189) 6.00 15.00
JSY AU ODDS 1:12 HOBBY
JSY AU PRINT RUN 99 SER.#'d SETS
EXCHANGE DEADLINE 9/30/2013
OVERALL 1-120 PLATE ODDS 1:110 HOBBY
1 Chipper Jones 1.00 2.50
2 Harmon Killebrew 1.00 2.50
3 Robin Roberts .60 1.50
4 Mark Teixeira .60 1.50
5 Todd Helton .60 1.50
6 Roy Halladay .60 1.50
7 Albert Pujols 1.25 3.00
8 Ryan Braun .60 1.50
9 Ryne Sandberg 2.00 5.00
10 Tony Perez .60 1.50
11 Jose Reyes .60 1.50
12 Al Kaline 1.00 2.50
13 Dustin Pedroia .75 2.00
14 Warren Spahn .60 1.50
15 Jacoby Ellsbury .75 2.00
16 Carl Yastrzemski 1.50 4.00
17 Jake Peavy .40 1.00
18 Carl Crawford .60 1.50
19 Reggie Jackson .60 1.50
20 Brian McCann .60 1.50
21 Ichiro Suzuki 1.25 3.00
22 Miguel Cabrera 1.00 2.50
23 Brooks Robinson .60 1.50
24 Ty Cobb 1.50 4.00
25 Christy Mathewson 1.00 2.50
26 Johnny Bench 1.00 2.50
27 Ozzie Smith 1.25 3.00
28 Bob Feller .60 1.50
29 Ken Griffey Jr. 2.00 5.00
30 Josh Hamilton .60 1.50
31 Adrian Gonzalez .75 2.00
32 Derek Jeter 2.50 6.00
33 Johnny Mize .60 1.50
34 Victor Martinez .60 1.50
35 Steve Carlton .60 1.50
36 Babe Ruth 2.50 6.00
37 Hunter Pence .60 1.50
38 Honus Wagner 1.00 2.50
39 Jorge Posada .60 1.50
40 Adam Dunn .60 1.50
41 Johan Santana .60 1.50
42 Andre Ethier .60 1.50
43 Phil Rizzuto .60 1.50
44 Justin Upton .60 1.50
45 Prince Fielder .60 1.50
46 Dave Winfield .60 1.50
47 Josh Beckett .40 1.00
48 Jackie Robinson 1.00 2.50
49 Walter Johnson 1.00 2.50
50 CC Sabathia .60 1.50
51 Ralph Kiner .60 1.50
52 Cole Hamels .75 2.00
53 Mark Buehrle .60 1.50
54 Ian Kinsler .60 1.50
55 Yogi Berra 1.00 2.50
56 Bobby Doerr .60 1.50
57 Roy Campanella 1.00 2.50
58 Alfonso Soriano .60 1.50
59 Tom Seaver .60 1.50
60 Hanley Ramirez .60 1.50
61 Mariano Rivera 1.25 3.00
62 Cy Young 1.00 2.50
63 Jimmie Foxx 1.00 2.50
64 Jim Palmer .60 1.50
65 Mickey Mantle 3.00 8.00
66 Pee Wee Reese .60 1.50
67 Justin Verlander 1.00 2.50
68 Zack Greinke .60 1.50
69 Jimmy Rollins .60 1.50
70 Felix Hernandez .60 1.50
71 Nolan Ryan 3.00 8.00
72 Ryan Howard .75 2.00
73 Manny Ramirez 1.00 2.50
74 Lou Brock .60 1.50
75 Mike Schmidt 1.50 4.00
76 Grady Sizemore .60 1.50
77 Alex Rodriguez 1.25 3.00
78 Joe Morgan .60 1.50
79 Eddie Mathews 1.00 2.50
80 Hideki Matsui 1.00 2.50
81 Mel Ott 1.00 2.50
82 Rogers Hornsby .60 1.50
83 Tris Speaker .60 1.50
84 Vladimir Guerrero .60 1.50
85 Evan Longoria .60 1.50
86 Dan Haren .40 1.00
87 Willie McCovey .60 1.50
88 Lou Gehrig 2.00 5.00
89 Tim Lincecum .60 1.50
90 Justin Morneau .60 1.50
91 Kevin Youkilis .40 1.00
92 B.J. Upton .60 1.50
93 Rickey Henderson 1.00 2.50
94 Roy Oswalt .60 1.50
95 Chase Utley .60 1.50
96 Lance Berkman .60 1.50
97 Matt Kemp .75 2.00
98 Dale Murphy 1.00 2.50
99 George Sisler .60 1.50
100 Nick Markakis .75 2.00
101 Thurman Munson 1.00 2.50
102 Dan Uggla .40 1.00
103 Matt Holliday 1.00 2.50
104 Bill Mazeroski .60 1.50
105 Joe Mauer .75 2.00
106 Chris Carpenter .60 1.50
107 David Wright .75 2.00
108 Ron Guidry .40 1.00
109 Roger Maris 1.00 2.50
110 Aaron Hill .40 1.00
111 Torii Hunter .40 1.00
112 Ubaldo Jimenez .40 1.00
113 Aramis Ramirez .40 1.00
114 Whitey Ford .60 1.50
115 Andrew McCutchen 1.00 2.50
116 Hank Greenberg 1.00 2.50
117 Dizzy Dean .60 1.50
118 Mark Fidrych .40 1.00
119 Bob Gibson .60 1.50
120 Johnny Damon .60 1.50
121 P.Sandoval Jsy AU 6.00 15.00
122 Denard Span Jsy AU 6.00 15.00
123 Colby Rasmus Jsy AU 6.00 15.00
124 C.Gomez Jsy AU EXCH 8.00 20.00
125 T.Hanson Jsy AU 6.00 15.00
126 Rick Porcello Jsy AU 6.00 15.00
128 Adam Jones Jsy AU 8.00 20.00
129 G.Beckham Jsy AU 10.00 25.00
130 Elvis Andrus Jsy AU 6.00 15.00
131 Adam Lind Jsy AU 6.00 15.00
132 Chris Young Jsy AU 6.00 15.00
134 Chris Coghlan Jsy AU 8.00 20.00
135 A.Escobar Jsy AU 8.00 20.00
136 Nelson Cruz Jsy AU 6.00 15.00
137 Neftali Feliz Jsy AU 6.00 15.00
139 J.Heyward Jsy AU RC 30.00 60.00
140 A.Jackson Jsy AU RC 8.00 20.00
141 S.Sizemore Jsy AU RC 6.00 15.00
142 C.Kershaw Jsy AU 40.00 100.00
143 Ike Davis Jsy AU RC 10.00 25.00
144 Josh Johnson Jsy AU 6.00 15.00
146 Andre Ethier Jsy AU 10.00 25.00
147 S.Castro Jsy AU RC 10.00 25.00
148 J.Happ Jsy AU 6.00 15.00
149 I.Kinsler Jsy AU EXCH 8.00 20.00
150 Will Venable Jsy AU 8.00 20.00
151 Chris Volstad Jsy AU 6.00 15.00
152 D.Stubbs Jsy AU RC 6.00 15.00
153 Chris Getz Jsy AU 6.00 15.00
155 D.McCutchen Jsy AU RC 6.00 15.00
157 A.McCutchen Jsy AU 40.00 80.00
158 Daniel Murphy Jsy AU 15.00 40.00
159 H.Kendrick Jsy AU 6.00 15.00
160 Billy Butler Jsy AU 8.00 20.00
162 J.Mejia Jsy AU RC 6.00 15.00
163 Trevor Cahill Jsy AU 10.00 25.00
164 W.Davis Jsy AU (RC) 6.00 15.00
165 Manny Parra Jsy AU EXCH 6.00 15.00
166 D.Storen Jsy AU RC 6.00 15.00
167 B.Matusz Jsy AU RC 6.00 15.00
169 E.Young Jr. Jsy AU (RC) 6.00 15.00
171 S.Strasburg Jsy AU RC 30.00 80.00
174 Alexei Ramirez Jsy AU 6.00 15.00
178 C.McGehee Jsy AU 6.00 15.00
182 Mark Reynolds Jsy AU 6.00 15.00
186 M.Stanton Jsy AU RC 40.00 80.00
188 C.Santana Jsy AU RC 6.00 15.00
189 M.Brantley Jsy AU RC 6.00 15.00

2010 Topps Triple Threads Emerald

*EMERALD 1-120: .6X TO 1.5X BASIC
1-120 ODDS 1:2 MINI
1-120 PRINT RUN 240 SER.#'d SETS
*EMERALD JSY AU: .4X TO 1X BASIC
EMERALD JSY AU ODDS 1:22 MINI
EM.JSY AU PRINT RUN 50 SER.#'d SETS

2010 Topps Triple Threads Gold

*GOLD 1-120: 1X TO 2.5X BASIC
1-120 ODDS 1:5 MINI
1-120 PRINT RUN 99 SER.#'d SETS
121-189 ODDS 1:44 HOBBY
121-189 PRINT RUN 25 SER.#'d SETS

2010 Topps Triple Threads Sepia

*SEPIA 1-120: .5X TO 1.2X BASIC
1-120 RANDOMLY INSERTED
1-120 PRINT RUN 525 SER.#'d SETS
*SEPIA JSY AU: .4X TO 1X BASIC
SEPIA JSY AU ODDS 1:15 MINI
SEP.JSY AU PRINT RUN 75 SER.#'d SETS

2010 Topps Triple Threads Autograph Relic Combos

STATED ODDS 1:98 MINI
STATED PRINT RUN 36 SER.#'d SETS
ARC1 Wright/Schm/Zimm 40.00 100.00
ARC2 Pujols/Fielder/Howard 150.00 300.00
ARC3 Hill/Cano/Pedroia 20.00 50.00
ARC4 Heyward/Jones/Upton 50.00 100.00
ARC5 Ford/Rivera/Berra 150.00 300.00
ARC6 Longoria/Beckham/Cabrera 60.00 120.00
ARC7 Price/Lester/Sabathia 30.00 60.00
ARC8 Porcello/Cabrera/Damon 40.00 80.00
ARC9 Varitek/Schilling/Ortiz 50.00 100.00
ARC10 Holliday/Braun/Wright 50.00 100.00
ARC11 John Lackey/Jon Lester/Jonathan Papelbon 20.00 50.00
ARC12 Dawson/Carter/Vlad 40.00 80.00
ARC13 Heyward/McCann/Murphy 75.00 150.00
AHC14 Howard/ARod/Pujols 200.00 400.00
ARC15 ARod/Ortiz/Manny 75.00 150.00

2010 Topps Triple Threads Autograph Relic Combos Sepia

*SEPIA: .4X TO 1X BASIC
STATED ODDS 1:130 MINI
STATED PRINT RUN 27 SER.#'d SETS

2010 Topps Triple Threads Autograph MLB Die Cut Relics

STATED ODDS 1:10 MINI
STATED PRINT RUN 18 SER.#'d SETS
ALL DC VARIATIONS PRICED EQUALLY
AD Adam Dunn 12.50 30.00
AD Andre Dawson 40.00 80.00
AG Adrian Gonzalez 8.00 20.00
AP Albert Pujols 200.00 300.00
AR Alex Rodriguez 100.00 175.00
BM Brian McCann 15.00 40.00
BS Bruce Sutter 15.00 40.00
BZ Ben Zobrist 15.00 40.00
CB Chad Billingsley 12.50 30.00
CC Carl Crawford 12.50 30.00
CF Chone Figgins 8.00 20.00
CL Cliff Lee 30.00 60.00
CP Carlos Pena 8.00 20.00
CS CC Sabathia 50.00 100.00
CY Carl Yastrzemski 40.00 80.00
DG Dwight Gooden 20.00 50.00
DM Dale Murphy 40.00 80.00
DO David Ortiz 15.00 40.00
DS Duke Snider 30.00 60.00
DW David Wright 40.00 80.00
EL Evan Longoria 30.00 60.00
FT Frank Thomas 75.00 150.00
GC Gary Carter 20.00 50.00
GK George Kell 15.00 40.00
HR Hanley Ramirez 12.50 30.00
JD Johnny Damon 30.00 60.00
JH Josh Hamilton 30.00 60.00
JH Jason Heyward 30.00 60.00
JL Jon Lester 8.00 20.00
JM Joe Morgan 20.00 50.00
MC Miguel Cabrera 50.00 100.00
MH Matt Holliday 20.00 50.00
MK Matt Kemp 12.50 30.00
MR Manny Ramirez 50.00 100.00
MT Miguel Tejada 8.00 20.00
NS Nick Swisher 30.00 60.00
PF Prince Fielder 12.50 30.00
RB Ryan Braun 20.00 50.00
RC Robinson Cano 30.00 60.00
RH Ryan Howard 12.00 30.00
RK Ralph Kiner 30.00 60.00
RZ Ryan Zimmerman 20.00 50.00
SM Stan Musial 60.00 120.00
SS Stephen Strasburg 150.00 250.00
SV Shane Victorino 30.00 60.00
VW Vernon Wells 10.00 25.00
WF Whitey Ford 30.00 60.00
CSC Curt Schilling 15.00 40.00
DWI Dave Winfield 30.00 60.00
MRI Mariano Rivera 100.00 175.00

2010 Topps Triple Threads Autograph MLB Die Cut Relics Gold

*GOLD: .5X TO 1.2X BASIC
STATED ODDS 1:19 MINI
STATED PRINT RUN 9 SER.#'d SETS
ALL DC VARIATIONS PRICED EQUALLY

2010 Topps Triple Threads Autograph Relics

STATED ODDS 1:10 MINI
STATED PRINT RUN 18 SER.#'d SETS
ALL DC VARIATIONS PRICED EQUALLY
AR1 Cliff Lee 30.00 60.00
AR2 Cliff Lee 30.00 60.00
AR3 Cliff Lee 30.00 60.00
AR4 Duke Snider 30.00 60.00
AR5 Duke Snider 30.00 60.00
AR6 Duke Snider 30.00 60.00
AR7 Gary Carter 20.00 50.00
AR8 Gary Carter 20.00 50.00
AR9 Gary Carter 20.00 50.00
AR10 Robinson Cano 30.00 60.00
AR11 Robinson Cano 30.00 60.00
AR12 Robinson Cano 30.00 60.00
AR13 Prince Fielder 15.00 40.00
AR14 Prince Fielder 15.00 40.00
AR15 Prince Fielder 15.00 40.00
AR16 Ryan Howard 30.00 60.00
AR17 Ryan Howard 30.00 60.00
AR18 Ryan Howard 30.00 60.00
AR19 Alex Rodriguez 100.00 175.00
AR20 Alex Rodriguez 100.00 175.00
AR21 Alex Rodriguez 100.00 175.00
AR22 Josh Hamilton 20.00 50.00
AR23 Josh Hamilton 20.00 50.00
AR24 Josh Hamilton 20.00 50.00
AR25 Chad Billingsley 12.50 30.00
AR26 Chad Billingsley 12.50 30.00
AR27 Chad Billingsley 12.50 30.00
AR28 Dustin Pedroia 15.00 40.00
AR29 Dustin Pedroia 15.00 40.00
AR30 Dustin Pedroia 15.00 40.00
AR31 Manny Ramirez 20.00 50.00
AR32 Manny Ramirez 20.00 50.00
AR33 Manny Ramirez 20.00 50.00
AR34 CC Sabathia 30.00 60.00
AR35 CC Sabathia 30.00 60.00
AR36 CC Sabathia 30.00 60.00
AR37 Jon Lester 12.50 30.00
AR38 Jon Lester 12.50 30.00
AR39 Jon Lester 12.50 30.00
AR40 Curt Schilling 15.00 40.00
AR41 Curt Schilling 15.00 40.00
AR42 Curt Schilling 15.00 40.00
AR43 Ryan Braun 12.50 30.00
AR44 Ryan Braun 12.50 30.00
AR45 Ryan Braun 12.50 30.00
AR46 David Wright 40.00 80.00
AR47 David Wright 40.00 80.00
AR48 David Wright 40.00 80.00
AR49 B.J. Upton 12.50 30.00
AR50 B.J. Upton 12.50 30.00
AR51 B.J. Upton 12.50 30.00
AR52 David Ortiz 15.00 40.00
AR53 David Ortiz 15.00 40.00
AR54 David Ortiz 15.00 40.00
AR55 Frank Thomas 60.00 120.00
AR56 Frank Thomas 60.00 120.00
AR57 Frank Thomas 60.00 120.00
AR58 Dave Winfield 30.00 60.00
AR59 Dave Winfield 30.00 60.00
AR60 Dave Winfield 30.00 60.00
AR61 John Lackey 20.00 50.00
AR62 John Lackey 20.00 50.00
AR63 John Lackey 20.00 50.00
AR64 Evan Longoria 40.00 80.00
AR65 Evan Longoria 40.00 80.00
AR66 Evan Longoria 40.00 80.00
AR67 Adam Dunn 8.00 20.00
AR68 Adam Dunn 8.00 20.00
AR69 Adam Dunn 8.00 20.00
AR70 Joe Morgan 20.00 50.00
AR71 Joe Morgan 20.00 50.00
AR72 Joe Morgan 20.00 50.00
AR73 Matt Cain 20.00 50.00
AR74 Matt Cain 20.00 50.00
AR75 Matt Cain 20.00 50.00
AR76 Dale Murphy 40.00 80.00
AR77 Dale Murphy 40.00 80.00
AR78 Dale Murphy 40.00 80.00
AR79 Whitey Ford 30.00 60.00
AR80 Whitey Ford 30.00 60.00
AR81 Whitey Ford 30.00 60.00
AR82 Michael Young 10.00 25.00
AR83 Michael Young 10.00 25.00
AR84 Michael Young 10.00 25.00
AR85 Matt Holliday 20.00 50.00
AR86 Matt Holliday 20.00 50.00
AR87 Matt Holliday 20.00 50.00
AR88 Ozzie Smith 30.00 60.00
AR89 Ozzie Smith 30.00 60.00
AR90 Ozzie Smith 30.00 60.00
AR91 Barry Larkin 50.00 100.00
AR92 Barry Larkin 50.00 100.00
AR93 Barry Larkin 50.00 100.00
AR94 Aramis Ramirez 8.00 20.00
AR95 Aramis Ramirez 8.00 20.00
AR96 Aramis Ramirez 8.00 20.00
AR97 Hanley Ramirez 12.50 30.00
AR98 Hanley Ramirez 12.50 30.00
AR99 Hanley Ramirez 12.50 30.00
AR100 Mariano Rivera 100.00 200.00
AR101 Mariano Rivera 100.00 200.00
AR102 Mariano Rivera 100.00 200.00
AR103 Reggie Jackson 50.00 100.00
AR104 Reggie Jackson 50.00 100.00
AR105 Reggie Jackson 50.00 100.00
AR106 Nolan Ryan 60.00 120.00
AR107 Nolan Ryan 60.00 120.00
AR108 Nolan Ryan 60.00 120.00
AR109 Torii Hunter 15.00 40.00
AR110 Torii Hunter 15.00 40.00
AR111 Torii Hunter 15.00 40.00
AR112 Albert Pujols 200.00 300.00
AR113 Albert Pujols 200.00 300.00
AR114 Albert Pujols 200.00 300.00
AR115 Shane Victorino 12.50 30.00
AR116 Shane Victorino 12.50 30.00
AR117 Shane Victorino 12.50 30.00
AR118 Justin Verlander 40.00 80.00
AR119 Justin Verlander 40.00 80.00
AR120 Justin Verlander 40.00 80.00
AR121 Miguel Cabrera 75.00 150.00
AR122 Miguel Cabrera 75.00 150.00
AR123 Miguel Cabrera 75.00 150.00
AR124 Adrian Gonzalez 12.50 30.00
AR125 Adrian Gonzalez 12.50 30.00
AR126 Adrian Gonzalez 12.50 30.00
AR127 Chone Figgins 8.00 20.00
AR128 Chone Figgins 8.00 20.00
AR129 Chone Figgins 8.00 20.00
AR130 Nick Swisher 8.00 20.00
AR131 Nick Swisher 8.00 20.00
AR132 Nick Swisher 8.00 20.00
AR133 Phil Hughes 20.00 50.00
AR134 Phil Hughes 20.00 50.00
AR135 Phil Hughes 20.00 50.00
AR136 Aaron Hill 10.00 25.00
AR137 Aaron Hill 10.00 25.00
AR138 Aaron Hill 10.00 25.00
AR139 Johnny Damon 30.00 60.00
AR140 Johnny Damon 30.00 60.00
AR141 Johnny Damon 30.00 60.00
AR142 Miguel Tejada 8.00 20.00
AR143 Miguel Tejada 8.00 20.00
AR144 Miguel Tejada 8.00 20.00
AR145 Vernon Wells 10.00 25.00
AR146 Vernon Wells 10.00 25.00
AR147 Vernon Wells 10.00 25.00
AR148 George Kell 15.00 40.00
AR149 George Kell 15.00 40.00
AR150 George Kell 15.00 40.00
AR151 Carlos Pena 8.00 20.00
AR152 Carlos Pena 8.00 20.00
AR153 Carlos Pena 8.00 20.00
AR154 Andre Dawson 40.00 80.00
AR155 Andre Dawson 40.00 80.00
AR156 Andre Dawson 40.00 80.00
AR157 Dwight Gooden 12.50 30.00
AR158 Dwight Gooden 12.50 30.00
AR159 Dwight Gooden 12.50 30.00
AR160 Ralph Kiner 30.00 60.00
AR161 Ralph Kiner 30.00 60.00
AR162 Ralph Kiner 30.00 60.00
AR163 Bobby Murcer 15.00 40.00
AR164 Bobby Murcer 15.00 40.00
AR165 Bobby Murcer 15.00 40.00
AR166 Tony Perez 30.00 60.00
AR167 Tony Perez 30.00 60.00
AR168 Tony Perez 30.00 60.00
AR169 Rich Harden 8.00 20.00
AR170 Rich Harden 8.00 20.00
AR171 Rich Harden 8.00 20.00
AR172 Joba Chamberlain 12.50 30.00
AR173 Joba Chamberlain 12.50 30.00
AR174 Joba Chamberlain 12.50 30.00
AR175 Cal Ripken Jr. 150.00 250.00
AR176 Cal Ripken Jr. 150.00 250.00
AR177 Cal Ripken Jr. 150.00 250.00
AR178 Carl Yastrzemski 40.00 80.00
AR179 Carl Yastrzemski 40.00 80.00
AR180 Carl Yastrzemski 40.00 80.00
AR181 Bruce Sutter 15.00 40.00
AR182 Bruce Sutter 15.00 40.00
AR183 Bruce Sutter 15.00 40.00
AR184 Stan Musial 100.00 200.00
AR185 Stan Musial 100.00 200.00
AR186 Stan Musial 100.00 200.00
AR187 Frank Robinson 30.00 60.00
AR188 Frank Robinson 30.00 60.00
AR189 Frank Robinson 30.00 60.00
AR190 Ryan Zimmerman 20.00 50.00
AR191 Ryan Zimmerman 20.00 50.00
AR192 Ryan Zimmerman 20.00 50.00
AR193 Felix Hernandez 40.00 80.00
AR194 Felix Hernandez 40.00 80.00
AR195 Felix Hernandez 40.00 80.00
AR196 Carl Crawford 12.50 30.00
AR197 Carl Crawford 12.50 30.00
AR198 Carl Crawford 12.50 30.00
AR199 Raul Ibanez 10.00 25.00
AR200 Raul Ibanez 10.00 25.00
AR201 Raul Ibanez 10.00 25.00
AR202 Brian McCann 12.50 30.00
AR203 Brian McCann 12.50 30.00
AR204 Brian McCann 12.50 30.00
AR205 Matt Garza 10.00 25.00
AR206 Matt Garza 10.00 25.00
AR207 Matt Garza 10.00 25.00
AR208 Chipper Jones 60.00 120.00
AR209 Chipper Jones 60.00 120.00
AR210 Chipper Jones 60.00 120.00
AR211 Jason Heyward 40.00 80.00
AR212 Jason Heyward 40.00 80.00
AR213 Jason Heyward 40.00 80.00
AR214 Stephen Strasburg 100.00 200.00
AR215 Stephen Strasburg 100.00 200.00
AR216 Stephen Strasburg 100.00 200.00
AR217 Al Kaline 30.00 80.00
AR218 Al Kaline 30.00 80.00
AR219 Al Kaline 30.00 80.00
AR220 Ryne Sandberg 50.00 100.00
AR221 Ryne Sandberg 50.00 100.00
AR222 Ryne Sandberg 50.00 100.00
AR226 Ivan Rodriguez 40.00 80.00
AR227 Ivan Rodriguez 40.00 80.00
AR228 Ivan Rodriguez 40.00 80.00
AR229 Alfonso Soriano 12.50 30.00
AR230 Alfonso Soriano 12.50 30.00
AR231 Alfonso Soriano 12.50 30.00
AR232 Ben Zobrist 12.00 30.00
AR233 Ben Zobrist 12.00 30.00
AR234 Ben Zobrist 12.00 30.00
AR235 Roberto Alomar 20.00 50.00
AR236 Roberto Alomar 20.00 50.00
AR237 Roberto Alomar 20.00 50.00
AR238 Tony Gwynn 30.00 60.00
AR239 Tony Gwynn 30.00 60.00
AR240 Tony Gwynn 30.00 60.00
AR241 Mike Schmidt 30.00 60.00
AR242 Mike Schmidt 30.00 60.00
AR243 Mike Schmidt 30.00 60.00
AR244 Matt Kemp 20.00 50.00
AR245 Matt Kemp 20.00 50.00
AR246 Matt Kemp 20.00 50.00
AR247 Johnny Bench 40.00 80.00
AR248 Johnny Bench 40.00 80.00
AR249 Johnny Bench 40.00 80.00
AR250 Ernie Banks 30.00 60.00
AR251 Ernie Banks 30.00 60.00
AR252 Ernie Banks 30.00 60.00
AR262 Ron Santo 60.00 120.00
AR263 Ron Santo 60.00 120.00
AR264 Ron Santo 60.00 120.00
AR265 Hunter Pence 12.50 30.00
AR266 Hunter Pence 12.50 30.00
AR267 Hunter Pence 12.50 30.00
AR274 Carlton Fisk 20.00 50.00
AR275 Carlton Fisk 20.00 50.00
AR276 Carlton Fisk 20.00 50.00
AR280 Shin-Soo Choo 20.00 50.00
AR281 Shin-Soo Choo 20.00 50.00
AR282 Shin-Soo Choo 20.00 50.00
AR283 Bernie Williams 60.00 120.00
AR284 Bernie Williams 60.00 120.00
AR286 Bernie Williams 60.00 120.00

2010 Topps Triple Threads Autograph Relics Gold

*GOLD: .5X TO 1.2X BASIC
STATED ODDS 1:19 MINI
STATED PRINT RUN 9 SER.#'d SETS
ALL DC VARIATIONS PRICED EQUALLY

2010 Topps Triple Threads Legend Relics

STATED ODDS 1:49 MINI
STATED PRINT RUN 36 SER.#'d SETS
RL1 Yogi Berra 20.00 50.00
RL2 Roy Campanella 20.00 50.00
RL3 Ty Cobb 60.00 120.00
RL4 Nolan Ryan 15.00 40.00
RL5 Johnny Bench 12.50 30.00
RL6 Jim Palmer 12.50 30.00
RL7 Whitey Ford 12.50 30.00
RL8 Jimmie Foxx 40.00 80.00
RL9 Lou Gehrig 100.00 175.00
RL10 Bob Gibson 15.00 40.00
RL11 Hank Greenberg 30.00 60.00
RL12 Rogers Hornsby 40.00 80.00
RL13 Ralph Kiner 15.00 40.00
RL14 Mickey Mantle 100.00 175.00
RL15 Roger Maris 50.00 100.00
RL16 Eddie Mathews 20.00 50.00
RL17 Johnny Mize 12.50 30.00
RL18 Thurman Munson 15.00 40.00
RL19 Stan Musial 30.00 60.00
RL20 Frank Robinson 12.50 30.00
RL21 Mel Ott 30.00 60.00
RL22 Pee Wee Reese 20.00 50.00
RL23 Phil Rizzuto 15.00 40.00
RL24 Jackie Robinson 40.00 80.00
RL25 Babe Ruth 350.00 500.00
RL26 Tom Seaver 12.50 30.00
RL27 George Sisler 30.00 60.00
RL28 Warren Spahn 20.00 50.00
RL29 Tris Speaker 20.00 50.00
RL30 Honus Wagner 50.00 100.00

2010 Topps Triple Threads Legend Relics Sepia

*SEPIA: .4X TO 1X BASIC
STATED ODDS 1:66 MINI
STATED PRINT RUN 27 SER.#'d SETS

2010 Topps Triple Threads MLB Die Cut Relics

STATED ODDS 1:10 MINI
STATED PRINT RUN 36 SER.#'d SETS
ALL DC VARIATIONS PRICED EQUALLY
AG Adrian Gonzalez 6.00 15.00
AK Al Kaline 15.00 40.00
CF Carlton Fisk 6.00 15.00
CJ Chipper Jones 12.50 30.00
CR Cal Ripken Jr. 12.50 30.00
CS Curt Schilling 6.00 15.00
CU Chase Utley 12.50 30.00
DJ Derek Jeter 30.00 60.00
DW David Wright 12.50 30.00
EL Evan Longoria 12.50 30.00
HR Hanley Ramirez 6.00 15.00
KY Kevin Youkilis 6.00 15.00
MC Miguel Cabrera 8.00 20.00
MR Manny Ramirez 12.50 30.00
MT Mark Teixeira 12.50 30.00
OC Orlando Cepeda 6.00 15.00
PF Prince Fielder 6.00 15.00
PM Paul Molitor 8.00 20.00
RH Rickey Henderson 30.00 60.00
RH Roy Halladay 15.00 40.00
SC Steve Carlton 8.00 20.00
TG Tony Gwynn 12.50 30.00
WS Willie Stargell 8.00 20.00
DWI Dave Winfield 8.00 20.00
SSC Shin-Soo Choo 10.00 25.00

2010 Topps Triple Threads MLB Die Cut Relics Emerald

*EMERALD: .5X TO 1.2X BASIC
STATED ODDS 1:19 MINI
STATED PRINT RUN 18 SER.#'d SETS
ALL DC VARIATIONS PRICED EQUALLY

2010 Topps Triple Threads MLB Die Cut Relics Sepia

*SEPIA: .4X TO 1X BASIC
STATED ODDS 1:13 MINI
STATED PRINT RUN 27 SER.#'d SETS
ALL DC VARIATIONS PRICED EQUALLY

2010 Topps Triple Threads Relic Combos

STATED ODDS 1:25 MINI
STATED PRINT RUN 36 SER.#'d SETS
RC1 Mauer/Killebrew/Morneau 20.00 50.00
RC2 Rivera/Posada/Pettitte 20.00 50.00
RC3 Tim Lincecum/Roy Halladay
Johan Santana 12.50 30.00
RC4 Pujols/Gibson/Musial 20.00 50.00
RC5 Ripken/Robinson/Palmer 15.00 40.00
RC6 Willie McCovey/Pablo Sandoval
Monte Irvin 15.00 40.00
RC7 Miggy/Teix/Morneau 15.00 40.00
RC8 Evan Longoria/David Wright
Ryan Zimmerman 12.50 30.00
RC9 Utley/Sandberg/Kinsler 12.50 30.00
RC10 Ramirez/Ripken/Tulowitzki 15.00 40.00
RC11 Matsui/Ichiro/Matsuzaka 30.00 60.00
RC12 David Wright/Aramis Ramirez
Pablo Sandoval 8.00 20.00
RC13 Heyward/Jones/McCann 15.00 40.00
RC14 Hunter Pence/Ryan Braun
Matt Holliday 10.00 25.00
RC15 Sandberg/Banks/Dawson 20.00 50.00
RC16 McCann/Mauer/Posada 12.50 30.00
RC17 Crawford/Henderson/Ellsbury 10.00 25.00
RC19 Zack Greinke/Cliff Lee
CC Sabathia 10.00 25.00
RC21 Ichiro/Ripken/Robinson 15.00 40.00
RC22 Rickey/Rickey/Rickey 12.00 30.00
RC23 Adrian Gonzalez
Ryan Zimmerman/Jimmy Rollins 8.00 20.00
RC24 Morneau/Pedroia/ARod 10.00 25.00
RC25 Dawson/Carter/Vlad 15.00 40.00
RC26 Bench/Mauer/Fisk 12.50 30.00
RC27 Guidry/Ford/Pettitte 15.00 40.00
RC28 Chipper Jones/Jorge Posada
Lance Berkman 12.50 30.00
RC29 Stntn/Strsbrg/Hywrd 20.00 50.00
RC30 Adam Jones/Brian Roberts
Nick Markakis 10.00 25.00
RC31 Mantle/Ruth/Maris 250.00 400.00
RC32 Mark Reynolds/Justin Upton
Stephen Drew 8.00 20.00
RC33 Wright/Carter/Bay 10.00 25.00
RC34 Vladimir Guerrero/David Ortiz
Manny Ramirez 8.00 20.00
RC35 Utley/Howard/Werth 30.00 60.00
RC36 Lincecum/Sandoval/Cain 15.00 40.00
RC37 Cruz/Hamilton/Kinsler 30.00 60.00
RC38 Ivan Rodriguez 15.00 40.00
RC39 Pujols/Hanley/ARod 15.00 40.00
RC40 Josh Hamilton
Adrian Gonzalez/Joe Mauer 10.00 25.00
RC41 ARod/Mauer/Upton 12.50 30.00
RC42 Reyes/Pedroia/Ichiro 12.50 30.00
RC43 Kaline/Cobb/Kell 40.00 80.00
RC44 Pujols/Howard/Prince 12.50 30.00
RC45 Teixeira/Cabrera/ARod 10.00 25.00
RC46 Schmidt/Stargell/Bench 20.00 50.00
RC47 Killebrew/Yaz/Robinson 12.50 30.00
RC48 Hernandez/CC/Verlander 12.50 30.00
RC50 Mariano Rivera/Curt Schilling
Cole Hamels 10.00 25.00
RC51 Ryan/Ryan/Ryan 30.00 60.00
RC52 Shane Victorino/Jose Reyes
Jimmy Rollins 8.00 20.00
RC53 Prince Fielder/Justin Morneau
Vladimir Guerrero 8.00 20.00
RC54 Justin Verlander/Rick Porcello
Jim Bunning 12.50 30.00
RC55 Josh Beckett/Jon Lester
John Lackey 10.00 25.00
RC56 Troy Tulowitzki/Jimmy Rollins
Hanley Ramirez 10.00 25.00
RC57 Upton/Ichiro/Sizemore 12.50 30.00
RC58 Sabathia/Greinke/Hernandez 12.00 30.00
RC59 Rivera/Eckersley/Gossage 15.00 40.00
RC60 ARod/ARod/ARod 10.00 25.00

2010 Topps Triple Threads Relic Combos Sepia

*SEPIA: .4X TO 1X BASIC
STATED ODDS 1:33 MINI
STATED PRINT RUN 27 SER.#'d SETS

2010 Topps Triple Threads Relic Combos Double

STATE ODDS 1:82 MINI
STATED PRINT RUN 36 SER.#'d SETS
RDC1 A.Pujols/J.Mauer 15.00 40.00
RDC2 A.Pujols/A.Rodriguez 30.00 60.00
RDC3 Kin/Gre/Mat/Kil/McC/Rob 50.00 100.00
RDC4 Puj/How/Hol/Car/Sch/Mur 15.00 40.00
RDC5 Ryan Howard 15.00 40.00
Matt Holliday
Albert Pujols
CC Sabathia
Josh Beckett
David Ortiz
RDC6 Miguel Cabrera 15.00 40.00
Justin Morneau
Kendry Morales
Ryan Howard
Albert Pujols
Prince Fielder
RDC7 Alex Rodriguez 15.00 40.00
Joe Mauer
Torii Hunter
Ryan Howard
Albert Pujols
Manny Ramirez
RDC8 Tim Lincecum 15.00 40.00
Roy Halladay
Johan Santana
Zack Greinke
Felix Hernandez
CC Sabathia
RDC9 Upt/Bra/Pen/Kem/McC/Hey 40.00 80.00
RDC10 Mau/Pos/Rod/Fis/Ben/Ber 15.00 40.00
RDC11 Adrian Gonzlez 15.00 40.00
Ryan Zimmerman
Jimmy Rollins
Matt Kemp
Shane Victorino
Yadier Molina
RDC12 Mau/Tei/Lon/Suz/Jon/Hunr 15.00 40.00
RDC13 Daw/Hen/Gos/Rip/Gwy/Sut 75.00 150.00
RDC14 Frank Robinson 15.00 40.00
Frank Robinson
RDC15 Lou Brock 15.00 40.00
Rickey Henderson
Jacoby Ellsbury
Carl Crawford
Jose Reyes
Jimmy Rollins
RDC16 Lin/Gre/Car/San/Sea/For 20.00 50.00
RDC17 Catfish Hunter 15.00 40.00
Thurman Munson
RDC18 How/Fie/Puj/Kil/Kin/Rob 40.00 80.00

2010 Topps Triple Threads Relic Combos Double Sepia

*SEPIA: .4X TO 1X BASIC
STATED ODDS 1:109 MINI
STATED PRINT RUN 27 SER.#'d SETS

2010 Topps Triple Threads Relics

STATED ODDS 1:10 MINI
STATED PRINT RUN 36 SER.#'d SETS
ALL DC VARIATIONS PRICED EQUALLY
R1 Albert Pujols 15.00 40.00
R2 Albert Pujols 15.00 40.00
R3 Albert Pujols 15.00 40.00
R4 Chase Utley 12.50 30.00
R5 Chase Utley 12.50 30.00
R6 Chase Utley 12.50 30.00
R7 Ichiro Suzuki 10.00 25.00
R8 Ichiro Suzuki 10.00 25.00
R9 Ichiro Suzuki 10.00 25.00
R10 Grady Sizemore 6.00 15.00
R11 Grady Sizemore 6.00 15.00
R12 Grady Sizemore 6.00 15.00
R13 Mark Teixeira 8.00 20.00
R14 Mark Teixeira 8.00 20.00
R15 Mark Teixeira 8.00 20.00
R16 Shin-Soo Choo 10.00 25.00
R17 Shin-Soo Choo 10.00 25.00
R18 Shin-Soo Choo 10.00 25.00
R22 Hanley Ramirez 6.00 15.00
R23 Hanley Ramirez 6.00 15.00
R24 Hanley Ramirez 6.00 15.00
R25 Evan Longoria 10.00 25.00
R26 Evan Longoria 10.00 25.00
R27 Evan Longoria 10.00 25.00
R28 David Wright 12.50 30.00
R29 David Wright 12.50 30.00
R30 David Wright 12.50 30.00
R31 Hunter Pence 6.00 15.00
R32 Hunter Pence 6.00 15.00
R33 Hunter Pence 6.00 15.00
R34 Joe Mauer 8.00 20.00
R35 Joe Mauer 8.00 20.00
R36 Joe Mauer 8.00 20.00
R37 Rickey Henderson 15.00 40.00
R38 Rickey Henderson 40.00 80.00
R39 Rickey Henderson 40.00 80.00
R40 Al Kaline 15.00 40.00
R41 Al Kaline 15.00 40.00
R42 Al Kaline 15.00 40.00
R43 Catfish Hunter 12.50 30.00
R44 Catfish Hunter 12.50 30.00
R45 Catfish Hunter 12.50 30.00
R46 Dave Winfield 8.00 20.00
R47 Dave Winfield 8.00 20.00
R48 Dave Winfield 8.00 20.00
R49 Carlton Fisk 12.50 30.00
R50 Carlton Fisk 12.50 30.00
R51 Carlton Fisk 12.50 30.00
R52 Curt Schilling 6.00 15.00
R53 Curt Schilling 6.00 15.00
R54 Curt Schilling 6.00 15.00
R58 Mike Schmidt 15.00 40.00
R58 Mike Schmidt 15.00 40.00
R59 Mike Schmidt 15.00 40.00
R61 Steve Carlton 8.00 20.00
R62 Steve Carlton 8.00 20.00
R63 Steve Carlton 8.00 20.00
R64 Orlando Cepeda 6.00 15.00
R65 Orlando Cepeda 6.00 15.00
R65 Orlando Cepeda 6.00 15.00
R67 Prince Fielder 8.00 20.00
R68 Prince Fielder 8.00 20.00
R69 Prince Fielder 8.00 20.00
R70 Ryne Sandberg 12.50 30.00
R71 Ryne Sandberg 12.50 30.00
R72 Ryne Sandberg 12.50 30.00
R73 Tony Gwynn 8.00 20.00
R74 Tony Gwynn 8.00 20.00
R75 Tony Gwynn 8.00 20.00
R75 Willie Stargell 10.00 25.00
R77 Willie Stargell 10.00 25.00
R78 Willie Stargell 10.00 25.00
R79 Miguel Cabrera 12.50 30.00
R80 Miguel Cabrera 12.50 30.00
R81 Miguel Cabrera 12.50 30.00
R82 George Kell 8.00 20.00
R83 George Kell 8.00 20.00
R84 George Kell 8.00 20.00
R85 Cal Ripken Jr. 15.00 40.00
R86 Cal Ripken Jr. 15.00 40.00
R87 Cal Ripken Jr. 15.00 40.00
R88 Joe Morgan 10.00 25.00
R89 Joe Morgan 10.00 25.00
R90 Joe Morgan 10.00 25.00
R91 Chipper Jones 12.50 30.00
R92 Chipper Jones 12.50 30.00
R93 Chipper Jones 12.50 30.00
R94 Paul Molitor 8.00 20.00
R95 Paul Molitor 8.00 20.00
R96 Paul Molitor 8.00 20.00
R97 Phil Niekro 10.00 25.00
R98 Phil Niekro 10.00 25.00
R99 Phil Niekro 10.00 25.00
R100 Manny Ramirez 12.50 30.00
R101 Manny Ramirez 12.50 30.00
R102 Manny Ramirez 12.50 30.00
R103 Kevin Youkilis 6.00 15.00
R104 Kevin Youkilis 6.00 15.00
R105 Kevin Youkilis 6.00 15.00
R106 Josh Beckett 8.00 20.00
R107 Josh Beckett 8.00 20.00
R108 Josh Beckett 8.00 20.00
R109 Victor Martinez 6.00 15.00
R110 Victor Martinez 6.00 15.00
R111 Victor Martinez 6.00 15.00
R112 Adam Dunn 8.00 20.00
R113 Adam Dunn 8.00 20.00
R114 Adam Dunn 8.00 20.00
R115 Justin Morneau 10.00 25.00
R116 Justin Morneau 10.00 25.00
R117 Justin Morneau 10.00 25.00
R118 Roy Halladay 8.00 20.00
R119 Roy Halladay 8.00 20.00
R120 Roy Halladay 8.00 20.00
R121 Andrew McCutchen 20.00 50.00
R122 Andrew McCutchen 20.00 50.00
R123 Andrew McCutchen 20.00 50.00
R124 Ryan Zimmerman 8.00 20.00
R125 Ryan Zimmerman 8.00 20.00
R126 Ryan Zimmerman 8.00 20.00
R127 Adrian Gonzalez 6.00 15.00
R128 Adrian Gonzalez 6.00 15.00
R129 Adrian Gonzalez 6.00 15.00
R130 Derek Jeter 30.00 60.00
R131 Derek Jeter 30.00 60.00
R132 Derek Jeter 30.00 60.00
R136 Reggie Jackson 15.00 40.00
R137 Reggie Jackson 15.00 40.00
R138 Reggie Jackson 15.00 40.00
R139 Monte Irvin 15.00 40.00
R140 Monte Irvin 15.00 40.00
R141 Monte Irvin 15.00 40.00

2010 Topps Triple Threads Relics Emerald

*EMERALD: .5X TO 1.2X BASIC
STATED ODDS 1:19 MINI
STATED PRINT RUN 18 SER.#'d SETS
ALL DC VARIATIONS PRICED EQUALLY

2010 Topps Triple Threads Relics Gold

*GOLD: .6X TO 1.5X BASIC
STATED ODDS 1:38 MINI
STATED PRINT RUN 9 SER.#'d SETS
ALL DC VARIATIONS PRICED EQUALLY

2010 Topps Triple Threads Relics Sepia

*SEPIA: .4X TO 1X BASIC
STATED ODDS 1:13 MINI
STATED PRINT RUN 27 SER.#'d SETS
ALL DC VARIATIONS PRICED EQUALLY

2010 Topps Triple Threads Rookie Rising Stars Autograph Relic Pairs

STATED ODDS 1:176 MINI
STATED PRINT RUN 50 SER.#'d SETS
RRARP1 S.Strasburg/J.Johnson 75.00 150.00
RRARP2 J.Heyward/T.Hanson 100.00 200.00
RRARP3 Gordon Beckham
Chris Coghlan 12.50 30.00
RRARP4 J.Upton/A.Jones 20.00 50.00
RRARP5 R.Porcello/M.Scherzer 30.00 80.00
RRARP6 S.Strasburg/J.Heyward 75.00 150.00

2011 Topps Triple Threads

COMP.SET w/o AU's (100) 40.00 80.00
COMMON CARD (1-100) .30 .75
1-100 PRINT RUN 1500 SER.#'d SETS
COMMON JSY AU RC (101-150) 5.00 12.00
JSY AU RC ODDS 1:11 HOBBY
JSY AU RC PRINT RUN 99 SER.#'d SETS
COMMON JSY AU (101-150) 5.00 12.00
JSY AU ODDS 1:11 HOBBY
JSY AU PRINT RUN 99 SER.#'d SETS
EXCHANGE DEADLINE 9/30/2014
OVERALL 1-100 PLATE ODDS 1:126 HOBBY
PLATE PRINT RUN 1 SET PER COLOR
BLACK-CYAN-MAGENTA-YELLOW ISSUED
NO PLATE PRICING DUE TO SCARCITY
1 Ryan Braun .50 1.25
2 Johnny Mize .50 1.25
3 Bert Blyleven .50 1.25
4 Lou Gehrig 1.50 4.00
5 Albert Pujols 1.00 2.50
6 Cliff Lee .50 1.25
7 Mickey Mantle 2.50 6.00
8 Cal Ripken Jr. 2.50 6.00
9 Dustin Pedroia .60 1.50
10 Nolan Ryan 2.50 6.00
11 Duke Snider .50 1.25
12 Shin-Soo Choo .50 1.25
13 Hanley Ramirez .50 1.25
14 Eddie Murray .50 1.25
15 Josh Hamilton .50 1.25
16 Chase Utley .50 1.25
17 Willie McCovey .50 1.25
18 Roy Campanella .75 2.00
19 Matt Kemp .60 1.50
20 Victor Martinez .50 1.25
21 Ozzie Smith 1.00 2.50
22 Kevin Youkilis .30 .75
23 Evan Longoria .50 1.25
24 Reggie Jackson .50 1.25
25 Jason Heyward .60 1.50
26 Ty Cobb 1.25 3.00
27 Babe Ruth 2.00 5.00
28 Clayton Kershaw 1.50 4.00
29 Andrew McCutchen .75 2.00
30 Justin Verlander .75 2.00
31 Joe Morgan .50 1.25
32 Carl Crawford .50 1.25
33 Johnny Bench .75 2.00
34 Robinson Cano .50 1.25
35 Mike Stanton .75 2.00
36 Honus Wagner .75 2.00
37 Troy Tulowitzki .75 2.00
38 Jackie Robinson .75 2.00
39 Ryan Zimmerman .50 1.25
40 Carlos Gonzalez .50 1.25
41 Ichiro Suzuki 1.00 2.50
42 Mike Schmidt 1.25 3.00
43 Carlton Fisk .50 1.25
44 Mark Teixeira .50 1.25
45 Tim Lincecum .50 1.25
46 Hank Aaron 1.50 4.00
47 Buster Posey 1.00 2.50
48 Jim Palmer .50 1.25
49 David Wright .60 1.50
50 Mel Ott .75 2.00
51 Brooks Robinson .50 1.25
52 Ryan Howard .60 1.50
53 Joe Mauer .60 1.50
54 Josh Johnson .50 1.25
55 Stan Musial 1.25 3.00
56 Derek Jeter 2.00 5.00
57 Ryne Sandberg 1.50 4.00
58 Pee Wee Reese .50 1.25
59 Bob Gibson .50 1.25
60 Carlos Santana .75 2.00
61 Jose Reyes .50 1.25
62 Paul Molitor .75 2.00
63 Frank Robinson .50 1.25
64 Darryl Strawberry .30 .75
65 Adrian Gonzalez .60 1.50
66 Christy Mathewson .75 2.00
67 Roy Halladay .50 1.25
68 Andre Dawson .50 1.25
69 George Sisler .50 1.25
70 Joey Votto .75 2.00
71 Roger Maris .75 2.00
72 Jimmie Foxx .75 2.00
73 Prince Fielder .50 1.25
74 Roberto Alomar .50 1.25
75 CC Sabathia .50 1.25
76 Rogers Hornsby .50 1.25
77 Ian Kinsler .50 1.25
78 Rickey Henderson .75 2.00
79 Andre Ethier .50 1.25
80 Thurman Munson .75 2.00
81 Matt Holliday .75 2.00
82 Walter Johnson .75 2.00
83 Jon Lester .50 1.25
84 Tom Seaver .50 1.25
85 Starlin Castro .50 1.25
86 Joe DiMaggio 1.50 4.00
87 Felix Hernandez .50 1.25
88 Monte Irvin .50 1.25
89 Cy Young .75 2.00
90 Barry Larkin .50 1.25
91 Tony Gwynn .75 2.00
92 Mariano Rivera 1.00 2.50
93 Clay Buchholz .30 .75
94 John Smoltz .75 2.00
95 Alex Rodriguez 1.00 2.50
96 Tris Speaker .50 1.25
97 Miguel Cabrera .75 2.00
98 Whitey Ford .50 1.25
99 Justin Morneau .50 1.25
100 Sandy Koufax 1.50 4.00
101 Buster Posey Bat AU 50.00 100.00
102 G.Beckham Jsy AU 6.00 15.00
103 Jay Bruce Bat AU 10.00 25.00
104 D.Valencia Bat AU 8.00 20.00
105 Neftali Feliz Jsy AU 5.00 12.00
106 Jose Tabata Jsy AU 5.00 12.00
107 Carlos Santana Jsy AU 5.00 12.00
108 Pablo Sandoval Jsy AU 6.00 15.00
109 Mitch Moreland Bat AU 5.00 12.00
110 Gio Gonzalez Jsy AU 10.00 25.00
111 Brett Wallace Bat AU 6.00 15.00
112 Chris Sale Jsy AU RC 10.00 25.00
113 Kyle Drabek Jsy AU RC 4.00 10.00
114 Starlin Castro Jsy AU 12.00 30.00
115 Austin Jackson Jsy AU 8.00 20.00
116 M.Scherzer Jsy AU 30.00 80.00
117 A.Chapman Jsy AU RC 20.00 50.00
118 A.McCutchen Jsy AU 30.00 60.00
119 Zach Britton Jsy AU RC 6.00 15.00
120 Bumgarner JSY AU 20.00 50.00
121 Mike Stanton Jsy AU 25.00 60.00
122 J.Heyward Jsy AU 12.00 30.00
123 F.Freeman Bat AU RC 60.00 150.00
124 Logan Morrison Bat AU 5.00 12.00
125 B.Belt Jsy AU RC 15.00 40.00
126 Brett Anderson Jsy AU 5.00 12.00
127 M.Pineda Jsy AU RC 12.00 30.00
128 Drew Stubbs Jsy AU 8.00 20.00
129 Elvis Andrus Jsy AU 12.50 30.00
130 Colby Rasmus Jsy AU 6.00 15.00
131 Chris Coghlan Jsy AU 5.00 12.00
132 T.Hanson Jsy AU 8.00 20.00
133 C.Kershaw Jsy AU 50.00 100.00
134 Brent Morel Jsy AU RC 5.00 12.00
135 Jaime Garcia Jsy AU 12.50 30.00
136 Hosmer Jsy AU RC EXCH 20.00 50.00
137 J.Hellickson Jsy AU RC 6.00 15.00
138 P.Alvarez Jsy AU RC 8.00 20.00
139 Gaby Sanchez Jsy AU 5.00 12.00
140 J.Arencibia Bat AU 8.00 20.00
141 Neil Walker Jsy AU 8.00 20.00
143 J.Zimmerman Bat AU 6.00 15.00
144 Ian Desmond Jsy AU 4.00 10.00
145 Rick Porcello Jsy AU 5.00 12.00
146 Daniel Bard Jsy AU 6.00 15.00
147A Alcides Escobar Jsy AU 8.00 20.00
147B Hank Conger Jsy AU RC EXCH 5.00 12.00
148 Brett Gardner Bat AU 15.00 40.00
149 Ike Davis Jsy AU 10.00 25.00
150 Carlos Gonzalez Jsy AU 12.50 30.00

2011 Topps Triple Threads Emerald

*EMERALD 1-100: .6X TO 1.5X BASIC
1-100 ODDS 1:3 MINI
1-100 PRINT RUN 249 SER.#'d SETS
*EMERALD JSY AU: .4X TO 1X BASIC
EMERALD JSY AU ODDS 1:21 MINI
EM.JSY AU PRINT RUN 50 SER.#'d SETS
EXCHANGE DEADLINE 9/30/2014

2011 Topps Triple Threads Gold

*GOLD 1-100: .75X TO 2X BASIC
1-100 ODDS 1:6 MINI
1-100 PRINT RUN 99 SER.#'d SETS
101-150 ODDS 1:41 HOBBY
101-150 PRINT RUN 25 SER.#'d SETS
NO 101-150 PRICING DUE TO SCARCITY
EXCHANGE DEADLINE 9/30/2014

2011 Topps Triple Threads Sepia

*SEPIA 1-100: .5X TO 1.2X BASIC
1-100 RANDOMLY INSERTED
1-100 PRINT RUN 625 SER.#'d SETS
*SEPIA JSY AU: .4X TO 1X BASIC
SEPIA JSY AU ODDS 1:14 MINI
SEP.JSY AU PRINT RUN 75 SER.#'d SETS
EXCHANGE DEADLINE 9/30/2014

2011 Topps Triple Threads Autograph Relic Combos

STATED ODDS 1:93 MINI
STATED PRINT RUN 36 SER.#'d SETS
EXCHANGE DEADLINE 9/30/2014
TTARC1 Alomar/Utley/Cano 50.00 100.00
TTARC2 Bench/Mauer/Posey 75.00 150.00
TTARC3 Walk/Gonz/Ubaldo EXCH 20.00 50.00
TTARC4 Schmidt/ARod/Longoria 75.00 150.00
TTARC5 McCovey/Howard/Prince 60.00 120.00
TTARC6 Ryno/Pedroia/Kinsler 40.00 80.00
TTARC7 Wright/Zimmer/Chip 60.00 120.00
TTARC8 Ryan/Halladay/Felix 100.00 200.00
TTARC9 Rick/Craw/Gard EXCH 30.00 60.00
TTARC10 Koufax/Kershaw/Aroldis 250.00 350.00
TTARC11 Braun/Grein/Prin EXCH 50.00 100.00
TTARC12 Musial/Holliday/Rasmus 25.00 60.00
TTARC13 Ryno/Daw/Cast EXCH 40.00 80.00
TTARC14 Strawberry/Heyward/Young 15.00 40.00
TTARC15 Gibson/Felix/Johnson 30.00 60.00

2011 Topps Triple Threads Autograph Relic Combos Sepia

*SEPIA: .4X TO 1X BASIC
STATED ODDS 1:124 MINI
STATED PRINT RUN 27 SER.#'d SETS
EXCHANGE DEADLINE 9/30/2014

2011 Topps Triple Threads Flashback Relics

STATED ODDS 1:56 MINI
STATED PRINT RUN 36 SER.#'d SETS
TTFR1 Mickey Mantle 60.00 150.00
TTFR2 Frank Robinson 12.50 30.00
TTFR3 Babe Ruth 175.00 350.00
TTFR4 Ozzie Smith 20.00 50.00
TTFR5 Nolan Ryan 15.00 40.00
TTFR6 Tony Gwynn 12.50 30.00
TTFR7 Mike Schmidt 15.00 40.00
TTFR8 Paul Molitor 12.50 30.00
TTFR9 Brooks Robinson 15.00 40.00
TTFR10 Hank Aaron 40.00 80.00
TTFR11 Willie McCovey 12.50 30.00
TTFR12 Stan Musial 20.00 50.00
TTFR13 Cal Ripken Jr. 30.00 60.00
TTFR14 Roger Maris 40.00 80.00
TTFR15 Reggie Jackson 12.50 30.00
TTFR16 Ryne Sandberg 12.50 30.00
TTFR17 Carlton Fisk 12.50 30.00
TTFR18 Jackie Robinson 30.00 60.00
TTFR19 Rickey Henderson 30.00 60.00
TTFR20 Johnny Bench 15.00 40.00
TTFR21 Lou Gehrig 75.00 150.00
TTFR22 Al Kaline 15.00 40.00
TTFR23 Ty Cobb 50.00 100.00
TTFR24 Rogers Hornsby 30.00 60.00
TTFR25 Sandy Koufax 75.00 150.00

2011 Topps Triple Threads Flashback Relics Sepia

*SEPIA: .4X TO 1X BASIC
STATED ODDS 1:75 MINI
STATED PRINT RUN 27 SER.#'d SETS

2011 Topps Triple Threads Legend Relics

STATED ODDS 1:94 MINI
STATED PRINT RUN 36 SER.#'d SETS
TTRL1 Ty Cobb 30.00 60.00
TTRL2 Brooks Robinson 12.50 30.00
TTRL3 Babe Ruth 150.00 300.00
TTRL4 Mike Schmidt 10.00 25.00
TTRL5 Joe DiMaggio 60.00 120.00
TTRL6 Johnny Bench 10.00 25.00
TTRL7 Mickey Mantle 75.00 150.00
TTRL8 Jackie Robinson 20.00 50.00
TTRL9 Jim Palmer 10.00 25.00
TTRL10 Lou Gehrig 75.00 150.00
TTRL11 Roy Campanella 12.50 30.00
TTRL12 Bob Gibson 10.00 25.00
TTRL13 Willie McCovey 10.00 25.00
TTRL14 Stan Musial 15.00 40.00
TTRL15 Hank Aaron 30.00 60.00

2011 Topps Triple Threads Legend Relics Sepia

*SEPIA: .4X TO 1X BASIC
STATED ODDS 1:124 MINI
STATED PRINT RUN 27 SER.#'D SETS

2011 Topps Triple Threads Relic Autographs

STATED ODDS 1:11 MINI
STATED PRINT RUN 18 SER.#'d SETS
ALL DC VARIATIONS PRICED EQUALLY
NO PRICING ON PLAYERS W/ONE DC VERSION
EXCHANGE DEADLINE 9/30/2014
TTAR4 Ubaldo Jimenez 10.00 25.00
TTAR5 Ubaldo Jimenez 10.00 25.00
TTAR6 Andre Dawson 15.00 40.00
TTAR7 Andre Dawson 15.00 40.00
TTAR9 Aroldis Chapman 30.00 80.00
TTAR10 Aroldis Chapman 30.00 80.00
TTAR11 Aroldis Chapman 30.00 80.00
TTAR12 Aroldis Chapman 30.00 80.00
TTAR13 Elvis Andrus 10.00 25.00
TTAR14 Johnny Cueto 8.00 20.00
TTAR15 Jay Bruce 20.00 50.00
TTAR16 Jeremy Hellickson 15.00 40.00
TTAR17 Andrew McCutchen 40.00 80.00
TTAR28 Justin Upton 12.50 30.00
TTAR29 Justin Upton 12.50 30.00
TTAR30 Luis Aparicio 12.50 30.00
TTAR31 Luis Aparicio 12.50 30.00
TTAR32 Juan Marichal 20.00 50.00
TTAR33 Juan Marichal 20.00 50.00
TTAR34 Carlos Santana 10.00 25.00
TTAR35 Carlos Santana 10.00 25.00
TTAR36 Carlos Santana 10.00 25.00
TTAR37 Carlos Santana 10.00 25.00
TTAR38 Carlos Santana 10.00 25.00
TTAR40 Tommy Hanson 8.00 20
TTAR41 Tommy Hanson 8.00 20
TTAR42 Tommy Hanson 8.00 20
TTAR43 Tommy Hanson 8.00 20
TTAR44 Roberto Alomar 15.00 40
TTAR45 Roberto Alomar 15.00 40
TTAR46 Elvis Andrus 10.00 25
TTAR47 Elvis Andrus 10.00 25
TTAR48 Elvis Andrus 10.00 25
TTAR49 Elvis Andrus 10.00 25
TTAR50 Max Scherzer 40.00 100
TTAR51 Max Scherzer 40.00 100
TTAR52 Max Scherzer 40.00 100
TTAR53 Max Scherzer 40.00 100
TTAR54 Jose Bautista 15.00 40.
TTAR55 Jose Bautista 15.00 40.
TTAR56 Jose Bautista 15.00 40.
TTAR57 Jose Bautista 15.00 40
TTAR58 Joe Morgan 10.00 25
TTAR59 Joe Morgan 10.00 25
TTAR60 Matt Garza 8.00 20
TTAR61 Matt Garza 8.00 20
TTAR62 Matt Garza 8.00 20.
TTAR63 Matt Garza 8.00 20.
TTAR66 Josh Johnson 8.00 20.
TTAR67 Josh Johnson 8.00 20.
TTAR68 Josh Johnson 8.00 20.
TTAR69 Josh Johnson 8.00 20.
TTAR70 Red Schoendienst 20.00 50.
TTAR71 Red Schoendienst 20.00 50.
TTAR72 Red Schoendienst 20.00 50.
TTAR73 Jason Heyward 30.00 60.
TTAR74 Jason Heyward 30.00 60.
TTAR76 Dustin Pedroia 30.00 60.
TTAR77 Dustin Pedroia 30.00 60.
TTAR78 Duke Snider 30.00 60.
TTAR79 Duke Snider 30.00 60.
TTAR80 Pablo Sandoval 12.50 30.
TTAR81 Pablo Sandoval 12.50 30.
TTAR82 Pablo Sandoval 12.50 30.
TTAR83 Pablo Sandoval 12.50 30.
TTAR84 Pablo Sandoval 12.50 30.
TTAR85 Angel Pagan 10.00 25.
TTAR86 Angel Pagan 10.00 25.
TTAR87 Angel Pagan 10.00 25.
TTAR88 Angel Pagan 10.00 25.
TTAR89 Angel Pagan 10.00 25.
TTAR90 Brian McCann 15.00 40.
TTAR91 Brian McCann 15.00 40.
TTAR92 Brian McCann 15.00 40.
TTAR94 Robinson Cano 20.00 50.
TTAR95 Robinson Cano 20.00 50.0
TTAR96 Aramis Ramirez 8.00 20.
TTAR97 Aramis Ramirez 8.00 20.
TTAR98 Aramis Ramirez 8.00 20.
TTAR99 Steve Garvey 20.00 50.
TTAR100 Steve Garvey 20.00 50.
TTAR101 David Wright 30.00 60.
TTAR102 David Wright 30.00 60.
TTAR103 John Smoltz 40.00 80.
TTAR104 John Smoltz 40.00 80.
TTAR105 Brooks Robinson 30.00 60.
TTAR106 Brooks Robinson 30.00 60.
TTAR107 Prince Fielder 12.00 30.
TTAR108 Prince Fielder 12.00 30.0
TTAR109 Trevor Cahill 8.00 20.0
TTAR110 Trevor Cahill 8.00 20.0
TTAR111 Trevor Cahill 8.00 20.0
TTAR112 Trevor Cahill 8.00 20.0
TTAR113 Trevor Cahill 8.00 20.0
TTAR117 Tim Hudson 15.00 40.0
TTAR118 Tim Hudson 15.00 40.0
TTAR119 Nick Markakis 10.00 25.0
TTAR120 Nick Markakis 10.00 25.0
TTAR121 Nick Markakis 10.00 25.0
TTAR122 Nick Markakis 10.00 25.0
TTAR124 Josh Hamilton 40.00 80.0
TTAR125 Josh Hamilton 40.00 80.0
TTAR129 Ozzie Smith 15.00 40.0
TTAR130 Ozzie Smith 15.00 40.0
TTAR131 Vernon Wells 8.00 20.0
TTAR132 Vernon Wells 8.00 20.0
TTAR133 Billy Butler 10.00 25.0
TTAR134 Billy Butler 10.00 25.0
TTAR135 Billy Butler 10.00 25.0
TTAR136 Billy Butler 10.00 25.0
TTAR138 Ryan Zimmerman 12.50 30.0
TTAR139 Ryan Zimmerman 12.50 30.0
TTAR140 Ryan Zimmerman 12.50 30.0
TTAR141 Miguel Cabrera 60.00 120.0
TTAR142 Miguel Cabrera 60.00 120.0
TTAR143 Jim Palmer 12.50 30.0
TTAR144 Jim Palmer 12.50 30.0
TTAR145 Adrian Gonzalez 15.00 40.0
TTAR146 Adrian Gonzalez 15.00 40.0
TTAR147 Andrew McCutchen 40.00 80.0
TTAR148 Andrew McCutchen 40.00 80.0
TTAR149 Andrew McCutchen 40.00 80.0
TTAR150 Andrew McCutchen 40.00 80.0
TTAR151 Neftali Feliz 8.00 20.0
TTAR152 Neftali Feliz 8.00 20.0
TTAR153 Neftali Feliz 8.00 20.0
TTAR154 Neftali Feliz 8.00 20.0
TTAR155 Neftali Feliz 8.00 20.0
TTAR158 Nelson Cruz 10.00 25.0
TTAR159 Nelson Cruz 10.00 25.0
TTAR160 Nelson Cruz 10.00 25.0
TTAR161 Nelson Cruz 10.00 25.0
TTAR162 Jonathan Papelbon 10.00 25.0
TTAR163 Jonathan Papelbon 10.00 25.0
TTAR165 Buster Posey 50.00 100.0
TTAR166 Buster Posey 50.00 100.0
TTAR167 Gordon Beckham 10.00 25.0

R168 Gordon Beckham 10.00 25.00
R169 Gordon Beckham 10.00 25.00
R170 Paul Molitor 15.00 40.00
R171 Paul Molitor 15.00 40.00
R172 Mike Stanton 30.00 60.00
R173 Mike Stanton 30.00 60.00
R174 Mike Stanton 30.00 60.00
R175 Jeremy Hellickson 15.00 40.00
R176 Jeremy Hellickson 15.00 40.00
R177 Jeremy Hellickson 15.00 40.00
R178 Jeremy Hellickson 15.00 40.00
R180 Joey Votto 20.00 50.00
R181 Joey Votto 20.00 50.00
R182 Cliff Lee 40.00 80.00
R183 Cliff Lee 40.00 80.00
R184 Ian Kinsler 12.50 30.00
R185 Ian Kinsler 12.50 30.00
R186 Ian Kinsler 12.50 30.00
R187 Ian Kinsler 12.50 30.00
R188 Adam Jones 12.50 30.00
R189 Adam Jones 12.50 30.00
R190 Adam Jones 12.50 30.00
R191 Adam Jones 12.50 30.00
R196 Manny Pacquiao 250.00 350.00
R197 Manny Pacquiao 250.00 350.00
R198 Manny Pacquiao 250.00 350.00
R201 Ryan Howard 30.00 60.00
R202 Ryan Howard 30.00 60.00
R203 Austin Jackson 12.50 30.00
R204 Austin Jackson 12.50 30.00
R205 Austin Jackson 12.50 30.00
R206 Austin Jackson 12.50 30.00
R209 Dan Uggla 15.00 40.00
R210 Dan Uggla 15.00 40.00
R211 Paul O'Neill 30.00 60.00
R212 Paul O'Neill 30.00 60.00
R213 Paul O'Neill 30.00 60.00
R214 Shane Victorino 15.00 40.00
R215 Shane Victorino 15.00 40.00
R216 Shane Victorino 15.00 40.00
R217 Shane Victorino 15.00 40.00
R218 Starlin Castro 20.00 50.00
R219 Starlin Castro 20.00 50.00
R220 Starlin Castro 20.00 50.00
R221 Starlin Castro 20.00 50.00
R222 Starlin Castro 20.00 50.00
R223 Johnny Cueto 8.00 20.00
R224 Johnny Cueto 8.00 20.00
R225 Johnny Cueto 8.00 20.00
R226 Johnny Cueto 8.00 20.00
R228 Fergie Jenkins 15.00 40.00
R229 Fergie Jenkins 15.00 40.00
R230 Andre Ethier 10.00 25.00
R231 Andre Ethier 10.00 25.00
R232 Andre Ethier 10.00 25.00
R233 Andre Ethier 10.00 25.00
R234 Bert Blyleven 15.00 40.00
R235 Bert Blyleven 15.00 40.00
R236 Bert Blyleven 15.00 40.00
R237 Hanley Ramirez 8.00 20.00
R238 Hanley Ramirez 8.00 20.00
R239 Rick Porcello 8.00 20.00
R240 Rick Porcello 8.00 20.00
R241 Rick Porcello 8.00 20.00
R242 Rick Porcello 8.00 20.00
R243 Albert Belle 10.00 25.00
R244 Albert Belle 10.00 25.00
R245 Albert Belle 10.00 25.00
R246 B.J. Upton 10.00 25.00
R247 B.J. Upton 10.00 25.00
R248 B.J. Upton 10.00 25.00
R249 B.J. Upton 10.00 25.00
R250 Matt Holliday 30.00 60.00
R251 Matt Holliday 30.00 60.00
R252 Al Kaline 30.00 80.00
R253 Al Kaline 30.00 80.00
R254 Adam Lind 8.00 20.00
R255 Adam Lind 8.00 20.00
R256 Adam Lind 8.00 20.00
R257 Adam Lind 8.00 20.00
R258 Adam Lind 8.00 20.00
R260 Jay Bruce 10.00 25.00
R261 Jay Bruce 10.00 25.00
R262 Jay Bruce 10.00 25.00
R263 Jay Bruce 10.00 25.00
R264 Heath Bell 8.00 20.00
R265 Heath Bell 8.00 20.00
R266 Heath Bell 8.00 20.00
R267 Heath Bell 8.00 20.00
R268 Darryl Strawberry 30.00 60.00
R269 Darryl Strawberry 30.00 60.00

2011 Topps Triple Threads Relic Autographs Gold

GOLD: .5X TO 1.2X BASIC
TATED ODDS 1:21 MINI
TATED PRINT RUN 9 SER.#'d SETS
LL DC VARIATIONS PRICED EQUALLY
O PRICING ON MANY DUE TO SCARCITY
XCHANGE DEADLINE 9/30/2014

2011 Topps Triple Threads Relic Combos

TATED ODDS 1:24 MINI
TATED PRINT RUN 36 SER.#'d SETS
TRC1 Rodriguez/Jeter/Cano 20.00 50.00
TRC2 Hanley/Tulo/Reyes 10.00 25.00
TRC3 Pujols/Votto/Cabrera 20.00 50.00
TRC4 Crawford/Gonzalez/Pedroia 8.00 20.00
TRC5 Long/Wright/Zimm 10.00 25.00
TRC6 Heyward/Jones/McCann 12.50 30.00
TRC7 Lincecum/Posey/Cain 20.00 50.00
TRC8 Howard/Utley/Rollins 15.00 40.00
TRC9 McCutchen/Upton/Kemp 8.00 20.00
TTRC10 Hamilton/Kinsler/Cruz 12.50 30.00
TTRC11 Jon Lester/CC Sabathia
David Price 6.00 15.00
TTRC12 Hamilton/Braun/Gonzalez 10.00 25.00
TTRC13 Halladay/Lee/Hamels 20.00 50.00
TTRC14 Stanton/Ramirez/Johnson 12.50 30.00
TTRC15 Ichiro/Hernandez/Figgins 10.00 25.00
TTRC16 Mauer/Posey/McCann 12.50 30.00
TTRC17 Verlan/Cabrera/VMart 15.00 40.00
TTRC18 Choo/Santana/Sizemore 8.00 20.00
TTRC19 Carlos Gonzalez
Troy Tulowitzki/Ubaldo Jimenez 6.00 15.00
TTRC20 Cano/Pedroia/Kinsler 10.00 25.00
TTRC21 Kershaw/Lester/Price 8.00 20.00
TTRC22 Chapman/Votto/Phillips 12.50 30.00
TTRC23 Mauer/Morneau/Liriano 10.00 25.00
TTRC24 Stanton/Heyward/Alvarez 10.00 25.00
TTRC25 Rivera/Sabathia/Hughes 12.50 30.00
TTRC26 Wright/Reyes/Davis 10.00 25.00
TTRC27 Pujols/Holliday/Rasmus 8.00 20.00
TTRC28 Brett Anderson
Trevor Cahill/Gio Gonzalez 6.00 15.00
TTRC29 Bautista/Morrow/Drabek 10.00 25.00
TTRC30 Halladay/Lince/Hernan 12.50 30.00
TTRC31 Walker/Morneau/Votto 12.50 30.00
TTRC32 Fisk/Posada/Posey 10.00 25.00
TTRC33 Jack/Straw/Beltran 12.50 30.00
TTRC34 McCov/How/Field 10.00 25.00
TTRC35 Maric/Lince/Cain 15.00 40.00
TTRC36 Aparicio/Reyes/Andrus 10.00 25.00
TTRC37 Morgan/Alomar/Cano 12.50 30.00
TTRC38 Murray/Teixeira/Jones 10.00 25.00
TTRC39 Campy/Mun/Mauer 15.00 40.00
TTRC40 Ruth/DiMaggio/Mantle 175.00 350.00
TTRC41 Robin/Longo/Zimm 10.00 25.00
TTRC42 Snider/Ethier/Kemp 12.50 30.00
TTRC43 Ryan/Hernandez/Jimenez 15.00 40.00
TTRC44 Sandberg/Castro/Ramirez 15.00 40.00
TTRC45 Schm/Rod/Longo 15.00 40.00
TTRC46 Scavor/Volquez/Cueto 10.00 25.00
TTRC47 Smith/Jeter/Rollins 10.00 25.00
TTRC48 Cobb/Ichiro/Cano 40.00 80.00
TTRC49 Foxx/Pujols/Howard 12.50 30.00
TTRC50 Koufax/Kershaw/Price 30.00 60.00
TTRC51 Dawson/Heyward/Gonzalez 8.00 20.00
TTRC52 Ripken/Jeter/Tulowitzki 20.00 50.00
TTRC53 Gib/Wain/Carp 12.50 30.00
TTRC54 Gwynn/Ichiro/Gonzalez 12.50 30.00
TTRC55 Hend/Craw/McCutch 15.00 40.00
TTRC56 Larkin/Ramirez/Tulowitzki 8.00 20.00
TTRC57 Molitor/Braun/Fielder 12.50 30.00
TTRC58 Musial/Holliday/Rasmus 10.00 25.00
TTRC59 Ford/Sabathia/Rivera 15.00 40.00
TTRC60 DiMaggio/Aaron/Koufax 75.00 150.00

2011 Topps Triple Threads Relic Combos Sepia

*SEPIA: .4X TO 1X BASIC
STATED ODDS 1:31 MINI
STATED PRINT RUN 27 SER.#'d SETS

2011 Topps Triple Threads Relic Combos Double

STATED ODDS 1:78 MINI
STATED PRINT RUN 27 SER.#'d SETS
TTRDC1 Shortstop Superstars 75.00 150.00
TTRDC2 J.Hamilton/J.Votto 30.00 60.00
TTRDC3 Outfield Legends 175.00 350.00
TTRDC4 Jered Weaver/Jon Lester/Felix
Hernandez/Roy Halladay
Tim Lincecum/Ubaldo Ji 20.00 50.00
TTRDC5 Dinger Kings 30.00 60.00
TTRDC6 Roy Halladay/Felix Hernandez 20.00 50.00
TTRDC7 Austin Jackson/Carlos Santana/Jason
Heyward/Buster Posey
Mike Stanton/Starl 20.00 50.00
TTRDC8 Slugging Second Basemen 40.00 80.00
TTRDC9 World Series Champions 100.00 200.00
TTRDC10 3 Time MVPs 100.00 200.00
TTRDC11 Hollywood Heroes 60.00 120.00
TTRDC12 J.DiMaggio/D.Jeter 100.00 200.00
TTRDC13 Light Tower Power 30.00 60.00
TTRDC14 All Time Aces 50.00 100.00
TTRDC15 Meet The Mets 40.00 80.00
TTRDC16 Cas/Gon/Pos/Price/Bau/Buc 20.00 50.00
TTRDC17 Red Sox Re-Load 30.00 60.00
TTRDC18 Throwing Cheese 40.00 80.00

2011 Topps Triple Threads Relic Combos Double Sepia

*SEPIA: .4X TO 1X BASIC
STATED ODDS 1:103 MINI
STATED PRINT RUN 27 SER.#'d SETS

2011 Topps Triple Threads Relics

STATED ODDS 1:11 MINI
STATED PRINT RUN 36 SER.#'d SETS
ALL DC VARIATIONS PRICED EQUALLY
TTR1 Derek Jeter 30.00 60.00
TTR2 Derek Jeter 30.00 60.00
TTR3 Derek Jeter 30.00 60.00
TTR4 Derek Jeter 30.00 60.00
TTR5 Ichiro Suzuki 12.50 30.00
TTR6 Ichiro Suzuki 12.50 30.00
TTR7 Ichiro Suzuki 12.50 30.00
TTR8 Ichiro Suzuki 12.50 30.00
TTR9 Carlos Gonzalez 5.00 12.00
TTR10 Carlos Gonzalez 5.00 12.00
TTR11 Carlos Gonzalez 5.00 12.00
TTR12 Carlos Gonzalez 5.00 12.00
TTR13 Roy Halladay 10.00 25.00
TTR14 Roy Halladay 10.00 25.00
TTR15 Roy Halladay 10.00 25.00
TTR16 Roy Halladay 10.00 25.00
TTR17 Starlin Castro 10.00 25.00
TTR18 Starlin Castro 10.00 25.00
TTR19 Starlin Castro 10.00 25.00
TTR20 Starlin Castro 10.00 25.00
TTR21 CC Sabathia 8.00 20.00
TTR22 CC Sabathia 8.00 20.00
TTR23 CC Sabathia 8.00 20.00
TTR24 Jose Bautista 5.00 12.00
TTR25 Jose Bautista 5.00 12.00
TTR26 Jose Bautista 5.00 12.00
TTR27 Jose Bautista 5.00 12.00
TTR28 Tim Lincecum 12.50 30.00
TTR29 Tim Lincecum 12.50 30.00
TTR30 Tim Lincecum 12.50 30.00
TTR31 Tim Lincecum 12.50 30.00
TTR32 Mark Teixeira 6.00 15.00
TTR33 Mark Teixeira 6.00 15.00
TTR34 Mark Teixeira 6.00 15.00
TTR35 Mark Teixeira 6.00 15.00
TTR36 Josh Johnson 5.00 12.00
TTR37 Josh Johnson 5.00 12.00
TTR38 Josh Johnson 5.00 12.00
TTR39 Josh Johnson 5.00 12.00
TTR40 Shin-Soo Choo 6.00 15.00
TTR41 Shin-Soo Choo 6.00 15.00
TTR42 Shin-Soo Choo 6.00 15.00
TTR43 Ryan Howard 8.00 20.00
TTR44 Ryan Howard 8.00 20.00
TTR45 Ryan Howard 8.00 20.00
TTR46 Ryan Howard 8.00 20.00
TTR47 Dustin Pedroia 10.00 25.00
TTR48 Dustin Pedroia 10.00 25.00
TTR49 Dustin Pedroia 10.00 25.00
TTR50 Dustin Pedroia 10.00 25.00
TTR51 Evan Longoria 6.00 15.00
TTR52 Evan Longoria 6.00 15.00
TTR53 Evan Longoria 6.00 15.00
TTR54 Evan Longoria 6.00 15.00
TTR55 Justin Morneau 6.00 15.00
TTR56 Justin Morneau 6.00 15.00
TTR57 Justin Morneau 6.00 15.00
TTR58 Hanley Ramirez 5.00 12.00
TTR59 Hanley Ramirez 5.00 12.00
TTR60 Hanley Ramirez 5.00 12.00
TTR61 Hanley Ramirez 5.00 12.00
TTR62 Alex Rodriguez 10.00 25.00
TTR63 Alex Rodriguez 10.00 25.00
TTR64 Alex Rodriguez 10.00 25.00
TTR65 Alex Rodriguez 10.00 25.00
TTR66 Joe Mauer 6.00 15.00
TTR67 Joe Mauer 6.00 15.00
TTR68 Joe Mauer 6.00 15.00
TTR69 Joe Mauer 6.00 15.00
TTR70 Joey Votto 12.50 30.00
TTR71 Joey Votto 12.50 30.00
TTR72 Joey Votto 12.50 30.00
TTR73 Joey Votto 12.50 30.00
TTR74 Chase Utley 8.00 20.00
TTR75 Chase Utley 8.00 20.00
TTR76 Chase Utley 8.00 20.00
TTR77 Prince Fielder 8.00 20.00
TTR78 Prince Fielder 8.00 20.00
TTR79 Prince Fielder 8.00 20.00
TTR80 Prince Fielder 8.00 20.00
TTR81 Robinson Cano 10.00 25.00
TTR82 Robinson Cano 10.00 25.00
TTR83 Robinson Cano 10.00 25.00
TTR84 Robinson Cano 10.00 25.00
TTR85 Carlos Santana 5.00 12.00
TTR86 Carlos Santana 5.00 12.00
TTR87 Carlos Santana 5.00 12.00
TTR88 Hunter Pence 6.00 15.00
TTR89 Hunter Pence 6.00 15.00
TTR90 Hunter Pence 6.00 15.00
TTR91 Kevin Youkilis 6.00 15.00
TTR92 Kevin Youkilis 6.00 15.00
TTR93 Kevin Youkilis 6.00 15.00
TTR94 David Wright 6.00 15.00
TTR95 David Wright 6.00 15.00
TTR96 David Wright 6.00 15.00
TTR97 David Wright 6.00 15.00
TTR98 Jon Lester 8.00 20.00
TTR99 Jon Lester 8.00 20.00
TTR100 Jon Lester 8.00 20.00
TTR101 Justin Upton 5.00 12.00
TTR102 Justin Upton 5.00 12.00
TTR103 Justin Upton 5.00 12.00
TTR104 Justin Upton 5.00 12.00
TTR105 Matt Holliday 6.00 15.00
TTR106 Matt Holliday 6.00 15.00
TTR107 Matt Holliday 6.00 15.00
TTR108 Miguel Cabrera 12.50 30.00
TTR109 Miguel Cabrera 12.50 30.00
TTR110 Miguel Cabrera 12.50 30.00
TTR111 Miguel Cabrera 12.50 30.00
TTR112 Jose Reyes 6.00 15.00
TTR113 Jose Reyes 6.00 15.00
TTR114 Jose Reyes 6.00 15.00
TTR115 Josh Hamilton 10.00 25.00
TTR116 Josh Hamilton 10.00 25.00
TTR117 Josh Hamilton 10.00 25.00
TTR118 Josh Hamilton 10.00 25.00
TTR119 Jason Heyward 8.00 20.00
TTR120 Jason Heyward 8.00 20.00
TTR121 Jason Heyward 8.00 20.00
TTR122 Matt Kemp 10.00 25.00
TTR123 Matt Kemp 10.00 25.00
TTR124 Matt Kemp 10.00 25.00
TTR125 Albert Pujols 10.00 25.00
TTR126 Albert Pujols 10.00 25.00
TTR127 Albert Pujols 10.00 25.00
TTR128 Felix Hernandez 6.00 15.00
TTR129 Felix Hernandez 6.00 15.00
TTR130 Felix Hernandez 6.00 15.00
TTR131 Felix Hernandez 6.00 15.00
TTR132 Ryan Braun 10.00 25.00
TTR133 Ryan Braun 10.00 25.00
TTR134 Ryan Braun 10.00 25.00
TTR135 Ryan Braun 10.00 25.00
TTR136 Troy Tulowitzki 8.00 20.00
TTR137 Troy Tulowitzki 8.00 20.00
TTR138 Troy Tulowitzki 8.00 20.00

2011 Topps Triple Threads Relics Emerald

*EMERALD: .5X TO 1.2X BASIC
STATED ODDS 1:21 MINI
STATED PRINT RUN 18 SER.#'d SETS
ALL DC VARIATIONS EQUALLY PRICED

2011 Topps Triple Threads Relics Gold

*GOLD: .6X TO 1.5X BASIC
STATED ODDS 1:41 MINI
STATED PRINT RUN 9 SER.#'d SETS
ALL DC VARIATIONS EQUALLY PRICED

2011 Topps Triple Threads Relics Sepia

*SEPIA: .4X TO 1X BASIC
STATED ODDS 1:14 MINI
STATED PRINT RUN 27 SER.#'d SETS
ALL DC VARIATIONS EQUALLY PRICED

2011 Topps Triple Threads Rookie Phenom Relic Pairs

STATED ODDS 1:168 MINI
STATED PRINT RUN 50 SER.#'d SETS
EXCHANGE DEADLINE 9/30/2014
RFPP1 Aroldis Chapman/Chris Sale 30.00 80.00
RFPP2 B.Posey/N.Feliz 30.00 80.00
RFPP3 Andrew McCutchen
Pedro Alvarez 25.00 60.00
RFPP4 J.Heyward/F.Freeman 25.00 60.00
RFPP5 Mike Stanton/Logan Morrison 25.00 60.00
RFPP6 Starlin Castro/Elvis Andrus 25.00 60.00

2011 Topps Triple Threads Unity Relic Autographs

STATED ODDS 1:6 MINI
STATED PRINT RUN 99 SER.#'d SETS
EXCHANGE DEADLINE 9/30/2014
TTUAR1 Martin Prado 6.00 15.00
TTUAR2 Chipper Jones 20.00 50.00
TTUAR3 Brian McCann 10.00 25.00
TTUAR4 Tim Hudson 6.00 15.00
TTUAR5 Mike Minor 6.00 15.00
TTUAR6 Jason Heyward 8.00 20.00
TTUAR7 Mike Minor 6.00 15.00
TTUAR8 Tommy Hanson 5.00 12.00
TTUAR9 Martin Prado 6.00 15.00
TTUAR10 Colby Rasmus 4.00 10.00
TTUAR11 Matt Holliday 15.00 40.00
TTUAR12 David Freese 10.00 25.00
TTUAR13 Ozzie Smith 20.00 50.00
TTUAR14 Colby Rasmus 4.00 10.00
TTUAR15 Jon Jay 5.00 12.00
TTUAR16 Jason Motte 8.00 20.00
TTUAR17 Allen Craig 6.00 15.00
TTUAR18 Jon Jay 5.00 12.00
TTUAR19 Marlon Byrd 4.00 10.00
TTUAR20 Andrew Cashner 4.00 10.00
TTUAR21 Randy Wells 4.00 10.00
TTUAR22 Marlon Byrd 4.00 10.00
TTUAR23 Aramis Ramirez 4.00 10.00
TTUAR24 Starlin Castro 6.00 15.00
TTUAR25 Marlon Byrd 4.00 10.00
TTUAR26 Tyler Colvin 4.00 10.00
TTUAR27 Andrew Cashner 4.00 10.00
TTUAR28 Pablo Sandoval 10.00 25.00
TTUAR29 Freddy Sanchez 5.00 12.00
TTUAR30 Cody Ross 10.00 25.00
TTUAR31 Pablo Sandoval 10.00 25.00
TTUAR32 Buster Posey 40.00 80.00
TTUAR33 Matt Cain 8.00 20.00
TTUAR34 Cody Ross 6.00 15.00
TTUAR35 Freddy Sanchez 5.00 12.00
TTUAR36 Brian Wilson 15.00 40.00
TTUAR37 Chris Coghlan 4.00 10.00
TTUAR38 Ricky Nolasco 8.00 20.00
TTUAR39 Logan Morrison 4.00 10.00
TTUAR40 Mike Stanton 15.00 40.00
TTUAR41 Hanley Ramirez 8.00 20.00
TTUAR42 Josh Johnson 5.00 12.00
TTUAR43 Gaby Sanchez 4.00 10.00
TTUAR44 Chris Coghlan 4.00 10.00
TTUAR45 Logan Morrison 4.00 10.00
TTUAR46 Angel Pagan 5.00 12.00
TTUAR47 Josh Thole 4.00 10.00
TTUAR48 Ike Davis 6.00 15.00
TTUAR49 Angel Pagan 5.00 12.00
TTUAR50 David Wright 12.50 30.00
TTUAR51 Darryl Strawberry 10.00 25.00
TTUAR52 Angel Pagan 5.00 12.00
TTUAR53 Josh Thole 4.00 10.00
TTUAR54 Jon Niese 5.00 12.00
TTUAR55 Jose Tabata 4.00 10.00
TTUAR56 Garrett Jones 6.00 15.00
TTUAR57 Neil Walker 5.00 12.00
TTUAR58 Jose Tabata 4.00 10.00
TTUAR59 Andrew McCutchen 20.00 50.00
TTUAR60 Pedro Alvarez 6.00 15.00
TTUAR61 Garrett Jones 6.00 15.00
TTUAR62 Neil Walker 5.00 12.00
TTUAR63 Daniel McCutchen 4.00 10.00
TTUAR64 Craig Gentry 6.00 15.00
TTUAR65 Elvis Andrus 6.00 15.00
TTUAR66 Ian Kinsler 10.00 25.00
TTUAR67 Josh Hamilton 30.00 60.00
TTUAR68 Mitch Moreland 5.00 12.00
TTUAR69 Neftali Feliz 6.00 15.00
TTUAR70 Nelson Cruz 6.00 15.00
TTUAR71 Mitch Moreland 6.00 15.00
TTUAR72 Derek Holland 6.00 15.00
TTUAR73 Chris Heisey 8.00 20.00
TTUAR74 Johnny Cueto 4.00 10.00
TTUAR75 Edinson Volquez 5.00 12.00
TTUAR76 Jay Bruce 10.00 25.00
TTUAR77 Johnny Cueto 6.00 15.00
TTUAR78 Aroldis Chapman 10.00 25.00
TTUAR79 Drew Stubbs 5.00 12.00
TTUAR80 Edinson Volquez 5.00 12.00
TTUAR81 Travis Wood 4.00 10.00
TTUAR82 Scott Sizemore 4.00 10.00
TTUAR83 Jhonny Peralta 5.00 12.00
TTUAR84 Ryan Perry 4.00 10.00
TTUAR85 Austin Jackson 8.00 20.00
TTUAR86 Daniel Schlereth 4.00 10.00
TTUAR87 Max Scherzer 20.00 50.00
TTUAR88 Austin Jackson 8.00 20.00
TTUAR89 Rick Porcello 5.00 12.00
TTUAR90 Jhonny Peralta 5.00 12.00
TTUAR91 Torii Hunter 8.00 20.00
TTUAR92 Kendrys Morales 4.00 10.00
TTUAR93 Jered Weaver 8.00 20.00
TTUAR94 Vernon Wells 4.00 10.00
TTUAR95 Kendrys Morales 4.00 10.00
TTUAR96 Jordan Walden 4.00 10.00
TTUAR97 Torii Hunter 8.00 20.00
TTUAR98 Hank Conger 4.00 10.00
TTUAR99 Dan Haren 5.00 12.00

2011 Topps Triple Threads Unity Relic Autographs Emerald

*EMERALD: .5X TO 1.2X BASIC
STATED ODDS 1:11 MINI
STATED PRINT RUN 50 SER.#'d SETS
EXCHANGE DEADLINE 9/30/2014

2011 Topps Triple Threads Unity Relic Autographs Gold

*GOLD: .5X TO 1.2X BASIC
STATED ODDS 1:21 MINI
STATED PRINT RUN 25 SER.#'d SETS
NO PRICING ON MOST DUE SCARCITY
EXCHANGE DEADLINE 9/30/2014

2011 Topps Triple Threads Unity Relic Autographs Sepia

*SEPIA: .4X TO 1X BASIC
STATED ODDS 1:7 MINI
STATED PRINT RUN 75 SER.#'d SETS
EXCHANGE DEADLINE 9/30/2014

2011 Topps Triple Threads Unity Relics

STATED ODDS 1:6 MINI
STATED PRINT RUN 36 SER.#'d SETS
TTUS80 Alfonso Soriano 4.00 10.00
TTUS81 Fergie Jenkins 5.00 12.00
TTUS83 Duke Snider 6.00 15.00
TTUS84 Clayton Kershaw 4.00 10.00
TTUS85 Sandy Koufax 30.00 60.00
TTUS86 Andre Ethier 4.00 10.00
TTUS87 Roy Campanella 8.00 20.00
TTUS88 Matt Kemp 4.00 10.00
TTUS89 Clayton Kershaw 4.00 10.00
TTUS90 Andre Ethier 4.00 10.00
TTUS91 Juan Marichal 4.00 10.00
TTUS92 Brian Wilson 6.00 15.00
TTUS93 Matt Cain 4.00 10.00
TTUS94 Willie McCovey 4.00 10.00
TTUS95 Tim Lincecum 6.00 15.00
TTUS96 Buster Posey 6.00 15.00
TTUS97 Willie McCovey 4.00 10.00
TTUS98 Tim Lincecum 6.00 15.00
TTUS99 Buster Posey 6.00 15.00
TTUSR1 Derek Jeter 10.00 25.00
TTUSR2 Reggie Jackson 6.00 15.00
TTUSR3 Mickey Mantle 30.00 60.00
TTUSR4 Reggie Jackson 6.00 15.00
TTUSR5 Babe Ruth 60.00 120.00
TTUSR6 Joe DiMaggio 30.00 60.00
TTUSR7 Lou Gehrig 50.00 100.00
TTUSR8 Joe DiMaggio 50.00 100.00
TTUSR9 Mariano Rivera 5.00 12.00
TTUS100 Carlos Santana 4.00 10.00
TTUS101 Shin-Soo Choo 4.00 10.00
TTUS102 Roberto Alomar 6.00 15.00
TTUS103 Grady Sizemore 4.00 10.00
TTUS104 Roberto Alomar 6.00 15.00
TTUS105 Albert Belle 5.00 12.00
TTUS106 Carlos Santana 4.00 10.00
TTUS107 Grady Sizemore 4.00 10.00
TTUS108 Albert Belle 5.00 12.00
TTUS109 Alex Rodriguez 6.00 15.00
TTUS110 Ichiro Suzuki 12.50 30.00
TTUS111 Felix Hernandez 4.00 10.00
TTUS112 Alex Rodriguez 6.00 15.00
TTUS113 Ichiro Suzuki 12.50 30.00
TTUS114 Felix Hernandez 4.00 10.00
TTUS115 Alex Rodriguez 6.00 15.00
TTUS116 Ichiro Suzuki 12.50 30.00
TTUS117 Felix Hernandez 4.00 10.00
TTUS118 Hanley Ramirez 4.00 10.00
TTUS119 Josh Johnson 4.00 10.00
TTUS120 Logan Morrison 4.00 10.00
TTUS121 Mike Stanton 5.00 12.00
TTUS122 Hanley Ramirez 4.00 10.00
TTUS123 Josh Johnson 4.00 10.00
TTUS124 Mike Stanton 5.00 12.00
TTUS125 Hanley Ramirez 4.00 10.00
TTUS126 Logan Morrison 4.00 10.00
TTUS127 Darryl Strawberry 4.00 10.00
TTUS128 Tom Seaver 5.00 12.00
TTUS129 Johan Santana 4.00 10.00
TTUS130 David Wright 6.00 15.00
TTUS131 Nolan Ryan 12.50 30.00
TTUS132 Jose Reyes 6.00 15.00
TTUS133 Tom Seaver 5.00 12.00
TTUS134 Jose Reyes 6.00 15.00
TTUS135 Darryl Strawberry 4.00 10.00
TTUS136 Nick Markakis 4.00 10.00
TTUS137 Eddie Murray 5.00 12.00
TTUS138 Adam Jones 4.00 10.00
TTUS139 Jim Palmer 4.00 10.00
TTUS140 Cal Ripken Jr. 10.00 25.00
TTUS141 Brooks Robinson 6.00 15.00
TTUS142 Frank Robinson 4.00 10.00
TTUS143 Brian Roberts 4.00 10.00
TTUS144 Brian Matusz 4.00 10.00
TTUS145 Mat Latos 4.00 10.00
TTUS146 Heath Bell 4.00 10.00
TTUS147 Tony Gwynn 6.00 15.00
TTUS148 Tony Gwynn 6.00 15.00
TTUS149 Ozzie Smith 6.00 15.00
TTUS150 Willie McCovey 4.00 10.00
TTUS151 Mat Latos 4.00 10.00
TTUS152 Tony Gwynn 6.00 15.00
TTUS153 Heath Bell 4.00 10.00
TTUS154 Mike Schmidt 6.00 15.00
TTUS155 Roy Halladay 8.00 20.00
TTUS156 Jimmy Rollins 4.00 10.00
TTUS157 Ryan Howard 5.00 12.00
TTUS158 Mike Schmidt 6.00 15.00
TTUS159 Chase Utley 4.00 10.00
TTUS160 Roy Halladay 8.00 20.00
TTUS161 Ryan Howard 5.00 12.00
TTUS162 Chase Utley 4.00 10.00
TTUS163 Andrew McCutchen 4.00 10.00
TTUS164 Jose Tabata 4.00 10.00
TTUS165 Pedro Alvarez 4.00 10.00
TTUS166 Honus Wagner 40.00 80.00
TTUS167 Andrew McCutchen 4.00 10.00
TTUS168 Jose Tabata 4.00 10.00
TTUS169 Andrew McCutchen 4.00 10.00
TTUS170 Jose Tabata 4.00 10.00
TTUS171 Pedro Alvarez 4.00 10.00
TTUS172 Michael Young 4.00 10.00
TTUS173 Nelson Cruz 4.00 10.00
TTUS174 Ian Kinsler 4.00 10.00
TTUS175 Nolan Ryan 12.50 30.00
TTUS176 Josh Hamilton 5.00 12.00
TTUS177 Alex Rodriguez 6.00 15.00
TTUS178 Vladimir Guerrero 4.00 10.00
TTUS179 Josh Hamilton 5.00 12.00
TTUS180 Ian Kinsler 4.00 10.00
TTUS181 Evan Longoria 4.00 10.00
TTUS182 David Price 4.00 10.00
TTUS183 B.J. Upton 4.00 10.00
TTUS184 Evan Longoria 4.00 10.00
TTUS185 David Price 4.00 10.00
TTUS186 B.J. Upton 4.00 10.00
TTUS187 Evan Longoria 4.00 10.00
TTUS188 David Price 4.00 10.00
TTUS189 Jeremy Hellickson 4.00 10.00
TTUS190 Nomar Garciaparra 6.00 15.00
TTUS191 David Ortiz 4.00 10.00
TTUS192 Kevin Youkilis 4.00 10.00
TTUS193 Jimmie Foxx 12.50 30.00
TTUS194 Jon Lester 4.00 10.00
TTUS195 Dustin Pedroia 4.00 10.00
TTUS196 Manny Ramirez 5.00 12.00
TTUS197 Carlton Fisk 5.00 12.00
TTUS199 Barry Larkin 6.00 15.00
TTUS200 Jay Bruce 4.00 10.00
TTUS201 Johnny Cueto 4.00 10.00
TTUS202 Johnny Bench 6.00 15.00
TTUS203 Joey Votto 5.00 12.00
TTUS204 Tom Seaver 5.00 12.00
TTUS205 Frank Robinson 4.00 10.00
TTUS206 Joe Morgan 4.00 10.00
TTUS207 Aroldis Chapman 5.00 12.00
TTUS208 Matt Holliday 4.00 10.00
TTUS209 Ubaldo Jimenez 4.00 10.00
TTUS210 Troy Tulowitzki 4.00 10.00
TTUS211 Larry Walker 4.00 10.00
TTUS212 Carlos Gonzalez 4.00 10.00
TTUS213 Todd Helton 4.00 10.00
TTUS214 Ubaldo Jimenez 4.00 10.00
TTUS215 Troy Tulowitzki 4.00 10.00
TTUS216 Larry Walker 4.00 10.00
TTUS217 Justin Verlander 6.00 15.00
TTUS218 Miguel Cabrera 6.00 15.00
TTUS219 Al Kaline 10.00 25.00
TTUS220 Ty Cobb 30.00 60.00
TTUS221 Miguel Cabrera 6.00 15.00
TTUS222 Al Kaline 10.00 25.00
TTUS223 Austin Jackson 4.00 10.00
TTUS224 Miguel Cabrera 6.00 15.00
TTUS225 Justin Verlander 6.00 15.00
TTUS226 Francisco Liriano 4.00 10.00
TTUS227 Joe Mauer 4.00 10.00
TTUS228 Justin Morneau 5.00 12.00
TTUS229 Bert Blyleven 5.00 12.00
TTUS230 Joe Mauer 4.00 10.00
TTUS231 Justin Morneau 5.00 12.00
TTUS233 Joe Mauer 4.00 10.00
TTUS234 Justin Morneau 5.00 12.00
TTUS235 Luis Aparicio 5.00 12.00
TTUS236 Gordon Beckham 4.00 10.00
TTUS237 John Danks 4.00 10.00
TTUS238 Carlton Fisk 5.00 12.00
TTUS239 Mark Buehrle 4.00 10.00
TTUS240 Paul Konerko 4.00 10.00
TTUS241 Alex Rios 4.00 10.00
TTUS242 Carlos Quentin 4.00 10.00
TTUS243 Alexei Ramirez 4.00 10.00
TTUS244 Justin Upton 4.00 10.00
TTUS245 Stephen Drew 4.00 10.00
TTUS246 Kelly Johnson 4.00 10.00
TTUS247 Justin Upton 4.00 10.00
TTUS248 Stephen Drew 4.00 10.00
TTUS249 Chris Young 4.00 10.00
TTUS250 Justin Upton 4.00 10.00
TTUS251 Stephen Drew 4.00 10.00
TTUS252 Miguel Montero 4.00 10.00
TTUS253 Stephen Strasburg 8.00 20.00
TTUS254 Ryan Zimmerman 4.00 10.00
TTUS255 Jayson Werth 4.00 10.00
TTUS256 Stephen Strasburg 8.00 20.00
TTUS257 Ryan Zimmerman 4.00 10.00
TTUS258 Jayson Werth 4.00 10.00
TTUS259 Stephen Strasburg 8.00 20.00
TTUS260 Ryan Zimmerman 4.00 10.00
TTUS261 Jayson Werth 4.00 10.00
TTUS262 Zack Greinke 4.00 10.00
TTUS263 Billy Butler 4.00 10.00
TTUS264 Joakim Soria 4.00 10.00
TTUS265 Billy Butler 4.00 10.00
TTUS266 Joakim Soria 4.00 10.00
TTUS267 Alex Gordon 4.00 10.00
TTUS268 Billy Butler 4.00 10.00
TTUS269 Joakim Soria 4.00 10.00
TTUS270 Alex Gordon 4.00 10.00
TTUSR10 Torii Hunter 4.00 10.00
TTUSR11 Kendrys Morales 4.00 10.00
TTUSR12 Jered Weaver 4.00 10.00
TTUSR13 Torii Hunter 4.00 10.00
TTUSR14 Nolan Ryan 12.50 30.00
TTUSR15 Reggie Jackson 6.00 15.00
TTUSR16 Torii Hunter 4.00 10.00
TTUSR17 Nolan Ryan 12.50 30.00
TTUSR18 Reggie Jackson 6.00 15.00
TTUSR19 Nolan Ryan 12.50 30.00
TTUSR20 Joe Morgan 4.00 10.00
TTUSR21 Hunter Pence 4.00 10.00
TTUSR22 Nolan Ryan 12.50 30.00
TTUSR23 Joe Morgan 4.00 10.00
TTUSR24 Lance Berkman 4.00 10.00
TTUSR25 Nolan Ryan 12.50 30.00
TTUSR26 Joe Morgan 4.00 10.00
TTUSR27 Hunter Pence 4.00 10.00
TTUSR28 Rickey Henderson 10.00 25.00
TTUSR29 Reggie Jackson 6.00 15.00
TTUSR30 Brett Anderson 4.00 10.00
TTUSR31 Rickey Henderson 10.00 25.00
TTUSR32 Reggie Jackson 6.00 15.00
TTUSR33 Rollie Fingers 4.00 10.00
TTUSR34 Rickey Henderson 10.00 25.00
TTUSR35 Rollie Fingers 4.00 10.00
TTUSR36 Kurt Suzuki 4.00 10.00
TTUSR37 Vernon Wells 4.00 10.00
TTUSR38 Paul Molitor 5.00 12.00
TTUSR39 Aaron Hill 4.00 10.00
TTUSR40 Roberto Alomar 6.00 15.00
TTUSR41 Roy Halladay 8.00 20.00
TTUSR42 Jose Bautista 4.00 10.00
TTUSR43 Roberto Alomar 6.00 15.00
TTUSR44 Roy Halladay 8.00 20.00
TTUSR45 Jose Bautista 4.00 10.00
TTUSR46 Hank Aaron 12.50 30.00
TTUSR47 Chipper Jones 6.00 15.00
TTUSR48 Brian McCann 4.00 10.00
TTUSR49 Hank Aaron 12.50 30.00
TTUSR50 John Smoltz 4.00 10.00
TTUSR51 Jason Heyward 4.00 10.00
TTUSR52 Hank Aaron 12.50 30.00
TTUSR53 Tommy Hanson 4.00 10.00
TTUSR54 Jason Heyward 4.00 10.00
TTUSR55 Paul Molitor 5.00 12.00
TTUSR56 Ryan Braun 6.00 15.00
TTUSR57 Prince Fielder 4.00 10.00
TTUSR58 Paul Molitor 5.00 12.00
TTUSR59 Ryan Braun 6.00 15.00
TTUSR60 Prince Fielder 4.00 10.00
TTUSR61 Paul Molitor 5.00 12.00
TTUSR62 Ryan Braun 6.00 15.00
TTUSR63 Yovani Gallardo 4.00 10.00
TTUSR64 Ozzie Smith 6.00 15.00
TTUSR65 Matt Holliday 4.00 10.00
TTUSR66 Bob Gibson 6.00 15.00
TTUSR67 Stan Musial 10.00 25.00
TTUSR68 Albert Pujols 10.00 25.00
TTUSR69 Rogers Hornsby 10.00 25.00
TTUSR70 Albert Pujols 10.00 25.00
TTUSR71 Adam Wainwright 4.00 10.00
TTUSR72 Johnny Mize 6.00 15.00
TTUSR73 Starlin Castro 4.00 10.00
TTUSR74 Fergie Jenkins 5.00 12.00
TTUSR75 Ryne Sandberg 8.00 20.00
TTUSR76 Andre Dawson 4.00 10.00
TTUSR77 Starlin Castro 4.00 10.00
TTUSR78 Ryne Sandberg 8.00 20.00
TTUSR79 Aramis Ramirez 4.00 10.00

2011 Topps Triple Threads Unity Relics Emerald

*EMERALD: .5X TO 1.2X BASIC
STATED ODDS 1:11 MINI
STATED PRINT RUN 18 SER.#'d SETS
ALL VERSIONS EQUALLY PRICED
SOME NOT PRICED DUE TO SCARCITY

2011 Topps Triple Threads Unity Relics Gold

*GOLD: .6X TO 1.5X BASIC
STATED ODDS 1:21 MINI
STATED PRINT RUN 9 SER.#'d SETS
ALL VERSIONS EQUALLY PRICED
SOME NOT PRICED DUE TO SCARCITY

2011 Topps Triple Threads Unity Relics Sepia

*SEPIA: .4X TO 1X BASIC

STATED ODDS 1:7 MINI
STATED PRINT RUN 27 SER.#'d SETS

2012 Topps Triple Threads

COMMON CARD (1-100) .30 .75
COMMON JSY AU RC (101-165) 5.00 12.00
JSY AU RC ODDS 1:10 MINI
JSY AU RC PRINT RUN 99 SER.#'d SETS
COMMON JSY AU (101-165) 5.00 12.00
JSY AU ODDS 1:10 MINI
JSY AU PRINT RUN 99 SER.#'d SETS
EXCHANGE DEADLINE 8/31/2015
OVERALL 1-100 PLATE ODDS 1:145 HOBBY
PLATE PRINT RUN 1 SET PER COLOR
BLACK-CYAN-MAGENTA-YELLOW ISSUED
NO PLATE PRICING DUE TO SCARCITY
1 Albert Pujols 1.00 2.50
2 Carlos Gonzalez .60 1.50
3 Adam Jones .60 1.50
4 Wade Boggs .50 1.25
5 Evan Longoria .60 1.50
6 Roberto Clemente 2.00 5.00
7 Mickey Mantle 2.50 6.00
8 Chase Utley .60 1.50
9 Dave Winfield .50 1.25
10 Buster Posey 1.00 2.50
11 Babe Ruth 2.00 5.00
12 Matt Kemp .60 1.50
13 Troy Tulowitzki .75 2.00
14 Matt Holliday .75 2.00
15 David Price .60 1.50
16 Jay Bruce .60 1.50
17 Alex Rodriguez 1.00 2.50
18 Reggie Jackson .50 1.25
19 Craig Kimbrel .60 1.50
20 Gary Carter .50 1.25
21 Don Mattingly 1.50 4.00
22 Ryan Braun .50 1.25
23 Giancarlo Stanton .75 2.00
24 Alex Gordon .60 1.50
25 Frank Robinson .50 1.25
26 Tim Lincecum .60 1.50
27 Justin Upton .60 1.50
28 CC Sabathia .60 1.50
29 Hunter Pence .60 1.50
30 Joe DiMaggio 1.50 4.00
31 Justin Verlander .75 2.00
32 Mike Schmidt 1.25 3.00
33 Ryan Zimmerman .60 1.50
34 Sandy Koufax 1.50 4.00
35 Hanley Ramirez .60 1.50
36 Jose Reyes .60 1.50
37 Lou Gehrig 1.50 4.00
38 Ian Kinsler .60 1.50
39 Felix Hernandez .60 1.50
40 Ichiro Suzuki 1.00 2.50
41 Tony Gwynn .75 2.00
42 David Ortiz .75 2.00
43 Miguel Cabrera .75 2.00
44 Tom Seaver .50 1.25
45 Jose Bautista .60 1.50
46 Josh Hamilton .60 1.50
47 Ty Cobb 1.25 3.00
48 David Freese .50 1.25
49 Dan Uggla .60 1.50
50 Andrew McCutchen .75 2.00
51 Stan Musial 1.25 3.00
52 Juan Marichal .50 1.25
53 Adrian Gonzalez .60 1.50
54 Nolan Ryan 2.50 6.00
55 Jacoby Ellsbury .60 1.50
56 Willie Mays 1.50 4.00
57 Eddie Mathews .75 2.00
58 Ryne Sandberg 1.50 4.00
59 Prince Fielder .60 1.50
60 Yogi Berra .75 2.00
61 Duke Snider .50 1.25
62 Kevin Youkilis .75 2.00
63 Willie McCovey .50 1.25
64 Carl Yastrzemski 1.25 3.00
65 Roger Maris .75 2.00
66 Adrian Beltre .75 2.00
67 Stephen Strasburg .75 2.00
68 Rickey Henderson .75 2.00
69 David Wright .60 1.50
70 Brian McCann .60 1.50
71 Jon Lester .50 1.25
72 Jered Weaver .60 1.50
73 Andre Dawson .50 1.25
74 Dustin Pedroia .60 1.50
75 Cole Hamels .60 1.50
76 Robinson Cano .60 1.50
77 Brooks Robinson .50 1.25
78 Curtis Granderson .60 1.50
79 Ozzie Smith 1.00 2.50
80 Pablo Sandoval .60 1.50
81 Cal Ripken Jr. 2.50 6.00
82 Mark Teixeira .60 1.50
83 Ryan Howard .60 1.50
84 Nelson Cruz .75 2.00
85 Bob Feller .50 1.25
86 Bob Gibson .50 1.25
87 Joe Mauer .60 1.50
88 Roy Halladay .60 1.50
89 Johnny Bench .75 2.00
90 George Brett 1.50 4.00
91 Paul Molitor .75 2.00
92 Derek Jeter 2.00 5.00
93 Carlton Fisk .50 1.25
94 Brandon Phillips .50 1.25
95 Clayton Kershaw 1.50 4.00
96 Joey Votto .75 2.00
97 Cliff Lee .60 1.50
98 Jackie Robinson .75 2.00
99 Mariano Rivera 1.00 2.50
100 Ken Griffey Jr. 1.50 4.00
101 Carlos Santana Jsy AU 6.00 15.00
102 Madison Bumgarner Jsy AU 30.00 80.00
103 Brandon Belt Jsy AU 8.00 20.00
104 Ben Revere Jsy AU 8.00 20.00
105 Dee Gordon Jsy AU EXCH 10.00 25.00
106 Derek Holland Jsy AU 6.00 15.00
107 Anthony Rizzo Jsy AU 12.00 30.00
108 Chris Sale Jsy AU 8.00 20.00
109 Drew Storen Jsy AU 6.00 15.00
110 Eduardo Nunez Jsy AU 5.00 12.00
111 Jason Kipnis Jsy AU 6.00 15.00
112 Jemile Weeks Jsy AU RC 6.00 15.00
113 Wilin Rosario Jsy AU RC 8.00 20.00
114 Jordan Walden Jsy AU 5.00 12.00
115 Mike Minor Jsy AU 4.00 10.00
116 Todd Frazier Jsy AU 8.00 20.00
117 Randall Delgado Jsy AU 5.00 12.00
118 Wilson Ramos Jsy AU 5.00 12.00
119 Yonder Alonso Jsy AU 6.00 15.00
120 Aroldis Chapman Jsy AU 10.00 25.00
121 Jacob Turner Jsy AU 8.00 20.00
122 Neftali Feliz Jsy AU 6.00 15.00
123 Drew Pomeranz Jsy AU RC 8.00 20.00
124 Ike Davis Jsy AU 8.00 20.00
125 Jason Heyward Jsy AU 10.00 25.00
126 Daniel Hudson Jsy AU 6.00 15.00
127 Jordan Zimmermann Jsy AU 6.00 15.00
129 Bryce Harper Jsy AU RC 150.00 300.00
131 Addison Reed Jsy AU RC 6.00 15.00
132 Tyler Pastornicky Jsy AU RC 6.00 15.00
134 Zack Cozart Jsy AU 6.00 15.00
135 B.Jackson Jsy AU RC EXCH 6.00 15.00
136 Devin Mesoraco Jsy AU RC 6.00 15.00
137 Vance Worley Jsy AU 6.00 15.00
138 Yoenis Cespedes Jsy AU RC 12.00 30.00
139 Yu Darvish Jsy AU RC 75.00 200.00
140 Jerry Sands Jsy AU 5.00 12.00
141 Ivan Nova Jsy AU 6.00 15.00
142 Matt Moore Jsy AU RC 10.00 25.00
143 Brett Lawrie Jsy AU RC 10.00 25.00
144 Jesus Montero Jsy AU RC 6.00 15.00
145 Mark Trumbo Jsy AU 6.00 15.00
146 Mike Trout Jsy AU 300.00 600.00
147 Michael Pineda Jsy AU 12.50 30.00
148 Dustin Ackley Jsy AU 6.00 15.00
149 Eric Hosmer Jsy AU 12.50 30.00
150 Freddie Freeman Jsy AU EXCH 12.50 30.00
151 Mike Moustakas Jsy AU 10.00 25.00
152 Starlin Castro Jsy AU 8.00 20.00
153 Paul Goldschmidt Jsy AU 20.00 50.00
154 Jeremy Hellickson Jsy AU 8.00 20.00
155 Matt Adams Jsy AU RC 15.00 40.00
156 Logan Morrison Jsy AU 5.00 12.00
157 Lonnie Chisenhall Jsy AU 6.00 15.00
158 Kyle Seager Jsy AU 6.00 15.00
159 Salvador Perez Jsy AU 15.00 40.00
160 J.D. Martinez Jsy AU 12.00 30.00
161 Cory Luebke Jsy AU 5.00 12.00
162 Danny Duffy Jsy AU 6.00 15.00
163 Kirk Nieuwenhuis Jsy AU RC 6.00 15.00
164 Jose Altuve Jsy AU 40.00 100.00
165 Julio Teheran Jsy AU 6.00 15.00

2012 Topps Triple Threads Amber

*AMBER: .75X TO 2X BASIC
STATED ODDS 1:5 MINI
STATED PRINT RUN 125 SER.#'d SETS

2012 Topps Triple Threads Emerald

*EMERALD 1-100: .6X TO 1.5X BASIC
1-100 ODDS 1:3 MINI
1-100 PRINT RUN 250 SER.#'d SETS
*EMERALD JSY AU: .4X TO 1X BASIC
EMERALD JSY AU ODDS 1:18 MINI
EM.JSY AU PRINT RUN 50 SER.#'d SETS
EXCHANGE DEADLINE 8/31/2015
128 Jarrod Parker Jsy AU 15.00 40.00
130 Trevor Bauer Jsy AU 15.00 40.00
133 Ryan Lavarnway Jsy AU 10.00 25.00
139 Yu Darvish Jsy AU 150.00 250.00

2012 Topps Triple Threads Gold

*GOLD 1-100: 1X TO 2.5X BASIC
1-100 ODDS 1:6 MINI
1-100 PRINT RUN 99 SER.#'d SETS
101-165 ODDS 1:36 HOBBY
101-165 PRINT RUN 25 SER.#'d SETS
NO 101-165 PRICING DUE TO SCARCITY
EXCHANGE DEADLINE 8/31/2015

2012 Topps Triple Threads Onyx

*ONYX: 2X TO 5X BASIC
STATED ODDS 1:12 MINI
STATED PRINT RUN 50 SER.#'d SETS

2012 Topps Triple Threads Sepia

*SEPIA 1-100: .5X TO 1.2X BASIC
1-100 RANDOMLY INSERTED
1-100 PRINT RUN 625 SER.#'d SETS
*SEPIA JSY AU: .4X TO 1X BASIC
SEPIA JSY AU ODDS 1:14 MINI
SEP.JSY AU PRINT RUN 75 SER.#'d SETS
EXCHANGE DEADLINE 08/31/2015
130 Trevor Bauer Jsy AU 15.00 40.00

2012 Topps Triple Threads Autograph Relic Combos

STATED ODDS 1:95 MINI
STATED PRINT RUN 36 SER.#'d SETS
EXCHANGE DEADLINE 8/31/2015
ARC1 Verland/Miggy/Prince 200.00 300.00
ARC2 Hamilton/Cruz/Napoli 15.00 40.00
ARC3 Dave Kingman/Ken Griffey Sr.
Greg Luzinski 20.00 50.00
ARC4 Fielder/Mattingly/Clark 100.00 200.00
ARC5 Cooper/Buckner/Clark 30.00 80.00
ARC6 George Bell/Andy Van Slyke
Ken Griffey Sr. 20.00 50.00
ARC7 Price/Hellickson/Moore 40.00 80.00
ARC8 Kershaw/Kemp/Ethier 75.00 150.00
ARC9 Cespedes/Montero/Trout 125.00 250.00
ARC10 Golds/Hosmer/Freeman 30.00 60.00
ARC11 Lawrie/ZimmerM/Freese 10.00 25.00
ARC12 Uggla/Heyward/McCann 20.00 50.00
ARC13 Aramis/Braun/Weeks 20.00 50.00
ARC14 Castro/Gordon/Andrus 20.00 50.00
ARC15 Santana/Weaver/Wilson 30.00 60.00
ARC16 Hanley/Stanton/Johnson 30.00 60.00
ARC17 Kershaw/Kemp/Gordon 50.00 100.00

2012 Topps Triple Threads Autograph Relic Combos Sepia

*SEPIA: .4X TO 1X BASIC
STATED ODDS 1:126 MINI
STATED PRINT RUN 27 SER.#'d SETS
EXCHANGE DEADLINE 8/31/2015

2012 Topps Triple Threads Flashback Relics

STATED ODDS 1:65 MINI
STATED PRINT RUN 36 SER.#'d SETS
FR1 Ty Cobb 50.00 100.00
FR2 Joe Morgan 12.50 30.00
FR3 Harmon Killebrew 20.00 50.00
FR4 Alex Rodriguez 12.50 30.00
FR5 Chipper Jones 50.00 100.00
FR6 David Ortiz 6.00 15.00
FR7 Cliff Lee 10.00 25.00
FR8 Roy Halladay 12.50 30.00
FR9 CC Sabathia 12.50 30.00
FR10 Mariano Rivera 15.00 40.00
FR11 Dave Winfield 8.00 20.00
FR12 Rickey Henderson 10.00 25.00
FR13 Albert Pujols 10.00 25.00
FR14 Paul Molitor 12.50 30.00
FR15 Johan Santana 10.00 25.00
FR16 Ozzie Smith 12.50 30.00
FR17 Jose Bautista 6.00 15.00
FR18 Derek Jeter 50.00 100.00
FR19 Tom Seaver 12.50 30.00
FR20 Tony Gwynn 12.50 30.00
FR21 Robin Yount 12.50 30.00
FR22 Cal Ripken Jr. 30.00 60.00
FR23 Gary Carter 15.00 40.00
FR24 Dwight Gooden 12.50 30.00
FR25 George Brett 20.00 50.00

2012 Topps Triple Threads Flashback Relics Sepia

*SEPIA: .4X TO 1X BASIC
STATED ODDS 1:86 MINI
STATED PRINT RUN 27 SER.#'D SETS

2012 Topps Triple Threads Legend Relics

STATED ODDS 1:81 MINI
STATED PRINT RUN 36 SER.#'d SETS
TTRL1 Joe Morgan 10.00 25.00
TTRL2 Rickey Henderson 15.00 40.00
TTRL3 Eddie Murray 12.50 30.00
TTRL4 Dave Winfield 10.00 25.00
TTRL5 Cal Ripken Jr. 40.00 80.00
TTRL6 Carl Yastrzemski 12.50 30.00
TTRL7 Roberto Clemente 60.00 120.00
TTRL8 Harmon Killebrew 15.00 40.00
TTRL9 Brooks Robinson 15.00 40.00
TTRL10 Willie Mays 40.00 80.00
TTRL11 Tony Gwynn 10.00 25.00
TTRL12 Sandy Koufax 50.00 100.00
TTRL13 Jackie Robinson 30.00 60.00
TTRL14 Ty Cobb 50.00 100.00
TTRL15 Joe DiMaggio 50.00 100.00
TTRL16 Mickey Mantle 60.00 120.00
TTRL17 Willie McCovey 10.00 25.00
TTRL18 Stan Musial 30.00 60.00
TTRL19 Mike Schmidt 12.50 30.00
TTRL20 George Brett 15.00 40.00

2012 Topps Triple Threads Legend Relics Sepia

*SEPIA: .4X TO 1X BASIC
STATED ODDS 1:107 MINI
STATED PRINT RUN 27 SER.#'d SETS

2012 Topps Triple Threads Relic Autographs

STATED ODDS 1:12 MINI
STATED PRINT RUN 18 SER.#'d SETS
ALL DC VARIATIONS PRICED EQUALLY
NO PRICING ON PLAYERS W/ONE DC VERSION
EXCHANGE DEADLINE 8/31/2015
TTAR1 Billy Butler 12.50 30.00
TTAR2 Billy Butler 12.50 30.00
TTAR3 Billy Butler 12.50 30.00
TTAR4 Steve Garvey 30.00 60.00
TTAR5 Steve Garvey 30.00 60.00
TTAR6 Steve Garvey 30.00 60.00
TTAR7 Steve Garvey 30.00 60.00
TTAR8 Steve Garvey 30.00 60.00
TTAR9 Yovani Gallardo 8.00 20.00
TTAR10 Yovani Gallardo 8.00 20.00
TTAR11 Yovani Gallardo 8.00 20.00
TTAR12 Yovani Gallardo 8.00 20.00
TTAR13 Yovani Gallardo 8.00 20.00
TTAR14 Tim Hudson 12.50 30.00
TTAR15 Tim Hudson 12.50 30.00
TTAR16 Tim Hudson 12.50 30.00
TTAR17 Tim Hudson 12.50 30.00
TTAR18 Tim Hudson 12.50 30.00
TTAR19 Tommy Hanson 8.00 20.00
TTAR20 Tommy Hanson 8.00 20.00
TTAR21 Tommy Hanson 8.00 20.00
TTAR22 Tommy Hanson 8.00 20.00
TTAR23 Tommy Hanson 8.00 20.00
TTAR24 Albert Belle 12.00 30.00
TTAR25 Albert Belle 12.00 30.00
TTAR26 Albert Belle 12.00 30.00
TTAR28 Andy Van Slyke 12.50 30.00
TTAR29 Andy Van Slyke 12.50 30.00
TTAR30 Andy Van Slyke 12.50 30.00
TTAR31 Carlos Gonzalez EXCH 12.50 30.00
TTAR32 Carlos Gonzalez EXCH 12.50 30.00
TTAR33 Carlos Gonzalez EXCH 12.50 30.00
TTAR34 Carlos Gonzalez EXCH 12.50 30.00
TTAR35 Carlos Gonzalez EXCH 12.50 30.00
TTAR36 Pablo Sandoval 15.00 40.00
TTAR37 Pablo Sandoval 15.00 40.00
TTAR38 Pablo Sandoval 15.00 40.00
TTAR39 Pablo Sandoval 15.00 40.00
TTAR40 Pablo Sandoval 15.00 40.00
TTAR41 Jose Bautista 20.00 50.00
TTAR42 Jose Bautista 20.00 50.00
TTAR43 Jose Bautista 20.00 50.00
TTAR44 Vida Blue 20.00 50.00
TTAR45 Vida Blue 20.00 50.00
TTAR46 Ryan Braun 40.00 80.00
TTAR47 Ryan Braun 10.00 25.00
TTAR48 Andre Ethier EXCH 10.00 25.00
TTAR49 Andre Ethier EXCH 10.00 25.00
TTAR50 Andre Ethier EXCH 10.00 25.00
TTAR51 Andre Ethier EXCH 10.00 25.00
TTAR52 Andre Ethier EXCH 6.00 15.00
TTAR54 Madison Bumgarner 30.00 80.00
TTAR55 Madison Bumgarner 30.00 80.00
TTAR56 Madison Bumgarner 30.00 80.00
TTAR57 Madison Bumgarner 30.00 80.00
TTAR58 Madison Bumgarner 30.00 80.00
TTAR59 Cecil Cooper 12.50 30.00
TTAR60 Cecil Cooper 12.50 30.00
TTAR61 Cecil Cooper 12.50 30.00
TTAR64 Orlando Cepeda 20.00 50.00
TTAR65 Orlando Cepeda 20.00 50.00
TTAR66 Orlando Cepeda 20.00 50.00
TTAR67 James Shields 8.00 20.00
TTAR68 James Shields 8.00 20.00
TTAR69 James Shields 8.00 20.00
TTAR70 James Shields 8.00 20.00
TTAR71 James Shields 8.00 20.00
TTAR72 Dennis Eckersley 15.00 40.00
TTAR73 Dennis Eckersley 15.00 40.00
TTAR76 George Bell 12.50 30.00
TTAR77 George Bell 12.50 30.00
TTAR81 Dale Murphy 40.00 80.00
TTAR82 Dale Murphy 40.00 80.00
TTAR83 Dale Murphy 40.00 80.00
TTAR84 Dale Murphy 40.00 80.00
TTAR86 Ian Kennedy 8.00 20.00
TTAR87 Ian Kennedy 8.00 20.00
TTAR88 Ian Kennedy 8.00 20.00
TTAR89 Ian Kennedy 8.00 20.00
TTAR90 Ian Kennedy 8.00 20.00
TTAR91 Ricky Romero 10.00 25.00
TTAR92 Ricky Romero 10.00 25.00
TTAR93 Giancarlo Stanton 30.00 60.00
TTAR94 Giancarlo Stanton 30.00 60.00
TTAR95 Giancarlo Stanton 30.00 60.00
TTAR96 Alex Gordon 15.00 40.00
TTAR97 Alex Gordon 15.00 40.00
TTAR98 C.J. Wilson 12.50 30.00
TTAR99 C.J. Wilson 12.50 30.00
TTAR100 C.J. Wilson 12.50 30.00
TTAR102 Cole Hamels 10.00 25.00
TTAR103 Cole Hamels 10.00 25.00
TTAR104 Cole Hamels 10.00 25.00
TTAR105 Cole Hamels 10.00 25.00
TTAR106 Eric Hosmer 15.00 40.00
TTAR107 Jered Weaver 15.00 40.00
TTAR108 Jered Weaver 15.00 40.00
TTAR109 Jered Weaver 15.00 40.00
TTAR110 Jered Weaver 15.00 40.00
TTAR111 Jered Weaver 15.00 40.00
TTAR115 Jon Lester 10.00 25.00
TTAR116 Jon Lester 10.00 25.00
TTAR117 Nelson Cruz 8.00 20.00
TTAR118 Nelson Cruz 8.00 20.00
TTAR119 Nelson Cruz 8.00 20.00
TTAR120 Nelson Cruz 8.00 20.00
TTAR121 Rickie Weeks 10.00 25.00
TTAR122 Rickie Weeks 10.00 25.00
TTAR123 Rickie Weeks 10.00 25.00
TTAR124 Billy Butler 10.00 25.00
TTAR125 Duke Snider 40.00 80.00
TTAR127 Billy Butler 10.00 25.00
TTAR128 Ike Davis 12.50 30.00
TTAR129 Ike Davis 12.50 30.00
TTAR130 Ike Davis 12.50 30.00
TTAR131 Steve Carlton 20.00 50.00
TTAR133 Clayton Kershaw 30.00 60.00
TTAR134 Clayton Kershaw 30.00 60.00
TTAR135 Clayton Kershaw 30.00 60.00
TTAR136 Clayton Kershaw 30.00 60.00
TTAR137 Clayton Kershaw 30.00 60.00
TTAR138 Ike Davis 12.50 30.00
TTAR139 Ike Davis 12.50 30.00
TTAR146 Gio Gonzalez 10.00 25.00
TTAR147 Gio Gonzalez 10.00 25.00
TTAR148 Gio Gonzalez 10.00 25.00
TTAR149 Gio Gonzalez 10.00 25.00
TTAR150 Gio Gonzalez 10.00 25.00
TTAR151 Luis Aparicio 15.00 40.00
TTAR152 Luis Aparicio 15.00 40.00
TTAR153 Luis Aparicio 15.00 40.00
TTAR154 Andrew McCutchen 20.00 50.00
TTAR155 Jim Rice 15.00 40.00
TTAR156 Jason Heyward 10.00 25.00
TTAR157 Jason Heyward 10.00 25.00
TTAR158 Jason Heyward 10.00 25.00
TTAR159 Jason Heyward 10.00 25.00
TTAR160 Jason Heyward 10.00 25.00
TTAR161 Greg Luzinski 12.50 30.00
TTAR162 Greg Luzinski 12.50 30.00
TTAR163 Greg Luzinski 12.50 30.00
TTAR164 Carl Crawford 10.00 25.00
TTAR165 Carl Crawford 10.00 25.00
TTAR166 Carl Crawford 10.00 25.00
TTAR167 David Freese 20.00 50.00
TTAR168 David Freese 20.00 50.00
TTAR169 David Freese 20.00 50.00
TTAR170 Ben Zobrist 12.00 30.00
TTAR171 Ben Zobrist 12.00 30.00
TTAR172 Ben Zobrist 12.00 30.00
TTAR173 Fergie Jenkins 15.00 40.00
TTAR174 Fergie Jenkins 15.00 40.00
TTAR175 Fergie Jenkins 15.00 40.00
TTAR177 Robinson Cano 20.00 50.00
TTAR178 Robinson Cano 20.00 50.00
TTAR179 Dan Uggla 10.00 25.00
TTAR180 Dan Uggla 10.00 25.00
TTAR181 Dan Uggla 10.00 25.00
TTAR182 Dan Uggla 10.00 25.00
TTAR183 Dan Uggla 10.00 25.00
TTAR185 Andre Dawson 20.00 50.00
TTAR186 Andre Dawson 20.00 50.00
TTAR187 Andre Dawson 20.00 50.00
TTAR188 Andy Pettitte 40.00 80.00
TTAR189 Andy Pettitte 40.00 80.00
TTAR190 Andy Pettitte 40.00 80.00
TTAR191 Andy Pettitte 40.00 80.00
TTAR192 Andy Pettitte 40.00 80.00
TTAR193 Al Kaline 40.00 100.00
TTAR194 Mike Morse 8.00 20.00
TTAR195 Mike Morse 8.00 20.00
TTAR196 Mike Morse 8.00 20.00
TTAR197 Mike Morse 8.00 20.00
TTAR198 Josh Johnson 8.00 20.00
TTAR199 Josh Johnson 8.00 20.00
TTAR200 Josh Johnson 8.00 20.00
TTAR201 Josh Johnson 8.00 20.00
TTAR202 Josh Johnson 8.00 20.00
TTAR203 Andrew McCutchen 20.00 50.00
TTAR208 Jim Rice 15.00 40.00
TTAR209 Jim Rice 15.00 40.00
TTAR210 Jim Rice 15.00 40.00
TTAR211 Maury Wills 15.00 40.00
TTAR212 Maury Wills 15.00 40.00
TTAR213 Maury Wills 15.00 40.00
TTAR217 Prince Fielder 50.00 100.00
TTAR218 Prince Fielder 50.00 100.00
TTAR219 Mike Napoli 10.00 25.00
TTAR220 Mike Napoli 10.00 25.00
TTAR221 Mike Napoli 10.00 25.00
TTAR222 Mike Napoli 10.00 25.00
TTAR223 Mike Napoli 10.00 25.00
TTAR225 Willie McCovey 40.00 80.00
TTAR226 Willie McCovey 40.00 80.00
TTAR227 Willie McCovey 40.00 80.00
TTAR228 Al Kaline 40.00 100.00
TTAR230 Brian McCann 15.00 40.00
TTAR231 Brian McCann 15.00 40.00
TTAR232 Brian McCann 15.00 40.00
TTAR233 Brian McCann 15.00 40.00
TTAR234 Brian McCann 15.00 40.00
TTAR235 Adam Jones 8.00 20.00
TTAR236 Adam Jones 8.00 20.00
TTAR237 Adam Jones 8.00 20.00
TTAR238 Adam Jones 8.00 20.00
TTAR242 Paul O'Neill 30.00 60.00
TTAR243 Paul O'Neill 30.00 60.00
TTAR244 Paul O'Neill 30.00 60.00
TTAR246 Felix Hernandez 30.00 60.00
TTAR247 Felix Hernandez 30.00 60.00
TTAR248 Felix Hernandez 30.00 60.00
TTAR249 Felix Hernandez 30.00 60.00
TTAR250 Will Clark 20.00 50.00
TTAR251 Will Clark 20.00 50.00
TTAR252 Will Clark 20.00 50.00
TTAR253 Carlton Fisk 20.00 50.00
TTAR254 Carlton Fisk 20.00 50.00
TTAR255 Carlton Fisk 20.00 50.00
TTAR256 Jose Bautista 12.50 30.00
TTAR257 Paul Molitor 20.00 50.00
TTAR258 Paul Molitor 40.00 80.00
TTAR259 Paul Molitor 20.00 50.00
TTAR261 Starlin Castro 20.00 50.00
TTAR262 Starlin Castro 20.00 50.00
TTAR263 Starlin Castro 20.00 50.00
TTAR264 Eric Hosmer 15.00 40.00
TTAR265 Eric Hosmer 15.00 40.00
TTAR266 David Price 15.00 40.00
TTAR267 David Price 15.00 40.00
TTAR268 David Price 15.00 40.00
TTAR269 David Price 15.00 40.00
TTAR270 Bryce Harper 200.00 300.00
TTAR271 Bryce Harper 200.00 300.00
TTAR272 Bryce Harper 200.00 300.00
TTAR273 Bryce Harper 200.00 300.00
TTAR274 Duke Snider 40.00 80.00
TTAR275 Duke Snider 40.00 80.00

2012 Topps Triple Threads Relic Autographs Gold

*GOLD: .5X TO 1.2X BASIC
STATED ODDS 1:24 MINI
STATED PRINT RUN 9 SER.#'d SETS
ALL DC VARIATIONS PRICED EQUALLY
NO PRICING ON MANY DUE TO SCARCITY
EXCHANGE DEADLINE 8/31/2015

2012 Topps Triple Threads Relic Combos

STATED ODDS 1:26 MINI
STATED PRINT RUN 36 SER.#'d SETS
RC1 Mantle/Musial/Yas 60.00 120.00
RC2 Jim Rice/Eddie Murray/Albert Belle 10.00 25.00
RC3 Brock/Henderson/Ichiro 15.00 40.00
RC4 Gwynn/Boggs/Ripken 30.00 60.00
RC5 Molitor/Sandb/Mattingly 12.50 30.00
RC6 Brooks/Schmidt/Boggs 15.00 40.00
RC7 Joe Morgan/Ryne Sandberg
Robinson Cano 12.50 30.00
RC8 Fisk/Thomas/Konerko 30.00 60.00
RC9 Carlton/Hamels/Lee 15.00 40.00
RC10 Carlton/Schmidt/Halla 10.00 25.00
RC11 Trout/Pujols/Weaver 30.00 60.00
RC12 Trout/Harper/Cespedes 75.00 150.00
RC13 Yas/Rice/Ellsbury 10.00 25.00
RC14 Kemp/Ethier/Kershaw 15.00 40.00
RC15 Dave Winfield/Jim Rice
Albert Belle 8.00 20.00
RC16 Mays/DiMaggio/Musial 50.00 100.00
RC17 Ruth/Gehrig/Mantle 175.00 350.00
RC18 David Price/James Shields
Matt Moore 8.00 20.00
RC19 Jeter/ARod/Cano 40.00 80.00
RC20 Ryan Braun/Ike Davis
Kevin Youkilis 8.00 20.00
RC21 Verland/Cabrera/Prince 30.00 60.00
RC22 Chipper/Uggla/Heyward 10.00 25.00
RC23 Jered Weaver/C.J. Wilson
Dan Haren 10.00 25.00
RC24 Longo/Zimmer/Chipper 12.50 30.00
RC25 Hamilton/Darvish/Kinsler 12.50 30.00
RC26 Ryan Zimmerman
Evan Longoria/David Wright 10.00 25.00
RC27 Hanley Ramirez/Evan Longoria
Ryan Zimmerman 10.00 25.00
RC28 Verland/Halla/Kershaw 15.00 40.00
RC29 Mantle/Yas/Musial 50.00 100.00
RC30 Killebrew/Carew/Mauer 20.00 50.00
RC31 Votto/Phillips/Bruce 30.00 60.00
RC32 Lincec/Cain/Bumg 20.00 50.00
RC33 Buster Posey/Joe Mauer
Mike Napoli 12.50 30.00
RC34 McCov/Mays/Cepeda 40.00 80.00
RC35 Tim Hudson/Tommy Hanson
Brandon Beachy 8.00 20.00
RC36 Hanley Ramirez/Jose Reyes
Giancarlo Stanton 8.00 20.00
RC37 Adrian Gonzalez/Dustin Pedroia
David Ortiz 10.00 25.00
RC38 Lincec/Stras/Verlander 20.00 50.00
RC39 CC Sabathia/Clayton Kershaw
Cliff Lee 10.00 25.00
RC40 Kiner/Stargell/McCutch 30.00 60.00
RC41 Billy Butler/Eric Hosmer
Alex Gordon 10.00 25.00
RC42 Nelson Cruz/Michael Young
Mike Napoli 8.00 20.00
RC43 Gard/Grander/Swish 15.00 40.00
RC44 Jose Bautista/Brett Lawrie
Ricky Romero 10.00 25.00
RC45 Jose Bautista/Matt Kemp
Ryan Braun 10.00 25.00
RC46 Harper/Stras/Zimmerm 15.00 40.00
RC47 Troy Tulowitzki/Carlos Gonzalez
Todd Helton 10.00 25.00
RC48 Ryan Zimmerman/David Freese
Evan Longoria 12.50 30.00
RC49 Tulo/Castro/Jeter 15.00 40.00
RC50 Justin Upton/Matt Kemp
Carlos Gonzalez 8.00 20.00
RC51 Trout/McCut/Upton 20.00 50.00
RC52 Ian Kinsler/Adrian Beltre
Michael Young 10.00 25.00
RC53 Ian Kinsler/Dustin Pedroia
Robinson Cano 8.00 20.00
RC54 Brooks/Murray/Ripken 40.00 80.00
RC55 O'Neill/Jeter/Rivera 30.00 60.00
RC56 Pettitte/Rivera/CC 15.00 40.00
RC57 Yovani Gallardo/Zack Greinke
Ryan Braun 8.00 20.00
RC58 Starg/VanSlyke/McCut 30.00 60.00
RC59 Mark Teixeira/Adrian Gonzalez
Prince Fielder 12.50 30.00
RC60 Hender/Morgan/Brock 12.00 30.00
RC61 Winfield/Murray/Matting 12.00 30.00
RC62 Cecil Cooper/Paul Molitor
Ryan Braun 12.00 30.00
RC63 Molitor/Boggs/Gwynn 10.00 25.00

2012 Topps Triple Threads Relic Combos Sepia

*SEPIA: .4X TO 1X BASIC
STATED ODDS 1:35 MINI
STATED PRINT RUN 27 SER.#'d SETS

2012 Topps Triple Threads Relics

STATED ODDS 1:9 MINI
STATED PRINT RUN 36 SER.#'d SETS
ALL DC VARIATIONS PRICED EQUALLY
TTR1 Roy Halladay 12.50 30.00
TTR2 Roy Halladay 12.50 30.00
TTR3 Roy Halladay 12.50 30.00
TTR4 David Price 8.00 20.00
TTR5 David Price 8.00 20.00
TTR6 David Price 8.00 20.00
TTR7 Ian Kinsler 5.00 12.00
TTR8 Ian Kinsler 5.00 12.00
TTR9 Ian Kinsler 5.00 12.
TTR10 Carlos Gonzalez 6.00 15.
TTR11 Carlos Gonzalez 6.00 15.
TTR12 Carlos Gonzalez 6.00 15.
TTR13 Freddie Freeman 5.00 12.
TTR14 Freddie Freeman 5.00 12.
TTR15 David Freese 12.50 30.
TTR16 David Freese 12.50 30.
TTR17 Tommy Hanson 5.00 12.
TTR18 Tommy Hanson 5.00 12.
TTR19 Starlin Castro 6.00 15.
TTR20 Starlin Castro 6.00 15.
TTR21 Starlin Castro 6.00 15.
TTR22 Joey Votto 12.50 30.
TTR23 Joey Votto 12.50 30.
TTR24 Joey Votto 12.50 30.
TTR25 C.J. Wilson 5.00 12.
TTR26 C.J. Wilson 5.00 12.
TTR27 C.J. Wilson 5.00 12.
TTR28 Madison Bumgarner 12.50 30.
TTR29 Madison Bumgarner 12.50 30.
TTR30 Madison Bumgarner 12.50 30.
TTR31 Andrew McCutchen 8.00 20.
TTR32 Andrew McCutchen 8.00 20.
TTR33 Andrew McCutchen 8.00 20.
TTR34 Zack Greinke 5.00 12.
TTR35 Zack Greinke 5.00 12.
TTR36 Zack Greinke 5.00 12.
TTR37 Stephen Strasburg 12.50 30.
TTR38 Stephen Strasburg 12.50 30.
TTR39 Stephen Strasburg 12.50 30.
TTR40 Matt Moore 5.00 12.
TTR41 Matt Moore 5.00 12.
TTR42 Jose Reyes 5.00 12.
TTR43 Jose Reyes 5.00 12.
TTR44 Jose Reyes 5.00 12.
TTR45 Yu Darvish 10.00 25.
TTR46 Nelson Cruz 5.00 12.
TTR47 Nelson Cruz 5.00 12.
TTR48 Nelson Cruz 5.00 12.
TTR49 Eric Hosmer 5.00 12.
TTR50 Eric Hosmer 5.00 12.
TTR51 Eric Hosmer 5.00 12.
TTR52 Cliff Lee 5.00 12.
TTR53 Cliff Lee 5.00 12.
TTR54 Cliff Lee 5.00 12.
TTR55 Justin Upton 5.00 12.
TTR56 Justin Upton 5.00 12.
TTR57 Justin Upton 5.00 12.
TTR58 Yovani Gallardo 5.00 12.
TTR59 Yovani Gallardo 5.00 12.
TTR60 Yovani Gallardo 5.00 12.
TTR61 Adrian Gonzalez 5.00 12.
TTR62 Adrian Gonzalez 5.00 12.
TTR63 Adrian Gonzalez 5.00 12.
TTR64 Cole Hamels 8.00 20.
TTR65 Cole Hamels 8.00 20.
TTR66 Cole Hamels 8.00 20.
TTR67 Josh Hamilton 8.00 20.
TTR68 Josh Hamilton 8.00 20.
TTR69 Josh Hamilton 8.00 20.
TTR70 Mike Trout 100.00 250.
TTR71 Mike Trout 100.00 250.
TTR72 Mike Trout 100.00 250.
TTR73 Jacoby Ellsbury 5.00 12.
TTR74 Jacoby Ellsbury 5.00 12.
TTR75 Jacoby Ellsbury 5.00 12.
TTR76 Mike Napoli 6.00 15.
TTR77 Mike Napoli 6.00 15.
TTR78 Mike Napoli 6.00 15.
TTR79 Clayton Kershaw 8.00 20.
TTR80 Clayton Kershaw 8.00 20.
TTR81 Clayton Kershaw 8.00 20.
TTR82 Dan Haren 5.00 12.
TTR83 Dan Haren 5.00 12.
TTR84 Dan Haren 5.00 12.
TTR85 Hanley Ramirez 5.00 12.
TTR86 Hanley Ramirez 5.00 12.
TTR87 Hanley Ramirez 5.00 12.
TTR88 Derek Jeter 20.00 50.
TTR89 Paul Goldschmidt 5.00 12.
TTR90 Paul Goldschmidt 5.00 12.
TTR91 Alex Gordon 6.00 15.
TTR92 Alex Gordon 6.00 15.
TTR93 Alex Gordon 6.00 15.
TTR94 Ryan Braun 8.00 20.
TTR95 Ryan Braun 8.00 20.
TTR96 Ryan Braun 8.00 20.
TTR97 Tim Lincecum 12.50 30.
TTR98 Tim Lincecum 12.50 30.
TTR99 Tim Lincecum 12.50 30.
TTR100 Shane Victorino 5.00 12.
TTR101 Shane Victorino 5.00 12.
TTR102 Shane Victorino 5.00 12.
TTR103 Carlos Santana 6.00 15.
TTR104 Carlos Santana 6.00 15.
TTR105 Carlos Santana 6.00 15.
TTR106 Evan Longoria 8.00 20.
TTR107 Evan Longoria 8.00 20.
TTR108 Evan Longoria 8.00 20.
TTR109 Adrian Beltre 5.00 12.
TTR110 Adrian Beltre 5.00 12.
TTR111 Adrian Beltre 5.00 12.
TTR112 Troy Tulowitzki 5.00 12.
TTR113 Troy Tulowitzki 5.00 12.
TTR114 Troy Tulowitzki 5.00 12.
TTR115 Matt Kemp 10.00 25.
TTR116 Matt Kemp 10.00 25.
TTR117 Matt Kemp 10.00 25.
TTR118 Dee Gordon 5.00 12.
TTR119 Dee Gordon 5.00 12.
TTR120 Dee Gordon 5.00 12.
TTR121 Felix Hernandez 6.00 15.

TR122 Felix Hernandez 6.00 15.00
TR123 Felix Hernandez 6.00 15.00
TR124 Gio Gonzalez 5.00 12.00
TR125 Gio Gonzalez 5.00 12.00
TR126 Gio Gonzalez 5.00 12.00
TR127 Miguel Cabrera 12.50 30.00
TR128 Miguel Cabrera 12.50 30.00
TR129 Miguel Cabrera 12.50 30.00
TR130 Jason Heyward 6.00 15.00
TR131 Jason Heyward 6.00 15.00
TR132 Jason Heyward 6.00 15.00
TR133 Albert Pujols 12.50 30.00
TR134 Mike Moustakas 5.00 12.00
TR135 Mike Moustakas 5.00 12.00
TR136 Mike Moustakas 5.00 12.00
TR137 Ryan Howard 6.00 15.00
TR138 Ryan Howard 6.00 15.00
TR139 Ryan Howard 6.00 15.00
TR140 David Ortiz 5.00 12.00
TR141 David Ortiz 5.00 12.00
TR142 David Ortiz 5.00 12.00
TR143 Buster Posey 10.00 25.00
TR144 Buster Posey 10.00 25.00
TR145 Buster Posey 10.00 25.00
TR146 Dustin Pedroia 6.00 15.00
TR147 Dustin Pedroia 6.00 15.00
TR148 Dustin Pedroia 6.00 15.00
TR149 Kevin Youkilis 5.00 12.00
TR150 Kevin Youkilis 5.00 12.00
TR151 Kevin Youkilis 5.00 12.00
TR152 Curtis Granderson 8.00 20.00
TR153 Curtis Granderson 8.00 20.00
TR154 Jimmy Rollins 6.00 15.00
TR155 Jimmy Rollins 6.00 15.00
TR156 Jimmy Rollins 6.00 15.00
TR157 Paul Konerko 6.00 15.00
TR158 Paul Konerko 6.00 15.00
TR159 Paul Konerko 6.00 15.00
TR160 Ian Kennedy 5.00 12.00
TR161 Ian Kennedy 5.00 12.00
TR162 Ian Kennedy 5.00 12.00
TR163 Jose Bautista 5.00 12.00
TR164 Robinson Cano 10.00 25.00
TR165 Freddie Freeman 5.00 12.00
TR166 David Freese 12.50 30.00
TR167 Tommy Hanson 5.00 12.00
TR168 Chipper Jones 15.00 40.00
TR169 Joe Mauer 6.00 15.00
TR170 Alex Rodriguez 10.00 25.00
TR171 Alex Rodriguez 10.00 25.00
TR172 Giancarlo Stanton 5.00 12.00
TR173 Dan Uggla 6.00 15.00
TR174 David Wright 10.00 25.00
TR175 Chipper Jones 15.00 40.00
TR176 David Wright 10.00 25.00
TR177 David Wright 10.00 25.00
TR178 Matt Moore 5.00 12.00
TR179 Bryce Harper 50.00 100.00
TR180 Brett Lawrie 8.00 20.00
TR181 Brett Lawrie 8.00 20.00
TR182 Brett Lawrie 8.00 20.00
TR183 Desmond Jennings 5.00 12.00
TR184 Desmond Jennings 5.00 12.00
TR185 Desmond Jennings 5.00 12.00
TR186 Chipper Jones 15.00 40.00

2012 Topps Triple Threads Relics Emerald

*EMERALD: .5X TO 1.2X BASIC
STATED ODDS 1:18 MINI
STATED PRINT RUN 18 SER.#'d SETS
ALL DC VARIATIONS EQUALLY PRICED
NO PRICING DUE TO SCARCITY ON SOME

2012 Topps Triple Threads Relics Gold

*GOLD: .6X TO 1.5X BASIC
STATED ODDS 1:35 MINI
STATED PRINT RUN 9 SER.#'d SETS
ALL DC VARIATIONS EQUALLY PRICED
NO PRICING ON SOME DUE TO SCARCITY

2012 Topps Triple Threads Relics Sepia

*SEPIA: .4X TO 1X BASIC
STATED ODDS 1:12 MINI
STATED PRINT RUN 27 SER.#'d SETS
ALL DC VARIATIONS EQUALLY PRICED

2012 Topps Triple Threads Unity Relic Autographs

STATED ODDS 1:6 MINI
PRINT RUNS BW/N 22-99 COPIES PER
NO SNIDER/22 PRICING AVAILABLE
ALL VERSIONS EQUALLY PRICED
EXCHANGE DEADLINE 8/31/2015
UAR1 Melky Cabrera 10.00 25.00
UAR2 Alex Avila 4.00 10.00
UAR3 Alex Avila 4.00 10.00
UAR4 Steve Garvey 8.00 20.00
UAR5 Allen Craig 12.50 30.00
UAR6 Anibal Sanchez 4.00 10.00
UAR7 Anibal Sanchez 4.00 10.00
UAR8 Aramis Ramirez 6.00 15.00
UAR9 Aroldis Chapman 12.50 30.00
UAR10 Mike Trout 250.00 600.00
UAR11 Billy Butler 5.00 12.00
UAR12 Brandon Belt 8.00 20.00
UAR13 Brandon Phillips 8.00 20.00
UAR14 Brennan Boesch EXCH 4.00 10.00
UAR15 Brennan Boesch EXCH 4.00 10.00
UAR16 Carlos Ruiz 5.00 12.00
UAR17 Carlos Ruiz 5.00 12.00
UAR18 Chris Heisey 5.00 12.00
UAR19 Chris Heisey 5.00 12.00
UAR20 Chris Sale 8.00 20.00
UAR21 Chris Sale 8.00 20.00
UAR22 Brett Lawrie 8.00 20.00
UAR23 Jesus Montero 8.00 20.00
UAR24 Jesus Montero 8.00 20.00
UAR25 Daniel Bard 5.00 12.00
UAR26 Daniel Bard 5.00 12.00
UAR27 Daniel Murphy 10.00 25.00
UAR28 Daniel Murphy 10.00 25.00
UAR29 Nick Markakis 4.00 10.00
UAR30 Nick Markakis 4.00 10.00
UAR31 Danny Espinosa EXCH 5.00 12.00
UAR32 Danny Espinosa EXCH 5.00 12.00
UAR33 Darryl Strawberry 10.00 25.00
UAR34 Dayan Viciedo EXCH 6.00 15.00
UAR35 Dayan Viciedo EXCH 6.00 15.00
UAR36 Doc Gooden 10.00 25.00
UAR37 Doc Gooden 10.00 25.00
UAR38 Michael Bourn EXCH 8.00 20.00
UAR39 Michael Bourn EXCH 8.00 20.00
UAR40 Hank Aaron/66 100.00 250.00
UAR41 Dustin Pedroia 12.50 30.00
UAR42 Elvis Andrus 5.00 12.00
UAR43 Emilio Bonifacio 4.00 10.00
UAR44 Emilio Bonifacio 4.00 10.00
UAR45 Ervin Santana 5.00 12.00
UAR46 Gaby Sanchez 4.00 10.00
UAR47 Gaby Sanchez 4.00 10.00
UAR48 Gary Carter 15.00 40.00
UAR49 Salvador Perez 12.00 30.00
UAR50 Henderson Alvarez 6.00 15.00
UAR51 Henderson Alvarez 6.00 15.00
UAR52 Tommy Hanson 6.00 15.00
UAR53 Tommy Hanson 6.00 15.00
UAR54 Ike Davis 5.00 12.00
UAR55 J.D. Martinez 12.00 30.00
UAR56 Josh Johnson 5.00 12.00
UAR57 Jason Motte 6.00 15.00
UAR58 J.D. Martinez 12.00 30.00
UAR59 Johnny Cueto 6.00 15.00
UAR60 Jon Jay 6.00 15.00
UAR61 Jordan Zimmermann 5.00 12.00
UAR62 Jose Valverde 4.00 10.00
UAR63 Jose Valverde 4.00 10.00
UAR64 Josh Thole 5.00 12.00
UAR65 Josh Thole 5.00 12.00
UAR66 Justin Masterson 6.00 15.00
UAR67 Lance Lynn 5.00 12.00
UAR68 Lance Lynn 5.00 12.00
UAR69 Logan Morrison 4.00 10.00
UAR70 David Justice 8.00 20.00
UAR71 David Justice 8.00 20.00
UAR72 Lucas Duda 6.00 15.00
UAR73 Lucas Duda 6.00 15.00
UAR74 David Justice 8.00 20.00
UAR75 Johnny Cueto 6.00 15.00
UAR76 Bryan LaHair 5.00 12.00
UAR77 Mike Minor 5.00 12.00
UAR78 Mike Minor 5.00 12.00
UAR79 Matt Garza 4.00 10.00
UAR80 Mitch Moreland 4.00 10.00
UAR81 Mitch Moreland 4.00 10.00
UAR82 Neftali Feliz 5.00 12.00
UAR83 Nyjer Morgan 4.00 10.00
UAR84 Nyjer Morgan 4.00 10.00
UAR85 Edwin Encarnacion 6.00 15.00
UAR86 Edwin Encarnacion 6.00 15.00
UAR87 R.A. Dickey 10.00 25.00
UAR88 Rickie Weeks 5.00 12.00
UAR89 Rickie Weeks 5.00 12.00
UAR90 Ruben Tejada 5.00 12.00
UAR91 Shaun Marcum 5.00 12.00
UAR92 Shaun Marcum 5.00 12.00
UAR93 Vance Worley 6.00 15.00
UAR94 Vance Worley 6.00 15.00
UAR95 Danny Duffy 5.00 12.00
UAR96 Danny Duffy 5.00 12.00
UAR97 Zack Cozart 5.00 12.00
UAR98 Evan Longoria 10.00 25.00
UAR99 Mike Moustakas 8.00 20.00
UAR100 Ruben Tejada 5.00 12.00
UAR101 Jason Kipnis 10.00 25.00
UAR103 Dexter Fowler 4.00 10.00
UAR104 Dexter Fowler 4.00 10.00
UAR105 R.A. Dickey 10.00 25.00
UAR106 Brandon McCarthy 4.00 10.00
UAR107 Brandon McCarthy 4.00 10.00
UAR108 Justin Masterson 6.00 15.00
UAR109 Jay Bruce 8.00 20.00
UAR110 Jose Altuve 40.00 100.00
UAR111 Jose Altuve 40.00 100.00
UAR112 Justin Masterson 6.00 15.00
UAR113 Bryan LaHair 5.00 12.00

2012 Topps Triple Threads Unity Relic Autographs Emerald

*EMERALD: .5X TO 1.2X BASIC
STATED ODDS 1:11 MINI
STATED PRINT RUN 50 SER.#'d SETS
EXCHANGE DEADLINE 8/31/2015
UAR40 Hank Aaron 100.00 250.00
UAR102 Duke Snider 15.00 40.00

2012 Topps Triple Threads Unity Relic Autographs Gold

*GOLD: .5X TO 1.2X BASIC
STATED ODDS 1:21 MINI
STATED PRINT RUN 25 SER.#'d SETS
NO PRICING ON MOST DUE SCARCITY
EXCHANGE DEADLINE 8/31/2015

2012 Topps Triple Threads Unity Relic Autographs Sepia

*SEPIA: .4X TO 1X BASIC
STATED ODDS 1:7 MINI
STATED PRINT RUN 75 SER.#'d SETS
EXCHANGE DEADLINE 8/31/2015

2012 Topps Triple Threads Unity Relics

STATED ODDS 1:6 MINI
STATED PRINT RUN 36 SER.#'d SETS
UR1 Dave Winfield 4.00 10.00
UR2 Dustin Pedroia 5.00 12.00
UR3 Dustin Pedroia 5.00 12.00
UR4 Paul Konerko 5.00 12.00
UR5 Paul Konerko 5.00 12.00
UR6 Paul Konerko 5.00 12.00
UR7 Jim Rice 4.00 10.00
UR8 Jim Rice 4.00 10.00
UR9 Prince Fielder 8.00 20.00
UR10 Dan Haren 4.00 10.00
UR11 Dan Haren 4.00 10.00
UR12 Dan Haren 4.00 10.00
UR13 Giancarlo Stanton 4.00 10.00
UR14 Giancarlo Stanton 4.00 10.00
UR15 Giancarlo Stanton 4.00 10.00
UR16 Carlos Gonzalez 4.00 10.00
UR17 Carlos Gonzalez 4.00 10.00
UR18 Carlos Gonzalez 4.00 10.00
UR19 Joe DiMaggio 30.00 60.00
UR20 Tony Gwynn 8.00 20.00
UR21 Ryan Howard 4.00 10.00
UR22 Ryan Howard 4.00 10.00
UR23 Ryan Howard 4.00 10.00
UR24 Mike Trout 40.00 100.00
UR25 Mike Trout 40.00 100.00
UR26 Mike Trout 40.00 100.00
UR27 Willie Mays 12.00 30.00
UR28 Jordan Zimmermann 4.00 10.00
UR29 Jordan Zimmermann 4.00 10.00
UR30 Jordan Zimmermann 4.00 10.00
UR31 Rickey Henderson 15.00 40.00
UR32 Rickey Henderson 15.00 40.00
UR33 Rickey Henderson 15.00 40.00
UR34 Zack Greinke 4.00 10.00
UR35 Zack Greinke 4.00 10.00
UR36 Zack Greinke 4.00 10.00
UR37 Paul Molitor 5.00 12.00
UR38 Paul Molitor 5.00 12.00
UR39 Kevin Youkilis 4.00 10.00
UR40 Kevin Youkilis 4.00 10.00
UR41 Kevin Youkilis 4.00 10.00
UR42 Tim Lincecum 6.00 15.00
UR43 Tim Lincecum 6.00 15.00
UR44 Tim Lincecum 6.00 15.00
UR45 Don Mattingly 10.00 25.00
UR46 David Wright 10.00 25.00
UR47 David Wright 10.00 25.00
UR48 David Wright 10.00 25.00
UR49 Derek Jeter 15.00 40.00
UR50 Derek Jeter 15.00 40.00
UR51 Derek Jeter 15.00 40.00
UR52 Tommy Hanson 4.00 10.00
UR53 Tommy Hanson 4.00 10.00
UR54 Tommy Hanson 4.00 10.00
UR55 Josh Johnson 4.00 10.00
UR56 Josh Johnson 4.00 10.00
UR57 Josh Johnson 4.00 10.00
UR58 Matt Kemp 6.00 15.00
UR59 Matt Kemp 6.00 15.00
UR60 Matt Kemp 6.00 15.00
UR61 Bob Lemon 5.00 12.00
UR62 Brett Gardner 4.00 10.00
UR63 Brett Gardner 4.00 10.00
UR64 Matt Moore 4.00 10.00
UR65 Matt Moore 4.00 10.00
UR66 Matt Moore 4.00 10.00
UR67 Andrew McCutchen 15.00 40.00
UR68 Andrew McCutchen 15.00 40.00
UR69 Andrew McCutchen 15.00 40.00
UR70 Paul O'Neill 6.00 15.00
UR71 Paul O'Neill 6.00 15.00
UR72 Todd Helton 4.00 10.00
UR73 Todd Helton 4.00 10.00
UR74 Todd Helton 4.00 10.00
UR75 Alex Gordon 4.00 10.00
UR76 Alex Gordon 4.00 10.00
UR77 Alex Gordon 4.00 10.00
UR78 Stan Musial 12.50 30.00
UR79 Carlos Santana 4.00 10.00
UR80 Carlos Santana 4.00 10.00
UR81 Carlos Santana 4.00 10.00
UR82 Willie Stargell 12.50 30.00
UR83 Curtis Granderson 4.00 10.00
UR84 Curtis Granderson 4.00 10.00
UR85 Curtis Granderson 4.00 10.00
UR86 Ichiro Suzuki 12.50 30.00
UR87 Ichiro Suzuki 12.50 30.00
UR88 Adrian Beltre 4.00 8.00
UR89 Adrian Beltre 4.00 10.00
UR90 Adrian Beltre 4.00 10.00
UR91 Mike Schmidt 8.00 20.00
UR92 Nelson Cruz 4.00 10.00
UR93 Nelson Cruz 4.00 10.00
UR94 Nelson Cruz 4.00 10.00
UR95 Clayton Kershaw 5.00 12.00
UR96 Clayton Kershaw 5.00 12.00
UR97 Clayton Kershaw 5.00 12.00
UR98 Ryan Braun 5.00 12.00
UR99 Ryan Braun 5.00 12.00
UR100 Ryan Braun 5.00 12.00
UR101 Albert Pujols 10.00 25.00
UR102 Albert Pujols 10.00 25.00
UR103 Justin Upton 4.00 10.00
UR104 Justin Upton 4.00 10.00
UR105 Justin Upton 4.00 10.00
UR106 Billy Butler 4.00 10.00
UR107 Billy Butler 4.00 10.00
UR108 Billy Butler 4.00 10.00
UR109 Madison Bumgarner 5.00 12.00
UR110 Madison Bumgarner 5.00 12.00
UR111 Madison Bumgarner 5.00 12.00
UR112 Starlin Castro 6.00 15.00
UR113 Starlin Castro 6.00 15.00
UR114 Steve Garvey 10.00 25.00
UR115 Frank Thomas 10.00 25.00
UR116 Freddie Freeman 4.00 10.00
UR117 Freddie Freeman 4.00 10.00
UR118 Freddie Freeman 4.00 10.00
UR119 Jimmy Rollins 6.00 15.00
UR120 Jimmy Rollins 6.00 15.00
UR121 Jimmy Rollins 6.00 15.00
UR122 Tim Hudson 4.00 10.00
UR123 Tim Hudson 4.00 10.00
UR124 Tim Hudson 4.00 10.00
UR125 Cole Hamels 4.00 10.00
UR126 Cole Hamels 4.00 10.00
UR127 Cole Hamels 4.00 10.00
UR128 Cal Ripken Jr. 15.00 40.00
UR129 Josh Hamilton 5.00 12.00
UR130 Josh Hamilton 5.00 12.00
UR131 Josh Hamilton 5.00 12.00
UR132 Warren Spahn 10.00 25.00
UR133 Gio Gonzalez 4.00 10.00
UR134 Gio Gonzalez 4.00 10.00
UR135 Gio Gonzalez 4.00 10.00
UR136 Brian McCann 4.00 10.00
UR137 Brian McCann 4.00 10.00
UR138 Brian McCann 4.00 10.00
UR139 Dustin Pedroia 5.00 12.00
UR140 Brooks Robinson 6.00 15.00
UR141 Brooks Robinson 6.00 15.00
UR142 George Brett 12.50 30.00
UR143 George Brett 12.50 30.00
UR144 Jemile Weeks 4.00 10.00
UR145 Adrian Gonzalez 4.00 10.00
UR146 Adrian Gonzalez 4.00 10.00
UR147 Adrian Gonzalez 4.00 10.00
UR148 David Freese 8.00 20.00
UR149 David Freese 8.00 20.00
UR150 David Freese 8.00 20.00
UR151 Roy Halladay 5.00 12.00
UR152 Roy Halladay 5.00 12.00
UR153 Troy Tulowitzki 4.00 10.00
UR154 Troy Tulowitzki 4.00 10.00
UR155 Troy Tulowitzki 4.00 10.00
UR156 Mariano Rivera 10.00 25.00
UR157 Mariano Rivera 10.00 25.00
UR158 Mariano Rivera 10.00 25.00
UR159 Ian Kinsler 4.00 10.00
UR160 Ian Kinsler 4.00 10.00
UR161 Ian Kinsler 4.00 10.00
UR162 Mat Latos 4.00 10.00
UR163 Mat Latos 4.00 10.00
UR164 Mat Latos 4.00 10.00
UR165 Johan Santana 4.00 10.00
UR166 Johan Santana 4.00 10.00
UR167 Johan Santana 4.00 10.00
UR168 Lou Gehrig 50.00 100.00
UR169 Chase Utley 4.00 10.00
UR170 Chase Utley 4.00 10.00
UR171 Chase Utley 4.00 10.00
UR172 Lance Berkman 4.00 10.00
UR173 Lance Berkman 4.00 10.00
UR174 Lance Berkman 4.00 10.00
UR175 Joe Morgan 4.00 10.00
UR176 Joe Morgan 4.00 10.00
UR177 Joe Morgan 4.00 10.00
UR178 Johnny Cueto 4.00 10.00
UR179 Johnny Cueto 4.00 10.00
UR180 Johnny Cueto 4.00 10.00
UR181 Yu Darvish 12.50 30.00
UR182 Eric Hosmer 4.00 10.00
UR183 Eric Hosmer 4.00 10.00
UR184 Eric Hosmer 4.00 10.00
UR185 Ben Zobrist 4.00 10.00
UR186 Ben Zobrist 4.00 10.00
UR187 Ben Zobrist 4.00 10.00
UR188 Hanley Ramirez 4.00 10.00
UR189 Hanley Ramirez 4.00 10.00
UR190 Hanley Ramirez 4.00 10.00
UR191 Ian Kennedy 4.00 10.00
UR192 Ian Kennedy 4.00 10.00
UR193 Ian Kennedy 4.00 10.00
UR194 Dan Uggla 4.00 10.00
UR195 Dan Uggla 4.00 10.00
UR196 Dan Uggla 4.00 10.00
UR197 Joey Votto 6.00 15.00
UR198 James Shields 4.00 10.00
UR199 James Shields 4.00 10.00
UR200 James Shields 4.00 10.00
UR201 Albert Belle 4.00 10.00
UR202 Albert Belle 4.00 10.00
UR203 Andy Pettitte 6.00 15.00
UR204 Andy Pettitte 6.00 15.00
UR205 Andy Pettitte 6.00 15.00
UR206 Bryce Harper 20.00 50.00
UR207 Jacoby Ellsbury 8.00 20.00
UR208 Jacoby Ellsbury 8.00 20.00
UR209 Jacoby Ellsbury 8.00 20.00
UR210 Mike Moustakas 4.00 10.00
UR211 Mike Moustakas 4.00 10.00
UR212 Mike Moustakas 4.00 10.00
UR213 Yovani Gallardo 4.00 10.00
UR214 Yovani Gallardo 4.00 10.00
UR215 Yovani Gallardo 4.00 10.00
UR216 Joey Votto 6.00 15.00
UR217 Alex Rodriguez 8.00 20.00
UR218 Alex Rodriguez 8.00 20.00
UR219 Jason Heyward 4.00 10.00
UR220 Jason Heyward 4.00 10.00
UR221 Jason Heyward 4.00 10.00
UR222 Miguel Cabrera 10.00 25.00
UR223 Miguel Cabrera 10.00 25.00
UR224 Miguel Cabrera 10.00 25.00
UR225 Ozzie Smith 10.00 25.00
UR226 Bobby Doerr 4.00 10.00
UR227 Bobby Doerr 4.00 10.00
UR228 Bobby Doerr 4.00 10.00
UR229 Matt Cain 5.00 12.00
UR230 Matt Cain 5.00 12.00
UR231 Matt Cain 5.00 12.00
UR232 Reggie Jackson 8.00 20.00
UR233 Torii Hunter 4.00 10.00
UR234 Torii Hunter 4.00 10.00
UR235 Torii Hunter 4.00 10.00
UR236 Brett Lawrie 6.00 15.00
UR237 Brett Lawrie 6.00 15.00
UR239 Felix Hernandez 4.00 10.00
UR240 Felix Hernandez 4.00 10.00
UR241 Felix Hernandez 4.00 10.00
UR242 Rod Carew 5.00 12.00
UR243 Lou Brock 6.00 15.00
UR244 Jered Weaver 4.00 10.00
UR245 Jered Weaver 4.00 10.00
UR246 Jered Weaver 4.00 10.00
UR247 Stephen Strasburg 6.00 15.00
UR248 Stephen Strasburg 6.00 15.00
UR249 Sandy Koufax 20.00 50.00
UR250 Cecil Cooper 4.00 10.00
UR251 Jose Bautista 4.00 10.00
UR252 Jose Bautista 4.00 10.00
UR253 Jose Bautista 4.00 10.00
UR254 Chipper Jones 8.00 20.00
UR255 Chipper Jones 8.00 20.00
UR256 Chipper Jones 8.00 20.00
UR257 Andre Ethier 4.00 10.00
UR258 Andre Ethier 4.00 10.00
UR259 Andre Ethier 4.00 10.00
UR260 Dustin Ackley 4.00 10.00
UR261 Dustin Ackley 4.00 10.00
UR262 Ryan Zimmerman 4.00 10.00
UR263 Ryan Zimmerman 4.00 10.00
UR264 Ryan Zimmerman 4.00 10.00
UR265 Nick Swisher 5.00 12.00
UR266 Harmon Killebrew 10.00 25.00
UR267 Brandon Beachy 4.00 10.00
UR268 Brandon Beachy 4.00 10.00
UR269 Brandon Beachy 4.00 10.00
UR270 Carlos Beltran 8.00 20.00
UR271 Carlos Beltran 8.00 20.00
UR272 Carlos Beltran 8.00 20.00
UR273 Robinson Cano 8.00 20.00
UR274 Robinson Cano 8.00 20.00
UR275 Robinson Cano 8.00 20.00
UR276 Jay Bruce 4.00 10.00
UR277 Jay Bruce 4.00 10.00
UR278 Jay Bruce 4.00 10.00
UR279 Eddie Murray 6.00 15.00
UR280 Eddie Murray 6.00 15.00
UR281 Anibal Sanchez 4.00 10.00
UR282 Anibal Sanchez 4.00 10.00
UR283 Anibal Sanchez 4.00 10.00
UR284 C.J. Wilson 4.00 10.00
UR285 C.J. Wilson 4.00 10.00
UR286 C.J. Wilson 4.00 10.00
UR287 Evan Longoria 5.00 12.00
UR288 Evan Longoria 5.00 12.00
UR289 Evan Longoria 5.00 12.00
UR290 Buster Posey 10.00 25.00
UR291 Buster Posey 10.00 25.00
UR292 Buster Posey 10.00 25.00
UR293 David Ortiz 4.00 10.00
UR294 David Ortiz 4.00 10.00
UR295 David Ortiz 4.00 10.00
UR296 Daniel Murphy 5.00 12.00
UR297 Justin Verlander 8.00 20.00
UR298 Justin Verlander 8.00 20.00
UR299 Justin Verlander 8.00 20.00
UR300 Ryne Sandberg 8.00 20.00
UR301 Mark Teixeira 4.00 10.00
UR302 Mark Teixeira 4.00 10.00
UR303 Mark Teixeira 4.00 10.00
UR304 Carl Yastrzemski 10.00 25.00
UR305 Carl Yastrzemski 10.00 25.00
UR306 David Price 4.00 10.00
UR307 David Price 4.00 10.00
UR308 David Price 4.00 10.00
UR309 Joey Votto 6.00 15.00
UR332 Joe Mauer 4.00 10.00

2012 Topps Triple Threads Unity Relics Emerald

*EMERALD: .5X TO 1.2X BASIC
STATED ODDS 1:11 MINI
STATED PRINT RUN 18 SER.#'d SETS
ALL VERSIONS EQUALLY PRICED
SOME NOT PRICED DUE TO SCARCITY

2012 Topps Triple Threads Unity Relics Gold

*GOLD: .6X TO 1.5X BASIC
STATED ODDS 1:21 MINI
STATED PRINT RUN 9 SER.#'d SETS
ALL VERSIONS EQUALLY PRICED
SOME NOT PRICED DUE TO SCARCITY

2012 Topps Triple Threads Unity Relics Sepia

*SEPIA: .4X TO 1X BASIC
STATED ODDS 1:7 MINI
STATED PRINT RUN 27 SER.#'d SETS

2013 Topps Triple Threads

JSY AU RC ODDS 1:10 MINI
JSY AU RC PRINT RUN 99 SER.#'d SETS
JSY AU ODDS 1:10 MINI
JSY AU PRINT RUN 99 SER.#'d SETS
EXCHANGE DEADLINE 10/31/2016
OVERALL 1-100 PLATE ODDS 1:145 HOBBY
PLATE PRINT RUN 1 SET PER COLOR
BLACK-CYAN-MAGENTA-YELLOW ISSUED
NO PLATE PRICING DUE TO SCARCITY
1 Ted Williams 1.50 4.00
2 Mike Mussina .60 1.50
3 Dustin Pedroia .60 1.50
4 Lou Gehrig 1.50 4.00
5 Albert Pujols 1.00 2.50
6 Justin Verlander .75 2.00
7 Ozzie Smith 1.00 2.50
8 David Wright .60 1.50
9 CC Sabathia .60 1.50
10 Babe Ruth 2.00 5.00
11 Craig Biggio .60 1.50
12 Ryan Zimmerman .60 1.50
13 Stephen Strasburg .75 2.00
14 Gary Carter .60 1.50
15 R.A. Dickey .60 1.50
16 Clayton Kershaw 1.50 4.00
17 Bob Gibson .60 1.50
18 Brooks Robinson .60 1.50
19 Derek Jeter 2.00 5.00
20 Matt Cain .60 1.50
21 George Brett 1.50 4.00
22 Nolan Ryan 2.50 6.00
23 David Ortiz .75 2.00
24 Ian Kinsler .60 1.50
25 Jose Bautista .60 1.50
26 Ryan Braun .60 1.50
27 Torii Hunter .50 1.25
28 Greg Maddux 1.00 2.50
29 Billy Butler .50 1.25
30 Jose Reyes .60 1.50
31 David Freese .50 1.25
32 Justin Upton .60 1.50
33 Yogi Berra .75 2.00
34 Tony Gwynn .75 2.00
35 Bo Jackson .75 2.00
36 Hanley Ramirez .60 1.50
37 Ryan Howard .60 1.50
38 Joey Votto .75 2.00
39 Harmon Killebrew .75 2.00
40 Tom Glavine .50 1.25
41 Roy Halladay .60 1.50
42 Jackie Robinson .75 2.00
43 John Smoltz .75 2.00
44 Hank Aaron 1.50 4.00
45 Cal Ripken Jr. 2.50 6.00
46 Bill Mazeroski .60 1.50
47 Reggie Jackson .60 1.50
48 Wade Boggs .60 1.50
49 Adrian Gonzalez .60 1.50
50 Johnny Bench .75 2.00
51 David Price .60 1.50
52 Joe Morgan .60 1.50
53 Willie Mays 1.50 4.00
54 Tim Lincecum .60 1.50
55 Whitey Ford .60 1.50
56 Albert Belle .50 1.25
57 Yu Darvish .75 2.00
58 Prince Fielder .60 1.50
59 Tom Seaver .60 1.50
60 Giancarlo Stanton .75 2.00
61 Buster Posey 1.00 2.50
62 Andrew McCutchen .75 2.00
63 Pablo Sandoval .60 1.50
64 Al Kaline .75 2.00
65 Troy Tulowitzki .75 2.00
66 Robinson Cano .60 1.50
67 Roberto Clemente 2.00 5.00
68 Rickey Henderson .75 2.00
69 Yasiel Puig RC 2.00 5.00
70 Evan Longoria .60 1.50
71 Matt Holliday .75 2.00
72 Joe DiMaggio 1.50 4.00
73 C.J. Wilson .50 1.25
74 Josh Hamilton .60 1.50
75 Ty Cobb 1.25 3.00
76 Justin Morneau .60 1.50
77 Mike Schmidt 1.25 3.00
78 Fred McGriff .60 1.50
79 Robin Yount .75 2.00
80 Willie Stargell .60 1.50
81 Bob Feller .60 1.50
82 Jimmie Foxx .75 2.00
83 Jered Weaver .60 1.50
84 Ernie Banks .75 2.00
85 Zack Greinke .60 1.50
86 Sandy Koufax 1.50 4.00
87 Frank Thomas .75 2.00
88 Miguel Cabrera .75 2.00
89 Mariano Rivera 1.00 2.50
90 Matt Kemp .60 1.50
91 Don Mattingly 1.50 4.00
92 Duke Snider .60 1.50
93 Felix Hernandez .60 1.50
94 Joe Mauer .60 1.50
95 Cole Hamels .60 1.50
96 James Shields .50 1.25
97 Carlos Gonzalez .60 1.50
98 Gio Gonzalez .60 1.50
99 Cliff Lee .60 1.50
100 Paul Molitor .75 2.00
101 Mike Trout JSY AU 100.00 250.00
102 K.Gausman JSY AU RC 10.00 25.00
103 N.Arenado JSY AU RC 60.00 150.00
104 Todd Frazier JSY AU 6.00 15.00
106 Salvador Perez JSY AU 12.00 30.00
107 Starlin Castro JSY AU 10.00 25.00
108 Tyler Skaggs JSY AU RC 5.00 12.00
109 M.Machado JSY AU RC 50.00 120.00
110 Josh Reddick JSY AU 8.00 20.00
111 Jurickson Profar JSY AU RC 12.50 30.00
112 Jarrod Parker JSY AU 5.00 12.00
113 Anthony Gose JSY AU 5.00 12.00
114 Alex Cobb JSY AU 5.00 12.00
116 Yonder Alonso JSY AU 5.00 12.00
117 H.Ryu JSY AU RC EXCH 20.00 50.00
118 Will Middlebrooks JSY AU 8.00 20.00
119 Brett Jackson JSY AU 5.00 12.00
120 Yasmani Grandal JSY AU 5.00 12.00
122 T.Rosenthal JSY AU RC 5.00 12.00
123 Wade Miley JSY AU 5.00 12.00
124 Andrew Cashner JSY AU 5.00 12.00
125 Felix Doubront JSY AU 5.00 12.00
126 Julio Teheran JSY AU 8.00 20.00
127 Yu Darvish JSY AU EXCH 40.00 100.00
128 Chris Archer JSY AU 6.00 15.00
129 Nate Eovaldi JSY AU 6.00 15.00
130 Derek Norris JSY AU 5.00 12.00
131 Josh Rutledge JSY AU 5.00 12.00
132 Mike Olt JSY AU RC 6.00 15.00
133 Devin Mesoraco JSY AU 5.00 12.00
134 Aaron Hicks JSY AU RC 5.00 12.00
135 Mark Trumbo JSY AU 6.00 15.00
136 Anthony Rizzo JSY AU 15.00 40.00
138 Brett Lawrie JSY AU 5.00 12.00
139 Jedd Gyorko JSY AU RC 5.00 12.00
140 Dylan Bundy JSY AU RC 15.00 40.00
141 Jeurys Familia JSY AU RC 5.00 12.00
142 Tommy Milone JSY AU 5.00 12.00
143 Matt Moore JSY AU 8.00 20.00
144 Shelby Miller JSY AU RC 12.50 30.00
145 Scott Diamond JSY AU 5.00 12.00
146 Starling Marte JSY AU 5.00 12.00
147 Michael Pineda JSY AU 5.00 12.00
148 Brad Jr. JSY AU RC EXCH 30.00 80.00
149 Matt Adams JSY AU 12.50 30.00
151 A.Garcia JSY AU RC EXCH 5.00 12.00
152 Jake Odorizzi JSY AU RC 5.00 12.00
153 D.Brown JSY AU EXCH 5.00 12.00
154 Freddie Freeman JSY AU 15.00 40.00
155 Jason Kipnis JSY AU 8.00 20.00
156 A.Rendon JSY AU RC 20.00 50.00
157 Kirk Nieuwenhuis JSY AU 5.00 12.00
158 Kris Medlen JSY AU EXCH 5.00 12.00
159 Paul Goldschmidt JSY AU 12.50 30.00
160 Tony Cingrani JSY AU RC 8.00 20.00
161 B.Harper JSY AU 75.00 150.00
162 Jean Segura JSY AU EXCH 10.00 25.00
163 Yoenis Cespedes JSY AU 10.00 25.00
164 Trevor Bauer JSY AU 6.00 15.00
165 Wily Peralta JSY AU 5.00 12.00
166 Wilin Rosario JSY AU 5.00 12.00
167 Didi Gregorius JSY AU RC 5.00 12.00
168 Wil Myers JSY AU RC 8.00 20.00
169 G.Cole JSY AU RC EXCH 10.00 25.00
170 Bruce Rondon JSY AU RC EXCH 5.00 12.00
171 Wheeler JSY AU RC EXCH 10.00 25.00

2013 Topps Triple Threads Amber

*AMBER: 1X TO 2.5X BASIC
STATED ODDS 1:5 MINI
STATED PRINT RUN 125 SER.#'d SETS
69 Yasiel Puig 12.50 30.00

2013 Topps Triple Threads Amethyst

*AMETHYST: .5X TO 1.2X BASIC
STATED PRINT RUN 650 SER.#'d SETS
69 Yasiel Puig 6.00 15.00

2013 Topps Triple Threads Emerald

*EMERALD 1-100: .6X TO 1.5X BASIC
1-100 STATED ODDS 1:3 MINI
1-100 PRINT RUN 250 SER.#'d SETS
*EMERALD JSY AU: .4X TO 1X BASIC
EMERALD JSY AU ODDS 1:18 MINI
EMER.JSY AU PRINT RUN 50 SER.#'d SETS
EXCHANGE DEADLINE 10/31/2016
69 Yasiel Puig 8.00 20.00

2013 Topps Triple Threads Gold

*GOLD: 2X TO 5X BASIC
STATED ODDS 1:6 MINI
STATED PRINT RUN 99 SER.#'d SETS
69 Yasiel Puig 20.00 50.00

2013 Topps Triple Threads Onyx

*ONYX: 2.5X TO 6X BASIC
STATED ODDS 1:12 MINI
STATED PRINT RUN 50 SER.#'d SETS
69 Yasiel Puig 25.00 60.00

2013 Topps Triple Threads Sapphire

*SAPPHIRE: 3X TO 8X BASIC
STATED ODDS 1:24 MINI
STATED PRINT RUN 25 SER.#'d SETS
19 Derek Jeter 30.00 60.00

2013 Topps Triple Threads Sepia

*SEPIA JSY AU: .4X TO 1X BASIC
STATED ODDS 1:12 MINI
STATED PRINT RUN 75 SER.#'d SETS
EXCHANGE DEADLINE 10/31/2016

2013 Topps Triple Threads Autograph Relic Combos

STATED ODDS 1:97 MINI
STATED PRINT RUN 36 SER.#'d SETS
EXCHANGE DEADLINE 10/31/2016
BPP Bggio/Phllps/Pdria
BSG Sgra/Braun/Gllrdo 30.00 60.00
CPC Phllps/Cngmi/Czart 15.00 40.00

GZZ R.Zim/J.Zim/Gnzlz	20.00	50.00
HTD Drvsh/Hrper/Trout	250.00	350.00
JGT Grffey/Thmas/Jcksn	250.00	350.00
JTH Jcksn/Hndrsn/Trout	200.00	400.00
KRM Krshw/Mrtnz/Ryu EXCH	100.00	200.00
MGM Gssge/Mssna/Mttngly	75.00	150.00
MGS Mddx/Smltz/Glvne EXCH	150.00	400.00
MHC Cobb/Hllcksn/Moore	15.00	40.00
MOG Ortz/Mrtnz/Grcparra	75.00	150.00
MRW Whler/Mller/Ryu EXCH	20.00	50.00
RDP Ryan/Drvsh/Prfar EXCH	100.00	200.00
SPR Prce/Ryu/Sale	30.00	60.00
WLM Lngria/Wrght/Mchdo	50.00	100.00
WMW Whler/Mrtnez/Wright	40.00	80.00

2013 Topps Triple Threads Autograph Relic Combos Sepia

*SEPIA: .4X TO 1X BASIC
STATED ODDS 1:130 MINI
STATED PRINT RUN 27 SER.#'d SETS
EXCHANGE DEADLINE 10/31/2016

2013 Topps Triple Threads Legend Relics

STATED ODDS 1:83 MINI
STATED PRINT RUN 36 SER.#'d SETS

BG Bob Gibson	12.50	30.00
BR Babe Ruth	100.00	200.00
CR Cal Ripken Jr.	30.00	60.00
FR Frank Robinson	20.00	50.00
HA Hank Aaron	30.00	60.00
HK Harmon Killebrew	12.50	30.00
JB Johnny Bench	12.50	30.00
JF Jimmie Foxx	20.00	50.00
JM Joe Morgan	8.00	20.00
JR Jackie Robinson	40.00	80.00
KG Ken Griffey Jr.	20.00	50.00
LG Lou Gehrig	60.00	120.00
NR Nolan Ryan	30.00	60.00
RC Roberto Clemente	60.00	120.00
RJ Reggie Jackson	12.50	30.00
SM Stan Musial	30.00	60.00
TC Ty Cobb	40.00	80.00
TW Ted Williams	40.00	80.00
WM Willie Mays	20.00	50.00
YB Yogi Berra	15.00	40.00

2013 Topps Triple Threads Legend Relics Sepia

*SEPIA: .4X TO 1X BASIC
STATED ODDS 1:110 MINI
STATED PRINT RUN 27 SER.#'D SETS

2013 Topps Triple Threads Relic Autographs

STATED ODDS 1:12 MINI
STATED PRINT RUN 18 SER.#'d SETS
ALL DC VARIATIONS PRICED EQUALLY
NO PRICING ON PLAYERS W/ONE DC VERSION
EXCHANGE DEADLINE 10/31/2016

AA1 Alex Avila	8.00	20.00
AA2 Alex Avila	8.00	20.00
AA3 Alex Avila	8.00	20.00
AA4 Alex Avila	8.00	20.00
AET1 Andre Ethier	12.50	30.00
AET2 Andre Ethier	12.50	30.00
AG1 Avisail Garcia	10.00	25.00
AG2 Avisail Garcia	10.00	25.00
AG3 Avisail Garcia	10.00	25.00
AG4 Avisail Garcia	10.00	25.00
AG5 Avisail Garcia	10.00	25.00
AGN1 Anthony Gose	8.00	20.00
AGN2 Anthony Gose	8.00	20.00
AGN3 Anthony Gose	8.00	20.00
AGN4 Anthony Gose	8.00	20.00
AR1 Anthony Rizzo	20.00	50.00
AR2 Anthony Rizzo	20.00	50.00
AR3 Anthony Rizzo	20.00	50.00
ARE1 Anthony Rendon	15.00	40.00
ARE2 Anthony Rendon	15.00	40.00
AS1 Anibal Sanchez	8.00	20.00
AS2 Anibal Sanchez	8.00	20.00
AS3 Anibal Sanchez	8.00	20.00
AS4 Anibal Sanchez	8.00	20.00
BG1 Brett Gardner	15.00	40.00
BG2 Brett Gardner	15.00	40.00
BGI1 Bob Gibson	15.00	40.00
BGI2 Bob Gibson	15.00	40.00
BGI3 Bob Gibson	20.00	50.00
BH1 Bryce Harper EXCH	100.00	200.00
BH2 Bryce Harper EXCH	100.00	200.00
BM1 Brian McCann	10.00	25.00
BM2 Brian McCann	10.00	25.00
BM3 Brian McCann	10.00	25.00
BM4 Brian McCann	10.00	25.00
BM5 Brian McCann	10.00	25.00
BPO1 Buster Posey	75.00	150.00
BPO2 Buster Posey	75.00	150.00
BPO3 Buster Posey	75.00	150.00
CA1 Chris Archer	10.00	25.00
CA2 Chris Archer	10.00	25.00
CA3 Chris Archer	10.00	25.00
CA4 Chris Archer	10.00	25.00
CB1 Craig Biggio	30.00	60.00
CB2 Craig Biggio	30.00	60.00
CKI1 Craig Kimbrel EXCH	40.00	80.00
CKI2 Craig Kimbrel EXCH	40.00	80.00
CKI3 Craig Kimbrel EXCH	40.00	80.00
CR1 Colby Rasmus	8.00	20.00
CR2 Colby Rasmus	8.00	20.00
CR3 Colby Rasmus	8.00	20.00
CR4 Colby Rasmus	8.00	20.00
CS1 Carlos Santana	8.00	20.00
CS2 Carlos Santana	8.00	20.00
CS3 Carlos Santana	8.00	20.00
DF1 Dexter Fowler	5.00	12.00
DF2 Dexter Fowler	5.00	12.00
DF3 Dexter Fowler	5.00	12.00
DF4 Dexter Fowler	5.00	12.00
DFR1 David Freese	15.00	40.00
DFR2 David Freese	15.00	40.00
DFR3 David Freese	15.00	40.00
DM1 Devin Mesoraco	10.00	25.00
DM2 Devin Mesoraco	10.00	25.00
DMA1 Don Mattingly	40.00	80.00
DMA2 Don Mattingly	40.00	80.00
DMA3 Don Mattingly	40.00	80.00
DN1 Derek Norris	5.00	12.00
DN2 Derek Norris	5.00	12.00
DN3 Derek Norris	5.00	12.00
DN4 Derek Norris	5.00	12.00
DO1 David Ortiz	50.00	100.00
DO2 David Ortiz	50.00	100.00
DO3 David Ortiz	50.00	100.00
DS1 Dave Stewart EXCH	8.00	20.00
DS2 Dave Stewart EXCH	8.00	20.00
DS3 Dave Stewart EXCH	8.00	20.00
DS4 Dave Stewart EXCH	8.00	20.00
DSN1 Duke Snider	20.00	50.00
DSN2 Duke Snider	20.00	50.00
DSN3 Duke Snider	20.00	50.00
DU1 Dan Uggla EXCH	6.00	15.00
DU2 Dan Uggla EXCH	6.00	15.00
DU3 Dan Uggla EXCH	6.00	15.00
DU4 Dan Uggla EXCH	6.00	15.00
DU5 Dan Uggla EXCH	6.00	15.00
DW1 David Wright	15.00	40.00
DW2 David Wright	15.00	40.00
DW3 David Wright	15.00	40.00
FF1 Freddie Freeman	15.00	40.00
FF2 Freddie Freeman	15.00	40.00
FH1 Felix Hernandez	20.00	50.00
FH2 Felix Hernandez	20.00	50.00
GG1 Gio Gonzalez	8.00	20.00
GG2 Gio Gonzalez	8.00	20.00
GS1 Gary Sheffield	10.00	25.00
GS2 Gary Sheffield	10.00	25.00
GS3 Gary Sheffield	10.00	25.00
GS4 Gary Sheffield	10.00	25.00
GST1 Giancarlo Stanton	15.00	40.00
GST2 Giancarlo Stanton	15.00	40.00
GST3 Giancarlo Stanton	15.00	40.00
GST4 Giancarlo Stanton	15.00	40.00
HA1 Hank Aaron	250.00	350.00
HA2 Hank Aaron	250.00	350.00
JBA1 Jose Bautista	10.00	25.00
JBA2 Jose Bautista	10.00	25.00
JBA3 Jose Bautista	10.00	25.00
JBE1 Johnny Bench	40.00	80.00
JBE2 Johnny Bench	40.00	80.00
JHE1 Jason Heyward	15.00	40.00
JHE2 Jason Heyward	15.00	40.00
JHE3 Jason Heyward	15.00	40.00
JK1 Jason Kipnis	12.00	30.00
JK2 Jason Kipnis	12.00	30.00
JK3 Jason Kipnis	12.00	30.00
JK4 Jason Kipnis	12.00	30.00
JK5 Jason Kipnis	12.00	30.00
JPA1 Jarrod Parker	6.00	15.00
JPA2 Jarrod Parker	6.00	15.00
JPA3 Jarrod Parker	6.00	15.00
JPA4 Jarrod Parker	6.00	15.00
JPO1 Johnny Podres EXCH	8.00	20.00
JPO2 Johnny Podres EXCH	8.00	20.00
JPO3 Johnny Podres EXCH	8.00	20.00
JPO4 Johnny Podres EXCH	8.00	20.00
JPR1 Jurickson Profar	20.00	50.00
JPR2 Jurickson Profar	20.00	50.00
JPR3 Jurickson Profar	20.00	50.00
JPR4 Jurickson Profar	20.00	50.00
JPR5 Jurickson Profar	20.00	50.00
JS1 Jean Segura	12.50	30.00
JS2 Jean Segura	12.50	30.00
JS3 Jean Segura	12.50	30.00
JU1 Justin Upton	12.50	30.00
JU2 Justin Upton	12.50	30.00
JU3 Justin Upton	12.50	30.00
JW1 Jered Weaver	10.00	25.00
JW2 Jered Weaver	10.00	25.00
JW3 Jered Weaver	10.00	25.00
KM1 Kris Medlen EXCH	10.00	25.00
KM2 Kris Medlen EXCH	10.00	25.00
MA1 Matt Adams	10.00	25.00
MC1 Matt Cain	20.00	50.00
MC2 Matt Cain	10.00	50.00
MC3 Matt Cain	20.00	50.00
MHO1 Matt Holliday EXCH	15.00	40.00
MHO2 Matt Holliday EXCH	15.00	40.00
MHO3 Matt Holliday EXCH	15.00	40.00
MIG1 Miguel Cabrera	75.00	150.00
MIG2 Miguel Cabrera	75.00	150.00
MIG3 Miguel Cabrera	75.00	150.00
MMA1 Manny Machado	50.00	100.00
MMA2 Manny Machado	50.00	100.00
MMA3 Manny Machado	50.00	100.00
MMA4 Manny Machado	20.00	50.00
MMA5 Manny Machado	20.00	50.00
MO1 Mike Olt	6.00	15.00
MO2 Mike Olt	6.00	15.00
MO3 Mike Olt	6.00	15.00
MO4 Mike Olt	6.00	15.00
MO5 Mike Olt	6.00	15.00
MS1 Mike Schmidt	40.00	80.00
MS2 Mike Schmidt	40.00	80.00
NG1 Nomar Garciaparra	30.00	60.00
NG2 Nomar Garciaparra	30.00	60.00
PF1 Prince Fielder EXCH	15.00	40.00
PF2 Prince Fielder EXCH	15.00	40.00
PF3 Prince Fielder EXCH	15.00	40.00
PG1 Paul Goldschmidt	12.50	30.00
PM1 Pedro Martinez EXCH	50.00	100.00
PM2 Pedro Martinez EXCH	50.00	100.00
RB1 Ryan Braun	12.50	30.00
RB2 Ryan Braun	12.50	30.00
RB3 Ryan Braun	12.50	30.00
RD1 R.A. Dickey	15.00	40.00
RD2 R.A. Dickey	15.00	40.00
RD3 R.A. Dickey	15.00	40.00
RH1 Rickey Henderson	60.00	120.00
RH2 Rickey Henderson	60.00	120.00
RJ1 Reggie Jackson EXCH	40.00	80.00
RJ2 Reggie Jackson EXCH	40.00	80.00
SM1 Starling Marte	15.00	40.00
SM2 Starling Marte	15.00	40.00
SM3 Starling Marte	15.00	40.00
SMA1 Shaun Marcum	5.00	12.00
SMA2 Shaun Marcum	5.00	12.00
SMA3 Shaun Marcum	5.00	12.00
SMI1 Shelby Miller	15.00	40.00
SMI2 Shelby Miller	15.00	40.00
SMI3 Shelby Miller	15.00	40.00
SP1 Salvador Perez	15.00	40.00
SP2 Salvador Perez	15.00	40.00
SP3 Salvador Perez	15.00	40.00
SP4 Salvador Perez	15.00	40.00
SP5 Salvador Perez	15.00	40.00
TG1 Tony Gwynn	30.00	60.00
TG2 Tony Gwynn	30.00	60.00
TH1 Tim Hudson	10.00	25.00
TH2 Tim Hudson	10.00	25.00
TH3 Tim Hudson	10.00	25.00
TH4 Tim Hudson	10.00	25.00
TH5 Tim Hudson	10.00	25.00
TM1 Tommy Milone	5.00	12.00
TM2 Tommy Milone	5.00	12.00
TM3 Tommy Milone	5.00	12.00
TM4 Tommy Milone	5.00	12.00
TS1 Tyler Skaggs	6.00	15.00
TS2 Tyler Skaggs	6.00	15.00
TS3 Tyler Skaggs	6.00	15.00
TS4 Tyler Skaggs	6.00	15.00
TS5 Tyler Skaggs	6.00	15.00
WM1 Wil Myers	20.00	50.00
WM2 Wil Myers	20.00	50.00
WM3 Wil Myers	20.00	50.00
WM4 Wil Myers	20.00	50.00
WM5 Wil Myers	20.00	50.00
WMI1 Will Middlebrooks	10.00	25.00
WMI2 Will Middlebrooks	10.00	25.00
WMI3 Will Middlebrooks	10.00	25.00
WMIL1 Wade Miley	5.00	12.00
WMIL2 Wade Miley	5.00	12.00
WMIL3 Wade Miley	5.00	12.00
WP1 Wily Peralta	10.00	25.00
WP2 Wily Peralta	10.00	25.00
WP3 Wily Peralta	10.00	25.00
WP4 Wily Peralta	10.00	25.00
YA1 Yonder Alonso	6.00	15.00
YA2 Yonder Alonso	6.00	15.00
YA3 Yonder Alonso	6.00	15.00
YC1 Yoenis Cespedes	15.00	40.00
YC2 Yoenis Cespedes	15.00	40.00
YC3 Yoenis Cespedes	15.00	40.00
YC4 Yoenis Cespedes	15.00	40.00
YD1 Yu Darvish EXCH	90.00	150.00
YD2 Yu Darvish EXCH	90.00	150.00
YD3 Yu Darvish EXCH	90.00	150.00
YD4 Yu Darvish EXCH	90.00	150.00
ZC1 Zack Cozart	6.00	15.00
ZC2 Zack Cozart	6.00	15.00
ZC3 Zack Cozart	6.00	15.00
ZC4 Zack Cozart	6.00	15.00

2013 Topps Triple Threads Relic Autographs Gold

*GOLD: .5X TO 1.2X BASIC
STATED ODDS 1:23 MINI
STATED PRINT RUN 9 SER.#'d SETS
ALL DC VARIATIONS PRICED EQUALLY
NO PRICING ON MANY DUE TO SCARCITY
EXCHANGE DEADLINE 10/31/2016

2013 Topps Triple Threads Relic Combos

STATED ODDS 1:24 MINI
STATED PRINT RUN 36 SER.#'d SETS

AHM Arcia/Mauer/Hcks	8.00	20.00
ATG Arndo/Tlwtzki/Gnzlz	6.00	15.00
BAP Bltre/Andrs/Prfar	8.00	20.00
BCA Cruz/Andrs/Bltre	8.00	20.00
BCL Bmgrnr/Lnccm/Cain	10.00	25.00
BEC Cbrra/Btsta/Encrncn	5.00	12.00
BHM Hlldy/Bltrn/Mlna	8.00	20.00
BHU Braun/Hrpr/Uptn	10.00	25.00
BJJ Brra/Jcksn/Jter	20.00	50.00
BUC Btsta/Uptn/Cspdes	5.00	12.00
CHD Drvsh/Cspdes/Hrpr	12.00	30.00
CJH Jcksn/Cspdes/Hndrsn	20.00	50.00
CKR Kmbrl/Rvra/Chpmn	15.00	40.00
CLS Cain/Lnccm/Sndvl	12.50	30.00
CMR Cstro/Rzzo/McGrff	8.00	20.00
CRN Rddck/Nrrs/Cspdes EXCH	15.00	40.00
FHS Frnkln/Sgar/Hrnndz	6.00	15.00
FPB Psey/Bnch/Fisk	20.00	50.00
FSH Sndvl/Frse/Hdley	6.00	15.00
GBV Grffy/Bnch/Vtto	30.00	60.00
GHJ Jcksn/Gwynn/Hndrsn	20.00	50.00
GMB Bggs/Mddlbrks/Grcprra	20.00	50.00
GRC Rzzo/Cstro/Grza	8.00	20.00
GRF Rzzo/Gldschmdt/Frman	8.00	20.00
HGA Alnso/Hdley/Gyrko	8.00	20.00
HHL Lee/Hlldy/Hmls	12.50	30.00
HMC Cngrni/Hrvy/Mller EXCH	8.00	20.00
HMF Mley/Frzier/Hrper	10.00	25.00
HRS Schmdt/Hwrd/Rllins	12.50	30.00
HSV Strsbrg/Hrvy/Vrlnder	12.50	30.00
HVF Hnter/Vrlndr/Fider	12.50	30.00
HWL Hdley/Wrght/Lngria	15.00	40.00
HWW Wrght/Whler/Hrvey	8.00	20.00
JRS Sbthia/Rdrgz/Jter	40.00	80.00
KGG Krshw/Grnke/Gnzlez	10.00	25.00
KKG Krshw/Kemp/Gnzlez	10.00	25.00
KMH Kmbrl/Hdsn/Mdlen	10.00	25.00
KSH Krshw/Hrvy/Strsbrg	15.00	40.00
LHH Hmels/Hwrd/Lee	10.00	25.00
LMP Price/Lngria/Moore	6.00	15.00
LRM Mchdo/Lngria/Rdrgz	15.00	40.00
MBH Braun/McCtchn/Hrper	12.50	30.00
MCR Mttngly/Cano/Rdrgz	12.50	30.00
MHU Uptn/McCtchn/Hnter	6.00	15.00
MML Mlna/Lynn/Mller	15.00	40.00
MPH Hrvy/Prfar/Mchdo	12.50	30.00
MPM Psey/McCvy/Mays	75.00	150.00
MPP Mlna/Psey/Prez	15.00	40.00
MRL Lynn/Mller/Rsnthl	10.00	25.00
MRR Ruiz/Rsrio/Msraco	5.00	12.00
NPM Npoli/Pdroia/Mddlbrks	12.50	30.00
OGS O'Nll/Shffld/Grndrsn	6.00	15.00
PCL Lnccm/Cain/Psey	15.00	40.00
PKG Kpns/Prfar/Gyrko	12.50	30.00
PRC Chpmn/Rvra/Pplbon	10.00	25.00
RTG Gnzlz/Tlwtzki/Rsrio	6.00	15.00
SBG Sgura/Gllrdo/Braun	5.00	12.00
SKL Sale/Krshw/Lee	8.00	20.00
SMC McCtchn/Clmnte/Strgll	75.00	150.00
SMF Frnkln/Sgura/Mchdo	12.50	30.00
SPK Sale/Psavy/Knrko	8.00	20.00
SPW Sbthia/Wlhlm/Pttitte	8.00	20.00
STJ Sgura/Tlwtzki/Jter	8.00	20.00
SVS Snchz/Schrzer/Vrlnder	15.00	40.00
THT Trmbo/Trout/Hmlton	15.00	40.00
UUH Uptn/Hywrd/Uptn	10.00	25.00
VGG Gldschmdt/Vtto/Gnzlez	10.00	25.00
ZGS Zmmrmnn/Strsbrg/Gnzlez	12.50	30.00
HGA1 Alnso/Hwrd/Gnzlz	5.00	12.00
MRR1 Mchdo/Rbnsn/Rpken	20.00	50.00

2013 Topps Triple Threads Relic Combos Sepia

*SEPIA: .4X TO 1X BASIC
STATED ODDS 1:32 MINI
STATED PRINT RUN 27 SER.#'d SETS

2013 Topps Triple Threads Relics

STATED ODDS 1:8 MINI
STATED PRINT RUN 36 SER.#'d SETS
ALL DC VARIATIONS PRICED EQUALLY

ABE1 Adrian Beltre	4.00	10.00
ABE2 Adrian Beltre	4.00	10.00
ABE3 Adrian Beltre	4.00	10.00
AC1 Aroldis Chapman	6.00	15.00
AC2 Aroldis Chapman	6.00	15.00
AC3 Aroldis Chapman	6.00	15.00
AD1 Adam Dunn	4.00	10.00
AD2 Adam Dunn	4.00	10.00
AD3 Adam Dunn	4.00	10.00
AE1 Andre Ethier	6.00	15.00
AE2 Andre Ethier	6.00	15.00
AE3 Andre Ethier	6.00	15.00
AG1 Adrian Gonzalez	6.00	15.00
AG2 Adrian Gonzalez	6.00	15.00
AG3 Adrian Gonzalez	6.00	15.00
AJ1 Adam Jones	8.00	20.00
AJ2 Adam Jones	8.00	20.00
AJ3 Adam Jones	8.00	20.00
AM1 Andrew McCutchen	10.00	25.00
AM2 Andrew McCutchen	10.00	25.00
AM3 Andrew McCutchen	10.00	25.00
AP1 Albert Pujols	10.00	25.00
AP2 Albert Pujols	10.00	25.00
AP3 Albert Pujols	10.00	25.00
AR1 Anthony Rizzo	5.00	12.00
AR2 Anthony Rizzo	5.00	12.00
AR3 Anthony Rizzo	5.00	12.00
ARO1 Alex Rodriguez	10.00	25.00
ARO2 Alex Rodriguez	10.00	25.00
ARO3 Alex Rodriguez	10.00	25.00
BB1 Billy Butler	4.00	10.00
BB2 Billy Butler	4.00	10.00
BB3 Billy Butler	4.00	10.00
BBE1 Brandon Beachy	4.00	10.00
BBE2 Brandon Beachy	4.00	10.00
BBE3 Brandon Beachy	4.00	10.00
BH1 Bryce Harper	10.00	25.00
CB1 Carlos Beltran	10.00	25.00
CB2 Carlos Beltran	10.00	25.00
CB3 Carlos Beltran	10.00	25.00
CBI1 Craig Biggio	8.00	20.00
CBI2 Craig Biggio	8.00	20.00
CBI3 Craig Biggio	8.00	20.00
CC1 Carl Crawford	4.00	10.00
CC2 Carl Crawford	4.00	10.00
CC3 Carl Crawford	4.00	10.00
CG1 Carlos Gonzalez	4.00	10.00
CG2 Carlos Gonzalez	4.00	10.00
CG3 Carlos Gonzalez	4.00	10.00
CGR1 Curtis Granderson	5.00	12.00
CGR2 Curtis Granderson	5.00	12.00
CGR3 Curtis Granderson	5.00	12.00
CH1 Cole Hamels	5.00	12.00
CH2 Cole Hamels	5.00	12.00
CH3 Cole Hamels	5.00	12.00
CHE1 Chase Headley	4.00	10.00
CHE2 Chase Headley	4.00	10.00
CHE3 Chase Headley	4.00	10.00
CK1 Craig Kimbrel	10.00	25.00
CK2 Craig Kimbrel	10.00	25.00
CK3 Craig Kimbrel	10.00	25.00
CL1 Cliff Lee	5.00	12.00
CL2 Cliff Lee	5.00	12.00
CL3 Cliff Lee	5.00	12.00
DF1 David Freese	5.00	12.00
DF2 David Freese	5.00	12.00
DF3 David Freese	5.00	12.00
DJ1 Derek Jeter	20.00	50.00
DJ2 Derek Jeter	20.00	50.00
DJ3 Derek Jeter	20.00	50.00
DM1 Don Mattingly	10.00	25.00
DM2 Don Mattingly	10.00	25.00
DM3 Don Mattingly	10.00	25.00
DO1 David Ortiz	8.00	20.00
DO2 David Ortiz	8.00	20.00
DO3 David Ortiz	8.00	20.00
DP1 Dustin Pedroia	8.00	20.00
DP2 Dustin Pedroia	8.00	20.00
DP3 Dustin Pedroia	8.00	20.00
DPR1 David Price	5.00	12.00
DPR2 David Price	5.00	12.00
DPR3 David Price	5.00	12.00
DW1 David Wright	8.00	20.00
DW2 David Wright	8.00	20.00
DW3 David Wright	8.00	20.00
EA1 Elvis Andrus	4.00	10.00
EA2 Elvis Andrus	4.00	10.00
EA3 Elvis Andrus	4.00	10.00
EL1 Evan Longoria	6.00	15.00
EL2 Evan Longoria	6.00	15.00
EL3 Evan Longoria	6.00	15.00
FH1 Felix Hernandez	8.00	20.00
FH2 Felix Hernandez	8.00	20.00
FH3 Felix Hernandez	8.00	20.00
FM1 Fred McGriff	6.00	15.00
FM2 Fred McGriff	6.00	15.00
FM3 Fred McGriff	6.00	15.00
GF1 George Foster	6.00	15.00
GF2 George Foster	6.00	15.00
GF3 George Foster	6.00	15.00
GG1 Gio Gonzalez	4.00	10.00
GG2 Gio Gonzalez	4.00	10.00
GG3 Gio Gonzalez	4.00	10.00
IK1 Ian Kinsler	4.00	10.00
IK2 Ian Kinsler	4.00	10.00
IK3 Ian Kinsler	4.00	10.00
JB1 Jose Bautista	4.00	10.00
JB2 Jose Bautista	4.00	10.00
JB3 Jose Bautista	4.00	10.00
JBR1 Jay Bruce	5.00	12.00
JBR2 Jay Bruce	5.00	12.00
JBR3 Jay Bruce	5.00	12.00
JC1 Johnny Cueto	5.00	12.00
JC2 Johnny Cueto	5.00	12.00
JC3 Johnny Cueto	5.00	12.00
JE1 Jacoby Ellsbury	6.00	15.00
JE2 Jacoby Ellsbury	6.00	15.00
JE3 Jacoby Ellsbury	6.00	15.00
JG1 Jedd Gyorko	4.00	10.00
JG2 Jedd Gyorko	4.00	10.00
JG3 Jedd Gyorko	4.00	10.00
JHA1 Josh Hamilton	4.00	10.00
JHA2 Josh Hamilton	4.00	10.00
JHA3 Josh Hamilton	4.00	10.00
JHE1 Jason Heyward	4.00	10.00
JHE2 Jason Heyward	4.00	10.00
JHE3 Jason Heyward	4.00	10.00
JP1 Jurickson Profar	5.00	12.00
JP2 Jurickson Profar	5.00	12.00
JR1 Jim Rice	6.00	15.00
JR2 Jim Rice	6.00	15.00
JR3 Jim Rice	6.00	15.00
JS1 John Smoltz	8.00	20.00
JS2 John Smoltz	8.00	20.00
JS3 John Smoltz	8.00	20.00
JV1 Justin Verlander	6.00	15.00
JV2 Justin Verlander	6.00	15.00
JV3 Justin Verlander	6.00	15.00
MB1 Madison Bumgarner	20.00	50.00
MB2 Madison Bumgarner	20.00	50.00
MB3 Madison Bumgarner	20.00	50.00
MC1 Miguel Cabrera	10.00	25.00
MC2 Miguel Cabrera	10.00	25.00
MC3 Miguel Cabrera	10.00	25.00
MCA1 Matt Cain	5.00	12.00
MCA2 Matt Cain	5.00	12.00
MCA3 Matt Cain	5.00	12.00
MH1 Matt Holliday	8.00	20.00
MH2 Matt Holliday	8.00	20.00
MH3 Matt Holliday	8.00	20.00
MK1 Matt Kemp	6.00	15.00
MK2 Matt Kemp	6.00	15.00
MK3 Matt Kemp	6.00	15.00
MM1 Mike Mussina	5.00	12.00
MM2 Mike Mussina	5.00	12.00
MM3 Mike Mussina	5.00	12.00
MR1 Mariano Rivera	25.00	60.00
MR2 Mariano Rivera	25.00	60.00
MR3 Mariano Rivera	25.00	60.00
MS1 Max Scherzer	6.00	15.00
MS2 Max Scherzer	6.00	15.00
MS3 Max Scherzer	6.00	15.00
NA1 Norichika Aoki	8.00	20.00
NA2 Norichika Aoki	8.00	20.00
NA3 Norichika Aoki	8.00	20.00
NC1 Nelson Cruz	4.00	10.00
NC2 Nelson Cruz	4.00	10.00
NC3 Nelson Cruz	4.00	10.00
NG1 Nomar Garciaparra	10.00	25.00
NG2 Nomar Garciaparra	10.00	25.00
NG3 Nomar Garciaparra	10.00	25.00
PF1 Prince Fielder	4.00	10.00
PF2 Prince Fielder	4.00	10.00
PF3 Prince Fielder	4.00	10.00
RB1 Ryan Braun	4.00	10.00
RB2 Ryan Braun	4.00	10.00
RB3 Ryan Braun	4.00	10.00
RC1 Robinson Cano	6.00	15.00
RC2 Robinson Cano	6.00	15.00
RC3 Robinson Cano	6.00	15.00
RD1 R.A. Dickey	5.00	12.00
RD2 R.A. Dickey	5.00	12.00
RD3 R.A. Dickey	5.00	12.00
RH1 Roy Halladay	5.00	12.00
RH2 Roy Halladay	5.00	12.00
RH3 Roy Halladay	5.00	12.00
RHO1 Ryan Howard	5.00	12.00
RHO2 Ryan Howard	5.00	12.00
RHO3 Ryan Howard	5.00	12.00
SC1 Starlin Castro	4.00	10.00
SC2 Starlin Castro	4.00	10.00
SC3 Starlin Castro	4.00	10.00
SS1 Stephen Strasburg	6.00	15.00
SS2 Stephen Strasburg	6.00	15.00
SS3 Stephen Strasburg	6.00	15.00
TC1 Tony Cingrani	6.00	15.00
TC2 Tony Cingrani	6.00	15.00
TC3 Tony Cingrani	6.00	15.00
TG1 Tom Glavine	6.00	15.00
TG2 Tom Glavine	6.00	15.00
TG3 Tom Glavine	6.00	15.00
TH1 Tim Hudson	4.00	10.00
TH2 Tim Hudson	4.00	10.00
TH3 Tim Hudson	4.00	10.00
TL1 Tim Lincecum	8.00	20.00
TL2 Tim Lincecum	8.00	20.00
TL3 Tim Lincecum	8.00	20.00
TS1 Tyler Skaggs EXCH	4.00	10.00
TS2 Tyler Skaggs EXCH	4.00	10.00
WC1 Will Clark	10.00	25.00
WC2 Will Clark	10.00	25.00
WC3 Will Clark	10.00	25.00
YC1 Yoenis Cespedes	6.00	15.00
YC2 Yoenis Cespedes	6.00	15.00
YC3 Yoenis Cespedes	6.00	15.00
YCE1 Yoenis Cespedes	6.00	15.00
YCE2 Yoenis Cespedes	6.00	15.00
YD1 Yu Darvish	10.00	25.00
YD2 Yu Darvish	10.00	25.00
YD3 Yu Darvish	10.00	25.00
ZG1 Zack Greinke	5.00	12.00
ZG2 Zack Greinke	5.00	12.00
ZG3 Zack Greinke	5.00	12.00

2013 Topps Triple Threads Relics Emerald

*EMERALD: .5X TO 1.2X BASIC
STATED ODDS 1:16 MINI
STATED PRINT RUN 18 SER.#'d SETS
ALL DC VARIATIONS EQUALLY PRICED
NO PRICING DUE TO SCARCITY ON SOME

2013 Topps Triple Threads Relics Gold

*GOLD: .6X TO 1.5X BASIC
STATED ODDS 1:31 MINI
STATED PRINT RUN 9 SER.#'d SETS
ALL DC VARIATIONS EQUALLY PRICED
NO PRICING ON SOME DUE TO SCARCITY

2013 Topps Triple Threads Relics Sepia

*SEPIA: .4X TO 1X BASIC
STATED ODDS 1:11 MINI
STATED PRINT RUN 27 SER.#'d SETS
ALL DC VARIATIONS EQUALLY PRICED

2013 Topps Triple Threads Unity Relic Autographs

STATED ODDS 1:6 MINI
STATED PRINT RUN 99 SER.#'d SETS
ALL VERSIONS EQUALLY PRICED
EXCHANGE DEADLINE 10/31/2016

AG1 Avisail Garcia EXCH	6.00	15.00
AG2 Avisail Garcia EXCH	6.00	15.00
AG3 Avisail Garcia EXCH	6.00	15.00
AR1 Anthony Rizzo	25.00	60.00
AS Anibal Sanchez EXCH	6.00	15.00
BP1 Brandon Phillips	6.00	15.00
BP2 Brandon Phillips	6.00	15.00
BP3 Brandon Phillips	6.00	15.00
CB Craig Biggio	12.50	30.00
CK Clayton Kershaw	25.00	60.00
CW1 C.J. Wilson	4.00	10.00
CW2 C.J. Wilson	4.00	10.00
CW3 C.J. Wilson	4.00	10.00
DG1 Didi Gregorius	4.00	10.00
DG2 Didi Gregorius	4.00	10.00
DG3 Didi Gregorius	4.00	10.00
DM1 Devin Mesoraco	4.00	10.00
DM2 Devin Mesoraco	4.00	10.00
DM3 Devin Mesoraco	4.00	10.00
DW David Wright	10.00	25.00
EG1 Evan Gattis	12.50	30.00
EG2 Evan Gattis	12.50	30.00
EG3 Evan Gattis	12.50	30.00
EL Evan Longoria	12.50	30.00
FD1 Felix Doubront	4.00	10.00
FD2 Felix Doubront	4.00	10.00
FD3 Felix Doubront	4.00	10.00
FD4 Felix Doubront	4.00	10.00
FD5 Felix Doubront	4.00	10.00
GS Giancarlo Stanton	20.00	50.00
HR1 Hyun-Jin Ryu EXCH	15.00	40.00
JBR1 Jay Bruce	8.00	20.00
JBR2 Jay Bruce	8.00	20.00
JC1 Johnny Cueto	4.00	10.00
JC2 Johnny Cueto	4.00	10.00
JC3 Johnny Cueto	4.00	10.0
JG1 Jedd Gyorko	4.00	10.0
JG2 Jedd Gyorko	4.00	10.0
JG3 Jedd Gyorko	4.00	10.0
JG4 Jedd Gyorko	4.00	10.0
JG5 Jedd Gyorko	4.00	10.0
JJ1 Jon Jay	4.00	10.0
JJ2 Jon Jay	4.00	10.0
JJ3 Jon Jay	4.00	10.0
JM1 J.D. Martinez	4.00	10.0
JM2 J.D. Martinez	4.00	10.0
JP1 Jurickson Profar	10.00	25.0
JP2 Jurickson Profar	10.00	25.0
JP3 Jurickson Profar	10.00	25.0
JP4 Jurickson Profar	10.00	25.0
JP5 Jurickson Profar	10.00	25.0
JRU1 Josh Rutledge	4.00	10.0
JRU2 Josh Rutledge	4.00	10.0
JRU3 Josh Rutledge	4.00	10.0
JU1 Justin Upton	8.00	20.0
JU2 Justin Upton	8.00	20.0
JU3 Justin Upton	8.00	20.0
JZ1 Jordan Zimmermann	5.00	12.0
JZ2 Jordan Zimmermann	5.00	12.0
JZ3 Jordan Zimmermann	5.00	12.0
JZ4 Jordan Zimmermann	5.00	12.0
JZ5 Jordan Zimmermann	5.00	12.0
KN1 Kirk Nieuwenhuis	4.00	10.0
KN2 Kirk Nieuwenhuis	4.00	10.0
KN3 Kirk Nieuwenhuis	4.00	10.0
LL1 Lance Lynn	5.00	12.0
LL2 Lance Lynn	5.00	12.0
LL3 Lance Lynn	5.00	12.0
MA1 Matt Adams	10.00	25.0
MA2 Matt Adams	10.00	25.0
MA3 Matt Adams	10.00	25.0
MC1 Matt Cain	6.00	15.0
MC2 Matt Cain	6.00	15.0
MM Mike Mussina EXCH	12.50	30.0
MO1 Mike Olt	4.00	10.0
MO2 Mike Olt	4.00	10.0
MO3 Mike Olt	4.00	10.0
MO4 Mike Olt	4.00	10.0
MO5 Mike Olt	4.00	10.0
MT1 Mark Trumbo	6.00	15.0
MT2 Mark Trumbo	6.00	15.0
MT3 Mark Trumbo	6.00	15.0
NG Nomar Garciaparra	15.00	40.0
PF Prince Fielder	12.00	30.0
PG1 Paul Goldschmidt	10.00	25.0
PG2 Paul Goldschmidt	10.00	25.0
PG3 Paul Goldschmidt	10.00	25.0
PG4 Paul Goldschmidt	10.00	25.0
PG5 Paul Goldschmidt	10.00	25.0
RD R.A. Dickey	8.00	20.0
SM1 Shelby Miller	8.00	20.0
SM2 Shelby Miller	8.00	20.0
SM3 Shelby Miller	8.00	20.0
SM4 Shelby Miller	8.00	20.0
SM5 Shelby Miller	8.00	20.0
TC1 Tony Cingrani	6.00	15.00
TC2 Tony Cingrani	6.00	15.00
TC3 Tony Cingrani	6.00	15.00
TC4 Tony Cingrani	6.00	15.00
TC5 Tony Cingrani	6.00	15.00
TG Tom Glavine EXCH	15.00	40.00
TS1 Tyler Skaggs	4.00	10.00
TS2 Tyler Skaggs	4.00	10.00
TS3 Tyler Skaggs	4.00	10.00
WM1 Will Middlebrooks	5.00	12.00
WM2 Will Middlebrooks	5.00	12.00
WM3 Will Middlebrooks	5.00	12.00
WM4 Will Middlebrooks	5.00	12.00
WM5 Will Middlebrooks	5.00	12.00
WMI1 Wade Miley	4.00	10.00
WMI2 Wade Miley	4.00	10.00
WP1 Wily Peralta	4.00	10.00
WP2 Wily Peralta	4.00	10.00
WP3 Wily Peralta	4.00	10.00
WR2 Wilin Rosario	4.00	10.00
YG1 Yovani Gallardo	4.00	10.00
YG2 Yovani Gallardo	4.00	10.00
ZC1 Zack Cozart	4.00	10.00
ZC2 Zack Cozart	4.00	10.00
ZC3 Zack Cozart	4.00	10.00

2013 Topps Triple Threads Unity Relic Autographs Emerald

*EMERALD: .5X TO 1.2X BASIC
STATED ODDS 1:11 MINI
STATED PRINT RUN 50 SER.#'d SETS
EXCHANGE DEADLINE 10/31/2016

2013 Topps Triple Threads Unity Relic Autographs Gold

*GOLD: .5X TO 1.2X BASIC
STATED ODDS 1:21 MINI
STATED PRINT RUN 25 SER.#'d SETS
NO PRICING ON MOST DUE SCARCITY
EXCHANGE DEADLINE 10/31/2016

2013 Topps Triple Threads Unity Relic Autographs Sapphire

*SAPPHIRE: 1X TO 2.5X BASIC
STATED ODDS 1:52 MINI
STATED PRINT RUN 10 SER.#'d SETS
NO PRICING ON MOST DUE SCARCITY
EXCHANGE DEADLINE 10/31/2016

2013 Topps Triple Threads Unity Relic Autographs Sepia

*SEPIA: .4X TO 1X BASIC
STATED ODDS 1:7 MINI
STATED PRINT RUN 75 SER.#'d SETS
EXCHANGE DEADLINE 10/31/2016

2013 Topps Triple Threads Unity Relics

TATED ODDS 1:6 MINI
TATED PRINT RUN 36 SER.#'d SETS
B1 Adrian Beltre 4.00 10.00
B2 Adrian Beltre 4.00 10.00
B3 Adrian Beltre 4.00 10.00
C1 Asdrubal Cabrera 4.00 10.00
C2 Asdrubal Cabrera 4.00 10.00
CR Allen Craig 10.00 25.00
D Adam Dunn 4.00 10.00
G Avisail Garcia 4.00 10.00
GN1 Anthony Gose 4.00 10.00
GN2 Anthony Gose 4.00 10.00
GO1 Adrian Gonzalez 4.00 10.00
GO2 Adrian Gonzalez 4.00 10.00
GO3 Adrian Gonzalez 4.00 10.00
GR Alex Gordon 4.00 10.00
H Aaron Hicks 4.00 10.00
J Austin Jackson 4.00 10.00
J2 Austin Jackson 4.00 10.00
J3 Austin Jackson 4.00 10.00
AM1 Andrew McCutchen 20.00 50.00
AM2 Andrew McCutchen 20.00 50.00
AM3 Andrew McCutchen 20.00 50.00
AP Albert Pujols 5.00 12.00
AP1 Andy Pettitte 4.00 10.00
AP2 Andy Pettitte 4.00 10.00
AP3 Andy Pettitte 4.00 10.00
ARE1 Anthony Rendon 4.00 10.00
ARO1 Alex Rodriguez 8.00 20.00
ARO2 Alex Rodriguez 8.00 20.00
ARO3 Alex Rodriguez 8.00 20.00
BB Brandon Beachy 4.00 10.00
BBU Billy Butler 4.00 10.00
BF Bob Feller 15.00 40.00
BG Brett Gardner 5.00 12.00
BH1 Bryce Harper 10.00 25.00
BH2 Bryce Harper 10.00 25.00
BJ1 Bo Jackson 10.00 25.00
BJ2 Bo Jackson 10.00 25.00
BJ3 Bo Jackson 10.00 25.00
BL1 Brett Lawrie 4.00 10.00
BL2 Brett Lawrie 4.00 10.00
BP1 Brandon Phillips 4.00 10.00
BP2 Brandon Phillips 4.00 10.00
BP3 Brandon Phillips 4.00 10.00
BPO Buster Posey 15.00 40.00
BR Brooks Robinson 12.50 30.00
BU B.J. Upton 4.00 10.00
BZ1 Ben Zobrist 4.00 10.00
BZ2 Ben Zobrist 4.00 10.00
CB1 Clay Buchholz 4.00 10.00
CB2 Clay Buchholz 4.00 10.00
CB3 Clay Buchholz 4.00 10.00
CBH1 Chad Billingsley 4.00 10.00
CBI1 Craig Biggio 5.00 12.00
CBI2 Craig Biggio 5.00 12.00
CBI3 Craig Biggio 5.00 12.00
CC1 CC Sabathia 4.00 10.00
CC2 CC Sabathia 4.00 10.00
CC3 CC Sabathia 4.00 10.00
CF1 Carlton Fisk 5.00 12.00
CF2 Carlton Fisk 5.00 12.00
CF3 Carlton Fisk 5.00 12.00
CG1 Carlos Gonzalez 4.00 10.00
CG2 Carlos Gonzalez 4.00 10.00
CG3 Carlos Gonzalez 4.00 10.00
CGR1 Curtis Granderson 4.00 10.00
CGR2 Curtis Granderson 4.00 10.00
CGR3 Curtis Granderson 4.00 10.00
CH Corey Hart 4.00 10.00
CH1 Chase Headley 4.00 10.00
CH2 Chase Headley 4.00 10.00
CH3 Chase Headley 4.00 10.00
CJ1 Chipper Jones 10.00 25.00
CJ2 Chipper Jones 10.00 25.00
CJ3 Chipper Jones 10.00 25.00
CK1 Craig Kimbrel 6.00 15.00
CK2 Craig Kimbrel 6.00 15.00
CKE Casey Kelly 4.00 10.00
CR1 Carlos Ruiz 4.00 10.00
CR2 Carlos Ruiz 4.00 10.00
CS1 Chris Sale 4.00 10.00
CS2 Chris Sale 4.00 10.00
CS3 Chris Sale 4.00 10.00
CSA Carlos Santana 4.00 10.00
CW1 C.J. Wilson 4.00 10.00
CW2 C.J. Wilson 4.00 10.00
CW3 C.J. Wilson 4.00 10.00
DE1 Dennis Eckersley 4.00 10.00
DF David Freese 5.00 12.00
DH Derek Holland 4.00 10.00
DJ1 Derek Jeter 12.50 30.00
DJ2 Derek Jeter 12.50 30.00
DJ3 Derek Jeter 12.50 30.00
DJE Desmond Jennings 4.00 10.00
DM1 Don Mattingly 12.50 30.00
DM2 Don Mattingly 12.50 30.00
DM3 Don Mattingly 12.50 30.00
DP1 Dustin Pedroia 5.00 12.00
DP2 Dustin Pedroia 5.00 12.00
DP3 Dustin Pedroia 5.00 12.00
DPR1 David Price 4.00 10.00
DPR2 David Price 4.00 10.00
DPR3 David Price 4.00 10.00
DS1 Don Sutton 4.00 10.00
DS2 Don Sutton 4.00 10.00
DS3 Don Sutton 4.00 10.00
EA1 Elvis Andrus 4.00 10.00
EA2 Elvis Andrus 4.00 10.00
EA3 Elvis Andrus 4.00 10.00
EB Ernie Banks 10.00 25.00
EE1 Edwin Encarnacion 4.00 10.00
EE2 Edwin Encarnacion 4.00 10.00
EH Eric Hosmer 4.00 10.00
EL1 Evan Longoria 4.00 10.00
EL2 Evan Longoria 4.00 10.00
EL3 Evan Longoria 4.00 10.00
EM Eddie Murray 8.00 20.00
FF Freddie Freeman 6.00 15.00
FH1 Felix Hernandez 4.00 10.00
FH2 Felix Hernandez 4.00 10.00
FH3 Felix Hernandez 4.00 10.00
FM1 Fred McGriff 5.00 12.00
FM2 Fred McGriff 5.00 12.00
FM3 Fred McGriff 5.00 12.00
GM1 Greg Maddux 10.00 25.00
GM2 Greg Maddux 10.00 25.00
GM3 Greg Maddux 10.00 25.00
GS Gary Sheffield 4.00 10.00
GS2 Gary Sheffield 4.00 10.00
GS3 Gary Sheffield 4.00 10.00
GST1 Giancarlo Stanton 5.00 12.00
GST2 Giancarlo Stanton 5.00 12.00
HW1 Hoyt Wilhelm 8.00 20.00
HW2 Hoyt Wilhelm 8.00 20.00
ID1 Ian Desmond 4.00 10.00
ID2 Ian Desmond 4.00 10.00
JB Johnny Bench 12.50 30.00
JBA1 Jose Bautista 4.00 10.00
JBA2 Jose Bautista 4.00 10.00
JBA3 Jose Bautista 4.00 10.00
JBR1 Jay Bruce 4.00 10.00
JBR2 Jay Bruce 4.00 10.00
JBR3 Jay Bruce 4.00 10.00
JBU1 Jim Bunning 6.00 15.00
JBU2 Jim Bunning 6.00 15.00
JC1 Johnny Cueto 4.00 10.00
JC2 Johnny Cueto 4.00 10.00
JC3 Johnny Cueto 4.00 10.00
JE1 Jacoby Ellsbury 6.00 15.00
JE2 Jacoby Ellsbury 6.00 15.00
JG Jedd Gyorko 5.00 12.00
JG1 Jaime Garcia 4.00 10.00
JG2 Jaime Garcia 4.00 10.00
JG3 Jaime Garcia 4.00 10.00
JH1 Josh Hamilton 4.00 10.00
JH2 Josh Hamilton 4.00 10.00
JH3 Josh Hamilton 4.00 10.00
JHE1 Jason Heyward 4.00 10.00
JHE2 Jason Heyward 4.00 10.00
JK Jason Kubel 4.00 10.00
JL1 Jon Lester 4.00 10.00
JL2 Jon Lester 4.00 10.00
JL3 Jon Lester 4.00 10.00
JM Justin Masterson 6.00 15.00
JMA Joe Mauer 5.00 12.00
JP1 Jake Peavy 4.00 10.00
JP2 Jake Peavy 4.00 10.00
JR1 Jim Rice 6.00 15.00
JR2 Jim Rice 6.00 15.00
JRO1 Jimmy Rollins 4.00 10.00
JRO2 Jimmy Rollins 4.00 10.00
JS Jean Segura 4.00 10.00
JS2 Jean Segura 4.00 10.00
JS3 Jean Segura 4.00 10.00
JT Jose Tabata 4.00 10.00
JU1 Justin Upton 4.00 10.00
JU2 Justin Upton 4.00 10.00
JU3 Justin Upton 4.00 10.00
JV1 Joey Votto 8.00 20.00
JV2 Joey Votto 8.00 20.00
JV3 Joey Votto 8.00 20.00
JVE1 Justin Verlander 5.00 12.00
JVE2 Justin Verlander 5.00 12.00
JVE3 Justin Verlander 5.00 12.00
JW1 Jayson Werth 4.00 10.00
JW2 Jayson Werth 4.00 10.00
JW3 Jayson Werth 4.00 10.00
JZ1 Jordan Zimmermann 4.00 10.00
KG1 Ken Griffey Jr. 10.00 25.00
KG2 Ken Griffey Jr. 10.00 25.00
KG3 Ken Griffey Jr. 10.00 25.00
KS Kyle Seager 5.00 12.00
LL Lance Lynn 5.00 12.00
MB1 Madison Bumgarner 10.00 25.00
MB2 Madison Bumgarner 10.00 25.00
MB3 Madison Bumgarner 10.00 25.00
MC1 Miguel Cabrera 8.00 20.00
MC2 Miguel Cabrera 8.00 20.00
MC3 Miguel Cabrera 8.00 20.00
MCA1 Matt Cain 4.00 10.00
MCA2 Matt Cain 4.00 10.00
MCA3 Matt Cain 4.00 10.00
MH1 Matt Harvey 5.00 12.00
MH2 Matt Harvey 5.00 12.00
MH3 Matt Harvey 5.00 12.00
MHO1 Matt Holliday 5.00 12.00
MHO2 Matt Holliday 5.00 12.00
MHO3 Matt Holliday 5.00 12.00
MJ Matt Joyce 4.00 10.00
MK1 Matt Kemp 4.00 10.00
MK2 Matt Kemp 4.00 10.00
MK3 Matt Kemp 4.00 10.00
ML1 Mat Latos 4.00 10.00
ML2 Mat Latos 4.00 10.00
ML3 Mat Latos 4.00 10.00
MMA1 Matt Moore 4.00 10.00
MMA2 Matt Moore 4.00 10.00
MMA3 Matt Moore 4.00 10.00
MMO Mike Moustakas 4.00 10.00
MMU1 Mike Mussina 4.00 10.00
MMU2 Mike Mussina 4.00 10.00
MMU3 Mike Mussina 4.00 10.00
MO Mike Olt 4.00 10.00
MO2 Mike Olt 4.00 10.00
MR1 Mariano Rivera 12.50 30.00
MR2 Mariano Rivera 12.50 30.00
MR3 Mariano Rivera 12.50 30.00
MS1 Max Scherzer 6.00 15.00
MS2 Max Scherzer 6.00 15.00
MS3 Max Scherzer 6.00 15.00
MSC Mike Schmidt 8.00 20.00
MT1 Mark Teixeira 4.00 10.00
MT2 Mark Teixeira 4.00 10.00
MT3 Mark Teixeira 4.00 10.00
NA1 Nolan Arenado 5.00 12.00
NA2 Nolan Arenado 5.00 12.00
NAO Norichika Aoki 6.00 15.00
NC Nelson Cruz 4.00 10.00
NG1 Nomar Garciaparra 6.00 15.00
NG2 Nomar Garciaparra 6.00 15.00
NG3 Nomar Garciaparra 6.00 15.00
NW Neil Walker 4.00 10.00
NW2 Neil Walker 4.00 10.00
NW3 Neil Walker 4.00 10.00
OC1 Orlando Cepeda 10.00 25.00
OC2 Orlando Cepeda 10.00 25.00
PA Pedro Alvarez 5.00 12.00
PF1 Prince Fielder 6.00 15.00
PF2 Prince Fielder 6.00 15.00
PF3 Prince Fielder 6.00 15.00
PK Paul Konerko 4.00 10.00
PM1 Paul Molitor 5.00 12.00
PM2 Paul Molitor 5.00 12.00
PM3 Paul Molitor 5.00 12.00
PN1 Phil Niekro 5.00 12.00
PN2 Phil Niekro 5.00 12.00
PN3 Phil Niekro 5.00 12.00
PO Paul O'Neill 4.00 10.00
PS1 Pablo Sandoval 4.00 10.00
PS2 Pablo Sandoval 4.00 10.00
PS3 Pablo Sandoval 4.00 10.00
RB1 Ryan Braun 4.00 10.00
RB2 Ryan Braun 4.00 10.00
RB3 Ryan Braun 4.00 10.00
RC1 Robinson Cano 5.00 12.00
RC2 Robinson Cano 5.00 12.00
RC3 Robinson Cano 5.00 12.00
RCL Roberto Clemente 40.00 80.00
RDI1 R.A. Dickey 4.00 10.00
RDI2 R.A. Dickey 4.00 10.00
RDI3 R.A. Dickey 4.00 10.00
RH1 Rickey Henderson 10.00 25.00
RH2 Rickey Henderson 10.00 25.00
RH3 Rickey Henderson 10.00 25.00
RHO Ryan Howard 4.00 10.00
RJ Reggie Jackson 6.00 15.00
RJ2 Reggie Jackson 6.00 15.00
RV Ryan Vogelsong 6.00 15.00
RW Rickie Weeks 4.00 10.00
RW2 Rickie Weeks 4.00 10.00
RY Robin Yount 6.00 15.00
RZ1 Ryan Zimmerman 4.00 10.00
RZ2 Ryan Zimmerman 4.00 10.00
RZ3 Ryan Zimmerman 4.00 10.00
SC1 Starlin Castro 4.00 10.00
SC2 Starlin Castro 4.00 10.00
SC3 Starlin Castro 4.00 10.00
SCH Shin-Soo Choo 6.00 15.00
SR1 Scott Rolen 4.00 10.00
SR2 Scott Rolen 4.00 10.00
SR3 Scott Rolen 4.00 10.00
SS1 Stephen Strasburg 6.00 15.00
SS2 Stephen Strasburg 6.00 15.00
SS3 Stephen Strasburg 6.00 15.00
TB Trevor Bauer 4.00 10.00
TC1 Tony Cingrani 4.00 10.00
TC2 Tony Cingrani 4.00 10.00
TG1 Tony Gwynn 10.00 25.00
TG2 Tony Gwynn 10.00 25.00
TG3 Tony Gwynn 10.00 25.00
TH Tim Hudson 4.00 10.00
TL1 Tim Lincecum 4.00 10.00
TL2 Tim Lincecum 4.00 10.00
TL3 Tim Lincecum 4.00 10.00
TT1 Troy Tulowitzki 4.00 10.00
TT2 Troy Tulowitzki 4.00 10.00
TT3 Troy Tulowitzki 4.00 10.00
UJ Ubaldo Jimenez 4.00 10.00
VM Victor Martinez 4.00 10.00
VM2 Victor Martinez 4.00 10.00
WM1 Wade Miley 4.00 10.00
WM2 Wade Miley 4.00 10.00
WM3 Wade Miley 4.00 10.00
WMC Willie McCovey 8.00 20.00
WS Willie Stargell 8.00 20.00
YA Yonder Alonso 4.00 10.00
YB Yogi Berra 6.00 15.00
YC1 Yoenis Cespedes 5.00 12.00
YC2 Yoenis Cespedes 5.00 12.00
YD1 Yu Darvish 10.00 25.00
YD2 Yu Darvish 10.00 25.00
YD3 Yu Darvish 10.00 25.00
YG1 Yovani Gallardo 4.00 10.00
YG2 Yovani Gallardo 4.00 10.00
YP3 Yasiel Puig 20.00 50.00

2013 Topps Triple Threads Unity Relics Emerald

*EMERALD: .5X TO 1.2X BASIC
STATED ODDS 1:11 MINI
STATED PRINT RUN 18 SER.#'d SETS
ALL VERSIONS EQUALLY PRICED
SOME NOT PRICED DUE TO SCARCITY

2013 Topps Triple Threads Unity Relics Gold

*GOLD: .6X TO 1.5X BASIC
STATED ODDS 1:21 MINI
STATED PRINT RUN 9 SER.#'d SETS
ALL VERSIONS EQUALLY PRICED
SOME NOT PRICED DUE TO SCARCITY

2013 Topps Triple Threads Unity Relics Sepia

*SEPIA: .4X TO 1X BASIC
STATED ODDS 1:7 MINI
STATED PRINT RUN 27 SER.#'d SETS

2014 Topps Triple Threads

COMP.SET w/o AU's (100) 100.00 200.00
JSY AU RC ODDS 1:12 MINI
JSY AU RC PRINT RUN 99 SER.#'d SETS
JSY AU ODDS 1:12 MINI
JSY AU PRINT RUN 99 SER.#'d SETS
EXCHANGE DEADLINE 9/30/2017
1-100 PLATE ODDS 1:109 MINI
102-160 PLATE ODDS 1:266 MINI
PLATE PRINT RUN 1 SET PER COLOR
BLACK-CYAN-MAGENTA-YELLOW ISSUED
NO PLATE PRICING DUE TO SCARCITY
1 Mike Trout 4.00 10.00
2 George Brett 1.50 4.00
3 Babe Ruth 2.00 5.00
4 Gerrit Cole .75 2.00
5 Joe DiMaggio 1.50 4.00
6 Yangervis Solarte RC .50 1.25
7 Ty Cobb 1.25 3.00
8 Roger Clemens 1.00 2.50
9 Yasiel Puig .75 2.00
10 Allen Craig .60 1.50
11 Justin Verlander .75 2.00
12 Al Kaline .75 2.00
13 Shin-Soo Choo .60 1.50
14 Evan Longoria .60 1.50
15 Josh Hamilton .60 1.50
16 Brooks Robinson .60 1.50
17 Carlos Beltran .60 1.50
18 Rickey Henderson .75 2.00
19 Paul Goldschmidt .75 2.00
20 Adrian Gonzalez .60 1.50
21 Robin Yount .75 2.00
22 Eddie Mathews .75 2.00
23 Tom Seaver .60 1.50
24 Mike Schmidt 1.25 3.00
25 Ted Williams 1.50 4.00
26 Jeff Bagwell .60 1.50
27 Willie Mays 1.50 4.00
28 Stephen Strasburg .75 2.00
29 Johnny Bench .75 2.00
30 Miguel Cabrera .75 2.00
31 Mike Piazza .75 2.00
32 Adrian Beltre .75 2.00
33 Jose Bautista .60 1.50
34 Pedro Martinez .60 1.50
35 Jose Abreu RC 4.00 10.00
36 Derek Jeter 2.00 5.00
37 Jon Singleton RC .60 1.50
38 Adam Jones .60 1.50
39 Ozzie Smith 1.00 2.50
40 John Smoltz .75 2.00
41 Masahiro Tanaka RC 1.50 4.00
42 Madison Bumgarner .60 1.50
43 Jacoby Ellsbury .60 1.50
44 Bryce Harper 1.25 3.00
45 Hyun-Jin Ryu .60 1.50
46 David Wright .60 1.50
47 Mariano Rivera 1.00 2.50
48 Robinson Cano .60 1.50
49 Max Scherzer .75 2.00
50 Roberto Clemente 2.00 5.00
51 Yoenis Cespedes .50 1.25
52 Carlos Gonzalez .60 1.50
53 Craig Kimbrel .60 1.50
54 Justin Upton .60 1.50
55 Ryan Braun .60 1.50
56 Ernie Banks .75 2.00
57 Chris Sale .75 2.00
58 Giancarlo Stanton .60 1.50
59 Matt Holliday .75 2.00
60 Joey Votto .75 2.00
61 Randy Johnson .75 2.00
62 Prince Fielder .60 1.50
63 Reggie Jackson .60 1.50
64 Felix Hernandez .60 1.50
65 Don Mattingly 1.50 4.00
66 Jackie Robinson .75 2.00
67 Jim Palmer .60 1.50
68 Gregory Polanco RC .75 2.00
69 Nolan Ryan 2.50 6.00
70 Bo Jackson .75 2.00
71 Pedro Alvarez .50 1.25
72 Albert Pujols 1.00 2.50
73 Dustin Pedroia .75 2.00
74 Jose Canseco .60 1.50
75 Sandy Koufax 1.50 4.00
76 Chris Davis .50 1.25
77 Jose Reyes .60 1.50
78 Joe Mauer .60 1.50
79 Yu Darvish .75 2.00
80 Mark McGwire 1.50 4.00
81 Greg Maddux 1.00 2.50
82 Hanley Ramirez .60 1.50
83 Ian Kinsler .60 1.50
84 Clayton Kershaw 1.50 4.00
85 Jose Fernandez .75 2.00
86 George Springer RC 2.00 5.00
87 Oscar Taveras RC .60 1.50
88 Jim Rice .60 1.50
89 Cliff Lee .60 1.50
90 Adam Wainwright .60 1.50
91 David Ortiz .75 2.00
92 Stan Musial 1.25 3.00
93 Freddie Freeman 1.00 2.50
94 Andrew McCutchen .75 2.00
95 Yadier Molina .75 2.00
96 Cal Ripken Jr. 2.50 6.00
97 Tony Gwynn .75 2.00
98 Troy Tulowitzki .75 2.00
99 Buster Posey 1.00 2.50
100 Ken Griffey Jr. 1.50 4.00
102 Jurickson Profar JSY AU EXCH 6.00 15.00
103 Josh Donaldson JSY AU 15.00 40.00
105 Kolten Wong JSY AU RC 8.00 20.00
107 Patrick Corbin JSY AU 6.00 15.00
108 Wilmer Flores JSY AU RC 8.00 20.00
109 Julio Teheran JSY AU 6.00 15.00
110 Enny Romero JSY AU RC 6.00 15.00
112 Tony Cingrani JSY AU 6.00 15.00
113 L.J. Hoes JSY AU 5.00 12.00
114 Tyler Chatwood JSY AU 5.00 12.00
115 Manny Machado JSY AU 20.00 50.00
116 Matt Adams JSY AU 8.00 20.00
117 Andrelton Simmons JSY AU 4.00 10.00
118 Casey Kelly JSY AU 6.00 15.00
119 Matt Carpenter JSY AU 10.00 25.00
120 Travis d'Arnaud JSY AU RC 12.00 30.00
121 Joe Kelly JSY AU 5.00 12.00
122 Jimmy Nelson JSY AU RC 6.00 15.00
123 Jonathan Schoop JSY AU RC 6.00 15.00
124 Christian Yelich JSY AU 25.00 60.00
126 Allen Webster JSY AU 5.00 12.00
127 Carlos Martinez JSY AU 10.00 25.00
128 Taijuan Walker JSY AU RC 12.00 30.00
129 Evan Gattis JSY AU 10.00 25.00
130 Yordano Ventura JSY AU RC 10.00 25.00
131 Chris Owings JSY AU RC 6.00 15.00
132 Zack Wheeler JSY AU 10.00 25.00
133 Kevin Gausman JSY AU 8.00 20.00
135 Junior Lake JSY AU 5.00 12.00
138 Mike Zunino JSY AU 5.00 12.00
139 Cody Asche JSY AU 10.00 25.00
140 Sonny Gray JSY AU 12.00 30.00
141 Michael Choice JSY AU RC 6.00 15.00
142 Taylor Jordan JSY AU (RC) 6.00 15.00
143 Shelby Miller JSY AU 8.00 15.00
145 Jake Odorizzi JSY AU 5.00 12.00
155 Marcell Ozuna JSY AU 8.00 20.00
157 Andrew Lambo JSY AU RC 6.00 15.00
158 Mike Olt JSY AU EXCH 5.00 12.00
160 John Ryan Murphy JSY AU RC 12.00 30.00

2014 Topps Triple Threads Amber

*AMBER: 1.2X TO 3X BASIC
*AMBER RC: 1.2X TO 3X BASIC RC
STATED ODDS 1:4 MINI
STATED PRINT RUN 125 SER.#'d SETS
35 Jose Abreu 10.00 25.00
36 Derek Jeter 10.00 25.00
96 Cal Ripken Jr. 6.00 15.00

2014 Topps Triple Threads Amethyst

*AMETHYST: .75X TO 2X BASIC
*AMETHYST RC: .75X TO 2X BASIC RC
RANDOM INSETS IN PACKS
STATED PRINT RUN 325 SER.#'d SETS
35 Jose Abreu 6.00 15.00
36 Derek Jeter 6.00 15.00
96 Cal Ripken Jr. 4.00 10.00

2014 Topps Triple Threads Black

*BLCK JSY AU: .5X TO 1.2X BASIC
*BLCK JSY AU RC: .5X TO 1.2X BASIC
STATED ODDS 1:31 MINI
STATED PRINT RUN 35 SER.#'d SETS
EXCHANGE DEADLINE 9/30/2017

2014 Topps Triple Threads Emerald

*EMRLD: .75X TO 2X BASIC
*EMRLD RC: .75X TO 2X BASIC RC
1-100 ODDS 1:2 MINI
1-100 PRINT RUN 250 SER.#'d SETS
*EMRLD JSY AU: .4X TO 1X BASIC
*EMRLD JSY AU RC: .4X TO 1X BASIC
102-160 ODDS 1:22 MINI
102-160 PRINT RUN 50 SER.#'d SETS
EXCHANGE DEADLINE 9/30/2017
35 Jose Abreu 6.00 15.00
36 Derek Jeter 6.00 15.00
96 Cal Ripken Jr. 4.00 10.00

2014 Topps Triple Threads Gold

*GOLD: 1.2X TO 3X BASIC
*GOLD RC: 1.2X TO 3X BASIC RC
STATED ODDS 1:5 MINI
STATED PRINT RUN 99 SER.#'d SETS
35 Jose Abreu 15.00 40.00
96 Cal Ripken Jr. 6.00 15.00

2014 Topps Triple Threads Onyx

*BLACK: 2X TO 5X BASIC
*BLACK RC: 2X TO 5X BASIC RC
STATED ODDS 1:9 MINI
STATED PRINT RUN 50 SER.#'d SETS
36 Derek Jeter 20.00 50.00

2014 Topps Triple Threads Sapphire

*SAPPHIRE: 2.5X TO 6X BASIC
*SAPPHIRE RC: 2.5X TO 6X BASIC RC
STATED ODDS 1:18 MINI
STATED PRINT RUN 25 SER.#'d SETS
1 Mike Trout 30.00 80.00
36 Derek Jeter 30.00 80.00
69 Nolan Ryan 30.00 80.00
75 Sandy Koufax 20.00 50.00
80 Mark McGwire 25.00 60.00
96 Cal Ripken Jr. 30.00 80.00

2014 Topps Triple Threads Sepia

*SEPIA JSY AU: .4X TO 1X BASIC
*SEPIA JSY AU RC: .4X TO 1X BASIC
STATED ODDS 1:15 MINI
STATED PRINT RUN 75 SER.#'d SETS
EXCHANGE DEADLINE 9/30/2017

2014 Topps Triple Threads Autograph Relic Combos

STATED ODDS 1:76 MINI
STATED PRINT RUN 36 SER.#'d SETS
EXCHANGE DEADLINE 9/30/2017
PRINTING PLATE ODDS 1:686 MINI
PLATE PRINT RUN 1 SET PER COLOR
BLACK-CYAN-MAGENTA-YELLOW ISSUED
NO PLATE PRICING DUE TO SCARCITY
TTARCCMS Myrs/Cbrr/Schrzr EXCH 60.00 150.00
TTARCCPD Cspds/Dnldsn/Prkr 15.00 40.00
TTARCCTJ Trt/Cspds/Jns 150.00 300.00
TTARCFSS Schrzr/Sl/Frndz 40.00 100.00
TTARCGFA Gldschmdt/Adms/Frmn 30.00 80.00
TTARCGMA McGwr/Almr/Griff Jr. 150.00 400.00
TTARCGMS Mddx/Smltz/Glvne 250.00 400.00
TTARCGRG Rns/Grrr/Gnzlz 25.00 60.00
TTARCHFG Glts/Hywrd/Frmn 30.00 80.00
TTARCLFS Santana/Longoria/Frazier 20.00 50.00
TTARCMLC Cobb/Longoria/Moore 20.00 50.00
TTARCMMW Miller/Wong/Martinez 20.00 50.00
TTARCMTM Trt/Myrs/Mchdo 100.00 200.00
TTARCPWH Mrtnz/Wrght/Pzza 60.00 150.00
TTARCSFK Schrzr/Krshw/Frnndz 75.00 150.00
TTARCVPF Phillips/Votto/Frazier 30.00 80.00

2014 Topps Triple Threads Autograph Relic Combos Emerald

*EMERALD: .5X TO 1.2X BASIC
STATED ODDS 1:151 MINI
STATED PRINT RUN 18 SER.#'d SETS
OVERALL 1-100 PLATE ODDS 1:109 MINI

2014 Topps Triple Threads Autograph Relic Combos Sepia

*SEPIA: .4X TO 1X BASIC
STATED ODDS 1:101 MINI
STATED PRINT RUN 27 SER.#'d SETS
OVERALL 1-100 PLATE ODDS 1:109 MINI

2014 Topps Triple Threads Legend Relics

STATED ODDS 1:61 MINI
STATED PRINT RUN 36 SER.#'d SETS
TTRLCR Cal Ripken Jr. 12.00 30.00
TTRLEM Eddie Mathews 15.00 40.00
TTRLHA Hank Aaron 50.00 100.00
TTRLJB Johnny Bench 10.00 25.00
TTRLJM Joe Morgan 12.00 30.00
TTRLKG Ken Griffey Jr. 20.00 50.00
TTRLMR Mariano Rivera 12.00 30.00
TTRLMS Mike Schmidt 10.00 25.00
TTRLNR Nolan Ryan 30.00 80.00
TTRLPM Pedro Martinez 12.00 30.00
TTRLRC Roberto Clemente 40.00 100.00
TTRLRCL Roger Clemens 10.00 25.00
TTRLRH Rickey Henderson 15.00 40.00
TTRLRJ Randy Johnson 15.00 40.00
TTRLSC Steve Carlton 12.00 30.00
TTRLTC Ty Cobb 30.00 80.00
TTRLTS Tom Seaver 12.00 30.00
TTRLTW Ted Williams 30.00 80.00
TTRLWM Willie Mays 40.00 80.00

2014 Topps Triple Threads Legend Relics Emerald

*EMERALD: .4X TO 1X BASIC
STATED ODDS 1:121 MINI
STATED PRINT RUN 18 SER.#'d SETS

2014 Topps Triple Threads Legend Relics Sepia

*SEPIA: .4X TO 1X BASIC
STATED ODDS 1:81 MINI
STATED PRINT RUN 27 SER.#'d SETS

2014 Topps Triple Threads Relic Autographs

STATED ODDS 1:10 MINI
STATED PRINT RUN 18 SER.#'d SETS
EXCHANGE DEADLINE 9/30/2017
PRINTING PLATE ODDS 1:43 MINI
PLATE PRINT RUN 1 SET PER COLOR
BLACK-CYAN-MAGENTA-YELLOW ISSUED
NO PLATE PRICING DUE TO SCARCITY
TTARAC1 Allen Craig 12.00 30.00
TTARAC2 Allen Craig 12.00 30.00
TTARAC3 Allen Craig 12.00 30.00
TTARAC4 Allen Craig 12.00 30.00
TTARAC5 Allen Craig 12.00 30.00
TTARAJ1 Adam Jones 15.00 40.00
TTARAR1 Anthony Rizzo 25.00 60.00
TTARAR2 Anthony Rizzo 25.00 60.00
TTARAR3 Anthony Rizzo 25.00 60.00
TTARBG1 Brett Gardner 10.00 25.00
TTARBG2 Brett Gardner 10.00 25.00
TTARBG3 Brett Gardner 10.00 25.00
TTARBH1 Bryce Harper 75.00 150.00
TTARBH2 Bryce Harper 75.00 150.00
TTARBH3 Bryce Harper 75.00 150.00
TTARBHA1 Billy Hamilton 15.00 40.00
TTARBHA2 Billy Hamilton 15.00 40.00
TTARBHA3 Billy Hamilton 15.00 40.00
TTARBHA4 Billy Hamilton 15.00 40.00
TTARBHA5 Billy Hamilton 15.00 40.00
TTARBM1 Brian McCann 15.00 40.00
TTARBM2 Brian McCann 15.00 40.00
TTARBM3 Brian McCann 15.00 40.00
TTARBP1 Brandon Phillips 8.00 20.00
TTARBP2 Brandon Phillips 8.00 20.00
TTARBP3 Brandon Phillips 8.00 20.00
TTARBZ1 Ben Zobrist 15.00 40.00
TTARBZ2 Ben Zobrist 15.00 40.00
TTARBZ3 Ben Zobrist 15.00 40.00
TTARCA1 Chris Archer 5.00 12.00
TTARCA2 Chris Archer 5.00 12.00
TTARCA3 Chris Archer 5.00 12.00
TTARCA4 Chris Archer 5.00 12.00
TTARCA5 Chris Archer 5.00 12.00
TTARCB1 Christian Bethancourt 5.00 12.00
TTARCB2 Christian Bethancourt 5.00 12.00
TTARCB3 Christian Bethancourt 5.00 12.00
TTARCB4 Christian Bethancourt 5.00 12.00
TTARCB5 Christian Bethancourt 5.00 12.00
TTARCH1 Cole Hamels 12.00 30.00
TTARCO1 Chris Owings 8.00 20.00
TTARCO2 Chris Owings 8.00 20.00
TTARCO3 Chris Owings 8.00 20.00
TTARCO4 Chris Owings 8.00 20.00
TTARCO5 Chris Owings 8.00 20.00
TTARCR1 Cal Ripken Jr. 60.00 150.00
TTARCR2 Cal Ripken Jr. 60.00 150.00
TTARCR3 Cal Ripken Jr. 60.00 150.00
TTARCS1 Chris Sale 15.00 40.00
TTARCS2 Chris Sale 15.00 40.00
TTARCS3 Chris Sale 15.00 40.00
TTARCSA1 Carlos Santana 6.00 15.00
TTARCSA2 Carlos Santana 6.00 15.00
TTARCSA3 Carlos Santana 6.00 15.00
TTARCSA4 Carlos Santana 6.00 15.00
TTARCSA5 Carlos Santana 6.00 15.00
TTARCW1 C.J. Wilson 8.00 20.00
TTARCW2 C.J. Wilson 8.00 20.00
TTARCW3 C.J. Wilson 8.00 20.00
TTARCY1 Christian Yelich 20.00 50.00
TTARCY2 Christian Yelich 20.00 50.00
TTARCY3 Christian Yelich 20.00 50.00
TTARDG1 Didi Gregorius 6.00 15.00
TTARDG2 Didi Gregorius 6.00 15.00
TTARDG3 Didi Gregorius 6.00 15.00
TTARDG4 Didi Gregorius 6.00 15.00
TTARDG5 Didi Gregorius 6.00 15.00
TTARDM1 Dale Murphy 30.00 80.00
TTARDM2 Dale Murphy 30.00 80.00
TTARDM3 Dale Murphy 30.00 80.00
TTARDMA1 Daisuke Matsuzaka 40.00 100.00
TTARDMA2 Daisuke Matsuzaka 40.00 100.00
TTARDMA3 Daisuke Matsuzaka 40.00 100.00
TTARDN1 Daniel Nava 12.00 30.00
TTARDN2 Daniel Nava 12.00 30.00
TTARDN3 Daniel Nava 12.00 30.00
TTARDN4 Daniel Nava 12.00 30.00
TTARDN5 Daniel Nava 12.00 30.00
TTARED1 Eric Davis 12.00 30.00
TTARED2 Eric Davis 12.00 30.00
TTARED3 Eric Davis 12.00 30.00
TTARED4 Eric Davis 12.00 30.00
TTARED5 Eric Davis 12.00 30.00
TTARFF1 Freddie Freeman 20.00 50.00
TTARFF2 Freddie Freeman 20.00 50.00
TTARFF3 Freddie Freeman 20.00 50.00
TTARFM1 Fred McGriff 12.00 30.00
TTARFM2 Fred McGriff 12.00 30.00
TTARFM3 Fred McGriff 12.00 30.00
TTARFV1 Fernando Valenzuela 40.00 100.00
TTARFV2 Fernando Valenzuela 40.00 100.00
TTARFV3 Fernando Valenzuela 40.00 100.00
TTARHA1 Hank Aaron 150.00 300.00
TTARHA2 Hank Aaron 150.00 300.00
TTARHA3 Hank Aaron 150.00 300.00
TTARJD1 Josh Donaldson 10.00 25.00
TTARJD2 Josh Donaldson 10.00 25.00
TTARJD3 Josh Donaldson 10.00 25.00
TTARJD4 Josh Donaldson 10.00 25.00
TTARJD5 Josh Donaldson 10.00 25.00
TTARJG1 Juan Gonzalez 25.00 60.00
TTARJG2 Juan Gonzalez 25.00 60.00
TTARJG3 Juan Gonzalez 25.00 60.00
TTARJH1 Jason Heyward 10.00 25.00
TTARJH2 Jason Heyward 10.00 25.00
TTARJH3 Jason Heyward 10.00 25.00
TTARJP1 Jarrod Parker 5.00 12.00
TTARJP2 Jarrod Parker 5.00 12.00
TTARJP3 Jarrod Parker 5.00 12.00
TTARJPR1 Jurickson Profar EXCH 10.00 25.00
TTARJPR2 Jurickson Profar EXCH 10.00 25.00
TTARJPR3 Jurickson Profar EXCH 10.00 25.00
TTARJR1 Jim Rice 12.00 30.00
TTARJR2 Jim Rice 12.00 30.00
TTARJR3 Jim Rice 12.00 30.00
TTARJS1 John Smoltz 25.00 60.00
TTARKG1 Ken Griffey Jr. 150.00 300.00
TTARKG2 Ken Griffey Jr. 150.00 300.00
TTARKG3 Ken Griffey Jr. 150.00 300.00
TTARKU1 Koji Uehara 30.00 80.00
TTARKU2 Koji Uehara 30.00 80.00
TTARKU3 Koji Uehara 30.00 80.00
TTARKW1 Kolten Wong 6.00 15.00
TTARLG1 Luis Gonzalez 8.00 20.00
TTARLG2 Luis Gonzalez 8.00 20.00
TTARLG3 Luis Gonzalez 8.00 20.00
TTARLH1 Livan Hernandez 5.00 12.00
TTARLH2 Livan Hernandez 5.00 12.00
TTARLH3 Livan Hernandez 5.00 12.00
TTARMA1 Matt Adams 10.00 25.00
TTARMA2 Matt Adams 10.00 25.00
TTARMA3 Matt Adams 10.00 25.00

TTARMA4 Matt Adams 10.00 25.00
TTARMA5 Matt Adams 10.00 25.00
TTARMC1 Miguel Cabrera EXCH 75.00 150.00
TTARMC2 Miguel Cabrera EXCH 75.00 150.00
TTARMC3 Miguel Cabrera EXCH 75.00 150.00
TTARMCA1 Matt Carpenter 15.00 40.00
TTARMCA2 Matt Carpenter 15.00 40.00
TTARMCA3 Matt Carpenter 15.00 40.00
TTARMCN1 Matt Cain 10.00 25.00
TTARMCN2 Matt Cain 10.00 25.00
TTARMCN3 Matt Cain 10.00 25.00
TTARMCU1 Michael Cuddyer 5.00 12.00
TTARMCU2 Michael Cuddyer 5.00 12.00
TTARMCU3 Michael Cuddyer 5.00 12.00
TTARMD1 Matt Davidson 6.00 15.00
TTARMD2 Matt Davidson 6.00 15.00
TTARMD3 Matt Davidson 6.00 15.00
TTARMM1 Mike Minor 6.00 15.00
TTARMM2 Mike Minor 6.00 15.00
TTARMM3 Mike Minor 6.00 15.00
TTARMM4 Mike Minor 6.00 15.00
TTARMM5 Mike Minor 6.00 15.00
TTARMMA1 Manny Machado 30.00 60.00
TTARMMA2 Manny Machado 30.00 60.00
TTARMMA3 Manny Machado 30.00 60.00
TTARMMC1 Mark McGwire 75.00 150.00
TTARMN1 Mike Napoli 10.00 25.00
TTARMN2 Mike Napoli 10.00 25.00
TTARMN3 Mike Napoli 10.00 25.00
TTARMP1 Mike Piazza 50.00 120.00
TTARMP2 Mike Piazza 50.00 120.00
TTARMP3 Mike Piazza 50.00 120.00
TTARMS1 Max Scherzer 30.00 80.00
TTARMW1 Michael Wacha EXCH 12.00 30.00
TTARMW2 Michael Wacha EXCH 12.00 30.00
TTARMW3 Michael Wacha EXCH 12.00 30.00
TTAROC1 Orlando Cepeda 20.00 50.00
TTAROC2 Orlando Cepeda 20.00 50.00
TTAROC3 Orlando Cepeda 20.00 50.00
TTAROH1 Orlando Hernandez EXCH 8.00 20.00
TTAROH2 Orlando Hernandez EXCH 8.00 20.00
TTAROH3 Orlando Hernandez EXCH 8.00 20.00
TTAROV1 Omar Vizquel 60.00 150.00
TTAROV2 Omar Vizquel 60.00 150.00
TTAROV3 Omar Vizquel 60.00 150.00
TTARPG1 Paul Goldschmidt 15.00 40.00
TTARPG2 Paul Goldschmidt 15.00 40.00
TTARPG3 Paul Goldschmidt 15.00 40.00
TTARRA1 Roberto Alomar 25.00 60.00
TTARRA2 Roberto Alomar 25.00 60.00
TTARRA3 Roberto Alomar 25.00 60.00
TTARRB1 Ryan Braun 12.00 30.00
TTARRB2 Ryan Braun 12.00 30.00
TTARRB3 Ryan Braun 12.00 30.00
TTARRC1 Roger Clemens 30.00 80.00
TTARRC2 Roger Clemens 30.00 80.00
TTARRC3 Roger Clemens 30.00 80.00
TTARRH1 Ryan Howard 20.00 50.00
TTARRJ1 Reggie Jackson 25.00 60.00
TTARSC1 Steve Carlton 12.00 30.00
TTARSG1 Sonny Gray 8.00 20.00
TTARSG2 Sonny Gray 8.00 20.00
TTARSG3 Sonny Gray 8.00 20.00
TTARSG4 Sonny Gray 8.00 20.00
TTARSG5 Sonny Gray 8.00 20.00
TTARSM1 Shelby Miller 10.00 25.00
TTARSM2 Shelby Miller 10.00 25.00
TTARSM3 Shelby Miller 10.00 25.00
TTARSMA1 Starling Marte 15.00 40.00
TTARSMA2 Starling Marte 15.00 40.00
TTARSMA3 Starling Marte 15.00 40.00
TTARSMA4 Starling Marte 15.00 40.00
TTARSMA5 Starling Marte 15.00 40.00
TTARSP1 Salvador Perez 12.00 30.00
TTARSP2 Salvador Perez 12.00 30.00
TTARSP3 Salvador Perez 12.00 30.00
TTARSP4 Salvador Perez 12.00 30.00
TTARSP5 Salvador Perez 12.00 30.00
TTARTC1 Tony Cingrani 6.00 15.00
TTARTC2 Tony Cingrani 6.00 15.00
TTARTC3 Tony Cingrani 6.00 15.00
TTARTC4 Tony Cingrani 6.00 15.00
TTARTC5 Tony Cingrani 6.00 15.00
TTARTF1 Todd Frazier 12.00 30.00
TTARTF2 Todd Frazier 12.00 30.00
TTARTF3 Todd Frazier 12.00 30.00
TTARTF4 Todd Frazier 12.00 30.00
TTARTF5 Todd Frazier 12.00 30.00
TTARTR1 Tim Raines 12.00 30.00
TTARTR2 Tim Raines 12.00 30.00
TTARTR3 Tim Raines 12.00 30.00
TTARTT1 Troy Tulowitzki 15.00 40.00
TTARTT2 Troy Tulowitzki 15.00 40.00
TTARTT3 Troy Tulowitzki 15.00 40.00
TTARVG1 Vladimir Guerrero 10.00 25.00
TTARVG2 Vladimir Guerrero 10.00 25.00
TTARVG3 Vladimir Guerrero 10.00 25.00
TTARWM1 Wil Myers 10.00 25.00
TTARWM2 Wil Myers 10.00 25.00
TTARWM3 Wil Myers 10.00 25.00
TTARYA1 Yonder Alonso 5.00 12.00
TTARYA2 Yonder Alonso 5.00 12.00
TTARYA3 Yonder Alonso 5.00 12.00
TTARYC1 Yoenis Cespedes 12.00 30.00
TTARYC2 Yoenis Cespedes 12.00 30.00
TTARYC3 Yoenis Cespedes 12.00 30.00
TTARZW1 Zack Wheeler 10.00 25.00
TTARZW2 Zack Wheeler 10.00 25.00
TTARZW3 Zack Wheeler 10.00 25.00
TTARZW4 Zack Wheeler 10.00 25.00
TTARZW5 Zack Wheeler 10.00 25.00

2014 Topps Triple Threads Relic Autographs Gold

*GOLD: .5X TO 1.2X BASIC
STATED ODDS 1:19 MINI
STATED PRINT RUN 9 SER.#'d SETS
SOME NOT PRICED DUE TO SCARCITY
EXCHANGE DEADLINE 9/30/2017

2014 Topps Triple Threads Relic Combos

STATED ODDS 1:24 MINI
STATED PRINT RUN 36 SER.#'d SETS
TTRCBAP Andrus/Profar/Beltre 8.00 20.00
TTRCBAS Alvarez/Sandoval/Beltre 8.00 20.00
TTRCBEC Btsta/Encrncn/Cbrra 10.00 25.00
TTRCBMC Cspds/McCtchn/Btsta 12.00 30.00
TTRCBSK Kpns/Sntna/Brn 8.00 20.00
TTRCCCC Cngrni/Chpmn/Cto 10.00 25.00
TTRCCHD Hrpr/Cspds/Drvsh 12.00 30.00
TTRCCMS Myrs/Schrzr/Cbrra 8.00 20.00
TTRCCPD Donaldson/Cespedes/Parker 8.00 20.00
TTRCDFE Encarnacion/Davis/Fielder 8.00 20.00
TTRCFHI Iwkma/Hrnndz/Frnkln 8.00 20.00
TTRCFRC Cstro/Rzzo/Fjkwa 10.00 25.00
TTRCFSH Sandoval/Headley/Freese 6.00 15.00
TTRCGCT Cspds/Trt/Gnzlz 20.00 50.00
TTRCGFA Freeman/Adams/Goldschmidt 10.00 25.00
TTRCGMA Almr/McGwre/Griff Jr. 20.00 50.00
TTRCGMG Goldschmidt
Miley/Gregorius 8.00 20.00
TTRCGRG Rns/Gnzlz/Grrro 10.00 25.00
TTRCHFG Heyward/Gattis/Freeman 10.00 25.00
TTRCHMM Mllr/Hlldy/Mlna 15.00 40.00
TTRCHSG Segura/Hart/Gomez 6.00 15.00
TTRCIDK Iwkma/Drvsh/Krda 10.00 25.00
TTRCIHW Iwkma/Wlkr/Hrnndz 12.00 30.00
TTRCJBS Bltrn/CC/Jeter 40.00 100.00
TTRCJPR Rvr/Psd/Jeter 30.00 80.00
TTRCKEP Puig/Ellis/Kemp 10.00 25.00
TTRCLHH Howard/Hamels/Lee 6.00 15.00
TTRCLMP Pice/Lngra/Mre 8.00 20.00
TTRCLUB Lee/Brown/Utley 8.00 20.00
TTRCMAC McCthn/Alvrz/Cole 20.00 50.00
TTRCMDJ Mchdo/Dvs/Jns 15.00 40.00
TTRCMEK Krda/McCnn/Ellsbry 12.00 30.00
TTRCMLC Cbb/Lngra/Mre 8.00 20.00
TTRCMMW Mlna/Mllr/Wnwrght 12.00 30.00
TTRCMMW1 Mllr/Mrtnz/Wong 15.00 40.00
TTRCNPM Pedroia/Middlebrooks/Napoli 8.00 20.00
TTRCPCL Cain/Lncm/Psey 10.00 25.00
TTRCPNC Papelbon/Chapman/Nathan 8.00 20.00
TTRCPWM Piazza/Martinez/Wright 8.00 20.00
TTRCRGA Alomar/Ramirez/Guerrero 8.00 20.00
TTRCRGS Strasburg/Gonzalez/Rodriguez 8.00 20.00
TTRCRPG Puig/Gordon/Ryu 8.00 20.00
TTRCSMF Sgra/Mchdo/Frnkln 6.00 15.00
TTRCSSS Schrzr/Sle/Stasbrg 10.00 25.00
TTRCSVS1 Schrzr/Vrlndr/Snchz 12.00 30.00
TTRCSYF Ylch/Stntn/Frnndz 10.00 25.00
TTRCTCG Tulowitzki/Gonzalez/Cuddyer 8.00 20.00
TTRCUUH Upton/Heyward/Upton 6.00 15.00
TTRCVFG Gonzalez/Freeman/Votto 10.00 25.00
TTRCVPF Philps/Vtto/Frzr 10.00 25.00
TTRCWHG Gnzlz/Wrth/Hrpr 12.00 30.00

2014 Topps Triple Threads Relic Combos Emerald

*EMERALD: .5X TO 1.2X BASIC
STATED ODDS 1:48 MINI
STATED PRINT RUN 18 SER.#'d SETS

2014 Topps Triple Threads Relic Combos Sepia

*SEPIA: .4X TO 1X BASIC
STATED ODDS 1:32 MINI
STATED PRINT RUN 27 SER.#'d SETS

2014 Topps Triple Threads Relic Combos Double

STATED ODDS 1:406 MINI
STATED PRINT RUN 18 SER.#'d SETS
TTRDC2 McC/Blt/Ell/Krd/Jtr/Sbt 75.00 150.00
TTRDC5 Frm/Vtt/Gnz/Cbr/Gld/Dvs 90.00 150.00
TTRDC8 Parker/Gray/Reddick/Cespedes
Donaldson/Lowrie 25.00 60.00
TTRDC12 Freeman/Gattis/Kimbrel/Heyward
Teheran/Simmons 30.00 80.00
TTRDC13 Cuddyer/Gonzalez/Rosario/Tulowitzki
Arenado/Morneau 30.00 80.00

2014 Topps Triple Threads Relics

STATED ODDS 1:9 MINI
STATED PRINT RUN 36 SER.#'d SETS
TTRAC1 Allen Craig 5.00 12.00
TTRAC2 Allen Craig 5.00 12.00
TTRAC3 Allen Craig 5.00 12.00
TTRAJ1 Adam Jones 8.00 20.00
TTRAJ2 Adam Jones 8.00 20.00
TTRAJ3 Adam Jones 8.00 20.00
TTRAR1 Anthony Rizzo 8.00 20.00
TTRAR2 Anthony Rizzo 8.00 20.00
TTRAR3 Anthony Rizzo 8.00 20.00
TTRBB1 Billy Butler 4.00 10.00
TTRBB2 Billy Butler 4.00 10.00
TTRBB3 Billy Butler 4.00 10.00
TTRBG1 Brett Gardner 10.00 25.00
TTRBG2 Brett Gardner 10.00 25.00
TTRBG3 Brett Gardner 10.00 25.00
TTRBHA1 Billy Hamilton 10.00 25.00
TTRBHA2 Billy Hamilton 10.00 25.00
TTRBHA3 Billy Hamilton 10.00 25.00
TTRBM1 Brian McCann 5.00 12.00
TTRBM2 Brian McCann 5.00 12.00
TTRBM3 Brian McCann 5.00 12.00
TTRBP1 Brandon Phillips 4.00 10.00
TTRBP2 Brandon Phillips 4.00 10.00
TTRBP3 Brandon Phillips 4.00 10.00
TTRBZ1 Ben Zobrist 5.00 12.00
TTRBZ2 Ben Zobrist 5.00 12.00
TTRBZ3 Ben Zobrist 5.00 12.00
TTRCA1 Chris Archer 4.00 10.00
TTRCA2 Chris Archer 4.00 10.00
TTRCA3 Chris Archer 4.00 10.00
TTRCB1 Christian Bethancourt 6.00 15.00
TTRCB2 Christian Bethancourt 6.00 15.00
TTRCB3 Christian Bethancourt 6.00 15.00
TTRCO1 Chris Owings 4.00 10.00
TTRCO2 Chris Owings 4.00 10.00
TTRCO3 Chris Owings 4.00 10.00
TTRCY1 Christian Yelich 8.00 20.00
TTRCY2 Christian Yelich 8.00 20.00
TTRCY3 Christian Yelich 8.00 20.00
TTRDJ1 Derek Jeter 40.00 100.00
TTRDJ2 Derek Jeter 40.00 100.00
TTRDJ3 Derek Jeter 40.00 100.00
TTRDMA1 Daisuke Matsuzaka 5.00 12.00
TTRDMA2 Daisuke Matsuzaka 5.00 12.00
TTRDMA3 Daisuke Matsuzaka 5.00 12.00
TTRDO1 David Ortiz 8.00 20.00
TTRDO2 David Ortiz 8.00 20.00
TTRDO3 David Ortiz 8.00 20.00
TTRFF1 Freddie Freeman 8.00 20.00
TTRFF2 Freddie Freeman 8.00 20.00
TTRFF3 Freddie Freeman 8.00 20.00
TTRFM1 Fred McGriff 5.00 12.00
TTRFM2 Fred McGriff 5.00 12.00
TTRFM3 Fred McGriff 5.00 12.00
TTRJD1 Josh Donaldson 5.00 12.00
TTRJD2 Josh Donaldson 5.00 12.00
TTRJD3 Josh Donaldson 5.00 12.00
TTRJG1 Juan Gonzalez 15.00 40.00
TTRJG2 Juan Gonzalez 15.00 40.00
TTRJG3 Juan Gonzalez 15.00 40.00
TTRJGR1 Jason Grilli 4.00 10.00
TTRJGR2 Jason Grilli 4.00 10.00
TTRJGR3 Jason Grilli 4.00 10.00
TTRJH1 Jason Heyward 5.00 12.00
TTRJH2 Jason Heyward 5.00 12.00
TTRJH3 Jason Heyward 5.00 12.00
TTRJP1 Jarrod Parker 4.00 10.00
TTRJP2 Jarrod Parker 4.00 10.00
TTRJP3 Jarrod Parker 4.00 10.00
TTRJPR1 Jurickson Profar 5.00 12.00
TTRJPR2 Jurickson Profar 5.00 12.00
TTRJPR3 Jurickson Profar 5.00 12.00
TTRJR1 Jim Rice 5.00 12.00
TTRJR2 Jim Rice 5.00 12.00
TTRJR3 Jim Rice 5.00 12.00
TTRKG1 Ken Griffey Jr. 12.00 30.00
TTRKG2 Ken Griffey Jr. 12.00 30.00
TTRKG3 Ken Griffey Jr. 12.00 30.00
TTRKW1 Kolten Wong 8.00 20.00
TTRKW2 Kolten Wong 8.00 20.00
TTRKW3 Kolten Wong 8.00 20.00
TTRMA1 Matt Adams 6.00 15.00
TTRMA2 Matt Adams 6.00 15.00
TTRMA3 Matt Adams 6.00 15.00
TTRMC1 Miguel Cabrera 12.00 30.00
TTRMC2 Miguel Cabrera 12.00 30.00
TTRMC3 Miguel Cabrera 12.00 30.00
TTRMCN1 Matt Cain 6.00 15.00
TTRMCN2 Matt Cain 6.00 15.00
TTRMCN3 Matt Cain 6.00 15.00
TTRMCU1 Michael Cuddyer 4.00 10.00
TTRMCU2 Michael Cuddyer 4.00 10.00
TTRMCU3 Michael Cuddyer 4.00 10.00
TTRMM1 Mike Minor 4.00 10.00
TTRMM2 Mike Minor 4.00 10.00
TTRMM3 Mike Minor 4.00 10.00
TTRMMC1 Mark McGwire 12.00 30.00
TTRMMC2 Mark McGwire 12.00 30.00
TTRMMC3 Mark McGwire 12.00 30.00
TTRMN1 Mike Napoli 4.00 10.00
TTRMN2 Mike Napoli 4.00 10.00
TTRMN3 Mike Napoli 4.00 10.00
TTRMRA1 Manny Ramirez 6.00 15.00
TTRMRA2 Manny Ramirez 6.00 15.00
TTRMRA3 Manny Ramirez 6.00 15.00
TTRMT1 Mike Trout 25.00 60.00
TTRMT2 Mike Trout 25.00 60.00
TTRMT3 Mike Trout 25.00 60.00
TTRMTA1 Masahiro Tanaka 20.00 50.00
TTRMTA2 Masahiro Tanaka 20.00 50.00
TTRMTA3 Masahiro Tanaka 20.00 50.00
TTROC1 Orlando Cepeda 6.00 15.00
TTROC2 Orlando Cepeda 6.00 15.00
TTROC3 Orlando Cepeda 6.00 15.00
TTROV1 Omar Vizquel 8.00 20.00
TTROV2 Omar Vizquel 8.00 20.00
TTROV3 Omar Vizquel 8.00 20.00
TTRPG1 Paul Goldschmidt 6.00 15.00
TTRPG2 Paul Goldschmidt 6.00 15.00
TTRPG3 Paul Goldschmidt 6.00 15.00
TTRRA1 Roberto Alomar 10.00 25.00
TTRRA2 Roberto Alomar 10.00 25.00
TTRRA3 Roberto Alomar 10.00 25.00
TTRRB1 Ryan Braun 5.00 12.00
TTRRB2 Ryan Braun 5.00 12.00
TTRRB3 Ryan Braun 5.00 12.00
TTRRC1 Roger Clemens 12.00 30.00
TTRRC2 Roger Clemens 12.00 30.00
TTRRC3 Roger Clemens 12.00 30.00
TTRSG1 Sonny Gray 5.00 12.00
TTRSG2 Sonny Gray 5.00 12.00
TTRSG3 Sonny Gray 5.00 12.00
TTRSMA1 Starling Marte 5.00 12.00
TTRSMA2 Starling Marte 5.00 12.00
TTRSMA3 Starling Marte 5.00 12.00
TTRTF1 Todd Frazier 5.00 12.00
TTRTF2 Todd Frazier 5.00 12.00
TTRTF3 Todd Frazier 5.00 12.00
TTRVG1 Vladimir Guerrero 5.00 12.00
TTRVG2 Vladimir Guerrero 5.00 12.00
TTRVG3 Vladimir Guerrero 5.00 12.00
TTRWM1 Wil Myers 4.00 10.00
TTRWM2 Wil Myers 4.00 10.00
TTRWM3 Wil Myers 4.00 10.00
TTRYA1 Yonder Alonso 4.00 10.00
TTRYA2 Yonder Alonso 4.00 10.00
TTRYA3 Yonder Alonso 4.00 10.00
TTRYC1 Yoenis Cespedes 8.00 20.00
TTRYC2 Yoenis Cespedes 8.00 20.00
TTRYC3 Yoenis Cespedes 8.00 20.00

2014 Topps Triple Threads Relics Emerald

*EMERALD: .5X TO 1.2X BASIC
STATED ODDS 1:17 MINI
STATED PRINT RUN 18 SER.#'d SETS

2014 Topps Triple Threads Relics Gold

*GOLD: .6X TO 1.5X BASIC
STATED ODDS 1:33 MINI
STATED PRINT RUN 9 SER.#'d SETS

2014 Topps Triple Threads Relics Sepia

*SEPIA: .4X TO 1X BASIC
STATED ODDS 1:11 MINI
STATED PRINT RUN 27 SER.#'d SETS

2014 Topps Triple Threads Rookie Autographs

RANDOM INSERTS IN PACKS
STATED PRINT RUN 100 SER.#'d SETS
EXCHANGE DEADLINE 9/30/2017
TRAAH Andrew Heaney 5.00 12.00
TRAEA Erisbel Arruebarrena 12.00 30.00
TRAEB Eddie Butler 5.00 12.00
TRAGP Gregory Polanco 10.00 25.00
TRAGS George Springer 10.00 25.00
TRAJA Jose Abreu 30.00 80.00
TRAJS Jon Singleton 6.00 15.00
TRANC Nick Castellanos 15.00 40.00
TRAOT Oscar Taveras 6.00 15.00
TRARE Roenis Elias 5.00 12.00
TRARO Rougned Odor 10.00 25.00
TRAYS Yangervis Solarte 5.00 12.00

2014 Topps Triple Threads Transparencies Relic Autographs

STATED ODDS 1:88 MINI
STATED PRINT RUN 25 SER.#'d SETS
EXCHANGE DEADLINE 9/30/2017
TTTAJ Adam Jones 12.00 30.00
TTTAP Albert Pujols 75.00 200.00
TTTBH Bryce Harper 100.00 200.00
TTTBP Buster Posey EXCH 25.00 60.00
TTTDP Dustin Pedroia EXCH 20.00 50.00
TTTDW David Wright 15.00 40.00
TTTFF Freddie Freeman EXCH 30.00 80.00
TTTGS Giancarlo Stanton 30.00 80.00
TTTJF Jose Fernandez EXCH 25.00 60.00
TTTJV Joey Votto 30.00 80.00
TTTMC Miguel Cabrera 30.00 80.00
TTTMS Max Scherzer 30.00 80.00
TTTPG Paul Goldschmidt 25.00 60.00
TTTRB Ryan Braun 15.00 40.00
TTTRC Robinson Cano 25.00 60.00
TTTTT Troy Tulowitzki 25.00 60.00
TTTYM Yadier Molina 60.00 120.00

2014 Topps Triple Threads Unity Relic Autographs

STATED ODDS 1:6 MINI
STATED PRINT RUN 99 SER.#'d SETS
EXCHANGE DEADLINE 9/30/2017
UAJRAB Albert Belle 5.00 12.00
UAJRAC Alex Cobb 4.00 10.00
UAJRACR Allen Craig 5.00 12.00
UAJRAE Adam Eaton 4.00 10.00
UAJRAG Adrian Gonzalez 10.00 25.00
UAJRAJ Adam Jones 6.00 15.00
UAJRBP Buster Posey 30.00 80.00
UAJRCHA Cole Hamels 5.00 12.00
UAJRCO Chris Owings 4.00 10.00
UAJRCO1 Chris Owings 4.00 10.00
UAJRCS Chris Sale 10.00 30.00
UAJRCSA Carlos Santana 5.00 12.00
UAJRDF David Freese 4.00 10.00
UAJRDG Didi Gregorius 5.00 12.00
UAJRDP Dustin Pedroia 15.00 40.00
UAJRDW David Wright 5.00 12.00
UAJRED Eric Davis 10.00 25.00
UAJREG Evan Gattis 4.00 10.00
UAJREL Evan Longoria 5.00 12.00
UAJREM Edgar Martinez 10.00 25.00
UAJRER Enny Romero 4.00 10.00
UAJRFF Freddie Freeman 10.00 25.00
UAJRFL Fred Lynn 10.00 25.00
UAJRFM Fred McGriff 6.00 15.00
UAJRFV Fernando Valenzuela 15.00 40.00
UAJRIR Ivan Rodriguez 6.00 15.00
UAJRJG Juan Gonzalez 6.00 15.00
UAJRJGR Jason Grilli 4.00 10.00
UAJRJH Josh Hamilton 12.00 30.00
UAJRJHE Jason Heyward 5.00 12.00
UAJRJO Jake Odorizzi 4.00 10.00
UAJRJP Jorge Posada 20.00 50.00
UAJRJPA Jarrod Parker 4.00 10.00
UAJRJPR Jurickson Profar 6.00 15.00
UAJRJR Jim Rice 10.00 25.00
UAJRJSA Jarrod Saltalamacchia 4.00 10.00
UAJRJSE Jean Segura 5.00 12.00
UAJRJT Julio Teheran 6.00 15.00
UAJRJV Joey Votto 15.00 40.00
UAJRKG Kevin Gausman 5.00 12.00
UAJRKM Kris Medlen 5.00 12.00
UAJRKS Kevin Siegrist 4.00 10.00
UAJRKU Koji Uehara 10.00 25.00
UAJRKW Kolten Wong 5.00 12.00
UAJRMA Matt Adams 6.00 15.00
UAJRMC Michael Cuddyer 4.00 10.00
UAJRMMA Manny Machado EXCH 20.00 50.00
UAJRMMO Matt Moore 5.00 12.00
UAJRMN Mike Napoli 8.00 20.00
UAJRMS Max Scherzer 12.00 30.00
UAJRMSC Mike Schmidt 20.00 50.00
UAJRNE Nathan Eovaldi 5.00 12.00
UAJRNG Nomar Garciaparra 10.00 25.00
UAJRNR Nolan Ryan 40.00 100.00
UAJRPC Patrick Corbin 5.00 12.00
UAJRPC1 Patrick Corbin 5.00 12.00
UAJRSCA Steve Carlton 12.00 30.00
UAJRPG Paul Goldschmidt 10.00 25.00
UAJRPM Pedro Martinez 25.00 60.00
UAJRRB Ryan Braun 8.00 20.00
UAJRRD R.A. Dickey 6.00 15.00
UAJRRN Ricky Nolasco 4.00 10.00
UAJRRZ Ryan Zimmerman 5.00 12.00
UAJRSC Starlin Castro 8.00 20.00
UAJRSG Sonny Gray 6.00 15.00
UAJRSM Shelby Miller 5.00 12.00
UAJRSMA Starling Marte 10.00 25.00
UAJRTC Tony Cingrani 5.00 12.00
UAJRTD Travis d'Arnaud 5.00 12.00
UAJRTD1 Travis d'Arnaud 5.00 12.00
UAJRTF Todd Frazier 5.00 12.00
UAJRTG Tom Glavine 15.00 40.00
UAJRTRA Tim Raines 4.00 10.00
UAJRVG Vladimir Guerrero 10.00 25.00
UAJRVG1 Vladimir Guerrero 10.00 25.00
UAJRWB Wade Boggs 12.00 30.00
UAJRWB1 Wade Boggs 12.00 30.00
UAJRWC Will Clark 12.00 30.00
UAJRWM Wil Myers 4.00 10.00
UAJRWR Wilin Rosario 4.00 10.00
UAJRYC Yoenis Cespedes 10.00 25.00
UAJRZW Zack Wheeler 5.00 12.00

2014 Topps Triple Threads Unity Relic Autographs Emerald

*EMERALD: .5X TO 1.2X BASIC
STATED ODDS 1:11 MINI
STATED PRINT RUN 50 SER.#'d SETS
EXCHANGE DEADLINE 9/30/2017

2014 Topps Triple Threads Unity Relic Autographs Gold

*GOLD: .6X TO 1.5X BASIC
STATED ODDS 1:22 MINI
STATED PRINT RUN 25 SER.#'d SETS
EXCHANGE DEADLINE 9/30/2017

2014 Topps Triple Threads Unity Relic Autographs Sepia

*SEPIA: .4X TO 1X BASIC
STATED ODDS 1:8 MINI
STATED PRINT RUN 75 SER.#'d SETS
EXCHANGE DEADLINE 9/30/2017

2014 Topps Triple Threads Unity Relics

STATED ODDS 1:6 MINI
UJRAA Albert Almora 6.00 15.00
UJRAB Adrian Beltre 6.00 15.00
UJRAC Aroldis Chapman 6.00 15.00
UJRACA Andrew Cashner 4.00 10.00
UJRACA1 Andrew Cashner 4.00 10.00
UJRACH Aroldis Chapman 6.00 15.00
UJRAD Andre Dawson 8.00 20.00
UJRADU Adam Dunn 5.00 12.00
UJRAE A.J. Ellis 4.00 10.00
UJRAE1 A.J. Ellis 4.00 10.00
UJRAE2 A.J. Ellis 4.00 10.00
UJRAEA Adam Eaton 4.00 10.00
UJRAES Alcides Escobar 5.00 12.00
UJRAG Alex Gordon 5.00 12.00
UJRAGO Adrian Gonzalez 5.00 12.00
UJRAJ Adam Jones 5.00 12.00
UJRAL Adam Lind 5.00 12.00
UJRAL1 Adam Lind 5.00 12.00
UJRAL2 Adam Lind 5.00 12.00
UJRAM Andrew McCutchen 25.00 60.00
UJRAP Albert Pujols 6.00 15.00
UJRAR Anthony Rizzo 12.00 30.00
UJRAR1 Anthony Rizzo 12.00 30.00
UJRARA Alexei Ramirez 5.00 12.00
UJRAW Adam Wainwright 5.00 12.00
UJRBHA Bryce Harper 10.00 25.00
UJRBJ Bo Jackson 10.00 25.00
UJRBL Brett Lawrie 5.00 12.00
UJRBLE Bob Lemon 10.00 25.00
UJRBM Brandon Morrow 4.00 10.00
UJRBMC Brian McCann 5.00 12.00
UJRBP Buster Posey 8.00 20.00
UJRBPH Brandon Phillips 4.00 10.00
UJRBPO Buster Posey 8.00 20.00
UJRBW Brett Wallace 4.00 10.00
UJRCB Chad Billingsley 5.00 12.00
UJRCBE Carlos Beltran 5.00 12.00
UJRCBI Craig Biggio 5.00 12.00
UJRCBU Clay Buchholz 4.00 10.00
UJRCG Carlos Gonzalez 5.00 12.00
UJRCGO Carlos Gonzalez 5.00 12.00
UJRCGO1 Carlos Gonzalez 5.00 12.00
UJRCGR Curtis Granderson 5.00 12.00
UJRCH Chris Heisey 4.00 10.00
UJRCH1 Chris Heisey 4.00 10.00
UJRCH2 Chris Heisey 4.00 10.00
UJRCL Cliff Lee 5.00 12.00
UJRCLU Cory Luebke 4.00 10.00
UJRCS CC Sabathia 10.00 25.00
UJRCSA CC Sabathia 10.00 25.00
UJRCSA1 Carlos Santana 5.00 12.00
UJRCSA2 Chris Sale 6.00 15.00
UJRCSA3 Carlos Santana 5.00 12.00
UJRCSE Chris Sale 6.00 15.00
UJRCW C.J. Wilson 4.00 10.00
UJRDB Domonic Brown 5.00 12.00
UJRDE Danny Espinosa 4.00 10.00
UJRDGD Dee Gordon 4.00 10.00
UJRDGO1 Dee Gordon 4.00 10.00
UJRDJ Desmond Jennings 5.00 12.00
UJRDJ1 Desmond Jennings 5.00 12.00
UJRDJE Derek Jeter 30.00 80.00
UJRDMA Don Mattingly 12.00 30.00
UJRDO David Ortiz 6.00 15.00
UJRDP Dustin Pedroia 6.00 15.00
UJRDS Drew Storen 4.00 10.00
UJRDST Drew Storen 4.00 10.00
UJRDW David Wright 5.00 12.00
UJREE Edwin Encarnacion 6.00 15.00
UJREG Evan Gattis 4.00 10.00
UJREL Evan Longoria 5.00 12.00
UJREM Eddie Murray 6.00 15.00
UJRFH Felix Hernandez 5.00 12.00
UJRFH1 Felix Hernandez 5.00 12.00
UJRFH2 Felix Hernandez 5.00 12.00
UJRFH3 Felix Hernandez 5.00 12.00
UJRFH4 Felix Hernandez 5.00 12.00
UJRFM Franklin Morales 4.00 10.00
UJRFMO Franklin Morales 4.00 10.00
UJRFV Fernando Valenzuela 10.00 25.00
UJRGB Gordon Beckham 4.00 10.00
UJRGB1 Gordon Beckham 4.00 10.00
UJRGC Gerrit Cole 6.00 15.00
UJRGCO Gerrit Cole 6.00 15.00
UJRGG Gio Gonzalez 5.00 12.00
UJRGG1 Gio Gonzalez 5.00 12.00
UJRGM Greg Maddux 12.00 30.00
UJRHC Hank Conger 4.00 10.00
UJRHI Hisashi Iwakuma 5.00 12.00
UJRHIW Hisashi Iwakuma 5.00 12.00
UJRHK Howie Kendrick 4.00 10.00
UJRHKU Hiroki Kuroda 5.00 12.00
UJRHR Hanley Ramirez 5.00 12.00
UJRHRY Hyun-jin Ryu 5.00 12.00
UJRIK Ian Kinsler 5.00 12.00
UJRIK1 Ian Kinsler 5.00 12.00
UJRIR Ivan Rodriguez 5.00 12.00
UJRJB Jackie Bradley Jr. 6.00 15.00
UJRJBE Josh Beckett 4.00 10.00
UJRJBR Jackie Bradley Jr. 6.00 15.00
UJRJCH Jhoulys Chacin 4.00 10.00
UJRJCU Johnny Cueto 5.00 12.00
UJRJD John Danks 4.00 10.00
UJRJD1 John Danks 4.00 10.00
UJRJDA John Danks 4.00 10.00
UJRJE Jacoby Ellsbury 5.00 12.00
UJRJF Jeurys Familia 5.00 12.00
UJRJG Jaime Garcia 5.00 12.00
UJRJH Jeremy Hellickson 4.00 10.00
UJRJHA Josh Hamilton 5.00 12.00
UJRJHY J.J. Hardy 4.00 10.00
UJRJK Jason Kipnis 5.00 12.00
UJRJK1 Jason Kipnis 5.00 12.00
UJRJL Junior Lake 4.00 10.00
UJRJL1 Junior Lake 4.00 10.00
UJRJLE Jon Lester 5.00 12.00
UJRJM Joe Mauer 5.00 12.00
UJRJMA Joe Mauer 5.00 12.00
UJRJMN Joe Morgan 8.00 20.00
UJRJMU Justin Morneau 5.00 12.00
UJRJN Joe Nathan 4.00 10.00
UJRJP Jorge Posada 5.00 12.00
UJRJPA James Paxton 6.00 15.00
UJRJPO Jordan Pacheco 4.00 10.00
UJRJR Josh Reddick 4.00 10.00
UJRJRU Josh Rutledge 4.00 10.00
UJRJS Justin Smoak 4.00 10.00
UJRJSM John Smoltz 6.00 15.00
UJRJT Jose Tabata 4.00 10.00
UJRJTA Jose Tabata 4.00 10.00
UJRJV Joey Votto 6.00 15.00
UJRJV1 Joey Votto 6.00 15.00
UJRJVE Jonny Venters 4.00 10.00
UJRJVL Justin Verlander 6.00 15.00
UJRJVO Joey Votto 6.00 15.00
UJRJWE Jayson Werth 5.00 12.00
UJRJZ Jordan Zimmermann 5.00 12.00
UJRKD Kyle Drabek 4.00 10.00
UJRKF Kyuji Fujikawa 5.00 12.00
UJRKFJ Kyuji Fujikawa 5.00 12.00
UJRKG Ken Griffey Jr. 25.00 60.00
UJRKGA Kevin Gausman 5.00 12.00
UJRKH Kelvin Herrera 4.00 10.00
UJRKM Kris Medlen 5.00 12.00
UJRKN Kirk Nieuwenhuis 4.00 10.00
UJRKW Kolten Wong 5.00 12.00
UJRKWO Kolten Wong 5.00 12.00
UJRLM Leonys Martin 4.00 10.00
UJRMA Matt Adams 5.00 12.00
UJRMB Michael Bourn 4.00 10.00
UJRMBO Michael Bourn 4.00 10.00
UJRMBO1 Michael Bourn 4.00 10.00
UJRMC Michael Cuddyer 4.00 10.00
UJRMCA1 Miguel Cabrera 6.00 15.00
UJRMCU Michael Cuddyer 4.00 10.00
UJRMD Matt Davidson 5.00 12.00
UJRMH Matt Holliday 10.00 25.00
UJRMIG Miguel Cabrera 6.00 15.00
UJRMK Matt Kemp 5.00 12.00
UJRML Mike Leake 4.00 10.00
UJRML1 Mike Leake 4.00 10.00
UJRMLA Mat Latos 5.00 12.00
UJRMM Mitch Moreland 4.00 10.00
UJRMMC Mark McGwire 15.00 40.00
UJRMMC1 Mark McGwire 15.00 40.00
UJRMMI Mike Minor 4.00 10.00
UJRMMO Matt Moore 5.00 12.00
UJRMN Mike Napoli 4.00 10.00
UJRMR Manny Ramirez 6.00 15.00
UJRMR1 Manny Ramirez 6.00 15.00
UJRMRI Mariano Rivera 8.00 20.00
UJRMSC Max Scherzer 6.00 15.00
UJRMT Mike Trout 15.00 40.00
UJRMTE Mark Teixeira 5.00 12.00
UJRMY Michael Young 4.00 10.00
UJRMZ Mike Zunino 4.00 10.00
UJRNA Nolan Arenado 8.00 20.00
UJRNA2 Nolan Arenado 8.00 20.00
UJRNF Nick Franklin 4.00 10.00
UJRNF1 Nick Franklin 4.00 10.00
UJRNF2 Nick Franklin 4.00 10.00
UJRNS Nick Swisher 5.00 12.00
UJRNS1 Nick Swisher 5.00 12.00
UJRNW Neil Walker 5.00 12.00
UJRPA Pedro Alvarez 4.00 10.00
UJRPAL Pedro Alvarez 4.00 10.00
UJRPB Peter Bourjos 4.00 10.00
UJRPC Patrick Corbin 5.00 12.00
UJRPG Paul Goldschmidt 5.00 12.00
UJRPK Paul Konerko 5.00 12.00
UJRPS Pablo Sandoval 5.00 12.00
UJRRB Ryan Braun 5.00 12.00
UJRRB1 Ryan Braun 5.00 12.00
UJRRH Rickey Henderson 6.00 15.00
UJRRHA Roy Halladay 5.00 12.00
UJRRR Ricky Romero 4.00 10.00
UJRRR1 Ricky Romero 4.00 10.00
UJRRZ Ryan Zimmerman 5.00 12.00
UJRSC Starlin Castro 4.00 10.00
UJRSC1 Starlin Castro 4.00 10.00
UJRSC2 Starlin Castro 4.00 10.00
UJRSC3 Starlin Castro 4.00 10.00
UJRSCH Shin-Soo Choo 5.00 12.00
UJRSD Scott Diamond 4.00 10.00
UJRSM Starling Marte 6.00 15.00
UJRSP Salvador Perez 5.00 12.00
UJRSS Stephen Strasburg 6.00 15.00
UJRSST Stephen Strasburg 6.00 15.00
UJRSV Shane Victorino 5.00 12.00
UJRTC1 Tony Cingrani 5.00 12.00
UJRTF Todd Frazier 5.00 12.00
UJRTFR Todd Frazier 5.00 12.00
UJRTHE Todd Helton 5.00 12.00
UJRTHU Torii Hunter 4.00 10.00
UJRTL Tim Lincecum 5.00 12.00
UJRTL1 Tim Lincecum 5.00 12.00
UJRTM Tommy Milone 4.00 10.00
UJRTR Trevor Rosenthal 5.00 12.00
UJRTT Troy Tulowitzki 5.00 12.00
UJRTW Taijuan Walker 5.00 12.00
UJRVG Vladimir Guerrero 5.00 12.00
UJRVG1 Vladimir Guerrero 5.00 12.00
UJRWB Wade Boggs 6.00 15.00
UJRWB1 Wade Boggs 6.00 15.00
UJRWB2 Wade Boggs 6.00 15.00
UJRXB Xander Bogaerts 12.00 30.00
UJRYC Yoenis Cespedes 6.00 15.00
UJRYM Yadier Molina 10.00 25.00
UJRYP Yasiel Puig 6.00 15.00
UJRYP1 Yasiel Puig 6.00 15.00
UJRZC1 Zack Cozart 4.00 10.00
UJRZG Zack Greinke 5.00 12.00
UJRZWH Zack Wheeler 5.00 12.00

2014 Topps Triple Threads Unity Relics Emerald

*EMERALD: .5X TO 1.2X BASIC
STATED ODDS 1:11 MINI
STATED PRINT RUN 18 SER.#'d SETS

2014 Topps Triple Threads Unity Relics Gold

*GOLD: .5X TO 1.5X BASIC
STATED ODDS 1:21 MINI
STATED PRINT RUN 9 SER.#'d SETS
NO PRICING ON MOST DUE TO SCARCITY

2014 Topps Triple Threads Unity Relics Sepia

*SEPIA: .4X TO 1X BASIC
STATED ODDS 1:7 MINI
STATED PRINT RUN 27 SER.#'d SETS

2015 Topps Triple Threads

COMP.SET w/o AU's (100) 100.00 200.00
JSY AU RC ODDS 1:11 MINI BOX
JSY AU RC PRINT RUN 99 SER.#'d SETS
JSY AU ODDS 1:11 MINI BOX
JSY AU PRINT RUN 99 SER.#'d SETS
EXCHANGE DEADLINE 9/30/2017
1-100 PLATE ODDS 1:114 MINI BOX
101-172 PLATE ODDS 1:267 MINI BOX
PLATE PRINT RUN 1 SET PER COLOR
BLACK-CYAN-MAGENTA-YELLOW ISSUED
NO PLATE PRICING DUE TO SCARCITY
1 Babe Ruth 1.50 4.00
2 Matt Kemp .50 1.25
3 Mike Schmidt 1.00 2.50
4 Johnny Bench .60 1.50
5 Paul Goldschmidt .60 1.50
6 Clayton Kershaw 1.25 3.00
7 Chris Sale .60 1.50
8 Reggie Jackson .50 1.25
9 Madison Bumgarner .50 1.25

Honus Wagner .60 1.50
Carlos Gomez .40 1.00
John Smoltz .60 1.50
Troy Tulowitzki .60 1.50
Cal Ripken Jr. 2.00 5.00
Francisco Lindor RC 4.00 10.00
Jose Abreu .60 1.50
Evan Longoria .50 1.25
Greg Maddux .75 2.00
Hank Aaron 1.25 3.00
Michael Brantley .50 1.25
Wade Boggs .50 1.25
Johnny Cueto .50 1.25
Miguel Cabrera .60 1.50
Nolan Ryan 2.00 5.00
Warren Spahn .50 1.25
David Price .50 1.25
Ted Williams 1.25 3.00
Devin Mesoraco .40 1.00
Edwin Encarnacion .60 1.50
Don Mattingly 1.25 3.00
Anthony Rizzo 1.00 2.50
Joe DiMaggio 1.25 3.00
Jose Altuve .50 1.25
Jose Fernandez .60 1.50
Joe Mauer .50 1.25
Carlos Gonzalez .50 1.25
Yordano Ventura .50 1.25
Bryce Harper 1.00 2.50
Cole Hamels .50 1.25
Mike Piazza .60 1.50
Adam Wainwright .50 1.25
Dave Winfield .50 1.25
Jason Heyward .50 1.25
Albert Pujols .75 2.00
Masahiro Tanaka .50 1.25
Steve Carlton .50 1.25
David Ortiz .60 1.50
Jacob deGrom .60 1.50
Mariano Rivera .75 2.00
Lou Gehrig 1.25 3.00
Freddie Freeman .75 2.00
Randy Johnson .60 1.50
Felix Hernandez .50 1.25
Chase Utley .50 1.25
Stan Musial 1.00 2.50
Jose Bautista .50 1.25
57 David Peralta .40 1.00
58 Adam Jones .50 1.25
59 Bo Jackson .60 1.50
60 Andrew McCutchen .60 1.50
61 Craig Biggio .50 1.25
62 Gregory Polanco .50 1.25
63 Satchel Paige .60 1.50
64 Mike Trout 3.00 8.00
65 Sean Doolittle .40 1.00
66 Giancarlo Stanton .60 1.50
67 Ozzie Smith .75 2.00
68 Whitey Ford .50 1.25
69 Frank Thomas .60 1.50
70 Craig Kimbrel .50 1.25
71 Wil Myers .40 1.00
72 Adrian Beltre .60 1.50
73 Kris Bryant RC 6.00 15.00
74 Rickey Henderson .60 1.50
75 Rod Carew .50 1.25
76 Jacoby Ellsbury .50 1.25
77 Jackie Robinson .60 1.50
78 Adrian Gonzalez .50 1.25
79 Buster Posey .75 2.00
80 Joey Gallo RC 1.25 3.00
81 Corey Kluber .50 1.25
82 Manny Machado .60 1.50
83 Chipper Jones .60 1.50
84 Robinson Cano .50 1.25
85 Alex Gordon .50 1.25
86 Addison Russell RC 2.00 5.00
87 Sonny Gray .50 1.25
88 Jonathan Lucroy .50 1.25
89 Yu Darvish .60 1.50
90 Daniel Murphy .50 1.25
91 Roger Clemens .75 2.00
92 Mark McGwire 1.00 2.50
93 Yasiel Puig .60 1.50
94 Carlos Correa RC 6.00 15.00
95 Byron Buxton RC 1.00 2.50
96 Ken Griffey Jr. 1.25 3.00
97 Barry Larkin .50 1.25
98 Anthony Rendon .60 1.50
99 Chris Archer .40 1.00
100 Derek Jeter 1.50 4.00
103 Bryce Brentz JSY AU RC 3.00 8.00
104 Edwin Escobar JSY AU RC 3.00 8.00
106 Kendall Graveman JSY AU RC 3.00 8.00
107 Dilson Herrera JSY AU RC 15.00 40.00
109 Rymer Liriano JSY AU RC 3.00 8.00
110 Daniel Norris JSY AU RC EXCH 3.00 8.00
111 Aaron Sanchez JSY AU 5.00 12.00
112 Arismendy Alcantara JSY AU 3.00 8.00
113 McCann JSY AU RC EXCH 5.00 12.00
114 Marcus Stroman JSY AU 4.00 10.00
116 Matt Barnes JSY AU RC 3.00 8.00
117 Dellin Betances JSY AU 6.00 15.00
118 Jarred Cosart JSY AU 3.00 8.00
123 Steven Moya JSY AU RC 6.00 15.00
124 Chris Owings JSY AU 3.00 8.00
125 Anthony Ranaudo JSY AU RC EXCH 3.00 8.00
126 Kolten Wong JSY AU 8.00 20.00
127 Gary Brown JSY AU RC 5.00 12.00
128 Sonny Gray JSY AU 8.00 20.00
129 Carlos Martinez JSY AU 6.00 15.00
131 Dalton Pompey JSY AU RC 5.00 12.00
132 Tyson Ross JSY AU 3.00 8.00
133 Taijuan Walker JSY AU 3.00 8.00
134 Javier Baez JSY AU RC 12.00 30.00
135 Nick Castellanos JSY AU 6.00 15.00
136 J.Pederson JSY AU RC 10.00 25.00
137 Jorge Soler JSY AU RC 5.00 12.00
138 Zack Wheeler JSY AU 4.00 10.00
139 Jacob deGrom JSY AU 12.00 30.00
141 R.Castillo JSY AU RC 4.00 10.00
142 Jose Fernandez JSY AU 20.00 50.00
153 Matt Adams JSY AU 6.00 15.00
155 Archie Bradley JSY AU 3.00 8.00
158 Syndergaard JSY AU RC 25.00 60.00
161 Shelby Miller JSY AU 4.00 10.00
163 G.Polanco JSY AU 12.00 30.00
164 Michael Wacha JSY AU 8.00 20.00
165 Wil Myers JSY AU 3.00 8.00
168 Alex Colome JSY AU (RC) 3.00 8.00
172 Addison Russell JSY AU 15.00 40.00

2015 Topps Triple Threads Amber

*AMBER VET: 1.2X TO 3X BASIC
*AMBER RC: .75X TO 2X BASIC RC
STATED ODDS 1:4 MINI BOX
STATED PRINT RUN 125 SER.#'d SETS

2015 Topps Triple Threads Amethyst

*AMETHYST VET: 1X TO 2.5X BASIC
*AMETHYST RC: .6X TO 1.5X BASIC RC
STATED ODDS 1:2 MINI BOX
STATED PRINT RUN 354 SER.#'d SETS

2015 Topps Triple Threads Black

*BLACK: .6X TO 1.5X BASIC
STATED ODDS 1:31 MINI BOX
STATED PRINT RUN 35 SER.#'d SETS
EXCHANGE DEADLINE 8/31/2017

2015 Topps Triple Threads Emerald

*EMERALD VET: 1X TO 2.5X BASIC
*EMERALD RC: .6X TO 1.5X BASIC RC
1-100 ODDS 1:2 MINI BOX
1-100 PRINT RUN 250 SER.#'d SETS
*EMERALD JSY AU: .5X TO 1.2X BASIC
JSY AU ODDS 1:22 MINI BOX
JSY AU PRINT RUN 50 SER.#'d SETS
EXCHANGE DEADLINE 8/31/2017

2015 Topps Triple Threads Gold

*GOLD VET: 1.5X TO 4X BASIC
*GOLD RC: 1X TO 2.5X BASIC RC
STATED ODDS 1:5 MINI BOX
STATED PRINT RUN 99 SER.#'d SETS

2015 Topps Triple Threads Onyx

*ONYX VET: 2.5X TO 6X BASIC
*ONYX RC: 1.5X TO 4X BASIC RC
STATED ODDS 1:10 MINI BOX
STATED PRINT RUN 50 SER.#'d SETS
100 Derek Jeter 20.00 50.00

2015 Topps Triple Threads Sapphire

*SAPPHIRE VET: 3X TO 8X BASIC
*SAPPHIRE RC: 2X TO 5X BASIC RC
STATED ODDS 1:19 MINI BOX
STATED PRINT RUN 25 SER.#'d SETS

2015 Topps Triple Threads Sepia

*SEPIA: .4X TO 1X BASIC
STATED ODDS 1:15 MINI BOX
STATED PRINT RUN 75 SER.#'d SETS
EXCHANGE DEADLINE 8/31/2017

2015 Topps Triple Threads Autograph Relic Combos

STATED ODDS 1:76 MINI BOX
STATED PRINT RUN 36 SER.#'d SETS
EXCHANGE DEADLINE 8/31/2017
*SEPIA/27: .4X TO 1X BASIC
*EMERALD/18: .5X TO 1.2 BASIC
TTARCAHC Hywrd/Adms/Crpntr 60.00 150.00
TTARCALB Lester/Rizzo/Baez 50.00 120.00
TTARCBFP Baez/Frnco/Pdrsn 15.00 40.00
TTARCDWW Whlr/dGrm/Wrght 60.00 150.00
TTARCEDP Encrncn/Pmpy/Dnldsn 30.00 80.00
TTARCFRG Frmn/Rizzo/Gnzlz 40.00 100.00
TTARCMSJ Smltz/Jnes/Mddx 125.00 250.00
TTARCMZF Mesoraco/Zunino/McCann 20.00 50.00
TTARCOPC Pdra/Cstllo/Ortz 60.00 150.00
TTARCRSP Sandoval/Porcello/Ramirez 20.00 50.00
TTARCSCT Tomas/Soler/Castillo 25.00 60.00

2015 Topps Triple Threads Legend Relics

STATED ODDS 1:64 MINI BOX
STATED PRINT RUN 36 SER.#'d SETS
*SEPIA/27: .4X TO 1X BASIC
*EMERALD/18: .4X TO 1X BASIC
TTRLCF Carlton Fisk 4.00 10.00
TTRLCR Cal Ripken Jr. 15.00 40.00
TTRLDM Don Mattingly 10.00 25.00
TTRLEW Early Wynn 4.00 10.00
TTRLFR Frank Robinson 6.00 15.00
TTRLFT Frank Thomas 15.00 40.00
TTRLHN Hal Newhouser 10.00 25.00
TTRLJM Juan Marichal 8.00 20.00
TTRLJPA Jorge Posada 4.00 10.00
TTRLJPR Jim Palmer 4.00 10.00
TTRLJS John Smoltz 5.00 12.00
TTRLMM Mark McGwire 8.00 20.00
TTRLMS Mike Schmidt 15.00 40.00
TTRLNR Nolan Ryan 15.00 40.00
TTRLRCS Roger Clemens 6.00 15.00
TTRLRCW Rod Carew 4.00 10.00
TTRLRJ Reggie Jackson 4.00 10.00
TTRLRS Ryne Sandberg 10.00 25.00
TTRLRY Robin Yount 12.00 30.00
TTRLTG Tony Gwynn 12.00 30.00

2015 Topps Triple Threads Relic Autographs

STATED ODDS 1:10 MINI BOX
STATED PRINT RUN 18 SER.#'d SETS
EXCHANGE DEADLINE 8/31/2017
*GOLD/9: .5X TO 1.2X BASIC
SOME GOLD NOT PRICED DUE TO SCARCITY
ALL VERSIONS EQUALLY PRICED
TTARAC1 Alex Colome 5.00 12.00
TTARAC2 Alex Colome 5.00 12.00
TTARAC3 Alex Colome 5.00 12.00
TTARAC4 Alex Colome 5.00 12.00
TTARAC5 Alex Colome 5.00 12.00
TTARAG1 Adrian Gonzalez 15.00 40.00
TTARAG2 Adrian Gonzalez 15.00 40.00
TTARAG3 Adrian Gonzalez 15.00 40.00
TTARAJ1 Adam Jones 15.00 40.00
TTARAJ2 Adam Jones 15.00 40.00
TTARAJ3 Adam Jones 15.00 40.00
TTARAR1 Anthony Rizzo 30.00 80.00
TTARAR2 Anthony Rizzo 30.00 80.00
TTARAR3 Anthony Rizzo 30.00 80.00
TTARAR4 Anthony Rizzo 30.00 80.00
TTARAR5 Anthony Rizzo 30.00 80.00
TTARBB1 Brandon Belt 12.00 30.00
TTARBB2 Brandon Belt 12.00 30.00
TTARBB3 Brandon Belt 12.00 30.00
TTARBHR1 Bryce Harper 150.00 250.00
TTARBHR2 Bryce Harper 150.00 250.00
TTARBHR3 Bryce Harper 150.00 250.00
TTARBHT1 Brock Holt 10.00 20.00
TTARBHT2 Brock Holt 10.00 20.00
TTARBHT3 Brock Holt 10.00 25.00
TTARBJ1 Bo Jackson 60.00 150.00
TTARBM1 Brian McCann 12.00 30.00
TTARBM2 Brian McCann 12.00 30.00
TTARBM3 Brian McCann 12.00 30.00
TTARBP1 Buster Posey 75.00 200.00
TTARBP2 Buster Posey 75.00 200.00
TTARBS1 Blake Swihart 15.00 40.00
TTARBS2 Blake Swihart 15.00 40.00
TTARBS3 Blake Swihart 15.00 40.00
TTARBS4 Blake Swihart 15.00 40.00
TTARBS5 Blake Swihart 15.00 40.00
TTARBZ1 Ben Zobrist 20.00 50.00
TTARCBN1 Charlie Blackmon 8.00 20.00
TTARCBN2 Charlie Blackmon 8.00 20.00
TTARCBN3 Charlie Blackmon 8.00 20.00
TTARCBN4 Charlie Blackmon 8.00 20.00
TTARCBO1 Craig Biggio 20.00 50.00
TTARCD1 Carlos Delgado 10.00 25.00
TTARCF1 Cliff Floyd 10.00 25.00
TTARCF2 Cliff Floyd 10.00 25.00
TTARCF3 Cliff Floyd 10.00 25.00
TTARCF4 Cliff Floyd 10.00 25.00
TTARCKW1 Clayton Kershaw 75.00 200.00
TTARCR1 Cal Ripken Jr. 75.00 200.00
TTARCR2 Cal Ripken Jr. 75.00 200.00
TTARCR3 Cal Ripken Jr. 75.00 200.00
TTARCSA1 CC Sabathia 12.00 30.00
TTARCSA2 CC Sabathia 12.00 30.00
TTARCSA3 CC Sabathia 12.00 30.00
TTARCSE1 Chris Sale 15.00 40.00
TTARCSE2 Chris Sale 15.00 40.00
TTARCSE3 Chris Sale 15.00 40.00
TTARCY1 Christian Yelich 20.00 50.00
TTARCY2 Christian Yelich 20.00 50.00
TTARCY3 Christian Yelich 20.00 50.00
TTARCY4 Christian Yelich 20.00 50.00
TTARCY5 Christian Yelich 20.00 50.00
TTARDE1 Dennis Eckersley 15.00 40.00
TTARDFE1 David Freese 8.00 20.00
TTARDFE2 David Freese 8.00 20.00
TTARDFE3 David Freese 8.00 20.00
TTARDG1 Didi Gregorius 15.00 40.00
TTARDG2 Didi Gregorius 15.00 40.00
TTARDG3 Didi Gregorius 15.00 40.00
TTARDG4 Didi Gregorius 15.00 40.00
TTARDG5 Didi Gregorius 15.00 40.00
TTARDMO1 Devin Mesoraco 5.00 12.00
TTARDMO2 Devin Mesoraco 5.00 12.00
TTARDMO3 Devin Mesoraco 5.00 12.00
TTARDMO4 Devin Mesoraco 5.00 12.00
TTARDMO5 Devin Mesoraco 5.00 12.00
TTARDMY1 Don Mattingly 50.00 120.00
TTARDO1 David Ortiz 30.00 80.00
TTARDO2 David Ortiz 30.00 80.00
TTARDO3 David Ortiz 30.00 80.00
TTARDP1 Dustin Pedroia 20.00 50.00
TTARDP2 Dustin Pedroia 20.00 50.00
TTARDP3 Dustin Pedroia 20.00 50.00
TTARDW1 David Wright 15.00 40.00
TTARDW2 David Wright 15.00 40.00
TTARDW3 David Wright 15.00 40.00
TTAREL1 Evan Longoria 12.00 30.00
TTAREL2 Evan Longoria 12.00 30.00
TTAREL3 Evan Longoria 12.00 30.00
TTARFF1 Freddie Freeman 10.00 25.00
TTARFF2 Freddie Freeman 10.00 25.00
TTARFF3 Freddie Freeman 10.00 25.00
TTARFR1 Frank Robinson 30.00 80.00
TTARFR2 Frank Robinson 30.00 80.00
TTARFT1 Frank Thomas 40.00 100.00
TTARGR1 Garrett Richards 6.00 15.00
TTARGR2 Garrett Richards 6.00 15.00
TTARGR3 Garrett Richards 6.00 15.00
TTARGR4 Garrett Richards 6.00 15.00
TTARHA1 Hank Aaron 150.00 250.00
TTARHA2 Hank Aaron 150.00 250.00
TTARHR1 Hanley Ramirez 10.00 25.00
TTARHR2 Hanley Ramirez 10.00 25.00
TTARHR3 Hanley Ramirez 10.00 25.00
TTARIR1 Ivan Rodriguez 20.00 50.00
TTARIS1 Ichiro Suzuki
TTARIS2 Ichiro Suzuki
TTARJBL1 Jeff Bagwell 60.00 150.00
TTARJD1 Josh Donaldson 30.00 80.00
TTARJD2 Josh Donaldson 30.00 80.00
TTARJD3 Josh Donaldson 30.00 80.00
TTARJHD1 Jason Heyward 20.00 50.00
TTARJHD2 Jason Heyward 20.00 50.00
TTARJHD3 Jason Heyward 20.00 50.00
TTARJL1 Jon Lester 20.00 50.00
TTARJL2 Jon Lester 20.00 50.00
TTARJL3 Jon Lester 20.00 50.00
TTARJM1 Joe Mauer 20.00 50.00
TTARJM2 Joe Mauer 20.00 50.00
TTARJM3 Joe Mauer 20.00 50.00
TTARJR1 Jim Rice 15.00 40.00
TTARJR2 Jim Rice 15.00 40.00
TTARKC1 Kole Calhoun 10.00 25.00
TTARKC2 Kole Calhoun 10.00 25.00
TTARKC3 Kole Calhoun 10.00 25.00
TTARKC4 Kole Calhoun 10.00 25.00
TTARKC5 Kole Calhoun 10.00 25.00
TTARKGS1 Ken Griffey Sr. 10.00 25.00
TTARKGS2 Ken Griffey Sr. 10.00 25.00
TTARKGS3 Ken Griffey Sr. 10.00 25.00
TTARKGS4 Ken Griffey Sr. 10.00 25.00
TTARLB1 Lou Brock 20.00 50.00
TTARLD1 Lucas Duda 10.00 25.00
TTARLD2 Lucas Duda 10.00 25.00
TTARLD3 Lucas Duda 10.00 25.00
TTARLD4 Lucas Duda 10.00 25.00
TTARLG1 Luis Gonzalez 8.00 20.00
TTARLG2 Luis Gonzalez 8.00 20.00
TTARLG3 Luis Gonzalez 8.00 20.00
TTARLG4 Luis Gonzalez 8.00 20.00
TTARMB1 Matt Barnes 5.00 12.00
TTARMB2 Matt Barnes 5.00 12.00
TTARMB3 Matt Barnes 5.00 12.00
TTARMCN1 Matt Cain 12.00 30.00
TTARMCN2 Matt Cain 12.00 30.00
TTARMCN3 Matt Cain 12.00 30.00
TTARMCR1 Matt Carpenter 12.00 30.00
TTARMCR2 Matt Carpenter 12.00 30.00
TTARMCR3 Matt Carpenter 12.00 30.00
TTARMCR4 Matt Carpenter 12.00 30.00
TTARMCR5 Matt Carpenter 12.00 30.00
TTARMR1 Mariano Rivera 100.00 250.00
TTARMR2 Mariano Rivera 100.00 250.00
TTARMS1 Marcus Semien 5.00 12.00
TTARMS2 Marcus Semien 5.00 12.00
TTARMS3 Marcus Semien 5.00 12.00
TTARMS4 Marcus Semien 5.00 12.00
TTARMS5 Marcus Semien 5.00 12.00
TTARMSH1 Matt Shoemaker 6.00 15.00
TTARMSH2 Matt Shoemaker 6.00 15.00
TTARMSH3 Matt Shoemaker 6.00 15.00
TTARMSH4 Matt Shoemaker 6.00 15.00
TTARMT1 Mike Trout 150.00 300.00
TTARMT2 Mike Trout 150.00 300.00
TTARMT3 Mike Trout 150.00 300.00
TTARMZ1 Mike Zunino 5.00 12.00
TTARMZ2 Mike Zunino 5.00 12.00
TTARMZ3 Mike Zunino 5.00 12.00
TTARMZ4 Mike Zunino 5.00 12.00
TTARNR1 Nolan Ryan 60.00 150.00
TTARNR2 Nolan Ryan 60.00 150.00
TTARNG Nomar Garciaparra 15.00 40.00
TTAROS1 Ozzie Smith 30.00 80.00
TTAROV1 Omar Vizquel 175.00 350.00
TTAROV2 Omar Vizquel 175.00 350.00
TTAROV3 Omar Vizquel 175.00 350.00
TTARPF1 Prince Fielder 15.00 40.00
TTARPF2 Prince Fielder 15.00 40.00
TTARPF3 Prince Fielder 15.00 40.00
TTARPG3 Paul Goldschmidt 20.00 50.00
TTARPS1 Pablo Sandoval 8.00 20.00
TTARPS2 Pablo Sandoval 8.00 20.00
TTARPS3 Pablo Sandoval 8.00 20.00
TTARRB1 Ryan Braun 10.00 25.00
TTARRB2 Ryan Braun 10.00 25.00
TTARRB3 Ryan Braun 10.00 25.00
TTARRCO1 Robinson Cano 15.00 40.00
TTARRCO2 Robinson Cano 15.00 40.00
TTARRCO3 Robinson Cano 15.00 40.00
TTARRCS1 Roger Clemens 40.00 100.00
TTARRCS2 Roger Clemens 40.00 100.00
TTARRHD1 Ryan Howard 10.00 25.00
TTARRHD2 Ryan Howard 10.00 25.00
TTARRHD3 Ryan Howard 10.00 25.00
TTARRJA1 Reggie Jackson 30.00 80.00
TTARRJA2 Reggie Jackson 30.00 80.00
TTARRJO1 Randy Johnson 75.00 150.00
TTARRJO2 Randy Johnson 75.00 150.00
TTARRP1 Rick Porcello 8.00 20.00
TTARRP2 Rick Porcello 8.00 20.00
TTARRP3 Rick Porcello 8.00 20.00
TTARRP4 Rick Porcello 8.00 20.00
TTARRS1 Ryne Sandberg 30.00 80.00
TTARSM1 Starling Marte 15.00 40.00
TTARSM2 Starling Marte 15.00 40.00
TTARSM3 Starling Marte 15.00 40.00
TTARSM4 Starling Marte 15.00 40.00
TTARSM5 Starling Marte 15.00 40.00
TTARTG1 Tom Glavine 12.00 30.00
TTARTT1 Troy Tulowitzki 10.00 25.00
TTARTT2 Troy Tulowitzki 10.00 25.00
TTARTT3 Troy Tulowitzki 10.00 25.00
TTARVG1 Vladimir Guerrero 12.00 30.00
TTARVG2 Vladimir Guerrero 12.00 30.00
TTARVG3 Vladimir Guerrero 12.00 30.00
TTARWP1 Wily Peralta 5.00 12.00
TTARWP2 Wily Peralta 5.00 12.00
TTARWP3 Wily Peralta 5.00 12.00
TTARWP4 Wily Peralta 5.00 12.00
TTARWP5 Wily Peralta 5.00 12.00
TTARYC1 Yoenis Cespedes 20.00 50.00
TTARYC2 Yoenis Cespedes 20.00 50.00
TTARYC3 Yoenis Cespedes 20.00 50.00
TTARZW1 Zack Wheeler 10.00 25.00
TTARZW2 Zack Wheeler 10.00 25.00
TTARZW3 Zack Wheeler 10.00 25.00
TTARZW4 Zack Wheeler 10.00 25.00

2015 Topps Triple Threads Relic Combos

STATED ODDS 1:25 MINI BOX
STATED PRINT RUN 36 SER.#'d SETS
*SEPIA/27: .4X TO 1X BASIC
*EMERALD/18: .5X TO 1.2X BASIC
TTRCACS Ackley/Seager/Cano 6.00 15.00
TTRCAHC Carpenter/Adams/Heyward 8.00 20.00
TTRCASR Abreu/Sale/Ramirez 8.00 20.00
TTRCBCH Cn/Hdsn/Bmgrnr 6.00 15.00
TTRCBFC Beltre/Fielder/Choo 8.00 20.00
TTRCBFT Tomas/Baez/Franco 8.00 20.00
TTRCBPB Bmgrnr/Blt/Psy 40.00 100.00
TTRCBRE Encarnacion/Bautista/Reyes 8.00 20.00
TTRCBTJ Jns/Btsta/Trt 20.00 50.00
TTRCCAM Cole/Alvarez/Melancon 8.00 20.00
TTRCCDC Castellanos/Donaldson Carpenter 6.00 15.00
TTRCCKC Knslr/Cbrra/Cspds 10.00 25.00
TTRCCSF Fernandez/Cishek/Stanton 6.00 15.00
TTRCCVM Cbrra/Vrlndr/Mrtnz 8.00 20.00
TTRCDHF Holland/Darvish/Feliz 8.00 20.00
TTRCDJM Mchdo/Jns/Dvs 20.00 50.00
TTRCDWW deGrm/Whlr/Wrght 8.00 20.00
TTRCEDP Dnldsn/Encrncn/Pmpy 20.00 50.00
TTRCFRG Frmn/Rzzo/Gnzlz 10.00 25.00
TTRCFSK Kimbrel/Simmons/Freeman 6.00 15.00
TTRCGAC Cbrra/Abru/Gldschmdt 8.00 20.00
TTRCGKP Puig/Krshw/Gnzlz 15.00 40.00
TTRCGOT Tomas/Owings/Goldschmidt 8.00 20.00
TTRCGRB Ramirez/Gomez/Braun 6.00 15.00
TTRCGTB Blackmon/Gonzalez/Tulowitzki 8.00 20.00
TTRCGVP Grdn/Vntra/Prz 12.00 30.00
TTRCHCI Iwakuma/Cano/Hernandez 6.00 15.00
TTRCHDW deGrm/Hrvy/Whlr 8.00 20.00
TTRCHJH Jay/Hlldy/Hywrd 10.00 25.00
TTRCHRZ Zmmrmn/Hrpr/Rndn 12.00 30.00
TTRCHSP Price/Hernandez/Sale 8.00 20.00
TTRCHUL Hamels/Utley/Lee 6.00 15.00
TTRCHVC Vtto/Cto/Hmltn 10.00 25.00
TTRCKGR Grnke/Ryu/Krshw 15.00 40.00
TTRCLJL Loney/Jennings/Longoria 6.00 15.00
TTRCMJS McCnn/Sbtha/Jtr 20.00 50.00
TTRCMMP McCtchn/Plnco/Mrte 15.00 40.00
TTRCMMZ McCann/Zunino/Mesoraco 6.00 15.00
TTRCMSJ Mddx/Jns/Smltz 25.00 60.00
TTRCOPC Ortz/Cstllo/Pdra 15.00 40.00
TTRCPJR Rvra/Psda/Jtr 25.00 60.00
TTRCPTH Trt/Pjls/Hmltn 20.00 50.00
TTRCRGB Reddick/Butler/Gray 6.00 15.00
TTRCRSP Porcello/Ramirez/Sandoval 6.00 15.00
TTRCSAS Springer/Singleton/Altuve 6.00 15.00
TTRCSCP Castillo/Pederson/Soler 10.00 25.00
TTRCSHM Mchdo/Schp/Hrdy 20.00 50.00
TTRCWML Wnwrght/Lynn/Mlna 10.00 25.00

2015 Topps Triple Threads Relics

STATED ODDS 1:9 MINI BOX
STATED PRINT RUN 36 SER.#'d SETS
*SEPIA/27: .4X TO 1X BASIC
*EMERALD/18: .5X TO 1.2X BASIC
*GOLD/9: .6X TO 1.5X BASIC
ALL VERSIONS EQUALLY PRICED
TTRAGN1 Alex Gordon 5.00 12.00
TTRAGN2 Alex Gordon 5.00 12.00
TTRAGZ1 Adrian Gonzalez 5.00 12.00
TTRAGZ2 Adrian Gonzalez 5.00 12.00
TTRAGZ3 Adrian Gonzalez 5.00 12.00
TTRAM1 Andrew McCutchen 12.00 30.00
TTRAM2 Andrew McCutchen 12.00 30.00
TTRAM3 Andrew McCutchen 12.00 30.00
TTRAP1 Albert Pujols 8.00 20.00
TTRAP2 Albert Pujols 8.00 20.00
TTRAP3 Albert Pujols 8.00 20.00
TTRAS1 Andrelton Simmons 8.00 20.00
TTRAWD1 Alex Wood 4.00 10.00
TTRAWD2 Alex Wood 4.00 10.00
TTRAWD3 Alex Wood 4.00 10.00
TTRAWT1 Adam Wainwright 6.00 15.00
TTRAWT2 Adam Wainwright 6.00 15.00
TTRAWT3 Adam Wainwright 6.00 15.00
TTRBM1 Brian McCann 5.00 12.00
TTRBM2 Brian McCann 5.00 12.00
TTRBM3 Brian McCann 5.00 12.00
TTRBP1 Buster Posey 8.00 20.00
TTRBP2 Buster Posey 8.00 20.00
TTRBP3 Buster Posey 8.00 20.00
TTRCBN1 Carlos Beltran 6.00 15.00
TTRCBN2 Carlos Beltran 6.00 15.00
TTRCBN3 Carlos Beltran 6.00 15.00
TTRCBZ1 Clay Buchholz 4.00 10.00
TTRCBZ2 Clay Buchholz 4.00 10.00
TTRCBZ3 Clay Buchholz 4.00 10.00
TTRCKL1 Craig Kimbrel 5.00 12.00
TTRCKL2 Craig Kimbrel 5.00 12.00
TTRCKL3 Craig Kimbrel 5.00 12.00
TTRCSA1 CC Sabathia 5.00 12.00
TTRCSA2 CC Sabathia 5.00 12.00
TTRCSA3 CC Sabathia 5.00 12.00
TTRCSE1 Chris Sale 6.00 15.00
TTRDJ1 Derek Jeter 20.00 50.00
TTRDJ2 Derek Jeter 20.00 50.00
TTRDJ3 Derek Jeter 20.00 50.00
TTRDO1 David Ortiz 8.00 20.00
TTRDO2 David Ortiz 8.00 20.00
TTRDO3 David Ortiz 8.00 20.00
TTRDPA1 Dustin Pedroia 6.00 15.00
TTRDPA2 Dustin Pedroia 6.00 15.00
TTRDPA3 Dustin Pedroia 6.00 15.00
TTRDPE1 David Price 10.00 25.00
TTRDPE2 David Price 10.00 25.00
TTRDPE3 David Price 10.00 25.00
TTRDW1 David Wright 5.00 12.00
TTRDW2 David Wright 5.00 12.00
TTRDW3 David Wright 5.00 12.00
TTRFF1 Freddie Freeman 8.00 20.00
TTRFF2 Freddie Freeman 8.00 20.00
TTRFF3 Freddie Freeman 8.00 20.00
TTRGS1 Giancarlo Stanton 6.00 15.00
TTRGS2 Giancarlo Stanton 6.00 15.00
TTRGS3 Giancarlo Stanton 6.00 15.00
TTRHP1 Hunter Pence 8.00 20.00
TTRHP2 Hunter Pence 8.00 20.00
TTRHP3 Hunter Pence 8.00 20.00
TTRHRR1 Hyun-Jin Ryu 6.00 15.00
TTRHRR2 Hyun-Jin Ryu 6.00 15.00
TTRHRR3 Hyun-Jin Ryu 6.00 15.00
TTRHRZ1 Hanley Ramirez 5.00 12.00
TTRHRZ2 Hanley Ramirez 5.00 12.00
TTRHRZ3 Hanley Ramirez 5.00 12.00
TTRIS1 Ichiro 12.00 30.00
TTRJB1 Javier Baez 30.00 80.00
TTRJB2 Javier Baez 30.00 80.00
TTRJB3 Javier Baez 30.00 80.00
TTRJD1 Jacob deGrom 6.00 15.00
TTRJD2 Jacob deGrom 6.00 15.00
TTRJD3 Jacob deGrom 6.00 15.00
TTRJE1 Jacoby Ellsbury 12.00 30.00
TTRJE2 Jacoby Ellsbury 12.00 30.00
TTRJE3 Jacoby Ellsbury 12.00 30.00
TTRJF1 Jose Fernandez 6.00 15.00
TTRJF2 Jose Fernandez 6.00 15.00
TTRJF3 Jose Fernandez 6.00 15.00
TTRJH1 Jason Heyward 6.00 15.00
TTRJH2 Jason Heyward 6.00 15.00
TTRJH3 Jason Heyward 6.00 15.00
TTRJS1 Jorge Soler 6.00 15.00
TTRJS2 Jorge Soler 6.00 15.00
TTRJS3 Jorge Soler 6.00 15.00
TTRJVO1 Joey Votto 8.00 20.00
TTRJVO2 Joey Votto 8.00 20.00
TTRJVO3 Joey Votto 8.00 20.00
TTRJVR1 Justin Verlander 8.00 20.00
TTRJVR2 Justin Verlander 8.00 20.00
TTRJVR3 Justin Verlander 8.00 20.00
TTRKB1 Kris Bryant 30.00 80.00
TTRKB2 Kris Bryant 30.00 80.00
TTRKB3 Kris Bryant 30.00 80.00
TTRLL1 Lance Lynn 4.00 10.00
TTRMC1 Miguel Cabrera 8.00 20.00
TTRMC2 Miguel Cabrera 8.00 20.00
TTRMC3 Miguel Cabrera 8.00 20.00
TTRMHO1 Matt Holliday 6.00 15.00
TTRMHO2 Matt Holliday 6.00 15.00
TTRMHO3 Matt Holliday 6.00 15.00
TTRMHY1 Matt Harvey 8.00 20.00
TTRMT1 Mike Trout 30.00 80.00
TTRMT2 Mike Trout 30.00 80.00
TTRMT3 Mike Trout 30.00 80.00
TTRMTA1 Masahiro Tanaka 8.00 20.00
TTRMTA2 Masahiro Tanaka 8.00 20.00
TTRMTX1 Mark Teixeira 6.00 15.00
TTRMTX2 Mark Teixeira 6.00 15.00
TTRMTX3 Mark Teixeira 6.00 15.00
TTRPF1 Prince Fielder 5.00 12.00
TTRPF2 Prince Fielder 5.00 12.00
TTRPF3 Prince Fielder 5.00 12.00
TTRPS1 Pablo Sandoval 6.00 15.00
TTRPS2 Pablo Sandoval 6.00 15.00
TTRPS3 Pablo Sandoval 6.00 15.00
TTRRB1 Ryan Braun 5.00 12.00
TTRRB2 Ryan Braun 5.00 12.00
TTRRB3 Ryan Braun 5.00 12.00
TTRRCA1 Rusney Castillo 5.00 12.00
TTRRCA2 Rusney Castillo 5.00 12.00
TTRRCO1 Robinson Cano 5.00 12.00
TTRRCO2 Robinson Cano 5.00 12.00
TTRRCO3 Robinson Cano 5.00 12.00
TTRSC1 Shin-Soo Choo 5.00 12.00
TTRSC2 Shin-Soo Choo 5.00 12.00
TTRSM1 Starling Marte 8.00 20.00
TTRSM2 Starling Marte 8.00 20.00
TTRSM3 Starling Marte 8.00 20.00
TTRSS1 Stephen Strasburg 6.00 15.00
TTRSS2 Stephen Strasburg 6.00 15.00
TTRSS3 Stephen Strasburg 6.00 15.00
TTRTT1 Troy Tulowitzki 6.00 15.00
TTRTT2 Troy Tulowitzki 6.00 15.00
TTRTT3 Troy Tulowitzki 6.00 15.00
TTRVM1 Victor Martinez 8.00 20.00
TTRXB1 Xander Bogaerts 8.00 20.00
TTRXB2 Xander Bogaerts 8.00 20.00
TTRXB3 Xander Bogaerts 8.00 20.00
TTRYD1 Yu Darvish 6.00 15.00
TTRYD2 Yu Darvish 6.00 15.00
TTRYD3 Yu Darvish 6.00 15.00
TTRYM1 Yadier Molina 10.00 25.00
TTRYM2 Yadier Molina 10.00 25.00
TTRYM3 Yadier Molina 10.00 25.00
TTRYP1 Yasiel Puig 6.00 15.00
TTRYP2 Yasiel Puig 6.00 15.00
TTRYV1 Yordano Ventura 5.00 12.00
TTRYV2 Yordano Ventura 5.00 12.00
TTRYV3 Yordano Ventura 5.00 12.00

2015 Topps Triple Threads Rookie Autographs

STATED ODDS 1:88 MINI BOX
STATED PRINT RUN 99 SER.#'d SETS
EXCHANGE DEADLINE 8/31/2017
RABBN Byron Buxton 20.00 50.00
RABFN Brandon Finnegan 4.00 10.00
RABS Blake Swihart 5.00 12.00
RACC Carlos Correa 40.00 100.00
RACR Carlos Rodon 10.00 25.00
RADT Devon Travis 4.00 10.00
RAFL Francisco Lindor 15.00 40.00
RAJGO Joey Gallo 20.00 50.00
RAJK Jung-Ho Kang 4.00 10.00
RAKB Kris Bryant 60.00 150.00
RAKP Kevin Plawecki 4.00 10.00
RAMFO Maikel Franco 12.00 30.00
RAMFZ Mike Foltynewicz 4.00 10.00
RAMJ Micah Johnson 4.00 10.00
RAMT Michael Taylor 4.00 10.00
RASM Steven Matz 10.00 25.00
RAYT Yasmany Tomas 5.00 12.00

2015 Topps Triple Threads Triple Threads

STATED ODDS 1:73 MINI BOX
STATED PRINT RUN 25 SER.#'d SETS
T3DAM Andrew McCutchen 60.00 150.00
T3DAP Albert Pujols 25.00 60.00
T3DBH Bryce Harper 60.00 150.00
T3DBP Buster Posey 60.00 150.00
T3DCB Craig Biggio 20.00 50.00
T3DCL Cliff Lee 15.00 40.00
T3DCR Cal Ripken Jr. 60.00 150.00
T3DDJ Derek Jeter 40.00 100.00
T3DDW David Wright 15.00 40.00
T3DJA Jose Abreu 12.00 30.00
T3DJB Jeff Bagwell 20.00 50.00
T3DJB Javier Baez 25.00 60.00
T3DJE Jacoby Ellsbury 15.00 40.00
T3DJPA Jorge Posada 20.00 50.00
T3DKG Ken Griffey Jr. 30.00 80.00
T3DMB Madison Bumgarner 25.00 60.00
T3DMC Miguel Cabrera 25.00 60.00
T3DMTA Masahiro Tanaka 15.00 40.00
T3DMTT Mike Trout 40.00 100.00
T3DRCA Rusney Castillo 15.00 40.00
T3DRCO Robinson Cano 15.00 40.00
T3DRJ Reggie Jackson 15.00 40.00
T3DSS Stephen Strasburg 12.00 30.00
T3DYD Yu Darvish 20.00 50.00
T3DYM Yadier Molina 25.00 60.00

2015 Topps Triple Threads Unity Relic Autographs

STATED ODDS 1:6 MINI BOX
STATED PRINT RUN 99 SER.#'d SETS
EXCHANGE DEADLINE 8/31/2017
*SEPIA/75: .4X TO 1X BASIC
*EMERALD/50: .5X TO 1.2X BASIC
*GOLD/25: .6X TO 1.5X BASIC
UAJRAA Arismendy Alcantara 4.00 10.00
UAJRAB Archie Bradley 4.00 10.00
UAJRAC Alex Colome 4.00 10.00
UAJRAG Adrian Gonzalez 8.00 20.00
UAJRAJ Adam Jones 6.00 15.00
UAJRAR Anthony Ranaudo 4.00 10.00
UAJRAS Aaron Sanchez 5.00 12.00
UAJRBBT Brandon Belt 5.00 12.00
UAJRBBZ Bryce Brentz 4.00 10.00
UAJRBC Brandon Crawford 5.00 12.00
UAJRBH Brock Holt 4.00 10.00
UAJRBS Blake Swihart 5.00 12.00
UAJRCC C.J. Cron 4.00 10.00
UAJRCG Carlos Gonzalez 6.00 15.00
UAJRCM Carlos Martinez 6.00 15.00
UAJRCSA CC Sabathia 8.00 20.00
UAJRCSE Chris Sale 8.00 20.00
UAJRCV Christian Vazquez 4.00 10.00
UAJRCY Christian Yelich 15.00 40.00
UAJRDB Dellin Betances 8.00 20.00
UAJRDF Dexter Fowler 5.00 12.00
UAJRDG Didi Gregorius 8.00 20.00
UAJRDM Devin Mesoraco 4.00 10.00
UAJRDN Daniel Norris 4.00 10.00
UAJRDNA Daniel Nava 4.00 10.00
UAJRDPA Dustin Pedroia 12.00 30.00
UAJRDPY Dalton Pompey 5.00 12.00
UAJREEN Edwin Encarnacion 6.00 15.00
UAJREER Edwin Escobar 4.00 10.00
UAJREG Evan Gattis 6.00 15.00
UAJRFF Freddie Freeman 6.00 15.00
UAJRGB Gary Brown 4.00 10.00
UAJRGR Garrett Richards 5.00 12.00
UAJRHR Hanley Ramirez 6.00 15.00
UAJRJA Jose Abreu 10.00 25.00
UAJRJB Javier Baez 10.00 25.00
UAJRJC Jarred Cosart 4.00 10.00
UAJRJD Jacob deGrom 15.00 40.00
UAJRJF Jose Fernandez 40.00 100.00
UAJRJHD Jason Heyward 5.00 12.00
UAJRJK Jung-Ho Kang 30.00 80.00
UAJRJLR Jon Lester 15.00 40.00
UAJRJLS Juan Lagares 4.00 10.00
UAJRJM James McCann 6.00 15.00
UAJRJP Joc Pederson 15.00 40.00
UAJRJPA Jose Pirela 4.00 10.00
UAJRJR Jason Rogers 4.00 10.00
UAJRJSR Jorge Soler 10.00 25.00
UAJRKG Kendall Graveman 4.00 10.00
UAJRKL Kyle Lobstein 4.00 10.00
UAJRKS Kyle Seager 4.00 10.00

UAJRKV Kennys Vargas 4.00 10.00
UAJRLG Luis Gonzalez 6.00 15.00
UAJRLS Luis Sardinas 4.00 10.00
UAJRMAS Matt Adams 4.00 10.00
UAJRMB Matt Barnes 4.00 10.00
UAJRMBS Matt Barnes 4.00 10.00
UAJRMCK Matt Clark 4.00 10.00
UAJRMCN Matt Cain 6.00 15.00
UAJRMCR Matt Carpenter 8.00 20.00
UAJRMG Mark Grace 10.00 25.00
UAJRMM Matt Moore 5.00 12.00
UAJRMS Matt Shoemaker 5.00 12.00
UAJRMSE Marcus Semien 4.00 10.00
UAJRMZ Mike Zunino 4.00 10.00
UAJROV Omar Vizquel 10.00 25.00
UAJRPG Paul Goldschmidt 10.00 25.00
UAJRRA R.J. Alvarez 4.00 10.00
UAJRRB Ryan Braun 8.00 20.00
UAJRRCA Robinson Cano 10.00 25.00
UAJRRCO Rusney Castillo 5.00 12.00
UAJRRL Rymer Liriano 4.00 10.00
UAJRROS Roberto Osuna 4.00 10.00
UAJRRP Rick Porcello 5.00 12.00
UAJRRZ Ryan Zimmerman 5.00 12.00
UAJRSG Sonny Gray 5.00 12.00
UAJRSGN Shane Greene 4.00 10.00
UAJRSMA Steven Moya 5.00 12.00
UAJRSMR Shelby Miller 6.00 15.00
UAJRSS Steven Souza Jr. 5.00 12.00
UAJRTW Taijuan Walker 4.00 10.00
UAJRWF Wilmer Flores 5.00 12.00
UAJRWP Wily Peralta 4.00 10.00
UAJRYT Yasmany Tomas 5.00 12.00
UAJRZW Zack Wheeler 5.00 12.00

2015 Topps Triple Threads Unity Relics

STATED ODDS 1:6 MINI BOX
STATED PRINT RUN 36 SER.#'d SETS
ALL VERSIONS EQUALLY PRICED
*SEPIA/27: .4X TO 1X BASIC
*EMERALD/18: .5X TO 1.2X BASIC
*GOLD/9: .6X TO 1.5X BASIC
UJRAB Adrian Beltre 5.00 12.00
UJRACA Aroldis Chapman 5.00 12.00
UJRACB Alex Cobb 3.00 8.00
UJRACH Aroldis Chapman 5.00 12.00
UJRAD Adam Dunn 4.00 10.00
UJRAEA Adam Eaton 3.00 8.00
UJRAEN Adam Eaton 3.00 8.00
UJRAGN Adrian Gonzalez 4.00 10.00
UJRAGO Adrian Gonzalez 4.00 10.00
UJRAGR Alex Gordon 4.00 10.00
UJRAGZ Adrian Gonzalez 4.00 10.00
UJRAJ Adam Jones 4.00 10.00
UJRAM Andrew McCutchen 5.00 12.00
UJRAPS Albert Pujols 6.00 15.00
UJRAPU Albert Pujols 6.00 15.00
UJRARO Anthony Rizzo 8.00 20.00
UJRASA Aaron Sanchez 4.00 10.00
UJRASZ Aaron Sanchez 4.00 10.00
UJRAWA Adam Wainwright 4.00 10.00
UJRAWD Alex Wood 3.00 8.00
UJRAWO Alex Wood 3.00 8.00
UJRAWT Adam Wainwright 4.00 10.00
UJRBD Brian Dozier 6.00 15.00
UJRBHN Billy Hamilton 4.00 10.00
UJRBMC Brian McCann 4.00 10.00
UJRBMN Brian McCann 4.00 10.00
UJRBPH Brandon Phillips 3.00 8.00
UJRBPP Brandon Phillips 3.00 8.00
UJRBPS Brandon Phillips 3.00 8.00
UJRBPY Buster Posey 6.00 15.00
UJRCBE Carlos Beltran 4.00 10.00
UJRCBL Charlie Blackmon 5.00 12.00
UJRCBN Carlos Beltran 4.00 10.00
UJRCBO Charlie Blackmon 5.00 12.00
UJRCC Chris Carter 3.00 8.00
UJRCDA Chris Davis 3.00 8.00
UJRCDN Corey Dickerson 3.00 8.00
UJRCDS Chris Davis 3.00 8.00
UJRCGO Carlos Gonzalez 4.00 10.00
UJRCGZ Carlos Gomez 3.00 8.00
UJRCH Cole Hamels 4.00 10.00
UJRCKL Craig Kimbrel 4.00 10.00
UJRCKR Corey Kluber 4.00 10.00
UJRCKW Clayton Kershaw 10.00 25.00
UJRCMA Carlos Martinez 4.00 10.00
UJRCMZ Carlos Martinez 4.00 10.00
UJRCOS Chris Owings 3.00 8.00
UJRCOW Chris Owings 3.00 8.00
UJRCSA Carlos Santana 4.00 10.00
UJRCSE Chris Sale 5.00 12.00
UJRCSL Chris Sale 5.00 12.00
UJRCU Chase Utley 4.00 10.00
UJRCYE Christian Yelich 6.00 15.00
UJRCYH Christian Yelich 6.00 15.00
UJRCYL Christian Yelich 6.00 15.00
UJRDBE Dellin Betances 4.00 10.00
UJRDBN Domonic Brown 4.00 10.00
UJRDBR Domonic Brown 4.00 10.00
UJRDBS Dellin Betances 4.00 10.00
UJRDF Doug Fister 3.00 8.00
UJRDHD Derek Holland 3.00 8.00
UJRDHO Derek Holland 3.00 8.00
UJRDJE Derek Jeter 25.00 60.00
UJRDJR Derek Jeter 25.00 60.00
UJRDJT Derek Jeter 25.00 60.00
UJRDNA Daniel Nava 3.00 8.00
UJRDNO Daniel Norris 3.00 8.00
UJRDNS Daniel Norris 3.00 8.00
UJRDNV Daniel Nava 3.00 8.00
UJRDO David Ortiz 5.00 12.00
UJRDPA Dustin Pedroia 5.00 12.00
UJRDPD Dustin Pedroia 5.00 12.00
UJRDPE David Price 4.00 10.00
UJRDPO Dalton Pompey 4.00 10.00
UJRDPY Dalton Pompey 4.00 10.00
UJRDWR David Wright 4.00 10.00
UJRDWT David Wright 4.00 10.00
UJREA Elvis Andrus 4.00 10.00
UJREEE Edwin Escobar 3.00 8.00
UJREEN Edwin Encarnacion 5.00 12.00
UJREER Edwin Escobar 3.00 8.00
UJREH Eric Hosmer 4.00 10.00
UJREL Evan Longoria 4.00 10.00
UJRFFN Freddie Freeman 6.00 15.00
UJRFFR Freddie Freeman 6.00 15.00
UJRFH Felix Hernandez 4.00 10.00
UJRGCE Gerrit Cole 5.00 12.00
UJRGCO Gerrit Cole 5.00 12.00
UJRGG Gio Gonzalez 4.00 10.00
UJRGSR George Springer 4.00 10.00
UJRGST Giancarlo Stanton 5.00 12.00
UJRHP Hunter Pence 6.00 15.00
UJRHRA Hanley Ramirez 4.00 10.00
UJRHRU Hyun-Jin Ryu 4.00 10.00
UJRHRY Hyun-Jin Ryu 4.00 10.00
UJRHRZ Hanley Ramirez 4.00 10.00
UJRID Ian Desmond 3.00 8.00
UJRIKI Ian Kinsler 4.00 10.00
UJRIKR Ian Kinsler 4.00 10.00
UJRJAE Jose Altuve 4.00 10.00
UJRJAU Jose Abreu 5.00 12.00
UJRJBA Javier Baez 25.00 60.00
UJRJBE Jay Bruce 4.00 10.00
UJRJBR Jay Bruce 4.00 10.00
UJRJBT Jose Bautista 4.00 10.00
UJRJBU Jay Bruce 4.00 10.00
UJRJBZ Javier Baez 25.00 60.00
UJRJC Johnny Cueto 4.00 10.00
UJRJD Josh Donaldson 10.00 25.00
UJRJDM Jacob deGrom 5.00 12.00
UJRJE Jacoby Ellsbury 4.00 10.00
UJRJF Jose Fernandez 5.00 12.00
UJRJGO Jedd Gyorko 3.00 8.00
UJRJGY Jedd Gyorko 3.00 8.00
UJRJHA Josh Hamilton 4.00 10.00
UJRJHD Jason Heyward 4.00 10.00
UJRJHE Jason Heyward 4.00 10.00
UJRJHN Josh Hamilton 4.00 10.00
UJRJHT Josh Hamilton 4.00 10.00
UJRJHY Jason Heyward 4.00 10.00
UJRJK Jason Kipnis 4.00 10.00
UJRJLA Juan Lagares 3.00 8.00
UJRJLR Jon Lester 5.00 12.00
UJRJLY Jonathan Lucroy 4.00 10.00
UJRJMA Joe Mauer 4.00 10.00
UJRJMC Jake McGee 3.00 8.00
UJRJME Jake McGee 3.00 8.00
UJRJMR Joe Mauer 4.00 10.00
UJRJR Jose Reyes 6.00 15.00
UJRJSA Jarrod Saltalamacchia 3.00 8.00
UJRJSG Jean Segura 3.00 8.00
UJRJSH Jonathan Schoop 3.00 8.00
UJRJSL Jarrod Saltalamacchia 3.00 8.00
UJRJSP Jonathan Schoop 3.00 8.00
UJRJSR Jorge Soler 5.00 12.00
UJRJSS James Shields 3.00 8.00
UJRJSU Jean Segura 4.00 10.00
UJRJTA Junichi Tazawa 3.00 8.00
UJRJTN Julio Teheran 4.00 10.00
UJRJTZ Junichi Tazawa 3.00 8.00
UJRJU Justin Upton 4.00 10.00
UJRJV Justin Verlander 5.00 12.00
UJRJVE Justin Verlander 5.00 12.00
UJRJVO Joey Votto 5.00 12.00
UJRJVR Justin Verlander 5.00 12.00
UJRJVT Joey Votto 5.00 12.00
UJRJZ Jordan Zimmermann 4.00 10.00
UJRKC Kole Calhoun 3.00 8.00
UJRKSE Kyle Seager 3.00 8.00
UJRKSR Kyle Seager 3.00 8.00
UJRKW Kolten Wong 4.00 10.00
UJRLD Lucas Duda 4.00 10.00
UJRLL Lance Lynn 3.00 8.00
UJRLMA Leonys Martin 3.00 8.00
UJRLMN Leonys Martin 3.00 8.00
UJRMAD Matt Adams 3.00 8.00
UJRMAS Matt Adams 3.00 8.00
UJRMBR Madison Bumgarner 8.00 20.00
UJRMBY Michael Brantley 4.00 10.00
UJRMCA Miguel Cabrera 6.00 15.00
UJRMCB Miguel Cabrera 6.00 15.00
UJRMCE Michael Choice 3.00 8.00
UJRMCH Michael Choice 3.00 8.00
UJRMCR Miguel Cabrera 6.00 15.00
UJRMHA Matt Harvey 4.00 10.00
UJRMHO Matt Holliday 5.00 12.00
UJRMHY Matt Holliday 5.00 12.00
UJRMK Matt Kemp 6.00 15.00
UJRMMI Mike Minor 3.00 8.00
UJRMMO Manny Machado 8.00 20.00
UJRMMR Mike Minor 3.00 8.00
UJRMMS Mike Moustakas 4.00 10.00
UJRMOA Marcell Ozuna 5.00 12.00
UJRMOL Mike Olt 3.00 8.00
UJRMOT Mike Olt 3.00 8.00
UJRMOZ Marcell Ozuna 5.00 12.00
UJRMPA Michael Pineda 3.00 8.00
UJRMPI Michael Pineda 3.00 8.00
UJRMS Max Scherzer 5.00 12.00
UJRMTA Mark Teixeira 6.00 15.00
UJRMTE Mark Teixeira 6.00 15.00
UJRMTT Mike Trout 20.00 50.00
UJRMW Michael Wacha 4.00 10.00
UJRMZO Mike Zunino 3.00 8.00
UJRMZU Mike Zunino 3.00 8.00
UJRNAI Norichika Aoki 10.00 25.00
UJRNAO Nolan Arenado 6.00 15.00
UJRNCA Nick Castellanos 5.00 12.00
UJRNCS Nick Castellanos 5.00 12.00
UJRNMA Nick Martinez 3.00 8.00
UJRNMZ Nick Martinez 3.00 8.00
UJRPAL Pedro Alvarez 3.00 8.00
UJRPAZ Pedro Alvarez 3.00 8.00
UJRPF Prince Fielder 4.00 10.00
UJRPG Paul Goldschmidt 5.00 12.00
UJRPS Pablo Sandoval 4.00 10.00
UJRRBA Ryan Braun 4.00 10.00
UJRRBN Ryan Braun 4.00 10.00
UJRRBR Ryan Braun 4.00 10.00
UJRRCA Robinson Cano 4.00 10.00
UJRRCL Rusney Castillo 5.00 12.00
UJRRCN Robinson Cano 4.00 10.00
UJRRCO Robinson Cano 4.00 10.00
UJRRCT Rusney Castillo 5.00 12.00
UJRRLI Rymer Liriano 3.00 8.00
UJRRLO Rymer Liriano 3.00 8.00
UJRRZI Ryan Zimmerman 4.00 10.00
UJRRZN Ryan Zimmerman 4.00 10.00
UJRSCA Starlin Castro 3.00 8.00
UJRSCO Shin-Soo Choo 4.00 10.00
UJRSG Sonny Gray 4.00 10.00
UJRSM Starling Marte 4.00 10.00
UJRSP Salvador Perez 4.00 10.00
UJRSS Stephen Strasburg 5.00 12.00
UJRSTA Sam Tuivailala 3.00 8.00
UJRSTU Sam Tuivailala 3.00 8.00
UJRTBA Trevor Bauer 5.00 12.00
UJRTBR Trevor Bauer 5.00 12.00
UJRTDA Travis d'Arnaud 4.00 10.00
UJRTDD Travis d'Arnaud 4.00 10.00
UJRTDR Travis d'Arnaud 4.00 10.00
UJRTF Todd Frazier 4.00 10.00
UJRTRO Tyson Ross 3.00 8.00
UJRTRS Tyson Ross 3.00 8.00
UJRTT Troy Tulowitzki 5.00 12.00
UJRTWA Taijuan Walker 3.00 8.00
UJRTWR Taijuan Walker 3.00 8.00
UJRVMA Victor Martinez 4.00 10.00
UJRVMT Victor Martinez 4.00 10.00
UJRVMZ Victor Martinez 4.00 10.00
UJRWFL Wilmer Flores 4.00 10.00
UJRWFS Wilmer Flores 4.00 10.00
UJRWPA Wily Peralta 3.00 8.00
UJRWPE Wily Peralta 3.00 8.00
UJRYC Yoenis Cespedes 4.00 10.00
UJRYD Yu Darvish 5.00 12.00
UJRYMA Yadier Molina 6.00 15.00
UJRYMO Yadier Molina 6.00 15.00
UJRYP Yasiel Puig 5.00 12.00
UJRYT Yasmany Tomas 5.00 12.00
UJRZG Zack Greinke 6.00 15.00
UJRZW Zack Wheeler 4.00 10.00

2016 Topps Triple Threads

COMP.SET w/o AU's (100) 75.00 200.00
JSY AU RC ODDS 1:12 MINI BOX
JSY AU RC PRINT RUN 99 SER.#'d SETS
JSY AU ODDS 1:12 MINI BOX
JSY AU PRINT RUN 99 SER.#'d SETS
EXCHANGE DEADLINE 8/31/2018
1-100 PLATE ODDS 1:115 MINI BOX
JSY AU PLATE ODDS 1:276 MINI BOX
PLATE PRINT RUN 1 SET PER COLOR
BLACK-CYAN-MAGENTA-YELLOW ISSUED
NO PLATE PRICING DUE TO SCARCITY
1 Ken Griffey Jr. 1.25 3.00
2 Frank Thomas .60 1.50
3 David Ortiz .60 1.50
4 Nolan Arenado .75 2.00
5 Mark McGwire 1.00 2.50
6 Albert Pujols .75 2.00
7 Satchel Paige .60 1.50
8 Ryan Braun .50 1.25
9 Hank Aaron 1.25 3.00
10 Blake Snell RC .75 2.00
11 David Wright .50 1.25
12 Justin Verlander .60 1.50
13 Honus Wagner .60 1.50
14 Paul Goldschmidt .60 1.50
15 Jose Fernandez .60 1.50
16 Jacob deGrom .60 1.50
17 Freddie Freeman .75 2.00
18 Chipper Jones .60 1.50
19 Lou Gehrig 1.25 3.00
20 Yasiel Puig .60 1.50
21 Reggie Jackson .50 1.25
22 Lorenzo Cain .40 1.00
23 Todd Frazier .50 1.25
24 Adam Jones .50 1.25
25 Eric Hosmer .50 1.25
26 Mookie Betts 1.00 2.50
27 Roberto Clemente 1.50 4.00
28 Kris Bryant .75 2.00
29 Ichiro Suzuki .75 2.00
30 Vladimir Guerrero .50 1.25
31 Wade Boggs .50 1.25
32 Kenta Maeda RC 1.25 3.00
33 Sandy Koufax 1.25 3.00
34 Willie Mays 1.25 3.00
35 Noah Syndergaard .50 1.25
36 Joey Votto .60 1.50
37 Clayton Kershaw 1.25 3.00
38 Cal Ripken Jr. 2.00 5.00
39 Sonny Gray .50 1.25
40 Miguel Cabrera .60 1.50
41 Max Scherzer .60 1.50
42 Nolan Ryan 2.00 5.00
43 Carl Yastrzemski 1.00 2.50
44 Prince Fielder .50 1.25
45 A.J. Reed RC .60 1.50
46 Zack Greinke .50 1.25
47 Ted Williams 1.25 3.00
48 Matt Harvey .50 1.25
49 Mike Piazza .60 1.50
50 Chris Archer .40 1.00
51 Buster Posey .75 2.00
52 Roger Clemens .75 2.00
53 George Brett 1.25 3.00
54 Manny Machado .60 1.50
55 Gerrit Cole .60 1.50
56 Bryce Harper 1.00 2.50
57 Randy Johnson .60 1.50
58 Aaron Nola RC 1.25 3.00
59 Dallas Keuchel .50 1.25
60 Jose Berrios RC .75 2.00
61 Jake Arrieta .50 1.25
62 Chris Sale .60 1.50
63 Edwin Encarnacion .60 1.50
64 Robinson Cano .50 1.25
65 Jose Abreu .60 1.50
66 Troy Tulowitzki .60 1.50
67 Stephen Strasburg .60 1.50
68 Giancarlo Stanton .60 1.50
69 Mike Trout 3.00 8.00
70 Felix Hernandez .50 1.25
71 Adrian Gonzalez .50 1.25
72 Lucas Giolito RC 1.00 2.50
73 Hunter Pence .50 1.25
74 Bo Jackson .60 1.50
75 Ozzie Smith .75 2.00
76 Justin Upton .50 1.25
77 Johnny Cueto .50 1.25
78 Jackie Robinson .60 1.50
79 Jason Heyward .50 1.25
80 Stan Musial 1.00 2.50
81 Yoenis Cespedes .60 1.50
82 John Smoltz .60 1.50
83 Andrew McCutchen .60 1.50
84 Matt Kemp .50 1.25
85 Josh Donaldson .50 1.25
86 Jose Altuve .60 1.50
87 George Springer .50 1.25
88 Carlos Gonzalez .50 1.25
89 Madison Bumgarner .60 1.50
90 David Price .50 1.25
91 Jose Bautista .50 1.25
92 Trevor Story RC 2.50 6.00
93 Carlos Correa .60 1.50
94 Anthony Rizzo 1.00 2.50
95 Nomar Mazara RC 1.00 2.50
96 Don Mattingly 1.25 3.00
97 Greg Maddux .75 2.00
98 Yu Darvish .60 1.50
99 Babe Ruth 1.50 4.00
100 Julio Urias RC 2.00 5.00
RFPBD Brandon Drury JSY AU RC 8.00 20.00
RFPBS Blake Swihart JSY AU 5.00 12.00
RFPCC Carlos Correa JSY AU 30.00 80.00
RFPCE Carl Edwards Jr. JSY AU RC 5.00 12.00
RFPCM Carlos Martinez JSY AU 4.00 10.00
RFPCR Carlos Rodon JSY AU 5.00 12.00
RFPCRE Colin Rea JSY AU RC 3.00 8.00
RFPCS Corey Seager JSY AU RC 25.00 60.00
RFPEI Ender Inciarte JSY AU 4.00 10.00
RFPER Eduardo Rodriguez JSY AU 3.00 8.00
RFPGB Greg Bird JSY AU RC 4.00 10.00
RFPGS George Springer JSY AU 6.00 15.00
RFPHO Hector Olivera JSY AU RC 4.00 10.00
RFPHOW Henry Owens JSY AU RC 4.00 10.00
RFPJB Justin Bour JSY AU 4.00 10.00
RFPJG Jon Gray JSY AU RC 4.00 10.00
RFPJH Jesse Hahn JSY AU 3.00 8.00
RFPJP Joc Pederson JSY AU 8.00 20.00
RFPJPA Joe Panik JSY AU 4.00 10.00
RFPJS Jorge Soler JSY AU 6.00 15.00
RFPKB Kris Bryant JSY AU 60.00 150.00
RFPKC Kaleb Cowart JSY AU RC 3.00 8.00
RFPKMA Ketel Marte JSY AU RC 6.00 15.00
RFPKP Kevin Plawecki JSY AU 3.00 8.00
RFPKS Kyle Schwarber JSY AU RC 30.00 80.00
RFPLS Luis Severino JSY AU RC 4.00 10.00
RFPMC Michael Conforto
JSY AU RC EXCH 15.00 40.00
RFPMD Matt Duffy JSY AU 3.00 8.00
RFPMF Maikel Franco JSY AU 4.00 10.00
RFPMS Miguel Sano JSY AU RC 5.00 12.00
RFPNS Noah Syndergaard JSY AU 15.00 40.00
RFPPO Peter O'Brien JSY AU RC 3.00 8.00
RFPRO Roberto Osuna JSY AU 3.00 8.00
RFPRR Rob Refsnyder JSY AU RC 4.00 10.00
RFPRS Richie Shaffer JSY AU RC 3.00 8.00
RFPSM Steven Matz JSY AU 4.00 10.00
RFPSP Stephen Piscotty JSY AU RC 5.00 12.00
RFPTT Trea Turner JSY AU RC 20.00 50.00

2016 Topps Triple Threads Amber

*AMBER VET: .75X TO 2X BASIC
*AMBER RC: .5X TO 1.2X BASIC RC
STATED ODDS 1:4 MINI BOX
STATED PRINT RUN 150 SER.#'d SETS

2016 Topps Triple Threads Amethyst

*AMETHYST VET: .6X TO 1.5X BASIC
*AMETHYST RC: .4X TO 1X BASIC RC
STATED ODDS 1:2 MINI BOX
STATED PRINT RUN 340 SER.#'d SETS

2016 Topps Triple Threads Emerald

*EMERALD VET: .6X TO 1.5X BASIC
*EMERALD RC: .4X TO 1X BASIC RC
*EMERALD JSY AU: .4X TO 1X BASIC RC
1-100 ODDS 1:2 MINI BOX
JSY AU ODDS 1:23 MINI BOX
1-100 PRINT RUN 250 SER.#'d SETS
JSY AU PRINT RUN 50 SER.#'d SETS
EXCHANGE DEADLINE 8/31/2018

2016 Topps Triple Threads Gold

*GOLD VET: 1X TO 2.5X BASIC
*GOLD RC: .6X TO 1.5X BASIC RC
STATED ODDS 1:5 MINI BOX
STATED PRINT RUN 99 SER.#'d SETS

2016 Topps Triple Threads Onyx

*ONYX VET: 2.5X TO 6X BASIC
*ONYX RC: 1.5X TO 4X BASIC RC
*ONYX JSY AU: .5X TO 1.2X BASIC RC
1-100 ODDS 1:10 MINI BOX
JSY AU ODDS 1:32 MINI BOX
1-100 PRINT RUN 50 SER.#'d SETS
JSY AU PRINT RUN 35 SER.#'d SETS
EXCHANGE DEADLINE 8/31/2018

2016 Topps Triple Threads Sapphire

*SAPPHIRE VET: 3X TO 8X BASIC
*SAPPHIRE RC: 2X TO 5X BASIC RC
STATED ODDS 1:19 MINI BOX
STATED PRINT RUN 25 SER.#'d SETS

2016 Topps Triple Threads Silver

*SILVER JSY AU: .4X TO 1X BASIC RC
STATED ODDS 1:15 MINI BOX
STATED PRINT RUN 75 SER.#'d SETS
EXCHANGE DEADLINE 8/31/2018

2016 Topps Triple Threads Autograph Relic Combos

STATED ODDS 1:82 MINI BOX
STATED PRINT RUN 36 SER.#'d SETS
EXCHANGE DEADLINE 8/31/2018
*SILVER/27: .4X TO 1X BASIC
*EMERALD/18: .5X TO 1.2 BASIC
TTARCBLR Ltr/Brynt/Rzzo 150.00 400.00
TTARCCAK Crra/Kchl/Altve 60.00 150.00
TTARCDCB Crwfrd/Belt/Dffy 20.00 50.00
TTARCHCI Cano/Iwkma/Hrnndz 30.00 80.00
TTARCHTS Hdly/Txra/Svrno 20.00 50.00
TTARCMPH Plnco/Hrrsn/Marte 25.00 60.00
TTARCOIF Inciarte/Freeman/Olivera 15.00 40.00
TTARCPSM Mda/Sger/Pdrsn 60.00 150.00
TTARCPTM Tms/Pllck/Mllr 15.00 40.00
TTARCPWM Wong/Mrtnz/Psctty 20.00 50.00
TTARCSHS Soler/Hywrd/Schwrbr 30.00 80.00
TTARCSMD deGrm/Syndrgrd/Mtz 60.00 150.00
TTARCSPP Prcllo/Pdra/Swhrt 25.00 60.00
TTARCTGG Trnr/Gnzlz/Grndl 25.00 60.00
TTARCTSE Encrncn/Strmn/Tlwtzki 25.00 60.00

2016 Topps Triple Threads Legend Relics

STATED ODDS 1:85 MINI BOX
STATED PRINT RUN 36 SER.#'d SETS
*SILVER/27: .4X TO 1X BASIC
*EMERALD/18: .4X TO 1X BASIC
TTRLBL Bob Lemon 10.00 25.00
TTRLCJ Chipper Jones 12.00 30.00
TTRLCR Cal Ripken Jr. 20.00 50.00
TTRLCY Carl Yastrzemski 30.00 80.00
TTRLEW Early Wynn 10.00 25.00
TTRLFT Frank Thomas 15.00 40.00
TTRLHA Hank Aaron 25.00 60.00
TTRLHN Hal Newhouser 8.00 20.00
TTRLHW Honus Wagner 50.00 120.00
TTRLJM Juan Marichal 8.00 20.00
TTRLJS John Smoltz 8.00 20.00
TTRLKG Ken Griffey Jr. 30.00 80.00
TTRLMP Mike Piazza 10.00 25.00
TTRLOS Ozzie Smith 12.00 30.00
TTRLPM Paul Molitor 8.00 20.00
TTRLRA Roberto Alomar 8.00 20.00
TTRLRC Roberto Clemente 60.00 150.00
TTRLRH Rickey Henderson 12.00 30.00
TTRLRS Ryne Sandberg 12.00 30.00
TTRLTW Ted Williams 50.00 120.00
TTRLWB Wade Boggs 8.00 20.00
TTRLWM Willie Mays 50.00 120.00
TTRLWS Willie Stargell 10.00 25.00

2016 Topps Triple Threads Relic Autographs

STATED ODDS 1:10 MINI BOX
STATED PRINT RUN 18 SER.#'d SETS
EXCHANGE DEADLINE 8/31/2018
*GOLD/9: .5X TO 1.2X BASIC
SOME GOLD NOT PRICED DUE TO SCARCITY
ALL VERSIONS EQUALLY PRICED
TTARAE1 Alcides Escobar 6.00 15.00
TTARAE2 Alcides Escobar 6.00 15.00
TTARAE3 Alcides Escobar 6.00 15.00
TTARAE4 Alcides Escobar 6.00 15.00
TTARAE5 Alcides Escobar 6.00 15.00
TTARAG1 Adrian Gonzalez 10.00 25.00
TTARAG2 Adrian Gonzalez 10.00 25.00
TTARAG3 Adrian Gonzalez 10.00 25.00
TTARAG4 Adrian Gonzalez 10.00 25.00
TTARAJ1 Adam Jones 15.00 40.00
TTARAJ2 Adam Jones 15.00 40.00
TTARAJ3 Adam Jones 15.00 40.00
TTARAJ4 Adam Jones 15.00 40.00
TTARAM1 Andrew Miller 12.00 30.00
TTARAM2 Andrew Miller 12.00 30.00
TTARAM3 Andrew Miller 12.00 30.00
TTARAM4 Andrew Miller 12.00 30.00
TTARAM5 Andrew Miller 12.00 30.00
TTARAP1 A.J. Pollock 10.00 25.00
TTARAP2 A.J. Pollock 10.00 25.00
TTARAP3 A.J. Pollock 10.00 25.00
TTARAP4 A.J. Pollock 10.00 25.00
TTARAP5 A.J. Pollock 10.00 25.00
TTARAR1 Anthony Rizzo 40.00 100.00
TTARAR2 Anthony Rizzo 40.00 100.00
TTARAR3 Anthony Rizzo 40.00 100.00
TTARAR4 Anthony Rizzo 40.00 100.00
TTARAR5 Anthony Rizzo 40.00 100.00
TTARAW1 Alex Wood 5.00 12.00
TTARAW2 Alex Wood 5.00 12.00
TTARAW3 Alex Wood 5.00 12.00
TTARAW4 Alex Wood 5.00 12.00
TTARAW5 Alex Wood 5.00 12.00
TTARBB1 Brandon Belt 10.00 25.00
TTARBC1 Brandon Crawford 15.00 40.00
TTARBC2 Brandon Crawford 15.00 40.00
TTARBC3 Brandon Crawford 15.00 40.00
TTARBC4 Brandon Crawford 15.00 40.00
TTARBC5 Brandon Crawford 15.00 40.00
TTARBH1 Bryce Harper 150.00 300.00
TTARBH2 Bryce Harper 150.00 300.00
TTARBHO1 Brock Holt 10.00 25.00
TTARBHO2 Brock Holt 10.00 25.00
TTARBHO3 Brock Holt 10.00 25.00
TTARBHO4 Brock Holt 10.00 25.00
TTARBHO5 Brock Holt 10.00 25.00
TTARBM1 Brian McCann 6.00 15.00
TTARBM2 Brian McCann 6.00 15.00
TTARBM3 Brian McCann 6.00 15.00
TTARBP1 Buster Posey 60.00 150.00
TTARCB1 Craig Biggio 25.00 60.00
TTARCD1 Kevin Costner 125.00 250.00
TTARCD2 Kevin Costner 125.00 250.00
TTARCDI1 Corey Dickerson 5.00 12.00
TTARCDI2 Corey Dickerson 5.00 12.00
TTARCDI3 Corey Dickerson 5.00 12.00
TTARCF1 Carlton Fisk 25.00 60.00
TTARCH1 Cole Hamels 10.00 25.00
TTARCK1 Clayton Kershaw 60.00 150.00
TTARCM1 Carlos Martinez 8.00 20.00
TTARCM2 Carlos Martinez 8.00 20.00
TTARCM3 Carlos Martinez 8.00 20.00
TTARCM4 Carlos Martinez 8.00 20.00
TTARCM5 Carlos Martinez 8.00 20.00
TTARCR1 Cal Ripken Jr. 75.00 200.00
TTARCS1 Curt Schilling 20.00 50.00
TTARCSA1 Chris Sale 10.00 25.00
TTARCSA2 Chris Sale 10.00 25.00
TTARCSA3 Chris Sale 10.00 25.00
TTARCSA4 Chris Sale 10.00 25.00
TTARCSH1 Curt Schilling 20.00 50.00
TTARCY1 Carl Yastrzemski 75.00 200.00
TTARCYE1 Christian Yelich 15.00 40.00
TTARCYE2 Christian Yelich 15.00 40.00
TTARCYE3 Christian Yelich 15.00 40.00
TTARCYE4 Christian Yelich 15.00 40.00
TTARCYE5 Christian Yelich 15.00 40.00
TTARDG1 Dee Gordon 8.00 20.00
TTARDG2 Dee Gordon 8.00 20.00
TTARDG3 Dee Gordon 8.00 20.00
TTARDG4 Dee Gordon 8.00 20.00
TTARDG5 Dee Gordon 8.00 20.00
TTARDK1 Dallas Keuchel 6.00 15.00
TTARDK2 Dallas Keuchel 6.00 15.00
TTARDK3 Dallas Keuchel 6.00 15.00
TTARDK4 Dallas Keuchel 6.00 15.00
TTARDK5 Dallas Keuchel 6.00 15.00
TTARDL1 Derrek Lee 8.00 20.00
TTARDL2 Derrek Lee 8.00 20.00
TTARDL3 Derrek Lee 8.00 20.00
TTARDL4 Derrek Lee 8.00 20.00
TTARDL5 Derrek Lee 8.00 20.00
TTARDO1 David Ortiz 75.00 200.00
TTAREE1 Edwin Encarnacion 12.00 30.00
TTAREI1 Ender Inciarte 8.00 20.00
TTAREI2 Ender Inciarte 8.00 20.00
TTAREI3 Ender Inciarte 8.00 20.00
TTAREI4 Ender Inciarte 8.00 20.00
TTAREI5 Ender Inciarte 8.00 20.00
TTAREL1 Evan Longoria 8.00 20.00
TTARFH1 Felix Hernandez 40.00 100.00
TTARGR1 Garrett Richards 6.00 15.00
TTARGR2 Garrett Richards 6.00 15.00
TTARGR3 Garrett Richards 6.00 15.00
TTARGR4 Garrett Richards 6.00 15.00
TTARGR5 Garrett Richards 6.00 15.00
TTARHA1 Hank Aaron 125.00 250.00
TTARI Ichiro Suzuki 200.00 400.00
TTARICH1 Ichiro Suzuki 200.00 400.00
TTARIS Ichiro Suzuki 200.00 400.00
TTARJA1 Jose Abreu 20.00 50.00
TTARJB1 Jeff Bagwell 30.00 80.00
TTARJB2 Jeff Bagwell 30.00 80.00
TTARJB3 Jeff Bagwell 30.00 80.00
TTARJB4 Jeff Bagwell 30.00 80.00
TTARJD1 Jacob deGrom 25.00 60.00
TTARJD2 Jacob deGrom 25.00 60.00
TTARJD3 Jacob deGrom 25.00 60.00
TTARJD4 Jacob deGrom 25.00 60.00
TTARJD5 Jacob deGrom 25.00 60.00
TTARJF1 Jeurys Familia 12.00 30.00
TTARJF2 Jeurys Familia 12.00 30.00
TTARJF3 Jeurys Familia 12.00 30.00
TTARJG1 Joey Gallo 20.00 50.00
TTARJH1 Jesse Hahn 5.00 12.00
TTARJH2 Jesse Hahn 5.00 12.00
TTARJHE1 Jason Heyward 12.00 30.00
TTARJHE2 Jason Heyward 12.00 30.00
TTARJHE3 Jason Heyward 12.00 30.00
TTARJHE4 Jason Heyward 12.00 30.
TTARJHE5 Jason Heyward 12.00 30.
TTARJL1 Jon Lester 40.00 100.
TTARJL2 Jon Lester 40.00 100
TTARJM1 J.D. Martinez 20.00 50.
TTARJM2 J.D. Martinez 20.00 50.
TTARJM3 J.D. Martinez 20.00 50.
TTARJM4 J.D. Martinez 20.00 50.
TTARJM5 J.D. Martinez 20.00 50.
TTARJR1 Jim Rice 12.00 30.
TTARJR2 Jim Rice 12.00 30.
TTARJRE1 J.T. Realmuto 20.00 50.
TTARJRE2 J.T. Realmuto 20.00 50.
TTARJRE3 J.T. Realmuto 20.00 50.
TTARJS1 James Shields 5.00 12.
TTARJS2 James Shields 5.00 12.
TTARJS3 James Shields 5.00 12.
TTARJS4 James Shields 5.00 12.
TTARJS5 James Shields 5.00 12.
TTARJSO1 Jorge Soler 10.00 25.
TTARJSO2 Jorge Soler 10.00 25.
TTARJSO3 Jorge Soler 10.00 25.
TTARJSO4 Jorge Soler 10.00 25.
TTARJSO5 Jorge Soler 10.00 25.
TTARJT1 Justin Turner 20.00 50.0
TTARJT2 Justin Turner 20.00 50.0
TTARKC1 Kole Calhoun 5.00 12.0
TTARKC2 Kole Calhoun 5.00 12.0
TTARKC3 Kole Calhoun 5.00 12.0
TTARKC4 Kole Calhoun 5.00 12.0
TTARKC5 Kole Calhoun 5.00 12.0
TTARKGM Ken Griffey Jr. 125.00 300.0
TTARKGR Ken Griffey Jr. 125.00 300.0
TTARKM1 Kendrys Morales 8.00 20.0
TTARKM2 Kendrys Morales 8.00 20.0
TTARKM3 Kendrys Morales 8.00 20.0
TTARKM4 Kendrys Morales 8.00 20.0
TTARKM5 Kendrys Morales 8.00 20.0
TTARKS1 Kyle Seager 10.00 25.0
TTARKS2 Kyle Seager 10.00 25.0
TTARKS3 Kyle Seager 10.00 25.0
TTARKS4 Kyle Seager 10.00 25.0
TTARKS5 Kyle Seager 10.00 25.0
TTARKW1 Kolten Wong 6.00 15.0
TTARKW2 Kolten Wong 6.00 15.0
TTARKW3 Kolten Wong 6.00 15.0
TTARKW4 Kolten Wong 6.00 15.0
TTARKW5 Kolten Wong 6.00 15.0
TTARMC2 Matt Carpenter 10.00 25.00
TTARMG1 Mark Grace 20.00 50.00
TTARMG2 Mark Grace 20.00 50.00
TTARMG3 Mark Grace 20.00 50.00
TTARMG4 Mark Grace 20.00 50.00
TTARMGR1 Mark Grace 20.00 50.00
TTARMH1 Matt Harvey 25.00 60.00
TTARMM1 Manny Machado 40.00 100.00
TTARMM2 Manny Machado 40.00 100.00
TTARMM3 Manny Machado 40.00 100.00
TTARMM4 Manny Machado 40.00 100.00
TTARMMC1 Mark McGwire 60.00 150.00
TTARMMG1 Mark McGwire 60.00 150.00
TTARMP1 Mike Piazza 50.00 120.00
TTARMPI1 Michael Pineda 5.00 12.00
TTARMPI2 Michael Pineda 5.00 12.00
TTARMPI3 Michael Pineda 5.00 12.00
TTARMPI4 Michael Pineda 5.00 12.00
TTARMPI5 Michael Pineda 5.00 12.00
TTARMPIA1 Mike Piazza 50.00 120.00
TTARMR1 Matt Reynolds 5.00 12.00
TTARMR2 Matt Reynolds 5.00 12.00
TTARMR3 Matt Reynolds 5.00 12.00
TTARMR4 Matt Reynolds 5.00 12.00
TTARMR5 Matt Reynolds 5.00 12.00
TTARMS1 Matt Shoemaker 6.00 15.00
TTARMS2 Matt Shoemaker 6.00 15.00
TTARMS3 Matt Shoemaker 6.00 15.00
TTARMS4 Matt Shoemaker 6.00 15.00
TTARMS5 Matt Shoemaker 6.00 15.00
TTARMSE3 Marcus Semien
TTARMST1 Marcus Stroman 10.00 25.00
TTARMST2 Marcus Stroman 10.00 25.00
TTARMST3 Marcus Stroman 10.00 25.00
TTARMST4 Marcus Stroman 10.00 25.00
TTARMST5 Marcus Stroman 10.00 25.00
TTARMT1 Mike Trout 150.00 250.00
TTARMW1 Michael Wacha
TTARMW2 Michael Wacha
TTARMW3 Michael Wacha
TTARMW4 Michael Wacha
TTARMW5 Michael Wacha
TTARNA1 Nolan Arenado 25.00 60.00
TTARNA2 Nolan Arenado 25.00 60.00
TTARNA3 Nolan Arenado 25.00 60.00
TTARNA4 Nolan Arenado 25.00 60.00
TTARNR1 Nolan Ryan
TTARPF1 Prince Fielder 8.00 20.00
TTARPM1 Paul Molitor 15.00 40.00
TTARRB1 Ryan Braun 15.00 40.00
TTARRC1 Roger Clemens 30.00 80.00
TTARRCA1 Rusney Castillo 5.00 12.00
TTARRCAN Robinson Cano 20.00 50.00
TTARRH1 Rickey Henderson 40.00 100.00
TTARRHE1 Rickey Henderson 40.00 100.00
TTARRI1 Raisel Iglesias 6.00 15.00
TTARRI2 Raisel Iglesias 6.00 15.00
TTARRJO1 Randy Johnson 40.00 100.00
TTARROL1 Rollie Fingers 10.00 25.00
TTARROL2 Rollie Fingers 10.00 25.00
TTARROL3 Rollie Fingers 10.00 25.00
TTARROL4 Rollie Fingers 10.00 25.00
TTARROL5 Rollie Fingers 10.00 25.00
TTARRS1 Ryne Sandberg 25.00 60.00
TTARSC1 Steve Carlton 15.00 40.00

ARSC2 Starlin Castro 25.00 60.00
ARSD1 Sean Doolittle 5.00 12.00
ARSD2 Sean Doolittle 5.00 12.00
ARSD3 Sean Doolittle 5.00 12.00
ARSG1 Sonny Gray 6.00 15.00
ARSG2 Sonny Gray 6.00 15.00
ARSG3 Sonny Gray 6.00 15.00
ARSG4 Sonny Gray 6.00 15.00
ARSG5 Sonny Gray 6.00 15.00
ARSM1 Starling Marte 10.00 25.00
ARSM2 Starling Marte 10.00 25.00
ARSM3 Starling Marte 10.00 25.00
ARSM4 Starling Marte 10.00 25.00
ARTEX1 Mark Teixeira 12.00 30.00
ARTEX2 Mark Teixeira 12.00 30.00
ARTEX3 Mark Teixeira 12.00 30.00
ARTEX4 Mark Teixeira 12.00 30.00
ARTT1 Troy Tulowitzki
ARWD1 Wade Davis 8.00 20.00
ARWD2 Wade Davis 8.00 20.00
ARWD3 Wade Davis 8.00 20.00
ARWD4 Wade Davis 8.00 20.00
ARWD5 Wade Davis 8.00 20.00
ARWM1 Wil Myers 10.00 25.00
ARYD1 Yu Darvish 40.00 100.00
ARYG1 Yasmani Grandal 10.00 25.00
ARYG2 Yasmani Grandal 10.00 25.00
ARYG3 Yasmani Grandal 10.00 25.00
ARYG4 Yasmani Grandal 10.00 25.00
ARYG5 Yasmani Grandal 10.00 25.00
ARYT1 Yasmany Tomas 5.00 12.00

2016 Topps Triple Threads Relic Combos

STATED ODDS 1:26 MINI BOX
STATED PRINT RUN 36 SER.#'d SETS
*SILVER/27: .4X TO 1X BASIC
*EMERALD/18: .5X TO 1.2X BASIC
TTRCHG Ichiro/Giffy/Hrnndz 25.00 60.00
TTRCBLR Brnt/Rzzo/Lstr 12.00 30.00
TTRCBLS Santana/Braun/Lucroy 6.00 15.00
TTRCBPC Cain/Bmgrnr/Psy 10.00 25.00
TTRCBTE Encrncn/Tulo/Btsta 12.00 30.00
TTRCBVP Bruce/Phillips/Votto 8.00 20.00
TTRCCMB Mllr/Chpmn/Btncs 12.00 30.00
TTRCCMH Cole/McCutchen/Harrison 8.00 20.00
TTRCCTE Ellsbury/Teixeira/Castro 6.00 15.00
TTRCDBE Bggs/Ellsbry/Dmn 10.00 25.00
TTRCDCB Belt/Duffy/Crawford 8.00 20.00
TTRCFBA Beltre/Fielder/Andrus 8.00 20.00
TTRCFSG Stanton/Fernandez/Gordon 6.00 15.00
TTRCFSI Stntn/Szki/Frnndz 15.00 40.00
TTRCGBP Grdn/Prz/Brtt 15.00 40.00
TTRCGHC Granderson/Harvey/Conforto 6.00 15.00
TTRCHCC Hernandez/Cruz/Cano 8.00 20.00
TTRCHTS Teixeira/Headley/Severino 6.00 15.00
TTRCICH Ichiro Suzuki 30.00 80.00
TTRCKCU Uptn/Knslr/Cbrra 5.00 12.00
TTRCKKL Lndr/Kpns/Klbr 15.00 40.00
TTRCKPS Sgr/Krshw/Puig 12.00 30.00
TTRCLBG Gonzalez/LeMahieu/Blackmon 8.00 20.00
TTRCMCH Holliday/Molina/Carpenter 8.00 20.00
TTRCMDJ Davis/Machado/Jones 6.00 15.00
TTRCMGJ Gausman/Machado/Jones 8.00 20.00
TTRCMKH Kang/Marte/Harrison 6.00 15.00
TTRCMKS Kemp/Myers/Shields 5.00 12.00
TTRCMRP Mrry/Plmr/Rpkn 30.00 80.00
TTRCMSB Buxton/Mauer/Sano 8.00 20.00
TTRCMSN Norris/Shields/Myers 5.00 12.00
TTRCPBO Owens/Buchholz/Price 6.00 15.00
TTRCPPC Psy/Crwfrd/Pnk 10.00 25.00
TTRCPSP Pdrsn/Sgr/Puig 10.00 25.00
TTRCPVH Hmltn/Vtto/Phllps 10.00 25.00
TTRCPWM Piscotty/Martinez/Wong 20.00 50.00
TTRCRGV Reddick/Gray/Vogt 6.00 15.00
TTRCRRB Brnt/Rssll/Rzzo 30.00 80.00
TTRCRRH Hywrd/Rzzo/Rssll 12.00 30.00
TTRCRSA Sale/Rodon/Abreu 6.00 15.00
TTRCSHS Hrpr/Strsbrg/Schrzr 10.00 25.00
TTRCSMD Syndrgrd/Matz/dGrm 12.00 30.00
TTRCSPP Pedroia/Porcello/Swihart 8.00 20.00
TTRCSSB Brnt/Slr/Schwrbr 20.00 50.00
TTRCTPC Clhn/Pjls/Trt 12.00 30.00
TTRCTSE Stroman/Encarnacion Tulowitzki 6.00 15.00
TTRCVCM Mrtnz/Vrlndr/Cbrra 12.00 30.00
TTRCVCP Ventura/Cain/Perez 6.00 15.00
TTRCVCU Cabrera/Verlander/Upton 8.00 20.00
TTRCWHC Harvey/Wright/Conforto 6.00 15.00

2016 Topps Triple Threads Relics

STATED ODDS 1:8 MINI BOX
STATED PRINT RUN 36 SER.#'d SETS
*SILVER/27: .4X TO 1X BASIC
*EMERALD/18: .5X TO 1.2X BASIC
*GOLD/9: .6X TO 1.5X BASIC
ALL VERSIONS EQUALLY PRICED
TTRI1 Ichiro Suzuki 6.00 15.00
TTRI2 Ichiro Suzuki 6.00 15.00
TTRAG1 Adrian Gonzalez 4.00 10.00
TTRAG2 Adrian Gonzalez 4.00 10.00
TTRAG3 Adrian Gonzalez 4.00 10.00
TTRAM1 Andrew McCutchen 6.00 15.00
TTRAM2 Andrew McCutchen 6.00 15.00
TTRAM3 Andrew McCutchen 6.00 15.00
TTRAP1 Albert Pujols 6.00 15.00
TTRAP2 Albert Pujols 6.00 15.00
TTRAP3 Albert Pujols 6.00 15.00
TTRAR1 Anthony Rizzo 8.00 20.00
TTRAR2 Anthony Rizzo 8.00 20.00
TTRAR3 Anthony Rizzo 8.00 20.00
TTRARU1 Addison Russell 5.00 12.00
TTRARU2 Addison Russell 5.00 12.00
TTRARU3 Addison Russell 5.00 12.00
TTRAW1 Adam Wainwright 4.00 10.00
TTRAW2 Adam Wainwright 4.00 10.00
TTRBG1 Brett Gardner 5.00 12.00
TTRBG2 Brett Gardner 5.00 12.00
TTRBH1 Bryce Harper 8.00 20.00
TTRBH2 Bryce Harper 8.00 20.00
TTRBM1 Brian McCann 4.00 10.00
TTRBM2 Brian McCann 4.00 10.00
TTRBP1 Brandon Phillips 3.00 8.00
TTRBP2 Brandon Phillips 3.00 8.00
TTRBP3 Brandon Phillips 3.00 8.00
TTRBPO1 Buster Posey 6.00 15.00
TTRBPO2 Buster Posey 6.00 15.00
TTRBPO3 Buster Posey 6.00 15.00
TTRCB1 Carlos Beltran 4.00 10.00
TTRCB2 Carlos Beltran 4.00 10.00
TTRCB3 Carlos Beltran 4.00 10.00
TTRCBI1 Craig Biggio 4.00 10.00
TTRCBI2 Craig Biggio 4.00 10.00
TTRCK1 Clayton Kershaw 10.00 25.00
TTRCK2 Clayton Kershaw 10.00 25.00
TTRCK3 Clayton Kershaw 10.00 25.00
TTRCM1 Carlos Martinez 4.00 10.00
TTRCM2 Carlos Martinez 4.00 10.00
TTRCR1 Cal Ripken Jr. 15.00 40.00
TTRCR2 Cal Ripken Jr. 15.00 40.00
TTRDL1 DJ LeMahieu 5.00 12.00
TTRDL2 DJ LeMahieu 5.00 12.00
TTRDO1 David Ortiz 8.00 20.00
TTRDO2 David Ortiz 8.00 20.00
TTRDO3 David Ortiz 8.00 20.00
TTRDP1 Dustin Pedroia 6.00 15.00
TTRDP2 Dustin Pedroia 6.00 15.00
TTRDP3 Dustin Pedroia 6.00 15.00
TTRDW1 David Wright 4.00 10.00
TTRDW2 David Wright 4.00 10.00
TTRDW3 David Wright 4.00 10.00
TTREL1 Evan Longoria 4.00 10.00
TTREL2 Evan Longoria 4.00 10.00
TTREL3 Evan Longoria 4.00 10.00
TTRFH1 Felix Hernandez 4.00 10.00
TTRFH2 Felix Hernandez 4.00 10.00
TTRFH3 Felix Hernandez 4.00 10.00
TTRGS1 Giancarlo Stanton 5.00 12.00
TTRGS2 Giancarlo Stanton 5.00 12.00
TTRGS3 Giancarlo Stanton 5.00 12.00
TTRHR1 Hanley Ramirez 4.00 10.00
TTRHR2 Hanley Ramirez 4.00 10.00
TTRHR3 Hanley Ramirez 4.00 10.00
TTRIR1 Ivan Rodriguez 6.00 15.00
TTRIR2 Ivan Rodriguez 6.00 15.00
TTRJA1 Jose Abreu 5.00 12.00
TTRJA2 Jose Abreu 5.00 12.00
TTRJA3 Jose Abreu 5.00 12.00
TTRJAL1 Jose Altuve 5.00 12.00
TTRJAL2 Jose Altuve 5.00 12.00
TTRJC1 Jose Canseco 10.00 25.00
TTRJC2 Jose Canseco 10.00 25.00
TTRJD1 Johnny Damon 4.00 10.00
TTRJD2 Johnny Damon 4.00 10.00
TTRJDE1 Jacob deGrom 5.00 12.00
TTRJDE2 Jacob deGrom 5.00 12.00
TTRJDE3 Jacob deGrom 5.00 12.00
TTRJF1 Jose Fernandez 6.00 15.00
TTRJF2 Jose Fernandez 6.00 15.00
TTRJF3 Jose Fernandez 6.00 15.00
TTRJH1 Josh Harrison 3.00 8.00
TTRJH2 Josh Harrison 3.00 8.00
TTRJK1 Jung Ho Kang 3.00 8.00
TTRJK2 Jung Ho Kang 3.00 8.00
TTRJL1 Jon Lester 4.00 10.00
TTRJL2 Jon Lester 4.00 10.00
TTRJL3 Jon Lester 4.00 10.00
TTRJLU1 Jonathan Lucroy 4.00 10.00
TTRJS1 Jorge Soler 5.00 12.00
TTRJS2 Jorge Soler 5.00 12.00
TTRJV1 Justin Verlander 5.00 12.00
TTRJV2 Justin Verlander 5.00 12.00
TTRJV3 Justin Verlander 5.00 12.00
TTRJVO1 Joey Votto 5.00 12.00
TTRJVO2 Joey Votto 5.00 12.00
TTRJVO3 Joey Votto 5.00 12.00
TTRKB1 Kris Bryant 25.00 60.00
TTRKB2 Kris Bryant 25.00 60.00
TTRKP1 Kevin Plawecki 3.00 8.00
TTRKS1 Kurt Suzuki 3.00 8.00
TTRKW1 Kolten Wong 4.00 10.00
TTRKW2 Kolten Wong 4.00 10.00
TTRLD1 Lucas Duda 4.00 10.00
TTRLD2 Lucas Duda 4.00 10.00
TTRMB1 Madison Bumgarner 4.00 10.00
TTRMC1 Miguel Cabrera 5.00 12.00
TTRMC2 Miguel Cabrera 5.00 12.00
TTRMC3 Miguel Cabrera 5.00 12.00
TTRMF1 Maikel Franco 4.00 10.00
TTRMF2 Maikel Franco 4.00 10.00
TTRMH1 Matt Harvey 4.00 10.00
TTRMH2 Matt Harvey 4.00 10.00
TTRMH3 Matt Harvey 4.00 10.00
TTRMM1 Manny Machado 6.00 15.00
TTRMM2 Manny Machado 6.00 15.00
TTRMM3 Manny Machado 6.00 15.00
TTRMMC1 Mark McGwire 8.00 20.00
TTRMMC2 Mark McGwire 8.00 20.00
TTRMP1 Mike Piazza 5.00 12.00
TTRMP2 Mike Piazza 5.00 12.00
TTRMS1 Max Scherzer 5.00 12.00
TTRMS2 Max Scherzer 5.00 12.00
TTRMT1 Masahiro Tanaka 4.00 10.00
TTRMT2 Masahiro Tanaka 4.00 10.00
TTRMT3 Masahiro Tanaka 4.00 10.00
TTRMTE1 Mark Teixeira 4.00 10.00
TTRMTE2 Mark Teixeira 4.00 10.00
TTRMTR1 Mike Trout 12.00 30.00
TTRMTR2 Mike Trout 12.00 30.00
TTRPF1 Prince Fielder 4.00 10.00
TTRPF2 Prince Fielder 4.00 10.00
TTRPF3 Prince Fielder 4.00 10.00
TTRPG1 Paul Goldschmidt 5.00 12.00
TTRPG2 Paul Goldschmidt 5.00 12.00
TTRPG3 Paul Goldschmidt 5.00 12.00
TTRPS1 Pablo Sandoval 4.00 10.00
TTRPS2 Pablo Sandoval 4.00 10.00
TTRPS3 Pablo Sandoval 4.00 10.00
TTRRC1 Robinson Cano 4.00 10.00
TTRRC2 Robinson Cano 4.00 10.00
TTRRC3 Robinson Cano 4.00 10.00
TTRRCA1 Rusney Castillo 3.00 8.00
TTRRCA2 Rusney Castillo 3.00 8.00
TTRRCA3 Rusney Castillo 3.00 8.00
TTRRCL1 Roger Clemens 6.00 15.00
TTRRH1 Ryan Howard 4.00 10.00
TTRRH2 Ryan Howard 4.00 10.00
TTRSC1 Shin-Soo Choo 4.00 10.00
TTRSC2 Shin-Soo Choo 4.00 10.00
TTRSM1 Steven Matz 4.00 10.00
TTRSM2 Steven Matz 4.00 10.00
TTRTD1 Travis d'Arnaud 4.00 10.00
TTRTD2 Travis d'Arnaud 4.00 10.00
TTRVG1 Vladimir Guerrero 4.00 10.00
TTRVM1 Victor Martinez 4.00 10.00
TTRVM2 Victor Martinez 4.00 10.00
TTRVM3 Victor Martinez 4.00 10.00
TTRYM1 Yadier Molina 6.00 15.00
TTRYM2 Yadier Molina 6.00 15.00
TTRYM3 Yadier Molina 6.00 15.00
TTRZW1 Zack Wheeler 4.00 10.00
TTRZW2 Zack Wheeler 4.00 10.00

2016 Topps Triple Threads Unity Jumbo Relic Autographs

STATED ODDS 1:6 MINI BOX
STATED PRINT RUN 99 SER.#'d SETS
EXCHANGE DEADLINE 8/31/2018
*SILVER/75: .4X TO 1X BASIC
*EMERALD/50: .5X TO 1.2X BASIC
*GOLD/25: .6X TO 1.5X BASIC
UAJRAC Alex Cobb 4.00 10.00
UAJRAE Alcides Escobar 5.00 12.00
UAJRAM Andrew Miller 8.00 20.00
UAJRAR Anthony Rizzo 30.00 80.00
UAJRARU Addison Russell 25.00 60.00
UAJRAW Alex Wood 4.00 10.00
UAJRBB Brandon Belt 5.00 12.00
UAJRBC Brandon Crawford 6.00 15.00
UAJRBD Brandon Drury 6.00 15.00
UAJRBH Brock Holt 4.00 10.00
UAJRCD Corey Dickerson 4.00 10.00
UAJRCE Carl Edwards Jr. 6.00 15.00
UAJRCM Carlos Martinez 5.00 12.00
UAJRCR Colin Rea 4.00 10.00
UAJRCRO Carlos Rodon 6.00 15.00
UAJRCS Corey Seager 25.00 60.00
UAJRCY Christian Yelich 15.00 40.00
UAJRDA Dariel Alvarez 4.00 10.00
UAJRDK Dallas Keuchel 5.00 12.00
UAJRDL DJ LeMahieu 12.00 30.00
UAJRDLE DJ LeMahieu 12.00 30.00
UAJRDTR Devon Travis 4.00 10.00
UAJREI Ender Inciarte 4.00 10.00
UAJRFM Frankie Montas 5.00 12.00
UAJRGB Greg Bird 5.00 12.00
UAJRGHO Greg Holland
UAJRGS George Springer 5.00 12.00
UAJRGSP George Springer 5.00 12.00
UAJRHO Hector Olivera 5.00 12.00
UAJRHOE Henry Owens 5.00 12.00
UAJRHOW Henry Owens 5.00 12.00
UAJRJC Jose Canseco 10.00 25.00
UAJRJCA Jose Canseco 10.00 25.00
UAJRJF Jeurys Familia 5.00 12.00
UAJRJH Jesse Hahn 4.00 10.00
UAJRJP Joc Pederson 5.00 12.00
UAJRJPAN Joe Panik 5.00 12.00
UAJRJR J.T. Realmuto 20.00 50.00
UAJRJS Jorge Soler 6.00 15.00
UAJRJSH James Shields 4.00 10.00
UAJRJT Justin Turner 25.00 60.00
UAJRKC Kole Calhoun 4.00 10.00
UAJRKCA Kole Calhoun 4.00 10.00
UAJRKGI Ken Giles 4.00 10.00
UAJRKH Kelvin Herrera 4.00 10.00
UAJRKMA Ketel Marte 8.00 20.00
UAJRKW Kolten Wong 5.00 12.00
UAJRKWO Kolten Wong 5.00 12.00
UAJRLS Luis Severino 5.00 12.00
UAJRMCO Michael Conforto 8.00 20.00
UAJRMD1 Matt Duffy 4.00 10.00
UAJRMD2 Matt Duffy 4.00 10.00
UAJRMDU Matt Duffy 4.00 10.00
UAJRMF Maikel Franco 5.00 12.00
UAJRMP Michael Pineda 4.00 10.00
UAJRMR Matt Reynolds 4.00 10.00
UAJRMRE Michael Reed 4.00 10.00
UAJRMS Marcus Semien 4.00 10.00
UAJRMSA Miguel Sano 6.00 15.00
UAJRMSE Marcus Semien 4.00 10.00
UAJRMSH Matt Shoemaker 5.00 12.00
UAJRMW Matt Wisler 4.00 10.00
UAJRMWA Michael Wacha 6.00 15.00
UAJRNE Nathan Eovaldi 5.00 12.00
UAJRNS Noah Syndergaard 10.00 25.00
UAJROV Omar Vizquel 6.00 15.00
UAJRRI Raisel Iglesias 5.00 12.00
UAJRRR Rob Refsnyder 5.00 12.00
UAJRSD Sean Doolittle 4.00 10.00
UAJRSDO Sean Doolittle 4.00 10.00
UAJRSM Steven Matz 5.00 12.00
UAJRSMA Starling Marte 5.00 12.00
UAJRSMT Steven Matz 5.00 12.00
UAJRYG Yasmani Grandal 4.00 10.00
UAJRYR Yadiel Rivera 4.00 10.00
UAJRZW Zack Wheeler 5.00 12.00

2016 Topps Triple Threads Unity Jumbo Relics

STATED ODDS 1:6 MINI BOX
STATED PRINT RUN 36 SER.#'d SETS
*SILVER/27: .4X TO 1X BASIC
*EMERALD/18: .5X TO 1.2X BASIC
*GOLD/9: .6X TO 1.5X BASIC
ALL VERSIONS EQUALLY PRICED
UJRABA Archie Bradley 3.00 8.00
UJRABD Archie Bradley 3.00 8.00
UJRABR Archie Bradley 3.00 8.00
UJRAGN Adrian Gonzalez 4.00 10.00
UJRAGO Adrian Gonzalez 4.00 10.00
UJRAGZ Adrian Gonzalez 4.00 10.00
UJRALP Albert Pujols 6.00 15.00
UJRALU Albert Pujols 6.00 15.00
UJRAMC Andrew McCutchen 6.00 15.00
UJRAMI Andrew Miller 4.00 10.00
UJRAML Andrew Miller 4.00 10.00
UJRAMR Andrew Miller 4.00 10.00
UJRAMU Andrew McCutchen 6.00 15.00
UJRANI Anthony Rizzo 8.00 20.00
UJRANR Anthony Rizzo 8.00 20.00
UJRAPJ Albert Pujols 6.00 15.00
UJRARE Addison Russell 5.00 12.00
UJRARI Anthony Rizzo 8.00 20.00
UJRARL Addison Russell 5.00 12.00
UJRARS Addison Russell 5.00 12.00
UJRARU Addison Russell 5.00 12.00
UJRARZ Anthony Rizzo 8.00 20.00
UJRAWA Adam Wainwright 4.00 10.00
UJRAWI Adam Wainwright 4.00 10.00
UJRBHA Bryce Harper 8.00 20.00
UJRBHL Brock Holt 3.00 8.00
UJRBHO Brock Holt 3.00 8.00
UJRBHT Brock Holt 3.00 8.00
UJRBMA Brian McCann 4.00 10.00
UJRBMC Brian McCann 4.00 10.00
UJRBMN Brian McCann 4.00 10.00
UJRBPH Brandon Phillips 3.00 8.00
UJRBPI Brandon Phillips 3.00 8.00
UJRBPL Brandon Phillips 3.00 8.00
UJRBPO Buster Posey 6.00 15.00
UJRBRA Bryce Harper 8.00 20.00
UJRBRH Bryce Harper 8.00 20.00
UJRBSH Blake Swihart 4.00 10.00
UJRBSI Blake Swihart 4.00 10.00
UJRBST Blake Swihart 4.00 10.00
UJRBSW Blake Swihart 4.00 10.00
UJRCBE Carlos Beltran 4.00 10.00
UJRCBL Carlos Beltran 4.00 10.00
UJRCDA Chris Davis 3.00 8.00
UJRCDV Chris Davis 3.00 8.00
UJRCGA Curtis Granderson 4.00 10.00
UJRCGN Carlos Gonzalez 4.00 10.00
UJRCGO Carlos Gonzalez 4.00 10.00
UJRCGR Curtis Granderson 4.00 10.00
UJRCKE Clayton Kershaw 10.00 25.00
UJRCMA Carlos Martinez 4.00 10.00
UJRCMR Carlos Martinez 4.00 10.00
UJRCSA Carlos Santana 4.00 10.00
UJRCSN Carlos Santana 4.00 10.00
UJRCST Carlos Santana 4.00 10.00
UJRCVA Christian Vazquez 3.00 8.00
UJRCVQ Christian Vazquez 3.00 8.00
UJRCVZ Christian Vazquez 3.00 8.00
UJRDAR David Wright 4.00 10.00
UJRDAW David Wright 4.00 10.00
UJRDBA Dellin Betances 4.00 10.00
UJRDBE Dellin Betances 4.00 10.00
UJRDBN Dellin Betances 4.00 10.00
UJRDBT Dellin Betances 4.00 10.00
UJRDKE Dallas Keuchel 4.00 10.00
UJRDOT David Ortiz 8.00 20.00
UJRDPD Dustin Pedroia 6.00 15.00
UJRDPE Dustin Pedroia 6.00 15.00
UJRDWR David Wright 4.00 10.00
UJRDWT David Wright 4.00 10.00
UJREAD Elvis Andrus 4.00 10.00
UJREAN Elvis Andrus 4.00 10.00
UJREAR Elvis Andrus 4.00 10.00
UJREEC Edwin Encarnacion 5.00 12.00
UJREEN Edwin Encarnacion 5.00 12.00
UJRELG Evan Longoria 4.00 10.00
UJRELN Evan Longoria 4.00 10.00
UJRELO Evan Longoria 4.00 10.00
UJRFHE Felix Hernandez 4.00 10.00
UJRGCE Gerrit Cole 5.00 12.00
UJRGCL Gerrit Cole 5.00 12.00
UJRGCO Gerrit Cole 5.00 12.00
UJRGGN Gio Gonzalez 4.00 10.00
UJRGGO Gio Gonzalez 4.00 10.00
UJRGGZ Gio Gonzalez 4.00 10.00
UJRGPA Gregory Polanco 4.00 10.00
UJRGPL Gregory Polanco 4.00 10.00
UJRGPO Gregory Polanco 4.00 10.00
UJRGSA Giancarlo Stanton 5.00 12.00
UJRGST Giancarlo Stanton 5.00 12.00
UJRHJR Hyun-Jin Ryu 4.00 10.00
UJRHRA Hanley Ramirez 4.00 10.00
UJRHRM Hanley Ramirez 4.00 10.00
UJRHRU Hyun-Jin Ryu 4.00 10.00
UJRHRY Hyun-Jin Ryu 4.00 10.00
UJRHRZ Hanley Ramirez 4.00 10.00
UJRICH Ichiro Suzuki 6.00 15.00
UJRICY Ichiro Suzuki 6.00 15.00
UJRIKI Ian Kinsler 4.00 10.00
UJRIKN Ian Kinsler 4.00 10.00
UJRIKS Ian Kinsler 4.00 10.00
UJRIRO Ivan Rodriguez 6.00 15.00
UJRJAB Javier Baez 6.00 15.00
UJRJAD Jacob deGrom 5.00 12.00
UJRJAE Jacob deGrom 5.00 12.00
UJRJBA Javier Baez 6.00 15.00
UJRJBE Javier Baez 6.00 15.00
UJRJBR Jay Bruce 4.00 10.00
UJRJBU Jay Bruce 4.00 10.00
UJRJBZ Javier Baez 6.00 15.00
UJRJDA Johnny Damon 4.00 10.00
UJRJDG Jacob deGrom 5.00 12.00
UJRJDM Johnny Damon 4.00 10.00
UJRJEB Jacoby Ellsbury 4.00 10.00
UJRJEL Jacoby Ellsbury 4.00 10.00
UJRJFE Jose Fernandez 6.00 15.00
UJRJFR Jose Fernandez 6.00 15.00
UJRJGA Joey Gallo 5.00 12.00
UJRJGL Joey Gallo 4.00 10.00
UJRJGO Joey Gallo 4.00 10.00
UJRJHA Josh Harrison 3.00 8.00
UJRJHR Josh Harrison 3.00 8.00
UJRJHS Josh Harrison 3.00 8.00
UJRJLA Juan Lagares 3.00 8.00
UJRJLE Jon Lester 4.00 10.00
UJRJLG Juan Lagares 3.00 8.00
UJRJLS Jon Lester 4.00 10.00
UJRJMA J.D. Martinez 5.00 12.00
UJRJMA Joe Mauer 4.00 10.00
UJRJMR J.D. Martinez 5.00 12.00
UJRJMT J.D. Martinez 5.00 12.00
UJRJMU Joe Mauer 4.00 10.00
UJRJVA Justin Verlander 5.00 12.00
UJRJVE Justin Verlander 5.00 12.00
UJRJVL Justin Verlander 5.00 12.00
UJRJVO Joey Votto 5.00 12.00
UJRJVR Justin Verlander 5.00 12.00
UJRJVT Joey Votto 5.00 12.00
UJRJYV Joey Votto 5.00 12.00
UJRKCA Kole Calhoun 3.00 8.00
UJRKCL Kole Calhoun 3.00 8.00
UJRKPA Kevin Plawecki 3.00 8.00
UJRKPL Kevin Plawecki 3.00 8.00
UJRKPW Kevin Plawecki 3.00 8.00
UJRKSE Kyle Seager 3.00 8.00
UJRKWG Kolten Wong 4.00 10.00
UJRKWN Kolten Wong 4.00 10.00
UJRKWO Kolten Wong 4.00 10.00
UJRKYS Kyle Seager 3.00 8.00
UJRLDA Lucas Duda 4.00 10.00
UJRLDD Lucas Duda 4.00 10.00
UJRLDU Lucas Duda 4.00 10.00
UJRLLN Lance Lynn 3.00 8.00
UJRLLY Lance Lynn 3.00 8.00
UJRMAA Matt Harvey 4.00 10.00
UJRMAC Manny Machado 6.00 15.00
UJRMAH Matt Harvey 4.00 10.00
UJRMAM Manny Machado 6.00 15.00
UJRMBE Mookie Betts 8.00 20.00
UJRMBM Madison Bumgarner 4.00 10.00
UJRMBT Mookie Betts 8.00 20.00
UJRMCA Matt Cain 4.00 10.00
UJRMCA Miguel Cabrera 5.00 12.00
UJRMCA Matt Carpenter 5.00 12.00
UJRMCB Miguel Cabrera 5.00 12.00
UJRMCE Miguel Cabrera 5.00 12.00
UJRMCI Matt Cain 4.00 10.00
UJRMCN Michael Conforto 5.00 12.00
UJRMCN Matt Cain 4.00 10.00
UJRMCO Michael Conforto 5.00 12.00
UJRMCP Matt Carpenter 5.00 12.00
UJRMCR Miguel Cabrera 5.00 12.00
UJRMCR Matt Carpenter 5.00 12.00
UJRMFA Maikel Franco 4.00 10.00
UJRMFR Maikel Franco 4.00 10.00
UJRMHA Matt Harvey 4.00 10.00
UJRMMC Mark Melancon 3.00 8.00
UJRMME Mark Melancon 3.00 8.00
UJRMML Mark Melancon 3.00 8.00
UJRMMY Mark McGwire 8.00 20.00
UJRMON Marcell Ozuna 5.00 12.00
UJRMOU Marcell Ozuna 5.00 12.00
UJRMOZ Marcell Ozuna 5.00 12.00
UJRMPD Michael Pineda 3.00 8.00
UJRMPI Michael Pineda 3.00 8.00
UJRMPN Michael Pineda 3.00 8.00
UJRMTA Masahiro Tanaka 4.00 10.00
UJRMTN Masahiro Tanaka 4.00 10.00
UJRMTR Mike Trout 12.00 30.00
UJRMZI Mike Zunino 3.00 8.00
UJRMZN Mike Zunino 3.00 8.00
UJRMZU Mike Zunino 3.00 8.00
UJRPFE Prince Fielder 4.00 10.00
UJRPFI Prince Fielder 4.00 10.00
UJRPSA Pablo Sandoval 4.00 10.00
UJRPSD Pablo Sandoval 4.00 10.00
UJRPSN Pablo Sandoval 4.00 10.00
UJRRCA Rusney Castillo 3.00 8.00
UJRRCS Rusney Castillo 3.00 8.00
UJRRCT Rusney Castillo 3.00 8.00
UJRRHO Ryan Howard 4.00 10.00
UJRRHW Ryan Howard 4.00 10.00
UJRSCH Shin-Soo Choo 4.00 10.00
UJRSCO Shin-Soo Choo 4.00 10.00
UJRSMA Starling Marte 4.00 10.00
UJRSMR Starling Marte 4.00 10.00
UJRSSC Shin-Soo Choo 4.00 10.00
UJRSSO Steven Souza Jr. 4.00 10.00
UJRSSU Steven Souza Jr. 4.00 10.00
UJRSSZ Steven Souza Jr. 4.00 10.00
UJRTLI Tim Lincecum 4.00 10.00
UJRTLN Tim Lincecum 4.00 10.00
UJRTRO Tyson Ross 3.00 8.00
UJRTRS Tyson Ross 3.00 8.00
UJRTWA Taijuan Walker 3.00 8.00
UJRTWK Taijuan Walker 3.00 8.00
UJRTWL Taijuan Walker 3.00 8.00
UJRTYR Tyson Ross 3.00 8.00
UJRVMA Victor Martinez 4.00 10.00
UJRVMR Victor Martinez 4.00 10.00
UJRVMT Victor Martinez 4.00 10.00
UJRVMZ Victor Martinez 4.00 10.00
UJRWFL Wilmer Flores 4.00 10.00
UJRWFO Wilmer Flores 4.00 10.00
UJRWFR Wilmer Flores 4.00 10.00
UJRWLM Wil Myers 3.00 8.00
UJRWME Wil Myers 3.00 8.00
UJRWMR Wil Myers 3.00 8.00
UJRWMS Wil Myers 3.00 8.00
UJRYCE Yoenis Cespedes 5.00 12.00
UJRYCS Yoenis Cespedes 5.00 12.00
UJRYGM Yan Gomes 3.00 8.00
UJRYGO Yan Gomes 3.00 8.00
UJRYML Yadier Molina 6.00 15.00
UJRYMN Yadier Molina 6.00 15.00
UJRYMO Yadier Molina 6.00 15.00
UJRYPG Yasiel Puig 5.00 12.00
UJRYPI Yasiel Puig 5.00 12.00
UJRYPU Yasiel Puig 5.00 12.00
UJRYVE Yordano Ventura 4.00 10.00
UJRYVN Yordano Ventura 4.00 10.00
UJRYVT Yordano Ventura 4.00 10.00
UJRZWE Zack Wheeler 4.00 10.00
UJRZWH Zack Wheeler 4.00 10.00
UJRZWL Zack Wheeler 4.00 10.00

2017 Topps Triple Threads

COMP.SET w/o AU's (100) 75.00 200.00
JSY AU RC ODDS 1:12 MINI BOX
JSY AU RC PRINT RUN 99 SER.#'d SETS
JSY AU ODDS 1:12 MINI BOX
JSY AU PRINT RUN 99 SER.#'d SETS
EXCHANGE DEADLINE 8/31/2019
1-100 PLATE ODDS 1:115 MINI BOX
JSY AU PLATE ODDS 1:278 MINI BOX
PLATE PRINT RUN 1 SET PER COLOR
BLACK-CYAN-MAGENTA-YELLOW ISSUED
NO PLATE PRICING DUE TO SCARCITY
1 Bryce Harper 1.00 2.50
2 Ken Griffey Jr. 1.25 3.00
3 Kris Bryant .75 2.00
4 Mike Trout 3.00 8.00
5 Paul Goldschmidt .60 1.50
6 Manny Machado .60 1.50
7 Mookie Betts 1.00 2.50
8 Anthony Rizzo 1.00 2.50
9 Kyle Schwarber .60 1.50
10 Joey Votto .60 1.50
11 Nolan Arenado .75 2.00
12 Miguel Cabrera .60 1.50
13 Justin Verlander .60 1.50
14 Carlos Correa .60 1.50
15 Eric Hosmer .50 1.25
16 Clayton Kershaw 1.25 3.00
17 Corey Seager .60 1.50
18 Julio Urias .60 1.50
19 Giancarlo Stanton .60 1.50
20 Ichiro .75 2.00
21 Noah Syndergaard .50 1.25
22 Masahiro Tanaka .50 1.25
23 Gary Sanchez .60 1.50
24 Buster Posey .75 2.00
25 Felix Hernandez .50 1.25
26 Robinson Cano .50 1.25
27 Aledmys Diaz .50 1.25
28 Yu Darvish .60 1.50
29 Josh Donaldson .50 1.25
30 Jose Bautista .50 1.25
31 Max Scherzer .60 1.50
32 Francisco Lindor .60 1.50
33 Chris Sale .60 1.50
34 Addison Russell .60 1.50
35 Javier Baez .75 2.00
36 Jacob deGrom .60 1.50
37 Andrew McCutchen .60 1.50
38 Wil Myers .50 1.25
39 Albert Pujols .75 2.00
40 Yoenis Cespedes .60 1.50
41 Jose Altuve .50 1.25
42 Jake Arrieta .50 1.25
43 Edwin Encarnacion .60 1.50
44 David Price .50 1.25
45 Ryan Braun .50 1.25
46 Freddie Freeman .75 2.00
47 Troy Tulowitzki .60 1.50
48 Matt Carpenter .60 1.50
49 Carlos Gonzalez .50 1.25
50 Adrian Beltre .60 1.50
51 Hunter Pence .50 1.25
52 Corey Kluber .50 1.25
53 Trea Turner .50 1.25
54 Kenta Maeda .50 1.25
55 Stephen Strasburg .60 1.50
56 Matt Kemp .50 1.25
57 David Wright .50 1.25
58 Xander Bogaerts .60 1.50
59 Adam Jones .50 1.25
60 Daniel Murphy .50 1.25
61 Roberto Clemente 1.50 4.00
62 Cal Ripken Jr. 2.00 5.00
63 Hank Aaron 1.25 3.00
64 Ted Williams 1.25 3.00
65 Jackie Robinson .60 1.50
66 Sandy Koufax 1.25 3.00
67 Babe Ruth 1.50 4.00
68 Ernie Banks .60 1.50
69 Derek Jeter 1.50 4.00
70 David Ortiz .60 1.50
71 Mark McGwire 1.00 2.50
72 Randy Johnson .60 1.50
73 Honus Wagner .60 1.50
74 Roger Maris .60 1.50
75 Ty Cobb 1.00 2.50
76 Lou Gehrig 1.25 3.00
77 Reggie Jackson .50 1.25
78 George Brett 1.25 3.00
79 Don Mattingly 1.25 3.00
80 Frank Thomas .60 1.50
81 Bo Jackson .60 1.50
82 Johnny Bench .60 1.50
83 Greg Maddux .75 2.00
84 Roger Clemens .75 2.00
85 Mike Piazza .60 1.50
86 Nolan Ryan 2.00 5.00
87 Brooks Robinson .50 1.25
88 Chipper Jones .60 1.50
89 Ozzie Smith .75 2.00
90 Carl Yastrzemski 1.00 2.50
91 George Springer .50 1.25
92 Zack Greinke .50 1.25
93 Pedro Martinez .50 1.25
94 Ryne Sandberg 1.25 3.00
95 Barry Larkin .50 1.25
96 Starling Marte .50 1.25
97 Chris Davis .40 1.00
98 Byron Buxton .50 1.25
99 Dustin Pedroia .60 1.50
100 John Smoltz .60 1.50
RPAAB Bregman JSY AU RC 20.00 50.00
RPAABE Bnntndi JSY AU RC EXCH 30.00 80.00
RPAAD Aledmys Diaz JSY AU 4.00 10.00
RPAAJ Judge JSY AU RC EXCH 75.00 200.00
RPAAN Nola JSY AU EXCH 10.00 25.00
RPAAR Alex Reyes JSY AU RC 6.00 15.00
RPAARU A.Russell JSY AU 10.00 25.00
RPAAT Andrew Toles JSY AU RC 3.00 8.00
RPABB Byron Buxton JSY AU 10.00 25.00
RPABS Blake Snell JSY AU 4.00 10.00
RPABSE Braden Shipley JSY AU RC 3.00 8.00
RPACF Carson Fulmer JSY AU RC 4.00 10.00
RPACS Seager JSY AU EXCH 20.00 50.00
RPADS Swnsn JSY AU RC EXCH 8.00 20.00
RPAGB Greg Bird JSY AU 4.00 10.00
RPAHD Hunter Dozier JSY AU RC 3.00 8.00
RPAHR Hunter Renfroe JSY AU RC 4.00 10.00
RPAJB Javier Baez JSY AU 15.00 40.00
RPAJC Jharel Cotton JSY AU RC 3.00 8.00
RPAJH Jeff Hoffman JSY AU RC 3.00 8.00
RPAJM Joe Musgrove JSY AU RC 3.00 8.00
RPAJT Jameson Taillon JSY AU 5.00 12.00
RPAJU Julio Urias JSY AU EXCH 5.00 12.00
RPAKS Kyle Schwarber JSY AU
RPALG Lucas Giolito JSY AU 15.00 40.00
RPALS Luis Severino JSY AU 10.00 25.00
RPAMF Michael Fulmer JSY AU 3.00 8.00
RPAMM Manny Margot JSY AU RC 4.00 10.00
RPAMS Miguel Sano JSY AU 4.00 10.00
RPARG Robert Gsellman JSY AU RC 3.00 8.00
RPARH Ryon Healy JSY AU RC 6.00 15.00
RPARQ Roman Quinn JSY AU RC 3.00 8.00
RPART Raimel Tapia JSY AU RC 4.00 10.00
RPASM Steven Matz JSY AU 4.00 10.00
RPASP Stephen Piscotty JSY AU 4.00 10.00
RPATA Tyler Austin JSY AU RC 8.00 20.00
RPATG Tyler Glasnow JSY AU RC 4.00 10.00
RPATS Trevor Story JSY AU 5.00 12.00
RPAWC W.Contreras JSY AU 10.00 25.00
RPAYG Gurriel JSY AU RC 10.00 25.00
RPAYM Moncada JSY AU RC 20.00 50.00

2017 Topps Triple Threads Amber

*AMBER VET: .75X TO 2X BASIC
STATED ODDS 1:4 MINI BOX
STATED PRINT RUN 150 SER.#'d SETS
69 Derek Jeter 5.00 12.00

2017 Topps Triple Threads Amethyst

*AMETHYST VET: .6X TO 1.5X BASIC
STATED ODDS 1:2 MINI BOX
STATED PRINT RUN 340 SER.#'d SETS
69 Derek Jeter 4.00 10.00

2017 Topps Triple Threads Emerald

*EMERALD VET: .6X TO 1.5X BASIC
*EMERALD JSY AU: .4X TO 1X BASIC RC
1-100 ODDS 1:2 MINI BOX
JSY AU ODDS 1:23 MINI BOX
1-100 PRINT RUN 250 SER.#'d SETS
JSY AU PRINT RUN 50 SER.#'d SETS
EXCHANGE DEADLINE 8/31/2019
69 Derek Jeter 4.00 10.00

2017 Topps Triple Threads Gold

*GOLD VET: 1X TO 2.5X BASIC
STATED ODDS 1:5 MINI BOX
STATED PRINT RUN 99 SER.#'d SETS
4 Mike Trout 6.00 15.00
61 Roberto Clemente 5.00 12.00
62 Cal Ripken Jr. 10.00 25.00
69 Derek Jeter 6.00 15.00
86 Nolan Ryan 8.00 20.00

2017 Topps Triple Threads Onyx

*ONYX VET: 1.5X TO 4X BASIC
*ONYX JSY AU: .5X TO 1.2X BASIC RC

1-100 ODDS 1:10 MINI BOX
JSY AU ODDS 1:32 MINI BOX
1-100 PRINT RUN 50 SER.#'d SETS
JSY AU PRINT RUN 35 SER.#'d SETS
EXCHANGE DEADLINE 8/31/2019
4 Mike Trout 10.00 25.00
61 Roberto Clemente 8.00 20.00
62 Cal Ripken Jr. 15.00 40.00
64 Ted Williams 8.00 20.00
69 Derek Jeter 12.00 30.00
78 George Brett 12.00 30.00
79 Don Mattingly 10.00 25.00
86 Nolan Ryan 12.00 30.00

2017 Topps Triple Threads Sapphire

*SAPPHIRE VET: 2.5X TO 6X BASIC
STATED ODDS 1:19 MINI BOX
STATED PRINT RUN 25 SER.#'d SETS
2 Ken Griffey Jr. 20.00 50.00
4 Mike Trout 20.00 50.00
61 Roberto Clemente 12.00 30.00
62 Cal Ripken Jr. 25.00 60.00
64 Ted Williams 12.00 30.00
69 Derek Jeter 50.00 120.00
78 George Brett 20.00 50.00
79 Don Mattingly 15.00 40.00
80 Frank Thomas 8.00 20.00
86 Nolan Ryan 20.00 50.00

2017 Topps Triple Threads Silver

*SILVER JSY AU: .4X TO 1X BASIC RC
STATED ODDS 1:16 MINI BOX
STATED PRINT RUN 75 SER.#'d SETS
EXCHANGE DEADLINE 8/31/2019

2017 Topps Triple Threads Autograph Relic Combos

STATED ODDS 1:82 HOBBY
STATED PRINT RUN 36 SER.#'d SETS
EXCHANGE DEADLINE 8/31/2019
*SILVER/27: .4X TO 1X BASIC
*EMERALD/18: .4X TO 1X BASIC
PRINTING PLATE ODDS 1:743 HOBBY
PLATE PRINT RUN 1 SET PER COLOR
BLACK-CYAN-MAGENTA-YELLOW ISSUED
NO PLATE PRICING DUE TO SCARCITY
ARCBBA Altve/Bgwll/Bggo EX 125.00 300.00
ARCBRS Schwrbr/Rssll/Baez EX 40.00 100.00
ARCBSK Bnntndi/Kmbrl/Sale EX 75.00 200.00
ARCBSU Urs/Bllngr/Sgr EX 125.00 300.00
ARCCAB Brgmn/Crra/Altve EX 75.00 200.00
ARCCAS Crra/Altve/Sprngr EX 60.00 150.00
ARCDSC dGrm/Sndrgrd/Cnfrto 50.00 120.00
ARCDSM Sndrgrd/Matz/dGrm 40.00 100.00
ARCJMM Mchdo/Jns/Mncni 30.00 80.00
ARCKSU Sgr/Urs/Krshw
ARCLGV Vtto/Grffy/Lrkn 125.00 300.00
ARCLKE Lndr/Klbr/Encrncn EX 50.00 120.00
ARCLKZ Zmmr/Lndr/Klbr
ARCPCD Psctty/Crpntr/Diaz 10.00 25.00
ARCRBS Rzzo/Schwrbr/Brnt EX 150.00 400.00
ARCRGB Grnlz/Rdrgz/Bltre 50.00 120.00
ARCRRM Mchdo/Rbnsn/Rpkn
ARCSAB Sprngr/Brgmn/Altve EX 60.00 150.00
ARCSJF Swnsn/Frmn/Jns EX 75.00 200.00
ARCSPB Bnntndi/Sale/Pdria

2017 Topps Triple Threads Legend Relics

STATED ODDS 1:85 HOBBY
STATED PRINT RUN 36 SER.#'d SETS
*SILVER/27: .4X TO 1X BASIC
*EMERALD/18: .4X TO 1X BASIC
RLCCJ Chipper Jones 10.00 25.00
RLCCR Cal Ripken Jr. 25.00 60.00
RLCCY Carl Yastrzemski
RLCDJ Derek Jeter 40.00 100.00
RLCFT Frank Thomas 10.00 25.00
RLCGB George Brett 25.00 60.00
RLCGM Greg Maddux 12.00 30.00
RLCJB Johnny Bench 12.00 30.00
RLCJS John Smoltz 10.00 25.00
RLCKG Ken Griffey Jr. 30.00 80.00
RLCMP Mike Piazza 10.00 25.00
RLCNR Nolan Ryan 30.00 80.00
RLCOS Ozzie Smith 12.00 30.00
RLCPM Pedro Martinez 8.00 20.00
RLCRH Rickey Henderson 12.00 30.00
RLCRJ Reggie Jackson 8.00 20.00
RLCRL Roger Clemens 10.00 25.00
RLCRS Ryne Sandberg 12.00 30.00
RLCSC Steve Carlton 10.00 25.00
RLCTW Ted Williams 40.00 100.00

2017 Topps Triple Threads Relic Autographs

STATED ODDS 1:9 HOBBY
STATED PRINT RUN 18 SER.#'d SETS
EXCHANGE DEADLINE 8/31/2019
*GOLD/9: .5X TO 1.2X BASIC
SOME GOLD NOT PRICED DUE TO SCARCITY
ALL VERSIONS EQUALLY PRICED
TTARAB1 Adrian Beltre 50.00 120.00
TTARAB2 Adrian Beltre 50.00 120.00
TTARAD1 Aledmys Diaz 6.00 15.00
TTARAD2 Aledmys Diaz 6.00 15.00
TTARAD3 Aledmys Diaz 6.00 15.00
TTARAD4 Aledmys Diaz 6.00 15.00
TTARAD5 Aledmys Diaz 6.00 15.00
TTARAJ1 Adam Jones 12.00 30.00
TTARAJ2 Adam Jones 12.00 30.00
TTARAJ3 Adam Jones 12.00 30.00
TTARAJ4 Adam Jones 12.00 30.00
TTARAJ5 Adam Jones 12.00 30.00
TTARAL01 Roberto Alomar 15.00 40.00
TTARAL02 Roberto Alomar 15.00 40.00
TTARAR1 Anthony Rizzo 30.00 80.00
TTARAR2 Anthony Rizzo 30.00 80.00
TTARAR3 Anthony Rizzo 30.00 80.00
TTARAR4 Anthony Rizzo 30.00 80.00
TTARAR5 Anthony Rizzo 30.00 80.00
TTARBA1 Bobby Abreu 12.00 30.00
TTARBA2 Bobby Abreu 12.00 30.00
TTARBB1 Brandon Belt 10.00 25.00
TTARBB2 Brandon Belt 10.00 25.00
TTARBH1 Bryce Harper 100.00 250.00
TTARBH2 Bryce Harper 100.00 250.00
TTARBP1 Buster Posey
TTARBZ1 Ben Zobrist
TTARBZ2 Ben Zobrist
TTARBZ3 Ben Zobrist
TTARBZ4 Ben Zobrist
TTARCB1 Craig Biggio 12.00 30.00
TTARCBE1 Cody Bellinger 75.00 200.00
TTARCBE2 Cody Bellinger 75.00 200.00
TTARCBE3 Cody Bellinger 75.00 200.00
TTARCBE4 Cody Bellinger 75.00 200.00
TTARCBE5 Cody Bellinger 75.00 200.00
TTARCC1 Carlos Correa 40.00 100.00
TTARCC2 Carlos Correa 40.00 100.00
TTARCF1 Carlton Fisk 15.00 40.00
TTARCK1 Corey Kluber 15.00 40.00
TTARCK2 Corey Kluber 15.00 40.00
TTARCK3 Corey Kluber 15.00 40.00
TTARCK4 Corey Kluber 15.00 40.00
TTARCKE1 Clayton Kershaw 75.00 200.00
TTARCKI1 Craig Kimbrel 15.00 40.00
TTARCKI2 Craig Kimbrel 15.00 40.00
TTARCKI3 Craig Kimbrel 15.00 40.00
TTARCKI4 Craig Kimbrel 15.00 40.00
TTARCKI5 Craig Kimbrel 15.00 40.00
TTARCRJ1 Cal Ripken Jr. 60.00 150.00
TTARCS1 Corey Seager 25.00 60.00
TTARCS2 Corey Seager 25.00 60.00
TTARCS3 Corey Seager 25.00 60.00
TTARCS4 Chris Sale 20.00 50.00
TTARCS5 Chris Sale 20.00 50.00
TTARCSA1 Chris Sale 20.00 50.00
TTARCSA2 Chris Sale 20.00 50.00
TTARCSA3 Chris Sale 20.00 50.00
TTARCY1 Carl Yastrzemski 40.00 100.00
TTARDA1 Daniel Murphy EXCH 20.00 50.00
TTARDA2 Daniel Murphy EXCH 20.00 50.00
TTARDB1 Dellin Betances 6.00 15.00
TTARDB2 Dellin Betances 6.00 15.00
TTARDB3 Dellin Betances 6.00 15.00
TTARDB4 Dellin Betances 6.00 15.00
TTARDB5 Dellin Betances 6.00 15.00
TTARDJ1 Derek Jeter 600.00 800.00
TTARDL1 Derrek Lee 8.00 20.00
TTARDL2 Derrek Lee 8.00 20.00
TTARDL3 Derrek Lee 8.00 20.00
TTARDM1 Don Mattingly 50.00 120.00
TTARDM2 Don Mattingly 50.00 120.00
TTARDM3 Daniel Murphy EXCH 20.00 50.00
TTARDM4 Daniel Murphy EXCH 20.00 50.00
TTARDM5 Daniel Murphy EXCH 20.00 50.00
TTARDO1 David Ortiz 40.00 100.00
TTARDP1 David Price 10.00 25.00
TTARDP2 David Price 10.00 25.00
TTARDP3 David Price 10.00 25.00
TTARDPE1 Dustin Pedroia 20.00 50.00
TTARDPE2 Dustin Pedroia 20.00 50.00
TTARDW1 Dave Winfield 25.00 60.00
TTARDW2 Dave Winfield 25.00 60.00
TTAREE1 Edwin Encarnacion 15.00 40.00
TTAREE2 Edwin Encarnacion 15.00 40.00
TTAREE3 Edwin Encarnacion 15.00 40.00
TTAREE4 Edwin Encarnacion 15.00 40.00
TTARET1 Eric Thames 8.00 20.00
TTARET2 Eric Thames 8.00 20.00
TTARET3 Eric Thames 8.00 20.00
TTARET4 Eric Thames 8.00 20.00
TTARET5 Eric Thames 8.00 20.00
TTARFF1 Freddie Freeman 20.00 50.00
TTARFF2 Freddie Freeman 20.00 50.00
TTARFF3 Freddie Freeman 20.00 50.00
TTARFL1 Francisco Lindor 30.00 80.00
TTARFL2 Francisco Lindor 30.00 80.00
TTARFL3 Francisco Lindor 30.00 80.00
TTARFL4 Francisco Lindor 30.00 80.00
TTARFM1 Floyd Mayweather 250.00 500.00
TTARFM2 Floyd Mayweather 250.00 500.00
TTARFT1 Frank Thomas 50.00 120.00
TTARFT2 Frank Thomas 50.00 120.00
TTARGS1 George Springer 12.00 30.00
TTARGS2 George Springer 12.00 30.00
TTARGS3 George Springer 12.00 30.00
TTARGS4 George Springer 12.00 30.00
TTARGS5 George Springer 12.00 30.00
TTARHA1 Hank Aaron 150.00 300.00
TTARIR1 Ivan Rodriguez 25.00 60.00
TTARIR2 Ivan Rodriguez 25.00 60.00
TTARIR3 Ivan Rodriguez 25.00 60.00
TTARI3 Ichiro 200.00 400.00
TTARJA1 Jose Altuve 25.00 60.00
TTARJA2 Jose Altuve 25.00 60.00
TTARJA3 Jose Altuve 25.00 60.00
TTARJA4 Jose Altuve 25.00 60.00
TTARJA5 Jose Altuve 25.00 60.00
TTARJAB1 Jose Abreu 25.00 60.00
TTARJB1 Javier Baez 20.00 50.00
TTARJB2 Javier Baez 20.00 50.00
TTARJB3 Javier Baez 20.00 50.00
TTARJB4 Javier Baez 20.00 50.00
TTARJB5 Javier Baez 20.00 50.00
TTARJBA1 Jeff Bagwell 30.00 80.00
TTARJBA2 Jeff Bagwell 30.00 80.00
TTARJBA3 Jeff Bagwell 30.00 80.00
TTARJBA4 Jeff Bagwell 30.00 80.00
TTARJD1 Josh Donaldson 20.00 50.00
TTARJD2 Josh Donaldson 20.00 50.00
TTARJD3 Josh Donaldson 20.00 50.00
TTARJDA1 Johnny Damon 20.00 50.00
TTARJDA2 Johnny Damon 20.00 50.00
TTARJDE1 Jacob deGrom 15.00 40.00
TTARJDE2 Jacob deGrom 15.00 40.00
TTARJDE3 Jacob deGrom 15.00 40.00
TTARJDE4 Jacob deGrom 15.00 40.00
TTARJDE5 Jacob deGrom 15.00 40.00
TTARJDM1 J.D. Martinez 10.00 25.00
TTARJDM2 J.D. Martinez 10.00 25.00
TTARJDM3 J.D. Martinez 10.00 25.00
TTARJDM4 J.D. Martinez 10.00 25.00
TTARJDM5 J.D. Martinez 10.00 25.00
TTARJE1 Jim Edmonds 30.00 80.00
TTARJE2 Jim Edmonds 30.00 80.00
TTARJE3 Jim Edmonds 30.00 80.00
TTARJG1 Joey Gallo 12.00 30.00
TTARJG2 Joey Gallo 12.00 30.00
TTARJG3 Joey Gallo 12.00 30.00
TTARJG4 Joey Gallo 12.00 30.00
TTARJG5 Joey Gallo 12.00 30.00
TTARJM1 Juan Marichal 20.00 50.00
TTARJM2 Juan Marichal 20.00 50.00
TTARJP1 Jim Palmer 10.00 25.00
TTARJP2 Jim Palmer 10.00 25.00
TTARJT1 Jim Thome 60.00 150.00
TTARJT2 Jim Thome 60.00 150.00
TTARJU1 Julio Urias 8.00 20.00
TTARJU2 Julio Urias 8.00 20.00
TTARJU3 Julio Urias 8.00 20.00
TTARJU4 Julio Urias 8.00 20.00
TTARJU5 Julio Urias 8.00 20.00
TTARJV1 Joey Votto 40.00 100.00
TTARJV2 Joey Votto 40.00 100.00
TTARKB1 Kris Bryant 75.00 200.00
TTARKB2 Kris Bryant 75.00 200.00
TTARKB3 Kris Bryant 75.00 200.00
TTARKGJ1 Ken Griffey Jr. 100.00 250.00
TTARKGJ2 Ken Griffey Jr. 100.00 250.00
TTARKK1 Kevin Kiermaier 6.00 15.00
TTARKK2 Kevin Kiermaier 6.00 15.00
TTARKK3 Kevin Kiermaier 6.00 15.00
TTARKK4 Kevin Kiermaier 6.00 15.00
TTARKK5 Kevin Kiermaier 6.00 15.00
TTARKM1 Kenta Maeda 20.00 50.00
TTARKM2 Kenta Maeda 20.00 50.00
TTARKM3 Kendrys Morales 5.00 12.00
TTARKM4 Kendrys Morales 5.00 12.00
TTARKM5 Kendrys Morales 5.00 12.00
TTARKMO1 Kendrys Morales 5.00 12.00
TTARKMO2 Kendrys Morales 5.00 12.00
TTARKS1 Kyle Seager 8.00 20.00
TTARKS2 Kyle Seager 8.00 20.00
TTARKS3 Kyle Seager 8.00 20.00
TTARKS4 Kyle Seager 8.00 20.00
TTARKS5 Kyle Seager 8.00 20.00
TTARMC1 Matt Carpenter 8.00 20.00
TTARMC2 Matt Carpenter 8.00 20.00
TTARMC3 Matt Carpenter 8.00 20.00
TTARMC4 Matt Carpenter 8.00 20.00
TTARMC5 Matt Carpenter 8.00 20.00
TTARMF1 Michael Fulmer 10.00 25.00
TTARMF2 Michael Fulmer 10.00 25.00
TTARMF3 Michael Fulmer 10.00 25.00
TTARMF4 Michael Fulmer 10.00 25.00
TTARMF5 Michael Fulmer 10.00 25.00
TTARMIKE1 Mike Piazza 50.00 120.00
TTARMIKE2 Mike Piazza 50.00 120.00
TTARMM1 Manny Machado 50.00 120.00
TTARMM2 Manny Machado 50.00 120.00
TTARMM3 Manny Machado 50.00 120.00
TTARMM4 Manny Machado 50.00 120.00
TTARMMC1 Mark McGwire 60.00 150.00
TTARMMC2 Mark McGwire 60.00 150.00
TTARMPI1 Michael Pineda 5.00 12.00
TTARMPI2 Michael Pineda 5.00 12.00
TTARMSA1 Miguel Sano EXCH 12.00 30.00
TTARMSA2 Miguel Sano EXCH 12.00 30.00
TTARMSA3 Miguel Sano EXCH 12.00 30.00
TTARMSA4 Miguel Sano EXCH 12.00 30.00
TTARMSA5 Miguel Sano EXCH 12.00 30.00
TTARMST1 Marcus Stroman 8.00 20.00
TTARMST2 Marcus Stroman 8.00 20.00
TTARMST3 Marcus Stroman 8.00 20.00
TTARMST4 Marcus Stroman 8.00 20.00
TTARMT1 Mike Trout EXCH 200.00 400.00
TTARNG1 Nomar Garciaparra 25.00 60.00
TTARNR1 Nolan Ryan 75.00 200.00
TTARNS1 Noah Syndergaard 20.00 50.00
TTARNS2 Noah Syndergaard 20.00 50.00
TTARNS3 Noah Syndergaard 20.00 50.00
TTARPG1 Paul Goldschmidt EXCH 20.00 50.00
TTARPG2 Paul Goldschmidt EXCH 20.00 50.00
TTARPG3 Paul Goldschmidt EXCH 20.00 50.00
TTARPG4 Paul Goldschmidt EXCH 20.00 50.00
TTARPG5 Paul Goldschmidt EXCH 20.00 50.00
TTARPK1 Paul Konerko 12.00 30.00
TTARRB1 Ryan Braun 10.00 25.00
TTARRC1 Roger Clemens 30.00 80.00
TTARRC2 Roger Clemens 30.00 80.00
TTARRCA1 Rod Carew 20.00 50.00
TTARRCA2 Rod Carew 20.00 50.00
TTARRF1 Rollie Fingers 12.00 30.00
TTARRF2 Rollie Fingers 12.00 30.00
TTARRH1 Rickey Henderson 40.00 100.00
TTARRHA1 Roy Halladay EXCH 25.00 60.00
TTARRHA2 Roy Halladay 25.00 60.00
TTARRHA3 Roy Halladay EXCH 25.00 60.00
TTARRHA4 Roy Halladay EXCH 25.00 60.00
TTARRHA5 Roy Halladay EXCH 25.00 60.00
TTARRJO1 Randy Johnson 40.00 100.00
TTARRJO2 Randy Johnson 40.00 100.00
TTARRS1 Ryne Sandberg 30.00 80.00
TTARRY1 Robin Yount 30.00 80.00
TTARRY2 Robin Yount 30.00 80.00
TTARSG1 Sonny Gray 6.00 15.00
TTARSG2 Sonny Gray 6.00 15.00
TTARSG3 Sonny Gray 6.00 15.00
TTARSG4 Sonny Gray 6.00 15.00
TTARSMA1 Steven Matz 6.00 15.00
TTARSMA2 Steven Matz 6.00 15.00
TTARSMA3 Steven Matz 6.00 15.00
TTARSMA4 Steven Matz 6.00 15.00
TTARSMA5 Steven Matz 6.00 15.00
TTARSP1 Stephen Piscotty 6.00 15.00
TTARSP2 Stephen Piscotty 6.00 15.00
TTARSP3 Stephen Piscotty 6.00 15.00
TTARSP4 Stephen Piscotty 6.00 15.00
TTARSP5 Stephen Piscotty 6.00 15.00
TTARTE1 Theo Epstein 75.00 200.00
TTARTE2 Theo Epstein 75.00 200.00
TTARTE3 Theo Epstein 75.00 200.00
TTARTR1 Tim Raines 20.00 50.00
TTARTR2 Tim Raines 20.00 50.00
TTARTS1 Trevor Story 10.00 25.00
TTARTS2 Trevor Story 10.00 25.00
TTARTS3 Trevor Story 10.00 25.00
TTARTS4 Trevor Story 10.00 25.00
TTARTS5 Trevor Story 10.00 25.00
TTARTT1 Trea Turner 15.00 40.00
TTARTT2 Trea Turner 15.00 40.00
TTARTT3 Trea Turner 15.00 40.00
TTARTT4 Trea Turner 15.00 40.00
TTARTT5 Trea Turner 15.00 40.00
TTARVG1 Vladimir Guerrero 20.00 50.00
TTARVG2 Vladimir Guerrero 20.00 50.00
TTARVG3 Vladimir Guerrero 20.00 50.00
TTARVG4 Vladimir Guerrero 20.00 50.00

2017 Topps Triple Threads Relic Combos

STATED ODDS 1:37 HOBBY
STATED PRINT RUN 36 SER.#'d SETS
*SILVER/27: .4X TO 1X BASIC
*EMERALD/18: .5X TO 1.2X BASIC
TTRCACB Crra/Brgmn/Altuve 15.00 40.00
TTRCACS Sprngr/Crra/Altuve 15.00 40.00
TTRCBBA Bggo/Altve/Bgwll 15.00 40.00
TTRCBBB Brdly/Betts/Bnntndi 15.00 40.00
TTRCBPH Pedroia/Bogaerts/Ramirez 8.00 20.00
TTRCBRR Baez/Rssll/Rizzo 12.00 30.00
TTRCBRS Rssll/Baez/Schwrbr 10.00 25.00
TTRCCPP Posey/Crwfrd/Pence 10.00 25.00
TTRCCST Tnka/Chpmn/Sanchez 8.00 20.00
TTRCDSH deGrom/Syndergaard/Harvey 8.00 20.00
TTRCGAB Gonzalez/Blackmon/Arenado 10.00 25.00
TTRCGHP Grdn/Hsmr/Perez 10.00 25.00
TTRCGSY Gordon/Stanton/Yelich 8.00 20.00
TTRCHCC Cruz/Hernandez/Cano 8.00 20.00
TTRCHTB Hrpr/Brynt/Trout 30.00 80.00
TTRCHVD Duvall/Votto/Hamilton 8.00 20.00
TTRCIGH Grffy/Ichro/Hrnndz 20.00 50.00
TTRCISY Ichiro/Stntn/Ylich 10.00 25.00
TTRCJMD Davis/Machado/Jones 8.00 20.00
TTRCKFS Kemp/Swanson/Freeman 8.00 20.00
TTRCLGV Votto/Griffey/Larkin 12.00 30.00
TTRCLKS Klbr/Lndr/Sntna 15.00 40.00
TTRCMCM Crpntr/Mlna/Mrtnz 10.00 25.00
TTRCMJJ Jtr/Jcksn/Mttngly 30.00 80.00
TTRCMKU Kershaw/Urias/Maeda 8.00 20.00
TTRCMMP Polanco/Marte/McCutchen 8.00 20.00
TTRCPGG Pollock/Greinke/Goldschmidt 8.00 20.00
TTRCPGP Pederson/Gonzalez/Puig 8.00 20.00
TTRCPSP Sale/Price/Porcello 8.00 20.00
TTRCRBS Rzzo/Schwrbr/Brnt 12.00 30.00
TTRCSAB Sprngr/Altve/Brgmn 10.00 25.00
TTRCSBM Mauer/Sano/Buxton 6.00 15.00
TTRCSFJ Frmn/Smoltz/Jones 12.00 30.00
TTRCSGA Gonzalez/Story/Arenado 10.00 25.00
TTRCSKU Krshw/Urias/Seager 10.00 25.00
TTRCSWC Syndergaard/Wright
Cespedes 8.00 20.00
TTRCTCG Cole/Glasnow/Taillon 8.00 20.00
TTRCUCM Cabrera/Upton/Martinez 8.00 20.00
TTRCVCU Verlander/Cabrera/Upton 6.00 15.00

2017 Topps Triple Threads Relics

STATED ODDS 1:9 MINI BOX
STATED PRINT RUN 36 SER.#'d SETS
*SILVER/27: .4X TO 1X BASIC
*EMERALD/18: .5X TO 1.2X BASIC
*GOLD/9: .6X TO 1.5X BASIC
ALL VERSIONS EQUALLY PRICED
TTRAC1 Aroldis Chapman 6.00 15.00
TTRAJ1 Adam Jones 3.00 8.00
TTRAJ2 Adam Jones 3.00 8.00
TTRAJ3 Adam Jones 3.00 8.00
TTRAM1 Andrew McCutchen 6.00 15.00
TTRAM2 Andrew McCutchen 6.00 15.00
TTRAM3 Andrew McCutchen 6.00 15.00
TTRAM4 Andrew McCutchen 6.00 15.00
TTRAM5 Andrew McCutchen 6.00 15.00
TTRAR1 Anthony Rizzo 6.00 15.00
TTRAR2 Anthony Rizzo 6.00 15.00
TTRAR3 Anthony Rizzo 6.00 15.00
TTRBH1 Bryce Harper 10.00 25.00
TTRBH2 Bryce Harper 10.00 25.00
TTRBP1 Buster Posey 8.00 20.00
TTRBP2 Buster Posey 8.00 20.00
TTRCA1 Corey Seager 6.00 15.00
TTRCA2 Corey Seager 6.00 15.00
TTRCA3 Corey Seager 6.00 15.00
TTRCC1 Carlos Correa 4.00 10.00
TTRCC2 Carlos Correa 4.00 10.00
TTRCC3 Carlos Correa 4.00 10.00
TTRCE1 Clayton Kershaw 8.00 20.00
TTRCE2 Clayton Kershaw 8.00 20.00
TTRCS1 Chris Sale 4.00 10.00
TTRCS2 Chris Sale 4.00 10.00
TTRCS3 Chris Sale 4.00 10.00
TTRCS4 Chris Sale 4.00 10.00
TTRCS5 Chris Sale 4.00 10.00
TTRDE1 Dustin Pedroia 5.00 12.00
TTRDE2 Dustin Pedroia 5.00 12.00
TTRDE3 Dustin Pedroia 5.00 12.00
TTRDJ1 Derek Jeter 40.00 100.00
TTRDJ2 Derek Jeter 40.00 100.00
TTRDO1 David Ortiz 6.00 15.00
TTRDO2 David Ortiz 6.00 15.00
TTRDW1 David Wright 3.00 8.00
TTRDW2 David Wright 3.00 8.00
TTRDW3 David Wright 3.00 8.00
TTREL1 Evan Longoria 3.00 8.00
TTREL2 Evan Longoria 3.00 8.00
TTREL3 Evan Longoria 3.00 8.00
TTRFF1 Freddie Freeman 5.00 12.00
TTRFF2 Freddie Freeman 5.00 12.00
TTRFF3 Freddie Freeman 5.00 12.00
TTRFH1 Felix Hernandez 5.00 12.00
TTRFH2 Felix Hernandez 5.00 12.00
TTRFH3 Felix Hernandez 5.00 12.00
TTRFH4 Felix Hernandez 5.00 12.00
TTRFH5 Felix Hernandez 5.00 12.00
TTRFL1 Francisco Lindor 6.00 15.00
TTRFL2 Francisco Lindor 6.00 15.00
TTRFL3 Francisco Lindor 6.00 15.00
TTRFL4 Francisco Lindor 6.00 15.00
TTRGP1 George Springer 5.00 12.00
TTRGP2 George Springer 5.00 12.00
TTRGP3 George Springer 5.00 12.00
TTRGS1 Gary Sanchez 4.00 10.00
TTRGS2 Gary Sanchez 4.00 10.00
TTRGS3 Gary Sanchez 4.00 10.00
TTRGT1 Giancarlo Stanton 4.00 10.00
TTRGT2 Giancarlo Stanton 4.00 10.00
TTRGT3 Giancarlo Stanton 4.00 10.00
TTRGT4 Giancarlo Stanton 4.00 10.00
TTRI1 Ichiro 8.00 20.00
TTRI2 Ichiro 8.00 20.00
TTRJD1 Josh Donaldson 6.00 15.00
TTRJD2 Josh Donaldson 6.00 15.00
TTRJD3 Josh Donaldson 6.00 15.00
TTRJE1 Jacob deGrom 4.00 10.00
TTRJE2 Jacob deGrom 4.00 10.00
TTRJE3 Jacob deGrom 4.00 10.00
TTRJE4 Jacob deGrom 4.00 10.00
TTRJE5 Jacob deGrom 4.00 10.00
TTRJL1 Jose Altuve 8.00 20.00
TTRJL2 Jose Altuve 8.00 20.00
TTRJL3 Jose Altuve 8.00 20.00
TTRJL4 Jose Altuve 8.00 20.00
TTRJL5 Jose Altuve 8.00 20.00
TTRJO1 Joey Votto 6.00 15.00
TTRJO2 Joey Votto 6.00 15.00
TTRJO3 Joey Votto 6.00 15.00
TTRJU1 Jose Bautista 4.00 10.00
TTRJU2 Jose Bautista 4.00 10.00
TTRJU3 Jose Bautista 4.00 10.00
TTRJV1 Justin Verlander 4.00 10.00
TTRJV2 Justin Verlander 4.00 10.00
TTRJV3 Justin Verlander 4.00 10.00
TTRJV4 Justin Verlander 4.00 10.00
TTRJV5 Justin Verlander 4.00 10.00
TTRJZ1 Javier Baez 5.00 12.00
TTRJZ2 Javier Baez 5.00 12.00
TTRJZ3 Javier Baez 5.00 12.00
TTRKB1 Kris Bryant 5.00 12.00
TTRKB2 Kris Bryant 5.00 12.00
TTRKB3 Kris Bryant 5.00 12.00
TTRKM1 Kenta Maeda 3.00 8.00
TTRKM2 Kenta Maeda 3.00 8.00
TTRMA1 Matt Carpenter 4.00 10.00
TTRMA2 Matt Carpenter 4.00 10.00
TTRMA3 Matt Carpenter 4.00 10.00
TTRMB1 Mookie Betts 6.00 15.00
TTRMB2 Mookie Betts 6.00 15.00
TTRMB3 Mookie Betts 6.00 15.00
TTRMB4 Mookie Betts 6.00 15.00
TTRMB5 Mookie Betts 6.00 15.00
TTRMC1 Miguel Cabrera 4.00 10.00
TTRMC2 Miguel Cabrera 4.00 10.00
TTRMC3 Miguel Cabrera 4.00 10.00
TTRMC4 Miguel Cabrera 4.00 10.00
TTRMC5 Miguel Cabrera 4.00 10.00
TTRMMA1 Manny Machado 5.00 12.00
TTRMMA2 Manny Machado 5.00 12.00
TTRMMA3 Manny Machado 5.00 12.00
TTRMMA4 Manny Machado 5.00 12.00
TTRMO1 Mike Trout 20.00 50.00
TTRMO2 Mike Trout 20.00 50.00
TTRMS1 Miguel Sano 3.00 8.00
TTRMS2 Miguel Sano 3.00 8.00
TTRMS3 Miguel Sano 3.00 8.00
TTRMS4 Miguel Sano 3.00 8.00
TTRMS5 Miguel Sano 3.00 8.00
TTRMT1 Masahiro Tanaka 3.00 8.00
TTRMT2 Masahiro Tanaka 3.00 8.00
TTRMT3 Masahiro Tanaka 3.00 8.00
TTRMT4 Masahiro Tanaka 3.00 8.00
TTRNA1 Nolan Arenado 5.00 12.00
TTRNA2 Nolan Arenado 5.00 12.00
TTRNA3 Nolan Arenado 5.00 12.00
TTRNA4 Nolan Arenado 5.00 12.00
TTRNA5 Nolan Arenado 5.00 12.00
TTRNS1 Noah Syndergaard 3.00 8.00
TTRNS2 Noah Syndergaard 3.00 8.00
TTRNS3 Noah Syndergaard 3.00 8.00
TTRNS4 Noah Syndergaard 3.00 8.00
TTRRC1 Robinson Cano 3.00 8.00
TTRRC2 Robinson Cano 3.00 8.00
TTRRC3 Robinson Cano 3.00 8.00
TTRRC4 Robinson Cano 3.00 8.00
TTRRC5 Robinson Cano 3.00 8.00
TTRWM1 Wil Myers 2.50 6.00
TTRXB1 Xander Bogaerts 4.00 10.00
TTRXB2 Xander Bogaerts 4.00 10.00
TTRXB3 Xander Bogaerts 4.00 10.00
TTRYC1 Yoenis Cespedes 5.00 12.00
TTRYC2 Yoenis Cespedes 5.00 12.00
TTRYC3 Yoenis Cespedes 5.00 12.00
TTRYC4 Yoenis Cespedes 5.00 12.00
TTRYC5 Yoenis Cespedes 5.00 12.00
TTRYM1 Yadier Molina 8.00 20.00
TTRYM2 Yadier Molina 8.00 20.00
TTRYM3 Yadier Molina 8.00 20.00
TTRYM4 Yadier Molina 8.00 20.00

2017 Topps Triple Threads Rookie Autographs

STATED ODDS 1:23 HOBBY
STATED PRINT RUN 99 SER.#'d SETS
EXCHANGE DEADLINE 8/31/2019
PRINTING PLATE ODDS 1:577 HOBBY
PLATE PRINT RUN 1 SET PER COLOR
BLACK-CYAN-MAGENTA-YELLOW ISSUED
NO PLATE PRICING DUE TO SCARCITY
*EMERALD/50: .4X TO 1X BASIC
*GOLD/25: .5X TO 1.2X BASIC
RAAG Amir Garrett 4.00 10.00
RABP Brett Phillips 5.00 12.00
RABZ Bradley Zimmer 6.00 15.00
RACA Christian Arroyo 6.00 15.00
RACB Cody Bellinger 60.00 150.00
RADF Derek Fisher 5.00 12.00
RADV Dan Vogelbach 5.00 12.00
RAFB Franklin Barreto 4.00 10.00
RAGC Gavin Cecchini 5.00 12.00
RAGM German Marquez 6.00 15.00
RAIH Ian Happ 8.00 20.00
RAJD Jose De Leon 4.00 10.00
RAJMO Jordan Montgomery 20.00 50.00
RAJW Jesse Winker 6.00 15.00
RALB Lewis Brinson 6.00 15.00
RALW Luke Weaver 5.00 12.00
RAMH Mitch Haniger 6.00 15.00
RASN Sean Newcomb 6.00 15.00
RATM Trey Mancini 12.00 30.00
RAYM Yoan Moncada 10.00 25.00

2017 Topps Triple Threads Unity Jumbo Relic Autographs

STATED ODDS 1:7 HOBBY
STATED PRINT RUN 99 SER.#'d SETS
EXCHANGE DEADLINE 8/31/2019
*SILVER/75: .4X TO 1X BASIC
*EMERALD/50: .5X TO 1.2X BASIC
*GOLD/25: .6X TO 1.5X BASIC
UAJRAB Aledmys Diaz 5.00 12.00
UAJRAD Adam Duvall 6.00 15.00
UAJRAG Amir Garrett 4.00 10.00
UAJRAI Andrew Benintendi 25.00 60.00
UAJRAM Alex Bregman 15.00 40.00
UAJRAO Alex Gordon 5.00 12.00
UAJRAR Anthony Rendon 8.00 20.00
UAJRAS Addison Russell 10.00 25.00
UAJRAU Adam Duvall 6.00 15.00
UAJRAZ Aledmys Diaz 5.00 12.00
UAJRCB Charlie Blackmon 8.00 20.00
UAJRCBL Charlie Blackmon 8.00 20.00
UAJRCI Corey Dickerson 4.00 10.00
UAJRCK Corey Kluber 10.00 25.00
UAJRCS Corey Seager 20.00 50.00
UAJRDB Dellin Betances 5.00 12.00
UAJRDF Dexter Fowler 5.00 12.00
UAJRDG Dee Gordon 4.00 10.00
UAJRDO Didi Gregorius 12.00 30.00
UAJRDP Drew Pomeranz 5.00 12.00
UAJRDR Didi Gregorius 12.00 30.00
UAJREN Ender Inciarte 8.00 20.00
UAJRGB Greg Bird 5.00 12.00
UAJRGD Greg Bird 5.00 12.00
UAJRGG Gary Sheffield 4.00 10.00
UAJRGH Gary Sheffield 4.00 10.00
UAJRGP George Springer 8.00 20.00
UAJRGS George Springer 8.00 20.00
UAJRHW Henry Owens 4.00 10.00
UAJRJA Jose Altuve EXCH 20.00 50.00
UAJRJB Justin Bour 5.00 12.00
UAJRJC Jose Canseco 10.00 25.00
UAJRJD Jacob deGrom 8.00 20.00
UAJRJE Jose Canseco 10.00 25.00
UAJRJF Jeurys Familia
UAJRJJ Javier Baez 12.00 30.00
UAJRJK Jameson Taillon 5.00 12.00
UAJRJM J.D. Martinez 6.00 15.00
UAJRJN Juan Gonzalez 5.00 12.00
UAJRJR Jon Gray 4.00 10.00
UAJRJS Jorge Soler 6.00 15.00
UAJRJU Joe Panik 5.00 12.00
UAJRJV Joe Panik 5.00 12.00
UAJRJY Joey Gallo 5.00 12.00
UAJRJZ Andrew Benintendi EXCH 25.00 60.00
UAJRKA Kenta Maeda 8.00 20.00
UAJRKD Khris Davis 6.00 15.00
UAJRKH Kelvin Herrera 4.00 10.00
UAJRKI Kevin Kiermaier 5.00 12.00
UAJRKK Kevin Kiermaier 5.00 12.00
UAJRKM Kendrys Morales 4.00 10.00
UAJRKR Kendall Graveman 4.00 10.00
UAJRKV Khris Davis 6.00 15.
UAJRLS Luis Severino 10.00 25.
UAJRMA Miguel Sano 5.00 12.
UAJRMC Matt Carpenter 6.00 15.
UAJRMD Matt Adams 4.00 10.
UAJRMI Michael Fulmer 4.00 10.
UAJRMM Michael Conforto 10.00 25.
UAJRMR Maikel Franco 5.00 12.
UAJRMU Michael Fulmer 4.00 10.
UAJRNS Noah Syndergaard 12.00 30.
UAJRRG Randal Grichuk 4.00 10.
UAJRRR Randal Grichuk 4.00 10.
UAJRSG Sonny Gray 5.00 12.0
UAJRSM Steven Matz 5.00 12.0
UAJRSP Stephen Piscotty 5.00 12.0
UAJRST Steven Matz 5.00 12.0
UAJRTM Trey Mancini 10.00 25.0
UAJRTR Trevor Story 6.00 15.0
UAJRTS Trevor Story 6.00 15.0
UAJRWC Willson Contreras 10.00 25.0
UAJRYG Yulieski Gurriel 8.00 20.0
UAJRZC Zack Cozart 4.00 10.0

2017 Topps Triple Threads Unit Jumbo Relics

STATED ODDS 1:6 HOBBY
STATED PRINT RUN 36 SER.#'d SETS
*SILVER/27: .4X TO 1X BASIC
*EMERALD/18: .5X TO 1.2X BASIC
*GOLD/9: .6X TO 1.5X BASIC
ALL VERSIONS EQUALLY PRICED
SJRAB Alex Bregman 5.00 12.0
SJRABI Andrew Benintendi 5.00 12.0
SJRABN Andrew Benintendi 5.00 12.0
SJRABR Alex Bregman 5.00 12.0
SJRAC Aroldis Chapman 6.00 15.0
SJRACH Aroldis Chapman 6.00 15.0
SJRADJ Adam Jones 3.00 8.0
SJRAG Adrian Gonzalez 3.00 8.0
SJRAJE Adam Jones 3.00 8.00
SJRAJO Adam Jones 3.00 8.0
SJRAMC Andrew McCutchen 6.00 15.0
SJRAMT Andrew McCutchen 6.00 15.0
SJRAMU Andrew McCutchen 6.00 15.00
SJRANR Anthony Rizzo 6.00 15.00
SJRAPJ Albert Pujols 5.00 12.0
SJRAPO Albert Pujols 5.00 12.0
SJRAPU Albert Pujols 5.00 12.00
SJRAR Alex Reyes 3.00 8.00
SJRARD Alex Rodriguez 8.00 20.00
SJRARE Alex Reyes 3.00 8.00
SJRARG Alex Rodriguez 8.00 20.00
SJRARI Anthony Rizzo 6.00 15.00
SJRARL Addison Russell 4.00 10.00
SJRARO Alex Rodriguez 8.00 20.00
SJRARR Addison Russell 4.00 10.00
SJRARU Addison Russell 4.00 10.00
SJRARZ Anthony Rizzo 6.00 15.00
SJRAW Adam Wainwright 3.00 8.00
SJRAWA Adam Wainwright 3.00 8.00
SJRAWI Adam Wainwright 3.00 8.00
SJRBB Byron Buxton 3.00 8.00
SJRBBU Byron Buxton 3.00 8.00
SJRBBX Byron Buxton 3.00 8.00
SJRBH Bryce Harper 10.00 25.00
SJRBP Buster Posey 8.00 20.00
SJRBPO Buster Posey 8.00 20.00
SJRBZ Ben Zobrist 3.00 8.00
SJRBZB Ben Zobrist 3.00 8.00
SJRBZO Ben Zobrist 3.00 8.00
SJRCC Carlos Correa 4.00 10.00
SJRCCO Carlos Correa 4.00 10.00
SJRCG Curtis Granderson 3.00 8.00
SJRCGN Carlos Gonzalez 3.00 8.00
SJRCGO Carlos Gonzalez 3.00 8.00
SJRCGR Curtis Granderson 3.00 8.00
SJRCGZ Carlos Gonzalez 3.00 8.00
SJRCH Cole Hamels 3.00 8.00
SJRCK Craig Kimbrel 3.00 8.00
SJRCKB Corey Kluber 3.00 8.00
SJRCKE Clayton Kershaw 8.00 20.00
SJRCKI Craig Kimbrel 3.00 8.00
SJRCKL Corey Kluber 3.00 8.00
SJRCKR Clayton Kershaw 8.00 20.00
SJRCKU Corey Kluber 3.00 8.00
SJRCO Carlos Correa 4.00 10.00
SJRCS Chris Sale 4.00 10.00
SJRCSA Chris Sale 4.00 10.00
SJRCSE Corey Seager 6.00 15.00
SJRCSL Chris Sale 4.00 10.00
SJRCY Christian Yelich 5.00 12.00
SJRCYE Christian Yelich 5.00 12.00
SJRDJ Derek Jeter 40.00 100.00
SJRDMP Daniel Murphy 3.00 8.00
SJRDMR Daniel Murphy 3.00 8.00
SJRDMU Daniel Murphy 3.00 8.00
SJRDO David Ortiz 6.00 15.00
SJRDOR David Ortiz 6.00 15.00
SJRDOT David Ortiz 6.00 15.00
SJRDP Dustin Pedroia 5.00 12.00
SJRDPC David Price 3.00 8.00
SJRDPD Dustin Pedroia 5.00 12.00
SJRDPE Dustin Pedroia 5.00 12.00
SJRDPI David Price 3.00 8.00
SJRDPO Dustin Pedroia 5.00 12.00
SJRDPR David Price 3.00 8.00
SJRDS Dansby Swanson 5.00 12.00
SJRDSW Dansby Swanson 5.00 12.00
SJRDW David Wright 3.00 8.00
SJRDWI David Wright 3.00 8.00
SJRDWR David Wright 3.00 8.00
SJREH Eric Hosmer 3.00 8.00
SJREHO Eric Hosmer 3.00 8.00

REHS Eric Hosmer 3.00 8.00
REL Evan Longoria 3.00 8.00
RELN Evan Longoria 3.00 8.00
RELO Evan Longoria 3.00 8.00
RFF Freddie Freeman 5.00 12.00
RFFE Freddie Freeman 5.00 12.00
RFFR Freddie Freeman 5.00 12.00
RFH Felix Hernandez 5.00 12.00
RFHE Felix Hernandez 5.00 12.00
RFHR Felix Hernandez 5.00 12.00
RFL Francisco Lindor 6.00 15.00
RFLI Francisco Lindor 6.00 15.00
RGAS Gary Sanchez 4.00 10.00
RGC Gerrit Cole 4.00 10.00
RGP Gregory Polanco 3.00 8.00
RGPO Gregory Polanco 3.00 8.00
RGRS Gary Sanchez 4.00 10.00
RGS Gary Sheffield 4.00 10.00
RGSA Giancarlo Stanton 4.00 10.00
RGSE Gary Sheffield 4.00 10.00
RGSF Gary Sheffield 4.00 10.00
RGSH Gary Sheffield 4.00 10.00
RGSI George Springer 5.00 12.00
RGSN Giancarlo Stanton 4.00 10.00
RGSP George Springer 5.00 12.00
RGSR George Springer 5.00 12.00
RGST Giancarlo Stanton 4.00 10.00
RGYS Gary Sanchez 4.00 10.00
RHP Hunter Pence 3.00 8.00
RHPE Hunter Pence 3.00 8.00
RHPN Hunter Pence 3.00 8.00
RHR Hanley Ramirez 3.00 8.00
RHRA Hanley Ramirez 3.00 8.00
RHRI Hanley Ramirez 3.00 8.00
RHRM Hanley Ramirez 3.00 8.00
SJRIK Ichiro 8.00 20.00
SJRIS Ichiro 8.00 20.00
SJRJA Jake Arrieta 3.00 8.00
SJRJAE Jake Arrieta 3.00 8.00
SJRJAL Jose Altuve 8.00 20.00
SJRJAR Jake Arrieta 3.00 8.00
SJRJAT Jose Altuve 8.00 20.00
SJRJAU Jose Altuve 8.00 20.00
SJRJB Jackie Bradley Jr. 4.00 10.00
SJRJBA Javier Baez 5.00 12.00
SJRJBE Javier Baez 5.00 12.00
SJRJBI Jose Bautista 4.00 10.00
SJRJBR Jackie Bradley Jr. 4.00 10.00
SJRJBT Jose Bautista 4.00 10.00
SJRJBU Jose Bautista 4.00 10.00
SJRJBZ Javier Baez 5.00 12.00
SJRJD Josh Donaldson 6.00 15.00
SJRJDE Jacob deGrom 4.00 10.00
SJRJDG Jacob deGrom 4.00 10.00
SJRJDN Josh Donaldson 6.00 15.00
SJRJDR Jacob deGrom 4.00 10.00
SJRJE Jacoby Ellsbury 6.00 15.00
SJRJEL Jacoby Ellsbury 6.00 15.00
SJRJH Jason Heyward 3.00 8.00
SJRJHE Jason Heyward 3.00 8.00
SJRJHY Jason Heyward 3.00 8.00
SJRJL Jon Lester 3.00 8.00
SJRJLL Jon Lester 3.00 8.00
SJRJM J.D. Martinez 6.00 15.00
SJRJMA J.D. Martinez 6.00 15.00
SJRJOV Joey Votto 6.00 15.00
SJRJS John Smoltz 8.00 20.00
SJRJT Jameson Taillon 3.00 8.00
SJRJU Julio Urias 4.00 10.00
SJRJUP Justin Upton 6.00 15.00
SJRJUT Justin Upton 6.00 15.00
SJRJV Justin Verlander 4.00 10.00
SJRJVA Justin Verlander 4.00 10.00
SJRJVE Justin Verlander 4.00 10.00
SJRJVL Justin Verlander 4.00 10.00
SJRJVO Joey Votto 6.00 15.00
SJRJVR Justin Verlander 4.00 10.00
SJRJVT Joey Votto 6.00 15.00
SJRKB Kris Bryant 5.00 12.00
SJRKBR Kris Bryant 5.00 12.00
SJRKM Kenta Maeda 3.00 8.00
SJRKMA Kenta Maeda 3.00 8.00
SJRKS Kyle Seager 2.50 6.00
SJRKSA Kyle Seager 2.50 6.00
SJRKSE Kyle Seager 2.50 6.00
SJRMB Mookie Betts 6.00 15.00
SJRMBE Mookie Betts 6.00 15.00
SJRMBS Mookie Betts 6.00 15.00
SJRMBT Mookie Betts 6.00 15.00
SJRMC Miguel Cabrera 4.00 10.00
SJRMCA Matt Carpenter 4.00 10.00
SJRMCB Miguel Cabrera 4.00 10.00
SJRMCE Miguel Cabrera 4.00 10.00
SJRMCP Matt Carpenter 4.00 10.00
SJRMCR Matt Carpenter 4.00 10.00
SJRMF Michael Fulmer 2.50 6.00
SJRMFU Michael Fulmer 2.50 6.00
SJRMGC Miguel Cabrera 4.00 10.00
SJRMH Matt Harvey 3.00 8.00
SJRMHA Matt Harvey 3.00 8.00
SJRMHR Matt Harvey 3.00 8.00
SJRMHV Matt Harvey 3.00 8.00
SJRMIC Miguel Cabrera 4.00 10.00
SJRMM Mark McGwire 10.00 25.00
SJRMMA Manny Machado 5.00 12.00
SJRMMC Manny Machado 5.00 12.00
SJRMMG Mark McGwire 10.00 25.00
SJRMS Miguel Sano 3.00 8.00
SJRMSA Miguel Sano 3.00 8.00
SJRMSN Miguel Sano 3.00 8.00
SJRMSR Marcus Stroman 3.00 8.00
SJRMST Marcus Stroman 3.00 8.00
SJRMT Mark Teixeira 3.00 8.00
SJRMTA Masahiro Tanaka 3.00 8.00
SJRMTE Mark Teixeira 3.00 8.00
SJRMTI Mark Teixeira 3.00 8.00
SJRMTK Masahiro Tanaka 3.00 8.00
SJRMTN Masahiro Tanaka 3.00 8.00
SJRMTR Mike Trout 20.00 50.00
SJRNA Nolan Arenado 5.00 12.00
SJRNAA Nolan Arenado 5.00 12.00
SJRNAR Nolan Arenado 5.00 12.00
SJRNC Nelson Cruz 4.00 10.00
SJRNCR Nelson Cruz 4.00 10.00
SJRNS Noah Syndergaard 3.00 8.00
SJRNSN Noah Syndergaard 3.00 8.00
SJRNSY Noah Syndergaard 3.00 8.00
SJRPG Paul Goldschmidt 5.00 12.00
SJRPGL Paul Goldschmidt 5.00 12.00
SJRPGO Paul Goldschmidt 5.00 12.00
SJRRB Ryan Braun 3.00 8.00
SJRRBA Ryan Braun 3.00 8.00
SJRRBR Ryan Braun 3.00 8.00
SJRRCA Robinson Cano 3.00 8.00
SJRRCN Robinson Cano 3.00 8.00
SJRRCO Robinson Cano 3.00 8.00
SJRRO Rougned Odor 3.00 8.00
SJRSM Starling Marte 6.00 15.00
SJRSMA Starling Marte 6.00 15.00
SJRSMR Starling Marte 6.00 15.00
SJRSP Salvador Perez 8.00 20.00
SJRSPC Stephen Piscotty 3.00 8.00
SJRSPI Stephen Piscotty 3.00 8.00
SJRSPS Stephen Piscotty 3.00 8.00
SJRTG Tyler Glasnow 3.00 8.00
SJRTGL Tyler Glasnow 3.00 8.00
SJRTL Tim Lincecum 3.00 8.00
SJRTS Trevor Story 4.00 10.00
SJRTSO Trevor Story 4.00 10.00
SJRTST Trevor Story 4.00 10.00
SJRTT Troy Tulowitzki 4.00 10.00
SJRVMA Victor Martinez 3.00 8.00
SJRVMR Victor Martinez 3.00 8.00
SJRVMT Victor Martinez 3.00 8.00
SJRWM Wil Myers 2.50 6.00
SJRWME Wil Myers 2.50 6.00
SJRWMY Wil Myers 2.50 6.00
SJRXB Xander Bogaerts 4.00 10.00
SJRXBG Xander Bogaerts 4.00 10.00
SJRXBO Xander Bogaerts 4.00 10.00
SJRYC Yoenis Cespedes 5.00 12.00
SJRYCE Yoenis Cespedes 5.00 12.00
SJRYCP Yoenis Cespedes 5.00 12.00
SJRYCS Yoenis Cespedes 5.00 12.00
SJRYG Yulieski Gurriel 4.00 10.00
SJRYGU Yulieski Gurriel 4.00 10.00
SJRYM Yadier Molina 8.00 20.00
SJRYML Yadier Molina 8.00 20.00
SJRYMO Yadier Molina 8.00 20.00

2017 Topps Triple Threads WBC Relic Combos

STATED ODDS 1:128 HOBBY
STATED PRINT RUN 36 SER.#'d SETS
*SILVER/27: .4X TO 1X BASIC
*EMERALD/18: .4X TO 1X BASIC
WBCACH Cbrra/Altve/Hrnndz 10.00 25.00
WBCBML Beltran/Lindor/Molina 10.00 25.00
WBCCAK Ian Kinsler 8.00 20.00
Brandon Crawford
Nolan Arenado
WBCGCA Altve/Gnzlz/Cbrra 10.00 25.00
WBCHPG Gldschmdt/Posey/Hsmr 8.00 20.00
WBCJSM Stntn/McCtchn/Jones 6.00 15.00
WBCLCB Correa/Lindor/Baez 15.00 40.00
WBCMCB Jose Bautista 6.00 15.00
Robinson Cano
Manny Machado
WBCPBG Grgrs/Bgrts/Prfr 15.00 40.00
WBCSYT Ymda/Skmto/Tstsgh 12.00 30.00

2017 Topps Triple Threads WBC Relics

STATED ODDS 1:64 HOBBY
STATED PRINT RUN 36 SER.#'d SETS
*SILVER/27: .4X TO 1X BASIC
*EMERALD/18: .4X TO 1X BASIC
WBCRAB Alex Bregman 8.00 20.00
WBCRAJ Adam Jones 6.00 15.00
WBCRAM Andrew McCutchen 12.00 30.00
WBCRBP Buster Posey 6.00 15.00
WBCRCC Carlos Correa 12.00 30.00
WBCRDG Didi Gregorius 10.00 25.00
WBCRFF Freddie Freeman 8.00 20.00
WBCRFH Felix Hernandez 4.00 10.00
WBCRGS Giancarlo Stanton 5.00 12.00
WBCRHS Hayato Sakamoto 12.00 30.00
WBCRJA Jose Altuve 4.00 10.00
WBCRJB Javier Baez 10.00 25.00
WBCRKT Kohsuke Tanaka 6.00 15.00
WBCRMC Miguel Cabrera 12.00 30.00
WBCRMM Manny Machado 8.00 20.00
WBCRNA Nolan Arenado 10.00 25.00
WBCRRC Robinson Cano 6.00 15.00
WBCRTY Tetsuto Yamada 6.00 15.00
WBCRYM Yadier Molina 10.00 25.00
WBCRYT Yoshitomo Tsutsugo 10.00 25.00

2018 Topps Triple Threads

COMP.SET w/o AU's (100) 75.00 200.00
JSY AU RC ODDS 1:13 MINI BOX
JSY AU RC PRINT RUN 99 SER.#'d SETS
JSY AU ODDS 1:13 MINI BOX
JSY AU PRINT RUN 99 SER.#'d SETS
EXCHANGE DEADLINE 8/31/2020
1-100 PLATE ODDS 1:116 MINI BOX
JSY AU PLATE ODDS 1:273 MINI BOX
PLATE PRINT RUN 1 SET PER COLOR
BLACK-CYAN-MAGENTA-YELLOW ISSUED
NO PLATE PRICING DUE TO SCARCITY
1 Bryce Harper 1.00 2.50
2 Charlie Blackmon .60 1.50
3 Kris Bryant .75 2.00
4 Mike Trout 3.00 8.00
5 Paul Goldschmidt .60 1.50
6 Manny Machado .60 1.50
7 Mookie Betts 1.00 2.50
8 Anthony Rizzo 1.00 2.50
9 Kyle Schwarber .60 1.50
10 Joey Votto .60 1.50
11 Nolan Arenado .75 2.00
12 Miguel Cabrera .60 1.50
13 Justin Verlander .60 1.50
14 Carlos Correa .60 1.50
15 Eric Hosmer .50 1.25
16 Clayton Kershaw 1.25 3.00
17 Corey Seager .60 1.50
18 Evan Longoria .50 1.25
19 Giancarlo Stanton .60 1.50
20 Ichiro .75 2.00
21 Noah Syndergaard .50 1.25
22 Masahiro Tanaka .50 1.25
23 Gary Sanchez .60 1.50
24 Buster Posey .75 2.00
25 Felix Hernandez .50 1.25
26 Robinson Cano .50 1.25
27 Nelson Cruz .60 1.50
28 Yu Darvish .60 1.50
29 Josh Donaldson .50 1.25
30 Andrew Benintendi .60 1.50
31 Max Scherzer .60 1.50
32 Francisco Lindor .60 1.50
33 Chris Sale .60 1.50
34 Addison Russell .60 1.50
35 Javier Baez .75 2.00
36 Jacob deGrom .60 1.50
37 Andrew McCutchen .60 1.50
38 Wil Myers .40 1.00
39 Albert Pujols .75 2.00
40 Michael Conforto .50 1.25
41 Jose Altuve .50 1.25
42 Justin Upton .50 1.25
43 Edwin Encarnacion .60 1.50
44 Cody Bellinger 1.25 3.00
45 Ryan Braun .50 1.25
46 Freddie Freeman .75 2.00
47 Marcus Stroman .50 1.25
48 Marcell Ozuna .60 1.50
49 Aaron Judge 1.50 4.00
50 Adrian Beltre .60 1.50
51 Luis Severino .50 1.25
52 Corey Kluber .50 1.25
53 Trea Turner .50 1.25
54 Byron Buxton .50 1.25
55 Stephen Strasburg .60 1.50
56 J.D. Martinez .60 1.50
57 Mariano Rivera .75 2.00
58 Xander Bogaerts .60 1.50
59 Adam Jones .50 1.25
60 Daniel Murphy .50 1.25
61 Roberto Clemente 1.50 4.00
62 Cal Ripken Jr. 2.00 5.00
63 Hank Aaron 1.25 3.00
64 Ted Williams 1.25 3.00
65 Jackie Robinson .60 1.50
66 Sandy Koufax 1.25 3.00
67 Babe Ruth 1.50 4.00
68 Ernie Banks .60 1.50
69 Derek Jeter 1.50 4.00
70 David Ortiz .60 1.50
71 Mark McGwire 1.00 2.50
72 Randy Johnson .60 1.50
73 Honus Wagner .60 1.50
74 Roger Maris .60 1.50
75 Ty Cobb 1.00 2.50
76 Lou Gehrig 1.25 3.00
77 Reggie Jackson .50 1.25
78 George Brett 1.25 3.00
79 Don Mattingly 1.25 3.00
80 Frank Thomas .60 1.50
81 Bo Jackson .60 1.50
82 Johnny Bench .60 1.50
83 Greg Maddux .75 2.00
84 Roger Clemens .75 2.00
85 Mike Piazza .60 1.50
86 Nolan Ryan 2.00 5.00
87 Bob Gibson .50 1.25
88 Chipper Jones .60 1.50
89 Ozzie Smith .75 2.00
90 Alex Bregman .60 1.50
91 George Springer .50 1.25
92 Zack Greinke .50 1.25
93 Pedro Martinez .50 1.25
94 Ryne Sandberg 1.25 3.00
95 Barry Larkin .50 1.25
96 Starling Marte .50 1.25
97 Chris Davis .40 1.00
98 Bartolo Colon .40 1.00
99 Dustin Pedroia .60 1.50
100 John Smoltz .60 1.50
RFPARAA Anthony Banda JSY AU RC 3.00 8.00
RFPARAB Bregman JSY AU EXCH 15.00 40.00
RFPARAV Verdugo JSY AU RC 10.00 25.00
RFPARBA Brian Anderson JSY AU RC 4.00 10.00
RFPARBB Byron Buxton JSY AU 5.00 12.00
RFPARBZ Bradley Zimmer JSY AU 3.00 8.00
RFPARCA Christian Arroyo JSY AU 3.00 8.00
RFPARCR Frazier JSY AU RC 6.00 15.00
RFPARCS Chance Sisco JSY AU RC 4.00 10.00
RFPARDF Derek Fisher JSY AU 3.00 8.00
RFPARFB Franklin Barreto JSY AU 3.00 8.00
RFPARFM Mejia JSY AU RC 6.00 15.00
RFPARGT Torres JSY AU RC 25.00 60.00
RFPARHR Hunter Renfroe JSY AU 4.00 10.00
RFPARIH Ian Happ JSY AU 4.00 10.00
RFPARJC J.P. Crawford JSY AU RC 5.00 12.00
RFPARJH Josh Hader JSY AU 6.00 15.00
RFPARJL Flaherty JSY AU RC 20.00 50.00
RFPARJW Jesse Winker JSY AU 3.00 8.00
RFPARLB Lewis Brinson JSY AU EXCH 3.00 8.00
RFPARLS Lucas Sims JSY AU RC 4.00 10.00
RFPARMF Max Fried JSY AU RC 12.00 30.00
RFPARMH Haniger JSY AU 10.00 25.00
RFPARMM Manny Margot JSY AU 3.00 8.00
RFPARMO Matt Olson JSY AU 8.00 20.00
RFPARND Nicky Delmonico JSY AU RC 3.00 8.00
RFPAROA Albies JSY AU RC 15.00 40.00
RFPARPD DeJong JSY AU 6.00 15.00
RFPARRA Acuna Jr. JSY AU RC 125.00 300.00
RFPARRD Devers JSY AU RC EXCH 25.00 60.00
RFPARRH Hoskins JSY AU RC 12.00 30.00
RFPARRM Ryan McMahon JSY AU RC 4.00 10.00
RFPARSA Sandy Alcantara JSY AU RC 3.00 8.00
RFPARSN Sean Newcomb JSY AU 4.00 10.00
RFPARTA Tyler Mahle JSY AU RC 4.00 10.00
RFPARTT Story JSY AU EXCH 6.00 15.00
RFPARTW Tyler Wade JSY AU RC 4.00 10.00
RFPARVR Robles JSY AU RC 15.00 40.00
RFPARWM Whit Merrifield JSY AU 5.00 12.00
RFPARZG Zack Granite JSY AU RC 3.00 8.00

2018 Topps Triple Threads Amber

*AMBER VET: .75X TO 2X BASIC
STATED ODDS 1:3 MINI BOX
STATED PRINT RUN 199 SER.#'d SETS

2018 Topps Triple Threads Amethyst

*AMETHYST VET: .6X TO 1.5X BASIC
STATED ODDS 1:2 MINI BOX
STATED PRINT RUN 299 SER.#'d SETS

2018 Topps Triple Threads Emerald

*EMERALD VET: .6X TO 1.5X BASIC
*EMERALD JSY AU: .4X TO 1X BASIC RC
1-100 ODDS 1:2 MINI BOX
JSY AU ODDS 1:23 MINI BOX
1-100 PRINT RUN 259 SER.#'d SETS
JSY AU PRINT RUN 50 SER.#'d SETS
EXCHANGE DEADLINE 8/31/2020

2018 Topps Triple Threads Gold

*GOLD VET: 1X TO 2.5X BASIC
STATED ODDS 1:5 MINI BOX
STATED PRINT RUN 99 SER.#'d SETS
62 Cal Ripken Jr. 8.00 20.00
86 Nolan Ryan 10.00 25.00

2018 Topps Triple Threads Onyx

*ONYX VET: 1.5X TO 4X BASIC
*ONYX JSY AU: .5X TO 1.2X BASIC RC
1-100 ODDS 1:10 MINI BOX
JSY AU ODDS 1:31 MINI BOX
1-100 PRINT RUN 50 SER.#'d SETS
JSY AU PRINT RUN 50 SER.#'d SETS
EXCHANGE DEADLINE 8/31/2020
4 Mike Trout 12.00 30.00
62 Cal Ripken Jr. 12.00 30.00
69 Derek Jeter 12.00 30.00
79 Don Mattingly 10.00 25.00
86 Nolan Ryan 12.00 30.00
RFPARDM Dominic Smith 4.00 10.00
RFPARLW Luke Weaver 5.00 12.00

2018 Topps Triple Threads Sapphire

*SAPPHIRE VET: 3X TO 8X BASIC
STATED ODDS 1:19 MINI BOX
STATED PRINT RUN 25 SER.#'d SETS
4 Mike Trout 20.00 50.00
62 Cal Ripken Jr. 20.00 50.00
69 Derek Jeter 20.00 50.00
79 Don Mattingly 20.00 50.00
86 Nolan Ryan 30.00 80.00

2018 Topps Triple Threads Silver

*SILVER JSY AU: .4X TO 1X BASIC RC
STATED ODDS 1:15 MINI BOX
STATED PRINT RUN 75 SER.#'d SETS
EXCHANGE DEADLINE 8/31/2020

2018 Topps Triple Threads Autograph Relic Combos

STATED ODDS 1:62 HOBBY
STATED PRINT RUN 36 SER.#'d SETS
EXCHANGE DEADLINE 8/31/2020
*SILVER/27: .4X TO 1X BASIC
*EMERALD/18: .4X TO 1X BASIC
PRINTING PLATE ODDS 1:442 HOBBY
PLATE PRINT RUN 1 SET PER COLOR
BLACK-CYAN-MAGENTA-YELLOW ISSUED
NO PLATE PRICING DUE TO SCARCITY
ARCADM Pettitte/Jeter/Rivera
ARCAJA Acuna/Albies/Jones 125.00 300.00
ARCAJG Brgmn/Altve/Sprngr EXCH 50.00 120.00
ARCAMS Trout/Pujols/Ohtani
ARCAMT Mncni/Mchdo/Jns EXCH 30.00 80.00
ARCATV Dawson/Raines/Vlad 40.00 100.00
ARCBCM Brooks/Cal/Machado EXCH 75.00 200.00
ARCBKJ Larkin/Bench/Votto 125.00 300.00
ARCCGD Frazier/Gregorius/Bird 20.00 50.00
ARCCJJ Altuve/Bagwell/Biggio 60.00 150.00
ARCFCJ Kluber/Lindor/Ramirez EXCH 50.00 120.00
ARCHIS Ichiro/Matsui/Ohtani
ARCIJA Beltre/Gonzalez/Rodriguez 40.00 100.00
ARCJAK Schwrbr/Baez/Rssll EXCH 30.00 80.00
ARCJCD Smoltz/Jones/Murphy 75.00 200.00
ARCJNM Conforto/deGrom/Syndgrd 40.00 100.00
ARCLGD Svrno/Grgrs/Trrs 40.00 100.00
ARCLKT Thme/Lndr/Klbr EXCH 40.00 100.00
ARCLPJ Lamb/Gldschmdt/Gnzlz 20.00 50.00
ARCMKM Davis/Chapman/Olson 40.00 100.00
ARCMYM Wcha/Mlna/Ozna EXCH 40.00 100.00
ARCOFD Swanson/Albies/Freeman 40.00 100.00
ARCPAB Williams/Posada/Pettitte 60.00 150.00
ARCRAK Sandberg/Bryant/Rizzo 100.00 250.00
ARCRDC Sale/Pdria/Dvrs EXCH 40.00 100.00
ARCTCE Thames/Shaw/Yelich 30.00 80.00
ARCTCT Stry/Blckmn/Andrsn EXCH 20.00 50.00
ARCYAD Smith/Rosario/Cespedes

2018 Topps Triple Threads Autograph Relics

STATED ODDS 1:10 HOBBY
STATED PRINT RUN 18 SER.#'d SETS
EXCHANGE DEADLINE 8/31/2020
*GOLD/9: .5X TO 1.2X BASIC
SOME GOLD NOT PRICED DUE TO SCARCITY
ALL VERSIONS EQUALLY PRICED
TTARAB1 Adrian Beltre 30.00 80.00
TTARAB2 Adrian Beltre 30.00 80.00
TTARAB3 Adrian Beltre 30.00 80.00
TTARABR1 Alex Bregman EXCH 20.00 50.00
TTARABR2 Alex Bregman EXCH 20.00 50.00
TTARABR3 Alex Bregman EXCH 20.00 50.00
TTARABR4 Alex Bregman EXCH 20.00 50.00
TTARABR5 Alex Bregman EXCH 20.00 50.00
TTARAD1 Andre Dawson 15.00 40.00
TTARAD2 Andre Dawson 15.00 40.00
TTARAD3 Andre Dawson 15.00 40.00
TTARAJ1 Aaron Judge 60.00 150.00
TTARAJ2 Aaron Judge 60.00 150.00
TTARAM1 Andrew McCutchen 20.00 50.00
TTARAM2 Andrew McCutchen 20.00 50.00
TTARAM3 Andrew McCutchen 20.00 50.00
TTARAM4 Andrew McCutchen 20.00 50.00
TTARAP1 Andy Pettitte 20.00 50.00
TTARAP2 Andy Pettitte 20.00 50.00
TTARAP3 Andy Pettitte 20.00 50.00
TTARAP4 Andy Pettitte 20.00 50.00
TTARAR1 Addison Russell 6.00 15.00
TTARAR2 Addison Russell 6.00 15.00
TTARARI1 Anthony Rizzo 25.00 60.00
TTARARI2 Anthony Rizzo 25.00 60.00
TTARARI3 Anthony Rizzo 25.00 60.00
TTARARI4 Anthony Rizzo 25.00 60.00
TTARBB1 Byron Buxton 10.00 25.00
TTARBB2 Byron Buxton 10.00 25.00
TTARBB3 Byron Buxton 10.00 25.00
TTARBD1 Brian Dozier 10.00 25.00
TTARBD2 Brian Dozier 10.00 25.00
TTARBD3 Brian Dozier 10.00 25.00
TTARBH1 Bryce Harper 75.00 200.00
TTARBH2 Bryce Harper 75.00 200.00
TTARBL1 Barry Larkin 20.00 50.00
TTARBL2 Barry Larkin 20.00 50.00
TTARBP1 Buster Posey
TTARCBI1 Craig Biggio 15.00 40.00
TTARCBI2 Craig Biggio 15.00 40.00
TTARCBI3 Craig Biggio 15.00 40.00
TTARCBL1 Charlie Blackmon 8.00 20.00
TTARCBL2 Charlie Blackmon 8.00 20.00
TTARCBL3 Charlie Blackmon 8.00 20.00
TTARCBL4 Charlie Blackmon 8.00 20.00
TTARCBL5 Charlie Blackmon 8.00 20.00
TTARCF1 Carlton Fisk 20.00 50.00
TTARCF2 Carlton Fisk 20.00 50.00
TTARCF3 Carlton Fisk 20.00 50.00
TTARCJ1 Chipper Jones 75.00 200.00
TTARCJ2 Chipper Jones 75.00 200.00
TTARCK1 Craig Kimbrel 15.00 40.00
TTARCK2 Craig Kimbrel 15.00 40.00
TTARCK3 Craig Kimbrel 15.00 40.00
TTARCK4 Craig Kimbrel 15.00 40.00
TTARCK5 Craig Kimbrel 15.00 40.00
TTARCKL1 Corey Kluber 10.00 25.00
TTARCKL2 Corey Kluber 10.00 25.00
TTARCKL3 Corey Kluber 10.00 25.00
TTARCKL4 Corey Kluber 10.00 25.00
TTARCKL5 Corey Kluber 10.00 25.00
TTARCR1 Cal Ripken Jr. 60.00 150.00
TTARCSA1 Chris Sale 20.00 50.00
TTARCSA2 Chris Sale 20.00 50.00
TTARCSA3 Chris Sale 20.00 50.00
TTARCSA4 Chris Sale 20.00 50.00
TTARCSA5 Chris Sale 20.00 50.00
TTARCY1 Christian Yelich 30.00 80.00
TTARCY2 Christian Yelich 30.00 80.00
TTARCY3 Christian Yelich 30.00 80.00
TTARCY4 Christian Yelich 30.00 80.00
TTARCY5 Christian Yelich 30.00 80.00
TTARDE1 Dennis Eckersley 12.00 30.00
TTARDE2 Dennis Eckersley 12.00 30.00
TTARDE3 Dennis Eckersley 12.00 30.00
TTARDE4 Dennis Eckersley 12.00 30.00
TTARDG1 Didi Gregorius 12.00 30.00
TTARDG2 Didi Gregorius 12.00 30.00
TTARDG3 Didi Gregorius 12.00 30.00
TTARDG4 Didi Gregorius 12.00 30.00
TTARDG5 Didi Gregorius 12.00 30.00
TTARDJ1 Derek Jeter 300.00 500.00
TTARDMA1 Don Mattingly 60.00 150.00
TTARDMA2 Don Mattingly 60.00 150.00
TTARDMU1 Dale Murphy 30.00 80.00
TTARDMU2 Dale Murphy 30.00 80.00
TTARDMU3 Dale Murphy 30.00 80.00
TTARDO1 David Ortiz 40.00 100.00
TTARDO2 David Ortiz 40.00 100.00
TTARFF1 Freddie Freeman 15.00 40.00
TTARFF2 Freddie Freeman 15.00 40.00
TTARFF3 Freddie Freeman 15.00 40.00
TTARFF4 Freddie Freeman 15.00 40.00
TTARFF5 Freddie Freeman 15.00 40.00
TTARFL1 Francisco Lindor 25.00 60.00
TTARFL2 Francisco Lindor 25.00 60.00
TTARFL3 Francisco Lindor 25.00 60.00
TTARFL4 Francisco Lindor 25.00 60.00
TTARFT1 Frank Thomas 40.00 100.00
TTARFT2 Frank Thomas 40.00 100.00
TTARFT3 Frank Thomas 40.00 100.00
TTARGS1 Gary Sanchez 20.00 50.00
TTARGS2 Gary Sanchez 20.00 50.00
TTARGS3 Gary Sanchez 20.00 50.00
TTARGS4 Gary Sanchez 20.00 50.00
TTARGS5 Gary Sanchez 20.00 50.00
TTARGSP1 George Springer 15.00 40.00
TTARGSP2 George Springer 15.00 40.00
TTARGSP3 George Springer 15.00 40.00
TTARGSP4 George Springer 15.00 40.00
TTARGSP5 George Springer 15.00 40.00
TTARHA1 Hank Aaron 200.00 400.00
TTARIH1 Ian Happ 6.00 15.00
TTARIH2 Ian Happ 6.00 15.00
TTARIH3 Ian Happ 6.00 15.00
TTARIH4 Ian Happ 6.00 15.00
TTARIH5 Ian Happ 6.00 15.00
TTARIR1 Ivan Rodriguez 15.00 40.00
TTARIR2 Ivan Rodriguez 15.00 40.00
TTARIR3 Ivan Rodriguez 15.00 40.00
TTARJA1 Jose Altuve 20.00 50.00
TTARJA2 Jose Altuve 20.00 50.00
TTARJA3 Jose Altuve 20.00 50.00
TTARJA4 Jose Altuve 20.00 50.00
TTARJA5 Jose Altuve 20.00 50.00
TTARJB1 Jeff Bagwell 25.00 60.00
TTARJB2 Jeff Bagwell 25.00 60.00
TTARJB3 Jeff Bagwell 25.00 60.00
TTARJB4 Jeff Bagwell 25.00 60.00
TTARJBA1 Javier Baez EXCH 20.00 50.00
TTARJBA2 Javier Baez EXCH 20.00 50.00
TTARJBA3 Javier Baez EXCH 20.00 50.00
TTARJBA4 Javier Baez EXCH 20.00 50.00
TTARJBA5 Javier Baez EXCH 20.00 50.00
TTARJC1 Jose Canseco 15.00 40.00
TTARJC2 Jose Canseco 15.00 40.00
TTARJC3 Jose Canseco 15.00 40.00
TTARJC4 Jose Canseco 15.00 40.00
TTARJD1 Jacob deGrom 25.00 60.00
TTARJD2 Jacob deGrom 25.00 60.00
TTARJD3 Jacob deGrom 25.00 60.00
TTARJD4 Jacob deGrom 25.00 60.00
TTARJD5 Jacob deGrom 25.00 60.00
TTARJDO1 Josh Donaldson 15.00 40.00
TTARJDO2 Josh Donaldson 15.00 40.00
TTARJDO3 Josh Donaldson 15.00 40.00
TTARJG1 Juan Gonzalez 20.00 50.00
TTARJG2 Juan Gonzalez 20.00 50.00
TTARJG3 Juan Gonzalez 20.00 50.00
TTARJR1 Jose Ramirez 20.00 50.00
TTARJR2 Jose Ramirez 20.00 50.00
TTARJR3 Jose Ramirez 20.00 50.00
TTARJR4 Jose Ramirez 20.00 50.00
TTARJS1 John Smoltz 25.00 60.00
TTARJS2 John Smoltz 25.00 60.00
TTARJS3 John Smoltz 25.00 60.00
TTARJT1 Jim Thome 25.00 60.00
TTARJT2 Jim Thome 25.00 60.00
TTARJT3 Jim Thome 25.00 60.00
TTARJU1 Justin Upton 6.00 15.00
TTARJU2 Justin Upton 6.00 15.00
TTARJU3 Justin Upton 6.00 15.00
TTARJU4 Justin Upton 6.00 15.00
TTARJV1 Joey Votto 30.00 80.00
TTARJV2 Joey Votto 30.00 80.00
TTARKB1 Kris Bryant 60.00 150.00
TTARKB2 Kris Bryant 60.00 150.00
TTARKB3 Kris Bryant 60.00 150.00
TTARKS1 Kyle Schwarber 12.00 30.00
TTARKS2 Kyle Schwarber 12.00 30.00
TTARKS3 Kyle Schwarber 12.00 30.00
TTARKS4 Kyle Schwarber 12.00 30.00
TTARKS5 Kyle Schwarber 12.00 30.00
TTARLS1 Luis Severino 12.00 30.00
TTARLS2 Luis Severino 12.00 30.00
TTARLS3 Luis Severino 12.00 30.00
TTARLS4 Luis Severino 12.00 30.00
TTARLS5 Luis Severino 12.00 30.00
TTARMM1 Mark McGwire 40.00 100.00
TTARMM2 Mark McGwire 40.00 100.00
TTARMMA1 Manny Machado 20.00 50.00
TTARMMA2 Manny Machado 20.00 50.00
TTARMMA3 Manny Machado 20.00 50.00
TTARMMA4 Manny Machado 20.00 50.00
TTARMP1 Mike Piazza 30.00 80.00
TTARMT1 Mike Trout 150.00 400.00
TTARMT2 Mike Trout 150.00 400.00
TTARNG1 Nomar Garciaparra 15.00 40.00
TTARNG2 Nomar Garciaparra 15.00 40.00
TTARNG3 Nomar Garciaparra 15.00 40.00
TTARNR1 Nolan Ryan 75.00 200.00
TTARNR2 Nolan Ryan 75.00 200.00
TTARNS1 Noah Syndergaard 12.00 30.00
TTARNS2 Noah Syndergaard 12.00 30.00
TTARNS3 Noah Syndergaard 12.00 30.00
TTARNS4 Noah Syndergaard 12.00 30.00
TTARNS5 Noah Syndergaard 12.00 30.00
TTAROS1 Ozzie Smith 25.00 60.00
TTAROS2 Ozzie Smith 25.00 60.00
TTAROS3 Ozzie Smith 25.00 60.00
TTARPG1 Paul Goldschmidt 20.00 50.00
TTARPG2 Paul Goldschmidt 20.00 50.00
TTARPG3 Paul Goldschmidt 20.00 50.00
TTARPG4 Paul Goldschmidt 20.00 50.00
TTARPG5 Paul Goldschmidt 20.00 50.00
TTARRA1 Roberto Alomar 20.00 50.00
TTARRA2 Roberto Alomar 20.00 50.00
TTARRA3 Roberto Alomar 20.00 50.00
TTARRC1 Rod Carew 15.00 40.00
TTARRC2 Rod Carew 15.00 40.00
TTARRC3 Rod Carew 15.00 40.00
TTARRF1 Rollie Fingers 12.00 30.00
TTARRH1 Rickey Henderson 30.00 80.00
TTARRH2 Rickey Henderson 30.00 80.00
TTARRJ1 Randy Johnson 40.00 100.00
TTARRY1 Robin Yount 30.00 80.00
TTARRY2 Robin Yount 30.00 80.00
TTARSG1 Sonny Gray 6.00 15.00
TTARSG2 Sonny Gray 6.00 15.00
TTARSG3 Sonny Gray 6.00 15.00
TTARSM1 Starling Marte 10.00 25.00
TTARSM2 Starling Marte 10.00 25.00
TTARSM3 Starling Marte 10.00 25.00
TTARSM4 Starling Marte 10.00 25.00
TTARSM5 Starling Marte 10.00 25.00
TTARSO1 Shohei Ohtani 300.00 500.00
TTARSO2 Shohei Ohtani 300.00 500.00
TTARSP1 Salvador Perez 15.00 40.00
TTARSP2 Salvador Perez 15.00 40.00
TTARSP3 Salvador Perez 15.00 40.00
TTARSP4 Salvador Perez 15.00 40.00
TTARSP5 Salvador Perez 15.00 40.00
TTARTG1 Tom Glavine 20.00 50.00
TTARTG2 Tom Glavine 20.00 50.00
TTARTH1 Torii Hunter 12.00 30.00
TTARTH2 Torii Hunter 12.00 30.00
TTARTH3 Torii Hunter 12.00 30.00
TTARTH4 Torii Hunter 12.00 30.00
TTARTM1 Trey Mancini 10.00 25.00
TTARTM2 Trey Mancini 10.00 25.00
TTARTM3 Trey Mancini 10.00 25.00
TTARTM4 Trey Mancini 10.00 25.00
TTARTM5 Trey Mancini 10.00 25.00
TTARTR1 Tim Raines 10.00 25.00
TTARTR2 Tim Raines 10.00 25.00
TTARTR3 Tim Raines 10.00 25.00
TTARVG1 Vladimir Guerrero 30.00 80.00
TTARVG2 Vladimir Guerrero 30.00 80.00
TTARVG3 Vladimir Guerrero 30.00 80.00
TTARWC1 Will Clark 40.00 100.00
TTARWC2 Will Clark 40.00 100.00
TTARWC3 Will Clark 40.00 100.00
TTARWC4 Will Clark 40.00 100.00
TTARWCO1 Willson Contreras 12.00 30.00
TTARWCO2 Willson Contreras 12.00 30.00
TTARWCO3 Willson Contreras 12.00 30.00
TTARWCO4 Willson Contreras 12.00 30.00
TTARWCO5 Willson Contreras 12.00 30.00
TTARYM1 Yadier Molina 40.00 100.00
TTARYM2 Yadier Molina 40.00 100.00
TTARYM3 Yadier Molina 40.00 100.00
TTARYM4 Yadier Molina 40.00 100.00
TTARYM5 Yadier Molina 40.00 100.00

2018 Topps Triple Threads Legend Relics

STATED ODDS 1:68 HOBBY
STATED PRINT RUN 36 SER.#'d SETS
*SILVER/27: .4X TO 1X BASIC
*EMERALD/18: .4X TO 1X BASIC
RLCCF Carlton Fisk 8.00 20.00
RLCCJ Chipper Jones 10.00 25.00
RLCCR Cal Ripken Jr. 20.00 50.00
RLCDJ Derek Jeter 25.00 60.00
RLCEB Ernie Banks 20.00 50.00
RLCFT Frank Thomas 12.00 30.00
RLCGM Greg Maddux 10.00 25.00
RLCJB Johnny Bench 12.00 30.00
RLCJS John Smoltz 10.00 25.00
RLCMM Mark McGwire 12.00 30.00
RLCMP Mike Piazza 10.00 25.00
RLCMR Mariano Rivera 10.00 25.00
RLCNR Nolan Ryan 20.00 50.00
RLCOS Ozzie Smith 10.00 25.00
RLCPM Pedro Martinez 8.00 20.00
RLCRC Roger Clemens 8.00 20.00
RLCRE Roberto Clemente 75.00 200.00
RLCRH Rickey Henderson 10.00 25.00
RLCRJ Reggie Jackson 8.00 20.00
RLCRS Ryne Sandberg 10.00 25.00
RLCTW Ted Williams 60.00 150.00
RLCWB Wade Boggs 10.00 25.00

2018 Topps Triple Threads Players Weekend Relics

STATED ODDS 1:142 HOBBY
STATED PRINT RUN 36 SER.#'d SETS
*SILVER/27: .4X TO 1X BASIC
*EMERALD/18: .4X TO 1X BASIC
PWAR Amed Rosario 5.00 12.00
PWBP Buster Posey 10.00 25.00
PWI Ichiro 20.00 50.00
PWKB Kris Bryant 20.00 50.00
PWKD Khris Davis 6.00 15.00
PWKS Kyle Schwarber 8.00 20.00
PWRB Ryan Braun 5.00 12.00
PWRD Rafael Devers 12.00 30.00
PWYM Yadier Molina 12.00 30.00

2018 Topps Triple Threads Relic Combos

STATED ODDS 1:33 HOBBY
STATED PRINT RUN 36 SER.#'d SETS
*SILVER/27: .4X TO 1X BASIC
*EMERALD/18: .5X TO 1.2X BASIC
RCCAGM Chapman/Sanchez/Tanaka 6.00 15.00
RCCAKK Rizzo/Schwrbr/Bryant 10.00 25.00
RCCAMT Mancini/Jones/Machado 6.00 15.00
RCCAPJ Goldschmidt/Lamb/Pollock 6.00 15.00

RCCAPZ Greinke/Pollock/Goldschmidt 6.00 15.00
RCCARJ Crawford/Nola/Hoskins 10.00 25.00
RCCBBE Lngria/Posey/Crawford 8.00 20.00
RCCBMK Harper/Bryant/Trout 30.00 80.00
RCCCAJ Hamels/Gallo/Beltre 6.00 15.00
RCCCCC Krshw/Bellinger/Seager 12.00 30.00
RCCCCK Krshw/Jansen/Seager 12.00 30.00
RCCCDC Sale/Price/Kimbrel 10.00 25.00
RCCCJJ Biggio/Bagwell/Altuve 10.00 25.00
RCCCMA Betts/Benintendi/Sale 20.00 50.00
RCCCNC Gonzalez/Blackmon/Arenado 8.00 20.00
RCCCYA Martinez/Reyes/Molina 6.00 15.00
RCCDDA Judge/Jeter/Mattingly 40.00 100.00
RCCDFO Albies/Frmn/Swanson 8.00 20.00
RCCDMA Bnntndi/Betts/Pedroia 15.00 40.00
RCCDYT Pham/Fowler/Molina 6.00 15.00
RCCFRN Hernandez/Cano/Cruz 6.00 15.00
RCCGAD Snchz/Grgrius/Judge 10.00 25.00
RCCIJA Gonzalez/Rodriguez/Beltre 6.00 15.00
RCCJAA Rizzo/Baez/Russell 10.00 25.00
RCCJBJ Votto/Larkin/Bench 10.00 25.00
RCCJCA Brgmn/Correa/Altuve 6.00 15.00
RCCJCJ Altuve/Vrlndr/Correa 6.00 15.00
RCCJGS Polanco/Marte/Bell 5.00 12.00
RCCJJA Sanchez/Smoak/Donaldson 5.00 12.00
RCCJMA Trout/Upton/Pujols 15.00 40.00
RCCJNS Sndrgrd/deGrom/Matz 10.00 25.00
RCCJWK Cntrra/Baez/Schwarber 8.00 20.00
RCCJYJ Turner/Puig/Pederson 6.00 15.00
RCCLMS Severino/Tanaka/Gray 5.00 12.00
RCCMBJ Buxton/Mauer/Sano 5.00 12.00
RCCMBS Schrzr/Harper/Strasburg 8.00 20.00
RCCNMM Cstllns/Cabrera/Fulmer 6.00 15.00
RCCSGJ Marte/Taillon/Polanco 5.00 12.00
RCCWMS Moustakas/Mrrfld/Perez 8.00 20.00
RCCYMA Conforto/Rosario/Cespedes 6.00 15.00

2018 Topps Triple Threads Relics

STATED ODDS 1:8 MINI BOX
STATED PRINT RUN 36 SER.#'d SETS
*SILVER/27: .4X TO 1X BASIC
*EMERALD/18: .5X TO 1.2X BASIC
*GOLD/9: .6X TO 1.5X BASIC
ALL VERSIONS EQUALLY PRICED
TTRAB1 Adrian Beltre 4.00 10.00
TTRAB2 Adrian Beltre 4.00 10.00
TTRABE1 Andrew Benintendi 10.00 25.00
TTRABE2 Andrew Benintendi 10.00 25.00
TTRAJE1 Adam Jones 3.00 8.00
TTRAJE2 Adam Jones 3.00 8.00
TTRAJE3 Adam Jones 3.00 8.00
TTRAJE4 Adam Jones 3.00 8.00
TTRAP1 Albert Pujols 5.00 12.00
TTRAP2 Albert Pujols 5.00 12.00
TTRAR1 Anthony Rizzo 6.00 15.00
TTRAR2 Anthony Rizzo 6.00 15.00
TTRAR3 Anthony Rizzo 6.00 15.00
TTRARU1 Addison Russell 3.00 8.00
TTRARU2 Addison Russell 3.00 8.00
TTRARU3 Addison Russell 3.00 8.00
TTRARU4 Addison Russell 3.00 8.00
TTRAW1 Adam Wainwright 3.00 8.00
TTRAW2 Adam Wainwright 3.00 8.00
TTRAW3 Adam Wainwright 3.00 8.00
TTRAW4 Adam Wainwright 3.00 8.00
TTRBB1 Byron Buxton 3.00 8.00
TTRBB2 Byron Buxton 3.00 8.00
TTRBB3 Byron Buxton 3.00 8.00
TTRBH1 Bryce Harper 6.00 15.00
TTRBH2 Bryce Harper 6.00 15.00
TTRBP1 Buster Posey 5.00 12.00
TTRBP2 Buster Posey 5.00 12.00
TTRCC1 Carlos Correa 4.00 10.00
TTRCC2 Carlos Correa 4.00 10.00
TTRCC3 Carlos Correa 4.00 10.00
TTRCG1 Carlos Gonzalez 3.00 8.00
TTRCG2 Carlos Gonzalez 3.00 8.00
TTRCG3 Carlos Gonzalez 3.00 8.00
TTRCKRS1 Clayton Kershaw 8.00 20.00
TTRCKRS2 Clayton Kershaw 8.00 20.00
TTRCR1 Cal Ripken Jr. 12.00 30.00
TTRCS1 Corey Seager 4.00 10.00
TTRCS2 Corey Seager 4.00 10.00
TTRCS3 Corey Seager 4.00 10.00
TTRCSA1 Chris Sale 4.00 10.00
TTRCSA2 Chris Sale 4.00 10.00
TTRCSA3 Chris Sale 4.00 10.00
TTRCSA4 Chris Sale 4.00 10.00
TTRCSA5 Chris Sale 4.00 10.00
TTRDJ1 Derek Jeter 20.00 50.00
TTRDJ2 Derek Jeter 20.00 50.00
TTRDO1 David Ortiz 6.00 15.00
TTRDO2 David Ortiz 6.00 15.00
TTRDP1 Dustin Pedroia 4.00 10.00
TTRDP2 Dustin Pedroia 4.00 10.00
TTRDP3 Dustin Pedroia 4.00 10.00
TTRDPR1 David Price 3.00 8.00
TTRDPR2 David Price 3.00 8.00
TTRDPR3 David Price 3.00 8.00
TTREL1 Evan Longoria 3.00 8.00
TTREL2 Evan Longoria 3.00 8.00
TTREL3 Evan Longoria 3.00 8.00
TTRFF1 Freddie Freeman 5.00 12.00
TTRFF2 Freddie Freeman 5.00 12.00
TTRFF3 Freddie Freeman 5.00 12.00
TTRGSA1 Gary Sanchez 4.00 10.00
TTRGSA2 Gary Sanchez 4.00 10.00
TTRGSA3 Gary Sanchez 4.00 10.00
TTRIK1 Ian Kinsler 3.00 8.00
TTRIK2 Ian Kinsler 3.00 8.00
TTRIK3 Ian Kinsler 3.00 8.00
TTRIK4 Ian Kinsler 3.00 8.00
TTRI1 Ichiro 6.00 15.00
TTRI2 Ichiro 6.00 15.00
TTRJAL1 Jose Altuve 3.00 8.00
TTRJAL2 Jose Altuve 3.00 8.00
TTRJAL3 Jose Altuve 3.00 8.00
TTRJAL4 Jose Altuve 3.00 8.00
TTRJAL5 Jose Altuve 3.00 8.00
TTRJBZ1 Javier Baez 8.00 20.00
TTRJBZ2 Javier Baez 8.00 20.00
TTRJBZ3 Javier Baez 8.00 20.00
TTRJBZ4 Javier Baez 8.00 20.00
TTRJBZ5 Javier Baez 8.00 20.00
TTRJD1 Josh Donaldson 3.00 8.00
TTRJD2 Josh Donaldson 3.00 8.00
TTRJD3 Josh Donaldson 3.00 8.00
TTRJDE1 Jacob deGrom 5.00 12.00
TTRJDE2 Jacob deGrom 5.00 12.00
TTRJDE3 Jacob deGrom 5.00 12.00
TTRJDE4 Jacob deGrom 5.00 12.00
TTRJDE5 Jacob deGrom 5.00 12.00
TTRJU1 Justin Upton 3.00 8.00
TTRJU2 Justin Upton 3.00 8.00
TTRJU3 Justin Upton 3.00 8.00
TTRJU4 Justin Upton 3.00 8.00
TTRJV1 Justin Verlander 4.00 10.00
TTRJV2 Justin Verlander 4.00 10.00
TTRJV3 Justin Verlander 4.00 10.00
TTRJV4 Justin Verlander 4.00 10.00
TTRJV5 Justin Verlander 4.00 10.00
TTRJVO1 Joey Votto 4.00 10.00
TTRJVO2 Joey Votto 4.00 10.00
TTRJVO3 Joey Votto 4.00 10.00
TTRKB1 Kris Bryant 8.00 20.00
TTRKB2 Kris Bryant 8.00 20.00
TTRKB3 Kris Bryant 8.00 20.00
TTRKM1 Kenta Maeda 3.00 8.00
TTRKM2 Kenta Maeda 3.00 8.00
TTRMB1 Mookie Betts 8.00 20.00
TTRMB2 Mookie Betts 8.00 20.00
TTRMB3 Mookie Betts 8.00 20.00
TTRMB4 Mookie Betts 8.00 20.00
TTRMB5 Mookie Betts 8.00 20.00
TTRMCB1 Miguel Cabrera 4.00 10.00
TTRMCB2 Miguel Cabrera 4.00 10.00
TTRMCB3 Miguel Cabrera 4.00 10.00
TTRMCB4 Miguel Cabrera 4.00 10.00
TTRMCB5 Miguel Cabrera 4.00 10.00
TTRMM1 Manny Machado 4.00 10.00
TTRMM2 Manny Machado 4.00 10.00
TTRMM3 Manny Machado 4.00 10.00
TTRMMG1 Mark McGwire 12.00 30.00
TTRMMG2 Mark McGwire 12.00 30.00
TTRMP1 Mike Piazza 6.00 15.00
TTRMS1 Marcus Stroman 3.00 8.00
TTRMS2 Marcus Stroman 3.00 8.00
TTRMS3 Marcus Stroman 3.00 8.00
TTRMS4 Marcus Stroman 3.00 8.00
TTRMSC1 Max Scherzer 4.00 10.00
TTRMSC2 Max Scherzer 4.00 10.00
TTRMSC3 Max Scherzer 4.00 10.00
TTRMTA1 Masahiro Tanaka 3.00 8.00
TTRMT1 Mike Trout 25.00 60.00
TTRMT2 Mike Trout 25.00 60.00
TTRMTA2 Masahiro Tanaka 3.00 8.00
TTRMTA3 Masahiro Tanaka 3.00 8.00
TTRMTA4 Masahiro Tanaka 3.00 8.00
TTRRB1 Ryan Braun 3.00 8.00
TTRRB2 Ryan Braun 3.00 8.00
TTRRB3 Ryan Braun 3.00 8.00
TTRSM1 Starling Marte 3.00 8.00
TTRSM2 Starling Marte 3.00 8.00
TTRSM3 Starling Marte 3.00 8.00
TTRSM4 Starling Marte 3.00 8.00
TTRSS1 Stephen Strasburg 4.00 10.00
TTRSS2 Stephen Strasburg 4.00 10.00
TTRSS3 Stephen Strasburg 4.00 10.00
TTRSS4 Stephen Strasburg 4.00 10.00
TTRSS5 Stephen Strasburg 4.00 10.00
TTRTST1 Trevor Story 3.00 8.00
TTRTST2 Trevor Story 3.00 8.00
TTRTST3 Trevor Story 3.00 8.00
TTRTST4 Trevor Story 3.00 8.00
TTRWM1 Wil Myers 2.50 6.00
TTRWM2 Wil Myers 2.50 6.00
TTRXB1 Xander Bogaerts 4.00 10.00
TTRXB2 Xander Bogaerts 4.00 10.00
TTRXB3 Xander Bogaerts 4.00 10.00
TTRYC1 Yoenis Cespedes 4.00 10.00
TTRYC2 Yoenis Cespedes 4.00 10.00
TTRYC3 Yoenis Cespedes 4.00 10.00
TTRYC4 Yoenis Cespedes 4.00 10.00
TTRYC5 Yoenis Cespedes 4.00 10.00
TTRYM1 Yadier Molina 6.00 15.00
TTRYM2 Yadier Molina 6.00 15.00
TTRYM3 Yadier Molina 6.00 15.00
TTRYM4 Yadier Molina 6.00 15.00

2018 Topps Triple Threads Rookie Autographs

STATED ODDS 1:29 MINI BOX
STATED PRINT RUN 99 SER.#'d SETS
EXCHANGE DEADLINE 8/31/2020
PRINTING PLATE ODDS 1:701 MINI BOX
PLATE PRINT RUN 1 SET PER COLOR
BLACK-CYAN-MAGENTA-YELLOW ISSUED
NO PLATE PRICING DUE TO SCARCITY
*EMERALD/50: .4X TO 1X BASIC
*GOLD/25: .5X TO 1.2X BASIC
RAAH Austin Hays 6.00 15.00
RAAM Austin Meadows EXCH 10.00 25.00
RACV Christian Villanueva 4.00 10.00
RADF Dustin Fowler 4.00 10.00
RAFR Fernando Romero 4.00 10.00
RAHB Harrison Bader 6.00 15.00
RAJH Jordan Hicks 8.00 20.00
RAJS Juan Soto 100.00 250.00
RALG Lourdes Gurriel Jr. 8.00 20.00
RAMA Miguel Andujar 20.00 50.00
RAMM Miles Mikolas 8.00 20.00
RAMS Mike Soroka 20.00 50.00
RANK Nick Kingham 4.00 10.00
RASK Scott Kingery 6.00 15.00
RASO Shohei Ohtani 250.00 500.00
RAWA Willy Adames 5.00 12.00
RAWB Walker Buehler 20.00 50.00

2018 Topps Triple Threads Unity Autograph Jumbo Relics

STATED ODDS 1:7 HOBBY
STATED PRINT RUN 99 SER.#'d SETS
EXCHANGE DEADLINE 8/31/2020
UAJRABR Alex Bregman EXCH 15.00 40.00
UAJRAD Adam Duvall 6.00 15.00
UAJRAE Alcides Escobar 5.00 12.00
UAJRAMED Amed Rosario 5.00 12.00
UAJRARO Amed Rosario 5.00 12.00
UAJRAV Adam Duvall 6.00 15.00
UAJRAW Alex Wood 4.00 10.00
UAJRBS Blake Snell 5.00 12.00
UAJRBSN Blake Snell 5.00 12.00
UAJRBZO Ben Zobrist 15.00 40.00
UAJRCA Christian Arroyo 4.00 10.00
UAJRCB Charlie Blackmon 6.00 15.00
UAJRCSA Chris Sale 15.00 40.00
UAJRCYH Christian Yelich 20.00 50.00
UAJRDB Dellin Betances EXCH 5.00 12.00
UAJRDBE Dellin Betances EXCH 5.00 12.00
UAJRDG Didi Gregorius 6.00 15.00
UAJRDP Drew Pomeranz 4.00 10.00
UAJRDPR David Price 12.00 30.00
UAJRDT Darryl Strawberry 8.00 20.00
UAJRET Eric Thames 5.00 12.00
UAJRGB Greg Bird 5.00 12.00
UAJRGI Greg Bird 5.00 12.00
UAJRHOS Rhys Hoskins 15.00 40.00
UAJRIH Ian Happ 5.00 12.00
UAJRIHA Ian Happ 5.00 12.00
UAJRIKS Ian Kinsler 5.00 12.00
UAJRJB Javier Baez EXCH 20.00 50.00
UAJRJBO Justin Bour 4.00 10.00
UAJRJE Jose Berrios 5.00 12.00
UAJRJG Juan Gonzalez 4.00 10.00
UAJRJH Josh Harrison 4.00 10.00
UAJRJHA Josh Harrison 4.00 10.00
UAJRJL Jake Lamb 5.00 12.00
UAJRJP Joc Pederson 5.00 12.00
UAJRJSM Justin Smoak 4.00 10.00
UAJRJU Jay Bruce 5.00 12.00
UAJRJW Jesse Winker 4.00 10.00
UAJRKD Khris Davis 6.00 15.00
UAJRKS Kyle Schwarber 10.00 25.00
UAJRKV Khris Davis 6.00 15.00
UAJRLSE Luis Severino 10.00 25.00
UAJRMA Matt Carpenter 6.00 15.00
UAJRMAR Marcell Ozuna 6.00 15.00
UAJRMCF Michael Conforto 6.00 15.00
UAJRMC Matt Carpenter 6.00 15.00
UAJRMCO Michael Conforto 6.00 15.00
UAJRMF Michael Fulmer 4.00 10.00
UAJRMG Marwin Gonzalez 4.00 10.00
UAJRMGO Marwin Gonzalez 4.00 10.00
UAJRMH Matt Chapman 6.00 15.00
UAJRML Matt Olson 4.00 10.00
UAJRMO Matt Olson 4.00 10.00
UAJRMOZ Marcell Ozuna 6.00 15.00
UAJRRHY Rhys Hoskins 15.00 40.00
UAJRRI Raisel Iglesias 5.00 12.00
UAJRRP Rafael Palmeiro 5.00 12.00
UAJRSD Sean Doolittle 4.00 10.00
UAJRSMO Justin Smoak 4.00 10.00
UAJRSP Stephen Piscotty 4.00 10.00
UAJRSPE Salvador Perez 10.00 25.00
UAJRSPZ Salvador Perez 10.00 25.00
UAJRTH Tommy Pham 4.00 10.00
UAJRTM Trey Mancini 5.00 12.00
UAJRTMA Trey Mancini 5.00 12.00
UAJRTP Tommy Pham 4.00 10.00
UAJRTS Travis Shaw 4.00 10.00
UAJRTY Trevor Story EXCH 6.00 15.00
UAJRWC Willson Contreras 6.00 15.00
UAJRWE Whit Merrifield 6.00 15.00
UAJRWM Whit Merrifield 6.00 15.00
UAJRYA Yonder Alonso 4.00 10.00
UAJRYGL Yasmani Grandal 4.00 10.00
UAJRZC Zack Cozart 4.00 10.00

2018 Topps Triple Threads Unity Autograph Jumbo Relics Emerald

*EMERALD: .5X TO 1.2X BASIC
STATED ODDS 1:13 HOBBY
STATED PRINT RUN 50 SER.#'d SETS
EXCHANGE DEADLINE 8/31/2020
UAJRAB Archie Bradley 5.00 12.00
UAJRAR Anthony Rendon 10.00 25.00
UAJRDS Domingo Santana 6.00 15.00
UAJREI Ender Inciarte 5.00 12.00
UAJRGR Garrett Richards 6.00 15.00
UAJRGSP George Springer 10.00 25.00
UAJRKSG Kyle Seager 5.00 12.00
UAJRPG Paul Goldschmidt 15.00 40.00
UAJRRO Roy Oswalt 6.00 15.00
UAJRTB Tim Beckham 6.00 15.00

2018 Topps Triple Threads Unity Autograph Jumbo Relics Gold

*GOLD: .6X TO 1.5X BASIC
STATED ODDS 1:22 HOBBY
STATED PRINT RUN 25 SER.#'d SETS
EXCHANGE DEADLINE 8/31/2020
UAJRAB Archie Bradley 6.00 15.00
UAJRAR Anthony Rendon 12.00 30.00
UAJRDS Domingo Santana 8.00 20.00
UAJREI Ender Inciarte 6.00 15.00
UAJRGR Garrett Richards 8.00 20.00
UAJRGSP George Springer 12.00 30.00
UAJRJV Joey Votto 25.00 60.00
UAJRKSG Kyle Seager 6.00 15.00
UAJRPG Paul Goldschmidt 20.00 50.00
UAJRRO Roy Oswalt 8.00 20.00
UAJRTB Tim Beckham 8.00 20.00

2018 Topps Triple Threads Unity Autograph Jumbo Relics Silver

*SILVER: .4X TO 1X BASIC
STATED ODDS 1:8 HOBBY
STATED PRINT RUN 75 SER.#'d SETS
EXCHANGE DEADLINE 8/31/2020
UAJRGSP George Springer 8.00 20.00
UAJRKSG Kyle Seager 4.00 10.00
UAJRPG Paul Goldschmidt 12.00 30.00

2018 Topps Triple Threads Unity Single Jumbo Relics

STATED ODDS 1:6 HOBBY
STATED PRINT RUN 36 SER.#'d SETS
*SILVER/27: .4X TO 1X BASIC
*EMERALD/18: .5X TO 1.2X BASIC
*GOLD/9: .6X TO 1.5X BASIC
ALL VERSIONS EQUALLY PRICED
SJRAB1 Andrew Benintendi 10.00 25.00
SJRAB2 Andrew Benintendi 10.00 25.00
SJRABL1 Adrian Beltre 4.00 10.00
SJRABL2 Adrian Beltre 4.00 10.00
SJRABR1 Alex Bregman 4.00 10.00
SJRABR2 Alex Bregman 4.00 10.00
SJRAC1 Aroldis Chapman 4.00 10.00
SJRAJ1 Aaron Judge 15.00 40.00
SJRAJO1 Adam Jones 3.00 8.00
SJRAJO2 Adam Jones 3.00 8.00
SJRAMC1 Andrew McCutchen 4.00 10.00
SJRAMC2 Andrew McCutchen 4.00 10.00
SJRAP1 Albert Pujols 5.00 12.00
SJRAP2 Albert Pujols 5.00 12.00
SJRAP3 Albert Pujols 5.00 12.00
SJRAPT1 Andy Pettitte 3.00 8.00
SJRARO1 Alex Rodriguez 6.00 15.00
SJRARO2 Alex Rodriguez 6.00 15.00
SJRARO3 Alex Rodriguez 6.00 15.00
SJRARU1 Addison Russell 3.00 8.00
SJRARU2 Addison Russell 3.00 8.00
SJRARU3 Addison Russell 3.00 8.00
SJRARZ1 Anthony Rizzo 6.00 15.00
SJRARZ2 Anthony Rizzo 6.00 15.00
SJRARZ3 Anthony Rizzo 6.00 15.00
SJRAW1 Adam Wainwright 3.00 8.00
SJRAW2 Adam Wainwright 3.00 8.00
SJRAW3 Adam Wainwright 3.00 8.00
SJRBB1 Byron Buxton 3.00 8.00
SJRBB2 Byron Buxton 3.00 8.00
SJRBB3 Byron Buxton 3.00 8.00
SJRBC1 Brandon Crawford 3.00 8.00
SJRBC2 Brandon Crawford 3.00 8.00
SJRBC3 Brandon Crawford 3.00 8.00
SJRBH1 Bryce Harper 6.00 15.00
SJRBL1 Barry Larkin 3.00 8.00
SJRBP1 Buster Posey 5.00 12.00
SJRBP2 Buster Posey 5.00 12.00
SJRCA1 Chris Archer 2.50 6.00
SJRCB1 Craig Biggio 3.00 8.00
SJRCC1 Carlos Correa 4.00 10.00
SJRCC2 Carlos Correa 4.00 10.00
SJRCC3 Carlos Correa 4.00 10.00
SJRCG1 Carlos Gonzalez 3.00 8.00
SJRCG2 Carlos Gonzalez 3.00 8.00
SJRCG3 Carlos Gonzalez 3.00 8.00
SJRCH1 Cole Hamels 3.00 8.00
SJRCJ1 Chipper Jones 6.00 15.00
SJRCKE1 Clayton Kershaw 8.00 20.00
SJRCKE2 Clayton Kershaw 8.00 20.00
SJRCKI1 Craig Kimbrel 3.00 8.00
SJRCKI2 Craig Kimbrel 3.00 8.00
SJRCM1 Carlos Martinez 3.00 8.00
SJRCR1 Cal Ripken Jr. 12.00 30.00
SJRCS1 Chris Sale 4.00 10.00
SJRCS2 Chris Sale 4.00 10.00
SJRCS3 Chris Sale 4.00 10.00
SJRCSE1 Corey Seager 4.00 10.00
SJRCY1 Christian Yelich 5.00 12.00
SJRCY2 Christian Yelich 5.00 12.00
SJRDG1 Didi Gregorius 3.00 8.00
SJRDJ1 Derek Jeter 20.00 50.00
SJRDM1 Don Mattingly 20.00 50.00
SJRDMU1 Daniel Murphy 3.00 8.00
SJRDO1 David Ortiz 6.00 15.00
SJRDO2 David Ortiz 6.00 15.00
SJRDO3 David Ortiz 6.00 15.00
SJRDP1 David Price 3.00 8.00
SJRDP2 David Price 3.00 8.00
SJRDP3 David Price 3.00 8.00
SJRDPE1 Dustin Pedroia 4.00 10.00
SJRDPE2 Dustin Pedroia 4.00 10.00
SJRDPE3 Dustin Pedroia 4.00 10.00
SJRDPE4 Dustin Pedroia 4.00 10.00
SJRDS1 Dansby Swanson 4.00 10.00
SJRDS2 Dansby Swanson 4.00 10.00
SJREE1 Edwin Encarnacion 4.00 10.00
SJREH1 Eric Hosmer 3.00 8.00
SJREH2 Eric Hosmer 3.00 8.00
SJREH3 Eric Hosmer 3.00 8.00
SJREL1 Evan Longoria 3.00 8.00
SJREL2 Evan Longoria 3.00 8.00
SJRFF1 Freddie Freeman 5.00 12.00
SJRFF2 Freddie Freeman 5.00 12.00
SJRFF3 Freddie Freeman 5.00 12.00
SJRFT1 Frank Thomas 10.00 25.00
SJRGP1 Gregory Polanco 3.00 8.00
SJRGP2 Gregory Polanco 3.00 8.00
SJRGS1 Gary Sanchez 4.00 10.00
SJRGS2 Gary Sanchez 4.00 10.00
SJRGS3 Gary Sanchez 4.00 10.00
SJRGSP1 George Springer 3.00 8.00
SJRGSP2 George Springer 3.00 8.00
SJRGSP3 George Springer 3.00 8.00
SJRHR1 Hanley Ramirez 3.00 8.00
SJRHR2 Hanley Ramirez 3.00 8.00
SJRHR3 Hanley Ramirez 3.00 8.00
SJRHR4 Hanley Ramirez 3.00 8.00
SJRIK1 Ian Kinsler 3.00 8.00
SJRIK2 Ian Kinsler 3.00 8.00
SJRIK3 Ian Kinsler 3.00 8.00
SJRI1 Ichiro 6.00 15.00
SJRI2 Ichiro 6.00 15.00
SJRI3 Ichiro 6.00 15.00
SJRI4 Ichiro 6.00 15.00
SJRJA1 Jake Arrieta 3.00 8.00
SJRJA2 Jake Arrieta 3.00 8.00
SJRJA3 Jake Arrieta 3.00 8.00
SJRJAL1 Jose Altuve 3.00 8.00
SJRJAL2 Jose Altuve 3.00 8.00
SJRJAL3 Jose Altuve 3.00 8.00
SJRJB1 Jackie Bradley Jr. 4.00 10.00
SJRJB2 Jackie Bradley Jr. 4.00 10.00
SJRJBZ1 Javier Baez 8.00 20.00
SJRJBZ2 Javier Baez 8.00 20.00
SJRJBZ3 Javier Baez 8.00 20.00
SJRJD1 Josh Donaldson 3.00 8.00
SJRJD2 Josh Donaldson 3.00 8.00
SJRJDE1 Jacob deGrom 5.00 12.00
SJRJDE2 Jacob deGrom 5.00 12.00
SJRJDE3 Jacob deGrom 5.00 12.00
SJRJG1 Joey Gallo 3.00 8.00
SJRJH1 Jason Heyward 3.00 8.00
SJRJH2 Jason Heyward 3.00 8.00
SJRJH3 Jason Heyward 3.00 8.00
SJRJL1 Jon Lester 3.00 8.00
SJRJL2 Jon Lester 3.00 8.00
SJRJM1 J.D. Martinez 4.00 10.00
SJRJM2 J.D. Martinez 4.00 10.00
SJRJT1 Jameson Taillon 3.00 8.00
SJRJU1 Justin Upton 3.00 8.00
SJRJU2 Justin Upton 3.00 8.00
SJRJU3 Justin Upton 3.00 8.00
SJRJU4 Justin Upton 3.00 8.00
SJRJU5 Justin Upton 3.00 8.00
SJRJV1 Justin Verlander 4.00 10.00
SJRJV2 Justin Verlander 4.00 10.00
SJRJV3 Justin Verlander 4.00 10.00
SJRJV4 Justin Verlander 4.00 10.00
SJRJV5 Justin Verlander 4.00 10.00
SJRJVO1 Joey Votto 4.00 10.00
SJRJVO2 Joey Votto 4.00 10.00
SJRJVO3 Joey Votto 4.00 10.00
SJRKB1 Kris Bryant 8.00 20.00
SJRKB2 Kris Bryant 8.00 20.00
SJRKD1 Khris Davis 4.00 10.00
SJRKM1 Kenta Maeda 3.00 8.00
SJRKM2 Kenta Maeda 3.00 8.00
SJRKS1 Kyle Seager 2.50 6.00
SJRKS2 Kyle Seager 2.50 6.00
SJRKS3 Kyle Seager 2.50 6.00
SJRLS1 Luis Severino 3.00 8.00
SJRLS2 Luis Severino 3.00 8.00
SJRMB1 Mookie Betts 8.00 20.00
SJRMB2 Mookie Betts 8.00 20.00
SJRMB3 Mookie Betts 8.00 20.00
SJRMB4 Mookie Betts 8.00 20.00
SJRMC1 Michael Conforto 3.00 8.00
SJRMC2 Michael Conforto 3.00 8.00
SJRMC3 Michael Conforto 3.00 8.00
SJRMCA1 Matt Carpenter 4.00 10.00
SJRMCA2 Matt Carpenter 4.00 10.00
SJRMCA3 Matt Carpenter 4.00 10.00
SJRMCB1 Miguel Cabrera 4.00 10.00
SJRMCB2 Miguel Cabrera 4.00 10.00
SJRMCB3 Miguel Cabrera 4.00 10.00
SJRMCB4 Miguel Cabrera 4.00 10.00
SJRMCB5 Miguel Cabrera 4.00 10.00
SJRMF1 Michael Fulmer 2.50 6.00
SJRMF2 Michael Fulmer 2.50 6.00
SJRMM1 Mark McGwire 12.00 30.00
SJRMM2 Mark McGwire 12.00 30.00
SJRMMC1 Manny Machado 4.00 10.00
SJRMMC2 Manny Machado 4.00 10.00
SJRMO1 Marcell Ozuna 4.00 10.00
SJRMO2 Marcell Ozuna 4.00 10.00
SJRMO3 Marcell Ozuna 4.00 10.00
SJRMOL1 Matt Olson 2.50 6.00
SJRMP1 Mike Piazza 6.00 15.00
SJRMS1 Max Scherzer 4.00 10.00
SJRMS2 Max Scherzer 4.00 10.00
SJRMS3 Max Scherzer 4.00 10.00
SJRMSA1 Miguel Sano 3.00 8.00
SJRMSA2 Miguel Sano 3.00 8.00
SJRMSA3 Miguel Sano 3.00 8.00
SJRMST1 Marcus Stroman 3.00 8.00
SJRMST2 Marcus Stroman 3.00 8.00
SJRMT1 Masahiro Tanaka 3.00 8.00
SJRMT2 Masahiro Tanaka 3.00 8.00
SJRMT3 Masahiro Tanaka 3.00 8.00
SJRMTR1 Mike Trout 25.00 60.00
SJRNC1 Nelson Cruz 4.00 10.00
SJRNC2 Nelson Cruz 4.00 10.00
SJRNS1 Noah Syndergaard 3.00 8.00
SJRNS2 Noah Syndergaard 3.00 8.00
SJRNS3 Noah Syndergaard 3.00 8.00
SJRPG1 Paul Goldschmidt 4.00 10.00
SJRPG2 Paul Goldschmidt 4.00 10.00
SJRPG3 Paul Goldschmidt 4.00 10.00
SJRPM1 Pedro Martinez 3.00 8.00
SJRRA1 Roberto Alomar 8.00 20.00
SJRRB1 Ryan Braun 3.00 8.00
SJRRB2 Ryan Braun 3.00 8.00
SJRRB3 Ryan Braun 3.00 8.00
SJRRC1 Roger Clemens 5.00 12.00
SJRRD1 Rafael Devers 8.00 20.00
SJRRH1 Rhys Hoskins 5.00 12.00
SJRRH2 Rhys Hoskins 5.00 12.00
SJRRO1 Rougned Odor 3.00 8.00
SJRRZ1 Ryan Zimmerman 3.00 8.00
SJRRZ2 Ryan Zimmerman 3.00 8.00
SJRSM1 Starling Marte 3.00 8.00
SJRSM2 Starling Marte 3.00 8.00
SJRSM3 Starling Marte 3.00 8.00
SJRSP1 Salvador Perez 3.00 8.00
SJRSP2 Salvador Perez 3.00 8.00
SJRSS1 Stephen Strasburg 4.00 10.00
SJRSS2 Stephen Strasburg 4.00 10.00
SJRSS3 Stephen Strasburg 4.00 10.00
SJRSS4 Stephen Strasburg 4.00 10.00
SJRTM1 Trey Mancini 3.00 8.00
SJRTM2 Trey Mancini 3.00 8.00
SJRTM3 Trey Mancini 3.00 8.00
SJRTS1 Trevor Story 4.00 10.00
SJRTS2 Trevor Story 4.00 10.00
SJRTS3 Trevor Story 4.00 10.00
SJRTTU1 Troy Tulowitzki 4.00 10.00
SJRVM1 Victor Martinez 3.00 8.00
SJRVM2 Victor Martinez 3.00 8.00
SJRWB1 Wade Boggs 10.00 25.00
SJRWC1 Willson Contreras 4.00 10.00
SJRWC2 Willson Contreras 4.00 10.00
SJRWC3 Willson Contreras 4.00 10.00
SJRWM1 Wil Myers 2.50 6.00
SJRWM2 Wil Myers 2.50 6.00
SJRWM3 Wil Myers 2.50 6.00
SJRXB1 Xander Bogaerts 4.00 10.00
SJRXB2 Xander Bogaerts 4.00 10.00
SJRXB3 Xander Bogaerts 4.00 10.00
SJRYC1 Yoenis Cespedes 4.00 10.00
SJRYC2 Yoenis Cespedes 4.00 10.00
SJRYC3 Yoenis Cespedes 4.00 10.00
SJRYC4 Yoenis Cespedes 4.00 10.00
SJRYG1 Yuli Gurriel 3.00 8.00
SJRYG2 Yuli Gurriel 3.00 8.00
SJRYM1 Yadier Molina 6.00 15.00
SJRYM2 Yadier Molina 6.00 15.00
SJRYM3 Yadier Molina 6.00 15.00

2019 Topps Triple Threads

JSY AU RC ODDS 1:XX MINI BOX
JSY AU RC PRINT RUN 99 SER.#'d SETS
JSY AU ODDS 1:XX MINI BOX
JSY AU PRINT RUN 99 SER.#'d SETS
EXCHANGE DEADLINE 8/31/2020
1-100 PLATE ODDS 1:XXX MINI BOX
JSY AU PLATE ODDS 1:XXX MINI BOX
PLATE PRINT RUN 1 SET PER COLOR
BLACK-CYAN-MAGENTA-YELLOW ISSUED
NO PLATE PRICING DUE TO SCARCITY
1 Noah Syndergaard .50 1.25
2 Bryce Harper 1.00 2.50
3 Todd Helton .50 1.25
4 Clayton Kershaw 1.25 3.00
5 Randy Johnson .60 1.50
6 Alex Gordon .50 1.25
7 Trevor Story .60 1.50
8 Jose Berrios .50 1.25
9 Jose Abreu .60 1.50
10 Jose Altuve .50 1.25
11 Roy Halladay .50 1.25
12 Roberto Alomar .50 1.25
13 Christian Yelich .75 2.00
14 Khris Davis .60 1.50
15 Andrew Benintendi .60 1.50
16 George Springer .50 1.25
17 Cody Bellinger 1.25 3.00
18 Tom Seaver .50 1.25
19 Blake Snell .50 1.25
20 Tony Gwynn .60 1.50
21 Gerrit Cole .60 1.50
22 Cal Ripken Jr. 2.00 5.00
23 Nolan Ryan 2.00 5.00
24 Francisco Lindor .60 1.50
25 George Brett 1.25 3.00
26 Kris Bryant .75 2.00
27 Trevor Bauer .60 1.50
28 Stephen Strasburg .60 1.50
29 Ken Griffey Jr. 1.25 3.00
30 Robin Yount .60 1.50
31 Derek Jeter 1.50 4.00
32 Don Mattingly 1.25 3.00
33 Ronald Acuna Jr. 3.00 8.00
34 Max Scherzer .60 1.50
35 Manny Machado .60 1.50
36 Willie Stargell .50 1.25
37 Ryne Sandberg 1.25 3.00
38 Josh Hader .40 1.00
39 Frank Thomas .60 1.50
40 Jim Thome .50 1.25
41 Ichiro Suzuki .75 2.00
42 Chipper Jones .60 1.50
43 Al Kaline .60 1.50
44 Trey Mancini .50 1.25
45 Aaron Nola .50 1.25
46 Ted Williams 1.25 3.00
47 Mark McGwire 1.00 2.50
48 Sandy Koufax 1.25 3.00
49 Albert Pujols .75 2.00
50 Jackie Robinson .60 1.50
51 Rhys Hoskins .75 2.00
52 Roberto Clemente 1.50 4.00
53 Yadier Molina .60 1.50
54 Zack Greinke .50 1.25
55 Andres Galarraga .50 1.25
56 Alex Bregman .60 1.50
57 Babe Ruth 1.50 4.00
58 Javier Baez .75 2.00
59 Mariano Rivera .75 2.00
60 Josh Bell .50 1.25
61 Jim Palmer .50 1.25
62 Aaron Judge 1.50 4.00
63 Barry Larkin .50 1.25
64 Buster Posey .75 2.00
65 Jose Ramirez .50 1.25
66 Justin Verlander .60 1.50
67 Yoan Moncada .60 1.50
68 Eddie Rosario .50 1.25
69 Wade Boggs .50 1.25
70 Anthony Rizzo 1.00 2.50
71 Roger Clemens .75 2.00
72 Rafael Devers .75 2.00
73 Mike Trout 3.00 8.00
74 John Smoltz .60 1.50
75 Hunter Dozier .40 1.00
76 Hank Aaron 1.25 3.00
77 Mike Piazza .60 1.50
78 Byron Buxton .50 1.25
79 Joey Votto .60 1.50
80 Nolan Arenado .75 2.00
81 Paul Goldschmidt .60 1.50
82 Willie McCovey .50 1.25
83 Ozzie Smith .75 2.00
84 J.D. Martinez .60 1.50
85 Gleyber Torres 1.25 3.00
86 Mookie Betts 1.00 2.50
87 Shohei Ohtani .75 2.00
88 Reggie Jackson .50 1.25
89 Vladimir Guerrero .50 1.25
90 Johnny Bench .60 1.50
91 Miguel Cabrera .60 1.50
92 Pedro Martinez .50 1.25
93 Carlos Correa .60 1.50
94 Ivan Rodriguez .50 1.25
95 Willie Mays 1.25 3.00
96 Juan Soto 2.00 5.00
97 David Ortiz .60 1.50
98 Michael Conforto .50 1.25
99 Jacob deGrom .60 1.50
100 Rickey Henderson .60 1.50
RFPARAG Aramis Garcia JSY AU RC 3.00 8.00
RFPARBK Brad Keller JSY AU 3.00 8.00
RFPARBN Brandon Nimmo JSY AU 4.00 10.00
RFPARCA Chance Adams JSY AU RC 3.00 8.00
RFPARCB Corbin Burnes JSY AU RC 5.00 12.00
RFPARCMU Cedric Mullins JSY AU RC 5.00 12.00
RFPARCS Chris Shaw JSY AU RC 5.00 12.00
RFPARCST C.Stewart JSY AU RC 6.00 15.00
RFPARDB David Bote JSY AU 8.00 20.00
RFPARDC Dylan Cozens JSY AU 3.00 8.00
RFPARDH Dakota Hudson JSY AU RC 4.00 10.00
RFPARDJ Danny Jansen JSY AU RC 3.00 8.00
RFPARDP Daniel Ponce de Leon JSY AU RC 5.00 12.00
RFPARDR Dereck Rodriguez JSY AU 3.00 8.00
RFPARFT F.Tatis Jr. JSY AU RC 150.00 400.00
RFPARGT G.Torres JSY AU EXCH 40.00 100.00
RFPARGU Gio Urshela JSY AU EXCH 20.00 50.00
RFPARIK Isiah Kiner-Falefa JSY AU 3.00 8.00
RFPARJA Jesus Aguilar JSY AU 3.00 8.00
RFPARJC Johan Camargo JSY AU 6.00 15.00
RFPARJSO Juan Soto JSY AU 40.00 100.00
RFPARKA Kolby Allard JSY AU RC 5.00 12.00
RFPARKH Hiura JSY AU RC EXCH 40.00 100.00
RFPARKK Kevin Kramer JSY AU RC 4.00 10.00
RFPARKW Kyle Wright JSY AU RC 5.00 12.00
RFPARLU Luis Urias JSY AU RC 10.00 25.00
RFPARMA Miguel Andujar JSY AU 15.00 40.00
RFPARMK M.Kopech JSY AU RC 12.00 30.00
RFPARMM Miles Mikolas JSY AU 5.00 12.00
RFPARNC Nick Ciuffo JSY AU RC 3.00 8.00
RFPAROA Ozzie Albies JSY AU 10.00 25.00
RFPARPA Pete Alonso JSY AU RC 60.00 150.00
RFPARRB Ryan Borucki JSY AU RC 3.00 8.00
RFPARRD Rafael Devers JSY AU 15.00 40.00
RFPARRO Ryan O'Hearn JSY AU 3.00 8.00
RFPARRT Rowdy Tellez JSY AU RC 6.00 15.00
RFPARRY Ryan Yarbrough JSY AU 3.00 8.00
RFPARSK Scott Kingery JSY AU 10.00 25.00
RFPARTO Tyler O'Neill JSY AU 4.00 10.00
RFPARTT Touki Toussaint JSY AU RC 4.00 10.00
RFPARVG Guerrero Jr. JSY AU RC 60.00 150.00
RFPARWA Willy Adames JSY AU 3.00 8.00
RFPARWAS W.Astudillo JSY AU RC 6.00 15.00
RFPARYK Yusei Kikuchi JSY AU RC 8.00 20.00

2019 Topps Triple Threads Amber

*AMBER VET: .75X TO 2X BASIC
STATED ODDS 1:XX MINI BOX
STATED PRINT RUN 199 SER.#'d SETS

2019 Topps Triple Threads Amethyst

*AMETHYST VET: .6X TO 1.5X BASIC
*AMETHYST JSY AU: .4X TO 1X BASIC RC
STATED ODDS 1:XX MINI BOX
JSY AU ODDS 1:XX MINI BOX
1-100 PRINT RUN 299 SER.#'d SETS
JSY AU PRINT RUN 75 SER.#'d SETS
EXCHANGE DEADLINE 8/31/2021

2019 Topps Triple Threads Citrine

TRINE VET: 1X TO 2.5X BASIC
ATED ODDS 1:XX MINI BOX
ATED PRINT RUN 75 SER.#'d SETS

2019 Topps Triple Threads Emerald

MERALD VET: .6X TO 1.5X BASIC
MERALD JSY AU: .4X TO 1X BASIC RC
100 ODDS 1:XX MINI BOX
Y AU ODDS 1:XX MINI BOX
100 PRINT RUN 259 SER.#'d SETS
Y AU PRINT RUN 50 SER.#'d SETS
CHANGE DEADLINE 8/31/2021

2019 Topps Triple Threads Gold

OLD VET: 1X TO 2.5X BASIC
ATED ODDS 1:XX MINI BOX
ATED PRINT RUN 99 SER.#'d SETS

019 Topps Triple Threads Onyx

ONYX VET: 1.5X TO 4X BASIC
ONYX JSY AU: .5X TO 1.2X BASIC RC
100 ODDS 1:XX MINI BOX
SY AU ODDS 1:XX MINI BOX
100 PRINT RUN 50 SER.#'d SETS
SY AU PRINT RUN 35 SER.#'d SETS
CHANGE DEADLINE 8/31/2021
FPARSO Shohei Ohtani JSY AU 100.00 250.00

2019 Topps Triple Threads Sapphire

SAPPHIRE VET: 2.5X TO 6X BASIC
TATED ODDS 1:XX MINI BOX
TATED PRINT RUN 25 SER.#'d SETS
9 Ken Griffey Jr. 20.00 50.00
1 Derek Jeter 25.00 60.00

2019 Topps Triple Threads Autograph Jumbo Relics

STATED ODDS 1:XX HOBBY
STATED PRINT RUN 99 SER.#'d SETS
EXCHANGE DEADLINE 8/31/2021
AUJRABE Andrew Benintendi 10.00 25.00
AUJRAG Andres Galarraga 5.00 12.00
AUJRAM Austin Meadows 5.00 12.00
AUJRAN Aaron Nola 8.00 20.00
AUJRAR Amed Rosario 5.00 12.00
AUJRBB Byron Buxton 8.00 20.00
AUJRBN Brandon Nimmo 5.00 12.00
AUJRBT Blake Treinen 4.00 10.00
AUJRCD Corey Dickerson 4.00 10.00
AUJRCF Clint Frazier 8.00 20.00
AUJRCK Corey Kluber 8.00 20.00
AUJRCM Charlie Morton 6.00 15.00
AUJRCSA Chris Sale 8.00 20.00
AUJRCV Christian Vazquez 5.00 12.00
AUJRCY Christian Yelich 30.00 80.00
AUJRDB David Bote 6.00 15.00
AUJRDC Dylan Cozens 4.00 10.00
AUJRDE Dennis Eckersley 12.00 30.00
AUJRDPR David Price 8.00 20.00
AUJRDR Dereck Rodriguez 4.00 10.00
AUJRET Eric Thames 4.00 10.00
AUJRFL Francisco Lindor 12.00 30.00
AUJRFV Felipe Vazquez 4.00 10.00
AUJRIH Ian Happ 20.00 50.00
AUJRJA Jesus Aguilar 4.00 10.00
AUJRJB Jose Berrios 5.00 12.00
AUJRJC Jose Canseco 6.00 15.00
AUJRJD Johnny Damon 10.00 25.00
AUJRJDM J.D. Martinez 10.00 25.00
AUJRJH Josh Hader 4.00 10.00
AUJRJHI Jordan Hicks 5.00 12.00
AUJRJJ Jeremy Jeffress 4.00 10.00
AUJRJM Jose Martinez 4.00 10.00
AUJRJR Jose Ramirez 5.00 12.00
AUJRJS Jean Segura 6.00 15.00
AUJRJT Jim Thome 20.00 50.00
AUJRKF Kyle Freeland 5.00 12.00
AUJRKS Kyle Schwarber 6.00 15.00
AUJRKW Kerry Wood 8.00 20.00
AUJRLG Luis Gonzalez 4.00 10.00
AUJRLGU Lourdes Gurriel Jr. 5.00 12.00
AUJRLM Lance McCullers Jr. 4.00 10.00
AUJRLS Luis Severino 8.00 20.00
AUJRLV Luke Voit 20.00 50.00
AUJRMA Miguel Andujar 6.00 15.00
AUJRMC Matt Chapman 6.00 15.00
AUJRMCL Mike Clevinger 5.00 12.00
AUJRMF Mike Foltynewicz 6.00 15.00
AUJRMH Mitch Haniger 5.00 12.00
AUJRMK Max Kepler 5.00 12.00
AUJRMMI Miles Mikolas 6.00 15.00
AUJRMO Matt Olson 4.00 10.00
AUJRNW Nick Williams 4.00 10.00
AUJROA Ozzie Albies 10.00 25.00
AUJRPC Patrick Corbin 6.00 15.00
AUJRPD Paul DeJong 6.00 15.00
AUJRRA Ronald Acuna Jr. 50.00 120.00
AUJRRD Rafael Devers 15.00 40.00
AUJRRH Rhys Hoskins 10.00 25.00
AUJRRI Raisel Iglesias 4.00 10.00
AUJRSD Sean Doolittle 6.00 15.00
AUJRSG Scooter Gennett 8.00 20.00
AUJRSK Scott Kingery 6.00 15.00
AUJRSMA Steven Matz 5.00 12.00
AUJRTA Tim Anderson 6.00 15.00
AUJRTB Trevor Bauer 6.00 15.00
AUJRTO Tyler O'Neill 5.00 12.00
AUJRTP Tommy Pham 4.00 10.00
AUJRTS Travis Shaw 4.00 10.00
AUJRWA Willy Adames 4.00 10.00
AUJRWM Whit Merrifield 6.00 15.00
AUJRXB Xander Bogaerts 15.00 40.00
AUJRYG Yuli Gurriel 8.00 20.00
AUJRZW Zack Wheeler 5.00 12.00

2019 Topps Triple Threads Autograph Jumbo Relics Amethyst

*AMETHYST: .4X TO 1X BASIC
STATED ODDS 1:XX HOBBY
STATED PRINT RUN 75 SER.#'d SETS
EXCHANGE DEADLINE 8/31/2021
AUJRCS CC Sabathia 20.00 50.00
AUJRJL Jake Lamb 5.00 12.00

2019 Topps Triple Threads Autograph Jumbo Relics Emerald

*EMERALD: .5X TO 1.2X BASIC
STATED ODDS 1:XX HOBBY
STATED PRINT RUN 50 SER.#'d SETS
EXCHANGE DEADLINE 8/31/2021
AUJRCS CC Sabathia 25.00 60.00
AUJRFB Franklin Barreto 5.00 12.00
AUJRJL Jake Lamb 6.00 15.00

2019 Topps Triple Threads Autograph Jumbo Relics Gold

*GOLD: .6X TO 1.5X BASIC
STATED ODDS 1:XX HOBBY
STATED PRINT RUN 25 SER.#'d SETS
EXCHANGE DEADLINE 8/31/2021
AUJRCS CC Sabathia 30.00 80.00
AUJRFB Franklin Barreto 6.00 15.00
AUJRJL Jake Lamb 8.00 20.00

2019 Topps Triple Threads Autograph Relic Combos

STATED ODDS 1:XX HOBBY
STATED PRINT RUN 36 SER.#'d SETS
EXCHANGE DEADLINE 8/31/2021
PRINTING PLATE ODDS 1:XXX HOBBY
PLATE PRINT RUN 1 SET PER COLOR
BLACK-CYAN-MAGENTA-YELLOW ISSUED
NO PLATE PRICING DUE TO SCARCITY
*AMETHYST/27: .4X TO 1X BASIC
ARCBRB Rosario/Buxton/Berrios 20.00 50.00
ARCBRS Bryant/Rizzo/Schwrbr 60.00 150.00
ARCCHS Cbrra/Stwrt/Harrison 30.00 80.00
ARCDSW Syndrgrd/deGrom/Whlr 40.00 100.00
ARCFAA Albies/Freeman/Acuna 100.00 250.00
ARCHKS Haniger/Seager/Kikuchi 15.00 40.00
ARCHTG Hiura/Tatis/Guerrero 150.00 400.00
ARCLKR Lindor/Ramirez/Kluber 30.00 80.00
ARCMGC Mlna/Crpntr/Gldschmdt 60.00 150.00
ARCMTU Urias/Tatis/Machado 100.00 250.00
ARCPDB Dvrs/Pdra/Bgrts EXCH 40.00 100.00
ARCPMC Molina/Contreras/Perez 40.00 100.00
ARCPRB IRod/Bltre/Plmro 30.00 80.00
ARCRNA Nimmo/Rosario/Alonso 60.00 150.00
ARCSAP Adames/Snell/Mdws 25.00 60.00
ARCSJJ Jones/Jones/Smoltz 60.00 150.00
ARCSMP Price/Sale/Martinez 25.00 60.00
ARCSSR Robles/Soto/Scherzer 75.00 200.00
ARCSST Svrno/Sbtha/Sanchez 40.00 100.00
ARCTOP Pujols/Ohtani/Trout
ARCYHA Yelich/Aguilar/Hader 30.00 80.00

2019 Topps Triple Threads Autograph Relic Combos Emerald

*EMERALD: .4X TO 1X BASIC
STATED ODDS 1:XXX HOBBY
STATED PRINT RUN 18 SER.#'d SETS
EXCHANGE DEADLINE 8/31/2021
ARCHHN Hskns/Nola/Hrpr EXCH 150.00 400.00
ARCIOK Kikuchi/Ichiro/Ohtani 200.00 500.00

2019 Topps Triple Threads Autograph Relics

STATED ODDS 1:XX HOBBY
STATED PRINT RUN 18 SER.#'d SETS
EXCHANGE DEADLINE 8/31/2021
*GOLD/9: .5X TO 1.2X BASIC
SOME GOLD NOT PRICED DUE TO SCARCITY
ALL VERSIONS EQUALLY PRICED
TTARAB1 Adrian Beltre 25.00 60.00
TTARAB2 Adrian Beltre 25.00 60.00
TTARABE1 Andrew Benintendi 20.00 50.00
TTARABE2 Andrew Benintendi 20.00 50.00
TTARABE3 Andrew Benintendi 20.00 50.00
TTARABE4 Andrew Benintendi 20.00 50.00
TTARAJ1 Andruw Jones 12.00 30.00
TTARAJ2 Andruw Jones 12.00 30.00
TTARAJ3 Andruw Jones 12.00 30.00
TTARAJ4 Andruw Jones 12.00 30.00
TTARAJ5 Andruw Jones 12.00 30.00
TTARAJU1 Aaron Judge 75.00 200.00
TTARALR1 Alex Rodriguez 60.00 150.00
TTARAM1 Austin Meadows 10.00 25.00
TTARAM2 Austin Meadows 10.00 25.00
TTARAM3 Austin Meadows 10.00 25.00
TTARAM4 Austin Meadows 10.00 25.00
TTARAM5 Austin Meadows 10.00 25.00
TTARAP1 Andy Pettitte 25.00 60.00
TTARAP2 Andy Pettitte 25.00 60.00
TTARAR1 Anthony Rizzo 15.00 40.00
TTARAR2 Anthony Rizzo 15.00 40.00
TTARARO1 Amed Rosario 8.00 20.00
TTARARO2 Amed Rosario 8.00 20.00
TTARARO3 Amed Rosario 8.00 20.00
TTARARO4 Amed Rosario 8.00 20.00
TTARARO5 Amed Rosario 8.00 20.00
TTARBB1 Bert Blyleven 8.00 20.00
TTARBB2 Bert Blyleven 8.00 20.00
TTARBBU1 Byron Buxton 10.00 25.00
TTARBBU2 Byron Buxton 10.00 25.00
TTARBBU3 Byron Buxton 10.00 25.00
TTARBBU4 Byron Buxton 10.00 25.00
TTARBBU5 Byron Buxton 10.00 25.00
TTARBP1 Buster Posey 40.00 100.00
TTARBS1 Blake Snell 8.00 20.00
TTARBS2 Blake Snell 8.00 20.00
TTARBS3 Blake Snell 8.00 20.00
TTARBS4 Blake Snell 8.00 20.00
TTARBS5 Blake Snell 8.00 20.00
TTARCJ1 Chipper Jones 50.00 120.00
TTARCJ2 Chipper Jones 50.00 120.00
TTARCK1 Corey Kluber 10.00 25.00
TTARCK2 Corey Kluber 10.00 25.00
TTARCKE1 Clayton Kershaw 40.00 100.00
TTARCKE2 Clayton Kershaw 40.00 100.00
TTARCS1 Chris Sale 12.00 30.00
TTARCS2 Chris Sale 12.00 30.00
TTARCS3 Chris Sale 12.00 30.00
TTARCS4 Chris Sale 12.00 30.00
TTARCS5 Chris Sale 12.00 30.00
TTARCSA1 CC Sabathia 30.00 80.00
TTARCSA2 CC Sabathia 30.00 80.00
TTARCSA3 CC Sabathia 30.00 80.00
TTARCSA4 CC Sabathia 30.00 80.00
TTARCSA5 CC Sabathia 30.00 80.00
TTARDC1 David Cone 15.00 40.00
TTARDC2 David Cone 15.00 40.00
TTARDC3 David Cone 15.00 40.00
TTARDC4 David Cone 15.00 40.00
TTARDC5 David Cone 15.00 40.00
TTARDG1 Didi Gregorius 10.00 25.00
TTARDG2 Didi Gregorius 10.00 25.00
TTARDG3 Didi Gregorius 10.00 25.00
TTARDO1 David Ortiz 30.00 80.00
TTARDO2 David Ortiz 30.00 80.00
TTARDP1 Dustin Pedroia 20.00 50.00
TTARDP2 Dustin Pedroia 20.00 50.00
TTARDP3 Dustin Pedroia 20.00 50.00
TTARDPR1 David Price 8.00 20.00
TTARDPR2 David Price 8.00 20.00
TTARDPR3 David Price 8.00 20.00
TTARDS1 Dansby Swanson 15.00 40.00
TTARDS2 Dansby Swanson 15.00 40.00
TTARDS3 Dansby Swanson 15.00 40.00
TTAREM1 Edgar Martinez 20.00 50.00
TTAREM2 Edgar Martinez 20.00 50.00
TTAREM3 Edgar Martinez 20.00 50.00
TTAREM4 Edgar Martinez 20.00 50.00
TTARER1 Eddie Rosario 10.00 25.00
TTARER2 Eddie Rosario 10.00 25.00
TTARER3 Eddie Rosario 10.00 25.00
TTARER4 Eddie Rosario 10.00 25.00
TTARER5 Eddie Rosario 10.00 25.00
TTARFF1 Freddie Freeman 20.00 50.00
TTARFL1 Francisco Lindor 25.00 60.00
TTARFL2 Francisco Lindor 25.00 60.00
TTARFL3 Francisco Lindor 25.00 60.00
TTARFL4 Francisco Lindor 25.00 60.00
TTARFL5 Francisco Lindor 25.00 60.00
TTARFV1 Felipe Vazquez 5.00 12.00
TTARFV2 Felipe Vazquez 5.00 12.00
TTARFV3 Felipe Vazquez 5.00 12.00
TTARFV4 Felipe Vazquez 5.00 12.00
TTARGC1 Gerrit Cole 25.00 60.00
TTARGC2 Gerrit Cole 25.00 60.00
TTARGC3 Gerrit Cole 25.00 60.00
TTARGC4 Gerrit Cole 25.00 60.00
TTARGC5 Gerrit Cole 25.00 60.00
TTARGS1 George Springer 20.00 50.00
TTARGS2 George Springer 20.00 50.00
TTARGS3 George Springer 20.00 50.00
TTARI Ichiro Suzuki 125.00 300.00
TTARIR1 Ivan Rodriguez 15.00 40.00
TTARIR2 Ivan Rodriguez 15.00 40.00
TTARIR3 Ivan Rodriguez 15.00 40.00
TTARJAL1 Jose Altuve 25.00 60.00
TTARJAL2 Jose Altuve 25.00 60.00
TTARJAL3 Jose Altuve 25.00 60.00
TTARJB1 Jose Berrios 12.00 30.00
TTARJB2 Jose Berrios 12.00 30.00
TTARJB3 Jose Berrios 12.00 30.00
TTARJB4 Jose Berrios 12.00 30.00
TTARJD1 Jacob deGrom 15.00 40.00
TTARJD2 Jacob deGrom 15.00 40.00
TTARJD3 Jacob deGrom 15.00 40.00
TTARJD4 Jacob deGrom 15.00 40.00
TTARJD5 Jacob deGrom 15.00 40.00
TTARJDA1 Johnny Damon 10.00 25.00
TTARJDA2 Johnny Damon 10.00 25.00
TTARJDA3 Johnny Damon 10.00 25.00
TTARJDA4 Johnny Damon 10.00 25.00
TTARJH1 Josh Hader 10.00 25.00
TTARJH2 Josh Hader 10.00 25.00
TTARJH3 Josh Hader 10.00 25.00
TTARJH4 Josh Hader 10.00 25.00
TTARJH5 Josh Hader 10.00 25.00
TTARJM1 J.D. Martinez 10.00 25.00
TTARJM2 J.D. Martinez 10.00 25.00
TTARJM3 J.D. Martinez 10.00 25.00
TTARJM4 J.D. Martinez 10.00 25.00
TTARJM5 J.D. Martinez 10.00 25.00
TTARJP1 Joc Pederson 8.00 20.00
TTARJP2 Joc Pederson 8.00 20.00
TTARJP3 Joc Pederson 8.00 20.00
TTARJR1 Jose Ramirez 6.00 15.00
TTARJR2 Jose Ramirez 6.00 15.00
TTARJR3 Jose Ramirez 6.00 15.00
TTARJR4 Jose Ramirez 6.00 15.00
TTARJSM1 John Smoltz 20.00 50.00
TTARJSO1 Juan Soto 50.00 120.00
TTARJSO2 Juan Soto 50.00 120.00
TTARJSO3 Juan Soto 50.00 120.00
TTARJV1 Joey Votto 30.00 80.00
TTARJV2 Joey Votto 30.00 80.00
TTARKB1 Kris Bryant 40.00 100.00
TTARKG1 Ken Griffey Jr. 100.00 250.00
TTARKS1 Kyle Schwarber 10.00 25.00
TTARKS2 Kyle Schwarber 10.00 25.00
TTARKS3 Kyle Schwarber 10.00 25.00
TTARKS4 Kyle Schwarber 10.00 25.00
TTARKS5 Kyle Schwarber 10.00 25.00
TTARKSE1 Kyle Seager 5.00 12.00
TTARKSE2 Kyle Seager 5.00 12.00
TTARKSE3 Kyle Seager 5.00 12.00
TTARKSE4 Kyle Seager 5.00 12.00
TTARKSE5 Kyle Seager 5.00 12.00
TTARLM1 Lance McCullers Jr. 8.00 20.00
TTARLM2 Lance McCullers Jr. 8.00 20.00
TTARLM3 Lance McCullers Jr. 8.00 20.00
TTARLM4 Lance McCullers Jr. 8.00 20.00
TTARLS1 Luis Severino 10.00 25.00
TTARLS2 Luis Severino 10.00 25.00
TTARLS3 Luis Severino 10.00 25.00
TTARLS4 Luis Severino 10.00 25.00
TTARMA1 Miguel Andujar 12.00 30.00
TTARMA2 Miguel Andujar 12.00 30.00
TTARMA3 Miguel Andujar 12.00 30.00
TTARMC1 Miguel Cabrera 25.00 60.00
TTARMC2 Miguel Cabrera 25.00 60.00
TTARMCA1 Matt Carpenter 10.00 25.00
TTARMCA2 Matt Carpenter 10.00 25.00
TTARMCA3 Matt Carpenter 10.00 2.00
TTARMM1 Manny Machado 20.00 50.00
TTARMM2 Manny Machado 20.00 50.00
TTARMM3 Manny Machado 20.00 50.00
TTARMMU1 Max Muncy 6.00 15.00
TTARMMU2 Max Muncy 6.00 15.00
TTARMMU3 Max Muncy 6.00 15.00
TTARMO1 Matt Olson 10.00 25.00
TTARMO2 Matt Olson 10.00 25.00
TTARMO3 Matt Olson 10.00 25.00
TTARMO4 Matt Olson 10.00 25.00
TTARMO5 Matt Olson 10.00 25.00
TTARMS1 Max Scherzer 30.00 80.00
TTARMS2 Max Scherzer 30.00 80.00
TTARMS3 Max Scherzer 30.00 80.00
TTARMS4 Max Scherzer 30.00 80.00
TTARMT1 Mike Trout 200.00 500.00
TTARMT2 Mike Trout 200.00 500.00
TTARNA1 Nolan Arenado 40.00 100.00
TTARNA2 Nolan Arenado 40.00 100.00
TTARNA3 Nolan Arenado 40.00 100.00
TTARNS1 Noah Syndergaard 12.00 30.00
TTARNS2 Noah Syndergaard 12.00 30.00
TTARNS3 Noah Syndergaard 12.00 30.00
TTARNS4 Noah Syndergaard 12.00 30.00
TTARNS5 Noah Syndergaard 12.00 30.00
TTAROA1 Ozzie Albies 15.00 40.00
TTAROA2 Ozzie Albies 15.00 40.00
TTAROA3 Ozzie Albies 15.00 40.00
TTAROA4 Ozzie Albies 15.00 40.00
TTAROA5 Ozzie Albies 15.00 40.00
TTARPG1 Paul Goldschmidt 20.00 50.00
TTARPG2 Paul Goldschmidt 20.00 50.00
TTARPG3 Paul Goldschmidt 20.00 50.00
TTARPG4 Paul Goldschmidt 20.00 50.00
TTARRA1 Ronald Acuna Jr. 60.00 150.00
TTARRA2 Ronald Acuna Jr. 60.00 150.00
TTARRA3 Ronald Acuna Jr. 60.00 150.00
TTARRA4 Ronald Acuna Jr. 60.00 150.00
TTARRD1 Rafael Devers 20.00 50.00
TTARRD2 Rafael Devers 20.00 50.00
TTARRD3 Rafael Devers 20.00 50.00
TTARRD4 Rafael Devers 20.00 50.00
TTARRH1 Rhys Hoskins 25.00 60.00
TTARRH2 Rhys Hoskins 25.00 60.00
TTARRH3 Rhys Hoskins 25.00 60.00
TTARRH4 Rhys Hoskins 25.00 60.00
TTARRHE Rickey Henderson 60.00 150.00
TTARSC1 Shin-Soo Choo 30.00 80.00
TTARSC2 Shin-Soo Choo 30.00 80.00
TTARSC3 Shin-Soo Choo 30.00 80.00
TTARSC4 Shin-Soo Choo 30.00 80.00
TTARSG1 Scooter Gennett 10.00 25.00
TTARSG2 Scooter Gennett 10.00 25.00
TTARSG3 Scooter Gennett 10.00 25.00
TTARSG4 Scooter Gennett 10.00 25.00
TTARSG5 Scooter Gennett 10.00 25.00
TTARSO1 Shohei Ohtani 75.00 200.00
TTARSO2 Shohei Ohtani 75.00 200.00
TTARSP1 Salvador Perez 12.00 30.00
TTARSP2 Salvador Perez 12.00 30.00
TTARSP3 Salvador Perez 12.00 30.00
TTARSP4 Salvador Perez 12.00 30.00
TTARSPI1 Stephen Piscotty 5.00 12.00
TTARSPI2 Stephen Piscotty 5.00 12.00
TTARSPI3 Stephen Piscotty 5.00 12.00
TTARSPI4 Stephen Piscotty 5.00 12.00
TTARSS1 Sammy Sosa 75.00 200.00
TTARTA1 Tim Anderson 8.00 20.00
TTARTA2 Tim Anderson 8.00 20.00
TTARTA3 Tim Anderson 8.00 20.00
TTARTA4 Tim Anderson 8.00 20.00
TTARTA5 Tim Anderson 8.00 20.00
TTARTB1 Trevor Bauer 8.00 20.00
TTARTB2 Trevor Bauer 8.00 20.00
TTARTB3 Trevor Bauer 8.00 20.00
TTARTB4 Trevor Bauer 8.00 20.00
TTARTG1 Tom Glavine 15.00 40.00
TTARTG2 Tom Glavine 15.00 40.00
TTARTG3 Tom Glavine 15.00 40.00
TTARTH1 Todd Helton 12.00 30.00
TTARTH2 Todd Helton 12.00 30.00
TTARTH3 Todd Helton 12.00 30.00
TTARTHU1 Torii Hunter 8.00 20.00
TTARTHU2 Torii Hunter 8.00 20.00
TTARTHU3 Torii Hunter 8.00 20.00
TTARTHU4 Torii Hunter 8.00 20.00
TTARTHU5 Torii Hunter 8.00 20.00
TTARTM1 Trey Mancini 6.00 15.00
TTARTM2 Trey Mancini 6.00 15.00
TTARTM3 Trey Mancini 6.00 15.00
TTARTM4 Trey Mancini 6.00 15.00
TTARTM5 Trey Mancini 6.00 15.00
TTARVR1 Victor Robles 10.00 25.00
TTARVR2 Victor Robles 10.00 25.00
TTARVR3 Victor Robles 10.00 25.00
TTARVR4 Victor Robles 10.00 25.00
TTARVR5 Victor Robles 10.00 25.00
TTARWB1 Walker Buehler 20.00 50.00
TTARWB2 Walker Buehler 20.00 50.00
TTARWB3 Walker Buehler 20.00 50.00
TTARWC1 Willson Contreras 10.00 25.00
TTARWC2 Willson Contreras 10.00 25.00
TTARWC3 Willson Contreras 10.00 25.00
TTARWC4 Willson Contreras 10.00 25.00
TTARWC5 Willson Contreras 10.00 25.00
TTARWM1 Whit Merrifield 10.00 25.00
TTARWM2 Whit Merrifield 10.00 25.00
TTARWM3 Whit Merrifield 10.00 25.00
TTARWM4 Whit Merrifield 10.00 25.00
TTARXB1 Xander Bogaerts 20.00 50.00
TTARXB2 Xander Bogaerts 20.00 50.00
TTARXB3 Xander Bogaerts 20.00 50.00
TTARXB4 Xander Bogaerts 20.00 50.00
TTARXB5 Xander Bogaerts 20.00 50.00

2019 Topps Triple Threads Legend Relics

STATED ODDS 1:XX HOBBY
STATED PRINT RUN 36 SER.#'d SETS
*SILVER/27: .4X TO 1X BASIC
*EMERALD/18: .4X TO 1X BASIC
RLCAD Andre Dawson 8.00 20.00
RLCBG Bob Gibson 15.00 40.00
RLCBL Barry Larkin 6.00 15.00
RLCCF Carlton Fisk 8.00 20.00
RLCCJ Chipper Jones 12.00 30.00
RLCCR Cal Ripken Jr. 12.00 30.00
RLCDJ Derek Jeter 25.00 60.00
RLCDO David Ortiz 8.00 20.00
RLCHA Hank Aaron
RLCI Ichiro Suzuki 15.00 40.00
RLCKG Ken Griffey Jr. 15.00 40.00
RLCMM Mark McGwire 12.00 30.00
RLCPM Pedro Martinez 6.00 15.00
RLCRA Roberto Alomar 10.00 25.00
RLCRC Rod Carew 6.00 15.00
RLCRCL Roberto Clemente
RLCRH Roy Halladay 15.00 40.00
RLCRJ Reggie Jackson 20.00 50.00
RLCRJO Randy Johnson 10.00 25.00
RLCSC Steve Carlton 8.00 20.00
RLCTG Tony Gwynn 12.00 30.00
RLCVG Vladimir Guerrero 6.00 15.00
RLCWB Wade Boggs 8.00 20.00

2019 Topps Triple Threads Pieces of the Game Autograph Relics

STATED ODDS 1:XX MINI BOX
STATED PRINT RUN 18 SER.#'d SETS
EXCHANGE DEADLINE 8/31/2021
PTGARAJ Aaron Judge 75.00 200.00
PTGARAR Anthony Rizzo 40.00 100.00
PTGARJA Jorge Alfaro 8.00 20.00
PTGARJD Jacob deGrom 25.00 60.00
PTGARJM J.D. Martinez 25.00 60.00
PTGARKB Kris Bryant 40.00 100.00
PTGAROA Ozzie Albies 20.00 50.00
PTGARPA Pete Alonso 60.00 150.00
PTGARRD Rafael Devers 20.00 50.00

2019 Topps Triple Threads Pieces of the Game Relics

STATED ODDS 1:XX MINI BOX
STATED PRINT RUN 18 SER.#'d SETS
PTGRAJ Aaron Judge 20.00 50.00
PTGRAR Anthony Rizzo 12.00 30.00
PTGRFT Fernando Tatis Jr. 25.00 60.00
PTGRJA Jorge Alfaro 3.00 8.00
PTGRJD Jacob deGrom 10.00 25.00
PTGRJM J.D. Martinez 10.00 25.00
PTGRKB Kris Bryant 15.00 40.00
PTGROA Ozzie Albies 10.00 25.00
PTGRPA Pete Alonso 50.00 120.00
PTGRRD Rafael Devers 12.00 30.00

2019 Topps Triple Threads Relic Combos

STATED ODDS 1:XX HOBBY
STATED PRINT RUN 36 SER.#'d SETS
*AMETHYST/27: .4X TO 1X BASIC
*EMERALD/18: .5X TO 1.2X BASIC
RCCAAF Acuna/Freeman/Albies 15.00 40.00
RCCAHN Nola/Hoskins/Arrieta 10.00 25.00
RCCBAC Bregman/Altuve/Correa 5.00 12.00
RCCBDP Pedroia/Devers/Bogaerts 6.00 15.00
RCCBMB Bnntndi/Mrtnz/Betts 8.00 20.00
RCCBRM Maeda/Buehler/Ryu 6.00 15.00
RCCCCF Cbrra/Fldr/Cstllns 8.00 20.00
RCCCDM Carpenter/DeJong/Martinez 5.00 12.00
RCCCSV McCllrs/Cole/Vrlndr 5.00 12.00
RCCDAS deGrom/Syndrgrd/Alonso 25.00 60.00
RCCDLP Davis/Laureano/Pinder 6.00 15.00
RCCFGH Frazier/Gardner/Hicks 6.00 15.00
RCCFMO Molina/Ozuna/Flaherty 5.00 12.00
RCCGIR Rodriguez/Griffey/Ichiro 20.00 50.00
RCCGLV Griffey/Votto/Larkin 25.00 60.00
RCCGPM Glavine/Mrtnz/Piazza 8.00 20.00
RCCHAS Story/Arenado/Helton 6.00 15.00
RCCHDW Hader/Woodruff/Davies 3.00 8.00
RCCHKF Harper/Franco/Kingery 25.00 60.00
RCCHSB Beckham/Santana/Haniger 4.00 10.00
RCCJSS Sanchez/Stanton/Judge 12.00 30.00
RCCKMP Meadows/Pham/Kiermaier 4.00 10.00
RCCLCH Contreras/Lester/Hamels 4.00 10.00
RCCLRS Lindor/Sntna/Ramirez 8.00 20.00
RCCMAG Mazara/Andrus/Gallo 4.00 10.00
RCCMMR Myers/Reyes/Margot 3.00 8.00
RCCMPD Dozier/Perez/Merrifield 5.00 12.00
RCCMPO Pedroia/Martinez/Ortiz 12.00 30.00
RCCMTH Tatis/Machado/Hosmer 12.00 30.00
RCCOTP Pujols/Ohtani/Trout 25.00 60.00
RCCPBV Vazquez/Bell/Polanco 4.00 10.00
RCCPCL Posey/Longoria/Crawford 6.00 15.00
RCCPJR Rivera/Pettitte/Jeter 30.00 80.00
RCCRBB Baez/Bryant/Rizzo 25.00 60.00
RCCRHB Buxton/Hunter/Rosario 4.00 10.00
RCCRMA Ripken/Alomar/Mancini 10.00 25.00
RCCRPR Plmro/ARod/IRod 8.00 20.00
RCCSAH Heyward/Schwarber/Almora Jr. 5.00 12.00
RCCSCR Conforto/Smith/Rosario 4.00 10.00
RCCSMG Glasnow/Morton/Snell 5.00 12.00
RCCSST Tanaka/Severino/Sabathia 4.00 10.00
RCCTGA Trrs/Andjr/Gregorius 10.00 25.00
RCCTGAL Alonso/Tatis/Guerrero 30.00 80.00
RCCTGM Griffey/McGwire/Thomas 30.00 80.00
RCCYCB Braun/Yelich/Cain 8.00 20.00

2019 Topps Triple Threads Relics

STATED ODDS 1:XX MINI BOX
STATED PRINT RUN 36 SER.#'d SETS
*SILVER/27: .4X TO 1X BASIC
*EMERALD/18: .5X TO 1.2X BASIC
*GOLD/9: .6X TO 1.5X BASIC
ALL VERSIONS EQUALLY PRICED
TTRAB Andrew Benintendi 5.00 12.00
TTRAB2 Andrew Benintendi 5.00 12.00
TTRAB3 Andrew Benintendi 5.00 12.00
TTRAB4 Andrew Benintendi 5.00 12.00
TTRABR Alex Bregman 4.00 10.00
TTRABR2 Alex Bregman 4.00 10.00
TTRABR3 Alex Bregman 4.00 10.00
TTRABR4 Alex Bregman 4.00 10.00
TTRAC Aroldis Chapman 4.00 10.00
TTRAC2 Aroldis Chapman 4.00 10.00
TTRAC3 Aroldis Chapman 4.00 10.00
TTRAJ Aaron Judge 10.00 25.00
TTRAM Austin Meadows 3.00 8.00
TTRAM2 Austin Meadows 3.00 8.00
TTRAM3 Austin Meadows 3.00 8.00
TTRAN Aaron Nola 3.00 8.00
TTRAN2 Aaron Nola 3.00 8.00
TTRAN3 Aaron Nola 3.00 8.00
TTRAR Anthony Rendon 4.00 10.00
TTRAR2 Anthony Rendon 4.00 10.00
TTRAR3 Anthony Rendon 4.00 10.00
TTRAR4 Anthony Rendon 4.00 10.00
TTRARO Amed Rosario 3.00 8.00
TTRARO2 Amed Rosario 3.00 8.00
TTRARO3 Amed Rosario 3.00 8.00
TTRARO4 Amed Rosario 3.00 8.00
TTRBB Byron Buxton 3.00 8.00
TTRBB2 Byron Buxton 3.00 8.00
TTRBB3 Byron Buxton 3.00 8.00
TTRBB4 Byron Buxton 3.00 8.00
TTRBP Buster Posey 5.00 12.00
TTRBP2 Buster Posey 5.00 12.00
TTRBP3 Buster Posey 5.00 12.00
TTRCB Cody Bellinger 8.00 20.00
TTRCC Carlos Correa 4.00 10.00
TTRCC2 Carlos Correa 4.00 10.00
TTRCC3 Carlos Correa 4.00 10.00
TTRCS CC Sabathia 3.00 8.00
TTRCS2 CC Sabathia 3.00 8.00
TTRDB Dellin Betances 3.00 8.00
TTRDB2 Dellin Betances 3.00 8.00
TTRDB3 Dellin Betances 3.00 8.00
TTRDB4 Dellin Betances 3.00 8.00
TTRDO David Ortiz 4.00 10.00
TTRDO2 David Ortiz 4.00 10.00
TTRDP Dustin Pedroia 4.00 10.00
TTRDP2 Dustin Pedroia 4.00 10.00
TTRDP3 Dustin Pedroia 4.00 10.00
TTRDP4 Dustin Pedroia 4.00 10.00
TTRDP5 Dustin Pedroia 4.00 10.00
TTRDPR David Price 3.00 8.00
TTRDPR2 David Price 3.00 8.00
TTRDPR3 David Price 3.00 8.00
TTREH Eric Hosmer 3.00 8.00
TTREH2 Eric Hosmer 3.00 8.00
TTREH3 Eric Hosmer 3.00 8.00
TTREL Evan Longoria 3.00 8.00
TTREL2 Evan Longoria 3.00 8.00
TTREL3 Evan Longoria 3.00 8.00
TTREL4 Evan Longoria 3.00 8.00
TTRER Eddie Rosario 3.00 8.00
TTRER2 Eddie Rosario 3.00 8.00
TTRER3 Eddie Rosario 3.00 8.00
TTRFL Francisco Lindor 6.00 15.00
TTRGC Gerrit Cole 4.00 10.00
TTRGC2 Gerrit Cole 4.00 10.00
TTRGC3 Gerrit Cole 4.00 10.00
TTRGP Gregory Polanco 3.00 8.00
TTRGP2 Gregory Polanco 3.00 8.00
TTRGP3 Gregory Polanco 3.00 8.00
TTRGP4 Gregory Polanco 3.00 8.00
TTRGP5 Gregory Polanco 3.00 8.00
TTRGS George Springer 3.00 8.00
TTRGS2 George Springer 3.00 8.00
TTRGST Giancarlo Stanton 4.00 10.00
TTRGST2 Giancarlo Stanton 4.00 10.00
TTRGST3 Giancarlo Stanton 4.00 10.00
TTRHD Hunter Dozier 2.50 6.00
TTRHD2 Hunter Dozier 2.50 6.00
TTRHD3 Hunter Dozier 2.50 6.00
TTRJA Jose Abreu 4.00 10.00
TTRJA2 Jose Abreu 4.00 10.00
TTRJA3 Jose Abreu 4.00 10.00
TTRJA4 Jose Abreu 4.00 10.00
TTRJA5 Jose Abreu 4.00 10.00
TTRJAL Jorge Alfaro 2.50 6.00
TTRJAL2 Jorge Alfaro 2.50 6.00
TTRJAL3 Jorge Alfaro 2.50 6.00
TTRJAR Jake Arrieta 3.00 8.00
TTRJAR2 Jake Arrieta 3.00 8.00
TTRJAR3 Jake Arrieta 3.00 8.00
TTRJAR4 Jake Arrieta 3.00 8.00
TTRJD Jacob deGrom 4.00 10.00
TTRJD2 Jacob deGrom 4.00 10.00
TTRJH Jason Heyward 3.00 8.00
TTRJH2 Jason Heyward 3.00 8.00
TTRJH3 Jason Heyward 3.00 8.00
TTRJL Jon Lester 3.00 8.00
TTRJL2 Jon Lester 3.00 8.00
TTRJL3 Jon Lester 3.00 8.00
TTRJLU Joey Lucchesi 2.50 6.00
TTRJLU2 Joey Lucchesi 2.50 6.00
TTRJLU3 Joey Lucchesi 2.50 6.00
TTRJOA Jose Altuve 3.00 8.00
TTRJOA2 Jose Altuve 3.00 8.00
TTRJOA3 Jose Altuve 3.00 8.00
TTRJOA4 Jose Altuve 3.00 8.00
TTRJS Juan Soto 6.00 15.00
TTRJS2 Juan Soto 6.00 15.00
TTRKG Ken Griffey Jr. 15.00 40.00
TTRKG2 Ken Griffey Jr. 15.00 40.00
TTRLC Luis Castillo 3.00 8.00
TTRLC2 Luis Castillo 3.00 8.00
TTRLC3 Luis Castillo 3.00 8.00
TTRLC4 Luis Castillo 3.00 8.00
TTRMA Miguel Andujar 4.00 10.00
TTRMA2 Miguel Andujar 4.00 10.00
TTRMB Mookie Betts 5.00 12.00
TTRMB2 Mookie Betts 5.00 12.00
TTRMB3 Mookie Betts 5.00 12.00
TTRMB4 Mookie Betts 5.00 12.00
TTRMB5 Mookie Betts 5.00 12.00
TTRMC Miguel Cabrera 4.00 10.00
TTRMC2 Miguel Cabrera 4.00 10.00
TTRMC3 Miguel Cabrera 4.00 10.00
TTRMC4 Miguel Cabrera 4.00 10.00
TTRMC5 Miguel Cabrera 4.00 10.00
TTRMM Manny Machado 4.00 10.00
TTRMM2 Manny Machado 4.00 10.00
TTRMO Matt Olson 2.50 6.00
TTRMO2 Matt Olson 2.50 6.00
TTRMO3 Matt Olson 2.50 6.00
TTRMOZ Marcell Ozuna 4.00 10.00
TTRMOZ2 Marcell Ozuna 4.00 10.00
TTRMOZ3 Marcell Ozuna 4.00 10.00
TTRMS Max Scherzer 4.00 10.00
TTRMS2 Max Scherzer 4.00 10.00
TTRNA Nolan Arenado 5.00 12.00
TTRNA2 Nolan Arenado 5.00 12.00
TTRNA3 Nolan Arenado 5.00 12.00
TTRNM Nomar Mazara 2.50 6.00
TTRNM2 Nomar Mazara 2.50 6.00
TTRNM3 Nomar Mazara 2.50 6.00
TTRNM4 Nomar Mazara 2.50 6.00
TTROA Ozzie Albies 4.00 10.00
TTROA2 Ozzie Albies 4.00 10.00
TTROA3 Ozzie Albies 4.00 10.00
TTROA4 Ozzie Albies 4.00 10.00
TTROA5 Ozzie Albies 4.00 10.00
TTRRA Roberto Alomar 8.00 20.00
TTRRA2 Roberto Alomar 8.00 20.00
TTRRB Ryan Braun 3.00 8.00
TTRRB2 Ryan Braun 3.00 8.00
TTRRB3 Ryan Braun 3.00 8.00
TTRRD Rafael Devers 5.00 12.00
TTRRD2 Rafael Devers 5.00 12.00
TTRRD3 Rafael Devers 5.00 12.00
TTRRD4 Rafael Devers 5.00 12.00
TTRRH Rhys Hoskins 6.00 15.00
TTRSK Scott Kingery 3.00 8.00
TTRSK2 Scott Kingery 3.00 8.00
TTRSK3 Scott Kingery 3.00 8.00
TTRSM Starling Marte 3.00 8.00
TTRSM2 Starling Marte 3.00 8.00
TTRSM3 Starling Marte 3.00 8.00
TTRSP Salvador Perez 3.00 8.00
TTRSP2 Salvador Perez 3.00 8.00
TTRSP3 Salvador Perez 3.00 8.00
TTRTM Trey Mancini 3.00 8.00
TTRTM2 Trey Mancini 3.00 8.00
TTRTM3 Trey Mancini 3.00 8.00
TTRWB Walker Buehler 5.00 12.00
TTRWB2 Walker Buehler 5.00 12.00
TTRWB3 Walker Buehler 5.00 12.00
TTRWC Willson Contreras 3.00 8.00
TTRWC2 Willson Contreras 3.00 8.00
TTRWM Wil Myers 2.50 6.00
TTRWM2 Wil Myers 2.50 6.00
TTRWM3 Wil Myers 2.50 6.00
TTRWM4 Wil Myers 2.50 6.00
TTRXB Xander Bogaerts 4.00 10.00
TTRXB2 Xander Bogaerts 4.00 10.00
TTRXB3 Xander Bogaerts 4.00 10.00
TTRXB4 Xander Bogaerts 4.00 10.00
TTRXB5 Xander Bogaerts 4.00 10.00

2019 Topps Triple Threads Rookie Autographs

STATED ODDS 1:XX MINI BOX
STATED PRINT RUN 99 SER.#'d SETS
EXCHANGE DEADLINE 8/31/2021
PRINTING PLATE ODDS 1:XXX MINI BOX

PLATE PRINT RUN 1 SET PER COLOR
BLACK-CYAN-MAGENTA-YELLOW ISSUED
NO PLATE PRICING DUE TO SCARCITY
*EMERALD/50: .4X TO 1X BASIC
*GOLD/25: .5X TO 1.2X BASIC
RAUAR Austin Riley 15.00 40.00
RAUBL Brandon Lowe 10.00 25.00
RAUCK Carter Kieboom 10.00 25.00
RAUDC Dylan Cozens 4.00 10.00
RAUDH Darwinzon Hernandez 4.00 10.00
RAUDJ Danny Jansen 4.00 10.00
RAUEJ Eloy Jimenez 20.00 50.00
RAUFT Fernando Tatis Jr. 125.00 300.00
RAUGH Garrett Hampson 4.00 10.00
RAUJD Jon Duplantier 4.00 10.00
RAUKS Kohl Stewart 5.00 12.00
RAULT Lane Thomas 6.00 15.00
RAUMS Myles Straw 6.00 15.00
RAUNL Nate Lowe 5.00 12.00
RAUNM Nick Margevicius 4.00 10.00
RAUNS Nick Senzel 15.00 40.00
RAUPA Pete Alonso 60.00 150.00
RAURB Ryan Borucki 4.00 10.00
RAURR Ronny Rodriguez 4.00 10.00
RAUSB Skye Bolt 5.00 12.00
RAUTB Ty Buttrey 6.00 15.00
RAUTE Thairo Estrada 8.00 20.00
RAUVG Vladimir Guerrero Jr. 50.00 120.00
RAUWA Willians Astudillo 4.00 10.00
RAUYK Yusei Kikuchi 6.00 15.00

2019 Topps Triple Threads Single Jumbo Relics

STATED ODDS 1:XX HOBBY
STATED PRINT RUN 36 SER.#'d SETS
*SILVER/27: .4X TO 1X BASIC
*EMERALD/18: .5X TO 1.2X BASIC
*GOLD/9: .6X TO 1.5X BASIC
ALL VERSIONS EQUALLY PRICED
SJRAB1 Andrew Benintendi 5.00 12.00
SJRAB2 Andrew Benintendi 5.00 12.00
SJRAB3 Andrew Benintendi 5.00 12.00
SJRABR1 Alex Bregman 4.00 10.00
SJRABR2 Alex Bregman 4.00 10.00
SJRABR3 Alex Bregman 4.00 10.00
SJRAC1 Aroldis Chapman 4.00 10.00
SJRAC2 Aroldis Chapman 4.00 10.00
SJRAC3 Aroldis Chapman 4.00 10.00
SJRAG1 Alex Gordon 3.00 8.00
SJRAG2 Alex Gordon 3.00 8.00
SJRAG3 Alex Gordon 3.00 8.00
SJRAJ1 Aaron Judge 10.00 25.00
SJRAJ2 Aaron Judge 10.00 25.00
SJRAM1 Adalberto Mondesi 3.00 8.00
SJRAM2 Adalberto Mondesi 3.00 8.00
SJRAN1 Aaron Nola 3.00 8.00
SJRAN2 Aaron Nola 3.00 8.00
SJRAP1 Albert Pujols 5.00 12.00
SJRAP2 Albert Pujols 5.00 12.00
SJRAP3 Albert Pujols 5.00 12.00
SJRAR1 Anthony Rendon 4.00 10.00
SJRAR2 Anthony Rendon 4.00 10.00
SJRARI1 Anthony Rizzo 6.00 15.00
SJRARI2 Anthony Rizzo 6.00 15.00
SJRARI3 Anthony Rizzo 6.00 15.00
SJRARI4 Anthony Rizzo 6.00 15.00
SJRARO1 Amed Rosario 3.00 8.00
SJRARO2 Amed Rosario 3.00 8.00
SJRARO3 Amed Rosario 3.00 8.00
SJRBB1 Byron Buxton 3.00 8.00
SJRBB2 Byron Buxton 3.00 8.00
SJRBB3 Byron Buxton 3.00 8.00
SJRBG1 Brett Gardner 3.00 8.00
SJRBG2 Brett Gardner 3.00 8.00
SJRBG3 Brett Gardner 3.00 8.00
SJRBP1 Buster Posey 5.00 12.00
SJRBP2 Buster Posey 5.00 12.00
SJRBP3 Buster Posey 5.00 12.00
SJRBP4 Buster Posey 5.00 12.00
SJRBS1 Blake Snell 3.00 8.00
SJRBS2 Blake Snell 3.00 8.00
SJRCB Cody Bellinger 12.00 30.00
SJRCC1 Carlos Carrasco 2.50 6.00
SJRCC2 Carlos Carrasco 2.50 6.00
SJRCCO1 Carlos Correa 4.00 10.00
SJRCCO2 Carlos Correa 4.00 10.00
SJRCCO3 Carlos Correa 4.00 10.00
SJRCF1 Clint Frazier 3.00 8.00
SJRCF2 Clint Frazier 3.00 8.00
SJRCH1 Cole Hamels 3.00 8.00
SJRCH2 Cole Hamels 3.00 8.00
SJRCS1 CC Sabathia 3.00 8.00
SJRCS2 CC Sabathia 3.00 8.00
SJRCS3 CC Sabathia 3.00 8.00
SJRCS4 CC Sabathia 3.00 8.00
SJRCSA1 Chris Sale 4.00 10.00
SJRCSA2 Chris Sale 4.00 10.00
SJRCSA3 Chris Sale 4.00 10.00
SJRCSA4 Chris Sale 4.00 10.00
SJRCY Christian Yelich 5.00 12.00
SJRDD1 David Dahl 2.50 6.00
SJRDD2 David Dahl 2.50 6.00
SJRDP1 Dustin Pedroia 4.00 10.00
SJRDP2 Dustin Pedroia 4.00 10.00
SJRDP3 Dustin Pedroia 4.00 10.00
SJRDP4 Dustin Pedroia 4.00 10.00
SJRDPR1 David Price 3.00 8.00
SJRDPR2 David Price 3.00 8.00
SJRDPR3 David Price 3.00 8.00
SJRDPR4 David Price 3.00 8.00
SJRDPR5 David Price 3.00 8.00
SJRDS1 Dominic Smith 2.50 6.00
SJRDS2 Dominic Smith 2.50 6.00
SJRDS3 Dominic Smith 2.50 6.00
SJRDS4 Dominic Smith 2.50 6.00
SJRDSW1 Dansby Swanson 4.00 10.00
SJRDSW2 Dansby Swanson 4.00 10.00
SJRDSW3 Dansby Swanson 4.00 10.00
SJREH1 Eric Hosmer 3.00 8.00
SJREH2 Eric Hosmer 3.00 8.00
SJREL1 Evan Longoria 3.00 8.00
SJREL2 Evan Longoria 3.00 8.00
SJREL3 Evan Longoria 3.00 8.00
SJRER1 Eddie Rosario 3.00 8.00
SJRER2 Eddie Rosario 3.00 8.00
SJRER3 Eddie Rosario 3.00 8.00
SJRES1 Eugenio Suarez 3.00 8.00
SJRES2 Eugenio Suarez 3.00 8.00
SJRES3 Eugenio Suarez 3.00 8.00
SJRFF1 Freddie Freeman 5.00 12.00
SJRFF2 Freddie Freeman 5.00 12.00
SJRFF3 Freddie Freeman 5.00 12.00
SJRFL1 Francisco Lindor 4.00 10.00
SJRFL2 Francisco Lindor 4.00 10.00
SJRFL3 Francisco Lindor 4.00 10.00
SJRFR1 Franmil Reyes 2.50 6.00
SJRFR2 Franmil Reyes 2.50 6.00
SJRGC1 Gerrit Cole 4.00 10.00
SJRGC2 Gerrit Cole 4.00 10.00
SJRGM1 German Marquez 2.50 6.00
SJRGM2 German Marquez 2.50 6.00
SJRGP1 Gregory Polanco 3.00 8.00
SJRGP2 Gregory Polanco 3.00 8.00
SJRGP3 Gregory Polanco 3.00 8.00
SJRGP4 Gregory Polanco 3.00 8.00
SJRGS1 Gary Sanchez 4.00 10.00
SJRGS2 Gary Sanchez 4.00 10.00
SJRGS3 Gary Sanchez 4.00 10.00
SJRGSP1 George Springer 3.00 8.00
SJRGSP2 George Springer 3.00 8.00
SJRGSP3 George Springer 3.00 8.00
SJRGSP4 George Springer 3.00 8.00
SJRGST1 Giancarlo Stanton 4.00 10.00
SJRGST2 Giancarlo Stanton 4.00 10.00
SJRGST3 Giancarlo Stanton 4.00 10.00
SJRHD1 Hunter Dozier 2.50 6.00
SJRHD2 Hunter Dozier 2.50 6.00
SJRJA1 Jose Abreu 4.00 10.00
SJRJA2 Jose Abreu 4.00 10.00
SJRJAL1 Jose Altuve 3.00 8.00
SJRJAL2 Jose Altuve 3.00 8.00
SJRJAR1 Jake Arrieta 3.00 8.00
SJRJAR2 Jake Arrieta 3.00 8.00
SJRJB1 Javier Baez 8.00 20.00
SJRJB2 Javier Baez 8.00 20.00
SJRJH1 Josh Hader 2.50 6.00
SJRJH2 Josh Hader 2.50 6.00
SJRJHE1 Jason Heyward 3.00 8.00
SJRJHE2 Jason Heyward 3.00 8.00
SJRJHE3 Jason Heyward 3.00 8.00
SJRJHI1 Jordan Hicks 3.00 8.00
SJRJHI2 Jordan Hicks 3.00 8.00
SJRJL1 Jon Lester 3.00 8.00
SJRJL2 Jon Lester 3.00 8.00
SJRJL3 Jon Lester 3.00 8.00
SJRJL4 Jon Lester 3.00 8.00
SJRJLU Joey Lucchesi 2.50 6.00
SJRJM1 J.D. Martinez 4.00 10.00
SJRJM2 J.D. Martinez 4.00 10.00
SJRJP1 Joc Pederson 3.00 8.00
SJRJP2 Joc Pederson 3.00 8.00
SJRJR1 Jose Ramirez 3.00 8.00
SJRJR2 Jose Ramirez 3.00 8.00
SJRJR3 Jose Ramirez 3.00 8.00
SJRJS01 Juan Soto 6.00 15.00
SJRJS02 Juan Soto 6.00 15.00
SJRJV Justin Verlander 4.00 10.00
SJRJV1 Joey Votto 4.00 10.00
SJRJV2 Joey Votto 4.00 10.00
SJRJV3 Joey Votto 4.00 10.00
SJRKB1 Kris Bryant 5.00 12.00
SJRKB2 Kris Bryant 5.00 12.00
SJRKD Khris Davis 4.00 10.00
SJRKM1 Kenta Maeda 3.00 8.00
SJRKM2 Kenta Maeda 3.00 8.00
SJRKS1 Kyle Schwarber 4.00 10.00
SJRKS2 Kyle Schwarber 4.00 10.00
SJRKS3 Kyle Schwarber 4.00 10.00
SJRKS4 Kyle Schwarber 4.00 10.00
SJRKSE1 Kyle Seager 2.50 6.00
SJRKSE2 Kyle Seager 2.50 6.00
SJRKSE3 Kyle Seager 2.50 6.00
SJRKW1 Kolten Wong 3.00 8.00
SJRKW2 Kolten Wong 3.00 8.00
SJRKW3 Kolten Wong 3.00 8.00
SJRLC1 Lorenzo Cain 2.50 6.00
SJRLC2 Lorenzo Cain 2.50 6.00
SJRLCA1 Luis Castillo 3.00 8.00
SJRLCA2 Luis Castillo 3.00 8.00
SJRLCA3 Luis Castillo 3.00 8.00
SJRLS1 Luis Severino 3.00 8.00
SJRLS2 Luis Severino 3.00 8.00
SJRLS3 Luis Severino 3.00 8.00
SJRLS4 Luis Severino 3.00 8.00
SJRMA1 Miguel Andujar 4.00 10.00
SJRMA2 Miguel Andujar 4.00 10.00
SJRMB1 Mookie Betts 5.00 12.00
SJRMB2 Mookie Betts 5.00 12.00
SJRMB3 Mookie Betts 5.00 12.00
SJRMC1 Miguel Cabrera 4.00 10.00
SJRMC2 Miguel Cabrera 4.00 10.00
SJRMC3 Miguel Cabrera 4.00 10.00
SJRMC4 Miguel Cabrera 4.00 10.00
SJRMC5 Miguel Cabrera 4.00 10.00
SJRMCO1 Michael Conforto 3.00 8.00
SJRMCO2 Michael Conforto 3.00 8.00
SJRMF1 Maikel Franco 3.00 8.00
SJRMF2 Maikel Franco 3.00 8.00
SJRMF3 Maikel Franco 3.00 8.00
SJRMFR1 Max Fried 4.00 10.00
SJRMFR2 Max Fried 4.00 10.00
SJRMFR3 Max Fried 4.00 10.00
SJRMM Manny Machado 4.00 10.00
SJRMO1 Marcell Ozuna 4.00 10.00
SJRMO2 Marcell Ozuna 4.00 10.00
SJRMS1 Max Scherzer 4.00 10.00
SJRMS2 Max Scherzer 4.00 10.00
SJRMS3 Max Scherzer 4.00 10.00
SJRMT1 Mike Trout 20.00 50.00
SJRMT2 Mike Trout 20.00 50.00
SJRNA1 Nolan Arenado 5.00 12.00
SJRNA2 Nolan Arenado 5.00 12.00
SJRNC1 Nicholas Castellanos 4.00 10.00
SJRNC2 Nicholas Castellanos 4.00 10.00
SJRNM1 Nomar Mazara 2.50 6.00
SJRNM2 Nomar Mazara 2.50 6.00
SJRNS1 Noah Syndergaard 3.00 8.00
SJRNS2 Noah Syndergaard 3.00 8.00
SJROA1 Ozzie Albies 4.00 10.00
SJROA2 Ozzie Albies 4.00 10.00
SJROA3 Ozzie Albies 4.00 10.00
SJRPG1 Paul Goldschmidt 4.00 10.00
SJRPG2 Paul Goldschmidt 4.00 10.00
SJRRA Ronald Acuna Jr. 15.00 40.00
SJRRB1 Ryan Braun 3.00 8.00
SJRRB2 Ryan Braun 3.00 8.00
SJRRD1 Rafael Devers 5.00 12.00
SJRRD2 Rafael Devers 5.00 12.00
SJRRD3 Rafael Devers 5.00 12.00
SJRRH1 Rhys Hoskins 6.00 15.00
SJRRH2 Rhys Hoskins 6.00 15.00
SJRRH3 Rhys Hoskins 6.00 15.00
SJRRP1 Rick Porcello 3.00 8.00
SJRRP2 Rick Porcello 3.00 8.00
SJRRP3 Rick Porcello 3.00 8.00
SJRRP4 Rick Porcello 3.00 8.00
SJRRT1 Raimel Tapia 2.50 6.00
SJRRT2 Raimel Tapia 2.50 6.00
SJRSK1 Scott Kingery 3.00 8.00
SJRSK2 Scott Kingery 3.00 8.00
SJRSK3 Scott Kingery 3.00 8.00
SJRSO Shohei Ohtani 5.00 12.00
SJRSP1 Salvador Perez 3.00 8.00
SJRSP2 Salvador Perez 3.00 8.00
SJRSP3 Salvador Perez 3.00 8.00
SJRSS1 Stephen Strasburg 4.00 10.00
SJRSS2 Stephen Strasburg 4.00 10.00
SJRTM1 Trey Mancini 3.00 8.00
SJRTM2 Trey Mancini 3.00 8.00
SJRTP1 Tommy Pham 2.50 6.00
SJRTP2 Tommy Pham 2.50 6.00
SJRTP3 Tommy Pham 2.50 6.00
SJRTS1 Trevor Story 4.00 10.00
SJRTS2 Trevor Story 4.00 10.00
SJRTS3 Trevor Story 4.00 10.00
SJRTT1 Trea Turner 3.00 8.00
SJRTT2 Trea Turner 3.00 8.00
SJRWB Walker Buehler 5.00 12.00
SJRWC1 Willson Contreras 3.00 8.00
SJRWC2 Willson Contreras 3.00 8.00
SJRWC3 Willson Contreras 3.00 8.00
SJRWM1 Whit Merrifield 4.00 10.00
SJRWM2 Whit Merrifield 4.00 10.00
SJRWM3 Whit Merrifield 4.00 10.00
SJRWMY1 Wil Myers 2.50 6.00
SJRWMY2 Wil Myers 2.50 6.00
SJRXB1 Xander Bogaerts 4.00 10.00
SJRXB2 Xander Bogaerts 4.00 10.00
SJRXB3 Xander Bogaerts 4.00 10.00
SJRXB4 Xander Bogaerts 4.00 10.00
SJRYM1 Yadier Molina 8.00 20.00
SJRYM2 Yadier Molina 8.00 20.00
SJRYP1 Yasiel Puig 4.00 10.00
SJRYP2 Yasiel Puig 4.00 10.00
SJRZD1 Zach Davies 2.50 6.00
SJRZD2 Zach Davies 2.50 6.00

2020 Topps Triple Threads

JSY AU RC ODDS 1:XX MINI BOX
JSY AU RC PRINT RUN 99 SER.#'d SETS
JSY AU ODDS 1:XX MINI BOX
JSY AU PRINT RUN 99 SER.#'d SETS
EXCHANGE DEADLINE 8/31/2022
1-100 PLATE ODDS 1:XXX MINI BOX
JSY AU PLATE ODDS 1:XXX MINI BOX
PLATE PRINT RUN 1 SET PER COLOR
BLACK-CYAN-MAGENTA-YELLOW ISSUED
NO PLATE PRICING DUE TO SCARCITY
1 Mike Trout 3.00 8.00
2 Albert Pujols .75 2.00
3 Shohei Ohtani .75 2.00
4 Anthony Rendon .60 1.50
5 Freddie Freeman .75 2.00
6 Yoshi Tsutsugo RC .75 2.00
7 Ronald Acuna Jr. 2.50 6.00
8 Chipper Jones .60 1.50
9 Cal Ripken Jr. 2.00 5.00
10 Hank Aaron 1.25 3.00
11 Rafael Devers .75 2.00
12 J.D. Martinez .60 1.50
13 Ted Williams 1.25 3.00
14 David Ortiz .60 1.50
15 Thurman Munson .60 1.50
16 Jackie Robinson .60 1.50
17 Nico Hoerner RC 2.50 6.00
18 Kris Bryant .75 2.00
19 Anthony Rizzo 1.00 2.50
20 Javier Baez .75 2.00
21 Ernie Banks .60 1.50
22 Ryne Sandberg 1.25 3.00
23 Frank Thomas .60 1.50
24 Luis Robert RC 6.00 15.00
25 Eloy Jimenez 1.25 3.00
26 Joey Votto .60 1.50
27 Johnny Bench .60 1.50
28 Barry Larkin .50 1.25
29 Aristides Aquino RC 1.25 3.00
30 Francisco Lindor .60 1.50
31 Shane Bieber .60 1.50
32 Nolan Arenado .75 2.00
33 Trevor Story .60 1.50
34 Miguel Cabrera .60 1.50
35 Justin Verlander .60 1.50
36 Jose Altuve .50 1.25
37 George Springer .50 1.25
38 Alex Bregman .60 1.50
39 Yordan Alvarez RC 3.00 8.00
40 Whit Merrifield .60 1.50
41 George Brett 1.25 3.00
42 Dave Winfield .50 1.25
43 Mookie Betts 1.25 3.00
44 Clayton Kershaw 1.25 3.00
45 Cody Bellinger 1.25 3.00
46 Sandy Koufax 1.25 3.00
47 Walker Buehler .75 2.00
48 Gavin Lux RC 4.00 10.00
49 Christian Yelich .75 2.00
50 Keston Hiura .75 2.00
51 Jacob deGrom .60 1.50
52 Pete Alonso 1.50 4.00
53 Robin Yount .60 1.50
54 Tom Seaver .50 1.25
55 Darryl Strawberry .40 1.00
56 Aaron Judge 1.50 4.00
57 Gleyber Torres 1.25 3.00
58 Derek Jeter 1.50 4.00
59 Don Mattingly 1.25 3.00
60 Mariano Rivera .75 2.00
61 Gerrit Cole 1.00 2.50
62 Babe Ruth 1.50 4.00
63 Lou Gehrig 1.25 3.00
64 Jesus Luzardo RC 1.25 3.00
65 Matt Chapman .60 1.50
66 Rickey Henderson .60 1.50
67 Mark McGwire 1.00 2.50
68 Rhys Hoskins .75 2.00
69 Andrew McCutchen .60 1.50
70 Bryce Harper 1.00 2.50
71 Mike Schmidt 1.00 2.50
72 Roberto Clemente 1.50 4.00
73 Ty Cobb 1.00 2.50
74 Honus Wagner .60 1.50
75 Manny Machado .60 1.50
76 Tony Gwynn .60 1.50
77 Fernando Tatis Jr. 2.50 6.00
78 Buster Posey .75 2.00
79 Will Clark .50 1.25
80 Willie Mays 1.25 3.00
81 Ichiro .75 2.00
82 Ken Griffey Jr. 1.25 3.00
83 Kyle Lewis RC 5.00 12.00
84 Randy Johnson .60 1.50
85 Paul Goldschmidt .60 1.50
86 Yadier Molina .60 1.50
87 Ozzie Smith .75 2.00
88 Shogo Akiyama RC 1.00 2.50
89 Brendan McKay RC 1.00 2.50
90 Nolan Ryan 2.00 5.00
91 Josh Donaldson .50 1.25
92 Bo Bichette RC 5.00 12.00
93 Roberto Alomar .50 1.25
94 Vladimir Guerrero Jr. 1.25 3.00
95 Max Scherzer .60 1.50
96 Stephen Strasburg .60 1.50
97 Juan Soto 2.00 5.00
98 Brooks Robinson .50 1.25
99 Mike Piazza .60 1.50
100 Reggie Jackson .50 1.25
RFPARAAQ A.Aquino JSY AU 12.00 30.00
RFPARAM Andres Munoz JSY AU RC 4.00 10.00
RFPARAN Austin Nola JSY AU RC 5.00 12.00
RFPARAP A.Puk JSY AU RC 6.00 15.00
RFPARAR A.Riley JSY AU 12.00 30.00
RFPARBBR Bobby Bradley JSY AU RC 5.00 12.00
RFPARBL B.Lowe JSY AU 8.00 20.00
RFPARBM B.McKay JSY AU 6.00 15.00
RFPARBR Brendan Rodgers JSY AU 5.00 12.00
RFPAREJ E.Jimenez JSY AU EXCH 20.00 50.00
RFPARGL G.Lux JSY AU EXCH 30.00 80.00
RFPARID I.Diaz JSY AU RC 8.00 20.00
RFPARJD Justin Dunn JSY AU RC 4.00 10.00
RFPARJDD J.Davis JSY AU 8.00 20.00
RFPARJL J.Luzardo JSY AU 10.00 25.00
RFPARJM J.McNeil JSY AU 12.00 30.00
RFPARJME J.Means JSY AU 6.00 15.00
RFPARJP Jorge Polanco JSY AU 4.00 10.00
RFPARJR Jake Rogers JSY AU RC 3.00 8.00
RFPARKN Kevin Newman JSY AU 4.00 10.00
RFPARLA L.Arraez JSY AU 8.00 20.00
RFPARLG L.Gurriel Jr. JSY AU 8.00 20.00
RFPARLR L.Robert JSY AU 100.00 250.00
RFPARLW L.Webb JSY AU RC 10.00 25.00
RFPARMC M.Chavis JSY AU 8.00 20.00
RFPARMG Mitch Garver JSY AU 5.00 12.00
RFPARMK M.King JSY AU RC 8.00 20.00
RFPARMS M.Soroka JSY AU 12.00 30.00
RFPARNL Nicky Lopez JSY AU 5.00 12.00
RFPARNS N.Senzel JSY AU 6.00 15.00
RFPARNSO N.Solak JSY AU RC 5.00 12.00
RFPARRL R.Laureano JSY AU 6.00 15.00
RFPARSB S.Brown JSY AU RC 6.00 15.00
RFPARSL Shed Long JSY AU 4.00 10.00
RFPARSM S.Murphy JSY AU RC 8.00 20.00
RFPARSN Sheldon Neuse JSY AU RC 4.00 10.00
RFPARTE T.Edman JSY AU 10.00 25.00
RFPARTES Thairo Estrada JSY AU 4.00 10.00
RFPARTZ T.J. Zeuch JSY AU RC 3.00 8.00
RFPARWS W.Smith JSY AU 10.00 25.00

2020 Topps Triple Threads Amber

*AMBER VET: .75X TO 2X BASIC
*AMBER RC: .5X TO 1.2X BASIC
STATED ODDS 1:XX MINI BOX
STATED PRINT RUN 199 SER.#'d SETS
24 Luis Robert 12.00 30.00

2020 Topps Triple Threads Amethyst

*AMETHYST VET: .75X TO 2X BASIC
*AMETHYST RC: .5X TO 1.2X BASIC
*AMETHYST JSY AU: .4X TO 1X BASIC RC
STATED ODDS 1:XX MINI BOX
JSY AU ODDS 1:XX MINI BOX
1-100 PRINT RUN 299 SER.#'d SETS
JSY AU PRINT RUN 75 SER.#'d SETS
EXCHANGE DEADLINE 8/31/2022
24 Luis Robert 12.00 30.00

2020 Topps Triple Threads Citrine

*CITRINE VET: 1X TO 2.5X BASIC
*CITRINE RC: .6X TO 1.5X BASIC
STATED ODDS 1:XX MINI BOX
STATED PRINT RUN 75 SER.#'d SETS
24 Luis Robert 25.00 60.00
72 Roberto Clemente 10.00 25.00
82 Ken Griffey Jr. 10.00 25.00
90 Nolan Ryan 8.00 20.00
92 Bo Bichette 15.00 40.00

2020 Topps Triple Threads Emerald

*EMERALD VET: .75X TO 2X BASIC
*EMERALD RC: .5X TO 1.2X BASIC
*EMERALD JSY AU: .4X TO 1X BASIC RC
1-100 ODDS 1:XX MINI BOX
JSY AU ODDS 1:XX MINI BOX
1-100 PRINT RUN 275 SER.#'d SETS
JSY AU PRINT RUN 50 SER.#'d SETS
EXCHANGE DEADLINE 8/31/2022
24 Luis Robert 12.00 30.00

2020 Topps Triple Threads Gold

*GOLD VET: 1X TO 2.5X BASIC
*GOLD RC: .6X TO 1.5X BASIC
STATED ODDS 1:XX MINI BOX
STATED PRINT RUN 99 SER.#'d SETS
24 Luis Robert 25.00 60.00
72 Roberto Clemente 10.00 25.00
82 Ken Griffey Jr. 10.00 25.00
90 Nolan Ryan 8.00 20.00
92 Bo Bichette 15.00 40.00

2020 Topps Triple Threads Onyx

*ONYX VET: 1.5X TO 4X BASIC
*ONYX RC: 1X TO 2.5X BASIC
*ONYX JSY AU: .5X TO 1.2X BASIC RC
1-100 ODDS 1:XX MINI BOX
JSY AU ODDS 1:XX MINI BOX
1-100 PRINT RUN 50 SER.#'d SETS
JSY AU PRINT RUN 35 SER.#'d SETS
EXCHANGE DEADLINE 8/31/2022
24 Luis Robert 40.00 100.00
72 Roberto Clemente 15.00 40.00
79 Will Clark 6.00 15.00
82 Ken Griffey Jr. 15.00 40.00
87 Ozzie Smith 8.00 20.00
90 Nolan Ryan 12.00 30.00
92 Bo Bichette 25.00 60.00

2020 Topps Triple Threads Sapphire

*SAPPHIRE VET: 2.5X TO 6X BASIC
*SAPPHIRE RC: 1.5X TO 4X BASIC
STATED ODDS 1:XX MINI BOX
STATED PRINT RUN 25 SER.#'d SETS
101-140 PRINT RUN 10 SER.#'d SETS
NO JSY AU PRICING DUE TO SCARCITY
EXCHANGE DEADLINE 8/31/2022
24 Luis Robert 60.00 150.00
58 Derek Jeter 20.00 50.00
66 Rickey Henderson 15.00 40.00
72 Roberto Clemente 25.00 60.00
79 Will Clark 10.00 25.00
82 Ken Griffey Jr. 25.00 60.00
87 Ozzie Smith 12.00 30.00
90 Nolan Ryan 20.00 50.00
92 Bo Bichette 40.00 100.00

2020 Topps Triple Threads Autograph Relic Combos

STATED ODDS 1:XX HOBBY
STATED PRINT RUN 36 SER.#'d SETS
EXCHANGE DEADLINE 8/31/2022
PRINTING PLATE ODDS 1:XXX HOBBY
PLATE PRINT RUN 1 SET PER COLOR
BLACK-CYAN-MAGENTA-YELLOW ISSUED
NO PLATE PRICING DUE TO SCARCITY
ARCBKB Brrs/Bxtn/Kplr 25.00 60.00
ARCBLM Bhlr/Lux/May 60.00 150.00
ARCBRS Sndbrg/Brnt/Rzzo
ARCCOL Chpmn/Olsn/Lzrdo 30.00 80.00
ARCCPL Psy/Clrk/Lnccm
ARCDSW Alnso/Wight/dGom
ARCFAA Jns/Acna/Mrphy 100.00 250.00
ARCFTB Thms/Bhrle/Fsk 100.00 250.00
ARCGVD Dmn/Vrtk/Grcprra
ARCHNR Nola/Hskns/Rlmto 60.00 150.00
ARCKBB Bhlr/Blingr/Krshw
ARCMDB Bgrts/Dvrs/Mrtnz 40.00 100.00
ARCMGF Flhrty/Gldschmdt/Mlna 75.00 200.00
ARCMLP Puk/Lzrdo/Mrphy EXCH 40.00 100.00
ARCPMS Prz/Mrrfld/Slr 30.00 80.00
ARCPRB Andrs/Rdigz/Bltre
ARCPWP Pttte/Wllms/Psda 100.00 250.00
ARCSAP Snll/Lowe/Mdws 30.00 80.00
ARCSBA Sprngr/Brgmn/Alvrz 50.00 120.00
ARCSDG Dwsn/Sndbrg/Grce
ARCSJG Jns/Smltz/Glvne
ARCSJM Jstce/Smltz/McGrff 50.00 120.00
ARCSLM Lux/Sgr/Mncy 75.00 200.00
ARCSRC Soto/Grrro Jr./Acna Jr. 200.00 500.00
ARCSSC Strsbrg/Crbn/Soto
ARCSWA Alnso/Wrght/Stawbrry 75.00 200.00
ARCTBY Bllngr/Trt/Ylch
ARCVGS Snzl/Vtto/Gray 40.00 100.00
ARCWHA Hltn/Arndo/Wlkr
ARCYYH Hra/Ynt/Ylch EXCH

2020 Topps Triple Threads Autograph Relic Combos Amethyst

*AMETHYST: .4X TO 1X BASIC
STATED ODDS 1:XX HOBBY
STATED PRINT RUN 27 SER.#'d SETS
EXCHANGE DEADLINE 8/31/2022
ARCCPL Psy/Clrk/Lnccm 125.00 300.00
ARCDSW Alnso/Wight/dGom 125.00 300.00
ARCGVD Dmn/Vrtk/Grcprra 50.00 120.00
ARCPRB Andrs/Rdigz/Bltre 50.00 120.00
ARCSDG Dwsn/Sndbrg/Grce 125.00 300.00
ARCWHA Hltn/Arndo/Wlkr 100.00 250.00

2020 Topps Triple Threads Autograph Relic Combos Emerald

*EMERALD: .4X TO 1X BASIC
STATED ODDS 1:XXX HOBBY
STATED PRINT RUN 18 SER.#'d SETS
EXCHANGE DEADLINE 8/31/2022
ARCBRS Sndbrg/Brnt/Rzzo 75.00 200.00
ARCCPL Psy/Clrk/Lnccm 125.00 300.00
ARCDSW Alnso/Wight/dGom 125.00 300.00
ARCGVD Dmn/Vrtk/Grcprra 50.00 120.00
ARCKBB Bhlr/Blingr/Krshw 200.00 500.00
ARCPRB Andrs/Rdigz/Bltre 50.00 120.00
ARCSDG Dwsn/Sndbrg/Grce 125.00 300.00
ARCSJG Jns/Smltz/Glvne 100.00 250.00
ARCSSC Strsbrg/Crbn/Soto 100.00 250.00
ARCWHA Hltn/Arndo/Wlkr 100.00 250.00
ARCYYH Hra/Ynt/Ylch EXCH 100.00 250.00

2020 Topps Triple Threads Autograph Relics

STATED ODDS 1:XX HOBBY
STATED PRINT RUN 18 SER.#'d SETS
EXCHANGE DEADLINE 8/31/2022
ALL VERSIONS EQUALLY PRICED
TTARAB1 Adrian Beltre
TTARAB2 Adrian Beltre
TTARABE1 Andrew Benintendi 12.00 30.00
TTARABE2 Andrew Benintendi 12.00 30.00
TTARABE3 Andrew Benintendi 12.00 30.00
TTARABE4 Andrew Benintendi 12.00 30.00
TTARABR1 Alex Bregman 20.00 50.00
TTARABR2 Alex Bregman 20.00 50.00
TTARABR3 Alex Bregman 20.00 50.00
TTARABR4 Alex Bregman 20.00 50.00
TTARABR5 Alex Bregman 20.00 50.00
TTARAJ1 Andruw Jones 20.00 50.00
TTARAJ2 Andruw Jones 20.00 50.00
TTARAJ3 Andruw Jones 20.00 50.00
TTARAJ4 Andruw Jones 20.00 50.00
TTARAJU1 Aaron Judge
TTARAJU2 Aaron Judge
TTARAM1 Austin Meadows 10.00 25.00
TTARAM2 Austin Meadows 10.00 25.00
TTARAM3 Austin Meadows 10.00 25.00
TTARAM4 Austin Meadows 10.00 25.00
TTARAMC1 Andrew McCutchen 50.00 120.00
TTARAMC2 Andrew McCutchen 50.00 120.00
TTARAMC3 Andrew McCutchen 50.00 12.00
TTARAP1 Andy Pettitte 20.00 50.00
TTARAP2 Andy Pettitte 20.00 50.00
TTARAP3 Andy Pettitte 20.00 50.00
TTARAR1 Anthony Rizzo
TTARAR2 Anthony Rizzo
TTARAS1 Alfonso Soriano 15.00 40.00
TTARAS2 Alfonso Soriano 15.00 40.00
TTARAS3 Alfonso Soriano 15.00 40.00
TTARAS4 Alfonso Soriano 15.00 40.00
TTARBB1 Bert Blyleven 12.00 30.00
TTARBB2 Bert Blyleven 12.00 30.00
TTARBH1 Bryce Harper
TTARBH2 Bryce Harper
TTARBW1 Bernie Williams 25.00 60.00
TTARBW2 Bernie Williams 25.00 60.00
TTARBW3 Bernie Williams 25.00 60.00
TTARCB1 Cody Bellinger 75.00 200.00
TTARCB2 Cody Bellinger 75.00 200.00
TTARCB3 Cody Bellinger 75.00 200.00
TTARCF1 Carlton Fisk 25.00 60.00
TTARCF2 Carlton Fisk 25.00 60.00
TTARCF3 Carlton Fisk 25.00 60.00
TTARCFE1 Cecil Fielder 25.00 60.00
TTARCFE2 Cecil Fielder 25.00 60.00
TTARCFE3 Cecil Fielder 25.00 60.00
TTARCJ1 Chipper Jones
TTARCJ2 Chipper Jones
TTARCKE1 Clayton Kershaw
TTARCKE2 Clayton Kershaw
TTARCRJ1 Cal Ripken Jr. 100.00 250.00
TTARCRJ2 Cal Ripken Jr. 100.00 250.00
TTARCSA1 CC Sabathia 20.00 50.00
TTARCSA2 CC Sabathia 20.00 50.00
TTARCSA3 CC Sabathia 20.00 50
TTARCY1 Christian Yelich EXCH 50.00 120
TTARCY2 Christian Yelich EXCH 50.00 120.
TTARCY3 Christian Yelich EXCH 50.00 120.
TTARCY4 Christian Yelich EXCH 50.00 120.
TTARDE1 Dennis Eckersley 15.00 40.
TTARDE2 Dennis Eckersley 15.00 40.
TTARDE3 Dennis Eckersley 15.00 40.
TTARDJ2 Derek Jeter
TTARDJL1 DJ LeMahieu 40.00 100.
TTARDJL2 DJ LeMahieu 40.00 100.
TTARDJL3 DJ LeMahieu 40.00 100.
TTARDJL4 DJ LeMahieu 40.00 100.
TTARDL1 Derrek Lee 10.00 25.
TTARDL2 Derrek Lee 10.00 25.
TTARDL3 Derrek Lee 10.00 25.0
TTARDO1 David Ortiz
TTARDO2 David Ortiz
TTARDP1 Dustin Pedroia 20.00 50.0
TTARDP2 Dustin Pedroia 20.00 50.0
TTARDP3 Dustin Pedroia 20.00 50.0
TTARDS1 Dansby Swanson 12.00 30.0
TTARDS2 Dansby Swanson 12.00 30.0
TTARDS3 Dansby Swanson 12.00 30.0
TTARDST1 Darryl Strawberry 20.00 50.0
TTARDST2 Darryl Strawberry 20.00 50.0
TTARDST3 Darryl Strawberry 20.00 50.0
TTARDST4 Darryl Strawberry 20.00 50.0
TTARDW1 David Wright 25.00 60.0
TTARDW2 David Wright 25.00 60.0
TTAREA1 Elvis Andrus 10.00 25.0
TTAREA2 Elvis Andrus 10.00 25.0
TTAREA3 Elvis Andrus 10.00 25.0
TTAREA4 Elvis Andrus 10.00 25.0
TTAREH1 Eric Hosmer 12.00 30.0
TTAREH2 Eric Hosmer 12.00 30.0
TTAREH3 Eric Hosmer 12.00 30.0
TTAREH4 Eric Hosmer 12.00 30.0
TTAREH5 Eric Hosmer 12.00 30.0
TTAREJ1 Eloy Jimenez
TTAREJ2 Eloy Jimenez
TTAREJ3 Eloy Jimenez
TTAREJ4 Eloy Jimenez
TTAREM1 Edgar Martinez 25.00 60.00
TTAREM2 Edgar Martinez 25.00 60.00
TTAREM3 Edgar Martinez 25.00 60.00
TTAREM4 Edgar Martinez 25.00 60.00
TTARFF1 Freddie Freeman 40.00 100.00
TTARFF2 Freddie Freeman 40.00 100.00
TTARFF3 Freddie Freeman 40.00 100.00
TTARFF4 Freddie Freeman 40.00 100.00
TTARFF5 Freddie Freeman 40.00 100.00
TTARFM1 Fred McGriff 25.00 60.00
TTARFM2 Fred McGriff 25.00 60.00
TTARFT1 Frank Thomas 40.00 100.00
TTARFT2 Frank Thomas 40.00 100.00
TTARFTJ1 Fernando Tatis Jr. 100.00 250.00
TTARFTJ2 Fernando Tatis Jr. 100.00 250.00
TTARFTJ3 Fernando Tatis Jr. 100.00 250.00
TTARFTJ4 Fernando Tatis Jr. 100.00 250.00
TTARFTJ5 Fernando Tatis Jr. 100.00 250.00
TTARGS1 George Springer 25.00 60.00
TTARGS2 George Springer 25.00 60.00
TTARGS3 George Springer 25.00 60.00
TTARGT1 Gleyber Torres 50.00 120.00
TTARGT2 Gleyber Torres 50.00 120.00
TTARGT3 Gleyber Torres 50.00 120.00
TTARIR1 Ivan Rodriguez 25.00 60.00
TTARIR2 Ivan Rodriguez 25.00 60.00
TTARIR3 Ivan Rodriguez 25.00 60.00
TTARI Ichiro
TTARJAL1 Jose Altuve 15.00 40.00
TTARJAL2 Jose Altuve 15.00 40.00
TTARJAL3 Jose Altuve 15.00 40.00
TTARJDA1 Johnny Damon 20.00 50.00
TTARJDA2 Johnny Damon 20.00 50.00
TTARJDA3 Johnny Damon 20.00 50.00
TTARJF1 Jack Flaherty 12.00 30.00
TTARJF2 Jack Flaherty 12.00 30.00
TTARJF3 Jack Flaherty 12.00 30.00
TTARJF4 Jack Flaherty 12.00 30.00
TTARJF5 Jack Flaherty 12.00 30.00
TTARJG1 Joey Gallo
TTARJG2 Joey Gallo
TTARJG3 Joey Gallo
TTARJG4 Joey Gallo
TTARJM1 J.D. Martinez 15.00 40.00
TTARJM2 J.D. Martinez 15.00 40.00
TTARJM3 J.D. Martinez 15.00 40.00
TTARJM4 J.D. Martinez 15.00 40.00
TTARJMA1 Joe Mauer 30.00 80.00
TTARJMA2 Joe Mauer 30.00 80.00
TTARJMA3 Joe Mauer 30.00 80.00
TTARJS1 Jorge Soler 8.00 20.00
TTARJS2 Jorge Soler 8.00 20.00
TTARJS3 Jorge Soler 8.00 20.00
TTARJS4 Jorge Soler 8.00 20.00
TTARJSM1 John Smoltz 30.00 80.00
TTARJSM2 John Smoltz 30.00 80.00
TTARJSO1 Juan Soto 60.00 150.00
TTARJSO2 Juan Soto 60.00 150.00
TTARJSO3 Juan Soto 60.00 150.00
TTARJSO4 Juan Soto 60.00 150.00
TTARJSO5 Juan Soto 60.00 150.00
TTARJT1 Jim Thome 40.00 100.00
TTARJT2 Jim Thome 40.00 100.00
TTARJV1 Joey Votto
TTARJV2 Joey Votto
TTARKB1 Kris Bryant 30.00 80.00
TTARKB2 Kris Bryant 30.00 80.00
TTARKGJ1 Ken Griffey Jr.
TTARKGJ2 Ken Griffey Jr.
TTARKH1 Keston Hiura 12.00 30.00

RKH2 Keston Hiura 12.00 30.00
RKH3 Keston Hiura 12.00 30.00
RKH4 Keston Hiura 12.00 30.00
RKL1 Kenny Lofton 30.00 80.00
RKL2 Kenny Lofton 30.00 80.00
RKL3 Kenny Lofton 30.00 80.00
RKL4 Kenny Lofton 30.00 80.00
RKS1 Kyle Schwarber 15.00 40.00
RKS2 Kyle Schwarber 15.00 40.00
RKS3 Kyle Schwarber 15.00 40.00
RKS4 Kyle Schwarber 15.00 40.00
RKS5 Kyle Schwarber 15.00 40.00
RLW1 Larry Walker 40.00 100.00
RLW2 Larry Walker 40.00 100.00
RLW3 Larry Walker 40.00 100.00
RLW4 Larry Walker 40.00 100.00
ARMC1 Miguel Cabrera
ARMC2 Miguel Cabrera
ARMCH1 Matt Chapman 12.00 30.00
ARMCH2 Matt Chapman 12.00 30.00
ARMCH3 Matt Chapman 12.00 30.00
ARMCH4 Matt Chapman 12.00 30.00
ARMG1 Mark Grace 20.00 50.00
ARMG2 Mark Grace 20.00 50.00
ARMG3 Mark Grace 20.00 50.00
ARMMC Mark McGwire
ARMMO1 Mike Moustakas 15.00 40.00
TARMMO2 Mike Moustakas 15.00 40.00
TARMMO3 Mike Moustakas 15.00 40.00
TARMMO4 Mike Moustakas 15.00 40.00
TARMMO5 Mike Moustakas 15.00 40.00
TARMMU1 Max Muncy 10.00 25.00
TARMMU2 Max Muncy 10.00 25.00
TARMMU3 Max Muncy 10.00 25.00
TARMMU4 Max Muncy 10.00 25.00
TARMO1 Matt Olson 8.00 20.00
TARMO2 Matt Olson 8.00 20.00
TARMO3 Matt Olson 8.00 20.00
TARMT1 Mike Trout 250.00 600.00
TARMT2 Mike Trout 250.00 600.00
TARMV1 Mo Vaughn 20.00 50.00
TARMV2 Mo Vaughn 20.00 50.00
TARMV3 Mo Vaughn 20.00 50.00
TARNA1 Nolan Arenado 30.00 80.00
TARNA2 Nolan Arenado 30.00 80.00
TARNA3 Nolan Arenado 30.00 80.00
TARNRY Nolan Ryan 75.00 200.00
TAROS1 Ozzie Smith 30.00 80.00
TAROS2 Ozzie Smith 30.00 80.00
TAROS3 Ozzie Smith 30.00 80.00
TTARPA1 Pete Alonso 40.00 100.00
TTARPA2 Pete Alonso 40.00 100.00
TTARPA3 Pete Alonso 40.00 100.00
TTARPC1 Patrick Corbin 8.00 20.00
TTARPC2 Patrick Corbin 8.00 20.00
TTARPC3 Patrick Corbin 8.00 20.00
TTARPC4 Patrick Corbin 8.00 20.00
TTARPC5 Patrick Corbin 8.00 20.00
TTARPG1 Paul Goldschmidt 15.00 40.00
TTARPG2 Paul Goldschmidt 15.00 40.00
TTARPG3 Paul Goldschmidt 15.00 40.00
TTARPG4 Paul Goldschmidt 15.00 40.00
TTARRA1 Ronald Acuna Jr. 75.00 200.00
TTARRA2 Ronald Acuna Jr. 75.00 200.00
TTARRA3 Ronald Acuna Jr. 75.00 200.00
TTARRA4 Ronald Acuna Jr. 75.00 200.00
TTARRA5 Ronald Acuna Jr. 75.00 200.00
TTARRAL1 Roberto Alomar 40.00 100.00
TTARRAL2 Roberto Alomar 40.00 100.00
TTARRD1 Rafael Devers 12.00 30.00
TTARRD2 Rafael Devers 12.00 30.00
TTARRD3 Rafael Devers 12.00 30.00
TTARRD4 Rafael Devers 12.00 30.00
TTARRD5 Rafael Devers 12.00 30.00
TTARRH1 Rhys Hoskins 20.00 50.00
TTARRH2 Rhys Hoskins 20.00 50.00
TTARRH3 Rhys Hoskins 20.00 50.00
TTARRH4 Rhys Hoskins 20.00 50.00
TTARRHE Rickey Henderson 75.00 200.00
TTARRS1 Ryne Sandberg
TTARRS2 Ryne Sandberg
TTARRY1 Robin Yount 40.00 100.00
TTARRY2 Robin Yount 40.00 100.00
TTARRYN1 Ryan Howard 20.00 50.00
TTARRYN2 Ryan Howard 20.00 50.00
TTARRYN3 Ryan Howard 20.00 50.00
TTARSC1 Shin-Soo Choo 25.00 60.00
TTARSC2 Shin-Soo Choo 25.00 60.00
TTARSC3 Shin-Soo Choo 25.00 60.00
TTARSC4 Shin-Soo Choo 25.00 60.00
TTARSCA1 Steve Carlton 25.00 60.00
TTARSCA2 Steve Carlton 25.00 60.00
TTARSCA3 Steve Carlton 25.00 60.00
TTARSGR1 Sonny Gray 15.00 40.00
TTARSGR2 Sonny Gray 15.00 40.00
TTARSGR3 Sonny Gray 15.00 40.00
TTARSGR4 Sonny Gray 15.00 40.00
TTARSO1 Shohei Ohtani 75.00 200.00
TTARSO2 Shohei Ohtani 75.00 200.00
TTARSR1 Scott Rolen 20.00 50.00
TTARSR2 Scott Rolen 20.00 50.00
TTARSR3 Scott Rolen 20.00 50.00
TTARSST1 Stephen Strasburg 30.00 80.00
TTARSST2 Stephen Strasburg 30.00 80.00
TTARSST3 Stephen Strasburg 30.00 80.00
TTARSST4 Stephen Strasburg 30.00 80.00
TTARSST5 Stephen Strasburg 30.00 80.00
TTARTB1 Trevor Bauer 25.00 60.00
TTARTB2 Trevor Bauer 25.00 60.00
TTARTB3 Trevor Bauer 25.00 60.00
TTARTB4 Trevor Bauer 25.00 60.00
TTARTG1 Tom Glavine 25.00 60.00
TTARTG2 Tom Glavine 25.00 60.00
TTARTG3 Tom Glavine 25.00 60.00
TTARTH1 Todd Helton 20.00 50.00
TTARTH2 Todd Helton 20.00 50.00
TTARTH3 Todd Helton 20.00 50.00
TTARTHU1 Torii Hunter
TTARTHU2 Torii Hunter
TTARTL1 Tim Lincecum
TTARTL2 Tim Lincecum
TTARTL3 Tim Lincecum
TTARTL4 Tim Lincecum
TTARTS1 Trevor Story EXCH 30.00 80.00
TTARTS2 Trevor Story EXCH 30.00 80.00
TTARTS3 Trevor Story EXCH 30.00 80.00
TTARTS4 Trevor Story EXCH 30.00 80.00
TTARTS5 Trevor Story EXCH 30.00 80.00
TTARVGJ1 Vladimir Guerrero Jr. 40.00 100.00
TTARVGJ2 Vladimir Guerrero Jr. 40.00 100.00
TTARVGJ3 Vladimir Guerrero Jr. 40.00 100.00
TTARVGJ4 Vladimir Guerrero Jr. 40.00 100.00
TTARVGJ5 Vladimir Guerrero Jr. 40.00 100.00
TTARVR1 Victor Robles 10.00 25.00
TTARVR2 Victor Robles 10.00 25.00
TTARVR3 Victor Robles 10.00 25.00
TTARVR4 Victor Robles 10.00 25.00
TTARWC1 Willson Contreras 12.00 3.00
TTARWC2 Willson Contreras 12.00 30.00
TTARWC3 Willson Contreras 12.00 30.00
TTARWC4 Willson Contreras 12.00 30.00
TTARWCL1 Will Clark 30.00 80.00
TTARWCL2 Will Clark 30.00 80.00
TTARXB1 Xander Bogaerts 25.00 60.00
TTARXB2 Xander Bogaerts 25.00 60.00
TTARXB3 Xander Bogaerts 25.00 60.00
TTARXB4 Xander Bogaerts 25.00 60.00
TTARXB5 Xander Bogaerts 25.00 60.00
TTARYM1 Yadier Molina 60.00 150.00
TTARYM2 Yadier Molina 60.00 150.00
TTARYM3 Yadier Molina 60.00 150.00
TTARYM4 Yadier Molina 60.00 150.00

2020 Topps Triple Threads Autograph Relics Gold

*GOLD: .5X TO 1.2X BASIC
STATED ODDS 1:XX HOBBY
STATED PRINT RUN 9 SER.#'d SETS
SOME NOT PRICED DUE TO SCARCITY
EXCHANGE DEADLINE 8/31/2022
TTARAB1 Adrian Beltre 40.00 100.00
TTARAJU1 Aaron Judge 125.00 300.00
TTARAR1 Anthony Rizzo 40.00 100.00
TTARBH1 Bryce Harper 125.00 300.00
TTARCJ1 Chipper Jones
TTARCKE1 Clayton Kershaw 75.00 200.00
TTARDO1 David Ortiz 40.00 100.00
TTARJG1 Joey Gallo 20.00 50.00
TTARJV1 Joey Votto 30.00 80.00
TTARMC1 Miguel Cabrera 60.00 150.00
TTARRS1 Ryne Sandberg 75.00 200.00
TTARTHU1 Torii Hunter 12.00 3.00

2020 Topps Triple Threads Legend Relics

STATED ODDS 1:XX HOBBY
STATED PRINT RUN 36 SER.#'d SETS
*SILVER/27: .4X TO 1X BASIC
RLCAR Alex Rodriguez 20.00 50.00
RLCBL Barry Larkin 12.00 30.00
RLCCJ Chipper Jones 15.00 40.00
RLCCR Cal Ripken Jr. 20.00 50.00
RLCI Ichiro 30.00 80.00
RLCJB Johnny Bench 20.00 50.00
RLCKG Ken Griffey Jr. 30.00 80.00
RLCLB Lou Brock 12.00 30.00
RLCMM Mark McGwire 12.00 30.00
RLCMP Mike Piazza 10.00 25.00
RLCMS Mike Schmidt 12.00 30.00
RLCPM Pedro Martinez 6.00 15.00
RLCRC Rod Carew 6.00 15.00
RLCRJ Reggie Jackson 12.00 30.00
RLCRJO Randy Johnson 10.00 25.00
RLCRY Robin Yount 10.00 25.00
RLCSC Steve Carlton 12.00 30.00
RLCTG Tony Gwynn 12.00 30.00

2020 Topps Triple Threads Legend Relics Amethyst

*AMETHYST: .4X TO 1X BASIC
STATED ODDS 1:XX HOBBY
STATED PRINT RUN 27 SER.#'d SETS
RLCTM Thurman Munson 40.00 100.00
RLCVG Ted Williams 40.00 100.00
RLCWM Willie Mays 40.00 100.00

2020 Topps Triple Threads Legend Relics Emerald

*EMERALD: .4X TO 1X BASIC
STATED ODDS 1:XX HOBBY
STATED PRINT RUN 18 SER.#'d SETS
RLCBG Bob Gibson 15.00 40.00
RLCTM Thurman Munson 40.00 100.00
RLCVG Ted Williams 40.00 100.00
RLCWM Willie Mays 40.00 100.00

2020 Topps Triple Threads Relic Combos

STATED ODDS 1:XX HOBBY
STATED PRINT RUN 36 SER.#'d SETS
*AMETHYST/27: .4X TO 1X BASIC
*EMERALD/18: .5X TO 1.2X BASIC
RCCACA Alvarez/Altuve/Correa 12.00 30.00
RCCAFA Acuna Jr./Albies/Freeman 20.00 50.00
RCCAGC Gallo/Andrus/Calhoun 5.00 12.00
RCCATG Guerrero Jr.
Tatis Jr./Acuna Jr. 40.00 100.00
RCCBAS Story/Arenado/Blackmon 6.00 15.00
RCCBDC Devers/Bogaerts/Chavis 10.00 25.00
RCCBGB Bichette/Guerrero Jr./Biggio 12.00 30.00
RCCBKR Rosario/Kepler/Berrios 8.00 20.00
RCCBMB Martinez/Benintendi/Bogaerts 6.00 15.00
RCCCJS Sanchez/Sabathia/Judge 15.00 40.00
RCCCOS Semien/Olson/Chapman 6.00 15.00
RCCCYH Hiura/Cain/Yelich 8.00 20.00
RCCDCL Davis/Chapman/Luzardo 6.00 15.00
RCCGIR Griffey Jr./Rodriguez/Ichiro 25.00 60.00
RCCGMF Molina/Flaherty/Goldschmidt 15.00 40.00
RCCGSM McKay/Snell/Glasnow 5.00 12.00
RCCGVB Gray/Bauer/Votto 15.00 40.00
RCCHHM Harper/McCutchen/Hoskins 20.00 50.00
RCCHNR Nola/Realmuto/Hoskins 20.00 50.00
RCCKBB Bellinger/Kershaw/Buehler 20.00 50.00
RCCLGV Votto/Griffey Jr./Larkin 25.00 60.00
RCCLMK Lowe/Kiermaier/Meadows 5.00 12.00
RCCLRS Lindor/Santana/Reyes 8.00 20.00
RCCMAJ Moncada/Jimenez/Abreu 15.00 40.00
RCCMCR Conforto/McNeil/Rosario 12.00 30.00
RCCMGT McGwire/Griffey Jr./Thomas 30.00 80.00
RCCMOP Pedroia/Martinez/Ortiz 15.00 40.00
RCCPBY Posey/Pence/Yaz 12.00 30.00
RCCPTO Trout/Ohtani/Pujols 30.00 80.00
RCCRBB Baez/Rizzo/Bryant 15.00 40.00
RCCRBC Rizzo/Baez/Contreras 12.00 30.00
RCCRRB Beltre/Rodriguez/Rodriguez 15.00 40.00
RCCRRM Ripken Jr./Murray/Robinson 15.00 40.00
RCCSHH Schwarber/Hoerner/Happ 12.00 30.00
RCCSJG Glavine/Jones/Smoltz 25.00 60.00
RCCSRO Riley/Soroka/Swanson 8.00 20.00
RCCSSS Scherzer/Strasburg/Corbin 8.00 20.00
RCCSTG Soto/Tatis Jr./Guerrero Jr. 25.00 60.00
RCCSVS Suarez/Senzel/Votto 10.00 25.00
RCCSWA Wright/Alonso/Strawberry 12.00 30.00
RCCTBY Trout/Bellinger/Yelich 30.00 80.00
RCCTJR Jimenez/Thomas/Robert 60.00 150.00
RCCTJS Stanton/Judge/Torres 20.00 50.00
RCCTSR Soto/Robles/Turner 10.00 25.00
RCCVBS Verlander/Springer/Bregman 8.00 20.00
RCCWHA Walker/Arenado/Helton 10.00 25.00

2020 Topps Triple Threads Relics

STATED ODDS 1:XX MINI BOX
STATED PRINT RUN 36 SER.#'d SETS
*SILVER/27: .4X TO 1X BASIC
*EMERALD/18: .5X TO 1.2X BASIC
*GOLD/9: .6X TO 1.5X BASIC
ALL VERSIONS EQUALLY PRICED
TTRAA1 Aristides Aquino 5.00 12.00
TTRAA2 Aristides Aquino 5.00 12.00
TTRAA3 Aristides Aquino 5.00 12.00
TTRAB Andrew Benintendi 4.00 10.00
TTRAB2 Andrew Benintendi 4.00 10.00
TTRAB3 Andrew Benintendi 4.00 10.00
TTRAB4 Andrew Benintendi 4.00 10.00
TTRABR Alex Bregman 4.00 10.00
TTRABR2 Alex Bregman 4.00 10.00
TTRABR3 Alex Bregman 4.00 10.00
TTRABR4 Alex Bregman 4.00 10.00
TTRAJ Aaron Judge 12.00 30.00
TTRAJ2 Aaron Judge 12.00 30.00
TTRAM Austin Meadows 3.00 8.00
TTRAM2 Austin Meadows 3.00 8.00
TTRAM3 Austin Meadows 3.00 8.00
TTRAN1 Aaron Nola 4.00 10.00
TTRAN2 Aaron Nola 4.00 10.00
TTRAN3 Aaron Nola 4.00 10.00
TTRARO Amed Rosario 3.00 8.00
TTRARO2 Amed Rosario 3.00 8.00
TTRARO3 Amed Rosario 3.00 8.00
TTRAUR1 Austin Riley 5.00 12.00
TTRAUR2 Austin Riley 5.00 12.00
TTRAUR3 Austin Riley 5.00 12.00
TTRBB1 Bo Bichette 10.00 25.00
TTRBB2 Bo Bichette 10.00 25.00
TTRBEL Josh Bell 3.00 8.00
TTRBEL2 Josh Bell 3.00 8.00
TTRBEL3 Josh Bell 3.00 8.00
TTRBH1 Bryce Harper 12.00 30.00
TTRBH2 Bryce Harper 12.00 30.00
TTRBL1 Brandon Lowe 4.00 10.00
TTRBL2 Brandon Lowe 4.00 10.00
TTRBL3 Brandon Lowe 4.00 10.00
TTRBP Buster Posey 5.00 12.00
TTRBP2 Buster Posey 5.00 12.00
TTRBP3 Buster Posey 5.00 12.00
TTRCB Cody Bellinger 6.00 15.00
TTRCB2 Cody Bellinger 6.00 15.00
TTRCB3 Cody Bellinger 6.00 15.00
TTRCB4 Cody Bellinger 6.00 15.00
TTRCS CC Sabathia 5.00 12.00
TTRCS2 CC Sabathia 5.00 12.00
TTRCS3 CC Sabathia 5.00 12.00
TTRCY Christian Yelich 6.00 15.00
TTRCY2 Christian Yelich 6.00 15.00
TTRCY3 Christian Yelich 6.00 15.00
TTRDD1 David Dahl 2.50 6.00
TTRDD2 David Dahl 2.50 6.00
TTRDD3 David Dahl 2.50 6.00
TTRDO David Ortiz 10.00 25.00
TTRDO2 David Ortiz 10.00 25.00
TTRDO3 David Ortiz 10.00 25.00
TTRDSW Dansby Swanson 6.00 15.00
TTRDSW2 Dansby Swanson 6.00 15.00
TTRDSW3 Dansby Swanson 6.00 15.00
TTRDSW4 Dansby Swanson 6.00 15.00
TTRFF1 Freddie Freeman 8.00 20.00
TTRFF2 Freddie Freeman 8.00 20.00
TTRFF3 Freddie Freeman 8.00 20.00
TTRFL Francisco Lindor 6.00 15.00
TTRFL2 Francisco Lindor 6.00 15.00
TTRFL3 Francisco Lindor 6.00 15.00
TTRFTJ Fernando Tatis Jr. 15.00 40.00
TTRFTJ2 Fernando Tatis Jr. 15.00 40.00
TTRFTJ3 Fernando Tatis Jr. 15.00 40.00
TTRGS George Springer 6.00 15.00
TTRGS2 George Springer 6.00 15.00
TTRGS3 George Springer 6.00 15.00
TTRGS4 George Springer 6.00 15.00
TTRGSA1 Gary Sanchez 5.00 12.00
TTRGSA2 Gary Sanchez 5.00 12.00
TTRGSA3 Gary Sanchez 5.00 12.00
TTRGSA4 Gary Sanchez 5.00 12.00
TTRGST Giancarlo Stanton 6.00 15.00
TTRGST2 Giancarlo Stanton 6.00 15.00
TTRGST3 Giancarlo Stanton 6.00 15.00
TTRJA Jose Abreu 6.00 15.00
TTRJA2 Jose Abreu 6.00 15.00
TTRJB1 Javier Baez 8.00 20.00
TTRJB2 Javier Baez 8.00 20.00
TTRJB3 Javier Baez 8.00 20.00
TTRJBE1 Jose Berrios 4.00 10.00
TTRJBE2 Jose Berrios 4.00 10.00
TTRJBE3 Jose Berrios 4.00 10.00
TTRJG1 Joey Gallo 4.00 10.00
TTRJG2 Joey Gallo 4.00 10.00
TTRJG3 Joey Gallo 4.00 10.00
TTRJMC1 Jeff McNeil 3.00 8.00
TTRJMC2 Jeff McNeil 3.00 8.00
TTRJMC3 Jeff McNeil 3.00 8.00
TTRJOA Jose Altuve 5.00 12.00
TTRJOA2 Jose Altuve 5.00 12.00
TTRJOA3 Jose Altuve 5.00 12.00
TTRJOA4 Jose Altuve 5.00 12.00
TTRJS Juan Soto 10.00 25.00
TTRJS2 Juan Soto 10.00 25.00
TTRJSO1 Jorge Soler 4.00 10.00
TTRJSO2 Jorge Soler 4.00 10.00
TTRJSO3 Jorge Soler 4.00 10.00
TTRJV1 Joey Votto 8.00 20.00
TTRJV2 Joey Votto 8.00 20.00
TTRJV3 Joey Votto 8.00 20.00
TTRKH Keston Hiura 5.00 12.00
TTRKH2 Keston Hiura 5.00 12.00
TTRKH3 Keston Hiura 5.00 12.00
TTRMC Miguel Cabrera 6.00 15.00
TTRMC2 Miguel Cabrera 6.00 15.00
TTRMC3 Miguel Cabrera 6.00 15.00
TTRMC4 Miguel Cabrera 6.00 15.00
TTRMCC1 Andrew McCutchen 6.00 15.00
TTRMCC2 Andrew McCutchen 10.00 25.00
TTRMCC3 Andrew McCutchen 6.00 15.00
TTRMCC4 Andrew McCutchen 6.00 15.00
TTRMCH1 Matt Chapman 6.00 15.00
TTRMCH2 Matt Chapman 6.00 15.00
TTRMCH3 Matt Chapman 6.00 15.00
TTRMCO1 Michael Conforto 5.00 12.00
TTRMCO2 Michael Conforto 5.00 12.00
TTRMCO3 Michael Conforto 5.00 12.00
TTRMK1 Max Kepler 6.00 15.00
TTRMK2 Max Kepler 6.00 15.00
TTRMK3 Max Kepler 6.00 15.00
TTRMO1 Matt Olson 2.50 6.00
TTRMO2 Matt Olson 2.50 6.00
TTRMO3 Matt Olson 2.50 6.00
TTRMS Max Scherzer 4.00 10.00
TTRMS2 Max Scherzer 4.00 10.00
TTRMSE1 Marcus Semien 2.50 6.00
TTRMSE2 Marcus Semien 2.50 6.00
TTRMSE3 Marcus Semien 2.50 6.00
TTRMT Mike Trout 40.00 100.00
TTRMT2 Mike Trout 40.00 100.00
TTRMT3 Mike Trout 40.00 100.00
TTRMT4 Mike Trout 40.00 100.00
TTRMTA1 Masahiro Tanaka 6.00 15.00
TTRMTA2 Masahiro Tanaka 6.00 15.00
TTRMTA3 Masahiro Tanaka 6.00 15.00
TTRNA Nolan Arenado 5.00 12.00
TTRNA2 Nolan Arenado 5.00 12.00
TTRNA3 Nolan Arenado 5.00 12.00
TTRNS1 Nick Senzel 4.00 10.00
TTRNS2 Nick Senzel 4.00 10.00
TTRNS3 Nick Senzel 4.00 10.00
TTROA Ozzie Albies 5.00 12.00
TTROA2 Ozzie Albies 5.00 12.00
TTROA3 Ozzie Albies 5.00 12.00
TTROA4 Ozzie Albies 5.00 12.00
TTRPD1 Paul DeJong 4.00 10.00
TTRPD2 Paul DeJong 4.00 10.00
TTRPD3 Paul DeJong 4.00 10.00
TTRRD Rafael Devers 5.00 12.00
TTRRD2 Rafael Devers 5.00 12.00
TTRRD3 Rafael Devers 5.00 12.00
TTRRD4 Rafael Devers 5.00 12.00
TTRRH Rhys Hoskins 5.00 12.00
TTRRH2 Rhys Hoskins 5.00 12.00
TTRRH3 Rhys Hoskins 5.00 12.00
TTRRIZ1 Anthony Rizzo 8.00 20.00
TTRRIZ2 Anthony Rizzo 8.00 20.00
TTRRIZ3 Anthony Rizzo 8.00 20.00
TTRSG1 Sonny Gray 3.00 8.00
TTRSG2 Sonny Gray 3.00 8.00
TTRSG3 Sonny Gray 3.00 8.00
TTRSTR1 Stephen Strasburg 5.00 12.00
TTRSTR2 Stephen Strasburg 5.00 12.00
TTRSTR3 Stephen Strasburg 5.00 12.00
TTRTS1 Trevor Story 4.00 10.00
TTRTS2 Trevor Story 4.00 10.00
TTRTS3 Trevor Story 4.00 10.00
TTRTS4 Trevor Story 4.00 10.00
TTRTT1 Trea Turner 3.00 8.00
TTRTT2 Trea Turner 3.00 8.00
TTRTT3 Trea Turner 5.00 12.00
TTRVGJ1 Vladimir Guerrero Jr. 8.00 20.00
TTRVGJ2 Vladimir Guerrero Jr. 8.00 20.00
TTRVGJ3 Vladimir Guerrero Jr. 8.00 20.00
TTRWC Willson Contreras 4.00 10.00
TTRWC2 Willson Contreras 4.00 10.00
TTRWC3 Willson Contreras 4.00 10.00
TTRXB Xander Bogaerts 6.00 15.00
TTRXB2 Xander Bogaerts 6.00 15.00
TTRXB3 Xander Bogaerts 6.00 15.00
TTRXB4 Xander Bogaerts 6.00 15.00
TTRYM1 Yadier Molina 15.00 40.00
TTRYM2 Yadier Molina 15.00 40.00
TTRYM3 Yadier Molina 15.00 40.00

2020 Topps Triple Threads Rookie Autographs

STATED ODDS 1:XXX HOBBY
STATED PRINT RUN 99 SER.#'d SETS
EXCHANGE DEADLINE 8/31/2022
PRINTING PLATE ODDS 1:XXX MINI BOX
PLATE PRINT RUN 1 SET PER COLOR
BLACK-CYAN-MAGENTA-YELLOW ISSUED
NO PLATE PRICING DUE TO SCARCITY
*EMERALD/50: .4X TO 1X BASIC
*GOLD/25: .5X TO 1.2X BASIC
RACAA Adbert Alzolay 6.00 15.00
RACAQ Aristides Aquino 10.00 25.00
RACAT Abraham Toro 5.00 12.00
RACBA Bryan Abreu 4.00 10.00
RACBB Bo Bichette EXCH 75.00 200.00
RACBM Brendan McKay 6.00 15.00
RACBQ Bobby Bradley 5.00 12.00
RACDC Dylan Cease 8.00 20.00
RACDM Dustin May 20.00 50.00
RACHH Hunter Harvey 6.00 15.00
RACJK James Karinchak 20.00 50.00
RACJS Josh Staumont 4.00 10.00
RACJU Jose Urquidy 5.00 12.00
RACJY Jordan Yamamoto 5.00 12.00
RACKH Kwang-Hyun Kim 15.00 40.00
RACLR Luis Robert 125.00 300.00
RACMB Mike Brosseau 8.00 20.00
RACMD Mauricio Dubon 6.00 15.00
RACMT Matt Thaiss 5.00 12.00
RACMZ Michel Baez 4.00 10.00
RACNH Nico Hoerner 15.00 40.00
RACNS Nick Solak 6.00 15.00
RACRA Randy Arozarena 75.00 200.00
RACRG Robel Garcia 4.00 10.00
RACSA Shogo Akiyama 8.00 20.00
RACSY Shun Yamaguchi 5.00 12.00
RACTGO Tony Gonsolin 10.00 25.00
RACYD Yonathan Daza 5.00 12.00
RACYT Yoshi Tsutsugo 10.00 25.00
RACZG Zac Gallen 8.00 20.00

2020 Topps Triple Threads Single Jumbo Relic Autographs

STATED ODDS 1:XX HOBBY
STATED PRINT RUN 99 SER.#'d SETS
EXCHANGE DEADLINE 8/31/2022
ASJRAA Aristides Aquino 12.00 30.00
ASJRAAL Adbert Alzolay 8.00 20.00
ASJRAB Andrew Benintendi 10.00 25.00
ASJRAC Aaron Civale 6.00 15.00
ASJRAN Aaron Nola 10.00 25.00
ASJRAR Austin Riley 12.00 30.00
ASJRAY Alex Young 4.00 10.00
ASJRBL Brandon Lowe 6.00 15.00
ASJRBM Brendan McKay 6.00 15.00
ASJRBR Bryan Reynolds 5.00 12.00
ASJRBRO Brendan Rodgers 6.00 15.00
ASJRBS Blake Snell 10.00 25.00
ASJRCB Cavan Biggio 8.00 20.00
ASJRCF Clint Frazier 10.00 25.00
ASJRCK Carter Kieboom 5.00 12.00
ASJRCP Chris Paddack 8.00 20.00
ASJRCS Corey Seager 25.00 60.00
ASJRDC Dylan Cease 8.00 20.00
ASJRDJ Danny Jansen 4.00 10.00
ASJRDP David Peralta 4.00 10.00
ASJRDS Dansby Swanson 12.00 30.00
ASJRDSM Dominic Smith 8.00 20.00
ASJRDV Daniel Vogelbach 4.00 10.00
ASJRES Eugenio Suarez 8.00 20.00
ASJRFT Fernando Tatis Jr. 75.00 200.00
ASJRGL Gavin Lux 20.00 50.00
ASJRIH Ian Happ 12.00 30.00
ASJRJF Jack Flaherty 8.00 20.00
ASJRJL Jesus Luzardo 8.00 20.00
ASJRJM Jeff McNeil 8.00 20.00
ASJRJR J.T. Realmuto 10.00 25.00
ASJRJRO Jake Rogers 4.00 10.00
ASJRJY Jordan Yamamoto 5.00 12.00
ASJRKN Kevin Newman 5.00 12.00
ASJRKT Kyle Tucker 8.00 20.00
ASJRLC Luis Castillo 8.00 20.00
ASJRLG Lourdes Gurriel Jr. 5.00 12.00
ASJRLV Luke Voit 10.00 25.00
ASJRMA Miguel Andujar 8.00 20.00
ASJRMCH Michael Chavis 5.00 12.00
ASJRMD Mauricio Dubon 10.00 25.00
ASJRMH Mitch Haniger 5.00 12.00
ASJRMK Max Kepler EXCH 8.00 20.00
ASJRMM Miles Mikolas 4.00 10.00
ASJRMS Mike Soroka 12.00 30.00
ASJRMT Matt Thaiss 5.00 12.00
ASJRNH Nico Hoerner 10.00 25.00
ASJRNS Nick Solak 6.00 15.00
ASJRNSE Nick Senzel 8.00 20.00
ASJRNSY Noah Syndergaard 10.00 25.00
ASJRPD Paul DeJong 6.00 15.00
ASJRRD Rafael Devers 12.00 30.00
ASJRRH Rhys Hoskins 8.00 20.00
ASJRRL Ramon Laureano 8.00 20.00
ASJRRM Ryan McMahon 4.00 10.00
ASJRRO Ryan O'Hearn 4.00 10.00
ASJRSA Shogo Akiyama 8.00 20.00
ASJRSB Seth Brown 4.00 10.00
ASJRSK Scott Kingery 5.00 12.00
ASJRSY Shun Yamaguchi EXCH 5.00 12.00
ASJRTA Tim Anderson 12.00 30.00
ASJRVR Victor Robles 8.00 20.00
ASJRWC Willson Contreras 8.00 20.00
ASJRWS Will Smith 10.00 25.00
ASJRXB Xander Bogaerts 12.00 30.00
ASJRYA Yordan Alvarez 30.00 80.00
ASJRYG Yasmani Grandal 4.00 10.00

2020 Topps Triple Threads Single Jumbo Relic Autographs Amethyst

*AMETHYST: .4X TO 1X BASIC
STATED ODDS 1:XX HOBBY
STATED PRINT RUN 75 SER.#'d SETS
EXCHANGE DEADLINE 8/31/2022
ASJRABR Alex Bregman 12.00 30.00
ASJRKH Keston Hiura 10.00 25.00
ASJRKL Kyle Lewis 30.00 80.00
ASJRMKO Michael Kopech 8.00 20.00
ASJRMO Matt Olson 6.00 15.00
ASJRPG Paul Goldschmidt 15.00 40.00
ASJRRA Ronald Acuna Jr. 50.00 120.00
ASJRTG Trent Grisham 123.00

2020 Topps Triple Threads Single Jumbo Relic Autographs Emerald

*EMERALD: .5X TO 1.2X BASIC
STATED ODDS 1:XX HOBBY
STATED PRINT RUN 50 SER.#'d SETS
EXCHANGE DEADLINE 8/31/2022
ASJRABR Alex Bregman 15.00 40.00
ASJRJA Jose Altuve EXCH 12.00 30.00
ASJRJH Josh Hader 5.00 12.00
ASJRKH Keston Hiura 12.00 30.00
ASJRKL Kyle Lewis 40.00 100.00
ASJRMKO Michael Kopech 10.00 25.00
ASJRMO Matt Olson 8.00 20.00
ASJRPG Paul Goldschmidt 20.00 50.00
ASJRRA Ronald Acuna Jr. 60.00 150.00
ASJRTG Trent Grisham 15.00 40.00
ASJRTM Trey Mancini 8.00 20.00
ASJRVG Vladimir Guerrero Jr. 25.00 60.00

2020 Topps Triple Threads Single Jumbo Relic Autographs Gold

*GOLD: .6X TO 1.5X BASIC
STATED ODDS 1:XX HOBBY
STATED PRINT RUN 25 SER.#'d SETS
EXCHANGE DEADLINE 8/31/2022
ASJRABR Alex Bregman 20.00 50.00
ASJRARO Amed Rosario 8.00
ASJRJA Jose Altuve EXCH 15.00 40.00
ASJRJH Josh Hader 6.00 15.00
ASJRKH Keston Hiura 15.00 40.00
ASJRKL Kyle Lewis 50.00 125.00
ASJRLR Luis Robert 125.00 300.00
ASJRMKO Michael Kopech 12.00 30.00
ASJRMO Matt Olson 10.00 25.00
ASJRPG Paul Goldschmidt 25.00 60.00
ASJRRA Ronald Acuna Jr. 75.00 200.00
ASJRTG Trent Grisham 20.00 50.00
ASJRTM Trey Mancini 10.00 25.00
ASJRVG Vladimir Guerrero Jr. 30.00 80.00

2020 Topps Triple Threads Single Jumbo Relics

STATED ODDS 1:XX HOBBY
STATED PRINT RUN 36 SER.#'d SETS
*SILVER/27: .4X TO 1X BASIC
*EMERALD/18: .5X TO 1.2X BASIC
*GOLD/9: .6X TO 1.5X BASIC
ALL VERSIONS EQUALLY PRICED
SJRAA Aristides Aquino 5.00 12.00
SJRAAL Adbert Alzolay 3.00 8.00
SJRAAQ Aristides Aquino 5.00 12.00
SJRAB Andrew Benintendi 4.00 10.00
SJRABE Alex Bregman 4.00 10.00
SJRABN Andrew Benintendi 4.00 10.00
SJRABR Alex Bregman 4.00 10.00
SJRAC Aroldis Chapman 4.00 10.00
SJRACH Aroldis Chapman 4.00 10.00
SJRAJ Aaron Judge 12.00 30.00
SJRAJU Aaron Judge 12.00 30.00
SJRAM Andrew McCutchen 6.00 15.00
SJRAMC Andrew McCutchen 6.00 15.00
SJRAME Austin Meadows 3.00 8.00
SJRAMU Andres Munoz 3.00 8.00
SJRAN Aaron Nola 4.00 10.00
SJRANO Aaron Nola 4.00 10.00
SJRAP A.J. Puk 5.00 12.00
SJRAPU A.J. Puk 5.00 12.00
SJRAR Anthony Rizzo 8.00 20.00
SJRARI Anthony Rizzo 8.00 20.00
SJRARL Austin Riley 5.00 12.00
SJRARO Amed Rosario 3.00 8.00
SJRARS Amed Rosario 3.00 8.00
SJRARY Austin Riley 5.00 12.00
SJRAV Alex Verdugo 6.00 15.00
SJRAVE Alex Verdugo 6.00 15.00
SJRBA Brian Anderson 2.50 6.00
SJRBB Bo Bichette 10.00 25.00
SJRBBI Bo Bichette 10.00 50.00
SJRBBR Bobby Bradley 3.00 8.00
SJRBH Bryce Harper 12.00 30.00
SJRBHA Bryce Harper 12.00 30.00
SJRBL Brandon Lowe 4.00 10.00
SJRBLO Brandon Lowe 4.00 10.00
SJRBM Brendan McKay 4.00 10.00
SJRBMC Brendan McKay 4.00 10.00
SJRBP Buster Posey 5.00 12.00
SJRBPO Buster Posey 5.00 12.00
SJRBR Bryan Reynolds 3.00 8.00
SJRBRD Brendan Rodgers 4.00 10.00
SJRBRE Bryan Reynolds 3.00 8.00
SJRBRO Brendan Rodgers 4.00 10.00
SJRBS Blake Snell 3.00 8.00
SJRBSN Blake Snell 3.00 8.00
SJRCB Cavan Biggio 5.00 12.00
SJRCBE Cody Bellinger 6.00 15.00
SJRCBI Cavan Biggio 5.00 12.00
SJRCC Carlos Correa 4.00 10.00
SJRCCO Carlos Correa 4.00 10.00
SJRCF Clint Frazier 3.00 8.00
SJRCFR Clint Frazier 3.00 8.00
SJRCK Clayton Kershaw 8.00 20.00
SJRCKB Carter Kieboom 3.00 8.00
SJRCKE Clayton Kershaw 8.00 20.00
SJRCKI Carter Kieboom 3.00 8.00
SJRCP Chris Paddack 4.00 10.00
SJRCPA Chris Paddack 4.00 10.00
SJRCS Chris Sale 4.00 10.00
SJRCSA Chris Sale 4.00 10.00
SJRCSE Corey Seager 6.00 15.00
SJRCSG Corey Seager 6.00 15.00
SJRCY Christian Yelich 6.00 15.00
SJRCYE Christian Yelich 6.00 15.00
SJRDC Dylan Cease 5.00 12.00
SJRDCE Dylan Cease 5.00 12.00
SJRDD David Dahl 2.50 6.00
SJRDDA David Dahl 2.50 6.00
SJRDL DJ LeMahieu 6.00 15.00
SJRDLE DJ LeMahieu 6.00 15.00
SJRDM Dustin May 8.00 20.00
SJRDMA Dustin May 8.00 20.00
SJRDP Dustin Pedroia 4.00 10.00
SJRDPE Dustin Pedroia 4.00 10.00
SJRDS Dansby Swanson 6.00 15.00
SJRDSW Dansby Swanson 6.00 15.00
SJRDV Daniel Vogelbach 2.50 6.00
SJREH Eric Hosmer 3.00 8.00
SJREHO Eric Hosmer 3.00 8.00
SJREJ Eloy Jimenez 5.00 12.00
SJREJI Eloy Jimenez 5.00 12.00
SJRER Eduardo Rodriguez 2.50 6.00
SJRERO Eduardo Rodriguez 2.50 6.00
SJRFF Freddie Freeman 8.00 20.00
SJRFFR Freddie Freeman 8.00 20.00
SJRFL Francisco Lindor 6.00 15.00
SJRFLI Francisco Lindor 6.00 15.00
SJRFT Fernando Tatis Jr. 15.00 40.00
SJRFTA Fernando Tatis Jr. 15.00 40.00
SJRGC Griffin Canning 4.00 10.00
SJRGL Gavin Lux 6.00 15.00
SJRGLU Gavin Lux 6.00 15.00
SJRGS George Springer 6.00 15.00
SJRGSA Gary Sanchez 5.00 12.00
SJRGSN Gary Sanchez 5.00 12.00
SJRGT Gleyber Torres 8.00 20.00
SJRGTO Gleyber Torres 8.00 20.00
SJRGU Gio Urshela 4.00 10.00
SJRHD Hunter Dozier 2.50 6.00
SJRHP Hunter Pence 3.00 8.00
SJRIH Ian Happ 6.00 15.00
SJRIHA Ian Happ 6.00 15.00
SJRIHH Ian Happ 6.00 15.00
SJRIHP Ian Happ 6.00 15.00
SJRJA Jose Altuve 5.00 12.00
SJRJAL Jose Altuve 5.00 12.00
SJRJB Javier Baez 8.00 20.00
SJRJBA Javier Baez 8.00 20.00
SJRJBE Jose Berrios 4.00 10.00
SJRJBR Jose Berrios 4.00 10.00
SJRJD Jacob deGrom 6.00 15.00
SJRJDE Jacob deGrom 6.00 15.00
SJRJDN Josh Donaldson 3.00 8.00
SJRJDO Josh Donaldson 3.00 8.00
SJRJF Jack Flaherty 6.00 15.00
SJRJFL Jack Flaherty 6.00 15.00
SJRJG Joey Gallo 4.00 10.00
SJRJH Josh Hader 2.50 6.00
SJRJHA Josh Hader 2.50 6.00
SJRJL Jesus Luzardo 5.00 12.00
SJRJLU Jesus Luzardo 5.00 12.00
SJRJM J.D. Martinez 4.00 10.00
SJRJMA J.D. Martinez 4.00 10.00
SJRJMC Jeff McNeil 3.00 8.00
SJRJMN Jeff McNeil 3.00 8.00
SJRJP Joc Pederson 4.00 10.00
SJRJPE Joc Pederson 4.00 10.00
SJRJR Jose Ramirez 3.00 8.00
SJRJRE J.T. Realmuto 6.00 15.00
SJRJSE Justus Sheffield 4.00 10.00
SJRJSH Justus Sheffield 4.00 10.00
SJRJSL Jorge Soler 4.00 10.00
SJRJT Jameson Taillon 3.00 8.00
SJRJU Julio Urias 8.00 20.00
SJRJUR Julio Urias 8.00 20.00
SJRKB Kris Bryant 5.00 12.00
SJRKBR Kris Bryant 5.00 12.00
SJRKD Khris Davis 4.00 10.00
SJRKDA Khris Davis 4.00 10.00
SJRKH Keston Hiura 5.00 12.00
SJRKHI Keston Hiura 5.00 12.00
SJRKL Kyle Lewis 10.00 25.00
SJRKLE Kyle Lewis 10.00 25.00
SJRKS Kyle Schwarber 4.00 10.00
SJRKSC Kyle Schwarber 4.00 10.00
SJRKT Kyle Tucker 3.00 8.00
SJRKTU Kyle Tucker 3.00 8.00
SJRLC Lorenzo Cain 2.50 6.00
SJRLCL Luis Castillo 3.00 8.00
SJRLCS Luis Castillo 3.00 8.00
SJRLG Lourdes Gurriel Jr. 3.00 8.00

Card	Low	High
SJRLGR Lourdes Gurriel Jr.	3.00	8.00
SJRLR Luis Robert	30.00	80.00
SJRLRO Luis Robert	30.00	80.00
SJRLS Luis Severino	3.00	8.00
SJRLSE Luis Severino	3.00	8.00
SJRLV Luke Voit	5.00	12.00
SJRLVO Luke Voit	5.00	12.00
SJRMA Miguel Andujar	4.00	10.00
SJRMAN Miguel Andujar	4.00	10.00
SJRMB Matt Boyd	5.00	12.00
SJRMC Mike Clevinger	3.00	8.00
SJRMCA Miguel Cabrera	6.00	15.00
SJRMCB Miguel Cabrera	6.00	15.00
SJRMCH Michael Chavis	3.00	8.00
SJRMCN Matt Chapman	6.00	15.00
SJRMCP Matt Chapman	6.00	15.00
SJRMCR Matt Carpenter	4.00	10.00
SJRMCT Matt Carpenter	4.00	10.00
SJRMCV Michael Chavis	3.00	8.00
SJRMD Mauricio Dubon	3.00	8.00
SJRMDU Mauricio Dubon	3.00	8.00
SJRMG Mitch Garver	2.50	6.00
SJRMH Mitch Haniger	3.00	8.00
SJRMHN Mitch Haniger	3.00	8.00
SJRMK Max Kepler	6.00	15.00
SJRMKE Max Kepler	6.00	15.00
SJRMKO Michael Kopech	5.00	12.00
SJRMKP Michael Kopech	5.00	12.00
SJRMM Max Muncy	3.00	8.00
SJRMMA Manny Machado	4.00	10.00
SJRMMN Manny Machado	4.00	10.00
SJRMMU Max Muncy	3.00	8.00
SJRMO Matt Olson	2.50	6.00
SJRMOL Matt Olson	2.50	6.00
SJRMSC Max Scherzer	4.00	10.00
SJRMSH Max Scherzer	4.00	10.00
SJRMSN Miguel Sano	3.00	8.00
SJRMSO Mike Soroka	4.00	10.00
SJRMSR Mike Soroka	4.00	10.00
SJRMSS Miguel Sano	3.00	8.00
SJRMT Mike Trout	40.00	100.00
SJRMTR Mike Trout	40.00	100.00
SJRNA Nolan Arenado	5.00	12.00
SJRNAR Nolan Arenado	5.00	12.00
SJRNH Nico Hoerner	6.00	15.00
SJRNHO Nico Hoerner	6.00	15.00
SJRNS Noah Syndergaard	3.00	8.00
SJRNSE Nick Senzel	4.00	10.00
SJRNSL Nick Solak	4.00	10.00
SJRNSN Nick Senzel	4.00	10.00
SJRNSO Nick Solak	4.00	10.00
SJRNSY Noah Syndergaard	3.00	8.00
SJROA Ozzie Albies	5.00	12.00
SJROAL Ozzie Albies	5.00	12.00
SJRPA Pete Alonso	6.00	15.00
SJRPAL Pete Alonso	6.00	15.00
SJRPC Patrick Corbin	3.00	8.00
SJRPCO Patrick Corbin	3.00	8.00
SJRPD Paul DeJong	4.00	10.00
SJRPDE Paul DeJong	4.00	10.00
SJRPG Paul Goldschmidt	5.00	12.00
SJRPGO Paul Goldschmidt	5.00	12.00
SJRRA Ronald Acuna Jr.	10.00	25.00
SJRRAC Ronald Acuna Jr.	10.00	25.00
SJRRD Rafael Devers	5.00	12.00
SJRRDE Rafael Devers	5.00	12.00
SJRRG Robel Garcia	2.50	6.00
SJRRGA Robel Garcia	2.50	6.00
SJRRH Rhys Hoskins	5.00	12.00
SJRRHO Rhys Hoskins	5.00	12.00
SJRRL Ramon Laureano	4.00	10.00
SJRRLA Ramon Laureano	4.00	10.00
SJRRM Ryan McMahon	2.50	6.00
SJRRMC Ryan McMahon	2.50	6.00
SJRSA Shogo Akiyama	4.00	10.00
SJRSAK Shogo Akiyama	4.00	10.00
SJRSB Seth Brown	2.50	6.00
SJRSG Sonny Gray	3.00	8.00
SJRSGR Sonny Gray	3.00	8.00
SJRSK Scott Kingery	3.00	8.00
SJRSKI Scott Kingery	3.00	8.00
SJRSM Sean Murphy	4.00	10.00
SJRSO Shohei Ohtani	6.00	15.00
SJRSOH Shohei Ohtani	6.00	15.00
SJRTA Tim Anderson	6.00	15.00
SJRTAN Tim Anderson	6.00	15.00
SJRTE Tommy Edman	4.00	10.00
SJRTED Tommy Edman	4.00	10.00
SJRTG Trent Grisham	6.00	15.00
SJRTGL Tyler Glasnow	2.50	6.00
SJRTGR Trent Grisham	6.00	15.00
SJRTM Trey Mancini	4.00	10.00
SJRTMA Trey Mancini	4.00	10.00
SJRTS Trevor Story	4.00	10.00
SJRTST Trevor Story	4.00	10.00
SJRTT Trea Turner	5.00	12.00
SJRTTU Trea Turner	5.00	12.00
SJRVG Vladimir Guerrero Jr.	8.00	20.00
SJRVR Victor Robles	5.00	12.00
SJRWA Willy Adames	2.50	6.00
SJRWB Walker Buehler	8.00	20.00
SJRWC Willson Contreras	4.00	10.00
SJRWM Whit Merrifield	4.00	10.00
SJRWS Will Smith	6.00	15.00
SJRXB Xander Bogaerts	6.00	15.00
SJRYA Yordan Alvarez	8.00	20.00
SJRYG Yasmani Grandal	2.50	6.00
SJRYM Yadier Molina	15.00	40.00
SJRYMC Yoan Moncada	4.00	10.00
SJRYMN Yoan Moncada	4.00	10.00
SJRYMO Yadier Molina	15.00	40.00
SJRVGU Vladimir Guerrero Jr.	8.00	20.00
SJRVRO Victor Robles	5.00	12.00
SJRWBU Walker Buehler	8.00	20.00
SJRWCN Willson Contreras	4.00	10.00
SJRWSM Will Smith	6.00	15.00
SJRXBO Xander Bogaerts	6.00	15.00
SJRYAL Yordan Alvarez	8.00	20.00
SJRYGI Yuli Gurriel	3.00	8.00
SJRYGR Yasmani Grandal	2.50	6.00
SJRYGU Yuli Gurriel	3.00	8.00

2020 Topps Triple Threads Touch 'Em All Relics

STATED ODDS 1:XX HOBBY
STATED PRINT RUN 18 SER.#'d SETS

Card	Low	High
TEARABB McKay/Meadows/Lowe	8.00	20.00
TEARAJE Gallo/Beltre/Andrus	12.00	30.00
TEARCNT Blckmn/Arndo/Stry	10.00	25.00
TEARDAM Txra/Rdrgz/Jeter	50.00	120.00
TEARGAJ Brgmn/Sprngr/Altve	15.00	40.00
TEARJVH Soto/Kndrck/Rbls	12.00	30.00
TEARMDK Vglbch/Hngr/Lws	15.00	40.00
TEARMMK Chapman/Olson/Davis	8.00	20.00
TEARXRA Bnntndi/Bgrts/Dvrs	15.00	40.00

1989 Upper Deck

This attractive 800-card standard-size set was introduced in 1989 as the premier issue by the then-fledgling Upper Deck company. Unlike other 1989 major releases, this set was issued in two separate series - a low series numbered 1-700 and a high series numbered 701-800. Cards were primarily issued in fin-wrapped low and high series foil packs, complete 800-card factory sets and 100-card high series factory sets. High series packs contained a mixture of both low and high series cards. Collectors should also note that many dealers consider that Upper Deck's "planned" production of 1,000,000 of each player was increased (perhaps even doubled) later in the year due to the explosion in popularity of the product. The cards feature slick paper stock, full color on both the front and the back and carry a hologram on the reverse to protect against counterfeiting. Subsets include Rookie Stars (1-26) and Collector's Choice art cards (668-693). The more significant variations involving changed photos or changed type are listed below. According to the company, the Murphy and Sheridan cards were corrected very early, after only two percent of the cards had been produced. Similarly, the Sheffield was corrected after 15 percent had been printed; Varsho, Gallego, and Schroeder were corrected after 20 percent; and Holton, Manrique, and Winningham were corrected 30 percent of the way through. Rookie Cards in the set include Jim Abbott, Sandy Alomar Jr., Dante Bichette, Craig Biggio, Steve Finley, Ken Griffey Jr., Randy Johnson, Gary Sheffield, John Smoltz and Todd Zeile. Cards with missing or duplicate holograms appear to be relatively common and are generally considered to be flawed copies that sell for substantial discounts.

Card	Low	High
COMPLETE SET (800)	25.00	60.00
COMP.FACT.SET (800)	25.00	60.00
COMPLETE LO SET (700)	15.00	40.00
COMPLETE HI SET (100)	6.00	15.00
COMP.HI FACT.SET (100)	6.00	15.00
1 Ken Griffey Jr. RC	30.00	80.00
2 Luis Medina RC	.08	.25
3 Tony Chance RC	.08	.25
4 Dave Otto	.08	.25
5 Sandy Alomar Jr. RC UER	.40	1.00
Born 6/16/66		
should be 6/18/66		
6 Rolando Roomes RC	.08	.25
7 Dave West RC	.08	.25
8 Cris Carpenter RC	.08	.25
9 Gregg Jefferies	.08	.25
10 Doug Dascenzo RC	.08	.25
11 Ron Jones RC	.08	.25
12 Luis DeLosSantos RC	.08	.25
13 Gary Sheffield COR RC	2.00	5.00
13A Gary Sheffield ERR	2.00	5.00
14 Mike Harkey RC	.08	.25
15 Lance Blankenship RC	.08	.25
16 William Brennan RC	.08	.25
17 John Smoltz RC	2.00	5.00
18 Ramon Martinez RC	.20	.50
19 Mark Lemke RC	.40	1.00
20 Juan Bell RC	.08	.25
21 Rey Palacios RC	.08	.25
22 Felix Jose RC	.08	.25
23 Van Snider RC	.08	.25
24 Dante Bichette RC	.40	1.00
25 Randy Johnson RC	4.00	10.00
26 Carlos Quintana RC	.08	.25
27 Star Rookie CL	.08	.25
28 Mike Schooler	.08	.25
29 Randy St.Claire	.08	.25
30 Jerald Clark RC	.08	.25
31 Kevin Gross	.08	.25
32 Dan Firova	.08	.25
33 Jeff Calhoun	.08	.25
34 Tommy Hinzo	.08	.25
35 Ricky Jordan RC	.20	.50
36 Larry Parrish	.08	.25
37 Bret Saberhagen UER	.15	.40
38 Mike Smithson	.08	.25
39 Dave Dravecky	.08	.25
40 Ed Romero	.08	.25
41 Jeff Musselman	.08	.25
42 Ed Hearn	.08	.25
43 Rance Mulliniks	.08	.25
44 Jim Eisenreich	.08	.25
45 Sil Campusano	.08	.25
46 Mike Krukow	.08	.25
47 Paul Gibson	.08	.25
48 Mike LaCoss	.08	.25
49 Larry Herndon	.08	.25
50 Scott Garrelts	.08	.25
51 Dwayne Henry	.08	.25
52 Jim Acker	.08	.25
53 Steve Sax	.08	.25
54 Pete O'Brien	.08	.25
55 Paul Runge	.08	.25
56 Rick Rhoden	.08	.25
57 John Dopson	.08	.25
58 Casey Candaele UER	.08	.25
No stats for Astros		
for '88 season		
59 Dave Righetti	.15	.40
60 Joe Hesketh	.08	.25
61 Frank DiPino	.08	.25
62 Tim Laudner	.08	.25
63 Jamie Moyer	.15	.40
64 Fred Toliver	.08	.25
65 Mitch Webster	.08	.25
66 John Tudor	.15	.40
67 John Cangelosi	.08	.25
68 Mike Devereaux	.08	.25
69 Brian Fisher	.08	.25
70 Mike Marshall	.08	.25
71 Zane Smith	.08	.25
72A Brian Holton ERR	.40	1.00
Photo actually		
Shawn Hillegas		
72B Brian Holton COR	.15	.40
73 Jose Guzman	.08	.25
74 Rick Mahler	.08	.25
75 John Shelby	.08	.25
76 Jim Deshaies	.08	.25
77 Bobby Meacham	.08	.25
78 Bryn Smith	.08	.25
79 Joaquin Andujar	.15	.40
80 Richard Dotson	.08	.25
81 Charlie Lea	.08	.25
82 Calvin Schiraldi	.08	.25
83 Les Straker	.08	.25
84 Les Lancaster	.08	.25
85 Allan Anderson	.08	.25
86 Junior Ortiz	.08	.25
87 Jesse Orosco	.08	.25
88 Felix Fermin	.08	.25
89 Dave Anderson	.08	.25
90 Rafael Belliard UER	.08	.25
Born '61 not '51		
91 Franklin Stubbs	.08	.25
92 Cecil Espy	.08	.25
93 Albert Hall	.08	.25
94 Tim Leary	.08	.25
95 Mitch Williams	.08	.25
96 Tracy Jones	.08	.25
97 Danny Darwin	.08	.25
98 Gary Ward	.08	.25
99 Neal Heaton	.08	.25
100 Jim Pankovits	.08	.25
101 Bill Doran	.08	.25
102 Tim Wallach	.08	.25
103 Joe Magrane	.08	.25
104 Ozzie Virgil	.08	.25
105 Alvin Davis	.08	.25
106 Tom Brookens	.08	.25
107 Shawon Dunston	.08	.25
108 Tracy Woodson	.08	.25
109 Nelson Liriano	.08	.25
110 Devon White UER	.15	.40
Doubles total 46		
should be 56		
111 Steve Balboni	.08	.25
112 Buddy Bell	.15	.40
113 German Jimenez	.08	.25
114 Ken Dayley	.08	.25
115 Andres Galarraga	.15	.40
116 Mike Scioscia	.15	.40
117 Gary Pettis	.08	.25
118 Ernie Whitt	.08	.25
119 Bob Boone	.15	.40
120 Ryne Sandberg	.60	1.50
121 Bruce Benedict	.08	.25
122 Hubie Brooks	.08	.25
123 Mike Moore	.08	.25
124 Wallace Johnson	.08	.25
125 Bob Horner	.15	.40
126 Chili Davis	.15	.40
127 Manny Trillo	.08	.25
128 Chet Lemon	.15	.40
129 John Cerutti	.08	.25
130 Orel Hershiser	.15	.40
131 Terry Pendleton	.15	.40
132 Jeff Blauser	.08	.25
133 Mike Fitzgerald	.08	.25
134 Henry Cotto	.08	.25
135 Gerald Young	.08	.25
136 Luis Salazar	.08	.25
137 Alejandro Pena	.08	.25
138 Jack Howell	.08	.25
139 Tony Fernandez	.08	.25
140 Mark Grace	.40	1.00
141 Ken Caminiti	.25	.60
142 Mike Jackson	.08	.25
143 Larry McWilliams	.08	.25
144 Andres Thomas	.08	.25
145 Nolan Ryan 3X	1.50	4.00
146 Mike Davis	.08	.25
147 DeWayne Buice	.08	.25
148 Jody Davis	.08	.25
149 Jesse Barfield	.15	.40
150 Matt Nokes	.08	.25
151 Jerry Reuss	.08	.25
152 Rick Cerone	.08	.25
153 Storm Davis	.08	.25
154 Marvell Wynne	.08	.25
155 Will Clark	.25	.60
156 Luis Aguayo	.08	.25
157 Willie Upshaw	.08	.25
158 Randy Bush	.08	.25
159 Ron Darling	.15	.40
160 Kal Daniels	.08	.25
161 Spike Owen	.08	.25
162 Luis Polonia	.08	.25
163 Kevin Mitchell UER	.15	.40
'88 total HR should be 19		
164 Dave Gallagher	.08	.25
165 Benito Santiago	.15	.40
166 Greg Gagne	.08	.25
167 Ken Phelps	.08	.25
168 Sid Fernandez	.08	.25
169 Bo Diaz	.08	.25
170 Cory Snyder	.08	.25
171 Eric Show	.08	.25
172 Robby Thompson	.08	.25
173 Marty Barrett	.08	.25
174 Dave Henderson	.08	.25
175 Ozzie Guillen	.15	.40
176 Barry Lyons	.08	.25
177 Kelvin Torve	.08	.25
178 Don Slaught	.08	.25
179 Steve Lombardozzi	.08	.25
180 Chris Sabo RC	.40	1.00
181 Jose Uribe	.08	.25
182 Shane Mack	.08	.25
183 Ron Karkovice	.08	.25
184 Todd Benzinger	.08	.25
185 Dave Stewart	.15	.40
186 Julio Franco	.15	.40
187 Ron Robinson	.08	.25
188 Wally Backman	.08	.25
189 Randy Velarde	.08	.25
190 Joe Carter	.15	.40
191 Bob Welch	.15	.40
192 Kelly Paris	.08	.25
193 Chris Brown	.08	.25
194 Rick Reuschel	.15	.40
195 Roger Clemens	.75	2.00
196 Dave Concepcion	.15	.40
197 Al Newman	.08	.25
198 Brook Jacoby	.08	.25
199 Mookie Wilson	.15	.40
200 Don Mattingly	1.00	2.50
201 Dick Schofield	.08	.25
202 Mark Gubicza	.08	.25
203 Gary Gaetti	.15	.40
204 Dan Pasqua	.08	.25
205 Andre Dawson	.15	.40
206 Chris Speier	.08	.25
207 Kent Tekulve	.08	.25
208 Rod Scurry	.08	.25
209 Scott Bailes	.08	.25
210 R.Henderson UER	.40	1.00
Throws Right		
211 Harold Baines	.15	.40
212 Tony Armas	.15	.40
213 Kent Hrbek	.15	.40
214 Darrin Jackson	.08	.25
215 George Brett	1.00	2.50
216 Rafael Santana	.08	.25
217 Andy Allanson	.08	.25
218 Brett Butler	.15	.40
219 Steve Jeltz	.08	.25
220 Jay Buhner	.15	.40
221 Bo Jackson	.40	1.00
222 Angel Salazar	.08	.25
223 Kirk McCaskill	.08	.25
224 Steve Lyons	.08	.25
225 Bert Blyleven	.15	.40
226 Scott Bradley	.08	.25
227 Bob Melvin	.08	.25
228 Ron Kittle	.08	.25
229 Phil Bradley	.08	.25
230 Tommy John	.15	.40
231 Greg Walker	.08	.25
232 Juan Berenguer	.08	.25
233 Pat Tabler	.08	.25
234 Terry Clark	.08	.25
235 Rafael Palmeiro	.40	1.00
236 Paul Zuvella	.08	.25
237 Willie Randolph	.15	.40
238 Bruce Fields	.08	.25
239 Mike Aldrete	.08	.25
240 Lance Parrish	.15	.40
241 Greg Maddux	1.00	2.50
242 John Moses	.08	.25
243 Melido Perez	.08	.25
244 Willie Wilson	.15	.40
245 Mark McLemore	.08	.25
246 Von Hayes	.08	.25
247 Matt Williams	.40	1.00
248 John Candelaria UER		
(Listed as Yankee for/part o	.08	.25
249 Harold Reynolds	.15	.40
250 Greg Swindell	.08	.25
251 Juan Agosto	.08	.25
252 Mike Felder	.08	.25
253 Vince Coleman	.08	.25
254 Larry Sheets	.08	.25
255 George Bell	.15	.40
256 Terry Steinbach	.15	.40
257 Jack Armstrong RC	.20	.50
258 Dickie Thon	.08	.25
259 Ray Knight	.15	.40
260 Darryl Strawberry	.15	.40
261 Doug Sisk	.08	.25
262 Alex Trevino	.08	.25
263 Jeffrey Leonard	.08	.25
264 Tom Henke	.08	.25
265 Ozzie Smith	.60	1.50
266 Dave Bergman	.08	.25
267 Tony Phillips	.08	.25
268 Mark Davis	.08	.25
269 Kevin Elster	.08	.25
270 Barry Larkin	.25	.60
271 Manny Lee	.08	.25
272 Tom Brunansky	.08	.25
273 Craig Biggio RC	2.50	6.00
274 Jim Gantner	.08	.25
275 Eddie Murray	.40	1.00
276 Jeff Reed	.08	.25
277 Tim Teufel	.08	.25
278 Rick Honeycutt	.08	.25
279 Guillermo Hernandez	.08	.25
280 John Kruk	.15	.40
281 Luis Alicea RC	.20	.50
282 Jim Clancy	.08	.25
283 Billy Ripken	.08	.25
284 Craig Reynolds	.08	.25
285 Robin Yount	.60	1.50
286 Jimmy Jones	.08	.25
287 Ron Oester	.08	.25
288 Terry Leach	.08	.25
289 Dennis Eckersley	.25	.60
290 Alan Trammell	.15	.40
291 Jimmy Key	.15	.40
292 Chris Bosio	.08	.25
293 Jose DeLeon	.08	.25
294 Jim Traber	.08	.25
295 Mike Scott	.15	.40
296 Roger McDowell	.08	.25
297 Garry Templeton	.15	.40
298 Doyle Alexander	.08	.25
299 Nick Esasky	.08	.25
300 Mark McGwire UER	2.00	5.00
301 Darryl Hamilton RC	.20	.50
302 Dave Smith	.08	.25
303 Rick Sutcliffe	.15	.40
304 Dave Stapleton	.08	.25
305 Alan Ashby	.08	.25
306 Pedro Guerrero	.15	.40
307 Ron Guidry	.15	.40
308 Steve Farr	.08	.25
309 Curt Ford	.08	.25
310 Claudell Washington	.08	.25
311 Tom Prince	.08	.25
312 Chad Kreuter RC	.20	.50
313 Ken Oberkfell	.08	.25
314 Jerry Browne	.08	.25
315 R.J. Reynolds	.08	.25
316 Scott Bankhead	.08	.25
317 Milt Thompson	.08	.25
318 Mario Diaz	.08	.25
319 Bruce Ruffin	.08	.25
320 Dave Valle	.08	.25
321A Gary Varsho ERR	.75	2.00
321B Gary Varsho COR	.08	.25
In road uniform		
322 Paul Mirabella	.08	.25
323 Chuck Jackson	.08	.25
324 Drew Hall	.08	.25
325 Don August	.08	.25
326 Israel Sanchez	.08	.25
327 Denny Walling	.08	.25
328 Joel Skinner	.08	.25
329 Danny Tartabull	.08	.25
330 Tony Pena	.08	.25
331 Jim Sundberg	.15	.40
332 Jeff D. Robinson	.08	.25
333 Oddibe McDowell	.08	.25
334 Jose Lind	.08	.25
335 Paul Kilgus	.08	.25
336 Juan Samuel	.08	.25
337 Mike Campbell	.08	.25
338 Mike Maddux	.08	.25
339 Darnell Coles	.08	.25
340 Bob Dernier	.08	.25
341 Rafael Ramirez	.08	.25
342 Scott Sanderson	.08	.25
343 B.J. Surhoff	.15	.40
344 Billy Hatcher	.08	.25
345 Pat Perry	.08	.25
346 Jack Clark	.15	.40
347 Gary Thurman	.08	.25
348 Tim Jones	.08	.25
349 Dave Winfield	.15	.40
350 Frank White	.15	.40
351 Dave Collins	.08	.25
352 Jack Morris	.15	.40
353 Eric Plunk	.08	.25
354 Leon Durham	.08	.25
355 Ivan DeJesus	.08	.25
356 Brian Holman RC	.08	.25
357A Dale Murphy ERR	12.50	30.00
357B Dale Murphy COR	.25	.60
358 Mark Portugal	.08	.25
359 Andy McGaffigan	.08	.25
360 Tom Glavine	.40	1.00
361 Keith Moreland	.08	.25
362 Todd Stottlemyre	.08	.25
363 Dave Leiper	.08	.25
364 Cecil Fielder	.15	.40
365 Carmelo Martinez	.08	.25
366 Dwight Evans	.25	.60
367 Kevin McReynolds	.08	.25
368 Rich Gedman	.08	.25
369 Len Dykstra	.15	.40
370 Jody Reed	.08	.25
371 Jose Canseco UER	.40	1.00
Strikeout total 391		
should be 491		
372 Rob Murphy	.08	.25
373 Mike Henneman	.08	.25
374 Walt Weiss	.08	.25
375 Rob Dibble RC	.40	1.00
376 Kirby Puckett	.40	1.00
Mark McGwire		
in background		
377 Dennis Martinez	.15	.40
378 Ron Gant	.15	.40
379 Brian Harper	.08	.25
380 Nelson Santovenia	.08	.25
381 Lloyd Moseby	.08	.25
382 Lance McCullers	.08	.25
383 Dave Stieb	.15	.40
384 Tony Gwynn	.50	1.25
385 Mike Flanagan	.08	.25
386 Bob Ojeda	.08	.25
387 Bruce Hurst	.08	.25
388 Dave Magadan	.08	.25
389 Wade Boggs	.25	.60
390 Gary Carter	.15	.40
391 Frank Tanana	.15	.40
392 Curt Young	.08	.25
393 Jeff Treadway	.08	.25
394 Darrell Evans	.15	.40
395 Glenn Hubbard	.08	.25
396 Chuck Cary	.08	.25
397 Frank Viola	.15	.40
398 Jeff Parrett	.08	.25
399 Terry Blocker	.08	.25
400 Dan Gladden	.08	.25
401 Louie Meadows RC	.08	.25
402 Tim Raines	.15	.40
403 Joey Meyer	.08	.25
404 Larry Andersen	.08	.25
405 Rex Hudler	.08	.25
406 Mike Schmidt	.75	2.00
407 John Franco	.15	.40
408 Brady Anderson RC	.40	1.00
409 Don Carman	.08	.25
410 Eric Davis	.15	.40
411 Bob Stanley	.08	.25
412 Pete Smith	.08	.25
413 Jim Rice	.15	.40
414 Bruce Sutter	.15	.40
415 Oil Can Boyd	.08	.25
416 Ruben Sierra	.15	.40
417 Mike LaValliere	.08	.25
418 Steve Buechele	.08	.25
419 Gary Redus	.08	.25
420 Scott Fletcher	.08	.25
421 Dale Sveum	.08	.25
422 Bob Knepper	.08	.25
423 Luis Rivera	.08	.25
424 Ted Higuera	.08	.25
425 Kevin Bass	.08	.25
426 Ken Gerhart	.08	.25
427 Shane Rawley	.08	.25
428 Paul O'Neill	.25	.60
429 Joe Orsulak	.08	.25
430 Jackie Gutierrez	.08	.25
431 Gerald Perry	.08	.25
432 Mike Greenwell	.08	.25
433 Jerry Royster	.08	.25
434 Ellis Burks	.15	.40
435 Ed Olwine	.08	.25
436 Dave Rucker	.08	.25
437 Charlie Hough	.15	.40
438 Bob Walk	.08	.25
439 Bob Brower	.08	.25
440 Barry Bonds	2.00	5.00
441 Tom Foley	.08	.25
442 Rob Deer	.08	.25
443 Glenn Davis	.08	.25
444 Dave Martinez	.08	.25
445 Bill Wegman	.08	.25
446 Lloyd McClendon	.08	.25
447 Dave Schmidt	.08	.25
448 Darren Daulton	.15	.40
449 Frank Williams	.08	.25
450 Don Aase	.08	.25
451 Lou Whitaker	.15	.40
452 Rich Gossage	.15	.40
453 Ed Whitson	.08	.25
454 Jim Walewander	.08	.25
455 Damon Berryhill	.08	.25
456 Tim Burke	.08	.25
457 Barry Jones	.08	.25
458 Joel Youngblood	.08	.25
459 Floyd Youmans	.08	.25
460 Mark Salas	.08	.25
461 Jeff Russell	.08	.25
462 Darrell Miller	.08	.25
463 Jeff Kunkel	.08	.25
464 Sherman Corbett RC	.08	.25
465 Curtis Wilkerson	.08	.25
466 Bud Black	.08	.25
467 Cal Ripken	1.25	3.00
468 John Farrell	.08	.25
469 Terry Kennedy	.08	.25
470 Tom Candiotti	.08	.25
471 Roberto Alomar	.40	1.00
472 Jeff M. Robinson	.08	.25
473 Vance Law	.08	.25
474 Randy Ready UER	.08	.25
Strikeout total 136		
should be 115		
475 Walt Terrell	.08	.25
476 Kelly Downs	.08	.25
477 Johnny Paredes	.08	.25
478 Shawn Hillegas	.08	.25
479 Bob Brenly	.08	.25
480 Otis Nixon	.08	.25
481 Johnny Ray	.08	.25
482 Geno Petralli	.08	.25
483 Stu Cliburn	.08	.25
484 Pete Incaviglia	.08	.25
485 Brian Downing	.15	.40
486 Jeff Stone	.08	.25
487 Carmen Castillo	.08	.25
488 Tom Niedenfuer	.08	.25
489 Jay Bell	.15	.40
490 Rick Schu	.08	.25
491 Jeff Pico	.08	.25
492 Mark Parent RC	.08	.25
493 Eric King	.08	.25
494 Al Nipper	.08	.25
495 Andy Hawkins	.08	.25
496 Daryl Boston	.08	.25
497 Ernie Riles	.08	.25
498 Pascual Perez	.08	.25
499 Bill Long UER		
(Games started total/70& should be	.08	.25
500 Kirt Manwaring	.08	.25
501 Chuck Crim	.08	.25
502 Candy Maldonado	.08	.25
503 Dennis Lamp	.08	.25
504 Glenn Braggs	.08	.25
505 Joe Price	.08	.25
506 Ken Williams	.08	.25
507 Bill Pecota	.08	.25
508 Rey Quinones	.08	.25
509 Jeff Bittiger	.08	.25
510 Kevin Seitzer	.08	.25
511 Steve Bedrosian	.08	.25
512 Todd Worrell	.08	.25
513 Chris James	.08	.25
514 Jose Oquendo	.08	.25
515 David Palmer	.08	.25
516 John Smiley	.08	.25
517 Dave Clark	.08	.25
518 Mike Dunne	.08	.25
519 Ron Washington	.08	.25
520 Bob Kipper	.08	.25
521 Lee Smith	.15	.40
522 Juan Castillo	.08	.25
523 Don Robinson	.08	.25
524 Kevin Romine	.08	.25
525 Paul Molitor	.15	.40
526 Mark Langston	.08	.25
527 Donnie Hill	.08	.25
528 Larry Owen	.08	.25
529 Jerry Reed	.08	.25
530 Jack McDowell	.15	.40
531 Greg Mathews	.08	.25
532 John Russell	.08	.25
533 Dan Quisenberry	.08	.25
534 Greg Gross	.08	.25
535 Danny Cox	.08	.25
536 Terry Francona	.15	.40
537 Andy Van Slyke	.25	.60
538 Mel Hall	.08	.25
539 Jim Gott	.08	.25
540 Doug Jones	.08	.25
541 Craig Lefferts	.08	.25
542 Mike Boddicker	.08	.25
543 Greg Brock	.08	.25
544 Atlee Hammaker	.08	.25
545 Tom Bolton	.08	.25
546 Mike Macfarlane RC	.20	.50
547 Rich Renteria	.08	.25
548 John Davis	.08	.25
549 Floyd Bannister	.08	.25
550 Mickey Brantley	.08	.25
551 Duane Ward	.08	.25
552 Dan Petry	.08	.25
553 Mickey Tettleton UER	.08	.25
Walks total 175		
should be 136		
554 Rick Leach	.08	.25
555 Mike Witt	.08	.25
556 Sid Bream	.08	.25
557 Bobby Witt	.08	.25
558 Tommy Herr	.08	.25
559 Randy Milligan	.08	.25
560 Jose Cecena	.08	.25
561 Mackey Sasser	.08	.25
562 Carney Lansford	.15	.40
563 Rick Aguilera	.08	.25
564 Ron Hassey	.08	.25
565 Dwight Gooden	.15	.40
566 Paul Assenmacher	.08	.25
567 Neil Allen	.08	.25
568 Jim Morrison	.08	.25
569 Mike Pagliarulo	.08	.25
570 Ted Simmons	.15	.40
571 Mark Thurmond	.08	.25
572 Fred McGriff	.25	.60
573 Wally Joyner	.15	.40
574 Jose Bautista RC	.08	.25
575 Kelly Gruber	.08	.25
576 Cecilio Guante	.08	.25
577 Mark Davidson	.08	.25
578 Bobby Bonilla UER	.15	.40

Total steals 2 in '87
should be 3
579 Mike Stanley .08 .25
580 Gene Larkin .08 .25
581 Stan Javier .08 .25
582 Howard Johnson .15 .40
583A Mike Gallego ERR .40 1.00
Front reversed
negative
583B Mike Gallego COR .40 1.00
584 David Cone .15 .40
585 Doug Jennings RC .08 .25
586 Charles Hudson .08 .25
587 Dion James .08 .25
588 Al Leiter .40 1.00
589 Charlie Puleo .08 .25
590 Roberto Kelly .08 .25
591 Thad Bosley .08 .25
592 Pete Stanicek .08 .25
593 Pat Borders RC .20 .50
594 Bryan Harvey RC .20 .50
595 Jeff Ballard .08 .25
596 Jeff Reardon .15 .40
597 Doug Drabek .08 .25
598 Edwin Correa .08 .25
599 Keith Atherton .08 .25
600 Dave LaPoint .08 .25
601 Don Baylor .15 .40
602 Tom Pagnozzi .08 .25
603 Tim Flannery .08 .25
604 Gene Walter .08 .25
605 Dave Parker .15 .40
606 Mike Diaz .08 .25
607 Chris Gwynn .08 .25
608 Odell Jones .08 .25
609 Carlton Fisk .25 .60
610 Jay Howell .08 .25
611 Tim Crews .08 .25
612 Keith Hernandez .15 .40
613 Willie Fraser .08 .25
614 Jim Eppard .08 .25
615 Jeff Hamilton .08 .25
616 Kurt Stillwell .08 .25
617 Tom Browning .08 .25
618 Jeff Montgomery .08 .25
619 Jose Rijo .15 .40
620 Jamie Quirk .08 .25
621 Willie McGee .15 .40
622 Mark Grant UER .08 .25
Glove on wrong hand
623 Bill Swift .08 .25
624 Orlando Mercado .08 .25
625 John Costello RC .08 .25
626 Jose Gonzalez .08 .25
627A Bill Schroeder ERR .25 .60
Back photo actually
Ronn Reynolds buckling
shin guards
627B Bill Schroeder COR .25 .60
628A Fred Manrique ERR .25 .60
Back photo actually
Ozzie Guillen throwing
628B Fred Manrique COR .08 .25
Swinging bat on back
629 Ricky Horton .08 .25
630 Dan Plesac .08 .25
631 Alfredo Griffin .08 .25
632 Chuck Finley .15 .40
633 Kirk Gibson .15 .40
634 Randy Myers .15 .40
635 Greg Minton .08 .25
636A Herm Winningham .40 1.00
ERR W1nningham
on back
636B Herm Winningham COR .08 .25
637 Charlie Leibrandt .08 .25
638 Tim Birtsas .08 .25
639 Bill Buckner .15 .40
640 Danny Jackson .08 .25
641 Greg Booker .08 .25
642 Jim Presley .08 .25
643 Gene Nelson .08 .25
644 Rod Booker .08 .25
645 Dennis Rasmussen .08 .25
646 Juan Nieves .08 .25
647 Bobby Thigpen .08 .25
648 Tim Belcher .08 .25
649 Mike Young .08 .25
650 Ivan Calderon .08 .25
651 Oswald Peraza RC .08 .25
652A Pat Sheridan ERR 6.00 15.00
652B Pat Sheridan COR .08 .25
653 Mike Morgan .08 .25
654 Mike Heath .08 .25
655 Jay Tibbs .08 .25
656 Fernando Valenzuela .15 .40
657 Lee Mazzilli .15 .40
658 Frank Viola AL CY .08 .25
659A Jose Canseco AL MVP .25 .60
Eagle logo in black
659B Jose Canseco AL MVP .25 .60
Eagle logo in blue
660 Walt Weiss AL ROY .08 .25
661 Orel Hershiser NL CY .08 .25
662 Kirk Gibson NL MVP .15 .40
663 Chris Sabo NL ROY .15 .40
664 Dennis Eckersley .15 .40
ALCS MVP
665 Orel Hershiser .15 .40
NLCS MVP
666 Kirk Gibson WS .40 1.00
667 Orel Hershiser WS MVP .08 .25
668 Wally Joyner TC .08 .25
669 Nolan Ryan TC .50 1.25
670 Jose Canseco TC .25 .60
671 Fred McGriff TC .15 .40
672 Dale Murphy TC .15 .40
673 Paul Molitor TC .08 .25
674 Ozzie Smith TC .40 1.00
675 Ryne Sandberg TC .40 1.00
676 Kirk Gibson TC .15 .40
677 Andres Galarraga TC .08 .25
678 Will Clark TC .15 .40
679 Cory Snyder TC .08 .25
680 Alvin Davis TC .08 .25
681 Darryl Strawberry TC .08 .25
682 Cal Ripken TC .40 1.00
683 Tony Gwynn TC .25 .60
684 Mike Schmidt TC .40 1.00
685 Andy Van Slyke TC
Pittsburgh Pirates/UER (96 Jun .15 .40
686 Ruben Sierra TC .08 .25
687 Wade Boggs TC .15 .40
688 Eric Davis TC .08 .25
689 George Brett TC .40 1.00
690 Alan Trammell TC .08 .25
691 Frank Viola TC .08 .25
692 Harold Baines TC .08 .25
Chicago White Sox
693 Don Mattingly TC .40 1.00
694 Checklist 1-100 .08 .25
695 Checklist 101-200 .08 .25
696 Checklist 201-300 .08 .25
697 Checklist 301-400 .08 .25
698 CL 401-500 UER .08 .25
467 Cal Ripkin Jr.
699 CL 501-600 UER .08 .25
543 Greg Booker
700 Checklist 601-700 .08 .25
701 Checklist 701-800 .08 .25
702 Jesse Barfield .15 .40
703 Walt Terrell .08 .25
704 Dickie Thon .08 .25
705 Al Leiter .40 1.00
706 Dave LaPoint .08 .25
707 Charlie Hayes RC .20 .50
708 Andy Hawkins .08 .25
709 Mickey Hatcher .08 .25
710 Lance McCullers .08 .25
711 Ron Kittle .08 .25
712 Bert Blyleven .15 .40
713 Rick Dempsey .08 .25
714 Ken Williams .08 .25
715 Steve Rosenberg .08 .25
716 Joe Skalski .08 .25
717 Spike Owen .08 .25
718 Todd Burns .08 .25
719 Kevin Gross .08 .25
720 Tommy Herr .08 .25
721 Rob Ducey .08 .25
722 Gary Green .08 .25
723 Gregg Olson RC .20 .50
724 Greg W. Harris RC .08 .25
725 Craig Worthington .08 .25
726 Tom Howard RC .08 .25
727 Dale Mohorcic .08 .25
728 Rich Yett .08 .25
729 Mel Hall .08 .25
730 Floyd Youmans .08 .25
731 Lonnie Smith .08 .25
732 Wally Backman .08 .25
733 Trevor Wilson RC .08 .25
734 Jose Alvarez RC .08 .25
735 Bob Milacki .08 .25
736 Tom Gordon RC .60 1.50
737 Wally Whitehurst RC .08 .25
738 Mike Aldrete .08 .25
739 Keith Miller .08 .25
740 Randy Milligan .08 .25
741 Jeff Parrett .08 .25
742 Steve Finley RC .75 2.00
743 Junior Felix RC .08 .25
744 Pete Harnisch RC .20 .50
745 Bill Spiers RC .20 .50
746 Hensley Meulens RC .08 .25
747 Juan Bell RC .08 .25
748 Steve Sax .08 .25
749 Phil Bradley .08 .25
750 Rey Quinones .08 .25
751 Tommy Gregg .08 .25
752 Kevin Brown .40 1.00
753 Derek Lilliquist RC .08 .25
754 Todd Zeile RC .40 1.00
755 Jim Abbott RC .75 2.00
756 Ozzie Canseco .08 .25
757 Nick Esasky .08 .25
758 Mike Moore .08 .25
759 Rob Murphy .08 .25
760 Rick Mahler .08 .25
761 Fred Lynn .15 .40
762 Kevin Blankenship .08 .25
763 Eddie Murray .40 1.00
764 Steve Searcy .08 .25
765 Jerome Walton RC .20 .50
766 Erik Hanson RC .20 .50
767 Bob Boone .15 .40
768 Edgar Martinez .40 1.00
769 Jose DeJesus .08 .25
770 Greg Briley .08 .25
771 Steve Peters .08 .25
772 Rafael Palmeiro .40 1.00
773 Jack Clark .15 .40
774 Nolan Ryan 1.50 4.00
775 Lance Parrish .15 .40
776 Joe Girardi RC .40 1.00
777 Willie Randolph .15 .40
778 Mitch Williams .08 .25
779 Dennis Cook RC .20 .50
780 Dwight Smith RC .20 .50
781 Lenny Harris RC .20 .50
782 Torey Lovullo RC .08 .25
783 Norm Charlton RC .20 .50
784 Chris Brown .08 .25
785 Todd Benzinger .08 .25
786 Shane Rawley .08 .25
787 Omar Vizquel RC 1.25 3.00
788 LaVel Freeman .08 .25
789 Jeffrey Leonard .08 .25
790 Eddie Williams .08 .25
791 Jamie Moyer .15 .40
792 Bruce Hurst UER .08 .25
World Series
793 Julio Franco .15 .40
794 Claudell Washington .08 .25
795 Jody Davis .08 .25
796 Oddibe McDowell .08 .25
797 Paul Kilgus .08 .25
798 Tracy Jones .08 .25
799 Steve Wilson .08 .25
800 Pete O'Brien .08 .25

1989 Upper Deck Sheets

These blank-backed, 8 1/2" by 11" sheets feature pictures of Upper Deck baseball cards and were distributed at conventions in Chicago and Washington, D.C. The sheets carried a production run number but not the total number produced. The sheets are listed below in chronological order.

COMPLETE SET (3) 15.00 40.00
1 10th National Sports Collectors Convention Chica 4.00 10.00
2 National Candy Wholesalers Expo Washington& D.C. 8.00 20.00
3 Sun-Times Card Show Chicago& Illinois Dec. 16-17 4.00 10.00

1990 Upper Deck

The 1990 Upper Deck set contains 800 standard-size cards issued in two series, low numbers (1-700) and high numbers (701-800). Cards were distributed in fin-wrapped low and high series foil packs, complete 800-card factory sets and 100-card high series factory sets. High series foil packs contained a mixture of low and high series cards. The front and back borders are white, and both sides feature full-color photos. The horizontally oriented backs have recent stats and anti-counterfeiting holograms. Team checklist cards are mixed in with the first 100 cards of the set. Rookie Cards in the set include Juan Gonzalez, David Justice, Ray Lankford, Dean Palmer, Sammy Sosa and Larry Walker. The high series contains a Nolan Ryan variation; all cards produced before August 12th only discuss Ryan's sixth no-hitter while the later-issue cards include a stripe honoring Ryan's 300th victory. Card 702 (Rookie Threats) was originally scheduled to be Mike Witt. A few Witt cards with 702 on back and checklist cards showing Witt as 702 escaped into early packs; they are characterized by a black rectangle covering much of the card's back.

COMPLETE SET (800) 10.00 25.00
COMP.FACT.SET (800) 10.00 25.00
COMPLETE LO SET (700) 10.00 25.00
COMPLETE HI SET (100) 2.00 5.00
COMP.HI FACT.SET (100) 2.00 4.00
1 Star Rookie Checklist .02 .10
2 Randy Nosek RC .02 .10
3 Tom Drees RC .02 .10
4 Curt Young .02 .10
5 Devon White TC .02 .10
6 Luis Salazar .02 .10
7 Von Hayes TC .02 .10
8 Jose Bautista .02 .10
9 Marquis Grissom RC .20 .50
10 Orel Hershiser TC .02 .10
11 Rick Aguilera .07 .20
12 Benito Santiago TC .02 .10
13 Deion Sanders .20 .50
14 Marvell Wynne .02 .10
15 Dave West .02 .10
16 Bobby Bonilla TC .02 .10
17 Sammy Sosa RC 1.25 3.00
18 Steve Sax TC .02 .10
19 Jack Howell .02 .10
20 Mike Schmidt SPEC .40 1.00
21 Robin Ventura .20 .50
22 Brian Meyer .02 .10
23 Blaine Beatty RC .02 .10
24 Ken Griffey Jr. TC .30 .75
25 Greg Vaughn .02 .10
26 Xavier Hernandez RC .02 .10
27 Jason Grimsley RC .02 .10
28 Eric Anthony RC .02 .10
29 Tim Raines TC UER .02 .10
30 David Wells .07 .20
31 Hal Morris .02 .10
32 Bo Jackson TC .07 .20
33 Kelly Mann RC .02 .10
34 Nolan Ryan SPEC .40 1.00
35 Scott Service UER
(Born Cincinati on/7/27/67& s .02 .10
36 Mark McGwire TC .30 .75
37 Tino Martinez .40 1.00
38 Chili Davis .07 .20
39 Scott Sanderson .02 .10
40 Kevin Mitchell TC .02 .10
41 Lou Whitaker TC .02 .10
42 Scott Coolbaugh RC .02 .10
43 Jose Cano RC .02 .10
44 Jose Vizcaino RC .08 .25
45 Bob Hamelin RC .08 .25
46 Jose Offerman RC .08 .25
47 Kevin Blankenship .02 .10
48 Kirby Puckett TC .10 .30
49 Tommy Greene UER RC .02 .10
50 Will Clark SPEC .07 .20
51 Rob Nelson .02 .10
52 Chris Hammond UER RC .02 .10
53 Joe Carter TC .02 .10
54A Ben McDonald ERR 2.00 5.00
54B Ben McDonald COR RC .08 .25
55 Andy Benes UER .07 .20
56 John Olerud RC .30 .75
57 Roger Clemens TC .30 .75
58 Tony Armas .02 .10
59 George Canale RC .02 .10
60A Mickey Tettleton TC ERR .75 2.00
60B Mickey Tettleton TC COR .02 .10
61 Mike Stanton RC .08 .25
62 Dwight Gooden TC .02 .10
63 Kent Mercker RC .08 .25
64 Francisco Cabrera .02 .10
65 Steve Avery .02 .10
66 Jose Canseco .10 .30
67 Matt Merullo .02 .10
68 Vince Coleman TC UER .02 .10
69 Ron Karkovice .02 .10
70 Kevin Maas RC .08 .25
71 Dennis Cook UER
(Shown with righty/glove on card .02 .10
72 Juan Gonzalez RC .60 1.50
73 Andre Dawson TC .02 .10
74 Dean Palmer RC .08 .25
75 Bo Jackson SPEC .07 .20
76 Rob Richie RC .02 .10
77 Bobby Rose UER
(Pickin& should/be pick in) .02 .10
78 Brian DuBois UER RC .02 .10
79 Ozzie Guillen TC .02 .10
80 Gene Nelson .02 .10
81 Bob McClure .02 .10
82 Julio Franco TC .02 .10
83 Greg Minton .02 .10
84 John Smoltz TC UER .10 .30
85 Willie Fraser .02 .10
86 Neal Heaton .02 .10
87 Kevin Tapani RC .08 .25
88 Mike Scott TC .02 .10
89A Jim Gott ERR .75 2.00
89B Jim Gott COR .02 .10
90 Lance Johnson .02 .10
91 Robin Yount TC UER .20 .50
92 Jeff Parrett .02 .10
93 Julio Machado RC .02 .10
94 Ron Jones .02 .10
95 George Bell TC .02 .10
96 Jerry Reuss .02 .10
97 Brian Fisher .02 .10
98 Kevin Ritz RC .02 .10
99 Barry Larkin TC .07 .20
100 Checklist 1-100 .02 .10
101 Gerald Perry .02 .10
102 Kevin Appier .07 .20
103 Julio Franco .07 .20
104 Craig Biggio .20 .50
105 Bo Jackson UER .20 .50
106 Junior Felix .02 .10
107 Mike Harkey .02 .10
108 Fred McGriff .20 .50
109 Rick Sutcliffe .07 .20
110 Pete O'Brien .02 .10
111 Kelly Gruber .02 .10
112 Dwight Evans .10 .30
113 Pat Borders .02 .10
114 Dwight Gooden .07 .20
115 Kevin Batiste RC .02 .10
116 Eric Davis .07 .20
117 Kevin Mitchell UER
(Career HR total 99&/should b .02 .10
118 Ron Oester .02 .10
119 Brett Butler .07 .20
120 Danny Jackson .02 .10
121 Tommy Gregg .02 .10
122 Ken Caminiti .07 .20
123 Kevin Brown .07 .20
124 George Brett .50 1.25
125 Mike Scott .02 .10
126 Cory Snyder .02 .10
127 George Bell .02 .10
128 Mark Grace .10 .30
129 Devon White .07 .20
130 Tony Fernandez .02 .10
131 Don Aase .02 .10
132 Rance Mulliniks .02 .10
133 Marty Barrett .02 .10
134 Nelson Liriano .02 .10
135 Mark Carreon .02 .10
136 Candy Maldonado .02 .10
137 Tim Birtsas .02 .10
138 Tom Brookens .02 .10
139 John Franco .07 .20
140 Mike LaCoss .02 .10
141 Jeff Treadway .02 .10
142 Pat Tabler .02 .10
143 Darrell Evans .07 .20
144 Rafael Ramirez .02 .10
145 Oddibe McDowell UER
(Misspelled Odibbe) .02 .10
146 Brian Downing .02 .10
147 Curt Wilkerson .02 .10
148 Ernie Whitt .02 .10
149 Bill Schroeder .02 .10
150 Domingo Ramos UER
(Says throws right&/but shows .02 .10
151 Rick Honeycutt .02 .10
152 Don Slaught .02 .10
153 Mitch Webster .02 .10
154 Tony Phillips .02 .10
155 Paul Kilgus .02 .10
156 Ken Griffey Jr. .75 2.00
157 Gary Sheffield .20 .50
158 Wally Backman .02 .10
159 B.J. Surhoff .07 .20
160 Louie Meadows .02 .10
161 Paul O'Neill .10 .30
162 Jeff McKnight RC .02 .10
163 Alvaro Espinoza .02 .10
164 Scott Scudder .02 .10
165 Jeff Reed .02 .10
166 Gregg Jefferies .07 .20
167 Barry Larkin .10 .30
168 Gary Carter .07 .20
169 Robby Thompson .02 .10
170 Rolando Roomes .02 .10
171 Mark McGwire .60 1.50
172 Steve Sax .02 .10
173 Mark Williamson .02 .10
174 Mitch Williams .02 .10
175 Brian Holton .02 .10
176 Rob Deer .02 .10
177 Tim Raines .07 .20
178 Mike Felder .02 .10
179 Harold Reynolds .07 .20
180 Terry Francona .07 .20
181 Chris Sabo .02 .10
182 Darryl Strawberry .07 .20
183 Willie Randolph .07 .20
184 Bill Ripken .02 .10
185 Mackey Sasser .02 .10
186 Todd Benzinger .02 .10
187 Kevin Elster UER
(16 homers in 1989&/should be 1 .02 .10
188 Jose Uribe .02 .10
189 Tom Browning .02 .10
190 Keith Miller .02 .10
191 Don Mattingly .50 1.25
192 Dave Parker .07 .20
193 Roberto Kelly UER .02 .10
194 Phil Bradley .02 .10
195 Ron Hassey .02 .10
196 Gerald Young .02 .10
197 Hubie Brooks .02 .10
198 Bill Doran .02 .10
199 Al Newman .02 .10
200 Checklist 101-200 .02 .10
201 Terry Puhl .02 .10
202 Frank DiPino .02 .10
203 Jim Clancy .02 .10
204 Bob Ojeda .02 .10
205 Alex Trevino .02 .10
206 Dave Henderson .02 .10
207 Henry Cotto .02 .10
208 Rafael Belliard UER
(Born 1961& not 1951) .02 .10
209 Stan Javier .02 .10
210 Jerry Reed .02 .10
211 Doug Dascenzo .02 .10
212 Andres Thomas .02 .10
213 Greg Maddux .30 .75
214 Mike Schooler .02 .10
215 Lonnie Smith .02 .10
216 Jose Rijo .02 .10
217 Greg Gagne .02 .10
218 Jim Gantner .02 .10
219 Allan Anderson .02 .10
220 Rick Mahler .02 .10
221 Jim Deshaies .02 .10
222 Keith Hernandez .07 .20
223 Vince Coleman .02 .10
224 David Cone .07 .20
225 Ozzie Smith .30 .75
226 Matt Nokes .02 .10
227 Barry Bonds .60 1.50
228 Felix Jose .02 .10
229 Dennis Powell .02 .10
230 Mike Gallego .02 .10
231 Shawon Dunston UER
('89 stats are/Andre Dawson's .02 .10
232 Ron Gant .07 .20
233 Omar Vizquel .20 .50
234 Derek Lilliquist .02 .10
235 Erik Hanson .02 .10
236 Kirby Puckett .20 .50
237 Bill Spiers .02 .10
238 Dan Gladden .02 .10
239 Bryan Clutterbuck .02 .10
240 John Moses .02 .10
241 Ron Darling .02 .10
242 Joe Magrane .02 .10
243 Dave Magadan .02 .10
244 Pedro Guerrero UER .02 .10
Misspelled Guerrero
245 Glenn Davis .02 .10
246 Terry Steinbach .02 .10
247 Fred Lynn .02 .10
248 Gary Redus .02 .10
249 Ken Williams .02 .10
250 Sid Bream .02 .10
251 Bob Welch UER
(2587 career strike-/outs& should .02 .10
252 Bill Buckner .02 .10
253 Carney Lansford .07 .20
254 Paul Molitor .07 .20
255 Jose DeJesus .02 .10
256 Orel Hershiser .07 .20
257 Tom Brunansky .02 .10
258 Mike Davis .02 .10
259 Jeff Ballard .02 .10
260 Scott Terry .02 .10
261 Sid Fernandez .02 .10
262 Mike Marshall .02 .10
263 Howard Johnson UER
(192 SO& should be 592) .02 .10
264 Kirk Gibson UER .07 .20
Charlotesville
265 Kevin McReynolds .02 .10
266 Cal Ripken .60 1.50
267 Ozzie Guillen UER .07 .20
268 Jim Traber .02 .10
269 Bobby Thigpen UER
(31 saves in 1989&/should be 3 .02 .10
270 Joe Orsulak .02 .10
271 Bob Boone .07 .20
272 Dave Stewart UER .07 .20
273 Tim Wallach .02 .10
274 Luis Aquino UER
(Says throws lefty&/but shows hi .02 .10
275 Mike Moore .02 .10
276 Tony Pena .02 .10
277 Eddie Murray .20 .50
278 Milt Thompson .02 .10
279 Alejandro Pena .02 .10
280 Ken Dayley .02 .10
281 Carmelo Castillo .02 .10
282 Tom Henke .02 .10
283 Mickey Hatcher .02 .10
284 Roy Smith .02 .10
285 Manny Lee .02 .10
286 Dan Pasqua .02 .10
287 Larry Sheets .02 .10
288 Garry Templeton .02 .10
289 Eddie Williams .02 .10
290 Brady Anderson .07 .20
291 Spike Owen .02 .10
292 Storm Davis .02 .10
293 Chris Bosio .02 .10
294 Jim Eisenreich .02 .10
295 Don August .02 .10
296 Jeff Hamilton .02 .10
297 Mickey Tettleton .02 .10
298 Mike Scioscia .02 .10
299 Kevin Hickey .02 .10
300 Checklist 201-300 .02 .10
301 Shawn Abner .02 .10
302 Kevin Bass .02 .10
303 Bip Roberts .02 .10
304 Joe Girardi .10 .30
305 Danny Darwin .02 .10
306 Mike Heath .02 .10
307 Mike Macfarlane .02 .10
308 Ed Whitson .02 .10
309 Tracy Jones .02 .10
310 Scott Fletcher .02 .10
311 Darnell Coles .02 .10
312 Mike Brumley .02 .10
313 Bill Swift .02 .10
314 Charlie Hough .07 .20
315 Jim Presley .02 .10
316 Luis Polonia .02 .10
317 Mike Morgan .02 .10
318 Lee Guetterman .02 .10
319 Jose Oquendo .02 .10
320 Wayne Tolleson .02 .10
321 Jody Reed .02 .10
322 Damon Berryhill .02 .10
323 Roger Clemens .60 1.50
324 Ryne Sandberg .30 .75
325 Benito Santiago UER .07 .20
326 Bret Saberhagen UER
(1140 hits& should be/1240; .07 .20
327 Lou Whitaker .07 .20
328 Dave Gallagher .02 .10
329 Mike Pagliarulo .02 .10
330 Doyle Alexander .02 .10
331 Jeffrey Leonard .02 .10
332 Torey Lovullo .02 .10
333 Pete Incaviglia .02 .10
334 Rickey Henderson .20 .50
335 Rafael Palmeiro .10 .30
336 Ken Hill .07 .20
337 Dave Winfield UER .07 .20
338 Alfredo Griffin .02 .10
339 Andy Hawkins .02 .10
340 Ted Power .02 .10
341 Steve Wilson .02 .10
342 Jack Clark UER
(916 BB& should be/1006; 1142 SO&.07 .20
343 Ellis Burks .10 .30
344 Tony Gwynn .25 .60
345 Jerome Walton UER
(Total At Bats 476&/should be .02 .10
346 Roberto Alomar .10 .30
347 Carlos Martinez UER
(Born 8/11/64& should/be 8/1 .02 .10
348 Chet Lemon .02 .10
349 Willie Wilson .02 .10
350 Greg Walker .02 .10
351 Tom Bolton .02 .10
352 German Gonzalez .02 .10
353 Harold Baines .07 .20
354 Mike Greenwell .02 .10
355 Ruben Sierra .07 .20
356 Andres Galarraga .07 .20
357 Andre Dawson .07 .20
358 Jeff Brantley .02 .10
359 Mike Bielecki .02 .10
360 Ken Oberkfell .02 .10
361 Kurt Stillwell .02 .10
362 Brian Holman .02 .10
363 Kevin Seitzer UER
(Career triples total/does not .02 .10
364 Alvin Davis .02 .10
365 Tom Gordon .07 .20
366 Bobby Bonilla UER
(Two steals in 1987&/should be .07 .20
367 Carlton Fisk .10 .30
368 Steve Carter UER .02 .10
Charlotesville
369 Joel Skinner .02 .10
370 John Cangelosi .02 .10
371 Cecil Espy .02 .10
372 Gary Wayne .02 .10
373 Jim Rice .07 .20
374 Mike Dyer RC .02 .10
375 Joe Carter .07 .20
376 Dwight Smith .02 .10
377 John Wetteland .20 .50
378 Ernie Riles .02 .10
379 Otis Nixon .02 .10
380 Vance Law .02 .10
381 Dave Bergman .02 .10
382 Frank White .07 .20
383 Scott Bradley .02 .10
384 Israel Sanchez UER
(Totals don't in-/clude '89 s .02 .10
385 Gary Pettis .02 .10
386 Donn Pall .02 .10
387 John Smiley .02 .10
388 Tom Candiotti .02 .10
389 Junior Ortiz .02 .10
390 Steve Lyons .02 .10
391 Brian Harper .02 .10
392 Fred Manrique .02 .10
393 Lee Smith .07 .20
394 Jeff Kunkel .02 .10
395 Claudell Washington .02 .10
396 John Tudor .02 .10
397 Terry Kennedy UER .02 .10
Career totals all
wrong
398 Lloyd McClendon .02 .10
399 Craig Lefferts .02 .10
400 Checklist 301-400 .02 .10
401 Keith Moreland .02 .10
402 Rich Gedman .02 .10
403 Jeff D. Robinson .02 .10
404 Randy Ready .02 .10
405 Rick Cerone .02 .10
406 Jeff Blauser .02 .10
407 Larry Andersen .02 .10
408 Joe Boever .02 .10
409 Felix Fermin .02 .10
410 Glenn Wilson .02 .10
411 Rex Hudler .02 .10
412 Mark Grant .02 .10
413 Dennis Martinez .07 .20
414 Darrin Jackson .02 .10
415 Mike Aldrete .02 .10
416 Roger McDowell .02 .10
417 Jeff Reardon .07 .20
418 Darren Daulton .07 .20
419 Tim Laudner .02 .10
420 Don Carman .02 .10
421 Lloyd Moseby .02 .10
422 Doug Drabek .02 .10
423 Lenny Harris UER
(Walks 2 in '89&/should be 20) .02 .10
424 Jose Lind .02 .10
425 Dave Wayne Johnson RC .02 .10
426 Jerry Browne .02 .10
427 Eric Yelding RC .02 .10
428 Brad Komminsk .02 .10
429 Jody Davis .02 .10
430 Mariano Duncan .02 .10
431 Mark Davis .02 .10
432 Nelson Santovenia .02 .10
433 Bruce Hurst .02 .10
434 Jeff Huson RC .02 .10
435 Chris James .02 .10
436 Mark Guthrie RC .02 .10
437 Charlie Hayes .02 .10
438 Shane Rawley .02 .10
439 Dickie Thon .02 .10
440 Juan Berenguer .02 .10
441 Kevin Romine .02 .10
442 Bill Landrum .02 .10
443 Todd Frohwirth .02 .10
444 Craig Worthington .02 .10

445 Fernando Valenzuela .07 .20
446 Albert Belle .20 .50
447 Ed Whited UER RC .02 .10
448 Dave Smith .02 .10
449 Dave Clark .02 .10
450 Juan Agosto .02 .10
451 Dave Valle .02 .10
452 Kent Hrbek .07 .20
453 Von Hayes .02 .10
454 Gary Gaetti .07 .20
455 Greg Briley .02 .10
456 Glenn Braggs .02 .10
457 Kirt Manwaring .02 .10
458 Mel Hall .02 .10
459 Brook Jacoby .02 .10
460 Pat Sheridan .02 .10
461 Rob Murphy .02 .10
462 Jimmy Key .07 .20
463 Nick Esasky .02 .10
464 Rob Ducey .02 .10
465 Carlos Quintana UER .02 .10
Internatinoal
466 Larry Walker RC .60 1.50
467 Todd Worrell .02 .10
468 Kevin Gross .02 .10
469 Terry Pendleton .07 .20
470 Dave Martinez .02 .10
471 Gene Larkin .02 .10
472 Len Dykstra UER .07 .20
473 Barry Lyons .02 .10
474 Terry Mulholland .02 .10
475 Chip Hale RC .02 .10
476 Jesse Barfield .02 .10
477 Dan Plesac .02 .10
478A Scott Garrelts ERR .75 2.00
478B Scott Garrelts COR .02 .10
479 Dave Righetti .02 .10
480 Gus Polidor UER
(Wearing 14 on front& but 10 on .02 .10
481 Mookie Wilson .07 .20
482 Luis Rivera .02 .10
483 Mike Flanagan .02 .10
484 Dennis Boyd .02 .10
485 John Cerutti .02 .10
486 John Costello .02 .10
487 Pascual Perez .02 .10
488 Tommy Herr .02 .10
489 Tom Foley .02 .10
490 Curt Ford .02 .10
491 Steve Lake .02 .10
492 Tim Teufel .02 .10
493 Randy Bush .02 .10
494 Mike Jackson .02 .10
495 Steve Jeltz .02 .10
496 Paul Gibson .02 .10
497 Steve Balboni .02 .10
498 Bud Black .02 .10
499 Dale Sveum .02 .10
500 Checklist 401-500 .02 .10
501 Tim Jones .02 .10
502 Mark Portugal .02 .10
503 Ivan Calderon .02 .10
504 Rick Rhoden .02 .10
505 Willie McGee .07 .20
506 Kirk McCaskill .02 .10
507 Dave LaPoint .02 .10
508 Jay Howell .02 .10
509 Johnny Ray .02 .10
510 Dave Anderson .02 .10
511 Chuck Crim .02 .10
512 Joe Hesketh .02 .10
513 Dennis Eckersley .07 .20
514 Greg Brock .02 .10
515 Tim Burke .02 .10
516 Frank Tanana .02 .10
517 Jay Bell .07 .20
518 Guillermo Hernandez .02 .10
519 Randy Kramer UER
(Codiroli misspelled/as Codorol .02 .10
520 Charles Hudson .02 .10
521 Jim Corsi .02 .10
522 Steve Rosenberg .02 .10
523 Cris Carpenter .02 .10
524 Matt Winters RC .02 .10
525 Melido Perez .02 .10
526 Chris Gwynn UER .02 .10
Albeguergue
527 Bert Blyleven UER .07 .20
528 Chuck Cary .02 .10
529 Daryl Boston .02 .10
530 Dale Mohorcic .02 .10
531 Geronimo Berroa .02 .10
532 Edgar Martinez .10 .30
533 Dale Murphy .10 .30
534 Jay Buhner .07 .20
535 John Smoltz .20 .50
536 Andy Van Slyke .10 .30
537 Mike Henneman .02 .10
538 Miguel Garcia .02 .10
539 Frank Williams .02 .10
540 R.J. Reynolds .02 .10
541 Shawn Hillegas .02 .10
542 Walt Weiss .02 .10
543 Greg Hibbard RC .02 .10
544 Nolan Ryan .75 2.00
545 Todd Zeile .07 .20
546 Hensley Meulens .02 .10
547 Tim Belcher .02 .10
548 Mike Witt .02 .10
549 Greg Cadaret UER
(Aquiring& should/be Acquiring) .02 .10
550 Franklin Stubbs .02 .10
551 Tony Castillo .02 .10
552 Jeff M. Robinson .02 .10
553 Steve Olin RC .08 .25
554 Alan Trammell .07 .20
555 Wade Boggs 4X .10 .30
556 Will Clark .10 .30
557 Jeff King .02 .10
558 Mike Fitzgerald .02 .10
559 Ken Howell .02 .10
560 Bob Kipper .02 .10
561 Scott Bankhead .02 .10
562A Jeff Innis ERR .75 2.00
562B Jeff Innis COR RC .02 .10
563 Randy Johnson .40 1.00
564 Wally Whitehurst .02 .10
565 Gene Harris .02 .10
566 Norm Charlton .02 .10
567 Robin Yount UER .30 .75
568 Joe Oliver .02 .10
569 Mark Parent .02 .10
570 John Farrell UER .02 .10
Loss total added wrong
571 Tom Glavine .10 .30
572 Rod Nichols .02 .10
573 Jack Morris .07 .20
574 Greg Swindell .02 .10
575 Steve Searcy .02 .10
576 Ricky Jordan .02 .10
577 Matt Williams .07 .20
578 Mike LaValliere .02 .10
579 Bryn Smith .02 .10
580 Bruce Ruffin .02 .10
581 Randy Myers .07 .20
582 Rick Wrona .02 .10
583 Juan Samuel .02 .10
584 Les Lancaster .02 .10
585 Jeff Musselman .02 .10
586 Rob Dibble .07 .20
587 Eric Show .02 .10
588 Jesse Orosco .02 .10
589 Herm Winningham .02 .10
590 Andy Allanson .02 .10
591 Dion James .02 .10
592 Carmelo Martinez .02 .10
593 Luis Quinones .02 .10
594 Dennis Rasmussen .02 .10
595 Rich Yett .02 .10
596 Bob Walk .02 .10
597A Andy McGaffigan ERR
(Photo actually/Rich Thompso .75 2.00
597B Andy McGaffigan COR .02 .10
598 Billy Hatcher .02 .10
599 Bob Knepper .02 .10
600 Checklist 501-600 UER
(599 Bob Kneppers) .02 .10
601 Joey Cora .07 .20
602 Steve Finley .07 .20
603 Kal Daniels UER
(12 hits in '87& should/be 123; .02 .10
604 Gregg Olson .07 .20
605 Dave Stieb .07 .20
606 Kenny Rogers .07 .20
607 Zane Smith .02 .10
608 Bob Geren UER .02 .10
Originally
609 Chad Kreuter .02 .10
610 Mike Smithson .02 .10
611 Jeff Wetherby RC .02 .10
612 Gary Mielke RC .02 .10
613 Pete Smith .02 .10
614 Jack Daugherty RC .02 .10
615 Lance McCullers .02 .10
616 Don Robinson .02 .10
617 Jose Guzman .02 .10
618 Steve Bedrosian .02 .10
619 Jamie Moyer .07 .20
620 Atlee Hammaker .02 .10
621 Rick Luecken RC .02 .10
622 Greg W. Harris .02 .10
623 Pete Harnisch .02 .10
624 Jerald Clark .02 .10
625 Jack McDowell .02 .10
626 Frank Viola .02 .10
627 Teddy Higuera .02 .10
628 Marty Pevey RC .02 .10
629 Bill Wegman .02 .10
630 Eric Plunk .02 .10
631 Drew Hall .02 .10
632 Doug Jones .02 .10
633 Geno Petralli UER .02 .10
Sacremento
634 Jose Alvarez .02 .10
635 Bob Milacki .02 .10
636 Bobby Witt .02 .10
637 Trevor Wilson .02 .10
638 Jeff Russell UER .02 .10
Shutout stats wrong
639 Mike Krukow .02 .10
640 Rick Leach .02 .10
641 Dave Schmidt .02 .10
642 Terry Leach .02 .10
643 Calvin Schiraldi .02 .10
644 Bob Melvin .02 .10
645 Jim Abbott .10 .30
646 Jaime Navarro .02 .10
647 Mark Langston UER/
Several errors in/stats total .02 .10
648 Juan Nieves .02 .10
649 Damaso Garcia .02 .10
650 Charlie O'Brien .02 .10
651 Eric King .02 .10
652 Mike Boddicker .02 .10
653 Duane Ward .02 .10
654 Bob Stanley .02 .10
655 Sandy Alomar Jr. .07 .20
656 Danny Tartabull UER .02 .10
657 Randy McCament RC .02 .10
658 Charlie Leibrandt .02 .10
659 Dan Quisenberry .02 .10
660 Paul Assenmacher .02 .10
661 Walt Terrell .02 .10
662 Tim Leary .02 .10
663 Randy Milligan .02 .10
664 Bo Diaz .02 .10
665 Mark Lemke UER
(Richmond misspelled/as Richmond .02 .10
666 Jose Gonzalez .02 .10
667 Chuck Finley UER
(Born 11/16/62& should/be 11/26 .07 .20
668 John Kruk .07 .20
669 Dick Schofield .02 .10
670 Tim Crews .02 .10
671 John Dopson .02 .10
672 John Orton RC .02 .10
673 Eric Hetzel .02 .10
674 Lance Parrish .02 .10
675 Ramon Martinez .02 .10
676 Mark Gubicza .02 .10
677 Greg Litton .02 .10
678 Greg Mathews .02 .10
679 Dave Dravecky .07 .20
680 Steve Farr .02 .10
681 Mike Devereaux .02 .10
682 Ken Griffey Sr. .07 .20
683A Jamie Weston ERR .75 2.00
683B Mickey Weston COR RC .02 .10
684 Jack Armstrong .02 .10
685 Steve Buechele .02 .10
686 Bryan Harvey .02 .10
687 Lance Blankenship .02 .10
688 Dante Bichette .07 .20
689 Todd Burns .02 .10
690 Dan Petry .02 .10
691 Kent Anderson .02 .10
692 Todd Stottlemyre .07 .20
693 Wally Joyner UER .07 .20
Several stats errors
694 Mike Rochford .02 .10
695 Floyd Bannister .02 .10
696 Rick Reuschel .02 .10
697 Jose DeLeon .02 .10
698 Jeff Montgomery .07 .20
699 Kelly Downs .02 .10
700A CL 601-700 ERR .75 2.00
700B Checklist 601-700 .02 .10
683 Mickey Weston
701 Jim Gott .02 .10
702 L.Walker/Grissom/DeSh .20 .50
703 Alejandro Pena .02 .10
704 Willie Randolph .07 .20
705 Tim Leary .02 .10
706 Chuck McElroy RC .02 .10
707 Gerald Perry .02 .10
708 Tom Brunansky .02 .10
709 John Franco .07 .20
710 Mark Davis .02 .10
711 David Justice RC .30 .75
712 Storm Davis .02 .10
713 Scott Ruskin RC .02 .10
714 Glenn Braggs .02 .10
715 Kevin Bearse RC .02 .10
716 Jose Nunez .02 .10
717 Tim Layana RC .02 .10
718 Greg Myers .02 .10
719 Pete O'Brien .02 .10
720 John Candelaria .02 .10
721 Craig Grebeck RC .02 .10
722 Shawn Boskie RC .02 .10
723 Jim Leyritz RC .08 .25
724 Bill Sampen RC .02 .10
725 Scott Radinsky RC .02 .10
726 Todd Hundley RC .08 .25
727 Scott Hemond RC .02 .10
728 Lenny Webster RC .02 .10
729 Jeff Reardon .07 .20
730 Mitch Webster .02 .10
731 Brian Bohanon RC .02 .10
732 Rick Parker RC .02 .10
733 Terry Shumpert RC .02 .10
734A Nolan Ryan 6th 1.25 3.00
734B Nolan Ryan 6th/300 .40 1.00
735 John Burkett .02 .10
736 Derrick May RC .02 .10
737 Carlos Baerga RC .08 .25
738 Greg Smith RC .02 .10
739 Scott Sanderson .02 .10
740 Joe Kraemer RC .02 .10
741 Hector Villanueva RC .02 .10
742 Mike Fetters RC .08 .25
743 Mark Gardner RC .02 .10
744 Matt Nokes .02 .10
745 Dave Winfield .07 .20
746 Delino DeShields RC .08 .25
747 Dann Howitt RC .02 .10
748 Tony Pena .02 .10
749 Oil Can Boyd .02 .10
750 Mike Benjamin RC .02 .10
751 Alex Cole RC .02 .10
752 Eric Gunderson RC .02 .10
753 Howard Farmer RC .02 .10
754 Joe Carter .07 .20
755 Ray Lankford RC .20 .50
756 Sandy Alomar Jr. .07 .20
757 Alex Sanchez .02 .10
758 Nick Esasky .02 .10
759 Stan Belinda RC .02 .10
760 Jim Presley .02 .10
761 Gary DiSarcina RC .08 .25
762 Wayne Edwards RC .02 .10
763 Pat Combs .02 .10
764 Mickey Pina RC .02 .10
765 Wilson Alvarez RC .08 .25
766 Dave Parker .07 .20
767 Mike Blowers RC .02 .10
768 Tony Phillips .02 .10
769 Pascual Perez .02 .10
770 Gary Pettis .02 .10
771 Fred Lynn .02 .10
772 Mel Rojas RC .02 .10
773 David Segui RC .20 .50
774 Gary Carter .07 .20
775 Rafael Valdez RC .02 .10
776 Glenallen Hill .02 .10
777 Keith Hernandez .07 .20
778 Billy Hatcher .02 .10
779 Marty Clary .02 .10
780 Candy Maldonado .02 .10
781 Mike Marshall .02 .10
782 Billy Jo Robidoux .02 .10
783 Mark Langston .02 .10
784 Paul Sorrento RC .08 .25
785 Dave Hollins RC .08 .25
786 Cecil Fielder .07 .20
787 Matt Young .02 .10
788 Jeff Huson .02 .10
789 Lloyd Moseby .02 .10
790 Ron Kittle .02 .10
791 Hubie Brooks .02 .10
792 Craig Lefferts .02 .10
793 Kevin Bass .02 .10
794 Bryn Smith .02 .10
795 Juan Samuel .02 .10
796 Sam Horn .02 .10
797 Randy Myers .07 .20
798 Chris James .02 .10
799 Bill Gullickson .02 .10
800 Checklist 701-800 .02 .10

1990 Upper Deck Jackson Heroes

This ten-card standard-size set was issued as an insert in 1990 Upper Deck High Number packs as part of the Upper Deck promotional giveaway of 2,500 officially signed and personally numbered Reggie Jackson cards. Signed cards ending with 00 have the words "Mr. October" added to the autograph. These cards cover Jackson's major league career. The complete set price refers only to the unautographed card set of ten. One-card packs of over-sized (3 1/2" by 5") versions of these cards were later inserted into retail blister repacks containing one foil pack each of 1993 Upper Deck Series I and II. These cards were later inserted into various forms of repackaging. The larger cards are also distinguishable by the Upper Deck Fifth Anniversary logo and "1993 Hall of Fame Inductee" logo on the front of the card. These over-sized cards were a limited edition of 10,000 numbered cards and have no extra value than the basic cards.

COMPLETE SET (10) 6.00 15.00
COMMON REGGIE (1-9) .60 1.50
RANDOM INSERTS IN HI SERIES
NNO Reggie Jackson Header 1.25 3.00
AU1 Reggie Jackson AU/2500 75.00 200.00

1990 Upper Deck Sheets

These blank-backed, 8 1/2" by 11" sheets feature pictures of Upper Deck baseball cards and were distributed at various specific events and times around the country. The sheets carried a production run number but not necessarily a total number produced. There were four regionally-issued sheets bound inside Street and Smith's 1990 Baseball Annual magazines to celebrate its 50th anniversary. The top five 1990 Upper Deck cards featured on all four sheets were the same: Carlton Fisk, Tim Raines, Jose Canseco and Will Clark. The Street and Smith sheets are listed below by their regions and regional players. The sheets are listed below in chronological order.

COMPLETE SET (5) 15.00 40.00
1 11th Annual National 3.00 8.00
Sports Collectors
Conventio
2 San Francisco 3.00 8.00
Conv. Center Show
Aug. 31-Sept. 3&
3 Street 8.00 20.00
Smith: West
Ken Griffey Jr.
Roberto Aloma
4 Street 3.00 8.00
Smith: East
Gregg Olson
Wade Boggs
Gregg
5 Street 3.00 8.00
Smith: Midwest
Tom Gordon
Pedro Guerrero#

1991 Upper Deck

This set marked the third year Upper Deck issued a 800-card standard-size set in two separate series of 700 and 100 cards respectively. Cards were distributed in low and high series foil packs and factory sets. The 100-card extended or high-number series was issued by Upper Deck several months after the release of their first series. For the first time in Upper Deck's three-year history, they did not issue a factory Extended set. The basic cards are made on the typical Upper Deck slick, white card stock and features full-color photos on both the front and the back. Subsets include Star Rookies (1-26), Team Cards (28-34, 43-49, 77-82, 95-99) and Top Prospects (50-76). Several other special achievement cards are seeded throughout the set. The team checklist (TC) cards in the set feature an attractive Vernon Wells drawing of a featured player for that particular team. Rookie Cards in this set include Jeff Bagwell, Luis Gonzalez, Chipper Jones, Eric Karros, and Mike Mussina. A special Michael Jordan card (numbered SP1) was randomly included in packs on a somewhat limited basis. The Hank Aaron hologram card was randomly inserted in the 1991 Upper Deck high number foil packs. Neither card is included in the price of the regular issue set though both are listed at the end of our checklist.

COMPLETE SET (800) 6.00 15.00
COMP.FACT.SET (800) 8.00 20.00
COMPLETE LO SET (700) 6.00 15.00
COMPLETE HI SET (100) 2.00 5.00
1 Star Rookie Checklist .01 .05
2 Phil Plantier RC .02 .10
3 D.J. Dozier .01 .05
4 Dave Hansen .01 .05
5 Maurice Vaughn .02 .10
6 Leo Gomez .01 .05
7 Scott Aldred .01 .05
8 Scott Chiamparino .01 .05
9 Lance Dickson RC .02 .10
10 Sean Berry RC .02 .10
11 Bernie Williams .08 .25
12 Brian Barnes UER RC .02 .10
13 Narciso Elvira RC .01 .05
14 Mike Gardiner RC .01 .05
15 Greg Colbrunn RC .08 .25
16 Bernard Gilkey .01 .05
17 Mark Lewis .01 .05
18 Mickey Morandini .01 .05
19 Charles Nagy .01 .05
20 Geronimo Pena .01 .05
21 Henry Rodriguez RC .08 .25
22 Scott Cooper .01 .05
23 Andujar Cedeno UER .01 .05
Shown batting left
back says right
24 Eric Karros RC .30 .75
25 Steve Decker UER RC .01 .05
26 Kevin Belcher RC .01 .05
27 Jeff Conine RC .20 .50
28 Dave Stewart TC .01 .05
29 Carlton Fisk TC .02 .10
30 Rafael Palmeiro TC .02 .10
31 Chuck Finley TC .01 .05
32 Harold Reynolds TC .01 .05
33 Bret Saberhagen TC .01 .05
34 Gary Gaetti TC .01 .05
35 Scott Leius .01 .05
36 Neal Heaton .01 .05
37 Terry Lee RC .01 .05
38 Gary Redus .01 .05
39 Barry Jones .01 .05
40 Chuck Knoblauch .02 .10
41 Larry Andersen .01 .05
42 Darryl Hamilton .01 .05
43 Mike Greenwell TC .01 .05
44 Kelly Gruber TC .01 .05
45 Jack Morris TC .01 .05
46 Sandy Alomar Jr. TC .01 .05
47 Gregg Olson TC .01 .05
48 Dave Parker TC .01 .05
49 Roberto Kelly TC .01 .05
50 Top Prospect Checklist .01 .05
51 Kyle Abbott .01 .05
52 Jeff Juden .01 .05
53 Todd Van Poppel UER RC .08 .25
54 Steve Karsay RC .08 .25
55 Chipper Jones RC 2.50 6.00
56 Chris Johnson UER RC .02 .10
57 John Ericks .01 .05
58 Gary Scott RC .01 .05
59 Kiki Jones .01 .05
60 Wil Cordero RC .02 .10
61 Royce Clayton .01 .05
62 Tim Costo RC .02 .10
63 Roger Salkeld .01 .05
64 Brook Fordyce RC .08 .25
65 Mike Mussina RC 1.00 2.50
66 Dave Staton RC .02 .10
67 Mike Lieberthal RC .20 .50
68 Kurt Miller RC .01 .05
69 Dan Peltier RC .02 .10
70 Greg Blosser .01 .05
71 Reggie Sanders RC .30 .75
72 Brent Mayne .01 .05
73 Rico Brogna .01 .05
74 Willie Banks .01 .05
75 Len Brutcher RC .01 .05
76 Pat Kelly RC .02 .10
77 Chris Sabo TC .01 .05
78 Ramon Martinez TC .01 .05
79 Matt Williams TC .01 .05
80 Roberto Alomar TC .02 .10
81 Glenn Davis TC .01 .05
82 Ron Gant TC .01 .05
83 Cecil Fielder FEAT .01 .05
84 Orlando Merced RC .02 .10
85 Domingo Ramos .01 .05
86 Tom Bolton .01 .05
87 Andres Santana .01 .05
88 John Dopson .01 .05
89 Kenny Williams .01 .05
90 Marty Barrett .01 .05
91 Tom Pagnozzi .01 .05
92 Carmelo Martinez .01 .05
93 Bobby Thigpen SAVE .01 .05
94 Barry Bonds TC .20 .50
95 Gregg Jefferies TC .01 .05
96 Tim Wallach TC .01 .05
97 Len Dykstra TC .01 .05
98 Pedro Guerrero TC .01 .05
99 Mark Grace TC .02 .10
100 Checklist 1-100 .01 .05
101 Kevin Elster .01 .05
102 Tom Brookens .01 .05
103 Mackey Sasser .01 .05
104 Felix Fermin .01 .05
105 Kevin McReynolds .01 .05
106 Dave Stieb .01 .05
107 Jeffrey Leonard .01 .05
108 Dave Henderson .01 .05
109 Sid Bream .01 .05
110 Henry Cotto .01 .05
111 Shawon Dunston .01 .05
112 Mariano Duncan .01 .05
113 Joe Girardi .01 .05
114 Billy Hatcher .01 .05
115 Greg Maddux .15 .40
116 Jerry Browne .01 .05
117 Juan Samuel .01 .05
118 Steve Olin .01 .05
119 Alfredo Griffin .01 .05
120 Mitch Webster .01 .05
121 Joel Skinner .01 .05
122 Frank Viola .02 .10
123 Cory Snyder .01 .05
124 Howard Johnson .01 .05
125 Carlos Baerga .01 .05
126 Tony Fernandez .01 .05
127 Dave Stewart .02 .10
128 Jay Buhner .02 .10
129 Mike LaValliere .01 .05
130 Scott Bradley .01 .05
131 Tony Phillips .01 .05
132 Ryne Sandberg .15 .40
133 Paul O'Neill .05 .15
134 Mark Grace .05 .15
135 Chris Sabo .01 .05
136 Ramon Martinez .01 .05
137 Brook Jacoby .01 .05
138 Candy Maldonado .01 .05
139 Mike Scioscia .01 .05
140 Chris James .01 .05
141 Craig Worthington .01 .05
142 Manny Lee .01 .05
143 Tim Raines .02 .10
144 Sandy Alomar Jr. .01 .05
145 John Olerud .02 .10
146 Ozzie Canseco .01 .05
With Jose
147 Pat Borders .01 .05
148 Harold Reynolds .02 .10
149 Tom Henke .01 .05
150 R.J. Reynolds .01 .05
151 Mike Gallego .01 .05
152 Bobby Bonilla .02 .10
153 Terry Steinbach .01 .05
154 Barry Bonds .40 1.00
155 Jose Canseco .05 .15
156 Gregg Jefferies .01 .05
157 Matt Williams .02 .10
158 Craig Biggio .05 .15
159 Daryl Boston .01 .05
160 Ricky Jordan .01 .05
161 Stan Belinda .01 .05
162 Ozzie Smith .15 .40
163 Tom Brunansky .01 .05
164 Todd Zeile .01 .05
165 Mike Greenwell .01 .05
166 Kal Daniels .01 .05
167 Kent Hrbek .02 .10
168 Franklin Stubbs .01 .05
169 Dick Schofield .01 .05
170 Junior Ortiz .01 .05
171 Hector Villanueva .01 .05
172 Dennis Eckersley .02 .10
173 Mitch Williams .01 .05
174 Mark McGwire .30 .75
175 Fernando Valenzuela 3X .02 .10
176 Gary Carter .02 .10
177 Dave Magadan .01 .05
178 Robby Thompson .01 .05
179 Bob Ojeda .01 .05
180 Ken Caminiti .02 .10
181 Don Slaught .01 .05
182 Luis Rivera .01 .05
183 Jay Bell .02 .10
184 Jody Reed .01 .05
185 Wally Backman .01 .05
186 Dave Martinez .01 .05
187 Luis Polonia .01 .05
188 Shane Mack .01 .05
189 Spike Owen .01 .05
190 Scott Bailes .01 .05
191 John Russell .01 .05
192 Walt Weiss .01 .05
193 Jose Oquendo .01 .05
194 Carney Lansford .02 .10
195 Jeff Huson .01 .05
196 Keith Miller .01 .05
197 Eric Yelding .01 .05
198 Ron Darling .01 .05
199 John Kruk .02 .10
200 Checklist 101-200 .01 .05
201 John Shelby .01 .05
202 Bob Geren .01 .05
203 Lance McCullers .01 .05
204 Alvaro Espinoza .01 .05
205 Mark Salas .01 .05
206 Mike Pagliarulo .01 .05
207 Jose Uribe .01 .05
208 Jim Deshaies .01 .05
209 Ron Karkovice .01 .05
210 Rafael Ramirez .01 .05
211 Donnie Hill .01 .05
212 Brian Harper .01 .05
213 Jack Howell .01 .05
214 Wes Gardner .01 .05
215 Tim Burke .01 .05
216 Doug Jones .01 .05
217 Hubie Brooks .01 .05
218 Tom Candiotti .01 .05
219 Gerald Perry .01 .05
220 Jose DeLeon .01 .05
221 Wally Whitehurst .01 .05
222 Alan Mills .01 .05
223 Alan Trammell .02 .10
224 Dwight Gooden .02 .10
225 Travis Fryman .02 .10
226 Joe Carter .02 .10
227 Julio Franco .02 .10
228 Craig Lefferts .01 .05
229 Gary Pettis .01 .05
230 Dennis Rasmussen .01 .05
231A Brian Downing ERR .01 .05
No position on front
231B Brian Downing COR .08 .25
DH on front
232 Carlos Quintana .01 .05
233 Gary Gaetti .02 .10
234 Mark Langston .01 .05
235 Tim Wallach .01 .05
236 Greg Swindell .01 .05
237 Eddie Murray .08 .25
238 Jeff Manto .01 .05
239 Lenny Harris .01 .05
240 Jesse Orosco .01 .05
241 Scott Lusader .01 .05
242 Sid Fernandez .01 .05
243 Jim Leyritz .01 .05
244 Cecil Fielder .02 .10
245 Darryl Strawberry .02 .10
246 Frank Thomas UER .08 .25
Comiskey Park
misspelled Comisky
247 Kevin Mitchell .01 .05
248 Lance Johnson .01 .05
249 Rick Reuschel .01 .05
250 Mark Portugal .01 .05
251 Derek Lilliquist .01 .05
252 Brian Holman .01 .05
253 Rafael Valdez UER .01 .05
Born 4/17/68
should be 12/17/67
254 B.J. Surhoff .02 .10
255 Tony Gwynn .10 .30
256 Andy Van Slyke .05 .15
257 Todd Stottlemyre .01 .05
258 Jose Lind .01 .05
259 Greg Myers .01 .05
260 Jeff Ballard .01 .05
261 Bobby Thigpen .01 .05
262 Jimmy Kremers .01 .05
263 Robin Ventura .02 .10
264 John Smoltz .05 .15
265 Sammy Sosa .08 .25
266 Gary Sheffield .02 .10
267 Len Dykstra .02 .10
268 Bill Spiers .01 .05
269 Charlie Hayes .01 .05
270 Brett Butler .02 .10
271 Bip Roberts .01 .05
272 Rob Deer .01 .05
273 Fred Lynn .01 .05
274 Dave Parker .02 .10
275 Andy Benes .01 .05

276 Glenallen Hill .01 .05
277 Steve Howard .01 .05
278 Doug Drabek .01 .05
279 Joe Oliver .01 .05
280 Todd Benzinger .01 .05
281 Eric King .01 .05
282 Jim Presley .01 .05
283 Ken Patterson .01 .05
284 Jack Daugherty .01 .05
285 Ivan Calderon .01 .05
286 Edgar Diaz .01 .05
287 Kevin Bass .01 .05
288 Don Carman .01 .05
289 Greg Brock .01 .05
290 John Franco .02 .10
291 Joey Cora .01 .05
292 Bill Wegman .01 .05
293 Eric Show .01 .05
294 Scott Bankhead .01 .05
295 Garry Templeton .01 .05
296 Mickey Tettleton .01 .05
297 Luis Sojo .01 .05
298 Jose Rijo .01 .05
299 Dave Johnson .01 .05
300 Checklist 201-300 .01 .05
301 Mark Grant .01 .05
302 Pete Harnisch .01 .05
303 Greg Olson .01 .05
304 Anthony Telford RC .01 .05
305 Lonnie Smith .01 .05
306 Chris Hoiles .01 .05
307 Bryn Smith .01 .05
308 Mike Devereaux .01 .05
309A Milt Thompson ERR .08 .25
Under yr information
has print dot
309B Milt Thompson COR .01 .05
Under yr information
says 86
310 Bob Melvin .01 .05
311 Luis Salazar .01 .05
312 Ed Whitson .01 .05
313 Charlie Hough .02 .10
314 Dave Clark .01 .05
315 Eric Gunderson .01 .05
316 Dan Petry .01 .05
317 Dante Bichette UER .02 .10
Assists misspelled
as assissts
318 Mike Heath .01 .05
319 Damon Berryhill .01 .05
320 Walt Terrell .01 .05
321 Scott Fletcher .01 .05
322 Dan Plesac .01 .05
323 Jack McDowell .01 .05
324 Paul Molitor .02 .10
325 Ozzie Guillen .02 .10
326 Gregg Olson .01 .05
327 Pedro Guerrero .02 .10
328 Bob Milacki .01 .05
329 John Tudor UER .01 .05
'90 Cardinals
should be '90 Dodgers
330 Steve Finley UER .02 .10
Born 3/12/65
should be 5/12
331 Jack Clark .02 .10
332 Jerome Walton .01 .05
333 Andy Hawkins .01 .05
334 Derrick May .01 .05
335 Roberto Alomar .05 .15
336 Jack Morris .02 .10
337 Dave Winfield .02 .10
338 Steve Searcy .01 .05
339 Chili Davis .02 .10
340 Larry Sheets .01 .05
341 Ted Higuera .01 .05
342 David Segui .01 .05
343 Greg Cadaret .01 .05
344 Robin Yount .15 .40
345 Nolan Ryan .40 1.00
346 Ray Lankford .02 .10
347 Cal Ripken .30 .75
348 Lee Smith .02 .10
349 Brady Anderson .02 .10
350 Frank DiPino .01 .05
351 Hal Morris .01 .05
352 Deion Sanders .05 .15
353 Barry Larkin .05 .15
354 Don Mattingly .25 .60
355 Eric Davis .02 .10
356 Jose Offerman .01 .05
357 Mel Rojas .01 .05
358 Rudy Seanez .01 .05
359 Oil Can Boyd .01 .05
360 Nelson Liriano .01 .05
361 Ron Gant .02 .10
362 Howard Farmer .01 .05
363 David Justice .02 .10
364 Delino DeShields .02 .10
365 Steve Avery .01 .05
366 David Cone .02 .10
367 Lou Whitaker .02 .10
368 Von Hayes .01 .05
369 Frank Tanana .01 .05
370 Tim Teufel .01 .05
371 Randy Myers .01 .05
372 Roberto Kelly .01 .05
373 Jack Armstrong .01 .05
374 Kelly Gruber .01 .05
375 Kevin Maas .01 .05
376 Randy Johnson .10 .30
377 David West .01 .05
378 Brent Knackert .01 .05
379 Rick Honeycutt .01 .05
380 Kevin Gross .01 .05
381 Tom Foley .01 .05
382 Jeff Blauser .01 .05
383 Scott Ruskin .01 .05
384 Andres Thomas .01 .05
385 Dennis Martinez .02 .10
386 Mike Henneman .01 .05
387 Felix Jose .01 .05
388 Alejandro Pena .01 .05
389 Chet Lemon .01 .05
390 Craig Wilson RC .01 .05
391 Chuck Crim .01 .05
392 Mel Hall .01 .05
393 Mark Knudson .01 .05
394 Norm Charlton .01 .05
395 Mike Felder .01 .05
396 Tim Layana .01 .05
397 Steve Frey .01 .05
398 Bill Doran .01 .05
399 Dion James .01 .05
400 Checklist 301-400 .01 .05
401 Ron Hassey .01 .05
402 Don Robinson .01 .05
403 Gene Nelson .01 .05
404 Terry Kennedy .01 .05
405 Todd Burns .01 .05
406 Roger McDowell .01 .05
407 Bob Kipper .01 .05
408 Darren Daulton .02 .10
409 Chuck Cary .01 .05
410 Bruce Ruffin .01 .05
411 Juan Berenguer .01 .05
412 Gary Ward .01 .05
413 Al Newman .01 .05
414 Danny Jackson .01 .05
415 Greg Gagne .01 .05
416 Tom Herr .01 .05
417 Jeff Parrett .01 .05
418 Jeff Reardon .02 .10
419 Mark Lemke .01 .05
420 Charlie O'Brien .01 .05
421 Willie Randolph .02 .10
422 Steve Bedrosian .01 .05
423 Mike Moore .01 .05
424 Jeff Brantley .01 .05
425 Bob Welch .01 .05
426 Terry Mulholland .01 .05
427 Willie Blair .01 .05
428 Darrin Fletcher .01 .05
429 Mike Witt .01 .05
430 Joe Boever .01 .05
431 Tom Gordon .01 .05
432 Pedro Munoz RC .02 .10
433 Kevin Seitzer .01 .05
434 Kevin Tapani .01 .05
435 Bret Saberhagen .02 .10
436 Ellis Burks .02 .10
437 Chuck Finley .02 .10
438 Mike Boddicker .01 .05
439 Francisco Cabrera .01 .05
440 Todd Hundley .01 .05
441 Kelly Downs .01 .05
442 Dann Howitt .01 .05
443 Scott Garrelts .01 .05
444 Rickey Henderson 3X .08 .25
445 Will Clark .05 .15
446 Ben McDonald .01 .05
447 Dale Murphy .05 .15
448 Dave Righetti .02 .10
449 Dickie Thon .01 .05
450 Ted Power .01 .05
451 Scott Coolbaugh .01 .05
452 Dwight Smith .01 .05
453 Pete Incaviglia .01 .05
454 Andre Dawson .02 .10
455 Ruben Sierra .02 .10
456 Andres Galarraga .02 .10
457 Alvin Davis .01 .05
458 Tony Castillo .01 .05
459 Pete O'Brien .01 .05
460 Charlie Leibrandt .01 .05
461 Vince Coleman .01 .05
462 Steve Sax .01 .05
463 Omar Olivares RC .02 .10
464 Oscar Azocar .01 .05
465 Joe Magrane .01 .05
466 Karl Rhodes .01 .05
467 Benito Santiago .02 .10
468 Joe Klink .01 .05
469 Sil Campusano .01 .05
470 Mark Parent .01 .05
471 Shawn Boskie UER .01 .05
Depleted misspelled
as depleated
472 Kevin Brown .02 .10
473 Rick Sutcliffe .02 .10
474 Rafael Palmeiro .05 .15
475 Mike Harkey .01 .05
476 Jaime Navarro .01 .05
477 Marquis Grissom UER .02 .10
DeShields misspelled
as DeSheilds
478 Marty Clary .01 .05
479 Greg Briley .01 .05
480 Tom Glavine .05 .15
481 Lee Guetterman .01 .05
482 Rex Hudler .01 .05
483 Dave LaPoint .01 .05
484 Terry Pendleton .02 .10
485 Jesse Barfield .01 .05
486 Jose DeJesus .01 .05
487 Paul Abbott RC .02 .10
488 Ken Howell .01 .05
489 Greg W. Harris .01 .05
490 Roy Smith .01 .05
491 Paul Assenmacher .01 .05
492 Geno Petralli .01 .05
493 Steve Wilson .01 .05
494 Kevin Reimer .01 .05
495 Bill Long .01 .05
496 Mike Jackson .01 .05
497 Oddibe McDowell .01 .05
498 Bill Swift .01 .05
499 Jeff Treadway .01 .05
500 Checklist 401-500 .01 .05
501 Gene Larkin .01 .05
502 Bob Boone .02 .10
503 Allan Anderson .01 .05
504 Luis Aquino .01 .05
505 Mark Guthrie .01 .05
506 Joe Orsulak .01 .05
507 Dana Kiecker .01 .05
508 Dave Gallagher .01 .05
509 Greg A. Harris .01 .05
510 Mark Williamson .01 .05
511 Casey Candaele .01 .05
512 Mookie Wilson .02 .10
513 Dave Smith .01 .05
514 Chuck Carr .01 .05
515 Glenn Wilson .01 .05
516 Mike Fitzgerald .01 .05
517 Devon White .02 .10
518 Dave Hollins .01 .05
519 Mark Eichhorn .01 .05
520 Otis Nixon .01 .05
521 Terry Shumpert .01 .05
522 Scott Erickson .01 .05
523 Danny Tartabull .01 .05
524 Orel Hershiser .02 .10
525 George Brett .25 .60
526 Greg Vaughn .01 .05
527 Tim Naehring .01 .05
528 Curt Schilling .08 .25
529 Chris Bosio .01 .05
530 Sam Horn .01 .05
531 Mike Scott .01 .05
532 George Bell .01 .05
533 Eric Anthony .01 .05
534 Julio Valera .01 .05
535 Glenn Davis .01 .05
536 Larry Walker UER .08 .25
Should have comma
after Expos in text
537 Pat Combs .01 .05
538 Chris Nabholz .01 .05
539 Kirk McCaskill .01 .05
540 Randy Ready .01 .05
541 Mark Gubicza .01 .05
542 Rick Aguilera .02 .10
543 Brian McRae RC .08 .25
544 Kirby Puckett .08 .25
545 Bo Jackson .08 .25
546 Wade Boggs .05 .15
547 Tim McIntosh .01 .05
548 Randy Milligan .01 .05
549 Dwight Evans .05 .15
550 Billy Ripken .01 .05
551 Erik Hanson .01 .05
552 Lance Parrish .02 .10
553 Tino Martinez .08 .25
554 Jim Abbott .05 .15
555 Ken Griffey Jr. UER .25 .60
556 Milt Cuyler .01 .05
557 Mark Leonard RC .01 .05
558 Jay Howell .01 .05
559 Lloyd Moseby .01 .05
560 Chris Gwynn .01 .05
561 Mark Whiten .01 .05
562 Harold Baines .02 .10
563 Junior Felix .01 .05
564 Darren Lewis .01 .05
565 Fred McGriff .05 .15
566 Kevin Appier .02 .10
567 Luis Gonzalez RC .30 .75
568 Frank White .02 .10
569 Juan Agosto .01 .05
570 Mike Macfarlane .01 .05
571 Bert Blyleven .02 .10
572 Ken Griffey Sr. .10 .30
Ken Griffey Jr.
573 Lee Stevens .01 .05
574 Edgar Martinez .05 .15
575 Wally Joyner .02 .10
576 Tim Belcher .01 .05
577 John Burkett .01 .05
578 Mike Morgan .01 .05
579 Paul Gibson .01 .05
580 Jose Vizcaino .01 .05
581 Duane Ward .01 .05
582 Scott Sanderson .01 .05
583 David Wells .02 .10
584 Willie McGee .02 .10
585 John Cerutti .01 .05
586 Danny Darwin .01 .05
587 Kurt Stillwell .01 .05
588 Rich Gedman .01 .05
589 Mark Davis .01 .05
590 Bill Gullickson .01 .05
591 Matt Young .01 .05
592 Bryan Harvey .01 .05
593 Omar Vizquel .05 .15
594 Scott Lewis RC .02 .10
595 Dave Valle .01 .05
596 Tim Crews .01 .05
597 Mike Bielecki .01 .05
598 Mike Sharperson .01 .05
599 Dave Bergman .01 .05
600 Checklist 501-600 .01 .05
601 Steve Lyons .01 .05
602 Bruce Hurst .01 .05
603 Donn Pall .01 .05
604 Jim Vatcher RC .01 .05
605 Dan Pasqua .01 .05
606 Kenny Rogers .02 .10
607 Jeff Schulz RC .01 .05
608 Brad Arnsberg .01 .05
609 Willie Wilson .01 .05
610 Jamie Moyer .02 .10
611 Ron Oester .01 .05
612 Dennis Cook .01 .05
613 Rick Mahler .01 .05
614 Bill Landrum .01 .05
615 Scott Scudder .01 .05
616 Tom Edens RC .01 .05
617 1917 Revisited .02 .10
White Sox vintage uniforms
618 Jim Gantner .01 .05
619 Darrel Akerfelds .01 .05
620 Ron Robinson .01 .05
621 Scott Radinsky .01 .05
622 Pete Smith .01 .05
623 Melido Perez .01 .05
624 Jerald Clark .01 .05
625 Carlos Martinez .01 .05
626 Wes Chamberlain RC .08 .25
627 Bobby Witt .01 .05
628 Ken Dayley .01 .05
629 John Barfield .01 .05
630 Bob Tewksbury .01 .05
631 Glenn Braggs .01 .05
632 Jim Neidlinger RC .01 .05
633 Tom Browning .01 .05
634 Kirk Gibson .02 .10
635 Rob Dibble .02 .10
636 Rickey Henderson SB .08 .25
Lou Brock
May 1 1991 on front
636A R.Henderson SB .08 .25
Lou Brock
no date on card
637 Jeff Montgomery .01 .05
638 Mike Schooler .01 .05
639 Storm Davis .01 .05
640 Rich Rodriguez RC .01 .05
641 Phil Bradley .01 .05
642 Kent Mercker .01 .05
643 Carlton Fisk .05 .15
644 Mike Bell RC .01 .05
645 Alex Fernandez .01 .05
646 Juan Gonzalez .08 .25
647 Ken Hill .01 .05
648 Jeff Russell .01 .05
649 Chuck Malone .01 .05
650 Steve Buechele .01 .05
651 Mike Benjamin .01 .05
652 Tony Pena .01 .05
653 Trevor Wilson .01 .05
654 Alex Cole .01 .05
655 Roger Clemens .30 .75
656 Mark McGwire BASH .15 .40
657 Joe Grahe RC .02 .10
658 Jim Eisenreich .01 .05
659 Dan Gladden .01 .05
660 Steve Farr .01 .05
661 Bill Sampen .01 .05
662 Dave Rohde .01 .05
663 Mark Gardner .01 .05
664 Mike Simms RC .01 .05
665 Moises Alou .02 .10
666 Mickey Hatcher .01 .05
667 Jimmy Key .02 .10
668 John Wetteland .02 .10
669 John Smiley .01 .05
670 Jim Acker .01 .05
671 Pascual Perez .01 .05
672 Reggie Harris UER .01 .05
Opportunity misspelled
as oppurtinty
673 Matt Nokes .01 .05
674 Rafael Novoa RC .01 .05
675 Hensley Meulens .01 .05
676 Jeff M. Robinson .01 .05
677 Ground Breaking .02 .10
New Comiskey Park;
Carlton Fisk and
Robin Ventura
678 Johnny Ray .01 .05
679 Greg Hibbard .01 .05
680 Paul Sorrento .01 .05
681 Mike Marshall .01 .05
682 Jim Clancy .01 .05
683 Rob Murphy .01 .05
684 Dave Schmidt .01 .05
685 Jeff Gray RC .01 .05
686 Mike Hartley .01 .05
687 Jeff King .01 .05
688 Stan Javier .01 .05
689 Bob Walk .01 .05
690 Jim Gott .01 .05
691 Mike LaCoss .01 .05
692 John Farrell .01 .05
693 Tim Leary .01 .05
694 Mike Walker .01 .05
695 Eric Plunk .01 .05
696 Mike Fetters .01 .05
697 Wayne Edwards .01 .05
698 Tim Drummond .01 .05
699 Willie Fraser .01 .05
700 Checklist 601-700 .01 .05
701 Mike Heath .01 .05
702 Gonzalez/Rhodes/Bagwell .40 1.00
703 Jose Mesa .01 .05
704 Dave Smith .01 .05
705 Danny Darwin .01 .05
706 Rafael Belliard .01 .05
707 Rob Murphy .01 .05
708 Terry Pendleton .02 .10
709 Mike Pagliarulo .01 .05
710 Sid Bream .01 .05
711 Junior Felix .01 .05
712 Dante Bichette .02 .10
713 Kevin Gross .01 .05
714 Luis Sojo .01 .05
715 Bob Ojeda .01 .05
716 Julio Machado .01 .05
717 Steve Farr .01 .05
718 Franklin Stubbs .01 .05
719 Mike Boddicker .01 .05
720 Willie Randolph .02 .10
721 Willie McGee .02 .10
722 Chili Davis .02 .10
723 Danny Jackson .01 .05
724 Cory Snyder .01 .05
725 Andre Dawson .08 .25
George Bell
Ryne Sandberg
726 Rob Deer .01 .05
727 Rich DeLucia RC .01 .05
728 Mike Perez RC .02 .10
729 Mickey Tettleton .01 .05
730 Mike Blowers .01 .05
731 Gary Gaetti .02 .10
732 Brett Butler .02 .10
733 Dave Parker .02 .10
734 Eddie Zosky .01 .05
735 Jack Clark .02 .10
736 Jack Morris .02 .10
737 Kirk Gibson .02 .10
738 Steve Bedrosian .01 .05
739 Candy Maldonado .01 .05
740 Matt Young .01 .05
741 Rich Garces RC .02 .10
742 George Bell .01 .05
743 Deion Sanders .05 .15
744 Bo Jackson .08 .25
745 Luis Mercedes RC .02 .10
746 Reggie Jefferson UER .01 .05
Throwing left on card;
back has throws right
747 Pete Incaviglia .01 .05
748 Chris Hammond .01 .05
749 Mike Stanton .01 .05
750 Scott Sanderson .01 .05
751 Paul Faries RC .01 .05
752 Al Osuna RC .01 .05
753 Steve Chitren RC .01 .05
754 Tony Fernandez .01 .05
755 Jeff Bagwell UER RC .60 1.50
756 Kirk Dressendorfer RC .02 .10
757 Glenn Davis .01 .05
758 Gary Carter .02 .10
759 Zane Smith .01 .05
760 Vance Law .01 .05
761 Denis Boucher RC .02 .10
762 Turner Ward RC .02 .10
763 Roberto Alomar .05 .15
764 Albert Belle .02 .10
765 Joe Carter .02 .10
766 Pete Schourek RC .02 .10
767 Heathcliff Slocumb RC .02 .10
768 Vince Coleman .01 .05
769 Mitch Williams .01 .05
770 Brian Downing .01 .05
771 Dana Allison RC .01 .05
772 Pete Harnisch .01 .05
773 Tim Raines .02 .10
774 Darryl Kile .02 .10
775 Fred McGriff .05 .15
776 Dwight Evans .05 .15
777 Joe Slusarski RC .01 .05
778 Dave Righetti .02 .10
779 Jeff Hamilton .01 .05
780 Ernest Riles .01 .05
781 Ken Dayley .01 .05
782 Eric King .01 .05
783 Devon White .02 .10
784 Beau Allred .01 .05
785 Mike Timlin RC .08 .25
786 Ivan Calderon .01 .05
787 Hubie Brooks .01 .05
788 Juan Agosto .01 .05
789 Barry Jones .01 .05
790 Wally Backman .01 .05
791 Jim Presley .01 .05
792 Charlie Hough .02 .10
793 Larry Andersen .01 .05
794 Steve Finley .02 .10
795 Shawn Abner .01 .05
796 Jeff M. Robinson .01 .05
797 Joe Bitker RC .01 .05
798 Eric Show .01 .05
799 Bud Black .01 .05
800 Checklist 701-800 .01 .05
HH1 Hank Aaron Hologram .60 1.50
SP1 Michael Jordan SP 12.00 30.00
SP2 R.Henderson/N.Ryan .75 2.00

1991 Upper Deck Aaron Heroes

These standard-size cards were issued in honor of Hall of Famer Hank Aaron and inserted in Upper Deck high number wax packs. Aaron autographed 2,500 of card number 27, which featured his portrait by noted sports artist Vernon Wells. The cards are numbered on the back in continuation of the Baseball Heroes set.

COMPLETE SET (10) 2.00 5.00
COMMON AARON (19-27) .20 .50
RANDOM INSERTS IN HI SERIES
NNO Hank Aaron Header SP .40 1.00
AU3 Hank Aaron AU/2500 75.00 200.00

1991 Upper Deck Heroes of Baseball

These standard-size cards were randomly inserted in Upper Deck Baseball Heroes wax packs. The fourth card features a color portrait of the three players by noted sports artist Vernon Wells. Each of the features heroes also signed 3,000 of each card for inclusion in this product.

COMPLETE SET (4) 10.00 25.00
RANDOM INSERTS IN HEROES FOIL
H1 Harmon Killebrew 3.00 8.00
H2 Gaylord Perry 2.00 5.00
H3 Fergie Jenkins 2.00 5.00
H4 Header 3.00 8.00
Art Card
AU1 Harmon Killebrew AU/3000 20.00 50.00
AU2 Gaylord Perry AU/3000 20.00 50.00
AU3 Fergie Jenkins AU/3000 12.00 30.00

1991 Upper Deck Ryan Heroes

This nine-card standard-size set was included in first series 1991 Upper Deck packs. The set which honors Nolan Ryan and is numbered as a continuation of the Baseball Heroes set which began with Reggie Jackson in 1990. This set honors Ryan's long career and his place in Baseball History. Card number 18 features the artwork of Vernon Wells while the other cards are photos. The complete set price below does not include the signed Ryan card of which only 2500 were made. Signed cards ending with 00 have the expression "Strikeout King" added. These Ryan cards were apparently issued on 100-card sheets with the following configuration: ten each of the nine Ryan Baseball Heroes cards, five Michael Jordan cards and five Baseball Heroes header cards. The Baseball Heroes header card is a standard size card which explains the continuation of the Baseball Heroes series on the back while the front just says Baseball Heroes.

COMPLETE SET (10) 2.00 5.00
COMMON RYAN (10-18) .20 .50
RANDOM INSERTS IN LO SERIES
NNO Nolan Ryan Header SP .40 1.00
AU2 Nolan Ryan AU/2500 100.00 200.00

1991 Upper Deck Silver Sluggers

The Upper Deck Silver Slugger set features nine players from each league, representing the nine batting positions on the team. The cards were issued one per 1991 Upper Deck jumbo pack. The cards measure the standard size. The cards are numbered on the back with an "SS" prefix.

COMPLETE SET (18) 6.00 15.00
ONE PER LO OR HI JUMBO PACK
SS1 Julio Franco .30 .75
SS2 Alan Trammell .30 .75
SS3 Rickey Henderson .75 2.00
SS4 Jose Canseco .50 1.25
SS5 Barry Bonds 3.00 8.00
SS6 Eddie Murray .75 2.00
SS7 Kelly Gruber .15 .40
SS8 Ryne Sandberg 1.25 3.00
SS9 Darryl Strawberry .30 .75
SS10 Ellis Burks .30 .75
SS11 Lance Parrish .30 .75
SS12 Cecil Fielder .30 .75
SS13 Matt Williams .30 .75
SS14 Dave Parker .30 .75
SS15 Bobby Bonilla .30 .75
SS16 Don Robinson .15 .40
SS17 Benito Santiago .30 .75
SS18 Barry Larkin .50 1.25

1991 Upper Deck Final Edition

The 1991 Upper Deck Final Edition boxed set contains 100 standard-size cards and showcases players who made major contributions during their team's late-season pennant drive. In addition to the late season traded and impact rookie cards (22-78), the set includes two special subsets: Diamond Skills cards (1-21), depicting the best Minor League prospects, and All-Star cards (80-99). Six assorted team logo hologram cards were issued with each set. The cards are numbered on the back with an F suffix. Among the outstanding Rookie Cards in this set are Ryan Klesko, Kenny Lofton, Pedro Martinez, Ivan Rodriguez, Jim Thome, Rondell White, and Dmitri Young.

COMP.FACT.SET (100) 3.00 8.00
1F R.Klesko .08 .25
R.Sanders CL
2F Pedro Martinez RC 4.00 10.00
3F Lance Dickson .01 .05
4F Royce Clayton .01 .05
5F Scott Bryant .01 .05
6F Dan Wilson RC .08 .25
7F Dmitri Young RC .30 .75
8F Ryan Klesko RC .20 .50
9F Tom Goodwin .01 .05
10F Rondell White RC .20 .50
11F Reggie Sanders .20 .50
12F Todd Van Poppel .01 .05
13F Arthur Rhodes RC .08 .25
14F Eddie Zosky .01 .05
15F Gerald Williams RC .08 .25
16F Robert Eenhoorn RC .02 .10
17F Jim Thome RC 4.00 10.00
18F Marc Newfield RC .02 .10
19F Kerwin Moore RC .02 .10
20F Jeff McNeely RC .02 .10
21F Frank Rodriguez RC .02 .10
22F Andy Mota RC .01 .05
23F Chris Haney RC .02 .10
24F Kenny Lofton RC .30 .75
25F Dave Nilsson RC .08 .25
26F Derek Bell .02 .10
27F Frank Castillo RC .08 .25
28F Candy Maldonado .01 .05
29F Chuck McElroy .01 .05
30F Chito Martinez RC .01 .05
31F Steve Howe .01 .05
32F Freddie Benavides RC .01 .05
33F Scott Kamieniecki RC .02 .10
34F Denny Neagle RC .08 .25
35F Mike Humphreys RC .02 .10
36F Mike Remlinger .01 .05
37F Scott Coolbaugh .01 .05
38F Darren Lewis .01 .05
39F Thomas Howard .01 .05
40F John Candelaria .01 .05
41F Todd Benzinger .01 .05
42F Wilson Alvarez .01 .05
43F Patrick Lennon RC .02 .10
44F Rusty Meacham RC .02 .10
45F Ryan Bowen RC .02 .10
46F Rick Wilkins RC .02 .10
47F Ed Sprague .01 .05
48F Bob Scanlan RC .01 .05
49F Tom Candiotti .01 .05
50F Dennis Martinez Perfect .02 .10
51F Oil Can Boyd .01 .05
52F Glenallen Hill .01 .05
53F Scott Livingstone RC .02 .10
54F Brian R.Hunter RC .08 .25
55F Ivan Rodriguez RC .75 2.00
56F Keith Mitchell RC .02 .10
57F Roger McDowell .01 .05
58F Otis Nixon .01 .05
59F Juan Bell .01 .05
60F Bill Krueger .01 .05
61F Chris Donnels RC .01 .05
62F Tommy Greene .01 .05
63F Doug Simons RC .01 .05
64F Andy Ashby RC .08 .25
65F Anthony Young RC .01 .05
66F Kevin Morton RC .01 .05
67F Bret Barberie RC .02 .10

68F Scott Servais RC	.08	.25
69F Ron Darling	.01	.05
70F Tim Burke	.01	.05
71F Vicente Palacios	.01	.05
72F Gerald Alexander RC	.01	.05
73F Reggie Jefferson	.01	.05
74F Dean Palmer	.02	.10
75F Mark Whiten	.01	.05
76F Randy Tomlin RC	.02	.10
77F Mark Wohlers RC	.08	.25
78F Brook Jacoby	.01	.05
79F K.Griffey Jr. R.Sandberg CL	.20	.50
80F Jack Morris AS	.01	.05
81F Sandy Alomar Jr. AS	.01	.05
82F Cecil Fielder AS	.01	.05
83F Roberto Alomar AS	.02	.10
84F Wade Boggs AS	.02	.10
85F Cal Ripken AS	.15	.40
86F Rickey Henderson AS	.05	.15
87F Ken Griffey Jr. AS	.10	.30
88F Dave Henderson AS	.01	.05
89F Danny Tartabull AS	.01	.05
90F Tom Glavine AS	.02	.10
91F Benito Santiago AS	.01	.05
92F Will Clark AS	.02	.10
93F Ryne Sandberg AS	.08	.25
94F Chris Sabo AS	.01	.05
95F Ozzie Smith AS	.08	.25
96F Ivan Calderon AS	.01	.05
97F Tony Gwynn AS	.05	.15
98F Andre Dawson AS	.01	.05
99F Bobby Bonilla AS	.01	.05
100F Checklist 1-100	.01	.05

1991 Upper Deck Comic Ball 2 Promos

These promo cards measure the standard size and are horizontally oriented. The fronts feature color photos of the players with Looney Tunes characters superimposed on the pictures. An orange banner on the top of each picture has the Looney Tunes and Upper Deck logos. The backs of all four cards form a composite cartoon in which Tweety is standing on the pitcher's mound as Sylvester drags it from the field. The cards are unnumbered and checklisted below by the date of distribution at the 1991 National Sports Collectors Convention in Anaheim.

COMPLETE SET (4)	5.00	12.00
1 The National 7/4/91 Nolan Ryan (with Daffy and Bugs Bunny)	2.00	5.00
2 The National 7/5/91 Reggie Jackson (with Taz)	1.00	2.50
3 The National 7/6/91 Nolan Ryan (with Speedy Gonzales)	2.00	5.00
4 The National 7/7/91 Reggie Jackson (with Elmer Fudd/Sylvester)	1.00	2.50

1991 Upper Deck Heroes of Baseball 5x7

1 Date sheet 5x7 Reggie Jackson Lou Brock Harmon	8.00	20.00

1991 Upper Deck Sheets

These 23 commemorative sheets were issued in 1991 to fans attending old-timers games preceding major league games. The sheets measure 8 1/2" by 11" and feature artist renderings of players from the teams recreated for the old-timers game. The front carries the individual production number out of the total number produced, but otherwise the sheets are unnumbered and so listed below in chronological order. The cover sheet was produced in two different versions, one numbered to 10,000, the other to 20,000. After the original 10,000 were produced, another 10,000 were needed for promotions.

COMPLETE SET (23)	75.00	150.00
1 Cover sheet Reggie Jackson/(20&000) Dates and s	2.00	5.00
2 Philadelphia Scholars Fund Sports Show Oct. 17&	6.00	15.00
3 Tribute to Baltimore Orioles Heroes April 21& 19	4.00	10.00
4 Tribute to Joe DiMaggio and Ted Williams in cele	4.00	10.00
5 Heroes of the '70s May 18& 1991 (22&000) Clevela	4.00	10.00
6 Atlanta Braves Heroes vs. National League Heroes	4.00	10.00
7 Oakland A's June 9& 1991 (22&000) Oakland Colise	4.00	10.00
8 World Series Heroes June 15& 1991 (47&000) Shea	2.50	6.00
9 Cincinnati Reds Heroes vs. World Series Heroes J	6.00	15.00
10 1981 American League Divisional Playoff Heroes J	2.50	6.00
11 A Tribute to All-Star Heroes Toronto July 8& 19	2.00	5.00
12 Tribute to Home Run Heroes July 14& 1991 (44&000	2.50	6.00
13 Pittsburgh Pirates July 20& 1991 (18&000) Three	4.00	10.00
14 Battle of Missouri July 21, 1991 (17,000) Busch	4.00	10.00
15 David vs. Goliath July 27& 1991 (17&000) Astrodo	4.00	10.00
16 45th Annual Old-Timer's Day Classic July 27& 199	2.50	6.00
17 1971 Phillies vs. Upper Deck Heroes Aug. 10& 199	2.50	6.00
18 Tribute to Hall of Famers Aug. 10& 1991 (17&000)	4.00	10.00
19 All-Star Joes vs. All-Star Bobs Aug. 16& 1991 (2	3.00	8.00
20 Giants Reunion with Newest Hall of Famer Aug. 18	2.50	6.00
21 American League vs. National League Aug. 24& 199	4.00	10.00
22 Tribute to 1971 Heroes Aug. 25& 1991 (32&000) Ti	3.00	8.00
23 10th Anniversary of Expos' Divisional Championsh	2.50	6.00

1992 Upper Deck

The 1992 Upper Deck set contains 800 standard-size cards issued in two separate series of 700 and 100 cards respectively. The cards were distributed in low and high series foil packs in addition to factory sets. Factory sets feature a unique gold-foil hologram on the card backs (in contrast to the silver hologram on foil pack cards). Special subsets included in the set are Star Rookies (1-27), Team Checklists (29-40/86-99), with player portraits by Vernon Wells Sr.; Top Prospects (52-77); Bloodlines (79-85), Diamond Skills (640-650/711-721) and Diamond Debuts (771-780). Rookie Cards in the set include Shawn Green, Brian Jordan and Manny Ramirez. A special card picturing Tom Selleck and Frank Thomas, commemorating the forgettable movie "Mr. Baseball", was randomly inserted into high series packs. A standard-size Ted Williams hologram card was randomly inserted into low series packs. By mailing in 15 low series foil wrappers, a completed order form, and a handling fee, the collector could receive an 8 1/2" by 11" numbered, black and white lithograph picturing Ted Williams in his batting swing.

COMPLETE SET (800)	10.00	25.00
COMPLETE LO SET (700)	8.00	20.00
COMPLETE HI SET (100)	2.00	5.00
1 J.Thome R.Klesko CL	.08	.25
2 Royce Clayton SR	.01	.05
3 Brian Jordan RC	.20	.50
4 Dave Fleming	.01	.05
5 Jim Thome	.08	.25
6 Jeff Juden SR	.01	.05
7 Roberto Hernandez SR	.01	.05
8 Kyle Abbott SR	.01	.05
9 Chris George SR	.01	.05
10 Rob Maurer SR RC	.01	.05
11 Donald Harris SR	.01	.05
12 Ted Wood SR	.01	.05
13 Patrick Lennon SR	.01	.05
14 Willie Banks SR	.01	.05
15 Roger Salkeld SR UER (Bill was his grand- father	.01	.05
16 Wil Cordero SR	.01	.05
17 Arthur Rhodes SR	.01	.05
18 Pedro Martinez	.40	1.00
19 Andy Ashby SR	.01	.05
20 Tom Goodwin SR	.01	.05
21 Braulio Castillo SR	.01	.05
22 Todd Van Poppel	.01	.05
23 Brian Williams RC	.01	.05
24 Ryan Klesko	.02	.10
25 Kenny Lofton	.05	.15
26 Derek Bell	.02	.10
27 Reggie Sanders	.02	.10
28 Dave Winfield's 400th	.01	.05
29 David Justice TC	.01	.05
30 Rob Dibble TC Cincinnati Reds	.01	.05
31 Craig Biggio TC	.02	.10
32 Eddie Murray TC	.05	.15
33 Fred McGriff TC	.02	.10
34 Willie McGee TC San Francisco Giants	.01	.05
35 Shawon Dunston TC Chicago Cubs	.01	.05
36 Delino DeShields TC	.01	.05
37 Howard Johnson TC New York Mets	.01	.05
38 John Kruk TC	.01	.05
39 Doug Drabek TC Pittsburgh Pirates	.01	.05
40 Todd Zeile TC	.01	.05
41 Steve Avery Playoff	.01	.05
42 Jeremy Hernandez RC	.01	.05
43 Doug Henry RC	.02	.10
44 Chris Donnels	.01	.05
45 Mo Sanford	.01	.05
46 Scott Kamieniecki	.01	.05
47 Mark Lemke	.01	.05
48 Steve Farr	.01	.05
49 Francisco Oliveras	.01	.05
50 Ced Landrum	.01	.05
51 R.White M.Newfield CL	.02	.10
52 Eduardo Perez RC	.08	.25
53 Tom Nevers TP	.01	.05
54 David Zancanaro TP	.01	.05
55 Shawn Green RC	.40	1.00
56 Mark Wohlers TP	.01	.05
57 Dave Nilsson	.01	.05
58 Dmitri Young	.02	.10
59 Ryan Hawblitzel RC	.02	.10
60 Raul Mondesi	.02	.10
61 Rondell White	.02	.10
62 Steve Hosey	.01	.05
63 Manny Ramirez RC	1.50	4.00
64 Marc Newfield	.01	.05
65 Jeromy Burnitz	.02	.10
66 Mark Smith RC	.02	.10
67 Joey Hamilton RC	.02	.10
68 Tyler Green RC	.02	.10
69 Jon Farrell RC	.02	.10
70 Kurt Miller TP	.01	.05
71 Jeff Plympton TP	.01	.05
72 Dan Wilson TP	.01	.05
73 Joe Vitiello RC	.02	.10
74 Rico Brogna TP	.01	.05
75 David McCarty RC	.08	.25
76 Bob Wickman	.08	.25
77 Carlos Rodriguez TP	.01	.05
78 Jim Abbott Stay In School	.02	.10
79 P.Martinez R.Martinez	.08	.25
80 Kevin Mitchell Keith Mitchell	.01	.05
81 Sandy Roberto Alomar	.02	.10
82 Ripken Brothers	.20	.50
83 Tony Chris Gwynn	.05	.15
84 D.Gooden G.Sheffield	.02	.10
85 K.Griffey Jr. w Family	.10	.30
86 Jim Abbott TC California Angels	.02	.10
87 Frank Thomas TC	.05	.15
88 Danny Tartabull TC Kansas City Royals	.01	.05
89 Scott Erickson TC Minnesota Twins	.01	.05
90 Rickey Henderson TC	.05	.15
91 Edgar Martinez TC	.02	.10
92 Nolan Ryan TC	.20	.50
93 Ben McDonald TC Baltimore Orioles	.01	.05
94 Ellis Burks TC Boston Red Sox	.01	.05
95 Greg Swindell TC Cleveland Indians	.01	.05
96 Cecil Fielder TC	.01	.05
97 Greg Vaughn TC	.01	.05
98 Kevin Maas TC New York Yankees	.01	.05
99 Dave Stieb TC Toronto Blue Jays	.01	.05
100 Checklist 1-100	.01	.05
101 Joe Oliver	.01	.05
102 Hector Villanueva	.01	.05
103 Ed Whitson	.01	.05
104 Danny Jackson	.01	.05
105 Chris Hammond	.01	.05
106 Ricky Jordan	.01	.05
107 Kevin Bass	.01	.05
108 Darrin Fletcher	.01	.05
109 Junior Ortiz	.01	.05
110 Tom Bolton	.01	.05
111 Jeff King	.01	.05
112 Dave Magadan	.01	.05
113 Mike LaValliere	.01	.05
114 Hubie Brooks	.01	.05
115 Jay Bell	.02	.10
116 David Wells	.02	.10
117 Jim Leyritz	.01	.05
118 Manuel Lee	.01	.05
119 Alvaro Espinoza	.01	.05
120 B.J. Surhoff	.02	.10
121 Hal Morris	.01	.05
122 Shawon Dawson	.01	.05
123 Chris Sabo	.01	.05
124 Andre Dawson	.02	.10
125 Eric Davis	.02	.10
126 Chili Davis	.02	.10
127 Dale Murphy	.05	.15
128 Kirk McCaskill	.01	.05
129 Terry Mulholland	.01	.05
130 Rick Aguilera	.02	.10
131 Vince Coleman	.01	.05
132 Andy Van Slyke	.05	.15
133 Gregg Jefferies	.01	.05
134 Barry Bonds	.40	1.00
135 Dwight Gooden	.02	.10
136 Dave Stieb	.01	.05
137 Albert Belle	.02	.10
138 Teddy Higuera	.01	.05
139 Jesse Barfield	.01	.05
140 Pat Borders	.01	.05
141 Bip Roberts	.01	.05
142 Rob Dibble	.02	.10
143 Mark Grace	.05	.15
144 Barry Larkin	.05	.15
145 Ryne Sandberg	.15	.40
146 Scott Erickson	.01	.05
147 Luis Polonia	.01	.05
148 John Burkett	.01	.05
149 Luis Sojo	.01	.05
150 Dickie Thon	.01	.05
151 Walt Weiss	.01	.05
152 Mike Scioscia	.01	.05
153 Mark McGwire	.25	.60
154 Matt Williams	.02	.10
155 Rickey Henderson	.08	.25
156 Sandy Alomar Jr.	.01	.05
157 Brian McRae	.01	.05
158 Harold Baines	.02	.10
159 Kevin Appier	.02	.10
160 Felix Fermin	.01	.05
161 Leo Gomez	.01	.05
162 Craig Biggio	.05	.15
163 Ben McDonald	.01	.05
164 Randy Johnson	.08	.25
165 Cal Ripken	.30	.75
166 Frank Thomas	.08	.25
167 Delino DeShields	.01	.05
168 Greg Gagne	.01	.05
169 Ron Karkovice	.01	.05
170 Charlie Leibrandt	.01	.05
171 Dave Righetti	.02	.10
172 Dave Henderson	.01	.05
173 Steve Decker	.01	.05
174 Darryl Strawberry	.02	.10
175 Will Clark	.05	.15
176 Ruben Sierra	.02	.10
177 Ozzie Smith	.15	.40
178 Charles Nagy	.01	.05
179 Gary Pettis	.01	.05
180 Kirk Gibson	.02	.10
181 Randy Milligan	.01	.05
182 Dave Valle	.01	.05
183 Chris Hoiles	.01	.05
184 Tony Phillips	.01	.05
185 Brady Anderson	.02	.10
186 Scott Fletcher	.01	.05
187 Gene Larkin	.01	.05
188 Lance Johnson	.01	.05
189 Greg Olson	.01	.05
190 Melido Perez	.01	.05
191 Lenny Harris	.01	.05
192 Terry Kennedy	.01	.05
193 Mike Gallego	.01	.05
194 Willie McGee	.02	.10
195 Juan Samuel	.01	.05
196 Jeff Huson	.02	.10
197 Alex Cole	.01	.05
198 Ron Robinson	.01	.05
199 Joel Skinner	.01	.05
200 Checklist 101-200	.01	.05
201 Kevin Reimer	.01	.05
202 Stan Belinda	.01	.05
203 Pat Tabler	.01	.05
204 Jose Guzman	.01	.05
205 Jose Lind	.01	.05
206 Spike Owen	.01	.05
207 Joe Orsulak	.01	.05
208 Charlie Hayes	.01	.05
209 Mike Devereaux	.01	.05
210 Mike Fitzgerald	.01	.05
211 Willie Randolph	.02	.10
212 Rod Nichols	.01	.05
213 Mike Boddicker	.01	.05
214 Bill Spiers	.01	.05
215 Steve Olin	.01	.05
216 David Howard	.01	.05
217 Gary Varsho	.01	.05
218 Mike Harkey	.01	.05
219 Luis Aquino	.01	.05
220 Chuck McElroy	.01	.05
221 Doug Drabek	.01	.05
222 Dave Winfield	.02	.10
223 Rafael Palmeiro	.05	.15
224 Joe Carter	.02	.10
225 Bobby Bonilla	.02	.10
226 Ivan Calderon	.01	.05
227 Gregg Olson	.01	.05
228 Tim Wallach	.01	.05
229 Terry Pendleton	.02	.10
230 Gilberto Reyes	.01	.05
231 Carlos Baerga	.01	.05
232 Greg Vaughn	.01	.05
233 Bret Saberhagen	.02	.10
234 Gary Sheffield	.02	.10
235 Mark Lewis	.01	.05
236 George Bell	.01	.05
237 Danny Tartabull	.01	.05
238 Willie Wilson	.01	.05
239 Doug Dascenzo	.01	.05
240 Bill Pecota	.01	.05
241 Julio Franco	.02	.10
242 Ed Sprague	.01	.05
243 Juan Gonzalez	.05	.15
244 Chuck Finley	.02	.10
245 Ivan Rodriguez	.08	.25
246 Len Dykstra	.02	.10
247 Deion Sanders	.05	.15
248 Dwight Evans	.05	.15
249 Larry Walker	.05	.15
250 Billy Ripken	.01	.05
251 Mickey Tettleton	.01	.05
252 Tony Pena	.01	.05
253 Benito Santiago	.02	.10
254 Kirby Puckett	.08	.25
255 Cecil Fielder	.02	.10
256 Howard Johnson	.01	.05
257 Andujar Cedeno	.01	.05
258 Jose Rijo	.01	.05
259 Al Osuna	.01	.05
260 Todd Hundley	.01	.05
261 Orel Hershiser	.02	.10
262 Ray Lankford	.02	.10
263 Robin Ventura	.02	.10
264 Felix Jose	.01	.05
265 Eddie Murray	.08	.25
266 Kevin Mitchell	.01	.05
267 Gary Carter	.02	.10
268 Mike Benjamin	.01	.05
269 Dick Schofield	.01	.05
270 Jose Uribe	.01	.05
271 Pete Incaviglia	.01	.05
272 Tony Fernandez	.01	.05
273 Alan Trammell	.02	.10
274 Tony Gwynn	.10	.30
275 Mike Greenwell	.01	.05
276 Jeff Bagwell	.08	.25
277 Frank Viola	.02	.10
278 Randy Myers	.01	.05
279 Ken Caminiti	.02	.10
280 Bill Doran	.01	.05
281 Dan Pasqua	.01	.05
282 Alfredo Griffin	.01	.05
283 Jose Oquendo	.01	.05
284 Kal Daniels	.01	.05
285 Bobby Thigpen	.01	.05
286 Robby Thompson	.01	.05
287 Mark Eichhorn	.01	.05
288 Mike Felder	.01	.05
289 Dave Gallagher	.01	.05
290 Dave Anderson	.01	.05
291 Mel Hall	.01	.05
292 Jerald Clark	.01	.05
293 Al Newman	.01	.05
294 Rob Deer	.01	.05
295 Matt Nokes	.01	.05
296 Jack Armstrong	.01	.05
297 Jim Deshaies	.01	.05
298 Jeff Innis	.01	.05
299 Jeff Reed	.01	.05
300 Checklist 201-300	.01	.05
301 Lonnie Smith	.01	.05
302 Jimmy Key	.02	.10
303 Junior Felix	.01	.05
304 Mike Heath	.01	.05
305 Mark Langston	.01	.05
306 Greg W. Harris	.01	.05
307 Brett Butler	.02	.10
308 Luis Rivera	.01	.05
309 Bruce Ruffin	.01	.05
310 Paul Faries	.01	.05
311 Terry Leach	.01	.05
312 Scott Brosius RC	.20	.50
313 Scott Leius	.01	.05
314 Harold Reynolds	.02	.10
315 Jack Morris	.02	.10
316 David Segui	.01	.05
317 Bill Gullickson	.01	.05
318 Todd Frohwirth	.01	.05
319 Mark Leiter	.01	.05
320 Jeff M. Robinson	.01	.05
321 Gary Gaetti	.02	.10
322 John Smoltz	.05	.15
323 Andy Benes	.01	.05
324 Kelly Gruber	.01	.05
325 Jim Abbott	.05	.15
326 John Kruk	.02	.10
327 Kevin Seitzer	.01	.05
328 Darrin Jackson	.01	.05
329 Kurt Stillwell	.01	.05
330 Mike Maddux	.01	.05
331 Dennis Eckersley	.02	.10
332 Dan Gladden	.01	.05
333 Jose Canseco	.05	.15
334 Kent Hrbek	.02	.10
335 Ken Griffey Sr.	.02	.10
336 Greg Swindell	.01	.05
337 Trevor Wilson	.01	.05
338 Sam Horn	.01	.05
339 Mike Henneman	.01	.05
340 Jerry Browne	.01	.05
341 Glenn Braggs	.01	.05
342 Tom Glavine	.05	.15
343 Wally Joyner	.02	.10
344 Fred McGriff	.05	.15
345 Ron Gant	.02	.10
346 Ramon Martinez	.01	.05
347 Wes Chamberlain	.01	.05
348 Terry Shumpert	.01	.05
349 Tim Teufel	.01	.05
350 Wally Backman	.01	.05
351 Joe Girardi	.01	.05
352 Devon White	.02	.10
353 Greg Maddux	.15	.40
354 Ryan Bowen	.01	.05
355 Roberto Alomar	.05	.15
356 Don Mattingly	.25	.60
357 Pedro Guerrero	.02	.10
358 Steve Sax	.01	.05
359 Joey Cora	.01	.05
360 Jim Gantner	.01	.05
361 Brian Barnes	.01	.05
362 Kevin McReynolds	.01	.05
363 Bret Barberie	.01	.05
364 David Cone	.02	.10
365 Dennis Martinez	.02	.10
366 Brian Hunter	.01	.05
367 Edgar Martinez	.05	.15
368 Steve Finley	.02	.10
369 Greg Briley	.01	.05
370 Jeff Blauser	.01	.05
371 Todd Stottlemyre	.01	.05
372 Luis Gonzalez	.02	.10
373 Rick Wilkins	.01	.05
374 Darryl Kile	.02	.10
375 John Olerud	.02	.10
376 Lee Smith	.02	.10
377 Kevin Maas	.01	.05
378 Dante Bichette	.02	.10
379 Tom Pagnozzi	.01	.05
380 Mike Flanagan	.01	.05
381 Charlie O'Brien	.01	.05
382 Dave Martinez	.01	.05
383 Keith Miller	.01	.05
384 Scott Ruskin	.01	.05
385 Kevin Elster	.01	.05
386 Alvin Davis	.01	.05
387 Casey Candaele	.01	.05
388 Pete O'Brien	.01	.05
389 Jeff Treadway	.01	.05
390 Scott Bradley	.01	.05
391 Mookie Wilson	.02	.10
392 Jimmy Jones	.01	.05
393 Candy Maldonado	.01	.05
394 Eric Yelding	.01	.05
395 Tom Henke	.01	.05
396 Franklin Stubbs	.01	.05
397 Milt Thompson	.01	.05
398 Mark Carreon	.01	.05
399 Randy Velarde	.01	.05
400 Checklist 301-400	.01	.05
401 Omar Vizquel	.05	.15
402 Joe Boever	.01	.05
403 Bill Krueger	.01	.05
404 Jody Reed	.01	.05
405 Mike Schooler	.01	.05
406 Jason Grimsley	.01	.05
407 Greg Myers	.01	.05
408 Randy Ready	.01	.05
409 Mike Timlin	.01	.05
410 Mitch Williams	.01	.05
411 Garry Templeton	.01	.05
412 Greg Cadaret	.01	.05
413 Donnie Hill	.01	.05
414 Wally Whitehurst	.01	.05
415 Scott Sanderson	.01	.05
416 Thomas Howard	.01	.05
417 Neal Heaton	.01	.05
418 Charlie Hough	.02	.10
419 Jack Howell	.01	.05
420 Greg Hibbard	.01	.05
421 Carlos Quintana	.01	.05
422 Kim Batiste	.01	.05
423 Paul Molitor	.02	.10
424 Ken Griffey Jr.	.20	.50
425 Phil Plantier	.01	.05
426 Denny Neagle	.02	.10
427 Von Hayes	.01	.05
428 Shane Mack	.01	.05
429 Darren Daulton	.02	.10
430 Dwayne Henry	.01	.05
431 Lance Parrish	.02	.10
432 Mike Humphreys	.01	.05
433 Tim Burke	.01	.05
434 Bryan Harvey	.01	.05
435 Pat Kelly	.01	.05
436 Ozzie Guillen	.02	.10
437 Bruce Hurst	.01	.05
438 Sammy Sosa	.08	.25
439 Dennis Rasmussen	.01	.05
440 Ken Patterson	.01	.05
441 Jay Buhner	.02	.10
442 Pat Combs	.01	.05
443 Wade Boggs	.05	.15
444 George Brett	.25	.60
445 Mo Vaughn	.02	.10
446 Chuck Knoblauch	.02	.10
447 Tom Candiotti	.01	.05
448 Mark Portugal	.01	.05
449 Mickey Morandini	.01	.05
450 Duane Ward	.01	.05
451 Otis Nixon	.01	.05
452 Bob Welch	.01	.05
453 Rusty Meacham	.01	.05
454 Keith Mitchell	.01	.05
455 Marquis Grissom	.02	.10
456 Robin Yount	.15	.40
457 Harvey Pulliam	.01	.05
458 Jose DeLeon	.01	.05
459 Mark Gubicza	.01	.05
460 Darryl Hamilton	.01	.05
461 Tom Browning	.01	.05
462 Monty Fariss	.01	.05
463 Jerome Walton	.01	.05
464 Paul O'Neill	.05	.15
465 Dean Palmer	.02	.10
466 Travis Fryman	.02	.10
467 John Smiley	.01	.05
468 Lloyd Moseby	.01	.05
469 John Wehner	.01	.05
470 Skeeter Barnes	.01	.05
471 Steve Chitren	.01	.05
472 Kent Mercker	.01	.05
473 Terry Steinbach	.01	.05
474 Andres Galarraga	.02	.10
475 Steve Avery	.01	.05
476 Tom Gordon	.01	.05
477 Cal Eldred	.01	.05
478 Omar Olivares	.01	.05
479 Julio Machado	.01	.05
480 Bob Milacki	.01	.05
481 Les Lancaster	.01	.05
482 John Candelaria	.01	.05
483 Brian Downing	.01	.05
484 Roger McDowell	.01	.05
485 Scott Scudder	.01	.05
486 Zane Smith	.01	.05
487 John Cerutti	.01	.05
488 Steve Buechele	.01	.05
489 Paul Gibson	.01	.05
490 Curtis Wilkerson	.01	.05
491 Marvin Freeman	.01	.05
492 Tom Foley	.01	.05
493 Juan Berenguer	.01	.05
494 Ernest Riles	.01	.05
495 Sid Bream	.01	.05
496 Chuck Crim	.01	.05
497 Mike Macfarlane	.01	.05
498 Dale Sveum	.01	.05
499 Storm Davis	.01	.05
500 Checklist 401-500	.01	.05
501 Jeff Reardon	.02	.10
502 Shawn Abner	.01	.05
503 Tony Fossas	.01	.05
504 Cory Snyder	.01	.05
505 Matt Young	.01	.05
506 Allan Anderson	.01	.05
507 Mark Lee	.01	.05
508 Gene Nelson	.01	.05
509 Mike Pagliarulo	.01	.05
510 Rafael Belliard	.01	.05
511 Jay Howell	.01	.05
512 Bob Tewksbury	.01	.05
513 Mike Morgan	.01	.05
514 John Franco	.02	.10
515 Kevin Gross	.01	.05
516 Lou Whitaker	.02	.10
517 Orlando Merced	.01	.05
518 Todd Benzinger	.01	.05
519 Gary Redus	.01	.05
520 Walt Terrell	.01	.05
521 Jack Clark	.02	.10
522 Dave Parker	.02	.10
523 Tim Naehring	.01	.05
524 Mark Whiten	.01	.05
525 Ellis Burks	.02	.10
526 Frank Castillo	.01	.05
527 Brian Harper	.01	.05
528 Brook Jacoby	.01	.05
529 Rick Sutcliffe	.02	.10
530 Joe Klink	.01	.05
531 Terry Bross	.01	.05
532 Jose Offerman	.01	.05
533 Todd Zeile	.01	.05
534 Eric Karros	.02	.10
535 Anthony Young	.01	.05
536 Milt Cuyler	.01	.05
537 Randy Tomlin	.01	.05
538 Scott Livingstone	.01	.05
539 Jim Eisenreich	.01	.05
540 Don Slaught	.01	.05
541 Scott Cooper	.01	.05
542 Joe Grahe	.01	.05
543 Tom Brunansky	.01	.05
544 Eddie Zosky	.01	.05
545 Roger Clemens	.20	.50
546 David Justice	.02	.10
547 Dave Stewart	.02	.10
548 David West	.01	.05
549 Dave Smith	.01	.05
550 Dan Plesac	.01	.05
551 Alex Fernandez	.01	.05
552 Bernard Gilkey	.01	.05
553 Jack McDowell	.01	.05
554 Tino Martinez	.05	.15
555 Bo Jackson	.08	.25
556 Bernie Williams	.05	.15
557 Mark Gardner	.01	.05
558 Glenallen Hill	.01	.05
559 Oil Can Boyd	.01	.05
560 Chris James	.01	.05
561 Scott Servais	.01	.05
562 Rey Sanchez RC	.08	.25
563 Paul McClellan	.01	.05
564 Andy Mota	.01	.05
565 Darren Lewis	.01	.05
566 Jose Melendez	.01	.05
567 Tommy Greene	.01	.05
568 Rich Rodriguez	.01	.05
569 Heathcliff Slocumb	.01	.05
570 Joe Hesketh	.01	.05
571 Carlton Fisk	.05	.15
572 Erik Hanson	.01	.05
573 Wilson Alvarez	.01	.05
574 Rheal Cormier	.01	.05
575 Tim Raines	.02	.10

576 Bobby Witt .01 .05
577 Roberto Kelly .01 .05
578 Kevin Brown .02 .10
579 Chris Nabholz .01 .05
580 Jesse Orosco .01 .05
581 Jeff Brantley .01 .05
582 Rafael Ramirez .01 .05
583 Kelly Downs .01 .05
584 Mike Simms .01 .05
585 Mike Remlinger .01 .05
586 Dave Hollins .01 .05
587 Larry Andersen .01 .05
588 Mike Gardiner .01 .05
589 Craig Lefferts .01 .05
590 Paul Assenmacher .01 .05
591 Bryn Smith .01 .05
592 Donn Pall .01 .05
593 Mike Jackson .01 .05
594 Scott Radinsky .01 .05
595 Brian Holman .01 .05
596 Geronimo Pena .01 .05
597 Mike Jeffcoat .01 .05
598 Carlos Martinez .01 .05
599 Geno Petralli .01 .05
600 Checklist 501-600 .01 .05
601 Jerry Don Gleaton .01 .05
602 Adam Peterson .01 .05
603 Craig Grebeck .01 .05
604 Mark Guthrie .01 .05
605 Frank Tanana .01 .05
606 Hensley Meulens .01 .05
607 Mark Davis .01 .05
608 Eric Plunk .01 .05
609 Mark Williamson .01 .05
610 Lee Guetterman .01 .05
611 Bobby Rose .01 .05
612 Bill Wegman .01 .05
613 Mike Hartley .01 .05
614 Chris Beasley .01 .05
615 Chris Bosio .01 .05
616 Henry Cotto .01 .05
617 Chico Walker .01 .05
618 Russ Swan .01 .05
619 Bob Walk .01 .05
620 Bill Swift .01 .05
621 Warren Newson .01 .05
622 Steve Bedrosian .01 .05
623 Ricky Bones .01 .05
624 Kevin Tapani .01 .05
625 Juan Guzman .01 .05
626 Jeff Johnson .01 .05
627 Jeff Montgomery .01 .05
628 Ken Hill .01 .05
629 Gary Thurman .01 .05
630 Steve Howe .01 .05
631 Jose DeJesus .01 .05
632 Kirk Dressendorfer .01 .05
633 Jaime Navarro .01 .05
634 Lee Stevens .01 .05
635 Pete Harnisch .01 .05
636 Bill Landrum .01 .05
637 Rich DeLucia .01 .05
638 Luis Salazar .01 .05
639 Rob Murphy .01 .05
640 J.Canseco .05 .15
R.Henderson CL
641 Roger Clemens DS .08 .25
642 Jim Abbott DS .02 .10
643 Travis Fryman DS .01 .05
644 Jesse Barfield DS .01 .05
645 Cal Ripken DS .15 .40
646 Wade Boggs DS .02 .10
647 Cecil Fielder DS .01 .05
648 Rickey Henderson DS .05 .15
649 Jose Canseco DS .02 .10
650 Ken Griffey Jr. DS .10 .30
651 Kenny Rogers .02 .10
652 Luis Mercedes .01 .05
653 Mike Stanton .01 .05
654 Glenn Davis .01 .05
655 Nolan Ryan .40 1.00
656 Reggie Jefferson .01 .05
657 Javier Ortiz .01 .05
658 Greg A. Harris .01 .05
659 Mariano Duncan .01 .05
660 Jeff Shaw .01 .05
661 Mike Moore .01 .05
662 Chris Haney .01 .05
663 Joe Slusarski .01 .05
664 Wayne Housie .01 .05
665 Carlos Garcia .01 .05
666 Bob Ojeda .01 .05
667 Bryan Hickerson RC .02 .10
668 Tim Belcher .01 .05
669 Ron Darling .01 .05
670 Rex Hudler .01 .05
671 Sid Fernandez .01 .05
672 Chito Martinez .01 .05
673 Pete Schourek .01 .05
674 Armando Reynoso RC .08 .25
675 Mike Mussina .08 .25
676 Kevin Morton .01 .05
677 Norm Charlton .01 .05
678 Danny Darwin .01 .05
679 Eric King .01 .05
680 Ted Power .01 .05
681 Barry Jones .01 .05
682 Carney Lansford .02 .10
683 Mel Rojas .01 .05
684 Rick Honeycutt .01 .05
685 Jeff Fassero .01 .05
686 Cris Carpenter .01 .05
687 Tim Crews .01 .05
688 Scott Terry .01 .05
689 Chris Gwynn .01 .05
690 Gerald Perry .01 .05
691 John Barfield .01 .05
692 Bob Melvin .01 .05
693 Juan Agosto .01 .05
694 Alejandro Pena .01 .05
695 Jeff Russell .01 .05
696 Carmelo Martinez .01 .05
697 Bud Black .01 .05
698 Dave Otto .01 .05
699 Billy Hatcher .01 .05
700 Checklist 601-700 .01 .05
701 Clemente Nunez RC .01 .05
702 M.Clark .01 .05
Osborne
Jordan
703 Mike Morgan .01 .05
704 Keith Miller .01 .05
705 Kurt Stillwell .01 .05
706 Damon Berryhill .01 .05
707 Von Hayes .01 .05
708 Rick Sutcliffe .02 .10
709 Hubie Brooks .01 .05
710 Ryan Turner RC .02 .10
711 B.Bonds .20 .50
A.Van Slyke CL
712 Jose Rijo DS .01 .05
713 Tom Glavine DS .02 .10
714 Shawon Dunston DS .01 .05
715 Andy Van Slyke DS .02 .10
716 Ozzie Smith DS .08 .25
717 Tony Gwynn DS .05 .15
718 Will Clark DS .02 .10
719 Marquis Grissom DS .01 .05
720 Howard Johnson DS .01 .05
721 Barry Bonds DS .20 .50
722 Kirk McCaskill .01 .05
723 Sammy Sosa Cubs .30 .75
724 George Bell .01 .05
725 Gregg Jefferies .01 .05
726 Gary DiSarcina .01 .05
727 Mike Bordick .01 .05
728 Eddie Murray 400 HR .05 .15
729 Rene Gonzales .01 .05
730 Mike Bielecki .01 .05
731 Calvin Jones .01 .05
732 Jack Morris .02 .10
733 Frank Viola .02 .10
734 Dave Winfield .02 .10
735 Kevin Mitchell .01 .05
736 Bill Swift .01 .05
737 Dan Gladden .01 .05
738 Mike Jackson .01 .05
739 Mark Carreon .01 .05
740 Kirt Manwaring .01 .05
741 Randy Myers .01 .05
742 Kevin McReynolds .01 .05
743 Steve Sax .01 .05
744 Wally Joyner .02 .10
745 Gary Sheffield .02 .10
746 Danny Tartabull .01 .05
747 Julio Valera .01 .05
748 Denny Neagle .02 .10
749 Lance Blankenship .01 .05
750 Mike Gallego .01 .05
751 Bret Saberhagen .02 .10
752 Ruben Amaro .02 .10
753 Eddie Murray .08 .25
754 Kyle Abbott .01 .05
755 Bobby Bonilla .02 .10
756 Eric Davis .02 .10
757 Eddie Taubensee RC .08 .25
758 Andres Galarraga .02 .10
759 Pete Incaviglia .01 .05
760 Tom Candiotti .01 .05
761 Tim Belcher .01 .05
762 Ricky Bones .01 .05
763 Bip Roberts .01 .05
764 Pedro Munoz .01 .05
765 Greg Swindell .01 .05
766 Kenny Lofton .05 .15
767 Gary Carter .02 .10
768 Charlie Hayes .01 .05
769 Dickie Thon .01 .05
770 Donovan Osborne DD CL .01 .05
771 Bret Boone .05 .15
772 Archi Cianfrocco RC .02 .10
773 Mark Clark RC .02 .10
774 Chad Curtis RC .08 .25
775 Pat Listach RC .08 .25
776 Pat Mahomes RC .08 .25
777 Donovan Osborne .01 .05
778 John Patterson RC .02 .10
779 Andy Stankiewicz DD .01 .05
780 Turk Wendell RC .08 .25
781 Bill Krueger .01 .05
782 Rickey Henderson 1000 .05 .15
783 Kevin Seitzer .01 .05
784 Dave Martinez .01 .05
785 John Smiley .01 .05
786 Matt Stairs RC .08 .25
787 Scott Scudder .01 .05
788 John Wetteland .02 .10
789 Jack Armstrong .01 .05
790 Ken Hill .01 .05
791 Dick Schofield .01 .05
792 Mariano Duncan .01 .05
793 Bill Pecota .01 .05
794 Mike Kelly RC .02 .10
795 Willie Randolph .02 .10
796 Butch Henry .01 .05
797 Carlos Hernandez .01 .05
798 Doug Jones .01 .05
799 Melido Perez .01 .05
800 Checklist 701-800 .01 .05
HH2 Ted Williams Holo .75 2.00
SP3 Deion Sanders FB/BB .40 1.00
SP4 F.Thomas .40 1.00
T.Selleck

1992 Upper Deck Gold Hologram

COMP.FACT.SET (800) 10.00 25.00
*STARS: .4X TO 1X BASIC CARDS
*ROOKIES: .4X TO 1X BASIC
ALL FACTORY CARDS FEATURE GOLD HOLO
DISTRIBUTED ONLY IN FACT.SET FORM

1992 Upper Deck Bench/Morgan Heroes

This standard size 10-card set was randomly inserted in 1992 Upper Deck high number packs. Both Bench and Morgan autographed 2,500 of card number 45, which displays a portrait by sports artist Vernon Wells. The fronts feature color photos of Bench (37-39), Morgan (40-42), or both (43-44) at various stages of their baseball careers.

COMPLETE SET (10) 6.00 15.00
COMMON BENCH/MORG (37-45) .60 1.50
RANDOM INSERTS IN HI SERIES PACKS
NNO Bench 1.00 2.50
Morgan Hdr SP
AU5 Bench/Morgan AU/2500 40.00 80.00

1992 Upper Deck College POY Holograms

This three-card standard-size set was randomly inserted in 1992 Upper Deck high series foil packs. This set features College Player of the Year winners for 1989 through 1991. The cards are numbered on the back with the prefix "CP".

COMPLETE SET (3) .75 2.00
RANDOM INSERTS IN HI SERIES
CP1 David McCarty .40 1.00
CP2 Mike Kelly .40 1.00
CP3 Ben McDonald .40 1.00

1992 Upper Deck Heroes of Baseball

Continuing a popular insert set introduced the previous year, Upper Deck produced four new commemorative cards, including three player cards and one portrait card by sports artist Vernon Wells. These cards were randomly inserted in 1992 Upper Deck baseball low number foil packs. Three thousand of each card were personally numbered and autographed by each player.

RANDOM INSERTS IN HEROES FOIL
H5 Vida Blue .75 2.00
H6 Lou Brock .75 2.00
H7 Rollie Fingers .75 2.00
H8 L.Brock .75 2.00
Blue
Fingers
AU5 Vida Blue AU/3000 8.00 20.00
AU6 Lou Brock AU/3000 15.00 40.00
AU7 R.Fingers AU/3000 6.00 15.00

1992 Upper Deck Heroes Highlights

To dealers participating in Heroes of Baseball Collectors shows, Upper Deck made available this ten-card insert standard-size set, which commemorates one of the greatest moments in the careers of ten of baseball's all-time players. The cards were primarily randomly inserted in high number packs sold at these shows. However at the first Heroes show in Anaheim, the cards were inserted into low number packs. The fronts feature color player photos with a shadowed strip for a three-dimensional effect. The player's name and the date of the great moment in the hero's career appear with a "Heroes Highlights" logo in a bottom border of varying shades of brown and blue-green. The backs have white borders and display a blue-green and brown bordered monument design accented with baseballs. The major portion of the design is parchment-textured and contains text highlighting a special moment in the player's career. The cards are numbered on the back with an "HI" prefix. The card numbering follows alphabetical order by player's name.

COMPLETE SET (10) 6.00 15.00
HI1 Bobby Bonds .20 .50
HI2 Lou Brock 1.25 3.00
HI3 Rollie Fingers .75 2.00
HI4 Bob Gibson 1.25 3.00
HI5 Reggie Jackson 1.50 4.00
HI6 Gaylord Perry .75 2.00
HI7 Robin Roberts .75 2.00
HI8 Brooks Robinson 1.50 4.00
HI9 Billy Williams .75 2.00
HI10 Ted Williams 2.50 6.00

1992 Upper Deck Home Run Heroes

This 26-card standard-size set was inserted one per pack into 1992 Upper Deck low series jumbo packs. The set spotlights the 1991 home run leaders from each of the 26 Major League teams.

COMPLETE SET (26) 5.00 12.00
ONE PER LO SERIES JUMBO
HR1 Jose Canseco .20 .50
HR2 Cecil Fielder .10 .30
HR3 Howard Johnson .05 .15
HR4 Cal Ripken 1.00 2.50
HR5 Matt Williams .10 .30
HR6 Joe Carter .10 .30
HR7 Ron Gant .10 .30
HR8 Frank Thomas .30 .75
HR9 Andre Dawson .10 .30
HR10 Fred McGriff .20 .50
HR11 Danny Tartabull .05 .15
HR12 Chili Davis .10 .30
HR13 Albert Belle .10 .30
HR14 Jack Clark .10 .30
HR15 Paul O'Neill .20 .50
HR16 Darryl Strawberry .10 .30
HR17 Dave Winfield .10 .30
HR18 Jay Buhner .10 .30
HR19 Juan Gonzalez .20 .50
HR20 Greg Vaughn .05 .15
HR21 Barry Bonds 1.25 3.00
HR22 Matt Nokes .05 .15
HR23 John Kruk .10 .30
HR24 Ivan Calderon .05 .15
HR25 Jeff Bagwell .30 .75
HR26 Todd Zeile .05 .15

1992 Upper Deck Scouting Report

Inserted one per high series jumbo pack, cards from this 25-card standard-size set feature outstanding prospects in baseball. Please note these cards are highly condition sensitive and are priced below in NmMt condition. Mint copies trade for premiums.

COMPLETE SET (25) 8.00 20.00
COMMON CARD (SR1-SR25) .40 1.00
ONE PER HI SERIES JUMBO
CONDITION SENSITIVE SET
SR1 Andy Ashby .40 1.00
SR2 Willie Banks .40 1.00
SR3 Kim Batiste .40 1.00
SR4 Derek Bell .40 1.00
SR5 Archi Cianfrocco .40 1.00
SR6 Royce Clayton .40 1.00
SR7 Gary DiSarcina .40 1.00
SR8 Dave Fleming .40 1.00
SR9 Butch Henry .40 1.00
SR10 Todd Hundley .40 1.00
SR11 Brian Jordan .40 1.00
SR12 Eric Karros .40 1.00
SR13 Pat Listach .40 1.00
SR14 Scott Livingstone .40 1.00
SR15 Kenny Lofton .40 1.00
SR16 Pat Mahomes .40 1.00
SR17 Denny Neagle .40 1.00
SR18 Dave Nilsson .40 1.00
SR19 Donovan Osborne .40 1.00
SR20 Reggie Sanders .40 1.00
SR21 Andy Stankiewicz .40 1.00
SR22 Jim Thome .75 2.00
SR23 Julio Valera .40 1.00
SR24 Mark Wohlers .40 1.00
SR25 Anthony Young .40 1.00

1992 Upper Deck Williams Best

This 20-card standard-size set contains Ted Williams' choices of best current and future hitters in the game. The cards were randomly inserted in Upper Deck high number foil packs. These cards are condition sensitive and priced below in NmMt condition. True mint condition copies do sell for more than these listed prices.

COMPLETE SET (20) 8.00 20.00
COMMON CARD (T1-T20) .10 .25
RANDOM INSERTS IN HI SERIES
CONDITION SENSITIVE SET
T1 Wade Boggs .30 .75
T2 Barry Bonds 2.00 5.00
T3 Jose Canseco .30 .75
T4 Will Clark .30 .75
T5 Cecil Fielder .20 .50
T6 Tony Gwynn .60 1.50
T7 Rickey Henderson .50 1.25
T8 Fred McGriff .30 .75
T9 Kirby Puckett .50 1.25
T10 Ruben Sierra .20 .50
T11 Roberto Alomar .30 .75
T12 Jeff Bagwell .50 1.25
T13 Albert Belle .20 .50
T14 Juan Gonzalez .30 .75
T15 Ken Griffey Jr. 1.00 2.50
T16 Chris Hoiles .08 .25
T17 David Justice .20 .50
T18 Phil Plantier .08 .25
T19 Frank Thomas .50 1.25
T20 Robin Ventura .20 .50

1992 Upper Deck Williams Heroes

This standard-size ten-card set was randomly inserted in 1992 Upper Deck low number foil packs. Williams autographed 2,500 of card 36, which displays his portrait by sports artist Vernon Wells. The cards are numbered on the back in continuation of the Upper Deck heroes series.

COMPLETE SET (10) 3.00 8.00
COMMON T.WILLIAMS (28-36) .20 .50
RANDOM INSERTS IN LO SERIES PACKS
NNO Ted Williams Header SP .75 2.00
AU4 Ted Williams AU/2500 300.00 500.00

1992 Upper Deck Williams Wax Boxes

These eight oversized blank-backed "cards," measuring approximately 5 1/4" by 7 1/4", were featured on the bottom panels of 1992 Upper Deck low series wax boxes. They are identical in design to the Williams Heroes insert cards, displaying color player photos in an oval frame. These boxes are unnumbered. We have checklisted them below according to the numbering of the Heroes cards.

COMMON PLAYER (28-35) .20 .50

1992 Upper Deck FanFest

As a title sponsor of the 1992 All-Star FanFest in San Diego, Upper Deck produced this 54-card standard size set to commemorate past, present, and future All-Stars Heroes of Major League Baseball. Sixty sets were packaged in a case, and each case had at least one gold foil set. Cards 1-10 feature ten Future Heroes that are, in Upper Deck's opinion, sure bets to make an upcoming team; cards 11-44 present active All-Star alumni; and cards 45-54 salute All-Star Heroes of the past with ten fan favorites.

COMP.FACT SET (54) 4.00 10.00
1 Steve Avery .02 .10
2 Ivan Rodriguez .30 .75
3 Jeff Bagwell .30 .75
4 Delino DeShields .07 .20
5 Royce Clayton .02 .10
6 Robin Ventura .20 .50
7 Phil Plantier .02 .10
8 Ray Lankford .07 .20
9 Juan Gonzalez .25 .60
10 Frank Thomas .30 .75
11 Roberto Alomar .20 .50
12 Sandy Alomar Jr. .07 .20
13 Wade Boggs .30 .75
14 Barry Bonds .50 1.25
15 Bobby Bonilla .02 .10
16 George Brett .60 1.50
17 Jose Canseco .25 .60
18 Will Clark .20 .50
19 Roger Clemens .60 1.50
20 Eric Davis .07 .20
21 Rob Dibble .07 .20
22 Cecil Fielder .07 .20
23 Dwight Gooden .07 .20
24 Ken Griffey Jr. .75 2.00
25 Tony Gwynn .60 1.50
26 Bryan Harvey .02 .10
27 Rickey Henderson .40 1.00
28 Howard Johnson .02 .10
29 Wally Joyner .07 .20
30 Barry Larkin .20 .50
31 Don Mattingly .60 1.50
32 Mark McGwire .60 1.50
33 Dale Murphy .20 .50
34 Rafael Palmeiro .20 .50
35 Kirby Puckett .40 1.00
36 Cal Ripken 1.25 3.00
37 Nolan Ryan 1.25 3.00
38 Chris Sabo .02 .10
39 Ryne Sandberg .60 1.50
40 Benito Santiago .07 .20
41 Ruben Sierra .07 .20
42 Ozzie Smith .60 1.50
43 Darryl Strawberry .07 .20
44 Robin Yount .30 .75
45 Rollie Fingers .07 .20
46 Reggie Jackson .20 .50
47 Billy Williams .07 .20
48 Lou Brock .20 .50
49 Gaylord Perry .07 .20
50 Ted Williams 1.25 3.00
51 Brooks Robinson .20 .50
52 Bob Gibson .20 .50
53 Bobby Bonds .07 .20
54 Robin Roberts .07 .20

1992 Upper Deck Heroes of Baseball 5x7

1 Ted Williams 20.00 50.00

1992 Upper Deck Sheets

The 35 commemorative sheets listed below in chronological order were issued by Upper Deck in 1992. The Upper Deck Heroes of Baseball made stops in all 26 MLB ballparks, as well as Mile High Stadium in Denver. They sponsored old-timer baseball games and donated $10,000 to the Baseball Assistance Team, a group dedicated to helping members of the baseball family that have fallen upon hard times. At each game a limited edition commemorative sheet was distributed. Four other commemorative sheets were produced in honor of other events. When the Orioles moved to Oriole Park at Camden Yards on April 6, Upper Deck distributed 17,000 individually numbered sheets free to fans. These sheets feature four artistic views of the new stadium. The first 1992 sheet listed below was issued at the Yankee Fan Festival held at the Jacob Javits Convention Center in New York Jan. 31-Feb. 2. Sheets 17 and 18 were issued at the All-Star Game in San Diego. Sheets 31 and 32 were inserted into retail repacks of eight 1992 Upper Deck foil packs. Displaying different player cards, sheets 33-34 are two different versions of the same sheet and list dates and locations of collectors shows. All the sheets measure 8 1/2" by 11" and most feature artist renderings of players from the teams recreated for the old-timers games. The front carries the individual production number out of the total number produced, but otherwise the sheets are unnumbered.

COMPLETE SET (35) 125.00 250.00
1 Yankee Fan Festival 6.00 15.00
Jan. 31-Feb. 2, 1992/12,500
Pictures regular-issue/1992 Upper Deck cards
Don Mattingly
Mel Hall
Pat Kelly
Matt Nokes
Alvaro Espinoza
Bernie Williams
2 Opening of Oriole Park 12.50 30.00
at Camden Yards
April 6, 1992 (17,000)
Features four artist
renderings of the Park
3 Toronto Blue Jays 2.00 5.00
April 25, 1992/52,000)
SkyDome
Bob Bailor
John Mayberry
Rick Bosetti
Balor Moore
Garth Iorg
4 '72 Upper Deck Heroes 3.00 8.00
vs. Atlanta Braves Heroes
May 1, 1992 (22,000)
Fulton County
Coliseum
Bruce Benedict
Darrell Evans
Glenn Hubbard
Dave Johnson
Reggie Jackson
5 Rangers Heroes vs. 2.50 6.00
White Sox Heroes
May 3, 1992 (22,000)
Comiskey Park
Bill Melton
Dick Allen
Wilbur Wood
Carlos May
Chuck Tanner MG
6 Silver Anniversary of 2.50 6.00
the Impossible Dream
May 16, 1992 (38,000)
Fenway Park
Jim Lonborg
George Scott
Carl Yastrzemski
Tony Conigliaro
Dick Williams MG
7 Nickname Heroes at 2.50 6.00
the 'Stick
May 17, 1992 (37,000)
Candlestick Park
Orlando Cepeda
Jim Davenport
Juan Marichal
Dave Kingman
John Montefusco
8 American League Heroes 3.00 8.00
vs. National League Heroes
May 30, 1992 (17,000)
Astrodome
Tony Oliva
Joe Niekro
Jose Cruz
Mark Fidrych
Jim Wynn
9 Harvey's Wallbangers 2.50 6.00
May 30, 1992 (32,000)
County Stadium
Ben Oglivie
Harvey Kuenn
Cecil Cooper
Gorman Thomas
10 30 Years of Mets 2.00 5.00
Baseball
June 13, 1992 (47,000)
Shea Stadium
Cleon Jones
Bud Harrelson
Rusty Staub
Jerry Koosman
Ed Kranepool
11 Cardinals' 100th 4.00 10.00
Anniversary
June 14, 1992 (22,000)
Busch Stadium
Red Schoendienst
Bob Gibson
Enos Slaughter
Lou Brock
12 N.L. Heroes 2.00 5.00
vs. American
League Heroes
June 20, 1992 (47,000)
Arlington Stadium
former Texas Rangers
Jim Sundberg
Toby Harrah
Jim Kern
Al Oliver
Jim Spencer
13 Record Setters 6.00 15.00
June 21, 1992 (52,000)
Anaheim Stadium
Nolan Ryan
Jim Abbott
Jimmie Reese CO
14 Cubs Heroes vs. 3.00 8.00
Reds Heroes
June 28, 1992 (27,000)
Riverfront Stadium
George Foster
Gary Nolan
Pedro Borbon
Cesar Cedeno
Bernie Carbo
15 The Record-Setting 2.50 6.00
Infield
July 5, 1992 (62,000)
Dodger Stadium
Bill Russell
Davey Lopes
Steve Garvey

Ron Cey
16 46th Annual Old-Timers 2.50 6.00
Day Classic
July 11, 1992 (50,000)
Yankee Stadium
Phil Rizzuto
Bobby Brown
Allie Reynolds
Hank Bauer
Tom Henrich
17 Heroes of Baseball 3.00 8.00
All-Star Game
July 13, 1992 (67,000)
Jack Murphy Stadium
Reggie Jackson
Rollie Fingers
Steve Garvey
Brooks Robinson
Bob Feller
18 All-Star Fanfest 6.00 15.00
July 13, 1992 (12,000)
Jack Murphy Stadium
Larry Doby
Steve Garvey
Rollie Fingers
This card measures 5 1/2-in by 8 1/2-in
19 All-Star Game Heroes 3.00 8.00
July 18, 1992 (27,000)
Three Rivers Stadium
Kent Tekulve
Frank Thomas
Elroy Face
Bob Veale
Chuck Tanner
20 Royals HOF Inductees 2.00 5.00
July 18-19, 1992 (42,000)
Royal Stadium
Fred Patek
Joe Burke GM
Larry Gura
21 More Than 100 Years of 3.00 8.00
Baseball in Montreal
July 26, 1992 (22,000)
Olympic Stadium
Claude Raymond
Duke Snider
Jean-Pierre Roy ANN
Rusty Staub
Steve Rogers
22 Seattle Mariners 2.50 6.00
Heroes of Baseball
July 26, 1992
Kingdome
23 A Tribute to 3.00 8.00
Rocky Colavito
Aug. 1, 1992 (22,000)
Municipal Stadium
24 '70s A's vs./'76 Phillies 3.00 8.00
Aug. 8, 1992 (44,000)
Veterans Stadium
Tug McGraw
Steve Carlton
Greg Luzinski
Larry Bowa
Dick Allen
25 Rollie Fingers 2.50 6.00
Hall of Fame Day
Aug. 9, 1992 (32,000)
County Stadium
26 200 Club 3.00 8.00
Aug. 9, 1992 (50,000)
Camden Yards
Luis Aparicio
J.R. Richard
Brooks Robinson
Milt Pappas
Bill Buckner
27 25th Anniversary of 4.00 10.00
the Oakland Athletics
Aug. 15, 1992 (22,000)
Oakland-Alameda
County Stadium
Jim(Catfish) Hunter
Reggie Jackson
Rollie Fingers
Vida Blue
Bert Campaneris
28 Chicago Cubs 2.00 5.00
August 16, 1982
Ron Santo
Ernie Banks
Randy Hundley
Billy Williams
Don Kessinger
29 Minnesota Twins 3.00 8.00
World Series Heroes
Aug. 23, 1992 (22,000)
Metrodome
Maury Wills
Bob Gibson
Zoilo Versalles
Jim(Mudcat) Grant
Tony Oliva
30 1972 Division Winners 3.00 8.00
Detroit Tigers
Aug. 30, 1992 (32,000)
Bert Campaneris
Aurelio Rodriguez
Sparky Anderson MG
Al Oliver
31 Upper Deck Authenticated 2.00 5.00
Salutes The Legends
Past, Present and Future
Nov. 13-15, 1992 (18,000)
Midwest Sports Collectors Show
List of Tri-Star Sports, Inc. shows
32 50 Year Anniversary of 4.00 10.00
the 1942 Triple Crown
Season by Ted Williams/(Numbered, but without total production number)
Ted Williams
33 Upper Deck Honors 3.00 8.00
Lou Brock
Vida Blue
Rollie Fingers/50,000
34 Upper Deck 2.00 5.00
Heroes of Baseball Shows
Rollie Fingers
Reggie Jackson
Gaylord Perry
Brooks Robinson
Ted Williams/76,400)
35 Upper Deck Heroes of 2.00 5.00
Baseball Shows
Bobby Bonds
Lou Brock
Bob Gibson
Robin Roberts
Billy Williams/76,400

1992 Upper Deck Team MVP Holograms

The 54 hologram cards in this standard size set feature the top offensive player and pitcher from each Major League team plus two checklist cards. Only 216,000 number sets were produced, and each set was packaged in a custom-designed box with protective sleeve and included a numbered certificate. To display the set, Upper Deck also made available a custom album through a mail-in offer for 10.00. Cards 1-2 feature the AL and NL MVPs (with checklists) while cards 3-54 are arranged in alphabetical order.

COMP. FACT SET (54) 6.00 15.00
1 Cal Ripken MVP .60 1.50
AL Checklist
2 Terry Pendleton MVP .02 .10
NL Checklist
3 Jim Abbott .07 .20
4 Roberto Alomar .20 .50
5 Kevin Appier .02 .10
6 Steve Avery .02 .10
7 Jeff Bagwell .30 .75
8 Albert Belle .07 .20
9 Andy Benes .02 .10
10 Wade Boggs .30 .75
11 Barry Bonds .50 1.25
12 George Brett .60 1.50
13 Ivan Calderon .02 .10
14 Jose Canseco .30 .75
15 Will Clark .20 .50
16 Roger Clemens .60 1.50
17 David Cone .10 .30
18 Doug Drabek .02 .10
19 Dennis Eckersley .25 .60
20 Scott Erickson .07 .20
21 Cecil Fielder .07 .20
22 Ken Griffey Jr. .75 2.00
23 Bill Gullickson .02 .10
24 Juan Guzman .02 .10
25 Pete Harnisch .02 .10
26 Howard Johnson .02 .10
27 Randy Johnson .30 .75
28 John Kruk .07 .20
29 Barry Larkin .20 .50
30 Greg Maddux .60 1.50
31 Dennis Martinez .07 .20
32 Ramon Martinez .02 .10
33 Don Mattingly .60 1.50
34 Jack McDowell .02 .10
35 Fred McGriff .10 .30
36 Paul Molitor .25 .60
37 Charles Nagy .02 .10
38 Gregg Olson .07 .20
39 Terry Pendleton .02 .10
40 Luis Polonia .02 .10
41 Kirby Puckett .25 .60
42 Dave Righetti .02 .10
43 Jose Rijo .02 .10
44 Cal Ripken 1.25 3.00
45 Nolan Ryan 1.25 3.00
46 Ryne Sandberg .60 1.50
47 Scott Sanderson .02 .10
48 Ruben Sierra .07 .20
49 Lee Smith .07 .20
50 Ozzie Smith .60 1.50
51 Darryl Strawberry .07 .20
52 Frank Thomas .30 .75
53 Bill Wegman .02 .10
54 Mitch Williams .02 .10

1993 Upper Deck

The 1993 Upper Deck set consists of two series of 420 standard-size cards. Special subsets featured include Star Rookies (1-29), Community Heroes (30-40), and American League Teammates (41-55), Top Prospects (421-449), Inside the Numbers (450-470), Team Stars (471-485), Award Winners (486-499), and Diamond Debuts (500-510). Derek Jeter is the only notable Rookie Card in this set. A special card (SP5) was randomly inserted in first series packs to commemorate the 3,000th hit of George Brett and Robin Yount. A special card (SP6) commemorating Nolan Ryan's last season was randomly inserted into second series packs. Both SP cards were inserted at a rate of one every 72 packs

COMPLETE SET (840) 15.00 40.00
COMP.FACT.SET (840) 20.00 50.00
COMPLETE SERIES 1 (420) 6.00 15.00
COMPLETE SERIES 2 (420) 10.00 25.00
SUBSET CARDS HALF VALUE OF BASE CARDS
SP CARDS STATED ODDS 1:72
1 Tim Salmon CL .07 .20
2 Mike Piazza 1.25 3.00
3 Rene Arocha RC .20 .50
4 Willie Greene .02 .10
5 Manny Alexander .02 .10
6 Dan Wilson .07 .20
7 Dan Smith .02 .10
8 Kevin Rogers .02 .10
9 Nigel Wilson .02 .10
10 Joe Vitko .02 .10
11 Tim Costo .02 .10
12 Alan Embree .02 .10
13 Jim Tatum RC .05 .15
14 Cris Colon .02 .10
15 Steve Hosey .02 .10
16 Sterling Hitchcock RC .20 .50
17 Dave Mlicki .02 .10
18 Jessie Hollins .02 .10
19 Bobby Jones .07 .20
20 Kurt Miller .02 .10
21 Melvin Nieves .02 .10
22 Billy Ashley .02 .10
23 J.T.Snow RC .30 .75
24 Chipper Jones .20 .50
25 Tim Salmon .10 .30
26 Tim Pugh RC .05 .15
27 David Nied .02 .10
28 Mike Trombley .02 .10
29 Javier Lopez .10 .30
30 Jim Abbott CH CL .07 .20
31 Jim Abbott CH .02 .10
32 Dale Murphy CH .10 .30
33 Tony Pena CH .02 .10
34 Kirby Puckett CH .10 .30
35 Harold Reynolds CH .02 .10
36 Cal Ripken CH .30 .75
37 Nolan Ryan CH .40 1.00
38 Ryne Sandberg CH .20 .50
39 Dave Stewart CH .02 .10
40 Dave Winfield CH .02 .10
41 M.McGwire .20 .50
J.Carter CL
42 R.Alomar .07 .20
J.Carter
43 Molitor .20 .50
Listach
Yount
44 C.Ripken .20 .50
B.Anderson
45 Belle .07 .20
Baerga
Thome
Lofton
46 C.Fielder .02 .10
M.Tettleton
47 R.Kelly .25 .60
D.Mattingly
48 R.Clemens .20 .50
F.Viola
49 R.Sierra .20 .50
M.McGwire
50 K.Puckett .10 .30
K.Hrbek
51 F.Thomas .10 .30
R.Ventura
52 Cans .10 .30
IRod
Gonz
Palmeiro
53 Lethal Lefties .07 .20
Mark Langston
Jim Abbott
Chuck F
54 Joyner .20 .50
Jefferies
Brett
55 K.Griffey .25 .60
Buhner
Mitchell
56 George Brett .50 1.25
57 Scott Cooper .02 .10
58 Mike Maddux .02 .10
59 Rusty Meacham .02 .10
60 Wil Cordero .02 .10
61 Tim Teufel .02 .10
62 Jeff Montgomery .02 .10
63 Scott Livingstone .02 .10
64 Doug Dascenzo .02 .10
65 Bret Boone .07 .20
66 Tim Wakefield .20 .50
67 Curt Schilling .07 .20
68 Frank Tanana .02 .10
69 Len Dykstra .07 .20
70 Derek Lilliquist .02 .10
71 Anthony Young .02 .10
72 Hipolito Pichardo .02 .10
73 Rod Beck .02 .10
74 Kent Hrbek .07 .20
75 Tom Glavine .10 .30
76 Kevin Brown .07 .20
77 Chuck Finley .07 .20
78 Bob Walk .02 .10
79 Rheal Cormier UER .02 .10
80 Rick Sutcliffe .07 .20
81 Harold Baines .07 .20
82 Lee Smith .07 .20
83 Geno Petralli .02 .10
84 Jose Oquendo .02 .10
85 Mark Gubicza .02 .10
86 Mickey Tettleton .02 .10
87 Bobby Witt .02 .10
88 Mark Lewis .02 .10
89 Kevin Appier .07 .20
90 Mike Stanton .02 .10
91 Rafael Belliard .02 .10
92 Kenny Rogers .07 .20
93 Randy Velarde .02 .10
94 Luis Sojo .02 .10
95 Mark Leiter .02 .10
96 Jody Reed .02 .10
97 Pete Harnisch .02 .10
98 Tom Candiotti .02 .10
99 Mark Portugal .02 .10
100 Dave Valle .02 .10
101 Shawon Dunston .02 .10
102 B.J. Surhoff .07 .20
103 Jay Bell .07 .20
104 Sid Bream .02 .10
105 Frank Thomas CL .10 .30
106 Mike Morgan .02 .10
107 Bill Doran .02 .10
108 Lance Blankenship .02 .10
109 Mark Lemke .02 .10
110 Brian Harper .02 .10
111 Brady Anderson .07 .20
112 Bip Roberts .02 .10
113 Mitch Williams .02 .10
114 Craig Biggio .10 .30
115 Eddie Murray .20 .50
116 Matt Nokes .02 .10
117 Lance Parrish .07 .20
118 Bill Swift .02 .10
119 Jeff Innis .02 .10
120 Mike LaValliere .02 .10
121 Hal Morris .02 .10
122 Walt Weiss .02 .10
123 Ivan Rodriguez .10 .30
124 Andy Van Slyke .10 .30
125 Roberto Alomar .10 .30
126 Robby Thompson .02 .10
127 Sammy Sosa .20 .50
128 Mark Langston .02 .10
129 Jerry Browne .02 .10
130 Chuck McElroy .02 .10
131 Frank Viola .07 .20
132 Leo Gomez .02 .10
133 Ramon Martinez .02 .10
134 Don Mattingly .50 1.25
135 Roger Clemens .40 1.00
136 Rickey Henderson .20 .50
137 Darren Daulton .07 .20
138 Ken Hill .02 .10
139 Ozzie Guillen .07 .20
140 Jerald Clark .02 .10
141 Dave Fleming .02 .10
142 Delino DeShields .02 .10
143 Matt Williams .07 .20
144 Larry Walker .07 .20
145 Ruben Sierra .07 .20
146 Ozzie Smith .30 .75
147 Chris Sabo .02 .10
148 Carlos Hernandez .02 .10
149 Pat Borders .02 .10
150 Orlando Merced .02 .10
151 Royce Clayton .02 .10
152 Kurt Stillwell .02 .10
153 Dave Hollins .02 .10
154 Mike Greenwell .02 .10
155 Nolan Ryan .75 2.00
156 Felix Jose .02 .10
157 Junior Felix .02 .10
158 Derek Bell .02 .10
159 Steve Buechele .02 .10
160 John Burkett .02 .10
161 Pat Howell .02 .10
162 Milt Cuyler .02 .10
163 Terry Pendleton .07 .20
164 Jack Morris .07 .20
165 Tony Gwynn .25 .60
166 Deion Sanders .10 .30
167 Mike Devereaux .02 .10
168 Ron Darling .02 .10
169 Orel Hershiser .07 .20
170 Mike Jackson .02 .10
171 Doug Jones .02 .10
172 Dan Walters .02 .10
173 Darren Lewis .02 .10
174 Carlos Baerga .02 .10
175 Ryne Sandberg .30 .75
176 Gregg Jefferies .02 .10
177 John Jaha .02 .10
178 Luis Polonia .02 .10
179 Kirt Manwaring .02 .10
180 Mike Magnante .02 .10
181 Billy Ripken .02 .10
182 Mike Moore .02 .10
183 Eric Anthony .02 .10
184 Lenny Harris .02 .10
185 Tony Pena .02 .10
186 Mike Felder .02 .10
187 Greg Olson .02 .10
188 Rene Gonzales .02 .10
189 Mike Bordick .02 .10
190 Mel Rojas .02 .10
191 Todd Frohwirth .02 .10
192 Darryl Hamilton .02 .10
193 Mike Fetters .02 .10
194 Omar Olivares .02 .10
195 Tony Phillips .02 .10
196 Paul Sorrento .02 .10
197 Trevor Wilson .02 .10
198 Kevin Gross .02 .10
199 Ron Karkovice .02 .10
200 Brook Jacoby .02 .10
201 Mariano Duncan .02 .10
202 Dennis Cook .02 .10
203 Daryl Boston .02 .10
204 Mike Perez .02 .10
205 Manuel Lee .02 .10
206 Steve Olin .02 .10
207 Charlie Hough .07 .20
208 Scott Scudder .02 .10
209 Charlie O'Brien .02 .10
210 Barry Bonds CL .30 .75
211 Jose Vizcaino .02 .10
212 Scott Leius .02 .10
213 Kevin Mitchell .02 .10
214 Brian Barnes .02 .10
215 Pat Kelly .02 .10
216 Chris Hammond .02 .10
217 Rob Deer .02 .10
218 Cory Snyder .02 .10
219 Gary Carter .07 .20
220 Danny Darwin .02 .10
221 Tom Gordon .02 .10
222 Gary Sheffield 2X .07 .20
223 Joe Carter .07 .20
224 Jay Buhner .07 .20
225 Jose Offerman .02 .10
226 Jose Rijo .02 .10
227 Mark Whiten .02 .10
228 Randy Milligan .02 .10
229 Bud Black .02 .10
230 Gary DiSarcina .02 .10
231 Steve Finley .07 .20
232 Dennis Martinez .07 .20
233 Mike Mussina .10 .30
234 Joe Oliver .02 .10
235 Chad Curtis .02 .10
236 Shane Mack .02 .10
237 Jaime Navarro .02 .10
238 Brian McRae .02 .10
239 Chili Davis .07 .20
240 Jeff King .02 .10
241 Dean Palmer .07 .20
242 Danny Tartabull .02 .10
243 Charles Nagy .02 .10
244 Ray Lankford .07 .20
245 Barry Larkin .10 .30
246 Steve Avery .02 .10
247 John Kruk .07 .20
248 Derrick May .02 .10
249 Stan Javier .02 .10
250 Roger McDowell .02 .10
251 Dan Gladden .02 .10
252 Wally Joyner .07 .20
253 Pat Listach .02 .10
254 Chuck Knoblauch .07 .20
255 Sandy Alomar Jr. .02 .10
256 Jeff Bagwell .10 .30
257 Andy Stankiewicz .02 .10
258 Darrin Jackson .02 .10
259 Brett Butler .07 .20
260 Joe Orsulak .02 .10
261 Andy Benes .02 .10
262 Kenny Lofton .07 .20
263 Robin Ventura .07 .20
264 Ron Gant .07 .20
265 Ellis Burks .07 .20
266 Juan Guzman .02 .10
267 Wes Chamberlain .02 .10
268 John Smiley .02 .10
269 Franklin Stubbs .02 .10
270 Tom Browning .02 .10
271 Dennis Eckersley .07 .20
272 Carlton Fisk .10 .30
273 Lou Whitaker .07 .20
274 Phil Plantier .02 .10
275 Bobby Bonilla .07 .20
276 Ben McDonald .02 .10
277 Bob Zupcic .02 .10
278 Terry Steinbach .02 .10
279 Terry Mulholland .02 .10
280 Lance Johnson .02 .10
281 Willie McGee .07 .20
282 Bret Saberhagen .07 .20
283 Randy Myers .02 .10
284 Randy Tomlin .02 .10
285 Mickey Morandini .02 .10
286 Brian Williams .02 .10
287 Tino Martinez .10 .30
288 Jose Melendez .02 .10
289 Jeff Huson .02 .10
290 Joe Grahe .02 .10
291 Mel Hall .02 .10
292 Otis Nixon .02 .10
293 Todd Hundley .02 .10
294 Casey Candaele .02 .10
295 Kevin Seitzer .02 .10
296 Eddie Taubensee .02 .10
297 Moises Alou .07 .20
298 Scott Radinsky .02 .10
299 Thomas Howard .02 .10
300 Kyle Abbott .02 .10
301 Omar Vizquel .10 .30
302 Keith Miller .02 .10
303 Rick Aguilera .02 .10
304 Bruce Hurst .02 .10
305 Ken Caminiti .07 .20
306 Mike Pagliarulo .02 .10
307 Frank Seminara .02 .10
308 Andre Dawson .07 .20
309 Jose Lind .02 .10
310 Joe Boever .02 .10
311 Jeff Parrett .02 .10
312 Alan Mills .02 .10
313 Kevin Tapani .02 .10
314 Darryl Kile .07 .20
315 Checklist 211-315 .07 .20
Will Clark
316 Mike Sharperson .02 .10
317 John Orton .02 .10
318 Bob Tewksbury .02 .10
319 Xavier Hernandez .02 .10
320 Paul Assenmacher .02 .10
321 John Franco .07 .20
322 Mike Timlin .02 .10
323 Jose Guzman .02 .10
324 Pedro Martinez .40 1.00
325 Bill Spiers .02 .10
326 Melido Perez .02 .10
327 Mike Macfarlane .02 .10
328 Ricky Bones .02 .10
329 Scott Bankhead .02 .10
330 Rich Rodriguez .02 .10
331 Geronimo Pena .02 .10
332 Bernie Williams .10 .30
333 Paul Molitor .07 .20
334 Carlos Garcia .02 .10
335 David Cone .07 .20
336 Randy Johnson .20 .50
337 Pat Mahomes .02 .10
338 Erik Hanson .02 .10
339 Duane Ward .02 .10
340 Al Martin .02 .10
341 Pedro Munoz .02 .10
342 Greg Colbrunn .02 .10
343 Julio Valera .02 .10
344 John Olerud .07 .20
345 George Bell .02 .10
346 Devon White .07 .20
347 Donovan Osborne .02 .10
348 Mark Gardner .02 .10
349 Zane Smith .02 .10
350 Wilson Alvarez .02 .10
351 Kevin Koslofski .02 .10
352 Roberto Hernandez .02 .10
353 Glenn Davis .02 .10
354 Reggie Sanders .07 .20
355 Ken Griffey Jr. .40 1.00
356 Marquis Grissom .07 .20
357 Jack McDowell .02 .10
358 Jimmy Key .07 .20
359 Stan Belinda .02 .10
360 Gerald Williams .02 .10
361 Sid Fernandez .02 .10
362 Alex Fernandez .02 .10
363 John Smoltz .10 .30
364 Travis Fryman .07 .20
365 Jose Canseco .10 .30
366 David Justice .07 .20
367 Pedro Astacio .02 .10
368 Tim Belcher .02 .10
369 Steve Sax .02 .10
370 Gary Gaetti .07 .20
371 Jeff Frye .02 .10
372 Bob Wickman .02 .10
373 Ryan Thompson .02 .10
374 David Hulse RC .05 .15
375 Cal Eldred .02 .10
376 Ryan Klesko .07 .20
377 Damion Easley .02 .10
378 John Kiely .02 .10
379 Jim Bullinger .02 .10
380 Brian Bohanon .02 .10
381 Rod Brewer .02 .10
382 Fernando Ramsey RC .05 .15
383 Sam Militello .02 .10
384 Arthur Rhodes .02 .10
385 Eric Karros .07 .20
386 Rico Brogna .02 .10
387 John Valentin .02 .10
388 Kerry Woodson .02 .10
389 Ben Rivera .02 .10
390 Matt Whiteside RC .05 .15
391 Henry Rodriguez .02 .10
392 John Wetteland .07 .20
393 Kent Mercker .02 .10
394 Bernard Gilkey .02 .10
395 Doug Henry .02 .10
396 Mo Vaughn .07 .20
397 Scott Erickson .02 .10
398 Bill Gullickson .02 .10
399 Mark Guthrie .02 .10
400 Dave Martinez .02 .10
401 Jeff Kent .20 .50
402 Chris Hoiles .02 .10
403 Mike Henneman .02 .10
404 Chris Nabholz .02 .10
405 Tom Pagnozzi .02 .10
406 Kelly Gruber .02 .10
407 Bob Welch .02 .10
408 Frank Castillo .02 .10
409 John Dopson .02 .10
410 Steve Farr .02 .10
411 Henry Cotto .02 .10
412 Bob Patterson .02 .10
413 Todd Stottlemyre .02 .10
414 Greg A. Harris .02 .10
415 Denny Neagle .07 .20
416 Bill Wegman .02 .10
417 Willie Wilson .02 .10
418 Terry Leach .02 .10
419 Willie Randolph .07 .20
420 Checklist 316-420 McGwire .10 .30
421 Calvin Murray CL .02 .10
422 Pete Janicki RC .05 .15
423 Todd Jones TP .07 .20
424 Mike Neill .02 .10
425 Carlos Delgado .20 .50
426 Jose Oliva .02 .10
427 Tyrone Hill .02 .10
428 Dmitri Young .07 .20
429 Derek Wallace RC .05 .15
430 Michael Moore RC .05 .15
431 Cliff Floyd .07 .20
432 Calvin Murray .02 .10
433 Manny Ramirez .30 .75
434 Marc Newfield .02 .10
435 Charles Johnson .07 .20
436 Butch Huskey .02 .10
437 Brad Pennington TP .02 .10
438 Ray McDavid RC .05 .15
439 Chad McConnell .02 .10
440 Midre Cummings RC .05 .15
441 Benji Gil .02 .10
442 Frankie Rodriguez .02 .10
443 Chad Mottola RC .05 .15
444 John Burke RC .05 .15
445 Michael Tucker .02 .10
446 Rick Greene .02 .10
447 Rich Becker .02 .10
448 Mike Robertson TP .02 .10
449 Derek Jeter RC ! 6.00 15.00
450 I.Rodriguez .10 .30
D.McCarty CL
451 Jim Abbott IN .07 .20
452 Jeff Bagwell IN .07 .20
453 Jason Bere IN .02 .10
454 Delino DeShields IN .02 .10
455 Travis Fryman IN .02 .10
456 Alex Gonzalez IN .02 .10
457 Phil Hiatt IN .02 .10
458 Dave Hollins IN .02 .10
459 Chipper Jones IN .10 .30
460 David Justice IN .02 .10
461 Ray Lankford IN .02 .10
462 David McCarty IN .02 .10
463 Mike Mussina IN .07 .20
464 Jose Offerman IN .02 .10
465 Dean Palmer IN .02 .10
466 Geronimo Pena IN .02 .10
467 Eduardo Perez IN .02 .10
468 Ivan Rodriguez IN .07 .20
469 Reggie Sanders IN .02 .10
470 Bernie Williams IN .07 .20
471 Bonds .30 .75
Williams
Clark CL
472 Madd .20 .50
Avery
Smolt
Glav
473 Red October .07 .20
Jose Rijo
Rob Dibble
Roberto Kelly#
474 Sheff .07 .20
Plant
Gwynn
McGrif
475 Biggio .07 .20
Drabek
Bagwell
476 Clark .30 .75
Bonds
Williams
477 Eric Davis .07 .20
Darryl Strawberry
478 Bich .07 .20
Nied
Galarraga
479 Maga .02 .10
Destr
Barbe
Conine
480 Wakefield .07 .20
Van Slyke
Bell
481 Griss .10 .30
DeSh
Mart

Walker
482 O.Smith .20 .50
Redbirds
483 Myers .20 .50
Sandberg
Grace
484 Big Apple Power Switch .10 .30
485 Kruk .02 .10
Holl
Dault
Dyks
486 Barry Bonds AW .30 .75
487 Dennis Eckersley AW .07 .20
488 Greg Maddux AW .20 .50
489 Dennis Eckersley AW .07 .20
490 Eric Karros AW .02 .10
491 Pat Listach AW .02 .10
492 Gary Sheffield AW .02 .10
493 Mark McGwire AW .25 .60
494 Gary Sheffield AW .02 .10
495 Edgar Martinez AW .07 .20
496 Fred McGriff AW .07 .20
497 Juan Gonzalez AW .02 .10
498 Darren Daulton AW .02 .10
499 Cecil Fielder AW .02 .10
500 Brent Gates CL .02 .10
501 Tavo Alvarez .02 .10
502 Rod Bolton .02 .10
503 John Cummings RC .05 .15
504 Brent Gates .02 .10
505 Tyler Green .02 .10
506 Jose Martinez RC .05 .15
507 Troy Percival .10 .30
508 Kevin Stocker .02 .10
509 Matt Walbeck RC .05 .15
510 Rondell White .07 .20
511 Billy Ripken .02 .10
512 Mike Moore .02 .10
513 Jose Lind .02 .10
514 Chito Martinez .02 .10
515 Jose Guzman .02 .10
516 Kim Batiste .02 .10
517 Jeff Tackett .02 .10
518 Charlie Hough .07 .20
519 Marvin Freeman .02 .10
520 Carlos Martinez .02 .10
521 Eric Young .02 .10
522 Pete Incaviglia .02 .10
523 Scott Fletcher .02 .10
524 Orestes Destrade .02 .10
525 Ken Griffey Jr. CL .25 .60
526 Ellis Burks .07 .20
527 Juan Samuel .02 .10
528 Dave Magadan .02 .10
529 Jeff Parrett .02 .10
530 Bill Krueger .02 .10
531 Frank Bolick .02 .10
532 Alan Trammell .07 .20
533 Walt Weiss .02 .10
534 David Cone .07 .20
535 Greg Maddux .30 .75
536 Kevin Young .07 .20
537 Dave Hansen .02 .10
538 Alex Cole .02 .10
539 Greg Hibbard .02 .10
540 Gene Larkin .02 .10
541 Jeff Reardon .07 .20
542 Felix Jose .02 .10
543 Jimmy Key .07 .20
544 Reggie Jefferson .02 .10
545 Gregg Jefferies .02 .10
546 Dave Stewart .07 .20
547 Tim Wallach .02 .10
548 Spike Owen .02 .10
549 Tommy Greene .02 .10
550 Fernando Valenzuela .07 .20
551 Rich Amaral .02 .10
552 Bret Barberie .02 .10
553 Edgar Martinez .10 .30
554 Jim Abbott .10 .30
555 Frank Thomas .20 .50
556 Wade Boggs .10 .30
557 Tom Henke .02 .10
558 Milt Thompson .02 .10
559 Lloyd McClendon .02 .10
560 Vinny Castilla .20 .50
561 Ricky Jordan .02 .10
562 Andujar Cedeno .02 .10
563 Greg Vaughn .02 .10
564 Cecil Fielder .07 .20
565 Kirby Puckett .20 .50
566 Mark McGwire .50 1.25
567 Barry Bonds .60 1.50
568 Jody Reed .02 .10
569 Todd Zeile .02 .10
570 Mark Carreon .02 .10
571 Joe Girardi .02 .10
572 Luis Gonzalez .07 .20
573 Mark Grace .10 .30
574 Rafael Palmeiro .10 .30
575 Darryl Strawberry .07 .20
576 Will Clark .10 .30
577 Fred McGriff .10 .30
578 Kevin Reimer .02 .10
579 Dave Righetti .07 .20
580 Juan Bell .02 .10
581 Jeff Brantley .02 .10
582 Brian Hunter .02 .10
583 Tim Naehring .02 .10
584 Glenallen Hill .02 .10
585 Cal Ripken .60 1.50
586 Albert Belle .07 .20
587 Robin Yount .30 .75
588 Chris Bosio .02 .10
589 Pete Smith .02 .10
590 Chuck Carr .02 .10
591 Jeff Blauser .02 .10
592 Kevin McReynolds .02 .10
593 Andres Galarraga .07 .20
594 Kevin Maas .02 .10
595 Eric Davis .07 .20
596 Brian Jordan .07 .20
597 Tim Raines .07 .20
598 Rick Wilkins .02 .10
599 Steve Cooke .02 .10
600 Mike Gallego .02 .10
601 Mike Munoz .02 .10
602 Luis Rivera .02 .10
603 Junior Ortiz .02 .10
604 Brent Mayne .02 .10
605 Luis Alicea .02 .10
606 Damon Berryhill .02 .10
607 Dave Henderson .02 .10
608 Kirk McCaskill .02 .10
609 Jeff Fassero .02 .10
610 Mike Harkey .02 .10
611 Francisco Cabrera .02 .10
612 Rey Sanchez .02 .10
613 Scott Servais .02 .10
614 Darrin Fletcher .02 .10
615 Felix Fermin .02 .10
616 Kevin Seitzer .02 .10
617 Bob Scanlan .02 .10
618 Billy Hatcher .02 .10
619 John Vander Wal .02 .10
620 Joe Hesketh .02 .10
621 Hector Villanueva .02 .10
622 Randy Milligan .02 .10
623 Tony Tarasco RC .05 .15
624 Russ Swan .02 .10
625 Willie Wilson .02 .10
626 Frank Tanana .02 .10
627 Pete O'Brien .02 .10
628 Lenny Webster .02 .10
629 Mark Clark .02 .10
630 Roger Clemens CL .20 .50
631 Alex Arias .02 .10
632 Chris Gwynn .02 .10
633 Tom Bolton .02 .10
634 Greg Briley .02 .10
635 Kent Bottenfield .02 .10
636 Kelly Downs .02 .10
637 Manuel Lee .02 .10
638 Al Leiter .07 .20
639 Jeff Gardner .02 .10
640 Mike Gardiner .02 .10
641 Mark Gardner .02 .10
642 Jeff Branson .02 .10
643 Paul Wagner .02 .10
644 Sean Berry .02 .10
645 Phil Hiatt .02 .10
646 Kevin Mitchell .02 .10
647 Charlie Hayes .02 .10
648 Jim Deshaies .02 .10
649 Dan Pasqua .02 .10
650 Mike Maddux .02 .10
651 Domingo Martinez RC .05 .15
652 Greg McMichael RC .05 .15
653 Eric Wedge RC .20 .50
654 Mark Whiten .02 .10
655 Roberto Kelly .02 .10
656 Julio Franco .07 .20
657 Gene Harris .02 .10
658 Pete Schourek .02 .10
659 Mike Bielecki .02 .10
660 Ricky Gutierrez .02 .10
661 Chris Hammond .02 .10
662 Tim Scott .02 .10
663 Norm Charlton .02 .10
664 Doug Drabek .02 .10
665 Dwight Gooden .07 .20
666 Jim Gott .02 .10
667 Randy Myers .02 .10
668 Darren Holmes .02 .10
669 Tim Spehr .02 .10
670 Bruce Ruffin .02 .10
671 Bobby Thigpen .02 .10
672 Tony Fernandez .02 .10
673 Darrin Jackson .02 .10
674 Gregg Olson .02 .10
675 Rob Dibble .07 .20
676 Howard Johnson .02 .10
677 Mike Lansing RC .20 .50
678 Charlie Leibrandt .02 .10
679 Kevin Bass .02 .10
680 Hubie Brooks .02 .10
681 Scott Brosius .07 .20
682 Randy Knorr .02 .10
683 Dante Bichette .07 .20
684 Bryan Harvey .02 .10
685 Greg Gohr .02 .10
686 Willie Banks .02 .10
687 Robb Nen .07 .20
688 Mike Scioscia .02 .10
689 John Farrell .02 .10
690 John Candelaria .02 .10
691 Damon Buford .02 .10
692 Todd Worrell .02 .10
693 Pat Hentgen .02 .10
694 John Smiley .02 .10
695 Greg Swindell .02 .10
696 Derek Bell .02 .10
697 Terry Jorgensen .02 .10
698 Jimmy Jones .02 .10
699 David Wells .07 .20
700 Dave Martinez .02 .10
701 Steve Bedrosian .02 .10
702 Jeff Russell .02 .10
703 Joe Magrane .02 .10
704 Matt Mieske .02 .10
705 Paul Molitor .07 .20
706 Dale Murphy .10 .30
707 Steve Howe .02 .10
708 Greg Gagne .02 .10
709 Dave Eiland .02 .10
710 David West .02 .10
711 Luis Aquino .02 .10
712 Joe Orsulak .02 .10
713 Eric Plunk .02 .10
714 Mike Felder .02 .10
715 Joe Klink .02 .10
716 Lonnie Smith .02 .10
717 Monty Fariss .02 .10
718 Craig Lefferts .02 .10
719 John Habyan .02 .10
720 Willie Blair .02 .10
721 Darnell Coles .02 .10
722 Mark Williamson .02 .10
723 Bryn Smith .02 .10
724 Greg W. Harris .02 .10
725 Graeme Lloyd RC .20 .50
726 Cris Carpenter .02 .10
727 Chico Walker .02 .10
728 Tracy Woodson .02 .10
729 Jose Uribe .02 .10
730 Stan Javier .02 .10
731 Jay Howell .02 .10
732 Freddie Benavides .02 .10
733 Jeff Reboulet .02 .10
734 Scott Sanderson .02 .10
735 Ryne Sandberg CL .20 .50
736 Archi Cianfrocco .02 .10
737 Daryl Boston .02 .10
738 Craig Grebeck .02 .10
739 Doug Dascenzo .02 .10
740 Gerald Young .02 .10
741 Candy Maldonado .02 .10
742 Joey Cora .02 .10
743 Don Slaught .02 .10
744 Steve Decker .02 .10
745 Blas Minor .02 .10
746 Storm Davis .02 .10
747 Carlos Quintana .02 .10
748 Vince Coleman .02 .10
749 Todd Burns .02 .10
750 Steve Frey .02 .10
751 Ivan Calderon .02 .10
752 Steve Reed RC .05 .15
753 Danny Jackson .02 .10
754 Jeff Conine .07 .20
755 Juan Gonzalez .07 .20
756 Mike Kelly .02 .10
757 John Doherty .02 .10
758 Jack Armstrong .02 .10
759 John Wehner .02 .10
760 Scott Bankhead .02 .10
761 Jim Tatum .02 .10
762 Scott Pose RC .05 .15
763 Andy Ashby .02 .10
764 Ed Sprague .02 .10
765 Harold Baines .07 .20
766 Kirk Gibson .07 .20
767 Troy Neel .02 .10
768 Dick Schofield .02 .10
769 Dickie Thon .02 .10
770 Butch Henry .02 .10
771 Junior Felix .02 .10
772 Ken Ryan RC .05 .15
773 Trevor Hoffman .20 .50
774 Phil Plantier .02 .10
775 Bo Jackson .20 .50
776 Benito Santiago .07 .20
777 Andre Dawson .07 .20
778 Bryan Hickerson .02 .10
779 Dennis Moeller .02 .10
780 Ryan Bowen .02 .10
781 Eric Fox .02 .10
782 Joe Kmak .02 .10
783 Mike Hampton .07 .20
784 Darrell Sherman RC .05 .15
785 J.T.Snow .10 .30
786 Dave Winfield .07 .20
787 Jim Austin .02 .10
788 Craig Shipley .02 .10
789 Greg Myers .02 .10
790 Todd Benzinger .02 .10
791 Cory Snyder .02 .10
792 David Segui .02 .10
793 Armando Reynoso .02 .10
794 Chili Davis .07 .20
795 Dave Nilsson .02 .10
796 Paul O'Neill .10 .30
797 Jerald Clark .02 .10
798 Jose Mesa .02 .10
799 Brain Holman .02 .10
800 Jim Eisenreich .02 .10
801 Mark McLemore .02 .10
802 Luis Sojo .02 .10
803 Harold Reynolds .07 .20
804 Dan Plesac .02 .10
805 Dave Stieb .02 .10
806 Tom Brunansky .02 .10
807 Kelly Gruber .02 .10
808 Bob Ojeda .02 .10
809 Dave Burba .02 .10
810 Joe Boever .02 .10
811 Jeremy Hernandez .02 .10
812 Tim Salmon TC .07 .20
813 Jeff Bagwell TC .07 .20
814 Dennis Eckersley TC .07 .20
815 Roberto Alomar TC .07 .20
816 Steve Avery TC .02 .10
817 Pat Listach TC .02 .10
818 Gregg Jefferies TC .02 .10
819 Sammy Sosa TC .20 .50
820 Darryl Strawberry TC .02 .10
821 Dennis Martinez TC .02 .10
822 Robby Thompson TC .02 .10
823 Albert Belle TC .07 .20
824 Randy Johnson TC .10 .30
825 Nigel Wilson TC .02 .10
826 Bobby Bonilla TC .02 .10
827 Glenn Davis TC .02 .10
828 Gary Sheffield TC .02 .10
829 Darren Daulton TC .02 .10
830 Jay Bell TC .02 .10
831 Juan Gonzalez TC .02 .10
832 Andre Dawson TC .02 .10
833 Hal Morris TC .02 .10
834 David Nied TC .02 .10
835 Felix Jose TC .02 .10
836 Travis Fryman TC .02 .10
837 Shane Mack TC .02 .10
838 Robin Ventura TC .02 .10
839 Danny Tartabull TC .02 .10
840 Roberto Alomar CL .07 .20
SP5 G.Brett .40 1.00
R.Yount
SP6 Nolan Ryan .75 2.00

1993 Upper Deck Gold Hologram

COMP.FACT.SET (840) 40.00 100.00
*STARS: 3X TO 8X BASIC CARDS
*ROOKIES: 3X TO 8X BASIC CARDS
ONE GOLD SET PER 15 CT FACT.SET CASE
ALL GOLD SETS MUST BE OPENED TO VERIFY
HOLOGRAM ON BACK IS GOLD
DISTRIBUTED ONLY IN FACT.SET FORM
449 Derek Jeter ! 60.00 150.00

1993 Upper Deck Clutch Performers

These 20 standard-size cards were inserted one every nine series II retail foil packs, as well as inserted one per series II retail jumbo packs. The cards are numbered on the back with an "R" prefix and appear in alphabetical order. These 20 cards represent Reggie Jackson's selection of players who have come through under pressure. Please note these cards are condition sensitive and trade for premium values if found in Mint.

COMPLETE SET (20) 8.00 20.00
SER.2 STAT.ODDS 1:9 RET, 1:1 RED JUMBO
CONDITION SENSITIVE SET
R1 Roberto Alomar .30 .75
R2 Wade Boggs .30 .75
R3 Barry Bonds 1.50 4.00
R4 Jose Canseco .30 .75
R5 Joe Carter .20 .50
R6 Will Clark .30 .75
R7 Roger Clemens 1.00 2.50
R8 Dennis Eckersley .20 .50
R9 Cecil Fielder .20 .50
R10 Juan Gonzalez .20 .50
R11 Ken Griffey Jr. 1.00 2.50
R12 Rickey Henderson .50 1.25
R13 Barry Larkin .30 .75
R14 Don Mattingly 1.25 3.00
R15 Fred McGriff .30 .75
R16 Terry Pendleton .20 .50
R17 Kirby Puckett .50 1.25
R18 Ryne Sandberg .75 2.00
R19 John Smoltz .30 .75
R20 Frank Thomas .50 1.25

1993 Upper Deck Fifth Anniversary

This 15-card standard-size set celebrates Upper Deck's five years in the sports card business.The cards are essentially reprinted versions of some of Upper Deck's most popular cards in the last five years. These cards were inserted one every nine second series hobby packs. The black-bordered fronts feature player photos that previously appeared on an Upper Deck card. The cards are numbered on the back with an "A" prefix. These cards are condition sensitive and trade for premium values in Mint.

COMPLETE SET (15) 6.00 15.00
SER.2 STATED ODDS 1:9 HOBBY
JUMBOS DISTRIBUTED IN RETAIL PACKS
CONDITION SENSITIVE SET
A1 Ken Griffey Jr. 1.00 2.50
A2 Gary Sheffield .20 .50
A3 Roberto Alomar .30 .75
A4 Jim Abbott .30 .75
A5 Nolan Ryan 2.00 5.00
A6 Juan Gonzalez .20 .50
A7 David Justice .20 .50
A8 Carlos Baerga .08 .25
A9 Reggie Jackson .30 .75
A10 Eric Karros .20 .50
A11 Chipper Jones .50 1.25
A12 Ivan Rodriguez .30 .75
A13 Pat Listach .08 .25
A14 Frank Thomas .50 1.25
A15 Tim Salmon .30 .75

1993 Upper Deck Future Heroes

Inserted in second series foil packs at a rate of one every nine pack; this set continues the Heroes insert set begun in the 1990 Upper Deck high-number set, this ten-card standard-size set features eight different "Future Heroes" along with a checklist and header card.

COMPLETE SET (10) 5.00 12.00
SER.2 STATED ODDS 1:9
55 Roberto Alomar .30 .75
56 Barry Bonds 1.50 4.00
57 Roger Clemens 1.00 2.50
58 Juan Gonzalez .20 .50
59 Ken Griffey Jr. 1.00 2.50
60 Mark McGwire 1.25 3.00
61 Kirby Puckett .50 1.25
62 Frank Thomas .50 1.25
63 Art Card .20 .50
NNO Header Card SP .08 .25

1993 Upper Deck Home Run Heroes

This 28-card standard-size set features the home run leader from each Major League team. Each 1993 first series 27-card jumbo pack contained one of these cards. The cards are numbered on the back with an "HR" prefix and the set is arranged in descending order according to the number of home runs.

COMPLETE SET (28) 6.00 15.00
ONE PER SER.1 JUMBO PACK
HR1 Juan Gonzalez .20 .50
HR2 Mark McGwire 1.25 3.00
HR3 Cecil Fielder .20 .50
HR4 Fred McGriff .30 .75
HR5 Albert Belle .20 .50
HR6 Barry Bonds 1.50 4.00
HR7 Joe Carter .20 .50
HR8 Darren Daulton .20 .50
HR9 Ken Griffey Jr. 1.00 2.50
HR10 Dave Hollins .08 .25
HR11 Ryne Sandberg .75 2.00
HR12 George Bell .08 .25
HR13 Danny Tartabull .08 .25
HR14 Mike Devereaux .08 .25
HR15 Greg Vaughn .08 .25
HR16 Larry Walker .20 .50
HR17 David Justice .20 .50
HR18 Terry Pendleton .20 .50
HR19 Eric Karros .20 .50
HR20 Ray Lankford .20 .50
HR21 Matt Williams .20 .50
HR22 Eric Anthony .08 .25
HR23 Bobby Bonilla .20 .50
HR24 Kirby Puckett .50 1.25
HR25 Mike Macfarlane .08 .25
HR26 Tom Brunansky .08 .25
HR27 Paul O'Neill .30 .75
HR28 Gary Gaetti .20 .50

1993 Upper Deck Iooss Collection

This 27-card standard-size set spotlights the work of famous sports photographer Walter Iooss Jr. by presenting 26 of the game's current greats in a candid photo set. The cards were inserted in series I retail foil packs at a rate of one every nine packs. They were also in retail jumbo packs at a rate of one in five packs. The cards are numbered on the back with a "WI" prefix. Please note these cards are condition sensitive and trade for premium values in Mint.

COMPLETE SET (27) 12.50 30.00
SER.1 STATED ODDS 1:9 RET, 1:5 JUM
CONDITION SENSITIVE SET
*JUMBO CARDS: 2X TO 5X BASIC IOOSS
JUMBOS DISTRIBUTED IN RETAIL PACKS
WI1 Tim Salmon .40 1.00
WI2 Jeff Bagwell .40 1.00
WI3 Mark McGwire 1.50 4.00
WI4 Roberto Alomar .40 1.00
WI5 Steve Avery .10 .30
WI6 Paul Molitor .25 .60
WI7 Ozzie Smith 1.00 2.50
WI8 Mark Grace .40 1.00
WI9 Eric Karros .25 .60
WI10 Delino DeShields .10 .30
WI11 Will Clark .40 1.00
WI12 Albert Belle .25 .60
WI13 Ken Griffey Jr. 1.25 3.00
WI14 Howard Johnson .10 .30
WI15 Cal Ripken 2.00 5.00
WI16 Fred McGriff .40 1.00
WI17 Darren Daulton .25 .60
WI18 Andy Van Slyke .40 1.00
WI19 Nolan Ryan 2.50 6.00
WI20 Wade Boggs .40 1.00
WI21 Barry Larkin .40 1.00
WI22 George Brett 1.50 4.00
WI23 Cecil Fielder .25 .60
WI24 Kirby Puckett .60 1.50
WI25 Frank Thomas .60 1.50
WI26 Don Mattingly 1.50 4.00
NNO Iooss Header .10 .30

1993 Upper Deck Mays Heroes

This standard-size ten-card set was randomly inserted in 1993 Upper Deck first series foil packs. The fronts feature color photos of Mays at various stages of his career that are partially contained within a black bordered circle. The cards are numbered in continuation of Upper Deck's Heroes series.

COMPLETE SET (10) 1.25 3.00
COMMON CARD (46-54/HDR) .20 .50
SER.1 STATED ODDS 1:9

1993 Upper Deck On Deck

Inserted one per series II jumbo packs, these 25 standard-size cards profile baseball's top players. The cards are numbered on the back with a "D" prefix in alphabetical order by name.

COMPLETE SET (25) 8.00 20.00
SER.2 STAT.ODDS 1:1 RED/BLUE JUMBO
D1 Jim Abbott .30 .75
D2 Roberto Alomar .30 .75
D3 Carlos Baerga .08 .25
D4 Albert Belle .20 .50
D5 Wade Boggs .30 .75
D6 George Brett 1.25 3.00
D7 Jose Canseco .30 .75
D8 Will Clark .30 .75
D9 Roger Clemens 1.00 2.50
D10 Dennis Eckersley .20 .50
D11 Cecil Fielder .20 .50
D12 Juan Gonzalez .20 .50
D13 Ken Griffey Jr. 1.00 2.50
D14 Tony Gwynn .60 1.50
D15 Bo Jackson .50 1.25
D16 Chipper Jones .50 1.25
D17 Eric Karros .20 .50
D18 Mark McGwire 1.25 3.00
D19 Kirby Puckett .50 1.25
D20 Nolan Ryan 2.00 5.00
D21 Tim Salmon .30 .75
D22 Ryne Sandberg .75 2.00
D23 Darryl Strawberry .20 .50
D24 Frank Thomas .50. 1.25
D25 Andy Van Slyke .30 .75

1993 Upper Deck Season Highlights

This 20-card standard-size insert set captures great moments of the 1992 Major League Baseball season. The cards were exclusively distributed in specially marked cases that were available only at Upper Deck Heroes of Baseball Card Shows and through the purchase of a specified quantity of second series cases. In these packs, the cards were inserted at a rate of one every nine. The cards are numbered on the back with an "HI" prefix in alphabetical order by player's name.

COMPLETE SET (20) 60.00 120.00
STATED ODDS 1:9 HOBBY SEASON HL
HI1 Roberto Alomar 2.00 5.00
HI2 Steve Avery .60 1.50
HI3 Harold Baines 1.25 3.00
HI4 Damon Berryhill .60 1.50
HI5 Barry Bonds 10.00 25.00
HI6 Bret Boone 1.25 3.00
HI7 George Brett 8.00 20.00
HI8 Francisco Cabrera .60 1.50
HI9 Ken Griffey Jr. 6.00 15.00
HI10 Rickey Henderson 3.00 8.00
HI11 Kenny Lofton 1.25 3.00
HI12 Mickey Morandini .60 1.50
HI13 Eddie Murray 3.00 8.00
HI14 David Nied .60 1.50
HI15 Jeff Reardon 1.25 3.00
HI16 Bip Roberts .60 1.50
HI17 Nolan Ryan 12.50 30.00
HI18 Ed Sprague .60 1.50
HI19 Dave Winfield 1.25 3.00
HI20 Robin Yount 5.00 12.00

1993 Upper Deck Then And Now

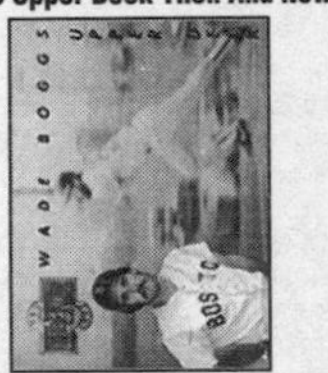

This 18-card, standard-size hologram set highlights veteran stars in their rookie year and today, reflecting on how they and the game have changed. Cards 1-9 were randomly inserted in series I foil packs; cards 10-18 were randomly inserted in series II foil packs. In either series, the cards were inserted one every 27 packs. The nine lithogram cards in the second series feature one card each of Hall of Famers Reggie Jackson, Mickey Mantle, and Willie Mays, as well as six active players. The cards are numbered on the back with a "TN" prefix and arranged alphabetically within subgroup according to player's last name.

COMPLETE SET (18) 10.00 25.00
COMPLETE SERIES 1 (9) 4.00 10.00
COMPLETE SERIES 2 (9) 6.00 15.00
STATED ODDS 1:27 HOBBY
TN1 Wade Boggs .50 1.25
TN2 George Brett 2.00 5.00
TN3 Rickey Henderson .75 2.00
TN4 Cal Ripken 2.50 6.00
TN5 Nolan Ryan 3.00 8.00
TN6 Ryne Sandberg 1.25 3.00
TN7 Ozzie Smith 1.25 3.00
TN8 Darryl Strawberry .30 .75
TN9 Dave Winfield .30 .75
TN10 Dennis Eckersley .30 .75
TN11 Tony Gwynn 1.00 2.50
TN12 Howard Johnson .15 .40
TN13 Don Mattingly 2.00 5.00
TN14 Eddie Murray .75 2.00
TN15 Robin Yount 1.25 3.00
TN16 Reggie Jackson 1.00 2.50
TN17 Mickey Mantle 5.00 12.00
TN18 Willie Mays 2.50 6.00

1993 Upper Deck Triple Crown

This ten-card, standard-size insert set highlights ten players who were selected by Upper Deck as having the best shot at winning Major League Baseball's Triple Crown. The cards were randomly inserted in series I hobby foil packs at a rate of one in 15. The cards are numbered on the back with a "TC" prefix and arranged alphabetically by player's last name.

COMPLETE SET (10) 5.00 12.00

STATED ODDS 1:15 HOBBY
TC1 Barry Bonds 1.50 4.00
TC2 Jose Canseco .30 .75
TC3 Will Clark .30 .75
TC4 Ken Griffey Jr. 1.00 2.50
TC5 Fred McGriff .30 .75
TC6 Kirby Puckett .50 1.25
TC7 Cal Ripken Jr. 1.50 4.00
TC8 Gary Sheffield .20 .50
TC9 Frank Thomas .50 1.25
TC10 Larry Walker .20 .50

1993 Upper Deck Adventures in Toon World

IT'S WAY COOLER! This new Upper Deck produced set definitely builds the success of the 'Comic Ball' series on. Indeed, nothing creates funnier stories than pairing Looney Tune characters with respected professional athletes. The base set is divided into 9-card subsets: 'Act 1' (A1S1-A1S9) through 'Act 10' (A10S1-A10S9); each of 18 scenes and with each card being double-sided with two different scenes.
COMPLETE SET (91) 10.00 25.00
COMMON CARD (1-90) .20 .50

1993 Upper Deck All-Time Heroes Preview

COMPLETE SET (4) 2.00 5.00
1 Ted Williams / Mickey Mantle .60 1.50
2 Reggie Jackson / Mickey Mantle .60 1.50
3 Ted Williams / Reggie Jackson .60 1.50
4 Reggie Jackson / Mickey Mantle / Ted Williams .60 1.50

1993 Upper Deck All-Time Heroes

This 165-card set of All-Time Heroes of Baseball is patterned after the T-202 Hassan Triple Folders cards, which first appeared in 1912. The cards measure approximately 2 1/4" by 5 1/4" and feature two side panels and a larger middle panel. The set consists of 130 regular cards and the Classic Combinations subset (131-165). The fronts feature candid or action photos of the featured player on the center panel, along with a portrait on one of the side panels and the B.A.T. (Baseball Assistance Team) logo on the other. The backs include player biographies and career highlights, as well as an explanation of the B.A.T. cause. The Classic Combinations subset have center panels that feature either artwork by Todd Reigle or a photograph of multiple greats. The side panels feature photos of two players. The backs include player biographies on the side panels, with the center panel detailing the association between the players. The foil packs contained 12 cards per pack. Each card is holographically enhanced. Reggie Jackson and Mickey Mantle were the spokespersons for this set and they are featured prominently on the front of the box. The grand prize for the set's mail-in contest was an actual, original set of T202 Hassan Triplefolders, which Upper Deck had purchased in the open hobby market expressly for the promotion.
COMPLETE SET (165) 10.00 25.00
1 Hank Aaron .75 2.00
2 Tommie Agee .02 .10
3 Bob Allison .02 .10
4 Matty Alou .02 .10
5 Sal Bando .02 .10
6 Hank Bauer .02 .10
7 Don Baylor .05 .15
8 Glenn Beckert .02 .10
9 Yogi Berra .40 1.00
10 Buddy Biancalana .02 .10
11 Jack Billingham .02 .10
12 Joe Black .05 .15
13 Paul Blair .02 .10
14 Steve Blass .02 .10
15 Ray Boone .02 .10
16 Lou Boudreau .08 .25
17 Ken Brett .02 .10
18 Nellie Briles .02 .10
19 Bobby Brown .05 .15
20 Bill Buckner .05 .15
21 Don Buford .02 .10
22 Al Bumbry .02 .10
23 Lew Burdette .05 .15
24 Jeff Burroughs .02 .10
25 Johnny Callison .02 .10
26 Bert Campaneris .02 .10
27 Rico Carty .02 .10
28 Dave Cash .02 .10
29 Cesar Cedeno .05 .15
30 Frank Chance .08 .25
31 Joe Charboneau .05 .15
32 Ty Cobb .75 2.00
33 Jerry Coleman .02 .10
34 Cecil Cooper .02 .10
35 Frankie Crosetti .02 .10
36 Alvin Dark .02 .10
37 Tommy Davis .02 .10
38 Dizzy Dean .20 .50
39 Doug DeCinces .02 .10
40 Bucky Dent .02 .10
41 Larry Dierker .02 .10
42 Larry Doby .15 .40
43 Moe Drabowsky .02 .10
44 Dave Dravecky .02 .10
45 Del Ennis .02 .10
46 Carl Erskine .05 .15
47 Johnny Evers .08 .25
48 Roy Face .02 .10
49 Rick Ferrell .08 .25
50 Mark Fidrych .05 .15
51 Curt Flood .05 .15
52 Whitey Ford .30 .75
53 George Foster .05 .15
54 Jimmie Foxx .20 .50
55 Jim Fregosi .02 .10
56 Phil Garner .05 .15
57 Ralph Garr .02 .10
58 Lou Gehrig 1.00 2.50
59 Bobby Grich .05 .15
60 Jerry Grote .02 .10
61 Harvey Haddix .02 .10
62 Toby Harrah .02 .10
63 Bud Harrelson .05 .15
64 Jim Hegan .02 .10
65 Gil Hodges .08 .25
66 Ken Holtzman .02 .10
67 Bob Horner .02 .10
68 Rogers Hornsby .20 .50
69 Carl Hubbell .15 .40
70 Ron Hunt .02 .10
71 Monte Irvin .07 .20
72 Reggie Jackson .30 .75
73 Larry Jansen .02 .10
74 Ferguson Jenkins .08 .25
75 Tommy John .05 .15
76 Cliff Johnson .02 .10
77 Davey Johnson .05 .15
78 Walter Johnson .20 .50
79 George Kell .07 .20
80 Don Kessinger .02 .10
81 Vern Law .02 .10
82 Dennis Leonard .02 .10
83 Johnny Logan .02 .10
84 Mickey Lolich .05 .15
85 Jim Lonborg .02 .10
86 Bill Madlock .02 .10
87 Mickey Mantle 2.00 5.00
88 Billy Martin .07 .20
89 Christy Mathewson .20 .50
90 Lee May .02 .10
91 Willie Mays .75 2.00
92 Bill Mazeroski .08 .25
93 Gil McDougald .05 .15
94 Sam McDowell .02 .10
95 Minnie Minoso .05 .15
96 Johnny Mize .07 .20
97 Rick Monday .02 .10
98 Wally Moon .02 .10
99 Manny Mota .02 .10
100 Bobby Murcer .02 .10
101 Ron Necciai .02 .10
102 Al Oliver .05 .15
103 Mel Ott .07 .20
104 Mel Parnell .02 .10
105 Jimmy Piersall .05 .15
106 Johnny Podres .02 .10
107 Bobby Richardson .05 .15
108 Robin Roberts .07 .20
109 Al Rosen .05 .15
110 Babe Ruth 2.00 5.00
111 Joe Sambito .02 .10
112 Manny Sanguillen .02 .10
113 Ron Santo .07 .20
114 Bill Skowron .02 .10
115 Enos Slaughter .08 .25
116 Warren Spahn .08 .25
117 Tris Speaker .08 .25
118 Frank Thomas .02 .10
119 Bobby Thomson .05 .15
120 Andre Thornton .02 .10
121 Marv Throneberry .02 .10
122 Luis Tiant .05 .15
123 Joe Tinker .08 .25
124 Honus Wagner .20 .50
125 Bill White .05 .15
126 Ted Williams 1.50 4.00
127 Earl Wilson .02 .10
128 Joe Wood .05 .15
129 Cy Young .20 .50
130 Richie Zisk .02 .10
131 Babe Ruth / Lou Gehrig .75 2.00
132 Ted Williams / Rogers Hornsby .40 1.00
133 Lou Gehrig / Babe Ruth .75 2.00
134 Babe Ruth / Mickey Mantle .75 2.00
135 Mickey Mantle / Reggie Jackson .50 1.25
136 Mel Ott / Carl Hubbell .05 .15
137 Mickey Mantle / Willie Mays .60 1.50
138 Cy Young / Walter Johnson .07 .20
139 Honus Wagner / Rogers Hornsby .07 .20
140 Mickey Mantle / Whitey Ford .50 1.25
141 Mickey Mantle / Billy Martin .50 1.25
142 Cy Young / Walter Johnson .07 .20
143 Christy Mathewson / Walter Johnson .07 .20
144 Warren Spahn / Christy Mathewson .07 .20
145 Honus Wagner / Ty Cobb .40 1.00
146 Babe Ruth / Ty Cobb .75 2.00
147 Joe Tinker / Johnny Evers .07 .20
148 Johnny Evers / Frank Chance .07 .20
149 Hank Aaron / Babe Ruth .75 2.00
150 Willie Mays / Hank Aaron .50 1.25
151 Babe Ruth / Willie Mays .75 2.00
152 Babe Ruth / Whitey Ford .50 1.25
153 Larry Doby / Minnie Minoso .02 .10
154 Joe Black / Monte Irvin .05 .15
155 Joe Wood / Christy Mathewson .05 .15
156 Christy Mathewson / Cy Young .07 .20
157 Cy Young / Joe Wood .05 .15
158 Cy Young / Whitey Ford .05 .15
159 Cy Young / Ferguson Jenkins .05 .15
160 Ty Cobb / Rogers Hornsby .40 1.00
161 Tris Speaker / Ted Williams .40 1.00
162 Rogers Hornsby / Ted Williams .40 1.00
163 Willie Mays / Monte Irvin .30 .75
164 Willie Mays / Bobby Thomson .30 .75
165 Reggie Jackson / Mickey Mantle .60 1.50

1993 Upper Deck All-Time Heroes T202 Reprints

Inserted in 1993 Upper Deck All-Time Heroes of Baseball foil packs at a stated rate of one in five, this ten-card set of reprints feature players from the 1912 Hassan "Triplefolders. The Hassan cigarette ads were replaced by the Upper Deck hologram and their designation of "T202" comes from their assignment in the American Card Catalog. The reprints are unnumbered and appear alphabetically
COMPLETE SET (10) 6.00 15.00
1 Art Devlin / Christy Mathewson .40 1.00
2 Hugh Jennings / Ty Cobb 1.00 2.50
3 John Kling / Cy Young .40 1.00
4 Jack Knight / Walter Johnson .40 1.00
5 John McGraw / Hugh Jennings .60 1.50
6 George Moriarty / Ty Cobb .75 2.00
7 Charles O'Leary / Ty Cobb .75 2.00
8 Charles O'Leary / Ty Cobb .75 2.00
9 Joe Tinker / Frank Chance 1.00 2.50
10 Joe Wood / Tris Speaker .40 1.00

1993 Upper Deck Clark Reggie Jackson

Issued to promote the reintroduction of the Reggie bar by the Clark Candy Co., these three standard-size cards highlight Jackson's career and feature on their fronts white-bordered color photos of Jackson as an Athletic and as a Yankee, with all team logos airbrushed out. The cards are numbered on the back with a "C" prefix. One card was inserted in each Reggie bar and Jackson autographed 200 cards that were randomly inserted into the candy bar packages.
COMPLETE SET (3) 2.00 5.00
COMMON CARD (C1-C3) .80 2.00
RJ Reggie Jackson AU Autograph card

1993 Upper Deck Diamond Gallery

This 38-card standard-size boxed set features two player action photos on its horizontal fronts. One is a hologram, the other is a color action shot of the player, which is displayed on the left side projecting from a baseball diamond design. In the hologram, the player's uniform number appears behind him. Two subsets are present in this set; cards 29-31 are Gallery Heroes subset, and cards 32-36 are Diamonds in the Rough. Also included in the set are the checklist bearing the production number out of 123,600 sets produced, and a mail-away card for the Diamond Gallery card album.
COMPLETE SET (38) 6.00 15.00
1 Tim Salmon .20 .50
2 Jeff Bagwell .30 .75
3 Mark McGwire .60 1.50
4 Roberto Alomar .20 .50
5 Terry Pendleton .02 .10
6 Robin Yount .20 .50
7 Ray Lankford .07 .20
8 Ryne Sandberg .60 1.50
9 Darryl Strawberry .07 .20
10 Marquis Grissom .07 .20
11 Barry Bonds .50 1.25
12 Carlos Baerga .02 .10
13 Ken Griffey Jr. .75 2.00
14 Benito Santiago .07 .20
15 Dwight Gooden .07 .20
16 Cal Ripken 1.25 3.00
17 Tony Gwynn .60 1.50
18 Dave Hollins .02 .10
19 Andy Van Slyke .02 .10
20 Juan Gonzalez .25 .60
21 Roger Clemens .60 1.50
22 Barry Larkin .20 .50
23 David Nied .02 .10
24 George Brett .60 1.50
25 Travis Fryman .07 .20
26 Kirby Puckett .40 1.00
27 Frank Thomas .30 .75
28 Don Mattingly .60 1.50
29 Rickey Henderson .40 1.00
30 Nolan Ryan 1.25 3.00
31 Ozzie Smith .60 1.50
32 Wil Cordero .02 .10
33 Phil Hiatt .02 .10
34 Mike Piazza 1.25 3.00
35 J.T. Snow .20 .50
36 Kevin Young .02 .10
NNO Checklist Card .02 .10
NNO Album Offer Card .02 .10

1993 Upper Deck Folder

This folder features four 1993 Upper Deck Triple Crown Contenders insert cards on the front. The back of the folder features the back of the cards involved. Inside the folder is room to place some of a collectors favorite cards.
1 Ken Griffey Jr. / Will Clark / Cal Ripken Jr / Kirby 1.00 2.50

1993 Upper Deck Sheets

The 31 commemorative sheets listed below in chronological order were issued by Upper Deck in 1993. The Upper Deck Heroes of Baseball made stops in MLB ballparks and sponsored old-timer baseball games preceding major league games. At each game a limited edition commemorative sheet was distributed. Commemorative sheets were produced in honor of other events. Days prior to the All-Star Game, sheets 16 and 17 were issued to fans who were at Camden Yards to watch the All-Star Workout. Sheet 19 was issued at the National in Chicago. Sheet 21 commemorates the World Children's Baseball Fair. And sheet 29 was handed out at by Upper Deck to collectors at various shows during the year. All the sheets measure 8 1/2" by 11" and most feature artist renderings of players from the teams recreated for the old-timers games. The front of each sheet carries the individual production number out of the total number produced, but otherwise the sheets are unnumbered.
COMPLETE SET (31) 100.00 200.00
1 Blue Jays Heroes vs. Upper Deck Heroes April 25& 2.50 6.00
2 Atlanta Braves Heroes vs. Upper Deck Award Winne 2.50 6.00
3 Upper Deck Heroes of Baseball vs. St. Louis Card 2.50 6.00
4 '69 Royals vs./'69 Twins May 22& 1993 (42&600)/ 2.50 6.00
5 Ewing M. Kauffman Induction into Royals Hall of 2.00 5.00
6 Upper Deck Heroes vs. Red Sox Heroes May 29& 199 3.00 8.00
7 Heroes of the '60s June 6& 1993 (31&600) Candles 2.50 6.00
8 125 Years of Cincinnati Baseball June 6& 1993 (5 1.50 4.00
9 Nickname Heroes Milwaukee County Stad. June 12& 2.50 6.00
10 20th Anniversary of the 1973 World Series June 1 2.50 6.00
11 Colorado Rockies Inaugural Season June 19& 1993 4.00 10.00
12 '83 Phillies vs./'83 Heroes June 19& 1993 (56&60 3.00 8.00
13 25 Years of Padres Baseball June 25& 1993 (41&60 2.50 6.00
14 White Sox 1983 Winning Ugly vs./1983 Baltimore O 2.50 6.00
15 All-Time Home Run Hitters July'4& 1993 (21&600)# 3.00 8.00
16 1993 Upper Deck All-Star FanFest Autograph Sheet .75 2.00
17 A Celebration of Early Black Baseball July 10& 1 3.00 8.00
18 Upper Deck Heroes of Baseball All-Star Game Jul 2.50 6.00
19 The 1993 National Chicago Upper Deck Five Year/ 2.00 5.00
20 1978 Yankees/22nd World Championship 2.50 6.00 July 24& 19
21 Astros All-Star Heroes Game July 24, 1993 Fergus .75 2.00
22 World Children's Baseball Fair July 31& 1993 (61 3.00 8.00
23 Reggie Jackson Hall of Fame Induction Aug. 1& 1 2.50 6.00
24 Seattle Mariners Salutes Heroes of the 70's/26,6 .75 2.00
25 A Tribute to Billy Ball Billy Martin Aug. 15& 1 2.50 6.00
26 25th Anniversary of the 1968 World Series August 4.00 10.00
27 The Expos' 25th Anniversary August 28& 1993 (41& 2.50 6.00
28 Florida Marlins Inaugural Season September 25& 1 3.00 8.00
29 Upper Deck Company Salutes the Heroes of Arlingt 1.50 4.00
30 Tribute to Cleveland Stadium October 2& 1993 (76 1.50 4.00
31 Upper Deck Heroes of Baseball Autograph Sheet N .75 2.00

1994 Upper Deck

The 1994 Upper Deck set was issued in two series of 280 and 270 standard-size cards for a total of 550. There are number of topical subsets including Star Rookies (1-30), Fantasy Team (31-40), The Future is Now (41-55), Home Field Advantage (267-294), Upper Deck Classic Alumni (295-299), Diamond Debuts (511-522) and Top Prospects (523-550). Three autograph cards were randomly inserted into first series retail packs. They are Ken Griffey Jr. (KG), Mickey Mantle (MM) and a combo card with Griffey and Mantle (GM). Though they lack serial-numbering, all three cards have an announced print run of 1,000 copies per. An Alex Rodriguez (298A) autograph card was randomly inserted into second series retail packs but production quantities were never divulged by the manufacturer. Rookie Cards include Michael Jordan (as an baseball player), Chan Ho Park, Alex Rodriguez and Billy Wagner. Many cards have been found with a significant variation on the back. The player's name, the horizontal bar containing the biographical information and the vertical bar containing the stats header are normally printed in copper-gold color. On the variation cards, these areas are printed in silver. It is not known exactly how many of the 550 cards have silver versions, nor has any premium been established for them. Also, all of the American League Home Field Advantage subset cards (numbers 281-294) are minor uncorrected errors because the Upper Deck logos on the front are missing the year "1994".
COMPLETE SET (550) 15.00 40.00
COMPLETE SERIES 1 (280) 10.00 25.00
COMPLETE SERIES 2 (270) 6.00 15.00
SUBSET CARDS HALF VALUE OF BASE CARDS
GRIFFEY/MANTLE AU INSERTS IN SER.1 RET.
A.RODRIGUEZ AU INSERT IN SER.2 RET.
1 Brian Anderson RC .15 .40
2 Shane Andrews .05 .15
3 James Baldwin .05 .15
4 Rich Becker .05 .15
5 Greg Blosser .05 .15
6 Ricky Bottalico RC .05 .15
7 Midre Cummings .05 .15
8 Carlos Delgado .20 .50
9 Steve Dreyer RC .05 .15
10 Joey Eischen .05 .15
11 Carl Everett .10 .30
12 Cliff Floyd .10 .30
13 Alex Gonzalez .05 .15
14 Jeff Granger .05 .15
15 Shawn Green .30 .75
16 Brian L.Hunter .05 .15
17 Butch Huskey .05 .15
18 Mark Hutton .05 .15
19 Michael Jordan RC 3.00 8.00
20 Steve Karsay .05 .15
21 Jeff McNeely .05 .15
22 Marc Newfield .05 .15
23 Manny Ramirez .30 .75
24 Alex Rodriguez RC 5.00 12.00
25 Scott Ruffcorn UER .05 .15
26 Paul Spoljaric UER .05 .15
27 Salomon Torres .05 .15
28 Steve Trachsel .05 .15
29 Chris Turner .05 .15
30 Gabe White .05 .15
31 Randy Johnson FT .20 .50
32 John Wetteland FT .05 .15
33 Mike Piazza FT .30 .75
34 Rafael Palmeiro FT .10 .30
35 Roberto Alomar FT .10 .30
36 Matt Williams FT .05 .15
37 Travis Fryman FT .05 .15
38 Barry Bonds FT .40 1.00
39 Marquis Grissom FT .05 .15
40 Albert Belle FT .10 .30
41 Steve Avery FUT .05 .15
42 Jason Bere FUT .05 .15
43 Alex Fernandez FUT .05 .15
44 Mike Mussina FUT .10 .30
45 Aaron Sele FUT .05 .15
46 Rod Beck FUT .05 .15
47 Mike Piazza FUT .30 .75
48 John Olerud FUT .05 .15
49 Carlos Baerga FUT .05 .15
50 Gary Sheffield FUT .05 .15
51 Travis Fryman FUT .05 .15
52 Juan Gonzalez FUT .05 .15
53 Ken Griffey Jr. FUT .40 1.00
54 Tim Salmon FUT .10 .30
55 Frank Thomas FUT .20 .50
56 Tony Phillips .05 .15
57 Julio Franco .10 .30
58 Kevin Mitchell .05 .15
59 Raul Mondesi .10 .30
60 Rickey Henderson .30 .75
61 Jay Buhner .05 .15
62 Bill Swift .05 .15
63 Brady Anderson .10 .30
64 Ryan Klesko .10 .30
65 Darren Daulton .10 .30
66 Damion Easley .05 .15
67 Mark McGwire .75 2.00
68 John Roper .05 .15
69 Dave Telgheder .05 .15
70 David Nied .05 .15
71 Mo Vaughn .10 .30
72 Tyler Green .05 .15
73 Dave Magadan .05 .15
74 Chili Davis .10 .30
75 Archi Cianfrocco .05 .15
76 Joe Girardi .05 .15
77 Chris Hoiles .05 .15
78 Ryan Bowen .05 .15
79 Greg Gagne .05 .15
80 Aaron Sele .05 .15
81 Dave Winfield .10 .30
82 Chad Curtis .05 .15
83 Andy Van Slyke .20 .50
84 Kevin Stocker .05 .15
85 Deion Sanders .20 .50
86 Bernie Williams .20 .50
87 John Smoltz .20 .50
88 Ruben Santana .05 .15
89 Dave Stewart .10 .30
90 Don Mattingly .75 2.00
91 Joe Carter .10 .30
92 Ryne Sandberg .50 1.25
93 Chris Gomez .05 .15
94 Tino Martinez .20 .50
95 Terry Pendleton .10 .30
96 Andre Dawson .10 .30
97 Wil Cordero .05 .15
98 Kent Hrbek .10 .30
99 John Olerud .10 .30
100 Kirt Manwaring .05 .15
101 Tim Bogar .05 .15
102 Mike Mussina .20 .50
103 Nigel Wilson .05 .15
104 Ricky Gutierrez .05 .15
105 Roberto Mejia .05 .15
106 Tom Pagnozzi .05 .15
107 Mike Macfarlane .05 .15
108 Jose Bautista .05 .15
109 Luis Ortiz .05 .15
110 Brent Gates .05 .15
111 Tim Salmon .20 .50
112 Wade Boggs .20 .50
113 Tripp Cromer .05 .15
114 Denny Hocking .05 .15
115 Carlos Baerga .05 .15
116 J.R. Phillips .05 .15
117 Bo Jackson .30 .75
118 Lance Johnson .05 .15
119 Bobby Jones .05 .15
120 Bobby Witt .05 .15
121 Ron Karkovice .05 .15
122 Jose Vizcaino .05 .15
123 Danny Darwin .05 .15
124 Eduardo Perez .05 .15
125 Brian Looney RC .05 .15
126 Pat Hentgen .05 .15
127 Frank Viola .10 .30
128 Darren Holmes .05 .15
129 Wally Whitehurst .05 .15
130 Matt Walbeck .05 .15
131 Albert Belle .10 .30
132 Steve Cooke .05 .15
133 Kevin Appier .10 .30
134 Joe Oliver .05 .15
135 Benji Gil .05 .15
136 Steve Buechele .05 .15
137 Devon White .10 .30
138 Sterling Hitchcock UER .05 .15
139 Phil Leftwich RC .05 .15
140 Jose Canseco .20 .50
141 Rick Aguilera .05 .15
142 Rod Beck .05 .15
143 Jose Rijo .05 .15
144 Tom Glavine .20 .50
145 Phil Plantier .05 .15
146 Jason Bere .05 .15
147 Jamie Moyer .10 .30
148 Wes Chamberlain .05 .15
149 Glenallen Hill .05 .15
150 Mark Whiten .05 .15
151 Bret Barberie .05 .15
152 Chuck Knoblauch .10 .30
153 Trevor Hoffman .20 .50
154 Rick Wilkins .05 .15
155 Juan Gonzalez .10 .30
156 Ozzie Guillen .10 .30
157 Jim Eisenreich .05 .15
158 Pedro Astacio .05 .15
159 Joe Magrane .05 .15
160 Ryan Thompson .05 .15
161 Jose Lind .05 .15
162 Jeff Conine .10 .30
163 Todd Benzinger .05 .15
164 Roger Salkeld .05 .15
165 Gary DiSarcina .05 .15
166 Kevin Gross .05 .15
167 Charlie Hayes .05 .15
168 Tim Costo .05 .15
169 Wally Joyner .10 .30
170 Johnny Ruffin .05 .15
171 Kirk Rueter .05 .15
172 Lenny Dykstra .10 .30
173 Ken Hill .05 .15
174 Mike Bordick .05 .15
175 Billy Hall .05 .15
176 Rob Butler .05 .15
177 Jay Bell .10 .30
178 Jeff Kent .20 .50
179 David Wells .10 .30
180 Dean Palmer .10 .30
181 Mariano Duncan .05 .15
182 Orlando Merced .05 .15
183 Brett Butler .10 .30
184 Milt Thompson .05 .15
185 Chipper Jones .30 .75
186 Paul O'Neill .20 .50
187 Mike Greenwell .05 .15
188 Harold Baines .10 .30
189 Todd Stottlemyre .05 .15
190 Jeromy Burnitz .10 .30
191 Rene Arocha .05 .15
192 Jeff Fassero .05 .15
193 Robby Thompson .05 .15
194 Greg W. Harris .05 .15
195 Todd Van Poppel .05 .15
196 Jose Guzman .05 .15
197 Shane Mack .05 .15
198 Carlos Garcia .05 .15
199 Kevin Roberson .05 .15
200 David McCarty .05 .15

201 Alan Trammell .10 .30
202 Chuck Carr .05 .15
203 Tommy Greene .05 .15
204 Wilson Alvarez .05 .15
205 Dwight Gooden .10 .30
206 Tony Tarasco .05 .15
207 Darren Lewis .05 .15
208 Eric Karros .10 .30
209 Chris Hammond .05 .15
210 Jeffrey Hammonds .05 .15
211 Rich Amaral .05 .15
212 Danny Tartabull .05 .15
213 Jeff Russell .05 .15
214 Dave Staton .05 .15
215 Kenny Lofton .10 .30
216 Manuel Lee .05 .15
217 Brian Koelling .05 .15
218 Scott Lydy .05 .15
219 Tony Gwynn .40 1.00
220 Cecil Fielder .10 .30
221 Royce Clayton .05 .15
222 Reggie Sanders .10 .30
223 Brian Jordan .10 .30
224 Ken Griffey Jr. .60 1.50
225 Fred McGriff .20 .50
226 Felix Jose .05 .15
227 Brad Pennington .05 .15
228 Chris Bosio .05 .15
229 Mike Stanley .05 .15
230 Willie Greene .05 .15
231 Alex Fernandez .05 .15
232 Brad Ausmus .20 .50
233 Darrell Whitmore .05 .15
234 Marcus Moore .05 .15
235 Allen Watson .05 .15
236 Jose Offerman .05 .15
237 Rondell White .10 .30
238 Jeff King .05 .15
239 Luis Alicea .05 .15
240 Dan Wilson .05 .15
241 Ed Sprague .05 .15
242 Todd Hundley .05 .15
243 Al Martin .05 .15
244 Mike Lansing .05 .15
245 Ivan Rodriguez .20 .50
246 Dave Fleming .05 .15
247 John Doherty .05 .15
248 Mark McLemore .05 .15
249 Bob Hamelin .05 .15
250 Curtis Pride RC .15 .40
251 Zane Smith .05 .15
252 Eric Young .05 .15
253 Brian McRae .05 .15
254 Tim Raines .10 .30
255 Javier Lopez .10 .30
256 Melvin Nieves .05 .15
257 Randy Myers .05 .15
258 Willie McGee .10 .30
259 Jimmy Key UER .10 .30
260 Tom Candiotti .05 .15
261 Eric Davis .10 .30
262 Craig Paquette .05 .15
263 Robin Ventura .10 .30
264 Pat Kelly .05 .15
265 Gregg Jefferies .05 .15
266 Cory Snyder .05 .15
267 David Justice HFA .05 .15
268 Sammy Sosa HFA .30 .75
269 Barry Larkin HFA .10 .30
270 Andres Galarraga HFA .05 .15
271 Gary Sheffield HFA .05 .15
272 Jeff Bagwell HFA .10 .30
273 Mike Piazza HFA .30 .75
274 Larry Walker HFA .05 .15
275 Bobby Bonilla HFA .05 .15
276 John Kruk HFA .05 .15
277 Jay Bell HFA .05 .15
278 Ozzie Smith HFA .30 .75
279 Tony Gwynn HFA .20 .50
280 Barry Bonds HFA .40 1.00
281 Cal Ripken HFA .50 1.25
282 Mo Vaughn HFA .05 .15
283 Tim Salmon HFA .10 .30
284 Frank Thomas HFA .20 .50
285 Albert Belle HFA .10 .30
286 Cecil Fielder HFA .05 .15
287 Wally Joyner HFA .05 .15
288 Greg Vaughn HFA .05 .15
289 Kirby Puckett HFA .20 .50
290 Don Mattingly HFA .40 1.00
291 Terry Steinbach HFA .05 .15
292 Ken Griffey Jr. HFA .40 1.00
293 Juan Gonzalez HFA .05 .15
294 Paul Molitor HFA .05 .15
295 Tavo Alvarez UDCA .05 .15
296 Matt Brunson UDCA .05 .15
297 Shawn Green UDCA .10 .30
298 Alex Rodriguez UDCA 2.00 5.00
299 Shannon Stewart UDCA .30 .75
300 Frank Thomas .30 .75
301 Mickey Tettleton .05 .15
302 Pedro Munoz .05 .15
303 Jose Valentin .05 .15
304 Orestes Destrade .05 .15
305 Pat Listach .05 .15
306 Scott Brosius .10 .30
307 Kurt Miller .05 .15
308 Rob Dibble .10 .30
309 Mike Blowers .05 .15
310 Jim Abbott .20 .50
311 Mike Jackson .05 .15
312 Craig Biggio .20 .50
313 Kurt Abbott RC .05 .15
314 Chuck Finley .10 .30
315 Andres Galarraga .10 .30
316 Mike Moore .05 .15
317 Doug Strange .05 .15
318 Pedro Martinez .30 .75
319 Kevin McReynolds .05 .15
320 Greg Maddux .50 1.25
321 Mike Henneman .05 .15
322 Scott Leius .05 .15
323 John Franco .10 .30
324 Jeff Blauser .05 .15
325 Kirby Puckett .30 .75
326 Darryl Hamilton .05 .15
327 John Smiley .05 .15
328 Derrick May .05 .15
329 Jose Vizcaino .05 .15
330 Randy Johnson .30 .75
331 Jack Morris .10 .30
332 Graeme Lloyd .05 .15
333 Dave Valle .05 .15
334 Greg Myers .05 .15
335 John Wetteland .10 .30
336 Jim Gott .05 .15
337 Tim Naehring .05 .15
338 Mike Kelly .05 .15
339 Jeff Montgomery .05 .15
340 Rafael Palmeiro .20 .50
341 Eddie Murray .30 .75
342 Xavier Hernandez .05 .15
343 Bobby Munoz .05 .15
344 Bobby Bonilla .10 .30
345 Travis Fryman .10 .30
346 Steve Finley .10 .30
347 Chris Sabo .05 .15
348 Armando Reynoso .05 .15
349 Ramon Martinez .05 .15
350 Will Clark .20 .50
351 Moises Alou .10 .30
352 Jim Thome .20 .50
353 Bob Tewksbury .05 .15
354 Andujar Cedeno .05 .15
355 Orel Hershiser .10 .30
356 Mike Devereaux .05 .15
357 Mike Perez .05 .15
358 Dennis Martinez .10 .30
359 Dave Nilsson .05 .15
360 Ozzie Smith .50 1.25
361 Eric Anthony .05 .15
362 Scott Sanders .05 .15
363 Paul Sorrento .05 .15
364 Tim Belcher .05 .15
365 Dennis Eckersley .10 .30
366 Mel Rojas .05 .15
367 Tom Henke .05 .15
368 Randy Tomlin .05 .15
369 B.J. Surhoff .10 .30
370 Larry Walker .10 .30
371 Joey Cora .05 .15
372 Mike Harkey .05 .15
373 John Valentin .05 .15
374 Doug Jones .05 .15
375 David Justice .10 .30
376 Vince Coleman .05 .15
377 David Hulse .05 .15
378 Kevin Seitzer .05 .15
379 Pete Harnisch .05 .15
380 Ruben Sierra .10 .30
381 Mark Lewis .05 .15
382 Bip Roberts .05 .15
383 Paul Wagner .05 .15
384 Stan Javier .05 .15
385 Barry Larkin .20 .50
386 Mark Portugal .05 .15
387 Roberto Kelly .05 .15
388 Andy Benes .05 .15
389 Felix Fermin .05 .15
390 Marquis Grissom .10 .30
391 Troy Neel .05 .15
392 Chad Kreuter .05 .15
393 Gregg Olson .05 .15
394 Charles Nagy .05 .15
395 Jack McDowell .05 .15
396 Luis Gonzalez .10 .30
397 Benito Santiago .10 .30
398 Chris James .05 .15
399 Terry Mulholland .05 .15
400 Barry Bonds .75 2.00
401 Joe Grahe .05 .15
402 Duane Ward .05 .15
403 John Burkett .05 .15
404 Scott Servais .05 .15
405 Bryan Harvey .05 .15
406 Bernard Gilkey .05 .15
407 Greg McMichael .05 .15
408 Tim Wallach .05 .15
409 Ken Caminiti .10 .30
410 John Kruk .10 .30
411 Darrin Jackson .05 .15
412 Mike Gallego .05 .15
413 David Cone .10 .30
414 Lou Whitaker .10 .30
415 Sandy Alomar Jr. .05 .15
416 Bill Wegman .05 .15
417 Pat Borders .05 .15
418 Roger Pavlik .05 .15
419 Pete Smith .05 .15
420 Steve Avery .05 .15
421 David Segui .05 .15
422 Rheal Cormier .05 .15
423 Harold Reynolds .10 .30
424 Edgar Martinez .20 .50
425 Cal Ripken 1.00 2.50
426 Jaime Navarro .05 .15
427 Sean Berry .05 .15
428 Bret Saberhagen .10 .30
429 Bob Welch .05 .15
430 Juan Guzman .05 .15
431 Cal Eldred .05 .15
432 Dave Hollins .05 .15
433 Sid Fernandez .05 .15
434 Willie Banks .05 .15
435 Darryl Kile .10 .30
436 Henry Rodriguez .05 .15
437 Tony Fernandez .05 .15
438 Walt Weiss .05 .15
439 Kevin Tapani .05 .15
440 Mark Grace .20 .50
441 Brian Harper .05 .15
442 Kent Mercker .05 .15
443 Anthony Young .05 .15
444 Todd Zeile .05 .15
445 Greg Vaughn .05 .15
446 Ray Lankford .10 .30
447 Dave Weathers .05 .15
448 Bret Boone .10 .30
449 Charlie Hough .10 .30
450 Roger Clemens .60 1.50
451 Mike Morgan .05 .15
452 Doug Drabek .05 .15
453 Danny Jackson .05 .15
454 Dante Bichette .10 .30
455 Roberto Alomar .20 .50
456 Ben McDonald .05 .15
457 Kenny Rogers .10 .30
458 Bill Gullickson .05 .15
459 Darrin Fletcher .05 .15
460 Curt Schilling .10 .30
461 Billy Hatcher .05 .15
462 Howard Johnson .05 .15
463 Mickey Morandini .05 .15
464 Frank Castillo .05 .15
465 Delino DeShields .05 .15
466 Gary Gaetti .10 .30
467 Steve Farr .05 .15
468 Roberto Hernandez .05 .15
469 Jack Armstrong .05 .15
470 Paul Molitor .10 .30
471 Melido Perez .05 .15
472 Greg Hibbard .05 .15
473 Jody Reed .05 .15
474 Tom Gordon .05 .15
475 Gary Sheffield .10 .30
476 John Jaha .05 .15
477 Shawon Dunston .05 .15
478 Reggie Jefferson .05 .15
479 Don Slaught .05 .15
480 Jeff Bagwell .20 .50
481 Tim Pugh .05 .15
482 Kevin Young .05 .15
483 Ellis Burks .10 .30
484 Greg Swindell .05 .15
485 Mark Langston .05 .15
486 Omar Vizquel .20 .50
487 Kevin Brown .10 .30
488 Terry Steinbach .05 .15
489 Mark Lemke .05 .15
490 Matt Williams .10 .30
491 Pete Incaviglia .05 .15
492 Karl Rhodes .05 .15
493 Shawn Green .30 .75
494 Hal Morris .05 .15
495 Derek Bell .05 .15
496 Luis Polonia .05 .15
497 Otis Nixon .05 .15
498 Ron Darling .05 .15
499 Mitch Williams .05 .15
500 Mike Piazza .60 1.50
501 Pat Meares .05 .15
502 Scott Cooper .05 .15
503 Scott Erickson .05 .15
504 Jeff Juden .05 .15
505 Lee Smith .10 .30
506 Bobby Ayala .05 .15
507 Dave Henderson .05 .15
508 Erik Hanson .05 .15
509 Bob Wickman .05 .15
510 Sammy Sosa .30 .75
511 Hector Carrasco .05 .15
512 Tim Davis .05 .15
513 Joey Hamilton .05 .15
514 Robert Eenhoorn .05 .15
515 Jorge Fabregas .05 .15
516 Tim Hyers RC .05 .15
517 John Hudek RC .05 .15
518 James Mouton .05 .15
519 Herbert Perry RC .05 .15
520 Chan Ho Park RC .30 .75
521 W.VanLandingham RC .05 .15
522 Paul Shuey DD .05 .15
523 Ryan Hancock RC .05 .15
524 Billy Wagner RC .75 2.00
525 Jason Giambi .30 .75
526 Jose Silva RC .05 .15
527 Terrell Wade RC .05 .15
528 Todd Dunn .05 .15
529 Alan Benes RC .15 .40
530 Brooks Kieschnick RC .05 .15
531 Todd Hollandsworth .05 .15
532 Brad Fullmer RC .15 .40
533 Steve Soderstrom RC .05 .15
534 Daron Kirkreit .05 .15
535 Arquimedez Pozo RC .05 .15
536 Charles Johnson .10 .30
537 Preston Wilson .10 .30
538 Alex Ochoa .05 .15
539 Derrek Lee RC 1.50 4.00
540 Wayne Gomes RC .05 .15
541 Jermaine Allensworth RC .05 .15
542 Mike Bell RC .05 .15
543 Trot Nixon RC .75 2.00
544 Pokey Reese .05 .15
545 Neifi Perez RC .15 .40
546 Johnny Damon .30 .75
547 Matt Brunson RC .05 .15
548 LaTroy Hawkins RC .15 .40
549 Eddie Pearson RC .05 .15
550 Derek Jeter 1.00 2.50
A298 Alex Rodriguez AU 30.00 80.00
P224 Ken Griffey Jr. Promo 1.00 2.50
GM1 Griff AU/Mant AU/1000 900.00 1200.00
KG1 K.Griffey Jr. AU/1000 75.00 150.00
MM1 M.Mantle AU/1000 450.00 650.00

1994 Upper Deck Electric Diamond

COMPLETE SET (550) 30.00 60.00
COMPLETE SERIES 1 (280) 15.00 40.00
COMPLETE SERIES 2 (270) 8.00 20.00
*STARS: .75X TO 2X BASIC CARDS
*ROOKIES: .6X TO 1.5X BASIC CARDS
ONE PER PACK/TWO PER MINI JUMBO

1994 Upper Deck Electric Diamond Silver Back

*SILVER: .4X TO 1X ELECTRIC DIAMOND

1994 Upper Deck Diamond Collection

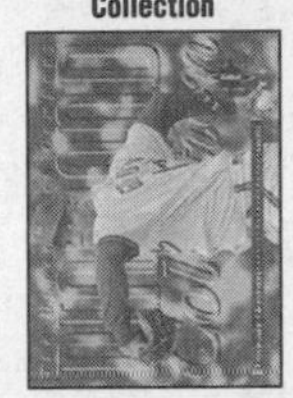

This 30-card standard-size set was inserted regionally in first series hobby packs at a rate of one in 18. The three regions are Central (C1-C10), East (E1-E10) and West (W1-W10). While each card has the same horizontal format, the color scheme differs by region. The Central cards have a blue background, the East green and the West a deep shade of red. Color player photos are superimposed over the backgrounds. Each card has, "The Upper Deck Diamond Collection" as part of the background. The backs have a small photo and career highlights.

COMPLETE SET (30) 100.00 200.00
COMPLETE CENTRAL (10) 30.00 80.00
COMPLETE EAST (10) 15.00 40.00
COMPLETE WEST (10) 25.00 60.00
SER.1 STATED ODDS 1:18 HOBBY REGIONAL
C1 Jeff Bagwell 1.50 4.00
C2 Michael Jordan 15.00 40.00
C3 Barry Larkin 1.50 4.00
C4 Kirby Puckett 2.50 6.00
C5 Manny Ramirez 2.50 6.00
C6 Ryne Sandberg 4.00 10.00
C7 Ozzie Smith 4.00 10.00
C8 Frank Thomas 2.50 6.00
C9 Andy Van Slyke 1.50 4.00
C10 Robin Yount 2.50 6.00
E1 Roberto Alomar 1.50 4.00
E2 Roger Clemens 5.00 12.00
E3 Len Dykstra 1.00 2.50
E4 Cecil Fielder 1.00 2.50
E5 Cliff Floyd 1.00 2.50
E6 Dwight Gooden 1.00 2.50
E7 David Justice 1.00 2.50
E8 Don Mattingly 6.00 15.00
E9 Cal Ripken 8.00 20.00
E10 Gary Sheffield 1.00 2.50
W1 Barry Bonds 6.00 15.00
W2 Andres Galarraga 1.00 2.50
W3 Juan Gonzalez 1.00 2.50
W4 Ken Griffey Jr. 5.00 12.00
W5 Tony Gwynn 3.00 8.00
W6 Rickey Henderson 2.50 6.00
W7 Bo Jackson 2.50 6.00
W8 Mark McGwire 6.00 15.00
W9 Mike Piazza 5.00 12.00
W10 Tim Salmon 1.50 4.00

1994 Upper Deck Griffey Jumbos

Measuring 4 7/8" by 6 13/16", these four Griffey cards serve as checklists for first series Upper Deck issues. They were issued one per first series hobby foil box. Card fronts have a full color photo with a small Griffey hologram. The first three cards provide a numerical, alphabetical and team organized checklist for the basic set. The fourth card is a checklist of inserts. Each card was printed in different quantities with CL1 the most plentiful and CL4 the more scarce. The backs are numbered with a CL prefix.

COMPLETE SET (4) 4.00 10.00
COMMON GRIFFEY (CL1-CL4) 1.25 3.00
ONE PER SEALED SER.1 HOBBY FOIL BOX

1994 Upper Deck Mantle Heroes

Randomly inserted in second series packs at a rate of one in 35, this 10-card standard-size set looks at various moments from The Mick's career. Metallic fronts feature a vintage photo with the card title at the bottom. The backs contain career highlights with a small scrapbook like photo. The numbering (64-72) is a continuation from previous Heroes sets.

COMPLETE SET (10) 15.00 40.00
COMMON CARD (64-72/HDR) 4.00 10.00
SER.2 STATED ODDS 1:35

1994 Upper Deck Mantle's Long Shots

Randomly inserted in first series retail packs at a rate of one in 18, this 21-card silver foil standard-size set features top longball hitters as selected by Mickey Mantle. The cards are numbered on the back with a "MM" prefix and sequenced in alphabetical order. Two trade cards, were also random inserts and were redeemable (expiration: December 31, 1994) for either the basic silver foil set version (Silver Trade card) or the Electric Diamond version (blue Trade card).

COMPLETE SET (21) 12.50 30.00
SER.1 STATED ODDS 1:18 RETAIL
ONE SET VIA MAIL PER SILVER TRADE CARD
*ED: .5X TO 1.2X BASIC MANTLE LS
ONE ED SET VIA MAIL PER BLUE TRD.CARD
MANTLE TRADES: RANDOM IN SER.1 HOB
MM1 Jeff Bagwell .60 1.50
MM2 Albert Belle .40 1.00
MM3 Barry Bonds 2.50 6.00
MM4 Jose Canseco .60 1.50
MM5 Joe Carter .40 1.00
MM6 Carlos Delgado .60 1.50
MM7 Cecil Fielder .40 1.00
MM8 Cliff Floyd .40 1.00
MM9 Juan Gonzalez .40 1.00
MM10 Ken Griffey Jr. 2.00 5.00
MM11 David Justice .40 1.00
MM12 Fred McGriff .60 1.50
MM13 Mark McGwire 2.50 6.00
MM14 Dean Palmer .40 1.00
MM15 Mike Piazza 2.00 5.00
MM16 Manny Ramirez 1.00 2.50
MM17 Tim Salmon .60 1.50
MM18 Frank Thomas 1.00 2.50
MM19 Mo Vaughn .40 1.00
MM20 Matt Williams .40 1.00
MM21 Mickey Mantle 6.00 15.00
NNO M.Mantle Silver Trade 2.50 6.00
NNO M.Mantle Blue EDTrade 6.00 15.00

1994 Upper Deck Next Generation

Randomly inserted in second series retail packs at a rate of one in 20, this 18-card standard-size set spotlights young established stars and promising prospects. The set is sequenced in alphabetical order. A Next Generation Electric Diamond Trade Card and a Next Generation Trade Card were seeded randomly in second series hobby packs. Each card could be redeemed for that set. Expiration date for redemption was October 31, 1994.

COMPLETE SET (18) 40.00 100.00
SER.2 STATED ODDS 1:20 RETAIL
ONE SET VIA MAIL PER TRADE CARD
TRADES: RANDOM INSERTS IN SER.2 HOB
1 Roberto Alomar 1.25 3.00
2 Carlos Delgado 1.25 3.00
3 Cliff Floyd .75 2.00
4 Alex Gonzalez .40 1.00
5 Juan Gonzalez .75 2.00
6 Ken Griffey Jr. 4.00 10.00
7 Jeffrey Hammonds .40 1.00
8 Michael Jordan 6.00 15.00
9 David Justice .75 2.00
10 Ryan Klesko .75 2.00
11 Javier Lopez .75 2.00
12 Raul Mondesi .75 2.00
13 Mike Piazza 4.00 10.00
14 Kirby Puckett 2.00 5.00
15 Manny Ramirez 2.00 5.00
16 Alex Rodriguez 6.00 15.00
17 Tim Salmon 1.25 3.00
18 Gary Sheffield .75 2.00
NNO Expired NG Trade Card .40 1.00

1994 Upper Deck Next Generation Electric Diamond

COMPLETE SET (18) 60.00 120.00
*ELEC.DIAM: .5X TO 1.2X BASIC NEXT.GEN.
ONE ED SET VIA MAIL PER ED TRADE CARD
TRADES: RANDOM INSERTS IN SER.2 HOBBY
8 Michael Jordan 10.00 25.00
16 Alex Rodriguez 6.00 15.00

1994 Upper Deck All-Star Jumbos

This 48-card boxed set captures the photography of Walter Iooss Jr. Iooss shot 42 of the 49 cards in the set. The set included an order form for an album. The cards are oversized, measuring 3 1/2" by 5 1/4". The full-bleed color player photos are edged on one side by a green stripe carrying the player's name. A special green foil All-Star logo appears in one of the lower corners. One set per 40-box case uses gold foil in place of green. The horizontal back has a thick black stripe carrying a small color photo and Iooss' comments on the left, with a career summary and another closeup photo on the remainder of the back. The set closes with six cards commemorating historic events during the 125-year history of baseball (43-48). Some dealers believe that gold production was limited to 1,200 sets.

COMP.FACT SET (48) 6.00 15.00
1 Ken Griffey Jr. .75 2.00
2 Ruben Sierra .02 .10
Todd Van Poppel
3 Bryan Harvey .15 .40
Gary Sheffield
4 Gregg Jefferies .07 .20
Brian Jordan
5 Ryne Sandberg .30 .75
6 Matt Williams .10 .30
John Burkett
7 Darren Daulton .07 .20
John Kruk
8 Don Mattingly .40 1.00
Wade Boggs
9 Pat Listach .02 .10
Greg Vaughn
10 Tim Salmon .15 .40
Eduardo Perez
11 Fred McGriff .10 .30
Tom Glavine
12 Mo Vaughn .07 .20
Andre Dawson
13 Brian McRae .02 .10
Kevin Appier
14 Kirby Puckett .40 1.00
Kent Hrbek
15 Cal Ripken .75 2.00
16 Roberto Alomar .15 .40
Paul Molitor
17 Tony Gwynn .40 1.00
Phil Plantier
18 Greg Maddux .50 1.25
Steve Avery
19 Mike Mussina .15 .40
Chris Hoiles
20 Randy Johnson .15 .40
21 Roger Clemens .40 1.00
Aaron Sele
22 Will Clark .15 .40
Dean Palmer
23 Cecil Fielder .07 .20
Travis Fryman
24 John Olerud .07 .20
Joe Carter
25 Juan Gonzalez .15 .40
26 Jose Rijo .10 .30
Barry Larkin
27 Andy Van Slyke .07 .20
Jeff King
28 Larry Walker .07 .20
Marquis Grissom
29 Kenny Lofton .07 .20
Albert Belle
30 Mark Grace .50 1.25
Sammy Sosa
31 Mike Piazza .60 1.50
32 Ramon Martinez .20 .50
Pedro Martinez
Orel Hershiser
33 David Justice .15 .40
Terry Pendleton
34 Ivan Rodriguez .20 .50
Jose Canseco
35 Barry Bonds .40 1.00
36 Jeff Bagwell .30 .75
Craig Biggio
37 Jay Bell .02 .10
Orlando Merced
38 Jeff Kent .07 .20
Dwight Gooden
39 Andres Galarraga .15 .40
Charlie Hayes
40 Frank Thomas .30 .75
41 Bobby Bonilla .02 .10
42 Jack McDowell .02 .10
Tim Raines
43 1869 Red Stockings .02 .10
44 Ty Cobb 25th Ann. .30 .75
45 Babe Ruth 50th Ann. .75 2.00
46 Mickey Mantle 75th Ann. .75 2.00
47 Reggie Jackson 125th Ann. .30 .75
48 Ken Griffey Jr. 125th Ann. .60 1.50
P48 Ken Griffey Jr. Promo 2.50 6.00

1994 Upper Deck All-Time Heroes

This set consists of 225 standard-size cards. According to Upper Deck, production was limited to 4,015 numbered cases. Special subsets featured are Off The Wire (1-18), All-Time Heroes (101-125), Diamond Legends (151-177), and Heroes of Baseball (208-224). Mickey Mantle and three other superstars (Reggie Jackson, Tom Seaver, and George Brett) each autographed 1,000 cards that were randomly inserted into packs. (Nolan Ryan had been expected to sign cards for this product but did not. Instead, Brett signed an additional 1,000 cards). According to Upper Deck, a signed card would be found in one of every 385 packs. A Reggie Jackson Promo card was distributed to dealers and hobby media to preview the set.

COMPLETE SET (225) 8.00 20.00
1 Ted Williams OW .20 .50
2 Johnny Vander Meer OW .02 .10
3 Lou Brock OW .10 .30
4 Lou Gehrig OW .20 .50
5 Hank Aaron OW .20 .50
6 Tommie Agee OW .02 .10
7 Mickey Mantle OW .40 1.00
8 Bill Mazeroski OW .07 .20
9 Reggie Jackson OW .10 .30
10 W.Mays .40 1.00
M.Mantle OW
11 Roy Campanella OW .07 .20
12 Harvey Haddix OW .02 .10
13 Jimmy Piersall OW .02 .10
14 Enos Slaughter OW .02 .10
15 Nolan Ryan OW .30 .75
16 Bobby Thomson OW .02 .10
17 Willie Mays OW .20 .50
18 Bucky Dent OW .02 .10
19 Joe Garagiola .07 .20
20 George Brett .50 1.25
21 Cecil Cooper .07 .20
22 Ray Boone .02 .10
23 King Kelly .07 .20
24 Willie Mays .40 1.00
25 Napoleon Lajoie .10 .30
26 Gil McDougald .07 .20
27 Nelson Briles .02 .10
28 Bucky Dent .07 .20
29 Manny Sanguillen .02 .10
30 Ty Cobb .30 .75
31 Jim Grant .02 .10
32 Del Ennis .02 .10
33 Ron Hunt .02 .10
34 Nolan Ryan .60 1.50
35 Christy Mathewson .10 .30
36 Robin Roberts .07 .20
37 Frank Crosetti .02 .10
38 Johnny Vander Meer .02 .10
39 Virgil Trucks .02 .10
40 Lou Gehrig .40 1.00
41 Luke Appling .07 .20
42 Rico Petrocelli .02 .10
43 Harry Walker .02 .10
44 Reggie Jackson .10 .30
45 Mel Ott .10 .30
46 Phil Cavarretta .07 .20
47 Larry Doby .07 .20
48 Johnny Mize .07 .20
49 Ralph Kiner .10 .30
50 Ted Williams .40 1.00
51 Bobby Thomson .07 .20
52 Joe Black .07 .20
53 Monte Irvin .07 .20
54 Bill Virdon .07 .20
55 Honus Wagner .20 .50
56 Herb Score .07 .20
57 Jerry Coleman .02 .10
58 Jimmie Foxx .10 .30
59 Roy Face .02 .10
60 Babe Ruth .60 1.50
61 Jimmy Piersall .07 .20
62 Ed Charles .02 .10
63 Johnny Podres .07 .20
64 Charlie Neal .02 .10
65 Bill White .07 .20
66 Bill Skowron .10 .30
67 Al Rosen .07 .20
68 Eddie Lopat .02 .10
69 Bud Harrelson .07 .20
70 Steve Carlton .07 .20
71 Vida Blue .02 .10
72 Don Newcombe .07 .20
73 Al Bumbry .02 .10

74 Bill Madlock .07 .20
75 Hank Aaron CL .10 .30
76 Bill Mazeroski .10 .30
77 Ron Cey .07 .20
78 Tommy John .07 .20
79 Lou Brock .10 .30
80 Walter Johnson .20 .50
81 Harvey Haddix .07 .20
82 Al Oliver .07 .20
83 Johnny Logan .07 .20
84 Dave Dravecky .07 .20
85 Tony Oliva .07 .20
86 Dave Kingman .07 .20
87 Luis Tiant .07 .20
88 Sal Bando .07 .20
89 Cesar Cedeno .07 .20
90 Warren Spahn .10 .30
91 Mickey Lolich .02 .10
92 Lew Burdette .07 .20
93 Hank Bauer .07 .20
94 Marv Throneberry .02 .10
95 Willie Stargell .10 .30
96 George Kell .07 .20
97 Ferguson Jenkins .07 .20
98 Al Kaline .20 .50
99 Billy Martin .10 .30
100 Mickey Mantle .75 2.00
101 1869 Red Stockings ATH .02 .10
102 King Kelly ATH .02 .10
103 Nap Lajoie ATH .07 .20
104 Christy Mathewson ATH .07 .20
105 Cy Young ATH .07 .20
106 Ty Cobb ATH .20 .50
107 Reggie Jackson CL .07 .20
108 Rogers Hornsby ATH .07 .20
109 Walter Johnson ATH .07 .20
110 Babe Ruth ATH .30 .75
111 Hack Wilson ATH .07 .20
112 Lou Gehrig ATH .20 .50
113 Ted Williams ATH .20 .50
114 Yogi Berra ATH .10 .30
115 Bobby Thomson ATH .02 .10
116 Mickey Mantle ATH .40 1.00
117 Willie Mays ATH .20 .50
118 Bill Mazeroski ATH .07 .20
119 Bob Gibson ATH .07 .20
120 1969 Miracle Mets ATH .20 .50
121 Hank Aaron ATH .20 .50
122 Reggie Jackson ATH .10 .30
123 George Brett ATH .25 .60
124 Steve Carlton ATH .02 .10
125 Nolan Ryan ATH .30 .75
126 Frank Thomas .07 .20
127 Sam McDowell .07 .20
128 Jim Lonborg .02 .10
129 Bert Campaneris .02 .10
130 Bob Gibson .10 .30
131 Bobby Richardson .07 .20
132 Bobby Grich .07 .20
133 Billy Pierce .07 .20
134 Enos Slaughter .07 .20
135 Honus Wagner CL .07 .20
136 Orlando Cepeda .07 .20
137 Rennie Stennett .02 .10
138 Gene Alley .02 .10
139 Manny Mota .02 .10
140 Rogers Hornsby .10 .30
141 Joe Charboneau .02 .10
142 Rick Ferrell .07 .20
143 Toby Harrah .02 .10
144 Hank Aaron .40 1.00
145 Yogi Berra .20 .50
146 Whitey Ford .10 .30
147 Roy Campanella .20 .50
148 Graig Nettles .07 .20
149 Bobby Brown .02 .10
150 Willie Mays CL .10 .30
151 Cy Young LGD .07 .20
152 Walter Johnson LGD .07 .20
153 Christy Mathewson LGD .07 .20
154 Warren Spahn LGD .10 .30
155 Steve Carlton LGD .02 .10
156 Bob Gibson LGD .07 .20
157 Whitey Ford LGD .07 .20
158 Yogi Berra LGD .10 .30
159 Roy Campanella LGD .07 .20
160 Lou Gehrig LGD .20 .50
161 Johnny Mize LGD .02 .10
162 Rogers Hornsby LGD .07 .20
163 Honus Wagner LGD .07 .20
164 Hank Aaron LGD .20 .50
165 Babe Ruth LGD .30 .75
166 Willie Mays LGD .20 .50
167 Reggie Jackson LGD .07 .20
168 Mickey Mantle LGD .40 1.00
169 Jimmie Foxx LGD .07 .20
170 Ted Williams LGD .20 .50
171 Mel Ott LGD .07 .20
172 Willie Stargell LGD .07 .20
173 Al Kaline LGD .07 .20
174 Ty Cobb LGD .20 .50
175 Nap Lajoie LGD .07 .20
176 Lou Brock LGD .10 .30
177 Tom Seaver LGD .07 .20
178 Mark Fidrych .07 .20
179 Don Baylor .07 .20
180 Tom Seaver .10 .30
181 Jerry Grote .02 .10
182 George Foster .02 .10
183 Buddy Bell .07 .20
184 Ralph Garr .07 .20
185 Steve Garvey .07 .20
186 Joe Torre .07 .20
187 Carl Erskine .10 .30
188 Tommy Davis .02 .10
189 Bill Buckner .07 .20
190 Hack Wilson .10 .30
191 Steve Blass .02 .10
192 Ken Brett .02 .10
193 Lee May .02 .10
194 Bob Horner .07 .20
195 Boog Powell .07 .20
196 Darrell Evans .07 .20
197 Paul Blair .07 .20
198 Johnny Callison .07 .20
199 Jimmie Reese .02 .10
200 Cy Young .20 .50
201 Ron Santo .07 .20
202 Rico Carty .02 .10
203 Ron Necciai .02 .10
204 Lou Boudreau .07 .20
205 Minnie Minoso .07 .20
206 Eddie Yost .02 .10
207 Tommie Agee .07 .20
208 Dave Kingman HB .02 .10
209 Tony Oliva HB .07 .20
210 Reggie Jackson HB .10 .30
211 Paul Blair HB .02 .10
212 Ferguson Jenkins HB .02 .10
213 Steve Garvey HB .07 .20
214 Bert Campaneris HB .02 .10
215 Orlando Cepeda HB .07 .20
216 Bill Madlock HB .02 .10
217 Rennie Stennett HB .02 .10
218 Frank Thomas HB .02 .10
219 Bob Gibson HB .07 .20
220 Lou Brock HB .10 .30
221 Rico Carty HB .02 .10
222 Mickey Mantle HB .40 1.00
223 Robin Roberts HB .07 .20
224 Manny Sanguillen HB .02 .10
225 Mickey Mantle CL .20 .50
P44 Reggie Jackson Promo 1.25 3.00

1994 Upper Deck All-Time Heroes 125th Anniversary

COMPLETE SET (225) 20.00 50.00
*STARS: 1.5X TO 4X BASIC CARDS
ONE PER PACK

1994 Upper Deck All-Time Heroes 1954 Archives

Measuring the standard-size, these three chase cards were randomly inserted in the foil packs at a ratio of one card per 30 ten-card foil packs. Cards numbered 1 and 250 of Ted Williams, which are similar in design to the two that were originally issued by Topps in 1954, were not included in that company's 1954 Archives edition due to the terms of his contract with Upper Deck. Like Williams, Mickey Mantle had an exclusive agreement with Upper Deck that precluded his appearance in the 1954 Topps Archives set. Mantle didn't even appear in the original 1954 Topps set due to his then exclusive contract with Bowman. This "card that never was" is similar to the original 1954 set design.

STATED ODDS 1:30
1 Ted Williams 12.00 30.00
250 Ted Williams 12.00 30.00
259 Mickey Mantle 15.00 40.00

1994 Upper Deck All-Time Heroes Autographs

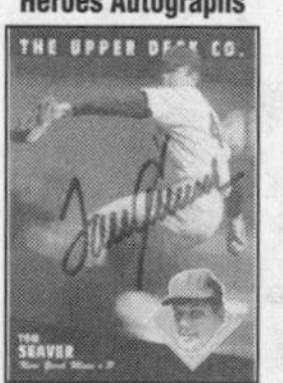

These four autograph cards were inserted one every 385 packs into the All-Time Heroes packs. Three players signed 1,000 cards while George Brett signed 2,000 cards since Nolan Ryan did not sign the 1,000 cards he had been expected to sign for this product. Each card came with a certification of authenticity on the back and could be registered with Upper Deck upon receipt.

STATED ODDS 1:385
PRINT RUNS B/WN 1000-2000 COPIES PER
CARDS ARE NOT SERIAL-NUMBERED
1 George Brett/2000 * 20.00 50.00
2 Reggie Jackson/1000 * 25.00 60.00
3 Mickey Mantle/1000 * 400.00 800.00
4 Tom Seaver/1000 * 20.00 50.00

1994 Upper Deck All-Time Heroes Next In Line

Capturing up and coming Minor League stars, this 20-card standard-size set was randomly inserted at a ratio of one in every 39 packs. Production was limited to 2,500 of each card. The fronts have a metallic finish with a color player cutout on the left, silhouetted by a blue-foil line. A black border on the right features the words "Next In Line," a color player headshot, and the player's name. The backs carry another color player photo, player information, and 1993 statistics. The cards are numbered on the back as "X of 20".

COMPLETE SET (20) 20.00 50.00
STATED ODDS 1:39
1 Mike Bell .75 2.00
2 Alan Benes .75 2.00
3 D.J. Boston .75 2.00
4 Johnny Damon 2.00 5.00
5 Brad Fullmer 1.25 3.00
6 LaTroy Hawkins 1.25 3.00
7 Derek Jeter 40.00 100.00
8 Daron Kirkreit .75 2.00
9 Trot Nixon 2.00 5.00
10 Alex Ochoa .75 2.00
11 Kirk Presley .75 2.00
12 Jose Silva .75 2.00
13 Terrell Wade .75 2.00
14 Billy Wagner 2.00 5.00
15 Glenn Williams .75 2.00
16 Preston Wilson 1.25 3.00
17 Wayne Gomes .75 2.00
18 Ben Grieve 1.25 3.00
19 Dustin Hermanson .75 2.00
20 Paul Wilson .75 2.00

1994 Upper Deck: The American Epic

This 80-card boxed standard-size set recounts the story behind the PBS documentary "Baseball: The American Epic," produced by Ken Burns and sponsored by GM. The suggested retail price for the set, including the storage container, was 19.95. It was available from leading retail stores, the QVC television network, direct mail solicitation, and the Upper Deck Authenticated catalog. Like the documentary, the set is divided into "nine innings" and arranged chronologically as follows: 1st Inning (the 19th century [1-10], 2nd Inning (the 1900s [11-20], 3rd Inning (the 1910s [21-29], 4th Inning (the 1920s [30-39], 5th Inning (the 1930s [40-49], 6th Inning (the 1940s [50-56], 7th Inning (the 1950s [57-64], 8th Inning (the 1960s [65-71], and 9th Inning (1970-present [72-80]. Three insert cards were included with the set. A Michael Jordan card was available for direct mail customers, a Babe Ruth card for retail customers and a Mickey Mantle card for QVC customers. These cards are horizontal, full-bleed cards with black and white player photos. The backs are black and white with player information. The set price applies to either of the three versions and includes either of the three inserts. Recently, some autographs of Mickey Mantle from this set have surfaced on one of the home shopping channels. Since no information on how these cards were issued, or whether they were actually inserted into packs is available we are not pricing or listing this card at this point. Any further information on this card is appreciated.

COMP.FACT SET (81) 6.00 15.00
1 Our Game .01 .05
2 Alexander Cartwright .02 .10
3 Henry Chadwick .01 .05
4 The Fair Sex .01 .05
5 Harry Wright .01 .05
6 Albert Goodwill Spalding .02 .10
7 Cap Anson .05 .15
8 Moses Fleetwood Walker/1884 .02 .10
9 King Kelly .02 .10
10 John Montgomery Ward/1890 .02 .10
11 Ty Cobb .50 1.25
12 John McGraw .05 .15
13 Rube Waddell .02 .10
14 Christy Mathewson .07 .20
15 Walter Johnson .20 .50
16 Alta Weiss .01 .05
17 Fred Merkle .01 .05
18 Take Me Out To The Ballgame .01 .05
19 John Henry(Pop) Lloyd .02 .10
20 Honus Wagner .30 .75
21 Woodrow Wilson .05 .15
22 Nap Lajoie .02 .10
23 Addie Joss .02 .10
24 Joe Wood .05 .15
25 Royal Rooters .01 .05
26 Ebbets Field .01 .05
27 Johnny Evers .02 .10
28 World War I .01 .05
29 Joe Jackson .40 1.00
30 Babe Ruth 1.25 3.00
31 George(Rube) Foster .01 .05
32 Ray Chapman .01 .05
33 Kenesaw M. Landis .01 .05
34 Yankee Stadium .01 .05
35 Rogers Hornsby .07 .20
36 Warren G. Harding .01 .05
37 Lou Gehrig .75 2.00
38 Grover C. Alexander .02 .10
39 House of David .01 .05
40 Satchel Paige .30 .75
41 Lefty Grove .02 .10
42 Jimmie Foxx .05 .15
43 Connie Mack .05 .15
44 Josh Gibson .07 .20
45 Dizzy Dean .02 .10
46 Carl Hubbell .02 .10
47 Franklin D. Roosevelt .05 .15
48 Bob Feller .02 .10
49 Cool Papa Bell .02 .10
50 Jackie Robinson .75 2.00
51 Ted Williams .75 2.00
52 Sym-phony Band .01 .05
53 Annabel Lee .01 .05
54 Hank Greenberg .02 .10
55 Branch Rickey .02 .10
56 Harry S. Truman .07 .20
57 Casey Stengel .07 .20
58 Bobby Thomson .02 .10
59 Dwight D. Eisenhower .05 .15
60 Mario Cuomo .02 .10
61 Buck O'Neil .02 .10
62 Yogi Berra .20 .50
63 Mickey Mantle 1.25 3.00
64 Don Larsen .02 .10
65 John F. Kennedy .60 1.50
66 Bill Mazeroski .02 .10
67 Roger Maris .07 .20
68 Frank Robinson .02 .10
69 Bob Gibson .02 .10
70 Tom Seaver/1969 .20 .50
71 Curt Flood .01 .05
72 Roberto Clemente .75 2.00
73 Luis Tiant .01 .05
74 Marvin Miller .01 .05
75 Reggie Jackson .20 .50
76 Willie(Pops) Stargell .02 .10
77 Pete Rose .20 .50
78 Bill Clinton .40 1.00
79 Nolan Ryan 1.00 2.50
80 George Brett .07 .20
BC1 Mickey Mantle 2.00 5.00
Home shopping insert
BC2 Michael Jordan 2.00 5.00
Direct mail insert
BC3 Babe Ruth 2.00 5.00
Retail insert

1994 Upper Deck: The American Epic GM

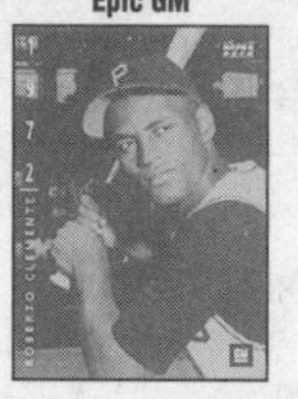

This nine-card set recounts part of the story behind the PBS documentary "Baseball: The American Epic," produced by Ken Burns and sponsored by GM. A GM Merchandise and Memorabilia Catalog was based on the American Epic series and available at GM dealers. The catalog included an offer for this nine-card set for 1.00. The GM logo appears in the lower right corner.

COMPLETE SET (9) 1.50 4.00
1 Hank Aaron .20 .50
2 Roberto Clemente .30 .75
3 Ty Cobb .20 .50
4 Hank Greenberg .02 .10
5 Mickey Mantle .50 1.25
6 Satchel Paige .08 .25
7 Jackie Robinson .30 .75
8 Babe Ruth .50 1.25
9 Ted Williams .30 .75

1994 Upper Deck: The American Epic Little Debbies

This 15-card set recounts part of the story behind the PBS documentary "Baseball: The American Epic," produced by Ken Burns. The cards could be ordered through an on-pack offer on Little Debbies cakes for 3.99. The Little Debbies logo appears on the bottom of the checklist card.

COMPLETE SET (15) 4.00 10.00
LD1 Our Game CL .02 .10
LD2 Alexander Cartwright .02 .10
LD3 King Kelly .02 .10
LD4 John McGraw .07 .20
LD5 Christy Mathewson .07 .20
LD6 Walter Johnson .10 .30
LD7 Ted Williams .60 1.50
LD8 Annabel Lee .02 .10
LD9 Jackie Robinson .40 1.00
LD10 Bobby Thomson .07 .20
LD11 Buck O'Neil .02 .10
LD12 Mickey Mantle .60 1.50
LD13 Bob Gibson .10 .30
LD14 Curt Flood .02 .10
LD15 Reggie Jackson .15 .40

1994 Upper Deck Commemorative Cards

1 1994 Launch Tour/2000 2.00 5.00
Wayne Gretzky
Reggie Jackson
Michael Jordan
Joe Montana

1994 Upper Deck Mantle Phone Cards

Upper Deck in conjunction with Global Telecommunication Solutions produced this set of 10 phone cards to honor Mickey Mantle, the greatest switch-hitter in baseball history. The set was issued in two five-card sets: series one in early October, and series two later that year. Each five-card set retailed for $59.95. Chronicling his career from 1951 until his 1974 Hall of Fame Induction, the set is a replica of the "Baseball Heroes" insert cards featured in the 1994 Upper Deck baseball series 2. Just 5,000 sets of series 1 were produced, with each card including a bonus one-minute Mantle highlight replay moment. As an added bonus, 500 1869 Cincinnati Red Stockings phone cards were randomly inserted in series two sets, while Upper Deck distributed its allotment to the first 450 orders received from hobby dealers. Only 2,000 Red Stocking cards were produced. The phone cards are unnumbered and checklisted below in chronological order.

COMPLETE SET (11) 25.00 60.00
COMMON CARD (1-10) 3.20 8.00
NNO0 1869 Cincinnati 4.00 10.00
Red Stockings

1994 Upper Deck Sheets

These ten 8 1/2" by 11" sheets were produced by Upper Deck. They were issued to commemorate various special events sponsored by Upper Deck. We have listed the production quantities when known.

COMPLETE SET (10) 15.00 40.00
1 Heroes of Baseball Day .75 2.00
The Ballpark in Arlington#
2 Tribute to the 1964 3.00 8.00
Season
June 4& 1994 (50&000)
3 Milwaukee Brewers .75 2.00
Silver Anniversary
June 25, 19
4 Hollywood Softball Game 2.50 6.00
June 26
5 Heroes of Baseball 2.50 6.00
All-Star Game
July 11& 1994 (
6 25th Anniversary of the
1969 Season and the 3.00 8.00
Mira
7 All-Time Homerun Kings 3.00 8.00
July 23
8 Baseball 125th Anniversary .75 2.00
August 6, 1994 (40,000
9 All Star Fanfest .75 2.00
Autograph Sheet/(Drawing of
ba
10 Upper Deck Authenticated .75 2.00
Triple Crown Winners/2,
11 UDA Ted Williams Career
Commemorative .75 2.00

1994 Upper Deck Top Ten Promo

This one-card Ken Griffey promo was issued to promote the never issued 1994 Upper Deck Top Ten set. The set which was supposed to honor the best players in baseball was never issued by Upper Deck due to the baseball strike in 1994.

P6 Ken Griffey Jr. 2.50 6.00

1995 Upper Deck

The 1995 Upper Deck baseball set was issued in two series of 225 cards for a total of 450. The cards were distributed in 12-card packs (36 per box) with a suggested retail price of $1.99. Subsets include Top Prospect (1-15, 251-265), 90's Midpoint (101-110), Star Rookie (211-240), and Diamond Debuts (241-250). Rookie Cards in this set include Hideo Nomo. Five randomly inserted Trade Cards were each redeemable for nine updated cards of new rookies or players who changed teams, comprising a 45-card Trade Redemption set. The Trade cards expired Feb 1, 1996. Autographed jumbo cards (Roger Clemens for series one, Alex Rodriguez for either series) were available through a wrapper redemption offer.

COMP.MASTER SET (495) 60.00 120.00
COMPLETE SET (450) 20.00 50.00
COMPLETE SERIES 1 (225) 10.00 25.00
COMPLETE SERIES 2 (225) 10.00 25.00
COMMON CARD (1-450) .05 .15
COMP.TRADE SET (45) 30.00 60.00
COMMON TRADE (451T-495T) .40 1.00
NINE TRADE CARDS PER TRADE EXCH.CARD
SUBSET CARDS HALF VALUE OF BASE CARDS
JUMBO AUS WERE REDEEMED W/WRAPPERS
1 Ruben Rivera .05 .15
2 Bill Pulsipher .05 .15
3 Ben Grieve .05 .15
4 Curtis Goodwin .05 .15
5 Damon Hollins .05 .15
6 Todd Greene .05 .15
7 Glenn Williams .05 .15
8 Bret Wagner .05 .15
9 Karim Garcia RC .05 .15
10 Nomar Garciaparra .75 2.00
11 Raul Casanova RC .05 .15
12 Matt Smith .05 .15
13 Paul Wilson .05 .15
14 Jason Isringhausen .10 .30
15 Reid Ryan .10 .30
16 Lee Smith .10 .30
17 Chili Davis .10 .30
18 Brian Anderson .05 .15
19 Gary DiSarcina .05 .15
20 Bo Jackson .30 .75
21 Chuck Finley .10 .30
22 Darryl Kile .10 .30
23 Shane Reynolds .05 .15
24 Tony Eusebio .05 .15
25 Craig Biggio .20 .50
26 Doug Drabek .05 .15
27 Brian L.Hunter .05 .15
28 James Mouton .05 .15
29 Geronimo Berroa .05 .15
30 Rickey Henderson .30 .75
31 Steve Karsay .05 .15
32 Steve Ontiveros .05 .15
33 Ernie Young .05 .15
34 Dennis Eckersley .10 .30
35 Mark McGwire .75 2.00
36 Dave Stewart .10 .30
37 Pat Hentgen .05 .15
38 Carlos Delgado .10 .30
39 Joe Carter .10 .30
40 Roberto Alomar .20 .50
41 John Olerud .10 .30
42 Devon White .10 .30
43 Roberto Kelly .05 .15
44 Jeff Blauser .05 .15
45 Fred McGriff .20 .50
46 Tom Glavine .20 .50
47 Mike Kelly .05 .15
48 Javier Lopez .10 .30
49 Greg Maddux .50 1.25
50 Matt Mieske .05 .15
51 Troy O'Leary .05 .15
52 Jeff Cirillo .05 .15
53 Cal Eldred .05 .15
54 Pat Listach .05 .15
55 Jose Valentin .05 .15
56 John Mabry .05 .15
57 Bob Tewksbury .05 .15
58 Brian Jordan .10 .30
59 Gregg Jefferies .05 .15
60 Ozzie Smith .50 1.25
61 Geronimo Pena .05 .15
62 Mark Whiten .05 .15
63 Rey Sanchez .05 .15
64 Willie Banks .05 .15
65 Mark Grace .20 .50
66 Randy Myers .05 .15
67 Steve Trachsel .05 .15
68 Derrick May .05 .15
69 Brett Butler .10 .30
70 Eric Karros .10 .30
71 Tim Wallach .05 .15
72 Delino DeShields .05 .15
73 Darren Dreifort .05 .15
74 Orel Hershiser .10 .30
75 Billy Ashley .05 .15
76 Sean Berry .05 .15
77 Ken Hill .05 .15
78 John Wetteland .10 .30
79 Moises Alou .10 .30
80 Cliff Floyd .10 .30
81 Marquis Grissom .10 .30
82 Larry Walker .10 .30
83 Rondell White .10 .30
84 William VanLandingham .05 .15
85 Matt Williams .10 .30
86 Rod Beck .05 .15
87 Darren Lewis .05 .15
88 Robby Thompson .05 .15
89 Darryl Strawberry .10 .30
90 Kenny Lofton .10 .30
91 Charles Nagy .05 .15
92 Sandy Alomar Jr. .05 .15
93 Mark Clark .05 .15
94 Dennis Martinez .10 .30
95 Dave Winfield .10 .30
96 Jim Thome .20 .50
97 Manny Ramirez .20 .50
98 Goose Gossage .10 .30
99 Tino Martinez .20 .50
100 Ken Griffey Jr. .60 1.50
101 Greg Maddux ANA .30 .75
102 Randy Johnson ANA .20 .50
103 Barry Bonds ANA .40 1.00
104 Juan Gonzalez ANA .05 .15
105 Frank Thomas ANA .20 .50
106 Matt Williams ANA .05 .15
107 Paul Molitor ANA .05 .15
108 Fred McGriff ANA .10 .30
109 Carlos Baerga ANA .05 .15
110 Ken Griffey Jr. ANA .40 1.00
111 Reggie Jefferson .05 .15
112 Randy Johnson .30 .75
113 Marc Newfield .05 .15
114 Robb Nen .10 .30
115 Jeff Conine .10 .30
116 Kurt Abbott .05 .15
117 Charlie Hough .10 .30
118 Dave Weathers .05 .15
119 Juan Castillo .05 .15
120 Bret Saberhagen .10 .30
121 Rico Brogna .05 .15
122 John Franco .10 .30
123 Todd Hundley .05 .15
124 Jason Jacome .05 .15
125 Bobby Jones .05 .15
126 Bret Barberie .05 .15
127 Ben McDonald .05 .15
128 Harold Baines .10 .30
129 Jeffrey Hammonds .05 .15
130 Mike Mussina .20 .50
131 Chris Hoiles .05 .15
132 Brady Anderson .10 .30
133 Eddie Williams .05 .15
134 Andy Benes .05 .15
135 Tony Gwynn .40 1.00
136 Bip Roberts .05 .15
137 Joey Hamilton .05 .15
138 Luis Lopez .05 .15
139 Ray McDavid .05 .15
140 Lenny Dykstra .10 .30
141 Mariano Duncan .05 .15
142 Fernando Valenzuela .10 .30
143 Bobby Munoz .05 .15
144 Kevin Stocker .05 .15
145 John Kruk .10 .30
146 Jon Lieber .05 .15
147 Zane Smith .05 .15
148 Steve Cooke .05 .15
149 Andy Van Slyke .20 .50
150 Jay Bell .10 .30
151 Carlos Garcia .05 .15
152 John Dettmer .05 .15
153 Darren Oliver .05 .15
154 Dean Palmer .10 .30
155 Otis Nixon .05 .15
156 Rusty Greer .10 .30
157 Rick Helling .05 .15
158 Jose Canseco .20 .50
159 Roger Clemens .60 1.50
160 Andre Dawson .10 .30
161 Mo Vaughn .10 .30
162 Aaron Sele .05 .15
163 John Valentin .05 .15
164 Brian R. Hunter .05 .15
165 Bret Boone .10 .30
166 Hector Carrasco .05 .15
167 Pete Schourek .05 .15
168 Willie Greene .05 .15
169 Kevin Mitchell .05 .15
170 Deion Sanders .20 .50
171 John Roper .05 .15
172 Charlie Hayes .05 .15
173 David Nied .05 .15
174 Ellis Burks .10 .30
175 Dante Bichette .10 .30
176 Marvin Freeman .05 .15
177 Eric Young .05 .15
178 David Cone .10 .30
179 Greg Gagne .05 .15
180 Bob Hamelin .05 .15
181 Wally Joyner .10 .30
182 Jeff Montgomery .05 .15
183 Jose Lind .05 .15
184 Chris Gomez .05 .15
185 Travis Fryman .10 .30
186 Kirk Gibson .10 .30
187 Mike Moore .05 .15
188 Lou Whitaker .10 .30
189 Sean Bergman .05 .15

190 Shane Mack .05 .15
191 Rick Aguilera .05 .15
192 Denny Hocking .05 .15
193 Chuck Knoblauch .10 .30
194 Kevin Tapani .05 .15
195 Kent Hrbek .10 .30
196 Ozzie Guillen .10 .30
197 Wilson Alvarez .05 .15
198 Tim Raines .10 .30
199 Scott Ruffcorn .05 .15
200 Michael Jordan 1.00 2.50
201 Robin Ventura .10 .30
202 Jason Bere .05 .15
203 Darrin Jackson .05 .15
204 Russ Davis .05 .15
205 Jimmy Key .10 .30
206 Jack McDowell .05 .15
207 Jim Abbott .20 .50
208 Paul O'Neill .20 .50
209 Bernie Williams .20 .50
210 Don Mattingly .75 2.00
211 Orlando Miller .05 .15
212 Alex Gonzalez .05 .15
213 Terrell Wade .05 .15
214 Jose Oliva .05 .15
215 Alex Rodriguez .75 2.00
216 Garret Anderson .10 .30
217 Alan Benes .05 .15
218 Armando Benitez .05 .15
219 Dustin Hermanson .05 .15
220 Charles Johnson .10 .30
221 Julian Tavarez .05 .15
222 Jason Giambi .20 .50
223 LaTroy Hawkins .05 .15
224 Todd Hollandsworth .05 .15
225 Derek Jeter .75 2.00
226 Hideo Nomo RC 1.00 2.50
227 Tony Clark .05 .15
228 Roger Cedeno .05 .15
229 Scott Stahoviak .05 .15
230 Michael Tucker .05 .15
231 Joe Rosselli .05 .15
232 Antonio Osuna .05 .15
233 Bob Higginson RC .30 .75
234 Mark Grudzielanek RC .30 .75
235 Ray Durham .10 .30
236 Frank Rodriguez .05 .15
237 Quilvio Veras .05 .15
238 Darren Bragg .05 .15
239 Ugueth Urbina .05 .15
240 Jason Bates .05 .15
241 David Bell .05 .15
242 Ron Villone .05 .15
243 Joe Randa .10 .30
244 Carlos Perez RC .15 .40
245 Brad Clontz .05 .15
246 Steve Rodriguez .05 .15
247 Joe Vitiello .05 .15
248 Ozzie Timmons .05 .15
249 Rudy Pemberton .05 .15
250 Marty Cordova .05 .15
251 Tony Graffanino .05 .15
252 Mark Johnson RC .15 .40
253 Tomas Perez RC .05 .15
254 Jimmy Hurst .05 .15
255 Edgardo Alfonzo .05 .15
256 Jose Malave .05 .15
257 Brad Radke RC .30 .75
258 Jon Nunnally .05 .15
259 Dilson Torres RC .05 .15
260 Esteban Loaiza .05 .15
261 Freddy Adrian Garcia RC .05 .15
262 Don Wengert .05 .15
263 Robert Person RC .15 .40
264 Tim Unroe RC .05 .15
265 Juan Acevedo RC .05 .15
266 Eduardo Perez .05 .15
267 Tony Phillips .05 .15
268 Jim Edmonds .20 .50
269 Jorge Fabregas .05 .15
270 Tim Salmon .20 .50
271 Mark Langston .05 .15
272 J.T. Snow .10 .30
273 Phil Plantier .05 .15
274 Derek Bell .05 .15
275 Jeff Bagwell .20 .50
276 Luis Gonzalez .10 .30
277 John Hudek .05 .15
278 Todd Stottlemyre .05 .15
279 Mark Acre .05 .15
280 Ruben Sierra .10 .30
281 Mike Bordick .05 .15
282 Ron Darling .05 .15
283 Brent Gates .05 .15
284 Todd Van Poppel .05 .15
285 Paul Molitor .10 .30
286 Ed Sprague .05 .15
287 Juan Guzman .05 .15
288 David Cone .10 .30
289 Shawn Green .10 .30
290 Marquis Grissom .10 .30
291 Kent Mercker .05 .15
292 Steve Avery .05 .15
293 Chipper Jones .30 .75
294 John Smoltz .20 .50
295 David Justice .10 .30
296 Ryan Klesko .10 .30
297 Joe Oliver .05 .15
298 Ricky Bones .05 .15
299 John Jaha .05 .15
300 Greg Vaughn .05 .15
301 Dave Nilsson .05 .15
302 Kevin Seitzer .05 .15
303 Bernard Gilkey .05 .15
304 Allen Battle .05 .15
305 Ray Lankford .10 .30
306 Tom Pagnozzi .05 .15
307 Allen Watson .05 .15
308 Danny Jackson .05 .15
309 Ken Hill .05 .15
310 Todd Zeile .05 .15
311 Kevin Roberson .05 .15
312 Steve Buechele .05 .15
313 Rick Wilkins .05 .15
314 Kevin Foster .05 .15
315 Sammy Sosa .30 .75
316 Howard Johnson .05 .15
317 Greg Hansell .05 .15
318 Pedro Astacio .05 .15
319 Rafael Bournigal .05 .15
320 Mike Piazza .50 1.25
321 Ramon Martinez .05 .15
322 Raul Mondesi .10 .30
323 Ismael Valdes .05 .15
324 Wil Cordero .05 .15
325 Tony Tarasco .05 .15
326 Roberto Kelly .05 .15
327 Jeff Fassero .05 .15
328 Mike Lansing .05 .15
329 Pedro Martinez .20 .50
330 Kirk Rueter .05 .15
331 Glenallen Hill .05 .15
332 Kirt Manwaring .05 .15
333 Royce Clayton .05 .15
334 J.R. Phillips .05 .15
335 Barry Bonds .75 2.00
336 Mark Portugal .05 .15
337 Terry Mulholland .05 .15
338 Omar Vizquel .20 .50
339 Carlos Baerga .05 .15
340 Albert Belle .10 .30
341 Eddie Murray .30 .75
342 Wayne Kirby .05 .15
343 Chad Ogea .05 .15
344 Tim Davis .05 .15
345 Jay Buhner .10 .30
346 Bobby Ayala .05 .15
347 Mike Blowers .05 .15
348 Dave Fleming .05 .15
349 Edgar Martinez .20 .50
350 Andre Dawson .10 .30
351 Darrell Whitmore .05 .15
352 Chuck Carr .05 .15
353 John Burkett .05 .15
354 Chris Hammond .05 .15
355 Gary Sheffield .10 .30
356 Pat Rapp .05 .15
357 Greg Colbrunn .05 .15
358 David Segui .05 .15
359 Jeff Kent .10 .30
360 Bobby Bonilla .10 .30
361 Pete Harnisch .05 .15
362 Ryan Thompson .05 .15
363 Jose Vizcaino .05 .15
364 Brett Butler .10 .30
365 Cal Ripken 1.00 2.50
366 Rafael Palmeiro .20 .50
367 Leo Gomez .05 .15
368 Andy Van Slyke .20 .50
369 Arthur Rhodes .05 .15
370 Ken Caminiti .10 .30
371 Steve Finley .10 .30
372 Melvin Nieves .05 .15
373 Andujar Cedeno .05 .15
374 Trevor Hoffman .10 .30
375 Fernando Valenzuela .10 .30
376 Ricky Bottalico .05 .15
377 Dave Hollins .05 .15
378 Charlie Hayes .05 .15
379 Tommy Greene .05 .15
380 Darren Daulton .10 .30
381 Curt Schilling .10 .30
382 Midre Cummings .05 .15
383 Al Martin .05 .15
384 Jeff King .05 .15
385 Orlando Merced .05 .15
386 Denny Neagle .10 .30
387 Don Slaught .05 .15
388 Dave Clark .05 .15
389 Kevin Gross .05 .15
390 Will Clark .20 .50
391 Ivan Rodriguez .20 .50
392 Benji Gil .05 .15
393 Jeff Frye .05 .15
394 Kenny Rogers .10 .30
395 Juan Gonzalez .10 .30
396 Mike Macfarlane .05 .15
397 Lee Tinsley .05 .15
398 Tim Naehring .05 .15
399 Tim Vanegmond .05 .15
400 Mike Greenwell .05 .15
401 Ken Ryan .05 .15
402 John Smiley .05 .15
403 Tim Pugh .05 .15
404 Reggie Sanders .10 .30
405 Barry Larkin .20 .50
406 Hal Morris .05 .15
407 Jose Rijo .05 .15
408 Lance Painter .05 .15
409 Joe Girardi .05 .15
410 Andres Galarraga .10 .30
411 Mike Kingery .05 .15
412 Roberto Mejia .05 .15
413 Walt Weiss .05 .15
414 Bill Swift .05 .15
415 Larry Walker .10 .30
416 Billy Brewer .05 .15
417 Pat Borders .05 .15
418 Tom Gordon .05 .15
419 Kevin Appier .10 .30
420 Gary Gaetti .10 .30
421 Greg Gohr .05 .15
422 Felipe Lira .05 .15
423 John Doherty .05 .15
424 Chad Curtis .05 .15
425 Cecil Fielder .10 .30
426 Alan Trammell .10 .30
427 David McCarty .05 .15
428 Scott Erickson .05 .15
429 Pat Mahomes .05 .15
430 Kirby Puckett .30 .75
431 Dave Stevens .05 .15
432 Pedro Munoz .05 .15
433 Chris Sabo .05 .15
434 Alex Fernandez .05 .15
435 Frank Thomas .30 .75
436 Roberto Hernandez .05 .15
437 Lance Johnson .05 .15
438 Jim Abbott .20 .50
439 John Wetteland .10 .30
440 Melido Perez .05 .15
441 Tony Fernandez .05 .15
442 Pat Kelly .05 .15
443 Mike Stanley .05 .15
444 Danny Tartabull .05 .15
445 Wade Boggs .20 .50
446 Robin Yount TRIB .50 1.25
447 Ryne Sandberg TRIB .50 1.25
448 Nolan Ryan TRIB 1.25 3.00
449 George Brett TRIB .75 2.00
450 Mike Schmidt TRIB .50 1.25
451 Jim Abbott TRADE .75 2.00
452 Danny Tartabull TRADE .40 1.00
453 Ariel Prieto TRADE .40 1.00
454 Scott Cooper TRADE .40 1.00
455 Tom Henke TRADE .40 1.00
456 Todd Zeile TRADE .40 1.00
457 Brian McRae TRADE .40 1.00
458 Luis Gonzalez TRADE .60 1.50
459 Jaime Navarro TRADE .40 1.00
460 Todd Worrell TRADE .40 1.00
461 Roberto Kelly TRADE .40 1.00
462 Chad Fonville TRADE .40 1.00
463 Shane Andrews TRADE .40 1.00
464 David Segui TRADE .40 1.00
465 Deion Sanders TRADE .75 2.00
466 Orel Hershiser TRADE .60 1.50
467 Ken Hill TRADE .40 1.00
468 Andy Benes TRADE .40 1.00
469 Terry Pendleton TRADE .60 1.50
470 Bobby Bonilla TRADE .60 1.50
471 Scott Erickson TRADE .40 1.00
472 Kevin Brown TRADE .60 1.50
473 Glenn Dishman TRADE .40 1.00
474 Phil Plantier TRADE .40 1.00
475 Gregg Jefferies TRADE .40 1.00
476 Tyler Green TRADE .40 1.00
477 Heathcliff Slocumb TRADE .40 1.00
478 Mark Whiten TRADE .40 1.00
479 Mickey Tettleton TRADE .40 1.00
480 Tim Wakefield TRADE .60 1.50
481 Vaughn Eshelman TRADE .40 1.00
482 Rick Aguilera TRADE .40 1.00
483 Erik Hanson TRADE .40 1.00
484 Willie McGee TRADE .60 1.50
485 Troy O'Leary TRADE .40 1.00
486 Benito Santiago TRADE .60 1.50
487 Darren Lewis TRADE .40 1.00
488 Dave Burba TRADE .40 1.00
489 Ron Gant TRADE .60 1.50
490 Bret Saberhagen TRADE .60 1.50
491 Vinny Castilla TRADE .60 1.50
492 Frank Rodriguez TRADE .40 1.00
493 Andy Pettitte TRADE .75 2.00
494 Ruben Sierra TRADE .60 1.50
495 David Cone TRADE .60 1.50
J159 R.Clemens Jumbo AU 15.00 40.00
J215 A.Rodriguez Jumbo AU 20.00 50.00
P100 Ken Griffey Jr. Promo 1.00 2.50

1995 Upper Deck Electric Diamond

COMPLETE SET (450) 50.00 100.00
COMPLETE SERIES 1 (225) 20.00 50.00
COMPLETE SERIES 2 (225) 25.00 60.00
*STARS: 1.25X TO 3X BASIC CARDS
*ROOKIES: 1X TO 2.5X BASIC CARDS
ONE PER RETAIL PACK/TWO PER MINI JUMBO

1995 Upper Deck Autographs

Trade cards to redeem these autographed issues were randomly seeded into second series packs. The actual signed cards share the same front design as the basic issue 1995 Upper Deck cards. The cards were issued along with a card signed in facsimile by Brain Burr of Upper Deck along with instructions on how to register these cards.

SER.2 STATED ODDS 1:72 HOBBY
AC1 Reggie Jackson 15.00 40.00
AC2 Willie Mays 75.00 200.00
AC3 Frank Robinson 8.00 20.00
AC4 Roger Clemens 15.00 40.00
AC5 Raul Mondesi 8.00 20.00

1995 Upper Deck Checklists

Each of these 10 cards features a star player(s) on the front and a checklist on the back. The cards were randomly inserted in hobby and retail packs at a rate of one in 17. The horizontal fronts feature a player photo along with a sentence about the 1994 highlight. The cards are numbered as "X" of 5 in the upper left.

COMPLETE SET (10) 5.00 12.00
COMPLETE SERIES 1 (5) 1.50 4.00
COMPLETE SERIES 2 (5) 3.00 8.00
STATED ODDS 1:17 ALL PACKS
1A Montreal Expos .10 .30
2A Fred McGriff .40 1.00
3A John Valentin .10 .30
4A Kenny Rogers .25 .60
5A Greg Maddux 1.00 2.50
1B Cecil Fielder .25 .60
2B Tony Gwynn .75 2.00
3B Greg Maddux 1.00 2.50
4B Randy Johnson .60 1.50
5B Mike Schmidt 1.00 2.50

1995 Upper Deck Predictor Award Winners

Cards from this set were inserted in hobby packs at a rate of approximately one in 30. This 40-card standard-size set features nine players and a Long Shot in each league for each of two categories -- MVP and Rookie of the Year. If the player pictured on the card won his category, the card was redeemable for a special foil version of all 20 Hobby Predictor cards. Winning cards are marked with a "W" in the checklist below. Both MVP winners for the season (Barry Larkin in the NL and Mo Vaughn in the AL) were not featured on their own Predictor cards and thus the Longshot card became the winner. Fronts are full-color player action photos. Backs include the rules of the contest. These cards were redeemable until December 31, 1995.

COMPLETE SET (40) 15.00 40.00
COMPLETE SERIES 1 (20) 8.00 20.00
COMPLETE SERIES 2 (20) 8.00 20.00
STATED ODDS 1:30 HOBBY
*EXCH: .5X TO 1.2X BASIC PREDICTOR AW
ONE EXCH.SET VIA MAIL PER PRED.WINNER
H1 Albert Belle .50 1.25
H2 Juan Gonzalez .50 1.25
H3 Ken Griffey Jr. 2.50 6.00
H4 Kirby Puckett 1.25 3.00
H5 Frank Thomas 1.25 3.00
H6 Jeff Bagwell .75 2.00
H7 Barry Bonds 3.00 8.00
H8 Mike Piazza 2.00 5.00
H9 Matt Williams .50 1.25
H10 MVP Wild Card W .25 .60
H11 Armando Benitez .25 .60
H12 Alex Gonzalez .25 .60
H13 Shawn Green .50 1.25
H14 Derek Jeter 12.00 30.00
H15 Alex Rodriguez 3.00 8.00
H16 Alan Benes .25 .60
H17 Brian L.Hunter .25 .60
H18 Charles Johnson .50 1.25
H19 Jose Oliva .25 .60
H20 ROY Wild Card .25 .60
H21 Cal Ripken 4.00 10.00
H22 Don Mattingly 3.00 8.00
H23 Roberto Alomar .75 2.00
H24 Kenny Lofton .50 1.25
H25 Will Clark .75 2.00
H26 Mark McGwire 3.00 8.00
H27 Greg Maddux 2.00 5.00
H28 Fred McGriff .75 2.00
H29 Andres Galarraga .50 1.25
H30 Jose Canseco .75 2.00
H31 Ray Durham .50 1.25
H32 Mark Grudzielanek 1.25 3.00
H33 Scott Ruffcorn .25 .60
H34 Michael Tucker .25 .60
H35 Garret Anderson .50 1.25
H36 Darren Bragg .25 .60
H37 Quilvio Veras .25 .60
H38 Hideo Nomo W 4.00 10.00
H39 Chipper Jones 1.25 3.00
H40 Marty Cordova W .25 .60

1995 Upper Deck Predictor League Leaders

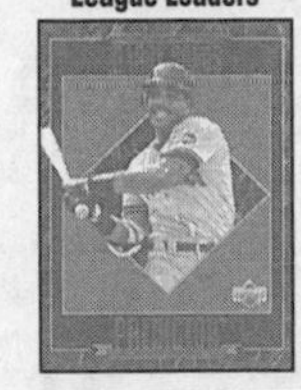

Cards from this 60-card standard size set were seeded exclusively in first and second series retail packs at a rate of 1:30 and ANCO packs at 1:17. Cards 1-30 were distributed in series one packs and cards 31-60 in series two packs. The set includes nine players and a Long Shot in each league for each of three categories -- Batting Average Leader, Home Run Leader and Runs Batted In Leader. If the player pictured on the card won his category, the card was redeemable for a special foil version of 30 Retail Predictor cards (based upon the first or second series that it was associated with). These cards were redeemable until December 31, 1995. Card fronts are full-color action photos of the player emerging from a marble diamond. Backs list the rules of the game. Winning cards are designated with a W in our listings and are in noticeably shorter supply than other cards from this set as the bulk of them were mailed in to Upper Deck (and destroyed) in exchange for the parallel card prizes.

COMPLETE SET (60) 40.00 100.00
COMPLETE SERIES 1 (30) 25.00 60.00
COMPLETE SERIES 2 (30) 15.00 40.00
STATED ODDS 1:30 RET, 1:17 ANCO
*EXCH: .5X TO 1.2X BASIC PREDICTOR LL
ONE EXCH.SET VIA MAIL PER PRED.WINNER
R1 Albert Belle W .50 1.25
R2 Jose Canseco .75 2.00
R3 Juan Gonzalez .50 1.25
R4 Ken Griffey Jr. 2.50 6.00
R5 Frank Thomas 1.25 3.00
R6 Jeff Bagwell .75 2.00
R7 Barry Bonds 3.00 8.00
R8 Fred McGriff .75 2.00
R9 Matt Williams .50 1.25
R10 HR Wild Card W .25 .60
R11 Albert Belle W .50 1.25
R12 Joe Carter .50 1.25
R13 Cecil Fielder .50 1.25
R14 Kirby Puckett 1.25 3.00
R15 Frank Thomas 1.25 3.00
R16 Jeff Bagwell .75 2.00
R17 Barry Bonds 3.00 8.00
R18 Mike Piazza 2.00 5.00
R19 Matt Williams .50 1.25
R20 RBI Wild Card W .25 .60
R21 Wade Boggs .75 2.00
R22 Kenny Lofton .50 1.25
R23 Paul Molitor .50 1.25
R24 Paul O'Neill .75 2.00
R25 Frank Thomas 1.25 3.00
R26 Jeff Bagwell .75 2.00
R27 Tony Gwynn W 1.50 4.00
R28 Gregg Jefferies .25 .60
R29 Hal Morris .25 .60
R30 Bat Wild Card W .25 .60
R31 Joe Carter .50 1.25
R32 Cecil Fielder .50 1.25
R33 Rafael Palmeiro .75 2.00
R34 Larry Walker .50 1.25
R35 Manny Ramirez .75 2.00
R36 Tim Salmon .75 2.00
R37 Mike Piazza 2.00 5.00
R38 Andres Galarraga .50 1.25
R39 David Justice .50 1.25
R40 Gary Sheffield .50 1.25
R41 Juan Gonzalez .50 1.25
R42 Jose Canseco .75 2.00
R43 Will Clark .75 2.00
R44 Rafael Palmeiro .75 2.00
R45 Ken Griffey Jr. 2.50 6.00
R46 Ruben Sierra .50 1.25
R47 Larry Walker .50 1.25
R48 Fred McGriff .75 2.00
R49 Dante Bichette W .50 1.25
R50 Darren Daulton .50 1.25
R51 Will Clark .75 2.00
R52 Ken Griffey Jr. 2.50 6.00
R53 Don Mattingly 3.00 8.00
R54 John Olerud .50 1.25
R55 Kirby Puckett 1.25 3.00
R56 Raul Mondesi .50 1.25
R57 Moises Alou .50 1.25
R58 Bret Boone .50 1.25
R59 Albert Belle .50 1.25
R60 Mike Piazza 2.00 5.00

1995 Upper Deck Ruth Heroes

Randomly inserted in second series hobby and retail packs at a rate of 1:34, this set of 10 standard-size cards celebrates the achievements of one of baseball's all-time greats. The set was issued on the Centennial of Ruth's birth. The numbering (73-81) is a continuation from previous Heroes sets.

COMPLETE SET (10) 40.00 100.00
COMMON CARD (73-81/HDR) 6.00 15.00
SER.2 STATED ODDS 1:34 HOBBY/RETAIL

1995 Upper Deck Special Edition

Inserted at a rate of one per pack, this 270 standard-size card set features full color action shots of players on a silver foil background. The back highlights the player's previous performance, including 1994 and career statistics. Another player photo is also featured on the back.

COMPLETE SET (270) 25.00 60.00
COMPLETE SERIES 1 (135) 12.50 30.00
COMPLETE SERIES 2 (135) 12.50 30.00
ONE PER HOBBY PACK
*SE GOLD STARS: 3X TO 8X HI COLUMN
*SE GOLD RC's: 2X TO 5X HI
SE GOLD ODDS 1:35 HOBBY
1 Cliff Floyd .30 .75
2 Wil Cordero .15 .40
3 Pedro Martinez .50 1.25
4 Larry Walker .30 .75
5 Derek Jeter 10.00 25.00
6 Mike Stanley .15 .40
7 Melido Perez .15 .40
8 Jim Leyritz .15 .40
9 Danny Tartabull .15 .40
10 Wade Boggs .50 1.25
11 Ryan Klesko .30 .75
12 Steve Avery .15 .40
13 Damon Hollins .15 .40
14 Chipper Jones .75 2.00
15 David Justice .30 .75
16 Glenn Williams .15 .40
17 Jose Oliva .15 .40
18 Terrell Wade .15 .40
19 Alex Fernandez .15 .40
20 Frank Thomas .75 2.00
21 Ozzie Guillen .30 .75
22 Roberto Hernandez .15 .40
23 Albie Lopez .15 .40
24 Eddie Murray .75 2.00
25 Albert Belle .30 .75
26 Omar Vizquel .50 1.25
27 Carlos Baerga .15 .40
28 Jose Rijo .15 .40
29 Hal Morris .15 .40
30 Reggie Sanders .30 .75
31 Jack Morris .30 .75
32 Raul Mondesi .30 .75
33 Karim Garcia .15 .40
34 Todd Hollandsworth .15 .40
35 Mike Piazza 1.25 3.00
36 Chan Ho Park .30 .75
37 Ramon Martinez .15 .40
38 Kenny Rogers .30 .75
39 Will Clark .50 1.25
40 Juan Gonzalez .30 .75
41 Ivan Rodriguez .50 1.25
42 Orlando Miller .15 .40
43 John Hudek .15 .40
44 Luis Gonzalez .30 .75
45 Jeff Bagwell .50 1.25
46 Cal Ripken 2.50 6.00
47 Mike Oquist .15 .40
48 Armando Benitez .15 .40
49 Ben McDonald .15 .40
50 Rafael Palmeiro .50 1.25
51 Curtis Goodwin .15 .40
52 Vince Coleman .15 .40
53 Tom Gordon .15 .40
54 Mike Macfarlane .15 .40
55 Brian McRae .15 .40
56 Matt Smith .15 .40
57 David Segui .15 .40
58 Paul Wilson .15 .40
59 Bill Pulsipher .15 .40
60 Bobby Bonilla .30 .75
61 Jeff Kent .30 .75
62 Ryan Thompson .15 .40
63 Jason Isringhausen .30 .75
64 Ed Sprague .15 .40
65 Paul Molitor .30 .75
66 Juan Guzman .15 .40
67 Alex Gonzalez .15 .40
68 Shawn Green .30 .75
69 Mark Portugal .15 .40
70 Barry Bonds 2.00 5.00
71 Robby Thompson .15 .40
72 Royce Clayton .15 .40
73 Ricky Bottalico .15 .40
74 Doug Jones .15 .40
75 Darren Daulton .30 .75
76 Gregg Jefferies .15 .40
77 Scott Cooper .15 .40
78 Nomar Garciaparra 1.25 3.00
79 Ken Ryan .15 .40
80 Mike Greenwell .15 .40
81 LaTroy Hawkins .15 .40
82 Rich Becker .15 .40
83 Scott Erickson .15 .40
84 Pedro Munoz .15 .40
85 Kirby Puckett .75 2.00
86 Orlando Merced .15 .40
87 Jeff King .15 .40
88 Midre Cummings .15 .40
89 Bernard Gilkey .15 .40
90 Ray Lankford .30 .75
91 Todd Zeile .15 .40
92 Alan Benes .15 .40
93 Bret Wagner .15 .40
94 Rene Arocha .15 .40
95 Cecil Fielder .30 .75
96 Alan Trammell .30 .75
97 Tony Phillips .15 .40
98 Junior Felix .15 .40
99 Brian Harper .15 .40
100 Greg Vaughn .15 .40
101 Ricky Bones .15 .40
102 Walt Weiss .15 .40
103 Lance Painter .15 .40
104 Roberto Mejia .15 .40
105 Andres Galarraga .30 .75
106 Todd Van Poppel .15 .40
107 Ben Grieve .15 .40
108 Brent Gates .15 .40
109 Jason Giambi .50 1.25
110 Ruben Sierra .30 .75
111 Terry Steinbach .15 .40
112 Chris Hammond .15 .40
113 Charles Johnson .30 .75
114 Jesus Tavarez .15 .40
115 Gary Sheffield .30 .75
116 Chuck Carr .15 .40
117 Bobby Ayala .15 .40
118 Randy Johnson .75 2.00
119 Edgar Martinez .50 1.25
120 Alex Rodriguez 2.00 5.00
121 Kevin Foster .15 .40
122 Kevin Roberson .15 .40
123 Sammy Sosa .75 2.00
124 Steve Trachsel .15 .40
125 Eduardo Perez .15 .40
126 Tim Salmon .50 1.25
127 Todd Greene .15 .40
128 Jorge Fabregas .15 .40
129 Mark Langston .15 .40
130 Mitch Williams .15 .40
131 Raul Casanova .15 .40
132 Mel Nieves .15 .40
133 Andy Benes .15 .40
134 Dustin Hermanson .15 .40
135 Trevor Hoffman .30 .75
136 Mark Grudzielanek .50 1.25
137 Ugueth Urbina .15 .40
138 Moises Alou .30 .75
139 Roberto Kelly .15 .40
140 Rondell White .30 .75
141 Paul O'Neill .50 1.25
142 Jimmy Key .30 .75
143 Jack McDowell .15 .40
144 Ruben Rivera .15 .40
145 Don Mattingly 2.00 5.00
146 John Wetteland .30 .75
147 Tom Glavine .50 1.25
148 Marquis Grissom .30 .75
149 Javier Lopez .30 .75
150 Fred McGriff .50 1.25
151 Greg Maddux 1.25 3.00
152 Chris Sabo .15 .40
153 Ray Durham .30 .75
154 Robin Ventura .30 .75
155 Jim Abbott .50 1.25
156 Jimmy Hurst .15 .40
157 Tim Raines .30 .75
158 Dennis Martinez .30 .75
159 Kenny Lofton .30 .75
160 Dave Winfield .30 .75
161 Manny Ramirez .50 1.25
162 Jim Thome .50 1.25
163 Barry Larkin .50 1.25
164 Bret Boone .30 .75
165 Deion Sanders .50 1.25
166 Ron Gant .30 .75
167 Benito Santiago .30 .75
168 Hideo Nomo 2.00 5.00
169 Billy Ashley .15 .40
170 Roger Cedeno .15 .40
171 Ismael Valdes .15 .40
172 Eric Karros .30 .75
173 Rusty Greer .30 .75
174 Rick Helling .15 .40
175 Nolan Ryan TRIB 3.00 8.00
176 Dean Palmer .30 .75
177 Phil Plantier .15 .40
178 Darryl Kile .30 .75
179 Derek Bell .15 .40
180 Doug Drabek .15 .40
181 Craig Biggio .50 1.25
182 Kevin Brown .30 .75
183 Harold Baines .30 .75
184 Jeffrey Hammonds .15 .40
185 Chris Hoiles .15 .40
186 Mike Mussina .50 1.25
187 Bob Hamelin .15 .40
188 Jeff Montgomery .15 .40
189 Michael Tucker .15 .40
190 George Brett TRIB 2.00 5.00
191 Edgardo Alfonzo .30 .75
192 Brett Butler .30 .75
193 Bobby Jones .15 .40
194 Todd Hundley .30 .75
195 Bret Saberhagen .30 .75
196 Pat Hentgen .15 .40
197 Roberto Alomar .50 1.25
198 David Cone .30 .75
199 Carlos Delgado .30 .75
200 Joe Carter .30 .75
201 Wm. VanLandingham .15 .40

202 Rod Beck .15 .40
203 J.R. Phillips .15 .40
204 Darren Lewis .15 .40
205 Matt Williams .30 .75
206 Lenny Dykstra .30 .75
207 Dave Hollins .15 .40
208 Mike Schmidt TRIB 1.25 3.00
209 Charlie Hayes .15 .40
210 Mo Vaughn .30 .75
211 Jose Malave .15 .40
212 Roger Clemens 1.50 4.00
213 Jose Canseco .50 1.25
214 Mark Whiten .15 .40
215 Marty Cordova .15 .40
216 Rick Aguilera .15 .40
217 Kevin Tapani .15 .40
218 Chuck Knoblauch .30 .75
219 Al Martin .15 .40
220 Jay Bell .30 .75
221 Carlos Garcia .15 .40
222 Freddy Adrian Garcia .15 .40
223 Jon Lieber .15 .40
224 Danny Jackson .15 .40
225 Ozzie Smith 1.25 3.00
226 Brian Jordan .30 .75
227 Ken Hill .15 .40
228 Scott Cooper .15 .40
229 Chad Curtis .15 .40
230 Lou Whitaker .30 .75
231 Kirk Gibson .30 .75
232 Travis Fryman .30 .75
233 Jose Valentin .15 .40
234 Dave Nilsson .15 .40
235 Cal Eldred .15 .40
236 Matt Mieske .15 .40
237 Bill Swift .15 .40
238 Marvin Freeman .15 .40
239 Jason Bates .15 .40
240 Larry Walker .30 .75
241 Dave Nied .15 .40
242 Dante Bichette .30 .75
243 Dennis Eckersley .30 .75
244 Todd Stottlemyre .15 .40
245 Rickey Henderson .75 2.00
246 Geronimo Berroa .15 .40
247 Mark McGwire 2.00 5.00
248 Quilvio Veras .15 .40
249 Terry Pendleton .30 .75
250 Andre Dawson .30 .75
251 Jeff Conine .30 .75
252 Kurt Abbott .15 .40
253 Jay Buhner .30 .75
254 Darren Bragg .15 .40
255 Ken Griffey Jr. 1.50 4.00
256 Tino Martinez .50 1.25
257 Mark Grace .50 1.25
258 Ryne Sandberg TRIB 1.25 3.00
259 Randy Myers .15 .40
260 Howard Johnson .15 .40
261 Lee Smith .30 .75
262 J.T. Snow .30 .75
263 Chili Davis .30 .75
264 Chuck Finley .30 .75
265 Eddie Williams .15 .40
266 Joey Hamilton .15 .40
267 Ken Caminiti .30 .75
268 Andujar Cedeno .15 .40
269 Steve Finley .30 .75
270 Tony Gwynn 1.00 2.50

1995 Upper Deck Steal of a Deal

This set was inserted in hobby and retail packs at a rate of approximately one in 34. This 15-card standard-size set focuses on players who were acquired through, according to Upper Deck, "astute trades" or low round draft picks. The cards are numbered in the upper left with an "SD" prefix.

COMPLETE SET (15) 30.00 80.00
SER.1 STATED ODDS 1:34 ALL PACKS
SD1 Mike Piazza 5.00 12.00
SD2 Fred McGriff 2.00 5.00
SD3 Kenny Lofton 1.25 3.00
SD4 Jose Oliva .60 1.50
SD5 Jeff Bagwell 2.00 5.00
SD6 R.Alomar 2.00 5.00
J.Carter
SD7 Steve Karsay .60 1.50
SD8 Ozzie Smith 5.00 12.00
SD9 Dennis Eckersley 1.25 3.00
SD10 Jose Canseco 2.00 5.00
SD11 Carlos Baerga .60 1.50
SD12 Cecil Fielder 1.25 3.00
SD13 Don Mattingly 8.00 20.00
SD14 Bret Boone 1.25 3.00
SD15 Michael Jordan 6.00 15.00

1995 Upper Deck Trade Exchange

These five cards were randomly inserted into second series Upper Deck packs. A collector could send in these cards and receive nine cards from the trade set for the base 1995 Upper Deck set (numbers 451-495). These cards were redeemable until February 1, 1996.

COMPLETE SET (5) 2.50 5.00
RANDOM INSERTS IN SERIES 2 PACKS
TC1 Orel Hershiser .60 1.50
TC2 Terry Pendleton .40 1.00
TC3 Benito Santiago .60 1.50
TC4 Kevin Brown .75 2.00
TC5 Gregg Jefferies .40 1.00

1995 Upper Deck/GTS Phone Cards

Upper Deck joined with GTS (Global Telecommunication Solutions Inc.) to produce a series of MLB player phone cards. Each card contained 15 minutes of long distance phone time and was priced at $12.00. Card numbers 1-5 were released March 1, April 15, and May 15, for a total of fifteen cards. Moreover, other cards were to be released later in the year. The cards are unnumbered and checklisted below in alphabetical order in two sections--the first five that were released (MLB1-MLB5) and then the other ten cards (MLB6-MLB15).

COMPLETE SET (15) 60.00 120.00
MLB1 Tony Gwynn 5.00 12.00
MLB2 Fred McGriff 1.25 3.00
MLB3 Frank Thomas 2.50 6.00
MLB4 Ken Griffey Jr. 6.00 15.00
MLB5 Cecil Fielder .75 2.00
MLB6 Roberto Alomar 2.00 5.00
MLB7 Jeff Bagwell 2.50 6.00
MLB8 Barry Bonds 4.00 10.00
MLB9 Roger Clemens 5.00 12.00
MLB10 David Justice 2.00 5.00
MLB11 Don Mattingly 5.00 12.00
MLB12 Kirby Puckett 3.00 8.00
MLB13 Cal Ripken 10.00 25.00
MLB14 Gary Sheffield 2.50 6.00
MLB15 Ozzie Smith 4.00 10.00

1995 Upper Deck Mantle Metallic Impressions

This eight-card set features vintage photos of career highlights of Mickey Mantle printed on metal cards. The backs carry information about the various stages of his career with a small stamp-like photo. The set was distributed in a collector's edition metal box containing a Certificate of Authenticity.

COMPLETE SET (10) 10.00 25.00
COMMON CARD (1-10) 1.25 3.00

1995 Upper Deck Sonic Heroes of Baseball

These standard-size cards were given out in three-card cello packs to customers who purchased a combo meal at participating Sonic Restaurants. The fronts feature black-and-white player photos with white borders. The words "Exclusive Edition" are printed in a blue bar at the top, with the player's name in a red bar directly below. The team name and the player's position appear on the bottom. The backs carry stats, career highlights, and sponsor and producer logos.

COMPLETE SET (20) 2.50 6.00
1 Whitey Ford .10 .30
2 Cy Young .15 .40
3 Babe Ruth .60 1.50
4 Lou Gehrig .30 .75
5 Mike Schmidt .15 .40
6 Nolan Ryan .60 1.50
7 Robin Yount .15 .40
8 Gary Carter .07 .20
9 Tom Seaver .10 .30
10 Reggie Jackson .10 .30
11 Bob Gibson .07 .20
12 Gil Hodges .10 .30
13 Monte Irvin .02 .10
14 Minnie Minoso .02 .10
15 Willie Stargell .07 .20
16 Al Kaline .07 .20
17 Joe Jackson .20 .50
18 Walter Johnson .15 .40
19 Ty Cobb .20 .50
20 Satchel Paige .10 .30

1995 Upper Deck Sports Drink Jackson

Upper Deck and Energy Foods have joined together to produce the Upper Deck Authentic Sports Drink. The drink was available in four flavors (lemon lime, madarin orange, fruit cooler and tropical berry), and each package included one of three Reggie Jackson Heroes cards. Six-bottle packages retail for $2.00. The cards are similar to those that were included with Reggie Candy Bars in 1993, and come with and without a gold facsimile autograph. The cards are numbered on the back "X of 3."

COMPLETE SET (3) 2.00 5.00
COMMON CARD (1-3) .80 2.00

1996 Upper Deck

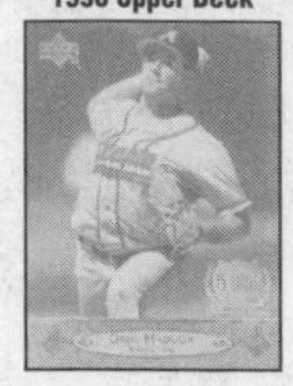

The 1996 Upper Deck set was issued in two series of 240 cards, and a 30 card update set, for a total of 510 cards. The cards were distributed in 10-card packs with a suggested retail price of $1.99, and 28 packs were contained in each box. Upper Deck issued 15,000 factory sets (containing all 510 cards) at season's end. In addition to being included in factory sets, the 30-card Update sets (U481-U510) were also available via mail through a wrapper exchange program. The attractive fronts of each basic card feature a full-bleed photo above a bronze foil bar that includes the player's name, team and position in a white oval. Subsets include Young at Heart (100-117), Beat the Odds (145-153), Postseason Checklist (218-222), Best of a Generation (370-387), Strange But True (415-423) and Managerial Salute Checklists (476-480). The only Rookie Card of note is Livan Hernandez.

COMPLETE SET (480) 15.00 40.00
COMP.FACT.SET (510) 25.00 60.00
COMPLETE SERIES 1 (240) 8.00 20.00
COMPLETE SERIES 2 (240) 8.00 20.00
COMMON CARD (1-480) .10 .30
COMP.UPDATE SET (30) 10.00 20.00
COMMON UPDATE (481U-510U) .20 .50
ONE UPDATE SET PER FACTORY SET
ONE UPDATE SET VIA SER.2 WRAP.OFFER
FACTORY SET PRINT RUN 15,000 SETS
SUBSET CARDS HALF VALUE OF BASE CARDS
1 Cal Ripken 2131 1.50 4.00
2 Eddie Murray 3000 Hits .20 .50
3 Mark Wohlers .10 .30
4 David Justice .10 .30
5 Chipper Jones .30 .75
6 Javier Lopez .10 .30
7 Mark Lemke .10 .30
8 Marquis Grissom .10 .30
9 Tom Glavine .20 .50
10 Greg Maddux .50 1.25
11 Manny Alexander .10 .30
12 Curtis Goodwin .10 .30
13 Scott Erickson .10 .30
14 Chris Hoiles .10 .30
15 Rafael Palmeiro .20 .50
16 Rick Krivda .10 .30
17 Jeff Manto .10 .30
18 Mo Vaughn .10 .30
19 Tim Wakefield .10 .30
20 Roger Clemens .60 1.50
21 Tim Naehring .10 .30
22 Troy O'Leary .10 .30
23 Mike Greenwell .10 .30
24 Stan Belinda .10 .30
25 John Valentin .10 .30
26 J.T. Snow .10 .30
27 Gary DiSarcina .10 .30
28 Mark Langston .10 .30
29 Brian Anderson .10 .30
30 Jim Edmonds .10 .30
31 Garret Anderson .10 .30
32 Orlando Palmeiro .10 .30
33 Brian McRae .10 .30
34 Kevin Foster .10 .30
35 Sammy Sosa .30 .75
36 Todd Zeile .10 .30
37 Jim Bullinger .10 .30
38 Luis Gonzalez .10 .30
39 Lyle Mouton .10 .30
40 Ray Durham .10 .30
41 Ozzie Guillen .10 .30
42 Alex Fernandez .10 .30
43 Brian Keyser .10 .30
44 Robin Ventura .10 .30
45 Reggie Sanders .10 .30
46 Pete Schourek .10 .30
47 John Smiley .10 .30
48 Jeff Brantley .10 .30
49 Thomas Howard .10 .30
50 Bret Boone .10 .30
51 Kevin Jarvis .10 .30
52 Jeff Branson .10 .30
53 Carlos Baerga .10 .30
54 Jim Thome .20 .50
55 Manny Ramirez .20 .50
56 Omar Vizquel .20 .50
57 Jose Mesa .10 .30
58 Julian Tavarez UER .10 .30
59 Orel Hershiser .10 .30
60 Larry Walker .10 .30
61 Bret Saberhagen .10 .30
62 Vinny Castilla .10 .30
63 Eric Young .10 .30
64 Bryan Rekar .10 .30
65 Andres Galarraga .10 .30
66 Steve Reed .10 .30
67 Chad Curtis .10 .30
68 Bobby Higginson .10 .30
69 Phil Nevin .10 .30
70 Cecil Fielder .10 .30
71 Felipe Lira .10 .30
72 Chris Gomez .10 .30
73 Charles Johnson .10 .30
74 Quilvio Veras .10 .30
75 Jeff Conine .10 .30
76 John Burkett .10 .30
77 Greg Colbrunn .10 .30
78 Terry Pendleton .10 .30
79 Shane Reynolds .10 .30
80 Jeff Bagwell .20 .50
81 Orlando Miller .10 .30
82 Mike Hampton .10 .30
83 James Mouton .10 .30
84 Brian L. Hunter .10 .30
85 Derek Bell .10 .30
86 Kevin Appier .10 .30
87 Joe Vitiello .10 .30
88 Wally Joyner .10 .30
89 Michael Tucker .10 .30
90 Johnny Damon .20 .50
91 Jon Nunnally .10 .30
92 Jason Jacome .10 .30
93 Chad Fonville .10 .30
94 Chan Ho Park .10 .30
95 Hideo Nomo .30 .75
96 Ismael Valdes .10 .30
97 Greg Gagne .10 .30
98 Diamondbacks-Devil Rays .30 .75
99 Raul Mondesi .10 .30
100 Dave Winfield YH .10 .30
101 Dennis Eckersley YH .10 .30
102 Andre Dawson YH .10 .30
103 Dennis Martinez YH .10 .30
104 Lance Parrish YH .10 .30
105 Eddie Murray YH .20 .50
106 Alan Trammell YH .10 .30
107 Lou Whitaker YH .10 .30
108 Ozzie Smith YH .30 .75
109 Paul Molitor YH .10 .30
110 Rickey Henderson YH .20 .50
111 Tim Raines YH .10 .30
112 Harold Baines YH .10 .30
113 Lee Smith YH .10 .30
114 Fernando Valenzuela YH .10 .30
115 Cal Ripken YH .50 1.25
116 Tony Gwynn YH .20 .50
117 Wade Boggs .20 .50
118 Todd Hollandsworth .10 .30
119 Dave Nilsson .10 .30
120 Jose Valentin .10 .30
121 Steve Sparks .10 .30
122 Chuck Carr .10 .30
123 John Jaha .10 .30
124 Scott Karl .10 .30
125 Chuck Knoblauch .10 .30
126 Brad Radke .10 .30
127 Pat Meares .10 .30
128 Ron Coomer .10 .30
129 Pedro Munoz .10 .30
130 Kirby Puckett .30 .75
131 David Segui .10 .30
132 Mark Grudzielanek .10 .30
133 Mike Lansing .10 .30
134 Sean Berry .10 .30
135 Rondell White .10 .30
136 Pedro Martinez .20 .50
137 Carl Everett .10 .30
138 Dave Mlicki .10 .30
139 Bill Pulsipher .10 .30
140 Jason Isringhausen .10 .30
141 Rico Brogna .10 .30
142 Edgardo Alfonzo .10 .30
143 Jeff Kent .10 .30
144 Andy Pettitte .20 .50
145 Mike Piazza BO .30 .75
146 Cliff Floyd BO .10 .30
147 Jason Isringhausen BO .10 .30
148 Tim Wakefield BO .10 .30
149 Chipper Jones BO .20 .50
150 Hideo Nomo BO .20 .50
151 Mark McGwire BO .40 1.00
152 Ron Gant BO .10 .30
153 Gary Gaetti BO .10 .30
154 Don Mattingly .75 2.00
155 Paul O'Neill .20 .50
156 Derek Jeter .75 2.00
157 Joe Girardi .10 .30
158 Ruben Sierra .10 .30
159 Jorge Posada .20 .50
160 Geronimo Berroa .10 .30
161 Steve Ontiveros .10 .30
162 George Williams .10 .30
163 Doug Johns .10 .30
164 Ariel Prieto .10 .30
165 Scott Brosius .10 .30
166 Mike Bordick .10 .30
167 Tyler Green .10 .30
168 Mickey Morandini .10 .30
169 Darren Daulton .10 .30
170 Gregg Jefferies .10 .30
171 Jim Eisenreich .10 .30
172 Heathcliff Slocumb .10 .30
173 Kevin Stocker .10 .30
174 Esteban Loaiza .10 .30
175 Jeff King .10 .30
176 Mark Johnson .10 .30
177 Denny Neagle .10 .30
178 Orlando Merced .10 .30
179 Carlos Garcia .10 .30
180 Brian Jordan .10 .30
181 Mike Morgan .10 .30
182 Mark Petkovsek .10 .30
183 Bernard Gilkey .10 .30
184 John Mabry .10 .30
185 Tom Henke .10 .30
186 Glenn Dishman .10 .30
187 Andy Ashby .10 .30
188 Bip Roberts .10 .30
189 Melvin Nieves .10 .30
190 Ken Caminiti .10 .30
191 Brad Ausmus .10 .30
192 Deion Sanders .20 .50
193 Jamie Brewington RC .10 .30
194 Glenallen Hill .10 .30
195 Barry Bonds .75 2.00
196 Wm. Van Landingham .10 .30
197 Mark Carreon .10 .30
198 Royce Clayton .10 .30
199 Joey Cora .10 .30
200 Ken Griffey Jr. .60 1.50
201 Jay Buhner .10 .30
202 Alex Rodriguez .60 1.50
203 Norm Charlton .10 .30
204 Andy Benes .10 .30
205 Edgar Martinez .20 .50
206 Juan Gonzalez .10 .30
207 Will Clark .20 .50
208 Kevin Gross .10 .30
209 Roger Pavlik .10 .30
210 Ivan Rodriguez .20 .50
211 Rusty Greer .10 .30
212 Angel Martinez .10 .30
213 Tomas Perez .10 .30
214 Alex Gonzalez .10 .30
215 Joe Carter .10 .30
216 Shawn Green .10 .30
217 Edwin Hurtado .10 .30
218 E.Martinez .10 .30
T.Pena CL
219 C.Jones .20 .50
B.Larkin CL
220 Orel Hershiser CL .10 .30
221 Mike Devereaux CL .10 .30
222 Tom Glavine CL .10 .30
223 Karim Garcia .10 .30
224 Arquimedez Pozo .10 .30
225 Billy Wagner .10 .30
226 John Wasdin .10 .30
227 Jeff Suppan .10 .30
228 Steve Gibralter .10 .30
229 Jimmy Haynes .10 .30
230 Ruben Rivera .10 .30
231 Chris Snopek .10 .30
232 Alex Ochoa .10 .30
233 Shannon Stewart .10 .30
234 Quinton McCracken .10 .30
235 Trey Beamon .10 .30
236 Billy McMillon .10 .30
237 Steve Cox .10 .30
238 George Arias .10 .30
239 Yamil Benitez .10 .30
240 Todd Greene .10 .30
241 Jason Kendall .10 .30
242 Brooks Kieschnick .10 .30
243 Osvaldo Fernandez RC .10 .30
244 Livan Hernandez RC .40 1.00
245 Rey Ordonez .10 .30
246 Mike Grace RC .10 .30
247 Jay Canizaro .10 .30
248 Bob Wolcott .10 .30
249 Jermaine Dye .10 .30
250 Jason Schmidt .20 .50
251 Mike Sweeney RC .40 1.00
252 Marcus Jensen .10 .30
253 Mendy Lopez .10 .30
254 Wilton Guerrero RC .10 .30
255 Paul Wilson .10 .30
256 Edgar Renteria .10 .30
257 Richard Hidalgo .10 .30
258 Bob Abreu .30 .75
259 Robert Smith RC .10 .30
260 Sal Fasano .10 .30
261 Enrique Wilson .10 .30
262 Rich Hunter RC .10 .30
263 Sergio Nunez .10 .30
264 Dan Serafini .10 .30
265 David Doster .10 .30
266 Ryan McGuire .10 .30
267 Scott Spiezio .10 .30
268 Rafael Orellano .10 .30
269 Steve Avery .10 .30
270 Fred McGriff .20 .50
271 John Smoltz .20 .50
272 Ryan Klesko .10 .30
273 Jeff Blauser .10 .30
274 Brad Clontz .10 .30
275 Roberto Alomar .20 .50
276 B.J. Surhoff .10 .30
277 Jeffrey Hammonds .10 .30
278 Brady Anderson .10 .30
279 Bobby Bonilla .10 .30
280 Cal Ripken 1.00 2.50
281 Mike Mussina .20 .50
282 Wil Cordero .10 .30
283 Mike Stanley .10 .30
284 Aaron Sele .10 .30
285 Jose Canseco .20 .50
286 Tom Gordon .10 .30
287 Heathcliff Slocumb .10 .30
288 Lee Smith .10 .30
289 Troy Percival .10 .30
290 Tim Salmon .20 .50
291 Chuck Finley .10 .30
292 Jim Abbott .20 .50
293 Chili Davis .10 .30
294 Steve Trachsel .10 .30
295 Mark Grace .20 .50
296 Rey Sanchez .10 .30
297 Scott Servais .10 .30
298 Jaime Navarro .10 .30
299 Frank Castillo .10 .30
300 Frank Thomas .30 .75
301 Jason Bere .10 .30
302 Danny Tartabull .10 .30
303 Darren Lewis .10 .30
304 Roberto Hernandez .10 .30
305 Tony Phillips .10 .30
306 Wilson Alvarez .10 .30
307 Jose Rijo .10 .30
308 Hal Morris .10 .30
309 Mark Portugal .10 .30
310 Barry Larkin .20 .50
311 Dave Burba .10 .30
312 Eddie Taubensee .10 .30
313 Sandy Alomar Jr. .10 .30
314 Dennis Martinez .10 .30
315 Albert Belle .10 .30
316 Eddie Murray .30 .75
317 Charles Nagy .10 .30
318 Chad Ogea .10 .30
319 Kenny Lofton .10 .30
320 Dante Bichette .10 .30
321 Armando Reynoso .10 .30
322 Walt Weiss .10 .30
323 Ellis Burks .10 .30
324 Kevin Ritz .10 .30
325 Bill Swift .10 .30
326 Jason Bates .10 .30
327 Tony Clark .10 .30
328 Travis Fryman .10 .30
329 Mark Parent .10 .30
330 Alan Trammell .10 .30
331 C.J. Nitkowski .10 .30
332 Jose Lima .10 .30
333 Phil Plantier .10 .30
334 Kurt Abbott .10 .30
335 Andre Dawson .10 .30
336 Chris Hammond .10 .30
337 Robb Nen .10 .30
338 Pat Rapp .10 .30
339 Al Leiter .10 .30
340 Gary Sheffield .10 .30
341 Todd Jones .10 .30
342 Doug Drabek .10 .30
343 Greg Swindell .10 .30
344 Tony Eusebio .10 .30
345 Craig Biggio .20 .50
346 Darryl Kile .10 .30
347 Mike Macfarlane .10 .30
348 Jeff Montgomery .10 .30
349 Chris Haney .10 .30
350 Bip Roberts .10 .30
351 Tom Goodwin .10 .30
352 Mark Gubicza .10 .30
353 Joe Randa .10 .30
354 Ramon Martinez .10 .30
355 Eric Karros .10 .30
356 Delino DeShields .10 .30
357 Brett Butler .10 .30
358 Todd Worrell .10 .30
359 Mike Blowers .10 .30
360 Mike Piazza .50 1.25
361 Ben McDonald .10 .30
362 Ricky Bones .10 .30
363 Greg Vaughn .10 .30
364 Matt Mieske .10 .30
365 Kevin Seitzer .10 .30
366 Jeff Cirillo .10 .30
367 LaTroy Hawkins .10 .30
368 Frank Rodriguez .10 .30
369 Rick Aguilera .10 .30
370 Roberto Alomar BG .10 .30
371 Albert Belle BG .10 .30
372 Wade Boggs BG .10 .30
373 Barry Bonds BG .40 1.00
374 Roger Clemens BG .30 .75
375 Dennis Eckersley BG .10 .30
376 Ken Griffey Jr. BG .40 1.00
377 Tony Gwynn BG .20 .50
378 Rickey Henderson BG .20 .50
379 Greg Maddux BG .30 .75
380 Fred McGriff BG .10 .30
381 Paul Molitor BG .10 .30
382 Eddie Murray BG .20 .50
383 Mike Piazza BG .30 .75
384 Kirby Puckett BG .20 .50
385 Cal Ripken BG .50 1.25
386 Ozzie Smith BG .30 .75
387 Frank Thomas BG .20 .50
388 Matt Walbeck .10 .30
389 Dave Stevens .10 .30
390 Marty Cordova .10 .30
391 Darrin Fletcher .10 .30
392 Cliff Floyd .10 .30
393 Mel Rojas .10 .30
394 Shane Andrews .10 .30
395 Moises Alou .10 .30
396 Carlos Perez .10 .30
397 Jeff Fassero .10 .30
398 Bobby Jones .10 .30
399 Todd Hundley .10 .30
400 John Franco .10 .30
401 Jose Vizcaino .10 .30
402 Bernard Gilkey .10 .30
403 Pete Harnisch .10 .30
404 Pat Kelly .10 .30
405 David Cone .10 .30
406 Bernie Williams .20 .50
407 John Wetteland .10 .30
408 Scott Kamieniecki .10 .30
409 Tim Raines .10 .30
410 Wade Boggs .20 .50
411 Terry Steinbach .10 .30
412 Jason Giambi .10 .30
413 Todd Van Poppel .10 .30
414 Pedro Munoz .10 .30
415 Eddie Murray SBT .20 .50
416 Dennis Eckersley SBT .10 .30
417 Bip Roberts SBT .10 .30
418 Glenallen Hill SBT .10 .30
419 John Hudek SBT .10 .30
420 Derek Bell SBT .10 .30
421 Larry Walker SBT .10 .30
422 Greg Maddux SBT .30 .75
423 Ken Caminiti SBT .10 .30
424 Brent Gates .10 .30
425 Mark McGwire .75 2.00
426 Mark Whiten .10 .30
427 Sid Fernandez .10 .30
428 Ricky Bottalico .10 .30
429 Mike Mimbs .10 .30
430 Lenny Dykstra .10 .30
431 Todd Zeile .10 .30
432 Benito Santiago .10 .30
433 Danny Miceli .10 .30
434 Al Martin .10 .30
435 Jay Bell .10 .30
436 Charlie Hayes .10 .30
437 Mike Kingery .10 .30
438 Paul Wagner .10 .30
439 Tom Pagnozzi .10 .30
440 Ozzie Smith .50 1.25
441 Ray Lankford .10 .30
442 Dennis Eckersley .10 .30
443 Ron Gant .10 .30
444 Alan Benes .10 .30
445 Rickey Henderson .30 .75
446 Jody Reed .10 .30
447 Trevor Hoffman .10 .30
448 Andujar Cedeno .10 .30
449 Steve Finley .10 .30
450 Tony Gwynn .40 1.00
451 Joey Hamilton .10 .30
452 Mark Leiter .10 .30
453 Rod Beck .10 .30
454 Kirt Manwaring .10 .30
455 Matt Williams .10 .30
456 Robby Thompson .10 .30
457 Shawon Dunston .10 .30
458 Russ Davis .10 .30
459 Paul Sorrento .10 .30
460 Randy Johnson .30 .75
461 Chris Bosio .10 .30
462 Luis Sojo .10 .30
463 Sterling Hitchcock .10 .30
464 Benji Gil .10 .30
465 Mickey Tettleton .10 .30
466 Mark McLemore .10 .30
467 Darryl Hamilton .10 .30
468 Ken Hill .10 .30
469 Dean Palmer .10 .30
470 Carlos Delgado .10 .30
471 Ed Sprague .10 .30
472 Otis Nixon .10 .30
473 Pat Hentgen .10 .30
474 Juan Guzman .10 .30
475 John Olerud .10 .30
476 Buck Showalter CL .10 .30
477 Bobby Cox CL .10 .30
478 Tommy Lasorda CL .10 .30
479 Buck Showalter CL .10 .30
480 Sparky Anderson CL .10 .30
481U Randy Myers .20 .50
482U Kent Mercker .20 .50
483U David Wells .30 .75
484U Kevin Mitchell .20 .50
485U Randy Velarde .20 .50
486U Ryne Sandberg 1.50 4.00
487U Doug Jones .20 .50
488U Terry Adams .20 .50
489U Kevin Tapani .20 .50
490U Harold Baines .30 .75
491U Eric Davis .30 .75
492U Julio Franco .30 .75
493U Jack McDowell .20 .50
494U Devon White .30 .75
495U Kevin Brown .30 .75
496U Rick Wilkins .20 .50
497U Sean Berry .20 .50
498U Keith Lockhart .20 .50
499U Mark Loretta .20 .50
500U Paul Molitor .30 .75
501U Roberto Kelly .20 .50
502U Lance Johnson .20 .50
503U Tino Martinez .50 1.25
504U Kenny Rogers .30 .75
505U Todd Stottlemyre .20 .50
506U Gary Gaetti .30 .75
507U Royce Clayton .20 .50
508U Andy Benes .20 .50
509U Wally Joyner .30 .75
510U Erik Hanson .20 .50
P100 Ken Griffey Jr Promo 1.50 4.00

1996 Upper Deck Blue Chip Prospects

Randomly inserted in first series retail packs at a rate of one in 72, this 20-card set, diecut on the top and bottom, features some of the best young stars in the majors against a bluish background.

COMPLETE SET (20) 40.00 100.00
SER.1 STATED ODDS 1:72
BC1 Hideo Nomo 4.00 10.00
BC2 Johnny Damon 2.50 6.00
BC3 Jason Isringhausen 1.50 4.00
BC4 Bill Pulsipher 1.50 4.00
BC5 Marty Cordova 1.50 4.00
BC6 Michael Tucker 1.50 4.00
BC7 John Wasdin 1.50 4.00
BC8 Karim Garcia 1.50 4.00
BC9 Ruben Rivera 1.50 4.00
BC10 Chipper Jones 4.00 10.00
BC11 Billy Wagner 1.50 4.00
BC12 Brooks Kieschnick 1.50 4.00
BC13 Alan Benes 1.50 4.00
BC14 Roger Cedeno 1.50 4.00
BC15 Alex Rodriguez 8.00 20.00
BC16 Jason Schmidt 2.50 6.00
BC17 Derek Jeter 10.00 25.00
BC18 Brian L.Hunter 1.50 4.00
BC19 Garret Anderson 1.50 4.00
BC20 Manny Ramirez 2.50 6.00

1996 Upper Deck Diamond Destiny

Issued one per Wal Mart pack, these 40 cards feature leading players of baseball. The cards have two photos on the front with the player's name listed on the bottom. The backs have another photo along with biographical information.

COMPLETE SET (40) 25.00 60.00
ONE PER UD TECH RETAIL PACK
*GOLD: 3X TO 8X BASIC DESTINY
GOLD ODDS 1:143 UD TECH RETAIL PACKS
*SILVER: 1X TO 2.5X BASIC DESTINY
SILVER ODDS 1:35 UD TECH RETAIL PACKS
DD1 Chipper Jones 1.00 2.50
DD2 Fred McGriff .60 1.50
DD3 John Smoltz .60 1.50
DD4 Ryan Klesko .40 1.00
DD5 Greg Maddux 1.50 4.00
DD6 Cal Ripken 3.00 8.00
DD7 Roberto Alomar .60 1.50
DD8 Eddie Murray .60 1.50
DD9 Brady Anderson .40 1.00
DD10 Mo Vaughn .40 1.00
DD11 Roger Clemens 1.25 3.00
DD12 Darin Erstad .40 1.00
DD13 Sammy Sosa 1.00 2.50
DD14 Frank Thomas 1.00 2.50
DD15 Barry Larkin .60 1.50
DD16 Albert Belle .40 1.00
DD17 Manny Ramirez .60 1.50
DD18 Kenny Lofton .40 1.00
DD19 Dante Bichette .40 1.00
DD20 Gary Sheffield .40 1.00
DD21 Jeff Bagwell .60 1.50
DD22 Hideo Nomo 1.00 2.50
DD23 Mike Piazza 1.00 2.50
DD24 Kirby Puckett 1.00 2.50
DD25 Paul Molitor 1.00 2.50
DD26 Chuck Knoblauch .40 1.00
DD27 Wade Boggs .60 1.50
DD28 Derek Jeter 2.50 6.00
DD29 Rey Ordonez .40 1.00
DD30 Mark McGwire 1.50 4.00
DD31 Ozzie Smith 1.25 3.00
DD32 Tony Gwynn 1.00 2.50
DD33 Barry Bonds 1.50 4.00
DD34 Matt Williams .40 1.00
DD35 Ken Griffey Jr. 2.00 5.00
DD36 Jay Buhner .40 1.00
DD37 Randy Johnson 1.00 2.50
DD38 Alex Rodriguez 1.25 3.00
DD39 Juan Gonzalez .40 1.00
DD40 Joe Carter .40 1.00

1996 Upper Deck Future Stock Prospects

Randomly inserted in packs at a rate of one in 6, this 20-card set highlights the top prospects who made their major league debuts in 1995. The cards are diecut at the top and feature a purple border surrounding the player's picture.

COMPLETE SET (20) 3.00 8.00
SER.1 STATED ODDS 1:6 HOB/RET
FS1 George Arias .40 1.00
FS2 Brian Barber .40 1.00
FS3 Trey Beamon .40 1.00
FS4 Yamil Benitez .40 1.00
FS5 Jamie Brewington .40 1.00
FS6 Tony Clark .40 1.00
FS7 Steve Cox .40 1.00
FS8 Carlos Delgado .40 1.00
FS9 Chad Fonville .40 1.00
FS10 Alex Ochoa .40 1.00
FS11 Curtis Goodwin .40 1.00
FS12 Todd Greene .40 1.00
FS13 Jimmy Haynes .40 1.00
FS14 Quinton McCracken .40 1.00
FS15 Billy McMillon .40 1.00
FS16 Chan Ho Park .40 1.00
FS17 Arquimedez Pozo .40 1.00
FS18 Chris Snopek .40 1.00
FS19 Shannon Stewart .40 1.00
FS20 Jeff Suppan .40 1.00

1996 Upper Deck Gameface

These Gameface cards were seeded at a rate of one per Upper Deck and Collector's Choice Wal Mart retail pack. The Upper Deck packs contained eight cards and the Collector's Choice packs contained sixteen cards. Both packs carried a suggested retail price of $1.50. The card fronts feature the player's photo surrounded by a "cloudy" white border along with a Gameface logo at the bottom.

COMPLETE SET (10) 5.00 12.00
ONE PER SPECIAL SER.2 RETAIL PACK
GF1 Ken Griffey Jr. .60 1.50
GF2 Frank Thomas .30 .75
GF3 Barry Bonds .75 2.00
GF4 Albert Belle .10 .30
GF5 Cal Ripken 1.00 2.50
GF6 Mike Piazza .50 1.25
GF7 Chipper Jones .30 .75
GF8 Matt Williams .10 .30
GF9 Hideo Nomo .30 .75
GF10 Greg Maddux .50 1.25

1996 Upper Deck Hot Commodities

Cards from this 20 card set double die-cut set were randomly inserted into series two Upper Deck packs at a rate of one in 37. The set features some of baseball's most popular players.

COMPLETE SET (20) 20.00 50.00
SER.2 STATED ODDS 1:36 HOB/RET/ANCO
HC1 Ken Griffey Jr. 5.00 12.00
HC2 Hideo Nomo 1.50 4.00
HC3 Roberto Alomar 1.00 2.50
HC4 Paul Wilson .60 1.50
HC5 Albert Belle .60 1.50
HC6 Manny Ramirez 1.00 2.50
HC7 Kirby Puckett 1.50 4.00
HC8 Johnny Damon 1.00 2.50
HC9 Randy Johnson 1.50 4.00
HC10 Greg Maddux 2.50 6.00
HC11 Chipper Jones 1.50 4.00
HC12 Barry Bonds 2.50 6.00
HC13 Mo Vaughn .60 1.50
HC14 Mike Piazza 1.50 4.00
HC15 Cal Ripken 5.00 12.00
HC16 Tim Salmon .60 1.50
HC17 Sammy Sosa 1.50 4.00
HC18 Kenny Lofton .60 1.50
HC19 Tony Gwynn 1.50 4.00
HC20 Frank Thomas 1.50 4.00

1996 Upper Deck V.J. Lovero Showcase

Upper Deck utilized photos from the files of V.J. Lovero to produce this set. The cards feature the photos along with a story of how Lovero took the photos. The cards are numbered with a "VJ" prefix. These cards were inserted at a rate of one every six packs.

COMPLETE SET (19) 10.00 25.00
SER.2 STATED ODDS 1:6 HOB/RET,1:3 ANCO
VJ1 Jim Abbott .50 1.25
VJ2 Hideo Nomo .75 2.00
VJ3 Derek Jeter 2.00 5.00
VJ4 Barry Bonds 2.00 5.00
VJ5 Greg Maddux 1.25 3.00
VJ6 Mark McGwire 2.00 5.00
VJ7 Jose Canseco .50 1.25
VJ8 Ken Caminiti .30 .75
VJ9 Raul Mondesi .30 .75
VJ10 Ken Griffey Jr. 1.50 4.00
VJ11 Jay Buhner .30 .75
VJ12 Randy Johnson .75 2.00
VJ13 Roger Clemens 1.50 4.00
VJ14 Brady Anderson .30 .75
VJ15 Frank Thomas .75 2.00
VJ16 G.And .30 .75
Edmonds
Salmon
VJ17 Mike Piazza 1.25 3.00
VJ18 Dante Bichette .30 .75
VJ19 Tony Gwynn 1.00 2.50

1996 Upper Deck Nomo Highlights

Los Angeles Dodgers star pitcher and Upper Deck spokesperson Hideo Nomo was featured in this special five card set. The cards were randomly seeded into second series packs at a rate of one in 24 and feature game action as well as descriptions of some of Nomo's key 1995 games.

COMPLETE SET (5) 8.00 20.00
COMMON CARD (1-5) 2.00 5.00
SER.2 STATED ODDS 1:24

1996 Upper Deck Power Driven

Randomly inserted in first series packs at a rate of one in 36, this 20-card set consists of embossed rainbow foil inserts of baseball's top power hitters.

COMPLETE SET (20) 60.00 120.00
SER.1 STATED ODDS 1:36 HOB/RET
PD1 Albert Belle 1.25 3.00
PD2 Barry Bonds 8.00 20.00
PD3 Jay Buhner 1.25 3.00
PD4 Jose Canseco 2.00 5.00
PD5 Cecil Fielder 1.25 3.00
PD6 Juan Gonzalez 1.25 3.00
PD7 Ken Griffey Jr. 6.00 15.00
PD8 Eric Karros 1.25 3.00
PD9 Fred McGriff 2.00 5.00
PD10 Mark McGwire 8.00 20.00
PD11 Rafael Palmeiro 2.00 5.00
PD12 Mike Piazza 5.00 12.00
PD13 Manny Ramirez 2.00 5.00
PD14 Tim Salmon 2.00 5.00
PD15 Reggie Sanders 1.25 3.00
PD16 Sammy Sosa 3.00 8.00
PD17 Frank Thomas 3.00 8.00
PD18 Mo Vaughn 1.25 3.00
PD19 Larry Walker 1.25 3.00
PD20 Matt Williams 1.25 3.00

1996 Upper Deck Predictor Hobby

Randomly inserted in both series hobby packs at a rate of one in 12, this 60-card predictor set offered six different 10-card parallel exchange sets for prizes as featured players competed for monthly milestones and awards. The fronts feature a cutout player photo against a pinstriped background surrounded by a gray marble border. Card backs feature game rules and guidelines. Winner cards are signified with a W in our listings and are in noticeably shorter supply since they had to be mailed in to Upper Deck (where they were destroyed) to claim your exchange cards. The deadline to mail in winning cards was November 18th, 1996.

COMPLETE SET (60) 25.00 60.00
COMPLETE SERIES 1 (30) 12.50 30.00
COMPLETE SERIES 2 (30) 12.50 30.00
STATED ODDS 1:12 HOBBY
EXPIRATION DATE: 11/18/96
*EXCHANGE: .4X TO 1X BASIC PREDICTOR
ONE EXCH.SET VIA MAIL PER PRED.WINNER
H1 Albert Belle .25 .60
H2 Kenny Lofton .25 .60
H3 Rafael Palmeiro .40 1.00
H4 Ken Griffey Jr. 1.25 3.00
H5 Tim Salmon .40 1.00
H6 Cal Ripken 2.00 5.00
H7 Mark McGwire 1.50 4.00
H8 Frank Thomas .60 1.50
H9 Mo Vaughn .25 .60
H10 AL Player of Month LS W .25 .60
H11 Roger Clemens 1.25 3.00
H12 David Cone .25 .60
H13 Jose Mesa .25 .60
H14 Randy Johnson .60 1.50
H15 Chuck Finley .25 .60
H16 Mike Mussina .40 1.00
H17 Kevin Appier .25 .60
H18 Kenny Rogers .60 1.50
H19 Lee Smith .25 .60
H20 AL Pitcher of Month LS W .25 .60
H21 George Arias .25 .60
H22 Jose Herrera .25 .60
H23 Tony Clark .25 .60
H24 Todd Greene .25 .60
H25 Derek Jeter 1.50 4.00
H26 Arquimedez Pozo .25 .60
H27 Matt Lawton .25 .60
H28 Shannon Stewart .25 .60
H29 Chris Snopek .25 .60
H30 AL Most Rookie Hits LS .25 .60
H31 Jeff Bagwell .40 1.00
H32 Dante Bichette W .25 .60
H33 Barry Bonds 1.50 4.00
H34 Tony Gwynn .75 2.00
H35 Chipper Jones .60 1.50
H36 Eric Karros .25 .60
H37 Barry Larkin .40 1.00
H38 Mike Piazza 1.00 2.50
H39 Matt Williams .25 .60
H40 NL Player of Month LS W .25 .60
H41 Osvaldo Fernandez .25 .60
H42 Tom Glavine .40 1.00
H43 Jason Isringhausen .25 .60
H44 Greg Maddux 1.00 2.50
H45 Pedro Martinez .40 1.00
H46 Hideo Nomo .60 1.50
H47 Pete Schourek .25 .60
H48 Paul Wilson .25 .60
H49 Mark Wohlers .25 .60
H50 NL Pitcher of Month LS W .25 .60
H51 Bob Abreu .60 1.50
H52 Trey Beamon .25 .60
H53 Yamil Benitez .25 .60
H54 Roger Cedeno W .25 .60
H55 Todd Hollandsworth .25 .60
H56 Marvin Benard .25 .60
H57 Jason Kendall .25 .60
H58 Brooks Kieschnick .25 .60
H59 Rey Ordonez .25 .60
H60 NL Most Rookie Hits LS W .25 .60

1996 Upper Deck Predictor Retail

Randomly inserted in both series retail packs at a rate of one in 12, this 60-card Predictor set offered six different 10-card parallel exchange sets as featured players competed for "monthly milestones and awards." The fronts feature a "cutout" player photo against a pinstriped background surrounded by a gray marble border. Card backs feature game rules and guidelines. Winner cards are signified with a W in our listings and are in noticeably shorter supply since they had to be mailed in to Upper Deck (where they were destroyed) to claim your exchange cards. The expiration date to send in cards was November 18th, 1996.

COMPLETE SET (60) 30.00 80.00
COMPLETE SERIES 1 (30) 15.00 40.00
COMPLETE SERIES 2 (30) 15.00 40.00
STATED ODDS 1:12 RETAIL
EXPIRATION DATE: 11/18/96
*EXCHANGE: .4X TO 1X BASIC PREDICTOR
ONE EXCH.SET VIA MAIL PER PRED.WINNER
R1 Albert Belle .25 .60
R2 Jay Buhner W .25 .60
R3 Juan Gonzalez .25 .60
R4 Ken Griffey Jr. 1.25 3.00
R5 Mark McGwire 1.50 4.00
R6 Rafael Palmeiro .40 1.00
R7 Tim Salmon .40 1.00
R8 Frank Thomas .60 1.50
R9 Mo Vaughn .25 .60
R10 AL Monthly HR LS W .25 .60
R11 Albert Belle .25 .60
R12 Jay Buhner .25 .60
R13 Jim Edmonds .25 .60
R14 Cecil Fielder .25 .60
R15 Ken Griffey Jr. 1.25 3.00
R16 Edgar Martinez .40 1.00
R17 Manny Ramirez .40 1.00
R18 Frank Thomas .60 1.50
R19 Mo Vaughn .25 .60
R20 AL Monthly RBI LS W .25 .60
R21 Roberto Alomar .40 1.00
R22 Carlos Baerga .25 .60
R23 Wade Boggs .40 1.00
R24 Ken Griffey Jr. 1.25 3.00
R25 Chuck Knoblauch .25 .60
R26 Kenny Lofton .25 .60
R27 Edgar Martinez .40 1.00
R28 Tim Salmon .40 1.00
R29 Frank Thomas .60 1.50
R30 AL Monthly Batting LS W .25 .60
R31 Dante Bichette .25 .60
R32 Barry Bonds 1.50 4.00
R33 Ron Gant .25 .60
R34 Chipper Jones .60 1.50
R35 Fred McGriff .40 1.00
R36 Mike Piazza 1.00 2.50
R37 Sammy Sosa W .60 1.50
R38 Larry Walker .25 .60
R39 Matt Williams .25 .60
R40 NL Monthly HR LS W .25 .60
R41 Jeff Bagwell .40 1.00
R42 Dante Bichette W .25 .60
R43 Barry Bonds 1.50 4.00
R44 Jeff Conine .25 .60
R45 Andres Galarraga .25 .60
R46 Mike Piazza 1.00 2.50
R47 Reggie Sanders .25 .60
R48 Sammy Sosa .60 1.50
R49 Matt Williams .25 .60
R50 NL Monthly RBI LS W .25 .60
R51 Jeff Bagwell .40 1.00
R52 Derek Bell .25 .60
R53 Dante Bichette .25 .60
R54 Craig Biggio .40 1.00
R55 Barry Bonds 1.50 4.00
R56 Bret Boone .25 .60
R57 Tony Gwynn .75 2.00
R58 Barry Larkin .40 1.00
R59 Mike Piazza 1.00 2.50
R60 NL Monthly Batting LS W .25 .60

1996 Upper Deck Ripken Collection

This 23 card set was issued across all the various Upper Deck brands. The cards were issued to commemorate Cal Ripken's career, which had been capped the previous season by the breaking of the consecutive game streak long held by Lou Gehrig. The cards were inserted at the following ratios: Cards 1-4 were in Collector Choice first series packs at a rate of one in 12. Cards 5-8 were inserted into Upper Deck series one packs at a rate of one in 24. Cards 9-12 were placed into second series Collector Choice packs at a rate of one in 12. Cards 13-17 were in second series Upper Deck packs at a rate of one in 24. And Cards 18-22 were in SP Packs at a rate of one in 45. The header card (number 23) was also inserted into only Collector Choice packs.

COMPLETE SET (23) 15.00 40.00
COMP.COLC SER.1 (5) 1.50 4.00
COMP.UD SER.1 (4) 3.00 8.00
COMP.COLC SER.2 (4) 1.25 3.00
COMP.UD SER.2 (5) 3.00 8.00
COMP.SP SET (5) 6.00 15.00
COMMON COLC (1-4/9-12) 1.25 3.00
COMMON UD (5-8/13-17) 2.50 6.00
COMMON SP (18-22) 4.00 10.00
CARDS 1-4 STATED ODDS 1:12 CC SER.1
CARDS 5-8 STATED ODDS 1:24 UD SER.1
CARDS 9-12 STATED ODDS 1:12 CC SER.2
CARDS 13-17 STATED ODDS 1:24 UD SER.2
CARDS 18-22 STATED ODDS 1:45 SP
NNO Cal Ripken Header COLC 1.25 3.00

1996 Upper Deck Ripken Collection Jumbos

COMP.FACT SET 8.00 20.00
COMMON CARD .40 1.00
1 Cal Ripken Jr. .75 2.00
after playing in 2130 consecutive
2 Cal Ripken Jr./13th consecutive year as American
1.00 2.50
6 Cal Ripken Jr. .60 1.50
Brian McRae sliding into second/1
22 Cal Ripken SP 1.00 2.50
Eddie Murray/1981

1996 Upper Deck Run Producers

This 20 card set was randomly inserted into series two packs at a rate of one every 71 packs. The cards are thermographically printed, which gives the card a rubber surface texture. The cards are double die-cut and are foil stamped. These cards are highly condition sensitive, often found with noticable chipping on the edges.

COMPLETE SET (20) 75.00 150.00
SER.2 ODDS 1:72 HOB/RET, 1:36 ANCO
CONDITION SENSITIVE SET
THIS SET PRICED IN NRMT CONDITION
RP1 Albert Belle 1.50 4.00
RP2 Dante Bichette 1.50 4.00
RP3 Barry Bonds 10.00 25.00
RP4 Jay Buhner 1.50 4.00
RP5 Jose Canseco 2.50 6.00
RP6 Juan Gonzalez 1.50 4.00
RP7 Ken Griffey Jr. 8.00 20.00
RP8 Tony Gwynn 5.00 12.00
RP9 Kenny Lofton 1.50 4.00
RP10 Edgar Martinez 2.50 6.00
RP11 Fred McGriff 2.50 6.00
RP12 Mark McGwire 10.00 25.00
RP13 Rafael Palmeiro 2.50 6.00
RP14 Mike Piazza 6.00 15.00
RP15 Manny Ramirez 2.50 6.00
RP16 Tim Salmon 2.50 6.00
RP17 Sammy Sosa 4.00 10.00
RP18 Frank Thomas 4.00 10.00
RP19 Mo Vaughn 1.50 4.00
RP20 Matt Williams 1.50 4.00

1996 Upper Deck All-Stars Jumbos

This 18-card set measures approximately 3 1/2" by 5" with a suggested retail blurb to price of $19.95 a set. The fronts feature borderless color player photos and are foil stamped with the official 1996 Major League Baseball All-Star game logo. The backs carry another player photo with player information and statistics. The cards are checklisted below in alphabetical order.

1 Roberto Alomar .30 .75
2 Sandy Alomar Jr. .15 .40
3 Jeff Bagwell .40 1.00
4 Albert Belle .15 .40
5 Dante Bichette .15 .40
6 Craig Biggio .25 .60
7 Wade Boggs .40 1.00
8 Barry Bonds .60 1.50
9 Ken Griffey Jr. 1.00 2.50
10 Tony Gwynn .75 2.00
11 Barry Larkin .30 .75
12 Kenny Lofton .25 .60
13 Charles Nagy .07 .20
14 Mike Piazza 1.25 3.00
15 Cal Ripken Jr. 1.50 4.00
16 John Smoltz .15 .40
17 Frank Thomas .40 1.00
18 Matt Williams .25 .60

1996 Upper Deck Meet the Stars Griffey Redemption

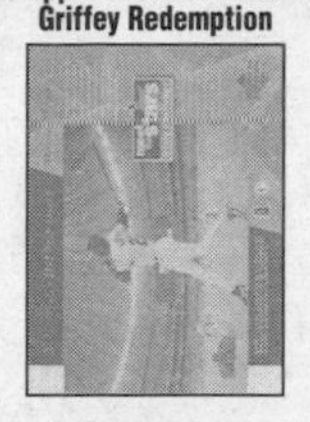

This one-card set features a postcard-size action photo of Ken Griffey Jr. with a "Magic Moment" from a 1995 Post-Season game printed on one side of the three-sided black-and-aqua border. The back is blank.

1 Ken Griffey Jr/1995 Post-Season 1.50 4.00

1996 Upper Deck Nomo Collection Jumbos

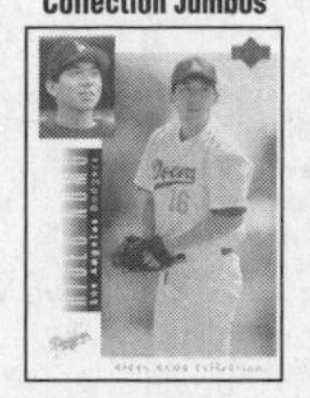

This 16-card set measures approximately 3 1/2" by 5" and features color action photos of Hideo Nomo with a small black-and-white head photo in the upper left. The backs carry a smaller black-and-white version of the front photo with a continuing story highlighting Nomo's major league career.

COMPLETE SET (16) 6.00 15.00
COMMON CARD (1-16) .40 1.00

1996 Upper Deck Nomo ROY Japanese

Produced by Upper Deck, this 3 1/2" by 5" card commemorates Hideo Nomo being named the Rookie-of-the-Year of the National League for 1995. The front features a color action player photo while the back displays a blue-tinted player portrait with player information in Japanese.

1 Hideo Nomo 2.00 5.00

1996 Upper Deck Sheet

This one 8 1/2" by 11" sheet was issued so fans at Fan Fest could have an item for players to sign at the show. The sheet has very little on the front so more signatures can be signed and the back is blank.

1 All-Star Fanfest .75 2.00
Autograph Sheet

1997 Upper Deck

The 1997 Upper Deck set was issued in two series (series one 1-240, series two 271-520). The 12-card packs retailed for $2.49 each. Many cards have dates on the front to identify when, and when possible, what significant event is pictured. The backs include a player photo, stats and a brief blurb to go with vital statistics. Subsets include Jackie Robinson Tribute (1-9), Strike Force (64-72), Defensive Gems (136-153), Global Impact (181-207), Season Highlight Checklists (214-222/316-324), Star Rookies (223-240/271-288), Capture the Flag (370-387), Griffey's Hot List (415-424) and Diamond Debuts (470-483). It's critical to note that the Griffey's Hot List subset cards (in an unannounced move by the manufacturer) were shortprinted (about 1:7 packs) in relation to other cards in the series two set. The comparatively low print run on these cards created a dramatic surge in demand amongst set collectors and the cards soared in value on the secondary market. A 30-card first series Update set (numbered 241-270) was available to collectors that mailed in 10 series one wrappers along with $3 for postage and handling. The Series One Update set is composed primarily of 1996 post-season highlights. An additional 30-card series two Trade set (numbered 521-550) was also released around the end of the season. It too was available to collectors that mailed in ten series two wrappers along with $3 for postage and handling. The Series Two Trade set is composed primarily of traded players pictured in their new uniforms and a selection of rookies and prospects highlighted by the inclusion of Jose Cruz Jr. and Hideki Irabu.

COMP.MASTER SET (550) 100.00 200.00
COMPLETE SET (490) 50.00 100.00
COMPLETE SERIES 1 (240) 15.00 40.00
COMPLETE SERIES 2 (250) 25.00 60.00
COMP.SER.2 w/o GHL (240) 10.00 25.00
COMMON (1-240/271-520) .10 .30
COMP.UPDATE SET (30) 40.00 80.00
COMMON UPDATE (241-270) .40 1.00
1 UPD.SET VIA MAIL PER 10 SER.1 WRAPS
COMMON GHL (415-424) .60 1.50
GHL 415-424 SER.2 ODDS APPROX. 1:7
COMP.TRADE SET (30) 8.00 20.00
COMMON TRADE (521-550) .20 .50
1 TRD.SET VIA MAIL PER 10 SER.2 WRAPS
COMP.SET (490) EXCLUDES UPD/TRD SETS
1 Jackie Robinson .20 .50
2 Jackie Robinson .20 .50
3 Jackie Robinson .20 .50
4 Jackie Robinson .20 .50
5 Jackie Robinson .20 .50
6 Jackie Robinson .20 .50
7 Jackie Robinson .20 .50
8 Jackie Robinson .20 .50
9 Jackie Robinson .20 .50
10 Chipper Jones .30 .75
11 Marquis Grissom .10 .30
12 Jermaine Dye .10 .30
13 Mark Lemke .10 .30
14 Terrell Wade .10 .30
15 Fred McGriff .20 .50
16 Tom Glavine .20 .50
17 Mark Wohlers .10 .30
18 Randy Myers .10 .30
19 Roberto Alomar .20 .50
20 Cal Ripken 1.00 2.50
21 Rafael Palmeiro .20 .50
22 Mike Mussina .20 .50
23 Brady Anderson .10 .30
24 Jose Canseco .20 .50
25 Mo Vaughn .10 .30
26 Roger Clemens .60 1.50
27 Tim Naehring .10 .30
28 Jeff Suppan .10 .30
29 Troy Percival .10 .30
30 Sammy Sosa .30 .75
31 Amaury Telemaco .10 .30
32 Rey Sanchez .10 .30
33 Scott Servais .10 .30
34 Steve Trachsel .10 .30
35 Mark Grace .20 .50
36 Wilson Alvarez .10 .30
37 Harold Baines .10 .30
38 Tony Phillips .10 .30
39 James Baldwin .10 .30
40 Frank Thomas UER .30 .75
41 Lyle Mouton .10 .30
42 Chris Snopek .10 .30
43 Hal Morris .10 .30
44 Eric Davis .10 .30
45 Barry Larkin .20 .50
46 Reggie Sanders .10 .30
47 Pete Schourek .10 .30
48 Lee Smith .10 .30
49 Charles Nagy .10 .30
50 Albert Belle .10 .30
51 Julio Franco .10 .30
52 Kenny Lofton .10 .30
53 Orel Hershiser .10 .30
54 Omar Vizquel .20 .50
55 Eric Young .10 .30
56 Curtis Leskanic .10 .30
57 Quinton McCracken .10 .30
58 Kevin Ritz .10 .30
59 Walt Weiss .10 .30
60 Dante Bichette .10 .30
61 Mark Lewis .10 .30
62 Tony Clark .10 .30
63 Travis Fryman .10 .30
64 John Smoltz SF .10 .30
65 Greg Maddux SF .30 .75
66 Tom Glavine SF .10 .30
67 Mike Mussina SF .10 .30
68 Andy Pettitte SF .10 .30
69 Mariano Rivera SF .20 .50
70 Hideo Nomo SF .10 .30
71 Kevin Brown SF .10 .30
72 Randy Johnson SF .20 .50
73 Felipe Lira .10 .30
74 Kimera Bartee .10 .30
75 Alan Trammell .10 .30
76 Kevin Brown .10 .30
77 Edgar Renteria .10 .30
78 Al Leiter .10 .30
79 Charles Johnson .10 .30
80 Andre Dawson .10 .30
81 Billy Wagner .10 .30
82 Donne Wall .10 .30
83 Jeff Bagwell .20 .50
84 Keith Lockhart .10 .30
85 Jeff Montgomery .10 .30
86 Tom Goodwin .10 .30
87 Tim Belcher .10 .30
88 Mike Macfarlane .10 .30
89 Joe Randa .10 .30
90 Brett Butler .10 .30
91 Todd Worrell .10 .30
92 Todd Hollandsworth .10 .30
93 Ismael Valdes .10 .30
94 Hideo Nomo .30 .75
95 Mike Piazza .50 1.25
96 Jeff Cirillo .10 .30
97 Ricky Bones .10 .30
98 Fernando Vina .10 .30

99 Ben McDonald .10 .30
100 John Jaha .10 .30
101 Mark Loretta .10 .30
102 Paul Molitor .10 .30
103 Rick Aguilera .10 .30
104 Marty Cordova .10 .30
105 Kirby Puckett .30 .75
106 Dan Naulty .10 .30
107 Frank Rodriguez .10 .30
108 Shane Andrews .10 .30
109 Henry Rodriguez .10 .30
110 Mark Grudzielanek .10 .30
111 Pedro Martinez .20 .50
112 Ugueth Urbina .10 .30
113 David Segui .10 .30
114 Rey Ordonez .10 .30
115 Bernard Gilkey .10 .30
116 Butch Huskey .10 .30
117 Paul Wilson .10 .30
118 Alex Ochoa .10 .30
119 John Franco .10 .30
120 Dwight Gooden .10 .30
121 Ruben Rivera .10 .30
122 Andy Pettitte .20 .50
123 Tino Martinez .20 .50
124 Bernie Williams .20 .50
125 Wade Boggs .20 .50
126 Paul O'Neill .20 .50
127 Scott Brosius .10 .30
128 Ernie Young .10 .30
129 Doug Johns .10 .30
130 Geronimo Berroa .10 .30
131 Jason Giambi .10 .30
132 John Wasdin .10 .30
133 Jim Eisenreich .10 .30
134 Ricky Otero .10 .30
135 Ricky Bottalico .10 .30
136 Mark Langston DG .10 .30
137 Greg Maddux DG .30 .75
138 Ivan Rodriguez DG .10 .30
139 Charles Johnson DG .10 .30
140 J.T. Snow DG .10 .30
141 Mark Grace DG .10 .30
142 Roberto Alomar DG .10 .30
143 Craig Biggio DG .10 .30
144 Ken Caminiti DG .10 .30
145 Matt Williams DG .10 .30
146 Omar Vizquel DG .10 .30
147 Cal Ripken DG .50 1.25
148 Ozzie Smith DG .30 .75
149 Rey Ordonez DG .10 .30
150 Ken Griffey Jr. DG .40 1.00
151 Devon White DG .10 .30
152 Barry Bonds DG .40 1.00
153 Kenny Lofton DG .10 .30
154 Mickey Morandini .10 .30
155 Gregg Jefferies .10 .30
156 Curt Schilling .10 .30
157 Jason Kendall .10 .30
158 Francisco Cordova .10 .30
159 Dennis Eckersley .10 .30
160 Ron Gant .10 .30
161 Ozzie Smith .50 1.25
162 Brian Jordan .10 .30
163 John Mabry .10 .30
164 Andy Ashby .10 .30
165 Steve Finley .10 .30
166 Fernando Valenzuela .10 .30
167 Archi Cianfrocco .10 .30
168 Wally Joyner .10 .30
169 Greg Vaughn .10 .30
170 Barry Bonds .75 2.00
171 William VanLandingham .10 .30
172 Marvin Benard .10 .30
173 Rich Aurilia .10 .30
174 Jay Canizaro .10 .30
175 Ken Griffey Jr. .60 1.50
176 Bob Wells .10 .30
177 Jay Buhner .10 .30
178 Sterling Hitchcock .10 .30
179 Edgar Martinez .20 .50
180 Rusty Greer .10 .30
181 Dave Nilsson GI .10 .30
182 Larry Walker GI .10 .30
183 Edgar Renteria GI .10 .30
184 Rey Ordonez GI .10 .30
185 Rafael Palmeiro GI .10 .30
186 Osvaldo Fernandez GI .10 .30
187 Raul Mondesi GI .10 .30
188 Manny Ramirez GI .10 .30
189 Sammy Sosa GI .20 .50
190 Robert Eenhoorn GI .10 .30
191 Devon White GI .10 .30
192 Hideo Nomo GI .10 .30
193 Mac Suzuki GI .10 .30
194 Chan Ho Park GI .10 .30
195 Fernando Valenzuela GI .10 .30
196 Andruw Jones GI .10 .30
197 Vinny Castilla GI .10 .30
198 Dennis Martinez GI .10 .30
199 Ruben Rivera GI .10 .30
200 Juan Gonzalez GI .10 .30
201 Roberto Alomar GI .10 .30
202 Edgar Martinez GI .10 .30
203 Ivan Rodriguez GI .10 .30
204 Carlos Delgado GI .10 .30
205 Andres Galarraga GI .10 .30
206 Ozzie Guillen GI .10 .30
207 Midre Cummings GI .10 .30
208 Roger Pavlik .10 .30
209 Darren Oliver .10 .30
210 Dean Palmer .10 .30
211 Ivan Rodriguez .20 .50
212 Otis Nixon .10 .30
213 Pat Hentgen .10 .30
214 Ozzie .20 .50
Dawson
Puckett HL
CL
215 Bonds .40 1.00
Sheff
Brady HL
CL
216 Ken Caminiti SH CL .10 .30
217 John Smoltz SH CL .10 .30
218 Eric Young SH CL .10 .30
219 Juan Gonzalez SH CL .10 .30
220 Eddie Murray SH CL .20 .50
221 Tommy Lasorda SH CL .10 .30
222 Paul Molitor SH CL .10 .30
223 Luis Castillo .10 .30
224 Justin Thompson .10 .30
225 Rocky Coppinger .10 .30
226 Jermaine Allensworth .10 .30
227 Jeff D'Amico .10 .30
228 Jamey Wright .10 .30
229 Scott Rolen .20 .50
230 Darin Erstad .10 .30
231 Marty Janzen .10 .30
232 Jacob Cruz .10 .30
233 Raul Ibanez .10 .30
234 Nomar Garciaparra .50 1.25
235 Todd Walker .10 .30
236 Brian Giles RC .60 1.50
237 Matt Beech .10 .30
238 Mike Cameron .10 .30
239 Jose Paniagua .10 .30
240 Andruw Jones .20 .50
241 Brant Brown UPD .40 1.00
242 Robin Jennings UPD .40 1.00
243 Willie Adams UPD .40 1.00
244 Ken Caminiti UPD .60 1.50
245 Brian Jordan UPD .60 1.50
246 Chipper Jones UPD 1.50 4.00
247 Juan Gonzalez UPD .60 1.50
248 Bernie Williams UPD 1.00 2.50
249 Roberto Alomar UPD 1.00 2.50
250 Bernie Williams UPD 1.00 2.50
251 David Wells UPD .60 1.50
252 Cecil Fielder UPD .60 1.50
253 Darryl Strawberry UPD .60 1.50
254 Andy Pettitte UPD 1.00 2.50
255 Javier Lopez UPD .60 1.50
256 Gary Gaetti UPD .60 1.50
257 Ron Gant UPD .60 1.50
258 Brian Jordan UPD .60 1.50
259 John Smoltz UPD 1.00 2.50
260 Greg Maddux UPD 3.00 8.00
261 Tom Glavine UPD 1.00 2.50
262 Andruw Jones UPD 1.00 2.50
263 Greg Maddux UPD 3.00 8.00
264 David Cone UPD .60 1.50
265 Jim Leyritz UPD .40 1.00
266 Andy Pettitte UPD 1.00 2.50
267 John Wetteland UPD .60 1.50
268 Dario Veras UPD .40 1.00
269 Neifi Perez UPD .40 1.00
270 Bill Mueller UPD 1.50 4.00
271 Vladimir Guerrero .30 .75
272 Dmitri Young .10 .30
273 Nerio Rodriguez RC .10 .30
274 Kevin Orie .10 .30
275 Felipe Crespo .10 .30
276 Danny Graves .10 .30
277 Rod Myers .10 .30
278 Felix Heredia RC .10 .30
279 Ralph Milliard .10 .30
280 Greg Norton .10 .30
281 Derek Wallace .10 .30
282 Trot Nixon .10 .30
283 Bobby Chouinard .10 .30
284 Jay Witasick .10 .30
285 Travis Miller .10 .30
286 Brian Bevil .10 .30
287 Bobby Estalella .10 .30
288 Steve Soderstrom .10 .30
289 Mark Langston .10 .30
290 Tim Salmon .20 .50
291 Jim Edmonds .10 .30
292 Garret Anderson .10 .30
293 George Arias .10 .30
294 Gary DiSarcina .10 .30
295 Chuck Finley .10 .30
296 Todd Greene .10 .30
297 Randy Velarde .10 .30
298 David Justice .10 .30
299 Ryan Klesko .10 .30
300 John Smoltz .20 .50
301 Javier Lopez .10 .30
302 Greg Maddux .50 1.25
303 Denny Neagle .10 .30
304 B.J. Surhoff .10 .30
305 Chris Hoiles .10 .30
306 Eric Davis .10 .30
307 Scott Erickson .10 .30
308 Mike Bordick .10 .30
309 John Valentin .10 .30
310 Heathcliff Slocumb .10 .30
311 Tom Gordon .10 .30
312 Mike Stanley .10 .30
313 Reggie Jefferson .10 .30
314 Darren Bragg .10 .30
315 Troy O'Leary .10 .30
316 John Mabry SH CL .10 .30
317 Mark Whiten SH CL .10 .30
318 Edgar Martinez SH CL .10 .30
319 Alex Rodriguez SH CL .30 .75
320 Mark McGwire SH CL .40 1.00
321 Hideo Nomo SH CL .10 .30
322 Todd Hundley SH CL .10 .30
323 Barry Bonds SH CL .40 1.00
324 Andruw Jones SH CL .10 .30
325 Ryne Sandberg .50 1.25
326 Brian McRae .10 .30
327 Frank Castillo .10 .30
328 Shawon Dunston .10 .30
329 Ray Durham .10 .30
330 Robin Ventura .10 .30
331 Ozzie Guillen .10 .30
332 Roberto Hernandez .10 .30
333 Albert Belle .10 .30
334 Dave Martinez .10 .30
335 Willie Greene .10 .30
336 Jeff Brantley .10 .30
337 Kevin Jarvis .10 .30
338 John Smiley .10 .30
339 Eddie Taubensee .10 .30
340 Bret Boone .10 .30
341 Kevin Seitzer .10 .30
342 Jack McDowell .10 .30
343 Sandy Alomar Jr. .10 .30
344 Chad Curtis .10 .30
345 Manny Ramirez .20 .50
346 Chad Ogea .10 .30
347 Jim Thome .20 .50
348 Mark Thompson .10 .30
349 Ellis Burks .10 .30
350 Andres Galarraga .10 .30
351 Vinny Castilla .10 .30
352 Kirt Manwaring .10 .30
353 Larry Walker .10 .30
354 Omar Olivares .10 .30
355 Bobby Higginson .10 .30
356 Melvin Nieves .10 .30
357 Brian Johnson .10 .30
358 Devon White .10 .30
359 Jeff Conine .10 .30
360 Gary Sheffield .10 .30
361 Robb Nen .10 .30
362 Mike Hampton .10 .30
363 Bob Abreu .20 .50
364 Luis Gonzalez .10 .30
365 Derek Bell .10 .30
366 Sean Berry .10 .30
367 Craig Biggio .20 .50
368 Darryl Kile .10 .30
369 Shane Reynolds .10 .30
370B Jeff Bagwell CF .10 .30
White back
370A Jeff Bagwell CF .10 .30
371B Ron Gant CF .10 .30
White back
371A Ron Gant CF .10 .30
372B Andy Benes CF .10 .30
White back
372A Andy Benes CF .10 .30
373B Gary Gaetti CF .10 .30
White back
373A Gary Gaetti CF .10 .30
374B Ramon Martinez CF .10 .30
White back
374A Ramon Martinez CF .10 .30
375B Raul Mondesi CF .10 .30
White back
375A Raul Mondesi CF .10 .30
376B Steve Finley CF .10 .30
White back
376A Steve Finley CF .10 .30
377B Ken Caminiti CF .10 .30
White back
377A Ken Caminiti CF .10 .30
378B Tony Gwynn CF .20 .50
White back
378A Tony Gwynn CF .20 .50
379B Dario Veras RC .10 .30
White back
379A Dario Veras RC .10 .30
380B Andy Pettitte CF .10 .30
White back
380A Andy Pettitte CF .10 .30
381B Ruben Rivera CF .10 .30
White back
381A Ruben Rivera CF .10 .30
382B David Cone CF .10 .30
White back
382A David Cone CF .10 .30
383B Roberto Alomar CF .10 .30
White back
383A Roberto Alomar CF .10 .30
384B Edgar Martinez CF .10 .30
White back
384A Edgar Martinez CF .10 .30
385B Griffey Jr CF Wht Back .40 1.00
385A Ken Griffey Jr. CF .40 1.00
386B McGwire CF Wht Back .40 1.00
386A Mark McGwire CF .40 1.00
387B Rusty Greer CF .10 .30
White back
387A Rusty Greer CF .10 .30
388 Jose Rosado .10 .30
389 Kevin Appier .10 .30
390 Johnny Damon .20 .50
391 Jose Offerman .10 .30
392 Michael Tucker .10 .30
393 Craig Paquette .10 .30
394 Bip Roberts .10 .30
395 Ramon Martinez .10 .30
396 Greg Gagne .10 .30
397 Chan Ho Park .10 .30
398 Karim Garcia .10 .30
399 Wilton Guerrero .10 .30
400 Eric Karros .10 .30
401 Raul Mondesi .10 .30
402 Matt Mieske .10 .30
403 Mike Fetters .10 .30
404 Dave Nilsson .10 .30
405 Jose Valentin .10 .30
406 Scott Karl .10 .30
407 Marc Newfield .10 .30
408 Cal Eldred .10 .30
409 Rich Becker .10 .30
410 Terry Steinbach .10 .30
411 Chuck Knoblauch .10 .30
412 Pat Meares .10 .30
413 Brad Radke .10 .30
414 Kirby Puckett UER .30 .75
415 Andruw Jones GHL SP .60 1.50
416 Chipper Jones GHL SP 1.00 2.50
417 Mo Vaughn GHL SP .60 1.50
418 Frank Thomas GHL SP 1.00 2.50
419 Albert Belle GHL SP .60 1.50
420 Mark McGwire GHL SP 3.00 8.00
421 Derek Jeter GHL SP 3.00 8.00
422 Alex Rodriguez GHL SP 2.00 5.00
423 Juan Gonzalez GHL SP .60 1.50
424 Ken Griffey Jr. GHL SP 2.50 6.00
425 Rondell White .10 .30
426 Darrin Fletcher .10 .30
427 Cliff Floyd .10 .30
428 Mike Lansing .10 .30
429 F.P. Santangelo .10 .30
430 Todd Hundley .10 .30
431 Mark Clark .10 .30
432 Pete Harnisch .10 .30
433 Jason Isringhausen .10 .30
434 Bobby Jones .10 .30
435 Lance Johnson .10 .30
436 Carlos Baerga .10 .30
437 Mariano Duncan .10 .30
438 David Cone .10 .30
439 Mariano Rivera .30 .75
440 Derek Jeter .75 2.00
441 Joe Girardi .10 .30
442 Charlie Hayes .10 .30
443 Tim Raines .10 .30
444 Darryl Strawberry .10 .30
445 Cecil Fielder .10 .30
446 Ariel Prieto .10 .30
447 Tony Batista .10 .30
448 Brent Gates .10 .30
449 Scott Spiezio .10 .30
450 Mark McGwire .75 2.00
451 Don Wengert .10 .30
452 Mike Lieberthal .10 .30
453 Lenny Dykstra .10 .30
454 Rex Hudler .10 .30
455 Darren Daulton .10 .30
456 Kevin Stocker .10 .30
457 Trey Beamon .10 .30
458 Midre Cummings .10 .30
459 Mark Johnson .10 .30
460 Al Martin .10 .30
461 Kevin Elster .10 .30
462 Jon Lieber .10 .30
463 Jason Schmidt .10 .30
464 Paul Wagner .10 .30
465 Andy Benes .10 .30
466 Alan Benes .10 .30
467 Royce Clayton .10 .30
468 Gary Gaetti .10 .30
469 Curt Lyons RC .10 .30
470 Eugene Kingsale DD .10 .30
471 Damian Jackson DD .10 .30
472 Wendell Magee DD .10 .30
473 Kevin L. Brown DD .10 .30
474 Raul Casanova DD .10 .30
475 Ramiro Mendoza RC .10 .30
476 Todd Dunn DD .10 .30
477 Chad Mottola DD .10 .30
478 Andy Larkin DD .10 .30
479 Jaime Bluma DD .10 .30
480 Mac Suzuki DD .10 .30
481 Brian Banks DD .10 .30
482 Desi Wilson DD .10 .30
483 Einar Diaz DD .10 .30
484 Tom Pagnozzi .10 .30
485 Ray Lankford .10 .30
486 Todd Stottlemyre .10 .30
487 Donovan Osborne .10 .30
488 Trevor Hoffman .10 .30
489 Chris Gomez .10 .30
490 Ken Caminiti .10 .30
491 John Flaherty .10 .30
492 Tony Gwynn .40 1.00
493 Joey Hamilton .10 .30
494 Rickey Henderson .30 .75
495 Glenallen Hill .10 .30
496 Rod Beck .10 .30
497 Osvaldo Fernandez .10 .30
498 Rick Wilkins .10 .30
499 Joey Cora .10 .30
500 Alex Rodriguez .50 1.25
501 Randy Johnson .30 .75
502 Paul Sorrento .10 .30
503 Dan Wilson .10 .30
504 Jamie Moyer .10 .30
505 Will Clark .20 .50
506 Mickey Tettleton .10 .30
507 John Burkett .10 .30
508 Ken Hill .10 .30
509 Mark McLemore .10 .30
510 Juan Gonzalez .10 .30
511 Bobby Witt .10 .30
512 Carlos Delgado .10 .30
513 Alex Gonzalez .10 .30
514 Shawn Green .10 .30
515 Joe Carter .10 .30
516 Juan Guzman .10 .30
517 Charlie O'Brien .10 .30
518 Ed Sprague .10 .30
519 Mike Timlin .10 .30
520 Roger Clemens .60 1.50
521 Eddie Murray TRADE .75 2.00
522 Jason Dickson TRADE .20 .50
523 Jim Leyritz TRADE .20 .50
524 Michael Tucker TRADE .20 .50
525 Kenny Lofton TRADE .30 .75
526 Jimmy Key TRADE .30 .75
527 Mel Rojas TRADE .20 .50
528 Deion Sanders TRADE .50 1.25
529 Bartolo Colon TRADE .30 .75
530 Matt Williams TRADE .30 .75
531 Marquis Grissom TRADE .30 .75
532 David Justice TRADE .30 .75
533 Bubba Trammell TRADE .30 .75
534 Moises Alou TRADE .30 .75
535 Bobby Bonilla TRADE .30 .75
536 Alex Fernandez TRADE .20 .50
537 Jay Bell TRADE .30 .75
538 Chili Davis TRADE .30 .75
539 Jeff King TRADE .20 .50
540 Todd Zeile TRADE .20 .50
541 John Olerud TRADE .30 .75
542 Jose Guillen TRADE .30 .75
543 Derrek Lee TRADE .50 1.25
544 Dante Powell TRADE .20 .50
545 J.T. Snow TRADE .30 .75
546 Jeff Kent TRADE .30 .75
547 Jose Cruz Jr. TRADE .30 .75
548 John Wetteland TRADE .30 .75
549 Orlando Merced TRADE .20 .50
550 Hideki Irabu TRADE .30 .75

1997 Upper Deck Amazing Greats

Randomly inserted in all first series packs at a rate of one in 69, this 20-card set features a horizontal design along with two player photos on the front. The cards feature translucent player images against a real wood grain stock.

SER.1 STATED ODDS 1:69
AG1 Ken Griffey Jr. 5.00 12.00
AG2 Roberto Alomar 1.50 4.00
AG3 Alex Rodriguez 3.00 8.00
AG4 Paul Molitor 2.50 6.00
AG5 Chipper Jones 2.50 6.00
AG6 Tony Gwynn 2.50 6.00
AG7 Kenny Lofton 1.00 2.50
AG8 Albert Belle 1.00 2.50
AG9 Matt Williams 1.00 2.50
AG10 Frank Thomas 2.50 6.00
AG11 Greg Maddux 4.00 10.00
AG12 Sammy Sosa 1.50 4.00
AG13 Kirby Puckett 2.50 6.00
AG14 Jeff Bagwell 1.50 4.00
AG15 Cal Ripken 8.00 20.00
AG16 Manny Ramirez 1.50 4.00
AG17 Barry Bonds 4.00 10.00
AG18 Mo Vaughn 1.00 2.50
AG19 Eddie Murray 1.50 4.00
AG20 Mike Piazza 2.50 6.00

1997 Upper Deck Blue Chip Prospects

This rare 20-card set, randomly inserted into series two packs, features color photos of high expectation prospects who are likely to have a big impact on Major League Baseball. Only 500 of this crash numbered, limited edition set was produced.

RANDOM INSERTS IN SER.2 PACKS
STATED PRINT RUN 500 SERIAL #'d SETS
BC1 Andruw Jones 15.00 40.00
BC2 Derek Jeter 40.00 80.00
BC3 Scott Rolen 15.00 40.00
BC4 Manny Ramirez 15.00 40.00
BC5 Todd Walker 10.00 25.00
BC6 Rocky Coppinger 6.00 15.00
BC7 Nomar Garciaparra 8.00 20.00
BC8 Darin Erstad 10.00 25.00
BC9 Jermaine Dye 10.00 25.00
BC10 Vladimir Guerrero 10.00 25.00
BC11 Edgar Renteria 10.00 25.00
BC12 Bob Abreu 15.00 40.00
BC13 Karim Garcia 6.00 15.00
BC14 Jeff D'Amico 6.00 15.00
BC15 Chipper Jones 10.00 25.00
BC16 Todd Hollandsworth 6.00 15.00
BC17 Andy Pettitte 15.00 40.00
BC18 Ruben Rivera 6.00 15.00
BC19 Jason Kendall 10.00 25.00
BC20 Alex Rodriguez 15.00 40.00

1997 Upper Deck Game Jersey

Randomly inserted in all first series packs at a rate of one in 800, this three-card set features swatches of real game-worn jerseys cut up and placed on the cards. These cards represent the first memorabilia insert cards to hit the baseball card market and thus carry a significant impact in the development of the hobby in the late 1990's.

SER.1 STATED ODDS 1:800
GJ1 Ken Griffey Jr. 500.00 1000.00
GJ2 Tony Gwynn 25.00 60.00
GJ3 Rey Ordonez 10.00 25.00

1997 Upper Deck Hot Commodities

Randomly inserted in series two packs at a rate of one in 13, this 20-card set features color player images on a flame background in a black border. The backs carry a player head photo, statistics, and a commentary by ESPN sportscaster Dan Patrick.

COMPLETE SET (20) 10.00 25.00
SER.2 STATED ODDS 1:13
HC1 Alex Rodriguez 1.00 2.50
HC2 Andruw Jones .30 .75
HC3 Derek Jeter 2.00 5.00
HC4 Frank Thomas .75 2.00
HC5 Ken Griffey Jr. 1.50 4.00
HC6 Chipper Jones .75 2.00
HC7 Juan Gonzalez .30 .75
HC8 Cal Ripken 2.50 6.00
HC9 John Smoltz .50 1.25
HC10 Mark McGwire 1.25 3.00
HC11 Barry Bonds 1.25 3.00
HC12 Albert Belle .30 .75
HC13 Mike Piazza .75 2.00
HC14 Manny Ramirez .50 1.25
HC15 Mo Vaughn .30 .75
HC16 Tony Gwynn .75 2.00
HC17 Vladimir Guerrero .50 1.25
HC18 Hideo Nomo .50 1.25
HC19 Greg Maddux 1.25 3.00
HC20 Kirby Puckett .75 2.00

1997 Upper Deck Long Distance Connection

Randomly inserted in series two packs at a rate of one in 35, this 20-card set features color player images of some of the League's top power hitters on backgrounds utilizing Light/FX technology. The backs carry the pictured player's statistics.

COMPLETE SET (20) 15.00 40.00
SER.2 STATED ODDS 1:35
LD1 Mark McGwire 1.50 4.00
LD2 Brady Anderson .60 1.50
LD3 Ken Griffey Jr. 3.00 8.00
LD4 Albert Belle .60 1.50
LD5 Juan Gonzalez .60 1.50
LD6 Andres Galarraga 1.00 2.50
LD7 Jay Buhner .60 1.50
LD8 Mo Vaughn .60 1.50
LD9 Barry Bonds 2.50 6.00
LD10 Gary Sheffield .60 1.50
LD11 Todd Hundley .60 1.50
LD12 Frank Thomas 1.50 4.00
LD13 Sammy Sosa 1.00 2.50
LD14 Rafael Palmeiro .60 1.50
LD15 Alex Rodriguez 2.00 5.00
LD16 Mike Piazza 1.50 4.00
LD17 Ken Caminiti .60 1.50
LD18 Chipper Jones 1.50 4.00
LD19 Manny Ramirez 1.00 2.50
LD20 Andruw Jones .60 1.50

1997 Upper Deck Memorable Moments

Cards from these sets were distributed exclusively in six-card retail Collector's Choice series one and two packs. Each pack contained one of ten different Memorable Moments inserts. Each set features a selection of top stars captured in highlights of season's gone by. Each card features wave-like die cut top and bottom borders wth gold foil.

COMPLETE SERIES 1 (10) 5.00 12.00
COMPLETE SERIES 2 (10) 5.00 12.00
A1 Andruw Jones .20 .50
A2 Chipper Jones .30 .75
A3 Cal Ripken 1.00 2.50
A4 Frank Thomas .30 .75
A5 Manny Ramirez .20 .50
A6 Mike Piazza .50 1.25
A7 Mark McGwire .75 2.00
A8 Barry Bonds .75 2.00
A9 Ken Griffey Jr. .60 1.50
A10 Alex Rodriguez .50 1.25
B1 Ken Griffey Jr. .60 1.50
B2 Albert Belle .10 .30
B3 Derek Jeter .75 2.00
B4 Greg Maddux .50 1.25
B5 Tony Gwynn .40 1.00
B6 Ryne Sandberg .50 1.25
B7 Juan Gonzalez .10 .30
B8 Roger Clemens .60 1.50
B9 Jose Cruz Jr. .10 .30
B10 Mo Vaughn .10 .30

1997 Upper Deck Power Package

Randomly inserted in all first series packs at a rate of one in 24, this 20-card set feaures some of the best longball hitters. The die cut cards feature some of baseball's leading power hitters.

COMPLETE SET (20) 30.00 80.00
SER.1 STATED ODDS 1:24
*JUMBOS: .2X TO .5X BASIC PP
JUMBOS ONE PER RETAIL JUMBO PACK
PP1 Ken Griffey Jr. 4.00 10.00
PP2 Joe Carter .75 2.00
PP3 Rafael Palmeiro 1.25 3.00
PP4 Jay Buhner .75 2.00
PP5 Sammy Sosa 2.00 5.00
PP6 Fred McGriff 1.25 3.00
PP7 Jeff Bagwell 1.25 3.00
PP8 Albert Belle .75 2.00
PP9 Matt Williams .75 2.00
PP10 Mark McGwire 5.00 12.00
PP11 Gary Sheffield .75 2.00
PP12 Tim Salmon 1.25 3.00
PP13 Ryan Klesko .75 2.00
PP14 Manny Ramirez 1.25 3.00
PP15 Mike Piazza 3.00 8.00
PP16 Barry Bonds 5.00 12.00
PP17 Mo Vaughn .75 2.00
PP18 Jose Canseco 1.25 3.00
PP19 Juan Gonzalez .75 2.00
PP20 Frank Thomas 2.00 5.00

1997 Upper Deck Predictor

Randomly inserted in series two packs at a rate of one in five, this 30-card set featues a color player photo alongside a series of bats. The collector could activate the card by scratching off one of the bats to predict the performance of the pictured player during a single game. If the player matches or exceeds the predicted performance, the card could be mailed in with $2 to receive a Totally Virtual high-tech cel-card of the player pictured on the front. The backs carry the rules of the game. The deadline to redeem these cards was November 22nd, 1997. Winners and Losers are specified in our checklist with a "W" or a "L" after the player's name.

COMPLETE SET (30) 12.50 30.00
*SCRATCH LOSER: .25X TO .6X UNSCRATCH
*EXCH.WIN: 1X TO 2.5X BASIC PREDICTOR
SER.2 STATED ODDS 1:5

1 Andruw Jones .25 .60
2 Chipper Jones .40 1.00
3 Greg Maddux .60 1.50
4 Fred McGriff .25 .60
5 John Smoltz .25 .60
6 Brady Anderson .15 .40
7 Cal Ripken 1.25 3.00
8 Mo Vaughn .15 .40
9 Sammy Sosa .40 1.00
10 Albert Belle .15 .40
11 Frank Thomas .40 1.00
12 Kenny Lofton .15 .40
13 Jim Thome .25 .60
14 Dante Bichette .15 .40
15 Andres Galarraga .15 .40
16 Gary Sheffield .15 .40
17 Hideo Nomo .40 1.00
18 Mike Piazza .60 1.50
19 Derek Jeter 1.00 2.50
20 Bernie Williams .25 .60
21 Mark McGwire 1.00 2.50
22 Ken Caminiti .15 .40
23 Tony Gwynn .50 1.25
24 Barry Bonds 1.00 2.50
25 Jay Buhner .15 .40
26 Ken Griffey Jr. .75 2.00
27 Alex Rodriguez .60 1.50
28 Juan Gonzalez .15 .40
29 Dean Palmer .15 .40
30 Roger Clemens .75 2.00

1997 Upper Deck Rock Solid Foundation

Randomly inserted in all first series packs at a rate of one in seven, this 20-card set features players 25 and under who have made an impact in the majors. The fronts feature a player photo against a "silver" type background. The backs give player information as well as another player photo and are numbered with a "RS" prefix.

COMPLETE SET (20) 15.00 40.00
SER.1 STATED ODDS 1:7
RS1 Alex Rodriguez 2.50 6.00
RS2 Rey Ordonez .60 1.50
RS3 Derek Jeter 4.00 10.00
RS4 Darin Erstad .60 1.50
RS5 Chipper Jones 1.50 4.00
RS6 Johnny Damon 1.00 2.50
RS7 Ryan Klesko .60 1.50
RS8 Charles Johnson .60 1.50
RS9 Andy Pettitte 1.00 2.50
RS10 Manny Ramirez 1.00 2.50
RS11 Ivan Rodriguez 1.00 2.50
RS12 Jason Kendall .60 1.50
RS13 Rondell White .60 1.50
RS14 Alex Ochoa .60 1.50
RS15 Javier Lopez .60 1.50
RS16 Pedro Martinez 1.00 2.50
RS17 Carlos Delgado .60 1.50
RS18 Paul Wilson .60 1.50
RS19 Alan Benes .60 1.50
RS20 Raul Mondesi .60 1.50

1997 Upper Deck Run Producers

Randomly inserted in series two packs at a rate of one in 69, this 24-card set features color player images on die-cut cards that actually look and feel like home plate. The backs carry player information and career statistics.

COMPLETE SET (24) 75.00 150.00
SER.2 STATED ODDS 1:69
RP1 Ken Griffey Jr. 8.00 20.00
RP2 Barry Bonds 10.00 25.00
RP3 Albert Belle 1.50 4.00
RP4 Mark McGwire 10.00 25.00
RP5 Frank Thomas 4.00 10.00
RP6 Juan Gonzalez 1.50 4.00
RP7 Brady Anderson 1.50 4.00
RP8 Andres Galarraga 1.50 4.00
RP9 Rafael Palmeiro 2.50 6.00
RP10 Alex Rodriguez 6.00 15.00
RP11 Jay Buhner 1.50 4.00
RP12 Gary Sheffield 1.50 4.00
RP13 Sammy Sosa 4.00 10.00
RP14 Dante Bichette 1.50 4.00
RP15 Mike Piazza 6.00 15.00
RP16 Manny Ramirez 2.50 6.00
RP17 Kenny Lofton 1.50 4.00
RP18 Mo Vaughn 1.50 4.00
RP19 Tim Salmon 2.50 6.00
RP20 Chipper Jones 4.00 10.00
RP21 Jim Thome 2.50 6.00
RP22 Ken Caminiti 1.50 4.00
RP23 Jeff Bagwell 2.50 6.00
RP24 Paul Molitor 1.50 4.00

1997 Upper Deck Star Attractions

These 20 cards were issued one per pack in special Upper Deck Memorabilia Madness packs. The Memorabilia Madness packs included various redemptions for signed 8 by 10 photos with the grand prize being a grouping of Ken Griffey Jr. signed jersey, baseball and 8 by 10 photo. The die cut cards feature the words "Star Attraction" on the top with the player and team identification on the sides. The backs have a photo and a brief blurb on the player. Cards numbered 1-10 were inserted in Upper Deck packs while cards numbered 11-20 were in Collectors Choice packs.

COMPLETE SET (20) 10.00 25.00
1-10 ONE PER UD MADNESS RETAIL PACK
11-20 ONE PER CC MADNESS RETAIL PACK
*GOLD: 2X TO 5X BASIC STAR ATT.
GOLD INSERTS IN UD/CC MADNESS RETAIL
1 Ken Griffey Jr. .75 2.00
2 Barry Bonds 1.00 2.50
3 Jeff Bagwell .25 .60
4 Nomar Garciaparra .60 1.50
5 Tony Gwynn .50 1.25
6 Roger Clemens .75 2.00
7 Chipper Jones .40 1.00
8 Tino Martinez .25 .60
9 Albert Belle .15 .40
10 Kenny Lofton .15 .40
11 Alex Rodriguez .60 1.50
12 Mark McGwire 1.00 2.50
13 Cal Ripken 1.25 3.00
14 Larry Walker .15 .40
15 Mike Piazza .60 1.50
16 Frank Thomas .40 1.00
17 Juan Gonzalez .15 .40
18 Greg Maddux .60 1.50
19 Jose Cruz Jr. .40 1.00
20 Mo Vaughn .15 .40

1997 Upper Deck Ticket To Stardom

Randomly inserted in all first series packs at a rate of one in 34, this 20-card set is designed in the form of a ticket and are designed to be matched. The horizontal fronts feature two player photos as well as using "light f/x technology and embossed player images.

SER.1 STATED ODDS 1:34
TS1 Chipper Jones 2.50 6.00
TS2 Jermaine Dye 1.00 2.50
TS3 Rey Ordonez 1.00 2.50
TS4 Alex Ochoa 1.00 2.50
TS5 Derek Jeter 6.00 15.00
TS6 Ruben Rivera 1.00 2.50
TS7 Billy Wagner 1.00 2.50
TS8 Jason Kendall 1.00 2.50
TS9 Darin Erstad 1.00 2.50
TS10 Alex Rodriguez 4.00 10.00
TS11 Bob Abreu 1.50 4.00
TS12 Richard Hidalgo 2.50 6.00
TS13 Karim Garcia 1.00 2.50
TS14 Andruw Jones 1.50 4.00
TS15 Carlos Delgado 1.00 2.50
TS16 Rocky Coppinger 1.00 2.50
TS17 Jeff D'Amico 1.00 2.50
TS18 Johnny Damon 1.50 4.00
TS19 John Wasdin 1.00 2.50
TS20 Manny Ramirez 1.50 4.00

1997 Upper Deck Ticket To Stardom Combos

COMPLETE SET (10) 10.00 25.00
TS1 C.Jones 1.25 3.00
A.Jones
TS2 R.Ordonez/K.Orie .75 2.00
TS3 D.Jeter/N.Garciaparra 2.00 5.00
TS4 B.Wagner/J.Kendall .75 2.00
TS5 D.Erstad/A.Rodriguez 1.50 4.00
TS6 B.Abreu/J.Guillen 1.00 2.50
TS7 W.Guerrero/V.Guerrero 1.00 2.50
TS8 C.Delgado/R.Coppinger 1.00 2.50
TS9 J.Dickson/J.Damon .75 2.00
TS10 B.Colon/M.Ramirez 1.00 2.50

1997 Upper Deck 1996 Award Winner Jumbos

This 23-card set measures approximately 3 1/2" by 5" and features borderless color player photos with gold and silver foil highlights of both American and National League award winners. The backs carry another player photo and statistics with a sentence about winning his award. The set was issued through retail outlets and television promotions with a suggested retail set price of $19.95.

COMP.FACT SET (23) 4.00 10.00
1 Alex Rodriguez 1.25 3.00
American League
2 Tony Gwynn 1.00 2.50
National League
3 Mark McGwire 1.25 3.00
American League
4 Andres Galarraga .40 1.00
National League
5 Albert Belle .30 .75
6 Andres Galarraga .40 1.00
7 Kenny Lofton .20 .50
8 Eric Young .08 .25
9 Andy Pettitte .30 .75
10 John Smoltz .30 .75
11 Roger Clemens 1.00 2.50
12 John Smoltz .40 1.00
13 Juan Guzman .08 .25
14 Kevin Brown .30 .75
15 John Wetteland .20 .50
16 Jeff Brantley .08 .25
National League SAVE CoLeader
17 Todd Worrell .08 .25
18 Derek Jeter 2.00 5.00
19 Todd Hollandsworth .08 .25
National League
20 Juan Gonzalez .50 1.25
21 Ken Caminiti .40 1.00
22 Pat Hentgen .20 .50
23 John Smoltz .40 1.00

1997 Upper Deck Chris Berman Rock 'N Roll Hall of Fame

This one-card set features a borderless color picture of Chris Berman performing and was given away at the Rock 'N Roll Hall of Fame as part of the party Chris Berman hosted for ESPN. The back displays a small head shot of Berman along with a list of players and nicknames under the heading, "Baseball Nickname Hall of Fame."

1 Chris Berman .40 1.00

1997 Upper Deck Home Team Heroes

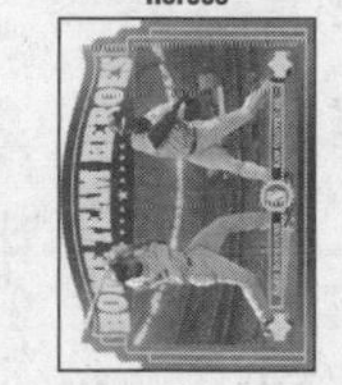

This 12-card set measures approximately 5" by 3 1/2" and features two color action embossed images of top players from the same team printed on a die-cut card with silver foil enhancements. The backs carry two small color action player photos with player information in paragraph form.

COMPLETE SET (12) 4.00 10.00
HT1 Alex Rodriguez 1.50 4.00
Ken Griffey Jr.
HT2 Bernie Williams .75 2.00
Derek Jeter
HT3 Bernard Gilkey .20 .50
Todd Hundley
HT4 Hideo Nomo .30 .75
Mike Piazza
HT5 Andruw Jones 1.00 2.50
Chipper Jones
HT6 John Smoltz 1.00 2.50
Greg Maddux
HT7 Mike Mussina 1.25 3.00
Cal Ripken Jr.
HT8 Andres Galarraga .30 .75
Dante Bichette
HT9 Juan Gonzalez .75 2.00
Ivan Rodriguez
HT10 Albert Belle .75 2.00
Frank Thomas
HT11 Kenny Lofton .30 .75
Manny Ramirez
HT12 Ken Caminiti .75 2.00
Tony Gwynn

1997 Upper Deck Ken Griffey Jr. Highlight Reels

This five-card hi-tech Diamond Vision set features actual MLB video footage of Ken Griffey Jr.'s most unbelievable plays. Each card was distributed in clamshell packaging for a suggested retail price of $9.99. The cards measure approximately 3.5" by 5" with each card containing over 20 frames of actual video footage of the player.

COMMON CARD (1-5) 4.00 10.00

1997 Upper Deck Shimano

This six-card set features color photos of top fishermen on a background of fish images with side and bottom aqua borders. The backs carry a smaller head photo and information about the pictured fisherman.

COMPLETE SET (6) 1.60 4.00
5 Jay Buhner .40 1.00
6 Tony Gwynn 1.20 3.00

1997 Upper Deck Sister Assumpta Trivia

This one-card set was introduced at the National in Cleveland, Ohio, on August 7, 1997, and is a tribute to Indians fan, Sister Mary Assumpta, who began baking chocolate chip cookies for the players in 1986. The front features the nun's picture holding a bat and a cookie. The back displays ten trivia questions with the answers printed upside down in a blue bar at the bottom.

1 Sister Mary Assumpta .20 .50

1998 Upper Deck

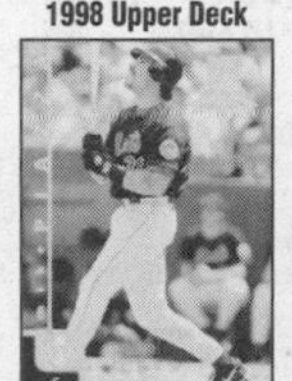

The 1998 Upper Deck set was issued in three series consisting of a 270-card first series, a 270-card second series and a 211-card third series. Each series was distributed in 12-card packs which carried a suggested retail price of $2.49. Card fronts feature game dated photographs of some of the season's most memorable moments. The following subsets are contained within the set: History in the Making (1-8/361-369), Griffey's Hot List (9-18), Define the Game (136-153), Season Highlights (244-252/532-540/748-750), Star Rookies (253-288/541-600), Postseason Headliners (415-432), Upper Echelon (451-459) and Eminent Prestige (601-630). The Eminent Prestige subset cards were slightly shortprinted (approximately 1:4 packs) and Upper Deck offered a free service to collectors trying to finish their Series three sets whereby Eminent Prestige cards were mailed to collectors who sent in proof of purchase of one-and-a-half boxes or more. The print run for Mike Piazza card number 681 was split exactly in half creating two shortprints: card number 681 (picturing Piazza as a New York Met) and card number 681A (picturing Piazza as a Florida Marlin). Both cards are exactly two times tougher to pull from packs than other regular issue Series three cards. The series three set is considered complete with both versions at 251 total cards. Notable Rookie Cards include Gabe Kapler and Magglio Ordonez.

COMPLETE SET (751) 100.00 200.00
COMPLETE SERIES 1 (270) 15.00 40.00
COMPLETE SERIES 2 (270) 15.00 40.00
COMPLETE SERIES 3 (211) 50.00 120.00
COMMON (1-600/631-750) .10 .30
COMMON EP (601-630) .75 2.00
EP SER.2 ODDS APPROXIMATELY 1:4
1 Tino Martinez HIST .10 .30
2 Jimmy Key HIST .10 .30
3 Jay Buhner HIST .10 .30
4 Mark Gardner HIST .10 .30
5 Greg Maddux HIST .30 .75
6 Pedro Martinez HIST .20 .50
7 Hideo Nomo HIST .20 .50
8 Sammy Sosa HIST .20 .50
9 Mark McGwire GHL .40 1.00
10 Ken Griffey Jr. GHL .40 1.00
11 Larry Walker GHL .10 .30
12 Tino Martinez GHL .10 .30
13 Mike Piazza GHL .30 .75
14 Jose Cruz Jr. GHL .10 .30
15 Tony Gwynn GHL .20 .50
16 Greg Maddux GHL .30 .75
17 Roger Clemens GHL .30 .75
18 Alex Rodriguez GHL .30 .75
19 Shigetoshi Hasegawa .10 .30
20 Eddie Murray .30 .75
21 Jason Dickson .10 .30
22 Darin Erstad .10 .30
23 Chuck Finley .10 .30
24 Dave Hollins .10 .30
25 Garret Anderson .10 .30
26 Michael Tucker .10 .30
27 Kenny Lofton .10 .30
28 Javier Lopez .10 .30
29 Fred McGriff .20 .50
30 Greg Maddux .50 1.25
31 Jeff Blauser .10 .30
32 John Smoltz .20 .50
33 Mark Wohlers .10 .30
34 Scott Erickson .10 .30
35 Jimmy Key .10 .30
36 Harold Baines .10 .30
37 Randy Myers .10 .30
38 B.J. Surhoff .10 .30
39 Eric Davis .10 .30
40 Rafael Palmeiro .20 .50
41 Jeffrey Hammonds .10 .30
42 Mo Vaughn .10 .30
43 Tom Gordon .10 .30
44 Tim Naehring .10 .30
45 Darren Bragg .10 .30
46 Aaron Sele .10 .30
47 Troy O'Leary .10 .30
48 John Valentin .10 .30
49 Doug Glanville .10 .30
50 Ryne Sandberg .50 1.25
51 Steve Trachsel .10 .30
52 Mark Grace .20 .50
53 Kevin Foster .10 .30
54 Kevin Tapani .10 .30
55 Kevin Orie .10 .30
56 Lyle Mouton .10 .30
57 Ray Durham .10 .30
58 Jaime Navarro .10 .30
59 Mike Cameron .10 .30
60 Albert Belle .10 .30
61 Doug Drabek .10 .30
62 Chris Snopek .10 .30
63 Eddie Taubensee .10 .30
64 Terry Pendleton .10 .30
65 Barry Larkin .20 .50
66 Willie Greene .10 .30
67 Deion Sanders .20 .50
68 Pokey Reese .10 .30
69 Jeff Shaw .10 .30
70 Jim Thome .20 .50
71 Orel Hershiser .10 .30
72 Omar Vizquel .20 .50
73 Brian Giles .10 .30
74 David Justice .10 .30
75 Bartolo Colon .10 .30
76 Sandy Alomar Jr. .10 .30
77 Neifi Perez .10 .30
78 Dante Bichette .10 .30
79 Vinny Castilla .10 .30
80 Eric Young .10 .30
81 Quinton McCracken .10 .30
82 Jamey Wright .10 .30
83 John Thomson .10 .30
84 Damion Easley .10 .30
85 Justin Thompson .10 .30
86 Willie Blair .10 .30
87 Raul Casanova .10 .30
88 Bobby Higginson .10 .30
89 Bubba Trammell .10 .30
90 Tony Clark .10 .30
91 Livan Hernandez .10 .30
92 Charles Johnson .10 .30
93 Edgar Renteria .10 .30
94 Alex Fernandez .10 .30
95 Gary Sheffield .10 .30
96 Moises Alou .10 .30
97 Tony Saunders .10 .30
98 Robb Nen .10 .30
99 Darryl Kile .10 .30
100 Craig Biggio .20 .50
101 Chris Holt .10 .30
102 Bob Abreu .10 .30
103 Luis Gonzalez .10 .30
104 Billy Wagner .10 .30
105 Brad Ausmus .10 .30
106 Chili Davis .10 .30
107 Tim Belcher .10 .30
108 Dean Palmer .10 .30
109 Jeff King .10 .30
110 Jose Rosado .10 .30
111 Mike Macfarlane .10 .30
112 Jay Bell .10 .30
113 Todd Worrell .10 .30
114 Chan Ho Park .10 .30
115 Raul Mondesi .10 .30
116 Brett Butler .10 .30
117 Greg Gagne .10 .30
118 Hideo Nomo .30 .75
119 Todd Zeile .10 .30
120 Eric Karros .10 .30
121 Cal Eldred .10 .30
122 Jeff D'Amico .10 .30
123 Antone Williamson .10 .30
124 Doug Jones .10 .30
125 Dave Nilsson .10 .30
126 Gerald Williams .10 .30
127 Fernando Vina .10 .30
128 Ron Coomer .10 .30
129 Matt Lawton .10 .30
130 Paul Molitor .10 .30
131 Todd Walker .10 .30
132 Rick Aguilera .10 .30
133 Brad Radke .10 .30
134 Bob Tewksbury .10 .30
135 Vladimir Guerrero .30 .75
136 Tony Gwynn DG .20 .50
137 Roger Clemens DG .30 .75
138 Dennis Eckersley DG .10 .30
139 Brady Anderson DG .10 .30
140 Ken Griffey Jr. DG .40 1.00
141 Derek Jeter DG .40 1.00
142 Ken Caminiti DG .10 .30
143 Frank Thomas DG .20 .50
144 Barry Bonds DG .40 1.00
145 Cal Ripken DG .50 1.25
146 Alex Rodriguez DG .30 .75
147 Greg Maddux DG .30 .75
148 Kenny Lofton DG .10 .30
149 Mike Piazza DG .30 .75
150 Mark McGwire DG .40 1.00
151 Andruw Jones DG .10 .30
152 Rusty Greer DG .10 .30
153 F.P. Santangelo DG .10 .30
154 Mike Lansing .10 .30
155 Lee Smith .10 .30
156 Carlos Perez .10 .30
157 Pedro Martinez .20 .50
158 Ryan McGuire .10 .30
159 F.P. Santangelo .10 .30
160 Rondell White .10 .30
161 Takashi Kashiwada RC .15 .40
162 Butch Huskey .10 .30
163 Edgardo Alfonzo .10 .30
164 John Franco .10 .30
165 Todd Hundley .10 .30
166 Rey Ordonez .10 .30
167 Armando Reynoso .10 .30
168 John Olerud .10 .30
169 Bernie Williams .20 .50
170 Andy Pettitte .20 .50
171 Wade Boggs .20 .50
172 Paul O'Neill .20 .50
173 Cecil Fielder .10 .30
174 Charlie Hayes .10 .30
175 David Cone .10 .30
176 Hideki Irabu .10 .30
177 Mark Bellhorn .10 .30
178 Steve Karsay .10 .30
179 Damon Mashore .10 .30
180 Jason McDonald .10 .30
181 Scott Spiezio .10 .30
182 Ariel Prieto .10 .30
183 Jason Giambi .10 .30
184 Wendell Magee .10 .30
185 Rico Brogna .10 .30
186 Garrett Stephenson .10 .30
187 Wayne Gomes .10 .30
188 Ricky Bottalico .10 .30
189 Mickey Morandini .10 .30
190 Mike Lieberthal .10 .30
191 Kevin Polcovich .10 .30
192 Francisco Cordova .10 .30
193 Kevin Young .10 .30
194 Jon Lieber .10 .30
195 Kevin Elster .10 .30
196 Tony Womack .10 .30
197 Lou Collier .10 .30
198 Mike Difelice RC .15 .40
199 Gary Gaetti .10 .30
200 Dennis Eckersley .10 .30
201 Alan Benes .10 .30
202 Willie McGee .10 .30
203 Ron Gant .10 .30
204 Fernando Valenzuela .10 .30
205 Mark McGwire .75 2.00
206 Archi Cianfrocco .10 .30
207 Andy Ashby .10 .30
208 Steve Finley .10 .30
209 Quilvio Veras .10 .30
210 Ken Caminiti .10 .30
211 Rickey Henderson .30 .75
212 Joey Hamilton .10 .30
213 Derrek Lee .20 .50
214 Bill Mueller .10 .30
215 Shawn Estes .10 .30
216 J.T. Snow .10 .30
217 Mark Gardner .10 .30
218 Terry Mulholland .10 .30
219 Dante Powell .10 .30
220 Jeff Kent .10 .30
221 Jamie Moyer .10 .30
222 Joey Cora .10 .30
223 Jeff Fassero .10 .30
224 Dennis Martinez .10 .30
225 Ken Griffey Jr. .60 1.50
226 Edgar Martinez .20 .50
227 Russ Davis .10 .30
228 Dan Wilson .10 .30
229 Will Clark .20 .50
230 Ivan Rodriguez .20 .50
231 Benji Gil .10 .30
232 Lee Stevens .10 .30
233 Mickey Tettleton .10 .30
234 Julio Santana .10 .30
235 Rusty Greer .10 .30
236 Bobby Witt .10 .30
237 Ed Sprague .10 .30
238 Pat Hentgen .10 .30
239 Kelvim Escobar .10 .30
240 Joe Carter .10 .30
241 Carlos Delgado .10 .30
242 Shannon Stewart .10 .30
243 Benito Santiago .10 .30
244 Tino Martinez SH .10 .30
245 Ken Griffey Jr. SH .40 1.00
246 Kevin Brown SH .10 .30
247 Ryne Sandberg SH .20 .50
248 Mo Vaughn SH .10 .30
249 Darryl Hamilton SH .10 .30
250 Randy Johnson SH .20 .50
251 Steve Finley SH .10 .30
252 Bobby Higginson SH .10 .30
253 Brett Tomko .10 .30
254 Mark Kotsay .10 .30
255 Jose Guillen .10 .30
256 Eli Marrero .10 .30
257 Dennis Reyes .10 .30
258 Richie Sexson .10 .30
259 Pat Cline .10 .30
260 Todd Helton .20 .50
261 Juan Melo .10 .30
262 Matt Morris .10 .30
263 Jeremi Gonzalez .10 .30
264 Jeff Abbott .10 .30
265 Aaron Boone .10 .30
266 Todd Dunwoody .10 .30
267 Jaret Wright .10 .30
268 Derrick Gibson .10 .30
269 Mario Valdez .10 .30
270 Fernando Tatis .10 .30
271 Craig Counsell .10 .30
272 Brad Rigby .10 .30
273 Danny Clyburn .10 .30
274 Brian Rose .10 .30
275 Miguel Tejada .30 .75
276 Jason Varitek .30 .75
277 Dave Dellucci RC .25 .60
278 Michael Coleman .10 .30
279 Adam Riggs .10 .30
280 Ben Grieve .10 .30
281 Brad Fullmer .10 .30
282 Ken Cloude .10 .30
283 Tom Evans .10 .30
284 Kevin Millwood RC .40 1.00
285 Paul Konerko .10 .30
286 Juan Encarnacion .10 .30
287 Chris Carpenter .10 .30
288 Tom Fordham .10 .30
289 Gary DiSarcina .10 .30
290 Tim Salmon .20 .50
291 Troy Percival .10 .30
292 Todd Greene .10 .30
293 Ken Hill .10 .30
294 Dennis Springer .10 .30
295 Jim Edmonds .10 .30
296 Allen Watson .10 .30
297 Brian Anderson .10 .30
298 Keith Lockhart .10 .30
299 Tom Glavine .20 .50
300 Chipper Jones .30 .75
301 Randall Simon .10 .30
302 Mark Lemke .10 .30
303 Ryan Klesko .10 .30
304 Denny Neagle .10 .30
305 Andruw Jones .20 .50
306 Mike Mussina .20 .50
307 Brady Anderson .10 .30
308 Chris Hoiles .10 .30
309 Mike Bordick .10 .30
310 Cal Ripken 1.00 2.50
311 Geronimo Berroa .10 .30
312 Armando Benitez .10 .30
313 Roberto Alomar .20 .50
314 Tim Wakefield .10 .30
315 Reggie Jefferson .10 .30
316 Jeff Frye .10 .30
317 Scott Hatteberg .10 .30
318 Steve Avery .10 .30
319 Robinson Checo .10 .30
320 Nomar Garciaparra .50 1.25
321 Lance Johnson .10 .30
322 Tyler Houston .10 .30
323 Mark Clark .10 .30
324 Terry Adams .10 .30
325 Sammy Sosa .30 .75
326 Scott Servais .10 .30
327 Manny Alexander .10 .30
328 Norberto Martin .10 .30
329 Scott Eyre .10 .30
330 Frank Thomas .30 .75
331 Robin Ventura .10 .30
332 Matt Karchner .10 .30
333 Keith Foulke .10 .30
334 James Baldwin .10 .30
335 Chris Stynes .10 .30
336 Bret Boone .10 .30
337 Jon Nunnally .10 .30
338 Dave Burba .10 .30
339 Eduardo Perez .10 .30
340 Reggie Sanders .10 .30
341 Mike Remlinger .10 .30
342 Pat Watkins .10 .30
343 Chad Ogea .10 .30
344 John Smiley .10 .30
345 Kenny Lofton .10 .30
346 Jose Mesa .10 .30
347 Charles Nagy .10 .30
348 Enrique Wilson .10 .30
349 Bruce Aven .10 .30
350 Manny Ramirez .20 .50
351 Jerry DiPoto .10 .30
352 Ellis Burks .10 .30
353 Kirt Manwaring .10 .30
354 Vinny Castilla .10 .30
355 Larry Walker .10 .30
356 Kevin Ritz .10 .30
357 Pedro Astacio .10 .30
358 Scott Sanders .10 .30
359 Deivi Cruz .10 .30
360 Brian L. Hunter .10 .30
361 Pedro Martinez HM .20 .50
362 Tom Glavine HM .10 .30
363 Willie McGee HM .10 .30
364 J.T. Snow HM .10 .30
365 Rusty Greer HM .10 .30
366 Mike Grace HM .10 .30
367 Tony Clark HM .10 .30

368 Ben Grieve HM .10 .30
369 Gary Sheffield HM .10 .30
370 Joe Oliver .10 .30
371 Todd Jones .10 .30
372 Frank Catalanotto RC .25 .60
373 Brian Moehler .10 .30
374 Cliff Floyd .10 .30
375 Bobby Bonilla .10 .30
376 Al Leiter .10 .30
377 Josh Booty .10 .30
378 Darren Daulton .10 .30
379 Jay Powell .10 .30
380 Felix Heredia .10 .30
381 Jim Eisenreich .10 .30
382 Richard Hidalgo .10 .30
383 Mike Hampton .10 .30
384 Shane Reynolds .10 .30
385 Jeff Bagwell .20 .50
386 Derek Bell .10 .30
387 Ricky Gutierrez .10 .30
388 Bill Spiers .10 .30
389 Jose Offerman .10 .30
390 Johnny Damon .20 .50
391 Jermaine Dye .10 .30
392 Jeff Montgomery .10 .30
393 Glendon Rusch .10 .30
394 Mike Sweeney .10 .30
395 Kevin Appier .10 .30
396 Joe Vitiello .10 .30
397 Ramon Martinez .10 .30
398 Darren Dreifort .10 .30
399 Wilton Guerrero .10 .30
400 Mike Piazza .50 1.25
401 Eddie Murray .30 .75
402 Ismael Valdes .10 .30
403 Todd Hollandsworth .10 .30
404 Mark Loretta .10 .30
405 Jeromy Burnitz .10 .30
406 Jeff Cirillo .10 .30
407 Scott Karl .10 .30
408 Mike Matheny .10 .30
409 Jose Valentin .10 .30
410 John Jaha .10 .30
411 Terry Steinbach .10 .30
412 Torii Hunter .10 .30
413 Pat Meares .10 .30
414 Marty Cordova .10 .30
415 Jaret Wright PH .10 .30
416 Mike Mussina PH .10 .30
417 John Smoltz PH .10 .30
418 Devon White PH .10 .30
419 Denny Neagle PH .10 .30
420 Livan Hernandez PH .10 .30
421 Kevin Brown PH .10 .30
422 Marquis Grissom PH .10 .30
423 Mike Mussina PH .10 .30
424 Eric Davis PH .10 .30
425 Tony Fernandez PH .10 .30
426 Moises Alou PH .10 .30
427 Sandy Alomar Jr. PH .10 .30
428 Gary Sheffield PH .10 .30
429 Jaret Wright PH .10 .30
430 Livan Hernandez PH .10 .30
431 Chad Ogea PH .10 .30
432 Edgar Renteria PH .10 .30
433 LaTroy Hawkins .10 .30
434 Rich Robertson .10 .30
435 Chuck Knoblauch .10 .30
436 Jose Vidro .10 .30
437 Dustin Hermanson .10 .30
438 Jim Bullinger .10 .30
439 Orlando Cabrera .10 .30
440 Vladimir Guerrero .30 .75
441 Ugueth Urbina .10 .30
442 Brian McRae .10 .30
443 Matt Franco .10 .30
444 Bobby Jones .10 .30
445 Bernard Gilkey .10 .30
446 Dave Mlicki .10 .30
447 Brian Bohanon .10 .30
448 Mel Rojas .10 .30
449 Tim Raines .10 .30
450 Derek Jeter .75 2.00
451 Roger Clemens UE .30 .75
452 Nomar Garciaparra UE .30 .75
453 Mike Piazza UE .30 .75
454 Mark McGwire UE .40 1.00
455 Ken Griffey Jr. UE .40 1.00
456 Larry Walker UE .10 .30
457 Alex Rodriguez UE .30 .75
458 Tony Gwynn UE .20 .50
459 Frank Thomas UE .20 .50
460 Tino Martinez .20 .50
461 Chad Curtis .10 .30
462 Ramiro Mendoza .10 .30
463 Joe Girardi .10 .30
464 David Wells .10 .30
465 Mariano Rivera .30 .75
466 Willie Adams .10 .30
467 George Williams .10 .30
468 Dave Telgheder .10 .30
469 Dave Magadan .10 .30
470 Matt Stairs .10 .30
471 Bill Taylor .10 .30
472 Jimmy Haynes .10 .30
473 Gregg Jefferies .10 .30
474 Midre Cummings .10 .30
475 Curt Schilling .10 .30
476 Mike Grace .10 .30
477 Mark Leiter .10 .30
478 Matt Beech .10 .30
479 Scott Rolen .20 .50
480 Jason Kendall .10 .30
481 Esteban Loaiza .10 .30
482 Jermaine Allensworth .10 .30
483 Mark Smith .10 .30
484 Jason Schmidt .10 .30
485 Jose Guillen .10 .30
486 Al Martin .10 .30
487 Delino DeShields .10 .30
488 Todd Stottlemyre .10 .30
489 Brian Jordan .10 .30
490 Ray Lankford .10 .30
491 Matt Morris .10 .30
492 Royce Clayton .10 .30
493 John Mabry .10 .30
494 Wally Joyner .10 .30
495 Trevor Hoffman .10 .30
496 Chris Gomez .10 .30
497 Sterling Hitchcock .10 .30
498 Pete Smith .10 .30
499 Greg Vaughn .10 .30
500 Tony Gwynn .40 1.00
501 Will Cunnane .10 .30
502 Darryl Hamilton .10 .30
503 Brian Johnson .10 .30
504 Kirk Rueter .10 .30
505 Barry Bonds .75 2.00
506 Osvaldo Fernandez .10 .30
507 Stan Javier .10 .30
508 Julian Tavarez .10 .30
509 Rich Aurilia .10 .30
510 Alex Rodriguez .50 1.25
511 David Segui .10 .30
512 Rich Amaral .10 .30
513 Raul Ibanez .10 .30
514 Jay Buhner .10 .30
515 Randy Johnson .30 .75
516 Heathcliff Slocumb .10 .30
517 Tony Saunders .10 .30
518 Kevin Elster .10 .30
519 John Burkett .10 .30
520 Juan Gonzalez .10 .30
521 John Wetteland .10 .30
522 Domingo Cedeno .10 .30
523 Darren Oliver .10 .30
524 Roger Pavlik .10 .30
525 Jose Cruz Jr. .10 .30
526 Woody Williams .10 .30
527 Alex Gonzalez .10 .30
528 Robert Person .10 .30
529 Juan Guzman .10 .30
530 Roger Clemens .60 1.50
531 Shawn Green .10 .30
532 F.Cordova .10 .30
R.Rincon
M.Smith SH
533 Nomar Garciaparra SH .30 .75
534 Roger Clemens SH .30 .75
535 Mark McGwire SH .40 1.00
536 Larry Walker SH .10 .30
537 Mike Piazza SH .30 .75
538 Curt Schilling SH .10 .30
539 Tony Gwynn SH .20 .50
540 Ken Griffey Jr. SH .40 1.00
541 Carl Pavano .10 .30
542 Shane Monahan .10 .30
543 Gabe Kapler RC .25 .60
544 Eric Milton .10 .30
545 Gary Matthews Jr. RC .25 .60
546 Mike Kinkade RC .10 .30
547 Ryan Christenson RC .10 .30
548 Corey Koskie RC .25 .60
549 Norm Hutchins .10 .30
550 Russell Branyan .10 .30
551 Masato Yoshii RC .15 .40
552 Jesus Sanchez RC .10 .30
553 Anthony Sanders .10 .30
554 Edwin Diaz .10 .30
555 Gabe Alvarez .10 .30
556 Carlos Lee RC .75 2.00
557 Mike Darr .10 .30
558 Kerry Wood .15 .40
559 Carlos Guillen .10 .30
560 Sean Casey .10 .30
561 Manny Aybar RC .10 .30
562 Octavio Dotel .10 .30
563 Jarrod Washburn .10 .30
564 Mark L. Johnson .10 .30
565 Ramon Hernandez .10 .30
566 Rich Butler RC .10 .30
567 Mike Caruso .10 .30
568 Cliff Politte .10 .30
569 Scott Elarton .10 .30
570 Magglio Ordonez RC 1.25 3.00
571 Adam Butler RC .10 .30
572 Marlon Anderson .10 .30
573 Julio Ramirez RC .10 .30
574 Darron Ingram RC .10 .30
575 Bruce Chen .10 .30
576 Steve Woodard .10 .30
577 Hiram Bocachica .10 .30
578 Kevin Witt .10 .30
579 Javier Vazquez .10 .30
580 Alex Gonzalez .10 .30
581 Brian Powell .10 .30
582 Wes Helms .10 .30
583 Ron Wright .10 .30
584 Rafael Medina .10 .30
585 Daryle Ward .10 .30
586 Geoff Jenkins .10 .30
587 Preston Wilson .10 .30
588 Jim Chamblee RC .10 .30
589 Mike Lowell RC .60 1.50
590 A.J. Hinch .10 .30
591 Francisco Cordero RC .25 .60
592 Rolando Arrojo RC .15 .40
593 Braden Looper .10 .30
594 Sidney Ponson .10 .30
595 Matt Clement .10 .30
596 Carlton Loewer .10 .30
597 Brian Meadows .10 .30
598 Danny Klassen .10 .30
599 Larry Sutton .10 .30
600 Travis Lee .10 .30
601 Randy Johnson EP 1.00 2.50
602 Greg Maddux EP 1.50 4.00
603 Roger Clemens EP 2.00 5.00
604 Jaret Wright EP .75 2.00
605 Mike Piazza EP 1.50 4.00
606 Tino Martinez EP .75 2.00
607 Frank Thomas EP 1.00 2.50
608 Mo Vaughn EP .75 2.00
609 Todd Helton EP .75 2.00
610 Mark McGwire EP 2.50 6.00
611 Jeff Bagwell EP .75 2.00
612 Travis Lee EP .75 2.00
613 Scott Rolen EP .75 2.00
614 Cal Ripken EP 3.00 8.00
615 Chipper Jones EP 1.00 2.50
616 Nomar Garciaparra EP 1.50 4.00
617 Alex Rodriguez EP 1.50 4.00
618 Derek Jeter EP 2.50 6.00
619 Tony Gwynn EP 1.25 3.00
620 Ken Griffey Jr. EP 2.00 5.00
621 Kenny Lofton EP .75 2.00
622 Juan Gonzalez EP .75 2.00
623 Jose Cruz Jr. EP .75 2.00
624 Larry Walker EP .75 2.00
625 Barry Bonds EP 2.50 6.00
626 Ben Grieve EP .75 2.00
627 Andruw Jones EP .75 2.00
628 Vladimir Guerrero EP 1.00 2.50
629 Paul Konerko EP .75 2.00
630 Paul Molitor EP .75 2.00
631 Cecil Fielder .10 .30
632 Jack McDowell .10 .30
633 Mike James .10 .30
634 Brian Anderson .10 .30
635 Jay Bell .10 .30
636 Devon White .10 .30
637 Andy Stankiewicz .10 .30
638 Tony Batista .10 .30
639 Omar Daal .10 .30
640 Matt Williams .10 .30
641 Brent Brede .10 .30
642 Jorge Fabregas .10 .30
643 Karim Garcia .10 .30
644 Felix Rodriguez .10 .30
645 Andy Benes .10 .30
646 Willie Blair .10 .30
647 Jeff Suppan .10 .30
648 Yamil Benitez .10 .30
649 Walt Weiss .10 .30
650 Andres Galarraga .10 .30
651 Doug Drabek .10 .30
652 Ozzie Guillen .10 .30
653 Joe Carter .10 .30
654 Dennis Eckersley .10 .30
655 Pedro Martinez .20 .50
656 Jim Leyritz .10 .30
657 Henry Rodriguez .10 .30
658 Rod Beck .10 .30
659 Mickey Morandini .10 .30
660 Jeff Blauser .10 .30
661 Ruben Sierra .10 .30
662 Mike Sirotka .10 .30
663 Pete Harnisch .10 .30
664 Damian Jackson .10 .30
665 Dmitri Young .10 .30
666 Steve Cooke .10 .30
667 Geronimo Berroa .10 .30
668 Shawon Dunston .10 .30
669 Mike Jackson .10 .30
670 Travis Fryman .10 .30
671 Dwight Gooden .10 .30
672 Paul Assenmacher .10 .30
673 Eric Plunk .10 .30
674 Mike Lansing .10 .30
675 Darryl Kile .10 .30
676 Luis Gonzalez .10 .30
677 Frank Castillo .10 .30
678 Joe Randa .10 .30
679 Bip Roberts .10 .30
680 Derrek Lee .20 .50
681 M.Piazza Mets SP 1.25 3.00
681A M.Piazza Marlins SP 1.25 3.00
682 Sean Berry .10 .30
683 Ramon Garcia .10 .30
684 Carl Everett .10 .30
685 Moises Alou .10 .30
686 Hal Morris .10 .30
687 Jeff Conine .10 .30
688 Gary Sheffield .10 .30
689 Jose Vizcaino .10 .30
690 Charles Johnson .10 .30
691 Bobby Bonilla .10 .30
692 Marquis Grissom .10 .30
693 Alex Ochoa .10 .30
694 Mike Morgan .10 .30
695 Orlando Merced .10 .30
696 David Ortiz .40 1.00
697 Brent Gates .10 .30
698 Otis Nixon .10 .30
699 Trey Moore .10 .30
700 Derrick May .10 .30
701 Rich Becker .10 .30
702 Al Leiter .10 .30
703 Chili Davis .10 .30
704 Scott Brosius .10 .30
705 Chuck Knoblauch .10 .30
706 Kenny Rogers .10 .30
707 Mike Blowers .10 .30
708 Mike Fetters .10 .30
709 Tom Candiotti .10 .30
710 Rickey Henderson .30 .75
711 Bob Abreu .10 .30
712 Mark Lewis .10 .30
713 Doug Glanville .10 .30
714 Desi Relaford .10 .30
715 Kent Mercker .10 .30
716 Kevin Brown .20 .50
717 James Mouton .10 .30
718 Mark Langston .10 .30
719 Greg Myers .10 .30
720 Orel Hershiser .10 .30
721 Charlie Hayes .10 .30
722 Robb Nen .10 .30
723 Glenallen Hill .10 .30
724 Tony Saunders .10 .30
725 Wade Boggs .20 .50
726 Kevin Stocker .10 .30
727 Wilson Alvarez .10 .30
728 Albie Lopez .10 .30
729 Dave Martinez .10 .30
730 Fred McGriff .20 .50
731 Quinton McCracken .10 .30
732 Bryan Rekar .10 .30
733 Paul Sorrento .10 .30
734 Roberto Hernandez .10 .30
735 Bubba Trammell .10 .30
736 Miguel Cairo .10 .30
737 John Flaherty .10 .30
738 Terrell Wade .10 .30
739 Roberto Kelly .10 .30
740 Mark McLemore .10 .30
741 Danny Patterson .10 .30
742 Aaron Sele .10 .30
743 Tony Fernandez .10 .30
744 Randy Myers .10 .30
745 Jose Canseco .20 .50
746 Darrin Fletcher .10 .30
747 Mike Stanley .10 .30
748 Marquis Grissom SH CL .10 .30
749 Fred McGriff SH CL .10 .30
750 Travis Lee SH CL .10 .30

1998 Upper Deck 3 x 5 Blow Ups

27 Kenny Lofton .30 .75
30 Greg Maddux 1.00 2.50
40 Rafael Palmeiro .50 1.25
50 Ryne Sandberg 1.25 3.00
60 Albert Belle .30 .75
65 Barry Larkin .50 1.25
67 Deion Sanders .50 1.25
95 Gary Sheffield .30 .75
130 Paul Molitor .75 2.00
135 Vladimir Guerrero .50 1.25
176 Hideki Irabu .30 .75
205 Mark McGwire 1.25 3.00
211 Rickey Henderson .75 2.00
225 Ken Griffey Jr. 1.50 4.00
230 Ivan Rodriguez .50 1.25

1998 Upper Deck 5 x 7 Blow Ups

310 Cal Ripken 2.50 6.00
320 Nomar Garciaparra .50 1.25
330 Frank Thomas .75 2.00
355 Larry Walker .50 1.25
385 Jeff Bagwell .50 1.25
400 Mike Piazza .75 2.00
450 Derek Jeter 2.00 5.00
500 Tony Gwynn .75 2.00
510 Alex Rodriguez 1.00 2.50
530 Roger Clemens 1.00 2.50

1998 Upper Deck 10th Anniversary Preview

Randomly inserted in Series one packs at the rate of one in five, this 60-card set features color player photos in a design similar to the inaugural 1989 Upper Deck series. The backs carry a photo of that player's previous Upper Deck card. A 10th Anniversary Ballot Card was inserted one in four packs which allowed the collector to vote for the players they wanted to see in the 1999 Upper Deck tenth anniversary series.

COMPLETE SET (60) 60.00 120.00
SER.1 STATED ODDS 1:5
COMP.RETAIL SET (60) 8.00 20.00
*RETAIL: .08X TO .2X BASIC 10TH ANN
RETAIL DISTRIBUTED AS FACTORY SET

1 Greg Maddux 2.00 5.00
2 Mike Mussina .75 2.00
3 Roger Clemens 2.50 6.00
4 Hideo Nomo 1.25 3.00
5 David Cone .50 1.25
6 Tom Glavine .75 2.00
7 Andy Pettitte .75 2.00
8 Jimmy Key .50 1.25
9 Randy Johnson 1.25 3.00
10 Dennis Eckersley .50 1.25
11 Lee Smith .50 1.25
12 John Franco .50 1.25
13 Randy Myers .50 1.25
14 Mike Piazza 2.00 5.00
15 Ivan Rodriguez .75 2.00
16 Todd Hundley .50 1.25
17 Sandy Alomar Jr. .50 1.25
18 Frank Thomas 1.25 3.00
19 Rafael Palmeiro .75 2.00
20 Mark McGwire 3.00 8.00
21 Mo Vaughn .50 1.25
22 Fred McGriff .75 2.00
23 Andres Galarraga .50 1.25
24 Mark Grace .75 2.00
25 Jeff Bagwell .75 2.00
26 Roberto Alomar .75 2.00
27 Chuck Knoblauch .50 1.25
28 Ryne Sandberg 2.00 5.00
29 Eric Young .50 1.25
30 Craig Biggio .75 2.00
31 Carlos Baerga .50 1.25
32 Robin Ventura .50 1.25
33 Matt Williams .50 1.25
34 Wade Boggs .75 2.00
35 Dean Palmer .50 1.25
36 Chipper Jones 1.25 3.00
37 Vinny Castilla .50 1.25
38 Ken Caminiti .50 1.25
39 Omar Vizquel .75 2.00
40 Cal Ripken 4.00 10.00
41 Derek Jeter 3.00 8.00
42 Alex Rodriguez 2.00 5.00
43 Barry Larkin .75 2.00
44 Mark Grudzielanek .50 1.25
45 Albert Belle .50 1.25
46 Manny Ramirez .75 2.00
47 Jose Canseco .75 2.00
48 Ken Griffey Jr. 2.50 6.00
49 Juan Gonzalez .50 1.25
50 Kenny Lofton .50 1.25
51 Sammy Sosa 1.25 3.00
52 Larry Walker .50 1.25
53 Gary Sheffield .50 1.25
54 Rickey Henderson 1.25 3.00
55 Tony Gwynn 1.50 4.00
56 Barry Bonds 3.00 8.00
57 Paul Molitor .50 1.25
58 Edgar Martinez .75 2.00
59 Chili Davis .50 1.25
60 Eddie Murray 1.25 3.00

1998 Upper Deck 10th Anniversary Preview Retail

COMPLETE SET (60) 8.00 20.00
*STARS: .08X TO .2X BASIC CARDS

1998 Upper Deck A Piece of the Action 1

Randomly inserted in first series packs at the rate of one in 2,500, cards from this set feature color photos of top players with pieces of actual game worn jerseys and/or game used bats embedded in the cards.

SER.1 STATED ODDS 1:2500
MULTI-COLOR PATCHES CARRY PREMIUMS

1 Jay Buhner Bat 10.00 25.00
2 Tony Gwynn Bat 15.00 40.00
3 Tony Gwynn Jersey 15.00 40.00
4 Todd Hollandsworth Bat 6.00 15.00
5 Todd Hollandsworth Jersey 6.00 15.00
6 Greg Maddux Jersey 30.00 60.00
7 Alex Rodriguez Bat 15.00 40.00
8 Alex Rodriguez Jersey 15.00 40.00
9 Gary Sheffield Bat 10.00 25.00
10 Gary Sheffield Jersey 10.00 25.00

1998 Upper Deck A Piece of the Action 2

Randomly seeded into second series packs at a rate of 1:2500, each of these four different cards features pieces of both game-used bats and jerseys incorporated into the design of the card. According to information provided on the media release, only 225 of each card was produced. The cards are numbered by the player's initials.

SER.2 STATED ODDS 1:2500
STATED PRINT RUN 225 SETS

AJ Andruw Jones 30.00 60.00
GS Gary Sheffield 15.00 40.00
JB Jay Buhner 15.00 40.00
RA Roberto Alomar 30.00 60.00

1998 Upper Deck A Piece of the Action 3

Randomly seeded into third series packs, each of these cards featured a jersey swatch embedded on the card. The portion of the bat which was in series two is now just a design element. Ken Griffey, Jr. signed 24 of these cards and they were inserted into the packs as well.

RANDOM INSERTS IN SER.3 PACKS
PRINT RUNS B/WN 200-300 #'d COPIES PER
GRIFFEY AU PRINT RUN 24 #'d CARDS
NO GRIFFEY AU PRICE DUE TO SCARCITY

BG Ben Grieve/200 10.00 25.00
JC Jose Cruz Jr./200 10.00 25.00
KG Ken Griffey Jr./300 15.00 40.00
TL Travis Lee/200 10.00 25.00
KGS Ken Griffey Jr. AU/24

1998 Upper Deck All-Star Credentials

Randomly inserted in packs at a rate of one in nine, this 30-card insert set features players who have the best chance of appearing in future All-Star games.

COMPLETE SET (30) 40.00 100.00
SER.3 STATED ODDS 1:9

AS1 Ken Griffey Jr. 2.50 6.00
AS2 Travis Lee .50 1.25
AS3 Ben Grieve .50 1.25
AS4 Jose Cruz Jr. .50 1.25
AS5 Andruw Jones .75 2.00
AS6 Craig Biggio .75 2.00
AS7 Hideo Nomo 1.25 3.00
AS8 Cal Ripken 4.00 10.00
AS9 Jaret Wright .50 1.25
AS10 Mark McGwire 3.00 8.00
AS11 Derek Jeter 3.00 8.00
AS12 Scott Rolen .75 2.00
AS13 Jeff Bagwell .75 2.00
AS14 Manny Ramirez .75 2.00
AS15 Alex Rodriguez 2.00 5.00
AS16 Chipper Jones 1.25 3.00
AS17 Larry Walker .50 1.25
AS18 Barry Bonds 3.00 8.00
AS19 Tony Gwynn 1.50 4.00
AS20 Mike Piazza 2.00 5.00
AS21 Roger Clemens 2.50 6.00
AS22 Greg Maddux 2.00 5.00
AS23 Jim Thome .75 2.00
AS24 Tino Martinez .75 2.00
AS25 Nomar Garciaparra 2.00 5.00
AS26 Juan Gonzalez .50 1.25
AS27 Kenny Lofton .50 1.25
AS28 Randy Johnson 1.25 3.00
AS29 Todd Helton .75 2.00
AS30 Frank Thomas 1.25 3.00

1998 Upper Deck Amazing Greats

Randomly inserted in Series one packs, this 30-card set features color photos of amazing players printed on a hi-tech plastic card. Only 2000 of this set were produced and are sequentially numbered.

COMPLETE SET (30) 200.00 400.00
STATED PRINT RUN 2000 SETS
*DIE CUTS: 1X TO 2.5X BASIC AMAZING
DIE CUT PRINT RUN 250 SERIAL #'d SETS
RANDOM INSERTS IN SER.1 PACKS

AG1 Ken Griffey Jr. 6.00 15.00
AG2 Derek Jeter 8.00 20.00
AG3 Alex Rodriguez 5.00 12.00
AG4 Paul Molitor 1.25 3.00
AG5 Jeff Bagwell 2.00 5.00
AG6 Larry Walker 1.25 3.00
AG7 Kenny Lofton 1.25 3.00
AG8 Cal Ripken 10.00 25.00
AG9 Juan Gonzalez 1.25 3.00
AG10 Chipper Jones 3.00 8.00
AG11 Greg Maddux 5.00 12.00
AG12 Roberto Alomar 2.00 5.00
AG13 Mike Piazza 5.00 12.00
AG14 Andres Galarraga 1.25 3.00
AG15 Barry Bonds 8.00 20.00
AG16 Andy Pettitte 2.00 5.00
AG17 Nomar Garciaparra 5.00 12.00
AG18 Tino Martinez 2.00 5.00
AG19 Tony Gwynn 4.00 10.00
AG20 Frank Thomas 3.00 8.00
AG21 Roger Clemens 6.00 15.00
AG22 Sammy Sosa 3.00 8.00
AG23 Jose Cruz Jr. 1.25 3.00
AG24 Manny Ramirez 2.00 5.00
AG25 Mark McGwire 8.00 20.00
AG26 Randy Johnson 3.00 8.00
AG27 Mo Vaughn 1.25 3.00
AG28 Gary Sheffield 1.25 3.00
AG29 Andruw Jones 2.00 5.00
AG30 Albert Belle 1.25 3.00

1998 Upper Deck Blue Chip Prospects

Randomly inserted in Series two packs, this 30-card set features color photos of some of the league's most impressive prospects printed on die-cut acetate cards. Only 2,000 of each card were produced.

COMPLETE SET (30) 30.00 60.00
RANDOM INSERTS IN SER.2 PACKS
STATED PRINT RUN 2000 SERIAL #'d SETS

BC1 Nomar Garciaparra 2.00 5.00
BC2 Scott Rolen 2.00 5.00
BC3 Jason Dickson 1.25 3.00
BC4 Darin Erstad 1.25 3.00
BC5 Brad Fullmer 1.25 3.00
BC6 Jaret Wright 1.25 3.00
BC7 Justin Thompson 1.25 3.00
BC8 Matt Morris 1.25 3.00
BC9 Fernando Tatis 1.25 3.00
BC10 Alex Rodriguez 4.00 10.00
BC11 Todd Helton 2.00 5.00
BC12 Andy Pettitte 2.00 5.00
BC13 Jose Cruz Jr. 1.25 3.00
BC14 Mark Kotsay 1.25 3.00
BC15 Derek Jeter 8.00 20.00
BC16 Paul Konerko 1.25 3.00
BC17 Todd Dunwoody 1.25 3.00
BC18 Vladimir Guerrero 2.00 5.00
BC19 Miguel Tejada 3.00 8.00
BC20 Chipper Jones 3.00 8.00
BC21 Kevin Orie 1.25 3.00
BC22 Juan Encarnacion 1.25 3.00
BC23 Brian Rose 1.25 3.00
BC24 Livan Hernandez 1.25 3.00
BC25 Andruw Jones 1.25 3.00
BC26 Brian Giles 1.25 3.00
BC27 Brett Tomko 1.25 3.00
BC28 Jose Guillen 1.25 3.00
BC29 Aaron Boone 1.25 3.00
BC30 Ben Grieve 1.25 3.00

1998 Upper Deck Clearly Dominant

Randomly inserted in Series two packs, this 30-card set features color head photos of top players with a black-and-white action shot in the background printed on Light F/X plastic stock. Only 250 sequentially numbered sets were produced.

RANDOM INSERTS IN SER.2 PACKS
STATED PRINT RUN 250 SERIAL #'d SETS

CD1 Mark McGwire 20.00 50.00
CD2 Derek Jeter 30.00 80.00
CD3 Alex Rodriguez 15.00 40.00
CD4 Paul Molitor 12.00 30.00
CD5 Jeff Bagwell 8.00 20.00
CD6 Ivan Rodriguez 8.00 20.00
CD7 Kenny Lofton 5.00 12.00
CD8 Cal Ripken 40.00 100.00
CD9 Albert Belle 5.00 12.00
CD10 Chipper Jones 12.00 30.00

CD11 Gary Sheffield 5.00 12.00
CD12 Roberto Alomar 8.00 20.00
CD13 Mo Vaughn 5.00 12.00
CD14 Andres Galarraga 8.00 20.00
CD15 Nomar Garciaparra 8.00 20.00
CD16 Randy Johnson 12.00 30.00
CD17 Mike Mussina 8.00 20.00
CD18 Greg Maddux 15.00 40.00
CD19 Tony Gwynn 12.00 30.00
CD20 Frank Thomas 12.00 30.00
CD21 Roger Clemens 15.00 40.00
CD22 Dennis Eckersley 8.00 20.00
CD23 Juan Gonzalez 5.00 12.00
CD24 Tino Martinez 5.00 12.00
CD25 Andruw Jones 5.00 12.00
CD26 Larry Walker 8.00 20.00
CD27 Ken Caminiti 5.00 12.00
CD28 Mike Piazza 12.00 30.00
CD29 Barry Bonds 20.00 50.00
CD30 Ken Griffey Jr. 25.00 60.00

1998 Upper Deck Destination Stardom

Randomly inserted in packs at a rate of one in five, this 60-card insert set features color action photos of today's star potential placed in a diamond-cut center with four colored corners. The cards are foil enhanced and die-cut.

COMPLETE SET (60) 40.00 100.00
SER.3 STATED ODDS 1:5
DS1 Travis Lee .40 1.00
DS2 Nomar Garciaparra 2.50 6.00
DS3 Alex Gonzalez .40 1.00
DS4 Richard Hidalgo .40 1.00
DS5 Jaret Wright .40 1.00
DS6 Mike Kinkade 1.25 3.00
DS7 Matt Morris .60 1.50
DS8 Gary Matthews Jr. 1.25 3.00
DS9 Brett Tomko .40 1.00
DS10 Todd Helton .75 2.00
DS11 Scott Elarton .40 1.00
DS12 Scott Rolen .75 2.00
DS13 Jose Cruz Jr. .40 1.00
DS14 Jarrod Washburn .40 1.00
DS15 Sean Casey .60 1.50
DS16 Magglio Ordonez 2.50 6.00
DS17 Gabe Alvarez .40 1.00
DS18 Todd Dunwoody .40 1.00
DS19 Kevin Witt .40 1.00
DS20 Ben Grieve .40 1.00
DS21 Daryle Ward .40 1.00
DS22 Matt Clement .60 1.50
DS23 Carlton Loewer .40 1.00
DS24 Javier Vazquez .60 1.50
DS25 Paul Konerko .60 1.50
DS26 Preston Wilson .60 1.50
DS27 Wes Helms .40 1.00
DS28 Derek Jeter 4.00 10.00
DS29 Corey Koskie 1.25 3.00
DS30 Russell Branyan .40 1.00
DS31 Vladimir Guerrero 1.25 3.00
DS32 Ryan Christenson .60 1.50
DS33 Carlos Lee 2.50 6.00
DS34 Dave Dellucci .75 2.00
DS35 Bruce Chen .40 1.00
DS36 Ricky Ledee .40 1.00
DS37 Ron Wright .40 1.00
DS38 Derrek Lee .75 2.00
DS39 Miguel Tejada 1.25 3.00
DS40 Brad Fullmer .40 1.00
DS41 Rich Butler .40 1.00
DS42 Chris Carpenter .60 1.50
DS43 Alex Rodriguez 2.50 6.00
DS44 Darron Ingram .60 1.50
DS45 Kerry Wood .60 1.50
DS46 Jason Varitek 1.25 3.00
DS47 Ramon Hernandez .40 1.00
DS48 Aaron Boone .60 1.50
DS49 Juan Encarnacion .40 1.00
DS50 A.J. Hinch .40 1.00
DS51 Mike Lowell 2.00 5.00
DS52 Fernando Tatis .40 1.00
DS53 Jose Guillen .60 1.50
DS54 Mike Caruso .40 1.00
DS55 Carl Pavano .60 1.50
DS56 Chris Clemons .40 1.00
DS57 Mark L. Johnson .40 1.00
DS58 Ken Cloude .40 1.00
DS59 Rolando Arrojo 1.25 3.00
DS60 Mark Kotsay .60 1.50

1998 Upper Deck Griffey Home Run Chronicles

Randomly inserted in first and second series packs at the rate of one in nine, this 56-card set features color photos of Ken Griffey Jr.'s 56 home runs of the 1997 season. The fronts of the Series one inserts have photos and a brief headline of each homer. The backs all have the same photo and more details about each homer. The cards are notated on the back with what date each homer was hit. Series two inserts feature game-dated photos from the actual games in which the homers were hit.

COMPLETE SET (56) 20.00 50.00
COMPLETE SERIES 1 (30) 10.00 25.00
COMPLETE SERIES 2 (26) 10.00 25.00
COMMON GRIFFEY (1-56) .75 2.00
SER.1 AND 2 STATED ODDS 1:9

1998 Upper Deck National Pride

Randomly inserted in Series one packs at the rate of one in 23, this 42-card set features color photos of some of the league's great players from countries other than the United States printed on die-cut rainbow foil cards. The backs carry player information.

SER.1 STATED ODDS 1:23
NP1 Dave Nilsson 2.00 5.00
NP2 Larry Walker 2.00 5.00
NP3 Edgar Renteria 2.00 5.00
NP4 Jose Canseco 3.00 8.00
NP5 Rey Ordonez 2.00 5.00
NP6 Rafael Palmeiro 3.00 8.00
NP7 Livan Hernandez 2.00 5.00
NP8 Andruw Jones 3.00 8.00
NP9 Manny Ramirez 3.00 8.00
NP10 Sammy Sosa 5.00 12.00
NP11 Raul Mondesi 2.00 5.00
NP12 Moises Alou 2.00 5.00
NP13 Pedro Martinez 3.00 8.00
NP14 Vladimir Guerrero 5.00 12.00
NP15 Chili Davis 2.00 5.00
NP16 Hideo Nomo 5.00 12.00
NP17 Hideki Irabu 2.00 5.00
NP18 Shigetoshi Hasegawa 2.00 5.00
NP19 Takashi Kashiwada 2.50 6.00
NP20 Chan Ho Park 2.00 5.00
NP21 Fernando Valenzuela 2.00 5.00
NP22 Vinny Castilla 2.00 5.00
NP23 Armando Reynoso 2.00 5.00
NP24 Karim Garcia 2.00 5.00
NP25 Marvin Benard 2.00 5.00
NP26 Mariano Rivera 5.00 12.00
NP27 Juan Gonzalez 2.00 5.00
NP28 Roberto Alomar 3.00 8.00
NP29 Ivan Rodriguez 3.00 8.00
NP30 Carlos Delgado 2.00 5.00
NP31 Bernie Williams 3.00 8.00
NP32 Edgar Martinez 3.00 8.00
NP33 Frank Thomas 5.00 12.00
NP34 Barry Bonds 12.50 30.00
NP35 Mike Piazza 8.00 20.00
NP36 Chipper Jones 5.00 12.00
NP37 Cal Ripken 15.00 40.00
NP38 Alex Rodriguez 8.00 20.00
NP39 Ken Griffey Jr. 10.00 25.00
NP40 Andres Galarraga 2.00 5.00
NP41 Omar Vizquel 3.00 8.00
NP42 Ozzie Guillen 2.00 5.00

1998 Upper Deck Power Deck Audio Griffey

In an effort to premier their new Power Deck Audio technology, Upper Deck created three special Ken Griffey Jr. cards (blue, green and silver backgrounds), each of which contained the same five minute interview with the Mariner's superstar. These cards were randomly seeded exclusively into test packs comprising only 10 percent of the total first series 1998 Upper Deck print run. The seeding ratios are as follows: blue 1:8, green 1:100 and silver 1:2400. Each test issue box contained a clear CD disc for which the card could be placed upon for playing on any common CD player. To play the card, the center hole had to be punched out. Prices below are for Mint unpunched cards. Punched out cards trade at twenty-five percent of the listed values.

GREY STATED ODDS 1:46
BLUE STATED ODDS 1:500
TEAL STATED ODDS 1:2400
1 Ken Griffey Jr. Grey 1.00 2.50
2 Ken Griffey Jr. Blue 6.00 15.00
3 Ken Griffey Jr. Teal 20.00 50.00

1998 Upper Deck Prime Nine

Randomly inserted in Series two packs at the rate of one in five, this 60-card set features color photos of the current most popular players printed on premium silver card stock.

COMPLETE SET (60) 40.00 100.00
COMMON GRIFFEY (1-7) .75 2.00
COMMON PIAZZA (8-14) .75 2.00
COMMON F.THOMAS (15-21) .50 1.25
COMMON MCGWIRE (22-28) 1.25 3.00
COMMON RIPKEN (29-35) 1.50 4.00
COMMON J.GONZALEZ (36-42) .20 .50
COMMON GWYNN (43-49) .60 1.50
COMMON BONDS (50-55) 1.25 3.00
COMMON MADDUX (56-60) .75 2.00
SER.2 STATED ODDS 1:5

1998 Upper Deck Retrospectives

Randomly inserted in series three packs at a rate of one in 24, this 30-card insert set takes a look back at the unforgettable careers of some of baseball's most valuable contributors. The fronts feature a color action photo from each player's rookie season.

SER.3 STATED ODDS 1:24 3.00 8.00
1 Dennis Eckersley 1.25 3.00
2 Rickey Henderson 3.00 8.00
3 Harold Baines 1.25 3.00
4 Cal Ripken 10.00 25.00
5 Tony Gwynn 4.00 10.00
6 Wade Boggs 2.00 5.00
7 Orel Hershiser 1.25 3.00
8 Joe Carter 1.25 3.00
9 Roger Clemens 6.00 15.00
10 Barry Bonds 8.00 20.00
11 Mark McGwire 8.00 20.00
12 Greg Maddux 5.00 12.00
13 Fred McGriff 2.00 5.00
14 Rafael Palmeiro 2.00 5.00
15 Craig Biggio 2.00 5.00
16 Brady Anderson 1.25 3.00
17 Randy Johnson 3.00 8.00
18 Gary Sheffield 1.25 3.00
19 Albert Belle 1.25 3.00
20 Ken Griffey Jr. 6.00 15.00
21 Juan Gonzalez 1.25 3.00
22 Larry Walker 1.25 3.00
23 Tino Martinez 2.00 5.00
24 Frank Thomas 3.00 8.00
25 Jeff Bagwell 2.00 5.00
26 Kenny Lofton 1.25 3.00
27 Mo Vaughn 1.25 3.00
28 Mike Piazza 5.00 12.00
29 Alex Rodriguez 5.00 12.00
30 Chipper Jones 3.00 8.00

1998 Upper Deck Rookie Edition Preview

Randomly inserted in Upper Deck Series two packs at an approximate rate of one in six, this 10-card set features color photos of players who were top rookies. The backs carry player information.

COMPLETE SET (10) 2.50 6.00
1 Nomar Garciaparra .75 2.00
2 Scott Rolen .30 .75
3 Mark Kotsay .20 .50
4 Todd Helton .30 .75
5 Paul Konerko .20 .50
6 Juan Encarnacion .20 .50
7 Brad Fullmer .20 .50
8 Miguel Tejada .50 1.25
9 Richard Hidalgo .20 .50
10 Ben Grieve .20 .50

1998 Upper Deck Tape Measure Titans

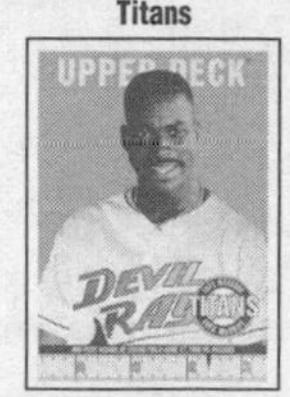

Randomly inserted in Series two packs at the rate of one in 23, this 30-card set features color photos of the league's most productive long-ball hitters printed on unique retro cards.

COMPLETE SET (30) 75.00 150.00
SER.2 STATED ODDS 1:23
*GOLD: .4X TO 1X BASIC TITAN
GOLD: RANDOM IN RETAIL PACKS
GOLD PRINT RUN 2667 SERIAL #'d SETS
1 Mark McGwire 8.00 20.00
2 Andres Galarraga 1.25 3.00
3 Jeff Bagwell 2.00 5.00
4 Larry Walker 1.25 3.00
5 Frank Thomas 3.00 8.00
6 Rafael Palmeiro 2.00 5.00
7 Nomar Garciaparra 5.00 12.00
8 Mo Vaughn 1.25 3.00
9 Albert Belle 1.25 3.00
10 Ken Griffey Jr. 6.00 15.00
11 Manny Ramirez 2.00 5.00
12 Jim Thome 2.00 5.00
13 Tony Clark 1.25 3.00
14 Juan Gonzalez 1.25 3.00
15 Mike Piazza 5.00 12.00
16 Jose Canseco 2.00 5.00
17 Jay Buhner 1.25 3.00
18 Alex Rodriguez 5.00 12.00
19 Jose Cruz Jr. 1.25 3.00
20 Tino Martinez 2.00 5.00
21 Carlos Delgado 1.25 3.00
22 Andruw Jones 2.00 5.00
23 Chipper Jones 3.00 8.00
24 Fred McGriff 2.00 5.00
25 Matt Williams 1.25 3.00
26 Sammy Sosa 3.00 8.00
27 Vinny Castilla 1.25 3.00
28 Tim Salmon 2.00 5.00
29 Ken Caminiti 1.25 3.00
30 Barry Bonds 8.00 20.00

1998 Upper Deck Unparalleled

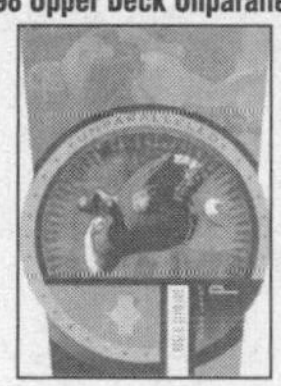

Randomly inserted in series three hobby packs only at a rate of one in 72, this 20-card insert set features color action photos on a high-tech designed card.

COMPLETE SET (20) 125.00 250.00
SER.3 STATED ODDS 1:72 HOBBY
1 Ken Griffey Jr. 8.00 20.00
2 Travis Lee 1.50 4.00
3 Ben Grieve 1.50 4.00
4 Jose Cruz Jr. 1.50 4.00
5 Nomar Garciaparra 6.00 15.00
6 Hideo Nomo 4.00 10.00
7 Kenny Lofton 1.50 4.00
8 Cal Ripken 12.50 30.00
9 Roger Clemens 8.00 20.00
10 Mike Piazza 6.00 15.00
11 Jeff Bagwell 2.50 6.00
12 Chipper Jones 4.00 10.00
13 Greg Maddux 6.00 15.00
14 Randy Johnson 4.00 10.00
15 Alex Rodriguez 6.00 15.00
16 Barry Bonds 10.00 25.00
17 Frank Thomas 4.00 10.00
18 Juan Gonzalez 1.50 4.00
19 Tony Gwynn 5.00 12.00
20 Mark McGwire 10.00 25.00

1998 Upper Deck Griffey Most Memorable Home Runs

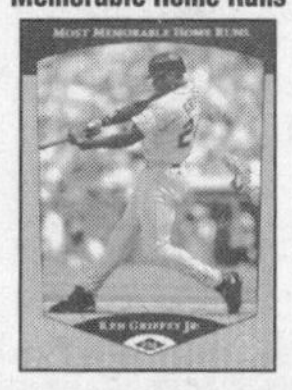

This 10-card set features color action photos of Ken Griffey Jr. hitting the most memorable home runs of his career printed on cards measuring approximately 3 1/2" by 5" with gold foil highlights. The backs carry another photo of the home run along with the date and why the home run was important in his career. Limited Edition Ken Griffey Jr. Autograph cards were randomly inserted in the set boxes. Also inserted was a special redemption card to be redeemed for an exclusive Ken Griffey Jr. 300th HR Commemorative Card or a special oversized card of equal or geater value.

COMMON CARD (1-10) .50 1.25

1998 Upper Deck Griffey Most Memorable Home Runs Autographed

Randomly inserted into boxes of Griffey Most Memorable Home Runs sets were these autographed cards. Ken Griffey Jr. signed 10 each of the cards in the set and the cards are all serial numbered on the front "x"/10. No pricing is available due to scarcity.

1 Ken Griffey Jr./4/10/89
2 Ken Griffey Jr./9/14/90
3 Ken Griffey Jr./7/14/92
4 Ken Griffey Jr./7/28/93
5 Ken Griffey Jr./6/30/94
6 Ken Griffey Jr./8/24/95
7 Ken Griffey Jr./10/8/95
8 Ken Griffey Jr./4/25/97
9 Ken Griffey Jr./9/7/97
10 Ken Griffey Jr./9/27/97

1998 Upper Deck Mark McGwire's Chase for 62

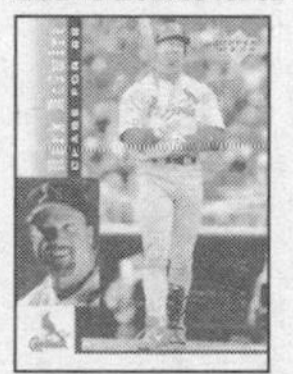

This 31-card set features color action photos of memorable moments in the 1998 season for Mark McGwire in his chase for 62 home runs. One oversized 3 1/2" by 5" commemorative card was included showing Big Mac's historical 61st and 62nd home runs. The set was distributed by the Home Shopping Network in a red box. The hobby box is yellow. The set carries a suggested retail price of $19.99. The oversize card is slightly different in each version (Home Shopping, Hobby and Retail) issued. However, there is no difference in the values of this card.

COMP.FACT SET (31) 6.00 15.00
COMMON CARD (1-30) .20 .50
4 Mark McGwire .40 1.00
Ken Griffey Jr.
NNO Mark McGwire/61st and 62nd homers 1.25 3.00

1998 Upper Deck McGwire Jumbo

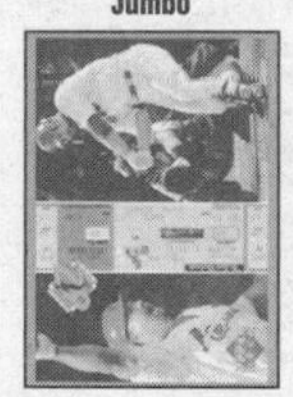
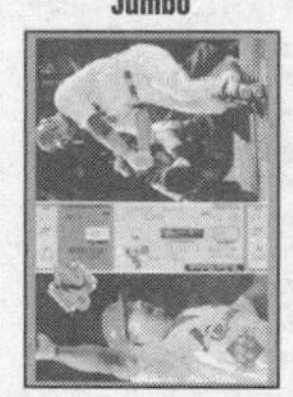

This one-card set measuring 3 1/2" by 5" commemorates Mark McGwire's 62nd Home Run. The front features two action player photos with a reproduction of a ticket stub from the game in the center with a red border. The card was originally offered on the Home Shopping Network and then sold to Hobby dealers. Only 16,200 of this card were produced and sequentially numbered.

1 Mark McGwire 6.00 15.00

1998 Upper Deck Richie Ashburn

This one-card set was distributed as a wrapper redemption at SportsFest 98 held in Philadelphia. The front features a color action photo of Richie Ashburn with a white border. The back carries the top part of the photo with career statistics and player information.

1 Richie Ashburn .75 2.00

1999 Upper Deck

This 525-card set was distributed in two separate series. Series one packs contained cards 1-255 and series two contained 266-535. Cards 256-265 were never created. Subsets are as follows: Star Rookies (1-18, 266-292), Foreign Focus (229-246), Season Highlights Checklists (247-255, 527-535), and Arms Race '99 (518-526). The product was distributed in 10-card packs with a suggested retail price of $2.99. Though not confirmed by Upper Deck, it's widely believed by dealers that broke a good deal of product that these subset cards were slightly short-printed in comparison to other cards in the set. Notable Rookie Cards include Pat Burrell. 100 signed 1989 Upper Deck Ken Griffey Jr. RC's were randomly seeded into series one packs. These signed cards are real 89 RC's and they contain an additional diamond shaped hologram on back signifying that UD has verified Griffey's signature. Approximately 350 Babe Ruth A Piece of History cards were randomly seeded into all series one packs at a rate of one in 15,000. 50 Babe Ruth A Piece of History 500 Club bat cards were randomly seeded into second series packs. Pricing for these bat cards can be referenced under 1999 Upper Deck A Piece of History 500 Club.

COMPLETE SET (525) 30.00 60.00
COMPLETE SERIES 1 (255) 15.00 40.00
COMPLETE SERIES 2 (270) 10.00 25.00
COMMON (19-255/293-535) .10 .30
COMMON SER.1 SR (1-18) .20 .50
COMMON SER.2 SR (266-292) .20 .50
CARDS 256-265 DO NOT EXIST
GRIFFEY 89 AU RANDOM IN SER.1 PACKS
RUTH SER.1 BAT LISTED UNDER '99 APH
RUTH SER.2 BAT LISTED W/APH 500 CLUB
1 Troy Glaus SR .40 1.00
2 Adrian Beltre SR .25 .60
3 Matt Anderson SR .20 .50
4 Eric Chavez SR .25 .60
5 Jin Ho Cho SR .20 .50
6 Robert Smith SR .20 .50
7 George Lombard SR .20 .50
8 Mike Kinkade SR .20 .50
9 Seth Greisinger SR .20 .50
10 J.D. Drew SR .25 .60
11 Aramis Ramirez SR .25 .60
12 Carlos Guillen SR .25 .60
13 Justin Baughman SR .20 .50
14 Jim Parque SR .20 .50
15 Ryan Jackson SR .20 .50
16 Ramon E.Martinez SR RC .20 .50
17 Orlando Hernandez SR .25 .60
18 Jeremy Giambi SR .20 .50
19 Gary DiSarcina .10 .30
20 Darin Erstad .10 .30
21 Troy Glaus .20 .50
22 Chuck Finley .10 .30
23 Dave Hollins .10 .30
24 Troy Percival .10 .30
25 Tim Salmon .20 .50
26 Brian Anderson .10 .30
27 Jay Bell .10 .30
28 Andy Benes .10 .30
29 Brent Brede .10 .30
30 David Dellucci .10 .30
31 Karim Garcia .10 .30
32 Travis Lee .10 .30
33 Andres Galarraga .10 .30
34 Ryan Klesko .10 .30
35 Keith Lockhart .10 .30
36 Kevin Millwood .10 .30
37 Denny Neagle .10 .30
38 John Smoltz .20 .50
39 Michael Tucker .10 .30
40 Walt Weiss .10 .30
41 Dennis Martinez .10 .30
42 Javy Lopez .10 .30
43 Brady Anderson .10 .30
44 Harold Baines .10 .30
45 Mike Bordick .10 .30
46 Roberto Alomar .20 .50
47 Scott Erickson .10 .30
48 Mike Mussina .20 .50
49 Cal Ripken 1.00 2.50
50 Darren Bragg .10 .30
51 Dennis Eckersley .10 .30
52 Nomar Garciaparra .50 1.25
53 Scott Hatteberg .10 .30
54 Troy O'Leary .10 .30
55 Bret Saberhagen .10 .30
56 John Valentin .10 .30
57 Rod Beck .10 .30
58 Jeff Blauser .10 .30
59 Brant Brown .10 .30
60 Mark Clark .10 .30
61 Mark Grace .20 .50
62 Kevin Tapani .10 .30
63 Henry Rodriguez .10 .30
64 Mike Cameron .10 .30
65 Mike Caruso .10 .30
66 Ray Durham .10 .30
67 Jaime Navarro .10 .30
68 Magglio Ordonez .10 .30
69 Mike Sirotka .10 .30
70 Sean Casey .10 .30
71 Barry Larkin .20 .50
72 Jon Nunnally .10 .30
73 Paul Konerko .10 .30
74 Chris Stynes .10 .30
75 Brett Tomko .10 .30
76 Dmitri Young .10 .30
77 Sandy Alomar Jr. .10 .30
78 Bartolo Colon .10 .30
79 Travis Fryman .10 .30
80 Brian Giles .10 .30
81 David Justice .10 .30
82 Omar Vizquel .20 .50
83 Jaret Wright .10 .30
84 Jim Thome .20 .50
85 Charles Nagy .10 .30
86 Pedro Astacio .10 .30
87 Todd Helton .20 .50
88 Darryl Kile .10 .30
89 Mike Lansing .10 .30
90 Neifi Perez .10 .30
91 John Thomson .10 .30
92 Larry Walker .10 .30
93 Tony Clark .10 .30
94 Deivi Cruz .10 .30
95 Damion Easley .10 .30
96 Brian L.Hunter .10 .30
97 Todd Jones .10 .30
98 Brian Moehler .10 .30
99 Gabe Alvarez .10 .30
100 Craig Counsell .10 .30
101 Cliff Floyd .10 .30
102 Livan Hernandez .10 .30
103 Andy Larkin .10 .30
104 Derrek Lee .20 .50
105 Brian Meadows .10 .30
106 Moises Alou .10 .30
107 Sean Berry .10 .30
108 Craig Biggio .20 .50
109 Ricky Gutierrez .10 .30
110 Mike Hampton .10 .30
111 Jose Lima .10 .30
112 Billy Wagner .10 .30
113 Hal Morris .10 .30
114 Johnny Damon .20 .50
115 Jeff King .10 .30
116 Jeff Montgomery .10 .30
117 Glendon Rusch .10 .30
118 Larry Sutton .10 .30
119 Bobby Bonilla .10 .30
120 Jim Eisenreich .10 .30
121 Eric Karros .10 .30
122 Matt Luke .10 .30
123 Ramon Martinez .10 .30
124 Gary Sheffield .10 .30
125 Eric Young .10 .30
126 Charles Johnson .10 .30
127 Jeff Cirillo .10 .30
128 Marquis Grissom .10 .30
129 Jeromy Burnitz .10 .30
130 Bob Wickman .10 .30
131 Scott Karl .10 .30
132 Mark Loretta .10 .30
133 Fernando Vina .10 .30
134 Matt Lawton .10 .30
135 Pat Meares .10 .30
136 Eric Milton .10 .30
137 Paul Molitor .10 .30
138 David Ortiz .30 .75
139 Todd Walker .10 .30
140 Shane Andrews .10 .30
141 Brad Fullmer .10 .30
142 Vladimir Guerrero .30 .75
143 Dustin Hermanson .10 .30
144 Ryan McGuire .10 .30
145 Ugueth Urbina .10 .30
146 John Franco .10 .30
147 Butch Huskey .10 .30
148 Bobby Jones .10 .30
149 John Olerud .10 .30
150 Rey Ordonez .10 .30
151 Mike Piazza .50 1.25
152 Hideo Nomo .30 .75
153 Masato Yoshii .10 .30
154 Derek Jeter .75 2.00
155 Chuck Knoblauch .10 .30
156 Paul O'Neill .20 .50
157 Andy Pettitte .20 .50
158 Mariano Rivera .30 .75
159 Darryl Strawberry .10 .30
160 David Wells .10 .30
161 Jorge Posada .20 .50
162 Ramiro Mendoza .10 .30
163 Miguel Tejada .10 .30
164 Ryan Christenson .10 .30
165 Rickey Henderson .30 .75
166 A.J. Hinch .10 .30
167 Ben Grieve .10 .30
168 Kenny Rogers .10 .30
169 Matt Stairs .10 .30
170 Bob Abreu .10 .30
171 Rico Brogna .10 .30
172 Doug Glanville .10 .30
173 Mike Grace .10 .30
174 Desi Relaford .10 .30
175 Scott Rolen .20 .50
176 Jose Guillen .10 .30
177 Francisco Cordova .10 .30
178 Al Martin .10 .30
179 Jason Schmidt .10 .30

Card	Low	High
180 Turner Ward	.10	.30
181 Kevin Young	.10	.30
182 Mark McGwire	.75	2.00
183 Delino DeShields	.10	.30
184 Eli Marrero	.10	.30
185 Tom Lampkin	.10	.30
186 Ray Lankford	.10	.30
187 Willie McGee	.10	.30
188 Matt Morris	.10	.30
189 Andy Ashby	.10	.30
190 Kevin Brown	.20	.50
191 Ken Caminiti	.10	.30
192 Trevor Hoffman	.10	.30
193 Wally Joyner	.10	.30
194 Greg Vaughn	.10	.30
195 Danny Darwin	.10	.30
196 Shawn Estes	.10	.30
197 Orel Hershiser	.10	.30
198 Jeff Kent	.10	.30
199 Bill Mueller	.10	.30
200 Robb Nen	.10	.30
201 J.T. Snow	.10	.30
202 Ken Cloude	.10	.30
203 Russ Davis	.10	.30
204 Jeff Fassero	.10	.30
205 Ken Griffey Jr.	.60	1.50
206 Shane Monahan	.10	.30
207 David Segui	.10	.30
208 Dan Wilson	.10	.30
209 Wilson Alvarez	.10	.30
210 Wade Boggs	.20	.50
211 Miguel Cairo	.10	.30
212 Bubba Trammell	.10	.30
213 Quinton McCracken	.10	.30
214 Paul Sorrento	.10	.30
215 Kevin Stocker	.10	.30
216 Will Clark	.20	.50
217 Rusty Greer	.10	.30
218 Rick Helling	.10	.30
219 Mark McLemore	.10	.30
220 Ivan Rodriguez	.20	.50
221 John Wetteland	.10	.30
222 Jose Canseco	.20	.50
223 Roger Clemens	.60	1.50
224 Carlos Delgado	.10	.30
225 Darrin Fletcher	.10	.30
226 Alex Gonzalez	.10	.30
227 Jose Cruz Jr.	.10	.30
228 Shannon Stewart	.10	.30
229 Rolando Arrojo FF	.10	.30
230 Livan Hernandez FF	.10	.30
231 Orlando Hernandez FF	.10	.30
232 Raul Mondesi FF	.10	.30
233 Moises Alou FF	.10	.30
234 Pedro Martinez FF	.20	.50
235 Sammy Sosa FF	.20	.50
236 Vladimir Guerrero FF	.30	.75
237 Bartolo Colon FF	.10	.30
238 Miguel Tejada FF	.10	.30
239 Ismael Valdes FF	.10	.30
240 Mariano Rivera FF	.20	.50
241 Jose Cruz Jr. FF	.10	.30
242 Juan Gonzalez FF	.10	.30
243 Ivan Rodriguez FF	.20	.50
244 Sandy Alomar Jr. FF	.10	.30
245 Roberto Alomar FF	.20	.50
246 Magglio Ordonez FF	.10	.30
247 Kerry Wood SH CL	.10	.30
248 Mark McGwire SH CL	.75	2.00
249 David Wells SH CL	.10	.30
250 Rolando Arrojo SH CL	.10	.30
251 Ken Griffey Jr. SH CL	.60	1.50
252 Trevor Hoffman SH CL	.10	.30
253 Travis Lee SH CL	.10	.30
254 Roberto Alomar SH CL	.10	.30
255 Sammy Sosa SH CL	.20	.50
266 Pat Burrell SR RC	1.25	3.00
267 Shea Hillenbrand SR RC	.60	1.50
268 Robert Fick SR	.20	.50
269 Roy Halladay SR	2.00	5.00
270 Ruben Mateo SR	.20	.50
271 Bruce Chen SR	.20	.50
272 Angel Pena SR	.20	.50
273 Michael Barrett SR	.20	.50
274 Kevin Witt SR	.20	.50
275 Damon Minor SR	.20	.50
276 Ryan Minor SR	.20	.50
277 A.J. Pierzynski SR	.25	.60
278 A.J. Burnett SR RC	.60	1.50
279 Dermal Brown SR	.20	.50
280 Joe Lawrence SR	.20	.50
281 Derrick Gibson SR	.20	.50
282 Carlos Febles SR	.20	.50
283 Chris Haas SR	.20	.50
284 Cesar King SR	.20	.50
285 Calvin Pickering SR	.20	.50
286 Mitch Meluskey SR	.20	.50
287 Carlos Beltran SR	.40	1.00
288 Ron Belliard SR	.20	.50
289 Jerry Hairston Jr. SR	.20	.50
290 Fernando Seguignol SR	.20	.50
291 Kris Benson SR	.20	.50
292 Chad Hutchinson SR RC	.25	.60
293 Jarrod Washburn	.10	.30
294 Jason Dickson	.10	.30
295 Mo Vaughn	.10	.30
296 Garret Anderson	.10	.30
297 Jim Edmonds	.10	.30
298 Ken Hill	.10	.30
299 Shigetoshi Hasegawa	.10	.30
300 Todd Stottlemyre	.10	.30
301 Randy Johnson	.30	.75
302 Omar Daal	.10	.30
303 Steve Finley	.10	.30
304 Matt Williams	.10	.30
305 Danny Klassen	.10	.30
306 Tony Batista	.10	.30
307 Brian Jordan	.10	.30
308 Greg Maddux	.50	1.25
309 Chipper Jones	.30	.75
310 Bret Boone	.10	.30
311 Ozzie Guillen	.10	.30
312 John Rocker	.10	.30
313 Tom Glavine	.20	.50
314 Andruw Jones	.20	.50
315 Albert Belle	.10	.30
316 Charles Johnson	.10	.30
317 Will Clark	.20	.50
318 B.J. Surhoff	.10	.30
319 Delino DeShields	.10	.30
320 Heathcliff Slocumb	.10	.30
321 Sidney Ponson	.10	.30
322 Juan Guzman	.10	.30
323 Reggie Jefferson	.10	.30
324 Mark Portugal	.10	.30
325 Tim Wakefield	.10	.30
326 Jason Varitek	.30	.75
327 Jose Offerman	.10	.30
328 Pedro Martinez	.20	.50
329 Trot Nixon	.10	.30
330 Kerry Wood	.10	.30
331 Sammy Sosa	.30	.75
332 Glenallen Hill	.10	.30
333 Gary Gaetti	.10	.30
334 Mickey Morandini	.10	.30
335 Benito Santiago	.10	.30
336 Jeff Blauser	.10	.30
337 Frank Thomas	.30	.75
338 Paul Konerko	.10	.30
339 Jaime Navarro	.10	.30
340 Carlos Lee	.10	.30
341 Brian Simmons	.10	.30
342 Mark Johnson	.10	.30
343 Jeff Abbott	.10	.30
344 Steve Avery	.10	.30
345 Mike Cameron	.10	.30
346 Michael Tucker	.10	.30
347 Greg Vaughn	.10	.30
348 Hal Morris	.10	.30
349 Pete Harnisch	.10	.30
350 Denny Neagle	.10	.30
351 Manny Ramirez	.20	.50
352 Roberto Alomar	.20	.50
353 Dwight Gooden	.10	.30
354 Kenny Lofton	.10	.30
355 Mike Jackson	.10	.30
356 Charles Nagy	.10	.30
357 Enrique Wilson	.10	.30
358 Russ Branyan	.10	.30
359 Richie Sexson	.10	.30
360 Vinny Castilla	.10	.30
361 Dante Bichette	.10	.30
362 Kirt Manwaring	.10	.30
363 Darryl Hamilton	.10	.30
364 Jamey Wright	.10	.30
365 Curtis Leskanic	.10	.30
366 Jeff Reed	.10	.30
367 Bobby Higginson	.10	.30
368 Justin Thompson	.10	.30
369 Brad Ausmus	.10	.30
370 Dean Palmer	.10	.30
371 Gabe Kapler	.10	.30
372 Juan Encarnacion	.10	.30
373 Karim Garcia	.10	.30
374 Alex Gonzalez	.10	.30
375 Braden Looper	.10	.30
376 Preston Wilson	.10	.30
377 Todd Dunwoody	.10	.30
378 Alex Fernandez	.10	.30
379 Mark Kotsay	.10	.30
380 Matt Mantei	.10	.30
381 Ken Caminiti	.10	.30
382 Scott Elarton	.10	.30
383 Jeff Bagwell	.20	.50
384 Derek Bell	.10	.30
385 Ricky Gutierrez	.10	.30
386 Richard Hidalgo	.10	.30
387 Shane Reynolds	.10	.30
388 Carl Everett	.10	.30
389 Scott Service	.10	.30
390 Jeff Suppan	.10	.30
391 Joe Randa	.10	.30
392 Kevin Appier	.10	.30
393 Shane Halter	.10	.30
394 Chad Kreuter	.10	.30
395 Mike Sweeney	.10	.30
396 Kevin Brown	.20	.50
397 Devon White	.10	.30
398 Todd Hollandsworth	.10	.30
399 Todd Hundley	.10	.30
400 Chan Ho Park	.10	.30
401 Mark Grudzielanek	.10	.30
402 Raul Mondesi	.10	.30
403 Ismael Valdes	.10	.30
404 Rafael Roque RC	.10	.30
405 Sean Berry	.10	.30
406 Kevin Barker	.10	.30
407 Dave Nilsson	.10	.30
408 Geoff Jenkins	.10	.30
409 Jim Abbott	.20	.50
410 Bobby Hughes	.10	.30
411 Corey Koskie	.10	.30
412 Rick Aguilera	.10	.30
413 LaTroy Hawkins	.10	.30
414 Ron Coomer	.10	.30
415 Denny Hocking	.10	.30
416 Marty Cordova	.10	.30
417 Terry Steinbach	.10	.30
418 Rondell White	.10	.30
419 Wilton Guerrero	.10	.30
420 Shane Andrews	.10	.30
421 Orlando Cabrera	.10	.30
422 Carl Pavano	.10	.30
423 Javier Vazquez	.10	.30
424 Chris Widger	.10	.30
425 Robin Ventura	.10	.30
426 Rickey Henderson	.30	.75
427 Al Leiter	.10	.30
428 Bobby Jones	.10	.30
429 Brian McRae	.10	.30
430 Roger Cedeno	.10	.30
431 Bobby Bonilla	.10	.30
432 Edgardo Alfonzo	.10	.30
433 Bernie Williams	.20	.50
434 Ricky Ledee	.10	.30
435 Chili Davis	.10	.30
436 Tino Martinez	.20	.50
437 Scott Brosius	.10	.30
438 David Cone	.10	.30
439 Joe Girardi	.10	.30
440 Roger Clemens	.60	1.50
441 Chad Curtis	.10	.30
442 Hideki Irabu	.10	.30
443 Jason Giambi	.10	.30
444 Scott Spiezio	.10	.30
445 Tony Phillips	.10	.30
446 Ramon Hernandez	.10	.30
447 Mike Macfarlane	.10	.30
448 Tom Candiotti	.10	.30
449 Billy Taylor	.10	.30
450 Bobby Estalella	.10	.30
451 Curt Schilling	.10	.30
452 Carlton Loewer	.10	.30
453 Marlon Anderson	.10	.30
454 Kevin Jordan	.10	.30
455 Ron Gant	.10	.30
456 Chad Ogea	.10	.30
457 Abraham Nunez	.10	.30
458 Jason Kendall	.10	.30
459 Pat Meares	.10	.30
460 Brant Brown	.10	.30
461 Brian Giles	.10	.30
462 Chad Hermansen	.10	.30
463 Freddy Adrian Garcia	.10	.30
464 Edgar Renteria	.10	.30
465 Fernando Tatis	.10	.30
466 Eric Davis	.10	.30
467 Darren Bragg	.10	.30
468 Donovan Osborne	.10	.30
469 Manny Aybar	.10	.30
470 Jose Jimenez	.10	.30
471 Kent Mercker	.10	.30
472 Reggie Sanders	.10	.30
473 Ruben Rivera	.10	.30
474 Tony Gwynn	.40	1.00
475 Jim Leyritz	.10	.30
476 Chris Gomez	.10	.30
477 Matt Clement	.10	.30
478 Carlos Hernandez	.10	.30
479 Sterling Hitchcock	.10	.30
480 Ellis Burks	.10	.30
481 Barry Bonds	.75	2.00
482 Marvin Benard	.10	.30
483 Kirk Rueter	.10	.30
484 F.P. Santangelo	.10	.30
485 Stan Javier	.10	.30
486 Jeff Kent	.10	.30
487 Alex Rodriguez	.50	1.25
488 Tom Lampkin	.10	.30
489 Jose Mesa	.10	.30
490 Jay Buhner	.10	.30
491 Edgar Martinez	.20	.50
492 Butch Huskey	.10	.30
493 John Mabry	.10	.30
494 Jamie Moyer	.10	.30
495 Roberto Hernandez	.10	.30
496 Tony Saunders	.10	.30
497 Fred McGriff	.20	.50
498 Dave Martinez	.10	.30
499 Jose Canseco	.20	.50
500 Rolando Arrojo	.10	.30
501 Esteban Yan	.10	.30
502 Juan Gonzalez	.10	.30
503 Rafael Palmeiro	.20	.50
504 Aaron Sele	.10	.30
505 Royce Clayton	.10	.30
506 Todd Zeile	.10	.30
507 Tom Goodwin	.10	.30
508 Lee Stevens	.10	.30
509 Esteban Loaiza	.10	.30
510 Joey Hamilton	.10	.30
511 Homer Bush	.10	.30
512 Willie Greene	.10	.30
513 Shawn Green	.10	.30
514 David Wells	.10	.30
515 Kelvim Escobar	.10	.30
516 Tony Fernandez	.10	.30
517 Pat Hentgen	.10	.30
518 Mark McGwire AR	.40	1.00
519 Ken Griffey Jr. AR	.40	1.00
520 Sammy Sosa AR	.20	.50
521 Juan Gonzalez AR	.10	.30
522 J.D. Drew AR	.10	.30
523 Chipper Jones AR	.20	.50
524 Alex Rodriguez AR	.30	.75
525 Mike Piazza AR	.30	.75
526 Nomar Garciaparra AR	.30	.75
527 Mark McGwire SH CL	.40	1.00
528 Sammy Sosa SH CL	.20	.50
529 Scott Brosius SH CL	.10	.30
530 Cal Ripken SH CL	.50	1.25
531 Barry Bonds SH CL	.40	1.00
532 Roger Clemens SH CL	.30	.75
533 Ken Griffey Jr. SH CL	.40	1.00
534 Alex Rodriguez SH CL	.30	.75
535 Curt Schilling SH CL	.10	.30
NNO K.Griffey Jr. '89 AU/100	900.00	1200.00

1999 Upper Deck Exclusives Level 1

*STARS: 10X TO 25X BASIC CARDS
*SER.1 STAR ROOK: 4X TO 10X BASIC SR
*SER.2 STAR ROOK: 6X TO 15X BASIC SR
RANDOM INSERTS IN ALL HOBBY PACKS
STATED PRINT RUN 100 SERIAL #'d SETS
CARDS 256-265 DO NOT EXIST

1999 Upper Deck 10th Anniversary Team

Randomly inserted in first series packs at the rate of one in four, this 30-card set features color photos of collectors' favorite players selected for this special All-Star team.

COMPLETE SET (30) 20.00 50.00
SER.1 STATED ODDS 1:4
*DOUBLES: 1.25X TO 3X BASIC 10TH ANN.
DOUBLES RANDOM INSERTS IN SER.1 PACKS
DOUBLES PRINT RUN 4000 SERIAL #'d SETS
*TRIPLES: 8X TO 20X BASIC 10TH ANN
TRIPLES RANDOM INSERTS IN SER.1 PACKS
TRIPLES PRINT RUN 100 SERIAL #'d SETS
HR'S RANDOM INSERTS IN SER.1 PACKS
HOME RUN PRINT RUN 1 SERIAL #'d SET
HR'S NOT PRICED DUE TO SCARCITY

Card	Low	High
X1 Mike Piazza	1.00	2.50
X2 Mark McGwire	1.50	4.00
X3 Roberto Alomar	.40	1.00
X4 Chipper Jones	.60	1.50
X5 Cal Ripken	2.00	5.00
X6 Ken Griffey Jr.	1.25	3.00
X7 Barry Bonds	1.50	4.00
X8 Tony Gwynn	.75	2.00
X9 Nolan Ryan	2.50	6.00
X10 Randy Johnson	.60	1.50
X11 Dennis Eckersley	.25	.60
X12 Ivan Rodriguez	.40	1.00
X13 Frank Thomas	.60	1.50
X14 Craig Biggio	.40	1.00
X15 Wade Boggs	.40	1.00
X16 Alex Rodriguez	1.00	2.50
X17 Albert Belle	.25	.60
X18 Juan Gonzalez	.25	.60
X19 Rickey Henderson	.60	1.50
X20 Greg Maddux	1.00	2.50
X21 Tom Glavine	.40	1.00
X22 Randy Myers	.25	.60
X23 Sandy Alomar Jr.	.25	.60
X24 Jeff Bagwell	.40	1.00
X25 Derek Jeter	1.50	4.00
X26 Matt Williams	.25	.60
X27 Kenny Lofton	.25	.60
X28 Sammy Sosa	.60	1.50
X29 Larry Walker	.25	.60
X30 Roger Clemens	1.25	3.00

1999 Upper Deck A Piece of History

This limited edition set features photos of Babe Ruth along with a bat chip from an actual game-used Louisville Slugger swung by him during the late 20's. Approximately 350 cards were made and seeded into packs at a rate of 1:15,000. Another insert card incorporates both a "cut" signature of Ruth along with a piece of his game-used bat. Only three of these cards were produced.

SER.1 STATED ODDS 1:15,000
PRINT RUN APPROXIMATELY 350 CARDS
B.RUTH AU RANDOM IN SER.1 PACKS
B.RUTH AU PRINT RUN 3 #'d CARDS
B.RUTH AU NOT PRICED DUE TO SCARCITY

Card	Low	High
PHLC Babe Ruth AU/3		
PH Babe Ruth	750.00	1000.00

1999 Upper Deck A Piece of History 500 Club

During the 1999 season, Upper Deck inserted into various products these cards which are cut up bats from all except one of the members of the 500 homer club. Mark McGwire asked that one of his bats not be included in this set, thus there was no Mark McGwire card in this grouping (until 2003 when McGwire signed a deal with Upper Deck). With the exception of Babe Ruth, approximately 350 of each card was produced. Only 50 Babe Ruth's were made. The cards were released in the following products: 1999 SP Authentic: Ernie Banks; 1999 SP Signature: Mel Ott; 1999 SPx: Willie Mays, 1999 UD Choice: Eddie Murray; 1999 UD Ionix: Frank Robinson; 1999 Upper Deck 2: Babe Ruth; 1999 Upper Deck Century Legends: Jimmie Foxx; 1999 Upper Deck Challengers for 70: Harmon Killebrew; 1999 Upper Deck HoloGrFx: Eddie Mathews and Willie McCovey; 1999 Upper Deck MVP: Mike Schmidt; 1999 Upper Deck Ovation: Mickey Mantle: 1999 Upper Deck Retro: Ted Williams; 2000 Black Diamond: Reggie Jackson; 2000 Upper Deck 1: Hank Aaron.

RANDOM INSERTS IN 1999-2000 UD BRANDS
PRINT RUN APPROXIMATELY 350 SETS

Card	Low	High
BR Babe Ruth/50		
EB Ernie Banks	50.00	120.00
EM Eddie Mathews	75.00	200.00
EM Eddie Murray	100.00	250.00
FR Frank Robinson	60.00	150.00
HA Hank Aaron	150.00	400.00
HK Harmon Killebrew	60.00	150.00
JF Jimmie Foxx	75.00	200.00
MM Mickey Mantle	300.00	600.00
MO Mel Ott	75.00	200.00
MS Mike Schmidt	60.00	150.00
RJ Reggie Jackson	50.00	120.00
TW Ted Williams	125.00	300.00
WM Willie Mays	125.00	300.00
WM Willie McCovey	60.00	150.00
ARM Aaron/Ruth/Mays SP		

1999 Upper Deck A Piece of History 500 Club Autographs

As part of the Upper Deck A Piece of History 500 Club Autograph promotion, Upper Deck had most of the living members of the 500 homer club sign a number of cards which matched their uniform number (except for Mantle of which is a true 1/1, features a cut signature and altered card front design from the other cards in the set). On some of the players, the cards are not priced due to scarcity. Each card is serial numbered on the front except Mantle. Each of these cards was issued in a separate UD brand from 1999.

RANDOM INSERTS IN 1999-2000 UD BRANDS
PRINT RUNS B/WN 3-44 COPIES PER
NO PRICING ON QTY OF 40 OR LESS

Card	Low	High
536HR Mickey Mantle/1		
EBAU Ernie Banks/14		
EMAU Eddie Mathews/41	500.00	800.00
FRAU Frank Robinson/20		
HAAU Hank Aaron/44	1500.00	1800.00
HKAU Harmon Killebrew/3		
MSAU Mike Schmidt/20		
RJAU Reggie Jackson/44	600.00	900.00
TWAU Ted Williams/9		
WMAU Willie Mays/24		
WMAU Willie McCovey/44	500.00	800.00

1999 Upper Deck Crowning Glory

Randomly inserted in first series packs at the rate of one in 23, this three-card set features color photos of players who reached major milestones during the '98 MLB season and printed on double sided cards.

COMPLETE SET (3) 25.00 60.00
RANDOM INSERTS IN SER.1 PACKS
*DOUBLES: .6X TO 1.5X BASIC CROWN
DOUBLES RANDOM INSERTS IN SER.1 PACKS
DOUBLES PRINT RUN 1000 SERIAL #'d SETS
*TRIPLES: 4X TO 10X BASIC CROWN
TRIPLES RANDOM INSERTS IN SER.1 PACKS
TRIPLES PRINT RUN 25 SERIAL #'d SETS
HR'S RANDOM INSERTS IN SER.1 PACKS
HOME RUNS PRINT RUN 1 SERIAL #'d SET
HOME RUNS NOT PRICED DUE TO SCARCITY

Card	Low	High
CG1 R.Clemens / K.Wood	6.00	15.00
CG2 M.McGwire / B.Bonds	8.00	20.00
CG3 K.Griffey Jr. / M.McGwire	8.00	20.00

1999 Upper Deck Forte

Randomly inserted in series two packs at the rate of one in 23, this 30-card set features color photos of the most collectible superstars captured on super premium cards with extensive rainbow foil coverage. Three limited parallel sets were also produced and randomly inserted into Series two packs. Forte Doubles was serially numbered to 2000; Forte Triples, to 100; and Forte Quadruples, to 10.

COMPLETE SET (30) 20.00 50.00
SER.2 STATED ODDS 1:23
*DOUBLES: .6X TO 1.5X BASIC FORTE
DOUBLES RANDOM INSERTS IN SER.2 PACKS
DOUBLES PRINT RUN 2000 SERIAL #'d SETS
*TRIPLES: 2X TO 5X BASIC FORTE
TRIPLES RANDOM INSERTS IN SER.2 PACKS
TRIPLES PRINT RUN 100 SERIAL #'d SETS
QUADS RANDOM INSERTS IN SER.2 PACKS
QUADRUPLES PRINT RUN 10 SERIAL #'d SETS
QUADRUPLES NOT PRICED DUE TO SCARCITY

Card	Low	High
F1 Darin Erstad	.40	1.00
F2 Troy Glaus	.40	1.00
F3 Mo Vaughn	.40	1.00
F4 Greg Maddux	1.25	3.00
F5 Andres Galarraga	.60	1.50
F6 Chipper Jones	1.00	2.50
F7 Cal Ripken	3.00	8.00
F8 Albert Belle	.40	1.00
F9 Nomar Garciaparra	.60	1.50
F10 Sammy Sosa	1.00	2.50
F11 Kerry Wood	.40	1.00
F12 Frank Thomas	1.00	2.50
F13 Jim Thome	.60	1.50
F14 Jeff Bagwell	.60	1.50
F15 Vladimir Guerrero	.60	1.50
F16 Mike Piazza	1.00	2.50
F17 Derek Jeter	2.50	6.00
F18 Ben Grieve	.40	1.00
F19 Eric Chavez	.40	1.00
F20 Scott Rolen	.60	1.50
F21 Mark McGwire	1.50	4.00
F22 J.D. Drew	.40	1.00
F23 Tony Gwynn	1.00	2.50
F24 Barry Bonds	1.50	4.00
F25 Alex Rodriguez	1.25	3.00
F26 Ken Griffey Jr.	2.00	5.00
F27 Ivan Rodriguez	.60	1.50
F28 Juan Gonzalez	.40	1.00
F29 Roger Clemens	1.25	3.00
F30 Andruw Jones	.40	1.00

1999 Upper Deck Game Jersey

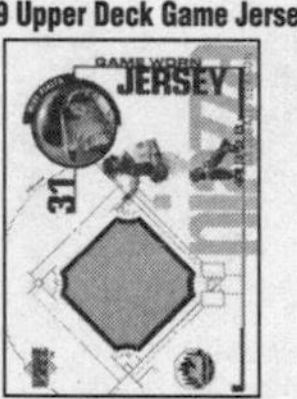

This set consists of 23 cards inserted in first and second series packs. Hobby packs contained Game Jersey hobby cards (signified in the listings with an H after the player's name) at a rate of 1:288. Hobby and retail packs contained much scarcer Game Jersey hobby/retail cards (signified with an H/R after the player's name in the listings below) at a rate of 1:2500. Each card features a piece of an actual game worn jersey. Five additional cards were signed by the athlete and serial numbered by hand to the player's respective jersey number. These rare signed Game Jersey cards are priced below but not considered part of the complete set.

H STATED ODDS 1:288 HOBBY
HR STATED ODDS 1:2500 HOBBY/RETAIL
H1 AND HR1 CARDS DIST.IN SER.1 PACKS
H2 AND HR2 CARDS DIST.IN SER.2 PACKS
AU'S RANDOM INSERTS IN PACKS
AU PRINT RUNS B/WN 24-34 COPIES PER
NO AU PRICING ON QTY OF 24 PER
COMP.SET DOES NOT INCLUDE AU CARDS

Card	Low	High
AB Adrian Beltre H1	4.00	10.00
AR Alex Rodriguez HR1	8.00	20.00
BF Brad Fullmer H2	4.00	10.00
BG Ben Grieve H1	4.00	10.00
BT Bubba Trammell H2	4.00	10.00
CJ Charles Johnson HR1	6.00	15.00
CJ Chipper Jones H2	8.00	20.00
DE Darin Erstad H1	6.00	15.00
EC Eric Chavez H2	6.00	15.00
FT Frank Thomas HR2	10.00	25.00
GM Greg Maddux HR2	12.50	30.00
IR Ivan Rodriguez H1	6.00	15.00
JD J.D. Drew H2	6.00	15.00
JG Juan Gonzalez HR1	6.00	15.00
JR Ken Griffey Jr. HR2	15.00	40.00
KG Ken Griffey Jr. H1	15.00	40.00
KW Kerry Wood HR1	6.00	15.00
MP Mike Piazza HR1	12.50	30.00
MR Manny Ramirez H2	6.00	15.00
NRA N.Ryan Astros H2	10.00	25.00
NRB N.Ryan Rangers HR2	10.00	25.00
SS Sammy Sosa H2	4.00	10.00
TH Todd Helton H2	6.00	15.00
TGW Tony Gwynn H2	6.00	15.00
TL Travis Lee H1	4.00	10.00
JDS J.Drew AU/8 H2		
JRS Ken Griffey Jr. AU/24 HR2		
KGAU Ken Griffey Jr. AU/24 H1		
KWAU K.Wood AU/34 HR1	150.00	250.00
NRAS N.Ryan AU/34 H2	500.00	800.00

1999 Upper Deck Ken Griffey Jr. Box Blasters

These ten 5" by 7" cards were inserted one per Upper Deck special retail boxes. The cards feature oversize reprints of the regular issue Ken Griffey Jr. Upper Deck cards during both his 10 year career and the 10 seasons Upper Deck has made cards for. We have numbered the cards 1-10 based on the year of the card's original issue.

COMPLETE SET (1-10) 20.00 50.00
COMMON CARD (1-10) 2.00 5.00

1999 Upper Deck Ken Griffey Jr. Box Blasters Autographs

Randomly seeded into one in every 64 special retail boxes, each of these attractive cards was signed by Ken Griffey Jr. The cards are over-sized 5" by 7" replicas of each of Griffey's basic issue Upper Deck cards from 1989-1999. The backs of the cards provide a certificate of authenticity from UD Chairman and CEO Richard McWilliam.

COMMON CARD (90-99) 50.00 100.00
STATED ODDS 1:64 SPECIAL RETAIL BOXES

Card	Low	High
KG1989 Ken Griffey Jr. AU89	150.00	250.00

1999 Upper Deck Immaculate Perception

Randomly inserted in Series one packs at the rate of one in 23, this 27-card set features top player photos printed on unique, foil-enhanced cards.

COMPLETE SET (27) 125.00 250.00
SER.1 STATED ODDS 1:23
*DOUBLES: .75X TO 2X BASIC IMM.PERC.
DOUBLES RANDOM INSERTS IN SER.1 PACKS
DOUBLES PRINT RUN 1000 SERIAL #'d SETS
*TRIPLES: 5X TO 12X BASIC IMM.PERC.
TRIPLES RANDOM INSERTS IN SER.1 PACKS
TRIPLES PRINT RUN 25 SERIAL #'d SETS
HR'S RANDOM INSERTS IN SER.1 PACKS
HOME RUNS PRINT RUN 1 SERIAL #'d SET
HOME RUNS NOT PRICED DUE TO SCARCITY

Card	Low	High
I1 Jeff Bagwell	2.00	5.00
I2 Craig Biggio	2.00	5.00
I3 Barry Bonds	8.00	20.00
I4 Roger Clemens	6.00	15.00
I5 Jose Cruz Jr.	1.25	3.00
I6 Nomar Garciaparra	5.00	12.00
I7 Tony Clark	1.25	3.00
I8 Ben Grieve	1.25	3.00
I9 Ken Griffey Jr.	6.00	15.00
I10 Tony Gwynn	4.00	10.00
I11 Randy Johnson	3.00	8.00
I12 Chipper Jones	3.00	8.00
I13 Travis Lee	1.25	3.00
I14 Kenny Lofton	1.25	3.00
I15 Greg Maddux	5.00	12.00
I16 Mark McGwire	8.00	20.00
I17 Hideo Nomo	3.00	8.00
I18 Mike Piazza	5.00	12.00
I19 Manny Ramirez	2.00	5.00
I20 Cal Ripken	10.00	25.00
I21 Alex Rodriguez	5.00	12.00
I22 Scott Rolen	2.00	5.00
I23 Frank Thomas	3.00	8.00
I24 Kerry Wood	1.25	3.00

25 Larry Walker 1.25 3.00
26 Vinny Castilla 1.25 3.00
27 Derek Jeter 8.00 20.00

1999 Upper Deck Textbook Excellence

Inserted one every 23 second series packs, these cards offer information on the skills of some of the game's most fundamentally sound performers.

COMPLETE SET (30) 20.00 50.00
SER.2 STATED ODDS 1:4
*DOUBLES: 1.5X TO 4X BASIC TEXTBOOK
DOUBLES RANDOM INSERTS IN SER.2 PACKS
DOUBLES PRINT RUN 2000 SERIAL #'d SETS
*TRIPLES: 6X TO 15X BASIC TEXTBOOK
TRIPLES RANDOM INSERTS IN SER.2 PACKS
TRIPLES PRINT RUN 100 SERIAL #'d SETS
QUADS RANDOM INSERTS IN SER.2 PACKS
QUADRUPLES PRINT RUN 10 SERIAL #'d SETS
QUADRUPLES NOT PRICED DUE TO SCARCITY
T1 Mo Vaughn .30 .75
T2 Greg Maddux 1.25 3.00
T3 Chipper Jones .75 2.00
T4 Andruw Jones .50 1.25
T5 Cal Ripken 2.50 6.00
T6 Albert Belle .30 .75
T7 Roberto Alomar .50 1.25
T8 Nomar Garciaparra 1.25 3.00
T9 Kerry Wood .30 .75
T10 Sammy Sosa .75 2.00
T11 Greg Vaughn .30 .75
T12 Jeff Bagwell .50 1.25
T13 Kevin Brown .50 1.25
T14 Vladimir Guerrero .75 2.00
T15 Mike Piazza 1.25 3.00
T16 Bernie Williams .50 1.25
T17 Derek Jeter 2.00 5.00
T18 Ben Grieve .30 .75
T19 Eric Chavez .20 .50
T20 Scott Rolen .50 1.25
T21 Mark McGwire 2.00 5.00
T22 David Wells .30 .75
T23 J.D. Drew .20 .50
T24 Tony Gwynn 1.00 2.50
T25 Barry Bonds 2.00 5.00
T26 Alex Rodriguez 1.25 3.00
T27 Ken Griffey Jr. 1.50 4.00
T28 Juan Gonzalez .30 .75
T29 Ivan Rodriguez .50 1.25
T30 Roger Clemens 1.50 4.00

1999 Upper Deck View to a Thrill

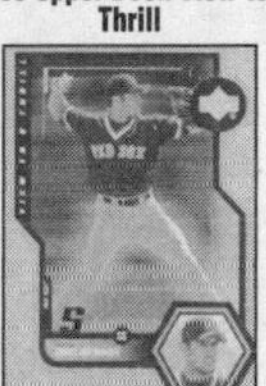

These cards, inserted one every seven second series packs feature special die-cuts and embossing and takes a new look at 30 of the best overall athletes in baseball.

COMPLETE SET (30) 40.00 100.00
SER.2 STATED ODDS 1:7
*DOUBLES: 1X TO 2.5X BASIC VIEW
DOUBLES RANDOM INSERTS IN SER.2 PACKS
DOUBLES PRINT RUN 2000 SERIAL #'d SETS
*TRIPLES: 4X TO 10X BASIC VIEW
TRIPLES RANDOM INSERTS IN SER.2 PACKS
TRIPLES PRINT RUN 100 SERIAL #'d SETS
QUADS RANDOM INSERTS IN SER.2 PACKS
QUADRUPLES PRINT RUN 10 SERIAL #'d SETS
QUADRUPLES NOT PRICED DUE TO SCARCITY
V1 Mo Vaughn .50 1.25
V2 Darin Erstad .50 1.25
V3 Travis Lee .50 1.25
V4 Chipper Jones 1.25 3.00
V5 Greg Maddux 2.00 5.00
V6 Gabe Kapler .50 1.25
V7 Cal Ripken 4.00 10.00
V8 Nomar Garciaparra 2.00 5.00
V9 Kerry Wood .50 1.25
V10 Frank Thomas 1.25 3.00
V11 Manny Ramirez .75 2.00
V12 Larry Walker .50 1.25
V13 Tony Clark .50 1.25
V14 Jeff Bagwell .75 2.00
V15 Craig Biggio .75 2.00
V16 Vladimir Guerrero 1.25 3.00
V17 Mike Piazza 2.00 5.00
V18 Bernie Williams .75 2.00
V19 Derek Jeter 3.00 8.00
V20 Ben Grieve .50 1.25
V21 Eric Chavez .30 .75
V22 Scott Rolen .75 2.00
V23 Mark McGwire 3.00 8.00
V24 Tony Gwynn 1.50 4.00
V25 Barry Bonds 3.00 8.00
V26 Ken Griffey Jr. 2.50 6.00
V27 Alex Rodriguez 2.00 5.00
V28 J.D. Drew .30 .75
V29 Juan Gonzalez .50 1.25
V30 Roger Clemens 2.50 6.00

1999 Upper Deck Wonder Years

Randomly inserted in Series one packs at the rate of one in seven, this 30-card set features color photos of top stars.

COMPLETE SET (30) 30.00 80.00
SER.1 STATED ODDS 1:7
*DOUBLES: 1X TO 2.5X BASIC WONDER
DOUBLES RANDOM INSERTS IN SER.1 PACKS
DOUBLES PRINT RUN 2000 SERIAL #'d SETS
*TRIPLES: 8X TO 20X BASIC WONDER
TRIPLES RANDOM INSERTS IN SER.1 PACKS
TRIPLES PRINT RUN 50 SERIAL #'d SETS
HR'S RANDOM INSERTS IN SER.1 PACKS
HOME RUNS PRINT RUN 1 SERIAL #'d SET
HOME RUNS NOT PRICED DUE TO SCARCITY
W1 Kerry Wood .50 1.25
W2 Travis Lee .50 1.25
W3 Jeff Bagwell .75 2.00
W4 Barry Bonds 3.00 8.00
W5 Roger Clemens 2.50 6.00
W6 Jose Cruz Jr. .50 1.25
W7 Andres Galarraga .50 1.25
W8 Nomar Garciaparra 2.00 5.00
W9 Juan Gonzalez .50 1.25
W10 Ken Griffey Jr. 2.50 6.00
W11 Tony Gwynn 1.50 4.00
W12 Derek Jeter 3.00 8.00
W13 Randy Johnson 1.25 3.00
W14 Andruw Jones .75 2.00
W15 Chipper Jones 1.25 3.00
W16 Kenny Lofton .50 1.25
W17 Greg Maddux 2.00 5.00
W18 Tino Martinez .75 2.00
W19 Mark McGwire 3.00 8.00
W20 Paul Molitor .50 1.25
W21 Mike Piazza 2.00 5.00
W22 Manny Ramirez .75 2.00
W23 Cal Ripken 4.00 10.00
W24 Alex Rodriguez 2.00 5.00
W25 Sammy Sosa 1.25 3.00
W26 Frank Thomas 1.25 3.00
W27 Mo Vaughn .50 1.25
W28 Larry Walker .50 1.25
W29 Scott Rolen .75 2.00
W30 Ben Grieve .50 1.25

1999 Upper Deck Employment Promo

This card was used as a promotional tool by Upper Deck to thank anyone who applied for a job there. The card features Upper Deck corporate spokesperson Ken Griffey Jr.

NNO Ken Griffey Jr. 1.00 2.50

1999 Upper Deck Ken Griffey Jr Santa

This one card was issued to Upper Deck employees as well as some of their direct dealers. The card features a photo of Griffey on the front along a swatch of the "Santa" hat he wore for the shoot. The back has a congratulatory message from Upper Deck.

1 Ken Griffey Jr. 25.00 60.00

1999 Upper Deck Mark McGwire Tribute

This 30 card standard-size set was released by Upper Deck in 1999 to commemorate Mark McGwire's 70 home run season in 1998. The set was issued in a lunch box and each card features a highlight from the 1998 season. There is an action shot on the front of the card along with a little inset portrait photo. The back gives big play to the date along with a description of what happened on that day.

COMPLETE SET 6.00 15.00
COMMON CARD .30 .75

1999 Upper Deck McGwire 500 Home Run Set

This 30 card box set honors Mark McGwire hitting his 500th homer during the 1999 season. The cards were issued in a special box which also commemorated the feat.

COMPLETE SET (30) 8.00 20.00
COMMON CARD (1-30) .30 .75

1999 Upper Deck/Kodak

NNO Mark McGwire

2000 Upper Deck

Upper Deck Series one was released in December, 1999 and offered 270 standard-size cards. The first series was distributed in 10 card packs with a SRP of $2.99 per pack. The second series was released in July, 2000 and offered 270 standard-size cards. The cards were issued in 24 pack boxes. Cards numbered 1-28 and 271-297 are Star Rookie subsets while cards numbered 262-270 and 532-540 feature 1999 season highlights and have checklists on back. Cards 523-531 feature the All-UD Team subset - a collection of top stars as selected by Upper Deck. Notable Rookie Cards include Kazuhiro Sasaki. Also, 350 1999 A Piece of History 500 Club Hank Aaron bat cards were randomly seeded into first series packs. In addition, Aaron signed and numbered 44 copies. Pricing for these bat cards can be referenced under 1999 Upper Deck A Piece of History 500 Club. Also, a selection of A Piece of History 3000 Club Hank Aaron memorabilia cards were randomly seeded into second series packs. 350 bat cards, 350 jersey cards, 100 hand-numbered, combination bat-jersey cards and forty-four hand-numbered, autographed, combination bat-jersey cards were produced. Pricing for these memorabilia cards can be referenced under 2000 Upper Deck A Piece of History 3000 Club.

COMPLETE SET (540) 20.00 50.00
COMPLETE SERIES 1 (270) 10.00 25.00
COMPLETE SERIES 2 (270) 10.00 25.00
COMMON CARD (1-540) .12 .30
COMMON SR (1-28/271-297) .20 .50
CARD 460 DOES NOT EXIST
1 Rick Ankiel SR .30 .75
2 Vernon Wells SR .20 .50
3 Ryan Anderson SR .20 .50
4 Ed Yarnall SR .20 .50
5 Brian McNichol SR .20 .50
6 Ben Petrick SR .20 .50
7 Kip Wells SR .20 .50
8 Eric Munson SR .20 .50
9 Matt Riley SR .20 .50
10 Peter Bergeron SR .20 .50
11 Eric Gagne SR .20 .50
12 Ramon Ortiz SR .20 .50
13 Josh Beckett SR .40 1.00
14 Alfonso Soriano SR .50 1.25
15 Jorge Toca SR .20 .50
16 Buddy Carlyle SR .20 .50
17 Chad Hermansen SR .20 .50
18 Matt Perisho SR .20 .50
19 Tomokazu Ohka SR RC .20 .50
20 Jacque Jones SR .20 .50
21 Josh Paul SR .20 .50
22 Dermal Brown SR .20 .50
23 Adam Kennedy SR .20 .50
24 Chad Harville SR .20 .50
25 Calvin Murray SR .20 .50
26 Chad Meyers SR .20 .50
27 Brian Cooper SR .20 .50
28 Troy Glaus .20 .50
29 Ben Molina .12 .30
30 Troy Percival .12 .30
31 Ken Hill .12 .30
32 Chuck Finley .12 .30
33 Todd Greene .12 .30
34 Tim Salmon .12 .30
35 Gary DiSarcina .12 .30
36 Luis Gonzalez .12 .30
37 Tony Womack .12 .30
38 Omar Daal .12 .30
39 Randy Johnson .30 .75
40 Erubiel Durazo .12 .30
41 Jay Bell .12 .30
42 Steve Finley .12 .30
43 Travis Lee .12 .30
44 Greg Maddux .40 1.00
45 Bret Boone .12 .30
46 Brian Jordan .12 .30
47 Kevin Millwood .12 .30
48 Odalis Perez .12 .30
49 Javy Lopez .12 .30
50 John Smoltz .30 .75
51 Bruce Chen .12 .30
52 Albert Belle .12 .30
53 Jerry Hairston Jr. .12 .30
54 Will Clark .20 .50
55 Sidney Ponson .12 .30
56 Charles Johnson .12 .30
57 Cal Ripken 1.00 2.50
58 Ryan Minor .12 .30
59 Mike Mussina .20 .50
60 Tom Gordon .12 .30
61 Jose Offerman .12 .30
62 Trot Nixon .12 .30
63 Pedro Martinez .20 .50
64 John Valentin .12 .30
65 Jason Varitek .30 .75
66 Juan Pena .12 .30
67 Troy O'Leary .12 .30
68 Sammy Sosa .30 .75
69 Henry Rodriguez .12 .30
70 Kyle Farnsworth .12 .30
71 Glenallen Hill .12 .30
72 Lance Johnson .12 .30
73 Mickey Morandini .12 .30
74 Jon Lieber .12 .30
75 Kevin Tapani .12 .30
76 Carlos Lee .12 .30
77 Ray Durham .12 .30
78 Jim Parque .12 .30
79 Bob Howry .12 .30
80 Magglio Ordonez .20 .50
81 Paul Konerko .12 .30
82 Mike Caruso .12 .30
83 Chris Singleton .12 .30
84 Sean Casey .12 .30
85 Barry Larkin .20 .50
86 Pokey Reese .12 .30
87 Eddie Taubensee .12 .30
88 Scott Williamson .12 .30
89 Jason LaRue .12 .30
90 Aaron Boone .12 .30
91 Jeffrey Hammonds .12 .30
92 Omar Vizquel .20 .50
93 Manny Ramirez .30 .75
94 Kenny Lofton .12 .30
95 Jaret Wright .12 .30
96 Einar Diaz .12 .30
97 Charles Nagy .12 .30
98 David Justice .12 .30
99 Richie Sexson .12 .30
100 Steve Karsay .12 .30
101 Todd Helton .20 .50
102 Dante Bichette .12 .30
103 Larry Walker .20 .50
104 Pedro Astacio .12 .30
105 Neifi Perez .12 .30
106 Brian Bohanon .12 .30
107 Edgard Clemente .12 .30
108 Dave Veres .12 .30
109 Gabe Kapler .12 .30
110 Juan Encarnacion .12 .30
111 Jeff Weaver .12 .30
112 Damion Easley .12 .30
113 Justin Thompson .12 .30
114 Brad Ausmus .12 .30
115 Frank Catalanotto .12 .30
116 Todd Jones .12 .30
117 Preston Wilson .12 .30
118 Cliff Floyd .12 .30
119 Mike Lowell .12 .30
120 Antonio Alfonseca .12 .30
121 Alex Gonzalez .12 .30
122 Braden Looper .12 .30
123 Bruce Aven .12 .30
124 Richard Hidalgo .12 .30
125 Mitch Meluskey .12 .30
126 Jeff Bagwell .20 .50
127 Jose Lima .12 .30
128 Derek Bell .12 .30
129 Billy Wagner .12 .30
130 Shane Reynolds .12 .30
131 Moises Alou .12 .30
132 Carlos Beltran .20 .50
133 Carlos Febles .12 .30
134 Jermaine Dye .12 .30
135 Jeremy Giambi .12 .30
136 Joe Randa .12 .30
137 Jose Rosado .12 .30
138 Chad Kreuter .12 .30
139 Jose Vizcaino .12 .30
140 Adrian Beltre .30 .75
141 Kevin Brown .12 .30
142 Ismael Valdes .12 .30
143 Angel Pena .12 .30
144 Chan Ho Park .20 .50
145 Mark Grudzielanek .12 .30
146 Jeff Shaw .12 .30
147 Geoff Jenkins .12 .30
148 Jeromy Burnitz .12 .30
149 Hideo Nomo .30 .75
150 Ron Belliard .12 .30
151 Sean Berry .12 .30
152 Mark Loretta .12 .30
153 Steve Woodard .12 .30
154 Joe Mays .12 .30
155 Eric Milton .12 .30
156 Corey Koskie .12 .30
157 Ron Coomer .12 .30
158 Brad Radke .12 .30
159 Terry Steinbach .12 .30
160 Cristian Guzman .12 .30
161 Vladimir Guerrero .20 .50
162 Wilton Guerrero .12 .30
163 Michael Barrett .12 .30
164 Chris Widger .12 .30
165 Fernando Seguignol .12 .30
166 Ugueth Urbina .12 .30
167 Dustin Hermanson .12 .30
168 Kenny Rogers .12 .30
169 Edgardo Alfonzo .12 .30
170 Orel Hershiser .12 .30
171 Robin Ventura .12 .30
172 Octavio Dotel .12 .30
173 Rickey Henderson .30 .75
174 Roger Cedeno .12 .30
175 John Olerud .12 .30
176 Derek Jeter .75 2.00
177 Tino Martinez .12 .30
178 Orlando Hernandez .12 .30
179 Chuck Knoblauch .12 .30
180 Bernie Williams .20 .50
181 Chili Davis .12 .30
182 David Cone .12 .30
183 Ricky Ledee .12 .30
184 Paul O'Neill .20 .50
185 Jason Giambi .12 .30
186 Eric Chavez .12 .30
187 Matt Stairs .12 .30
188 Miguel Tejada .20 .50
189 Olmedo Saenz .12 .30
190 Tim Hudson .20 .50
191 John Jaha .12 .30
192 Randy Velarde .12 .30
193 Rico Brogna .12 .30
194 Mike Lieberthal .12 .30
195 Marlon Anderson .12 .30
196 Bob Abreu .12 .30
197 Ron Gant .12 .30
198 Randy Wolf .12 .30
199 Desi Relaford .12 .30
200 Doug Glanville .12 .30
201 Warren Morris .12 .30
202 Kris Benson .12 .30
203 Kevin Young .12 .30
204 Brian Giles .12 .30
205 Jason Schmidt .12 .30
206 Ed Sprague .12 .30
207 Francisco Cordova .12 .30
208 Mark McGwire .50 1.25
209 Jose Jimenez .12 .30
210 Fernando Tatis .12 .30
211 Kent Bottenfield .12 .30
212 Eli Marrero .12 .30
213 Edgar Renteria .12 .30
214 Joe McEwing .12 .30
215 J.D. Drew .12 .30
216 Tony Gwynn .30 .75
217 Gary Matthews Jr. .12 .30
218 Eric Owens .12 .30
219 Damian Jackson .12 .30
220 Reggie Sanders .12 .30
221 Trevor Hoffman .20 .50
222 Ben Davis .12 .30
223 Shawn Estes .12 .30
224 F.P. Santangelo .12 .30
225 Livan Hernandez .12 .30
226 Ellis Burks .12 .30
227 J.T. Snow .12 .30
228 Jeff Kent .12 .30
229 Robb Nen .12 .30
230 Marvin Benard .12 .30
231 Ken Griffey Jr. .60 1.50
232 John Halama .12 .30
233 Gil Meche .12 .30
234 David Bell .12 .30
235 Brian Hunter .12 .30
236 Jay Buhner .12 .30
237 Edgar Martinez .20 .50
238 Jose Mesa .12 .30
239 Wilson Alvarez .12 .30
240 Wade Boggs .20 .50
241 Fred McGriff .20 .50
242 Jose Canseco .20 .50
243 Kevin Stocker .12 .30
244 Roberto Hernandez .12 .30
245 Bubba Trammell .12 .30
246 John Flaherty .12 .30
247 Ivan Rodriguez .20 .50
248 Rusty Greer .12 .30
249 Rafael Palmeiro .20 .50
250 Jeff Zimmerman .12 .30
251 Royce Clayton .12 .30
252 Todd Zeile .12 .30
253 John Wetteland .12 .30
254 Ruben Mateo .12 .30
255 Kelvim Escobar .12 .30
256 David Wells .12 .30
257 Shawn Green .12 .30
258 Homer Bush .12 .30
259 Shannon Stewart .12 .30
260 Carlos Delgado .12 .30
261 Roy Halladay .20 .50
262 Fernando Tatis SH CL .12 .30
263 Jose Jimenez SH CL .12 .30
264 Tony Gwynn SH CL .30 .75
265 Wade Boggs SH CL .20 .50
266 Cal Ripken SH CL 1.00 2.50
267 David Cone SH CL .12 .30
268 Mark McGwire SH CL .50 1.25
269 Pedro Martinez SH CL .20 .50
270 Nomar Garciaparra SH CL .20 .50
271 Nick Johnson SR .20 .50
272 Mark Quinn SR .20 .50
273 Roosevelt Brown SR .20 .50
274 Terrence Long SR .20 .50
275 Jason Marquis SR .20 .50
276 Kazuhiro Sasaki SR RC .50 1.25
277 Aaron Myette SR .20 .50
278 Danys Baez SR RC .20 .50
279 Travis Dawkins SR .20 .50
280 Mark Mulder SR .20 .50
281 Chris Haas SR .20 .50
282 Milton Bradley SR .20 .50
283 Brad Penny SR .20 .50
284 Rafael Furcal SR .30 .75
285 Luis Matos SR RC .20 .50
286 Victor Santos SR RC .20 .50
287 Rico Washington SR RC .20 .50
288 Rob Bell SR .20 .50
289 Joe Crede SR .20 .50
290 Pablo Ozuna SR .20 .50
291 Wascar Serrano SR RC .20 .50
292 Sang-Hoon Lee SR RC .20 .50
293 Chris Wakeland SR RC .20 .50
294 Luis Rivera SR RC .20 .50
295 Mike Lamb SR RC .20 .50
296 Wily Mo Pena SR .20 .50
297 Mike Meyers SR RC .30 .75
298 Mo Vaughn .12 .30
299 Darin Erstad .12 .30
300 Garret Anderson .12 .30
301 Tim Belcher .12 .30
302 Scott Spiezio .12 .30
303 Kent Bottenfield .12 .30
304 Orlando Palmeiro .12 .30
305 Jason Dickson .12 .30
306 Matt Williams .12 .30
307 Brian Anderson .12 .30
308 Hanley Frias .12 .30
309 Todd Stottlemyre .12 .30
310 Matt Mantei .12 .30
311 David Dellucci .12 .30
312 Armando Reynoso .12 .30
313 Bernard Gilkey .12 .30
314 Chipper Jones .30 .75
315 Tom Glavine .20 .50
316 Quilvio Veras .12 .30
317 Andruw Jones .12 .30
318 Bobby Bonilla .12 .30
319 Reggie Sanders .12 .30
320 Andres Galarraga .20 .50
321 George Lombard .12 .30
322 John Rocker .12 .30
323 Wally Joyner .12 .30
324 B.J. Surhoff .12 .30
325 Scott Erickson .12 .30
326 Delino DeShields .12 .30
327 Jeff Conine .12 .30
328 Mike Timlin .12 .30
329 Brady Anderson .12 .30
330 Mike Bordick .12 .30
331 Harold Baines .20 .50
332 Nomar Garciaparra .20 .50
333 Bret Saberhagen .12 .30
334 Ramon Martinez .12 .30
335 Donnie Sadler .12 .30
336 Wilton Veras .12 .30
337 Mike Stanley .12 .30
338 Brian Rose .12 .30
339 Carl Everett .12 .30
340 Tim Wakefield .20 .50
341 Mark Grace .20 .50
342 Kerry Wood .12 .30
343 Eric Young .12 .30
344 Jose Nieves .12 .30
345 Ismael Valdes .12 .30
346 Joe Girardi .20 .50
347 Damon Buford .12 .30
348 Ricky Gutierrez .12 .30
349 Frank Thomas .30 .75
350 Brian Simmons .12 .30
351 James Baldwin .12 .30
352 Brook Fordyce .12 .30
353 Jose Valentin .12 .30
354 Mike Sirotka .12 .30
355 Greg Norton .12 .30
356 Dante Bichette .12 .30
357 Deion Sanders .20 .50
358 Ken Griffey Jr. .60 1.50
359 Denny Neagle .12 .30
360 Dmitri Young .12 .30
361 Pete Harnisch .12 .30
362 Michael Tucker .12 .30
363 Roberto Alomar .20 .50
364 Dave Roberts .12 .30
365 Jim Thome .20 .50
366 Bartolo Colon .12 .30
367 Travis Fryman .12 .30
368 Chuck Finley .12 .30
369 Russell Branyan .12 .30
370 Alex Ramirez .12 .30
371 Jeff Cirillo .12 .30
372 Jeffrey Hammonds .12 .30
373 Scott Karl .12 .30
374 Brent Mayne .12 .30
375 Tom Goodwin .12 .30
376 Jose Jimenez .12 .30
377 Rolando Arrojo .12 .30
378 Terry Shumpert .12 .30
379 Juan Gonzalez .12 .30
380 Bobby Higginson .12 .30
381 Tony Clark .12 .30
382 Dave Mlicki .12 .30
383 Deivi Cruz .12 .30
384 Brian Moehler .12 .30
385 Dean Palmer .12 .30
386 Luis Castillo .12 .30
387 Mike Redmond .12 .30
388 Alex Fernandez .12 .30
389 Brant Brown .12 .30
390 Dave Berg .12 .30
391 A.J. Burnett .12 .30
392 Mark Kotsay .12 .30
393 Craig Biggio .20 .50
394 Daryle Ward .12 .30
395 Lance Berkman .20 .50
396 Roger Cedeno .12 .30
397 Scott Elarton .12 .30
398 Octavio Dotel .12 .30
399 Ken Caminiti .12 .30
400 Johnny Damon .20 .50
401 Mike Sweeney .12 .30
402 Jeff Suppan .12 .30
403 Rey Sanchez .12 .30
404 Blake Stein .12 .30
405 Ricky Bottalico .12 .30
406 Jay Witasick .12 .30
407 Shawn Green .12 .30
408 Orel Hershiser .12 .30
409 Gary Sheffield .12 .30
410 Todd Hollandsworth .12 .30
411 Terry Adams .12 .30
412 Todd Hundley .12 .30
413 Eric Karros .12 .30
414 F.P. Santangelo .12 .30
415 Alex Cora .20 .50
416 Marquis Grissom .12 .30
417 Henry Blanco .12 .30
418 Jose Hernandez .12 .30
419 Kyle Peterson .12 .30
420 John Snyder RC .12 .30
421 Bob Wickman .12 .30
422 Jamey Wright .12 .30
423 Chad Allen .12 .30
424 Todd Walker .12 .30
425 J.C. Romero RC .12 .30
426 Butch Huskey .12 .30
427 Jacque Jones .12 .30
428 Matt Lawton .12 .30
429 Rondell White .12 .30
430 Jose Vidro .12 .30
431 Hideki Irabu .12 .30
432 Javier Vazquez .12 .30
433 Lee Stevens .12 .30
434 Mike Thurman .12 .30
435 Geoff Blum .12 .30
436 Mike Hampton .12 .30
437 Mike Piazza .30 .75
438 Al Leiter .12 .30
439 Derek Bell .12 .30
440 Armando Benitez .12 .30
441 Rey Ordonez .12 .30
442 Todd Zeile .12 .30
443 Roger Clemens .40 1.00
444 Ramiro Mendoza .12 .30
445 Andy Pettitte .20 .50
446 Scott Brosius .12 .30
447 Mariano Rivera .40 1.00
448 Jim Leyritz .12 .30
449 Jorge Posada .20 .50
450 Omar Olivares .12 .30
451 Ben Grieve .12 .30
452 A.J. Hinch .12 .30
453 Gil Heredia .12 .30
454 Kevin Appier .12 .30
455 Ryan Christenson .12 .30
456 Ramon Hernandez .12 .30
457 Scott Rolen .20 .50
458 Alex Arias .12 .30
459 Andy Ashby .12 .30
461 Robert Person .12 .30
462 Paul Byrd .12 .30
463 Curt Schilling .20 .50
464 Mike Jackson .12 .30
465 Jason Kendall .12 .30
466 Pat Meares .12 .30
467 Bruce Aven .12 .30
468 Todd Ritchie .12 .30
469 Wil Cordero .12 .30
470 Aramis Ramirez .12 .30
471 Andy Benes .12 .30
472 Ray Lankford .12 .30
473 Fernando Vina .12 .30
474A Jim Edmonds .12 .30
474B Kevin Jordan .12 .30
475 Craig Paquette .12 .30
476 Pat Hentgen .12 .30
477 Darryl Kile .12 .30
478 Sterling Hitchcock .12 .30
479 Ruben Rivera .12 .30
480 Ryan Klesko .12 .30
481 Phil Nevin .12 .30
482 Woody Williams .12 .30
483 Carlos Hernandez .12 .30
484 Brian Meadows .12 .30
485 Bret Boone .12 .30
486 Barry Bonds .50 1.25
487 Russ Ortiz .12 .30
488 Bobby Estalella .12 .30
489 Rich Aurilia .12 .30
490 Bill Mueller .12 .30
491 Joe Nathan .12 .30
492 Russ Davis .12 .30
493 John Olerud .12 .30
494 Alex Rodriguez .40 1.00
495 Freddy Garcia .12 .30
496 Carlos Guillen .12 .30
497 Aaron Sele .12 .30
498 Brett Tomko .12 .30
499 Jamie Moyer .12 .30

500 Mike Cameron .12 .30
501 Vinny Castilla .12 .30
502 Gerald Williams .12 .30
503 Mike DiFelice .12 .30
504 Ryan Rupe .12 .30
505 Greg Vaughn .12 .30
506 Miguel Cairo .12 .30
507 Juan Guzman .12 .30
508 Jose Guillen .12 .30
509 Gabe Kapler .12 .30
510 Rick Helling .12 .30
511 David Segui .12 .30
512 Doug Davis .12 .30
513 Justin Thompson .12 .30
514 Chad Curtis .12 .30
515 Tony Batista .12 .30
516 Billy Koch .12 .30
517 Raul Mondesi .12 .30
518 Joey Hamilton .12 .30
519 Darrin Fletcher .12 .30
520 Brad Fullmer .12 .30
521 Jose Cruz Jr. .12 .30
522 Kevin Witt .12 .30
523 Mark McGwire AUT .50 1.25
524 Roberto Alomar AUT .20 .50
525 Chipper Jones AUT .30 .75
526 Derek Jeter AUT .75 2.00
527 Ken Griffey Jr. AUT .60 1.50
528 Sammy Sosa AUT .30 .75
529 Manny Ramirez AUT .30 .75
530 Ivan Rodriguez AUT .20 .50
531 Pedro Martinez AUT .20 .50
532 Mariano Rivera CL .40 1.00
533 Sammy Sosa CL .30 .75
534 Cal Ripken CL 1.00 2.50
535 Vladimir Guerrero CL .20 .50
536 Tony Gwynn CL .30 .75
537 Mark McGwire CL .50 1.25
538 Bernie Williams CL .20 .50
539 Pedro Martinez CL .20 .50
540 Ken Griffey Jr. CL .60 1.50

2000 Upper Deck Exclusives Gold

NO PRICING DUE TO SCARCITY

2000 Upper Deck Exclusives Silver

*EXC.SILV: 8X TO 20X BASIC CARDS
*SR: 5X TO 12X BASIC SR
STATED PRINT RUN 100 SERIAL #'d SETS
CARD 460 DOES NOT EXIST
JORDAN AND EDMONDS BOTH NUMBER 474

2000 Upper Deck 2K Plus

Inserted one every 23 first series packs, these 12 cards feature some players who are expected to be stars in the beginning of the 21st century.

COMPLETE SET (12) 8.00 20.00
*SINGLES: 2X TO 5X BASE CARD HI
SER.1 STATED ODDS 1:23
*DIE CUTS: 2.5X TO 6X BASIC 2K PLUS
DIE CUTS RANDOM INSERTS IN SER.1 HOBBY
DIE CUTS PRINT RUN 100 SERIAL #'d SETS
GOLD DIE CUTS RANDOM IN SER.1 HOBBY
GOLD DIE CUT PRINT RUN 1 SERIAL #'d SET
GOLD DC NOT PRICED DUE TO SCARCITY
2K1 Ken Griffey Jr. 2.00 5.00
2K2 J.D. Drew .40 1.00
2K3 Derek Jeter 2.50 6.00
2K4 Nomar Garciaparra .60 1.50
2K5 Pat Burrell .40 1.00
2K6 Ruben Mateo .40 1.00
2K7 Carlos Beltran .60 1.50
2K8 Vladimir Guerrero .60 1.50
2K9 Scott Rolen .60 1.50
2K10 Chipper Jones 1.00 2.50
2K11 Alex Rodriguez 1.25 3.00
2K12 Magglio Ordonez .60 1.50

2000 Upper Deck A Piece of History 3000 Club

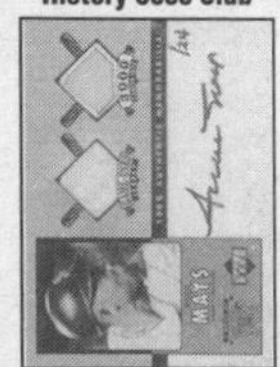

During the 2000 and early 2001 season, Upper Deck inserted a selection of memorabilia cards celebrating members of the 3000 hit club. Approximately 350 of each bat or jersey card was produced. In addition, a wide array of scarce, hand-numbered, autographed cards and combination memorabilia cards were made available. Complete print run information for these cards is provided in our checklist. The cards were released in the following products: 2000 SP Authentic: Tris Speaker and Paul Waner; 2000 SPx: Ty Cobb; 2000 UD Ionix: Roberto Clemente; 2000 Upper Deck 2: Hank Aaron; 2000 Upper Deck Gold Reserve: Al Kaline; 2000 Upper Deck Hitter's Club: Wade Boggs and Tony Gwynn; 2000 Upper Deck HoloGrFx: George Brett and Robin Yount; 2000 Upper Deck Legends: Paul Molitor and Carl Yastrzemski; 2000 Upper Deck MVP: Stan Musial; 2000 Upper Deck Ovation: Willie Mays; 2000 Upper Deck Pros and Prospects: Lou Brock and Rod Carew; 2000 Upper Deck Yankees Legends: Dave Winfield; 2001 Upper Deck: Eddie Murray and Cal Ripken. Exchange cards were seeded into packs for the following cards: Al Kaline Bat AU, Eddie Murray Bat AU, Cal Ripken Bat and Cal Ripken Bat-Jsy. The deadline to exchange the Kaline card was April 10th, 2001 and the Murray/Ripken cards was August 22nd, 2001.

STATED PRINT RUNS LISTED BELOW
NO PRICING ON QTY OF 33 OR LESS
AKB A.Kaline Bat/400 12.00 30.00
BGB Boggs/Gwynn Bat/99 75.00 150.00
BYB Brett/Yount Bat/99 75.00 150.00
BYJ Brett/Yount Jersey/99 125.00 200.00
CRB C.Ripken Bat/350 12.00 30.00
CRJ C.Ripken Jersey/350 10.00 25.00
CRJB C.Ripken Bat-Jsy/100 30.00 60.00
CYB C.Yaz Bat/350 15.00 40.00
CYJ C.Yaz Jersey/350 10.00 25.00
CYJB C.Yaz Bat-Jsy/100 50.00 100.00
DWB D.Winf. Bat/350 10.00 25.00
DWJ D.Winf. Jersey/350 10.00 25.00
DWJB D.Winf. Bat-Jsy/100 40.00 80.00
EMB E.Murray Bat/350 12.00 30.00
EMJ E.Murray Jersey/350 20.00 50.00
EMJB E.Murray Bat-Jsy/100 12.50 30.00
GBB G.Brett Bat/350 25.00 60.00
GBJ G.Brett Jersey/350 20.00 50.00
HAB H.Aaron Bat/350 25.00 60.00
HABS H.Aaron Bat-Jsy AU/44 800.00 1200.00
HAJ H.Aaron Jersey/350 25.00 60.00
HAJB H.Aaron Bat-Jsy/100 125.00 250.00
LBB L.Brock Bat/350 15.00 40.00
LBJ L.Brock Jsy/350 15.00 40.00
LBJB L.Brock Bat-Jsy/100 40.00 80.00
PMB P.Molitor Bat/350 10.00 25.00
PWB P.Waner Bat/350 12.00 30.00
RCAB R.Carew Bat/350 12.50 30.00
RCAJ R.Carew Jsy/350 10.00 25.00
RCABJ R.Carew Bat-Jsy/100 30.00 60.00
RCLB R.Clemente Bat/350 40.00 80.00
RYB R.Yount Bat/350 20.00 50.00
RYJ R.Yount Jersey/350 20.00 50.00
SMB S.Musial Bat/350 12.00 30.00
SMJ S.Musial Jersey/350 15.00 40.00
SMJB S.Musial Bat-Jsy/100 75.00 150.00
TCB Ty Cobb Bat/350 60.00 150.00
TGB T.Gwynn Bat/350 12.00 30.00
TGBC T.Gwynn Bat-Cap/50 75.00 150.00
TSB T.Speaker Bat/350 15.00 40.00
WBB W.Boggs Bat/350 12.00 30.00
WBBC W.Boggs Bat-Cap/50 50.00 100.00
WMB W.Mays Bat/300 30.00 60.00
WMJ W.Mays Jersey/350 30.00 60.00
WMJB W.Mays Bat-Jsy/50 150.00 250.00

2000 Upper Deck Cooperstown Calling

Randomly inserted into Upper Deck Series two packs at one in 23, this 15-card insert features players that will be going to Cooperstown after they retire from baseball. Card backs carry a "CC" prefix.

COMPLETE SET (15) 15.00 40.00
SER.2 STATED ODDS 1:23
CC1 Roger Clemens 1.25 3.00
CC2 Cal Ripken 3.00 8.00
CC3 Ken Griffey Jr. 2.00 5.00
CC4 Mike Piazza 1.00 2.50
CC5 Tony Gwynn 1.00 2.50
CC6 Sammy Sosa 1.00 2.50
CC7 Jose Canseco .60 1.50
CC8 Larry Walker .60 1.50
CC9 Barry Bonds 1.50 4.00
CC10 Greg Maddux 1.25 3.00
CC11 Derek Jeter 2.50 6.00
CC12 Mark McGwire 1.50 4.00
CC13 Randy Johnson 1.00 2.50
CC14 Frank Thomas 1.00 2.50
CC15 Jeff Bagwell .60 1.50

2000 Upper Deck e-Card

Inserted as a two-pack box-topper in Upper Deck Series two, this six-card insert features cards that can be viewed over the Upper Deck website. Cards feature a serial number that is to be typed in a the Upper Deck website to reveal that card. Card backs carry an "E" prefix.

COMPLETE SET (6) 4.00 10.00
TWO PER SER.2 BOX CHIPTOPPER
E1 Ken Griffey Jr. 1.25 3.00
E2 Alex Rodriguez .75 2.00
E3 Cal Ripken Jr. 2.00 5.00
E4 Jeff Bagwell .40 1.00
E5 Barry Bonds 1.00 2.50
E6 Manny Ramirez .60 1.50

2000 Upper Deck eVolve Autograph

Lucky participants in Upper Deck's E-Card program received special upgraded E-Cards available by checking the UD website (www.upperdeck.com) and entering their basic E-Card serial code (printed on the front of each basic E-Card). When viewed on the Upper Deck website, if an autographed card of the depicted player appeared, the bearer of the base card could then exchange their basic E-Card and receive the signed upgrade via mail. Only 200 serial numbered E-Card Autograph sets were produced. Signed E-Cards all have an ES prefix on the card numbers.

EXCH.CARD AVAIL.VIA WEBSITE PROGRAM
STATED PRINT RUN 200 SERIAL #'d SETS
ES1 Ken Griffey Jr. 40.00 100.00
ES2 Alex Rodriguez 25.00 60.00
ES3 Cal Ripken 50.00 100.00
ES4 Jeff Bagwell 20.00 50.00
ES5 Barry Bonds 40.00 100.00
ES6 Manny Ramirez 12.00 50.00

2000 Upper Deck eVolve Game Jersey

Lucky participants in Upper Deck's E-Card program received special upgraded E-Cards available by checking the UD website (www.upperdeck.com) and entering their basic E-Card serial code (printed on the front of each basic E-Card). When viewed on the Upper Deck website, if a jersey card of the depicted player appeared, the bearer of the base card could then exchange their basic E-Card and receive the Game Jersey upgrade via mail. The cards closely parallel basic 2000 Game Jerseys that were distributed in first and second series packs except for the gold foil "e-volve" logo on front. Only 300 serial numbered E-Card Jersey sets were produced with each card being serial -numbered by hand in blue ink sharpie at the bottom right front corner. Unsigned E-Card Game Jerseys all have an EJ prefix on the card numbers.

EXCH.CARD AVAIL.VIA WEBSITE PROGRAM
STATED PRINT RUN 300 SERIAL #'d SETS
EJ1 Ken Griffey Jr. 10.00 25.00
EJ2 Alex Rodriguez 10.00 25.00
EJ3 Cal Ripken 10.00 25.00
EJ4 Jeff Bagwell 10.00 25.00
EJ5 Barry Bonds 10.00 25.00
EJ6 Manny Ramirez 10.00 25.00

2000 Upper Deck eVolve Game Jersey Autograph

Lucky participants in Upper Deck's E-Card program received special upgraded E-Cards available by checking the UD website (www.upperdeck.com) and entering their basic E-Card serial code (printed on the front of each basic E-Card). When viewed on the Upper Deck website, if an autographed card of the depicted player appeared, the bearer of the base card could then exchange their basic E-Card and receive the signed jersey upgrade via mail. A mere 50 serial numbered sets were produced. Signed jersey E-Cards all have an ESJ prefix on the card numbers.

EXCH.CARD AVAIL.VIA WEBSITE PROGRAM
STATED PRINT RUN 50 SERIAL #'d SETS
ESJ1 Ken Griffey Jr. 50.00 120.00
ESJ2 Alex Rodriguez 100.00 250.00
ESJ3 Cal Ripken 75.00 200.00
ESJ4 Jeff Bagwell 40.00 100.00
ESJ5 Barry Bonds 75.00 200.00
ESJ6 Manny Ramirez 60.00 150.00

2000 Upper Deck Faces of the Game

Inserted one every 11 first series packs, these 20 cards feature leading players captured by exceptional photography.

COMPLETE SET (20) 20.00 50.00
SER.1 STATED ODDS 1:11
*DIE CUTS: 3X TO 8X BASIC FACES
DIE CUTS RANDOM INSERTS IN SER.1 HOBBY
DIE CUTS PRINT RUN 100 SERIAL #'d SETS
GOLD DIE CUTS RANDOM IN SER.1 HOBBY
GOLD DIE CUT PRINT RUN 1 SERIAL #'d SET
GOLD DC NOT PRICED DUE TO SCARCITY
F1 Ken Griffey Jr. 2.00 5.00
F2 Mark McGwire 1.50 4.00
F3 Sammy Sosa 1.00 2.50
F4 Alex Rodriguez 1.25 3.00
F5 Manny Ramirez 1.00 2.50
F6 Derek Jeter 2.50 6.00
F7 Jeff Bagwell .60 1.50
F8 Roger Clemens 1.25 3.00
F9 Scott Rolen .60 1.50
F10 Tony Gwynn 1.00 2.50
F11 Nomar Garciaparra .60 1.50
F12 Randy Johnson 1.00 2.50
F13 Greg Maddux 1.25 3.00
F14 Mike Piazza 1.00 2.50
F15 Frank Thomas 1.00 2.50
F16 Cal Ripken 3.00 8.00
F17 Ivan Rodriguez .60 1.50
F18 Mo Vaughn .40 1.00
F19 Chipper Jones 1.00 2.50
F20 Sean Casey .40 1.00

2000 Upper Deck Five-Tool Talents

Randomly inserted into packs at one in 11, this 15-card insert features players that possess all of the tools needed to succeed in the Major Leagues. Card backs carry a "FT" prefix.

COMPLETE SET (15) 10.00 25.00
SER.2 STATED ODDS 1:11
FT1 Vladimir Guerrero .60 1.50
FT2 Barry Bonds 1.50 4.00
FT3 Jason Kendall .40 1.00
FT4 Derek Jeter 2.50 6.00
FT5 Ken Griffey Jr. 2.00 5.00
FT6 Andruw Jones .40 1.00
FT7 Bernie Williams .60 1.50
FT8 Jose Canseco .60 1.50
FT9 Scott Rolen .60 1.50
FT10 Shawn Green .40 1.00
FT11 Nomar Garciaparra .60 1.50
FT12 Jeff Bagwell .60 1.50
FT13 Larry Walker .60 1.50
FT14 Chipper Jones 1.00 2.50
FT15 Alex Rodriguez 1.25 3.00

2000 Upper Deck Game Ball

Randomly inserted into packs at one in 287, this 10-card insert features game-used baseballs from the depicted players. Card backs carry a "B" prefix.

SER.2 STATED ODDS 1:287
BAJ Andruw Jones 4.00 10.00
BAR Alex Rodriguez 6.00 15.00
BBW Bernie Williams 4.00 10.00
BDJ Derek Jeter 15.00 40.00
BJB Jeff Bagwell 4.00 10.00
BKG Ken Griffey Jr. 15.00 40.00
BMM Mark McGwire 8.00 20.00
BRC Roger Clemens 6.00 15.00
BTG Tony Gwynn 6.00 15.00
BVG Vladimir Guerrero 4.00 10.00

2000 Upper Deck Game Jersey

These cards feature swatches of jerseys of various major league stars. The cards with an "H" after the player names are available only in hobby packs at a rate of one every 288 first series and 1:287 second series. The cards which have an "HR" after the player names are available in either hobby or retail packs at a rate of one every 2500 packs.

H1 SER.1 STATED ODDS 1:288 HOBBY
HR1 SER.1 ODDS 1:2500 HOBBY/RETAIL
HR2 SER.2 ODDS 1:287 HOBBY/RETAIL
AJ Andruw Jones HR2 2.50 6.00
AR Alex Rodriguez H1 8.00 20.00
AR Alex Rodriguez HR2 8.00 20.00
BG Ben Grieve HR2 2.50 6.00
CJ Chipper Jones HR1 6.00 15.00
CR Cal Ripken HR1 8.00 20.00
CY Tom Glavine H1 4.00 10.00
DC David Cone HR2 2.50 6.00
DJ Derek Jeter H1 15.00 40.00
EC Eric Chavez HR2 2.50 6.00
EM Edgar Martinez HR2 4.00 10.00
FT Frank Thomas H1 6.00 15.00
FT Frank Thomas HR2 6.00 15.00
GK Gabe Kapler HR1 2.50 6.00
GM Greg Maddux HR1 8.00 20.00
GM Greg Maddux HR2 8.00 20.00
GV Greg Vaughn HR1 2.50 6.00
JB Jeff Bagwell H1 4.00 10.00
JC Jose Canseco HR1 4.00 10.00
JR Ken Griffey Jr. H1 12.00 30.00
KG Ken Griffey Jr. Reds HR2 12.00 30.00
KM Kevin Millwood HR2 2.50 6.00
MH Mike Hampton HR2 2.50 6.00
MP Mike Piazza H1 6.00 15.00
MR Manny Ramirez HR1 6.00 15.00
MV Mo Vaughn HR2 2.50 6.00
MW Matt Williams HR2 2.50 6.00
PM Pedro Martinez H1 4.00 10.00
RJ Randy Johnson HR2 6.00 15.00
RV Robin Ventura HR2 2.50 6.00
SA Sandy Alomar Jr. HR2 2.50 6.00
TG Tony Gwynn HR2 6.00 15.00
TH Todd Helton HR1 4.00 10.00
TH Todd Helton HR2 4.00 10.00
VG Vladimir Guerrero HR1 4.00 10.00
TGL Tom Glavine HR2 4.00 10.00
TRG Troy Glaus H1 2.50 6.00
TRG Troy Glaus HR2 2.50 6.00

2000 Upper Deck Game Jersey Autograph

Randomly inserted into Upper Deck Series two hobby packs, this insert set features autographed game-used jersey cards from some of the hottest players in major league baseball. Card backs carry an "H" prefix. A few autographs were not available in packs and had to be exchanged for signed cards. These cards had to be returned to Upper Deck by March 6th, 2001.

EXCHANGE DEADLINE 03/06/01
HAR Alex Rodriguez 40.00 100.00
HBB Barry Bonds 60.00 150.00
HCR Cal Ripken 50.00 100.00
HDJ Derek Jeter 300.00 600.00
HIR Ivan Rodriguez 20.00 50.00
HJB Jeff Bagwell 25.00 60.00
HJC Jose Canseco 12.00 30.00
HJK Jason Kendall 6.00 15.00
HKG K.Griffey Jr. Reds 50.00 120.00
HMR Manny Ramirez 15.00 40.00
HPO Paul O'Neill 30.00 60.00
HSR Scott Rolen 6.00 15.00
HVG Vladimir Guerrero 15.00 40.00

2000 Upper Deck Game Jersey Autograph Numbered

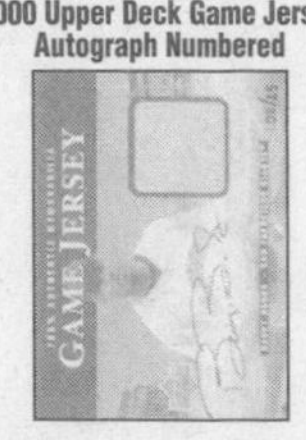

Randomly inserted into Upper Deck hobby packs, this insert set features autographed game-used jersey cards of the hottest players in baseball. Please note that these cards are hand-numbered on front in blue ink sharpie pen to the depicted players jersey number. Due to scarcity, some of these cards are not priced. A few cards were available via exchange: Series one exchange cards had to be redeemed by July 15th, 2000 while series two exchange cards were to be redeemed by March 6th, 2001. Cards tagged with an H1 or H2 suffix in the description were distributed exclusively in first and second series hobby packs. Cards tagged with an HR1 or HR2 suffix were distributed in hobby and retail packs. The "hobby-only" cards carry an "HN" prefix for the numbering on the back of each card (i.e. Scott Rolen is HN-SR). In addition, each of these cards features a congratulations from UD President Richard McWilliams with the reference to the card being "crash numbered". These two differences make these scarce numbered inserts easy to legitimize against possible fakes whereby unscrupulous parties may have numbered the cards themselves on front (not very tough to do given the cards were hand-numbered by UD). Unfortunately, the hobby-retail cards do not carry these key differences in design. It's believed that these Numbered inserts feature a gold hologram on back (lower left corner) rather than the silver hologram featured on the more common non-Numbered Game Jersey Autograph cards. Nonetheless, buyers are encouraged to exercise extreme caution for fakes when purchasing the hobby-retail versions of these cards.

H1 CARDS DIST.IN SER.1 HOBBY ONLY
HR1 CARDS DIST.IN SER.1 HOBBY & RETAIL
H2 CARDS DIST.IN SER.2 HOBBY ONLY
HR2 CARDS DIST.IN SER.2 HOBBY & RETAIL
PRINT RUNS B/WN 2-51 COPIES PER
NO PRICING ON QTY OF 25 OR LESS
SER.1 EXCHANGE DEADLINE 07/15/00
SER.2 EXCHANGE DEADLINE 03/06/01
FT Frank Thomas/35 HR2 75.00 200.00
GM Greg Maddux/31 HR2 100.00 200.00
JC Jose Canseco/33 H2 50.00 120.00
KG Ken Griffey Jr. Reds/30 H2 150.00 400.00
MV Mo Vaughn/42 HR2 30.00 60.00
RJ Randy Johnson/51 HR2 125.00 200.00
VG Vladimir Guerrero/27 H2 75.00 200.00
TGl Tom Glavine/47 HR2 50.00 100.00

2000 Upper Deck Game Jersey Patch

Randomly inserted into series one packs at one in 10,000 and series two packs at a rate of 1:7500, these cards feature game-worn uniform patches.

SER.1 STATED ODDS 1:10,000
SER.2 STATED ODDS 1:7500
1 OF 1 PATCH PRINT RUN 1 SERIAL #'d SET
NO 1 OF 1 PATCH PRICING AVAILABLE
PAJ Andruw Jones 2 50.00 100.00
PAR Alex Rodriguez 1 50.00 100.00
PAR Alex Rodriguez 2 50.00 100.00
PBB Barry Bonds 2 100.00 250.00
PBG Ben Grieve 2 20.00 50.00
PCJ Chipper Jones 1 50.00 100.00
PCR Cal Ripken 1 75.00 150.00
PCR Cal Ripken 2 75.00 150.00
PCY Tom Glavine 1 50.00 100.00
PDC David Cone 30.00 60.00
PDJ Derek Jeter 1 75.00 150.00
PDJ Derek Jeter 2 75.00 150.00
PEC Eric Chavez 1 30.00 60.00
PFT Frank Thomas 1 30.00 80.00
PGK Gabe Kapler 1 30.00 60.00
PGM Greg Maddux 1 60.00 120.00
PGM Greg Maddux 2 60.00 120.00
PGV Greg Vaughn 1 20.00 50.00
PIR Ivan Rodriguez 2 50.00 100.00
PJB Jeff Bagwell 1 60.00 150.00
PJC Jose Canseco 1 50.00 100.00
PJR Ken Griffey Jr. 1 75.00 150.00
PKG Ken Griffey Jr. Reds 2 75.00 150.00
PMP Mike Piazza 1 60.00 120.00
PMR Manny Ramirez 1 50.00 100.00
PMR Manny Ramirez 2 50.00 100.00
PMV Mo Vaughn 2 30.00 60.00
PMW Matt Williams 2 30.00 60.00
PPM Pedro Martinez 1 50.00 100.00
PRJ Randy Johnson 2 50.00 100.00
PSR Scott Rolen 2 50.00 100.00
PTG Tony Gwynn 2 50.00 100.00
PTH Todd Helton 1 50.00 100.00
PTRG Troy Glaus 1 30.00 60.00
PTRG Troy Glaus 2 30.00 60.00
PVG Vladimir Guerrero 1 60.00 120.00
PVG Vladimir Guerrero 2 60.00 120.00

2000 Upper Deck Hit Brigade

Inserted into first series packs at a rate of one in eight, these 15 cards feature some of the best hitters. These cards are printed in etched foil.

COMPLETE SET (15) 12.50 30.00
SER.1 STATED ODDS 1:8
*DIE CUTS: 3X TO 8X BASIC HIT BRIGADE
DIE CUTS RANDOM INSERTS IN SER.1 PACKS
DIE CUTS PRINT RUN 100 SERIAL #'d SETS
GOLD DIE CUTS RANDOM IN SER.1 PACKS
GOLD DIE CUT PRINT RUN 1 SERIAL #'d SET
GOLD DC NOT PRICED DUE TO SCARCITY
H1 Ken Griffey Jr. 2.00 5.00
H2 Tony Gwynn 1.00 2.50
H3 Alex Rodriguez 1.25 3.00
H4 Derek Jeter 2.50 6.00
H5 Mike Piazza 1.00 2.50
H6 Sammy Sosa 1.00 2.50
H7 Juan Gonzalez .40 1.00
H8 Scott Rolen .60 1.50
H9 Nomar Garciaparra .60 1.50
H10 Barry Bonds 1.50 4.00
H11 Craig Biggio .60 1.50
H12 Chipper Jones 1.00 2.50
H13 Frank Thomas 1.00 2.50
H14 Larry Walker .60 1.50
H15 Mark McGwire 1.50 4.00

2000 Upper Deck Hot Properties

Randomly inserted into Upper Deck series two packs at one in 11, this 15-card insert features the major league's top prospects. Card backs carry a "HP" prefix.

COMPLETE SET (15) 2.00 5.00
SER.2 STATED ODDS 1:11
HP1 Carlos Beltran .30 .75
HP2 Rick Ankiel .30 .75
HP3 Sean Casey .20 .50
HP4 Preston Wilson .20 .50
HP5 Vernon Wells .20 .50
HP6 Pat Burrell .20 .50
HP7 Eric Chavez .20 .50
HP8 J.D. Drew .20 .50
HP9 Alfonso Soriano .50 1.25
HP10 Gabe Kapler .20 .50
HP11 Rafael Furcal .30 .75
HP12 Ruben Mateo .20 .50
HP13 Corey Koskie .20 .50
HP14 Kip Wells .20 .50
HP15 Ramon Ortiz .20 .50

2000 Upper Deck Legendary Cuts

Randomly inserted into Upper Deck series two packs, this eight-card insert features cut-signatures from some of the all-time great players of the 20th Century. Please note that only one set was produced of this insert.

NO PRICING DUE TO SCARCITY

2000 Upper Deck Pennant Driven

Randomly inserted into packs at one in four, this 10-card insert features players that are driven to win the pennant. Card backs carry a "PD" prefix.

COMPLETE SET (10) 4.00 10.00
SER.2 STATED ODDS 1:4
PD1 Derek Jeter 1.25 3.00
PD2 Roberto Alomar .30 .75
PD3 Chipper Jones .50 1.25
PD4 Jeff Bagwell .30 .75
PD5 Roger Clemens .60 1.50
PD6 Nomar Garciaparra .30 .75
PD7 Manny Ramirez .50 1.25
PD8 Mike Piazza .50 1.25
PD9 Ivan Rodriguez .30 .75
PD10 Randy Johnson .50 1.25

2000 Upper Deck People's Choice

Randomly inserted into second series packs at one in 23, this 15-card set features players that people have voted as their favorites to watch. Card backs carry a "PC" prefix.

COMPLETE SET (15) 12.50 30.00
SER.2 STATED ODDS 1:23
PC1 Mark McGwire 1.50 4.00
PC2 Nomar Garciaparra .60 1.50
PC3 Derek Jeter 2.50 6.00
PC4 Shawn Green .40 1.00
PC5 Manny Ramirez 1.00 2.50
PC6 Pedro Martinez .60 1.50
PC7 Ivan Rodriguez .60 1.50
PC8 Alex Rodriguez 1.25 3.00
PC9 Juan Gonzalez .40 1.00
PC10 Ken Griffey Jr. 2.00 5.00
PC11 Sammy Sosa 1.00 2.50
PC12 Jeff Bagwell .60 1.50
PC13 Chipper Jones 1.00 2.50
PC14 Cal Ripken 3.00 8.00
PC15 Mike Piazza 1.00 2.50

2000 Upper Deck Power MARK

Inserted one every 23 first series packs, these 10 cards all feature Mark McGwire.

COMPLETE SET (10) 25.00 50.00
COMMON CARD (MC1-MC10) 2.50 6.00
SER.1 STATED ODDS 1:23
*DIE CUTS: 3X TO 8X BASIC POWER MARK
DIE CUTS RANDOM INSERTS IN SER.1 HOBBY
DIE CUTS PRINT RUN 100 SERIAL #'d SETS
GOLD DIE CUTS RANDOM IN SER.1 HOBBY
GOLD DIE CUT PRINT RUN 1 SERIAL #'d SET
GOLD DC NOT PRICED DUE TO SCARCITY

2000 Upper Deck Power Rally

Inserted one every 11 first series packs, these 15 cards feature baseball's leading power hitters.

COMPLETE SET (15) 10.00 25.00
SER.1 STATED ODDS 1:11
*DIE CUTS: 5X TO 12X BASIC POWER RALLY
DIE CUTS RANDOM INSERTS IN SER.1 PACKS
DIE CUTS PRINT RUN 100 SERIAL #'d SETS
GOLD DIE CUTS RANDOM IN SER.1 PACKS
GOLD DIE CUT PRINT RUN 1 SERIAL #'d SET
GOLD DC NOT PRICED DUE TO SCARCITY
P1 Ken Griffey Jr. 1.50 4.00
P2 Mark McGwire 1.25 3.00
P3 Sammy Sosa .75 2.00
P4 Jose Canseco .50 1.25
P5 Juan Gonzalez .30 .75
P6 Bernie Williams .50 1.25
P7 Jeff Bagwell .50 1.25
P8 Chipper Jones .75 2.00
P9 Vladimir Guerrero .50 1.25
P10 Mo Vaughn .30 .75
P11 Derek Jeter 2.00 5.00
P12 Mike Piazza .75 2.00
P13 Barry Bonds 1.25 3.00
P14 Alex Rodriguez 1.00 2.50
P15 Nomar Garciaparra .50 1.25

2000 Upper Deck PowerDeck Inserts

These CD's were inserted into packs at two different rates. PD1 through PD 8 were inserted at a rate of one every 23 packs while PD9 through PD 11 were inserted at a rate of one every 287 packs. Due to problems at the manufacturer, the Alex Rodriguez CD was not inserted into the first series packs so a collector could acquire one of those by sending in a UPC code on the bottom of the 2000 Upper Deck first series boxes. Also, some of the 1999 Upper Deck PowerDeck CD's were mistakenly inserted into this product. Those CD's are priced under the 1999 Upper Deck PowerDeck listings. Finally, Ken Griffey Jr., Reggie Jackson and Mark McGwire have all been confirmed as short prints by representatives at Upper Deck.

COMPLETE SET (11) 15.00 40.00
SER.1 1-8 STATED ODDS 1:23
SER.1 9-11 STATED ODDS 1:287
PD1 Ken Griffey Jr. 2.00 5.00
PD2 Cal Ripken 3.00 8.00
PD3 Mark McGwire 1.50 4.00
PD4 Tony Gwynn 1.00 2.50
PD5 Roger Clemens 1.25 3.00
PD6 Alex Rodriguez 1.25 3.00
PD7 Sammy Sosa 1.00 2.50
PD8 Derek Jeter 2.50 6.00
PD9 Ken Griffey Jr. SP 4.00 10.00
PD10 Mark McGwire SP 3.00 8.00
PD11 Reggie Jackson SP 1.25 3.00

2000 Upper Deck Prime Performers

Randomly inserted into series two packs at one in eight, this 10-card insert features players that are prime performers. Card backs carry a "PP" prefix.

COMPLETE SET (10) 2.50 6.00
SER.2 STATED ODDS 1:8
PP1 Manny Ramirez .40 1.00
PP2 Pedro Martinez .25 .60
PP3 Carlos Delgado .15 .40
PP4 Ken Griffey Jr. .75 2.00
PP5 Derek Jeter 1.00 2.50
PP6 Chipper Jones .40 1.00
PP7 Sean Casey .15 .40

PP8 Shawn Green .15 .40
PP9 Sammy Sosa .40 1.00
PP10 Alex Rodriguez .50 1.25

2000 Upper Deck Statitude

Inserted one every four packs, these 30 cards feature some of the most statistically dominant players in baseball.

COMPLETE SET (30) 12.50 30.00
SER.1 STATED ODDS 1:4
*DIE CUTS: 6X TO 15X BASIC STATITUDE
DIE CUTS RANDOM INSERTS IN SER.1 RETAIL
DIE CUTS PRINT RUN 100 SERIAL #'d SETS
GOLD DIE CUTS RANDOM IN SER.1 RETAIL
GOLD DIE CUT PRINT RUN 1 SERIAL #'d SET
GOLD DC NOT PRICED DUE TO SCARCITY
S1 Mo Vaughn .25 .60
S2 Matt Williams .25 .60
S3 Travis Lee .25 .60
S4 Chipper Jones .60 1.50
S5 Greg Maddux .75 2.00
S6 Gabe Kapler .25 .60
S7 Cal Ripken 2.00 5.00
S8 Nomar Garciaparra .40 1.00
S9 Sammy Sosa .60 1.50
S10 Frank Thomas .60 1.50
S11 Manny Ramirez .60 1.50
S12 Larry Walker .40 1.00
S13 Ivan Rodriguez .40 1.00
S14 Jeff Bagwell .40 1.00
S15 Craig Biggio .40 1.00
S16 Vladimir Guerrero .40 1.00
S17 Mike Piazza .60 1.50
S18 Bernie Williams .40 1.00
S19 Derek Jeter 1.50 4.00
S20 Jose Canseco .40 1.00
S21 Eric Chavez .25 .60
S22 Scott Rolen .40 1.00
S23 Mark McGwire 1.00 2.50
S24 Tony Gwynn .60 1.50
S25 Barry Bonds 1.00 2.50
S26 Ken Griffey Jr. 1.25 3.00
S27 Alex Rodriguez .75 2.00
S28 J.D. Drew .25 .60
S29 Juan Gonzalez .25 .60
S30 Roger Clemens .75 2.00

2000 Upper Deck Subway Series

This 30-card box set was released shortly after the 2000 World Series, in mid-November. The set features 13 New York Yankee players, 13 New York Met players and four Subway Series Flashback cards. Each set also included one 3x5 Commemorative 2000 World Series Championship card. Each set carried a suggested retail price of $19.99.

COMP. FACT SET (30) 6.00 15.00
NY1 Derek Jeter .50 1.25
NY2 Bernie Williams .12 .30
NY3 Roger Clemens .25 .60
NY4 Paul O'Neill .12 .30
NY5 Tino Martinez .07 .20
NY6 Jorge Posada .12 .30
NY7 David Justice .07 .20
NY8 Andy Pettitte .12 .30
NY9 Orlando Hernandez .07 .20
NY10 Mariano Rivera .25 .60
NY11 Scott Brosius .07 .20
NY12 Dwight Gooden .07 .20
NY13 Jose Canseco .12 .30
NY14 Mike Hampton .07 .20
NY15 Al Leiter .07 .20
NY16 Armando Benitez .07 .20
NY17 Bobby Jones .07 .20
NY18 Mike Piazza .20 .50
NY19 Todd Zeile .07 .20
NY20 Edgardo Alfonzo .07 .20
NY21 Mike Bordick .07 .20
NY22 Robin Ventura .07 .20
NY23 Jay Payton .07 .20
NY24 Timo Perez .12 .30
NY25 John Franco .07 .20
NY26 Turk Wendell .07 .20
NY27 Mickey Mantle .60 1.50
NY28 Don Larsen .07 .20
NY29 Jackie Robinson .20 .50
NY30 Pee Wee Reese .12 .30
NNO New York Yankees 3x5 .30 .60

2000 Upper Deck Hawaii

These cards were issued by Upper Deck and given away at the Kit Young annual conference in Hawaii in 2000. These cards feature autographs of four athletes Upper Deck brought over to the conference. Each player signed a card serial numbered to 500. The card featuring all four players signed was not included in the factory set, but 100 cards featuring all four players were also signed and distributed. Two Kit Young cards were also included with the factory sets.

COMPLETE SET (6) 160.00 400.00
TS Tom Seaver AU 25.00 60.00
GAU Julius Erving AU/100 200.00 500.00
Gordie Howe AU
Joe Namath AU
Tom Seaver AU

2001 Upper Deck

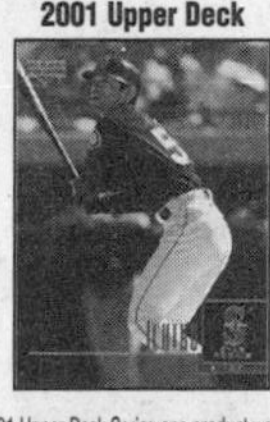

The 2001 Upper Deck Series one product was released in November, 2000 and featured a 270-card base set. Series two (entitled Mid-Summer Classic) was released in June, 2001 and featured a 180-card base set. The complete set is broken into subsets as follows: Star Rookies (1-45/271-300), basic cards (46-261/301-444), and Season Highlight checklists (262-270/445-450). Each pack contained 8-cards and carried a suggested retail price of $2.99. Key Rookie Cards in the set include Albert Pujols and Ichiro Suzuki. Also, a selection of A Piece of History 3000 Club Eddie Murray and Cal Ripken memorabilia cards were randomly seeded into series one packs. 350 bat cards, 350 jersey cards and 100 hand-numbered, combination bat-jersey cards were produced for each player. In addition, thirty-three autographed, hand-numbered, combination bat-jersey Eddie Murray cards and eight autographed, hand-numbered, combination bat-jersey Cal Ripken cards were produced. The Ripken Bat, Ripken Bat-Jsy Combo and Murray Bat-Jsy Combo Autograph were all exchange cards. The deadline to send in the exchange cards was August 22nd, 2001. Pricing for these memorabilia cards can be referenced under 2000 Upper Deck A Piece of History 3000 Club.

COMPLETE SET (450) 90.00 150.00
COMPLETE SERIES 1 (270) 20.00 40.00
COMPLETE SERIES 2 (180) 60.00 100.00
COMMON (46-270/300-450) .10 .30
COMMON SR (1-45/271-300) .20 .50
1 Jeff DaVanon SR .20 .50
2 Aubrey Huff SR .20 .50
3 Pasqual Coco SR .20 .50
4 Barry Zito SR .25 .60
5 Augie Ojeda SR .20 .50
6 Chris Richard SR .20 .50
7 Josh Phelps SR .20 .50
8 Kevin Nicholson SR .20 .50
9 Juan Guzman SR .20 .50
10 Brandon Kolb SR .20 .50
11 Johan Santana SR 3.00 8.00
12 Josh Kalinowski SR .20 .50
13 Tike Redman SR .20 .50
14 Ivanon Coffie SR .20 .50
15 Chad Durbin SR .20 .50
16 Derrick Turnbow SR .20 .50
17 Scott Downs SR .20 .50
18 Jason Grilli SR .20 .50
19 Mark Buehrle SR .25 .60
20 Paxton Crawford SR .20 .50
21 Bronson Arroyo SR .40 1.00
22 Tomas De la Rosa SR .20 .50
23 Paul Rigdon SR .20 .50
24 Rob Ramsay SR .20 .50
25 Damian Rolls SR .20 .50
26 Jason Conti SR .20 .50
27 John Parrish SR .20 .50
28 Geraldo Guzman SR .20 .50
29 Tony Mota SR .20 .50
30 Luis Rivas SR .20 .50
31 Brian Tollberg SR .20 .50
32 Adam Bernero SR .20 .50
33 Michael Cuddyer SR .20 .50
34 Josue Espada SR .20 .50
35 Joe Lawrence SR .20 .50
36 Chad Moeller SR .20 .50
37 Nick Bierbrodt SR .20 .50
38 DeWayne Wise SR .20 .50
39 Javier Cardona SR .20 .50
40 Hiram Bocachica SR .20 .50
41 Giuseppe Chiaramonte SR .20 .50
42 Alex Cabrera SR .20 .50
43 Jimmy Rollins SR .20 .50
44 Pat Flury SR RC .20 .50
45 Leo Estrella SR .20 .50
46 Darin Erstad .10 .30
47 Seth Etherton .10 .30
48 Troy Glaus .10 .30
49 Brian Cooper .10 .30
50 Tim Salmon .10 .30
51 Adam Kennedy .10 .30
52 Bengie Molina .10 .30
53 Jason Giambi .10 .30
54 Miguel Tejada .10 .30
55 Tim Hudson .10 .30
56 Eric Chavez .10 .30
57 Terrence Long .10 .30
58 Jason Isringhausen .10 .30
59 Ramon Hernandez .10 .30
60 Raul Mondesi .10 .30
61 David Wells .10 .30
62 Shannon Stewart .10 .30
63 Tony Batista .10 .30
64 Brad Fullmer .10 .30
65 Chris Carpenter .10 .30
66 Homer Bush .10 .30
67 Gerald Williams .10 .30
68 Miguel Cairo .10 .30
69 Ryan Rupe .10 .30
70 Greg Vaughn .10 .30
71 John Flaherty .10 .30
72 Dan Wheeler .10 .30
73 Fred McGriff .20 .50
74 Roberto Alomar .20 .50
75 Bartolo Colon .10 .30
76 Kenny Lofton .10 .30
77 David Segui .10 .30
78 Omar Vizquel .20 .50
79 Russ Branyan .10 .30
80 Chuck Finley .10 .30
81 Manny Ramirez UER .20 .50
82 Alex Rodriguez .40 1.00
83 John Halama .10 .30
84 Mike Cameron .10 .30
85 David Bell .10 .30
86 Jay Buhner .10 .30
87 Aaron Sele .10 .30
88 Rickey Henderson .30 .75
89 Brook Fordyce .10 .30
90 Cal Ripken 1.00 2.50
91 Mike Mussina .20 .50
92 Delino DeShields .10 .30
93 Melvin Mora .10 .30
94 Sidney Ponson .10 .30
95 Brady Anderson .10 .30
96 Ivan Rodriguez .20 .50
97 Ricky Ledee .10 .30
98 Rick Helling .10 .30
99 Ruben Mateo .10 .30
100 Luis Alicea .10 .30
101 John Wetteland .10 .30
102 Mike Lamb .10 .30
103 Carl Everett .10 .30
104 Troy O'Leary .10 .30
105 Wilton Veras .10 .30
106 Pedro Martinez .20 .50
107 Rolando Arrojo .10 .30
108 Scott Hatteberg .10 .30
109 Jason Varitek .30 .75
110 Jose Offerman .10 .30
111 Carlos Beltran .10 .30
112 Johnny Damon .20 .50
113 Mark Quinn .10 .30
114 Rey Sanchez .10 .30
115 Mac Suzuki .10 .30
116 Jermaine Dye .10 .30
117 Chris Fussell .10 .30
118 Jeff Weaver .10 .30
119 Dean Palmer .10 .30
120 Robert Fick .10 .30
121 Brian Moehler .10 .30
122 Damion Easley .10 .30
123 Juan Encarnacion .10 .30
124 Tony Clark .10 .30
125 Cristian Guzman .10 .30
126 Matt LeCroy .10 .30
127 Eric Milton .10 .30
128 Jay Canizaro .10 .30
129 David Ortiz .30 .75
130 Brad Radke .10 .30
131 Jacque Jones .10 .30
132 Magglio Ordonez .10 .30
133 Carlos Lee .10 .30
134 Mike Sirotka .10 .30
135 Ray Durham .10 .30
136 Paul Konerko .10 .30
137 Charles Johnson .10 .30
138 James Baldwin .10 .30
139 Jeff Abbott .10 .30
140 Roger Clemens .60 1.50
141 Derek Jeter .75 2.00
142 David Justice .10 .30
143 Ramiro Mendoza .10 .30
144 Chuck Knoblauch .10 .30
145 Orlando Hernandez .10 .30
146 Alfonso Soriano .20 .50
147 Jeff Bagwell .20 .50
148 Julio Lugo .10 .30
149 Mitch Meluskey .10 .30
150 Jose Lima .10 .30
151 Richard Hidalgo .10 .30
152 Moises Alou .10 .30
153 Scott Elarton .10 .30
154 Andruw Jones .20 .50
155 Quilvio Veras .10 .30
156 Greg Maddux .50 1.25
157 Brian Jordan .10 .30
158 Andres Galarraga .10 .30
159 Kevin Millwood .10 .30
160 Rafael Furcal .10 .30
161 Jeromy Burnitz .10 .30
162 Jimmy Haynes .10 .30
163 Mark Loretta .10 .30
164 Ron Belliard .10 .30
165 Richie Sexson .10 .30
166 Kevin Barker .10 .30
167 Jeff D'Amico .10 .30
168 Rick Ankiel .10 .30
169 Mark McGwire .75 2.00
170 J.D. Drew .10 .30
171 Eli Marrero .10 .30
172 Darryl Kile .10 .30
173 Edgar Renteria .10 .30
174 Will Clark .20 .50
175 Eric Young .10 .30
176 Mark Grace .20 .50
177 Jon Lieber .10 .30
178 Damon Buford .10 .30
179 Kerry Wood .10 .30
180 Rondell White .10 .30
181 Joe Girardi .10 .30
182 Curt Schilling .10 .30
183 Randy Johnson .30 .75
184 Steve Finley .10 .30
185 Kelly Stinnett .10 .30
186 Jay Bell .10 .30
187 Matt Mantei .10 .30
188 Luis Gonzalez .10 .30
189 Shawn Green .10 .30
190 Todd Hundley .10 .30
191 Chan Ho Park .10 .30
192 Adrian Beltre .10 .30
193 Mark Grudzielanek .10 .30
194 Gary Sheffield .10 .30
195 Tom Goodwin .10 .30
196 Lee Stevens .10 .30
197 Javier Vazquez .10 .30
198 Milton Bradley .10 .30
199 Vladimir Guerrero .30 .75
200 Carl Pavano .10 .30
201 Orlando Cabrera .10 .30
202 Tony Armas Jr. .10 .30
203 Jeff Kent .10 .30
204 Calvin Murray .10 .30
205 Ellis Burks .10 .30
206 Barry Bonds .75 2.00
207 Russ Ortiz .10 .30
208 Marvin Benard .10 .30
209 Joe Nathan .10 .30
210 Preston Wilson .10 .30
211 Cliff Floyd .10 .30
212 Mike Lowell .10 .30
213 Ryan Dempster .10 .30
214 Brad Penny .10 .30
215 Mike Redmond .10 .30
216 Luis Castillo .10 .30
217 Derek Bell .10 .30
218 Mike Hampton .10 .30
219 Todd Zeile .10 .30
220 Robin Ventura .10 .30
221 Mike Piazza .50 1.25
222 Al Leiter .10 .30
223 Edgardo Alfonzo .10 .30
224 Mike Bordick .10 .30
225 Phil Nevin .10 .30
226 Ryan Klesko .10 .30
227 Adam Eaton .10 .30
228 Eric Owens .10 .30
229 Tony Gwynn .40 1.00
230 Matt Clement .10 .30
231 Wiki Gonzalez .10 .30
232 Robert Person .10 .30
233 Doug Glanville .10 .30
234 Scott Rolen .20 .50
235 Mike Lieberthal .10 .30
236 Randy Wolf .10 .30
237 Bob Abreu .10 .30
238 Pat Burrell .10 .30
239 Bruce Chen .10 .30
240 Kevin Young .10 .30
241 Todd Ritchie .10 .30
242 Adrian Brown .10 .30
243 Chad Hermansen .10 .30
244 Warren Morris .10 .30
245 Kris Benson .10 .30
246 Jason Kendall .10 .30
247 Pokey Reese .10 .30
248 Rob Bell .10 .30
249 Ken Griffey Jr. .60 1.50
250 Sean Casey .10 .30
251 Aaron Boone .10 .30
252 Pete Harnisch .10 .30
253 Barry Larkin .20 .50
254 Dmitri Young .10 .30
255 Todd Hollandsworth .10 .30
256 Pedro Astacio .10 .30
257 Todd Helton .20 .50
258 Terry Shumpert .10 .30
259 Neifi Perez .10 .30
260 Jeffrey Hammonds .10 .30
261 Ben Petrick .10 .30
262 Mark McGwire SH .40 1.00
263 Derek Jeter SH .40 1.00
264 Sammy Sosa SH .20 .50
265 Cal Ripken SH .50 1.25
266 Pedro Martinez SH .20 .50
267 Barry Bonds SH .40 1.00
268 Fred McGriff SH .10 .30
269 Randy Johnson SH .20 .50
270 Darin Erstad SH .10 .30
271 Ichiro Suzuki SR RC 6.00 15.00
272 Wilson Betemit SR RC .75 2.00
273 Corey Patterson SR .20 .50
274 Sean Douglass SR RC .20 .50
275 Mike Penney SR RC .20 .50
276 Nate Teut SR RC .20 .50
277 Ricardo Rodriguez SR RC .20 .50
278 Brandon Duckworth SR RC .20 .50
279 Rafael Soriano SR RC .20 .50
280 Juan Diaz SR RC .20 .50
281 Horacio Ramirez SR RC .25 .60
282 Tsuyoshi Shinjo SR RC .25 .60
283 Keith Ginter SR .20 .50
284 Esix Snead SR RC .20 .50
285 Erick Almonte SR RC .20 .50
286 Travis Hafner SR RC 2.00 5.00
287 Jason Smith SR RC .20 .50
288 Jackson Melian SR RC .20 .50
289 Tyler Walker SR RC .20 .50
290 Jason Standridge SR .20 .50
291 Juan Uribe SR RC .25 .60
292 Adrian Hernandez SR RC .20 .50
293 Jason Michaels SR RC .20 .50
294 Jason Hart SR .20 .50
295 Albert Pujols SR RC 25.00 60.00
296 Morgan Ensberg SR RC .75 2.00
297 Brandon Inge SR .20 .50
298 Jesus Colome SR .20 .50
299 Kyle Kessel SR RC .20 .50
300 Timo Perez SR .20 .50
301 Mo Vaughn .10 .30
302 Ismael Valdes .10 .30
303 Glenallen Hill .10 .30
304 Garret Anderson .10 .30
305 Johnny Damon .20 .50
306 Jose Ortiz .10 .30
307 Mark Mulder .10 .30
308 Adam Piatt .10 .30
309 Gil Heredia .10 .30
310 Mike Sirotka .10 .30
311 Carlos Delgado .10 .30
312 Alex Gonzalez .10 .30
313 Jose Cruz Jr. .10 .30
314 Darrin Fletcher .10 .30
315 Ben Grieve .10 .30
316 Vinny Castilla .10 .30
317 Wilson Alvarez .10 .30
318 Brent Abernathy .10 .30
319 Ellis Burks .10 .30
320 Jim Thome .20 .50
321 Juan Gonzalez .10 .30
322 Ed Taubensee .10 .30
323 Travis Fryman .10 .30
324 John Olerud .10 .30
325 Edgar Martinez .20 .50
326 Freddy Garcia .10 .30
327 Bret Boone .20 .50
328 Kazuhiro Sasaki .10 .30
329 Albert Belle .10 .30
330 Mike Bordick .10 .30
331 David Segui .10 .30
332 Pat Hentgen .10 .30
333 Alex Rodriguez .40 1.00
334 Andres Galarraga .10 .30
335 Gabe Kapler .10 .30
336 Ken Caminiti .10 .30
337 Rafael Palmeiro .20 .50
338 Manny Ramirez Sox .20 .50
339 David Cone .10 .30
340 Nomar Garciaparra .50 1.25
341 Trot Nixon .10 .30
342 Derek Lowe .10 .30
343 Roberto Hernandez .10 .30
344 Mike Sweeney .10 .30
345 Carlos Febles .10 .30
346 Jeff Suppan .10 .30
347 Roger Cedeno .10 .30
348 Bobby Higginson .10 .30
349 Deivi Cruz .10 .30
350 Mitch Meluskey .10 .30
351 Matt Lawton .10 .30
352 Mark Redman .10 .30
353 Jay Canizaro .10 .30
354 Corey Koskie .10 .30
355 Matt Kinney .10 .30
356 Frank Thomas .30 .75
357 Sandy Alomar Jr. .10 .30
358 David Wells .10 .30
359 Jim Parque .10 .30
360 Chris Singleton .10 .30
361 Tino Martinez .20 .50
362 Paul O'Neill .20 .50
363 Mike Mussina .20 .50
364 Bernie Williams .20 .50
365 Andy Pettitte .20 .50
366 Mariano Rivera .30 .75
367 Brad Ausmus .10 .30
368 Craig Biggio .20 .50
369 Lance Berkman .10 .30
370 Shane Reynolds .10 .30
371 Chipper Jones .30 .75
372 Tom Glavine .20 .50
373 B.J. Surhoff .10 .30
374 John Smoltz .20 .50
375 Rico Brogna .10 .30
376 Geoff Jenkins .10 .30
377 Jose Hernandez .10 .30
378 Tyler Houston .10 .30
379 Henry Blanco .10 .30
380 Jeffrey Hammonds .10 .30
381 Jim Edmonds .10 .30
382 Fernando Vina .10 .30
383 Andy Benes .10 .30
384 Ray Lankford .10 .30
385 Dustin Hermanson .10 .30
386 Todd Hundley .10 .30
387 Sammy Sosa .30 .75
388 Tom Gordon .10 .30
389 Bill Mueller .10 .30
390 Ron Coomer .10 .30
391 Matt Stairs .10 .30
392 Mark Grace .20 .50
393 Matt Williams .10 .30
394 Todd Stottlemyre .10 .30
395 Tony Womack .10 .30
396 Erubiel Durazo .10 .30
397 Reggie Sanders .10 .30
398 Andy Ashby .10 .30
399 Eric Karros .10 .30
400 Kevin Brown .10 .30
401 Darren Dreifort .10 .30
402 Fernando Tatis .10 .30
403 Jose Vidro .10 .30
404 Peter Bergeron .10 .30
405 Geoff Blum .10 .30
406 J.T. Snow .10 .30
407 Livan Hernandez .10 .30
408 Robb Nen .10 .30
409 Bobby Estalella .10 .30
410 Rich Aurilia .10 .30
411 Eric Davis .10 .30
412 Charles Johnson .10 .30
413 Alex Gonzalez .10 .30
414 A.J. Burnett .10 .30
415 Antonio Alfonseca .10 .30
416 Derrek Lee .20 .50
417 Jay Payton .10 .30
418 Kevin Appier .10 .30
419 Steve Trachsel .10 .30
420 Rey Ordonez .10 .30
421 Darryl Hamilton .10 .30
422 Ben Davis .10 .30
423 Damian Jackson .10 .30
424 Mark Kotsay .10 .30
425 Trevor Hoffman .10 .30
426 Travis Lee .10 .30
427 Omar Daal .10 .30
428 Paul Byrd .10 .30
429 Reggie Taylor .10 .30
430 Brian Giles .10 .30
431 Derek Bell .10 .30
432 Francisco Cordova .10 .30
433 Pat Meares .10 .30
434 Scott Williamson .10 .30
435 Jason LaRue .10 .30
436 Michael Tucker .10 .30
437 Wilton Guerrero .10 .30
438 Mike Hampton .10 .30
439 Ron Gant .10 .30
440 Jeff Cirillo .10 .30
441 Denny Neagle .10 .30
442 Larry Walker .10 .30
443 Juan Pierre .10 .30
444 Todd Walker .10 .30
445 Jason Giambi SH CL .10 .30
446 Jeff Kent SH CL .10 .30
447 Mariano Rivera SH CL .20 .50
448 Edgar Martinez SH CL .10 .30
449 Troy Glaus SH CL .10 .30
450 Alex Rodriguez SH CL .25 .60

2001 Upper Deck Exclusives Gold

*STARS: 30X TO 80X BASIC CARDS
*SR STARS: 15X TO 40X BASIC SR
*SR ROOKIES: 15X TO 40X BASIC SR
STATED PRINT RUN 25 SERIAL #'d SETS
11 Johan Santana SR 25.00 60.00

2001 Upper Deck Exclusives Silver

STARS: 12.5X TO 30X BASIC CARDS
*SR YNG.STARS: 6X TO 15X BASIC
*SR RC's: 6X TO 15X BASIC SR
STATED PRINT RUN 100 SERIAL #'d SETS
11 Johan Santana SR 10.00 25.00

2001 Upper Deck 1971 All-Star Game Salute

Inserted in second series packs at a rate of one in 288, these 12 memorabilia cards feature players who participated in the 1971 All-Star Game which was highlighted by Reggie Jackson's home run off the light tower at Tiger Stadium.

SER.2 STATED ODDS 1:288
ASBR Brooks Robinson Bat 8.00 20.00
ASFR Frank Robinson Jsy 6.00 15.00
ASHA Hank Aaron Bat 12.50 30.00
ASHA Hank Aaron Jsy 12.50 30.00
ASJB Johnny Bench Bat 8.00 20.00
ASJB Johnny Bench Jsy 8.00 20.00
ASLA Luis Aparicio Jsy 6.00 15.00
ASLB Lou Brock Bat 8.00 20.00
ASRC Roberto Clemente Jsy 25.00 60.00
ASRJ Reggie Jackson Jsy 8.00 20.00
ASTM Thurman Munson Jsy 15.00 40.00
ASTS Tom Seaver Jsy 8.00 20.00

2001 Upper Deck All-Star Heroes Memorabilia

Randomly inserted in second series packs, these 14 cards feature a mix of past and present players who have starred in All-Star Games. Since each player was issued to a different amount, we have notated that information in our checklist.

PRINT RUNS B/WN 36-2000 COPIES PER
ASHAR A.Rodriguez Bat/1998 6.00 15.00
ASHBR Babe Ruth Bat/1933 75.00 150.00
ASHCR C.Ripken Bat/1991 10.00 25.00
ASHDJ D.Jeter Base/2000 10.00 25.00
ASHKG K.Griffey Jr. Bat/1992 15.00 40.00
ASHMM M.Mantle Jsy/54 150.00 400.00
ASHMP M.Piazza Base/1996 6.00 15.00
ASHRC R.Clemens Jsy/1986 4.00 15.00
ASHRJ R.Johnson Jsy/1993 6.00 15.00
ASHSS S.Sosa Jsy/2000 10.00 25.00
ASHTG T.Gwynn Jsy/1994 6.00 15.00
ASHTP T.Perez Bat/1967 4.00 10.00
ASHROC R.Clemente Bat/1961 20.00 50.00

2001 Upper Deck Big League Beat

Randomly inserted into packs at one in three, this 20-card insert features some of the most prolific players in the Major Leagues. Card backs carry a "BB" prefix.

COMPLETE SET (20) 8.00 20.00
SER.1 STATED ODDS 1:3
BB1 Barry Bonds .75 2.00
BB2 Nomar Garciaparra .50 1.25
BB3 Mark McGwire .75 2.00
BB4 Roger Clemens .60 1.50
BB5 Chipper Jones .30 .75
BB6 Jeff Bagwell .20 .50
BB7 Sammy Sosa .30 .75
BB8 Cal Ripken 1.00 2.50
BB9 Randy Johnson .30 .75
BB10 Carlos Delgado .20 .50
BB11 Manny Ramirez .20 .50
BB12 Derek Jeter .75 2.00
BB13 Tony Gwynn .40 1.00
BB14 Pedro Martinez .20 .50
BB15 Jose Canseco .20 .50
BB16 Frank Thomas .30 .75
BB17 Alex Rodriguez .40 1.00
BB18 Bernie Williams .20 .50
BB19 Greg Maddux .50 1.25
BB20 Rafael Palmeiro .20 .50

2001 Upper Deck Big League Challenge Game Jerseys

Issued at a rate of one in 288 second series packs, these 11 cards feature jersey pieces from participants in the 2001 Big League Challenge home run hitting contest.

SER.2 STATED ODDS 1:288
BLCBB Barry Bonds 5.00 12.00
BLCFT Frank Thomas 3.00 8.00
BLCGS Gary Sheffield 1.25 3.00
BLCJC Jose Canseco 2.00 5.00
BLCJE Jim Edmonds 2.00 5.00
BLCMP Mike Piazza 3.00 8.00
BLCRH Richard Hidalgo 1.25 3.00
BLCRP Rafael Palmeiro 2.00 5.00
BLCSF Steve Finley 1.25 3.00
BLCTG Troy Glaus 1.25 3.00
BLCTH Todd Helton 2.00 5.00

2001 Upper Deck e-Card

Inserted as a two-pack box-topper, this six-card insert features cards that can be viewed over the Upper Deck website. Cards feature a serial number that is to be typed in a the Upper Deck website to reveal that card. Card backs carry an "E" prefix.

COMPLETE SET (12) 7.50 15.00
COMPLETE SERIES 1 (6) 3.00 6.00
COMPLETE SERIES 2 (6) 5.00 10.00
STATED ODDS 1:12
E1 Andruw Jones .40 1.00
E2 Alex Rodriguez .50 1.25
E3 Frank Thomas .40 1.00
E4 Todd Helton .40 1.00
E5 Troy Glaus .40 1.00
E6 Barry Bonds 1.00 2.50
E7 Alex Rodriguez .50 1.25
E8 Ken Griffey Jr. .75 2.00
E9 Sammy Sosa .40 1.00
E10 Gary Sheffield .40 1.00
E11 Barry Bonds 1.00 2.50
E12 Andruw Jones .40 1.00

2001 Upper Deck eVolve Autograph

Lucky participants in Upper Deck's E-Card program received special upgraded E-Cards available by checking the UD website (www.upperdeck.com) and entering their basic E-Card serial code (printed on the front of each basic E-Card). When viewed on the Upper Deck website, if an autographed card of the depicted player appeared, the bearer of the base card could then exchange their basic E-Card and receive the signed upgrade via mail. Only 200 serial numbered E-Card Autograph sets were produced. Signed E-Cards all have an ES prefix on the card numbers.

EXCH.CARD AVAIL.VIA WEBSITE PROGRAM
STATED PRINT RUN 200 SERIAL #'d SETS
ESAJ Andruw Jones S1 10.00 25.00
ESAJ Andruw Jones S2 10.00 25.00
ESAR Alex Rodriguez S1 20.00 50.00
ESAR Alex Rodriguez S2 20.00 50.00
ESBB Barry Bonds S1 60.00 120.00
ESBB Barry Bonds S2 60.00 120.00
ESFT Frank Thomas S1 30.00 60.00
ESGS Gary Sheffield S2 6.00 15.00
ESKG Ken Griffey Jr. S2 40.00 100.00
ESSS Sammy Sosa S2 30.00 60.00
ESTG Troy Glaus S1 6.00 15.00
ESTH Todd Helton S1 6.00 15.00

2001 Upper Deck eVolve Game Jersey

Lucky participants in Upper Deck's E-Card program received special upgraded E-Cards available by checking the UD website (www.upperdeck.com) and entering their basic E-Card serial code (printed on the front of each basic E-Card). When viewed on the Upper Deck website, if a jersey card of the depicted player appeared, the bearer of the base card could then exchange their basic E-Card and receive the Game Jersey upgrade via mail. The cards closely parallel basic 2000 Game Jerseys that were distributed in first and second series packs except for the gold foil "e-volve" logo on front. Only 300 serial numbered E-Card Jersey sets were produced with each card being serial -numbered by hand in blue ink sharpie at the bottom right front corner. Unsigned E-Card Game Jerseys all have an EJ prefix on the card numbers.

EXCH.CARD AVAIL.VIA WEBSITE PROGRAM
PRINT RUNS B/WN 200-300 COPIES PER
EJAJ Andruw Jones S1 6.00 15.00
EJAJ Andruw Jones S2 6.00 15.00
EJAR Alex Rodriguez S1 8.00 20.00
EJAR Alex Rodriguez S2 8.00 20.00
EJBB Barry Bonds S1 12.50 30.00
EJBB Barry Bonds S2 12.50 30.00
EJFT Frank Thomas S1 6.00 15.00
EJGS Gary Sheffield S2 4.00 10.00
EJKG Ken Griffey Jr. S2/300 10.00 25.00
EJSS Sammy Sosa S2 6.00 15.00
EJTG Troy Glaus S1 4.00 10.00
EJTH Todd Helton S1 6.00 15.00
EJKG Ken Griffey Jr. S1/200 10.00 25.00

2001 Upper Deck eVolve Game Jersey Autograph

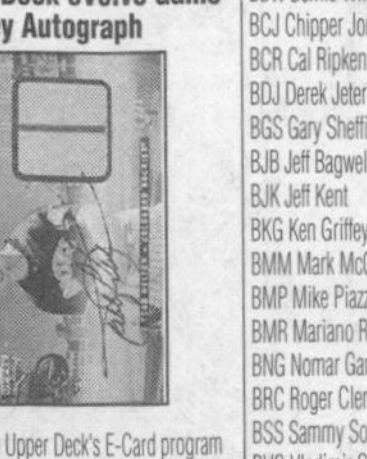

Lucky participants in Upper Deck's E-Card program received special upgraded E-Cards available by checking the UD website (www.upperdeck.com) and entering their basic E-Card serial code (printed on the front of each basic E-Card). When viewed on the Upper Deck website, if an autographed card of the depicted player appeared, the bearer of the base card could then exchange their basic E-Card and receive the signed jersey upgrade via mail. A mere 50 serial numbered sets were produced. Signed jersey E-Cards all have an ESJ prefix on the card numbers.

EXCH.CARD AVAIL.VIA WEBSITE PROGRAM
STATED PRINT RUN 50 SERIAL #'d SETS
ESJAJ Andruw Jones S1 10.00 25.00
ESJAJ Andruw Jones S2 10.00 25.00
ESJAR Alex Rodriguez S1 15.00 40.00
ESJAR Alex Rodriguez S2 15.00 40.00
ESJBB Barry Bonds S1 125.00 250.00
ESJBB Barry Bonds S2 125.00 250.00
ESJFT Frank Thomas S1 40.00 80.00
ESJGS Gary Sheffield S2 10.00 25.00
ESJKG Ken Griffey Jr. S2 60.00 120.00
ESJSS Sammy Sosa S2 30.00 80.00
ESJTG Troy Glaus S1 30.00 60.00
ESJTH Todd Helton S1 30.00 60.00

2001 Upper Deck Franchise

Inserted at a rate of one in 36 second series packs, these 10 cards feature players who are considered the money players for their franchise.

COMPLETE SET (10) 25.00 60.00
SER.2 STATED ODDS 1:36
F1 Frank Thomas 1.50 4.00
F2 Mark McGwire 4.00 10.00
F3 Ken Griffey Jr. 3.00 8.00
F4 Manny Ramirez Sox 1.50 4.00
F5 Alex Rodriguez 2.00 5.00
F6 Greg Maddux 2.50 6.00
F7 Sammy Sosa 1.50 4.00
F8 Derek Jeter 4.00 10.00
F9 Mike Piazza 2.50 6.00
F10 Vladimir Guerrero 1.50 4.00

2001 Upper Deck Game Ball 1

Randomly inserted into packs, this 18-card insert features game-used baseballs from the depicted players. Card backs carry a "B" prefix. Please note that only 100 serial numbered sets were produced.

STATED PRINT RUN 100 SERIAL #'d SETS
BAJ Andruw Jones 15.00 40.00
BAR Alex Rodriguez Mariners 30.00 60.00
BBB Barry Bonds 10.00 25.00
BDJ Derek Jeter 40.00 80.00
BIR Ivan Rodriguez 15.00 40.00
BJG Jason Giambi 10.00 25.00
BJG Jeff Bagwell 15.00 40.00
BKG Ken Griffey Jr. 10.00 25.00
BMM Mark McGwire 75.00 150.00
BMP Mike Piazza 30.00 60.00
BRA Rick Ankiel 10.00 25.00
BRJ Randy Johnson 15.00 40.00
BSG Shawn Green 10.00 25.00
BSS Sammy Sosa 15.00 40.00
BTH Todd Helton 15.00 40.00
BTOG Tony Gwynn 15.00 40.00
BTRG Troy Glaus 10.00 25.00
BVG Vladimir Guerrero 15.00 40.00

2001 Upper Deck Game Ball 2

Inserted into second series packs at a rate of one in 288 , this 18-card insert features game-used baseballs from the depicted players. Card backs carry a "B" prefix. The Nomar Garciaparra card was short printed and has been notated as such in our checklist.

SER.2 STATED ODDS 1:288
BAJ Andruw Jones 6.00 15.00
BAR Alex Rodriguez Rangers 10.00 25.00
BBB Barry Bonds 15.00 40.00
BBW Bernie Williams 6.00 15.00
BCJ Chipper Jones 6.00 15.00
BCR Cal Ripken 15.00 40.00
BDJ Derek Jeter 12.00 30.00
BGS Gary Sheffield 4.00 10.00
BJB Jeff Bagwell 6.00 15.00
BJK Jeff Kent 4.00 10.00
BKG Ken Griffey Jr. 10.00 25.00
BMM Mark McGwire 20.00 50.00
BMP Mike Piazza 10.00 25.00
BMR Mariano Rivera 6.00 15.00
BNG Nomar Garciaparra SP 15.00 40.00
BRC Roger Clemens 10.00 25.00
BSS Sammy Sosa 6.00 15.00
BVG Vladimir Guerrero 6.00 15.00

2001 Upper Deck Game Jersey

These cards feature swatches of jerseys of various major league stars. These cards were available in either series one hobby or retail packs at a rate of one every 288 packs. Card backs carry a "C" prefix.

SER.1 STATED ODDS 1:288 HOB/RET
CAJ Andruw Jones 10.00 25.00
CAR Alex Rodriguez 10.00 25.00
CBW Bernie Williams 10.00 25.00
CCR Cal Ripken 20.00 50.00
CDJ Derek Jeter 12.50 30.00
CFT Fernando Tatis 6.00 15.00
CIR Ivan Rodriguez 10.00 25.00
CKG Ken Griffey Jr. 15.00 40.00
CMR Manny Ramirez 10.00 25.00
CMW Matt Williams 6.00 15.00
CNRA Nolan Ryan Astros 12.00 30.00
CNRR Nolan Ryan Rangers 12.00 30.00
CPO Paul O'Neill 10.00 25.00
CRV Robin Ventura 6.00 15.00
CSK Sandy Koufax 40.00 80.00
CTG Tony Gwynn 10.00 25.00
CTH Todd Helton 10.00 25.00
CTIH Tim Hudson 6.00 15.00

2001 Upper Deck Game Jersey Autograph 1

These cards feature both autographs and swatches of jerseys from various major league stars. The cards which have an "H1" after the player names are available in series one hobby packs at a rate of one in every 288 packs. Card backs carry a "H" prefix. The following cards were distributed in packs as exchange cards: Alex Rodriguez, Jeff Bagwell, Ken Griffey Jr., Mike Hampton and Rick Ankiel. The deadline to exchange these cards was August 7th, 2001.

SER.1 STATED ODDS 1:288 HOBBY
HAR Alex Rodriguez 20.00 50.00
HBB Barry Bonds 60.00 120.00
HFT Frank Thomas 40.00 80.00
HGM Greg Maddux 75.00 150.00
HJB Jeff Bagwell 20.00 50.00
HJC Jose Canseco 20.00 50.00
HJD J.D. Drew 6.00 15.00
HJG Jason Giambi 6.00 15.00
HJL Javy Lopez 6.00 15.00
HKG Ken Griffey Jr. 50.00 100.00
HMH Mike Hampton 6.00 15.00
HNRA Nolan Ryan Angels 40.00 100.00
HNRM Nolan Ryan Mets 40.00 100.00
HRA Rick Ankiel 12.50 30.00
HRJ Randy Johnson 30.00 60.00
HRP Rafael Palmeiro 10.00 25.00
HSC Sean Casey 6.00 15.00
HSG Shawn Green 10.00 25.00

2001 Upper Deck Game Jersey Autograph 2

These cards feature both autographs and swatches of jerseys from various major league stars. The cards which have an "H2" after the player names are available in series one hobby packs at a rate of one in every 288 packs. Card backs carry a "H" prefix. Please note a few of the players were issued in lesser quantites and we have notated those as SP's. The following players packed out as exchange cards: Alex Rodriguez and Ken Griffey Jr. The deadline for exchange was June 26th, 2006.

SER.2 STATED ODDS 1:288 HOBBY
EXCHANGE DEADLINE 06/26/06
AJ Andruw Jones 6.00 15.00
AR Alex Rodriguez 25.00 60.00
BB Barry Bonds 40.00 80.00
CJ Chipper Jones 40.00 80.00
CR Cal Ripken SP 60.00 120.00
GS Gary Sheffield 6.00 15.00
IR Ivan Rodriguez SP 15.00 40.00
JB Johnny Bench 20.00 50.00
JC Jose Canseco 20.00 50.00
KG Ken Griffey Jr. 60.00 120.00
NR Nolan Ryan 75.00 150.00
RC Roger Clemens 20.00 50.00
SS Sammy Sosa SP 15.00 40.00
TG Troy Glaus 20.00 50.00

2001 Upper Deck Game Jersey Autograph Numbered

These cards feature both autographs and swatches of jerseys from various major league stars. The cards which have an "H" after the player names are only available in series one hobby packs, while the cards with a "C" can be found in either series one hobby or retail packs. Hobby cards feature gold backgrounds and say "Signed Game Jersey" on front. Hobby/Retail cards feature white backgrounds and simply say "Game Jersey" on front. These cards are individually serial numbered to the depicted player's jersey number. The following players packed out as exchange cards: Alex Rodriguez, Ken Griffey Jr., Jeff Bagwell, Mike Hampton and Rick Ankiel. The exchange deadline was August 7th, 2001.

PRINT RUNS LISTED BELOW
NO PRICING ON QTY OF 25 OR LESS
CKG Ken Griffey Jr./30 125.00 250.00
CNRA N.Ryan Astros/34 175.00 300.00
CNRR N.Ryan Rangers/34 175.00 300.00
CSK Sandy Koufax/32 600.00 1000.00
HFT Frank Thomas/35 75.00 150.00
HGM Greg Maddux/31 175.00 300.00
HJC Jose Canseco/33 50.00 100.00
HKG Ken Griffey Jr./30 125.00 250.00
HMH Mike Hampton/32 30.00 60.00
HNRA N.Ryan Angels/30 200.00 350.00
HNRM N.Ryan Mets/30 250.00 400.00
HRA Rick Ankiel/66 30.00 60.00
HRJ Randy Johnson/51 125.00 200.00

2001 Upper Deck Game Jersey Combo

Randomly inserted into series one packs, these 13 cards feature dual player game-worn uniform patches. Card backs carry both players initials as numbering. Please note that there were only 50 serial numbered sets produced.

STATED PRINT RUN 50 SERIAL #'d SETS
AJKG A.Jones 10.00 25.00
K.Griffey Jr.
BBJC B.Bonds 50.00 100.00
J.Canseco
BBKG B.Bonds 50.00 100.00
K.Griffey Jr.
DJAR D.Jeter 30.00 60.00
A.Rodriguez
FTJB F.Thomas 20.00 50.00
J.Bagwell
IRRP I.Rodriguez 20.00 50.00
R.Palmeiro
JDRA J.Drew 15.00 40.00
R.Ankiel
NRAR N.Ryan Astro-Rgr 60.00 120.00
NRMA N.Ryan Mets-Angels 60.00 120.00
RATH R.Ankiel 15.00 40.00
T.Hudson
RJGM R.Johnson 30.00 60.00
G.Maddux
TGCR T.Gwynn 50.00 100.00
C.Ripken
VGMR V.Guerrero 20.00 50.00
M.Ramirez

2001 Upper Deck Game Jersey Patch

Randomly inserted into series one packs at one in 7500 and series 2 packs at 1:5000, these cards feature game-worn uniform patches. Card backs carry a "P" prefix.

SER.1 STATED ODDS 1:7500
SER.2 STATED ODDS 1:5000
PAR Alex Rodriguez S1 30.00 60.00
PAR Alex Rodriguez S2 30.00 60.00
PBB Barry Bonds S1 75.00 150.00
PBB Barry Bonds S2 75.00 150.00
PCJ Chipper Jones S2 50.00 100.00
PCR Cal Ripken S1 40.00 100.00
PCR Cal Ripken S2 40.00 100.00
PDJ Derek Jeter S1 75.00 150.00
PFT Frank Thomas S1 50.00 100.00
PIR Ivan Rodriguez S1 30.00 60.00
PIR Ivan Rodriguez S2 30.00 60.00
PJB Johnny Bench S2 50.00 100.00
PJB Jeff Bagwell S1 40.00 80.00
PJC Jose Canseco S1 40.00 80.00
PJG Jason Giambi S1 30.00 60.00
PKG Ken Griffey Jr. S1 30.00 60.00
PKG Ken Griffey Jr. S2 30.00 60.00
PNRA N.Ryan Astros S1 30.00 60.00
PNRR N.Ryan Rangers S1 30.00 60.00
PNRR N.Ryan Rangers S2 30.00 60.00
PRA Rick Ankiel S1 15.00 40.00
PRP Rafael Palmeiro S1 15.00 40.00
PSS Sammy Sosa S2 15.00 40.00
PTG Tony Gwynn S1 50.00 100.00

2001 Upper Deck Game Jersey Patch Autograph Numbered

Randomly inserted into series one hobby packs, these cards feature both autographs and game-worn uniform patches. Card backs carry a "SP" prefix. Please note that these cards are hand-numbered to the depicted players jersey number. All of these cards packed out as exchange cards with a redemption deadline of 8/07/01.

PRINT RUNS B/WN 3-66 COPIES PER
SPKG Ken Griffey Jr./30 300.00 500.00
SPRA Rick Ankiel/66 40.00 80.00

2001 Upper Deck Home Run Derby Heroes

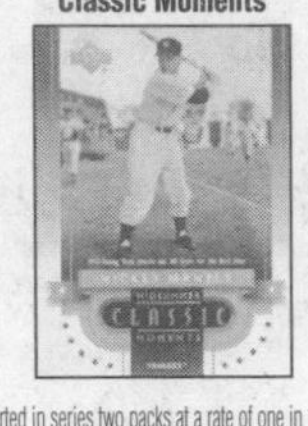

Inserted in second series packs at a rate of one in 36, these 10 cards features a look back at some of the most explosive performances from past Home Run Derby competitions.

COMPLETE SET (10) 20.00 50.00
SER.2 STATED ODDS 1:36
HD1 Mark McGwire 99 4.00 10.00
HD2 Sammy Sosa 00 1.50 4.00
HD3 Frank Thomas 96 1.50 4.00
HD4 Cal Ripken 91 5.00 12.00
HD5 Tino Martinez 97 1.00 2.50
HD6 Ken Griffey Jr. 99 3.00 8.00
HD7 Barry Bonds 96 4.00 10.00
HD8 Albert Belle 95 .75 2.00
HD9 Mark McGwire 92 4.00 10.00
HD10 Juan Gonzalez 93 .75 2.00

2001 Upper Deck Home Run Explosion

Randomly inserted into series one packs at one in 12, this 15-card insert features players that are among the league leaders in homeruns every year. Card backs carry a "HR" prefix.

COMPLETE SET (15) 15.00 40.00
SER.1 STATED ODDS 1:12
HR1 Mark McGwire 2.00 5.00
HR2 Chipper Jones .75 2.00
HR3 Jeff Bagwell .50 1.25
HR4 Carlos Delgado .40 1.00
HR5 Barry Bonds 2.00 5.00
HR6 Troy Glaus .40 1.00
HR7 Sammy Sosa .75 2.00
HR8 Alex Rodriguez 1.00 2.50
HR9 Mike Piazza 1.25 3.00
HR10 Vladimir Guerrero .75 2.00
HR11 Ken Griffey Jr. 1.50 4.00
HR12 Frank Thomas .75 2.00
HR13 Ivan Rodriguez .50 1.25
HR14 Jason Giambi .40 1.00
HR15 Carl Everett .40 1.00

2001 Upper Deck Midseason Superstar Summit

Inserted in series two packs at a rate of one in 24, these 15 cards feature some of the most dominant players of the 2000 season.

COMPLETE SET (15) 25.00 60.00
SER.2 STATED ODDS 1:24
MS1 Derek Jeter 4.00 10.00
MS2 Sammy Sosa 1.50 4.00
MS3 Jeff Bagwell 1.00 2.50
MS4 Tony Gwynn 2.00 5.00
MS5 Alex Rodriguez 2.00 5.00
MS6 Greg Maddux 2.50 6.00
MS7 Jason Giambi .75 2.00
MS8 Mark McGwire 4.00 10.00
MS9 Barry Bonds 4.00 10.00
MS10 Ken Griffey Jr. 3.00 8.00
MS11 Carlos Delgado .75 2.00
MS12 Troy Glaus .75 2.00
MS13 Todd Helton 1.00 2.50
MS14 Manny Ramirez Sox 1.00 2.50
MS15 Jeff Kent .75 2.00

2001 Upper Deck Midsummer Classic Moments

Inserted in series two packs at a rate of one in 12, these 20 cards feature some of the most memorable moments from All Star Game history.

COMPLETE SET (20) 15.00 40.00
SER.2 STATED ODDS 1:12
CM1 Joe DiMaggio 36 1.25 3.00
CM2 Joe DiMaggio 51 1.25 3.00
CM3 Mickey Mantle 52 2.50 6.00
CM4 Mickey Mantle 68 2.50 6.00
CM5 Roger Clemens 86 1.50 4.00
CM6 Mark McGwire 87 2.00 5.00
CM7 Cal Ripken 91 2.50 6.00
CM8 Ken Griffey Jr. 92 1.50 4.00
CM9 Randy Johnson 93 .75 2.00
CM10 Tony Gwynn 94 1.00 2.50
CM11 Fred McGriff 94 .50 1.25
CM12 Hideo Nomo 95 .75 2.00
CM13 Jeff Conine 95 .40 1.00
CM14 Mike Piazza 96 1.25 3.00
CM15 Sandy Alomar Jr. 97 .40 1.00
CM16 Alex Rodriguez 98 .75 2.00
CM17 Roberto Alomar 98 .50 1.25
CM18 Pedro Martinez 99 .50 1.25
CM19 Andres Galarraga 00 .40 1.00
CM20 Derek Jeter 00 1.50 4.00

2001 Upper Deck People's Choice

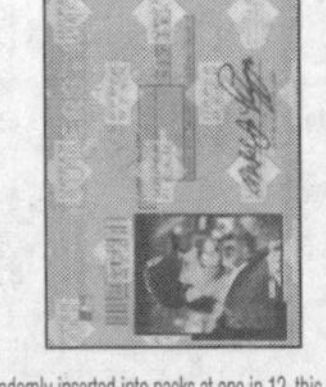

Inserted one per 24 series two packs, these 15 cards feature the players who fans want to see the most.

COMPLETE SET (15) 30.00 80.00
SER.2 STATED ODDS 1:24
PC1 Alex Rodriguez 2.00 5.00
PC2 Ken Griffey Jr. 3.00 8.00
PC3 Mark McGwire 4.00 10.00
PC4 Todd Helton 1.00 2.50
PC5 Manny Ramirez 1.00 2.50
PC6 Mike Piazza 2.50 6.00
PC7 Vladimir Guerrero 1.50 4.00
PC8 Randy Johnson 1.50 4.00
PC9 Cal Ripken 5.00 12.00
PC10 Andruw Jones 1.00 2.50
PC11 Sammy Sosa 1.50 4.00
PC12 Derek Jeter 4.00 10.00
PC13 Pedro Martinez 1.00 2.50
PC14 Frank Thomas 1.50 4.00
PC15 Nomar Garciaparra 2.50 6.00

2001 Upper Deck Rookie Roundup

Randomly inserted into series one packs at one in six, this 10-card insert features some of the younger players in Major League baseball. Card backs carry a "RR" prefix.

COMPLETE SET (10) 2.00 5.00
SER.1 STATED ODDS 1:6
RR1 Rick Ankiel .20 .50
RR2 Adam Kennedy .20 .50
RR3 Mike Lamb .20 .50
RR4 Adam Eaton .20 .50
RR5 Rafael Furcal .30 .75
RR6 Pat Burrell .30 .75
RR7 Adam Piatt .20 .50
RR8 Eric Munson .20 .50
RR9 Brad Penny .20 .50
RR10 Mark Mulder .30 .75

2001 Upper Deck Subway Series Game Jerseys

While the set name seemed to indicate that these cards were from jerseys worn during the 2000 World series, they were actually swatches from regular-season game jerseys.

SER.2 STATED ODDS 1:144 HOBBY
CARDS ERRONEOUSLY STATE W.SERIES USE
SSAL Al Leiter 2.00 5.00
SSAP Andy Pettitte 3.00 8.00
SSBW Bernie Williams 3.00 8.00
SSEA Edgardo Alfonzo 2.00 5.00
SSJF John Franco 2.00 5.00
SSJP Jay Payton 2.00 5.00
SSOH Orlando Hernandez 2.00 5.00
SSPO Paul O'Neill 3.00 8.00
SSRC Roger Clemens 8.00 20.00
SSTP Timo Perez 2.00 5.00

2001 Upper Deck Superstar Summit

Randomly inserted into packs at one in 12, this 15-card insert features the Major League's top superstar caliber players. Card backs carry a "SS" prefix.

COMPLETE SET (15) 20.00 50.00
SER.1 STATED ODDS 1:12
SS1 Derek Jeter 2.00 5.00
SS2 Randy Johnson .75 2.00
SS3 Barry Bonds 2.00 5.00
SS4 Frank Thomas .75 2.00
SS5 Cal Ripken 2.50 6.00
SS6 Pedro Martinez .75 2.00
SS7 Ivan Rodriguez .75 2.00
SS8 Mike Piazza 1.25 3.00
SS9 Mark McGwire 2.00 5.00
SS10 Manny Ramirez Sox .75 2.00
SS11 Ken Griffey Jr. 1.50 4.00
SS12 Sammy Sosa .75 2.00
SS13 Alex Rodriguez 1.00 2.50
SS14 Chipper Jones .75 2.00
SS15 Nomar Garciaparra 1.25 3.00

2001 Upper Deck UD's Most Wanted

Randomly inserted into packs at one in 14, this 15-card insert features players that are in high demand on the collectibles market. Card backs carry a "MW" prefix.

COMPLETE SET (15) 10.00 25.00
SER.1 STATED ODDS 1:14
MW1 Mark McGwire 1.50 4.00
MW2 Cal Ripken 3.00 8.00
MW3 Ivan Rodriguez .60 1.50
MW4 Pedro Martinez .60 1.50
MW5 Sammy Sosa .60 1.50
MW6 Tony Gwynn 1.00 2.50
MW7 Vladimir Guerrero 1.00 2.50
MW8 Derek Jeter 2.50 6.00
MW9 Mike Piazza 1.00 2.50
MW10 Chipper Jones 1.00 2.50
MW11 Alex Rodriguez 1.25 3.00
MW12 Barry Bonds 1.50 4.00
MW13 Jeff Bagwell .60 1.50
MW14 Frank Thomas 1.00 2.50
MW15 Nomar Garciaparra .60 1.50

2001 Upper Deck Pinstripe Exclusives DiMaggio

This 56-card set features a wide selection of cards focusing on Yankees legend Joe DiMaggio. The cards were distributed in special three-card foil wrapped packs, exclusively seeded into 2001 SP Game Bat Milestone, SP Game-Used, SPx, Upper Deck Decade 1970's, Upper Deck Gold Glove, Upper

Deck Legends, Upper Deck Ovation and Upper Deck Sweet Spot hobby boxes at a rate of one pack per sealed box.
COMPLETE SET (56) 30.00 60.00
COMMON CARD (JD1-JD56) .60 1.50
ONE PACK PER SP BAT MILESTONE BOX
ONE PACK PER SP GAME-USED HOBBY BOX
ONE PACK PER SPX HOBBY BOX
ONE PACK PER UD DECADE 1970 HOBBY BOX
ONE PACK PER UD GOLD GLOVE HOBBY BOX
ONE PACK PER UD LEGENDS HOBBY BOX
ONE PACK PER UD OVATION HOBBY BOX
ONE PACK PER UD SWEET SPOT HOBBY BOX

2001 Upper Deck Pinstripe Exclusives DiMaggio Memorabilia

Randomly seeded into special three-card Pinstripe Exclusives DiMaggio foil packs (of which were distributed exclusively in 2001 SP Game Bat Milestone, SP Game-Used, SPx, Upper Deck Decade 1970's, Upper Deck Gold Glove, Upper Deck Legends, Upper Deck Ovation and Upper Deck Sweet Spot Sweet Spot hobby boxes) were a selection of scarce game-used memorabilia and autograph cut cards featuring Joe DiMaggio. Each card is serial-numbered and features either a game-used bat chip, jersey swatch or autograph cut.
COMMON BAT (B1-B9) 30.00 60.00
COMMON JERSEY (J1-J9) 20.00 50.00
SUFFIX 1 CARDS DIST.IN SWEET SPOT
SUFFIX 2 CARDS DIST.IN OVATION
SUFFIX 3 CARDS DIST.IN SPX
SUFFIX 4 CARDS DIST.IN SP GAME USED
SUFFIX 5 CARDS DIST.IN LEGENDS
SUFFIX 6 CARDS DIST.IN DECADE 1970
SUFFIX 7 CARDS DIST.IN SP BAT MILE
SUFFIX 8 CARDS DIST.IN UD GOLD GLOVE
BAT 1-9 PRINT RUN 100 SERIAL #'d SETS
BAT-CUT 1-8 PRINT RUN 5 SERIAL #'d SETS
COMBO 1-8 PRINT RUN 50 SERIAL #'D SETS
CUT 1-8 PRINT RUN 5 SERIAL #'d SETS
JERSEY 1-8 PRINT RUN 100 SERIAL #'d SETS
CJ1 DiMag. 300.00 600.00
Gehrig Pants/50
CJ2 DiMag. 175.00 300.00
Mantle Jsy/50
CJ3 DiMag. 100.00 200.00
Griffey Jsy/50
CJ4 DiMag. 150.00 250.00
DiMag. Jsy/50
CJ5 DiMag. 150.00 300.00
Mantle Jsy/50
CJ6 DiMag. 150.00 300.00
Mantle Jsy/50

2001 Upper Deck Pinstripe Exclusives Mantle

This 56-card set features a wide selection of cards focusing on Yankees legend Mickey Mantle. The cards were distributed in special three-card foil wrapped packs, seeded into 2001 Upper Deck Series 2, Upper Deck Hall of Famers, Upper Deck MVP and Upper Deck Vintage hobby boxes at a rate of one pack per 24 ct. box.
COMPLETE SET (56) 50.00 100.00
COMMON CARD (MM1-MM56) 1.00 2.50
ONE PACK PER UD SER.2 HOBBY BOX
ONE PACK PER UD HOF'ers HOBBY BOX
ONE PACK PER UD MVP HOBBY BOX
ONE PACK PER UD VINTAGE HOBBY BOX

2001 Upper Deck Pinstripe Exclusives Mantle Memorabilia

Randomly seeded into special three-card Pinstripe Exclusives Mantle foil packs (of which were distributed in hobby boxes of 2001 SP Authentic, 2001 SP Game Bat Milestone, 2001 Upper Deck series 2, 2001 Upper Deck Hall of Famers, 2001 Upper Deck Legends of New York, 2001 Upper Deck MVP and 2001 Upper Deck Vintage) were a selection of scarce game-used memorabilia and autograph cut cards featuring Mickey Mantle. Each card is serial-numbered and features either a game-used bat chip, jersey swatch or autograph cut.
COMMON BAT (B1-B4) 75.00 150.00
COMMON JERSEY (J1-J7) 100.00 200.00
COMMON BAT CUT (BC1-BC4)
COMMON CUT (C1-C4)
SUFFIX 1 CARDS DIST.IN UD VINTAGE
SUFFIX 2 CARDS DIST.IN UD HOF'ers
SUFFIX 3 CARDS DIST.IN UD MVP
SUFFIX 4 CARDS DIST.IN UD SER.2
SUFFIX 5 CARDS DIST. IN SP AUTH
SUFFIX 6 CARDS DIST. IN SP GAME BAT MILE
SUFFIX 7 CARDS DIST. IN UD LEG OF NY
BAT 1-9 PRINT RUN 100 SERIAL #'d SETS
BAT-CUT 1-4 PRINT RUN 7 SERIAL #'d SETS
COMBO 1-6 PRINT RUN 50 SERIAL #'d SETS
CUT 1-4 PRINT RUN 7 SERIAL #'D SETS
JERSEY 1-7 PRINT RUN 100 SERIAL #'d SETS
CJ1 Mantle 175.00 300.00
Maris Jsy/50
CJ2 Mantle 150.00 250.00
DiMag Jsy/50
CJ3 Mantle 75.00 150.00
Griffey Jsy/50
CJ4 Mantle 175.00 300.00
Maris Jsy/50
CJ5 Mantle 150.00 250.00
DiMag Jsy/50
CJ6 Mantle 150.00 250.00
DiMag Jsy 50
CJ7 Mantle 150.00 250.00
DiMag Jsy 50

2001 Upper Deck Gwynn

This five-card standard-size set was issued by Upper Deck to honor Tony Gwynn during his final days as an active player. These cards feature shots of Tony Gwynn along with a blurb on the back and career stats. Each card also has a "Thanks Tony" logo on the bottom left corner.
COMPLETE SET 10.00 25.00
COMMON CARD 2.00 5.00

2001 Upper Deck Collectibles Ichiro Tribute to 51

This set was issued by Upper Deck to commemorate both the sensational rookie season of Ichiro Suzuki and the signing of Suzuki to an Upper Deck spokesman contract. Cards numbered I1 through I20 are regular cards while I21 through I25 are milestone cards. The set was issued in a box which contained these 25 cards as well as as a special bonus jumbo commemorative card. The set originally retailed for $19.95.
COMPLETE FACT. SET (26) 8.00 20.00
COMMON ICHIRO (I1-I25) .30 .75
XX Ichiro Suzuki/3 1/2 x 5
commemorative card .80 2.00

2001 Upper Deck DiMaggio Kit Young Game Bat

These cards were passed out to paid attendees of the 2001 Kit Young Hawaii Trade Conference on the day of Tuesday, February 27th (during day one of the popular Meet the Industry session). The basic card features a piece of bat in the shape of the classic NY logo that was used by Joe DiMaggio in an official Major League Baseball game. Each card was presented in a special silver foil Kit Young Hawaii wrapper. Please note that each pack also contained a special card explaining Upper Deck's 2001 Pinstripe Exclusive Promotion. Five lucky attendees got one of the rare autograph cut variation cards. Please note that each basic card is serial numbered to 450 in gold foil on the back.
KYJD1 Joe DiMaggio Bat/450 25.00 60.00
KYJD2 Joe DiMaggio Bat/450 25.00 60.00

2001 Upper Deck Store Ichiro

This one card set, which measures approximately 3 1/2" by 5" feature a thank- you note from Ichiro on the front and information on some of the ways to purchase Ichiro items on the back.
COMPLETE SET

2001 Upper Deck Subway Series Heroes

These four cards were distributed exclusively to paid attendees of the 2001 Kit Young Trade Show in Hawaii that took place in late February of that year. Each card was handed out on a different day of the week long trade show. The cards measure the standard 2 1/2" by 3 1/2" dimensions and feature a vintage era black and white image on a horizontal card front. Each player signed his cards in blue sharpie on front. Only 450 sets were produced and each card is serial numbered to that figure in gold foil on back.
COMPLETE SET (4) 50.00 100.00
KYSS1 Don Larsen 6.00 15.00
KYSS2 Whitey Ford 20.00 40.00
KYSS3 Johnny Podres 5.00 10.00
KYSS4 Duke Snider 20.00 40.00

2001 Upper Deck Twizzlers

This 10-card standard-size set features players involved in the 2001 Big League Challenge contest which was traditionally held before spring training. These cards were available in Twizzler packaging. In addition to the cards, an album, with a $2 cost, was available to sleeve each card.
COMPLETE SET (10)
COMMON CARD

2002 Upper Deck

The 500 card first series set was issued in November, 2001. The 245-card second series set was issued in May, 2002. The cards were issued in eight card packs with 24 packs to a box. Subsets include Star Rookies (cards numbered 1-50, 501-545), World Stage (cards numbered 461-480), Griffey Gallery (481-490) and Checklists (491-500, 736-745) and Year of the Record (726-735). Star Rookies were inserted at a rate of one per pack into second series packs, making them 1.75X times tougher to pull than veteran second series cards.
COMPLETE SET (745) 50.00 100.00
COMPLETE SERIES 1 (500) 40.00 80.00
COMPLETE SERIES 2 (245) 10.00 25.00
COMMON (51-500/546-745) .10 .30
COMMON SR (1-50/501-545) .40 1.00
SR 501-545 ONE PER SER.2 PACK
1 Mark Prior SR .75 2.00
2 Mark Teixeira SR 3.00 8.00
3 Brian Roberts SR .75 2.00
4 Jason Romano SR .40 1.00
5 Dennis Stark SR .40 1.00
6 Oscar Salazar SR .40 1.00
7 John Patterson SR .40 1.00
8 Shane Loux SR .40 1.00
9 Marcus Giles SR .40 1.00
10 Juan Cruz SR .40 1.00
11 Jorge Julio SR .40 1.00
12 Adam Dunn SR .40 1.00
13 Delvin James SR .40 1.00
14 Jeremy Affeldt SR .40 1.00
15 Tim Raines Jr. SR .40 1.00
16 Luke Hudson SR .40 1.00
17 Todd Sears SR .40 1.00
18 George Perez SR .40 1.00
19 Wilmy Caceres SR .40 1.00
20 Abraham Nunez SR .40 1.00
21 Mike Amrhein SR RC .40 1.00
22 Carlos Hernandez SR .40 1.00
23 Scott Hodges SR .40 1.00
24 Brandon Knight SR .40 1.00
25 Geoff Goetz SR .40 1.00
26 Carlos Garcia SR .40 1.00
27 Luis Pineda SR .40 1.00
28 Chris Gissell SR .40 1.00
29 Jae Weong Seo SR .40 1.00
30 Paul Phillips SR .40 1.00
31 Cory Aldridge SR .40 1.00
32 Aaron Cook SR RC .40 1.00
33 Rendy Espina SR RC .40 1.00
34 Jason Phillips SR .40 1.00
35 Carlos Silva SR .40 1.00
36 Ryan Mills SR .40 1.00
37 Pedro Santana SR .40 1.00
38 John Grabow SR .40 1.00
39 Cody Ransom SR .40 1.00
40 Orlando Woodards SR .40 1.00
41 Bud Smith SR .40 1.00
42 Junior Guerrero SR .40 1.00
43 David Brous SR .40 1.00
44 Steve Green SR .40 1.00
45 Brian Rogers SR .40 1.00
46 Juan Figueroa SR RC .40 1.00
47 Nick Punto SR .40 1.00
48 Junior Herndon SR .40 1.00
49 Justin Kaye SR .40 1.00
50 Jason Karnuth SR .40 1.00
51 Troy Glaus .10 .30
52 Bengie Molina .10 .30
53 Ramon Ortiz .10 .30
54 Adam Kennedy .10 .30
55 Jarrod Washburn .10 .30
56 Troy Percival .10 .30
57 David Eckstein .10 .30
58 Ben Weber .10 .30
59 Larry Barnes .10 .30
60 Ismael Valdes .10 .30
61 Benji Gil .10 .30
62 Scott Schoeneweis .10 .30
63 Pat Rapp .10 .30
64 Jason Giambi .10 .30
65 Mark Mulder .10 .30
66 Ron Gant .10 .30
67 Johnny Damon .20 .50
68 Adam Piatt .10 .30
69 Jermaine Dye .10 .30
70 Jason Hart .10 .30
71 Eric Chavez .10 .30
72 Jim Mecir .10 .30
73 Barry Zito .10 .30
74 Jason Isringhausen .10 .30
75 Jeremy Giambi .10 .30
76 Olmedo Saenz .10 .30
77 Terrence Long .10 .30
78 Ramon Hernandez .10 .30
79 Chris Carpenter .10 .30
80 Raul Mondesi .10 .30
81 Carlos Delgado .10 .30
82 Billy Koch .10 .30
83 Vernon Wells .10 .30
84 Darrin Fletcher .10 .30
85 Homer Bush .10 .30
86 Pasqual Coco .10 .30
87 Shannon Stewart .10 .30
88 Chris Woodward .10 .30
89 Joe Lawrence .10 .30
90 Esteban Loaiza .10 .30
91 Cesar Izturis .10 .30
92 Kelvim Escobar .10 .30
93 Greg Vaughn .10 .30
94 Brent Abernathy .10 .30
95 Tanyon Sturtze .10 .30
96 Steve Cox .10 .30
97 Aubrey Huff .10 .30
98 Jesus Colome .10 .30
99 Ben Grieve .10 .30
100 Esteban Yan .10 .30
101 Joe Kennedy .10 .30
102 Felix Martinez .10 .30
103 Nick Bierbrodt .10 .30
104 Damian Rolls .10 .30
105 Russ Johnson .10 .30
106 Toby Hall .10 .30
107 Roberto Alomar .20 .50
108 Bartolo Colon .10 .30
109 John Rocker .10 .30
110 Juan Gonzalez .10 .30
111 Einar Diaz .10 .30
112 Chuck Finley .10 .30
113 Kenny Lofton .10 .30
114 Danys Baez .10 .30
115 Travis Fryman .10 .30
116 C.C. Sabathia .10 .30
117 Paul Shuey .10 .30
118 Marty Cordova .10 .30
119 Ellis Burks .10 .30
120 Bob Wickman .10 .30
121 Edgar Martinez .20 .50
122 Freddy Garcia .10 .30
123 Ichiro Suzuki .60 1.50
124 John Olerud .10 .30
125 Gil Meche .10 .30
126 Dan Wilson .10 .30
127 Aaron Sele .10 .30
128 Kazuhiro Sasaki .10 .30
129 Mark McLemore .10 .30
130 Carlos Guillen .10 .30
131 Al Martin .10 .30
132 David Bell .10 .30
133 Jay Buhner .10 .30
134 Stan Javier .10 .30
135 Tony Batista .10 .30
136 Jason Johnson .10 .30
137 Brook Fordyce .10 .30
138 Mike Kinkade .10 .30
139 Willis Roberts .10 .30
140 David Segui .10 .30
141 Josh Towers .10 .30
142 Jeff Conine .10 .30
143 Chris Richard .10 .30
144 Pat Hentgen .10 .30
145 Melvin Mora .10 .30
146 Jerry Hairston Jr. .10 .30
147 Calvin Maduro .10 .30
148 Brady Anderson .10 .30
149 Alex Rodriguez .40 1.00
150 Kenny Rogers .10 .30
151 Chad Curtis .10 .30
152 Ricky Ledee .10 .30
153 Rafael Palmeiro .20 .50
154 Rob Bell .10 .30
155 Rick Helling .10 .30
156 Doug Davis .10 .30
157 Mike Lamb .10 .30
158 Gabe Kapler .10 .30
159 Jeff Zimmerman .10 .30
160 Bill Haselman .10 .30
161 Tim Crabtree .10 .30
162 Carlos Pena .10 .30
163 Nomar Garciaparra .50 1.25
164 Shea Hillenbrand .10 .30
165 Hideo Nomo .30 .75
166 Manny Ramirez .20 .50
167 Jose Offerman .10 .30
168 Scott Hatteberg .10 .30
169 Trot Nixon .10 .30
170 Darren Lewis .10 .30
171 Derek Lowe .10 .30
172 Troy O'Leary .10 .30
173 Tim Wakefield .10 .30
174 Chris Stynes .10 .30
175 John Valentin .10 .30
176 David Cone .10 .30
177 Neifi Perez .10 .30
178 Brent Mayne .10 .30
179 Dan Reichert .10 .30
180 A.J. Hinch .10 .30
181 Chris George .10 .30
182 Mike Sweeney .10 .30
183 Jeff Suppan .10 .30
184 Roberto Hernandez .10 .30
185 Joe Randa .10 .30
186 Paul Byrd .10 .30
187 Luis Ordaz .10 .30
188 Kris Wilson .10 .30
189 Dee Brown .10 .30
190 Tony Clark .10 .30
191 Matt Anderson .10 .30
192 Robert Fick .10 .30
193 Juan Encarnacion .10 .30
194 Dean Palmer .10 .30
195 Victor Santos .10 .30
196 Damion Easley .10 .30
197 Jose Lima .10 .30
198 Deivi Cruz .10 .30
199 Roger Cedeno .10 .30
200 Jose Macias .10 .30
201 Jeff Weaver .10 .30
202 Brandon Inge .10 .30
203 Brian Moehler .10 .30
204 Brad Radke .10 .30
205 Doug Mientkiewicz .10 .30
206 Cristian Guzman .10 .30
207 Corey Koskie .10 .30
208 LaTroy Hawkins .10 .30
209 J.C. Romero .10 .30
210 Chad Allen .10 .30
211 Torii Hunter .10 .30
212 Travis Miller .10 .30
213 Joe Mays .10 .30
214 Todd Jones .10 .30
215 David Ortiz .30 .75
216 Brian Buchanan .10 .30
217 A.J. Pierzynski .10 .30
218 Carlos Lee .10 .30
219 Gary Glover .10 .30
220 Jose Valentin .10 .30
221 Aaron Rowand .10 .30
222 Sandy Alomar Jr. .10 .30
223 Herbert Perry .10 .30
224 Jon Garland .10 .30
225 Mark Buehrle .10 .30
226 Chris Singleton .10 .30
227 Kip Wells .10 .30
228 Ray Durham .10 .30
229 Joe Crede .10 .30
230 Keith Foulke .10 .30
231 Royce Clayton .10 .30
232 Andy Pettitte .20 .50
233 Derek Jeter .75 2.00
234 Jorge Posada .20 .50
235 Roger Clemens .60 1.50
236 Paul O'Neill .20 .50
237 Nick Johnson .10 .30
238 Gerald Williams .10 .30
239 Mariano Rivera .30 .75
240 Alfonso Soriano .10 .30
241 Ramiro Mendoza .10 .30
242 Mike Mussina .20 .50
243 Luis Sojo .10 .30
244 Scott Brosius .10 .30
245 David Justice .10 .30
246 Wade Miller .10 .30
247 Brad Ausmus .10 .30
248 Jeff Bagwell .20 .50
249 Daryle Ward .10 .30
250 Shane Reynolds .10 .30
251 Chris Truby .10 .30
252 Billy Wagner .10 .30
253 Craig Biggio .20 .50
254 Moises Alou .10 .30
255 Vinny Castilla .10 .30
256 Tim Redding .10 .30
257 Roy Oswalt .10 .30
258 Julio Lugo .10 .30
259 Chipper Jones .30 .75
260 Greg Maddux .50 1.25
261 Ken Caminiti .10 .30
262 Kevin Millwood .10 .30
263 Keith Lockhart .10 .30
264 Rey Sanchez .10 .30
265 Jason Marquis .10 .30
266 Brian Jordan .10 .30
267 Steve Karsay .10 .30
268 Wes Helms .10 .30
269 B.J. Surhoff .10 .30
270 Wilson Betemit .10 .30
271 John Smoltz .20 .50
272 Rafael Furcal .10 .30
273 Jeromy Burnitz .10 .30
274 Jimmy Haynes .10 .30
275 Mark Loretta .10 .30
276 Jose Hernandez .10 .30
277 Paul Rigdon .10 .30
278 Alex Sanchez .10 .30
279 Chad Fox .10 .30
280 Devon White .10 .30
281 Tyler Houston .10 .30
282 Ronnie Belliard .10 .30
283 Luis Lopez .10 .30
284 Ben Sheets .10 .30
285 Curtis Leskanic .10 .30
286 Henry Blanco .10 .30
287 Mark McGwire .75 2.00
288 Edgar Renteria .10 .30
289 Matt Morris .10 .30
290 Gene Stechschulte .10 .30
291 Dustin Hermanson .10 .30
292 Eli Marrero .10 .30
293 Albert Pujols .60 1.50
294 Luis Saturria .10 .30
295 Bobby Bonilla .10 .30
296 Garrett Stephenson .10 .30
297 Jim Edmonds .10 .30
298 Rick Ankiel .10 .30
299 Placido Polanco .10 .30
300 Dave Veres .10 .30
301 Sammy Sosa .30 .75
302 Eric Young .10 .30
303 Kerry Wood .10 .30
304 Jon Lieber .10 .30
305 Joe Girardi .10 .30
306 Fred McGriff .20 .50
307 Jeff Fassero .10 .30
308 Julio Zuleta .10 .30
309 Kevin Tapani .10 .30
310 Rondell White .10 .30
311 Julian Tavarez .10 .30
312 Tom Gordon .10 .30
313 Corey Patterson .10 .30
314 Bill Mueller .10 .30
315 Randy Johnson .30 .75
316 Chad Moeller .10 .30
317 Tony Womack .10 .30
318 Erubiel Durazo .10 .30
319 Luis Gonzalez .10 .30
320 Brian Anderson .10 .30
321 Reggie Sanders .10 .30
322 Greg Colbrunn .10 .30
323 Robert Ellis .10 .30
324 Jack Cust .10 .30
325 Bret Prinz .10 .30
326 Steve Finley .10 .30
327 Byung-Hyun Kim .10 .30
328 Albie Lopez .10 .30
329 Gary Sheffield .10 .30
330 Mark Grudzielanek .10 .30
331 Paul LoDuca .10 .30
332 Tom Goodwin .10 .30
333 Andy Ashby .10 .30
334 Hiram Bocachica .10 .30
335 Dave Hansen .10 .30
336 Kevin Brown .10 .30
337 Marquis Grissom .10 .30
338 Terry Adams .10 .30
339 Chan Ho Park .10 .30
340 Adrian Beltre .10 .30
341 Luke Prokopec .10 .30
342 Jeff Shaw .10 .30
343 Vladimir Guerrero .30 .75
344 Orlando Cabrera .10 .30
345 Tony Armas Jr. .10 .30
346 Michael Barrett .10 .30
347 Geoff Blum .10 .30
348 Ryan Minor .10 .30
349 Peter Bergeron .10 .30
350 Graeme Lloyd .10 .30
351 Jose Vidro .10 .30
352 Javier Vazquez .10 .30
353 Matt Blank .10 .30
354 Masato Yoshii .10 .30
355 Carl Pavano .10 .30
356 Barry Bonds .75 2.00
357 Shawon Dunston .10 .30
358 Livan Hernandez .10 .30
359 Felix Rodriguez .10 .30
360 Pedro Feliz .10 .30
361 Calvin Murray .10 .30
362 Robb Nen .10 .30
363 Marvin Benard .10 .30
364 Russ Ortiz .10 .30
365 Jason Schmidt .10 .30
366 Rich Aurilia .10 .30
367 John Vander Wal .10 .30
368 Benito Santiago .10 .30
369 Ryan Dempster .10 .30
370 Charles Johnson .10 .30
371 Alex Gonzalez .10 .30
372 Luis Castillo .10 .30
373 Mike Lowell .10 .30
374 Antonio Alfonseca .10 .30
375 A.J. Burnett .10 .30
376 Brad Penny .10 .30
377 Jason Grilli .10 .30
378 Derrek Lee .20 .50
379 Matt Clement .10 .30
380 Eric Owens .10 .30
381 Vladimir Nunez .10 .30
382 Cliff Floyd .10 .30
383 Mike Piazza .50 1.25
384 Lenny Harris .10 .30
385 Glendon Rusch .10 .30
386 Todd Zeile .10 .30
387 Al Leiter .10 .30
388 Armando Benitez .10 .30
389 Alex Escobar .10 .30
390 Kevin Appier .10 .30
391 Matt Lawton .10 .30
392 Bruce Chen .10 .30
393 John Franco .10 .30
394 Tsuyoshi Shinjo .10 .30
395 Rey Ordonez .10 .30
396 Joe McEwing .10 .30
397 Ryan Klesko .10 .30
398 Brian Lawrence .10 .30
399 Kevin Walker .10 .30
400 Phil Nevin .10 .30
401 Bubba Trammell .10 .30
402 Wiki Gonzalez .10 .30
403 D'Angelo Jimenez .10 .30
404 Rickey Henderson .30 .75
405 Mike Darr .10 .30
406 Trevor Hoffman .10 .30
407 Damian Jackson .10 .30
408 Santiago Perez .10 .30
409 Cesar Crespo .10 .30
410 Robert Person .10 .30
411 Travis Lee .10 .30
412 Scott Rolen .20 .50
413 Turk Wendell .10 .30
414 Randy Wolf .10 .30
415 Kevin Jordan .10 .30
416 Jose Mesa .10 .30
417 Mike Lieberthal .10 .30
418 Bobby Abreu .10 .30
419 Tomas Perez .10 .30
420 Doug Glanville .10 .30
421 Reggie Taylor .10 .30
422 Jimmy Rollins .10 .30
423 Brian Giles .10 .30
424 Rob Mackowiak .10 .30
425 Bronson Arroyo .10 .30
426 Kevin Young .10 .30
427 Jack Wilson .10 .30
428 Adrian Brown .10 .30
429 Chad Hermansen .10 .30
430 Jimmy Anderson .10 .30
431 Aramis Ramirez .10 .30
432 Todd Ritchie .10 .30
433 Pat Meares .10 .30
434 Warren Morris .10 .30
435 Derek Bell .10 .30
436 Ken Griffey Jr. .60 1.50
437 Elmer Dessens .10 .30
438 Ruben Rivera .10 .30
439 Jason LaRue .10 .30
440 Sean Casey .10 .30
441 Pete Harnisch .10 .30
442 Danny Graves .10 .30
443 Aaron Boone .10 .30
444 Dmitri Young .10 .30
445 Brandon Larson .10 .30
446 Pokey Reese .10 .30
447 Todd Walker .10 .30
448 Juan Castro .10 .30
449 Todd Helton .20 .50
450 Ben Petrick .10 .30
451 Juan Pierre .10 .30
452 Jeff Cirillo .10 .30
453 Juan Uribe .10 .30
454 Brian Bohanon .10 .30
455 Terry Shumpert .10 .30
456 Mike Hampton .10 .30
457 Shawn Chacon .10 .30
458 Adam Melhuse .10 .30
459 Greg Norton .10 .30
460 Gabe White .10 .30
461 Ichiro Suzuki WS .30 .75
462 Carlos Delgado WS .10 .30
463 Manny Ramirez WS .20 .50
464 Miguel Tejada WS .10 .30
465 Tsuyoshi Shinjo WS .10 .30
466 Bernie Williams WS .10 .30
467 Juan Gonzalez WS .10 .30
468 Andruw Jones WS .10 .30
469 Ivan Rodriguez WS .10 .30
470 Larry Walker WS .10 .30
471 Hideo Nomo WS .10 .30
472 Albert Pujols WS .30 .75
473 Pedro Martinez WS .20 .50
474 Vladimir Guerrero WS .20 .50
475 Tony Batista WS .10 .30
476 Kazuhiro Sasaki WS .10 .30
477 Richard Hidalgo WS .10 .30
478 Carlos Lee WS .10 .30
479 Roberto Alomar WS .10 .30
480 Rafael Palmeiro WS .10 .30
481 Ken Griffey Jr. GG .40 1.00
482 Ken Griffey Jr. GG .40 1.00
483 Ken Griffey Jr. GG .40 1.00
484 Ken Griffey Jr. GG .40 1.00
485 Ken Griffey Jr. GG .40 1.00
486 Ken Griffey Jr. GG .40 1.00
487 Ken Griffey Jr. GG .40 1.00
488 Ken Griffey Jr. GG .40 1.00
489 Ken Griffey Jr. GG .40 1.00
490 Ken Griffey Jr. GG .40 1.00
491 Barry Bonds CL .40 1.00
492 Hideo Nomo CL .10 .30
493 Ichiro Suzuki CL .30 .75
494 Cal Ripken CL .50 1.25
495 Tony Gwynn CL .20 .50
496 Randy Johnson CL .20 .50
497 A.J. Burnett CL .10 .30
498 Rickey Henderson CL .20 .50
499 Albert Pujols CL .30 .75
500 Luis Gonzalez CL .10 .30
501 Brandon Puffer SR RC .40 1.00
502 Rodrigo Rosario SR RC .40 1.00
503 Tom Shearn SR RC .40 1.00
504 Reed Johnson SR RC .60 1.50
505 Chris Baker SR RC .40 1.00
506 John Ennis SR RC .40 1.00
507 Luis Martinez SR RC .40 1.00
508 So Taguchi SR RC .60 1.50
509 Scotty Layfield SR RC .40 1.00
510 Francis Beltran SR RC .40 1.00
511 Brandon Backe SR RC .60 1.50
512 Doug Devore SR RC .40 1.00
513 Jeremy Ward SR RC .40 1.00
514 Jose Valverde SR RC 1.25 3.00
515 P.J. Bevis SR RC .40 1.00
516 Victor Alvarez SR RC .40 1.00
517 Kazuhisa Ishii SR RC .60 1.50
518 Jorge Nunez SR RC .40 1.00
519 Eric Good SR RC .40 1.00
520 Ron Calloway SR RC .40 1.00
521 Val Pascucci SR RC .40 1.00
522 Nelson Castro SR RC .40 1.00
523 Deivis Santos SR .40 1.00
524 Luis Ugueto SR RC .40 1.00
525 Matt Thornton SR RC .40 1.00
526 Hansel Izquierdo SR RC .40 1.00

527 Tyler Yates SR RC .40 1.00
528 Mark Corey SR RC .40 1.00
529 Jaime Cerda SR RC .40 1.00
530 Satoru Komiyama SR RC .40 1.00
531 Steve Bechler SR RC .40 1.00
532 Ben Howard SR RC .40 1.00
533 Anderson Machado SR RC .40 1.00
534 Jorge Padilla SR RC .40 1.00
535 Eric Junge SR RC .40 1.00
536 Adrian Burnside SR RC .40 1.00
537 Mike Gonzalez SR RC .40 1.00
538 Josh Hancock SR RC .50 1.25
539 Colin Young SR RC .40 1.00
540 Rene Reyes SR RC .40 1.00
541 Cam Esslinger SR RC .40 1.00
542 Tim Kalita SR RC .40 1.00
543 Kevin Frederick SR RC .40 1.00
544 Kyle Kane SR RC .40 1.00
545 Edwin Almonte SR RC .40 1.00
546 Aaron Sele .10 .30
547 Garret Anderson .10 .30
548 Darin Erstad .10 .30
549 Brad Fullmer .10 .30
550 Kevin Appier .10 .30
551 Tim Salmon .20 .50
552 David Justice .10 .30
553 Billy Koch .10 .30
554 Scott Hatteberg .10 .30
555 Tim Hudson .10 .30
556 Miguel Tejada .10 .30
557 Carlos Pena .10 .30
558 Mike Sirotka .10 .30
559 Jose Cruz Jr. .10 .30
560 Josh Phelps .10 .30
561 Brandon Lyon .10 .30
562 Luke Prokopec .10 .30
563 Felipe Lopez .10 .30
564 Jason Standridge .10 .30
565 Chris Gomez .10 .30
566 John Flaherty .10 .30
567 Jason Tyner .10 .30
568 Bobby Smith .10 .30
569 Wilson Alvarez .10 .30
570 Matt Lawton .10 .30
571 Omar Vizquel .20 .50
572 Jim Thome .20 .50
573 Brady Anderson .10 .30
574 Alex Escobar .10 .30
575 Russell Branyan .10 .30
576 Bret Boone .10 .30
577 Ben Davis .10 .30
578 Mike Cameron .10 .30
579 Jamie Moyer .10 .30
580 Ruben Sierra .10 .30
581 Jeff Cirillo .10 .30
582 Marty Cordova .10 .30
583 Mike Bordick .10 .30
584 Brian Roberts .10 .30
585 Luis Matos .10 .30
586 Geronimo Gil .10 .30
587 Jay Gibbons .10 .30
588 Carl Everett .10 .30
589 Ivan Rodriguez .20 .50
590 Chan Ho Park .10 .30
591 Juan Gonzalez .10 .30
592 Hank Blalock .20 .50
593 Todd Van Poppel .10 .30
594 Pedro Martinez .20 .50
595 Jason Varitek .30 .75
596 Tony Clark .10 .30
597 Johnny Damon Sox .20 .50
598 Dustin Hermanson .10 .30
599 John Burkett .10 .30
600 Carlos Beltran .10 .30
601 Mark Quinn .10 .30
602 Chuck Knoblauch .10 .30
603 Michael Tucker .10 .30
604 Carlos Febles .10 .30
605 Jose Rosado .10 .30
606 Dmitri Young .10 .30
607 Bobby Higginson .10 .30
608 Craig Paquette .10 .30
609 Mitch Meluskey .10 .30
610 Wendell Magee .10 .30
611 Mike Rivera .10 .30
612 Jacque Jones .10 .30
613 Luis Rivas .10 .30
614 Eric Milton .10 .30
615 Eddie Guardado .10 .30
616 Matt LeCroy .10 .30
617 Mike Jackson .10 .30
618 Magglio Ordonez .10 .30
619 Frank Thomas .30 .75
620 Rocky Biddle .10 .30
621 Paul Konerko .10 .30
622 Todd Ritchie .10 .30
623 Jon Rauch .10 .30
624 John Vander Wal .10 .30
625 Rondell White .10 .30
626 Jason Giambi .10 .30
627 Robin Ventura .10 .30
628 David Wells .10 .30
629 Bernie Williams .20 .50
630 Lance Berkman .10 .30
631 Richard Hidalgo .10 .30
632 Greg Zaun .10 .30
633 Jose Vizcaino .10 .30
634 Octavio Dotel .10 .30
635 Morgan Ensberg .10 .30
636 Andruw Jones .20 .50
637 Tom Glavine .20 .50
638 Gary Sheffield .10 .30
639 Vinny Castilla .10 .30
640 Javy Lopez .10 .30
641 Albie Lopez .10 .30
642 Geoff Jenkins .10 .30
643 Jeffrey Hammonds .10 .30
644 Alex Ochoa .10 .30
645 Richie Sexson .10 .30
646 Eric Young .10 .30
647 Glendon Rusch .10 .30
648 Tino Martinez .20 .50
649 Fernando Vina .10 .30
650 J.D. Drew .10 .30
651 Woody Williams .10 .30
652 Darryl Kile .10 .30
653 Jason Isringhausen .10 .30
654 Moises Alou .10 .30
655 Alex Gonzalez .10 .30
656 Delino DeShields .10 .30
657 Todd Hundley .10 .30
658 Chris Stynes .10 .30
659 Jason Bere .10 .30
660 Curt Schilling .10 .30
661 Craig Counsell .10 .30
662 Mark Grace .20 .50
663 Matt Williams .10 .30
664 Jay Bell .10 .30
665 Rick Helling .10 .30
666 Shawn Green .10 .30
667 Eric Karros .10 .30
668 Hideo Nomo .30 .75
669 Omar Daal .10 .30
670 Brian Jordan .10 .30
671 Cesar Izturis .10 .30
672 Fernando Tatis .10 .30
673 Lee Stevens .10 .30
674 Tomo Ohka .10 .30
675 Brian Schneider .10 .30
676 Brad Wilkerson .10 .30
677 Bruce Chen .10 .30
678 Tsuyoshi Shinjo .10 .30
679 Jeff Kent .10 .30
680 Kirk Rueter .10 .30
681 J.T. Snow .10 .30
682 David Bell .10 .30
683 Reggie Sanders .10 .30
684 Preston Wilson .10 .30
685 Vic Darensbourg .10 .30
686 Josh Beckett .10 .30
687 Pablo Ozuna .10 .30
688 Mike Redmond .10 .30
689 Scott Strickland .10 .30
690 Mo Vaughn .10 .30
691 Roberto Alomar .20 .50
692 Edgardo Alfonzo .10 .30
693 Shawn Estes .10 .30
694 Roger Cedeno .10 .30
695 Jeromy Burnitz .10 .30
696 Ray Lankford .10 .30
697 Mark Kotsay .10 .30
698 Kevin Jarvis .10 .30
699 Bobby Jones .10 .30
700 Sean Burroughs .10 .30
701 Ramon Vazquez .10 .30
702 Pat Burrell .10 .30
703 Marlon Byrd .10 .30
704 Brandon Duckworth .10 .30
705 Marlon Anderson .10 .30
706 Vicente Padilla .10 .30
707 Kip Wells .10 .30
708 Jason Kendall .10 .30
709 Pokey Reese .10 .30
710 Pat Meares .10 .30
711 Kris Benson .10 .30
712 Armando Rios .10 .30
713 Mike Williams .10 .30
714 Barry Larkin .20 .50
715 Adam Dunn .10 .30
716 Juan Encarnacion .10 .30
717 Scott Williamson .10 .30
718 Wilton Guerrero .10 .30
719 Chris Reitsma .10 .30
720 Larry Walker .10 .30
721 Denny Neagle .10 .30
722 Todd Zeile .10 .30
723 Jose Ortiz .10 .30
724 Jason Jennings .10 .30
725 Tony Eusebio .10 .30
726 Ichiro Suzuki YR .30 .75
727 Barry Bonds YR .40 1.00
728 Randy Johnson YR .20 .50
729 Albert Pujols YR .30 .75
730 Roger Clemens YR .30 .75
731 Sammy Sosa YR .20 .50
732 Alex Rodriguez YR .25 .60
733 Chipper Jones YR .20 .50
734 Rickey Henderson YR .20 .50
735 Ichiro Suzuki YR .30 .75
736 Luis Gonzalez SH CL .10 .30
737 Derek Jeter SH CL .40 1.00
738 Ichiro Suzuki SH CL .30 .75
739 Barry Bonds SH CL .40 1.00
740 Curt Schilling SH CL .10 .30
741 Shawn Green SH CL .10 .30
742 Jason Giambi SH CL .10 .30
743 Roberto Alomar SH CL .10 .30
744 Larry Walker SH CL .10 .30
745 Mark McGwire SH CL .40 1.00

2002 Upper Deck 2001 Greatest Hits

Issued into first series packs at a rate of one in 14, these 10 cards feature some of the leading hitters during the 2001 season.
COMPLETE SET (10) 15.00 40.00
SER.1 STATED ODDS 1:14
GH1 Barry Bonds 2.50 6.00
GH2 Ichiro Suzuki 2.00 5.00
GH3 Albert Pujols 2.00 5.00
GH4 Mike Piazza 1.50 4.00
GH5 Alex Rodriguez 1.25 3.00
GH6 Mark McGwire 2.50 6.00
GH7 Manny Ramirez 1.00 2.50
GH8 Ken Griffey Jr. 2.00 5.00
GH9 Sammy Sosa 1.00 2.50
GH10 Derek Jeter 2.50 6.00

2002 Upper Deck A Piece of History 500 Club

Randomly inserted in 2002 Upper Deck second series packs, this card features a bat slice from Mark McGwire and continues the Upper Deck A Piece of History set begun in 1999. Though lacking actual serial-numbering, according to Upper Deck this card was printed to a stated print run of 350 copies.
RANDOM INSERTS IN SER.2 PACKS
STATED PRINT RUN 350 SETS
MMC Mark McGwire 150.00 300.00

2002 Upper Deck A Piece of History 500 Club Autograph

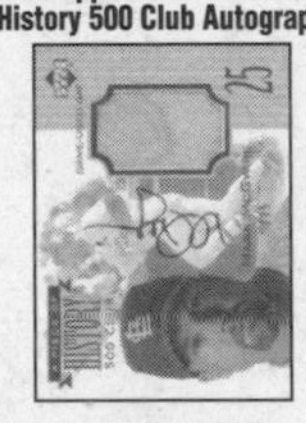

Randomly inserted in 2002 Upper Deck second series packs, this card features a bat slice from Mark McGwire and an authentic autograph and continues the Upper Deck A Piece of History set begun in 1999. This card was printed to a stated print run of 25 serial numbered sets.

2002 Upper Deck AL Centennial Memorabilia

Inserted into first series packs at a rate of one in 144, these 10 cards feature memorabilia from some of the leading players in American League history. The bat jersey cards were produced in smaller quantities than the jersey cards and we have notated those cards with SP's in our checklist.
SER.1 STATED ODDS 1:144
SP INFO PROVIDED BY UPPER DECK
ALBBR Babe Ruth Bat SP 30.00 80.00
ALBJD Joe DiMaggio Bat SP 40.00 80.00
ALBMM Mickey Mantle Bat SP 40.00 80.00
ALJAR Alex Rodriguez Jsy 6.00 15.00
ALJCR Cal Ripken Jsy 10.00 25.00
ALJFT Frank Thomas Jsy 6.00 15.00
ALJIR Ivan Rodriguez Jsy 6.00 15.00
ALJNR Nolan Ryan Jsy 10.00 25.00
ALJPM Pedro Martinez Jsy 6.00 15.00
ALJRA Roberto Alomar Jsy 6.00 15.00

2002 Upper Deck All-Star Home Run Derby Game Jersey

Inserted into first series packs at a rate of one in 288, these seven cards feature jersey swatches from these players who participated in the Home Run Derby. A couple of the jerseys were from regular use and we have notated that information in our checklist.
SER.1 STATED ODDS 1:288
HR DERBY SWATCHES UNLESS SPECIFIED
GOLD RANDOM INSERTS IN PACKS
GOLD PRINT RUN 25 SERIAL #'d SETS
NO GOLD PRICING DUE TO SCARCITY
ASAR Alex Rodriguez 10.00 25.00
ASBRB Bret Boone 6.00 15.00
ASJG1 Jason Giambi 6.00 15.00
ASJG2 Jason Giambi A's 6.00 15.00
ASSS1 Sammy Sosa 8.00 20.00
ASSS2 Sammy Sosa Cubs 8.00 20.00
ASTH Todd Helton 6.00 15.00

2002 Upper Deck All-Star Salute Game Jersey

Inserted into first series packs at a rate of one in 288, these nine cards feature game jersey swatches of some of the most exciting All-Star performers.
SER.1 STATED ODDS 1:288
GOLD RANDOM INSERTS IN PACKS
GOLD PRINT RUN 25 SERIAL #'d SETS
NO GOLD PRICING DUE TO SCARCITY
SJAR1 Alex Rodriguez Mariners 10.00 25.00
SJAR2 Alex Rodriguez Rangers 10.00 25.00
SJDE Dennis Eckersley 6.00 15.00
SJDS Don Sutton 6.00 15.00
SJIS Ichiro Suzuki 20.00 50.00
SJKG Ken Griffey Jr. 12.50 30.00
SJLB Lou Boudreau 6.00 15.00
SJNF Nellie Fox 6.00 15.00
SJSA Sparky Anderson 6.00 15.00

2002 Upper Deck Authentic McGwire

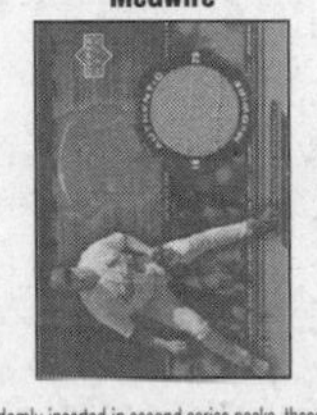

Randomly inserted in second series packs, these two cards feature authentic memorabilia from Mark McGwire's career. These cards have a stated print run of 70 serial numbered sets.
RANDOM INSERTS IN SER.2 PACKS
STATED PRINT RUN 70 SERIAL #'d SETS
AMB Mark McGwire Bat 12.00 30.00
AMJ Mark McGwire Jsy 12.00 30.00

2002 Upper Deck Big Fly Zone

Issued into first series packs at a rate of one in 14, these 10 cards feature some of the leading power hitters in the game.
COMPLETE SET (10) 12.50 30.00
SER.1 STATED ODDS 1:14
Z1 Mark McGwire 2.50 6.00
Z2 Ken Griffey Jr. 2.00 5.00
Z3 Manny Ramirez .60 1.50
Z4 Sammy Sosa 1.00 2.50
Z5 Todd Helton .60 1.50
Z6 Barry Bonds 2.50 6.00
Z7 Luis Gonzalez .60 1.50
Z8 Alex Rodriguez 1.25 3.00
Z9 Carlos Delgado .60 1.50
Z10 Chipper Jones 1.00 2.50

2002 Upper Deck Breakout Performers

Issued into first series packs at a rate of one in 14, these 10 cards feature players who had breakout seasons in 2001.
COMPLETE SET (10) 10.00 25.00
SER.1 STATED ODDS 1:14
BP1 Ichiro Suzuki 2.00 5.00
BP2 Albert Pujols 2.00 5.00
BP3 Doug Mientkiewicz .60 1.50
BP4 Lance Berkman .60 1.50
BP5 Tsuyoshi Shinjo .60 1.50
BP6 Ben Sheets .60 1.50
BP7 Jimmy Rollins .60 1.50
BP8 J.D. Drew .60 1.50
BP9 Bret Boone .60 1.50
BP10 Alfonso Soriano .60 1.50

2002 Upper Deck Championship Caliber

Inserted into first series packs at a rate of one in 23, these six cards feature players who have all earned World Series rings.
COMPLETE SET (6) 8.00 20.00
SER.1 STATED ODDS 1:23
CC1 Derek Jeter 2.50 6.00
CC2 Roberto Alomar .60 1.50
CC3 Chipper Jones 1.00 2.50
CC4 Gary Sheffield .60 1.50
CC5 Roger Clemens 2.00 5.00
CC6 Greg Maddux 1.50 4.00

2002 Upper Deck Championship Caliber Swatch

Inserted in second series packs at a stated rate of one in 288, these 14 cards feature not only players who have been on World Champions but also a game-worn swatch. A few players were issued in shorter supply and we have notated that information in our checklist.
SER.2 STATED ODDS 1:288
SP INFO PROVIDED BY UPPER DECK
AP Andy Pettitte 6.00 15.00
BL Barry Larkin 6.00 15.00
BW Bernie Williams 6.00 15.00
CF Cliff Floyd 4.00 10.00
CHJ Charles Johnson 4.00 10.00
CS Curt Schilling 4.00 10.00
JO John Olerud 4.00 10.00
JP Jorge Posada 6.00 15.00
KB Kevin Brown SP 6.00 15.00
RJ Randy Johnson 6.00 15.00
TM Tino Martinez 6.00 15.00

2002 Upper Deck Chasing History

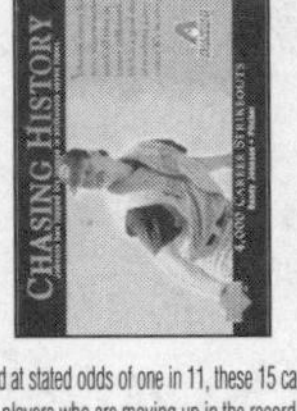

Inserted at stated odds of one in 11, these 15 cards feature players who are moving up in the record books.
COMPLETE SET (15) 15.00 40.00
SER.2 STATED ODDS 1:11
CH1 Sammy Sosa 1.25 3.00
CH2 Ken Griffey Jr. 2.50 6.00
CH3 Roger Clemens 2.50 6.00
CH4 Barry Bonds 3.00 8.00
CH5 Rafael Palmeiro .75 2.00
CH6 Andres Galarraga .75 2.00
CH7 Juan Gonzalez .75 2.00
CH8 Roberto Alomar .75 2.00
CH9 Randy Johnson 1.25 3.00
CH10 Jeff Bagwell .75 2.00
CH11 Fred McGriff .75 2.00
CH12 Matt Williams .75 2.00
CH13 Greg Maddux 2.00 5.00
CH14 Robb Nen .75 2.00
CH15 Kenny Lofton .75 2.00

2002 Upper Deck Combo Memorabilia

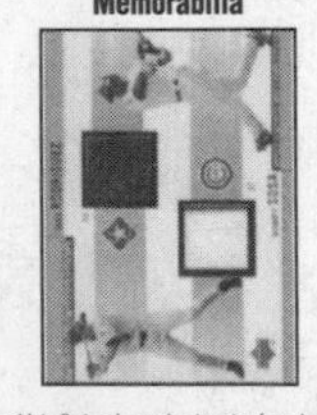

Issued into first series packs at a rate of one in 288, these seven cards feature two pieces of game-used memorabilia from players who have something in common.
SER.1 STATED ODDS 1:288
SP INFO PROVIDED BY UPPER DECK
GOLD RANDOM INSERTS IN PACKS
GOLD PRINT RUN 25 SERIAL #'d SETS
NO GOLD PRICING DUE TO SCARCITY
BDM DiMag Bat/Mantle Bat SP 40.00 100.00
BRG A.Rod Bat/Griffey Jr. Bat 10.00 25.00
JBS Bonds Jsy/S.Sosa Jsy 12.00 30.00
JHK Hasegawa Jsy/Kim Jsy 6.00 15.00
JRC Ryan Jsy/Clemens Jsy 10.00 25.00
JRM Ryan Jsy/Pedro Jsy 25.00 50.00
JRS A.Rod Jsy/Sosa Jsy 15.00 40.00

2002 Upper Deck Double Game Worn Gems

Randomly inserted in second series retail packs, these 12 cards feature two teammates along with pieces of game used memorabilia. These cards have a stated print run of 450 serial numbered sets, except for the Martinez/Ichiro card of which only 150 #'d copies were issued.
RANDOM INSERTS IN SERIES 2 RETAIL
STATED PRINT RUN 450 SERIAL #'d SETS
DGAP R.Alomar/M.Piazza 10.00 25.00
DGDF C.Delgado/S.Stewart 6.00 15.00
DGDH J.Dye/T.Hudson 6.00 15.00
DGGS L.Gonzalez/C.Schilling 6.00 15.00
DGKG J.Kendall/B.Giles 6.00 15.00
DGMM K.Millwood/G.Maddux 10.00 25.00
DGNK P.Nevin/R.Klesko 6.00 15.00
DGPL R.Person/M.Lieberthal 6.00 15.00
DGPN C.Park/H.Nomo 20.00 50.00
DGTO F.Thomas/M.Ordonez 8.00 20.00
DGVB O.Vizquel/R.Branyan 6.00 15.00

2002 Upper Deck Double Game Worn Gems Gold

RANDOM INSERTS IN SERIES 2 RETAIL
STATED PRINT RUN 100 SERIAL #'d SETS
DGAP R.Alomar/M.Piazza 20.00 50.00
DGDF C.Delgado/S.Stewart 12.50 30.00
DGDH J.Dye/T.Hudson 12.50 30.00
DGGS L.Gonzalez/C.Schilling 12.50 30.00
DGKG J.Kendall/B.Giles 12.50 30.00
DGMI E.Martinez/I.Suzuki SP/40 50.00 100.00
DGMM K.Millwood/G.Maddux 20.00 50.00
DGNK P.Nevin/R.Klesko 12.50 30.00
DGPL R.Person/M.Lieberthal 12.50 30.00
DGPN C.Park/H.Nomo 40.00 100.00
DGTO F.Thomas/M.Ordonez 15.00 40.00
DGVB O.Vizquel/R.Branyan 12.50 30.00

2002 Upper Deck First Timers Game Jersey

Inserted into first series hobby packs at a rate of one in 288 hobby packs, these nine cards feature players who have never been featured on a Upper Deck game jersey card before.
SER.1 STATED ODDS 1:288 HOBBY
FTAP Albert Pujols 20.00 50.00
FTCP Corey Patterson 4.00 10.00
FTEM Eric Milton 4.00 10.00
FTFG Freddy Garcia 4.00 10.00
FTJM Joe Mays 4.00 10.00
FTML Matt Lawton 4.00 10.00
FTOD Omar Daal 4.00 10.00
FTRB Russell Branyan 4.00 10.00
FTSS Shannon Stewart 4.00 10.00

2002 Upper Deck Game Base

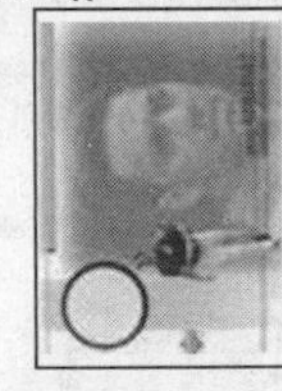

Inserted into first series packs at a rate of one in 288, these 22 cards feature authentic pieces of bases used in official Major League games.
SER.1 STATED ODDS 1:288
SP INFO PROVIDED BY UPPER DECK
BAJ Andruw Jones 6.00 15.00
BAR Alex Rodriguez 8.00 20.00
BBB Barry Bonds 12.50 30.00
BCD Carlos Delgado 4.00 10.00
BCJ Chipper Jones 6.00 15.00
BCR Cal Ripken 15.00 40.00
BDJ Derek Jeter 12.50 30.00
BIR Ivan Rodriguez 6.00 15.00
BIS Ichiro Suzuki 20.00 50.00
BJG Jason Giambi 4.00 10.00
BJG Juan Gonzalez 4.00 10.00
BKG Ken Griffey Jr. 8.00 20.00
BKS Kazuhiro Sasaki 4.00 10.00
BLG Luis Gonzalez 4.00 10.00
BMM Mark McGwire 20.00 50.00
BMP Mike Piazza 6.00 15.00
BRC Roger Clemens 10.00 25.00
BSG Shawn Green 4.00 10.00
BSS Sammy Sosa 6.00 15.00
BTG Troy Glaus 4.00 10.00
CBMJ McGwire 30.00 60.00
Jeter SP
CBRG A.Rod 15.00 40.00
Griffey Jr. SP

2002 Upper Deck Game Jersey

Randomly inserted in packs, these 11 cards feature some of today's star players along with a game-worn swatch of the featured player.
RANDOM INSERTS IN SER.2 HOBBY
STATED PRINT RUN 350 SERIAL #'d SETS
AB Adrian Beltre 4.00 10.00
CS Curt Schilling 4.00 10.00
FT Frank Thomas 6.00 15.00
JC Jeff Cirillo Pants 4.00 10.00
KG Ken Griffey Jr. 6.00 15.00
MP Mike Piazza Pants 6.00 15.00
PW Preston Wilson 4.00 10.00
SR Scott Rolen 4.00 10.00
SS Sammy Sosa 4.00 10.00
TB Tony Batista 4.00 10.00
TH Tim Hudson 4.00 10.00

2002 Upper Deck Game Jersey Autograph

Randomly inserted into first series hobby packs, these 12 cards feature not only a game jersey swatch but also an authentic autograph of the player featured. These cards are serial numbered to 200. The following players did not return their signed cards in time for release in the packs and those cards had an exchange deadline of November 19, 2004: Andruw Jones, Albert Pujols and Ken Griffey Jr.
RANDOM INSERTS IN SER.1 HOBBY PACKS
STATED PRINT RUN 200 SERIAL #'d SETS
EXCHANGE DEADLINE 11/19/04
JAJ Andruw Jones 20.00 50.00
JAP Albert Pujols 150.00 250.00
JBB Barry Bonds 40.00 80.00
JCD Carlos Delgado 8.00 20.00
JCR Cal Ripken 75.00 150.00
JGS Gary Sheffield 20.00 50.00
JIS Ichiro Suzuki 450.00 900.00
JJG Jason Giambi 8.00 20.00
JKG Ken Griffey Jr. 60.00 120.00
JNR Nolan Ryan 75.00 150.00
JPW Preston Wilson 8.00 20.00
JRF Rafael Furcal 8.00 20.00

2002 Upper Deck Game Jersey Patch

Inserted at a rate of one in 2,500 first series packs, these cards feature a jersey patch from the star players featured.
LOGO SER.1 STATED ODDS 1:2500
NUMBER SER.1 STATED ODDS 1:2500
STRIPES SER.1 STATED ODDS 1:2500
PLAR Alex Rodriguez L 40.00 80.00
PLBB Barry Bonds L 40.00 80.00
PLCR Cal Ripken L 60.00 120.00
PLJG Jason Giambi L 20.00 50.00
PLKG Ken Griffey Jr. L 50.00 120.00
PLPM Pedro Martinez L 40.00 80.00
PLSS Sammy Sosa L 40.00 80.00
PNAR Alex Rodriguez N 40.00 80.00
PNBB Barry Bonds N 40.00 80.00
PNCR Cal Ripken N 60.00 120.00
PNJG Jason Giambi N 20.00 50.00
PNKG Ken Griffey Jr. N 50.00 120.00
PNPM Pedro Martinez N 40.00 80.00
PNSS Sammy Sosa N 40.00 80.00
PSAR Alex Rodriguez S 40.00 80.00
PSBB Barry Bonds S 40.00 80.00
PSCR Cal Ripken S 60.00 120.00
PSJG Jason Giambi S 20.00 50.00
PSKG Ken Griffey Jr. S 50.00 120.00
PSPM Pedro Martinez S 40.00 80.00
PSSS Sammy Sosa S 40.00 80.00

2002 Upper Deck Game Worn Gems

Inserted in second series retail packs at a stated rate of one in 48 retail packs, these 31 cards feature leading stars along a game-used memorabilia piece. A few cards were issued in shorter supply and those cards are notated in our checklist with an SP. Cards notated with an SP are not priced due to market scarcity.
SER.2 STATED ODDS 1:48 RETAIL
SP INFO PROVIDED BY UPPER DECK
NO SP PRICING DUE TO SCARCITY
GAS Aaron Sele 4.00 10.00
GCD Carlos Delgado 4.00 10.00
GCJ Chipper Jones 6.00 15.00
GCR Cal Ripken 20.00 50.00
GCS Curt Schilling 4.00 10.00
GEC Eric Chavez 4.00 10.00
GEM Edgar Martinez 6.00 15.00
GEM Eric Milton 4.00 10.00
GFT Frank Thomas 6.00 15.00
GGM Greg Maddux 6.00 15.00
GIR Ivan Rodriguez 6.00 15.00
GJG Juan Gonzalez 4.00 10.00
GJK Jason Kendall 4.00 10.00
GJM Joe Mays 4.00 10.00
GPN Phil Nevin 4.00 10.00
GRA Roberto Alomar 6.00 15.00
GRP Robert Person 4.00 10.00
GRY Robin Yount 6.00 15.00
GSR Scott Rolen 6.00 15.00
GTG Tom Glavine 6.00 15.00
GTM Tino Martinez 6.00 15.00

02 Upper Deck Global Swatch Game Jersey

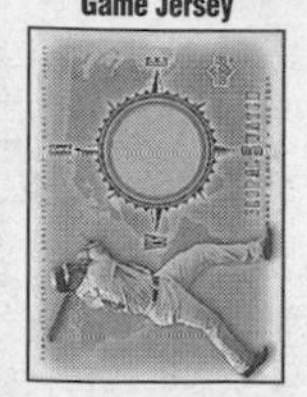

ed at a rate of one in 144 first series packs, these ards feature swatches of game jerseys worn by ers who were born outside the continental United es.

.1 STATED ODDS 1:144

Card	Low	High
K Byung-Hyun Kim	4.00	10.00
D Carlos Delgado	4.00	10.00
P Chan Ho Park	4.00	10.00
N Hideo Nomo	10.00	25.00
S Ichiro Suzuki	10.00	25.00
S Kazuhiro Sasaki	4.00	10.00
MR Manny Ramirez	6.00	15.00
Y Masato Yoshii	4.00	10.00
H Shigetoshi Hasegawa	4.00	10.00
S Tsuyoshi Shinjo	4.00	10.00

2002 Upper Deck Peoples Choice Game Jersey

erted in second series hobby packs at a stated rate ne in 24, these 39 cards feature some of the most ular player in baseball along with a game-worn morablila swatch. A few cards were in lesser ntity and we have notated those cards with an SP ur checklist.

.2 STATED ODDS 1:24 HOBBY
INFO PROVIDED BY UPPER DECK

Card	Low	High
G Andres Galarraga SP	6.00	15.00
P Andy Pettitte	6.00	15.00
R Alex Rodriguez	6.00	15.00
G Brian Giles	4.00	10.00
W Bernie Williams	6.00	15.00
D Carlos Delgado	4.00	10.00
J Charles Johnson	4.00	10.00
S Curt Schilling	4.00	10.00
DL Derek Lowe	4.00	10.00
W David Wells	4.00	10.00
B Ellis Burks SP	6.00	15.00
T Frank Thomas	6.00	15.00
GM Greg Maddux	6.00	15.00
I Hideki Irabu	4.00	10.00
JG Juan Gonzalez	4.00	10.00
JN Jeff Nelson	4.00	10.00
JS J.T. Snow	4.00	10.00
JBA Jeff Bagwell	6.00	15.00
JBU Jeromy Burnitz	4.00	10.00
KG Ken Griffey Jr.	8.00	20.00
MP Mike Piazza	6.00	15.00
MS Mike Stanton	4.00	10.00
MW Matt Williams SP	6.00	15.00
MRA Manny Ramirez	6.00	15.00
MRI Mariano Rivera	6.00	15.00
OD Omar Daal	4.00	10.00
OV Omar Vizquel	6.00	15.00
RF Rafael Furcal	4.00	10.00
RO Rey Ordonez	4.00	10.00
RP Rafael Palmeiro SP	10.00	25.00
RP Robert Person SP	6.00	15.00
RV Robin Ventura	4.00	10.00
SH Sterling Hitchcock	4.00	10.00
SS Sammy Sosa	6.00	15.00
TG Tony Gwynn	6.00	15.00
TM Tino Martinez	6.00	15.00
TR Tim Raines Sr.	4.00	10.00
TS Tim Salmon	6.00	15.00
TSh Tsuyoshi Shinjo	4.00	10.00

2002 Upper Deck Return of the Ace

serted into second series packs at a stated rate of e in 11 packs, these 15 cards feature some of day's leading pitchers.

Card	Low	High
MPLETE SET (15)	12.50	30.00
R.2 STATED ODDS 1:11		
1 Randy Johnson	1.25	3.00
2 Greg Maddux	2.00	5.00
3 Pedro Martinez	.75	2.00
4 Freddy Garcia	.75	2.00
5 Matt Morris	.75	2.00
6 Mark Mulder	.75	2.00
RA7 Wade Miller	.75	2.00
RA8 Kevin Brown	.75	2.00
RA9 Roger Clemens	2.50	6.00
RA10 Jon Lieber	.75	2.00
RA11 C.C. Sabathia	.75	2.00
RA12 Tim Hudson	.75	2.00
RA13 Curt Schilling	.75	2.00
RA14 Al Leiter	.75	2.00
RA15 Mike Mussina	.75	2.00

2002 Upper Deck Sons of Summer Game Jersey

Inserted at a stated rate of one in 288 second series packs, these eight cards feature some of the best players in the game along with a game jersey swatch. According to Upper Deck, the Pedro Martinez card was issued in shorter supply.

SER.2 STATED ODDS 1:288
SP INFO PROVIDED BY UPPER DECK

Card	Low	High
SSAR Alex Rodriguez	8.00	20.00
SSGM Greg Maddux	8.00	20.00
SSJB Jeff Bagwell	8.00	20.00
SSJG Juan Gonzalez	6.00	15.00
SSMP Mike Piazza	8.00	20.00
SSPM Pedro Martinez SP	10.00	25.00
SSRA Roberto Alomar	8.00	20.00
SSRC Roger Clemens	12.50	30.00

2002 Upper Deck Superstar Summit I

Inserted into first series packs at a rate of one in 23, these six cards feature the most popular players in the game.

Card	Low	High
COMPLETE SET (6)	10.00	25.00
SER.1 STATED ODDS 1:23		
SS1 Sammy Sosa	1.50	4.00
SS2 Alex Rodriguez	1.25	3.00
SS3 Mark McGwire	2.50	6.00
SS4 Barry Bonds	2.50	6.00
SS5 Mike Piazza	1.50	4.00
SS6 Ken Griffey Jr.	2.00	5.00

2002 Upper Deck Superstar Summit II

Inserted into second series packs at a rate of one in 11, these fifteen cards feature the most popular players in the game.

Card	Low	High
COMPLETE SET (15)	25.00	60.00
SER.2 STATED ODDS 1:11		
SS1 Alex Rodriguez	1.50	4.00
SS2 Jason Giambi	1.25	3.00
SS3 Vladimir Guerrero	1.25	3.00
SS4 Randy Johnson	1.25	3.00
SS5 Chipper Jones	1.25	3.00
SS6 Ichiro Suzuki	2.50	6.00
SS7 Sammy Sosa	1.25	3.00
SS8 Greg Maddux	2.00	5.00
SS9 Ken Griffey Jr.	2.50	6.00
SS10 Todd Helton	1.25	3.00
SS11 Barry Bonds	3.00	8.00
SS12 Derek Jeter	3.00	8.00
SS13 Mike Piazza	2.00	5.00
SS14 Ivan Rodriguez	1.25	3.00
SS15 Frank Thomas	1.25	3.00

2002 Upper Deck UD Plus Hobby

Issued as a two-card box topper in second series Upper Deck packs, these 100 cards could be exchanged for Joe DiMaggio or Mickey Mantle jersey cards if a collector finished the entire set. These cards were numbered to a stated print run of 1125 serial numbered sets. Hobby cards feature silver foil accents on front (unlike the Retail UD Plus cards - of which feature bronze fronts and backs). These cards could be exchanged until May 16, 2003.

ONE 2-CARD PACK PER SER.2 HOBBY BOX
STATED PRINT RUN 1125 SERIAL #'d SETS
COMP.SET CAN BE EXCH.FOR JSY CARD
HOBBY CARDS ARE SILVER

Card	Low	High
UD1 Darin Erstad	2.00	5.00
UD2 Troy Glaus	2.00	5.00
UD3 Tim Hudson	2.00	5.00
UD4 Jermaine Dye	2.00	5.00
UD5 Barry Zito	2.00	5.00
UD6 Carlos Delgado	2.00	5.00
UD7 Shannon Stewart	2.00	5.00
UD8 Greg Vaughn	2.00	5.00
UD9 Jim Thome	2.00	5.00
UD10 C.C. Sabathia	2.00	5.00
UD11 Ichiro Suzuki	5.00	12.00
UD12 Edgar Martinez	2.00	5.00
UD13 Bret Boone	2.00	5.00
UD14 Freddy Garcia	2.00	5.00
UD15 Matt Thornton	2.00	5.00
UD16 Jeff Conine	2.00	5.00
UD17 Steve Bechler	2.00	5.00
UD18 Rafael Palmeiro	2.00	5.00
UD19 Juan Gonzalez	2.00	5.00
UD20 Alex Rodriguez	3.00	8.00
UD21 Ivan Rodriguez	2.00	5.00
UD22 Carl Everett	2.00	5.00
UD23 Manny Ramirez	2.00	5.00
UD24 Nomar Garciaparra	4.00	10.00
UD25 Pedro Martinez	2.00	5.00
UD26 Mike Sweeney	2.00	5.00
UD27 Chuck Knoblauch	2.00	5.00
UD28 Dmitri Young	2.00	5.00
UD29 Bobby Higginson	2.00	5.00
UD30 Dean Palmer	2.00	5.00
UD31 Doug Mientkiewicz	2.00	5.00
UD32 Corey Koskie	2.00	5.00
UD33 Brad Radke	2.00	5.00
UD34 Cristian Guzman	2.00	5.00
UD35 Frank Thomas	2.50	6.00
UD36 Magglio Ordonez	2.00	5.00
UD37 Carlos Lee	2.00	5.00
UD38 Roger Clemens	5.00	12.00
UD39 Bernie Williams	2.00	5.00
UD40 Derek Jeter	6.00	15.00
UD41 Jason Giambi	2.00	5.00
UD42 Mike Mussina	2.00	5.00
UD43 Jeff Bagwell	2.00	5.00
UD44 Lance Berkman	2.00	5.00
UD45 Wade Miller	2.00	5.00
UD46 Greg Maddux	4.00	10.00
UD47 Chipper Jones	2.50	6.00
UD48 Andruw Jones	2.00	5.00
UD49 Gary Sheffield	2.00	5.00
UD50 Richie Sexson	2.00	5.00
UD51 Albert Pujols	5.00	12.00
UD52 J.D. Drew	2.00	5.00
UD53 Matt Morris	2.00	5.00
UD54 Jim Edmonds	2.00	5.00
UD55 So Taguchi	2.00	5.00
UD56 Sammy Sosa	2.50	6.00
UD57 Fred McGriff	2.00	5.00
UD58 Kerry Wood	2.00	5.00
UD59 Moises Alou	2.00	5.00
UD60 Randy Johnson	2.50	6.00
UD61 Luis Gonzalez	2.00	5.00
UD62 Mark Grace	2.00	5.00
UD63 Curt Schilling	2.00	5.00
UD64 Matt Williams	2.00	5.00
UD65 Kevin Brown	2.00	5.00
UD66 Brian Jordan	2.00	5.00
UD67 Shawn Green	2.00	5.00
UD68 Hideo Nomo	5.00	12.00
UD69 Kazuhisa Ishii	2.00	5.00
UD70 Vladimir Guerrero	2.50	6.00
UD71 Jose Vidro	2.00	5.00
UD72 Eric Good	2.00	5.00
UD73 Barry Bonds	6.00	15.00
UD74 Jeff Kent	2.00	5.00
UD75 Rich Aurilia	2.00	5.00
UD76 Deivis Santos	2.00	5.00
UD77 Preston Wilson	2.00	5.00
UD78 Cliff Floyd	2.00	5.00
UD79 Josh Beckett	2.00	5.00
UD80 Hansel Izquierdo	2.00	5.00
UD81 Mike Piazza	4.00	10.00
UD82 Roberto Alomar	2.00	5.00
UD83 Mo Vaughn	2.00	5.00
UD84 Jeromy Burnitz	2.00	5.00
UD85 Phil Nevin	2.00	5.00
UD86 Ryan Klesko	2.00	5.00
UD87 Bobby Abreu	2.00	5.00
UD88 Scott Rolen	2.00	5.00
UD89 Jimmy Rollins	2.00	5.00
UD90 Jason Kendall	2.00	5.00
UD91 Brian Giles	2.00	5.00
UD92 Aramis Ramirez	2.00	5.00
UD93 Ken Griffey Jr.	5.00	12.00
UD94 Sean Casey	2.00	5.00
UD95 Barry Larkin	2.00	5.00
UD96 Adam Dunn	2.00	5.00
UD97 Todd Helton	2.00	5.00
UD98 Larry Walker	2.00	5.00
UD99 Mike Hampton	2.00	5.00
UD100 Rene Reyes	2.00	5.00

2002 Upper Deck UD Plus Memorabilia Moments Game Uniform

These cards were available only through a mail exchange. Collectors who finished the UD Plus set earliest had an opportunity to receive cards with game-used jersey swatches of either Mickey Mantle or Joe DiMaggio. These cards were issued to a stated print run of 25 serial numbred sets. The deadline to redeem these cards was 5/16/03. Due to market scarcity, no pricing will be provided for these cards.

Card	Low	High
COMMON DIMAGGIO (1-5)	60.00	120.00
COMMON MANTLE (1-5)	100.00	200.00

AVAILABLE VIA MAIL EXCHANGE
STATED PRINT RUN 25 SERIAL #'d SETS

2002 Upper Deck World Series Heroes Memorabilia

Issued into first series packs at a rate of one in 288 hobby packs, these eight cards feature memorabilia from players who had star moments in the World Series.

SER.1 STATED ODDS 1:288 HOBBY
SP INFO PROVIDED BY UPPER DECK

Card	Low	High
BDJ Derek Jeter Base SP	10.00	25.00
BES Enos Slaughter Bat	6.00	15.00
BJD Joe DiMaggio Bat SP	50.00	100.00
BKP Kirby Puckett Bat	10.00	25.00
BMM Mickey Mantle Bat	30.00	80.00
SBM Bill Mazeroski Jsy	15.00	40.00
SCF Carlton Fisk Jsy	8.00	20.00
SDL Don Larsen Jsy	8.00	20.00
SJC Joe Carter Jsy	6.00	15.00

2002 Upper Deck Yankee Dynasty Memorabilia

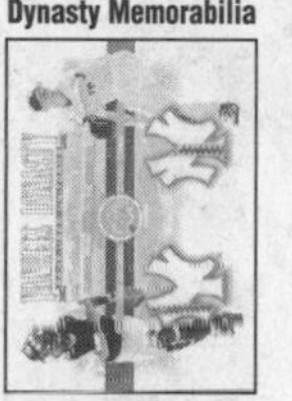

Issued into first series packs at a rate of one in 144, these 13 cards feature two pieces of game-worn memorabilia from various members of the Yankees Dynasty.

SER.1 STATED ODDS 1:144
SP INFO PROVIDED BY UPPER DECK

Card	Low	High
YBCJ Clemens/Jeter Base SP	75.00	150.00
YBJW Jeter/Bernie Base SP	30.00	60.00
YJBJ S.Brosius/D.Justice Jsy	10.00	25.00
YJBT W.Boggs/J.Torre Jsy	10.00	25.00
YJCP R.Clemens/J.Posada Jsy	10.00	25.00
YJDM J.DiMag/M.Mantle Jsy	75.00	150.00
YJGC J.Girardi/D.Cone Jsy	10.00	25.00
YJKR C.Knoblauch/T.Raines Jsy	10.00	25.00
YJOM P.O'Neill/T.Martinez Jsy	10.00	25.00
YJPR A.Pettitte/M.Rivera Jsy	12.00	30.00
YJRK W.Randolph/C.Knob Jsy	10.00	25.00
YJWG D.Wells/D.Gooden Jsy	10.00	25.00
YJWO B.Williams/P.O'Neill Jsy	10.00	25.00

2002 Upper Deck Ichiro Mini Playmaker

This five card standard-size set features Japanese sensation Ichiro Suzuki. The fronts have the "Mini Play-maker" logo on the upper left and this set was issued by Upper Deck Collectibles. The fronts have the 51 Ichiro on the bottom, while the backs have some information about Ichiro's sensational 2001 rookie season.

Card	Low	High
COMPLETE SET	8.00	20.00
COMMON CARD	1.50	4.00

2002 Upper Deck Mark McGwire Employee Game Jersey

This one card set features Upper Deck spokesperson Mark McGwire. The front has two photos of McGwire along with a game-worn jersey swatch while the back has some words thanking the UD employees for their hard work. This card was issued to a stated print run of 350 serial numbered sets and was distributed as a bonus to Upper Deck employees.

Card	Low	High
UDCMM Mark McGwire		150.00

2002 Upper Deck Mark McGwire Holiday Card

This one-card set, which measures 3" by 5" features a photo of Mark McGwire on the front hitting a snowball, while the back gives Upper Deck's message that everyone should enjoy a happy holiday season.

Card	Low	High
1 Mark McGwire	2.00	5.00

2002 Upper Deck Twizzlers

Card	Low	High
3 Nomar Garciaparra	1.00	2.50
4 Nomar Garciaparra	1.00	2.50

2003 Upper Deck

The 270 card first series was released in November, 2002. The 270 card second series was released in June, 2003. The final 60 cards were released as part of an special boxed insert in the 2004 Upper Deck Series one product. The first tw series cards were issued in eight card packs which came 24 packs to a box and 12 boxes to a case with an SRP of $3 per pack. Cards numbered from 1 through 30 featured leading rookie prospects while cards numbered from 261 through 270 featured checklist cards honoring the leading events of the 2002 season. In the second series the following subsets were issued: Cards numbered 501 through 530 feature Star Rookies while cards numbered 531 through 540 feature Season Highlight fronts and checklist backs. Due to an error in printing, card 19 was originally intended to feature Marcos Scutaro but the card was erroneosuly numbered as card 96. Thus, the set features two card 96's (Scutaro and Nomar Garciaparra) and no card number 19.

Card	Low	High
COMPLETE SET (540)	25.00	50.00
COMPLETE SERIES 1 (270)	8.00	20.00
COMPLETE SERIES 2 (270)	8.00	20.00
COMP.UPDATE SET (60)	5.00	12.00
COMMON (31-500/531-600)	.12	.30
COMMON (1-30/347/501-530)	.40	1.00
COMMON RC (541-600)	.20	.50

SR 1-30/501-530 ARE NOT SHORT PRINTS
CARD 19 DOES NOT EXIST
SCUTARO/NOMAR ARE BOTH CARD 96
541-600 ISSUED IN 04 UD1 HOBBY BOXES
UPDATE SET EXCH 1:240 '04 UD1 RETAIL
UPDATE SET EXCH.DEADLINE 11/10/06

Card	Low	High
1 John Lackey SR	.60	1.50
2 Alex Cintron SR	.40	1.00
3 Jose Leon SR	.40	1.00
4 Bobby Hill SR	.40	1.00
5 Brandon Larson SR	.40	1.00
6 Raul Gonzalez SR	.40	1.00
7 Ben Broussard SR	.40	1.00
8 Earl Snyder SR	.40	1.00
9 Ramon Santiago SR	.40	1.00
10 Jason Lane SR	.40	1.00
11 Keith Ginter SR	.40	1.00
12 Kirk Saarloos SR	.40	1.00
13 Juan Brito SR	.40	1.00
14 Runelvys Hernandez SR	.40	1.00
15 Shawn Sedlacek SR	.40	1.00
16 Jayson Durocher SR	.40	1.00
17 Kevin Frederick SR	.40	1.00
18 Zach Day SR	.40	1.00
20 Marcus Thames SR	.40	1.00
21 Esteban German SR	.40	1.00
22 Brett Myers SR	.40	1.00
23 Oliver Perez SR	.40	1.00
24 Dennis Tankersley SR	.40	1.00
25 Julius Matos SR	.40	1.00
26 Jake Peavy SR	.40	1.00
27 Eric Cyr SR	.40	1.00
28 Mike Crudale SR	.40	1.00
29 Josh Pearce SR	.40	1.00
30 Carl Crawford SR	.60	1.50
31 Tim Salmon	.12	.30
32 Troy Glaus	.12	.30
33 Adam Kennedy	.12	.30
34 David Eckstein	.12	.30
35 Ben Molina	.12	.30
36 Jarrod Washburn	.12	.30
37 Ramon Ortiz	.12	.30
38 Eric Chavez	.12	.30
39 Miguel Tejada	.20	.50
40 Adam Piatt	.12	.30
41 Jermaine Dye	.12	.30
42 Olmedo Saenz	.12	.30
43 Tim Hudson	.20	.50
44 Barry Zito	.20	.50
45 Billy Koch	.12	.30
46 Shannon Stewart	.12	.30
47 Kelvim Escobar	.12	.30
48 Jose Cruz Jr.	.12	.30
49 Vernon Wells	.12	.30
50 Roy Halladay	.20	.50
51 Esteban Loaiza	.12	.30
52 Eric Hinske	.12	.30
53 Steve Cox	.12	.30
54 Brent Abernathy	.12	.30
55 Ben Grieve	.12	.30
56 Aubrey Huff	.12	.30
57 Jared Sandberg	.12	.30
58 Paul Wilson	.12	.30
59 Tanyon Sturtze	.12	.30
60 Jim Thome	.20	.50
61 Omar Vizquel	.20	.50
62 C.C. Sabathia	.20	.50
63 Chris Magruder	.12	.30
64 Ricky Gutierrez	.12	.30
65 Einar Diaz	.12	.30
66 Danys Baez	.12	.30
67 Ichiro Suzuki	.40	1.00
68 Ruben Sierra	.12	.30
69 Carlos Guillen	.12	.30
70 Mark McLemore	.12	.30
71 Dan Wilson	.12	.30
72 Jamie Moyer	.12	.30
73 Joel Pineiro	.12	.30
74 Edgar Martinez	.20	.50
75 Tony Batista	.12	.30
76 Jay Gibbons	.12	.30
77 Chris Singleton	.12	.30
78 Melvin Mora	.12	.30
79 Geronimo Gil	.12	.30
80 Rodrigo Lopez	.12	.30
81 Jorge Julio	.12	.30
82 Rafael Palmeiro	.20	.50
83 Juan Gonzalez	.12	.30
84 Mike Young	.12	.30
85 Hideki Irabu	.12	.30
86 Chan Ho Park	.20	.50
87 Kevin Mench	.12	.30
88 Doug Davis	.12	.30
89 Pedro Martinez	.20	.50
90 Shea Hillenbrand	.12	.30
91 Derek Lowe	.12	.30
92 Jason Varitek	.30	.75
93 Tony Clark	.12	.30
94 John Burkett	.12	.30
95 Frank Castillo	.12	.30
96A Nomar Garciaparra	.20	.50
96B Marcos Scutaro SR	2.50	6.00
97 Rickey Henderson	.30	.75
98 Mike Sweeney	.12	.30
99 Carlos Febles	.12	.30
100 Mark Quinn	.12	.30
101 Raul Ibanez	.20	.50
102 A.J. Hinch	.12	.30
103 Paul Byrd	.12	.30
104 Chuck Knoblauch	.12	.30
105 Dmitri Young	.12	.30
106 Randall Simon	.12	.30
107 Brandon Inge	.12	.30
108 Damion Easley	.12	.30
109 Carlos Pena	.20	.50
110 George Lombard	.12	.30
111 Juan Acevedo	.12	.30
112 Torii Hunter	.12	.30
113 Doug Mientkiewicz	.12	.30
114 David Ortiz	.30	.75
115 Eric Milton	.12	.30
116 Eddie Guardado	.12	.30
117 Cristian Guzman	.12	.30
118 Corey Koskie	.12	.30
119 Magglio Ordonez	.20	.50
120 Mark Buehrle	.20	.50
121 Todd Ritchie	.12	.30
122 Jose Valentin	.12	.30
123 Paul Konerko	.20	.50
124 Carlos Lee	.12	.30
125 Jon Garland	.12	.30
126 Jason Giambi	.12	.30
127 Derek Jeter	.75	2.00
128 Roger Clemens	.40	1.00
129 Raul Mondesi	.12	.30
130 Jorge Posada	.20	.50
131 Rondell White	.12	.30
132 Robin Ventura	.12	.30
133 Mike Mussina	.20	.50
134 Jeff Bagwell	.20	.50
135 Craig Biggio	.20	.50
136 Morgan Ensberg	.12	.30
137 Richard Hidalgo	.12	.30
138 Brad Ausmus	.12	.30
139 Roy Oswalt	.20	.50
140 Carlos Hernandez	.12	.30
141 Shane Reynolds	.12	.30
142 Gary Sheffield	.12	.30
143 Andruw Jones	.12	.30
144 Tom Glavine	.20	.50
145 Rafael Furcal	.12	.30
146 Javy Lopez	.12	.30
147 Vinny Castilla	.12	.30
148 Marcus Giles	.12	.30
149 Kevin Millwood	.12	.30
150 Jason Marquis	.12	.30
151 Ruben Quevedo	.12	.30
152 Ben Sheets	.12	.30
153 Geoff Jenkins	.12	.30
154 Jose Hernandez	.12	.30
155 Glendon Rusch	.12	.30
156 Jeffrey Hammonds	.12	.30
157 Alex Sanchez	.12	.30
158 Jim Edmonds	.20	.50
159 Tino Martinez	.12	.30
160 Albert Pujols	.40	1.00
161 Eli Marrero	.12	.30
162 Woody Williams	.12	.30
163 Fernando Vina	.12	.30
164 Jason Isringhausen	.12	.30
165 Jason Simontacchi	.12	.30
166 Kerry Robinson	.12	.30
167 Sammy Sosa	.30	.75
168 Juan Cruz	.12	.30
169 Fred McGriff	.20	.50
170 Antonio Alfonseca	.12	.30
171 Jon Lieber	.12	.30
172 Mark Prior	.20	.50
173 Moises Alou	.12	.30
174 Matt Clement	.12	.30
175 Mark Bellhorn	.12	.30
176 Randy Johnson	.30	.75
177 Luis Gonzalez	.12	.30
178 Tony Womack	.12	.30
179 Mark Grace	.20	.50
180 Junior Spivey	.12	.30
181 Byung Hyun Kim	.12	.30
182 Danny Bautista	.12	.30
183 Brian Anderson	.12	.30
184 Shawn Green	.12	.30
185 Brian Jordan	.12	.30
186 Eric Karros	.12	.30
187 Andy Ashby	.12	.30
188 Cesar Izturis	.12	.30
189 Dave Roberts	.20	.50
190 Eric Gagne	.12	.30
191 Kazuhisa Ishii	.12	.30
192 Adrian Beltre	.30	.75
193 Vladimir Guerrero	.20	.50
194 Tony Armas Jr.	.12	.30
195 Bartolo Colon	.12	.30
196 Troy O'Leary	.12	.30
197 Tomo Ohka	.12	.30
198 Brad Wilkerson	.12	.30
199 Orlando Cabrera	.12	.30
200 Barry Bonds	.50	1.25
201 David Bell	.12	.30
202 Tsuyoshi Shinjo	.12	.30
203 Benito Santiago	.12	.30
204 Livan Hernandez	.12	.30
205 Jason Schmidt	.12	.30
206 Kirk Rueter	.12	.30
207 Ramon E. Martinez	.12	.30
208 Mike Lowell	.12	.30
209 Luis Castillo	.12	.30
210 Derrek Lee	.12	.30
211 Andy Fox	.12	.30
212 Eric Owens	.12	.30
213 Charles Johnson	.12	.30
214 Brad Penny	.12	.30
215 A.J. Burnett	.12	.30
216 Edgardo Alfonzo	.12	.30
217 Roberto Alomar	.20	.50
218 Rey Ordonez	.12	.30
219 Al Leiter	.12	.30
220 Roger Cedeno	.12	.30
221 Timo Perez	.12	.30
222 Jeromy Burnitz	.12	.30
223 Pedro Astacio	.12	.30
224 Joe McEwing	.12	.30
225 Ryan Klesko	.12	.30
226 Ramon Vazquez	.12	.30
227 Mark Kotsay	.12	.30
228 Bubba Trammell	.12	.30
229 Wiki Gonzalez	.12	.30
230 Trevor Hoffman	.20	.50
231 Ron Gant	.12	.30
232 Bob Abreu	.12	.30
233 Marlon Anderson	.12	.30
234 Jeremy Giambi	.12	.30
235 Jimmy Rollins	.20	.50
236 Mike Lieberthal	.12	.30
237 Vicente Padilla	.12	.30
238 Randy Wolf	.12	.30
239 Pokey Reese	.12	.30
240 Brian Giles	.12	.30
241 Jack Wilson	.12	.30
242 Mike Williams	.12	.30
243 Kip Wells	.12	.30
244 Rob Mackowiak	.12	.30
245 Craig Wilson	.12	.30
246 Adam Dunn	.20	.50
247 Sean Casey	.12	.30
248 Todd Walker	.12	.30
249 Corky Miller	.12	.30
250 Ryan Dempster	.12	.30
251 Reggie Taylor	.12	.30
252 Aaron Boone	.12	.30
253 Larry Walker	.20	.50
254 Jose Ortiz	.12	.30
255 Todd Zeile	.12	.30
256 Bobby Estalella	.12	.30
257 Juan Pierre	.12	.30
258 Terry Shumpert	.12	.30
259 Mike Hampton	.12	.30
260 Denny Stark	.12	.30
261 Shawn Green SH CL	.12	.30
262 Derek Lowe SH CL	.12	.30
263 Barry Bonds SH CL	.50	1.25
264 Mike Cameron SH CL	.12	.30
265 Luis Castillo SH CL	.12	.30
266 Vladimir Guerrero SH CL	.20	.50
267 Jason Giambi SH CL	.12	.30
268 Eric Gagne SH CL	.12	.30
269 Magglio Ordonez SH CL	.20	.50
270 Jim Thome SH CL	.20	.50
271 Garret Anderson	.12	.30

272 Troy Percival .12 .30
273 Brad Fullmer .12 .30
274 Scott Spiezio .12 .30
275 Darin Erstad .12 .30
276 Francisco Rodriguez .20 .50
277 Kevin Appier .12 .30
278 Shawn Wooten .12 .30
279 Eric Owens .12 .30
280 Scott Hatteberg .12 .30
281 Terrence Long .12 .30
282 Mark Mulder .12 .30
283 Ramon Hernandez .12 .30
284 Ted Lilly .12 .30
285 Erubiel Durazo .12 .30
286 Mark Ellis .12 .30
287 Carlos Delgado .12 .30
288 Orlando Hudson .12 .30
289 Chris Woodward .12 .30
290 Mark Hendrickson .12 .30
291 Josh Phelps .12 .30
292 Ken Huckaby .12 .30
293 Justin Miller .12 .30
294 Travis Lee .12 .30
295 Jorge Sosa .12 .30
296 Joe Kennedy .12 .30
297 Carl Crawford .20 .50
298 Toby Hall .12 .30
299 Rey Ordonez .12 .30
300 Brandon Phillips .12 .30
301 Matt Lawton .12 .30
302 Ellis Burks .12 .30
303 Bill Selby .12 .30
304 Travis Hafner .12 .30
305 Milton Bradley .12 .30
306 Karim Garcia .12 .30
307 Cliff Lee .75 2.00
308 Jeff Cirillo .12 .30
309 John Olerud .12 .30
310 Kazuhiro Sasaki .12 .30
311 Freddy Garcia .12 .30
312 Bret Boone .12 .30
313 Mike Cameron .12 .30
314 Ben Davis .12 .30
315 Randy Winn .12 .30
316 Gary Matthews Jr. .12 .30
317 Jeff Conine .12 .30
318 Sidney Ponson .12 .30
319 Jerry Hairston .12 .30
320 David Segui .12 .30
321 Scott Erickson .12 .30
322 Marty Cordova .12 .30
323 Hank Blalock .12 .30
324 Herbert Perry .12 .30
325 Alex Rodriguez .40 1.00
326 Carl Everett .12 .30
327 Einar Diaz .12 .30
328 Ugueth Urbina .12 .30
329 Mark Teixeira .20 .50
330 Manny Ramirez .30 .75
331 Johnny Damon .20 .50
332 Trot Nixon .12 .30
333 Tim Wakefield .20 .50
334 Casey Fossum .12 .30
335 Todd Walker .12 .30
336 Jeremy Giambi .12 .30
337 Bill Mueller .12 .30
338 Ramiro Mendoza .12 .30
339 Carlos Beltran .20 .50
340 Jason Grimsley .12 .30
341 Brent Mayne .12 .30
342 Angel Berroa .12 .30
343 Albie Lopez .12 .30
344 Michael Tucker .12 .30
345 Bobby Higginson .12 .30
346 Shane Halter .12 .30
347 Jeremy Bonderman RC 1.50 4.00
348 Eric Munson .12 .30
349 Andy Van Hekken .12 .30
350 Matt Anderson .12 .30
351 Jacque Jones .12 .30
352 A.J. Pierzynski .12 .30
353 Joe Mays .12 .30
354 Brad Radke .12 .30
355 Dustan Mohr .12 .30
356 Bobby Kielty .12 .30
357 Michael Cuddyer .12 .30
358 Luis Rivas .12 .30
359 Frank Thomas .30 .75
360 Joe Borchard .12 .30
361 D'Angelo Jimenez .12 .30
362 Bartolo Colon .12 .30
363 Joe Crede .12 .30
364 Miguel Olivo .12 .30
365 Billy Koch .12 .30
366 Bernie Williams .20 .50
367 Nick Johnson .12 .30
368 Andy Pettitte .20 .50
369 Mariano Rivera .40 1.00
370 Alfonso Soriano .20 .50
371 David Wells .12 .30
372 Drew Henson .12 .30
373 Juan Rivera .12 .30
374 Steve Karsay .12 .30
375 Jeff Kent .12 .30
376 Lance Berkman .20 .50
377 Octavio Dotel .12 .30
378 Julio Lugo .12 .30
379 Jason Lane .12 .30
380 Wade Miller .12 .30
381 Billy Wagner .12 .30
382 Brad Ausmus .12 .30
383 Mike Hampton .12 .30
384 Chipper Jones .30 .75
385 John Smoltz .30 .75
386 Greg Maddux .40 1.00
387 Javy Lopez .12 .30
388 Robert Fick .12 .30
389 Mark DeRosa .12 .30
390 Russ Ortiz .12 .30
391 Julio Franco .12 .30
392 Richie Sexson .12 .30
393 Eric Young .12 .30
394 Robert Machado .12 .30
395 Mike DeJean .12 .30
396 Todd Ritchie .12 .30
397 Royce Clayton .12 .30
398 Nick Neugebauer .12 .30
399 J.D. Drew .12 .30
400 Edgar Renteria .12 .30
401 Scott Rolen .20 .50
402 Matt Morris .12 .30
403 Garrett Stephenson .12 .30
404 Eduardo Perez .12 .30
405 Mike Matheny .12 .30
406 Miguel Cairo .12 .30
407 Brett Tomko .12 .30
408 Bobby Hill .12 .30
409 Troy O'Leary .12 .30
410 Corey Patterson .12 .30
411 Kerry Wood .12 .30
412 Eric Karros .12 .30
413 Hee Seop Choi .12 .30
414 Alex Gonzalez .12 .30
415 Matt Clement .12 .30
416 Mark Grudzielanek .12 .30
417 Curt Schilling .20 .50
418 Steve Finley .12 .30
419 Craig Counsell .12 .30
420 Matt Williams .12 .30
421 Quinton McCracken .12 .30
422 Chad Moeller .12 .30
423 Lyle Overbay .12 .30
424 Miguel Batista .12 .30
425 Paul Lo Duca .12 .30
426 Kevin Brown .12 .30
427 Hideo Nomo .30 .75
428 Fred McGriff .20 .50
429 Joe Thurston .12 .30
430 Odalis Perez .12 .30
431 Darren Dreifort .12 .30
432 Todd Hundley .12 .30
433 Dave Roberts .20 .50
434 Jose Vidro .12 .30
435 Javier Vazquez .12 .30
436 Michael Barrett .12 .30
437 Fernando Tatis .12 .30
438 Peter Bergeron .12 .30
439 Endy Chavez .12 .30
440 Orlando Hernandez .12 .30
441 Marvin Benard .12 .30
442 Rich Aurilia .12 .30
443 Pedro Feliz .12 .30
444 Robb Nen .12 .30
445 Ray Durham .12 .30
446 Marquis Grissom .12 .30
447 Damian Moss .12 .30
448 Edgardo Alfonzo .12 .30
449 Juan Pierre .12 .30
450 Braden Looper .12 .30
451 Alex Gonzalez .12 .30
452 Justin Wayne .12 .30
453 Josh Beckett .12 .30
454 Juan Encarnacion .12 .30
455 Ivan Rodriguez .20 .50
456 Todd Hollandsworth .12 .30
457 Cliff Floyd .12 .30
458 Rey Sanchez .12 .30
459 Mike Piazza .30 .75
460 Mo Vaughn .12 .30
461 Armando Benitez .12 .30
462 Tsuyoshi Shinjo .12 .30
463 Tom Glavine .20 .50
464 David Cone .12 .30
465 Phil Nevin .12 .30
466 Sean Burroughs .12 .30
467 Jake Peavy .12 .30
468 Brian Lawrence .12 .30
469 Mark Loretta .12 .30
470 Dennis Tankersley .12 .30
471 Jesse Orosco .12 .30
472 Jim Thome .20 .50
473 Kevin Millwood .12 .30
474 David Bell .12 .30
475 Pat Burrell .12 .30
476 Brandon Duckworth .12 .30
477 Jose Mesa .12 .30
478 Marlon Byrd .12 .30
479 Reggie Sanders .12 .30
480 Jason Kendall .12 .30
481 Aramis Ramirez .12 .30
482 Kris Benson .12 .30
483 Matt Stairs .12 .30
484 Kevin Young .12 .30
485 Kenny Lofton .12 .30
486 Austin Kearns .12 .30
487 Barry Larkin .20 .50
488 Jason LaRue .12 .30
489 Ken Griffey Jr. .60 1.50
490 Danny Graves .12 .30
491 Russell Branyan .12 .30
492 Reggie Taylor .12 .30
493 Jimmy Haynes .12 .30
494 Charles Johnson .12 .30
495 Todd Helton .20 .50
496 Juan Uribe .12 .30
497 Preston Wilson .12 .30
498 Chris Stynes .12 .30
499 Jason Jennings .12 .30
500 Jay Payton .12 .30
501 Hideki Matsui SR RC 2.00 5.00
502 Jose Contreras SR RC 1.00 2.50
503 Brandon Webb SR RC 1.25 3.00
504 Robby Hammock SR RC .40 1.00
505 Matt Kata SR RC .40 1.00
506 Tim Olson SR RC .40 1.00
507 Michael Hessman SR RC .40 1.00
508 Jon Leicester SR RC .40 1.00
509 Todd Wellemeyer SR RC .40 1.00
510 David Sanders SR RC .40 1.00
511 Josh Stewart SR RC .40 1.00
512 Luis Ayala SR RC .40 1.00
513 Clint Barmes SR RC 1.00 2.50
514 Josh Willingham SR RC 1.25 3.00
515 Alejandro Machado SR RC .40 1.00
516 Felix Sanchez SR RC .40 1.00
517 Willie Eyre SR RC .40 1.00
518 Brent Hoard SR RC .40 1.00
519 Lew Ford SR RC .40 1.00
520 Termel Sledge SR RC .40 1.00
521 Jeremy Griffiths SR RC .40 1.00
522 Phil Seibel SR RC .40 1.00
523 Craig Brazell SR RC .40 1.00
524 Prentice Redman SR RC .40 1.00
525 Jeff Duncan SR RC .40 1.00
526 Shane Bazzell SR RC .40 1.00
527 Bernie Castro SR RC .40 1.00
528 Rett Johnson SR RC .40 1.00
529 Bobby Madritsch SR RC .40 1.00
530 Rocco Baldelli SR .40 1.00
531 Alex Rodriguez SH CL .40 1.00
532 Eric Chavez SH CL .12 .30
533 Miguel Tejada SH CL .20 .50
534 Ichiro Suzuki SH CL .40 1.00
535 Sammy Sosa SH CL .30 .75
536 Barry Zito SH CL .20 .50
537 Darin Erstad SH CL .20 .50
538 Alfonso Soriano SH CL .20 .50
539 Troy Glaus SH CL .12 .30
540 Nomar Garciaparra SH CL .20 .50
541 Bo Hart RC .20 .50
542 Dan Haren RC 1.00 2.50
543 Ryan Wagner RC .20 .50
544 Rich Harden .20 .50
545 Dontrelle Willis .12 .30
546 Jerome Williams .12 .30
547 Bobby Crosby .12 .30
548 Greg Jones RC .20 .50
549 Todd Linden .12 .30
550 Byung-Hyun Kim .12 .30
551 Rickie Weeks RC .60 1.50
552 Jason Roach RC .20 .50
553 Oscar Villarreal RC .20 .50
554 Justin Duchscherer .12 .30
555 Chris Capuano RC .20 .50
556 Josh Hall RC .12 .30
557 Luis Matos .12 .30
558 Miguel Ojeda RC .20 .50
559 Kevin Ohme RC .20 .50
560 Julio Manon RC .20 .50
561 Kevin Correia RC .20 .50
562 Delmon Young RC 1.25 3.00
563 Aaron Boone .12 .30
564 Aaron Looper RC .20 .50
565 Mike Neu RC .20 .50
566 Aquilino Lopez RC .20 .50
567 Jhonny Peralta .12 .30
568 Duaner Sanchez .12 .30
569 Stephen Randolph RC .20 .50
570 Nate Bland RC .20 .50
571 Chin-Hui Tsao .12 .30
572 Michel Hernandez RC .20 .50
573 Rocco Baldelli .12 .30
574 Robb Quinlan .12 .30
575 Aaron Heilman .12 .30
576 Jae Weong Seo .12 .30
577 Joe Borowski .12 .30
578 Chris Bootcheck .12 .30
579 Michael Ryan RC .20 .50
580 Mark Malaska RC .20 .50
581 Jose Guillen .12 .30
582 Josh Towers .12 .30
583 Tom Gregorio RC .20 .50
584 Edwin Jackson RC .30 .75
585 Jason Anderson .12 .30
586 Jose Reyes .30 .75
587 Miguel Cabrera 1.50 4.00
588 Nate Bump .12 .30
589 Jeremy Burnitz .12 .30
590 David Ross .12 .30
591 Chase Utley .20 .50
592 Brandon Webb .40 1.00
593 Masao Kida .12 .30
594 Jimmy Journell .12 .30
595 Eric Young .12 .30
596 Tony Womack .12 .30
597 Amaury Telemaco .12 .30
598 Rickey Henderson .30 .75
599 Esteban Loaiza .12 .30
600 Sidney Ponson .12 .30

2003 Upper Deck Gold

COMP.FACT.SET (60) 15.00 40.00
*GOLD: 2X TO 5X BASIC
*GOLD: 1.25X TO 3X BASIC RC'S
ONE GOLD SET PER 12 CT HOBBY CASE

2003 Upper Deck A Piece of History 500 Club

This card, which continues the Upper Deck A Piece of History 500 club set which began in 1999, was randomly inserted into second series packs. These cards were issued to a stated print run of 350 cards.
RANDOM INSERT IN SERIES 2 PACKS
STATED PRINT RUN 350 CARDS
SS Sammy Sosa 30.00 60.00

2003 Upper Deck AL All-Star Swatches

Inserted into first series retail packs at a stated rate of one in 144, these 13 cards feature game-used uniform swatches of players who had made the AL All-Star game during their career.
SERIES 1 STATED ODDS 1:144 RETAIL
AP Andy Pettitte 6.00 15.00
AS Aaron Sele 4.00 10.00
CE Carl Everett 4.00 10.00
CF Chuck Finley 4.00 10.00
JG Juan Gonzalez 4.00 10.00
JM Joe Mays 4.00 10.00
JP Jorge Posada 6.00 15.00
MC Mike Cameron 4.00 10.00
MO Magglio Ordonez 4.00 10.00
MR Mariano Rivera 6.00 15.00
MS Mike Sweeney 4.00 10.00
RD Ray Durham 4.00 10.00
TF Travis Fryman 4.00 10.00

2003 Upper Deck Big League Breakdowns

Inserted into series one packs at a stated rate of one in eight, these 15 cards feature some of the leading hitters in the game.
COMPLETE SET (15) 10.00 25.00
SERIES 1 STATED ODDS 1:8
BL1 Troy Glaus .40 1.00
BL2 Miguel Tejada .60 1.50
BL3 Chipper Jones 1.00 2.50
BL4 Torii Hunter .40 1.00
BL5 Nomar Garciaparra .60 1.50
BL6 Sammy Sosa 1.00 2.50
BL7 Todd Helton .60 1.50
BL8 Lance Berkman .60 1.50
BL9 Shawn Green .40 1.00
BL10 Vladimir Guerrero .60 1.50
BL11 Jason Giambi .40 1.00
BL12 Derek Jeter 2.50 6.00
BL13 Barry Bonds 1.50 4.00
BL14 Ichiro Suzuki 1.25 3.00
BL15 Alex Rodriguez 1.25 3.00

2003 Upper Deck Chase for 755

Inserted into first series packs at a stated rate of one in eight, these 15 cards feature players who are considered to have some chance of surpassing Hank Aaron's career home run total.
COMPLETE SET (15) 8.00 20.00
SERIES 1 STATED ODDS 1:8
C1 Troy Glaus .40 1.00
C2 Andruw Jones .40 1.00
C3 Manny Ramirez 1.00 2.50
C4 Sammy Sosa 1.00 2.50
C5 Ken Griffey Jr. 2.00 5.00
C6 Adam Dunn .60 1.50
C7 Todd Helton .60 1.50
C8 Lance Berkman .60 1.50
C9 Jeff Bagwell .60 1.50
C10 Shawn Green .40 1.00
C11 Vladimir Guerrero .60 1.50
C12 Barry Bonds 1.50 4.00
C13 Alex Rodriguez 1.25 3.00
C14 Juan Gonzalez .40 1.00
C15 Carlos Delgado .40 1.00

2003 Upper Deck Game Swatches

Inserted into first series packs at a stated rate of one in 72, these 25 cards feature game-used memorabilia swatches. A few cards were printed to a lesser quantity and we have notated those cards in our checklist.
SERIES 1 STATED ODDS 1:72 HOBBY/RETAIL
HJAR Alex Rodriguez 6.00 15.00
HJBW Bernie Williams 4.00 10.00
HJCC C.C. Sabathia 3.00 8.00
HJCD Carlos Delgado SP 6.00 15.00
HJCP Carlos Pena 3.00 8.00
HJCS Curt Schilling SP/100 6.00 15.00
HJGM Greg Maddux 4.00 10.00
HJMM Mike Mussina 4.00 10.00
HJMO Magglio Ordonez 3.00 8.00
HJMP Mike Piazza SP 10.00 25.00
HJSB Sean Burroughs SP 6.00 15.00
HJSS Sammy Sosa 4.00 10.00
RJAD Adam Dunn 3.00 8.00
RJDE Darin Erstad 3.00 8.00
RJEM Edgar Martinez 4.00 10.00
RJFT Frank Thomas 4.00 10.00
RJIR Ivan Rodriguez 4.00 10.00
RJJD J.D. Drew 3.00 8.00
RJJE Jim Edmonds 3.00 8.00
RJJG Jason Giambi 3.00 8.00
RJJK Jeff Kent 3.00 8.00
RJKG Ken Griffey Jr. 6.00 15.00
RJRC Roger Clemens 8.00 20.00
RJRJ Randy Johnson 4.00 10.00
RJTH Tim Hudson 3.00 8.00

2003 Upper Deck Leading Swatches

SERIES 2 STATED ODDS 1:24 HOB/1:48 RET
SP INFO PROVIDED BY UPPER DECK
SP'S ARE NOT SERIAL-NUMBERED
*GOLD: .75X TO 2X BASIC SWATCHES
*GOLD: .6X TO 1.5X BASIC SP SWATCHES
*GOLD MATSUI HR: .75X TO 1.5X BASIC HR
*GOLD MATSUI RBI: .6X TO 1.2X BASIC RBI
GOLD RANDOM INSERTS IN SER.2 PACKS
GOLD PRINT RUN 100 SERIAL #'d SETS
AB Adrian Beltre GM 3.00 8.00
AD Adam Dunn RUN 3.00 8.00
AD1 Adam Dunn BB SP 4.00 10.00
AJ Andruw Jones HR 4.00 10.00
AJ1 Andruw Jones AB SP 6.00 15.00
AP Andy Pettitte WIN SP 6.00 15.00
AR Alex Rodriguez HR 6.00 15.00
AR1 Alex Rodriguez RBI 6.00 15.00
AS Alfonso Soriano SB 3.00 8.00
AS1 Alfonso Soriano RUN 3.00 8.00
AS2 Aaron Sele WIN 3.00 8.00
BA Bobby Abreu 2B 3.00 8.00
BG Brian Giles HR 3.00 8.00
BG1 Brian Giles OBP 3.00 8.00
BW Bernie Williams 333 AVG 4.00 10.00
BW1 Bernie Williams 339 AVG 4.00 10.00
BZ Barry Zito WIN 3.00 8.00
CD Carlos Delgado RBI 3.00 8.00
CJ Chipper Jones AVG-RBI 4.00 10.00
CP Corey Patterson HR 3.00 8.00
CS Curt Schilling WIN 3.00 8.00
EC Eric Chavez HR 3.00 8.00
GA Garret Anderson RBI 3.00 8.00
GM Greg Maddux 2.62 ERA 4.00 10.00
GM1 Greg Maddux 1.56 ERA SP 6.00 15.00
GO Juan Gonzalez RBI 3.00 8.00
HM Hideki Matsui HR 15.00 40.00
HM1 Hideki Matsui RBI SP 20.00 50.00
HN Hideo Nomo WIN 6.00 15.00
IR Ivan Rodriguez AVG 4.00 10.00
IS Ichiro Suzuki HIT 10.00 25.00
IS1 Ichiro Suzuki SB SP 10.00 25.00
JB Jeff Bagwell RBI 4.00 10.00
JB1 Jeff Bagwell SLG SP 6.00 15.00
JD J.D. Drew RBI 3.00 8.00
JE Jim Edmonds RUN 3.00 8.00
JG Jason Giambi HR 3.00 8.00
JG1 Jason Giambi SLG 3.00 8.00
JL Javy Lopez NLCS 3.00 8.00
JP Jay Payton 3B 3.00 8.00
JS J.T. Snow GLV 3.00 8.00
JT Jim Thome HR 4.00 10.00
JT1 Jim Thome SLG 4.00 10.00
KE Jason Kendall RUN 3.00 8.00
KG Ken Griffey Jr. 40 HR 6.00 15.00
KG1 Ken Griffey Jr. 56 HR SP 8.00 20.00
KI Kazuhisa Ishii K 3.00 8.00
KS Kazuhiro Sasaki SV 3.00 8.00
KW Kerry Wood K 3.00 8.00
LB Lance Berkman HR 3.00 8.00
LG Luis Gonzalez RUN 3.00 8.00
LW Larry Walker AVG 3.00 8.00
MP Mike Piazza HR 6.00 15.00
MP1 Mike Piazza SLG 6.00 15.00
MR Manny Ramirez AVG 4.00 10.00
MSL Mike Sweeney AVG 3.00 8.00
MSW Mike Stanton Pants GM 3.00 8.00
MT Miguel Tejada RBI 3.00 8.00
MT1 Miguel Tejada GM SP 4.00 10.00
OV Omar Vizquel SAC 4.00 10.00
PB Pat Burrell HR 3.00 8.00
PB1 Pat Burrell RBI 3.00 8.00
PM Pedro Martinez K 4.00 10.00
RC Roger Clemens K 6.00 15.00
RC1 Roger Clemens ERA 6.00 15.00
RJ Randy Johnson K 4.00 10.00
RJ1 Randy Johnson ERA 4.00 10.00
RO Roy Oswalt WIN 3.00 8.00
RO1 Roy Oswalt PCT SP 4.00 10.00
RP Rafael Palmeiro RBI 4.00 10.00
RP1 Rafael Palmeiro 2B 4.00 10.00
SG Shawn Green HR 3.00 8.00
SG1 Shawn Green TB 3.00 8.00
SR Scott Rolen HR 4.00 10.00
SS Sammy Sosa 49 HR 4.00 10.00
SS1 Sammy Sosa 50 HR SP/170 6.00 15.00
TB Tony Batista HR 3.00 8.00
TG Troy Glaus HR 3.00 8.00
THE Todd Helton RBI 4.00 10.00
THU Tim Hudson IP 3.00 8.00
THU1 Tim Hudson GM SP 4.00 10.00
TP Troy Percival SV 3.00 8.00
VG Vladimir Guerrero HIT 4.00 10.00

2003 Upper Deck Lineup Time Jerseys

Inserted into first series hobby packs at a stated rate of one in 96, these 10 cards feature game-used uniform swatches from some of the leading players in the game. A couple of cards were printed to a smaller quantity and we have notated those cards with an SP in our checklist.
SERIES 1 STATED ODDS 1:96 HOBBY
BW Bernie Williams 4.00 10.00
CD Carlos Delgado 3.00 8.00
GM Greg Maddux 4.00 10.00
IS Ichiro Suzuki 15.00 40.00
JD J.D. Drew 3.00 8.00
JT Jim Thome 4.00 10.00
RC Roger Clemens SP 10.00 25.00
RJ Randy Johnson SP 8.00 20.00
SG Shawn Green 3.00 8.00
TH Todd Helton 4.00 10.00

2003 Upper Deck Magical Performances

SERIES 2 STATED ODDS 1:96 HOBBY
*GOLD: .6X TO 1.5X BASIC MAGIC
GOLD RANDOM INSERTS IN SER.2 PACKS
GOLD PRINT RUN 50 SERIAL #'d SETS
DUPE STARS EQUALLY VALUED
MP1 Hideki Matsui 6.00 15.00
MP2 Ken Griffey Jr. 6.00 15.00
MP3 Ichiro Suzuki 4.00 10.00
MP4 Ken Griffey Jr. 6.00 15.00
MP5 Hideo Nomo 3.00 8.00
MP6 Mickey Mantle 10.00 25.00
MP7 Ken Griffey Jr. 6.00 15.00
MP8 Barry Bonds 5.00 12.00
MP9 Mickey Mantle 10.00 25.00
MP10 Tom Seaver 2.00 5.00
MP11 Mike Piazza 3.00 8.00
MP12 Roger Clemens 4.00 10.00
MP13 Nolan Ryan 10.00 25.00
MP14 Nomar Garciaparra 2.00 5.00
MP15 Ernie Banks 3.00 8.00
MP16 Stan Musial 5.00 12.00
MP17 Mickey Mantle 10.00 25
MP18 Nolan Ryan 10.00 25
MP19 Nolan Ryan 10.00 25
MP20 Mickey Mantle 10.00 25
MP21 Ichiro Suzuki 4.00 10
MP22 Nolan Ryan 10.00 25
MP23 Tom Seaver 2.00 5
MP24 Ken Griffey Jr. 6.00 15
MP25 Hideo Nomo 3.00 8
MP26 Ken Griffey Jr. 6.00 15
MP27 Mark McGwire 5.00 12
MP28 Barry Bonds 5.00 12
MP29 Alex Rodriguez 4.00 10
MP30 Nolan Ryan 10.00 25
MP31 Mark McGwire 5.00 12.
MP32 Nolan Ryan 10.00 25
MP33 Sammy Sosa 3.00 8
MP34 Ichiro Suzuki 4.00 10
MP35 Barry Bonds 5.00 12
MP36 Derek Jeter 8.00 20
MP37 Roger Clemens 4.00 10
MP38 Jason Giambi 1.25 3.
MP39 Mickey Mantle 10.00 25.
MP40 Ted Williams 6.00 15
MP41 Ted Williams 6.00 15.
MP42 Ted Williams 6.00 15.

2003 Upper Deck Mark of Greatness Autograph Jerseys

Randomly inserted into first series packs, these th cards feature authenitically signed Mark McGwire cards. There are three different versions of this ca which were all signed to a different print run, and have notated that information in our checklist.
RANDOM INSERTS IN SERIES 1 PACKS
STATED PRINT RUNS LISTED BELOW
CARD MOG IS NOT SERIAL NUMBERED
MOG M.McGwire/400 * 125.00 250.
MOGS M.McGwire Silver/70 250.00 400.

2003 Upper Deck Masters wit the Leather

COMPLETE SET (12) 8.00 20.
SERIES 2 STATED ODDS 1:12
L1 Darin Erstad .40 1.
L2 Andruw Jones .40 1.
L3 Greg Maddux 1.25 3.
L4 Nomar Garciaparra .60 1.
L5 Torii Hunter .40 1.
L6 Roberto Alomar .60 1.
L7 Derek Jeter 2.50 6.
L8 Eric Chavez .40 1.
L9 Ichiro Suzuki 1.25 3.
L10 Jim Edmonds .60 1.
L11 Scott Rolen .60 1.
L12 Alex Rodriguez 1.25 3.

2003 Upper Deck Matsui Mani

COMMON CARD (HM1-HM18) 2.00 5.
NO MANIA 25 PRICING AVAILABLE
HM1 Hideki Matsui 2.00 5.
HM2 Hideki Matsui 2.00 5.
HM3 Hideki Matsui 2.00 5.
HM4 Hideki Matsui 2.00 5.
HM5 Hideki Matsui 2.00 5.
HM6 Hideki Matsui 2.00 5.
HM7 Hideki Matsui 2.00 5.
HM8 Hideki Matsui 2.00 5.
HM9 Hideki Matsui 2.00 5.
HM10 Hideki Matsui 2.00 5.
HM11 Hideki Matsui 2.00 5.
HM12 Hideki Matsui 2.00 5.
HM13 Hideki Matsui 2.00 5.
HM14 Hideki Matsui 2.00 5.
HM15 Hideki Matsui 2.00 5.
HM16 Hideki Matsui 2.00 5.
HM17 Hideki Matsui 2.00 5.
HM18 Hideki Matsui 2.00 5.

2003 Upper Deck Mid-Summer Stars Swatches

rted into first series packs at a stated rate of one ?, these 23 cards feature a mix of players who e all during the season. A few cards do not re jersey swatches and we have notated that mation in our checklist. In addition, a few cards issued to a smaller quantity and we have ed those cards with an SP in our checklist.

ES 1 STATED ODDS 1:72
ndruw Jones 4.00 10.00
Alex Rodriguez 6.00 15.00
Barry Zito 3.00 8.00
Carlos Delgado 3.00 8.00
Curt Schilling 3.00 8.00
Darin Erstad 3.00 8.00
David Wells 3.00 8.00
Edgar Martinez 4.00 10.00
Freddy Garcia 3.00 8.00
Frank Thomas 4.00 10.00
Hideo Nomo 8.00 20.00
Ichiro Suzuki Turtleneck SP 20.00 50.00
im Edmonds SP * 4.00 10.00
Juan Gonzalez Pants 3.00 8.00
Kazuhiro Sasaki 3.00 8.00
Mike Piazza 6.00 15.00
Manny Ramirez 4.00 10.00
Roger Clemens 6.00 15.00
Randy Johnson Shirt 4.00 10.00
Robin Ventura 4.00 10.00
Shawn Green SP 4.00 10.00
Sammy Sosa 4.00 10.00
Tom Glavine 4.00 10.00

2003 Upper Deck NL All-Star Swatches

erted into first series hobby packs at a stated rate one in 72, these 12 cards feature game-used morabilia swatch of players who had participated he All-Star game for the National League.

RIES 1 STATED ODDS 1:72 HOBBY
Al Leiter 3.00 8.00
Cliff Floyd 3.00 8.00
Curt Schilling 3.00 8.00
Fred McGriff 4.00 10.00
Jose Vidro 3.00 8.00
Mike Hampton 3.00 8.00
Matt Morris 3.00 8.00
Ryan Klesko 3.00 8.00
Sean Casey 3.00 8.00
Tom Glavine 4.00 10.00
Tony Gwynn 6.00 15.00
Trevor Hoffman 3.00 8.00

003 Upper Deck National Pride Memorabilia

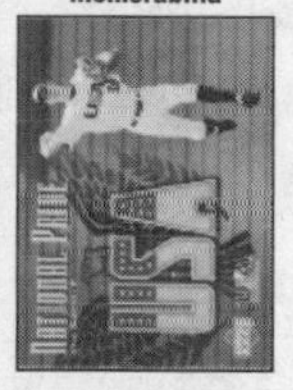

RIES 2 ODDS 1:24 HOBBY/1:48 RETAIL
PRINT RUNS PROVIDED BY UPPER DECK
'S ARE NOT SERIAL-NUMBERED
FEATURE PANTS UNLESS NOTED
Abe Alvarez 1.50 4.00
Aaron Hill 5.00 12.00
A.J. Hinch Jsy 1.50 4.00
A.Kearns Right Jsy 1.50 4.00
1 A.Kearns Left Jsy SP/250 6.00 15.00
Bobby Hill Field Jsy 1.50 4.00
1 Bobby Hill Run Jsy SP/100 8.00 20.00
Brad Sullivan Wind Up 1.50 4.00
1 Brad Sullivan Throw SP/250 6.00 15.00
Bob Zimmermann 1.50 4.00
Chad Cordero 1.50 4.00
Conor Jackson 5.00 12.00
Carlos Quentin 5.00 12.00
Clint Sammons 1.50 4.00
Dustin Pedroia 5.00 12.00
Eric Milton White Jsy 1.50 4.00
1 Eric Milton Blue Jsy SP/50 8.00 20.00
Eric Patterson 1.50 4.00
Grant Johnson 1.50 4.00
Huston Street 2.50 6.00
J.Jones White Jsy 1.50 4.00
1 J.Jones Blue Jsy SP/250 6.00 15.00
Jason Jennings Jsy 1.50 4.00
Kyle Bakker 1.50 4.00
A K.Saarloos Red Jsy 1.50 4.00
L Kyle Sleeth 1.50 4.00
A1 K.Saarloos Grey Jsy SP/250 6.00 15.00
Landon Powell 1.50 4.00
Michael Aubrey 4.00 10.00
Mark Jurich 1.50 4.00
Mark Prior Pinstripes Jsy 2.50 6.00
1 Mark Prior Grey Jsy SP/100 10.00 25.00
Philip Humber 1.50 4.00
Robert Fick Jsy 1.50 4.00

RO R.Oswalt Behind Jsy 2.50 6.00
RO1 R.Oswalt Beside Jsy SP/100 8.00 20.00
RW R.Weeks Glove-Chest 5.00 12.00
SB Sean Burroughs 1.50 4.00
SC Shane Costa 1.50 4.00
SF Sam Fuld 1.50 4.00
WL Wes Littleton 1.50 4.00

2003 Upper Deck Piece of the Action Game Ball

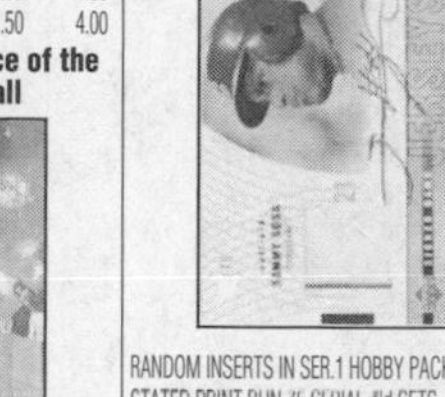

SERIES 2 ODDS 1:288 HOBBY/1:576 RETAIL
PRINT RUNS B/WN 10-175 COPIES PER
PRINT RUNS PROVIDED BY UPPER DECK
CARDS ARE NOT SERIAL-NUMBERED
NO PRICING ON QTY OF 25 OR LESS
AB Adrian Beltre/100 4.00 10.00
ARA Aramis Ramirez/100 4.00 10.00
ARO Alex Rodriguez/100 10.00 25.00
BA Bobby Abreu/125 4.00 10.00
BB Barry Bonds/125 15.00 40.00
BG Brian Giles/100 4.00 10.00
BW Bernie Williams/125 6.00 15.00
CJ Chipper Jones/62 10.00 25.00
CS Curt Schilling/100 4.00 10.00
DE Darin Erstad/125 4.00 10.00
DJ Derek Jeter/65 15.00 40.00
EM Edgar Martinez/125 6.00 15.00
FG Freddy Garcia/100 4.00 10.00
FT Frank Thomas/150 6.00 15.00
GA Garret Anderson/150 4.00 10.00
GS Gary Sheffield/100 4.00 10.00
HN Hideo Nomo/100 15.00 40.00
JG Juan Gonzalez/100 4.00 10.00
JK Jason Kendall/100 4.00 10.00
JT Jim Thome/125 6.00 15.00
JV Jose Vidro/100 4.00 10.00
KB Kevin Brown/100 4.00 10.00
KE Jeff Kent/150 4.00 10.00
KS Kazuhiro Sasaki/100 4.00 10.00
LG Luis Gonzalez/100 4.00 10.00
LW Larry Walker/150 4.00 10.00
MP Mike Piazza/150 10.00 25.00
PB Pat Burrell/150 4.00 10.00
PM Pedro Martinez/150 6.00 15.00
PN Phil Nevin/75 6.00 15.00
RJ Randy Johnson/100 6.00 15.00
RK Ryan Klesko/75 6.00 15.00
RP Rafael Palmeiro/150 6.00 15.00
RS Richie Sexson/160 4.00 10.00
SG Shawn Green/175 4.00 10.00
SS Sammy Sosa/85 10.00 25.00
TG Troy Glaus/150 4.00 10.00
THE Todd Helton/100 6.00 15.00
THO Trevor Hoffman/150 4.00 10.00
VG Vladimir Guerrero/50 10.00 25.00

2003 Upper Deck Piece of the Action Game Ball Gold

*GOLD: 1X TO 2.5X GAME BALL p/r 150-175
*GOLD: 1X TO 2.5X GAME BALL p/r 100-125
*GOLD: .6X TO 1.5X GAME BALL p/r 50-85
RANDOM INSERTS IN SERIES 2 PACKS
STATED PRINT RUN 50 SERIAL #'d SETS
IR Ivan Rodriguez 15.00 40.00

2003 Upper Deck Signed Game Jerseys

Randomly inserted into first series packs, these seven cards feature not only game-used memorabilia swatches but also an authentic autograph of the player. We have notated the print run for each card next to the player's name. In addition, Ken Griffey Jr. did not sign cards in time for inclusion into packs and those cards could be redeemed until February 11th, 2006.

PRINT RUNS B/WN 150-350 COPIES PER
AR Alex Rodriguez/350 40.00 80.00
CR Cal Ripken/350 30.00 80.00
JG Jason Giambi/350 20.00 50.00
KG Ken Griffey Jr./350 40.00 80.00
MM Mark McGwire/150 250.00 400.00
RC Roger Clemens/350 25.00 60.00
SS Sammy Sosa/150 40.00 80.00

2003 Upper Deck Signed Game Jerseys Silver

RANDOM INSERTS IN SER.1 HOBBY PACKS
STATED PRINT RUN 75 SERIAL #'d SETS
JG Jason Giambi 30.00 60.00

2003 Upper Deck Slammin Sammy Autograph Jerseys

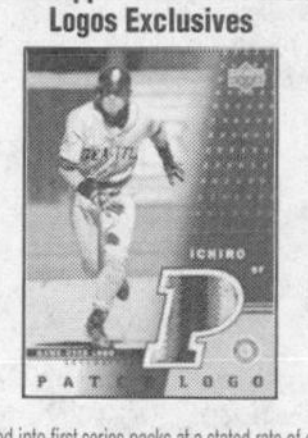

Randomly inserted into first series packs, these three cards feature authentically signed Sammy Sosa cards. Each of these cards also have a game-worn uniform swatch on them. There are three different versions of this card, which were all signed to a different print run, and we have notated that information in our checklist.

RANDOM INSERTS IN SERIES 1 PACKS
PRINT RUNS B/WN 25-384 COPIES PER
NO PRICING ON QTY OF 25 OR LESS
SST Sammy Sosa/384 40.00 80.00
SSTS Sammy Sosa Silver/66 125.00 200.00

2003 Upper Deck Star-Spangled Swatches

Inserted into first series packs at a stated rate of one in 72, these 16 cards feature game-worn uniform swatches of players who were on the USA National Team.

SERIES 1 STATED ODDS 1:72
AH Aaron Hill H 3.00 8.00
BS Brad Sullivan H 3.00 8.00
CC Chad Cordero H 3.00 8.00
CJ Conor Jackson Pants R 4.00 10.00
CQ Carlos Quentin H 4.00 10.00
DP Dustin Pedroia R 4.00 20.00
EP Eric Patterson H 3.00 8.00
GJ Grant Johnson H 3.00 8.00
HS Huston Street R 3.00 8.00
KB Kyle Bakker R 2.00 5.00
KS Kyle Sleeth R 3.00 8.00
LP Landon Powell R 3.00 8.00
MA Michael Aubrey H 3.00 8.00
PH Philip Humber R 3.00 8.00
RW Rickie Weeks H 6.00 15.00
SC Shane Costa R 2.00 5.00

2003 Upper Deck Superior Sluggers

Inserted into second series packs at a stated rate of one in eight, these cards feature a mix of active and retired players known for their extra base power while batting.

COMPLETE SET (18) 12.50 30.00
SERIES 2 STATED ODDS 1:8
S1 Troy Glaus .40 1.00
S2 Chipper Jones 1.00 2.50
S3 Manny Ramirez 1.00 2.50
S4 Ken Griffey Jr. 2.00 5.00
S5 Jim Thome .60 1.50
S6 Todd Helton .60 1.50
S7 Lance Berkman .60 1.50
S8 Derek Jeter 2.50 6.00
S9 Vladimir Guerrero .60 1.50
S10 Mike Piazza 1.00 2.50
S11 Hideki Matsui 2.00 5.00
S12 Barry Bonds 1.50 4.00
S13 Mickey Mantle 3.00 8.00
S14 Alex Rodriguez 1.25 3.00
S15 Ted Williams 2.00 5.00
S16 Carlos Delgado .40 1.00
S17 Frank Thomas 1.00 2.50
S18 Adam Dunn .60 1.50

2003 Upper Deck Triple Game Jersey

Randomly inserted into first series packs, these nine cards feature three game-worn uniform swatches of teammates. These cards were issued to a stated print run of anywhere from 25 to 150 serial numbered sets depending on which group the card belongs to. Please note the cards from group C are not priced due to market scarcity.

GROUP A 150 SERIAL #'d SETS
GROUP B 75 SERIAL #'d SETS
GROUP C 25 SERIAL #'d SETS
NO GROUP C PRICING DUE TO SCARCITY
ARZ Johnson/Schilling/L.Gonz A 20.00 50.00
ATL Chipper/Maddux/Sheff B 12.00 30.00
CHC Sosa/Alou/Wood B 20.00 50.00
CIN Griffey/Casey/Dunn A 10.00 25.00
HOU Bagwell/Berkman/Biggio A 20.00 50.00
NYM Piazza/Alomar/Vaughn B 20.00 50.00
SEA Ichiro/Garcia/Boone B 60.00 120.00
TEX Palmeiro/A-Rod/Gonzalez A 20.00 50.00

2003 Upper Deck UD Bonus

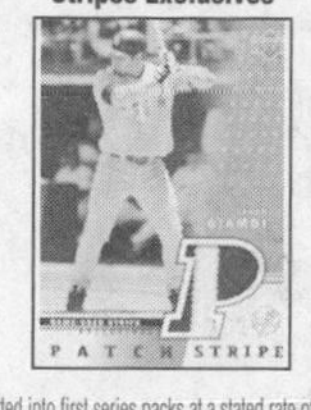

Inserted into second series packs at a stated rate of one in 288, these are copies of various recent year Upper Deck cards which were repurchased for insertion in 2003 Upper Deck 2nd series. Please note that these cards were all stamped with a "UD Bonus" logo. Each of these cards were issued to differening print runs and we have notated the print runs next to the player's name in our checklist.

SER.2 STATED ODDS 1:288 HOBBY
PRINT RUNS B/WN 2-201 COPIES PER
NO PRICING ON QTY OF 40 OR LESS
2 Josh Beckett 01 TP AU/55 12.50 30.00
3 C.Beltran 00 SPA AU/118 6.00 15.00
6 Barry Bonds 01 P P Jsy/117 10.00 25.00
7 Lou Brock 00 LGD AU/198 10.00 25.00
8 Gary Carter 00 LGD AU/63 20.00 50.00
12 Roger Clemens 01 P P Jsy/117 6.00 15.00
13 A.Dawson 00 LGD AU/140 6.00 15.00
14 J.D. Drew 00 SPA AU/55 8.00 20.00
15 Rollie Fingers 00 LGD AU/116 6.00 15.00
16 Rafael Furcal 00 SPA AU/87 6.00 15.00
18 Jason Giambi 00 SPA AU/106 6.00 15.00
20 Jason Giambi 01 P P Jsy/97 4.00 10.00
21 Troy Glaus 00 SPA AU/110 10.00 25.00
28 Brandon Inge 01 TP AU/113 4.00 10.00
43 D.Mientkiewicz 00 BD Jsy/57 4.00 10.00
44 Dale Murphy 00 LGD AU/91 10.00 25.00
46 Jim Palmer 00 LGD AU/121 6.00 15.00
47 P.Reese 01 HOF Jsy/46 6.00 15.00
53 C.C. Sabathia 01 TP AU/64 8.00 20.00
56 Ben Sheets 01 TP AU/60 8.00 20.00
58 Alf Soriano 00 SPA AU/80 10.00 25.00
59 Sammy Sosa 01 P P Jsy/77 6.00 15.00
63 Dave Winfield 00 YL Bat/53 4.00 10.00
64 B.Will/Ichiro 01 P/P Bat/87 20.00 50.00
65 Sosa/L.Gonz 01 P/P Bat/61 6.00 15.00

2003 Upper Deck UD Patch Logos

Inserted into first series packs at a stated rate of one in 7500, these eight cards feature game-used patch pieces. Each card has a print run between 41 and 54 and we have notated that print run information next to the player's name in our checklist.

CJ Chipper Jones/52 50.00 120.00
FT Frank Thomas/52 50.00 120.00
GM Greg Maddux/50 60.00 150.00
KI Kazuhisa Ishii/54 20.00 50.00
RJ Randy Johnson/50 50.00 120.00

2003 Upper Deck UD Patch Logos Exclusives

Inserted into first series packs at a stated rate of one in 7500, these ten cards feature game-used patch pieces. Each card has a print run between nine and 61 and we have notated that print run information next to the player's name in our checklist. The cards with a print run of 25 or fewer are not priced due to market scarcity.

KG Ken Griffey Jr./50 75.00 150.00
MP Mike Piazza/61 60.00 120.00
SS Sammy Sosa/60 15.00 40.00

2003 Upper Deck UD Patch Numbers

Inserted into first series packs at a stated rate of one in 7500, these six cards feature game-used patch number pieces. Each card has a print run between 27 and 90 and we have notated that print run information next to the player's name in our checklist.

SERIES 1 STATED ODDS 1:7500
PRINT RUNS B/WN 27-91 COPIES PER
CARDS ARE NOT SERIAL-NUMBERED
NO PRICING ON QTY OF 40 OR LESS
BW Bernie Williams/66 40.00 80.00
FT Frank Thomas/91 40.00 80.00
KI Kazuhisa Ishii/63 30.00 60.00
RJ Randy Johnson/90 40.00 80.00

2003 Upper Deck UD Patch Numbers Exclusives

Inserted into first series packs at a stated rate of one in 7500, these six cards feature game-used patch number pieces. Each card has a print run between 56 and 100 and we have notated that print run information next to the player's name in our checklist.

SERIES 1 STATED ODDS 1:7500
PRINT RUNS B/WN 56-100 COPIES PER
CARDS ARE NOT SERIAL-NUMBERED
AR Alex Rodriguez/56 75.00 150.00
JG Jason Giambi/68 30.00 60.00
KG Ken Griffey Jr./97 50.00 100.00
MG Mark McGwire/60 150.00 250.00
SS Sammy Sosa/100 40.00 80.00

2003 Upper Deck UD Patch Stripes

Inserted into first series packs at a stated rate of one in 7500, these seven cards feature game-used patch striped pieces. Each card has a print run between 43 and 73 and we have notated that print run information next to the player's name in our checklist.

SERIES 1 STATED ODDS 1:7500
PRINT RUNS B/WN 43-73 COPIES PER
CARDS ARE NOT SERIAL-NUMBERED
BW Bernie Williams/58 40.00 80.00
CJ Chipper Jones/58 40.00 80.00
FT Frank Thomas/58 40.00 80.00
JB Jeff Bagwell/73 40.00 80.00
KI Kazuhisa Ishii/58 30.00 60.00
RJ Randy Johnson/58 40.00 80.00

2003 Upper Deck UD Patch Stripes Exclusives

Inserted into first series packs at a stated rate of one in 7500, these seven cards feature game-used patch striped pieces. Each card has a print run between 63 and 66 and we have notated that print run information next to the player's name in our checklist.

SERIES 1 STATED ODDS 1:7500
PRINT RUNS B/WN 63-66 COPIES PER
CARDS ARE NOT SERIAL-NUMBERED
AR Alex Rodriguez/63 60.00 120.00
IS Ichiro Suzuki/63 150.00 250.00
JG Jason Giambi/66 30.00 60.00
KG Ken Griffey Jr./63 60.00 120.00
MG Mark McGwire/63 150.00 250.00
SS Sammy Sosa/63 60.00 120.00

2003 Upper Deck UD Superstar Slam Jerseys

Inserted into first series hobby packs at a stated rate of one in 48, these 10 cards feature game-used jersey pieces of the featured players.

SERIES 1 STATED ODDS 1:48 HOBBY
AR Alex Rodriguez 6.00 15.00
CJ Chipper Jones 4.00 10.00
FT Frank Thomas 4.00 10.00
JB Jeff Bagwell 4.00 10.00
JG Jason Giambi 3.00 8.00
KG Ken Griffey Jr. 6.00 15.00
LG Luis Gonzalez 3.00 8.00
MP Mike Piazza 6.00 15.00
SS Sammy Sosa 4.00 10.00
JGO Juan Gonzalez 3.00 8.00

2003 Upper Deck Gary Carter Hawaii Autograph

This one card set was distibuted at the Hawaii Trade Show conference. This card features an authentic autograph of recently inducted Hall of Famer Gary Carter.

DISTRIBUTED AT 2003 HAWAII CONFERENCE
GC Gary Carter 20.00 50.00

2003 Upper Deck Star Rookie Hawaii

This card was produced to commemorate the Yankees signing of Japanese slugger Hideki Matsui. The card was distributed in February, 2003 to select attendees of the Kit Young Hawaii Trade Conference. It's estimated that only about 300 copies were produced. The card carries an HM number on back.

HM Hideki Matsui 30.00 80.00

2003 Upper Deck Star Rookie Sportsfest

This six-card set was distibuted at the Chicago Sportsfest show in June, 2003. These cards were available if a collector opened a 2003 Upper Deck full box at the Upper Deck booth during the show. The collectors received not just this set but the first liscenced LeBron James card as well as a six-card football set. Since these cards are unnumbered, we have sequenced them in alphabetical order by first name.

COMPLETE SET 2.50 6.00
AM Alejandro Machado .40 1.00
HB Hank Blalock .40 1.00
HC Hee Seop Choi .40 1.00
HM Hideki Matsui 2.00 5.00
RB Rocco Baldelli .40 1.00
RH Runelvys Hernandez .40 1.00

2003 Upper Deck Magazine

As a bonus to buyers of the Upper Deck magazine produced by Krause Publications late in 2003, a nine-card perforated sheet featuring players basically signed to Upper Deck exclusives was included. When the cards were perforated, these cards measured the standard size. Please note that all of these cards have a "UD" prefix.

COMPLETE SET (9) 8.00 20.00
UD2 Hideki Matsui 1.50 4.00
UD4 Ichiro Suzuki 1.25 3.00
UD7 Mickey Mantle 1.50 4.00

2004 Upper Deck

The 270-card first series was released in November, 2003. The cards were issued in eight-card hobby packs with an $3 SRP which came 24 packs to a box and 12 boxes to a case. These cards were also issued in nine-card retail packs also with a $3 SRP which came 24 packs to a box and 12 boxes to a case. Please note that insert cards were much more prevalent in the hobby packs. The following subsets were included in the first series: Super Rookies (1-30); Season Highlights Checklists (261-270). In addition, please note that the Super Rookie cards were not short printed. The second series, also of 270 cards, was released in June 2004. That series was highlighted by the following subsets: Season Highlights Checklists (471-480), Super Rookies (481-540). In addition, an update set was issued as a complete set with the 2005 Upper Deck I product. Those cards feature a mix of players who changed teams and Rookie Cards.

COMPLETE SERIES 1 (270) 20.00 50.00
COMPLETE SERIES 2 (270) 20.00 50.00
COMP.UPDATE SET (50) 7.50 15.00
COMMON (31-480/541-565) .10 .30
COMMON (1-30/481-540) .40 1.00
1-30/481-540 ARE NOT SHORT PRINTS
COMMON CARD (566-590) .20 .50
541-590 ONE SET PER '05 UD1 HOBBY BOX
UPDATE SET EXCH 1:480 '05 UD1 RETAIL
UPDATE SET EXCH.DEADLINE TBD
1 Dontrelle Willis SR .40 1.00
2 Edgar Gonzalez SR .40 1.00
3 Jose Reyes SR .60 1.50
4 Jae Weong Seo SR .40 1.00
5 Miguel Cabrera SR 1.00 2.50
6 Jesse Foppert SR .40 1.00
7 Mike Neu SR .40 1.00
8 Michael Nakamura SR .40 1.00
9 Luis Ayala SR .40 1.00
10 Jared Sandberg SR .40 1.00
11 Jhonny Peralta SR .40 1.00
12 Wil Ledezma SR .40 1.00
13 Jason Roach SR .40 1.00
14 Kirk Saarloos SR .40 1.00
15 Cliff Lee SR .60 1.50
16 Bobby Hill SR .40 1.00
17 Lyle Overbay SR .40 1.00
18 Josh Hall SR .40 1.00
19 Joe Thurston SR .40 1.00
20 Matt Kata SR .40 1.00
21 Jeremy Bonderman SR .40 1.00
22 Julio Manon SR .40 1.00
23 Rodrigo Rosario SR .40 1.00
24 Robby Hammock SR .40 1.00
25 David Sanders SR .40 1.00
26 Miguel Ojeda SR .40 1.00
27 Mark Teixeira SR .60 1.50
28 Franklyn German SR .40 1.00
29 Ken Harvey SR .40 1.00
30 Xavier Nady SR .40 1.00
31 Tim Salmon .12 .30
32 Troy Glaus .12 .30
33 Adam Kennedy .12 .30
34 David Eckstein .12 .30
35 Ben Molina .12 .30
36 Jarrod Washburn .12 .30
37 Ramon Ortiz .12 .30
38 Eric Chavez .12 .30
39 Miguel Tejada .20 .50
40 Chris Singleton .12 .30
41 Jermaine Dye .12 .30
42 John Halama .12 .30
43 Tim Hudson .20 .50
44 Barry Zito .20 .50
45 Ted Lilly .12 .30
46 Bobby Kielty .12 .30
47 Kelvim Escobar .12 .30
48 Josh Phelps .12 .30
49 Vernon Wells .12 .30
50 Roy Halladay .20 .50
51 Orlando Hudson .12 .30
52 Eric Hinske .12 .30
53 Brandon Backe .12 .30
54 Dewon Brazelton .12 .30
55 Ben Grieve .12 .30
56 Aubrey Huff .12 .30
57 Toby Hall .12 .30

58 Rocco Baldelli	.12	.30
59 Al Martin	.12	.30
60 Brandon Phillips	.12	.30
61 Omar Vizquel	.20	.50
62 C.C. Sabathia	.20	.50
63 Milton Bradley	.12	.30
64 Ricky Gutierrez	.12	.30
65 Matt Lawton	.12	.30
66 Danys Baez	.12	.30
67 Ichiro Suzuki	.40	1.00
68 Randy Winn	.12	.30
69 Carlos Guillen	.12	.30
70 Mark McLemore	.12	.30
71 Dan Wilson	.12	.30
72 Jamie Moyer	.12	.30
73 Joel Pineiro	.12	.30
74 Edgar Martinez	.20	.50
75 Tony Batista	.12	.30
76 Jay Gibbons	.12	.30
77 Jeff Conine	.12	.30
78 Melvin Mora	.12	.30
79 Geronimo Gil	.12	.30
80 Rodrigo Lopez	.12	.30
81 Jorge Julio	.12	.30
82 Rafael Palmeiro	.20	.50
83 Juan Gonzalez	.12	.30
84 Mike Young	.12	.30
85 Alex Rodriguez	.40	1.00
86 Einar Diaz	.12	.30
87 Kevin Mench	.12	.30
88 Hank Blalock	.12	.30
89 Pedro Martinez	.20	.50
90 Byung-Hyun Kim	.12	.30
91 Derek Lowe	.12	.30
92 Jason Varitek	.30	.75
93 Manny Ramirez	.30	.75
94 John Burkett	.12	.30
95 Todd Walker	.12	.30
96 Nomar Garciaparra	.20	.50
97 Trot Nixon	.12	.30
98 Mike Sweeney	.12	.30
99 Carlos Febles	.12	.30
100 Mike MacDougal	.12	.30
101 Raul Ibanez	.20	.50
102 Jason Grimsley	.12	.30
103 Chris George	.12	.30
104 Brent Mayne	.12	.30
105 Dmitri Young	.12	.30
106 Eric Munson	.12	.30
107 A.J. Hinch	.12	.30
108 Andres Torres	.12	.30
109 Bobby Higginson	.12	.30
110 Shane Halter	.12	.30
111 Matt Walbeck	.12	.30
112 Torii Hunter	.12	.30
113 Doug Mientkiewicz	.12	.30
114 Lew Ford	.12	.30
115 Eric Milton	.12	.30
116 Eddie Guardado	.12	.30
117 Cristian Guzman	.12	.30
118 Corey Koskie	.12	.30
119 Magglio Ordonez	.20	.50
120 Mark Buehrle	.20	.50
121 Billy Koch	.12	.30
122 Jose Valentin	.12	.30
123 Paul Konerko	.20	.50
124 Carlos Lee	.12	.30
125 Jon Garland	.12	.30
126 Jason Giambi	.12	.30
127 Derek Jeter	.75	2.00
128 Roger Clemens	.40	1.00
129 Andy Pettitte	.20	.50
130 Jorge Posada	.20	.50
131 David Wells	.12	.30
132 Hideki Matsui	.50	1.25
133 Mike Mussina	.20	.50
134 Jeff Bagwell	.20	.50
135 Craig Biggio	.20	.50
136 Morgan Ensberg	.12	.30
137 Richard Hidalgo	.12	.30
138 Brad Ausmus	.12	.30
139 Roy Oswalt	.20	.50
140 Billy Wagner	.12	.30
141 Octavio Dotel	.12	.30
142 Gary Sheffield	.12	.30
143 Andruw Jones	.12	.30
144 John Smoltz	.30	.75
145 Rafael Furcal	.12	.30
146 Javy Lopez	.12	.30
147 Shane Reynolds	.12	.30
148 Horacio Ramirez	.12	.30
149 Mike Hampton	.12	.30
150 Jung Bong	.12	.30
151 Ruben Quevedo	.12	.30
152 Ben Sheets	.12	.30
153 Geoff Jenkins	.12	.30
154 Royce Clayton	.12	.30
155 Glendon Rusch	.12	.30
156 John Vander Wal	.12	.30
157 Scott Podsednik	.12	.30
158 Jim Edmonds	.20	.50
159 Tino Martinez	.20	.50
160 Albert Pujols	.40	1.00
161 Matt Morris	.12	.30
162 Woody Williams	.12	.30
163 Edgar Renteria	.12	.30
164 Jason Isringhausen	.12	.30
165 Jason Simontacchi	.12	.30
166 Kerry Robinson	.12	.30
167 Sammy Sosa	.30	.75
168 Joe Borowski	.12	.30
169 Tony Womack	.12	.30
170 Antonio Alfonseca	.12	.30
171 Corey Patterson	.12	.30
172 Mark Prior	.20	.50
173 Moises Alou	.12	.30
174 Matt Clement	.12	.30
175 Randall Simon	.12	.30
176 Randy Johnson	.30	.75
177 Luis Gonzalez	.12	.30
178 Craig Counsell	.12	.30
179 Miguel Batista	.12	.30
180 Steve Finley	.12	.30
181 Brandon Webb	.12	.30
182 Danny Bautista	.12	.30
183 Oscar Villarreal	.12	.30
184 Shawn Green	.12	.30
185 Brian Jordan	.12	.30
186 Fred McGriff	.20	.50
187 Andy Ashby	.12	.30
188 Rickey Henderson	.30	.75
189 Dave Roberts	.20	.50
190 Eric Gagne	.12	.30
191 Kazuhisa Ishii	.12	.30
192 Adrian Beltre	.30	.75
193 Vladimir Guerrero	.20	.50
194 Livan Hernandez	.12	.30
195 Ron Calloway	.12	.30
196 Sun Woo Kim	.12	.30
197 Wil Cordero	.12	.30
198 Brad Wilkerson	.12	.30
199 Orlando Cabrera	.12	.30
200 Barry Bonds	.50	1.25
201 Ray Durham	.12	.30
202 Andres Galarraga	.20	.50
203 Benito Santiago	.12	.30
204 Jose Cruz Jr.	.12	.30
205 Jason Schmidt	.12	.30
206 Kirk Rueter	.12	.30
207 Felix Rodriguez	.12	.30
208 Mike Lowell	.12	.30
209 Luis Castillo	.12	.30
210 Derrek Lee	.12	.30
211 Andy Fox	.12	.30
212 Tommy Phelps	.12	.30
213 Todd Hollandsworth	.12	.30
214 Brad Penny	.12	.30
215 Juan Pierre	.12	.30
216 Mike Piazza	.30	.75
217 Jae Weong Seo	.12	.30
218 Ty Wigginton	.12	.30
219 Al Leiter	.12	.30
220 Roger Cedeno	.12	.30
221 Timo Perez	.12	.30
222 Aaron Heilman	.12	.30
223 Pedro Astacio	.12	.30
224 Joe McEwing	.12	.30
225 Ryan Klesko	.12	.30
226 Brian Giles	.12	.30
227 Mark Kotsay	.12	.30
228 Brian Lawrence	.12	.30
229 Rod Beck	.12	.30
230 Trevor Hoffman	.20	.50
231 Sean Burroughs	.12	.30
232 Bob Abreu	.12	.30
233 Jim Thome	.20	.50
234 David Bell	.12	.30
235 Jimmy Rollins	.20	.50
236 Mike Lieberthal	.12	.30
237 Vicente Padilla	.12	.30
238 Randy Wolf	.12	.30
239 Reggie Sanders	.12	.30
240 Jason Kendall	.12	.30
241 Jack Wilson	.12	.30
242 Jose Hernandez	.12	.30
243 Kip Wells	.12	.30
244 Carlos Rivera	.12	.30
245 Craig Wilson	.12	.30
246 Adam Dunn	.20	.50
247 Sean Casey	.12	.30
248 Danny Graves	.12	.30
249 Ryan Dempster	.12	.30
250 Barry Larkin	.20	.50
251 Reggie Taylor	.12	.30
252 Wily Mo Pena	.12	.30
253 Larry Walker	.20	.50
254 Mark Sweeney	.12	.30
255 Preston Wilson	.12	.30
256 Jason Jennings	.12	.30
257 Charles Johnson	.12	.30
258 Jay Payton	.12	.30
259 Chris Stynes	.12	.30
260 Juan Uribe	.12	.30
261 Hideki Matsui SH CL	.50	1.25
262 Barry Bonds SH CL	.50	1.25
263 Dontrelle Willis SH CL	.12	.30
264 Kevin Millwood SH CL	.12	.30
265 Billy Wagner SH CL	.12	.30
266 Rocco Baldelli SH CL	.12	.30
267 Roger Clemens SH CL	.40	1.00
268 Rafael Palmeiro SH CL	.20	.50
269 Miguel Cabrera SH CL	.30	.75
270 Jose Contreras SH CL	.12	.30
271 Aaron Sele	.12	.30
272 Bartolo Colon	.12	.30
273 Darin Erstad	.12	.30
274 Francisco Rodriguez	.20	.50
275 Garret Anderson	.12	.30
276 Jose Guillen	.12	.30
277 Troy Percival	.12	.30
278 Alex Cintron	.12	.30
279 Casey Fossum	.12	.30
280 Elmer Dessens	.12	.30
281 Jose Valverde	.12	.30
282 Matt Mantei	.12	.30
283 Richie Sexson	.12	.30
284 Roberto Alomar	.20	.50
285 Shea Hillenbrand	.12	.30
286 Chipper Jones	.30	.75
287 Greg Maddux	.40	1.00
288 J.D. Drew	.12	.30
289 Marcus Giles	.12	.30
290 Mike Hessman	.12	.30
291 John Thomson	.12	.30
292 Russ Ortiz	.12	.30
293 Adam Loewen	.12	.30
294 Jack Cust	.12	.30
295 Jerry Hairston Jr.	.12	.30
296 Kurt Ainsworth	.12	.30
297 Luis Matos	.12	.30
298 Marty Cordova	.12	.30
299 Sidney Ponson	.12	.30
300 Bill Mueller	.12	.30
301 Curt Schilling	.20	.50
302 David Ortiz	.30	.75
303 Johnny Damon	.20	.50
304 Keith Foulke Sox	.12	.30
305 Pokey Reese	.12	.30
306 Scott Williamson	.12	.30
307 Tim Wakefield	.20	.50
308 Alex S. Gonzalez	.12	.30
309 Aramis Ramirez	.12	.30
310 Carlos Zambrano	.20	.50
311 Juan Cruz	.12	.30
312 Kerry Wood	.12	.30
313 Kyle Farnsworth	.12	.30
314 Aaron Rowand	.12	.30
315 Esteban Loaiza	.12	.30
316 Frank Thomas	.30	.75
317 Joe Borchard	.12	.30
318 Joe Crede	.12	.30
319 Miguel Olivo	.12	.30
320 Willie Harris	.12	.30
321 Aaron Harang	.12	.30
322 Austin Kearns	.12	.30
323 Brandon Claussen	.12	.30
324 Brandon Larson	.12	.30
325 Ryan Freel	.12	.30
326 Ken Griffey Jr.	.60	1.50
327 Ryan Wagner	.12	.30
328 Alex Escobar	.12	.30
329 Coco Crisp	.12	.30
330 David Riske	.12	.30
331 Jody Gerut	.12	.30
332 Josh Bard	.12	.30
333 Travis Hafner	.12	.30
334 Chin-Hui Tsao	.12	.30
335 Denny Stark	.12	.30
336 Jeromy Burnitz	.12	.30
337 Shawn Chacon	.12	.30
338 Todd Helton	.20	.50
339 Vinny Castilla	.12	.30
340 Alex Sanchez	.12	.30
341 Carlos Pena	.20	.50
342 Fernando Vina	.12	.30
343 Jason Johnson	.12	.30
344 Matt Anderson	.12	.30
345 Mike Maroth	.12	.30
346 Rondell White	.12	.30
347 A.J. Burnett	.12	.30
348 Alex Gonzalez	.12	.30
349 Armando Benitez	.12	.30
350 Carl Pavano	.12	.30
351 Hee Seop Choi	.12	.30
352 Ivan Rodriguez	.20	.50
353 Josh Beckett	.12	.30
354 Josh Willingham	.20	.50
355 Adam Everett	.12	.30
356 Brandon Duckworth	.12	.30
357 Jason Lane	.12	.30
358 Jeff Kent	.12	.30
359 Jeriome Robertson	.12	.30
360 Lance Berkman	.20	.50
361 Wade Miller	.12	.30
362 Aaron Guiel	.12	.30
363 Angel Berroa	.12	.30
364 Carlos Beltran	.20	.50
365 David DeJesus	.12	.30
366 Desi Relaford	.12	.30
367 Joe Randa	.12	.30
368 Runelvys Hernandez	.12	.30
369 Edwin Jackson	.12	.30
370 Hideo Nomo	.30	.75
371 Jeff Weaver	.12	.30
372 Juan Encarnacion	.12	.30
373 Odalis Perez	.12	.30
374 Paul Lo Duca	.12	.30
375 Robin Ventura	.12	.30
376 Bill Hall	.12	.30
377 Chad Moeller	.12	.30
378 Chris Capuano	.12	.30
379 Junior Spivey	.12	.30
380 Rickie Weeks	.12	.30
381 Wes Helms	.12	.30
382 Brad Radke	.12	.30
383 Jacque Jones	.12	.30
384 Joe Mays	.12	.30
385 Joe Nathan	.12	.30
386 Johan Santana	.20	.50
387 Nick Punto	.12	.30
388 Shannon Stewart	.12	.30
389 Carl Everett	.12	.30
390 Claudio Vargas	.12	.30
391 Jose Vidro	.12	.30
392 Nick Johnson	.12	.30
393 Rocky Biddle	.12	.30
394 Tony Armas Jr.	.12	.30
395 Braden Looper	.12	.30
396 Cliff Floyd	.12	.30
397 Jason Phillips	.12	.30
398 Mike Cameron	.12	.30
399 Tom Glavine	.20	.50
400 Kenny Lofton	.12	.30
401 Alfonso Soriano	.20	.50
402 Bernie Williams	.20	.50
403 Javier Vazquez	.12	.30
404 Jon Lieber	.12	.30
405 Jose Contreras	.12	.30
406 Kevin Brown	.12	.30
407 Mariano Rivera	.40	1.00
408 Arthur Rhodes	.12	.30
409 Eric Byrnes	.12	.30
410 Erubiel Durazo	.12	.30
411 Graham Koonce	.12	.30
412 Marco Scutaro	.20	.50
413 Mark Mulder	.12	.30
414 Mark Redman	.12	.30
415 Rich Harden	.12	.30
416 Brett Myers	.12	.30
417 Chase Utley	.20	.50
418 Kevin Millwood	.12	.30
419 Marlon Byrd	.12	.30
420 Pat Burrell	.12	.30
421 Placido Polanco	.12	.30
422 Tim Worrell	.12	.30
423 Jason Bay	.20	.50
424 Josh Fogg	.12	.30
425 Kris Benson	.12	.30
426 Mike Gonzalez	.12	.30
427 Oliver Perez	.12	.30
428 Tike Redman	.12	.30
429 Adam Eaton	.12	.30
430 Ismael Valdes	.12	.30
431 Jake Peavy	.12	.30
432 Khalil Greene	.20	.50
433 Mark Loretta	.12	.30
434 Phil Nevin	.12	.30
435 Ramon Hernandez	.12	.30
436 A.J. Pierzynski	.12	.30
437 Edgardo Alfonzo	.12	.30
438 J.T. Snow	.12	.30
439 Jerome Williams	.12	.30
440 Marquis Grissom	.12	.30
441 Robb Nen	.12	.30
442 Bret Boone	.12	.30
443 Freddy Garcia	.12	.30
444 Gil Meche	.12	.30
445 John Olerud	.12	.30
446 Rich Aurilia	.12	.30
447 Shigetoshi Hasegawa	.12	.30
448 Bo Hart	.12	.30
449 Danny Haren	.12	.30
450 Jason Marquis	.12	.30
451 Marlon Anderson	.12	.30
452 Scott Rolen	.20	.50
453 So Taguchi	.12	.30
454 Carl Crawford	.20	.50
455 Delmon Young	.20	.50
456 Geoff Blum	.12	.30
457 Jesus Colome	.12	.30
458 Jonny Gomes	.12	.30
459 Lance Carter	.12	.30
460 Robert Fick	.12	.30
461 Chan Ho Park	.20	.50
462 Francisco Cordero	.12	.30
463 Jeff Nelson	.12	.30
464 Jeff Zimmerman	.12	.30
465 Kenny Rogers	.12	.30
466 Aquilino Lopez	.12	.30
467 Carlos Delgado	.12	.30
468 Frank Catalanotto	.12	.30
469 Reed Johnson	.12	.30
470 Pat Hentgen	.12	.30
471 Curt Schilling SH CL	.12	.30
472 Gary Sheffield SH CL	.12	.30
473 Javier Vazquez SH CL	.12	.30
474 Kazuo Matsui SH CL	.20	.50
475 Kevin Brown SH CL	.12	.30
476 Rafael Palmeiro SH CL	.20	.50
477 Richie Sexson SH CL	.12	.30
478 Roger Clemens SH CL	.40	1.00
479 Vladimir Guerrero SH CL	.20	.50
480 Alex Rodriguez SH CL	.40	1.00
481 Jake Woods SR RC	.40	1.00
482 Tim Bittner SR RC	.40	1.00
483 Brandon Medders SR RC	.40	1.00
484 Casey Daigle SR RC	.40	1.00
485 Jerry Gil SR RC	.40	1.00
486 Mike Gosling SR RC	.40	1.00
487 Jose Capellan SR RC	.40	1.00
488 Onil Joseph SR RC	.40	1.00
489 Roman Colon SR RC	.40	1.00
490 Dave Crouthers SR RC	.40	1.00
491 Eddy Rodriguez SR RC	.40	1.00
492 Franklyn Gracesqui SR RC	.40	1.00
493 Jamie Brown SR RC	.40	1.00
494 Jerome Gamble SR RC	.40	1.00
495 Tim Hamulack SR RC	.40	1.00
496 Carlos Vasquez SR RC	.40	1.00
497 Renyel Pinto SR RC	.40	1.00
498 Ronny Cedeno SR RC	.40	1.00
499 Enemencio Pacheco SR RC	.40	1.00
500 Ryan Meaux SR RC	.40	1.00
501 Ryan Wing SR RC	.40	1.00
502 Shingo Takatsu SR RC	.40	1.00
503 William Bergolla SR RC	.40	1.00
504 Ivan Ochoa SR RC	.40	1.00
505 Mariano Gomez SR RC	.40	1.00
506 Justin Hampson SR RC	.40	1.00
507 Justin Huisman SR RC	.40	1.00
508 Scott Dohmann SR RC	.40	1.00
509 Donnie Kelly SR RC	.60	1.50
510 Chris Aguila SR RC	.40	1.00
511 Lincoln Holdzkom SR RC	.40	1.00
512 Freddy Guzman SR RC	.40	1.00
513 Hector Gimenez SR RC	.40	1.00
514 Jorge Vasquez SR RC	.40	1.00
515 Jason Frasor SR RC	.40	1.00
516 Chris Saenz SR RC	.40	1.00
517 Dennis Sarfate SR RC	.40	1.00
518 Colby Miller SR RC	.40	1.00
519 Jason Bartlett SR RC	1.25	3.00
520 Chad Bentz SR RC	.40	1.00
521 Josh Labandeira SR RC	.40	1.00
522 Shawn Hill SR RC	.40	1.00
523 Kazuo Matsui SR RC	.60	1.50
524 Carlos Hines SR RC	.40	1.00
525 Mike Vento SR RC	.40	1.00
526 Scott Proctor SR RC	.40	1.00
527 Sean Henn SR RC	.40	1.00
528 David Aardsma SR RC	.40	1.00
529 Ian Snell SR RC	.40	1.00
530 Mike Johnston SR RC	.40	1.00
531 Akinori Otsuka SR RC	.40	1.00
532 Rusty Tucker SR RC	.40	1.00
533 Justin Knoedler SR RC	.40	1.00
534 Merkin Valdez SR RC	.40	1.00
535 Greg Dobbs SR RC	.40	1.00
536 Justin Leone SR RC	.40	1.00
537 Shawn Camp SR RC	.40	1.00
538 Edwin Moreno SR RC	.40	1.00
539 Angel Chavez SR RC	.40	1.00
540 Jesse Harper SR RC	.40	1.00
541 Alex Rodriguez	.40	1.00
542 Roger Clemens	.40	1.00
543 Andy Pettitte	.20	.50
544 Vladimir Guerrero	.20	.50
545 David Wells	.12	.30
546 Derrek Lee	.12	.30
547 Carlos Beltran	.20	.50
548 Orlando Cabrera Sox	.12	.30
549 Paul Lo Duca	.12	.30
550 Dave Roberts	.20	.50
551 Guillermo Mota	.12	.30
552 Steve Finley	.12	.30
553 Juan Encarnacion	.12	.30
554 Larry Walker	.20	.50
555 Ty Wigginton	.12	.30
556 Doug Mientkiewicz	.12	.30
557 Roberto Alomar	.20	.50
558 B.J. Upton	.20	.50
559 Brad Penny	.12	.30
560 Hee Seop Choi	.12	.30
561 David Wright	.25	.60
562 Nomar Garciaparra	.20	.50
563 Felix Rodriguez	.12	.30
564 Victor Zambrano	.12	.30
565 Kris Benson	.12	.30
566 Aarom Baldiris SR RC	.20	.50
567 Joey Gathright SR RC	.20	.50
568 Charles Thomas SR RC	.20	.50
569 Brian Dallimore SR RC	.20	.50
570 Chris Oxspring SR RC	.20	.50
571 Chris Shelton SR RC	.20	.50
572 Dioner Navarro SR RC	.30	.75
573 Edwardo Sierra SR RC	.20	.50
574 Fernando Nieve SR RC	.20	.50
575 Frank Francisco SR RC	.20	.50
576 Jeff Bennett SR RC	.20	.50
577 Justin Lehr SR RC	.20	.50
578 John Gall SR RC	.20	.50
579 Jorge Sequea SR RC	.20	.50
580 Justin Germano SR RC	.20	.50
581 Kazuhito Tadano SR RC	.20	.50
582 Kevin Cave SR RC	.20	.50
583 Jesse Crain SR RC	.30	.75
584 Luis A. Gonzalez SR RC	.20	.50
585 Michael Wuertz SR RC	.20	.50
586 Orlando Rodriguez SR RC	.20	.50
587 Phil Stockman SR RC	.20	.50
588 Ramon Ramirez SR RC	.20	.50
589 Roberto Novoa SR RC	.20	.50
590 Scott Kazmir SR RC	1.00	2.50

2004 Upper Deck Glossy

COMP.FACT.SET (590)	70.00	100.00

*GLOSSY: .75X TO 2X BASIC
ISSUED ONLY IN FACTORY SET FORM

2004 Upper Deck A Piece of History 500 Club

SERIES 1 STATED ODDS 1:8700
STATED PRINT RUN 350 SERIAL #'D CARDS

504HR Rafael Palmeiro	150.00	300.00

2004 Upper Deck Authentic Stars Jersey

SERIES 1 ODDS 1:48 HOBBY, 1:96 RETAIL
*GOLD: .75X TO 2X BASIC AS JSY
GOLD RANDOM INSERTS IN SERIES 1 PACKS
GOLD PRINT RUN 100 SERIAL #'d SETS

AJ Andruw Jones	4.00	10.00
AP Albert Pujols	6.00	15.00
AR Alex Rodriguez	4.00	10.00
AS Alfonso Soriano	3.00	8.00
BA Bob Abreu	3.00	8.00
BW Bernie Williams	4.00	10.00
BZ Barry Zito	3.00	8.00
CD Carlos Delgado	3.00	8.00
CJ Chipper Jones	4.00	10.00
CS Curt Schilling	3.00	8.00
DE Darin Erstad	3.00	8.00
EC Eric Chavez	3.00	8.00
FT Frank Thomas	4.00	10.00
GM Greg Maddux	4.00	10.00
HB Hank Blalock	3.00	8.00
HM Hideki Matsui	8.00	20.00
IR Ivan Rodriguez	4.00	10.00
IS Ichiro Suzuki	10.00	25.00
JB Jeff Bagwell	4.00	10.00
JD J.D. Drew	3.00	8.00
JG Jason Giambi	3.00	8.00
JH Josh Beckett	3.00	8.00
JK Jeff Kent	3.00	8.00
KG Ken Griffey Jr.	6.00	15.00
LW Larry Walker	3.00	8.00
MI Mike Piazza	4.00	10.00
MP Mark Prior	4.00	10.00
MT Mark Teixeira	4.00	10.00
PM Pedro Martinez	4.00	10.00
PN Phil Nevin	3.00	8.00
RB Rocco Baldelli	3.00	8.00
RC Roger Clemens	6.00	15.00
RJ Randy Johnson	4.00	10.00
RO Roberto Alomar	4.00	10.00
SG Shawn Green	3.00	8.00
SS Sammy Sosa	4.00	10.00
TG Troy Glaus	3.00	8.00
TH Todd Helton	4.00	10.00
TL Tom Glavine	4.00	10.00
TM Tino Martinez	4.00	10.00
TO Torii Hunter	3.00	8.00
VG Vladimir Guerrero	4.00	10.00

2004 Upper Deck Authentic Stars Jersey Update

UPDATE GU ODDS 1:12 '04 UPDATE SETS
STATED PRINT RUN 75 SERIAL #'d SETS

AK Austin Kearns	4.00	10.00
CB Carlos Beltran	4.00	10.00
DJ Derek Jeter	8.00	20.00
HA Roy Halladay	4.00	10.00
HN Hideo Nomo	10.00	25.00
HU Tim Hudson	4.00	10.00
JE Jim Edmonds	4.00	10.00
JR Jose Reyes	4.00	10.00
JT Jim Thome	6.00	15.00
KW Kerry Wood	4.00	10.00
LB Lance Berkman	4.00	10.00
MO Magglio Ordonez	4.00	10.00
MR Manny Ramirez	6.00	15.00
OS Roy Oswalt	4.00	10.00
PW Preston Wilson	4.00	10.00
RF Rafael Furcal	4.00	10.00
RH Rich Harden	4.00	10.00
RP Rafael Palmeiro	6.00	15.00
SR Scott Rolen	6.00	15.00
TE Miguel Tejada	4.00	10.00
VW Vernon Wells	4.00	10.00
WE Brandon Webb	4.00	10.00

2004 Upper Deck Awesome Honors

COMPLETE SET (10)	8.00	20.00
SERIES 2 STATED ODDS 1:12 H/R		
1 Albert Pujols	1.25	3.00
2 Alex Rodriguez	1.25	3
3 Angel Berroa	.40	1
4 Dontrelle Willis	.40	1
5 Eric Gagne	.40	1
6 Garret Anderson	.40	1
7 Ivan Rodriguez	.60	1
8 Josh Beckett	.40	1
9 Mariano Rivera	1.25	3
10 Roy Halladay	.60	1

2004 Upper Deck Awesome Honors Jersey

*GOLD: .6X TO 1.5X BASIC
GOLD PRINT RUN 165 SERIAL #'d SETS
OVERALL SER.2 GU ODDS 1:12 H, 1:24 R

AJ Andruw Jones GG	3.00	8
AP Albert Pujols PC	6.00	15
AP1 Albert Pujols HA	6.00	15
AP2 Albert Pujols POM	6.00	15
AR Alex Rodriguez MVP	5.00	12
AR1 Alex Rodriguez GG	5.00	12
AR2 Alex Rodriguez HA	5.00	12
AR3 Alex Rodriguez POM	5.00	12
AS Alfonso Soriano POM	2.00	5.
BB Bret Boone GG	2.00	5.
BM Ben Molina GG	2.00	5.
DL Derrek Lee GG	3.00	8
DW Dontrelle Willis ROY	3.00	8
EC Eric Chavez GG	2.00	5
EG Eric Gagne CY	2.00	5.
EG1 Eric Gagne RA	2.00	5.
EM Edgar Martinez POM	3.00	8.
GA Garret Anderson AS MVP	2.00	5.
HU Torii Hunter GG	2.00	5.
IR Ivan Rodriguez NLCS MVP	3.00	8
IS Ichiro Suzuki GG	10.00	25.
JB Josh Beckett WS MVP	2.00	5.
JE Jim Edmonds GG	2.00	5.
JG Jason Giambi POM	2.00	5.
JM Jamie Moyer MAN	2.00	5.
JO John Olerud GG	2.00	5.
JS John Smoltz MAN	3.00	8.
JT Jim Thome POM	3.00	8.
LC Luis Castillo GG	2.00	5.
MC Mike Cameron GG	2.00	5.
MH Mike Hampton GG	2.00	5.
MO Magglio Ordonez POM	2.00	5.
MR Mariano Rivera ALCS MVP	3.00	8.
MU Mike Mussina GG	3.00	8.
RH Roy Halladay CY	2.00	5.
SR Scott Rolen GG	3.00	8.
TH Todd Helton POM	3.00	8.
VG Vladimir Guerrero POM	3.00	8.

2004 Upper Deck Awesome Honors Jersey Update

UPDATE GU ODDS 1:12 '04 UPDATE SETS
STATED PRINT RUN 75 SERIAL #'d SETS

AB Angel Berroa	4.00	10.
AP Albert Pujols	10.00	25.
AS Alfonso Soriano	4.00	10.
BE Adrian Beltre	4.00	10.
BG Brian Giles	4.00	10.
DL Derrek Lee	6.00	15.
EG Eric Gagne	4.00	10.
GS Gary Sheffield	4.00	10.
IR Ivan Rodriguez	6.00	15.
JM Joe Mauer	4.00	10.
KB Kevin Brown	4.00	10.
KM Kazuo Matsui	4.00	10.
MC Miguel Cabrera	6.00	15.
PE Andy Pettitte	6.00	15.
RC Roger Clemens	10.00	25.
RS Richie Sexson	4.00	10.
SC Curt Schilling	6.00	15.
SP Scott Podsednik	4.00	10.
VA Javier Vazquez	4.00	10.

2004 Upper Deck First Pitch Inserts

SERIES 1 STATED ODDS 1:72
CARD SP9 DOES NOT EXIST

LeBron James 10.00 25.00
Gordie Howe 4.00 10.00
) Ernie Banks 4.00 10.00
l General Tommy Franks 2.00 5.00
2 Ben Affleck 4.00 10.00
3 Halle Berry UER 4.00 10.00
l George H.W. Bush 2.00 5.00
5 George W. Bush 4.00 10.00

04 Upper Deck Game Winners Bat

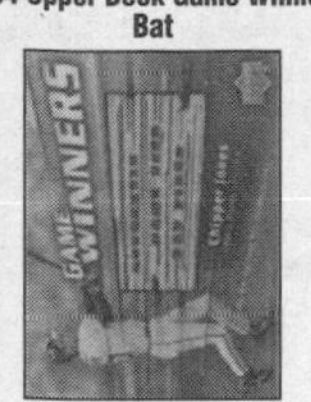

LD: .6X TO 1.5X BASIC
D PRINT RUN 50 SERIAL #'d SETS
RALL SER.2 GU ODDS 1:12 H, 1:24 R
Alex Gonzalez 3.00 8.00
Andruw Jones 4.00 10.00
Albert Pujols 8.00 20.00
Alfonso Soriano 3.00 8.00
Bobby Abreu 3.00 8.00
Bernie Williams 4.00 10.00
Chipper Jones 4.00 10.00
Corey Patterson 3.00 8.00
Darin Erstad 3.00 8.00
Derek Jeter 10.00 25.00
Gary Sheffield 3.00 8.00
Hank Blalock 3.00 8.00
Hideki Matsui 12.50 30.00
Torii Hunter 3.00 8.00
van Rodriguez 4.00 10.00
Jeff Bagwell 4.00 10.00
Jim Edmonds 3.00 8.00
Jason Giambi 3.00 8.00
Jorge Posada 4.00 10.00
Jim Thome 4.00 10.00
Miguel Cabrera 4.00 10.00
Mike Lowell 3.00 8.00
Magglio Ordonez 3.00 8.00
Mike Piazza 6.00 15.00
Mark Teixeira 4.00 10.00
Rafael Furcal 3.00 8.00
Ramon Hernandez 3.00 8.00
Ryan Klesko 3.00 8.00
Shawn Green 3.00 8.00
Scott Rolen 4.00 10.00
Miguel Tejada 3.00 8.00
Troy Glaus 3.00 8.00
Todd Helton 4.00 10.00
Trot Nixon 3.00 8.00
Vladimir Guerrero 4.00 10.00

2004 Upper Deck Going Deep Bat

RIES 1 ODDS 1:288 HOB, 1:576 RET
PRINT RUNS B/WN 12-123 COPIES PER
PRINT RUNS PROVIDED BY UPPER DECK
PRICING ON QTY OF 41 OR LESS
LD RANDOM INSERTS IN PACKS
LD PRINT RUN 50 SERIAL #'d SETS
GOLD PRICING DUE TO SCARCITY
Albert Pujols 10.00 25.00
Alfonso Soriano SP/53 4.00 10.00
Bob Abreu SP/110 4.00 10.00
Bernie Williams SP/56 6.00 15.00
Craig Biggio SP/89 6.00 15.00
Chipper Jones SP/69 6.00 15.00
Curt Schilling SP/57 4.00 10.00
Darin Erstad 4.00 10.00
Doug Mientkiewicz SP/123 4.00 10.00
Garret Anderson 4.00 10.00
Hideki Matsui SP/70 15.00 40.00
Hideo Nomo 6.00 15.00
Jeff Bagwell SP/92 6.00 15.00
Jim Edmonds SP 4.00 10.00
Javy Lopez SP/77 4.00 10.00
A Jorge Posada 6.00 15.00
O Jay Payton SP/100 4.00 10.00
Jim Thome 6.00 15.00
Ken Griffey Jr. SP 12.00 30.00
Kerry Wood SP/108 4.00 10.00
O Magglio Ordonez 4.00 10.00
P Mike Piazza 6.00 15.00
Omar Vizquel SP/115 6.00 15.00
A Rich Aurilia SP/102 4.00 10.00
B Rocco Baldelli SP 4.00 10.00
F Rafael Furcal SP 4.00 10.00
H Rickey Henderson SP/77 6.00 15.00
O Roberto Alomar 6.00 15.00
C Sandy Alomar Jr. SP/95 4.00 10.00
G Shawn Green SP/100 4.00 10.00
R Scott Rolen SP/77 6.00 15.00
G Troy Glaus SP/113 4.00 10.00
H Torii Hunter SP/115 4.00 10.00

2004 Upper Deck Headliners Jersey

SERIES 1 ODDS 1:48 HOBBY, 1:96 RETAIL
SP PRINT RUNS B/WN 97-153 COPIES PER
SP PRINT RUNS PROVIDED BY UPPER DECK
*GOLD: .75X TO 2X BASIC
*GOLD: .4X TO 1X BASIC SP p/r 97-153
GOLD RANDOM INSERTS IN SERIES 1 PACKS
GOLD PRINT RUN 100 SERIAL #'d SETS
AD Adam Dunn 2.50 6.00
BK Byung-Hyun Kim AS 1.50 4.00
BS Benito Santiago AS 1.50 4.00
CS Curt Schilling 2.50 6.00
GM Greg Maddux 5.00 12.00
HM Hideki Matsui 6.00 15.00
IS Ichiro Suzuki SP/153 15.00 40.00
JB Josh Beckett 1.50 4.00
JD Joe DiMaggio SP/153 20.00 50.00
JE Jim Edmonds 2.50 6.00
JH Jose Hernandez AS 1.50 4.00
JR Jimmy Rollins AS 2.50 6.00
JS Junior Spivey AS 1.50 4.00
JT Jim Thome 2.50 6.00
JV Jose Vidro AS 1.50 4.00
KG Ken Griffey Jr. 8.00 20.00
LB Lance Berkman 2.50 6.00
LC Luis Castillo AS 1.50 4.00
LG Luis Gonzalez 1.50 4.00
MA Mariano Rivera 5.00 12.00
MB Mark Buehrle AS 2.50 6.00
ML Mike Lowell AS 1.50 4.00
MM Mickey Mantle SP/97 30.00 80.00
MO Magglio Ordonez 2.50 6.00
MR Manny Ramirez 4.00 10.00
MS Matt Morris AS 1.50 4.00
MT Miguel Tejada 2.50 6.00
MU Mike Mussina 2.50 6.00
MY Mike Sweeney AS 1.50 4.00
PK Paul Konerko AS 2.50 6.00
PM Pedro Martinez 2.50 6.00
RF Robert Fick AS 1.50 4.00
RH Roy Halladay AS 2.50 6.00
RK Ryan Klesko 1.50 4.00
RO Roy Oswalt 2.50 6.00
SG Shawn Green 1.50 4.00
TB Tony Batista AS 1.50 4.00
TG Tom Glavine 2.50 6.00
TH Trevor Hoffman AS 2.50 6.00
TW Ted Williams SP/153 20.00 50.00
VG Vladimir Guerrero SP/153 6.00 15.00

2004 Upper Deck Derek Jeter Bonus

COMMON CARD (1-25) 2.00 5.00
1-25 THREE PER JETER BONUS PACK
COMMON JSY (26-32) 15.00 40.00
26-32 JSY PRINT RUN 99 #'d SETS
COMMON AU (33-37) 100.00 175.00
33-37 AU PRINT RUN 50 #'d SETS
38-42 AU JSY PRINT RUN 10 #'d SETS
AU JSY NO PRICING DUE TO SCARCITY
26-42 RANDOM IN JETER BONUS PACKS
ONE JETER BONUS PACK PER FACT.SET

2004 Upper Deck Magical Performances

SERIES 1 STATED ODDS 1:96 HOBBY
GOLD RANDOM INSERTS IN SER.1 HOBBY
GOLD STATED ODDS 1:1300 RETAIL
GOLD PRINT RUN 50 SERIAL #'d SETS
NO GOLD PRICING DUE TO SCARCITY
1 Mickey Mantle USC HR 12.00 30.00
2 Mickey Mantle 56 Triple Crown 12.00 30.00
3 Joe DiMaggio 56th Game 8.00 20.00
4 Joe DiMaggio Slides Home 8.00 20.00
5 Derek Jeter The Flip 10.00 25.00
6 Derek Jeter 00 AS MVP 10.00 25.00
7 R.Clemens 300 Win/4000 K 5.00 12.00
8 Roger Clemens 20-1 5.00 12.00
9 Alfonso Soriano Walkoff 2.50 6.00
10 Andy Pettitte 96 2.50 6.00
11 Hideki Matsui Grand Slam 6.00 15.00
12 Mike Mussina 1-Hitter 2.50 6.00
13 Jorge Posada ALDS HR 2.50 6.00
14 Jason Giambi Grand Slam 1.50 4.00
15 David Wells Perfect 1.50 4.00
16 Mariano Rivera 99 WS MVP 5.00 12.00
17 Yogi Berra 12 K's 4.00 10.00
18 Phil Rizzuto 50 MVP 2.50 6.00
19 Whitey Ford 61 CY 2.50 6.00
20 Jose Contreras 1st Win 1.50 4.00
21 Catfish Hunter Free Agent 2.50 6.00
22 Mickey Mantle Cycle 12.00 30.00
23 M.Mantle HR's Both Sides 12.00 30.00
24 Joe DiMaggio 3-Time MVP 8.00 20.00
25 Joe DiMaggio Cycle 8.00 20.00
26 Derek Jeter 7 Seasons 10.00 25.00
27 Derek Jeter Mr. November 10.00 25.00
28 Roger Clemens 1-Hitter 5.00 12.00
29 Roger Clemens 01 CY 5.00 12.00
30 Alfonso Soriano HR Record 2.50 6.00
31 Andy Pettitte ALCS 2.50 6.00
32 Hideki Matsui 4 Hits 6.00 15.00
33 Mike Mussina 1st Postseason 2.50 6.00
34 Jorge Posada 40 Doubles 2.50 6.00
35 Jason Giambi 200th HR 1.50 4.00
36 David Wells 3-Hitter 1.50 4.00
37 Mariano Rivera Saves 3 5.00 12.00
38 Yogi Berra 3-Time MVP 4.00 10.00
39 Phil Rizzuto Broadcasting 2.50 6.00
40 Whitey Ford 10 WS Wins 2.50 6.00
41 Jose Contreras 2 Hits 1.50 4.00
42 Catfish Hunter 200th Win 2.50 6.00

2004 Upper Deck Matsui Chronicles

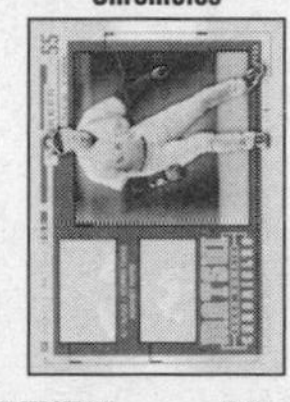

COMPLETE SET (60) 30.00 60.00
COMMON CARD (HM1-HM60) .75 2.00
ONE PER SERIES 1 RETAIL PACK

2004 Upper Deck National Pride

SERIES 1 STATED ODDS 1:6
1 Justin Orenduff .40 1.00
2 Micah Owings .25 .60
3 Steven Register .25 .60
4 Huston Street .40 1.00
5 Justin Verlander 2.50 6.00
6 Jered Weaver 1.00 2.50
7 Matt Campbell .25 .60
8 Stephen Head .25 .60
9 Mark Romanczuk .25 .60
10 Jeff Clement .40 1.00
11 Mike Nickeas .25 .60
12 Tyler Greene .25 .60
13 Paul Janish .40 1.00
14 Jeff Larish .25 .60
15 Eric Patterson .25 .60
16 Dustin Pedroia 1.25 3.00
17 Michael Griffin .25 .60
18 Brent Lillibridge .25 .60
19 Danny Putnam .25 .60
20 Seth Smith .40 1.00

2004 Upper Deck National Pride Jersey 1

SERIES 1 ODDS 1:24 HOBBY, 1:48 RETAIL
1 Justin Orenduff 2.00 5.00
2 Micah Owings 2.00 5.00
3 Steven Register 2.00 5.00
4 Huston Street 2.50 6.00
5 Justin Verlander 10.00 25.00
6 Jered Weaver 5.00 12.00
7 Matt Campbell 2.00 5.00
8 Stephen Head 2.00 5.00
9 Mark Romanczuk 2.00 5.00
10 Jeff Clement 4.00 10.00
11 Mike Nickeas 2.00 5.00
12 Tyler Greene 2.00 5.00
13 Paul Janish 2.00 5.00
14 Jeff Larish 2.00 5.00
15 Eric Patterson 2.00 5.00
16 Dustin Pedroia 2.00 5.00
17 Michael Griffin 2.00 5.00
18 Brent Lillibridge 2.00 5.00
19 Danny Putnam 2.00 5.00
20 Seth Smith 3.00 8.00
21 Justin Orenduff SP 3.00 8.00
22 Micah Owings SP 3.00 8.00
23 Steven Register SP 3.00 8.00
24 Huston Street SP 3.00 8.00
25 Justin Verlander SP 10.00 25.00
26 Jered Weaver SP 6.00 15.00
27 Matt Campbell SP 3.00 8.00
28 Stephen Head SP 3.00 8.00
29 Mark Romanczuk SP 3.00 8.00
30 Jeff Clement SP 5.00 12.00
31 Mike Nickeas SP 3.00 8.00
32 Tyler Greene SP 3.00 8.00
33 Paul Janish SP 3.00 8.00
34 Jeff Larish SP 3.00 8.00
35 Eric Patterson SP 3.00 8.00
36 Dustin Pedroia SP 3.00 8.00
37 Michael Griffin SP 3.00 8.00
38 Brent Lillibridge SP 3.00 8.00
39 Danny Putnam SP 3.00 8.00
40 Seth Smith SP 4.00 10.00
41 Delmon Young SP 6.00 15.00
42 Rickie Weeks SP 4.00 10.00

2004 Upper Deck National Pride Memorabilia 2

OVERALL SER.2 GU ODDS 1:12 H, 1:24 R
BBJ Brian Bruney Jsy 2.00 5.00
CBJ Chris Burke Jsy 2.00 5.00
CBP Chris Burke Pants 2.00 5.00
DUJ Justin Duchscherer Jsy 2.00 5.00
DUP Justin Duchscherer Pants 2.00 5.00
ERJ Eddie Rodriguez CO Jsy 2.00 5.00
ERP Eddie Rodriguez CO Pants 2.00 5.00
EYJ Ernie Young Jsy 2.00 5.00
GGJ Gabe Gross Jsy 2.00 5.00
GKJ Graham Koonce Jsy 2.00 5.00
GKP Graham Koonce Pants 2.00 5.00
GLJ Gerald Laird Jsy 2.00 5.00
GSJ Grady Sizemore Jsy 3.00 8.00
GSP Grady Sizemore Pants 3.00 8.00
HRJ Horacio Ramirez Jsy 2.00 5.00
HRP Horacio Ramirez Pants 2.00 5.00
JBJ John Van Benschoten Jsy 2.00 5.00
JBP John Van Benschoten Pants 2.00 5.00
JCJ Jesse Crain Jsy 3.00 8.00
JCP Jesse Crain Pants 3.00 8.00
JDJ J.D. Durbin Jsy 2.00 5.00
JGJ John Grabow Jsy 2.00 5.00
JHJ J.J. Hardy Jsy 2.00 5.00
JLJ Justin Leone Jsy 3.00 8.00
JLP Justin Leone Pants 3.00 8.00
JMJ Joe Mauer Jsy 6.00 15.00
JMP Joe Mauer Pants 6.00 15.00
JRJ Jeremy Reed Jsy 4.00 10.00
JSJ Jason Stanford Jsy 2.00 5.00
JSP Jason Stanford Pants 2.00 5.00
MLJ Mike Lamb Jsy 2.00 5.00
MRJ Mike Rouse Jsy 2.00 5.00
MRP Mike Rouse Pants 2.00 5.00
RMP Ryan Madson Pants 2.00 5.00
RRJ Royce Ring Jsy 2.00 5.00
RRP Royce Ring Pants 2.00 5.00
TBJ Thad Bosley CO Jsy 2.00 5.00
TWJ Todd Williams Jsy 2.00 5.00

2004 Upper Deck Peak Performers Jersey

*GOLD: .6X TO 1.5X BASIC
GOLD PRINT RUN 165 SERIAL #'d SETS
OVERALL SER.2 GU ODDS 1:12 H, 1:24 R
AP Albert Pujols 6.00 15.00
AS Alfonso Soriano 2.00 5.00
BE Josh Beckett 2.00 5.00
BP Brandon Phillips 2.00 5.00
CB Craig Biggio 3.00 8.00
CD Carlos Delgado 2.00 5.00
CS Curt Schilling 3.00 8.00
EG Eric Gagne 2.00 5.00
FT Frank Thomas 3.00 8.00
HB Hank Blalock 2.00 5.00
HM Hideki Matsui 10.00 25.00
HN Hideo Nomo 3.00 8.00
IR Ivan Rodriguez 3.00 8.00
IS Ichiro Suzuki 10.00 25.00
JB Jeff Bagwell 3.00 8.00
JR Jose Reyes 2.00 5.00
JT Jim Thome 3.00 8.00
KG Ken Griffey Jr. 6.00 15.00
KW Kerry Wood 2.00 5.00
LB Lance Berkman 2.00 5.00
LC Luis Castillo 2.00 5.00
MM Mike Mussina 3.00 8.00
MO Magglio Ordonez 2.00 5.00
MP Mark Prior 3.00 8.00
MT Miguel Tejada 2.00 5.00
OV Omar Vizquel 3.00 8.00
PB Pat Burrell 2.00 5.00
PE Andy Pettitte 3.00 8.00
PL Paul Lo Duca 2.00 5.00
PM Pedro Martinez 3.00 8.00
RF Rafael Furcal 2.00 5.00
RP Rafael Palmeiro 3.00 8.00
SA C.C. Sabathia 2.00 5.00
SG Shawn Green 2.00 5.00
SR Scott Rolen 3.00 8.00
TH Todd Helton 3.00 8.00
VG Vladimir Guerrero 3.00 8.00
VW Vernon Wells 2.00 5.00

2004 Upper Deck Famous Quotes

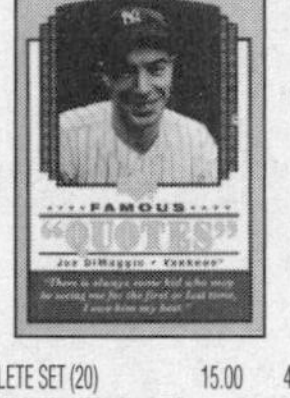

COMPLETE SET (20) 15.00 40.00
SERIES 2 STATED ODDS 1:6 H/R
1 Al Lopez .40 1.00
2 Bob Feller .60 1.50
3 Bob Gibson .60 1.50
4 Brooks Robinson .60 1.50
5 Cal Ripken 3.00 8.00
6 Carl Yastrzemski 1.00 2.50
7 Earl Weaver .60 1.50
8 Eddie Mathews 1.00 2.50
9 Ernie Banks 1.00 2.50
10 Greg Maddux 1.25 3.00
11 Joe DiMaggio 2.00 5.00
12 Mickey Mantle 3.00 8.00
13 Nolan Ryan 3.00 8.00
14 Stan Musial 1.50 4.00
15 Ted Williams 2.00 5.00
16 Tom Seaver .60 1.50
17 Tommy Lasorda .60 1.50
18 Warren Spahn .60 1.50
19 Whitey Ford .60 1.50
20 Yogi Berra 1.00 2.50

2004 Upper Deck Signature Stars Black Ink 1

Please note that Roger Clemens did not return his cards in time for pack-out and those cards could be redeemed until November 10, 2006.
SER.1 ODDS 1:288 H,1:24 UPD BOX, 1:1800 R
PRINT RUNS B/WN 18-479 COPIES PER
NO PRICING ON QTY OF 25 OR LESS
EXCHANGE DEADLINE 11/10/06
AG Andres Galarraga/248 6.00 15.00
AH Aaron Heilman/49 10.00 25.00
BK Billy Koch/429 4.00 10.00
CR Cal Ripken/69 125.00 200.00
DR1 Dave Roberts/278 5.00 12.00
JRA Joe Randa/271 6.00 15.00
KI Kazuhisa Ishii/58 10.00 25.00
MO Magglio Ordonez/377 6.00 15.00
MU Mike Mussina/68 15.00 40.00
NG Nomar Garciaparra/69 60.00 120.00
NR1 Nolan Ryan/69 75.00 150.00
RA Rich Aurilia/479 4.00 10.00
RH1 Rich Harden/163 6.00 15.00
TH Torii Hunter/374 6.00 15.00
VG Vladimir Guerrero/68 30.00 60.00

2004 Upper Deck Signature Stars Black Ink 2

OVERALL SER.2 SIG ODDS 1:288 H, 1:1500 R
PRINT RUNS B/WN 43-450 COPIES PER
BB Bret Boone/43 15.00 40.00
BW Brandon Webb/60 6.00 15.00
DB Dewon Brazelton/96 4.00 10.00
DR2 Dave Roberts/450 5.00 12.00
DS Darryl Strawberry/160 10.00 25.00
DW Dontrelle Willis/160 10.00 25.00
EC Eric Chavez/60 10.00 25.00
EG Eric Gagne/160 10.00 25.00
JC Jose Canseco/160 15.00 40.00
JV Javier Vazquez/60 10.00 25.00
KG Ken Griffey Jr./450 40.00 80.00
MT Mark Teixeira/200 6.00 15.00
RH2 Rich Harden/65 10.00 25.00
RW Rickie Weeks/65 10.00 25.00

2004 Upper Deck Signature Stars Blue Ink 1

SER.1 ODDS 1:288 H,1:24 UPD BOX, 1:1800 R
STATED PRINT RUN 25 SERIAL #'d SETS
MATSUI PRINT RUN 324 SERIAL #'d CARDS
NO PRICING ON QTY OF 25 OR LESS
EXCHANGE DEADLINE 11/10/06
HM Hideki Matsui/324 175.00 300.00

2004 Upper Deck Signature Stars Blue Ink 2

OVERALL SER.2 SIG ODDS 1:288 H, 1:1500 R
PRINT RUNS B/WN 20-95 COPIES PER
NO PRICING ON QTY OF 25 OR LESS
NR2 Nolan Ryan/95 40.00 80.00

2004 Upper Deck Signature Stars Gold

SER.1 ODDS 1:288 H, 1:24 MINI, 1:1800 R
STATED PRINT RUN 99 SERIAL #'d SETS
ALL EXCEPT MATSUI FEATURE BLUE INK
NO PRICING DUE TO SCARCITY
EXCHANGE DEADLINE 11/10/06

2004 Upper Deck Super Patch Logos 2

OVERALL SERIES 2 ODDS 1:2500 H/R
PRINT RUNS B/WN 8-34 COPIES PER
PRINT RUNS PROVIDED BY UPPER DECK
CARDS ARE NOT SERIAL-NUMBERED
NO PRICING DUE TO SCARCITY

2004 Upper Deck Super Patches Logos 1

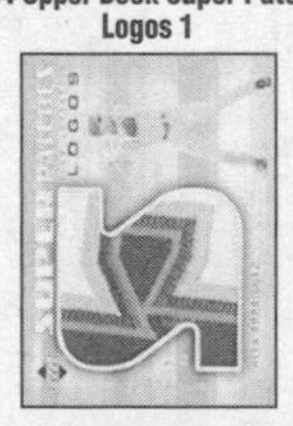

OVERALL PATCH SERIES 1 ODDS 1:7500
PRINT RUNS B/WN 8-25 COPIES PER
PRINT RUNS PROVIDED BY UPPER DECK
NO PRICING DUE TO SCARCITY

2004 Upper Deck Super Patch Numbers 2

OVERALL SERIES 2 ODDS 1:2500 H/R
PRINT RUNS B/WN 2-45 COPIES PER
PRINT RUNS PROVIDED BY UPPER DECK
CARDS ARE NOT SERIAL-NUMBERED
NO PRICING DUE TO SCARCITY

2004 Upper Deck Super Patches Numbers 1

OVERALL PATCH SERIES 1 ODDS 1:7500
PRINT RUNS B/WN 10-25 COPIES PER
PRINT RUNS PROVIDED BY UPPER DECK
NO PRICING DUE TO SCARCITY

2004 Upper Deck Super Patch Stripes 2

OVERALL SERIES 2 ODDS 1:2500 H/R
PRINT RUNS B/WN 6-65 COPIES PER
PRINT RUNS PROVIDED BY UPPER DECK
CARDS ARE NOT SERIAL-NUMBERED
NO PRICING DUE TO SCARCITY

2004 Upper Deck Super Patches Stripes 1

OVERALL PATCH SERIES 1 ODDS 1:7500
PRINT RUNS B/WN 25-40 COPIES PER
PRINT RUNS PROVIDED BY UPPER DECK
NO PRICING DUE TO SCARCITY

2004 Upper Deck Super Sluggers

COMPLETE SET (30) 10.00 25.00
ONE PER SERIES 2 RETAIL PACK
1 Albert Pujols 1.00 2.50
2 Alex Rodriguez 1.00 2.50
3 Alfonso Soriano .50 1.25
4 Andruw Jones .30 .75
5 Bret Boone .30 .75
6 Carlos Delgado .30 .75
7 Edgar Renteria .30 .75
8 Eric Chavez .30 .75
9 Frank Thomas .75 2.00
10 Garret Anderson .30 .75
11 Gary Sheffield .30 .75
12 Jason Giambi .30 .75
13 Javy Lopez .30 .75
14 Jeff Bagwell .50 1.25
15 Jim Edmonds .50 1.25
16 Jim Thome .50 1.25
17 Jorge Posada .50 1.25
18 Lance Berkman .50 1.25
19 Magglio Ordonez .50 1.25
20 Manny Ramirez .75 2.00
21 Mike Lowell .30 .75
22 Nomar Garciaparra .50 1.25
23 Preston Wilson .30 .75
24 Rafael Palmeiro .50 1.25
25 Richie Sexson .30 .75
26 Sammy Sosa .75 2.00
27 Shawn Green .30 .75
28 Todd Helton .50 1.25
29 Vernon Wells .30 .75
30 Vladimir Guerrero .50 1.25

2004 Upper Deck Twenty-Five Salute

COMPLETE SET (10) 4.00 10.00
SERIES 1 STATED ODDS 1:12
1 Barry Bonds 1.50 4.00
2 Troy Glaus .40 1.00
3 Andruw Jones .40 1.00
4 Jay Gibbons .40 1.00
5 Jeremy Giambi .40 1.00
6 Jason Giambi .40 1.00
7 Jim Thome .60 1.50
8 Rafael Palmeiro .60 1.50
9 Carlos Delgado .40 1.00
10 Dmitri Young .40 1.00

2004 Upper Deck Chevron

This 12-card standard-size set was issued by Upper Deck in conjunction with Chevron gas stations. The cards are in the design of the basic 2004 Upper Deck set except that there is a clean outta here logo added to the front.

COMPLETE SET .75 2.00
1 Andruw Jones .10 .25
2 Hank Blalock .10 .25
3 Jeff Bagwell .15 .40
4 Vladimir Guerrero .15 .40
5 Shawn Green .10 .25
6 Mike Lowell .10 .25
7 Aubrey Huff .10 .25
8 Richie Sexson .10 .25
9 Brian Giles .10 .25
10 Bret Boone .10 .25
11 A.J. Pierzynski .10 .25
12 Eric Chavez .10 .25

2004 Upper Deck Holiday Card

This one card set, which measures approximately 6 1/4" by 4 1/2" was issued by Upper Deck to wish hobby media, dealers and collectors a happy holiday. The front features a superimposed shot of five Yankee greats while the back has holiday wishes from Upper Deck.

HH4 Babe Ruth 5.00 12.00
Lou Gehrig
Joe DiMaggio
Mickey Mantle
Derek Jeter

2004 Upper Deck Pepsi Get Out There and Play

NNO Sammy Sosa 1.25 3.00

2004 Upper Deck Sportsfest

These cards were issued in groups of five over the course of three days at the 2004 Sportsfest card show in Chicago. Collectors would receive a group of 5 each day in exchange for 10 Upper Deck card wrappers that carried and SRP valued of $2.99 or higher. A 16th card was issued as an exchange card good for the first pick in the 2004 NBA draft.

STATED PRINT RUN 500 SER.#'d SETS
SF4 Ken Griffey Jr. 2.00 5.00
SF5 Ichiro Suzuki 1.50 4.00
SF6 Derek Jeter 4.00 10.00
SF7 Mickey Mantle 2.50 6.00
SF8 Joe DiMaggio 2.00 5.00

2005 Upper Deck Sportsfest

STATED PRINT RUN 750 SER.#'d SETS
MLB1 Ken Griffey Jr. 2.00 5.00
MLB2 Mark Prior .60 1.50
MLB3 Derek Jeter 2.50 6.00
MLB4 Carlos Beltran .60 1.50
MLB5 Albert Pujols 1.25 3.00
MLB6 Curt Schilling .60 1.50

2006 Upper Deck Sportsfest

MLB1 Ken Griffey Jr. 1.50 4.00
MLB2 Derek Jeter 2.00 5.00
MLB3 Albert Pujols 1.00 2.50
MLB4 Miguel Cabrera .75 2.00
MLB5 Scott Podsednik .30 .75
MLB6 Derrek Lee .30 .75

2007 Upper Deck Sportsfest

UNPRICED AUTO PRINT RUN 3 TO 5 SETS
SF1 Cal Ripken Jr. 3.00 8.00
SF2 Ken Griffey Jr. 1.50 4.00
SF3 Derek Jeter 2.00 5.00
SF4 Kei Igawa .75 2.00
SF5 Daisuke Matsuzaka 1.25 3.00
SF6 Derrek Lee .30 .75

2004 Upper Deck Sunkist

This six-card set was attached to packages of Sunkist oranges. These standard-size cards featured players dressed up in their little league uniforms while backs feature information about the player's little league days along with an health hint.

COMPLETE SET (6) 1.25 3.00
1 Rollie Fingers .30 .75
2 Gary Carter .30 .75
3 Mark McGwire .75 2.00
4 Mickey Morandini
5 Paul O'Neill .30 .75
6 Dave Stieb .20 .50

2005 Upper Deck

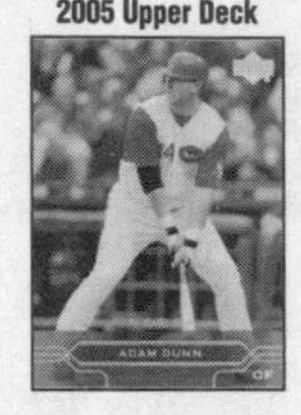

This 300-card first series was released in November, 2004. The set was issued in 10-card hobby packs with an $3 SRP which came 24 packs to a box and 12 boxes to a case. The set was also issued in 10-card retail packs which also had a $3 SRP and came 24 packs to a box and 12 boxes to a case. The hobby and retail packs are differentiated as there is different insert odds depending on which class of pack it is. Subsets include: Super Rookies (211-260); Team Leaders (261-290) and Pennant Race (291-300). The 200-card second series was released in June, 2004 and had the following subsets: Super Rookies (431-450); Bound for Glory (451-470) and Team Checklists (471-500).

COMPLETE SET (500) 20.00 50.00
COMPLETE SERIES 1 (300) 10.00 25.00
COMPLETE SERIES 2 (200) 10.00 25.00
COMMON CARD (1-500) .10 .30
COMMON (211-250/426-450) .25 .60
OVERALL PLATES SER.1 ODDS 1:1080 H
PLATES PRINT RUN 1 #'d SET PER COLOR
BLACK-CYAN-MAGENTA-YELLOW ISSUED
NO PLATES PRICING DUE TO SCARCITY
1 Casey Kotchman .12 .30
2 Chone Figgins .12 .30
3 David Eckstein .12 .30
4 Jarrod Washburn .12 .30
5 Robb Quinlan .12 .30
6 Troy Glaus .12 .30
7 Vladimir Guerrero .20 .50
8 Brandon Webb .20 .50
9 Danny Bautista .12 .30
10 Luis Gonzalez .12 .30
11 Matt Kata .12 .30
12 Randy Johnson .30 .75
13 Robby Hammock .12 .30
14 Shea Hillenbrand .12 .30
15 Adam LaRoche .12 .30
16 Andruw Jones .12 .30
17 Horacio Ramirez .12 .30
18 John Smoltz .30 .75
19 Johnny Estrada .12 .30
20 Mike Hampton .12 .30
21 Rafael Furcal .12 .30
22 Brian Roberts .12 .30
23 Javy Lopez .12 .30
24 Jay Gibbons .12 .30
25 Jorge Julio .12 .30
26 Melvin Mora .12 .30
27 Miguel Tejada .20 .50
28 Rafael Palmeiro .20 .50
29 Derek Lowe .12 .30
30 Jason Varitek .30 .75
31 Kevin Youkilis .12 .30
32 Manny Ramirez .30 .75
33 Curt Schilling .20 .50
34 Pedro Martinez .20 .50
35 Trot Nixon .12 .30
36 Corey Patterson .12 .30
37 Derrek Lee .12 .30
38 LaTroy Hawkins .12 .30
39 Mark Prior .20 .50
40 Matt Clement .12 .30
41 Moises Alou .12 .30
42 Sammy Sosa .30 .75
43 Aaron Rowand .12 .30
44 Carlos Lee .12 .30
45 Jose Valentin .12 .30
46 Juan Uribe .12 .30
47 Magglio Ordonez .20 .50
48 Mark Buehrle .20 .50
49 Paul Konerko .20 .50
50 Adam Dunn .20 .50
51 Barry Larkin .20 .50
52 D'Angelo Jimenez .12 .30
53 Danny Graves .12 .30
54 Paul Wilson .12 .30
55 Sean Casey .12 .30
56 Wily Mo Pena .12 .30
57 Ben Broussard .12 .30
58 C.C. Sabathia .20 .50
59 Casey Blake .12 .30
60 Cliff Lee .20 .50
61 Matt Lawton .12 .30
62 Omar Vizquel .20 .50
63 Victor Martinez .20 .50
64 Charles Johnson .12 .30
65 Joe Kennedy .12 .30
66 Jeromy Burnitz .12 .30
67 Matt Holliday .30 .75
68 Preston Wilson .12 .30
69 Royce Clayton .12 .30
70 Shawn Estes .12 .30
71 Bobby Higginson .12 .30
72 Brandon Inge .12 .30
73 Carlos Guillen .12 .30
74 Dmitri Young .12 .30
75 Eric Munson .12 .30
76 Jeremy Bonderman .12 .30
77 Ugueth Urbina .12 .30
78 Josh Beckett .12 .30
79 Dontrelle Willis .12 .30
80 Jeff Conine .12 .30
81 Juan Pierre .12 .30
82 Luis Castillo .12 .30
83 Miguel Cabrera .30 .75
84 Mike Lowell .12 .30
85 Andy Pettitte .20 .50
86 Brad Lidge .12 .30
87 Carlos Beltran .20 .50
88 Craig Biggio .20 .50
89 Jeff Bagwell .20 .50
90 Roger Clemens .40 1.00
91 Roy Oswalt .20 .50
92 Benito Santiago .12 .30
93 Jeremy Affeldt .12 .30
94 Juan Gonzalez .12 .30
95 Ken Harvey .12 .30
96 Mike MacDougal .12 .30
97 Mike Sweeney .12 .30
98 Zack Greinke .30 .75
99 Adrian Beltre .30 .75
100 Alex Cora .20 .50
101 Cesar Izturis .12 .30
102 Eric Gagne .12 .30
103 Kazuhisa Ishii .12 .30
104 Milton Bradley .12 .30
105 Shawn Green .12 .30
106 Danny Kolb .12 .30
107 Ben Sheets .12 .30
108 Brooks Kieschnick .12 .30
109 Craig Counsell .12 .30
110 Geoff Jenkins .12 .30
111 Lyle Overbay .12 .30
112 Scott Podsednik .12 .30
113 Corey Koskie .12 .30
114 Johan Santana .20 .50
115 Joe Mauer .25 .60
116 Justin Morneau .20 .50
117 Lew Ford .12 .30
118 Matt LeCroy .12 .30
119 Torii Hunter .12 .30
120 Brad Wilkerson .12 .30
121 Chad Cordero .12 .30
122 Livan Hernandez .12 .30
123 Jose Vidro .12 .30
124 Termel Sledge .12 .30
125 Tony Batista .12 .30
126 Zach Day .12 .30
127 Al Leiter .12 .30
128 Jae Weong Seo .12 .30
129 Jose Reyes .20 .50
130 Kazuo Matsui .12 .30
131 Mike Piazza .30 .75
132 Todd Zeile .12 .30
133 Cliff Floyd .12 .30
134 Alex Rodriguez .40 1.00
135 Derek Jeter .75 2.00
136 Gary Sheffield .12 .30
137 Hideki Matsui .50 1.25
138 Jason Giambi .12 .30
139 Jorge Posada .20 .50
140 Mike Mussina .20 .50
141 Barry Zito .20 .50
142 Bobby Crosby .12 .30
143 Octavio Dotel .12 .30
144 Eric Chavez .12 .30
145 Jermaine Dye .12 .30
146 Mark Kotsay .12 .30
147 Tim Hudson .20 .50
148 Billy Wagner .12 .30
149 Bobby Abreu .12 .30
150 David Bell .12 .30
151 Jim Thome .20 .50
152 Jimmy Rollins .20 .50
153 Mike Lieberthal .12 .30
154 Randy Wolf .12 .30
155 Craig Wilson .12 .30
156 Daryle Ward .12 .30
157 Jack Wilson .12 .30
158 Jason Kendall .12 .30
159 Kip Wells .12 .30
160 Oliver Perez .12 .30
161 Rob Mackowiak .12 .30
162 Brian Giles .12 .30
163 Brian Lawrence .12 .30
164 David Wells .12 .30
165 Jay Payton .12 .30
166 Ryan Klesko .12 .30
167 Sean Burroughs .12 .30
168 Trevor Hoffman .20 .50
169 Brett Tomko .12 .30
170 J.T. Snow .12 .30
171 Jason Schmidt .12 .30
172 Kirk Rueter .12 .30
173 A.J. Pierzynski .12 .30
174 Pedro Feliz .12 .30
175 Ray Durham .12 .30
176 Eddie Guardado .12 .30
177 Edgar Martinez .20 .50
178 Ichiro Suzuki .40 1.00
179 Jamie Moyer .12 .30
180 Joel Pineiro .12 .30
181 Randy Winn .12 .30
182 Raul Ibanez .20 .50
183 Albert Pujols .40 1.00
184 Edgar Renteria .12 .30
185 Jason Isringhausen .12 .30
186 Jim Edmonds .20 .50
187 Matt Morris .12 .30
188 Reggie Sanders .12 .30
189 Tony Womack .12 .30
190 Aubrey Huff .12 .30
191 Danys Baez .12 .30
192 Carl Crawford .20 .50
193 Jose Cruz Jr. .12 .30
194 Rocco Baldelli .12 .30
195 Tino Martinez .20 .50
196 Dewon Brazelton .12 .30
197 Alfonso Soriano .20 .50
198 Brad Fullmer .12 .30
199 Gerald Laird .12 .30
200 Hank Blalock .12 .30
201 Laynce Nix .12 .30
202 Mark Teixeira .20 .50
203 Michael Young .12 .30
204 Alexis Rios .12 .30
205 Eric Hinske .12 .30
206 Miguel Batista .12 .30
207 Orlando Hudson .12 .30
208 Roy Halladay .20 .50
209 Ted Lilly .12 .30
210 Vernon Wells .12 .30
211 Aarom Baldiris SR .25 .60
212 B.J. Upton SR .40 1.00
213 Dallas McPherson SR .25 .60
214 Brian Dallimore SR .25 .60
215 Chris Oxspring SR .25 .60
216 Chris Shelton SR .25 .60
217 David Wright SR .50 1.25
218 Edwardo Sierra SR .25 .60
219 Fernando Nieve SR .25 .60
220 Frank Francisco SR .25 .60
221 Jeff Bennett SR .25 .60
222 Justin Lehr SR .25 .60
223 John Gall SR .25 .60
224 Jorge Sequea SR .25 .60
225 Justin Germano SR .25 .60
226 Kazuhito Tadano SR .25 .60
227 Kevin Cave SR .25 .60
228 Joe Blanton SR .25 .60
229 Luis A. Gonzalez SR .25 .60
230 Michael Wuertz SR .25 .60
231 Mike Rouse SR .25 .60
232 Nick Regilio SR .25 .60
233 Orlando Rodriguez SR .25 .60
234 Phil Stockman SR .25 .60
235 Ramon Ramirez SR .25 .60
236 Roberto Novoa SR .25 .60
237 Dioner Navarro SR .25 .60
238 Tim Bausher SR .25 .60
239 Logan Kensing SR .25 .60
240 Andy Green SR .25 .60
241 Brad Halsey SR .25 .60
242 Charles Thomas SR .25 .60
243 George Sherrill SR .25 .60
244 Jesse Crain SR .25 .60
245 Jimmy Serrano SR .25 .60
246 Joe Horgan SR .25 .60
247 Chris Young SR .40 1.00
248 Joey Gathright SR .25 .60
249 Gavin Floyd SR .25 .60
250 Ryan Howard SR .50 1.25
251 Lance Cormier SR .25 .60
252 Matt Treanor SR .25 .60
253 Jeff Francis SR .25 .60
254 Nick Swisher SR .40 1.00
255 Scott Atchison SR .25 .60
256 Travis Blackley SR .25 .60
257 Travis Smith SR .25 .60
258 Yadier Molina SR .60 1.50
259 Jeff Keppinger SR .25 .60
260 Scott Kazmir SR .60 1.50
261 G.Anderson .20 .50
V.Guerrero TL
262 L.Gonzalez .30 .75
R.Johnson TL
263 A.Jones .30 .75
C.Jones TL
264 M.Tejada .20 .50
R.Palmeiro TL
265 C.Schilling .30 .75
M.Ramirez TL
266 M.Prior .30 .75
S.Sosa TL
267 F.Thomas .30 .75
M.Ordonez TL
268 B.Larkin .60 1.50
K.Griffey Jr. TL
269 C.Sabathia .20 .50
V.Martinez TL
270 J.Burnitz .20 .50
T.Helton TL
271 D.Young .20 .50
I.Rodriguez TL
272 J.Beckett .30 .75
M.Cabrera TL
273 J.Bagwell .40 1.00
R.Clemens TL
274 K.Harvey .12 .30
M.Sweeney TL
275 A.Beltre .30 .75
E.Gagne TL
276 B.Sheets .12 .30
G.Jenkins TL
277 J.Mauer .25 .60
T.Hunter TL
278 J.Vidro .12 .30
L.Hernandez TL
279 K.Matsui .30 .75
M.Piazza TL
280 A.Rodriguez .75 2.00
D.Jeter TL
281 E.Chavez .20 .50
T.Hudson TL
282 B.Abreu .20 .50
J.Thome TL
283 C.Wilson .12 .30
J.Kendall TL
284 B.Giles .12 .30
P.Nevin TL
285 A.Pierzynski .12 .30
J.Schmidt TL
286 B.Boone .40 1.00
I.Suzuki TL
287 A.Pujols .40 1.00
S.Rolen TL
288 A.Huff .20 .50
T.Martinez TL
289 H.Blalock .20 .50
M.Teixeira TL
290 C.Delgado .20 .50
R.Halladay TL
291 Vladimir Guerrero PR .20 .50
292 Curt Schilling PR .20 .50
293 Mark Prior PR .20 .50
294 Josh Beckett PR .12 .30
295 Roger Clemens PR .40 1.00
296 Derek Jeter PR .75 2.00
297 Eric Chavez PR .12 .30
298 Jim Thome PR .20 .50
299 Albert Pujols PR .40 1.00
300 Hank Blalock PR .12 .30
301 Bartolo Colon .12 .30
302 Darin Erstad .12 .30
303 Garret Anderson .12 .30
304 Orlando Cabrera .12 .30
305 Steve Finley .12 .30
306 Javier Vazquez .12 .30
307 Russ Ortiz .12 .30
308 Chipper Jones .30 .75
309 Marcus Giles .12 .30
310 Raul Mondesi .12 .30
311 B.J. Ryan .12 .30
312 Luis Matos .12 .30
313 Sidney Ponson .12 .30
314 Bill Mueller .12 .30
315 David Ortiz .30 .75
316 Johnny Damon .20 .50
317 Keith Foulke .12 .30
318 Mark Bellhorn .12 .30
319 Wade Miller .12 .30
320 Aramis Ramirez .12 .30
321 Carlos Zambrano .20 .50
322 Greg Maddux .40 1.00
323 Kerry Wood .12 .30
324 Nomar Garciaparra .20 .50
325 Todd Walker .12 .30
326 Frank Thomas .30 .75
327 Freddy Garcia .12 .30
328 Joe Crede .12 .30
329 Jose Contreras .12 .30
330 Orlando Hernandez .12 .30
331 Shingo Takatsu .12 .30
332 Austin Kearns .12 .30
333 Eric Milton .12 .30
334 Ken Griffey Jr. .60 1.50
335 Aaron Boone .12 .30
336 David Riske .12 .30
337 Jake Westbrook .12 .30
338 Kevin Millwood .12 .30
339 Travis Hafner .12 .30
340 Aaron Miles .12 .30
341 Jeff Baker .12 .30
342 Todd Helton .20 .50
343 Garrett Atkins .12 .30
344 Carlos Pena .20 .50
345 Ivan Rodriguez .20 .50
346 Rondell White .12 .30
347 Troy Percival .12 .30
348 A.J. Burnett .12 .30
349 Carlos Delgado .20 .50
350 Guillermo Mota .12 .30
351 Paul Lo Duca .12 .30
352 Jason Lane .12 .30
353 Lance Berkman .20 .50
354 Angel Berroa .12 .30
355 David DeJesus .12 .30
356 Ruben Gotay .12 .30
357 Jose Lima .12 .30
358 Brad Penny .12 .30
359 J.D. Drew .12 .30
360 Jayson Werth .12 .30
361 Jeff Kent .12 .30
362 Odalis Perez .12 .30
363 Brady Clark .12 .30
364 Junior Spivey .12 .30
365 Rickie Weeks .12 .30
366 Jacque Jones .12 .30
367 Joe Nathan .12 .30
368 Nick Punto .12 .30
369 Shannon Stewart .12 .30
370 Doug Mientkiewicz .12 .30
371 Kris Benson .12 .30
372 Tom Glavine .20 .50
373 Victor Zambrano .12 .30
374 Bernie Williams .20 .50
375 Carl Pavano .12 .30
376 Jaret Wright .12 .30
377 Kevin Brown .12 .30
378 Mariano Rivera .40 1.00
379 Danny Haren .12 .30
380 Eric Byrnes .12 .30
381 Erubiel Durazo .12 .30
382 Rich Harden .12 .30
383 Brett Myers .12 .30
384 Chase Utley .20 .50
385 Marlon Byrd .12 .30
386 Pat Burrell .12 .30
387 Placido Polanco .12 .30
388 Freddy Sanchez .12 .30
389 Jason Bay .12 .30
390 Josh Fogg .12 .30
391 Adam Eaton .12 .30
392 Jake Peavy .12 .30
393 Khalil Greene .12 .30
394 Mark Loretta .12 .30
395 Phil Nevin .12 .30
396 Ramon Hernandez .12 .30
397 Woody Williams .12 .30
398 Armando Benitez .12 .30
399 Edgardo Alfonzo .12 .30
400 Marquis Grissom .12 .30
401 Mike Matheny .12 .30
402 Richie Sexson .12 .30
403 Bret Boone .12 .30
404 Gil Meche .12 .30
405 Chris Carpenter .20 .50
406 Jeff Suppan .12 .30
407 Larry Walker .20 .50
408 Mark Grudzielanek .12 .30
409 Mark Mulder .12 .30
410 Scott Rolen .20 .50
411 Josh Phelps .12 .30
412 Jonny Gomes .12 .30
413 Francisco Cordero .12 .30
414 Kenny Rogers .12 .30
415 Richard Hidalgo .12 .30
416 Dave Bush .12 .30
417 Frank Catalanotto .12 .30
418 Gabe Gross .12 .30
419 Guillermo Quiroz .12 .30
420 Reed Johnson .12 .30
421 Cristian Guzman .12 .30
422 Esteban Loaiza .12 .30
423 Jose Guillen .12 .30
424 Nick Johnson .12 .30
425 Vinny Castilla .12 .30
426 Pete Orr SR RC .40 1.00
427 Tadahito Iguchi SR RC .40 1.00
428 Jeff Baker SR .25 .60
429 Marcos Carvajal SR RC .25 .60
430 Justin Verlander SR RC 5.00 12.00
431 Luke Scott SR RC .60 1.50
432 Willy Taveras SR .25 .60
433 Ambiorix Burgos SR RC .25 .60
434 Andy Sisco SR .25 .60
435 Denny Bautista SR .25 .60
436 Mark Teahen SR .25 .60
437 Ervin Santana SR .25 .60
438 Dennis Houlton SR RC .25 .60
439 Philip Humber SR RC .60 1.50
440 Steve Schmoll SR RC .25 .60
441 J.J. Hardy SR .25 .60
442 Ambiorix Concepcion SR RC .25 .60
443 Dae-Sung Koo SR RC .25 .60
444 Andy Phillips SR .25 .60
445 Dan Meyer SR .25 .60
446 Huston Street SR .25 .60
447 Keiichi Yabu SR RC .25 .60
448 Jeff Niemann SR RC .60 1.50
449 Jeremy Reed SR .25 .60
450 Tony Blanco SR .25 .60
451 Albert Pujols BG .40 1.00
452 Alex Rodriguez BG .40 1.00
453 Curt Schilling BG .20 .50
454 Derek Jeter BG .75 2.00
455 Greg Maddux BG .40 1.00
456 Ichiro Suzuki BG .40 1.00
457 Ivan Rodriguez BG .20 .50
458 Jeff Bagwell BG .20 .50
459 Jim Thome BG .20 .50
460 Ken Griffey Jr. BG .60 1.50
461 Manny Ramirez BG .30 .75
462 Mike Mussina BG .20 .50
463 Mike Piazza BG .30 .75
464 Pedro Martinez BG .20 .50
465 Rafael Palmeiro BG .20 .50
466 Randy Johnson BG .30 .75
467 Roger Clemens BG .40 1.00
468 Sammy Sosa BG .30 .75
469 Todd Helton BG .20 .50
470 Vladimir Guerrero BG .20 .50
471 Vladimir Guerrero TC .20 .50
472 Shawn Green TC .12 .30
473 John Smoltz TC .30 .75
474 Miguel Tejada TC .20 .50
475 Curt Schilling TC .20 .50
476 Mark Prior TC .20 .50
477 Frank Thomas TC .30 .75
478 Ken Griffey Jr. TC .60 1.50
479 C.C. Sabathia TC .20
480 Todd Helton TC .20
481 Ivan Rodriguez TC .20
482 Miguel Cabrera TC .30
483 Roger Clemens TC .40 1
484 Mike Sweeney TC .12
485 Eric Gagne TC .12
486 Ben Sheets TC .12
487 Johan Santana TC .20
488 Mike Piazza TC .30
489 Derek Jeter TC .75 2
490 Eric Chavez TC .12
491 Jim Thome TC .20
492 Craig Wilson TC .12
493 Jake Peavy TC .12
494 Jason Schmidt TC .12
495 Ichiro Suzuki TC .40 1.
496 Albert Pujols TC .40 1
497 Carl Crawford TC .20
498 Mark Teixeira TC .20
499 Vernon Wells TC .12
500 Jose Vidro TC .12

2005 Upper Deck Blue

*BLUE 300-425/451-500: 4X TO 10X BASIC
*BLUE 426-450: 2.5X TO 6X BASIC
OVERALL SER.2 PARALLEL ODDS 1:12 H
STATED PRINT RUN 150 SERIAL #'d SETS

2005 Upper Deck Emerald

*EMER 300-425/451-500: 12.5X TO 30X BASIC
OVERALL SER.2 PARALLEL ODDS 1:12 H
STATED PRINT RUN 25 SERIAL #'d SETS
NO PRICING AVAILABLE ON 426-450

2005 Upper Deck Gold

*GOLD 300-425/451-500: 5X TO 12X BASIC
*GOLD 426-450: 3X TO 8X BASIC
OVERALL SER.2 PARALLEL ODDS 1:12 H
STATED PRINT RUN 99 SERIAL #'d SETS

2005 Upper Deck Retro

*RETRO: 1.25X TO 3X BASIC
ONE RETRO BOX PER SER.1 HOBBY CASE
SER.1 HOBBY CASES CONTAIN 12 BOXES
OVERALL PLATES SER.1 ODDS 1:1080 H
PLATES PRINT RUN 1 #'d SET PER COLOR
BLACK-CYAN-MAGENTA-YELLOW ISSUED
NO PLATES PRICING DUE TO SCARCITY

2005 Upper Deck 4000 Strikeo

RANDOM INSERTS IN SERIES 1 PACKS
STATED PRINT RUN 4000 SERIAL #'d SETS
CRCJ Carlton 8.00 20.0
Ryan
Clem
Randy

2005 Upper Deck Baseball Heroes Jeter

COMPLETE SET (10) 12.50 30.0
COMMON CARD (91-99) 1.50 4.0
SERIES 1 STATED ODDS 1:6 H/R

2005 Upper Deck Flyball

E PER '05 PRO SIGS PACK

ohan Santana	.15	.40
andy Johnson	.25	.60
edro Martinez	.15	.40
ason Schmidt	.10	.25
urt Schilling	.15	.40
oger Clemens	.30	.75
ric Gagne	.10	.25
Mariano Rivera	.30	.75
Mike Piazza	.25	.60
Ivan Rodriguez	.15	.40
Albert Pujols	.30	.75
Todd Helton	.15	.40
Jim Thome	.15	.40
Alfonso Soriano	.15	.40
Jeff Kent	.10	.25
Bret Boone	.10	.25
Scott Rolen	.15	.40
Alex Rodriguez	.30	.75
Adrian Beltre	.25	.60
Nomar Garciaparra	.15	.40
Derek Jeter	.60	1.50
Miguel Tejada	.15	.40
Manny Ramirez	.25	.60
Adam Dunn	.15	.40
Miguel Cabrera	.25	.60
Jim Edmonds	.15	.40
Ken Griffey Jr.	.50	1.25
Vladimir Guerrero	.15	.40
Ichiro Suzuki	.30	.75
Sammy Sosa	.25	.60
Gary Sheffield	.10	.25
Roy Oswalt	.15	.40
Carlos Zambrano	.15	.40
Mark Prior	.15	.40
Tim Hudson	.15	.40
Kerry Wood	.10	.25
Joe Nathan	.10	.25
Brad Lidge	.10	.25
Jason Isringhausen	.10	.25
Armando Benitez	.10	.25
Keith Foulke	.10	.25
Octavio Dotel	.10	.25
Trevor Hoffman	.15	.40
Johnny Estrada	.10	.25
Victor Martinez	.15	.40
Jason Varitek	.25	.60
Paul Lo Duca	.10	.25
Jason Kendall	.10	.25
Michael Barrett	.10	.25
Mike Lieberthal	.10	.25
3 Carlos Delgado	.10	.25
9 Derrek Lee	.10	.25
0 Jason Giambi	.10	.25
Rafael Palmeiro	.15	.40
2 David Ortiz	.25	.60
3 Jeff Bagwell	.15	.40
4 Paul Konerko	.15	.40
5 Mark Loretta	.10	.25
6 Ray Durham	.10	.25
7 Luis Castillo	.10	.25
8 Marcus Giles	.10	.25
9 Adam Kennedy	.10	.25
0 Jose Vidro	.10	.25
2 Eric Chavez	.10	.25
4 Vinny Castilla	.10	.25
5 Hank Blalock	.10	.25
7 Michael Young	.10	.25
8 Carlos Guillen	.10	.25
9 Jimmy Rollins	.15	.40
0 Rafael Furcal	.10	.25
1 Edgar Renteria	.10	.25
2 Alex Gonzalez	.10	.25
3 Carlos Lee	.10	.25
4 Hideki Matsui	.40	1.00
5 Craig Biggio	.15	.40
7 Moises Alou	.10	.25
8 Chipper Jones	.25	.60
9 Andruw Jones	.10	.25
0 Corey Patterson	.10	.25
1 Torii Hunter	.10	.25
2 Carl Crawford	.15	.40
3 Steve Finley	.10	.25
5 J.D. Drew	.10	.25
6 Brian Giles	.10	.25
7 Lance Berkman	.15	.40
8 Shawn Green	.10	.25
9 Larry Walker	.15	.40
00 Magglio Ordonez	.15	.40
01 Mark Mulder	.10	.25
02 Oliver Perez	.10	.25
04 Carl Pavano	.10	.25
05 Matt Clement	.10	.25
06 Bartolo Colon	.10	.25
07 Roy Halladay	.15	.40
09 Javier Vazquez	.10	.25
10 Josh Beckett	.10	.25
11 Tom Gordon	.10	.25
12 Francisco Rodriguez	.15	.40
13 Guillermo Mota	.10	.25
114 Juan Rincon	.10	.25
115 Steve Kline	.10	.25
116 Ray King	.10	.25
117 Giovanni Carrara	.10	.25
118 Akinori Otsuka	.10	.25
119 Kyle Farnsworth	.10	.25
121 Brandon Inge	.10	.25
123 Yadier Molina	.25	.60
124 Miguel Olivo	.10	.25
125 Joe Mauer	.20	.50
126 Rod Barajas	.10	.25
127 Aubrey Huff	.10	.25
128 Travis Hafner	.10	.25
129 Phil Nevin	.10	.25
130 Pedro Feliz	.10	.25
131 Lyle Overbay	.10	.25
132 Carlos Pena	.15	.40
133 Craig Wilson	.10	.25
134 Brad Wilkerson	.10	.25
135 Mike Sweeney	.10	.25
138 Todd Walker	.10	.25
139 D'Angelo Jimenez	.10	.25
140 Jose Reyes	.15	.40
141 Juan Uribe	.10	.25
142 Mark Bellhorn	.10	.25
143 Orlando Hudson	.10	.25
144 Tony Womack	.10	.25
146 Aaron Miles	.10	.25
147 Miguel Cairo	.10	.25
148 Ken Griffey Jr.	.50	1.25
149 Casey Blake	.10	.25
150 Chone Figgins	.10	.25
151 Mike Lowell	.10	.25
152 Shea Hillenbrand	.10	.25
153 Corey Koskie	.10	.25
154 David Bell	.10	.25
155 Eric Hinske	.10	.25
157 Morgan Ensberg	.10	.25
158 Cesar Izturis	.10	.25
159 Julio Lugo	.10	.25
160 Jose Valentin	.10	.25
161 Omar Vizquel	.15	.40
162 Bobby Crosby	.10	.25
163 Khalil Greene	.10	.25
164 Angel Berroa	.10	.25
165 David Eckstein	.10	.25
166 Christian Guzman	.10	.25
167 Kaz Matsui	.10	.25
168 Lew Ford	.10	.25
169 Geoff Jenkins	.10	.25
171 Jason Bay	.10	.25
173 Reggie Sanders	.10	.25
174 Pat Burrell	.10	.25
176 Cliff Floyd	.10	.25
177 Ryan Klesko	.10	.25
178 Luis Gonzalez		
179 Jose Guillen	.10	.25
180 Mike Cameron	.10	.25
181 Vernon Wells	.10	.25
182 Aaron Rowand	.10	.25
183 Scott Podsednik	.10	.25
186 Bernie Williams	.15	.40
187 Mark Kotsay	.10	.25
188 Milton Bradley	.10	.25
189 Garret Anderson	.10	.25
190 Preston Wilson		
191 Wily Mo Pena	.10	.25
192 Jeromy Burnitz	.10	.25
193 Jermaine Dye	.10	.25
194 Jose Cruz Jr.	.10	.25
195 Richard Hidalgo	.10	.25
196 Derek Jeter	.60	1.50
197 Juan Encarnacion	.10	.25
198 Bobby Higginson	.10	.25
199 Alex Rios	.10	.25
200 Austin Kearns	.10	.25
201 Yogi Berra	.25	.60
202 Harmon Killebrew	.25	.60
203 Joe Morgan	.15	.40
204 Ernie Banks	.25	.60
205 Mike Schmidt	.50	1.25
206 Mickey Mantle	.75	2.00
207 Ted Williams	.50	1.25
208 Babe Ruth	.60	1.50
209 Nolan Ryan	.75	2.00
210 Bob Gibson	.15	.40

2005 Upper Deck Game Jersey

SERIES 2 OVERALL GU ODDS 1:8
SP INFO PROVIDED BY UPPER DECK

AB Adrian Beltre	3.00	8.00
AP Albert Pujols	6.00	15.00
AS Alfonso Soriano	3.00	8.00
CB Carlos Beltran SP	3.00	8.00
CJ Chipper Jones	4.00	10.00
CS Curt Schilling	4.00	10.00
DJ Derek Jeter	8.00	20.00
DO David Ortiz SP	4.00	10.00
DW David Wright	6.00	15.00
EC Eric Chavez	3.00	8.00
EG Eric Gagne	3.00	8.00
FT Frank Thomas	4.00	10.00
GM Greg Maddux SP	4.00	10.00
HB Hank Blalock	3.00	8.00
HE Todd Helton	4.00	10.00
HU Torii Hunter	3.00	8.00
IR Ivan Rodriguez	4.00	10.00
JB Jeff Bagwell SP	4.00	10.00
JK Jeff Kent	3.00	8.00
JS Johan Santana SP	4.00	10.00
JT Jim Thome SP	4.00	10.00
KG Ken Griffey Jr. SP	6.00	15.00
KW Kerry Wood	3.00	8.00
LB Lance Berkman	3.00	8.00
MC Miguel Cabrera	4.00	10.00
MM Mark Mulder	3.00	8.00
MP Mark Prior	4.00	10.00
MR Manny Ramirez SP	4.00	10.00
MT Mark Teixeira SP	4.00	10.00
PI Mike Piazza	4.00	10.00
PM Pedro Martinez	4.00	10.00
RC Roger Clemens	4.00	10.00
RJ Randy Johnson SP	4.00	10.00
SM John Smoltz	4.00	10.00
SR Scott Rolen	4.00	10.00
SS Sammy Sosa	4.00	10.00
TE Miguel Tejada	3.00	8.00
TG Troy Glaus	3.00	8.00
TH Tim Hudson	3.00	8.00
VG Vladimir Guerrero	4.00	10.00

2005 Upper Deck Hall of Fame Plaques

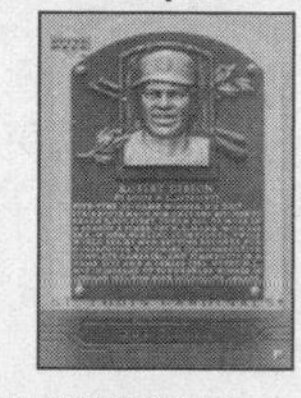

SERIES 1 STATED ODDS 1:36 H/R

16 Ernie Banks	2.50	6.00
17 Yogi Berra	2.50	6.00
18 Whitey Ford	1.50	4.00
19 Bob Gibson	1.50	4.00
20 Willie McCovey	1.50	4.00
21 Stan Musial	4.00	10.00
22 Nolan Ryan	8.00	20.00
23 Mike Schmidt	5.00	12.00
24 Tom Seaver	1.50	4.00
25 Robin Yount	2.50	6.00

2005 Upper Deck Marquee Attractions Jersey

SER.1 OVERALL GU ODDS 1:12 H

AD Adam Dunn	3.00	8.00
AJ Andruw Jones	4.00	10.00
AP Albert Pujols	6.00	15.00
BE Josh Beckett	3.00	8.00
BG Brian Giles	3.00	8.00
BW Billy Wagner	3.00	8.00
CD Carlos Delgado	3.00	8.00
CJ Chipper Jones	4.00	10.00
CS Curt Schilling	4.00	10.00
DJ Derek Jeter	8.00	20.00
DW Dontrelle Willis	3.00	8.00
EG Eric Gagne	3.00	8.00
GM Greg Maddux	5.00	12.00
HM Hideki Matsui	10.00	25.00
HN Hideo Nomo	4.00	10.00
HO Trevor Hoffman	3.00	8.00
IR Ivan Rodriguez	4.00	10.00
IS Ichiro Suzuki	10.00	25.00
JB Jeff Bagwell	4.00	10.00
JG Jason Giambi	3.00	8.00
JM Joe Mauer	4.00	10.00
JS Jason Schmidt	3.00	8.00
JT Jim Thome	4.00	10.00
KB Kevin Brown	3.00	8.00
KM Kazuo Matsui	3.00	8.00
KW Kerry Wood	3.00	8.00
MC Miguel Cabrera	4.00	10.00
MP Mark Prior	4.00	10.00
MT Miguel Tejada	3.00	8.00
PE Andy Pettitte	4.00	10.00
PI Mike Piazza	4.00	10.00
PM Pedro Martinez	4.00	10.00
PW Preston Wilson	3.00	8.00
RC Roger Clemens	5.00	12.00
RJ Randy Johnson	4.00	10.00
SG Shawn Green	3.00	8.00
SS Sammy Sosa	4.00	10.00
TH Todd Helton	4.00	10.00
VG Vladimir Guerrero	4.00	10.00

2005 Upper Deck Marquee Attractions Jersey Gold

*GOLD: .6X TO 1.5X BASIC
SER.1 OVERALL GU ODDS 1:12 H

GA Garret Anderson	5.00	12.00
RO Roy Oswalt	5.00	12.00

2005 Upper Deck Matinee Idols Jersey

SER.1 OVERALL GU ODDS 1:12 H, 1:24 R
SP INFO PROVIDED BY UPPER DECK

BB Bret Boone SP	4.00	10.00
BE Josh Beckett	3.00	8.00
BW Billy Wagner	3.00	8.00
BZ Barry Zito	3.00	8.00
CD Carlos Delgado	3.00	8.00
CJ Chipper Jones	4.00	10.00
CR Cal Ripken	15.00	40.00
CS Curt Schilling	4.00	10.00
DJ Derek Jeter	8.00	20.00
DW Dontrelle Willis	3.00	8.00
EC Eric Chavez	3.00	8.00
GS Gary Sheffield	3.00	8.00
HB Hank Blalock	3.00	8.00
HU Torii Hunter	3.00	8.00
JB Jeff Bagwell	4.00	10.00
JE Jim Edmonds	3.00	8.00
JG Jason Giambi	3.00	8.00
JT Jim Thome	4.00	10.00
KG Ken Griffey Jr.	6.00	15.00
KW Kerry Wood	3.00	8.00
ML Mike Lowell	4.00	10.00
MM Mike Mussina	4.00	10.00
MP Mark Prior	4.00	10.00
MT Mark Teixeira	4.00	10.00
NR Nolan Ryan	15.00	40.00
PB Pat Burrell	3.00	8.00
PI Mike Piazza	4.00	10.00
RB Rocco Baldelli	3.00	8.00
RC Roger Clemens	5.00	12.00
RH Roy Halladay	3.00	8.00
RJ Randy Johnson	4.00	10.00
RW Rickie Weeks	3.00	8.00
SG Shawn Green	3.00	8.00
SR Scott Rolen	4.00	10.00
SS Sammy Sosa	4.00	10.00
TG Troy Glaus	3.00	8.00
TH Todd Helton	4.00	10.00
TS Tom Seaver	6.00	15.00
VG Vladimir Guerrero	4.00	10.00
VW Vernon Wells	3.00	8.00

2005 Upper Deck Milestone Materials

SERIES 2 OVERALL GU ODDS 1:8

AP Albert Pujols	6.00	15.00
BA Jeff Bagwell	4.00	10.00
BC Bobby Crosby	3.00	8.00
CB Carlos Beltran	3.00	8.00
CS Curt Schilling	4.00	10.00
DO David Ortiz	4.00	10.00
EG Eric Gagne	3.00	8.00
GM Greg Maddux	4.00	10.00
JB Jason Bay	3.00	8.00
JP Jake Peavy	3.00	8.00
JS Johan Santana	4.00	10.00
JT Jim Thome	4.00	10.00
KG Ken Griffey Jr.	6.00	15.00
MR Manny Ramirez	4.00	10.00
MT Mark Teixeira	4.00	10.00
RJ Randy Johnson	4.00	10.00
RP Rafael Palmeiro	4.00	10.00
TE Miguel Tejada	3.00	8.00
VG Vladimir Guerrero	4.00	10.00

2005 Upper Deck Origins Jersey

SER.1 OVERALL GU ODDS 1:12 H, 1:24 R

AB Adrian Beltre	4.00	10.00
AJ Andruw Jones	1.50	4.00
AP Albert Pujols	5.00	12.00
AS Alfonso Soriano	2.50	6.00
BG Brian Giles	1.50	4.00
BU B.J. Upton	2.50	6.00
CB Carlos Beltran	2.50	6.00
EG Eric Gagne	1.50	4.00
GA Garret Anderson	1.50	4.00
GM Greg Maddux	5.00	12.00
HM Hideki Matsui	6.00	15.00
HN Hideo Nomo	4.00	10.00
IR Ivan Rodriguez	2.50	6.00
IS Ichiro Suzuki	5.00	12.00
JG Juan Gonzalez	1.50	4.00
JK Jeff Kent	1.50	4.00
JL Javy Lopez	1.50	4.00
JP Jorge Posada	2.50	6.00
JR Jose Reyes	2.50	6.00
JS Jason Schmidt	1.50	4.00
JV Javier Vazquez	1.50	4.00
KM Kazuo Matsui	1.50	4.00
LB Lance Berkman	2.50	6.00
LG Luis Gonzalez	1.50	4.00
MC Miguel Cabrera	4.00	10.00
MM Mark Mulder	1.50	4.00
MO Magglio Ordonez	2.50	6.00
MR Manny Ramirez	4.00	10.00
MT Miguel Tejada	2.50	6.00
PE Jake Peavy	1.50	4.00
PM Pedro Martinez	2.50	6.00
PW Preston Wilson	1.50	4.00
RF Rafael Furcal	1.50	4.00
RP Rafael Palmeiro	2.50	6.00
RS Richie Sexson	1.50	4.00
SS Sammy Sosa	4.00	10.00
TH Tim Hudson	2.50	6.00
VG Vladimir Guerrero	2.50	6.00

2005 Upper Deck Rewind to 1997 Jersey

SER.2 STATED ODDS 1:288 H, 1:480 R
PRINT RUNS B/WN 100-150 COPIES PER
CARDS ARE NOT SERIAL-NUMBERED
PRINT RUN INFO PROVIDED BY UD

AJ Andruw Jones	15.00	40.00
CJ Chipper Jones	15.00	40.00
CR Cal Ripken	20.00	50.00
CS Curt Schilling Phils	10.00	25.00
DJ Derek Jeter	20.00	50.00
FT Frank Thomas	15.00	40.00
GM Greg Maddux Braves	15.00	40.00
IR Ivan Rodriguez Rgr	15.00	40.00
JB Jeff Bagwell	15.00	40.00
JS John Smoltz	15.00	40.00
JT Jim Thome Indians	15.00	40.00
KG Ken Griffey Jr. M's	60.00	120.00
MP Mike Piazza Dgr	15.00	40.00
MR Manny Ramirez Indians	15.00	40.00
PM Pedro Martinez Expos	15.00	40.00
RJ Randy Johnson M's	15.00	40.00
SR Scott Rolen Phils Pants	15.00	40.00
TG Tony Gwynn	15.00	40.00
VG Vladimir Guerrero Expos	15.00	40.00
WC Will Clark Rgr	15.00	40.00

2005 Upper Deck Season Opener MLB Game-Worn Jersey Collection

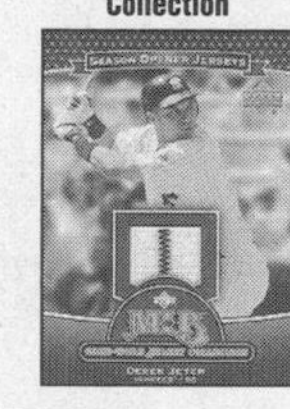

STATED ODDS 1:8

AB Angel Berroa	2.00	5.00
AD Adam Dunn	2.00	5.00
AJ Andruw Jones	3.00	8.00
CD Carlos Delgado	2.00	5.00
CP Corey Patterson	2.00	5.00
DJ Derek Jeter	10.00	25.00
EB Eric Byrnes	2.00	5.00
EH Eric Hinske	2.00	5.00
JB Josh Beckett	2.00	5.00
JG Jody Gerut	2.00	5.00
JT Jim Thome	3.00	8.00
MO Magglio Ordonez	2.00	5.00
MT Michael Tucker	2.00	5.00
PM Pedro Martinez	3.00	8.00
RB Rocco Baldelli	2.00	5.00
RK Ryan Klesko	2.00	5.00
SG Shawn Green	2.00	5.00
SR Scott Rolen	3.00	8.00

2005 Upper Deck Signature Stars Hobby

SERIES 1 STATED ODDS 1:288 HOBBY
SP INFO PROVIDED BY UPPER DECK

BC Bobby Crosby	6.00	15.00
BS Ben Sheets	6.00	15.00
CR Cal Ripken SP	60.00	150.00
DW Dontrelle Willis	6.00	15.00
DY Delmon Young	10.00	25.00
HB Hank Blalock	6.00	15.00
JL Javy Lopez	6.00	15.00
JM Joe Mauer	20.00	50.00
KG Ken Griffey Jr.	60.00	150.00
KW Kerry Wood	10.00	25.00
LF Lew Ford	4.00	10.00
MC Miguel Cabrera	20.00	50.00

2005 Upper Deck Signature Stars Retail

NO PRICING DUE TO SCARCITY
SERIES 1 STATED ODDS 1:480 RETAIL
SP INFO PROVIDED BY UPPER DECK

2005 Upper Deck Super Patch Logo

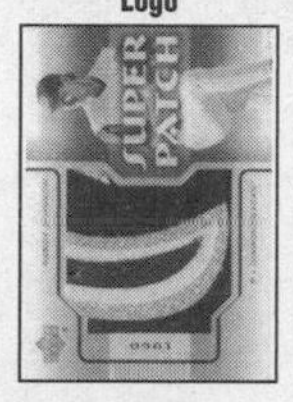

SER.1 OVERALL GU ODDS 1:12 H, 1:24 R
PRINT RUNS B/WN 8-34 COPIES PER
CARDS ARE NOT SERIAL-NUMBERED
PRINT RUNS PROVIDED BY UPPER DECK

2005 Upper Deck Wingfield Collection

COMPLETE SET (20)	15.00	40.00
SERIES 1 STATED ODDS 1:9 H/R		
1 Eddie Mathews	1.25	3.00
2 Ernie Banks	1.25	3.00
3 Joe DiMaggio	2.50	6.00
4 Mickey Mantle	4.00	10.00
5 Pee Wee Reese	.75	2.00
6 Phil Rizzuto	.75	2.00
7 Stan Musial	2.00	5.00
8 Ted Williams	2.50	6.00
9 Bob Feller	.75	2.00
10 Whitey Ford	.75	2.00
11 Willie Stargell	.75	2.00
12 Yogi Berra	1.25	3.00
13 Roy Campanella	.75	2.00
14 Franklin D. Roosevelt	.50	1.25
15 Harry Truman	.50	1.25
16 Dwight D. Eisenhower	.50	1.25
17 John F. Kennedy	1.25	3.00
18 Lyndon Johnson	.50	1.25
19 Richard Nixon	.50	1.25
20 Thurman Munson	.75	2.00

2005 Upper Deck World Series Heroes

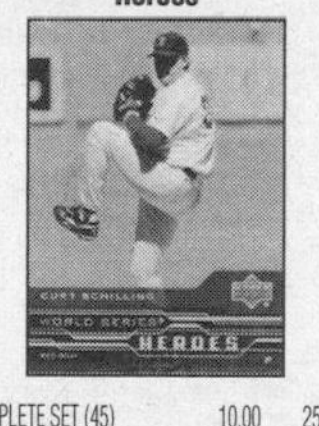

COMPLETE SET (45)	10.00	25.00
SERIES 1 STATED ODDS 1:1 RETAIL		
1 Garret Anderson	.20	.50
2 Troy Glaus	.20	.50
3 Vladimir Guerrero	.30	.75
4 Andruw Jones	.20	.50
5 Chipper Jones	.50	1.25
6 Curt Schilling	.30	.75
7 Keith Foulke	.20	.50
8 Manny Ramirez	.50	1.25
9 Nomar Garciaparra	.30	.75
10 Pedro Martinez	.30	.75
11 Kerry Wood	.20	.50
12 Mark Prior	.30	.75
13 Sammy Sosa	.50	1.25
14 Frank Thomas	.50	1.25
15 Magglio Ordonez	.30	.75
16 Dontrelle Willis	.20	.50
17 Josh Beckett	.20	.50
18 Miguel Cabrera	.50	1.25
19 Jeff Bagwell	.30	.75
20 Lance Berkman	.30	.75
21 Roger Clemens	.60	1.50
22 Eric Gagne	.20	.50
23 Torii Hunter	.20	.50
24 Mike Piazza	.50	1.25
25 Alex Rodriguez	.60	1.50
26 Derek Jeter	1.25	3.00
27 Gary Sheffield	.20	.50
28 Hideki Matsui	.75	2.00
29 Jason Giambi	.20	.50
30 Jorge Posada	.30	.75
31 Kevin Brown	.20	.50
32 Mariano Rivera	.60	1.50
33 Mike Mussina	.30	.75
34 Eric Chavez	.20	.50
35 Mark Mulder	.20	.50
36 Tim Hudson	.30	.75
37 Billy Wagner	.20	.50
38 Jim Thome	.30	.75
39 Brian Giles	.20	.50
40 Jason Schmidt	.20	.50
41 Albert Pujols	.60	1.50
42 Scott Rolen	.30	.75
43 Alfonso Soriano	.30	.75
44 Hank Blalock	.20	.50
45 Mark Teixeira	.30	.75

2005 Upper Deck Chicago National

This six-card standard-size set was distributed as a give-away during the 2005 National Sports Collectors Convention. Each of these cards feature a current Chicago baseball player and were issued to a stated print run of 750 serial numbered sets.

COMPLETE SET (6)	2.50	6.00
DISTRIBUTED AT '05 CHICAGO NSCC		
STATED PRINT RUN 750 SERIAL #'d SETS		
MLB1 Mark Prior	.60	1.50
MLB2 Greg Maddux	1.25	3.00
MLB3 Derrek Lee	.40	1.00
MLB4 Kerry Wood	.40	1.00
MLB5 Tadahito Iguchi	.60	1.50
MLB6 Paul Konerko	.60	1.50

2005 Upper Deck Sunkist

This five-card set, which was inserted one per package of Sunkist oranges, featured five great retired players. The fronts have a posed shot of the player along with the Upper Deck logo in the upper right corner. The back has information about the player as well as food tips.

COMPLETE SET (5)	2.50	6.00
1 Mickey Mantle	1.50	4.00
2 Stan Musial	.75	2.00
3 Roger Maris	.50	1.25
4 Roberto Clemente	1.25	3.00
5 Bob Gibson	.30	.75

2006 Upper Deck

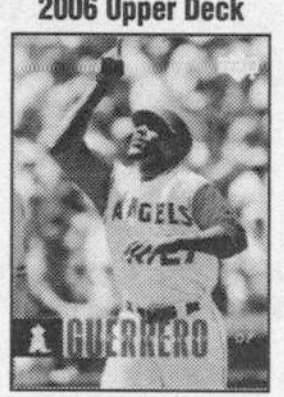

This 1,252-card set was issued over three series in 2006. The first series was released in April, the second series in August, and the Update set in December. All three series were issued in eight-card packs with an $2.99 SRP. These cards came 24 packs to a box and 12 boxes to a case. The first two series were sequenced in alphabetical team order, with the players in first name alphabetical order in the first series as well. However, if the player was traded, he was still sequenced as if he were with his 2005 team. The second series was just sequenced in alphabetical team order. Cards 871-900 were checklists while cards 901-999 featured 2006 rookies. The final cards in this set feature a mix of players with new teams and more 2006 rookies. Cards numbered 1221–1250 were also checklist cards sequenced in alphabetical team order and were printed to stated odds of one in two update packs. Jason Repko card number 245 was not issued in packs; however, when the Upper Deck Fat Packs, which included series one and two cards that situation was rectified. However, the Repko card was issued as card number 283.

COMPLETE SET (1250)	375.00	600.00
COMPLETE SERIES 1 (500)	125.00	200.00
COMPLETE SERIES 2 (500)	125.00	200.00

COMPLETE UPDATE (250) 125.00 200.00
COMP.UPDATE w/o SP's (200) 30.00 50.00
COMMON CARD (1-1250) .15 .40
1-500 ISSUED IN SERIES 1 PACKS
501-1000 ISSUED IN SERIES 2 PACKS
1001-1250 ISSUED IN UPDATE PACKS
BAKER & REPKO BOTH CARD 283
1001-1250 SP STATED ODDS 1:2
SP: 1005/1013/1021/1037/1045/1061/1069
SP: 1077/1093/1101/1117/1125/1133/1149
SP: 1157/1173/1181/1189/1205/1213
SP: 1221-1250
4 MATCHED PLATES 1:2 SER.2 HOBBY CASES
PLATE PRINT RUN 1 SET PER COLOR
BLACK-CYAN-MAGENTA-YELLOW ISSUED
NO PLATE PRICING DUE TO SCARCITY
EXQUISITE EXCH 1 PER SER.2 HOBBY CASE
EXQUISITE EXCH RANDOM IN UPD.CASES
EXQUISITE EXCH DEADLINE 07/27/07
1 Adam Kennedy .15 .40
2 Bartolo Colon .15 .40
3 Bengie Molina .15 .40
4 Casey Kotchman .15 .40
5 Chone Figgins .15 .40
6 Dallas McPherson .15 .40
7 Darin Erstad .15 .40
8 Ervin Santana .15 .40
9 Francisco Rodriguez .25 .60
10 Garret Anderson .15 .40
11 Jarrod Washburn .15 .40
12 John Lackey .25 .60
13 Juan Rivera .15 .40
14 Orlando Cabrera .15 .40
15 Paul Byrd .15 .40
16 Steve Finley .15 .40
17 Vladimir Guerrero .25 .60
18 Alex Cintron .15 .40
19 Brandon Lyon .15 .40
20 Brandon Webb .25 .60
21 Chad Tracy .15 .40
22 Chris Snyder .15 .40
23 Claudio Vargas .15 .40
24 Conor Jackson .25 .60
25 Craig Counsell .15 .40
26 Javier Vazquez .15 .40
27 Jose Valverde .15 .40
28 Luis Gonzalez .15 .40
29 Royce Clayton .15 .40
30 Russ Ortiz .15 .40
31 Shawn Green .15 .40
32 Dustin Nippert (RC) .30 .75
33 Tony Clark .15 .40
34 Troy Glaus .15 .40
35 Adam LaRoche .15 .40
36 Andruw Jones .15 .40
37 Craig Hansen RC .75 2.00
38 Chipper Jones .40 1.00
39 Horacio Ramirez .15 .40
40 Jeff Francoeur .40 1.00
41 John Smoltz .40 1.00
42 Joey Devine RC .30 .75
43 Johnny Estrada .15 .40
44 Anthony Lerew (RC) .30 .75
45 Julio Franco .15 .40
46 Kyle Farnsworth .15 .40
47 Marcus Giles .15 .40
48 Mike Hampton .15 .40
49 Rafael Furcal .15 .40
50 Chuck James (RC) .30 .75
51 Tim Hudson .25 .60
52 B.J. Ryan .15 .40
53 Bernie Castro (RC) .30 .75
54 Brian Roberts .15 .40
55 Walter Young (RC) .30 .75
56 Daniel Cabrera .15 .40
57 Eric Byrnes .15 .40
58 Alejandro Freire RC .30 .75
59 Erik Bedard .15 .40
60 Javy Lopez .15 .40
61 Jay Gibbons .15 .40
62 Jorge Julio .15 .40
63 Luis Matos .15 .40
64 Melvin Mora .15 .40
65 Miguel Tejada .25 .60
66 Rafael Palmeiro .25 .60
67 Rodrigo Lopez .15 .40
68 Sammy Sosa .40 1.00
69 Alejandro Machado (RC) .30 .75
70 Bill Mueller .15 .40
71 Bronson Arroyo .15 .40
72 Curt Schilling .25 .60
73 David Ortiz .40 1.00
74 David Wells .15 .40
75 Edgar Renteria .15 .40
76 Ryan Jorgensen RC .30 .75
77 Jason Varitek .40 1.00
78 Johnny Damon .25 .60
79 Keith Foulke .15 .40
80 Kevin Youkilis .15 .40
81 Manny Ramirez .40 1.00
82 Matt Clement .15 .40
83 Hanley Ramirez (RC) .50 1.25
84 Tim Wakefield .25 .60
85 Trot Nixon .15 .40
86 Wade Miller .15 .40
87 Aramis Ramirez .15 .40
88 Carlos Zambrano .25 .60
89 Corey Patterson .15 .40
90 Derrek Lee .15 .40
91 Geovany Soto (RC) .75 2.00
92 Greg Maddux .50 1.25
93 Jeromy Burnitz .15 .40
94 Jerry Hairston .15 .40
95 Kerry Wood .15 .40
96 Mark Prior .25 .60
97 Matt Murton .15 .40
98 Michael Barrett .15 .40
99 Neifi Perez .15 .40
100 Nomar Garciaparra .25 .60
101 Rich Hill .40 1.00
102 Ryan Dempster .15 .40
103 Todd Walker .15 .40
104 A.J. Pierzynski .15 .40
105 Aaron Rowand .15 .40
106 Bobby Jenks .15 .40
107 Carl Everett .15 .40
108 Dustin Hermanson .15 .40
109 Frank Thomas .40 1.00
110 Freddy Garcia .15 .40
111 Jermaine Dye .15 .40
112 Joe Crede .15 .40
113 Jon Garland .15 .40
114 Jose Contreras .15 .40
115 Juan Uribe .15 .40
116 Mark Buehrle .25 .60
117 Orlando Hernandez .15 .40
118 Paul Konerko .25 .60
119 Scott Podsednik .15 .40
120 Tadahito Iguchi .15 .40
121 Aaron Harang .15 .40
122 Adam Dunn .25 .60
123 Austin Kearns .15 .40
124 Brandon Claussen .15 .40
125 Chris Denorfia (RC) .30 .75
126 Edwin Encarnacion .40 1.00
127 Miguel Perez (RC) .30 .75
128 Felipe Lopez .15 .40
129 Jason LaRue .15 .40
130 Ken Griffey Jr. .75 2.00
131 Chris Booker (RC) .30 .75
132 Luke Hudson .15 .40
133 Jason Bergmann RC .30 .75
134 Ryan Freel .15 .40
135 Sean Casey .15 .40
136 Wily Mo Pena .15 .40
137 Aaron Boone .15 .40
138 Ben Broussard .15 .40
139 Ryan Garko (RC) .30 .75
140 C.C. Sabathia .25 .60
141 Casey Blake .15 .40
142 Cliff Lee .25 .60
143 Coco Crisp .15 .40
144 David Riske .15 .40
145 Grady Sizemore .25 .60
146 Jake Westbrook .15 .40
147 Jhonny Peralta .15 .40
148 Josh Bard .15 .40
149 Kevin Millwood .15 .40
150 Ronnie Belliard .15 .40
151 Scott Elarton .15 .40
152 Travis Hafner .15 .40
153 Victor Martinez .25 .60
154 Aaron Cook .15 .40
155 Aaron Miles .15 .40
156 Brad Hawpe .15 .40
157 Mike Esposito (RC) .30 .75
158 Chin-Hui Tsao .15 .40
159 Clint Barmes .15 .40
160 Cory Sullivan .15 .40
161 Garrett Atkins .15 .40
162 J.D. Closser .15 .40
163 Jason Jennings .15 .40
164 Jeff Baker .15 .40
165 Jeff Francis .15 .40
166 Luis A. Gonzalez .15 .40
167 Matt Holliday .40 1.00
168 Todd Helton .25 .60
169 Bradon Inge .15 .40
170 Carlos Guillen .15 .40
171 Carlos Pena .25 .60
172 Chris Shelton .15 .40
173 Craig Monroe .15 .40
174 Curtis Granderson .30 .75
175 Dmitri Young .15 .40
176 Ivan Rodriguez .25 .60
177 Jason Johnson .15 .40
178 Jeremy Bonderman .15 .40
179 Magglio Ordonez .25 .60
180 Mark Woodyard (RC) .30 .75
181 Nook Logan .15 .40
182 Omar Infante .15 .40
183 Placido Polanco .15 .40
184 Chris Heintz RC .30 .75
185 A.J. Burnett .15 .40
186 Alex Gonzalez .15 .40
187 Josh Johnson (RC) .75 2.00
188 Carlos Delgado .15 .40
189 Dontrelle Willis .15 .40
190 Josh Wilson (RC) .30 .75
191 Jason Vargas .15 .40
192 Jeff Conine .15 .40
193 Jeremy Hermida .15 .40
194 Josh Beckett .15 .40
195 Juan Encarnacion .15 .40
196 Juan Pierre .15 .40
197 Luis Castillo .15 .40
198 Miguel Cabrera .40 1.00
199 Mike Lowell .15 .40
200 Paul Lo Duca .15 .40
201 Todd Jones .15 .40
202 Adam Everett .15 .40
203 Andy Pettitte .25 .60
204 Brad Ausmus .15 .40
205 Brad Lidge .15 .40
206 Brandon Backe .15 .40
207 Charlton Jimerson (RC) .30 .75
208 Chris Burke .15 .40
209 Craig Biggio .25 .60
210 Dan Wheeler .15 .40
211 Jason Lane .15 .40
212 Jeff Bagwell .25 .60
213 Lance Berkman .25 .60
214 Luke Scott .15 .40
215 Morgan Ensberg .15 .40
216 Roger Clemens .50 1.25
217 Roy Oswalt .25 .60
218 Willy Taveras .15 .40
219 Andres Blanco .15 .40
220 Angel Berroa .15 .40
221 Ruben Gotay .15 .40
222 David DeJesus .15 .40
223 Emil Brown .15 .40
224 J.P. Howell .15 .40
225 Jeremy Affeldt .15 .40
226 Jimmy Gobble .15 .40
227 John Buck .15 .40
228 Jose Lima .15 .40
229 Mark Teahen .15 .40
230 Matt Stairs .15 .40
231 Mike MacDougal .15 .40
232 Mike Sweeney .15 .40
233 Runelvys Hernandez .15 .40
234 Terrence Long .15 .40
235 Zack Greinke .25 .60
236 Ron Flores RC .30 .75
237 Brad Penny .15 .40
238 Cesar Izturis .15 .40
239 D.J. Houlton .15 .40
240 Derek Lowe .15 .40
241 Eric Gagne .15 .40
242 Hee Seop Choi .15 .40
243 J.D. Drew .15 .40
244 Jason Phillips .15 .40
245 Jason Repko .15 .40
246 Jayson Werth .25 .60
247 Jeff Kent .15 .40
248 Jeff Weaver .15 .40
249 Milton Bradley .15 .40
250 Odalis Perez .15 .40
251 Hong-Chih Kuo (RC) .75 2.00
252 Oscar Robles .15 .40
253 Ben Sheets .15 .40
254 Bill Hall .15 .40
255 Brady Clark .15 .40
256 Carlos Lee .15 .40
257 Chris Capuano .15 .40
258 Nelson Cruz (RC) 1.25 3.00
259 Derrick Turnbow .15 .40
260 Doug Davis .15 .40
261 Geoff Jenkins .15 .40
262 J.J. Hardy .15 .40
263 Lyle Overbay .15 .40
264 Prince Fielder .75 2.00
265 Rickie Weeks .15 .40
266 Russell Branyan .15 .40
267 Tomo Ohka .15 .40
268 Jonah Bayliss RC .30 .75
269 Brad Radke .15 .40
270 Carlos Silva .15 .40
271 Francisco Liriano (RC) .75 2.00
272 Jacque Jones .15 .40
273 Joe Mauer .25 .60
274 Travis Bowyer (RC) .30 .75
275 Joe Nathan .15 .40
276 Johan Santana .25 .60
277 Justin Morneau .25 .60
278 Kyle Lohse .15 .40
279 Lew Ford .15 .40
280 Matt LeCroy .15 .40
281 Michael Cuddyer .15 .40
282 Nick Punto .15 .40
283a Scott Baker .15 .40
283b Jason Repko UER .15 .40
284 Shannon Stewart .15 .40
285 Torii Hunter .15 .40
286 Braden Looper .15 .40
287 Carlos Beltran .25 .60
288 Cliff Floyd .15 .40
289 David Wright .30 .75
290 Doug Mientkiewicz .15 .40
291 Anderson Hernandez (RC) .30 .75
292 Jose Reyes .25 .60
293 Kazuo Matsui .15 .40
294 Kris Benson .15 .40
295 Miguel Cairo .15 .40
296 Mike Cameron .15 .40
297 Robert Andino RC .30 .75
298 Mike Piazza .40 1.00
299 Pedro Martinez .25 .60
300 Tom Glavine .25 .60
301 Victor Diaz .15 .40
302 Tim Hamulack (RC) .30 .75
303 Alex Rodriguez .50 1.25
304 Bernie Williams .25 .60
305 Carl Pavano .15 .40
306 Chien-Ming Wang .25 .60
307 Derek Jeter 1.00 2.50
308 Gary Sheffield .15 .40
309 Hideki Matsui .40 1.00
310 Jason Giambi .15 .40
311 Jorge Posada .25 .60
312 Kevin Brown .15 .40
313 Mariano Rivera .50 1.25
314 Matt Lawton .15 .40
315 Mike Mussina .25 .60
316 Randy Johnson .40 1.00
317 Robinson Cano .25 .60
318 Mike Vento (RC) .30 .75
319 Tino Martinez .15 .40
320 Tony Womack .15 .40
321 Barry Zito .25 .60
322 Bobby Crosby .15 .40
323 Bobby Kielty .15 .40
324 Dan Johnson .15 .40
325 Danny Haren .15 .40
326 Eric Chavez .15 .40
327 Erubiel Durazo .15 .40
328 Huston Street .15 .40
329 Jason Kendall .15 .40
330 Jay Payton .15 .40
331 Joe Blanton .15 .40
332 Joe Kennedy .15 .40
333 Kirk Saarloos .15 .40
334 Mark Kotsay .15 .40
335 Nick Swisher .25 .60
336 Rich Harden .15 .40
337 Scott Hatteberg .15 .40
338 Billy Wagner .15 .40
339 Bobby Abreu .15 .40
340 Brett Myers .15 .40
341 Chase Utley .25 .60
342 Danny Sandoval RC .30 .75
343 David Bell .15 .40
344 Gavin Floyd .15 .40
345 Jim Thome .25 .60
346 Jimmy Rollins .25 .60
347 Jon Lieber .15 .40
348 Kenny Lofton .15 .40
349 Mike Lieberthal .15 .40
350 Pat Burrell .15 .40
351 Randy Wolf .15 .40
352 Ryan Howard .30 .75
353 Vicente Padilla .15 .40
354 Bryan Bullington (RC) .30 .75
355 J.J. Furmaniak (RC) .30 .75
356 Craig Wilson .15 .40
357 Matt Capps (RC) .30 .75
358 Tom Gorzelanny (RC) .30 .75
359 Jack Wilson .15 .40
360 Jason Bay .15 .40
361 Jose Mesa .15 .40
362 Josh Fogg .15 .40
363 Kip Wells .15 .40
364 Steve Stemle RC .30 .75
365 Oliver Perez .15 .40
366 Rob Mackowiak .15 .40
367 Ronny Paulino (RC) .30 .75
368 Tike Redman .15 .40
369 Zach Duke .15 .40
370 Adam Eaton .15 .40
371 Scott Feldman RC .30 .75
372 Brian Giles .15 .40
373 Brian Lawrence .15 .40
374 Damian Jackson .15 .40
375 Dave Roberts .25 .60
376 Jake Peavy .15 .40
377 Joe Randa .15 .40
378 Khalil Greene .15 .40
379 Mark Loretta .15 .40
380 Ramon Hernandez .15 .40
381 Robert Fick .15 .40
382 Ryan Klesko .15 .40
383 Trevor Hoffman .25 .60
384 Woody Williams .15 .40
385 Xavier Nady .15 .40
386 Armando Benitez .15 .40
387 Brad Hennessey .15 .40
388 Brian Myrow RC .30 .75
389 Edgardo Alfonzo .15 .40
390 J.T. Snow .15 .40
391 Jeremy Accardo RC .30 .75
392 Jason Schmidt .15 .40
393 Lance Niekro .15 .40
394 Matt Cain 1.00 2.50
395 Dan Ortmeier (RC) .30 .75
396 Moises Alou .15 .40
397 Doug Clark (RC) .30 .75
398 Omar Vizquel .25 .60
399 Pedro Feliz .15 .40
400 Randy Winn .15 .40
401 Ray Durham .15 .40
402 Adrian Beltre .40 1.00
403 Eddie Guardado .15 .40
404 Felix Hernandez .25 .60
405 Gil Meche .15 .40
406 Ichiro Suzuki .50 1.25
407 Jamie Moyer .15 .40
408 Jeff Nelson .15 .40
409 Jeremy Reed .15 .40
410 Joel Pineiro .15 .40
411 Jaime Bubela (RC) .30 .75
412 Raul Ibanez .25 .60
413 Rickie Sexson .15 .40
414 Ryan Franklin .15 .40
415 Willie Bloomquist .15 .40
416 Yorvit Torrealba .15 .40
417 Yuniesky Betancourt .15 .40
418 Jeff Harris RC .30 .75
419 Albert Pujols .50 1.25
420 Chris Carpenter .25 .60
421 David Eckstein .15 .40
422 Jason Isringhausen .15 .40
423 Jason Marquis .15 .40
424 Adam Wainwright (RC) .50 1.25
425 Jim Edmonds .25 .60
426 Ryan Theriot RC 1.00 2.50
427 Chris Duncan (RC) .50 1.25
428 Mark Grudzielanek .15 .40
429 Mark Mulder .15 .40
430 Matt Morris .15 .40
431 Reggie Sanders .15 .40
432 Scott Rolen .25 .60
433 Tyler Johnson (RC) .30 .75
434 Yadier Molina .40 1.00
435 Alex S. Gonzalez .15 .40
436 Aubrey Huff .15 .40
437 Tim Corcoran RC .30 .75
438 Carl Crawford .25 .60
439 Casey Fossum .15 .40
440 Danys Baez .15 .40
441 Edwin Jackson .15 .40
442 Joey Gathright .15 .40
443 Jonny Gomes .15 .40
444 Jorge Cantu .15 .40
445 Julio Lugo .15 .40
446 Nick Green .15 .40
447 Rocco Baldelli .15 .40
448 Scott Kazmir .25 .60
449 Seth McClung .15 .40
450 Toby Hall .15 .40
451 Travis Lee .15 .40
452 Craig Breslow RC .30 .75
453 Alfonso Soriano .25 .60
454 Chris R. Young .15 .40
455 David Dellucci .15 .40
456 Francisco Cordero .15 .40
457 Gary Matthews .15 .40
458 Hank Blalock .15 .40
459 Juan Dominguez .15 .40
460 Josh Rupe (RC) .30 .75
461 Kenny Rogers .15 .40
462 Kevin Mench .15 .40
463 Laynce Nix .15 .40
464 Mark Teixeira .25 .60
465 Michael Young .15 .40
466 Richard Hidalgo .15 .40
467 Jason Botts (RC) .30 .75
468 Aaron Hill .15 .40
469 Alex Rios .15 .40
470 Corey Koskie .15 .40
471 Chris Demaria RC .30 .75
472 Eric Hinske .15 .40
473 Frank Catalanotto .15 .40
474 John-Ford Griffin (RC) .30 .75
475 Gustavo Chacin .15 .40
476 Josh Towers .15 .40
477 Miguel Batista .15 .40
478 Orlando Hudson .15 .40
479 Reed Johnson .15 .40
480 Roy Halladay .25 .60
481 Shaun Marcum (RC) .30 .75
482 Shea Hillenbrand .15 .40
483 Ted Lilly .15 .40
484 Vernon Wells .15 .40
485 Brad Wilkerson .15 .40
486 Darrell Rasner (RC) .30 .75
487 Chad Cordero .15 .40
488 Cristian Guzman .15 .40
489 Esteban Loaiza .15 .40
490 John Patterson .15 .40
491 Jose Guillen .15 .40
492 Jose Vidro .15 .40
493 Livan Hernandez .15 .40
494 Marlon Byrd .15 .40
495 Nick Johnson .15 .40
496 Preston Wilson .15 .40
497 Ryan Church .15 .40
498 Ryan Zimmerman (RC) 1.00 2.50
499 Tony Armas Jr. .15 .40
500 Vinny Castilla .15 .40
501 Andy Green .15 .40
502 Damion Easley .15 .40
503 Eric Byrnes .15 .40
504 Jason Grimsley .15 .40
505 Jeff DaVanon .15 .40
506 Johnny Estrada .15 .40
507 Luis Vizcaino .15 .40
508 Miguel Batista .15 .40
509 Orlando Hernandez .15 .40
510 Orlando Hudson .15 .40
511 Terry Mulholland .15 .40
512 Chris Reitsma .15 .40
513 Edgar Renteria .15 .40
514 John Thomson .15 .40
515 Jorge Sosa .15 .40
516 Oscar Villarreal .15 .40
517 Pete Orr .15 .40
518 Ryan Langerhans .15 .40
519 Todd Pratt .15 .40
520 Wilson Betemit .15 .40
521 Brian Jordan .15 .40
522 Lance Cormier .15 .40
523 Matt Diaz .15 .40
524 Mike Remlinger .15 .40
525 Bruce Chen .15 .40
526 Chris Gomez .15 .40
527 Chris Ray .15 .40
528 Corey Patterson .15 .40
529 David Newhan .15 .40
530 Ed Rogers (RC) .30 .75
531 John Halama .15 .40
532 Kris Benson .15 .40
533 LaTroy Hawkins .15 .40
534 Raul Chavez .15 .40
535 Alex Cora .25 .60
536 Alex Gonzalez .15 .40
537 Coco Crisp .15 .40
538 David Riske .15 .40
539 Doug Mirabelli .15 .40
540 Josh Beckett .15 .40
541 J.T. Snow .15 .40
542 Mike Timlin .15 .40
543 Julian Tavarez .15 .40
544 Rudy Seanez .15 .40
545 Wily Mo Pena .15 .40
546 Bob Howry .15 .40
547 Glendon Rusch .15 .40
548 Henry Blanco .15 .40
549 Jacque Jones .15 .40
550 Jerome Williams .15 .40
551 John Mabry .15 .40
552 Juan Pierre .15 .40
553 Scott Eyre .15 .40
554 Scott Williamson .15 .40
555 Wade Miller .15 .40
556 Will Ohman .15 .40
557 Alex Cintron .15 .40
558 Rob Mackowiak .15 .40
559 Brandon McCarthy .15 .40
560 Chris Widger .15 .40
561 Cliff Politte .15 .40
562 Javier Vazquez .15 .40
563 Jim Thome .25 .60
564 Matt Thornton .15 .40
565 Neal Cotts .15 .40
566 Pablo Ozuna .15 .40
567 Ross Gload .15 .40
568 Brandon Phillips .15 .40
569 Bronson Arroyo .15 .40
570 Dave Williams .15 .40
571 David Ross .15 .40
572 David Weathers .15 .40
573 Eric Milton .15 .40
574 Javier Valentin .15 .40
575 Kent Mercker .15 .40
576 Matt Belisle .15 .40
577 Paul Wilson .15 .40
578 Rich Aurilia .15 .40
579 Rick White .15 .40
580 Scott Hatteberg .15 .40
581 Todd Coffey .15 .40
582 Bob Wickman .15 .40
583 Danny Graves .15 .40
584 Eduardo Perez .15 .40
585 Guillermo Mota .15 .40
586 Jason Davis .15 .40
587 Jason Johnson .15 .40
588 Jason Michaels .15 .40
589 Rafael Betancourt .15 .40
590 Ramon Vazquez .15 .40
591 Scott Sauerbeck .15 .40
592 Todd Hollandsworth .15 .40
593 Brian Fuentes .15 .40
594 Danny Ardoin .15 .40
595 David Cortes .15 .40
596 Eli Marrero .15 .40
597 Jamey Carroll .15 .40
598 Jason Smith .15 .40
599 Josh Fogg .15 .40
600 Miguel Ojeda .15 .40
601 Mike DeJean .15 .40
602 Ray King .15 .40
603 Omar Quintanilla (RC) .30 .75
604 Zach Day .15 .40
605 Fernando Rodney .15 .40
606 Kenny Rogers .15 .40
607 Mike Maroth .15 .40
608 Nate Robertson .15 .40
609 Todd Jones .15 .40
610 Vance Wilson .15 .40
611 Bobby Seay .15 .40
612 Chris Spurling .15 .40
613 Roman Colon .15 .40
614 Jason Grilli .15 .40
615 Marcus Thames .15 .40
616 Ramon Santiago .15 .40
617 Alfredo Amezaga .15 .40
618 Brian Moehler .15 .40
619 Chris Aguila .15 .40
620 Franklyn German .15 .40
621 Joe Borowski .15 .40
622 Logan Kensing (RC) .30 .75
623 Matt Treanor .15 .40
624 Miguel Olivo .15 .40
625 Sergio Mitre .15 .40
626 Todd Wellemeyer .15 .40
627 Wes Helms .15 .40
628 Chad Qualls .15 .40
629 Eric Bruntlett .15 .40
630 Mike Gallo .15 .40
631 Mike Lamb .15 .40
632 Orlando Palmeiro .15 .40
633 Russ Springer .15 .40
634 Dan Wheeler .15 .40
635 Eric Munson .15 .40
636 Preston Wilson .15 .40
637 Trever Miller .15 .40
638 Ambiorix Burgos .15 .40
639 Andy Sisco .15 .40
640 Denny Bautista .15 .40
641 Doug Mientkiewicz .15 .40
642 Elmer Dessens .15 .40
643 Esteban German .15 .40
644 Joe Nelson (RC) .30 .75
645 Mark Grudzielanek .15 .40
646 Mark Redman .15 .40
647 Mike Wood .15 .40
648 Paul Bako .15 .40
649 Reggie Sanders .15 .40
650 Scott Elarton .15 .40
651 Shane Costa .15 .40
652 Tony Graffanino .15 .40
653 Jason Bulger (RC) .30 .75
654 Chris Bootcheck (RC) .30 .75
655 Esteban Yan .15 .40
656 Hector Carrasco .15 .40
657 J.C. Romero .15 .40
658 Jeff Weaver .15 .40
659 Jose Molina .15
660 Kelvim Escobar .15
661 Maicer Izturis .15
662 Robb Quinlan .15
663 Scot Shields .15
664 Tim Salmon .15
665 Bill Mueller .15
666 Brett Tomko .15
667 Dioner Navarro .15
668 Jae Seo .15
669 Jose Cruz Jr. .15
670 Kenny Lofton .15
671 Lance Carter .15
672 Nomar Garciaparra .25
673 Olmedo Saenz .15
674 Rafael Furcal .15
675 Ramon Martinez .15
676 Ricky Ledee .15
677 Sandy Alomar Jr. .15
678 Yhency Brazoban .15
679 Corey Koskie .15
680 Dan Kolb .15
681 Gabe Gross .15
682 Jeff Cirillo .15
683 Matt Wise .15
684 Rick Helling .15
685 Chad Moeller .15
686 Dave Bush .15
687 Jorge De La Rosa .15
688 Justin Lehr .15
689 Jason Bartlett .15
690 Jesse Crain .15
691 Juan Rincon .15
692 Luis Castillo .15
693 Mike Redmond .15
694 Rondell White .15
695 Tony Batista .15
696 Juan Castro .15
697 Luis Rodriguez .15
698 Matt Guerrier .15
699 Willie Eyre (RC) .30
700 Aaron Heilman .15
701 Billy Wagner .15
702 Carlos Delgado .15
703 Chad Bradford .15
704 Chris Woodward .15
705 Darren Oliver .15
706 Duaner Sanchez .15
707 Endy Chavez .15
708 Jorge Julio .15
709 Jose Valentin .15
710 Julio Franco .15
711 Paul Lo Duca .15
712 Ramon Castro .15
713 Steve Trachsel .15
714 Victor Zambrano .15
715 Xavier Nady .15
716 Andy Phillips .15
717 Bubba Crosby .15
718 Jaret Wright .15
719 Kelly Stinnett .15
720 Kyle Farnsworth .15
721 Mike Myers .15
722 Octavio Dotel .15
723 Ron Villone .15
724 Scott Proctor .15
725 Shawn Chacon .15
726 Tanyon Sturtze .15
727 Adam Melhuse .15
728 Brad Halsey .15
729 Esteban Loaiza .15
730 Frank Thomas .40
731 Jay Witasick .15
732 Justin Duchscherer .15
733 Kiko Calero .15
734 Marco Scutaro .25
735 Mark Ellis .15
736 Milton Bradley .15
737 Aaron Fultz .15
738 Aaron Rowand .15
739 Geoff Geary .15
740 Arthur Rhodes .15
741 Chris Coste RC .75
742 Rheal Cormier .15
743 Ryan Franklin .15
744 Ryan Madson .15
745 Sal Fasano .15
746 Tom Gordon .15
747 Abraham Nunez .15
748 David Dellucci .15
749 Julio Santana .15
750 Shane Victorino .15
751 Damaso Marte .15
752 Freddy Sanchez .15
753 Humberto Cota .15
754 Jeromy Burnitz .15
755 Joe Randa .15
756 Jose Castillo .15
757 Mike Gonzalez .15
758 Ryan Doumit .15
759 Sean Burnett .15
760 Sean Casey .15
761 Ian Snell .15
762 John Grabow .15
763 Jose Hernandez .15
764 Roberto Hernandez .15
765 Ryan Vogelsong .15
766 Victor Santos .15
767 Adrian Gonzalez .30
768 Alan Embree .15
769 Brian Sweeney (RC) .30
770 Chan Ho Park .25
771 Clay Hensley .15

Dewon Brazelton .15 .40
Doug Brocail .15 .40
Eric Young .15 .40
Geoff Blum .15 .40
Josh Bard .15 .40
Mark Bellhorn .15 .40
Mike Cameron .15 .40
Mike Piazza .40 1.00
Rob Bowen .15 .40
Scott Cassidy .15 .40
Scott Linebrink .15 .40
Shawn Estes .15 .40
Terrmel Sledge .15 .40
Vinny Castilla .15 .40
Jeff Fassero .15 .40
Jose Vizcaino .15 .40
Mark Sweeney .15 .40
Matt Morris .15 .40
Steve Finley .15 .40
Tim Worrell .15 .40
Jamey Wright .15 .40
Jason Ellison .15 .40
Noah Lowry .15 .40
Steve Kline .15 .40
Todd Greene .15 .40
Carl Everett .15 .40
George Sherrill .15 .40
J.J. Putz .15 .40
Jake Woods .15 .40
Jose Lopez .15 .40
Julio Mateo .15 .40
Mike Morse .15 .40
Rafael Soriano .15 .40
Roberto Petagine .15 .40
Aaron Miles .15 .40
Braden Looper .15 .40
Gary Bennett .15 .40
Hector Luna .15 .40
Jeff Suppan .15 .40
1 John Rodriguez .15 .40
2 Josh Hancock .15 .40
3 Juan Encarnacion .15 .40
4 Larry Bigbie .15 .40
5 Scott Spiezio .15 .40
6 Sidney Ponson .15 .40
7 So Taguchi .15 .40
8 Brian Meadows .15 .40
9 Damon Hollins .15 .40
0 Dan Miceli .15 .40
1 Doug Waechter .15 .40
2 Jason Childers RC .30 .75
3 Josh Paul .15 .40
4 Julio Lugo .15 .40
5 Mark Hendrickson .15 .40
6 Sean Burroughs .15 .40
7 Shawn Camp .15 .40
8 Travis Harper .15 .40
9 Ty Wigginton .15 .40
0 Adam Eaton .15 .40
1 Adrian Brown .15 .40
2 Akinori Otsuka .15 .40
3 Antonio Alfonseca .15 .40
4 Brad Wilkerson .15 .40
5 D'Angelo Jimenez .15 .40
6 Gerald Laird .15 .40
7 Joaquin Benoit .15 .40
8 Kameron Loe .15 .40
9 Kevin Millwood .15 .40
0 Mark DeRosa .15 .40
1 Phil Nevin .15 .40
2 Rod Barajas .15 .40
3 Vicente Padilla .15 .40
4 A.J. Burnett .15 .40
5 Bengie Molina .15 .40
6 Gregg Zaun .15 .40
47 John McDonald .15 .40
8 Lyle Overbay .15 .40
49 Russ Adams .15 .40
50 Troy Glaus .15 .40
51 Vinny Chulk .15 .40
52 B.J. Ryan .15 .40
53 Justin Speier .15 .40
54 Pete Walker .15 .40
55 Scott Downs .15 .40
56 Scott Schoeneweis .15 .40
57 Alfonso Soriano .25 .60
58 Brian Schneider .15 .40
59 Daryle Ward .15 .40
60 Felix Rodriguez .15 .40
61 Gary Majewski .15 .40
62 Joey Eischen .15 .40
63 Jon Rauch .15 .40
64 Marlon Anderson .15 .40
65 Matt LeCroy .15 .40
66 Mike Stanton .15 .40
67 Ramon Ortiz .15 .40
68 Robert Fick .15 .40
69 Royce Clayton .15 .40
70 Ryan Drese .15 .40
71 Vladimir Guerrero CL .25 .60
72 Craig Biggio CL .25 .60
73 Barry Zito CL .25 .60
74 Vernon Wells CL .15 .40
75 Chipper Jones CL .40 1.00
76 Prince Fielder CL .75 2.00
77 Albert Pujols CL .50 1.25
78 Greg Maddux CL .50 1.25
79 Carl Crawford CL .25 .60
80 Brandon Webb CL .25 .60
81 J.D. Drew CL .25 .60
82 Jason Schmidt CL .15 .40
83 Victor Martinez CL .25 .60
84 Ichiro Suzuki CL .50 1.25
885 Miguel Cabrera CL .40 1.00
886 David Wright CL .30 .75
887 Alfonso Soriano CL .25 .60
888 Miguel Tejada CL .25 .60
889 Khalil Greene CL .15 .40
890 Ryan Howard CL .30 .75
891 Jason Bay CL .15 .40
892 Mark Teixeira CL .25 .60
893 Manny Ramirez CL .40 1.00
894 Ken Griffey Jr. CL .75 2.00
895 Todd Helton CL .25 .60
896 Angel Berroa CL .15 .40
897 Ivan Rodriguez CL .25 .60
898 Johan Santana CL .25 .60
899 Paul Konerko CL .25 .60
900 Derek Jeter CL 1.00 2.50
901 Macay McBride (RC) .30 .75
902 Tony Pena (RC) .30 .75
903 Peter Moylan RC .30 .75
904 Aaron Rakers (RC) .30 .75
905 Chris Britton RC .30 .75
906 Nick Markakis (RC) .60 1.50
907 Sendy Rleal RC .30 .75
908 Val Majewski (RC) .30 .75
909 Jermaine Van Buren (RC) .30 .75
910 Jonathan Papelbon (RC) 1.50 4.00
911 Angel Pagan (RC) .30 .75
912 David Aardsma (RC) .30 .75
913 Sean Marshall (RC) .30 .75
914 Brian Anderson (RC) .30 .75
915 Freddie Bynum (RC) .30 .75
916 Fausto Carmona (RC) .30 .75
917 Kelly Shoppach (RC) .30 .75
918 Choo Freeman (RC) .30 .75
919 Ryan Shealy (RC) .30 .75
920 Joel Zumaya (RC) .75 2.00
921 Jordan Tata RC .30 .75
922 Justin Verlander (RC) 2.50 6.00
923 Carlos Martinez RC .30 .75
924 Chris Resop (RC) .30 .75
925 Dan Uggla (RC) .50 1.25
926 Eric Reed (RC) .30 .75
927 Hanley Ramirez .50 1.25
928 Yusmeiro Petit (RC) .30 .75
929 Josh Willingham (RC) .50 1.25
930 Mike Jacobs (RC) .30 .75
931 Reggie Abercrombie (RC) .30 .75
932 Ricky Nolasco (RC) .30 .75
933 Scott Olsen (RC) .30 .75
934 Fernando Nieve (RC) .30 .75
935 Taylor Buchholz (RC) .30 .75
936 Cody Ross (RC) .75 2.00
937 James Loney (RC) .50 1.25
938 Takashi Saito RC .50 1.25
939 Tim Hamulack .30 .75
940 Chris Demaria .30 .75
941 Jose Capellan (RC) .30 .75
942 David Gassner (RC) .30 .75
943 Jason Kubel (RC) .30 .75
944 Brian Bannister (RC) .30 .75
945 Mike Thompson RC .30 .75
946 Cole Hamels (RC) 1.00 2.50
947 Paul Maholm (RC) .30 .75
948 John Van Benschoten (RC) .30 .75
949 Nate McLouth (RC) .30 .75
950 Ben Johnson (RC) .30 .75
951 Josh Barfield (RC) .30 .75
952 Travis Ishikawa (RC) .50 1.25
953 Jack Taschner (RC) .30 .75
954 Kenji Johjima RC .75 2.00
955 Skip Schumaker (RC) .30 .75
956 Ruddy Lugo (RC) .30 .75
957 Jason Hammel (RC) .75 2.00
958 Chris Roberson (RC) .30 .75
959 Fabio Castro RC .30 .75
960 Ian Kinsler (RC) 1.00 2.50
961 John Koronka (RC) .30 .75
962 Brandon Watson (RC) .30 .75
963 Jon Lester RC 1.25 3.00
964 Ben Hendrickson (RC) .30 .75
965 Martin Prado (RC) .50 1.25
966 Erick Aybar (RC) .30 .75
967 Bobby Livingston (RC) .30 .75
968 Ryan Spilborghs (RC) .30 .75
969 Tommy Murphy (RC) .30 .75
970 Howie Kendrick (RC) .60 1.50
971 Casey Janssen RC .30 .75
972 Michael O'Connor RC .30 .75
973 Conor Jackson (RC) .50 1.25
974 Jeremy Hermida (RC) .30 .75
975 Renyel Pinto (RC) .30 .75
976 Prince Fielder (RC) 1.50 4.00
977 Kevin Frandsen (RC) .30 .75
978 Ty Taubenheim RC .50 1.25
979 Rich Hill (RC) .75 2.00
980 Jonathan Broxton (RC) .30 .75
981 Jamie Shields RC 1.00 2.50
982 Carlos Villanueva RC .30 .75
983 Boone Logan RC .30 .75
984 Brian Wilson RC 5.00 12.00
985 Andre Ethier (RC) 1.00 2.50
986 Mike Napoli RC .50 1.25
987 Agustin Montero (RC) .30 .75
988 Jack Hannahan RC .30 .75
989 Boof Bonser (RC) .50 1.25
990 Carlos Ruiz (RC) .30 .75
991 Jason Botts .30 .75
992 Kendry Morales (RC) .75 2.00
993 Alay Soler RC .30 .75
994 Santiago Ramirez (RC) .30 .75
995 Saul Rivera (RC) .30 .75
996 Anthony Reyes (RC) .30 .75
997 Matt Kemp (RC) .75 2.00
998 Jae Kuk Ryu RC .30 .75
999 Lastings Milledge (RC) .30 .75
NNO Exquisite Redemption
1000 Jered Weaver (RC) 1.00 2.50
1001 Stephen Drew (RC) .60 1.50
1002 Carlos Quentin (RC) .50 1.25
1003 Livan Hernandez .15 .40
1004 Chris B. Young (RC) .75 2.00
1005 Alberto Callaspo SP (RC) 1.25 3.00
1006 Enrique Gonzalez (RC) .30 .75
1007 Tony Pena (RC) .30 .75
1008 Bob Melvin MG .15 .40
1009 Fernando Tatis .15 .40
1010 Willy Aybar (RC) .30 .75
1011 Ken Ray (RC) .30 .75
1012 Scott Thorman (RC) .30 .75
1013 Eric Hinske SP 1.25 3.00
1014 Kevin Barry (RC) .30 .75
1015 Bobby Cox MG .15 .40
1016 Phil Stockman (RC) .30 .75
1017 Brayan Pena (RC) .30 .75
1018 Adam Loewen (RC) .30 .75
1019 Brandon Fahey RC .30 .75
1020 Jim Hoey RC .30 .75
1021 Kurt Birkins SP RC 1.25 3.00
1022 Jim Johnson RC 1.25 3.00
1023 Sam Perlozzo MG .15 .40
1024 Cory Morris RC .30 .75
1025 Hayden Penn (RC) .30 .75
1026 Javy Lopez .15 .40
1027 Dustin Pedroia (RC) 8.00 20.00
1028 Kason Gabbard (RC) .30 .75
1029 David Pauley (RC) .30 .75
1030 Kyle Snyder .15 .40
1031 Terry Francona MG .15 .40
1032 Craig Breslow .30 .75
1033 Bryan Corey (RC) .30 .75
1034 Manny Delcarmen (RC) .30 .75
1035 Carlos Marmol RC 1.00 2.50
1036 Buck Coats (RC) .30 .75
1037 Ryan O'Malley SP RC 1.25 3.00
1038 Angel Guzman (RC) .30 .75
1039 Ronny Cedeno .15 .40
1040 Juan Mateo RC .30 .75
1041 Cesar Izturis .15 .40
1042 Les Walrond (RC) .30 .75
1043 Geovany Soto .75 2.00
1044 Sean Tracey (RC) .30 .75
1045 Ozzie Guillen MG SP 1.25 3.00
1046 Royce Clayton .15 .40
1047 Norris Hopper RC .30 .75
1048 Bill Bray (RC) .30 .75
1049 Jerry Narron MG .15 .40
1050 Brendan Harris (RC) .30 .75
1051 Brian Shackelford .15 .40
1052 Jeremy Sowers (RC) .30 .75
1053 Joe Inglett RC .30 .75
1054 Brian Slocum (RC) .30 .75
1055 Andrew Brown (RC) .30 .75
1056 Rafael Perez RC .30 .75
1057 Edward Mujica RC .30 .75
1058 Andy Marte (RC) .30 .75
1059 Shin-Soo Choo (RC) .50 1.25
1060 Jeremy Guthrie (RC) .30 .75
1061 Franklin Gutierrez SP (RC) 1.25 3.00
1062 Kazuo Matsui .15 .40
1063 Chris Iannetta RC .30 .75
1064 Manny Corpas RC .30 .75
1065 Clint Hurdle MG .15 .40
1066 Ramon Ramirez (RC) .30 .75
1067 Sean Casey .15 .40
1068 Zach Miner (RC) .30 .75
1069 Brent Clevlen SP (RC) 2.00 5.00
1070 Bob Wickman .15 .40
1071 Jim Leyland MG .15 .40
1072 Alexis Gomez (RC) .30 .75
1073 Anibal Sanchez (RC) .30 .75
1074 Taylor Tankersley (RC) .30 .75
1075 Eric Wedge MG .15 .40
1076 Jonah Bayliss .30 .75
1077 Paul Hoover SP (RC) 1.25 3.00
1078 Eddie Guardado .15 .40
1079 Cody Ross .75 2.00
1080 Aubrey Huff .15 .40
1081 Jason Hirsh (RC) .30 .75
1082 Brandon League .15 .40
1083 Matt Albers (RC) .30 .75
1084 Chris Sampson RC .30 .75
1085 Phil Garner MG .15 .40
1086 J.R. House (RC) .30 .75
1087 Ryan Shealy .15 .40
1088 Stephen Andrade (RC) .30 .75
1089 Bob Keppel (RC) .30 .75
1090 Buddy Bell MG .15 .40
1091 Justin Huber (RC) .30 .75
1092 Paul Phillips (RC) .30 .75
1093 Greg Jones SP (RC) 1.25 3.00
1094 Jeff Mathis (RC) .30 .75
1095 Dustin Moseley (RC) .30 .75
1096 Joe Saunders (RC) .30 .75
1097 Reggie Willits RC .75 2.00
1098 Mike Scioscia MG .15 .40
1099 Greg Maddux .50 1.25
1100 Wilson Betemit .15 .40
1101 Chad Billingsley SP (RC) 2.00 5.00
1102 Russell Martin (RC) .50 1.25
1103 Grady Little MG .15 .40
1104 David Bell .15 .40
1105 Kevin Mench .15 .40
1106 Laynce Nix .15 .40
1107 Chris Barnwell RC .30 .75
1108 Tony Gwynn Jr. (RC) .30 .75
1109 Corey Hart (RC) .30 .75
1110 Zach Jackson (RC) .30 .75
1111 Francisco Cordero .15 .40
1112 Joe Winkelsas (RC) .30 .75
1113 Ned Yost MG .15 .40
1114 Matt Garza (RC) .30 .75
1115 Chris Heintz .15 .40
1116 Pat Neshek RC 3.00 8.00
1117 Josh Rabe SP RC 1.25 3.00
1118 Mike Rivera .15 .40
1119 Ron Gardenhire MG .15 .40
1120 Shawn Green .15 .40
1121 Oliver Perez .15 .40
1122 Heath Bell .15 .40
1123 Bartolome Fortunato (RC) .30 .75
1124 Anderson Garcia RC .30 .75
1125 John Maine SP (RC) 2.00 5.00
1126 Henry Owens RC .30 .75
1127 Mike Pelfrey RC .75 2.00
1128 Royce Ring (RC) .30 .75
1129 Willie Randolph MG .15 .40
1130 Bobby Abreu .15 .40
1131 Craig Wilson .15 .40
1132 T.J. Beam (RC) .30 .75
1133 Colter Bean SP (RC) 1.25 3.00
1134 Melky Cabrera (RC) .50 1.25
1135 Mitch Jones (RC) .30 .75
1136 Jeffrey Karstens RC .30 .75
1137 Wil Nieves (RC) .30 .75
1138 Kevin Reese (RC) .30 .75
1139 Kevin Thompson (RC) .30 .75
1140 Jose Veras RC .30 .75
1141 Joe Torre MG .25 .60
1142 Jeremy Brown (RC) .30 .75
1143 Santiago Casilla (RC) .30 .75
1144 Shane Komine RC .50 1.25
1145 Mike Rouse (RC) .30 .75
1146 Jason Windsor (RC) .30 .75
1147 Ken Macha MG .15 .40
1148 Jamie Moyer .15 .40
1149 Phil Nevin SP 1.25 3.00
1150 Eude Brito (RC) .30 .75
1151 Fabio Castro .15 .40
1152 Jeff Conine .15 .40
1153 Scott Mathieson (RC) .30 .75
1154 Brian Sanches (RC) .30 .75
1155 Matt Smith RC .30 .75
1156 Joe Thurston (RC) .30 .75
1157 Marlon Anderson SP 1.25 3.00
1158 Xavier Nady .15 .40
1159 Shawn Chacon .15 .40
1160 Rajai Davis (RC) .30 .75
1161 Yurendell DeCaster (RC) .30 .75
1162 Marty McLeary (RC) .30 .75
1163 Chris Duffy .15 .40
1164 Josh Sharpless RC .30 .75
1165 Jim Tracy MG .15 .40
1166 David Wells .15 .40
1167 Russell Branyan .15 .40
1168 Todd Walker .15 .40
1169 Paul McAnulty (RC) .30 .75
1170 Bruce Bochy MG .25 .60
1171 Shea Hillenbrand .15 .40
1172 Eliezer Alfonzo RC .30 .75
1173 Justin Knoedler SP (RC) 1.25 3.00
1174 Jonathan Sanchez (RC) .75 2.00
1175 Travis Smith (RC) .30 .75
1176 Cha-Seung Baek .15 .40
1177 T.J. Bohn (RC) .30 .75
1178 Emiliano Fruto RC .30 .75
1179 Sean Green RC .30 .75
1180 Jon Huber RC .30 .75
1181 Adam Jones SP RC 6.00 15.00
1182 Mark Lowe (RC) .30 .75
1183 Eric O'Flaherty RC .30 .75
1184 Preston Wilson .15 .40
1185 Mike Hargrove MG .15 .40
1186 Jeff Weaver .15 .40
1187 Ronnie Belliard .15 .40
1188 John Gall (RC) .30 .75
1189 Josh Kinney SP RC 1.25 3.00
1190 Tony LaRussa MG .25 .60
1191 Scott Dunn (RC) .30 .75
1192 B.J. Upton .15 .40
1193 Jon Switzer (RC) .30 .75
1194 Ben Zobrist (RC) 1.50 4.00
1195 Joe Maddon .15 .40
1196 Carlos Lee .15 .40
1197 Matt Stairs .15 .40
1198 Nick Masset (RC) .30 .75
1199 Nelson Cruz 1.25 3.00
1200 Francisco Rosario (RC) .30 .75
1201 Wes Littleton (RC) .30 .75
1202 Drew Meyer (RC) .30 .75
1203 John Rheinecker (RC) .30 .75
1204 Robinson Tejeda .15 .40
1205 Jeremy Accardo SP 1.25 3.00
1206 Luis Figueroa RC .30 .75
1207 John Hattig (RC) .30 .75
1208 Dustin McGowan (RC) .30 .75
1209 Ryan Roberts RC .30 .75
1210 Davis Romero (RC) .30 .75
1211 Ty Taubenheim .50 1.25
1212 John Gibbons MG .15 .40
1213 Shawn Hill SP (RC) 1.25 3.00
1214 Brandon Harper RC .30 .75
1215 Travis Hughes (RC) .30 .75
1216 Chris Schroder RC .30 .75
1217 Austin Kearns .15 .40
1218 Felipe Lopez .15 .40
1219 Roy Corcoran RC .30 .75
1220 Melvin Dorta RC .30 .75
1221 Brandon Webb CL SP 1.25 3.00
1222 Andruw Jones CL SP .75 2.00
1223 Miguel Tejada CL SP 1.25 3.00
1224 David Ortiz CL SP 2.00 5.00
1225 Derrek Lee CL SP .75 2.00
1226 Jim Thome CL SP 1.25 3.00
1227 Ken Griffey Jr. CL SP 4.00 10.00
1228 Travis Hafner CL SP .75 2.00
1229 Todd Helton CL SP 1.25 3.00
1230 Magglio Ordonez CL SP 1.25 3.00
1231 Miguel Cabrera CL SP 2.00 5.00
1232 Lance Berkman CL SP 1.25 3.00
1233 Mike Sweeney CL SP .75 2.00
1234 Vladimir Guerrero CL SP 1.25 3.00
1235 Nomar Garciaparra CL SP 1.25 3.00
1236 Prince Fielder CL SP 4.00 10.00
1237 Johan Santana CL SP 1.25 3.00
1238 Pedro Martinez CL SP 1.25 3.00
1239 Derek Jeter CL SP 5.00 12.00
1240 Barry Zito CL SP 1.25 3.00
1241 Ryan Howard CL SP 1.50 4.00
1242 Jason Bay CL SP .75 2.00
1243 Trevor Hoffman CL SP 1.25 3.00
1244 Jason Schmidt CL SP .75 2.00
1245 Ichiro Suzuki CL SP 2.50 6.00
1246 Albert Pujols CL SP 2.50 6.00
1247 Carl Crawford CL SP 1.25 3.00
1248 Mark Teixeira CL SP 1.25 3.00
1249 Vernon Wells CL SP .75 2.00
1250 Alfonso Soriano CL SP 1.25 3.00

2006 Upper Deck Gold

*GOLD 1-1000: 2X TO 5X BASIC
*GOLD 1-1000: 1X TO 2.5X BASIC RC's
*GOLD 1001-1250: 3X TO 8X BASIC
*GOLD 1001-1250: 1.5X TO 4X BASIC RC'S
*GOLD 1001-1220: .15X TO .4X BASIC SP
COMMON (1221-1250) 1.25 3.00
SEMIS 1221-1250 2.00 5.00
UNLISTED 1221-1250 3.00 8.00
1-500 FIVE #'d INSERTS PER SER.1 HOB.BOX
501-1000 SER.2 ODDS 1:8 H, RANDOM IN RET
1001-1250 UPDATE ODDS 1:24 RET
1-1000 PRINT RUN 299 SERIAL #'d SETS
1001-1250 PRINT RUN 99 SERIAL #'d SETS
984 Brian Wilson 20.00 50.00
1181 Adam Jones 8.00 20.00

2006 Upper Deck Silver Spectrum

*501-1000: 3X TO 8X BASIC
*501-1000: 1.5X TO 4X BASIC RC's
1-500 FIVE #'d INSERTS PER SER.1 HOB.BOX
501-1000 SER.2 ODDS1:24 H,RANDOM IN RET
1-500 PRINT RUN 25 SERIAL #'d SETS
501-1000 PRINT RUN 99 SERIAL #'d SETS
1-500 NO PRICING DUE TO SCARCITY

2006 Upper Deck Ozzie Smith SABR San Diego

1 Ozzie Smith 1.25 3.00

2006 Upper Deck Rookie Foil Silver

*SILVER: 1X TO 2.5X BASIC
2-3 PER SER.2 RC PACK
ONE RC PACK PER SER.2 HOBBY BOX
3-CARDS PER SEALED RC PACK
STATED PRINT RUN 399 SERIAL #'d SETS
*GOLD: 1.5X TO 4X BASIC
GOLD RANDOM IN SER.2 RC PACKS
GOLD PRINT RUN 99 SERIAL #'d SETS
PLAT.RANDOM IN SER.2 RC PACKS
PLATINUM PRINT RUN 15 #'d SETS
NO PLATINUM PRICING DUE TO SCARCITY
AU PLATES RANDOM IN RC PACKS
AU PLATE PRINT RUN 1 SET PER COLOR
BLACK-CYAN-MAGENTA-YELLOW ISSUED
NO AU PLATE PRICING DUE TO SCARCITY
AU PLATES ISSUED FOR 28 OF 100 FOILS
SEE BECKETT.COM FOR AU PLATE CL

2006 Upper Deck All-Time Legends

TWO PER SERIES 2 FAT PACK
AT1 Ty Cobb 1.50 4.00
AT2 Lou Gehrig 2.00 5.00
AT3 Babe Ruth 2.50 6.00
AT4 Jimmie Foxx 1.00 2.50
AT5 Honus Wagner 1.00 2.50
AT6 Lou Brock .60 1.50
AT7 Joe Morgan .60 1.50
AT8 Christy Mathewson 1.00 2.50
AT9 Walter Johnson 1.00 2.50
AT10 Mike Schmidt 1.50 4.00
AT11 Al Kaline 1.00 2.50
AT12 Robin Yount 1.00 2.50
AT13 Johnny Bench 1.00 2.50
AT14 Yogi Berra 1.00 2.50
AT15 Rod Carew .60 1.50
AT16 Bob Feller .60 1.50
AT17 Carlton Fisk .60 1.50
AT18 Bob Gibson .60 1.50
AT19 Cy Young 1.00 2.50
AT20 Reggie Jackson .60 1.50
AT21 Jackie Robinson 1.00 2.50
AT22 Harmon Killebrew 1.00 2.50
AT23 Mickey Cochrane .60 1.50
AT24 Eddie Mathews 1.00 2.50
AT25 Bill Mazeroski .60 1.50
AT26 Willie McCovey .60 1.50
AT27 Eddie Murray .60 1.50
AT28 Lefty Grove .60 1.50
AT29 Jim Palmer .60 1.50
AT30 Pee Wee Reese .60 1.50
AT31 Phil Rizzuto .60 1.50
AT32 Brooks Robinson .60 1.50
AT33 Nolan Ryan 3.00 8.00
AT34 Tom Seaver .60 1.50
AT35 Ozzie Smith 1.25 3.00
AT36 Roy Campanella 1.00 2.50
AT37 Thurman Munson 1.00 2.50
AT38 Mel Ott .40 1.00
AT39 Satchel Paige 1.00 2.50
AT40 Rogers Hornsby .60 1.50

2006 Upper Deck All-Upper Deck Team

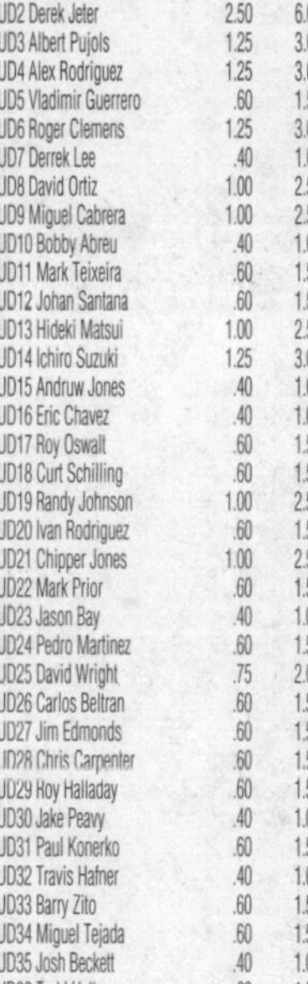

TWO PER SERIES 1 FAT PACK
UD1 Ken Griffey Jr. 2.00 5.00
UD2 Derek Jeter 2.50 6.00
UD3 Albert Pujols 1.25 3.00
UD4 Alex Rodriguez 1.25 3.00
UD5 Vladimir Guerrero .60 1.50
UD6 Roger Clemens 1.25 3.00
UD7 Derrek Lee .40 1.00
UD8 David Ortiz 1.00 2.50
UD9 Miguel Cabrera 1.00 2.50
UD10 Bobby Abreu .40 1.00
UD11 Mark Teixeira .60 1.50
UD12 Johan Santana .60 1.50
UD13 Hideki Matsui 1.00 2.50
UD14 Ichiro Suzuki 1.25 3.00
UD15 Andruw Jones .40 1.00
UD16 Eric Chavez .40 1.00
UD17 Roy Oswalt .60 1.50
UD18 Curt Schilling .60 1.50
UD19 Randy Johnson 1.00 2.50
UD20 Ivan Rodriguez .60 1.50
UD21 Chipper Jones 1.00 2.50
UD22 Mark Prior .60 1.50
UD23 Jason Bay .40 1.00
UD24 Pedro Martinez .60 1.50
UD25 David Wright .75 2.00
UD26 Carlos Beltran .60 1.50
UD27 Jim Edmonds .60 1.50
UD28 Chris Carpenter .60 1.50
UD29 Roy Halladay .60 1.50
UD30 Jake Peavy .40 1.00
UD31 Paul Konerko .60 1.50
UD32 Travis Hafner .40 1.00
UD33 Barry Zito .60 1.50
UD34 Miguel Tejada .60 1.50
UD35 Josh Beckett .40 1.00
UD36 Todd Helton .60 1.50
UD37 Dontrelle Willis .40 1.00
UD38 Manny Ramirez 1.00 2.50
UD39 Mariano Rivera 1.25 3.00
UD40 Jeff Kent .40 1.00

2006 Upper Deck Amazing Greats

SER.1 ODDS 1:6 HOBBY, 1:12 RETAIL
*GOLD: .6X TO 1.5X BASIC
FIVE #'d INSERTS PER SER.1 HOBBY BOX
GOLD STATED PRINT RUN 699 SERIAL #'d SETS
AB Adrian Beltre 1.25 3.00
AJ Andruw Jones .50 1.25
AP Albert Pujols 1.50 4.00
AS Alfonso Soriano .75 2.00
BA Bobby Abreu .75 2.00
CB Carlos Beltran .75 2.00
CC Carl Crawford .75 2.00
CJ Chipper Jones 1.25 3.00
CL Carlos Lee .50 1.25
CP Corey Patterson .50 1.25
CS Curt Schilling .75 2.00
DJ Derek Jeter 3.00 8.00
DO David Ortiz 1.25 3.00
DW Dontrelle Willis .50 1.25
EG Eric Gagne .50 1.25
FT Frank Thomas 1.25 3.00
GM Greg Maddux 1.50 4.00
GS Gary Sheffield .50 1.25
HE Todd Helton .75 2.00
IR Ivan Rodriguez .75 2.00
JB Jeff Bagwell .75 2.00
JD Johnny Damon .75 2.00
JE Jim Edmonds .75 2.00
JG Jason Giambi .75 2.00
JJ Jacque Jones .50 1.25
JL Javy Lopez .50 1.25
JR Jose Reyes .75 2.00
JS Johan Santana .75 2.00
JT Jim Thome .75 2.00
KG Ken Griffey Jr. 2.50 6.00
KW Kerry Wood .50 1.25
MC Miguel Cabrera 1.25 3.00
MP Mike Piazza 1.25 3.00
MR Manny Ramirez 1.25 3.00
MT Mark Teixeira .75 2.00
PK Paul Konerko .75 2.00
PM Pedro Martinez .75 2.00
PR Mark Prior .75 2.00
RC Roger Clemens 1.50 4.00
RF Rafael Furcal .50 1.25
RJ Randy Johnson 1.25 3.00
RO Roy Oswalt .75 2.00
RP Rafael Palmeiro .75 2.00
SM John Smoltz 1.25 3.00
SR Scott Rolen .75 2.00
SS Sammy Sosa 1.25 3.00
TE Miguel Tejada .75 2.00
TG Tom Glavine .75 2.00
TH Tim Hudson .75 2.00
WR David Wright 1.00 2.50

2006 Upper Deck Amazing Greats Materials

SER.1 ODDS 1:48 HOBBY, 1:288 RETAIL
AB Adrian Beltre Jsy 3.00 8.00
AJ Andruw Jones Jsy 4.00 10.00
AP Albert Pujols Jsy 6.00 15.00
AS Alfonso Soriano Jsy 3.00 8.00
BA Bobby Abreu Jsy 3.00 8.00
CB Carlos Beltran Jsy 3.00 8.00
CC Carl Crawford Jsy 3.00 8.00
CJ Chipper Jones Jsy 4.00 10.00
CL Carlos Lee Jsy 3.00 8.00
CP Corey Patterson Jsy 3.00 8.00
CS Curt Schilling Jsy 4.00 10.00
DJ Derek Jeter Jsy 10.00 25.00
DO David Ortiz Jsy 4.00 10.00
DW Dontrelle Willis Jsy 3.00 8.00
EG Eric Gagne Jsy 3.00 8.00
FT Frank Thomas Jsy 4.00 10.00
GM Greg Maddux Jsy 4.00 10.00
GS Gary Sheffield Jsy 3.00 8.00
TH Todd Helton Jsy 4.00 10.00
IR Ivan Rodriguez Jsy 4.00 10.00
JB Jeff Bagwell Jsy 4.00 10.00
JD Johnny Damon Jsy 4.00 10.00
JE Jim Edmonds Jsy 3.00 8.00
JG Jason Giambi Jsy 3.00 8.00
JJ Jacque Jones Jsy 3.00 8.00
JL Javy Lopez Jsy 3.00 8.00
JR Jose Reyes Jsy 3.00 8.00
JS Johan Santana Jsy 4.00 10.00
JT Jim Thome Jsy 4.00 10.00
KG Ken Griffey Jr. Jsy 6.00 15.00
KW Kerry Wood Jsy 3.00 8.00
MC Miguel Cabrera Jsy 4.00 10.00
MP Mike Piazza Jsy 4.00 10.00
MR Manny Ramirez Jsy 4.00 10.00
MT Mark Teixeira Jsy 4.00 10.00
PK Paul Konerko Jsy 3.00 8.00
PM Pedro Martinez Jsy 4.00 10.00
PR Mark Prior Jsy 3.00 8.00
RC Roger Clemens Jsy 6.00 15.00
RF Rafael Furcal Jsy 3.00 8.00
RJ Randy Johnson Pants 4.00 10.00
RO Roy Oswalt Jsy 3.00 8.00
RP Rafael Palmeiro Jsy 4.00 10.00
SM John Smoltz Jsy 4.00 10.00
SR Scott Rolen Jsy 4.00 10.00
SS Sammy Sosa Jsy 4.00 10.00
TE Miguel Tejada Jsy 3.00 8.00
TG Tom Glavine Jsy 4.00 10.00
TH Tim Hudson Jsy 3.00 8.00
WR David Wright Jsy 4.00 10.00

2006 Upper Deck Diamond Collection

SER.1 ODDS 1:6 HOBBY, 1:12 RETAIL
*GOLD: .6X TO 1.5X BASIC
FIVE #'d INSERTS PER SER.1 HOBBY BOX
GOLD PRINT RUN 699 SERIAL #'d SETS
AE Adam Eaton .50 1.25
AH Aubrey Huff .50 1.25
AK Adam Kennedy .50 1.25
AL Moises Alou .50 1.25
AO Akinori Otsuka .50 1.25
BC Bobby Crosby .50 1.25
BR Brad Radke .50 1.25
CC C.C. Sabathia .75 2.00
CK Casey Kotchman .50 1.25
CO Jose Contreras .50 1.25
CP Carl Pavano .50 1.25
CS Chris Shelton .50 1.25
DJ Derek Jeter 3.00 8.00
DO David Ortiz 1.25 3.00
EC Eric Chavez .50 1.25
EJ Edwin Jackson .50 1.25
FG Freddy Garcia .50 1.25
GM Greg Maddux 1.50 4.00
GO Juan Gonzalez .50 1.25
IR Ivan Rodriguez .75 2.00
JB Jeff Bagwell .75 2.00
JC Jesse Crain .50 1.25
JD Johnny Damon .75 2.00
JE Jim Edmonds .75 2.00
JG Jose Guillen .50 1.25
JJ Jacque Jones .50 1.25
JK Jason Kendall .50 1.25
JP Jorge Posada .75 2.00
JS John Smoltz 1.25 3.00
JT Jim Thome .75 2.00
JW Jayson Werth .75 2.00
KE Austin Kearns .50 1.25
KG Ken Griffey Jr. 2.50 6.00
KL Kenny Lofton .50 1.25
KM Kevin Millwood .50 1.25
LA Matt Lawton .50 1.25
LO Mike Lowell .50 1.25
MA Kazuo Matsui .50 1.25
MC Mike Cameron .50 1.25
MH Mike Hampton .50 1.25
ML Mike Lieberthal .50 1.25
NJ Nick Johnson .50 1.25
OC Orlando Cabrera .50 1.25
PL Paul Lo Duca .50 1.25
PW Preston Wilson .50 1.25
RB Rocco Baldelli .50 1.25
RJ Randy Johnson 1.25 3.00
SF Steve Finley .50 1.25
SK Scott Kazmir .75 2.00
SS Shannon Stewart .50 1.25

2006 Upper Deck Diamond Collection Materials

SER.1 ODDS 1:48 HOBBY, 1:288 RETAIL
AE Adam Eaton Jsy 3.00 8.00
AH Aubrey Huff Jsy 3.00 8.00
AK Adam Kennedy Jsy 3.00 8.00
AL Moises Alou Jsy 3.00 8.00
AO Akinori Otsuka Jsy 3.00 8.00
BC Bobby Crosby Jsy 3.00 8.00
BR Brad Radke Jsy 3.00 8.00
CC C.C. Sabathia Jsy 3.00 8.00
CK Casey Kotchman Jsy 3.00 8.00
CO Jose Contreras Jsy 3.00 8.00
CP Carl Pavano Jsy 3.00 8.00
CS Chris Shelton Jsy 4.00 10.00
DJ Derek Jeter Jsy 10.00 25.00
DO David Ortiz Jsy 4.00 10.00
EC Eric Chavez Jsy 3.00 8.00
EJ Edwin Jackson Jsy 3.00 8.00
FG Freddy Garcia Jsy 3.00 8.00
GM Greg Maddux Jsy 4.00 10.00
GO Juan Gonzalez Jsy 3.00 8.00
IR Ivan Rodriguez Jsy 4.00 10.00
JB Jeff Bagwell Jsy 4.00 10.00
JC Jesse Crain Jsy 3.00 8.00
JD Johnny Damon Jsy 4.00 10.00
JE Jim Edmonds Jsy 3.00 8.00
JG Jose Guillen Jsy 3.00 8.00
JJ Jacque Jones Jsy 3.00 8.00
JK Jason Kendall Jsy 3.00 8.00
JP Jorge Posada Jsy 4.00 10.00
JS John Smoltz Jsy 4.00 10.00
JT Jim Thome Jsy 4.00 10.00
JW Jayson Werth Jsy 3.00 8.00
KE Austin Kearns Jsy 3.00 8.00
KG Ken Griffey Jr. Jsy 6.00 15.00
KL Kenny Lofton Jsy 3.00 8.00
KM Kevin Millwood Jsy 3.00 8.00
LA Matt Lawton Jsy 3.00 8.00
LO Mike Lowell Jsy 3.00 8.00
MA Kazuo Matsui Jsy 3.00 8.00
MC Mike Cameron Jsy 3.00 8.00
MH Mike Hampton Jsy 3.00 8.00
ML Mike Lieberthal Jsy 3.00 8.00
NJ Nick Johnson Jsy 3.00 8.00
OC Orlando Cabrera Jsy 3.00 8.00
PL Paul Lo Duca Jsy 3.00 8.00
PW Preston Wilson Jsy 3.00 8.00
RB Rocco Baldelli Jsy 3.00 8.00
RJ Randy Johnson Pants 4.00 10.00
SF Steve Finley Jsy 3.00 8.00
SK Scott Kazmir Jsy 3.00 8.00
SS Shannon Stewart Jsy 3.00 8.00

2006 Upper Deck Diamond Debut

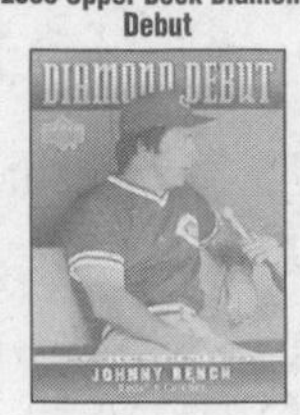

STATED ODDS 1:4 WAL MART PACKS
1-40 ISSUED IN SERIES 1 PACKS
41-82 ISSUED IN SERIES 2 PACKS
DD1 Tadahito Iguchi .60 1.50
DD2 Huston Street .60 1.50
DD3 Norihiro Nakamura .60 1.50
DD4 Chien-Ming Wang 1.00 2.50
DD5 Pedro Lopez
DD6 Robinson Cano 1.00 2.50
DD7 Tim Stauffer .60 1.50
DD8 Ervin Santana .60 1.50
DD9 Brandon McCarthy .60 1.50
DD10 Hayden Penn .60 1.50
DD11 Derek Jeter 4.00 10.00
DD12 Ken Griffey Jr. 3.00 8.00
DD13 Prince Fielder 3.00 8.00
DD14 Edwin Encarnacion 1.50 4.00
DD15 Scott Olsen .60 1.50
DD16 Chris Resop .60 1.50
DD17 Justin Verlander 5.00 12.00
DD18 Melky Cabrera 1.00 2.50
DD19 Jeff Francoeur 1.50 4.00
DD20 Yuniesky Betancourt .60 1.50
DD21 Conor Jackson 1.00 2.50
DD22 Felix Hernandez 1.00 2.50
DD23 Anthony Reyes .60 1.50
DD24 John-Ford Griffin .60 1.50
DD25 Adam Wainwright 1.00 2.50
DD26 Ryan Garko .60 1.50
DD27 Ryan Zimmerman 2.00 5.00
DD28 Tom Seaver 1.00 2.50
DD29 Johnny Bench 1.50 4.00
DD30 Reggie Jackson 1.00 2.50
DD31 Rod Carew 1.00 2.50
DD32 Nolan Ryan 5.00 12.00
DD33 Richie Ashburn 1.00 2.50
DD34 Yogi Berra 1.50 4.00
DD35 Lou Brock 1.00 2.50
DD36 Carlton Fisk 1.00 2.50
DD37 Joe Morgan 1.00 2.50
DD38 Bob Gibson 1.00 2.50
DD39 Willie McCovey 1.00 2.50
DD40 Harmon Killebrew 1.50 4.00
DD41 Takashi Saito 1.00 2.50
DD42 Kenji Johjima 1.50 4.00
DD43 Joel Zumaya 1.50 4.00
DD44 Dan Uggla 1.00 2.50
DD45 Taylor Buchholz .60 1.50
DD46 Josh Barfield .60 1.50
DD47 Brian Bannister .60 1.50
DD48 Nick Markakis 1.25 3.00
DD49 Carlos Martinez .60 1.50
DD50 Macay McBride .60 1.50
DD51 Brian Anderson .60 1.50
DD52 Freddie Bynum .60 1.50
DD53 Kelly Shoppach .60 1.50
DD54 Choo Freeman .60 1.50
DD55 Ryan Shealy .60 1.50
DD56 Chris Resop .60 1.50
DD57 Hanley Ramirez 1.00 2.50
DD58 Mike Jacobs .60 1.50
DD59 Cody Ross 1.50 4.00
DD60 Jose Capellan .60 1.50
DD61 David Gassner .60 1.50
DD62 Jason Kubel .60 1.50
DD63 Jered Weaver 2.00 5.00
DD64 Paul Maholm .60 1.50
DD65 Nate McLouth .60 1.50
DD66 Ben Johnson .60 1.50
DD67 Jack Taschner .60 1.50
DD68 Skip Schumaker .60 1.50
DD69 Brandon Watson .60 1.50
DD70 David Wright 1.25 3.00
DD71 David Ortiz 1.50 4.00
DD72 Alex Rodriguez 2.00 5.00
DD73 Johan Santana 1.00 2.50
DD74 Greg Maddux 2.00 5.00
DD75 Ichiro Suzuki 2.00 5.00
DD76 Albert Pujols 2.00 5.00
DD77 Hideki Matsui 1.50 4.00
DD78 Vladimir Guerrero 1.00 2.50
DD79 Pedro Martinez 1.00 2.50
DD80 Mike Schmidt 2.50 6.00
DD81 Al Kaline 1.50 4.00
DD82 Robin Yount 1.50 4.00

2006 Upper Deck First Class Cuts

RANDOM INSERTS IN SERIES 1 PACKS
STATED PRINT RUN 1 SERIAL #'d SET
NO PRICING DUE TO SCARCITY

2006 Upper Deck First Class Legends

COMMON RUTH (1-20) 1.25 3.00
COMMON COBB (21-40) .75 2.00
COMMON WAGNER (41-60 .40 1.00
COMMON MATHEWSON (61-80) .40 1.00
COMMON W.JOHNSON (81-100) .40 1.00
SER.1 STATED ODDS 1:6 HOBBY
SER.2 ODDS APPROX. 1:12 HOBBY
*GOLD: .75X TO 2X BASIC
GOLD PRINT RUN 699 SERIAL #'d SETS
*SILVER SPECTRUM: 1.25X TO 3X BASIC
SILVER SPEC. PRINT RUN 99 SERIAL #'d SETS
FIVE #'d INSERTS PER SER.1 HOBBY BOX
GOLD-SILVER AVAIL ONLY IN SER.1 PACKS

2006 Upper Deck Collect the Mascots

COMPLETE SET (3) .40 1.00
ISSUED IN 06 UD 1 AND 2 FAT PACKS
MLB1 Wally the Green Monster .20 .50
MLB2 Phillie Phanatic .20 .50
MLB3 Mr. Met .20 .50

2006 Upper Deck Inaugural Images

SER.2 ODDS 1:8 H, RANDOM IN RETAIL
II1 Sung-Heon Hong .75 2.00
II2 Yulieski Gourriel 1.50 4.00
II3 Tsuyoshi Nishioka 3.00 8.00
II4 Miguel Cabrera 1.25 3.00
II5 Yung Chi Chen .75 2.00
II6 Ormari Romero .50 1.25
II7 Ken Griffey Jr. 2.50 6.00
II8 Bernie Williams .75 2.00
II9 Daniel Cabrera .50 1.25
II10 David Ortiz 1.25 3.00
II11 Alex Rodriguez 1.50 4.00
II12 Frederich Cepeda .50 1.25
II13 Derek Jeter 3.00 8.00
II14 Jorge Cantu .50 1.25
II15 Alexi Ramirez 3.00 8.00
II16 Yoandy Garlobo .50 1.25
II17 Koji Uehara 1.50 4.00
II18 Nobuhiko Matsunaka .75 2.00
II19 Tomoya Satozaki .75 2.00
II20 Seung Yeop Lee .75 2.00
II21 Yulieski Gourriel 1.50 4.00
II22 Adrian Beltre 1.25 3.00
II23 Ken Griffey Jr. 2.50 6.00
II24 Jong Beom Lee .50 1.25
II25 Ichiro Suzuki 1.50 4.00
II26 Yoandy Garlobo .50 1.25
II27 Daisuke Matsuzaka 1.50 4.00
II28 Yadel Marti .50 1.25
II29 Chan Ho Park .75 2.00
II30 Daisuke Matsuzaka 1.50 4.00

2006 Upper Deck INKredible

SER.2 ODDS 1:288 H, RANDOM IN RETAIL
UPDATE ODDS 1:24 RETAIL
SP INFO/PRINT RUNS PROVIDED BY UD
SP * INFO PROVIDED BY BECKETT
SP's ARE NOT SERIAL-NUMBERED
NO PRICING ON QTY OF 36 OR LESS
AB Ambiorix Burgos UPD SP * 6.00 15.00
AH Aaron Harang UPD 4.00 10.00
AJ Adam Jones UPD 12.00 30.00
AP Angel Pagan UPD 6.00 15.00
AR2 Alex Rios UPD SP 15.00 40.00
AR Alexis Rios 6.00 15.00
BA Brandon Backe UPD 4.00 10.00
BB Ben Broussard UPD 6.00 15.00
BC Brandon Claussen UPD 4.00 10.00
BM Brandon McCarthy UPD SP 6.00 15.00
BM Brett Myers SP/72 * 6.00 15.00
BR Brian Roberts 6.00 15.00
BR2 Brian Roberts UPD 6.00 15.00
BW Brian Wilson UPD 10.00 25.00
CA Miguel Cabrera 20.00 50.00
CB Colter Bean UPD 4.00 10.00
CC Coco Crisp UPD 5.00 12.00
CC Carl Crawford 6.00 15.00
CC2 Carl Crawford UPD 6.00 15.00
CD Chris Duffy UPD 4.00 10.00
CI Cesar Izturis UPD SP * 6.00 15.00
CK Casey Kotchman 4.00 10.00
CK2 Casey Kotchman UPD 4.00 10.00
CL Cliff Lee UPD 4.00 10.00
CO Chad Cordero 6.00 15.00
CO2 Chad Cordero UPD SP 6.00 15.00
CW C.J. Wilson UPD 6.00 15.00
DJ Derek Jeter 75.00 150.00
DJ2 Derek Jeter UPD SP 125.00 250.00
DR Darrell Rasner UPD 4.00 10.00
DW David Wright SP/91 * 8.00 20.00
EA Erick Aybar UPD 4.00 10.00
EB Eude Brito UPD 6.00 15.00
EG Eric Gagne UPD SP 30.00 60.00
GC Gustavo Chacin UPD 4.00 10.00
GF Gavin Floyd UPD 4.00 10.00
JB Joe Blanton 6.00 15.00
JC Jesse Crain 4.00 10.00
JD Jermaine Dye UPD 6.00 15.00
JH John Hattig UPD 4.00 10.00
JH J.J. Hardy 4.00 10.00
JJ Jorge Julio UPD SP 6.00 15.00
JM Joe Mauer SP/91 * 15.00 40.00
JO Jacque Jones UPD 6.00 15.00
JP Jhonny Peralta UPD 4.00 10.00
JR Juan Rivera UPD SP 10.00 25.00
JR Jeremy Reed 4.00 10.00
JV Justin Verlander SP/91 * 12.50 30.00
KG Ken Griffey Jr. 40.00 80.00
KG2 Ken Griffey Jr. UPD SP 40.00 80.00
KR Ken Ray UPD 4.00 10.00
KY Kevin Youkilis 6.00 15.00
KY2 Kevin Youkilis UPD 6.00 15.00
LN Leo Nunez UPD 4.00 10.00
LO Lyle Overbay SP/91 * 6.00 15.00
MH Matt Holliday UPD 8.00 20.00
MM Matt Murton UPD 10.00 25.00
MO Justin Morneau 10.00 25.00
MR Mike Rouse UPD 4.00 10.00
MT Mark Teahen UPD 6.00 15.00
MT Mark Teixeira 10.00 25.00
MV Mike Vento UPD 4.00 10.00
NG Nomar Garciaparra 30.00 60.00
NL Noah Lowry UPD 6.00 15.00
NS Nick Swisher UPD 6.00 15.00
PA John Patterson UPD 4.00 10.00
PE Joel Peralta UPD 4.00 10.00
PI Joel Pineiro UPD 4.00 10.00
RE Jose Reyes SP/91 * 8.00 20.00
RF Ryan Freel UPD 6.00 15.00
RG Ryan Garko UPD 4.00 10.00
RP Ronny Paulino UPD 6.00 15.00
RS Ryan Shealy UPD 6.00 15.00
RZ Ryan Zimmerman SP/91 * 10.00 25.00
SK Scott Kazmir 8.00 20.00
TH Travis Hafner 10.00 25.00
TI Tadahito Iguchi SP/91 * 20.00 50.00
TI2 Tadahito Iguchi UPD SP 30.00 60.00
VM Victor Martinez 6.00 15.00
WI Dontrelle Willis 10.00 25.00
YB Yuniesky Betancourt UPD 4.00 10.00
YM Yadier Molina UPD 20.00 50.00
ZM Zach Miner UPD 4.00 10.00

2006 Upper Deck Derek Jeter Spell and Win

COMPLETE SET (5) 6.00 15.00
COMMON CARD (1-5) 1.25 3.00
RANDOM IN SER.2 WAL-MART PACKS

2006 Upper Deck Player Highlights

SER.2 ODDS 1:6 H, RANDOM IN RETAIL
PH1 Andruw Jones .40 1.00
PH2 Manny Ramirez 1.00 2.50
PH3 Travis Hafner .40 1.00
PH4 Johnny Damon .60 1.50
PH5 Miguel Cabrera 1.00 2.50
PH6 Chris Carpenter .60 1.50
PH7 Derrek Lee .40 1.00
PH8 Jason Bay .40 1.00
PH9 Jason Varitek 1.00 2.50
PH10 Ryan Howard .75 2.00
PH11 Mark Teixeira .60 1.50
PH12 Carlos Delgado .40 1.00
PH13 Bartolo Colon .40 1.00
PH14 David Wright .75 2.00
PH15 Miguel Tejada .60 1.50
PH16 Mike Piazza 1.00 2.50
PH17 Paul Konerko .60 1.50
PH18 Jermaine Dye .40 1.00
PH19 Ichiro Suzuki 1.25 3.00
PH20 Brad Wilkerson .40 1.00
PH21 Hideki Matsui 1.00 2.50
PH22 Albert Pujols 1.25 3.00
PH23 Chris Burke .40 1.00
PH24 Derek Jeter 2.50 6.00
PH25 Brian Roberts .40 1.00
PH26 David Ortiz 1.00 2.50
PH27 Alex Rodriguez 1.25 3.00
PH28 Ken Griffey Jr. 2.00 5.00
PH29 Prince Fielder 2.00 5.00
PH30 Bobby Abreu .40 1.00
PH31 Vladimir Guerrero .60 1.50
PH32 Tadahito Iguchi .40 1.00
PH33 Jose Reyes .60 1.50
PH34 Scott Podsednik .40 1.00
PH35 Gary Sheffield .40 1.00

2006 Upper Deck Run Producers

SER.2 ODDS 1:8 H, RANDOM IN RETAIL
RP1 Ty Cobb 1.50 4.00
RP2 Derrek Lee .40 1.00
RP3 Andruw Jones .40 1.00
RP4 David Ortiz 1.00 2.50
RP5 Lou Gehrig 2.00 5.00
RP6 Ken Griffey Jr. 2.00 5.00
RP7 Albert Pujols 1.25 3.00
RP8 Derek Jeter 2.50 6.00
RP9 Manny Ramirez 1.00 2.50
RP10 Alex Rodriguez 1.25 3.00
RP11 Gary Sheffield .40 1.00
RP12 Miguel Cabrera 1.00 2.50
RP13 Hideki Matsui 1.00 2.50
RP14 Vladimir Guerrero .60 1.50
RP15 David Wright .75 2.00
RP16 Mike Schmidt 1.50 4.00
RP17 Mark Teixeira .60 1.50
RP18 Babe Ruth 2.50 6.00
RP19 Jimmie Foxx 1.00 2.50
RP20 Honus Wagner 1.00 2.50

2006 Upper Deck Season Highlights

ISSUED IN 06 UD 1 AND 2 FAT PACKS
SH1 Albert Pujols 1.25 3.00
SH2 Ken Griffey Jr. 2.00 5.00
SH3 Travis Hafner .40 1.00
SH4 David Ortiz 1.00 2.50
SH5 David Ortiz 1.00 2.50
SH6 Ryan Howard .75 2.00
SH7 Chase Utley .60 1.50
SH8 Manny Ramirez 1.00 2.50
SH9 Barry Zito .60 1.50
SH10 Roger Clemens 1.25 3.00
SH11 Francisco Liriano 1.00 2.50
SH12 Jered Weaver 1.25 3.00
SH13 Roy Halladay .60 1.50
SH14 Johan Santana .60 1.50
SH15 Tom Glavine .60 1.50
SH16 Pedro Martinez .60 1.50
SH17 Mike Piazza 1.00 2.50
SH18 Alfonso Soriano .60 1.50
SH19 Miguel Cabrera 1.00 2.50
SH20 Vladimir Guerrero .60 1.50
SH21 Joe Mauer .60 1.50
SH22 Ryan Zimmerman 1.25 3.00
SH23 Carlos Delgado .40 1.00
SH24 Jim Thome .60 1.50
SH25 Jermaine Dye .40 1.00
SH26 Derek Jeter 2.50 6.00
SH27 Ivan Rodriguez .60 1.50
SH28 Bobby Abreu .40 1.00
SH29 Greg Maddux 1.25 3.00
SH30 Alex Rodriguez 1.25 3.00

2006 Upper Deck Signature Sensations

SER.1 ODDS 1:288 HOBBY, 1:1920 RETAIL
SP INFO PROVIDED BY UPPER DECK
AL Al Leiter 6.00 15.00
AM Aaron Miles 4.00 10.00
AR Aaron Rowand 6.00 15.00
BA Bronson Arroyo 6.00 15.00
CS Cory Sullivan 4.00 10.00
GA Garrett Atkins 4.00 10.00
JE Johnny Estrada 4.00 10.00
JJ Josh Johnson 4.00 10.00
JS Jeff Suppan 4.00 10.00
JV Joe Valentine 4.00 10.00
KC Kiko Calero 4.00 10.00
NP Nick Punto 6.00 15.00
SB Scott Baker 6.00 15.00
TR Travis Hafner 6.00 15.00
YM Yadier Molina 20.00 50.00

2006 Upper Deck Speed To Burn

SER.2 ODDS 1:12 H, RANDOM IN RETAIL
CARDS 2/10/13 DO NOT EXIST
SB1 Lou Brock .60 1.50
SB3 Alfonso Soriano .60 1.50
SB4 Carl Crawford .60 1.50
SB5 Chone Figgins .40 1.00
SB6 Ichiro Suzuki 1.25 3.00
SB7 Jose Reyes .60 1.50
SB8 Juan Pierre .40 1.00
SB9 Scott Podsednik .40 1.00
SB11 Alex Rodriguez 1.25 3.00
SB12 David Wright .75 2.00
SB14 Bobby Abreu .40 1.00
SB15 Brian Roberts .40 1.00

2006 Upper Deck Star Attractions

COMPLETE UPDATE (50) 20.00 50.00
SER.1 MINORS .50 1.25
SER.1 SEMIS .75 2.00
SER.1 UNLISTED 1.25 3.00
SER.1 ODDS 1:6 HOBBY, 1:12 RETAIL
UPDATE ODDS 1:2 RETAIL
*GOLD: .6X TO 1.5X BASIC
FIVE #'d INSERTS PER SER.1 HOBBY BOX
GOLD PRINT RUN 699 SERIAL #'d SETS
*SILVER: 1.25X TO 3X BASIC
ONE #'d INSERT PER UPDATE BOX
SILVER PRINT RUN 99 SERIAL #'d SETS
AB Adrian Beltre 1.00 2.50
AE Andre Ethier UPD 1.25 3.00
AH Aubrey Huff .40 1.00
AJ Andruw Jones .40 1.00
AJ Adam Jones UPD 4.00 10.00
AL Adam Loewen UPD .40 1.00
AM Andy Marte UPD .40 1.00
AN Anibal Sanchez UPD .40 1.00
AP Andy Pettitte .60 1.50
AR Anthony Reyes UPD .40 1.00
AS Alfonso Soriano .60 1.50
AW Adam Wainwright UPD .60 1.50
BA Bobby Abreu .40 1.00
BI Chad Billingsley UPD .60 1.50
BR Brian Anderson UPD .40 1.00
BZ Barry Zito .60 1.50
CB Carlos Beltran .60 1.50
CD Carlos Delgado .40 1.00
CH Cole Hamels UPD 1.25 3.00
CJ Chipper Jones 1.00 2.50
CL Carlos Lee .40 1.00
CO Conor Jackson UPD .60 1.50
CQ Carlos Quentin UPD .60 1.50
CS Curt Schilling .60 1.50
CY Chris Young UPD 1.00 2.50
DJ Derek Jeter 2.50 6.00
DL Derrek Lee .40 1.00
DM Dustin McGowan UPD .40 1.00
DO David Ortiz 1.00 2.50
DP Dustin Pedroia UPD 10.00 25.00
DU Dan Uggla UPD .60 1.50
DW Dontrelle Willis .40 1.00
EA Erick Aybar UPD .40 1.00
EG Eric Gagne .40 1.00
FL Francisco Liriano UPD 1.00 2.50
FT Frank Thomas 1.00 2.50
GA Garret Anderson .40 1.00
GM Greg Maddux 1.25 3.00
GR Khalil Greene .40 1.00
GS Gary Sheffield .40 1.00
GU Jose Guillen .40 1.00
HI Jason Hirsh UPD .40 1.00
HK Howie Kendrick UPD .75 2.00
HP Hayden Penn UPD .40 1.00
HR Hanley Ramirez UPD .60 1.50
HU Justin Huber UPD .40 1.00
JA Chuck James UPD .40 1.00
JB Josh Beckett .40 1.00
JC Jose Contreras .40 1.00
JD Johnny Damon .60 1.50
JE Jim Edmonds .60 1.50
JG Jason Giambi .40 1.00
JH Jeremy Hermida UPD .40 1.00
JJ Josh Johnson UPD 1.00 2.50
JJ Jacque Jones .40 1.00
JK Jason Kubel UPD .40 1.00
JL Javy Lopez .40 1.00
JM Joe Mauer .60 1.50
JO Josh Barfield UPD .40 1
JP Jorge Posada .60 1
JR Jose Reyes .60 1
JS Jason Schmidt .40 1
JV Justin Verlander UPD 3.00 8.
JW Jered Weaver UPD 1.25 3.
JZ Joel Zumaya UPD 1.00 2.
KG Ken Griffey Jr. 2.00 5.
KJ Kenji Johjima UPD 1.00 2.
KM Kendry Morales UPD 1.00 2.
KW Kerry Wood .40 1.
LB Lance Berkman .60 1.
LE Jon Lester UPD 1.50 4.
LM Lastings Milledge UPD .40 1.
MA Jeff Mathis UPD .40 1.
MC Matt Cain UPD 2.50 6.
MK Matt Kemp UPD 1.00 2.
MM Mark Mulder .40 1.
MO Magglio Ordonez .60 1.
MP Mark Prior .60 1.
MR Manny Ramirez 1.00 2.
MT Mark Teixeira .60 1.
NM Nick Markakis UPD .75 2.
PA Jonathan Papelbon UPD 2.00 5.
PE Mike Pelfrey UPD 1.00 2.
PF Prince Fielder UPD 2.00 5.
PM Pedro Martinez .60 1.
PU Albert Pujols 1.25 3.
RC Ronny Cedeno UPD .40 1.
RH Rich Harden .40 1.
RM Russell Martin UPD .60 1.
RZ Ryan Zimmerman UPD 1.25 3.
SD Stephen Drew UPD .75 2.
SG Shawn Green .40 1.
SM John Smoltz 1.00 2.
SO Scott Olsen UPD .40 1.
SW Jeremy Sowers UPD .40 1.
TG Tony Gwynn Jr. UPD .40 1.
TH Torii Hunter .40 1.
TI Tadahito Iguchi .40 1.
WA Willy Aybar UPD .40 1.
WR David Wright .75 2.

2006 Upper Deck Star Attractions Swatches

SER.1 ODDS 1:48 HOBBY, 1:288 RETAIL
AB Adrian Beltre Jsy 3.00 8.0
AH Aubrey Huff Jsy 3.00 8.0
AJ Andruw Jones Jsy 4.00 10.0
AP Andy Pettitte Jsy 4.00 10.0
AS Alfonso Soriano Jsy 3.00 8.0
BA Bobby Abreu Jsy 3.00 8.0
BZ Barry Zito Jsy 3.00 8.0
CB Carlos Beltran Jsy 3.00 8.0
CD Carlos Delgado Jsy 3.00 8.0
CJ Chipper Jones Jsy 4.00 10.0
CL Carlos Lee Jsy 3.00 8.0
CS Curt Schilling Jsy 4.00 10.0
DJ Derek Jeter Jsy 10.00 25.0
DL Derrek Lee Jsy 4.00 10.0
DO David Ortiz Jsy 4.00 10.0
DW Dontrelle Willis Jsy 3.00 8.0
EG Eric Gagne Jsy 3.00 8.0
FT Frank Thomas Jsy 4.00 10.0
GA Garret Anderson Jsy 3.00 8.0
GM Greg Maddux Jsy 4.00 10.0
GR Khalil Greene Jsy 4.00 10.0
GS Gary Sheffield Jsy 3.00 8.0
GU Jose Guillen Jsy 3.00 8.0
JB Josh Beckett Jsy 3.00 8.0
JC Jose Contreras Jsy 3.00 8.0
JD Johnny Damon Jsy 4.00 10.0
JE Jim Edmonds Jsy 3.00 8.0
JG Jason Giambi Jsy 3.00 8.0
JJ Jacque Jones Jsy 3.00 8.0
JL Javy Lopez Jsy 3.00 8.0
JM Joe Mauer Jsy 4.00 10.0
JP Jorge Posada Jsy 4.00 10.0
JR Jose Reyes Jsy 3.00 8.0
JS Jason Schmidt Jsy 3.00 8.0
KG Ken Griffey Jr. Jsy 6.00 15.0
KW Kerry Wood Jsy 3.00 8.0
LB Lance Berkman Jsy 3.00 8.0
MM Mark Mulder Jsy 3.00 8.0
MO Magglio Ordonez Jsy 3.00 8.0
MP Mark Prior Jsy 3.00 8.0
MR Manny Ramirez Jsy 4.00 10.0
MT Mark Teixeira Jsy 4.00 10.0
PM Pedro Martinez Jsy 4.00 10.0
PU Albert Pujols Jsy 6.00 15.0
RH Rich Harden Jsy 3.00 8.0
SG Shawn Green Jsy 3.00 8.0
SM John Smoltz Jsy 4.00 10.0
TH Torii Hunter Jsy 3.00 8.0
TI Tadahito Iguchi Jsy 4.00 10.0
WR David Wright Jsy 4.00 10.0

2006 Upper Deck Team Pride

ER.1 ODDS 1:6 HOBBY, 1:12 RETAIL
GOLD: .6X TO 1.5X BASIC
VE #'d INSERTS PER SER.1 HOBBY BOX
OLD PRINT RUN 699 SERIAL #'d SETS
H Aubrey Huff .50 1.25
J Andruw Jones .50 1.25
P Albert Pujols 1.50 4.00
A Bobby Abreu .50 1.25
W Bernie Williams .75 2.00
Z Barry Zito .75 2.00
C C.C. Sabathia .75 2.00
D Carlos Delgado .50 1.25
J Chipper Jones 1.25 3.00
K Casey Kotchman .50 1.25
S Curt Schilling .75 2.00
J Derek Jeter 3.00 8.00
O David Ortiz 1.25 3.00
W Dontrelle Willis .50 1.25
C Eric Chavez .50 1.25
G Eric Gagne .50 1.25
T Frank Thomas 1.25 3.00
A Garret Anderson .50 1.25
M Greg Maddux 1.50 4.00
R Khalil Greene .50 1.25
R Ivan Rodriguez .75 2.00
B Jeff Bagwell .75 2.00
D Johnny Damon .75 2.00
E Jim Edmonds .75 2.00
M Jamie Moyer .50 1.25
P Jorge Posada .75 2.00
R Jose Reyes .75 2.00
S John Smoltz 1.25 3.00
T Jim Thome .75 2.00
V Jose Vidro .50 1.25
F Keith Foulke .50 1.25
KG Ken Griffey Jr. 2.50 6.00
KW Kerry Wood .50 1.25
LC Luis Castillo .50 1.25
LG Luis Gonzalez .50 1.25
LO Mike Lowell .50 1.25
MA Joe Mauer .75 2.00
ME Morgan Ensberg .50 1.25
ML Mike Lieberthal .50 1.25
MP Mark Prior .75 2.00
MS Mike Sweeney .50 1.25
MY Michael Young .50 1.25
NJ Nick Johnson .50 1.25
PE Andy Pettitte .75 2.00
RB Rocco Baldelli .50 1.25
RH Rich Harden .50 1.25
RK Ryan Klesko .50 1.25
SC Sean Casey .50 1.25
TH Trevor Hoffman .75 2.00
VA Jason Varitek 1.25 3.00

2006 Upper Deck Team Pride Materials

SER.1 ODDS 1:48 HOBBY, 1:288 RETAIL
AH Aubrey Huff Jsy 3.00 8.00
AJ Andruw Jones Jsy 4.00 10.00
AP Albert Pujols Jsy 6.00 15.00
BA Bobby Abreu Jsy 3.00 8.00
BW Bernie Williams Jsy 4.00 10.00
BZ Barry Zito Jsy 3.00 8.00
CC C.C. Sabathia Jsy 3.00 8.00
CD Carlos Delgado Jsy 3.00 8.00
CJ Chipper Jones Jsy 4.00 10.00
CK Casey Kotchman Jsy 3.00 8.00
CS Curt Schilling Jsy 4.00 10.00
DJ Derek Jeter Jsy 10.00 25.00
DO David Ortiz Jsy 4.00 10.00
DW Dontrelle Willis Jsy 3.00 8.00
EC Eric Chavez Jsy 3.00 8.00
EG Eric Gagne Jsy 3.00 8.00
FT Frank Thomas Jsy 4.00 10.00
GA Garret Anderson Jsy 3.00 8.00
GM Greg Maddux Jsy 4.00 10.00
GR Khalil Greene Jsy 4.00 10.00
IR Ivan Rodriguez Jsy 4.00 10.00
JB Jeff Bagwell Jsy 4.00 10.00
JD Johnny Damon Jsy 4.00 10.00
JE Jim Edmonds Jsy 3.00 8.00
JM Jamie Moyer Jsy 3.00 8.00
JP Jorge Posada Jsy 4.00 10.00
JR Jose Reyes Jsy 3.00 8.00
JS John Smoltz Jsy 4.00 10.00
JT Jim Thome Jsy 4.00 10.00
JV Jose Vidro Jsy 3.00 8.00
KF Keith Foulke Jsy 3.00 8.00
KG Ken Griffey Jr. Jsy 6.00 15.00
KW Kerry Wood Jsy 3.00 8.00
LC Luis Castillo Jsy 3.00 8.00
LG Luis Gonzalez Jsy 3.00 8.00
LO Mike Lowell Jsy 3.00 8.00
MA Joe Mauer Jsy 4.00 10.00
ME Morgan Ensberg Jsy 3.00 8.00
ML Mike Lieberthal Jsy 3.00 8.00
MP Mark Prior Jsy 3.00 8.00
MS Mike Sweeney Jsy 3.00 8.00
MY Michael Young Jsy 3.00 8.00
NJ Nick Johnson Jsy 3.00 8.00
PE Andy Pettitte Jsy 4.00 10.00
RB Rocco Baldelli Jsy 3.00 8.00
RH Rich Harden Jsy 3.00 8.00
RK Ryan Klesko Jsy 3.00 8.00
SC Sean Casey Jsy 3.00 8.00
TH Trevor Hoffman Jsy 3.00 8.00
VA Jason Varitek Jsy 4.00 10.00

2006 Upper Deck UD Game Materials

SER.1 ODDS 1:24 HOBBY, 1:24 RETAIL
SER.2 GU ODDS 1:24 H, RANDOM IN RETAIL
SP INFO PROVIDED BY UPPER DECK
SER.1 PATCH ODDS 1:288 H, 1:1500 R
SER.2 PATCH RANDOM IN HOBBY/RETAIL
SER.2 PATCH PRINT RUN 11 SETS
SER.2 PATCH PRINT RUN PROVIDED BY UD
NO PATCH PRICING DUE TO SCARCITY
AB Adrian Beltre Bat S2 5.00 12.00
AD Adam Dunn Jsy S2 3.00 8.00
AJ Andruw Jones Pants S1 2.00 5.00
AP1 Andy Pettitte Jsy S2 3.00 8.00
AP2 Albert Pujols Pants S1 6.00 15.00
AS Alfonso Soriano Jsy S1 3.00 8.00
BA Bobby Abreu Jsy S2 2.00 5.00
BI Craig Biggio Jsy S2 3.00 8.00
BR Brian Roberts Jsy S1 2.00 5.00
BZ Barry Zito Jsy S2 3.00 8.00
CB Carlos Beltran Jsy S2 3.00 8.00
CD Carlos Delgado Jsy S2 2.00 5.00
CJ Chipper Jones Pants S1 5.00 12.00
CL Carlos Lee Jsy S2 2.00 5.00
CP Corey Patterson Jsy S1 2.00 5.00
CS Curt Schilling Jsy S1 3.00 8.00
DJ1 Derek Jeter Jsy S1 10.00 25.00
DJ2 Derek Jeter Jsy S2 10.00 25.00
DL Derrek Lee Pants S1 2.00 5.00
DO David Ortiz Jsy S1 5.00 12.00
DW Dontrelle Willis Jsy S1 2.00 5.00
EC Eric Chavez Jsy S1 2.00 5.00
EG Eric Gagne Jsy S1 2.00 5.00
FT Frank Thomas Jsy S1 5.00 12.00
GA Garrett Atkins Jsy S2 2.00 5.00
GM Greg Maddux Jsy S1 6.00 15.00
GR Khalil Greene Jsy S2 2.00 5.00
GS Gary Sheffield Jsy S2 2.00 5.00
HA Travis Hafner Jsy S2 2.00 5.00
HB Hank Blalock Jsy S2 2.00 5.00
IR Ivan Rodriguez Jsy S1 3.00 8.00
JB1 Jeff Bagwell Pants S1 3.00 8.00
JB2 Josh Beckett Jsy S2 2.00 5.00
JD1 Johnny Damon Jsy S1 3.00 8.00
JD2 Johnny Damon Jsy S2 3.00 8.00
JE Jim Edmonds Jsy S1 3.00 8.00
JG Jason Giambi Jsy S1 2.00 5.00
JJ Jacque Jones Jsy S1 2.00 5.00
JL Javy Lopez Jsy S2 2.00 5.00
JM Joe Mauer Jsy S2 3.00 8.00
JP Jake Peavy Jsy S1 2.00 5.00
JR Jose Reyes Jsy S2 3.00 8.00
JS Johan Santana Pants S1 3.00 8.00
JT Jim Thome Jsy S1 3.00 8.00
JV Jason Varitek Jsy S2 5.00 12.00
KG1 Ken Griffey Jr. Jsy S1 6.00 15.00
KG2 Ken Griffey Jr. Jsy S2 6.00 15.00
KW Kerry Wood Jsy S2 2.00 5.00
MC Miguel Cabrera Pants S1 6.00 15.00
MM Mike Mussina Pants S2 3.00 8.00
MO Magglio Ordonez Jsy S2 3.00 8.00
MP1 Mike Piazza Jsy S1 5.00 12.00
MP2 Mike Piazza Bat S2 5.00 12.00
MR Manny Ramirez Jsy S1 5.00 12.00
MT Mark Teixeira Jsy S1 3.00 8.00
MY Michael Young Jsy S2 2.00 5.00
PF Prince Fielder Jsy S2 6.00 15.00
PK Paul Konerko Jsy S2 3.00 8.00
PM Pedro Martinez Pants S1 3.00 8.00
PO Jorge Posada Jsy S1 3.00 8.00
PR Mark Prior Jsy S1 3.00 8.00
RC Roger Clemens Jsy S1 6.00 15.00
RF Rafael Furcal Jsy S1 2.00 5.00
RH1 Roy Halladay Jsy S1 3.00 8.00
RH2 Ryan Howard Jsy S2 4.00 10.00
RO Roy Oswalt Jsy S2 3.00 8.00
RP Rafael Palmeiro Jsy S1 3.00 8.00
RW Rickie Weeks Jsy S2 2.00 5.00
RZ Ryan Zimmerman Jsy S2 6.00 15.00
SC Sean Casey Jsy S2 2.00 5.00
SI Grady Sizemore Jsy S2 3.00 8.00
SM John Smoltz Jsy S1 5.00 12.00
SR Scott Rolen Jsy S1 3.00 8.00
TE Miguel Tejada Pants S1 3.00 8.00
TG Tom Glavine Jsy S2 3.00 8.00
TH Todd Helton Jsy S2 3.00 8.00
TI Tadahito Iguchi Jsy S2 2.00 5.00
VG Vladimir Guerrero Jsy S1 3.00 8.00
VM Victor Martinez Jsy S2 3.00 8.00
WR David Wright Pants S1 4.00 10.00

2006 Upper Deck WBC Collection Jersey

SER.2 GU ODDS 1:24 H, RANDOM IN RETAIL
SER.2 PATCH RANDOM IN HOBBY/RETAIL
PATCH PRINT RUN 8 SETS
PATCH PRINT RUN PROVIDED BY UD
NO PATCH PRICING DUE TO SCARCITY
AI Akinori Iwamura 8.00 20.00
AJ Andruw Jones 8.00 20.00
AP Albert Pujols 15.00 40.00
AR Alex Rodriguez 20.00 50.00
AS Alfonso Soriano 6.00 15.00
CB Carlos Beltran 6.00 15.00
CD Carlos Delgado 6.00 15.00
CH Chin-Lung Hu 50.00 100.00
CL Carlos Lee 4.00 10.00
DL Derrek Lee 6.00 15.00
DM Daisuke Matsuzaka 10.00 25.00
DO David Ortiz 10.00 25.00
EB Erik Bedard 6.00 15.00
EP Eduardo Paret 10.00 25.00
FC Frederich Cepeda 10.00 25.00
FG Freddy Garcia 6.00 15.00
FR Jeff Francoeur 15.00 40.00
GL Guangbiao Liu 6.00 15.00
GY Guogan Yang 6.00 15.00
HS Chia-Hsien Hseih 40.00 80.00
HT Hitoshi Tamura 20.00 50.00
IR Ivan Rodriguez 8.00 20.00
IS Ichiro Suzuki 125.00 250.00
JB Jason Bay 6.00 15.00
JD Johnny Damon 6.00 15.00
JF Jeff Francis 6.00 15.00
JG Jason Grilli 4.00 10.00
JH Justin Huber 6.00 15.00
JL Jong Beom Lee 6.00 15.00
JM Justin Morneau 4.00 10.00
JP Jin Man Park 6.00 15.00
JS Johan Santana 10.00 25.00
JV Jason Varitek 10.00 25.00
KG Ken Griffey Jr. 15.00 40.00
KU Koji Uehara 6.00 15.00
MC Miguel Cabrera 6.00 15.00
ME Michel Enriquez 10.00 25.00
MF Maikel Folch 10.00 25.00
MK Munenori Kawasaki 20.00 50.00
MO Michihiro Ogasawara 20.00 50.00
MP Mike Piazza 20.00 50.00
MS Min Han Son 6.00 15.00
MT Mark Teixeira 6.00 15.00
NM Nobuhiko Matsunaka 30.00 60.00
OP Oliver Perez 4.00 10.00
PE Ariel Pestano 10.00 25.00
PL Pedro Lazo 10.00 25.00
RC Roger Clemens 12.50 30.00
SW Shunsuke Watanabe 30.00 60.00
TC Tai-San Chang 10.00 25.00
TE Miguel Tejada 6.00 15.00
TN Tsuyoshi Nishioka 30.00 60.00
TW Tsuyoshi Wada 30.00 60.00
VC Vinny Castilla 6.00 15.00
VM Victor Martinez 6.00 15.00
WL Wei-Chu Lin 75.00 150.00
WP Wei-Lun Pan 10.00 25.00
WW Wei Wang 6.00 15.00
YG Yuliesky Gourriel 15.00 40.00
YM Yunieski Maya 10.00 25.00

2007 Upper Deck

This 1024-card set was issued over two series. In addition, a 20-card Rookie Exchange set was also produced and numbered sequentially at the beginning of the second series. The first series was released in March, 2007 and the second series was released in June, 2007. The cards were released in both hobby and retail packs. The hobby packs contained 15 cards per pack which came 16 packs to a box and 12 boxes to a case. Cards numbered 1-50 and 501-520 are rookie subsets while cards numbered 471-500 are checklist cards. There was a Rookie Exchange card for cards 501-520 which was redeemable until February 27, 2010. The rest of the set is sequenced alphabetically by what team the player featured was playing for when the individual series went to press.

COMPLETE SET (1020) 200.00 300.00
COMP.SET w/o RC EXCH (1000) 120.00 200.00
COMP.SER.1 w/o RC EXCH (500) 40.00 80.00
COMP.SER.2 w/o RC EXCH (500) 80.00 120.00
COMMON CARD (1-1020) .15 .40
STATED PRINT RUN'X SER.#'d SETS
COMMON ROOKIE .30 .75
COMMON ROOKIE (501-520) 1.00 2.50
1-500 ISSUED IN SERIES 1 PACKS
501-1020 ISSUED IN SERIES 2 PACKS
MATSUZAKA JSY RANDOMLY INSERTED
NO MATSUZAKA JSY PRICING AVAILABLE
OVERALL PLATE SER.1 ODDS 1:192 H
OVERALL PLATE SER.2 ODDS 1:96 H
PLATE PRINT RUN 1 SET PER COLOR
BLACK-CYAN-MAGENTA-YELLOW ISSUED
NO PLATE PRICING DUE TO SCARCITY
ROOKIE EXCH APPX. 1-2 PER CASE
ROOKIE EXCH DEADLINE 02/27/2010
1 Doug Slaten RC .30 .75
2 Miguel Montero (RC) .30 .75
3 Brian Burres (RC) .30 .75
4 Devern Hansack RC .30 .75
5 David Murphy (RC) .30 .75
6 Jose Reyes RC .30 .75
7 Scott Moore (RC) .30 .75
8 Josh Fields (RC) .30 .75
9 Chris Stewart RC .30 .75
10 Jerry Owens (RC) .30 .75
11 Ryan Sweeney (RC) .30 .75
12 Kevin Kouzmanoff (RC) .30 .75
13 Jeff Baker (RC) .30 .75
14 Justin Hampson (RC) .30 .75
15 Jeff Salazar (RC) .30 .75
16 Alvin Colina RC .75 2.00
17 Troy Tulowitzki (RC) 1.00 2.50
18 Andrew Miller RC 1.25 3.00
19 Mike Rabelo RC .30 .75
20 Jose Diaz (RC) .30 .75
21 Angel Sanchez RC .30 .75
22 Ryan Braun RC .30 .75
23 Delwyn Young (RC) .30 .75
24 Drew Anderson RC .30 .75
25 Dennis Sarfate (RC) .30 .75
26 Vinny Rottino (RC) .30 .75
27 Glen Perkins (RC) .30 .75
28 Alexi Casilla RC .50 1.25
29 Philip Humber (RC) .30 .75
30 Andy Cannizaro RC .30 .75
31 Jeremy Brown .15 .40
32 Sean Henn (RC) .30 .75
33 Brian Rogers .15 .40
34 Carlos Maldonado (RC) .30 .75
35 Juan Morillo (RC) .30 .75
36 Fred Lewis (RC) .50 1.25
37 Patrick Misch (RC) .30 .75
38 Billy Sadler (RC) .30 .75
39 Ryan Feierabend (RC) .30 .75
40 Cesar Jimenez RC .30 .75
41 Oswaldo Navarro RC .30 .75
42 Travis Chick (RC) .30 .75
43 Delmon Young (RC) .75 2.00
44 Shawn Riggans (RC) .30 .75
45 Brian Stokes (RC) .30 .75
46 Juan Salas (RC) .30 .75
47 Joaquin Arias (RC) .30 .75
48 Adam Lind (RC) .30 .75
49 Beltran Perez (RC) .30 .75
50 Brett Campbell RC .30 .75
51 Brian Roberts .15 .40
52 Miguel Tejada .25 .60
53 Brandon Fahey .15 .40
54 Jay Gibbons .15 .40
55 Corey Patterson .15 .40
56 Nick Markakis .30 .75
57 Ramon Hernandez .15 .40
58 Kris Benson .15 .40
59 Adam Loewen .15 .40
60 Erik Bedard .15 .40
61 Chris Ray .15 .40
62 Chris Britton .15 .40
63 Daniel Cabrera .15 .40
64 Sendy Rleal .15 .40
65 Manny Ramirez .40 1.00
66 David Ortiz .40 1.00
67 Gabe Kapler .15 .40
68 Alex Cora .25 .60
69 Dustin Pedroia .30 .75
70 Trot Nixon .15 .40
71 Doug Mirabelli .15 .40
72 Mark Loretta .15 .40
73 Curt Schilling .25 .60
74 Jonathan Papelbon .40 1.00
75 Tim Wakefield .25 .60
76 Jon Lester .25 .60
77 Craig Hansen .15 .40
78 Keith Foulke .15 .40
79 Jermaine Dye .15 .40
80 Jim Thome .25 .60
81 Tadahito Iguchi .15 .40
82 Rob Mackowiak .15 .40
83 Brian Anderson .15 .40
84 Juan Uribe .15 .40
85 A.J. Pierzynski .15 .40
86 Alex Cintron .15 .40
87 Jon Garland .15 .40
88 Jose Contreras .15 .40
89 Neal Cotts .15 .40
90 Bobby Jenks .15 .40
91 Mike MacDougal .15 .40
92 Javier Vazquez .15 .40
93 Travis Hafner .15 .40
94 Jhonny Peralta .15 .40
95 Ryan Garko .15 .40
96 Victor Martinez .25 .60
97 Hector Luna .15 .40
98 Casey Blake .15 .40
99 Jason Michaels .15 .40
100 Shin-Soo Choo .25 .60
101 C.C. Sabathia .25 .60
102 Paul Byrd .15 .40
103 Jeremy Sowers .15 .40
104 Cliff Lee .25 .60
105 Rafael Betancourt .15 .40
106 Francisco Cruceta .15 .40
107 Sean Casey .15 .40
108 Brandon Inge .15 .40
109 Placido Polanco .15 .40
110 Omar Infante .15 .40
111 Ivan Rodriguez .25 .60
112 Magglio Ordonez .25 .60
113 Craig Monroe .15 .40
114 Marcus Thames .15 .40
115 Justin Verlander .40 1.00
116 Todd Jones .15 .40
117 Kenny Rogers .15 .40
118 Joel Zumaya .15 .40
119 Jeremy Bonderman .15 .40
120 Nate Robertson .15 .40
121 Mark Teahen .15 .40
122 Ryan Shealy .15 .40
123 Mitch Maier RC .30 .75
124 Doug Mientkiewicz .15 .40
125 Mark Grudzielanek .15 .40
126 Shane Costa .15 .40
127 John Buck .15 .40
128 Reggie Sanders .15 .40
129 Mike Sweeney .15 .40
130 Mark Redman .15 .40
131 Todd Wellemeyer .15 .40
132 Scott Elarton .15 .40
133 Ambiorix Burgos .15 .40
134 Joe Nelson .15 .40
135 Howie Kendrick .15 .40
136 Chone Figgins .15 .40
137 Orlando Cabrera .15 .40
138 Maicer Izturis .15 .40
139 Jose Molina .15 .40
140 Vladimir Guerrero .25 .60
141 Darin Erstad .15 .40
142 Juan Rivera .15 .40
143 Jered Weaver .25 .60
144 John Lackey .25 .60
145 Joe Saunders .15 .40
146 Bartolo Colon .15 .40
147 Scot Shields .15 .40
148 Francisco Rodriguez .25 .60
149 Justin Morneau .25 .60
150 Jason Bartlett .15 .40
151 Luis Castillo .15 .40
152 Nick Punto .15 .40
153 Shannon Stewart .15 .40
154 Michael Cuddyer .15 .40
155 Jason Kubel .15 .40
156 Joe Mauer .30 .75
157 Francisco Liriano .30 .75
158 Joe Nathan .15 .40
159 Dennys Reyes .15 .40
160 Brad Radke .15 .40
161 Boof Bonser .15 .40
162 Juan Rincon .15 .40
163 Derek Jeter 1.00 2.50
164 Jason Giambi .15 .40
165 Robinson Cano .25 .60
166 Andy Phillips .15 .40
167 Bobby Abreu .15 .40
168 Gary Sheffield .15 .40
169 Bernie Williams .25 .60
170 Melky Cabrera .15 .40
171 Mike Mussina .25 .60
172 Chien-Ming Wang .25 .60
173 Mariano Rivera .50 1.25
174 Scott Proctor .15 .40
175 Jaret Wright .15 .40
176 Kyle Farnsworth .15 .40
177 Eric Chavez .15 .40
178 Bobby Crosby .15 .40
179 Frank Thomas .40 1.00
180 Dan Johnson .15 .40
181 Marco Scutaro .25 .60
182 Nick Swisher .25 .60
183 Milton Bradley .15 .40
184 Jay Payton .15 .40
185 Joe Blanton .15 .40
186 Barry Zito .25 .60
187 Rich Harden .15 .40
188 Esteban Loaiza .15 .40
189 Huston Street .15 .40
190 Chad Gaudin .15 .40
191 Richie Sexson .15 .40
192 Yuniesky Betancourt .15 .40
193 Willie Bloomquist .15 .40
194 Ben Broussard .15 .40
195 Kenji Johjima .40 1.00
196 Ichiro Suzuki .50 1.25
197 Raul Ibanez .25 .60
198 Chris Snelling .15 .40
199 Felix Hernandez .25 .60
200 Cha-Seung Baek .15 .40
201 Joel Pineiro .15 .40
202 Julio Mateo .15 .40
203 J.J. Putz .15 .40
204 Rafael Soriano .15 .40
205 Jorge Cantu .15 .40
206 B.J. Upton .15 .40
207 Ty Wigginton .15 .40
208 Greg Norton .15 .40
209 Dioner Navarro .15 .40
210 Carl Crawford .25 .60
211 Jonny Gomes .15 .40
212 Damon Hollins .15 .40
213 Scott Kazmir .25 .60
214 Casey Fossum .15 .40
215 Ruddy Lugo .15 .40
216 James Shields .15 .40
217 Tyler Walker .15 .40
218 Shawn Camp .15 .40
219 Mark Teixeira .25 .60
220 Hank Blalock .15 .40
221 Ian Kinsler .25 .60
222 Jerry Hairston Jr. .15 .40
223 Gerald Laird .15 .40
224 Carlos Lee .15 .40
225 Gary Matthews .15 .40
226 Mark DeRosa .15 .40
227 Kip Wells .15 .40
228 Akinori Otsuka .15 .40
229 Vicente Padilla .15 .40
230 John Koronka .15 .40
231 Kevin Millwood .15 .40
232 Wes Littleton .15 .40
233 Troy Glaus .15 .40
234 Lyle Overbay .15 .40
235 Aaron Hill .15 .40
236 John McDonald .15 .40
237 Bengie Molina .15 .40
238 Vernon Wells .15 .40
239 Reed Johnson .15 .40
240 Frank Catalanotto .15 .40
241 Roy Halladay .25 .60
242 B.J. Ryan .15 .40
243 Gustavo Chacin .15 .40
244 Scott Downs .15 .40
245 Casey Janssen .15 .40
246 Justin Speier .15 .40
247 Stephen Drew .15 .40
248 Conor Jackson .15 .40
249 Orlando Hudson .15 .40
250 Chad Tracy .15 .40
251 Johnny Estrada .15 .40
252 Luis Gonzalez .15 .40
253 Eric Byrnes .15 .40
254 Carlos Quentin .15 .40
255 Brandon Webb .25 .60
256 Claudio Vargas .15 .40
257 Juan Cruz .15 .40
258 Jorge Julio .15 .40
259 Luis Vizcaino .15 .40
260 Livan Hernandez .15 .40
261 Chipper Jones .40 1.00
262 Edgar Renteria .15 .40
263 Adam LaRoche .15 .40
264 Willy Aybar .15 .40
265 Brian McCann .15 .40
266 Ryan Langerhans .15 .40
267 Jeff Francoeur .40 1.00
268 Matt Diaz .15 .40
269 Tim Hudson .25 .60
270 John Smoltz .40 1.00
271 Oscar Villarreal .15 .40
272 Horacio Ramirez .15 .40
273 Bob Wickman .15 .40
274 Chad Paronto .15 .40
275 Derrek Lee .15 .40
276 Ryan Theriot .15 .40
277 Cesar Izturis .15 .40
278 Ronny Cedeno .15 .40
279 Michael Barrett .15 .40
280 Juan Pierre .15 .40
281 Jacque Jones .15 .40
282 Matt Murton .15 .40
283 Carlos Zambrano .25 .60
284 Mark Prior .25 .60
285 Rich Hill .15 .40
286 Sean Marshall .15 .40
287 Ryan Dempster .15 .40
288 Ryan O'Malley .15 .40
289 Scott Hatteberg .15 .40
290 Brandon Phillips .15 .40
291 Edwin Encarnacion .40 1.00
292 Rich Aurilia .15 .40
293 David Ross .15 .40
294 Ken Griffey Jr. .75 2.00
295 Ryan Freel .15 .40
296 Chris Denorfia .15 .40
297 Bronson Arroyo .15 .40
298 Aaron Harang .15 .40
299 Brandon Claussen .15 .40
300 Todd Coffey .15 .40
301 David Weathers .15 .40
302 Eric Milton .15 .40
303 Todd Helton .25 .60
304 Clint Barmes .15 .40
305 Kazuo Matsui .15 .40
306 Jamey Carroll .15 .40
307 Yorvit Torrealba .15 .40
308 Matt Holliday .40 1.00
309 Choo Freeman .15 .40
310 Brad Hawpe .15 .40
311 Jason Jennings .15 .40
312 Jeff Francis .15 .40
313 Josh Fogg .15 .40
314 Aaron Cook .15 .40
315 Ubaldo Jimenez (RC) 1.00 2.50
316 Manny Corpas .15 .40
317 Miguel Cabrera .40 1.00
318 Dan Uggla .15 .40
319 Hanley Ramirez .25 .60
320 Wes Helms .15 .40
321 Miguel Olivo .15 .40
322 Jeremy Hermida .15 .40
323 Cody Ross .15 .40
324 Josh Willingham .25 .60
325 Dontrelle Willis .15 .40
326 Anibal Sanchez .15 .40
327 Josh Johnson .40 1.00
328 Jose Garcia RC .30 .75
329 Joe Borowski .15 .40
330 Taylor Tankersley .15 .40
331 Lance Berkman .25 .60
332 Craig Biggio .25 .60
333 Aubrey Huff .15 .40
334 Adam Everett .15 .40
335 Brad Ausmus .15 .40
336 Willy Taveras .15 .40
337 Luke Scott .15 .40
338 Chris Burke .15 .40
339 Roger Clemens .50 1.25
340 Andy Pettitte .25 .60
341 Brandon Backe .15 .40
342 Hector Gimenez (RC) .30 .75
343 Brad Lidge .15 .40
344 Dan Wheeler .15 .40
345 Nomar Garciaparra .25 .60
346 Rafael Furcal .15 .40
347 Wilson Betemit .15 .40
348 Julio Lugo .15 .40
349 Russell Martin .15 .40
350 Andre Ethier .25 .60
351 Matt Kemp .30 .75
352 Kenny Lofton .15 .40
353 Brad Penny .15 .40
354 Derek Lowe .15 .40
355 Chad Billingsley .25 .60
356 Greg Maddux .50 1.25
357 Takashi Saito .15 .40
358 Jonathan Broxton .15 .40
359 Prince Fielder .25 .60
360 Rickie Weeks .15 .40
361 Bill Hall .15 .40
362 J.J. Hardy .15 .40
363 Jeff Cirillo .15 .40
364 Tony Gwynn Jr. .15 .40
365 Corey Hart .15 .40
366 Laynce Nix .15 .40
367 Doug Davis .15 .40
368 Ben Sheets .15 .40
369 Chris Capuano .15 .40
370 Dave Bush .15 .40
371 Derrick Turnbow .15 .40
372 Francisco Cordero .15 .40
373 Jose Reyes .25 .60
374 Carlos Delgado .15 .40
375 Julio Franco .15 .40
376 Jose Valentin .15 .40
377 Paul LoDuca .15 .40
378 Carlos Beltran .25 .60
379 Shawn Green .15 .40
380 Lastings Milledge .25 .60
381 Endy Chavez .15 .40
382 Pedro Martinez .25 .60
383 John Maine .15 .40
384 Orlando Hernandez .15 .40
385 Steve Trachsel .15 .40
386 Billy Wagner .15 .40
387 Ryan Howard .30 .75
388 Chase Utley .25 .60
389 Jimmy Rollins .25 .60
390 Chris Coste .15 .40
391 Jeff Conine .15 .40
392 Aaron Rowand .15 .40
393 Shane Victorino .15 .40
394 David Dellucci .15 .40
395 Cole Hamels .30 .75
396 Jamie Moyer .15 .40
397 Ryan Madson .15 .40
398 Brett Myers .15 .40
399 Tom Gordon .15 .40
400 Geoff Geary .15 .40
401 Freddy Sanchez .15 .40
402 Xavier Nady .15 .40
403 Jose Castillo .15 .40
404 Joe Randa .15 .40
405 Jason Bay .25 .60
406 Chris Duffy .15 .40
407 Jose Bautista .25 .60
408 Ronny Paulino .15 .40
409 Ian Snell .15 .40
410 Zach Duke .15 .40
411 Tom Gorzelanny .15 .40
412 Shane Youman RC .30 .75
413 Mike Gonzalez .15 .40
414 Matt Capps .15 .40
415 Adrian Gonzalez .30 .75
416 Josh Barfield .15 .40
417 Todd Walker .15 .40
418 Khalil Greene .15 .40
419 Mike Piazza .40 1.00
420 Dave Roberts .25 .60
421 Mike Cameron .15 .40
422 Geoff Blum .15 .40
423 Jake Peavy .15 .40
424 Chris R. Young .15 .40
425 Woody Williams .15 .40
426 Clay Hensley .15 .40
427 Cla Meredith .15 .40
428 Trevor Hoffman .25 .60
429 Shea Hillenbrand .15 .40
430 Pedro Feliz .15 .40
431 Ray Durham .15 .40
432 Mark Sweeney .15 .40

Card	Low	High
433 Eliezer Alfonzo	.15	.40
434 Moises Alou	.15	.40
435 Steve Finley	.15	.40
436 Todd Linden	.15	.40
437 Jason Schmidt	.15	.40
438 Matt Cain	.25	.60
439 Noah Lowry	.15	.40
440 Brad Hennessey	.15	.40
441 Armando Benitez	.15	.40
442 Jonathan Sanchez	.15	.40
443 Albert Pujols	.50	1.25
444 Ronnie Belliard	.15	.40
445 David Eckstein	.15	.40
446 Aaron Miles	.15	.40
447 Yadier Molina	.40	1.00
448 Jim Edmonds	.25	.60
449 Chris Duncan	.15	.40
450 Juan Encarnacion	.15	.40
451 Chris Carpenter	.25	.60
452 Jeff Suppan	.15	.40
453 Jason Marquis	.15	.40
454 Jeff Weaver	.15	.40
455 Jason Isringhausen	.15	.40
456 Braden Looper	.15	.40
457 Ryan Zimmerman	.25	.60
458 Nick Johnson	.15	.40
459 Felipe Lopez	.15	.40
460 Brian Schneider	.15	.40
461 Alfonso Soriano	.25	.60
462 Austin Kearns	.15	.40
463 Ryan Church	.15	.40
464 Alex Escobar	.15	.40
465 Ramon Ortiz	.15	.40
466 Tony Armas	.15	.40
467 Michael O'Connor	.15	.40
468 Chad Cordero	.15	.40
469 Jon Rauch	.15	.40
470 Pedro Astacio	.15	.40
471 Miguel Tejada CL	.25	.60
472 David Ortiz CL	.40	1.00
473 Jermaine Dye CL	.15	.40
474 Travis Hafner CL	.15	.40
475 Magglio Ordonez CL	.25	.60
476 Mark Teahen CL	.15	.40
477 Vladimir Guerrero CL	.25	.60
478 Justin Morneau CL	.25	.60
479 Derek Jeter CL	1.00	2.50
480 Nick Swisher CL	.25	.60
481 Ichiro Suzuki CL	.50	1.25
482 Scott Kazmir CL	.25	.60
483 Mark Teixeira CL	.25	.60
484 Vernon Wells CL	.15	.40
485 Brandon Webb CL	.25	.60
486 Andruw Jones CL	.15	.40
487 Carlos Zambrano CL	.25	.60
488 Adam Dunn CL	.25	.60
489 Matt Holliday CL	.40	1.00
490 Miguel Cabrera CL	.40	1.00
491 Lance Berkman CL	.25	.60
492 Nomar Garciaparra CL	.25	.60
493 Prince Fielder CL	.25	.60
494 Carlos Beltran CL	.25	.60
495 Ryan Howard CL	.30	.75
496 Jason Bay CL	.25	.60
497 Adrian Gonzalez CL	.30	.75
498 Matt Cain CL	.25	.60
499 Albert Pujols CL	.50	1.25
500 Ryan Zimmerman CL	.25	.60
501a D.Matsuzaka Suit RC	20.00	50.00
501b D.Matsuzaka Throwing RC	6.00	15.00
502 Kei Igawa RC	1.50	4.00
503 Akinori Iwamura RC	2.50	6.00
504 Alex Gordon RC	6.00	15.00
505 Matt Chico (RC)	1.00	2.50
506 John Danks RC	1.00	2.50
507 Elijah Dukes RC	1.00	2.50
508 Gustavo Molina RC	1.00	2.50
509 Joakim Soria RC	2.50	6.00
510 Jay Marshall RC	2.50	6.00
511 Travis Buck (RC)	1.00	2.50
512 Brandon Wood (RC)	1.00	2.50
513 Kevin Cameron RC	1.00	2.50
514 Jared Burton RC	2.50	6.00
515 Kory Casto (RC)	1.00	2.50
516 Joe Smith RC	1.00	2.50
517 Jose Garcia	1.00	2.50
518 Hunter Pence (RC)	6.00	15.00
519 Felix Pie (RC)	1.00	2.50
520 Zach Segovia (RC)	1.00	2.50
521 Randy Johnson	.40	1.00
522 Brandon Lyon	.15	.40
523 Robby Hammock	.15	.40
524 Micah Owings (RC)	.30	.75
525 Doug Davis	.15	.40
526 Brian Barden RC	.30	.75
527 Alberto Callaspo	.15	.40
528 Stephen Drew	.15	.40
529 Chris Young	.15	.40
530 Edgar Gonzalez	.15	.40
531 Brandon Medders	.15	.40
532 Tony Pena	.15	.40
533 Jose Valverde	.15	.40
534 Chris Snyder	.15	.40
535 Tony Clark	.15	.40
536 Scott Hairston	.15	.40
537 Jeff DaVanon	.15	.40
538 Randy Johnson CL	.40	1.00
539 Mark Redman	.15	.40
540 Andruw Jones	.15	.40
541 Rafael Soriano	.15	.40
542 Scott Thorman	.15	.40
543 Chipper Jones	.40	1.00
544 Mike Gonzalez	.15	.40
545 Lance Cormier	.15	.40
546 Kyle Davies	.15	.40
547 Mike Hampton	.15	.40
548 Chuck James	.15	.40
549 Macay McBride	.15	.40
550 Tanyon Sturtze	.15	.40
551 Tyler Yates	.15	.40
552 Pete Orr	.15	.40
553 Craig Wilson	.15	.40
554 Chris Woodward	.15	.40
555 Kelly Johnson	.15	.40
556 Chipper Jones CL	.40	1.00
557 Chad Bradford	.15	.40
558 John Parrish	.15	.40
559 Jeremy Guthrie	.15	.40
560 Steve Trachsel	.15	.40
561 Scott Williamson	.15	.40
562 Jaret Wright	.15	.40
563 Paul Bako	.15	.40
564 Chris Gomez	.15	.40
565 Melvin Mora	.15	.40
566 Freddie Bynum	.15	.40
567 Aubrey Huff	.15	.40
568 Jay Payton	.15	.40
569 Miguel Tejada	.25	.60
570 Kurt Birkins	.15	.40
571 Danys Baez	.15	.40
572 Brian Roberts CL	.15	.40
573 Josh Beckett	.15	.40
574 Matt Clement	.15	.40
575 Hideki Okajima RC	2.00	5.00
576 Javier Lopez	.15	.40
577 Joel Pineiro	.15	.40
578 J.C. Romero	.15	.40
579 Kyle Snyder	.15	.40
580 Julian Tavarez	.15	.40
581 Mike Timlin	.15	.40
582 Jason Varitek	.40	1.00
583 Mike Lowell	.15	.40
584 Kevin Youkilis	.15	.40
585 Coco Crisp	.15	.40
586 J.D. Drew	.15	.40
587 Eric Hinske	.15	.40
588 Wily Mo Pena	.15	.40
589 Julio Lugo	.15	.40
590 David Ortiz	.40	1.00
591 Manny Ramirez	.40	1.00
592 Daisuke Matsuzaka CL	1.50	4.00
593 Scott Eyre	.15	.40
594 Angel Guzman	.15	.40
595 Bob Howry	.15	.40
596 Ted Lilly	.15	.40
597 Juan Mateo	.15	.40
598 Wade Miller	.15	.40
599 Carlos Zambrano	.25	.60
600 Will Ohman	.15	.40
601 Michael Wuertz	.15	.40
602 Henry Blanco	.15	.40
603 Aramis Ramirez	.15	.40
604 Cliff Floyd	.15	.40
605 Kerry Wood	.15	.40
606 Alfonso Soriano	.25	.60
607 Daryle Ward	.15	.40
608 Jason Marquis	.15	.40
609 Mark DeRosa	.15	.40
610 Neal Cotts	.15	.40
611 Derrek Lee	.15	.40
612 Aramis Ramirez CL	.15	.40
613 David Aardsma	.15	.40
614 Mark Buehrle	.25	.60
615 Nick Masset	.15	.40
616 Andrew Sisco	.15	.40
617 Matt Thornton	.15	.40
618 Toby Hall	.15	.40
619 Joe Crede	.15	.40
620 Paul Konerko	.25	.60
621 Darin Erstad	.15	.40
622 Pablo Ozuna	.15	.40
623 Scott Podsednik	.15	.40
624 Jim Thome	.25	.60
625 Jermaine Dye	.15	.40
626 Jim Thome CL	.25	.60
627 Adam Dunn	.25	.60
628 Bill Bray	.15	.40
629 Alex Gonzalez	.15	.40
630 Josh Hamilton (RC)	4.00	10.00
631 Matt Belisle	.15	.40
632 Rheal Cormier	.15	.40
633 Kyle Lohse	.15	.40
634 Eric Milton	.15	.40
635 Kirk Saarloos	.15	.40
636 Mike Stanton	.15	.40
637 Javier Valentin	.15	.40
638 Juan Castro	.15	.40
639 Jeff Conine	.15	.40
640 Jon Coutlangus (RC)	.30	.75
641 Ken Griffey Jr.	.75	2.00
642 Ken Griffey Jr. CL	.75	2.00
643 Fernando Cabrera	.15	.40
644 Fausto Carmona	.15	.40
645 Jason Davis	.15	.40
646 Aaron Fultz	.15	.40
647 Roberto Hernandez	.15	.40
648 Jake Westbrook	.15	.40
649 Kelly Shoppach	.15	.40
650 Josh Barfield	.15	.40
651 Andy Marte	.15	.40
652 Joe Inglett	.15	.40
653 David Dellucci	.15	.40
654 Joe Borowski	.15	.40
655 Franklin Gutierrez	.15	.40
656 Trot Nixon	.15	.40
657 Grady Sizemore	.25	.60
658 Mike Rouse	.15	.40
659 Travis Hafner	.15	.40
660 Victor Martinez	.25	.60
661 C.C. Sabathia	.25	.60
662 Grady Sizemore CL	.25	.60
663 Jeremy Affeldt	.15	.40
664 Taylor Buchholz	.15	.40
665 Brian Fuentes	.15	.40
666 Latroy Hawkins	.15	.40
667 Byung-Hyun Kim	.15	.40
668 Brian Lawrence	.15	.40
669 Rodrigo Lopez	.15	.40
670 Jeff Francis	.15	.40
671 Chris Ianetta	.15	.40
672 Garrett Atkins	.15	.40
673 Todd Helton	.25	.60
674 Steve Finley	.15	.40
675 John Mabry	.15	.40
676 Willy Taveras	.15	.40
677 Jason Hirsh	.15	.40
678 Ramon Ramirez	.15	.40
679 Matt Holliday	.40	1.00
680 Todd Helton CL	.25	.60
681 Roman Colon	.15	.40
682 Chad Durbin	.15	.40
683 Jason Grilli	.15	.40
684 Wilfredo Ledezma	.15	.40
685 Mike Maroth	.15	.40
686 Jose Mesa	.15	.40
687 Justin Verlander	.40	1.00
688 Fernando Rodney	.15	.40
689 Vance Wilson	.15	.40
690 Carlos Guillen	.15	.40
691 Neifi Perez	.15	.40
692 Curtis Granderson	.30	.75
693 Gary Sheffield	.15	.40
694 Justin Verlander CL	.40	1.00
695 Kevin Gregg	.15	.40
696 Logan Kensing	.15	.40
697 Randy Messenger	.15	.40
698 Sergio Mitre	.15	.40
699 Ricky Nolasco	.15	.40
700 Scott Olsen	.15	.40
701 Renyel Pinto	.15	.40
702 Matt Treanor	.15	.40
703 Alfredo Amezaga	.15	.40
704 Aaron Boone	.15	.40
705 Mike Jacobs	.15	.40
706 Miguel Cabrera	.40	1.00
707 Joe Borchard	.15	.40
708 Jorge Julio	.15	.40
709 Rick Vanden Hurk RC	.30	.75
710 Lee Gardner (RC)	.30	.75
711 Matt Lindstrom (RC)	.30	.75
712 Henry Owens	.15	.40
713 Hanley Ramirez	.25	.60
714 Alejandro De Aza RC	.50	1.25
715 Hanley Ramirez CL	.25	.60
716 Dave Borkowski	.15	.40
717 Jason Jennings	.15	.40
718 Trever Miller	.15	.40
719 Roy Oswalt	.25	.60
720 Wandy Rodriguez	.15	.40
721 Humberto Quintero	.15	.40
722 Morgan Ensberg	.15	.40
723 Mike Lamb	.15	.40
724 Mark Loretta	.15	.40
725 Jason Lane	.15	.40
726 Carlos Lee	.15	.40
727 Orlando Palmeiro	.15	.40
728 Woody Williams	.15	.40
729 Chad Qualls	.15	.40
730 Lance Berkman	.25	.60
731 Rick White	.15	.40
732 Chris Sampson	.15	.40
733 Carlos Lee CL	.15	.40
734 Jorge De La Rosa	.15	.40
735 Octavio Dotel	.15	.40
736 Jimmy Gobble	.15	.40
737 Zack Greinke	.25	.60
738 Luke Hudson	.15	.40
739 Gil Meche	.15	.40
740 Joel Peralta	.15	.40
741 Odalis Perez	.15	.40
742 David Riske	.15	.40
743 Jason LaRue	.15	.40
744 Tony Pena	.15	.40
745 Esteban German	.15	.40
746 Ross Gload	.15	.40
747 Emil Brown	.15	.40
748 David DeJesus	.15	.40
749 Brandon Duckworth	.15	.40
750 Alex Gordon CL	.50	1.25
751 Jered Weaver	.25	.60
752 Vladimir Guerrero	.25	.60
753 Hector Carrasco	.15	.40
754 Kelvim Escobar	.15	.40
755 Darren Oliver	.15	.40
756 Dustin Moseley	.15	.40
757 Ervin Santana	.15	.40
758 Mike Napoli	.15	.40
759 Shea Hillenbrand	.15	.40
760 Casey Kotchman	.15	.40
761 Reggie Willits	.15	.40
762 Robb Quinlan	.15	.40
763 Garret Anderson	.15	.40
764 Gary Matthews	.15	.40
765 Justin Speier	.15	.40
766 Jered Weaver CL	.25	.60
767 Joe Beimel	.15	.40
768 Yhency Brazoban	.15	.40
769 Elmer Dessens	.15	.40
770 Mark Hendrickson	.15	.40
771 Hong-Chih Kuo	.15	.40
772 Jason Schmidt	.15	.40
773 Brett Tomko	.15	.40
774 Randy Wolf	.15	.40
775 Mike Liberthal	.15	.40
776 Marlon Anderson	.15	.40
777 Jeff Kent	.15	.40
778 Ramon Martinez	.15	.40
779 Olmedo Saenz	.15	.40
780 Luis Gonzalez	.15	.40
781 Juan Pierre	.15	.40
782 Jason Repko	.15	.40
783 Nomar Garciaparra	.25	.60
784 Wilson Valdez	.15	.40
785 Jason Schmidt CL	.15	.40
786 Greg Aquino	.15	.40
787 Brian Shouse	.15	.40
788 Jeff Suppan	.15	.40
789 Carlos Villanueva	.15	.40
790 Matt Wise	.15	.40
791 Johnny Estrada	.15	.40
792 Craig Counsell	.15	.40
793 Tony Graffanino	.15	.40
794 Corey Koskie	.15	.40
795 Claudio Vargas	.15	.40
796 Brady Clark	.15	.40
797 Gabe Gross	.15	.40
798 Geoff Jenkins	.15	.40
799 Kevin Mench	.15	.40
800 Bill Hall CL	.15	.40
801 Sidney Ponson	.15	.40
802 Jesse Crain	.15	.40
803 Matt Guerrier	.15	.40
804 Pat Neshek	.30	.75
805 Ramon Ortiz	.15	.40
806 Johan Santana	.25	.60
807 Carlos Silva	.15	.40
808 Mike Redmond	.15	.40
809 Jeff Cirillo	.15	.40
810 Luis Rodriguez	.15	.40
811 Lew Ford	.15	.40
812 Torii Hunter	.15	.40
813 Jason Tyner	.15	.40
814 Rondell White	.15	.40
815 Justin Morneau	.25	.60
816 Joe Mauer	.30	.75
817 Johan Santana CL	.25	.60
818 David Newhan	.15	.40
819 Aaron Sele	.15	.40
820 Ambiorix Burgos	.15	.40
821 Pedro Feliciano	.15	.40
822 Tom Glavine	.25	.60
823 Aaron Heilman	.15	.40
824 Guillermo Mota	.15	.40
825 Jose Reyes	.25	.60
826 Oliver Perez	.15	.40
827 Duaner Sanchez	.15	.40
828 Scott Schoeneweis	.15	.40
829 Ramon Castro	.15	.40
830 Damion Easley	.15	.40
831 David Wright	.30	.75
832 Moises Alou	.15	.40
833 Carlos Beltran	.25	.60
834 Dave Williams	.15	.40
835 David Wright CL	.30	.75
836 Brian Bruney	.15	.40
837 Mike Myers	.15	.40
838 Carl Pavano	.15	.40
839 Andy Pettitte	.25	.60
840 Luis Vizcaino	.15	.40
841 Jorge Posada	.25	.60
842 Miguel Cairo	.15	.40
843 Doug Mientkiewicz	.15	.40
844 Derek Jeter	1.00	2.50
845 Alex Rodriguez	.50	1.25
846 Johnny Damon	.25	.60
847 Hideki Matsui	.40	1.00
848 Josh Phelps	.15	.40
849 Phil Hughes (RC)	1.50	4.00
850 Roger Clemens	.50	1.25
851 Jason Giambi CL	.15	.40
852 Kiko Calero	.15	.40
853 Justin Duchscherer	.15	.40
854 Alan Embree	.15	.40
855 Todd Walker	.15	.40
856 Rich Harden	.15	.40
857 Dan Haren	.15	.40
858 Joe Kennedy	.15	.40
859 Jason Kendall	.15	.40
860 Adam Melhuse	.15	.40
861 Mark Ellis	.15	.40
862 Bobby Kielty	.15	.40
863 Mark Kotsay	.15	.40
864 Shannon Stewart	.15	.40
865 Mike Piazza	.40	1.00
866 Mike Piazza CL	.40	1.00
867 Antonio Alfonseca	.15	.40
868 Carlos Ruiz	.15	.40
869 Adam Eaton	.15	.40
870 Freddy Garcia	.15	.40
871 Jon Lieber	.15	.40
872 Matt Smith	.15	.40
873 Rod Barajas	.15	.40
874 Wes Helms	.15	.40
875 Abraham Nunez	.15	.40
876 Pat Burrell	.15	.40
877 Jayson Werth	.25	.60
878 Greg Dobbs	.15	.40
879 Joseph Bisenius RC	.30	.75
880 Michael Bourn (RC)	.50	1.25
881 Chase Utley	.25	.60
882 Ryan Howard	.30	.75
883 Chase Utley CL	.25	.60
884 Tony Armas	.15	.40
885 Shawn Chacon	.15	.40
886 John Grabow	.15	.40
887 Paul Maholm	.15	.40
888 Damaso Marte	.15	.40
889 Salomon Torres	.15	.40
890 Humberto Cota	.15	.40
891 Ryan Doumit	.15	.40
892 Adam LaRoche	.15	.40
893 Jack Wilson	.15	.40
894 Nate McLouth	.15	.40
895 Brad Eldred	.15	.40
896 Jonah Bayliss	.15	.40
897 Juan Perez RC	.30	.75
898 Jason Bay	.25	.60
899 Adam LaRoche CL	.15	.40
900 Doug Brocail	.15	.40
901 Scott Cassidy	.15	.40
902 Scott Linebrink	.15	.40
903 Greg Maddux	.50	1.25
904 Jake Peavy	.15	.40
905 Mike Thompson	.15	.40
906 David Wells	.15	.40
907 Josh Bard	.15	.40
908 Rob Bowen	.15	.40
909 Marcus Giles	.15	.40
910 Russell Branyan	.15	.40
911 Jose Cruz	.15	.40
912 Termel Sledge	.15	.40
913 Trevor Hoffman	.25	.60
914 Brian Giles	.15	.40
915 Trevor Hoffman CL	.25	.60
916 Vinnie Chulk	.15	.40
917 Kevin Correia	.15	.40
918 Tim Lincecum RC	5.00	12.00
919 Matt Morris	.15	.40
920 Russ Ortiz	.15	.40
921 Barry Zito	.25	.60
922 Bengie Molina	.15	.40
923 Rich Aurilia	.15	.40
924 Omar Vizquel	.25	.60
925 Jason Ellison	.15	.40
926 Ryan Klesko	.15	.40
927 Dave Roberts	.25	.60
928 Randy Winn	.15	.40
929 Barry Zito CL	.25	.60
930 Miguel Batista	.15	.40
931 Horacio Ramirez	.15	.40
932 Chris Reitsma	.15	.40
933 George Sherrill	.15	.40
934 Jarrod Washburn	.15	.40
935 Jeff Weaver	.15	.40
936 Jake Woods	.15	.40
937 Adrian Beltre	.40	1.00
938 Jose Lopez	.15	.40
939 Ichiro Suzuki	.50	1.25
940 Jose Vidro	.15	.40
941 Jose Guillen	.15	.40
942 Sean White RC	.30	.75
943 Brandon Morrow RC	1.50	4.00
944 Felix Hernandez	.25	.60
945 Felix Hernandez CL	.25	.60
946 Randy Flores	.15	.40
947 Ryan Franklin	.15	.40
948 Kelvin Jimenez RC	.30	.75
949 Tyler Johnson	.15	.40
950 Mark Mulder	.15	.40
951 Anthony Reyes	.15	.40
952 Russ Springer	.15	.40
953 Brad Thompson	.15	.40
954 Adam Wainwright	.25	.60
955 Kip Wells	.15	.40
956 Gary Bennett	.15	.40
957 Adam Kennedy	.15	.40
958 Scott Rolen	.25	.60
959 Scott Spiezio	.15	.40
960 So Taguchi	.15	.40
961 Preston Wilson	.15	.40
962 Skip Schumaker	.15	.40
963 Albert Pujols	.50	1.25
964 Chris Carpenter	.25	.60
965 Chris Carpenter CL	.25	.60
966 Edwin Jackson	.15	.40
967 Jae Kuk Ryu	.15	.40
968 Jae Seo	.15	.40
969 Jon Switzer	.15	.40
970 Josh Paul	.15	.40
971 Ben Zobrist	.25	.60
972 Rocco Baldelli	.15	.40
973 Scott Kazmir	.25	.60
974 Carl Crawford	.25	.60
975 Delmon Young CL	.25	.60
976 Bruce Chen	.15	.40
977 Joaquin Benoit	.15	.40
978 Scott Feldman	.25	.60
979 Eric Gagne	.15	.40
980 Kameron Loe	.15	.40
981 Brandon McCarthy	.15	.40
982 Robinson Tejeda	.15	.40
983 C.J. Wilson	.15	.40
984 Mark Teixeira	.25	.60
985 Michael Young	.15	.40
986 Kenny Lofton	.15	.40
987 Brad Wilkerson	.15	.40
988 Nelson Cruz	.40	1.00
989 Sammy Sosa	.40	1.00
990 Michael Young CL	.15	.40
991 Vernon Wells	.15	.40
992 Matt Stairs	.15	.40
993 Jeremy Accardo	.15	.40
994 A.J. Burnett	.15	.40
995 Jason Frasor	.15	.40
996 Roy Halladay	.25	.60
997 Shaun Marcum	.15	.40
998 Tomo Ohka	.15	.40
999 Josh Towers	.15	.40
1000 Gregg Zaun	.15	.40
1001 Royce Clayton	.15	.40
1002 Jason Smith	.15	.40
1003 Alex Rios	.15	.40
1004 Frank Thomas	.40	1.00
1005 Roy Halladay CL	.25	.60
1006 Jesus Flores RC	.30	.75
1007 Dmitri Young	.15	.40
1008 Ray King	.15	.40
1009 Micah Bowie	.15	.40
1010 Shawn Hill	.15	.40
1011 John Patterson	.15	.40
1012 Levale Speigner RC	.30	.75
1013 Ryan Wagner	.15	.40
1014 Jerome Williams	.15	.40
1015 Ryan Zimmerman	.25	.60
1016 Cristian Guzman	.15	.40
1017 Nook Logan	.15	.40
1018 Chris Snelling	.15	.40
1019 Ronnie Belliard	.15	.40
1020 Nick Johnson CL	.15	.40

2007 Upper Deck Gold

*GOLD: 3X TO 8X BASIC
*GOLD RC: 2.5X TO 6X BASIC RC
STATED ODDS 1:16 HOBBY
RANDOM INSERTS IN RETAIL PACKS
STATED PRINT RUN 75 SER.#'d SETS

Card	Low	High
18 Andrew Miller	10.00	25.00
163 Derek Jeter	10.00	25.00
172 Chien-Ming Wang	10.00	25.00
196 Ichiro Suzuki	6.00	15.00
443 Albert Pujols	10.00	25.00
479 Derek Jeter CL	10.00	25.00
481 Ichiro Suzuki CL	6.00	15.00
499 Albert Pujols CL	10.00	25.00

2007 Upper Deck 1989 Reprints

Card	Low	High
COMPLETE SET (26)	20.00	50.00
STATED ODDS 1:4 HOBBY		
AK Al Kaline	1.25	3.00
BF Bob Feller	.75	2.00
BR Babe Ruth	3.00	8.00
CA Rod Carew	.75	2.00
CF Carlton Fisk	.75	2.00
CM Christy Mathewson	1.25	3.00
CS Casey Stengel	.75	2.00
CY Cy Young	1.25	3.00
DR Don Drysdale	.75	2.00
FR Frank Robinson	.75	2.00
GE Lou Gehrig	2.50	6.00
HW Honus Wagner	1.25	3.00
JB Johnny Bench	1.25	3.00
JF Jimmie Foxx	1.25	3.00
JR Jackie Robinson	1.25	3.00
LG Lefty Grove	.75	2.00
MO Mel Ott	.75	2.00
RC Roy Campanella	1.25	3.00
RH Rogers Hornsby	.75	2.00
RJ Reggie Jackson	.75	2.00
RO Brooks Robinson	.75	2.00
SM Stan Musial	2.00	5.00
SP Satchel Paige	1.25	3.00
TC Ty Cobb	2.00	5.00
TM Thurman Munson	1.25	3.00
WJ Walter Johnson	1.25	3.00

2007 Upper Deck 1989 Rookie Reprints

STATED ODDS 1:4 HOBBY
OVERALL PRINTING PLATE ODDS 1:96 H
PLATE PRINT RUN 1 SET PER COLOR
BLACK-CYAN-MAGENTA-YELLOW ISSUED
NO PLATE PRICING DUE TO SCARCITY

Card	Low	High
AD Alejandro De Aza	1.00	2.50
AG Alex Gordon	2.00	5.00
AI Akinori Iwamura	1.50	4.00
AS Angel Sanchez	.60	1.50
BB Brian Barden	.60	1.50
BI Joseph Bisenius	.60	1.50
BM Brandon Morrow	3.00	8.00
BN Jared Burton	.60	1.50
BU Jamie Burke	.60	1.50
CJ Cesar Jimenez	.60	1.50
CS Chris Stewart	.60	1.50
CW Chase Wright	1.50	4.00
DK Don Kelly	.60	1.50
DM Daisuke Matsuzaka	2.50	6.00
DY Delmon Young	1.00	2.50
ED Elijah Dukes	1.00	2.50
FP Felix Pie	.60	1.50
GM Gustavo Molina	.60	1.50
HG Hector Gimenez	.60	1.50
HO Hideki Okajima	3.00	8.00
JA Joaquin Arias	.60	1.50
JB Jeff Baker	.60	1.50
JD John Danks	1.00	2.50
JF Jesus Flores	.60	1.50
JG Jose Garcia	.60	1.50
JH Josh Hamilton	2.00	5.00
JM Jay Marshall	.60	1.50
JP Juan Perez	.60	1.50
JS Joe Smith	.60	1.50
KC Kevin Cameron	.60	1.50
KI Kei Igawa	1.50	4.00
KK Kevin Kouzmanoff	.60	1.50
KO Kory Casto	.60	1.50
LG Lee Gardner	.60	1.50
LS Levale Speigner	.60	1.50
MB Michael Bourn	1.00	2.50
MC Matt Chico	.60	1.50
ML Matt Lindstrom	.60	1.50
MM Miguel Montero	.60	1.50
MO Micah Owings	.60	1.50
MR Mike Rabelo	.60	1.50
RB Ryan Z. Braun	.60	1.50
SA Juan Salas	.60	1.50
SH Sean Henn	.60	1.50
SL Doug Slaten	.60	1.50
SO Joakim Soria	.60	1.50
ST Brian Stokes	.60	1.50
TB Travis Buck	.60	1.50
TT Troy Tulowitzki	2.00	5.00
ZS Zack Segovia	.60	1.50

2007 Upper Deck 1989 Rookie Reprints Signatures

RANDOM INSERTS IN PACKS
STATED PRINT RUN 5 SERIAL #'d SETS
NO PRICING DUE TO SCARCITY

2007 Upper Deck Cal Ripken Jr. Chronicles

Card	Low	High
COMMON RIPKEN	2.50	6.00

STATED ODDS 1:8 H, 1:72 R
PRINTING PLATE ODDS 1:192 H
PLATE PRINT RUN 1 SET PER COLOR
BLACK-CYAN-MAGENTA-YELLOW ISSUED
NO PLATE PRICING DUE TO SCARCITY

2007 Upper Deck Cooperstown Calling

Card	Low	High
COMMON CARD	2.50	6.00

STATED ODDS 1:4 WAL MART PACKS
OVERALL PRINTING PLATE ODDS 1:96 H
PLATE PRINT RUN 1 SET PER COLOR
BLACK-CYAN-MAGENTA-YELLOW ISSUED
NO PLATE PRICING DUE TO SCARCITY

2007 Upper Deck Cooperstown Calling Signatures

STATED ODDS 1:1440 WAL-MART PACKS
NO PRICING DUE TO SCARCITY

2007 Upper Deck Iron Men

Card	Low	High
COMMON CARD (1-50)	2.50	6.00
IM1 C.Ripken Jr./L.Gehrig	2.00	5.00
IM2 C.Ripken Jr./L.Gehrig	2.00	5.00
IM3 C.Ripken Jr./L.Gehrig	2.00	5.00
IM4 C.Ripken Jr./L.Gehrig	2.00	5.00
IM5 C.Ripken Jr./L.Gehrig	2.00	5.00

M6 C.Ripken Jr./L.Gehrig 2.00 5.00
M7 C.Ripken Jr./L.Gehrig 2.00 5.00
M8 C.Ripken Jr./L.Gehrig 2.00 5.00
M9 C.Ripken Jr./L.Gehrig 2.00 5.00
M10 C.Ripken Jr./L.Gehrig 2.00 5.00
M11 C.Ripken Jr./L.Gehrig 2.00 5.00
M12 C.Ripken Jr./L.Gehrig 2.00 5.00
M13 C.Ripken Jr./L.Gehrig 2.00 5.00
M14 C.Ripken Jr./L.Gehrig 2.00 5.00
M15 C.Ripken Jr./L.Gehrig 2.00 5.00
M16 C.Ripken Jr./L.Gehrig 2.00 5.00
M17 C.Ripken Jr./L.Gehrig 2.00 5.00
M18 C.Ripken Jr./L.Gehrig 2.00 5.00
M19 C.Ripken Jr./L.Gehrig 2.00 5.00
M20 C.Ripken Jr./L.Gehrig 2.00 5.00
M21 C.Ripken Jr./L.Gehrig 2.00 5.00
M22 C.Ripken Jr./L.Gehrig 2.00 5.00
M23 C.Ripken Jr./L.Gehrig 2.00 5.00
M24 C.Ripken Jr./L.Gehrig 2.00 5.00
M25 C.Ripken Jr./L.Gehrig 2.00 5.00
M26 C.Ripken Jr./L.Gehrig 2.00 5.00
M27 C.Ripken Jr./L.Gehrig 2.00 5.00
M28 C.Ripken Jr./L.Gehrig 2.00 5.00
M29 C.Ripken Jr./L.Gehrig 2.00 5.00
M30 C.Ripken Jr./L.Gehrig 2.00 5.00
M31 C.Ripken Jr./L.Gehrig 2.00 5.00
M32 C.Ripken Jr./L.Gehrig 2.00 5.00
M33 C.Ripken Jr./L.Gehrig 2.00 5.00
M34 C.Ripken Jr./L.Gehrig 2.00 5.00
M35 C.Ripken Jr./L.Gehrig 2.00 5.00
M36 C.Ripken Jr./L.Gehrig 2.00 5.00
M37 C.Ripken Jr./L.Gehrig 2.00 5.00
M38 C.Ripken Jr./L.Gehrig 2.00 5.00
M39 C.Ripken Jr./L.Gehrig 2.00 5.00
M40 C.Ripken Jr./L.Gehrig 2.00 5.00
M41 C.Ripken Jr./L.Gehrig 2.00 5.00
M42 C.Ripken Jr./L.Gehrig 2.00 5.00
M43 C.Ripken Jr./L.Gehrig 2.00 5.00
M44 C.Ripken Jr./L.Gehrig 2.00 5.00
M45 C.Ripken Jr./L.Gehrig 2.00 5.00
M46 C.Ripken Jr./L.Gehrig 2.00 5.00
M47 C.Ripken Jr./L.Gehrig 2.00 5.00
M48 C.Ripken Jr./L.Gehrig 2.00 5.00
M49 C.Ripken Jr./L.Gehrig 2.00 5.00
M50 C.Ripken Jr./L.Gehrig 2.00 5.00

2007 Upper Deck Ken Griffey Jr. Chronicles

COMMON GRIFFEY 2.00 5.00
STATED ODDS 1:8 H, 1:72 R
PRINTING PLATE ODDS 1:192 H
PLATE PRINT RUN 1 SET PER COLOR
BLACK-CYAN-MAGENTA-YELLOW ISSUED
NO PLATE PRICING DUE TO SCARCITY

2007 Upper Deck MLB Rookie Card of the Month

COMPLETE SET (9) 8.00 20.00
ROM1 Daisuke Matsuzaka 1.00 2.50
ROM2 Fred Lewis .40 1.00
ROM3 Hunter Pence .75 2.00
ROM4 Ryan Braun 1.25 3.00
ROM5 Tim Lincecum 1.25 3.00
ROM6 Joba Chamberlain .40 1.00
ROM7 Troy Tulowitzki .75 2.00
ROMAL Dustin Pedroia .50 1.25
ROMNL Ryan Braun 1.25 3.00

2007 Upper Deck MVP Potential

STATED ODDS 2:1 FAT PACKS
MVP1 Stephen Drew .40 1.00
MVP2 Brian McCann .40 1.00
MVP3 Adam LaRoche .40 1.00
MVP4 Brian Roberts .40 1.00
MVP5 Manny Ramirez 1.00 2.50
MVP6 David Ortiz 1.00 2.50
MVP7 J.D. Drew .40 1.00
MVP8 Alfonso Soriano .60 1.50
MVP9 Aramis Ramirez .40 1.00
MVP10 Derrek Lee .40 1.00
MVP11 Jermaine Dye .40 1.00
MVP12 Paul Konerko .60 1.50
MVP13 Jim Thome .60 1.50
MVP14 Adam Dunn .60 1.50
MVP15 Travis Hafner .40 1.00
MVP16 Victor Martinez .60 1.50
MVP17 Grady Sizemore .60 1.50
MVP18 Garrett Atkins .40 1.00
MVP19 Matt Holliday 1.00 2.50
MVP20 Magglio Ordonez .60 1.50
MVP21 Miguel Cabrera 1.00 2.50
MVP22 Hanley Ramirez .60 1.50
MVP23 Dan Uggla .40 1.00
MVP24 Lance Berkman .60 1.50
MVP25 Carlos Lee .40 1.00
MVP26 Jered Weaver .60 1.50
MVP27 Nomar Garciaparra .60 1.50
MVP28 Rafael Furcal .40 1.00
MVP29 Prince Fielder .60 1.50
MVP30 Joe Mauer .75 2.00
MVP31 Johan Santana .60 1.50
MVP32 David Wright .75 2.00
MVP33 Jose Reyes .60 1.50
MVP34 Carlos Beltran .60 1.50
MVP35 Robinson Cano .60 1.50
MVP36 Derek Jeter 2.50 6.00
MVP37 Bobby Abreu .40 1.00
MVP38 Johnny Damon .60 1.50
MVP39 Nick Swisher .60 1.50
MVP40 Chase Utley .60 1.50
MVP41 Jason Bay .60 1.50
MVP42 Adrian Gonzalez .75 2.00
MVP43 Adrian Beltre 1.00 2.50
MVP44 Scott Rolen .60 1.50
MVP45 Carl Crawford .60 1.50
MVP46 Mark Teixeira .60 1.50
MVP47 Michael Young .40 1.00
MVP48 Vernon Wells .40 1.00
MVP49 Roy Halladay .60 1.50
MVP50 Ryan Zimmerman .60 1.50

2007 Upper Deck MVP Predictors

STATED ODDS 1:16 H, 1:240 R
MVP1 Miguel Tejada 2.00 5.00
MVP2 David Ortiz 4.00 10.00
MVP3 Manny Ramirez 2.00 5.00
MVP4 Jermaine Dye 2.00 5.00
MVP5 Jim Thome 2.00 5.00
MVP6 Paul Konerko 2.00 5.00
MVP7 Travis Hafner 2.00 5.00
MVP8 Grady Sizemore 2.00 5.00
MVP9 Victor Martinez 2.00 5.00
MVP10 Magglio Ordonez 2.00 5.00
MVP11 Justin Verlander 2.00 5.00
MVP12 Vladimir Guerrero 4.00 10.00
MVP13 Jered Weaver 2.00 5.00
MVP14 Justin Morneau 2.00 5.00
MVP15 Joe Mauer 2.00 5.00
MVP16 Johan Santana 2.00 5.00
MVP17 Alex Rodriguez 6.00 15.00
MVP18 Derek Jeter 12.50 30.00
MVP19 Jason Giambi 2.00 5.00
MVP20 Johnny Damon 3.00 8.00
MVP21 Bobby Abreu 2.00 5.00
MVP22 American League Field 6.00 15.00
MVP23 Frank Thomas 3.00 8.00
MVP24 Eric Chavez 2.00 5.00
MVP25 Ichiro Suzuki 2.00 5.00
MVP26 Adrian Beltre 2.00 5.00
MVP27 Carl Crawford 2.00 5.00
MVP28 Scott Kazmir 2.00 5.00
MVP29 Mark Teixeira 2.00 5.00
MVP30 Michael Young 2.00 5.00
MVP31 Carlos Lee 2.00 5.00
MVP32 Vernon Wells 2.00 5.00
MVP33 Roy Halladay 2.00 5.00
MVP34 Troy Glaus 2.00 5.00
MVP35 Stephen Drew 2.00 5.00
MVP36 Chipper Jones 2.00 5.00
MVP37 Andruw Jones 2.00 5.00
MVP38 Adam LaRoche 2.00 5.00
MVP39 Derrek Lee 3.00 8.00
MVP40 Aramis Ramirez 2.00 5.00
MVP41 Adam Dunn 2.00 5.00
MVP42 Ken Griffey Jr. 15.00 40.00
MVP43 Matt Holliday 2.50 6.00
MVP44 Garrett Atkins 2.00 5.00
MVP45 Miguel Cabrera 2.00 5.00
MVP46 Hanley Ramirez 2.00 5.00
MVP47 Dan Uggla 2.00 5.00
MVP48 Lance Berkman 2.00 5.00
MVP49 Roy Oswalt 2.00 5.00
MVP50 Nomar Garciaparra 2.00 5.00
MVP51 J.D. Drew 2.00 5.00
MVP52 Rafael Furcal 2.00 5.00
MVP53 Prince Fielder 15.00 40.00
MVP54 Bill Hall 3.00 8.00
MVP55 Jose Reyes 4.00 10.00
MVP56 Carlos Beltran 2.00 5.00
MVP57 Carlos Delgado 2.00 5.00
MVP58 David Wright 4.00 10.00
MVP59 National League Field 6.00 15.00
MVP60 Chase Utley 3.00 8.00
MVP61 Ryan Howard 6.00 15.00
MVP62 Jimmy Rollins 2.00 5.00
MVP63 Jason Bay 2.00 5.00
MVP64 Freddy Sanchez 2.00 5.00
MVP65 Adrian Gonzalez 2.00 5.00
MVP66 Albert Pujols 10.00 25.00
MVP67 Scott Rolen 2.00 5.00
MVP68 Chris Carpenter 2.00 5.00
MVP69 Alfonso Soriano 4.00 10.00
MVP70 Ryan Zimmerman 2.00 5.00

2007 Upper Deck Postseason Predictors

STATED ODDS 1:16 H, 1:240 R
PP1 Arizona Diamondbacks 2.00 5.00
PP2 Atlanta Braves 4.00 10.00
PP3 Baltimore Orioles 2.00 5.00
PP4 Boston Red Sox 10.00 25.00
PP5 Chicago Cubs 6.00 15.00
PP6 Chicago White Sox 4.00 10.00
PP7 Cincinnati Reds 2.00 5.00
PP8 Cleveland Indians 4.00 10.00
PP9 Colorado Rockies 2.00 5.00
PP10 Detroit Tigers 6.00 15.00
PP11 Florida Marlins 2.00 5.00
PP12 Houston Astros 2.00 5.00
PP13 Kansas City Royals 2.00 5.00
PP14 Los Angeles Angels 6.00 15.00
PP15 Los Angeles Dodgers 4.00 10.00
PP16 Milwaukee Brewers 2.00 5.00
PP17 Minnesota Twins 6.00 15.00
PP18 New York Mets 10.00 25.00
PP19 New York Yankees 12.50 30.00
PP20 Oakland Athletics 4.00 10.00
PP21 Philadelphia Phillies 4.00 10.00
PP22 Pittsburgh Pirates 2.00 5.00
PP23 San Diego Padres 4.00 10.00
PP24 San Francisco Giants 4.00 10.00
PP25 Seattle Mariners 2.00 5.00
PP26 St. Louis Cardinals 6.00 15.00
PP27 Tampa Bay Devil Rays 2.00 5.00
PP28 Texas Rangers 2.00 5.00
PP29 Toronto Blue Jays 2.00 5.00
PP30 Washington Nationals 2.00 5.00

2007 Upper Deck Rookie of the Year Predictor

STATED ODDS 1:16 HOBBY, 1:96 RETAIL
OVERALL PRINTING PLATE ODDS 1:96 H
PLATE PRINT RUN 1 SET PER COLOR
BLACK-CYAN-MAGENTA-YELLOW ISSUED
NO PLATE PRICING DUE TO SCARCITY
ROY1 Doug Slaten 1.25 3.00
ROY2 Miguel Montero 1.25 3.00
ROY3 Joseph Bisenius 1.25 3.00
ROY4 Kory Casto 1.25 3.00
ROY5 Jesus Flores 1.25 3.00
ROY6 John Danks 1.25 3.00
ROY7 Daisuke Matsuzaka 12.50 30.00
ROY8 Matt Lindstrom 1.25 3.00
ROY9 Chris Stewart 1.25 3.00
ROY10 Kevin Cameron 1.25 3.00
ROY11 Hideki Okajima 6.00 15.00
ROY12 Levale Speigner 1.25 3.00
ROY13 Kevin Kouzmanoff 1.25 3.00
ROY14 Jeff Baker 1.25 3.00
ROY15 Don Kelly 1.25 3.00
ROY16 Troy Tulowitzki 4.00 10.00
ROY17 Felix Pie 4.00 10.00
ROY18 Cesar Jimenez 1.25 3.00
ROY19 Alejandro De Aza 1.25 3.00
ROY20 Jose Garcia 1.25 3.00
ROY21 Micah Owings 1.25 3.00
ROY22 Josh Hamilton 30.00 60.00
ROY23 Brian Barden 1.25 3.00
ROY24 Jamie Burke 1.25 3.00
ROY25 Mike Rabelo 1.25 3.00
ROY26 Elijah Dukes 2.00 5.00
ROY27 Travis Buck 1.25 3.00
ROY28 Kei Igawa 2.00 5.00
ROY29 Sean Henn 1.25 3.00
ROY30 American League Field 10.00 25.00
ROY31 National League Field 10.00 25.00
ROY32 Michael Bourn 1.25 3.00
ROY33 Alex Gordon 10.00 25.00
ROY34 Chase Wright 2.00 5.00
ROY35 Matt Chico 1.25 3.00
ROY36 Joe Smith 1.25 3.00
ROY37 Lee Gardner 1.25 3.00
ROY38 Gustavo Molina 1.25 3.00
ROY39 Jared Burton 1.25 3.00
ROY40 Jay Marshall 1.25 3.00
ROY41 Brandon Morrow 1.25 3.00
ROY42 Akinori Iwamura 4.00 10.00
ROY43 Delmon Young 2.00 5.00
ROY44 Juan Salas 1.25 3.00
ROY45 Zack Segovia 1.25 3.00
ROY46 Brian Stokes 1.25 3.00
ROY47 Joaquin Arias 1.25 3.00
ROY48 Hector Gimenez 1.25 3.00
ROY49 Ryan Z. Braun 1.25 3.00
ROY50 Juan Perez 1.25 3.00

2007 Upper Deck Star Power

COMMON CARD .40 1.00
SEMISTARS .60 1.50
UNLISTED STARS 1.00 2.50
STATED ODDS 2:1 FAT PACKS
AJ Andruw Jones .60 1.50
AP Albert Pujols 2.00 5.00
AR Alex Rodriguez 1.50 4.00
BR Brian Roberts .40 1.00
BZ Barry Zito .40 1.00
CA Chris Carpenter .40 1.00
CB Carlos Beltran .40 1.00
CC Carl Crawford .40 1.00
CJ Chipper Jones 1.00 2.50
CS Curt Schilling .60 1.50
CU Chase Utley 1.00 2.50
CZ Carlos Zambrano .40 1.00
DA Johnny Damon .60 1.50
DJ Derek Jeter 2.50 6.00
DO David Ortiz 1.00 2.50
DW Dontrelle Willis .40 1.00
FS Freddy Sanchez .40 1.00
FT Frank Thomas 1.00 2.50
HA Roy Halladay .40 1.00
HO Trevor Hoffman .40 1.00
IS Ichiro Suzuki 1.50 4.00
JB Jason Bay .40 1.00
JD Jermaine Dye .40 1.00
JM Joe Mauer .60 1.50
JP Jake Peavy .40 1.00
JR Jose Reyes .40 1.00
JS Johan Santana .60 1.50
JT Jim Thome .60 1.50
JU Justin Morneau .40 1.00
JV Justin Verlander 1.00 2.50
KG Ken Griffey Jr. 2.00 5.00
KR Kenny Rogers .40 1.00
LB Lance Berkman .40 1.00
MA Matt Cain .60 1.50
MC Miguel Cabrera .60 1.50
MH Matt Holliday .50 1.25
MO Magglio Ordonez .40 1.00
MR Manny Ramirez .60 1.50
MT Mark Teixeira .60 1.50
MY Michael Young .40 1.00
NG Nomar Garciaparra 1.00 2.50
NS Nick Swisher .40 1.00
PF Prince Fielder 1.00 2.50
RH Ryan Howard 1.50 4.00
RO Roy Oswalt .40 1.00
RZ Ryan Zimmerman 1.00 2.50
SM John Smoltz .60 1.50
TH Travis Hafner .40 1.00
VG Vladimir Guerrero 1.00 2.50
WR David Wright 1.50 4.00

2007 Upper Deck Star Rookies

SR1 Adam Lind .40 1.00
SR2 Akinori Iwamura 1.00 2.50
SR3 Alexi Casilla .60 1.50
SR4 Alex Gordon 1.25 3.00
SR5 Matt Chico .40 1.00
SR6 John Danks .60 1.50
SR7 Angel Sanchez .40 1.00
SR8 Elijah Dukes .60 1.50
SR9 Brian Burres .40 1.00
SR10 Gustavo Molina .40 1.00
SR11 Chris Stewart .40 1.00
SR12 Daisuke Matsuzaka 1.50 4.00
SR13 Joakim Soria .40 1.00
SR14 Delmon Young .60 1.50
SR15 Jay Marshall .40 1.00
SR16 Travis Buck .40 1.00
SR17 Doug Slaten .40 1.00
SR18 Don Kelly .40 1.00
SR19 Kevin Cameron .40 1.00
SR20 Glen Perkins .40 1.00
SR21 Hector Gimenez .40 1.00
SR22 Jeff Baker .40 1.00
SR23 Jared Burton .40 1.00
SR24 Kory Casto .40 1.00
SR25 Joe Smith .40 1.00
SR26 Joaquin Arias .40 1.00
SR27 Dallas Braden 2.50 6.00
SR28 Jon Knott .40 1.00
SR29 Jose Garcia .40 1.00
SR30 Jamie Burke .40 1.00
SR31 Zach Segovia .40 1.00
SR32 Felix Pie .40 1.00
SR33 Juan Salas .40 1.00
SR34 Kei Igawa 1.00 2.50
SR35 Philip Hughes 1.00 2.50
SR36 Kevin Kouzmanoff .40 1.00
SR37 Michael Bourn .60 1.50
SR38 Miguel Montero .40 1.00
SR39 Mike Rabelo .40 1.00
SR40 Josh Hamilton 1.25 3.00
SR41 Micah Owings .40 1.00
SR42 Alejandro De Aza .60 1.50
SR43 Brian Barden .40 1.00
SR44 Andy Gonzalez .40 1.00
SR45 Chase Wright 1.00 2.50
SR46 Sean Henn .40 1.00
SR47 Rick Vanden Hurk .40 1.00
SR48 Troy Tulowitzki 1.25 3.00
SR49 Rocky Cherry 1.00 2.50
SR50 Jesus Flores .40 1.00

2007 Upper Deck Star Signings

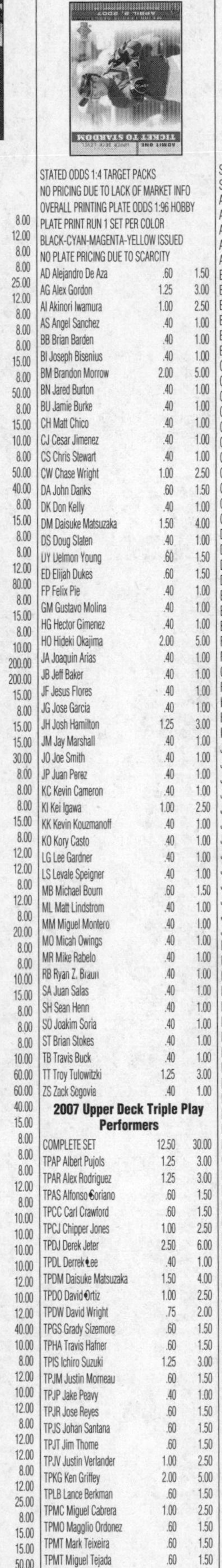

SER.1 ODDS 1:16 HOBBY, 1:960 RETAIL
SER.2 ODDS 1:16 HOBBY, 1:960 RETAIL
SP INFO PROVIDED BY UPPER DECK
EXCH DEADLINE 02/27/2010
AB Ambiorix Burgos 3.00 8.00
AB Adrian Beltre S2 SP 5.00 12.00
AC Alberto Callaspo S2 3.00 8.00
AC Aaron Cook 3.00 8.00
AG Alex Gordon S2 10.00 25.00
AH Aubrey Huff SP 5.00 12.00
AR Alex Rios 3.00 8.00
AS Angel Sanchez S2 3.00 8.00
BA Jeff Baker S2 3.00 8.00
BA Bobby Abreu 6.00 15.00
BB Brian Burres S2 3.00 8.00
BE Josh Beckett S2 SP 20.00 50.00
BL Joe Blanton 3.00 8.00
BO Jeremy Bonderman 6.00 15.00
BO Ben Broussard S2 4.00 10.00
BR Brandon Backe 3.00 8.00
BU B.J. Upton S2 SP 20.00 50.00
CB Craig Biggio S2 SP 15.00 40.00
CC Carl Crawford S2 SP 3.00 8.00
CJ Conor Jackson 6.00 15.00
CO Chad Cordero 3.00 8.00
CP Corey Patterson 3.00 8.00
CR Coco Crisp SP 5.00 12.00
CR Cal Ripken Jr. S2 SP 30.00 80.00
CS Chris Shelton 3.00 8.00
CY Chris Young SP 6.00 15.00
DC Daniel Cabrera SP 3.00 8.00
DH Danny Haren 4.00 10.00
DJ Derek Jeter 100.00 200.00
DJ Derek Jeter S2 100.00 200.00
DL Derrek Lee SP 6.00 15.00
DU Chris Duffy 3.00 8.00
DY Delmon Young S2 SP 6.00 15.00
ED Elijah Dukes S2 6.00 15.00
FH Felix Hernandez S2 12.00 30.00
GA Garrett Atkins 3.00 8.00
GC Gustavo Chacin 3.00 8.00
HS Huston Street 3.00 8.00
HU Torii Hunter 6.00 15.00
IK Ian Kinsler S2 SP 3.00 8.00
IS Ian Snell S2 5.00 12.00
IS Ian Snell SP 5.00 12.00
JA Jeremy Accardo 3.00 8.00
JB Jason Bergmann SP 5.00 12.00
JD Joey Devine 3.00 8.00
JD J.D. Drew S2 SP 8.00 20.00
JG Jonny Gomes 3.00 8.00
JJ Jorge Julio 3.00 8.00
JK Jason Kubel 4.00 10.00
JM Justin Morneau 6.00 15.00
JN Joe Nathan 3.00 8.00
JS Jason Bay 3.00 8.00
JW Jake Westbrook 3.00 8.00
KF Keith Foulke 4.00 10.00
KG Ken Griffey Jr. 30.00 60.00
KG Ken Griffey Jr. S2 SP 30.00 60.00
KI Kei Igawa S2 SP 15.00 40.00
KJ Kelly Johnson S2 6.00 15.00
KM Kevin Mench 3.00 8.00
KS Kirk Saarloos 3.00 8.00
KY Kevin Youkilis 3.00 8.00
LN Laynce Nix SP 5.00 12.00
LO Lyle Overbay 3.00 8.00
MA Matt Cain SP 4.00 10.00
MH Matt Holliday 4.00 10.00
MK Mark Kotsay 4.00 10.00
MM Melvin Mora 4.00 10.00
MT Mark Teahen SP 5.00 12.00
NC Nelson Cruz S2 4.00 10.00
NM Nate McLouth SP 5.00 12.00
OP Oliver Perez S2 SP 15.00 40.00
RA Chris Ray S2 4.00 10.00
RC Ryan Church 3.00 8.00
RF Rafael Furcal SP 5.00 12.00
RG Ryan Garko 4.00 10.00
RI Juan Rivera SP 5.00 12.00
RJ Reed Johnson 3.00 8.00
RO Aaron Rowand SP 5.00 12.00
RU Carlos Ruiz 5.00 12.00
SA Juan Salas S2 3.00 8.00
SC Sean Casey SP 5.00 12.00
SD Stephen Drew 10.00 25.00
SH Sean Henn S2 3.00 8.00
SP Scott Podsednik SP 6.00 15.00
TI Tadahito Iguchi 6.00 15.00
VE Justin Verlander 20.00 50.00
WM Wily Mo Pena 6.00 15.00
XN Xavier Nady 4.00 10.00
YB Yuniesky Betancourt 4.00 10.00
YO Chris Young S2 10.00 25.00
ZS Zack Segovia S2 3.00 8.00

2007 Upper Deck Ticket to Stardom

STATED ODDS 1:4 TARGET PACKS
NO PRICING DUE TO LACK OF MARKET INFO
OVERALL PRINTING PLATE ODDS 1:96 HOBBY
PLATE PRINT RUN 1 SET PER COLOR
BLACK-CYAN-MAGENTA-YELLOW ISSUED
NO PLATE PRICING DUE TO SCARCITY
AD Alejandro De Aza .60 1.50
AG Alex Gordon 1.25 3.00
AI Akinori Iwamura 1.00 2.50
AS Angel Sanchez .40 1.00
BB Brian Barden .40 1.00
BI Joseph Bisenius .40 1.00
BM Brandon Morrow 2.00 5.00
BN Jared Burton .40 1.00
BU Jamie Burke .40 1.00
CH Matt Chico .40 1.00
CJ Cesar Jimenez .40 1.00
CS Chris Stewart .40 1.00
CW Chase Wright 1.00 2.50
DA John Danks .60 1.50
DK Don Kelly .40 1.00
DM Daisuke Matsuzaka 1.50 4.00
DS Doug Slaten .40 1.00
DY Delmon Young .60 1.50
ED Elijah Dukes .60 1.50
FP Felix Pie .40 1.00
GM Gustavo Molina .40 1.00
HG Hector Gimenez .40 1.00
HO Hideki Okajima 2.00 5.00
JA Joaquin Arias .40 1.00
JB Jeff Baker .40 1.00
JF Jesus Flores .40 1.00
JG Jose Garcia .40 1.00
JH Josh Hamilton 1.25 3.00
JM Jay Marshall .40 1.00
JO Joe Smith .40 1.00
JP Juan Perez .40 1.00
KC Kevin Cameron .40 1.00
KI Kei Igawa 1.00 2.50
KK Kevin Kouzmanoff .40 1.00
KO Kory Casto .40 1.00
LG Lee Gardner .40 1.00
LS Levale Speigner .40 1.00
MB Michael Bourn .60 1.50
ML Matt Lindstrom .40 1.00
MM Miguel Montero .40 1.00
MO Micah Owings .40 1.00
MR Mike Rabelo .40 1.00
RB Ryan Z. Braun .40 1.00
SA Juan Salas .40 1.00
SH Sean Henn .40 1.00
SO Joakim Soria .40 1.00
ST Brian Stokes .40 1.00
TB Travis Buck .40 1.00
TT Troy Tulowitzki 1.25 3.00
ZS Zack Segovia .40 1.00

2007 Upper Deck Triple Play Performers

COMPLETE SET 12.50 30.00
TPAP Albert Pujols 1.25 3.00
TPAR Alex Rodriguez 1.25 3.00
TPAS Alfonso Soriano .60 1.50
TPCC Carl Crawford .60 1.50
TPCJ Chipper Jones 1.00 2.50
TPDJ Derek Jeter 2.50 6.00
TPDL Derrek Lee .40 1.00
TPDM Daisuke Matsuzaka 1.50 4.00
TPDO David Ortiz 1.00 2.50
TPDW David Wright .75 2.00
TPGS Grady Sizemore .60 1.50
TPHA Travis Hafner .60 1.50
TPIS Ichiro Suzuki 1.25 3.00
TPJM Justin Morneau .60 1.50
TPJP Jake Peavy .40 1.00
TPJR Jose Reyes .60 1.50
TPJS Johan Santana .60 1.50
TPJT Jim Thome .60 1.50
TPJV Justin Verlander 1.00 2.50
TPKG Ken Griffey 2.00 5.00
TPLB Lance Berkman .60 1.50
TPMC Miguel Cabrera 1.00 2.50
TPMO Magglio Ordonez .60 1.50
TPMT Mark Teixeira .60 1.50
TPMT Miguel Tejada .60 1.50
TPPF Prince Fielder .60 1.50
TPRH Ryan Howard .75 2.00
TPRJ Randy Johnson 1.00 2.50
TPTH Todd Helton .40 1.00
TPVG Vladimir Guerrero .60 1.50

2007 Upper Deck UD Game Materials

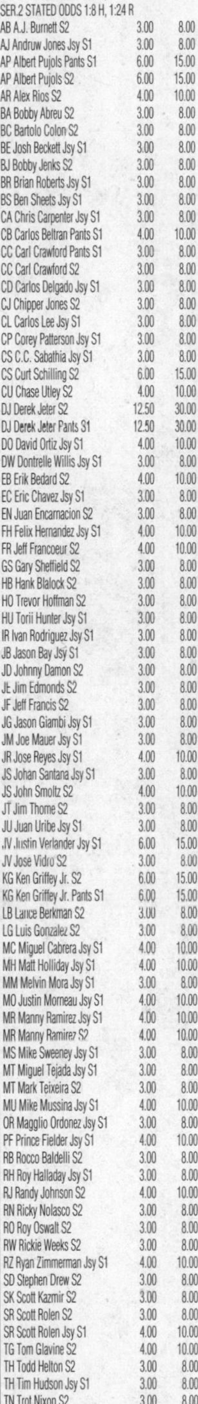

SER.1 STATED ODDS 1:8 H, 1:24 R
SER.2 STATED ODDS 1:8 H, 1:24 R
AB A.J. Burnett S2 3.00 8.00
AJ Andruw Jones Jsy S1 3.00 8.00
AP Albert Pujols Pants S1 6.00 15.00
AP Albert Pujols S2 6.00 15.00
AR Alex Rios S2 4.00 10.00
BA Bobby Abreu S2 3.00 8.00
BC Bartolo Colon S2 3.00 8.00
BE Josh Beckett Jsy S1 3.00 8.00
BJ Bobby Jenks S2 3.00 8.00
BR Brian Roberts Jsy S1 3.00 8.00
BS Ben Sheets Jsy S1 3.00 8.00
CA Chris Carpenter Jsy S1 3.00 8.00
CB Carlos Beltran Pants S1 4.00 10.00
CC Carl Crawford Pants S1 3.00 8.00
CC Carl Crawford S2 3.00 8.00
CD Carlos Delgado Jsy S1 3.00 8.00
CJ Chipper Jones S2 3.00 8.00
CL Carlos Lee Jsy S1 3.00 8.00
CP Corey Patterson Jsy S1 3.00 8.00
CS C.C. Sabathia Jsy S1 3.00 8.00
CS Curt Schilling S2 6.00 15.00
CU Chase Utley S2 4.00 10.00
DJ Derek Jeter S2 12.50 30.00
DJ Derek Jeter Pants S1 12.50 30.00
DO David Ortiz Jsy S1 4.00 10.00
DW Dontrelle Willis Jsy S1 3.00 8.00
EB Erik Bedard S2 4.00 10.00
EC Eric Chavez Jsy S1 3.00 8.00
EN Juan Encarnacion S2 3.00 8.00
FH Felix Hernandez Jsy S1 4.00 10.00
FR Jeff Francoeur S2 4.00 10.00
GS Gary Sheffield S2 3.00 8.00
HB Hank Blalock S2 3.00 8.00
HO Trevor Hoffman S2 3.00 8.00
HU Torii Hunter Jsy S1 3.00 8.00
IR Ivan Rodriguez Jsy S1 3.00 8.00
JB Jason Bay Jsy S1 3.00 8.00
JD Johnny Damon S2 3.00 8.00
JE Jim Edmonds S2 3.00 8.00
JF Jeff Francis S2 3.00 8.00
JG Jason Giambi Jsy S1 3.00 8.00
JM Joe Mauer Jsy S1 3.00 8.00
JR Jose Reyes Jsy S1 4.00 10.00
JS Johan Santana Jsy S1 3.00 8.00
JS John Smoltz S2 4.00 10.00
JT Jim Thome S2 3.00 8.00
JU Juan Uribe Jsy S1 3.00 8.00
JV Justin Verlander Jsy S1 6.00 15.00
JV Jose Vidro S2 3.00 8.00
KG Ken Griffey Jr. S2 6.00 15.00
KG Ken Griffey Jr. Pants S1 6.00 15.00
LB Lance Berkman S2 3.00 8.00
LG Luis Gonzalez S2 3.00 8.00
MC Miguel Cabrera Jsy S1 4.00 10.00
MH Matt Holliday Jsy S1 4.00 10.00
MM Melvin Mora Jsy S1 3.00 8.00
MO Justin Morneau Jsy S1 4.00 10.00
MR Manny Ramirez Jsy S1 4.00 10.00
MR Manny Ramirez S2 4.00 10.00
MS Mike Sweeney Jsy S1 3.00 8.00
MT Miguel Tejada Jsy S1 3.00 8.00
MT Mark Teixeira S2 3.00 8.00
MU Mike Mussina Jsy S1 4.00 10.00
OR Magglio Ordonez Jsy S1 3.00 8.00
PF Prince Fielder Jsy S1 4.00 10.00
RB Rocco Baldelli S2 3.00 8.00
RH Roy Halladay Jsy S1 3.00 8.00
RJ Randy Johnson S2 4.00 10.00
RN Ricky Nolasco S2 3.00 8.00
RO Roy Oswalt S2 3.00 8.00
RW Rickie Weeks S2 3.00 8.00
RZ Ryan Zimmerman Jsy S1 4.00 10.00
SD Stephen Drew S2 3.00 8.00
SK Scott Kazmir S2 3.00 8.00
SR Scott Rolen S2 3.00 8.00
SR Scott Rolen Jsy S1 4.00 10.00
TG Tom Glavine S2 4.00 10.00
TH Todd Helton S2 3.00 8.00
TH Tim Hudson Jsy S1 3.00 8.00
TN Trot Nixon S2 3.00 8.00
VG Vladimir Guerrero S2 4.00 10.00
VM Victor Martinez Jsy S1 3.00 8.00
ZD Zach Duke S2 3.00 8.00

2007 Upper Deck UD Game Patch

STATED ODDS 1:192 H, 1:2500 R
AJ Andruw Jones 15.00 40.00
AP Albert Pujols 40.00 80.00
BE Josh Beckett 10.00 25.00
BR Brian Roberts 10.00 25.00
BS Ben Sheets 10.00 25.00
CA Chris Carpenter 15.00 40.00
CB Carlos Beltran 15.00 40.00
CC Carl Crawford 10.00 25.00
CD Carlos Delgado 10.00 25.00
CL Carlos Lee 10.00 25.00
CP Corey Patterson 10.00 25.00
CS C.C. Sabathia 10.00 25.00
DJ Derek Jeter 40.00 80.00
DO David Ortiz 20.00 50.00
DW Dontrelle Willis 10.00 25.00
EC Eric Chavez 10.00 25.00
FH Felix Hernandez 15.00 40.00
HU Torii Hunter 15.00 40.00
IR Ivan Rodriguez 15.00 40.00
JB Jason Bay 15.00 40.00
JG Jason Giambi 15.00 40.00
JM Joe Mauer 15.00 40.00
JR Jose Reyes 20.00 50.00
JS Johan Santana 15.00 40.00
JU Juan Uribe 10.00 25.00
KG Ken Griffey Jr. 40.00 80.00
MC Miguel Cabrera 15.00 40.00
MH Matt Holliday 12.50 30.00
MM Melvin Mora 10.00 25.00
MO Justin Morneau 10.00 25.00
MR Manny Ramirez 20.00 50.00
MS Mike Sweeney 10.00 25.00
MT Miguel Tejada 10.00 25.00
MU Mike Mussina 10.00 25.00
OR Magglio Ordonez 10.00 25.00
PF Prince Fielder 15.00 40.00
RH Roy Halladay 10.00 25.00
RZ Ryan Zimmerman 20.00 50.00
SR Scott Rolen 20.00 50.00
TH Tim Hudson 10.00 25.00
VM Victor Martinez 15.00 40.00

2008 Upper Deck

This 400-card first series was released in February, 2008. The set was issued into the hobby in 20-card packs, with an $4.99 SRP, which came 16 packs to a box and 12 boxes to a case. Cards numbered 1-300 feature veterans in team nickname alphabetical order while cards numbered 301-350 feature 2007 rookies in alphabetical order. The first series concludes with team checklist cards (also in team nickname alphabetical order) from cards 351-380 and 20 highlight cards from 381-400.

COMPLETE SET (799) 50.00 100.00
COMP.SER.1 (1-400) 20.00 50.00
COMP.SER.2 (401-799) 20.00 50.00
COMMON CARD (1-799) .15 .40
COMMON ROOKIE (1-799) .40 1.00
1 Joe Saunders .15 .40
2 Kelvim Escobar .25 .60
3 Jered Weaver .25 .60
4 Justin Speier .25 .60
5 Scot Shields .25 .60
6 Mike Napoli .25 .60
7 Orlando Cabrera .25 .60
8 Casey Kotchman .15 .40
9 Vladimir Guerrero .25 .60
10 Garret Anderson .15 .40
11 Roy Oswalt .25 .60
12 Wandy Rodriguez .15 .40
13 Woody Williams .25 .60
14 Chad Qualls .15 .40
15 Brian Moehler .15 .40
16 Mark Loretta .25 .60
17 Brad Ausmus .15 .40
18 Ty Wigginton .25 .60
19 Carlos Lee .15 .40
20 Hunter Pence .25 .60
21 Dan Haren .15 .40
22 Lenny DiNardo .25 .60
23 Chad Gaudin .25 .60
24 Huston Street .25 .60
25 Andrew Brown .15 .40
26 Mike Piazza .40 1.00
27 Jack Cust .15 .40
28 Mark Ellis .15 .40
29 Shannon Stewart .15 .40
30 Travis Buck .25 .60
31 Shaun Marcum .15 .40
32 A.J. Burnett .15 .40
33 Jesse Litsch .25 .60
34 Casey Janssen .15 .40
35 Jeremy Accardo .25 .60
36 Gregg Zaun .15 .40
37 Aaron Hill .15 .40
38 Frank Thomas .40 1.00
39 Matt Stairs .15 .40
40 Vernon Wells .15 .40
41 Tim Hudson .25 .60
42 Chuck James .15 .40
43 Buddy Carlyle .15 .40
44 Rafael Soriano .15 .40
45 Peter Moylan .15 .40
46 Brian McCann .25 .60
47 Edgar Renteria .15 .40
48 Mark Teixeira .25 .60
49 Willie Harris .15 .40
50 Andruw Jones .15 .40
51 Ben Sheets .15 .40
52 Dave Bush .15 .40
53 Yovani Gallardo .15 .40
54 Francisco Cordero .15 .40
55 Matt Wise .15 .40
56 Johnny Estrada .15 .40
57 Prince Fielder .25 .60
58 J.J. Hardy .15 .40
59 Corey Hart .15 .40
60 Geoff Jenkins .15 .40
61 Adam Wainwright .25 .60
62 Joel Pineiro .15 .40
63 Brad Thompson .15 .40
64 Jason Isringhausen .15 .40
65 Troy Percival .15 .40
66 Yadier Molina .40 1.00
67 Albert Pujols .50 1.25
68 David Eckstein .15 .40
69 Jim Edmonds .25 .60
70 Rick Ankiel .15 .40
71 Ted Lilly .15 .40
72 Rich Hill .15 .40
73 Jason Marquis .15 .40
74 Carlos Marmol .25 .60
75 Ryan Dempster .15 .40
76 Jason Kendall .15 .40
77 Aramis Ramirez .15 .40
78 Ryan Theriot .15 .40
79 Alfonso Soriano .25 .60
80 Jacque Jones .15 .40
81 James Shields .15 .40
82 Andy Sonnanstine .15 .40
83 Scott Dohmann .15 .40
84 Al Reyes .15 .40
85 Dioner Navarro .15 .40
86 B.J. Upton .25 .60
87 Carlos Pena .25 .60
88 Brendan Harris .15 .40
89 Josh Wilson .15 .40
90 Jonny Gomes .15 .40
91 Brandon Webb .25 .60
92 Micah Owings .15 .40
93 Livan Hernandez .15 .40
94 Doug Slaten .15 .40
95 Brandon Lyon .15 .40
96 Miguel Montero .15 .40
97 Stephen Drew .15 .40
98 Mark Reynolds .15 .40
99 Conor Jackson .15 .40
100 Chris B. Young .15 .40
101 Chad Billingsley .25 .60
102 Derek Lowe .15 .40
103 Mark Hendrickson .15 .40
104 Takashi Saito .15 .40
105 Rudy Seanez .15 .40
106 Russell Martin .15 .40
107 Jeff Kent .15 .40
108 Nomar Garciaparra .25 .60
109 Matt Kemp .30 .75
110 Juan Pierre .15 .40
111 Matt Cain .25 .60
112 Barry Zito .25 .60
113 Kevin Correia .15 .40
114 Brad Hennessey .15 .40
115 Jack Taschner .15 .40
116 Bengie Molina .15 .40
117 Ryan Klesko .15 .40
118 Omar Vizquel .25 .60
119 Dave Roberts .25 .60
120 Rajai Davis .15 .40
121 Fausto Carmona .15 .40
122 Jake Westbrook .15 .40
123 Cliff Lee .25 .60
124 Rafael Betancourt .15 .40
125 Joe Borowski .15 .40
126 Victor Martinez .25 .60
127 Travis Hafner .15 .40
128 Ryan Garko .15 .40
129 Kenny Lofton .15 .40
130 Franklin Gutierrez .15 .40
131 Felix Hernandez .25 .60
132 Jeff Weaver .15 .40
133 J.J. Putz .15 .40
134 Brandon Morrow .15 .40
135 Sean Green .15 .40
136 Kenji Johjima .15 .40
137 Jose Vidro .15 .40
138 Richie Sexson .15 .40
139 Ichiro Suzuki .50 1.25
140 Ben Broussard .15 .40
141 Sergio Mitre .15 .40
142 Scott Olsen .15 .40
143 Rick Vanden Hurk .15 .40
144 Justin Miller .15 .40
145 Lee Gardner .15 .40
146 Miguel Olivo .15 .40
147 Hanley Ramirez .25 .60
148 Mike Jacobs .15 .40
149 Josh Willingham .25 .60
150 Alfredo Amezaga .15 .40
151 John Maine .15 .40
152 Tom Glavine .25 .60
153 Orlando Hernandez .15 .40
154 Billy Wagner .15 .40
155 Aaron Heilman .15 .40
156 David Wright .25 .60
157 Luis Castillo .15 .40
158 Shawn Green .15 .40
159 Damion Easley .15 .40
160 Carlos Delgado .15 .40
161 Shawn Hill .15 .40
162 Mike Bacsik .15 .40
163 John Lannan .15 .40
164 Chad Cordero .15 .40
165 Jon Rauch .15 .40
166 Jesus Flores .15 .40
167 Dmitri Young .15 .40
168 Cristian Guzman .15 .40
169 Austin Kearns .15 .40
170 Nook Logan .15 .40
171 Erik Bedard .15 .40
172 Daniel Cabrera .15 .40
173 Chris Ray .15 .40
174 Danys Baez .15 .40
175 Chad Bradford .15 .40
176 Ramon Hernandez .15 .40
177 Miguel Tejada .25 .60
178 Freddie Bynum .15 .40
179 Corey Patterson .15 .40
180 Aubrey Huff .15 .40
181 Chris Young .15 .40
182 Greg Maddux .50 1.25
183 Clay Hensley .15 .40
184 Kevin Cameron .15 .40
185 Doug Brocail .15 .40
186 Josh Bard .15 .40
187 Kevin Kouzmanoff .15 .40
188 Geoff Blum .15 .40
189 Milton Bradley .15 .40
190 Brian Giles .15 .40
191 Jamie Moyer .15 .40
192 Kyle Kendrick .15 .40
193 Kyle Lohse .15 .40
194 Antonio Alfonseca .15 .40
195 Ryan Madson .15 .40
196 Chris Coste .15 .40
197 Chase Utley .25 .60
198 Tadahito Iguchi .15 .40
199 Aaron Rowand .15 .40
200 Shane Victorino .15 .40
201 Paul Maholm .15 .40
202 Ian Snell .15 .40
203 Shane Youman .15 .40
204 Damaso Marte .15 .40
205 Shawn Chacon .15 .40
206 Ronny Paulino .15 .40
207 Jack Wilson .15 .40
208 Adam LaRoche .15 .40
209 Ryan Doumit .15 .40
210 Xavier Nady .15 .40
211 Kevin Millwood .15 .40
212 Brandon McCarthy .15 .40
213 Joaquin Benoit .15 .40
214 Wes Littleton .15 .40
215 Mike Wood .15 .40
216 Gerald Laird .15 .40
217 Hank Blalock .15 .40
218 Ian Kinsler .25 .60
219 Marlon Byrd .15 .40
220 Brad Wilkerson .15 .40
221 Tim Wakefield .25 .60
222 Daisuke Matsuzaka .25 .60
223 Julian Tavarez .15 .40
224 Hideki Okajima .15 .40
225 Manny Delcarmen .15 .40
226 Doug Mirabelli .15 .40
227 Dustin Pedroia .25 .60
228 Mike Lowell .15 .40
229 Manny Ramirez .40 1.00
230 Coco Crisp .15 .40
231 Bronson Arroyo .15 .40
232 Matt Belisle .15 .40
233 Jared Burton .15 .40
234 David Weathers .15 .40
235 Mike Gosling .15 .40
236 David Ross .15 .40
237 Jeff Keppinger .15 .40
238 Edwin Encarnacion .40 1.00
239 Ken Griffey Jr. .75 2.00
240 Adam Dunn .25 .60
241 Jeff Francis .15 .40
242 Jason Hirsh .15 .40
243 Josh Fogg .15 .40
244 Manny Corpas .15 .40
245 Jeremy Affeldt .15 .40
246 Yorvit Torrealba .15 .40
247 Todd Helton .25 .60
248 Kazuo Matsui .15 .40
249 Brad Hawpe .15 .40
250 Willy Taveras .15 .40
251 Brian Bannister .15 .40
252 Zack Greinke .25 .60
253 Kyle Davies .15 .40
254 David Riske .15 .40
255 Joel Peralta .15 .40
256 John Buck .15 .40
257 Mark Grudzielanek .15 .40
258 Ross Gload .15 .40
259 Billy Butler .15 .40
260 David DeJesus .15 .40
261 Jeremy Bonderman .15 .40
262 Chad Durbin .15 .40
263 Andrew Miller .25 .60
264 Bobby Seay .15 .40
265 Todd Jones .15 .40
266 Brandon Inge .15 .40
267 Sean Casey .15 .40
268 Placido Polanco .15 .40
269 Gary Sheffield .15 .40
270 Magglio Ordonez .25 .60
271 Matt Garza .15 .40
272 Boof Bonser .15 .40
273 Scott Baker .15 .40
274 Joe Nathan .15 .40
275 Dennys Reyes .15 .40
276 Joe Mauer .30 .75
277 Michael Cuddyer .15 .40
278 Jason Bartlett .15 .40
279 Torii Hunter .15 .40
280 Jason Tyner .15 .40
281 Mark Buehrle .25 .60
282 Jon Garland .15 .40
283 Jose Contreras .15 .40
284 Matt Thornton .15 .40
285 Ryan Bukvich .15 .40
286 Juan Uribe .15 .40
287 Jim Thome .25 .60
288 Scott Podsednik .15 .40
289 Jerry Owens .15 .40
290 Jermaine Dye .15 .40
291 Andy Pettitte .25 .60
292 Phil Hughes .15 .40
293 Mike Mussina .25 .60
294 Joba Chamberlain .15 .40
295 Brian Bruney .15 .40
296 Jorge Posada .25 .60
297 Derek Jeter 1.00 2.50
298 Jason Giambi .15 .40
299 Johnny Damon .25 .60
300 Melky Cabrera .15 .40
301 Jonathan Albaladejo RC .60 1.50
302 Josh Anderson (RC) .40 1.00
303 Wladimir Balentien (RC) .40 1.00
304 Josh Banks (RC) .40 1.00
305 Daric Barton (RC) .40 1.00
306 Jerry Blevins RC .60 1.50
307 Emilio Bonifacio RC 1.00 2.50
308 Lance Broadway (RC) .40 1.00
309 Clay Buchholz (RC) .60 1.50
310 Billy Buckner (RC) .40 1.00
311 Jeff Clement (RC) .60 1.50
312 Willie Collazo RC .60 1.50
313 Ross Detwiler RC .60 1.50
314 Sam Fuld RC 1.25 3.00
315 Harvey Garcia (RC) .40 1.00
316 Alberto Gonzalez RC .60 1.50
317 Ryan Hanigan RC .60 1.50
318 Kevin Hart (RC) .40 1.00
319 Luke Hochevar RC .60 1.50
320 Chin-Lung Hu (RC) .40 1.00
321 Rob Johnson (RC) .40 1.00
322 Radhames Liz RC .60 1.50
323 Ian Kennedy RC 1.00 2.50
324 Joe Koshansky (RC) .40 1.00
325 Donny Lucy (RC) .40 1.00
326 Justin Maxwell RC .40 1.00
327 Jonathan Meloan RC .60 1.50
328 Luis Mendoza (RC) .40 1.00
329 Jose Morales (RC) .40 1.00
330 Nyjer Morgan (RC) .40 1.00
331 Carlos Muniz RC .60 1.50
332 Bill Murphy (RC) .40 1.00
333 Josh Newman RC .60 1.50
334 Ross Ohlendorf RC .60 1.50
335 Troy Patton (RC) .40 1.00
336 Felipe Paulino RC .60 1.50
337 Steve Pearce RC 2.00 5.00
338 Heath Phillips RC .60 1.50
339 Justin Ruggiano RC .60 1.50
340 Clint Sammons (RC) .40 1.00
341 Bronson Sardinha (RC) .40 1.00
342 Chris Seddon (RC) .40 1.00
343 Seth Smith (RC) .40 1.00
344 Mitch Stetter RC .60 1.50
345 Dave Davidson RC .60 1.50
346 Rich Thompson RC .60 1.50
347 J.R. Towles RC .60 1.50
348 Eugenio Velez RC .40 1.00
349 Joey Votto (RC) 1.50 4.00
350 Bill White RC .40 1.00
351 Vladimir Guerrero CL .25 .60
352 Lance Berkman CL .25 .60
353 Dan Haren CL .15 .40
354 Frank Thomas CL .40 1.00
355 Chipper Jones CL .40 1.00
356 Prince Fielder CL .25 .60
357 Albert Pujols CL .50 1.25
358 Alfonso Soriano CL .25 .60
359 B.J. Upton CL .25 .60
360 Eric Byrnes CL .15 .40
361 Russell Martin CL .15 .40
362 Tim Lincecum CL .25 .60
363 Grady Sizemore CL .25 .60
364 Ichiro Suzuki CL .50 1.25
365 Hanley Ramirez CL .25 .60
366 David Wright CL .25 .60
367 Ryan Zimmerman CL .25 .60
368 Nick Markakis CL .30 .75
369 Jake Peavy CL .15 .40
370 Ryan Howard CL .25 .60
371 Freddy Sanchez CL .15 .40
372 Michael Young CL .15 .40
373 David Ortiz CL .40 1.00
374 Ken Griffey Jr. CL .75 2.00
375 Matt Holliday CL .40 1.00
376 Brian Bannister CL .15 .40
377 Magglio Ordonez CL .25 .60
378 Johan Santana CL .25 .60
379 Jim Thome CL .25 .60
380 Alex Rodriguez CL .50 1.25
381 Alex Rodriguez HL .50 1.25
382 Brandon Webb HL .25 .60
383 Chone Figgins HL .15 .40
384 Clay Buchholz HL .25 .60
385 Curtis Granderson HL .25 .60
386 Frank Thomas HL .40 1.00
387 Fred Lewis HL .15 .40
388 Garret Anderson HL .15 .40
389 J.R. Towles HL .25 .60
390 Jake Peavy HL .15 .40
391 Jim Thome HL .25 .60
392 Jimmy Rollins HL .25 .60
393 Johan Santana HL .25 .60
394 Justin Verlander HL .40 1.00
395 Mark Buehrle HL .15 .40
396 Matt Holliday HL .40 1.00
397 Jarrod Saltalamacchia HL .15 .40
398 Sammy Sosa HL .40 1.00
399 Tom Glavine HL .25 .60
400 Trevor Hoffman HL .25 .60
401 Dan Haren .15 .40
402 Randy Johnson .40 1.00
403 Chris Burke .15 .40
404 Orlando Hudson .15 .40
405 Justin Upton .25 .60
406 Eric Byrnes .15 .40
407 Doug Davis .15 .40
408 Chad Tracy .15 .40
409 Tom Glavine .25 .60
410 Kelly Johnson .15 .40
411 Chipper Jones .40 1.00
412 Matt Diaz .15 .40
413 Jeff Francoeur .25 .60
414 Mark Kotsay .15 .40
415 John Smoltz .40 1.00
416 Tyler Yates .15 .40
417 Yunel Escobar .15 .40
418 Mike Hampton .15 .40
419 Luke Scott .15 .40
420 Adam Jones .25 .60
421 Jeremy Guthrie .15 .40
422 Nick Markakis .30 .75
423 Jay Payton .15 .40
424 Brian Roberts .15 .40
425 Melvin Mora .15 .40
426 Adam Loewen .15 .40
427 Luis Hernandez .15 .40
428 Steve Trachsel .15 .40
429 Josh Beckett .15 .40
430 Jon Lester .25 .60
431 Curt Schilling .25 .60
432 Jonathan Papelbon .25 .60
433 Jason Varitek .40 1.00
434 David Ortiz .40 1.00
435 Jacoby Ellsbury .30 .75
436 Julio Lugo .15 .40
437 Sean Casey .15 .40
438 Kevin Youkilis .15 .40
439 J.D. Drew .15 .40
440 Alex Cora .25 .60
441 Derrek Lee .15 .40
442 Carlos Zambrano .25 .60
443 Sean Marshall .15 .40
444 Matt Murton .15 .40
445 Kerry Wood .15 .40
446 Felix Pie .15 .40
447 Mark DeRosa .15 .40
448 Ronny Cedeno .15 .40
449 Jon Lieber .15 .40
450 Geovany Soto .40 1.00
451 Gavin Floyd .15 .40
452 Bobby Jenks .15 .40
453 Scott Linebrink .15 .40
454 Javier Vazquez .15 .40
455 A.J. Pierzynski .15 .40
456 Orlando Cabrera .25 .60
457 Joe Crede .15 .40
458 Josh Fields .15 .40
459 Paul Konerko .25 .60
460 Brian Anderson .15 .40
461 Nick Swisher .25 .60
462 Carlos Quentin .15 .40
463 Homer Bailey .25 .60
464 Francisco Cordero .15 .40
465 Aaron Harang .15 .40
466 Alex Gonzalez .15 .40
467 Brandon Phillips .15 .40
468 Ryan Freel .15 .40
469 Scott Hatteberg .15 .40
470 Juan Castro .15 .40
471 Norris Hopper .15 .40
472 Josh Barfield .15 .40
473 Casey Blake .15 .40
474 Paul Byrd .15 .40
475 Grady Sizemore .25 .60
476 Jason Michaels .15 .40
477 Jhonny Peralta .15 .40
478 Asdrubal Cabrera .25 .60
479 David Dellucci .15 .40
480 C.C. Sabathia .25 .60
481 Andy Marte .15 .40
482 Troy Tulowitzki .40 1.00
483 Matt Holliday .40 1.00
484 Garrett Atkins .15 .40
485 Aaron Cook .15 .40
486 Brian Fuentes .15 .40
487 Ryan Spilborghs .15 .40
488 Ubaldo Jimenez .15 .40
489 Jayson Nix .15 .40
490 Nate Robertson .15 .40
491 Kenny Rogers .15 .40
492 Justin Verlander .40 1.00
493 Dontrelle Willis .15 .40
494 Joel Zumaya .15 .40
495 Ivan Rodriguez .25 .60
496 Miguel Cabrera .40 1.00
497 Carlos Guillen .15 .40
498 Edgar Renteria .15 .40
499 Curtis Granderson .25 .60
500 Jacque Jones .15 .40
501 Marcus Thames .15 .40
502 Josh Johnson .25 .60
503 Jeremy Hermida .15 .40
504 Dan Uggla .15 .40
505 Mark Hendrickson .15 .40
506 Luis Gonzalez .15 .40
507 Dallas McPherson .15 .40
508 Cody Ross .15 .40
509 Matt Treanor .15 .40
510 Andrew Miller .25 .60
511 Jorge Cantu .15 .40
512 Kazuo Matsui .15 .40
513 Lance Berkman .25 .60
514 Darin Erstad .15 .40
515 Miguel Tejada .25 .60
516 Jose Valverde .15 .40
517 Geoff Blum .15 .40
518 Reggie Abercrombie .15 .40
519 Brandon Backe .15 .40
520 Michael Bourn .15 .40
521 Gil Meche .15 .40
522 Brett Tomko .15 .40
523 Miguel Olivo .15 .40
524 Shane Costa .15 .40
525 Joey Gathright .15 .40
526 Mark Teahen .15 .40
527 Alex Gordon .25 .60
528 Tony Pena .15 .40
529 Jose Guillen .15 .40
530 Torii Hunter .15 .40
531 Ervin Santana .15 .40
532 Francisco Rodriguez .25 .60
533 Howie Kendrick .15 .40
534 Reggie Willits .15 .40
535 John Lackey .25 .60
536 Gary Matthews .15 .40
537 Jon Garland .15 .40
538 Kendry Morales .15 .40
539 Chone Figgins .15 .40
540 Andruw Jones .15 .40
541 Jason Schmidt .15 .40
542 James Loney .15 .40
543 Andre Ethier .25 .60
544 Rafael Furcal .15 .40
545 Brad Penny .15 .40
546 Hong-Chih Kuo .15 .40
547 Jonathan Broxton .15 .40
548 Esteban Loaiza .15 .40
549 Delwyn Young .15 .40
550 Mike Cameron .15 .40
551 Ryan Braun .25 .60
552 Rickie Weeks .15 .40
553 Bill Hall .15 .40
554 Tony Gwynn Jr. .15 .40
555 Eric Gagne .15 .40
556 Jeff Suppan .15 .40
557 Chris Capuano .15 .40
558 Derrick Turnbow .15 .40
559 Jason Kendall .15 .40
560 Livan Hernandez .15 .40
561 Philip Humber .15 .40
562 Francisco Liriano .15 .40
563 Pat Neshek .25 .60
564 Adam Everett .15 .40
565 Brendan Harris .15 .40
566 Justin Morneau .25 .60
567 Craig Monroe .15 .40
568 Carlos Gomez .15 .40
569 Delmon Young .25 .60
570 Mike Lamb .15 .40
571 Oliver Perez .15 .40
572 Jose Reyes .25 .60
573 Moises Alou .15 .40
574 Carlos Beltran .25 .60
575 Endy Chavez .15 .40
576 Ryan Church .15 .40
577 Pedro Martinez .25 .60
578 Johan Santana .25 .60
579 Mike Pelfrey .15 .40
580 Brian Schneider .15 .40
581 Joe Smith .15 .40
582 Matt Wise .15 .40
583 Duaner Sanchez .15 .40
584 Ramon Castro .15 .40
585 Kei Igawa .15 .40
586 Mariano Rivera .50 1.25
587 Chien-Ming Wang .25 .60
588 Wilson Betemit .15 .40
589 Robinson Cano .25 .60
590 Alex Rodriguez .50 1.25
591 Bobby Abreu .15 .40
592 Shelley Duncan .15 .40
593 Hideki Matsui .40 1.00
594 Kyle Farnsworth .15 .40
595 Joe Blanton .15 .40
596 Bobby Crosby .15 .40
597 Eric Chavez .15 .40
598 Dan Johnson .15 .40
599 Rich Harden .15 .40
600 Justin Duchscherer .15 .40
601 Kurt Suzuki .15 .40
602 Chris Denorfia .15 .40
603 Emil Brown .15 .40
604 Ryan Howard .25 .60
605 Jimmy Rollins .25 .60
606 Pedro Feliz .15 .40
607 Adam Eaton .15 .40
608 Brad Lidge .15 .40
609 Brett Myers .15 .40
610 Pat Burrell .15 .40
611 So Taguchi .15 .40
612 Geoff Jenkins .15 .40
613 Tom Gordon .15 .40
614 Zach Duke .15 .40
615 Matt Morris .15 .40
616 Tom Gorzelanny .15 .40
617 Jason Bay .25 .60
618 Chris Duffy .15 .40
619 Freddy Sanchez .15 .40
620 Jose Bautista .25 .60
621 Nyjer Morgan .15 .40
622 Matt Capps .15 .40
623 Paul Maholm .15 .40
624 Tadahito Iguchi .15 .40
625 Adrian Gonzalez .25 .60
626 Jim Edmonds .25 .60
627 Jake Peavy .15 .40
628 Khalil Greene .15 .40
629 Trevor Hoffman .25 .60
630 Mark Prior .25 .60
631 Randy Wolf .15 .40
632 Michael Barrett .15 .40
633 Scott Hairston .15 .40
634 Tim Lincecum .25 .60
635 Noah Lowry .15 .40
636 Rich Aurilia .15 .40
637 Aaron Rowand .15 .40
638 Randy Winn .15 .40
639 Daniel Ortmeier .15 .40
640 Ray Durham .15 .40
641 Brian Wilson .40 1.00
642 Adrian Beltre .40 1.00
643 Jeremy Reed .15 .40
644 Jarrod Washburn .15 .40
645 Yuniesky Betancourt .15 .40
646 Jose Lopez .15 .40
647 Raul Ibanez .25 .60
648 Mike Morse .15 .40
649 Erik Bedard .15 .40
650 Brad Wilkerson .15 .40
651 Chris Carpenter .25 .60
652 Mark Mulder .15 .40
653 Juan Encarnacion .15 .40
654 Skip Schumaker .15 .40
655 Troy Glaus .25 .60
656 Anthony Reyes .15 .40
657 Cesar Izturis .15 .40
658 Adam Kennedy .15 .40
659 Chris Duncan .15 .40
660 Matt Clement .15 .40
661 Scott Kazmir .25 .60
662 Troy Percival .15 .40
663 Akinori Iwamura .15 .40
664 Carl Crawford .25 .60
665 Cliff Floyd .15 .40
666 Jason Bartlett .15 .40
667 Rocco Baldelli .15 .40
668 Matt Garza .15 .40
669 Edwin Jackson .15 .40
670 Vicente Padilla .15 .40
671 Josh Hamilton .25 .60
672 Jason Botts .15 .40
673 Milton Bradley .15 .40
674 Michael Young .15 .40
675 Eddie Guardado .15 .40
676 David Murphy .15 .40
677 Ramon Vazquez .15 .40
678 Ben Broussard .15 .40
679 C.J. Wilson .15 .40
680 Jason Jennings .15 .40
681 Gustavo Chacin .15 .40
682 BJ Ryan .15 .40
683 David Eckstein .15 .40
684 Alex Rios .15 .40
685 John McDonald .15 .40
686 Rod Barajas .15 .40
687 Lyle Overbay .15 .40
688 Scott Rolen .25 .60
689 Reed Johnson .15 .40
690 Marco Scutaro .25 .60
691 Lastings Milledge .15 .40
692 Johnny Estrada .15 .40
693 Paul Lo Duca .15 .40
694 Ryan Zimmerman .25 .60
695 Odalis Perez .15 .40
696 Wily Mo Pena .15 .40
697 Elijah Dukes .15 .40
698 Aaron Boone .25 .60
699 Ronnie Belliard .15 .40
700 Nick Johnson .15 .40
701 Randor Bierd RC .40 1.00
702 Brian Barton RC .60 1.50
703 Brian Bass (RC) .40 1.00
704 Brian Bocock RC .40 1.00
705 Gregor Blanco (RC) .40 1.00
706 Callix Crabbe (RC) .40 1.00
707 Johnny Cueto RC 1.00 2.50
708 Kosuke Fukudome RC 4.00 10.00
708b K.Fukudome Japanese 40.00 80.00
709 Scott Kazmir SH .25 .60
710 Steve Holm RC .40 1.00
711 Fernando Hernandez RC .40 1.00
712 Elliot Johnson (RC) .40 1.00
713 Masahide Kobayashi RC .60 1.50
714 Hiroki Kuroda RC 1.00 2.50
715 Blake DeWitt (RC) .60 1.50
716 Kyle McClellan RC .40 1.00
717 Evan Meek RC .40 1.00
718 Denard Span (RC) .60 1.50
719 Darren O'Day RC .40 1.00
720 Alexei Ramirez RC 1.25 3.00

Alex Romero (RC) .60 1.50
Clete Thomas RC .60 1.50
Matt Tolbert RC .60 1.50
Ramon Troncoso RC .40 1.00
Matt Tupman RC .40 1.00
Rico Washington (RC) .40 1.00
7 Randy Wells RC .60 1.50
8 Wesley Wright RC .40 1.00
Yasuhiko Yabuta RC .60 1.50
Alex Rodriguez SH .50 1.25
Andruw Jones SH .15 .40
2 C.C. Sabathia SH .25 .60
3 Carlos Beltran SH .25 .60
4 David Wright SH .25 .60
5 Derrek Lee SH .15 .40
6 Dustin Pedroia SH .25 .60
7 Grady Sizemore SH .25 .60
8 Greg Maddux SH .50 1.25
9 Ichiro Suzuki SH .50 1.25
0 Ivan Rodriguez SH .25 .60
1 Jake Peavy SH .15 .40
2 Jimmy Rollins SH .25 .60
3 Johan Santana SH .25 .60
4 Josh Beckett SH .15 .40
5 Kevin Youkilis SH .15 .40
6 Matt Holliday SH .40 1.00
7 Mike Lowell SH .15 .40
8 Ryan Braun SH .25 .60
9 Torii Hunter SH .15 .40
0 Alex Rodriguez SH .50 1.25
1 Torii Hunter CL .15 .40
2 Miguel Tejada CL .25 .60
3 Huston Street CL .25 .60
4 Scott Rolen CL .25 .60
5 Tom Glavine CL .25 .60
6 Ryan Braun CL .25 .60
7 Troy Glaus CL .25 .60
8 Carlos Zambrano CL .25 .60
9 Carl Crawford CL .25 .60
60 Dan Haren CL .15 .40
61 Andruw Jones CL .15 .40
62 Barry Zito CL .25 .60
63 Victor Martinez CL .25 .60
64 Erik Bedard CL .15 .40
65 Josh Willingham CL .25 .60
66 Johan Santana CL .25 .60
67 Dmitri Young CL .15 .40
68 Brian Roberts CL .15 .40
69 Jim Edmonds CL .25 .60
70 Jimmy Rollins CL .25 .60
71 Jason Bay CL .25 .60
72 Josh Hamilton CL .25 .60
73 Josh Beckett CL .15 .40
74 Aaron Harang CL .15 .40
775 Troy Tulowitzki CL .40 1.00
776 Jose Guillen CL .15 .40
777 Miguel Cabrera CL .40 1.00
778 Joe Mauer CL .30 .75
779 Nick Swisher CL .25 .60
780 Derek Jeter CL 1.00 2.50
781 Brandon Webb SH .25 .60
782 Brian Roberts SH .15 .40
783 C.C. Sabathia SH .25 .60
784 Carl Crawford SH .25 .60
785 Curtis Granderson SH .25 .60
786 David Ortiz SH .40 1.00
787 Ichiro Suzuki SH .50 1.25
788 Jake Peavy SH .15 .40
789 Jimmy Rollins SH .25 .60
790 Joe Borowski SH .15 .40
791 Johan Santana SH .25 .60
792 John Lackey SH .25 .60
793 Jose Reyes SH .25 .60
794 Jose Valverde SH .15 .40
795 Josh Beckett SH .15 .40
796 Juan Pierre SH .15 .40
797 Magglio Ordonez SH .25 .60
798 Matt Holliday SH .40 1.00
799 Prince Fielder SH .25 .60

2008 Upper Deck Gold

*GOLD VET: 4X TO 10X BASIC
*GOLD RC: 3X TO 8X BASIC
RANDOM INSERTS IN PACKS
STATED PRINT RUN 99 SER. #'d SETS
708 Kosuke Fukudome 50.00 100.00

2008 Upper Deck A Piece of History 500 Club

STATED ODDS 1:192 HOBBY
EXCHANGE DEADLINE 1/14/2010

FT Frank Thomas 15.00 40.00
JT Jim Thome 15.00 40.00

2008 Upper Deck All Rookie Team Signatures

STATED ODDS 1:80 H, 1:7500 R
AI Akinori Iwamura 10.00 25.00
AL Adam Lind 3.00 8.00
BB Billy Butler 5.00 12.00
BU Brian Burres 3.00 8.00
DY Delmon Young 6.00 15.00
HA Justin Hampson 3.00 8.00
JH Josh Hamilton 12.50 30.00
KC Kevin Cameron 3.00 8.00
KK Kyle Kendrick 6.00 15.00
MB Michael Bourn 3.00 8.00
MF Mike Fontenot 5.00 12.00
MO Micah Owings 5.00 12.00
RB Ryan Braun 10.00 25.00
SO Joakim Soria 3.00 8.00

2008 Upper Deck Derek Jeter O-Pee-Chee Reprints

STATED ODDS 1:6 TARGET
DJ1 Derek Jeter 1.50 4.00
DJ2 Derek Jeter 1.50 4.00
DJ3 Derek Jeter 1.50 4.00
DJ4 Derek Jeter 1.50 4.00
DJ5 Derek Jeter 1.50 4.00
DJ6 Derek Jeter 1.50 4.00
DJ7 Derek Jeter 1.50 4.00
DJ8 Derek Jeter 1.50 4.00
DJ9 Derek Jeter 1.50 4.00
DJ10 Derek Jeter 1.50 4.00
DJ11 Derek Jeter 1.50 4.00
DJ12 Derek Jeter 1.50 4.00
DJ13 Derek Jeter 1.50 4.00
DJ14 Derek Jeter 1.50 4.00
DJ15 Derek Jeter 1.50 4.00

2008 Upper Deck Diamond Collection

COMPLETE SET (20) 6.00 15.00
1 Adam LaRoche .40 1.00
2 Brian McCann .60 1.50
3 Bronson Arroyo .40 1.00
4 Chad Billingsley .60 1.50
5 Chin-Lung Hu .40 1.00
6 Felix Pie .40 1.00
7 Garrett Atkins .40 1.00
8 Homer Bailey .60 1.50
9 Ian Kennedy 1.00 2.50
10 James Shields .40 1.00
11 Jarrod Saltalamacchia .40 1.00
12 Manny Corpas .40 1.00
13 Mark Ellis .40 1.00
14 Micah Owings .40 1.00
15 Nick Swisher .60 1.50
16 Rich Hill .40 1.00
17 Russell Martin .40 1.00
18 Ryan Theriot .40 1.00
19 Steve Pearce 2.00 5.00
20 Victor Martinez .60 1.50

2008 Upper Deck Hit Brigade

HB1 Albert Pujols 1.25 3.00
HB2 Alex Rodriguez 1.25 3.00
HB3 David Ortiz 1.00 2.50
HB4 David Wright .60 1.50
HB5 Derek Jeter 2.50 6.00
HB6 Derrek Lee .40 1.00
HB7 Freddy Sanchez .40 1.00
HB8 Hanley Ramirez .60 1.50
HB9 Ichiro Suzuki 1.25 3.00
HB10 Joe Mauer .75 2.00
HB11 Magglio Ordonez .60 1.50
HB12 Matt Holliday 1.00 2.50
HB13 Miguel Cabrera 1.00 2.50
HB14 Todd Helton .60 1.50
HB15 Vladimir Guerrero .60 1.50

2008 Upper Deck Hot Commodities

COMPLETE SET (50) 8.00 20.00
STATED ODDS 2:1 WALMART/FAT PACKS
HC1 Miguel Tejada .60 1.50
HC2 Daisuke Matsuzaka .60 1.50
HC3 David Ortiz 1.00 2.50
HC4 Manny Ramirez 1.00 2.50
HC5 Alex Rodriguez 1.25 3.00
HC6 Derek Jeter 2.50 6.00
HC7 Carl Crawford .60 1.50
HC8 Alex Rios .40 1.00
HC9 Jim Thome .60 1.50
HC10 Grady Sizemore .60 1.50
HC11 Travis Hafner .40 1.00
HC12 Victor Martinez .60 1.50
HC13 Justin Verlander 1.00 2.50
HC14 Magglio Ordonez .60 1.50
HC15 Gary Sheffield .40 1.00
HC16 Alex Gordon .60 1.50
HC17 Justin Morneau .60 1.50
HC18 Johan Santana .60 1.50
HC19 Vladimir Guerrero .60 1.50
HC20 Dan Haren .40 1.00
HC21 Ichiro Suzuki 1.25 3.00
HC22 Mark Teixeira .60 1.50
HC23 Chipper Jones 1.00 2.50
HC24 John Smoltz 1.00 2.50
HC25 Miguel Cabrera 1.00 2.50
HC26 Hanley Ramirez .60 1.50
HC27 Jose Reyes .60 1.50
HC28 David Wright .60 1.50
HC29 Carlos Beltran .60 1.50
HC30 Ryan Howard .60 1.50
HC31 Chase Utley .60 1.50
HC32 Ryan Zimmerman .60 1.50
HC33 Aramis Ramirez .40 1.00
HC34 Derrek Lee .40 1.00
HC35 Alfonso Soriano .60 1.50
HC36 Ken Griffey Jr. 2.00 5.00
HC37 Adam Dunn .60 1.50
HC38 Carlos Lee .40 1.00
HC39 Lance Berkman .60 1.50
HC40 Prince Fielder .60 1.50
HC41 Ryan Braun .60 1.50
HC42 Jason Bay .60 1.50
HC43 Albert Pujols 1.25 3.00
HC44 Brandon Webb .60 1.50
HC45 Matt Holliday 1.00 2.50
HC46 Brad Penny .40 1.00
HC47 Russell Martin .40 1.00
HC48 Trevor Hoffman .60 1.50
HC49 Jake Peavy .40 1.00
HC50 Tim Lincecum .60 1.50

2008 Upper Deck Infield Power

RANDOM INSERTS IN RETAIL PACKS
AB Adrian Beltre .60 1.50
AG Alex Gordon .40 1.00
AP Albert Pujols .75 2.00
AR Aramis Ramirez .25 .60
BP Brandon Phillips .25 .60
BR Brian Roberts .25 .60
CJ Chipper Jones .60 1.50
CP Carlos Pena .40 1.00
CU Chase Utley .40 1.00
DJ Derek Jeter 1.50 4.00
DW David Wright .40 1.00
GA Garrett Atkins .25 .60
GO Adrian Gonzalez .40 1.00
HK Howie Kendrick .25 .60
HR Hanley Ramirez .40 1.00
JI Jimmy Rollins .40 1.00
JK Jeff Kent .25 .60
JM Justin Morneau .40 1.00
JR Jose Reyes .40 1.00
LB Lance Berkman .40 1.00
MC Miguel Cabrera .60 1.50
ML Mike Lowell .25 .60
MT Mark Teixeira .40 1.00
PF Prince Fielder .40 1.00
PK Paul Konerko .40 1.00
RG Ryan Garko .25 .60
RH Ryan Howard .60 1.50
RO Alex Rodriguez .75 2.00
RZ Ryan Zimmerman .40 1.00
TT Troy Tulowitzki .60 1.50

2008 Upper Deck Inkredible

STATED ODDS 1:80 H, 1:7500 R
AL Adam Lind 3.00 8.00
CP Corey Patterson 3.00 8.00
CR Cody Ross 6.00 15.00
DL Derrek Lee 6.00 15.00
EA Erick Aybar 3.00 8.00
IK Ian Kinsler 5.00 12.00
IR Ivan Rodriguez 20.00 50.00
JB Josh Barfield 5.00 12.00
JH Jason Hammel 3.00 8.00
JS James Shields 3.00 8.00
KE Ian Kennedy 5.00 12.00
LS Luke Scott 3.00 8.00
MJ Mike Jacobs 5.00 12.00
RC Ryan Church 3.00 8.00
RL Ruddy Lugo 3.00 8.00
RS Ryan Shealy 3.00 8.00
RT Ryan Theriot 6.00 15.00
SO Jorge Sosa 5.00 12.00
TB Taylor Buchholz 3.00 8.00

2008 Upper Deck Milestone Memorabilia

STATED ODDS 1:192 HOBBY
GS Gary Sheffield 4.00 10.00
KG Ken Griffey Jr. 6.00 15.00
TG Tom Glavine 6.00 15.00
TH Trevor Hoffman 4.00 10.00

2008 Upper Deck Mr. November

STATED ODDS 1:6 TARGET
1 Derek Jeter 1.50 4.00
2 Derek Jeter 1.50 4.00
3 Derek Jeter 1.50 4.00
4 Derek Jeter 1.50 4.00
5 Derek Jeter 1.50 4.00
6 Derek Jeter 1.50 4.00
7 Derek Jeter 1.50 4.00
8 Derek Jeter 1.50 4.00
9 Derek Jeter 1.50 4.00
10 Derek Jeter 1.50 4.00
11 Derek Jeter 1.50 4.00
12 Derek Jeter 1.50 4.00
13 Derek Jeter 1.50 4.00
14 Derek Jeter 1.50 4.00
15 Derek Jeter 1.50 4.00

2008 Upper Deck O-Pee-Chee

COMPLETE SET (50) 30.00 60.00
STATED ODDS 1:2 HOBBY
AG Alex Gordon .60 1.50
AP Albert Pujols 1.25 3.00
AR Alex Rodriguez 1.25 3.00
BP Brad Penny .40 1.00
BR Babe Ruth 2.50 6.00
BU B.J. Upton .60 1.50
BW Brandon Webb .60 1.50
CD Chris Duncan .40 1.00
CJ Chipper Jones 1.00 2.50
CL Carlos Lee .40 1.00
CP Carlos Pena .60 1.50
CU Chase Utley .60 1.50
CY Chris Young .40 1.00
DH Dan Haren .40 1.00
DJ Derek Jeter 2.50 6.00
DL Derrek Lee .40 1.00
DM Daisuke Matsuzaka .60 1.50
DO David Ortiz 1.00 2.50
DW David Wright .60 1.50
EB Erik Bedard .40 1.00
ER Edgar Renteria .40 1.00
GS Gary Sheffield .40 1.00
HP Hunter Pence .60 1.50
HR Hanley Ramirez .60 1.50
IS Ichiro Suzuki 1.25 3.00
JB Jason Bay .60 1.50
JJ J.J. Putz .40 1.00
JM Justin Morneau .60 1.50
JP Jake Peavy .40 1.00
JR Jose Reyes .60 1.50
JS Johan Santana .60 1.50
JT Jim Thome .60 1.50
JW Jered Weaver .60 1.50
KG Ken Griffey Jr. 2.00 5.00
MC Miguel Cabrera 1.00 2.50
MH Matt Holliday 1.00 2.50
MO Magglio Ordonez .60 1.50
MR Manny Ramirez 1.00 2.50
MT Mark Teixeira .60 1.50
NL Noah Lowry .40 1.00
PF Prince Fielder .60 1.50
PH Brandon Phillips .40 1.00
RA Aramis Ramirez .40 1.00
RB Ryan Braun .60 1.50
RH Ryan Howard .60 1.50
RM Russell Martin .40 1.00
RZ Ryan Zimmerman .60 1.50
TH Todd Helton .60 1.50
VG Vladimir Guerrero .60 1.50
VW Vernon Wells .40 1.00

2008 Upper Deck Presidential Predictors

COMP SET w/o HILLARY (8) 15.00 40.00
STATED ODDS 1:6 H,1:6 R,1:10 WAL MART
PP1 Rudy Giuliani 2.00 5.00
PP2 John Edwards 2.00 5.00
PP3 John McCain 2.00 5.00
PP4 Barack Obama 4.00 10.00
PP5 Mitt Romney 2.00 5.00
PP6 Fred Thompson 2.00 5.00
PP7 Hillary Clinton SP 40.00 80.00
PP8 A.Gore/G.Bush 2.00 5.00
PP9 Wild Card 2.00 5.00
PV1 Barack Obama Victor 4.00 10.00
PP15 Sarah Palin 40.00 80.00
PP16 Joe Biden 10.00 25.00

2008 Upper Deck Presidential Running Mate Predictors

PP7B H.Clinton/B.Obama 10.00 25.00
PP7H H.Clinton/B.Obama 60.00 120.00
PP10 B.Obama/J.McCain 4.00 10.00
PP10A J.McCain/H.Clinton 4.00 10.00
PP11 B.Obama/J.McCain 4.00 10.00
PP11A J.McCain/H.Clinton 2.00 5.00
PP12 B.Obama/J.McCain 4.00 10.00
PP12A J.McCain/H.Clinton 2.00 5.00
PP13 B.Obama/J.McCain 4.00 10.00
PP13A J.McCain/H.Clinton 2.00 5.00
PP14 B.Obama/J.McCain 4.00 10.00
PP14A J.McCain/H.Clinton 2.00 5.00
PP15 B.Obama/J.McCain 150.00 300.00

2008 Upper Deck Rookie Debut

COMPLETE SET (30) 12.50 30.00
1 Emilio Bonifacio 1.00 2.50
2 Billy Buckner .40 1.00
3 Brandon Jones 1.00 2.50
4 Clay Buchholz .60 1.50
5 Lance Broadway .40 1.00
6 Joey Votto 1.50 4.00
7 Ryan Hanigan .60 1.50
8 Seth Smith .40 1.00
9 Joe Koshansky .40 1.00
10 Chris Seddon .40 1.00
11 J.R. Towles .60 1.50
12 Luke Hochevar .60 1.50
13 Chin-Lung Hu .40 1.00
14 Sam Fuld 1.25 3.00
15 Jose Morales .40 1.00
16 Carlos Muniz .60 1.50
17 Ian Kennedy 1.00 2.50
18 Alberto Gonzalez .60 1.50
19 Jonathan Albaladejo .60 1.50
20 Daric Barton .40 1.00
21 Jerry Blevins .60 1.50
22 Steve Pearce 2.00 5.00
23 Dave Davidson .60 1.50
24 Eugenio Velez .40 1.00
25 Erick Threets .40 1.00
26 Bronson Sardinha .40 1.00
27 Wladimir Balentien .40 1.00
28 Justin Ruggiano .60 1.50
29 Luis Mendoza .40 1.00
30 Justin Maxwell .40 1.00

2008 Upper Deck Season Highlights Signatures

STATED ODDS 1:80 H, 1:7500 R
BB Brian Bannister 6.00 15.00
BF Ben Francisco 3.00 8.00
CG Curtis Granderson 6.00 15.00
CS Curt Schilling 20.00 50.00
FL Fred Lewis 3.00 8.00
JS Jarrod Saltalamacchia 5.00 12.00
JW Josh Willingham 3.00 8.00
KK Kevin Kouzmanoff 3.00 8.00
MO Micah Owings 5.00 12.00
MR Mark Reynolds 6.00 15.00
MT Miguel Tejada 12.50 30.00
RB Ryan Braun 20.00 50.00
RS Ryan Spilborghs 6.00 15.00

2008 Upper Deck Signature Sensations

STATED ODDS 1:80 H, 1:7500 R
AE Andre Ethier 3.00 8.00
AK Austin Kearns 5.00 12.00
AM Aaron Miles 5.00 12.00
BB Boof Bonser 3.00 8.00
BH Brendan Harris 3.00 8.00
BM Brandon McCarthy 3.00 8.00
CB Cha-Seung Baek 3.00 8.00
DL Derrek Lee 6.00 15.00
IR Ivan Rodriguez 30.00 60.00
JP Joel Peralta 3.00 8.00
JS James Shields 3.00 8.00
JV John Van Benschoten 3.00 8.00
LS Luke Scott 3.00 8.00
MC Matt Cain 8.00 20.00
NS Nick Swisher 5.00 12.00
RA Reggie Abercrombie 3.00 8.00
SM Sean Marshall 3.00 8.00
YP Yusmeiro Petit 3.00 8.00

2008 Upper Deck Signs of History Cut Signatures

BH Benjamin Harrison/45 700.00 1000.00
GC Grover Cleveland/30 600.00 850.00
GF Gerald Ford/75 100.00 200.00
HT Harry Truman/47 400.00 700.00
JC Jimmy Carter/49 150.00 300.00
RH Rutherford B. Hayes/75 400.00 650.00
WT William H. Taft/50 500.00 750.00
NNO Exchange Card 700.00 1000.00

2008 Upper Deck Star Attractions

SA1 B.J. Upton .60 1.50
SA2 Carl Crawford .60 1.50
SA3 Chris B. Young .40 1.00
SA4 John Maine .40 1.00
SA5 Jonathan Papelbon .60 1.50
SA6 Nick Markakis .75 2.00
SA7 Prince Fielder .60 1.50
SA8 Takashi Saito .40 1.00
SA9 Tom Gorzelanny .40 1.00
SA10 Troy Tulowitzki 1.00 2.50

2008 Upper Deck StarQuest

SER.1 ODDS 1:1 RETAIL/TARGET
SER.1 ODDS 1:1 WAL MART
*UNCOMMON: .4X TO 1X COMMON
SER.1 UNC ODDS 1:4 RETAIL/TARGET
SER.1 UNC ODDS 1:6 WAL MART
*RARE: .6X TO 1.5X COMMON
SER.1 RARE ODDS 1:8 RETAIL/TARGET
SER.1 RARE ODDS 1:12 WAL MART
*SUPER: 1X TO 2.5X COMMON
SER.1 SUPER ODDS 1:16 RETAIL/TARGET
SER.1 SUPER ODDS 1:24 WAL MART
*ULTRA: 1.5X TO 4X BASIC
SER.1 ULTRA ODDS 1:24 RETAIL/TARGET
SER.1 ULTRA ODDS 1:36 WAL MART
1 Ichiro Suzuki 1.25 3.00
2 Ryan Braun .60 1.50
3 Prince Fielder .60 1.50
4 Ken Griffey Jr. 2.00 5.00
5 Vladimir Guerrero .60 1.50
6 Travis Hafner .40 1.00
7 Matt Holliday 1.00 2.50
8 Ryan Howard .60 1.50
9 Derek Jeter 2.50 6.00
10 Chipper Jones 1.00 2.50
11 Carlos Lee .40 1.00
12 Justin Morneau .60 1.50
13 Magglio Ordonez .60 1.50
14 David Ortiz 1.00 2.50
15 Jake Peavy .40 1.00
16 Albert Pujols 1.25 3.00
17 Hanley Ramirez .60 1.50
18 Manny Ramirez 1.00 2.50
19 Jose Reyes .60 1.50
20 Alex Rodriguez 1.25 3.00
21 Johan Santana .60 1.50
22 Grady Sizemore .60 1.50
23 Alfonso Soriano .60 1.50
24 Mark Teixeira .60 1.50
25 Frank Thomas 1.00 2.50
26 Jim Thome .60 1.50
27 Chase Utley .60 1.50
28 Brandon Webb .60 1.50
29 David Wright .60 1.50
30 Michael Young .40 1.00
31 Adam Dunn .60 1.50
32 Albert Pujols 1.25 3.00
33 Alex Rodriguez 1.25 3.00
34 B.J. Upton .60 1.50
35 C.C. Sabathia .60 1.50
36 Carlos Beltran .60 1.50
37 Carlos Pena .60 1.50
38 Cole Hamels .75 2.00
39 Curtis Granderson .60 1.50
40 Daisuke Matsuzaka .60 1.50
41 David Ortiz 1.00 2.50
42 Derek Jeter 2.50 6.00
43 Derrek Lee .40 1.00
44 Eric Byrnes .40 1.00
45 Felix Hernandez .60 1.50
46 Ichiro Suzuki 1.25 3.00
47 Jeff Francoeur .60 1.50
48 Jimmy Rollins .60 1.50
49 Joe Mauer .75 2.00
50 John Smoltz 1.00 2.50
51 Ken Griffey Jr. 2.00 5.00
52 Lance Berkman .60 1.50
53 Miguel Cabrera 1.00 2.50
54 Paul Konerko .60 1.50
55 Pedro Martinez .60 1.50
56 Randy Johnson 1.00 2.50
57 Russell Martin .40 1.00
58 Troy Tulowitzki 1.00 2.50
59 Vernon Wells .40 1.00
60 Vladimir Guerrero .60 1.50

2008 Upper Deck Superstar Scrapbooks

SS1 Albert Pujols 1.25 3.00
SS2 Alex Rodriguez 1.25 3.00
SS3 Chase Utley .60 1.50
SS4 Chipper Jones 1.00 2.50
SS5 David Ortiz 1.00 2.50
SS6 Derek Jeter 2.50 6.00
SS7 Ichiro Suzuki 1.25 3.00
SS8 Johan Santana .60 1.50
SS9 Jose Reyes .60 1.50
SS10 Ken Griffey Jr. 2.00 5.00
SS11 Manny Ramirez 1.00 2.50
SS12 Prince Fielder .60 1.50
SS13 Randy Johnson 1.00 2.50
SS14 Ryan Howard .60 1.50
SS15 Vladimir Guerrero .60 1.50

2008 Upper Deck The House That Ruth Built

STATED ODDS 1:4 WAL MART BLISTER
STATED ODDS 1:6 WAL MART BLASTER
SILVER INSERTED IN WAL MART PACKS
SILVER PRINT RUN 1 SER.#'d SET
NO SILVER PRICING DUE TO SCARCITY
HRB1 Babe Ruth 1.50 4.00
HRB2 Babe Ruth 1.50 4.00
HRB3 Babe Ruth 1.50 4.00
HRB4 Babe Ruth 1.50 4.00
HRB5 Babe Ruth 1.50 4.00
HRB6 Babe Ruth 1.50 4.00
HRB7 Babe Ruth 1.50 4.00
HRB8 Babe Ruth 1.50 4.00
HRB9 Babe Ruth 1.50 4.00
HRB10 Babe Ruth 1.50 4.00
HRB11 Babe Ruth 1.50 4.00
HRB12 Babe Ruth 1.50 4.00
HRB13 Babe Ruth 1.50 4.00
HRB14 Babe Ruth 1.50 4.00
HRB15 Babe Ruth 1.50 4.00
HRB16 Babe Ruth 1.50 4.00
HRB17 Babe Ruth 1.50 4.00
HRB18 Babe Ruth 1.50 4.00
HRB19 Babe Ruth 1.50 4.00
HRB20 Babe Ruth 1.50 4.00
HRB21 Babe Ruth 1.50 4.00
HRB22 Babe Ruth 1.50 4.00
HRB23 Babe Ruth 1.50 4.00
HRB24 Babe Ruth 1.50 4.00
HRB25 Babe Ruth 1.50 4.00

2008 Upper Deck UD Autographs

STATED ODDS 1:80 H, 1:7500 R
CD Chris Duffy 3.00 8.00
CS Curt Schilling 20.00 50.00
JK Jeff Karstens 3.00 8.00
JP Joel Peralta 3.00 8.00
JS Jorge Sosa 5.00 12.00
JV John Van Benschoten 3.00 8.00
KI Kei Igawa 6.00 15.00
KS Kelly Shoppach 3.00 8.00
LS Luke Scott 3.00 8.00
MC Manny Corpas 6.00 15.00
MP Mike Pelfrey 5.00 12.00
MT Miguel Tejada 12.50 30.00
NM Nate McLouth 6.00 15.00
RH Ramon Hernandez 5.00 12.00
SA Kirk Saarloos 3.00 8.00
SF Scott Feldman 4.00 10.00

SH James Shields 3.00 8.00
SR Saul Rivera 3.00 8.00
SS Skip Schumaker 8.00 20.00

2008 Upper Deck UD Game Materials

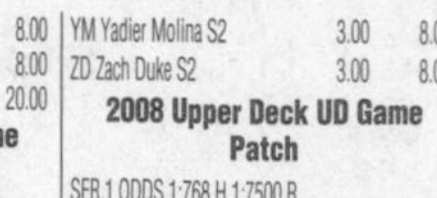

SER.1 ODDS 1:32 HOBBY,1:96 RETAIL
SER.1 ODDS 1:40 WAL MART BLASTER
SER.1 ODDS 1:96 TARGET/WM BLISTER
AJ Andruw Jones S2 3.00 8.00
AP Albert Pujols S2 6.00 15.00
BB Boof Bonser S2 3.00 8.00
BM Brandon McCarthy S2 3.00 8.00
BP Brandon Phillips S2 3.00 8.00
BR Brian Roberts 3.00 8.00
BU B.J. Upton S2 3.00 8.00
BZ Barry Zito S2 3.00 8.00
CA Matt Cain S2 3.00 8.00
CB Chris Burke S2 3.00 8.00
CB Carlos Beltran 3.00 8.00
CC Coco Crisp 3.00 8.00
CC Chris Carpenter S2 3.00 8.00
CD Chris Duncan S2 3.00 8.00
CG Carlos Guillen 3.00 8.00
CJ Conor Jackson S2 3.00 8.00
CL Cliff Lee S2 3.00 8.00
CQ Carlos Quentin S2 3.00 8.00
CU Michael Cuddyer S2 3.00 8.00
DC Daniel Cabrera 3.00 8.00
DJ Derek Jeter 8.00 20.00
DJ Derek Jeter S2 8.00 20.00
DL Derrek Lee S2 3.00 8.00
DO David Ortiz S2 4.00 10.00
DO David Ortiz 4.00 10.00
DW Dontrelle Willis 3.00 8.00
DW David Wells S2 3.00 8.00
EC Eric Chavez S2 3.00 8.00
EG Eric Gagne 3.00 8.00
ES Ervin Santana S2 3.00 8.00
FH Felix Hernandez S2 3.00 8.00
FL Francisco Liriano S2 3.00 8.00
FR Francisco Rodriguez S2 3.00 8.00
FS Freddy Sanchez S2 3.00 8.00
GA Garrett Atkins S2 3.00 8.00
GC Gustavo Chacin 1.50 4.00
GJ Geoff Jenkins 3.00 8.00
GL Troy Glaus S2 3.00 8.00
GM Gil Meche S2 3.00 8.00
GO Jonny Gomes S2 3.00 8.00
HR Hanley Ramirez S2 3.00 8.00
IR Ivan Rodriguez S2 3.00 8.00
JB Jeremy Bonderman S2 3.00 8.00
JB Jason Bay 3.00 8.00
JD Justin Duchscherer 3.00 8.00
JD Jermaine Dye S2 3.00 8.00
JG Jason Giambi S2 3.00 8.00
JH Jeremy Hermida S2 3.00 8.00
JJ Josh Johnson S2 3.00 8.00
JL James Loney S2 3.00 8.00
JP Jonathan Papelbon S2 4.00 10.00
JP Jake Peavy 4.00 10.00
JR Jeremy Reed S2 3.00 8.00
JS Jason Schmidt S2 3.00 8.00
JS Jeremy Sowers 3.00 8.00
JV Jason Varitek 4.00 10.00
JV Justin Verlander S2 3.00 8.00
JW Jered Weaver S2 3.00 8.00
KG Khalil Greene S2 3.00 8.00
KJ Kenji Johjima S2 3.00 8.00
KM Kazuo Matsui 3.00 8.00
KW Kerry Wood S2 3.00 8.00
MC Miguel Cabrera S2 4.00 10.00
ME Melky Cabrera S2 3.00 8.00
ME Morgan Ensberg 3.00 8.00
MG Marcus Giles S2 3.00 8.00
MJ Mike Jacobs S2 3.00 8.00
MK Masumi Kuwata 3.00 8.00
MM Melvin Mora 3.00 8.00
MN Mike Napoli S2 3.00 8.00
MP Mark Prior S2 3.00 8.00
MS Mike Sweeney 3.00 8.00
MY Michael Young 3.00 8.00
MY Brett Myers S2 3.00 8.00
OL Scott Olsen S2 3.00 8.00
PA Jonathan Papelbon 4.00 10.00
PE Mike Pelfrey S2 3.00 8.00
PF Prince Fielder S2 4.00 10.00
PK Paul Konerko S2 3.00 8.00
RC Ryan Church S2 3.00 8.00
RD Ray Durham S2 3.00 8.00
RF Ryan Freel S2 3.00 8.00
RH Roy Halladay 3.00 8.00
RJ Reed Johnson S2 3.00 8.00
RQ Robb Quinlan S2 3.00 8.00
RW Rickie Weeks S2 3.00 8.00
RZ Ryan Zimmerman S2 4.00 10.00
SK Scott Kazmir S2 3.00 8.00
SO Jeremy Sowers S2 3.00 8.00
TG Tom Glavine S2 3.00 8.00
TS Takashi Saito 3.00 8.00
VW Vernon Wells S2 3.00 8.00
WI Dontrelle Willis S2 3.00 8.00
YM Yadier Molina S2 3.00 8.00
ZD Zach Duke S2 3.00 8.00

2008 Upper Deck UD Game Patch

SER.1 ODDS 1:768 H,1:7500 R
AJ Andruw Jones S2 8.00 20.00
AP Albert Pujols S2 20.00 50.00
BB Boof Bonser S2 8.00 20.00
BM Brandon McCarthy S2 8.00 20.00
BP Brandon Phillips S2 8.00 20.00
BR Brian Roberts 8.00 20.00
BU B.J. Upton S2 8.00 20.00
BZ Barry Zito S2 8.00 20.00
CA Matt Cain S2 8.00 20.00
CB Chris Burke S2 8.00 20.00
CB Carlos Beltran 8.00 20.00
CC Coco Crisp 8.00 20.00
CC Chris Carpenter S2 8.00 20.00
CD Chris Duncan S2 8.00 20.00
CG Carlos Guillen 8.00 20.00
CJ Conor Jackson S2 8.00 20.00
CL Cliff Lee S2 8.00 20.00
CQ Carlos Quentin S2 8.00 20.00
CU Michael Cuddyer S2 8.00 20.00
DC Daniel Cabrera 8.00 20.00
DJ Derek Jeter 50.00 100.00
DJ Derek Jeter S2 50.00 100.00
DL Derrek Lee S2 8.00 20.00
DO David Ortiz S2 12.50 30.00
DO David Ortiz 12.50 30.00
DW Dontrelle Willis 8.00 20.00
DW David Wells S2 8.00 20.00
EC Eric Chavez S2 8.00 20.00
EG Eric Gagne 8.00 20.00
ES Ervin Santana S2 8.00 20.00
FH Felix Hernandez S2 8.00 20.00
FL Francisco Liriano S2 8.00 20.00
FR Francisco Rodriguez S2 8.00 20.00
FS Freddy Sanchez S2 8.00 20.00
GA Garrett Atkins S2 8.00 20.00
GC Gustavo Chacin 8.00 20.00
GJ Geoff Jenkins 8.00 20.00
GL Troy Glaus S2 8.00 20.00
GM Gil Meche S2 8.00 20.00
GO Jonny Gomes S2 8.00 20.00
HR Hanley Ramirez S2 8.00 20.00
IR Ivan Rodriguez S2 8.00 20.00
JB Jeremy Bonderman S2 8.00 20.00
JB Jason Bay 8.00 20.00
JD Justin Duchscherer 8.00 20.00
JD Jermaine Dye S2 8.00 20.00
JG Jason Giambi S2 8.00 20.00
JH Jeremy Hermida S2 8.00 20.00
JJ Josh Johnson S2 8.00 20.00
JL James Loney S2 8.00 20.00
JP Jonathan Papelbon S2 12.50 30.00
JP Jake Peavy 12.50 30.00
JR Jeremy Reed S2 8.00 20.00
JS Jason Schmidt S2 8.00 20.00
JS Jeremy Sowers 8.00 20.00
JV Jason Varitek 12.50 30.00
JV Justin Verlander S2 8.00 20.00
JW Jered Weaver S2 8.00 20.00
KG Khalil Greene S2 8.00 20.00
KJ Kenji Johjima S2 8.00 20.00
KM Kazuo Matsui 8.00 20.00
KW Kerry Wood S2 8.00 20.00
MC Miguel Cabrera S2 12.50 30.00
ME Melky Cabrera S2 8.00 20.00
ME Morgan Ensberg 8.00 20.00
MG Marcus Giles S2 8.00 20.00
MJ Mike Jacobs S2 8.00 20.00
MK Masumi Kuwata 8.00 20.00
MM Melvin Mora 8.00 20.00
MN Mike Napoli S2 8.00 20.00
MP Mark Prior S2 8.00 20.00
MS Mike Sweeney 8.00 20.00
MY Michael Young 8.00 20.00
MY Brett Myers S2 8.00 20.00
OL Scott Olsen S2 8.00 20.00
PA Jonathan Papelbon 12.50 30.00
PE Mike Pelfrey S2 8.00 20.00
PF Prince Fielder S2 12.50 30.00
PK Paul Konerko S2 8.00 20.00
RC Ryan Church S2 8.00 20.00
RD Ray Durham S2 8.00 20.00
RF Ryan Freel S2 8.00 20.00
RH Roy Halladay 8.00 20.00
RJ Reed Johnson S2 8.00 20.00
RQ Robb Quinlan S2 8.00 20.00
RW Rickie Weeks S2 8.00 20.00
RZ Ryan Zimmerman S2 12.50 30.00
SK Scott Kazmir S2 8.00 20.00
SO Jeremy Sowers S2 8.00 20.00
TG Tom Glavine S2 8.00 20.00
TS Takashi Saito 8.00 20.00
VW Vernon Wells S2 8.00 20.00
WI Dontrelle Willis S2 8.00 20.00
YM Yadier Molina S2 8.00 20.00
ZD Zach Duke S2 8.00 20.00

2008 Upper Deck UD Game Materials 1997

SER.1 ODDS 1:32 HOBBY,1:96 RETAIL
SER.1 ODDS 1:40 WAL MART BLASTER
SER.1 ODDS 1:96 TARGET/WM BLISTER
AP Albert Pujols 8.00 20.00
BC Bobby Crosby 3.00 8.00
BG Brian Giles 3.00 8.00
BR B.J. Ryan 3.00 8.00
BS Ben Sheets 3.00 8.00
CH Cole Hamels S2 3.00 8.00
CS Curt Schilling 4.00 10.00
DL Derek Lowe 3.00 8.00
DO David Ortiz 4.00 10.00
DO David Ortiz S2 4.00 10.00
DU Dan Uggla S2 3.00 8.00
GJ Geoff Jenkins 3.00 8.00
HK Hong-Chih Kuo 4.00 10.00
IR Ivan Rodriguez 4.00 10.00
JB Joe Blanton 3.00 8.00
JC Joe Crede 3.00 8.00
JJ Josh Johnson 3.00 8.00
JM Justin Morneau S2 3.00 8.00
JP Jonathan Papelbon S2 4.00 10.00
JS James Shields 3.00 8.00
JV Justin Verlander S2 3.00 8.00
JW Jake Westbrook 3.00 8.00
JZ Joel Zumaya S2 3.00 8.00
LM Lastings Milledge 3.00 8.00
MC Miguel Cabrera 4.00 10.00
MO Magglio Ordonez 4.00 10.00
NM Nick Markakis 4.00 10.00
PE Andy Pettitte 4.00 10.00
PF Prince Fielder S2 4.00 10.00
PO Jorge Posada S2 3.00 8.00
RB Rocco Baldelli 3.00 8.00
TH Todd Helton 4.00 10.00
VG Vladimir Guerrero S2 3.00 8.00
VM Victor Martinez 3.00 8.00
XN Xavier Nady 3.00 8.00

2008 Upper Deck UD Game Materials 1997 Patch

SER.1 ODDS 1:768 H,1:7500 R
AP Albert Pujols 15.00 40.00
BC Bobby Crosby 8.00 20.00
BG Brian Giles 8.00 20.00
BR BJ Ryan 8.00 20.00
BS Ben Sheets 8.00 20.00
CH Cole Hamels S2 8.00 20.00
CS Curt Schilling 12.50 30.00
DL Derek Lowe 8.00 20.00
DO David Ortiz 12.50 30.00
DO David Ortiz S2 12.50 30.00
DU Dan Uggla S2 8.00 20.00
GJ Geoff Jenkins 8.00 20.00
HK Hong-Chih Kuo 8.00 20.00
IR Ivan Rodriguez 12.50 30.00
JB Joe Blanton 8.00 20.00
JC Joe Crede 8.00 20.00
JJ Josh Johnson 8.00 20.00
JM Justin Morneau S2 8.00 20.00
JP Jonathan Papelbon S2 12.50 30.00
JS James Shields 8.00 20.00
JV Justin Verlander S2 8.00 20.00
JW Jake Westbrook 8.00 20.00
JZ Joel Zumaya S2 8.00 20.00
LM Lastings Milledge 8.00 20.00
MC Miguel Cabrera 12.50 30.00
MO Magglio Ordonez 12.50 30.00
NM Nick Markakis 12.50 30.00
PE Andy Pettitte 12.50 30.00
PF Prince Fielder S2 12.50 30.00
PO Jorge Posada S2 8.00 20.00
RB Rocco Baldelli 8.00 20.00
TH Todd Helton 12.50 30.00
VG Vladimir Guerrero S2 8.00 20.00
VM Victor Martinez 8.00 20.00
XN Xavier Nady 8.00 20.00

2008 Upper Deck UD Game Materials 1998

SER.1 ODDS 1:32 HOBBY,1:96 RETAIL
SER.1 ODDS 1:40 WAL MART BLASTER
SER.1 ODDS 1:96 TARGET/WM BLISTER
AJ Andruw Jones S2 3.00 8.00
BH Bill Hall 3.00 8.00
BS Ben Sheets 3.00 8.00
CD Chris Duncan S2 3.00 8.00
CF Chone Figgins 3.00 8.00
CZ Carlos Zambrano 3.00 8.00
DJ Derek Jeter S2 10.00 25.00
DL Derrek Lee S2 3.00 8.00
EG Eric Gagne 3.00 8.00
FC Fausto Carmona 3.00 8.00
FH Felix Hernandez 4.00 10.00
GM Greg Maddux S2 5.00 12.00
GS Grady Sizemore 4.00 10.00
HB Hank Blalock 3.00 8.00
IS Ian Snell 3.00 8.00
JE Johnny Estrada 3.00 8.00
JJ Jacque Jones 3.00 8.00
JK Jason Kendall 3.00 8.00
JS Johan Santana 4.00 10.00
KM Kevin Millwood 3.00 8.00
MB Mark Buehrle 3.00 8.00
MG Marcus Giles 3.00 8.00
NM Nick Markakis 4.00 10.00
PK Paul Konerko 3.00 8.00
RM Russell Martin S2 3.00 8.00
RO Roy Oswalt S2 3.00 8.00
TH Travis Hafner S2 3.00 8.00
VG Vladimir Guerrero S2 3.00 8.00
VM Victor Martinez S2 3.00 8.00
VM Victor Martinez 3.00 8.00

2008 Upper Deck UD Game Materials 1998 Patch

SER.1 ODDS 1:768 H,1:7500 R
AJ Andruw Jones S2 8.00 20.00
BH Bill Hall 8.00 20.00
BS Ben Sheets 8.00 20.00
CD Chris Duncan S2 8.00 20.00
CF Chone Figgins 8.00 20.00
CZ Carlos Zambrano 8.00 20.00
DJ Derek Jeter S2 20.00 50.00
DL Derrek Lee S2 8.00 20.00
EG Eric Gagne 8.00 20.00
FC Fausto Carmona 8.00 20.00
FH Felix Hernandez 12.50 30.00
GM Greg Maddux S2 12.50 30.00
GS Grady Sizemore 12.50 30.00
HB Hank Blalock 8.00 20.00
IS Ian Snell 8.00 20.00
JE Johnny Estrada 8.00 20.00
JJ Jacque Jones 8.00 20.00
JK Jason Kendall 8.00 20.00
JS Johan Santana 12.50 30.00
KM Kevin Millwood 8.00 20.00
MB Mark Buehrle 8.00 20.00
MG Marcus Giles 8.00 20.00
NM Nick Markakis 12.50 30.00
PK Paul Konerko 8.00 20.00
RM Russell Martin S2 8.00 20.00
RO Roy Oswalt S2 8.00 20.00
TH Travis Hafner S2 8.00 20.00
VG Vladimir Guerrero S2 8.00 20.00
VM Victor Martinez S2 8.00 20.00
VM Victor Martinez 8.00 20.00

2008 Upper Deck UD Game Materials 1999

SER.1 ODDS 1:32 HOBBY,1:96 RETAIL
SER.1 ODDS 1:40 WAL MART BLASTER
SER.1 ODDS 1:96 TARGET/WM BLISTER
BR Brian Roberts 3.00 8.00
BU B.J. Upton S2 3.00 8.00
BW Brandon Webb S2 3.00 8.00
CA Matt Cain S2 3.00 8.00
CD Chris Duffy 3.00 8.00
CJ Chipper Jones 4.00 10.00
CS C.C. Sabathia 3.00 8.00
DL Derrek Lee 3.00 8.00
DO David Ortiz S2 4.00 10.00
DW David Wells 3.00 8.00
EB Erik Bedard 3.00 8.00
FS Freddy Sanchez 3.00 8.00
HR Hanley Ramirez S2 3.00 8.00
JB Jason Bay 3.00 8.00
JD Johnny Damon 3.00 8.00
JG Jeremy Guthrie 3.00 8.00
JH J.J. Hardy 3.00 8.00
JK Jason Kubel 3.00 8.00
JM Joe Mauer S2 3.00 8.00
JP Jorge Posada 4.00 10.00
KG Khalil Greene S2 3.00 8.00
KJ Kenji Johjima 3.00 8.00
KM Kendry Morales 3.00 8.00
MC Miguel Cabrera S2 3.00 8.00
MT Mark Teixeira 4.00 10.00
NM Nick Markakis S2 3.00 8.00
RW Rickie Weeks 3.00 8.00
TE Miguel Tejada 3.00 8.00
TH Travis Hafner 3.00 8.00
TH Torii Hunter S2 3.00 8.00

2008 Upper Deck UD Game Materials 1999 Patch

SER.1 ODDS 1:768 H,1:7500 R
BR Brian Roberts 8.00 20.00
BU B.J. Upton S2 8.00 20.00
BW Brandon Webb S2 8.00 20.00
CA Matt Cain S2 8.00 20.00
CD Chris Duffy 8.00 20.00
CJ Chipper Jones 12.50 30.00
CS C.C. Sabathia 8.00 20.00
DL Derrek Lee 8.00 20.00
DO David Ortiz S2 12.50 30.00
DW David Wells 8.00 20.00
EB Erik Bedard 8.00 20.00
FS Freddy Sanchez 8.00 20.00
HR Hanley Ramirez S2 8.00 20.00
JB Jason Bay 8.00 20.00
JD Johnny Damon 8.00 20.00
JG Jeremy Guthrie 8.00 20.00
JH J.J. Hardy 8.00 20.00
JK Jason Kubel 8.00 20.00
JM Joe Mauer S2 8.00 20.00
JP Jorge Posada 12.50 30.00
KG Khalil Greene S2 8.00 20.00
KJ Kenji Johjima 8.00 20.00
KM Kendry Morales 8.00 20.00
MC Miguel Cabrera S2 8.00 20.00
MT Mark Teixeira 12.50 30.00
NM Nick Markakis S2 8.00 20.00
RW Rickie Weeks 8.00 20.00
TE Miguel Tejada 8.00 20.00
TH Travis Hafner 8.00 20.00
TH Torii Hunter S2 8.00 20.00

2008 Upper Deck Superstar

COMPLETE SET (10) 6.00 15.00
STATED ODDS 3:1 SUPER PACKS
9 Vladimir Guerrero .40 1.00
48 Mark Teixeira .40 1.00
57 Prince Fielder .40 1.00
67 Albert Pujols .75 2.00
139 Ichiro Suzuki .75 2.00
147 Hanley Ramirez .40 1.00
156 David Wright .40 1.00
239 Ken Griffey Jr. 1.25 3.00
270 Magglio Ordonez .40 1.00
297 Derek Jeter 1.50 4.00

2008 Upper Deck USA Junior National Team

USJR1 Eric Hosmer 6.00 15.00
USJR2 Garrison Lassiter 1.25 3.00
USJR3 Harold Martinez 1.25 3.00
USJR4 J.P. Ramirez 1.25 3.00
USJR5 Jeff Malm 2.00 5.00
USJR6 Jordan Swagerty 1.25 3.00
USJR7 Kyle Buchanan 1.25 3.00
USJR8 Kyle Skipworth 2.00 5.00
USJR9 L.J. Hoes 1.25 3.00
USJR10 Matthew Purke 1.25 3.00
USJR11 Mychal Givens 1.25 3.00
USJR12 Nick Maronde 1.25 3.00
USJR13 Riccio Torrez 1.25 3.00
USJR14 Robbie Grossman 2.00 5.00
USJR15 Ryan Weber 1.25 3.00
USJR16 T.J. House 1.25 3.00
USJR17 Tim Melville 1.25 3.00
USJR18 Tyler Hibbs 1.25 3.00
USJR19 Tyler Stovall 1.25 3.00
USJR20 Tyler Wilson 1.25 3.00

2008 Upper Deck USA Junior National Team Autographs

PRINT RUNS B/WN 133-500 COPIES PER
EH Eric Hosmer/238 5.00 12.00
GL Garrison Lassiter/375 4.00 10.00
HI Tyler Hibbs/375 4.00 10.00
HM Harold Martinez/237 4.00 10.00
JM Jeff Malm/375 4.00 10.00
JR J.P. Ramirez/239 4.00 10.00
JS Jordan Swagerty/350 4.00 10.00
KB Kyle Buchanan/375 4.00 10.00
KS Kyle Skipworth/177 4.00 10.00
LH L.J. Hoes/158 4.00 10.00
MG Mychal Givens/209 4.00 10.00
MP Matthew Purke/375 4.00 10.00
NM Nick Maronde/166 4.00 10.00
RG Robbie Grossman/155 4.00 10.00
RT Riccio Torrez/500 4.00 10.00
RW Ryan Weber/375 4.00 10.00
TH T.J. House/147 4.00 10.00
TM Tim Melville/133 4.00 10.00
TS Tyler Stovall/375 4.00 10.00
TW Tyler Wilson/375 4.00 10.00

2008 Upper Deck USA Junior National Team Autographs Blue

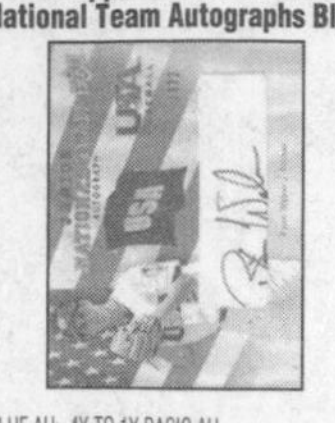

*BLUE AU: .4X TO 1X BASIC AU
PRINT RUNS B/WN 75-400 COPIES PER
EH Eric Hosmer/75 10.00 25.00
GL Garrison Lassiter/175 4.00 10.00
HI Tyler Hibbs/400 4.00 10.00
HM Harold Martinez/275 4.00 10.00
JM Jeff Malm/175 4.00 10.00
JR J.P. Ramirez/90 4.00 10.00
JS Jordan Swagerty/195 4.00 10.00
KB Kyle Buchanan/175 4.00 10.00
LH L.J. Hoes/300 4.00 10.00
MG Mychal Givens/309 4.00 10.00
MP Matthew Purke/390 4.00 10.00
NM Nick Maronde/100 4.00 10.00
RG Robbie Grossman/175 4.00 10.00
RT Riccio Torrez/400 4.00 10.00
RW Ryan Weber/392 4.00 10.00
TH T.J. House/75 4.00 10.00
TM Tim Melville/330 4.00 10.00
TS Tyler Stovall/186 4.00 10.00
TW Tyler Wilson/75 4.00 10.00

2008 Upper Deck USA Junior National Team Autographs Red

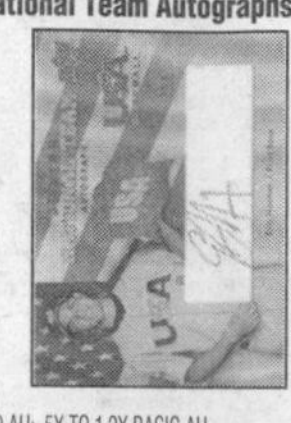

*RED AU: .5X TO 1.2X BASIC AU
PRINT RUNS B/WN 50-150 COPIES PER
EH Eric Hosmer/50 30.00 80.00

2008 Upper Deck USA Junior National Team Jerseys

EH Eric Hosmer 6.00 15.00
GL Garrison Lassiter 3.00 8.00
HI Tyler Hibbs 3.00 8.00
HM Harold Martinez 3.00 8.00
JM Jeff Malm 3.00 8.00
JR J.P. Ramirez 3.00 8.00
JS Jordan Swagerty 3.00 8.00
KB Kyle Buchanan 3.00 8.00
KS Kyle Skipworth 4.00 10.00
LH L.J. Hoes 3.00 8.00
MG Mychal Givens 3.00 8.00
MP Matthew Purke 3.00 8.00
NM Nick Maronde 3.00 8.00
RG Robbie Grossman 3.00 8.00
RT Riccio Torrez 3.00 8.00
RW Ryan Weber 3.00 8.00
TH T.J. House 3.00 8.00
TM Tim Melville 3.00 8.00
TS Tyler Stovall 3.00 8.00
TW Tyler Wilson 3.00 8.00

2008 Upper Deck USA Junior National Team Jerseys Autographs Black

PRINT RUNS B/WN 99-400 COPIES PER
EH Eric Hosmer/100 15.00 40.00
GL Garrison Lassiter/226 4.00 10.00
HI Tyler Hibbs/222 4.00 10.00
HM Harold Martinez/99 4.00 10.00
JM Jeff Malm/258 4.00 10.00
JR J.P. Ramirez/99 4.00 10.00
JS Jordan Swagerty/199 4.00 10.00
KB Kyle Buchanan/205 4.00 10.00
KS Kyle Skipworth/99 4.00 10.00
LH L.J. Hoes/150 4.00 10.00
MG Mychal Givens/99 4.00 10.00
MP Matthew Purke/209 4.00 10.00
NM Nick Maronde/99 4.00 10.00
RG Robbie Grossman/150 4.00 10.00
RT Riccio Torrez/400 4.00 10.00
RW Ryan Weber/222 4.00 10.00
TH T.J. House/149 4.00 10.00
TM Tim Melville/175 4.00 10.00
TS Tyler Stovall/199 4.00 10.00
TW Tyler Wilson/199 4.00 10.00

2008 Upper Deck USA Junior National Team Jerseys Autographs Blue

*JSY BLUE: .4X TO 1X JSY BLACK
PRINT RUNS B/WN 50-400 COPIES PER
EH Eric Hosmer/121 15.00 40.00
GL Garrison Lassiter/172 4.00 10.00
HI Tyler Hibbs/392 4.00 10.00
HM Harold Martinez/375 4.00 10.00
JM Jeff Malm/107 4.00 10.00
JR J.P. Ramirez/200 4.00 10.00
RW Ryan Weber/400 4.00 10.00

2008 Upper Deck USA Junior National Team Jerseys Autographs Red

*JSY RED: .5X TO 1.2X JSY BLACK
PRINT RUNS B/WN 25-150 COPIES PER
NO PRICING ON QTY 25 OR LESS
EH Eric Hosmer/50 20.00 50.00
GL Garrison Lassiter/50 5.00 12.00
HI Tyler Hibbs/75 5.00 12.00
HM Harold Martinez/50 5.00 12.00
JM Jeff Malm/75 5.00 12.00
JR J.P. Ramirez/50 5.00 12.00
JS Jordan Swagerty/60 5.00 12.00
KB Kyle Buchanan/85 5.00 21.00
LH L.J. Hoes/60 5.00 12.00
MG Mychal Givens/60 5.00 12.00
MP Matthew Purke/74 5.00 12.00
RG Robbie Grossman/50 5.00 12.00
RT Riccio Torrez/150 5.00 12.00
RW Ryan Weber/50 5.00 12.00
TH T.J. House/50 5.00 12.00
TM Tim Melville/50 5.00 12.00
TS Tyler Stovall/85 5.00 12.00
TW Tyler Wilson/85 5.00 12.00

2008 Upper Deck USA Junior National Team Patch

*PATCH 99: .5X TO 1.2X BASIC JSY
STATED PRINT RUN 99 SER.#'d SETS
EH Eric Hosmer 8.00 20.00
KS Kyle Skipworth 6.00 15.00

2008 Upper Deck USA Junior National Team Patch Autographs

STATED PRINT RUN 99 SER.#'d SETS
EH Eric Hosmer 20.00 50.00
GL Garrison Lassiter 6.00 15.00
HI Tyler Hibbs 6.00 15.00
HM Harold Martinez 6.00 15.00
JM Jeff Malm 6.00 15.00
JR J.P. Ramirez 6.00 15.00
JS Jordan Swagerty 6.00 15.00
KB Kyle Buchanan 6.00 15.00
KS Kyle Skipworth 10.00 25.00
LH L.J. Hoes 6.00 15.00
MG Mychal Givens 6.00 15.00
MP Matthew Purke 6.00 15.00
NM Nick Maronde 6.00 15.00
RG Robbie Grossman 6.00 15.00
RT Riccio Torrez 6.00 15.00
RW Ryan Weber 6.00 15.00
TH T.J. House 6.00 15.00
TM Tim Melville 6.00 15.00
TS Tyler Stovall 6.00 15.00
TW Tyler Wilson 6.00 15.00

2008 Upper Deck USA National Team

USA1 Brett Hunter 1.25 3.00
USA2 Brian Matusz 1.25 3.00
USA3 Brett Wallace 1.25 3.00
USA4 Cody Satterwhite 1.25 3.00
USA5 Danny Espinosa 1.25 3.00
USA6 Eric Surkamp 1.25 3.00
USA7 Jordan Danks 1.25 3.00
USA8 Jeremy Hamilton 1.25 3.00
USA9 Joe Kelly 1.25 3.00
USA10 Jordy Mercer 1.25 3.00
USA11 Josh Romanski 1.25 3.00
USA12 Justin Smoak 1.25 3.00
USA13 Jacob Thompson 1.25 3.00
USA14 Logan Forsythe 1.25 3.00
USA15 Lance Lynn 1.25 3.00
USA16 Mike Minor 1.25 3.00
USA17 Pedro Alvarez 1.25 3.00
USA18 Petey Paramore 1.25 3.00
USA19 Ryan Berry 1.25 3.00
USA20 Ryan Flaherty 1.25 3.00
USA21 Roger Kieschnick 1.25 3.00
USA22 Seth Frankoff 1.25 3.00
USA23 Scott Gorgen 1.25 3.00
USA24 Tommy Medica 1.25 3.00
USA25 Tyson Ross 1.25 3.00

2008 Upper Deck USA National Team Autographs

PRINT RUNS B/WN 183-500 COPIES PER
BH Brett Hunter/297 4.00 10.00
BM Brian Matusz/264 10.00 25.00
BW Brett Wallace/183 6.00 15.00
CS Cody Satterwhite/375 4.00 10.00
DE Danny Espinosa/311 12.50 30.00
JD Jordan Danks/311 4.00 10.00
JH Jeremy Hamilton/375 4.00 10.00
JK Joe Kelly/457 4.00 10.00
JM Jordy Mercer/375 4.00 10.00
JR Josh Romanski/375 4.00 10.00
JS Justin Smoak/345 10.00 25.00
JT Jacob Thompson/267 4.00 10.00
LF Logan Forsythe/201 5.00 12.00
LL Lance Lynn/425 4.00 10.00
MM Mike Minor/375 6.00 15.00
PA Pedro Alvarez/205 6.00 15.00
PP Petey Paramore/237 4.00 10.00
RB Ryan Berry/375 4.00 10.00
RF Ryan Flaherty/244 4.00 10.00
RK Roger Kieschnick/272 4.00 10.00
TM Tommy Medica/487 4.00 10.00
TR Tyson Ross/500 4.00 10.00

2008 Upper Deck USA National Team Autographs Blue

*BLUE AU: .4X TO 1X BASIC AU
PRINT RUNS B/WN 50-204 COPIES PER
BH Brett Hunter/129 4.00 10.00
BM Brian Matusz/50 15.00 40.00
BW Brett Wallace/75 6.00 15.00
CS Cody Satterwhite/131 4.00 10.00
DE Danny Espinosa/75 12.50 30.00
ES Eric Surkamp/117 4.00 10.00
JD Jordan Danks/75 6.00 15.00
JH Jeremy Hamilton/204 4.00 10.00
JK Joe Kelly/125 4.00 10.00
JM Jordy Mercer/175 4.00 10.00
JR Josh Romanski/175 4.00 10.00
JS Justin Smoak/60 20.00 50.00
JT Jacob Thompson/105 4.00 10.00
LF Logan Forsythe/75 5.00 12.00
MM Mike Minor/175 6.00 15.00
PA Pedro Alvarez/75 8.00 20.00
PP Petey Paramore/175 4.00 10.00
RB Ryan Berry/175 4.00 10.00
RF Ryan Flaherty/75 4.00 10.00
RK Roger Kieschnick/113 5.00 12.00
SF Seth Frankoff/175 4.00 10.00
SG Scott Gorgen/175 4.00 10.00
TM Tommy Medica/175 4.00 10.00
TR Tyson Ross/75 4.00 10.00

2008 Upper Deck USA National Team Autographs Red

*RED AU: .5X TO 1.2X BASIC AU
STATED PRINT RUN 50 SER.#'d SETS
BM Brian Matusz 15.00 40.00
BW Brett Wallace 6.00 15.00
JD Jordan Danks 6.00 15.00
LF Logan Forsythe 5.00 12.00
LL Lance Lynn 6.00 15.00
RF Ryan Flaherty 4.00 10.00
TR Tyson Ross 4.00 10.00

2008 Upper Deck USA National Team Highlights

H1 Game 1 1.00 2.50
H2 Game 2 1.00 2.50
H3 Game 3 1.00 2.50
H4 Game 4 1.00 2.50
H5 Game 5 1.00 2.50

2008 Upper Deck USA National Team Jerseys

BH Brett Hunter 3.00 8.00
BM Brian Matusz 3.00 8.00
BW Brett Wallace 3.00 8.00
CS Cody Satterwhite 3.00 8.00
DE Danny Espinosa 4.00 10.00
ES Eric Surkamp 3.00 8.00
JD Jordan Danks 3.00 8.00
JH Jeremy Hamilton 3.00 8.00
JK Joe Kelly 3.00 8.00
JM Jordy Mercer 3.00 8.00
JR Josh Romanski 3.00 8.00
JS Justin Smoak 5.00 12.00
JT Jacob Thompson 3.00 8.00
LF Logan Forsythe 3.00 8.00
LL Lance Lynn 3.00 8.00
MM Mike Minor 3.00 8.00
PA Pedro Alvarez 4.00 10.00
PP Petey Paramore 3.00 8.00
RB Ryan Berry 3.00 8.00
RF Ryan Flaherty 3.00 8.00
RK Roger Kieschnick 3.00 8.00
SF Seth Frankoff 3.00 8.00
SG Scott Gorgen 3.00 8.00
TM Tommy Medica 3.00 8.00
TR Tyson Ross 3.00 8.00

2008 Upper Deck USA National Team Jerseys Autographs Black

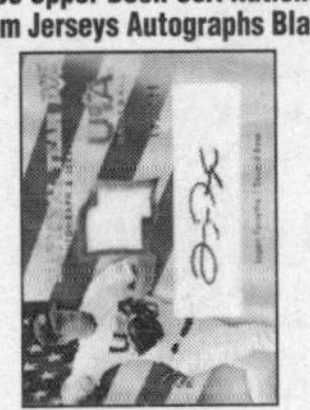

PRINT RUNS B/WN 99-400 COPIES PER
BH Brett Hunter/99 4.00 10.00
BM Brian Matusz/181 20.00 50.00
BW Brett Wallace/199 4.00 10.00
CS Cody Satterwhite/273 6.00 15.00
DE Danny Espinosa/130 10.00 25.00
JD Jordan Danks/99 6.00 15.00
JH Jeremy Hamilton/271 4.00 10.00
JK Joe Kelly/300 4.00 10.00
JM Jordy Mercer/287 4.00 10.00
JR Josh Romanski/311 4.00 10.00
JS Justin Smoak/199 12.50 30.00
JT Jacob Thompson/199 4.00 10.00
LF Logan Forsythe/199 4.00 10.00
LL Lance Lynn/149 4.00 10.00
MM Mike Minor/359 4.00 10.00
PA Pedro Alvarez/275 5.00 12.00
PP Petey Paramore/199 4.00 10.00
RB Ryan Berry/284 4.00 10.00
RF Ryan Flaherty/149 6.00 15.00
RK Roger Kieschnick/199 4.00 10.00
TM Tommy Medica/400 4.00 10.00
TR Tyson Ross/400 4.00 10.00

2008 Upper Deck USA National Team Jerseys Autographs Blue

*BLUE JSY AU: .4X TO 1X BLACK JSY AU
PRINT RUNS B/WN 69-292 COPIES PER
ES Eric Surkamp/200 4.00 10.00
SF Seth Frankoff/69 4.00 10.00
SG Scott Gorgen/247 4.00 10.00

2008 Upper Deck USA National Team Jerseys Autographs Red

*RED JSY AU: .5X TO 1.2X BASIC JSY AU
PRINT RUNS B/WN 50-182 COPIES PER
ES Eric Surkamp/50 5.00 12.00
LL Lance Lynn/50 5.00 12.00
PA Pedro Alvarez/50 8.00 20.00
SF Seth Frankoff/50 5.00 12.00
SG Scott Gorgen/50 5.00 12.00

2008 Upper Deck USA National Team Patch

*PATCH: .5X TO 1.2X BASIC JSY
STATED PRINT RUN 99 SER.#'d SETS
BM Brian Matusz 15.00 40.00
LL Lance Lynn 10.00 25.00
PA Pedro Alvarez 10.00 25.00

2008 Upper Deck USA National Team Patch Autographs

STATED PRINT RUN 99 SER.#'d SETS
BH Brett Hunter 6.00 15.00
BM Brian Matusz 30.00 60.00
BW Brett Wallace 12.50 30.00
CS Cody Satterwhite 15.00 40.00
DE Danny Espinosa 8.00 20.00
ES Eric Surkamp 6.00 15.00
JD Jordan Danks 8.00 20.00
JH Jeremy Hamilton 6.00 15.00
JK Joe Kelly 6.00 15.00
JM Jordy Mercer 6.00 15.00
JR Josh Romanski 6.00 15.00
JS Justin Smoak 10.00 25.00
JT Jacob Thompson 6.00 15.00
LF Logan Forsythe 6.00 15.00
LL Lance Lynn 10.00 25.00
MM Mike Minor 8.00 20.00
PA Pedro Alvarez 12.50 30.00
PP Petey Paramore 6.00 15.00
RB Ryan Berry 6.00 15.00
RF Ryan Flaherty 6.00 15.00
RK Roger Kieschnick 6.00 15.00
SF Seth Frankoff 6.00 15.00
SG Scott Gorgen 6.00 15.00
TM Tommy Medica 6.00 15.00
TR Tyson Ross 10.00 25.00

2008 Upper Deck Sportsfest

COMPLETE SET (12) 15.00 40.00
UNPRICED AUTO PRINT RUN 5 SETS
SF1 Ken Griffey Jr. 1.25 3.00
SF5 Daisuke Matsuzaka 1.00 2.50
SF9 Derek Jeter 1.50 4.00

2008 Upper Deck Yankee Stadium Legacy Collection

COMMON CLEMENS 1.50 4.00
COMMON DIMAGGIO 2.50 6.00
COMMON GEHRIG 2.50 6.00
COMMON JETER 3.00 8.00
COMMON MATTINGLY 2.50 6.00
COMMON RODRIGUEZ 1.50 4.00
COMMON RUTH 3.00 8.00
1-6661 ISSUED IN VARIOUS 08 UD PRODUCTS
6662-6742 ISSUED IN 2009 UD1
1 Babe Ruth 10.00 25.00

2008 Upper Deck Yankee Stadium Legacy Collection Historical Moments

473 Notre Dame v. Army 1.50 4.00
1198 Joe Louis 1.25 3.00
1288 Joe DiMaggio 2.00 5.00
2835 1958 NFL Championship 1.50 4.00
2946 Whitey Ford 1.50 4.00
3407 Pope Paul VI 1.25 3.00
4131 Muhammad Ali v. Ken Norton 2.00 5.00
4181 Reggie Jackson 1.50 4.00
5404 U2 1.25 3.00
6710 2008 MLB All Star Game 1.50 4.00

2008 Upper Deck Yankee Stadium Legacy Collection Memorabilia

AP Andy Pettitte 6.00 15.00
BD Bill Dickey 6.00 15.00
BM Billy Martin 10.00 25.00
BR Babe Ruth 200.00 500.00
CL Roger Clemens 6.00 15.00
CS Casey Stengel 10.00 25.00
CW Chien-Ming Wang 6.00 15.00
DE Bucky Dent 4.00 10.00
DJ Derek Jeter 12.00 30.00
DM Don Mattingly 10.00 25.00
DW Dave Winfield 6.00 15.00
EH Elston Howard 6.00 15.00
FC Frankie Crosetti 10.00 25.00
GG Goose Gossage 6.00 15.00
GM Gil McDougald 6.00 15.00
GN Graig Nettles 6.00 15.00
GS Gary Sheffield 4.00 10.00
JA Reggie Jackson 6.00 15.00
JC Joba Chamberlain 4.00 10.00
JD Joe DiMaggio 75.00 200.00
JG Jason Giambi 4.00 10.00
JP Joe Pepitone 10.00 25.00
LG Lou Gehrig 125.00 300.00
LP Lou Piniella 50.00 120.00
MC Melky Cabrera 4.00 10.00
MM Mike Mussina 6.00 15.00
MU Bobby Murcer 4.00 10.00
ON Paul O'Neill 6.00 15.00
PN Phil Niekro 6.00 15.00
PO Jorge Posada 6.00 15.00
RC Robinson Cano 6.00 15.00
RE Allie Reynolds 10.00 25.00
RG Ron Guidry 6.00 15.00
RJ Randy Johnson 6.00 15.00
RM Roger Maris 10.00 25.00
SL Sparky Lyle 4.00 10.00
TH Tommy Henrich 10.00 25.00
TM Thurman Munson 10.00 25.00
WB Wade Boggs 6.00 15.00
WF Whitey Ford 10.00 25.00
WR Willie Randolph 4.00 10.00
YB Yogi Berra 10.00 25.00

2009 Upper Deck

This set was released on February 3, 2009. The base set consists of 500 cards.
COMP.SER 1 SET w/o #0 (500) 40.00 80.00
COMP.SER 2 SET w/SP RC (506) 75.00 150.00
COMP.SER 2 SET w/o SP RC (500) 50.00 100.00
COMMON CARD (1-1000) .15 .40
COMMON RC (1-1000) .40 1.00
COMMON RC (1001-1006) 1.25 3.00
0 Joe DiMaggio SP 40.00 80.00
1 Randy Johnson .40 1.00
2 Conor Jackson .15 .40
3 Brandon Webb .25 .60
4 Dan Haren .15 .40
5 Orlando Hudson .15 .40
6 Stephen Drew .15 .40
7 Mark Reynolds .15 .40
8 Eric Byrnes .15 .40
9 Justin Upton .25 .60
10 Chris B. Young .15 .40
11 Max Scherzer .40 1.00
12 Alex Romero .15 .40
13 Chad Tracy .15 .40
14 Brandon Lyon .15 .40
15 Adam Dunn .25 .60
16 David Eckstein .15 .40
17 Jair Jurrjens .15 .40
18 Mike Hampton .15 .40
19 Brandon Jones .15 .40
20 Tom Glavine .25 .60
21 John Smoltz .40 1.00
22 Chipper Jones .40 1.00
23 Yunel Escobar .15 .40
24 Kelly Johnson .15 .40
25 Brian McCann .25 .60
26 Jeff Francoeur .25 .60
27 Tim Hudson .25 .60
28 Casey Kotchman .15 .40
29 Nick Markakis .30 .75
30 Brian Roberts .15 .40
31 Jeremy Guthrie .15 .40
32 Ramon Hernandez .15 .40
33 Adam Jones .25 .60
34 Luke Scott .15 .40
35 Aubrey Huff .15 .40
36 Daniel Cabrera .15 .40
37 George Sherrill .15 .40
38 Melvin Mora .15 .40
39 Jay Payton .15 .40
40 Mark Kotsay .15 .40
41 David Ortiz .40 1.00
42 Jacoby Ellsbury .30 .75
43 Coco Crisp .15 .40
44 J.D. Drew .15 .40
45 Daisuke Matsuzaka .25 .60
46 Josh Beckett .15 .40
47 Curt Schilling .25 .60
48 Clay Buchholz .15 .40
49 Dustin Pedroia .30 .75
50 Julio Lugo .15 .40
51 Mike Lowell .15 .40
52 Jonathan Papelbon .25 .60
53 Jason Varitek .40 1.00
54 Hideki Okajima .15 .40
55 Jon Lester .25 .60
56 Tim Wakefield .25 .60
57 Kevin Youkilis .15 .40
58 Jason Bay .25 .60
59 Justin Masterson .15 .40
60 Jeff Samardzija .25 .60
61 Alfonso Soriano .25 .60
62 Derrek Lee .15 .40
63 Aramis Ramirez .15 .40
64 Kerry Wood .15 .40
65 Jim Edmonds .25 .60
66 Kosuke Fukudome .25 .60
67 Geovany Soto .25 .60
68 Ted Lilly .15 .40
69 Carlos Zambrano .25 .60
70 Ryan Theriot .15 .40
71 Mark DeRosa .25 .60
72 Ronny Cedeno .15 .40
73 Ryan Dempster .15 .40
74 Jon Lieber .15 .40
75 Rich Hill .15 .40
76 Rich Harden .15 .40
77 Alexei Ramirez .25 .60
78 Nick Swisher .25 .60
79 Carlos Quentin .15 .40
80 Jermaine Dye .15 .40
81 Paul Konerko .25 .60
82 Orlando Cabrera .15 .40
83 Joe Crede .25 .60
84 Jim Thome .25 .60
85 Gavin Floyd .15 .40
86 Javier Vazquez .15 .40
87 Mark Buehrle .25 .60
88 Bobby Jenks .15 .40
89 Brian Anderson .15 .40
90 A.J. Pierzynski .15 .40
91 Jose Contreras .15 .40
92 Juan Uribe .15 .40
93a Ken Griffey Jr. .75 2.00
93b K.Griffey Jr. SEA 20.00 50.00
94 Chris Dickerson .15 .40
95 Brandon Phillips .15 .40
96 Aaron Harang .15 .40
97 Bronson Arroyo .15 .40
98 Edinson Volquez .15 .40
99 Johnny Cueto .25 .60
100 Edwin Encarnacion .40 1.00
101 Jeff Keppinger .15 .40
102 Joey Votto .40 1.00
103 Jay Bruce .25 .60
104 Ryan Freel .15 .40
105 Travis Hafner .15 .40
106 Victor Martinez .25 .60
107 Grady Sizemore .25 .60
108 Cliff Lee .25 .60
109 Ryan Garko .15 .40
110 Jhonny Peralta .15 .40
111 Franklin Gutierrez .15 .40
112 Fausto Carmona .15 .40
113 Jeff Baker .15 .40
114 Troy Tulowitzki .40 1.00
115 Matt Holliday .40 1.00
116 Todd Helton .25 .60
117 Ubaldo Jimenez .15 .40
118 Brian Fuentes .15 .40
119 Willy Taveras .15 .40
120 Aaron Cook .15 .40
121 Jason Grilli .15 .40
122 Garrett Atkins .15 .40
123 Jeff Francis .15 .40
124 Ryan Spilborghs .15 .40
125 Armando Galarraga .15 .40
126 Miguel Cabrera .40 1.00
127 Placido Polanco .15 .40
128 Edgar Renteria .15 .40
129 Carlos Guillen .15 .40
130 Gary Sheffield .15 .40
131 Curtis Granderson .30 .75
132 Marcus Thames .15 .40
133 Magglio Ordonez .25 .60
134 Jeremy Bonderman .15 .40
135 Dontrelle Willis .15 .40
136 Kenny Rogers .15 .40
137 Justin Verlander .40 1.00
138 Nate Robertson .15 .40
139 Todd Jones .15 .40
140 Joel Zumaya .15 .40
141 Hanley Ramirez .25 .60
142 Jeremy Hermida .15 .40
143 Mike Jacobs .15 .40
144 Andrew Miller .25 .60
145 Josh Willingham .25 .60
146 Luis Gonzalez .15 .40
147 Dan Uggla .15 .40
148 Scott Olsen .15 .40
149 Josh Johnson .25 .60
150 Darin Erstad .15 .40
151 Hunter Pence .25 .60
152 Roy Oswalt .25 .60
153 Lance Berkman .25 .60
154 Carlos Lee .15 .40
155 Michael Bourn .15 .40
156 Kazuo Matsui .15 .40
157 Miguel Tejada .25 .60
158 Ty Wigginton .15 .40
159 Jose Valverde .15 .40
160 J.R. Towles .15 .40
161 Brandon Backe .15 .40
162 Randy Wolf .15 .40
163 Mike Aviles .15 .40
164 Brian Bannister .15 .40
165 Zack Greinke .25 .60
166 Gil Meche .15 .40
167 Alex Gordon .25 .60
168 Tony Pena .15 .40
169 Luke Hochevar .15 .40
170 Mark Grudzielanek .15 .40
171 Jose Guillen .15 .40
172 Billy Butler .15 .40
173 David DeJesus .15 .40
174 Joey Gathright .15 .40
175 Mark Teahen .15 .40
176 Joakim Soria .15 .40
177 Mark Teixeira .25 .60
178 Vladimir Guerrero .25 .60
179 Torii Hunter .15 .40
180 Jered Weaver .25 .60
181 Chone Figgins .15 .40
182 Francisco Rodriguez .25 .60
183 Garret Anderson .15 .40
184 Howie Kendrick .15 .40
185 John Lackey .25 .60
186 Ervin Santana .15 .40
187 Joe Saunders .15 .40
188 Gary Matthews .15 .40
189 Jon Garland .15 .40
190 Nick Adenhart .15 .40
191 Manny Ramirez .40 1.00
192 Casey Blake .15 .40
193 Chad Billingsley .25 .60
194 Russell Martin .15 .40
195 Matt Kemp .30 .75
196 James Loney .15 .40
197 Jeff Kent .15 .40
198 Nomar Garciaparra .25 .60
199 Rafael Furcal .15 .40
200 Andruw Jones .15 .40
201 Andre Ethier .25 .60
202 Takashi Saito .15 .40
203 Brad Penny .15 .40
204 Hiroki Kuroda .15 .40
205 Jonathan Broxton .15 .40
206 Chin-Lung Hu .15 .40
207 Juan Pierre .15 .40
208 Blake DeWitt .15 .40
209 Derek Lowe .15 .40
210 Clayton Kershaw .75 2.00
211 Greg Maddux .50 1.25
212 CC Sabathia .25 .60
213 Yovani Gallardo .15 .40
214 Ryan Braun .25 .60
215 Prince Fielder .25 .60
216 Corey Hart .15 .40
217 Bill Hall .15 .40
218 Rickie Weeks .15 .40
219 Mike Cameron .15 .40
220 Ben Sheets .15 .40
221 Jason Kendall .15 .40
222 J.J. Hardy .15 .40
223 Jeff Suppan .15 .40
224 Ray Durham .15 .40
225 Denard Span .15 .40
226 Carlos Gomez .15 .40
227 Joe Mauer .30 .75
228 Justin Morneau .25 .60
229 Michael Cuddyer .15 .40
230 Joe Nathan .15 .40
231 Kevin Slowey .25 .60
232 Delmon Young .25 .60
233 Jason Kubel .15 .40
234 Craig Monroe .15 .40
235 Livan Hernandez .15 .40
236 Francisco Liriano .15 .40
237 Pat Neshek .25 .60
238 Boof Bonser .15 .40
239 Nick Blackburn .15 .40
240 Daniel Murphy RC 1.50 4.00
241 Nick Evans .15 .40
242 Jose Reyes .25 .60
243 David Wright .30 .75
244 Carlos Delgado .15 .40
245 Luis Castillo .15 .40
246 Ryan Church .15 .40
247 Carlos Beltran .25 .60
248 Moises Alou .15 .40
249 Pedro Martinez .25 .60
250 Johan Santana .25 .60
251 John Maine .15 .40
252 Endy Chavez .15 .40
253 Oliver Perez .15 .40
254 Brian Schneider .15 .40
255 Fernando Tatis .15 .40
256 Mike Pelfrey .15 .40
257 Billy Wagner .15 .40
258 Ramon Castro .15 .40
259 Ivan Rodriguez .25 .60
260 Alex Rodriguez .50 1.25
261 Derek Jeter 1.00 2.50
262 Robinson Cano .25 .60
263 Jason Giambi .15 .40
264 Bobby Abreu .15 .40
265 Johnny Damon .25 .60
266 Melky Cabrera .15 .40
267 Hideki Matsui .40 1.00
268 Jorge Posada .25 .60
269 Joba Chamberlain .15 .40
270 Ian Kennedy .15 .40
271 Mike Mussina .25 .60
272 Andy Pettitte .25 .60
273 Mariano Rivera .50 1.25
274 Chien-Ming Wang .25 .60
275 Phil Hughes .15 .40
276 Xavier Nady .15 .40
277 Richie Sexson .15 .40
278 Brad Ziegler .15 .40
279 Justin Duchscherer .15 .40
280 Eric Chavez .15 .40
281 Bobby Crosby .15 .40
282 Mark Ellis .15 .40
283 Daric Barton .15 .40
284 Frank Thomas .40 1.00
285 Emil Brown .15 .40
286 Huston Street .15 .40
287 Jack Cust .15 .40
288 Kurt Suzuki .15 .40
289 Joe Blanton .15 .40
290 Ryan Howard .30 .75
291 Chase Utley .25 .60
292 Jimmy Rollins .25 .60
293 Pedro Feliz .15 .40
294 Pat Burrell .15 .40
295 Geoff Jenkins .15 .40
296 Shane Victorino .15 .40
297 Brett Myers .15 .40
298 Brad Lidge .15 .40
299 Cole Hamels .30 .75
300 Jamie Moyer .15 .40
301 Adam Eaton .15 .40
302 Matt Stairs .15 .40
303 Nate McLouth .15 .40
304 Ian Snell .15 .40
305 Matt Capps .15 .40
306 Freddy Sanchez .15 .40
307 Ryan Doumit .15 .40
308 Adam LaRoche .15 .40
309 Jack Wilson .15 .40
310 Tom Gorzelanny .15 .40
311 Jody Gerut .15 .40
312 Jake Peavy .15 .40
313 Chris Young .15 .40
314 Trevor Hoffman .25 .60
315 Adrian Gonzalez .30 .75
316 Chase Headley .15 .40
317 Khalil Greene .15 .40
318 Kevin Kouzmanoff .15 .40
319 Brian Giles .15 .40
320 Josh Bard .15 .40
321 Scott Hairston .15 .40
322 Barry Zito .25 .60
323 Tim Lincecum .25 .60
324 Matt Cain .25 .60
325 Brian Wilson .40 1.00
326 Aaron Rowand .15 .40
327 Randy Winn .15 .40
328 Omar Vizquel .25 .60
329 Bengie Molina .15 .40
330 Fred Lewis .15 .40
331 Erik Bedard .15 .40
332 Felix Hernandez .25 .60
333 Ichiro Suzuki .50 1.25
334 J.J. Putz .15 .40
335 Raul Ibanez .25 .60
336 Adrian Beltre .40 1.00
337 Jose Vidro .15 .40
338 Jeff Clement .15 .40
339 Kenji Johjima .25 .60
340 Wladimir Balentien .15 .40
341 Jose Lopez .15 .40
342 Kyle Lohse .15 .40
343 Albert Pujols .50 1.25
344 Troy Glaus .15 .40
345 Chris Carpenter .25 .60
346 Adam Kennedy .15 .40
347 Rick Ankiel .15 .40
348 Adam Wainwright .25 .60
349 Jason Isringhausen .15 .40
350 Chris Duncan .15 .40
351 Skip Schumaker .15 .40
352 Mark Mulder .15 .40
353 Todd Wellemeyer .15 .40
354 Cesar Izturis .15 .40
355 Ryan Ludwick .25 .60
356 Yadier Molina .40 1.00
357 Braden Looper .15 .40
358 B.J. Upton .25 .60
359 Carl Crawford .25 .60
360 Evan Longoria .25 .60
361 James Shields .15 .40
362 Scott Kazmir .15 .40
363 Carlos Pena .25 .60
364 Akinori Iwamura .15 .40
365 Jonny Gomes .15 .40
366 Cliff Floyd .15 .40
367 Troy Percival .15 .40
368 Edwin Jackson .15 .40
369 Matt Garza .15 .40
370 Eric Hinske .15 .40
371 Rocco Baldelli .15 .40
372 Chris Davis .25 .60
373 Marlon Byrd .15 .40
374 Michael Young .15 .40
375 Ian Kinsler .25 .60
376 Josh Hamilton .25 .60
377 Hank Blalock .15 .40
378 Milton Bradley .15 .40
379 Kevin Millwood .15 .40
380 Vicente Padilla .15 .40
381 Jarrod Saltalamacchia .15 .40
382 Jesse Litsch .15 .40
383 Roy Halladay .25 .60
384 A.J. Burnett .15 .40
385 Dustin McGowan .15 .40
386 Scott Rolen .25 .60
387 Alex Rios .15 .40
388 Vernon Wells .15 .40
389 Shannon Stewart .15 .40
390 B.J. Ryan .15 .40
391 Lyle Overbay .15 .40
392 Elijah Dukes .15 .40
393 Lastings Milledge .15 .40
394 Chad Cordero .15 .40
395 Ryan Zimmerman .25 .60
396 Austin Kearns .15 .40

397 Wily Mo Pena .15 .40
398 Ronnie Belliard .15 .40
399 Cristian Guzman .15 .40
400 Jesus Flores .15 .40
401a David Price RC .75 2.00
401b David Price White Uni SP 50.00 100.00
402 Matt Antonelli RC .60 1.50
403 Jonathon Niese RC .60 1.50
404 Phil Coke RC .60 1.50
405 Jason Pridie (RC) .40 1.00
406 Mark Saccomanno RC .40 1.00
407 Freddy Sandoval (RC) .40 1.00
408 Travis Snider RC .60 1.50
409 Matt Tuiasosopo (RC) .40 1.00
410 Will Venable RC .40 1.00
411 Brad Nelson (RC) .40 1.00
412 Aaron Cunningham RC .40 1.00
413 Wilkin Castillo RC .40 1.00
414 Robert Parnell RC .60 1.50
415 Conor Gillaspie RC 1.00 2.50
416 Dexter Fowler (RC) .60 1.50
417 George Kottaras (RC) .40 1.00
418 Josh Roenicke RC .40 1.00
419 Luis Valbuena RC .60 1.50
420 Casey McGehee (RC) .40 1.00
421 Mat Gamel RC 1.00 2.50
422 Greg Golson (RC) .40 1.00
423 Alfredo Aceves RC .60 1.50
424 Michael Bowden (RC) .40 1.00
425 Kila Kaaihue (RC) .60 1.50
426 Josh Geer (RC) .40 1.00
427 James Parr (RC) .40 1.00
428 Chris Lambert (RC) .40 1.00
429 Fernando Perez (RC) .40 1.00
430 Josh Whitesell RC .60 1.50
431 Pedroia/Dice-K/Beckett TL .30 .75
432 Howard/Hamels/Rollins TL .30 .75
433 Reyes/Wright/Delgado TL .30 .75
434 Rodriguez/Jeter/Mussina TL 1.00 2.50
435 Carlos Quentin/Gavin Floyd
Javier Vazquez TL .15 .40
436 Ludwick/Pujols/Wellem TL .50 1.25
437 Cabrera/Grand/Verlander .40 1.00
438 Adrian Gonzalez/Jake Peavy
Brian Giles TL .30 .75
439 Braun/Fielder/Sheets TL .25 .60
440 Cliff Lee/Grady Sizemore
Jhonny Peralta TL .25 .60
441 Josh Hamilton/Ian Kinsler
Vicente Padilla TL .25 .60
442 Jorge Cantu/Hanley Ramirez
Ricky Nolasco TL .25 .60
443 Carlos Pena/Akinori Iwamura
B.J. Upton TL .25 .60
444 Jack Cust/Dana Eveland
Kurt Suzuki TL .15 .40
445 Alfonso Soriano/Ryan Dempster
Aramis Ramirez TL .25 .60
446 Lance Berkman/Roy Oswalt
Miguel Tejada TL .25 .60
447 Matt Holliday/Aaron Cook
Willy Taveras TL .40 1.00
448 Nate McLouth .15 .40
Adam LaRoche
Paul Maholm TL
449 Brian Roberts/Aubrey Huff
Jeremy Guthrie TL .15 .40
450 Justin Morneau/Joe Mauer
Carlos Gomez TL .30 .75
451 Ibanez/Ichiro/King Felix TL .50 1.25
452 Chipper Jones/Jair Jurrjens
Brian McCann TL .40 1.00
453 Brandon Webb/Dan Haren
Stephen Drew TL .25 .60
454 Lincecum/Winn/Molina TL .25 .60
455 Roy Halladay/A.J. Burnett
Alex Rios TL .25 .60
456 Edinson Volquez/Brandon Phillips
Edwin Encarnacion TL .40 1.00
457 Chad Billingsley/Matt Kemp
James Loney TL .30 .75
458 Ervin Santana/Vladimir Guerrero
Francisco Rodriguez TL .25 .60
459 Zack Greinke/Gil Meche
David DeJesus TL .25 .60
460 Tim Redding/Cristian Guzman
Lastings Milledge TL .15 .40
461 Carlos Zambrano HL .25 .60
462 Jon Lester HL .25 .60
463 Jim Thome HL .25 .60
464 Ken Griffey Jr. HL .75 2.00
465 Manny Ramirez HL .40 1.00
466 Derek Jeter HL 1.00 2.50
467 Josh Hamilton HL .25 .60
468 Francisco Rodriguez HL .25 .60
469 Alex Rodriguez HL .50 1.25
470 J.D. Drew HL .15 .40
471 David Wright CL .30 .75
472 Chase Utley CL .25 .60
473 Chipper Jones CL .40 1.00
474 Cristian Guzman CL .15 .40
475 Hanley Ramirez CL .25 .60
476 CC Sabathia CL .25 .60
477 Lance Berkman CL .25 .60
478 Alfonso Soriano CL .25 .60
479 Albert Pujols CL .50 1.25
480 Nate McLouth CL .15 .40
481 Brandon Phillips CL .15 .40
482 Adrian Gonzalez CL .30 .75
483 Brandon Webb CL .25 .60
484 Manny Ramirez CL .40 1.00
485 Tim Lincecum CL .25 .60
486 Matt Holliday CL .40 1.00

487 Dustin Pedroia CL .30 .75
488 Alex Rodriguez CL .50 1.25
489 Evan Longoria CL .25 .60
490 Roy Halladay CL .25 .60
491 Nick Markakis CL .30 .75
492 Grady Sizemore CL .25 .60
493 Carlos Quentin CL .15 .40
494 Joakim Soria CL .15 .40
495 Miguel Cabrera CL .40 1.00
496 Joe Mauer CL .30 .75
497 Francisco Rodriguez CL .25 .60
498 Jack Cust CL .15 .40
499 Ichiro Suzuki CL .50 1.25
500 Josh Hamilton CL .25 .60
501 Brandon Webb .25 .60
502 Miguel Montero .15 .40
503 Tony Pena .15 .40
504 Jon Rauch .15 .40
505 Augie Ojeda .15 .40
506 Yusmeiro Petit .15 .40
507 Chris Snyder .15 .40
508 Chris B. Young .15 .40
509 Doug Slaten .15 .40
510 Tony Clark .15 .40
511 Justin Upton .25 .60
512 Chad Qualls .15 .40
513 Doug Davis .15 .40
514 Eric Byrnes .15 .40
515 Conor Jackson .15 .40
516 Mike Gonzalez .15 .40
517 Josh Anderson .15 .40
518 Tom Glavine .25 .60
519 Clint Sammons .15 .40
520 Martin Prado .15 .40
521 Jorge Campillo .15 .40
522 Omar Infante .15 .40
523 Javier Vazquez .15 .40
524 Jo Jo Reyes .15 .40
525 Gregor Blanco .15 .40
526 Rafael Soriano .15 .40
527 Manny Acosta .15 .40
528 Chipper Jones .40 1.00
529 Buddy Carlyle .15 .40
530 Radhames Liz .15 .40
531 Scott Moore .15 .40
532 Jim Johnson .15 .40
533 Oscar Salazar .15 .40
534 Nick Markakis .30 .75
535 Brian Roberts .15 .40
536 Jeremy Guthrie .15 .40
537 Adam Jones .25 .60
538 Chris Ray .15 .40
539 Aubrey Huff .15 .40
540 Ty Wigginton .25 .60
541 Dennis Sarfate .15 .40
542 Melvin Mora .15 .40
543 Chris Waters .15 .40
544 John Smoltz .40 1.00
545 Brad Penny .15 .40
546 Josh Bard .15 .40
547 Takashi Saito .15 .40
548 Jacoby Ellsbury .30 .75
549 Jeff Bailey .15 .40
550 Ramon Ramirez .15 .40
551 Daisuke Matsuzaka .25 .60
552 Josh Beckett .15 .40
553 Jed Lowrie .15 .40
554 Dustin Pedroia .30 .75
555 David Ortiz .40 1.00
556 Jonathan Van Every .15 .40
557 Jonathan Papelbon .25 .60
558 Manny Delcarmen .15 .40
559 Hideki Okajima .15 .40
560 Jon Lester .25 .60
561 Javier Lopez .15 .40
562 Kevin Youkilis .15 .40
563 Jason Varitek .40 1.00
564 Milton Bradley .15 .40
565 Mike Fontenot .15 .40
566 Micah Hoffpauir .15 .40
567 Sean Marshall .15 .40
568 Alfonso Soriano .25 .60
569 Neal Cotts .15 .40
570 Kosuke Fukudome .25 .60
571 Reed Johnson .15 .40
572 Carlos Marmol .25 .60
573 Chad Gaudin .15 .40
574 Rich Harden .15 .40
575 Ted Lilly .15 .40
576 Carlos Zambrano .25 .60
577 Ryan Theriot .15 .40
578 Ryan Dempster .15 .40
579 Matt Thornton .15 .40
580 Jerry Owens .15 .40
581 Alexei Ramirez .25 .60
582 John Danks .15 .40
583 Carlos Quentin .15 .40
584 D.J. Carrasco .15 .40
585 Dewayne Wise .15 .40
586 Clayton Richard .15 .40
587 Brent Lillibridge .15 .40
588 Jim Thome .25 .60
589 Chris Getz .15 .40
590 Octavio Dotel .15 .40
591 Mark Buehrle .25 .60
592 Bobby Jenks .15 .40
593 Joey Votto .40 1.00
594 Jay Bruce .25 .60
595 David Weathers .15 .40
596 Bill Bray .15 .40
597 Mike Lincoln .15 .40
598 Norris Hopper .15 .40
599 Alex Gonzalez .15 .40

600 Jerry Hairston Jr. .15 .40
601 Brandon Phillips .15 .40
602 Aaron Harang .15 .40
603 Bronson Arroyo .15 .40
604 Edinson Volquez .15 .40
605 Ryan Hanigan .15 .40
606 Jared Burton .15 .40
607 Aaron Laffey .15 .40
608 Kerry Wood .15 .40
609 Shin-Soo Choo .25 .60
610 David Dellucci .15 .40
611 Mark DeRosa .25 .60
612 Masahide Kobayashi .15 .40
613 Rafael Perez .15 .40
614 Grady Sizemore .25 .60
615 Cliff Lee .25 .60
616 Ben Francisco .15 .40
617 Jensen Lewis .15 .40
618 Joe Smith .15 .40
619 Asdrubal Cabrera .25 .60
620 Brad Hawpe .15 .40
621 Chris Iannetta .15 .40
622 Clint Barmes .15 .40
623 Seth Smith .15 .40
624 Aaron Cook .15 .40
625 Troy Tulowitzki .40 1.00
626 Todd Helton .25 .60
627 Taylor Buchholz .15 .40
628 Jason Marquis .15 .40
629 Ian Stewart .15 .40
630 Ryan Speier .15 .40
631 Manny Corpas .15 .40
632 Yorvit Torrealba .15 .40
633 Fernando Rodney .15 .40
634 Justin Verlander .40 1.00
635 Bobby Seay .15 .40
636 Clete Thomas .15 .40
637 Placido Polanco .15 .40
638 Ramon Santiago .15 .40
639 Adam Everett .15 .40
640 Gary Sheffield .15 .40
641 Curtis Granderson .30 .75
642 Freddy Dolsi .15 .40
643 Magglio Ordonez .25 .60
644 Zach Miner .15 .40
645 Brandon Inge .15 .40
646 Dallas McPherson .15 .40
647 Anibal Sanchez .15 .40
648 Jorge Cantu .15 .40
649 John Baker .15 .40
650 Wes Helms .15 .40
651 Ricky Nolasco .15 .40
652 Chris Volstad .15 .40
653 Renyel Pinto .15 .40
654 Alfredo Amezaga .15 .40
655 Cameron Maybin .15 .40
656 Matt Lindstrom .15 .40
657 Cody Ross .15 .40
658 Logan Kensing .15 .40
659 Tim Byrdak .15 .40
660 Reggie Abercrombie .15 .40
661 Geoff Blum .15 .40
662 Humberto Quintero .15 .40
663 Doug Brocail .15 .40
664 Roy Oswalt .25 .60
665 Lance Berkman .25 .60
666 Carlos Lee .15 .40
667 Latroy Hawkins .15 .40
668 Geoff Geary .15 .40
669 Brian Moehler .15 .40
670 Wandy Rodriguez .15 .40
671 Esteban German .15 .40
672 Ross Gload .15 .40
673 Joakim Soria .15 .40
674 Kyle Farnsworth .15 .40
675 Ryan Shealy .15 .40
676 Mike Aviles .15 .40
677 John Buck .15 .40
678 Zack Greinke .25 .60
679 John Bale .15 .40
680 Alex Gordon .25 .60
681 Coco Crisp .15 .40
682 Miguel Olivo .15 .40
683 Alberto Callaspo .15 .40
684 Kyle Davies .15 .40
685 Brandon Wood .15 .40
686 Erick Aybar .15 .40
687 Robb Quinlan .15 .40
688 Bobby Abreu .15 .40
689 Jose Arredondo .15 .40
690 Juan Rivera .15 .40
691 Kendry Morales .15 .40
692 Vladimir Guerrero .25 .60
693 Darren Oliver .15 .40
694 Jeff Mathis .15 .40
695 Maicer Izturis .15 .40
696 Mike Napoli .15 .40
697 Reggie Willits .15 .40
698 Scot Shields .15 .40
699 John Lackey .25 .60
700 Manny Ramirez .40 1.00
701 Danny Ardoin .15 .40
702 Orlando Hudson .15 .40
703 Hong-Chih Kuo .15 .40
704 Mark Loretta .15 .40
705 Cory Wade .15 .40
706 Casey Blake .15 .40
707 Eric Stults .15 .40
708 Jason Schmidt .15 .40
709 Chad Billingsley .25 .60
710 Russell Martin .15 .40
711 Matt Kemp .30 .75
712 James Loney .15 .40

713 Rafael Furcal .15 .40
714 Ramon Troncoso .15 .40
715 Jonathan Broxton .15 .40
716 Hiroki Kuroda .15 .40
717 Andre Ethier .25 .60
718 Corey Hart .15 .40
719 Mitch Stetter .15 .40
720 Manny Parra .15 .40
721 Dave Bush .15 .40
722 Trevor Hoffman .25 .60
723 Tony Gwynn .15 .40
724 Chris Duffy .15 .40
725 Seth McClung .15 .40
726 J.J. Hardy .15 .40
727 David Riske .15 .40
728 Todd Coffey .15 .40
729 Rickie Weeks .15 .40
730 Mike Rivera .15 .40
731 Carlos Villanueva .15 .40
732 Ryan Braun .25 .60
733 Nick Punto .15 .40
734 Francisco Liriano .15 .40
735 Craig Breslow .15 .40
736 Matt Macri .15 .40
737 Scott Baker .15 .40
738 Jesse Crain .15 .40
739 Brendan Harris .15 .40
740 Alexi Casilla .15 .40
741 Nick Blackburn .15 .40
742 Brian Buscher .15 .40
743 Denard Span .15 .40
744 Mike Redmond .15 .40
745 Joe Mauer .30 .75
746 Carlos Gomez .15 .40
747 Matt Guerrier .15 .40
748 Joe Nathan .15 .40
749 Livan Hernandez .15 .40
750 Ryan Church .15 .40
751 Carlos Beltran .25 .60
752 Jeremy Reed .15 .40
753 Oliver Perez .15 .40
754 Duaner Sanchez .15 .40
755 J.J. Putz .15 .40
756 Mike Pelfrey .15 .40
757 Brian Schneider .15 .40
758 Francisco Rodriguez .25 .60
759 John Maine .15 .40
760 Daniel Murphy .60 1.50
761 Johan Santana .25 .60
762 Jose Reyes .25 .60
763 David Wright .30 .75
764 Carlos Delgado .15 .40
765 Pedro Feliciano .15 .40
766 Derek Jeter 1.00 2.50
767 Brian Bruney .15 .40
768 A.J. Burnett .15 .40
769 Andy Pettitte .25 .60
770 Nick Swisher .25 .60
771 Damaso Marte .15 .40
772 Edwar Ramirez .15 .40
773 CC Sabathia .25 .60
774 Chien-Ming Wang .25 .60
775 Mariano Rivera .50 1.25
776 Mark Teixeira .25 .60
777 Joba Chamberlain .15 .40
778 Jose Veras .15 .40
779 Hideki Matsui .40 1.00
780 Jose Molina .15 .40
781 Alex Rodriguez .50 1.25
782 Michael Wuertz .15 .40
783 Orlando Cabrera .15 .40
784 Sean Gallagher .15 .40
785 Dallas Braden .25 .60
786 Gio Gonzalez .25 .60
787 Rajai Davis .15 .40
788 Brad Ziegler .15 .40
789 Matt Holliday .40 1.00
790 Jack Cust .15 .40
791 Santiago Casilla .15 .40
792 Jason Giambi .15 .40
793 Joey Devine .15 .40
794 Travis Buck .15 .40
795 Justin Duchscherer .15 .40
796 Rob Bowen .15 .40
797 Andrew Brown .15 .40
798 Ryan Sweeney .15 .40
799 Jimmy Rollins .25 .60
800 Chad Durbin .15 .40
801 Clay Condrey .15 .40
802 Chris Coste .15 .40
803 Ryan Madson .15 .40
804 Chan Ho Park .25 .60
805 Carlos Ruiz .15 .40
806 Kyle Kendrick .15 .40
807 Jayson Werth .25 .60
808 Cole Hamels .30 .75
809 Brad Lidge .15 .40
810 Greg Dobbs .15 .40
811 Scott Eyre .15 .40
812 Eric Bruntlett .15 .40
813 Ryan Howard .30 .75
814 Chase Utley .25 .60
815 Paul Maholm .15 .40
816 Andy LaRoche .15 .40
817 Brandon Moss .15 .40
818 Nyjer Morgan .15 .40
819 John Grabow .15 .40
820 Tom Gorzelanny .15 .40
821 Steve Pearce .40 1.00
822 Sean Burnett .15 .40
823 Tyler Yates .15 .40
824 Zach Duke .15 .40
825 Matt Capps .15 .40

826 Ross Ohlendorf .15 .40
827 Nate McLouth .15 .40
828 Adrian Gonzalez .30 .75
829 Heath Bell .15 .40
830 Luis Rodriguez .15 .40
831 Kevin Kouzmanoff .15 .40
832 Edgar Gonzalez .15 .40
833 Cha-Seung Baek .15 .40
834 Cla Meredith .15 .40
835 Justin Hampson .25 .60
836 Nick Hundley .15 .40
837 Mike Adams .15 .40
838 Jake Peavy .15 .40
839 Chris Young .15 .40
840 Brian Giles .15 .40
841 Steve Holm .15 .40
842 Dave Roberts .25 .60
843 Travis Ishikawa .15 .40
844 Pablo Sandoval .30 .75
845 Emmanuel Burriss .15 .40
846 Nate Schierholtz .15 .40
847 Randy Johnson .40 1.00
848 Kevin Frandsen .15 .40
849 Edgar Renteria .15 .40
850 Jack Taschner .15 .40
851 Tim Lincecum .25 .60
852 Alex Hinshaw .15 .40
853 Jonathan Sanchez .15 .40
854 Eugenio Velez .15 .40
855a K.Griffey Jr. 09 SEA .75 2.00
855b K.Griffey Jr. 89 SEA 12.00 30.00
855c K.Griffey Jr. 90 SEA 12.00 30.00
855d K.Griffey Jr. 91 SEA 12.00 30.00
855e K.Griffey Jr. 92 SEA 12.00 30.00
855f K.Griffey Jr. 93 SEA 12.00 30.00
855g K.Griffey Jr. 94 SEA 12.00 30.00
855h K.Griffey Jr. 95 SEA 12.00 30.00
855i K.Griffey Jr. 96 SEA 12.00 30.00
855j K.Griffey Jr. 97 SEA 12.00 30.00
855k K.Griffey Jr. 98 SEA 12.00 30.00
855l K.Griffey Jr. 99 SEA 12.00 30.00
855m K.Griffey Jr. 00 CIN 12.00 30.00
855n K.Griffey Jr. 01 CIN 12.00 30.00
855o K.Griffey Jr. 02 CIN 12.00 30.00
855p K.Griffey Jr. 03 CIN 12.00 30.00
855q K.Griffey Jr. 04 CIN 12.00 30.00
855r K.Griffey Jr. 05 CIN 12.00 30.00
855s K.Griffey Jr. 06 CIN 12.00 30.00
855t K.Griffey Jr. 07 CIN 12.00 30.00
855u K.Griffey Jr. 08 CHI 12.00 30.00
856 Garrett Olson .15 .40
857 Cesar Jimenez .15 .40
858 Bryan LaHair .40 1.00
859 Franklin Gutierrez .15 .40
860 Brandon Morrow .15 .40
861 Roy Corcoran .15 .40
862 Carlos Silva .15 .40
863 Kenji Johjima .25 .60
864 Jarrod Washburn .15 .40
865 Felix Hernandez .25 .60
866 Ichiro Suzuki .50 1.25
867 Miguel Batista .15 .40
868 Yuniesky Betancourt .15 .40
869 Adrian Beltre .40 1.00
870 Ryan Rowland-Smith .15 .40
871 Khalil Greene .15 .40
872 Kyle McClellan .15 .40
873 Ryan Franklin .25 .60
874 Brian Barton .15 .40
875 Josh Kinney .15 .40
876 Ryan Ludwick .25 .60
877 Brendan Ryan .15 .40
878 Albert Pujols .50 1.25
879 Troy Glaus .15 .40
880 Joel Pineiro .15 .40
881 Jason LaRue .15 .40
882 Yadier Molina .40 1.00
883 Adam Wainwright .25 .60
884 Chris Perez .15 .40
885 Adam Kennedy .15 .40
886 Akinori Iwamura .15 .40
887 J.P. Howell .15 .40
888 Ben Zobrist .25 .60
889 Gabe Gross .15 .40
890 Matt Joyce .15 .40
891 Dan Wheeler .15 .40
892 Willie Aybar .15 .40
893 Jason Bartlett .15 .40
894 Dioner Navarro .15 .40
895 Andy Sonnanstine .15 .40
896 B.J. Upton .25 .60
897 Chad Bradford .15 .40
898 Evan Longoria .25 .60
899 Shawn Riggans .15 .40
900 Scott Kazmir .15 .40
901 Grant Balfour .15 .40
902 Josh Hamilton .25 .60
903 Frank Francisco .15 .40
904 Frank Catalanotto .15 .40
905 German Duran .15 .40
906 Brandon Boggs .15 .40
907 Matt Harrison .15 .40
908 David Murphy .15 .40
909 Nelson Cruz .40 1.00
910 Joaquin Benoit .15 .40
911 Taylor Teagarden .15 .40
912 Joaquin Arias .15 .40
913 Kevin Millwood .15 .40
914 Ian Kinsler .25 .60
915 T.J. Beam .15 .40
916 Marco Scutaro .25 .60
917 Adam Lind .15 .40
918 John McDonald .15 .40

919 Scott Downs .15 .40
920 Rod Barajas .15 .40
921 Joe Inglett .15 .40
922 Alex Rios .15 .40
923 David Purcey .15 .40
924 Roy Halladay .25 .60
925 Jason Frasor .15 .40
926 Shaun Marcum .15 .40
927 Aaron Hill .15 .40
928 Adam Dunn .25 .60
929 Shawn Hill .15 .40
930 Steven Shell .15 .40
931 Saul Rivera .15 .40
932 Josh Willingham .25 .60
933 John Lannan .15 .40
934 Joel Hanrahan .25 .60
935 Daniel Cabrera .15 .40
936 Willie Harris .15 .40
937 Wil Nieves .15 .40
938 Nick Johnson .15 .40
939 Garrett Mock .15 .40
940 Anderson Hernandez .15 .40
941 Koji Uehara RC 1.00 2.50
942 Kenshin Kawakami RC .60 1.50
943 Jason Motte (RC) .60 1.50
944 Elvis Andrus RC 1.00 2.50
945 Rick Porcello RC 1.25 3.00
946 Colby Rasmus (RC) .60 1.50
947 Shairon Martis RC .60 1.50
948 Ricky Romero (RC) .60 1.50
949 Kevin Jepsen (RC) .40 1.00
950 James McDonald RC 1.00 2.50
951 Joe Mauer AW .30 .75
952 Carlos Pena AW .25 .60
953 Dustin Pedroia AW .30 .75
954 Adrian Beltre AW .40 1.00
955 Michael Young AW .15 .40
956 Torii Hunter AW .15 .40
957 Grady Sizemore AW .25 .60
958 Ichiro Suzuki AW .50 1.25
959 Yadier Molina AW .40 1.00
960 Adrian Gonzalez AW .30 .75
961 Brandon Phillips AW .15 .40
962 David Wright AW .30 .75
963 Jimmy Rollins AW .25 .60
964 Nate McLouth AW .15 .40
965 Carlos Beltran AW .25 .60
966 Shane Victorino AW .15 .40
967 Cliff Lee AW .25 .60
968 Brad Lidge AW .15 .40
969 Evan Longoria AW .25 .60
970 Geovany Soto AW .25 .60
971 Francisco Rodriguez CL .25 .60
972 Raul Ibanez CL .25 .60
973 Derek Lowe CL .15 .40
974 Scott Olsen CL .15 .40
975 Josh Johnson CL .25 .60
976 Prince Fielder CL .25 .60
977 Mike Hampton CL .15 .40
978 Kevin Gregg CL .15 .40
979 Rick Ankiel CL .15 .40
980 Nate McLouth CL .15 .40
981 Ramon Hernandez CL .15 .40
982 David Eckstein CL .15 .40
983 Felipe Lopez CL .15 .40
984 Clayton Kershaw CL .75 2.00
985 Randy Johnson CL .40 1.00
986 Huston Street CL .15 .40
987 Rocco Baldelli CL .15 .40
988 Mark Teixeira CL .25 .60
989 Pat Burrell CL .15 .40
990 Vernon Wells CL .15 .40
991 Cesar Izturis CL .15 .40
992 Kerry Wood CL .15 .40
993 Wilson Betemit CL .15 .40
994 Mike Jacobs CL .15 .40
995 Gerald Laird CL .15 .40
996 Justin Morneau CL .25 .60
997 Brian Fuentes CL .15 .40
998 Jason Giambi CL .15 .40
999 Endy Chavez CL .15 .40
1000 Michael Young CL .15 .40
1001 Brett Anderson SP RC 2.00 5.00
1002 Trevor Cahill SP RC 3.00 8.00
1003 Jordan Schafer SP (RC) 2.00 5.00
1004 Trevor Crowe SP RC 1.25 3.00
1005 Everth Cabrera SP RC 2.00 5.00
1006 Ryan Perry SP RC 3.00 8.00
SP1 M.Buehrle PG SP 6.00 15.00
SP2 Obama/Pujols ASG SP 2.50 6.00
SP3 D.Jeter ATHK SP 12.50 30.00

2009 Upper Deck Gold

*GOLD VET: 5X TO 12X BASIC VET
*GOLD RC: 2X TO 5X BASIC RC
RANDOM INSERTS IN PACKS
STATED PRINT RUN 99 SER.#'d SETS

2009 Upper Deck 1989 Design

RANDOM INSERTS IN PACKS
801 Ken Griffey Jr. 25.00 60.00
802 Randy Johnson 6.00 15.00
803 Ronald Reagan 12.50 30.00
804 George H.W. Bush 30.00 60.00

2009 Upper Deck A Piece of History 500 Club

RANDOM INSERTS IN PACKS
MR Manny Ramirez 12.50 30.00

2009 Upper Deck A Piece of History 600 Club

RANDOM INSERTS IN PACKS
600KG Ken Griffey Jr. 12.00 30.00

2009 Upper Deck Derek Jeter 1993 Buyback Autograph

RANDOM INSERTS IN PACKS
STATED PRINT RUN 93 SER.#'d SETS
449 Derek Jeter/93 200.00 400.0

2009 Upper Deck Goodwin Champions Preview

RANDOM INSERTS IN PACKS
GCP1 Joe DiMaggio 5.00 12.0
GCP2 Tony Gwynn 3.00 8.0
GCP3 Cole Hamels 3.00 8.0
GCP4 Laird Hamilton 1.25 3.0
GCP5 Gordie Howe 6.00 15.0
GCP6 Ichiro Suzuki 3.00 8.0
GCP7 Derek Jeter 6.00 15.0
GCP8 Michael Jordan 6.00 15.0
GCP9 Barack Obama 6.00 15.0
GCP10 Albert Pujols 5.00 12.0
GCP11 Cal Ripken Jr. 10.00 25.0
GCP12 Bill Rodgers 1.25 3.0

2009 Upper Deck Griffey-Jordan

RANDOM INSERTS IN PACKS
KGMJ K.Griffey Jr./M.Jordan 20.00 50.0

2009 Upper Deck Historic Firsts

COMMON CARD .75 2.00
ODDS 1:4 HOB,1:6 RET,1:10 BLAST
HF1 Barack Obama 4.00 10.00
HF4 Republican Woman Runs As VP 2.00 5.00
HF11 Bo The First Puppy 10.00 25.00

2009 Upper Deck Historic Predictors

COMMON CARD .75 2.00
ODDS 1:4 HOB,1:6 RET,1:10 BLAST

2009 Upper Deck Inkredible

ODDS 1:17 HOB,1:1000 RET,1:1980 BLAST
EXCHANGE DEADLINE 1/12/2011
AC Aaron Cook 4.00 10.00
AE Andre Ethier 3.00 8.00
AG Alberto Gonzalez S2 3.00 8.00
AI Akinori Iwamura 6.00 15.00
AK Austin Kearns 3.00 8.00
AL Aaron Laffey 3.00 8.00
AR Bronson Arroyo 3.00 8.00
AR Alexei Ramirez S2 3.00 8.00
BA Brian Bannister 3.00 8.00
BA Burke Badenhop S2 3.00 8.00
BB Billy Butler 10.00 25.00
BB Brian Barton S2 3.00 8.00
BI Brian Bixler S2 3.00 8.00
BJ Jay Bruce S2 10.00 25.00
BK Bobby Korecky S2 4.00 10.00
BL Joe Blanton 6.00 15.00
BO Boof Bonser 3.00 8.00
BP Brandon Phillips 5.00 12.00
BR Brian Bruney 3.00 8.00
BR Brandon Jones S2 4.00 10.00
BW Billy Wagner 15.00 40.00
CA Chris Capuano 20.00 50.00
CB Craig Breslow 3.00 8.00
CC Chad Cordero 3.00 8.00
CD Chris Duffy 3.00 8.00
CG Carlos Gomez 8.00 20.00
CH Cole Hamels 50.00 100.00
CH Corey Hart S2 3.00 8.00
CR Chris Resop 3.00 8.00
CS Clint Sammons S2 3.00 8.00
CT Clete Thomas S2 10.00 25.00
DE David Eckstein 4.00 10.00
DL Derek Lowe 8.00 20.00
DM David Murphy 3.00 8.00
DP Dustin Pedroia S2 20.00 50.00
DU Dan Uggla 3.00 8.00
EA Erick Aybar 3.00 8.00
ED Elijah Dukes 3.00 8.00
ED Elijah Dukes S2 3.00 8.00
ET Eider Torres S2 5.00 12.00
EV Edinson Volquez 6.00 15.00
FC Fausto Carmona 4.00 10.00

Felix Hernandez 15.00 40.00
Garrett Atkins 4.00 10.00
Gavin Floyd 3.00 8.00
Glen Perkins 3.00 8.00
Gregorio Petit S2 3.00 8.00
Greg Smith S2 4.00 10.00
Tony Gwynn Mil 5.00 12.00
Brendan Harris 3.00 8.00
Jonathan Herrera S2 4.00 10.00
Hernan Iribarren S2 4.00 10.00
Ian Kinsler 10.00 25.00
Ian Kennedy S2 6.00 15.00
Joaquin Arias S2 3.00 8.00
Jeff Baker 3.00 8.00
Jason Bay S2 10.00 25.00
Jack Cust 3.00 8.00
Jeff Francoeur 3.00 8.00
Jeremy Hermida S2 4.00 10.00
Jeff Francis 4.00 10.00
Jeremy Guthrie 15.00 40.00
Josh Hamilton 30.00 60.00
J.A. Happ S2 3.00 8.00
Jeff Keppinger 4.00 10.00
James Loney 8.00 20.00
Jed Lowrie S2 3.00 8.00
M John Maine 30.00 60.00
M John Maine S2 6.00 15.00
J Joe Nathan 3.00 8.00
Joey Gathright 3.00 8.00
Jonathan Albaladejo S2 4.00 10.00
P Jonathan Papelbon 10.00 25.00
S James Shields 4.00 10.00
S Joe Smith S2 4.00 10.00
W Jered Weaver 5.00 12.00
G K.Griffey Jr. EXCH 100.00 200.00
G Ken Griffey Jr. S2 100.00 200.00
H Kevin Hart S2 4.00 10.00
J Kelly Johnson S2 3.00 8.00
K Kevin Kouzmanoff 4.00 10.00
M Kyle McClellan S2 4.00 10.00
S Kevin Slowey S2 6.00 15.00
A Adam LaRoche 6.00 15.00
B Lance Broadway S2 3.00 8.00
C Luke Carlin S2 5.00 12.00
J John Lackey 5.00 12.00
M Luis Mendoza S2 3.00 8.00
S Luke Scott 3.00 8.00
MA Matt Chico 3.00 8.00
MA Michael Aubrey S2 5.00 12.00
MB Marlon Byrd 3.00 8.00
MB Mitchell Boggs S2 10.00 25.00
MC Matt Cain 6.00 15.00
ME Mark Ellis 3.00 8.00
ME Mark Ellis S2 3.00 8.00
MI Michael Bourn 4.00 10.00
ML Matt Lindstrom S2 3.00 8.00
MO Dustin Moseley 3.00 8.00
MR Mike Rabelo S2 3.00 8.00
MT Mark Teahen 4.00 10.00
MU David Murphy S2 3.00 8.00
NB Nick Blackburn S2 3.00 8.00
NL Noah Lowry S2 3.00 8.00
NM Nick Markakis 10.00 25.00
NM Nyjer Morgan S2 4.00 10.00
NS Nick Swisher 6.00 15.00
OW Micah Owings 3.00 8.00
PA Mike Parisi S2 3.00 8.00
PF Prince Fielder 6.00 15.00
RB Ryan Braun 6.00 15.00
RG Ryan Garko 3.00 8.00
RH Ramon Hernandez 6.00 15.00
RH Ramon Hernandez S2 6.00 15.00
RM Russell Martin S2 3.00 8.00
RO Ross Ohlendorf S2 5.00 12.00
RT Ryan Theriot 6.00 15.00
RT Ramon Troncoso S2 5.00 12.00
SD Stephen Drew 4.00 10.00
SH Steve Holm S2 3.00 8.00
SM Sean Marshall 4.00 10.00
SO Andy Sonnanstine 3.00 8.00
TB Taylor Buchholz 4.00 10.00
TG Tom Gorzelanny 20.00 50.00
UJ Ubaldo Jimenez 5.00 12.00
VR Vinny Rottino S2 3.00 8.00
WI Josh Willingham 3.00 8.00
WW Wesley Wright S2 3.00 8.00
XN Xavier Nady 3.00 8.00
YE Yunel Escobar 6.00 15.00

2009 Upper Deck Ken Griffey Jr. 1989 Buyback Gold

RANDOM INSERTS IN PACKS
NNO Ken Griffey Jr. 15.00 40.00

2009 Upper Deck O-Pee-Chee

ODDS 1:6 HOB,1:30 RET,1:90 BLAST
*MINI: 1X TO 2.5X BASIC
MINI ODDS 1:48 HOB,1:240 RET,1:720 BLAST
OPC1 Albert Pujols 1.50 4.00
OPC2 Alex Rodriguez 1.50 4.00
OPC3 Alfonso Soriano .75 2.00
OPC4 B.J. Upton .75 2.00
OPC5 Brandon Webb .75 2.00
OPC6 CC Sabathia .75 2.00
OPC7 Carl Crawford .75 2.00
OPC8 Carlos Beltran .75 2.00
OPC9 Carlos Quentin .50 1.25
OPC10 Chase Utley .75 2.00
OPC11 Chien-Ming Wang .75 2.00
OPC12 Chipper Jones 1.25 3.00
OPC13 Daisuke Matsuzaka .75 2.00
OPC14 David Ortiz 1.25 3.00
OPC15 David Wright 1.00 2.50
OPC16 Derek Jeter 3.00 8.00
OPC17 Derrek Lee .50 1.25
OPC18 Evan Longoria .75 2.00
OPC19 Felix Hernandez .75 2.00
OPC20 Frank Thomas 1.25 3.00
OPC21 Grady Sizemore .75 2.00
OPC22 Greg Maddux 1.50 4.00
OPC23 Hanley Ramirez .75 2.00
OPC24 Ichiro Suzuki 1.50 4.00
OPC25 Jake Peavy .50 1.25
OPC26 Jimmy Rollins .75 2.00
OPC27 Joba Chamberlain .50 1.25
OPC28 Joe Mauer 1.00 2.50
OPC29 Johan Santana .75 2.00
OPC30 John Smoltz 1.25 3.00
OPC31 Jose Reyes .75 2.00
OPC32 Josh Beckett .50 1.25
OPC33 Josh Hamilton .75 2.00
OPC34 Ken Griffey Jr. 2.50 6.00
OPC35 Kosuke Fukudome .75 2.00
OPC36 Lance Berkman .75 2.00
OPC37 Magglio Ordonez .75 2.00
OPC38 Manny Ramirez 1.25 3.00
OPC39 Mark Teixeira .75 2.00
OPC40 Matt Holliday 1.25 3.00
OPC41 Matt Kemp 1.00 2.50
OPC42 Miguel Cabrera 1.25 3.00
OPC43 Prince Fielder .75 2.00
OPC44 Randy Johnson 1.25 3.00
OPC45 Rick Ankiel .50 1.25
OPC46 Russell Martin .50 1.25
OPC47 Ryan Braun .75 2.00
OPC48 Ryan Howard 1.00 2.50
OPC49 Travis Hafner .50 1.25
OPC50 Vladimir Guerrero .75 2.00

2009 Upper Deck O-Pee-Chee 1977 Preview

RANDOM INSERTS IN PACKS
OPC1 Prince Fielder .75 2.00
OPC2 Russell Martin .50 1.25
OPC3 Vladimir Guerrero .75 2.00
OPC4 Joe Mauer 1.00 2.50
OPC5 Justin Morneau .75 2.00
OPC6 Dustin Pedroia 1.00 2.50
OPC7 Mark Teixeira .75 2.00
OPC8 Tim Lincecum .75 2.00
OPC9 Jimmy Rollins .75 2.00
OPC10 Carlos Lee .50 1.25
OPC11 Hanley Ramirez .75 2.00
OPC12 Chipper Jones 1.25 3.00
OPC13 Matt Holliday 1.25 3.00
OPC14 Travis Hafner .50 1.25
OPC15 Magglio Ordonez .75 2.00
OPC16 Carlos Quentin .50 1.25
OPC17 Derrek Lee .50 1.25
OPC18 Aramis Ramirez .50 1.25
OPC19 Randy Johnson 1.25 3.00
OPC20 Brandon Webb .75 2.00
OPC21 Josh Hamilton .75 2.00
OPC22 CC Sabathia .75 2.00
OPC23 Carlos Beltran .75 2.00
OPC24 Adrian Gonzalez 1.00 2.50
OPC25 Jake Peavy .50 1.25
OPC26 Matt Kemp 1.00 2.50
OPC27 Joba Chamberlain .50 1.25
OPC28 Jonathan Papelbon .75 2.00
OPC29 Carlos Zambrano .75 2.00
OPC30 Jay Bruce .75 2.00
OPC31 Albert Pujols 1.50 4.00
OPC32 Alex Rodriguez 1.50 4.00
OPC33 Alfonso Soriano .75 2.00
OPC34 Chase Utley .75 2.00
OPC35 Daisuke Matsuzaka .75 2.00
OPC36 David Ortiz 1.25 3.00
OPC37 David Wright 1.00 2.50
OPC38 Derek Jeter 3.00 8.00
OPC39 Evan Longoria .75 2.00
OPC40 Grady Sizemore .75 2.00
OPC41 Ichiro Suzuki 1.50 4.00
OPC42 Johan Santana .75 2.00
OPC43 Jose Reyes .75 2.00
OPC44 Josh Beckett .50 1.25
OPC45 Ken Griffey Jr. 2.50 6.00
OPC46 Lance Berkman .75 2.00
OPC47 Manny Ramirez 1.25 3.00
OPC48 Miguel Cabrera 1.25 3.00
OPC49 Ryan Braun .75 2.00
OPC50 Ryan Howard 1.00 2.50

2009 Upper Deck Rivals

ODDS 1:12 HOB,1:50 RET,1:240 BLAST
R1 Jose Reyes/Jimmy Rollins .75 2.00
R2 D.Ortiz/D.Jeter 3.00 8.00
R3 A.Pujols/D.Lee 1.50 4.00
R4 Russell Martin/Bengie Molina .50 1.25
R5 Travis Hafner/Jim Thome .75 2.00
R6 Carlos Zambrano/CC Sabathia .75 2.00
R7 D.Wright/A.Rodriguez 1.50 4.00
R8 Josh Beckett/Scott Kazmir .50 1.25
R9 Vladimir Guerrero/Manny Ramirez 1.25 3.00
R10 Carlos Quentin/Alfonso Soriano .75 2.00
R11 L.Berkman/A.Pujols 1.50 4.00
R12 A.Rodriguez/E.Longoria 1.50 4.00
R13 Jake Peavy/Chad Billingsley .75 2.00
R14 Brandon Webb/Matt Kemp 1.00 2.50
R15 Johan Santana/Chipper Jones 1.25 3.00
R16 Jim Thome/Justin Morneau .75 2.00
R17 M.Cabrera/J.Mauer 1.25 3.00
R18 Hanley Ramirez/Jose Reyes .75 2.00
R19 R.Halladay/J.Chamberlain .75 2.00
R20 Josh Hamilton/Roy Oswalt .75 2.00
R21 T.Lincecum/J.Cust .75 2.00
R22 A.Pujols/P.Fielder 1.50 4.00
R23 F.Rodriguez/I.Suzuki 1.50 4.00
R24 D.Matsuzaka/N.Markakis 1.00 2.50
R25 Grady Sizemore/Jay Bruce .75 2.00

2009 Upper Deck Stars of the Game

ODDS 1:12 HOB,1:50 RET,1:240 BLAST
GGAP Albert Pujols 1.50 4.00
GGAR Alex Rodriguez 1.50 4.00
GGAS Alfonso Soriano .75 2.00
GGBW Brandon Webb .75 2.00
GGCJ Chipper Jones 1.25 3.00
GGCS CC Sabathia .75 2.00
GGCU Chase Utley .75 2.00
GGDJ Derek Jeter 3.00 8.00
GGDO David Ortiz 1.25 3.00
GGDP Dustin Pedroia 1.00 2.50
GGDW David Wright 1.00 2.50
GGEL Evan Longoria .75 2.00
GGGS Grady Sizemore .75 2.00
GGHR Hanley Ramirez .75 2.00
GGIS Ichiro Suzuki 1.50 4.00
GGJH Josh Hamilton .75 2.00
GGJR Jose Reyes .75 2.00
GGJS Johan Santana .75 2.00
GGLB Lance Berkman .75 2.00
GGMC Miguel Cabrera 1.25 3.00
GGMR Manny Ramirez 1.25 3.00
GGRB Ryan Braun .75 2.00
GGRH Ryan Howard 1.00 2.50
GGTL Tim Lincecum .75 2.00
GGVG Vladimir Guerrero .75 2.00

2009 Upper Deck StarQuest Common Purple

STATED ODDS 2:1 FAT PACK
*SILVER: .4X TO 1X PURPLE
SILVER ODDS 1:4 RETAIL,3:1 SUPER
*BLUE: .4X TO 1X PURPLE
BLUE ODDS 1:8 RET,1:32 BLAST,1:3 SUP
*GOLD: 5X TO 1.2X PURPLE
GLD ODDS 1:12 RET,1:48 BLAST,1:4 SUP
*EMERALD: .75X TO 2X PURPLE
EMLD ODDS 1:24 RET,1:96 BLAST,1:8 SUP
*BLACK: 1.2X TO 3X PURPLE
BLK ODDS 1:48 RET,1:192 BLAST,1:12 SUP
SQ1 Albert Pujols 1.50 4.00
SQ2 Alex Rodriguez 1.50 4.00
SQ3 Alfonso Soriano .75 2.00
SQ4 Chipper Jones 1.25 3.00
SQ5 Chase Utley .75 2.00
SQ6 Derek Jeter 3.00 8.00
SQ7 Daisuke Matsuzaka .75 2.00
SQ8 David Ortiz 1.25 3.00
SQ9 David Wright 1.00 2.50
SQ10 Grady Sizemore .75 2.00
SQ11 Hanley Ramirez .75 2.00
SQ12 Ichiro Suzuki 1.50 4.00
SQ13 Josh Beckett .50 1.25
SQ14 Jake Peavy .50 1.25
SQ15 Jose Reyes .75 2.00
SQ16 Johan Santana .75 2.00
SQ17 Ken Griffey Jr. 2.50 6.00
SQ18 Lance Berkman .75 2.00
SQ19 Miguel Cabrera 1.25 3.00
SQ20 Matt Holliday 1.25 3.00
SQ21 Manny Ramirez 1.25 3.00
SQ22 Prince Fielder .75 2.00
SQ23 Ryan Braun .75 2.00
SQ24 Ryan Howard 1.00 2.50
SQ25 Vladimir Guerrero .75 2.00
SQ26 B.J. Upton .75 2.00
SQ27 Brandon Phillips .50 1.25
SQ28 Brandon Webb .75 2.00
SQ29 Brian McCann .75 2.00
SQ30 Carl Crawford .75 2.00
SQ31 Carlos Beltran .75 2.00
SQ32 Carlos Quentin .50 1.25
SQ33 Chien-Ming Wang .75 2.00
SQ34 Cliff Lee .75 2.00
SQ35 Cole Hamels 1.00 2.50
SQ36 Curtis Granderson 1.00 2.50
SQ37 David Price 1.00 2.50
SQ38 Dustin Pedroia 1.00 2.50
SQ39 Evan Longoria .75 2.00
SQ40 Francisco Liriano .50 1.25
SQ41 Geovany Soto .75 2.00
SQ42 Ian Kinsler .75 2.00
SQ43 Jay Bruce .75 2.00
SQ44 Jimmy Rollins .75 2.00
SQ45 Jonathan Papelbon .75 2.00
SQ46 Josh Hamilton .75 2.00
SQ47 Justin Morneau .75 2.00
SQ48 Kevin Youkilis .50 1.25
SQ49 Nick Markakis 1.00 2.50
SQ50 Tim Lincecum .75 2.00

2009 Upper Deck StarQuest Turquoise

*TURQUOISE: .4X TO 1X PURPLE

2009 Upper Deck UD Game Jersey

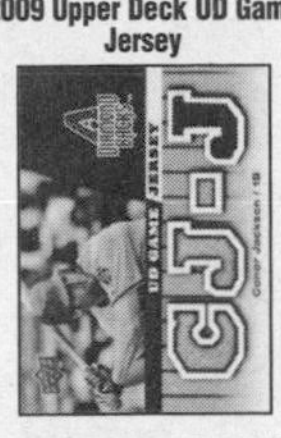

STATED ODDS 1:19 HOB,1:24 RET,1:9 BLAST
GJAD Adam Dunn 2.50 6.00
GJAE Andre Ethier 2.50 6.00
GJAG Adrian Gonzalez 3.00 8.00
GJAH Aaron Harang 1.50 4.00
GJAI Akinori Iwamura 1.50 4.00
GJAN Rick Ankiel 1.50 4.00
GJAP Albert Pujols 5.00 12.00
GJAR Aaron Rowand 1.50 4.00
GJAS Alfonso Soriano 2.50 6.00
GJBA Rocco Baldelli Pants 1.50 4.00
GJBE Josh Beckett 1.50 4.00
GJBH Bill Hall 1.50 4.00
GJBM Brian McCann 2.50 6.00
GJBP Brandon Phillips 1.50 4.00
GJBR Brian Bass 1.50 4.00
GJBU B.J. Upton 2.50 6.00
GJBW Billy Wagner 1.50 4.00
GJCB Chad Billingsley 2.50 6.00
GJCD Chris Duncan 1.50 4.00
GJCH Chin-Lung Hu 1.50 4.00
GJCJ Chipper Jones 4.00 10.00
GJCL Clay Buchholz 1.50 4.00
GJCO Corey Hart 1.50 4.00
GJCS CC Sabathia 2.50 6.00
GJCT Clay Timpner 1.50 4.00
GJCW Chien-Ming Wang 2.50 6.00
GJDA Johnny Damon 2.50 6.00
GJDB Daric Barton 1.50 4.00
GJDH Dan Haren 1.50 4.00
GJDJ Derek Jeter 10.00 25.00
GJDL Derrek Lee 1.50 4.00
GJDM David Murphy 1.50 4.00
GJDO David Ortiz 4.00 10.00
GJDU Dan Uggla 1.50 4.00
GJGA Garrett Atkins 1.50 4.00
GJGM Greg Maddux 5.00 12.00
GJGO Alex Gordon 2.50 6.00
GJGR Curtis Granderson 3.00 8.00
GJGS Grady Sizemore 2.50 6.00
GJHA Cole Hamels 3.00 8.00
GJHI Aaron Hill 1.50 4.00
GJHJ Josh Hamilton 2.50 6.00
GJIK Ian Kennedy 1.50 4.00
GJJA Conor Jackson 1.50 4.00
GJJD J.D. Drew 1.50 4.00
GJJF Jeff Francis 1.50 4.00
GJJG Jeremy Guthrie 1.50 4.00
GJJH Jeremy Hermida 1.50 4.00
GJJJ Josh Johnson 2.50 6.00
GJJL James Loney 1.50 4.00
GJJM John Maine 1.50 4.00
GJJN Joe Nathan 1.50 4.00
GJJO John Lackey 2.50 6.00
GJJP Jake Peavy 1.50 4.00
GJJT J.R. Towles 1.50 4.00
GJJU Justin Upton 2.50 6.00
GJJV Jason Varitek 4.00 10.00
GJJW Josh Willingham 2.50 6.00
GJKG Ken Griffey Jr. 10.00 25.00
GJKI Ian Kinsler 2.50 6.00
GJKK Kevin Kouzmanoff 1.50 4.00
GJKY Kevin Youkilis 1.50 4.00
GJLA A.LaRoche UER 1.50 4.00
GJMC Matt Cain 2.50 6.00
GJMK Matt Kemp 3.00 8.00
GJMT Mark Teahen 1.50 4.00
GJNB Nick Blackburn 1.50 4.00
GJNM Nick Markakis 3.00 8.00
GJNS Nick Swisher 2.50 6.00
GJPA Jonathan Papelbon 2.50 6.00
GJPB Pat Burrell 1.50 4.00
GJPE Jhonny Peralta 1.50 4.00
GJPH Phil Hughes 1.50 4.00
GJPK Paul Konerko 2.50 6.00
GJRA Aramis Ramirez 1.50 4.00
GJRB Ryan Braun 2.50 6.00
GJRF Rafael Furcal 1.50 4.00
GJRH Rich Harden 1.50 4.00
GJRM Russell Martin 1.50 4.00
GJRO Roy Halladay 2.50 6.00
GJRW Rickie Weeks 1.50 4.00
GJRZ Ryan Zimmerman 2.50 6.00
GJSA Jarrod Saltalamacchia 1.50 4.00
GJSM Greg Smith 1.50 4.00
GJSO Joakim Soria 1.50 4.00
GJSP Scott Podsednik 1.50 4.00
GJTG Tom Glavine 2.50 6.00
GJTH Tim Hudson 2.50 6.00
GJTR Travis Hafner 1.50 4.00
GJTT Troy Tulowitzki 4.00 10.00
GJVM Victor Martinez 2.50 6.00
GJWE Jered Weaver 2.50 6.00

2009 Upper Deck UD Game Jersey Autographs

RANDOM INSERTS IN PACKS
PRINT RUNS B/WN 5-99 COPIES PER
NO PRICING ON QTY 25 OR LESS
GJAG Adrian Gonzalez/99 12.50 30.00
GJAH Aaron Harang/99 5.00 12.00
GJAK Austin Kearns/99 5.00 12.00
GJBM Brian McCann/99 10.00 25.00
GJBP Brandon Phillips/99 12.50 30.00
GJBR Brian Bass/99 5.00 12.00
GJBW Billy Wagner/35 10.00 25.00
GJCB Chad Billingsley/99 10.00 25.00
GJCD Chris Duncan/99 12.50 30.00
GJCH Chin-Lung Hu/99 12.50 30.00
GJCO Corey Hart/99 15.00 40.00
GJDB Daric Barton/99 6.00 15.00
GJGA Garrett Atkins/99 5.00 12.00
GJGO Alex Gordon/49 8.00 20.00
GJHJ Josh Hamilton/99 15.00 40.00
GJIK Ian Kennedy/35 5.00 12.00
GJJA Conor Jackson/49 8.00 20.00
GJJH Jeremy Hermida/99 6.00 15.00
GJJL James Loney/99 10.00 25.00
GJJN Joe Nathan/99 6.00 15.00
GJJO John Lackey/99 6.00 15.00
GJJT J.R. Towles/99 5.00 12.00
GJJW Josh Willingham/99 5.00 12.00
GJKG Ken Griffey Jr./99 50.00 100.00
GJKI Ian Kinsler/99 8.00 20.00
GJKK Kevin Kouzmanoff/99 5.00 12.00
GJKY Kevin Youkilis/99 20.00 50.00
GJLA Adam LaRoche/99 6.00 15.00
GJMC Matt Cain/99 15.00 40.00
GJMK Matt Kemp/25 20.00 50.00
GJMM Melvin Mora/99 5.00 12.00
GJMT Mark Teahen/99 6.00 15.00
GJNB Nick Blackburn/99 10.00 25.00
GJNM Nick Markakis/99 12.50 30.00
GJNS Nick Swisher/99 6.00 15.00
GJRM Russell Martin/35 10.00 25.00
GJRZ Ryan Zimmerman/50 12.50 30.00
GJSA Jarrod Saltalamacchia/99 5.00 12.00
GJSM Greg Smith/99 6.00 15.00
GJTR Travis Hafner/99 6.00 15.00
GJTT Troy Tulowitzki/99 6.00 15.00

2009 Upper Deck UD Game Jersey Dual

RANDOM INSERTS IN PACKS
PRINT RUNS B/WN 37-149 COPIES PER
GJAD Adam Dunn/149 4.00 10.00
GJAE Andre Ethier/149 4.00 10.00
GJAG Adrian Gonzalez/149 4.00 10.00
GJAH Aaron Harang/149 4.00 10.00
GJAI Akinori Iwamura/88 4.00 10.00
GJAN Rick Ankiel/149 5.00 12.00
GJAP Albert Pujols/149 10.00 25.00
GJAR Aaron Rowand/149 4.00 10.00
GJAS Alfonso Soriano/149 4.00 10.00
GJBA Rocco Baldelli/50 3.00 8.00
GJBM Brian McCann/149 4.00 10.00
GJBP Brandon Phillips/149 3.00 8.00
GJBR Brian Bass/149 3.00 8.00
GJBU B.J. Upton/149 3.00 8.00
GJBW Billy Wagner/149 5.00 12.00
GJCB Chad Billingsley/149 4.00 10.00
GJCC Carl Crawford/149 4.00 10.00
GJCD Chris Duncan/148 4.00 10.00
GJCH Chin-Lung Hu/149 4.00 10.00
GJCJ Chipper Jones/149 5.00 12.00
GJCL Clay Buchholz/149 4.00 10.00
GJCS CC Sabathia/149 5.00 12.00
GJCW Chien-Ming Wang/149 6.00 15.00
GJDB Daric Barton/149 4.00 10.00
GJDH Dan Haren/149 3.00 8.00
GJDJ Derek Jeter/139 12.50 30.00
GJDL Derrek Lee/149 3.00 8.00
GJDO David Ortiz/149 3.00 8.00
GJDU Dan Uggla/149 3.00 8.00
GJGO Alex Gordon/149 5.00 12.00
GJGR Curtis Granderson/149 4.00 10.00
GJHA Cole Hamels/149 6.00 15.00
GJHJ Josh Hamilton/149 10.00 25.00
GJIK Ian Kennedy/149 3.00 8.00
GJJA Conor Jackson/149 3.00 8.00
GJJD J.D. Drew/112 4.00 10.00
GJJF Jeff Francis/149 3.00 8.00
GJJG Jeremy Guthrie/149 3.00 8.00
GJJH Jeremy Hermida/149 3.00 8.00
GJJJ Josh Johnson/149 3.00 8.00
GJJL James Loney/149 5.00 12.00
GJJM John Maine/149 5.00 12.00
GJJN Joe Nathan/149 3.00 8.00
GJJO John Lackey/149 3.00 8.00
GJJT J.R. Towles/149 3.00 8.00
GJJU Justin Upton/149 5.00 12.00
GJJV Jason Varitek/149 5.00 12.00
GJJW Josh Willingham/149 3.00 8.00
GJKG Ken Griffey Jr./50 12.50 30.00
GJKI Ian Kinsler/75 3.00 8.00
GJKK Kevin Kouzmanoff/149 3.00 8.00
GJKY Kevin Youkilis/149 5.00 12.00
GJLA Adam LaRoche/75 5.00 12.00
GJMC Matt Cain/149 4.00 10.00
GJMK Matt Kemp/149 4.00 10.00
GJMM Melvin Mora/149 3.00 8.00
GJMT Mark Teahen/149 3.00 8.00
GJNB Nick Blackburn/149 3.00 8.00
GJNM Nick Markakis/149 4.00 10.00
GJPA Jonathan Papelbon/149 4.00 10.00
GJPB Pat Burrell/37 15.00 40.00
GJPE Jhonny Peralta/125 3.00 8.00
GJPH Phil Hughes/149 4.00 10.00
GJPK Paul Konerko/149 4.00 10.00
GJRA Aramis Ramirez/149 3.00 8.00
GJRB Ryan Braun/149 6.00 15.00
GJRF Rafael Furcal/149 4.00 10.00
GJRH Rich Harden/149 3.00 8.00
GJRM Russell Martin/149 5.00 12.00
GJRO Roy Halladay/50 6.00 15.00
GJRW Rickie Weeks/149 3.00 8.00
GJRZ Ryan Zimmerman/149 3.00 8.00
GJSO Joakim Soria/75 4.00 10.00
GJSP Scott Podsednik/149 3.00 8.00
GJTH Tim Hudson/149 5.00 12.00
GJTT Troy Tulowitzki/149 5.00 12.00
GJWE Jered Weaver/149 3.00 8.00

2009 Upper Deck UD Game Jersey Triple

RANDOM INSERTS IN PACKS
PRINT RUNS B/WN 15-100 COPIES PER
NO PRICING ON QTY 25 OR LESS
GJAD Adam Dunn/99 5.00 12.00
GJAG Adrian Gonzalez/99 5.00 12.00
GJAH Aaron Harang/99 5.00 12.00
GJAN Rick Ankiel/99 6.00 15.00
GJAP Albert Pujols/99 6.00 15.00
GJAS Alfonso Soriano/79 5.00 12.00
GJBH Bill Hall/73 4.00 10.00
GJBM Brian McCann/99 5.00 12.00
GJBR Brian Bass/65 4.00 10.00
GJBU B.J. Upton/99 4.00 10.00
GJCB Chad Billingsley/99 5.00 12.00
GJCC Carl Crawford/99 4.00 10.00
GJCD Chris Duncan/99 5.00 12.00
GJCH Chin-Lung Hu/99 5.00 12.00
GJCJ Chipper Jones/99 8.00 20.00
GJCO Corey Hart/63 5.00 12.00
GJCS CC Sabathia/99 6.00 15.00
GJCW Chien-Ming Wang/99 8.00 20.00
GJDB Daric Barton/99 5.00 12.00
GJDH Dan Haren/99 4.00 10.00
GJDJ Derek Jeter/69 15.00 40.00
GJDO David Ortiz/99 4.00 10.00
GJGA Garrett Atkins/99 4.00 10.00
GJGO Alex Gordon/99 6.00 15.00
GJGR Curtis Granderson/99 5.00 12.00
GJGS Grady Sizemore/99 5.00 12.00
GJHI Aaron Hill/44 5.00 12.00
GJHJ Josh Hamilton/83 12.50 30.00
GJIK Ian Kennedy/99 4.00 10.00
GJJA Conor Jackson/99 4.00 10.00
GJJD J.D. Drew/58 5.00 12.00
GJJF Jeff Francis/99 4.00 10.00
GJJG Jeremy Guthrie/99 4.00 10.00
GJJH Jeremy Hermida/99 4.00 10.00
GJJL James Loney/99 5.00 12.00
GJJM John Maine/99 6.00 15.00
GJJN Joe Nathan/99 4.00 10.00
GJJT J.R. Towles/99 4.00 10.00
GJJU Justin Upton/99 6.00 15.00
GJJV Jason Varitek/66 6.00 15.00
GJKI Ian Kinsler/43 4.00 10.00
GJKK Kevin Kouzmanoff/99 4.00 10.00
GJKY Kevin Youkilis/99 6.00 15.00
GJMC Matt Cain/99 5.00 12.00
GJMK Matt Kemp/99 5.00 12.00
GJMT Mark Teahen/99 4.00 10.00
GJNB Nick Blackburn/91 4.00 10.00
GJNM Nick Markakis/100 5.00 12.00
GJPA Jonathan Papelbon/100 5.00 12.00
GJPE Jhonny Peralta/53 4.00 10.00
GJPH Phil Hughes/66 5.00 12.00
GJPK Paul Konerko/83 5.00 12.00
GJRA Aramis Ramirez/99 4.00 10.00
GJRB Ryan Braun/99 8.00 20.00
GJRH Rich Harden/99 4.00 10.00
GJRM Russell Martin/99 6.00 15.00
GJRW Rickie Weeks/99 4.00 10.00
GJRZ Ryan Zimmerman/99 4.00 10.00
GJSM Greg Smith/66 4.00 10.00
GJSO Joakim Soria/50 5.00 12.00
GJSP Scott Podsednik/65 4.00 10.00
GJTH Tim Hudson/50 6.00 15.00
GJTR Travis Hafner/99 5.00 12.00
GJTT Troy Tulowitzki/99 6.00 15.00
GJWE Jered Weaver/66 4.00 10.00

2009 Upper Deck UD Game Materials

RANDOM INSERTS IN PACKS
GMAH Aaron Harang 3.00 8.00
GMAJ Andruw Jones 2.50 6.00
GMAP Albert Pujols 6.00 15.00
GMAR Alex Romero 2.50 6.00
GMBA Josh Barfield 2.50 6.00
GMBB Brian Bocock 2.50 6.00
GMBC Bartolo Colon 2.50 6.00
GMBH Bill Hall 2.50 6.00
GMBI Brandon Inge 2.50 6.00
GMBM Brian McCann 3.00 8.00
GMBP Brandon Phillips 3.00 8.00
GMCB Chris Burke 2.50 6.00
GMCD Carlos Delgado 3.00 8.00
GMCH Chin-Lung Hu 2.50 6.00
GMCL Carlos Lee 2.50 6.00
GMCM Colt Morton 2.50 6.00
GMCR Bobby Crosby 2.50 6.00
GMCY Chris Young 3.00 8.00
GMDB Daric Barton 2.50 6.00
GMDE Darin Erstad 2.50 6.00
GMDL Derrek Lee 2.50 6.00
GMDM Daisuke Matsuzaka 3.00 8.00
GMDU Chris Duncan 2.50 6.00
GMEC Eric Chavez 2.50 6.00
GMED Jim Edmonds 3.00 8.00
GMEG Eric Gagne 2.50 6.00
GMFH Felix Hernandez 4.00 10.00
GMFS Freddy Sanchez 2.50 6.00
GMHB Hank Blalock 2.50 6.00
GMHE Ramon Hernandez 2.50 6.00
GMHI Hernan Iribarren 2.50 6.00
GMHK Hong-Chih Kuo 2.50 6.00
GMIK Ian Kinsler 3.00 8.00
GMJB Jason Bay 4.00 10.00
GMJE Jeff Baker 2.50 6.00
GMJG Jason Giambi 3.00 8.00
GMJH Josh Hamilton 3.00 8.00
GMJK Jason Kubel 2.50 6.00
GMJP Jhonny Peralta 2.50 6.00
GMJW Jake Westbrook 2.50 6.00
GMKG Ken Griffey Jr. 6.00 15.00
GMKJ Kelly Johnson 2.50 6.00
GMKM Kendry Morales 2.50 6.00
GMLM Lastings Milledge 2.50 6.00
GMMK Matt Kemp 15.00 40.00
GMMM Melvin Mora 2.50 6.00
GMMP Mark Prior 2.50 6.00
GMNM Nyjer Morgan 2.50 6.00
GMPK Paul Konerko 2.50 6.00
GMRA Aramis Ramirez 3.00 8.00
GMRB Rocco Baldelli 2.50 6.00
GMRF Rafael Furcal 3.00 8.00
GMTG Troy Glaus 2.50 6.00
GMTT Troy Tulowitzki 2.50 6.00
GMTW Tim Wakefield 3.00 8.00
GMUG Dan Uggla 2.50 6.00
GMVM Victor Martinez 3.00 8.00
GMYE Yunel Escobar 2.50 6.00
GMYG Yovani Gallardo 2.50 6.00
GMZG Zack Greinke 4.00 10.00

2009 Upper Deck UD Game Materials Autographs

RANDOM INSERTS IN PACKS
PRINT RUNS B/WN 5-99 COPIES PER
GMAH Aaron Harang/76 5.00 12.00
GMAR Alex Romero/72 4.00 10.00
GMBA Josh Barfield/69 4.00 10.00
GMBB Brian Bocock/61 4.00 10.00
GMBH Bill Hall/99 6.00 15.00
GMBM Brian McCann/71 15.00 40.00
GMBP Brandon Phillips/99 8.00 20.00
GMCB Chad Billingsley/99 15.00 40.00
GMCH Chin-Lung Hu/99 5.00 12.00
GMCM Colt Morton/99 4.00 10.00
GMDB Daric Barton/99 6.00 15.00
GMDU Chris Duncan/99 6.00 15.00
GMJE Jeff Baker/99 4.00 10.00
GMJS Jarrod Saltalamacchia/99 4.00 10.00
GMKJ Kelly Johnson/99 6.00 15.00
GMMK Matt Kemp/99 10.00 25.00
GMMM Melvin Mora/99 6.00 15.00
GMNM Nyjer Morgan/99 4.00 10.00
GMYG Yovani Gallardo/99 10.00 25.00

2009 Upper Deck USA 18U National Team

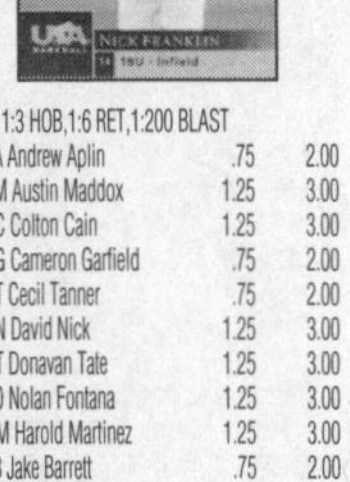

ODDS 1:3 HOB,1:6 RET,1:200 BLAST
18UAA Andrew Aplin .75 2.00
18UAM Austin Maddox 1.25 3.00
18UCC Colton Cain 1.25 3.00
18UCG Cameron Garfield .75 2.00
18UCT Cecil Tanner .75 2.00
18UDN David Nick 1.25 3.00
18UDT Donavan Tate 1.25 3.00
18UFO Nolan Fontana 1.25 3.00
18UHM Harold Martinez 1.25 3.00
18UJB Jake Barrett .75 2.00
18UJM Jeff Malm .75 2.00
18UJT Jacob Turner 3.00 8.00
18UME Jonathan Meyer .75 2.00
18UMP Matthew Purke .75 2.00
18UMS Max Stassi 1.25 3.00

18UNF Nick Franklin	2.00	5.00
18URW Ryan Weber	.75	2.00
18UWH Wes Hatton	.75	2.00

2009 Upper Deck USA 18U National Team Jersey

STATED ODDS 1:96 HOB,1:1715 RET,1:3163 BLAST

18UAA Andrew Aplin	4.00	10.00
18UAM Austin Maddox	4.00	10.00
18UCC Colton Cain	2.50	6.00
18UCG Cameron Garfield	4.00	10.00
18UCT Cecil Tanner	2.50	6.00
18UDN David Nick	2.50	6.00
18UDT Donavan Tate	4.00	10.00
18UFO Nolan Fontana	4.00	10.00
18UHM Harold Martinez	4.00	10.00
18UJB Jake Barrett	2.50	6.00
18UJM Jeff Malm	2.50	6.00
18UJT Jacob Turner	4.00	10.00
18UME Jonathan Meyer	2.50	6.00
18UMP Matthew Purke	4.00	10.00
18UMS Max Stassi	4.00	10.00
18UNF Nick Franklin	2.50	6.00
18URW Ryan Weber	2.50	6.00
18UWH Wes Hatton	4.00	10.00

2009 Upper Deck USA National Team

RANDOM INSERTS IN PACKS

AG A.J. Griffin	1.25	3.00
AO Andrew Oliver	.75	2.00
BS Blake Smith	.75	2.00
CC Christian Colon	1.25	3.00
CH Chris Hernandez	.75	2.00
DD Derek Dietrich	2.00	5.00
HM Hunter Morris	.75	2.00
JC Jared Clark	.75	2.00
JF Josh Fellhauer	.75	2.00
KD Kentrail Davis	1.25	3.00
KG Kyle Gibson	2.00	5.00
KV Kendal Volz	1.25	3.00
MD Matt den Dekker	1.25	3.00
MG Micah Gibbs	.75	2.00
ML Mike Leake	2.50	6.00
MM Mike Minor	1.25	3.00
RJ Ryan Jackson	.75	2.00
RL Ryan Lipkin	.75	2.00
SS Stephen Strasburg	4.00	10.00
SW Scott Woodward	.75	2.00
TL Tyler Lyons	1.25	3.00
TM Tommy Mendonca	.75	2.00

2009 Upper Deck USA National Team Autographs

RANDOM INSERTS IN PACKS

AG A.J. Griffin	3.00	8.00
AO Andrew Oliver	3.00	8.00
BS Blake Smith	3.00	8.00
CC Christian Colon	4.00	10.00
CH Chris Hernandez	3.00	8.00
DD Derek Dietrich	8.00	20.00
HM Hunter Morris	3.00	8.00
JF Josh Fellhauer	3.00	8.00
KD Kentrail Davis	4.00	10.00
KV Kendal Volz	3.00	8.00
MD Matt den Dekker	4.00	10.00
MG Micah Gibbs	4.00	10.00
ML Mike Leake	6.00	15.00
MM Mike Minor	4.00	10.00
RJ Ryan Jackson	3.00	8.00
RL Ryan Lipkin	3.00	8.00
TL Tyler Lyons	3.00	8.00

2009 Upper Deck USA National Team Jerseys

AG A.J. Griffin	3.00	8.00
AO Andrew Oliver	3.00	8.00
BS Blake Smith	3.00	8.00
CC Christian Colon	3.00	8.00
CH Chris Hernandez	3.00	8.00
DD Derek Dietrich	3.00	8.00
HM Hunter Morris	3.00	8.00
JF Josh Fellhauer	3.00	8.00
KD Kentrail Davis	3.00	8.00
KG Kyle Gibson	3.00	8.00
KR Kevin Rhoderick	3.00	8.00
KV Kendal Volz	3.00	8.00
MD Matt den Dekker	3.00	8.00
MG Micah Gibbs	3.00	8.00
ML Mike Leake	4.00	10.00
MM Mike Minor	3.00	8.00
RJ Ryan Jackson	3.00	8.00
RL Ryan Lipkin	3.00	8.00
SS Stephen Strasburg	5.00	12.00
TL Tyler Lyons	3.00	8.00

2009 Upper Deck USA National Team Jersey Autographs

RANDOM INSERTS IN PACKS
STATED PRINT RUN 225 SER.#'d SETS

AG A.J. Griffin	4.00	10.00
AO Andrew Oliver	4.00	10.00
BS Blake Smith	6.00	15.00
CC Christian Colon	8.00	20.00
CH Chris Hernandez	5.00	12.00
DD Derek Dietrich	8.00	20.00
HM Hunter Morris	5.00	12.00
JF Josh Fellhauer	5.00	12.00
KD Kentrail Davis	4.00	10.00
KG Kyle Gibson	15.00	40.00
KR Kevin Rhoderick	4.00	10.00
KV Kendal Volz	4.00	10.00
MD Matt den Dekker	4.00	10.00
MG Micah Gibbs	4.00	10.00
ML Mike Leake	4.00	10.00
MM Mike Minor	6.00	12.00
RJ Ryan Jackson	4.00	10.00
RL Ryan Lipkin	4.00	10.00
SS Stephen Strasburg	40.00	100.00
TL Tyler Lyons	4.00	10.00

2009 Upper Deck USA National Team Retrospective

ODDS 1:8 HOB,1:36 RET,1:108 BLAST

USA1 Matt Brown	.75	2.00
USA2 Stephen Strasburg	4.00	10.00
USA3 Jayson Nix	.75	2.00
USA4 Brian Duensing	1.25	3.00
USA5 Jake Arrieta	2.00	5.00
USA6 Dexter Fowler	1.25	3.00
USA7 Casey Weathers	.75	2.00
USA8 Mike Koplove	.75	2.00
USA9 Jason Donald	.75	2.00
USA10 Taylor Teagarden	.75	2.00
USA11 Kevin Jepsen	.75	2.00
USA12 Matt LaPorta	1.25	3.00
USA13 Team USA Wins Bronze Medal	.75	2.00
USA14 Team USA Wins Third Olympic Medal	.75	2.00

2010 Upper Deck

COMPLETE SET (609)	25.00	60.00
COMMON CARD (2-40)	.50	1.25
COMMON CARD (1/41-600)	.15	.40

C EQUALS COMMON VARIATION
R EQUALS RARE VARIATION
S EQUALS SUPER RARE VARIATION
U EQUALS ULTRA RARE VARIATION

1 Star Rookie CL	.15	.40
2 Daniel McCutchen RC	.75	2.00
3 Eric Young Jr. (RC)	.50	1.25
4 Michael Brantley RC	.75	2.00
5 Brian Matusz RC	1.25	3.00
6 Ian Desmond (RC)	.75	2.00
7 Carlos Carrasco (RC)	1.25	3.00
8 Dustin Richardson RC	.50	1.25
9 Tyler Flowers RC	.75	2.00
10 Drew Stubbs RC	1.25	3.00
11 Reid Gorecki (RC)	.75	2.00
12 Tommy Manzella (RC)	.50	1.25
13 Wade Davis (RC)	.75	2.00
14 Esmil Rogers RC	.50	1.25
15 Michael Dunn RC	.50	1.25
16 Luis Durango RC	.50	1.25
17 Juan Francisco RC	.75	2.00
18 Ernesto Frieri RC	.50	1.25
19 Tyler Colvin RC	.75	2.00
20 Armando Gabino RC	.50	1.25
21 Adam Moore RC	.50	1.25
22 Cesar Ramos (RC)	.50	1.25
23 Chris Johnson RC	.75	2.00
24 Chris Pettit RC	.50	1.25
25 Brandon Allen (RC)	.50	1.25
26 Brad Kilby RC	.50	1.25
27 Dusty Hughes RC	.50	1.25
28 Buster Posey RC	4.00	10.00
29 Kevin Richardson (RC)	.50	1.25
30 Josh Thole RC	.75	2.00
31 John Hester RC	.50	1.25
32 Kyle Phillips RC	.50	1.25
33 Neil Walker (RC)	.75	2.00
34 Matt Carson (RC)	.50	1.25
35 Pedro Strop RC	1.25	3.00
36 Pedro Viola RC	.50	1.25
37 Daniel Runzler RC	.75	2.00
38 Henry Rodriguez RC	.50	1.25
39 Justin Turner RC	2.50	6.00
40 Madison Bumgarner RC	4.00	10.00
41 Chris B. Young	.15	.40
42A Justin Upton	.25	.60
43 Conor Jackson	.15	.40
44 Augie Ojeda	.15	.40
45 Mark Reynolds	.15	.40
46 Miguel Montero	.15	.40
47 Max Scherzer	.40	1.00
48 Doug Slaten	.15	.40
49 Chad Qualls	.15	.40
50 Dan Haren	.15	.40
51 Juan Gutierrez	.15	.40
52 Doug Davis	.15	.40
53 Leo Rosales	.15	.40
54 Chad Tracy	.15	.40
55 Stephen Drew	.15	.40
56 Jordan Schafer	.15	.40
57 Rafael Soriano	.15	.40
58 Javier Vazquez	.15	.40
59 Brandon Jones	.15	.40
60 Matt Diaz	.15	.40
61 Jair Jurrjens	.15	.40
62 Adam LaRoche	.15	.40
63 Martin Prado	.15	.40
64 Omar Infante	.15	.40
65 Chipper Jones	.40	1.00
66A Yunel Escobar	.15	.40
67 David Ross	.15	.40
68 Derek Lowe	.15	.40
69 James Parr	.15	.40
70 Kenshin Kawakami	.25	.60
71 Kris Medlen	.25	.60
72 Ryan Church	.15	.40
73 Nate McLouth	.15	.40
74 Adam Jones	.25	.60
75 Luke Scott	.15	.40
76 Nolan Reimold	.15	.40
77 Felix Pie	.15	.40
78 Lou Montanez	.15	.40
79 Ty Wigginton	.15	.40
80 Cesar Izturis	.15	.40
81 Robert Andino	.15	.40
82 Chad Moeller	.15	.40
83A Koji Uehara	.15	.40
84 Matt Wieters	.40	1.00
85 Jim Johnson	.15	.40
86 Chris Ray	.15	.40
87 Danys Baez	.15	.40
88 David Hernandez	.15	.40
89 Jeremy Guthrie	.15	.40
90 Rich Hill	.15	.40
91 Dustin Pedroia	.30	.75
92 David Ortiz	.40	1.00
93 J.D. Drew	.15	.40
94 Jeff Bailey	.15	.40
95 Kevin Youkilis	.15	.40
96 Clay Buchholz	.15	.40
97 Jed Lowrie	.15	.40
98 Mike Lowell	.15	.40
99 George Kottaras	.15	.40
100 Takashi Saito	.15	.40
101 Hideki Okajima	.15	.40
102 Jason Varitek	.40	1.00
103 Jon Lester	.25	.60
104A Josh Beckett	.15	.40
105 Daniel Bard	.15	.40
106 Jonathan Papelbon	.25	.60
107 Nick Green	.15	.40
108 Kevin Gregg	.15	.40
109A Ryan Theriot	.15	.40
110A Kosuke Fukudome	.25	.60
111 Derrek Lee	.15	.40
112 Bobby Scales	.15	.40
113 Aramis Ramirez	.15	.40
114 Aaron Miles	.15	.40
115 Mike Fontenot	.15	.40
116 Koyie Hill	.15	.40
117 Carlos Zambrano	.25	.60
118 Jeff Samardzija	.15	.40
119 Randy Wells	.15	.40
120 Sean Marshall	.15	.40
121 Carlos Marmol	.25	.60
122 Ryan Dempster	.15	.40
123 Reed Johnson	.15	.40
124 Jake Fox	.15	.40
125 Tony Pena	.15	.40
126 Carlos Quentin	.15	.40
127 A.J. Pierzynski	.15	.40
128 Scott Podsednik	.15	.40
129A Alexei Ramirez	.25	.60
130 Paul Konerko	.25	.60
131 Josh Fields	.15	.40
132 Alex Rios	.15	.40
133 Matt Thornton	.15	.40
134 Mark Buehrle	.25	.60
135 Scott Linebrink	.15	.40
136 Freddy Garcia	.15	.40
137 John Danks	.15	.40
138 Bobby Jenks	.15	.40
139 Gavin Floyd	.15	.40
140 DJ Carrasco	.15	.40
141 Jake Peavy	.15	.40
142 Justin Lehr	.15	.40
143 Wladimir Balentien	.15	.40
144 Laynce Nix	.15	.40
145 Chris Dickerson	.15	.40
146A Joey Votto	.40	1.00
147 Paul Janish	.15	.40
148 Brandon Phillips	.15	.40
149 Scott Rolen	.25	.60
150 Ryan Hanigan	.15	.40
151 Edinson Volquez	.15	.40
152 Arthur Rhodes	.15	.40
153 Micah Owings	.15	.40
154 Ramon Hernandez	.15	.40
155 Francisco Cordero	.15	.40
156 Bronson Arroyo	.15	.40
157 Jared Burton	.15	.40
158 Homer Bailey	.15	.40
159 Travis Hafner	.15	.40
160 Grady Sizemore	.25	.60
161 Matt LaPorta	.15	.40
162 Jeremy Sowers	.15	.40
163 Trevor Crowe	.15	.40
164 Asdrubal Cabrera	.25	.60
165A Shin-Soo Choo	.25	.60
166 Kelly Shoppach	.15	.40
167 Kerry Wood	.15	.40
168 Jake Westbrook	.15	.40
169 Fausto Carmona	.15	.40
170 Aaron Laffey	.15	.40
171 Justin Masterson	.15	.40
172 Jhonny Peralta	.15	.40
173 Jensen Lewis	.15	.40
174 Luis Valbuena	.15	.40
175 Jason Giambi	.15	.40
176 Ryan Spilborghs	.15	.40
177 Seth Smith	.15	.40
178 Matt Murton	.15	.40
179 Dexter Fowler	.25	.60
180A Troy Tulowitzki	.40	1.00
181 Ian Stewart	.15	.40
182 Omar Quintanilla	.15	.40
183 Clint Barmes	.15	.40
184 Garrett Atkins	.15	.40
185 Chris Iannetta	.15	.40
186 Huston Street	.15	.40
187 Franklin Morales	.15	.40
188 Todd Helton	.25	.60
189 Carlos Gonzalez	.25	.60
190 Aaron Cook	.15	.40
191 Jason Hammel	.25	.60
192 Edwin Jackson	.15	.40
193 Clete Thomas	.15	.40
194 Marcus Thames	.15	.40
195 Ryan Raburn	.15	.40
196 Fernando Rodney	.15	.40
197 Adam Everett	.15	.40
198A Brandon Inge	.25	.60
199 Miguel Cabrera	.40	1.00
200 Gerald Laird	.15	.40
201 Joel Zumaya	.15	.40
202 Curtis Granderson	.30	.75
203 Justin Verlander	.40	1.00
204 Bobby Seay	.15	.40
205 Nate Robertson	.15	.40
206 Rick Porcello	.25	.60
207 Ryan Perry	.15	.40
208 Fu-Te Ni	.25	.60
209 Cody Ross	.15	.40
210 Jeremy Hermida	.15	.40
211 Alfredo Amezaga	.15	.40
212A Chris Coghlan	.15	.40
213 Wes Helms	.15	.40
214 Emilio Bonifacio	.15	.40
215 Ricky Nolasco	.15	.40
216 Anibal Sanchez	.15	.40
217 Josh Johnson	.25	.60
218 Burke Badenhop	.15	.40
219 Kiko Calero	.15	.40
220 Renyel Pinto	.15	.40
221 Andrew Miller	.25	.60
222 Hanley Ramirez	.25	.60
223 Gaby Sanchez	.15	.40
224 Hunter Pence	.25	.60
225 Carlos Lee	.15	.40
226A Michael Bourn	.15	.40
227 Kazuo Matsui	.15	.40
228 Darin Erstad	.15	.40
229 Lance Berkman	.25	.60
230 Humberto Quintero	.15	.40
231 J.R. Towles	.15	.40
232 Wesley Wright	.15	.40
233 Jose Valverde	.15	.40
234 Wandy Rodriguez	.15	.40
235 Roy Oswalt	.25	.60
236 Latroy Hawkins	.15	.40
237 Bud Norris	.15	.40
238 Alberto Arias	.15	.40
239 Billy Butler	.15	.40
240 Jose Guillen	.15	.40
241 David DeJesus	.15	.40
242 Willie Bloomquist	.15	.40
243 Mike Aviles	.15	.40
244 Alberto Callaspo	.15	.40
245 John Buck	.15	.40
246 Joakim Soria	.15	.40
247 Zack Greinke	.25	.60
248 Miguel Olivo	.15	.40
249 Kyle Davies	.15	.40
250 Juan Cruz	.15	.40
251 Luke Hochevar	.15	.40
252 Brian Bannister	.15	.40
253 Robinson Tejeda	.15	.40
254 Kyle Farnsworth	.15	.40
255 John Lackey	.25	.60
256 Torii Hunter	.15	.40
257 Chone Figgins	.15	.40
258 Kevin Jepsen	.15	.40
259 Reggie Willits	.15	.40
260 Kendry Morales	.15	.40
261 Howie Kendrick	.15	.40
262 Erick Aybar	.15	.40
263 Brandon Wood	.15	.40
264 Maicer Izturis	.15	.40
265 Mike Napoli	.15	.40
266 Jeff Mathis	.15	.40
267A Jered Weaver	.25	.60
268 Joe Saunders	.15	.40
269 Ervin Santana	.15	.40
270 Brian Fuentes	.15	.40
271 Jose Arredondo	.15	.40
272 Chad Billingsley	.25	.60
273 Juan Pierre	.15	.40
274 Matt Kemp	.30	.75
275 Randy Wolf	.15	.40
276 Doug Mientkiewicz	.15	.40
277 James Loney	.15	.40
278 Casey Blake	.15	.40
279 Rafael Furcal	.15	.40
280 Blake DeWitt	.15	.40
281 Russell Martin	.15	.40
282 Jeff Weaver	.15	.40
283 Cory Wade	.15	.40
284 Eric Stults	.15	.40
285 George Sherrill	.15	.40
286 Hiroki Kuroda	.15	.40
287 Hong-Chih Kuo	.15	.40
288A Clayton Kershaw	.75	2.00
289 Corey Hart	.15	.40
290 Jody Gerut	.15	.40
291A Ryan Braun	.25	.60
292 Mike Cameron	.15	.40
293 Casey McGehee	.15	.40
294 Mat Gamel	.15	.40
295 J.J. Hardy	.15	.40
296 Braden Looper	.15	.40
297 Yovani Gallardo	.15	.40
298 Mike Rivera	.15	.40
299 Carlos Villanueva	.15	.40
300 Jeff Suppan	.15	.40
301 Mitch Stetter	.15	.40
302 David Riske	.15	.40
303 Manny Parra	.15	.40
304 Seth McClung	.15	.40
305 Todd Coffey	.15	.40
306 Joe Mauer	.30	.75
307 Delmon Young	.25	.60
308 Michael Cuddyer	.15	.40
309 Matt Tolbert	.15	.40
310 Nick Punto	.15	.40
311 Jason Kubel	.15	.40
312 Brendan Harris	.15	.40
313 Brian Buscher	.15	.40
314 Kevin Slowey	.15	.40
315 Glen Perkins	.15	.40
316 Joe Nathan	.15	.40
317 Nick Blackburn	.15	.40
318 Jesse Crain	.15	.40
319 Matt Guerrier	.15	.40
320 Scott Baker	.15	.40
321 Anthony Swarzak	.15	.40
322 Jon Rauch	.15	.40
323A David Wright	.30	.75
324 Jeremy Reed	.15	.40
325 Angel Pagan	.15	.40
326 Jose Reyes	.25	.60
327 Jeff Francoeur	.25	.60
328 Luis Castillo	.15	.40
329 Daniel Murphy	.30	.75
330 Omir Santos	.15	.40
331 John Maine	.15	.40
332 Brian Schneider	.15	.40
333 Johan Santana	.25	.60
334 Francisco Rodriguez	.25	.60
335 Tim Redding	.15	.40
336 Mike Pelfrey	.15	.40
337 Bobby Parnell	.15	.40
338 Pat Misch	.15	.40
339 Pedro Feliciano	.15	.40
340 Nick Swisher	.25	.60
341 Melky Cabrera	.15	.40
342 Mark Teixeira	.25	.60
343 CC Sabathia	.25	.60
344 Ramiro Pena	.15	.40
345 Derek Jeter	1.00	2.50
346 Andy Pettitte	.25	.60
347A Jorge Posada	.25	.60
348 Francisco Cervelli	.15	.40
349 Chien-Ming Wang	.25	.60
350A Mariano Rivera	.50	1.25
351 Phil Hughes	.15	.40
352 Phil Coke	.15	.40
353 A.J. Burnett	.15	.40
354 Jose Molina	.15	.40
355 Jonathan Albaladejo	.15	.40
356 Ryan Sweeney	.15	.40
357 Jack Cust	.15	.40
358 Rajai Davis	.15	.40
359 Andrew Bailey	.15	.40
360 Aaron Cunningham	.15	.40
361 Adam Kennedy	.15	.40
362 Mark Ellis	.15	.40
363 Daric Barton	.15	.40
364 Kurt Suzuki	.15	.40
365 Brad Ziegler	.15	.40
366 Michael Wuertz	.15	.40
367 Josh Outman	.15	.40
368 Edgar Gonzalez	.15	.40
369 Joey Devine	.15	.40
370 Craig Breslow	.15	.40
371 Trevor Cahill	.15	.40
372 Brett Anderson	.15	.40
373 Scott Hairston	.15	.40
374 Jayson Werth	.25	.60
375 Raul Ibanez	.25	.60
376A Chase Utley	.25	.60
377 Greg Dobbs	.15	.40
378 Eric Bruntlett	.15	.40
379 Shane Victorino	.25	.60
380 Jimmy Rollins	.25	.60
381 Jack Taschner	.15	.40
382 Ryan Madson	.15	.40
383 Brad Lidge	.15	.40
384 J.A. Happ	.25	.60
385 Cole Hamels	.30	.75
386 Carlos Ruiz	.15	.40
387 JC Romero	.15	.40
388 Kyle Kendrick	.15	.40
389 Chad Durbin	.15	.40
390 Cliff Lee	.25	.60
391 Delwyn Young	.15	.40
392 Brandon Moss	.15	.40
393 Ramon Vazquez	.15	.40
394 Andy LaRoche	.15	.40
395 Jason Jaramillo	.15	.40
396 Ross Ohlendorf	.15	.40
397 Paul Maholm	.15	.40
398 Jeff Karstens	.15	.40
399 Charlie Morton	.40	1.00
400 Zach Duke	.15	.40
401 Jesse Chavez	.15	.40
402 Lastings Milledge	.15	.40
403 Matt Capps	.15	.40
404 Evan Meek	.15	.40
405 Ryan Doumit	.15	.40
406 Drew Macias	.15	.40
407 Chase Headley	.15	.40
408A Tony Gwynn Jr.	.15	.40
409 Kevin Kouzmanoff	.15	.40
410 Edgar Gonzalez	.15	.40
411 David Eckstein	.15	.40
412 Everth Cabrera	.15	.40
413 Nick Hundley	.15	.40
414 Chris Young	.15	.40
415 Luis Perdomo	.15	.40
416 Edward Mujica	.15	.40
417 Clayton Richard	.15	.40
418A Luke Gregerson	.15	.40
419 Heath Bell	.15	.40
420 Kevin Correia	.15	.40
421 Cha-Seung Baek	.15	.40
422 Joe Thatcher	.15	.40
423 Luis Rodriguez	.15	.40
424 Bengie Molina	.15	.40
425 Ryan Garko	.15	.40
426 Nate Schierholtz	.15	.40
427 Aaron Rowand	.15	.40
428 Eugenio Velez	.15	.40
429 Pablo Sandoval	.25	.60
430 Edgar Renteria	.15	.40
431 Kevin Frandsen	.15	.40
432 Rich Aurilia	.15	.40
433 Jonathan Sanchez	.15	.40
434 Barry Zito	.25	.60
435 Brian Wilson	.40	1.00
436 Merkin Valdez	.15	.40
437 Juan Uribe	.15	.40
438 Brandon Medders	.15	.40
439 Noah Lowry	.15	.40
440 Tim Lincecum	.25	.60
441 Jeremy Affeldt	.15	.40
442 Russell Branyan	.15	.40
443 Ian Snell	.15	.40
444 Franklin Gutierrez	.15	.40
445 Ken Griffey Jr.	.75	2.00
446 Matt Tuiasosopo	.15	.40
447 Jose Lopez	.15	.40
448 Michael Saunders	.25	.60
449 Ryan Rowland-Smith	.15	.40
450 Carlos Silva	.15	.40
451A Ichiro Suzuki	.50	1.25
452 Brandon Morrow	.15	.40
453 Chris Jakubauskas	.15	.40
454 Felix Hernandez	.25	.60
455 David Aardsma	.15	.40
456 Mark Lowe	.15	.40
457 Rob Johnson	.15	.40
458 Garrett Olson	.15	.40
459 Ryan Ludwick	.15	.40
460 Colby Rasmus	.25	.60
461 Brendan Ryan	.15	.40
462 Skip Schumaker	.15	.40
463 Albert Pujols	.50	1.25
464 Joe Thurston	.15	.40
465 Julio Lugo	.15	.40
466A Yadier Molina	.40	1.00
467 Adam Wainwright	.25	.60
468 Brad Thompson	.15	.40
469 Dennys Reyes	.15	.40
470 Mitchell Boggs	.15	.40
471 Jason Motte	.15	.40
472 Kyle McClellan	.15	.40
473 Kyle Lohse	.15	.40
474 Chris Carpenter	.25	.60
475 Ryan Franklin	.15	.40
476 Fernando Perez	.15	.40
477 Ben Zobrist	.25	.60
478 Evan Longoria	.25	.60
479 Gabe Gross	.15	.40
480 Pat Burrell	.15	.40
481 Carlos Pena	.25	.60
482 Jason Bartlett	.15	.40
483 Willie Aybar	.15	.40
484 Dioner Navarro	.15	.40
485 Dan Wheeler	.15	.40
486 Andy Sonnanstine	.15	.40
487 James Shields	.15	.40
488 Jeff Niemann	.15	.40
489 J.P. Howell	.15	.40
490 Grant Balfour	.15	.40
491 David Price	.30	.75
492 Matt Garza	.15	.40
493 David Murphy	.15	.40
494 Nelson Cruz	.40	1.00
495 Michael Young	.15	.40
496 Ian Kinsler	.25	.60
497 Chris Davis	.25	.60
498A Elvis Andrus	.25	.60
499 Taylor Teagarden	.15	.40
500 Jarrod Saltalamacchia	.15	.40
501 CJ Wilson	.15	.40
502 Derek Holland	.15	.40
503 Darren O'Day	.15	.40
504 Brandon McCarthy	.15	.40
505 Scott Feldman	.15	.40
506 Jason Jennings	.15	.40
507 Eddie Guardado	.15	.40
508 Frank Francisco	.15	.40
509 Marlon Byrd	.15	.40
510 Scott Downs	.15	.40
511 Adam Lind	.25	.60
512 Brett Cecil	.15	.40
513 Travis Snider	.15	.40
514 Ricky Romero	.15	.40
515 Lyle Overbay	.15	.40
516 Aaron Hill	.15	.40
517 Jose Bautista	.25	[illegible]
518 Michael Barrett	.15	.4
519 Roy Halladay	.25	[illegible]
520 Brian Tallet	.15	.4
521 Marc Rzepczynski	.15	.4
522 Robert Ray	.15	.4
523 Dustin McGowan	.15	.4
524 Shaun Marcum	.15	.4
525 Jesse Litsch	.15	.4
526 Josh Willingham	.25	.6
527 Nyjer Morgan	.15	.4
528 Adam Dunn	.25	.6
529 Ryan Zimmerman	.25	.6
530 Willie Harris	.15	.4
531 Wil Nieves	.15	.4
532 Ron Villone	.15	.4
533 Livan Hernandez	.15	.4
534 Austin Kearns	.15	.4
535 Alberto Gonzalez	.15	.4
536 Shairon Martis	.15	.4
537 Ross Detwiler	.15	.4
538 Garrett Mock	.15	.4
539 Mike MacDougal	.15	.4
540 Jason Bergmann	.15	.4
541 Arizona Diamondbacks BP	.15	.4
542 Atlanta Braves BP	.15	.40
543 Baltimore Orioles BP	.15	.40
544 Boston Red Sox BP	.25	.60
545 Chicago Cubs BP	.25	.60
546 Chicago White Sox BP	.15	.40
547 Cincinnati Reds BP	.15	.40
548 Cleveland Indians BP	.15	.40
549 Colorado Rockies BP	.15	.40
550 Detroit Tigers BP	.15	.40
551 Florida Marlins BP	.15	.40
552 Houston Astros BP	.15	.40
553 Kansas City Royals BP	.15	.40
554 Los Angeles Angels BP	.15	.40
555 Los Angeles Dodgers BP	.25	.60
556 Milwaukee Brewers BP	.15	.40
557 Minnesota Twins BP	.15	.40
558 New York Mets BP	.25	.60
559 New York Yankees BP	.40	1.00
560 Oakland Athletics BP	.15	.40
561 Philadelphia Phillies	.15	.40
562 Pittsburgh Pirates	.15	.40
563 San Diego Padres	.15	.40
564 San Francisco Giants	.15	.40
565 St. Louis Cardinals	.25	.60
566 Seattle Mariners	.15	.40
567 Tampa Bay Rays	.15	.40
568 Texas Rangers	.15	.40
569 Toronto Blue Jays	.15	.40
570 Washington Nationals	.15	.40
571 Arizona Diamondbacks CL	.15	.40
572 Atlanta Braves CL	.15	.40
573 Baltimore Orioles CL	.15	.40
574 Boston Red Sox CL	.25	.60
575 Chicago Cubs CL	.25	.60
576 Chicago White Sox CL	.15	.40
577 Cincinnati Reds CL	.15	.40
578 Cleveland Indians CL	.15	.40
579 Colorado Rockies CL	.15	.40
580 Detroit Tigers CL	.15	.40
581 Florida Marlins CL	.15	.40
582 Houston Astros CL	.15	.40
583 Kansas City Royals CL	.15	.40
584 Los Angeles Angels CL	.15	.40
585 Los Angeles Dodgers CL	.25	.60
586 Milwaukee Brewers CL	.15	.40
587 Minnesota Twins CL	.15	.40
588 New York Mets CL	.25	.60
589 New York Yankees CL	.40	1.00
590 Oakland Athletics CL	.15	.40
591 Philadelphia Phillies CL	.15	.40
592 Pittsburgh Pirates CL	.15	.40
593 San Diego Padres CL	.15	.40
594 San Francisco Giants CL	.15	.40
595 St. Louis Cardinals CL	.25	.60
596 Seattle Mariners CL	.15	.40
597 Tampa Bay Rays CL	.15	.40
598 Texas Rangers CL	.15	.40
599 Toronto Blue Jays CL	.15	.40
600 Washington Nationals CL	.15	.40
R1 Pete Rose ATHK SP	12.50	30.00
R2 Pos/Jet/Riv/Pet SP	60.00	120.00
R3 Joe Jackson SP	20.00	50.00

2010 Upper Deck Gold

*GOLD 2-40: 4X TO 10X BASIC RC
*GOLD 1/41-600: 12X TO 30X BASIC VET
STATED PRINT RUN 99 SER.#'d SETS

28 Buster Posey	40.00	100.00

2010 Upper Deck 2000 Star Rookie Update

541 Mark Buehrle	3.00	8.00
542 Miguel Cabrera	5.00	12.00
543 Jorge Cantu	2.00	5.00
544 Carl Crawford	3.00	8.00
545 Adam Dunn	3.00	8.00
546 Adrian Gonzalez	4.00	10.00
547 Matt Holliday	5.00	12.00
548 Brandon Inge	3.00	8.00
549 Roy Oswalt	3.00	8.00
550 Carlos Pena	3.00	8.00
551 Brandon Phillips	2.00	5.00
552 Francisco Rodriguez	3.00	8.00
553 Jimmy Rollins	3.00	8.00
554 Aaron Rowand	2.00	5.00
555 CC Sabathia	3.00	8.00
556 Johan Santana	3.00	8.00
557 Grady Sizemore	3.00	8.00
558 Adam Wainwright	3.00	8.00

Michael Young 2.00 5.00
Carlos Zambrano 3.00 8.00

2010 Upper Deck A Piece of History 500 Club

Gary Sheffield 15.00 40.00

2010 Upper Deck All World

W1 Albert Pujols 1.25 3.00
W2 Carlos Beltran .60 1.50
W3 Carlos Lee .40 1.00
W4 Chien-Ming Wang .60 1.50
W5 Daisuke Matsuzaka .60 1.50
W6 Derek Jeter 2.50 6.00
W7 Felix Hernandez .60 1.50
W8 Hanley Ramirez .60 1.50
W9 Ichiro Suzuki 1.25 3.00
W10 Johan Santana .60 1.50
W11 Justin Morneau .60 1.50
W12 Kendry Morales .40 1.00
W13 Magglio Ordonez .60 1.50
W14 Russell Martin .40 1.00
W15 Vladimir Guerrero .60 1.50

2010 Upper Deck Baseball Heroes

0 Joe DiMaggio 1.50 4.00
H1 Joe DiMaggio 1.50 4.00
H2 Joe DiMaggio 1.50 4.00
H3 Joe DiMaggio 1.50 4.00
H4 Joe DiMaggio 1.50 4.00
H5 Joe DiMaggio 1.50 4.00
H6 Joe DiMaggio 1.50 4.00
H7 Joe DiMaggio 1.50 4.00
H8 Joe DiMaggio 1.50 4.00

2010 Upper Deck Baseball Heroes 20th Anniversary Art

BHA1 Ken Griffey Jr. 2.00 5.00
BHA2 Derek Jeter 2.50 6.00
BHA3 Evan Longoria .60 1.50
BHA4 Hanley Ramirez .60 1.50
BHA5 David Price .75 2.00
BHA6 Jon Lester .60 1.50
BHA7 Nick Markakis .75 2.00
BHA8 Cole Hamels .75 2.00
BHA9 Jonathan Papelbon .60 1.50
BHA10 Chipper Jones 1.00 2.50

2010 Upper Deck Baseball Heroes 20th Anniversary Art Autographs

STATED PRINT RUN 90 SER.#'d SETS
BHA1 Ken Griffey Jr. 125.00 250.00
BHA2 Derek Jeter 100.00 200.00
BHA3 Evan Longoria 15.00 40.00
BHA5 David Price 12.50 30.00
BHA7 Nick Markakis 30.00 60.00
BHA8 Cole Hamels 20.00 50.00
BHA9 Jonathan Papelbon 6.00 15.00

2010 Upper Deck Baseball Heroes DiMaggio Cut Signature

STATED PRINT RUN 56 SER.#'d SETS
JD Joe DiMaggio 300.00 500.00

2010 Upper Deck Celebrity Predictors

CP1/CP2 Jennifer Aniston/John Mayer 1.50 4.00
CP3/CP4 Cameron Diaz
Justin Timberlake 1.50 4.00
CP5/CP6 Megan Fox/Shia LaBeouf 1.50 4.00
CP7/CP8 Katie Holmes/Tom Cruise 1.50 4.00
CP11/CP12 Anna Kournikova
Enrique Iglesias 1.50 4.00
CP13/CP14 Mariah Carey/Nick Cannon 1.50 4.00
CP15/CP16 Rob Pattinson
Kristen Stewart 1.50 4.00
CP17/CP18 A.Jolie/B.Pitt 6.00 15.00
CP19/CP20 C.Ronaldo/P.Hilton 6.00 15.00
CP9/CP10 Chris Martin
Gwyneth Paltrow 1.50 4.00

2010 Upper Deck Portraits

*GOLD: 1.5X TO 4X BASIC
GOLD PRINT RUN 99 SER.#'d SETS
SE1 Justin Upton .60 1.50
SE2 Dan Haren .40 1.00
SE3 Chipper Jones 1.00 2.50
SE4 Yunel Escobar .40 1.00
SE5 Derek Lowe .40 1.00
SE6 Nick Markakis .75 2.00
SE7 Brian Roberts .40 1.00
SE8 Koji Uehara .40 1.00
SE9 Josh Beckett .40 1.00
SE10 Jon Lester .60 1.50
SE11 David Ortiz 1.00 2.50
SE12 Jason Varitek 1.00 2.50
SE13 Carlos Zambrano .60 1.50
SE14 Kosuke Fukudome .60 1.50
SE15 Aramis Ramirez .40 1.00
SE16 Mark Buehrle .60 1.50
SE17 Paul Konerko .60 1.50
SE18 Carlos Quentin .40 1.00
SE19 Joey Votto 1.00 2.50
SE20 Brandon Phillips .40 1.00
SE21 Edinson Volquez .40 1.00
SE22 Shin-Soo Choo .60 1.50
SE23 Kerry Wood .40 1.00
SE24 Grady Sizemore .60 1.50
SE25 Troy Tulowitzki 1.00 2.50
SE26 Aaron Cook .40 1.00
SE27 Todd Helton .60 1.50
SE28 Justin Verlander 1.00 2.50
SE29 Miguel Cabrera 1.00 2.50
SE30 Rick Porcello .60 1.50
SE31 Chris Coghlan .40 1.00
SE32 Josh Johnson .60 1.50
SE33 Carlos Lee .40 1.00
SE34 Lance Berkman .60 1.50
SE35 Roy Oswalt .60 1.50
SE36 Zack Greinke .60 1.50
SE37 Billy Butler .40 1.00
SE38 Joakim Soria .40 1.00
SE39 Jered Weaver .60 1.50
SE40 Torii Hunter .40 1.00
SE41 Kendry Morales .40 1.00
SE42 Chone Figgins .40 1.00
SE43 Russell Martin .40 1.00
SE44 Clayton Kershaw 2.00 5.00
SE45 Matt Kemp .75 2.00
SE46 Hiroki Kuroda .40 1.00
SE47 Alcides Escobar .60 1.50
SE48 Yovani Gallardo .40 1.00
SE49 Ryan Braun .60 1.50
SE50 Justin Morneau .60 1.50
SE51 Joe Nathan .40 1.00
SE52 Michael Cuddyer .40 1.00
SE53 Johan Santana .60 1.50
SE54 David Wright .75 2.00
SE55 Jose Reyes .60 1.50
SE56 Francisco Rodriguez .60 1.50
SE57 Mark Teixeira .60 1.50
SE58 Derek Jeter 2.50 6.00
SE59 Mariano Rivera 1.25 3.00
SE60 A.J. Burnett .40 1.00
SE61 Jorge Posada .60 1.50
SE62 Jack Cust .40 1.00
SE63 Mark Ellis .40 1.00
SE64 Andrew Bailey .40 1.00
SE65 Chase Utley .60 1.50
SE66 Cole Hamels .75 2.00
SE67 Raul Ibanez .60 1.50
SE68 Jimmy Rollins .60 1.50
SE69 Ryan Doumit .40 1.00
SE70 Zach Duke .40 1.00
SE71 Tony Gwynn Jr. .40 1.00
SE72 Chris Young .40 1.00
SE73 Heath Bell .40 1.00
SE74 Barry Zito .60 1.50
SE75 Pablo Sandoval .60 1.50
SE76 Aaron Rowand .40 1.00
SE77 Tim Lincecum .60 1.50
SE78 Felix Hernandez .60 1.50
SE79 Ichiro Suzuki 1.25 3.00
SE80 Franklin Gutierrez .40 1.00
SE81 Albert Pujols 1.25 3.00
SE82 Adam Wainwright .60 1.50
SE83 Chris Carpenter .60 1.50
SE84 Colby Rasmus .60 1.50
SE85 Yadier Molina 1.00 2.50
SE86 Evan Longoria .60 1.50
SE87 Jeff Niemann .40 1.00
SE88 James Shields .40 1.00
SE89 Carlos Pena .60 1.50
SE90 Scott Feldman .40 1.00
SE91 Michael Young .40 1.00
SE92 Ian Kinsler .60 1.50
SE93 Elvis Andrus .60 1.50
SE94 Ricky Romero .40 1.00
SE95 Roy Halladay .60 1.50
SE96 Adam Lind .60 1.50
SE97 Aaron Hill .40 1.00
SE98 Ryan Zimmerman .60 1.50
SE99 Adam Dunn .60 1.50
SE100 Nyjer Morgan .40 1.00

2010 Upper Deck Portraits Gold

*GOLD: 1.5X TO 4X BASIC
STATED PRINT RUN 99 SER.#'d SETS

2010 Upper Deck Pure Heat

PH1 Adrian Gonzalez .75 2.00
PH2 Albert Pujols 1.25 3.00
PH3 Alex Rodriguez 1.25 3.00
PH4 Cole Hamels .75 2.00
PH5 CC Sabathia .60 1.50
PH6 Evan Longoria .60 1.50
PH7 Josh Beckett .40 1.00
PH8 Joe Mauer .75 2.00
PH9 Justin Verlander 1.00 2.50
PH10 Manny Ramirez 1.00 2.50
PH11 Mark Teixeira .60 1.50
PH12 Prince Fielder .60 1.50
PH13 Ryan Howard .75 2.00
PH14 Tim Lincecum .60 1.50
PH15 Troy Tulowitzki 1.00 2.50

2010 Upper Deck Season Biography

SB1 Derek Lowe .40 1.00
SB2 Johan Santana .60 1.50
SB3 Aaron Rowand .40 1.00
SB4 Koji Uehara .40 1.00
SB5 Everth Cabrera .40 1.00
SB6 Miguel Cabrera 1.00 2.50
SB7 Justin Verlander 1.00 2.50
SB8 Evan Longoria .60 1.50
SB9 Orlando Hudson .40 1.00
SB10 Zach Duke .40 1.00
SB11 Ken Griffey Jr. 2.00 5.00
SB12 Ian Kinsler .60 1.50
SB13 Tim Wakefield .60 1.50
SB14 Grady Sizemore .60 1.50
SB15 Gary Sheffield .40 1.00
SB16 Tim Lincecum .60 1.50
SB17 Randy Johnson 1.00 2.50
SB18 Dustin Pedroia .75 2.00
SB19 Ryan Braun .60 1.50
SB20 Dan Haren .40 1.00
SB21 Dave Bush .40 1.00
SB22 Carlos Pena .60 1.50
SB23 Albert Pujols 1.25 3.00
SB24 Jacoby Ellsbury .75 2.00
SB25 Dexter Fowler .60 1.50
SB26 Ryan Howard .75 2.00
SB27 Jorge Cantu .40 1.00
SB28 Yovani Gallardo .40 1.00
SB29 Evan Longoria .60 1.50
SB30 Matt Garza .40 1.00
SB31 Jake Peavy .40 1.00
SB32 Jason Marquis .40 1.00
SB33 Carl Crawford .60 1.50
SB34 Zack Greinke .60 1.50
SB35 Vicente Padilla .40 1.00
SB36 Manny Ramirez 1.00 2.50
SB37 Hanley Ramirez .60 1.50
SB38 Alex Rodriguez 1.25 3.00
SB39 Joe Saunders .40 1.00
SB40 Torii Hunter .40 1.00
SB41 Brett Cecil .40 1.00
SB42 Ryan Zimmerman .60 1.50
SB43 Derek Holland .40 1.00
SB44 Ryan Zimmerman .60 1.50
SB45 Torii Hunter .40 1.00
SB46 Jimmy Rollins .60 1.50
Barack Obama
SB47 Alex Rodriguez 1.25 3.00
SB48 Ivan Rodriguez .60 1.50
SB49 Clayton Kershaw 2.00 5.00
SB50 Jake Peavy .40 1.00
SB51 Jason Kendall .40 1.00
SB52 Mark Teixeira .60 1.50
SB53 David Ortiz 1.00 2.50
SB54 Joe Mauer .75 2.00
SB55 Raul Ibanez .60 1.50
SB56 Kenshin Kawakami .60 1.50
SB57 Nelson Cruz 1.00 2.50
SB58 Alex Gonzalez .40 1.00
SB59 Freddy Sanchez .40 1.00
SB60 Chris B. Young .40 1.00
SB61 Rick Porcello .60 1.50
SB62 Nolan Reimold .40 1.00
SB63 Scott Feldman .40 1.00
SB64 Ryan Howard .75 2.00
SB65 Ryan Dempster .40 1.00
SB66 Jamie Moyer .40 1.00
SB67 Jim Thome .60 1.50
SB68 Roy Halladay .60 1.50
SB69 Jeff Niemann .40 1.00
SB70 Randy Johnson 1.00 2.50
SB71 Jonathan Broxton .40 1.00
SB72 Carlos Zambrano .60 1.50
SB73 Jon Lester .60 1.50
SB74 Alfonso Soriano .60 1.50
SB75 Dan Haren .40 1.00
SB76 Vin Mazzaro .40 1.00
SB77 Sean West .40 1.00
SB78 Andre Ethier .60 1.50
SB79 Colby Rasmus .60 1.50
SB80 Jim Thome .60 1.50
SB81 Tim Lincecum .60 1.50
SB82 Miguel Tejada .60 1.50
SB83 Torii Hunter .40 1.00
SB84 Albert Pujols 1.25 3.00
SB85 Todd Helton .60 1.50
SB86 Jered Weaver .60 1.50
SB87 Prince Fielder .60 1.50
SB88 Robinson Cano .60 1.50
SB89 Ivan Rodriguez .60 1.50
SB90 Tommy Hanson .40 1.00
SB91 Kenshin Kawakami .60 1.50
SB92 Jeff Weaver .40 1.00
SB93 Albert Pujols 1.25 3.00
SB94 B.J. Upton .60 1.50
SB95 Trevor Cahill .40 1.00
SB96 Tim Lincecum .60 1.50
SB97 Troy Tulowitzki 1.00 2.50
SB98 Jermaine Dye .40 1.00
SB99 Lance Berkman .60 1.50
SB100 Hanley Ramirez .60 1.50
SB101 Alex Rodriguez 1.25 3.00
SB102 Albert Pujols 1.25 3.00
SB103 Tommy Hanson .40 1.00
SB104 Zack Greinke .60 1.50
SB105 Brandon Phillips .40 1.00
SB106 Dallas Braden .60 1.50
SB107 Joey Votto 1.00 2.50
SB108 Albert Pujols 1.25 3.00
SB109 Adam Dunn .60 1.50
SB110 Ricky Nolasco .40 1.00
SB111 Ted Lilly .40 1.00
SB112 Vladimir Guerrero .60 1.50
SB113 Ryan Spilborghs .40 1.00
SB114 Garrett Atkins .40 1.00
SB115 Jonathan Sanchez .40 1.00
SB116 Josh Beckett .40 1.00
SB117 Kurt Suzuki .40 1.00
SB118 Ichiro Suzuki 1.25 3.00
Barack Obama
SB119 Ryan Howard .75 2.00
SB120 Marc Rzepczynski .40 1.00
SB121 Clayton Kershaw 2.00 5.00
SB122 Roy Halladay .60 1.50
SB123 Jason Marquis .40 1.00
SB124 Manny Ramirez 1.00 2.50
SB125 Scott Hairston .40 1.00
SB126 A.J. Burnett .40 1.00
SB127 Mark Buehrle .60 1.50
SB128 Jeremy Sowers .40 1.00
SB129 Chone Figgins .40 1.00
SB130 Cliff Lee .60 1.50
SB131 Michael Young .40 1.00
SB132 Josh Willingham .60 1.50
SB133 Pablo Sandoval .60 1.50
SB134 Cliff Lee .60 1.50
SB135 Aaron Hill .40 1.00
SB136 Bud Norris .40 1.00
SB137 Neftali Feliz .40 1.00
SB138 Chase Utley .60 1.50
SB139 Fausto Carmona .40 1.00
SB140 Barry Zito .60 1.50
SB141 Jered Weaver .60 1.50
SB142 Roy Halladay .60 1.50
SB143 Wandy Rodriguez .40 1.00
SB144 Mark Teixeira .60 1.50
SB145 Vladimir Guerrero .60 1.50
SB146 Adrian Gonzalez .75 2.00
SB147 Tim Lincecum .60 1.50
SB148 Pedro Martinez .60 1.50
SB149 Felix Pie .40 1.00
SB150 Jim Thome .60 1.50
SB151 Derek Jeter 2.50 6.00
SB152 Gregg Zaun .40 1.00
SB153 Ian Kinsler .60 1.50
SB154 Brandon Inge .60 1.50
SB155 Hanley Ramirez .60 1.50
SB156 Russell Branyan .40 1.00
SB157 Pedro Martinez .60 1.50
SB158 Michael Cuddyer .40 1.00
SB159 Jake Fox .40 1.00
SB160 John Smoltz 1.00 2.50
SB161 Ryan Howard .75 2.00
SB162 Matt LaPorta .40 1.00
SB163 Joe Saunders .40 1.00
SB164 Tony Gwynn Jr. .40 1.00
SB165 Carlos Ruiz .40 1.00
SB166 Edgar Renteria .40 1.00
SB167 Josh Hamilton .60 1.50
SB168 Tim Hudson .60 1.50
SB169 Garrett Jones .40 1.00
SB170 Landon Powell .40 1.00
SB171 Casey McGehee .40 1.00
SB172 Ichiro Suzuki 1.25 3.00
SB173 Daniel Murphy .75 2.00
SB174 Jon Lester .60 1.50
SB175 Derrek Lee .40 1.00
SB176 Mark Buehrle .60 1.50
SB177 Mark Teixeira .60 1.50
SB178 Brad Penny .40 1.00
SB179 Wade LeBlanc .40 1.00
SB180 Micah Hoffpauir .40 1.00
SB181 Ian Desmond .60 1.50
SB182 Derek Jeter 2.50 6.00
SB183 Brian Matusz 1.00 2.50
SB184 Ichiro Suzuki 1.25 3.00
SB185 Josh Johnson .60 1.50
SB186 Luis Durango .40 1.00
SB187 Jody Gerut .40 1.00
SB188 Francisco Rodriguez .60 1.50
SB189 Jake Peavy .40 1.00
SB190 Mariano Rivera 1.25 3.00
SB191 Sonia Sotomayor .40 1.00
SB192 Willy Aybar .40 1.00
SB193 Wade Davis .60 1.50
SB194 Ceasar Ramos .40 1.00
SB195 Kevin Millwood .40 1.00
SB196 Andres Torres .40 1.00
SB197 Willy Aybar .40 1.00
SB198 Clayton Kershaw 2.00 5.00
SB199 Justin Verlander 1.00 2.50
SB200 Alexi Casilla .40 1.00

2010 Upper Deck Signature Sensations

AA Aaron Rowand 8.00 20.00
AE Alcides Escobar 5.00 12.00
AH Aaron Harang 8.00 20.00
AI Akinori Iwamura 8.00 20.00
AL Andy LaRoche 6.00 15.00
AR Alex Romero 3.00 8.00
AS Anibal Sanchez 4.00 10.00
BA Burke Badenhop 3.00 8.00
BB Brian Bixler 5.00 12.00
BO Jeremy Bonderman 15.00 40.00
CB Clay Buchholz 6.00 15.00
CF Chone Figgins 4.00 10.00
CH Chase Headley 3.00 8.00
CK Clayton Kershaw 50.00 100.00
CL Carlos Lee 3.00 8.00
DE David Eckstein 5.00 12.00
DJ Derek Jeter 200.00 500.00
DO Darren O'Day 4.00 10.00
DP Dustin Pedroia 12.50 30.00
DS Denard Span 4.00 10.00
DU Dan Uggla 6.00 15.00
DV Donald Veal 5.00 12.00
EB Emilio Bonifacio 3.00 8.00
ED Elijah Dukes 3.00 8.00
EM Evan Meek 12.50 30.00
EV Eugenio Velez 4.00 10.00
FP Felix Pie 8.00 20.00
HE Jeremy Hermida 3.00 8.00
HJ Josh Hamilton 8.00 20.00
HP Hunter Pence 5.00 12.00
JA Jonathan Albaladejo 3.00 8.00
JC Johnny Cueto 4.00 10.00
JH J.A. Happ 8.00 20.00
JL Jesse Litsch 4.00 10.00
JM John Maine 3.00 8.00
JO Joaquin Arias 3.00 8.00
JP Jonathan Papelbon 8.00 20.00
JW Josh Willingham 3.00 8.00
KG Khalil Greene 6.00 15.00
KH Kevin Hart 4.00 10.00
KJ Kelly Johnson 3.00 8.00
KK Kevin Kouzmanoff 3.00 8.00
KS Kevin Slowey 6.00 15.00
KY Kevin Youkilis 10.00 25.00
MB Marlon Byrd 3.00 8.00
MG Mat Gamel 4.00 10.00
MO Micah Owings 5.00 12.00
MP Mike Pelfrey 5.00 12.00
NY Nyjer Morgan 4.00 10.00
PA Felipe Paulino 3.00 8.00
PF Prince Fielder 10.00 25.00
RA Alexei Ramirez 6.00 15.00
RH Roy Halladay 30.00 60.00
RM Russell Martin 6.00 15.00
RO Ross Ohlendorf 5.00 12.00
RT Ryan Theriot 10.00 25.00
SK Scott Kazmir 15.00 40.00
SM Sean Marshall 3.00 8.00
TE Miguel Tejada 3.00 8.00
TP Troy Patton 3.00 8.00
TR Ramon Troncoso 3.00 8.00
TS Takashi Saito 10.00 25.00
VO Edinson Volquez 4.00 10.00
WW Wesley Wright 3.00 8.00
YE Yunel Escobar 5.00 12.00
YG Yovani Gallardo 6.00 15.00
ZD Zach Duke 5.00 12.00

2010 Upper Deck Supreme Blue

*BLUE: 1.5X TO 4X BASIC
S37 Tim Lincecum 4.00 10.00

2010 Upper Deck Supreme Green

S1 Dan Haren .60 1.50
S2 Chipper Jones 1.50 4.00
S3 Tommy Hanson .60 1.50
S4 Adam Jones 1.00 2.50
S5 Jonathan Papelbon 1.00 2.50
S6 Dustin Pedroia 1.25 3.00
S7 Kevin Youkilis .60 1.50
S8 Jason Bay 1.00 2.50
S9 Alfonso Soriano 1.00 2.50
S10 Paul Konerko 1.00 2.50
S11 Mark Buehrle 1.00 2.50
S12 Joey Votto 1.50 4.00
S13 Grady Sizemore 1.00 2.50
S14 Travis Hafner .60 1.50
S15 Troy Tulowitzki 1.50 4.00
S16 Jason Marquis .60 1.50
S17 Brandon Inge 1.00 2.50
S18 Justin Verlander 1.50 4.00
S19 Josh Johnson 1.00 2.50
S20 Carlos Lee .60 1.50
S21 Billy Butler .60 1.50
S22 Vladimir Guerrero 1.00 2.50
S23 Torii Hunter .60 1.50
S24 Manny Ramirez 1.50 4.00
S25 Ryan Braun 1.00 2.50
S26 Michael Cuddyer .60 1.50
S27 Joe Mauer 1.25 3.00
S28 Carlos Beltran 1.00 2.50
S29 David Wright 1.25 3.00
S30 Hideki Matsui 1.50 4.00
S31 Derek Jeter 4.00 10.00
S32 CC Sabathia 1.00 2.50
S33 Kurt Suzuki .60 1.50
S34 Ryan Howard 1.25 3.00
S35 Cole Hamels 1.25 3.00
S36 Mat Latos 1.00 2.50
S37 Tim Lincecum 1.00 2.50
S38 Pablo Sandoval 1.00 2.50
S39 Ichiro Suzuki 2.00 5.00
S40 Matt Holliday 1.50 4.00
S41 Yadier Molina 1.50 4.00
S42 Colby Rasmus 1.00 2.50
S43 Evan Longoria 1.00 2.50
S44 Carlos Pena 1.00 2.50
S45 Carl Crawford 1.00 2.50
S46 Ian Kinsler 1.00 2.50
S47 Josh Hamilton 1.00 2.50
S48 Scott Feldman .60 1.50
S49 Roy Halladay 1.00 2.50
S50 Ryan Zimmerman 1.00 2.50
S51 Justin Upton 1.00 2.50
S52 Mark Reynolds .60 1.50
S53 Brian McCann 1.00 2.50
S54 Nick Markakis 1.25 3.00
S55 Matt Wieters 1.50 4.00
S56 Jacoby Ellsbury 1.25 3.00
S57 David Ortiz 1.50 4.00
S58 Josh Beckett .60 1.50
S59 Carlos Zambrano 1.00 2.50
S60 Gordon Beckham .60 1.50
S61 Jay Bruce 1.00 2.50
S62 Shin-Soo Choo 1.00 2.50
S63 Todd Helton 1.00 2.50
S64 Dexter Fowler 1.00 2.50
S65 Miguel Cabrera 1.50 4.00
S66 Curtis Granderson 1.25 3.00
S67 Hanley Ramirez 1.00 2.50
S68 Dan Uggla .60 1.50
S69 Lance Berkman 1.00 2.50
S70 Zack Greinke 1.00 2.50
S71 Chone Figgins .60 1.50
S72 John Lackey 1.00 2.50
S73 Russell Martin .60 1.50
S74 Matt Kemp 1.25 3.00
S75 Prince Fielder 1.00 2.50
S76 Yovani Gallardo .60 1.50
S77 Justin Morneau 1.00 2.50
S78 Jose Reyes 1.00 2.50
S79 Johan Santana 1.00 2.50
S80 Francisco Rodriguez 1.00 2.50
S81 Johnny Damon 1.00 2.50
S82 Mark Teixeira 1.00 2.50
S83 Mariano Rivera 2.00 5.00
S84 Alex Rodriguez 2.00 5.00
S85 Cliff Lee 1.00 2.50
S86 Chase Utley 1.00 2.50
S87 Shane Victorino 1.00 2.50
S88 Zach Duke .60 1.50
S89 Andrew McCutchen 1.50 4.00
S90 Adrian Gonzalez 1.25 3.00
S91 Matt Cain 1.00 2.50
S92 Ken Griffey Jr. 3.00 8.00
S93 Felix Hernandez 1.00 2.50
S94 Albert Pujols 2.00 5.00
S95 Adam Wainwright 1.00 2.50
S96 David Price 1.25 3.00
S97 B.J. Upton 1.00 2.50
S98 Michael Young .60 1.50
S99 Adam Lind 1.00 2.50
S100 Adam Dunn 1.00 2.50

2010 Upper Deck Tape Measure Shots

TMS1 Mark Reynolds .40 1.00
TMS2 Raul Ibanez .60 1.50
TMS3 Joey Votto 1.00 2.50
TMS4 Adam Dunn .60 1.50
TMS5 Josh Hamilton .60 1.50
TMS6 Adrian Gonzalez .75 2.00
TMS7 Miguel Montero .40 1.00
TMS8 Trent Smith .40 1.00
TMS9 Nelson Cruz 1.00 2.50
TMS10 Carlos Pena .60 1.50
TMS11 Albert Pujols 1.25 3.00
TMS12 Pablo Sandoval .60 1.50
TMS13 Josh Willingham .60 1.50
TMS14 Manny Ramirez 1.00 2.50
TMS15 Prince Fielder .60 1.50
TMS16 Jermaine Dye .40 1.00
TMS17 Brandon Inge .60 1.50
TMS18 Lance Berkman .60 1.50
TMS19 Kelly Shoppach .40 1.00
TMS20 Ian Stewart .40 1.00
TMS21 Magglio Ordonez .60 1.50
TMS22 Michael Cuddyer .40 1.00
TMS23 Ryan Howard .75 2.00
TMS24 Troy Tulowitzki 1.00 2.50
TMS25 Colby Rasmus .60 1.50

2010 Upper Deck UD Game Jersey

AE Andre Ethier 2.00 5.00
AG Alex Gordon 2.00 5.00
AJ Adam Jones 2.00 5.00
AP Albert Pujols 4.00 10.00
AR Aramis Ramirez 1.25 3.00
BE Josh Beckett 1.25 3.00
BI Brandon Inge 2.00 5.00
BM Brandon Morrow 1.25 3.00
BO John Bowker 1.25 3.00
BR Ryan Braun 2.00 5.00
BU B.J. Upton 2.00 5.00
BZ Barry Zito 2.00 5.00
CA Matt Cain 2.00 5.00
CB Clay Buchholz 1.25 3.00
CC Chris Carpenter 2.00 5.00
CF Chone Figgins 1.25 3.00
CG Curtis Granderson 2.50 6.00
CH Cole Hamels 2.50 6.00
CJ Chipper Jones 3.00 8.00
CR Carl Crawford 2.00 5.00
CU Chase Utley 2.00 5.00
CY Chris Young 1.25 3.00
DA Johnny Damon 2.00 5.00
DE David Eckstein 1.25 3.00
DH Dan Haren 1.25 3.00
DJ Derek Jeter 8.00 20.00
DL Derrek Lee 1.25 3.00
DO David Ortiz 3.00 8.00
EJ Edwin Jackson 1.25 3.00
EL Evan Longoria 2.00 5.00
EM Evan Meek 1.25 3.00
EV Eugenio Velez 1.25 3.00
FC Fausto Carmona 1.25 3.00
FH Felix Hernandez 2.00 5.00
FL Francisco Liriano 1.25 3.00
FN Fu-Te Ni 2.00 5.00
FR Fernando Rodney 1.25 3.00
GA Armando Galarraga 1.25 3.00
GO Adrian Gonzalez 2.50 6.00
GS Grady Sizemore 2.00 5.00
HB Hank Blalock 1.25 3.00
HE Chase Headley 1.25 3.00
HK Howie Kendrick 1.25 3.00
HR Hanley Ramirez 2.00 5.00
IK Ian Kinsler 2.00 5.00
JB Jeremy Bonderman 1.25 3.00
JD Jermaine Dye 1.25 3.00
JE Jacoby Ellsbury 2.50 6.00
JH Josh Hamilton 2.00 5.00
JN Jayson Nix 1.25 3.00
JP Jonathan Papelbon 2.00 5.00
JR Jimmy Rollins 2.00 5.00
JS Johan Santana 2.00 5.00
JU Justin Morneau 2.00 5.00
JV Jason Varitek 3.00 8.00
KE Kendry Morales 1.25 3.00
KF Kosuke Fukudome 2.00 5.00
KG Ken Griffey Jr. 6.00 15.00
KH Kevin Hart 1.25 3.00
KK Kevin Kouzmanoff 1.25 3.00
KM Kevin Millwood 1.25 3.00
KY Kevin Youkilis 1.25 3.00
MA Max Scherzer 3.00 8.00
MB Mark Buehrle 2.00 5.00
MC Michael Cuddyer 1.25 3.00
MI Miguel Cabrera 3.00 8.00
MK Matt Kemp 2.50 6.00
ML Matt LaPorta 1.25 3.00
MM Melvin Mora 1.25 3.00
MO Magglio Ordonez 2.00 5.00
MR Mariano Rivera 4.00 10.00
MT Matt Tolbert 1.25 3.00
MY Michael Young 1.25 3.00
NM Nick Markakis 2.50 6.00
PF Prince Fielder 2.00 5.00
PH Phil Hughes 1.25 3.00
PM Pedro Martinez 2.00 5.00
PO Jorge Posada 2.00 5.00
RC Robinson Cano 2.00 5.00
RE Jose Reyes 2.00 5.00
RH Roy Halladay 2.00 5.00
RI Raul Ibanez 2.00 5.00
RM Russell Martin 1.25 3.00
RO Alex Rodriguez 4.00 10.00
RT Ramon Troncoso 1.25 3.00
RW Randy Wells 1.25 3.00
RZ Ryan Zimmerman 2.00 5.00
SC Shin-Soo Choo 2.00 5.00
SD Stephen Drew 1.25 3.00
SK Scott Kazmir 1.25 3.00
TH Travis Hafner 1.25 3.00
TL Tim Lincecum 2.00 5.00
TO Todd Helton 2.00 5.00
TT Troy Tulowitzki 3.00 8.00
UP Justin Upton 2.00 5.00
VE Justin Verlander 3.00 8.00
VG Vladimir Guerrero 2.00 5.00
WW Wesley Wright 1.25 3.00
YY Yasuhiko Yabuta 1.25 3.00
ZG Zack Greinke 2.00 5.00

2009 Upper Deck Goodwin Champions

COMMON CARD (1-150) .15 .40
COMMON NIGHT 5.00 12.00
COMMON SP (151-190) 1.25 3.00
151-190 STATED ODDS 1:2 HOBBY
COMMON SUPER SP (191-210) 1.50 4.00
SUPER SP MINORS 1.50 4.00
SUPER SP SEMIS 1.50 4.00
SUPER SP UNLISTED 1.50 4.00
191-210 STATED ODDS 1:10 HOBBY
PLATES RANDOMLY INSERTED
PLATE PRINT RUN 1 SET PER COLOR
BLACK-CYAN-MAGENTA-YELLOW ISSUED
NO PLATE PRICING DUE TO SCARCITY
1a K.Griffey Jr. Day .75 2.00
1b K.Griffey Jr. Night SP 10.00 25.00
2 Derek Jeter 1.00 2.50
3 Jon Lester .25 .60
4 Jorge Posada .25 .60
5 Albert Pujols .50 1.25
6 Chipper Jones .40 1.00
7a R.Sandberg Day .75 2.00
7b R.Sandberg Night SP 6.00 15.00
8 Johnny Damon .25 .60
9 Carlos Delgado .15 .40
10 Vladimir Guerrero .25 .60
11 Johnny Bench .40 1.00
12 Matt Cain .25 .60
13 Bill Skowron CL .15 .40
14 Donovan Bailey .15 .40
15 Dick Allen CL .15 .40
16 Abraham Lincoln .25 .60
17 Rollie Fingers .25 .60
18 Bo Jackson CL .40 1.00
19 Scott Kazmir .15 .40
20a Grady Sizemore Day .25 .60
20b G.Sizemore Night SP 5.00 12.00
21 Ian Kinsler .25 .60
22 Jim Palmer .25 .60
23 Kevin Youkilis .15 .40
24 O.J. Mayo .20 .50
25 Hunter Pence .25 .60
26 Hiroki Kuroda .15 .40
27 Derrek Lee .15 .40
28 Brian McCann .25 .60
29 Carlos Quentin .15 .40
30 Al Kaline .40 1.00
31 Hanley Ramirez .25 .60
32 Josh Hamilton .25 .60
33 Jeff Samardzija .25 .60
34 Alexander Ovechkin 1.25 3.00
35 Clayton Kershaw .75 2.00
36 Lyndon Johnson .15 .40
37 Whitey Ford .25 .60
38 Carey Price 1.00 2.50
39 Jay Bruce .25 .60
40 Phil Niekro .25 .60
41 Ted Williams .75 2.00
42 Justin Upton .25 .60
43 Cole Hamels .30 .75
44a B.Obama Day .40 1.00
44b B.Obama Night SP 8.00 20.00
45 Peyton Manning .50 1.25
46 Jim Thome .25 .60
47 Nick Markakis .30 .75
48 Joe Carter CL .15 .40
49 Ryan Braun .25 .60
50 Mike Schmidt .60 1.50
51 Carlos Beltran .25 .60
52 Nolan Ryan 1.25 3.00
53 Anderson Silva .50 1.25
54 Kosuke Fukudome .25 .60
55 Chad Reed .15 .40
56a O.Smith Day .50 1.25
56b O.Smith Night SP 8.00 20.00
57 Eli Manning .40 1.00
58 CC Sabathia .25 .60
59 Evan Longoria .25 .60
60 Matt Garza .15 .40
61 Michael Beasley .40 1.00
62 Yogi Berra .40 1.00
63 Brian Roberts .15 .40
64 Alex Rodriguez .50 1.25
65a T.Woods Day 1.50 4.00
65b T.Woods Night SP 12.50 30.00
66 Buffalo Bill Cody .15 .40
67 Josh Beckett .15 .40

68 Matt Ryan .40 1.00
69a I.Suzuki Day .50 1.25
69b I.Suzuki Night SP 8.00 20.00
70 Chuck Liddell .50 1.25
71 Adrian Gonzalez .30 .75
72 David Wright .30 .75
73 LeBron James 1.50 4.00
74a G.Lopez Day .15 .40
74b G.Lopez Night SP 5.00 12.00
75 Carlton Fisk .25 .60
76 Joe Mauer .30 .75
77 Manny Ramirez .40 1.00
78 Jason Varitek .40 1.00
79 John Lackey .25 .60
80 Ivan Rodriguez .25 .60
81 Wayne Gretzky 2.00 5.00
82 Justin Morneau .25 .60
83 Akinori Iwamura .15 .40
84 Joe Lewis .40 1.00
85 Lance Berkman .25 .60
86 Brooks Robinson .25 .60
87a A.Pettitte Day .25 .60
87b A.Pettitte Night SP 5.00 12.00
88 Peggy Fleming .15 .40
89 Joe DiMaggio .75 2.00
90 Jonathan Toews .60 1.50
91 Todd Helton .25 .60
92 Dennis Eckersley .25 .60
93 Daisuke Matsuzaka .25 .60
94 Adrian Peterson .60 1.50
95 Alfonso Soriano .25 .60
96 Paul Molitor .40 1.00
97 Johan Santana .25 .60
98 Jason Giambi .15 .40
99 Ben Roethlisberger .50 1.25
100 Chase Utley .25 .60
101a C.Ripken Jr. Day 1.25 3.00
101b C.Ripken Jr. Night SP 10.00 25.00
102 Curtis Granderson .30 .75
103 James Shields .15 .40
104 Nate McLouth .15 .40
105 Evelyn Ng .40 1.00
106a R.Howard Day .30 .75
106b R.Howard Night SP 6.00 15.00
107 Joe Nathan .15 .40
108 Tim Lincecum .25 .60
109 Chad Billingsley .25 .60
110 Matt Holliday .40 1.00
111 Kevin Garnett .60 1.50
112 Robin Roberts .25 .60
113 Jose Reyes .25 .60
114 Michael Jordan 8.00 20.00
115a S.Jones Day .40 1.00
115b S.Jones Night SP 5.00 12.00
116 Kristi Yamaguchi .25 .60
117 Carlos Zambrano .25 .60
118 Bucky Dent CL .15 .40
119 Carl Yastrzemski .60 1.50
120 Stephen Drew .15 .40
121 Dustin Pedroia .30 .75
122 Jonathan Papelbon .25 .60
123 B.J. Upton .25 .60
124 Steve Carlton .25 .60
125 Chris Johnson .40 1.00
126a T.Tulowitzki Day .40 1.00
126b T.Tulowitzki Night SP 5.00 12.00
127 Francisco Liriano .15 .40
128 Bill Rodgers .15 .40
129 Laird Hamilton .15 .40
130 Brandon Webb .25 .60
131 Miguel Cabrera .40 1.00
132a C.Wang Day .25 .60
132b C.Wang Night SP 5.00 12.00
133 Joba Chamberlain .15 .40
134 Felix Hernandez .25 .60
135 Tony Gwynn .40 1.00
136 Roy Oswalt .25 .60
137 Prince Fielder .25 .60
138 Gary Sheffield .15 .40
139 Koji Uehara RC .40 1.00
140a G.Howe Day 1.00 2.50
140b G.Howe Night SP 5.00 12.00
141 Bobby Orr 1.00 2.50
142 Zack Greinke .25 .60
143 Derrick Rose .50 1.25
144 Cliff Lee .25 .60
145 Joey Votto .40 1.00
146 Phil Hellmuth .40 1.00
147 Mark Teixeira .25 .60
148 David Price RC .30 .75
149 Ryan Ludwick .25 .60
150 David Ortiz .40 1.00
151 Cory Wade SP 1.25 3.00
152 Roy White SP 1.25 3.00
153 Jed Lowrie SP .75 2.00
154 Gavin Floyd SP 1.25 3.00
155 Justin Masterson SP .75 2.00
156 Travis Hafner SP 1.25 3.00
157 Kelly Shoppach SP 1.25 3.00
158 David Purcey SP 1.25 3.00
159 Howie Kendrick SP 1.25 3.00
160 Mike Parsons SP 1.25 3.00
161 Jeremy Bloom SP 1.25 3.00
162 Dave Scott SP 1.25 3.00
163 Nyjer Morgan SP 1.25 3.00
164 Chris Volstad SP 1.25 3.00
165 Barry Zito SP 2.00 5.00
166 Adrian Beltre SP 3.00 8.00
167 Mark Zupan SP 1.25 3.00
168 Victor Martinez SP 1.25 3.00
169 Eric Chavez SP 1.25 3.00
170 Chris Perez SP 1.25 3.00
171 Jered Weaver SP 2.00 5.00
172 Justin Verlander SP 2.00 5.00
173 Adam Lind SP 1.25 3.00
174 Corky Carroll SP 1.25 3.00
175 Ryan Zimmerman SP 1.25 3.00
176 Josh Willingham SP 2.00 5.00
177 Graig Nettles SP 1.25 3.00
178 Jonathan Albaladejo SP 1.25 3.00
179 Ted Martin SP 1.25 3.00
180 Bill Hall SP 1.25 3.00
181 Brad Hawpe SP 1.25 3.00
182 John Maine SP 1.25 3.00
183 Tom Curren SP 1.25 3.00
184 Ken Griffey Sr. CL SP 1.25 3.00
185 Josh Johnson SP 2.00 5.00
186 Phil Hughes SP .75 2.00
187 Joe Alexander SP 1.25 3.00
188 Fausto Carmona SP 1.25 3.00
189 Daniel Murphy SP RC 2.00 5.00
190 Alex Hinshaw SP 1.25 3.00
191 Clayton Richard SP 1.50 4.00
192 Sparky Lyle CL SP 1.50 4.00
193 Don Gay SP 1.50 4.00
194 Aramis Ramirez SP 1.50 4.00
195 Gaylord Perry CL SP 2.50 6.00
196 Carlos Lee SP 1.50 4.00
197 Paul Konerko SP 2.50 6.00
198 Kent Hrbek CL SP 1.50 4.00
199 Chris B. Young SP 1.50 4.00
200 Roy Halladay SP 1.50 4.00
201 Geovany Soto SP 1.50 4.00
202 Chone Figgins SP 1.50 4.00
203 Joe Pepitone CL SP 1.50 4.00
204 Mark Allen SP 1.50 4.00
205 Garrett Atkins SP 1.50 4.00
206 Ken Shamrock SP 1.50 4.00
207 Jermaine Dye SP 1.50 4.00
208 Don Newcombe CL SP 1.50 4.00
209 Rick Cerone CL SP 1.50 4.00
210 Adam Jones SP 1.50 4.00

2009 Upper Deck Goodwin Champions Mini

COMPLETE SET (192) 75.00 150.00
*MINI 1-150: 1X TO 2.5X BASIC
APPX.MINI ODDS ONE PER PACK
PLATES RANDOMLY INSERTED
PLATE PRINT RUN 1 SET PER COLOR
BLACK-CYAN-MAGENTA-YELLOW ISSUED
NO PLATE PRICING DUE TO SCARCITY
211 Brian Giles EXT .60 1.50
212 Robinson Cano EXT 1.00 2.50
213 Erik Bedard EXT .60 1.50
214 James Loney EXT .60 1.50
215 Jimmy Rollins EXT 1.00 2.50
216 Joakim Soria EXT .60 1.50
217 Jeremy Guthrie EXT .60 1.50
218 Adam Wainwright EXT 1.00 2.50
219 B.J. Ryan EXT .60 1.50
220 Aaron Cook EXT .60 1.50
221 Aaron Harang EXT .60 1.50
222 Mariano Rivera EXT 2.00 5.00
223 Freddy Sanchez EXT .60 1.50
224 Ryan Dempster EXT .60 1.50
225 Jacoby Ellsbury EXT 1.25 3.00
226 Russell Martin EXT .60 1.50
227 Ervin Santana EXT .60 1.50
228 Nomar Garciaparra EXT 1.00 2.50
229 Chris Young EXT .60 1.50
230 Jair Jurrjens EXT .60 1.50
231 Francisco Cordero EXT .60 1.50
232 Bobby Crosby EXT .60 1.50
233 Rich Harden EXT .60 1.50
234 Cameron Maybin EXT .60 1.50
235 Conor Jackson EXT .60 1.50
236 Jake Peavy EXT .60 1.50
237 Brad Ziegler EXT .60 1.50
238 Aaron Rowand EXT .60 1.50
239 Carl Crawford EXT 1.00 2.50
240 Mark Buehrle EXT 1.00 2.50
241 Carlos Guillen EXT .60 1.50
242 Alex Rios EXT .60 1.50
243 Vernon Wells EXT .60 1.50
244 Bobby Jenks EXT .60 1.50
245 Rick Ankiel EXT .60 1.50
246 Alex Gordon EXT 1.00 2.50
247 Paul Maholm EXT .60 1.50
248 Carlos Gomez EXT .60 1.50
249 Brad Lidge EXT .60 1.50
250 Hideki Okajima EXT .60 1.50
251 Michael Bourn EXT .60 1.50
252 Jhonny Peralta EXT .60 1.50

2009 Upper Deck Goodwin Champions Mini Black Border

*MINI BLK 1-150: 1.5X TO 4X BASE
*MINI BLK 211-252: .75X TO 2X MINI
RANDOM INSERTS IN PACKS

2009 Upper Deck Goodwin Champions Mini Foil

*MINI FOIL 1-150: 3X TO 8X BASE
*MINI FOIL 211-252: 1.5X TO 4X MINI
RANDOM INSERTS IN PACKS
ANNCD PRINT RUN OF 88 TOTAL SETS

2009 Upper Deck Goodwin Champions Animal Series

RANDOM INSERTS IN PACKS
AS1 King Cobra 2.00 5.00
AS2 Dodo Bird 2.00 5.00
AS3 Tasmanian Devil 2.00 5.00
AS4 Komodo Dragon 2.00 5.00
AS5 Bald Eagle 2.00 5.00
AS6 Great White Shark 2.00 5.00
AS7 Gorilla 2.00 5.00
AS8 Bengal Tiger 2.00 5.00
AS9 Killer Whale 2.00 5.00
AS10 Giant Panda 2.00 5.00

2009 Upper Deck Goodwin Champions Autographs

STATED ODDS 1:20 HOBBY
EXCHANGE DEADLINE 8/31/2011
AG Adrian Gonzalez/45 * 10.00 25.00
AH Alex Hinshaw 4.00 10.00
AK Al Kaline/50 * 40.00 100.00
AL Jonathan Albaladejo 4.00 10.00
BD Bucky Dent 8.00 20.00
BL Jeremy Bloom 5.00 12.00
BO Bobby Orr/25 * 90.00 150.00
BR Bill Rodgers 4.00 10.00
BS Bill Skowron 10.00 25.00
CB Chad Billingsley 6.00 15.00
CC Corky Carroll 10.00 25.00
CE Rick Cerone 4.00 10.00
CF Chone Figgins 4.00 10.00
CJ Chipper Jones/25 * 100.00 200.00
CK Clayton Kershaw/50 * 30.00 60.00
CL Carlos Lee 4.00 10.00
CP Chris Perez 5.00 12.00
CR Clayton Richard 4.00 10.00
CV Chris Volstad 4.00 10.00
CW Cory Wade 4.00 10.00
DA Dick Allen 12.50 30.00
DE Dennis Eckersley/50 * 10.00 25.00
DG Don Gay 5.00 12.00
DJ Derek Jeter/25 * 175.00 300.00
DM Daniel Murphy 10.00 25.00
DN Don Newcombe 6.00 15.00
DO Donovan Bailey 10.00 25.00
DP Dustin Pedroia 12.50 30.00
DS Dave Scott 5.00 12.00
EC Eric Chavez/50 * 5.00 12.00
EL Evan Longoria/25 * 100.00 250.00
EN Evelyn Ng 5.00 12.00
FH F.Hernandez EXCH 15.00 40.00
GA Garrett Atkins 4.00 10.00
GF Gavin Floyd 4.00 10.00
GK Kevin Garnett/25 * 50.00 100.00
GS Sizemore/50 * 10.00 25.00
GY Ken Griffey Sr. 8.00 20.00
HP Hunter Pence/50 * 12.50 30.00
HR Hanley Ramirez 4.00 10.00
JA Joe Alexander 6.00 15.00
JB Jay Bruce 4.00 10.00
JC Joe Carter/45 * 15.00 40.00
JE Jed Lowrie 5.00 12.00
JJ Josh Johnson 8.00 20.00
JL Joe Lewis 4.00 10.00
JM John Maine 4.00 10.00
JO Jon Lester/25 * 60.00 120.00
JS James Shields 4.00 10.00
JU Justin Masterson 6.00 15.00
JW Josh Willingham 4.00 10.00
KH Kent Hrbek 15.00 40.00
KU Koji Uehara/25 * 50.00 100.00
KY Kevin Youkilis 8.00 20.00
LA Ryan Braun/50 * 30.00 60.00
LH Laird Hamilton 20.00 50.00
LO Gerry Lopez 10.00 25.00
MA Mark Allen 5.00 12.00
MC Matt Cain 6.00 15.00
MG Matt Garza 5.00 12.00
MJ Michael Jordan/23 * 500.00 700.00
MN Nate McLouth 4.00 10.00
MZ Mark Zupan 5.00 12.00
NM Nick Markakis 6.00 15.00
OS Ozzie Smith/50 * 40.00 80.00
PA Mike Parsons 6.00 15.00
PD David Price 6.00 15.00
PF Prince Fielder/50 * 8.00 20.00
PH Phil Hellmuth 6.00 15.00
PJ Jonathan Papelbon 6.00 15.00
PK Paul Konerko 10.00 25.00
PM Paul Molitor/50 * 10.00 25.00
PU David Purcey 4.00 10.00
RB Brooks Robinson/50 * 12.50 30.00
RC Chad Reed 10.00 25.00
RF Rollie Fingers/50 * 10.00 25.00
RH Roy Halladay/50 * 50.00 100.00
RW Roy White 4.00 10.00
SC Steve Carlton 10.00 25.00
SD Stephen Drew/50 * 8.00 20.00
SK Kelly Shoppach 4.00 10.00
SL Sparky Lyle 5.00 12.00
SO Geovany Soto 10.00 25.00
TC Tom Curren 12.50 30.00
TM Ted Martin 4.00 10.00
TT Troy Tulowitzki 10.00 25.00
WF Whitey Ford/25 * 75.00 150.00
YA Kristi Yamaguchi/49 * 50.00 100.00
ZG Zack Greinke/25 * 15.00 40.00

2009 Upper Deck Goodwin Champions Citizens of the Century

RANDOM INSERTS IN PACKS
CC1 Hillary Clinton 2.00 5.00
CC2 Bill Clinton 2.00 5.00
CC3 Tony Blair 2.00 5.00
CC4 Princess Diana 2.50 6.00
CC5 Barack Obama 3.00 8.00
CC6 Ronald Reagan 2.00 5.00
CC7 Mikhail Gorbachev 2.00 5.00
CC8 Al Gore 2.00 5.00
CC9 Pope John Paul II 2.00 5.00
CC10 Winston Churchill 2.00 5.00

2009 Upper Deck Goodwin Champions Citizens of the Day

RANDOM INSERTS IN PACKS
CD1 Susan B. Anthony 2.00 5.00
CD2 P.T. Barnum 2.00 5.00
CD3 Cap Anson 2.50 6.00
CD4 Theodore Roosevelt 2.00 5.00
CD5 John D. Rockefeller 2.00 5.00
CD6 King Kelly 2.50 6.00
CD7 Will Rogers 2.00 5.00
CD8 Grover Cleveland 2.00 5.00
CD9 Scott Joplin 2.00 5.00
CD10 Sitting Bull 2.00 5.00
CD11 Bram Stoker 2.00 5.00
CD12 Wyatt Earp 2.00 5.00
CD13 Claude Monet 2.00 5.00
CD14 Queen Victoria 2.00 5.00
CD15 Grigori Rasputin 2.00 5.00

2009 Upper Deck Goodwin Champions Entomology

RANDOM INSERTS IN PACKS
EXCHANGE DEADLINE 8/31/2011
ENT5 BD Butterfly EXCH 60.00 120.00
ENT14 Strawberry Bluff EXCH 90.00 150.00
NNO EXCH Card 75.00 150.00

2009 Upper Deck Goodwin Champions Landmarks

RANDOM INSERTS IN PACKS
EXCHANGE DEADLINE 8/31/2011
TT RMS Titanic Coal 75.00 150.00
NNO EXCH Card 60.00 120.00

2009 Upper Deck Goodwin Champions Memorabilia

STATED ODDS 1:10 HOBBY
EXCHANGE DEADLINE 8/31/2011
AB Adrian Beltre 3.00 8.00
AI Akinori Iwamura 1.25 3.00
AJ Adam Jones 2.00 5.00
BE Johnny Bench 3.00 8.00
BH Bill Hall 1.25 3.00
BJ Bo Jackson 3.00 8.00
BM Brian McCann 2.00 5.00
BR Brian Roberts 1.25 3.00
BW Brandon Webb 2.00 5.00
BZ Barry Zito 2.00 5.00
CB Chad Billingsley 2.00 5.00
CD Carlos Delgado 1.25 3.00
CF Carlton Fisk 2.00 5.00
CG Curtis Granderson 2.50 6.00
CH Cole Hamels 2.50 6.00
CJ Chipper Jones 3.00 8.00
CL Carlos Lee 1.25 3.00
CR Cal Ripken Jr. 10.00 25.00
CU Chase Utley/100 * 5.00 12.00
CW Chien-Ming Wang 2.00 5.00
CY Carl Yastrzemski 5.00 12.00
CZ Carlos Zambrano 2.00 5.00
DA Johnny Damon 2.00 5.00
DJ Derek Jeter 8.00 20.00
DL Derrek Lee 1.25 3.00
DM Daisuke Matsuzaka 1.25 3.00
DO David Ortiz 3.00 8.00
DR Derrick Rose 5.00 12.00
EC Eric Chavez 1.25 3.00
FC Fausto Carmona 1.25 3.00
FH Felix Hernandez 2.00 5.00
FI Chone Figgins 1.25 3.00
FL Francisco Liriano 1.25 3.00
GN Graig Nettles 2.00 5.00
GP Gaylord Perry 2.00 5.00
GR Ken Griffey Jr. 6.00 15.00
HA Brad Hawpe 1.25 3.00
HK Hiroki Kuroda 1.25 3.00
HP Hunter Pence 2.00 5.00
IK Ian Kinsler 2.00 5.00
JA James Shields 1.25 3.00
JB Josh Beckett 1.25 3.00
JD Jermaine Dye 1.25 3.00
JH Jonathan Albaladejo 1.25 3.00
JL John Lackey 2.00 5.00
JM Joe Mauer 2.50 6.00
JN Joe Nathan 1.25 3.00
JP Jim Palmer 2.00 5.00
JR Jose Reyes/100 * 4.00 10.00
JT Jim Thome 2.00 5.00
JU Justin Upton 2.00 5.00
JV Jason Varitek 3.00 8.00
JW Jered Weaver 2.00 5.00
KE Howie Kendrick 1.25 3.00
KF Kosuke Fukudome 2.00 5.00
KG Kevin Garnett 6.00 15.00
LE Cliff Lee 2.00 5.00
LJ LeBron James 15.00 40.00
MA John Maine 1.25 3.00
MB Michael Beasley 4.00 10.00
MC Miguel Cabrera 3.00 8.00
MJ Michael Jordan/50 * 30.00 60.00
MO Justin Morneau 2.00 5.00
MS Mike Schmidt 5.00 12.00
NM Nick Markakis 2.50 6.00
OM O.J. Mayo 2.00 5.00
PA Jonathan Papelbon 2.00 5.00
PF Prince Fielder 2.00 5.00
PH Phil Hughes 2.00 5.00
PK Paul Konerko 2.00 5.00
PO Jorge Posada 2.00 5.00
PU Albert Pujols 4.00 10.00
RA Aramis Ramirez 1.25 3.00
RB Ryan Braun 2.00 5.00
RH Roy Halladay 2.00 5.00
RO Roy Oswalt 2.00 5.00
RS Ryne Sandberg 6.00 15.00
RZ Manny Ramirez 3.00 8.00
SC Steve Carlton 2.00 5.00
SK Scott Kazmir 1.25 3.00
TG Tony Gwynn 3.00 8.00
TH Todd Helton 2.00 5.00
TL Tim Lincecum 2.00 5.00
TR Travis Hafner 1.25 3.00
TT Troy Tulowitzki 3.00 8.00
TW Ted Williams/40 * 20.00 50.00
VE Justin Verlander 3.00 8.00
VG Vladimir Guerrero 2.00 5.00
VM Victor Martinez 2.00 5.00
WD Tiger Woods 15.00 40.00
WF Whitey Ford 2.00 5.00
YB Yogi Berra 3.00 8.00
YO Chris B. Young 1.25 3.00
ZG Zack Greinke 2.00 5.00

2009 Upper Deck Goodwin Champions Thoroughbred Hair Cuts

RANDOM INSERTS IN PACKS
EXCHANGE DEADLINE 8/31/2011
AA1 Afleet Alex 20.00 50.00
AA2 Afleet Alex 20.00 50.00
FC1 Funny Cide 20.00 50.00
FC2 Funny Cide 20.00 50.00
SJ1 Smarty Jones 20.00 50.00
SJ2 Smarty Jones 20.00 50.00

2011 Upper Deck Goodwin Champions

COMP.SET w/o VAR (210) 40.00 80.00
COMP.SET w/o SP's (150) 10.00 25.00
COMMON SP (151-190) 1.00 2.50
151-190 SP ODDS 1:3 HOBBY
COMMON SP (191-210) 1.50 4.00
191-210 SP ODDS 1:12 HOBBY
COMMON VARIATION SP 4.00 10.00
1A King Kelly .15 .40
1B Kelly Lightning SP 4.00 10.00
11 Greg Maddux .30 .75
16 Don Mattingly .50 1.25
19A Lou Brock .20 .50
19B L.Brock/J.Carter SP 4.00 10.00
24 Miller Huggins .15 .40
25 Manny Machado .30 .75
38 Nolan Ryan .75 2.00
39 Addie Joss .15 .40
41 Whitey Ford .20 .50
43 Stan Musial .40 1.00
46 Ryne Sandberg .50 1.25
50 Steve Carlton .20 .50
56 Jim Rice .20 .50
64 Johnny Bench .25 .60
68 Hugh Jennings .15 .40
69 Wilbert Robinson .15 .40
94 Ozzie Smith .40 1.00
95 Willie Keeler .15 .40
103 Rube Waddell .15 .40
112 Mike Schmidt .40 1.00
116 John Lamb .15 .40
119 Cap Anson .20 .50
120 Tony Perez .15 .40
126 Jose Canseco .20 .50
128 Bob Gibson .20 .50
140 John McGraw .15 .40
146 Carlton Fisk .20 .50
152 Jack Chesbro SP 1.00 2.50
158 Charles Comiskey SP 1.00 2.50
163 Ed Delahanty SP 1.00 2.50
178 Dennis Oil Can Boyd SP 1.00 2.50
181 Buck Ewing SP 1.00 2.50
184 Dan Brouthers SP 1.00 2.50
189 Eddie Plank SP 1.00 2.50
194 Rube Foster SP 1.50 4.00
195 John Montgomery Ward SP 1.50 4.00
209 Albert Spalding SP 1.50 4.00
210 Abner Doubleday SP 1.50 4.00

2011 Upper Deck Goodwin Champions Mini

*1-150 MINI: 1X TO 2.5X BASIC
1-150 MINI ODDS 1:4 HOBBY
COMMON CARD (211-231) .60 1.50
211-231 MINI ODDS 1:13 HOBBY
PRINTING PLATES RANDOMLY INSERTED
PLATE PRINT RUN 1 SET PER COLOR
BLACK-CYAN-MAGENTA-YELLOW ISSUED
NO PLATE PRICING DUE TO SCARCITY
211 Matt Packer SP .60 1.50
212 Gary Brown SP 1.00 2.50
213 Ramon Morla SP .60 1.50
214 Aaron Crow SP .60 1.50
215 Ryan Lavarnaway SP .60 1.50
216 Michael Choice SP .60 1.50
217 Matt Lipka SP .60 1.50
218 Aaron Hicks SP .60 1.50
219 Peter Tago SP .60 1.50
220 Jurickson Profar SP .60 1.50
221 Cody Hawn SP .60 1.50
222 Carlos Perez SP .60 1.50
223 Robinson Yambati SP .60 1.50
224 Mike Olt SP .75 2.00
225 LeVon Washington SP .75 2.00
226 Kyle Parker SP .75 2.00
227 Jonathan Garcia SP .60 1.50
228 Yordano Ventura SP 2.00 5.00
229 Delino DeShields Jr. SP .75 2.00
230 Collin Cowgill SP .60 1.50
231 Kyle Skipworth SP .60 1.50

2011 Upper Deck Goodwin Champions Mini Black

*1-150 MINI BLACK: 1.2X TO 3X BASIC
1-150 MINI BLACK ODDS 1:13 HOBBY
*211-231 MINI BLK: .6X TO 1.5X BASIC MINI
211-231 MINI BLACK ODDS 1:46 HOBBY

2011 Upper Deck Goodwin Champions Mini Foil

*1-150 MINI FOIL: 2.5X TO 6X BASIC
1-150 ANNCD PRINT RUN OF 89
*211-231 MINI FOIL : 1X TO 2.5X BASIC MINI
211-231 ANNCD PRINT RUN OF 178
PRINT RUNS PROVIDED BY UD
38 Nolan Ryan 12.50 30.00

2011 Upper Deck Goodwin Champions Autographs

Please note that the Dwayne De Rosario card in this set was issued in the 2014 Upper Deck Goodwin Champions product.
GROUP A ODDS 1:1577 HOBBY
GROUP B ODDS 1:729 HOBBY
GROUP C ODDS 1:339 HOBBY
GROUP D ODDS 1:246 HOBBY
GROUP E ODDS 1:72 HOBBY
GROUP F ODDS 1:35 HOBBY
OVERALL AUTO ODDS 1:20 HOBBY
EXCHANGE DEADLINE 6/7/2013
CA Steve Carlton C 10.00 25.00
CF Carlton Fisk B 12.00 30.00
CH Cody Hawn F 4.00 10.00
JB Johnny Bench A 40.00 80.00
JG Jonathan Garcia F 4.00 10.00
JL John Lamb F 4.00 10.00
JR Jim Rice D 8.00 20.00
KV Kolbrin Vitek F 4.00 10.00
LO Lou Brock B 20.00 50.00
LW LeVon Washington E 4.00 10.00
MM Manny Machado C 20.00 50.00
MO Mike Olt F 5.00 12.00
MU Stan Musial B 75.00 150.00
NR Nolan Ryan A
OC Dennis Oil Can Boyd E 6.00 15.00
PE Carlos Perez F 4.00 10.00
PT Peter Tago F 4.00 8.00
RL Ryan Lavarnway D 8.00 20.00
RM Ramon Morla F 4.00 10.00
RS Ryne Sandberg B 20.00 50.00
RY Robinson Yambati F 4.00 10.00
TP Tony Perez D 10.00 25.00
WF Whitey Ford B 15.00 40.00
YV Yordano Ventura F 8.00 20.00

2011 Upper Deck Goodwin Champions Figures of Sport

COMP.SET. w/o SP's (14) 10.00 25.00
COMMON CARD (1-14) .60 1.50
1-14 STATED ODDS 1:21 HOBBY
15-18 SP ODDS 1:300 HOBBY
FS11 Bo Jackson 1.25 3.00
FS12 Ozzie Smith 1.25 3.00
FS17 Nolan Ryan SP 5.00 12.00

2011 Upper Deck Goodwin Champions Memorabilia

GROUP A ODDS 1:14,613 HOBBY
GROUP B ODDS 1:179 HOBBY
GROUP C ODDS 1:31 HOBBY
GROUP D ODDS 1:22 HOBBY
KS Kyle Skipworth D 3.00 8.00
MC Michael Choice D 3.00 8.00
MM Manny Machado D 3.00 8.00
PT Peter Tago D 3.00 8.00

2011 Upper Deck Goodwin Champions Memorabilia Dual

GROUP A ODDS 1:87,680 HOBBY
GROUP B ODDS 1:8768 HOBBY
GROUP C ODDS 1:2923 HOBBY
GROUP D ODDS 1:877 HOBBY
GROUP E ODDS 1:585 HOBBY
NO GROUP A PRICING AVAILABLE
MM Manny Machado E 6.00 15.00

2012 Upper Deck Goodwin Champions

COMP.SET w/o VAR (210) 25.00 50.00
COMP.SET w/o SP's (150) 10.00 25.00
151-190 SP ODDS 1:3 HOBBY, BLASTER
191-210 SP ODDS 1:12 HOBBY, BLASTER
6 Carlton Fisk .20 .50
15 Billy Beane .15 .40
22 Greg Maddux .30 .75
25 Sam Thompson .15 .40
27 Mike Schmidt .40 1.00
29 Johnny Bench .25 .60
38 Billy Hamilton .15 .40
53A Lou Brock .20 .50
53B Lou Brock Horizontal SP 6.00 15.00
55A Al Kaline .25 .60
55B Kaline/Nixon/Palmer SP 6.00 15.00
75 Jack Morris .15 .40
81 Whitey Ford .20 .50
84 Don Mattingly .50 1.25
101 Ryne Sandberg .50 1.25
107A Ernie Banks .25 .60
107B Ernie Banks Horizontal SP 4.00 10.00
108 Nolan Ryan .75 2.00
109 John Kruk .15 .40
110 Jim O'Rourke .15 .40
113 Steve Carlton .20 .50
127A Dennis Eckersley .20 .50
127B Dennis Eckersley Horizontal SP 4.00 10.00
133 Bob Gibson .20 .50
139 Shoeless Joe Jackson .25 .60
145A Pete Rose .60 1.50
145B Pete Rose w/Rolls Royce SP 8.00 20.00
152 Stan Musial SP 1.00 2.50
153 Ross Youngs SP 1.00 2.50
159 Ross Barnes SP 1.00 2.50
160 Pud Galvin SP 1.00 2.50
163 Ned Hanlon SP 1.00 2.50
164 Mike Donlin SP 1.00 2.50
171 Pat Moran SP 1.00 2.50
180 Ozzie Smith SP 1.00 2.50
182 Deacon White SP 1.00 2.50
183 Joe McGinnity SP 1.00 2
184 Ned Williamson SP 1.00 2
189 Kid Gleason SP 1.00 2
190 Sherry McGee SP 1.00 2.
197 William Wrigley Jr. SP 1.50 4.
204 Charles Ebbetts SP 1.50 4.
205 Joe Start SP 1.50 4.

2012 Upper Deck Goodwin Champions Mini

*1-150 MINI: 1X TO 2.5X BASIC CARDS
1-150 MINI STATED ODDS 1:2 HOBBY, BLASTER
211-231 MINI ODDS 1:2 HOBBY, BLASTER
211 Christian Yelich .60 1.5
212 Cesar Puello .60 1.5
213 Matthew Andriese .60 1.5
214 Matt Lipka .60 1.5
215 Gauntlett Eldemire .75 2.0
216 Nick Bucci .60 1.5
217 Jared Hoying .60 1.5
218 Zach Walters .60 1.5
219 Aaron Altherr .60 1.5
220 Marcell Ozuna .60 1.5
221 Wilin Rosario .60 1.5
222 Billy Hamilton 2.00 5.0
223 Reggie Golden .60 1.5
224 Matt Szczur 1.25 3.0
225 Jake Hager .60 1.5
226 Nick Kingham .60 1.5
227 Marcus Knecht .60 1.5
228 Michael Choice .75 2.0
229 Cody Buckel .60 1.50
230 Matt Packer .60 1.50
231 Will Swanner .60 1.50

2012 Upper Deck Goodwin Champions Mini Foil

*1-150 MINI FOIL: 2.5X TO 6X BASIC
1-150 MINI FOIL ANNCD. PRINT RUN 99
*211-231 MINI FOIL: 1X TO 2.5X BASIC MINI
211-231 MINI FOIL ANNCD. PRINT RUN 199

2012 Upper Deck Goodwin Champions Mini Green

*1-150 MINI GREEN: 1.25X TO 3X BASIC
*211-231 MINI GREEN: .6X TO 1.5X BASIC MINI
TWO MINI GREEN PER HOBBY BOX
ONE MINI GREEN PER BLASTER

2012 Upper Deck Goodwin Champions Mini Green Blank Back

UNPRICED DUE TO SCARCITY

2012 Upper Deck Goodwin Champions Autographs

GROUP A ODDS 1:1,977
GROUP B ODDS 1:353
GROUP C ODDS 1:264
GROUP D ODDS 1:185
GROUP E ODDS 1:82
GROUP F ODDS 1:36
OVERALL AUTO ODDS 1:20
EXCHANGE DEADLINE 7/12/2014
AAA Aaron Altherr F 4.00 10.00
ABH Billy Hamilton E 10.00 25.00
ACB Cody Buckel F 4.00 10.00
ACF Carlton Fisk B 8.00 20.00
ACH Michael Choice F 4.00 10.00
ACY Christian Yelich D 30.00 80.00
ADB Don Mattingly B 30.00 60.00
ADE Dennis Eckersley B 6.00 15.00
AEB Ernie Banks/Liz Banks 25.00 50.00
AGE Gauntlett Eldemire F 4.00 10.00
AHR Jake Hager F 4.00 10.00
AJH Jared Hoying E 4.00 10.00
AJM Jack Morris C 6.00 15.00
AMK Marcus Knecht F 4.00 10.00
AMO Marcell Ozuna E 4.00 10.00
AMP Matt Packer F 4.00 10.00
AMS Mike Schmidt B 12.50 30.00
ANK Nick Kingham F 4.00 10.00
ANR Nolan Ryan A 100.00 200.00
APR Pete Rose B 30.00 60.00
ARG Reggie Golden E 4.00 10.00
AWR Wilin Rosario E 4.00 10.00
AWS Will Swanner F 4.00 10.00

2012 Upper Deck Goodwin Champions Memorabilia

GROUP A ODDS 1:10,631
GROUP B ODDS 1:4,784
GROUP C ODDS 1:302
GROUP D ODDS 1:118
GROUP E ODDS 1:36
GROUP F ODDS 1:23
MJJ Shoeless Joe Jackson B 40.00 80.00

2012 Upper Deck Goodwin Champions Memorabilia Dual

GROUP A ODDS 1:95,680
GROUP B ODDS 1:31,893
GROUP C ODDS 1:2,514
GROUP D ODDS 1:1,306
GROUP E ODDS 1:520
NO PRICING ON GROUP A
M2JJ Shoeless Joe Jackson B 150.00 300.00

2013 Upper Deck Goodwin Champions

COMP. SET w/o VAR (210) 25.00 60.00
COMP. SET w/o SPs (150) 8.00 20.00
151-190 SP ODDS 1:3 HOBBY,BLASTER
191-210 SP ODDS 1:12 HOBBY,BLASTER
OVERALL VARIATION ODDS 1:320 H, 1:1,200 B
GROUP A ODDS 1:4,800
GROUP B ODDS 1:2,400
GROUP C ODDS 1:1,400
6 Ozzie Smith .25 .60

Andre Dawson .20 .50
Ernie Banks .25 .60
Reggie Jackson .30 .75
Pete Rose .60 1.50
Johnny Bench .30 .75
Jim Rice .25 .60
Darryl Strawberry .20 .50
Keith Hernandez .15 .40
Mark McGwire .40 1.00
Rafael Palmeiro .25 .60
Kent Hrbek .15 .40
Juan Gonzalez .20 .50
Jim Abbott .25 .60
A Paul O'Neill .15 .40
9B P.O'Neill/O.Smith SP
01 Tony Gwynn .30 .75
11 Fred Lynn .20 .50
13 Steve Carlton .25 .60
15 Tim Salmon .20 .50
19 Jay Buhner .15 .40
24 Edgar Martinez .15 .40
26A Kenny Lofton .20 .50
26B K.Lofton/W.Moon SP 12.00 30.00
28 Frank Thomas .30 .75
36 John Olerud .25 .60
41 Nolan Ryan .75 2.00
42 Mike Schmidt .30 .75
51 Harry Stovey SP 1.00 2.50
52 John Clarkson SP 1.00 2.50
53 Mike Donovan SP 1.00 2.50
55 Ed Killian SP 1.00 2.50
57 Jake Beckley SP 1.00 2.50
58 Harry Wright SP 1.00 2.50
59 Mickey Welch SP 1.00 2.50
61 Tommy McCarthy SP 1.00 2.50
69 Tim Keefe SP 1.00 2.50
70 Jimmy Collins SP 1.00 2.50
78 George Wright SP 1.00 2.50
79 Amos Rusie SP 1.00 2.50
183 Bid McPhee SP 1.00 2.50
198 Jake Daubert SP 1.50 4.00
199 Lave Cross SP 1.50 4.00
209 Roger Connor SP 1.50 4.00

2013 Upper Deck Goodwin Champions Mini

*1-150 MINI: 1X TO 2.5X BASIC CARDS
7 MINIS PER HOBBY BOX, 4 MINIS PER BLASTER
211 Bobby Bundy .60 1.50
212 Nick Castellanos .60 1.50
214 Yao-Lin Wang .75 2.00
215 Matt Davidson .75 2.00
216 Zach Lee .75 2.00
217 Kevin Pillar .60 1.50
219 Kyle Parker .60 1.50
220 Nick Bucci .60 1.50
221 Clayton Blackburn .75 2.00
222 Matthew Andriese .60 1.50
224 Kolten Wong .75 2.00
225 Alen Hanson .75 2.00

2013 Upper Deck Goodwin Champions Mini Canvas

*1-150 MINI CANVAS: 2.5X TO 6X BASIC CARDS
1-150 MINI CANVAS ANNCD. PRINT RUN 99
*211-225 MINI CANVAS: 1X TO 2.5 BASIC MINI
211-225 MINI CANVAS ANNCD. PRINT RUN 198

2013 Upper Deck Goodwin Champions Mini Green

STATED ODDS 1:12 HOBBY, 1:15 BLASTER
STATED SP ODDS 1:60 HOBBY, 1:72 BLASTER

2013 Upper Deck Goodwin Champions Autographs

OVERALL ODDS 1:20
GROUP A ODDS 1:7,517
GROUP B ODDS 1:1,224
GROUP C ODDS 1:489
GROUP D ODDS 1:142
GROUP E ODDS 1:206
GROUP F ODDS 1:28
AAH Alen Hanson G 4.00 10.00
AAN Matthew Andriese F 4.00 10.00
AEM Edgar Martinez D 10.00 25.00
AGO Juan Gonzalez D 15.00 40.00
AJA Jim Abbott G 6.00 15.00
AJB Jay Buhner E 6.00 15.00
AJO John Olerud E 5.00 12.00
AJR Jim Rice D 6.00 15.00
AKH Kent Hrbek G 6.00 15.00
AKL Kenny Lofton D 6.00 15.00
AKW Kolten Wong G 5.00 12.00
AMD Matt Davidson G 4.00 10.00
AME Mark McGwire B 175.00 300.00
ANB Nick Bucci G 4.00 10.00
APL Kevin Pillar G 4.00 10.00
APO Paul O'Neill D 10.00 25.00
ARJ Reggie Jackson B 20.00 50.00
ARP Rafael Palmeiro D 12.00 30.00
ATG Tony Gwynn D 12.00 30.00
ATS Tim Salmon F 4.00 10.00
DJ Doc Jacobs/100 8.00 20.00

2013 Upper Deck Goodwin Champions Sport Royalty Autographs

OVERALL ODDS 1:1,161
GROUP A ODDS 1:7,473
GROUP B ODDS 1:4,171
GROUP C ODDS 1:2,050
SRANR Nolan Ryan A

2014 Upper Deck Goodwin Champions

COMPLETE SET w/o AU's(180) 40.00 100.00
COMPLETE SET w/o SP's(155) 12.00 30.00
131-155 SP ODDS 1:3 HOBBY,BLAST
156-180 SP ODDS 1:12 HOB/1:12 BLAST
AU ODDS 1:60 HOB/1:720 BLAST
NOLA AU ODDS 1:860 '15 PACKS
NOLA AU ISSUED IN '15 GOODWIN
1 Frank Thomas .25 .60
4 Ron Cey .15 .40
28 Troy Glaus .15 .40
66 Bob Horner .15 .40
69 Steve Garvey .15 .40
83 Robin Ventura .15 .40
89 Ken Griffey Jr. .50 1.25
93 Tony Gwynn .25 .60
108 Pete Rose .50 1.25
112 Roger Clemens .30 .75
115 Will Clark .20 .50
120B Kidd/Clemens SP 4.00 10.00
126 Nolan Ryan .75 2.00
129 Mark McGwire .50 1.25
133 Oyster Burns SP 1.00 2.50
137 Cristobal Torriente SP 1.00 2.50
143 King Kelly SP 1.00 2.50
146 Buck Ewing SP 1.00 2.50
148 Jose Mendez SP 1.00 2.50
149 Fred Dunlap SP 1.00 2.50
152 Tip O'Neill SP 1.00 2.50
156 Babe Siebert SP 1.50 4.00
157 Urban Shocker SP 1.50 4.00
158 Jim McCormick SP 1.50 4.00
161 Cap Anson SP 1.50 4.00
165 Pete Browning SP 1.50 4.00
171 Dan Brouthers SP 1.50 4.00
173 Miller Huggins SP 1.50 4.00
175 Jack Chesbro SP 1.50 4.00
178 Joe Kelley SP 1.50 4.00
180 George Davis SP 1.50 4.00
181 Byron Buxton AU 12.00 30.00
182 Miguel Sano AU 6.00 15.00
183 Chris Anderson AU 3.00 8.00
184 Travis Demeritte AU 3.00 8.00
185 Roberto Osuna AU 3.00 8.00
186 Raul Mondesi Jr. AU 6.00 15.00
187 Jorge Alfaro AU 3.00 8.00
188 Corey Black AU 3.00 8.00
189 Breyvic Valera AU 3.00 8.00
190 Jacob May AU 3.00 8.00
191 Jonathan Gray AU 3.00 8.00
192 Joey Gallo AU 10.00 25.00
193 Zach Borenstein AU 3.00 8.00
194 Bryan Mitchell AU 3.00 8.00
195 Joc Pederson AU 5.00 12.00
196 Nola AU Issued in '15 8.00 20.00
197 Miguel Almonte AU 3.00 8.00
198 Eduardo Rodriguez AU 3.00 8.00
199 Marten Gasparini AU 3.00 8.00
200 Micker Adolfo Zapata AU 6.00 15.00

2014 Upper Deck Goodwin Champions Mini

*1-130 MINI: .75X TO 2X BASIC
COMMON CARD (131-180) .50 1.25
7 MINIS PER HOBBY 4 PER BLASTER

2014 Upper Deck Goodwin Champions Mini Canvas

*1-130 MINI CANVAS: 2X TO 5X BASIC
COMMON CARD (131-180) 1.25 3.00
RANDOM INSERTS IN PACKS
1 Frank Thomas 3.00 8.00
89 Ken Griffey Jr. 12.00 30.00
93 Tony Gwynn 5.00 12.00
108 Pete Rose 4.00 10.00
126 Nolan Ryan 10.00 25.00
129 Mark McGwire 8.00 20.00

2014 Upper Deck Goodwin Champions Mini Green

*1-130 MINI GREEN: 1X TO 2.5X BASIC
COMMON CARD (131-180) .60 1.50
STATED ODDS 1:10 HOB/1:12 BLAST

2014 Upper Deck Goodwin Champions Autographs

GROUP A ODDS 1:54,400 HOBBY
GROUP B ODDS 1:6590 HOBBY
GROUP C ODDS 1:17,525 HOBBY
GROUP D ODDS 1:1280 HOBBY
GROUP E ODDS 1:410 HOBBY
GROUP F ODDS 1:135 HOBBY
GROUP G ODDS 1:42 HOBBY
'16 STATED ODDS 1:4352 HOBBY
AFT Frank Thomas D 40.00 80.00
AGA Steve Garvey F 6.00 15.00
AHO Bob Horner F 3.00 8.00
AKG Ken Griffey Jr. D 75.00 150.00
ANR Nolan Ryan C
ARC Roger Clemens
ARO Pete Rose C
ARV Robin Ventura F 5.00 12.00

2014 Upper Deck Goodwin Champions Goudey

COMPLETE SET (52) 25.00 60.00
BB ODDS 1:13 HOB/1:32 BLAST
BK ODDS 1:25 HOB/1:60 BLAST
FB ODDS 1:25 HOB/1:60 BLAST
HK ODDS 1:33 HOB/1:80 BLAST
GOLF ODDS 1:33 HOB/1:80 BLAST
MISC SPORT ODDS 1:100 HOB/1:240 BLAST
HISTORY ODDS 1:40 HOB/1:96 BLAST
1 Will Clark .50 1.25
2 Mark McGwire 1.25 3.00
3 Ken Griffey Jr. 1.25 3.00
4 Nolan Ryan 2.00 5.00
5 Johnny Bench .60 1.50
6 Reggie Jackson .50 1.25
7 Carlton Fisk .50 1.25
8 Mike Schmidt 1.00 2.50
9 Paul O'Neill .50 1.25
10 Edgar Martinez .50 1.25

2014 Upper Deck Goodwin Champions Goudey Autographs

GROUP A ODDS 1:7200 HOBBY
GROUP B ODDS 1:4800 HOBBY
GROUP C ODDS 1:1650 HOBBY
GROUP D ODDS 1:1200 HOBBY
'16 GROUP A ODDS 1:21,760 HOBBY
'16 GROUP B ODDS 1:8369 HOBBY
2 Mark McGwire C 100.00 200.00
3 Ken Griffey Jr. B 90.00 150.00
5 Johnny Bench C 20.00 50.00
6 Reggie Jackson C 15.00 40.00
7 Carlton Fisk D 12.00 30.00
8 Mike Schmidt C 20.00 50.00
9 Paul O'Neill D 12.00 30.00
10 Edgar Martinez D 20.00 50.00

2014 Upper Deck Goodwin Champions Memorabilia

GROUP A ODDS 1:5140
GROUP B ODDS 1:685
GROUP C ODDS 1:80
GROUP D ODDS 1:18
MGR Jonathan Gray D 2.50 6.00
MJG Joey Gallo D 2.50 6.00
MMZ Micker Adolfo Zapata D 4.00 10.00
MOS Roberto Osuna D 2.50 6.00
MPE Joc Pederson D 3.00 8.00

2014 Upper Deck Goodwin Champions Memorabilia Premium

*PREMIUM: .75X TO 2X BASIC
RANDOM INSERTS IN PACKS
PRINT RUNS B/WN 10-50 COPIES PER
NO PRICING ON QTY 15 OR LESS
MGR Jonathan Gray/50 5.00 12.00
MMG Marten Gasparini/50

2014 Upper Deck Goodwin Champions Sport Royalty Autographs

GROUP A ODDS 1:17,130 HOBBY
GROUP B ODDS 1:4670 HOBBY
GROUP C ODDS 1:2855 HOBBY
GROUP D ODDS 1:1070 HOBBY
'16 GROUP A ODDS 1:21,760 HOBBY
'16 GROUP B ODDS 1:5440 HOBBY
SRAKG Ken Griffey Jr. C 75.00 150.00
SRAMM Mark McGwire A

2015 Upper Deck Goodwin Champions

COMPLETE SET w/o AU's(150) 25.00 60.00
COMPLETE SET w/o SP's(100) 6.00 15.00
131-155 SP ODDS APPX. 1:3 PACKS
156-180 SP ODDS 1:8 PACKS
GROUP A AU ODDS 1:755 PACKS
GROUP B AU ODDS 1:65 PACKS
PRINTING PLATES RANDOMLY INSERTED
PLATE PRINT RUN 1 SET PER COLOR
BLACK-CYAN-MAGENTA-YELLOW ISSUED
NO PLATE PRICING DUE TO SCARCITY
EXCHANGE DEADLINE 6/10/2017
3 John McGraw .15 .40
46 Kenesaw Landis .15 .40
47 Mark McGwire .50 1.25
48 Nolan Ryan .75 2.00
70 Candy Cummings .15 .40
82 Ken Griffey Jr. .50 1.25
93 Eddie Plank .15 .40
95 Roger Bresnahan .15 .40
119 Mark McGwire SP 1.50 4.00
129 Ken Griffey Jr. SP 2.00 5.00
137 Nolan Ryan SP 3.00 8.00
151 D.Dahl AU A EXCH 5.00 12.00
152 Michael Feliz AU B 2.50 6.00
153 Austin Meadows AU B 4.00 10.00
154 Colin Moran AU B 2.50 6.00
155 Sean Newcomb AU B 2.50 6.00
156 Jose Berrios AU B 3.00 8.00
157 Rob Kaminsky AU B 2.50 6.00
158 Blake Snell AU B 2.50 6.00
159 Raimel Tapia AU B 2.50 6.00
160 Matt Olson AU B 4.00 10.00
161 J.Thompson AU A EXCH 5.00 12.00
162 Jorge Mateo AU B 4.00 10.00
163 D.Garcia AU A EXCH 5.00 12.00
165 Bobby Bradley AU B 2.50 6.00

2015 Upper Deck Goodwin Champions Mini

*MINI 1-100: 1X TO 2.5X BASIC
*MINI 101-125: .3X TO .75X BASIC
*MINI 126-150: .25X TO .6X BASIC
STATED ODDS THREE PER BOX

2015 Upper Deck Goodwin Champions Mini Canvas

*CANVAS 1-100: 2X TO 5X BASIC
*CANVAS 101-125: .6X TO 1.5X BASIC
*CANVAS 126-150: .5X TO 1.2X BASIC
RANDOM INSERTS IN PACKS
ANNCD PRINT RUN OF 99 COPIES PER

2015 Upper Deck Goodwin Champions Mini Cloth Lady Luck

*LUCK 1-100: 2.5X TO 6X BASIC
*LUCK 101-125: .75X TO 2X BASIC
*LUCK 126-150: .6X TO 1.5X BASIC
RANDOM INSERTS IN PACKS
STATED PRINT RUN 50 SER.#'d SETS

2015 Upper Deck Goodwin Champions Mini Leather Magician

*MAGICIAN 1-100: 6X TO 15X BASIC
*MAGICIAN 101-125: 2X TO 5X BASIC
*MAGICIAN 126-150: 1.5X TO 4X BASIC
RANDOM INSERTS IN PACKS
STATED PRINT RUN 15 SER.#'d SETS

2015 Upper Deck Goodwin Champions Autographs

GROUP A ODDS 1:6830 PACKS
GROUP B ODDS 1:780 PACKS
GROUP C ODDS 1:685 PACKS
GROUP D ODDS 1:350 PACKS
GROUP E ODDS 1:150 PACKS
GROUP F ODDS 1:65 PACKS
'16 GROUP A ODDS 1:14,836 PACKS
'16 GROUP B ODDS 1:1106 PACKS
EXCHANGE DEADLINE 6/10/2017
ANR Nolan Ryan A EXCH

2015 Upper Deck Goodwin Champions Autographs Black and White

GROUP A ODDS 1:24,800 PACKS
GROUP B ODDS 1:7630 PACKS
GROUP C ODDS 1:5670 PACKS
GROUP D ODDS 1:6615 PACKS
OVERALL B/W ODDS 1:2000 PACKS
EXCHANGE DEADLINE 6/10/2017
126 Nolan Ryan A
142 Mark McGwire B

2015 Upper Deck Goodwin Champions Autographs Inscriptions

RANDOM INSERTS IN PACKS
PRINT RUNS B/WN 2-298 COPIES PER
NO PRICING ON QTY 16 OR LESS
EXCHANGE DEADLINE 6/10/2017

2015 Upper Deck Goodwin Champions Goudey

COMPLETE SET (60) 15.00 40.00
1-40 STATED ODDS 1:5 PACKS
41-60 STATED ODDS 1:20 PACKS
6 Ken Griffey Jr. 1.25 3.00

2015 Upper Deck Goodwin Champions Goudey Sport Royalty Autographs

GROUP A ODDS 1:24,960 PACKS
GROUP B ODDS 1:9985 PACKS
GROUP C ODDS 1:3995 PACKS
OVERALL GOUDEY ODDS 1:2560 PACKS
'16 STATED ODDS 1:32,640 HOBBY
EXCHANGE DEADLINE 6/10/2017
SRALB Larry Bird

2015 Upper Deck Goodwin Champions Memorabilia

GROUP A ODDS 1:1420 PACKS
GROUP B ODDS 1:175 PACKS
GROUP C ODDS 1:28 PACKS
MBE Jose Berrios Shirt C 2.50 6.00
MRT Raimel Tapia Shirt C 2.50 6.00

2015 Upper Deck Goodwin Champions Memorabilia Premium Series

*PREMIUM: .6X TO 1.5X BASIC
RANDOM INSERTS IN PACKS
PRINT RUNS B/WN 10-75 COPIES PER
NO PRICING ON QTY 15 OR LESS

2016 Upper Deck Goodwin Champions

COMPLETE SET w/o SP's(100) 6.00 15.00
101-150 SP ODDS 1:4 HOBBY
SP1 STATED ODDS 1:1280 HOBBY
PRINTING PLATES RANDOMLY INSERTED
PLATE PRINT RUN 1 SET PER COLOR
BLACK-CYAN-MAGENTA-YELLOW ISSUED
NO PLATE PRICING DUE TO SCARCITY
12 Tom Glavine .20 .50
62 Tom Glavine .20 .50
107 Tom Glavine BW SP .50 1.25

2016 Upper Deck Goodwin Champions Mini

*MINI 1-100: 1X TO 2.5X BASIC
*MINI BW 101-150: .4X TO 1X BASIC BW
STATED ODDS 1:4 HOBBY

2016 Upper Deck Goodwin Champions Mini Canvas

*CANVAS 1-100: 1.2X TO 3X BASIC
*CANVAS BW 101-150: .5X TO 1.2X BASIC BW
STATED ODDS 1:12 HOBBY

2016 Upper Deck Goodwin Champions Mini Cloth Lady Luck

*CLOTH 1-100: 5X TO 12X BASIC
*CLOTH BW 101-150: 2X TO 5X BASIC BW
RANDOM INSERTS IN PACKS
STATED PRINT RUN 25 SER.#'d SETS

2016 Upper Deck Goodwin Champions Goudey

COMPLETE SET (50) 12.00 30.00
STATED ODDS 1:4 PACKS
PRINTING PLATES RANDOMLY INSERTED
PLATE PRINT RUN 1 SET PER COLOR
BLACK-CYAN-MAGENTA-YELLOW ISSUED
NO PLATE PRICING DUE TO SCARCITY
35 Tom Glavine .40 1.00

2016 Upper Deck Goodwin Champions Goudey Autographs

GROUP A STATED ODDS 1:119,716 PACKS
GROUP B STATED ODDS 1:30,784 PACKS
GROUP C STATED ODDS 1:7280 PACKS
GROUP D STATED ODDS 1:1796 PACKS
GROUP E STATED ODDS 1:1247 PACKS
GROUP F STATED ODDS 1:630 PACKS
EXCHANGE DEADLINE 6/21/2018
GATG Tom Glavine D 10.00 25.00

2016 Upper Deck Goodwin Champions Goudey Sport Royalty Autographs

GROUP A STATED ODDS 1:200,192 PACKS
GROUP B STATED ODDS 1:52,682 PACKS
GROUP C STATED ODDS 1:19,627 PACKS
GROUP D STATED ODDS 1:3168 PACKS
EXCHANGE DEADLINE 6/21/2018
SRTG Tom Glavine D 12.00 30.00

2017 Upper Deck Goodwin Champions

COMPLETE SET w/o SP's(100) 6.00 15.00
101-150 SP ODDS 1:4 HOBBY
SP1 STATED ODDS 1:1280 HOBBY
PRINTING PLATES RANDOMLY INSERTED
PLATE PRINT RUN 1 SET PER COLOR
BLACK-CYAN-MAGENTA-YELLOW ISSUED
NO PLATE PRICING DUE TO SCARCITY
49 Kevin Maitan .25 1.00
99 Kevin Maitan .25 1.00
149 Kevin Maitan BW SP .60 1.50

2017 Upper Deck Goodwin Champions Mini

*MINI 1-100: .6X TO 1.5X BASIC
*MINI BW 101-150: .4X TO 1X BASIC BW
STATED ODDS 1:4 HOBBY

2017 Upper Deck Goodwin Champions Mini Canvas

*CANVAS 1-100: 1.2X TO 3X BASIC
*CANVAS BW 101-150: .75X TO 2X BASIC BW
RANDOM INSERTS IN PACKS

2017 Upper Deck Goodwin Champions Mini Cloth Lady Luck

*CLOTH 1-100: 5X TO 12X BASIC
*CLOTH BW 101-150: 3X TO 8X BASIC BW
RANDOM INSERTS IN PACKS
STATED PRINT RUN 25 SER.#'d SETS

2017 Upper Deck Goodwin Champions Autographs

GROUP A 1:25,933 HOBBY
GROUP B 1:4914 HOBBY
GROUP C 1:3154 HOBBY
GROUP D 1:546 HOBBY
GROUP E 1:419 HOBBY
GROUP F 1:99 HOBBY
AKM Kevin Maitan F 8.00 20.00

2017 Upper Deck Goodwin Champions Autographs Inscriptions

RANDOM INSERTS IN PACKS
PRINT RUNS B/WN 5-650 COPIES PER
NO PRICING ON QTY 15 OR LESS
AKM Kevin Maitan/50 15.00 40.00

2017 Upper Deck Goodwin Champions Goudey

COMPLETE SET (25) 10.00 25.00
STATED ODDS 1:8 PACKS
PRINTING PLATES RANDOMLY INSERTED
PLATE PRINT RUN 1 SET PER COLOR
BLACK-CYAN-MAGENTA-YELLOW ISSUED
NO PLATE PRICING DUE TO SCARCITY
G24 Kevin Maitan .75 2.00

2017 Upper Deck Goodwin Champions Goudey Memorabilia

STATED GROUP A ODDS 1:2,288 HOBBY
STATED GROUP B ODDS 1:161 HOBBY
*PREMIUM/35-65: .5X TO 1.2X BASIC
*PREMIUM/25: 1X TO 2.5X BASIC
GMKM Kevin Maitan B 2.50 6.00

2017 Upper Deck Goodwin Champions Memorabilia

STATED GROUP A ODDS 1:1,285 HOBBY
STATED GROUP B ODDS 1:1,573 HOBBY
STATED GROUP C ODDS 1:541 HOBBY
STATED GROUP D ODDS 1:198 HOBBY
STATED GROUP E ODDS 1:51 HOBBY
*PREMIUM/35-65: .5X TO 1.2X BASIC
*PREMIUM/25: 1X TO 2.5X BASIC
MKM Kevin Maitan E 2.50 6.00

2017 Upper Deck Goodwin Champions Memorabilia Dual Swatch

STATED GROUP A ODDS 1:4061 HOBBY
STATED GROUP B ODDS 1:1218 HOBBY
STATED GROUP C ODDS 1:1248 HOBBY
STATED GROUP D ODDS 1:435 HOBBY
*PREMIUM/25: 1X TO 2.5X BASIC
M2KM Kevin Maitan D 2.50 6.00

2018 Upper Deck Goodwin Champions Autographs

GROUP A 1:107,323 HOBBY
GROUP B 1:53,661 HOBBY
GROUP C 1:17,887 HOBBY
GROUP D 1:3960 HOBBY
GROUP E 1:1239 HOBBY
GROUP F 1:715 HOBBY
GROUP G 1:390 HOBBY
GROUP H 1:236 HOBBY
GROUP I 1:101 HOBBY
ASO Shohei Ohtani B 300.00 600.00

2018 Upper Deck Goodwin Champions Autographs Inscriptions

RANDOM INSERTS IN PACKS
PRINT RUNS B/WN 5-53 COPIES PER
NO PRICING ON QTY 15 OR LESS

2018 Upper Deck Goodwin Champions Goudey Autographs

GROUP A 1:110,880 HOBBY
GROUP B 1:20,921 HOBBY
GROUP C 1:11,314 HOBBY
GROUP D 1:1724 HOBBY
GROUP E 1:736 HOBBY
GASO Shohei Ohtani B 150.00 300.00

2018 Upper Deck Goodwin Champions Goudey Sport Royalty Autographs

GROUP A ODDS 1:116,880 HOBBY
GROUP B ODDS 1:8588 HOBBY
NO GROUP A PRICING DUE TO SCARCITY

2018 Upper Deck Goodwin Champions Splash of Color Autographs

GROUP A ODDS 1:211,200 HOBBY
GROUP B ODDS 1:15,304 HOBBY
GROUP C RANDOMLY INSERTED
GROUP D ODDS 1:10,667 HOBBY
GROUP E ODDS 1:8123 HOBBY
GROUP F ODDS 1:4735 HOBBY
GROUP G ODDS 1:3771 HOBBY
NO GROUP A PRICING DUE TO SCARCITY
SCASO Shohei Ohtani B 300.00 600.00

2019 Upper Deck Goodwin Champions

COMPLETE SET (150) 12.00 30.00
COMPLETE SET w/o SP's(100) 6.00 15.00
101-150 SP ODDS 1:4 HOBBY
PRINTING PLATES RANDOMLY INSERTED
PLATE PRINT RUN 1 SET PER COLOR
BLACK-CYAN-MAGENTA-YELLOW ISSUED
NO PLATE PRICING DUE TO SCARCITY
49 Victor Robles .30 .75
99 Victor Robles .30 .75
149 Victor Robles SP .50 1.25

2019 Upper Deck Goodwin Champions Goudey

COMPLETE SET (50) 10.00 25.00
STATED ODDS 1:4 HOBBY
PRINTING PLATES RANDOMLY INSERTED
PLATE PRINT RUN 1 SET PER COLOR
BLACK-CYAN-MAGENTA-YELLOW ISSUED
NO PLATE PRICING DUE TO SCARCITY
*MINI: .5X TO 1.2X BASIC
*MINI WOOD: .75X TO 2X BASIC
G47 Victor Robles .40 1.00

2019 Upper Deck Goodwin Champions Goudey Memorabilia

GMVR Victor Robles D

2019 Upper Deck Goodwin Champions Splash of Color Autographs

SCAVR Victor Robles

2019 Upper Deck Goodwin Champions Memorabilia

MVR Victor Robles C

2019 Upper Deck Goodwin Champions Mini

*MINI 1-100: .6X TO 1.5X BASIC
APPX. ODDS 1:4 HOBBY

2019 Upper Deck Goodwin Champions Mini Wood Lumberjack

*MINI WOOD 1-100: 1X TO 2.5X BASIC
APPX. ODDS 1:20 HOBBY, 1:20 EPACK

2019 Upper Deck Goodwin Champions Splash of Color 3D

LSVR Victor Robles T2

2019 Upper Deck Goodwin Champions Splash of Color Memorabilia

SMVR Victor Robles B

2020 Upper Deck Goodwin Champions

101-150 SP ODDS 1:4 HOBBY
PRINTING PLATES RANDOMLY INSERTED
PLATE PRINT RUN 1 SET PER COLOR
NO PLATE PRICING DUE TO SCARCITY
7 Casey Mize .60 1.50
30 Wander Franco 2.00 5.00
45 Jasson Dominguez 2.50 6.00
57 Casey Mize .60 1.50
80 Wander Franco 2.00 5.00
95 Jasson Dominguez 2.50 6.00
107 Casey Mize 1.00 2.50
130 Wander Franco 3.00 8.00
145 Jasson Dominguez 4.00 10.00

2020 Upper Deck Goodwin Champions '11 Goodwin Champions

RANDOM INSERTS IN PACKS
30 Wander Franco 10.00 25.00
45 Jasson Dominguez 25.00 60.00

2020 Upper Deck Goodwin Champions Autographs

GROUP A ODDS 1:35,401 HOBBY
GROUP B ODDS 1:25,287 HOBBY
GROUP C ODDS 1:6627 HOBBY
GROUP D ODDS 1:1535 HOBBY
GROUP E ODDS 1:981 HOBBY
GROUP F ODDS 1:284 HOBBY
GROUP G ODDS 1:146 HOBBY
GROUP H ODDS 1:129 HOBBY
EXCHANGE DEADLINE 12/31/22
ACM Casey Mize E 15.00 40.00
AJD Jasson Dominguez C 100.00 250.00
AWF Wander Franco D EXCH 40.00 100.00

2020 Upper Deck Goodwin Champions Autographs Inscriptions

INSCRIPTION/75-200: .6X TO 1.5X BASIC
INSCRIPTION/25: .75X TO 2X BASIC
RANDOM INSERTS IN PACKS
PRINT RUNS B/WN 25-200 COPIES PER
EXCHANGE DEADLINE 12/31/22
AJD Jasson Dominguez 300.00 600.00
Martian/20

2020 Upper Deck Goodwin Champions Dual Swatch Memorabilia

STATED ODDS 1:300 HOBBY; 1:600 EPACK
M2CM Casey Mize 4.00 10.00

2020 Upper Deck Goodwin Champions Dual Swatch Memorabilia Premium

PREMIUM/35: .8X TO 2X BASIC
RANDOM INSERTS IN PACKS
STATED PRINT RUN 35 SER.#'d SETS

2020 Upper Deck Goodwin Champions Fanimation

STATED ODDS 1:2540 HOBBY; 1:2540 EPACK
F7 Wander Franco 40.00 100.00

2020 Upper Deck Goodwin Champions Goudey

STATED ODDS 1:4 HOBBY; 1:4 EPACK
*MINI 1-100: .5X TO 1.2X BASIC
*MINI WOOD 1-100: .75X TO 2X BASIC
G7 Casey Mize .75 2.00
G30 Wander Franco 2.50 6.00
G45 Jasson Dominguez 3.00 8.00

2020 Upper Deck Goodwin Champions Goudey Autographs

GROUP A ODDS 1:7842 HOBBY
GROUP B ODDS 1:1511 HOBBY
EXCHANGE DEADLINE 12/31/22
GAJD Jasson Dominguez A 100.00 250.00

2020 Upper Deck Goodwin Champions Goudey Memorabilia

STATED ODDS 1:300 HOBBY; 1:600 EPACK
GMCM Casey Mize 4.00 10.00
GMJD Jasson Dominguez 8.00 20.00
GMWF Wander Franco 8.00 20.00

2020 Upper Deck Goodwin Champions Goudey Memorabilia Premium

PREMIUM/50: .8X TO 2X BASIC
RANDOM INSERTS IN PACKS
STATED PRINT RUN 50 SER.#'d SETS
GMJD Jasson Dominguez 20.00 50.00

2020 Upper Deck Goodwin Champions Goudey Sport Royalty Dual Swatch Memorabilia

STATED ODDS 1:2880 HOBBY; 1:2880 EPACK
SRM2WF Wander Franco 8.00 20.00

2020 Upper Deck Goodwin Champions Goudey Sport Royalty Memorabilia

STATED ODDS 1:300 HOBBY; 1:600 EPACK
SRMWF Wander Franco 8.00 20.00

2020 Upper Deck Goodwin Champions Horizontal Autographs

GROUP A ODDS 1:20,295 HOBBY
GROUP B ODDS 1:4832 HOBBY
GROUP C ODDS 1:2585 HOBBY
GROUP D ODDS 1:1532 HOBBY
GROUP E ODDS 1:782 HOBBY
GROUP F ODDS 1:385 HOBBY
EXCHANGE DEADLINE 12/31/22
HACM Casey Mize D 15.00 40.00
HAJD Jasson Dominguez C 100.00 250.00
HAWF Wander Franco C EXCH 40.00 100.00

2020 Upper Deck Goodwin Champions Memorabilia

GROUP A ODDS 1:29211 EXCH
GROUP B ODDS 1:2434 EXCH
GROUP C ODDS 1:2921 EXCH
GROUP D ODDS 1:2142 EXCH
GROUP E ODDS 1:42 EXCH
MCM Casey Mize E 4.00 10.00
MDO Jasson Dominguez E 8.00 20.00
MWF Wander Franco E 6.00 15.00

2020 Upper Deck Goodwin Champions Memorabilia Premium

PREMIUM/25-65: .8X TO 2X BASIC
RANDOM INSERTS IN PACKS
PRINT RUNS B/WN 25-65 COPIES PER
MDO Jasson Dominguez/65 20.00 50.00

2020 Upper Deck Goodwin Champions Splash of Color Autographs

GROUP A ODDS 1:44,742 HOBBY
GROUP B ODDS 1:4873 HOBBY
GROUP C ODDS 1:1806 HOBBY
EXCHANGE DEADLINE 12/31/22
SCACM Casey Mize B 15.00 40.00
SCAJD Jasson Dominguez A 100.00 250.00
SCAWF Wander Franco B EXCH 40.00 100.00

2020 Upper Deck Goodwin Champions Splash of Color Memorabilia

GROUP A ODDS 1:3351 HOBBY
GROUP B ODDS 1:1510 HOBBY
GROUP C ODDS 1:1416 HOBBY
SMJD Jasson Dominguez B 8.00 20.00
SMWF Wander Franco C 8.00 20.00

2020 Upper Deck Goodwin Champions Splash of Color Memorabilia Premium

PREMIUM/25: .8X TO 2X BASIC
RANDOM INSERTS IN PACKS
STATED PRINT RUN 25 SER.#'d SETS
SMJD Jasson Dominguez 40.00 100.00

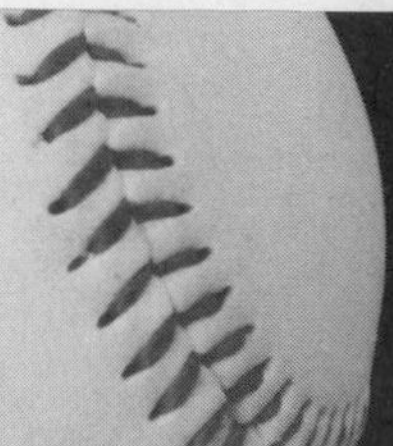

MINOR LEAGUE

2011 Topps Heritage Minors

COMPLETE SET (250) 100.00 200.00
COMP.SET w/o SP's (200) 20.00 50.00
COMMON CARD (1-200) .12 .30
COMMON SP (201-250) .60 1.50
SP STATED ODDS 1:4 HOBBY
PRINTING PLATE ODDS 1:407 HOBBY
PLATE PRINT RUN 1 SET PER COLOR
BLACK-CYAN-MAGENTA-YELLOW ISSUED
NO PLATE PRICING DUE TO SCARCITY
1 Andrelton Simmons .30 .75
2 Stetson Allie .20 .50
3 Chris Archer .25 .60
4 Manny Banuelos .30 .75
5 Dellin Betances .30 .75
6 Wil Myers .20 .50
7 Michael Choice .20 .50
8 Zack Cox .20 .50
9 Travis D'Arnaud .20 .50
10 Julio Rodriguez .12 .30
11 Delino DeShields Jr. .12 .30
12 Matt Dominguez .20 .50
13 Kyle Gibson .20 .50
14 Wily Peralta .12 .30
15 Grant Green .12 .30
16 Bryce Harper 12.00 30.00
17 Cody Hawn .20 .50
18 Luis Heredia .12 .30
19 Aaron Hicks .20 .50
20 Blake Tekotte .12 .30
21 Brett Jackson .20 .50
22 Casey Kelly .12 .30
23 Brett Lawrie .50 1.25
24 Justin O'Conner .12 .30
25 Starling Marte .30 .75
26 Tyler Matzek .20 .50
27 Devin Mesoraco .30 .75
28 Shelby Miller .60 1.50
29 Jesus Montero .12 .30
30 Mike Montgomery .20 .50
31 Peter Tago .12 .30
32 Taijuan Walker .30 .75
33 Carlos Perez .12 .30
34 Anthony Ranaudo .30 .75
35 Derek Norris .12 .30
36 Austin Romine .12 .30
37 Jean Segura .50 1.25
38 Tony Sanchez .20 .50
39 Gary Sanchez .60 1.50
40 Matt Miller .12 .30
41 Jeff Locke .30 .75
42 Garin Cecchini .30 .75
43 John Lamb .12 .30
44 Mike Trout 40.00 100.00
45 Jacob Turner .50 1.25
46 Arodys Vizcaino .20 .50
47 Adam Bailey .12 .30
48 Alex Wimmers .12 .30
49 Christian Yelich 2.50 6.00
50 Josh Zeid .12 .30
51 Austin Adams .12 .30
52 Ehire Adrianza .12 .30
53 Nolan Arenado .60 1.50
54 Phillippe Aumont .12 .30
55 Yasmani Grandal .20 .50
56 Luke Bailey .12 .30
57 Nino Leyja .12 .30
58 Keyviuis Sampson .12 .30
59 Cory Spangenberg .20 .50
60 Nate Baker .12 .30
61 Jake Skole .12 .30
62 Tim Beckham .30 .75
63 Engel Beltre .12 .30
64 Miguel Sano .25 .60
65 Jesse Biddle .20 .50
66 Seth Blair .12 .30
67 Andrew Brackman .12 .30
68 Drake Britton .12 .30
69 Tommy Shirley .12 .30
70 Gary Brown .30 .75
71 Nick Bucci .12 .30
72 Trystan Magnuson .12 .30
73 Michael Burgess .20 .50
74 Dan Klein .20 .50
75 Jordan Pacheco .12 .30
76 Nick Castellanos .60 1.50
77 Simon Castro .12 .30
78 Garrett Gould .12 .30
79 Brian Cavazos-Galvez .12 .30
80 Josh Sale .20 .50
81 Darrell Ceciliani .12 .30
82 Chevez Clarke .12 .30
83 Maikel Cleto .12 .30
84 A.J. Cole .20 .50
85 Alex Colome .12 .30
86 Christian Colon .12 .30
87 Austin Ross .20 .50
88 Tyler Thornburg .20 .50
89 Jarred Cosart .20 .50
90 Kaleb Cowart .20 .50
91 Sean Coyle .20 .50
92 Charlie Culberson .12 .30
93 Jordan Swagerty .20 .50
94 James Darnell .12 .30
95 Matt Davidson .20 .50
96 Khris Davis .60 1.50
97 Dimaster Delgado .12 .30
98 Mel Rojas Jr. .12 .30
99 Miguel De Los Santos .12 .30
100 Jaff Decker .12 .30
101 Kellin Deglan .12 .30
102 Zack Wheeler .40 1.00
103 Matt Den Dekker .20 .50
104 Garrett Richards .30 .75
105 Danny Duffy .20 .50
106 Adam Eaton .30 .75
107 Nathan Eovaldi .30 .75
108 Robbie Erlin .20 .50
109 Daniel Fields .12 .30
110 Kyle Skipworth .12 .30
111 Ryan Flaherty .12 .30
112 Wilmer Flores .20 .50
113 Mike Foltynewicz .12 .30
114 Adys Portillo .12 .30
115 Nick Franklin .20 .50
116 Reymond Fuentes .12 .30
117 John Gast .12 .30
118 Scooter Gennett .30 .75
119 Mychal Givens .12 .30
120 Todd Glaesmann .12 .30
121 Anthony Gose .20 .50
122 JP Ramirez .12 .30
123 Kevin Kiermaier .30 .75
124 Angelo Gumbs .12 .30
125 Jedd Gyorko .30 .75
126 Jason Hagerty .12 .30
127 Jeudy Valdez .12 .30
128 Brody Colvin .12 .30
129 Billy Hamilton .25 .60
130 Matt Harvey .75 2.00
131 Kyle Russell .20 .50
132 Jason Stoffel .12 .30
133 Kyle Higashioka .12 .30
134 L.J. Hoes .20 .50
135 Alan Horne .12 .30
136 Ryan Jackson .12 .30
137 Luke Jackson .20 .50
138 Jiwan James .12 .30
139 Justin Wilson .12 .30
140 Chad Jenkins .12 .30
141 Tyrell Jenkins .20 .50
142 James Jones .12 .30
143 Joe Kelly .12 .30
144 Max Kepler .40 1.00
145 Jonathan Villar .30 .75
146 Ydwin Villegas .12 .30
147 Kolbrin Vitek .20 .50
148 Josh Vitters .20 .50
149 Everett Williams .12 .30
150 Hak-Ju Lee .12 .30
151 Zach Lee .20 .50
152 Jake Lemmerman .20 .50
153 Joe Leonard .20 .50
154 Jonathan Singleton .20 .50
155 Matt Lipka .20 .50
156 Rymer Liriano .30 .75
157 Marcus Littlewood .12 .30
158 Domingo Santana .30 .75
159 Matt Lollis .20 .50
160 Barret Loux .12 .30
161 Manny Machado 1.25 3.00
162 Yordy Cabrera .12 .30
163 Francisco Martinez .12 .30
164 Carlos Martinez .30 .75
165 Chance Ruffin .12 .30
166 Travis Mattair .12 .30
167 Edward Salcedo .12 .30
168 Trevor May .12 .30
169 Deck McGuire .12 .30
170 Adam Warren .20 .50
171 Jio Mier .12 .30
172 Carlos Perez .12 .30
173 Matt Moore .30 .75
174 Hunter Morris .12 .30
175 Jimmy Nelson .12 .30
176 Steve Parker .12 .30
177 Jake Odorizzi .12 .30
178 Andrew Oliver .12 .30
179 Mike Olt .20 .50
180 Juan Oramas .12 .30
181 Neil Ramirez .12 .30
182 Eury Perez .12 .30
183 Francisco Peguero .12 .30
184 Martin Perez .30 .75
185 Chris Withrow .12 .30
186 Asher Wojciechowski .12 .30
187 Drew Pomeranz .20 .50
188 Tony Wolters .12 .30
189 Jurickson Profar .30 .75
190 Cesar Puello .20 .50
191 Wilin Rosario .12 .30
192 JC Ramirez .12 .30
193 Elmer Reyes .12 .30
194 Trevor Reckling .12 .30
195 Edinson Rincon .12 .30
196 Clint Robinson .12 .30
197 Jerry Sullivan .12 .30
198 Yorman Rodriguez .20 .50
199 Allen Webster .20 .50
200 Robbie Ray .12 .30
201 Stetson Allie SP 1.00 2.50
202 Dellin Betances SP 1.50 4.00
203 Danny Duffy SP 1.00 2.50
204 Zack Cox SP 1.00 2.50
205 Travis D'Arnaud SP 1.00 2.50
206 Anthony Gose SP 1.00 2.50
207 Delino DeShields Jr. SP .60 1.50
208 Matt Dominguez SP 1.00 2.50
209 Kyle Gibson SP 1.00 2.50
210 Grant Green SP .60 1.50
211 Bryce Harper SP 12.00 30.00
212 Cody Hawn SP 1.00 2.50
213 Luis Heredia SP .60 1.50
214 Aaron Hicks SP 1.00 2.50
215 Brett Jackson SP 1.00 2.50
216 Casey Kelly SP .60 1.50
217 Rymer Liriano SP 1.50 4.00
218 Jeff Locke SP 1.50 4.00
219 Manny Machado SP 6.00 15.00
220 Starling Marte SP 1.50 4.00
221 Tyler Matzek SP 1.00 2.50
222 Shelby Miller SP 3.00 8.00
223 Jesus Montero SP .60 1.50
224 Mike Montgomery SP 1.00 2.50
225 Wil Myers SP 1.00 2.50
226 Derek Norris SP .60 1.50
227 Carlos Perez SP .60 1.50
228 Jurickson Profar SP 1.50 4.00
229 Anthony Ranaudo SP 1.50 4.00
230 Austin Romine SP .60 1.50
231 Mike Foltynewicz SP .60 1.50
232 Tony Sanchez SP 1.00 2.50
233 Gary Sanchez SP 3.00 8.00
234 Miguel Sano SP 1.25 3.00
235 Jean Segura SP 2.50 6.00
236 Kyle Skipworth SP .60 1.50
237 Nathan Eovaldi SP 1.50 4.00
238 Cory Spangenberg SP 1.00 2.50
239 Mike Trout SP 75.00 200.00
240 Jacob Turner SP 2.50 6.00
241 Arodys Vizcaino SP 1.00 2.50
242 Alex Wimmers SP .60 1.50
243 Christian Yelich SP 12.00 30.00
244 Josh Zeid SP .60 1.50
245 Mel Rojas Jr. SP .60 1.50
246 Sean Coyle SP 1.00 2.50
247 Yordy Cabrera SP .60 1.50
248 Matt Moore SP 1.50 4.00
249 Matt Harvey SP 4.00 10.00
250 Peter Tago SP .60 1.50

2011 Topps Heritage Minors Black Border

*BLACK 1-200: 4X TO 10X BASIC
STATED ODDS 1:28 HOBBY
STATED PRINT RUN 62 SER.#'d SETS
6 Wil Myers 12.50 30.00
16 Bryce Harper 40.00 80.00
44 Mike Trout 600.00 1200.00
161 Manny Machado 10.00 25.00
173 Matt Moore 30.00 60.00
201 Stetson Allie 2.00 5.00
202 Dellin Betances 3.00 8.00
203 Danny Duffy 2.00 5.00
204 Zack Cox 2.00 5.00
205 Travis D'Arnaud 2.00 5.00
206 Anthony Gose 2.00 5.00
207 Delino DeShields Jr. 1.25 3.00
208 Matt Dominguez 2.00 5.00
209 Kyle Gibson 2.00 5.00
210 Grant Green 1.25 3.00
211 Bryce Harper 20.00 50.00
212 Cody Hawn 2.00 5.00
213 Luis Heredia 1.25 3.00
214 Aaron Hicks 2.00 5.00
215 Brett Jackson 2.00 5.00
216 Casey Kelly 1.25 3.00
217 Rymer Liriano 3.00 8.00
218 Jeff Locke 3.00 8.00
219 Manny Machado 10.00 25.00
220 Starling Marte 3.00 8.00
221 Tyler Matzek 2.00 5.00
222 Shelby Miller 6.00 15.00
223 Jesus Montero 1.25 3.00
224 Mike Montgomery 2.00 5.00
225 Wil Myers 12.50 30.00
226 Derek Norris 1.25 3.00
227 Carlos Perez 1.25 3.00
228 Jurickson Profar 3.00 8.00
229 Anthony Ranaudo 3.00 8.00
230 Austin Romine 1.25 3.00
231 Mike Foltynewicz 1.25 3.00
232 Tony Sanchez 2.00 5.00
233 Gary Sanchez 6.00 15.00
234 Miguel Sano 2.50 6.00
235 Jean Segura 5.00 12.00
236 Kyle Skipworth 1.25 3.00
237 Nathan Eovaldi 3.00 8.00
238 Cory Spangenberg 2.00 5.00
239 Mike Trout 500.00 1000.00
240 Jacob Turner 5.00 12.00
241 Arodys Vizcaino 2.00 5.00
242 Alex Wimmers 1.25 3.00
243 Christian Yelich 25.00 60.00
244 Josh Zeid 1.25 3.00
245 Mel Rojas Jr. 1.25 3.00
246 Sean Coyle 2.00 5.00
247 Yordy Cabrera 1.25 3.00
248 Matt Moore 30.00 60.00
249 Matt Harvey 8.00 20.00
250 Peter Tago 1.25 3.00

2011 Topps Heritage Minors Blue Tint

*BLUE: 3X TO 8X BASIC
STATED ODDS 1:9 HOBBY
STATED PRINT RUN 620 SER.#'d SETS
16 Bryce Harper 10.00 25.00
173 Matt Moore 2.50 6.00

2011 Topps Heritage Minors Green Tint

*GREEN: 3X TO 8X BASIC
STATED ODDS 1:14 HOBBY
STATED PRINT RUN 620 SER.#'d SETS

2011 Topps Heritage Minors Red Tint

*RED: 3X TO 8X BASIC
STATED ODDS 1:9 HOBBY
STATED PRINT RUN 620 SER.#'d SETS
44 Mike Trout 100.00 250.00

2011 Topps Heritage Minors Bryce Harper Game Used Base

STATED ODDS 1:396 HOBBY
BH Bryce Harper 12.00 30.00

2011 Topps Heritage Minors Bryce Harper Game Used Base Blue Tint

STATED ODDS 1:1369 HOBBY
STATED PRINT RUN 299 SER.#'d SETS
BH Bryce Harper 12.00 30.00

2011 Topps Heritage Minors Bryce Harper Game Used Base Green Tint

STATED ODDS 1:17,675 HOBBY
STATED PRINT RUN 25 SER.#'d SETS
NO PRICING DUE TO SCARCITY

2011 Topps Heritage Minors Bryce Harper Game Used Base Red Tint

STATED ODDS 1:4181 HOBBY
STATED PRINT RUN 99 SER.#'d SETS
BH Bryce Harper 15.00 40.00

2011 Topps Heritage Minors Bryce Harper Jumbo Patch Autograph

STATED ODDS 1:388,920 HOBBY
STATED PRINT RUN 1 SER.#'d SET
NO PRICING DUE TO SCARITY

2011 Topps Heritage Minors Clubhouse Collection Relics

STATED ODDS 1:35 HOBBY
AB Adam Bailey 3.00 8.00
AG Anthony Gose 3.00 8.00
AP Adys Portillo 3.00 8.00
AS Andrelton Simmons 3.00 8.00
AV Arodys Vizcaino 3.00 8.00
BH Bryce Harper 10.00 25.00
CC Christian Colon 3.00 8.00
DD Dimaster Delgado 3.00 8.00
JL John Lamb 3.00 8.00
JL Joe Leonard 3.00 8.00
MF Mike Foltynewicz 3.00 8.00
RL Rymer Liriano 3.00 8.00
SA Stetson Allie 3.00 8.00
TD Travis D'Arnaud 3.00 8.00
WM Wil Myers 6.00 15.00
DDS Delino DeShields Jr. 3.00 8.00

2011 Topps Heritage Minors Clubhouse Collection Relics Blue Tint

*BLUE: .5X TO 1.2X BASIC
STATED ODDS 1:131 HOBBY
STATED PRINT RUN 199 SER.#'d SETS
BH Bryce Harper 15.00 40.00

2011 Topps Heritage Minors Clubhouse Collection Relics Green Tint

*GREEN: .5X TO 1.2X BASIC
STATED ODDS 1:566 HOBBY
STATED PRINT RUN 50 SER.#'d SETS
BH Bryce Harper 30.00 80.00

2011 Topps Heritage Minors Clubhouse Collection Relics Red Tint

*RED: .5X TO 1.2X BASIC
STATED ODDS 1:270 HOBBY
STATED PRINT RUN 99 SER.#'d SETS
BH Bryce Harper 20.00 50.00

2011 Topps Heritage Minors Real One Autographs

STATED ODDS 1:14 HOBBY
HARPER STATED ODDS 1:2663 HOBBY
PRINT RUNS B/WN 154-861 COPIES PER
PRINTING PLATE ODDS 1:2991 HOBBY
HARPER PLATE ODDS 1:97,230 HOBBY
PLATE PRINT RUN 1 SET PER COLOR
BLACK-CYAN-MAGENTA-YELLOW ISSUED
NO PLATE PRICING DUE TO SCARCITY
EXCHANGE DEADLINE 9/30/2014
AA Austin Adams EXCH 4.00 10.00
AG Avisail Garcia 3.00 8.00
AP Andy Parrino EXCH 3.00 8.00
BC Brad Chalk 3.00 8.00
BH Bryce Harper 250.00 500.00
BT Blake Tekotte 3.00 8.00
CB Charles Brewer 4.00 10.00
CG Chris Gloor 3.00 8.00
CS Cody Stanley 3.00 8.00
CW Cole White 3.00 8.00
DH Deunte Heath 3.00 8.00
DK David Kopp 3.00 8.00
DO Danny Otero 3.00 8.00
DS Davis Stoneburner 3.00 8.00
DW Dakota Watts 3.00 8.00
FM Francisco Martinez 3.00 8.00
GR Garrett Richards EXCH 6.00 15.00
JD Justin Dalles 3.00 8.00
JH Jordan Henry 3.00 8.00
JP Jon Pettibone 10.00 25.00
JP Joc Pederson 6.00 15.00
JS Jerry Sullivan 6.00 15.00
JS Jordan Swagerty EXCH 6.00 15.00
JW Joe Wieland 4.00 10.00
LJ Luke Jackson 4.00 10.00
LL Leon Landry EXCH 5.00 12.00
NA Nolan Arenado EXCH 20.00 50.00
RA Robbie Aviles 3.00 8.00
RB Ryan Berry 3.00 8.00
RS Robbie Shields 3.00 8.00
SB Sean Black 4.00 10.00
SL Steve Lombardozzi EXCH 8.00 20.00
SW Stefan Welch 3.00 8.00
TF Tim Federowicz 3.00 8.00
TM Trystan Magnuson EXCH 4.00 10.00
TS Tommy Shirley 3.00 8.00
VC Vinnie Catricala EXCH 60.00 120.00
BBO Brett Bochy 4.00 10.00
BBR Brad Brach 8.00 20.00
BPE Blake Perry 3.00 8.00
BPO Brian Pointer 3.00 8.00
DBU Dan Burkhart 4.00 10.00
DJT Dickie Joe Thon EXCH 8.00 20.00
EC1 Evan Crawford P 3.00 8.00
EC2 Evan Crawford OF 3.00 8.00
JMA Justin Marks 3.00 8.00
JMU Jonathan Musser 3.00 8.00
SCS Scott Shuman 3.00 8.00
STS Steven Souza 4.00 10.00
TTH Tony Thompson 3.00 8.00

2011 Topps Heritage Minors Real One Autographs Blue Tint

*BLUE: .5X TO 1.2X BASIC
STATED ODDS 1:122 HOBBY
HARPER ODDS 1:16,205 HOBBY
STATED PRINT RUN 99 SER.#'d SETS
HARPER PRINT RUN 25 SER.#'d SETS
NO HARPER PRICING DUE TO SCARCITY
EXCHANGE DEADLINE 9/30/2014

2012 Topps Heritage Minors Black

*BLACK 1-200: 6X TO 15X BASIC
*BLACK SP 201-225: .5X TO 1.2X BASIC SP
STATED ODDS 1:8 HOBBY
STATED PRINT RUN 96 SER.#'d SETS
99 Evan Gattis 50.00 100.00

2012 Topps Heritage Minors Clubhouse Collection Relics

STATED ODDS 1:31 HOBBY
BH Billy Hamilton 4.00 10.00
BM Brad Miller 3.00 8.00
CB Christian Bethancourt 4.00 10.00
CBU Cody Buckel 3.00 8.00
CO Chris Owings 3.00 8.00
CS Cory Spangenberg 3.00 8.00
DB Dylan Bundy 8.00 20.00
FL Francisco Lindor 4.00 10.00
GS George Springer 4.00 10.00
JB Jackie Bradley Jr. 5.00 12.00
JS Jonathan Singleton 4.00 10.00
KW Kolten Wong 6.00 15.00
MB Matt Barnes 3.00 8.00
MC Michael Choice 4.00 10.00
NC Nick Castellanos 5.00 12.00
OT Oscar Taveras 6.00 15.00
RL Rymer Liriano 3.00 8.00
TJ Tommy Joseph 4.00 10.00
TW Taijuan Walker 3.00 8.00
XB Xander Bogaerts 10.00 25.00

2012 Topps Heritage Minors Clubhouse Collection Relics Black

*BLACK: .6X TO 1.5X BASIC
STATED ODDS 1:173 HOBBY
STATED PRINT RUN 50 SER.#'d SETS

2012 Topps Heritage Minors Manufactured Cap Logo

STATED ODDS 1:94 HOBBY
EXCHANGE DEADLINE 08/31/2015
AB Archie Bradley EXCH 8.00 20.00
AC A.J. Cole EXCH 5.00 12.00
AG Anthony Gose EXCH 5.00 12.00
AH Aaron Hicks EXCH 10.00 25.00
AP Adys Portillo EXCH 5.00 12.00
AR Anthony Rendon EXCH 15.00 40.00
BB Bryce Brentz EXCH 8.00 20.00
BG Brian Goodwin EXCH 10.00 25.00
BM Brad Miller EXCH 8.00 20.00
CB Cody Buckel EXCH 6.00 15.00
CC Chun-Hsiu Chen EXCH 8.00 20.00
CJ Cody Johnson EXCH 6.00 15.00
CK Casey Kelly EXCH 6.00 15.00
CS Carlos Sanchez EXCH 5.00 12.00
DB Dylan Bundy EXCH 40.00 80.00
DL Donald Lutz EXCH 10.00 25.00
EC Edwin Carl EXCH 10.00 25.00
ER Eddie Rosario EXCH 8.00 20.00
FL Francisco Lindor EXCH 10.00 25.00
GC Gerrit Cole EXCH 12.50 30.00
GS George Springer EXCH 10.00 25.00
JB Jackie Bradley Jr. EXCH 10.00 25.00
JF Jeurys Familia EXCH 8.00 20.00
JS Jonathan Schoop EXCH 8.00 20.00
JSE Jean Segura EXCH 10.00 25.00
KS Kevan Smith EXCH 6.00 15.00
MD Matt Davidson EXCH 5.00 12.00
MH Miles Head EXCH 5.00 12.00
MM Mikie Mahtook EXCH 8.00 20.00
MO Marcell Ozuna EXCH 6.00 15.00
MW Mason Williams EXCH 10.00 25.00
NC Nick Castellanos EXCH 10.00 25.00
ND Nick Delmonico EXCH 20.00 50.00
OA Oswaldo Arcia EXCH 8.00 20.00
PM Pratt Maynard EXCH 6.00 15.00
RBR Rob Brantly EXCH 15.00 40.00
RE Robbie Erlin EXCH 6.00 15.00
RM Rafael Montero EXCH 15.00 40.00
TC Tony Cingrani EXCH 6.00 15.00
TCO Tyler Collins EXCH 10.00 25.00
TJ Taylor Jungmann EXCH 8.00 20.00
TS Trevor Story EXCH 8.00 20.00
TT Tyler Thornburg EXCH 8.00 20.00
ZD Zeke DeVoss EXCH 6.00 15.00
ZL Zach Lee EXCH 40.00 80.00

2012 Topps Heritage Minors Prospect Performers

COMPLETE SET (25) 15.00 40.00
STATED ODDS 1:4 HOBBY
AB Archie Bradley .40 1.00
AH Aaron Hicks .60 1.50
BH Billy Hamilton .75 2.00
CK Casey Kelly .60 1.50
CS Cory Spangenberg .60 1.50
CY Christian Yelich 5.00 12.00
DB Dylan Bundy 1.25 3.00
DH Danny Hultzen 1.00 2.50
FL Francisco Lindor 4.00 10.00
GB Gary Brown .60 1.50
GC Gerrit Cole 4.00 10.00
GS Gary Sanchez 2.00 5.00
HL Hak-Ju Lee .60 1.50
JM Jake Marisnick .75 2.00
JP Jurickson Profar .75 2.00
JS Jonathan Singleton .75 2.00
JT Jameson Taillon .75 2.00
MM Manny Machado 4.00 10.00
MO Mike Olt .75 2.00
MS Miguel Sano .75 2.00
NA Nolan Arenado 2.00 5.00
NC Nick Castellanos 2.00 5.00
RL Rymer Liriano .60 1.50
TA Tyler Austin 1.00 2.50
TS Tyler Skaggs 1.00 2.50

2012 Topps Heritage Minors Real One Autographs

STATED ODDS 1:15 HOBBY
PRINTING PLATE ODDS 1:2898 HOBBY
PLATE PRINT RUN 1 SET PER COLOR
BLACK-CYAN-MAGENTA-YELLOW ISSUED
NO PLATE PRICING DUE TO SCARCITY
EXCHANGE DEADLINE 08/31/2015
AS Aaron Sanchez 6.00 15.00
CB Charles Brewer 3.00 8.00
CC Cheslor Cuthbert 4.00 10.00
CH Chris Heston 10.00 25.00
CO Chris Owings 4.00 10.00
DB Dylan Bundy 50.00 100.00
DC Daniel Corcino 4.00 10.00
DS Daniel Straily 6.00 15.00
DV David Vidal 6.00 15.00
DVE Drew Vettleson 3.00 8.00
DW Dakota Watts 3.00 8.00
GP Guillermo Pimentel 3.00 8.00
JB Jed Bradley 3.00 8.00
JF Jeurys Familia 4.00 10.00
JG Jonathan Galvez 3.00 8.00
JP Joc Pederson 6.00 15.00
JPR J.P. Ramirez 3.00 8.00
JR Julio Rodriguez 3.00 8.00
JS Jerry Sullivan 3.00 8.00
JT Joe Testa 4.00 10.00
KC Kes Carter 4.00 10.00
KW Kolten Wong 6.00 15.00
LJ Luke Jackson 3.00 8.00
LM Levi Michael 4.00 10.00
MM Mikie Mahtook 3.00 8.00
MMO Mike Montgomery 3.00 8.00
MP Matthew Purke 4.00 10.00
ND Nick Delmonico 5.00 12.00
PM Pratt Maynard 4.00 10.00
RH Ryan Hafner 5.00 12.00
RL Rymer Liriano 6.00 15.00
RR Robbie Ray 3.00 8.00
RS Rob Segedin 3.00 8.00
SC Sean Coyle 3.00 8.00
SG Steven Geltz 3.00 8.00
SN Sean Nolin 3.00 8.00
SV Sebastian Valle 3.00 8.00
TB Tyler Bortnick 3.00 8.00
TC Tyler Collins 3.00 8.00
TN Telvin Nash 3.00 8.00

2012 Topps Heritage Minors Real One Autographs Black

*BLACK: .75X TO 2X BASIC
STATED ODDS 1:89 HOBBY
PRINT RUNS B/WN 10-50 SER.#'d SETS
NO PRICING ON QTY 25 OR LESS
EXCHANGE DEADLINE 08/31/2015

2013 Topps Heritage Minors

SP ODDS 1:6 HOBBY
VAR SP ODDS 1:89 HOBBY
PRINTING PLATE ODDS 1:222 HOBBY
PLATE PRINT RUN 1 SET PER COLOR
BLACK-CYAN-MAGENTA-YELLOW ISSUED
NO PLATE PRICING DUE TO SCARCITY
1A Miguel Sano .25 .60
1B M.Sano Btg SP 8.00 20.00
2 Gorman Erickson .12 .30
3A David Dahl .25 .60
3B David Dahl VAR SP 6.00 15.00
4 J.R. Murphy .12 .30
5 Luis Heredia .25 .60
6 J.R. Graham .20 .50
7 Gus Schlosser .12 .30
8 Christian Vazquez .12 .30
9 Victor Sanchez .25 .60
10 Henry Owens .25 .60
11 Parker Bridwell .20 .50
12 Keury de la Cruz .20 .50
13 Kevin Plawecki .20 .50
14 Victor Roache .25 .60
15 Mitch Brown .20 .50
16 Austin Aune .25 .60
17 Taylor Dugas .25 .60
18 Rafael Montero .30 .75
19 Bobby Bundy .20 .50
20 Matt Davidson .25 .60
21 John Lamb .12 .30
22 Gary Brown .20 .50
23 Rougned Odor .50 1.25
24 Mike Freeman .12 .30
25 Greg Bird .25 .60
26 Delino DeShields .20 .50
27 Joe Wendle .12 .30
28 Mark Montgomery .30 .75
29 Kyle Smith .20 .50
30 Clayton Blackburn .30 .75
31 Stryker Trahan .20 .50
32 Ryan O'Sullivan .12 .30
33 Trevor Story .75 2.00
34 Chad Bettis .20 .50
35 Jesse Winker .12 .30
36 Archie Bradley .20 .50
37 Cody Anderson .25 .60
38 Jed Bradley .20 .50
39 Julio Rodriguez .12 .30
40 Mike Piazza .20 .50
41A Jonathan Schoop .20 .50
41B Schoop Blue bkgrnd SP 8.00 20.00
42 Stefen Romero .20 .50
43 Tyler Naquin .25 .60
44 Bryce Brentz .20 .50
45 Brandon Meredith .20 .50
46 Corey Oswalt .30 .75
47 Clay Schrader .20 .50
48 Jon Lucas .20 .50
49 Lee Orr .12 .30
50A Xander Bogaerts .60 1.50
50B X.Bogaerts Wht Jsy SP 20.00 50.00
51A Patrick Leonard .20 .50
51B Patrick Leonard VAR SP 6.00 15.00
52 Peter O'Brien .25 .60
53 Steve Bean .30 .75
54 Bryan Brickhouse .20 .50
55 Jimmy Nelson .20 .50
56 Arismendy Alcantara .30 .75
57 Miles Head .25 .60
58 Robert Stephenson .20 .50
59 Domingo Santana .30 .75
60 Cory Vaughn .20 .50
61 Daniel Corcino .20 .50
62 Joey Gallo .60 1.50
63A Raul Mondesi .60 1.50
63B Raul Mondesi VAR SP 6.00 15.00
64A Mason Williams .25 .60
64B Mason Williams VAR SP 6.00 15.00
65 Jake Thompson .20 .50
66 Jonathan Singleton .25 .60
67 Ethan Martin .20 .50
68 Tanner Rahier .25 .60
69 Gary Sanchez .60 1.50
70 Nick Martinez .12 .30
71 Adam Morgan .20 .50
72 Danny Salazar .40 1.00
73 Yordano Ventura .25 .60
74 Nick Castellanos .60 1.50
75A Tyler Austin .30 .75
75B Tyler Austin VAR SP 6.00 15.00
76 Dillon Howard .30 .75
77 Blake Perry .12 .30
78 Bruce Maxwell .12 .30
79A Jorge Soler .40 1.00
79B J.Soler Btg SP 10.00 25.00
80 Joe Panik .30 .75
81 Kyle Zimmer .25 .60
82 Eddie Butler .20 .50
83 Jorge Alfaro .40 1.00
84 Danry Vasquez .20 .50
85 Francisco Lindor 1.25 3.00
86 Edwin Carl .20 .50
87 Justin Nicolino .20 .50
88 Rio Ruiz .20 .50
89 James Ramsey .12 .30
90 Eduardo Rodriguez .60 1.50
91 Dilson Herrera .60 1.50
92 Matt Olson .30 .75
93 Taylor Guerrieri .20 .50
94 Brian Johnson .12 .30
95A Corey Seager .75 2.00
95B Corey Seager VAR SP 6.00 15.00
96 Tommy Joseph .40 1.00
97 Kyle Lotzkar .12 .30
98 Roberto Osuna .20 .50
99 Vance Albitz .30 .75
100A Byron Buxton .50 1.25
100B B.Buxton Grey Jsy SP 20.00 50.00
101 Lucas Giolito .30 .75
102 Jose Berrios .30 .75
103 Kyle Waldrop .12 .30
104 Hak-Ju Lee .20 .50
105 Erik Johnson .20 .50
106 Micah Johnson .25 .60
107 Andrew Susac .20 .50
108 Enny Romero .12 .30
109 Kyle Parker .20 .50
110 Eric Haase .20 .50
111 Wilmer Flores .25 .60
112 Adalberto Mejia .20 .50
113 Ronny Rodriguez .20 .50
114 Lewis Brinson .25 .60
115 Edward Salcedo .12 .30
116 Nick Travieso .25 .60
117 Sean Gilmartin .20 .50
118A Lance McCullers .20 .50
118B Lance McCullers VAR SP 6.00 15.00
119 Gavin Cecchini .25 .60
120 Max Kepler .40 1.00
121 Anthony Garcia .30 .75
122 Luis Merejo .20 .50
123 Xavier Scruggs .30 .75

124 Anthony Ranaudo .12 .30
125 Matthew Skole .25 .60
126 Nolan Fontana .25 .60
127A Jameson Taillon .25 .60
127B Jameson Taillon VAR SP 6.00 15.00
128 Matt Lipka .20 .50
129 Josh Bell .40 1.00
130 James Paxton .25 .60
131 Matt Barnes .25 .60
132 Ty Hensley .25 .60
133 Trevor May .12 .30
134 Dante Bichette .25 .60
135 David Holmberg .20 .50
136 C.J. Edwards .30 .75
137 Roman Quinn .30 .75
138 Rock Shoulders .20 .50
139 Noah Syndergaard .25 .60
140 Stephen Piscotty .40 1.00
141 Ross Stripling .20 .50
142 Matt Andriese .20 .50
143 Kevin Pillar .12 .30
144 Chad Smith .20 .50
145 Patrick Kivlehan .20 .50
146 Richie Shaffer .20 .50
147 Marcus Stroman .30 .75
148 Joe Ross .20 .50
149A Eddie Rosario .40 1.00
149B Eddie Rosario VAR SP 6.00 15.00
150A Carlos Correa 2.00 5.00
150B C.Correa Blk glvs SP 10.00 25.00
151 Corey Black .25 .60
152 Michael Fulmer .30 .75
153 Tyrone Taylor .20 .50
154 Gregory Polanco .40 1.00
155 Stetson Allie .30 .75
156 Cory Spangenberg 1.50 4.00
157 Kyle Crick .30 .75
158 Maikel Franco .30 .75
159 Nick Tropeano .20 .50
160A Javier Baez .75 2.00
160B J.Baez Look left SP 8.00 20.00
161 Eury Perez .25 .60
162 Mauricio Cabrera .20 .50
163 Nik Turley .20 .50
164 Zach Jones .12 .30
165 Barrett Barnes .20 .50
166 Cesar Hernandez .20 .50
167 Levi Michael .20 .50
168 Dorssys Paulino .25 .60
169 Garrett Gould .20 .50
170 Dillon Maples .12 .30
171 Brooks Pounders .12 .30
172 D.J. Davis .25 .60
173 Kaleb Cowart .25 .60
174 Nick Williams .25 .60
175 Joc Pederson .30 .75
176 Gioskar Amaya .20 .50
177 Jorge Bonifacio .25 .60
178 Mike O'Neill .20 .50
179 Michael Choice .20 .50
180 Jose Ramirez 1.50 4.00
181 Luis Mateo .25 .60
182 Rafael De Paula .20 .50
183 Jorge Polanco .20 .50
184 Clay Holmes .12 .30
185 Deven Marrero .20 .50
186 Angelo Gumbs .12 .30
187 Alen Hanson .25 .60
188 Lucas Sims .25 .60
189A Taijuan Walker .25 .60
189B Taijuan Walker VAR SP 6.00 15.00
190 Brett Bochy .20 .50
191 Robby Rowland .12 .30
192 Taylor Jungmann .20 .50
193 Brandon Nimmo .30 .75
194 Rymer Liriano .20 .50
195 Max Fried .75 2.00
196 Jesse Biddle .25 .60
197 Alex Meyer .20 .50
198A Kolten Wong .20 .50
198B Wong Bat off shlder SP 10.00 25.00
199 Cody Buckel .20 .50
200A Oscar Taveras .25 .60
200B O.Taveras Btg SP 12.50 30.00
201 Christian Yelich SP 8.00 20.00
202 C.J. Cron SP 2.50 6.00
203A Addison Russell SP 3.00 8.00
203B A.Russell Look left SP 8.00 20.00
204A Andrew Heaney SP 2.50 6.00
204B Andrew Heaney VAR SP 6.00 15.00
205 Adam Conley SP 2.00 5.00
206 A.J. Cole SP 2.50 6.00
207 Dan Vogelbach SP 3.00 8.00
208 Chris Stratton SP 2.00 5.00
209 Chris Owings SP 1.25 3.00
210A Albert Almora SP 4.00 10.00
210B Albert Almora VAR SP 6.00 15.00
211A Carlos Sanchez SP 2.00 5.00
211B Carlos Sanchez VAR SP 6.00 15.00
212 Chase Golden Thunder SP 3.00 8.00
213A Courtney Hawkins SP 2.00 5.00
213B Courtney Hawkins VAR SP 6.00 15.00
214 Christian Bethancourt SP 3.00 8.00
215 Chris Reed SP 2.00 5.00
216A Bubba Starling SP 2.50 6.00
216B B.Starling Btg SP 10.00 25.00
217 A.J. Jimenez SP 1.25 3.00
218 Clint Coulter SP 2.00 5.00
219 Brian Goodwin SP 2.50 6.00
220 Austin Hedges SP 2.50 6.00
221 Slade Heathcott SP 2.00 5.00
222 Aaron Sanchez SP 2.50 6.00
223 Andrew Aplin SP 2.00 5.00
224 Blake Swihart SP 2.50 6.00
225 George Springer SP 8.00 20.00

2013 Topps Heritage Minors Black

*BLACK 1-200: 4X TO 10X BASIC
*BLACK 201-225: .5X TO 1.2X BASIC
STATED ODDS 1:11 HOBBY
STATED PRINT RUN 96 SER.#'d SETS

2013 Topps Heritage Minors Venezuelan

*VENEZUELAN 1-200: 4X TO 10X BASIC
*VENEZUELAN 201-225: .5X TO 1.2X BASIC
STATED ODDS 1:24 HOBBY

2013 Topps Heritage Minors '64 Bazooka

COMPLETE SET (25) 15.00 40.00
STATED ODDS 1:6 HOBBY
AA Albert Almora 1.00 2.50
AM Alex Meyer .50 1.25
BB Byron Buxton 1.25 3.00
BS Bubba Starling .60 1.50
CB Cody Buckel .50 1.25
CC C.J. Cron .60 1.50
DS Domingo Santana .75 2.00
FL Francisco Lindor 3.00 8.00
GP Gregory Polanco 1.00 2.50
GS George Springer 2.00 5.00
GSA Gary Sanchez 1.50 4.00
HL Hak-Ju Lee .50 1.25
JB Javier Baez 2.00 5.00
JM Jake Marisnick .60 1.50
JP Joc Pederson .75 2.00
KC Kyle Crick .75 2.00
KW Kolten Wong .60 1.50
KZ Kyle Zimmer .60 1.50
MB Matt Barnes .60 1.50
MD Matt Davidson .60 1.50
MS Miguel Sano .60 1.50
MW Mason Williams .60 1.50
NC Nick Castellanos 1.50 4.00
TA Tyler Austin .75 2.00
XB Xander Bogaerts 1.50 4.00

2013 Topps Heritage Minors Clubhouse Collection Dual Relics

STATED PRINT RUN 25 SER.#'d SETS
EXCHANGE DEADLINE 9/30/2016
LM H.Lee/B.Miller 20.00 50.00
LP J.Pederson/R.Liriano 10.00 25.00
PB G.Brown/J.Panik 30.00 60.00
SS G.Springer/J.Singleton 10.00 25.00

2013 Topps Heritage Minors Clubhouse Collection Relics

STATED ODDS 1:30 HOBBY
EXCHANGE DEADLINE 9/30/2016
AM Alex Meyer 3.00 8.00
BB Bryce Brentz 4.00 10.00
BH Billy Hamilton 5.00 12.00
BM Brad Miller EXCH 3.00 8.00
CB Cody Buckel 3.00 8.00
CC Corey Dickerson 3.00 8.00
CO Chris Owings 3.00 8.00
CR Chris Reed 3.00 8.00
CS Cory Spangenberg 3.00 8.00
CSA Carlos Sanchez 3.00 8.00
ER Enny Romero 3.00 8.00
GB Gary Brown 3.00 8.00
GS George Springer 3.00 8.00
HJL Hak-Ju Lee 3.00 8.00
JG J.R. Graham 3.00 8.00
JM Jake Marisnick 3.00 8.00
JP Joe Panik 3.00 8.00
JPE Joc Pederson 3.00 8.00
JS Jonathan Singleton 3.00 8.00
MC Michael Choice 3.00 8.00
MD Matt Davidson 3.00 8.00
NF Nick Franklin 3.00 8.00
RL Rymer Liriano 3.00 8.00
WF Wilmer Flores 3.00 8.00
XB Xander Bogaerts 8.00 20.00

2013 Topps Heritage Minors Clubhouse Collection Relics Black

*BLACK: .6X TO 1.5X BASIC
STATED ODDS 1:177 HOBBY
STATED PRINT RUN 50 SER.#'d SETS
EXCHANGE DEADLINE 9/30/2016

2013 Topps Heritage Minors Manufactured Hat Logo

STATED ODDS 1:96 HOBBY
AH Alen Hanson 6.00 15.00
AM Raul Mondesi 8.00 20.00
BJ Brian Johnson 5.00 12.00
CB Clayton Blackburn 10.00 25.00
CC Carlos Correa 15.00 40.00
CS Corey Seager 8.00 20.00
DD David Dahl 5.00 12.00
DH Dilson Herrera 5.00 12.00
DP Dorssys Paulino 5.00 12.00
DS Domingo Santana 5.00 12.00
DV Danry Vasquez 5.00 12.00
EJ Erik Johnson 8.00 20.00
HO Henry Owens 6.00 15.00
JB Jed Bradley 8.00 20.00
JG Joey Gallo 6.00 15.00
JN Justin Nicolino 5.00 12.00
JS Jonathan Schoop 6.00 15.00
KP Kevin Plawecki 5.00 12.00
KW Kolten Wong 6.00 15.00
LH Luis Heredia 8.00 20.00
MF Max Fried 5.00 12.00
MH Miles Head 6.00 15.00
MJ Micah Johnson 5.00 12.00
MM Mark Montgomery 6.00 15.00
MO Matt Olson 5.00 12.00
MS Matthew Skole 8.00 20.00
NS Noah Syndergaard 6.00 15.00
RM Rafael Montero 8.00 20.00
RO Roberto Osuna 8.00 20.00
RQ Roman Quinn 5.00 12.00
RR Ronny Rodriguez 6.00 15.00
RS Rock Shoulders 10.00 25.00
TD Tyler Dugas 5.00 12.00
TG Taylor Guerrieri 5.00 12.00
TM Trevor May 6.00 15.00
TN Tyler Naquin 8.00 20.00
TS Trevor Story 6.00 15.00
TT Tyrone Taylor 8.00 20.00
VS Victor Sanchez 5.00 12.00
AHE Austin Hedges 6.00 15.00
AMO Adam Morgan 8.00 20.00
CBE Christian Bethancourt 8.00 20.00
CCR C.J. Cron 5.00 12.00
DDA D.J. Davis 8.00 20.00
DHO David Holmberg 5.00 12.00
JBE Jose Berrios 8.00 20.00
JBO Jorge Bonifacio 6.00 15.00
JSO Jorge Soler 8.00 20.00
MST Marcus Stroman 10.00 25.00
RSC Richie Shaffer 8.00 20.00

2013 Topps Heritage Minors Real One Autographs

STATED ODDS 1:14 HOBBY
PRINTING PLATE ODDS 1:3705 HOBBY
PLATE PRINT RUN 1 SET PER COLOR
BLACK-CYAN-MAGENTA-YELLOW ISSUED
NO PLATE PRICING DUE TO SCARCITY
EXCHANGE DEADLINE 9/30/2016
AG Anthony Garcia 3.00 8.00
AGU Angelo Gumbs 3.00 8.00
AM Adalberto Mejia 3.00 8.00
BB Bobby Bundy 3.00 8.00
BBO Brett Bochy 3.00 8.00
BBU Byron Buxton 90.00 150.00
BM Brandon Meredith 3.00 8.00
BMA Bruce Maxwell 3.00 8.00
BP Brooks Pounders 3.00 8.00
CB Chad Bettis 3.00 8.00
CO Corey Oswalt 3.00 8.00
CS Clay Schrader 3.00 8.00
CV Christian Vazquez 10.00 25.00
DS Danny Salazar 5.00 12.00
GE Gorman Erickson 3.00 8.00
JR Jose Ramirez 25.00 60.00
JW Joe Wendle 3.00 8.00
MA Matt Andriese 3.00 8.00
MF Mike Freeman 3.00 8.00
MK Max Kepler 12.00 30.00
ML Matt Lipka 3.00 8.00
MON Mike O'Neill 3.00 8.00
NM Nick Martinez 3.00 8.00
PB Parker Bridwell 3.00 8.00
ROS Ryan O'Sullivan 3.00 8.00
RS Ross Stripling 3.00 8.00

2013 Topps Heritage Minors Real One Autographs Black

*BLACK: .75X TO 2X BASIC
STATED ODDS 1:8447 HOBBY
STATED PRINT RUN 50 SER.#'d SETS
EXCHANGE DEADLINE 09/30/2016

2013 Topps Heritage Minors Road to the Show

STATED ODDS 1:4 HOBBY
AA Albert Almora 1.00 2.50
AB Archie Bradley .50 1.25
AH Alen Hanson .60 1.50
AHD Austin Hedges .60 1.50
AHE Andrew Heaney .60 1.50
AM Raul Mondesi 1.50 4.00
AR Addison Russell .75 2.00
AS Aaron Sanchez .60 1.50
BB Byron Buxton 1.25 3.00
BS Bubba Starling .60 1.50
CB Clayton Blackburn .75 2.00
CC Carlos Correa 5.00 12.00
CCR C.J. Cron .60 1.50
CH Courtney Hawkins .50 1.25
CS Corey Seager 2.00 5.00
CST Chris Stratton .50 1.25
DD David Dahl .60 1.50
DDA D.J. Davis .60 1.50
DP Dorssys Paulino .60 1.50
DS Danny Salazar 1.00 2.50
FL Francisco Lindor 3.00 8.00
GS Gary Sanchez 1.50 4.00
JB Jose Berrios .75 2.00
JBA Javier Baez 2.00 5.00
JBI Jesse Biddle .60 1.50
JG Joey Gallo 1.50 4.00
JN Justin Nicolino .50 1.25
JP Joe Panik .75 2.00
JS Jorge Soler 1.00 2.50
KC Kyle Crick .75 2.00
KW Kolten Wong .50 1.25
KZ Kyle Zimmer .60 1.50
LB Lewis Brinson .60 1.50
LH Luis Heredia .60 1.50
LM Lance McCullers .50 1.25
LS Lucas Sims .60 1.50
MF Max Fried 2.00 5.00
MS Miguel Sano .60 1.50
MWI Mason Williams .60 1.50
NS Noah Syndergaard .60 1.50
RQ Roman Quinn .75 2.00
RR Rio Ruiz .50 1.25
RS Robert Stephenson .50 1.25
SH Slade Heathcott .50 1.25
TA Tyler Austin .75 2.00
TG Taylor Guerrieri .50 1.25
TN Tyler Naquin .60 1.50
TW Taijuan Walker .60 1.50
VR Victor Roache .60 1.50
VS Victor Sanchez .60 1.50

2014 Topps Heritage Minors

COMP.SET w/ SPs (250) 50.00 120.00
COMP.SET w/o SP VAR (225) 20.00 50.00
SP RANDOMLY INSERTED
VAR SP RANDOMLY INSERTED
PRINTING PLATES RANDOMLY INSERTED
PLATE PRINT RUN 1 SET PER COLOR
BLACK-CYAN-MAGENTA-YELLOW ISSUED
NO PLATE PRICING DUE TO SCARCITY
1A Carlos Correa .60 1.50
1B C.Correa w/ball SP 10.00 25.00
2 Nick Ahmed .12 .30
3 Andrew Susac .15 .40
4 Dalton Pompey .20 .50
5 Stryker Trahan .12 .30
6 Lucas Giolito .20 .50
7 Yeison Asencio .12 .30
8 Alen Hanson .12 .30
9A Gary Sanchez .40 1.00
9B Snchz Blue gear SP 20.00 50.00
10A Byron Buxton .15 .40
10B B.Buxton w/glv SP 12.00 30.00
11 Trevor Story .50 1.25
12 David Dahl .15 .40
13 Cam Bedrosian .12 .30
14 Tyler Austin .12 .30
15 Daniel Corcino .15 .40
16 Kyle Crick .12 .30
17 Zach Lee .12 .30
18 Max Fried .50 1.25
19 Matt Wisler .12 .30
20A Miguel Sano .15 .40
20B M.Sano Bunting SP 8.00 20.00
21 Clayton Blackburn .20 .50
22 Corey Seager .50 1.25
23 Raul Mondesi .40 1.00
24 Roberto Osuna .12 .30
25 Luis Heredia .12 .30
26 Kohl Stewart .12 .30
27 Mike Foltynewicz .12 .30
28 Edwin Escobar .12 .30
29 Lucas Sims .12 .30
30A Kris Bryant 8.00 20.00
30B Bryant Grn bckgrnd SP 20.00 50.00
31 D.J. Peterson .12 .30
32 Nick Kingham .15 .40
33 Braden Shipley .12 .30
34 Joey Gallo .25 .60
35 Chris Stratton .12 .30
36A Javier Baez .50 1.25
36B J.Baez Portrait SP 10.00 25.00
37 Nick Delmonico .12 .30
38 Reese McGuire .12 .30
39 Courtney Hawkins .12 .30
40 Francisco Lindor .75 2.00
41 Josh Bell .25 .60
42 Brian Goodwin .12 .30
43 Christian Binford .12 .30
44 Jesus Galindo .12 .30
45 Nick Travieso .12 .30
46 Tommy La Stella .12 .30
47 Michael Fulmer .20 .50
48 Jorge Bonifacio .12 .30
49 Victor Roache .12 .30
50 Archie Bradley .12 .30
51 Pierce Johnson .15 .40
52 Blake Swihart .15 .40
53 Trevor Williams .12 .30
54 Avery Romero .12 .30
55A Julio Urias .60 1.50
55B J.Urias Leg up SP 12.00 30.00
56 Amed Rosario .20 .50
57A Lance McCullers .12 .30
57B L.McCul Facing right SP 6.00 15.00
58 Daniel Norris .15 .40
59 Brandon Nimmo .25 .60
60 Christian Walker .25 .60
61 Tim Anderson .25 .60
62 Lewis Brinson .20 .50
63 Dan Vogelbach .20 .50
64 Mitch Haniger .20 .50
65 Richie Shaffer .20 .50
66 Luis Mateo .15 .40
67 Jake Thompson .12 .30
68 Jorge Polanco .12 .30
69 Breyvic Valera .12 .30
70 Mark Appel .15 .40
71 Daniel Robertson .15 .40
72 Carson Kelly .20 .50
73 Matt Olson .20 .50
74 Domingo Santana .20 .50
75 Sam Selman .12 .30
76 Jesmuel Valentin .12 .30
77 Walker Weickel .12 .30
78 Patrick Wisdom .12 .30
79 Angelo Gumbs .12 .30
80A Albert Almora .20 .50
80B Almora Batting SP 8.00 20.00
81 Jose Rondon .12 .30
82 Adam Walker .12 .30
83 Clint Coulter .12 .30
84 Gabriel Guerrero .12 .30
85 Jairo Beras .12 .30
86 Kevin Plawecki .12 .30
87 Mason Melotakis .12 .30
88A Jose Berrios .20 .50
88B J.Berrios Leg up SP 10.00 25.00
89 Jesse Winker .15 .40
90A Clint Frazier .50 1.25
90B Frazier Bttng helmet SP 10.00 25.00
91 Josh Hader .30 .75
92 Austin Wilson .12 .30
93 Kyle Parker .15 .40
94 Rio Ruiz .12 .30
95 Renato Nunez .25 .60
96 Blake Snell .15 .40
97 Dante Bichette Jr. .15 .40
98 Jeff Ames .12 .30
99 Kean Wong .12 .30
100A Austin Meadows .20 .50
100B Meadows No bat SP 10.00 25.00
101 Mitch Gueller .12 .30
102 Luke Jackson .12 .30
103 J.P. Crawford .12 .30
104 Hunter Renfroe .15 .40
105 David Goforth .12 .30
106 Trevor May .12 .30
107 Dominic Smith .12 .30
108A Trey Ball .12 .30
108B T.Ball Facing right SP 6.00 15.00
109A A.J. Cole .12 .30
109B A.Cole Red jersey SP 6.00 15.00
110A Oscar Taveras .15 .40
110B O.Taveras No bat SP 15.00 40.00
111 Hunter Harvey .12 .30
112A Bubba Starling .15 .40
112B B.Starling w/glv SP 12.00 30.00
113 Nick Williams .15 .40
114 Mason Williams .12 .30
115 Gavin Cecchini .12 .30
116 Garin Cecchini .12 .30
117 Phil Ervin .12 .30
118 Dorssys Paulino .12 .30
119 Joe Panik .20 .50
120 Jonathan Singleton .12 .30
121 Alberto Tirado .15 .40
122 Billy McKinney .15 .40
123A Hunter Dozier .12 .30
123B H.Dozier w/bat SP 8.00 20.00
124 Jose Peraza .12 .30
125 Jason Hursh .12 .30
126 Vincent Velasquez .20 .50
127 Chris Anderson .12 .30
128 Alex Gonzalez .12 .30
129 Christian Arroyo .75 2.00
130A Alex Meyer .12 .30
130B A.Meyer w/ball SP 6.00 15.00
131 Eric Jagielo .12 .30
132 Rob Kaminsky .12 .30
133 Travis Demeritte .15 .40
134 Manny Ramirez .20 .50
135 Andrew Thurman .12 .30
136 Justin Williams .15 .40
137 Teddy Stankiewicz .12 .30
138 Cody Reed .12 .30
139 Gosuke Katoh .20 .50
140A Andrew Heaney .12 .30
140B Heaney Wall bckgrnd SP 6.00 15.00
141 Oscar Mercado .20 .50
142 Devin Williams .30 .75
143 Ryan McMahon .12 .30
144 Akeem Bostick .12 .30
145 Isiah Kiner-Falefa .20 .50
146 Andrew Knapp .12 .30
147 Tom Windle .12 .30
148 Tyler Danish .12 .30
149 Mikie Mahtook .12 .30
150A Henry Owens .15 .40
150B Owens Glv at chest SP 8.00 20.00
151 Chris Beck .12 .30
152 Christian Villanueva .12 .30
153 Keenyn Walker .12 .30
154 Mark Lamm .12 .30
155 Phil Wetherell .12 .30
156 Dylan Unsworth .12 .30
157 Kenny Wilson .12 .30
158 Jamie Westbrook .12 .30
159 Robert Hefflinger .12 .30
160A Joc Pederson .20 .50
160B J.Pederson w/bat SP 8.00 20.00
161 Levon Washington .12 .30
162 Tommy Murphy .12 .30
163 Michael Feliz .15 .40
164 Rangel Ravelo .12 .30
165 Wyatt Mathisen .12 .30
166 Tim Cooney .25 .60
167 Alex Reyes .20 .50
168 Michael Taylor .15 .40
169 Logan Vick .12 .30
170 Eddie Butler .12 .30
171 Brett Phillips .15 .40
172 Delta Cleary .12 .30
173 Jonathan Reynoso .12 .30
174 Greg Bird .15 .40
175 Aaron Judge 12.00 30.00
176 Rob Whalen .20 .50
177 Mac Williamson .15 .40
178 Thomas Coyle .12 .30
179 Tyler Naquin .15 .40
180 Jameson Taillon .12 .30
181 Shawn Pleffner .12 .30
182 Kyle Waldrop .12 .30
183 Peter O'Brien .15 .40
184 Sam Moll .12 .30
185 Dane Phillips .12 .30
186 Cory Spangenberg .12 .30
187 Tanner Rahier .12 .30
188 Dilson Herrera .20 .50
189 Orlando Arcia .20 .50
190A C.J. Edwards .15 .40
190B Edwards Gray jersey SP 8.00 20.00
191 Anthony Ranaudo .12 .30
192 Austin Hedges .12 .30
193A Jesse Biddle .15 .40
193B Biddle Tossing ball SP 10.00 25.00
194 Delino DeShields .12 .30
195 Eduardo Rodriguez .15 .40
196 Justin Nicolino .12 .30
197 Preston Tucker .20 .50
198 Matt Barnes .12 .30
199A Arismendy Alcantara .12 .30
199B Alcantara White jersey SP 8.00 20.00
200 Eddie Rosario .25 .60
201 Stephen Piscotty SP 1.25 3.00
202 Miguel Almonte SP 1.00 2.50
203 Jeremy Barfield SP 1.00 2.50
204 Brandon Drury SP 1.00 2.50
205 Marco Gonzales SP 1.50 4.00
206 Micah Johnson SP 1.00 2.50
207 Patrick Kivlehan SP 1.00 2.50
208 Taylor Lindsey SP 1.00 2.50
209 Manuel Margot SP 1.50 4.00
210 James Ramsey SP 1.00 2.50
211 Sean Manaea SP 1.00 2.50
212 Maikel Franco SP 1.25 3.00
213 Jorge Soler SP 2.00 5.00
214 Jorge Alfaro SP 1.25 3.00
215A Tyler Glasnow SP 1.50 4.00
215B J.Alfaro w/ bat SP 8.00 20.00
216 Addison Russell SP 1.50 4.00
217 Mookie Betts SP 50.00 120.00
218 Jonathan Gray SP 1.25 3.00
219 Gregory Polanco SP 1.50 4.00
220 Aaron Sanchez SP 1.00 2.50
221 Colin Moran SP 1.00 2.50
222 Ben Lively SP 1.00 2.50
223 Kyle Zimmer SP 1.00 2.50
224 Robert Stephenson SP 1.00 2.50
225 Noah Syndergaard SP 1.25 3.00

2014 Topps Heritage Minors Black

*BLACK 1-200: 5X TO 12X BASIC
*BLACK 201-225: .6X TO 1.5X BASIC
RANDOM INSERTS IN PACKS
STATED PRINT RUN 105 SER.#'d SETS
30 Kris Bryant 12.00 30.00
175 Aaron Judge 60.00 150.00

2014 Topps Heritage Minors Lime Green

*GREEN 1-200: 4X TO 10X BASIC
*GREEN 201-225: .5X TO 1.2X BASIC
RANDOM INSERTS IN PACKS
30 Kris Bryant 10.00 25.00
175 Aaron Judge 50.00 120.00

2014 Topps Heritage Minors Clubhouse Collection Patches

RANDOM INSERTS IN PACKS
STATED PRINT RUN 15 SER.#'d SETS
CCPAA Albert Almora 12.00 30.00
CCPAH Austin Hedges 8.00 20.00
CCPAHE Andrew Heaney 8.00 20.00
CCPAM Alex Meyer 8.00 20.00
CCPAR Addison Russell 12.00 30.00
CCPARA Anthony Ranaudo 8.00 20.00
CCPBG Brian Goodwin 8.00 20.00
CCPBN Brandon Nimmo 12.00 30.00
CCPCM Colin Moran 8.00 20.00
CCPFL Francisco Lindor 50.00 125.00
CCPKB Kris Bryant 30.00 80.00
CCPKC Kyle Crick 8.00 20.00
CCPYA Yeison Asencio 8.00 20.00

2014 Topps Heritage Minors Clubhouse Collection Relics

RANDOM INSERTS IN PACKS
*BLACK: .6X TO 1.5X BASIC
BLACK RANDOMLY INSERTED
BLACK PRINT RUN 99 SER.#'d SETS
CCRAA Albert Almora 3.00 8.00
CCRAH Austin Hedges 2.00 5.00
CCRAHE Andrew Heaney 2.00 5.00
CCRAM Alex Meyer 2.00 5.00
CCRAR Addison Russell 3.00 8.00
CCRBG Brian Goodwin 2.00 5.00
CCRBN Brandon Nimmo 3.00 8.00
CCRCM Colin Moran 2.00 5.00
CCRCS Corey Seager 8.00 20.00
CCRCW Christian Walker 4.00 10.00
CCRFL Francisco Lindor 12.00 30.00
CCRJS Jorge Soler 4.00 10.00
CCRKB Kris Bryant 12.00 30.00
CCRKC Kyle Crick 2.00 5.00
CCRYA Yeison Asencio 2.00 5.00

2014 Topps Heritage Minors Flashbacks

COMPLETE SET (20) 8.00 20.00
RANDOM INSERTS IN PACKS
FBAA Albert Almora .50 1.25
FBAR Addison Russell .50 1.25
FBBB Byron Buxton .40 1.00
FBCE C.J. Edwards .40 1.00
FBER Eddie Rosario .60 1.50
FBHO Henry Owens .40 1.00
FBJA Jorge Alfaro .40 1.00
FBJB Jesse Biddle .40 1.00
FBJG Joey Gallo .60 1.50
FBJS Jorge Soler .60 1.50
FBJU Julio Urias 1.50 4.00
FBKC Kyle Crick .30 .75
FBKZ Kyle Zimmer .30 .75
FBMB Mookie Betts 6.00 15.00
FBMF Maikel Franco .40 1.00
FBMFR Max Fried 1.25 3.00
FBRH Rosell Herrera .50 1.25
FBRM Raul Mondesi 1.00 2.50
FBRS Robert Stephenson .30 .75
FBTG Tyler Glasnow .50 1.25

2014 Topps Heritage Minors Make Your Pro Debut

RANDOM INSERTS IN PACKS
PDAS Alan Strout 2.00 5.00

2014 Topps Heritage Minors Manufactured Cap Logo

RANDOM INSERTS IN PACKS
MPAC A.J. Cole 5.00 12.00
MPAH Austin Hedges 5.00 12.00
MPAHE Andrew Heaney 5.00 12.00
MPAM Austin Meadows 6.00 15.00
MPAR Anthony Ranaudo 5.00 12.00
MPARU Addison Russell 10.00 25.00
MPAS Andrew Susac 6.00 15.00
MPAW Austin Wilson 5.00 12.00
MPBB Byron Buxton 10.00 25.00
MPBD Brandon Drury 5.00 12.00
MPBL Ben Lively 5.00 12.00
MPBN Brandon Nimmo 8.00 20.00
MPBS Braden Shipley 5.00 12.00
MPCC Carlos Correa 8.00 20.00
MPCF Clint Frazier 8.00 20.00
MPCK Carson Kelly 8.00 20.00
MPCR Cody Reed 5.00 12.00
MPCS Corey Seager 8.00 20.00
MPDD David Dahl 6.00 15.00
MPEB Eddie Butler 5.00 12.00
MPEJ Eric Jagielo 10.00 25.00
MPFL Francisco Lindor 30.00 80.00
MPGP Gregory Polanco 8.00 20.00
MPGS Gary Sanchez 15.00 40.00
MPHH Hunter Harvey 5.00 12.00
MPHO Henry Owens 6.00 15.00
MPHR Hunter Renfroe 6.00 15.00
MPJA Jorge Alfaro 6.00 15.00
MPJB Jorge Bonifacio 5.00 12.00
MPJBA Javier Baez 8.00 20.00
MPJC J.P. Crawford 5.00 12.00
MPJP Joc Pederson 8.00 20.00
MPJR James Ramsey 5.00 12.00
MPKB Kris Bryant 12.00 30.00
MPKS Kohl Stewart 5.00 12.00
MPLG Lucas Giolito 10.00 25.00
MPLH Luis Heredia 5.00 12.00
MPMA Miguel Almonte 5.00 12.00
MPMG Marco Gonzales 8.00 20.00
MPMJ Micah Johnson 5.00 12.00
MPMM Manuel Margot 6.00 15.00
MPMS Miguel Sano 6.00 15.00
MPNA Nick Ahmed 5.00 12.00
MPNK Nick Kingham 6.00 15.00
MPOT Oscar Taveras 10.00 25.00
MPPE Phil Ervin 5.00 12.00
MPTA Tim Anderson 10.00 25.00
MPTD Tyler Danish 5.00 12.00
MPTDE Travis Demeritte 6.00 15.00
MPTS Trevor Story 20.00 50.00

2014 Topps Heritage Minors Mystery Redemptions

EXCHANGE DEADLINE 9/30/2017
MR1 Tyler Kolek 15.00 40.00
MR2 Kyle Schwarber 30.00 80.00

2014 Topps Heritage Minors Real One Autographs

RANDOM INSERTS IN PACKS
EXCHANGE DEADLINE 9/30/2017
PRINTING PLATES RANDOMLY INSERTED
PLATE PRINT RUN 1 SET PER COLOR
BLACK-CYAN-MAGENTA-YELLOW ISSUED
NO PLATE PRICING DUE TO SCARCITY
ROAAR Alex Reyes 4.00 10.00
ROABL Ben Lively 2.50 6.00
ROABP Brett Phillips 3.00 8.00
ROACF Clint Frazier 12.00 30.00
ROADP Dalton Pompey 4.00 10.00
ROADU Dylan Unsworth 2.50 6.00
ROAGP Gregory Polanco 12.00 30.00
ROAIK Isiah Kiner-Falefa 4.00 10.00
ROAJB Jorge Bonifacio 2.50 6.00
ROAJW Jamie Westbrook 2.50 6.00
ROAKW Kenny Wilson 2.50 6.00
ROALV Logan Vick 2.50 6.00
ROALW LeVon Washington 2.50 6.00
ROAMF Michael Feliz 3.00 8.00
ROAMG Mitch Gueller 2.50 6.00
ROAML Mark Lamm 2.50 6.00
ROAMM Mikie Morin 2.50 6.00
ROAMT Michael Taylor 3.00 8.00
ROAPW Phil Wetherell 2.50 6.00
ROARH Robert Hefflinger 2.50 6.00
ROARR Rangel Ravelo 2.50 6.00
ROARW Rob Whalen 2.50 6.00
ROASP Shawn Pleffner 2.50 6.00
ROATC Tim Cooney 2.50 6.00
ROATM Tommy Murphy 2.50 6.00
ROAWM Wyatt Mathisen 2.50 6.00

2014 Topps Heritage Minors Real One Autographs Black

*BLACK: .75X TO 2X BASIC
RANDOM INSERTS IN PACKS
STATED PRINT RUN 35 SER.#'d SETS
EXCHANGE DEADLINE 9/30/2017

2014 Topps Heritage Minors Real One Autographs Dual

RANDOM INSERTS IN PACKS
STATED PRINT RUN 15 SER.#'d SETS
EXCHANGE DEADLINE 9/30/2017
PRINTING PLATES RANDOMLY INSERTED
PLATE PRINT RUN 1 SET PER COLOR
BLACK-CYAN-MAGENTA-YELLOW ISSUED
NO PLATE PRICING DUE TO SCARCITY
RDOABD H.Dozier/J.Bonifacio 15.00 40.00
RDOACR A.Reyes/T.Cooney 25.00 60.00
RDOACW P.Wisdom/T.Cooney 15.00 40.00
RDOADH C.Hawkins/T.Danish 15.00 40.00
RDOAFM C.Frazier/A.Meadows 40.00 100.00
RDOAGT M.Taylor/L.Giolito 25.00 60.00
RDOALH R.Hefflinger/M.Lamm 15.00 40.00
RDOAMM T.Murphy/W.Mathisen 15.00 40.00
RDOAMW T.Williams/C.Moran 15.00 40.00
RDOAPS D.Phillips/C.Spangenberg 15.00 40.00

2014 Topps Heritage Minors Road to the Show

COMPLETE SET (50) 20.00 50.00
RANDOM INSERTS IN PACKS
RTTSAW Adam Walker .40 1.00
RTTSBL Ben Lively .40 1.00
RTTSBP Brett Phillips .50 1.25
RTTSBS Blake Snell .50 1.25
RTTSCB Chris Beck .40 1.00
RTTSCC Clint Coulter .40 1.00
RTTSCH Courtney Hawkins .40 1.00
RTTSCK Carson Kelly .60 1.50
RTTSCS Corey Seager 1.50 4.00
RTTSDP D.J. Peterson .40 1.00
RTTSDS Dominic Smith .40 1.00
RTTSEJ Eric Jagielo .40 1.00
RTTSGC Gavin Cecchini .40 1.00
RTTSHD Hunter Dozier .40 1.00
RTTSHH Hunter Harvey .40 1.00
RTTSHR Hunter Renfroe .50 1.25
RTTSJG Jonathan Gray .50 1.25
RTTSJR Jose Rondon .40 1.00
RTTSJT Jake Thompson .40 1.00
RTTSJV Jesmuel Valentin .40 1.00
RTTSJW Jesse Winker .50 1.25
RTTSKS Kohl Stewart .40 1.00
RTTSLG Lucas Giolito .60 1.50
RTTSLH Luis Heredia .40 1.00
RTTSLJ Luke Jackson .40 1.00
RTTSLM Luis Mateo .50 1.25
RTTSLV Logan Vick .40 1.00
RTTSLW Levon Washington .40 1.00
RTTSMF Michael Fulmer .60 1.50
RTTSMH Mitch Haniger .60 1.50
RTTSMM Mikie Mahtook .40 1.00
RTTSND Nick Delmonico .40 1.00
RTTSNW Nick Williams .50 1.25
RTTSPW Phil Wetherell .40 1.00
RTTSRM Raul Mondesi 1.25 3.00
RTTSRO Roberto Osuna .40 1.00
RTTSRS Richie Shaffer .40 1.00
RTTSSS Sam Selman .40 1.00
RTTSST Stryker Trahan .40 1.00
RTTSTC Thomas Coyle .40 1.00
RTTSTM Tommy Murphy .40 1.00
RTTSTS Trevor Story 1.50 4.00
RTTSWM Wyatt Mathisen .40 1.00
RTTSBST Bubba Starling .50 1.25
RTTSCBI Christian Binford .40 1.00
RTTSCST Chris Stratton .40 1.00
RTTSDPA Dorssys Paulino .40 1.00
RTTSJWI Justin Williams .50 1.25
RTTSMAP Mark Appel .50 1.25
RTTSRMC Reese McGuire .40 1.00

2015 Topps Heritage Minors

COMPLETE SET (225) 50.00 120.00
COMP.SET w/ SPs (200) 20.00 50.00
STATED SP ODDS 1:6 HOBBY
STATED PLATE ODDS 1:214 HOBBY
STATED LL PLATE ODDS 1:3927 HOBBY
PLATE PRINT RUN 1 SET PER COLOR
BLACK-CYAN-MAGENTA-YELLOW ISSUED
NO PLATE PRICING DUE TO SCARCITY
1 Julio Urias .40 1.00
2 Rob Kaminsky .12 .30
3 Reese McGuire .12 .30
4 Ozhaino Albies 1.25 3.00
5 Nick Kingham .12 .30
6 Tony Kemp .12 .30
7 Kyle Zimmer .12 .30
8 Alex Reyes .15 .40
9 Jose De Leon .20 .50
10 Sean Reid-Foley .15 .40
11 Max White .12 .30
12 Austin Voth .12 .30
13 Jordan Betts .12 .30
14 Lucas Sims .12 .30
15 Daniel Alvarez .12 .30
16 Luis Ortiz .12 .30
17 Jacob Dahlstrand .12 .30
18 Drew Dosch .12 .30
19 Jace Fry .12 .30
20 Carlos Asuaje .12 .30
21 Robert Refsnyder .15 .40
22 Cole Tucker .12 .30
23 Sean Manaea .20 .50
24 Steven Matz .20 .50
25 Nick Gordon .15 .40
26 Ty Blach .12 .30
27 Nick Ciuffo .12 .30
28 Austin Wilson .12 .30
29 Wes Parsons .12 .30
30 Tyrell Jenkins .15 .40
31 Austin Dean .12 .30
32 Tayron Guerrero .12 .30
33 Manuel Margot .12 .30
34 Hunter Dozier .12 .30
35 Monte Harrison .20 .50
36 Spencer Turnbull .12 .30
37 Billy McKinney .15 .40
38 Derek Fisher .15 .40
39 Chase Vallot .12 .30
40 Ryan Merritt .12 .30
41 Albert Almora .15 .40
42 Frankie Montas .15 .40
43 Dominic Smith .12 .30
44 Brian Anderson .12 .30
45 Zech Lemond .12 .30
46 Michael Conforto .15 .40
47 Brett Graves .12 .30
48 Keury Mella .12 .30
49 Jorge Mateo .40 1.00

50 Lucas Giolito .25 .60
51 Jake Reed .12 .30
52 Greg Bird .15 .40
53 Dustin DeMuth .12 .30
54 James Dykstra .12 .30
55 Touki Toussaint .15 .40
56 Derek Hill .15 .40
57 Jake Gatewood .12 .30
58 Clint Coulter .12 .30
59 Natanael Delgado .12 .30
60 Jorge Lopez .12 .30
61 Amed Rosario .20 .50
62 Courtney Hawkins .12 .30
63 Duane Underwood Jr. .12 .30
64 Brent Honeywell .20 .50
65 Sean Newcomb .15 .40
66 J.D. Davis .20 .50
67 Erich Weiss .12 .30
68 Buddy Borden .12 .30
69 Trevor Gott .12 .30
70 Adam Walker .12 .30
71 Tyrone Taylor .12 .30
72 Alex Meyer .12 .30
73 Grant Hockin .12 .30
74 Chance Sisco .25 .60
75 Joe Gatto .12 .30
76 Forrest Wall .12 .30
77 Rowdy Tellez .20 .50
78 Alen Hanson .12 .30
79 Deven Marrero .12 .30
80 Danny Burawa .12 .30
81 Rio Ruiz .12 .30
82 Renato Nunez .25 .60
83 Daniel Robertson .12 .30
84 Braxton Davidson .12 .30
85 Nick Howard .20 .50
86 Jameson Taillon .15 .40
87 Andrew Velazquez .12 .30
88 Sam Travis .25 .60
89 Magneuris Sierra .20 .50
90 Colin Moran .12 .30
91 Dan Vogelbach .20 .50
92 Ricardo Sanchez .12 .30
93 Alex Blandino .12 .30
94 Trey Michalczewski .12 .30
95 Franklin Barreto .15 .40
96 Grant Holmes .15 .40
97 Domingo Leyba .12 .30
98 Drew Ward .12 .30
99 Daniel Carbonell .12 .30
100 Kyle Schwarber .50 1.25
101 Teoscar Hernandez .40 1.00
102 Kyle Waldrop .12 .30
103 Mallex Smith .20 .50
104 Austin Kubitza .12 .30
105 Blake Snell .15 .40
106 Tyler Naquin .15 .40
107 Jack Flaherty .20 .50
108 Daniel Mengden .12 .30
109 Roman Quinn .20 .50
110 Jon Gray .12 .30
111 Mitch Haniger .12 .30
112 Gleyber Torres 4.00 10.00
113 Chad Pinder .15 .40
114 Clint Frazier .50 1.25
115 Tim Anderson .25 .60
116 Amir Garrett .12 .30
117 Avery Romero .12 .30
118 Jordan Luplow .12 .30
119 Michael Gettys .15 .40
120 Luke Jackson .12 .30
121 Raimel Tapia .20 .50
122 Trey Supak .12 .30
123 Jordy Lara .12 .30
124 Tyler Danish .12 .30
125 B.J. Boyd .12 .30
126 David Dahl .15 .40
127 D.J. Peterson .12 .30
128 Michael Chavis .30 .75
129 Jake Thompson .12 .30
130 Kyle Crick .15 .40
131 Jake Cave .12 .30
132 Lewis Thorpe .12 .30
133 Bobby Bradley .15 .40
134 Seth Mejias-Brean .12 .30
135 Rafael Devers .75 2.00
136 Willy Adames .20 .50
137 Justin Nicolino .12 .30
138 Marcos Molina .12 .30
139 Alec Grosser .12 .30
140 Alex Verdugo .20 .50
141 Foster Griffin .12 .30
142 Brandon Nimmo .20 .50
143 Travis Demeritte .15 .40
144 Brian Johnson .12 .30
145 Carson Sands .12 .30
146 Nick Wells .12 .30
147 Brett Phillips .12 .30
148 Lewis Brinson .20 .50
149 Gary Sanchez .40 1.00
150 Luis Severino .15 .40
151 Nick Burdi .12 .30
152 Kyle Freeland .15 .40
153 Jorge Polanco .12 .30
154 Matt Wisler .12 .30
155 Sam Howard .12 .30
156 Aaron Blair .12 .30
157 Peter O'Brien .20 .50
158 Brandon Drury .12 .30
159 Alberto Tirado .12 .30
160 Tim Berry .12 .30
161 Juan Herrera .12 .30
162 Miguel Almonte .12 .30
163 James Ramsey .12 .30
164 Raul Mondesi .15 .40
165 Ryan McMahon .12 .30
166 Erik Gonzalez .12 .30
167 Ben Lively .12 .30
168 Harold Ramirez .15 .40
169 Spencer Kieboom .12 .30
170 Mark Zagunis .12 .30
171 Justin O'Conner .12 .30
172 Jen-Ho Tseng .12 .30
173 Michael Kopech .30 .75
174 Bradley Zimmer .20 .50
175 Nick Williams .15 .40
176 Nick Travieso .12 .30
177 Parker Bridwell .12 .30
178 Kodi Medeiros .12 .30
179 Jesse Winker .12 .30
180 Max Pentecost .12 .30
181 Orlando Arcia .15 .40
182 Eric Haase .12 .30
183 Stephen Piscotty .15 .40
184 Logan Moon .12 .30
185 Joe Sclafani .12 .30
186 Chris Ellis .12 .30
187 Joey Curletta .15 .40
188 Pierce Johnson .12 .30
189 Chris Anderson .12 .30
190 Jake Stinnett .12 .30
191 Sikula/Burgos/Drake LL .12 .30
192 Wang/Fioro/Heston LL .12 .30
193 Cooney/Owens/Senzatela LL .15 .40
194 Johnson/Glasnow/Sparkman LL .15 .40
195 Blair/Lively/Cole LL .12 .30
196 Bautista/Peraza/Smith LL .20 .50
197 Olsn/Brynt/Kemp LL 1.00 2.50
198 Brynt/Smith/Ptrsn LL 1.00 2.50
199 Gllo/Olsn/Brynt LL 1.00 2.50
200 Lara/Souza Jr./Sisco LL .25 .60
201 Miguel Sano SP 1.25 3.00
202 Alex Jackson SP 1.25 3.00
203 Braden Shipley SP 1.00 2.50
204 Matt Olson SP 1.25 3.00
205 Jorge Alfaro SP 1.50 4.00
206 Nomar Mazara SP 1.50 4.00
207 Tyler Beede SP 1.25 3.00
208 J.P. Crawford SP 1.00 2.50
209 Aaron Nola SP 1.50 4.00
210 Hunter Renfroe SP 1.50 4.00
211 Robert Stephenson SP 1.00 2.50
212 Austin Meadows SP 1.50 4.00
213 Kohl Stewart SP 1.00 2.50
214 A.J. Reed SP 1.25 3.00
215 Henry Owens SP 1.00 2.50
216 Jose Berrios SP 1.50 4.00
218 Josh Bell SP 2.00 5.00
219 Mark Appel SP 1.00 2.50
220 Hunter Harvey SP 1.50 4.00
221 Tyler Glasnow SP 1.25 3.00
222 Jose Peraza SP 1.00 2.50
223 Carl Edwards Jr. SP 1.50 4.00
224 Aaron Judge SP 15.00 40.00
225 Corey Seager SP 4.00 10.00
317 Tyler Kolek UER SP 1.00 2.50
Should be card #217

2015 Topps Heritage Minors Blue

*BLUE: 1.5X TO 4X BASIC
STATED ODDS 1:8 HOBBY

2015 Topps Heritage Minors Gum Damage

*BLUE 1-190: 2X TO 5X BASIC
*BLUE 191-200: 2.5X TO 6X BASIC
1-190 ODDS 1:17 HOBBY
191-200 ODDS 1:322 HOBBY

2015 Topps Heritage Minors Orange

*ORANGE: 6X TO 15X BASIC
1-190 ODDS 1:34 HOBBY
191-200 ODDS 1:641 HOBBY
STATED PRINT RUN 25 SER.#'d SETS
197 Olsn/Brynt/Kemp LL 10.00 25.00
198 Brynt/Smith/Ptrsn LL 10.00 25.00
199 Gllo/Olsn/Brynt LL 10.00 25.00

2015 Topps Heritage Minors Clubhouse Collection Relics

STATED ODDS 1:29 HOBBY
PRINTING PLATE ODDS 1:2220
PLATE PRINT RUN 1 SET PER COLOR
NO PLATE PRICING DUE TO SCARCITY
*BLUE/50: .6X TO 1.5X BASIC
*ORANGE/25: 1X TO 2.5X BASIC
CCRAJ Aaron Judge 10.00 25.00
CCRAM Alex Meyer 2.00 5.00
CCRBB Byron Buxton 3.00 8.00
CCRBN Brandon Nimmo 3.00 8.00
CCRCE Chris Ellis 2.00 5.00
CCRCS Corey Seager 5.00 12.00
CCRDP D.J. Peterson 2.00 5.00
CCRFM Frankie Montas 2.50 6.00
CCRHD Hunter Dozier 2.00 5.00
CCRHR Hunter Renfroe 3.00 8.00
CCRJB Josh Bell 4.00 10.00
CCRJG Joe Gatto 2.00 5.00
CCRJN Justin Nicolino 2.00 5.00
CCRJU Julio Urias 6.00 15.00
CCRMA Mark Appel 2.00 5.00
CCRMS Miguel Sano 4.00 10.00
CCRPO Peter O'Brien 3.00 8.00
CCRRS Robert Stephenson 2.00 5.00

2015 Topps Heritage Minors Clubhouse Collection Relics Autographs

STATED ODDS 1:325 HOBBY
PRINT RUNS B/WN 31-50 COPIES PER
*ORANGE/25: .5X TO 1.2X BASIC
CCARAJ Aaron Judge/50 40.00 100.00
CCARAM Alex Meyer/50 8.00 20.00
CCARBD Brandon Drury/50 10.00 25.00
CCARDP D.J. Peterson/50 8.00 20.00
CCARJN Justin Nicolino/50 8.00 20.00
CCARJW Jesse Winker/50 10.00 25.00
CCARPO Peter O'Brien/50 12.00 30.00
CCARRQ Roman Quinn/31 15.00 40.00

2015 Topps Heritage Minors Looming Legacy Autographs

STATED ODDS 1:696 HOBBY
PRINT RUNS B/WN 15-35 COPIES PER
PRINTING PLATE ODDS 1:4375 HOBBY
PLATE PRINT RUN 1 SET PER COLOR
NO PLATE PRICING DUE TO SCARCITY
LLAAJ Andruw Jones/35 10.00 25.00
LLACF Cliff Floyd/35 10.00 25.00
LLAJG Juan Gonzalez/35 10.00 25.00
LLAJS John Smoltz/15 25.00 60.00
LLANG Nomar Garciaparra/35 30.00 80.00
LLAOV Omar Vizquel/35 25.00 60.00
LLARW Rondell White/35 15.00 40.00
LLAVG Vladimir Guerrero/15 30.00 80.00

2015 Topps Heritage Minors Minor Miracles

COMPLETE SET (25) 10.00 25.00
STATED ODDS 1:8 HOBBY
MM1 Carlos Correa 2.00 5.00
MM2 Robert Refsnyder .50 1.25
MM3 Mike Hessman .40 1.00
MM4 Jon Griffin .40 1.00
MM5 Spokane Indians .40 1.00
MM6 Clinton LumberKings .40 1.00
MM7 Dante Bichette Jr. .50 1.25
MM8 Fresno Grizzlies .40 1.00
MM9 Kyle Schwarber 1.50 4.00
MM10 Tyler Glasnow .50 1.25
MM11 Lucas Sims .40 1.00
MM12 Cody Scarpetta .40 1.00
MM13 Lewis Brinson .60 1.50
MM14 Mark Zagunis .40 1.00
MM15 Darnell Sweeney .40 1.00
MM16 Hudson Valley Renegades .40 1.00
MM17 Justin Williams .40 1.00
MM18 Tyler Glasnow .50 1.25
MM19 Corey Seager 1.50 4.00
MM20 Henry Owens .40 1.00
MM21 Robert Stephenson .40 1.00
MM22 Mallex Smith .60 1.50
MM23 Matt Olson .50 1.25
MM24 Sean Newcomb .50 1.25
MM25 Mark Appel .40 1.00

2015 Topps Heritage Minors Mystery Redemptions

STATED ODDS 1:401 HOBBY
EXCHANGE DEADLINE 9/30/2017
MR1 Dansby Swanson 20.00 50.00
MR2 Brendan Rodgers 20.00 50.00

2015 Topps Heritage Minors Real One Autographs

STATED ODDS 1:19 HOBBY
PRINTING PLATE ODDS 1:970
PLATE PRINT RUN 1 SET PER COLOR
NO PLATE PRICING DUE TO SCARCITY
*BLUE/50: .6X TO 1.5X BASIC
ROA10 Sean Reid-Foley 3.00 8.00
ROA17 Jacob Dahlstrand 2.50 6.00
ROA29 Wes Parsons 2.50 6.00
ROA39 Chase Vallot 2.50 6.00
ROA45 Zech Lemond 2.50 6.00
ROA67 Erich Weiss 2.50 6.00
ROA68 Buddy Borden 2.50 6.00
ROA73 Grant Hockin 2.50 6.00
ROA75 Joe Gatto 2.50 6.00
ROA80 Danny Burawa 2.50 6.00
ROA84 Braxton Davidson 2.50 6.00
ROA100 Kyle Schwarber 60.00 150.00
ROA108 Daniel Mengden 2.50 6.00
ROA119 Michael Gettys 3.00 8.00
ROA122 Trey Supak 2.50 6.00
ROA125 B.J. Boyd 2.50 6.00
ROA145 Carson Sands 2.50 6.00
ROA146 Nick Wells 2.50 6.00
ROA150 Luis Severino 10.00 25.00
ROA156 Aaron Blair 6.00 15.00
ROA168 Harold Ramirez 3.00 8.00
ROA185 Joe Sclafani 2.50 6.00
ROA186 Chris Ellis 2.50 6.00
ROA187 Joey Curletta 3.00 8.00

2015 Topps Heritage Minors Real One Autographs Orange

*ORANGE: .75X TO 2X BASIC
STATED ODDS 1:156 HOBBY
STATED PRINT RUN 25 SER.#'d SETS
ROA50 Lucas Giolito 15.00 40.00

2015 Topps Heritage Minors Road to The Show

COMPLETE SET (50) 20.00 50.00
STATED ODDS 1:4 HOBBY
RTTS1 Julio Urias 1.25 3.00
RTTS2 Tyler Naquin .50 1.25
RTTS3 Josh Bell .75 2.00
RTTS4 Brett Graves .40 1.00
RTTS5 Orlando Arcia .50 1.25
RTTS6 Michael Conforto .50 1.25
RTTS7 Nick Ciuffo .40 1.00
RTTS8 Natanael Delgado .40 1.00
RTTS9 Buddy Borden .40 1.00
RTTS10 Willy Adames .60 1.50
RTTS11 Jake Reed .40 1.00
RTTS12 Nick Burdi .50 1.25
RTTS13 Amir Garrett .40 1.00
RTTS14 Hunter Harvey .40 1.00
RTTS15 Nomar Mazara .60 1.50
RTTS16 Grant Holmes .50 1.25
RTTS17 Alex Verdugo .60 1.50
RTTS18 Sean Newcomb .50 1.25
RTTS19 Brian Anderson .40 1.00
RTTS20 Zech Lemond .40 1.00
RTTS21 A.J. Reed .50 1.25
RTTS22 J.D. Davis .50 1.25
RTTS23 Rowdy Tellez .60 1.50
RTTS24 Clint Frazier 1.50 4.00
RTTS25 Bradley Zimmer .60 1.50
RTTS26 Chad Pinder .50 1.25
RTTS27 Raimel Tapia .60 1.50
RTTS28 Ryan McMahon .40 1.00
RTTS29 Alex Reyes .50 1.25
RTTS30 Rob Kaminsky .40 1.00
RTTS31 Drew Ward .40 1.00
RTTS32 Daniel Carbonell .50 1.25
RTTS33 Braxton Davidson .40 1.00
RTTS34 Alec Grosser .40 1.00
RTTS35 Ozhaino Albies 4.00 10.00
RTTS36 Ty Blach .50 1.25
RTTS37 Manuel Margot .40 1.00
RTTS38 Sam Travis .75 2.00
RTTS39 Tyler Beede .50 1.25
RTTS40 Gleyber Torres 6.00 15.00
RTTS41 Jake Stinnett .40 1.00
RTTS42 Marcos Molina .40 1.00
RTTS43 Aaron Judge 6.00 15.00
RTTS44 Jake Cave .40 1.00
RTTS45 Chris Anderson .40 1.00
RTTS46 Domingo Leyba .40 1.00
RTTS47 Derek Hill .50 1.25
RTTS48 Spencer Turnbull .40 1.00
RTTS49 Trey Michalczewski .40 1.00
RTTS50 James Dykstra .40 1.00

2016 Topps Heritage Minors

COMPLETE SET (228)
COMP.SET w/ SPs (215) 30.00 80.00
COMP.SET w/o SPs (200) 25.00 60.00
STATED SP ODDS 1:6 HOBBY
STATED SIG VAR ODDS 1:123 HOBBY
STATED ERR ODDS 1:818 HOBBY
1A Dansby Swanson .40 1.00
1B Swanson Sig Var 6.00 15.00
2 Erick Fedde .12 .30
3 Justus Sheffield .25 .60
4 Jacob Faria .15 .40
5 Chad Pinder .12 .30
6 Derek Fisher .12 .30
7 Kevin Newman .20 .50
8 Cornelius Randolph .12 .30
9 Franklyn Kilome .15 .40
10 Scott Kingery .20 .50
11 Dawel Lugo .12 .30
12 Jake Bauers .20 .50
13 Ricardo Pinto .15 .40
14 Ian Clarkin .12 .30
15 Renato Nunez .25 .60
16 Ryan McMahon .12 .30
17 Francis Martes .15 .40
18 Brady Aiken .30 .75
19 Alex Jackson .12 .30
20 Domingo Acevedo .20 .50
21 Raimel Tapia .15 .40
22 Christian Arroyo .40 1.00
23 Mike Soroka .40 1.00
24 Samuel Coonrod .12 .30
25A Austin Meadows .20 .50
25B Austin Meadows Signature Variation 3.00 8.00
26 Hunter Harvey .12 .30
27 Roman Quinn .20 .50
28 Ozzie Albies .50 1.25
29 Rob Kaminsky .12 .30
30 Jose Marmolejos-Diaz .12 .30
31 D.J. Peterson .12 .30
32A Andrew Benintendi .40 1.00
32B Benintendi Sig Var 8.00 20.00
33 Manuel Margot .12 .30
34 David Thompson .15 .40
35 Felix Jorge .12 .30
36 Joe Musgrove .12 .30
37 David Hess .12 .30
38 Jaime Schultz .12 .30
39 Rafael Bautista .12 .30
40 Jen-Ho Tseng .12 .30
41 Andrew Sopko .12 .30
42 Isan Diaz .30 .75
43 Ryan Mountcastle .20 .50
44 Beau Burrows .12 .30
45A Nick Gordon .12 .30
45B Gordon ERR Blank Back 8.00 20.00
46 Lucio Ortiz .12 .30
47 Cody Bellinger 6.00 15.00
48 Josh Sborz .20 .50
49 Mikey White .12 .30
50 Lewis Brinson .20 .50
51 Sean Reid-Foley .15 .40
52 Yusniel Diaz .40 1.00
53 Yairo Munoz .12 .30
54 Harold Ramirez .15 .40
55 David Denson .12 .30
56 Anthony Alford .12 .30
57 Osvaldo Abreu .12 .30
58A Taylor O'Neill .12 .30
58B O'Neill ERR Grn Bat 8.00 20.00
59 Brett Phillips .12 .30
60 Enyel De los Santos .20 .50
61 Eloy Jimenez .50 1.25
62 Hunter Renfroe .15 .40
63 Sam Travis .25 .60
64 Mark Appel .15 .40
65 Chih-Wei Hu .15 .40
66 Matt Olson .20 .50
67 Todd Hankins .12 .30
68 Mitch Keller .15 .40
69 Austin Riley .40 1.00
70 Austin Gomber .12 .30
71 Conner Greene .12 .30
72 Domingo Leyba .12 .30
73 Lucas Sims .12 .30
74 Jorge Alfaro .20 .50
75 Jack Flaherty .20 .50
76 George Iskenderian .12 .30
77 Daniel Robertson .12 .30
78 Max Fried .20 .50
79 Brian Mundell .12 .30
80 Jahmai Jones .15 .40
81 Wuilmer Becerra .12 .30
82 Jalen Miller .15 .40
83 Paul DeJong .75 2.00
84 Josh Naylor .15 .40
85 Ian Happ .25 .60
86 Ryan Williams .12 .30
87 Kyle Freeland .15 .40
88 Harrison Bader .20 .50
89 Phil Bickford .12 .30
90 Adam Brett Walker II .12 .30
91A Jose De Leon .12 .30
91B De Leon Sig Var 4.00 10.00
92 Austin Dean .12 .30
93 Junior Fernandez .20 .50
94 Brent Honeywell .20 .50
95A Dominic Smith .12 .30
95B Dominic Smith Signature Variation 2.00 5.00
96 Jose Rondon .12 .30
97 Jorge Mateo .15 .40
98 Jason Martin .12 .30
99 Nate Smith .12 .30
100A Clint Frazier .50 1.25
100B Frazier Sig Var 8.00 20.00
101 David Paulino .15 .40
102 Duane Underwood .12 .30
103 Forrest Wall .12 .30
104 Daniel Poncedeleon .12 .30
105 Sam Howard .12 .30
106 Nick Williams .15 .40
107 Hoy-Jun Park .15 .40
108 Billy McKinney .15 .40
109 Demi Orimoloye .12 .30
110 Dillon Tate .15 .40
111 Trey Michalczewski .12 .30
112 Kolby Allard .12 .30
113 Braden Shipley .12 .30
114 Nolan Watson .12 .30
115 Raul Alcantara .12 .30
116 Magneuris Sierra .40 1.00
117 Daz Cameron .12 .30
118 Corey Zangari .12 .30
119 Jeff Hoffman .15 .40
120 Anthony Banda .12 .30
121 Tyler Alexander .12 .30
122 Jharel Cotton .12 .30
123 Mike Gerber .12 .30
124 Rowdy Tellez .20 .50
125 Nick Burdi .12 .30
126 Willie Calhoun .40 1.00
127 Trey Mancini .40 1.00
128A Yeudy Garcia .12 .30
128B Garcia ERR Gaci 8.00 20.00
129 Dustin Fowler .15 .40
130 James Kaprielian .15 .40
131 Jordan Guerrero .12 .30
132 Lucius Fox .20 .50
133 Touki Toussaint .15 .40
134 John Norwood .12 .30
135 Luis Liberato .12 .30
136 Gavin Cecchini .12 .30
137 Jake Thompson .12 .30
138 Yandy Diaz .25 .60
139 Victor Alcantara .12 .30
140 Jose Pujols .12 .30
141 Grant Holmes .15 .40
142 Kodi Medeiros .12 .30
143 Joe Jimenez .15 .40
144 Kyle Tucker .50 1.25
145 Ruddy Giron .12 .30
146 Alex Blandino .12 .30
147 Mauricio Dubon .15 .40
148 Jermaine Palacios .15 .40
149 Ariel Jurado .12 .30
150A Sean Newcomb .15 .40
150B Sean Newcomb Signature Variation 2.50 6.00
151 Richie Martin .12 .30
152 Jacob Nottingham .12 .30
153 Bobby Bradley .15 .40
154 Andrew Suarez .15 .40
155 Tyler Beede .15 .40
156 Amed Rosario .20 .50
157 Amir Garrett .12 .30
158 Andrew Stevenson .12 .30
159 Mac Marshall .12 .30
160 Jesse Winker .12 .30
161 Tyler Stephenson .12 .30
162 Connor Sadzeck .12 .30
163 Luis Carpio .20 .50
164 Dylan Cease .30 .75
165 Ronald Acuna 25.00 60.00
166 Javier Guerra .12 .30
167 Bradley Zimmer .20 .50
168 Kyle Zimmer .12 .30
169 Tyrell Jenkins .12 .30
170 Alex Verdugo .20 .50
171 Mark Zagunis .12 .30
172 Roniel Raudes .20 .50
173 Jose Taveras .15 .40
174 Kohl Stewart .12 .30
175 Sandy Alcantara .15 .40
176 German Marquez .20 .50
177 Josh Staumont .15 .40
178 Willy Adames .20 .50
179A Victor Robles .50 1.25
179B Robles Sig Var 6.00 15.00
180 Chance Sisco .25 .60
181 Reynaldo Lopez .12 .30
182 Sal Romano .12 .30
183 Andrew Knapp .12 .30
184 Rhys Hoskins .50 1.25
185 Jeimer Candelario .15 .40
186A Orlando Arcia .15 .40
186B Orlando Arcia Signature Variation 2.50 6.00
187 Ke'Bryan Hayes .12 .30
188 Jon Harris .15 .40
189 Reese McGuire .12 .30
190A J.P. Crawford .12 .30
190B J.P. Crawford Signature Variation 2.00 5.00
191 A.J. Reed Tyler O'Neill Jabari Blash LL .15 .40
192 Adam Engel Jorge Mateo Yefri Perez LL .15 .40
193 Brett Phillips A.J. Reed Derek Fisher LL .12 .30
194 Adam Brett Walker II Peter O'Brien A.J. Reed LL .12 .30
195 Jose Martinez Jermaine Palacios Michael Pierson LL .15 .40
196 Josh Michalec Zack Weiss Zac Curtis LL .12 .30
197 Richard Bleier Taylor Rogers Pat Dean LL .15 .40
198 Terry Doyle Jacob Faria Austin Coley LL .12 .30
199 Blake Snell David Oca Williams Ramirez LL .15 .40
200 Jaime Schultz Jose Berrios Sean Newcomb LL .15 .40
201 Christin Stewart SP 1.25 3.00
202 Brendan Rodgers SP 1.50 4.00
203 Anderson Espinoza SP 1.00 2.50
204 David Dahl SP 1.25 3.00
205 Drew Jackson SP 1.00 2.50
206 Franklin Barreto SP 1.00 2.50
207 Rafael Devers SP 6.00 15.00
208 Carson Fulmer SP 1.00 2.50
209 Gleyber Torres SP 10.00 25.00
210 Aaron Judge SP 12.00 30.00
211 Alex Reyes SP 1.25 3.00
212 Tyler Jay SP 1.00 2.50
213 Josh Hader SP 1.25 3.00
214 Alex Bregman SP 3.00 8.00
215 Yoan Moncada SP 3.00 8.00

2016 Topps Heritage Minors Blue

*BLUE: 3X TO 8X BASIC
STATED ODDS 1:10 HOBBY
STATED PRINT RUN 99 SER.#'d SETS
165 Ronald Acuna 60.00 150.00

2016 Topps Heritage Minors Peach

*PEACH: 6X TO 15X BASIC
STATED ODDS 1:37 HOBBY
STATED PRINT RUN 25 SER.#'d SETS
165 Ronald Acuna 125.00 300.00

2016 Topps Heritage Minors '67 Mint Relics

STATED ODDS 1:93 HOBBY
STATED PRINT RUN 99 SER.#'d SETS
*PEACH/25: .6X TO 1.5X BASIC
67MAA Anthony Alford 4.00 10.00
67MAB Alex Bregman 10.00 25.00
67MABE Andrew Benintendi 10.00 25.00
67MAE Anderson Espinoza 3.00 8.00
67MBP Brett Phillips 3.00 8.00
67MBR Brendan Rodgers 6.00 15.00
67MBZ Bradley Zimmer 5.00 12.00
67MDD David Dahl 4.00 10.00
67MDS Dansby Swanson 10.00 25.00
67MFB Franklin Barreto 3.00 8.00
67MFM Francis Martes 4.00 10.00
67MGT Gleyber Torres 6.00 15.00
67MJDL Jose De Leon 3.00 8.00
67MJM Jorge Mateo 6.00 15.00
67MKT Kyle Tucker 12.00 30.00
67MMM Manuel Margot 3.00 8.00
67MOA Ozzie Albies 12.00 30.00
67MSN Sean Newcomb 4.00 10.00
67MVR Victor Robles 6.00 15.00
67MYM Yoan Moncada 8.00 20.00

2016 Topps Heritage Minors '67 Topps Stickers

COMPLETE SET (50) 10.00 25.00
STATED ODDS 1:3 HOBBY
1 Brendan Rodgers .30 .75
2 Alex Reyes .25 .60
3 Brett Phillips .20 .50
4 Dansby Swanson .60 1.50
5 Chih-Wei Hu .25 .60
6 Kyle Zimmer .20 .50
7 Nick Williams .25 .60
8 Kodi Medeiros .20 .50
9 Christian Arroyo .60 1.50
10 Adam Brett Walker II .20 .50
11 Andrew Benintendi .60 1.50
12 Tyler Stephenson .20 .50
13 Mark Appel .30 .75
14 Sean Newcomb .25 .60
15 Renato Nunez .40 1.00
16 Amir Garrett .20 .50
17 Billy McKinney .25 .60
18 Kyle Freeland .25 .60
19 Grant Holmes .25 .60
20 Austin Dean .20 .50
21 Nick Gordon .20 .50
22 Andrew Stevenson .20 .50
23 Tyler O'Neill .25 .60
24 Jon Harris .20 .50
25 Derek Fisher .20 .50
26 James Kaprielian .25 .60
27 Domingo Leyba .20 .50
28 Hunter Harvey .20 .50
29 Yoan Moncada .50 1.25
30 Mike Gerber .20 .50
31 Alex Bregman 1.25 3.00
32 Taylor Ward .25 .60
33 Hornsby .30 .75
34 Bumble .30 .75
35 Ted E. Tourist .30 .75
36 Mason .30 .75
37 Splash .30 .75
38 Phinley .30 .75
39 Screwball .30 .75
40 Webbly .30 .75
41 Big Lug .30 .75
42 South Paw .30 .75
43 Tim E. Gator .30 .75
44 Rip Tide .30 .75
45 Reedy Rip'it .30 .75
46 Mr. Shucks .30 .75
47 Wool E. Bull .30 .75
48 Bingo .30 .75
49 Champ .30 .75
50 Rally Shark .30 .75

2016 Topps Heritage Minors Attribtues Autographs

STATED ODDS 1:1794 HOBBY
STATED PRINT RUN 20 SER.#'d SETS
AAAR A.J. Reed 15.00 40.00
AARE Alex Reyes 20.00 50.00
AABR Brendan Rodgers 40.00 100.00
AADS Dansby Swanson 60.00 150.00
AADT Dillon Tate 20.00 50.00
AAJM Jorge Mateo 12.00 30.00
AAOA Orlando Arcia 12.00 30.00

2016 Topps Heritage Minors Clubhouse Collection Relics

STATED ODDS 1:26 HOBBY
PRINTING PLATE ODDS 1:3317 HOBBY
PLATE PRINT RUN 1 SET PER COLOR
NO PLATE PRICING DUE TO SCARCITY
*PEACH/25: 1.5X TO 4X BASIC
CCRAB Alex Blandino 2.00 5.00
CCRAG Amir Garrett 2.00 5.00
CCRAJ Aaron Judge 12.00 30.00
CCRAM Austin Meadows 3.00 8.00
CCRAR Alex Reyes 2.50 6.00
CCRCA Christian Arroyo 6.00 15.00
CCRCF Clint Frazier 5.00 12.00
CCRDS Dominic Smith 2.00 5.00
CCRHH Hunter Harvey 2.00 5.00
CCRJB Josh Bell 4.00 10.00
CCRJC J.P. Crawford 2.00 5.00
CCRLS Lucas Sims 2.00 5.00
CCRMO Matt Olson 4.00 10.00
CCROA Orlando Arcia 2.50 6.00
CCRRD Rafael Devers 4.00 10.00
CCRRN Renato Nunez 4.00 10.00
CCRRT Raimel Tapia 2.50 6.00

2016 Topps Heritage Minors Looming Legacy Autographs

STATED ODDS 1:1794 HOBBY
PRINT RUNS B/WN 5-50 COPIES PER
NO PRICING ON QTY 10 OR LESS
LLADK Dallas Keuchel/50 12.00 30.00
LLADP Dustin Pedroia/25 60.00 150.00
LLAEL Evan Longoria/20 30.00 80.00

2016 Topps Heritage Minors Minor Miracles

COMPLETE SET (15) 4.00 10.00
STATED ODDS 1:6 HOBBY
MM1 Jordan Patterson .20 .50
MM2 James Dykstra .20 .50
MM3 Derek Fisher .20 .50
MM4 Amir Garrett .20 .50
MM5 A.J. Reed .30 .75
MM6 Joey Rickard .20 .50
MM7 Biloxi Shuckers .25 .60
MM8 Louisville Bats .25 .60
MM9 Arkansas Travelers .25 .60
MM10 Mike Hessman .25 .60
MM11 Savannah Sand Gnats .25 .60
MM12 Lucas Giolito .30 .75
MM13 Corpus Christi Hooks .25 .60
MM14 J.P. Crawford .20 .50
MM15 Ariel Jurado .20 .50

2016 Topps Heritage Minors Mystery Redemptions

STATED ODDS 1:461 HOBBY
MR1 Mickey Moniak 40.00 100.00
MR2 Jason Groome 10.00 25.00

2016 Topps Heritage Minors Real One Autographs

STATED ODDS 1:23 HOBBY
*BLUE/50: .6X TO 1.5X BASIC
*PEACH/25: .75X TO 2X BASIC
ROAABE Andrew Benintendi 40.00 100.00
ROAABR Alex Bregman 30.00 80.00
ROAAE Anderson Espinoza 2.50 6.00
ROAAJ Ariel Jurado 2.50 6.00
ROAAR A.J. Reed 3.00 8.00
ROAARE Alex Reyes 8.00 20.00
ROAARI Austin Riley 20.00 50.00
ROABP Brett Phillips 2.50 6.00
ROABR Brendan Rodgers 10.00 25.00
ROADJ Drew Jackson 2.50 6.00
ROADS Dansby Swanson 40.00 100.00
ROADT Dillon Tate 5.00 12.00
ROAFM Francis Martes 3.00 8.00
ROAJM Jorge Mateo 3.00 8.00
ROAKA Kolby Allard 4.00 10.00
ROANW Nolan Watson 2.50 6.00
ROAOAL Ozzie Albies 10.00 25.00
ROAOAR Orlando Arcia 3.00 8.00
ROAPB Phil Bickford 2.50 6.00
ROATT Touki Toussaint 3.00 8.00

2017 Topps Heritage Minors

COMP.SET w/o SPs (200) 30.00 80.00
STATED SP ODDS 1:6 HOBBY
STATED SIG VAR ODDS 1:328 HOBBY
STATED ERR ODDS 1:820 HOBBY
1A Amed Rosario .20 .50
1B Rosario Sig Var 10.00 25.00
2 Stephen Gonsalves .12 .30
3 Ramon Laureano .75 2.00
4 Micker Adolfo .25 .60
5 Andrew Sopko .12 .30
6 Akil Baddoo .15 .40
7 Jazz Chisholm .50 1.25
8 Leody Taveras .40 1.00
9 Erick Fedde .12 .30
10A Mickey Moniak .30 .75
10B Moniak Sig Var 8.00 20.00
10C Moniak TN Green 15.00 40.00
11 P.J. Conlon .12 .30
12 Buddy Reed .12 .30
13 JoJo Romero .30 .75
14 Freddy Peralta .20 .50
15 Scott Kingery .20 .50
16 Rowdy Tellez .20 .50
17 Touki Toussaint .15 .40
18 Ryan Helsley .15 .40
19 Luis Alexander Basabe .20 .50
20 Kevin Newman .20 .50
21 Adonis Medina .20 .50
22 Bryan Reynolds .20 .50
23 Khalil Lee .20 .50
24 Eric Lauer .15 .40
25A Jason Groome .25 .60
25B Groome Sig Var 6.00 15.00
25C Groome TN ERR 12.00 30.00
26 T.J. Zeuch .12 .30
27 Meibrys Viloria .12 .30
28 Dylan Cozens .12 .30
29 Justin Dunn .12 .30
30 Greg Allen .20 .50
31 David Thompson .15 .40
32 Andrew Suarez .12 .30
33 Chance Adams .20 .50
34 Logan Shore .15 .40
35 Jon Duplantier .20 .50
36 Yusniel Diaz .40 1.00
37 Luis Urias .50 1.25
38 Tyler Badamo .12 .30
39 Willy Adames .15 .40
40 Desmond Lindsay .12 .30
41 Franklin Perez .20 .50
42 Taylor Clarke .12 .30
43 Franklyn Kilome .15 .40
44 Shed Long .12 .30
45 Will Smith .30 .75
46 Cody Sedlock .12 .30
47 Kevin Maitan .30 .75
48 Hudson Potts .15 .40
49 Alex Kirilloff .30 .75
50A Nick Senzel .40 1.00
50B Senzel Sig Var 12.00 30.00
50C Senzell TN White 12.00 30.00
51 Mike Soroka .40 1.00
52 Juan Soto 2.50 6.00
53 Bryson Brigman .12 .30
54 Jack Flaherty .20 .50
55 Felix Jorge .12 .30
56 Brent Honeywell .15 .40
57 Anthony Banda .12 .30
58 Andy Yerzy .12 .30
59 Will Craig .12 .30
60 Trevor Clifton .12 .30
61 Luis Ortiz .12 .30
62 Anderson Tejeda .12 .30
63 Nick Solak .30 .75
64 Wuilmer Becerra
65 Nick Williams .15 .40
66 Peter Alonso 1.25 3.00
67 Richard Urena .20 .50
68 Brady Aiken .20 .50
69 Bobby Dalbec .30 .75
70 Vladimir Gutierrez .12 .30
71 Anfernee Grier .12 .30
72 Daulton Jefferies .15 .40
73A Blake Rutherford .20 .50
73B Rutherford Sig Var 6.00 15.00
74 Sheldon Neuse .15 .40
75A Clint Frazier .25 .60
75B Frazier Sig Var 8.00 20.00
75C Frazier TN Blue 15.00 40.00
76 Sixto Sanchez .30 .75
77 Max Fried .50 1.25
78 Chris Okey .12 .30
79 Estevan Florial .75 2.00
80 Yu-Cheng Chang .20 .50
81 J.P. Crawford .12 .30
82 Nonie Williams .12 .30

83 Ryan Mountcastle .20 .50
84 Will Benson .12 .30
85 Logan Allen .12 .30
86 C.J. Hinojosa .12 .30
87 Alex Verdugo .20 .50
88 A.J. Puckett .12 .30
89 J.B. Woodman .25 .60
90 Isan Diaz .30 .75
91 Zack Collins .15 .40
92 Ben Bowden .12 .30
93 Rob Kaminsky .12 .30
94 Alex Speas .12 .30
95 Cal Quantrill .12 .30
96 Jake Bauers .15 .40
97 Cole Ragans .12 .30
98 Bobby Bradley .15 .40
99 Fernando Tatis Jr. 6.00 15.00
100A Gleyber Torres 2.00 5.00
100B Torres Sig Var 12.00 30.00
100C Torres TN Blue 25.00 60.00
101 Taylor Ward .15 .40
102 Taylor Trammell .20 .50
103 Ozzie Albies .50 1.25
104 Gavin Lux .75 2.00
105 Jordan Sheffield .12 .30
106 Alec Hansen .12 .30
107 Fernando Romero .12 .30
108 Ryan O'Hearn .25 .60
109 Andrew Calica .12 .30
110A Mitch Keller .15 .40
110B Keller TN Black 20.00 50.00
111 Delvin Perez .20 .50
112 Austin Hays .30 .75
113 Jose Taveras .15 .40
114 Oscar De La Cruz .12 .30
115 Kyle Funkhouser .15 .40
116 Jesus Sanchez .60 1.50
117 Andy Ibanez .12 .30
118 Domingo Acevedo .12 .30
119 Ronnie Dawson .12 .30
120 Jacob Nix .12 .30
121 Dylan Carlson .75 2.00
122 Dash Winningham .20 .50
123 Mitchell White .20 .50
124 Jose Albertos .30 .75
125A Eloy Jimenez .50 1.25
125B Jimenez Sig Var 8.00 20.00
125C Jimenez TN Yel 8.00 20.00
126 Keibert Ruiz .40 1.00
127 Jorge Ona .15 .40
128 Chance Sisco .25 .60
129 Forrest Whitley .40 1.00
130 Kyle Tucker .25 .60
131 Braxton Garrett .12 .30
132 Tomas Nido .12 .30
133 Phil Bickford .12 .30
134 Jacob Heyward .12 .30
135 Trent Clark .12 .30
136 Luiz Gohara .12 .30
137 Tyler O'Neill .15 .40
138 Marcos Diplan .12 .30
139 Ariel Jurado .12 .30
140 Kohl Stewart .12 .30
141 Jaime Schultz .12 .30
142 Willie Calhoun .20 .50
143 Dillon Tate .12 .30
144 Roniel Raudes .12 .30
145 Josh Ockimey .20 .50
146 Randy Arozarena 2.50 6.00
147 Ryan McMahon .12 .30
148 Patrick Weigel .12 .30
149 Kyle Zimmer .12 .30
150A Corey Ray .15 .40
150B Ray TN White 10.00 25.00
151 Keegan Akin .15 .40
152 Juan Hillman .12 .30
153 Michael Kopech .25 .60
154 Andrew Stevenson .15 .40
155 Thomas Szapucki .15 .40
156 Matt Thaiss .12 .30
157 Harrison Bader .20 .50
158 Tyler Jay .12 .30
159 Sandy Alcantara .15 .40
160 Lewin Diaz .12 .30
161 Josh Staumont .12 .30
162 Walker Buehler .30 .75
163 Yadier Alvarez .20 .50
164 Rhys Hoskins .50 1.25
165 Sean Reid-Foley .12 .30
166 Carter Kieboom .20 .50
167 Francisco Rios .12 .30
168 Cristian Pache .60 1.50
169 Brandon Woodruff .12 .30
170 Austin Riley .40 1.00
171 Christin Stewart .15 .40
172 Zack Burdi .12 .30
173 Franklin Barreto .12 .30
174 Yanio Perez .12 .30
175 Angel Perdomo .12 .30
176 T.J. Friedl .12 .30
177A Austin Meadows .20 .50
177B Meadows Sig Var 10.00 25.00
178 Lucas Erceg .15 .40
179 Dominic Smith .12 .30
180 Bo Bichette .50 1.25
181 Dane Dunning .12 .30
182 Grant Holmes .12 .30
183 Casey Gillaspie .12 .30
184 Corbin Burnes .20 .50
185 Tyler Beede .12 .30
186 Nick Neidert .12 .30
187 Jahmai Jones .12 .30
188 Colton Welker .12 .30
189 Kolby Allard .12 .30
190A Rafael Devers .25 .60
190B Devers Sig Var 12.00 30.00
191 Coz/Chap/Hosk LL .50 1.25
192 Eric Jenkins .40 1.00
Rafael Bautista
Zack Granite
SB LL
193 Mauricio Dubon .20 .50
Greg Allen
Dylan Cozens
Runs LL
194 Hosk/Jens/Coz LL .50 1.25
195 Viloria/Ruiz/Dckrsn LL .40 1.00
196 Alejandro Chacin .12 .30
Joe Jimenez
Matt Carasiti
Saves LL
197 Anthony Vasquez .12 .30
Chris Volstad
Parker French
IP LL
198 Shawn Morimando .15 .40
Ben Lively
Chase De Jong
Pitching LL
199 Caleb Dirks .12 .30
Ben Holmes
Danny Barnes
ERA LL
200 Jaime Schultz .12 .30
Brandon Woodruff
Josh Staumont
K LL
201 Tim Tebow SP 6.00 15.00
202 Ronald Acuna SP 12.00 30.00
203 Nick Gordon SP 1.00 2.50
204 Anderson Espinoza SP 1.00 2.50
205 Matt Manning SP 1.50 4.00
206 Dawel Lugo SP 1.00 2.50
207 Kyle Lewis SP 2.00 5.00
208 Triston McKenzie SP 1.00 2.50
209 Justus Sheffield SP 1.50 4.00
210 Jorge Mateo SP 1.00 2.50
211 Dylan Cease SP 2.50 6.00
212 Brendan Rodgers SP 1.25 3.00
213 Lourdes Gurriel Jr. SP 1.50 4.00
214 Ian Anderson SP 2.50 6.00
215 Vladimir Guerrero Jr. SP 15.00 40.00
216 Francisco Mejia SP 1.50 4.00
217 Jordan Hicks SP 2.00 5.00
218 A.J. Puk SP 1.50 4.00
219 Riley Pint SP 1.00 2.50
220 Victor Robles SP 2.50 6.00

2017 Topps Heritage Minors Blue

*BLUE: 2.5X TO 6X BASIC
STATED ODDS 1:17 HOBBY
STATED PRINT RUN 99 SER.#'d SETS
99 Fernando Tatis Jr. 40.00 100.00

2017 Topps Heritage Minors Error Variation Autographs

STATED ODDS 1:1285 HOBBY
PRINT RUNS B/WN 25-50 COPIES PER
EXCHANGE DEADLINE 9/30/19
25 Jay Groome/50
50 Nick Senzel/25 40.00 100.00
75 Clint Frazier/50 60.00 150.00
100 Gleyber Torres/50 75.00 200.00
125 Eloy Jimenez/50 30.00 80.00
150 Corey Ray/50

2017 Topps Heritage Minors Gray

*GRAY: 5X TO 12X BASIC
STATED ODDS 1:66 HOBBY
STATED PRINT RUN 25 SER.#'d SETS
99 Fernando Tatis Jr. 125.00 300.00

2017 Topps Heritage Minors Green

*GREEN: 3X TO 8X BASIC
STATED ODDS 1:33 HOBBY
STATED PRINT RUN 50 SER.#'d SETS
99 Fernando Tatis Jr. 60.00 150.00

2017 Topps Heritage Minors No First Name

*NO NAME: 4X TO 10X BASIC
STATED ODDS 1:47 HOBBY
99 Fernando Tatis Jr. 100.00 250.00

2017 Topps Heritage Minors '68 Discs

COMPLETE SET (40) 15.00 40.00
STATED ODDS 1:5 HOBBY
68TDC1 Mickey Moniak .75 2.00
68TDC2 Alec Hansen .30 .75
68TDC3 Roniel Raudes .30 .75
68TDC4 Sandy Alcantara .40 1.00
68TDC5 Grant Holmes .30 .75
68TDC6 Gleyber Torres 5.00 12.00
68TDC7 Yadier Alvarez .50 1.25
68TDC8 Kolby Allard .30 .75
68TDC9 Michael Kopech .60 1.50
68TDC10 Eloy Jimenez 1.25 3.00
68TDC11 Blake Rutherford .50 1.25
68TDC12 Cody Sedlock .30 .75
68TDC13 Ariel Jurado .30 .75
68TDC14 Tyler O'Neill .40 1.00
68TDC15 Cal Quantrill .30 .75
68TDC16 Bobby Bradley .40 1.00
68TDC17 Kyle Tucker .60 1.50
68TDC18 Scott Kingery .50 1.25
68TDC19 Lucas Erceg .40 1.00
68TDC20 Luis Castillo 1.00 2.50
68TDC21 Bo Bichette 1.25 3.00
68TDC22 Josh Ockimey .50 1.25
68TDC23 Nick Solak .75 2.00
68TDC24 Rafael Devers .60 1.50
68TDC25 Vladimir Guerrero Jr. 4.00 10.00
68TDC26 Sasquatch .30 .75
68TDC27 Bolt .30 .75
68TDC28 Bernie .30 .75
68TDC29 Dewd .30 .75
68TDC30 Ted E. Tourist .30 .75
68TDC31 Marty .30 .75
68TDC32 Fang .30 .75
68TDC33 Buster T. Bison .30 .75
68TDC34 Shelldon .30 .75
68TDC35 Kaboom .30 .75
68TDC36 Tim Tebow 2.50 6.00
68TDC37 Jorge Mateo .30 .75
68TDC38 Homer The Dragon .30 .75
68TDC39 Charlie T. RiverDog .30 .75
68TDC40 Gizmo .30 .75

2017 Topps Heritage Minors '68 Mint Gray Quarter

STATED ODDS 1:547 HOBBY
STATED PRINT RUN 25 SER.#'d SETS
68MAM Austin Meadows 10.00 25.00
68MAP A.J. Puk 8.00 20.00
68MAR Amed Rosario 12.00 30.00
68MBR Blake Rutherford 12.00 30.00
68MBRO Brendan Rodgers 8.00 20.00
68MCR Corey Ray 8.00 20.00
68MEJ Eloy Jimenez 10.00 25.00
68MFM Francisco Mejia 10.00 25.00
68MGT Gleyber Torres 15.00 40.00
68MJC J.P. Crawford 6.00 15.00
68MJM Jorge Mateo 6.00 15.00
68MKA Kolby Allard 6.00 15.00
68MKL Kyle Lewis 8.00 20.00
68MMM Mickey Moniak 15.00 40.00
68MNS Nick Senzel 12.00 30.00
68MOA Ozzie Albies 15.00 40.00
68MRA Ronald Acuna 15.00 40.00
68MRD Rafael Devers 25.00 60.00
68MTM Triston McKenzie 10.00 25.00
68MTT Tim Tebow 75.00 200.00
68MVGJ Vladimir Guerrero Jr. 30.00 80.00
68MVR Victor Robles 12.00 30.00
68MYA Yadier Alvarez 15.00 40.00
68MZC Zack Collins 8.00 20.00

2017 Topps Heritage Minors '68 Mint Nickel

STATED ODDS 1:138 HOBBY
STATED PRINT RUN 99 SER.#'d SETS
68MAM Austin Meadows 6.00 15.00
68MAP A.J. Puk 5.00 12.00
68MAR Amed Rosario 8.00 20.00
68MBR Blake Rutherford 8.00 20.00
68MBRO Brendan Rodgers 5.00 12.00
68MCR Corey Ray 5.00 12.00
68MEJ Eloy Jimenez 6.00 15.00
68MFM Francisco Mejia 6.00 15.00
68MGT Gleyber Torres 10.00 25.00
68MJC J.P. Crawford 4.00 10.00
68MJM Jorge Mateo 4.00 10.00
68MKA Kolby Allard 4.00 10.00
68MKL Kyle Lewis 5.00 12.00
68MMM Mickey Moniak 10.00 25.00
68MNS Nick Senzel 8.00 20.00
68MOA Ozzie Albies 10.00 25.00
68MRA Ronald Acuna 10.00 25.00
68MRD Rafael Devers 8.00 20.00
68MTM Triston McKenzie 6.00 15.00
68MTT Tim Tebow 15.00 40.00
68MVGJ Vladimir Guerrero Jr. 20.00 50.00
68MVR Victor Robles 8.00 20.00
68MYA Yadier Alvarez 10.00 25.00
68MZC Zack Collins 5.00 12.00

2017 Topps Heritage Minors '68 Topps Game Mascots

COMPLETE SET (20) 12.00 30.00
STATED ODDS 1:9 HOBBY
1 Tim E. Gator .60 1.50
2 Mason .60 1.50
3 Striker .60 1.50
4 Robbie the Redbird .60 1.50
5 Slugger .60 1.50
6 Skipper .60 1.50
7 Rascal .60 1.50
8 Blooper .60 1.50
9 Homer .60 1.50
10 Sluggo .60 1.50
11 Stu .60 1.50
12 Wool E. Bull .60 1.50
13 Big Lug .60 1.50
14 Splash .60 1.50
15 Bernie .60 1.50
16 Bucky the Beaver .60 1.50
17 Heater .60 1.50
18 Webbly .60 1.50
19 Hornsby .60 1.50
20 South Paw .60 1.50

2017 Topps Heritage Minors Baseball America All Stars

COMPLETE SET (20) 10.00 25.00
STATED ODDS 1:6 HOBBY
BAAM Austin Meadows .50 1.25
BABR Brendan Rodgers .40 1.00
BACR Corey Ray .40 1.00
BAEJ Eloy Jimenez 1.25 3.00
BAFM Francis Martes .30 .75
BAGT Gleyber Torres 5.00 12.00
BAKA Kolby Allard .30 .75
BAKN Kevin Newman .50 1.25
BAKT Kyle Tucker .60 1.50
BALT Leody Taveras 1.00 2.50
BAMM Mickey Moniak .75 2.00
BANG Nick Gordon .30 .75
BANS Nick Senzel 1.00 2.50
BARA Ronald Acuna 5.00 12.00
BARD Rafael Devers .60 1.50
BATM Triston McKenzie .30 .75
BATO Tyler O'Neill .40 1.00
BAVG Vladimir Guerrero Jr. 4.00 10.00
BAVR Victor Robles .75 2.00
BABRU Blake Rutherford .50 1.25

2017 Topps Heritage Minors Clubhouse Collection Relics

STATED ODDS 1:29 HOBBY
*GREEN/99: .5X TO 1.2X BASIC
*BLUE/50: .6X TO 1.5X BASIC
*GRAY/25: .75X TO 2X BASIC
CCRAM Austin Meadows 3.00 8.00
CCRAR Amed Rosario 3.00 8.00
CCRAV Alex Verdugo 3.00 8.00
CCRBH Brent Honeywell 2.50 6.00
CCRCS Christin Stewart 2.50 6.00
CCRDC Dylan Cozens 2.00 5.00
CCRDS Dominic Smith 2.00 5.00
CCRDT Dillon Tate 2.00 5.00
CCREJ Eloy Jimenez 4.00 10.00
CCRFB Franklin Barreto 2.00 5.00
CCRFM Francisco Mejia 3.00 8.00
CCRGT Gleyber Torres 5.00 12.00
CCRHB Harrison Bader 4.00 10.00
CCRJC J.P. Crawford 2.00 5.00
CCRJM Jorge Mateo 2.00 5.00
CCRMK Michael Kopech 4.00 10.00
CCRRD Rafael Devers 4.00 10.00
CCRRM Ryan McMahon 2.00 5.00
CCRTO Tyler O'Neill 2.50 6.00
CCRTT Tim Tebow 10.00 25.00
CCRTW Taylor Ward 2.50 6.00
CCRWA Willy Adames 2.50 6.00
CCRWC Willie Calhoun 3.00 8.00

2017 Topps Heritage Minors Fantastic Feats Autographs

STATED ODDS 1:537 HOBBY
PRINT RUNS B/WN 30-99 COPIES PER
EXCHANGE DEADLINE 9/30/19
*GRAY/25: .5X TO 1.2X BASIC
FFAAR Amed Rosario/30 20.00 50.00
FFACF Clint Frazier/25 75.00 200.00
FFADC Dylan Cozens/40 6.00 15.00
FFAEJ Eloy Jimenez/30 15.00 40.00
FFAGT Gleyber Torres/25 60.00 150.00
FFAJG Jason Groome/40 8.00 20.00
FFAKL Kyle Lewis/99 15.00 40.00
FFANS Nick Senzel/15 20.00 50.00
FFATM Triston McKenzie/60 6.00 15.00

2017 Topps Heritage Minors Looming Legacy Autographs

PRINT RUNS B/WN 4-20 COPIES PER
NO PRICING ON QTY 10 OR LESS
EXCHANGE DEADLINE 9/30/19
LLACS Chris Sale
LLAMM Manny Machado/20 60.00 150.00

2017 Topps Heritage Minors Real One Autographs

STATED ODDS 1:24 HOBBY
*BLUE/75: .5X TO 1.2X BASIC
*GRAY/25: .75X TO 2X BASIC
ROAAE Anderson Espinoza 5.00 12.00
ROAAR Amed Rosario 15.00 40.00
ROAAS Andrew Stevenson 3.00 8.00
ROABD Bobby Dalbec 6.00 15.00
ROABR Blake Rutherford 12.00 30.00
ROACA Chance Adams 5.00 12.00
ROACF Clint Frazier 30.00 80.00
ROACR Corey Ray 10.00 25.00
ROADC Dylan Cozens 6.00 15.00
ROAEJ Eloy Jimenez 30.00 80.00
ROAFB Franklin Barreto 4.00 10.00
ROAFRI Francisco Rios 2.50 6.00
ROAGT Gleyber Torres 50.00 120.00
ROAJG Jason Groome 10.00 25.00
ROAJH Jacob Heyward 2.50 6.00
ROAJM Jorge Mateo 8.00 20.00
ROAJS Justus Sheffield 8.00 20.00
ROAKM Kevin Maitan 10.00 25.00
ROALGJ Lourdes Gurriel Jr. 4.00 10.00
ROALT Leody Taveras 6.00 15.00
ROANS Nick Senzel
ROANSO Nick Solak 6.00 15.00
ROAPA Peter Alonso 50.00 120.00
ROAPC P.J. Conlon 2.50 6.00
ROARA Ronald Acuna 125.00 300.00
ROASN Sean Newcomb 4.00 10.00
ROATC Trevor Clifton 2.50 6.00
ROATF T.J. Friedl 4.00 10.00
ROATM Triston McKenzie 8.00 20.00

2017 Topps Heritage Nolan Ryan Highlights

COMPLETE SET (5) 5.00 12.00
STATED HN ODDS 1:24 HOBBY
NRH1 Nolan Ryan 1.50 4.00
NRH2 Nolan Ryan 1.50 4.00
NRH3 Nolan Ryan 1.50 4.00
NRH4 Nolan Ryan 1.50 4.00
NRH5 Nolan Ryan 1.50 4.00

2017 Topps Heritage Now and Then

COMPLETE SET (15) 8.00 20.00
STATED HN ODDS 1:8 HOBBY
NT1 Wil Myers .40 1.00
NT2 Bryce Harper 1.00 2.50
NT3 Andrew Benintendi 1.25 3.00
NT4 Francisco Lindor .60 1.50
NT5 Mike Trout 3.00 8.00
NT6 Manny Margot .40 1.00
NT7 Yoenis Cespedes .60 1.50
NT8 Dansby Swanson 1.00 2.50
NT9 Ichiro .75 2.00
NT10 Aaron Judge 3.00 8.00
NT11 Trea Turner .50 1.25
NT12 Eric Thames .50 1.25
NT13 Buster Posey .75 2.00
NT14 Cody Bellinger 2.50 6.00
NT15 Ryan Zimmerman .50 1.25

2017 Topps Heritage Rookie Performers

COMPLETE SET (15) 8.00 20.00
STATED HN ODDS 1:8 HOBBY
RPAB Andrew Benintendi 1.25 3.00
RPABR Alex Bregman 1.50 4.00
RPAJ Aaron Judge 4.00 10.00
RPBZ Bradley Zimmer .50 1.25
RPCA Christian Arroyo .60 1.50
RPCB Cody Bellinger 2.50 6.00
RPDD David Dahl .50 1.25
RPDS Dansby Swanson 1.00 2.50
RPHR Hunter Renfroe .50 1.25
RPLW Luke Weaver .50 1.25
RPOA Orlando Arcia .60 1.50
RPRH Ryon Healy .50 1.25
RPTG Tyler Glasnow .50 1.25
RPYG Yulieski Gurriel .60 1.50
RPYM Yoan Moncada 1.25 3.00

2018 Topps Heritage Minors

COMPLETE SET (220) 60.00 150.00
COMP.SET w/o SPs (200) 30.00 80.00
1 Vladimir Guerrero Jr. 1.25 3.00
2 DL Hall .12 .30
3 Justin Williams .12 .30
4 Brandon Marsh .15 .40
5 Will Smith .30 .75
6 Franklin Perez .12 .30
7 Domingo Acevedo .12 .30
8 Jeren Kendall .15 .40
9 Alex Faedo .20 .50
10 Mickey Moniak .30 .75
11 Kyle Tucker .25 .60
12 David Peterson .15 .40
13 Jon Duplantier .12 .30
14 Jordan Humphreys .12 .30
15 Aramis Ademan .20 .50
16 Brendon Little .12 .30
17 Jorge Ona .12 .30
18 Riley Pint .12 .30
19 Tanner Houck .30 .75
20 Oneil Cruz .20 .50
21 Dylan Cozens .12 .30
22 Colton Welker .12 .30
23 Sam Carlson .15 .40
24 Yadier Alvarez .15 .40
25 Hunter Greene .40 1.00
26 Brian Miller .12 .30
27 J.B. Bukauskas .12 .30
28 Genesis Cabrera .20 .50
29 Jorge Mateo .12 .30
30 Taylor Ward .15 .40
31 Shed Long .12 .30
32 Ke'Bryan Hayes .12 .30
33 Edward Cabrera .12 .30
34 Tyler Jay .12 .30
35 Cedric Mullins .20 .50
36 Cal Quantrill .12 .30
37 Jeisson Rosario .20 .50
38 Adonis Medina .20 .50
39 Max Schrock .12 .30
40 Blake Rutherford .15 .40
41 Akil Baddoo .15 .40
42 MJ Melendez .12 .30
43 Matt Hall .12 .30
44 Gavin Lux .40 1.00
45 Alex Lange .12 .30
46 Carter Kieboom .20 .50
47 Jose Albertos .12 .30
48 Adolis Garcia .15 .40
49 Kyle Funkhouser .15 .40
50 Eloy Jimenez .50 1.25
51 Trevor Stephan .12 .30
52 Spencer Howard .12 .30
53 Daniel Johnson .12 .30
54 Bo Bichette .50 1.25
55 Gavin Sheets .15 .40
56 Mike Miller .20 .50
57 Aramis Garcia .12 .30
58 Dane Dunning .12 .30
59 Pavin Smith .12 .30
60 Luis Medina .20 .50
61 Josh Naylor .15 .40
62 Charcer Burks .12 .30
63 Bryan Mata .15 .40
64 Nelson Velazquez .12 .30
65 Zack Collins .15 .40
66 Nick Solak .30 .75
67 Randy Arozarena 1.00 2.50
68 Ian Anderson .30 .75
69 Steven Duggar .12 .30
70 Ryan Borucki .12 .30
71 Stephen Gonsalves .12 .30
72 Drew Waters .30 .75
73 Isaac Paredes .60 1.50
74 Leody Taveras .15 .40
75 Mike Shawaryn .12 .30
76 Nicky Lopez .12 .30
77 Enyel De Los Santos .15 .40
78 Sam Hilliard .30 .75
79 Adbert Alzolay .15 .40
80 Isan Diaz .30 .75
81 Shane Baz .15 .40
82 Luis Garcia .25 .60
83 Oscar De La Cruz .12 .30
84 Quentin Holmes .12 .30
85 Andres Gimenez .15 .40
86 Freicer Perez .25 .60
87 Nick Allen .12 .30
88 Austin Beck .15 .40
89 DJ Peters .30 .75
90 Danny Jansen .20 .50
91 Jorge Guzman .12 .30
92 JoJo Romero .15 .40
93 Jazz Chisholm .30 .75
94 Estevan Florial .20 .50
95 Yasel Antuna .25 .60
96 Sheldon Neuse .12 .30
97 Jeter Downs .20 .50
98 McKenzie Mills .12 .30
99 Tristen Lutz .15 .40
100 Fernando Tatis Jr. 1.00 2.50
101 Nick Senzel .40 1.00
102 Brusdar Graterol .25 .60
103 MacKenzie Gore .25 .60
104 Franklyn Kilome .15 .40
105 Stuart Fairchild .15 .40
106 Lazaro Armenteros .25 .60
107 Drew Ellis .15 .40
108 Pete Alonso 1.25 3.00
109 Nick Pratto .15 .40
110 Yu Chang .15 .40
111 Yordan Alvarez 5.00 12.00
112 LoLo Sanchez .15 .40
113 Riley Adams .15 .40
114 Dylan Cease .30 .75
115 Monte Harrison .12 .30
116 Mark Vientos .20 .50
117 Rogelio Armenteros .12 .30
118 Matt Thaiss .12 .30
119 Brian Mundell .12 .30
120 Miguelangel Sierra .12 .30
121 Justin Dunn .15 .40
122 Khalil Lee .12 .30
123 Mitch Keller .15 .40
124 Corbin Burnes .20 .50
125 Michael Gigliotti .12 .30
126 Alex Kirilloff .20 .50
127 Brent Rooker .15 .40
128 Foster Griffin .12 .30
129 Johan Mieses .20 .50
130 Kyle Young .15 .40
131 Adam Haseley .20 .50
132 Cavan Biggio .25 .60
133 Cristian Pache .60 1.50
134 Mike Baumann .12 .30
135 Heliot Ramos .20 .50
136 Brendan Rodgers .15 .40
137 Zack Littell .12 .30
138 Beau Burrows .15 .40
139 TJ Zeuch .12 .30
140 Wander Javier .15 .40
141 Kyle Lewis .25 .60
142 Nick Neidert .12 .30
143 Gregory Soto .12 .30
144 Sean Murphy .20 .50
145 Zack Burdi .12 .30
146 Evan White .20 .50
147 Logan Allen .12 .30
148 Griffin Canning .12 .30
149 Evan Steele .15 .40
150 Royce Lewis .50 1.25
151 Nick Gordon .12 .30
152 Blayne Enlow .12 .30
153 Corey Ray .15 .40
154 Dillon Tate .12 .30
155 Cionel Perez .12 .30
156 Kolby Allard .12 .30
157 Pedro Avila .12 .30
158 Michael Kopech .25 .60
159 Garrett Hampson .20 .50
160 Luis Urias .25 .60
161 Ryan Vilade .12 .30
162 Matt Manning .20 .50
163 Joey Wentz .15 .40
164 Bryse Wilson .20 .50
165 Greg Deichmann .15 .40
166 Daulton Varsho .15 .40
167 David Fletcher .40 1.00
168 Bobby Bradley .15 .40
169 Albert Abreu .12 .30
170 Christin Stewart .15 .40
171 Ronnie Dawson .12 .30
172 Michael Barash .12 .30
173 Darwinzon Hernandez .30 .75
174 Chance Adams .20 .50
175 Nate Pearson .30 .75
176 Shaun Anderson .12 .30
177 Matt Sauer .12 .30
178 Kyle Muller .12 .30
179 Chris Seise .12 .30
180 Tim Tebow 1.25 3.00
181 Vladimir Guerrero Jr. AS 1.25 3.00
182 MacKenzie Gore AS .25 .60
183 Leody Taveras AS .15 .40
184 Brendan Rodgers AS .15 .40
185 Royce Lewis AS .50 1.25
186 Eloy Jimenez AS .50 1.25
187 Estevan Florial AS .20 .50
188 Hunter Greene AS .40 1.00
189 Mitch Keller AS .15 .40
190 Fernando Tatis Jr. AS 1.00 2.50
191 A.J. Reed .20 .50
Renato Nunez
Austin Hays
192 Jorge Mateo .12 .30
Wes Rogers
Johnny Davis
193 Christian Walker .20 .50
Garrett Hampson
Blake Perkins
194 Seth Brown .20 .50
Viosergy Rosa
Christian Walker
195 Miller/Hiura/Longo .30 .75
196 Griep/Ramsey/Beato .12 .30
197 Chirinos/Knapp/Bieber 1.50 4.00
198 Adams/Littell/Griffin .20 .50
199 Jon Duplantier .12 .30
Merandy Gonzalez
Dakota Mekkes
200 A.J. Puk .15 .40
Alec Hansen
Triston McKenzie
201 Brendan McKay SP 1.25 3.00
202 Taylor Trammell SP 1.25 3.00
203 Seuly Matias SP 1.50 4.00
204 Alec Hansen SP .75 2.00
205 Ryan Mountcastle SP 1.25 3.00
206 Kyle Wright SP 2.00 5.00
207 Jesus Sanchez SP .75 2.00
208 Mitchell White SP .75 2.00
209 Adrian Morejon SP .75 2.00
210 Michel Baez SP .75 2.00
211 Sixto Sanchez SP 2.00 5.00
212 Wander Javier SP 1.00 2.50
213 Jahmai Jones SP .75 2.00
214 Austin Riley SP 2.50 6.00
215 Jesus Luzardo SP 1.25 3.00
216 Mickey Moniak SP 2.00 5.00
217 Keibert Ruiz SP 2.50 6.00
218 Justus Sheffield SP 1.00 2.50
219 Keston Hiura SP 2.00 5.00
220 Jo Adell SP 2.50 6.00

2018 Topps Heritage Minors Black

*BLACK: 4X TO 10X BASIC
STATED ODDS 1:40 HOBBY
STATED PRINT RUN 50 SER.#'d SETS
1 Vladimir Guerrero Jr. 20.00 50.00
181 Vladimir Guerrero Jr. AS 20.00 50.00

2018 Topps Heritage Minors Blue

*BLUE: 3X TO 8X BASIC
STATED ODDS 1:20 HOBBY
STATED PRINT RUN 99 SER.#'d SETS
1 Vladimir Guerrero Jr. 15.00 40.00
181 Vladimir Guerrero Jr. AS 15.00 40.00

2018 Topps Heritage Minors Circle Color Variations

STATED ODDS 1:396 HOBBY
1 Vladimir Guerrero Jr. 40.00 100.00
25 Hunter Greene 10.00 25.00
28 Genesis Cabrera
50 Eloy Jimenez 15.00 40.00
94 Estevan Florial 5.00 12.00
131 Adam Haseley
136 Brendan Rodgers 12.00 30.00
150 Royce Lewis 25.00 60.00
158 Michael Kopech 6.00 15.00
180 Tim Tebow 50.00 120.00

2018 Topps Heritage Minors Glossy Front

*GLOSSY: 1.5X TO 4X BASIC
THREE PER BOX TOPPER

2018 Topps Heritage Minors Magenta Back

*MAGENTA BACK: 5X TO 12X BASIC
STATED ODDS 1:40 HOBBY
1 Vladimir Guerrero Jr. 25.00 60.00
181 Vladimir Guerrero Jr. AS 25.00 60.00

2018 Topps Heritage Minors Team Color Change

*CLR CHNG: 6X TO 15X BASIC
STATED ODDS 1:80 HOBBY
STATED PRINT RUN 25 SER.#'d SETS
1 Vladimir Guerrero Jr. 30.00 80.00
181 Vladimir Guerrero Jr. AS 30.00 80.00

2018 Topps Heritage Minors Image Variation Autographs

STATED ODDS 1:1556 HOBBY
STATED PRINT RUN 50 SER.#'d SETS
EXCHANGE DEADLINE 9/30/2020
75 Royce Lewis 50.00 120.00
86 Brendan McKay 30.00 80.00
132 Hunter Greene 50.00 120.00

2018 Topps Heritage Minors Image Variations

STATED ODDS 1:396 HOBBY
1 Vladimir Guerrero Jr. 40.00 100.00
13 Jon Duplantier 10.00 25.00
50 Eloy Jimenez 15.00 40.00
54 Bo Bichette
94 Estevan Florial 5.00 12.00
103 MacKenzie Gore 6.00 15.00
123 Mitch Keller
150 Royce Lewis 25.00 60.00
160 Luis Urias 10.00 25.00
180 Tim Tebow 50.00 120.00

2018 Topps Heritage Minors '69 Collector Cards

COMPLETE SET (20) 10.00 25.00
STATED ODDS 1:6 HOBBY
69CCBB Bo Bichette .75 2.00
69CCBR Brendan Rodgers .25 .60
69CCCR Corey Ray .25 .60
69CCEF Estevan Florial .30 .75
69CCEJ Eloy Jimenez .75 2.00
69CCFTJ Fernando Tatis Jr. 1.50 4.00
69CCGC Genesis Cabrera .30 .75
69CCHG Hunter Greene .60 1.50
69CCJL Jesus Luzardo .30 .75
69CCKT Kyle Tucker .40 1.00
69CCLT Leody Taveras .25 .60
69CCLU Luis Urias .40 1.00
69CCMG MacKenzie Gore .40 1.00
69CCMK Mitch Keller .25 .60
69CCMKO Michael Kopech .40 1.00
69CCNS Nick Senzel .60 1.50
69CCRL Royce Lewis .75 2.00
69CCTM Triston McKenzie .20 .50
69CCTT Tim Tebow 2.00 5.00
69CCVGJ Vladimir Guerrero Jr. 2.00 5.00

2018 Topps Heritage Minors '69 Deckle Edge

COMPLETE SET (30) 15.00 40.00
STATED ODDS 1:5 HOBBY
*COLOR: 4X TO 10X BASIC
1 Tim Tebow 2.00 5.00
2 Colton Welker .20 .50
3 Matt Manning .30 .75
4 MacKenzie Gore .40 1.00
5 Ryan Vilade .20 .50
6 Leody Taveras .25 .60
7 Justin Dunn .25 .60
8 Mitch Keller .25 .60
9 Corbin Burnes .30 .75
10 Vladimir Guerrero Jr. 2.00 5.00
11 Eloy Jimenez .75 2.00
12 Genesis Cabrera .30 .75
13 Jose Albertos .20 .50
14 Estevan Florial .30 .75
15 Heliot Ramos .30 .75
16 Jorge Mateo .20 .50
17 Josh Naylor .25 .60
18 Seuly Matias .40 1.00
19 Adbert Alzolay .25 .60
20 Fernando Tatis Jr. 1.50 4.00
21 Bo Bichette .75 2.00
22 Kolby Allard .20 .50
23 Daulton Varsho .25 .60
24 Brendan Rodgers .25 .60
25 Hunter Greene .60 1.50
26 Brandon Marsh .25 .60
27 Jesus Luzardo .30 .75
28 Trevor Stephan .20 .50
29 Mickey Moniak .50 1.25
30 Royce Lewis .75 2.00

2018 Topps Heritage Minors '69 Deckle Edge Autographs

STATED ODDS 1:187 HOBBY
STATED PRINT RUN 99 SER.#'d SETS
EXCHANGE DEADLINE 9/30/2020
*COLOR/25: .6X TO 1.5X BASIC
DEAAG Andres Gimenez 8.00 20.00
DEABM Brendan McKay 15.00 40.00
DEABR Brent Rooker 8.00 20.00
DEACB Corbin Burnes 10.00 25.00
DEADE Drew Ellis 8.00 20.00
DEAFP Franklin Perez 6.00 15.00
DEAGD Greg Deichmann 8.00 20.00
DEAHG Hunter Greene 40.00 100.00
DEAHR Heliot Ramos 10.00 25.00
DEAJK Jeren Kendall 8.00 20.00
DEAKR Keibert Ruiz 15.00 40.00
DEAMB Michel Baez 6.00 15.00
DEAMG MacKenzie Gore 12.00 30.00
DEAMV Mark Vientos 10.00 25.00
DEANL Nicky Lopez 6.00 15.00
DEARL Royce Lewis 25.00 60.00
DEARM Ryan Mountcastle 10.00 25.00
DEASD Shane Dieber 10.00 25.00

2018 Topps Heritage Minors '69 Mint Black Quarter

STATED ODDS 1:294 HOBBY
STATED PRINT RUN 50 SER.#'d SETS
69MBB Bo Bichette 12.00 30.00
69MBM Brendan McKay 5.00 12.00
69MCS Chris Shaw 3.00 8.00
69MCW Colton Welker 3.00 8.00
69MEF Estevan Florial 12.00 30.00
69MEJ Eloy Jimenez 12.00 30.00
69MFT Fernando Tatis Jr. 25.00 60.00
69MHG Hunter Greene 12.00 30.00
69MHR Heliot Ramos 5.00 12.00
69MJD Jeter Downs 5.00 12.00
69MJG Jay Groome 4.00 10.00
69MJW Joey Wentz 4.00 10.00
69MKH Keston Hiura 8.00 20.00
69MKM Kevin Maitan 4.00 10.00
69MKR Keibert Ruiz 10.00 25.00
69MKT Kyle Tucker 6.00 15.00
69MLT Leody Taveras 4.00 10.00
69MMG MacKenzie Gore 6.00 15.00
69MMK Mitch Keller 4.00 10.00
69MMKO Michael Kopech 6.00 15.00
69MMM Mickey Moniak 8.00 20.00
69MNP Nick Pratto 4.00 10.00
69MRL Royce Lewis 20.00 50.00
69MRM Ryan Mountcastle 5.00 12.00
69MTH Tanner Houck 8.00 20.00
69MTT Taylor Trammell 5.00 12.00
69MVG Vladimir Guerrero Jr. 30.00 80.00

2018 Topps Heritage Minors '69 Mint Nickel

STATED ODDS 1:149 HOBBY
STATED PRINT RUN 99 SER.#'d SETS
69MBB Bo Bichette 12.00 30.00
69MBM Brendan McKay 5.00 12.00
69MCS Chris Shaw 3.00 8.00
69MCW Colton Welker 3.00 8.00
69MEF Estevan Florial 12.00 30.00
69MEJ Eloy Jimenez 12.00 30.00
69MFT Fernando Tatis Jr. 25.00 60.00
69MHG Hunter Greene 12.00 30.00
69MHR Heliot Ramos 5.00 12.00
69MJD Jeter Downs 5.00 12.00
69MJG Jay Groome 4.00 10.00
69MJW Joey Wentz 4.00 10.00

69MKH Keston Hiura 8.00 20.00
69MKM Kevin Maitan 4.00 10.00
69MKR Keibert Ruiz 10.00 25.00
69MKT Kyle Tucker 6.00 15.00
69MLT Leody Taveras 4.00 10.00
69MMG MacKenzie Gore 6.00 15.00
69MMK Mitch Keller 4.00 10.00
69MMKO Michael Kopech 6.00 15.00
69MMM Mickey Moniak 8.00 20.00
69MNP Nick Pratto 4.00 10.00
69MRL Royce Lewis 20.00 50.00
69MRM Ryan Mountcastle 5.00 12.00
69MTH Tanner Houck 8.00 20.00
69MTT Taylor Trammell 5.00 12.00
69MVG Vladimir Guerrero Jr. 30.00 80.00

2018 Topps Heritage Minors Bazooka Autographs

STATED ODDS 1:1109 HOBBY
STATED PRINT RUN 50 SER.#'d SETS
EXCHANGE DEADLINE 9/30/2020
BABM Brendan McKay 20.00 50.00
BAHG Hunter Greene
BAHR Heliot Ramos 20.00 50.00
BAJA Jo Adell 75.00 200.00
BARL Royce Lewis
BARM Ryan Mountcastle 20.00 50.00

2018 Topps Heritage Minors Clubhouse Collection Relics

STATED ODDS 1:30 HOBBY
*BLUE/99: .5X TO 1.2X BASIC
*BLACK/50: .6X TO 1.5X BASIC
*ORANGE/25: 1.5X TO 4X BASIC
CCRAA Adbert Alzolay 2.50 6.00
CCRAR Austin Riley 4.00 10.00
CCRBB Bo Bichette 8.00 20.00
CCRBBI Braden Bishop 2.00 5.00
CCRCQ Cal Quantrill 2.00 5.00
CCRCR Corey Ray 2.50 6.00
CCRCS Chris Shaw 2.00 5.00
CCRDA Domingo Acevedo 2.00 5.00
CCREF Estevan Florial 4.00 10.00
CCREJ Eloy Jimenez 8.00 20.00
CCRJD Jon Duplantier 2.00 5.00
CCRJN Josh Naylor 2.50 6.00
CCRJS Justus Sheffield 2.50 6.00
CCRKT Kyle Tucker 4.00 10.00
CCRLU Luis Urias 4.00 10.00
CCRMK Michael Kopech 4.00 10.00
CCRMKE Mitch Keller 2.50 6.00
CCRMS Mike Soroka 6.00 15.00
CCRNG Nick Gordon 2.00 5.00
CCRRM Ryan Mountcastle 3.00 8.00
CCRSN Sheldon Neuse 2.00 5.00
CCRTE Thairo Estrada 5.00 12.00
CCRTM Triston McKenzie 2.00 5.00
CCRTT Touki Toussaint 2.50 6.00
CCRVGJ Vladimir Guerrero Jr. 10.00 25.00
CCRYA Yadier Alvarez 2.50 6.00
CCRYOA Yordan Alvarez 10.00 25.00

2018 Topps Heritage Minors Dual Autographs

STATED ODDS 1:1949 HOBBY
STATED PRINT RUN 20 SER.#'d SETS
EXCHANGE DEADLINE 9/30/2020
HDAAM Marsh/Adell EXCH 75.00 200.00
HDAGG Greene/Gore
HDAGV Gimenez/Vientos 50.00 120.00
HDAHB Burnes/Hiura 40.00 100.00
HDALR Rooker/Lewis 60.00 150.00
HDARK Ruiz/Kendall EXCH 50.00 120.00
HDASE Smith/Ellis EXCH 30.00 80.00

2018 Topps Heritage Minors Real One Autographs

STATED ODDS 1:29 HOBBY
EXCHANGE DEADLINE 9/30/2020
*BLUE/99: .6X TO 1.5X BASIC
*BLACK/50: .75X TO 2X BASIC
*CLR CHNG/25: 1X TO 2.5X BASIC
ROAAG Andres Gimenez 3.00 8.00
ROABM Brendan McKay 6.00 15.00
ROABMA Brandon Marsh 3.00 8.00
ROABR Brent Rooker 6.00 15.00
ROACB Corbin Burnes 4.00 10.00
ROADE Drew Ellis 3.00 8.00
ROAFP Franklin Perez 2.50 6.00
ROAGD Greg Deichmann 3.00 8.00
ROAGS Gregory Soto 2.50 6.00
ROAHG Hunter Greene 25.00 60.00
ROAHR Heliot Ramos 6.00 15.00
ROAJA Jo Adell EXCH 50.00 120.00
ROAJD Jeter Downs 4.00 10.00
ROAJH Jordan Humphreys 2.50 6.00
ROAJK Jeren Kendall EXCH 3.00 8.00
ROAJW Joey Wentz 3.00 8.00
ROAKH Keston Hiura 20.00 50.00
ROAKR Keibert Ruiz 10.00 25.00
ROALG Luis Guillorme 2.50 6.00
ROAMB Michel Baez EXCH 2.50 6.00
ROAMG MacKenzie Gore 20.00 50.00
ROAMGO Merandy Gonzalez 2.50 6.00
ROAMV Mark Vientos 6.00 15.00
ROANL Nicky Lopez 2.50 6.00
ROAPS Pavin Smith 2.50 6.00
ROARL Royce Lewis 40.00 100.00
ROARM Ryan Mountcastle 4.00 10.00
ROASB Shane Bieber 12.00 30.00
ROASC Sam Carlson 3.00 8.00
ROASL Shed Long 5.00 12.00
ROATL Tristen Lutz 3.00 8.00
ROAYA Yordan Alvarez 60.00 150.00

2019 Topps Heritage Minors

COMPLETE SET (220) 60.00 150.00
COMP.SET w/o SPs (200) 25.00 60.00
STATED SP ODDS 1:6 HOBBY
1 Wander Franco 2.00 5.00
2 Melvin Adon .20 .50
3 Michael King .15 .40
4 Moises Gomez .20 .50
5 Aramis Ademan .12 .30
6 Brandon Marsh .12 .30
7 Ryan McKenna .12 .30
8 Brailyn Marquez .30 .75
9 Matt Vierling .20 .50
10 Alejandro Kirk .20 .50
11 Jonathan Ornelas .15 .40
12 Ryan Mountcastle .15 .40
13 Daulton Varsho .12 .30
14 Gabriel Cancel .20 .50
15 Chad Spanberger .12 .30
16 DL Hall .12 .30
17 Domingo Acevedo .12 .30
18 William Contreras .15 .40
19 Isiah Gilliam .15 .40
20 Shervyen Newton .20 .50
21 Mitchell White .12 .30
22 Jahmai Jones .12 .30
23 Nolan Gorman .40 1.00
24 Ali Sanchez .12 .30
25 Lyon Richardson .15 .40
26 Osvaldo Duarte
27 Spencer Howard .12 .30
28 Bobby Dalbec .30 .75
29 Joey Bart .40 1.00
30 Jackson Kowar .12 .30
31 Owen Miller .15 .40
32 Tim Tebow
33 Cal Mitchell .20 .50
34 Matthew Liberatore .12 .30
35 Israel Pineda .20 .50
36 Matt Manning .20 .50
37 Deivi Garcia .60 1.50
38 Bo Naylor .12 .30
39 Jeter Downs .20 .50
40 Garrett Whitlock .12 .30
41 Dane Dunning .12 .30
42 Jose Suarez .12 .30
43 Ethan Hankins .15 .40
44 Diosbel Arias .12 .30
45 Alex Scherff .20 .50
46 Brent Honeywell .15 .40
47 A.J. Puk .15 .40
48 Adonis Medina .20 .50
49 Kyle Funkhouser .12 .30
50 Casey Mize .30 .75
51 Anderson Tejeda .15 .40
52 Drew Waters .40 1.00
53 Khalil Lee .12 .30
54 Julio Pablo Martinez .12 .30
55 Denyi Reyes .15 .40
56 Vidal Brujan .75 2.00
57 Jordan Yamamoto .20 .50
58 Sean Murphy .15 .40
59 Yordan Alvarez .75 2.00
60 Isaac Paredes .40 1.00
61 Logan Allen .12 .30
62 Cal Raleigh .12 .30
63 Zack Collins .15 .40
64 Yusniel Diaz .20 .50
65 Freudis Nova .20 .50
66 Will Stewart .12 .30
67 Luis Garcia .50 1.25
68 Adam Haseley .20 .50
69 Hansel Moreno .12 .30
70 Vince Fernandez .15 .40
71 Abraham Toro .20 .50
72 Gage Canning .12 .30
73 Tyler Freeman .12 .30
74 Gavin Lux .40 1.00
75 Mitch Keller .15 .40
76 Sixto Sanchez .15 .40
77 Parker Meadows .15 .40
78 Leonardo Jimenez .20 .50
79 Corey Ray .12 .30
80 Casey Golden .20 .50
81 Sandro Fabian .12 .30
82 Andres Gimenez .15 .40
83 Dean Kremer .15 .40
84 Daz Cameron .12 .30
85 Anthony Kay .12 .30
86 Grant Lavigne .15 .40
87 Alex Faedo .15 .40
88 Evan White .20 .50
89 Jonathan Hernandez .12 .30
90 Alex Kirilloff .20 .50
91 Brusdar Graterol .15 .40
92 Taylor Trammell .15 .40
93 Franklin Perez .12 .30
94 Brewer Hicklen .20 .50
95 Eric Pardinho .15 .40
96 Oneil Cruz .20 .50
97 Keegan Thompson .12 .30
98 Blaze Alexander .12 .30
99 Esteury Ruiz .15 .40
100 Royce Lewis .25 .60
101 Colton Welker .12 .30
102 Logan Gilbert .20 .50
103 Nick Neidert .12 .30
104 Aaron Civale .20 .50
105 Jazz Chisholm .30 .75
106 Matt Mercer .12 .30
107 Nate Pearson .30 .75
108 Pedro Castellanos .12 .30
109 Rylan Bannon .15 .40
110 Beau Burrows .12 .30
111 Jose Devers .20 .50
112 Brendan McKay .20 .50
113 Cory Heitler .12 .30
114 Jo Adell .40 1.00
115 Derian Cruz .12 .30
116 Sean Hjelle .15 .40
117 Jesus Luzardo .20 .50
118 Brock Burke .12 .30
119 MacKenzie Gore .25 .60
120 Adrian Morejon .12 .30
121 Julio Rodriguez 1.00 2.50
122 Luken Baker .15 .40
123 Telmito Agustin .15 .40
124 Jarred Kelenic .50 1.25
125 Joey Wentz .12 .30
126 Dustin May .40 1.00
127 Izzy Wilson .12 .30
128 Ryan Costello .15 .40
129 Triston Casas .50 1.25
130 Tirso Ornelas .12 .30
131 Cristian Santana .20 .50
132 Kyle Lewis .25 .60
133 Alec Bohm .50 1.25
134 Hans Crouse .12 .30
135 Kyle Muller .12 .30
136 Austin Beck .12 .30
137 Conner Capel .15 .40
138 Forrest Whitley .20 .50
139 Bryan Abreu .20 .50
140 Jordyn Adams .15 .40
141 Justin Dunn .12 .30
142 Grayson Rodriguez .25 .60
143 Brice Turang .15 .40
144 Mateo Gil .15 .40
145 Miguel Amaya .20 .50
146 Brent Rooker .15 .40
147 Kevin Smith .12 .30
148 Kyle Isbel .15 .40
149 Ryan Weathers .12 .30
150 Kristian Robinson .30 .75
151 Nick Madrigal .40 1.00
152 Ian Anderson .30 .75
153 Ronny Mauricio .30 .75
154 Luis Robert 1.25 3.00
155 Dylan Cease .30 .75
156 Genesis Cabrera .20 .50
157 Seth Beer .30 .75
158 Peter Lambert .20 .50
159 Lazaro Armenteros .15 .40
160 Austin Riley .60 1.50
161 MJ Melendez
162 Daniel Johnson .12 .30
163 Clarke Schmidt .20 .50
164 Roberto Ramos .15 .40
165 J.B. Bukauskas .12 .30
166 Cristian Javier .15 .40
167 Anthony Seigler .20 .50
168 Briam Campusano .12 .30
169 Leody Taveras .12 .30
170 Travis Swaggerty .20 .50
171 DJ Peters .20 .50
172 Konnor Pilkington .12 .30
173 Brock Deatherage .12 .30
174 Albert Abreu .12 .30
175 Edward Cabrera .20 .50
176 Brendan Rodgers .20 .50
177 Jordan Groshans .25 .60
178 Joe Jacques .12 .30
179 Estevan Florial .20 .50
180 Victor Victor Mesa
181 Alex Kirilloff AS .20 .50
182 Joey Bart AS .40 1.00
183 Matthew Liberatore AS .12 .30
184 Royce Lewis AS .25 .60
185 MacKenzie Gore AS .25 .60
186 Jarred Kelenic AS .50 1.25
187 Jo Adell AS .40 1.00
188 Ke'Bryan Hayes AS .12 .30
189 Keston Hiura AS .40 1.00
190 Wander Franco AS 2.00 5.00
191 Garica/Arias/Stevenson LL .50 1.25
192 Craig/Dalbec/Santana LL .30 .75
193 Dalbec/Isabel/Golden LL .30 .75
194 Dakota Mekkes .15 .40
Tommy Eveld
Colin Poche LL
195 Keegan Akin .12 .30
Logan Allen
Scott Moss LL
196 Taylor Widener .15 .40
Conner Menez
Dean Kremer LL
197 Bichette/Boswell/Brujan LL .75 2.00
198 Ruiz/Brujan/Reed LL .75 2.00
199 Garcia/King/Marvel LL .20 .50
200 Addison Russ .12 .30
Nate Griep
Matt Pierpont LL
201 Bo Bichette SP 2.00 5.00
202 Nick Gordon SP .60 1.50
203 Adbert Alzolay SP .60 1.50
204 Jonathan India SP .75 2.00
205 Heliot Ramos SP 1.00 2.50
206 Andres Gimenez SP .75 2.00
207 Cristian Pache SP 1.50 4.00
208 Ronaldo Hernandez SP .60 1.50
209 Nolan Jones SP 1.00 2.50
210 Keibert Ruiz SP 1.50 4.00
211 Cavan Biggio SP 3.00 8.00
212 Andrew Knizner SP 1.00 2.50
213 Bryan Mata SP .60 1.50
214 Brady Singer SP 1.25 3.00
215 Nico Hoerner SP 2.00 5.00
216 Ke'Bryan Hayes SP .60 1.50
217 Jesus Sanchez SP .60 1.50
218 Buddy Reed SP .60 1.50
219 Seuly Matias SP .75 2.00
220 Elehuris Montero SP 1.00 2.50

2019 Topps Heritage Minors Black

*BLACK: 4X TO 10X BASIC
STATED ODDS 1:49 HOBBY
STATED PRINT RUN 50 SER.#'d SETS
1 Wander Franco 25.00 60.00
50 Casey Mize 8.00 20.00
59 Yordan Alvarez 50.00 120.00

2019 Topps Heritage Minors Blue

*BLUE: 3X TO 8X BASIC
STATED ODDS 1:25 HOBBY
STATED PRINT RUN 99 SER.#'d SETS
1 Wander Franco 20.00 50.00
50 Casey Mize 6.00 15.00
59 Yordan Alvarez 40.00 100.00

2019 Topps Heritage Minors Missing Player Name Variations

STATED ODDS 1:486 HOBBY
1 Wander Franco 40.00 100.00
23 Nolan Gorman 12.00 30.00
32 Tim Tebow 15.00 40.00
50 Casey Mize 10.00 25.00
54 Julio Pablo Martinez 4.00 10.00
98 Blaze Alexander 4.00 10.00
124 Jarred Kelenic 15.00 40.00
154 Luis Robert 20.00 50.00
173 Brock Deatherage 4.00 10.00
180 Victor Victor Mesa 8.00 20.00

2019 Topps Heritage Minors Image Variations

STATED ODDS 1:486 HOBBY
1 Wander Franco 40.00 100.00
23 Nolan Gorman 12.00 30.00
32 Tim Tebow 20.00 50.00
50 Casey Mize 10.00 25.00
114 Jo Adell 15.00 40.00
119 MacKenzie Gore 10.00 25.00
126 Dustin May 12.00 30.00
133 Alec Bohm 15.00 40.00
154 Luis Robert 20.00 50.00
180 Victor Victor Mesa 8.00 20.00

2019 Topps Heritage Minors Image Variation Autographs

STATED ODDS 1:1894 HOBBY
STATED PRINT RUN 50 SER.#'d SETS
EXCHANGE DEADLINE 9/30/2021
2 Keibert Ruiz 10.00 25.00
36 Julio Pablo Martinez 4.00 10.00
43 Nolan Gorman 25.00 60.00
50 Casey Mize 10.00 25.00
72 Wander Franco EXCH 125.00 300.00
150 Joey Bart 40.00 100.00

2019 Topps Heritage Minors '70 Mint

STATED ODDS 1:197 HOBBY
STATED PRINT RUN 99 SER.#'d SETS
BLACK/50: .5X TO 1.2X BASIC
70MRAB Alec Bohm 8.00 20.00
70MRAG Andres Gimenez 4.00 10.00
70MRBG Brusdar Graterol 5.00 12.00
70MRBS Brady Singer 4.00 10.00
70MRDM Dustin May 8.00 20.00
70MRDW Drew Waters 8.00 20.00
70MREF Estevan Florial 4.00 10.00
70MRJA Jo Adell 8.00 20.00
70MRJB Joey Bart 8.00 20.00
70MRJI Jonathan India 3.00 8.00
70MRJK Jarred Kelenic 8.00 20.00
70MRJL Jesus Luzardo 4.00 10.00
70MRJPM Julio Pablo Martinez 2.50 6.00
70MRKHA Ke'Bryan Hayes 2.50 6.00
70MRKR Keibert Ruiz 6.00 15.00
70MRLR Luis Robert 25.00 60.00
70MRMG MacKenzie Gore 5.00 12.00
70MRML Matthew Liberatore 2.50 6.00
70MRMM Matt Manning 6.00 15.00
70MRNJ Nolan Jones 4.00 10.00
70MRNM Nick Madrigal 8.00 20.00
70MRRH Ronaldo Hernandez 2.50 6.00
70MRRL Royce Lewis 5.00 12.00
70MRSM Sean Murphy 3.00 8.00
70MRWF Wander Franco 12.00 30.00

2019 Topps Heritage Minors '70 Super Boxloader

ONE PER HOBBY BOX
SBBT Brice Turang .60 1.50
SBCM Casey Mize 1.25 3.00
SBEM Elehuris Montero .75 2.00
SBJB Joey Bart 1.50 4.00
SBJI Jonathan India .60 1.50
SBJK Jarred Kelenic 2.00 5.00
SBJPM Julio Pablo Martinez .50 1.25
SBKR Keibert Ruiz 1.25 3.00
SBLG Luis Garcia 2.00 5.00
SBNG Nolan Gorman 1.50 4.00
SBNH Nico Hoerner 1.50 4.00
SBNL Nathaniel Lowe .60 1.50
SBNM Nick Madrigal 1.50 4.00
SBRH Ronaldo Hernandez .50 1.25
SBRM Ronny Mauricio 1.25 3.00
SBSB Seth Beer 1.25 3.00
SBSM Seuly Matias .60 1.50
SBTC Triston Casas 2.00 5.00
SBTL Trevor Larnach 1.25 3.00
SBWF Wander Franco 8.00 20.00

2019 Topps Heritage Minors '70 Super Boxloader Autographs

STATED ODDS 1:71 HOBBY BOXES
STATED PRINT RUN 25 SER.#'d SETS
EXCHANGE DEADLINE 9/30/2021
SBBT Brice Turang
SBCM Casey Mize 40.00 100.00
SBEM Elehuris Montero
SBJB Joey Bart 30.00 80.00
SBJI Jonathan India 6.00 15.00
SBJK Jarred Kelenic
SBJPM Julio Pablo Martinez
SBKR Keibert Ruiz
SBNG Nolan Gorman
SBNH Nico Hoener 20.00 50.00
SBNM Nick Madrigal
SBRH Ronaldo Hernandez
SBRM Ronny Mauricio
SBSB Seth Beer 12.00 30.00
SBSM Seuly Matias 12.00 30.00
SBWF Wander Franco EXCH 125.00 300.00

2019 Topps Heritage Minors Bazooka Autographs

STATED ODDS 1:1578 HOBBY
STATED PRINT RUN 50 SER.#'d SETS
EXCHANGE DEADLINE 9/30/2021
BAJB Joey Bart 40.00 100.00
BAKR Keibert Ruiz 10.00 25.00
BAMA Miguel Amaya 15.00 40.00
BASM Seuly Matias
BATC Triston Casas 20.00 50.00
BAWF Wander Franco EXCH 125.00 300.00

2019 Topps Heritage Minors Clubhouse Collection Relics

STATED ODDS 1:27 HOBBY
*BLUE/99: .5X TO 1.2X BASIC
*BLACK/50: .6X TO 1.5X BASIC
*ORANGE/25: 1.5X TO 4X BASIC
CCRAG Andres Gimenez 2.50 6.00
CCRAK Alex Kirilloff 3.00 8.00
CCRBB Bo Bichette 5.00 12.00
CCRBD Bobby Dalbec 5.00 12.00
CCRBM Bryan Mata 2.00 5.00
CCRBRE Buddy Reed 2.00 5.00
CCRCP Cristian Pache 4.00 10.00
CCRCR Corey Ray 2.00 5.00
CCRDA Domingo Acevedo 2.00 5.00
CCRDC Dylan Cease 5.00 12.00
CCREF Estevan Florial 3.00 8.00
CCREW Evan White 3.00 8.00
CCRHR Heliot Ramos 3.00 8.00
CCRJA Jo Adell 4.00 10.00
CCRJH Jonathan Hernandez 2.00 5.00
CCRJS Jesus Sanchez 2.00 5.00
CCRKH Ke'Bryan Hayes 2.00 5.00
CCRKL Kyle Lewis 4.00 10.00
CCRKLE Khalil Lee 2.00 5.00
CCRKR Keibert Ruiz 5.00 12.00
CCRLR Luis Robert 10.00 25.00
CCRMA Miguel Amaya 3.00 8.00
CCRMAD Melvin Adon 3.00 8.00
CCRNG Nick Gordon 2.00 5.00
CCRNH Nico Hoerner 4.00 10.00
CCRNP Nate Pearson 5.00 12.00
CCRRH Ronaldo Hernandez 2.00 5.00
CCRSM Seuly Matias 2.50 6.00
CCRTM Triston McKenzie 2.00 5.00
CCRYA Yordan Alvarez 6.00 15.00

2019 Topps Heritage Minors Fantastic Feats

STATED ODDS 1:6 HOBBY
FF1 Tim Tebow .30 .75
FF2 Wander Franco 3.00 8.00
FF3 Dustin May .60 1.50
FF4 Jarred Kelenic .75 2.00
FF5 Luis Robert 2.00 5.00
FF6 Seuly Matias .25 .60
FF7 Ke'Bryan Hayes .20 .50
FF8 Andrew Knizner .30 .75
FF9 Adbert Alzolay .20 .50
FF10 Andres Gimenez .25 .60
FF11 Bo Bichette .60 1.50
FF12 Elehuris Montero .30 .75
FF13 Jo Adell .60 1.50
FF14 Jesus Sanchez .20 .50
FF15 Bryan Mata .20 .50
FF16 MacKenzie Gore .40 1.00
FF17 Cavan Biggio 1.00 2.50
FF18 Nolan Gorman .60 1.50
FF19 Alec Bohm .75 2.00
FF20 Joey Bart .60 1.50

2019 Topps Heritage Minors Fresh On The Scene

STATED ODDS 1:5 HOBBY
FOS1 Wander Franco 3.00 8.00
FOS2 Triston Casas .75 2.00
FOS3 Luis Garcia .75 2.00
FOS4 Brock Deatherage .20 .50
FOS5 Miguel Amaya .30 .75
FOS6 Jonathan India .25 .60
FOS7 Seth Beer .50 1.25
FOS8 Kris Bubic .30 .75
FOS9 Matthew Liberatore .20 .50
FOS10 Anthony Seigler .30 .75
FOS11 Brice Turang .25 .60
FOS12 Joey Bart .60 1.50
FOS13 Elehuris Montero .30 .75
FOS14 Greyson Jenista .25 .60
FOS15 Jarred Kelenic .75 2.00
FOS16 Jake McCarthy .30 .75
FOS17 Blaze Alexander .20 .50
FOS18 Nico Hoerner .60 1.50
FOS19 Julio Rodriguez 1.50 4.00
FOS20 Casey Mize .50 1.25
FOS21 Tristan Pompey .25 .60
FOS22 Nolan Gorman .60 1.50
FOS23 Nick Madrigal .60 1.50
FOS24 Trevor Larnach .50 1.25
FOS25 Alek Thomas .30 .75
FOS26 Luken Baker .25 .60
FOS27 Julio Pablo Martinez .20 .50
FOS28 Owen Miller .25 .60
FOS29 Alec Bohm .75 2.00
FOS30 Victor Victor Mesa .40 1.00

2019 Topps Heritage Minors Fresh On The Scene Autographs

STATED ODDS 1:240 HOBBY
STATED PRINT RUN 99 SER.#'d SETS
EXCHANGE DEADLINE 9/30/2021
FOSAAS Anthony Seigler 5.00 12.00
FOSABD Brock Deatherage 5.00 12.00
FOSABT Brice Turang 4.00 10.00
FOSACM Casey Mize 15.00 40.00
FOSAEM Elehuris Montero 5.00 12.00
FOSAGJ Greyson Jenista 10.00 25.00
FOSAJB Joey Bart 30.00 80.00
FOSAJI Jonathan India 4.00 10.00
FOSAJK Jarred Kelenic 15.00 40.00
FOSAJM Jake McCarthy 5.00 12.00
FOSAJPM Julio Pablo Martinez 3.00 8.00
FOSAMA Miguel Amaya 5.00 12.00
FOSANG Nolan Gorman 20.00 50.00
FOSANH Nico Hoerner 10.00 25.00
FOSANM Nick Madrigal 10.00 25.00
FOSAOM Owen Miller 5.00 12.00
FOSASB Seth Beer 8.00 20.00
FOSATC Triston Casas 15.00 40.00
FOSATL Trevor Larnach 8.00 20.00
FOSAWF Wander Franco EXCH 40.00 100.00

2019 Topps Heritage Minors Real One Autographs

STATED ODDS 1:26 HOBBY
EXCHANGE DEADLINE 9/30/2021
*BLUE/99: .5X TO 1.2X BASIC
*BLACK/50: .6X TO 1.5X BASIC
*CLR CHNG/25: .75X TO 2X BASIC
ROAAK Andrew Knizner 5.00 12.00
ROAAS Anthony Seigler 8.00 20.00
ROAAT Alek Thomas 5.00 12.00
ROABD Brock Deatherage 3.00 8.00
ROABT Brice Turang 4.00 10.00
ROACC Carlos Cortes 3.00 8.00
ROACM Casey Mize 20.00 50.00
ROAEM Elehuris Montero 5.00 12.00
ROAGJ Greyson Jenista 4.00 10.00
ROAGW Garrett Whitlock 3.00 8.00
ROAJB Joey Bart 40.00 100.00
ROAJG Jordan Groshans 6.00 15.00
ROAJI Jonathan India 4.00 10.00
ROAJK Jarred Kelenic 20.00 50.00
ROAJM Jake McCarthy 5.00 12.00
ROAJPM Julio Pablo Martinez 5.00 12.00
ROAKM Keibert Ruiz 6.00 15.00
ROALB Luken Baker 4.00 10.00
ROAMA Miguel Amaya 8.00 20.00
ROANG Nolan Gorman 20.00 50.00
ROANH Nico Hoerner 10.00 25.00
ROANM Nick Madrigal 10.00 25.00
ROAOM Owen Miller 4.00 10.00
ROARB Rylan Bannon 4.00 10.00
ROARH Ronaldo Hernandez 3.00 8.00
ROARM Ronny Mauricio 12.00 30.00
ROASB Seth Beer 10.00 25.00
ROASM Seuly Matias 6.00 15.00
ROATC Triston Casas 10.00 25.00
ROATL Trevor Larnach 8.00 20.00
ROATP Tristan Pompey 4.00 10.00
ROATS Travis Swaggerty 5.00 12.00
ROAWF Wander Franco EXCH 75.00 200.00

2019 Topps Heritage Minors Real One Dual Autographs

STATED ODDS 1:2367 HOBBY
STATED PRINT RUN 20 SER.#'d SETS
EXCHANGE DEADLINE 9/30/2021
RODABM Bannon/McKenna 20.00 50.00
RODABR Bart/Ruiz 50.00 12.00
RODAFL Franco/Liberatore EXCH 125.00 300.00
RODAGB Baker/Gorman
RODAHA Hoerner/Amaya EXCH 60.00 150.00
RODAIG Gorman/India 30.00 80.00
RODAMD Deatherage/Mize
RODAML Liberatore/Mize

2020 Topps Heritage Minors

COMMON SP (201-220) .60 1.50
SP SEMIS .75 2.00
SP UNLISTED 1.00 2.50
STATED SP ODDS 1:6 HOBBY
1 Wander Franco 1.25 3.00
2 Alex Kirilloff .25 .60
3 Kody Hoese .40 1.00
4 Sherten Apostel .60 1.50
5 Alexander Canario .12 .30
6 Gilberto Jimenez .60 1.50
7 Brenton Doyle .60 1.50
8 Hunter Bishop .25 .60
9 George Kirby .20 .50
10 Victor Mesa Jr. .30 .75
11 Victor Victor Mesa .20 .50
12 Sean Hjelle .20 .50
13 Bo Naylor .15 .40
14 Julio Rodriguez .75 2.00
15 Gabriel Cancel .20 .50
16 Jake Sanford .20 .50
17 Ronny Mauricio .30 .75
18 Brandon Marsh .12 .30
19 Grae Kessinger .20 .50
20 Drew Waters .30 .75
21 Ian Anderson .30 .75
22 Logan Gilbert .15 .40
23 Grant Gambrell .15 .40
24 Dominic Fletcher .12 .30
25 Heliot Ramos .20 .50
26 Taylor Trammell .15 .40
27 Alek Thomas .15 .40
28 Brent Honeywell .15 .40
29 Tommy Henry .15 .40
30 Tyler Stephenson .12 .30
31 Jordan Balazovic .25 .60
32 Logan Driscoll .20 .50
33 Simeon Woods Richardson .20 .50
34 Hunter Greene .20 .50
35 Tahnaj Thomas .12 .30
36 Jordyn Adams .15 .40
37 Jordan Groshans .25 .60
38 Mason Martin .25 .60
39 Jose Garcia .12 .30
40 George Valera .25 .60
41 Ezequiel Duran .25 .60
42 DL Hall .12 .30
43 Luis Garcia .20 .50
44 Keibert Ruiz .30 .75
45 Orelvis Martinez .30 .75
46 Matthew Lugo .20 .50
47 Geraldo Perdomo .12 .30
48 Nick Lodolo .20 .50
49 Tyler Freeman .15 .40
50 Matthew Liberatore .15 .40
51 Jesus Sanchez .12 .30
52 Max Lazar .15 .40
53 Liover Peguero .20 .50
54 Corbin Carroll .20 .50
55 Bryse Wilson .15 .40
56 Monte Harrison .12 .30
57 Andres Gimenez .15 .40
58 Brice Turang .12 .30
59 Ivan Herrera .20 .50
60 Mark Vientos .12 .30
61 Ryan Mountcastle .20 .50
62 Kris Bubic .20 .50
63 Ryan Rolison .12 .30
64 Brayan Rocchio .50 1.25
65 Brailyn Marquez .30 .75
66 Shane Baz .12 .30
67 Niko Hulsizer .30 .75
68 Alek Manoah .15 .40
69 Brent Rooker .15 .40
70 Sixto Sanchez .20 .50
71 Jackson Kowar .12 .30
72 Daniel Espino .15 .40
73 Grant Lavigne .12 .30
74 Aaron Bracho .12 .30
75 Brennan Malone .12 .30
76 Michael Busch .30 .75
77 Adam Kloffenstein .20 .50
78 Keoni Cavaco .12 .30
79 Kyle Muller .12 .30
80 Glenallen Hill Jr. .20 .50
81 Leody Taveras .12 .30
82 J.B. Bukauskas .12 .30
83 Matt Wallner .25 .60
84 Antonio Cabello .40 1.00
85 Matthew Allan .25 .60
86 Quinn Priester .20 .50
87 Anthony Volpe .50 1.25
88 Ryan Weathers .12 .30
89 Peyton Burdick .50 1.25
90 Cal Raleigh .12 .30
91 Blake Walston .20 .50
92 Gunnar Henderson .15 .40
93 Kyle Isbel .12 .30
94 Austin Beck .15 .40
95 Daniel Johnson .12 .30
96 Miguel Vargas .30 .75
97 Parker Meadows .15 .40
98 Bryce Ball .60 1.50
99 Yusniel Diaz .20 .50
100 Daz Cameron .12 .30
101 Brandon Bielak .12 .30
102 Daniel Lynch .12 .30
103 Riley Greene .50 1.25
104 Braden Shewmake .20 .50
105 Aaron Ashby .12 .30
106 Sam Huff .25 .60
107 Brock Deatherage .15 .40
108 Matt Manning .15 .40
109 Royce Lewis .30 .75
110 Forrest Whitley .12 .30
111 T.J. Sikkema .12 .30
112 Luis Patino .20 .50
113 Marco Luciano .50 1.25
114 Spencer Howard .50 1.25
115 Vidal Brujan .40 1.00
116 Kristian Robinson .40 1.00
117 Grayson Rodriguez .20 .50
118 Ke'Bryan Hayes .12 .30
119 Oneil Cruz .15 .40
120 Jazz Chisholm .30 .75
121 Dylan Carlson .50 1.25
122 Luis Campusano .20 .50
123 JJ Goss .12 .30
124 Deivi Garcia .50 1.25
125 Brennen Davis .25 .60
126 Tarik Skubal .60 1.50
127 Nolan Jones .20 .50
128 Trevor Larnach .25 .60
129 Alec Bohm .75 2.00
130 Triston Casas .30 .75
131 Tim Tebow .20 .50
132 Daulton Varsho .12 .30
133 Travis Swaggerty .15 .40
134 Jhoan Duran .12 .30
135 Evan White .12 .30
136 Miguel Amaya .15 .40
137 Edward Cabrera .20 .50
138 Josiah Gray .20 .50
139 William Contreras .15 .40
140 Lewin Diaz .12 .30
141 Isaac Paredes .20 .50
142 Bryan Mata .12 .30
143 Clarke Schmidt .20 .50
144 Estevan Florial .20 .50
145 Luis Gil .20 .50
146 Jonathan Stiever .12 .30
147 Ethan Hankins .15 .40
148 Khalil Lee .12 .30
149 Brady Singer .15 .40
150 Ulrich Bojarski .12 .30
151 Freudis Nova .12 .30
152 Jordan Brewer .12 .30
153 Jeremiah Jackson .12 .30
154 Jorge Mateo .12 .30
155 C.J. Chatham .15 .40
156 Cole Winn .12 .30
157 Jared Oliva .30 .75
158 Gabriel Rodriguez .25 .60
159 Seth Beer .25 .60
160 Michael Toglia .12 .30
161 Terrin Vavra .25 .60
162 Ildemaro Vargas .12 .30
163 Bobby Dalbec .30 .75
164 Jonathan India .15 .40
165 Greg Jones .15 .40
166 Owen Miller .12 .30
167 Luis Matos .20 .50
168 Josh Lowe .12 .30
169 Jackson Rutledge .20 .50
170 Elehuris Montero .15 .40
171 Chase Strumpf .25 .60
172 Kameron Misner .20 .50
173 Francisco Alvarez .40 1.00
174 Hudson Head .60 1.50
175 Bryson Stott .30 .75
176 Gabriel Arias .20 .50
177 Miguel Hiraldo .40 1.00
178 Hudson Potts .12 .30
179 Shane McClanahan .15 .40
180 Canaan Smith .20 .50
181 Triston McKenzie .20 .50
182 Andy Pages .15 .40
183 Edward Olivares .20 .50
184 Vargas/Rea/Abrams .50 1.25
185 Castro/Martin/Rojas .25 .60
186 Gettys/Martin/Hernandez .25 .60
187 Ober/Gudino/Marklund .12 .30
188 Campbell/Lowther/File .12 .30
189 Ryan/Skubal/Bubic .30 .80
190 Gettys/Rojas/Castro .12 .30
191 Fargas/Heath/Lee .12 .30
192 Kingham/Robles/Parsons .12 .30
193 Griep/Eckelman/Ratliff .12 .30
194 Abiatal Avelino HL .12 .30
Hits Walk-Off
195 Cristhian Adames HL .12 .30
Hits Go-Ahead Home Run
196 Enderson Franco HL .12 .30
Seals the Series with Five-Out Save
197 Sacramento River Cats HL .12 .30
Celebrate!
198 Bobby Bradley HL .15 .40
Home Run Lifts Clippers
199 Ryan Lavarnway HL .12 .30
Blasts Two Home Runs
200 Bradley Zimmer HL .12 .30
Hits Go-Ahead Three-Run Homer
201 Adley Rutschman SP 4.00 10.00
202 Bobby Witt Jr. SP 5.00 12.00
203 Josh Jung SP 1.50 4.00
204 Jarren Duran SP 2.50 6.00
205 MacKenzie Gore SP 1.25 3.00
206 Cristian Pache SP 2.00 5.00
207 Joey Bart SP 2.00 5.00
208 Jeter Downs SP 1.00 2.50
209 Casey Mize SP 2.00 5.00
210 Xavier Edwards SP 2.50 6.00
211 Andrew Vaughn SP 2.50 6.00
212 CJ Abrams SP 2.50 6.00
213 Jarred Kelenic SP 4.00 10.00
214 Shea Langeliers SP 1.25 3.00
215 Nick Madrigal SP 2.00 5.00
216 JJ Bleday SP 2.00 5.00
217 Jo Adell SP 2.50 6.00
218 Brett Baty SP 2.00 5.00
219 Nolan Gorman SP 1.25 3.00
220 Nate Pearson SP 1.25 3.00

2020 Topps Heritage Minors Missing Facsimile Variations

STATED ODDS 1:552 HOBBY
1 Wander Franco 12.00 30.00
2 Alex Kirilloff 8.00 20.00
11 Victor Mesa Jr. 3.00 8.00
14 Julio Rodriguez 10.00 25.00
103 Riley Greene 10.00 25.00
104 Braden Shewmake 2.00 5.00
106 Sam Huff 8.00 20.00
109 Royce Lewis 12.00 30.00
110 Forrest Whitley 6.00 15.00
131 Tim Tebow 15.00 40.00

2020 Topps Heritage Minors Image Variations

STATED ODDS 1:552 HOBBY
1 Wander Franco 25.00 60.00
11 Victor Mesa Jr. 6.00 15.00
14 Julio Rodriguez 30.00 80.00
103 Riley Greene 12.00 30.00
104 Braden Shewmake 15.00 40.00
106 Sam Huff 30.00 80.00
109 Royce Lewis 12.00 30.00
129 Alec Bohm 15.00 40.00
131 Tim Tebow 40.00 100.00
204 Nate Pearson 5.00 12.00

2020 Topps Heritage Minors Image Variation Autographs

STATED ODDS 1:2204 HOBBY
STATED PRINT RUN 50 SER.#'d SETS
EXCHANGE DEADLINE 9/30/22
36 Andrew Vaughn 20.00 50.00

50 Bobby Witt Jr. 100.00 250.00
77 JJ Bleday 25.00 60.00
102 Vidal Brujan 15.00 40.00
150 Adley Rutschman 100.00 250.00
171 Riley Greene 40.00 100.00

2020 Topps Heritage Minors Clubhouse Collection Relics

STATED ODDS 1:28 HOBBY
*BLUE/99: .5X TO 1.2X BASIC
*BLACK/50: .6X TO 1.5X BASIC
*ORANGE/25: 1X TO 2.5X BASIC
CCRAA Adbert Alzolay 2.00 5.00
CCRAB Alec Bohm 6.00 15.00
CCRAT Alek Thomas 2.00 5.00
CCRBZ Jordan Balazovic 3.00 8.00
CCRCP Cristian Pache 5.00 12.00
CCRDC Dylan Carlson 4.00 10.00
CCRDG Deivi Garcia 6.00 15.00
CCRDH DL Hall 1.50 4.00
CCRDV Daulton Varsho 1.50 4.00
CCRGR Grayson Rodriguez 2.50 6.00
CCRHR Heliot Ramos 2.50 6.00
CCRIP Isaac Paredes 2.50 6.00
CCRJA Jo Adell 6.00 15.00
CCRJB Joey Bart 5.00 12.00
CCRJC Jazz Chisholm 4.00 10.00
CCRJD Jarren Duran 4.00 10.00
CCRJK Jarred Kelenic 5.00 12.00
CCRLP Luis Patino 2.50 6.00
CCRMA Miguel Amaya 2.00 5.00
CCRMG MacKenzie Gore 3.00 8.00
CCRNG Nolan Gorman 5.00 12.00
CCRNJ Nolan Jones 2.50 6.00
CCRNM Nick Madrigal 5.00 12.00
CCRNP Nate Pearson 3.00 8.00
CCRRH Ronaldo Hernandez 1.50 4.00
CCRRL Royce Lewis 4.00 10.00
CCRSH Sam Huff 4.00 10.00
CCRSS Sixto Sanchez 2.50 6.00
CCRTT Taylor Trammell 2.00 5.00
CCRWF Wander Franco 8.00 80.00

2020 Topps Heritage Minors Futures of the Pastime Autograph Relics

STATED ODDS 1:3683 HOBBY
STATED PRINT RUN 25 SER.#'d SETS
EXCHANGE DEADLINE 9/30/22

2020 Topps Heritage Minors Real One Autographs

STATED ODDS 1:22 HOBBY
EXCHANGE DEADLINE 9/30/22
ROAAP Andy Pages 4.00 10.00
ROAAR Adley Rutschman 50.00 120.00
ROAAV Andrew Vaughn 15.00 40.00
ROABB Brett Baty 15.00 40.00
ROABS Braden Shewmake 6.00 15.00
ROACC Corbin Carroll 8.00 20.00
ROAEL Ethan Lindow 4.00 10.00
ROAFA Francisco Alvarez 15.00 40.00
ROAHB Hunter Bishop EXCH
ROAJA Jacob Amaya 4.00 10.00
ROAJD Jarren Duran 6.00 15.00
ROAJJ Josh Jung 8.00 20.00
ROAJR Jackson Rutledge 3.00 8.00
ROAKC Keoni Cavaco 3.00 8.00
ROALP Luis Patino 8.00 20.00
ROAMV Miguel Vargas 6.00 15.00
ROAPB Peyton Burdick 5.00 12.00
ROARG Riley Greene 20.00 50.00
ROASH Sam Huff 10.00 25.00
ROASL Shea Langeliers 10.00 25.00
ROATS Tarik Skubal 8.00 20.00
ROAVB Vidal Brujan 10.00 25.00
ROAWW Will Wilson 4.00 10.00
ROAXE Xavier Edwards 6.00 15.00
ROAAVO Anthony Volpe 12.00 30.00
ROABST Bryson Stott 12.00 30.00
ROABWJ Bobby Witt Jr. 50.00 120.00
ROAGHJ Glenallen Hill Jr. 5.00 12.00
ROAJJB JJ Bleday 15.00 40.00
ROAMLA Max Lazar 4.00 10.00

2020 Topps Heritage Minors Real One Autographs Blue

*BLUE/99: .5X TO 1.2X BASIC
STATED ODDS 1:215 HOBBY
STATED PRINT RUN 99 SER.#'d SETS
EXCHANGE DEADLINE 9/30/22
ROAFA Francisco Alvarez 25.00 60.00
ROAHB Hunter Bishop EXCH 20.00 50.00
ROASH Sam Huff 15.00 40.00

2020 Topps Heritage Minors Real One Autographs Image Border Removal

*NO BRDR/25: .8X TO 2X BASIC
STATED ODDS 1:712 HOBBY
STATED PRINT RUN 25 SER.#'d SETS
EXCHANGE DEADLINE 9/30/22
ROAFA Francisco Alvarez 40.00 100.00
ROAHB Hunter Bishop EXCH 30.00 80.00
ROARG Riley Greene 50.00 120.00
ROASH Sam Huff 40.00 100.00
ROABST Bryson Stott 30.00 80.00

2020 Topps Heritage Minors Real One Autographs White

*WHITE/50: .6X TO 1.5X BASIC
STATED ODDS 1:356 HOBBY
STATED PRINT RUN 50 SER.#'d SETS
EXCHANGE DEADLINE 9/30/22
ROAFA Francisco Alvarez 30.00 80.00
ROAHB Hunter Bishop EXCH 25.00 60.00
ROARG Riley Greene 40.00 100.00
ROASH Sam Huff 20.00 50.00
ROABST Bryson Stott 25.00 60.00

2020 Topps Heritage Minors '71 Bazooka Numbered Test Cards

STATED ODDS 1:6 HOBBY
1 Wander Franco 2.50 6.00
2 Adley Rutschman 1.50 4.00
3 Jarren Duran 1.00 2.50
4 MacKenzie Gore .50 1.25
5 Nolan Gorman .50 1.25
6 JJ Bleday .75 2.00
7 Bobby Witt Jr. 1.25 3.00
8 Andrew Vaughn 1.00 2.50
9 Jarred Kelenic 1.50 4.00
10 Royce Lewis .60 1.50
11 Casey Mize .75 2.00
12 Nick Madrigal .75 2.00
13 Joey Bart .75 2.00
14 Nate Pearson .50 1.25
15 Riley Greene 1.00 2.50
16 Alec Bohm 1.50 4.00
17 Josh Jung .60 1.50
18 Tim Tebow .40 1.00
19 Xavier Edwards 1.00 2.50
20 Shea Langeliers .50 1.25

2020 Topps Heritage Minors '71 Greatest Moments Autographs

STATED ODDS 1:XX HOBBY
STATED PRINT RUN 25 SER.#'d SETS
EXCHANGE DEADLINE 9/30/22
71GMAP Andy Pages 10.00 25.00
71GMAR Adley Rutschman 40.00 100.00
71GMAV Andrew Vaughn 20.00 50.00
71GMBS Braden Shewmake 30.00 80.00
71GMJD Jarren Duran 20.00 50.00
71GMRG Riley Greene 40.00 100.00
71GMSH Sam Huff
71GMSL Shea Langeliers 10.00 25.00
71GMVB Vidal Brujan
71GMXE Xavier Edwards
71GMAVO Anthony Volpe 20.00 50.00
71GMBWJ Bobby Witt Jr.
71GMJJB JJ Bleday

2020 Topps Heritage Minors '71 Greatest Moments Boxloader

STATED ODDS 1 PER BOX
1 Adley Rutschman 3.00 8.00
2 JJ Bleday 1.50 4.00
3 Bobby Witt Jr. 2.50 6.00
4 Andrew Vaughn 2.00 5.00
5 Riley Greene 2.00 5.00
6 CJ Abrams 2.00 5.00
7 Shea Langeliers 1.00 2.50
8 Sam Huff 1.00 2.50
9 Vidal Brujan 1.50 4.00
10 Xavier Edwards 2.00 5.00
11 Isaac Paredes .75 2.00
12 Jarren Duran 2.00 5.00
13 Braden Shewmake .75 2.00
14 Anthony Volpe 2.00 5.00
15 Andy Pages .60 1.50
16 Wander Franco 5.00 12.00
17 MacKenzie Gore 1.00 2.50
18 Jo Adell 2.00 5.00
19 Casey Mize 1.50 4.00
20 Royce Lewis 1.25 3.00

2020 Topps Heritage Minors '71 Mint Relics

STATED ODDS 1:279 HOBBY
STATED PRINT RUN 99 SER.#'d SETS
*BLACK/50: .6X TO 1.5X BASIC
71MRAR Adley Rutschman 12.00 30.00
71MRAV Andrew Vaughn 8.00 20.00
71MRBB Brett Baty 8.00 20.00
71MRBW Bobby Witt Jr. 12.00 30.00
71MRCA CJ Abrams 8.00 20.00
71MRDE Daniel Espino 2.50 6.00
71MRHB Hunter Bishop 4.00 10.00
71MRJB JJ Bleday 6.00 15.00
71MRJD Joey Bart 6.00 15.00
71MRJJ Josh Jung 10.00 25.00
71MRJK Jarred Kelenic 6.00 15.00
71MRJR Julio Rodriguez 12.00 30.00
71MRJT Jeter Downs 3.00 8.00
71MRKH Kody Hoese 6.00 15.00
71MRML Marco Luciano 8.00 20.00
71MRNG Nolan Gorman 12.00 30.00
71MRNL Nick Lodolo 3.00 8.00
71MRRG Riley Greene 8.00 20.00
71MRTS Tarik Skubal 10.00 25.00
71MRVO Anthony Volpe 12.00 30.00

2020 Topps Heritage Minors '71 Scratch Off

STATED ODDS 1:5 HOBBY
1 Adley Rutschman 1.50 4.00
2 JJ Bleday .75 2.00
3 Bobby Witt Jr. 1.25 3.00
4 Andrew Vaughn 1.00 2.50
5 Sam Huff .50 1.25
6 Francisco Alvarez .75 2.00
7 Xavier Edwards 1.00 2.50
8 Luis Patino .40 1.00
9 Will Wilson .30 .75
10 Isaac Paredes .40 1.00
11 Jarren Duran 1.00 2.50
12 Braden Shewmake .40 1.00
13 Tarik Skubal 1.25 3.00
14 Anthony Volpe 1.00 2.50
15 Andy Pages .30 .75
16 Peyton Burdick 1.00 2.50
17 Brady McConnell .30 .75
18 Matthew Lugo .40 1.00
19 Grant Gambrell .30 .75
20 Canaan Smith .40 1.00
21 Riley Greene 1.00 2.50
22 CJ Abrams 1.00 2.50
23 Shea Langeliers .50 1.25
24 Hunter Bishop .50 1.25
25 Vidal Brujan .75 2.00
26 Jordan Balazovic .50 1.25
27 Miguel Vargas .60 1.50
28 Jacob Amaya 1.00 2.50
29 Glenallen Hill Jr. .40 1.00
30 Max Lazar .30 .75

2020 Topps Heritage Minors '71 Topps All Star Rookie Autographs

STATED ODDS 1:1577 HOBBY
STATED PRINT RUN 50 SER.#'d SETS
EXCHANGE DEADLINE 9/30/22
71AAAV Andrew Vaughn 15.00 40.00
71AABS Braden Shewmake 6.00 15.00
71AAPB Peyton Burdick 15.00 40.00
71AARG Riley Greene 50.00 120.00
71AASH Sam Huff 15.00 40.00
71AATS Tarik Skubal 20.00 50.00
71AAAVO Anthony Volpe 25.00 60.00
71AABWJ Bobby Witt Jr. 50.00 120.00

2010 Topps Pro Debut

COMPLETE SET (440) 75.00 150.00
COMP.SER.1 SET (220) 40.00 80.00
COMP.SER 2.SET (220) 40.00 80.00
COMMON CARD .15 .40
PLATE ODDS 1:312 HOBBY
1 Pedro Alvarez .40 1.00
2 Aaron Hicks .40 1.00
3 Destin Hood .25 .60
4 Grant Desme .25 .60
5 Craig Kimbrel 1.00 2.50
6 Tim Melville .25 .60
7 Christian Bethancourt .25 .60
8 Brett Wallace .40 1.00
9 Chris Smith .15 .40
10 Kyle Skipworth .25 .60
11 James Jones .25 .60
12 Ryan Westmoreland .15 .40
13 Eric Hosmer 1.25 3.00
14 Casper Wells .15 .40
15 Tim Beckham .60 1.50
16 Robbie Weinhardt .15 .40
17 Jason Castro .40 1.00
18 Cutter Dykstra .15 .40
19 Pete Hissey .15 .40
20 Zach Braddock .15 .40
21 Ross Seaton .25 .60
22 Derrik Gibson .15 .40
23 Ryan Flaherty .15 .40
24 Randall Delgado .25 .60
25 Jefry Marte .15 .40
26 Justin Smoak .50 1.25
27 Jemile Weeks .25 .60
28 Yonder Alonso .40 1.00
29 Ethan Martin .40 1.00
30 Brett Lawrie .60 1.50
31 David Cooper .25 .60
32 Reese Havens .25 .60
33 Casey Kelly .75 2.00
34 David Adams .15 .40
35 Jeremy Bleich .15 .40
36 Brett DeVall .15 .40
37 Stephen Fife .15 .40
38 Garrison Lassiter .25 .60
39 Che-Hsuan Lin .25 .60
40 Kyle Lobstein .15 .40
41 Jordan Lyles .25 .60
42 Brett Marshall .15 .40
43 Wade Miley .25 .60
44 D.J. Mitchell .15 .40
45 Robbie Ross .25 .60
46 Carlos Paulino .15 .40
47 Carlos Triunfel .25 .60
48 Robbie Widlansky .15 .40
49 Myrio Richard .15 .40
50 Josh Phegley .25 .60
51 Trevor Holder .15 .40
52 Steve Baron .15 .40
53 Matt Davidson .50 1.25
54 Kyle Seager .40 1.00
55 Aaron Miller .15 .40
56 Jerry Sullivan .15 .40
57 Tyler Skaggs .40 1.00
58 Evan Chambers .25 .60
59 Garrett Richards .40 1.00
60 Chris Dominguez .40 1.00
61 Mike Belfiore .15 .40
62 Miles Head .40 1.00
63 Guillermo Pimentel .15 .40
64 Kyle Heckathorn .15 .40
65 Patrick Schuster .15 .40
66 Tyler Kehrer .15 .40
67 Erik Davis .15 .40
68 Jeff Kobernus .15 .40
69 Andrew Doyle .25 .60
70 Rich Poythress .15 .40
71 Melky Mesa .25 .60
72 Everett Williams .15 .40
73 Shelby Miller .75 2.00
74 Jose Alvarez .15 .40
75 Mark Cohoon .15 .40
76 Brett Jackson .50 1.25
77 Slade Heathcott .50 1.25
78 Yan Gomes .25 .60
79 Nick Franklin .40 1.00
80 Rex Brothers .15 .40
81 Blake Smith .15 .40
82 Keyvius Sampson .40 1.00
83 Chris Dwyer .15 .40
84 Leandro Castro .15 .40
85 Luke Murton .15 .40
86 Kent Matthes .15 .40
87 Nolan Arenado 2.50 6.00
88 Angelo Songco .15 .40
89 Trayce Thompson .40 1.00
90 Chris Owings .15 .40
91 Jason Stoffel .25 .60
92 Eric Smith .15 .40
93 Edwin Gomez .15 .40
94 Steven Inch .15 .40
95 Jason Kipnis .60 1.50
96 Tucker Barnhart .15 .40
97 Ryan Wheeler .25 .60
98 Sean Ochinko .15 .40
99 Josh Fellhauer .15 .40
100 Michael Ohlman .15 .40
101 Garrett Gould .15 .40
102 Nate Freiman .15 .40
103 Jonathan Singleton .40 1.00
104 Jordan Pacheco .40 1.00
105 Yorman Rodriguez .15 .40
106 DeAngelo Mack .25 .60
107 Dillon Baird .15 .40
108 Chris McGuiness .15 .40
109 Max Walla .15 .40
110 Brian Ruggiano .15 .40
111 Thomas Neal .25 .60
112 Cameron Garfield .15 .40
113 Tyson Gillies .40 1.00
114 Kelly Dugan .15 .40
115 Alexander Colome .40 1.00
116 Martin Perez .40 1.00
117 J.R. Murphy .25 .60
118 Pedro Figueroa .15 .40
119 James Darnell .25 .60
120 Alex Wilson .15 .40
121 Sebastian Valle .25 .60
122 Kiel Roling .15 .40
123 D.J. Lemahieu 1.50 4.00
124 Hak-Ju Lee .25 .60
125 Corban Joseph .15 .40
126 Brock Holt .15 .40
127 Chris Archer .50 1.25
128 Donnie Joseph .15 .40
129 Tom Milone .15 .40
130 Wade Gaynor .15 .40
131 Bryce Stowell .15 .40
132 Tyler Ladendorf .15 .40
133 Ben Paulsen .15 .40
134 Yohan Flande .15 .40
135 James McOwen .15 .40
136 Wil Myers .25 .60
137 Jason Van Kooten .15 .40
138 Jeff Malm .15 .40
139 Drew Cumberland .15 .40
140 Caleb Thielbar .25 .60
141 Sean Ratliff .15 .40
142 Paolo Espino .15 .40
143 Seth Loman .15 .40
144 Seth Lintz .15 .40
145 Steve Lombardozzi .25 .60
146 Chris Kessinger .15 .40
147 Randal Grichuk .40 1.00
148 Devin Goodwin .15 .40
149 Darrell Ceciliani .15 .40
150 Roberto De La Cruz .15 .40
151 Brooks Raley .15 .40
152 Brian Cavazos-Galvez .40 1.00
153 Jesus Brito .15 .40
154 Tony Sanchez .40 1.00
155 Matt Hobgood .40 1.00
156 Graham Stoneburner .25 .60
157 Kirk Nieuwenhuis .15 .40
158 Brock Bond .25 .60
159 D.J. Wabick .15 .40
160 Mike Minor .25 .60
161 Brett Pill .60 1.50
162 Ari Ronick .15 .40
163 Ryan Lavarnway .60 1.50
164 Drew Storen .25 .60
165 Isaias Velasquez .15 .40
166 Barry Butera .15 .40
167 Grant Green .15 .40
168 Zack Von Rosenberg .15 .40
169 Tony Delmonico .15 .40
170 Bobby Borchering .25 .60
171 A.J. Pollock .40 1.00
172 Kyle Conley .25 .60
173 Shaver Hansen .15 .40
174 Jiovanni Mier .25 .60
175 Jimmy Paredes .40 1.00
176 Alexia Amarista .15 .40
177 Jared Mitchell .25 .60
178 Marquise Cooper .15 .40
179 Damon Sublett .25 .60
180 Todd Glaesmann .15 .40
181 Mike Trout 50.00 120.00
182 Gustavo Nunez .15 .40
183 Eric Arnott .15 .40
184 Joe Kelly .15 .40
185 Matt Helm .15 .40
186 Reymond Fuentes .25 .60
187 Jason Thompson .15 .40
188 Tim Wheeler .25 .60
189 Rebel Ridling .15 .40
190 Keon Broxton .15 .40
191 Ian Krol .15 .40
192 Alex Torres .15 .40
193 Ben Tootle .15 .40
194 Craig Clark .60 1.50
195 David Hale .40 1.00
196 Brett Wallach .15 .40
197 Jeremy Hefner .15 .40
198 Marty Popham .15 .40
199 Donald Hume • .15 .40
200 Zelous Wheeler .15 .40
201 Brandon Douglas .15 .40
202 Manuel Banuelos .60 1.50
203 Robbie Erlin .40 1.00
204 Billy Nowlin .15 .40
205 Ozzie Lewis .15 .40
206 Jon Michael Redding .15 .40
207 Josh Harrison .15 .40
208 Johermyn Chavez .15 .40
209 Jose Pirela .25 .60
210 Bryan Pounds .15 .40
211 Phil Joon Jang .15 .40
212 Dan Kapala .15 .40
213 Marc Sorensen .15 .40
214 Jordan Lennerton .15 .40
215 Corey Kemp .15 .40
216 David Phelps .15 .40
217 Erik Crichton .15 .40
218 Josh Walter .15 .40
219 Alfredo Marte .15 .40
220 Evan Sharpley .15 .40
221 Jesus Montero .15 .40
222 Tanner Scheppers .40 1.00
223 Jose Iglesias .50 1.25
224 Jacob Skole .25 .60
225 Arodys Vizcaino .40 1.00
226 Kyle Colligan .15 .40
227 Todd Frazier .50 1.25
228 Mike Foltynewicz .40 1.00
229 Chris Balcom-Miller .25 .60
230 Zach Wheeler .50 1.25
231 Donnie Roach .15 .40
232 Kellin Deglan .15 .40
233 Riaan Spanjer-Furstenburg .15 .40
234 Ryan Goins .15 .40
235 Trey McNutt .15 .40
236 Matt Lipka .60 1.50
237 Max Stassi .25 .60
238 Tanner Bushue .25 .60
239 Marc Krauss .15 .40
240 Taylor Lindsey .25 .60
241 Juan Carlos Sulbaran .15 .40
242 Michael Kirkman .15 .40
243 Freddie Freeman 2.00 5.00
244 Ryan Bolden .15 .40
245 Paul Goldschmidt 10.00 25.00
246 Roger Kieschnick .15 .40
247 David Nick .15 .40
248 Wendell Soto .15 .40
249 Louis Coleman .15 .40
250 Robinson Lopez .15 .40
251 A.J. Morris .15 .40
252 Drew Robinson .15 .40
253 Mycal Jones .15 .40
254 Patrick Keating .15 .40
255 Collin Cowgill .15 .40
256 Nick Bartolone .15 .40
257 Tyler Stovall .15 .40
258 Billy Hamilton .40 1.00
259 David Holmberg .25 .60
260 Cito Culver .25 .60
261 Max Russell .15 .40
262 Jose Ramirez .25 .60
263 Kentrail Davis .15 .40
264 James Baldwin III .15 .40
265 Jeremy Hellickson .40 1.00
266 Jeurys Familia .40 1.00
267 Will Middlebrooks .25 .60
268 Christian Carmichael .25 .60
269 Cesar Puello .15 .40
270 Daniel Fields .15 .40
271 Mike Hessman .15 .40
272 Bryce Brentz .40 1.00
273 Anthony Hewitt .15 .40
274 Mark Serrano .15 .40
275 Kyle Gibson .60 1.50
276 Andrelton Simmons .60 1.50
277 Telvin Nash .25 .60
278 Jonathan Meyer .15 .40
279 Dimaster Delgado .15 .40
280 Christopher Hawkins .15 .40
281 Danny Duffy .25 .60
282 Jorge Reyes .15 .40
283 Pat Corbin .50 1.25
284 Jordan Akins .15 .40
285 Kendal Volz .15 .40
286 Jonathan Garcia .15 .40
287 Aaron Crow .25 .60
288 Marcus Knecht .15 .40
289 Zach Lutz .15 .40
290 John Lamb .40 1.00
291 Wellington Castillo .15 .40
292 Brodie Greene .15 .40
293 Robert Stock .15 .40
294 Julio Morban .15 .40
295 Ryan Dent .15 .40
296 Tyler Waldron .15 .40
297 B.J. Hermsen .15 .40
298 T.J. House .15 .40
299 Jay Jackson .15 .40
300 Nicholas Longmire .25 .60
301 Tyreace House .15 .40
302 David Cales .15 .40
303 Tommy Joseph .50 1.25
304 Brett Nicholas .15 .40
305 Adeiny Hechavarria .15 .40
306 Marcos Vechionacci .15 .40
307 Dustin Ackley .25 .60
308 Jesse Biddle .25 .60
309 Donavan Tate .15 .40
310 Danny Rosenbaum .25 .60
311 Matt Bashore .25 .60
312 Asher Wojciechowski .40 1.00
313 Alex White .25 .60
314 Francisco Peguero .15 .40
315 Nick Hagadone .15 .40
316 Jacob Petricka .15 .40
317 Dee Gordon .30 .75
318 Gustavo Pierre .15 .40
319 Michael Montgomery .25 .60
320 Tyler Vail .15 .40
321 Adam Warren .40 1.00
322 Billy Bullock .15 .40
323 Derek Norris .25 .60
324 Cory Vaughn .25 .60
325 Connor Hoehn .15 .40
326 Casey Crosby .15 .40
327 Aaron Sanchez .60 1.50
328 Daniel Descalso .15 .40
329 Jarred Cosart .25 .60
330 Zach Britton .50 1.25
331 Noah Syndergaard .60 1.50
332 Ben Jukich .15 .40
333 Victor Black .15 .40
334 Michael Moustakas .40 1.00
335 Taijuan Walker .40 1.00
336 Ryan Jackson .15 .40
337 Austin Romine .25 .60
338 Josh Harrison .15 .40
339 Ralston Cash .15 .40
340 Casey Coleman .25 .60
341 Jack Spradlin .15 .40
342 Daryl Jones .15 .40
343 Mike Antonio .15 .40
344 Josh Vitters .15 .40
345 Jordany Valdespin .15 .40
346 Travis D'Arnaud .25 .60
347 Christian Bisson .15 .40
348 Matt Clark .15 .40
349 Xavier Avery .15 .40
350 Hector Noesi .25 .60
351 David Filak .15 .40
352 Hank Conger .15 .40
353 Devin Mesoraco .40 1.00
354 Daniel Moskos .15 .40
355 Christian Colon .25 .60
356 Adrian Ortiz .15 .40
357 Wynn Pelzer .15 .40
358 Jurickson Profar .40 1.00
359 Justin O'Conner .15 .40
360 Justin Greene .15 .40
361 Bryan Morris .15 .40
362 Jarrod Parker .40 1.00
363 Henry Ramos .40 1.00
364 Lars Anderson .25 .60
365 Todd Cunningham .25 .60
366 Michael Taylor .25 .60
367 Eddie Rosario 1.25 3.00
368 Tomas Telis .15 .40
369 Chris Carter .25 .60
370 Niko Goodrum .50 1.25
371 Kyle Russell .15 .40
372 Matthew Moore 1.25 3.00
373 L.J. Hoes .15 .40
374 Joe Leonard .15 .40
375 James Leverton .15 .40
376 Matt Gorgen .15 .40
377 Erik Komatsu .15 .40
378 Hunter Morris .15 .40
379 Matt Cline .25 .60
380 Su-Min Jung .15 .40
381 Jacob Turner .60 1.50
382 Jedd Gyorko .25 .60
383 Chris Kirkland .15 .40
384 Cody Rogers .15 .40
385 Anthony Vasquez .15 .40
386 Cody Hawn .25 .60
387 Miguel Velazquez .15 .40
388 Tom Stuifbergen .15 .40
389 Jason Stidham .15 .40
390 Stephen Pryor .15 .40
391 Justin Bour .40 1.00
392 Khris Davis .75 2.00
393 Edward Salcedo .15 .40
394 Rett Varner .15 .40
395 Steven Souza .25 .60
396 Mark Sobolewski .15 .40
397 Michael Pineda .40 1.00
398 Jared Simon .15 .40
399 Anderson Hidalgo .15 .40
400 Scooter Gennett .30 .75
401 Kyle Drabek .25 .60
402 Seth Rosin .25 .60
403 Kyle Rose .15 .40
404 Darin Ruf .60 1.50
405 Brian Diemer .15 .40
406 Chad Bettis .15 .40
407 Justin Bloxom .15 .40
408 Jerry Sands .40 1.00
409 Martin Perez .40 1.00
410 Derek Dietrich .40 1.00
411 Chris McGuiness .15 .40
412 Juan Lagares .50 1.25
413 Robert Rowland .15 .40
414 Jake Thompson .15 .40
415 Brian Conley .15 .40
416 Bo Greenwell .15 .40
417 Derrick Robinson .15 .40
418 Michael Kvasnicka .25 .60
419 Garabez Rosa .15 .40
420 Casey Frawley .15 .40
421 Bobby Doran .15 .40
422 Zoilo Almonte 1.25 3.00
423 Ian Gac .15 .40
424 Phillippe Aumont .15 .40
425 Ben Heath .15 .40
426 J.D. Martinez 1.50 4.00
427 Chris Murrill .15 .40
428 Desmond Jennings .25 .60
429 Jason Martinson .15 .40
430 Eliezer Mesa .15 .40
431 Peter Bourjos .25 .60
432 Ryan Berry .15 .40
433 Cole Leonida .15 .40
434 Wilmer Flores .25 .60
435 Russell Wilson 6.00 15.00
436 Brandon Belt .40 1.00
437 T.J. McFarland .15 .40
438 Bruce Billings .15 .40
439 Casey Haerther .15 .40
440 Mike McDade .15 .40

2010 Topps Pro Debut Blue

*BLUE 1-220: 2X TO 5X BASIC
*BLUE 221-440: 1.2X TO 3X BASIC
SER.2 ODDS 1:4 HOBBY
SER.1 PRINT RUN 259 SER.#'d SETS
SER.2 PRINT RUN 369 SER.#'d SETS
181 Mike Trout 200.00 400.00
202 Manuel Banuelos 3.00 8.00
435 Russell Wilson 15.00 40.00

2010 Topps Pro Debut Gold

*GOLD: 4X TO 10X BASIC
SER.2 ODDS 1:25 HOBBY
STATED PRINT RUN 50 SER.#'d SET
181 Mike Trout 600.00 1200.00
435 Russell Wilson 25.00 60.00

2010 Topps Pro Debut AFLAC Debut Cut Autographs

SER.1 PRINT RUN 106 SER.#'d SETS
SER.2 PRINT RUN 200 SER.#'d SETS
AH Aaron Hicks 30.00 60.00
AS Aaron Sanchez S2 10.00 25.00
BD Brett DeVall 10.00 25.00
BH B.J. Hermsen 15.00 40.00
BL Braxton Lane 8.00 20.00
CB Cameron Bedrosian S2 8.00 20.00
CC Christian Colon S2 10.00 25.00
CK Chevez Clarke S2 8.00 20.00
CM Clark Murphy 8.00 20.00
CR Cameron Rupp S2 8.00 20.00
DD Derek Dietrich S2 10.00 25.00
DH Destin Hood 10.00 25.00
DL D.J. Lemahieu 10.00 25.00
DT Daniel Tuttle 12.50 30.00
EM Ethan Martin 12.50 30.00
EW Everett Williams 8.00 20.00
GL Garrison Lassiter 8.00 20.00
HM Hunter Morris S2 8.00 20.00
IK Ian Krol 10.00 25.00
JC Jarred Cosart S2 6.00 15.00
JS Jonathan Singleton 60.00 120.00
JT Jacob Turner S2 8.00 20.00
JT Jason Thompson 8.00 20.00
KH Kyrell Hudson 12.50 30.00
KK Kevin Keyes S2 8.00 20.00
KS Keyvius Sampson 12.50 30.00
KS Kyle Skipworth 8.00 20.00
ML Matt Lipka S2 8.00 20.00
RG Reggie Golden S2 8.00 20.00
SH Slade Heathcott 20.00 50.00
TB Tim Beckham 10.00 25.00
TM Tim Melville 10.00 25.00

2010 Topps Pro Debut Double-A All-Stars

COMPLETE SET (30) 10.00 25.00
DA1 Miguel Abreu .60 1.50
DA2 Deik Scram .40 1.00
DA3 Quintin Berry .60 1.50
DA4 Michael Taylor .60 1.50
DA5 Carlos Santana 1.25 3.00
DA6 Alex Avila .60 1.50
DA7 Marvin Lowrance .40 1.00
DA8 Nick Weglarz .60 1.50
DA9 Neil Sellers .40 1.00
DA10 Jonathan Tucker .40 1.00
DA11 Jason Delaney .40 1.00
DA12 Beau Mills .40 1.00
DA13 Brian Friday .40 1.00
DA14 Joe Savery .40 1.00
DA15 Danny Moskos .40 1.00
DA16 Brock Bond .60 1.50
DA17 Brian Dinkelman .40 1.00
DA18 Eduardo Nunez 1.00 2.50
DA19 Reegie Corona .40 1.00
DA20 Jorge Jimenez .40 1.00
DA21 Brian Dopirak .40 1.00
DA22 Jorge Vazquez .40 1.00
DA23 Whitney Robbins .40 1.00
DA24 Eddy Martinez - Esteve .40 1.00
DA25 Rene Tosoni .60 1.50
DA26 Lars Anderson .60 1.50
DA27 D.J. Wabick .40 1.00
DA28 Brian Jeroloman .40 1.00
DA29 Jesus Montero .40 1.00
DA30 Zach McAllister .60 1.50

2010 Topps Pro Debut Futures Game Jersey

SER.1 PRINT RUN 139 SER.#'d SETS
SER.2 PRINT RUN 199 SER.#'d SETS
SER.2 ODDS 1:28 HOBBY
SER.2 GOLD ODDS 1:220 HOBBY
GOLD PRINT RUN 25 SER.#'d SETS
AE Alcides Escobar 4.00 10.00
AL Alex Liddi S2 4.00 10.00
AL Alex Liddi 4.00 10.00
AR Austin Romine S2 4.00 10.00
AS Anthony Slama S2 3.00 8.00
AT Alex Torres S2 3.00 8.00
BC Barbaro Canizares 3.00 8.00
BJ Brett Jackson S2 5.00 12.00
BL Brett Lawrie S2 8.00 20.00
BL Brad Lincoln 4.00 10.00
BLA Brett Lawrie 8.00 20.00
BM Bryan Morris S2 3.00 8.00
BM Brian Matusz 6.00 15.00
BR Ben Revere S2 10.00 25.00
BW Brett Wallace 4.00 10.00
CC Chun Chen S2 4.00 10.00
CC Chris Carter 4.00 10.00
CF Christian Friedrich S2 4.00 10.00
CH Chris Heisey 10.00 25.00
CK Casey Kelly 12.50 30.00
CL Chia-Jen Lo 6.00 15.00
CP Carlos Peguero S2 4.00 10.00
CS Carlos Santana 4.00 10.00
CT Chris Tillman 4.00 10.00
DB Domonic Brown S2 6.00 15.00
DC Drew Cumberland S2 3.00 8.00
DD Danny Duffy 10.00 25.00
DE Danny Espinosa S2 3.00 8.00
DE Danny Espinosa 3.00 8.00
DG Dee Gordon S2 4.00 10.00
DJ Desmond Jennings S2 6.00 15.00
DJ Desmond Jennings 6.00 15.00
DJO Daryl Jones 4.00 10.00
DV Dayan Viciedo 6.00 15.00
EH Eric Hosmer S2 4.00 10.00
EP Eury Perez S2 3.00 8.00
ES Eduardo Sanchez S2 3.00 8.00
EY Eric Young Jr. 4.00 10.00
FP Francisco Peguero S2 3.00 8.00
FS Francisco Samuel 3.00 8.00
GG Grant Green S2 5.00 12.00
GH Gorkys Hernandez S2 4.00 10.00
HA Henderson Alvarez S2 3.00 8.00
HC Hank Conger S2 6.00 15.00
HJ Hak-Ju Lee S2 5.00 12.00
HN Hector Noesi S2 4.00 10.00
JC Jhoulys Chacin 4.00 10.00
JF Jeurys Familia S2 4.00 10.00
JH Jeremy Hellickson S2 12.50 30.00
JH Jason Heyward 30.00 60.00
JL Jordan Lyles S2 4.00 10.00
JM Jesus Montero 6.00 15.00
JP Jarrod Parker 4.00 10.00
JS Jason Castro 5.00 12.00
JS Juancarlos Sulbaran 4.00 10.00
JT Julio Teheran S2 8.00 20.00
JT Junichi Tazawa 4.00 10.00
JV Josh Vitters 5.00 12.00
JW Jemile Weeks 4.00 10.00
KD Kyle Drabek 5.00 12.00
KK Kyeong Kang 4.00 10.00
LC Lonnie Chisenhall S2 4.00 10.00
LD Luis Durango 4.00 10.00
LJ Luis Jimenez S2 3.00 8.00
LM Logan Morrison S2 6.00 15.00
LS Leyson Septimo 3.00 0.00
MB Madison Bumgarner 10.00 25.00
ML Mat Latos 4.00 10.00
MM Mike Minor S2 5.00 12.00
MMO Mike Moustakas S2 6.00 15.00
MS Mike Stanton 6.00 15.00
MT Mike Trout S2 75.00 150.00
NF Neftali Feliz 5.00 12.00
NW Nick Weglarz 4.00 10.00
OM Ozzie Martinez S2 4.00 10.00
PA Pedro Alvarez 10.00 25.00
PB Pedro Baez S2 3.00 8.00
PB Pedro Baez 4.00 10.00
PC Pedro Ciriaco S2 8.00 20.00
PV Philippe Valiquette S2 4.00 10.00
RT Rene Tosoni 4.00 10.00
SC Simon Castro S2 4.00 10.00
SC Starlin Castro 8.00 20.00
SM Shelby Miller S2 10.00 25.00
SP Stolmy Pimentel S2 4.00 10.00
SS Scott Sizemore 4.00 10.00
TF Tyler Flowers 4.00 10.00
TG Tyson Gillies 5.00 12.00
TM Trystan Magnuson S2 4.00 10.00
TR Trevor Reckling 5.00 12.00
TS Tanner Scheppers S2 3.00 8.00
WF Wilmer Flores 4.00 10.00
WR Wilin Rosario S2 3.00 8.00
WRA Wilkin Ramirez S2 3.00 8.00
YA Yonder Alonso S2 4.00 10.00
YF Yohan Flande 4.00 10.00
ZB Zach Britton S2 8.00 20.00
ZW Zach Wheeler S2 10.00 25.00

2010 Topps Pro Debut Hall of Fame Stars

COMPLETE SET (10) 8.00 20.00
HOF1 Jackie Robinson 1.00 2.50
HOF2 Babe Ruth 2.50 6.00
HOF3 Phil Rizzuto .60 1.50
HOF4 Stan Musial 1.50 4.00
HOF5 Pee Wee Reese .60 1.50
HOF6 Carl Yastrzemski 1.50 4.00
HOF7 Mickey Mantle 3.00 8.00
HOF8 Joe Morgan .60 1.50
HOF9 Jim Palmer .60 1.50
HOF10 Jimmie Foxx 1.00 2.50

2010 Topps Pro Debut Prospect Autographs

SER.2 ODDS 1:14 HOBBY
*BLUE: .5X TO 1.2X BASIC
SER.2 BLUE ODDS 1:115 HOBBY
BLUE PRINT RUN 199 SER.#'d SETS
*GOLD: .6X TO 1.5X BASIC
SER.2 GOLD ODDS 1:458 HOBBY
GOLD PRINT RUN 50 SER.#'d SETS

SER.2 RED ODDS 1:22,900 HOBBY
RED PRINT RUN 1 SER.#'d SET
SER.2 PLATE ODDS 1:5710 HOBBY
AC Andrew Cashner 4.00 10.00
AH Anthony Hewitt 3.00 8.00
AL Andrew Liebel 3.00 8.00
BJ Brett Jackson S2 3.00 8.00
CB Charlie Blackmon S2 8.00 20.00
CD Chase D'Arnaud 5.00 12.00
DC David Cook S2 3.00 8.00
GH Greg Halman S2 3.00 8.00
JA Jay Austin S2 3.00 8.00
JF Jeremy Farrell 3.00 8.00
JG Johnny Giavotella S2 3.00 8.00
JL Jeff Locke 5.00 12.00
JM Jenrry Mejia 4.00 10.00
JM Jesus Montero S2 3.00 8.00
JT John Tolisano S2 3.00 8.00
LC Lonnie Chisenhall 5.00 12.00
LF Logan Forsythe 3.00 8.00
MM Mike Montgomery 3.00 8.00
NV Niko Vasquez 3.00 8.00
RC Ryan Chaffee 3.00 8.00
RK Ryan Kalish 6.00 15.00
SG Steve Garrison S2 3.00 8.00
SP Shane Peterson 3.00 8.00
SP Shane Peterson S2 3.00 8.00
TJ Travis Jones 3.00 8.00
TS T.J. Steele S2 3.00 8.00
WS Will Smith 3.00 8.00
MMO Michael Moustakas 5.00 12.00
SHE Steven Hensley S2 3.00 8.00

2010 Topps Pro Debut Single-A All-Stars

COMPLETE SET (30) 10.00 25.00
SA1 Zoilo Almonte 3.00 8.00
SA2 Welinton Ramirez .40 1.00
SA3 Jimmy Paredes 1.00 2.50
SA4 John Murrian .60 1.50
SA5 Ryan Westmoreland .40 1.00
SA6 Sean Ochinko .40 1.00
SA7 Tyler Kelly .40 1.00
SA8 Cory Burns .40 1.00
SA9 Brian Kemp .40 1.00
SA10 Tyler Bortnick .40 1.00
SA11 Levi Carolus .40 1.00
SA12 Neil Medchill .60 1.50
SA13 Jacob Smith .40 1.00
SA14 Mitchell Clegg .60 1.50
SA15 Jose Alvarez .40 1.00
SA16 Leandro Castro .40 1.00
SA17 Sean Nicol .40 1.00
SA18 Sam Honeck .60 1.50
SA19 Francisco Murillo .40 1.00
SA20 Alan Ahmady .60 1.50
SA21 Chase Austin .40 1.00
SA22 J.D. Martinez 4.00 10.00
SA23 Luis Rivera .60 1.50
SA24 Russell Dixon .40 1.00
SA25 Francisco Soriano .40 1.00
SA26 Brock Holt .40 1.00
SA27 Michael Rockett .60 1.50
SA28 Deangelo Mack .60 1.50
SA29 Mark Cohoon .40 1.00
SA30 Kyle Jensen .40 1.00

2010 Topps Pro Debut Triple-A All-Stars

COMPLETE SET (30) 10.00 25.00
TA1 Austin Jackson .60 1.50
TA2 Jorge Padilla .40 1.00
TA3 Drew Stubbs 1.00 2.50
TA4 Shelley Duncan .40 1.00
TA5 Jordan Brown .40 1.00
TA6 Justin Huber .40 1.00
TA7 Fernando Cabrera .40 1.00
TA8 Nelson Figueroa .40 1.00
TA9 Zach Kroenke .40 1.00
TA10 Jose Vaquedano .40 1.00
TA11 Reid Brignac .40 1.00
TA12 Erik Kratz .60 1.50
TA13 Seth Bynum .40 1.00
TA14 Drew Carpenter .40 1.00
TA15 Eric Young Jr. .40 1.00
TA16 Rusty Ryal .40 1.00
TA17 Matt Murton .40 1.00
TA18 Michael Ryan .40 1.00
TA19 Randy Ruiz .40 1.00
TA20 Bryan LaHair 1.00 2.50
TA21 Terry Evans .40 1.00
TA22 Chad Huffman .40 1.00
TA23 Justin Lehr .40 1.00
TA24 Brendan Katin .40 1.00
TA25 Esteban German .40 1.00
TA26 Charlie Haeger .40 1.00
TA27 R.J. Swindle .40 1.00
TA28 Jay Marshall .40 1.00
TA29 Jeremy Hill .40 1.00
TA30 Jess Todd .40 1.00

2011 Topps Pro Debut

COMPLETE SET (330) 60.00 120.00
COMMON CARD .15 .40
PRINTING PLATE ODDS 1:267 HOBBY
PLATE PRINT RUN 1 SET PER COLOR
BLACK-CYAN-MAGENTA-YELLOW ISSUED
NO PLATE PRICING DUE TO SCARCITY
1 Eric Hosmer 1.00 2.50
2 Jameson Taillon .25 .60
3 Josh Ashenbrenner .25 .60
4 Aaron Hicks .25 .60
5 Felix Perez .15 .40
6 Kyle Gibson .25 .60
7 J.R. Bradley .15 .40
8 Bobby Borchering .25 .60
9 Jared Mitchell .25 .60
10 Justin Bencsko .25 .60
11 Wil Myers .25 .60
12 Cody Hawn .25 .60
13 Gary Sanchez .75 2.00
14 Kirk Nieuwenhuis .15 .40
15 Oswaldo Arcia .15 .40
16 Aaron Altherr .15 .40
17 Brandon Short .25 .60
18 Jason Martinson .15 .40
19 Ethan Martin .15 .40
20 Cameron Rupp .15 .40
21 Jorge Padron .25 .60
22 J.C. Menna .15 .40
23 Avisail Garcia .25 .60
24 Jason Kipnis .50 1.25
25 Bryan Mitchell .25 .60
26 Evan Chambers .15 .40
27 Jonathan Singleton .25 .60
28 Jason Townsend .40 1.00
29 Steve Crnkovich .15 .40
30 Darian Sandford .15 .40
31 Christopher Hawkins .15 .40
32 Kolbrin Vitek .25 .60
33 Aaron Shipman .15 .40
34 Jared Rogers .15 .40
35 Robert Anston .15 .40
36 Tyler Thornburg .25 .60
37 Jemile Weeks .25 .60
38 Mason Williams .40 1.00
39 Francisco Martinez .15 .40
40 Mike Montgomery .25 .60
41 Adalberto Santos .15 .40
42 Vincent Velasquez .40 1.00
43 Freddy Galvis .15 .40
44 Matt Thomson .15 .40
45 Alex Lavisky .15 .40
46 Kaleb Cowart .25 .60
47 Drake Britton .15 .40
48 Garrison Lassiter .25 .60
49 Jordan Pratt .15 .40
50 John Gast .15 .40
51 Derek Norris .15 .40
52 Michael Taylor .15 .40
53 Christian Yelich 5.00 12.00
54 LeVon Washington .25 .60
55 Rob Brantly .40 1.00
56 Mickey Wiswall .15 .40
57 Tommy Kahnle .40 1.00
58 Thomas Mittelstaedt .15 .40
59 Michael Sandoval .15 .40
60 Rex Brothers .15 .40
61 Yasmani Grandal .25 .60
62 Joc Pederson .50 1.25
63 Max Kepler .50 1.25
64 Adrian Salcedo .25 .60
65 Hak-Ju Lee .15 .40
66 Jordan Cooper .25 .60
67 Casey Kelly .15 .40
68 Eric Groff .15 .40
69 Conor Mullee .15 .40
70 Kurtis Muller .15 .40
71 Jared Lakind .25 .60
72 Daniel Tillman .15 .40
73 Madison Younginer .15 .40
74 Alex Wimmers .15 .40
75 Manny Machado 1.50 4.00
76 Ryan Delgado .15 .40
77 Matt Davidson .25 .60
78 K.C. Hobson .15 .40
79 Cody Scarpetta .15 .40
80 Oscar Taveras .40 1.00
81 Miguel De Los Santos .15 .40
82 Cam Bedrosian .15 .40
83 Scott Rembisz .15 .40
84 Austin Wates .40 1.00
85 Kellen Sweeney .25 .60
86 Rich Poythress .15 .40
87 Blake Kelso .25 .60
88 Keon Broxton .15 .40
89 Jose Iglesias .25 .60
90 Kyle Ryan .25 .60
91 Leslie Anderson .15 .40
92 Jaren Matthews .15 .40
93 Kyle Greenwalt .15 .40
94 Nick Franklin .25 .60
95 Cole Nelson .15 .40
96 Yordy Cabrera .15 .40
97 Tyler Pastornicky .25 .60
98 Brice Cutspec .15 .40
99 Brandon Guyer .25 .60
100 Nolan Arenado .75 2.00
101 Chris Lofton .15 .40
102 Tyler Holt .15 .40
103 D'Vontrey Richardson .15 .40
104 Victor Lara .15 .40
105 Carlos Gutierrez .15 .40
106 Trent Mummey .15 .40
107 Stolmy Pimentel .15 .40
108 James Robinson .25 .60
109 James Baldwin .15 .40
110 Nick Castellanos .75 2.00
111 P.J. Polk .15 .40
112 David Filak .15 .40
113 Jimmy Nelson .15 .40
114 Zack Cox .25 .60
115 Cody Buckel .25 .60
116 Philip Gosselin .15 .40
117 Tyler Austin .40 1.00
118 Grant Green .15 .40
119 Jabari Blash .15 .40
120 Miguel Sano .30 .75
121 Adam Gaylord .15 .40
122 Dan Adamson .25 .60
123 Will Middlebrooks .25 .60
124 Chris Jarrett .15 .40
125 Aaron Senne .15 .40
126 Tim Melville .15 .40
127 Colin Bates .15 .40
128 Scott Schebler .40 1.00
129 Julio Pimentel .15 .40
130 Cody Stanley .15 .40
131 Nick Weglarz .15 .40
132 Chuckie Jones .15 .40
133 Daniel Fields .15 .40
134 Tony Sanchez .25 .60
135 Tanner Bushue .15 .40
136 Ben Heath .15 .40
137 Kenneth Allison .15 .40
138 Brandon Laird .25 .60
139 Erik Komatsu .15 .40
140 Cory Brownsten .15 .40
141 Alex Kaminsky .25 .60
142 Eddie Rosario .50 1.25
143 Wily Peralta .15 .40
144 Josh Vitters .25 .60
145 Paul Goldschmidt 1.50 4.00
146 Edward Salcedo .15 .40
147 Niko Goodrum .40 1.00
148 Todd Cunningham .25 .60
149 Jaff Decker .15 .40
150 Kyle Skipworth .15 .40
151 Cameron Roth .40 1.00
152 Donn Roach .15 .40
153 Ismael Guillon .15 .40
154 Michael Choice .25 .60
155 Noel Cuevas .15 .40
156 Jiovanni Mier .15 .40
157 Nathan Aaron .25 .60
158 Sebastian Valle .15 .40
159 Mike Olt .25 .60
160 Drew Lee .25 .60
161 Jeff Locke .40 1.00
162 Yadiel Rivera .15 .40
163 Tyler Matzek .25 .60
164 J.T. Realmuto 8.00 20.00
165 Tyler Saladino .25 .60
166 Yasser Gomez .15 .40
167 William Beckwith .15 .40
168 Stephen Hunt .25 .60
169 Chad James .15 .40
170 Trayce Thompson .40 1.00
171 Dane Amedee .15 .40
172 Anthony Bryant .15 .40
173 Kyle Waldrop .25 .60
174 Colton Cain .15 .40
175 Matt Valaika .15 .40
176 Kurt Fleming .15 .40
177 Johermyn Chavez .15 .40
178 Jose Dore .15 .40
179 J.D. Ashbrook .15 .40
180 Oscar Tejada .15 .40
181 Jonathan Burns .15 .40
182 Trevor May .15 .40
183 Brodie Greene .15 .40
184 Henderson Alvarez .15 .40
185 Dallas Poulk .15 .40
186 Carlos Perez .15 .40
187 Wes Hodges .15 .40
188 Jacob Petricka .25 .60
189 Ralston Cash .15 .40
190 Matt Dominguez .25 .60
191 Robbie Erlin .25 .60
192 Adam Bailey .15 .40
193 Jiwan James .15 .40
194 Cheslor Cuthbert .15 .40
195 Matt Den Dekker .25 .60
196 Bryce Harper 10.00 25.00
197 Drew Poulk .15 .40
198 Brian McConkey .25 .60
199 Reggie Golden .15 .40
200 Brad Hand .15 .40
201 Ryan Fisher .15 .40
202 Delino DeShields .15 .40
203 Devin Mesoraco .40 1.00
204 Quincy Latimore .15 .40
205 Cory Vaughn .15 .40
206 Lonnie Chisenhall .25 .60
207 Andrelton Simmons .40 1.00
208 Junior Arias .15 .40
209 Jesus Montero .15 .40
210 Nicholas Bartolone .15 .40
211 Jarrett Martin .25 .60
212 Jordan Danks .40 1.00
213 Taylor Lindsey .15 .40
214 Chad Lewis .15 .40
215 Rangel Ravelo .15 .40
216 Elliot Soto .15 .40
217 Riley Hornback .15 .40
218 Max Stassi .15 .40
219 Brian Guinn .15 .40
220 Reymond Fuentes .15 .40
221 Brandon Decker .15 .40
222 Hunter Ackerman .15 .40
223 Drew Robinson .15 .40
224 Jacob Turner .60 1.50
225 Ronald Torreyes .50 1.25
226 Ryan LaMarre .15 .40
227 Marcus Knecht .15 .40
228 Guillermo Pimentel .25 .60
229 Rob Rasmussen .15 .40
230 Ryan Broussard .15 .40
231 Yordano Ventura .25 .60
232 Tyrell Jenkins .25 .60
233 Anthony Rizzo 1.50 4.00
234 Brett Oberholtzer .15 .40
235 Brian Pointer .15 .40
236 Blake Forsythe .15 .40
237 Byron Aird .15 .40
238 Mike Kickham .15 .40
239 L.J. Hoes .25 .60
240 Jeff Barfield .15 .40
241 Carlos Perez .15 .40
242 Felix Sterling .15 .40
243 Scott Copeland .40 1.00
244 Austin Romine .15 .40
245 Luis Sardinas .15 .40
246 D.J. LeMahieu 2.00 5.00
247 Jason Knapp .15 .40
248 Tyler Skaggs .40 1.00
249 Brad Boxberger .15 .40
250 Charly Bashara .15 .40
251 Robby Rowland .15 .40
252 Todd Frazier .50 1.25
253 Matt Moore .40 1.00
254 Adam Eaton .40 1.00
255 Chris Archer .30 .75
256 Jake Oester .15 .40
257 Jean Segura .60 1.50
258 Bryan Altman .15 .40
259 Austin Ross .25 .60
260 Kendal Volz .15 .40
261 Marc Krauss .15 .40
262 Stephen Pryor .15 .40
263 Mike Trout 75.00 200.00
264 Ryan Kussmaul .75 2.00
265 Casey Upperman .15 .40
266 Sean Coyle .25 .60
267 Robert Morey .15 .40
268 Eury Perez .15 .40
269 Chris Marrero .15 .40
270 Travis d'Arnaud .25 .60
271 Rene Oriental .15 .40
272 Angelo Gumbs .15 .40
273 Sam Tuivailala .15 .40
274 Anthony Gose .25 .60
275 Dallas Beeler .15 .40
276 Lucas Bailey .15 .40
277 Ryan Pineda .15 .40
278 Ryan Brett .25 .60
279 Brennan Smith .25 .60
280 David Vidal .40 1.00
281 Heath Hembree .15 .40
282 Matt Abraham .15 .40
283 Chris Owings .15 .40
284 Cameron Satterwhite .15 .40
285 Arodys Vizcaino .25 .60
286 Wilin Rosario .15 .40
287 Khris Davis .75 2.00
288 Derek Eitel .15 .40
289 Chase Whitley .75 2.00
290 Fautino De Los Santos .15 .40
291 Patrick Lawson .15 .40
292 Nicholas Struck .15 .40
293 Ryan Berry .15 .40
294 Zack Cozart .40 1.00
295 Christian Bethancourt .15 .40
296 Matt Miller .15 .40
297 Brandon Drury .40 1.00
298 Chase Burnette .15 .40
299 Jonathan Correa .15 .40
300 Nate Roberts .15 .40
301 Shelby Miller .75 2.00
302 Brett Jackson .25 .60
303 Hunter Morris .15 .40
304 Aaron Kurcz .15 .40
305 Kendrick Perkins .15 .40
306 Austin Reed .15 .40
307 Starling Marte .40 1.00
308 Mel Rojas Jr. .15 .40
309 Joe Leonard .25 .60
310 Salvador Perez .60 1.50
311 Kentrail Davis .15 .40
312 J.J. Hoover .15 .40
313 Gary Brown .40 1.00
314 Zack Von Rosenberg .15 .40
315 Marcus Nidiffer .15 .40
316 Chris Dominguez .25 .60
317 Scott Alexander .15 .40
318 Thomas Keeling .15 .40
319 Henry Ramos .15 .40
320 Drew Heid .15 .40
321 Dustin Geiger .15 .40
322 Kevin Kiermaier .40 1.00
323 Juan Carlos Linares .15 .40
324 Matthew Suschak .15 .40
325 Dixon Machado .15 .40
326 Chevez Clarke .15 .40
327 Drew Maggi .15 .40
328 Ryan Copeland .15 .40
329 Matt Curry .40 1.00
330 J.R. Murphy .15 .40

2011 Topps Pro Debut Blue

*BLUE: 3X TO 8X BASIC
STATED ODDS 1:4 HOBBY
STATED PRINT RUN 309 SER.#'d SETS
80 Oscar Taveras 10.00 25.00
196 Bryce Harper 25.00 60.00
263 Mike Trout 200.00 500.00

2011 Topps Pro Debut Gold

*GOLD: 5X TO 12X BASIC
STATED ODDS 1:22 HOBBY
STATED PRINT RUN 50 SER.#'d SETS
1 Eric Hosmer 12.50 30.00
2 Jameson Taillon 12.50 30.00
80 Oscar Taveras 40.00 100.00
196 Bryce Harper 60.00 150.00
263 Mike Trout 400.00 800.00

2011 Topps Pro Debut Debut Cuts

STATED ODDS 1:296 HOBBY
PRINT RUNS B/WN 33-130 COPIES PER
AH Aaron Hicks/95 10.00 25.00
BD Brett DeVall/78 6.00 15.00
CB Cam Bedrosian/33 6.00 15.00
CM Clark Murphy/122 6.00 15.00
DH Destin Hood/130 6.00 15.00
EM Ethan Martin/130 6.00 15.00
GL Garrison Lassiter/122 8.00 20.00
JC Jarred Cosart/33 10.00 25.00
KS Kyle Skipworth/122 8.00 20.00
RG Reggie Golden/33 15.00 40.00
TM Tim Melville/122 6.00 15.00
TW Tony Wolters/95 10.00 25.00
YC Yordy Cabrera/95 6.00 15.00

2011 Topps Pro Debut Double-A All Stars

COMPLETE SET (45) 15.00 40.00
STATED ODDS 1:4 HOBBY
PRINTING PLATE ODDS 1:882 HOBBY
PLATE PRINT RUN 1 SET PER COLOR
BLACK-CYAN-MAGENTA-YELLOW ISSUED
NO PLATE PRICING DUE TO SCARCITY
DA1 Kyle Gibson .60 1.50
DA2 Trystan Magnuson .40 1.00
DA3 Josh Stinson 1.00 2.50
DA4 Austin Romine .40 1.00
DA5 Matt Rizzotti 1.00 2.50
DA6 Kirk Nieuwenhuis .40 1.00
DA7 Eric Thames 2.00 5.00
DA8 Zach Britton 1.00 2.50
DA9 Lonnie Chisenhall .60 1.50
DA10 Thomas Neal .40 1.00
DA11 Joey Butler .40 1.00
DA12 Johnny Giavotella .40 1.00
DA13 Mike Moustakas 1.00 2.50
DA14 Willin Rosario .40 1.00
DA15 Adron Chambers .40 1.00
DA16 Simon Castro .40 1.00
DA17 Jordan Lyles .40 1.00
DA18 Koby Clemens .40 1.00
DA19 Corey Brown .40 1.00
DA20 Matt Dominguez .60 1.50
DA21 Brandon Tripp .40 1.00
DA22 Carlos Peguero .60 1.50
DA23 Brett Lawrie 1.50 4.00
DA24 Alex Liddi .40 1.00
DA25 Carlos Triunfel .40 1.00
DA26 Mauricio Robles .40 1.00
DA27 Collin Cowgill .40 1.00
DA28 Darin Mastroianni .40 1.00
DA29 Chase d'Arnaud .40 1.00
DA30 Matt Hague .60 1.50
DA31 Joshua Collmenter .40 1.00
DA32 Cedric Hunter .40 1.00
DA33 Jake Kahaulelio .60 1.50
DA34 Robinson Chirinos .40 1.00
DA35 Chris Marrero .40 1.00
DA36 Mike Nickeas .40 1.00
DA37 Pedro Beato .40 1.00
DA38 Rudy Owens .40 1.00
DA39 John Drennen 1.25 3.00
DA40 Ryan Mount 1.25 3.00
DA41 Carlos Hernandez .60 1.50
DA42 Craig Italiano .40 1.00
DA43 Matt Lawson .40 1.00
DA44 Steve Clevenger .40 1.00
DA45 Drew Anderson .40 1.00

2011 Topps Pro Debut Materials

STATED ODDS 1:13 HOBBY
GOLD PRINT RUN 25 SER.#'d SETS
NO GOLD PRICING DUE TO SCARCITY
RED PRINT RUN 5 SER.#'d SETS
NO RED PRICING DUE TO SCARCITY
PATCH PRINT RUN 5 SER.#'d SETS
NO PATCH PRICING DUE TO SCARCITY
LOGO PRINT RUN 1 SER.#'d SET
NO LOGO PRICING DUE TO SCARCITY
AC Angel Castillo 2.50 6.00
BB Brandon Belt 4.00 10.00
BJ Brett Jackson 3.00 8.00
CA Chris Archer 2.50 6.00
DG Dee Gordon 2.50 6.00
DS Domingo Santana 2.50 6.00
JB Jesse Biddle 3.00 8.00
JS Jerry Sands 3.00 8.00
JV Josh Vitters 2.50 6.00
MB Michael Burgess 2.50 6.00
MM Mike Moustakas 3.00 8.00
MT Mike Trout 40.00 100.00
NF Nick Franklin 2.50 6.00
TS Tony Sanchez 3.00 8.00
ZB Zach Britton 3.00 8.00

2011 Topps Pro Debut Materials Gold

*GOLD: .5X TO 1.2X BASIC
STATED ODDS 1:470 HOBBY
STATED PRINT RUN 50 SER.#'d SETS

2011 Topps Pro Debut Side By Side Autographs

STATED ODDS 1:458
GOLD ODDS 1:1283 HOBBY
GOLD PRINT RUN 25 SER.#'d SETS
NO GOLD PRICING DUE TO SCARCITY
RED ODDS 1:32,000 HOBBY
RED PRINT RUN 1 SER.#'d SET
NO RED PRICING DUE TO SCARCITY
PRINTING PLATE ODDS 1:2520 HOBBY
PLATE PRINT RUN 1 SET PER COLOR
BLACK-CYAN-MAGENTA-YELLOW ISSUED
NO PLATE PRICING DUE TO SCARCITY
BH Michael Burgess/Wes Hodges 4.00 10.00
GM F.Galvis/J.Mier 10.00 25.00
GU K.Greenwalt/P.Urckfitz 6.00 15.00
MB J.Mitchell/M.Burgess 5.00 12.00
MC F.Martinez/K.Cowart 8.00 20.00
MM M.Montgomery/M.Moore 30.00 60.00
PM Chris Parmelee/Chris Marrero 4.00 10.00
RG Tanner Robles/Robbie Grossman 4.00 10.00
RR B.Rowell/D.Robinson 6.00 15.00
RV R.Adams/N.Vasquez 8.00 20.00

2011 Topps Pro Debut Single-A All Stars

COMPLETE SET (45) 15.00 40.00
STATED ODDS 1:4 HOBBY
PRINTING PLATE ODDS 1:882 HOBBY
PLATE PRINT RUN 1 SET PER COLOR
BLACK-CYAN-MAGENTA-YELLOW ISSUED
NO PLATE PRICING DUE TO SCARCITY
SA1 Jordan Pacheco .40 1.00
SA2 Brandon Belt 1.00 2.50
SA3 Corban Joseph .40 1.00
SA4 Brett Jackson .60 1.50
SA5 Kyle Skipworth .40 1.00
SA6 Eric Hosmer 2.50 6.00
SA7 Will Middlebrooks .60 1.50
SA8 Brandon Short .60 1.50
SA9 Michael Burgess .60 1.50
SA10 Tyson Auer .40 1.00
SA11 Jerry Sands 1.00 2.50
SA12 Hak-Ju Lee .40 1.00
SA13 Mike Trout 10.00 25.00
SA14 Aaron Hicks .60 1.50
SA15 Chun-Hsiu Chen 1.00 2.50
SA16 Tyler Skaggs 1.00 2.50
SA17 Allen Webster .60 1.50
SA18 Jacob Turner 1.50 4.00
SA19 Quincy Latimore .40 1.00
SA20 Erik Komatsu .40 1.00
SA21 Ryan Lavarnway 1.50 4.00
SA22 Blake Tekotte .40 1.00
SA23 J.J. Hoover .40 1.00
SA24 Josh Satin .40 1.00
SA25 Stephen Vogt .60 1.50
SA26 Jeff Locke 1.00 2.50
SA27 J.D. Martinez 2.50 6.00
SA28 Destin Hood 1.00 2.50
SA29 Jonathan Villar 1.00 2.50
SA30 Ian Gac .60 1.50
SA31 Robbie Erlin .60 1.50
SA32 Alexander Colome .40 1.00
SA33 Matt Davidson .60 1.50
SA34 Casey Haerther .40 1.00
SA35 Robbie Ross .60 1.50
SA36 Tyson Van Winkle .40 1.00
SA37 Max Stassi .40 1.00
SA38 Jean Segura 1.50 4.00
SA39 Nick Franklin .60 1.50
SA40 Rafael Ynoa .40 1.00
SA41 Bo Greenwell 1.25 3.00
SA42 Brad Brach .40 1.00
SA43 Rich Poythress .40 1.00
SA44 Jon Gilmore 1.25 3.00
SA45 Tyler Chatwood .40 1.00

2011 Topps Pro Debut Solo Signatures

GROUP A ODDS 1:26
GROUP B ODDS 1:48
GROUP C ODDS 1:239
RED ODDS 1:14,700 HOBBY
RED PRINT RUN 1 SER.#'d SET
NO RED PRICING DUE TO SCARCITY
PRINTING PLATE ODDS 1:2520 HOBBY
PLATE PRINT RUN 1 SET PER COLOR
BLACK-CYAN-MAGENTA-YELLOW ISSUED
NO PLATE PRICING DUE TO SCARCITY
CC Cito Culver 6.00 15.00
CN Chris Nowak 3.00 8.00
CS Cody Scarpetta 3.00 8.00
DB Dan Brewer 5.00 12.00
FD Fautino De Los Santos 3.00 8.00
FG Freddy Galvis 4.00 10.00
GG Garrett Gould 3.00 8.00
JB Jesse Biddle 6.00 15.00
JD Jaff Decker 4.00 10.00
JP Julio Pimental 3.00 8.00
JZ Josh Zeid 3.00 8.00
KD Khris Davis 10.00 25.00
KG Kyle Greenwalt 3.00 8.00
MC Michael Choice 5.00 12.00
OP Omar Poveda 3.00 8.00
RA Ryan Adams 3.00 8.00
RL Ryan Larvarnway 8.00 20.00
RP Rich Poythress 3.00 8.00
SH Slade Heathcott 3.00 8.00
TF Thomas Field 3.00 8.00
WH Wes Hodges 3.00 8.00
ZA Zach McAllister 3.00 8.00
AWE Allen Webster 3.00 8.00
DBR David Bromberg 3.00 8.00

2011 Topps Pro Debut Solo Signatures Blue

*BLUE: .5X TO 1.2X BASIC
STATED ODDS 1:74 HOBBY
STATED PRINT RUN 199 SER.#'d SETS

2011 Topps Pro Debut Solo Signatures Gold

*GOLD: .6X TO 1.5X BASIC
STATED ODDS 1:294 HOBBY
STATED PRINT RUN 50 SER.#'d SETS

2011 Topps Pro Debut Triple-A All Stars

COMPLETE SET (10) 6.00 15.00
STATED ODDS 1:16 HOBBY
PRINTING PLATE ODDS 1:882 HOBBY
PLATE PRINT RUN 1 SET PER COLOR
BLACK-CYAN-MAGENTA-YELLOW ISSUED
NO PLATE PRICING DUE TO SCARCITY
TA1 Brock Bond .75 2.00
TA2 Brandon Dickson .75 2.00
TA3 Dustin Martin .75 2.00
TA4 Chase Lambin 1.25 3.00
TA5 Wes Timmons .75 2.00
TA6 Bubba Bells .75 2.00
TA7 Jose Constanza .75 2.00
TA8 Matt Miller .75 2.00
TA9 Doug Deeds .75 2.00
TA10 Jesus Montero .75 2.00

2012 Topps Pro Debut

COMP.SET w/o VAR (220) 30.00 60.00
VAR SP ODDS 1:169 HOBBY
PRINTING PLATE ODDS 1:196 HOBBY
PLATE PRINT RUN 1 SET PER COLOR
BLACK-CYAN-MAGENTA-YELLOW ISSUED
NO PLATE PRICING DUE TO SCARCITY
1 Dante Bichette Jr. .20 .50
2 Nestor Molina .15 .40
3 Keenyn Walker .15 .40
4 C.J. Cron .20 .50
5A Mike Olt .20 .50
6 Tyler Collins .20 .50
7 Matthew Szczur .15 .40
8 Ryan Brett .20 .50
9 Sean Gilmartin .15 .40
10 Barret Loux .15 .40
11 Kevin Matthews .15 .40
12 Nick Ramirez .20 .50
13 Jiwan James .20 .50
14 Kevin Patterson .25 .60
15 Bryson Myles .15 .40
16A Manny Machado 1.00 2.50
16B Manny Machado VAR SP 75.00 150.00
17 Luis Jimenez .15 .40
18A Julio Rodriguez .15 .40
18B Julio Rodriguez VAR SP 15.00 40.00
19 Chase Davidson .25 .60
20 Jeremy Williams .25 .60
21 Casey Kelly .15 .40
22A Oscar Taveras .25 .60
23 Garin Cecchini .20 .50
24A Christian Yelich 1.25 3.00
25 Mike Montgomery .15 .40
26 A.J. Jimenez .15 .40
27 Gregory Pron .40 1.00
28A Shelby Miller .30 .75
29 Allen Webster .20 .50
30 Bryson Smith .15 .40
31 Scott Snodgress .15 .40
32 Martin Perez .25 .60
33 Andrew Clark .15 .40
34 Trayce Thompson .25 .60
35 Jett Bandy .15 .40
36 Blake Hassebrock .15 .40
37A Eddie Rosario .30 .75
38 Henry Rodriguez .15 .40
39 Drew Vettleson .15 .40
40A Jake Marisnick .20 .50
40B Jake Marisnick VAR SP 10.00 25.00
41 Josh Parr .15 .40
42A Mason Williams .25 .60
42B Mason Williams VAR SP 20.00 50.00
43A Noah Syndergaard .20 .50
44 Nick Franklin .20 .50
45A Jean Segura .20 .50
45B Jean Segura VAR SP 20.00 50.00
46 Trevor Story .60 1.50
47 Jace Peterson .20 .50
48 Yazy Arbelo .15 .40
49 Kevin Pillar .20 .50
50A Jonathan Galvez .15 .40
51 Alexi Amarista .15 .40
52A Gary Brown .15 .40
52B Gary Brown VAR SP 15.00 40.00
53 Dean Green .15 .40
54 Cody Martin .15 .40
55 Bubba Starling .20 .50
56 Hak-Ju Lee .15 .40
57 Shawn Payne .20 .50
58 Grant Buckner .20 .50
59A Joe Panik .25 .60
60 Tim Shibuya .15 .40
61 Edward Salcedo .15 .40
62 Tanner Peters .15 .40
63 Zack Cox .15 .40
64A Miguel Sano .20 .50
64B Miguel Sano VAR SP 20.00 50.00
65 Taylor Motter .15 .40
66 Brandon Eckerle .15 .40
67 Tony Cingrani .30 .75
68 Cameron Hobson .15 .40
69 Sonny Gray .25 .60
70 Jonathan Griffin .15 .40
71 John Cornely .15 .40
72A Taylor Lindsey .15 .40
73A Jonathan Singleton .20 .50
73B Jonathan Singleton VAR SP 8.00 20.00
74 Sean Buckley .15 .40
75 Christopher Grayson .15 .40
76A Nick Castellanos .50 1.25
76B Nick Castellanos VAR SP 15.00 40.00
77 Ajay Meyer .15 .40
78A Taijuan Walker .20 .50
78B Taijuan Walker VAR SP 8.00 20.00
79 Zach Cone .20 .50
80 Jorge Vega-Rosado .20 .50
81A Jurickson Profar .20 .50
81B Jurickson Profar VAR SP 15.00 40.00
82 Nicholas Cuckovich .15 .40
83 Joe Terdoslavich .20 .50
84A Xander Bogaerts .60 1.50
84B Xander Bogaerts VAR SP 15.00 40.00
85 Steven Proscia .20 .50
86A Travis d'Arnaud .20 .50
87A Manny Banuelos .20 .50
87B Manny Banuelos VAR SP 10.00 25.00
88 Jeurys Familia .25 .60
89 Matt Davidson .20 .50
90 Chad James .15 .40
91 Kyle Hald .25 .60
92 Kyle Hallock .20 .50
93 Matthew Williams .25 .60
94 Drew Hutchison .20 .50
95 John Hellweg .15 .40
96 Anthony Ranaudo .20 .50
97 Daniel Corcino .20 .50
98 Christian Bethancourt .15 .40
99 Samuel Mende .15 .40
100A Trevor Bauer .50 1.25
100B Trevor Bauer VAR SP 40.00 80.00
101A Will Middlebrooks .20 .50
101B Will Middlebrooks VAR SP 15.00 40.00
102 Robbie Ray .15 .40
103A Bryce Brentz .15 .40
103B Bryce Brentz VAR SP 15.00 40.00
104 John Pedrotty .15 .40
105 Mike Murray .15 .40
106 Phillips Castillo .25 .60
107 Travis Taijeron .15 .40
108A Tim Wheeler .20 .50
108B Tim Wheeler VAR SP 10.00 25.00
109A Keyvius Sampson .15 .40
110 Jaff Decker .15 .40
111 Martin Peguero .25 .60
112 Abel Baker .15 .40
113A Rymer Liriano .15 .40
114 Gerrit Cole 1.00 2.50
115 Richard Espy .15 .40
116 Jake Hager .15 .40
117 Tommy Joseph .30 .75
118 Kelby Tomlinson .15 .40
119 Brennan May .15 .40
120A Matt Adams .20 .50
120B Matt Adams VAR SP 30.00 60.00
121 Taylor Siemens .15 .40
122 Mark Haddow .15 .40
123 Gary Sanchez .50 1.25
124 Daniel Paolini .15 .40
125 Justin Boudreaux .15 .40
126 Kole Calhoun .20 .50
127 Kyle Kubitza .15 .40
128A John Lamb .15 .40
129A Trevor May .15 .40
129B Trevor May VAR SP 15.00 40.00
130 Tyrell Jenkins .20 .50
131 O'Koyea Dickson .20 .50
132 Casey Crosby .20 .50
133A Tyler Thornburg .20 .50
134 Matt Den Dekker .20 .50
135 Guillermo Pimentel .15 .40
136 J.R. Graham .15 .40
137 Justin Nicolino .20 .50
138 Rafael Lopez .15 .40
139A Brian Dozier .50 1.25
139B Brian Dozier VAR SP 15.00 40.00
140 Kevan Smith .20 .50
141 Kevin Quackenbush .15 .40
142 Cheslor Cuthbert .15 .40
143 Dan Rosenbaum .20 .50
144 Heath Hembree .20 .50
145 Bryce Harper 5.00 12.00
146 Dan Bennett .15 .40
147 Carlos Martinez .25 .60
148 Matthew Summers .15 .40
149 Jake Odorizzi .20 .50
150 Justice French .15 .40
151 Keith Hessler .15 .40
152 Telvin Nash .15 .40
153 Gary Apelian .15 .40
154 Jason Van Skike .15 .40
155 Paul Hoilman .15 .40
156A Cory Spangenberg .15 .40
156B Cory Spangenberg VAR SP 15.00 40.00
157 Nick Urbanus .15 .40
158A Jordan Swagerty .15 .40
158B Jordan Swagerty VAR SP 30.00 60.00
159 Wilmer Flores .20 .50
160A Zack Wheeler .30 .75
161A Starling Marte .20 .50
161B Starling Marte VAR SP 15.00 40.00
162 Javier Baez .60 1.50
163 Todd McInnis .15 .40
164 Jose Ramirez 1.50 4.00
165 Cody Buckel .15 .40
166 Brandon Jacobs .20 .50
167 Tyler Rahmatulla .15 .40
168 Brett Krill .20 .50
169 D'Andre Toney .15 .40
170 Nicholas Tropeano .15 .40
171 Brandon Drury .25 .60
172 Deck McGuire .15 .40
173 Terrance Gore .15 .40
174A Robbie Erlin .20 .50
174B Robbie Erlin VAR SP 10.00 25.00
175A Scooter Gennett .25 .60
175B Scooter Gennett VAR SP 8.00 20.00
176 Kyle Waldrop .15 .40
177 Didi Gregorius 1.25 3.00
178A Matt Harvey 1.00 2.50
178B Matt Harvey VAR SP 10.00 25.00
179 James Paxton .25 .60
180 Ryan Jones .15 .40
181 James Allen .15 .40
182 Jeremy Patton .15 .40
183 A.J. Cole .20 .50
184 Branden Pinder .30 .75
185 Ryan Rua .20 .50
186 Andrelton Simmons .25 .60
187 Matthew Skole .20 .50
188 Chris Archer .15 .40
189 Trey McNutt .15 .40
190 Kes Carter .15 .40
191 Frazier Hall .15 .40
192 David Buchanan .20 .50
193 Jamal Austin .15 .40
194 Bryce Ortega .15 .40
195 Travis Shaw .20 .50
196 Chad Bettis .15 .40
197 Jabari Blash .15 .40
198 Jarred Cosart .15 .40

199 Daniel Muno .15 .40
200A Tyler Skaggs .25 .60
200B Tyler Skaggs VAR SP 10.00 25.00
201A Jedd Gyorko .20 .50
201B Jedd Gyorko VAR SP 8.00 20.00
202A Michael Choice .15 .40
203 Benjamin McMahan .20 .50
204 Zeke DeVoss .15 .40
205A Nolan Arenado .50 1.25
205B Nolan Arenado VAR SP 12.50 30.00
206 Robbie Grossman .15 .40
207A Anthony Gose .20 .50
207B Anthony Gose VAR SP 8.00 20.00
208 Joc Pederson .25 .60
209A Billy Hamilton .20 .50
209B Billy Hamilton VAR SP 40.00 80.00
210 Matthew Murray .15 .40
211 Jonathan Schoop .15 .40
212 Devin Shines .20 .50
213 Juan Perez .15 .40
214 Marcell Ozuna .40 1.00
215A Wil Myers .20 .50
215B Wil Myers VAR SP 30.00 60.00
216 Cameron Seitzer .15 .40
217 Alfredo Silverio .15 .40
218 Jonathon Berti .15 .40
219A Vincent Catricala .15 .40
220A Jameson Taillon .20 .50
220B Jameson Taillon VAR SP 8.00 20.00

2012 Topps Pro Debut Gold

*GOLD: 4X TO 10X BASIC
STATED ODDS 1:20 HOBBY
STATED PRINT RUN 50 SER.#'d SETS
145 Bryce Harper 20.00 50.00

2012 Topps Pro Debut Autographs

STATED ODDS 1:14 HOBBY
PRINTING PLATE ODDS 1:2117 HOBBY
PLATE PRINT RUN 1 SET PER COLOR
BLACK-CYAN-MAGENTA-YELLOW ISSUED
NO PLATE PRICING DUE TO SCARCITY
AA Alexi Amarista 5.00 12.00
AS Andrelton Simmons 10.00 25.00
AW Allen Webster 3.00 8.00
BH Blake Hassebrock 3.00 8.00
CB Chad Bettis 3.00 8.00
CC Casey Crosby 5.00 12.00
CP Carlos Perez 3.00 8.00
CT Charlie Tilson 3.00 8.00
DG Didi Gregorius 15.00 40.00
DH Drew Hutchison 4.00 10.00
DR Dan Rosenbaum 3.00 8.00
HH Heath Hembree 5.00 12.00
JH Jake Hager 3.00 8.00
JP Joe Panik 6.00 15.00
KC Kes Carter 3.00 8.00
KM Kevin Matthews 3.00 8.00
KW Keenyn Walker 3.00 8.00
LJ Luis Jimenez 3.00 8.00
ML Matt Lipka 3.00 8.00
RG Robbie Grossman 3.00 8.00
SB Sean Buckley 3.00 8.00
SG Sean Gilmartin 3.00 8.00
SP Steven Proscia 3.00 8.00
TT Trayce Thompson 3.00 8.00
ZC Zach Cone 3.00 8.00
KWA Kyle Waldrop 3.00 8.00

2012 Topps Pro Debut Autographs Gold

*GOLD: .6X TO 1.5X BASIC
STATED ODDS 1:169 HOBBY
STATED PRINT RUN 50 SER.#'d SETS

2012 Topps Pro Debut Minor League All-Stars

COMPLETE SET (50) 30.00 60.00
STATED ODDS 1:3 HOBBY
AG Anthony Gose 1.00 2.50
AS Andrelton Simmons 1.25 3.00
BH Bryce Harper 12.00 30.00
BJ Brandon Jacobs 1.00 2.50
CB Chad Bettis .75 2.00
CC Chih-Hsien Chiang .75 2.00
CK Casey Kelly .75 2.00
CM Carlos Martinez 1.25 3.00
CY Christian Yelich 6.00 15.00
DB David Buchanan 1.00 2.50
DC Daniel Corcino 1.00 2.50
GB Gary Brown .75 2.00
HH Heath Hembree 1.00 2.50
HL Hak-Ju Lee .75 2.00
JC Jarred Cosart .75 2.00
JG Jedd Gyorko 1.00 2.50
JM Jake Marisnick 1.00 2.50
JO Jake Odorizzi 1.00 2.50
JP James Paxton 1.25 3.00
JR Julio Rodriguez .75 2.00
JS Jean Segura 1.25 3.00
JT Jameson Taillon 1.00 2.50
KS Keyvius Sampson .75 2.00
MA Matt Adams 1.00 2.50
MC Michael Choice .75 2.00
MH Matt Harvey 5.00 12.00
MM Mike McDade .50 1.25
MO Mike Olt 1.00 2.50
MS Matthew Szczur 1.00 2.50
NA Nolan Arenado 2.50 6.00
RL Rymer Liriano .75 2.00
SG Scooter Gennett 1.25 3.00
SM Shelby Miller 1.50 4.00
TM Trevor May .75 2.00
TS Tyler Skaggs 1.25 3.00
TT Tyler Thornburg 1.00 2.50
TW Tim Wheeler 1.00 2.50
VC Vinnie Catricala .75 2.00
WM Will Middlebrooks 1.00 2.50
YA Yazy Arbelo .75 2.00
ZW Zack Wheeler 1.50 4.00
AJJ A.J. Jimenez .75 2.00
BHK Blake Hassebrock .75 2.00
JPA Joe Panik 1.25 3.00
JPR Jurickson Profar 1.00 2.50
JSC Jonathan Schoop .75 2.00
JTE Joe Terdoslavich 1.00 2.50
MMO Manny Machado 5.00 12.00
SMA Starling Marte 1.00 2.50
TTH Trayce Thompson 1.25 3.00

2012 Topps Pro Debut Minor League Manufactured Cap Logo

STATED ODDS 1:90 HOBBY
AC A.J. Cole 6.00 15.00
AG Anthony Gose 10.00 25.00
BB Bryce Brentz 12.50 30.00
BH Billy Hamilton 10.00 25.00
BJ Brett Jackson 6.00 15.00
CB Christian Bethancourt 8.00 20.00
CS Cory Spangenberg 12.50 30.00
CY Christian Yelich 8.00 20.00
GB Gary Brown 10.00 25.00
GC Garin Cecchini 6.00 15.00
GS Gary Sanchez 10.00 25.00
HH Heath Hembree 6.00 15.00
HL Hak-Ju Lee 10.00 25.00
JB Javier Baez 15.00 40.00
JC Jarred Cosart 10.00 25.00
JG Jedd Gyorko 8.00 20.00
JM Jake Marisnick 8.00 20.00
JP Joe Panik 6.00 15.00
JS Jonathan Singleton 8.00 20.00
JT Jameson Taillon 10.00 25.00
MB Manny Banuelos 10.00 25.00
MC Michael Choice 6.00 15.00
MH Matt Harvey 12.50 30.00
MM Manny Machado 10.00 25.00
MO Mike Olt 12.50 30.00
MP Martin Perez 6.00 15.00
MS Miguel Sano 10.00 25.00
NA Nolan Arenado 10.00 25.00
OT Oscar Taveras 20.00 50.00
RG Robbie Grossman 6.00 15.00
RL Rymer Liriano 8.00 20.00
SM Shelby Miller 12.50 30.00
TB Tim Beckham 8.00 20.00
TL Taylor Lindsey 8.00 20.00
TM Trevor May 10.00 25.00
TN Telvin Nash 10.00 25.00
TS Tyler Skaggs 8.00 20.00
TW Tim Wheeler 8.00 20.00
WF Wilmer Flores 8.00 20.00
WM Will Middlebrooks 12.50 30.00
XB Xander Bogaerts 8.00 20.00
JGR Jonathan Griffin 6.00 15.00
JPA James Paxton 8.00 20.00
JPR Jurickson Profar 10.00 25.00
JSE Jean Segura 8.00 20.00
MMO Mike Montgomery 8.00 20.00
SMA Starling Marte 8.00 20.00
TMC Trey McNutt 6.00 15.00
TWA Taijuan Walker 8.00 20.00
WMY Wil Myers 8.00 20.00

2012 Topps Pro Debut Minor League Materials

STATED ODDS 1:17 HOBBY
AG Anthony Gose 3.00 8.00
AH Aaron Hicks 2.50 6.00
AS Alfredo Silverio 2.50 6.00
BH Bryce Harper 10.00 25.00
BJ Brett Jackson 3.00 8.00
CC Chih-Hsien Chiang 3.00 8.00
CM Carlos Martinez 2.50 6.00
DH Danny Hultzen 6.00 15.00
FM Francisco Martinez 3.00 8.00
GB Gary Brown 3.00 8.00
GC Gerrit Cole 5.00 12.00
GG Grant Green 2.50 6.00
GI Manny Machado 4.00 10.00
HL Hak-Ju Lee 2.50 6.00
JC Jarred Cosart 4.00 10.00
JL Junior Lake 6.00 15.00
JM Jefry Marte 2.50 6.00
JP James Paxton 5.00 12.00
JS Jean Segura 2.50 6.00
KG Kyle Gibson 2.50 6.00
KM Kevin Mattison 2.50 6.00
KS Kyle Skipworth 2.50 6.00
MA Matt Adams 5.00 12.00
MC Michael Choice 2.50 6.00
MH Matt Harvey 8.00 20.00
MP Martin Perez 2.50 6.00
MS Matt Szczur 6.00 15.00
NA Nolan Arenado 2.50 6.00
RW Ryan Wheeler 2.50 6.00
SM Shelby Miller 3.00 8.00
SV Sebastian Valle 3.00 8.00
TB Tim Beckham 2.50 6.00
TS Tyler Skaggs 2.50 6.00
TW Tim Wheeler 2.50 6.00
WM Wil Myers 6.00 15.00
XA Xavier Avery 3.00 8.00
JPA Joe Panik 4.00 10.00
JPR Jurickson Profar 5.00 12.00
JSC Jonathan Schoop 3.00 8.00
SMA Starling Marte 3.00 8.00
WMI Will Middlebrooks 4.00 10.00

2012 Topps Pro Debut Minor League Materials Gold

*GOLD: .5X TO 1.2X BASIC
STATED ODDS 1:103 HOBBY
STATED PRINT RUN 50 SER.#'d SETS

2012 Topps Pro Debut Side By Side Dual Autographs

STATED ODDS 1:446 HOBBY
PRINT RUNS B/WN 6-50 COPIES PER
NO PRICING ON QTY 6
PRINTING PLATE ODDS 1:4812 HOBBY
PLATE PRINT RUN 1 SET PER COLOR
BLACK-CYAN-MAGENTA-YELLOW ISSUED
NO PLATE PRICING DUE TO SCARCITY
AS M.Adams/J.Swagerty 12.50 30.00
BW Kyle Waldrop 10.00 25.00
Sean Buckley
CG Michael Choice 10.00 25.00
Sonny Gray
GP S.Gilmartin/C.Perez 15.00 40.00
JB B.Jacobs/J.Bradley Jr. 25.00 60.00
JT T.Jenkins/C.Tilson 10.00 25.00
MC Kevin Matthews 10.00 25.00
Zach Cone
MG Starling Marte 10.00 25.00
Robbie Grossman
WT Walker/Thompson 12.50 30.00
CGR Tyler Collins 10.00 25.00
Dean Green

2013 Topps Pro Debut

COMP.SET.w/o VAR (220) 30.00 60.00
VAR SP ODDS 1:324 HOBBY
TIM KANE ODDS 1:2434 HOBBY
PRINTING PLATE ODDS 1:276 HOBBY
VARIATION PLATE ODDS 1:4050 HOBBY
PLATE PRINT RUN 1 SET PER COLOR
BLACK-CYAN-MAGENTA-YELLOW ISSUED
NO PLATE PRICING DUE TO SCARCITY
1 Oscar Taveras .30 .75
2 Arismendy Alcantara .40 1.00
3 Kyle Zimmer .30 .75
4A Carlos Correa 2.50 6.00
4B Carlos Correa SP 50.00 100.00
5 C.J. Cron .30 .75
6 Nick Williams .30 .75
7 Kyle Parker .25 .60
8 Gavin Cecchini .30 .75
9 Will Lamb .15 .40
10 Nathan Karns .25 .60
11 Matt Stites .25 .60
12A Mason Williams .30 .75
12B Mason Williams SP 15.00 40.00
13 Keon Barnum .25 .60
14 Mike Zunino .40 1.00
15 Adam Morgan .25 .60
16 A.J. Cole .30 .75
17 Max Kepler .50 1.25
18 Jorge Polanco .25 .60
19 A.J. Jimenez .15 .40
20 Alex Colome .25 .60
21 Robert Haney .25 .60
22 Oswaldo Arcia .25 .60
23 Albert Almora .50 1.25
24 Sonny Gray .40 1.00
25 Lance McCullers .25 .60
26 Daniel Corcino .25 .60
27 Michael Kickham .25 .60
28 Robert Stephenson .25 .60
29 Stryker Trahan .25 .60
30 Anthony Alford .25 .60
31 Luigi Rodriguez .25 .60
32 Brian Goodwin .30 .75
33 Zoilo Almonte .30 .75
34 Richie Shaffer .25 .60
35A Yasiel Puig 1.00 2.50
35B Yasiel Puig SP 75.00 150.00
36 Adalberto Mondesi .75 2.00
37 Courtney Hawkins .25 .60
38 Allen Webster .30 .75
39 Nick Travieso .30 .75
40 Blake Snell .30 .75
41 Clayton Blackburn .40 1.00
42 Brandon Nimmo .40 1.00
43 Matt Wisler .25 .60
44 Dylan Cozens .25 .60
45 Jimmy Nelson .25 .60
46 Ty Hensley .30 .75
47 Michael Fulmer .40 1.00
48 Kevin Pillar .15 .40
49 Taylor Lindsey .25 .60
50 Zack Wheeler .50 1.25
51 Rio Ruiz .25 .60
52 Wyatt Mathisen .25 .60
53A Carlos Martinez .40 1.00
53B Carlos Martinez SP 20.00 50.00
54 Cody Buckel .25 .60
55 Matt Magill .25 .60
56 Bralin Jackson .15 .40
57 Alen Hanson .30 .75
58 Miles Head .30 .75
59 Tyler Austin .40 1.00
60 C.J. Edwards .40 1.00
61A Matt Barnes .30 .75
61B Matt Barnes SP 20.00 50.00
62 Carlos Sanchez .25 .60
63 Nick Tropeano .25 .60
64 Patrick Kivlehan .25 .60
65 Taylor Jungmann .25 .60
66 Miguel Sano .30 .75
67 Rougned Odor .60 1.50
68 Deven Marrero .25 .60
69 Brad Miller .30 .75
70 Renato Nunez .50 1.25
71 Mauricio Cabrera .25 .60
72 Aaron Sanchez .30 .75
73 Christian Bethancourt .40 1.00
74 James Paxton .30 .75
75 Edwin Carl .25 .60
76 Alex Wood .30 .75
77 Michael Goodnight .40 1.00
78 Enny Romero .15 .40
79 Ethan Martin .25 .60
80 Rock Shoulders .25 .60
81 Justin Nicolino .25 .60
82 Ji-Man Choi .30 .75
83 Shawon Dunston Jr. .15 .40
84 Eury Perez .30 .75
85 Tyrone Taylor .25 .60
86 Gary Brown .25 .60
87 Andrew Aplin .25 .60
88 Gioskar Amaya .25 .60
89 Jesse Biddle .30 .75
90A Gary Sanchez .75 2.00
90B Gary Sanchez SP 8.00 20.00
91 Yeison Asencio .25 .60
92 Erik Johnson .25 .60
93 Trevor Story 1.00 2.50
94 Jonathan Singleton .30 .75
95 Jonathan Pettibone .40 1.00
96 Lucas Sims .30 .75
97 Julio Morban .15 .40
98 Keon Broxton .25 .60
99 Hak-Ju Lee .25 .60
100 Gerrit Cole 1.50 4.00
101 Matt Curry .25 .60
102 Maikel Franco .40 1.00
103 Corey Seager 1.00 2.50
104 George Springer 1.00 2.50
105 Danny Hultzen .30 .75
106A David Dahl .30 .75
106B David Dahl SP 12.50 30.00
107 Joe Ross .25 .60
108 Jabari Blash .25 .60
109 Eddie Rosario .50 1.25
110 Kaleb Cowart .30 .75
111 Marcell Ozuna .60 1.50
112 Fu-Lin Kuo .30 .75
113 Sam Selman .25 .60
114 Jose Peraza .25 .60
115 Jonathan Schoop .25 .60
116 Austin Hedges .30 .75
117 Aaron Westlake .15 .40
118 Lewis Brinson .30 .75
119 Eddie Butler .25 .60
120A Nick Castellanos .75 2.00
120B Nick Castellanos SP 10.00 25.00
121 Kyle Lotzkar .15 .40
122 Jake Barrett .25 .60
123 Michael Perez .25 .60
124 Mark Montgomery .40 1.00
125 Javier Baez 1.00 2.50
126 Luis Mateo .25 .60
127 Christian Yelich 2.00 5.00
128 Stephen Piscotty .50 1.25
129 Dorssys Paulino .30 .75
130 Matt Olson .40 1.00
131 Yordano Ventura .30 .75
132 Roberto Osuna .25 .60
133 Claudio Custodio .25 .60
134 Patrick Leonard .25 .60
135 Chris Reed .25 .60
136 Luis Merejo .25 .60
137 Delino DeShields .25 .60
138 Will Swanner .15 .40
139 R.J. Alvarez .25 .60
140 Luis Sardinas .25 .60
141A Archie Bradley .25 .60
141B Archie Bradley SP 10.00 25.00
142 Matt Davidson .30 .75
143 Scooter Gennett .40 1.00
144 Kolten Wong .25 .60
145 Lisalverto Bonilla .30 .75
146 Michael Choice .25 .60
147A Jameson Taillon .30 .75
147B Jameson Taillon SP 10.00 25.00
148 Wilmer Flores .30 .75
149 Adam Conley .25 .60
150A Byron Buxton .60 1.50
150B Byron Buxton SP 30.00 60.00
151 Chih Fang Pan .15 .40
152 Mike Piazza .25 .60
153 Kyle Crick .40 1.00
154 Gregory Polanco .50 1.25
155 Nestor Molina .25 .60
156 Noah Syndergaard .30 .75
157 Jae-Hoon Ha .15 .40
158 Matthew Skole .30 .75
159 Austin Wright .25 .60
160 Danry Vasquez .25 .60
161 Mike O'Neill .40 1.00
162 Trayce Thompson .40 1.00
163 Max Fried 1.00 2.50
164 Clint Coulter .25 .60
165 Nicholas Martinez .15 .40
166 Jorge Bonifacio .30 .75
167 Francisco Lindor 1.50 4.00
168 Chris Stratton .25 .60
169A Bubba Starling .30 .75
169B Bubba Starling SP 40.00 80.00
170 Anthony Rendon 1.25 3.00
171 D.J. Davis .30 .75
172 Jeimer Candelario .30 .75
173 Eduardo Rodriguez .75 2.00
174 Jake Marisnick .30 .75
175 Jose Berrios .40 1.00
176 Alberto Tirado .15 .40
177 Alex Meyer .25 .60
178 Vance Albitz .40 1.00
179 Mark Bordonaro .50 1.25
180 Tyler Naquin .30 .75
181 Pat Light .25 .60
182 Dan Vogelbach .40 1.00
183 Julio Rodriguez .15 .40
184 Henry Owens .30 .75
185 Stefen Romero .25 .60
186 Bryce Brentz .25 .60
187 Andrew Heaney .30 .75
188 Scott Savastano .15 .40
189 Blake Swihart .30 .75
190 Trevor May .15 .40
191 Josh Bell .50 1.25
192 Joey Gallo .75 2.00
193 Jorge Soler .50 1.25
194 Angelo Gumbs .15 .40
195 Tommy Joseph .50 1.25
196 Andres Santiago .15 .40
197 Michael Wacha .30 .75
198A Billy Hamilton .30 .75
198B Billy Hamilton SP 20.00 50.00
199 Austin Aune .30 .75
200 Travis d'Arnaud .30 .75
201 Taylor Guerrieri .25 .60
202 Sean Gilmartin .25 .60
203 Seth Rosin .40 1.00
204 Nolan Arenado 1.25 3.00
205 Sean Nolin .30 .75
206A Taijuan Walker .30 .75
206B Taijuan Walker SP 8.00 20.00
207 Jorge Alfaro .50 1.25
208 Addison Russell .40 1.00
209 Jake Thompson .25 .60
210 Joc Pederson .40 1.00
211 Andre Rienzo .25 .60
212 J.R. Graham .25 .60
213 Kevin Gausman .40 1.00
214 Mitch Brown .25 .60
215 Hunter Morris .30 .75
216 Keury de la Cruz .25 .60
217 Grant Green .40 1.00
218 Roman Quinn .40 1.00
219 Joe Panik .40 1.00
220A Xander Bogaerts .75 2.00
220B Xander Bogaerts SP 20.00 50.00
TK Tim Kane SP 12.50 30.00

2013 Topps Pro Debut Gold

*GOLD: 4X TO 10X BASIC
STATED ODDS 1:22 HOBBY
STATED PRINT RUN 50 SER.#'d SETS
102 Maikel Franco 12.50 30.00
219 Joe Panik 12.50 30.00

2013 Topps Pro Debut Autographs

STATED ODDS 1:14 HOBBY
PRINTING PLATE ODDS 1:2340 HOBBY
PLATE PRINT RUN 1 SET PER COLOR
BLACK-CYAN-MAGENTA-YELLOW ISSUED
NO PLATE PRICING DUE TO SCARCITY
EXCHANGE DEADLINE 06/30/2016
AC Alex Colome 3.00 8.00
AJ A.J. Jimenez 3.00 8.00
AS Andres Santiago 3.00 8.00
AT Alberto Tirado 3.00 8.00
AW Austin Wright 3.00 8.00
BJ Bralin Jackson 3.00 8.00
CC Claudio Custodio 4.00 10.00
DC Dylan Cozens 6.00 15.00
EP Eury Perez 3.00 8.00
FK Fu-Lin Kuo 4.00 10.00
JP Jose Peraza 3.00 8.00
JPE Jonathan Pettibone 5.00 12.00
JPO Jorge Polanco 3.00 8.00
KB Keon Broxton 3.00 8.00
LB Lisalverto Bonilla 3.00 8.00
LM Luis Merejo 3.00 8.00
LR Luigi Rodriguez 4.00 10.00
MC Matt Curry 3.00 8.00
MP Mike Piazza 3.00 8.00
NM Nicholas Martinez 4.00 10.00
NMO Nestor Molina 3.00 8.00
OT Oscar Taveras 90.00 150.00
RO Rougned Odor 6.00 15.00
RS Rock Shoulders 4.00 10.00
SD Shawon Dunston Jr. 3.00 8.00
WL Will Lamb 3.00 8.00
YA Yeison Asencio 3.00 8.00

2013 Topps Pro Debut Autographs Gold

*GOLD: .6X TO 1.5X BASIC
STATED ODDS 1:194 HOBBY
STATED PRINT RUN 50 SER.#'d SETS
EXCHANGE DEADLINE 06/30/2016
DC Dylan Cozens 15.00 40.00
JPE Jonathan Pettibone 15.00 40.00

2013 Topps Pro Debut Mascots

COMMON CARD 4.00 10.00
STATED ODDS 1:46 HOBBY
STATED PRINT RUN 120 SER.#'d SETS
A Abner 4.00 10.00
B Belle the Ballpark Diva 5.00 12.00
H Homer 4.00 10.00
J Johnny Fort 4.00 10.00
K KaBoom 4.00 10.00
L Looie 4.00 10.00
M Marty 4.00 10.00
O Orbit 4.00 10.00
S Snappy 4.00 10.00
BB Buddy Bat 4.00 10.00
BG Bubba Grape 4.00 10.00
BI Bingo 4.00 10.00
BIG Big L 4.00 10.00
BL Blooper 4.00 10.00
BM Boomer 4.00 10.00
BO Bolt 4.00 10.00
BTB Buster T. Bison 4.00 10.00
CH Charlie the Chukar 4.00 10.00
CR Crash West 4.00 10.00
CW C. Wolf 4.00 10.00
GTG Guilford the Grasshopper 4.00 10.00
HO Hootz 6.00 15.00
HRH Hamilton R. Head 4.00 10.00
LEL Lou E. Loon 4.00 10.00
LO Louie 4.00 10.00
LOE Louie the Lumberking 4.00 10.00
MAM Miss-A-Miracle 4.00 10.00
MM Mr. Moon 4.00 10.00
MU Muddy the Mudcat 4.00 10.00
MUG Mugsy 4.00 10.00
OZE Ozzie 4.00 10.00
OZI Ozzie the Cougar 4.00 10.00
RR Rockey Redbird 6.00 15.00
RS Rally Shark 4.00 10.00
RTRB Rascal the River Bandit 4.00 10.00
SA Sandy the Seagull 6.00 15.00
SK Skipper 4.00 10.00
SO Southpaw 4.00 10.00
SP Splash 4.00 10.00
ST Strike 4.00 10.00
STF Sox the Fox 4.00 10.00
TEG Tim E. Gator 4.00 10.00
US Uncle Sam 4.00 10.00
WEB Wool E. Bull 4.00 10.00

2013 Topps Pro Debut Mascots Gold

*GOLD: .5X TO 1.2X BASIC
STATED ODDS 1:110 HOBBY
STATED PRINT RUN 50 SER.#'d SETS

2013 Topps Pro Debut Minor League Manufactured Hat Logo

STATED ODDS 1:65 HOBBY
STATED PRINT RUN 75 SER.#'d SETS
PRINTING PLATE ODDS 1:1217 HOBBY
PLATE PRINT RUN 1 SET PER COLOR
BLACK-CYAN-MAGENTA-YELLOW ISSUED
NO PLATE PRICING DUE TO SCARCITY
AB Archie Bradley 5.00 12.00
AC Alex Colome 6.00 15.00
AH Andrew Heaney 10.00 25.00
AMY Alex Meyer 5.00 12.00
AR Addison Russell 8.00 20.00
AS Aaron Sanchez 8.00 20.00
BB Byron Buxton 15.00 40.00
BH Billy Hamilton 10.00 25.00
CH Courtney Hawkins 8.00 20.00
CST Chris Stratton 10.00 25.00
DDE Delino DeShields 6.00 15.00
DM Deven Marrero 6.00 15.00
DV Dan Vogelbach 6.00 15.00
ER Eduardo Rodriguez 5.00 12.00
FL Francisco Lindor 8.00 20.00
GB Gary Brown 8.00 20.00
GP Gregory Polanco 12.50 30.00
GS George Springer 10.00 25.00
HJL Hak-Ju Lee 6.00 15.00
HO Henry Owens 5.00 12.00
JA Jorge Alfaro 5.00 12.00
JB Jesse Biddle 10.00 25.00
JMC Ji-Man Choi 5.00 12.00
JMN Julio Morban 5.00 12.00
JP Joe Panik 8.00 20.00
JR Joe Ross 6.00 15.00
JT Jameson Taillon 10.00 25.00
KC Kyle Crick 8.00 20.00
KCO Kaleb Cowart 6.00 15.00
KG Kevin Gausman 10.00 25.00
KP Kyle Parker 6.00 15.00
KZ Kyle Zimmer 6.00 15.00
MB Matt Barnes 5.00 12.00
MD Matt Davidson 5.00 12.00
MMG Matt Magill 5.00 12.00
MO Marcell Ozuna 5.00 12.00
MP Michael Perez 5.00 12.00
MZ Mike Zunino 12.50 30.00
NK Nathan Karns 5.00 12.00
OA Oswaldo Arcia 8.00 20.00
RS Robert Stephenson 10.00 25.00
SG Scooter Gennett 5.00 12.00
SP Stephen Piscotty 10.00 25.00
TA Tyler Austin 6.00 15.00
TD Travis d'Arnaud 8.00 20.00
WF Wilmer Flores 10.00 25.00
XB Xander Bogaerts 15.00 40.00
YP Yasiel Puig 15.00 40.00
YV Yordano Ventura 5.00 12.00
ZW Zack Wheeler 8.00 20.00

2013 Topps Pro Debut Minor League Materials

STATED ODDS 1:32 HOBBY
AM Alfredo Marte 2.50 6.00
AME Alex Meyer 2.50 6.00
AP Ariel Pena 2.50 6.00
CFP Chih Fang Pan 2.50 6.00
CR Chris Reed 2.50 6.00
CS Carlos Sanchez 2.50 6.00
ER Enny Romero 2.50 6.00
JHH Jae-Hoon Ha 2.50 6.00
JR Julio Rodriguez 2.50 6.00
KL Kyle Lotzkar 2.50 6.00
LB Lisalverto Bonilla 2.50 6.00
WF Wilmer Flores 2.50 6.00

2013 Topps Pro Debut Minor League Materials Gold

*GOLD: .5X TO 1.2X BASIC
STATED ODDS 1:405 HOBBY
STATED PRINT RUN 50 SER.#'d SETS

2013 Topps Pro Debut Side By Side Dual Autographs

STATED ODDS 1:486 HOBBY
STATED PRINT RUN 50 SER.#'d SETS
PRINTING PLATE ODDS 1:6085 HOBBY
PLATE PRINT RUN 1 SET PER COLOR
BLACK-CYAN-MAGENTA-YELLOW ISSUED
NO PLATE PRICING DUE TO SCARCITY
EXCHANGE DEADLINE 06/30/2016
CK C.Custodio/F.Kuo 12.50 30.00
DS Dunston/Shoulders EXCH 15.00 40.00
LM Will Lamb 6.00 15.00
Nicholas Martinez
LO W.Lamb/R.Odor 15.00 40.00
OC Ozuna/Conley EXCH 10.00 25.00
PM J.Peraza/L.Merejo 10.00 25.00
PO Jose Peraza 6.00 15.00
Rougned Odor
PP J.Polanco/J.Peraza 10.00 25.00
TJ A.Tirado/A..Jimenez 10.00 25.00
WP A.Wright/J.Pettibone 12.50 30.00

2014 Topps Pro Debut

COMP.SET.w/o VAR (220) 40.00 80.00
VAR SP ODDS 1:249 HOBBY
PRINTING PLATE ODDS 1:199 HOBBY
PLATE PRINT RUN 1 SET PER COLOR
BLACK-CYAN-MAGENTA-YELLOW ISSUED
NO PLATE PRICING DUE TO SCARCITY
1A Byron Buxton .20 .50
1B Buxton SP Run 20.00 50.00
2 Chadd Krist .15 .40
3 Stephen Perez .15 .40
4 Lou Trivino .20 .50
5 Nestor Molina .15 .40
6 Trae Arbet .15 .40
7 Jeremy Barfield .15 .40
8 Tyler Danish .15 .40
9 Garrett Smith .15 .40
10 Nick Martinez .15 .40
11 Mike Freeman .15 .40
12 Nick Ahmed .15 .40
13A Clint Frazier .00 1.50
13B Frazier SP Run 20.00 50.00
14 Dominic Smith .15 .40
15 Gavin Cecchini .15 .40
16 Kevin Plawecki .15 .40
17 Michael Fulmer .25 .60
18 T.J. Chism .15 .40
19 L.J. Mazzilli .15 .40
20 John Gant .15 .40
21 Akeel Morris .15 .40
22 Amed Rosario .25 .60
23 Trevor Story .60 1.50
24 David Dahl .20 .50
25 Gus Schlosser .15 .40
26 Tyler Austin .15 .40
27 Kyle Crick .15 .40
28A Max Fried .60 1.50
28B Fried SP Hands together 10.00 25.00
29 Clayton Blackburn .25 .60
30 Corey Seager .60 1.50
31 Raul Mondesi .50 1.25
32 Roberto Osuna .15 .40
33 Luis Heredia .15 .40
34A Kohl Stewart .15 .40
34B Stewart SP Hands together 6.00 15.00
35 Dorssys Paulino .15 .40
36 Joey Gallo .30 .75
37 Luis Sardinas .15 .40
38 Steven Matz .30 .75
39 Courtney Hawkins .15 .40
40 Josh Bell .30 .75
41A Tyler Glasnow .25 .60
41B Glasnow SP Ball visable 10.00 25.00
42 Roman Quinn .25 .60
43 Jorge Bonifacio .15 .40
44 Victor Roache .15 .40
45 Stryker Trahan .15 .40
46 Adam Walker .15 .40
47 Rougned Odor .30 .75
48 Daniel Norris .20 .50
49 Brandon Nimmo .25 .60
50 Mark Appel .20 .50
51 Tyler Naquin .20 .50
52 Lewis Brinson .25 .60
53 Dan Vogelbach .25 .60
54 Parker Bridwell .15 .40
55 Jonathan Crawford .15 .40
56 Daniel Robertson .20 .50
57 Carson Kelly .25 .60
58 Matt Olson .25 .60
59 Nolan Fontana .15 .40
60 Bubba Starling .20 .50
61A Albert Almora .25 .60
61B Almora SP Facing right 12.00 30.00
62 Oscar Mercado .25 .60
63 Jesmuel Valentin .15 .40
64 Angelo Gumbs .15 .40
66 Hunter Harvey .15 .40
67 Tim Berry .15 .40
68 Blake Swihart .20 .50
69 Deven Marrero .15 .40
70 Keury De La Cruz .15 .40
71 Mookie Betts 3.00 8.00
72 Rafael De Paula .15 .40
73 Eric Jagielo .15 .40
74 Richie Shaffer .15 .40
75 Brandon Martin .15 .40
76 Arismendy Alcantara .15 .40
77 Garin Cecchini .15 .40
78 Christian Lopes .15 .40
79 Keon Barnum .15 .40
80 Logan Bawcom .15 .40
81 Jacob May .20 .50
82 Micah Johnson .15 .40
83 A.J. Jimenez .15 .40
84 Luigi Rodriguez .15 .40
85 Tony Wolters .15 .40
86 LeVon Washington .15 .40
87 Devon Travis .15 .40
88 Corey Knebel .15 .40
89 Hunter Dozier .15 .40
90 Miguel Almonte .15 .40
91 Elier Hernandez .15 .40
92 Jose Berrios .25 .60
93 Patrick Wisdom .15 .40
94 Jorge Polanco .15 .40
95 Eddie Butler .15 .40
96 Stephen Gonsalves .15 .40
97 Felix Jorge .15 .40
98 Lance McCullers .15 .40
99 Delino DeShields .15 .40
100A Carlos Correa .75 2.00
100B Correa SP #1 jersey 15.00 40.00
101 Mike Foltynewicz .15 .40
102 Rio Ruiz .15 .40
103 Andrew Thurman .15 .40
104 Gregory Polanco .25 .60
105 Alex Yarbrough .15 .40
106 R.J. Alvarez .15 .40
107 Zach Borenstein .20 .50
108 Kyle Simon .15 .40
109 Michael Ynoa .15 .40
110 Renato Nunez .30 .75
111 B.J. Boyd .15 .40
112 Austin Wilson .15 .40
113 Gabriel Guerrero .15 .40
114 Luiz Gohara .15 .40
115 Tyler Marlette .15 .40
116 Edwin Diaz .30 .75
117 Patrick Kivlehan .15 .40
118 Guillermo Pimentel .15 .40
119 Ketel Marte .30 .75
120 Nomar Mazara .40 1.00
121 Travis Demeritte .20 .50
122 Nick Williams .20 .50
123 Alec Asher .15 .40
124 Eduardo Rodriguez .20 .50
125 Jason Hursh .15 .40
126 Kyle Hunter .15 .40
127 Kyle Kubitza .15 .40
128A Colin Moran .15 .40
128B Moran SP Fldng 12.00 30.00
129 Adam Weisenburger .15 .40
130 Avery Romero .15 .40
131 Jeff Urlaub .15 .40
132 Dan Black .15 .40
133A J.P. Crawford .15 .40
133B Crawford SP Run 10.00 25.00
134 Cord Sandberg .15 .40
135 Andrew Knapp .15 .40
136 Tim Anderson .30 .75
137 Mike Morin .15 .40
139 Andy Burns .15 .40
140A Eddie Rosario .30 .75
140B Rosario SP w/bat 10.00 25.00
141 C.J. Edwards .20 .50
142 Jeimer Candelario .20 .50
143 Gioskar Amaya .15 .40
144A Robert Stephenson .15 .40
144B Stephen SP Hands together 10.00 25.00
145 Nicholas Travieso .15 .40
146 Stephen Piscotty .20 .50
147 Ismael Guillon .15 .40
148 James Hoyt .15 .40
149 Orlando Arcia .25 .60
150 Austin Meadows .25 .60
151 Clint Coulter .15 .40
152 Mitch Haniger .25 .60
153 Sam Selman .15 .40
154 Alen Hanson .15 .40
155 Reese McGuire .15 .40
156 Barrett Barnes .15 .40
157 David Goforth .15 .40
158 Willy Garcia .15 .40
159 Jin-De Jhang .15 .40
160 Jon Prosinski .15 .40
161 Marco Gonzales .25 .60
162 Rob Kaminsky .15 .40
163 Bruce Maxwell .15 .40
164 Braden Shipley .15 .40
165 Jake Lamb .25 .60
166 Brandon Drury .15 .40
167A Jonathan Gray .20 .50
167B Gray SP Holding glv 15.00 40.00
168 Rosell Herrera .25 .60
169 Mike Bolsinger .15 .40
170 Jayson Aquino .15 .40
171 Zach Lee .15 .40
172 Julio Urias .75 2.00
173 Chris Anderson .15 .40
174 Tom Windle .15 .40
175 Derek Law .20 .50
176 Scott Schebler .25 .60
177 James Baldwin .15 .40
178 A.J. Cole .15 .40
179 Austin Hedges .15 .40
180 Rymer Liriano .15 .40
181 Jeff Johnson .15 .40
182 Hunter Renfroe .20 .50
183 Matt Ramsey .15 .40
184 Zach Eflin .20 .50
185 Chris Stratton .15 .40
186 Christian Arroyo 1.00 2.50
187 Edwin Escobar .15 .40
188 Ty Blach .15 .40
189 Andrew Susac .20 .50
190 Ryder Jones .15 .40
191 Gosuke Katoh .25 .60
192A Gary Sanchez .50 1.25
192B Sanchez SP Run 15.00 40.00
193 Mason Williams .15 .40
194A Aaron Sanchez .15 .40
194B Sanchez SP Dugout 12.00 30.00
195A Henry Owens .20 .50
195B Owens SP Arm forward 10.00 25.00
196 Jorge Soler .30 .75
197 Cody Reed .15 .40
198 Sam Moll .15 .40
199 Logan Vick .15 .40
200 Lucas Giolito .25 .60
201 Raul Alcantara .15 .40
202 Thomas Coyle .15 .40
203 Isiah Kiner-Falefa .25 .60

204 Shawn Pleffner .15 .40
205 Kyle Waldrop .15 .40
206 Peter O'Brien .20 .50
207 Greg Bird .20 .50
208 Bryan Brickhouse .15 .40
209 Orlando Calixte .15 .40
210 Paul Blackburn .15 .40
211 Dillon Maples .15 .40
212 Jamie Callahan .15 .40
213 Brian Johnson .15 .40
214 James Ramsey .15 .40
215 Clay Holmes .15 .40
216 Max White .15 .40
217 Julio Morban .15 .40
218 Yeison Asencio .15 .40
219 Travis Jankowski .15 .40
220 Jorge Alfaro .20 .50
221 Jesus Galindo .15 .40
222 Dilson Herrera .25 .60

2014 Topps Pro Debut Gold

*GOLD: 5X TO 12X BASIC
STATED ODDS 1:17 HOBBY
STATED PRINT RUN 50 SER.#'d SETS
133 J.P. Crawford 6.00 15.00

2014 Topps Pro Debut Silver

*SILVER: 4X TO 10X BASIC
STATED ODDS 1:34 HOBBY
STATED PRINT RUN 25 SER.#'d SETS

2014 Topps Pro Debut Autographs

STATED ODDS 1:15 HOBBY
PRINTING PLATE ODDS 1:1870 HOBBY
PLATE PRINT RUN 1 SET PER COLOR
BLACK-CYAN-MAGENTA-YELLOW ISSUED
NO PLATE PRICING DUE TO SCARCITY
PDAAB Andy Burns 2.50 6.00
PDAAW Adam Weisenburger 2.50 6.00
PDACF Clint Frazier 15.00 40.00
PDACK Chadd Krist 2.50 6.00
PDADB Dan Black 2.50 6.00
PDADG David Goforth 2.50 6.00
PDADL Derek Law 3.00 8.00
PDAGS Garrett Smith 2.50 6.00
PDAJH James Hoyt 2.50 6.00
PDAJJ Jeff Johnson 2.50 6.00
PDAJU Jeff Urlaub 2.50 6.00
PDAKH Kyle Hunter 2.50 6.00
PDAKS Kyle Simon 2.50 6.00
PDAKW Kyle Waldrop 2.50 6.00
PDALB Logan Bawcom 2.50 6.00
PDALT Lou Trivino 3.00 8.00
PDAMB Mike Bolsinger 2.50 6.00
PDAMF Mike Freeman 2.50 6.00
PDAMR Matt Ramsey 2.50 6.00
PDANA Nick Ahmed 2.50 6.00
PDANM Nick Martinez 2.50 6.00
PDASP Stephen Perez 2.50 6.00
PDATA Trae Arbet 2.50 6.00
PDATC Thomas Coyle 2.50 6.00
PDATG Trevor Gretzky 2.50 6.00

2014 Topps Pro Debut Autographs Gold

*GOLD: .6X TO 1.5X BASIC
STATED ODDS 1:149 HOBBY
STATED PRINT RUN 50 SER.#'d SETS

2014 Topps Pro Debut Autographs Silver

*SILVER: .75X TO 2X BASIC
STATED ODDS 1:299 HOBBY
STATED PRINT RUN 25 SER.#'d SETS

2014 Topps Pro Debut Debut Duds Jerseys

STATED ODDS 1:38
DDAA Arismendy Alcantara 2.50 6.00
DDAC A.J. Cole 2.50 6.00
DDAH Austin Hedges 2.50 6.00
DDAJ A.J. Jimenez 2.50 6.00
DDBN Brandon Nimmo 4.00 10.00
DDCC Carlos Contreras 2.50 6.00
DDCR C.J. Riefenhauser 2.50 6.00
DDCW Christian Walker 5.00 12.00
DDDD Delino DeShields 2.50 6.00
DDDH Dilson Herrera 4.00 10.00
DDEB Eddie Butler 2.50 6.00
DDER Eduardo Rodriguez 3.00 8.00
DDGC Garin Cecchini 2.50 6.00
DDJG Jesus Galindo 2.50 6.00
DDJM James McCann 4.00 10.00
DDKC Kyle Crick 2.50 6.00
DDMA Miguel Almonte 2.50 6.00
DDMY Michael Ynoa 2.50 6.00
DDRD Rafael De Paula 2.50 6.00
DDYA Yeison Asencio 2.50 6.00

2014 Topps Pro Debut Debut Duds Jerseys Gold

*GOLD: .5X TO 1.2X BASIC
STATED ODDS 1:187 HOBBY
STATED PRINT RUN 50 SER.#'d SETS

2014 Topps Pro Debut Debut Duds Jerseys Silver

*SILVER: .6X TO 1.5X BASIC
STATED ODDS 1:374 HOBBY
STATED PRINT RUN 25 SER.#'d SETS

2014 Topps Pro Debut Mascots

STATED ODDS 1:76 HOBBY
STATED PRINT RUN 99 SER.#'d SETS
MMAB Abner 4.00 10.00
MMBB Buster T. Bison 4.00 10.00
MMBG Bubba Grape 4.00 10.00
MMBI Bingo 4.00 10.00
MMBL Big L 4.00 10.00
MMBO Boomer 4.00 10.00
MMCC Charlie the Chukar 4.00 10.00
MMGG Guilford the Grasshopper 4.00 10.00
MMHO Homer 4.00 10.00
MMJO Johnny 4.00 10.00
MMLL Lou E. Loon 4.00 10.00
MMLO Looie 4.00 10.00
MMMO Mr. Moon 4.00 10.00
MMOC Ozzie the Cougar 4.00 10.00
MMRR Rockey the Rockin' Redbird 4.00 10.00
MMSF Sox the Fox 4.00 10.00
MMSN Snappy D. Turtle 4.00 10.00
MMSO Southpaw 4.00 10.00
MMSP Splash 4.00 10.00
MMSS Sandy the Seagull 8.00 20.00
MMUS Uncle Slam 4.00 10.00
MMWB Wool E. Bull 4.00 10.00
MMBBA Buddy Bat 4.00 10.00
MMBLO Blooper 4.00 10.00
MMBOL Bolt 4.00 10.00

2014 Topps Pro Debut Mascots Gold

*GOLD: .5X TO 1.2X BASIC
STATED ODDS 1:150 HOBBY
STATED PRINT RUN 50 SER.#'d SETS

2014 Topps Pro Debut Minor League Manufactured Hat Logo

STATED ODDS 1:38 HOBBY
PRINTING PLATE ODDS 1:936 HOBBY
PLATE PRINT RUN 1 SET PER COLOR
BLACK-CYAN-MAGENTA-YELLOW ISSUED
NO PLATE PRICING DUE TO SCARCITY
MHAA Albert Almora 5.00 12.00
MHAC A.J. Cole 3.00 8.00
MHAS Andrew Susac 4.00 10.00
MHAT Andrew Toles 4.00 10.00
MHAW Adam Walker 3.00 8.00
MHAY Alex Yarbrough 3.00 8.00
MHBS Bubba Starling 4.00 10.00
MHCC Carlos Correa 15.00 40.00
MHCM Colin Moran 3.00 8.00
MHCS Chris Stratton 3.00 8.00
MHDG Dustin Geiger 3.00 8.00
MHDR Daniel Robertson 4.00 10.00
MHER Eddie Rosario 6.00 15.00
MHFJ Felix Jorge 3.00 8.00
MHGB Greg Bird 4.00 10.00
MHGN Gift Ngoepe 3.00 8.00
MHGP Gregory Polanco 5.00 12.00
MHHM Hoby Milner 4.00 10.00
MHHO Henry Owens 4.00 10.00
MHJB Jorge Bonifacio 3.00 8.00
MHJJ Jin-De Jhang 3.00 8.00
MHJU Julio Urias 15.00 40.00
MHKC Kyle Crick 3.00 8.00
MHKD Kentrail Davis 3.00 8.00
MHKV Kenny Vargas 3.00 8.00
MHLB Lewis Brinson 5.00 12.00
MHLR Luigi Rodriguez 3.00 8.00
MHLW Levon Washington 3.00 8.00
MHMB Mookie Betts 60.00 150.00
MHMF Mike Foltynewicz 3.00 8.00
MHMH Mitch Haniger 5.00 12.00
MHMM Mike Montgomery 3.00 8.00
MHMR Matt Ramsey 3.00 8.00
MHNA Nick Ahmed 3.00 8.00
MHNF Nolan Fontana 3.00 8.00
MHNM Nestor Molina 3.00 8.00
MHPK Patrick Kivlehan 3.00 8.00
MHSM Seth Mejias-Brean 3.00 8.00
MHST Stryker Trahan 3.00 8.00
MHTB Tim Berry 3.00 8.00
MHTM Tyler Marlette 3.00 8.00
MHTS Trevor Story 12.00 30.00
MHZE Zach Eflin 4.00 10.00
MHZL Zach Lee 3.00 8.00
MHCSE Corey Seager 12.00 30.00
MHJHA Justin Haley 3.00 8.00
MHJUR Jose Urena 4.00 10.00
MHMMI Mikie Mahtook 3.00 8.00
MHSMA Steven Matz 6.00 15.00
MHTBU Ty Buttrey 3.00 8.00

2014 Topps Pro Debut Side By Side Dual Autographs

STATED ODDS 1:936 HOBBY
STATED PRINT RUN 20 SER.#'d SETS
PRINTING PLATE ODDS 1:4680 HOBBY
PLATE PRINT RUN 1 SET PER COLOR
BLACK-CYAN-MAGENTA-YELLOW ISSUED
NO PLATE PRICING DUE TO SCARCITY
SSABC O.Calixte/J.Bonifacio 12.00 30.00
SSABH B.Barnes/C.Holmes 6.00 15.00
SSABM D.Maples/P.Blackburn 10.00 25.00
SSANO R.Nunez/M.Olson 12.00 30.00
SSAOB P.O'Brien/G.Bird 15.00 40.00
SSAOM B.Maxwell/M.Olson 12.00 30.00
SSAPR S.Piscotty/J.Ramsey 20.00 50.00

2015 Topps Pro Debut

COMP.SET w/o VAR (200) 25.00 60.00
VAR SP ODDS 1:190 HOBBY
PRINTING PLATE ODDS 1:247 HOBBY
PLATE PRINT RUN 1 SET PER COLOR
BLACK-CYAN-MAGENTA-YELLOW ISSUED
NO PLATE PRICING DUE TO SCARCITY
1A Kris Bryant 1.00 2.50
1B Bryant SP Fcng rght 20.00 50.00
2 Tayron Guerrero .15 .40
3 Josh Hader .15 .40
4 Mike Papi .15 .40
5 Alex Verdugo .25 .60
6 Robert Stephenson .15 .40
7 Brian Johnson .15 .40
8 Manuel Margot .15 .40
9 Justin O'Conner .15 .40
10 Wyatt Mathisen .15 .40
11 Kyle Zimmer .15 .40
12 Peter O'Brien .25 .60
13 Conrad Gregor .15 .40
14 Francisco Lindor 1.00 2.50
15 Tim Berry .15 .40
16 Grant Holmes .20 .50
17 Julio Urias .50 1.25
18 Steven Matz .25 .60
19 Raul Mondesi .20 .50
20 Adam Conley .15 .40
21 Luis Severino .20 .50
22 Willy Adames .25 .60
23 Hunter Dozier .15 .40
24 Forrest Wall .15 .40
25A Alex Jackson .20 .50
25B Jackson SP Bat down 4.00 10.00
26 Christian Arroyo .50 1.25
27 Tyler Beede .20 .50
28 Cody Reed .20 .50
29 Bradley Zimmer .25 .60
30 Trey Supak .15 .40
31 Foster Griffin .15 .40
32 Rob Whalen .15 .40
33 Corey Seager .60 1.50
34 Blake Swihart .20 .50
35 Lucas Sims .15 .40
36 Aaron Blair .15 .40
37 Kyle Waldrop .15 .40
38 Reese McGuire .15 .40
39 J.P. Crawford .15 .40
40 Tyler Danish .15 .40
41 Kohl Stewart .15 .40
42 Cameron Varga .15 .40
43 Brett Phillips .15 .40
44 Max Pentecost .15 .40
45 Matt Imhof .15 .40
46 Brandon Drury .15 .40
47 Jesse Biddle .20 .50
48 Renato Nunez .30 .75
49 Marcos Molina .15 .40
50 Byron Buxton .25 .60
51 Carson Sands .15 .40
52 Tyrone Taylor .15 .40
53 Orlando Arcia .20 .50
54 Lance McCullers .15 .40
55 Tim Anderson .30 .75
56 A.J. Cole .15 .40
57 A.J. Reed .20 .50
58 Jose Peraza .15 .40
59 Patrick Kivlehan .15 .40
60 Garrett Fulenchek .15 .40
61 Touki Toussaint .20 .50
62A Michael Conforto .20 .50
62B Conforto SP Red hat 20.00 50.00
63 Jose De Leon .25 .60
64 Rosell Herrera .15 .40
65 Clint Coulter .15 .40
66 Michael Chavis .40 1.00
67 Jesse Winker .15 .40
68 Kodi Medeiros .15 .40
69 David Dahl .20 .50
70 Raimel Tapia .25 .60
71 Ryan Castellani .15 .40
72 Taylor Sparks .15 .40
73 Dane Phillips .15 .40
74 Dan Black .15 .40
75 Lucas Giolito .30 .75
76 Julio Morban .15 .40
77 Jacob Lindgren .20 .50
78 Trey Ball .15 .40
79 Austin Meadows .25 .60
80 Tommy Coyle .15 .40
81 Robby Hefflinger .15 .40
82 Zech Lemond .15 .40
83 Christian Binford .15 .40
84 Mark Appel .15 .40
85 Drew Ward .15 .40
86 Brandon Nimmo .25 .60
87 Justin Twine .15 .40
88 Braden Shipley .15 .40
89 Joe Gatto .15 .40
90 Nomar Mazara .25 .60
91 Stephen Piscotty .20 .50
92A Joey Gallo .30 .75
92B Gallo SP Look up 6.00 15.00
93 Mike Freeman .15 .40
94 Cole Tucker .15 .40
95 Eddie Rosario .30 .75
96 Kyle Freeland .20 .50
97 Jose Queliz .15 .40
98 Kyle Crick .20 .50
99 Jacob Gatewood .15 .40
100 Kyle Schwarber .60 1.50
101 Spencer Adams .15 .40
102 Matt Wisler .15 .40
103 Sean Manaea .15 .40
104 Nick Wells .15 .40
105 Jon Gray .15 .40
106 Albert Almora .20 .50
107 Justin Nicolino .15 .40
108 Alex Meyer .15 .40
109 Sean Reid-Foley .20 .50
110 Austin DeCarr .15 .40
111 Jordy Lara .15 .40
112 Alex Gonzalez .25 .60
113 Monte Harrison .25 .60
114 Pierce Johnson .15 .40
115 Sean Coyle .15 .40
116 Trea Turner .50 1.25
117 Robert Refsnyder .20 .50
118 Ti'Quan Forbes .15 .40
119 T.J. Chism .15 .40
120 Max White .15 .40
121 Jack Flaherty .25 .60
122 Dominic Smith .15 .40
123 Eduardo Rodriguez .15 .40
124 Nestor Molina .15 .40
125A Carlos Correa .75 2.00
125B Correa SP No helmet 15.00 40.00
126 C.J. Edwards .25 .60
127 Tyler Naquin .20 .50
128 Jake Bauers .25 .60
129 Reynaldo Lopez .20 .50
130 Grant Hockin .15 .40
131 Phil Ervin .15 .40
132 Nick Howard .25 .60
133 Stephen Perez .15 .40
134 Jose Berrios .25 .60
135 Greg Bird .20 .50
136 Trevor Williams .15 .40
137 Micah Johnson .15 .40
138 Michael Kopech .40 1.00
139 Jake Stinnett .15 .40
140 Alex Blandino .15 .40
141 Derek Hill .20 .50
142 Tyler Glasnow .20 .50
143 Henry Owens .15 .40
144 Blake Anderson .15 .40
145 Ozhaino Albies 1.50 4.00
146 Matt Chapman .25 .60
147 Gary Sanchez .50 1.25
148 Luis Ortiz .15 .40
149 Austin Hedges .15 .40
150A Carlos Rodon .25 .60
150B Rodon SP Hldng glve 5.00 12.00
151 Casey Gillaspie .25 .60
152 Billy McKinney .20 .50
153 Francelis Montas .20 .50
154 Rob Kaminsky .15 .40
155 Jhoan Urena .15 .40
156 Gabby Guerrero .15 .40
157 Archie Bradley .15 .40
158 Michael Gettys .20 .50
159 Aaron Judge 8.00 20.00
160 Miguel Sano .20 .50
161 Derek Fisher .20 .50
162 Chris Ellis .15 .40
163 Noah Syndergaard .30 .75
164 Kevin Plawecki .15 .40
165 Hunter Renfroe .25 .60
166A Aaron Nola .25 .60
166B Nola SP No ball 20.00 50.00
167 Eric Jagielo .15 .40
168 JaCoby Jones .20 .50
169 Tanner Rahier .15 .40
170A Addison Russell .50 1.25
170B Russell SP Bttng 15.00 40.00
171 Sean Newcomb .20 .50
172 Jorge Alfaro .25 .60
173 Luke Jackson .15 .40
174 Ben Klimesh .15 .40
175A Nick Gordon .20 .50
175B Gordon SP Thrwng 15.00 40.00
176 Matt Olson .20 .50
177 Andrew Aplin .15 .40
178 Miguel Almonte .15 .40
179 Roman Quinn .25 .60
180 Braxton Davidson .15 .40
181 Nick Burdi .20 .50
182 Courtney Hawkins .15 .40
183 Drew Vettleson .15 .40
184 Michael Lorenzen .15 .40
185 Rafael Devers 1.00 2.50
186 Justus Sheffield .30 .75
187 Josh Bell .30 .75
188 Patrick Wisdom .15 .40
189 D.J. Peterson .15 .40
190 Jameson Taillon .20 .50
191 Nick Williams .20 .50
192 Cody Decker .25 .60
193 Colin Moran .15 .40
194 Chance Sisco .30 .75
195 Alex Reyes .20 .50
196 Luke Weaver .25 .60
197 Hunter Harvey .15 .40
198 Alen Hanson .15 .40
199 Clint Frazier .60 1.50
200A Tyler Kolek .15 .40
200B Kolek SP Glv at face 12.00 30.00

2015 Topps Pro Debut Gold

*GOLD: 4X TO 10X BASIC
STATED ODDS 1:20 HOBBY
STATED PRINT RUN 50 SER.#'d SETS
1 Kris Bryant 30.00 80.00

2015 Topps Pro Debut Orange

*ORANGE: 5X TO 12X BASIC
STATED ODDS 1:40 HOBBY
STATED PRINT RUN 25 SER.#'d SETS
1 Kris Bryant 40.00 100.00

2015 Topps Pro Debut Autographs

STATED ODDS 1:16 HOBBY
*GOLD/50: .5X TO 1.2X BASIC
*ORNGE/25: .75X TO 2X BASIC
1 Kris Bryant 150.00 250.00
4 Mike Papi 2.50 6.00
10 Wyatt Mathisen 2.50 6.00
13 Conrad Gregor 2.50 6.00
24 Forrest Wall 2.50 6.00
40 Tyler Danish 2.50 6.00
45 Matt Imhof 2.50 6.00
57 A.J. Reed 3.00 8.00
73 Dane Phillips 2.50 6.00
74 Dan Black 2.50 6.00
76 Julio Morban 2.50 6.00
77 Jacob Lindgren 3.00 8.00
80 Tommy Coyle 2.50 6.00
81 Robby Hefflinger 2.50 6.00
87 Justin Twine 2.50 6.00
93 Mike Freeman 2.50 6.00
118 Ti'Quan Forbes 2.50 6.00
120 Max White 2.50 6.00
121 Jack Flaherty 4.00 10.00
124 Nestor Molina 2.50 6.00
128 Jake Bauers 4.00 10.00
131 Phil Ervin 2.50 6.00
133 Stephen Perez 2.50 6.00
139 Jake Stinnett 2.50 6.00
142 Tyler Glasnow 15.00 40.00
144 Blake Anderson 2.50 6.00
153 Francelis Montas 3.00 8.00
169 Tanner Rahier 2.50 6.00
174 Ben Klimesh 2.50 6.00
175 Nick Gordon 12.00 30.00
177 Andrew Aplin 2.50 6.00
180 Braxton Davidson 2.50 6.00
181 Nick Burdi 3.00 8.00
183 Drew Vettleson 2.50 6.00
186 Justus Sheffield 5.00 12.00
188 Patrick Wisdom 2.50 6.00

2015 Topps Pro Debut Distinguished Debuts

COMPLETE SET (25) 10.00 25.00
STATED ODDS 1:6 HOBBY
PRINTING PLATE ODDS 1:1884 HOBBY
PLATE PRINT RUN 1 SET PER COLOR
BLACK-CYAN-MAGENTA-YELLOW ISSUED
NO PLATE PRICING DUE TO SCARCITY
*GOLD/50: 1.2X TO 3X BASIC
*ORNGE/25: 1.5X TO 4X BASIC
DD1 Michael Conforto .50 1.25
DD2 Nick Gordon .50 1.25
DD3 Tyler Kolek .40 1.00
DD4 Carlos Rodon .60 1.50
DD5 Kyle Schwarber 1.50 4.00
DD6 Alex Jackson .50 1.25
DD7 Aaron Nola .60 1.50
DD8 Kyle Freeland .50 1.25
DD9 Max Pentecost .40 1.00
DD10 Kodi Medeiros .40 1.00
DD11 Tyler Beede .50 1.25
DD12 Sean Newcomb .50 1.25
DD13 Touki Toussaint .50 1.25
DD14 Casey Gillaspie .60 1.50
DD15 Bradley Zimmer .60 1.50
DD16 Grant Holmes .50 1.25
DD17 Derek Hill .50 1.25
DD18 Cole Tucker .40 1.00
DD19 Matt Chapman .60 1.50
DD20 Michael Chavis 1.00 2.50
DD21 Alex Blandino .40 1.00
DD22 Jacob Gatewood .40 1.00
DD23 Braxton Davidson .40 1.00
DD24 Alex Verdugo .60 1.50
DD25 Rafael Devers 2.50 6.00

2015 Topps Pro Debut Dual Affiliation Autographs

STATED ODDS 1:536 HOBBY
PRINT RUNS B/WN 9-35 COPIES PER
NO PRICING ON QTY 9
PRINTING PLATE ODDS 1:4587 HOBBY
PLATE PRINT RUN 1 SET PER COLOR
NO PLATE PRICING DUE TO SCARCITY
DAAAJ Anderson/Johnson 15.00 40.00
DAAGA Alfaro/Gallo 30.00 60.00
DAAGC Cole/Giolito 15.00 40.00
DAAKM Kivlehan/Morban 8.00 20.00
DAALH Lorenzen/Howard 12.00 30.00
DAARK Piscotty/Kaminsky 10.00 25.00
DAASP Sheffield/Papi 15.00 40.00
DAAWF Flaherty/Wisdom 12.00 30.00

2015 Topps Pro Debut Fragments of the Farm

STATED ODDS 1:63 HOBBY
PRINTING PLATE ODDS 1:3139 HOBBY
PLATE PRINT RUN 1 SET PER COLOR
BLACK-CYAN-MAGENTA-YELLOW ISSUED
NO PLATE PRICING DUE TO SCARCITY
*GOLD/50: .5X TO 1.2X BASIC
FFAR Addison Russell 6.00 15.00
FFCS Corey Seager 10.00 25.00
FFGB Gwinnett Braves Base 2.50 6.00
FFGD Greenville Drive Ballpark Seat 2.50 6.00
FFHR Hunter Renfroe 4.00 10.00
FFJC J.P. Crawford 6.00 15.00
FFLCC Lake County Captains Championship Flag 2.50 6.00
FFLCO Lake County Captains Mascot Relic 2.50 6.00
FFML Michael Lorenzen 5.00 12.00
FFPBW Pensacola Blue Wahoos Infield Dirt 2.50 6.00
FFRB Braves Rubber 5.00 12.00
FFRRE Round Rock Express Ballpark Seat 2.50 6.00
FFSIY Yankees Mat 6.00 15.00
FFTD Drillers Netting 5.00 12.00
FFWBR Wilmington Blue Rocks Ticket 2.50 6.00
FFWC Williamsport Crosscutters Store Sign 2.50 6.00

2015 Topps Pro Debut Make Your Pro Debut

STATED ODDS 1:250 HOBBY
PDTB Tyler Badger 3.00 8.00

2015 Topps Pro Debut Minor League Mascots

STATED ODDS 1:100 HOBBY
PRINTING PLATE ODDS 1:1884 HOBBY
PLATE PRINT RUN 1 SET PER COLOR
BLACK-CYAN-MAGENTA-YELLOW ISSUED
NO PLATE PRICING DUE TO SCARCITY
MLM1 Ted E. Tourist 4.00 10.00
MLM2 Mr. Moon 4.00 10.00
MLM3 Sandy 4.00 10.00
MLM4 Buster T. Bison 4.00 10.00
MLM5 Homer 4.00 10.00
MLM6 Phinley 4.00 10.00
MLM7 Wool E. Bull 4.00 10.00
MLM8 Miss-A-Miracle 4.00 10.00
MLM9 Gizmo 4.00 10.00
MLM10 Reedy Rip'It 4.00 10.00
MLM11 Bernie 4.00 10.00
MLM12 Cubbie Bear 4.00 10.00
MLM13 Tim E. Gator 4.00 10.00
MLM14 Kaboom 4.00 10.00
MLM15 Big Lug 4.00 10.00
MLM16 Big Mo 4.00 10.00
MLM17 Splash Pelican 4.00 10.00
MLM18 Nutzy 4.00 10.00
MLM19 Oggie 4.00 10.00
MLM20 Homer 4.00 10.00
MLM21 Bumble 4.00 10.00
MLM22 Strike 4.00 10.00
MLM23 Roxy 4.00 10.00
MLM24 Boomer 4.00 10.00
MLM25 Rocky Bluewinkle 4.00 10.00

2015 Topps Pro Debut Pennant Patches

STATED ODDS 1:29 HOBBY
*GOLD/50: .5X TO 1.2X BASIC
PPAJ Alex Jackson 5.00 12.00
PPAN Aaron Nola 5.00 12.00
PPBB Byron Buxton 6.00 15.00
PPBN Brandon Nimmo 5.00 12.00
PPBS Braden Shipley 2.50 6.00
PPBSW Blake Swihart 6.00 15.00
PPCC Carlos Correa 6.00 15.00
PPCF Clint Frazier 10.00 25.00
PPCR Carlos Rodon 6.00 15.00
PPCS Corey Seager 6.00 15.00
PPDH Derek Hill 3.00 8.00
PPDP D.J. Peterson 2.50 6.00
PPFL Francisco Lindor 15.00 40.00
PPGH Grant Holmes 3.00 8.00
PPHH Hunter Harvey 2.50 6.00
PPHO Henry Owens 2.50 6.00
PPJB Josh Bell 6.00 15.00
PPJC J.P. Crawford 6.00 15.00
PPJG Joey Gallo 6.00 15.00
PPJP Jose Peraza 2.50 6.00
PPJT Jameson Taillon 6.00 15.00
PPJU Julio Urias 8.00 20.00
PPKC Kyle Crick 6.00 15.00
PPKS Kohl Stewart 5.00 12.00
PPKSC Kyle Schwarber 10.00 25.00
PPKZ Kyle Zimmer 2.50 6.00
PPLG Lucas Giolito 5.00 12.00
PPLS Lucas Sims 2.50 6.00
PPMA Mark Appel 2.50 6.00
PPMC Michael Conforto 3.00 8.00
PPMW Matt Wisler 5.00 12.00
PPNG Nick Gordon 6.00 15.00
PPNS Noah Syndergaard 6.00 15.00
PPRK Rob Kaminsky 5.00 12.00
PPRS Robert Stephenson 2.50 6.00
PPRT Raimel Tapia 4.00 10.00
PPSN Sean Newcomb 3.00 8.00
PPSP Stephen Piscotty 5.00 12.00
PPTA Tim Anderson 5.00 12.00
PPTG Tyler Glasnow 3.00 8.00
PPTK Tyler Kolek 2.50 6.00
PPTT Touki Toussaint 3.00 8.00

2015 Topps Pro Debut Promo Night Uniforms

COMPLETE SET (20) 12.00 30.00
STATED ODDS 1:12 HOBBY
PNAR A.J. Reed .75 2.00
PNBD Brandon Drury .60 1.50
PNCC Clint Coulter .60 1.50
PNCD Cody Decker 1.00 2.50
PNDC Daniel Carbonell .75 2.00
PNFP Fernando Perez .60 1.50
PNGB Greg Bird .75 2.00
PNJP Jorge Polanco .60 1.50
PNJU Jhoan Urena .60 1.50
PNKC Keury De La Cruz .60 1.50
PNMA Miguel Andujar 2.00 5.00
PNMC Michael Conforto .75 2.00
PNMR Manny Ramirez 1.00 2.50
PNMS Miguel Sano .75 2.00
PNMW Mike Wright .60 1.50
PNNM Nomar Mazara 1.00 2.50
PNNW Nick Williams .75 2.00
PNPC D.J. Peterson .60 1.50
PNRW Rowan Wick .60 1.50
PNTA Tim Anderson 1.25 3.00

2016 Topps Pro Debut

COMP.SET w/o VAR (200) 25.00 60.00
PLATE PRINT RUN 1 SET PER COLOR
NO PLATE PRICING DUE TO SCARCITY
1 Dansby Swanson .50 1.25
2 Renato Nunez .30 .75
3 Jake Thompson .15 .40
4 Omar Garcia .15 .40
5 Trey Mancini .50 1.25
6 Jacob Nottingham .15 .40
7 Mallex Smith .15 .40
8A Orlando Arcia .20 .50
8B Arcia SP dugout 8.00 20.00
9 Kevin Padlo .15 .40
10 Luiz Gohara .15 .40
11 Tyler Alexander .15 .40
12 Derek Fisher .15 .40
13 Cody Ponce .15 .40
14 Jorge Alfaro .25 .60
15 Brent Honeywell .25 .60
16 Kevin Kramer .20 .50
17 Gavin Cecchini .15 .40
18 Nathan Kirby .20 .50
19 Ke'Bryan Hayes .15 .40
20 Jomar Reyes .25 .60
21 Brandon Nimmo .25 .60
22 Willy Adames .25 .60
23A Brendan Rodgers .25 .60
23B Rodgers SP Bttng 12.00 30.00
24 Spencer Adams .15 .40
25A Jose Berrios .20 .50
25B Berrios SP Blck jrsy 8.00 20.00
26 Alex Verdugo .25 .60
27 Mark Zagunis .15 .40
28 Kyle Tucker .60 1.50
29 Jeff Hoffman .20 .50
30 Victor Robles .60 1.50
31 Edwin Diaz .30 .75
32 Tate Matheny .20 .50
33 Cornelius Randolph .15 .40
34 Nomar Mazara .25 .60
35 Tim Anderson .60 1.50
36 Tyler Kolek .20 .50
37 Ruddy Giron .15 .40
38 Jesse Winker .15 .40
39 Jorge Mateo .20 .50
40 Colin Moran .15 .40
41 Trent Clark .15 .40
42 Mark Appel .15 .40
43 Lewis Brinson .25 .60
44 Eloy Jimenez .60 1.50
45 Mike Nikorak .15 .40
46 Cody Bellinger 6.00 15.00
47 Eric Jenkins .15 .40
48 Luke Weaver .25 .60
49 Austin Meadows .25 .60
50A J.P. Crawford .15 .40
50B Crawford SP Glasses 12.00 30.00
51 Sean Newcomb .20 .50
52 Luis Ortiz .15 .40
53 Alen Hanson .20 .50
54 Gleyber Torres 2.50 6.00
55 Yeudy Garcia .15 .40
56 Chad Sobotka .15 .40
57 Tyler Beede .20 .50
58 Tyler Stephenson .15 .40
59 Jack Flaherty .25 .60
60 David Dahl .20 .50
61 Christin Stewart .20 .50
62 Paul DeJong 1.00 2.50
63 Manuel Margot .15 .40
64 Nick Travieso .15 .40
65 Anderson Espinoza .15 .40
66 Rob Kaminsky .15 .40
67 Daniel Robertson .15 .40
68 Christian Arroyo .50 1.25
69 Phil Bickford .15 .40
70 Chris Shaw .25 .60
71 Duane Underwood .15 .40
72 Rafael Bautista .15 .40
73 Bryce Denton .25 .60
74 Touki Toussaint .20 .50
75 Blake Snell .20 .50
76 Jose De Leon .15 .40
77 Tyler Nevin .25 .60
78 Brett Phillips .15 .40
79 Trey Michalczewski .15 .40
80 Kyle Zimmer .15 .40
81 Stone Garrett .15 .40
82 Juan Hillman .15 .40
83 J.D. Davis .20 .50
84 Corey Black .15 .40
85 Beau Burrows .15 .40
86 C.J. McElroy .15 .40
87 Wei-Chieh Huang .15 .40
88 Kevin Newman .25 .60
89 Alex Jackson .20 .50
90 Todd Hankins .15 .40
91 Alex Young .20 .50
92 Antonio Santillan .15 .40
93 Aaron Blair .15 .40
94 Kyle Holder .20 .50
95 Kyle Freeland .20 .50
96 Amed Rosario .25 .60
97 D.J. Stewart .15 .40
98 Stephen Gonsalves .15 .40
99 Kolby Allard .15 .40
100A Lucas Giolito .25 .60
100B Giolito SP Ball waist 10.00 25.00
101 Justus Sheffield .30 .75
102 Antonio Senzatela .15 .40
103 Andrew Moore .20 .50
104 Spencer Turnbull .15 .40
105 Mariano Rivera .20 .50
106 Zack Erwin .15 .40
107 Amir Garrett .15 .40
108 Ryan McMahon .15 .40
109 Nick Williams .20 .50
110 Drew Finley .15 .40
111 Sean Manaea .15 .40
112 Reynaldo Lopez .15 .40
113 Francis Martes .20 .50
114 Matt Chapman .25 .60
115 Daz Cameron .15 .40
116 Josh Staumont .20 .50
117 Kohl Stewart .15 .40
118 Jharel Cotton .15 .40
119 Dillon Tate .20 .50
120 Bobby Bradley .20 .50
121 Garrett Whitley .20 .50
122 Michael Soroka .50 1.25
123 Clint Frazier .60 1.50
124 Ozzie Albies .60 1.50
125A Tyler Glasnow .20 .50
125B Glasnow SP Arm back 8.00 20.00
126 Rafael Devers .50 1.25
127 Andrew Suarez .20 .50
128 Austin Riley .50 1.25
129 Donnie Dewees .20 .50
130 Anthony Alford .15 .40
131 Jahmai Jones .20 .50
132 Desmond Lindsay .25 .60
133 Lucas Herbert .15 .40
134 Keury Mella .15 .40
135 Nick Neidert .15 .40
136 Raimel Tapia .20 .50
137 Billy McKinney .20 .50
138 Bradley Zimmer .25 .60
139 Peter Lambert .15 .40
140 James Kaprielian .20 .50
141 Gareth Morgan .15 .40
142A Alex Bregman 1.00 2.50
142B Bregman SP Glasses 20.00 50.00
143 Jesus Tinoco .15 .40
144 Jeff Degano .20 .50
145 Austin Dean .15 .40
146 Robert Stephenson .15 .40
147A Carson Fulmer .15 .40
147B Fulmer SP Glv out 6.00 15.00
148 Dominic Smith .15 .40
149 Brett Lilek .15 .40
150 Ariel Jurado .15 .40
151 Alex Reyes .20 .50
152A Andrew Benintendi .50 1.25
152B Bnntndi SP w/Bat 25.00 60.00
153 Braden Shipley .15 .40
154 Nick Gordon .15 .40
155 Pierce Johnson .15 .40
156 Miguel Angel Sierra .30 .75
157 Mike Hessman .20 .50
158 Taylor Ward .20 .50
159 Hunter Renfroe .20 .50
160 Sean Reid-Foley .20 .50
161 Dakota Chalmers .15 .40
162 Tanner Rainey .15 .40
163 Ashe Russell .15 .40
164 Taylor Clarke .15 .40
165 Javier Guerra .15 .40
166 Tyler Jay .15 .40
167 Jordan Guerrero .15 .40
168 Josh Sborz .25 .60
169 Jermaine Palacios .20 .50
170 Jake Bauers .25 .60
171 Albert Almora .20 .50
172 Josh Naylor .20 .50
173 Forrest Wall .15 .40
174 Willson Contreras 1.00 2.50
175 Drew Jackson .15 .40
176 Nick Plummer .20 .50
177 Franklyn Kilome .20 .50
178 Jarlin Garcia .15 .40
179 Andrew Stevenson .15 .40
180 Domingo Acevedo .25 .60
181 A.J. Reed .15 .40
182 Chad Pinder .15 .40
183 Harold Ramirez .20 .50
184 Aaron Judge 4.00 10.00
185 Ian Happ .30 .75
186 David Denson .15 .40
187 Aaron Wilkerson .15 .40
188 Josh Bell .30 .75
189 Tyler O'Neill .20 .50
190 Richie Martin .15 .40
191 Michael Fulmer .25 .60
192 Willie Calhoun .50 1.25
193 Lucas Sims .15 .40
194 Cole Tucker .15 .40
195 Jake Woodford .15 .40
196 Mike Clevinger .30 .75
197A Franklin Barreto .15 .40
197B Barreto SP Bttng 6.00 15.00
198 Braden Bishop .15 .40
199 Grant Holmes .20 .50
200 Julio Urias .50 1.25

2016 Topps Pro Debut Gold

*GOLD: 3X TO 8X BASIC
STATED PRINT RUN 50 SER.#'d SETS

2016 Topps Pro Debut Orange

*ORANGE: 4X TO 10X BASIC
STATED PRINT RUN 25 SER.#'d SETS

2016 Topps Pro Debut Autographs

4 Omar Garcia 2.50 6.00
7 Mallex Smith 8.00 20.00
13 Cody Ponce 2.50 6.00
19 Ke'Bryan Hayes 5.00 12.00
24 Spencer Adams 2.50 6.00
32 Tate Matheny 3.00 8.00
39 Jorge Mateo 3.00 8.00
56 Chad Sobotka 2.50 6.00
65 Anderson Espinoza 2.50 6.00
74 Touki Toussaint 3.00 8.00
79 Trey Michalczewski 2.50 6.00
86 C.J. McElroy 2.50 6.00
101 Justus Sheffield 5.00 12.00
104 Spencer Turnbull 2.50 6.00
128 Austin Riley 10.00 25.00
129 Donnie Dewees 3.00 8.00
132 Desmond Lindsay 4.00 10.00
141 Gareth Morgan 2.50 6.00
155 Pierce Johnson 2.50 6.00
157 Mike Hessman 3.00 8.00
175 Drew Jackson 2.50 6.00
183 Harold Ramirez 3.00 8.00
184 Aaron Judge 75.00 200.00

2016 Topps Pro Debut Autographs Gold

*GOLD: .5X TO 1.2X BASIC
STATED PRINT RUN 50 SER.#'d SETS
8 Orlando Arcia 12.00 30.00

15 Brent Honeywell 5.00 12.00
25 Jose Berrios 10.00 25.00
30 Victor Robles 15.00 40.00
54 Gleyber Torres 20.00 50.00
75 Blake Snell 8.00 20.00
100 Lucas Giolito 10.00 25.00
119 Dillon Tate 8.00 20.00
124 Ozzie Albies 50.00 120.00
130 Anthony Alford 6.00 15.00
151 Alex Reyes 20.00 50.00
152 Andrew Benintendi 30.00 80.00

2016 Topps Pro Debut Autographs Orange

*ORANGE: .75X TO 2X BASIC
STATED PRINT RUN 25 SER.#'d SETS
8 Orlando Arcia 20.00 50.00
15 Brent Honeywell 8.00 20.00
25 Jose Berrios 15.00 40.00
30 Victor Robles 25.00 60.00
54 Gleyber Torres 30.00 80.00
75 Blake Snell 12.00 30.00
100 Lucas Giolito 15.00 40.00
119 Dillon Tate 12.00 30.00
124 Ozzie Albies 75.00 200.00
130 Anthony Alford 10.00 25.00
142 Alex Bregman 100.00 250.00
151 Alex Reyes 30.00 80.00
152 Andrew Benintendi 50.00 120.00

2016 Topps Pro Debut Distinguished Debuts

COMPLETE SET (25) 10.00 25.00
PLATE PRINT RUN 1 SET PER COLOR
NO PLATE PRICING DUE TO SCARCITY
*GOLD/50: 1.2X TO 3X BASIC
*ORNGE/25: 1.5X TO 4X BASIC
DD1 Dansby Swanson 1.00 2.50
DD2 Alex Bregman 2.00 5.00
DD3 Brendan Rodgers .50 1.25
DD4 Dillon Tate .40 1.00
DD5 Kyle Tucker 1.25 3.00
DD6 Tyler Jay .30 .75
DD7 Andrew Benintendi 1.00 2.50
DD8 Carson Fulmer .30 .75
DD9 Ian Happ .60 1.50
DD10 Cornelius Randolph .30 .75
DD11 Tyler Stephenson .30 .75
DD12 Josh Naylor .40 1.00
DD13 Garrett Whitley .40 1.00
DD14 Kolby Allard .30 .75
DD15 Trent Clark .30 .75
DD16 James Kaprielian .40 1.00
DD17 Phil Bickford .30 .75
DD18 Kevin Newman .50 1.25
DD19 Richie Martin .30 .75
DD20 Ashe Russell .30 .75
DD21 Beau Burrows .30 .75
DD22 Nick Plummer .40 1.00
DD23 D.J. Stewart .30 .75
DD24 Taylor Ward .40 1.00
DD25 Mike Nikorak .30 .75

2016 Topps Pro Debut Dual Affiliation Autographs

STATED PRINT RUN 25 SER.#'d SETS
PLATE PRINT RUN 1 SET PER COLOR
NO PLATE PRICING DUE TO SCARCITY
DAAAM T.Michalczewski/S.Adams 6.00 15.00
DAAAP C.Ponce/O.Arcia 20.00 50.00
DAAAS O.Albies/M.Smith 30.00 80.00
DAABE A.Espinoza/A.Benintendi 50.00 120.00
DAAGT G.Torres/D.Dewees 12.00 30.00
DAAHR K.Hayes/H.Ramirez 8.00 20.00
DAAHS B.Snell/B.Honeywell 10.00 25.00
DAAMJ A.Judge/J.Mateo
DAART D.Tate/B.Rodgers 10.00 25.00

2016 Topps Pro Debut Fragments of the Farm

PLATE PRINT RUN 1 SET PER COLOR
NO PLATE PRICING DUE TO SCARCITY
*GOLD/50: .5X TO 1.2X BASIC
FOTFCC Game-Used Home Plate from Huntington Park 2.00 5.00
Columbus Clippers
FOTFCCL Game-Used Base from Huntington Park 2.00 5.00
Columbus Clippers
FOTFEPC 2015 Triple-A Championship Game Ticket 2.00 5.00
El Paso Chihuahuas
FOTFFRR Pink in the Park Promotional Jersey 2.00 5.00
Frisco RoughRiders
FOTFHS Outfield Wall from Metro Bank Park 2.00 5.00
Harrisburg Senators
FOTFLCC Jobu Hair 15.00 40.00
FOTFLCCA Game-Used Home Plate from Classic Park 2.00 5.00
Lake County Captains
FOTFMBP Promotional Foam Finger 2.00 5.00
Myrtle Beach Pelicans
FOTFMRH Game-Used Base from Security Bank Ballpark 2.00 5.00
Midland RockHounds
FOTFRB Game-Used Base from State Mutual Stadium 2.00 5.00
Rome Braves
FOTFRFS Orange RVA Promotional Jersey 2.00 5.00
Richmond Flying Squirrels
FOTFRRE Ugly Christmas Sweater Promotional Jersey 2.00 5.00
Round Rock Express
FOTFRRW Team Stock Cert 3.00 8.00
FOTFTD Field Tarp from Oneok Field 2.00 5.00
Tulsa Drillers
FOTFTMH Stadium Seat Back from Fifth Third Field 2.00 5.00
Toledo Mud Hens
FOTFWCC Game Day Shirt from Director of Smiles 2.00 5.00
Rhashan
Williamsport Crosscutters

2016 Topps Pro Debut Make Your Pro Debut

PDCB Christian Byrnes 3.00 8.00

2016 Topps Pro Debut Minor League Mascots

STATED PRINT RUN 75 SER.#'d SETS
PLATE PRINT RUN 1 SET PER COLOR
NO PLATE PRICING DUE TO SCARCITY
MLM1 Baby Bear 3.00 8.00
MLM2 Barley 3.00 8.00
MLM3 Bernie 3.00 8.00
MLM5 Buddy 3.00 8.00
MLM6 Bumble 3.00 8.00
MLM7 C. Wolf 3.00 8.00
MLM8 Candy 3.00 8.00
MLM9 Champ 3.00 8.00
MLM10 Cubbie 3.00 8.00
MLM12 Homer 3.00 8.00
MLM14 Hornsby 3.00 8.00
MLM16 Marty 3.00 8.00
MLM17 Mr. Moon 3.00 8.00
MLM18 Phinley 3.00 8.00
MLM19 Rally Shark 3.00 8.00
MLM20 Reedy Rip'It 3.00 8.00
MLM22 Splash Pelican 3.00 8.00
MLM23 Ted E. Tourist 3.00 8.00
MLM24 Webbly 3.00 8.00
MLM25 Wool E. Bull 3.00 8.00

2016 Topps Pro Debut Pennant Patches

*GOLD/50: .5X TO 1.2X BASIC
PPAB Alex Bregman 8.00 20.00
PPABE Andrew Benintendi 8.00 20.00
PPAG Amir Garrett 2.00 5.00
PPAJ Aaron Judge 10.00 25.00
PPAJR A.J. Reed 2.00 5.00
PPAM Austin Meadows 3.00 8.00
PPAR Ashe Russell 2.00 5.00
PPARE Alex Reyes 2.50 6.00
PPBR Brendan Rodgers 6.00 15.00
PPBS Blake Snell 4.00 10.00
PPBZ Bradley Zimmer 4.00 10.00
PPCF Clint Frazier 4.00 10.00
PPCFU Carson Fulmer 2.00 5.00
PPDC Daz Cameron 2.00 5.00
PPDS Dansby Swanson 8.00 20.00
PPDT Dillon Tate 2.50 6.00
PPFB Franklin Barreto 2.00 5.00
PPGH Grant Holmes 2.50 6.00
PPGT Gleyber Torres 8.00 20.00
PPJA Jorge Alfaro 3.00 8.00
PPJB Jose Berrios 2.50 6.00
PPJC J.P. Crawford 2.00 5.00
PPJDL Jose De Leon 2.00 5.00
PPJM Jorge Mateo 5.00 12.00
PPJU Julio Urias 6.00 15.00
PPKA Kolby Allard 2.00 5.00
PPLG Lucas Giolito 5.00 12.00
PPMM Manuel Margot 2.00 5.00
PPNG Nick Gordon 2.00 5.00
PPNM Nomar Mazara 3.00 8.00
PPOA Orlando Arcia 4.00 10.00
PPOAL Ozzie Albies 8.00 20.00
PPRD Rafael Devers 4.00 10.00
PPRS Robert Stephenson 2.00 5.00
PPTG Tyler Glasnow 4.00 10.00
PPTJ Tyler Jay 2.00 5.00
PPTK Tyler Kolek 2.50 6.00
PPTM Trey Mancini 6.00 15.00
PPVR Victor Robles 6.00 15.00

2016 Topps Pro Debut Pro Production Autographs

PRINT RUNS B/WN 10-25 COPIES PER
NO PRICING ON QTY 20 OR LESS
PLATE PRINT RUN 1 SET PER COLOR
NO PLATE PRICING DUE TO SCARCITY
PPAAA Anthony Alford/25
PPAAJ Aaron Judge/25
PPAAM Austin Meadows/25 25.00 60.00
PPABZ Bradley Zimmer/25 10.00 25.00
PPACF Carson Fulmer/25 6.00 15.00
PPADS Dansby Swanson/25
PPADSM Dominic Smith/25 12.00 30.00
PPAJB Jose Berrios/25 8.00 20.00
PPAJH Jeff Hoffman/25 8.00 20.00
PPAJM Jorge Mateo/25 8.00 20.00
PPAJN Josh Naylor/25 10.00 25.00
PPAKA Kolby Allard/25 15.00 40.00
PPAWA Willy Adames/25

2016 Topps Pro Debut Promo Night Uniforms

COMPLETE SET (20) 15.00 40.00
PNU1 Brooklyn Cyclones 1.25 3.00
PNU2 Fort Myers Miracle 1.25 3.00
PNU3 El Paso Chihuahuas 1.25 3.00
PNU4 Louisville Bats 1.25 3.00
PNU5 Lakewood BlueClaws 1.25 3.00
PNU6 Durham Bulls 1.25 3.00
PNU7 Lehigh Valley IronPigs 1.25 3.00
PNU8 Ogden Raptors 1.25 3.00
PNU9 Richmond Flying Squirrels 1.25 3.00
PNU10 Myrtle Beach Pelicans 1.25 3.00
PNU11 Aberdeen IronBirds 1.25 3.00
PNU12 Rochester Red Wings 1.25 3.00
PNU13 Altoona Curve 1.25 3.00
PNU14 Frederick Keys 1.25 3.00
PNU15 Eugene Emeralds 1.25 3.00
PNU16 Norfolk Tides 1.25 3.00
PNU17 Midland RockHounds 1.25 3.00
PNU18 Fresno Grizzlies 1.25 3.00
PNU19 Everett AquaSox 1.25 3.00
PNU20 Johnson City Cardinals 1.25 3.00

2017 Topps Pro Debut

COMP.SET.w/o VAR (200) 25.00 60.00
SP ODDS 1:101 HOBBY
TEBOW SP ODDS 1:505 HOBBY
1A Mickey Moniak .40 1.00
1B Mickey Moniak SP hand up .40 1.00
2 Buddy Reed .15 .40
3 Alex Kirilloff .40 1.00
4 Trevor Clifton .15 .40
5 Heath Quinn .20 .50
6 Andrew Sopko .15 .40
7 Conner Greene .15 .40
8 Ben Bowden .15 .40
9 Ryan McMahon .15 .40
10 Desmond Lindsay .15 .40
11 Lewis Brinson .25 .60
12 Justin Maese .15 .40
13 Sandy Alcantara .20 .50
14 Brady Aiken .40 1.00
15 Rafael Devers .30 .75
16 Dylan Carlson 1.00 2.50
17 Franklin Barreto .15 .40
18 Jon Harris .20 .50
19 Josh Morgan .15 .40
20 Roniel Raudes .15 .40
21 Jack Flaherty .25 .60
22 Angel Perdomo .15 .40
23 Jorge Mateo .15 .40
24 Ian Happ .30 .75
25A Amed Rosario .25 .60
25B Rosario SP Bttng 2.50 6.00
26 Spencer Adams .15 .40
27 A.J. Puk .25 .60
28 Nick Neidert .15 .40
29 David Thompson .20 .50
30 Jordan Stephens .15 .40
31 Cavan Biggio .30 .75
32 Brent Honeywell .20 .50
33 Nolan Jones .25 .60
34 Forrest Whitley .50 1.25
35 Felix Jorge .15 .40
36 Ian Anderson .40 1.00
37 Isan Diaz .40 1.00
38 Triston McKenzie .15 .40
39 Adonis Medina .25 .60
40 Bo Bichette .60 1.50
41 Peter Alonso 1.50 4.00
42 Yadier Alvarez .25 .60
43 Tyler Jay .15 .40
44 P.J. Conlon .15 .40
45 DJ Peters .40 1.00
46 Demi Orimoloye .15 .40
47 Tyler O'Neill .20 .50
48 Will Benson .15 .40
49 Joshua Lowe .15 .40
50A Brendan Rodgers .20 .50
50B Rodgers SP Thrwng 6.00 15.00
51 Franklin Perez .25 .60
52 Jordan Sheffield .15 .40
53 Kolby Allard .15 .40
54 Victor Robles .40 1.00
55 Sean Reid-Foley .15 .40
56 TJ Zeuch .15 .40
57 Rosell Herrera .15 .40
58 Matt Manning .25 .60
59 Luis Urias .60 1.50
60 C.J. Chatham .20 .50
61 Ben Rortvedt .20 .50
62 Nick Gordon .15 .40
63 Bryse Wilson .25 .60
64 Bryan Reynolds .25 .60
65 Bobby Bradley .20 .50
66 Kevin Newman .25 .60
67 Delvin Perez .25 .60
68 Luis Ortiz .15 .40
69 Josh Ockimey .25 .60
70 Andrew Stevenson .20 .50
71 Jose Pujols .20 .50
72 Vladimir Guerrero Jr. 40.00 100.00
73 Ronnie Dawson .15 .40
74 Garrett Hampson .25 .60
75 Matt Chapman .25 .60
76 Jake Bauers .20 .50
77 Cole Stobbe .15 .40
78A Ozzie Albies .60 1.50
78B Albies SP Thrwng 6.00 15.00
79 Chance Sisco .30 .75
80 Wuilmer Becerra .15 .40
81 Henry Centeno .15 .40
82 Luis Alexander Basabe .25 .60
83 Kyle Lewis .30 .75
84 Mitch Keller .20 .50
85 Justus Sheffield .25 .60
86 Brian Mundell .15 .40
87 Nick Solak .40 1.00
88 Freddy Peralta .25 .60
89 Reggie Lawson .15 .40
90 Cole Ragans .15 .40
91 Jose Taveras .20 .50
92 Matt Hall .15 .40
93 Josh Rogers .20 .50
94 Josh Staumont .15 .40
95 Tyler Beede .15 .40
96 Alex Verdugo .25 .60
97 Andy Ibanez .15 .40
98 Yu-Cheng Chang .25 .60
99 Leody Taveras .50 1.25
100A Austin Meadows .25 .60
100B Meadows SP Bttng 2.50 6.00
101 Alec Hansen .15 .40
102 Cal Quantrill .15 .40
103 Zack Collins .20 .50
104 Tim Lynch .20 .50
105 Will Craig .15 .40
106 Anthony Alford .15 .40
107 Blake Rutherford .25 .60
108 Dylan Cozens .15 .40
109 Hudson Potts .20 .50
110 Khalil Lee .25 .60
111 Trent Clark .15 .40
112 Taylor Trammell .25 .60
113 Thomas Szapucki .20 .50
114 Mauricio Dubon .20 .50
115 Josh Hader .15 .40
116 Mitchell White .25 .60
117 Gavin Lux 1.00 2.50
118 Dylan Cease .40 1.00
119 Brett Cumberland .25 .60
120 Christian Arroyo .25 .60
121 Willy Adames .20 .50
122 Dane Dunning .15 .40
123 Patrick Weigel .15 .40
124A Gleyber Torres 2.50 6.00
124B Torres SP Hlmt 25.00 60.00
125 Jen-Ho Tseng .15 .40
126 Anfernee Grier .15 .40
127 Taylor Clarke .15 .40
128 Jahmai Jones .15 .40
129 Bradley Zimmer .20 .50
130 Chris Okey .15 .40
131 Luis Castillo .50 1.25
132 Kyle Muller .15 .40
133 Rhys Hoskins .60 1.50
134 Daulton Jefferies .20 .50
135 James Kaprielian .15 .40
136 Taylor Ward .20 .50
137 Thomas Jones .15 .40
138A Jason Groome .30 .75
138B Groome SP Red jrsy 3.00 8.00
139 Nolan Martinez .15 .40
140 Francis Martes .15 .40
141 Will Smith .40 1.00
142 Dustin Fowler .20 .50
143 Richie Martin .15 .40
144 Riley Pint .15 .40
145 Cody Bellinger 2.50 6.00
146 Mike Soroka .50 1.25
147 Franklyn Kilome .20 .50
148 Kyle Tucker .30 .75
149 Fernando Romero .15 .40
150A Nick Senzel .50 1.25
150B Senzel SP Thrwng 5.00 12.00
151 Andy Yerzy .15 .40
152 Raudy Read .20 .50
153 Richard Urena .25 .60
154 Keegan Akin .20 .50
155 Ronald Acuna 6.00 15.00
156 Sean Newcomb .20 .50
157 Dakota Hudson .25 .60
158 Brett Phillips .20 .50
159 Michael Kopech .30 .75
160 Jesse Winker .15 .40
161 Jake Fraley .15 .40
162 Matt Thaiss .15 .40
163 Harrison Bader .25 .60
164 Casey Gillaspie .15 .40
165 Anderson Espinoza .15 .40
166 Josh Naylor .20 .50
167 Phil Bickford .15 .40
168 Akil Baddoo .20 .50
169 Francisco Rios .15 .40
170 Cristian Alvarado .15 .40
171 Yusniel Diaz .50 1.25
172 Francisco Mejia .25 .60
173 Joe Rizzo .15 .40
174 Clint Frazier .30 .75
175 Justin Dunn .15 .40
176 Alex Speas .15 .40
177 Chance Adams .25 .60
178 Christin Stewart .20 .50
179 Sheldon Neuse .20 .50
180 Connor Jones .20 .50
181 Dominic Smith .15 .40
182 Nick Williams .20 .50
183 Eloy Jimenez .60 1.50
184 T.J. Friedl .15 .40
185 Amir Garrett .15 .40
186 Carter Kieboom .25 .60
187 Corey Ray .20 .50
188 Zack Burdi .15 .40
189 Willie Calhoun .25 .60
190 Beau Burrows .15 .40
191 Stephen Gonsalves .15 .40
192 Robert Tyler .15 .40
193 Bobby Dalbec .40 1.00
194 Bryson Brigman .15 .40
195 Eric Lauer .20 .50
196 Luis Carpio .15 .40
197 Grant Holmes .15 .40
198 Cody Sedlock .15 .40
199 Derek Fisher .20 .50
200A J.P. Crawford .15 .40
200B Crawford SP Red jrsy 5.00 12.00
PDTT Tim Tebow SP 100.00 250.00

2017 Topps Pro Debut Green

*GREEN: 2X TO 5X BASIC
STATED ODDS 1:11 HOBBY
STATED PRINT RUN 99 SER.#'d SETS

2017 Topps Pro Debut Orange

*ORANGE: 4X TO 10X BASIC
STATED ODDS 1:41 HOBBY
STATED PRINT RUN 25 SER.#'d SETS

2017 Topps Pro Debut Autographs

STATED ODDS 1:19 HOBBY
EXCHANGE DEADLINE 5/31/2019
*GREEN/99: .5X TO 1.2X BASIC
*ORANGE/25: .75X TO 2X BASIC
1 Mickey Moniak 30.00 80.00
7 Conner Greene 2.50 6.00
15 Rafael Devers 25.00 60.00
20 Roniel Raudes 2.50 6.00
23 Jorge Mateo 5.00 12.00
24 Ian Happ 20.00 50.00
33 Nolan Jones 4.00 10.00
36 Ian Anderson 10.00 25.00
37 Isan Diaz 6.00 15.00
38 Triston McKenzie 2.50 6.00
41 Peter Alonso 50.00 120.00
48 Will Benson 2.50 6.00
49 Joshua Lowe 2.50 6.00
50 Brendan Rodgers 25.00 60.00
67 Delvin Perez 6.00 15.00
82 Luis Alexander Basabe 4.00 10.00
83 Kyle Lewis 20.00 50.00
84 Mitch Keller 3.00 8.00
85 Justus Sheffield 4.00 10.00
87 Nick Solak 6.00 15.00
90 Cole Ragans 2.50 6.00
97 Andy Ibanez 2.50 6.00
103 Zack Collins 3.00 8.00
105 Will Craig 2.50 6.00
106 Anthony Alford 2.50 6.00
108 Dylan Cozens 6.00 15.00
113 Thomas Szapucki 3.00 8.00
114 Mauricio Dubon 3.00 8.00
123 Patrick Weigel 2.50 6.00
128 Jahmai Jones 2.50 6.00
129 Bradley Zimmer
131 Luis Castillo 8.00 20.00
138 Jason Groome 10.00 25.00
144 Riley Pint 2.50 6.00
148 Kyle Tucker 5.00 12.00
149 Fernando Romero 2.50 6.00
150 Nick Senzel 25.00 60.00
152 Raudy Read 3.00 8.00
156 Sean Newcomb 3.00 8.00
163 Harrison Bader 4.00 10.00
165 Anderson Espinoza 2.50 6.00
167 Phil Bickford 2.50 6.00
172 Francisco Mejia 4.00 10.00
175 Justin Dunn 5.00 12.00
183 Eloy Jimenez 20.00 50.00
184 T.J. Friedl 2.50 6.00
186 Carter Kieboom 8.00 20.00
187 Corey Ray 15.00 40.00
193 Bobby Dalbec 6.00 15.00
198 Cody Sedlock 2.50 6.00

2017 Topps Pro Debut Ben's Biz

COMPLETE SET (15) 5.00 12.00
STATED ODDS 1:8 HOBBY
BBB1 Toastman .60 1.50
BBB2 Erik the Peanut Guy .60 1.50
BBB3 Toilet Paper First Pitch .60 1.50
BBB4 The Crazy Hot Dog Vendor .60 1.50
BBB5 The CLAWlossal .60 1.50
BBB6 Peter "Pedro" Bragan, Jr. .60 1.50
BBB7 Wally Walnut .60 1.50
Shelley the Pistachio
Al Almond
BBB8 Synagogue-turned-team store .60 1.50
BBB9 Paul "Super Churros Man" Cerda .60 1.50
BBB10 Jamestown's John .60 1.50
BBB11 The Uh-Huh Guy .60 1.50
BBB12 Fred Costello .60 1.50
BBB13 Todd "Parney" Parnell .60 1.50
BBB14 Heads of State .60 1.50
BBB15 Whitewall Ninja .60 1.50

2017 Topps Pro Debut Fragments of The Farm Relics

STATED ODDS 1:37 HOBBY
*GOLD/50: .5X TO 1.2X BASIC
FOTFAC Steamer MASCOT Uniform 2.00 5.00
FOTFAT Dickey-Stephens Park Tarp 2.00 5.00
FOTFBB 16 Regions Field Season Tickets 2.00 5.00
FOTFBK Wilmer Flores Bobblehead Giveaway 2.00 5.00
FOTFCC Huntington Park BASE 2.00 5.00
FOTFCK 16 Triple-A All-Star Banner 2.00 5.00
FOTFCM Muddy the Mudcat MASCOT Tail 2.00 5.00
FOTFDB Durham Bulls Athletic Park Backstop Netting 2.00 5.00
FOTFDBU Original Durham Bulls Athletic Park Bulls Sign 2.00 5.00
FOTFFF Game-Issued Inaugural Jersey 2.00 5.00
FOTFFR Dr. Pepper Ballpark Mound Rubber 2.00 5.00
FOTFGLL Midwest League Championship Celebration Cork 2.00 5.00
FOTFIC Principal Park Flag 2.00 5.00
FOTFLH Clavin Falwell Field Mound Rubber 2.00 5.00
FOTFLL South Atlantic League All-Star Game Patch 2.00 5.00
FOTFMBP Deuce the MASCOT Bat Dog Game-Worn Collar 2.00 5.00
FOTFMR Security Bank Park Mound Rubber 2.00 5.00
FOTFOSC Werner Park BASE 2.00 5.00
FOTFQCRB Modern Woodmen Park Mound Rubber 2.00 5.00
FOTFRB State Mutual Stadium Dugout Railing Pad 2.00 5.00
FOTFRFS 16 Sunday Brunch Games Cap 2.00 5.00
FOTFRRW Opening Day at Silver Stadium Tickets from April '96 2.00 5.00
FOTFTD ONEOK Field Home Dugout Padding 2.00 5.00
FOTFTMH Fifth Third Field BASE 2.00 5.00
FOTFWC Boomer MASCOT Fur 2.00 5.00
FOTFWCR BB&T Ballpark Parking Banner 2.00 5.00

2017 Topps Pro Debut In The Wings

COMPLETE SET (15) 6.00 15.00
STATED ODDS 1:8 HOBBY
*GOLD/50: 2X TO 5X BASIC
*ORANGE/25: 3X TO 8X BASIC
ITWAM Austin Meadows .40 1.00
ITWAR Amed Rosario .40 1.00
ITWBZ Bradley Zimmer .30 .75
ITWCF Clint Frazier .50 1.25
ITWDC Dylan Cozens .25 .60
ITWDS Dominic Smith .25 .60
ITWGT Gleyber Torres 4.00 10.00
ITWIH Ian Happ .50 1.25
ITWJH Josh Hader .25 .60
ITWLB Lewis Brinson .40 1.00
ITWNS Nick Senzel .75 2.00
ITWOA Ozzie Albies 1.00 2.50
ITWRD Rafael Devers .50 1.25
ITWRH Rhys Hoskins 1.00 2.50
ITWSN Sean Newcomb .30 .75

2017 Topps Pro Debut In The Wings Autographs

STATED ODDS 1:969 HOBBY
PRINT RUNS B/WN 10-25 COPIES PER
NO PRICING ON QTY 10
EXCHANGE DEADLINE 5/31/2019
ITWDC Dylan Cozens/25 20.00 50.00
ITWDS Dominic Smith/25 20.00 50.00
ITWGT Gleyber Torres/25 60.00 150.00
ITWLB Lewis Brinson/25 15.00 40.00
ITWNS Nick Senzel/25 15.00 40.00
ITWOA Ozzie Albies/25 15.00 40.00
ITWRD Rafael Devers/25 50.00 120.00
ITWSN Sean Newcomb/25 6.00 15.00

2017 Topps Pro Debut Make Your Pro Debut

STATED ODDS 1:270 HOBBY
PDNY Nick Yohanek 2.50 6.00

2017 Topps Pro Debut Pennant Patches

STATED ODDS 1:68 HOBBY
STATED PRINT RUN 99 SER.#'d SETS
*GOLD/50: .5X TO 1.2X BASIC
PPAE Anderson Espinoza 2.50 6.00
PPAK Alex Kirilloff 5.00 12.00
PPAM Austin Meadows 4.00 10.00
PPAP A.J. Puk 4.00 10.00
PPBR Brendan Rodgers 3.00 8.00
PPCB Cody Bellinger 10.00 25.00
PPCF Clint Frazier 5.00 12.00
PPCQ Cal Quantrill 2.50 6.00
PPCS Cody Sedlock 5.00 12.00
PPEJ Eloy Jimenez 5.00 12.00
PPIA Ian Anderson 6.00 15.00
PPIH Ian Happ 6.00 15.00
PPJC J.P. Crawford 2.50 6.00
PPJD Justin Dunn 5.00 12.00
PPJG Jason Groome 5.00 12.00
PPKA Kolby Allard 2.50 6.00
PPKN Kevin Newman 4.00 10.00
PPLB Lewis Brinson 4.00 10.00
PPMK Mitch Keller 3.00 8.00
PPMM Mickey Moniak 6.00 15.00
PPMMA Matt Manning 4.00 10.00
PPMT Matt Thaiss 2.50 6.00
PPNS Nick Senzel 6.00 15.00
PPRD Rafael Devers 5.00 12.00
PPRP Riley Pint 2.50 6.00
PPSN Sean Newcomb 3.00 8.00
PPTJ Tyler Jay 5.00 12.00
PPVR Victor Robles 6.00 15.00
PPWA Willy Adames 3.00 8.00
PPZC Zack Collins 3.00 8.00

2017 Topps Pro Debut Pro Production Autographs

STATED ODDS 1:330 HOBBY
PRINT RUNS B/WN 5-30 COPIES PER
NO PRICING ON QTY 15 OR LESS
EXCHANGE DEADLINE 5/31/2019
PPAAK Alex Kirilloff/30 12.00 30.00
PPABZ Bradley Zimmer/22 12.00 30.00
PPACR Corey Ray/20 10.00 25.00
PPACS Cody Sedlock/30 10.00 25.00
PPAFME Francisco Mejia/30 20.00 50.00
PPAFW Forrest Whitley/30 10.00 25.00
PPAGH Grant Holmes/30 10.00 25.00
PPAIH Ian Happ/30 20.00 50.00
PPAJD Justin Dunn/30 10.00 25.00
PPAJG Jason Groome/30 25.00 60.00
PPAJH Josh Hader
PPAJM Jorge Mateo/30 12.00 30.00
PPAMK Mitch Keller/30 12.00 30.00
PPARD Rafael Devers/30 25.00 60.00
PPARP Riley Pint/20 12.00 30.00
PPASN Sean Newcomb/30 6.00 15.00
PPATC Trent Clark/30 12.00 30.00
PPAZC Zack Collins/30 8.00 25.00

2017 Topps Pro Debut Promo Night Uniform Relics

STATED ODDS 1:85 HOBBY
STATED PRINT RUN 99 SER.#'d SETS
*GOLD/50: .5X TO 1.2X BASIC
PNR50N 50 Seasons in Reading Night 4.00 10.00
Reading Fightin Phils
PNRDEN Dora the Explorer Day 4.00 10.00
Wisconsin Timber Rattlers
PNREN Elvis Night 4.00 10.00
Toledo Mud Hens
PNRFBN Ferris Bueller Night 4.00 10.00
Midland RockHounds
PNRGBN Good Burger Night 4.00 10.00
Sacramento River Cats
PNRGN Ghostbusters Night 4.00 10.00
Birmingham Barons
PNRHIN Home Improvement Night 4.00 10.00
Wilmington Blue Rocks
PNRHJN Hockey Jersey Night 4.00 10.00
Pensacola Blue Wahoos
PNRHSN High School Spirit Night 4.00 10.00
Fort Wayne TinCaps
PNRLN Latin Night 4.00 10.00
Reno Aces
PNRMAS Military Appreciation Series 4.00 10.00
Charlotte Knights
PNRMMN Myrtle Beach Mermen Night 4.00 10.00
Myrtle Beach Pelicans
PNRNHN Hope for New Hampshire Night 4.00 10.00
New Hampshire Fisher Cats
PNRPIN Pink in the Park Night 4.00 10.00
Oklahoma City Dodgers
PNRPPN Purple Power Night 4.00 10.00
West Virginia Power
PNRPRN Paint the Park Red Night 4.00 10.00
St. Lucie Mets
PNRSN Superheroes Night 4.00 10.00
Tri-City Valleycats
PNRTGN Top Gun Night 4.00 10.00
Potomac Nationals
PNRTJN Team Jana Night 4.00 10.00
Round Rock Express
PNRTT Taco Tuesdays 4.00 10.00
Fresno Grizzlies
PNRTTN Tracktown Night 4.00 10.00
Eugene Emeralds
PNRVGN Video Game Night 4.00 10.00
Jackson Generals
PNRWFN Wizard of Funner Night 4.00 10.00
Bowling Green Hot Rods
PNRWWN Where's Waldo Night 4.00 10.00
Tri-City Valleycats

2017 Topps Pro Debut Promo Night Uniforms

COMPLETE SET (15) 5.00 12.00
STATED ODDS 1:6 HOBBY
PNEN Elvis Night .60 1.50
Toledo Mud Hens
PNGN Ghostbusters Night .60 1.50
Birmingham Barons
PNSN Superheroes Night .60 1.50
Tri-City Valleycats
PNTT Taco Tuesdays .60 1.50
Fresno Grizzlies
PN50N 50 Seasons in Reading Night .60 1.50
Reading Fightin Phils
PNDEN Dora the Explorer Day .60 1.50
Wisconsin Timber Rattlers
PNFBN Ferris Bueller Night .60 1.50
Midland RockHounds
PNHIN Home Improvement Night .60 1.50
Wilmington Blue Rocks
PNHJN Hockey Jersey Night .60 1.50
Pensacola Blue Wahoos
PNMAS Military Appreciation Series .60 1.50
Charlotte Knights
PNMMN Myrtle Beach Mermen Night .60 1.50
Myrtle Beach Pelicans
PNNHN Hope for New Hampshire Night .60 1.50
New Hampshire Fisher Cats
PNPIN Pink in the Park Night .60 1.50
Oklahoma City Dodgers
PNTGN Top Gun Night .60 1.50
Potomac Nationals
PNVGN Video Game Night .60 1.50
Jackson Generals

2017 Topps Pro Debut Wave of the Future Autographs

STATED ODDS 1:794 HOBBY
PRINT RUNS B/WN 13-25 COPIES PER
NO PRICING ON QTY 13
EXCHANGE DEADLINE 5/31/2019
WFAAE Anderson Espinoza/25 5.00 12.00
WFADC Dylan Cozens/25 25.00 60.00
WFAGT Gleyber Torres/25 60.00 150.00
WFAIA Ian Anderson/25
WFAJD Justin Dunn/25 8.00 20.00
WFAJM Jorge Mateo/25 12.00 30.00
WFALT Leodys Taveras/25 20.00 50.00
WFAMM Mickey Moniak/25 50.00 120.00
WFASN Sean Newcomb/25

2018 Topps Pro Debut

COMPLETE SET (200) 25.00 60.00
1 Ronald Acuna 3.00 8.00
2 Domingo Acevedo .15 .40
3 Josh Ockimey .15 .40
4 Sam Carlson .20 .50
5 Jordan Humphreys .15 .40
6 Carter Kieboom .25 .60
7 Corbin Burnes .25 .60
8 Greg Deichmann .20 .50
9 Mitchell White .15 .40
10 Matt Manning .25 .60
11 Michel Baez .15 .40
12 Anderson Tejeda .20 .50
13 Kyle Wright .40 1.00
14 Michael Kopech .30 .75
15 Jay Groome .20 .50
16 Justus Sheffield .20 .50
17 Paul Balestrieri .15 .40
18 Kolby Allard .15 .40
19 Chris Shaw .15 .40
20 Vladimir Guerrero Jr. 1.50 4.00
21 Blayne Enlow .15 .40
22 Dylan Cozens .15 .40
23 MacKenzie Gore .30 .75
24 Austin Meadows .25 .60
25 Hunter Greene .50 1.25
26 Bryse Wilson .25 .60
27 Glenn Otto .15 .40
28 P.J. Conlon .15 .40
29 J.J. Matijevic .20 .50
30 Brent Rooker .20 .50
31 Isan Diaz .40 1.00
32 Forrest Whitley .25 .60
33 Nick Solak .40 1.00
34 Matt Tabor .15 .40
35 Sixto Sanchez .40 1.00
36 Jesus Luzardo .25 .60
37 Jesus Sanchez .15 .40
38 Ibandel Isabel .25 .60
39 Kelvin Gutierrez .15 .40
40 Nick Pratto .20 .50
41 Albert Abreu .15 .40
42 Nick Allen .15 .40
43 Caden Lemons .15 .40
44 Mike Soroka .50 1.25
45 D.L. Hall .15 .40
46 Adam Haseley .25 .60
47 Shed Long .15 .40
48 Willy Adames .20 .50
49 Tyler Freeman .15 .40
50 Gleyber Torres 1.50 4.00
51 Zac Lowther .20 .50
52 Alec Hansen .15 .40
53 Eloy Jimenez .60 1.50
54 Daulton Varsho .20 .50
55 Fernando Tatis Jr. 1.25 3.00
56 Bo Bichette .60 1.50
57 Ke'Bryan Hayes .15 .40
58 Yadier Alvarez .20 .50
59 Kade McClure .15 .40
60 Kyle Tucker .30 .75
61 Zack Littell .15 .40
62 Jo Adell .50 1.25
63 Drew Waters .40 1.00
64 Tyler Stephenson .15 .40
65 Logan Allen .15 .40
66 Luis Urias .30 .75
67 Matt McCann .15 .40
68 Keibert Ruiz .50 1.25
69 Chance Adams .25 .60
70 Adbert Alzolay .20 .50
71 Ryan Vilade .15 .40
72 Joey Morgan .20 .50
73 Kevin Merrell .20 .50
74 Merandy Gonzalez .15 .40
75 Jacob Pearson .15 .40
76 Evan White .25 .60
77 Yusniel Diaz .50 1.25
78 Brian Miller .15 .40
79 Ronald Guzman .15 .40
80 Cal Mitchell .25 .60
81 Matt Thaiss .15 .40
82 Jahmai Jones .15 .40
83 David Peterson .20 .50
84 Ian Anderson .40 1.00
85 Samir Duenez .15 .40
86 Nate Pearson .40 1.00
87 Drew Ellis .20 .50
88 Yu-Cheng Chang .20 .50
89 Austin Beck .20 .50
90 Logan Warmoth .20 .50
91 Fred Costello .15 .40
92 Will Craig .15 .40
93 Miguelangel Sierra .15 .40
94 Dylan Cease .40 1.00
95 Oscar De La Cruz .15 .40
96 Khalil Lee .15 .40
97 Mitch Keller .20 .50
98 Jose Gomez .15 .40
99 JoJo Romero .20 .50
100 Royce Lewis .60 1.50
101 Cedric Mullins .25 .60
102 Pete Alonso 1.50 4.00
103 Tristen Lutz .20 .50
104 Chris Seise .15 .40
105 Hagen Danner .15 .40
106 Colton Welker .15 .40
107 Sean Murphy .25 .60
108 Quentin Holmes .15 .40
109 Dane Dunning .15 .40
110 Jacob Heatherly .15 .40
111 Michael Chavis .25 .60
112 Brett Netzer .25 .60
113 Derby .40 1.00
114 Todd "Parney" Parnell .25 .60
115 Jeren Kendall .20 .50
116 Luis Campusano .20 .50
117 Brendan McKay .25 .60
118 Dennis Santana .15 .40
119 Taylor Trammell .25 .60
120 Mark Vientos .25 .60
121 Jacob Gonzalez .30 .75
122 Jordan Hicks .30 .75
123 Tyler O'Neill .25 .60
124 Andres Gimenez .20 .50
125 Chris Rodriguez .15 .40
126 Braden Bishop .15 .40
127 Brendan Rodgers .20 .50
128 Franklin Perez .15 .40
129 Matt Hall .15 .40
130 Stuart Fairchild .20 .50
131 Bobby Bradley .20 .50
132 Luis Ortiz .15 .40
133 Juan Soto 3.00 8.00
134 Lewin Diaz .15 .40
135 Blake Rutherford .20 .50

136 Hans Crouse .25 .60
137 J.B. Bukauskas .15 .40
138 Toastman .25 .60
139 Jorge Ona .15 .40
140 Daniel Johnson .15 .40
141 Nick Senzel .50 1.25
142 Jon Duplantier .15 .40
143 Cole Brannen .20 .50
144 Quinn Brodey .15 .40
145 Jeter Downs .25 .60
146 Jose Siri .15 .40
147 DJ Peters .40 1.00
148 Bubba Thompson .25 .60
149 Tommy Doyle .15 .40
150 Heliot Ramos .25 .60
151 Corey Ray .20 .50
152 Jake Burger .15 .40
153 Jazz Chisholm .40 1.00
154 Lazaro Armenteros .30 .75
155 Brandon Marsh .20 .50
156 Anderson Espinoza .15 .40
157 Austin Riley .50 1.25
158 Corbin Martin .15 .40
159 Kyle Lewis .30 .75
160 Cole Ragans .15 .40
161 Stephen Gonsalves .15 .40
162 Riley Mahan .15 .40
163 Leody Taveras .20 .50
164 Conner Uselton .25 .60
165 Erik the Peanut Guy .25 .60
166 Mickey Moniak .40 1.00
167 Pavin Smith .15 .40
168 Gavin Sheets .20 .50
169 MJ Melendez .15 .40
170 Brent Honeywell .25 .60
171 Triston McKenzie .15 .40
172 Spencer Howard .15 .40
173 Tanner Houck .40 1.00
174 Adam Hall .25 .60
175 Scott Kingery .25 .60
176 Sam Howard .15 .40
177 Taylor Walls .15 .40
178 Kevin Maitan .20 .50
179 Thairo Estrada .40 1.00
180 Jake Bauers .20 .50
181 Bryan Reynolds .25 .60
182 Zach Kirtley .20 .50
183 Josh Lowe .15 .40
184 Nick Gordon .15 .40
185 Darick Hall .15 .40
186 Adrian Morejon .15 .40
187 Estevan Florial .25 .60
188 Cristian Pache .75 2.00
189 Kacy Clemens .20 .50
190 Keston Hiura .40 1.00
191 D.J. Stewart .15 .40
192 Jorge Guzman .15 .40
193 Justin Dunn .20 .50
194 A.J. Puk .20 .50
195 Fernando Romero .15 .40
196 Jorge Mateo .15 .40
197 Connor Wong .25 .60
198 Shane Baz .20 .50
199 Delvin Perez .15 .40
200 Tim Tebow 1.50 4.00

2018 Topps Pro Debut Green

*GREEN: 2.5X TO 6X BASIC
STATED ODDS 1:XX HOBBY
STATED PRINT RUN 99 SER.#'d SETS

2018 Topps Pro Debut Orange

*ORANGE: 5X TO 12X BASIC
STATED ODDS 1:XX HOBBY
STATED PRINT RUN 25 SER.#'d SETS
1 Ronald Acuna 30.00 80.00
20 Vladimir Guerrero Jr. 30.00 80.00
50 Gleyber Torres 25.00 60.00
200 Tim Tebow 25.00 60.00

2018 Topps Pro Debut Photo Variations

STATED ODDS 1:XX HOBBY
1 Ronald Acuna 30.00 80.00
14 Michael Kopech 6.00 15.00
20 Vladimir Guerrero Jr. 30.00 80.00
23 MacKenzie Gore 12.00 30.00
25 Hunter Greene 6.00 15.00
46 Adam Haseley 6.00 15.00
50 Gleyber Torres 20.00 50.00
62 Jo Adell 6.00 15.00
89 Austin Beck 10.00 25.00
100 Royce Lewis 10.00 25.00
117 Brendan McKay 10.00 25.00
127 Brendan Rodgers 6.00 15.00
152 Jake Burger 6.00 15.00
167 Pavin Smith 6.00 15.00
200 Tim Tebow 30.00 80.00

2018 Topps Pro Debut Autographs

STATED ODDS 1:XX HOBBY
EXCHANGE DEADLINE 5/31/2020
*GREEN/99: .5X TO 1.2X BASIC
*ORANGE/25: .75X TO 2X BASIC
1 Ronald Acuna 75.00 200.00
6 Carter Kieboom 10.00 25.00
7 Corbin Burnes 4.00 10.00
8 Greg Deichmann 3.00 8.00
11 Michel Baez 4.00 10.00
12 Anderson Tejeda 3.00 8.00
13 Kyle Wright 6.00 15.00
14 Michael Kopech 5.00 12.00
15 Jay Groome 3.00 8.00
16 Justus Sheffield 8.00 20.00
21 Blayne Enlow 2.50 6.00
23 MacKenzie Gore 12.00 30.00
25 Hunter Greene 20.00 50.00
29 J.J. Matijevic 3.00 8.00
30 Brent Rooker 3.00 8.00
40 Nick Pratto 3.00 8.00
46 Adam Haseley 4.00 10.00
49 Tyler Freeman 2.50 6.00
50 Gleyber Torres 25.00 60.00
51 Zac Lowther 3.00 8.00
59 Kade McClure 2.50 6.00
61 Zack Littell 2.50 6.00
62 Jo Adell 40.00 100.00
63 Drew Waters 10.00 25.00
68 Keibert Ruiz 12.00 30.00
70 Adbert Alzolay 6.00 15.00
71 Ryan Vilade 2.50 6.00
74 Merandy Gonzalez 2.50 6.00
87 Drew Ellis 3.00 8.00
89 Austin Beck 6.00 15.00
97 Mitch Keller 5.00 12.00
100 Royce Lewis
102 Pete Alonso 60.00 150.00
103 Tristen Lutz 3.00 8.00
104 Chris Seise 2.50 6.00
106 Colton Welker 2.50 6.00
107 Sean Murphy 10.00 25.00
108 Quentin Holmes 2.50 6.00
115 Jeren Kendall 6.00 15.00
117 Brendan McKay 20.00 50.00
118 Dennis Santana 2.50 6.00
119 Taylor Trammell 4.00 10.00
120 Mark Vientos 4.00 10.00
122 Jordan Hicks 6.00 15.00
124 Andres Gimenez 3.00 8.00
125 Chris Rodriguez 2.50 6.00
127 Brendan Rodgers 10.00 25.00
135 Blake Rutherford 3.00 8.00
136 Hans Crouse 4.00 10.00
143 Cole Brannen 3.00 8.00
145 Jeter Downs 8.00 20.00
150 Heliot Ramos 4.00 10.00
152 Jake Burger 2.50 6.00
166 Mickey Moniak 10.00 25.00
167 Pavin Smith 2.50 6.00
168 Gavin Sheets 3.00 8.00
169 MJ Melendez 2.50 6.00
178 Kevin Maitan 10.00 25.00
185 Darick Hall 2.50 6.00
188 Cristian Pache 12.00 30.00
189 Kacy Clemens 3.00 8.00
190 Keston Hiura
192 Jorge Guzman 2.50 6.00
194 A.J. Puk 3.00 8.00
198 Shane Baz 5.00 12.00

2018 Topps Pro Debut Ben's Biz

COMPLETE SET (9) 3.00 8.00
COMMON CARD .40 1.00
STATED ODDS 1:8 HOBBY
BBBA Ace .40 1.00
BBBC Chompers .40 1.00
BBBBB Belly Buster .40 1.00
BBBEG Eclipse Game .40 1.00
BBBSM Sean McCall .40 1.00
BBBBBLR Ben's Biz Lazy River .40 1.00
BBBSDB Steve the Dancing Batboy .40 1.00
BBBSMI Susan Mielnik .40 1.00
BBBTAB Tremor .40 1.00
Aaron Bishop

2018 Topps Pro Debut Distinguished Debut Medallions

STATED ODDS 1:XX HOBBY
STATED PRINT RUN 99 SER.#'d SETS
*GOLD/50: .5X TO 1.2X BASIC
DDAB Austin Beck 2.50 6.00
DDAH Adam Haseley 3.00 8.00
DDBM Brendan McKay 3.00 8.00
DDBR Brent Rooker 2.50 6.00
DDCB Cole Brannen 2.50 6.00
DDDE Drew Ellis 2.50 6.00
DDEW Evan White 3.00 8.00
DDGD Greg Deichmann 2.50 6.00
DDGS Gavin Sheets 2.50 6.00
DDHC Hans Crouse 3.00 8.00
DDHG Hunter Greene 5.00 12.00
DDHR Heliot Ramos 3.00 8.00
DDJA Jo Adell 5.00 12.00
DDJB Jake Burger 2.00 5.00
DDJBU J.B. Bukauskas 2.00 5.00
DDJD Jeter Downs 3.00 8.00
DDJK Jeren Kendall 5.00 12.00
DDKC Kacy Clemens 2.50 6.00
DDKH Keston Hiura 5.00 12.00
DDKM Kevin Maitan 5.00 12.00
DDKW Kyle Wright 5.00 12.00
DDMG MacKenzie Gore 4.00 10.00
DDMM MJ Melendez 2.00 5.00
DDMV Mark Vientos 3.00 8.00
DDNP Nick Pratto 2.50 6.00
DDPS Pavin Smith 2.00 5.00
DDQH Quentin Holmes 2.00 5.00
DDRL Royce Lewis 5.00 12.00
DDRV Ryan Vilade 2.00 5.00
DDSB Shane Baz 2.50 6.00

2018 Topps Pro Debut Fragments of the Farm Relics

RANDOM INSERTS IN PACKS
*GREEN/99: .5X TO 1.2X BASIC
*GOLD/50: .6X TO 1.5X BASIC
FOTFAA Adbert Alzolay 4.00 10.00
FOTFBB Rowdy Tellez 2.00 5.00
FOTFCF Andres Gimenez 2.50 6.00
FOTFES Christin Stewart 2.50 6.00
FOTFGR Tommy Doyle 2.00 5.00
FOTFHS Drew Ward 2.00 5.00
FOTFSC Austin Voth 2.00 5.00
FOTFSLM Tim Tebow 6.00 15.00
FOTFTD Yusniel Diaz 6.00 15.00
FOTFWC Jhailyn Ortiz 4.00 10.00
FOTFWIC Kyle Young 4.00 10.00
FOTFBRP Luis Guillorme 2.00 5.00
FOTFGCT Royce Lewis 6.00 15.00
FOTFGJR Ryan Vilade 2.00 5.00
FOTFHVR Brendan McKay 4.00 10.00
FOTFOSC Christian Binford 2.00 5.00
FOTFQCR J.J. Matijevic 2.50 6.00
FOTFSCS Zach Kirtley 2.50 6.00

2018 Topps Pro Debut Make Your Pro Debut

STATED ODDS 1:XXX HOBBY
PDJS John Springstube 2.50 6.00

2018 Topps Pro Debut MILB Leaps and Bounds

COMPLETE SET (25) 10.00 25.00
STATED ODDS 1:XX HOBBY
*GREEN/99: 1.2X TO 3X BASIC
*ORANGE/25: 2.5X TO 6X BASIC
LBAA Adbert Alzolay .30 .75
LBAG Andres Gimenez .30 .75
LBAP A.J. Puk .30 .75
LBBB Bo Bichette 1.00 2.50
LBCB Corbin Burnes .40 1.00
LBCK Carter Kieboom .40 1.00
LBCP Cristian Pache 1.25 3.00
LBFT Fernando Tatis Jr. 2.00 5.00
LBGT Gleyber Torres 2.50 6.00
LBJG Jorge Guzman .25 .60
LBJH Jordan Hicks .50 1.25
LBJS Jesus Sanchez .25 .60
LBKR Keibert Ruiz .75 2.00
LBLU Luis Urias .50 1.25
LBMB Michel Baez .25 .60
LBMC Michael Chavis .40 1.00
LBMK Michael Kopech .50 1.25
LBRM Ryan Mountcastle .40 1.00
LBSK Scott Kingery .40 1.00
LBSS Sixto Sanchez .60 1.50
LBTM Triston McKenzie .25 .60
LBTT Taylor Trammell .40 1.00
LBYD Yusniel Diaz .75 2.00
LBZL Zack Littell .25 .60
LBJSH Justus Sheffield .30 .75

2018 Topps Pro Debut MILB Leaps and Bounds Autographs

STATED ODDS 1:XX HOBBY
STATED PRINT RUN 50 SER.#'d SETS
EXCHANGE DEADLINE 5/31/2020
LBAA Adbert Alzolay 4.00 10.00
LBAG Andres Gimenez 4.00 10.00
LBAP A.J. Puk 4.00 10.00
LBCB Corbin Burnes 5.00 12.00
LBCK Carter Kieboom 12.00 30.00
LBCP Cristian Pache 20.00 50.00
LBGT Gleyber Torres 75.00 200.00
LBJG Jorge Guzman 10.00 25.00
LBJH Jordan Hicks 10.00 25.00
LBJSH Justus Sheffield 8.00 20.00
LBKR Keibert Ruiz 15.00 40.00
LBMB Michel Baez 3.00 8.00
LBMK Michael Kopech 12.00 30.00
LBRM Ryan Mountcastle 25.00 60.00
LBZL Zack Littell 8.00 20.00

2018 Topps Pro Debut Promo Night Uniform Relics

STATED ODDS 1:XX HOBBY
STATED PRINT RUN 99 SER.#'d SETS
*GOLD/50: .5X TO 1.2X BASIC
PNRAMG Reading Fightin Phils 5.00 12.00
PNRBCN Fort Wayne TinCaps 5.00 12.00
PNRBTN Toledo Mud Hens 5.00 12.00
PNRCAN Danville Braves 5.00 12.00
PNRCSC Columbia Fireflies 25.00 60.00
PNRFAN New Hampshire Fisher Cats 5.00 12.00
PNRMAN Richmond Flying Squirrels 5.00 12.00
PNRPCN Arkansas Travelers 5.00 12.00
PNRPSN Tacoma Rainiers 5.00 12.00
PNRRLN Everett AquaSox 5.00 12.00
PNRSCN Wisconsin Timber Rattlers 5.00 12.00
PNRSCR Aberdeen Iron Birds 5.00 12.00

2018 Topps Pro Debut Promo Night Uniforms

STATED ODDS 1:XX HOBBY
PNAMG Reading Fightin Phils .40 1.00
PNBCN Fort Wayne TinCaps .40 1.00
PNBTN Toledo Mud Hens .40 1.00
PNCAN Danville Braves .40 1.00
PNCSC Columbia Fireflies .40 1.00
PNFAN New Hampshire Fisher Cats .40 1.00
PNMAN Richmond Flying Squirrels .40 1.00
PNPCN Arkansas Travelers .40 1.00
PNPSN Tacoma Rainiers .40 1.00
PNRLN Everett AquaSox .40 1.00
PNSCN Wisconsin Timber Rattlers .40 1.00
PNSCR Aberdeen Iron Birds .40 1.00

2018 Topps Pro Debut Splash of the Future Autographs

RANDOM INSERTS IN PACKS
PRINT RUNS B/WN 20-45 COPIES PER
EXCHANGE DEADLINE 3/31/2020
SOFAA Adbert Alzolay/45* 4.00 10.00
SOFBM Brendan McKay/30* 30.00 80.00
SOFCK Carter Kieboom/45* 25.00 60.00
SOFCP Cristian Pache/45* 15.00 40.00
SOFGT Gleyber Torres/45* 50.00 120.00
SOFHG Hunter Greene/20* 50.00 120.00
SOFHR Heliot Ramos/45* 5.00 12.00
SOFJA Jo Adell/45* 20.00 50.00
SOFJB Jake Burger/45* 10.00 25.00
SOFJD Jeter Downs/45* 15.00 40.00
SOFJG Jay Groome/45* 4.00 10.00
SOFJS Justus Sheffield/35* 10.00 25.00
SOFKH Keston Hiura/45* 25.00 60.00
SOFKM Kevin Maitan/45* 12.00 30.00
SOFKR Keibert Ruiz/45* 25.00 60.00
SOFMK Mitch Keller/45* 15.00 40.00
SOFMKO Michael Kopech/45* 10.00 25.00
SOFNP Nick Pratto/45* 10.00 25.00
SOFNS Nick Senzel/20* 25.00 60.00
SOFRA Ronald Acuna/40* 40.00 100.00
SOFRL Royce Lewis/20* 40.00 100.00
SOFRV Ryan Vilade/45* 3.00 8.00

2018 Topps Pro Debut Splash of the Future Autographs Orange

*ORANGE: .5X TO 1.2X BASIC
RANDOM INSERTS IN PACKS
STATED PRINT RUN 25 SER.#'d SETS
EXCHANGE DEADLINE 3/31/2020
SOFRA Ronald Acuna 125.00 300.00

2019 Topps Pro Debut

1 Vladimir Guerrero Jr. 1.00 2.50
2 Brock Burke .15 .40
3 Tirso Ornelas .15 .40
4 Mason McReaken .15 .40
5 Esteury Ruiz .20 .50
6 Jonathan India .20 .50
7 Edward Cabrera .25 .60
8 Sean Hjelle .20 .50
9 Joey Bart .50 1.25
10 DL Hall .15 .40
11 Yadier Alvarez .15 .40
12 Shane McClanahan .20 .50
13 Grayson Rodriguez .30 .75
14 Dane Dunning .15 .40
15 Kevin Maitan .20 .50
16 Parker Meadows .20 .50
17 Jordyn Adams .20 .50
18 Jake McCarthy .25 .60
19 Simeon Woods Richardson .20 .50
20 Anderson Tejeda .20 .50
21 Daz Cameron .15 .40
22 Brendan Rodgers .25 .60
23 Matt Manning .25 .60
24 Cristian Santana .25 .60
25 Fernando Tatis Jr. 1.50 4.00
26 Dustin May .50 1.25
27 Albert Abreu .15 .40
28 Lenny Torres .20 .50
29 Alek Thomas .25 .60
30 Nolan Jones .25 .60
31 Griffin Canning .25 .60
32 Pete Alonso 1.25 3.00
33 Adonis Medina .25 .60
34 Bo Bichette .50 1.25
35 Micah Bello .25 .60
36 Carter Kieboom .25 .60
37 Alex Kirilloff .25 .60
38 Rylan Bannon .20 .50
39 Seuly Matias .20 .50
40 Griffin Roberts .15 .40
41 Jose Suarez .15 .40
42 Yusniel Diaz .25 .60
43 Hunter Greene .25 .60
44 Drew Waters .50 1.25
45 Adrian Morejon .15 .40
46 Jayson Schroeder .15 .40
47 Terrin Vavra .30 .75
48 Dylan Cease .40 1.00
49 Ian Anderson .40 1.00
50 Wander Franco 2.50 6.00
51 Ronny Mauricio .40 1.00
52 Ryan McKenna .15 .40
53 Spencer Howard .15 .40
54 Aaron Civale .25 .60
55 Sheldon Neuse .15 .40
56 Bobby Dalbec .40 1.00
57 Keibert Ruiz .40 1.00
58 Jazz Chisholm .40 1.00
59 Daulton Varsho .15 .40
60 Nick Senzel .50 1.25
61 Yordan Alvarez 1.00 2.50
62 Peter Lambert .25 .60
63 Estevan Florial .25 .60
64 Brusdar Graterol .20 .50
65 Nick Decker .30 .75
66 Kyle Lewis .30 .75
67 Mike Siani .25 .60
68 Heliot Ramos .25 .60
69 Trevor Larnach .40 1.00
70 Logan Webb .25 .60
71 Mickey Moniak .40 1.00
72 Jesus Luzardo .25 .60
73 Cristian Javier .20 .50
74 Royce Lewis .30 .75
75 Michael Chavis .25 .60
76 Jesus Sanchez .15 .40
77 Nick Schnell .15 .40
78 Forrest Whitley .25 .60
79 Josh Breaux .20 .50
80 Andres Gimenez .20 .50
81 Oneil Cruz .25 .60
82 Adam Haseley .25 .60
83 Ryan Weathers .15 .40
84 Ryan Costello .20 .50
85 Clarke Schmidt .25 .60
86 Andrew Bechtold .15 .40
87 Reggie Lawson .15 .40
88 Andrew Knizner .25 .60
89 Cole Roederer .50 1.25
90 Leody Taveras .15 .40
91 Logan Allen .15 .40
92 Jeter Downs .25 .60
93 Justin Dunn .15 .40
94 Tanner Dodson .20 .50
95 Kyle Isbel .20 .50
96 Grant Lavigne .20 .50
97 Chris Paddack .30 .75
98 Ronaldo Hernandez .15 .40
99 Jeremiah Jackson .25 .60
100 Eloy Jimenez .60 1.50
101 Taylor Widener .15 .40
102 Luis Robert 1.50 4.00
103 Michael Donadio .40 1.00
104 Kevin Smith .15 .40
105 Keegan Thompson .15 .40
106 Owen Miller .20 .50
107 Connor Scott .20 .50
108 Izzy Wilson .20 .50
109 Tim Cate .15 .40
110 Beau Burrows .15 .40
111 Daniel Lynch .20 .50
112 Jordan Groshans .30 .75
113 Jake Wong .15 .40
114 Triston McKenzie .15 .40
115 Greyson Jenista .20 .50
116 Jonathan Hernandez .15 .40
117 Seth Beer .40 1.00
118 Keston Hiura .50 1.25
119 Brendan McKay .25 .60
120 Brice Turang .20 .50
121 Nick Sandlin .15 .40
122 Matt Mercer .15 .40
123 Blake Rutherford .15 .40
124 Luis Garcia .20 .50
125 Nick Madrigal .50 1.25
126 Cadyn Grenier .20 .50
127 Colton Welker .15 .40
128 Anthony Seigler .25 .60
129 Jeremy Eierman .20 .50
130 Jonathan Ornelas .20 .50
131 Corey Ray .15 .40
132 Will Stewart .15 .40
133 Casey Golden .25 .60
134 Ke'Bryan Hayes .15 .40
135 Gavin Lux .50 1.25
136 Kris Bubic .25 .60
137 Mitch Keller .20 .50
138 Brandon Marsh .15 .40
139 Sean Murphy .20 .50
140 Joe Gray Jr. .20 .50
141 Jo Adell .50 1.25
142 Akil Baddoo .20 .50
143 Eli Morgan .15 .40
144 Triston Casas .60 1.50
145 Matthew Liberatore .15 .40
146 Mason Martin .30 .75
147 Ryder Green .40 1.00
148 Will Smith .40 1.00
149 Grant Little .15 .40
150 Shed Long .25 .60
151 Nate Pearson .40 1.00
152 Taylor Trammell .20 .50
153 Chad Spanberger .15 .40
154 Braden Bishop .20 .50
155 Hans Crouse .15 .40
156 Gabriel Cancel .25 .60
157 Daniel Johnson .15 .40
158 Alec Bohm .60 1.50
159 Carlos Cortes .15 .40
160 Austin Riley .75 2.00
161 Derian Cruz .15 .40
162 Blaze Alexander .15 .40
163 Tommy Romero .20 .50
164 Brennen Davis .60 1.50
165 Luken Baker .20 .50
166 Osiris Johnson .20 .50
167 Genesis Cabrera .25 .60
168 Michel Baez .15 .40
169 Julio Pablo Martinez .15 .40
170 Durbin Feltman .15 .40
171 Franklin Perez .15 .40
172 Khalil Lee .15 .40
173 MacKenzie Gore .30 .75
174 Tristan Pompey .20 .50
175 Jarred Kelenic .60 1.50
176 Kody Clemens .20 .50
177 Travis Swaggerty .25 .60
178 Brewer Hicklen .25 .60
179 Ford Proctor .20 .50
180 Jackson Kowar .15 .40
181 Will Banfield .15 .40
182 Elehuris Montero .25 .60
183 Sixto Sanchez .20 .50
184 Nico Hoerner .50 1.25
185 Darwinzon Hernandez .15 .40
186 Bo Naylor .15 .40
187 Miguel Amaya .25 .60
188 Jameson Hannah .20 .50
189 Roberto Ramos .20 .50
190 Braxton Ashcraft .15 .40
191 Nolan Gorman .50 1.25
192 Jon Duplantier .15 .40
193 Cristian Pache .40 1.00
194 Freudis Nova .25 .60
195 Ryan Jeffers .30 .75
196 Evan White .25 .60
197 Ryan Mountcastle .20 .50
198 Josh Stowers .30 .75
199 Alex Faedo .20 .50
200 Casey Mize .40 1.00

2019 Topps Pro Debut Gold

*GOLD: 2X TO 5X BASIC
STATED ODDS 1:38 HOBBY
STATED PRINT RUN 50 SER.#'d SETS
1 Vladimir Guerrero Jr. 15.00 40.00
61 Yordan Alvarez 20.00 50.00

2019 Topps Pro Debut Green

*GREEN: 1.2X TO 3X BASIC
STATED ODDS 1:19 HOBBY
STATED PRINT RUN 99 SER.#'d SETS
61 Yordan Alvarez 12.00 30.00

2019 Topps Pro Debut Orange

*ORANGE: 4X TO 10X BASIC
STATED ODDS 1:75 HOBBY
STATED PRINT RUN 25 SER.#'d SETS
1 Vladimir Guerrero Jr. 100.00 250.00

2019 Topps Pro Debut Image Variations

STATED ODDS 1:XX HOBBY
1 Vladimir Guerrero Jr. 10.00 25.00
9 Joey Bart 5.00 12.00
22 Brendan Rodgers 4.00 10.00
25 Fernando Tatis Jr. 15.00 40.00
34 Bo Bichette 5.00 12.00
37 Alex Kirilloff 8.00 20.00
50 Wander Franco 20.00 50.00
57 Keibert Ruiz 5.00 12.00
60 Nick Senzel 6.00 15.00
74 Royce Lewis 3.00 8.00
100 Eloy Jimenez 6.00 15.00
125 Nick Madrigal 5.00 12.00
175 Jarred Kelenic 6.00 15.00
191 Nolan Gorman 5.00 12.00
200 Casey Mize 4.00 10.00

2019 Topps Pro Debut 10 Year Anniversary Reprints

COMPLETE SET (5) 2.50 6.00
STATED ODDS 1:24 HOBBY
PD10BH Bryce Harper .60 1.50
PD10FL Francisco Lindor .40 1.00
PD10KB Kris Bryant .50 1.25
PD10MB Mookie Betts .60 1.50
PD10MT Mike Trout 2.00 5.00

2019 Topps Pro Debut Autographs

STATED ODDS 1:20 HOBBY
*GREEN/99: .5X TO 1.2X BASIC
*ORANGE/25: .75X TO 2X BASIC
1 Vladimir Guerrero Jr. 60.00 150.00
2 Brock Burke 2.50 6.00
6 Jonathan India 3.00 8.00
8 Sean Hjelle 3.00 8.00
9 Joey Bart 30.00 80.00
17 Jordyn Adams 3.00 8.00
18 Jake McCarthy 4.00 10.00
24 Cristian Santana 4.00 10.00
25 Fernando Tatis Jr. 50.00 120.00
29 Alek Thomas 4.00 10.00
36 Carter Kieboom 6.00 15.00
38 Rylan Bannon 3.00 8.00
39 Seuly Matias 3.00 8.00
50 Wander Franco 50.00 120.00
51 Ronny Mauricio 6.00 15.00
53 Spencer Howard 2.50 6.00
55 Sheldon Neuse 2.50 6.00
56 Bobby Dalbec 6.00 15.00
57 Keibert Ruiz 6.00 15.00
61 Yordan Alvarez 40.00 100.00
63 Estevan Florial 4.00 10.00
70 Logan Webb 4.00 10.00
74 Royce Lewis 20.00 50.00
88 Andrew Knizner 5.00 12.00
91 Logan Allen 2.50 6.00
96 Grant Lavigne 5.00 12.00
98 Ronaldo Hernandez 2.50 6.00
99 Jeremiah Jackson 4.00 10.00
100 Eloy Jimenez 12.00 30.00
101 Taylor Widener 2.50 6.00
102 Luis Robert 40.00 100.00
105 Keegan Thompson 2.50 6.00
109 Tim Cate 2.50 6.00
111 Daniel Lynch 3.00 8.00
115 Greyson Jenista 3.00 8.00
117 Seth Beer 6.00 15.00
120 Brice Turang 6.00 15.00
124 Luis Garcia 3.00 8.00
125 Nick Madrigal 10.00 25.00
128 Anthony Seigler 4.00 10.00
137 Mitch Keller 3.00 8.00
138 Brandon Marsh 2.50 6.00
140 Joe Gray Jr. 3.00 8.00
141 Jo Adell 15.00 40.00
144 Triston Casas 6.00 15.00
145 Matthew Liberatore 2.50 6.00
148 Will Smith 15.00 40.00
153 Chad Spanberger 2.50 6.00
154 Braden Bishop 3.00 8.00
155 Hans Crouse 2.50 6.00
158 Alec Bohm 12.00 30.00
162 Blaze Alexander 2.50 6.00
165 Luken Baker 3.00 8.00
166 Osiris Johnson 3.00 8.00
167 Genesis Cabrera 4.00 10.00
169 Julio Pablo Martinez 2.50 6.00
173 MacKenzie Gore 8.00 20.00
174 Tristan Pompey 3.00 8.00
175 Jarred Kelenic 10.00 25.00
176 Kody Clemens 3.00 8.00
177 Travis Swaggerty 4.00 10.00
178 Brewer Hicklen 4.00 10.00
180 Jackson Kowar 2.50 6.00
181 Will Banfield 2.50 6.00
182 Elehuris Montero 6.00 15.00
184 Nico Hoerner 8.00 20.00
187 Miguel Amaya 8.00 20.00
189 Roberto Ramos 3.00 8.00
191 Nolan Gorman 20.00 50.00
193 Cristian Pache 12.00 30.00
194 Freudis Nova 4.00 10.00
196 Evan White 4.00 10.00
198 Josh Stowers 5.00 12.00
200 Casey Mize 25.00 60.00

2019 Topps Pro Debut Autographs Gold

*GOLD: .6X TO 1.5X BASIC
STATED ODDS 1:124 HOBBY
STATED PRINT RUN 50 SER.#'d SETS
76 Jesus Sanchez 4.00 10.00
102 Luis Robert 100.00 250.00

2019 Topps Pro Debut Ben's Biz

COMPLETE SET (5) 2.50 6.00
STATED ODDS 1:24 HOBBY
BBBBE BenEverywhere .60 1.50
BBBMC Mr. Celery .60 1.50
BBBMF McCormick Field .60 1.50
BBBPJ Peg Johnston .60 1.50
BBBRTR Roscoe the Rooster .60 1.50

2019 Topps Pro Debut Distinguished Debut Medallions

STATED ODDS 1:126 HOBBY
STATED PRINT RUN 99 SER.#'d SETS
*GOLD/50: .5X TO 1.2X BASIC
DDAB Alec Bohm 4.00 10.00
DDAS Anthony Seigler 1.50 4.00
DDBN Bo Naylor 1.00 2.50
DDBT Brice Turang 1.25 3.00
DDCG Cadyn Grenier 1.25 3.00
DDCM Casey Mize 2.50 6.00
DDCS Connor Scott 1.25 3.00
DDDL Daniel Lynch 1.25 3.00
DDEH Ethan Hankins 1.25 3.00
DDGR Grayson Rodriguez 2.00 5.00
DDJA Jordyn Adams 1.25 3.00
DDJB Joey Bart 3.00 8.00
DDJG Jordan Groshans 2.00 5.00
DDJI Jonathan India 1.25 3.00
DDJK Jarred Kelenic 4.00 10.00
DDJKO Jackson Kowar 1.00 2.50
DDJM Jake McCarthy 1.50 4.00
DDKB Kris Bubic 1.50 4.00
DDML Matthew Liberatore 1.00 2.50
DDNG Nolan Gorman 3.00 8.00
DDNH Nico Hoerner 3.00 8.00
DDNM Nick Madrigal 3.00 8.00
DDNS Nick Schnell 1.00 2.50
DDRR Ryan Rolison 1.00 2.50
DDRW Ryan Weathers 1.00 2.50
DDSB Seth Beer 2.50 6.00
DDSM Shane McClanahan 1.25 3.00
DDTC Triston Casas 4.00 10.00
DDTL Trevor Larnach 2.50 6.00
DDTS Travis Swaggerty 1.50 4.00

2019 Topps Pro Debut Fragments of the Farm Relics

STATED ODDS 1:16 HOBBY
*GREEN/99: .5X TO 1.2X BASIC
*GOLD/50: .6X TO 1.5X BASIC
FOFAG Heliot Ramos 3.00 8.00
FOFBGR Tommy Romero 2.50 6.00
FOFCC Yu Chang 2.50 6.00
FOFCL Shao-Ching Chiang 2.50 6.00
FOFCOL Oscar Mercado 5.00 12.00
FOFFR Jonathan Hernandez 2.00 5.00
FOFHAS Daniel Johnson 2.00 5.00
FOFHR Ronaldo Hernandez 2.00 5.00
FOFHS Carter Kieboom 3.00 8.00
FOFLC Will Benson 2.00 5.00
FOFMO Alek Thomas 3.00 8.00
FOFMR Andrew Knizner 3.00 8.00
FOFPN Luis Garcia 4.00 10.00
FOFTD Dustin May 4.00 10.00
FOFTR Tristen Lutz 2.50 6.00
FOFTRT Domingo Acevedo 2.00 5.00
FOFTT Albert Abreu 2.00 5.00
FOFWC Matt Vierling 3.00 8.00

2019 Topps Pro Debut Future Cornerstones Autographs

STATED ODDS 1:387 HOBBY
PRINT RUNS B/WN 20-60 COPIES PER
*ORANGE/25: .5X TO 1.2X BASIC
FCAAB Alec Bohm/25 30.00 80.00
FCABM Brandon Marsh/60 8.00 20.00
FCACK Carter Kieboom/50 10.00 25.00
FCACM Casey Mize/20 40.00 100.00
FCACP Cristian Pache/50 15.00 40.00
FCAEJ Eloy Jimenez/20 40.00 100.00
FCAEW Evan White/50 5.00 12.00
FCAFTJ Fernando Tatis Jr./20 100.00 250.00
FCAJA Jo Adell/40 20.00 50.00
FCAJB Joey Bart/25 40.00 100.00
FCAJD Jon Duplantier/60 3.00 8.00
FCAJI Jonathan India/30 15.00 40.00
FCAKR Keibert Ruiz/40 10.00 25.00
FCALG Luis Garcia/50 4.00 10.00
FCAMA Miguel Amaya/50 10.00 25.00
FCAMG MacKenzie Gore/20 20.00 50.00
FCAMK Mitch Keller/40 4.00 10.00
FCANG Nolan Gorman/50 20.00 50.00
FCANM Nick Madrigal/25 30.00 80.00
FCARM Ronny Mauricio/50 10.00 25.00
FCASMA Seuly Matias/60 6.00 15.00
FCASS Sixto Sanchez/50 4.00 10.00
FCAVGJ Vladimir Guerrero Jr./20 100.00 250.00
FCAWF Wander Franco/30 75.00 200.00

2019 Topps Pro Debut Make Your Pro Debut

STATED ODDS 1:498 HOBBY
PDTW Tim Watts 2.00 5.00

2019 Topps Pro Debut MILB Leaps and Bounds

STATED ODDS 1:6 HOBBY
*GREEN/99: 1X TO 2.5X BASIC
*ORANGE/25: 2X TO 5X BASIC
LBAG Andres Gimenez .30 .75
LBAK Alex Kirilloff .40 1.00
LBBD Bobby Dalbec .60 1.50
LBBM Brandon Marsh .25 .60
LBCK Carter Kieboom .40 1.00
LBCP Chris Paddack .50 1.25
LBCPA Cristian Pache .60 1.50
LBDC Dylan Cease .60 1.50
LBDM Dustin May .75 2.00
LBEM Elehuris Montero .40 1.00
LBEW Evan White .40 1.00
LBGC Griffin Canning .40 1.00
LBJA Jo Adell .75 2.00
LBJD Justin Dunn .25 .60
LBJL Jesus Luzardo .40 1.00
LBLA Logan Allen .25 .60
LBLG Luis Garcia .30 .75
LBMA Miguel Amaya .40 1.00
LBPA Pete Alonso 2.00 5.00
LBRH Ronaldo Hernandez .25 .60
LBSM Sean Murphy .30 .75
LBTW Taylor Widener .25 .60
LBVGJ Vladimir Guerrero Jr. 1.50 4.00
LBWF Wander Franco 4.00 10.00
LBYA Yordan Alvarez 1.50 4.00

2019 Topps Pro Debut MILB Leaps and Bounds Autographs

STATED ODDS 1:504 HOBBY
PRINT RUNS B/WN 25-50 COPIES PER
LBBD Bobby Dalbec/50 10.00 25.00
LBBM Brandon Marsh/50 8.00 20.00
LBCK Carter Kieboom/25 8.00 20.00
LBCPA Cristian Pache/25 20.00 50.00
LBDM Dustin May/25 15.00 40.00
LBEM Elehuris Montero/50 10.00 25.00
LBEW Evan White/50 5.00 12.00
LBGC Griffin Canning/50 15.00 40.00
LBJA Jo Adell/25 25.00 60.00
LBLA Logan Allen/50 6.00 15.00
LBLG Luis Garcia/50 4.00 10.00
LBMA Miguel Amaya/50 5.00 12.00
LBRH Ronaldo Hernandez/50 3.00 8.00
LBSM Sean Murphy/50 4.00 10.00
LBTW Taylor Widener/50 3.00 8.00
LBVGJ Vladimir Guerrero Jr./25 100.00 250.00
LBWF Wander Franco/25 60.00 150.00
LBYA Yordan Alvarez/50 20.00 50.00

2019 Topps Pro Debut Promo Night Uniform Relics

STATED ODDS 1:377 HOBBY
STATED PRINT RUN 99 SER.#'d SETS
*GOLD/50: .5X TO 1.2X BASIC
PNR90N Carolina Mudcats 4.00 10.00
PNRCAN Oklahoma City Dodgers 4.00 10.00
PNRHHN Jackson Generals 4.00 10.00
PNRLEN Williamsport Crosscutters 4.00 10.00
PNRMTN Missoula Osprey 4.00 10.00
PNRPLN Frisco RoughRiders 4.00 10.00
PNRSSN Williamsport Crosscutters 4.00 10.00
PNRUSN Bowling Green Hot Rods 4.00 10.00
PNRUTN Tennessee Smokies 4.00 10.00
PNRZON Columbia Fireflies 4.00 10.00

2019 Topps Pro Debut Promo Night Uniforms

COMPLETE SET (10) 2.50 6.00
STATED ODDS 1:6 HOBBY
PN90N Carolina Mudcats .40 1.00
PNCAN Oklahoma City Dodgers .40 1.00
PNGPN Rochester Red Wings .40 1.00
PNHHN Jackson Generals .40 1.00
PNLEN Williamsport Crosscutters .40 1.00
PNMTN Missoula Osprey .40 1.00
PNSSN Williamsport Crosscutters .40 1.00
PNUSN Bowling Green Hot Rods .40 1.00
PNUTN Tennessee Smokies .40 1.00
PNZON Columbia Fireflies .40 1.00

2020 Topps Pro Debut

PD1 Wander Franco 1.50 4.00
PD2 Deivi Garcia .60 1.50
PD3 Grae Kessinger .25 .60
PD4 Julio Pablo Martinez .15 .40
PD5 Kyle Stowers .15 .40
PD6 Elehuris Montero .20 .50
PD7 Blaze Alexander .15 .40
PD8 Bobby Dalbec .40 1.00
PD9 Andy Pages .20 .50
PD10 Josh Jung .40 1.00
PD11 Grayson Rodriguez .25 .60
PD12 Jacob Amaya .60 1.50
PD13 Niko Hulsizer .40 1.00
PD14 Keoni Cavaco .15 .40
PD15 Brock Deatherage .20 .50
PD16 Ian Anderson .40 1.00
PD17 Isaac Paredes .25 .60
PD18 Logan Gilbert .20 .50
PD19 Jordan Groshans .30 .75
PD20 Ulrich Bojarski .15 .40
PD21 Daulton Varsho .15 .40
PD22 Ronaldo Hernandez .15 .40
PD23 Ryan Garcia .15 .40
PD24 Brailyn Marquez .40 1.00
PD25 Adley Rutschman 1.00 2.50
PD26 Alek Thomas .20 .50
PD27 Diego Cartaya .30 .75
PD28 Jasseel De La Cruz .25 .60
PD29 Chase Strumpf .30 .75
PD30 Tyler Freeman .20 .50
PD31 Nasim Nunez .15 .40
PD32 Jarren Duran .60 1.50
PD33 Zack Thompson .15 .40
PD34 Matt Manning .20 .50
PD35 Shane McClanahan .20 .50
PD36 Logan Wyatt .25 .60
PD37 Bryson Stott .40 1.00
PD38 Michael Busch .40 1.00
PD39 Alec Marsh .20 .50
PD40 Ethan Small .20 .50
PD41 Aaron Shortridge .15 .40
PD42 Noah Song .20 .50
PD43 Alex Speas .15 .40
PD44 Shane Baz .15 .40

PD45 Gus Varland .15 .40
PD46 Alex Faedo .20 .50
PD47 Tim Tebow .75 2.00
PD48 Aaron Ashby .15 .40
PD49 Ryan Mountcastle .25 .60
PD50 Bobby Witt Jr. .75 2.00
PD51 Rece Hinds .20 .50
PD52 Spencer Howard .60 1.50
PD53 Grant Little .15 .40
PD54 Drew Waters .40 1.00
PD55 Heliot Ramos .25 .60
PD56 Lewin Diaz .15 .40
PD57 Luis Patino .25 .60
PD58 Nate Pearson .30 .75
PD59 Davis Wendzel .20 .50
PD60 Cristian Pache .50 1.25
PD61 Sherten Apostel .75 2.00
PD62 Brennen Davis .30 .75
PD63 Glenallen Hill Jr. .25 .60
PD64 Francisco Alvarez .50 1.25
PD65 Ke'Bryan Hayes .15 .40
PD66 Josh Wolf .25 .60
PD67 Xavier Edwards .60 1.50
PD68 Daniel Espino .20 .50
PD69 Will Wilson .20 .50
PD70 Victor Mesa Jr. .40 1.00
PD71 Taylor Trammell .20 .50
PD72 Nick Lodolo .25 .60
PD73 Seth Johnson .15 .40
PD74 Nick Quintana .30 .75
PD75 Tommy Henry .20 .50
PD76 Grant Gambrell .20 .50
PD77 Josh Smith .30 .75
PD78 Ethan Lindow .20 .50
PD79 Ryne Nelson .20 .50
PD80 Ronny Mauricio .40 1.00
PD81 Kendall Williams .25 .60
PD82 Chris Vallimont .15 .40
PD83 Greg Jones .20 .50
PD84 Forrest Whitley .15 .40
PD85 Logan Driscoll .25 .60
PD86 Michael Toglia .15 .40
PD87 Wilfred Astudillo .20 .50
PD88 Andres Gimenez .20 .50
PD89 Brennan Malone .20 .50
PD90 Kyren Paris .15 .40
PD91 Victor Victor Mesa .25 .60
PD92 Matthew Thompson .20 .50
PD93 Jonathan India .20 .50
PD94 Canaan Smith .25 .60
PD95 Jackson Rutledge .25 .60
PD96 Hunter Bishop .30 .75
PD97 Josiah Gray .25 .60
PD98 Miguel Vargas .40 1.00
PD99 Triston McKenzie .25 .60
PD100 Jo Adell .60 1.50
PD101 Aaron Schunk .30 .75
PD102 Anthony Volpe .60 1.50
PD103 Blake Walston .25 .60
PD104 Matthew Lugo .25 .60
PD105 John Doxakis .25 .60
PD106 Damon Jones .20 .50
PD107 Hunter Greene .25 .60
PD108 Riley Greene .60 1.50
PD109 Dominic Fletcher .15 .40
PD110 Logan Davidson .20 .50
PD111 Julio Rodriguez 1.00 2.50
PD112 Alvaro Seijas .15 .40
PD113 Luis Garcia .60 1.50
PD114 Matt Wallner .30 .75
PD115 Dylan File .15 .40
PD116 Everson Pereira .40 1.00
PD117 Kody Hoese .50 1.25
PD118 Joe Ryan .15 .40
PD119 MacKenzie Gore .30 .75
PD120 Yusniel Diaz .25 .60
PD121 Kyle Muller .15 .40
PD122 Gabriel Cancel .20 .50
PD123 Brandon Williamson .25 .60
PD124 Andrew Vaughn .60 1.50
PD125 Alec Bohm 1.00 2.50
PD126 JJ Goss .15 .40
PD127 Gabriel Moreno .25 .60
PD128 Max Lazar .20 .50
PD129 Jesus Sanchez .15 .40
PD130 Jake Sanford .25 .60
PD131 Brady McConnell .20 .50
PD132 Briam Campusano .15 .40
PD133 Luis Matos .25 .60
PD134 Matt Canterino .20 .50
PD135 Shea Langeliers .30 .75
PD136 Triston Casas .40 1.00
PD137 Hector Figueroa .15 .40
PD138 Jordan Balazovic .30 .75
PD139 Joshua Mears .30 .75
PD140 Freudis Nova .15 .40
PD141 Corbin Carroll .25 .60
PD142 Dylan Carlson .60 1.50
PD143 Joey Cantillo .15 .40
PD144 Jerar Encarnacion .50 1.25
PD145 T.J. Sikkema .15 .40
PD146 Jeremy Pena .40 1.00
PD147 Brady Singer .20 .50
PD148 Daniel Lynch .15 .40
PD149 Matt Gorski .25 .60
PD150 Casey Mize .50 1.25
PD151 Quinn Priester .25 .60
PD152 Ryan Jensen .20 .50
PD153 Hans Crouse .15 .40
PD154 Oneil Cruz .20 .50
PD155 DL Hall .15 .40
PD156 Nick Madrigal .50 1.25
PD157 Jared Triolo .20 .50
PD158 George Kirby .25 .60
PD159 Edward Cabrera .25 .60
PD160 Sam Huff .30 .75
PD161 Joey Bart .50 1.25
PD162 Tyler Baum .15 .40
PD163 Alex Kirilloff .30 .75
PD164 Nolan Gorman .30 .75
PD165 Sammy Siani .15 .40
PD166 Austin Hansen .20 .50
PD167 Jeter Downs .25 .60
PD168 Sixto Sanchez .25 .60
PD169 George Valera .30 .75
PD170 Kameron Misner .25 .60
PD171 Gunnar Henderson .20 .50
PD172 Nolan Jones .25 .60
PD173 Drey Jameson .15 .40
PD174 Braden Shewmake .20 .50
PD175 Antonio Cabello .50 1.25
PD176 Antoine Kelly .30 .75
PD177 Brett Baty .50 1.25
PD178 Cameron Cannon .30 .75
PD179 Marco Luciano .60 1.50
PD180 Evan White .15 .40
PD181 Alek Manoah .20 .50
PD182 Kevin Smith .15 .40
PD183 Bryan Mata .15 .40
PD184 Orelvis Martinez .40 1.00
PD185 JJ Bleday .50 1.25
PD186 Adam Hall .20 .50
PD187 Luis Campusano .25 .60
PD188 Oscar Gonzalez .40 1.00
PD189 Keibert Ruiz .40 1.00
PD190 Trevor Larnach .30 .75
PD191 Jarred Kelenic 1.00 2.50
PD192 CJ Abrams .60 1.50
PD193 Tarik Skubal .75 2.00
PD194 Jackson Kowar .15 .40
PD195 Royce Lewis .40 1.00
PD196 Kristian Robinson .50 1.25
PD197 Beau Philip .25 .60
PD198 Ruben Cardenas .20 .50
PD199 Vidal Brujan .50 1.25
PD200 Brayan Rocchio .60 1.50

2020 Topps Pro Debut Blue

*BLUE: 1X TO 2.5X BASIC
STATED ODDS 1:20 HOBBY
STATED PRINT RUN 150 SER.#'d SETS
PD3 Grae Kessinger 5.00 12.00
PD47 Tim Tebow 4.00 10.00
PD50 Bobby Witt Jr. 8.00 20.00
PD124 Andrew Vaughn 3.00 8.00
PD179 Marco Luciano 4.00 10.00

2020 Topps Pro Debut Gold

*GOLD: 2X TO 5X BASIC
STATED ODDS 1:59 HOBBY
STATED PRINT RUN 50 SER.#'d SETS
PD1 Wander Franco 15.00 40.00
PD3 Grae Kessinger 15.00 40.00
PD25 Adley Rutschman 20.00 50.00
PD32 Jarren Duran 6.00 15.00
PD47 Tim Tebow 15.00 40.00
PD50 Bobby Witt Jr. 20.00 50.00
PD62 Brennen Davis 5.00 12.00
PD65 Ke'Bryan Hayes 4.00 10.00
PD100 Jo Adell 8.00 20.00
PD108 Riley Greene 6.00 15.00
PD111 Julio Rodriguez 20.00 50.00
PD117 Kody Hoese 10.00 25.00
PD124 Andrew Vaughn 8.00 20.00
PD125 Alec Bohm 10.00 25.00
PD142 Dylan Carlson 12.00 30.00
PD160 Sam Huff 8.00 20.00
PD179 Marco Luciano 10.00 25.00
PD184 Orelvis Martinez 8.00 20.00
PD196 Kristian Robinson 8.00 20.00

2020 Topps Pro Debut Green

*GREEN: 1.2X TO 3X BASIC
STATED ODDS 1:30 HOBBY
STATED PRINT RUN 99 SER.#'d SETS
PD1 Wander Franco 8.00 20.00
PD3 Grae Kessinger 6.00 15.00
PD47 Tim Tebow 8.00 20.00
PD50 Bobby Witt Jr. 10.00 25.00
PD108 Riley Greene 4.00 10.00
PD124 Andrew Vaughn 5.00 12.00
PD160 Sam Huff 5.00 12.00
PD179 Marco Luciano 5.00 12.00
PD184 Orelvis Martinez 2.00 5.00

2020 Topps Pro Debut Orange

*ORANGE: 4X TO 10X BASIC
STATED ODDS 1:117 HOBBY
STATED PRINT RUN 25 SER.#'d SETS
PD1 Wander Franco 30.00 80.00
PD2 Deivi Garcia 15.00 40.00
PD3 Grae Kessinger 30.00 80.00
PD10 Josh Jung 10.00 25.00
PD25 Adley Rutschman 40.00 100.00
PD32 Jarren Duran 12.00 30.00
PD47 Tim Tebow 30.00 100.00
PD50 Bobby Witt Jr. 40.00 100.00
PD58 Nate Pearson 8.00 20.00
PD62 Brennen Davis 10.00 25.00
PD65 Ke'Bryan Hayes 15.00 40.00
PD70 Victor Mesa Jr. 6.00 15.00
PD91 Victor Victor Mesa 6.00 15.00
PD100 Jo Adell 12.00 30.00
PD108 Riley Greene 12.00 30.00
PD111 Julio Rodriguez 40.00 100.00
PD117 Kody Hoese 20.00 50.00
PD124 Andrew Vaughn 15.00 40.00
PD125 Alec Bohm 20.00 50.00
PD142 Dylan Carlson 25.00 60.00
PD160 Sam Huff 15.00 40.00
PD179 Marco Luciano 20.00 50.00
PD184 Orelvis Martinez 20.00 50.00
PD196 Kristian Robinson 15.00 40.00

2020 Topps Pro Debut Image Variations

STATED ODDS 1:195 HOBBY
PD1 Wander Franco 15.00 40.00
PD25 Adley Rutschman 25.00 60.00
PD50 Bobby Witt Jr. 15.00 40.00
PD58 Nate Pearson 15.00 40.00
PD91 Victor Victor Mesa 6.00 15.00
PD100 Jo Adell 15.00 40.00
PD108 Riley Greene 15.00 40.00
PD124 Andrew Vaughn 10.00 25.00
PD150 Casey Mize 12.00 30.00
PD161 Joey Bart 15.00 40.00
PD185 JJ Bleday 10.00 25.00
PD191 Jarred Kelenic 10.00 25.00
PD192 CJ Abrams 6.00 15.00
PD193 Tarik Skubal 12.00 30.00
PD195 Royce Lewis 12.00 30.00

2020 Topps Pro Debut Chrome

STATED ODDS 6 PER JUMBO
PDC1 Wander Franco 5.00 12.00
PDC2 Deivi Garcia 2.00 5.00
PDC3 Grae Kessinger .75 2.00
PDC4 Julio Pablo Martinez .50 1.25
PDC5 Kyle Stowers .50 1.25
PDC6 Elehuris Montero .60 1.50
PDC7 Blaze Alexander .50 1.25
PDC8 Bobby Dalbec 1.25 3.00
PDC9 Andy Pages .60 1.50
PDC10 Josh Jung 1.25 3.00
PDC11 Grayson Rodriguez .75 2.00
PDC12 Jacob Amaya 2.00 5.00
PDC13 Niko Hulsizer 1.25 3.00
PDC14 Keoni Cavaco .50 1.25
PDC15 Brock Deatherage .60 1.50
PDC16 Ian Anderson 1.25 3.00
PDC17 Isaac Paredes .75 2.00
PDC18 Logan Gilbert .60 1.50
PDC19 Jordan Groshans 1.00 2.50
PDC20 Ulrich Bojarski .50 1.25
PDC21 Daulton Varsho .50 1.25
PDC22 Ronaldo Hernandez .50 1.25
PDC23 Ryan Garcia .50 1.25
PDC24 Brailyn Marquez 1.25 3.00
PDC25 Adley Rutschman 5.00 12.00
PDC26 Alek Thomas .60 1.50
PDC27 Diego Cartaya 1.00 2.50
PDC28 Jasseel De La Cruz .75 2.00
PDC29 Chase Strumpf 1.00 2.50
PDC30 Tyler Freeman .60 1.50
PDC31 Nasim Nunez .50 1.25
PDC32 Jarren Duran 2.00 5.00
PDC33 Zack Thompson .50 1.25
PDC34 Matt Manning .60 1.50
PDC35 Shane McClanahan .60 1.50
PDC36 Logan Wyatt .75 2.00
PDC37 Bryson Stott 1.25 3.00
PDC38 Michael Busch 1.25 3.00
PDC39 Alec Marsh .60 1.50
PDC40 Ethan Small .60 1.50
PDC41 Aaron Shortridge .50 1.25
PDC42 Noah Song .60 1.50
PDC43 Alex Speas .50 1.25
PDC44 Shane Baz .50 1.25
PDC45 Gus Varland .50 1.25
PDC46 Alex Faedo .60 1.50
PDC47 Tim Tebow 2.00 5.00
PDC48 Aaron Ashby .50 1.25
PDC49 Ryan Mountcastle .75 2.00
PDC50 Bobby Witt Jr. 2.50 6.00
PDC51 Rece Hinds .60 1.50
PDC52 Spencer Howard 2.00 5.00
PDC53 Grant Little .50 1.25
PDC54 Drew Waters 1.25 3.00
PDC55 Heliot Ramos .75 2.00
PDC56 Lewin Diaz 1.00 2.50
PDC57 Luis Patino .75 2.00
PDC58 Nate Pearson 1.00 2.50
PDC59 Davis Wendzel .60 1.50
PDC60 Cristian Pache 1.50 4.00
PDC61 Sherten Apostel 2.50 6.00
PDC62 Brennen Davis 1.00 2.50
PDC63 Glenallen Hill Jr. .75 2.00
PDC64 Francisco Alvarez 4.00 10.00
PDC65 Ke'Bryan Hayes .50 1.25
PDC66 Josh Wolf .75 2.00
PDC67 Xavier Edwards 1.50 4.00
PDC68 Daniel Espino .60 1.50
PDC69 Will Wilson .60 1.50
PDC70 Victor Mesa Jr. 1.25 3.00
PDC71 Taylor Trammell .60 1.50
PDC72 Nick Lodolo .75 2.00
PDC73 Seth Johnson .50 1.25
PDC74 Nick Quintana 1.00 2.50
PDC75 Tommy Henry .60 1.50
PDC76 Grant Gambrell .60 1.50
PDC77 Josh Smith 1.00 2.50
PDC78 Ethan Lindow .60 1.50
PDC79 Ryne Nelson .60 1.50
PDC80 Ronny Mauricio 1.25 3.00
PDC81 Kendall Williams .75 2.00
PDC82 Chris Vallimont .50 1.25
PDC83 Greg Jones .60 1.50
PDC84 Forrest Whitley .50 1.25
PDC85 Logan Driscoll .75 2.00
PDC86 Michael Toglia .50 1.25
PDC87 Wilfred Astudillo .60 1.50
PDC88 Andres Gimenez .60 1.50
PDC89 Brennan Malone .50 1.25
PDC90 Kyren Paris .50 1.25
PDC91 Victor Victor Mesa .75 2.00
PDC92 Matthew Thompson .60 1.50
PDC93 Jonathan India .60 1.50
PDC94 Canaan Smith .75 2.00
PDC95 Jackson Rutledge .75 2.00
PDC96 Hunter Bishop 1.00 2.50
PDC97 Josiah Gray .75 2.00
PDC98 Miguel Vargas 1.25 3.00
PDC99 Triston McKenzie .75 2.00
PDC100 Jo Adell 4.00 10.00
PDC101 Aaron Schunk 1.00 2.50
PDC102 Anthony Volpe 2.00 5.00
PDC103 Blake Walston .75 2.00
PDC104 Matthew Lugo .75 2.00
PDC105 John Doxakis .50 1.25
PDC106 Damon Jones .60 1.50
PDC107 Hunter Greene .75 2.00
PDC108 Riley Greene 2.50 6.00
PDC109 Dominic Fletcher .50 1.25
PDC110 Logan Davidson .60 1.50
PDC111 Julio Rodriguez 3.00 8.00
PDC112 Alvaro Seijas .50 1.25
PDC113 Luis Garcia 2.00 5.00
PDC114 Matt Wallner 1.00 2.50
PDC115 Dylan File .50 1.25
PDC116 Everson Pereira 2.00 5.00
PDC117 Kody Hoese 1.50 4.00
PDC118 Joe Ryan .50 1.25
PDC119 MacKenzie Gore 1.00 2.50
PDC120 Yusniel Diaz .75 2.00
PDC121 Kyle Muller .50 1.25
PDC122 Gabriel Cancel .60 1.50
PDC123 Brandon Williamson .75 2.00
PDC124 Andrew Vaughn 2.00 5.00
PDC125 Alec Bohm 3.00 8.00
PDC126 JJ Goss .50 1.25
PDC127 Gabriel Moreno .75 2.00
PDC128 Max Lazar .60 1.50
PDC129 Jesus Sanchez .50 1.25
PDC130 Jake Sanford .75 2.00
PDC131 Brady McConnell .60 1.50
PDC132 Briam Campusano .50 1.25
PDC133 Luis Matos .75 2.00
PDC134 Matt Canterino .60 1.50
PDC135 Shea Langeliers 1.00 2.50
PDC136 Triston Casas 1.25 3.00
PDC137 Hector Figueroa .50 1.25
PDC138 Jordan Balazovic 1.00 2.50
PDC139 Joshua Mears 1.00 2.50
PDC140 Freudis Nova .50 1.25
PDC141 Corbin Carroll .75 2.00
PDC142 Dylan Carlson 2.00 5.00
PDC143 Joey Cantillo .50 1.25
PDC144 Jerar Encarnacion 1.50 4.00
PDC145 T.J. Sikkema .50 1.25
PDC146 Jeremy Pena 1.25 3.00
PDC147 Brady Singer .60 1.50
PDC148 Daniel Lynch .50 1.25
PDC149 Matt Gorski .75 2.00
PDC150 Casey Mize 1.50 4.00
PDC151 Quinn Priester .75 2.00
PDC152 Ryan Jensen .60 1.50
PDC153 Hans Crouse .50 1.25
PDC154 Oneil Cruz .60 1.50
PDC155 DL Hall .50 1.25
PDC156 Nick Madrigal 1.50 4.00
PDC157 Jared Triolo .75 2.00
PDC158 George Kirby .75 2.00
PDC159 Edward Cabrera .75 2.00
PDC160 Sam Huff 1.00 2.50
PDC161 Joey Bart 3.00 8.00
PDC162 Tyler Baum .50 1.25
PDC163 Alex Kirilloff 1.00 2.50
PDC164 Nolan Gorman 1.00 2.50
PDC165 Sammy Siani .50 1.25
PDC166 Austin Hansen .60 1.50
PDC167 Jeter Downs .75 2.00
PDC168 Sixto Sanchez .75 2.00
PDC169 George Valera 1.00 2.50
PDC170 Kameron Misner .75 2.00
PDC171 Gunnar Henderson .60 1.50
PDC172 Nolan Jones .75 2.00
PDC173 Drey Jameson .50 1.25
PDC174 Braden Shewmake .75 2.00
PDC175 Antonio Cabello 1.50 4.00
PDC176 Antoine Kelly 1.00 2.50
PDC177 Brett Baty 1.50 4.00
PDC178 Cameron Cannon 1.00 2.50
PDC179 Marco Luciano 2.00 5.00
PDC180 Evan White .50 1.25
PDC181 Alek Manoah .60 1.50
PDC182 Kevin Smith .50 1.25
PDC183 Bryan Mata .50 1.25
PDC184 Orelvis Martinez 1.25 3.00
PDC185 JJ Bleday 1.50 4.00
PDC186 Adam Hall .60 1.50
PDC187 Luis Campusano .75 2.00
PDC188 Oscar Gonzalez 1.25 3.00
PDC189 Keibert Ruiz 1.25 3.00
PDC190 Trevor Larnach 1.00 2.50
PDC191 Jarred Kelenic 2.50 6.00
PDC192 CJ Abrams 2.00 5.00
PDC193 Tarik Skubal 2.50 6.00
PDC194 Jackson Kowar .50 1.25
PDC195 Royce Lewis 1.25 3.00
PDC196 Kristian Robinson 1.50 4.00
PDC197 Beau Philip .75 2.00
PDC198 Ruben Cardenas .60 1.50
PDC199 Vidal Brujan .75 2.00
PDC200 Brayan Rocchio 2.00 5.00

2020 Topps Pro Debut Chrome Gold Refractors

*GOLD REF: 1X TO 2.5X BASIC
STATED ODDS 1:5 JUMBO
STATED PRINT RUN 75 SER.#'d SETS
PDC25 Adley Rutschman 20.00 50.00
PDC47 Tim Tebow 8.00 20.00
PDC56 Lewin Diaz 5.00 12.00
PDC64 Francisco Alvarez 12.00 30.00
PDC100 Jo Adell 12.00 30.00
PDC108 Riley Greene 15.00 40.00
PDC161 Joey Bart 12.00 30.00
PDC191 Jarred Kelenic 12.00 30.00
PDC196 Kristian Robinson 5.00 12.00

2020 Topps Pro Debut Chrome Orange Refractors

*GOLD REF: 2X TO 5X BASIC
STATED ODDS 1:11 JUMBO
STATED PRINT RUN 25 SER.#'d SETS
PDC25 Adley Rutschman 40.00 100.00
PDC47 Tim Tebow 15.00 40.00
PDC56 Lewin Diaz 15.00 40.00
PDC64 Francisco Alvarez 25.00 60.00
PDC100 Jo Adell 40.00 100.00
PDC108 Riley Greene 30.00 80.00
PDC161 Joey Bart 25.00 60.00
PDC191 Jarred Kelenic 25.00 60.00
PDC196 Kristian Robinson 12.00 30.00

2020 Topps Pro Debut Chrome Refractors

*REF: .8X TO 2X BASIC
STATED ODDS 1:3 JUMBO
STATED PRINT RUN 99 SER.#'d SETS
PDC25 Adley Rutschman 15.00 40.00
PDC47 Tim Tebow 6.00 15.00
PDC56 Lewin Diaz 4.00 10.00
PDC100 Jo Adell 10.00 25.00
PDC108 Riley Greene 8.00 20.00
PDC161 Joey Bart 10.00 25.00
PDC191 Jarred Kelenic 8.00 20.00

2020 Topps Pro Debut Copa de La Diversion

STATED ODDS 1:6 HOBBY
CODJ Daniel Johnson .25 .60
COFG Foster Griffin .25 .60
COJG Jose Gomez .25 .60
COLR Luis Robert 2.50 6.00
COLV Luis Vazquez .25 .60
COSM Seth Martinez .25 .60
COZR Zach Reks .40 1.00

2020 Topps Pro Debut Copa de La Diversion Relics

STATED ODDS 1:49 HOBBY
PRINT RUN BTW 764-1089 COPIES PER
CORAT Forrest Whitley 2.00 5.00
CORDJ Daniel Johnson 2.00 5.00
CORFG Foster Griffin 2.00 5.00
CORJG Jose Gomez 2.00 5.00
CORLR Luis Robert 15.00 40.00
CORLV Luis Vazquez 2.00 5.00
CORSM Seth Martinez 2.00 5.00
CORZR Zach Reks 3.00 8.00

2020 Topps Pro Debut Copa de La Diversion Relics Gold

*GOLD: .6X TO 1.5X BASIC
STATED ODDS 1:1149 HOBBY
STATED PRINT RUN 50 SER.#'d SETS
CORDJ Daniel Johnson 4.00 10.00
CORLR Luis Robert 40.00 100.00
CORLV Luis Vazquez 15.00 40.00

2020 Topps Pro Debut Distinguished Debut Medallions

STATED ODDS 1:150 HOBBY
STATED PRINT RUN 99 SER.#'d SETS
DDAM Alek Manoah 1.25 3.00
DDAR Adley Rutschman 6.00 15.00
DDAV Anthony Volpe 4.00 10.00
DDBB Brett Baty 3.00 8.00
DDBS Bryson Stott 2.50 6.00
DDBW Blake Walston 1.50 4.00
DDCC Corbin Carroll 1.50 4.00
DDDE Daniel Espino 1.25 3.00
DDES Ethan Small 1.25 3.00
DDGJ Greg Jones 1.25 3.00
DDGK George Kirby 1.50 4.00
DDHB Hunter Bishop 2.00 5.00
DDJJ Josh Jung 2.50 6.00
DDJR Jackson Rutledge 1.50 4.00
DDKC Keoni Cavaco 1.00 2.50
DDKH Kody Hoese 3.00 8.00
DDLD Logan Davidson 1.25 3.00
DDMT Michael Toglia 1.00 2.50
DDNL Nick Lodolo 1.50 4.00
DDQP Quinn Priester 1.50 4.00
DDRG Riley Greene 4.00 10.00
DDRJ Ryan Jensen 1.25 3.00
DDSL Shea Langeliers 2.00 5.00
DDWW Will Wilson 1.25 3.00
DDZT Zack Thompson 1.00 2.50
DDAVA Andrew Vaughn 4.00 10.00
DDBSH Braden Shewmake 1.50 4.00
DDBWJ Bobby Witt Jr. 5.00 12.00
DDCJA CJ Abrams 4.00 10.00
DDJJB JJ Bleday 3.00 8.00

2020 Topps Pro Debut Distinguished Debut Medallions Gold

*GOLD: .5X TO 1.2X BASIC
STATED ODDS 1:291 HOBBY
STATED PRINT RUN 50 SER.#'d SETS
DDBWJ Bobby Witt Jr. 15.00 40.00

2020 Topps Pro Debut Fragments of the Farm Relics

*GREEN/99: .5X TO 1.2X BASIC
*GOLD/50: .6X TO 1.5X BASIC
STATED ODDS 1:31 HOBBY
FFBW Nate Pearson 4.00 10.00
FFFF Max Lazar 2.50 6.00
FFFL Brice Turang 2.00 5.00
FFJB Joey Bart 6.00 15.00
FFLJ Kyle Stowers 2.00 5.00
FFMS Bryson Stott 5.00 12.00
FFOD Bobby Dalbec 5.00 12.00
FFON CJ Abrams 8.00 20.00
FFPT Gray Fenter 2.50 6.00
FFRM Ronny Mauricio 5.00 12.00
FFTS Adam Hall 2.50 6.00
FFFDF Briam Campusano 2.00 5.00
FFMFN Carlos Cortes 2.00 5.00
FFMNJ Luis Garcia 8.00 20.00
FFODC Luis Garcia 3.00 8.00
FFSWN Nick Gordon 3.00 8.00

2020 Topps Pro Debut Future Cornerstones Autographs

STATED ODDS 1:380 HOBBY
PRINT RUN BTW 20-99 COPIES PER
FCAAR Adley Rutschman 30.00 80.00
FCAAV Andrew Vaughn 12.00 30.00
FCABD Bobby Dalbec 6.00 15.00
FCACM Casey Mize 20.00 50.00
FCAGR Grayson Rodriguez 20.00 50.00
FCAHG Hunter Greene 25.00 60.00
FCAJA Jo Adell 30.00 80.00
FCAJB Joey Bart 20.00 50.00
FCAJG Jordan Groshans 12.00 30.00
FCAJK Jarred Kelenic 25.00 60.00
FCAJR Julio Rodriguez 25.00 60.00
FCALG Logan Gilbert 12.00 30.00
FCAMG MacKenzie Gore 20.00 50.00
FCAML Matthew Liberatore 10.00 25.00
FCAMM Matt Manning 25.00 60.00
FCARG Riley Greene 25.00 60.00
FCARL Royce Lewis 15.00 40.00
FCASH Spencer Howard 12.00 30.00
FCASS Sixto Sanchez 20.00 50.00
FCATS Tarik Skubal 20.00 50.00
FCAWF Wander Franco 50.00 120.00
FCABWJ Bobby Witt Jr. 50.00 120.00
FCACJA CJ Abrams 30.00 80.00

2020 Topps Pro Debut Future Cornerstones Autographs Orange

*ORANGE: .6X TO 1.5X p/r 85
*ORANGE: .4X TO 1X p/r 20
STATED ODDS 1:1243 HOBBY
STATED PRINT RUN 25 SER.#'d SETS
FCAAR Adley Rutschman 60.00 150.00
FCABD Bobby Dalbec 12.00 30.00
FCAJB Joey Bart 40.00 100.00
FCAJR Julio Rodriguez 75.00 200.00
FCAMG MacKenzie Gore 40.00 100.00
FCABWJ Bobby Witt Jr. 100.00 250.00

2020 Topps Pro Debut Make Your Pro Debut

COMMON CARD 2.00 5.00
STATED ODDS 1:772 HOBBY
PDCN Caleb Neilson 3.00 8.00

2020 Topps Pro Debut Ready for Flight

STATED ODDS 1:6 HOBBY
*GREEN/99: 1.2X TO 3X BASIC
*ORANGE/25: 2.5X TO 6X BASIC
RFFAB Alec Bohm 1.50 4.00
RFFAK Alex Kirilloff .50 1.25
RFFBD Bobby Dalbec .60 1.50
RFFCM Casey Mize .75 2.00
RFFCP Cristian Pache .75 2.00
RFFDC Dylan Carlson 1.00 2.50
RFFEW Evan White .25 .60
RFFFW Forrest Whitley .25 .60
RFFIA Ian Anderson .60 1.50
RFFJA Jo Adell 1.00 2.50
RFFJI Jonathan India .30 .75
RFFJS Jesus Sanchez .25 .60
RFFKH Ke'Bryan Hayes .25 .60
RFFLG Logan Gilbert .30 .75
RFFMG MacKenzie Gore .50 1.25
RFFMM Matt Manning .30 .75
RFFNJ Nolan Jones .40 1.00
RFFNM Nick Madrigal .75 2.00
RFFNP Nate Pearson .50 1.25
RFFRH Ronaldo Hernandez .25 .60
RFFRL Royce Lewis .60 1.50
RFFRM Ryan Mountcastle .40 1.00
RFFSS Sixto Sanchez .40 1.00
RFFTF Tyler Freeman .30 .75
RFFYD Yusniel Diaz .40 1.00

2020 Topps Pro Debut Ready for Flight Autographs

STATED ODDS 1:1507 HOBBY
STATED PRINT RUN 40 SER.#'d SETS
RFFAB Alec Bohm 25.00 60.00
RFFBD Bobby Dalbec 8.00 20.00
RFFCM Casey Mize 20.00 50.00
RFFEW Evan White 12.00 30.00
RFFJA Jo Adell 60.00 150.00
RFFMG MacKenzie Gore 25.00 60.00
RFFMM Matt Manning 20.00 50.00
RFFNM Nick Madrigal 15.00 40.00
RFFRH Ronaldo Hernandez 4.00 10.00
RFFRL Royce Lewis
RFFRM Ryan Mountcastle 20.00 50.00
RFFTF Tyler Freeman

2020 Topps Pro Debut Tape-Measure Power

STATED ODDS 1:12 HOBBY
TMPAK Alex Kirilloff .50 1.25
TMPAR Adley Rutschman 1.50 4.00
TMPAV Andrew Vaughn 1.00 2.50
TMPDC Dylan Carlson 1.00 2.50
TMPEW Evan White .25 .60
TMPJB Joey Bart .75 2.00
TMPJK Jarred Kelenic 1.50 4.00
TMPJR Julio Rodriguez 1.50 4.00
TMPNG Nolan Gorman .50 1.25
TMPSH Sam Huff .50 1.25

2020 Topps Pro Debut Tape-Measure Power Autographs

STATED ODDS 1:2470 HOBBY
STATED PRINT RUN 40 SER.#'d SETS
TMPAR Adley Rutschman 40.00 100.00
TMPAV Andrew Vaughn 15.00 40.00
TMPEW Evan White 15.00 40.00
TMPJB Joey Bart 20.00 50.00
TMPJK Jarred Kelenic 20.00 50.00
TMPJR Julio Rodriguez 25.00 60.00
TMPSH Sam Huff 8.00 20.00

2020 Topps Pro Debut Autographs

STATED ODDS 1:18 HOBBY
PD1 Wander Franco 40.00 100.00
PD2 Deivi Garcia 10.00 25.00
PD4 Julio Pablo Martinez 2.50 6.00
PD6 Elehuris Montero 3.00 8.00
PD7 Blaze Alexander 2.50 6.00
PD12 Jacob Amaya 6.00 15.00
PD13 Niko Hulsizer 6.00 15.00
PD14 Keoni Cavaco 2.50 6.00
PD15 Brock Deatherage 3.00 8.00
PD20 Ulrich Bojarski 2.50 6.00
PD24 Brailyn Marquez 6.00 15.00
PD25 Adley Rutschman 20.00 50.00
PD27 Diego Cartaya 8.00 20.00
PD31 Nasim Nunez 2.50 6.00
PD32 Jarren Duran 10.00 25.00
PD36 Logan Wyatt 4.00 10.00
PD39 Alec Marsh 3.00 8.00
PD41 Aaron Shortridge 2.50 6.00
PD45 Gus Varland 2.50 6.00
PD46 Alex Faedo 3.00 8.00
PD49 Ryan Mountcastle 4.00 10.00
PD50 Bobby Witt Jr. 40.00 100.00
PD51 Rece Hinds 3.00 8.00
PD57 Luis Patino 8.00 20.00
PD61 Sherten Apostel 10.00 25.00
PD63 Glenallen Hill Jr. 4.00 10.00
PD66 Josh Wolf 4.00 10.00
PD68 Daniel Espino 3.00 8.00
PD70 Victor Mesa Jr. 6.00 15.00
PD72 Nick Lodolo 4.00 10.00
PD73 Seth Johnson 2.50 6.00
PD74 Nick Quintana 5.00 12.00
PD75 Tommy Henry 3.00 8.00
PD76 Grant Gambrell 3.00 8.00
PD77 Josh Smith 5.00 12.00
PD79 Ryne Nelson 3.00 8.00
PD80 Ronny Mauricio 6.00 15.00
PD81 Kendall Williams 4.00 10.00
PD83 Greg Jones 3.00 8.00
PD85 Logan Driscoll 4.00 10.00
PD89 Brennan Malone 2.50 6.00
PD90 Kyren Paris 2.50 6.00
PD91 Victor Victor Mesa 4.00 10.00
PD92 Matthew Thompson 3.00 8.00
PD94 Canaan Smith 5.00 12.00
PD95 Jackson Rutledge 5.00 12.00
PD97 Josiah Gray 4.00 10.00
PD100 Jo Adell 25.00 60.00
PD101 Aaron Schunk 5.00 12.00
PD102 Anthony Volpe 12.00 30.00
PD104 Matthew Lugo 4.00 10.00
PD108 Riley Greene 25.00 60.00
PD109 Dominic Fletcher 2.50 6.00
PD114 Matt Wallner 5.00 12.00
PD116 Everson Pereira 6.00 15.00
PD117 Kody Hoese 8.00 20.00
PD118 Joe Ryan 2.50 6.00
PD122 Gabriel Cancel 4.00 10.00
PD123 Brandon Williamson 4.00 10.00
PD124 Andrew Vaughn 15.00 40.00
PD125 Alec Bohm 12.00 30.00
PD126 JJ Goss 2.50 6.00
PD130 Jake Sanford 4.00 10.00
PD132 Briam Campusano 2.50 6.00
PD134 Matt Canterino 3.00 8.00
PD138 Jordan Balazovic 5.00 12.00
PD139 Joshua Mears 5.00 12.00
PD140 Freudis Nova 2.50 6.00
PD143 Joey Cantillo 2.50 6.00
PD145 T.J. Sikkema 2.50 6.00
PD149 Matt Gorski 4.00 10.00
PD150 Casey Mize 15.00 40.00
PD157 Jared Triolo 4.00 10.00
PD158 George Kirby 4.00 10.00
PD160 Sam Huff 5.00 12.00
PD161 Joey Bart 12.00 30.00
PD170 Kameron Misner 6.00 15.00
PD171 Gunnar Henderson 3.00 8.00
PD173 Drey Jameson 2.50 6.00
PD177 Brett Baty 8.00 20.00
PD178 Cameron Cannon 5.00 12.00
PD179 Marco Luciano 10.00 25.00
PD184 Orelvis Martinez 6.00 15.00
PD185 JJ Bleday 8.00 20.00
PD186 Adam Hall 3.00 8.00
PD189 Keibert Ruiz 3.00 8.00
PD190 Trevor Larnach 5.00 12.00
PD191 Jarred Kelenic 12.00 30.00
PD192 CJ Abrams 15.00 40.00
PD193 Tarik Skubal 8.00 20.00
PD197 Beau Philip 4.00 10.00
PD200 Brayan Rocchio 5.00 12.00

2020 Topps Pro Debut Autographs Blue

*BLUE: .5X TO 1.2X BASIC
STATED ODDS 1:82 HOBBY
STATED PRINT RUN 150 SER.#'d SETS
PD104 Matthew Lugo 6.00 15.00
PD196 Kristian Robinson 10.00 25.00

2020 Topps Pro Debut Autographs Gold

*GOLD: .6X TO 1.5X BASIC
STATED ODDS 1:153 HOBBY
STATED PRINT RUN 50 SER.#'d SETS
PD15 Brock Deatherage 10.00 25.00
PD25 Adley Rutschman 30.00 80.00
PD27 Diego Cartaya 20.00 50.00
PD36 Logan Wyatt 15.00 40.00
PD49 Ryan Mountcastle 8.00 20.00
PD57 Luis Patino 15.00 40.00
PD80 Ronny Mauricio 12.00 30.00
PD100 Jo Adell 40.00 100.00
PD102 Anthony Volpe 25.00 60.00
PD104 Matthew Lugo 8.00 20.00
PD170 Kameron Misner 15.00 40.00
PD179 Marco Luciano 30.00 80.00
PD184 Orelvis Martinez 12.00 30.00
PD196 Kristian Robinson 20.00 50.00

2020 Topps Pro Debut Autographs Green

*GREEN: .5X TO 1.2X BASIC
STATED ODDS 1:99 HOBBY
STATED PRINT RUN 99 SER.#'d SETS
PD36 Logan Wyatt 8.00 20.00
PD102 Anthony Volpe 20.00 50.00
PD104 Matthew Lugo 6.00 15.00
PD179 Marco Luciano 25.00 60.00
PD196 Kristian Robinson 10.00 25.00

2020 Topps Pro Debut Autographs Orange

*ORANGE: 2.5X TO 6X BASIC
STATED ODDS 1:292 HOBBY
STATED PRINT RUN 25 SER.#'d SETS
PD15 Brock Deatherage 12.00 30.00
PD25 Adley Rutschman 40.00 100.00
PD27 Diego Cartaya 25.00 60.00
PD36 Logan Wyatt 20.00 50.00
PD49 Ryan Mountcastle 10.00 25.00
PD57 Luis Patino 40.00 100.00
PD80 Ronny Mauricio 20.00 50.00
PD100 Jo Adell 60.00 150.00
PD102 Anthony Volpe 30.00 80.00
PD104 Matthew Lugo 10.00 25.00
PD116 Everson Pereira 15.00 40.00
PD124 Andrew Vaughn 40.00 100.00
PD170 Kameron Misner 20.00 50.00
PD179 Marco Luciano 40.00 100.00
PD184 Orelvis Martinez 25.00 60.00
PD196 Kristian Robinson 25.00 60.00

2002 USA Baseball National Team

This set, which was issued as a fund raiser for USA baseball was available through the USA baseball web site for an SRP of $19.99. Each factory set contained regular issue cards and one autograph and one jersey card. According to USA Baseball, no more than 10,000 sets were printed.

COMP FACT SET (32) 10.00 25.00
COMPLETE SET (30) 6.00 15.00
STATED PRINT RUN 10,000 SETS
FACTORY SET PRICE IS FOR SEALED SET
PRODUCED BY UPPER DECK
1 Chad Cordero .75 2.00
2 Philip Humber .60 1.50
3 Grant Johnson .40 1.00
4 Wes Littleton .30 .75
5 Kyle Sleeth .30 .75
6 Huston Street .75 2.00
7 Brad Sullivan .30 .75
8 Bob Zimmermann .20 .50
9 Abe Alvarez .30 .75
10 Kyle Bakker .20 .50
11 Clint Sammons .30 .75
12 Landon Powell .30 .75
13 Michael Aubrey .40 1.00
14 Aaron Hill .40 1.00
15 Conor Jackson 1.00 2.50
16 Eric Patterson .40 1.00
17 Dustin Pedroia 1.00 2.50
18 Rickie Weeks 1.50 4.00
19 Shane Costa .20 .50
20 Mark Jurich .20 .50
21 Sam Fuld .60 1.50
22 Carlos Quentin 1.00 2.50
23 Ryan Garko .50 1.25
24 Lelo Prado .20 .50
25 Terry Alexander .20 .50
26 Sunny Golloway .20 .50
27 Terry Rupp CO .20 .50
28 Team USA .20 .50
29 Team USA w Flag .20 .50
30 Team USA Checklist .20 .50

2002 USA Baseball National Team Jerseys

Inserted one per Team USA factory set, these 22 cards featured game worn swatches from members of Team USA. Each of these cards were issued to a stated print run of 475 serial numbered sets.

AA Abe Alvarez 4.00 10.00
AH Aaron Hill 4.00 10.00
BS Brad Sullivan 4.00 10.00
BZ Bob Zimmermann 3.00 8.00
CC Chad Cordero 6.00 15.00
CJ Conor Jackson 8.00 20.00
CQ Carlos Quentin 8.00 20.00
CS Clint Sammons 4.00 10.00
DP Dustin Pedroia 6.00 15.00
EP Eric Patterson 4.00 10.00
GJ Grant Johnson 4.00 10.00
HS Huston Street 8.00 20.00
KB Kyle Bakker 3.00 8.00
KS Kyle Sleeth 4.00 10.00
LP Landon Powell 4.00 10.00
MA Michael Aubrey 4.00 10.00

MJ Mark Jurich 3.00 8.00
PH Philip Humber 4.00 10.00
RW Rickie Weeks 10.00 25.00
SC Shane Costa 3.00 8.00
SF Sam Fuld 5.00 12.00
WL Wes Littleton 4.00 10.00

2002 USA Baseball National Team Signatures

Inserted one per Team USA factory set, these 27 cards feature signatures of Team USA alumni. Each of these cards were issued to a stated print run of 375 serial numbered sets.
ONE PER FACTORY SET
STATED PRINT RUN 375 SERIAL #'d SETS
BC Bobby Crosby 4.00 10.00
BD Ben Diggins 4.00 10.00
CE Clint Everts 4.00 10.00
CK Casey Kotchman 10.00 25.00
DK David Krynzel 4.00 10.00
JB Josh Bard 4.00 10.00
JF Jeff Francoeur 12.50 30.00
JH J.J. Hardy 6.00 15.00
JJ Jacque Jones 4.00 10.00
JK Josh Karp 4.00 10.00
JL James Loney 6.00 15.00
JM Joe Mauer 20.00 50.00
JS Jason Stanford 4.00 10.00
JW Justin Wayne 4.00 10.00
KD Keoni DeRenne 4.00 10.00
KH Koyie Hill 4.00 10.00
LD Lenny Dinardo 4.00 10.00
MG Mike Gosling 4.00 10.00
MH Matt Holliday 10.00 25.00
MP Mark Prior 8.00 20.00
MW Matt Whitney 4.00 10.00
PS Phil Seibel 4.00 10.00
RH Ryan Howard 30.00 60.00
SB Sean Burnett 4.00 10.00
SN Shane Nance 4.00 10.00
WB Willie Bloomquist 8.00 20.00
ZS Zack Segovia 4.00 10.00

2003 USA Baseball National Team

This 30-card factory set was issued at a SRP of $30 and featured 27 player cards along with two signature cards and one signed jersey card per factory set. This set honored players who were involved with the 2003 USA baseball team as well as the coaches.
COMP.FACT.SET (30) 30.00 50.00
COMPLETE SET (27) 6.00 15.00
FACTORY SET PRICE IS FOR SEALED SETS
PRODUCED BY UPPER DECK
1 Justin Orenduff .40 1.00
2 Micah Owings .30 .75
3 Steven Register .20 .50
4 Huston Street .75 2.00
5 Justin Verlander 8.00 20.00
6 Jered Weaver 1.25 3.00
7 Matt Campbell .20 .50
8 Stephen Head .30 .75
9 Mark Romanczuk .20 .50
10 Jeff Clement .75 2.00
11 Mike Nickeas .30 .75
12 Tyler Greene .40 1.00
13 Paul Janish .30 .75
14 Jeff Larish .30 .75
15 Eric Patterson .40 1.00
16 Dustin Pedroia .60 1.50
17 Michael Griffin .20 .50
18 Brent Lillibridge .20 .50
19 Danny Putnam .40 1.00
20 Seth Smith .50 1.25
21 Ray Tanner CO .20 .50
22 Dick Cooke CO .20 .50
23 Mark Scalf CO .20 .50
24 Mike Weathers CO .20 .50
25 Team Card .20 .50
26 Commemorative Card .20 .50
27 Checklist .20 .50

2003 USA Baseball National Team Signatures Blue

*BLUE AU: .5X TO 1.2X RED AU
TWO BLUE/RED AUTOS PER FACTORY SET
STATED PRINT RUN 250 SERIAL #'d SETS
5 Justin Verlander 40.00 100.00

2003 USA Baseball National Team Signatures Red

TWO BLUE/RED AUTOS PER FACTORY SET
STATED PRINT RUN 750 SERIAL #'d SETS
1 Justin Orenduff 5.00 12.00
2 Micah Owings 4.00 10.00
3 Steven Register 3.00 8.00
4 Huston Street 8.00 20.00
5 Justin Verlander 30.00 80.00
6 Jered Weaver 8.00 20.00
7 Matt Campbell 3.00 8.00
8 Stephen Head 4.00 10.00
9 Mark Romanczuk 3.00 8.00
10 Jeff Clement 8.00 20.00
11 Mike Nickeas 4.00 10.00
12 Tyler Greene 5.00 12.00
13 Paul Janish 5.00 12.00
14 Jeff Larish 4.00 10.00
15 Eric Patterson 5.00 12.00
16 Dustin Pedroia 15.00 40.00
17 Michael Griffin 3.00 8.00
18 Brent Lillibridge 3.00 8.00
19 Danny Putnam 5.00 12.00
20 Seth Smith 5.00 12.00

2003 USA Baseball National Team Signed Jersey Blue

*BLUE JSY: .5X TO 1.2X RED JSY
ONE BLUE/RED AU JSY PER FACTORY SET
STATED PRINT RUN 150 SERIAL #'d SETS

2003 USA Baseball National Team Signed Jersey Red

ONE BLUE/RED AU JSY PER FACTORY SET
STATED PRINT RUN 350 SERIAL #'d SETS
1 Justin Orenduff 6.00 15.00
2 Micah Owings 5.00 12.00
3 Steven Register 3.00 8.00
4 Huston Street 10.00 25.00
5 Justin Verlander 60.00 150.00
6 Jered Weaver 6.00 15.00
7 Matt Campbell 3.00 8.00
8 Stephen Head 5.00 12.00
9 Mark Romanczuk 3.00 8.00
10 Jeff Clement 6.00 15.00
11 Mike Nickeas 5.00 12.00
12 Tyler Greene 6.00 15.00
13 Paul Janish 6.00 15.00
14 Jeff Larish 5.00 12.00
15 Eric Patterson 6.00 15.00
16 Dustin Pedroia 12.50 30.00
17 Michael Griffin 3.00 8.00
18 Brent Lillibridge 3.00 8.00
19 Danny Putnam 6.00 15.00
20 Seth Smith 6.00 15.00

2004 USA Baseball 25th Anniversary

This 204-card set was issued as a factory release from Upper Deck. The set featuring 200 player cards, 3 autographs and one game-jersey set was issued with an $49.99 SRP.
COMP.FACT.SET (204) 40.00 50.00
COMPLETE SET (200) 10.00 25.00
COMMON CARD (1-200) .08 .25
COMMON RC YR .08 .25
ISSUED IN FACTORY SET FORM
PRODUCED BY UPPER DECK
1 Jim Abbott .10 .25
2 Brent Abernathy .10 .25
3 Kurt Ainsworth .10 .25
4 Abe Alvarez .10 .25
5 Matt Anderson .10 .25
6 Jeff Austin .10 .25
7 Justin Wayne .10 .25
8 Scott Bankhead .10 .25
9 Josh Bard .10 .25
10 Michael Barrett .10 .25
11 Mark Bellhorn .10 .25
12 Buddy Bell .10 .25
13 Andy Benes .10 .25
14 Kris Benson .10 .25
15 Peter Bergeron .10 .25
16 Rocky Biddle .10 .25
17 Casey Blake .10 .25
18 Willie Bloomquist .10 .25
19 Jeremy Bonderman .10 .25
20 Jeff Weaver .10 .25
21 Joe Borchard .10 .25
22 Rickie Weeks .10 .25
23 Rob Bowen .10 .25
24 Milton Bradley .10 .25
25 Dan Wheeler .10 .25
26 Ben Broussard .10 .25
27 Brian Bruney .10 .25
28 Mark Budzinski .10 .25
29 Kirk Bullinger .10 .25
30 Chris Burke .10 .25
31 Sean Burnett .10 .25
32 Jeromy Burnitz .10 .25
33 Pat Burrell .10 .25
34 Sean Burroughs .10 .25
35 Paul Byrd .10 .25
36 Chris Capuano .10 .25
37 Scott Cassidy .10 .25
38 Will Clark .15 .40
39 Chad Cordero .10 .25
40 Carl Crawford .15 .40
41 Bobby Crosby .10 .25
42 Brad Wilkerson .10 .25
43 Michael Cuddyer .10 .25
44 Ben Davis .10 .25
45 Gookie Dawkins .10 .25
46 Rod Dedeaux .10 .25
47 R.A. Dickey .15 .40
48 Ben Diggins .10 .25
49 Lenny DiNardo .10 .25
50 Ryan Drese .10 .25
51 Tim Drew .10 .25
52 Todd Williams .10 .25
53 Justin Duchscherer .10 .25
54 J.D. Durbin .10 .25
55 Scott Elarton .10 .25
56 Adam Everett .10 .25
57 Dan Wilson .10 .25
58 Steve Finley .10 .25
59 Casey Fossum .10 .25
60 Terry Francona .10 .25
61 Ryan Franklin .10 .25
62 Ryan Freel .10 .25
63 John VanBenschoten .10 .25
64 Nomar Garciaparra .15 .40
65 Chris George .10 .25
66 Jody Gerut .10 .25
67 Jason Giambi .10 .25
68 Matt Ginter .10 .25
69 Troy Glaus .10 .25
70 Tom Goodwin .10 .25
71 Mike Gosling .10 .25
72 Danny Graves .10 .25
73 Shawn Green .10 .25
74 Khalil Greene .15 .40
75 Todd Greene .10 .25
76 Seth Greisinger .10 .25
77 Gabe Gross .10 .25
78 Jeffrey Hammonds .10 .25
79 Aaron Heilman .10 .25
80 Paul Wilson .10 .25
81 Todd Helton .15 .40
82 Dustin Hermanson .10 .25
83 Bobby Hill .10 .25
84 Koyie Hill .10 .25
85 A.J. Hinch .10 .25
86 Matt Holliday .25 .60
87 Ted Wood .10 .25
88 Ken Huckaby .10 .25
89 Orlando Hudson .10 .25
90 Ernie Young .10 .25
91 Jason Jennings .10 .25
92 Charles Johnson .10 .25
93 Jacque Jones .10 .25
94 Matt Kata .10 .25
95 Austin Kearns .10 .25
96 Adam Kennedy .10 .25
97 Brooks Kieschnick .10 .25
98 Jesse Crain .15 .40
99 Scott Kazmir .50 1.25
100 Billy Koch .10 .25
101 Paul Konerko .15 .40
102 Graham Koonce .10 .25
103 Casey Kotchman .10 .25
104 Chris Snyder .10 .25
105 Nick Swisher .15 .40
106 Gerald Laird .10 .25
107 Barry Larkin .15 .40
108 Mike Lamb .10 .25
109 Tommy Lasorda .15 .40
110 Matt LeCroy .10 .25
111 Travis Lee .10 .25
112 Justin Leone .10 .25
113 John Vanderwal .10 .25
114 Braden Looper .10 .25
115 Shane Loux .10 .25
116 Ryan Ludwick .10 .25
117 Jason Varitek .25 .60
118 Ryan Madson .10 .25
119 Dave Magadan .10 .25
120 Tino Martinez .15 .40
121 Joe Mauer .20 .50
122 David McCarty .10 .25
123 Robin Ventura .10 .25
124 Jack McDowell .10 .25
125 Todd Walker .10 .25
126 Mark McGwire .40 1.00
127 Gil Meche .10 .25
128 Doug Mientkiewicz .10 .25
129 Matt Morris .10 .25
130 Warren Morris .10 .25
131 Mark Mulder .10 .25
132 Calvin Murray .10 .25
133 Eric Munson .10 .25
134 Mike Mussina .15 .40
135 Xavier Nady .10 .25
136 Shane Nance .10 .25
137 Mike Neill .10 .25
138 Augie Ojeda .10 .25
139 John Olerud .10 .25
140 Gregg Olson .10 .25
141 Roy Oswalt .15 .40
142 Jim Parque .10 .25
143 John Patterson .10 .25
144 Brad Penny .10 .25
145 Jay Powell .10 .25
146 Mark Prior .15 .40
147 Horacio Ramirez .10 .25
148 Jon Rauch .10 .25
149 Jeremy Reed .10 .25
150 Bob Watson .10 .25
151 Matt Riley .10 .25
152 Brian Roberts .10 .25
153 Dave Roberts .15 .40
154 Frank Robinson .15 .40
155 J.C. Romero .10 .25
156 David Ross .10 .25
157 Cory Vance .10 .25
158 Kirk Saarloos .10 .25
159 Anthony Sanders .10 .25
160 Dane Sardinha .10 .25
161 Bobby Seay .10 .25
162 Phil Seibel .10 .25
163 Aaron Sele .10 .25
164 Ben Sheets .10 .25
165 Paul Shuey .10 .25
166 Grady Sizemore .15 .40
167 Reggie Smith .10 .25
168 John Smoltz .25 .60
169 Zach Sorenson .10 .25
170 Scott Spezio .10 .25
171 Ed Sprague .10 .25
172 Jason Stanford .10 .25
173 Dave Stewart .10 .25
174 Scott Stewart .10 .25
175 B.J. Surhoff .10 .25
176 Bill Swift .10 .25
177 Mike Tonis .10 .25
178 Jason Tyner .10 .25
179 Michael Tucker .10 .25
180 B.J. Upton .15 .40
181 Eric Valent .10 .25
182 Ron Villone .10 .25
183 00 Team beats Cuba GM .08 .25
184 Jim Abbott GM .10 .25
185 1996 Atlanta GM .08 .25
186 1984 Los Angeles GM .08 .25
187 Mient .15 .40
Las
Sheets
Neill GM
188 Mike Neill Hit GM .10 .25
189 96 Olympic Team GM .08 .25
190 Nomar Garciaparra GM .15 .40
191 03 Nat'l Team GM .08 .25
192 95 Jr. Nat'l Team GM .08 .25
193 99 Jr. Nat'l Team GM .08 .25
194 98 Youth Nat'l Team GM .08 .25
195 Mark McGwire GM .40 1.00
196 00 Nat'l Team GM .08 .25
197 Stanford University GM .08 .25
198 Mike Neill HR GM .10 .25
199 Marcus Jensen GM .10 .25
200 Joe Mauer GM .20 .50

2004 USA Baseball 25th Anniversary Game Jersey

ONE PER FACTORY SET
PRINT RUNS B/WN 50-850 #'d COPIES PER
AE Adam Everett/850 2.00 5.00
BB Brian Bruney/195 2.00 5.00
BS Ben Sheets/850 3.00 8.00
BW Brad Wilkerson/850 2.00 5.00
CB Chris Burke/850 3.00 8.00
DH Dustin Hermanson/850 2.00 5.00
DM Doug Mientkiewicz/850 3.00 8.00
DS Dave Stewart/850 3.00 8.00
EM Eric Munson/50 6.00 15.00
FR Frank Robinson/850 4.00 10.00
GG Gabe Gross/850 2.00 5.00
GK Graham Koonce/850 2.00 5.00
GL Gerald Laird/150 2.00 5.00
GS Grady Sizemore/850 4.00 10.00
HR Horacio Ramirez/850 2.00 5.00
JD Justin Duchscherer/850 2.00 5.00
JG Jason Giambi/850 3.00 8.00
JL Justin Leone/850 3.00 8.00
JM Joe Mauer/850 3.00 8.00
JR Jon Rauch/850 2.00 5.00
JV John VanBenschoten/850 2.00 5.00
JW Jeff Weaver/850 2.00 5.00
KA Kurt Ainsworth/850 2.00 5.00
MH Matt Holliday/850 5.00 12.00
MP Mark Prior/550 4.00 10.00
MR Mike Rouse/130 2.00 5.00
RE Jeremy Reed/850 3.00 8.00
RO Roy Oswalt/850 3.00 8.00
SB Sean Burroughs/850 2.00 5.00
XN Xavier Nady/850 2.00 5.00

2004 USA Baseball 25th Anniversary Signatures Black Ink

OVERALL AU ODDS 3 PER FACTORY SET
PRINT RUNS B/WN 20-510 COPIES PER
NO MCGWIRE PRICING DUE TO SCARCITY
ABB Jim Abbott/180 12.50 30.00
ABE Brent Abernathy/360 4.00 10.00
AIN Kurt Ainsworth/360 4.00 10.00
ALV Abe Alvarez/360 6.00 15.00
AND Matt Anderson/360 4.00 10.00
AUS Jeff Austin/360 4.00 10.00
BANK Scott Bankhead/360 4.00 10.00
BARD Josh Bard/350 4.00 10.00
BARR Michael Barrett/360 4.00 10.00
BEN Andy Benes/350 4.00 10.00
BELL Buddy Bell/81 10.00 25.00
BENS Kris Benson/180 6.00 15.00
BERG Peter Bergeron/360 4.00 10.00
BLA Casey Blake/180 4.00 10.00
BLO Willie Bloomquist/175 6.00 15.00
BON Jeremy Bonderman/150 6.00 15.00
BOR Joe Borchard/350 4.00 10.00
BRO Ben Broussard/210 4.00 10.00
BRU Brian Bruney/160 4.00 10.00
BRAD Milton Bradley/360 6.00 15.00
BU Sean Burnett/180 4.00 10.00
BUD Mark Budzinski/360 4.00 10.00
BUR Pat Burrell/360 6.00 15.00
BULL Kirk Bullinger/360 4.00 10.00
BURK Chris Burke/350 6.00 15.00
BURN Jeromy Burnitz/360 6.00 15.00
BURR Sean Burroughs/360 4.00 10.00
BYRD Paul Byrd/360 4.00 10.00
CAP Chris Capuano/150 4.00 10.00
CASS Scott Cassidy/360 4.00 10.00
CLA Will Clark/60 30.00 60.00
COR Chad Cordero/360 6.00 15.00
CR Jesse Crain/180 6.00 15.00
CRA Carl Crawford/60 15.00 40.00
CUD Michael Cuddyer/370 6.00 15.00
DAV Ben Davis/344 4.00 10.00
DED Rod Dedeaux/29 20.00 50.00
DIC R.A. Dickey/180 30.00 60.00
DIG Ben Diggins/180 4.00 10.00
DIN Lenny DiNardo/150 4.00 10.00
DRA Danny Graves/360 4.00 10.00
DRE Ryan Drese/180 4.00 10.00
DREW Tim Drew/360 4.00 10.00
DUR J.D. Durbin/180 4.00 10.00
DUCH Justin Duchscherer/210 4.00 10.00
ELAR Scott Elarton/180 4.00 10.00
EVER Adam Everett/360 4.00 10.00
FIN Steve Finley/360 6.00 15.00
FOSS Casey Fossum/320 4.00 10.00
FRA Ryan Franklin/360 4.00 10.00
FRE Ryan Freel/360 4.00 10.00
FRAN Terry Francona/150 15.00 60.00
GEO Chris George/360 4.00 10.00
GER Jody Gerut/350 4.00 10.00
GIN Matt Ginter/179 4.00 10.00
GIAM Jason Giambi/60 20.00 60.00
GLA Troy Glaus/120 15.00 40.00
GOS Mike Gosling/150 4.00 10.00
GR Shawn Green/150 6.00 15.00
GRE Khalil Greene/180 10.00 25.00
GRO Gabe Gross/150 4.00 10.00
GREE Todd Greene/120 6.00 15.00
GREI Seth Greisinger/360 4.00 10.00
HAM Jeffrey Hammonds/150 4.00 10.00
HEIL Aaron Heilman/350 4.00 10.00
HELT Todd Helton/71 15.00 40.00
HERM Dustin Hermanson/150 4.00 10.00
HI Bobby Hill/360 4.00 10.00
HIN A.J. Hinch/360 4.00 10.00
HILL Koyie Hill/150 4.00 10.00
HUD Orlando Hudson/360 4.00 10.00
HUCK Ken Huckaby/360 4.00 10.00
JENN Jason Jennings/350 4.00 10.00
JON Jacque Jones/150 6.00 15.00
KAZ Scott Kazmir/360 6.00 15.00
KATA Matt Kata/350 4.00 10.00
KENN Adam Kennedy/150 4.00 10.00
KIES Brooks Kieschnick/360 4.00 10.00
KON Paul Konerko/179 10.00 25.00
KOO Graham Koonce/360 4.00 10.00
KOCH Billy Koch/71 10.00 25.00
KOTC Casey Kotchman/150 6.00 15.00
LAR Barry Larkin/60 30.00 150.00
LAMB Mike Lamb/360 4.00 10.00
LEC Matt LeCroy/360 4.00 10.00
LEE Travis Lee/360 4.00 10.00
LEO Justin Leone/150 6.00 15.00
LOO Braden Looper/360 4.00 10.00
LOUX Shane Loux/360 4.00 10.00
MAD Ryan Madson/360 4.00 10.00
MAG Dave Magadan/360 4.00 10.00
MAU Joe Mauer/360 12.00 30.00
MART Tino Martinez/360 10.00 25.00
MCC David McCarty/360 6.00 15.00
MCDO Jack McDowell/60 10.00 25.00
MEC Gil Meche/360 4.00 10.00
MIE Doug Mientkiewicz/300 6.00 15.00
MOR Matt Morris/150 6.00 15.00
MORR Warren Morris/360 4.00 10.00
MUL Mark Mulder/180 6.00 15.00
MUN Eric Munson/510 4.00 10.00
MURR Calvin Murray/360 4.00 10.00
MUSS Mike Mussina/60 20.00 100.00
NAN Shane Nance/150 4.00 10.00
NADY Xavier Nady/360 4.00 10.00
NEI Mike Neill/360 4.00 10.00
OJE Augie Ojeda/360 4.00 10.00
OLE John Olerud/360 10.00 25.00
OLS Gregg Olson/180 4.00 10.00
OSW Roy Oswalt/350 6.00 15.00
PARQ Jim Parque/360 4.00 10.00
PATT John Patterson/210 4.00 10.00
PEN Brad Penny/360 4.00 10.00
POW Jay Powell/180 4.00 10.00
PRI Mark Prior/350 4.00 10.00
RAM Horacio Ramirez/150 4.00 10.00
RAU Jon Rauch/359 4.00 10.00
REED Jeremy Reed/180 12.50 30.00
RIL Matt Riley/60 10.00 25.00
ROB Brian Roberts/60 15.00 40.00
ROM J.C. Romero/360 4.00 10.00
ROBE Dave Roberts/360 8.00 20.00
ROSS David Ross/360 6.00 15.00
SAR Dane Sardinha/360 4.00 10.00
SAAR Kirk Saarloos/360 4.00 10.00
SAND Anthony Sanders/360 4.00 10.00
SEI Phil Seibel/150 4.00 10.00
SEAY Bobby Seay/360 4.00 10.00
SELE Aaron Sele/360 4.00 10.00
SHE Ben Sheets/143 10.00 25.00
SHU Paul Shuey/360 4.00 10.00
SIZE Grady Sizemore/160 10.00 25.00
SMI Reggie Smith/360 6.00 15.00
SMO John Smoltz/360 12.50 30.00
SNY Chris Snyder/360 4.00 10.00
SPI Scott Spiezio/360 4.00 10.00
SPR Ed Sprague/360 4.00 10.00
STE Dave Stewart/180 6.00 15.00
STEW Scott Stewart/360 4.00 10.00
SUR B.J. Surhoff/60 15.00 40.00
SWI Nick Swisher/360 10.00 25.00
SWIF Bill Swift/360 4.00 10.00
TON Mike Tonis/350 4.00 10.00
TUCK Michael Tucker/150 4.00 10.00
TYN Jason Tyner/360 4.00 10.00
VAL Eric Valent/360 4.00 10.00
VAN Cory Vance/360 4.00 10.00
VAR Jason Varitek/360 15.00 40.00
VANB John VanBenschoten/180 4.00 10.00
VAND John Vanderwal/360 4.00 10.00
VENT Robin Ventura/360 6.00 15.00
WAT Bob Watson/150 4.00 10.00
WAY Justin Wayne/150 4.00 10.00
WALK Todd Walker/60 10.00 25.00
WEA Jeff Weaver/360 6.00 15.00
WEEK Rickie Weeks/360 6.00 15.00
WHEE Dan Wheeler/360 6.00 15.00
WI Dan Wilson/360 6.00 15.00
WIL Paul Wilson/360 4.00 10.00
WOOD Ted Wood/330 4.00 10.00
YOUN Ernie Young/350 4.00 10.00
VILL Ron Villone/359 4.00 10.00
WILL Todd Williams/360 4.00 10.00

2004 USA Baseball 25th Anniversary Signatures Blue Ink

*p/r 130-150: .4X TO 1X BLK p/r 300-510
*p/r 130-150: .4X TO 1X BLK p/r 143-210
*p/r 80-120: .4X TO 1X BLK p/r 300-510
*p/r 80-120: .4X TO 1X BLK p/r 143-210
*p/r 40-60: .6X TO 1.5X BLK p/r 300-510
*p/r 40-60: .6X TO 1.5X BLK p/r 143-210
*p/r 40-60: .4X TO 1X BLK p/r 71-120
*p/r 20-30: .75X TO 2X BLK p/r 143-210
*p/r 20-30: .5X TO 1.2X BLK p/r 71-120
*p/r 20-30: .4X TO 1X BLK p/r 60
*p/r 20-30: .4X TO 1X BLK p/r 20-29
*p/r 18: .6X TO 1.5X BLK p/r 71-120
OVERALL AU ODDS 3 PER FACTORY SET
PRINT RUNS B/WN 6-510 COPIES PER
NO PRICING ON QTY OF 6 OR LESS
BOW Rob Bowen/510 4.00 10.00
DIC R.A. Dickey/60 40.00 100.00
FRAN Terry Francona/40 15.00 80.00
GAR Nomar Garciaparra/60 6.00 15.00
GRE Khalil Greene/60 15.00 40.00
KEAR Austin Kearns/110 6.00 15.00
LAS Tommy Lasorda/30 20.00 50.00
LUD Ryan Ludwick/450 8.00 20.00
MAU Joe Mauer/120 12.00 30.00
ROBI Frank Robinson/30 12.50 30.00
SOR Zach Sorenson/450 4.00 10.00
STAN Jason Stanford/450 4.00 10.00
SWI Nick Swisher/110 10.00 25.00
UPT B.J. Upton/120 15.00 40.00

2004 USA Baseball 25th Anniversary Signatures Red Ink

*p/r 40-60: .6X TO 1.5X BLK p/r 300-510
*p/r 40-60: .6X TO 1.5X BLK p/r 143-210
*p/r 20-30: .75X TO 2X BLK p/r 300-510
*p/r 20-30: .75X TO 2X BLK p/r 143-210
*p/r 20-30: .5X TO 1.2X BLK p/r 71-120
OVERALL AU ODDS 3 PER FACTORY SET
PRINT RUNS B/WN 3-60 COPIES PER
NO PRICING ON QTY OF 10 OR LESS
CRO Bobby Crosby/60 10.00 25.00
GAR Nomar Garciaparra/30 25.00 60.00
KEAR Austin Kearns/30 10.00 25.00
LUD Ryan Ludwick/50 12.50 30.00
SOR Zach Sorenson/50 6.00 15.00
STAN Jason Stanford/50 6.00 15.00
SWI Nick Swisher/30 20.00 50.00
UPT B.J. Upton/20 20.00 50.00

2004-05 USA Baseball National Team

COMP.FACT SET (28) 30.00 50.00
COMPLETE SET (23) 5.00 12.00
COMMON CARD (28-50) .15 .40
CL 28-50 PICKS UP FROM 03 UD USA SET
28 Alex Gordon .50 1.25
29 Brett Hayes .15 .40
30 Cesar Ramos .15 .40
31 Chris Valaika .15 .40
32 Daniel Bard .15 .40
33 Drew Stubbs .40 1.00
34 Ian Kennedy .40 1.00
35 J. Brent Cox .15 .40
36 Jed Lowrie .15 .40
37 Jeff Clement .25 .60
38 Joey Devine .15 .40
39 John Mayberry Jr. .40 1.00
40 Luke Hochevar .50 1.25
41 Mark Romanczuk .15 .40
42 Mike Pelfrey .40 1.00
43 Ricky Romero .25 .60
44 Ryan Zimmerman .75 2.00
45 Stephen Kahn .15 .40
46 Taylor Teagarden .25 .60
47 Travis Buck .15 .40
48 Trevor Crowe .15 .40
49 Troy Tulowitzki 2.00 5.00
50 Team Checklist .15 .40

2004-05 USA Baseball National Team Alumni Signatures Black

PRINT RUNS B/WN 330-360 COPIES PER
*BLUE: .5X TO 1.2X BLACK SIG
*BLUE RC YR: .6X TO 1.5X BLACK SIG
BLUE PRINT RUNS B/WN 100-120 PER
GREEN PRINT RUN 2 SERIAL #'d SETS
NO GREEN PRICING DUE TO SCARCITY
OVERALL ALUMNI AU ODDS TWO PER BOX
AH Aaron Hill/350 6.00 15.00
AS Andy Sisco/360 3.00 8.00
BB Bobby Brownlie/360 2.50 6.00
BO Bryan Opdyke/350 3.00 8.00
BS Brad Sullivan/350 3.00 8.00
BU Bryan Bullington/350 3.00 8.00
BZ Bob Zimmermann/360 3.00 8.00
CB Chad Billingsley/360 5.00 12.00
CJ C.J. Bressoud/360 3.00 8.00
CL Chris Lubanski/360 3.00 8.00
CM Casey Myers/360 3.00 8.00
CQ Carlos Quentin/350 8.00 20.00
CT Chuck Tiffany/360 6.00 15.00
DM Drew Meyer/360 3.00 8.00
DS Denard Span/360 3.00 8.00
DY Delmon Young/360 8.00 20.00
GA Jake Gautreau/360 3.00 8.00
GG Geoff Goetz/360 3.00 8.00
IS Ian Stewart/360 4.00 10.00
JA Conor Jackson/350 8.00 20.00
JG John Gall/350 3.00 8.00
JH Javi Herrera/360 3.00 8.00
JM Josh McKinley/360 3.00 8.00
JS Jarrod Saltalamacchia/350 8.00 20.00
JW Josh Wilson/360 3.00 8.00
KH Kevin Howard/360 3.00 8.00
KS Kyle Sleeth/350 4.00 10.00
LM Lastings Milledge/360 6.00 15.00
MA Michael Aubrey/360 6.00 15.00
MC Matt Chico/360 3.00 8.00
MR Michael Rogers/360 3.00 8.00
MS Matt Smith/360 3.00 8.00
MY Corey Myers/360 3.00 8.00
PO Pat Osborn/360 UER 3.00 8.00
RG Ryan Garko/360 6.00 15.00
RO Mike Rouse/330 3.00 8.00
SC Shane Costa/360 3.00 8.00
TB Tagg Bozied/360 3.00 8.00
TG Tyrell Godwin/360 3.00 8.00
TR Tony Richie/330 3.00 8.00

2004-05 USA Baseball National Team Alumni Signatures Red

*RED p/r 50: .75X TO 2X BLACK SIG
*RED p/r 20-30: 1X TO 2.5X BLACK SIG
*RED p/r 18: 1.5X TO 4X BLACK SIG
OVERALL ALUMNI AU ODDS TWO PER BOX
PRINT RUNS B/WN 18-50 COPIES PER
NO RC YR PRICING ON QTY OF 30 OR LESS
TB Tagg Bozied/20 30.00 60.00

2004-05 USA Baseball National Team Signatures Black

STATED PRINT RUN 595 SERIAL #'d SETS
*BLUE: .5X TO 1.2X BLACK SIG
BLUE PRINT RUN 250 SERIAL #'d SETS
*RED: .75X TO 2X BLACK SIG
RED PRINT RUN 100 SERIAL #'d SETS
OVERALL AU ODDS TWO PER BOX
21 Alex Gordon 10.00 25.00
22 Brett Hayes 4.00 10.00
23 Cesar Ramos 5.00 12.00
24 Chris Valaika 4.00 10.00
25 Daniel Bard 4.00 10.00
26 Drew Stubbs 6.00 15.00
27 Ian Kennedy 5.00 12.00
28 J. Brent Cox 5.00 12.00
29 Jed Lowrie 6.00 15.00
30 Jeff Clement 8.00 20.00
31 Joey Devine 5.00 12.00
32 John Mayberry Jr. 6.00 15.00
33 Luke Hochevar 10.00 25.00
34 Mark Romanczuk 4.00 10.00
35 Mike Pelfrey 10.00 25.00
36 Ricky Romero 8.00 20.00
37 Ryan Zimmerman 8.00 20.00
38 Stephen Kahn 4.00 10.00
39 Taylor Teagarden 5.00 12.00
40 Travis Buck 5.00 12.00
41 Trevor Crowe 4.00 10.00
42 Troy Tulowitzki 12.50 30.00

2004-05 USA Baseball National Team Signatures Jersey Black

*BLACK JSY: .6X TO 1.5X BLACK SIG
OVERALL AU-JSY ODDS ONE PER BOX
STATED PRINT RUN 275 SERIAL #'d SETS
21 Alex Gordon 10.00 25.00
27 Ian Kennedy 8.00 20.00

2004-05 USA Baseball National Team Signatures Jersey Blue

*BLUE JSY: .75X TO 2X BLACK SIG
OVERALL AU-JSY ODDS ONE PER BOX
STATED PRINT RUN 150 SERIAL #'d SETS
27 Ian Kennedy 10.00 25.00

2004-05 USA Baseball National Team Signatures Jersey Red

*RED JSY: 2X TO 5X BLACK SIG
OVERALL AU-JSY ODDS ONE PER BOX
STATED PRINT RUN 50 SERIAL #'d SETS
27 Ian Kennedy 30.00 60.00
35 Mike Pelfrey 20.00 50.00
37 Ryan Zimmerman 20.00 50.00

2005-06 USA Baseball Junior National Team

COMP.FACT.SET (25) 20.00 30.00
COMPLETE SET (21) 4.00 10.00
COMMON CARD (74-94) .20 .50
STATED PRINT RUN 10,000 SETS
74 Grant Green .20 .50
75 Greg Peavey .20 .50
76 Brett Anderson .50 1.25
77 Jason Taylor .20 .50
78 Josh Thrailkill .20 .50
79 Max Sapp .20 .50
80 Kevin Rhoderick .20 .50
81 Sean Ratliff .20 .50
82 Jeremy Bleich .20 .50
83 Scott Schauer .20 .50
84 Dellin Betances .60 1.50
85 Torre Langley .20 .50
86 Clayton Kershaw 5.00 12.00
87 Leonardo Ware .20 .50
88 Dwight Childs .20 .50
89 Adrian Cardenas .20 .50
90 Shawn Tolleson .20 .50
91 Tyson Ross .30 .75
92 Marcus Lemon .20 .50
93 Lars Anderson .30 .75
94 Team Checklist .20 .50

2005-06 USA Baseball Junior National Team Signature Black

STATED PRINT RUN 495 SERIAL #'d SETS
GREEN PRINT RUN 2 SERIAL #'d SETS
NO GREEN PRICING DUE TO SCARCITY
ONE AUTO PER SEALED FACTORY SET
AC Adrian Cardenas 4.00 10.00
BA Brett Anderson 5.00 12.00
CK Clayton Kershaw 125.00 250.00
DB Dellin Betances 6.00 15.00
DC Dwight Childs 4.00 10.00
GG Grant Green 5.00 12.00
GP Greg Peavey 4.00 10.00
JB Jeremy Bleich 4.00 10.00
JL Josh Thrailkill 4.00 10.00
JT Jason Taylor 4.00 10.00
KR Kevin Rhoderick 4.00 10.00
LA Lars Anderson 6.00 15.00
LW Leonardo Ware 4.00 10.00
ML Marcus Lemon 5.00 12.00
MS Max Sapp 5.00 12.00
SR Sean Ratliff 4.00 10.00
SR Scott Schauer 4.00 10.00
ST Shawn Tolleson 4.00 10.00
TL Torre Langley 5.00 12.00
TR Tyson Ross 4.00 10.00

2005-06 USA Baseball Junior National Team Vision of the Future

ONE VISION PER SEALED FACTORY SET
SP's 6X TOUGHER THAN REGULAR CARDS
SP INFO PROVIDED BY USA BASEBALL
SP CL: 24-25/40-42
23 Grant Green .75 2.00
24 Greg Peavey SP 1.00 2.50
25 Brett Anderson SP 2.50 6.00
26 Jason Taylor .75 2.00
27 Josh Thrailkill .75 2.00
28 Max Sapp .75 2.00
29 Kevin Rhoderick .75 2.00
30 Sean Ratliff .75 2.00
31 Jeremy Bleich .75 2.00
32 Scott Schauer .75 2.00
33 Dellin Betances 2.50 6.00
34 Torre Langley .75 2.00
35 Clayton Kershaw 12.00 30.00
36 Leonardo Ware .75 2.00
37 Dwight Childs .75 2.00
38 Adrian Cardenas .75 2.00
39 Shawn Tolleson .75 2.00
40 Tyson Ross SP 1.50 4.00
41 Marcus Lemon SP 1.00 2.50
42 Lars Anderson SP 1.50 4.00

2005-06 USA Baseball Junior National Team Across the Nation Dual Signatures Black

STATED PRINT RUN 250 SERIAL #'d SETS
*BLUE: .6X TO 1.5X BLACK
BLUE PRINT RUN 100 SERIAL #'d SETS
GREEN PRINT RUN 2 SERIAL #'d SETS
NO GREEN PRICING DUE TO SCARCITY
RED PRINT RUN 16 SERIAL #'d SETS
NO RED PRICING DUE TO SCARCITY
ONE DUAL AUTO PER SEALED FACT.SET
1 C.Kershaw 40.00 100.00
S.Tolleson
2 Lars Anderson 5.00 12.00
Grant Green
3 Dwight Childs 4.00 10.00
Scott Schauer
4 Leonard Ware 6.00 15.00
Torre Langley
5 Adrian Cardenas 4.00 10.00
Marcus Lemon
6 Dellin Betances 4.00 10.00
Jason Taylor
7 Sean Ratliff 4.00 10.00
Kevin Rhoderick
8 Jeremy Bleich 4.00 10.00
Josh Thrailkill

2005-06 USA Baseball Junior National Team Future Category Leaders Dual Signatures Black

STATED PRINT RUN 250 SERIAL #'d SETS
*BLUE: .6X TO 1.5X BLACK
BLUE PRINT RUN 100 SERIAL #'d SETS
GREEN PRINT RUN 2 SERIAL #'d SETS
NO GREEN PRICING DUE TO SCARCITY
RED PRINT RUN 16 SERIAL #'d SETS
NO RED PRICING DUE TO SCARCITY
ONE DUAL AUTO PER SEALED FACT.SET
1 L.Ware/A.Cardenas 4.00 10.00
2 M.Sapp/L.Anderson 10.00 25.00
3 L.Ware/J.Taylor 4.00 10.00
4 M.Sapp/T.Langley 6.00 15.00
5 M.Lemon/S.Ratliff 6.00 15.00
6 B.Anderson/D.Betances 6.00 15.00
7 K.Rhoderick/G.Peavey 4.00 10.00
8 S.Tolleson/T.Ross 4.00 10.00
9 J.Bleich/J.Thrailkill 4.00 10.00
10 C.Kershaw/D.Betances 40.00 100.00
11 G.Green/M.Lemon 6.00 15.00
12 M.Sapp/S.Tolleson 6.00 15.00
13 B.Anderson/G.Peavey 6.00 15.00

2005-06 USA Baseball Junior National Team Future Match-Ups Dual Signatures Black

STATED PRINT RUN 250 SERIAL #'d SETS
*BLUE: .6X TO 1.5X BLACK
BLUE PRINT RUN 100 SERIAL #'d SETS
GREEN PRINT RUN 2 SERIAL #'d SETS
NO GREEN PRICING DUE TO SCARCITY
RED PRINT RUN 16 SERIAL #'d SETS
NO RED PRICING DUE TO SCARCITY
ONE DUAL AUTO PER SEALED FACT.SET
1 B.Anderson/T.Langley 10.00 25.00
2 T.Ross/D.Childs 4.00 10.00
3 C.Kershaw 40.00 100.00
A.Cardenas
4 S.Schauer/K.Rhoderick 4.00 10.00
5 J.Thrailkill/J.Taylor 4.00 10.00
6 G.Peavey/D.Childs 4.00 10.00
7 T.Ross/L.Anderson 10.00 25.00
8 S.Schauer/J.Bleich 4.00 10.00

2005-06 USA Baseball Junior National Team Opening Day Jersey Signature Blue

STATED PRINT RUN 360 SERIAL #'d SETS
GREEN PRINT RUN 2 SERIAL #'d SETS
NO GREEN PRICING DUE TO SCARCITY
*RED: .75X TO 2X BLUE
RED PRINT RUN 100 SERIAL #'d SETS
ONE AU-GU PER SEALED FACTORY SET
AC Adrian Cardenas 10.00 25.00
BA Brett Anderson 5.00 12.00
CK Clayton Kershaw 75.00 150.00
DB Dellin Betances 5.00 12.00
DC Dwight Childs 5.00 12.00
GG Grant Green 8.00 20.00
GP Greg Peavey 5.00 12.00
JB Jeremy Bleich 5.00 12.00
JL Josh Thrailkill 5.00 12.00
JT Jason Taylor 5.00 12.00
KR Kevin Rhoderick 5.00 12.00
LA Lars Anderson 10.00 25.00

W Leonardo Ware 5.00 12.00
L Marcus Lemon 8.00 20.00
S Max Sapp 8.00 20.00
R Sean Ratliff 5.00 12.00
R Scott Schauer 5.00 12.00
T Shawn Tolleson 5.00 12.00
L Torre Langley 8.00 20.00
R Tyson Ross 5.00 12.00

2005-06 USA Baseball National Team

COMP.FACT.SET (27) 20.00 30.00
COMPLETE SET (23) 6.00 15.00
COMMON CARD (51-73) .20 .50
STATED PRINT RUN 10,000 SETS
51 Ian Kennedy .50 1.25
52 Kyle McCulloch .20 .50
53 Mark Melancon .20 .50
54 Jonah Nickerson .30 .75
55 Chris Perez .30 .75
56 Max Scherzer 2.50 6.00
57 Sean Doolittle .20 .50
58 Kevin Gunderson .20 .50
59 David Price .60 1.50
60 Joe Savery .20 .50
61 J.P. Arencibia .50 1.25
62 Brian Jeroloman .20 .50
63 Matt Wieters .60 1.50
64 Adam Davis .20 .50
65 Blake Davis .20 .50
66 Wes Hodges .20 .50
67 Matt LaPorta .60 1.50
68 Josh Rodriguez .20 .50
69 Jon Jay .50 1.25
70 Hunter Mense .20 .50
71 Shane Robinson .20 .50
72 Drew Stubbs .50 1.25
73 Team Checklist .20 .50

2005-06 USA Baseball National Team Signature Black

STATED PRINT RUN 475 SERIAL #'d SETS
GREEN PRINT RUN 2 SERIAL #'d SETS
NO GREEN PRICING DUE TO SCARCITY
ONE AUTO PER SEALED FACTORY SET
AD Adam Davis 3.00 8.00
BD Blake Davis 3.00 8.00
BJ Brian Jeroloman 3.00 8.00
CP Chris Perez 3.00 8.00
DP David Price 15.00 40.00
DS Drew Stubbs 8.00 20.00
HM Hunter Mense 3.00 8.00
IK Ian Kennedy 5.00 12.00
JA J.P. Arencibia 5.00 12.00
JJ Jon Jay 5.00 12.00
JN Jonah Nickerson 3.00 8.00
JR Josh Rodriguez 3.00 8.00
JS Joe Savery 4.00 10.00
KG Kevin Gunderson 3.00 8.00
KM Kyle McCulloch 3.00 8.00
ML Matt LaPorta 10.00 25.00
MM Mark Melancon 3.00 8.00
MS Max Scherzer 60.00 150.00
MW Matt Wieters 8.00 20.00
SD Sean Doolittle 5.00 12.00
SR Shane Robinson 4.00 10.00
WH Wes Hodges 4.00 10.00

2005-06 USA Baseball National Team Vision of the Future

ONE VISION PER SEALED FACTORY SET
SP's 6X TOUGHER THAN REGULAR CARDS
SP INFO PROVIDED BY USA BASEBALL
SP CL: 1/6/9/17/19
1 Ian Kennedy SP 2.50 6.00
2 Kyle McCulloch .75 2.00
3 Mark Melancon .75 2.00
4 Jonah Nickerson 1.25 3.00
5 Chris Perez 1.25 3.00
6 Max Scherzer SP 12.00 30.00
7 Sean Doolittle .75 2.00
8 Kevin Gunderson .75 2.00
9 David Price SP 3.00 8.00
10 Joe Savery .75 2.00
11 J.P. Arencibia 2.00 5.00
12 Brian Jeroloman .75 2.00
13 Matt Wieters 3.00 8.00
14 Adam Davis .75 2.00
15 Blake Davis .75 2.00
16 Wes Hodges .75 2.00
17 Matt LaPorta SP 3.00 8.00
18 Josh Rodriguez .75 2.00
19 Jon Jay SP 2.00 5.00
20 Hunter Mense .75 2.00
21 Shane Robinson .75 2.00
22 Drew Stubbs 2.00 5.00

2005-06 USA Baseball National Team Collegiate Connections Dual Signatures Black

STATED PRINT RUN 250 SERIAL #'d SETS
*BLUE: .6X TO 1.5X BLACK
BLUE PRINT RUN 75 SERIAL #'d SETS
GREEN PRINT RUN 2 SERIAL #'d SETS
NO GREEN PRICING DUE TO SCARCITY
RED PRINT RUN 16 SERIAL #'d SETS
NO RED PRICING DUE TO SCARCITY
1 K.McCulloch/D.Stubbs 8.00 20.00
2 J.Nickerson/K.Gunderson 4.00 10.00
3 C.Perez/J.Jay 4.00 10.00
4 M.Scherzer/H.Mense 40.00 100.00
5 J.Savery/J.Rodriguez 6.00 15.00
6 B.Jeroloman/A.Davis 4.00 10.00

2005-06 USA Baseball National Team Future Match-Ups Dual Signatures Black

STATED PRINT RUN 250 SERIAL #'d SETS
*BLUE: .6X TO 1.5X BLACK
BLUE PRINT RUN 75 SERIAL #'d SETS
GREEN PRINT RUN 2 SERIAL #'d SETS
NO GREEN PRICING DUE TO SCARCITY
RED PRINT RUN 16 SERIAL #'d SETS
NO RED PRICING DUE TO SCARCITY
ONE DUAL AUTO PER SEALED FACT.SET
1 D.Price/D.Stubbs 10.00 25.00
2 M.Melancon/B.Davis 4.00 10.00
3 J.Savery/B.Jeroloman 6.00 15.00
4 C.Perez/H.Mense 10.00 25.00
5 W.Hodges/J.Nickerson 6.00 15.00
6 W.Hodges/M.Scherzer 40.00 100.00
7 J.Savery/J.Jay 6.00 15.00
8 K.McCulloch/W.Hodges 6.00 15.00
9 S.Doolittle/S.Robinson 6.00 15.00
10 J.Nickerson/B.Jeroloman 4.00 10.00
11 M.Scherzer/M.LaPorta 40.00 100.00

2005-06 USA Baseball National Team Leaders Dual Signatures Black

STATED PRINT RUN 250 SERIAL #'d SETS
*BLUE: .6X TO 1.5X BLACK
BLUE PRINT RUN 75 SERIAL #'d SETS
GREEN PRINT RUN 2 SERIAL #'d SETS
NO GRFFN PRICING DUE TO SCARCITY
RED PRINT RUN 16 SERIAL #'d SETS
NO RED PRICING DUE TO SCARCITY
ONE DUAL AUTO PER SEALED FACT.SET
1 J.Arencibia/S.Doolittle 4.00 10.00
2 J.Arencibia/A.Davis 4.00 10.00
3 M.LaPorta/M.Wieters 6.00 15.00
4 J.Jay/S.Robinson 6.00 15.00
5 J.Rodriguez/S.Doolittle 6.00 15.00
6 J.Arencibia/M.LaPorta 4.00 10.00
7 K.McCulloch/I.Kennedy 6.00 15.00
8 M.Melancon/C.Perez 4.00 10.00
9 D.Price/I.Kennedy 15.00 40.00
10 K.Gunderson/D.Price 12.00 30.00
11 K.Gunderson/M.Melancon 4.00 10.00
12 B.Davis/A.Davis 4.00 10.00
13 I.Kennedy/D.Stubbs 8.00 20.00

2005-06 USA Baseball National Team Opening Day Jersey Signature Blue

STATED PRINT RUN 350 SERIAL #'d SETS
GREEN PRINT RUN 2 SERIAL #'d SETS
NO GREEN PRICING DUE TO SCARCITY
ONE AU-GU PER SEALED FACTORY SET
AD Adam Davis 4.00 10.00
BD Blake Davis 4.00 10.00
BJ Brian Jeroloman 4.00 10.00
CP Chris Perez 4.00 10.00
DP David Price 15.00 40.00
DS Drew Stubbs 8.00 20.00
HM Hunter Mense 4.00 10.00
IK Ian Kennedy 6.00 15.00
JA J.P. Arencibia 5.00 12.00
JJ Jon Jay 6.00 15.00
JN Jonah Nickerson 4.00 10.00
JR Josh Rodriguez 4.00 10.00
JS Joe Savery 6.00 15.00
KG Kevin Gunderson 4.00 10.00
KM Kyle McCulloch 4.00 10.00
ML Matt LaPorta 12.50 30.00
MM Mark Melancon 4.00 10.00
MS Max Scherzer 60.00 150.00
MW Matt Wieters 10.00 25.00
SD Sean Doolittle 6.00 15.00
SR Shane Robinson 6.00 15.00
WH Wes Hodges 6.00 15.00

2005-06 USA Baseball National Team Opening Day Jersey Signature Red

*RED: .75X TO 2X BLUE
ONE AU-GU PER SEALED FACTORY SET
STATED PRINT RUN 100 SERIAL #'d SETS
DP David Price 15.00 40.00
ML Matt LaPorta 20.00 50.00

2006-07 USA Baseball

This fifty-card set featured members of the 2006 USA National Team and 2006 USA Junior National Team. These cards were included as part of a factory set which also included four autographed cards of Team USA players. two autographed game-used jersey cards of those same players. two parallel cards, one other autograph card, which included alumni players and one "Bound for Beijing" game-used relic card. The suggested retail price on the factory set price was $49.99 and these sets were packed 24 to a case.
COMPLETE SET (50) 10.00 25.00
COMMON CARD (1-30) .20 .50
1 Jemile Weeks .30 .75
2 Brandon Crawford .50 1.25
3 Julio Borbon .30 .75
4 Roger Kieschnick .30 .75
5 Preston Clark .20 .50
6 Zack Cozart .60 1.50
7 David Price 1.25 3.00
8 Darwin Barney 1.00 2.50
9 Daniel Moskos .20 .50
10 Ross Detwiler .30 .75
11 Cole St. Clair .20 .50
12 Tim Federowicz .30 .75
13 Nick Hill .20 .50
14 Sean Doolittle .20 .50
15 Pedro Alvarez .50 1.25
16 Tommy Hunter .30 .75
17 Nick Schmidt .20 .50
18 Jake Arrieta .50 1.25
19 Todd Frazier .60 1.50
20 Andrew Brackman .30 .75
21 J.P. Arencibia .40 1.00
22 Wes Roemer .20 .50
23 Casey Weathers .20 .50
24 National Team Coaches .20 .50
25 Jemile Weeks BTI .30 .75
26 Julio Borbon BTI .30 .75
27 Commodore Connection BTI 1.25 3.00
28 J.Arencibia 1.25 3.00
D.Price BTI
29 Nick Hill BTI .20 .50
30 National Team CL .20 .50
31 Hunter Morris .20 .50
32 Matt Newman .20 .50
33 Matt Dominguez .50 1.25
34 Daniel Elorriaga-Matra .20 .50
35 Jarrod Parker .50 1.25
36 Neil Ramirez .20 .50
37 Blake Beavan .30 .75
38 Mike Moustakas .60 1.50
39 Justin Jackson .30 .75
40 Christian Colon .30 .75
41 Michael Main .20 .50
42 Tim Alderson .20 .50
43 Kevin Rhoderick .20 .50
44 Freddie Freeman 3.00 8.00
45 Matt Harvey 2.50 6.00
46 Victor Sanchez .20 .50
47 Greg Peavey .20 .50
48 Tommy Medica .20 .50
49 Junior National Team Coaches .20 .50
50 Junior National Team CL .20 .50

2006-07 USA Baseball Foil

COMPLETE SET (41) 20.00 50.00
*FOIL: 75X TO 2X BASIC
STATED ODDS 1:1 BOX SETS

2006-07 USA Baseball 1st Round Draft Pick Signatures Black

OVERALL DP AU ODDS 1:3 BOX SETS
CARDS SER.#'d B/WN 11-350 COPIES PER
ANNOUNCED PRINT RUNS LISTED BELOW
PRINT RUNS PROVIDED BY USA BASEBALL
NO PRICING ON QTY 25 OR LESS
2 Jeff Clement/200 * 3.00 8.00
3 Ricky Romero/200 * 3.00 8.00
5 Drew Stubbs/200 * 5.00 12.00
7 Trevor Crowe/200 * 4.00 10.00
8 John Mayberry Jr./200 * 3.00 8.00
9 Ian Kennedy/200 * 4.00 10.00
10 Max Sapp/200 3.00 8.00
11 Daniel Bard/200 * 3.00 8.00
16 Cesar Ramos/200 * 3.00 8.00
20 Jed Lowrie/200 * 4.00 10.00

2006-07 USA Baseball 1st Round Draft Pick Signatures Blue

*BLUE: .5 TO 1.2X BLACK
OVERALL DP AU ODDS 1:3 BOX SETS
CARDS SER.#'d B/WN 11-350 COPIES PER
ANNOUNCED PRINT RUNS LISTED BELOW
PRINT RUNS PROVIDED BY USA BASEBALL
NO PRICING ON QTY 25 OR LESS
5 Drew Stubbs/100 * 5.00 12.00
9 Ian Kennedy/100 * 4.00 10.00
12 Matt Campbell/100 4.00 10.00
14 Tyler Greene/100 * 5.00 12.00
15 Justin Orenduff/100 3.00 8.00

2006-07 USA Baseball 1st Round Draft Pick Signatures Red

*RED: .6 TO 1.5X BLACK
OVERALL DP AU ODDS 1:3 BOX SETS
CARDS SER.#'d B/WN 11-350 COPIES PER
ANNOUNCED PRINT RUNS LISTED BELOW
PRINT RUNS PROVIDED BY USA BASEBALL
NO PRICING ON QTY 25 OR LESS
5 Drew Stubbs/50 * 6.00 15.00
9 Ian Kennedy/50 * 4.00 10.00

2006-07 USA Baseball 2004 Youth Junior Signatures

STATED ODDS 1:4 BOX SETS
STATED PRINT RUN 475 SER.#'d SETS
1 Brandon Snyder 3.00 8.00
2 Justin Upton 10.00 25.00
3 Sean O'Sullivan 4.00 10.00
4 Andrew McCutchen 12.00 30.00
5 Jonathon Niese 6.00 15.00
6 Steven Figueroa 3.00 8.00
7 Chris Marrero 6.00 15.00
8 Colton Willems 3.00 8.00
9 Chris Huseby 3.00 8.00
10 Hank Conger 5.00 12.00

2006-07 USA Baseball Bound for Beijing Materials

STATED ODDS 1:1 BOX SETS
PATCH ODDS 1:60 BOX SETS
PATCH PRINT RUNS B/WN 4-20 COPIES PER
NO PATCH PRICING DUE TO SCARCITY
1 Kevin Slowey Jsy 3.00 8.00
2 Nick Adenhart Jsy 6.00 15.00
3 Mike Bacsik Jsy 3.00 8.00
4 Greg Smith Jsy 3.00 8.00
5 Nick Ungs Hat SP 4.00 10.00
6 Lee Gronkiewicz Jsy 3.00 8.00
7 J. Brent Cox Jsy 3.00 8.00
8 Jeff Farnsworth Jsy 3.00 8.00
9 Kurt Suzuki Jsy 3.00 8.00
10 Jarrod Saltalamacchia Hat SP 10.00 25.00
11 Matt Tupman Hat SP 4.00 10.00
12 Brandon Wood Jsy 3.00 8.00
13 Mike Kinkade Hat SP 4.00 10.00
14 Bobby Hill Jsy 3.00 8.00
15 Mark Reynolds Jsy 3.00 8.00
16 Billy Butler Hat SP 6.00 15.00
17 Chad Allen Hat SP 6.00 15.00

2006-07 USA Baseball Bound for Beijing Signatures

STATED ODDS 1:12 BOX SETS
STATED PRINT RUN 50 SER.#'d SETS
1 Kevin Slowey 30.00 60.00
2 Nick Adenhart 12.50 30.00
3 Mike Bacsik 3.00 8.00
4 Greg Smith 8.00 20.00
5 Nick Ungs 3.00 8.00
6 Lee Gronkiewicz 3.00 8.00
7 J. Brent Cox 6.00 15.00
8 Jeff Farnsworth 3.00 8.00
9 Kurt Suzuki 6.00 15.00
10 Jarrod Saltalamacchia 20.00 50.00
11 Matt Tupman 3.00 8.00
12 Brandon Wood 15.00 40.00
13 Mike Kinkade 3.00 8.00
14 Bobby Hill 6.00 15.00
15 Mark Reynolds 40.00 80.00
16 Billy Butler 30.00 60.00
18 Davey Johnson 6.00 15.00

2006-07 USA Baseball Signatures Black

STATED PRINT RUN 595 SER.#'d SETS
ACTION/PORTRAIT PRINT RUN INFO
PROVIDED BY USA BASEBALL
BLUE PRINT RUN B/WN 100-275 PER
GREEN PRINT RUN 2 SER.#'d SETS
NO GREEN PRICING DUE TO SCARCITY
RED PRINT RUN 100 SER.#'d SETS
OVERALL AU ODDS 4:1 BOX SETS
1a J.Weeks Action/545 * 3.00 8.00
2 Brandon Crawford 6.00 15.00
3a J.Borbon Action/545 * 4.00 10.00
4 Roger Kieschnick 3.00 8.00
5 Preston Clark 3.00 8.00
6 Zack Cozart 6.00 15.00
7a D.Price Action/545 * 10.00 25.00
8 Darwin Barney 4.00 10.00
9 Daniel Moskos 3.00 8.00
10 Ross Detwiler 4.00 10.00
11 Cole St. Clair 3.00 8.00
12 Tim Federowicz 3.00 8.00
13 Nick Hill 3.00 8.00
14 Sean Doolittle 4.00 10.00
15 Pedro Alvarez 4.00 10.00
16 Tommy Hunter 6.00 15.00
17a N.Schmidt Action/545 * 6.00 15.00
18 Jake Arrieta 30.00 80.00
19 Todd Frazier 6.00 15.00
20 J.P. Arencibia 4.00 10.00
21 Wes Roemer 5.00 12.00
22 Casey Weathers 3.00 8.00
23 Hunter Morris 5.00 12.00
24 Matt Newman 3.00 8.00
25a M.Dominguez Action/545 * 8.00 20.00
26 Daniel Elorriaga-Matra 3.00 8.00
27 Jarrod Parker 4.00 10.00
28 Neil Ramirez 3.00 8.00
29a B.Beavan Action/545 * 6.00 15.00
30 Mike Moustakas 5.00 12.00
31a J.Jackson Action/545 * 4.00 10.00
32 Christian Colon 4.00 10.00
33 Michael Main 4.00 10.00
34 Tim Alderson 5.00 12.00
35 Kevin Rhoderick 3.00 8.00
36 Freddie Freeman 40.00 100.00
37a M.Harvey Action/545 * 20.00 50.00
38 Victor Sanchez 3.00 8.00
39 Greg Peavey 3.00 8.00
40 Tommy Medica 3.00 8.00

2006-07 USA Baseball Signatures Blue

*BLUE: .5X TO 1.2X BLACK
OVERALL AU ODDS 4:1 BOX SETS
PRINT RUNS B/WN 100-275 COPIES PER
3 Julio Borbon 8.00 20.00
7 David Price 10.00 25.00
10 Ross Detwiler 6.00 15.00
15 Pedro Alvarez 5.00 12.00
29 Blake Beavan 8.00 20.00
30 Mike Moustakas 6.00 15.00

2006-07 USA Baseball Signatures Red

*RED: .6X TO 1.5X BLACK
OVERALL AU ODDS 4:1 BOX SETS
STATED PRINT RUN 100 SER.#'d SETS
7 David Price 20.00 50.00
10 Ross Detwiler 8.00 20.00
15 Pedro Alvarez 30.00 60.00
19 Todd Frazier 12.50 30.00
22 Casey Weathers 6.00 15.00
27 Jarrod Parker 10.00 25.00
30 Mike Moustakas 6.00 15.00
33 Michael Main 8.00 20.00

2006-07 USA Baseball Signatures Jersey Black

PRINT RUN B/WN 90-295 SER.#'d SETS
BLUE PRINT RUNS B/WN 50-150 PER
GREEN PRINT RUN 2 SER.#'d SETS
NO GREEN PRICING DUE TO SCARCITY
RED PRINT RUN B/WN 30-50 COPIES PER
OVERALL JSY AU ODDS 2:1 BOX SETS
1 Jemile Weeks 6.00 15.00
2 Brandon Crawford 6.00 15.00
3 Julio Borbon 5.00 12.00
4 Roger Kieschnick 4.00 10.00
5 Preston Clark 4.00 10.00
6 Zack Cozart 8.00 20.00
7 David Price 8.00 20.00
8 Darwin Barney 8.00 20.00
9 Daniel Moskos 8.00 20.00
10 Ross Detwiler 5.00 12.00
11 Cole St. Clair 4.00 10.00
12 Tim Federowicz 4.00 10.00
13 Nick Hill 4.00 10.00
14 Sean Doolittle 5.00 12.00
15 Pedro Alvarez 4.00 10.00
16 Tommy Hunter 6.00 15.00
17 Nick Schmidt 6.00 15.00
18 Jake Arrieta 30.00 80.00
19 Todd Frazier 10.00 25.00
20 Andrew Brackman 30.00 60.00
21 J.P. Arencibia 5.00 12.00
22 Wes Roemer 4.00 10.00
23 Casey Weathers 4.00 10.00
24 Huntor Morris 5.00 12.00
25 Matt Newman 4.00 10.00
26 Matt Dominguez 5.00 12.00
27 Daniel Elorriaga-Matra 4.00 10.00
28 Jarrod Parker 10.00 25.00
29 Neil Ramirez 4.00 10.00
30 Blake Beavan 8.00 20.00
31 Mike Moustakas 4.00 10.00
32 Justin Jackson 4.00 10.00
33 Christian Colon 6.00 15.00
34 Michael Main 6.00 15.00
35 Tim Alderson 3.00 8.00
36 Kevin Rhoderick 4.00 10.00
37 Freddie Freeman 30.00 80.00
38 Matt Harvey 30.00 60.00
39 Victor Sanchez 4.00 10.00
40 Greg Peavey 4.00 10.00
41 Tommy Medica 4.00 10.00

2006-07 USA Baseball Signatures Jersey Red

*RED: 1.25X TO 3X BLACK
OVERALL JSY AU ODDS 2:1 BOX SETS
PRINT RUNS B/WN 30-50 COPIES PER
15 Pedro Alvarez 15.00 40.00

2006-07 USA Baseball Today and Tomorrow Signatures Black

STATED PRINT RUN 295 SER.#'d SETS
*BLUE: .5X TO 1.2X BASIC
BLUE PRINT RUN 150 SER.#'d SETS
GREEN PRINT RUN 2 SER.#'d SETS
NO GREEN PRICING DUE TO SCARCITY
RED PRINT RUN 25 SER.#'d SETS
NO RED PRICING DUE TO SCARCITY
OVERALL TT AUTO ODDS 1:2 BOX SETS
1 D.Price/M.Harvey 50.00 100.00
2 D.Moskos/B.Beavan 5.00 12.00
3 R.Detwiler/N.Ramirez 5.00 12.00
4 P.Clark/T.Medica 5.00 12.00
5 S.Doolittle/F.Freeman 12.00 30.00
6 J.Weeks/C.Colon 5.00 12.00
7 P.Alvarez/M.Dominguez 6.00 15.00
8 T.Frazier/J.Jackson 8.00 20.00
9 D.Barney/M.Moustakas 6.00 15.00
10 J.Borbon/M.Main 5.00 12.00
11 R.Kieschnick/V.Sanchez 4.00 10.00

2008 USA Baseball

COMPLETE SET (60) 8.00 20.00
COMMON CARD .25 .60
ONE COMPLETE SET PER BOX
1 Pedro Alvarez .60 1.50
2 Ryan Berry .25 .60
3 Jordan Danks .60 1.50
4 Danny Espinosa .40 1.00
5 Ryan Flaherty .40 1.00
6 Logan Forsythe .25 .60
7 Seth Frankoff .25 .60
8 Scott Gorgen .25 .60
9 Jeremy Hamilton .25 .60
10 Brett Hunter .25 .60
11 Joe Kelly .25 .60
12 Roger Kieschnick .40 1.00
13 Lance Lynn .60 1.50
14 Brian Matusz .60 1.50
15 Tommy Medica .25 .60
16 Jordy Mercer .25 .60
17 Mike Minor .60 1.50
18 Petey Paramore .40 1.00
19 Josh Romanski .40 1.00
20 Tyson Ross .40 1.00
21 Cody Satterwhite .40 1.00
22 Justin Smoak .75 2.00
23 Eric Surkamp .25 .60
24 Jacob Thompson .40 1.00
25 Brett Wallace .60 1.50
26 Nat Team Coaches .25 .60
27 National Team CL .25 .60
28 Game 1 .25 .60
29 Game 2 .25 .60
30 Game 3 .25 .60
31 Game 4 .25 .60
32 Game 5 .25 .60
33 Kyle Buchanan .25 .60
34 Mychal Givens .25 .60
35 Robbie Grossman .40 1.00
36 Tyler Hibbs .25 .60
37 L.J. Hoes .25 .60
38 Eric Hosmer 2.00 5.00
39 T.J. House .25 .60
40 Garrison Lassiter .25 .60
41 Jeff Malm .40 1.00
42 Nick Maronde .25 .60
43 Harold Martinez .25 .60
44 Tim Melville .25 .60
45 Matthew Purke .25 .60
46 J.P. Ramirez .25 .60
47 Kyle Skipworth .40 1.00
48 Tyler Stovall .25 .60
49 Jordan Swagerty .25 .60
50 Riccio Torrez .25 .60
51 Ryan Weber .25 .60
52 Tyler Wilson .25 .60
53 Jr. Team Coaches .25 .60
54 Junior Team CL .25 .60
55 Andrew Aplin .25 .60
Justin Charles
Matt Davidson
56 Robert Refsnyder .25 .60
Max Stassi
Zach Vincej
57 Colton Cain .40 1.00
Randal Grichuk
Zach Lee
58 A.J. Cole .25 .60
Nolan Fontana
Nick Franklin
59 Nate Gonzalez .25 .60
Austin Maddox
Steven Rodriguez
60 Luke Bailey .25 .60
Richie Shaffer
Jacob Tillotson

2008 USA Baseball Battleground Autographs

OVERALL AUTO ODDS 7 PER BOX
BG1 Ber/Lynn/Mat/Ross/Thomp 20.00 50.00
BG2 Hunter/Kelly/Minor/Satter 12.50 30.00
BG3 Alvarez/Ham/Smoak/Wallace 10.00 25.00
BG4 Danny Espinosa 10.00 25.00
Ryan Flaherty
Jordy Mercer
BG5 Jordan Danks 10.00 25.00
Logan Forsythe
Roger Kieschnick
Josh Romanski
BG6 T.Medica/P.Paramore 10.00 25.00

2008 USA Baseball Bound for Beijing II Signature Jersey

OVERALL AUTO ODDS 7 PER BOX
STATED PRINT RUN 50 SER.#'d SETS
NO PRICING ON MANY
DUE TO LACK OF MARKET INFO
WC1 Bryan Anderson 6.00 15.00
WC4 Chris Booker 4.00 10.00
WC5 Tyler Colvin 12.50 30.00
WC6 Brian Duensing 6.00 15.00
WC7 Lee Gronkiewicz 4.00 10.00
WC8 Michael Hollimon 4.00 10.00
WC15 Josh Outman 6.00 15.00
WC17 Chris Perez 12.50 30.00
WC20 Steven Shell 4.00 10.00
WC22 Dallas Trahern 4.00 10.00

2008 USA Baseball Camo Cloth Jerseys

OVERALL GU ODDS 2 PER BOX
CC1 Pedro Alvarez 5.00 12.00
CC2 Ryan Berry 3.00 8.00
CC3 Jordan Danks 3.00 8.00
CC4 Danny Espinosa 3.00 8.00
CC5 Ryan Flaherty 3.00 8.00
CC6 Logan Forsythe 3.00 8.00
CC7 Jeremy Hamilton 3.00 8.00
CC8 Brett Hunter 3.00 8.00
CC9 Joe Kelly 3.00 8.00
CC10 Roger Kieschnick 3.00 8.00
CC11 Lance Lynn 3.00 8.00
CC12 Brian Matusz 4.00 10.00
CC13 Tommy Medica 3.00 8.00
CC14 Jordy Mercer 3.00 8.00
CC15 Mike Minor 3.00 8.00
CC16 Petey Paramore 3.00 8.00
CC17 Josh Romanski 3.00 8.00
CC18 Tyson Ross 3.00 8.00
CC19 Cody Satterwhite 3.00 8.00
CC20 Justin Smoak 5.00 12.00
CC21 Jacob Thompson 3.00 8.00
CC22 Brett Wallace 3.00 8.00

2008 USA Baseball Japanese Collegiate All-Stars Jerseys

OVERALL GU ODDS 2 PER BOX
JN1 Sho Aranami 3.00 8.00
JN2 Takeshi Hosoyamada 3.00 8.00
JN3 Takahiro Iwamoto 3.00 8.00
JN4 Tomoyuki Kaida 3.00 8.00
JN5 Mikinori Kato 4.00 10.00
JN6 Testsuya Kokubo 3.00 8.00
JN7 Keijiro Matsumoto 3.00 8.00
JN8 Shirou Mori 3.00 8.00
JN9 Shinya Muramatsu 3.00 8.00
JN10 Ryoji Nakata 3.00 8.00
JN11 Hiroki Nakazawa 3.00 8.00
JN12 Tomohisa Nemoto 3.00 8.00
JN13 Shota Oba 4.00 10.00
JN14 Takashi Ogino 3.00 8.00
JN15 Shota Ohno 3.00 8.00
JN16 Yuki Saitoh 40.00 80.00
JN17 Ryo Sakakibara 3.00 8.00
JN18 Yukinaga Tanaka 3.00 8.00
JN19 Shingo Tatsumi 3.00 8.00
JN20 Hiroki Uemoto 3.00 8.00
JN21 Shota Waizumi 3.00 8.00
JN22 Noriharu Yamazaki 3.00 8.00

2008 USA Baseball Japanese Collegiate All-Stars Signatures

OVERALL AUTO ODDS 7 PER BOX
STATED PRINT RUN 50 SER.#'d SETS
JN1 Sho Aranami 20.00 50.00
JN2 Takeshi Hosoyamada 30.00 60.00
JN3 Takahiro Iwamoto 30.00 60.00
JN4 Tomoyuki Kaida 30.00 60.00
JN5 Mikinori Kato 40.00 80.00
JN6 Testsuya Kokubo 30.00 60.00
JN7 Keijiro Matsumoto 60.00 120.00
JN8 Shirou Mori 20.00 50.00
JN9 Shinya Muramatsu 30.00 60.00
JN10 Ryoji Nakata 20.00 50.00
JN11 Hiroki Nakazawa 20.00 50.00
JN12 Tomohisa Nemoto 20.00 50.00
JN13 Shota Oba 50.00 100.00
JN14 Takashi Ogino 20.00 50.00
JN15 Shota Ohno 20.00 50.00
JN16 Yuki Saitoh 400.00 700.00
JN17 Ryo Sakakibara 20.00 50.00
JN18 Yukinaga Tanaka 20.00 50.00
JN19 Shingo Tatsumi 50.00 100.00
JN20 Hiroki Uemoto 40.00 80.00
JN21 Shota Waizumi 20.00 50.00
JN22 Noriharu Yamazaki 20.00 50.00

2008 USA Baseball Junior National Team On-Card Signatures

OVERALL AUTO ODDS 7 PER BOX
PLATE PRINT RUN 1 SET PER COLOR
BLACK-CYAN-MAGENTA ISSUED
PLATES FOR FRONT AND BACK ISSUED
PLATES ARE AUTOGRAPHED
NO PLATE PRICING DUE TO SCARCITY
82 Kyle Buchanan 3.00 8.00
83 Mychal Givens 3.00 8.00
84 Robbie Grossman 3.00 8.00
85 Tyler Hibbs 3.00 8.00
86 L.J. Hoes 3.00 8.00
87 Eric Hosmer 15.00 40.00
88 T.J. House 3.00 8.00
89 Garrison Lassiter 3.00 8.00
90 Jeff Malm 3.00 8.00
91 Nick Maronde 3.00 8.00
92 Harold Martinez 3.00 8.00
93 Tim Melville 3.00 8.00
94 Matthew Purke 3.00 8.00
95 J.P. Ramirez 3.00 8.00
96 Kyle Skipworth 3.00 8.00
97 Tyler Stovall 3.00 8.00
98 Jordan Swagerty 3.00 8.00
99 Riccio Torrez 3.00 8.00
100 Ryan Weber 3.00 8.00
101 Tyler Wilson 3.00 8.00

2008 USA Baseball Junior National Team Signatures Black

OVERALL AUTO ODDS 7 PER BOX
STATED PRINT RUN 249 SER.#'d SETS
*BLUE AUTO: .4X TO 1X BLACK AUTO
BLUE PRINT RUN 150 SER.#'d SETS
GREEN PRINT RUN 2 SER.#'d SETS
NO GREEN PRICING DUE TO SCARCITY
*RED AUTO: .75X TO 2X BLACK AUTO
RED PRINT RUN 50 SER.#'d SETS
UE1 Kyle Buchanan 3.00 8.00
UE2 Mychal Givens 3.00 8.00
UE3 Robbie Grossman 3.00 8.00
UE4 Tyler Hibbs 3.00 8.00
UE5 L.J. Hoes 3.00 8.00
UE6 Eric Hosmer 12.50 30.00
UE7 T.J. House 3.00 8.00
UE8 Garrison Lassiter 3.00 8.00
UE9 Jeff Malm 3.00 8.00
UE10 Nick Maronde 3.00 8.00
UE11 Harold Martinez 3.00 8.00
UE12 Tim Melville 3.00 8.00
UE13 Matthew Purke 3.00 8.00
UE14 J.P. Ramirez 3.00 8.00
UE15 Kyle Skipworth 3.00 8.00
UE16 Tyler Stovall 3.00 8.00
UE17 Jordan Swagerty 3.00 8.00
UE18 Riccio Torrez 3.00 8.00
UE19 Ryan Weber 3.00 8.00
UE20 Tyler Wilson 3.00 8.00

2008 USA Baseball Junior National Team Signature Jersey Black

OVERALL AUTO ODDS 7 PER BOX
STATED PRINT RUN 195 SER.#'d SETS
*BLUE JSY AU: .5X TO 1.2X BLACK JSY AU
BLUE PRINT RUN 75 SER.#'d SETS
GREEN PRINT RUN 2 SER.#'d SETS
NO GREEN PRICING DUE TO SCARCITY
RED PRINT RUN 25 SER.#'d SETS
NO RED PRICING DUE TO SCARCITY
UI1 Kyle Buchanan 4.00 10.00
UI2 Mychal Givens 4.00 10.00
UI3 Robbie Grossman 4.00 10.00
UI4 Tyler Hibbs 4.00 10.00
UI5 L.J. Hoes 4.00 10.00
UI6 Eric Hosmer 8.00 20.00
UI7 T.J. House 4.00 10.00
UI8 Garrison Lassiter 4.00 10.00
UI9 Jeff Malm 4.00 10.00
UI10 Nick Maronde 4.00 10.00
UI11 Harold Martinez 4.00 10.00
UI12 Tim Melville 4.00 10.00
UI13 Matthew Purke 6.00 15.00
UI14 J.P. Ramirez 4.00 10.00
UI15 Kyle Skipworth 4.00 10.00
UI16 Tyler Stovall 4.00 10.00
UI17 Jordan Swagerty 4.00 10.00
UI18 Riccio Torrez 4.00 10.00
UI19 Ryan Weber 4.00 10.00
UI20 Tyler Wilson 4.00 10.00

2008 USA Baseball National Team On-Card Signatures

OVERALL AUTO ODDS 7 PER BOX
PLATE PRINT RUN 1 SET PER COLOR
BLACK-CYAN-MAGENTA ISSUED
PLATES FOR FRONT AND BACK ISSUED
PLATES ARE AUTOGRAPHED
NO PLATE PRICING DUE TO SCARCITY
61 Pedro Alvarez 6.00 15.00
62 Ryan Berry 3.00 8.00
63 Jordan Danks 3.00 8.00
64 Danny Espinosa 6.00 15.00
65 Ryan Flaherty 3.00 8.00
66 Logan Forsythe 3.00 8.00
67 Jeremy Hamilton 3.00 8.00
68 Brett Hunter 3.00 8.00
69 Joe Kelly 3.00 8.00
70 Roger Kieschnick 3.00 8.00
71 Brian Matusz 10.00 25.00
72 Tommy Medica 3.00 8.00
73 Jordy Mercer 3.00 8.00
74 Mike Minor 12.50 30.00
75 Petey Paramore 3.00 8.00
76 Josh Romanski 3.00 8.00
77 Tyson Ross 3.00 8.00
78 Cody Satterwhite 3.00 8.00
79 Justin Smoak 15.00 40.00
80 Jacob Thompson 3.00 8.00
81 Brett Wallace 12.50 30.00
83 B.Matusz/J.Romanski 10.00 25.00
84 C.Satterwhite/L.Lynn 6.00 15.00
85 P.Paramore/B.Wallace 6.00 15.00
86 J.Danks/R.Kieschnick 6.00 15.00
87 R.Kieschnick/P.Alvarez 12.50 30.00

2008 USA Baseball National Team Question and Answer Signatures

OVERALL AUTO ODDS 7 PER BOX
ALL VARIATIONS EQUAL VALUE
BH1 Brett Hunter 5.00 12.00
BH2 Brett Hunter 5.00 12.00
BH3 Brett Hunter 5.00 12.00
BH4 Brett Hunter 5.00 12.00
BH5 Brett Hunter 5.00 12.00
BM1 Brian Matusz 10.00 25.00
BM2 Brian Matusz 10.00 25.00
BM3 Brian Matusz 10.00 25.00
BM4 Brian Matusz 10.00 25.00
BM5 Brian Matusz 10.00 25.00
BW1 Brett Wallace 10.00 25.00
BW2 Brett Wallace 10.00 25.00
BW3 Brett Wallace 10.00 25.00
BW4 Brett Wallace 10.00 25.00
BW5 Brett Wallace 10.00 25.00
CS1 Cody Satterwhite 10.00 25.00
CS2 Cody Satterwhite 10.00 25.00
CS3 Cody Satterwhite 10.00 25.00
CS4 Cody Satterwhite 10.00 25.00
CS5 Cody Satterwhite 10.00 25.00
DE1 Danny Espinosa 10.00 25.00
DE2 Danny Espinosa 10.00 25.00
DE3 Danny Espinosa 10.00 25.00
DE4 Danny Espinosa 10.00 25.00
DE5 Danny Espinosa 10.00 25.00
JD1 Jordan Danks 6.00 15.00
JD2 Jordan Danks 6.00 15.00
JD3 Jordan Danks 6.00 15.00
JD4 Jordan Danks 6.00 15.00
JD5 Jordan Danks 6.00 15.00
JH1 Jeremy Hamilton 5.00 12.00
JH2 Jeremy Hamilton 5.00 12.00
JH3 Jeremy Hamilton 5.00 12.00
JH4 Jeremy Hamilton 5.00 12.00
JH5 Jeremy Hamilton 5.00 12.00
JK1 Joe Kelly 5.00 12.00
JK2 Joe Kelly 5.00 12.00
JK3 Joe Kelly 5.00 12.00
JK4 Joe Kelly 5.00 12.00
JK5 Joe Kelly 5.00 12.00
JM1 Jordy Mercer 5.00 12.00
JM2 Jordy Mercer 5.00 12.00
JM3 Jordy Mercer 5.00 12.00
JM4 Jordy Mercer 5.00 12.00
JM5 Jordy Mercer 5.00 12.00
JR1 Josh Romanski 5.00 12.00
JR2 Josh Romanski 5.00 12.00
JR3 Josh Romanski 5.00 12.00
JR4 Josh Romanski 5.00 12.00
JR5 Josh Romanski 5.00 12.00
JS1 Justin Smoak 30.00 60.00
JS2 Justin Smoak 30.00 60.00
JS3 Justin Smoak 30.00 60.00
JS4 Justin Smoak 30.00 60.00
JS5 Justin Smoak 30.00 60.00
JT1 Jacob Thompson 5.00 12.00
JT2 Jacob Thompson 5.00 12.00
JT3 Jacob Thompson 5.00 12.00
JT4 Jacob Thompson 5.00 12.00
JT5 Jacob Thompson 5.00 12.00
LF1 Logan Forsythe 5.00 12.00
LF2 Logan Forsythe 5.00 12.00
LF3 Logan Forsythe 5.00 12.00
LF4 Logan Forsythe 5.00 12.00
LF5 Logan Forsythe 5.00 12.00
MM1 Mike Minor 5.00 12.00
MM2 Mike Minor 5.00 12.00
MM3 Mike Minor 5.00 12.00
MM4 Mike Minor 5.00 12.00
MM5 Mike Minor 5.00 12.00
PA1 Pedro Alvarez 6.00 15.00
PA2 Pedro Alvarez 6.00 15.00
PA3 Pedro Alvarez 6.00 15.00
PA4 Pedro Alvarez 6.00 15.00
PA5 Pedro Alvarez 6.00 15.00
PP1 Petey Paramore 5.00 12.00
PP2 Petey Paramore 5.00 12.00
PP3 Petey Paramore 5.00 12.00
PP4 Petey Paramore 5.00 12.00
PP5 Petey Paramore 5.00 12.00
RB1 Ryan Berry 5.00 12.00
RB2 Ryan Berry 5.00 12.00
RB3 Ryan Berry 5.00 12.00
RB4 Ryan Berry 5.00 12.00
RB5 Ryan Berry 5.00 12.00

RF1 Ryan Flaherty 6.00 15.00
RF2 Ryan Flaherty 6.00 15.00
RF3 Ryan Flaherty 6.00 15.00
RF4 Ryan Flaherty 6.00 15.00
RF5 Ryan Flaherty 6.00 15.00
RK1 Roger Kieschnick 6.00 15.00
RK2 Roger Kieschnick 6.00 15.00
RK3 Roger Kieschnick 6.00 15.00
RK4 Roger Kieschnick 6.00 15.00
RK5 Roger Kieschnick 6.00 15.00
TM1 Tommy Medica 5.00 12.00
TM2 Tommy Medica 5.00 12.00
TM3 Tommy Medica 5.00 12.00
TM4 Tommy Medica 5.00 12.00
TM5 Tommy Medica 5.00 12.00
TR1 Tyson Ross 5.00 12.00
TR2 Tyson Ross 5.00 12.00
TR3 Tyson Ross 5.00 12.00
TR4 Tyson Ross 5.00 12.00
TR5 Tyson Ross 5.00 12.00

2008 USA Baseball National Team Signatures Black

OVERALL AUTO ODDS 7 PER BOX
STATED PRINT RUN 249 SER.#'d SETS
*BLUE AUTO: .4X TO 1X BLACK AUTO
BLUE PRINT RUN 150 SER.#'d SETS
GREEN PRINT RUN 2 SER.#'d SETS
NO GREEN PRICING DUE TO SCARCITY
*RED AUTO: .75X TO 2X BLACK AUTO
RED PRINT RUN 50 SER.#'d SETS
1 Pedro Alvarez 10.00 25.00
2 Ryan Berry 3.00 8.00
3 Jordan Danks 3.00 8.00
4 Danny Espinosa 6.00 15.00
5 Ryan Flaherty 3.00 8.00
6 Logan Forsythe 3.00 8.00
7 Seth Frankoff 3.00 8.00
8 Scott Gorgen 3.00 8.00
9 Jeremy Hamilton 3.00 8.00
10 Brett Hunter 3.00 8.00
11 Joe Kelly 3.00 8.00
12 Roger Kieschnick 3.00 8.00
13 Lance Lynn 8.00 20.00
14 Brian Matusz 6.00 15.00
15 Tommy Medica 3.00 8.00
16 Jordy Mercer 3.00 8.00
17 Mike Minor 8.00 20.00
18 Petey Paramore 3.00 8.00
19 Josh Romanski 3.00 8.00
20 Tyson Ross 3.00 8.00
21 Cody Satterwhite 3.00 8.00
22 Justin Smoak 10.00 25.00
23 Jacob Thompson 3.00 8.00
24 Brett Wallace 8.00 20.00
25 Eric Surkamp 3.00 8.00

2008 USA Baseball National Team Signature Jersey Black

OVERALL AUTO ODDS 7 PER BOX
STATED PRINT RUN 195 SER.#'d SETS
*BLUE JSY AU: .5X TO 1.2X BLACK JSY AU
BLUE PRINT RUN 75 SER.#'d SETS
GREEN PRINT RUN 2 SER.#'d SETS
NO GREEN PRICING DUE TO SCARCITY
RED PRINT RUN 25 SER.#'d SETS
NO RED PRICING DUE TO SCARCITY
1 Pedro Alvarez 6.00 15.00
2 Ryan Berry 4.00 10.00
3 Jordan Danks 4.00 10.00
4 Danny Espinosa 6.00 15.00
5 Ryan Flaherty 4.00 10.00
6 Logan Forsythe 4.00 10.00
7 Seth Frankoff 4.00 10.00
8 Scott Gorgen 4.00 10.00
9 Jeremy Hamilton 4.00 10.00
10 Brett Hunter 4.00 10.00
11 Joe Kelly 4.00 10.00
12 Roger Kieschnick 4.00 10.00
13 Lance Lynn 8.00 20.00
14 Brian Matusz 20.00 50.00
15 Tommy Medica 4.00 10.00
16 Jordy Mercer 4.00 10.00
17 Mike Minor 10.00 25.00
18 Petey Paramore 4.00 10.00
19 Josh Romanski 4.00 10.00
20 Tyson Ross 4.00 10.00
21 Cody Satterwhite 4.00 10.00
22 Justin Smoak 8.00 20.00
23 Jacob Thompson 4.00 10.00
24 Brett Wallace 10.00 25.00
25 Eric Surkamp 4.00 10.00

2008 USA Baseball Today and Tomorrow Signatures Black

COMMON CARD 3.00 8.00
OVERALL AUTO ODDS 7 PER BOX
STATED PRINT RUN 295 SER.#'d SETS
*BLUE AUTO: .5X TO 1.2X BLACK AUTO
BLUE PRINT RUN 150 SER.#'d SETS
GREEN PRINT RUN 2 SER.#'d SETS
NO GREEN PRICING DUE TO SCARCITY
RED PRINT RUN 25 SER.#'d SETS
NO RED PRICING DUE TO SCARCITY
TT1 B.Matusz/T.Melville 4.00 10.00
TT2 Jacob Thompson/Nick Maronde 3.00 8.00
TT3 Brett Hunter/T.J. House 3.00 8.00
TT4 Petey Paramore/Jordan Swagerty 3.00 8.00
TT5 J.Smoak/E.Hosmer 8.00 20.00
TT6 R.Flaherty/R.Torrez 4.00 10.00
TT7 P.Alvarez/H.Martinez 6.00 15.00
TT8 D.Espinosa/M.Givens 5.00 12.00
TT9 Jordan Danks/L.J. Hoes 3.00 8.00
TT10 Kieschnick/Grossman 4.00 10.00
TT11 Logan Forsythe/J.P. Ramirez 3.00 8.00
TT12 B.Wallace/K.Skipworth 8.00 20.00

2008 USA Baseball Youth National Team Signature Jersey Black

OVERALL AUTO ODDS 7 PER BOX
STATED PRINT RUN 295 SER.#'d SETS
YE1 Andrew Aplin 8.00 20.00
YE2 Luke Bailey 4.00 10.00
YE3 Colton Cain 4.00 10.00
YE4 Justin Charles 4.00 10.00
YE5 A.J. Cole 4.00 10.00
YE6 Matt Davidson 6.00 15.00
YE7 Nolan Fontana 4.00 10.00
YE8 Nick Franklin 8.00 20.00
YE9 Nate Gonzalez 5.00 12.00
YE10 Randal Grichuk 10.00 25.00
YE11 Zach Lee 6.00 15.00
YE12 Austin Maddox 4.00 10.00
YE13 Robert Refsnyder 20.00 50.00
YE14 Steven Rodriguez 4.00 10.00
YE15 Richie Shaffer 5.00 12.00
YE16 Max Stassi 4.00 10.00
YE17 Jacob Tillotson 4.00 10.00
YE18 Zach Vincej 5.00 12.00

2008-09 USA Baseball

This set was released on January 28, 2009. The base set consists of 47 cards.
COMPLETE SET (47) 20.00 50.00
ONE COMPLETE SET PER BOX
1 Jared Clark .40 1.00
2 Tommy Mendonca .40 1.00
3 Christian Colon .60 1.50
4 Kentrail Davis .60 1.50
5 Matt den Dekker .60 1.50
6 Derek Dietrich 1.00 2.50
7 Josh Fellhauer .60 1.50
8 Micah Gibbs .60 1.50
9 Kyle Gibson .60 1.50
10 A.J. Griffin .60 1.50
11 Chris Hernandez .60 1.50
12 Ryan Jackson .60 1.50
13 Mike Leake 1.00 2.50
14 Ryan Lipkin .40 1.00
15 Tyler Lyons .60 1.50
16 Mike Minor 1.00 2.50
17 Hunter Morris .40 1.00
18 Andrew Oliver .60 1.50
19 Scott Woodward .40 1.00
20 Blake Smith .60 1.50
21 Stephen Strasburg 10.00 25.00
22 Kendal Volz .60 1.50
23 Andrew Aplin .60 1.50
24 Austin Maddox .60 1.50
25 Colton Cain .40 1.00
26 Cameron Garfield .40 1.00
27 Cecil Tanner .40 1.00
28 David Nick .40 1.00
29 Donavan Tate .60 1.50
30 Nick Franklin 1.00 2.50
31 Harold Martinez .40 1.00
32 Jake Barrett .40 1.00
33 Jeff Malm .40 1.00
34 Jonathan Meyer .40 1.00
35 Matthew Purke .40 1.00
36 Max Stassi 1.00 2.50
37 Nolan Fontana .60 1.50
38 Ryan Weber .40 1.00
39 Jacob Turner 1.50 4.00
40 Wes Hatton .40 1.00
41 Delmonico/Pfeifer/Tago .60 1.50
42 Buckel/Camarena/Child .60 1.50
43 Kelly/Radziewski/Van Alstine .40 1.00
44 Rodriguez/Littlewood/Wolters .40 1.00
45 Mason/Lorenzen/Lipka 1.50 4.00
46 Montgomery/Allen/Lopes .40 1.00
47 Bryce Harper 75.00 200.00

2008-09 USA Baseball 16U National Team Jersey Patch Autographs

OVERALL AUTO ODDS 7 PER BOX
STATED PRINT RUN 50 SER.#'d SETS
BH Bryce Harper 1000.00 1500.00
BR Bryan Radziewski 10.00 25.00
CA Daniel Camarena 15.00 40.00
CB Cody Buckel 12.50 30.00
CL Christian Lopes 75.00 150.00
DC Dan Child 8.00 20.00
JR Jake Rodriguez 12.50 30.00
LI Marcus Littlewood 8.00 20.00
LO Michael Lorenzen 60.00 120.00
MK Michael Kelly 8.00 20.00
ML Matt Lipka 30.00 60.00
ND Nicky Delmonico 15.00 40.00
PP Philip Pfeifer 20.00 50.00
PT Peter Tago 10.00 25.00
TW Tony Wolters 10.00 25.00
WA Will Allen 12.50 30.00

2008-09 USA Baseball 18U National Team Jerseys

OVERALL MEM ODDS 6 PER BOX
STATED PRINT RUN 179 SER.#'d SETS
18UAA Andrew Aplin 2.50 6.00
18UAM Austin Maddox 2.50 6.00
18UCC Colton Cain 2.50 6.00
18UCG Cameron Garfield 2.50 6.00
18UCT Cecil Tanner 2.50 6.00
18UDN David Nick 2.50 6.00
18UDT Donavan Tate 6.00 15.00
18UFO Nolan Fontana 2.50 6.00
18UHM Harold Martinez 3.00 8.00
18UJB Jake Barrett 3.00 8.00
18UJM Jeff Malm 2.50 6.00
18UJT Jacob Turner 2.50 6.00
18UME Jonathan Meyer 2.50 6.00
18UMP Matthew Purke 3.00 8.00
18UMS Max Stassi 6.00 15.00
18UNF Nick Franklin 4.00 10.00
18URW Ryan Weber 3.00 8.00
18UWH Wes Hatton 3.00 8.00

2008-09 USA Baseball 18U National Team Jersey Autographs Blue

OVERALL AUTO ODDS 7 PER BOX
STATED PRINT RUN 99 SER.#'d SETS
18UAA Andrew Aplin 6.00 15.00
18UAM Austin Maddox 10.00 25.00
18UCC Colton Cain 6.00 15.00
18UCG Cameron Garfield 5.00 12.00
18UCT Cecil Tanner 5.00 12.00
18UDN David Nick 5.00 12.00
18UDT Donavan Tate 10.00 25.00
18UFO Nolan Fontana 5.00 12.00
18UHM Harold Martinez 6.00 15.00
18UJB Jake Barrett 10.00 25.00
18UJM Jeff Malm 5.00 12.00
18UJT Jacob Turner 20.00 50.00
18UME Jonathan Meyer 5.00 12.00
18UMP Matthew Purke 15.00 40.00
18UMS Max Stassi 15.00 40.00
18UNF Nick Franklin 6.00 15.00
18URW Ryan Weber 6.00 15.00
18UWH Wes Hatton 8.00 20.00

2008-09 USA Baseball 18U National Team Patch

OVERALL MEM ODDS 6 PER SET
STATED PRINT RUN 65 SER.#'d SETS
18UAA Andrew Aplin 4.00 10.00
18UAM Austin Maddox 4.00 10.00
18UCC Colton Cain 5.00 12.00
18UCG Cameron Garfield 4.00 10.00
18UDN David Nick 4.00 10.00
18UDT Donavan Tate 20.00 50.00
18UFO Nolan Fontana 4.00 10.00
18UHM Harold Martinez 5.00 12.00
18UJB Jake Barrett 4.00 10.00
18UJM Jeff Malm 4.00 10.00
18UJT Jacob Turner 6.00 15.00
18UME Jonathan Meyer 4.00 10.00
18UMP Matthew Purke 5.00 12.00
18UMS Max Stassi 12.50 30.00
18UNF Nick Franklin 4.00 10.00
18URW Ryan Weber 4.00 10.00
18UWH Wes Hatton 4.00 10.00

2008-09 USA Baseball 18U National Team Patch Autographs

OVERALL AUTO ODDS 7 PER SET
STATED PRINT RUN 30 SER.#'d SETS
18UAA Andrew Aplin 10.00 25.00
18UAM Austin Maddox 8.00 20.00
18UCC Colton Cain 10.00 25.00
18UCT Cecil Tanner 6.00 15.00
18UDN David Nick 6.00 15.00
18UDT Donavan Tate 50.00 100.00
18UFO Nolan Fontana 15.00 40.00
18UHM Harold Martinez 12.50 30.00
18UJB Jake Barrett 6.00 15.00
18UJM Jeff Malm 6.00 15.00
18UJT Jacob Turner 6.00 15.00
18UME Jonathan Meyer 6.00 15.00
18UMP Matthew Purke 10.00 25.00
18UMS Max Stassi 30.00 60.00
18UNF Nick Franklin 15.00 40.00
18URW Ryan Weber 6.00 15.00

2008-09 USA Baseball 18U National Team Q and A Autographs

OVERALL AUTO ODDS 7 PER SET
PRINT RUNS B/WN 20-104 COPIES PER
18QAAA Andrew Aplin/100 6.00 15.00
18QAAM Austin Maddox/100 10.00 25.00
18QACC Colton Cain/100 4.00 10.00
18QACT Cecil Tanner/99 10.00 25.00
18QADN David Nick/100 4.00 10.00
18QADT Donavan Tate/97 20.00 50.00
18QAFR Nick Franklin/87 10.00 25.00
18QAJM Jeff Malm/99 8.00 20.00
18QAME Jonathan Meyer/97 6.00 15.00
18QAMP Matthew Purke/100 12.50 30.00
18QAMS Max Stassi/20 20.00 50.00
18QANF Nolan Fontana/100 8.00 20.00
18QATU Jacob Turner/100 20.00 50.00
18QAWH Wes Hatton/100 10.00 25.00

2008-09 USA Baseball Autographs Gold

OVERALL AUTO ODDS 7 PER SET
STATED PRINT RUN 175 COPIES PER
61 Christian Colon 8.00 20.00
63 Matt den Dekker 6.00 15.00
64 Derek Dietrich 10.00 25.00
65 Josh Fellhauer 4.00 10.00
66 Micah Gibbs 5.00 12.00
67 Kyle Gibson 10.00 25.00
68 A.J. Griffin 4.00 10.00
69 Chris Hernandez 5.00 12.00
70 Ryan Jackson 4.00 10.00
71 Mike Leake 20.00 50.00
72 Ryan Lipkin 8.00 20.00
73 Tyler Lyons 4.00 10.00
74 Mike Minor 6.00 15.00
75 Hunter Morris 8.00 20.00
76 Andrew Oliver 6.00 15.00
78 Blake Smith 5.00 12.00
79 Stephen Strasburg 50.00 120.00
80 Kendal Volz 5.00 12.00
81 Andrew Aplin 6.00 15.00
82 Jake Barrett 5.00 12.00
85 Colton Cain 4.00 10.00
87 Nolan Fontana 4.00 10.00
88 Nick Franklin 6.00 15.00
89 Cameron Garfield 4.00 10.00
92 Wes Hatton 4.00 10.00
98 Austin Maddox 6.00 15.00
99 Jeff Malm 4.00 10.00
102 Jonathan Meyer 4.00 10.00
106 David Nick 4.00 10.00
107 Matthew Purke 8.00 20.00
108 Max Stassi 10.00 25.00
109 Cecil Tanner 8.00 20.00
110 Donavan Tate 8.00 20.00
113 Jacob Turner 10.00 25.00

2008-09 USA Baseball Chinese Taipei Jerseys

OVERALL MEM ODDS 6 PER BOX
STATED PRINT RUN 479 SER.#'d SETS
CTCH Chih-Pei Huang 2.50 6.00
CTCL Chia-Jen Lo 5.00 12.00
CTEH Erh-Hang Hsu 3.00 8.00
CTHL Hung-Cheng Lai 2.50 6.00
CTHU Chin-Lung Huang 4.00 10.00
CTHY Hsien-Hsien Yang 4.00 10.00
CTKC Kai-Wen Cheng 4.00 10.00
CTKL Ken-Wei Lin 2.50 6.00
CTLC Chih-Hsiang Lin 2.50 6.00
CTLI Kun-Sheng Lin 3.00 8.00
CTMT Ming-Chueh Tsai 4.00 10.00
CTPL Po-Kai Lai 2.50 6.00
CTTT Tsung-Hsuan Tseng 2.50 6.00
CTWC Wei-Jen Cheng 3.00 8.00
CTWL Wen-Yang Liao 3.00 8.00
CTWW Wei-Chung Wang 3.00 8.00
CTYC Yuan-Chin Chu 4.00 10.00
CTYH Yu-Chi Hsiao 3.00 8.00

2008-09 USA Baseball Chinese Taipei Patch

OVERALL MEM ODDS 6 PER SET
PRINT RUNS B/WN 6-75 COPIES PER
NO KEN-WEI LIN PRICING AVAILABLE
CTCH Chih-Pei Huang/69 8.00 20.00
CTCL Chia-Jen Lo/31 8.00 20.00
CTHL Hung-Cheng Lai/65 5.00 12.00
CTKC Kai-Wen Cheng/75 10.00 25.00
CTLC Chih-Hsiang Lin/62 10.00 25.00
CTMT Ming-Chueh Tsai/75 5.00 12.00
CTWC Wei-Jen Cheng/60 5.00 12.00
CTWW Wei-Chung Wang/75 8.00 20.00
CTYC Yuan-Chin Chu/75 5.00 12.00
CTYH Yu-Chi Hsiao/75 5.00 12.00

2008-09 USA Baseball Chinese Taipei Patch Autographs

OVERALL AUTO ODDS 7 PER SET
STATED PRINT RUN 55 SER.#'d SETS
CTCH Chih-Pei Huang 8.00 20.00
CTCL Chia-Jen Lo 10.00 25.00
CTEH Erh-Hang Hsu 8.00 20.00
CTHL Hung-Cheng Lai 20.00 50.00
CTHU Chin-Lung Huang 8.00 20.00
CTHY Hsien-Hsien Yang 6.00 15.00
CTKC Kai-Wen Cheng 50.00 100.00
CTKL Ken-Wei Lin 6.00 15.00
CTLC Chih-Hsiang Lin 6.00 15.00
CTLI Kun-Sheng Lin 20.00 50.00
CTMT Ming-Chueh Tsai 8.00 20.00
CTPL Po-Kai Lai 8.00 20.00
CTTT Tsung-Hsuan Tseng 15.00 40.00
CTWC Wei-Jen Cheng 8.00 20.00
CTWL Wen-Yang Liao 6.00 15.00
CTWW Wei-Chung Wang 20.00 50.00
CTYC Yuan-Chin Chu 8.00 20.00
CTYH Yu-Chi Hsiao 8.00 20.00

2008-09 USA Baseball National Team Jerseys

OVERALL MEM ODDS 6 PER SET
STATED PRINT RUN 149 SER.#'d SETS
NTAG A.J. Griffin 3.00 8.00
NTAO Andrew Oliver 4.00 10.00
NTBS Blake Smith 5.00 12.00
NTCC Christian Colon 4.00 10.00
NTCH Chris Hernandez 4.00 10.00
NTDD Derek Dietrich 4.00 10.00
NTHM Hunter Morris 4.00 10.00
NTJC Jared Clark 3.00 8.00
NTJF Josh Fellhauer 4.00 10.00
NTKD Kentrail Davis 3.00 8.00
NTKG Kyle Gibson 4.00 10.00
NTKV Kendal Volz 4.00 10.00
NTMD Matt den Dekker 3.00 8.00
NTMG Micah Gibbs 3.00 8.00
NTML Mike Leake 5.00 12.00
NTMM Mike Minor 4.00 10.00
NTRJ Ryan Jackson 4.00 10.00
NTRL Ryan Lipkin 5.00 12.00
NTSS Stephen Strasburg 30.00 60.00
NTSW Scott Woodward 3.00 8.00
NTTL Tyler Lyons 3.00 8.00
NTTM Tommy Mendonca 5.00 12.00

2008-09 USA Baseball National Team Jersey Autographs Blue

OVERALL AUTO ODDS 7 PER SET
STATED PRINT RUN 99 SER.#'d SETS
NTAG A.J. Griffin 10.00 25.00
NTBS Blake Smith 6.00 15.00
NTCC Christian Colon 12.50 30.00
NTCH Chris Hernandez 5.00 12.00
NTDD Derek Dietrich 12.50 30.00
NTHM Hunter Morris 12.50 30.00
NTJF Josh Fellhauer 5.00 12.00
NTKD Kentrail Davis 10.00 25.00
NTKG Kyle Gibson 8.00 20.00
NTKV Kendal Volz 6.00 15.00
NTMD Matt den Dekker 6.00 15.00
NTMG Micah Gibbs 5.00 12.00
NTML Mike Leake 15.00 40.00
NTMM Mike Minor 10.00 25.00
NTRJ Ryan Jackson 10.00 25.00
NTRL Ryan Lipkin 6.00 15.00
NTTL Tyler Lyons 5.00 12.00

2008-09 USA Baseball National Team Jersey Patch

OVERALL MEM ODDS 6 PER SET
STATED PRINT RUN 50 SER.#'d SETS
NTDD Derek Dietrich 6.00 15.00
NTKD Kentrail Davis 6.00 15.00
NTKV Kendal Volz 4.00 10.00
NTMD Matt den Dekker 4.00 10.00
NTML Mike Leake 5.00 12.00
NTRJ Ryan Jackson 6.00 15.00
NTSS Stephen Strasburg 125.00 250.00
NTSW Scott Woodward 4.00 10.00
NTTM Tommy Mendonca 8.00 20.00

2008-09 USA Baseball National Team Jersey Patch Autographs

OVERALL AUTO ODDS 7 PER SET
STATED PRINT RUN 30 SER.#'d SETS
NTAG A.J. Griffin 6.00 15.00
NTCH Chris Hernandez 6.00 15.00
NTDD Derek Dietrich 15.00 40.00
NTHM Hunter Morris 8.00 20.00
NTJF Josh Fellhauer 6.00 15.00
NTKD Kentrail Davis 20.00 50.00
NTKG Kyle Gibson 20.00 50.00
NTKV Kendal Volz 8.00 20.00
NTMD Matt den Dekker 8.00 20.00
NTML Mike Leake 40.00 80.00
NTMM Mike Minor 20.00 50.00
NTRJ Ryan Jackson 8.00 20.00
NTRL Ryan Lipkin 6.00 15.00
NTTL Tyler Lyons 6.00 15.00

2008-09 USA Baseball National Team Patriotic Patches

OVERALL MEM ODDS 6 PER SET
STATED PRINT RUN 50 SER.#'d SETS
PPABA Brett Anderson 40.00 80.00
PPABB Brian Barden 8.00 20.00
PPABK Brandon Knight 8.00 20.00
PPABN Blaine Neal 6.00 15.00
PPADF Dexter Fowler 30.00 60.00
PPAJA Jake Arrieta 75.00 150.00
PPAJC Jeremy Cummings 8.00 20.00
PPAJD Jason Donald 20.00 50.00
PPAJG John Gall 6.00 15.00
PPAKJ Kevin Jepsen 15.00 40.00
PPALM Lou Marson 30.00 60.00
PPAMK Mike Koplove 8.00 20.00
PPAML Matt LaPorta 30.00 60.00
PPANS Nate Schierholtz 12.50 30.00
PPASS Stephen Strasburg 100.00 250.00
PPATI Terry Tiffee 6.00 15.00
PPATT Taylor Teagarden 15.00 40.00

2008-09 USA Baseball National Team Q and A Autographs

OVERALL AUTO ODDS 7 PER SET
PRINT RUNS B/WN 20-102 COPIES PER
QAAG A.J. Griffin/100 5.00 12.00
QAAO Andrew Oliver/20 8.00 20.00
QABS Blake Smith/99 5.00 12.00
QACC Christian Colon/100 10.00 25.00
QACH Chris Hernandez/100 5.00 12.00
QADD Derek Dietrich/99 15.00 40.00
QAHM Hunter Morris/101 10.00 25.00
QAJF Josh Fellhauer/98 8.00 20.00
QAKG Kyle Gibson/100 6.00 15.00
QAKV Kendal Volz/100 6.00 15.00
QAMD Matt den Dekker/99 10.00 25.00
QAMG Micah Gibbs/100 8.00 20.00
QAML Mike Leake/101 15.00 40.00
QAMM Mike Minor/100 15.00 40.00
QATL Tyler Lyons/100 5.00 12.00

2008-09 USA Baseball National Team Retrospective

COMPLETE SET (13) 6.00 15.00
ONE SET PER BOX
USA1 Matt Brown .25 .60
USA2 Stephen Strasburg 6.00 15.00
USA3 Jayson Nix .25 .60
USA4 Brian Duensing .40 1.00
USA5 Jake Arrieta 1.50 4.00
USA6 Dexter Fowler .40 1.00
USA7 Casey Weathers .25 .60
USA8 Mike Koplove .25 .60
USA9 Jason Donald .25 .60
USA10 Taylor Teagarden .40 1.00
USA11 Kevin Jepsen .25 .60
USA12 Matt LaPorta .40 1.00
USA13 Team USA Wins Third Olympic Medal .25 .60

2009-10 USA Baseball

COMP.SET w/o SPs (59) 12.50 30.00
COMMON CARD (1-59) .40 1.00
COMMON AUTO (61-116) 3.00 8.00
FIVE AUTOS PER BOX
AU ANNCD PRINT RUN 502 SER.#'d SETS
COMMON PATCH (119-136) 3.00 8.00
ONE PATCH OR PATCH AU PER BOX
PATCH PRINT RUN 65 SER.#'d SETS
USA1 Trevor Bauer 2.00 5.00
USA2 Christian Colon .60 1.50
USA3 Cody Wheeler .40 1.00
USA4 Chad Bettis .40 1.00
USA5 Bryce Brentz 1.00 2.50
USA6 Nick Pepitone .40 1.00
USA7 Michael Choice .60 1.50
USA8 Gerrit Cole 3.00 8.00
USA9 Sonny Gray 1.00 2.50
USA10 Tyler Holt .40 1.00
USA11 T.J. Walz .40 1.00
USA12 Rick Hague .40 1.00
USA13 Drew Pomeranz 1.25 3.00
USA14 Blake Forsythe .40 1.00
USA15 Matt Newman .40 1.00
USA16 Casey McGrew .40 1.00
USA17 Brad Miller .40 1.00
USA18 Yasmani Grandal .60 1.50
USA19 Kolten Wong .60 1.50
USA20 Tony Zych .40 1.00
USA21 Andy Wilkins .40 1.00
USA22 Asher Wojciechowski .60 1.50
USA23 Cody Buckel .40 1.00
USA24 Nick Castellanos 1.50 4.00
USA25 Garin Cecchini 1.25 3.00
USA26 Sean Coyle .40 1.00
USA27 Nicky Delmonico .60 1.50
USA28 Kevin Gausman 1.25 3.00
USA29 Cory Hahn .40 1.00
USA30 Bryce Harper 10.00 25.00
USA31 Kavin Keyes .40 1.00
USA32 Manny Machado 2.50 6.00
USA33 Connor Mason .40 1.00
USA34 Ladson Montgomery .40 1.00
USA35 Phillip Pfeifer .40 1.00
USA36 Brian Ragira .60 1.50
USA37 Robbie Ray .40 1.00
USA38 Kyle Ryan .40 1.00
USA39 Jameson Taillon .60 1.50
USA40 A.J. Vanegas .40 1.00
USA41 Karsten Whitson .60 1.50
USA42 Tony Wolters .40 1.00
USA43 Albert Almora .60 1.50
USA44 Shaun Chase .40 1.00
USA45 Austin Cousino .40 1.00
USA46 Dylan Davis .40 1.00
USA47 Parker French .40 1.00
USA48 Cory Geisler .40 1.00
USA49 Courtney Hawkins .60 1.50
USA50 C.J. Hinojosa .40 1.00
USA51 John Hochstatter .40 1.00
USA52 Hayden Hurst .40 1.00
USA53 Ricardo Jacquez .40 1.00
USA54 Kevin Kramer .40 1.00
USA55 Francisco Lindor 4.00 10.00
USA56 Kenny Mathews .40 1.00
USA57 Evan Powell .60 1.50
USA58 Christopher Rivera .40 1.00
USA59 JoMarcos Woods .40 1.00
USA61 Trevor Bauer AU 4.00 10.00
USA62 Christian Colon AU 8.00 20.00
USA63 Cody Wheeler AU 3.00 8.00
USA64 Chad Bettis AU 3.00 8.00
USA65 Bryce Brentz AU 8.00 20.00
USA66 Nick Pepitone AU 3.00 8.00
USA67 Michael Choice AU 3.00 8.00
USA68 Gerrit Cole AU 10.00 25.00
USA69 Sonny Gray AU 8.00 20.00
USA70 Tyler Holt AU 3.00 8.00
USA71 T.J. Walz AU 4.00 10.00
USA72 Rick Hague AU 3.00 8.00
USA73 Drew Pomeranz AU 8.00 20.00
USA74 Blake Forsythe AU 4.00 10.00
USA75 Matt Newman AU 3.00 8.00
USA76 Casey McGrew AU 4.00 10.00
USA77 Brad Miller AU 8.00 20.00
USA78 Yasmani Grandal AU 10.00 25.00
USA79 Kolten Wong AU 8.00 20.00
USA80 Tony Zych AU 4.00 10.00
USA81 Andy Wilkins AU 3.00 8.00
USA82 Asher Wojciechowski AU 5.00 12.00
USA83 Bryce Harper AU 100.00 200.00
USA85 Cody Buckel AU 4.00 10.00
USA89 A.J. Vanegas AU 3.00 8.00
USA90 L.Montgomery AU 4.00 10.00
USA91 Karsten Whitson AU 5.00 12.00
USA95 Connor Mason AU 4.00 10.00
USA96 Garin Cecchini AU 5.00 12.00
USA98 Jameson Taillon AU 8.00 20.00
USA100 Sean Coyle AU 3.00 8.00
USA102 Kyle Ryan AU 3.00 8.00
USA105 Kevin Gausman AU 8.00 20.00
USA106 Robbie Ray AU 3.00 8.00
USA107 Nicky Delmonico AU 3.00 8.00
USA108 Cory Hahn AU 3.00 8.00
USA110 Nick Castellanos AU 8.00 20.00
USA113 Manny Machado AU 40.00 80.00
USA115 Phillip Pfeifer AU 3.00 8.00
USA116 Brian Ragira AU 5.00 12.00
USA119 Albert Almora Jsy 4.00 10.00
USA120 Shaun Chase Jsy 3.00 8.00
USA121 Austin Cousino Jsy 3.00 8.00
USA122 Dylan Davis Jsy 3.00 8.00
USA123 Parker French Jsy 4.00 10.00
USA124 Cory Geisler Jsy 3.00 8.00
USA126 C.J. Hinojosa Jsy 3.00 8.00
USA127 John Hochstatter Jsy 3.00 8.00
USA129 Ricardo Jacquez Jsy 4.00 10.00
USA130 Kevin Kramer Jsy 3.00 8.00
USA132 Francisco Lindor Jsy 15.00 40.00
USA134 Evan Powell Jsy 5.00 12.00
USA135 Christopher Rivera Jsy 3.00 8.00
USA136 JoMarcos Woods Jsy 4.00 10.00

2009-10 USA Baseball Patch Autograph Parallel

ONE PATCH OR PATCH AU PER BOX
STATED PRINT RUN 99 SER.#'d SETS
USA61 Trevor Bauer 6.00 15.00
USA62 Christian Colon 20.00 50.00
USA63 Cody Wheeler 4.00 10.00
USA64 Chad Bettis 8.00 20.00
USA65 Bryce Brentz 12.50 30.00
USA66 Nick Pepitone 5.00 12.00
USA67 Michael Choice 6.00 15.00
USA68 Gerrit Cole 30.00 60.00
USA69 Sonny Gray 6.00 15.00
USA70 Tyler Holt 4.00 10.00
USA71 T.J. Walz 10.00 25.00
USA72 Rick Hague 6.00 15.00
USA73 Drew Pomeranz 20.00 50.00
USA74 Blake Forsythe 5.00 12.00
USA75 Matt Newman 4.00 10.00
USA76 Casey McGrew 12.50 30.00
USA77 Brad Miller 15.00 40.00
USA78 Yasmani Grandal 20.00 50.00
USA79 Kolten Wong 30.00 60.00
USA80 Tony Zych 5.00 12.00
USA81 Andy Wilkins 5.00 12.00
USA82 Asher Wojciechowski 5.00 12.00
USA83 Bryce Harper 300.00 500.00
USA85 Cody Buckel 10.00 25.00
USA86 Tony Wolters 8.00 20.00
USA89 A.J. Vanegas 4.00 10.00
USA90 Ladson Montgomery 6.00 15.00
USA91 Karsten Whitson 6.00 15.00
USA95 Connor Mason 6.00 15.00
USA96 Garin Cecchini 8.00 20.00
USA98 Jameson Taillon 60.00 120.00
USA100 Sean Coyle 10.00 25.00
USA105 Kevin Gausman 12.50 30.00
USA106 Robbie Ray 10.00 25.00
USA107 Nicky Delmonico 8.00 20.00
USA108 Cory Hahn 5.00 12.00
USA110 Nick Castellanos 10.00 25.00
USA113 Manny Machado 25.00 60.00
USA115 Phillip Pfeifer 8.00 20.00
USA116 Brian Ragira 6.00 15.00

2009-10 USA Baseball 16U National Team Jersey Autographs

OVERALL ONE JSY AU PER BOX SET
STATED PRINT RUN 149 SER.#'d SETS
GREEN PRINT RUN 2 SER.#'d SETS
NO GRN PRICING DUE TO SCARCITY
RED PRINT RUN 25 SER.#'d SETS
NO RED PRICING DUE TO SCARCITY
AA Albert Almora 15.00 40.00
AC Austin Cousino 8.00 20.00
CG Cory Geisler 4.00 10.00
CH Courtney Hawkins 12.50 30.00
CR Christopher Rivera 4.00 10.00
DD Dylan Davis 4.00 10.00
EP Evan Powell 4.00 10.00
FL Francisco Lindor 40.00 100.00
HH Hayden Hurst 4.00 10.00
HI C.J. Hinojosa 4.00 10.00
JH John Hochstatter 4.00 10.00
JW JoMarcos Woods 10.00 25.00
KK Kevin Kramer 5.00 12.00
KM Kenny Mathews 4.00 10.00
PF Parker French 4.00 10.00
RJ Ricardo Jacquez 4.00 10.00
SC Shaun Chase 5.00 12.00

2009-10 USA Baseball 16U National Team Jerseys

TWO JSY CARDS PER BOX
AA Albert Almora 3.00 8.00
AC Austin Cousino 3.00 8.00
CG Cory Geisler 3.00 8.00
CH Courtney Hawkins 3.00 8.00
CR Christopher Rivera 3.00 8.00
DD Dylan Davis 3.00 8.00
EP Evan Powell 3.00 8.00
FL Francisco Lindor 8.00 20.00
HH Hayden Hurst 3.00 8.00
HI C.J. Hinojosa 3.00 8.00
JH John Hochstatter 3.00 8.00
JW JoMarcos Woods 3.00 8.00
KK Kevin Kramer 3.00 8.00
KM Kenny Mathews 3.00 8.00
PF Parker French 3.00 8.00
RJ Ricardo Jacquez 3.00 8.00
SC Shaun Chase 3.00 8.00

2009-10 USA Baseball 16U National Team Patch Autographs

ONE PATCH OR PATCH AU PER BOX
STATED PRINT RUN 35 SER.#'d SETS
AA Albert Almora 12.00 30.00
AC Austin Cousino 10.00 25.00
CG Cory Geisler 5.00 12.00
CH Courtney Hawkins 15.00 40.00
CR Christopher Rivera 8.00 20.00
DD Dylan Davis 8.00 20.00
EP Evan Powell 5.00 12.00
FL Francisco Lindor 75.00 200.00
HH Hayden Hurst 6.00 15.00
HI C.J. Hinojosa 10.00 25.00
JH John Hochstatter 5.00 12.00
JW JoMarcos Woods 12.50 30.00
KK Kevin Kramer 5.00 12.00
KM Kenny Mathews 12.50 30.00
PF Parker French 10.00 25.00
SC Shaun Chase 10.00 25.00

2009-10 USA Baseball 18U National Team Big Sigs

FIVE AUTOS PER BOX
STATED PRINT RUN 75 SER.#'d SETS
GOLD PRINT RUN 25 SER.#'d SETS
NO GOLD PRICING DUE TO SCARCITY
AV A.J. Vanegas 3.00 8.00
BH Bryce Harper 150.00 300.00
BR Brian Ragira 4.00 10.00
CB Cody Buckel 6.00 15.00
CH Cory Hahn 3.00 8.00
CM Connor Mason 3.00 8.00
GC Garin Cecchini 3.00 8.00
JT Jameson Taillon 10.00 25.00
KG Kevin Gausman 10.00 25.00
KR Kyle Ryan 4.00 10.00
KW Karsten Whitson 12.50 30.00
LM Ladson Montgomery 3.00 8.00
MM Manny Machado 40.00 80.00
NC Nick Castellanos 10.00 25.00
ND Nicky Delmonico 4.00 10.00
PP Phillip Pfeifer 3.00 8.00
RR Robbie Ray 4.00 10.00
SC Sean Coyle 5.00 12.00
TW Tony Wolters 4.00 10.00

2009-10 USA Baseball 18U National Team Inscriptions Autographs

FIVE AUTOS PER BOX
STATED PRINT RUN 162 SER.#'d SETS
GREEN PRINT RUN 2 SER.#'d SETS
NO GREEN PRICING DUE TO SCARCITY
RED PRINT RUN 15 SER.#'d SETS
NO RED PRICING DUE TO SCARCITY
AV A.J. Vanegas 4.00 10.00
BH Bryce Harper 125.00 250.00
BR Brian Ragira 10.00 25.00
CB Cody Buckel 5.00 12.00
CH Cory Hahn 3.00 8.00
CM Connor Mason 3.00 8.00
GC Garin Cecchini 10.00 25.00
JT Jameson Taillon 8.00 20.00
KG Kevin Gausman 10.00 25.00
KR Kyle Ryan 3.00 8.00
KW Karsten Whitson 5.00 12.00
LM Ladson Montgomery 3.00 8.00
NC Nick Castellanos 10.00 25.00
ND Nicky Delmonico 4.00 10.00
PP Phillip Pfeifer 3.00 8.00
RR Robbie Ray 4.00 10.00
SC Sean Coyle 8.00 20.00
TW Tony Wolters 8.00 20.00

2009-10 USA Baseball 18U National Team Jersey Autographs

OVERALL ONE JSY AU PER BOX SET
PRINT RUNS B/WN 28-149 COPIES PER
GREEN PRINT RUN 2 SER.#'d SETS
NO GRN PRICING DUE TO SCARCITY
RED PRINT RUN 25 SER.#'d SETS
NO RED PRICING DUE TO SCARCITY
AV A.J. Vanegas/32 4.00 10.00
BH Bryce Harper/149 150.00 300.00
BR Brian Ragira/149 15.00 40.00
CB Cody Buckel/28 5.00 12.00
CM Connor Mason/97 8.00 20.00
JT Jameson Taillon/149 30.00 60.00
KG Kevin Gausman/149 10.00 25.00
KK Kavin Keyes/149 4.00 10.00
KR Kyle Ryan/149 4.00 10.00
KW Karsten Whitson/37 12.50 30.00
LM Ladson Montgomery/62 4.00 10.00
MM Manny Machado/149 50.00 100.00
NC Nick Castellanos/36 12.00 30.00
ND Nicky Delmonico/149 4.00 10.00
PP Phillip Pfeifer/39 5.00 12.00
RR Robbie Ray/149 5.00 12.00
SC Sean Coyle/149 8.00 20.00
TW Tony Wolters/149 10.00 25.00

2009-10 USA Baseball 18U National Team Jerseys

TWO JSY CARDS PER BOX
AV A.J. Vanegas 3.00 8.00
BH Bryce Harper 12.00 30.00
BR Brian Ragira 3.00 8.00
CB Cody Buckel 3.00 8.00
CH Cory Hahn 3.00 8.00
CM Connor Mason 3.00 8.00
GC Garin Cecchini 3.00 8.00
JT Jameson Taillon 6.00 15.00
KG Kevin Gausman 3.00 8.00
KK Kavin Keyes 3.00 8.00
KR Kyle Ryan 3.00 8.00
KW Karsten Whitson 3.00 8.00
LM Ladson Montgomery 3.00 8.00
MM Manny Machado 8.00 20.00
NC Nick Castellanos 5.00 12.00
ND Nicky Delmonico 3.00 8.00
PP Phillip Pfeifer 3.00 8.00
RR Robbie Ray 3.00 8.00
SC Sean Coyle 3.00 8.00
TW Tony Wolters 3.00 8.00

2009-10 USA Baseball 18U National Team Patch Autographs

ONE PATCH OR PATCH AU PER BOX
STATED PRINT RUN 35 SER.#'d SETS
AV A.J. Vanegas 6.00 15.00
BH Bryce Harper 300.00 500.00
BR Brian Ragira 5.00 12.00
CB Cody Buckel 10.00 25.00
CH Cory Hahn 4.00 10.00
CM Connor Mason 10.00 25.00
GC Garin Cecchini 8.00 20.00
KG Kevin Gausman 10.00 25.00
KK Kavin Keyes 6.00 15.00
KR Kyle Ryan 4.00 10.00
KW Karsten Whitson 20.00 50.00
LM Ladson Montgomery 4.00 10.00
MM Manny Machado 60.00 120.00
NC Nick Castellanos 30.00 60.00
ND Nicky Delmonico 10.00 25.00
RR Robbie Ray 4.00 10.00
SC Sean Coyle 15.00 40.00
TW Tony Wolters 5.00 12.00

2009-10 USA Baseball 18U National Team Q And A Autographs

FIVE AUTOS PER BOX

STATED PRINT RUN 65 SER.#'d SETS
AV A.J. Vanegas 4.00 10.00
BH Bryce Harper 125.00 250.00
BR Brian Ragira 10.00 25.00
CB Cody Buckel 5.00 12.00
CH Cory Hahn 4.00 10.00
CM Connor Mason 6.00 15.00
GC Garin Cecchini 5.00 12.00
JT Jameson Taillon 15.00 40.00
KG Kevin Gausman 10.00 25.00
KR Kyle Ryan 4.00 10.00
KW Karsten Whitson 6.00 15.00
MM Manny Machado 12.00 30.00
NC Nick Castellanos 12.50 30.00
ND Nicky Delmonico 6.00 15.00
PP Phillip Pfeifer 4.00 10.00
RR Robbie Ray 5.00 12.00
SC Sean Coyle 5.00 12.00
TW Tony Wolters 5.00 12.00

2009-10 USA Baseball National Team Big Sigs

FIVE AUTOS PER BOX
STATED PRINT RUN 75 SER.#'d SETS
GOLD PRINT RUN 25 SER.#'d SETS
NO GOLD PRICING DUE TO SCARCITY
AW Andy Wilkins 3.00 8.00
BB Bryce Brentz 8.00 20.00
BF Blake Forsythe 5.00 12.00
BM Brad Miller 8.00 20.00
CB Chad Bettis 3.00 8.00
CC Christian Colon 5.00 12.00
CM Casey McGrew 8.00 20.00
CW Cody Wheeler 3.00 8.00
DP Drew Pomeranz 15.00 40.00
GC Gerrit Cole 12.50 30.00
KW Kolten Wong 10.00 25.00
MC Michael Choice 12.50 30.00
MN Matt Newman 4.00 10.00
NP Nick Pepitone 3.00 8.00
RH Rick Hague 4.00 10.00
SG Sonny Gray 6.00 15.00
TB Trevor Bauer 8.00 20.00
TH Tyler Holt 4.00 10.00
TW T.J. Walz 5.00 12.00
TZ Tony Zych 8.00 20.00
WO Asher Wojciechowski 3.00 8.00
YG Yasmani Grandal 12.50 30.00

2009-10 USA Baseball National Team Inscriptions Autographs

FIVE AUTOS PER BOX
STATED PRINT RUN 162 SER.#'d SETS
GREEN PRINT RUN 2 SER.#'d SETS
NO GREEN PRICING DUE TO SCARCITY
RED PRINT RUN 25 SER.#'d SETS
NO RED PRICING DUE TO SCARCITY
AW Andy Wilkins 8.00 20.00
BB Bryce Brentz 10.00 25.00
BF Blake Forsythe 4.00 10.00
BM Brad Miller 3.00 8.00
CB Chad Bettis 3.00 8.00
CC Christian Colon 5.00 12.00
CM Casey McGrew 4.00 10.00
CW Cody Wheeler 4.00 10.00
DP Drew Pomeranz 6.00 15.00
GC Gerrit Cole 10.00 25.00
KW Kolten Wong 10.00 25.00
MC Michael Choice 4.00 10.00
MN Matt Newman 3.00 8.00
NP Nick Pepitone 3.00 8.00
RH Rick Hague 4.00 10.00
SG Sonny Gray 6.00 15.00
TB Trevor Bauer 4.00 10.00
TH Tyler Holt 4.00 10.00
TW T.J. Walz 5.00 12.00
TZ Tony Zych 5.00 12.00
WO Asher Wojciechowski 4.00 10.00
YG Yasmani Grandal 8.00 20.00

2009-10 USA Baseball National Team Jersey Autographs

OVERALL ONE JSY AU PER BOX SET
STATED PRINT RUN 149 SER.#'d SETS
GREEN PRINT RUN 2 SER.#'d SETS
NO GRN PRICING DUE TO SCARCITY
RED PRINT RUN 25 SER.#'d SETS
NO RED PRICING DUE TO SCARCITY
AW Andy Wilkins 5.00 12.00
BB Bryce Brentz 12.50 30.00
BF Blake Forsythe 5.00 12.00
BM Brad Miller 4.00 10.00
CB Chad Bettis 4.00 10.00
CC Christian Colon 12.50 30.00
CM Casey McGrew 4.00 10.00
CW Cody Wheeler 4.00 10.00
DP Drew Pomeranz 5.00 12.00
GC Gerrit Cole 8.00 20.00
KW Kolten Wong 8.00 20.00
MC Michael Choice 10.00 25.00
MN Matt Newman 4.00 10.00
NP Nick Pepitone 4.00 10.00
RH Rick Hague 5.00 12.00
SG Sonny Gray 12.50 30.00
TB Trevor Bauer 30.00 60.00
TH Tyler Holt 4.00 10.00
TW T.J. Walz 5.00 12.00
TZ Tony Zych 5.00 12.00
WO Asher Wojciechowski 6.00 15.00
YG Yasmani Grandal 8.00 20.00

2009-10 USA Baseball National Team Jerseys

TWO JSY CARDS PER BOX
AW Andy Wilkins 3.00 8.00
BB Bryce Brentz 3.00 8.00
BF Blake Forsythe 3.00 8.00
BM Brad Miller 3.00 8.00
CB Chad Bettis 3.00 8.00
CC Christian Colon 4.00 10.00
CM Casey McGrew 3.00 8.00
CW Cody Wheeler 3.00 8.00
DP Drew Pomeranz 4.00 10.00
GC Gerrit Cole 5.00 12.00
KW Kolten Wong 3.00 8.00
MC Michael Choice 4.00 10.00
MN Matt Newman 3.00 8.00
NP Nick Pepitone 3.00 8.00
RH Rick Hague 3.00 8.00
SG Sonny Gray 3.00 8.00
TB Trevor Bauer 3.00 8.00
TH Tyler Holt 3.00 8.00
TW T.J. Walz 3.00 8.00
TZ Tony Zych 3.00 8.00
WO Asher Wojciechowski 3.00 8.00
YG Yasmani Grandal 4.00 10.00

2009-10 USA Baseball National Team Patch Autographs

ONE PATCH OR PATCH AU PER BOX
STATED PRINT RUN 35 SER.#'d SETS
AW Andy Wilkins 5.00 12.00
BB Bryce Brentz 20.00 50.00
BF Blake Forsythe 5.00 12.00
BM Brad Miller 20.00 50.00
CB Chad Bettis 6.00 15.00
CC Christian Colon 15.00 40.00
CM Casey McGrew 5.00 12.00
CW Cody Wheeler 10.00 25.00
DP Drew Pomeranz 15.00 40.00
GC Gerrit Cole 20.00 50.00
KW Kolten Wong 5.00 12.00
MC Michael Choice 20.00 50.00
MN Matt Newman 4.00 10.00
NP Nick Pepitone 4.00 10.00
RH Rick Hague 4.00 10.00
TB Trevor Bauer 30.00 60.00
TH Tyler Holt 8.00 20.00
TW T.J. Walz 10.00 25.00
WO Asher Wojciechowski 10.00 25.00
YG Yasmani Grandal 15.00 45.00

2009-10 USA Baseball National Team Q And A Autographs

FIVE AUTOS PER BOX
STATED PRINT RUN 65 SER.#'d SETS
AW Asher Wojciechowski 6.00 15.00
BB Bryce Brentz 8.00 20.00
BF Blake Forsythe 6.00 15.00
CB Chad Bettis 4.00 10.00
CC Christian Colon 4.00 10.00
CM Casey McGrew 10.00 25.00
CW Cody Wheeler 4.00 10.00
DP Drew Pomeranz 10.00 25.00
GC Gerrit Cole 12.50 30.00
KW Kolten Wong 5.00 12.00
MC Michael Choice 6.00 15.00
MN Matt Newman 5.00 12.00
NP Nick Pepitone 4.00 10.00
RH Rick Hague 5.00 12.00
SG Sonny Gray 4.00 10.00
TB Trevor Bauer 12.50 30.00
TH Tyler Holt 5.00 12.00
TW T.J. Walz 6.00 15.00
TZ Tony Zych 4.00 10.00
WI Andy Wilkins 5.00 12.00
YG Yasmani Grandal 12.50 30.00

2010 USA Baseball

COMPLETE SET (65) 12.50 30.00
COMMON CARD .20 .50
PRINTING PLATES RANDOMLY INSERTED
USA1 Albert Almora .60 1.50
USA2 Daniel Camarena .20 .50
USA3 Nicky Delmonico .30 .75
USA4 John Hochstatter .20 .50
USA5 Francisco Lindor 1.50 4.00
USA6 Marcus Littlewood .30 .75
USA7 Christian Lopes .30 .75
USA8 Michael Lorenzen .20 .50
USA9 Dillon Maples .20 .50
USA10 Lance McCullers .30 .75
USA11 Christian Montgomery .20 .50
USA12 Henry Owens .30 .75
USA13 Phillip Pfeifer III .20 .50
USA14 Brian Ragira .20 .50
USA15 John Simms .30 .75
USA16 Elvin Soto .20 .50
USA17 Bubba Starling .30 .75
USA18 Blake Swihart .50 1.25
USA19 AJ Vanegas .30 .75
USA20 Tony Wolters .30 .75
USA21 Ricardo Jacquez .20 .50
USA22 Tyler Anderson .30 .75
USA23 Matt Barnes .50 1.25
USA24 Jackie Bradley Jr. .75 2.00
USA25 Gerrit Cole 2.00 5.00
USA26 Alex Dickerson .20 .50
USA27 Jason Esposito .50 1.25
USA28 Nolan Fontana .30 .75
USA29 Sean Gilmartin .30 .75
USA30 Sonny Gray .50 1.25
USA31 Brian Johnson .20 .50
USA32 Andrew Maggi .20 .50
USA33 Mikie Mahtook .50 1.25
USA34 Scott McGough .50 1.25
USA35 Brad Miller .50 1.25
USA36 Brett Mooneyham .50 1.25
USA37 Peter O'Brien .50 1.25
USA38 Nick Ramirez .30 .75
USA39 Noe Ramirez .30 .75
USA40 Steve Rodriguez .30 .75
USA41 George Springer 1.25 3.00
USA42 Kyle Winkler .50 1.25
USA43 Ryan Wright .20 .50
USA44 Anthony Rendon 1.50 4.00
USA45 Albert Almora .60 1.50
USA46 Cole Billingsley .30 .75
USA47 Sean Brady .20 .50
USA48 Marc Brakeman .20 .50
USA49 Alex Bregman 2.50 6.00
USA50 Ryan Burr .50 1.25
USA51 Chris Chinea .30 .75
USA52 Troy Conyers .20 .50
USA53 Zach Green .20 .50
USA54 Carson Kelly .60 1.50
USA55 Timmy Lopes .20 .50
USA56 Adrian Marin .30 .75
USA57 Chris Okey .20 .50
USA58 Matt Olson 1.50 4.00
USA59 Ivan Pelaez .20 .50
USA60 Felipe Perez .20 .50
USA61 Nelson Rodriguez .30 .75
USA62 Corey Seager 2.50 6.00
USA63 Lucas Sims .50 1.25
USA64 Nick Travieso .30 .75
USA65 Sheldon Neuse .30 .75

2010 USA Baseball Autographs

A production error resulted in 20 cards in this set being numbered "A-TBD". We have cataloged these cards in alphabetical order - immediately following #A42 - starting with #ATBD1 and concluding with #ATBD20.
OVERALL AUTO ODDS 7 PER BOX SET
#ATBD CARDS IN ALPHABETICAL ORDER
A1 AJ Vanegas 4.00 10.00
A2 Albert Almora 10.00 25.00
A3 Blake Swihart 6.00 15.00
A4 Brian Ragira 4.00 10.00
A5 Christian Lopes 4.00 10.00
A6 Christian Montgomery 4.00 10.00
A7 Daniel Camarena 4.00 10.00
A8 Bubba Starling 10.00 25.00
A9 Dillon Maples 4.00 10.00
A10 Elvin Soto 4.00 10.00
A11 Francisco Lindor 30.00 80.00
A12 Henry Owens 4.00 10.00
A13 John Hochstatter 4.00 10.00
A14 John Simms 4.00 10.00
A15 Lance McCullers 6.00 15.00
A16 Marcus Littlewood 4.00 10.00
A17 Michael Lorenzen 4.00 10.00
A18 Nicky Delmonico 4.00 10.00
A19 Philip Pfeifer III 4.00 10.00
A20 Tony Wolters 4.00 10.00
A21 Tyler Anderson 4.00 10.00
A22 Matt Barnes 4.00 10.00
A23 Jackie Bradley Jr. 8.00 20.00
A24 Gerrit Cole 12.00 30.00
A25 Alex Dickerson 4.00 10.00
A26 Nolan Fontana 4.00 10.00
A27 Sean Gilmartin 4.00 10.00
A28 Sonny Gray 12.00 30.00
A29 Brian Johnson 4.00 10.00
A30 Andrew Maggi 4.00 10.00
A31 Mikie Mahtook 10.00 25.00
A32 Scott McGough 4.00 10.00
A33 Brad Miller 4.00 10.00
A34 Brett Mooneyham 5.00 12.00
A35 Peter O'Brien 4.00 10.00
A36 Nick Ramirez 4.00 10.00
A37 Noe Ramirez 4.00 10.00
A38 Jason Esposito 4.00 10.00
A39 Steve Rodriguez 4.00 10.00
A40 George Springer 15.00 40.00
A41 Kyle Winkler 4.00 10.00
A42 Ryan Wright 4.00 10.00
ATBD1 Albert Almora 4.00 10.00
ATBD2 Cole Billingsley 4.00 10.00
ATBD3 Sean Brady 4.00 10.00
ATBD4 Marc Brakeman 4.00 10.00
ATBD5 Alex Bregman 12.00 30.00
ATBD6 Ryan Burr 4.00 10.00
ATBD7 Chris Chinea 4.00 10.00
ATBD8 Troy Conyers 4.00 10.00
ATBD9 Zach Green 4.00 10.00
ATBD10 Carson Kelly 5.00 12.00
ATBD11 Timmy Lopes 4.00 10.00
ATBD12 Adrian Marin 4.00 10.00
ATBD13 Chris Okey 4.00 10.00
ATBD14 Matt Olson 20.00 50.00
ATBD15 Ivan Pelaez 4.00 10.00
ATBD16 Felipe Perez 4.00 10.00
ATBD17 Nelson Rodriguez 4.00 10.00
ATBD18 Corey Seager 50.00 120.00
ATBD19 Lucas Sims 4.00 10.00
ATBD20 Nick Travieso 8.00 20.00

2010 USA Baseball Autographs Red

*RED: .75X TO 2X BASIC AUTO
OVERALL AUTO ODDS SEVEN PER BOX SET
STATED PRINT RUN 99 SER.#'d SETS

2010 USA Baseball Triple Jersey Autographs

OVERALL AUTO ODDS 7 PER BOX SET
STATED PRINT RUN 219 SER.#'d SETS
AA Albert Almora 12.00 30.00
AD Alex Dickerson 5.00 12.00
AM Andrew Maggi 5.00 12.00
AV AJ Vanegas 5.00 12.00
BJ Brian Johnson 5.00 12.00
BM Brad Miller 5.00 12.00
BMO Brett Mooneyham 5.00 12.00
BR Brian Ragira 5.00 12.00
BS Bubba Starling 10.00 25.00
BSW Blake Swihart 10.00 25.00
CL Christian Lopes 5.00 12.00
DC Daniel Camarena 5.00 12.00
DM Dillon Maples 5.00 12.00
ES Elvin Soto 5.00 12.00
FL Francisco Lindor 20.00 50.00
GC Gerrit Cole 12.00 30.00
GS George Springer 15.00 40.00
HO Henry Owens 4.00 10.00
JB Jackie Bradley Jr. 40.00 100.00
JE Jason Esposito 5.00 12.00
JH John Hochstatter 5.00 12.00
JS John Simms 5.00 12.00
KW Kyle Winkler 5.00 12.00
LM Lance McCullers 8.00 20.00
MB Matt Barnes 8.00 20.00
ML Marcus Littlewood 6.00 15.00
MLO Michael Lorenzen 5.00 12.00
MM Mikie Mahtook 8.00 20.00
ND Nicky Delmonico 8.00 20.00
NF Nolan Fontana 5.00 12.00
NR Nick Ramirez 5.00 12.00
NRA Noe Ramirez 5.00 12.00
PO Peter O'Brien 5.00 12.00
PP Phillip Pfeifer III 5.00 12.00
RW Ryan Wright 5.00 12.00
SG Sean Gilmartin 6.00 15.00
SGR Sonny Gray 10.00 25.00
SM Scott McGough 5.00 12.00
SR Steve Rodriguez 5.00 12.00
TA Tyler Anderson 5.00 12.00
TW Tony Wolters 5.00 12.00

2010 USA Baseball Triple Jerseys

OVERALL MEM ODDS 3 PER BOX SET
AA Albert Almora 3.00 8.00
AB Alex Bregman 3.00 8.00
AD Alex Dickerson 3.00 8.00
AM Andrew Maggi 3.00 8.00
AV AJ Vanegas 3.00 8.00
BJ Brian Johnson 3.00 8.00
BM Brad Miller 3.00 8.00
BR Brian Ragira 3.00 8.00
BS Bubba Starling 6.00 15.00
CB Cole Billingsley 3.00 8.00
CC Chris Chinea 3.00 8.00
CK Carson Kelly 3.00 8.00
CL Christian Lopes 3.00 8.00
CO Chris Okey 3.00 8.00
CS Corey Seager 5.00 12.00
DC Daniel Camarena 3.00 8.00
DM Dillon Maples 3.00 8.00
ES Elvin Soto 3.00 8.00
FL Francisco Lindor 3.00 8.00
FP Felipe Perez 3.00 8.00
GC Gerrit Cole 4.00 10.00
GS George Springer 5.00 12.00
HO Henry Owens 3.00 8.00
IP Ivan Pelaez 3.00 8.00
JB Jackie Bradley Jr. 4.00 10.00
JE Jason Esposito 3.00 8.00
JH John Hochstatter 3.00 8.00
JS John Simms 3.00 8.00
KW Kyle Winkler 3.00 8.00
LM Lance McCullers 3.00 8.00
LS Lucas Sims 3.00 8.00
MB Matt Barnes 3.00 8.00
ML Marcus Littlewood 3.00 8.00
MM Mikie Mahtook 3.00 8.00
MO Matt Olson 4.00 10.00
ND Nicky Delmonico 3.00 8.00
NF Nolan Fontana 3.00 8.00
NR Nick Ramirez 3.00 8.00
PO Peter O'Brien 3.00 8.00
PP Phillip Pfeifer III 3.00 8.00
RB Ryan Burr 3.00 8.00
RJ Ricardo Jacquez 3.00 8.00
RW Ryan Wright 3.00 8.00
SB Sean Brady 3.00 8.00
SG Sean Gilmartin 3.00 8.00
SM Scott McGough 3.00 8.00
SN Sheldon Neuse 3.00 8.00
SR Steve Rodriguez 3.00 8.00
TA Tyler Anderson 3.00 8.00
TC Troy Conyers 3.00 8.00
TL Timmy Lopes 3.00 8.00
TW Tony Wolters 3.00 8.00
ZG Zach Green 3.00 8.00
AMA Adrian Marin 3.00 8.00
BMO Brett Mooneyham 3.00 8.00
BSW Blake Swihart 3.00 8.00
MBR Marc Brakeman 3.00 8.00
MLO Michael Lorenzen 3.00 8.00
NRA Noe Ramirez 3.00 8.00
NRO Nelson Rodriguez 3.00 8.00
SGR Sonny Gray 3.00 8.00

2010 USA Baseball Triple Patch Autographs

OVERALL AUTO ODDS SEVEN PER BOX SET
STATED PRINT RUN 50 SER.#'d SETS
AA Albert Almora 20.00 50.00
AD Alex Dickerson 20.00 50.00
AM Andrew Maggi 8.00 20.00
AV AJ Vanegas 8.00 20.00
BJ Brian Johnson 8.00 20.00
BM Brad Miller 15.00 40.00
BMO Brett Mooneyham 10.00 25.00
BR Brian Ragira 10.00 25.00
BS Bubba Starling 60.00 120.00
BSW Blake Swihart 50.00 100.00
CL Christian Lopes 10.00 25.00
DC Daniel Camarena 12.50 30.00
DM Dillon Maples 8.00 20.00
ES Elvin Soto 15.00 40.00
FL Francisco Lindor 75.00 200.00
GC Gerrit Cole 10.00 25.00
GS George Springer 30.00 80.00
HO Henry Owens 20.00 50.00
JB Jackie Bradley Jr. 60.00 150.00
JE Jason Esposito 10.00 25.00
JH John Hochstatter 12.50 30.00
JS John Simms 15.00 40.00
KW Kyle Winkler 8.00 20.00
LM Lance McCullers 15.00 40.00
MB Matt Barnes 10.00 25.00
ML Marcus Littlewood 8.00 20.00
MLO Michael Lorenzen 12.50 30.00
MM Mikie Mahtook 10.00 25.00
ND Nicky Delmonico 10.00 25.00
NF Nolan Fontana 8.00 20.00
NR Nick Ramirez 10.00 25.00
NRA Noe Ramirez 8.00 20.00
PO Peter O'Brien 20.00 50.00
PP Phillip Pfeifer III 15.00 40.00
RW Ryan Wright 8.00 20.00
SG Sean Gilmartin 30.00 60.00
SGR Sonny Gray 10.00 25.00
SM Scott McGough 15.00 40.00
SR Steve Rodriguez 8.00 20.00
TA Tyler Anderson 10.00 25.00
TW Tony Wolters 10.00 25.00

2011 USA Baseball

COMPLETE SET (61) 6.00 15.00
COMMON CARD .20 .50
PLATE PRINT RUN 1 SET PER COLOR
BLACK-CYAN-MAGENTA-YELLOW ISSUED
NO PLATE PRICING DUE TO SCARCITY
USA1 Mark Appel .50 1.25
USA2 D.J. Baxendale .30 .75
USA3 Josh Elander .20 .50
USA4 Chris Elder .20 .50
USA5 Dominic Ficociello .20 .50
USA6 Nolan Fontana .20 .50
USA7 Kevin Gausman .75 2.00
USA8 Brian Johnson .20 .50
USA9 Branden Kline .20 .50
USA10 Corey Knebel .20 .50
USA11 Michael Lorenzen .20 .50
USA12 David Lyon .20 .50
USA13 Deven Marrero .50 1.25
USA14 Hoby Milner .20 .50
USA15 Andrew Mitchell .20 .50
USA16 Tom Murphy .20 .50
USA17 Tyler Naquin .40 1.00
USA18 Matt Reynolds .30 .75
USA19 Brady Rodgers .20 .50
USA20 Marcus Stroman .50 1.25
USA21 Michael Wacha .60 1.50
USA22 Erich Weiss .20 .50
USA23 William Abreu .30 .75
USA24 Tyler Alamo .20 .50
USA25 Bryson Brigman .20 .50
USA26 Nick Ciuffo .20 .50
USA27 Trevor Clifton .20 .50
USA28 Zack Collins .30 .75
USA29 Joe DeMers .20 .50
USA30 Steven Farinaro .20 .50
USA31 Jake Jarvis .20 .50
USA32 Austin Meadows .75 2.00
USA33 Hunter Mercado-Hood .20 .50
USA34 Dom Nunez .20 .50
USA35 Arden Pabst .20 .50
USA36 Christian Pelaez .20 .50
USA37 Carson Sands .20 .50
USA38 Jordan Sheffield .20 .50
USA39 Keegan Thompson .20 .50
USA40 Touki Toussaint .30 .75
USA41 Riley Unroe .20 .50
USA42 Matt Vogel .20 .50
USA43 Albert Almora .30 .75
USA44 Alex Bregman 1.25 3.00
USA45 Gavin Cecchini .30 .75
USA46 Troy Conyers .20 .50
USA47 Carson Kelly .30 .75
USA48 Chase DeJong .40 1.00
USA49 Carson Fulmer .40 1.00
USA50 Cole Irvin .30 .75
USA51 Jeremy Martinez .20 .50
USA52 Walker Weickel .20 .50
USA53 Chris Okey .20 .50
USA54 Cody Poteet .20 .50
USA55 Nelson Rodriguez .30 .75
USA56 Hunter Virant .20 .50
USA57 Addison Russell .60 1.50
USA58 Clate Schmidt .20 .50
USA59 Mikey White .20 .50
USA60 Jesse Winker .20 .50
USA61 Joey Gallo 1.00 2.50

2011 USA Baseball Autographs

OVERALL SEVEN AUTOS PER HOBBY SET
A1 Mark Appel 6.00 15.00
A2 D.J. Baxendale 5.00 12.00
A3 Josh Elander 4.00 10.00
A4 Chris Elder 3.00 8.00
A5 Dominic Ficociello 4.00 10.00
A6 Nolan Fontana 4.00 10.00
A7 Kevin Gausman 6.00 15.00
A8 Brian Johnson 3.00 8.00
A9 Branden Kline 3.00 8.00
A10 Corey Knebel 3.00 8.00
A11 Michael Lorenzen 3.00 8.00
A12 David Lyon 3.00 8.00
A13 Deven Marrero 6.00 15.00
A14 Hoby Milner 3.00 8.00
A15 Andrew Mitchell 3.00 8.00
A16 Tom Murphy 3.00 8.00
A17 Tyler Naquin 10.00 25.00
A18 Matt Reynolds 3.00 8.00
A19 Brady Rodgers 3.00 8.00
A20 Marcus Stroman 3.00 8.00
A21 Michael Wacha 5.00 12.00
A22 Erich Weiss 3.00 8.00
A23 William Abreu 4.00 10.00
A24 Tyler Alamo 4.00 10.00
A25 Bryson Brigman 4.00 10.00
A26 Nick Ciuffo 4.00 10.00
A27 Trevor Clifton 3.00 8.00
A28 Zack Collins 4.00 10.00
A29 Joe DeMers 5.00 12.00
A30 Steven Farinaro 4.00 10.00
A31 Jake Jarvis 3.00 8.00
A32 Austin Meadows 15.00 40.00
A33 Hunter Mercado-Hood 3.00 8.00
A34 Dom Nunez 3.00 8.00
A35 Arden Pabst 4.00 10.00
A36 Christian Pelaez 3.00 8.00
A37 Carson Sands 4.00 10.00
A38 Jordan Sheffield 4.00 10.00
A39 Keegan Thompson 4.00 10.00
A40 Touki Toussaint 6.00 15.00
A41 Riley Unroe 4.00 10.00
A42 Matt Vogel 4.00 10.00
A43 Albert Almora 5.00 12.00
A44 Alex Bregman 15.00 40.00
A45 Gavin Cecchini 5.00 12.00
A46 Troy Conyers 3.00 8.00
A48 Chase DeJong 3.00 8.00
A50 Carson Fulmer 3.00 8.00
A51 Joey Gallo 10.00 25.00
A55 Cole Irvin 3.00 8.00
A56 Carson Kelly 4.00 10.00
A57 Jeremy Martinez 3.00 8.00
A59 Chris Okey 3.00 8.00
A60 Cody Poteet 3.00 8.00
A61 Nelson Rodriguez 3.00 8.00
A63A David Dahl 10.00 25.00
A63B Addison Russell 12.00 30.00
A64 Clate Schmidt 4.00 10.00
A66 Hunter Virant 3.00 8.00
A67 Walker Weickel 3.00 8.00
A68 Mikey White 3.00 8.00
A70 Jesse Winker 4.00 10.00

2011 USA Baseball Autographs Red

*RED: .6X TO 1.5X BASIC
OVERALL SEVEN AUTOS PER HOBBY SET
STATED PRINT RUN 99 SER.#'d SETS

2011 USA Baseball Triple Jersey Autographs

OVERALL SEVEN AUTOS PER HOBBY SET
STATED PRINT RUNS B/WN 64-214 PER
AA Albert Almora/214 6.00 15.00
AB Alex Bregman/214 20.00 50.00
AM Andrew Mitchell/214 4.00 10.00
AM Austin Meadows/64 20.00 50.00
AP Arden Pabst/64 4.00 10.00
AR Addison Russell/214 15.00 40.00
BB Bryson Brigman/64 6.00 15.00
BJ Brian Johnson/214 4.00 10.00
BK Branden Kline/214 4.00 10.00
BK Corey Knebel/214 4.00 10.00
BR Brady Rodgers/214 4.00 10.00
CD Chase DeJong/214 4.00 10.00
CE Chris Elder/214 4.00 10.00
CF Carson Fulmer/214 10.00 25.00
CI Cole Irvin/214 4.00 10.00
CKE Carson Kelly/214 4.00 10.00
CO Chris Okey/214 4.00 10.00
CP Cody Poteet/214 4.00 10.00
CPZ Christian Pelaez/64 4.00 10.00
CS Clate Schmidt/214 4.00 10.00
CSA Carson Sands/64 5.00 12.00
DB D.J. Baxendale/214 6.00 15.00
DF Dominic Ficociello/214 4.00 10.00
DL David Lyon/214 4.00 10.00
DM Deven Marrero/214 4.00 10.00
DN Dom Nunez/64 5.00 12.00
DT Touki Toussaint/64 10.00 25.00
EW Erich Weiss/214 4.00 10.00
GC Gavin Cecchini/214 6.00 15.00
HM Hoby Milner/214 4.00 10.00
HMH Hunter Mercado-Hood/64 4.00 10.00
HV Hunter Virant/214 4.00 10.00
JD Joe DeMers/64 8.00 20.00
JE Josh Elander/214 5.00 12.00
JG Joey Gallo/214 10.00 25.00
JJ Jake Jarvis/64 4.00 10.00
JM Jeremy Martinez/214 6.00 15.00
JS Jordan Sheffield/64 4.00 10.00
JW Jesse Winker/214 4.00 10.00
KG Kevin Gausman/214 4.00 10.00
KT Keegan Thompson/64 8.00 20.00
MA Mark Appel/214 6.00 15.00
ML Michael Lorenzen/214 4.00 10.00
MR Matt Reynolds/214 4.00 10.00
MS Marcus Stroman/214 4.00 10.00
MV Matt Vogel/64 5.00 12.00
MW Michael Wacha/214 10.00 25.00
MWH Mikey White/214 4.00 10.00
NC Nick Ciuffo/64 6.00 15.00
NF Nolan Fontana/214 4.00 10.00
NR Nelson Rodriguez/214 4.00 10.00
RU Riley Unroe/64 4.00 10.00
SF Steven Farinaro/64 5.00 12.00
TA Tyler Alamo/64 4.00 10.00
TC Troy Conyers/214 4.00 10.00
TCL Trevor Clifton/64 6.00 15.00
TM Tom Murphy/214 4.00 10.00
TN Tyler Naquin/214 4.00 10.00
WA William Abreu/64 8.00 20.00
WW Walker Weickel/214 5.00 12.00
ZC Zack Collins/64 5.00 12.00

2011 USA Baseball Triple Jerseys

OVERALL MEM ODDS 3 PER HOBBY SET
STATED PRINT RUN 240 SER.#'d SETS
AA Albert Almora 3.00 8.00
AB Alex Bregman 3.00 8.00
AM Andrew Mitchell 3.00 8.00
AP Arden Pabst 3.00 8.00
AR Addison Russell 5.00 12.00
BB Bryson Brigman 3.00 8.00
BJ Brian Johnson 3.00 8.00
BK Branden Kline 3.00 8.00
BR Brady Rodgers 3.00 8.00
CD Chase DeJong 3.00 8.00
CE Chris Elder 3.00 8.00
CF Carson Fulmer 4.00 10.00
CI Cole Irvin 3.00 8.00
CK Corey Knebel 3.00 8.00
CO Chris Okey 3.00 8.00
CP Cody Poteet 3.00 8.00
CS Clate Schmidt 3.00 8.00
DB D.J. Baxendale 3.00 8.00
DF Dominic Ficociello 4.00 10.00
DL David Lyon 3.00 8.00
DM Deven Marrero 3.00 8.00
DN Dom Nunez 3.00 8.00
DT Touki Toussaint 3.00 8.00
EW Erich Weiss 3.00 8.00
GC Gavin Cecchini 3.00 8.00
HM Hoby Milner 3.00 8.00
HV Hunter Virant 3.00 8.00
JD Joe DeMers 3.00 8.00
JE Josh Elander 3.00 8.00
JG Joey Gallo 6.00 15.00
JJ Jake Jarvis 3.00 8.00
JM Jeremy Martinez 3.00 8.00
JS Jordan Sheffield 3.00 8.00
JW Jesse Winker 3.00 8.00
KG Kevin Gausman 4.00 10.00
KT Keegan Thompson 3.00 8.00
MA Mark Appel 4.00 10.00
ML Michael Lorenzen 3.00 8.00
MR Matt Reynolds 3.00 8.00
MS Marcus Stroman 3.00 8.00
MV Matt Vogel 3.00 8.00
MW Michael Wacha 5.00 12.00
NC Nick Ciuffo 3.00 8.00
NF Nolan Fontana 3.00 8.00
NR Nelson Rodriguez 3.00 8.00
RU Riley Unroe 3.00 8.00
SF Steven Farinaro 3.00 8.00
TA Tyler Alamo 3.00 8.00
TC Troy Conyers 3.00 8.00
TM Tom Murphy 3.00 8.00
TN Tyler Naquin 3.00 8.00
WA William Abreu 3.00 8.00
WW Walker Weickel 3.00 8.00
ZC Zack Collins 3.00 8.00
AME Austin Meadows 6.00 15.00
CKE Carson Kelly 3.00 8.00
CPZ Christian Pelaez 3.00 8.00
CSA Carson Sands 3.00 8.00
HMH Hunter Mercado-Hood 3.00 8.00
MWH Mikey White 3.00 8.00
TCL Trevor Clifton 3.00 8.00

2012 USA Baseball

COMPLETE SET (65) 12.50 30.00
COMP.SET PRICE INCLUDES CHECKLISTS
1 David Berg .20 .50
2 Kris Bryant 8.00 20.00
3 Dan Child .20 .50
4 Michael Conforto 1.25 3.00
5 Austin Cousino .20 .50
6 Jonathon Crawford .30 .75
7 Kyle Farmer .30 .75
8 Johnny Field .30 .75
9 Adam Frazier .20 .50
10 Marco Gonzales .50 1.25
11 Brett Hambright .20 .50
12 Jordan Hankins .20 .50
13 Michael Lorenzen .30 .75
14 D.J. Peterson .20 .50
15 Colton Plaia .20 .50
16 Adam Plutko .20 .50
17 Jake Reed .30 .75
18 Carlos Rodon .75 2.00
19 Ryne Stanek .75 2.00
20 Jose Trevino .20 .50
21 Trea Turner 1.00 2.50
22 Bobby Wahl .20 .50
23 Trevor Williams .30 .75
24 Willie Abreu .30 .75
25 Christian Arroyo 2.00 5.00
26 Cavan Biggio .75 2.00
27 Ryan Boldt .50 1.25
28 Bryson Brigman .30 .75
29 Ian Clarkin .50 1.25
30 Kevin Davis .20 .50
31 Stephen Gonsalves .30 .75
32 Connor Heady .30 .75
33 John Kilichowski .20 .50
34 Jeremy Martinez .30 .75
35 Reese McGuire .60 1.50
36 Dom Nunez .20 .50
37 Chris Okey .20 .50
38 Ryan Olson .20 .50
39 Carson Sands .20 .50
40 Dominic Taccolini .20 .50
41 Keegan Thompson .20 .50
42 Garrett Williams .30 .75
43 John Aiello .30 .75
44 Nick Anderson .20 .50
45 Luken Baker .50 1.25
46 Solomon Bates .20 .50
47 Chris Betts .20 .50
48 Danny Casals .30 .75
49 Chris Cullen .30 .75
50 Kyle Dean .30 .75
51 Bailey Falter .20 .50
52 Isaak Gutierrez .20 .50
53 Nico Hoerner .60 1.50
54 Parker Kelly .50 1.25
55 Nick Madrigal .60 1.50
56 Austin Moore
57 Jio Orozco .20 .50
58 Kyle Robeniol .30 .75
59 Blake Rutherford .60 1.50
60 Cole Sands .20 .50
61 Kyle Tucker 2.00 5.00
62 Coby Weaver .30 .75

2012 USA Baseball 15U National Team Dual Jerseys

STATED PRINT RUN 49 SER.#'d SETS
3 Luken Baker 4.00 10.00
7 Chris Cullen 4.00 10.00
8 Kyle Dean 3.00 8.00
11 Nico Hoerner 4.00 10.00
13 Nick Madrigal 5.00 12.00
14 Austin Moore 4.00 10.00
16 Kyle Robeniol 4.00 10.00
18 Cole Sands 3.00 8.00
19 Kyle Tucker 5.00 12.00
20 Coby Weaver 4.00 10.00

2012 USA Baseball 15U National Team Dual Jerseys Signatures

STATED PRINT RUN 49 SER.#'d SETS
2 Nick Anderson 4.00 10.00
3 Luken Baker 6.00 15.00
4 Solomon Bates 6.00 15.00
5 Chris Betts 4.00 10.00
6 Danny Casals 4.00 10.00
7 Chris Cullen 4.00 10.00
8 Kyle Dean 10.00 25.00
9 Bailey Falter 6.00 15.00
10 Isaak Gutierrez 4.00 10.00
11 Nico Hoerner 8.00 20.00
12 Parker Kelly 4.00 10.00
13 Nick Madrigal 6.00 15.00
14 Austin Moore 4.00 10.00
15 Jio Orozco 4.00 10.00
16 Kyle Robeniol 4.00 10.00
18 Cole Sands 4.00 10.00
19 Kyle Tucker 10.00 25.00
20 Coby Weaver 6.00 15.00

2012 USA Baseball 15U National Team Jersey Signatures

STATED PRINT RUN 99 SER.#'d SETS
1 John Aiello 4.00 10.00
3 Luken Baker 5.00 12.00
4 Solomon Bates 4.00 10.00
5 Chris Betts 5.00 12.00
6 Danny Casals 8.00 20.00
7 Chris Cullen 4.00 10.00
8 Kyle Dean 4.00 10.00
9 Bailey Falter 4.00 10.00
10 Isaak Gutierrez 4.00 10.00
12 Parker Kelly 20.00 50.00
14 Austin Moore 5.00 12.00
15 Jio Orozco 4.00 10.00
16 Kyle Robeniol 4.00 10.00
17 Blake Rutherford 6.00 15.00
18 Cole Sands 4.00 10.00
19 Kyle Tucker 10.00 25.00
20 Coby Weaver 4.00 10.00

2012 USA Baseball 15U National Team Jerseys

STATED PRINT RUN 99 SER.#'d SETS
1 John Aiello 4.00 10.00
2 Nick Anderson 3.00 8.00
4 Solomon Bates 3.00 8.00
5 Chris Betts 3.00 8.00
6 Danny Casals 3.00 8.00
7 Chris Cullen 3.00 8.00
8 Kyle Dean 3.00 8.00
9 Bailey Falter 3.00 8.00
10 Isaak Gutierrez 3.00 8.00
12 Parker Kelly 3.00 8.00
13 Nick Madrigal 4.00 10.00
14 Austin Moore 3.00 8.00
15 Jio Orozco 3.00 8.00
16 Kyle Robeniol 3.00 8.00
17 Blake Rutherford 3.00 8.00
18 Cole Sands 3.00 8.00
19 Kyle Tucker 5.00 12.00
20 Coby Weaver 3.00 8.00

2012 USA Baseball 15U National Team Patches

*PATCH: .6X TO 1.5X BASIC
STATED PRINT RUN 35 SER.#'d SETS

2012 USA Baseball 15U National Team Patches Signatures

STATED PRINT RUN 35 SER.#'d SETS
1 John Aiello 5.00 12.00
2 Nick Anderson 5.00 12.00
4 Solomon Bates 8.00 20.00
7 Chris Cullen 10.00 25.00
12 Parker Kelly 10.00 25.00
13 Nick Madrigal 8.00 20.00
15 Jio Orozco 5.00 12.00
17 Blake Rutherford 12.00 30.00
18 Cole Sands 10.00 25.00
19 Kyle Tucker 20.00 50.00
20 Coby Weaver 8.00 20.00

2012 USA Baseball 15U National Team Profile Signatures

STATED PRINT RUN 100 SER.#'d SETS
1 John Aiello 6.00 15.00
2 Nick Anderson 5.00 12.00
3 Luken Baker 4.00 10.00
4 Solomon Bates 4.00 10.00
5 Chris Betts 5.00 12.00
6 Danny Casals 4.00 10.00
7 Chris Cullen 4.00 10.00
8 Kyle Dean 4.00 10.00
9 Bailey Falter 4.00 10.00
10 Isaak Gutierrez 4.00 10.00

11 Nico Hoerner 12.00 30.00
12 Parker Kelly 8.00 20.00
13 Nick Madrigal 6.00 15.00
14 Austin Moore 6.00 15.00
16 Kyle Robeniol 4.00 10.00
17 Blake Rutherford 6.00 15.00
18 Cole Sands 4.00 10.00
19 Kyle Tucker 10.00 25.00

2012 USA Baseball 15U National Team Signatures

STATED PRINT RUN 299 SER.#'d SETS
1 John Aiello 3.00 8.00
2 Nick Anderson 4.00 10.00
3 Luken Baker 4.00 10.00
4 Solomon Bates 3.00 8.00
5 Chris Betts 6.00 15.00
6 Danny Casals 3.00 8.00
7 Chris Cullen 5.00 12.00
8 Kyle Dean 5.00 12.00
9 Bailey Falter 3.00 8.00
10 Isaak Gutierrez 3.00 8.00
11 Nico Hoerner 12.00 30.00
12 Parker Kelly 3.00 8.00
13 Nick Madrigal 6.00 15.00
14 Austin Moore 3.00 8.00
15 Jio Orozco 4.00 10.00
16 Kyle Robeniol 3.00 8.00
17 Blake Rutherford 8.00 20.00
18 Cole Sands 3.00 8.00
19 Kyle Tucker 12.00 30.00
20 Coby Weaver 3.00 8.00

2012 USA Baseball 18U National Team America's Best Signatures

STATED PRINT RUN 100 SER.#'d SETS
2 Christian Arroyo 25.00 60.00
3 Cavan Biggio 10.00 25.00
5 Bryson Brigman 4.00 10.00
6 Ian Clarkin 10.00 25.00
7 Kevin Davis 4.00 10.00
8 Stephen Gonsalves 4.00 10.00
9 Connor Heady 4.00 10.00
11 Jeremy Martinez 4.00 10.00
13 Reese McGuire 8.00 20.00
14 Dom Nunez 6.00 15.00
15 Chris Okey 4.00 10.00
17 Carson Sands 4.00 10.00
18 Dominic Taccolini 8.00 20.00
19 Keegan Thompson 4.00 10.00
20 Garrett Williams 4.00 10.00

2012 USA Baseball 18U National Team Dual Jersey

STATED PRINT RUN 75 SER.#'d SETS
2 Christian Arroyo 3.00 8.00
4 Ryan Boldt 3.00 8.00
6 Ian Clarkin 6.00 15.00
9 Connor Heady 3.00 8.00
11 Jeremy Martinez 5.00 12.00
12 Reese McGuire 4.00 10.00
13 Dom Nunez 4.00 10.00
14 Chris Okey 3.00 8.00
15 Ryan Olson 3.00 8.00
16 Carson Sands 3.00 8.00
18 Keegan Thompson 3.00 8.00
19 Garrett Williams 5.00 12.00

2012 USA Baseball 18U National Team Dual Jerseys Signatures

STATED PRINT RUN 99 SER.#'d SETS
1 Willie Abreu 8.00 20.00
2 Christian Arroyo 20.00 50.00
3 Cavan Biggio 10.00 25.00
4 Ryan Boldt 6.00 15.00
5 Bryson Brigman 5.00 12.00
6 Ian Clarkin 15.00 40.00
7 Kevin Davis 6.00 15.00
8 Stephen Gonsalves 8.00 20.00
9 Connor Heady 5.00 12.00
10 John Kilichowski 5.00 12.00
11 Jeremy Martinez 6.00 15.00
12 Reese McGuire 5.00 12.00
13 Dom Nunez 6.00 15.00
14 Chris Okey 6.00 15.00
15 Ryan Olson 5.00 12.00
16 Carson Sands 5.00 12.00
17 Dominic Taccolini 6.00 15.00
18 Keegan Thompson 6.00 15.00
19 Garrett Williams 6.00 15.00

2012 USA Baseball 18U National Team Jersey Signatures

STATED PRINT RUN 99 SER.#'d SETS
1 Willie Abreu 8.00 20.00
2 Christian Arroyo 20.00 50.00
3 Cavan Biggio 10.00 25.00
4 Ryan Boldt 8.00 20.00
5 Bryson Brigman 5.00 12.00
6 Ian Clarkin 5.00 12.00
7 Kevin Davis 6.00 15.00
8 Stephen Gonsalves 6.00 15.00
9 Connor Heady 5.00 12.00
10 John Kilichowski 5.00 12.00
11 Jeremy Martinez 6.00 15.00
12 Reese McGuire 5.00 12.00
13 Dom Nunez 6.00 15.00
14 Chris Okey 6.00 15.00
15 Ryan Olson 5.00 12.00
16 Carson Sands 5.00 12.00
17 Dominic Taccolini 5.00 12.00
18 Keegan Thompson 6.00 15.00
19 Garrett Williams 5.00 12.00

2012 USA Baseball 18U National Team Jerseys

STATED PRINT RUN 99 SER.#'d SETS
1 Willie Abreu 3.00 8.00
3 Cavan Biggio 4.00 10.00
4 Ryan Boldt 3.00 8.00
5 Bryson Brigman 3.00 8.00
6 Ian Clarkin 4.00 10.00
7 Kevin Davis 3.00 8.00
10 John Kilichowski 3.00 8.00
11 Jeremy Martinez 3.00 8.00
12 Reese McGuire 3.00 8.00
14 Chris Okey 3.00 8.00
15 Ryan Olson 3.00 8.00
16 Carson Sands 3.00 8.00
17 Dominic Taccolini 3.00 8.00
18 Keegan Thompson 3.00 8.00

2012 USA Baseball 18U National Team Patches

*PATCH: .6X TO 1.5X BASIC
STATED PRINT RUN 35 SER.#'d SETS

2012 USA Baseball 18U National Team Patches Signatures

STATED PRINT RUN 35 SER.#'d SETS
1 Willie Abreu 8.00 20.00
2 Christian Arroyo 20.00 50.00
7 Kevin Davis 6.00 15.00
8 Stephen Gonsalves 10.00 25.00
9 Connor Heady 10.00 25.00
10 John Kilichowski 6.00 15.00
11 Jeremy Martinez 12.00 30.00
12 Reese McGuire 12.00 30.00
14 Chris Okey 8.00 20.00
16 Carson Sands 6.00 15.00
17 Dominic Taccolini 6.00 15.00

2012 USA Baseball 18U National Team Signatures

STATED PRINT RUN 349 SER.#'d SETS
1 Willie Abreu 5.00 12.00
2 Christian Arroyo 20.00 50.00
3 Cavan Biggio 10.00 25.00
4 Ryan Boldt 6.00 15.00
5 Bryson Brigman 3.00 8.00
6 Kevin Davis 4.00 10.00
7 Stephen Gonsalves 3.00 8.00
8 Connor Heady 3.00 8.00
9 John Kilichowski 4.00 10.00
10 Ian Clarkin 3.00 8.00
11 Jeremy Martinez 3.00 8.00
13 Reese McGuire 4.00 10.00
14 Dom Nunez 3.00 8.00
15 Chris Okey 4.00 10.00
16 Ryan Olson 4.00 10.00
17 Carson Sands 4.00 10.00
18 Dominic Taccolini 3.00 8.00
19 Keegan Thompson 4.00 10.00
20 Garrett Williams 5.00 12.00

2012 USA Baseball Collegiate National Team Collegiate Marks Signatures

STATED PRINT RUN 100 SER.#'d SETS
1 David Berg 3.00 8.00
2 Kris Bryant 60.00 150.00
3 Dan Child 5.00 12.00
4 Michael Conforto 20.00 50.00
5 Austin Cousino 6.00 15.00
6 Jonathon Crawford 10.00 25.00
7 Kyle Farmer 3.00 8.00
8 Johnny Field 3.00 8.00
9 Adam Frazier 4.00 10.00
10 Marco Gonzales 6.00 15.00
11 Brett Hambright 3.00 8.00
13 Michael Lorenzen 10.00 25.00
14 D.J. Peterson 8.00 20.00
15 Colton Plaia 4.00 10.00
16 Adam Plutko 8.00 20.00
17 Jake Reed 5.00 12.00
18 Carlos Rodon 10.00 25.00
19 Ryne Stanek 3.00 8.00
20 Trea Turner 15.00 40.00
21 Bobby Wahl 4.00 10.00
22 Trevor Williams 3.00 8.00

2012 USA Baseball Collegiate National Team Dual Jerseys

STATED PRINT RUN 75 SER.#'d SETS
1 David Berg 3.00 8.00
2 Kris Bryant 25.00 60.00
3 Dan Child 3.00 8.00
4 Michael Conforto 6.00 15.00
5 Austin Cousino 3.00 8.00
7 Kyle Farmer 4.00 10.00
8 Johnny Field 3.00 8.00
10 Marco Gonzales 3.00 8.00
11 Brett Hambright 3.00 8.00
12 Jordan Hankins 3.00 8.00
13 Michael Lorenzen 3.00 8.00
14 D.J. Peterson 3.00 8.00
15 Colton Plaia 3.00 8.00
16 Adam Plutko 3.00 8.00
17 Jake Reed 3.00 8.00
18 Carlos Rodon 4.00 10.00
19 Ryne Stanek 4.00 10.00
20 Jose Trevino 3.00 8.00
22 Bobby Wahl 4.00 10.00

2012 USA Baseball Collegiate National Team Dual Jerseys Signatures

STATED PRINT RUN 99 SER.#'d SETS
1 David Berg 5.00 12.00
2 Kris Bryant 60.00 150.00
3 Dan Child 5.00 12.00
4 Michael Conforto 20.00 50.00
5 Austin Cousino 8.00 20.00
6 Jonathon Crawford 6.00 15.00
7 Kyle Farmer 8.00 20.00
8 Johnny Field 5.00 12.00
9 Adam Frazier 6.00 15.00
10 Marco Gonzales 6.00 15.00
11 Brett Hambright 5.00 12.00
12 Jordan Hankins 5.00 12.00
13 Michael Lorenzen 5.00 12.00
14 D.J. Peterson 6.00 15.00
15 Colton Plaia 5.00 12.00
16 Adam Plutko 5.00 12.00
17 Jake Reed 8.00 20.00
18 Carlos Rodon 10.00 25.00
19 Ryne Stanek 6.00 15.00
20 Jose Trevino 5.00 12.00
21 Trea Turner 15.00 40.00
22 Bobby Wahl 8.00 20.00
23 Trevor Williams 5.00 12.00

2012 USA Baseball Collegiate National Team Jersey Signatures

STATED PRINT RUN 99 SER.#'d SETS
1 David Berg 5.00 12.00
2 Kris Bryant 60.00 150.00
3 Dan Child 5.00 12.00
4 Michael Conforto 20.00 50.00
5 Austin Cousino 8.00 20.00
6 Jonathon Crawford 6.00 15.00
7 Kyle Farmer 6.00 15.00
8 Johnny Field 5.00 12.00
9 Adam Frazier 6.00 15.00
10 Marco Gonzales 6.00 15.00
11 Brett Hambright 5.00 12.00
12 Jordan Hankins 5.00 12.00
13 Michael Lorenzen 6.00 15.00
14 D.J. Peterson 8.00 20.00
15 Colton Plaia 5.00 12.00
16 Adam Plutko 5.00 12.00
17 Jake Reed 5.00 12.00
18 Carlos Rodon 10.00 25.00
19 Ryne Stanek 10.00 25.00
20 Jose Trevino 5.00 12.00
21 Trea Turner 15.00 40.00
22 Bobby Wahl 5.00 12.00
23 Trevor Williams 5.00 12.00

2012 USA Baseball Collegiate National Team Jerseys

STATED PRINT RUN 99 SER.#'d SETS
1 David Berg 3.00 8.00
2 Kris Bryant 12.00 30.00
3 Dan Child 3.00 8.00
4 Michael Conforto 6.00 15.00
5 Austin Cousino 4.00 10.00
6 Jonathon Crawford 4.00 10.00
7 Kyle Farmer 3.00 8.00
8 Johnny Field 3.00 8.00
9 Adam Frazier 3.00 8.00
10 Marco Gonzales 3.00 8.00
11 Brett Hambright 3.00 8.00
12 Jordan Hankins 3.00 8.00
14 D.J. Peterson 3.00 8.00
15 Colton Plaia 3.00 8.00
16 Adam Plutko 3.00 8.00
17 Jake Reed 3.00 8.00
18 Carlos Rodon 4.00 10.00
19 Ryne Stanek 4.00 10.00
20 Jose Trevino 3.00 8.00
21 Trea Turner 6.00 15.00
22 Bobby Wahl 4.00 10.00
23 Trevor Williams 3.00 8.00

2012 USA Baseball Collegiate National Team Patches

*PATCH: .6X TO 1.5X BASIC
STATED PRINT RUN 35 SER.#'d SETS

2012 USA Baseball Collegiate National Team Patches Signatures

STATED PRINT RUN 35 SER.#'d SETS
2 Kris Bryant 125.00 300.00
3 Dan Child 6.00 15.00
4 Michael Conforto 25.00 60.00
5 Austin Cousino 10.00 25.00
6 Jonathon Crawford 6.00 15.00
9 Adam Frazier 6.00 15.00
11 Brett Hambright 6.00 15.00
12 Jordan Hankins 6.00 15.00
13 Michael Lorenzen 8.00 20.00
14 D.J. Peterson 10.00 25.00
15 Colton Plaia 6.00 15.00
16 Adam Plutko 8.00 20.00
17 Jake Reed 15.00 40.00
18 Carlos Rodon 30.00 60.00
19 Ryne Stanek 40.00 80.00
21 Trea Turner 20.00 50.00
22 Bobby Wahl 8.00 20.00

2012 USA Baseball Collegiate National Team Signatures

STATED PRINT RUN 399 SER.#'d SETS
1 David Berg 4.00 10.00
2 Kris Bryant 50.00 120.00
3 Dan Child 3.00 8.00
4 Michael Conforto 20.00 50.00
5 Austin Cousino 8.00 20.00
6 Jonathon Crawford 3.00 8.00
7 Kyle Farmer 5.00 12.00
8 Johnny Field 3.00 8.00
9 Adam Frazier 3.00 8.00
10 Marco Gonzales 6.00 15.00
11 Brett Hambright 4.00 10.00
12 Jordan Hankins 3.00 8.00
13 Michael Lorenzen 3.00 8.00
14 D.J. Peterson 4.00 10.00
15 Colton Plaia 3.00 8.00
16 Adam Plutko 3.00 8.00
17 Jake Reed 3.00 8.00
18 Carlos Rodon 12.00 30.00
19 Ryne Stanek 3.00 8.00
20 Trea Turner 10.00 25.00
21 Bobby Wahl 3.00 8.00
22 Trevor Williams 3.00 8.00

2012 USA Baseball Team Photo Checklists

COMMON CARD .20 .50
CARDS ARE UNNUMBERED
1 Collegiate National Team .20 .50
2 18U National Team .20 .50
3 15U National Team .20 .50

2013 USA Baseball

COMPLETE (65) 12.50 30.00
COMP.SET PRICE INCLUDES CHECKLISTS
1 Tyler Beede .40 1.00
2 David Berg .30 .75
3 Skye Bolt .40 1.00
4 Alex Bregman 1.25 3.00
5 Ryan Burr .40 1.00
6 Matt Chapman 1.50 4.00
7 Michael Conforto .60 1.50
8 Austin Cousino .30 .75
9 Chris Diaz .30 .75
10 Riley Ferrell .30 .75
11 Brandon Finnegan .60 1.50
12 Grayson Greiner .20 .50
13 Erick Fedde .20 .50
14 Matt Imhof .20 .50
15 Daniel Mengden .30 .75
16 Preston Morrison .30 .75
17 Carlos Rodon .75 2.00
18 Kyle Schwarber 1.25 3.00
19 Taylor Sparks .30 .75
20 Tommy Thorpe .30 .75
21 Sam Travis .60 1.50
22 Trea Turner 1.00 2.50
23 Luke Weaver 1.00 2.50
24 Bradley Zimmer .50 1.25
25 Brady Aiken 1.25 3.00
26 Bryson Brigman .30 .75
27 Joe DeMers .20 .50
28 Alex Destino .20 .50
29 Jack Flaherty 1.25 3.00
30 Marvin Gorgas .20 .50
31 Adam Haseley .60 1.50
32 Scott Hurst .20 .50
33 Kel Johnson .50 1.25
34 Trace Loehr .20 .50
35 Mac Marshall .20 .50
36 Keaton McKinney .30 .75
37 Jacob Nix .20 .50
38 Luis Ortiz .30 .75
39 Jakson Reetz .75 2.00
40 Michael Rivera .20 .50
41 JJ Schwarz .30 .75
42 Justus Sheffield .60 1.50
43 Lane Thomas .20 .50
44 Cole Tucker .20 .50
45 Nick Allen .40 1.00
46 Jordan Butler .30 .75
47 Daniel Cabrera 1.25 3.00
48 Sam Ferri .20 .50
49 Isaak Gutierrez .30 .75
50 Brandon Martorano .20 .50
51 Mickey Moniak .30 .75
52 Christian Moya .30 .75
53 Manuel Perez .20 .50
54 Todd Peterson .20 .50
55 Logan Pouelsen .20 .50
56 Nick Pratto .30 .75
57 Ben Ramirez .20 .50
58 DJ Roberts .20 .50
59 Matthew Rudick .20 .50
60 Blake Sabol .30 .75
61 Chase Strumpf .75 2.00
62 Mason Thompson .30 .75
63 Andrew Vaughn 1.00 2.50

2013 USA Baseball 15U National Team Dual Jerseys Signatures

STATED PRINT RUN 35 SER.#'d SETS
1 Nick Allen
2 Jordan Butler
3 Daniel Cabrera 6.00 15.00
4 Sam Ferri
5 Isaak Gutierrez 3.00 8.00
6 Brandon Martorano
7 Mickey Moniak 20.00 50.00
8 Christian Moya
9 Manuel Perez
10 Todd Peterson 5.00 12.00
11 Logan Pouelsen
12 Nick Pratto
13 Ben Ramirez 8.00 20.00
14 DJ Roberts
15 Matthew Rudick
16 Blake Sabol 5.00 12.00
17 Chase Strumpf 20.00 50.00
18 Mason Thompson
19 Andrew Vaughn 15.00 40.00

2013 USA Baseball 15U National Team Jersey Signatures

STATED PRINT RUN 99 SER.#'d SETS
1 Nick Allen 5.00 12.00
2 Jordan Butler
3 Daniel Cabrera 6.00 15.00
4 Sam Ferri 5.00 12.00
5 Isaak Gutierrez 4.00 10.00
6 Brandon Martorano 5.00 12.00
7 Mickey Moniak 15.00 40.00
8 Christian Moya
9 Manuel Perez 4.00 10.00
10 Todd Peterson 4.00 10.00
11 Logan Pouelsen
12 Nick Pratto 5.00 12.00
13 Ben Ramirez 5.00 12.00
14 DJ Roberts 4.00 10.00
15 Matthew Rudick
16 Blake Sabol 4.00 10.00
17 Chase Strumpf
18 Mason Thompson 4.00 10.00
19 Andrew Vaughn 15.00 40.00

2013 USA Baseball 15U National Team Jerseys

STATED PRINT RUN 199 SER.#'d SETS
1 Nick Allen 2.50 6.00
2 Jordan Butler 2.50 6.00
3 Daniel Cabrera 5.00 12.00
4 Sam Ferri 2.50 6.00
5 Isaak Gutierrez 2.50 6.00
6 Brandon Martorano 2.50 6.00
7 Mickey Moniak 6.00 15.00
8 Christian Moya 2.50 6.00
9 Manuel Perez 2.50 6.00
10 Todd Peterson 2.50 6.00
11 Logan Pouelsen 2.50 6.00
12 Nick Pratto 2.50 6.00
13 Ben Ramirez 2.50 6.00
14 DJ Roberts
15 Matthew Rudick 2.50 6.00
16 Blake Sabol 2.50 6.00
17 Chase Strumpf 2.50 6.00
18 Mason Thompson 2.50 6.00
19 Andrew Vaughn 4.00 10.00

2013 USA Baseball 15U National Team Patches

*PATCHES: .6X TO 1.5X BASIC
STATED PRINT RUN 35 SER.#'d SETS

2013 USA Baseball 15U National Team Profile Signatures

STATED PRINT RUN 100 SER.#'d SETS
1 Nick Allen 4.00 10.00
2 Jordan Butler
3 Daniel Cabrera 8.00 20.00
4 Sam Ferri 4.00 10.00
5 Isaak Gutierrez 4.00 10.00
6 Brandon Martorano 6.00 15.00
7 Mickey Moniak 20.00 50.00
8 Christian Moya
9 Manuel Perez
10 Todd Peterson
11 Logan Pouelsen
12 Nick Pratto
13 Ben Ramirez 4.00 10.00
14 DJ Roberts
15 Matthew Rudick 4.00 10.00
16 Blake Sabol 4.00 10.00
17 Chase Strumpf 15.00 40.00
18 Mason Thompson 4.00 10.00
19 Andrew Vaughn 15.00 40.00

2013 USA Baseball 15U National Team Signatures

STATED PRINT RUN 299 SER.#'d SETS
1 Nick Allen 4.00 10.00
2 Jordan Butler 4.00 10.00
3 Daniel Cabrera 6.00 15.00
4 Sam Ferri 4.00 10.00
5 Isaak Gutierrez
6 Brandon Martorano 5.00 12.00
7 Mickey Moniak 20.00 50.00
8 Christian Moya 4.00 10.00
9 Manuel Perez 4.00 10.00
10 Todd Peterson 4.00 10.00
11 Logan Pouelsen 4.00 10.00
12 Nick Pratto 4.00 10.00
13 Ben Ramirez 4.00 10.00
14 DJ Roberts 4.00 10.00
15 Matthew Rudick 4.00 10.00
16 Blake Sabol 4.00 10.00
17 Chase Strumpf 8.00 20.00
18 Mason Thompson 4.00 10.00
19 Andrew Vaughn 10.00 25.00

2013 USA Baseball 18U National Team America's Best Signatures

STATED PRINT RUN 100 SER.#'d SETS
1 Brady Aiken 20.00 50.00
2 Bryson Brigman
3 Joe DeMers 4.00 10.00
4 Alex Destino 4.00 10.00
5 Jack Flaherty 4.00 10.00
6 Marvin Gorgas
7 Adam Haseley
8 Scott Hurst 4.00 10.00
9 Kel Johnson 8.00 20.00
10 Trace Loehr 4.00 10.00
11 Mac Marshall
12 Keaton McKinney 8.00 20.00
13 Jacob Nix 5.00 12.00
14 Luis Ortiz 4.00 10.00
15 Jakson Reetz 10.00 25.00
16 Michael Rivera 4.00 10.00
17 JJ Schwarz 5.00 12.00
18 Justus Sheffield 8.00 20.00
19 Lane Thomas 6.00 15.00
20 Cole Tucker

2013 USA Baseball 18U National Team Dual Jerseys Signatures

1 Brady Aiken
2 Bryson Brigman
3 Joe DeMers 4.00 10.00
4 Alex Destino
5 Jack Flaherty
6 Marvin Gorgas
7 Adam Haseley
8 Scott Hurst
9 Kel Johnson
10 Trace Loehr 5.00 12.00
11 Mac Marshall 4.00 10.00
12 Keaton McKinney 6.00 15.00
13 Jacob Nix 4.00 10.00
14 Luis Ortiz 8.00 20.00
15 Jakson Reetz 10.00 25.00
16 Michael Rivera
17 JJ Schwarz
18 Justus Sheffield 8.00 20.00
19 Lane Thomas 5.00 12.00
20 Cole Tucker 4.00 10.00

2013 USA Baseball 18U National Team Jersey Signatures

STATED PRINT RUN 125 SER.#'d SETS
1 Brady Aiken 10.00 25.00
2 Bryson Brigman
3 Joe DeMers 4.00 10.00
4 Alex Destino 4.00 10.00
5 Jack Flaherty 5.00 12.00
6 Marvin Gorgas
7 Adam Haseley 4.00 10.00
8 Scott Hurst 4.00 10.00
9 Kel Johnson
10 Trace Loehr
11 Mac Marshall 5.00 12.00
12 Keaton McKinney 4.00 10.00
13 Jacob Nix 4.00 10.00
14 Luis Ortiz 4.00 10.00
15 Jakson Reetz 12.00 30.00
16 Michael Rivera 4.00 10.00
17 JJ Schwarz
18 Justus Sheffield 6.00 15.00
19 Lane Thomas 6.00 15.00
20 Cole Tucker

2013 USA Baseball 18U National Team Jerseys

STATED PRINT RUN 35 SER.#'d SETS
1 Brady Aiken 8.00 20.00
2 Bryson Brigman 2.50 6.00
3 Joe DeMers 2.50 6.00
4 Alex Destino 2.50 6.00
5 Jack Flaherty 2.50 6.00
6 Marvin Gorgas 2.50 6.00
7 Adam Haseley 2.50 6.00
8 Scott Hurst 2.50 6.00
9 Kel Johnson 2.50 6.00
10 Trace Loehr 2.50 6.00
11 Mac Marshall 2.50 6.00
12 Keaton McKinney
13 Jacob Nix 4.00 10.00
14 Luis Ortiz 2.50 6.00
15 Jakson Reetz 6.00 15.00
16 Michael Rivera 2.50 6.00
17 JJ Schwarz 2.50 6.00
18 Justus Sheffield 2.50 6.00
19 Lane Thomas 2.50 6.00
20 Cole Tucker 2.50 6.00

2013 USA Baseball 18U National Team Patches

*PATCHES: .6X TO 1.5X BASIC
STATED PRINT RUN 35 SER.#'d SETS

2013 USA Baseball 18U National Team Signatures

STATED PRINT RUN 499 SER.#'d SETS
1 Brady Aiken 15.00 40.00
2 Bryson Brigman 4.00 10.00
3 Joe DeMers 4.00 10.00
4 Alex Destino 4.00 10.00
5 Jack Flaherty 4.00 10.00
6 Marvin Gorgas 4.00 10.00
7 Adam Haseley 4.00 10.00
8 Scott Hurst 4.00 10.00
9 Kel Johnson 6.00 15.00
10 Trace Loehr 4.00 10.00
11 Mac Marshall 4.00 10.00
12 Keaton McKinney 5.00 12.00
13 Jacob Nix 4.00 10.00
14 Luis Ortiz 5.00 12.00
15 Jakson Reetz 20.00 50.00
16 Michael Rivera 4.00 10.00
17 JJ Schwarz 4.00 10.00
18 Justus Sheffield 4.00 10.00
19 Lane Thomas 4.00 10.00
20 Cole Tucker 4.00 10.00

2013 USA Baseball 18U National Team Winning Combinations Signatures

STATED PRINT RUN 50 SER.#'d SETS
2 M.Marshall/K.Johnson 12.50 30.00
5 K.McKinney/J.Reetz 20.00 50.00

2013 USA Baseball Collegiate Classic Signatures

STATED PRINT RUN 50 SER.#'d SETS
1 Tyler Beede
2 David Berg 8.00 20.00
3 Skye Bolt 20.00 50.00
4 Alex Bregman 20.00 50.00
5 Ryan Burr
6 Matt Chapman
7 Michael Conforto 30.00 80.00
8 Austin Cousino
9 Chris Diaz
10 Riley Ferrell
11 Brandon Finnegan
12 Grayson Greiner 6.00 15.00
13 Erick Fedde 12.50 30.00
14 Matt Imhof 6.00 15.00
15 Daniel Mengden
16 Preston Morrison 6.00 15.00
17 Carlos Rodon 40.00 80.00
18 Kyle Schwarber 40.00 100.00
19 Taylor Sparks 15.00 40.00
20 Tommy Thorpe 6.00 15.00
21 Sam Travis 10.00 25.00
22 Trea Turner 10.00 25.00
23 Luke Weaver 10.00 25.00
24 Bradley Zimmer 15.00 40.00

2013 USA Baseball Collegiate Connections Signatures

STATED PRINT RUN 50 SER.#'d SETS
1 C.Rodon/T.Turner 50.00 100.00
2 R.Ferrell/D.Mengden
3 B.Finnegan/P.Morrison 20.00 50.00
4 S.Travis/K.Schwarber 40.00 100.00

2013 USA Baseball Collegiate National Team Dual Jerseys Signatures

STATED PRINT RUN 35 SER.#'d SETS
1 Tyler Beede 20.00 50.00
2 David Berg
3 Skye Bolt 10.00 25.00
4 Alex Bregman
5 Ryan Burr
6 Matt Chapman 12.00 30.00
7 Michael Conforto
8 Austin Cousino
9 Chris Diaz 4.00 10.00
10 Riley Ferrell
11 Brandon Finnegan 25.00 60.00
12 Grayson Greiner
13 Erick Fedde
14 Matt Imhof
15 Daniel Mengden
16 Preston Morrison 10.00 25.00
17 Carlos Rodon 15.00 40.00
18 Kyle Schwarber 50.00 120.00
19 Taylor Sparks
20 Tommy Thorpe
21 Sam Travis
22 Trea Turner
23 Luke Weaver 6.00 15.00
24 Bradley Zimmer

2013 USA Baseball Collegiate National Team Jersey Signatures

STATED PRINT RUN 99 SER.#'d SETS
1 Tyler Beede
2 David Berg 4.00 10.00
3 Skye Bolt 6.00 15.00
4 Alex Bregman 12.50 30.00
5 Ryan Burr 4.00 10.00
6 Matt Chapman 12.00 30.00
7 Michael Conforto 20.00 50.00
8 Austin Cousino
9 Chris Diaz 4.00 10.00
10 Riley Ferrell
11 Brandon Finnegan 25.00 60.00
12 Grayson Greiner
13 Erick Fedde
14 Matt Imhof 4.00 10.00
15 Daniel Mengden 4.00 10.00
16 Preston Morrison 4.00 10.00
17 Carlos Rodon 15.00 40.00
18 Kyle Schwarber 40.00 100.00
19 Taylor Sparks
20 Tommy Thorpe 10.00 25.00
21 Sam Travis 6.00 15.00
22 Trea Turner 15.00 40.00
23 Luke Weaver 6.00 15.00
24 Bradley Zimmer 5.00 12.00

2013 USA Baseball Collegiate National Team Jerseys

STATED PRINT RUN 35 SER.#'d SETS
1 Tyler Beede 3.00 8.00
2 David Berg 2.50 6.00
3 Skye Bolt 5.00 12.00
4 Alex Bregman 5.00 12.00
5 Ryan Burr 2.50 6.00
6 Matt Chapman 2.50 6.00
7 Michael Conforto 5.00 12.00
8 Austin Cousino 2.50 6.00
9 Chris Diaz 3.00 8.00
10 Riley Ferrell 3.00 8.00
11 Brandon Finnegan 3.00 8.00
12 Grayson Greiner 2.50 6.00
13 Erick Fedde 2.50 6.00
14 Matt Imhof 2.50 6.00
15 Daniel Mengden 2.50 6.00
16 Preston Morrison 2.50 6.00
17 Carlos Rodon 5.00 12.00
18 Kyle Schwarber 8.00 20.00
19 Taylor Sparks 2.50 6.00
20 Tommy Thorpe 2.50 6.00
21 Sam Travis 2.50 6.00
22 Trea Turner 5.00 12.00
23 Luke Weaver 3.00 8.00
24 Bradley Zimmer 2.50 6.00

2013 USA Baseball Collegiate National Team Jerseys Jumbo

STATED PRINT RUN 49 SER.#'d SETS
1 Tyler Beede
2 David Berg 4.00 10.00
3 Skye Bolt
4 Alex Bregman 8.00 20.00
5 Ryan Burr 4.00 10.00
6 Matt Chapman
7 Michael Conforto 6.00 15.00
8 Austin Cousino 4.00 10.00
9 Chris Diaz
10 Riley Ferrell
11 Brandon Finnegan
12 Grayson Greiner 4.00 10.00
13 Erick Fedde 5.00 12.00
14 Matt Imhof 4.00 10.00
15 Daniel Mengden
16 Preston Morrison
17 Carlos Rodon
18 Kyle Schwarber
19 Taylor Sparks 4.00 10.00
20 Tommy Thorpe
21 Sam Travis 5.00 12.00
22 Trea Turner 8.00 20.00
23 Luke Weaver
24 Bradley Zimmer

2013 USA Baseball Collegiate National Team Patches

*PATCHES: .6X TO 1.5X BASIC
STATED PRINT RUN 35 SER.#'d SETS

2013 USA Baseball Collegiate National Team Signatures

STATED PRINT RUN 399 SER.#'d SETS
1 Tyler Beede 12.00 30.00
2 David Berg 4.00 10.00
3 Skye Bolt 10.00 25.00
4 Alex Bregman 8.00 20.00
5 Ryan Burr 4.00 10.00
6 Matt Chapman 10.00 25.00
7 Michael Conforto 12.00 30.00
8 Austin Cousino 5.00 12.00
9 Chris Diaz 4.00 10.00
10 Riley Ferrell 4.00 10.00
11 Brandon Finnegan 4.00 10.00
12 Grayson Greiner 4.00 10.00
13 Erick Fedde 5.00 12.00
14 Matt Imhof 8.00 20.00
15 Daniel Mengden 4.00 10.00
16 Preston Morrison 5.00 12.00
17 Carlos Rodon 20.00 50.00
18 Kyle Schwarber 20.00 50.00
19 Taylor Sparks 4.00 10.00
20 Tommy Thorpe 4.00 10.00
21 Sam Travis 5.00 12.00
22 Trea Turner 15.00 40.00
23 Luke Weaver 5.00 12.00
24 Bradley Zimmer 10.00 25.00

2013 USA Baseball Curtain Call

1 David Berg .40 1.00
2 Alex Bregman 1.50 4.00
3 Michael Conforto .75 2.00
4 Austin Cousino .40 1.00
5 Carlos Rodon 1.00 2.50
6 Isaak Gutierrez .40 1.00
7 Joe DeMers .25 .60
8 Trea Turner 1.25 3.00

2013 USA Baseball Select Preview Blue Prizms

STATED PRINT RUN 199 SER.#'d SETS
1 Tyler Beede 2.00 5.00
2 David Berg 1.50 4.00
3 Skye Bolt 2.00 5.00
4 Alex Bregman 6.00 15.00
5 Ryan Burr 2.00 5.00
6 Matt Chapman 8.00 20.00
7 Michael Conforto 3.00 8.00
8 Austin Cousino 1.50 4.00
9 Chris Diaz 1.50 4.00
10 Riley Ferrell 1.50 4.00
11 Brandon Finnegan 3.00 8.00
12 Grayson Greiner 1.00 2.50
13 Erick Fedde 1.00 2.50
14 Matt Imhof 1.00 2.50
15 Daniel Mengden 1.50 4.00
16 Preston Morrison 1.50 4.00
17 Carlos Rodon 4.00 10.00
18 Kyle Schwarber 6.00 15.00
19 Taylor Sparks 1.50 4.00
20 Tommy Thorpe 1.50 4.00
21 Sam Travis 3.00 8.00
22 Trea Turner 5.00 12.00
23 Luke Weaver 5.00 12.00
24 Bradley Zimmer 2.50 6.00
25 Brady Aiken 6.00 15.00
26 Bryson Brigman 1.50 4.00
27 Joe DeMers 1.00 2.50
28 Alex Destino 1.00 2.50
29 Jack Flaherty 6.00 15.00
30 Marvin Gorgas 1.00 2.50
31 Adam Haseley 3.00 8.00
32 Scott Hurst 1.00 2.50
33 Kel Johnson 2.50 6.00
34 Trace Loehr 1.00 2.50
35 Mac Marshall 1.00 2.50
36 Keaton McKinney 1.50 4.00
37 Jacob Nix 1.00 2.50
38 Luis Ortiz 1.50 4.00
39 Jakson Reetz 4.00 10.00
40 Michael Rivera 1.00 2.50
41 JJ Schwarz 1.50 4.00
42 Justus Sheffield 3.00 8.00
43 Lane Thomas 1.00 2.50
44 Cole Tucker 1.00 2.50
45 Nick Allen 2.00 5.00
46 Jordan Butler 1.50 4.00
47 Daniel Cabrera 6.00 15.00
48 Sam Ferri 1.00 2.50
49 Isaak Gutierrez 1.50 4.00
50 Brandon Martorano 1.00 2.50
51 Mickey Moniak 1.50 4.00
52 Christian Moya 1.50 4.00
53 Manuel Perez 1.00 2.50
54 Todd Peterson 1.00 2.50
55 Logan Pouelsen 1.00 2.50
56 Nick Pratto 1.50 4.00
57 Ben Ramirez 1.00 2.50
58 DJ Roberts 1.00 2.50
59 Matthew Rudick 1.00 2.50
60 Blake Sabol 1.50 4.00
61 Chase Strumpf 4.00 10.00
62 Mason Thompson 1.50 4.00
63 Andrew Vaughn 5.00 12.00
64 Tyler Beede 2.00 5.00
65 David Berg 1.50 4.00

56 Skye Bolt 2.00 5.00
57 Alex Bregman 6.00 15.00
58 Ryan Burr 2.00 5.00
59 Matt Chapman 8.00 20.00
70 Michael Conforto 3.00 8.00
71 Austin Cousino 1.50 4.00
72 Chris Diaz 1.50 4.00
73 Riley Ferrell 1.50 4.00
74 Brandon Finnegan 3.00 8.00
75 Grayson Greiner 1.00 2.50
76 Erick Fedde 1.00 2.50
77 Matt Imhof 1.00 2.50
78 Daniel Mengden 1.50 4.00
79 Preston Morrison 1.50 4.00
80 Carlos Rodon 4.00 10.00
81 Kyle Schwarber 6.00 15.00
82 Taylor Sparks 1.50 4.00
83 Tommy Thorpe 1.50 4.00
84 Sam Travis 3.00 8.00
85 Trea Turner 5.00 12.00
86 Luke Weaver 5.00 12.00
87 Bradley Zimmer 2.50 6.00
88 Brady Aiken 6.00 15.00
89 Bryson Brigman 1.50 4.00
90 Alex Destino 1.00 2.50
91 Jack Flaherty 6.00 15.00
92 Adam Haseley 3.00 8.00
93 Scott Hurst 1.00 2.50
94 Kel Johnson 2.50 6.00
95 Trace Loehr 1.00 2.50
96 Mac Marshall 1.00 2.50
97 Jakson Reetz 4.00 10.00
98 Michael Rivera 1.00 2.50
99 JJ Schwarz 1.50 4.00
100 Cole Tucker 1.00 2.50

2013 USA Baseball Team Photo Checklists

1 Collegiate National Team .20 .50
2 18U National Team .20 .50
3 15U National Team .20 .50

2013 USA Baseball USA Baseball In Action

1 Carlos Rodon 1.00 2.50
2 Michael Conforto .75 2.00
3 David Berg .40 1.00
4 Bryson Brigman .40 1.00
5 Isaak Gutierrez .40 1.00
6 Alex Bregman 1.50 4.00
7 Skye Bolt .50 1.25

2013 USA Baseball Champions

COMP.SET w/o SP's (150) 10.00 25.00
1 Ozzie Smith .40 1.00
2 Rod Dedeaux .20 .50
3 Terry Francona .20 .50
4 Joe Carter .20 .50
5 Wally Joyner .20 .50
6 Tyler Anderson .20 .50
7 Frank Viola .20 .50
8 Jeff King .12 .30
9 Jack McDowell .20 .50
10 Will Clark .25 .60
11 Mark McGwire .50 1.25
12 Barry Larkin .25 .60
13 Mike Mussina .25 .60
14 Chipper Jones .30 .75
15 Frank Thomas .30 .75
16 Jim Abbott .20 .50
17 Robin Ventura .20 .50
18 Ty Griffin .12 .30
19 Tino Martinez .25 .60
20 Ben McDonald .20 .50
21 Derrek Lee .12 .30
22 Shawn Green .20 .50
23 Nomar Garciaparra .25 .60
24 Jason Varitek .30 .75
25 Warren Morris .12 .30
26 Pat Burrell .20 .50
27 Ben Sheets .20 .50
28 Tommy Lasorda .25 .60
29 Ken Griffey Jr. .60 1.50
30 Chipper Jones .30 .75
31 Roger Clemens .40 1.00
32 Troy Glaus .20 .50
33 Frank Robinson .25 .60
34 Mike Schmidt .50 1.25
35 Reggie Smith .12 .30
36 Mark Mulder .20 .50
37 Tino Martinez .25 .60
38 Bob Watson .12 .30
39 Grant Green .30 .75
40 Davey Johnson .12 .30
41 Ken Griffey Jr. .60 1.50
42 Tim Melville .12 .30
43 Michael Main .12 .30
44 Nick Delmonico .25 .60
45 Cole Green .12 .30
46 Riccio Torrez .12 .30
47 Seth Blair .20 .50
48 Brett Mooneyham .12 .30
49 Francisco Lindor 1.25 3.00
50 Mac Williamson .30 .75
51 Mychal Givens .12 .30
52 David Nick .12 .30
53 Neil Ramirez .12 .30
54 A.J. Cole .25 .60
55 Zach Lee .25 .60
56 Randal Grichuk .30 .75
57 Richie Shaffer .20 .50
58 Robert Refsnyder .25 .60
59 Jordan Swagerty .12 .30
60 Cody Buckel .20 .50
61 Christian Lopes .12 .30
62 Austin Maddox .12 .30
63 Nick Castellanos .60 1.50
64 Nick Franklin .25 .60
65 Matt Purke .12 .30
66 Tommy Mendonca .12 .30
67 Mikie Mahtook .12 .30
68 Robbie Grossman .20 .50
69 Matt Lipka .20 .50
70 Jeff Malm .12 .30
71 Cameron Garfield .12 .30
72 Harold Martinez .20 .50
73 Kyle Gibson .30 .75
74 Hunter Morris .25 .60
75 Christian Colon .20 .50
76 Derek Dietrich .25 .60
77 Blake Swihart .25 .60
78 Michael Kelly .12 .30
79 Courtney Hawkins .20 .50
80 Sean Coyle .20 .50
81 Kevin Gausman .30 .75
82 Nick Castellanos .60 1.50
83 Garin Cecchini .20 .50
84 Jameson Taillon .25 .60
85 Tony Wolters .12 .30
86 Bryce Brentz .20 .50
87 Michael Choice .20 .50
88 Albert Almora .40 1.00
89 Zach Lee .25 .60
90 Kolten Wong .20 .50
91 Carson Kelly .25 .60
92 Lance McCullers .20 .50
93 Corey Seager .75 2.00
94 Lucas Sims .25 .60
95 Felipe Perez .12 .30
96 Zach Green .12 .30
97 Matt Olson .30 .75
98 Tim Lopes .12 .30
99 Adrian Marin .12 .30
100 Bubba Starling .25 .60
101 Henry Owens .25 .60
102 Dillon Maples .12 .30
103 Matt Barnes .25 .60
104 Brad Miller .25 .60
105 Nick Travieso .25 .60
106 Gerrit Cole 1.25 3.00
108 Sonny Gray .30 .75
109 Alex Dickerson .12 .30
110 Peter O'Brien .25 .60
111 Kyle Winkler .12 .30
112 George Springer .75 2.00
113 Nolan Fontana .25 .60
114 Chase De Jong .25 .60
115 David Dahl .25 .60
116 Joey Gallo .60 1.50
117 Addison Russell .30 .75
118 Jesse Winker .12 .30
119 Walker Weickel .12 .30
120 Tyler Naquin .25 .60
121 Hoby Milner .20 .50
122 Michael Wacha .25 .60
123 Deven Marrero .20 .50
125 Brady Rodgers .12 .30
126 David Berg .40 1.00
127 Kris Bryant 6.00 15.00
128 Dan Child .40 1.00
129 Michael Conforto .75 2.00
130 Austin Cousino .40 1.00
131 Jonathon Crawford .40 1.00
132 Kyle Farmer .25 .60
133 Johnny Field .40 1.00
134 Adam Frazier .25 .60
135 Marco Gonzales .60 1.50
136 Brett Hambright .25 .60
137 Jordan Hankins .25 .60
138 Michael Lorenzen .50 1.25
139 D.J. Peterson .40 1.00
140 Colton Plaia .25 .60
141 Adam Plutko .25 .60
142 Jake Reed .25 .60
143 Carlos Rodon 1.00 2.50
144 Ryne Stanek .75 2.00
145 Jose Trevino .25 .60
146 Trea Turner 1.25 3.00
147 Bobby Wahl .25 .60
148 Trevor Williams .40 1.00
149 Willie Abreu .40 1.00
150 Christian Arroyo 2.50 6.00
151 Cavan Biggio 1.00 2.50
152 Ryan Boldt .40 1.00
153 Bryson Brigman .40 1.00
154 Ian Clarkin .40 1.00
155 Kevin Davis .40 1.00
156 Stephen Gonsalves .40 1.00
157 Connor Heady .25 .60
158 John Kilichowski .25 .60
159 Jeremy Martinez .25 .60
160 Reese McGuire .50 1.25
161 Dom Nunez .25 .60
162 Chris Okey .25 .60
163 Ryan Olson .25 .60
164 Carson Sands .25 .60
165 Dominic Taccolini .25 .60
166 Keegan Thompson .25 .60
167 Garrett Williams .25 .60
168 John Aiello .50 1.25
169 Nick Anderson .40 1.00
170 Luken Baker .60 1.50
171 Solomon Bates .40 1.00
172 Chris Betts .40 1.00
173 Danny Casals .40 1.00
174 Chris Cullen .40 1.00
175 Kyle Dean .40 1.00
176 Bailey Falter .25 .60
177 Isaak Gutierrez .40 1.00
178 Nico Hoerner .75 2.00
179 Parker Kelly .40 1.00
180 Nick Madrigal .75 2.00
181 Austin Moore .25 .60
182 Jio Orozco .25 .60
183 Kyle Robeniol .25 .60
184 Blake Rutherford .75 2.00
185 Cole Sands .25 .60
186 Kyle Tucker 1.00 2.50
187 Coby Weaver .25 .60

2013 USA Baseball Champions National Team Mirror Blue

*MIRROR BLUE: 1.5X TO 4X BASIC
STATED PRINT RUN 299 SER.#'d SETS

2013 USA Baseball Champions National Team Mirror Green

*MIRROR GREEN: 2X TO 5X BASIC
STATED PRINT RUN 199 SER.#'d SETS

2013 USA Baseball Champions National Team Mirror Red

*MIRROR RED: 1.2X TO 3X BASIC
STATED PRINT RUN 499 SER.#'d SETS

2013 USA Baseball Champions Diamond Kings

STATED PRINT RUN 399 SER.#'d SETS
1 Frank Thomas 1.50 4.00
2 Jim Abbott 1.00 2.50
3 Pat Burrell 1.00 2.50
4 Nomar Garciaparra 1.25 3.00
5 Ken Griffey Jr. 3.00 8.00
6 Gerrit Cole 6.00 15.00
7 Bubba Starling 1.25 3.00
8 Michael Conforto 2.00 5.00
9 Reese McGuire 1.25 3.00
10 Isaak Gutierrez 1.00 2.50
11 Tommy Lasorda 1.25 3.00
13 Joey Gallo 3.00 8.00
14 Barry Larkin 1.25 3.00
15 Joe Carter 1.00 2.50
16 Carlos Rodon 2.50 6.00

2013 USA Baseball Champions Game Gear Bats

1 Kris Bryant 10.00 25.00
2 Michael Conforto 3.00 8.00
3 Austin Cousino 3.00 8.00
4 Kyle Farmer 3.00 8.00
5 Johnny Field 3.00 8.00
6 Marco Gonzales 3.00 8.00
7 Brett Hambright 3.00 8.00
8 Jordan Hankins 3.00 8.00
9 Michael Lorenzen 3.00 8.00
10 D.J. Peterson 3.00 8.00
11 Colton Plaia 3.00 8.00
12 Jose Trevino 3.00 8.00
13 Trea Turner 3.00 8.00

2013 USA Baseball Champions Game Gear Jerseys

1 David Dahl 3.00 8.00
2 Addison Russell 4.00 10.00
3 Deven Marrero 3.00 8.00
4 Albert Almora 3.00 8.00
5 Brady Rodgers 3.00 8.00
6 Branden Kline 3.00 8.00
7 Brian Johnson 3.00 8.00
8 Matt Reynolds 3.00 8.00
9 Marcus Stroman 3.00 8.00
10 Josh Elander 3.00 8.00
11 Kevin Gausman 4.00 10.00
12 Hoby Milner 3.00 8.00
13 Joey Gallo 4.00 10.00
14 Michael Wacha 3.00 8.00
15 Chase De Jong 3.00 8.00
16 Carson Sands 3.00 8.00
17 Jesse Winker 3.00 8.00
18 Nolan Fontana 3.00 8.00
19 Tyler Naquin 3.00 8.00
20 Walker Weickel 3.00 8.00
21 Tom Murphy 3.00 8.00
22 Gavin Cecchini 3.00 8.00
23 Carson Kelly 3.00 8.00
24 Nick Travieso 3.00 8.00
25 David Berg 3.00 8.00
26 Kris Bryant 12.00 30.00
27 Dan Child 3.00 8.00
28 Michael Conforto 3.00 8.00
29 Austin Cousino 3.00 8.00
30 Jonathon Crawford 3.00 8.00
31 Kyle Farmer 3.00 8.00
32 Johnny Field 3.00 8.00
33 Adam Frazier 3.00 8.00
34 Marco Gonzales 3.00 8.00
35 Jordan Hankins 3.00 8.00
36 Michael Lorenzen 3.00 8.00
37 D.J. Peterson 3.00 8.00
38 Colton Plaia 3.00 8.00
39 Adam Plutko 3.00 8.00
40 Jake Reed 3.00 8.00
41 Carlos Rodon 6.00 15.00
42 Ryne Stanek 3.00 8.00
43 Trea Turner 3.00 8.00
44 Christian Arroyo 3.00 8.00
45 Cavan Biggio 3.00 8.00
46 Ryan Boldt 3.00 8.00
47 Ian Clarkin 3.00 8.00
48 Gerrit Cole 4.00 10.00
49 Kolten Wong 3.00 8.00
50 Michael Choice 4.00 10.00
52 Corey Seager 4.00 10.00
53 Randal Grichuk 3.00 8.00
54 Matt Purke 3.00 8.00
55 Richie Shaffer 3.00 8.00
56 Mac Williamson 4.00 10.00
57 Adrian Marin 3.00 8.00
58 Courtney Hawkins 3.00 8.00
59 Hunter Morris 3.00 8.00
60 George Springer 3.00 8.00
61 Sonny Gray 3.00 8.00
62 Neil Ramirez 3.00 8.00

2013 USA Baseball Champions Game Gear Jerseys Prime

*PRIME: .6X TO 1.5X BASIC
PRINT RUNS B/WN 3-99 COPIES PER
NO RODGERS PRICING AVAILABLE
4 Albert Almora/99 8.00 20.00
41 Carlos Rodon/99 12.00 30.00

2013 USA Baseball Champions Highlights

1 Rod Dedeaux .60 1.50
2 Tino Martinez .75 2.00
3 Jim Abbott .60 1.50
4 Tommy Lasorda .75 2.00
5 Ben Sheets .60 1.50
6 Mike Neill .40 1.00
7 Willie Abreu .60 1.50
8 Davey Johnson .40 1.00
9 Steve Reich .40 1.00
10 Cavan Biggio 1.50 4.00
11 Nomar Garciaparra .75 2.00

2013 USA Baseball Champions Legends Certified Die-Cuts

STATED PRINT RUN 699 SER.#'d SETS
1 Ben Sheets 1.25 3.00
2 Matt Purke .75 2.00
3 Ty Griffin .75 2.00
4 Roger Clemens 2.50 6.00
6 Terry Francona 1.25 3.00
7 Ken Griffey Jr. 4.00 10.00
8 Will Clark 1.50 4.00
9 Nick Castellanos 4.00 10.00
10 Michael Choice 1.25 3.00
11 Jim Abbott 1.25 3.00
12 Shawn Green 1.25 3.00
13 Sonny Gray 2.00 5.00
14 Barry Larkin 1.50 4.00
15 Rod Dedeaux 1.25 3.00
16 Jack McDowell 1.25 3.00
17 Carlos Rodon 3.00 8.00
18 Joe Carter 1.25 3.00
19 Nomar Garciaparra 1.50 4.00
20 Addison Russell 2.00 5.00
21 Joey Gallo 4.00 10.00
22 Jameson Taillon 1.50 4.00
23 Ben McDonald 1.25 3.00
24 Troy Glaus 1.25 3.00
25 Mike Mussina 1.50 4.00
26 Michael Wacha 1.50 4.00
27 David Dahl 1.50 4.00
28 Mark McGwire 3.00 8.00
29 Robin Ventura 1.25 3.00
30 Gerrit Cole 8.00 20.00
31 Tino Martinez 1.50 4.00
32 Frank Thomas 2.00 5.00
33 Tommy Lasorda 1.50 4.00
34 Pat Burrell 1.25 3.00
35 Jason Varitek 2.00 5.00
36 D.J. Peterson 1.25 3.00
37 Chipper Jones 2.00 5.00
38 Reese McGuire 1.50 4.00

2013 USA Baseball Champions Legends Certified Die-Cuts Mirror Blue

*MIRROR BLUE: .6X TO 1.5X BASIC
STATED PRINT RUN 199 SER.#'d SETS

2013 USA Baseball Champions Legends Certified Die-Cuts Mirror Green

*MIRROR GREEN: .6X TO 1.5X BASIC
STATED PRINT RUN 199 SER.#'d SETS

2013 USA Baseball Champions Legends Certified Die-Cuts Mirror Red

*MIRROR RED: .5X TO 1.2X BASIC
STATED PRINT RUN 299 SER.#'d SETS

2013 USA Baseball Champions National Team Certified Signatures

PRINT RUNS B/WN 26-299 COPIES PER
EXCHANGE DEADLINE 11/29/2014
1 David Berg/299 3.00 8.00
2 Kris Bryant/299 50.00 120.00
3 Dan Child/299
4 Michael Conforto/299 15.00 40.00
5 Austin Cousino/299 3.00 8.00
6 Jonathon Crawford/299 8.00 20.00
7 Kyle Farmer/299 3.00 8.00
8 Johnny Field/299 4.00 10.00
9 Adam Frazier/299 4.00 10.00
10 Marco Gonzales/299 5.00 12.00
11 Brett Hambright/299 3.00 8.00
12 Jordan Hankins/299 3.00 8.00
13 Michael Lorenzen/299 3.00 8.00
14 D.J. Peterson/299 8.00 20.00
15 Colton Plaia/299 3.00 8.00
16 Adam Plutko/299 3.00 8.00
17 Jake Reed/299 3.00 8.00
18 Carlos Rodon/299 10.00 25.00
19 Ryne Stanek/299 4.00 10.00
20 Jose Trevino/299 3.00 8.00
21 Trea Turner/299 10.00 25.00
22 Bobby Wahl/299 8.00 20.00
23 Trevor Williams/299 3.00 8.00
24 Willie Abreu /299 3.00 8.00
25 Christian Arroyo/299 12.00 30.00
26 Cavan Biggio/299 10.00 25.00
27 Ryan Boldt/299 3.00 8.00
28 Bryson Brigman/299 3.00 8.00
29 Ian Clarkin/28 5.00 12.00
30 Kevin Davis/299 3.00 8.00
31 Stephen Gonsalves/299 3.00 8.00
32 Connor Heady/299 3.00 8.00
33 John Kilichowski/261 3.00 8.00
34 Jeremy Martinez/299 3.00 8.00
35 Reese McGuire/299 3.00 8.00
36 Dom Nunez/299 3.00 8.00
37 Chris Okey/299 3.00 8.00
38 Ryan Olson/299 3.00 8.00
39 Carson Sands/299 3.00 8.00
40 Dominic Taccolini/299 3.00 8.00
41 Keegan Thompson/299 3.00 8.00
42 Garrett Williams/273 3.00 8.00
43 John Aiello/26
44 Nick Anderson/26
45 Luken Baker/26
46 Solomon Bates/26
47 Chris Betts/26
48 Danny Casals/26
49 Chris Cullen/26
50 Kyle Dean/26
51 Bailey Falter/26
52 Isaak Gutierrez/26
53 Nico Hoerner/26
54 Parker Kelly/26
55 Nick Madrigal/26
56 Austin Moore/26
57 Jio Orozco/26
58 Kyle Robeniol/26
59 Blake Rutherford/28
60 Cole Sands/26
61 Kyle Tucker/26
62 Coby Weaver/26

2013 USA Baseball Champions National Team Certified Signatures Mirror Red

PRINT RUNS B/WN 20-49 COPIES PER
EXCHANGE DEADLINE 11/29/2014
1 David Berg
2 Kris Bryant 60.00 150.00
3 Dan Child
4 Michael Conforto 25.00 60.00
5 Austin Cousino
6 Jonathon Crawford
7 Kyle Farmer 5.00 12.00
8 Johnny Field 6.00 15.00
9 Adam Frazier 6.00 15.00
10 Marco Gonzales 10.00 25.00
11 Brett Hambright
12 Jordan Hankins 5.00 12.00
13 Michael Lorenzen 5.00 12.00
14 D.J. Peterson 8.00 20.00
15 Colton Plaia
16 Adam Plutko 5.00 12.00
17 Jake Reed
18 Carlos Rodon
19 Ryne Stanek 6.00 15.00
20 Jose Trevino 5.00 12.00
21 Trea Turner 12.00 30.00
22 Bobby Wahl 12.50 30.00
23 Trevor Williams 5.00 12.00
24 Willie Abreu 5.00 12.00
25 Christian Arroyo 15.00 40.00
26 Cavan Biggio
27 Ryan Boldt 4.00 10.00
28 Bryson Brigman 5.00 12.00
29 Ian Clarkin 8.00 20.00
30 Kevin Davis 5.00 12.00
31 Stephen Gonsalves 5.00 12.00
32 Connor Heady 5.00 12.00
33 John Kilichowski 5.00 12.00
34 Jeremy Martinez
35 Reese McGuire 5.00 12.00
36 Dom Nunez 12.50 30.00
37 Chris Okey
38 Ryan Olson 5.00 12.00
39 Carson Sands
40 Dominic Taccolini
41 Keegan Thompson
42 Garrett Williams 5.00 12.00
43 John Aiello 8.00 20.00
44 Nick Anderson 5.00 12.00
45 Luken Baker 5.00 12.00
46 Solomon Bates 5.00 12.00
47 Chris Betts 5.00 12.00
48 Danny Casals
49 Chris Cullen 5.00 12.00
50 Kyle Dean 8.00 20.00
51 Bailey Falter
52 Isaak Gutierrez 5.00 12.00
53 Nico Hoerner
54 Parker Kelly 5.00 12.00
55 Nick Madrigal 5.00 12.00
56 Austin Moore
57 Jio Orozco 5.00 12.00
58 Kyle Robeniol 5.00 12.00
59 Blake Rutherford 5.00 12.00
60 Cole Sands 5.00 12.00
61 Kyle Tucker 15.00 40.00
62 Coby Weaver 5.00 12.00

2013 USA Baseball Champions Pride

1 Rod Dedeaux .60 1.50
2 Tino Martinez .75 2.00
3 Jason Varitek 1.00 2.50
4 Ken Griffey Jr. 2.00 5.00
5 Gerrit Cole 4.00 10.00
6 Reese McGuire .75 2.00
7 Nomar Garciaparra .75 2.00
8 Nick Castellanos 2.00 5.00
9 Jameson Taillon .75 2.00
10 Jim Abbott .60 1.50
11 Ben McDonald .60 1.50
12 Carlos Rodon 1.50 4.00
13 Matt Purke .40 1.00
14 Michael Choice .60 1.50
15 Michael Conforto 1.25 3.00
16 Ben Sheets .60 1.50
17 Addison Russell 1.00 2.50
18 Frank Thomas 1.00 2.50
19 Chipper Jones 1.00 2.50
20 Jack McDowell .60 1.50
21 Mark McGwire 1.50 4.00
22 Robin Ventura .60 1.50
24 Troy Glaus .60 1.50
25 Will Clark .75 2.00
26 Isaak Gutierrez .60 1.50

2013 USA Baseball Champions Stars and Stripes Signatures

PRINT RUNS B/WN 50-999 COPIES PER
EXCHANGE DEADLINE 11/29/2014
1 Grant Green/700 EXCH 3.00 8.00
2 David Nick/971 3.00 8.00
3 J.P. Ramirez/949 EXCH 3.00 8.00
4 Ozzie Smith/125 10.00 25.00
5 Terry Francona/223 8.00 20.00
6 Michael Kelly/700 3.00 8.00
7 Brett Mooneyham/799 3.00 8.00
8 Joe Carter/198 6.00 15.00
9 Frank Viola/473 5.00 12.00
10 Brant Ust/573 3.00 8.00
11 Wally Joyner/400 3.00 8.00
12 Tyler Anderson/750 3.00 8.00
13 Jake Barrett/855 3.00 8.00
14 Jack McDowell/364 5.00 12.00
15 Marcus Littlewood/673 3.00 8.00
16 Riccio Torrez/722 3.00 8.00
17 Will Clark/250 10.00 25.00
18 Mark McGwire/73 40.00 100.00
19 Blake Swihart/792 3.00 8.00
20 Barry Larkin/125 20.00 50.00
21 Jeff King/773 3.00 8.00
22 Joe Girardi/74 6.00 15.00
23 Tommy Mendonca/673 3.00 8.00
24 Derrek Lee/473 4.00 10.00
25 Brady Rodgers/659 3.00 8.00
26 Mike Mussina/175 4.00 10.00
27 Frank Thomas/200 20.00 50.00
28 Ben McDonald/500 4.00 10.00
29 Jim Abbott/425 4.00 10.00
30 Robin Ventura/400 4.00 10.00
31 Tino Martinez/223 4.00 10.00
32 Mychal Givens/971 3.00 8.00
33 Ty Griffin/700 3.00 8.00
34 Nick Delmonico/500 EXCH 3.00 8.00
35 Shawn Green/229 4.00 10.00
36 Zach Green/855 3.00 8.00
37 Cameron Garfield/950 3.00 8.00
38 Nomar Garciaparra/149 8.00 20.00
39 Jason Varitek/573 EXCH 10.00 25.00
41 Robbie Grossman/999 EXCH 3.00 8.00
42 Warren Morris/473 3.00 8.00
43 Pat Burrell/200 6.00 15.00
44 Mikie Mahtook/600 3.00 8.00
45 Mark Mulder/473 3.00 8.00
46 Tommy Lasorda/250 12.00 30.00
47 Ben Sheets/473 4.00 10.00
48 Garin Cecchini/671 6.00 15.00
49 Sean Coyle/750 5.00 12.00
50 Francisco Lindor/250 12.00 30.00
51 Kyle Winkler/700 3.00 8.00
52 Mac Williamson/616 6.00 15.00
53 Neil Ramirez/499 EXCH 3.00 8.00
54 Ken Griffey Jr./100 60.00 150.00
55 Roger Clemens/73 20.00 50.00
56 Johnny Damon/125 8.00 20.00
57 Jordan Swagerty/700 3.00 8.00
58 Zach Lee/700 3.00 8.00
59 Randal Grichuk/873 4.00 10.00
60 Richie Shaffer/575 3.00 8.00
61 Robert Refsnyder/700 4.00 10.00
62 Nolan Fontana/610 3.00 8.00
63 Matt Lipka/973 3.00 8.00
64 Cody Buckel/676 3.00 8.00
65 Christian Lopes/672 3.00 8.00
66 Matt Purke/700 3.00 8.00
67 Austin Maddox/836 4.00 10.00
68 Hunter Morris/873 3.00 8.00
69 Bryce Brentz/873 3.00 8.00
70 Michael Choice/749 3.00 8.00
71 Kolten Wong/549 4.00 10.00
72 Nick Castellanos/573 3.00 8.00
73 Jameson Taillon/800 4.00 10.00
74 Chipper Jones/50 30.00 80.00
75 Corey Seager/250 25.00 60.00
76 Carson Kelly/769 4.00 10.00
77 Lucas Sims/235 3.00 8.00
78 Adrian Marin/489 3.00 8.00
79 Tim Lopes/875 3.00 8.00
80 Lance McCullers/238 5.00 12.00
81 Bubba Starling/75 3.00 8.00
82 Gerrit Cole/250 3.00 8.00
84 George Springer/499 8.00 20.00
85 Bob Watson/473 3.00 8.00
86 Sonny Gray/620 5.00 12.00
87 Sean Gilmartin/423 3.00 8.00
88 Peter O'Brien/398 4.00 10.00
89 Kevin Gausman/250 3.00 8.00
90 Joey Gallo/400 6.00 15.00
91 David Dahl/110 5.00 12.00
92 Addison Russell/350 6.00 15.00
93 Jesse Winker/625 3.00 8.00
94 Walker Weickel/300 3.00 8.00
95 Deven Marrero/420 3.00 8.00
96 Courtney Hawkins/181 3.00 8.00
97 Tyler Naquin/649 3.00 8.00
98 Michael Wacha/709 3.00 8.00
99 Chase De Jong/175 5.00 12.00
100 Frank Robinson/50 10.00 25.00

2014 USA Baseball

COMPLETE SET (81) 20.00 50.00
COMP.SET INCLUDES ACTION/CL/FIELD
1 James Kaprielian .60 1.50
2 Jake Lemoine .30 .75
3 Ryan Burr .40 1.00
4 Carson Fulmer .30 .75
5 DJ Stewart .50 1.25
6 Chris Okey .30 .75
7 Alex Bregman 1.25 3.00
8 Dansby Swanson 2.00 5.00
9 Blake Trahan .30 .75
10 Thomas Eshelman .40 1.00
11 Kyle Funkhouser .40 1.00
12 A.J. Minter .40 1.00
13 Nicholas Banks .30 .75
14 Zack Collins .50 1.25
15 Mark Mathias .40 1.00
16 Bryan Reynolds 1.00 2.50
17 Taylor Ward .50 1.25
18 Justin Garza .30 .75
19 Tyler Jay .40 1.00
20 Tate Matheny .40 1.00
21 Trey Killian .30 .75
22 Bailey Ober .30 .75
23 Andrew Moore .40 1.00
24 Christin Stewart .40 1.00
25 Dillon Tate .50 1.25
26 Elih Marrero .30 .75
27 Max Wotell .40 1.00
28 Kyle Molnar .30 .75
29 Kolby Allard .60 1.50
30 Luken Baker .50 1.25
31 Austin Bergner .40 1.00
32 Kale Breaux .50 1.25
33 Daz Cameron 1.00 2.50
34 Trenton Clark .40 1.00
35 Joe DeMers .30 .75
36 Gray Fenter .30 .75
37 Mitchell Hansen .30 .75
38 Ke'Bryan Hayes .50 1.25
39 Lucas Herbert .30 .75
40 Peter Lambert .30 .75
41 Xavier LeGrant .30 .75
42 Nick Madrigal .60 1.50
43 Blake Rutherford .60 1.50
44 Austin Smith .30 .75
45 L.T. Tolbert .30 .75
46 Brice Turang 1.00 2.50
47 Cordell Dunn Jr. .30 .75
48 Jacob Blas .30 .75
49 Hunter Greene 1.00 2.50
50 Devin Ortiz .30 .75
51 Royce Lewis .75 2.00
52 Kristofer Armstrong .30 .75
53 Ryan Vilade .60 1.50
54 Thomas Burbank .40 1.00
55 Christopher Martin 1.00 2.50
56 Justin Bullock .40 1.00
57 Mark Vientos .50 1.25
58 Noah Campbell .30 .75
59 Raymond Gil .30 .75
60 Doug Nikhazy .30 .75
61 John Dearth .30 .75
62 Steven Williams .30 .75
63 Hugh Fisher .40 1.00
64 Alejandro Toral .50 1.25
65 Blake Paugh .40 1.00

2014 USA Baseball Red and Blue Prizms

*RB PRIZMS: 1.2X TO 3X BASIC
STATED PRINT RUN 149 SER.#'d SETS

2014 USA Baseball 15U National Team Black Gold Signatures

RANDOM INSERTS IN FACTORY SETS
STATED PRINT RUN 49 SER.#'d SETS
46 Brice Turang 12.00 30.00
47 Cordell Dunn Jr. 4.00 10.00
48 Jacob Blas 4.00 10.00
49 Hunter Greene 12.00 30.00
50 Devin Ortiz 4.00 10.00
51 Royce Lewis 25.00 60.00
52 Kristofer Armstrong 4.00 10.00
53 Ryan Vilade 8.00 20.00
54 Thomas Burbank 5.00 12.00
55 Christopher Austin Martin 20.00 50.00
56 Justin Bullock 5.00 12.00
57 Mark Vientos 6.00 15.00
58 Noah Campbell 4.00 10.00
59 Raymond Gil 4.00 10.00
60 Doug Nikhazy 4.00 10.00
61 John Dearth 4.00 10.00
62 Steven Williams 4.00 10.00
63 Hugh Fisher 5.00 12.00
64 Alejandro Toral 6.00 15.00
65 Blake Paugh 5.00 12.00

2014 USA Baseball 15U National Team Game Ball Signatures

46 Brice Turang
47 Cordell Dunn Jr.
48 Jacob Blas
49 Hunter Greene
50 Devin Ortiz
51 Royce Lewis
52 Kristofer Armstrong
53 Ryan Vilade
54 Thomas Burbank
55 Christopher Austin Martin
56 Justin Bullock
57 Mark Vientos
58 Noah Campbell
59 Raymond Gil
60 Doug Nikhazy
61 John Dearth
62 Steven Williams
63 Hugh Fisher
64 Alejandro Toral
65 Blake Paugh

2014 USA Baseball 15U National Team Jerseys

RANDOM INSERTS IN FACTORY SETS
STATED PRINT RUN 99 SER.#'d SETS
*JUMBO/49: .5X TO 1.2X BASIC
*PRIME/30-35: .6X TO 1.5X BASIC
46 Brice Turang 6.00 15.00
47 Cordell Dunn Jr. 2.00 5.00
48 Jacob Blas 2.00 5.00
49 Hunter Greene 6.00 15.00
50 Devin Ortiz 2.00 5.00
51 Royce Lewis 5.00 12.00
52 Kristofer Armstrong 2.00 5.00
53 Ryan Vilade 4.00 10.00
54 Thomas Burbank 2.50 6.00
55 Christopher Austin Martin 4.00 10.00
56 Justin Bullock 2.50 6.00
57 Mark Vientos 3.00 8.00
58 Noah Campbell 2.00 5.00
59 Raymond Gil 2.00 5.00
60 Doug Nikhazy 2.00 5.00
61 John Dearth 2.00 5.00
62 Steven Williams 2.00 5.00
63 Hugh Fisher 2.50 6.00
64 Alejandro Toral 3.00 8.00
65 Blake Paugh 2.50 6.00

2014 USA Baseball 15U National Team Jerseys Signatures

RANDOM INSERTS IN FACTORY SETS
STATED PRINT RUN 99 SER.#'d SETS
46 Brice Turang 10.00 25.00
47 Cordell Dunn Jr. 3.00 8.00
48 Jacob Blas 3.00 8.00
49 Hunter Greene 10.00 25.00
50 Devin Ortiz 3.00 8.00
51 Royce Lewis 20.00 50.00
52 Kristofer Armstrong 3.00 8.00
53 Ryan Vilade 6.00 15.00
54 Thomas Burbank 4.00 10.00
55 Christopher Austin Martin 15.00 40.00
56 Justin Bullock 4.00 10.00
57 Mark Vientos 5.00 12.00
58 Noah Campbell 3.00 8.00
59 Raymond Gil 3.00 8.00
60 Doug Nikhazy 3.00 8.00
61 John Dearth 3.00 8.00
62 Steven Williams 3.00 8.00
63 Hugh Fisher 4.00 10.00
64 Alejandro Toral 5.00 12.00
65 Blake Paugh 4.00 10.00

2014 USA Baseball 15U National Team Signatures

RANDOM INSERTS IN FACTORY SETS
STATED PRINT RUN 299 SER.#'d SETS
46 Brice Turang 12.00 30.00
47 Cordell Dunn Jr. 3.00 8.00
48 Jacob Blas 3.00 8.00
49 Hunter Greene 25.00 60.00
50 Devin Ortiz 3.00 8.00
51 Royce Lewis 15.00 40.00
52 Kristofer Armstrong 3.00 8.00
53 Ryan Vilade 6.00 15.00
54 Thomas Burbank 4.00 10.00
55 Christopher Austin Martin 15.00 40.00
56 Justin Bullock 4.00 10.00
57 Mark Vientos 5.00 12.00
58 Noah Campbell 3.00 8.00
59 Raymond Gil 3.00 8.00
60 Doug Nikhazy 3.00 8.00
61 John Dearth 3.00 8.00
62 Steven Williams 3.00 8.00
63 Hugh Fisher 4.00 10.00
64 Alejandro Toral 5.00 12.00
65 Blake Paugh 4.00 10.00

2014 USA Baseball 18U National Team Black Gold Signatures

RANDOM INSERTS IN FACTORY SETS
STATED PRINT RUN 49 SER.#'d SETS
26 Elih Marrero 4.00 10.00
27 Max Wotell 5.00 12.00
28 Kyle Molnar 4.00 10.00
29 Kolby Allard 8.00 20.00
30 Luken Baker 6.00 15.00
31 Austin Bergner 5.00 12.00
32 Kale Breaux 6.00 15.00
33 Daz Cameron 5.00 12.00
34 Trenton Clark 5.00 12.00
35 Joe DeMers 4.00 10.00
36 Gray Fenter 4.00 10.00
37 Mitchell Hansen 4.00 10.00
38 Ke'Bryan Hayes 6.00 15.00
39 Lucas Herbert 4.00 10.00
40 Peter Lambert 4.00 10.00
41 Xavier LeGrant 4.00 10.00
42 Nick Madrigal 8.00 20.00
43 Blake Rutherford 8.00 20.00
44 Austin Smith 4.00 10.00
45 L.T. Tolbert 4.00 10.00

2014 USA Baseball 18U National Team Jerseys

RANDOM INSERTS IN FACTORY SETS
STATED PRINT RUN 99 SER.#'d SETS
*PRIME/35: .6X TO 1.5X BASIC
*JUMBO/49: .5X TO 1.2X BASIC
26 Elih Marrero 2.00 5.00
27 Max Wotell 2.50 6.00
28 Kyle Molnar 2.00 5.00
29 Kolby Allard 4.00 10.00
30 Luken Baker 3.00 8.00
31 Austin Bergner 2.50 6.00
32 Kale Breaux 3.00 8.00
33 Daz Cameron 6.00 15.00
34 Trenton Clark 2.50 6.00
35 Joe DeMers 2.00 5.00

36 Gray Fenter 2.00 5.00
37 Mitchell Hansen 2.00 5.00
38 Ke'Bryan Hayes 3.00 8.00
39 Lucas Herbert 2.00 5.00
40 Peter Lambert 2.00 5.00
41 Xavier LeGrant 2.00 5.00
42 Nick Madrigal 4.00 10.00
43 Blake Rutherford 4.00 10.00
44 Austin Smith 2.00 5.00
45 L.T. Tolbert 2.00 5.00

2014 USA Baseball 18U National Team Jerseys Signatures

RANDOM INSERTS IN FACTORY SETS
STATED PRINT RUN 99 SER.#'d SETS
26 Elih Marrero 3.00 8.00
27 Max Wotell 4.00 10.00
28 Kyle Molnar 3.00 8.00
29 Kolby Allard 6.00 15.00
30 Luken Baker 8.00 20.00
31 Austin Bergner 4.00 10.00
32 Kale Breaux 5.00 12.00
33 Daz Cameron 5.00 12.00
34 Trenton Clark 4.00 10.00
35 Joe DeMers 3.00 8.00
36 Gray Fenter 3.00 8.00
37 Mitchell Hansen 3.00 8.00
38 Ke'Bryan Hayes 5.00 12.00
39 Lucas Herbert 3.00 8.00
40 Peter Lambert 3.00 8.00
41 Xavier LeGrant 3.00 8.00
42 Nick Madrigal 10.00 25.00
43 Blake Rutherford 6.00 15.00
44 Austin Smith 3.00 8.00
45 L.T. Tolbert 3.00 8.00

2014 USA Baseball 18U National Team Signatures

RANDOM INSERTS IN FACTORY SETS
STATED PRINT RUN 499 SER.#'d SETS
AB Austin Bergner 4.00 10.00
AS Austin Smith 3.00 8.00
BR Blake Rutherford 10.00 25.00
DZ Daz Cameron 6.00 15.00
EM Elih Marrero 3.00 8.00
GF Gray Fenter 3.00 8.00
JM Joe DeMers 3.00 8.00
KA Kolby Allard 4.00 10.00
KB Kale Breaux 5.00 12.00
KH Ke'Bryan Hayes 5.00 12.00
KM Kyle Molnar 3.00 8.00
LB Luken Baker 5.00 12.00
LH Lucas Herbert 3.00 8.00
LT L.T. Tolbert 3.00 8.00
MH Mitchell Hansen 3.00 8.00
MW Max Wotell 4.00 10.00
NM Nick Madrigal 10.00 25.00
PL Peter Lambert 3.00 8.00
TC Trenton Clark 4.00 10.00
XL Xavier LeGrant 3.00 8.00

2014 USA Baseball Collegiate National Team Black Gold Signatures

RANDOM INSERTS IN FACTORY SETS
STATED PRINT RUN 49 SER.#'d SETS
1 James Kaprielian 8.00 20.00
2 Jake Lemoine 4.00 10.00
3 Ryan Burr 5.00 12.00
4 Carson Fulmer 4.00 10.00
5 DJ Stewart 6.00 15.00
6 Chris Okey 4.00 10.00
7 Alex Bregman 15.00 40.00
8 Dansby Swanson 40.00 100.00
9 Blake Trahan 4.00 10.00
10 Thomas Eshelman 5.00 12.00
11 Kyle Funkhouser 5.00 12.00
12 A.J. Minter 5.00 12.00
13 Nicholas Banks 4.00 10.00
14 Zack Collins 6.00 15.00
15 Mark Mathias 5.00 12.00
16 Bryan Reynolds 12.00 30.00
17 Taylor Ward 6.00 15.00
18 Justin Garza 4.00 10.00
19 Tyler Jay 5.00 12.00
20 Tate Matheny 5.00 12.00
21 Trey Killian 4.00 10.00
22 Bailey Ober 4.00 10.00
23 Andrew Moore 5.00 12.00
24 Christin Stewart 5.00 12.00
25 Dillon Tate 6.00 15.00

2014 USA Baseball Collegiate National Team Game Ball Signatures

RANDOM INSERTS IN FACTORY SETS
PRINT RUNS B/WN 20-99 COPIES PER
NO PRICING ON QTY 20
1 James Kaprielian/99 6.00 15.00
2 Jake Lemoine/99 3.00 8.00
3 Ryan Burr/99 4.00 10.00
4 Carson Fulmer/99 12.00 30.00
5 DJ Stewart/99 5.00 12.00
6 Chris Okey/99 3.00 8.00
7 Alex Bregman/99 12.00 30.00
8 Dansby Swanson/99 25.00 60.00
9 Blake Trahan/99 3.00 8.00
10 Thomas Eshelman/99 4.00 10.00
11 Kyle Funkhouser/99 4.00 10.00
12 A.J. Minter/99 4.00 10.00
13 Nicholas Banks/99 3.00 8.00
14 Zack Collins/99 5.00 12.00
15 Mark Mathias/99 4.00 10.00
16 Bryan Reynolds/99 10.00 25.00
17 Taylor Ward/99 5.00 12.00
18 Justin Garza/99 3.00 8.00
19 Tyler Jay/99 4.00 10.00
20 Tate Matheny/99 4.00 10.00
21 Trey Killian/99 3.00 8.00
23 Andrew Moore/99 4.00 10.00
24 Christin Stewart/99 4.00 10.00
25 Dillon Tate/99 5.00 12.00

2014 USA Baseball Collegiate National Team Jerseys

RANDOM INSERTS IN FACTORY SETS
STATED PRINT RUN 99 SER.#'d SETS
*JUMBO/49: .5X TO 1.2X BASIC
*PRIME/35: .6X TO 1.5X BASIC
1 James Kaprielian 4.00 10.00
2 Jake Lemoine 2.00 5.00
3 Ryan Burr 2.50 6.00
4 Carson Fulmer 2.00 5.00
5 DJ Stewart 3.00 8.00
6 Chris Okey 2.00 5.00
7 Alex Bregman 8.00 20.00
8 Dansby Swanson 6.00 15.00
9 Blake Trahan 2.00 5.00
10 Thomas Eshelman 2.50 6.00
11 Kyle Funkhouser 2.50 6.00
12 A.J. Minter 2.50 6.00
13 Nicholas Banks 2.00 5.00
14 Zack Collins 3.00 8.00
15 Mark Mathias 2.50 6.00
16 Bryan Reynolds 6.00 15.00
17 Taylor Ward 3.00 8.00
18 Justin Garza 2.00 5.00
19 Tyler Jay 2.50 6.00
20 Tate Matheny 2.50 6.00
21 Trey Killian 2.00 5.00
22 Bailey Ober 2.00 5.00
23 Andrew Moore 2.50 6.00
24 Christin Stewart 2.50 6.00
25 Dillon Tate 3.00 8.00

2014 USA Baseball Collegiate National Team Jerseys Signatures

1 James Kaprielian 6.00 15.00
2 Jake Lemoine 3.00 8.00
3 Ryan Burr 4.00 10.00
4 Carson Fulmer 3.00 8.00
5 DJ Stewart 5.00 12.00
6 Chris Okey 3.00 8.00
7 Alex Bregman 12.00 30.00
8 Dansby Swanson 30.00 80.00
9 Blake Trahan 3.00 8.00
10 Thomas Eshelman 4.00 10.00
11 Kyle Funkhouser 4.00 10.00
12 A.J. Minter 4.00 10.00
13 Nicholas Banks 3.00 8.00
14 Zack Collins 5.00 12.00
15 Mark Mathias 4.00 10.00
16 Bryan Reynolds 10.00 25.00
17 Taylor Ward 5.00 12.00
18 Justin Garza 3.00 8.00
19 Tyler Jay 4.00 10.00
20 Tate Matheny 4.00 10.00
21 Trey Killian 3.00 8.00
22 Bailey Ober 3.00 8.00
23 Andrew Moore 4.00 10.00
24 Christin Stewart 4.00 10.00
25 Dillon Tate 5.00 12.00

2014 USA Baseball Collegiate National Team Signatures

RANDOM INSERTS IN FACTORY SETS
STATED PRINT RUN 499 SER.#'d SETS
1 James Kaprielian 6.00 15.00
2 Jake Lemoine 3.00 8.00
3 Ryan Burr 4.00 10.00
4 Carson Fulmer 8.00 20.00
5 DJ Stewart 5.00 12.00
6 Chris Okey 3.00 8.00
7 Alex Bregman 12.00 30.00
8 Dansby Swanson 20.00 50.00
9 Blake Trahan 3.00 8.00
10 Thomas Eshelman 4.00 10.00
11 Kyle Funkhouser 4.00 10.00
12 A.J. Minter 4.00 10.00
13 Nicholas Banks 3.00 8.00
14 Zack Collins 5.00 12.00
15 Mark Mathias 4.00 10.00
16 Bryan Reynolds 10.00 25.00
17 Taylor Ward 5.00 12.00
18 Justin Garza 3.00 8.00
19 Tyler Jay 4.00 10.00
20 Tate Matheny 4.00 10.00
21 Trey Killian 3.00 8.00
22 Bailey Ober 3.00 8.00
23 Andrew Moore 4.00 10.00
24 Christin Stewart 4.00 10.00
25 Dillon Tate 5.00 12.00

2014 USA Baseball Game Action

1 Christin Stewart .40 1.00
2 Carson Fulmer .30 .75
3 James Kaprielian .60 1.50
4 Kyle Funkhouser .40 1.00
5 Justin Garza .30 .75
6 Dillon Tate .50 1.25
7 Alex Bregman 1.25 3.00
8 Ryan Burr .40 1.00
9 DJ Stewart .50 1.25
10 Thomas Eshelman .40 1.00
11 Mark Mathias .40 1.00
12 Blake Trahan .30 .75

2014 USA Baseball Team Checklists

THREE PER BOX SET
1 Collegiate National Team .30 .75
2 18U National Team .30 .75
3 15U National Team .30 .75

2014 USA Baseball USA Baseball Field

ONE PER BOX SET
1 USA Baseball Field .30 .75

2015 USA Baseball

1 USA Baseball Field .30 .75
2 Collegiate National Team .30 .75
3 18U National Team .30 .75
4 15U National Team .30 .75
5 Nick Banks .40 1.00
6 Bryson Brigman .30 .75
7 Zack Burdi .40 1.00
8 Corey Ray .50 1.25
9 Bobby Dalbec 1.50 4.00
10 Anfernee Grier .40 1.00
11 Garrett Hampson .60 1.50
12 KJ Harrison .60 1.50
13 Ryan Hendrix .30 .75
14 Tanner Houck 1.50 4.00
15 Ryan Howard .40 1.00
16 Zach Jackson .40 1.00
17 Daulton Jefferies .40 1.00
18 Anthony Kay .40 1.00
19 Brendan McKay 1.25 3.00
20 Stephen Nogosek .30 .75
21 Chris Okey .30 .75
22 A.J. Puk .60 1.50
23 Buddy Reed .30 .75
24 JJ Schwarz .40 1.00
25 Mike Shawaryn .40 1.00
26 Logan Shore .40 1.00
27 Robert Tyler .30 .75
28 Matt Thaiss .50 1.25
29 Michael Amditis .30 .75
30 Ian Anderson 1.50 4.00
31 Daniel Bakst .30 .75
32 William Benson .40 1.00
33 Austin Bergner .30 .75
34 Jordan Butler .30 .75
35 Hagen Danner .60 1.50
36 Braxton Garrett .50 1.25
37 Kevin Gowdy .50 1.25
38 Hunter Greene 1.00 2.50
39 Cooper Johnson .30 .75
40 Reggie Lawson .30 .75
41 Morgan McCullough .30 .75
42 Mickey Moniak 1.00 2.50
43 Nicholas Pratto .40 1.00
44 Nicholas Quintana .60 1.50
45 Ryan Rolison .60 1.50
46 Blake Rutherford .60 1.50
47 Cole Stobbe .30 .75
48 Forrest Whitley 1.25 3.00
49 Branden Boissiere .30 .75
50 Colton Bowman .30 .75
51 Gabe Briones .30 .75
52 C.J. Brown .30 .75
53 Kendrick Calilao .40 1.00
54 Triston Casas 1.25 3.00
55 Joseph Charles .30 .75
56 Jonathan Childress .30 .75
57 Jaden Fein .40 1.00
58 Ryder Green .75 2.00
59 Rohan Handa .30 .75
60 Jared Hart .30 .75
61 Jeremiah Jackson .50 1.25
62 Justyn-Henry Malloy .30 .75
63 Chris McElvain .30 .75
64 Zachary Morgan .30 .75
65 Connor Ollio .30 .75
66 Lyon Richardson .50 1.25
67 Luis Tuero .30 .75
68 Brandon Walker .30 .75
69 Tony Jacob .30 .75
70 A.J. Puk GA .60 1.50
71 Austin Bergner GA .30 .75
72 Blake Rutherford GA .60 1.50
73 Bobby Dalbec GA 1.50 4.00
74 Chris Okey GA .30 .75
75 Corey Ray GA .50 1.25
76 Kevin Gowdy GA .50 1.25
77 Mickey Moniak GA 1.00 2.50
78 Nick Banks GA .40 1.00
79 Robert Tyler GA .30 .75
80 Zach Jackson GA .40 1.00

2015 USA Baseball 14U National Team Jerseys Signatures

1 Matthew Allan/49
2 Adam Bloebaum/50
3 Adam Crampton/50
4 Joseph Cruz/49
5 J.J. Cruz/36
6 Jasiah Dixon/49
7 Michael Dixon/49
8 Damon Fountain/19
9 Dorian Gonzalez/48
10 Mac Guscette/47
11 Joshua Hahn/49
12 Anthony Hall/50
13 Maurice Hampton/50
14 Albert Hernandez/50
15 Tony Jacob/40
16 Michael Brooks/50
17 Jared Jones/49
18 Zane Keener/49
19 Kellen Kozlowski/47
20 Brooks Lee/48
21 Ethan Long/50
22 Skyler Loverink/50
23 Brandon Madrigal/48
24 Joseph Naranjo/50
25 Aaron Nixon/50
26 Colton Olasin/50
27 Riley O'Sullivan/50
28 Joshua Pakola/49
29 Sean Rimmer/50
30 Mason Roach/50
31 Paul Roche/47
32 Ben Rozenblum/49
33 Hudson Sapp/16
34 Dylan Tanner/50
35 Anthony Volpe/50
36 Joseph Wilkinson/50
37 Nate Wohlgemuth/47
38 Bronson Yager/48
39 Carter Young/50

2015 USA Baseball 15U National Team Jerseys

1 Branden Boissiere
2 Colton Bowman
3 Gabe Briones
4 C.J. Brown
6 Triston Casas
7 Joseph Charles
8 Jonathan Childress
9 Jaden Fein
10 Ryder Green
11 Rohan Handa
12 Jared Hart
13 Jeremiah Jackson
14 Justyn-Henry Malloy
15 Chris McElvain
16 Zachary Morgan
17 Connor Ollio
18 Lyon Richardson
19 Luis Tuero
20 Brandon Walker
21 Tony Jacob

2015 USA Baseball 15U National Team Jerseys Signatures

1 Branden Boissiere/99
2 Colton Bowman/99
3 Gabe Briones/99
4 C.J. Brown/99
6 Triston Casas/99
7 Joseph Charles/99
8 Jonathan Childress/99
9 Jaden Fein/99
10 Ryder Green/99
11 Rohan Handa/99
12 Jared Hart/99
13 Jeremiah Jackson/70
14 Justyn-Henry Malloy/99
15 Chris McElvain/99
16 Zachary Morgan/99
17 Connor Ollio/99
18 Lyon Richardson/99
19 Luis Tuero/99
20 Brandon Walker/99
21 Tony Jacob/98

2015 USA Baseball 15U National Team Signatures

OVERALL AUTO ODDS 7 PER BOX
*RED/25: .5X TO 1.2X BASIC
1 Branden Boissiere 2.50 6.00
2 Colton Bowman 4.00 10.00
3 Gabe Briones 4.00 10.00
4 C.J. Brown 4.00 10.00
5 Kendrick Calilao 3.00 8.00
6 Triston Casas 12.00 30.00
7 Joseph Charles 2.50 6.00
8 Jonathan Childress 2.50 6.00
9 Jaden Fein 4.00 10.00
10 Ryder Green 4.00 10.00
11 Rohan Handa 2.50 6.00
12 Jared Hart 3.00 8.00
13 Jeremiah Jackson 6.00 15.00
14 Justyn-Henry Malloy 10.00 25.00
15 Chris McElvain 6.00 15.00
16 Zachary Morgan 3.00 8.00
17 Connor Ollio 2.50 6.00
18 Lyon Richardson 2.50 6.00
19 Luis Tuero 4.00 10.00
20 Brandon Walker 3.00 8.00
21 Tony Jacob 6.00 15.00

2015 USA Baseball 17U National Team Jerseys Signatures

1 Leo Nierenberg/50
2 Troy Claunch/50
3 Brice Turang/50
4 Brandon McCabe/50
5 Brian Gursky/50
6 M.J. Melendez/50
7 Coleman Brannen/50
8 Jack Carey/50
9 Matthew Sauer/50
10 Tanner Burns/49
11 Jason Rooks/43
12 Jonathan Stroman/50
13 Kevin Abel/50
14 Raymond Gil/50
15 Graham Ashcraft/50
16 Altoon Coleman/50
17 John Samuel Shenker/50
18 Jayson Gonzalez/50
19 Kyle Hurt/48
20 Matthew Rudick/49
21 Will Wilson/50
22 Jose Ciccarello/50
23 Conner Uselton/50
24 Steven Williams/50
25 Weston Bizzle/50
26 Nick Kahle/50
27 Tristan Hanoian/50
28 Tyler Ahearn/50
29 Michael Rothenberg/50
30 Carlos Lomeli/50
31 Danny Zimmerman/50
32 Tyler Thompson/50
33 Garrett Gooden/50
34 Ray Gaither/49
35 Nick Brueser/50
36 Robert Touron/50
37 Tremaine Spears/49
38 Mitchell Stone/50
39 Darren Nelson/50
40 Boyd Vander Kooi/49

2015 USA Baseball 18U National Team Jerseys

1 Michael Amditis
2 Ian Anderson
3 Daniel Bakst
4 William Benson
5 Austin Bergner
6 Jordan Butler
7 Hagen Danner
8 Braxton Garrett
9 Kevin Gowdy
10 Hunter Greene
11 Cooper Johnson
12 Reggie Lawson
13 Morgan McCullough
14 Mickey Moniak
15 Nicholas Pratto
16 Nicholas Quintana
17 Ryan Rolison
18 Blake Rutherford
19 Cole Stobbe
20 Forrest Whitley

2015 USA Baseball 18U National Team Jerseys Signatures

1 Michael Amditis
2 Ian Anderson
3 Daniel Bakst
4 William Benson
5 Austin Bergner
6 Jordan Butler
7 Hagen Danner
8 Braxton Garrett
9 Kevin Gowdy
10 Hunter Greene
11 Cooper Johnson
12 Reggie Lawson
13 Morgan McCullough
14 Mickey Moniak
15 Nicholas Pratto
16 Nicholas Quintana
17 Ryan Rolison
18 Blake Rutherford
19 Cole Stobbe
20 Forrest Whitley

2015 USA Baseball 18U National Team Signatures

1 Michael Amditis
2 Ian Anderson
3 Daniel Bakst
4 William Benson
5 Austin Bergner
6 Jordan Butler
7 Hagen Danner
8 Braxton Garrett
9 Kevin Gowdy
10 Hunter Greene
11 Cooper Johnson
12 Reggie Lawson
13 Morgan McCullough
14 Mickey Moniak 20.00 50.00
15 Nicholas Pratto
16 Nicholas Quintana
17 Ryan Rolison
18 Blake Rutherford
19 Cole Stobbe
20 Forrest Whitley

2015 USA Baseball Chinese Taipei All Stars Signatures

1 Chung Yu Chen
2 Hao Wei Chang
3 Tzu Hong Chen
4 Chu Lin
5 Po Jung Wang
6 Min Hsun Chang
7 Yi Chih Huang
8 Yu Wei Kao
9 Shih Ying Peng
10 Wei Fan Tsai
11 Chih Chieh Su
12 Tzu Peng Huang
13 Yi Hung Chen
14 Wei Chih Lin
15 Tai Chun Yang
16 Sung Hsun Wu
17 Kai Wen Cheng
18 Tsung Hsien Lee
19 Ming Chien Lin
21 Chih Hsien Lin
22 Kai Hsiang Hsu
23 Yu Ning Tsao

2015 USA Baseball Chinese Taipei All Stars Signatures Materials

1 Chung Yu Chen
2 Hao Wei Chang
3 Tzu Hong Chen
4 Chu Lin
5 Po Jung Wang
6 Min Hsun Chang
7 Yi Chih Huang
9 Shih Ying Peng
10 Wei Fan Tsai
11 Chih Chieh Su
12 Tzu Peng Huang
13 Yi Hung Chen
14 Wei Chih Lin
15 Tai Chun Yang
16 Sung Hsun Wu
17 Kai Wen Cheng
18 Tsung Hsien Lee
19 Ming Chien Lin
21 Chih Hsien Lin
22 Kai Hsiang Hsu

2015 USA Baseball Collegiate National Team Jerseys

OVERALL MEM ODDS TWO PER BOX
STATED PRINT RUN 99 SER.#'d SETS
*JUMBO/49: .5X TO 1.2X BASIC
*PRIME/35: .6X TO 1.5X BASIC
1 Nick Banks 2.50 6.00
2 Bryson Brigman 2.00 5.00
3 Zack Burdi 2.50 6.00
4 Corey Ray 3.00 8.00
5 Bobby Dalbec 10.00 25.00
6 Anfernee Grier 2.50 6.00
7 Garrett Hampson 4.00 10.00
8 KJ Harrison 4.00 10.00
9 Ryan Hendrix 2.00 5.00
10 Tanner Houck 10.00 25.00
11 Ryan Howard 2.50 6.00
12 Zach Jackson 2.50 6.00
13 Daulton Jefferies 2.50 6.00
14 Anthony Kay 2.50 6.00
15 Brendan McKay 8.00 20.00
16 Stephen Nogosek 2.00 5.00
17 Chris Okey 2.00 5.00
18 A.J. Puk 4.00 10.00
19 Buddy Reed 2.00 5.00
20 JJ Schwarz 2.50 6.00
21 Mike Shawaryn 2.50 6.00
22 Logan Shore 2.50 6.00
23 Robert Tyler 2.00 5.00
24 Matt Thaiss 3.00 8.00

2015 USA Baseball Collegiate National Team Jerseys Signatures

1 Nick Banks/99
2 Bryson Brigman/99
3 Zack Burdi/99
4 Corey Ray/99
5 Bobby Dalbec/99
6 Anfernee Grier/99
7 Garrett Hampson/79
8 KJ Harrison/80
9 Ryan Hendrix/99
10 Tanner Houck/99
11 Ryan Howard/99
12 Zach Jackson/99
13 Daulton Jefferies/99
14 Anthony Kay/99
15 Brendan McKay/99
16 Stephen Nogosek/99
17 Chris Okey/99
18 A.J. Puk/99
19 Buddy Reed/99
20 JJ Schwarz/99
21 Mike Shawaryn/99
22 Logan Shore/99
23 Robert Tyler/99
24 Matt Thaiss/99

2015 USA Baseball Collegiate National Team Signatures

1 Nick Banks
2 Bryson Brigman
3 Zack Burdi
4 Corey Ray
6 Bobby Dalbec
7 Anfernee Grier
8 Garrett Hampson
9 KJ Harrison
10 Ryan Hendrix
11 Tanner Houck
12 Ryan Howard
13 Zach Jackson
14 Daulton Jefferies
16 Anthony Kay
17 Brendan McKay
18 Stephen Nogosek
19 Chris Okey
21 A.J. Puk
23 Buddy Reed
25 JJ Schwarz
26 Mike Shawaryn
27 Logan Shore
28 Robert Tyler
29 Matt Thaiss

2015 USA Baseball Crown Royale

1 Nick Banks
2 Bryson Brigman
3 Zack Burdi
4 Corey Ray
5 Bobby Dalbec
6 Anfernee Grier
7 Garrett Hampson
8 KJ Harrison
9 Ryan Hendrix
10 Tanner Houck
11 Ryan Howard
12 Zach Jackson
13 Daulton Jefferies
14 Anthony Kay
15 Brendan McKay
16 Stephen Nogosek
17 Chris Okey
18 A.J. Puk
19 Buddy Reed
20 JJ Schwarz
21 Mike Shawaryn
22 Logan Shore
23 Robert Tyler
24 Matt Thaiss
25 Michael Amditis
26 Ian Anderson
27 Daniel Bakst
28 William Benson
29 Austin Bergner
30 Jordan Butler
31 Hagen Danner
32 Braxton Garrett
33 Kevin Gowdy
34 Hunter Greene
35 Cooper Johnson
36 Reggie Lawson
37 Morgan McCullough
38 Mickey Moniak
39 Nicholas Pratto
40 Nicholas Quintana
41 Ryan Rolison
42 Blake Rutherford
43 Cole Stobbe
44 Forrest Whitley
45 Dansby Swanson

2015 USA Baseball Crown Royale Signatures Silver

1 Nick Banks
2 Bryson Brigman
3 Zack Burdi
4 Corey Ray
5 Bobby Dalbec
6 Anfernee Grier
7 Garrett Hampson
8 KJ Harrison
9 Ryan Hendrix
10 Tanner Houck
11 Ryan Howard
12 Zach Jackson
13 Daulton Jefferies
14 Anthony Kay
15 Brendan McKay
16 Stephen Nogosek
17 Chris Okey
18 A.J. Puk
19 Buddy Reed
20 JJ Schwarz
21 Mike Shawaryn
22 Logan Shore
23 Robert Tyler
24 Matt Thaiss
25 Michael Amditis
26 Ian Anderson
27 Daniel Bakst
28 William Benson
29 Austin Bergner
30 Jordan Butler
31 Hagen Danner
32 Braxton Garrett
33 Kevin Gowdy
34 Hunter Greene
35 Cooper Johnson
36 Reggie Lawson
37 Morgan McCullough
38 Mickey Moniak
39 Nicholas Pratto
40 Nicholas Quintana
41 Ryan Rolison
42 Blake Rutherford
43 Cole Stobbe
44 Forrest Whitley

2015 USA Baseball Stars and Stripes

COMPLETE SET (100) 8.00 20.00
1 A.J. Cole .12 .30
2 A.J. Minter .15 .40
3 Addison Russell .40 1.00
4 Albert Almora .15 .40
5 Alejandro Toral .20 .50
6 Alex Bregman .50 1.25
7 Andrew Moore .15 .40
8 Austin Bergner .12 .30
9 Austin Smith .12 .30
10 Bailey Ober .12 .30
11 Blake Paugh .12 .30
12 Blake Rutherford .25 .60
13 Blake Swihart .15 .40
14 Blake Trahan .12 .30
15 Bradley Zimmer .20 .50
16 Brice Turang .40 1.00
17 Bryan Reynolds .40 1.00
18 Carlos Rodon .20 .50
19 Carson Fulmer .12 .30
20 Chris Okey .12 .30
21 Christin Stewart .15 .40
22 Christopher Austin Martin .40 1.00
23 Cole Tucker .12 .30
24 Cordell Dunn Jr. .12 .30
25 Corey Seager .50 1.25
26 Courtney Hawkins .12 .30
27 D.J. Peterson .12 .30
28 Dansby Swanson .75 2.00
29 David Dahl .15 .40
30 Daz Cameron .20 .50
31 Deven Marrero .12 .30
32 Devin Ortiz .12 .30
33 Dillon Tate .15 .40
34 DJ Stewart .15 .40
35 Doug Nikhazy .12 .30
36 Austin Meadows .20 .50
37 Elih Marrero .12 .30
38 Erick Fedde .12 .30
39 Francisco Lindor .75 2.00
40 Gray Fenter .12 .30
41 Henry Owens .12 .30
42 Hugh Fisher .12 .30
43 Hunter Greene .40 1.00
44 J.P. Crawford .12 .30
45 Jack Flaherty .20 .50
46 Jacob Blas .12 .30
47 Jake Lemoine .12 .30
48 James Kaprielian .20 .50
49 Jameson Taillon .15 .40
50 Jesse Winker .12 .30
51 Joe DeMers .12 .30
52 Justus Sheffield .25 .60
53 John Dearth .12 .30
54 Justin Bullock .15 .40
55 Justin Garza .12 .30
56 Kale Breaux .20 .50
57 Ke'Bryan Hayes .20 .50
58 Kolby Allard .12 .30
59 Kris Bryant .75 2.00
60 Kristofer Armstrong .12 .30
61 Kyle Funkhouser .15 .40
62 Kyle Molnar .12 .30
63 Kyle Schwarber .50 1.25
64 L.T. Tolbert .12 .30
65 Lucas Herbert .12 .30
66 Lucas Sims .12 .30
67 Luis Ortiz .12 .30
68 Luke Weaver .20 .50
69 Luken Baker .20 .50
70 Mark Mathias .15 .40
71 Mark Vientos .20 .50
72 Matt Chapman .20 .50
73 Matt Olson .15 .40
74 Max Wotell .12 .30
75 Michael Conforto .15 .40
76 Mitchell Hansen .12 .30
77 Nicholas Banks .12 .30
78 Nick Madrigal .25 .60
79 Nick Travieso .12 .30
80 Noah Campbell .12 .30
81 Peter Lambert .12 .30
82 Peter O'Brien .20 .50
83 Raymond Gil .12 .30
84 Robert Refsnyder .15 .40
85 Royce Lewis .30 .75
86 Ryan Burr .12 .30
87 Ryan Vilade .25 .60
88 Steven Williams .12 .30
89 Tate Matheny .12 .30
90 Taylor Ward .20 .50
91 Thomas Burbank .12 .30
92 Thomas Eshelman .12 .30
93 Trea Turner .40 1.00
94 Trenton Clark .12 .30
95 Trey Killian .12 .30
96 Tyler Beede .15 .40
97 Tyler Jay .12 .30
98 Tyler Naquin .15 .40
99 Xavier LeGrant .12 .30
100 Zack Collins .15 .40

2015 USA Baseball Stars and Stripes Longevity

*LONGEVITY: 1X TO 2.5X BASIC
RANDOM INSERTS IN PACKS

2015 USA Baseball Stars and Stripes Longevity Holofoil

*LONGEVITY HOLO: 2.5X TO 6X BASIC
RANDOM INSERTS IN PACKS
STATED PRINT RUN 99 SER.#'d SETS

2015 USA Baseball Stars and Stripes Longevity Retail Gold

*LONG.RET.GOLD: .75X TO 2X BASIC
RANDOM INSERTS IN PACKS

2015 USA Baseball Stars and Stripes Longevity Ruby

*LONGEVITY RUBY: 2X TO 5X BASIC
RANDOM INSERTS IN PACKS
STATED PRINT RUN 199 SER.#'d SETS

2015 USA Baseball Stars and Stripes Longevity Sapphire

*LONG.SAPPHIRE: 3X TO 8X BASIC
RANDOM INSERTS IN PACKS
STATED PRINT RUN 49 SER.#'d SETS

2015 USA Baseball Stars and Stripes Longevity Team Logo Gold

*LONGEVITY GOLD: 4X TO 10X BASIC
RANDOM INSERTS IN PACKS
STATED PRINT RUN 25 SER.#'d SETS
59 Kris Bryant 20.00 50.00

2015 USA Baseball Stars and Stripes Champions

COMPLETE SET (25) 12.00 30.00
RANDOM INSERTS IN PACKS
*FOIL/99: .6X TO 1.5X BASIC
*HOLOFOIL/25: 1X TO 2.5X BASIC
1 Kolby Allard .50 1.25
2 Luken Baker .75 2.00
3 Alex Bregman 2.00 5.00
4 Daz Cameron .75 2.00
5 Trenton Clark .50 1.25
6 David Dahl .60 1.50
7 Joe DeMers .50 1.25
8 Carson Fulmer .50 1.25
9 Kyle Funkhouser .60 1.50
10 Blake Swihart .60 1.50
11 Mitchell Hansen .50 1.25
12 Tyler Jay .50 1.25
13 James Kaprielian .75 2.00
14 Jake Lemoine .50 1.25
15 Kyle Molnar .50 1.25
16 Matt Olson .60 1.50
17 Robert Refsnyder .60 1.50
18 Addison Russell 1.50 4.00
19 Corey Seager 2.00 5.00
20 Austin Smith .50 1.25
21 Christin Stewart .60 1.50

22 DJ Stewart .60 1.50
23 Dansby Swanson 3.00 8.00
24 Dillon Tate .60 1.50
25 Jesse Winker .50 1.25

2015 USA Baseball Stars and Stripes Crusade Blue

RANDOM INSERTS IN PACKS
1 A.J. Cole .40 1.00
2 A.J. Minter .50 1.25
3 Addison Russell 1.25 3.00
4 Albert Almora .50 1.25
5 Alejandro Toral .60 1.50
6 Alex Bregman 1.50 4.00
7 Andrew Moore .50 1.25
8 Austin Bergner .40 1.00
9 Austin Smith .40 1.00
10 Bailey Ober .40 1.00
11 Blake Paugh .40 1.00
12 Blake Rutherford .75 2.00
13 Blake Swihart .50 1.25
14 Blake Trahan .40 1.00
15 Bradley Zimmer .60 1.50
16 Brice Turang 1.25 3.00
17 Bryan Reynolds 1.25 3.00
18 Carlos Rodon .60 1.50
19 Carson Fulmer .40 1.00
20 Chris Okey .40 1.00
21 Christin Stewart .50 1.25
22 Christopher Austin Martin 1.25 3.00
23 Cole Tucker .40 1.00
24 Cordell Dunn Jr. .40 1.00
25 Corey Seager 1.50 4.00
26 Frank Thomas .60 1.50
27 D.J. Peterson .40 1.00
28 Dansby Swanson 2.50 6.00
29 David Dahl .50 1.25
30 Daz Cameron .60 1.50
31 Deven Marrero .40 1.00
32 Devin Ortiz .40 1.00
33 Dillon Tate .50 1.25
34 DJ Stewart .50 1.25
35 Doug Nikhazy .40 1.00
36 Austin Meadows .60 1.50
37 Elih Marrero .40 1.00
38 Erick Fedde .40 1.00
39 Francisco Lindor 2.50 6.00
40 Gray Fenter .40 1.00
41 Henry Owens .40 1.00
42 Hugh Fisher .40 1.00
43 Hunter Greene 1.25 3.00
44 Mark McGwire 1.00 2.50
45 Jack Flaherty .60 1.50
46 Jacob Blas .40 1.00
47 Jake Lemoine .40 1.00
48 James Kaprielian .60 1.50
49 Jameson Taillon .50 1.25
50 Jesse Winker .40 1.00
51 Joe DeMers .40 1.00
52 Justus Sheffield .75 2.00
53 John Dearth .40 1.00
54 Justin Bullock .50 1.25
55 Justin Garza .40 1.00
56 Kale Breaux .60 1.50
57 Ke'Bryan Hayes .60 1.50
58 Kolby Allard .40 1.00
59 Kris Bryant 2.50 6.00
60 Kristofer Armstrong .40 1.00
61 Kyle Funkhouser .50 1.25
62 Kyle Molnar .40 1.00
63 Kyle Schwarber 1.50 4.00
64 L.T. Tolbert .40 1.00
65 Lucas Herbert .40 1.00
66 Lucas Sims .40 1.00
67 Luis Ortiz .40 1.00
68 Luke Weaver .60 1.50
69 Luken Baker .60 1.50
70 Mark Mathias .50 1.25
71 Mark Vientos .60 1.50
72 Matt Chapman .60 1.50
73 Matt Olson .50 1.25
74 Max Wotell .40 1.00
75 Michael Conforto .50 1.25
76 Mitchell Hansen .40 1.00
77 Nicholas Banks .40 1.00
78 Nick Madrigal .75 2.00
79 Nick Travieso .40 1.00
80 Noah Campbell .40 1.00
81 Peter Lambert .40 1.00
82 Peter O'Brien .60 1.50
83 Raymond Gil .40 1.00
84 Robert Refsnyder .50 1.25
85 Royce Lewis 1.00 2.50
86 Ryan Burr .40 1.00
87 Ryan Vilade .75 2.00
88 Steven Williams .40 1.00
89 Tate Matheny .40 1.00
90 Taylor Ward .60 1.50
91 Thomas Burbank .40 1.00
92 Thomas Eshelman .40 1.00
93 Trea Turner 1.25 3.00
94 Trenton Clark .40 1.00
95 Trey Killian .40 1.00
96 Tyler Beede .50 1.25
97 Tyler Jay .40 1.00
98 Tyler Naquin .50 1.25
99 Xavier LeGrant .40 1.00
100 Zack Collins .50 1.25

2015 USA Baseball Stars and Stripes Crusade Gold

*GOLD: 1X TO 2.5X BASIC
RANDOM INSERTS IN PACKS
STATED PRINT RUN 25 SER.#'d SETS
26 Frank Thomas 15.00 40.00
44 Mark McGwire 25.00 60.00

2015 USA Baseball Stars and Stripes Crusade Red

*RED: .6X TO 1.5X BASIC
RANDOM INSERTS IN PACKS
STATED PRINT RUN 99 SER.#'d SETS
26 Frank Thomas 10.00 25.00
44 Mark McGwire 15.00 40.00

2015 USA Baseball Stars and Stripes Crusade Red and Blue

*RED-BLUE: .75X TO 2X BASIC
RANDOM INSERTS IN PACKS
STATED PRINT RUN 49 SER.#'d SETS
26 Frank Thomas 12.00 30.00
44 Mark McGwire 20.00 50.00

2015 USA Baseball Stars and Stripes Diamond Kings

COMPLETE SET (25) 12.00 30.00
RANDOM INSERTS IN PACKS
1 Mark McGwire 1.00 2.50
2 Frank Thomas .60 1.50
3 Fred Lynn .40 1.00
4 Blake Swihart .50 1.25
5 Carlos Rodon .60 1.50
6 Corey Seager 1.50 4.00
7 Addison Russell 1.25 3.00
8 A.J. Cole .40 1.00
9 D.J. Peterson .40 1.00
10 Dansby Swanson 2.50 6.00
11 David Dahl .50 1.25
12 Daz Cameron .60 1.50
13 Francisco Lindor 2.50 6.00
14 Henry Owens .40 1.00
15 J.P. Crawford .40 1.00
16 Jesse Winker .40 1.00
17 Jameson Taillon .50 1.25
18 Kris Bryant 2.50 6.00
19 Kyle Schwarber 1.50 4.00
20 Matt Olson .50 1.25
21 Michael Conforto .50 1.25
22 Robert Refsnyder .50 1.25
23 Trea Turner 1.25 3.00
24 Tyler Naquin .50 1.25
25 Trenton Clark .40 1.00

2015 USA Baseball Stars and Stripes Diamond Kings Foil

*FOIL: .6X TO 1.5.X BASIC
RANDOM INSERTS IN PACKS
STATED PRINT RUN 99 SER.#'d SETS
2 Frank Thomas 10.00 25.00

2015 USA Baseball Stars and Stripes Diamond Kings Holofoil

*HOLOFOIL: 1X TO 2.5X BASIC
RANDOM INSERTS IN PACKS
STATED PRINT RUN 25 SER.#'d SETS
2 Frank Thomas 15.00 40.00
18 Kris Bryant 20.00 50.00

2015 USA Baseball Stars and Stripes Fireworks

COMPLETE SET (25) 12.00 30.00
RANDOM INSERTS IN PACKS
1 Kris Bryant 2.50 6.00
2 Francisco Lindor 2.50 6.00
3 Matt Olson .50 1.25
4 Peter O'Brien .60 1.50
5 Courtney Hawkins .40 1.00
6 Corey Seager 1.50 4.00
7 D.J. Peterson .40 1.00
8 Kyle Schwarber 1.50 4.00
9 Addison Russell 1.25 3.00
10 Blake Swihart .50 1.25
11 Robert Refsnyder .50 1.25
12 David Dahl .50 1.25
13 Daz Cameron .60 1.50
14 Trenton Clark .40 1.00
15 Luken Baker .60 1.50
16 Lucas Herbert .40 1.00
17 Matt Chapman .60 1.50
18 Zack Collins .50 1.25
19 Christin Stewart .50 1.25
20 Mark McGwire 1.00 2.50
21 Jesse Winker .40 1.00
22 Michael Conforto .50 1.25
23 Nicholas Banks .40 1.00
24 Bradley Zimmer .60 1.50
25 Albert Almora .50 1.25

2015 USA Baseball Stars and Stripes Fireworks Foil

*FOIL: .6X TO 1.5.X BASIC
RANDOM INSERTS IN PACKS
STATED PRINT RUN 99 SER.#'d SETS
20 Mark McGwire 15.00 40.00

2015 USA Baseball Stars and Stripes Fireworks Holofoil

*HOLOFOIL: 1X TO 2.5X BASIC
RANDOM INSERTS IN PACKS
STATED PRINT RUN 25 SER.#'d SETS
1 Kris Bryant 20.00 50.00
20 Mark McGwire 25.00 60.00

2015 USA Baseball Stars and Stripes Game Gear Materials

*LONGEVITY: .5X TO 1.2X p/r 65-299
*LONGEVITY: .4X TO 1X p/r 25-49
*LONG.HOLO: .5X TO 1.2X p/r 65-299
*LONG.HOLO: .4X TO 1X p/r 25-49
*LONG.SAPP: .5X TO 1.2X p/r 65-299
*LONG.SAPP: .4X TO 1X p/r 25-49
RANDOM INSERTS IN PACKS
PRINT RUNS B/WN 25-299 COPIES PER
NO PRICING ON QTY 19 OR LESS
2 A.J. Minter/299 2.50 6.00
3 Addison Russell/25 8.00 20.00
4 Albert Almora/299 2.50 6.00
5 Alejandro Toral/299 3.00 8.00
6 Alex Bregman/299 8.00 20.00
7 Andrew Moore/299 2.50 6.00
8 Austin Bergner/299 2.00 5.00
9 Austin Meadows/89 3.00 8.00
10 Austin Smith/299 2.00 5.00
11 Bailey Ober/299 2.00 5.00
12 Blake Paugh/299 2.00 5.00
13 Blake Rutherford/299 4.00 10.00
14 Blake Trahan/299 2.00 5.00
15 Bradley Zimmer/299 3.00 8.00
16 Brice Turang/299 6.00 15.00
17 Bryan Reynolds/299 6.00 15.00
18 Carlos Rodon/299 5.00 12.00
19 Carson Fulmer/299 2.00 5.00
20 Chris Okey/299 2.00 5.00
21 Christin Stewart/299 2.50 6.00
22 Christopher Austin Martin/299 6.00 15.00
24 Cordell Dunn Jr./99 2.00 5.00
25 Courtney Hawkins/49 2.50 6.00
26 D.J. Peterson/299 2.00 5.00
27 Dansby Swanson/99 5.00 12.00
29 Daz Cameron/229 3.00 8.00
31 Devin Ortiz/299 2.00 5.00
32 Dillon Tate/299 2.50 6.00
33 DJ Stewart/299 2.50 6.00
34 Doug Nikhazy/299 2.00 5.00
35 Reese McGuire/299 2.00 5.00
38 Francisco Lindor/299 12.00 30.00
39 Gray Fenter/299 2.00 5.00
40 Hugh Fisher/299 2.00 5.00
41 Hunter Greene/99 6.00 15.00
42 Jack Flaherty/299 3.00 8.00
43 Jacob Blas/299 2.00 5.00
44 Jake Lemoine/299 2.00 5.00
45 James Kaprielian/299 3.00 8.00
47 Joe DeMers/299 2.00 5.00
48 Joey Gallo/25 5.00 12.00
49 John Dearth/299 2.00 5.00
50 Justin Bullock/299 2.50 6.00
51 Justin Garza/299 2.00 5.00
52 Justus Sheffield/99 4.00 10.00
53 Kale Breaux/299 3.00 8.00
54 Ke'Bryan Hayes/278 3.00 8.00
55 Kolby Allard/299 2.00 5.00
57 Kristofer Armstrong/125 2.00 5.00
58 Kyle Funkhouser/299 2.50 6.00
59 Kyle Molnar/299 2.00 5.00
61 L.T. Tolbert/129 2.00 5.00
62 Lance McCullers/299 2.00 5.00
63 Lucas Herbert/298 2.00 5.00
64 Lucas Sims/39 2.50 6.00
65 Luis Ortiz/65 2.00 5.00
66 Luke Weaver/175 3.00 8.00
67 Luken Baker/299 3.00 8.00
68 Ian Clarkin/99 2.00 5.00
69 Mark Mathias/299 2.50 6.00
70 Mark Vientos/299 3.00 8.00
71 Matt Chapman/299 3.00 8.00
72 Matt Olson/99 4.00 10.00
73 Max Wotell/299 2.00 5.00
74 Michael Conforto/299 2.50 6.00
75 Michael Lorenzen/299 2.00 5.00
76 Mitchell Hansen/299 2.00 5.00
77 Nicholas Banks/299 2.00 5.00
78 Nick Madrigal/299 4.00 10.00
80 Noah Campbell/299 2.00 5.00
81 Peter Lambert/299 2.00 5.00
82 Peter O'Brien/299 3.00 8.00
83 Raymond Gil/299 2.00 5.00
84 Robert Refsnyder/99 2.50 6.00
85 Royce Lewis/299 5.00 12.00
86 Ryan Burr/299 2.00 5.00
87 Ryan Vilade/299 4.00 10.00
88 Steven Williams/299 2.00 5.00
89 Tate Matheny/299 2.00 5.00
90 Taylor Ward/299 3.00 8.00
91 Thomas Burbank/299 2.00 5.00
92 Thomas Eshelman/299 2.00 5.00
93 Trea Turner/299 6.00 15.00
94 Trenton Clark/25 2.50 6.00
95 Trey Killian/299 2.00 5.00
96 Tyler Beede/299 2.50 6.00
97 Tyler Jay/299 2.00 5.00
99 Xavier LeGrant/299 2.00 5.00
100 Zack Collins/299 2.50 6.00

2015 USA Baseball Stars and Stripes Game Gear Materials Longevity Ruby

*RUBY p/r 99-299: .4X TO 1X p/r 65-299
*RUBY p/r 99-299: .3X TO .8X p/r 25-49
*RUBY p/r 25-49: .4X TO 1X p/r 25-49
RANDOM INSERTS IN PACKS
PRINT RUNS B/WN 5-299 COPIES PER
NO PRICING ON ON QTY 10 OR LESS
56 Kris Bryant/149 5.00 15.00

2015 USA Baseball Stars and Stripes Game Gear Materials Signatures

RANDOM INSERTS IN PACKS
PRINT RUNS B/WN 10-99 COPIES PER
NO PRICING ON QTY 10 OR LESS
*HOLOFOIL: .5X TO 1.2X p/r 89-99
*HOLOFOIL: .4X TO 1X p/r 25-49
*LONG.p/r 25-49: .5X TO 1.2X p/r 89-99
*LONG.p/r 25-49: .4X TO 1X p/r 25-49
*RUBY: .5X TO 1.2X p/r 89-99
*RUBY: .4X TO 1X p/r 25-49
*SAPPHIRE: .5X TO 1.2X p/r 89-99
*SAPPHIRE: .4X TO 1X p/r 25-49
2 A.J. Minter/99 4.00 10.00
3 Addison Russell/25 20.00 50.00
4 Albert Almora/99
5 Alejandro Toral/49 6.00 15.00
6 Alex Bregman/99 8.00 20.00
7 Andrew Moore/99 4.00 10.00
8 Austin Bergner/99 6.00 15.00
9 Austin Meadows/99 6.00 15.00
10 Austin Smith/99 3.00 8.00
11 Bailey Ober/99 3.00 8.00
13 Blake Rutherford/99 6.00 15.00
14 Blake Trahan/99 3.00 8.00
15 Bradley Zimmer/99 5.00 12.00
17 Bryan Reynolds/99 10.00 25.00
18 Carlos Rodon/99 10.00 25.00
19 Carson Fulmer/99 12.00 30.00
20 Chris Okey/99 3.00 8.00
21 Christin Stewart/99 4.00 10.00
22 Christopher Austin Martin/99 10.00 25.00
25 Courtney Hawkins/25 4.00 10.00
26 D.J. Peterson/99 3.00 8.00
27 Dansby Swanson/99 20.00 50.00
29 Daz Cameron/99 10.00 25.00
32 Dillon Tate/99 4.00 10.00
33 DJ Stewart/99 4.00 10.00
35 Reese McGuire/99 3.00 8.00
36 Elih Marrero/99 3.00 8.00
38 Francisco Lindor/99 20.00 50.00
39 Gray Fenter/99 3.00 8.00
42 Jack Flaherty/99 5.00 12.00
43 Jacob Blas/98 3.00 8.00
44 Jake Lemoine/99 3.00 8.00
45 James Kaprielian/99 8.00 20.00
47 Joe DeMers/99 3.00 8.00
51 Justin Garza/99 3.00 8.00
52 Justus Sheffield/99 6.00 15.00
53 Kale Breaux/99 5.00 12.00
54 Ke'Bryan Hayes/99 5.00 12.00
55 Kolby Allard/99 3.00 8.00
56 Kris Bryant/99 75.00 150.00
58 Kyle Funkhouser/99 4.00 10.00
59 Kyle Molnar/99 3.00 8.00
61 L.T. Tolbert/99 3.00 8.00
62 Lance McCullers/99 3.00 8.00
63 Lucas Herbert/99 3.00 8.00
64 Lucas Sims/99 3.00 8.00
65 Luis Ortiz/99 3.00 8.00
66 Luke Weaver/99 5.00 12.00
67 Luken Baker/99 5.00 12.00
68 Ian Clarkin/99 3.00 8.00
69 Mark Mathias/99 4.00 10.00
71 Matt Chapman/99 5.00 12.00
72 Matt Olson/99 8.00 20.00
73 Max Wotell/99 3.00 8.00
74 Michael Conforto/99 8.00 20.00
75 Michael Lorenzen/99 3.00 8.00
76 Mitchell Hansen/99 3.00 8.00
77 Nicholas Banks/99 3.00 8.00
78 Nick Madrigal/99 6.00 15.00
79 Nick Travieso/99 3.00 8.00
81 Peter Lambert/99 3.00 8.00
82 Peter O'Brien/89 5.00 12.00
84 Robert Refsnyder/99
86 Ryan Burr/99 3.00 8.00
89 Tate Matheny/99 3.00 8.00
90 Taylor Ward/99 5.00 12.00
92 Thomas Eshelman/99 3.00 8.00
93 Trea Turner/99 10.00 25.00
94 Trenton Clark/99 3.00 8.00
95 Trey Killian/99 3.00 8.00
96 Tyler Beede/99 4.00 10.00
97 Tyler Jay/99 3.00 8.00
99 Xavier LeGrant/99 3.00 8.00
100 Zack Collins/99 4.00 10.00

2015 USA Baseball Stars and Stripes Jersey Signatures

RANDOM INSERTS IN PACKS
PRINT RUN B/WN 5-99 COPIES PER
NO PRICING ON QTY 10 OR LESS
*PRIME: .6X TO 1.5X BASIC
2 A.J. Minter/82 4.00 10.00
6 Alex Bregman/99 15.00 40.00
7 Andrew Moore/99 4.00 10.00
8 Austin Bergner/95 3.00 8.00
9 Austin Meadows/99 6.00 15.00
10 Austin Smith/95 3.00 8.00
13 Blake Rutherford/95 6.00 15.00
14 Blake Trahan/99 3.00 8.00
15 Bradley Zimmer/99 5.00 12.00
17 Bryan Reynolds/99 10.00 25.00
19 Carson Fulmer/80 25.00 60.00
20 Chris Okey/99 3.00 8.00
21 Christin Stewart/99 4.00 10.00
26 D.J. Peterson/99 3.00 8.00
27 Dansby Swanson/99 30.00 80.00
29 Daz Cameron/95 12.00 30.00
32 Dillon Tate/91 4.00 10.00
33 DJ Stewart/99 4.00 10.00
36 Elih Marrero/99 3.00 8.00
38 Francisco Lindor/99 20.00 50.00
39 Gray Fenter/96 3.00 8.00
44 Jake Lemoine/94 3.00 8.00
45 James Kaprielian/99 10.00 25.00
47 Joe DeMers/95 3.00 8.00
51 Justin Garza/99 3.00 8.00
52 Justus Sheffield/99 6.00 15.00
53 Kale Breaux/99 5.00 12.00
54 Ke'Bryan Hayes/95 5.00 12.00
55 Kolby Allard/95 10.00 25.00
56 Kris Bryant/99 60.00 150.00
58 Kyle Funkhouser/99 8.00 20.00
59 Kyle Molnar/99 3.00 8.00
61 L.T. Tolbert/95 3.00 8.00
62 Lance McCullers/93 3.00 8.00
63 Lucas Herbert/95 3.00 8.00
64 Lucas Sims/99 3.00 8.00
65 Luis Ortiz/99 3.00 8.00
67 Luken Baker/95 6.00 15.00
69 Mark Mathias/99 4.00 10.00
71 Matt Chapman/99 5.00 12.00
72 Matt Olson/99 8.00 20.00
73 Max Wotell/88 3.00 8.00
76 Mitchell Hansen/96 3.00 8.00
77 Nicholas Banks/99 3.00 8.00
78 Nick Madrigal/95 6.00 15.00
79 Nick Travieso/25 4.00 10.00
81 Peter Lambert/94 3.00 8.00
84 Robert Refsnyder/99 6.00 15.00
86 Ryan Burr/99 3.00 8.00
89 Tate Matheny/99 3.00 8.00
90 Taylor Ward/99 5.00 12.00
92 Thomas Eshelman/99 6.00 15.00
93 Trea Turner/98 10.00 25.00
94 Trenton Clark/97 10.00 25.00
95 Trey Killian/98 3.00 8.00
96 Tyler Beede/99 4.00 10.00
97 Tyler Jay/99 3.00 8.00
99 Xavier LeGrant/92 3.00 8.00
100 Zack Collins/99 4.00 10.00

2015 USA Baseball Stars and Stripes Longevity Signatures

RANDOM INSERTS IN PACKS
PRINT RUNS B/WN 3-299 COPIES PER
NO PRICING ON QTY 18 OR LESS
*HOLOFOIL: .4X TO 1X p/r 37
*HOLOFOIL: .5X TO 1.2X p/r 61-299
*RUBY p/r 99: .4X TO 1X p/r 61-299
*RUBY p/r 49: .5X TO 1.2X p/r 61-299
*RUBY p/r 49: .4X TO 1X p/r 37
*SAPPHIRE: .4X TO 1X p/r 37
*SAPPHIRE: .5X TO 1.2X p/r 61-299
1 A.J. Cole/299 3.00 8.00
2 A.J. Minter/299 4.00 10.00
3 Addison Russell/99 15.00 40.00
4 Albert Almora/213 4.00 10.00
5 Alejandro Toral/61 10.00 25.00
6 Alex Bregman/299 12.00 30.00
7 Andrew Moore/299 4.00 10.00
8 Austin Bergner/171 3.00 8.00
9 Austin Smith/170 3.00 8.00
10 Bailey Ober/192 3.00 8.00
12 Blake Rutherford/186 12.00 30.00
13 Blake Swihart/299 5.00 12.00
14 Blake Trahan/299 3.00 8.00
15 Bradley Zimmer/299 5.00 12.00
17 Bryan Reynolds/299 10.00 25.00
18 Carlos Rodon/99 5.00 12.00
19 Carson Fulmer/299 3.00 8.00
20 Chris Okey/299 3.00 8.00
21 Christin Stewart/285 4.00 10.00
23 Cole Tucker/299 5.00 12.00
25 Corey Seager/85 20.00 50.00
26 Courtney Hawkins/299 3.00 8.00
27 D.J. Peterson/299 3.00 8.00
28 Dansby Swanson/299 15.00 40.00
30 Daz Cameron/175 8.00 20.00
31 Deven Marrero/299 3.00 8.00
33 Dillon Tate/299 4.00 10.00
34 DJ Stewart/299 4.00 10.00
36 Reese McGuire/299 5.00 12.00
37 Elih Marrero/37 4.00 10.00
38 Erick Fedde/99
40 Gray Fenter/184 3.00 8.00
41 Henry Owens/299 6.00 15.00
44 J.P. Crawford/112 8.00 20.00
45 Jack Flaherty/97 5.00 12.00
47 Jake Lemoine/299 3.00 8.00
48 James Kaprielian/299 5.00 12.00
49 Jameson Taillon/299 4.00 10.00
50 Jesse Winker/299 5.00 12.00
51 Joe DeMers/167 3.00 8.00
55 Justin Garza/299 3.00 8.00
56 Kale Breaux/201 5.00 12.00
57 Ke'Bryan Hayes/193 5.00 12.00
58 Kolby Allard/200 3.00 8.00
59 Kris Bryant/177 75.00 200.00
61 Kyle Funkhouser/299 4.00 10.00
62 Kyle Molnar/189 3.00 8.00
63 Kyle Schwarber/299 8.00 20.00
64 L.T. Tolbert/287 3.00 8.00
65 Lucas Herbert/235 3.00 8.00
67 Luis Ortiz/99 3.00 8.00
68 Luke Weaver/299 5.00 12.00
69 Luken Baker/188 5.00 12.00
70 Mark Mathias/299 4.00 10.00
72 Matt Chapman/199 5.00 12.00
73 Matt Olson/299 8.00 20.00
74 Max Wotell/201 3.00 8.00
75 Michael Conforto/66 15.00 40.00
76 Mitchell Hansen/168 3.00 8.00
77 Nicholas Banks/299 3.00 8.00
78 Nick Madrigal/218 10.00 25.00
79 Nick Travieso/299 3.00 8.00
81 Peter Lambert/185 3.00 8.00
82 Peter O'Brien/299 5.00 12.00
84 Robert Refsnyder/299 4.00 10.00
86 Ryan Burr/299 3.00 8.00
89 Tate Matheny/270 3.00 8.00
90 Taylor Ward/299 5.00 12.00
92 Thomas Eshelman/299 6.00 15.00
93 Trea Turner/299 10.00 25.00
94 Trenton Clark/299 3.00 8.00
95 Trey Killian/299 3.00 8.00
96 Tyler Beede/299 4.00 10.00
97 Tyler Jay/299 3.00 8.00
98 Tyler Naquin/299 6.00 15.00
99 Xavier LeGrant/162 3.00 8.00
100 Zack Collins/299 4.00 10.00

2015 USA Baseball Stars and Stripes Quad Materials

RANDOM INSERTS IN PACKS
PRINT RUNS B/WN 10-99 COPIES PER
NO PRICING ON QTY 10
1 Gllo/Brnt/Olsn/O'Brn 20.00 50.00
3 Swnsn/Cmrn/Allrd/Fnkhsr 10.00 25.00
6 Flmr/Lmn/Allrd/Fnkhsr 4.00 10.00
12 Rynlds/Flmer/Swnsn/Bde 20.00 50.00

2015 USA Baseball Stars and Stripes Silhouettes Bats

RANDOM INSERTS IN PACKS
PRINT RUN B/WN 10-69 COPIES PER
NO PRICING ON QTY 21 OR LESS
6 Alex Bregman/25 12.00 30.00
15 Bradley Zimmer/25 5.00 12.00
21 Christin Stewart/49 4.00 10.00
27 Dansby Swanson/69 15.00 40.00
33 DJ Stewart/65 3.00 8.00
42 Jack Flaherty/25 5.00 12.00
69 Mark Mathias/69 3.00 8.00
71 Matt Chapman/25 5.00 12.00
74 Michael Conforto/45 4.00 10.00
89 Tate Matheny/69 2.50 6.00
90 Taylor Ward/69 4.00 10.00
93 Trea Turner/47 10.00 25.00

2015 USA Baseball Stars and Stripes Silhouettes Jerseys

RANDOM INSERTS IN PACKS
PRINT RUN B/WN 1-99 COPIES PER
NO PRICING ON QTY 14 OR LESS
*PRIME p/r 25-63: .6X TO 1.5X
2 A.J. Minter/99 3.00 8.00
4 Albert Almora/99 3.00 8.00
5 Alejandro Toral/99 4.00 10.00
6 Alex Bregman/99 10.00 25.00
7 Andrew Moore/85 3.00 8.00
8 Austin Bergner/79 2.50 6.00
9 Austin Meadows/99 4.00 10.00
10 Austin Smith/99 2.50 6.00
11 Bailey Ober/99 2.50 6.00
12 Blake Paugh/99 2.50 6.00
13 Blake Rutherford/99 5.00 12.00
14 Blake Trahan/99 2.50 6.00
15 Bradley Zimmer/49 5.00 12.00
16 Brice Turang/99 8.00 20.00
17 Bryan Reynolds/99 8.00 20.00
18 Carlos Rodon/99 4.00 10.00
19 Carson Fulmer/99 2.50 6.00
20 Chris Okey/99 2.50 6.00
21 Christin Stewart/99 3.00 8.00
22 Christopher Austin Martin/79 8.00 20.00
24 Cordell Dunn Jr./39 3.00 8.00
25 Courtney Hawkins/25 3.00 8.00
26 D.J. Peterson/25 3.00 8.00
31 Devin Ortiz/99 2.50 6.00
32 Dillon Tate/99 3.00 8.00
33 DJ Stewart/99 3.00 8.00
34 Doug Nikhazy/49 3.00 8.00
35 Reese McGuire/99 2.50 6.00
36 Elih Marrero/99 2.50 6.00
38 Francisco Lindor/25 20.00 50.00
39 Gray Fenter/99 2.50 6.00
40 Hugh Fisher/99 2.50 6.00
41 Hunter Greene/39 10.00 25.00
42 Jack Flaherty/40 5.00 12.00
43 Jacob Blas/99 2.50 6.00
44 Jake Lemoine/99 2.50 6.00
45 James Kaprielian/99 4.00 10.00
47 Joe DeMers/99 2.50 6.00
49 John Dearth/99 2.50 6.00
50 Justin Bullock/25 4.00 10.00
51 Justin Garza/99 2.50 6.00
52 Justus Sheffield/49 6.00 15.00
53 Kale Breaux/59 4.00 10.00
54 Ke'Bryan Hayes/99 4.00 10.00
57 Kristofer Armstrong/99 2.50 6.00
58 Kyle Funkhouser/99 3.00 8.00
59 Kyle Molnar/99 2.50 6.00
61 L.T. Tolbert/25 3.00 8.00
62 Lance McCullers/49 3.00 8.00
63 Lucas Herbert/49 3.00 8.00
64 Lucas Sims/99 2.50 6.00
65 Luis Ortiz/49 3.00 8.00
66 Luke Weaver/99 4.00 10.00
67 Luken Baker/99 4.00 10.00
68 Ian Clarkin/31 3.00 8.00
69 Mark Mathias/99 3.00 8.00
70 Mark Vientos/99 4.00 10.00
71 Matt Chapman/99 4.00 10.00
72 Matt Olson/99 5.00 12.00
73 Max Wotell/99 2.50 6.00
74 Michael Conforto/99 3.00 8.00
75 Michael Lorenzen/99 2.50 6.00
76 Mitchell Hansen/99 2.50 6.00
77 Nicholas Banks/99 2.50 6.00
78 Nick Madrigal/99 5.00 12.00
80 Noah Campbell/99 2.50 6.00
81 Peter Lambert/99 2.50 6.00
82 Peter O'Brien/99 4.00 10.00
83 Raymond Gil/99 2.50 6.00
84 Robert Refsnyder/99 3.00 8.00
85 Royce Lewis/99 6.00 15.00
86 Ryan Burr/99 2.50 6.00
87 Ryan Vilade/99 5.00 12.00
88 Steven Williams/99 2.50 6.00
89 Tate Matheny/99 2.50 6.00
90 Taylor Ward/99 4.00 10.00
91 Thomas Burbank/99 2.50 6.00
92 Thomas Eshelman/99 2.50 6.00
93 Trea Turner/99 8.00 20.00
95 Trey Killian/25 3.00 8.00
96 Tyler Beede/35 4.00 10.00
97 Tyler Jay/99 2.50 6.00
99 Xavier LeGrant/99 2.50 6.00
100 Zack Collins/99 3.00 8.00

2015 USA Baseball Stars and Stripes Silhouettes Signature Bats

RANDOM INSERTS IN PACKS
PRINT RUNS B/WN 10-49 COPIES PER
NO PRICING ON QTY 12 OR LESS
6 Alex Bregman/25 15.00 40.00
14 Blake Trahan/49 4.00 10.00
15 Bradley Zimmer/25 6.00 15.00
21 Christin Stewart/49 5.00 12.00
27 Dansby Swanson/49 25.00 60.00
33 DJ Stewart/49 5.00 12.00
42 Jack Flaherty/25 6.00 15.00
69 Mark Mathias/49 5.00 12.00
71 Matt Chapman/25 6.00 15.00
74 Michael Conforto/25 12.00 30.00
89 Tate Matheny/49 4.00 10.00
90 Taylor Ward/49 6.00 15.00
93 Trea Turner/25 12.00 30.00

2015 USA Baseball Stars and Stripes Silhouettes Signature Jerseys

RANDOM INSERTS IN PACKS
PRINT RUN B/WN 1-99 COPIES PER
NO PRICING ON QTY 22 OR LESS
*PRIME: .6X TO 1.5X BASIC
2 A.J. Minter/99 4.00 10.00
4 Albert Almora/99 10.00 25.00
5 Alejandro Toral/25 6.00 15.00
6 Alex Bregman/99 8.00 20.00
7 Andrew Moore/99 4.00 10.00
8 Austin Bergner/99 3.00 8.00
9 Austin Meadows/99 10.00 25.00
10 Austin Smith/99 3.00 8.00
11 Bailey Ober/99 3.00 8.00
12 Blake Paugh/25 4.00 10.00
13 Blake Rutherford/99 12.00 30.00
14 Blake Trahan/99 3.00 8.00
15 Bradley Zimmer/25
16 Brice Turang/25 12.00 30.00
17 Bryan Reynolds/99 10.00 25.00
18 Carlos Rodon/99 5.00 12.00
19 Carson Fulmer/99
20 Chris Okey/99 3.00 8.00
21 Christin Stewart/99 4.00 10.00
22 Christopher Austin Martin/25 12.00 30.00
24 Cordell Dunn Jr./25 4.00 10.00
25 Courtney Hawkins/25 4.00 10.00
26 D.J. Peterson/25 4.00 10.00
27 Dansby Swanson/99 30.00 80.00
29 Daz Cameron/92 12.00 30.00
31 Devin Ortiz/99 3.00 8.00
32 Dillon Tate/99 4.00 10.00
33 DJ Stewart/99 4.00 10.00
34 Doug Nikhazy/49 4.00 10.00
35 Reese McGuire/99 3.00 8.00
36 Elih Marrero/99 3.00 8.00
38 Francisco Lindor/25 12.00 30.00
39 Gray Fenter/99 3.00 8.00
40 Hugh Fisher/99 3.00 8.00
42 Jack Flaherty/25 6.00 15.00
43 Jacob Blas/25 4.00 10.00
44 Jake Lemoine/99 3.00 8.00
45 James Kaprielian/99 5.00 12.00
47 Joe DeMers/99 3.00 8.00
49 John Dearth/99 3.00 8.00
51 Justin Garza/99 3.00 8.00
52 Justus Sheffield/49 8.00 20.00
53 Kale Breaux/99 5.00 12.00
54 Ke'Bryan Hayes/99 5.00 12.00
55 Kolby Allard/99 10.00 25.00
57 Kristofer Armstrong/49 4.00 10.00
58 Kyle Funkhouser/99 6.00 15.00
59 Kyle Molnar/99 3.00 8.00
61 L.T. Tolbert/25 4.00 10.00
62 Lance McCullers/49 4.00 10.00
63 Lucas Herbert/49 4.00 10.00
64 Lucas Sims/99 3.00 8.00
65 Luis Ortiz/43 4.00 10.00
66 Luke Weaver/99 5.00 12.00
67 Luken Baker/99 5.00 12.00
68 Ian Clarkin/49 4.00 10.00
69 Mark Mathias/99 4.00 10.00
70 Mark Vientos/99 5.00 12.00
71 Matt Chapman/25 6.00 15.00
72 Matt Olson/99 8.00 20.00
73 Max Wotell/99 3.00 8.00
74 Michael Conforto/99 15.00 40.00
76 Mitchell Hansen/99 3.00 8.00
77 Nicholas Banks/99 3.00 8.00
78 Nick Madrigal/99 6.00 15.00
79 Nick Travieso/49 4.00 10.00
80 Noah Campbell/25 4.00 10.00
81 Peter Lambert/98 3.00 8.00
82 Peter O'Brien/55 5.00 12.00
84 Robert Refsnyder/99
86 Ryan Burr/99 3.00 8.00
88 Steven Williams/99 3.00 8.00
89 Tate Matheny/99 3.00 8.00
90 Taylor Ward/99 5.00 12.00
91 Thomas Burbank/99 3.00 8.00
92 Thomas Eshelman/99 8.00 20.00
93 Trea Turner/99 15.00 40.00
95 Trey Killian/25 4.00 10.00
96 Tyler Beede/49 5.00 12.00
97 Tyler Jay/99 3.00 8.00
99 Xavier LeGrant/99 3.00 8.00
100 Zack Collins/99 4.00 10.00

2015 USA Baseball Stars and Stripes Statistical Standouts

COMPLETE SET (25) 12.00 30.00
RANDOM INSERTS IN PACKS
*FOIL/99: .6X TO 1.5X BASIC
1 Christin Stewart .60 1.50
2 Carson Fulmer .50 1.25
3 James Kaprielian .75 2.00
4 Kyle Funkhouser .60 1.50
5 Trenton Clark .50 1.25
6 Luken Baker .75 2.00
7 Ke'Bryan Hayes .75 2.00
8 Nick Madrigal 1.00 2.50
9 Daz Cameron .75 2.00
10 Mitchell Hansen .50 1.25
11 Lucas Herbert .50 1.25
12 Joe DeMers .50 1.25
13 Kyle Molnar .50 1.25
14 Peter Lambert .50 1.25
15 Kolby Allard .50 1.25
16 Corey Seager 2.00 5.00
17 A.J. Cole .50 1.25
18 David Dahl .60 1.50
19 Henry Owens .50 1.25
20 Kyle Schwarber 2.00 5.00
21 Kris Bryant 3.00 8.00
22 Matt Olson .60 1.50
23 D.J. Peterson .50 1.25
24 Nick Travieso .50 1.25
25 Robert Refsnyder .60 1.50

2015 USA Baseball Stars and Stripes Statistical Standouts Holofoil

*HOLOFOIL: 1X TO 2.5X BASIC
RANDOM INSERTS IN PACKS
STATED PRINT RUN 25 SER.#'d SETS
21 Kris Bryant 20.00 50.00

2017 USA Baseball Stars and Stripes

COMPLETE SET (100) 40.00 100.00
1 USA Baseball Collegiate CL .25 .60
2 USA Baseball 18U CL .25 .60
3 USA Baseball 15U CL .25 .60
4 Darren McCaughan .30 .75
5 Seth Beer 1.00 2.50
6 J.B. Bukauskas .40 1.00
7 Jake Burger .50 1.25
8 Tyler Johnson .30 .75
9 Alex Faedo .40 1.00
10 TJ Friedl .25 .60
11 Dalton Guthrie .40 1.00
12 Devin Hairston .30 .75
13 KJ Harrison .40 1.00
14 Keston Hiura 1.25 3.00
15 Tanner Houck 1.25 3.00
16 Jeren Kendall .50 1.25
17 Alex Lange .40 1.00
18 Brendan McKay 1.00 2.50
19 Glenn Otto .25 .60
20 David Peterson .30 .75
21 Mike Rivera .25 .60
22 Evan Skoug .30 .75
23 Ricky Tyler Thomas .25 .60
24 Taylor Walls .25 .60
25 Tim Cate .30 .75
26 Evan White .40 1.00
27 Kyle Wright .75 2.00
28 Nick Allen .30 .75
29 Hans Crouse .60 1.50
30 Hagen Danner .30 .75
31 Hunter Greene .75 2.00
32 Quentin Holmes .30 .75
33 Royce Lewis 2.00 5.00
34 Nick Pratto .40 1.00
35 Logan Allen .25 .60
36 Shane Baz .40 1.00
37 Jordan Butler .25 .60
38 Blayne Enlow .30 .75
39 M.J. Melendez .40 1.00
40 Mitchell Stone .25 .60
41 CJ Van Eyk .25 .60
42 Ryan Vilade .40 1.00
43 Patrick Bailey .75 2.00
44 Calvin Mitchell .50 1.25
45 Mike Siani .30 .75
46 Brice Turang .75 2.00
47 Triston Casas 1.00 2.50
48 Carter Young .40 1.00
49 Nelson Berkwich .25 .60
50 Coleman Brigman .30 .75
51 Gabe Briones .25 .60
52 Christian Cairo .25 .60
53 Justin Campbell .30 .75
54 Jasiah Dixon .40 1.00
55 Cade Doughty .40 1.00
56 Sammy Faltine .25 .60
57 Nick Gorby .25 .60
58 Tony Jacob .25 .60
59 Jared Jones .25 .60
60 Ethan Long .25 .60
61 Zach Martinez .30 .75
62 Joe Naranjo .25 .60
63 Colton Olasin .50 1.25
64 Wesley Scott .30 .75
65 Landon Sims .30 .75
66 Anthony Volpe .75 2.00
67 Nate Wohlgemuth .40 1.00
68 Bobby Dalbec .60 1.50
69 Ian Anderson .60 1.50
70 Corey Ray .30 .75
71 A.J. Puk .40 1.00
72 Braxton Garrett .25 .60
73 Zack Collins .30 .75
74 William Benson .25 .60
75 Matt Thaiss .25 .60
76 Forrest Whitley .75 2.00
77 Blake Rutherford .40 1.00
78 Zack Burdi .25 .60
79 Anthony Kay .25 .60
80 Daulton Jefferies .30 .75
81 Robert Tyler .25 .60
82 Anfernee Grier .25 .60
83 Kevin Gowdy .30 .75
84 Chris Okey .25 .60
85 Logan Shore .30 .75
86 Buddy Reed .25 .60
87 Bryan Reynolds .40 1.00

88 Reggie Lawson .25 .60
89 Cole Stobbe .25 .60
90 Garrett Hampson .40 1.00
91 Bryson Brigman .25 .60
92 Zach Jackson .25 .60
93 Mark McGwire .60 1.50
94 Frank Thomas .40 1.00
95 Alex Bregman 1.00 2.50
96 Dansby Swanson .60 1.50
97 Ken Griffey Jr. .75 2.00
98 Todd Helton .30 .75
99 Barry Larkin .30 .75
100 Roger Clemens .50 1.25

2017 USA Baseball Stars and Stripes Longevity

1 USA Baseball Collegiate CL .30 .75
2 USA Baseball 18U CL .30 .75
3 USA Baseball 15U CL .30 .75
4 Darren McCaughan .40 1.00
5 Seth Beer 1.25 3.00
6 J.B. Bukauskas .50 1.25
7 Jake Burger .60 1.50
8 Tyler Johnson .40 1.00
9 Alex Faedo .50 1.25
10 TJ Friedl .30 .75
11 Dalton Guthrie .50 1.25
12 Devin Hairston .40 1.00
13 KJ Harrison .50 1.25
14 Keston Hiura 1.50 4.00
15 Tanner Houck 1.50 4.00
16 Jeren Kendall .60 1.50
17 Alex Lange .50 1.25
18 Brendan McKay 1.25 3.00
19 Glenn Otto .30 .75
20 David Peterson .40 1.00
21 Mike Rivera .30 .75
22 Evan Skoug .40 1.00
23 Ricky Tyler Thomas .30 .75
24 Taylor Walls .30 .75
25 Tim Cate .40 1.00
26 Evan White .50 1.25
27 Kyle Wright 1.00 2.50
28 Nick Allen .40 1.00
29 Hans Crouse .75 2.00
30 Hagen Danner .40 1.00
31 Hunter Greene 1.00 2.50
32 Quentin Holmes .40 1.00
33 Royce Lewis 2.50 6.00
34 Nick Pratto .50 1.25
35 Logan Allen .30 .75
36 Shane Baz .50 1.25
37 Jordan Butler .30 .75
38 Blayne Enlow .40 1.00
39 M.J. Melendez .50 1.25
40 Mitchell Stone .30 .75
41 CJ Van Eyk .30 .75
42 Ryan Vilade .50 1.25
43 Patrick Bailey 1.00 2.50
44 Calvin Mitchell .60 1.50
45 Mike Siani .40 1.00
46 Brice Turang 1.00 2.50
47 Triston Casas 1.25 3.00
48 Carter Young .50 1.25
49 Nelson Berkwich .30 .75
50 Coleman Brigman .40 1.00
51 Gabe Briones .30 .75
52 Christian Cairo .30 .75
53 Justin Campbell .40 1.00
54 Jasiah Dixon .50 1.25
55 Cade Doughty .50 1.25
56 Sammy Faltine .30 .75
57 Nick Gorby .30 .75
58 Tony Jacob .30 .75
59 Jared Jones .30 .75
60 Ethan Long .30 .75
61 Zach Martinez .40 1.00
62 Joe Naranjo .30 .75
63 Colton Olasin .60 1.50
64 Wesley Scott .40 1.00
65 Landon Sims .40 1.00
66 Anthony Volpe 1.00 2.50
67 Nate Wohlgemuth .50 1.25
68 Bobby Dalbec .75 2.00
69 Ian Anderson .75 2.00
70 Corey Ray .40 1.00
71 A.J. Puk .50 1.25
72 Braxton Garrett .30 .75
73 Zack Collins .40 1.00
74 William Benson .30 .75
75 Matt Thaiss .30 .75
76 Forrest Whitley 1.00 2.50
77 Blake Rutherford .50 1.25
78 Zack Burdi .30 .75
79 Anthony Kay .30 .75
80 Daulton Jefferies .40 1.00
81 Robert Tyler .30 .75
82 Anfernee Grier .30 .75
83 Kevin Gowdy .40 1.00
84 Chris Okey .30 .75
85 Logan Shore .40 1.00
86 Buddy Reed .30 .75
87 Bryan Reynolds .50 1.25
88 Reggie Lawson .30 .75
89 Cole Stobbe .30 .75
90 Garrett Hampson .50 1.25
91 Bryson Brigman .30 .75
92 Zach Jackson .30 .75
93 Mark McGwire .75 2.00
94 Frank Thomas .50 1.25
95 Alex Bregman 1.25 3.00
96 Dansby Swanson .75 2.00
97 Ken Griffey Jr. 1.00 2.50
98 Todd Helton .40 1.00
99 Barry Larkin .40 1.00
100 Roger Clemens .60 1.50

2017 USA Baseball Stars and Stripes Longevity Holofoil

*HOLO: 1.2X TO 3X BASIC
RANDOM INSERTS IN PACKS
STATED PRINT RUN 99 COPIES PER

2017 USA Baseball Stars and Stripes Longevity Parallel

*PARALLEL: .5X TO 1.2X BASIC
RANDOM INSERTS IN PACKS

2017 USA Baseball Stars and Stripes Longevity Ruby

*RUBY: .75X TO 2X BASIC
RANDOM INSERTS IN PACKS
STATED PRINT RUN 249 COPIES PER

2017 USA Baseball Stars and Stripes Longevity Sapphire

*SAPPHIRE: 1.5X TO 4X BASIC
RANDOM INSERTS IN PACKS
STATED PRINT RUN 49 COPIES PER

2017 USA Baseball Stars and Stripes Longevity Team Logo Gold

*GOLD: 2X TO 5X BASIC
RANDOM INSERTS IN PACKS
STATED PRINT RUN 25 COPIES PER

2017 USA Baseball Stars and Stripes 14U Signatures

PRINT RUNS B/WN 349-399 COPIES PER
*BLACK/25: .6X TO 1.5X BASIC
1 Chad Abel/399 2.50 6.00
2 Matthew Bardowell/399 2.50 6.00
3 Sam Brady/399 2.50 6.00
4 Pete Crow-Armstrong/399 10.00 25.00
5 Jordan Daphney/399 2.50 6.00
6 Michael Davinni/399 2.50 6.00
7 Davis Diaz/399 2.50 6.00
8 Kendall Diggs/399 2.50 6.00
9 Oscar Estrada/399 2.50 6.00
10 Hunter Haas/399 4.00 10.00
11 Jackson Miller/399 2.50 6.00
12 Robert Moore/349 2.50 6.00
13 Emilio Morales/399 2.50 6.00
14 Matt Morello/399 2.50 6.00
15 Nathan Nankil/399 2.50 6.00
16 Logan Ott/399 2.50 6.00
17 Eli Paton/399 4.00 10.00
18 Nicholas Regalado/399 4.00 10.00
19 Roc Riggio/399 2.50 6.00
20 Christian Rodriguez/399 2.50 6.00
21 Shane Stafford/399 2.50 6.00
22 Quinn Sullivan/399 2.50 6.00
23 Tommy Troy/399 2.50 6.00
24 Cooper Vest/399 2.50 6.00
25 Zavien Watson/399 5.00 12.00
26 Parker Welch/399 2.50 6.00
27 Nick Yorke/399 4.00 10.00
28 Nelson Berkwich/399 2.50 6.00
29 Nicholas Bitsko/399 4.00 10.00
30 Michael Brooks/399 2.50 6.00
31 Irving Carter/399 2.50 6.00
32 Dylan Castaneda/399 2.50 6.00
33 Lucas Costello/399 2.50 6.00
34 Dylan Crews/399 4.00 10.00
35 Jonathan Cymrot/399 2.50 6.00
36 Kevin Garcia/399 2.50 6.00
37 Jacob Gonzalez/399 8.00 20.00
38 Lucas Gordon/399 3.00 8.00
39 Mac Guscette/399 3.00 8.00
40 Rawley Hector/399 4.00 10.00
41 Max Hitman/399 2.50 6.00
42 Jonathan Huff/399 2.50 6.00
43 Jayden Melendez/399 4.00 10.00
44 Cole Smith/399 2.50 6.00
45 Masyn Winn/399 2.50 6.00
46 Nate Wohlgemuth/399 4.00 10.00
47 Ethan Wood/399 4.00 10.00

2017 USA Baseball Stars and Stripes 15U Signatures

RANDOM INSERTS IN PACKS
STATED PRINT RUN 199 SER.#'d SETS
*BLACK/25: .6X TO 1.5X BASIC
1 Nelson Berkwich 2.50 6.00
2 Coleman Brigman 3.00 8.00
3 Gabe Briones 2.50 6.00
4 Christian Cairo 2.50 6.00
5 Justin Campbell 3.00 8.00
6 Jasiah Dixon 4.00 10.00
7 Cade Doughty 4.00 10.00
8 Sammy Faltine 2.50 6.00
9 Nick Gorby 2.50 6.00
10 Tony Jacob 2.50 6.00
11 Jared Jones 2.50 6.00
12 Ethan Long 2.50 6.00
13 Zach Martinez 3.00 8.00
14 Joe Naranjo 2.50 6.00
15 Colton Olasin 5.00 12.00
16 Wesley Scott 3.00 8.00
17 Landon Sims 3.00 8.00
18 Anthony Volpe 8.00 20.00
19 Nate Wohlgemuth 4.00 10.00
20 Carter Young 4.00 10.00

2017 USA Baseball Stars and Stripes 17U Signatures

RANDOM INSERTS IN PACKS
PRINT RUNS B/WN 399-499 COPIES PER
*BLACK/25: .6X TO 1.5X BASIC
1 Randall Abshier/399 2.50 6.00
2 Thomas Burbank/399 2.50 6.00
3 Elijah Cabell/399 4.00 10.00
4 Triston Casas/499 10.00 25.00
5 Zachary Chalmers/399 2.50 6.00
6 Chandler Champlain/399 2.50 6.00
7 Ethan Hankins/399 2.50 6.00
9 Charlie Loust/399 2.50 6.00
10 Justyn-Henry Malloy/399 2.50 6.00
11 Sean Mullen/399 4.00 10.00
12 Kameron Ojeda/399 2.50 6.00
13 Austin Schultz/399 10.00 25.00
14 Christian Scott/399 2.50 6.00
15 Isaiah Thomas/399 2.50 6.00
16 Luis Tuero/499 3.00 8.00
17 Jose Varela/399 2.50 6.00
18 Justin Willis/399 3.00 8.00
19 Gage Workman/399 4.00 10.00
20 Kerry Wright/399 2.50 6.00
21 Branden Boissiere/499 2.50 6.00
22 Tony Bullard/399 2.50 6.00
23 Brandon Comia/399 2.50 6.00
24 Sam Faith/399 2.50 6.00
25 Hunter Goodwin/399 2.50 6.00
26 Riley Greene/399 10.00 25.00
27 Daniel Grillo/399 2.50 6.00
28 Nick Hansen/399 2.50 6.00
29 Cole Henry/399 2.50 6.00
30 Jake Holland/399 2.50 6.00
31 Jeremiah Jackson/499 8.00 20.00
32 Carlos Lomeli/399 4.00 10.00
33 Jake Moberg/399 2.50 6.00
34 Holden Powell/399 2.50 6.00
35 Kumar Rocker/399 6.00 15.00
36 Calvin Schapira/399 3.00 8.00
37 Connor Scott/399 8.00 20.00
38 Brice Turang/499 8.00 20.00
39 Austin Wells/399 10.00 25.00
40 Ryan Wimbush/399 2.50 6.00

2017 USA Baseball Stars and Stripes 18U Connections Signatures

RANDOM INSERTS IN PACKS
STATED PRINT RUN 25 SER.#'d SETS
1 H.Danner/N.Pratto 25.00 60.00
2 Q.Holmes/R.Lewis
3 H.Greene/N.Allen

2017 USA Baseball Stars and Stripes 18U Signatures

RANDOM INSERTS IN PACKS
STATED PRINT RUN 499 SER.#'d SETS
1 Nick Allen 3.00 8.00
2 Hans Crouse 6.00 15.00
3 Hagen Danner 3.00 8.00
4 Hunter Greene 20.00 50.00
5 Quentin Holmes 3.00 8.00
6 Royce Lewis 10.00 25.00
7 Nick Pratto 4.00 10.00
8 Logan Allen 2.50 6.00
9 Shane Baz 4.00 10.00
11 Jordan Butler 2.50 6.00
15 Blayne Enlow 3.00 8.00
22 M.J. Melendez 4.00 10.00
28 Mitchell Stone 2.50 6.00
30 CJ Van Eyk 2.50 6.00
31 Ryan Vilade 4.00 10.00
34 Patrick Bailey 5.00 12.00
37 Jarred Kelenic 12.00 30.00
38 Mike Siani 3.00 8.00
39 Brice Turang 8.00 20.00

2017 USA Baseball Stars and Stripes Alumni Signatures

RANDOM INSERTS IN PACKS
STATED PRINT RUN 25 SER.#'d SETS
1 Mark McGwire
2 Frank Thomas 20.00 50.00
3 Alex Bregman 15.00 40.00
5 Ken Griffey Jr. 75.00 200.00

2017 USA Baseball Stars and Stripes College Connections Signatures

RANDOM INSERTS IN PACKS
STATED PRINT RUN 25 SER.#'d SETS
1 J.Burger/S.Beer 25.00 60.00
2 A.Faedo/J.Bukauskas 20.00 50.00
3 T.Houck/A.Lange
4 K.Harrison/B.McKay 20.00 50.00
5 J.Kendall/K.Wright 20.00 50.00
6 E.Skoug/M.Rivera
7 D.Guthrie/M.Rivera
8 B.McKay/D.Hairston
9 J.Kendall/S.Beer 50.00 120.00
10 J.Burger/K.Harrison

2017 USA Baseball Stars and Stripes College Signatures

RANDOM INSERTS IN PACKS
STATED PRINT RUN 499 SER.#'d SETS
*BLACK/25: .6X TO 1.5X BASIC
1 Darren McCaughan 3.00 8.00
2 Seth Beer 5.00 12.00
3 J.B. Bukauskas 4.00 10.00
4 Jake Burger 8.00 20.00
5 Tyler Johnson 3.00 8.00
6 Alex Faedo 4.00 10.00
7 TJ Friedl 2.50 6.00
8 Dalton Guthrie 4.00 10.00
9 Devin Hairston 3.00 8.00
10 KJ Harrison 4.00 10.00
11 Keston Hiura 8.00 20.00
12 Tanner Houck 12.00 30.00
13 Jeren Kendall 6.00 15.00
14 Alex Lange 4.00 10.00
15 Brendan McKay 10.00 25.00
16 Glenn Otto 2.50 6.00
17 David Peterson 3.00 8.00
18 Mike Rivera 2.50 6.00
19 Evan Skoug 3.00 8.00
20 Ricky Tyler Thomas 2.50 6.00
21 Taylor Walls 2.50 6.00
23 Evan White 4.00 10.00
24 Kyle Wright 8.00 20.00

2017 USA Baseball Stars and Stripes Jumbo Swatch Black Gold Silhouette Jersey Signatures

RANDOM INSERTS IN PACKS
PRINT RUNS B/WN 5-99 COPIES PER
NO PRICING ON QTY 5
1 Darren McCaughan/86 4.00 10.00
2 Seth Beer/79 15.00 40.00
3 J.B. Bukauskas/72 12.00 30.00
4 Jake Burger/64 6.00 15.00
5 Tyler Johnson/82 4.00 10.00
6 Alex Faedo/79 5.00 12.00
7 TJ Friedl/77 3.00 8.00
8 Dalton Guthrie/71 5.00 12.00
9 Devin Hairston/89 4.00 10.00
10 KJ Harrison/64 5.00 12.00
11 Keston Hiura/73 15.00 40.00
12 Tanner Houck/79 15.00 40.00
13 Jeren Kendall/64 6.00 15.00
14 Alex Lange/68 5.00 12.00
15 Brendan McKay/56 10.00 25.00
16 Glenn Otto/89 3.00 8.00
17 David Peterson/89 4.00 10.00
18 Mike Rivera/79 3.00 8.00
19 Evan Skoug/79 4.00 10.00
20 Ricky Tyler Thomas/82 3.00 8.00
21 Taylor Walls/79 3.00 8.00
22 Tim Cate/88 4.00 10.00
23 Evan White/79 5.00 12.00
24 Kyle Wright/73 10.00 25.00
25 Nick Allen/79 4.00 10.00
26 Hans Crouse/79 8.00 20.00
27 Hagen Danner/64 4.00 10.00
28 Hunter Greene/64 10.00 25.00
29 Quentin Holmes/64 6.00 15.00
30 Royce Lewis/62 10.00 25.00
31 Nick Pratto/64 5.00 12.00
32 Logan Allen/89 3.00 8.00
33 Shane Baz/78 5.00 12.00
34 Jordan Butler/87 3.00 8.00
35 Blayne Enlow/87 4.00 10.00
36 M.J. Melendez/79 5.00 12.00
37 Mitchell Stone/86 3.00 8.00
38 CJ Van Eyk/88 3.00 8.00
39 Ryan Vilade/79 5.00 12.00
40 Patrick Bailey/59 6.00 15.00
42 Mike Siani/68 4.00 10.00
43 Brice Turang/99 10.00 25.00
45 Triston Casas/99 6.00 15.00
46 Nelson Berkwich/99 3.00 8.00
47 Coleman Brigman/89 4.00 10.00
48 Gabe Briones/89 3.00 8.00
49 Christian Cairo/88 3.00 8.00
50 Justin Campbell/80 4.00 10.00
51 Jasiah Dixon/82 5.00 12.00
52 Cade Doughty/88 5.00 12.00
53 Sammy Faltine/89 3.00 8.00
54 Nick Gorby/89 3.00 8.00
55 Tony Jacob/87 3.00 8.00
56 Jared Jones/80 3.00 8.00
57 Ethan Long/85 3.00 8.00
59 Joe Naranjo/89
60 Colton Olasin/88 6.00 15.00
61 Wesley Scott/89 4.00 10.00
62 Landon Sims/84 4.00 10.00
63 Anthony Volpe/88 10.00 25.00
64 Nate Wohlgemuth/99 5.00 12.00
65 Carter Young/85 5.00 12.00
92 Randall Abshier/44 3.00 8.00
93 Thomas Burbank/36 3.00 8.00
94 Elijah Cabell/44 10.00 25.00
95 Triston Casas/24 10.00 25.00
96 Zachary Chalmers/43 3.00 8.00
97 Chandler Champlain/44 3.00 8.00
98 Ethan Hankins/44 4.00 10.00
100 Charlie Loust/44 3.00 8.00
101 Justyn-Henry Malloy/44 3.00 8.00
102 Sean Mullen/44
103 Kameron Ojeda/43 3.00 8.00
104 Austin Schultz/44 10.00 25.00
105 Christian Scott/44 3.00 8.00
106 Isaiah Thomas/43 3.00 8.00
107 Luis Tuero/44 4.00 10.00
108 Jose Varela/44 3.00 8.00
109 Justin Willis/44
110 Gage Workman/44 5.00 12.00
111 Kerry Wright/43 3.00 8.00
112 Branden Boissiere/44
113 Tony Bullard/44
114 Brandon Comia/44 3.00 8.00
115 Sam Faith/44 3.00 8.00
116 Hunter Goodwin/42 3.00 8.00
117 Riley Greene/43 12.00 30.00
118 Daniel Grillo/44 3.00 8.00
119 Nick Hansen/44 3.00 8.00
120 Cole Henry/44 3.00 8.00
121 Jake Holland/41 3.00 8.00
122 Jeremiah Jackson/34 8.00 20.00
123 Carlos Lomeli/44
124 Jake Moberg/44
125 Holden Powell/43 3.00 8.00
126 Kumar Rocker/41 15.00 40.00
127 Calvin Schapira/44
128 Connor Scott/44 10.00 25.00
129 Brice Turang/34 10.00 25.00
130 Austin Wells/43 12.00 30.00
131 Ryan Wimbush/44 3.00 8.00
132 Chad Abel/44 3.00 8.00
133 Matthew Bardowell/44 3.00 8.00
134 Sam Brady/39
135 Pete Crow-Armstrong/44 12.00 30.00
136 Jordan Daphney/43 3.00 8.00
137 Michael Davinni/43 3.00 8.00
138 Davis Diaz/44 3.00 8.00
139 Kendall Diggs/44 3.00 8.00
140 Oscar Estrada/43 10.00 25.00
141 Hunter Haas/44 8.00 20.00
142 Jackson Miller/44 3.00 8.00
143 Robert Moore/34 3.00 8.00
144 Emilio Morales/44 3.00 8.00
145 Matt Morello/40 3.00 8.00
146 Nathan Nankil/44 3.00 8.00
147 Logan Ott/44 5.00 12.00
148 Eli Paton/44
149 Nicholas Regalado/44 5.00 12.00
150 Roc Riggio/44 3.00 8.00
151 Christian Rodriguez/44 3.00 8.00
152 Shane Stafford/44 3.00 8.00
153 Quinn Sullivan/39 3.00 8.00
154 Tommy Troy/43 8.00 20.00
155 Cooper Vest/44 3.00 8.00
156 Zavien Watson/44
157 Parker Welch/43 3.00 8.00
158 Nick Yorke/38
159 Nelson Berkwich/34 3.00 8.00
160 Nicholas Bitsko/43
161 Michael Brooks/44 3.00 8.00
162 Irving Carter/44
163 Dylan Castaneda/44 3.00 8.00
164 Lucas Costello/44
165 Dylan Crews/43 5.00 12.00
166 Jonathan Cymrot/42 3.00 8.00
167 Kevin Garcia/44 3.00 8.00
168 Jacob Gonzalez/44 6.00 15.00
169 Lucas Gordon/44 4.00 10.00
170 Mac Guscette/44 4.00 10.00
171 Rawley Hector/43 5.00 12.00
172 Max Hitman/44
173 Jonathan Huff/43 3.00 8.00
174 Jayden Melendez/44 5.00 12.00
175 Cole Smith/40 3.00 8.00
176 Masyn Winn/44 3.00 8.00
177 Nate Wohlgemuth/30 5.00 12.00
178 Ethan Wood/38 10.00 25.00

2017 USA Baseball Stars and Stripes Jumbo Swatch Silhouette Bat Signatures

RANDOM INSERTS IN PACKS
PRINT RUNS B/WN 10-199 COPIES PER
NO PRICING ON QTY 10
2 Seth Beer/99 15.00 40.00
4 Jake Burger/99 6.00 15.00
7 TJ Friedl/99 3.00 8.00
8 Dalton Guthrie/99 5.00 12.00
10 KJ Harrison/99 5.00 12.00
11 Keston Hiura/99 8.00 20.00
13 Jeren Kendall/99 6.00 15.00
15 Brendan McKay/99 15.00 40.00
18 Mike Rivera/99 3.00 8.00
19 Evan Skoug/99 4.00 10.00
21 Taylor Walls/99 3.00 8.00
23 Evan White/99 5.00 12.00
25 Nick Allen/99 4.00 10.00
27 Hagen Danner/99 4.00 10.00
28 Hunter Greene/99 25.00 60.00
29 Quentin Holmes/99 6.00 15.00
30 Royce Lewis/99 12.00 30.00
31 Nick Pratto/99 5.00 12.00
36 M.J. Melendez/99 5.00 12.00
39 Ryan Vilade/99 5.00 12.00
40 Patrick Bailey/99 6.00 15.00
42 Mike Siani/99 4.00 10.00
45 Triston Casas/99 6.00 15.00
67 Corey Ray/25 4.00 10.00
83 Buddy Reed/25 3.00 8.00
91 Dansby Swanson/49 20.00 50.00
190 TJ Friedl/49 3.00 8.00

2017 USA Baseball Stars and Stripes Jumbo Swatch Silhouette Jersey Signatures

RANDOM INSERTS IN PACKS
PRINT RUNS B/WN 1-199 COPIES PER
NO PRICING ON QTY 15 OR LESS
*PRIME/20-25: .6X TO 1.5X BASIC
1 Darren McCaughan/199 4.00 10.00
2 Seth Beer/199 15.00 40.00
3 J.B. Bukauskas/199 10.00 25.00
4 Jake Burger/199 6.00 15.00
5 Tyler Johnson/199 4.00 10.00
6 Alex Faedo/199 5.00 12.00
7 TJ Friedl/193 3.00 8.00
8 Dalton Guthrie/199 5.00 12.00
9 Devin Hairston/199 4.00 10.00
10 KJ Harrison/199 5.00 12.00
11 Keston Hiura/199 8.00 20.00
12 Tanner Houck/199 15.00 40.00
13 Jeren Kendall/199 6.00 15.00
14 Alex Lange/199 5.00 12.00
15 Brendan McKay/199 10.00 25.00
16 Glenn Otto/199 3.00 8.00
17 David Peterson/199 4.00 10.00
18 Mike Rivera/199 3.00 8.00
19 Evan Skoug/199 4.00 10.00
20 Ricky Tyler Thomas/199 3.00 8.00
21 Taylor Walls/199 3.00 8.00
22 Tim Cate/199 4.00 10.00
23 Evan White/199 5.00 12.00
24 Kyle Wright/199 10.00 25.00
25 Nick Allen/199 4.00 10.00
26 Hans Crouse/199 8.00 20.00
27 Hagen Danner/199 4.00 10.00
28 Hunter Greene/199 10.00 25.00
29 Quentin Holmes/199 6.00 15.00
30 Royce Lewis/199 12.00 30.00
31 Nick Pratto/199 5.00 12.00
32 Logan Allen/199 3.00 8.00
33 Shane Baz/199 5.00 12.00
34 Jordan Butler/199 3.00 8.00
35 Blayne Enlow/199 4.00 10.00
36 M.J. Melendez/199 5.00 12.00
37 Mitchell Stone/199 3.00 8.00
38 CJ Van Eyk/199 3.00 8.00
39 Ryan Vilade/199 5.00 12.00
40 Patrick Bailey/199 6.00 15.00
42 Mike Siani/199 4.00 10.00
43 Brice Turang/199 10.00 25.00
44 Kyle Funkhouser/46 4.00 10.00
45 Triston Casas/199 6.00 15.00
46 Nelson Berkwich/99 3.00 8.00
47 Coleman Brigman/199 4.00 10.00
48 Gabe Briones/199 3.00 8.00
49 Christian Cairo/199 3.00 8.00
50 Justin Campbell/199 4.00 10.00
51 Jasiah Dixon/199 5.00 12.00
52 Cade Doughty/199 5.00 12.00
53 Sammy Faltine/199 3.00 8.00
54 Nick Gorby/194 3.00 8.00
55 Tony Jacob/199 3.00 8.00
56 Jared Jones/195 3.00 8.00
57 Ethan Long/199 3.00 8.00
58 Zach Martinez/199 4.00 10.00
59 Joe Naranjo/99
60 Colton Olasin/199 6.00 15.00
61 Wesley Scott/185 4.00 10.00
62 Landon Sims/156 4.00 10.00
63 Anthony Volpe/199 10.00 25.00
64 Nate Wohlgemuth/99 5.00 12.00
65 Carter Young/199 8.00 20.00
66 Ian Anderson/84 6.00 15.00
67 Corey Ray/108 4.00 10.00
68 A.J. Puk/127 5.00 12.00
69 Braxton Garrett/90 3.00 8.00
70 Zack Collins/68 4.00 10.00
71 William Benson/89 3.00 8.00
72 Matt Thaiss/133 3.00 8.00
73 Forrest Whitley/49 10.00 25.00
74 Blake Rutherford/61 12.00 30.00
75 Zack Burdi/143 3.00 8.00
76 Anthony Kay/139 3.00 8.00
77 Daulton Jefferies/143 4.00 10.00
78 Robert Tyler/128 3.00 8.00
79 Anfernee Grier/142 3.00 8.00
80 Kevin Gowdy/75 4.00 10.00
81 Chris Okey/199 3.00 8.00
82 Logan Shore/199 4.00 10.00
83 Buddy Reed/118 3.00 8.00
85 Reggie Lawson/49
86 Cole Stobbe/49 3.00 8.00
87 Garrett Hampson/142 5.00 12.00
88 Bryson Brigman/128 3.00 8.00
89 Zach Jackson/49 3.00 8.00
90 Alex Bregman/49 15.00 40.00
92 Randall Abshier/49 3.00 8.00
93 Thomas Burbank/49 3.00 8.00
94 Elijah Cabell/49
95 Triston Casas/49 6.00 15.00
96 Zachary Chalmers/49 3.00 8.00
97 Chandler Champlain/49 3.00 8.00
98 Ethan Hankins/49 4.00 10.00
100 Charlie Loust/49 3.00 8.00
101 Justyn-Henry Malloy/49 3.00 8.00
102 Sean Mullen/49
103 Kameron Ojeda/49 3.00 8.00
104 Austin Schultz/49
105 Christian Scott/49 3.00 8.00
106 Isaiah Thomas/49 3.00 8.00
107 Luis Tuero/49 4.00 10.00
108 Jose Varela/49 3.00 8.00
109 Justin Willis/49
110 Gage Workman/49 5.00 12.00
111 Kerry Wright/49
112 Branden Boissiere/49 3.00 8.00
113 Tony Bullard/49
114 Brandon Comia/49 3.00 8.00
115 Sam Faith/49 3.00 8.00
116 Hunter Goodwin/49 3.00 8.00
117 Riley Greene/49 12.00 30.00
118 Daniel Grillo/49 3.00 8.00
119 Nick Hansen/49 3.00 8.00
120 Cole Henry/49 3.00 8.00
121 Jake Holland/49 3.00 8.00
122 Jeremiah Jackson/49 8.00 20.00
123 Carlos Lomeli/49
124 Jake Moberg/49
125 Holden Powell/49 3.00 8.00
126 Kumar Rocker/49 25.00 60.00
127 Calvin Schapira/49
128 Connor Scott/49 10.00 25.00
129 Brice Turang/49 10.00 25.00
130 Austin Wells/49 12.00 30.00
131 Ryan Wimbush/49 3.00 8.00
132 Chad Abel/49 3.00 8.00
133 Matthew Bardowell/49 3.00 8.00
134 Sam Brady/49
135 Pete Crow-Armstrong/49 12.00 30.00
136 Jordan Daphney/49 3.00 8.00
137 Michael Davinni/49 3.00 8.00
138 Davis Diaz/49 3.00 8.00
139 Kendall Diggs/49
140 Oscar Estrada/49 10.00 25.00
141 Hunter Haas/49 8.00 20.00
142 Jackson Miller/49 3.00 8.00
143 Robert Moore/49 3.00 8.00
144 Emilio Morales/49 3.00 8.00
145 Matt Morello/49 3.00 8.00
146 Nathan Nankil/49 3.00 8.00
147 Logan Ott/49 5.00 12.00
148 Eli Paton/49
149 Nicholas Regalado/49 5.00 12.00
150 Roc Riggio/49 3.00 8.00
151 Christian Rodriguez/49 3.00 8.00
152 Shane Stafford/49
153 Quinn Sullivan/49 3.00 8.00
154 Tommy Troy/49 8.00 20.00
155 Cooper Vest/49 3.00 8.00
156 Zavien Watson/49
157 Parker Welch/49 3.00 8.00
158 Nick Yorke/49
159 Nelson Berkwich/49 3.00 8.00
160 Nicholas Bitsko/49
161 Michael Brooks/49 3.00 8.00
162 Irving Carter/49 3.00 8.00
163 Dylan Castaneda/49 3.00 8.00
164 Lucas Costello/44
165 Dylan Crews/49 5.00 12.00
166 Jonathan Cymrot/49 3.00 8.00
167 Kevin Garcia/49 3.00 8.00
168 Jacob Gonzalez/49 6.00 15.00
169 Lucas Gordon/49 4.00 10.00
170 Mac Guscette/49 4.00 10.00
171 Rawley Hector/49 5.00 12.00
172 Max Hitman/49
173 Jonathan Huff/49 3.00 8.00
174 Jayden Melendez/49 5.00 12.00
175 Cole Smith/49 3.00 8.00
176 Masyn Winn/49 3.00 8.00
177 Nate Wohlgemuth/49 5.00 12.00
178 Ethan Wood/49 10.00 25.00
179 Bobby Dalbec/99 8.00 20.00
180 Jeren Kendall/49 6.00 15.00
181 Alex Faedo/49 4.00 10.00
182 Hunter Greene/49 10.00 25.00
183 Tanner Houck/49 15.00 40.00
184 J.B. Bukauskas/49 10.00 25.00
185 Kyle Wright/49 10.00 25.00
186 Quentin Holmes/49 6.00 15.00
187 Brendan McKay/49 10.00 25.00
188 Jake Burger/49 6.00 15.00
189 Hagen Danner/49 4.00 10.00
190 TJ Friedl/49 3.00 8.00
192 Hans Crouse/49 8.00 20.00
193 Carson Fulmer/25 3.00 8.00
194 Nick Banks/199 3.00 8.00
195 Alex Lange/49 4.00 10.00
196 Royce Lewis/49 10.00 25.00
197 KJ Harrison/49 5.00 12.00
198 Nick Pratto/49 5.00 12.00
200 Shane Baz/49 5.00 12.00

2017 USA Baseball Stars and Stripes Material Signatures

RANDOM INSERTS IN PACKS
PRINT RUNS B/WN 1-199 COPIES PER
NO PRICING ON QTY 15 OR LESS
*PRIME/25: .6X TO 1.5X BASIC
1 Darren McCaughan/299 3.00 8.00
2 Seth Beer/199 15.00 40.00
3 J.B. Bukauskas/199 10.00 25.00
4 Jake Burger/99 6.00 15.00
5 Tyler Johnson/299 4.00 10.00
6 Alex Faedo/199 5.00 12.00
7 TJ Friedl/99 3.00 8.00
8 Dalton Guthrie/199 5.00 12.00
9 Devin Hairston/299 4.00 10.00
10 KJ Harrison/299 5.00 12.00
11 Keston Hiura/199 8.00 20.00
12 Tanner Houck/299 15.00 40.00
13 Jeren Kendall/99 6.00 15.00
14 Alex Lange/199 5.00 12.00
15 Brendan McKay/299 10.00 25.00
16 Glenn Otto/299 3.00 8.00
17 David Peterson/299 4.00 10.00
18 Mike Rivera/199 3.00 8.00
19 Evan Skoug/199 4.00 10.00
20 Ricky Tyler Thomas/299 3.00 8.00
21 Taylor Walls/199 3.00 8.00
22 Tim Cate/199 4.00 10.00
23 Evan White/199 5.00 12.00
24 Kyle Wright/199 4.00 10.00
25 Nick Allen/299 4.00 10.00
26 Hans Crouse/299 8.00 20.00
27 Hagen Danner/299 4.00 10.00
28 Hunter Greene/299 20.00 50.00
29 Quentin Holmes/299 4.00 10.00
30 Royce Lewis/299 12.00 30.00
31 Nick Pratto/299 5.00 12.00
32 Logan Allen/299 3.00 8.00
33 Shane Baz/299 5.00 12.00
34 Jordan Butler/299 3.00 8.00
35 Blayne Enlow/299 4.00 10.00
36 M.J. Melendez/299 5.00 12.00
37 Mitchell Stone/299 3.00 8.00
38 CJ Van Eyk/299 3.00 8.00
39 Ryan Vilade/299 5.00 12.00
40 Patrick Bailey/299 6.00 15.00
42 Mike Siani/299 4.00 10.00
43 Brice Turang/299 6.00 15.00
44 Bobby Dalbec/125 8.00 20.00
45 Triston Casas/299 12.00 30.00
46 Nelson Berkwich/99 3.00 8.00
47 Coleman Brigman/99 4.00 10.00
48 Gabe Briones/199 3.00 8.00
49 Christian Cairo/99 3.00 8.00
50 Justin Campbell/99 4.00 10.00
51 Jasiah Dixon/99 5.00 12.00
52 Cade Doughty/99 5.00 12.00
53 Sammy Faltine/99
54 Nick Gorby/99 3.00 8.00
55 Tony Jacob/199 3.00 8.00
56 Jared Jones/99 3.00 8.00
57 Ethan Long/99 3.00 8.00
58 Zach Martinez/99 4.00 10.00
59 Joe Naranjo/99
60 Colton Olasin/99 6.00 15.00
61 Wesley Scott/99 4.00 10.00
62 Landon Sims/99 4.00 10.00
63 Anthony Volpe/99 6.00 15.00
64 Nate Wohlgemuth/199 5.00 12.00
65 Carter Young/99 8.00 20.00
66 Ian Anderson/99 6.00 15.00
67 Corey Ray/99 4.00 10.00
68 A.J. Puk/99 5.00 12.00
69 Braxton Garrett/99 3.00 8.00
70 Zack Collins/99 4.00 10.00
71 William Benson/99 3.00 8.00
72 Matt Thaiss/99 3.00 8.00
73 Forrest Whitley/99 10.00 25.00
74 Blake Rutherford/99 12.00 30.00
75 Zack Burdi/99 3.00 8.00
76 Anthony Kay/99 3.00 8.00
77 Daulton Jefferies/99 4.00 10.00
78 Robert Tyler/99 3.00 8.00
79 Anfernee Grier/99 3.00 8.00
80 Kevin Gowdy/99 4.00 10.00
81 Chris Okey/99 3.00 8.00
82 Logan Shore/99 4.00 10.00
83 Buddy Reed/99 3.00 8.00
85 Reggie Lawson/99
86 Cole Stobbe/99 3.00 8.00
87 Garrett Hampson/99 5.00 12.00
88 Bryson Brigman/99 3.00 8.00
89 Zach Jackson/99 3.00 8.00
92 Alex Bregman/99 8.00 20.00
95 Carson Fulmer/234 3.00 8.00

2017 USA Baseball Stars and Stripes Quad Materials

RANDOM INSERTS IN PACKS
PRINT RUNS B/WN 5-199 COPIES PER
NO PRICING ON QTY 5
*PRIME/25: 1X TO 2.5X BASIC
1 Mc/Gr/Ho/Ke/199 8.00 20.00
2 Fa/Wr/Ho/Bu/199 8.00 20.00
3 Bu/Ha/Ho/Le/199 4.00 10.00
4 En/Da/Cr/Gr/199 5.00 12.00
5 La/Ba/Mc/Pe/199 4.00 10.00
6 Sk/Ha/Pr/Wh/199 2.50 6.00
7 Sk/Me/Ri/Ba/199 5.00 12.00
8 Ha/Gu/Bu/Wa/199 3.00 8.00
9 Vi/Tu/Al/Ca/199 4.00 10.00
10 Mc/Th/Pe/Ca/199 4.00 10.00
11 Mil/Ho/Le/Si/199 12.00 30.00
12 Ra/Co/Pu/Th/199 2.50 6.00

2017 USA Baseball Stars and Stripes Tools of the Trade Jerseys

RANDOM INSERTS IN PACKS
PRINT RUNS B/WN 99-199 COPIES PER
*PRIME/25: .5X TO 1.2X BASIC
1 Darren McCaughan/199 2.50 6.00
2 Seth Beer/199 8.00 20.00
3 J.B. Bukauskas/199 3.00 8.00
4 Jake Burger/199 4.00 10.00
5 Tyler Johnson/199 2.50 6.00
6 Alex Faedo/199 3.00 8.00
7 TJ Friedl/199 2.00 5.00
8 Dalton Guthrie/199 3.00 8.00
9 Devin Hairston/199 2.50 6.00
10 KJ Harrison/199 3.00 8.00
11 Keston Hiura/199 6.00 15.00
12 Tanner Houck/199 5.00 12.00
13 Jeren Kendall/199 6.00 15.00
14 Alex Lange/199 3.00 8.00
15 Brendan McKay/199 8.00 20.00
16 Glenn Otto/199 2.00 5.00
17 David Peterson/199 2.50 6.00
18 Mike Rivera/199 2.00 5.00
19 Evan Skoug/199 2.50 6.00
20 Ricky Tyler Thomas/199 2.00 5.00
21 Taylor Walls/199 2.00 5.00
22 Tim Cate/199 2.50 6.00
23 Evan White/199 6.00 15.00
24 Kyle Wright/199 6.00 15.00
25 Nick Allen/199 2.50 6.00
26 Hans Crouse/199 5.00 12.00
27 Hagen Danner/199 2.50 6.00
28 Hunter Greene/199 6.00 15.00
29 Quentin Holmes/199 2.50 6.00
30 Royce Lewis/199 15.00 40.00
31 Nick Pratto/199 3.00 8.00
32 Logan Allen/199 2.00 5.00
33 Shane Baz/199 3.00 8.00
34 Jordan Butler/199 2.00 5.00
35 Blayne Enlow/199 2.50 6.00
36 M.J. Melendez/199 3.00 8.00
37 Mitchell Stone/199 2.00 5.00
38 CJ Van Eyk/199 2.00 5.00
39 Ryan Vilade/199 3.00 8.00
40 Patrick Bailey/199 6.00 15.00
41 Calvin Mitchell/199 4.00 10.00
42 Mike Siani/199 2.50 6.00
43 Brice Turang/199 6.00 15.00
44 Triston Casas/199 8.00 20.00
45 Nelson Berkwich/199 2.00 5.00
46 Coleman Brigman/99 2.50 6.00
47 Gabe Briones/199 2.00 5.00
48 Christian Cairo/99 2.00 5.00
49 Justin Campbell/199 2.50 6.00
50 Jasiah Dixon/199 3.00 8.00
51 Cade Doughty/199 3.00 8.00
52 Sammy Faltine/199 2.00 5.00
53 Nick Gorby/199 2.00 5.00
54 Tony Jacob/199 2.00 5.00
55 Jared Jones/199 2.00 5.00
56 Ethan Long/199 2.00 5.00
57 Zach Martinez/199 2.50 6.00
58 Joe Naranjo/199 2.00 5.00
59 Colton Olasin/199 4.00 10.00
60 Wesley Scott/199 2.50 6.00
61 Landon Sims/199 2.50 6.00
62 Anthony Volpe/199 6.00 15.00
63 Nate Wohlgemuth/199 3.00 8.00
64 Carter Young/199 3.00 8.00

2017 USA Baseball Stars and Stripes Trios Materials

RANDOM INSERTS IN PACKS
STATED PRINT RUN 199 SER.#'d SETS
*PRIME/25: 1X TO 2.5X BASIC
1 Ken/Hol/Lew 6.00 15.00
2 Gre/Fae/Hou 5.00 12.00
3 McK/Pet/Pra 6.00 15.00
4 Bur/Gre/Har 5.00 12.00
5 Dan/Buk/Wri 5.00 12.00
6 Dan/Cro/Gre 6.00 15.00
7 Ken/Bee/Fri 6.00 15.00
8 Harrison/White/Hiura 8.00 20.00
9 Buk/Fae/Hou 8.00 20.00
10 McK/Bur/Ken 5.00 12.00
11 Whitley/Anderson/Burdi 5.00 12.00
12 Puk/Kay/Gar 2.50 6.00
13 Rut/Ray/Ben 2.50 6.00
14 Cas/Tur/Gre 5.00 12.00
15 Bre/Ful/Swa 8.00 20.00

2018 USA Baseball Stars and Stripes

COMPLETE SET (100) 25.00 60.00
1 USA Baseball Collegiate CL .25 .60
2 Andrew Vaughn .75 2.00
3 Braden Shewmake .75 2.00
4 Bryce Tucker .25 .60
5 Cadyn Grenier .30 .75
6 Casey Mize 2.00 5.00
7 Dallas Woolfolk .25 .60
8 Gianluca Dalatri .25 .60
9 Grant Koch .25 .60
10 Jake McCarthy .40 1.00
11 Jeremy Eierman .30 .75
12 Johnny Aiello .25 .60
13 Jon Olsen .25 .60
14 Konnor Pilkington .30 .75
15 Nick Madrigal 1.50 4.00
16 Nick Meyer .30 .75
17 Nick Sprengel .25 .60
18 Patrick Raby .30 .75
19 Ryley Gilliam .30 .75
20 Sean Wymer .25 .60
21 Seth Beer 1.00 2.50
22 Steele Walker .30 .75
23 Steven Gingery .30 .75
24 Tim Cate .40 1.00
25 Travis Swaggerty .75 2.00
26 Tyler Frank .25 .60
27 Tyler Holton .30 .75
28 USA Baseball 18U CL .25 .60
29 Alek Thomas 1.00 2.50
30 Anthony Seigler .60 1.50
31 Brandon Dieter .25 .60
32 Brice Turang .75 2.00
33 Carter Young .25 .60
34 Cole Wilcox .40 1.00
35 Ethan Hankins .30 .75
36 Jarred Kelenic 2.50 6.00
37 Joseph Menefee .30 .75
38 JT Ginn .30 .75
39 Kumar Rocker .60 1.50
40 Landon Marceaux .25 .60
41 Mason Denaburg .30 .75
42 Matthew Liberatore .30 .75
43 Michael Siani .30 .75
44 Nolan Gorman 1.50 4.00
45 Raynel Delgado .60 1.50
46 Ryan Weathers .30 .75
47 Triston Casas 2.00 5.00
48 Will Banfield .25 .60
49 USA Baseball 15U CL .25 .60
50 Alejandro Rosario .50 1.25
51 Alek Boychuk .25 .60
52 Davis Diaz .25 .60
53 Dylan Crews .30 .75
54 Giuseppe Ferraro .25 .60
55 Grant Taylor .30 .75
56 Jackson Miller .25 .60
57 Joshua Hartle .30 .75
58 Lucas Gordon .25 .60
59 Mac Guscette .25 .60
60 Masyn Winn .25 .60
61 Michael Brooks .25 .60
62 Michael Flores .30 .75
63 Nelson Berkwich .25 .60
64 Pete Crow-Armstrong .75 2.00
65 Petey Halpin .40 1.00
66 Rawley Hector .30 .75
67 Robert Moore .25 .60
68 Roc Riggio .30 .75
69 Tanner Witt .25 .60
70 Royce Lewis 1.00 2.50
71 Brendan McKay .40 1.00
72 Kyle Wright .60 1.50
73 Adam Haseley .40 1.00
74 Keston Hiura .60 1.50
75 Jake Burger .25 .60
76 Shane Baz .30 .75
77 Nick Pratto .30 .75
78 J.B. Bukauskas .25 .60
79 Evan White .40 1.00
80 Alex Faedo .40 1.00
81 David Peterson .30 .75
82 Jeren Kendall .30 .75
83 Tanner Houck .60 1.50
84 Alex Lange .25 .60
85 Ryan Vilade .25 .60
86 M.J. Melendez .25 .60
87 Mark Vientos .40 1.00
88 Hagen Danner .25 .60
89 Quentin Holmes .25 .60
90 Hans Crouse .40 1.00
91 Brendan McKay .40 1.00
92 Blayne Enlow .25 .60
93 Taylor Walls .25 .60
94 Nick Allen .25 .60
95 KJ Harrison .40 1.00
96 Scott Hurst .30 .75
97 Alex Rodriguez .50 1.25
98 Frank Thomas .40 1.00
99 Ken Griffey Jr. .75 2.00
100 Mark McGwire .60 1.50

2018 USA Baseball Stars and Stripes Longevity

COMPLETE SET (100) 30.00 80.00
1 USA Baseball Collegiate CL .30 .75
2 Andrew Vaughn 1.00 2.50
3 Braden Shewmake 1.00 2.50
4 Bryce Tucker .30 .75
5 Cadyn Grenier .40 1.00
6 Casey Mize 2.50 6.00
7 Dallas Woolfolk .30 .75
8 Gianluca Dalatri .30 .75
9 Grant Koch .30 .75
10 Jake McCarthy .50 1.25
11 Jeremy Eierman .40 1.00
12 Johnny Aiello .30 .75
13 Jon Olsen .30 .75
14 Konnor Pilkington .40 1.00
15 Nick Madrigal 2.00 5.00
16 Nick Meyer .40 1.00
17 Nick Sprengel .30 .75
18 Patrick Raby .40 1.00
19 Ryley Gilliam .40 1.00
20 Sean Wymer .30 .75
21 Seth Beer 1.25 3.00
22 Steele Walker .40 1.00
23 Steven Gingery .40 1.00
24 Tim Cate .50 1.25
25 Travis Swaggerty 1.00 2.50
26 Tyler Frank .30 .75
27 Tyler Holton .40 1.00
28 USA Baseball 18U CL .30 .75
29 Alek Thomas 1.25 3.00
30 Anthony Seigler .75 2.00
31 Brandon Dieter .30 .75
32 Brice Turang 1.00 2.50
33 Carter Young .30 .75
34 Cole Wilcox .50 1.25
35 Ethan Hankins .40 1.00
36 Jarred Kelenic 3.00 8.00
37 Joseph Menefee .40 1.00
38 JT Ginn .40 1.00
39 Kumar Rocker .75 2.00
40 Landon Marceaux .30 .75
41 Mason Denaburg .40 1.00
42 Matthew Liberatore .40 1.00
43 Michael Siani .40 1.00
44 Nolan Gorman 2.00 5.00
45 Raynel Delgado .75 2.00
46 Ryan Weathers .40 1.00
47 Triston Casas 2.50 6.00
48 Will Banfield .30 .75
49 USA Baseball 15U CL .30 .75
50 Alejandro Rosario .60 1.50
51 Alek Boychuk .30 .75
52 Davis Diaz .30 .75
53 Dylan Crews .40 1.00
54 Giuseppe Ferraro .30 .75
55 Grant Taylor .40 1.00
56 Jackson Miller .30 .75
57 Joshua Hartle .40 1.00
58 Lucas Gordon .30 .75
59 Mac Guscette .30 .75
60 Masyn Winn .30 .75
61 Michael Brooks .30 .75
62 Michael Flores .40 1.00
63 Nelson Berkwich .30 .75
64 Pete Crow-Armstrong 1.00 2.50
65 Petey Halpin .50 1.25
66 Rawley Hector .40 1.00
67 Robert Moore .30 .75
68 Roc Riggio .40 1.00
69 Tanner Witt .30 .75
70 Royce Lewis 1.25 3.00
71 Brendan McKay .50 1.25
72 Kyle Wright .75 2.00
73 Adam Haseley .50 1.25
74 Keston Hiura .75 2.00
75 Jake Burger .30 .75
76 Shane Baz .40 1.00
77 Nick Pratto .40 1.00
78 J.B. Bukauskas .30 .75
79 Evan White .50 1.25
80 Alex Faedo .50 1.25
81 David Peterson .40 1.00
82 Jeren Kendall .40 1.00
83 Tanner Houck .75 2.00
84 Alex Lange .30 .75
85 Ryan Vilade .30 .75
86 M.J. Melendez .30 .75
87 Mark Vientos .50 1.25
88 Hagen Danner .30 .75
89 Quentin Holmes .30 .75
90 Hans Crouse .50 1.25
91 Brendan McKay .50 1.25
92 Blayne Enlow .30 .75
93 Taylor Walls .30 .75
94 Nick Allen .30 .75
95 KJ Harrison .50 1.25
96 Scott Hurst .40 1.00
97 Alex Rodriguez .60 1.50
98 Frank Thomas .50 1.25
99 Ken Griffey Jr. 1.00 2.50
100 Mark McGwire .75 2.00

2018 USA Baseball Stars and Stripes Longevity Gold Team Logo

*GOLD: 2X TO 5X BASIC
RANDOM INSERTS IN PACKS
STATED PRINT RUN 25 COPIES PER

2018 USA Baseball Stars and Stripes Longevity Holofoil

*HOLO: 1.2X TO 3X BASIC
RANDOM INSERTS IN PACKS
STATED PRINT RUN 99 COPIES PER

2018 USA Baseball Stars and Stripes Longevity Parallel

*PARALLEL: .5X TO 1.2X BASIC
RANDOM INSERTS IN PACKS

2018 USA Baseball Stars and Stripes Longevity Ruby

*RUBY: .75X TO 2X BASIC
RANDOM INSERTS IN PACKS
STATED PRINT RUN 249 COPIES PER

2018 USA Baseball Stars and Stripes Longevity Sapphire

*SAPPHIRE: 1.5X TO 4X BASIC
RANDOM INSERTS IN PACKS
STATED PRINT RUN 49 COPIES PER

2018 USA Baseball Stars and Stripes 14U Signatures

RANDOM INSERTS IN PACKS
PRINT RUNS B/WN 100-371 COPIES PER
*BLACK/21-23: .6X TO 1.5X BASIC
1 Blake Burke/174
2 Brady House/179 3.00 8.00
3 Cody Schrier/196
4 Collin Reuter/196
5 Cooper Kinney/176
6 Daniel Corona Jr./143 3.00 8.00
7 Davis Diaz/325 2.50 6.00
8 Deston Worthy/193 3.00 8.00
9 Diego Prieto/197 2.50 6.00
10 Eddie King Jr./192 3.00 8.00
11 Eldridge Armstrong III/192 2.50 6.00
13 Jacob Galloway/196
14 Jakob Schardt/185 2.50 6.00
15 Joseph Collier/180 4.00 10.00
16 Joshua Alger/174 2.50 6.00
17 Joshua Hartle/299 3.00 8.00
18 Joshua Reis/187
19 Josiah Chavez/181 2.50 6.00
20 Logan Forsythe/180
21 Luke Leto/184 12.00 30.00
22 Marcus Franco/175 2.50 6.00
23 Mario Bejarano/188 2.50 6.00
24 Nicholas DeMarco/193 2.50 6.00
25 Nicholas Kurtz/178 2.50 6.00
26 Preston Herce/100 2.50 6.00
27 Ray Cebulski/196 2.50 6.00
28 Ryan Bertran/191 2.50 6.00
29 Ryan Clifford/153 3.00 8.00
30 Stephen Hood/173 3.00 8.00
31 Thomas DiLandri/183 3.00 8.00
32 Thomas Splaine/178 3.00 8.00
33 Trevor Haskins/194 2.50 6.00
34 Trey Duffield/371 3.00 8.00
35 Tyler Avery/159 2.50 6.00
14NTTC Tyler Collins/193 2.50 6.00
37 Tyler Fullman/144 3.00 8.00
38 Tyree Reed/184 2.50 6.00
39 William Overton/182 2.50 6.00
40 Zachary Torres/192 3.00 8.00

2018 USA Baseball Stars and Stripes 15U Signatures

RANDOM INSERTS IN PACKS
PRINT RUNS B/WN 146-199 COPIES PER
*BLACK/25: .6X TO 1.5X BASIC
1 Alejandro Rosario/189 5.00 12.00
2 Alek Boychuk/195
3 Davis Diaz/199 2.50 6.00
4 Dylan Crews/194 3.00 8.00
5 Giuseppe Ferraro/146 2.50 6.00
6 Grant Taylor/199 3.00 8.00
7 Jackson Miller/194 2.50 6.00
8 Joshua Hartle/149 3.00 8.00
9 Lucas Gordon/190 2.50 6.00
10 Mac Guscette/189 2.50 6.00
11 Masyn Winn/190 2.50 6.00
12 Michael Brooks/189 2.50 6.00
13 Michael Flores/187 3.00 8.00
14 Nelson Berkwich/192 2.50 6.00
15 Pete Crow-Armstrong/187 5.00 12.00
16 Petey Halpin/192 4.00 10.00
17 Rawley Hector/188 3.00 8.00
18 Robert Moore/190 2.50 6.00
19 Roc Riggio/188 3.00 8.00
20 Tanner Witt/191 2.50 6.00

2018 USA Baseball Stars and Stripes 17U Signatures

RANDOM INSERTS IN PACKS
PRINT RUNS B/WN 141-499 COPIES PER
*BLACK/25: .6X TO 1.5X BASIC
1 Anthony Volpe/233 5.00 12.00
2 Blake Shapen/190
3 Bobby Witt Jr./181 20.00 50.00
4 Brandon Walker/495 2.50 6.00
5 Cade Doughty/178 2.50 6.00
6 Carter Young/499 2.50 6.00
7 Charles Burroughs/185 2.50 6.00
8 Christian Cairo/193 3.00 8.00
9 CJ Abrams/194 8.00 20.00
10 Coleman Brigman/184
11 Conagher Sands/186 2.50 6.00
12 Cooper Benson/184 8.00 20.00
13 Dillon Carter/186 2.50 6.00
14 Dutch Landis/184 2.50 6.00
15 Ethan Hearn/192
16 Grant Leader/192 8.00 20.00
17 Ian Mejia/185 2.50 6.00
18 Isaiah Bennett/189 3.00 8.00
19 Jaden Woodson/183 2.50 6.00
20 Jake Holland/171 3.00 8.00
21 Jamir Simpson/177 2.50 6.00
22 Jason Brandow/182 2.50 6.00
23 Joseph Charles/398 2.50 6.00
24 Joseph Naranjo/184 2.50 6.00
25 Josh Spiegel/174 2.50 6.00
26 Joshua Hahn/191 2.50 6.00
27 Matthew Allan/176 2.50 6.00
28 Matthew Thompson/175 3.00 8.00
29 Michael Carpentier Jr./192 2.50 6.00
30 Michael Limoncelli/191 2.50 6.00
31 Nate Wohlgemuth/173 2.50 6.00
32 Nolan Crisp/191 3.00 8.00
33 Raynel Delgado/499 3.00 8.00
34 Rece Hinds/141 10.00 25.00
35 Sam Siani/183 3.00 8.00
36 Spencer Jones/184 2.50 6.00
37 Stephen Wilmer/185 2.50 6.00
38 Victor Mederos/182 2.50 6.00
39 Wesley Scott/172 2.50 6.00
40 Zachary Martinez/209 2.50 6.00

2018 USA Baseball Stars and Stripes 18U Connections Signatures

RANDOM INSERTS IN PACKS
STATED PRINT RUN 25 SER.#'d SETS
1 K.Rocker/E.Hankins 30.00 80.00
2 B.Turang/N.Gorman 40.00 100.00
10 K.Rocker/B.Turang 30.00 80.00

2018 USA Baseball Stars and Stripes 18U Signatures Black Ink

RANDOM INSERTS IN PACKS
STATED PRINT RUN 499 SER.#'d SETS
*BLUE/25: .6X TO 1.5X BASIC
1 Will Banfield 2.50 6.00
3 Triston Casas 4.00 10.00
MD Mason Denaburg 3.00 8.00
9 Brandon Dieter 2.50 6.00
11 JT Ginn 3.00 8.00
12 Nolan Gorman 6.00 15.00
16 Ethan Hankins 3.00 8.00
19 Jarred Kelenic 10.00 25.00
21 Matthew Liberatore 3.00 8.00
22 Landon Marceaux 2.50 6.00
23 Anthony Seigler 5.00 12.00
24 Joseph Menefee 3.00 8.00
27 Kumar Rocker 8.00 20.00
28 Raynel Delgado 3.00 8.00
30 Michael Siani 4.00 10.00
31 Alek Thomas 4.00 10.00
33 Brice Turang 8.00 20.00
35 Ryan Weathers 3.00 8.00
37 Cole Wilcox 4.00 10.00
40 Carter Young 2.50 6.00

2018 USA Baseball Stars and Stripes Alumni Signatures

RANDOM INSERTS IN PACKS
STATED PRINT RUN 25 SER.#'d SETS
3 Mark McGwire 30.00 80.00
5 Roger Clemens
6 Nomar Garciaparra 15.00 40.00
7 Todd Helton 15.00 40.00
10 Barry Larkin 15.00 40.00
12 Alex Rodriguez
13 Frank Thomas

2018 USA Baseball Stars and Stripes Chinese Taipei Material Signatures

RANDOM INSERTS IN PACKS
PRINT RUNS B/WN 3-47 COPIES PER
NO PRICING ON QTY 11 OR LESS
8 Yen Ching Lu/47

2018 USA Baseball Stars and Stripes College Connections Signatures Blue Ink

RANDOM INSERTS IN PACKS
STATED PRINT RUN 25 SER.#'d SETS
1 C.Grenier/N.Madrigal 50.00 125.00
3 J.McCarthy/S.Beer 40.00 100.00
4 S.Gingery/K.Pilkington 10.00 25.00
5 J.Eierman/S.Beer 40.00 100.00
8 N.Meyer/J.McCarthy 12.00 30.00

2018 USA Baseball Stars and Stripes College Signatures Black Ink

RANDOM INSERTS IN PACKS
STATED PRINT RUN 499 SER.#'d SETS
*BLUE/25: .6X TO 1.5X BASIC
AV Andrew Vaughn 10.00 25.00
BSH Braden Shewmake 8.00 20.00
BT Bryce Tucker 2.50 6.00
CG Cadyn Grenier 3.00 8.00
CM Casey Mize 10.00 25.00
DW Dallas Woolfolk 2.50 6.00
GD Gianluca Dalatri 2.50 6.00
GK Grant Koch 2.50 6.00
JE Jeremy Eierman 3.00 8.00
JM Jake McCarthy 4.00 10.00
JO Jon Olsen 2.50 6.00
KP Konnor Pilkington 3.00 8.00
NMA Nick Madrigal 15.00 40.00
NME Nick Meyer 3.00 8.00
NS Nick Sprengel 2.50 6.00
PR Patrick Raby 3.00 8.00
RG Ryley Gilliam 3.00 8.00
SB Seth Beer 12.00 30.00
SG Steven Gingery 3.00 8.00
SWA Steele Walker 3.00 8.00
SWY Sean Wymer 2.50 6.00
TC Tim Cate 4.00 10.00
TF Tyler Frank 2.50 6.00
TH Tyler Holton 3.00 8.00
TS Travis Swaggerty 3.00 8.00

2018 USA Baseball Stars and Stripes Jumbo Materials

RANDOM INSERTS IN PACKS
PRINT RUNS B/WN 72-299 COPIES PER
*PRIME/20-25: .6X TO 1.5X BASIC
1 Andrew Vaughn/299 10.00 25.00
2 Braden Shewmake/299 6.00 15.00
3 Bryce Tucker/299 2.00 5.00
4 Cadyn Grenier/299 2.50 6.00
5 Casey Mize/299 6.00 15.00
6 Dallas Woolfolk/299 2.00 5.00
7 Gianluca Dalatri/299 2.00 5.00
8 Grant Koch/299 2.00 5.00
9 Jake McCarthy/299 3.00 8.00
10 Jeremy Eierman/299 2.50 6.00
11 Johnny Aiello/205 2.00 5.00
12 Jon Olsen/299 2.00 5.00
13 Konnor Pilkington/299 2.50 6.00
14 Nick Madrigal/237 12.00 30.00
15 Nick Meyer/299 2.50 6.00
16 Nick Sprengel/299 2.00 5.00
17 Patrick Raby/299 2.50 6.00
18 Ryley Gilliam/299 2.50 6.00
19 Sean Wymer/299 2.00 5.00
20 Seth Beer/299 10.00 25.00
21 Steele Walker/299 2.50 6.00
22 Steven Gingery/299 2.50 6.00
23 Tim Cate/299 3.00 8.00
24 Travis Swaggerty/299 6.00 15.00
25 Tyler Frank/299 2.00 5.00
26 Tyler Holton/299 2.50 6.00
27 Alek Thomas/299 4.00 10.00
28 Anthony Seigler/290 5.00 12.00
29 Brandon Dieter/299 2.00 5.00
30 Brice Turang/299 6.00 15.00
31 Carter Young/299 4.00 10.00
32 Cole Wilcox/299 3.00 8.00
33 Ethan Hankins/299 2.50 6.00
34 Jarred Kelenic/299 8.00 20.00
35 Joseph Menefee/228 2.50 6.00
36 JT Ginn/299 2.50 6.00
37 Kumar Rocker/299 5.00 12.00
38 Landon Marceaux/299 2.00 5.00
39 Mason Denaburg/72 2.50 6.00
40 Matthew Liberatore/299 2.50 6.00
41 Michael Siani/299 2.50 6.00
42 Nolan Gorman/299 12.00 30.00
43 Raynel Delgado/299 5.00 12.00
44 Ryan Weathers/299 2.50 6.00
45 Triston Casas/299 15.00 40.00
46 Will Banfield/190 2.00 5.00
47 Royce Lewis/299 8.00 20.00
48 Brendan McKay/299 3.00 8.00
49 Kyle Wright/285 5.00 12.00
50 Adam Haseley/72 3.00 8.00

2018 USA Baseball Stars and Stripes Material Signatures

RANDOM INSERTS IN PACKS
PRINT RUNS B/WN 99-299 COPIES PER
*PRIME/21-25: .6X TO 1.5X BASIC
1 Andrew Vaughn/299 10.00 25.00
2 Braden Shewmake/299 10.00 25.00
3 Bryce Tucker/299 3.00 8.00
4 Cadyn Grenier/299 4.00 10.00
5 Casey Mize/299 10.00 25.00
6 Dallas Woolfolk/299 3.00 8.00
7 Gianluca Dalatri/299 3.00 8.00
8 Grant Koch/299 3.00 8.00
9 Jake McCarthy/299 5.00 12.00
10 Jeremy Eierman/299 4.00 10.00
11 Johnny Aiello/299 3.00 8.00
12 Jon Olsen/299 3.00 8.00
13 Konnor Pilkington/299 4.00 10.00
14 Nick Madrigal/299 20.00 50.00
15 Nick Meyer/299 4.00 10.00
16 Nick Sprengel/299 3.00 8.00
17 Patrick Raby/299 4.00 10.00
18 Ryley Gilliam/299 4.00 10.00
19 Sean Wymer/299 3.00 8.00
20 Seth Beer/299 15.00 40.00
21 Steele Walker/299 4.00 10.00
22 Steven Gingery/299 4.00 10.00
23 Tim Cate/299 5.00 12.00
24 Travis Swaggerty/299 4.00 10.00
25 Tyler Frank/299 3.00 8.00
26 Tyler Holton/299 4.00 10.00
27 Alek Thomas/299 5.00 12.00
28 Anthony Seigler/299 8.00 20.00
29 Brandon Dieter/299 3.00 8.00
30 Brice Turang/299 10.00 25.00
31 Carter Young/299 3.00 8.00
32 Cole Wilcox/299 5.00 12.00
33 Ethan Hankins/299 4.00 10.00
34 Jarred Kelenic/299 12.00 30.00
35 Joseph Menefee/199 4.00 10.00
36 JT Ginn/299 4.00 10.00
37 Kumar Rocker/299 4.00 10.00
38 Landon Marceaux/299 3.00 8.00
39 Mason Denaburg/299 4.00 10.00
40 Matthew Liberatore/299 4.00 10.00
41 Michael Siani/299 5.00 12.00
42 Nolan Gorman/299 15.00 40.00
43 Raynel Delgado/299 4.00 10.00
44 Ryan Weathers/299 4.00 10.00
45 Triston Casas/299 8.00 20.00
46 Will Banfield/299 3.00 8.00
47 Alejandro Rosario/150 6.00 15.00
48 Alek Boychuk/146 3.00 8.00
49 Davis Diaz/186 3.00 8.00
50 Dylan Crews/199 4.00 10.00
51 Giuseppe Ferraro/193 3.00 8.00
52 Grant Taylor/150 4.00 10.00
53 Jackson Miller/289 3.00 8.00
54 Joshua Hartle/99 4.00 10.00
55 Lucas Gordon/199 3.00 8.00
56 Mac Guscette/199 3.00 8.00
57 Masyn Winn/199 3.00 8.00
58 Michael Brooks/199 3.00 8.00
59 Michael Flores/199 4.00 10.00
60 Nelson Berkwich/249 3.00 8.00
61 Pete Crow-Armstrong/199 6.00 15.00
62 Petey Halpin/199 5.00 12.00
63 Rawley Hector/199 4.00 10.00
64 Robert Moore/199 3.00 8.00
65 Roc Riggio/199 4.00 10.00
66 Tanner Witt/199 3.00 8.00

2018 USA Baseball Stars and Stripes Silhouettes Black Gold Signature Jerseys

RANDOM INSERTS IN PACKS
PRINT RUNS B/WN 25-99 COPIES PER
1 Andrew Vaughn/89 10.00 25.00
2 Braden Shewmake/84 10.00 25.00
3 Bryce Tucker/89 3.00 8.00
4 Cadyn Grenier/84 4.00 10.00
5 Casey Mize/89 25.00 60.00
6 Dallas Woolfolk/89 3.00 8.00
7 Gianluca Dalatri/91 3.00 8.00
8 Grant Koch/89 3.00 8.00
9 Jake McCarthy/84 5.00 12.00
10 Jeremy Eierman/87 4.00 10.00
11 Johnny Aiello/94 3.00 8.00
12 Jon Olsen/89 3.00 8.00
13 Konnor Pilkington/89 4.00 10.00
14 Nick Madrigal/89 20.00 50.00
15 Nick Meyer/89 4.00 10.00
16 Nick Sprengel/89 3.00 8.00
17 Patrick Raby/89 4.00 10.00
18 Ryley Gilliam/89 4.00 10.00
19 Sean Wymer/89 3.00 8.00
20 Seth Beer/89 15.00 40.00
21 Steele Walker/84 4.00 10.00
22 Steven Gingery/88 4.00 10.00
23 Tim Cate/89 5.00 12.00
24 Travis Swaggerty/84 10.00 25.00
25 Tyler Frank/99 3.00 8.00
26 Tyler Holton/89 4.00 10.00
27 Alek Thomas/84 5.00 12.00
28 Anthony Seigler/70 8.00 20.00
29 Brandon Dieter/84 3.00 8.00
30 Brice Turang/94 10.00 25.00
31 Carter Young/69 3.00 8.00
32 Cole Wilcox/89 5.00 12.00
33 Ethan Hankins/89 4.00 10.00
34 Jarred Kelenic/99 10.00 25.00
35 Joseph Menefee/39 4.00 10.00
36 JT Ginn/89 4.00 10.00
37 Kumar Rocker/89 8.00 20.00
38 Landon Marceaux/89 3.00 8.00
39 Mason Denaburg/89 4.00 10.00
40 Matthew Liberatore/89 4.00 10.00
41 Michael Siani/84 5.00 12.00
42 Nolan Gorman/84 20.00 50.00
43 Raynel Delgado/49 4.00 10.00
44 Ryan Weathers/89 4.00 10.00
45 Triston Casas/99 8.00 20.00
46 Will Banfield/85 3.00 8.00
47 Alejandro Rosario/89 6.00 15.00
48 Alek Boychuk/89 3.00 8.00
49 Davis Diaz/49 3.00 8.00
50 Dylan Crews/89 4.00 10.00
51 Giuseppe Ferraro/89 3.00 8.00
52 Grant Taylor/89 4.00 10.00
53 Jackson Miller/89 3.00 8.00
54 Joshua Hartle/64 4.00 10.00
55 Lucas Gordon/89 3.00 8.00
56 Mac Guscette/89 3.00 8.00
57 Masyn Winn/89 3.00 8.00
58 Michael Brooks/89 3.00 8.00
59 Michael Flores/89 4.00 10.00
60 Nelson Berkwich/89 3.00 8.00
61 Pete Crow-Armstrong/89 6.00 15.00
62 Petey Halpin/89 5.00 12.00
63 Rawley Hector/89 4.00 10.00
64 Robert Moore/89 3.00 8.00
65 Roc Riggio/89 4.00 10.00
66 Tanner Witt/89 3.00 8.00
67 Anthony Volpo/39 6.00 15.00
68 Blake Shapen/39 3.00 8.00
69 Bobby Witt Jr./49 20.00 50.00
70 Brandon Walker/44 3.00 8.00
71 Cade Doughty/39 3.00 8.00
72 Carter Young/49 3.00 8.00
73 Charles Burroughs/39 3.00 8.00
74 Christian Cairo/39 4.00 10.00
75 CJ Abrams/39 12.00 30.00
76 Coleman Brigman/39 6.00 15.00
77 Conagher Sands/39 3.00 8.00
78 Cooper Benson/39 3.00 8.00
79 Dillon Carter/39 3.00 8.00
80 Dutch Landis/39 3.00 8.00
81 Ethan Hearn/39
82 Grant Leader/39 6.00 15.00
83 Ian Mejia/39 3.00 8.00
84 Isaiah Bennett/39 4.00 10.00
85 Jaden Woodson/39 3.00 8.00
86 Jake Holland/39 4.00 10.00
87 Jamir Simpson/39 3.00 8.00
88 Jason Brandow/39 3.00 8.00
89 Joseph Charles/49 3.00 8.00
90 Joseph Naranjo/39 3.00 8.00
91 Josh Spiegel/39 3.00 8.00
92 Joshua Hahn/39 3.00 8.00
93 Matthew Allan/39 3.00 8.00
94 Matthew Thompson/39 4.00 10.00
95 Michael Carpentier Jr./39 3.00 8.00
96 Michael Limoncelli/39 3.00 8.00
97 Nate Wohlgemuth/39 3.00 8.00
98 Nolan Crisp/39 4.00 10.00
99 Raynel Delgado/49 4.00 10.00
100 Rece Hinds/44 12.00 30.00
101 Sam Siani/39 4.00 10.00
102 Spencer Jones/39 3.00 8.00
103 Stephen Wilmer/39 3.00 8.00
104 Victor Mederos/39 3.00 8.00
105 Wesley Scott/39 3.00 8.00
106 Zachary Martinez/74 3.00 8.00
107 Blake Burke/39 3.00 8.00
108 Brady House/39 4.00 10.00
109 Cody Schrier/39 3.00 8.00
110 Collin Reuter/39 3.00 8.00
111 Cooper Kinney/39 3.00 8.00
112 Daniel Corona Jr./39 4.00 10.00
113 Davis Diaz/49 3.00 8.00
114 Deston Worthy/39 4.00 10.00
115 Diego Prieto/39 3.00 8.00
116 Eddie King Jr./39 3.00 8.00
117 Eldridge Armstrong III/39 3.00 8.00
119 Jacob Galloway/43 8.00 20.00
120 Jakob Schardt/39 3.00 8.00
121 Joseph Collier/39 10.00 25.00
122 Joshua Alger/39 3.00 8.00
123 Joshua Hartle/64 4.00 10.00
124 Joshua Reis/39
125 Josiah Chavez/39 3.00 8.00
126 Logan Forsythe/39 3.00 8.00
127 Luke Leto/39
128 Marcus Franco/39 3.00 8.00
129 Mario Bejarano/25 5.00 12.00
130 Nicholas DeMarco/39 3.00 8.00
131 Nicholas Kurtz/39 3.00 8.00
132 Preston Herce/49 3.00 8.00
133 Ray Cebulski/39 3.00 8.00
134 Ryan Bertran/39 3.00 8.00
135 Ryan Clifford/29 4.00 10.00
136 Stephen Hood/39 4.00 10.00
137 Thomas DiLandri/39 4.00 10.00
138 Thomas Splaine/39 4.00 10.00
139 Trevor Haskins/39 3.00 8.00
140 Trey Duffield/39 4.00 10.00
141 Tyler Avery/39 3.00 8.00
142 Tyler Collins/39 3.00 8.00
143 Tyler Fullman/45 4.00 10.00
144 Tyree Reed/37 3.00 8.00
145 William Overton/39 3.00 8.00
146 Zachary Torres/44 4.00 10.00

2018 USA Baseball Stars and Stripes Silhouettes Signature Bats

RANDOM INSERTS IN PACKS
PRINT RUNS B/WN 20-49 COPIES PER
2 Braden Shewmake/49 10.00 25.00
4 Cadyn Grenier/25 6.00 15.00
9 Jake McCarthy/49 5.00 12.00
10 Jeremy Eierman/49 4.00 10.00
21 Steele Walker/49 4.00 10.00
24 Travis Swaggerty/49 10.00 25.00
27 Alek Thomas/49 5.00 12.00
28 Anthony Seigler/49 8.00 20.00
29 Brandon Dieter/49 3.00 8.00
30 Brice Turang/49 10.00 25.00
31 Carter Young/35 3.00 8.00
34 Jarred Kelenic/49 30.00 80.00
41 Michael Siani/49 5.00 12.00
42 Nolan Gorman/49 20.00 50.00
43 Raynel Delgado/49 4.00 10.00
45 Triston Casas/49 8.00 20.00
46 Will Banfield/49 3.00 8.00
72 Carter Young/35 3.00 8.00
99 Raynel Delgado/49 4.00 10.00
147 Royce Lewis/20 15.00 40.00
148 Brendan McKay/49 5.00 12.00
151 Keston Hiura/49 8.00 20.00
152 Jake Burger/39 3.00 8.00
154 Nick Pratto/31 4.00 10.00
156 Evan White/49 5.00 12.00
163 M.J. Melendez/43 3.00 8.00
165 Hagen Danner/49 3.00 8.00
166 Quentin Holmes/39 3.00 8.00
170 Taylor Walls/20 5.00 12.00
171 Nick Allen/33 3.00 8.00
172 KJ Harrison/39 5.00 12.00

2018 USA Baseball Stars and Stripes Silhouettes Signature Jerseys

RANDOM INSERTS IN PACKS
PRINT RUNS B/WN 49-199 COPIES PER
*PRIME/20-25: .6X TO 1.5X BASIC
1 Andrew Vaughn/199 10.00 25.00
2 Braden Shewmake/199 10.00 25.00
3 Bryce Tucker/199 3.00 8.00
4 Cadyn Grenier/199 4.00 10.00
5 Casey Mize/199 10.00 25.00
6 Dallas Woolfolk/199 3.00 8.00
7 Gianluca Dalatri/199 3.00 8.00
8 Grant Koch/199 3.00 8.00
9 Jake McCarthy/199 5.00 12.00
10 Jeremy Eierman/199 4.00 10.00
11 Johnny Aiello/199 3.00 8.00
12 Jon Olson/199 3.00 8.00
13 Konnor Pilkington/199 4.00 10.00
14 Nick Madrigal/199 8.00 20.00
15 Nick Meyer/199 4.00 10.00
16 Nick Sprengel/199 3.00 8.00
17 Patrick Raby/199 4.00 10.00
18 Ryley Gilliam/199 4.00 10.00
19 Sean Wymer/199 3.00 8.00
20 Seth Beer/199 15.00 40.00
21 Steele Walker/199 4.00 10.00
22 Steven Gingery/199 4.00 10.00
23 Tim Cate/199 5.00 12.00
24 Travis Swaggerty/199 10.00 25.00
25 Tyler Frank/199 3.00 8.00
26 Tyler Holton/199 4.00 10.00
27 Alek Thomas/199 5.00 12.00
28 Anthony Seigler/199 8.00 20.00
29 Brandon Dieter/199 3.00 8.00
30 Brice Turang/199 10.00 25.00
31 Carter Young/199 3.00 8.00
32 Cole Wilcox/199 5.00 12.00
33 Ethan Hankins/199 4.00 10.00
34 Jarred Kelenic/199 10.00 25.00
35 Joseph Menefee/150 4.00 10.00
36 JT Ginn/199 4.00 10.00
37 Kumar Rocker/199 12.00 30.00
38 Landon Marceaux/199 3.00 8.00
39 Mason Denaburg/199 4.00 10.00
40 Matthew Liberatore/199 4.00 10.00
41 Michael Siani/199 5.00 12.00
42 Nolan Gorman/199 20.00 50.00
43 Raynel Delgado/199 4.00 10.00
44 Ryan Weathers/199 4.00 10.00
45 Triston Casas/199 8.00 20.00
46 Will Banfield/199 3.00 8.00
47 Alejandro Rosario/199 6.00 15.00
48 Alek Boychuk/199 3.00 8.00
49 Davis Diaz/99 3.00 8.00
50 Dylan Crews/142 4.00 10.00
51 Giuseppe Ferraro/199 3.00 8.00
52 Grant Taylor/189 4.00 10.00
53 Jackson Miller/52 3.00 8.00
54 Joshua Hartle/149 4.00 10.00
55 Lucas Gordon/149 3.00 8.00
56 Mac Guscette/149 3.00 8.00
57 Masyn Winn/149 3.00 8.00
58 Michael Brooks/149 3.00 8.00
59 Michael Flores/149 4.00 10.00
60 Nelson Berkwich/179 3.00 8.00
61 Pete Crow-Armstrong/149 6.00 15.00
62 Petey Halpin/149 5.00 12.00
63 Rawley Hector/149 4.00 10.00
64 Robert Moore/149 3.00 8.00
65 Roc Riggio/149 4.00 10.00
66 Tanner Witt/149 3.00 8.00
67 Anthony Volpe/150 6.00 15.00
68 Blake Shapen/199 3.00 8.00
69 Bobby Witt Jr./199 10.00 25.00
70 Brandon Walker/84 3.00 8.00
71 Cade Doughty/199 3.00 8.00
72 Carter Young/199 3.00 8.00
73 Charles Burroughs/199 3.00 8.00
74 Christian Cairo/199 4.00 10.00
75 CJ Abrams/199 12.00 30.00
76 Coleman Brigman/199 6.00 15.00
77 Conagher Sands/199 3.00 8.00
78 Cooper Benson/199 3.00 8.00
79 Dillon Carter/199 3.00 8.00
80 Dutch Landis/199 3.00 8.00
81 Ethan Hearn/199
82 Grant Leader/199 6.00 15.00
83 Ian Mejia/199 3.00 8.00
84 Isaiah Bennett/199 4.00 10.00
85 Jaden Woodson/199 3.00 8.00
86 Jake Holland/199 4.00 10.00
87 Jamir Simpson/199 3.00 8.00
88 Jason Brandow/199 3.00 8.00
89 Joseph Charles/199 3.00 8.00
90 Joseph Naranjo/199 3.00 8.00
91 Josh Spiegel/199 3.00 8.00
92 Joshua Hahn/199 3.00 8.00
93 Matthew Allan/199 3.00 8.00
94 Matthew Thompson/199 4.00 10.00
95 Michael Carpentier Jr./199 3.00 8.00
96 Michael Limoncelli/199 3.00 8.00
97 Nate Wohlgemuth/199 3.00 8.00
98 Nolan Crisp/199 4.00 10.00
99 Raynel Delgado/199 4.00 10.00
100 Rece Hinds/199 12.00 30.00
101 Sam Siani/199 4.00 10.00
102 Spencer Jones/199 3.00 8.00
103 Stephen Wilmer/199 3.00 8.00
104 Victor Mederos/199 3.00 8.00
105 Wesley Scott/199 3.00 8.00
106 Zachary Martinez/199 3.00 8.00
107 Blake Burke/199 3.00 8.00
108 Brady House/199 4.00 10.00
109 Cody Schrier/199 3.00 8.00
110 Collin Reuter/199 3.00 8.00
111 Cooper Kinney/199 3.00 8.00
112 Daniel Corona Jr./199 4.00 10.00
113 Davis Diaz/99 3.00 8.00
114 Deston Worthy/199 4.00 10.00
115 Diego Prieto/199 3.00 8.00
116 Eddie King Jr./199 3.00 8.00
117 Eldridge Armstrong III/199 3.00 8.00
119 Jacob Galloway/199 8.00 20.00
120 Jakob Schardt/199 3.00 8.00
121 Joseph Collier/199 10.00 25.00
122 Joshua Alger/199 3.00 8.00
123 Joshua Hartle/149 4.00 10.00
124 Joshua Reis/199
125 Josiah Chavez/199 3.00 8.00
126 Logan Forsythe/199 3.00 8.00
127 Luke Leto/199
128 Marcus Franco/199 3.00 8.00
129 Mario Bejarano/199 3.00 8.00
130 Nicholas DeMarco/199 3.00 8.00
131 Nicholas Kurtz/199 3.00 8.00
132 Preston Herce/199 3.00 8.00
133 Ray Cebulski/199 3.00 8.00
134 Ryan Bertran/199 3.00 8.00
135 Ryan Clifford/199 4.00 10.00
136 Stephen Hood/199 4.00 10.00
137 Thomas DiLandri/199 4.00 10.00
138 Thomas Splaine/199 4.00 10.00
139 Trevor Haskins/199 3.00 8.00
141 Tyler Avery/199 3.00 8.00
142 Tyler Collins/199 3.00 8.00

143 Tyler Fullman/199 4.00 10.00
144 Tyree Reed/199 3.00 8.00
145 William Overton/199 3.00 8.00
146 Zachary Torres/194 4.00 10.00
147 Royce Lewis/199 10.00 25.00
148 Brendan McKay/199 5.00 12.00
149 Kyle Wright/199 8.00 20.00
151 Keston Hiura/137 10.00 25.00
152 Jake Burger/195 3.00 8.00
153 Shane Baz/199 4.00 10.00
154 Nick Pratto/84 4.00 10.00
155 J.B. Bukauskas/121 3.00 8.00
156 Evan White/161 5.00 12.00
157 Alex Faedo/199 5.00 12.00
158 David Peterson/199 4.00 10.00
159 Jeren Kendall/166 4.00 10.00
160 Tanner Houck/199 8.00 20.00
161 Alex Lange/199 3.00 8.00
162 Ryan Vilade/168 3.00 8.00
163 M.J. Melendez/199 3.00 8.00
165 Hagen Danner/199 3.00 8.00
166 Quentin Holmes/199 3.00 8.00
167 Hans Crouse/153 5.00 12.00
169 Blayne Enlow/199 3.00 8.00
170 Taylor Walls/49 3.00 8.00
171 Nick Allen/82 3.00 8.00
172 KJ Harrison/103 5.00 12.00

2018 USA Baseball Stars and Stripes Stars and Stripes Alumni Signatures

RANDOM INSERTS IN PACKS
STATED PRINT RUN 299 SER.#'d SETS
1 Bobby Witt 4.00 10.00
3 Kyle Tucker 4.00 10.00
4 David Matranga 4.00 10.00

2018 USA Baseball Stars and Stripes Tools of the Trade

RANDOM INSERTS IN PACKS
PRINT RUNS B/WN 199-299 COPIES PER
*PRIME/20-25: .6X TO 1.5X BASIC
1 Andrew Vaughn/299 10.00 25.00
2 Braden Shewmake/299 6.00 15.00
3 Bryce Tucker/299 2.00 5.00
4 Cadyn Grenier/299 2.50 6.00
5 Casey Mize/299 6.00 15.00
6 Dallas Woolfolk/299 2.00 5.00
7 Gianluca Dalatri/299 2.00 5.00
8 Grant Koch/299 2.00 5.00
9 Jake McCarthy/299 3.00 8.00
10 Jeremy Eierman/299 2.50 6.00
11 Johnny Aiello/290 2.00 5.00
12 Jon Olsen/299 2.00 5.00
13 Konnor Pilkington/299 2.50 6.00
14 Nick Madrigal/205 12.00 30.00
15 Nick Meyer/299 2.50 6.00
16 Nick Sprengel/299 2.00 5.00
17 Patrick Raby/299 2.50 6.00
18 Ryley Gilliam/299 2.50 6.00
19 Sean Wymer/299 2.00 5.00
20 Seth Beer/299 10.00 25.00
21 Steele Walker/299 2.50 6.00
22 Steven Gingery/299 2.50 6.00
23 Tim Cate/299 3.00 8.00
24 Travis Swaggerty/299 3.00 8.00
25 Tyler Frank/299 2.00 5.00
26 Tyler Holton/299 2.50 6.00
27 Alek Thomas/299 4.00 10.00
28 Anthony Seigler/299 5.00 12.00
29 Brandon Dieter/299 2.00 5.00
30 Brice Turang/299 6.00 15.00
31 Carter Young/299 4.00 10.00
32 Cole Wilcox/299 3.00 8.00
33 Ethan Hankins/299 2.50 6.00
34 Jarred Kelenic/299 8.00 20.00
35 Joseph Menefee/205 2.50 6.00
36 JT Ginn/299 2.50 6.00
37 Kumar Rocker/299 5.00 12.00
38 Landon Marceaux/260 2.00 5.00
39 Mason Denaburg/199 2.50 6.00
40 Matthew Liberatore/299 2.50 6.00
41 Michael Siani/299 2.50 6.00
42 Nolan Gorman/299 12.00 30.00
43 Raynel Delgado/299 5.00 12.00
44 Ryan Weathers/299 2.50 6.00
45 Triston Casas/299 15.00 40.00
46 Will Banfield/299 2.00 5.00
47 Royce Lewis/299 8.00 20.00
48 Brendan McKay/299 3.00 8.00
49 Kyle Wright/205 5.00 12.00
50 Adam Haseley/149 3.00 8.00

2019 USA Baseball Stars and Stripes

COMPLETE SET (100)
1 USA Baseball Collegiate Team Checklist .30
.75
2 Kyle Brnovich .30 .75
3 Matt Cronin .30 .75
4 Mason Feole .30 .75
5 Dominic Fletcher .30 .75
6 Josh Jung 1.00 2.50
7 Shea Langeliers .60 1.50
8 Andre Pallante .40 1.00
9 Adley Rutschman 2.00 5.00
10 Braden Shewmake 1.00 2.50
11 Bryson Stott 1.00 2.50
12 Spencer Torkelson 4.00 10.00
13 Andrew Vaughn 1.00 2.50
14 Max Meyer 1.00 2.50
15 Tanner Burns .50 1.25
16 Zack Thompson .50 1.25
17 Zack Hess .30 .75
18 Zach Watson .50 1.25
19 Will Wilson .50 1.25
20 Drew Parrish .30 .75
21 Parker Caracci .30 .75
22 John Doxakis .50 1.25
23 Graeme Stinson .30 .75
24 Kenyon Yovan .30 .75
25 Jake Agnos .50 1.25
26 Daniel Cabrera 1.25 3.00
27 Bryant Packard .50 1.25
28 USA Baseball 18U Team Checklist .30 .75
29 CJ Abrams 1.50 4.00
30 Tyler Callihan .40 1.00
31 Corbin Carroll .50 1.25
32 Riley Cornelio .30 .75
33 Pete Crow-Armstrong 1.00 2.50
34 Riley Greene 1.25 3.00
35 Ryan Hawks .30 .75
36 Dylan Crews .40 1.00
37 Sammy Faltine
38 Jared Kelley .30 .75
39 Jack Leiter .40 1.00
40 Brennan Malone .30 .75
41 Jacob Meador .30 .75
42 Timmy Manning .50 1.25
43 Max Rajcic .30 .75
44 Yohandy Morales .30 .75
45 Avery Short .30 .75
46 Drew Romo .75 2.00
47 Anthony Volpe 1.00 2.50
48 Bobby Witt Jr. 1.25 3.00
49 USA Baseball 15U Team Checklist .30 .75
50 Ryan Spikes .30 .75
51 Davis Diaz .30 .75
52 Ryan Rolison .30 .75
53 Tyree Reed .30 .75
54 Rheego McIntosh .30 .75
55 Karson Bowen .30 .75
56 Justin Colon .40 1.00
57 Gage Ziehl .30 .75
58 Cale Lansville .30 .75
59 Ryan Clifford .30 .75
60 Samuel Dutton .30 .75
61 Joseph Brown .30 .75
62 Cody Schrier .30 .75
63 Charlie Saum .30 .75
64 Luke Leto .60 1.50
65 Andrew Painter .50 1.25
66 Brady House .50 1.25
67 Joshua Hartle .30 .75
68 Christian Little .30 .75
69 Thomas DiLandri .30 .75
70 Casey Mize .75 2.00
71 Nick Madrigal 1.00 2.50
72 Jarred Kelenic 1.25 3.00
73 Ryan Weathers .30 .75
74 Travis Swaggerty .50 1.25
75 Connor Scott .40 1.00
76 Matthew Liberatore .30 .75
77 Nico Hoerner 1.00 2.50
78 Nolan Gorman 1.00 2.50
79 Brice Turang .40 1.00
80 Anthony Seigler .50 1.25
81 Triston Casas 1.25 3.00
82 Mason Denaburg .40 1.00
83 Seth Beer .75 2.00
84 Ethan Hankins .40 1.00
85 Cadyn Grenier .40 1.00
86 Jake McCarthy .50 1.25
87 Steele Walker .40 1.00
88 Riley Greene 1.25 3.00
89 Bobby Witt Jr. 1.25 3.00
90 Zack Thompson .50 1.25
91 Shea Langeliers .60 1.50
92 Adley Rutschman 2.00 5.00
93 CJ Abrams 1.50 4.00
94 Josh Jung 1.00 2.50
95 Bryson Stott 1.00 2.50
96 Brennan Malone .30 .75
97 Dominic Fletcher .30 .75
98 Graeme Stinson .30 .75
99 Braden Shewmake 1.00 2.50
100 Zach Watson .50 1.25

2019 USA Baseball Stars and Stripes Longevity

COMPLETE SET (100)

2019 USA Baseball Stars and Stripes Longevity Gold Team Logo

*GOLD: 2X TO 5X BASIC
RANDOM INSERTS IN PACKS
STATED PRINT RUN 25 COPIES PER

2019 USA Baseball Stars and Stripes Longevity Holofoil

*HOLO: 1.2X TO 3X BASIC
RANDOM INSERTS IN PACKS
STATED PRINT RUN 99 COPIES PER

2019 USA Baseball Stars and Stripes Longevity Parallel

*PARALLEL: .5X TO 1.2X BASIC
RANDOM INSERTS IN PACKS

2019 USA Baseball Stars and Stripes Longevity Ruby

*RUBY: .75X TO 2X BASIC
RANDOM INSERTS IN PACKS
STATED PRINT RUN 249 COPIES PER

2019 USA Baseball Stars and Stripes Longevity Sapphire

*SAPPHIRE: 1.5X TO 4X BASIC
RANDOM INSERTS IN PACKS
STATED PRINT RUN 49 COPIES PER

2019 USA Baseball Stars and Stripes 15U Signatures

RANDOM INSERTS IN PACKS
STATED PRINT RUN 299 SER.#'d SETS
*BLACK/25: .6X TO 1.5X BASIC
1 Ryan Spikes 2.50 6.00
2 Davis Diaz 2.50 6.00
4 Tyree Reed 2.50 6.00
5 Rheego McIntosh 2.50 6.00
6 Karson Bowen 2.50 6.00
7 Justin Colon 3.00 8.00
8 Gage Ziehl 2.50 6.00
9 Cale Lansville 2.50 6.00
10 Ryan Clifford 2.50 6.00
11 Samuel Dutton 2.50 6.00
12 Joseph Brown 2.50 6.00
13 Cody Schrier 2.50 6.00
14 Charlie Saum 2.50 6.00
15 Luke Leto 5.00 12.00
16 Andrew Painter 4.00 10.00
17 Brady House 4.00 10.00
18 Joshua Hartle 2.50 6.00
19 Christian Little 2.50 6.00
20 Thomas DiLandri 2.50 6.00

2019 USA Baseball Stars and Stripes 16U Signatures

RANDOM INSERTS IN PACKS
PRINT RUNS B/WN 53-399 COPIES PER
*BLACK/25: .6X TO 1.5X BASIC
1 Philip Abner/166 2.50 6.00
2 Walter Ahuna/169 2.50 6.00
3 Matthew Bardowell/165 2.50 6.00
4 Hunter Barnhart/399 2.50 6.00
5 Braylon Bishop/183 2.50 6.00
6 Nick Bitsko/166 2.50 6.00
7 Irving Carter/166 2.50 6.00
8 Dylan Crews/399 3.00 8.00
9 Jonathan Cymrot/174 2.50 6.00
10 Joe Dixon/170 2.50 6.00
11 Ross Dunn/165 2.50 6.00
12 Alex Edmondson/165 2.50 6.00
13 Landen Looper/165 2.50 6.00
14 Hunter Haas/180
15 Miles Halligan/176 2.50 6.00
16 Petey Halpin/167 5.00 12.00
17 Rawley Hector/166 2.50 6.00
18 Cason Henry/176 2.50 6.00
19 Jesse Herrera III/168 2.50 6.00
20 Reece Holbrook/177
21 Sam Hunt/165 2.50 6.00
22 Kennedy Jones/165 2.50 6.00
23 Jordan Lawlar/165 2.50 6.00
24 Caleb Lomavita/169 2.50 6.00
25 Evan Maldonado/176 2.50 6.00
26 Marcelo Mayer/173 2.50 6.00
27 Jayden Melendez/53 2.50 6.00
28 Ian Moller/168 4.00 10.00
29 Christian Moore/168 3.00 8.00
30 Robert Moore/183 2.50 6.00
31 Izaac Pacheco/166 2.50 6.00
32 Roc Riggio/177 2.50 6.00
33 Austin Stracener/174 2.50 6.00
34 Grant Taylor/166 2.50 6.00
35 Hunter Teplansky/176 2.50 6.00
36 Jabin Trosky/177 4.00 10.00
37 Tanner Witt/167 3.00 8.00

2019 USA Baseball Stars and Stripes 17U Signatures

RANDOM INSERTS IN PACKS
PRINT RUNS B/WN 147-499 COPIES PER
*BLACK/23-25: .6X TO 1.5X BASIC
1 Mick Abel/166 4.00 10.00
2 Nelson Berkwich/160 2.50 6.00
3 Drew Bowser/167 2.50 6.00
4 Alek Boychuk/168
5 Enrique Bradfield/174 2.50 6.00
6 Jack Bulger/166 2.50 6.00
7 Max Carlson/168 2.50 6.00
8 Gavin Casas/166 2.50 6.00
9 Kellum Clark/167 2.50 6.00
10 Nate Clow/178 2.50 6.00
11 Dylan Crews/410 3.00 8.00
12 Pete Crow-Armstrong/499 5.00 12.00
13 Jamar Fairweather/170 2.50 6.00
14 Brandon Fields/174 2.50 6.00
15 Dax Fulton/147 2.50 6.00
16 Alex Greene/174 2.50 6.00
17 Austin Hendrick/178 6.00 15.00
18 Jared Jones/176 3.00 8.00
19 Colton Keith/166 3.00 8.00
20 Jared Kelley/499 5.00 12.00
21 Christian Knapczyk/183 2.50 6.00
22 Avery Mabe/153 2.50 6.00
23 Nolan McLean/178
24 Victor Mederos/166 2.50 6.00
25 Yohandy Morales/499 2.50 6.00
26 Aaron Nixon/168 3.00 8.00
27 Liam Norris/166 2.50 6.00
28 Jack O'Dowd/174 2.50 6.00
29 Caleb Pendleton/175 2.50 6.00
30 Brett Percival/166 2.50 6.00
31 Jackson Phipps/167 3.00 8.00
32 Max Rajcic/499 2.50 6.00
33 Jordan Rollins/175
34 Drew Romo/499 6.00 15.00
35 Blake Shapen/170 2.50 6.00
36 Josh Shuler/171 2.50 6.00
37 Carson Tucker/176 10.00 25.00
38 Anthony Volpe/499 8.00 20.00
39 Masyn Winn/183 3.00 8.00
40 Nate Wohlgemuth/169 2.50 6.00
41 Carter Young/219 2.50 6.00
42 Macauley Horvath/171 2.50 6.00

2019 USA Baseball Stars and Stripes 18U Connections Signatures Blue Ink

RANDOM INSERTS IN PACKS
STATED PRINT RUN 25 SER.#'d SETS
3 Witt Jr/Abrams 20.00 50.00
10 Witt/Witt Jr. 20.00 50.00

2019 USA Baseball Stars and Stripes 18U Signatures Black Ink

RANDOM INSERTS IN PACKS
STATED PRINT RUN 499 SER.#'d SETS
*BLUE/25: .6X TO 1.5X BASIC
1 CJ Abrams 10.00 25.00
6 Tyler Callihan 3.00 8.00
7 Corbin Carroll 4.00 10.00
9 Riley Cornelio 2.50 6.00
10 Pete Crow-Armstrong 5.00 12.00
13 Sammy Faltine
15 Riley Greene 10.00 25.00
17 Ryan Hawks 2.50 6.00
23 Jared Kelley 2.50 6.00
24 Jack Leiter 8.00 20.00
25 Brennan Malone 2.50 6.00
26 Jacob Meador 2.50 6.00
33 Max Rajcic 2.50 6.00
36 Avery Short 2.50 6.00
39 Anthony Volpe 8.00 20.00
42 Bobby Witt Jr. 15.00 40.00
45 Dylan Crews 3.00 8.00
46 Timmy Manning 4.00 10.00
47 Yohandy Morales 2.50 6.00
48 Drew Romo 6.00 15.00

2019 USA Baseball Stars and Stripes Alumni 40th Anniversary Signatures

RANDOM INSERTS IN PACKS
PRINT RUNS B/WN 25-199 COPIES PER
1 Alex Rodriguez/25 50.00 120.00
2 David Matranga/199 3.00 8.00
11 Roger Clemens/25

2019 USA Baseball Stars and Stripes Alumni Signatures

RANDOM INSERTS IN PACKS
STATED PRINT RUN 25 SER.#'d SETS
1 Ken Griffey Jr.
4 Mike Mussina 12.00 30.00

2019 USA Baseball Stars and Stripes Chinese Taipei Silhouettes Signatures Jerseys Prime

RANDOM INSERTS IN PACKS
PRINT RUNS B/WN 1-20 COPIES PER
NO PRICING ON QTY 19 OR LESS
2 Chien Lung Huang/20 25.00 60.00
3 Chia Chun Tang/20
4 Yu Hsiang Lin/20 6.00 15.00
7 Tsung Hao Wang/20
8 Hsiang Ying Wang/20
9 Wei Fan Tsai/20 6.00 15.00
13 Chia Wei Huang/20
19 Chun Kai Liao/20
20 Chien Ming Chiang/20

2019 USA Baseball Stars and Stripes College Connections Signatures Blue Ink

RANDOM INSERTS IN PACKS
STATED PRINT RUN 25 SER.#'d SETS
3 Zach Watson
Zack Hess
5 Adley Rutschman
Shea Langeliers
6 Braden Shewmake 12.00 30.00
Josh Jung
8 Andre Pallante
Kyle Brnovich
9 Mason Feole 8.00 20.00
Zack Thompson
10 Andrew Vaughn
Bryson Stott
12 Braden Shewmake
John Doxakis
13 Dominic Fletcher
Matt Cronin

2019 USA Baseball Stars and Stripes College Signatures Black Ink

RANDOM INSERTS IN PACKS
STATED PRINT RUN 499 SER.#'d SETS
*BLUE/25: .6X TO 1.5X BASIC
1 Kyle Brnovich 2.50 6.00
2 Matt Cronin 2.50 6.00
3 Mason Feole 2.50 6.00
4 Dominic Fletcher 2.50 6.00
5 Josh Jung 8.00 20.00
6 Shea Langeliers 5.00 12.00
7 Andre Pallante 3.00 8.00
8 Adley Rutschman 25.00 60.00
10 Braden Shewmake 8.00 20.00
11 Bryson Stott 8.00 20.00
12 Spencer Torkelson 25.00 60.00
13 Andrew Vaughn 10.00 25.00
15 Max Meyer 6.00 15.00
16 Tanner Burns 4.00 10.00
18 Zack Thompson 4.00 10.00
21 Zack Hess 2.50 6.00
23 Zach Watson 4.00 10.00
24 Will Wilson 4.00 10.00
25 Drew Parrish 2.50 6.00
29 Parker Caracci 2.50 6.00
30 John Doxakis 4.00 10.00
33 Graeme Stinson 2.50 6.00
34 Kenyon Yovan 2.50 6.00
35 Jake Agnos 4.00 10.00
36 Daniel Cabrera 10.00 25.00
37 Bryant Packard 4.00 10.00

2019 USA Baseball Stars and Stripes Jumbo Materials

RANDOM INSERTS IN PACKS
PRINT RUN B/TW 25-299 COPIES PER
1 Kyle Brnovich/299 2.00 5.00
2 Matt Cronin/299 2.00 5.00
3 Mason Feole/299 2.00 5.00
4 Dominic Fletcher/299 2.00 5.00
5 Josh Jung/299 6.00 15.00
6 Shea Langeliers/299 4.00 10.00
7 Andre Pallante/299 2.50 6.00
8 Adley Rutschman/299 10.00 25.00
9 Braden Shewmake/299 6.00 15.00
10 Bryson Stott/299 6.00 15.00
11 Spencer Torkelson/299 10.00 25.00
12 Andrew Vaughn/299 6.00 15.00
13 Max Meyer/299 6.00 15.00
14 Tanner Burns/299 3.00 8.00
15 Zack Thompson/299 3.00 8.00
16 Zack Hess/299 2.00 5.00
17 Zach Watson/299 3.00 8.00
18 Will Wilson/299 3.00 8.00
19 Drew Parrish/299 2.00 5.00
20 Parker Caracci/299 2.00 5.00
21 John Doxakis/299 3.00 8.00
22 Graeme Stinson/299 2.00 5.00
23 Kenyon Yovan/299 2.00 5.00
24 Jake Agnos/299 3.00 8.00
25 Daniel Cabrera/299 8.00 20.00
26 Bryant Packard/299 3.00 8.00
27 CJ Abrams/135 10.00 25.00
28 Tyler Callihan/179 2.50 6.00
29 Corbin Carroll/63 3.00 8.00
30 Riley Cornelio/171 2.00 5.00
31 Pete Crow-Armstrong/166 4.00 10.00
32 Riley Greene/182 8.00 20.00
33 Ryan Hawks/171 2.00 5.00
34 Sammy Faltine/49
35 Yohandy Morales/179 2.00 5.00
36 Jared Kelley/171 2.00 5.00
37 Jack Leiter/171 2.50 6.00
38 Brennan Malone/166 2.00 5.00
39 Jacob Meador/170 2.00 5.00
40 Bobby Witt Jr./166 8.00 20.00
41 Max Rajcic/171 2.00 5.00
42 Riley Greene/81 8.00 20.00
43 Avery Short/171 2.00 5.00
44 Drew Romo/166 5.00 12.00
45 Anthony Volpe/166 6.00 15.00
46 Bobby Witt Jr./25 8.00 20.00
47 Shea Langeliers/43 4.00 10.00
48 Dylan Crews/25 2.50 6.00
49 Adley Rutschman/53 10.00 25.00
50 Timmy Manning/25 3.00 8.00

2019 USA Baseball Stars and Stripes Material Signatures

RANDOM INSERTS IN PACKS
PRINT RUNS B/WN 53-199 COPIES PER
*PRIME/20-25: .6X TO 1.5X BASIC
1 Kyle Brnovich/299 3.00 8.00
2 Matt Cronin/299 3.00 8.00
3 Mason Feole/299 3.00 8.00
4 Dominic Fletcher/299 3.00 8.00
5 Josh Jung/299 8.00 20.00
6 Shea Langeliers/37 12.00 30.00
7 Andre Pallante/299 4.00 10.00
8 Adley Rutschman/84 25.00 60.00
9 Braden Shewmake/299 10.00 25.00
10 Bryson Stott/234 6.00 15.00
11 Spencer Torkelson/299 25.00 60.00
12 Andrew Vaughn/299 8.00 20.00
13 Max Meyer/299 10.00 25.00
14 Tanner Burns/299 5.00 12.00
15 Zack Thompson/299 5.00 12.00
16 Zack Hess/299 3.00 8.00
17 Zach Watson/234 5.00 12.00
18 Will Wilson/299 5.00 12.00
19 Drew Parrish/299 3.00 8.00
20 Parker Caracci/299 3.00 8.00
21 John Doxakis/299 5.00 12.00
22 Graeme Stinson/299 3.00 8.00
23 Kenyon Yovan/299 3.00 8.00
24 Jake Agnos/299 5.00 12.00
25 Daniel Cabrera/299 12.00 30.00
26 Bryant Packard/299 5.00 12.00
27 CJ Abrams/299 6.00 15.00
28 Tyler Callihan/299 4.00 10.00
29 Corbin Carroll/299 5.00 12.00
30 Riley Cornelio/299 3.00 8.00
31 Pete Crow-Armstrong/299 6.00 15.00
32 Riley Greene/225 15.00 40.00
33 Ryan Hawks/299 3.00 8.00
34 Timmy Manning/299 5.00 12.00
35 Sammy Faltine/299
36 Jared Kelley/299 3.00 8.00
37 Jack Leiter/299 4.00 10.00
38 Brennan Malone/299 3.00 8.00
39 Jacob Meador/299 3.00 8.00
40 Yohandy Morales/299 3.00 8.00
41 Max Rajcic/299 3.00 8.00
42 Bobby Witt Jr./224 12.00 30.00
43 Avery Short/299 3.00 8.00
44 Riley Greene/225 12.00 30.00
45 Anthony Volpe/299 10.00 25.00
46 Bobby Witt Jr./224 12.00 30.00
47 Drew Romo/299 8.00 20.00
48 Dylan Crews/299 4.00 10.00
50 Adley Rutschman/84 25.00 60.00

2019 USA Baseball Stars and Stripes Silhouettes Black Gold Signatures Jerseys

RANDOM INSERTS IN PACKS
PRINT RUNS B/WN 25-99 COPIES PER
*PRIME/20-25: .6X TO 1.5X BASIC
1 Kyle Brnovich/89 3.00 8.00
2 Matt Cronin/89 3.00 8.00
3 Mason Feole/89 3.00 8.00
4 Dominic Fletcher/54 3.00 8.00
5 Josh Jung/54 10.00 25.00
6 Shea Langeliers/44 12.00 30.00
7 Andre Pallante/89 4.00 10.00
8 Adley Rutschman/44 50.00 120.00
9 Braden Shewmake/44 10.00 25.00
10 Bryson Stott/45 10.00 25.00
11 Spencer Torkelson/84 40.00 100.00
12 Andrew Vaughn/85 10.00 25.00
13 Max Meyer/89 10.00 25.00
14 Tanner Burns/89 5.00 12.00
15 Zack Thompson/54 5.00 12.00
16 Zack Hess/89 3.00 8.00
17 Zach Watson/44 5.00 12.00
18 Will Wilson/89 5.00 12.00
19 Drew Parrish/89 3.00 8.00
20 Parker Caracci/89 3.00 8.00
21 John Doxakis/89 5.00 12.00
22 Graeme Stinson/51 3.00 8.00
23 Kenyon Yovan/89 3.00 8.00
24 Jake Agnos/79 5.00 12.00
25 Daniel Cabrera/89 12.00 30.00
26 Bryant Packard/89 5.00 12.00
27 CJ Abrams/44 12.00 30.00
28 Tyler Callihan/54 4.00 10.00
29 Corbin Carroll/84 5.00 12.00
30 Riley Cornelio/89 3.00 8.00
31 Pete Crow-Armstrong/44 6.00 15.00
32 Riley Greene/54 12.00 30.00
33 Ryan Hawks/89 3.00 8.00
34 Timmy Manning/89 5.00 12.00
36 Jared Kelley/38 3.00 8.00
37 Jack Leiter/89 4.00 10.00
38 Brennan Malone/54 3.00 8.00
39 Jacob Meador/89 3.00 8.00
40 Sammy Faltine/89
41 Max Rajcic/38 3.00 8.00
42 Yohandy Morales/33 3.00 8.00
43 Avery Short/89 3.00 8.00
44 Drew Romo/38 8.00 20.00
45 Anthony Volpe/38 10.00 25.00
46 Bobby Witt Jr./54 12.00 30.00
47 Ryan Spikes/89 3.00 8.00
48 Davis Diaz/99 3.00 8.00
49 T.R. Williams/74 4.00 10.00
50 Tyree Reed/89 3.00 8.00
51 Rheego McIntosh/89 3.00 8.00
52 Karson Bowen/54 3.00 8.00
53 Justin Colon/89 4.00 10.00
54 Gage Ziehl/88 3.00 8.00
55 Cale Lansville/89 3.00 8.00
56 Ryan Clifford/89 3.00 8.00
57 Samuel Dutton/89 3.00 8.00
58 Joseph Brown/54 3.00 8.00
59 Cody Schrier/89 3.00 8.00
60 Charlie Saum/89 3.00 8.00
61 Luke Leto/89 6.00 15.00
62 Andrew Painter/89 5.00 12.00
63 Brady House/89 5.00 12.00
64 Joshua Hartle/85 3.00 8.00
65 Christian Little/89 3.00 8.00
66 Thomas DiLandri/89 3.00 8.00
67 Mick Abel/48 5.00 12.00
68 Nelson Berkwich/48 3.00 8.00
69 Drew Bowser/48 3.00 8.00
70 Alek Boychuk/48
71 Enrique Bradfield/48 3.00 8.00
72 Jack Bulger/48 3.00 8.00
73 Max Carlson/48 3.00 8.00
74 Gavin Casas/48 3.00 8.00
75 Kellum Clark/48 3.00 8.00
76 Nate Clow/48 3.00 8.00
77 Dylan Crews/99 4.00 10.00
78 Pete Crow-Armstrong/88 6.00 15.00
79 Jamar Fairweather/48 3.00 8.00
80 Brandon Fields/48 3.00 8.00
81 Dax Fulton/44 3.00 8.00
82 Alex Greene/48 3.00 8.00
83 Austin Hendrick/48 8.00 20.00
84 Jared Jones/48 4.00 10.00
85 Colton Keith/48 4.00 10.00
86 Jared Kelley/99 3.00 8.00
87 Christian Knapczyk/48 3.00 8.00
88 Avery Mabe/48 3.00 8.00
89 Nolan McLean/47
90 Victor Mederos/48 3.00 8.00
91 Yohandy Morales/99 3.00 8.00
92 Aaron Nixon/48 4.00 10.00
93 Liam Norris/48 3.00 8.00
94 Jack O'Dowd/48 3.00 8.00
95 Caleb Pendleton/48 3.00 8.00
96 Brett Percival/48 3.00 8.00
97 Jackson Phipps/47 4.00 10.00
98 Max Rajcic/99 3.00 8.00
99 Jordan Rollins/48
100 Drew Romo/99 8.00 20.00
101 Blake Shapen/48 3.00 8.00
102 Josh Shuler/48 3.00 8.00
103 Carson Tucker/48 12.00 30.00
104 Anthony Volpe/99 10.00 25.00
105 Masyn Winn/48 4.00 10.00
106 Nate Wohlgemuth/48 3.00 8.00
107 Carter Young/48 3.00 8.00
108 Macauley Horvath/48 3.00 8.00
109 Philip Abner/48 3.00 8.00
110 Walter Ahuna/48 3.00 8.00
111 Matthew Bardowell/48 3.00 8.00
113 Braylon Bishop/48 3.00 8.00
114 Nick Bitsko/48 3.00 8.00
115 Irving Carter/48 3.00 8.00
116 Dylan Crews/86 4.00 10.00
117 Jonathan Cymrot/48 3.00 8.00
118 Joe Dixon/48 3.00 8.00
119 Ross Dunn/48 3.00 8.00
120 Alex Edmondson/48 3.00 8.00
121 Landen Looper/48 3.00 8.00
122 Hunter Haas/48
123 Miles Halligan/48 3.00 8.00
124 Petey Halpin/48 6.00 15.00
125 Rawley Hector/48 3.00 8.00
126 Cason Henry/48 3.00 8.00
127 Jesse Herrera III/45 3.00 8.00
128 Reece Holbrook/48
129 Sam Hunt/48 3.00 8.00
130 Kennedy Jones/46 3.00 8.00
131 Jordan Lawlar/48 3.00 8.00
132 Caleb Lomavita/48 3.00 8.00
133 Evan Maldonado/48 3.00 8.00
134 Marcelo Mayer/48 3.00 8.00
135 Jayden Melendez/48 3.00 8.00
136 Ian Moller/48
137 Christian Moore/48 4.00 10.00
138 Robert Moore/48 3.00 8.00
139 Izaac Pacheco/48 3.00 8.00
140 Roc Riggio/48 3.00 8.00
141 Austin Stracener/48 3.00 8.00
142 Grant Taylor/48 3.00 8.00
143 Hunter Teplansky/48 3.00 8.00
144 Jabin Trosky/47 5.00 12.00
145 Tanner Witt/48 4.00 10.00
152 Karson Bowen/30 3.00 8.00
153 Joseph Brown/30 3.00 8.00
187 Riley Greene/25 12.00 30.00
188 Bobby Witt Jr./25 12.00 30.00
189 Zack Thompson/25 5.00 12.00
190 Shea Langeliers/25 12.00 30.00
191 Adley Rutschman/25 50.00 120.00
192 CJ Abrams/25 12.00 30.00
193 Josh Jung/25 10.00 25.00
194 Bryson Stott/25 10.00 25.00
195 Brennan Malone/25 3.00 8.00
196 Dominic Fletcher/25 3.00 8.00
197 Graeme Stinson/25 3.00 8.00
198 Braden Shewmake/25 10.00 25.00
199 Zach Watson/25 5.00 12.00
200 Tyler Callihan/25 4.00 10.00

2019 USA Baseball Stars and Stripes Silhouettes Signatures Bats

RANDOM INSERTS IN PACKS
STATED PRINT RUN 49 SER.#'d SETS
6 Shea Langeliers 15.00 40.00
8 Adley Rutschman 50.00 120.00
9 Braden Shewmake 12.00 30.00
10 Bryson Stott 10.00 25.00
11 Spencer Torkelson 50.00 120.00
12 Andrew Vaughn 25.00 60.00
17 Zach Watson 6.00 15.00
27 CJ Abrams 15.00 40.00
29 Corbin Carroll 6.00 15.00
31 Pete Crow-Armstrong 8.00 20.00
42 Yohandy Morales 4.00 10.00
190 Shea Langeliers 15.00 40.00
191 Adley Rutschman 50.00 210.00
192 CJ Abrams 15.00 40.00
194 Bryson Stott 12.00 30.00
198 Braden Shewmake 12.00 30.00
199 Zach Watson 6.00 15.00

2019 USA Baseball Stars and Stripes Silhouettes Signatures Jerseys

RANDOM INSERTS IN PACKS
PRINT RUNS B/WN 53-199 COPIES PER
*PRIME/20-25: .6X TO 1.5X BASIC
1 Kyle Brnovich/199 3.00 8.00
2 Matt Cronin/199 3.00 8.00
3 Mason Feole/199 3.00 8.00
4 Dominic Fletcher/199 3.00 8.00
5 Josh Jung/199 10.00 25.00
6 Shea Langeliers/199 12.00 30.00
7 Andre Pallante/199 4.00 10.00
8 Adley Rutschman/199 20.00 50.00
9 Braden Shewmake/199 10.00 25.00
10 Bryson Stott/199 10.00 25.00
11 Spencer Torkelson/199 40.00 100.00
12 Andrew Vaughn/199 8.00 20.00
13 Max Meyer/199 10.00 25.00
14 Tanner Burns/199 5.00 12.00
15 Zack Thompson/199 5.00 12.00
16 Zack Hess/199 3.00 8.00
17 Zach Watson/199 5.00 12.00
18 Will Wilson/199 6.00 15.00
19 Drew Parrish/199 3.00 8.00
20 Parker Caracci/199 3.00 8.00
21 John Doxakis/199 5.00 12.00
22 Graeme Stinson/199 3.00 8.00
23 Kenyon Yovan/199 3.00 8.00
24 Jake Agnos/199 5.00 12.00
25 Daniel Cabrera/199 12.00 30.00
26 Bryant Packard/199 5.00 12.00
27 CJ Abrams/199 12.00 30.00
28 Tyler Callihan/199 4.00 10.00
29 Corbin Carroll/199 5.00 12.00
30 Riley Cornelio/199 3.00 8.00
31 Pete Crow-Armstrong/199 6.00 15.00
32 Riley Greene/199 12.00 30.00
33 Ryan Hawks/199 3.00 8.00
34 Timmy Manning/199 5.00 12.00
35 Dylan Crews/199 4.00 10.00
36 Jared Kelley/199 3.00 8.00
37 Jack Leiter/199 4.00 10.00
38 Brennan Malone/199 3.00 8.00
39 Jacob Meador/199 3.00 8.00
40 Sammy Faltine/199
41 Max Rajcic/199 3.00 8.00
42 Yohandy Morales/199 3.00 8.00
43 Avery Short/199 3.00 8.00
44 Drew Romo/199 8.00 20.00
45 Anthony Volpe/199 10.00 25.00
46 Bobby Witt Jr./199 12.00 30.00
47 Ryan Spikes/199 3.00 8.00
48 Davis Diaz/199 3.00 8.00
49 T.R. Williams/199 4.00 10.00
50 Tyree Reed/199 3.00 8.00
51 Rheego McIntosh/199 3.00 8.00
52 Karson Bowen/199 3.00 8.00
53 Justin Colon/199 4.00 10.00
54 Gage Ziehl/199 3.00 8.00
55 Cale Lansville/199 3.00 8.00
56 Ryan Clifford/199 3.00 8.00
57 Samuel Dutton/199 3.00 8.00
58 Joseph Brown/199 3.00 8.00
59 Cody Schrier/199 3.00 8.00
60 Charlie Saum/199 3.00 8.00
61 Luke Leto/199 6.00 15.00
62 Andrew Painter/199 5.00 12.00
63 Brady House/199 5.00 12.00
64 Joshua Hartle/199 3.00 8.00
65 Christian Little/199 3.00 8.00
66 Thomas DiLandri/199 3.00 8.00
67 Mick Abel/199 6.00 15.00
68 Nelson Berkwich/199 3.00 8.00
69 Drew Bowser/199 3.00 8.00
70 Alek Boychuk/199
71 Enrique Bradfield/199 3.00 8.00
72 Jack Bulger/199 3.00 8.00
73 Max Carlson/199 3.00 8.00
74 Gavin Casas/199 3.00 8.00
75 Kellum Clark/199 3.00 8.00
76 Nate Clow/199 3.00 8.00
77 Dylan Crews/199 4.00 10.00
78 Pete Crow-Armstrong/199 6.00 15.00
79 Jamar Fairweather/199 3.00 8.00
80 Brandon Fields/199
81 Dax Fulton/199 3.00 8.00
82 Alex Greene/199 3.00 8.00
83 Austin Hendrick/199 8.00 20.00
84 Jared Jones/199 4.00 10.00
85 Colton Keith/199 4.00 10.00
86 Jared Kelley/199 3.00 8.00
87 Christian Knapczyk/199 3.00 8.00
88 Avery Mabe/199 3.00 8.00
89 Nolan McLean/199
90 Victor Mederos/199 3.00 8.00
91 Yohandy Morales/199 3.00 8.00
92 Aaron Nixon/199 4.00 10.00
93 Liam Norris/199
94 Jack O'Dowd/199 3.00 8.00
95 Caleb Pendleton/199 3.00 8.00
96 Brett Percival/199 3.00 8.00
97 Jackson Phipps/199 4.00 10.00
98 Max Rajcic/199 3.00 8.00
99 Jordan Rollins/199
100 Drew Romo/199 8.00 20.00
101 Blake Shapen/199 3.00 8.00
102 Josh Shuler/199 3.00 8.00
103 Carson Tucker/199 12.00 30.00
104 Anthony Volpe/199 10.00 25.00
105 Masyn Winn/199 4.00 10.00
106 Nate Wohlgemuth/199 3.00 8.00
107 Carter Young/199 3.00 8.00
108 Macauley Horvath/199 3.00 8.00
109 Philip Abner/199 3.00 8.00
110 Walter Ahuna/199 3.00 8.00
111 Matthew Bardowell/199 3.00 8.00
113 Braylon Bishop/199 3.00 8.00
114 Nick Bitsko/199 3.00 8.00
115 Irving Carter/199 3.00 8.00
116 Dylan Crews/199 4.00 10.00
117 Jonathan Cymrot/199 3.00 8.00
118 Joe Dixon/199 3.00 8.00
119 Ross Dunn/199 3.00 8.00
120 Alex Edmondson/199
121 Landen Looper/199 3.00 8.00
122 Hunter Haas/199
123 Miles Halligan/199 3.00 8.00
124 Petey Halpin/199
125 Rawley Hector/199 3.00 8.00
126 Cason Henry/199 3.00 8.00
127 Jesse Herrera III/199 3.00 8.00
128 Reece Holbrook/199
129 Sam Hunt/199 3.00 8.00
130 Kennedy Jones/199 3.00 8.00
131 Jordan Lawlar/199 3.00 8.00
132 Caleb Lomavita/199 3.00 8.00
133 Evan Maldonado/199 3.00 8.00
134 Marcelo Mayer/199 3.00 8.00
135 Jayden Melendez/199 3.00 8.00
136 Ian Moller/199
137 Christian Moore/199 4.00 10.00
138 Robert Moore/199 3.00 8.00
139 Izaac Pacheco/199 3.00 8.00
140 Roc Riggio/199 3.00 8.00
141 Austin Stracener/199 3.00 8.00
142 Grant Taylor/199 3.00 8.00
143 Hunter Teplansky/199 3.00 8.00
144 Jabin Trosky/199
145 Tanner Witt/199
147 Nathan Aguilar/65 3.00 8.00
148 Jaden Anderson/71 3.00 8.00
149 Tyler Avery/57 3.00 8.00
150 Brandon Barriera/65
151 Casey Borba/65
152 Karson Bowen/61 3.00 8.00
153 Joseph Brown/61 3.00 8.00
154 Ryan Cainzos/66
155 Kai Caranto/57 3.00 8.00
156 Abel Castrejon/66
157 Cutter Coffey/55
158 Justin Crawford/69
159 Kyle Crow/61
160 Dylan Cupp/57
161 Demitri Diamant/57 3.00 8.00
162 Evan Dobias/67
163 Owen Egan/58
164 Duke Ekstrom/57
165 Jamie Felix/66

166 Termarr Johnson/66
167 Dylan Lina/60
168 Kaden Martin/57
169 Anthony Martinez/57
170 Jackson McKenzie/57
171 Steven Milam/68
172 Aidan Miller/74 3.00 8.00
173 Derrick Mitchell/57
174 Mason Neville/57
175 Christopher Paciolla/57
176 Alvaro Partida Lora/71
177 Jacob Randolph/57
178 Michael Rocha/57
179 Louis Rodriguez/64
180 Mikey Romero/56
181 Marcos Rosales/66
182 Logan Saloman/57 3.00 8.00
183 Christopher Scinta/57
184 Andrew Villalobos/69
185 Ethan Watson/57 3.00 8.00
186 Abraham Zapata/53 3.00 8.00
187 Riley Greene/199 12.00 30.00
188 Bobby Witt Jr./199 12.00 30.00
189 Zack Thompson/199 5.00 12.00
190 Shea Langeliers/199 12.00 30.00
191 Adley Rutschman/199 20.00 50.00
192 CJ Abrams/199 12.00 30.00
193 Josh Jung/199 10.00 25.00
194 Bryson Stott/199 10.00 25.00
195 Brennan Malone/199 3.00 8.00
196 Dominic Fletcher/199 3.00 8.00
197 Graeme Stinson/199 3.00 8.00
198 Braden Shewmake/199 10.00 25.00
199 Zach Watson/199 5.00 12.00
200 Tyler Callihan/199 4.00 10.00

2020 USA Baseball Stars and Stripes

1 USA Baseball Collegiate CL .30 .75
2 Patrick Bailey 1.00 2.50
3 Reid Detmers .75 2.00
4 Colton Cowser .40 1.00
5 Asa Lacy 2.00 5.00
6 Austin Martin 1.00 2.50
7 Max Meyer 1.25 3.00
8 Garrett Mitchell 2.50 6.00
9 Spencer Torkelson 3.00 8.00
10 Cole Wilcox .40 1.00
11 Alika Williams .40 1.00
12 Logan Allen .30 .75
13 Andrew Abbott .30 .75
14 Tyler Brown .50 1.25
15 Burl Carraway .75 2.00
16 Justin Foscue 1.25 3.00
17 Nick Loftin .50 1.25
18 Doug Nikhazy .30 .75
19 Tanner Allen .30 .75
20 Alec Burleson .50 1.25
21 Cade Cavalli .60 1.50
22 Jeff Criswell .50 1.25
23 Nick Frasso .30 .75
24 Heston Kjerstad 1.50 4.00
25 Luke Waddell .30 .75
26 Chris McMahon .40 1.00
27 Casey Opitz .50 1.25
28 USA Baseball 18U CL .30 .75
29 Alejandro Rosario .50 1.25
30 Austin Hendrick 3.00 8.00
31 Ben Hernandez .50 1.25
32 Drew Romo .75 2.00
33 Colby Halter .30 .75
34 Drew Bowser .30 .75
35 Lucas Dunn .30 .75
36 Hunter Haas .40 1.00
37 Jack Bulger .30 .75
38 Jason Savacool .50 1.25
39 Kyle Harrison .75 2.00
40 Lucas Gordon .30 .75
41 Max Rajcic .30 .75
42 Mick Abel .50 1.25
43 Milan Tolentino .50 1.25
44 Nate Savino .40 1.00
45 Nolan McLean .30 .75
46 Robert Hassell 2.50 6.00
47 Tyler Soderstrom 1.25 3.00
48 Pete Crow-Armstrong 1.00 2.50
49 Rawley Hector .30 .75
50 USA Baseball 15U CL .30 .75
51 Benjamin Reiland .60 1.50
52 Steven Milam .30 .75
53 Drew Burress .30 .75
54 Aidan Miller .50 1.25
55 Colton Wombles .60 1.50
56 Termarr Johnson .60 1.50
57 Mikey Romero .30 .75
58 Karson Bowen .30 .75
59 Brandon Barriera .30 .75
60 Spencer Butt .30 .75
61 Duke Ekstrom .30 .75
62 Brandon Olivera .30 .75
63 Kai Caranto .30 .75
64 Joseph Brown .30 .75
65 Ethan McElvain .30 .75
66 Louis Rodriguez .30 .75
67 Logan Saloman .30 .75
68 Dylan Lina .40 1.00
69 Matthew Matthijs .50 1.25
70 Nolan Schubart .30 .75
71 Spencer Torkelson 3.00 8.00
72 Pete Crow-Armstrong 1.00 2.50
73 Austin Martin 1.00 2.50
74 Asa Lacy 2.00 5.00
75 Garrett Mitchell 2.50 6.00
76 Cole Wilcox .40 1.00
77 Mick Abel .50 1.25
78 Reid Detmers .75 2.00
79 Austin Hendrick 3.00 8.00
80 Patrick Bailey 1.00 2.50
81 Drew Romo .75 2.00
82 Nate Savino .40 1.00
83 Heston Kjerstad 1.50 4.00
84 Robert Hassell 2.50 6.00
85 Max Meyer 1.25 3.00
86 Cade Cavalli .60 1.50
87 Adley Rutschman 2.00 5.00
88 Bobby Witt Jr. 1.50 4.00
89 Andrew Vaughn 1.25 3.00
90 Riley Greene 1.25 3.00
91 CJ Abrams 1.25 3.00
92 Josh Jung .75 2.00
93 Shea Langeliers .60 1.50
94 Bryson Stott .75 2.00
95 Will Wilson .40 1.00
96 Corbin Carroll .50 1.25
97 Zack Thompson .30 .75
98 Braden Shewmake .50 1.25
99 Anthony Volpe 1.25 3.00
100 Brennan Malone .30 .75

2020 USA Baseball Stars and Stripes Longevity

COMPLETE SET (100)
1 USA Baseball Collegiate CL .30 .75
2 Patrick Bailey 1.00 2.50
3 Reid Detmers .75 2.00
4 Colton Cowser .40 1.00
5 Asa Lacy 2.00 5.00
6 Austin Martin 1.00 2.50
7 Max Meyer 1.25 3.00
8 Garrett Mitchell 2.50 6.00
9 Spencer Torkelson 3.00 8.00
10 Cole Wilcox .40 1.00
11 Alika Williams .40 1.00
12 Logan Allen .30 .75
13 Andrew Abbott .30 .75
14 Tyler Brown .50 1.25
15 Burl Carraway .75 2.00
16 Justin Foscue 1.25 3.00
17 Nick Loftin .50 1.25
18 Doug Nikhazy .30 .75
19 Tanner Allen .30 .75
20 Alec Burleson .50 1.25
21 Cade Cavalli .60 1.50
22 Jeff Criswell .50 1.25
23 Nick Frasso .30 .75
24 Heston Kjerstad 1.50 4.00
25 Luke Waddell .30 .75
26 Chris McMahon .40 1.00
27 Casey Opitz .50 1.25
28 USA Baseball 18U CL .30 .75
29 Alejandro Rosario .50 1.25
30 Austin Hendrick 3.00 8.00
31 Ben Hernandez .50 1.25
32 Drew Romo .75 2.00
33 Colby Halter .30 .75
34 Drew Bowser .30 .75
35 Lucas Dunn .30 .75
36 Hunter Haas .40 1.00
37 Jack Bulger .30 .75
38 Jason Savacool .50 1.25
39 Kyle Harrison .75 2.00
40 Lucas Gordon .30 .75
41 Max Rajcic .30 .75
42 Mick Abel .50 1.25
43 Milan Tolentino .50 1.25
44 Nate Savino .40 1.00
45 Nolan McLean .30 .75
46 Robert Hassell 2.50 6.00
47 Tyler Soderstrom 1.25 3.00
48 Pete Crow-Armstrong 1.00 2.50
49 Rawley Hector .30 .75
50 USA Baseball 15U CL .30 .75
51 Benjamin Reiland .60 1.50
52 Steven Milam .30 .75
53 Drew Burress .30 .75
54 Aidan Miller .50 1.25
55 Colton Wombles .60 1.50
56 Termarr Johnson .60 1.50
57 Mikey Romero .30 .75
58 Karson Bowen .30 .75
59 Brandon Barriera .30 .75
60 Spencer Butt .30 .75
61 Duke Ekstrom .30 .75
62 Brandon Olivera .30 .75
63 Kai Caranto .30 .75
64 Joseph Brown .30 .75
65 Ethan McElvain .30 .75
66 Louis Rodriguez .30 .75
67 Logan Saloman .30 .75
68 Dylan Lina .40 1.00
69 Matthew Matthijs .50 1.25
70 Nolan Schubart .30 .75
71 Spencer Torkelson 3.00 8.00
72 Pete Crow-Armstrong 1.00 2.50
73 Austin Martin 1.00 2.50
74 Asa Lacy 2.00 5.00
75 Garrett Mitchell 2.50 6.00
76 Cole Wilcox .40 1.00
77 Mick Abel .50 1.25
78 Reid Detmers .75 2.00
79 Austin Hendrick 3.00 8.00
80 Patrick Bailey 1.00 2.50
81 Drew Romo .75 2.00
82 Nate Savino .40 1.00
83 Heston Kjerstad 1.50 4.00
84 Robert Hassell 2.50 6.00
85 Max Meyer 1.25 3.00
86 Cade Cavalli .60 1.50
87 Adley Rutschman 2.00 5.00
88 Bobby Witt Jr. 1.50 4.00
89 Andrew Vaughn 1.25 3.00
90 Riley Greene 1.25 3.00
91 CJ Abrams 1.25 3.00
92 Josh Jung .75 2.00
93 Shea Langeliers .60 1.50
94 Bryson Stott .75 2.00
95 Will Wilson .40 1.00
96 Corbin Carroll .50 1.25
97 Zack Thompson .30 .75
98 Braden Shewmake .50 1.25
99 Anthony Volpe 1.25 3.00
100 Brennan Malone .30 .75

2020 USA Baseball Stars and Stripes Longevity Gold Team Logo

*GOLD: 2X TO 5X BASIC
RANDOM INSERTS IN PACKS
STATED PRINT RUN 25 COPIES PER

2020 USA Baseball Stars and Stripes Longevity Parallel

*PARALLEL: .5X TO 1.2X BASIC
RANDOM INSERTS IN PACKS

2020 USA Baseball Stars and Stripes Longevity Ruby

*RUBY: .75X TO 2X BASIC
RANDOM INSERTS IN PACKS
STATED PRINT RUN 249 COPIES PER

2020 USA Baseball Stars and Stripes Longevity Sapphire

*SAPPHIRE: 1.5X TO 4X BASIC
RANDOM INSERTS IN PACKS
STATED PRINT RUN 49 COPIES PER

2020 USA Baseball Stars and Stripes 15U Signatures

RANDOM INSERTS IN PACKS
PRINT RUNS B/WN 234-299 COPIES PER
*BLACK/25: .6X TO 1.5X BASIC
1 Benjamin Reiland/299 5.00 12.00
2 Steven Milam/299 6.00 15.00
3 Drew Burress/299 2.50 6.00
4 Aidan Miller/299 4.00 10.00
5 Colton Wombles/299 8.00 20.00
6 Termarr Johnson/299 5.00 12.00
7 Mikey Romero/299 2.50 6.00
8 Karson Bowen/299 2.50 6.00
9 Brandon Barriera/299 2.50 6.00
10 Spencer Butt/234 2.50 6.00
11 Duke Ekstrom/299 2.50 6.00
12 Brandon Olivera/299 2.50 6.00
13 Kai Caranto/236 2.50 6.00
14 Joseph Brown/299 2.50 6.00
15 Ethan McElvain/299 2.50 6.00
16 Louis Rodriguez/299 6.00 15.00
17 Logan Saloman/299 2.50 6.00
18 Dylan Lina/299 3.00 8.00
19 Matthew Matthijs/299 4.00 10.00
20 Nolan Schubart/299 2.50 6.00

2020 USA Baseball Stars and Stripes 16U Development Program Signatures

RANDOM INSERTS IN PACKS
PRINT RUNS B/WN 166-269 COPIES PER
*BLACK/25: .6X TO 1.5X BASIC
1 Carson Applegate/170 2.50 6.00
2 Jesse Bullard/179 2.50 6.00
3 Korbyn Dickerson/179 2.50 6.00
4 Thomas DiLandri/250 2.50 6.00
5 Tyler Gough/176 2.50 6.00
6 Blaise Grove/170 2.50 6.00
7 Joshua Hartle/217 2.50 6.00
8 Cooper Kinney/170 2.50 6.00
9 Nicholas Kurtz/170 2.50 6.00
10 Cale Lansville/249 3.00 8.00
11 Gabriel Miranda/170 2.50 6.00
12 Jaron Nevarez/180 2.50 6.00
13 Tyree Reed/269 5.00 12.00
14 William Rogers/171 2.50 6.00
15 Michael Saumell/178 2.50 6.00
16 Chase Spencer/170 2.50 6.00
17 Sal Stewart/172 2.50 6.00
18 Tyler White/170 2.50 6.00
19 Carter Boyd/170 2.50 6.00
20 Lorenzo Carrier/170 3.00 8.00
21 Calvert Clark/172 2.50 6.00
22 Ryan Clifford/199 2.50 6.00
23 Daniel Corona Jr./200 2.50 6.00
24 Davis Diaz/262 2.50 6.00
25 Samuel Dutton/254 4.00 10.00
26 Jake Geis/170 2.50 6.00
27 Rafael Gross/166 2.50 6.00
28 Trevor Hopkins/180 2.50 6.00
29 Jack Holman/170 2.50 6.00
30 David Horn/170 3.00 8.00
31 Jayson Jones/171 2.50 6.00
32 Gage Jump/178 4.00 10.00
33 Kyndon Lovell/180 2.50 6.00
34 Malcolm Moore/179 8.00 20.00
35 Devin Obee/170 2.50 6.00
36 Gavin Ochoa/173 3.00 8.00
37 Xavier Perez/184 2.50 6.00

2020 USA Baseball Stars and Stripes 17U Development Program Signatures

RANDOM INSERTS IN PACKS
PRINT RUNS B/WN 99-499 COPIES PER
*BLACK/25: .6X TO 1.5X BASIC
1 Philip Abner/171 2.50 6.00
2 Jackson Baumeister/169 8.00 20.00
3 Mike Bello/169 2.50 6.00
4 Braylon Bishop/187 4.00 10.00
5 Nick Bitsko/169 8.00 20.00
6 Mark Black/179 2.50 6.00
7 Michael Braswell/179 2.50 6.00
8 Maddux Bruns/169 2.50 6.00
9 Irving Carter/169 2.50 6.00
10 Ryan Clifford/220 2.50 6.00
11 Pete Crow-Armstrong/99 8.00 20.00
12 Michael Davinni/169 2.50 6.00
13 Kade Grundy/171 2.50 6.00
14 Joshua Hartle/217 2.50 6.00
15 Rawley Hector/231 2.50 6.00
16 Brady House/247 10.00 25.00
17 Sam Hunt/170 2.50 6.00
18 Jordan Lawlar/179 3.00 8.00
19 Christian Little/247 4.00 10.00
20 Joseph Mack/170 2.50 6.00
21 Marcelo Mayer/170 2.50 6.00
22 Michael Morales/170 5.00 12.00
23 Maxwell Muncy/179 2.50 6.00
24 Izaac Pacheco/170 4.00 10.00
25 Andrew Painter/248 2.50 6.00
26 Joshua Pearson/176 2.50 6.00
27 Kurtis Reid/182 2.50 6.00
28 Roc Riggio/179 5.00 12.00
29 Alejandro Rosario/499 4.00 10.00
30 Charlie Saum/247 2.50 6.00
31 Cody Schrier/247 2.50 6.00
32 Brock Selvidge/170 2.50 6.00
33 Noah Smith/179 2.50 6.00
34 Ryan Spikes/260 2.50 6.00
35 Austin Stracener/189 2.50 6.00
36 Grant Taylor/169 2.50 6.00
37 Hunter Teplansky/170 2.50 6.00
39 Tyler Wiederstein/171 2.50 6.00
40 Luke Leto/246 8.00 20.00

2020 USA Baseball Stars and Stripes 18U Signatures Black Ink

RANDOM INSERTS IN PACKS
STATED PRINT RUN 499 SER.#'d SETS
*BLUE/25: .6X TO 1.5X BASIC
2 Alejandro Rosario 4.00 10.00
5 Austin Hendrick 8.00 20.00
6 Ben Hernandez 4.00 10.00
7 Drew Romo 5.00 12.00
12 Colby Halter 2.50 6.00
15 Drew Bowser 2.50 6.00
20 Hunter Haas 3.00 8.00
21 Jack Bulger 2.50 6.00
25 Jason Savacool 4.00 10.00
29 Kyle Harrison 6.00 15.00
30 Lucas Gordon 2.50 6.00
34 Max Rajcic 2.50 6.00
35 Mick Abel 4.00 10.00
36 Milan Tolentino 4.00 10.00
37 Nate Savino 3.00 8.00
38 Nolan McLean 2.50 6.00
40 Robert Hassell 20.00 50.00
43 Tyler Soderstrom 10.00 25.00
45 Pete Crow-Armstrong 8.00 20.00
46 Rawley Hector 2.50 6.00

2020 USA Baseball Stars and Stripes 40th Anniversary Signatures

RANDOM INSERTS IN PACKS
PRINT RUNS B/WN 5-25 COPIES PER
NO PRICING ON QTY 10 OR LESS
1 Brendan McKay/25 15.00 40.00
4 Chipper Jones/25 25.00 60.00
7 Frank Thomas/25 30.00 80.00
10 Ken Griffey Jr./25 100.00 250.00
13 David Ross/25

2020 USA Baseball Stars and Stripes Chinese Taipei U18 Signatures

RANDOM INSERTS IN PACKS
1 Yuan-Tai Hsu 6.00 15.00
2 Yu-Cheng Liu 8.00 20.00

2020 USA Baseball Stars and Stripes CNT Connections Signatures Blue Ink

RANDOM INSERTS IN PACKS
STATED PRINT RUN 25 SER.#'d SETS
3 A.Williams/S.Torkelson 30.00 80.00
4 J.Foscue/T.Allen 8.00 20.00
5 A.Lacy/P.Bailey 8.00 20.00

2020 USA Baseball Stars and Stripes CNT Signatures Black Ink

RANDOM INSERTS IN PACKS
STATED PRINT RUN 499 SER.#'d SETS
*BLUE/25: .6X TO 1.5X BASIC
1 Patrick Bailey 5.00 12.00
3 Reid Detmers 6.00 15.00
5 Colton Cowser 3.00 8.00
6 Asa Lacy 10.00 25.00
7 Austin Martin 12.00 30.00
8 Max Meyer 6.00 15.00
11 Spencer Torkelson 20.00 50.00
12 Cole Wilcox 3.00 8.00
13 Alika Williams 3.00 8.00
15 Logan Allen 2.50 6.00
16 Andrew Abbott 2.50 6.00
17 Tyler Brown 4.00 10.00
18 Burl Carraway 6.00 15.00
20 Justin Foscue 6.00 15.00
21 Nick Loftin 4.00 10.00
23 Doug Nikhazy 2.50 6.00
25 Tanner Allen 2.50 6.00
27 Alec Burleson 4.00 10.00
28 Cade Cavalli 5.00 12.00
29 Jeff Criswell 4.00 10.00
30 Nick Frasso 2.50 6.00
31 Heston Kjerstad 10.00 25.00
35 Luke Waddell 2.50 6.00
37 Chris McMahon 3.00 8.00
38 Casey Opitz 4.00 10.00

2020 USA Baseball Stars and Stripes Jumbo Materials

RANDOM INSERTS IN PACKS
1 Patrick Bailey 6.00 15.00
2 Reid Detmers 5.00 12.00
3 Colton Cowser 2.50 6.00
4 Asa Lacy 4.00 10.00
5 Austin Martin 6.00 15.00
6 Max Meyer 8.00 20.00
7 Garrett Mitchell 4.00 10.00
8 Spencer Torkelson 20.00 50.00
9 Cole Wilcox 2.50 6.00
10 Alika Williams 2.50 6.00
11 Logan Allen 2.00 5.00
12 Andrew Abbott 2.00 5.00
13 Tyler Brown 3.00 8.00
14 Burl Carraway 5.00 12.00
15 Justin Foscue 8.00 20.00
16 Nick Loftin 3.00 8.00
17 Doug Nikhazy 2.00 5.00
18 Tanner Allen 2.00 5.00
19 Alec Burleson 3.00 8.00
20 Cade Cavalli 4.00 10.00
21 Jeff Criswell 3.00 8.00
22 Nick Frasso 2.00 5.00
23 Heston Kjerstad 4.00 10.00
24 Luke Waddell 2.00 5.00
25 Chris McMahon 2.50 6.00
26 Casey Opitz 3.00 8.00

2020 USA Baseball Stars and Stripes Material Signatures

RANDOM INSERTS IN PACKS
PRINT RUN B/WN 39-399 COPIES PER
*PRIME/25: .6X TO 1.5X BASIC
1 Patrick Bailey/293 6.00 15.00
2 Reid Detmers/281 8.00 20.00
3 Colton Cowser/399 4.00 10.00
4 Asa Lacy/293 10.00 25.00
5 Austin Martin/267 15.00 40.00
6 Max Meyer/399 5.00 12.00
7 Garrett Mitchell/39 25.00 60.00
8 Spencer Torkelson/199 20.00 50.00
9 Cole Wilcox/395 4.00 10.00
10 Alika Williams/368 4.00 10.00
11 Logan Allen/399 3.00 8.00
12 Andrew Abbott/399 3.00 8.00
13 Tyler Brown/224 5.00 12.00
14 Burl Carraway/399 8.00 20.00
15 Justin Foscue/221 8.00 20.00
16 Nick Loftin/222 5.00 12.00
17 Doug Nikhazy/222 3.00 8.00
18 Tanner Allen/228 3.00 8.00
19 Alec Burleson/368 5.00 12.00
20 Cade Cavalli/330 6.00 15.00
21 Jeff Criswell/222 5.00 12.00
22 Nick Frasso/219 3.00 8.00
23 Heston Kjerstad/274 15.00 40.00
24 Luke Waddell/358 3.00 8.00
25 Chris McMahon/222 4.00 10.00
26 Casey Opitz/399 5.00 12.00
27 Alejandro Rosario/399 5.00 12.00
28 Austin Hendrick/399 8.00 20.00
29 Ben Hernandez/399 5.00 12.00
30 Drew Romo/399 8.00 20.00
31 Colby Halter/399 3.00 8.00
32 Drew Bowser/399 3.00 8.00
33 Lucas Dunn/399 3.00 8.00
34 Hunter Haas/399 4.00 10.00
35 Jack Bulger/399 3.00 8.00
36 Jason Savacool/399 5.00 12.00
37 Kyle Harrison/399 3.00 8.00
38 Lucas Gordon/399 3.00 8.00
39 Max Rajcic/399 3.00 8.00
40 Mick Abel/399 5.00 12.00
41 Milan Tolentino/399 5.00 12.00
42 Nate Savino/399 4.00 10.00
43 Nolan McLean/399 3.00 8.00
44 Robert Hassell/399 25.00 60.00
45 Tyler Soderstrom/399 12.00 30.00
46 Pete Crow-Armstrong/399 10.00 25.00
47 Rawley Hector/299 3.00 8.00
48 Spencer Torkelson/123 20.00 50.00

2020 USA Baseball Stars and Stripes Silhouettes Black Gold Signature Jerseys

RANDOM INSERTS IN PACKS
PRINT RUN B/WN 23-92 COPIES PER
1 Patrick Bailey/49 6.00 15.00
2 Reid Detmers/39 6.00 15.00
3 Colton Cowser/89 4.00 10.00
4 Asa Lacy/39 10.00 25.00
5 Austin Martin/25 25.00 60.00
6 Max Meyer/40 12.00 30.00
7 Garrett Mitchell/92 25.00 60.00
8 Spencer Torkelson/39 20.00 50.00
9 Cole Wilcox/39 4.00 10.00
10 Alika Williams/84 4.00 10.00
11 Logan Allen/89 3.00 8.00
12 Andrew Abbott/89 3.00 8.00
13 Tyler Brown/89 5.00 12.00
14 Burl Carraway/89 8.00 20.00
15 Justin Foscue/89 8.00 2.00
16 Nick Loftin/89 5.00 12.00
17 Doug Nikhazy/76 3.00 8.00
18 Tanner Allen/89 3.00 8.00
19 Alec Burleson/84 5.00 12.00
20 Cade Cavalli/39 6.00 15.00
21 Jeff Criswell/89 5.00 12.00
22 Nick Frasso/89 3.00 8.00
23 Heston Kjerstad/39 15.00 40.00
24 Luke Waddell/84 3.00 8.00
25 Chris McMahon/89 4.00 10.00
26 Casey Opitz/84 5.00 12.00
27 Alejandro Rosario/59 5.00 12.00
28 Austin Hendrick/49 30.00 80.00
29 Ben Hernandez/89 5.00 12.00
30 Drew Romo/49 8.00 20.00
31 Colby Halter/84 3.00 8.00
32 Drew Bowser/89 3.00 8.00
33 Lucas Dunn/89 3.00 8.00
34 Hunter Haas/84 4.00 10.00
35 Jack Bulger/84 3.00 8.00
36 Jason Savacool/89 5.00 12.00
37 Kyle Harrison/89 3.00 8.00
38 Lucas Gordon/89 3.00 8.00
39 Max Rajcic/89 3.00 8.00
40 Mick Abel/49 5.00 12.00
41 Milan Tolentino/84 5.00 12.00
42 Nate Savino/49 4.00 10.00
43 Nolan McLean/89 3.00 8.00
44 Robert Hassell/49 25.00 60.00
45 Tyler Soderstrom/89 12.00 30.00
46 Pete Crow-Armstrong/25 15.00 40.00
47 Rawley Hector/49 3.00 8.00
48 Benjamin Reiland/50 6.00 15.00
49 Steven Milam/89 3.00 8.00
50 Drew Burress/89 3.00 8.00
51 Aidan Miller/84 5.00 12.00
52 Colton Wombles/89 6.00 15.00
53 Termarr Johnson/89 6.00 15.00
54 Mikey Romero/89 3.00 8.00
55 Karson Bowen/89 3.00 8.00
56 Brandon Barriera/89 3.00 8.00
57 Spencer Butt/49 3.00 8.00
58 Duke Ekstrom/89 3.00 8.00
59 Brandon Olivera/42 3.00 8.00
60 Kai Caranto/25 5.00 12.00
61 Joseph Brown/89 3.00 8.00
62 Ethan McElvain/85 3.00 8.00
63 Louis Rodriguez/89 3.00 8.00
64 Logan Saloman/89 3.00 8.00
65 Dylan Lina/89 4.00 10.00
66 Matthew Matthijs/89 5.00 12.00
67 Nolan Schubart/89 3.00 8.00
68 Philip Abner/44 3.00 8.00
69 Jackson Baumeister/44 10.00 25.00
70 Mike Bello/44 3.00 8.00
71 Braylon Bishop/44 5.00 12.00
72 Nick Bitsko/44 10.00 25.00
73 Mark Black/44 3.00 8.00
74 Michael Braswell/44 3.00 8.00
75 Maddux Bruns/44 3.00 8.00
76 Irving Carter/40 3.00 8.00
77 Ryan Clifford/49 3.00 8.00
78 Pete Crow-Armstrong/35 10.00 25.00
79 Michael Davinni/44 3.00 8.00
80 Kade Grundy/44 3.00 8.00
81 Joshua Hartle/40 3.00 8.00
82 Rawley Hector/79 3.00 8.00
83 Brady House/43 8.00 20.00
84 Sam Hunt/44 3.00 8.00
85 Jordan Lawlar/44 4.00 10.00
86 Christian Little/39 5.00 12.00
87 Joseph Mack/44 3.00 8.00
88 Marcelo Mayer/44 3.00 8.00
89 Michael Morales/44 6.00 15.00
90 Maxwell Muncy/44 3.00 8.00
91 Izaac Pacheco/44 5.00 12.00
92 Andrew Painter/39 3.00 8.00
93 Joshua Pearson/44 3.00 8.00
94 Kurtis Reid/44 3.00 8.00
95 Roc Riggio/39 6.00 15.00
96 Alejandro Rosario/59 5.00 12.00
97 Charlie Saum/39 3.00 8.00
98 Cody Schrier/39 3.00 8.00
99 Brock Selvidge/44 3.00 8.00
100 Noah Smith/44 3.00 8.00
101 Ryan Spikes/39 3.00 8.00
102 Austin Stracener/39 3.00 8.00
103 Grant Taylor/39 3.00 8.00
104 Hunter Teplansky/44 3.00 8.00
106 Tyler Wiederstein/44 3.00 8.00
107 Luke Leto/39 20.00 50.00
108 Carson Applegate/44 3.00 8.00
109 Jesse Bullard/44 3.00 8.00
110 Korbyn Dickerson/44 10.00 25.00
111 Thomas DiLandri/39 3.00 8.00
112 Tyler Gough/44 3.00 8.00
113 Blaise Grove/44 3.00 8.00
114 Joshua Hartle/38 3.00 8.00
115 Cooper Kinney/44 3.00 8.00
116 Nicholas Kurtz/44 3.00 8.00
117 Cale Lansville/39 4.00 10.00
118 Gabriel Miranda/44 3.00 8.00
119 Jaron Nevarez/44 3.00 8.00
120 Tyree Reed/39 6.00 15.00
121 William Rogers/44 3.00 8.00
122 Michael Saumell/44 3.00 8.00
123 Chase Spencer/44 3.00 8.00
124 Sal Stewart/44 3.00 8.00
125 Tyler White/44 3.00 8.00
126 Carter Boyd/44 3.00 8.00
127 Lorenzo Carrier/44 4.00 10.00
128 Calvert Clark/44 3.00 8.00
129 Ryan Clifford/29 3.00 8.00
130 Daniel Corona Jr./49 3.00 8.00
131 Davis Diaz/51 3.00 8.00
132 Samuel Dutton/39 5.00 12.00
133 Jake Geis/44 3.00 8.00
134 Rafael Gross/44 3.00 8.00
135 Trevor Haskins/44 3.00 8.00
136 Jack Holman/44 3.00 8.00
137 David Horn/44 4.00 10.00
138 Jayson Jones/44 3.00 8.00
139 Gage Jump/44 5.00 12.00
140 Kyndon Lovell/44 3.00 8.00
141 Malcolm Moore/44 5.00 12.00
142 Devin Obee/44 3.00 8.00
143 Gavin Ochoa/44 4.00 10.00
144 Xavier Perez/44 3.00 8.00
146 Spencer Butt/45 3.00 8.00
165 Kai Caranto/57 3.00 8.00
175 Brandon Olivera/42 3.00 8.00
177 Benjamin Reiland/39 6.00 15.00
185 Spencer Torkelson/40 20.00 50.00
186 Pete Crow-Armstrong/47 10.00 25.00
187 Austin Martin/64 15.00 40.00
188 Asa Lacy/40 10.00 25.00
190 Cole Wilcox/40 4.00 10.00
191 Mick Abel/23 8.00 20.00
192 Reid Detmers/40 6.00 15.00
193 Austin Hendrick/30 30.00 80.00
194 Patrick Bailey/40 6.00 15.00
195 Drew Romo/35 8.00 20.00
196 Nate Savino/30 4.00 10.00
197 Heston Kjerstad/44 15.00 40.00
198 Robert Hassell/30 25.00 60.00
199 Max Meyer/39 12.00 30.00
200 Cade Cavalli/40 6.00 15.00

2020 USA Baseball Stars and Stripes Silhouettes Signature Jerseys

RANDOM INSERTS IN PACKS
PRINT RUN B/WN 39-299 COPIES PER
*BATS/39-49: .4X TO 1X BASIC
*BATS/25: .6X TO 1.5X BASIC
*PRIME/21-25: .6X TO 1.5X BASIC
1 Patrick Bailey/199 6.00 15.00
2 Reid Detmers/150 6.00 15.00
3 Colton Cowser/212 4.00 10.00
4 Asa Lacy/199 10.00 25.00
5 Austin Martin/99 15.00 40.00
6 Max Meyer/227 10.00 25.00
7 Garrett Mitchell/39 25.00 60.00
8 Spencer Torkelson/199 20.00 50.00
9 Cole Wilcox/299 4.00 10.00
10 Alika Williams/199 4.00 10.00
11 Logan Allen/299 3.00 8.00
12 Andrew Abbott/213 3.00 8.00
13 Tyler Brown/199 5.00 12.00
14 Burl Carraway/146 8.00 20.00
15 Justin Foscue/199 8.00 20.00
16 Nick Loftin/199 5.00 12.00
17 Doug Nikhazy/199 3.00 8.00
18 Tanner Allen/199 3.00 8.00
19 Alec Burleson/199 5.00 12.00
20 Cade Cavalli/79 6.00 15.00
21 Jeff Criswell/199 5.00 12.00
22 Nick Frasso/199 3.00 8.00
23 Heston Kjerstad/99 15.00 40.00
24 Luke Waddell/199 3.00 8.00
25 Chris McMahon/199 4.00 10.00
26 Casey Opitz/166 5.00 12.00
27 Alejandro Rosario/299 5.00 12.00
28 Austin Hendrick/299 30.00 80.00
29 Ben Hernandez/299 5.00 12.00
30 Drew Romo/299 8.00 20.00
31 Colby Halter/299 3.00 8.00
32 Drew Bowser/197 3.00 8.00
33 Lucas Dunn/299 3.00 8.00
34 Hunter Haas/299 4.00 10.00
35 Jack Bulger/299 3.00 8.00
36 Jason Savacool/299 5.00 12.00
37 Kyle Harrison/299 3.00 8.00
38 Lucas Gordon/299 3.00 8.00
39 Max Rajcic/299 3.00 8.00
40 Mick Abel/299 5.00 12.00
41 Milan Tolentino/299 5.00 12.00
42 Nate Savino/299 4.00 10.00
43 Nolan McLean/299 3.00 8.00
44 Robert Hassell/299 25.00 60.00
45 Tyler Soderstrom/299 12.00 30.00
46 Pete Crow-Armstrong/224 10.00 25.00
47 Rawley Hector/199 3.00 8.00
48 Benjamin Reiland/197 6.00 15.00
49 Steven Milam/199 3.00 8.00
50 Drew Burress/199 3.00 8.00
51 Aidan Miller/199 5.00 12.00
52 Colton Wombles/199 6.00 15.00
53 Termarr Johnson/199 6.00 15.00
54 Mikey Romero/199 3.00 8.00
55 Karson Bowen/199 3.00 8.00
56 Brandon Barriera/199 3.00 8.00
57 Spencer Butt/199 3.00 8.00
58 Duke Ekstrom/199 3.00 8.00
59 Brandon Olivera/259 3.00 8.00
60 Kai Caranto/199 3.00 8.00
61 Joseph Brown/199 3.00 8.00
62 Ethan McElvain/199 3.00 8.00
63 Louis Rodriguez/199 3.00 8.00
64 Logan Saloman/199 3.00 8.00
65 Dylan Lina/199 4.00 10.00
66 Matthew Matthijs/199 5.00 12.00
67 Nolan Schubart/199 3.00 8.00
68 Philip Abner/199 3.00 8.00
69 Jackson Baumeister/199 10.00 25.00
70 Mike Bello/199 3.00 8.00
71 Braylon Bishop/199 5.00 12.00
72 Nick Bitsko/199 10.00 25.00
73 Mark Black/199 3.00 8.00
74 Michael Braswell/199 3.00 8.00
75 Maddux Bruns/199 3.00 8.00
76 Irving Carter/199 3.00 8.00
77 Ryan Clifford/199 3.00 8.00
78 Pete Crow-Armstrong/208 10.00 25.00
79 Michael Davinni/199 3.00 8.00
80 Kade Grundy/199 3.00 8.00
81 Joshua Hartle/199 3.00 8.00
82 Rawley Hector/199 3.00 8.00
83 Brady House/199 8.00 20.00
84 Sam Hunt/199 3.00 8.00
85 Jordan Lawlar/199 4.00 10.00
86 Christian Little/199 5.00 12.00
87 Joseph Mack/199 3.00 8.00
88 Marcelo Mayer/199 3.00 8.00
89 Michael Morales/199 6.00 15.00
90 Maxwell Muncy/199 3.00 8.00
91 Izaac Pacheco/199 5.00 12.00
92 Andrew Painter/199 3.00 8.00
93 Joshua Pearson/199 3.00 8.00
94 Kurtis Reid/199 3.00 8.00
95 Roc Riggio/199 6.00 15.00
96 Alejandro Rosario/205 5.00 12.00
97 Charlie Saum/199 3.00 8.00
98 Cody Schrier/199 3.00 8.00
99 Brock Selvidge/199 3.00 8.00
100 Noah Smith/199 3.00 8.00
101 Ryan Spikes/199 3.00 8.00
102 Austin Stracener/199 3.00 8.00
103 Grant Taylor/199 3.00 8.00
104 Hunter Teplansky/199 3.00 8.00
106 Tyler Wiederstein/199 3.00 8.00
107 Luke Leto/199 12.00 30.00
108 Carson Applegate/199 3.00 8.00
109 Jesse Bullard/199 3.00 8.00
110 Korbyn Dickerson/199 10.00 25.00
111 Thomas DiLandri/199 3.00 8.00
112 Tyler Gough/199 3.00 8.00
113 Blaise Grove/199 3.00 8.00
114 Joshua Hartle/199 3.00 8.00
115 Cooper Kinney/199 3.00 8.00
116 Nicholas Kurtz/199 3.00 8.00
117 Cale Lansville/199 4.00 10.00
118 Gabriel Miranda/199 3.00 8.00
119 Jaron Nevarez/199 3.00 8.00
120 Tyree Reed/199 6.00 15.00
121 William Rogers/199 3.00 8.00
122 Michael Saumell/199 3.00 8.00
123 Chase Spencer/199 3.00 8.00
124 Sal Stewart/199 3.00 8.00
125 Tyler White/199 3.00 8.00
126 Carter Boyd/199 3.00 8.00
127 Lorenzo Carrier/199 4.00 10.00
128 Calvert Clark/199 3.00 8.00
129 Ryan Clifford/199 3.00 8.00
130 Daniel Corona Jr./199 3.00 8.00
131 Davis Diaz/199 3.00 8.00
132 Samuel Dutton/199 5.00 12.00
133 Jake Geis/199 3.00 8.00
134 Rafael Gross/199 3.00 8.00
135 Trevor Haskins/199 3.00 8.00
136 Jack Holman/199 3.00 8.00
137 David Horn/199 4.00 10.00
138 Jayson Jones/199 3.00 8.00
139 Gage Jump/199 5.00 12.00
140 Kyndon Lovell/199 3.00 8.00
141 Malcolm Moore/199 5.00 12.00
142 Devin Obee/199 3.00 8.00
143 Gavin Ochoa/199 4.00 10.00
144 Xavier Perez/199 3.00 8.00
145 Trent Abel/71 3.00 8.00
146 Spencer Butt/199 3.00 8.00
147 Angel Cepeda/66 3.00 8.00
148 Brandon Chang/62 3.00 8.00
149 Justin Cuellar/54 6.00 15.00
150 Ian Duarte/71 5.00 12.00
151 Owen Egan/65 3.00 8.00
152 Miles Ghossein/62 3.00 8.00
153 Gavin Grahovac/62 5.00 12.00
154 Christian Grino/62 4.00 10.00
155 Ryder Helfrick/56 3.00 8.00
156 Cayne Killion/58 3.00 8.00
157 Trenton Lape/71 4.00 10.00
158 Chris Newstrom/62 3.00 8.00
159 Keilon Parnell/56 3.00 8.00
160 Luca Reyes/62 3.00 8.00
161 CJ Rice/65 4.00 10.00
162 Cole Stokes/56 3.00 8.00
163 Sam Ward/68 3.00 8.00
164 Eric Bitoni/62 3.00 8.00
165 Kai Caranto/199 3.00 8.00
166 Justin Corless/73 3.00 8.00
167 Derek Curiel/63 5.00 12.00
168 Andrew Dunford/66 3.00 8.00
169 TJ Dunsford Jr./51 3.00 8.00
170 Colt Emerson/62 8.00 20.00
171 Keondre Fields/68 3.00 8.00
172 Jaydon Kea/69 3.00 8.00
173 Jonathan Mendez/60 3.00 8.00
174 Andre Modugno/62 5.00 12.00
175 Brandon Olivera/249 3.00 8.00
176 Bryce Rainer/70 3.00 8.00
177 Benjamin Reiland/275 6.00 15.00
178 Dillon Roberts/59 3.00 8.00
179 Ty Southisene/70 3.00 8.00
180 Nolan Stevens/53 3.00 8.00
181 Ralphy Velazquez/62 6.00 15.00
182 Brooks Wright/62 5.00 12.00
183 Carson Dean/54 3.00 8.00
184 Connor Crisp/70 3.00 8.00
185 Spencer Torkelson/199 20.00 50.00
186 Pete Crow-Armstrong/199 10.00 25.00
187 Austin Martin/149 15.00 40.00
188 Asa Lacy/95 10.00 25.00
190 Cole Wilcox/299 4.00 10.00
191 Mick Abel/224 5.00 12.00
192 Reid Detmers/150 6.00 15.00
193 Austin Hendrick/239 30.00 80.00
194 Patrick Bailey/199 6.00 15.00
195 Drew Romo/299 8.00 20.00
196 Nate Savino/299 4.00 10.00
197 Heston Kjerstad/199 15.00 40.00
198 Robert Hassell/241 25.00 60.00
199 Max Meyer/199 12.00 30.00
200 Cade Cavalli/199 6.00 15.00

ACKNOWLEDGMENTS

Each year, we refine the process of developing the most accurate and up-to-date information for this book. We believe this year's Annual is our best yet. Thanks again to all the contributors nationwide (listed below) as well as our staff here in Dallas.

Those who have worked closely with us on this and many other books have again proven themselves invaluable: Ed Allan, Frank and Vivian Barning, Levi Bleam and Jim Fleck (707 Sportscards), T. Scott Brandon, Peter Brennan, Ray Bright, Card Collectors Co., Dwight Chapin, Theo Chen, Barry Colla, Dick DeCourcy, Bill and Diane Dodge, Brett Domue, Ben Ecklar, Dan Even, David Festberg, Gean Paul Figari, Steve Freedman, Gervise Ford, Larry and Jeff Fritsch, Tony Galovich, Dick Gilkeson, Steve Gold (AU Sports), Bill Goodwin, Mike and Howard Gordon, George Grauer, Steve Green (STB Sports), John Greenwald, Wayne Grove, Bill Henderson, Jerry and Etta Hersh, Mike Hersh, Dan Hitt, Neil Hoppenworth, Keith Hower, Hunt Auction, Mike Jaspersen, Steven Judd, Jay and Mary Kasper (Jay's Emporium), Jerry Katz, Eddie Kelly, Pete Kennedy, Rich Klein, David Kohler (SportsCards Plus), Terry Knouse (Tik and Tik), Tom Layberger, Tom Leon, Robert Lifson (Robert Edward Auctions), Lew Lipset (Four Base Hits), Mike Livingston, Leon Luckey, Mark Macrae, Bill Madden, Bill Mastro, Doug Allen and Ron Oser (Mastro Auctions), Dr.William McAvoy, Michael McDonald, Mid-Atlantic Sports Cards (Bill Bossert), Gary Mills, Ernie Montella, Brian Morris, Mike Mosier (Columbia City Collectibles Co.), B.A. Murry, Ralph Nozaki, Oldies and Goodies (Nigel Spill), Oregon Trail Auctions, Jack Pollard, David Porter, Jeff Prillaman, Pat Quinn, Jerald Reichstein, Gavin Riley, Clifton Rouse, John Rumierz, Grant Sandground, Pat Blandford, Lonn Passon and Kevin Savage (Sports Gallery), Gary Sawatski and Jim Justus (The Wizards of Odd), Mike Schechter, Bill and Darlene Shafer, Dave Sliepka, Barry Sloate, John E. Spalding, Phil Spector, Rob Springs, Ted Taylor, Lee Temanson, Topps (Clay Luraschi), Tim Trout, Ed Twombly, Upper Deck (Don Williams and Chris Carlin), Wayne Varner, Bill Vizas, Waukesha Sportscards, Dave Weber, Brian and Mike Wentz (BMWCards), Bill Wesslund (Portland Sports Card Co.), Kit Young, Rick Young, Ted Zanidakis, Robert Zanze (Z-Cards and Sports), Bill Zimpleman and Dean Zindler. Finally we give a special acknowledgment to the late Dennis W. Eckes, "Mr. Sport Americana." The success of the Beckett Price Guides has always been the result of a team effort.

It is very difficult to be "accurate" - one can only do one's best. But this job is especially difficult since we're shooting at a moving target: Prices are fluctuating all the time. Having several full-time pricing experts has definitely proven to be better than just one, and I thank all of them for working together to provide you, our readers, with the most accurate prices possible.

Many people have provided price input, illustrative material, checklist verifications, errata, and/or background information. We should like to individually thank AbD Cards (Dale Wesolewski), Action Card Sales, Jerry Adamic, Johnny and Sandy Adams, Mehdi Ahlei, Alex's MVP Cards & Comics, Will Allison, Dennis Anderson, Ed Anderson, Shane Anderson, Ellis Anmuth, Alan Applegate, Ric Apter, Clyde Archer, Randy Archer, Burl Armstrong, Neil Armstrong, Barry Arnold, Carlos Ayala, B and J Sportscards, Jeremy Bachman, Dave Bailey, Ball Four Cards (Frank and Steve Pemper), Bob Bartosz, Jay Behrens, Bubba Bennett, Carl Berg, David Berman, Beulah Sports (Jeff Blatt), B..J. Sportscollectables, Al Blumkin, David Boedicker (The Wild Pitch Inc.), Louis Bollman, Tim Bond, Terry Boyd, Dan Brandenberry, Jeff Breitenfield, John Brigandi, Scott Brockleman, John Broggi, D.Bruce Brown, Virgil Burns, Greg Bussineau, David Byer, California Card Co., Capital Cards, Danny Cariseo, Carl Carlson (C.T.S.), Jim Carr, Brian Cataquet, Ira Cetron, Sandy Chan, Ric Chandgie, Ray Cherry, Bigg Wayne Christian, Ryan Christoff (Thanks for the help with Cuban Cards), Josh Chidester, Michael and Abe Citron, Dr. Jeffrey Clair, Michael Cohen, Tom Cohoon (Cardboard Dreams), Gary Collett, Jay Conti, Brian Coppola, Rick Cosmen (RC Card Co.), Lou Costanzo (Champion Sports), Mike Coyne, Tony Craig (T.C. Card Co.), Solomon Cramer, Kevin Crane, Taylor Crane, Chad Cripe, Scott Crump, Allen Custer, Dave Dame, Scott Dantio, Dee's Baseball Cards (Dee Robinson), Joe Delgrippo, Mike DeLuca, Ken Dinerman (California Cruizers), Rob DiSalvatore, Cliff Dolgins, Discount Dorothy, Richard Dolloff, Darren Duet, Joe Donato, Jerry Dong, Pat Dorsey, Double Play Baseball Cards, Joe Drelich, Richard Duglin (Baseball Cards-N-More), The Dugout, Ken Edick (Home Plate of Utah), Brad Englehardt, Terry Falkner, Mike and Chris Fanning, David Fela, Linda Ferrigno and Mark Mezzardi, Jay Finglass, A.J. Firestone, Scott Flatto, Bob Flitter, Fremont Fong, Paul Franzetti, Ron Frasier, Tom Freeman, Bob Frye, Bill Fusaro, Chris Gala, David Garza, David Gaumer, Georgetown Card Exchange, David Giove, Dick Goddard, Jeff Goldstein, Ron Gomez, Rich Gove, Paul Griggs, Jay and Jan Grinsby, Bob Grissett, Gerry Guenther, Neil Gubitz, Hall's Nostalgia, Gregg Hara, Lyman and Brett Hardeman (OldCardboard.com), Todd Harrell, Robert Harrison, Steve Hart, Floyd Haynes (H and H Baseball Cards), Kevin Heffner, Joel Hellman, Peter Henrici, Ron Hetrick, Hit and Run Cards (Jon, David, and Kirk Peterson), Vinny Ho, Paul Holstein, Johnny Hustle Card Co., John Inouye, Vern Isenberg, Dale Jackson, Marshall Jackson, Mike Jardina, Paul Jastrzembski, Jeff's Sports Cards, Donn Jennings Cards, George Johnson, Craig Jones, Chuck Juliana, Nick Kardoulias, Scott Kashner, Frank and Rose Katen, Steven J Kerno, Kevin's Kards, Kingdom Collectibles, Inc., John Klassnik, Steve Kluback, Don Knutsen, Gregg Kohn, Mike Kohlhas, Bob & Bryan Kornfield, Josh Krasner, Carl and Maryanne Laron, Bill Larsen, Howard Lau, Richard S. Lawrence, William Lawrence, Brent Lee, Morley Leeking, Irv Lerner, Larry and Sally Levine, Simeon Lipman, Larry Loeschen (A and J Sportscards), Neil Lopez, Kendall Loyd (Orlando Sportscards South), Steve Lowe, Leon Luckey, Ray Luurs, Jim Macie, Peter Maltin, Paul Marchant, Brian Marcy, Scott Martinez, James S. Maxwell Jr., McDag Productions Inc., Bob McDonald, Tony McLaughlin, Mendal Mearkle, Carlos Medina, Ken Melanson, William Mendel, Blake Meyer (Lone Star Sportscards), Tim Meyer, Joe Michalowicz, Lee Milazzo, Cary S. Miller, George Miller, Wayne Miller, Dick Millerd, Frank Mineo, Mitchell's Baseball Cards, John Morales, Paul Moss, William Munn, Mark Murphy, Robert Nappe, National Sportscard Exchange, Roger Neufeldt, Steve Novella, Bud Obermeyer, John O'Hara, Glenn Olson, Scott Olson, Luther Owen, Earle Parrish, Clay Pasternack, Michael Perrotta, Bobby Plapinger, Tom Pfirrmann, Don Phlong, Loran Pulver, Bob Ragonese, Bryan Rappaport, Don and Tom Ras, Robert M. Ray, Phil Regli, Rob Resnick, Dave Reynolds, David Ring, Carson Ritchey, Bill Rodman, Craig Roehrig, Mike Sablow, Terry Sack, Thomas Salem, Barry Sanders, Jon Sands, Tony Scarpa, John Schad, Dave Schau (Baseball Cards), Marc Scully, Masa Shinohara, Eddie Silard, Mike Slepcevic, Sam Sliheet, Art Smith, Cary Smith, Jerry Smolin, Lynn and Todd Solt, Jerry Sorice, Don Spagnolo, Sports Card Fan-Attic, The Sport Hobbyist, Norm Stapleton, Bill Steinberg, Lisa Stellato (Never Enough Cards), Rob Stenzel, Jason Stern, Andy Stoltz, Rob Stenzel, Bill Stone, Ted Straka, Tim Strandberg (East Texas Sports Cards), Edward Strauss, Strike Three, Richard Strobino, Kevin Struss, Superior Sport Card, Dr. Richard Swales, Steve Taft, George Tahinos, Ian Taylor, The Thirdhand Shoppe, Dick Thompson, Brent Thornton, Paul Thornton, Jim and Sally Thurtell, Bud Tompkins (Minnesota Connection), Philip J. Tremont, Ralph Triplette, Umpire's Choice Inc., Eric Unglaub, David Vargha, Hoyt Vanderpool, Steven Wagman, T. Wall, Gary A. Walter, Adam Warshaw, Dave Weber, Joe and John Weisenburger (The Wise Guys), Richard West, Mike Wheat, Louise and Richard Wiercinski, Don Williams (Robin's Nest of Dolls), Jeff Williams, John Williams, Kent Williams, Craig Williamson, Richard Wong, Rich Wojtasick, John Wolf Jr., Jay Wolt (Cavalcade of Sports), Eric Wu, Joe Yanello, Peter Yee, Tom Zocco, Mark Zubrensky and Tim Zwick.

Every year we make active solicitations for expert input. We are particularly appreciative of help (however extensive or cursory) provided for this volume. We receive many inquiries, comments and questions regarding material within this book. In fact, each and every one is read and digested. Time constraints, however, prevent us from personally replying. But keep sharing your knowledge. Your letters and input are part of the "big picture" of hobby information we can pass along to readers in our books and magazines. Even though we cannot respond to each letter or email, you are making significant contributions to the hobby through your interest and comments.

The effort to continually refine and improve this book also involves a growing number of people and types of expertise on our home team. Our company boasts a substantial Collectibles Data Group, which strengthens our ability to provide comprehensive analysis of the marketplace. CDG capably handled numerous technical details and provided able assistance in the preparation of this edition.

The Beckett baseball specialists are Brian Fleischer (Senior Market Analyst) and Sam Zimmer (Market Analyst). Their pricing analysis and careful proofreading were key contributions to the accuracy of this annual. They were ably assisted by the rest of the Market Analysts: Jeff Camay, Lloyd Almonguera, Kristian Redulla, Justin Grunert, Matt Bible, Eric Norton, Steve Dalton and Badz Mercader.

The price gathering and analytical talents of this fine group of hobbyists have helped make our Beckett team stronger, while making this guide and its companion monthly Price Guide more widely recognized as the hobby's most reliable and relied upon sources of pricing information. Surajpal Singh Bisht, Hemant Tiwari and Hritik Godara were responsible for layout of the book. Daniel Moscoso was responsible for the majority of the card images. The reason this book looks as good as it does is due to their hard work and expertise.

In the years since this guide debuted, Beckett Media has grown beyond any rational expectation. Many talented and hardworking individuals have been instrumental in this growth and success. Our whole team is to be congratulated for what we have accomplished.